Published in Nashville, Tennessee, by Thomas Nelson, Inc.

© 1994 by Thomas Nelson Publishers, Inc.
© 1983 by Old-Time Gospel Hour

Library of Congress Cataloging-in-Publication Data

Liberty Bible commentary.
  The KJV parallel Bible commentary / Jerry Falwell, executive editor : Edward Hindson, Woodrow Michael Kroll, general editors.
    p. cm.
  Includes bibliographical references.
  ISBN 0-8407-1848-9
  1. Bible—Commentaries. I. Falwell, Jerry. II. Hindson, Edward E. III. Kroll, Woodrow Michael, 1944– . IV. Bible, English, Authorized. 1994. V. Title.
BS491.2.L53 1994
220.7′7—dc20   94–11668
                                                              CIP

Printed in the United States of America.
1 2 3 4 5 6 7 8 — 00 99 98 97 96 95 94

THE
K·J·V
PARALLEL
BIBLE
COMMENTARY

Edward E. Hindson, Th.D., D.Min.
Woodrow Michael Kroll, Th.D.
General Editors

THOMAS NELSON PUBLISHERS
Nashville • Atlanta • London • Vancouver

TABLE OF CONTENTS

(**Bibliographies**—following the commentary on each book. An asterisk(*) denotes suggested readings for in-depth study.)

PUBLISHER'S PREFACE

The KJV Parallel Bible Commentary offers you the convenience of a thorough evangelical commentary on the whole Bible, along with the complete text of Scripture in a parallel column. When you open the *Commentary*, you will find—all on the same page—both verse-by-verse commentary and the complete verses of Scripture. Forty-eight quality maps located conveniently throughout the volume help you visualize key events of biblical history, and a brief Introduction and Outline for each book provide valuable information for effective Bible study.

This commentary is designed to meet the needs of pastors, teachers, and ordinary Bible readers and students alike. It draws upon the work of Bible scholars, and provides references to their works in Bibliographies for those who wish to carry their study further. However, the aim of the *Commentary* is not merely to *inform*, but to comment on Scriptures in such a way that prayerful readers may be *transformed* by the power of God's word.

Many capable Bible scholars and teachers have contributed to *The KJV Parallel Bible Commentary*. While each has been allowed the freedom of his personal views, all share a firm faith in these fundamental beliefs of evangelical Christianity: the inerrant inspiration of Scripture; the virgin birth and deity of Jesus Christ; and His vicarious atonement, bodily resurrection, and literal Second Coming. All commentary further reflects the contributors' shared emphasis on the evangelistic mandate of the church, the importance of individual conversion to Jesus Christ, and a premillennial understanding of Bible prophecy.

With *The KJV Parallel Bible Commentary* you are encouraged not only to consider the careful commentary of devout Bible scholars, but also to be like the noble Bereans of old, who both heard the word spoken to them and also "searched the scriptures daily, whether those things were so" (Acts 17:11). *The KJV Parallel Bible Commentary* goes forth with the prayer that our Lord Jesus Christ will use it as a means of instructing His church for many generations to come.

CONTRIBUTORS

James A. Borland, Th.D. Exodus, Leviticus, Daniel, Gospel of Luke, Philemon
Professor, Liberty University
B.A., Los Angeles Baptist College; M.Div., Los Angeles Baptist Theological Seminary;
Th.M., Talbot Theological Seminary; Th.D., Grace Theological Seminary.

Benjamin C. Chapman, Ph.D. I-II Samuel; Biblical Language Editor, I-II Thessalonians, Epistles
of Peter, John, Jude
Former Professor of Religion, Liberty University
B.R.E., Grand Rapids Baptist College; B.D., M.R.E., Grand Rapids Baptist Seminary;
Th.M., Calvin Theological Seminary; Ph.D., Bob Jones University. Additional graduate study
at the University of Michigan and the University of Manitoba (Canada).

Edward G. Dobson, D.D. Ezra, Nehemiah, Esther, Gospel of John
Senior Minister, Calvary Church, Grand Rapids, Michigan
B.A., M.A., Bob Jones University; D.D., California Graduate School of Theology; Doctoral
student at the University of Virginia.

Jerry Falwell, D.D., D.Litt. Executive Editor
Chancellor of Liberty University & Liberty Baptist Theological Seminary
Th.G. Baptist Bible College; D.D., Tennessee Temple University; D.Litt., California Gradu-
ate School of Theology.

Charles L. Feinberg, Th.D., Ph.D. Revelation
Former Visiting Professor, Liberty Baptist Theological Seminary
B.A., University of Pittsburgh; Th.B., Th.M., Th.D., Dallas Theological Seminary; M.A.,
Southern Methodist University; Ph.D., Johns Hopkins University.

Paul R. Fink, Th.D. Minor Prophets
Chairman and Professor of Pastoral Ministries and Biblical Studies, Liberty University
B.A., Columbia Bible College; Th.M., Dallas Theological Seminary; Ed.S., University of
Southern California; Th.D., Dallas Theological Seminary. Additional graduate study at Pur-
due University.

James Freerkson, Th.D. Hebrews
Professor of Biblical Studies, Liberty Baptist Theological Seminary
B.A., Pillsbury Baptist College; M.Div., Th.M., Central Baptist Theological Seminary;
Th.D., Grace Theological Seminary.

Harvey D. Hartman, Th.D. I-II Kings, I-II Chronicles
Associate Professor of Biblical Studies, Liberty University
B.A., Calvary Bible College; M.Div., Th.D., Grace Theological Seminary. Additional gradu-
ate study at the Hebrew Union College Nelson Glueck School of Archaeology (Israel).

Ronald E. Hawkins, Ed.D., D.Min. Proverbs, Ecclesiastes, Song of Solomon
Dean, Liberty Baptist Theological Seminary
B.A., Barrington College; M.Div., Gordon-Conwell Theological Seminary; D.Min., Westmin-
ster Theological Seminary; Ed.D., Virginia Polytechnic Institute and State University.

Edward E. Hindson, Th.D., D.Min. General Editor, Judges, Ruth, Isaiah, Gospel of Matthew
Vice President, There's Hope Ministries; Minister of Biblical Studies, Rehoboth Baptist
Church
B.A., William Tyndale College; M.A., Trinity Evangelical Divinity School; Th.M., Grace
Theological Seminary; Th.D., Trinity Graduate School of Theology; D.Min., Westminster
Theological Seminary; D.Litt. (Hon.), California Graduate School of Theology. Additional
graduate study at Acadia University (Canada) and the University of South Africa.

Elmer A. Jantz, Th.M. Ezekiel
   Former Associate Professor of Religion, Liberty University; Retired
   B.A., Tabor College; Th.M., Dallas Theological Seminary; M.Ed., University of Colorado.

F. Gerald Kroll, Th.D. Jeremiah, Lamentations
   Senior Pastor, Heritage Baptist Church, Lynchburg, Virginia
   B.A., Barrington College; M.Div., Gordon-Conwell Theological Seminary; D.Min., Westminster Theological Seminary. Additional graduate study at Dallas Theological Seminary.

Woodrow Michael Kroll, Th.D. General Editor, Joshua, Psalms, Romans
   General Director and Bible Teacher, Back to the Bible
   B.A., Barrington College; M.Div., Gordon-Conwell Theological Seminary; Th.M., Th.D., Geneva Theological Seminary. Additional graduate study at Harvard Divinity School; Princeton Theological Seminary; the University of Strasbourg (France).

William E. Matheny, Ph.D. Job
   Professor of Religion, Liberty University & Theological Seminary
   B.S., University of Illinois; M.Div., Southwestern Baptist Theological Seminary; M.A., Ph.D., Texas Christian University.

Daniel R. Mitchell, Th.D. I-II Corinthians
   Professor of Theology, Liberty Baptist Theological Seminary
   B.A., Washington Bible College; Th.M., Capital Bible Seminary; S.T.M., Dallas Theological Seminary; Th.D., Dallas Theological Seminary.

Edward R. Roustio, Th.D. Galatians, Ephesians, Philippians, Colossians
   Former Associate Professor of Religion, Liberty University
   A.B., William Jewell College; Th.M., Southern Baptist Theological Seminary; Th.M., Th.D., Central Baptist Theological Seminary.

Stephen R. Schrader, Th.D. Genesis
   Dean of Biblical Studies & Theology, Trinity College & Seminary
   B.S., Evansville University; M.Div., Th.M., Th.D., Grace Theological Seminary.

James D. Stevens, S.T.M., D.Min. Gospel of Mark, James
   Professor and Associate Dean of Religion, Liberty University
   B.A., Bob Jones University; M.Div., Grace Theological Seminary; S.T.M., Dallas Theological Seminary; M.Ed., Lynchburg College; D.Min., Trinity Evangelical Divinity School. Additional graduate study at Eastern Michigan University and the University of Virginia.

Elmer L. Towns, D.Min., D.D. Deuteronomy
   Professor and Dean, School of Religion, Liberty University
   B.A., Northwestern College; M.A., Southern Methodist University; Th.M., Dallas Theological Seminary; M.R.E., Garrett Theological Seminary; D.D., Baptist Bible College; D.Min., Fuller Theological Seminary.

C. Sumner Wemp, D.D. I-II Timothy, Titus
   Former Vice President and Professor of Religion, Liberty University; Retired
   B.A., Sanford University; Th.M., Dallas Theological Seminary;
   D.D., California Graduate School of Theology.

Harold L. Willmington, D.D., D.Min. Numbers, Acts of the Apostles
   Vice President, Liberty University; Dean, Liberty Bible Institute
   Dip., Moody Bible Institute; B.A., Culver-Stockton College; D.D., California Graduate School of Theology; D.Min., Trinity Evangelical Divinity School. Additional graduate study at Dallas Theological Seminary and Ashland Theological Seminary.

MAP SUPPLEMENTS

LIST OF ABBREVIATIONS

Gen	Genesis	Nah	Nahum
Ex	Exodus	Hab	Habakkuk
Lev	Leviticus	Zeph	Zephaniah
Num	Numbers	Hag	Haggai
Deut	Deuteronomy	Zech	Zechariah
Josh	Joshua	Mal	Malachi
Jud	Judges	Mt	Matthew
Ruth	Ruth	Mk	Mark
I Sam	I Samuel	Lk	Luke
II Sam	II Samuel	Jn	John
I Kgs	I Kings	Acts	Acts
II Kgs	II Kings	Rom	Romans
I Chr	I Chronicles	I Cor	I Corinthians
II Chr	II Chronicles	II Cor	II Corinthians
Ezr	Ezra	Gal	Galatians
Neh	Nehemiah	Eph	Ephesians
Est	Esther	Phil	Philippians
Job	Job	Col	Colossians
Ps	Psalms	I Thess	I Thessalonians
Prov	Proverbs	II Thess	II Thessalonians
Eccl	Ecclesiastes	I Tim	I Timothy
Song	Song of Solomon	II Tim	II Timothy
Isa	Isaiah	Tit	Titus
Jer	Jeremiah	Phm	Philemon
Lam	Lamentations	Heb	Hebrews
Ezk	Ezekiel	Jas	James
Dan	Daniel	I Pet	I Peter
Hos	Hosea	II Pet	II Peter
Joel	Joel	I Jn	I John
Amos	Amos	II Jn	II John
Ob	Obadiah	III Jn	III John
Jon	Jonah	Jude	Jude
Mic	Micah	Rev	Revelation

Adv. Her.	*Against Heresies*, Irenaus
ANET	*Ancient Near Eastern Texts*, J. B. Pritchard
Antiq.	*Antiquities of the Jews*, Josephus
Aram	Aramaic
ASV	American Standard Version
AV	Authorized Version
BDB	*Hebrew and English Lexicon of the Old Testament*, Francis Brown, S. R. Driver, and Charles Briggs
ca.	around
cf.	compare
ch.	chapter
Chal	Chaldee
chs.	chapters
Eccl. Hist.	*Ecclesiastical History*, Eusebius
Ed.	Editor
e.g.	for example
Eng	English
ff.	verses/pages following
Gr	Greek
Heb	Hebrew

i.e.	for example
I Macc	I Maccabees
II Macc	II Maccabees
JAOS	*Journal of the American Oriental Society*
JBL	*Journal of Biblical Literature*
JNES	*Journal of Near Eastern Studies*
Lat	Latin
LXX	Septuagint
lit.	literally
MS	Manuscript
MSS	Manuscripts
NASB	New American Standard Bible
NBD	*New Bible Dictionary*, J. D. Douglas
NEB	New English Bible
NIV	New International Version
NKJV	New King James Version
NPOT	*New Perspectives on the Old Testament*, J. Barton Payne
NT	New Testament
OT	Old Testament
p.	page
pp.	pages
POTT	*People of the Old Testament Times*, D. J. Wiseman
RSV	Revised Standard Version
RV	Revised Version
SAOC	*Studies in Ancient Oriental Civilization*
trans.	translator/translation
TDOT	*Theological Dictionary of the Old Testament*, G. Botterweck and H. Ringgren
viz.	namely
vs	versus
vs.	verse
vss.	verses
Wars	*Jewish Wars*, Josephus
ZPBD	*Zondervan Pictorial Bible Dictionary*
ZPEB	*Zondervan Pictoral Encyclopedia of the Bible*

ORIGINAL LANGUAGE TRANSLITERATIONS

Hebrew Consonants	Hebrew Vowels	Greek Consonants and Vowels
א = '	ָ = a	α = a
ב = b	ָ = a	β = b
ג = g	ֶ = e	γ = g
ד = d	ֵ = ē	δ = d
ה = h	ֵ = ē	ε = e
ו = w	ִי = ī	ζ = z
ז = z	ִ = i	η = ē
ח = ch	ֹ = ō	θ = th
ט = t	ֹ = ō	ι = i
י = y	ֻ = u	κ = k
כ = k	וּ = ū	λ = l
ל = l	ְ = e	μ = m
מ = m		ν = n
נ = n		ξ = x
ס = s		ο = o
ע = '		π = p
פ = p		ρ = r
צ = ts		σ = s
ק = q		τ = t
ר = r		υ = y
שׂ = s		φ = ph
שׁ = sh		χ = ch
ת = t		ψ = ps
		ω = ō

Note: The Hebrew Dagesh Lene and Dagesh Forte are
not indicated. Every vocal Shewa is indicated by
short e; silent Shewa is not indicated. In Greek, ι
subscript is not indicated, and in diphthongs υ is
indicated as u.

THE

K·J·V

PARALLEL BIBLE COMMENTARY

OLD TESTAMENT

GENESIS

INTRODUCTION

The book of Genesis is a thoroughly unique document. It is not the only ancient literary work to survive the centuries of time, but it stands head and shoulders above all the others. It transcends the primitive mythologies of the ancient Near East and stands as a divine account of earth's earliest ages.

The scope of this book is broad. The fifty chapters of Genesis cover a time period from the creation of the world to the death of Joseph ca. 1804 B.C. In these chapters the reader will find a storehouse of wealth regarding God, mankind, man's sin and rebellion, and God's grace and mercy. Where in the annals of history can be found so complete a selection of literature? The great questions of life are answered in Genesis: (1) where have I come from? (1:1); (2) why am I here? (15:6); and (3) where am I going? (25:8).

The theological questions treated in Genesis are numerous. Here, both origins and consummations are discussed; and the problem of evil is addressed. The fall of man is described, and the promise of God's salvation is recorded. The doctrines of creation, imputation, justification, atonement, depravity, grace, wrath, sovereignty, responsibility, and even more are all addressed in this book.

The personal accounts of great men, women, and families of God are recorded in Genesis. The lives of Adam and Eve, Abraham and Sarah, Jacob, Esau, Joseph, and Pharaoh are all written in detail. Genesis paints an accurate picture of man as he really is. In Genesis the love of Jacob and Rachel, the jealousy of Cain, the faith of Abraham, the failure of Lot, the unbelief of Abraham and Sarah, the faithfulness of Abraham's servant, the conniving of Rebekah and Jacob, and the steadfastness of the young man Joseph are recorded. Character sketches are provided of Adam the sinner, Cain the murderer, Noah the sailor, Nimrod the hunter, Abraham the intercessor, Isaac the welldigger, Jacob the supplanter, and Joseph the dreamer.

Genesis is informative in its content, beautiful in its arrangement, and inspiring in its appeal. There is something of value for everyone. Genesis has appeal to the scientist, the historian, the theologian, the housewife, the farmer, the traveler, and the man or woman of God. It is a fitting beginning for God's story of His love for mankind, the *Book of Beginnings* (Lat *Liber Genesis*). And we must approach it as a revelation of the mind of God to the minds of men.

Title. Genesis did not originate as a separate book under that name. Its status as a separate book in the canon of Scripture came later. "The title arose during the production, through an obvious need, of a translation of the Old Testament into the widely used Greek of the fourth and third centuries B.C., at which time the work of Moses had already been divided into the first five books of the Bible, now called the Pentateuch. The Greek translators already had before them these separate books and while the first book was titled *Berē'shīt* (*In the beginning*) in the Hebrew, the name *Genesis* derives from the Greek γενεσέως (*geneseōs*, gen. pl. of γενέσις of the Greek translation called the Septuagint, LXX) through the Vulgate of Jerome whose work translated the Greek title as *Liber Genesis*, derived from 2:4, 'This is the book of the *geneseōs* of heaven and earth'" (Harold G. Stigers, *A Commentary on Genesis*, p. 7).

The Hebrew title for Genesis is similar to the titles for the books of Exodus-Deuteronomy, in that the first significant word(s) are representative of the title. This was a common practice in the ancient Near East. Another example of it is the Babylonian creation story, which is entitled *Enūma Eliš* (meaning when on high) and begins with the words *Enūma eliš*. Thus, the antiquity of the whole Pentateuch is attested by the titles of its books.

Since the main theme of the writing consists of origins (origins of the created universe, origins of man, origins of the nations, etc.), the title Genesis, meaning origins, has been adopted by most translations of the Bible.

Authorship. With very few exceptions, until the nineteenth century, Jewish and Christian scholars alike held to the Mosaic authorship of Genesis. The Jews of Palestine and of the dispersion were unanimous in their belief that Moses wrote Genesis. This stance is reflected in the Samaritan Pentateuch, the Palestinian Talmud, the Apocrypha (cf. Eccles 45:4; II Macc 7:30), the writings of Philo (*Life of Moses* 3:39), and Josephus (*Antiq.* 4:8:45; *Contra Apion* I.8). The early church fathers were equally convinced of Mosaic authorship.

In the seventeenth century the philosopher Spinoza raised a question concerning the authorship of Genesis, and this led to what is now known as Higher Criticism of the Bible. With the rise of deism in the 1790's, the age of Hegelian dialecticism, and the inroads of Darwinian evolutionism in the nineteenth century, most liberal critics now have abandoned the Mosaic authorship of Genesis, and indeed of the entire Pentateuch, in favor of a hodgepodge view known as the Documentary Theory, or the Developmental Hypothesis. This theory was even extended to include Joshua, calling for the Hexateuch as a name for the now first six books of the Old Testament.

This theory uses the initials JEDP to identify what it considers to be four different hands involved in the composition of the Pentateuch, and specifically Genesis. The J manuscript was named from the writer's supposed use of the divine name Yahweh, or Jehovah (ca. 850 B.C.). The E document was named after the author's supposed use of the name Elohim for God (ca. 750 B.C.). The D document, which includes the major part of Deuteronomy, was believed to have been written around 621 B.C. and concocted by Josiah. The P document was supposedly the work of a priestly writer in the post-exilic age. Thus, the liberal view is that Moses was not the author of Genesis (or the Pentateuch), but that different writers, writing at different times and from different perspectives concerning God, were responsible for the composition of the book of Genesis.

This theory has been gradually revised until each of the four sources has been subdivided. J, for example, is commonly divided into J^1, J^2, and J^3; and additional sources have been postulated. They include an S document (Seir-Edom), an L document (Lay), and a K document (Kenite). These have been carefully defended, but not widely accepted.

"The traditional documentary theory began to change once Scandinavian scholars stressed the role of oral tradition in the origin of Scripture. In view of this and recent archaeological discoveries, some theorists conceded that some of the material had to be early, concluding that the documents merely represent streams of tradition and may be chronologically parallel. Most modern commentators, however, adhere to the traditional documentary analysis. They may disagree on the dates of sources or traditions, but they generally agree on a multiplicity of authors" (John J. Davis, *Paradise to Prison*, pp. 22-23).

The conservative scholar will totally reject this approach. The two basic presuppositions of the liberal critic rest upon the belief in evolution and the denial of the possibility of supernatural revelation (see Gleason Archer's work, *A Survey of Old Testament Introduction*, pp. 73-165 for the history of the documentary hypothesis and a thorough rejection of its tenets). There is no valid reason to reject Mosaic authorship. The Pentateuch itself attests to his authorship (cf. Ex 17:14; 24:4; 34:27; Num 33:1-2; Deut 31:9), and Old Testament allusions outside of the Pentateuch abound (cf. Josh 1:7-8; 8:31-32; I Kgs 2:3; II Kgs 14:6; 21:8; see also Ezr 6:18; Neh 13:1; Dan 9:11-13; Mal 4:4). New Testament references to Mosaic authorship are not lacking, either (see Mt 19:8; Mk 12:26; Jn 1:45; 5:46-47; Acts 3:22; Rom 10:5). What can be inclusively said of the Pentateuch can particularly be said of Genesis.

Both internal and external evidence suggests that Moses wrote the book of Genesis, and indeed the entire Pentateuch (for an excellent discussion of the subject see John J. Davis, pp. 24-26).

Ancient Near East Similarities. A real problem for many scholars centers in the alleged similarities between the literary form and content of Genesis and the ancient Near Eastern mythologies, particularly the Babylonian mythologies. "Under the heavy pressure of the prestigious scholarship of the late nineteenth and the twentieth century, the approach has become all but unanimous by now: Genesis 1-11 is primeval history reflecting its Near Eastern origins (mainly Babylonian) from which it was borrowed. Any modern appraisal of this section of Scripture must thereby reflect these philological and mythological connections" (Walter Kaiser, "The Literary Form of Genesis 1-11," in *New Perspectives on the Old Testament* [*NPOT*], p. 51).

Principally, the subjects discussed are common to the literature and culture of both groups. They are as follows: (1) the so-called four accounts of creation, including 1:1-2:4a; 2:4b-2:25; Prov 8:22-31; and allusions found in the prophetic and poetical books of the Old Testament; (2) the Serpent and the Garden of Eden, chapter 3 (Ezk 28:12-19); (3) the Cain and Abel conflict, chapter 4; (4) the genealogies of chapter 5 and 11:10-32; (5) the sons of God marrying the daughters of men, 6:1-4; (6) the Flood, 6:5-9:10; (7) the Curse of Canaan, 9:20-29; (8) the Table of Nations, chapter 10; and (9) the Tower of Babel, 11:1-9.

For each of these subjects or topics there are similarities to a greater or lesser degree. The two most famous are the *Gilgamesh Epic* (Babylonian flood) and the *Enuma Elish* (Babylonian Genesis or creation account). "For the Garden of Eden there is the Sumerian Dilmun Poem, the myth of Enki and Ninhursag, and the Akkadian myth of Adapa. The Cain and Abel story is seen in the contest of Dumuzi, shepherd-god, and Enkimdu, the farmer-god. The Weld-Blundell prism or the Sumerian king list is said to reflect our genealogical list; while the themes of the sons of god, the ethnological details on Canaan and the seventy nations, and finally the tower of Babel are all seen as being authentically Babylonian or at least Near Eastern in their origin" (Kaiser, pp. 51-52).

The Babylonian account of creation, the *Enuma Elish*, taken from the initial words of the document *When on high* was written on seven clay tablets. It was discovered between A.D. 1848 and 1876 at the great library of Ashurbanipal at Nineveh (who reigned about 668-630 B.C.). Archaeologists Austen H. Layar, Jormuzd Rassam, and George Adam Smith played key roles in its discovery.

The creation account tells how the gods first appeared before the beginning of things and framed the heavens above and the earth below. According to the epic, Apsu, a male freshwater ocean, mated with Tiamat, a female saltwater ocean. Their offspring, who were lesser deities, irritated Apsu with their noise; and thus, he decided to destroy them. In his attempt, Apsu himself was destroyed by one of these deities, Marduk, the god of wisdom. This action enraged Tiamat who gave birth to a host of dragons to fight Marduk. After a fierce battle, Marduk prevailed and took one half of Tiamat's body to make the heavens and the other half to make the earth.

Although this Babylonian epic of creation is comparable to the Hebrew in some respects (seven tablets corresponding to seven days of creation, Tiamat and *tehōm*, and the word *firmament*), nevertheless the contrasts are much greater. "While *Enuma Elish* is one of the more important witnesses to Babylonian cosmology, it is not primarily a creation epic. Its purpose is obviously to honor Marduk as the greatest of all gods. . . . Another purpose of the epic may have been to exalt the city of Babylon; it does relate the origin of the city (VI:45-73)" (Davis, p. 69; see also Alexander Heidel, *The Babylonian Genesis*, p. 10ff., for an excellent critique by a first-class Assyriologist and a Christian). Davis discusses the Hebrew *tehōm* and its relationship with Tiamat on page 46ff.

In the *Enuma Elish* there is rampant polytheism,

whereas in Genesis there is calm monotheism. In the Babylonian account creation was effected by force, but in Genesis it came into being as the plan and design of a gracious God (for an impressive list of differences, see Davis, p. 71).

However one explains the similarities between ancient cosmologies and the Bible, one thing seems eminently clear; and that is that the Genesis account is without real parallel. Heidel says, "These exalted conceptions in the biblical account of creation give it a depth and dignity unparalleled in any cosmogony known to us from Babylonia or Assyria" (pp. 139-140).

A similar account of the fall of man has been seen in the Adapa Myth on four Babylonian fragments, three of which came from the library of Ashurbanipal at Nineveh, and the fourth from the archives of King Amenhotep IV of Egypt at Tell el-Amarna. In each account, that of Adapa and Genesis 3, the hero is tempted; in each he could obtain immortality by eating a certain food; in each, toil and suffering are inflicted upon the man and woman for disobedience; in each, their eyes are opened through eating the food. But the Old Testament account is again far superior. There is no polytheism and no falsehood to accomplish the purpose of God. In the Old Testament Jehovah is righteous; in the Adapa Myth the god Ea is un-righteous.

A parallel account of the Great Deluge was also discovered at the library of Ashurbanipal in Nineveh. Written on twelve tablets, the *Gilgamesh Epic* records a remarkably similar account of the Great Flood on tablet eleven. The key figure is a young ruler named Gilgamesh, who was part god and part man. The first ten tablets deal mainly with the adventures of Gilgamesh and his friend Enkidu. At the death of Enkidu, Gilgamesh crossed the waters of death in a boat looking for immortality. Here he encountered Utnapishtim (the lord of life), who tells him the story of the Great Flood. Utnapishtim, the Babylonian Noah, built a boat, weathered the flood (which lasted six days and nights), and upon settling to a mountain-top, sent out a dove, a swallow, and then a raven to test the receding of the waters.

Again, similarities can be observed between the Genesis account and the Babylonian story. The deluge is sent from God or the gods; the hero is given divine instruction on building a boat; the hero and his family are delivered from the flood; worship and sacrifice follow the flood. But the dissimilarities are much greater than the similarities. The purpose of the flood is different in the two accounts; the Babylonian gods are given to caprice and whim; the morality of the gods is so despicable that it is hardly distinguishable from that of the morally-bankrupt man. In the *Gilgamesh Epic* when Utnapishtim offered sacrifices of thanksgiving, the gods hovered around the sacrifice like flies, hardly an activity befitting deity.

These similarities, however remote, may be explained in that they have a common source, i.e., the truth. The creation story, the fall of man, the great flood, were all historical events that gave rise to variant traditions. Unger says, "Early races of men wherever they wandered took with them these earliest traditions of mankind, and in varying latitudes and climes, have modified them according to their religions and mode of thought. Modifications, as time proceeded, resulted in the corruption of the original pure tradition. The Genesis account is not only the purest, but everywhere bears the unmistakable impress of divine inspiration when compared with the extravagances and corruptions of other accounts. The biblical narrative, we may conclude, represents the original form these traditions must have assumed" (Merrill F. Unger, *Archaeology and the Old Testament*, p. 36).

One must be careful about the concept of the original pure tradition, since Moses did not write the account until ca. 1440 B.C.; and many years had transpired before God gave the inspired account. Yet, there may have been an account that passed on from Noah and his sons (cf. 6:9 and 10:1 and the meaning of the term generations which will be discussed in the commentary section; see Davis, pp. 69-72 for a full discussion).

Chronological Framework. With the popularization of the theory of evolution and the discovery of the Java man, the Peking man, and the Neanderthal man, the question of the chronological framework of the book of Genesis has become a contested issue. How is the conservative Christian to fit all the years of history asserted by L. S. B. Leakey and others (for man to evolve to his present state) into the chronology and genealogical lists of chapters 5 and 10-11? Liberal scholars do not take the chronologies seriously, but conservative scholars have advanced various means of bringing our understanding of the genealogies in line with what we know the facts to be.

There are those who believe that the names given in chapter 5 not only represent an individual but his direct line by primogeniture as well. This interpretation allows for the figures to be added end to end, instead of overlapping. Thus, when Adam is said to have lived 930 years, it is a figure used to indicate that Adam and his family or dynasty were in a position of leadership for 930 years; and then the man Seth and his family superseded Adam's governmental leadership. This method allows for a grand total of 8,227 years between the birth of Adam and the Flood.

A second interpretation is the literalist interpretation, in which there are no gaps presented between generations and the total number of years from Adam to the Flood is 1,656 years. The total number of years from the Flood to the birth of Abraham would be 290 years, making the total of 1,946 years from Adam to Abraham. This is the method used by Archbishop James Ussher, working with the genealogical tables of Genesis 5 and 10-11, wherein he computed the date of creation as 4004 B.C. and the date of Abraham a little after 2000 B.C.

It should be noted that the chronology of events from the time of creation to the early years of Abraham is extremely difficult to determine. There are at least two reasons: (1) the Bible provides no controllable statistical data that apply to the problem of absolute chronology and (2) most of the

3

events took place in the preliterate period for which we have no written documents (Davis, p. 28). This relates especially to the time period before 3000 B.C. The only guides we have are archaeological data and typological materials, and modern scholarship has properly rejected Ussher's dates for creation and the Noachic flood. One of his reasons for setting these dates was his *a priori* belief of a 2000-year cycle from Creation to Abraham, then another 2000 years from Abraham to Christ, then 2000 years from Christ to the Rapture, and then 1000 years for the Millennium. Thus, the facts themselves did not lead him to these dates.

The genealogies of chapters 5 and 11 have been regarded by many as sufficient to establish an absolute chronology; but this assumption has proved inadequate, because the genealogies of the Bible are not designed to provide such statistical information. William Henry Green's statement is foundational. "It can scarcely be necessary to adduce proof to one who has even a superficial acquaintance with the genealogies of the Bible, that these are frequently abbreviated by the omission of unimportant names. In fact, abridgment is the general rule, induced by the indisposition of the sacred writers to incumber their pages with more names than were necessary for their immediate purpose. This is so constantly the case, and the reason for it is so obvious, that the occurrence of it need create no surprise anywhere, and we are at liberty to suppose it whenever anything in the circumstances of the case favors that belief" (W. H. Green, "Primeval Chronology," *Classical Evangelical Essays in Old Testament Interpretation*, pp. 13, 14; see also Kitchen, *Ancient Orient and Old Testament*, p. 37; R. Laird Harris, *Man: God's Eternal Creation*, pp. 68-71; John C. Whitcomb and Henry M. Morris, *The Genesis Flood*, p. 474; and Allis, *The Five Books of Moses*, pp. 295-298).

If Moses had intended these genealogies to be used for chronological purposes, he probably would have provided a numerical summation at the end of each list. It should also be noted that neither Moses nor any other inspired writer deduces a chronology from these genealogies. Scripture itself nowhere computes the time that elapsed from the Creation to the Flood, or from the Flood to the descent into Egypt by Jacob and his family. But it does, however, give the time for the period from the descent into Egypt to the Exodus (Ex 12:40) and the period from the Exodus to the building of the Temple (I Kgs 6:1). In addition, if these lists were intended for chronological purposes, why are numbers that have little relation to these purposes introduced?

It should also be noted that not all of the postdiluvian patriarchs are listed in the present Hebrew text of chapter 11. According to Luke's genealogy of Mary, the name "Cainan" appears between "Salah" and "Arphaxad" (Lk 3:35-36). This one omission makes it impossible to fix the date of the Great Flood. It is quite obvious the term "son of", or the phrase translated "begat", does not always imply direct descent (father and son relationship), not even in the New Testament, Matthew 1:1. If the genealogy of chapter 11 is complete, only 292

years separate the Flood from the birth of Abraham. Shem, the son of Noah, lived for 502 years after the Flood; and on this calculation he would have outlived Abraham, along with Shelah and Eber (cf. Josh 24:2, 14-15). The Flood would have occurred ca. 2458 B.C., when in fact, writing and history go well back into the fourth millennium according to most scholars (conservative and liberal). Yet, a worldwide flood would have destroyed any writing tablets. Chapter 11, then, must have gaps of considerable magnitude; and it is equally probable that the genealogy of chapter 5 is incomplete. Therefore, it is impossible to establish a firm date for the Creation or the Flood (Davis, p. 30).

There is evidence in stratified mounds in Mesopotamia and Palestine that demonstrates an unbroken sequence of occupation as far back as 7000 B.C. The archaeologists base their calculations on stratigraphy, pottery typology, carbon 14, and certain other technical methods of dating. "Since primitive cultures apparently appeared worldwide approximately 12,000 to 10,000 B.C., the flood might have occurred sometime prior to that" (Davis, p. 31). The amount of time which elapsed between Adam and Noah is even more difficult to calculate.

Where does all of this leave the serious student of Scripture? "On one hand are the extravagant estimates of evolutionary geologists, ranging anywhere from 100,000,000 to 24,000,000 years, and on the other are far lower ones which range from 100,000 to 4,974 years. This wide range of figures makes it evident that at the present time a specific date for the origin of either the earth or man cannot be fixed with certainty" (Davis, p. 31). The only way it could, would be to adopt one of two presuppositions. The first is that of the uniformitarian geologist, that all natural processes have remained essentially uniform. If this assumption is not allowed, then all modern chemical and radiological dating techniques are suspect; and the scientist must apply other means of establishing a time sequence for earth history. The second presupposition is that the genealogies of chapters 5 and 11 are sequential and unbroken, providing a fully dependable foundation for a chronological structure. Neither of the presuppositions can be adhered to for support. "The geological record of earth history points to major catastrophes which have sufficiently interrupted natural processes to render any general, unbroken uniformitarianism untenable. And because genealogies in Scripture are notorious for their schematic arrangement and omissions, the second presupposition is equally untenable" (Davis, p. 31). But there is no problem with adopting the stance of an early and recent creation, say somewhere around 10,000 B.C., which is diametrically opposed to the evolutionary basis of the uniformitarian geologist who would make the earth millions of years old. But there is no need on the part of the conservative to capitulate to the so-called evidence of science to bring about a harmonization of Scripture and science. The Bible reveals there has been a limited uniformitarianism since the Flood; the world before that perished in the Flood.

The Days of Creation. The duration of God's creative activity has provoked no small amount of discussion among Bible interpreters. How long were the days of creation? In addition to the use of the word "Day" in 1:5, 8, 13, 19, 23, and 31, where it describes the days of creation, it is used in at least four ways in the first two chapters of Genesis. In 1:14, 16, and 18, it refers to the twelve-hour period of daylight, as opposed to night. A solar day of twenty-four hours is the subject in 1:14. There is a reference to the period of light that began with the creation of light on the first creative day in 1:5; and the final use is that of the entire, six-day creative period in 2:4. Students of Genesis have advocated four basic interpretations.

1. The first theory believed by many scholars is that the creative days of Genesis 1 were literal twenty-four-hour days. This is the normal understanding of the Genesis account. The particular expressions such as light and darkness, day and night, evening and morning, seem to require such an interpretation. Also, it should be noted that every single occurrence of the word *yōm* where it is used to summarize one of the creative days is accompanied by the numerical adjective. It is always, the evening and morning were one day (Heb *yōm 'echad*), or there was evening and there was morning, a second day (*yōm shēnī*). This is very significant, because throughout the Old Testament *yōm* is never used figuratively (that is, to refer to something other than a normal day) with the numerical adjective (see John C. Whitcomb, Jr., "The Science of Historical Geology in the Light of the Biblical Doctrine of Mature Creation," *Westminster Theological Journal, Fall, 1973* and Weston Fields, *Unformed and Unfilled,* p. 176). Also "we must assume that the seventh day was a literal day because Adam and Eve lived through it before God drove them out of the Garden. Surely, he would not have cursed the earth during the seventh day which he blessed and sanctified (2:1-3; Ex 31:12-17)" (Whitcomb, p. 68). And Exodus 20:11 seems to be very explicit when Moses records that within ". . . six days the LORD made the heaven and earth, the sea, and all that in them is. . . ." God uses this expression for a pattern of Israel's work week of six literal days and then one literal twenty-four-hour day of rest. Fields lists all of the lexical categories for the use of *yōm* in the Old Testament, and there is no support for identifying the days of Genesis as long periods of time (Fields, pp. 170-172).

2. The second theory is called the day-age or geologic day theory. It attempts to correlate the geological ages with the seven days in chapter 1. The days are interpreted metaphorically, rather than literally. Thus, the phrase "the evening and the morning" is a figure for beginning and ending. Cole says, "Evening presents the picture of the gradual completion of the work of each creative period, succeeded by a morning of renewed activity" (*Creation and Science,* p. 92). Ramm says Exodus 20:11 "simply means that the human week of seven days takes its rise from the divine week of seven creative epochs" (*Science and Scripture,* p. 214). There are several arguments used by such proponents. They say from 1:12, ". . . the earth brought forth grass, and herb yielding seed after his kind, and the tree yielding fruit . . . ," that much more time than a mere twenty-four hours is required. Secondly, they assert that since the sun was not created until the fourth day, or that the law of the limitation of solar measure was not established, so the days of creation could well have been much longer than twenty-four hours. Yet, there may well have been a rotation of the earth in relation to a light source, which would have accounted for the day-night distinction in 1:5. Hebrews 4:1-11, where the seventh day of creation is referred to as a period of indefinite length, is also cited in support of this theory. If the seventh day was an age, the first six days must also be ages, they conclude. "The mention of the creation Sabbath is proof of the symbolic character of the creation day" (Sir Robert Anderson, *Bible and Modern Criticism,* p. 124). Ramm also appeals to the "great array of geologists and theologians who accept the metaphorical interpretation of the word day" and he concludes that "the case for the literal day cannot be conclusive nor the objections to the metaphorical interpretation too serious" (p. 213).

The real fallacy of this theory is that it rests on very scanty evidence. "The lexical exility on which it is based is almost unbelievable; consequently, we must conclude that it springs from presuppositions, a fact transparent even to the casual reader. Its defenders, too, even to a greater extent than gap theorists, have been bullied by science into abandoning the *prima facie* meaning of the creation account for a more scientifically palatable (at least in their thinking) interpretation" (Fields, pp. 165-166). Many day-age theorists are also theistic evolutionists and progressive creationists.

3. The third theory contends that the days of creation were separated by long ages. Creation "need not be taken consecutively but may be understood as separated by long ages. Each day would then indicate a normal, twenty-four-hour period, by the time of the arrival of which, the major phenomena which God had been creating since the previously mentioned day, had at length come into being . . ." (J. Barton Payne, "Theistic Evolution and the Hebrew of Genesis 1-2," *Bulletin of the Evangelical Society 8 (1965),* p. 87). Urquhart observed that, with the exception of the sixth day, *yōm* has the indefinite form. As a result, he supposes the days were not consecutive, but were actually separated by long ages (*The Bible: Its Structure and Purpose,* 2:69-70). Thus, each creative day came when the events previously discussed were completed. "This viewpoint has very few adherents because it severely strains the Hebrew text. If Moses had intended to describe nonconsecutive days, it would seem he could have done so with more clarity. Also, this theory regards the days as times only of completion of divine creation, while the writer of Genesis appears to describe the beginning of creative activity as well as the completion of it on each day" (Davis, p. 54).

4. A fourth theory upholds the Creation as a series of visions. It contends that "creation was revealed in six days, not performed in six days. . . . that the six days are pictorial-revelatory days, not literal days nor age days. The days are means of communicating to man the great fact that God is creator, and that He is creator of all" (Ramm, p. 222). Advocates of this position hold to the fact that as God revealed the future by visions, it is also logical that He revealed the unknown past by visions.

There are at least three good arguments against this view. There is no linguistic evidence to indicate that chapter 1 is a series of visions, rather than a historical narrative. Exodus 20:11 contradicts this theory when it relates that God "made heaven and earth, the sea, and all that in them is," not that He revealed His creation of heaven and earth. And finally, apart from the questionable example of Daniel 7:1ff., past events are normally revealed in literal, historical narratives. Visions are not used.

The Great Deluge. While there are many scholars who believe that the Noachic flood was simply a local phenomenon, it is a better scientific, theological, and biblical position to believe that the Flood in Noah's day was a universal, globe-encircling watery disaster. Many modern scholars have abandoned a global flood for a local one due to the catastrophism which is implicit in a universal flood. This is thought to be out of harmony with the current views of the earth's origin and early history. Some argue for a flood confined to the Mesopotamian valley which killed all animal and human life outside the ark. This is based upon the assumption, which is impossible to defend, that man and animals never migrated beyond that valley. Ramm argues that animal and human life were more widespread than the Flood and that it was eliminated only where the Flood occurred. Ramm says in his work *The Christian View of Science and Scripture*, that "the entire record must be interpreted phenomenally. If the flood is local, though spoken of in universal terms, so the destruction of man is local though spoken of in universal terms. The record neither affirms nor denies that man existed beyond the Mesopotamian valley. Noah certainly was not a preacher of righteousness to the peoples of Africa, of India, of China or of America, places where there is evidence for the existence of man many thousands of years before the flood (10,000 to 15,000 years in America)" (pp. 239-240).

The terms that tend to be indicative of universal effects of the Flood are regarded by Ramm as restrictive, or local, in extent. He also contends that the universality of flood traditions does not prove a universal flood. He contends that these may only be local and unrelated flood accounts. Ramm asserts "there is no known geological data to support those who defend a universal flood" (p. 243). "The principal concern of those advocating a local flood is to escape the geological implications of a universal flood. That the language could apply to a universal deluge they readily admit. They contend, however, that since the terms need not be universally applied, the account should be conformed to geological opinion" (Davis, p. 124).

Words such as *all, every,* and *whole* may be used in a restricted sense as in Luke 2:1; but it should be acknowledged just as readily that they may also have universal connotations, as is also obvious in Matthew 28:18-20. Thus, it is clear that the context, both general and immediate, must be studied before a meaning is to be rendered. Whitcomb and Morris cite at least seven good reasons that indicate a universal flood in *The Genesis Flood*, pp. 1-35 and 116ff.

1. *The depth of the Flood.* According to 7:19, the flood waters covered ". . . all the high hills, that were under the whole heaven. . . ." All the mountains were covered, and these were covered by at least 15 cubits of water, or about 23 feet, which was the approximate draft of the ark. Since water seeks its own level, even if the mountains were only 5000 to 6000 feet high, the whole earth would have been covered.

2. *The duration of the Flood.* It is indicated that the waters prevailed on the whole earth for five months and that it was seven more months before Noah could land and get out of the ark in the mountains of Ararat. Surely, a flood that lasts 371 days is a universal flood.

3. *The geology of the Flood.* Scripture relates the fact that it not only rained, but according to 7:11 ". . . all the fountains of the great deep . . ." were ". . . broken up. . . ." *Tehōm* most likely refers to the immense subterranean and suboceanic foundations upon which the then known world rested. This geological phenomenon probably lasted 150 days (cf. 8:2).

4. *The size of the ark.* The ark had 95,700 square feet of deck space and was certainly not designed for a local flood. Its total volume would have been at least 1,396,000 cubic feet, or at least 522 modern railroad stock cars.

5. *The need for an ark of this magnitude.* This would certainly indicate the universality of the Flood. If the Flood were local, why would an ark be necessary at all? Why couldn't God have told Noah to take a camel ride down the road to a safe place before the Flood came?

6. *The testimony of the Apostle Peter.* In II Peter 3:3-7, the apostle gives witness to one of the most important truths relating the Flood with the Creation account and the revelation of a final, universal judgment. "The apostle Peter answered skeptics concerning the end times by pointing to two events which undeniably occurred and which could not be explained by naturalistic uniformitarianism: creation ('there were heavens from old, and an earth . . . by the word of God', ASV) and the flood ('the world that then was, being overflowed with water, perished', ASV). Peter specifically compared the flood with the second coming of Christ and the final destruction of the world. Since creation and the final destruction of the world are universal, the flood of Noah must also have been universal" (Davis, p. 125).

7. *The purpose of the Flood.* The Flood was used to judge the sinfulness of the whole human race (cf. 6:5-7, 11-13). Nothing but a universal flood would have fulfilled this purpose. God also covenanted with Noah that He would not destroy this world with another such flood. Yet, there have been many local floods where individuals have perished, thus if the Flood had been a local one, then God

has broken His word. But if the Flood was universal, then He has not broken His word. Finally, the Lord Jesus clearly stated that all men were destroyed in the Flood according to Luke 17:26-30. In light of the longevity of the pre-Flood patriarchs (ch. 5) and the known settlement patterns (which are widespread), it is most likely that before the Flood man was spread out geographically, so that only a universal flood would have accomplished God's purpose.

OUTLINE

COMMENTARY

I. THE EARLY BEGINNINGS. 1:1-11:32.

A. The Creation. 1:1-2:25.

IN the beginning God created the heaven and the earth.

1:1. In the beginning. Most of the controversy concerning 1:1 centers around the translation and grammatical import of the first two words in the Hebrew text. The first word (Heb *berē'shīt*) is rendered as the above translation. If *berē'shīt* is in the absolute state and *bara'* (**created**) is a finite verb, then the translation is as it has been traditionally rendered, an independent clause: **In the beginning God created.** This translation is the basis for the view of *creatio ex nihilo*. If, on the other hand, *berē'shīt* is to be understood as being in the construct state, it would be translated as a dependent temporal clause, implying the existence of matter related in verse 2: When God began to create, or In the beginning when God created. Rashi, a well-known Jewish scholar (ca.

7

A.D. 1105), was one of the first to propose the dependent clause translation. There are basically two main differences in interpretation among those who take this stance. First, there are those who follow Rashi when he considers verse 1 as the *protasis:* When God began to create (or In the beginning of God's creation/creating). Then, verse 2 is the *parenthesis:* the earth being/was. . . . Finally, verse 3 is the *apodosis:* God said, Let there be light. Adherents to this view include Ewald, Albright, Eissfeldt, Orlinsky, Speiser, Unger, and Bauer. A slightly different translation, but one which is still based upon the construct state of *berēʾshīt,* is proposed by the Jewish scholar Abraham Ibn Ezra (ca. A.D. 1167). In contrast to Rashi, who considered verse 3 the main clause, Ibn Ezra considered verse 2 to be the main clause. Thus the following form would be given to the verses: the *protasis* would be 1:1: When God began to create, and the *apodosis* would be 1:2: the earth was void and without form. The implications of translating 1:1 as a dependent clause should be made known to all Christians. If this translation is adopted, it means that *creatio ex nihilo* is forever removed from Scripture. "If this exegesis is correct, the writer teaches a dualism. He thinks of a dark watery chaos existing before creation began, and gives it the mythical name *Tehom* (the Deep) which is evidently the Hebrew equivalent of the Babylonian Tiamat" ("Creation," *Encyclopaedia of Religion and Ethics,* 1928, III). This extreme view represents most liberal opinion, even though it does not represent the ideas of all who defend the dependent clause interpretation. In addition to the exclusion of *creatio ex nihilo* from Genesis, this interpretation presents another great problem. The problem is that it has the earth in existence at the time of God's creating. "The only solution to this (assuming one accepts the dependent clause view) is to resort, as Unger has done, to the proposition of the gap theorists by which all the acts of Genesis 1:3 and following are made to refer to a recreation or 'refashioning' the earth and its sidereal heavens at a much later period in geological history" (Fields, p. 161 citing *Unger's Bible Handbook,* p. 37 and his article in *Bibliotheca Sacra,* 115 in January of 1958, entitled, "Rethinking the Genesis Creation Account"). Actually, Unger makes 1:1 refer to the period of refashioning. So, Unger places a gap, complete with the fall of Satan, before 1:1. Speiser also recognizes the problems of translating this as a dependent clause, but still translates: When God set about to create heaven and earth, the earth being a formless waste. . . . (*Genesis,* p. 12). Whereas von Rad rejects the dependent clause interpretation, insisting that while both may be syntactically possible, they are not theologically (*Genesis,* p. 46). "In our opinion, the only way to escape the pantheistic notion of the eternality of matter and still not have Genesis 1:1 refer to the original creation, is to put some sort of a gap before Genesis 1:1 as Unger has done. But other Scripture seems to disallow this view, as we now proceed to show" (Fields, pp. 161-162). Exodus 20:11 and 31:17 certainly define the chronological limits of interpretation and translation for both 1:1 and 1:2. Moses wrote both Genesis and Exodus; and he said in Exodus 20:11, ". . . in six days the LORD made heaven and earth, the sea, and all that in them is, and rested on the seventh day. . . ." Certainly, this confines the limits of creation. Everything had to happen within those six days! It is the whole universe and everything in it that the verse speaks of when it says ". . . heaven and earth. . . ." The Hebrews did not have one word for universe, so they used this expression. "It is this universe and all its contents which were created in six days. God, through Moses, could not have been more explicit!" (Fields, p. 163). It is not a question of how God could have done it, but of how He says He did it. **God.** The Hebrew word for God is *ʾelōhīm,* a masculine plural noun that emphasizes His majestic power and glory. The noun's root is generally agreed to mean power, strength, glory. The Amarna tablets (ca. 1375 B.C.) have this same type of plural used when vassal kings addressed the Pharaoh of Egypt, indicating his majesty and power, or his being the summation of deity. Thus, it is not explicit that at this time this form refers to the Trinity, which is basically a New Testament revelation. Also, the term does not reflect polytheism, as the verb is a third masculine singular form. "Implicit in this verse are important statements concerning God's nature and character, statements which refute at least six fundamental heresies. The first is atheism, the view that God does not exist. The Bible offers no philosophical argument for the existence of God; it assumes His existence and views everything in the light of that assumption. The second is polytheism. The singular form of the key verb indicates that the Hebrews believed in one God and not many. There is no evidence that Israel's religion evolved from animism through polytheism and henotheism before it reached ethical monotheism. Third, this verse opposes a radical materialism which holds matter to be eternal. Without preexisting material God brought the earth—that is, matter—into existence. Fourth, since God is clearly distinguished from His creation, this verse clearly denies pantheism. Fifth, the supernatural origin of the earth and the universe refutes naturalism; God is the Architect and Creator of all that exists. Finally, the uniqueness of this concept of origins in ancient literature makes untenable the position that special revelation is nonexistent or impossible. Human reason and inquiry, while valid, are seriously limited; the problem of origins, therefore, is best solved in the light of biblical truth" (Davis, p. 42). **Created.** The Hebrew verb *bara'* is the best Hebrew word to convey the idea of an absolute creation, or *creatio ex nihilo*. In the *qal* stem, this verb is employed exclusively in the Old Testament for God's activity; and the subject of the verb is never man. "God is said to create 'the wind' (Amos 4:13), 'a clean heart' (Ps 51:10), and 'new heavens and a new earth' (Isa 65:17). Genesis 1 emphasizes three great beginnings, each initiated by God (cf. 1:21, 27)" (Davis, p. 40). Another Hebrew verb used interchangeably with *bara'*, is *'asah,* meaning essentially "to do or make." Many writers reject this last statement, but the evidence is overwhelming. Notice that in 1:1 it states that God **created** (*bara'*) the heavens and the earth, while in Exodus 20:11 and Nehemiah 9:6 it is related that God *made* (*'asah*) the heaven(s) and the earth (see also 2:2, 3, 4; Ex 34:10; Job 9:9; Prov 8:26; Ps 95:5; 100:3; Isa 41:20; 43:7; 45:7; an even clearer example is found in 1:21, 25). In spite of this, some interpreters continue to maintain that *'asah* can refer "only to the reforming of previously existing material" (Davis, p. 41 citing Barnhouse, *The New Scofield Reference Bible*). Proponents of the gap theory have a special interest in maintaining the distinction between these two verbs, but the issue will be discussed later. A third Hebrew verb is employed in 2:7, where God is said to have **formed** (*yatsar*) man out of the dust of the ground. **The heaven and the earth.** This is a reference to the universe. **Heaven** may refer to the three heavens of Scripture (cf. II Cor 12:2): the atmospheric heaven, the heaven of outer space, and the realm of angels. Apparently, the angels were created at the very beginning of the first day of creation week; for they were already on hand to rejoice at the creation of the earth (Job 38:7).

2 And the earth was without form, and void; and darkness *was* upon the face of the deep. And the Spirit of God moved upon the face of the waters.

2. And the earth was without form, and void. Some understand a gap of an indeterminate period of time between verses 1 and 2 and translate "became" rather than "was". The reference is to the traditional Gap Theory described as follows: "In the far distant, dateless past God created a perfect heaven and perfect earth. Satan was ruler of the earth which was peopled by a race of 'men' without any souls. Eventually, Satan, who dwelled in a garden of Eden composed of minerals (Ezk 28:13), rebelled by desiring to become like God (Isa 14). Because of Satan's fall, sin entered the universe and brought on the earth God's judgment

9

in the form of a flood (indicated by the water of 1:2), and then a global ice-age when the light and heat from the sun were somehow removed. All the plant, animal, and human fossils upon the earth today date from this 'Lucifer's flood' and do not bear any genetic relationship with the plants, animals, and fossils living upon the earth today. The biblical proofs for this theory are as follows: The verb *hāyᵉtâ* in Genesis 1:2 should be translated 'became' or 'had become,' not 'was.' The words *tōhû wābōhû* (without form and void) represent a sinful, and, therefore, not an original state of the earth. Furthermore, Isaiah 45:18 states that God did not make the earth '*tōhû*,' so the earth which Genesis 1:2 describes as *tōhû* could not possibly be the originally created one. There must be a sharp distinction, particularly in Genesis 1 and 2, between the Hebrew verb '*asa bara*' ('made' and 'created'). The darkness of Genesis 1:2 represents an evil state since God is light. This state of darkness, therefore, must have been a result of judgment, not perfect creation. God told Adam to replenish the earth (Gen 1:28), so it must have been filled previously. The Garden of Eden in Ezekiel 28 is different from the one in Genesis so that the Genesis Eden must be the second one" (Fields, pp. 7-8).

The vast ages of the geologic timetable are thought to have occurred during this interval, so that the fossils, plants and animals that are found in the crust of the earth today are relics of the originally perfect world that was destroyed before the six literal days of creation (or, better, re-creation) as recorded in 1:3-31. The Gap Theory, or Ruin-reconstruction theory, has been widely accepted among evangelical Christians. The motive has been to harmonize the vast time periods of earth history which are demanded by uniformitarian geologists. Chalmers (ca. 1780-1847) popularized the theory; it was elaborated by Pember ca. 1870, and then canonized by the *Scofield Reference Bible*. The 1917 edition supported the theory in chapter 1, and the 1967 edition only mentioned it in Isaiah 45. Field's work is an excellent treatise designed to demolish, once and for all, of the above assertions. It should be read by every concerned Christian. Suffice it to say, 1:2*a* is a noun clause used circumstantially, making or expressing the circumstances concomitant to the principal statement. The translation is best conveyed by: "Now, the earth was without form and void."

The original Gap Theory can be proved or disproved merely on the basis of what type of clauses these are in verse 2. This means that 1:2 is a description of the earth as it was created originally, not how it became at a time subsequent to creation. The circumstantial noun clause and the *waw* disjunctive also demonstrate this point. The Septuagint indicates the disjunctive by *de* in 1:2; 2:6, 10, and 12. In all four cases it describes the preceding conditions. In other words, the initial creation was formless and empty, a condition soon remedied. The phrase means that at this point in God's creative activity the earth was yet unfashioned and uninhabited (note Isa 45:18 where it says, ". . . he created it not in vain, *tōhû*, he formed it to be inhabited"). **And darkness was upon the face of the deep.** Darkness is not always a symbol of evil in the Bible. Psalm 104:19-24 makes it quite clear that physical darkness (the absence of visible light) is not to be considered inherently evil or as the result of divine judgment. It conveys the fact that God makes the darkness and the night for animals to find their prey. The deep is not a reference to the mythological Babylonian monster Tiamat, as has been alleged, but simply waters. **And the Spirit of God moved upon the face of the waters.** Recent interpreters have suggested that the verse ought to be translated, "An awesome wind sweeping over the water" (cf. Speiser, p. 3 and p. 5 note 2). But the context demands otherwise. It seems to be a reference to the third person of the Godhead (cf. Job 26:13; Ps 104:30). The Spirit is the subject of the verb, which is an active

3 ¶And God said, Let there be light: and there was light.

4 And God saw the light, that *it was* good: and God divided the light from the darkness.

5 And God called the light Day, and the darkness he called Night. And the evening and the morning were the first day.

participle that means "hovering over" (cf. Deut 32:11). Thus, the Spirit of God is seen hovering over, protecting, and participating in the creation of God the Father. John 1:1-3 and Colossians 1:16 make it clear that more than one person of the Godhead was involved in creation.

3-5. And God said. The jussive form of the Hebrew verb is very significant in Genesis 1 as it functions as a third person command (cf. vss. 6, 9, 14). This suggests a divine plan and purpose for the creation, not the result of mere accident or chance. Neither is it seen to be self-sustaining or self-perpetuating. It also demonstrates God's power. God merely spoke creation into existence by the word of His mouth. The psalmist says, ". . . he spake, and it was done; he commanded, and it stood fast" (Ps 33:9). We are reminded in Hebrews that "Through faith we understand that the worlds were framed by the word of God . . ." (Heb 11:3). Each of the six days begins with the announcement, **Let there be light: and there was light.** This light is not the sun, which was created on the fourth day according to verse 16; it must have been some fixed light source outside the earth. In reference to that light, the rotating earth passed through a day-night cycle. Our Lord wrought miracles while He was on earth through His words, and in almost every case the miracle occurred instantaneously after He spoke; Mark 8:25 is the only recorded exception. Whatever the light was, **God saw the light, that it was good.** Therefore, He divided the light from the darkness and called the light **Day,** and the darkness **he called Night.** The word **day** is used in three different senses in Genesis: (1) a twelve-hour period of light (1:5, 14, 16, 18); (2) a twenty-four-hour period; and (3) the entire creative week (2:4); the qualifying phrase, **And the evening and the morning were the first day,** indicates beyond any doubt that the word, as it is used here, is a twenty-four-hour period of time (see Introduction).

6 ¶And God said, Let there be a firmament in the midst of the waters, and let it divide the waters from the waters.

7 And God made the firmament, and divided the waters which *were* under the firmament from the waters which *were* above the firmament: and it was so.

8 And God called the firmament Heaven. And the evening and the morning were the second day.

6-8. On the second day of God's creative activity, He said, **Let there be a firmament in the midst of the waters, and let it divide the waters from the waters.** The word for **firmament** comes from a verb that means "to beat, stamp, beat out, and spread out." The noun in this instance is best rendered by an expanse. Whitcomb and Morris suggest that God suspended a vast body of water in vapor form over the earth, protecting it from the destructive rays of the sun (p. 229). This would accomplish two things: it would provide a means for the longevity attested to in chapter 5, and it would also provide a water source for the Flood in 6-9. This theory is an attempt to explain the tropical conditions that existed on the early earth. One must note that the term **firmament** in verse 8 must include the area above the canopy, or this suspended vapor body, as well as below it. This must be so, because in verse 17 God set the sun and moon **in the firmament of the heaven to give light upon the earth,** seemingly the same as in verse 8 when it says, **And God called the firmament Heaven.** With a second **evening** and **morning,** another day of creative activity was ended.

9 ¶And God said, Let the waters under the heaven be gathered together unto one place, and let the dry *land* appear: and it was so.

10 And God called the dry *land* Earth; and the gathering together of the waters called he Seas: and God saw that *it was* good.

11 And God said, Let the earth bring forth grass, the herb yielding seed, *and* the fruit tree yielding fruit after his kind, whose seed *is* in itself, upon the earth: and it was so.

12 And the earth brought forth grass, *and* herb yielding seed after his kind, and the tree yielding fruit, whose seed

9-13. On the third day dry land appeared, initiated by the spoken word of God. The waters under the heaven were told to gather into one place in order to **let the dry land appear.** The word **land** is in italics because it does not appear in the original text. **The dry** (Heb *hayabashah*) is the common term used to describe solid ground (cf. Ex 14:16, 22, 29; 15:19; Josh 4:22; Jon 1:9, 13; 2:10). At the voice of God's command, the waters obeyed; **and it was so.** Not only did God call the dry land into existence; but He also named it **Earth,** and the waters He named **Seas.** The dry land was called **Earth** (Heb *'erets*) because that word bears a meaning which may refer to that which is lower. It is in opposition to the firmament above, literally the heights of verse 8. The **Seas** (Heb *yamīm*) is used in the very broad sense to include every body of water, even lakes and rivers (cf. Ps

11

was in itself, after his kind: and God saw that *it was* good.

13 And the evening and the morning were the third day.

14 ¶And God said, Let there be lights in the firmament of the heaven to divide the day from the night; and let them be for signs, and for seasons, and for days, and years:

15 And let them be for lights in the firmament of the heaven to give light upon the earth: and it was so.

16 And God made two great lights; the greater light to rule the day, and the lesser light to rule the night: *he made* the stars also.

17 And God set them in the firmament of the heaven to give light upon the earth,

18 And to rule over the day and over the night, and to divide the light from the darkness: and God saw that *it was* good.

19 And the evening and the morning were the fourth day.

33:7-9). Von Rad notes that "in the ancient oriental view the act of giving a name meant, above all, the exercise of a sovereign right (cf. II Kgs 23:34; 24:17). Thus the naming of this and all subsequent creative works once more expresses graphically God's claim of lordship over the creatures" (*Genesis*, p. 53). **And God saw that it was good.** The word contains less an aesthetic judgment than the designation of purpose and correspondence. It resembles, therefore, though with much more restraint, the content of Psalm 104:31; Psalm 104 tells not so much of the beauty as of the marvelous purpose and order of the Creation (note the significance of this in 2:19).

In association with the creation of the dry ground, God commanded, **Let the earth bring forth grass, the herb yielding seed, and the fruit tree yielding fruit after his kind, whose seed is in itself.** This was the second work of God on the third day. It was again initiated by the divinely spoken word, **And God said.** "The expression 'let the earth bring forth' does not allow, as some have contended, for evolution. On the contrary, the biblical order of trees before marine organisms contradicts the concept of trees evolving from marine organisms" (Davis, p. 63). Whitcomb and Morris assert that according to verse 12 God produced a functioning and mature creation. The plants were created as mature, self-reproducing biological units with their own seed. This would give an appearance of age, both to the plants, and to man (pp. 232-233). Each family could reproduce only **after his kind.** There are fixed boundaries beyond which reproductive variations cannot go; but it is impossible to know whether **kind** is to be equated with families, genera, or some other category of biological classification. Moses uses the term **kind** in thirty out of the thirty-one times it is used in the Old Testament. Payne says that, "while *mîn* does not . . . require the separate creation of God of each species, it does require at least the separate creation of families within orders" ("The Concept of 'Kinds' in Scripture," *Journal of the American Scientific Affiliation*, 10 (1958)). Chapter 1 verse 12 records that God's command was completely obeyed by His creation: **The earth brought forth grass, and herb yielding seed after his kind, and the tree yielding fruit . . . and God saw that it was good.** Thus, at the close of these miraculous events, **the evening and the morning were the third day.**

14-19. These verses record the formation of the sun, moon, and stars on the fourth day. Here again is a reversal of order from that proposed by the evolutionists. According to Genesis, God created the earth on the first day, and then the sun on day number four. According to the evolutionist, the earth was thrown off from the sun or bore some other relationship to the sun. Nonetheless, **God said, Let there be lights in the firmament of the heaven to divide the day from the night.** The threefold purpose of placing the light in the firmament was: (1) **To divide the day from the night;** (2) **for signs;** and (3) **for seasons.** The light-dark sequence on the earth is now dependent on the sun, instead of the **light** created on the first day. Yet, some would distinguish between *bara'* and *'asah* so as to say that at this point in time God merely instituted the sun, moon, and stars in the firmament to function in a particular way relative to earth. Yet, there is no distinction between these two verbs; nor if they were only to appear at this time, having been created on day one, Moses would have used the verb to **appear** as he did in verse 9. The **signs** are not those frequently appealed to by modern astrologers, but rather related to faith (Ps 8:1-4; Rom 1:14-20), weather (Mt 16:2, 3), prophecy (Mt 2:2; Lk 21:25), and judgment (Joel 2:30-31; Mt 24:29).

And God made two great lights; the greater light to rule the day, and the lesser light to rule the night. It is obvious that the writer is speaking from his vantage point here on earth, or from the standpoint of astronomy. The sun and moon are clearly not the greater lights of the universe. The language of appearance is common in the Old Testament and is in no way unscientific or prescientific. The moon is merely a light reflector, and the sun is only a medium-sized star. Yet, as the writer would gaze into the sky of the ancient Orient, he would note the sun dominated those skies by day and the moon by night; and his description of that phenomenon is perfectly acceptable. **And the evening and the morning were the fourth day.**

20 ¶And God said, Let the waters bring forth abundantly the moving creature that hath life, and fowl *that* may fly above the earth in the open firmament of heaven.

21 And God created great whales, and every living creature that moveth, which the waters brought forth abundantly, after their kind, and every winged fowl after his kind: and God saw that *it was* good.

22 And God blessed them, saying, Be fruitful, and multiply, and fill the waters in the seas, and let fowl multiply in the earth.

23 And the evening and the morning were the fifth day.

20-23. On the fifth day God created the fish and the fowl. Again, He brought them forth by His mere command, **Let the waters bring forth abundantly the moving creature that hath life, and fowl that may fly above the earth.** This command should not imply that the waters themselves produced marine life; but at the command of God, the existing waters suddenly teemed with swimming creatures. The translation is somewhat misleading; a literal rendering is: Let the waters swarm with swarms of living creatures. Skinner said, "More probably the sense is simply *teem with*, indicating the place or element in which the swarming creatures abound" (*Genesis*, p. 27). This verse also implies that aquatic life and fowl appeared simultaneously. Such a statement contradicts the evolutionary sequence that reptiles must have appeared before birds and thus functions as another nail in the coffin of evolutionary theory.

Specifically, **God created great whales,** the largest animals that ever lived, including the great extinct reptilian dinosaurs. They are warm-blooded mammals. Scripture completely contradicts the theory of evolution, which claims that the first animals in the oceans were sub-microscopic, single-celled creatures. In addition to this, evolutionists claim that whales had to evolve from four-legged land mammals, which in turn had to evolve from cold-blooded marine creatures. A better rendering of **whales** would be great sea monsters (Heb *hatannînim hagedōlîm*). This would include other great fish as well as whales. It is used to describe the serpent (Ex 7:9-10, 12), the dragon (Isa 51:9; Ezk 29:3), and the sea-monster (Ps 148:7). All kinds of marine creatures and each **winged fowl** were said to have been brought forth abundantly **after his kind.**

God blessed these forms of marine life and fowl and commanded them saying, **Be fruitful, and multiply, and fill the waters in the seas, and let fowl multiply in the earth** (cf. vs. 28). With that blessing, and the passing of another evening and morning, the close of God's fifth day of creation was concluded.

24 ¶And God said, Let the earth bring forth the living creature after his kind, cattle, and creeping thing, and beast of the earth after his kind: and it was so.

25 And God made the beast of the earth after his kind, and cattle after their kind, and every thing that creepeth upon the earth after his kind: and God saw that *it was* good.

24-25. And God said, Let the earth bring forth the living creature. On this sixth day of creation God formed all the terrestrial animals. These included **cattle,** as representative of all four-footed beasts (cf. Gen 47:18; Ex 13:12), every **creeping thing,** including all kinds of insects (cf. Lev 11:20-23), and **beast of the earth,** i.e., the wild, roving, carnivorous beasts of the forest. Once again, each of these three orders was to produce only **after his kind.**

In this verse is a latent proof that the days of Genesis were literal twenty-four-hour days. The flowering plants were created on the third day, but the insects were not until the sixth day. If there were millions of years encompassed in, or between, each of these days, how could these flowering plants have survived without the insects to pollinate? In fact, how could they have survived until the fourth day, during which the sun was created, if these two **days** were separated by millions of years? When God completed the creation of the cattle, the creeping things, and the beasts of the earth, He **saw that it was good** and was pleased.

26 ¶And God said, Let us make man in our image, after our likeness: and let them have dominion over the fish of the sea, and over the fowl of the air, and over the cattle, and over all the earth,

26-28. As the creative activity of the sixth day continues, God brings His creation to a grand finale. **And God said, Let us make man in our image.** The **us** has been a subject of no small debate. Some of the explanations have included: (1) a reference to polytheism; (2) an indication of the Trinity; (3) a plural of

13

and over every creeping thing that creepeth upon the earth.

27 So God created man in his *own* image, in the image of God created he him; male and female created he them.

28 And God blessed them, and God said unto them, Be fruitful, and multiply, and replenish the earth, and subdue it: and have dominion over the fish of the sea, and over the fowl of the air, and over every living thing that moveth upon the earth.

29 ¶And God said, Behold, I have given you every herb bearing seed, which *is* upon the face of all the earth, and every tree, in the which *is* the fruit of a tree yielding seed; to you it shall be for meat.

30 And to every beast of the earth, and to every fowl of the air, and to every thing that creepeth upon the earth, wherein *there is* life, *I have given* every green herb for meat: and it was so.

31 And God saw every thing that he had made, and, behold, *it was* very

deliberation; (4) a plural of majesty; (5) a plural of the fulness of attributes and powers; and (6) God addressing angelic beings in heaven. Keil and Delitzsch are most likely right as they "regard it as *pluralis majestatis*—an interpretation which comprehends in its deepest and most intensive form (God speaking of Himself and with Himself in the plural number, not *reverentiae causa*, but with reference to the fullness of the divine powers and essences which He possesses) the truth that lies at the foundation of the trinitarian view, viz., that the potencies concentrated in the absolute Divine Being are something more than powers and attributes of God. . ." (*Genesis I*, p. 62). The **image** and the **likeness** are to be taken as synonymous terms (Feinberg, "The Image of God," *Bibliotheca Sacra* 129 (1972) p. 237). They are interchangeable in 5:3. It is not a reference to God's physical appearance, for God is non-corporeal. Jacob prefers the Lordship idea, while Eichdrodt believes it refers to the Personhood or Self-conscious Being concept. Ryrie almost combines both, indicating that man was created in a natural and moral likeness to God. When he sinned, he lost the moral likeness, which was his sinlessness. But at the same time, he still retains the natural likeness of intellect, emotions, and will (cf. Gen 9:6; Jas 3:9). The moral likeness is presently being formed in every believer who allows God's Spirit to conform him to the image of God's Son by His Spirit (cf. Rom 8:28-29; II Cor 3:18; Eph 4:24; Col 3:10).

And let them have dominion indicates that from the moment of his creation man was fully capable of exercising control over his environment. It did not take millions of years for man to evolve in his search for self-identity and self-consciousness, for the dominion was the direct consequence of being created in the image of God. Man was created with dominion over all living creatures (vs. 26). **Male and female** were both created in the image of God, indicating an equality of position with reference to the image. Man was also **blessed** by God and commanded to **Be fruitful, and multiply, and replenish the earth.** These three commands involve procreation, the union of man and woman to populate the earth (cf. 9:1; 11:8, 9; Isa 45:18). **Replenish** would be better rendered as **fill the earth,** indicating the first time. It cannot be used in support of the re-fashioning of an already judged earth, for the lexicon indicates it always means to fill something the first time, not a refilling, as the Ruin-constructionists or Gap theorists may assert. Man was also commanded to **subdue** the earth. The verb means, to tread upon. This implies a degree of sovereignty, control, and direction over nature (cf. Ps 8:6). With the fall of man in chapter 3 came a curse upon the ground and the animal kingdom; thus, man's control is not what Adam's was before his sin. In 2:15 God put Adam in the garden and commanded him **to dress it and to keep it.** From the very beginning it was God's plan that man work and be a fully responsible steward of God's creation. "This sublime creature, with his unbelievable privileges and heavy responsibilities, was to live and move in kingly fashion" (Yates, "Genesis," *The Wycliffe Bible Commentary*, p. 4).

29-31. In conclusion, God gave to man **every herb bearing seed,** and **every tree, in the which is the fruit of a tree yielding seed** for man to draw his sustenance. The word **every** is indicative of the rich bounty bestowed (cf. 2:16). If 9:3-4 be held at the side of this explanation, the contrast implies that animal food was not permitted. Three classes of animal life were given vegetation for eating as well: the beasts of the earth, the fowl of the air, and the creeping things upon the earth. **And God saw every thing that he had made, and, behold, it was very good.** Not just good, but exceedingly good. This statement makes it impossible to believe that the earth had already fallen under the control of Satan or that the planet was covered with the fossil remains of a pre-Adamic race that had fallen. This is the seventh

good. And the evening and the morning were the sixth day.

CHAPTER 2

THUS the heavens and the earth were finished, and all the host of them.

2 And on the seventh day God ended his work which he had made; and he rested on the seventh day from all his work which he had made.

3 And God blessed the seventh day, and sanctified it: because that in it he had rested from all his work which God created and made.

4 ¶These *are* the generations of the heavens and of the earth when they were created, in the day that the LORD God made the earth and the heavens,

5 And every plant of the field before it was in the earth, and every herb of the field before it grew: for the LORD God had not caused it to rain upon the earth, and *there was* not a man to till the ground.

6 But there went up a mist from the earth, and watered the whole face of the ground.

7 And the LORD God formed man *of* the dust of the ground, and breathed into his nostrils the breath of life; and man became a living soul.

time the word **good** is used in this portion of the narrative. God simply surveyed the six days of His creative activity and noted how exceedingly wonderful His creation was. **And the evening and the morning were the sixth day.** Thus ended the creation of God.

2:1-3. Thus the heavens and the earth were finished, and all the host of them. The elaborateness and completeness of God's finished work is emphasized by **all the host of them.** Nothing new has been created since the sixth day; note the first law of thermodynamics, that this is a closed continuum. **Host** may refer to stars (Neh 9:6) or angels (I Kgs 22:19), but here it is probably simply a reference to all the things that God created. Then God **rested.** We should not conceive of God's rest on the seventh day as a necessary assumption of a posture of quiet repose because of the sheer exhaustion of His six days of creative work. The verb means to cease or to desist from work in this case. To say that God rested is an anthropomorphism, a description of God's activity in terms conducive to man's understanding. The omnipotent God who ". . . **fainteth not, neither is weary . . .**" (Isa 40:28) did not cease from His labors on the seventh day because He needed a rest. The Hebrew word is *shabat*, the name of the day that was later given to Israel as a time of cessation from normal activities (Ex 16:29; 20:10-11; Deut 5:15; Jer 17:21; Amos 8:5). **And God blessed the seventh day, and sanctified it.** This must have been a twenty-four-hour period in analogy with the previous six and the testimony of Exodus 20:11. God has been engaged in the **work** of providence since the creation week (Jn 5:17, ". . . My Father worketh hitherto and I work"); and there is no clear evidence (the testimony of Scripture) that God commanded man to observe the Sabbath until the days of Moses. Only 8:10-12 and 29:27-28, with 29:30, give a reference to a seven-day week. It was just before the giving of the Ten Commandments that God prepared Israel for the Sabbath law by permitting them only six days to gather manna (Ex 16:23).

4-7. These are the generations. This is the first of ten section headings in Genesis (cf. 5:1; 6:9; 10:1; 11:10; 11:27; 25:12; 25:19; 36:1; 37:2). The term **generations** actually is better rendered as "histories of," and the phrase is foundational to the structure of the book. It is a reference to earlier accounts that were passed on by believers and finally employed by Moses under guidance of God Himself for inscripturation. We have no way of knowing how much was actually used in the Genesis account; but in 5:1 there is a reference to the **book of the generations of Adam,** which certainly demands a written record. Leupold says, "It never tells how things or persons came into being. It tells what happened after such things or such persons had appeared on the scene" (*Genesis*, p. 110). Kaiser relates, "This could well indicate the author's free admission of his dependence upon sources and lists, just as the writers of the Old Testament historical books give us a veritable string of sources which they consulted as they moved from one historical period to another. Particularly instructive is the appearance of this identical formula at the end of the book of Ruth, which also gives us a list of ten generations and brings the reader down to the writer's own day, i.e., the Davidic era. One should compare Luke's historical and literary method as he began to write his Gospel under the revelation and inspiration of the Triune God (Lk 1:1-4)" (*NPOT*, p. 60). It is an after-the-fact record of the lives of those who grace the pages of the book of Genesis.

In verse 4b it is recorded **in the day that the LORD God made the earth and the heavens.** Here is the first mention of the name for God, **the LORD.** Literally, it is YHWH (probably pronounced *Yahweh*), the most significant name for God in the Old Testament. Its use so early in Genesis does not indicate a separate creation account using a source document J, based on the critic's misinterpretation of Exodus 6:3. Rather, it is now being employed in contrast to the *'Elōhīm* of chapter 1 (the powerful God) to indicate its twofold meaning: (1) the active, self-existent One (since the word is connected with the verb meaning "to be") (Ex 3:14) and (2) Israel's Redeemer (Ex 6:6). "The name occurs 6,823 times in the O.T. and is especially associated with God's holiness (Lev 11:44-45), His hatred of sin (6:3-7), and His gracious provision of redemption (Isa 53:1, 5, 6, 10)" (Ryrie, *Study Bible*, p. 9). Verses 4b and 5 take us back into the time of the work of creation, more particularly to the time before the work of the third day began, and draw our attention to certain details, which, being details, could hardly have been inserted in chapter 1. Certain types of plant life, those which require the attentive care of man in greater measure, had not sprung up. In verse 5b it is said, "God had not yet caused rain to descend upon the earth; also, man did not exist as yet to till the ground." The fact that not all vegetation is meant appears from the distinctive terms employed (Leupold, p. 112). The opening phrase of verse 4b *beyōm*, is to be rendered as it so often is "at the time" and not "in the day" (Leupold and Ryrie). Though not mentioned specifically, the types of vegetation under consideration here grew up only in Paradise; for the account centers around Paradise throughout the rest of the chapter. The two initial clauses of verse 5 are correlative: "when God made heaven and earth neither was there a shrub . . . nor had any plant sprouted" (Leupold, p. 112). The conjunction translated **before** in verse 5 is the adverb "not yet." So a good translation of 4bff. would be: "At the time the LORD God made the earth and the heavens, then no shrub of the field was as yet in the earth . . . nor had any plant sprouted."

But there went up a mist from the earth, and watered the whole face of the ground. The translation **mist** is pure conjecture. In the Septuagint it is translated by *plēgē* (i.e., fountain, spring). In the *Chicago Assyrian Dictionary* an *ēdū* is an onrush of water, high water. Harris takes it as a water-course. An *ēdū* was an inundation that overflowed the city of Babylon on the lower Euphrates. Thus, it is probably not a **mist**, but an irrigated canal. Note in verse 10 the root verb of verse 6 **to water** is used of an irrigative type of watering with relation to the four rivers. The verb **went up** is used of the Nile River in Amos 8:8 and 9:5. As is described in 2:15, this was part of Adam's work: to keep the garden well irrigated and watered for these special types of plants.

And the LORD God formed man of the dust of the ground. God **formed** man by molding, or shaping, him of a particular substance. This was the corporeal, or material, part of man, the ground. The Hebrew words for man, *'adam*, and ground, *'adamah*, are similar (cf. I Cor 15:47); but his life came from the breath of God, **and breathed into his nostrils the breath of life.** God had previously breathed the heavens into existence by His omnipotent word (Ps 33:6). Later, He would breathe out the Holy Scriptures (II Tim 3:16). But here He breathes the breath of life into the lifeless body of the first man, the non-corporeal, non-material part of man. Such a breath could only come from God, the Giver of life. **And man became a living soul.** A better translation would be "a living creature or person," as the phrase (identical) is also used of animals (1:21, 24). Thus, **soul** is not a reference to the concept of body, soul/spirit, but rather to the fact man became a **living** being. Man is distinguished from animals by being created in the image of God. The **ground** or **dust** is not merely a symbol of the animal kingdom, as theistic evolutionists maintain, but is actual earth as the use of the same word in 3:19 indicates (see Davis, pp. 76-77).

8-14. And the LORD God planted a garden eastward in Eden. As God prepared the earth for the man; so, too, He prepared the man for the earth. The garden was designed to be

8 ¶And the LORD God planted a garden eastward in Eden; and there he put the man whom he had formed.

9 And out of the ground made the LORD God to grow every tree that is pleasant to the sight, and good for food; the tree of life also in the midst of the garden, and the tree of knowledge of good and evil.

10 And a river went out of Eden to water the garden; and from thence it was parted, and became into four heads.

11 The name of the first is Pī'sŏn: that is it which compasseth the whole land of Hăv'i-lah, where there is gold;

12 And the gold of that land is good: there is bdellium and the onyx stone.

13 And the name of the second river is Gī'hŏn: the same is it that compasseth the whole land of Ē-thī-ō'pĭ-a.

14 And the name of the third river is Hĭd'de-kĕl: that is it which goeth toward the east of Assyria. And the fourth river is Eū-phrā'tēs.

15 And the LORD God took the man, and put him into the garden of Eden to dress it and to keep it.

16 And the LORD God commanded the man, saying, Of every tree of the garden thou mayest freely eat:

17 But of the tree of the knowledge of good and evil, thou shalt not eat of it: for in the day that thou eatest thereof thou shalt surely die.

the home of man, and it was apparently lush and perfect. God caused every kind of tree that was both pleasant to the eyes and good for food to grow in the garden. But two trees in particular were designed especially for man (vs. 9). These two trees were **the tree of life . . . and the tree of knowledge of good and evil.** Leupold notes, "Both trees are mentioned because both were there and both were destined for a very definite purpose. The tree of life, as appears from 3:22, would have served its purpose in the events of the victory of man in the first temptation or thereafter. Its existence shows that God had made ample provision for man's good. Since, however, it never came to be used, it at once very properly recedes into the background after the first mention of it and is alluded to only after the Fall in 3:22" (Vol. I, p. 119).

Also **a river went out of Eden to water the garden;** and as it exited from Eden, it parted **into four heads.** Much speculation has emerged with regard to the identification of these rivers. The **Pison,** which flowed around the land of **Havilah,** a land especially known for its gold, and the **Gihon,** which flowed around the whole land of **Ethiopia,** are less known to us today than the **Hiddekel** (the modern Tigris; cf. Dan 10:4) and the **Euphrates.** It is entirely possible that these four rivers are no longer in existence and that the topography of the entire earth was transformed by the Flood. Should that be the case, Noah may have named the present Tigris and Euphrates rivers after two of the rivers he remembered before the Flood. It is futile to try and identify the exact location of the garden out of which these rivers flowed. A tablet discovered in Babylonia in 1885 reads "Sippar in Eden" (see Ira M. Price, *The Monuments and the Old Testament*, p. 110); and it is now generally agreed that the oldest known civilization centered in and about the region of Mesopotamia, the land between the rivers. Beyond this, an identification of the location of Eden is impossible.

15-17. And the LORD God took the man, and put him into the garden of Eden to dress it and to keep it. Man's position in the garden was the fulfillment of a need described in 2:5. To **dress** (from a root meaning to serve) and to **keep** (to look after or to have charge of) the garden was an activity that, unlike the type of work associated with the earth after the curse (cf. 3:17-18), was rewarded by productivity and enjoyment. There is no sense in which the second word indicates a guarding of the garden against evil, as even Delitzsch and Whitelaw surmise. Everything is still **very good** at this stage; sin does not enter until chapter 3. Adam became the caretaker of the garden, but with one distinct prohibition. **And the LORD God commanded the man, saying, Of every tree of the garden thou mayest freely eat: But of the tree of the knowledge of good and evil, thou shalt not eat of it.** The complete freedom of man in the garden was restricted only by this one prohibition. Since man was yet in a state of unconfirmed holiness, God chose to test the moral constitution of His creation by placing him in a perfect environment, with but one restriction. As God had created him, man was able not to sin. If he had not sinned, he would have been confirmed in righteousness and would subsequently not have been able to sin. Instead, he disobeyed God, died spiritually, and fell into a state that made him not able not to sin. God warned Adam, **in the day that thou eatest thereof thou shalt surely die.** Just as the emphasis upon eating of **every tree** was indicated by **freely** (the Hebrew construction depicting certainty), so the negative is expressed by the strongest form of prohibition in Hebrew (you shall never eat), as in the Ten Commandments. The results of eating are also expressed by a construction that relates the certainty of death (in the day that thou eatest thou shalt certainly die). The death depicted is not a physical death, but spiritual death which is a separation from God and this occurred **in the day** they ate recorded in 3:5.

18 ¶And the LORD God said, It is not good that the man should be alone; I will make him an help meet for him.

19 And out of the ground the LORD God formed every beast of the field, and every fowl of the air; and brought them unto Adam to see what he would call them: and whatsoever Adam called every living creature, that was the name thereof.

20 And Adam gave names to all cattle, and to the fowl of the air, and to every beast of the field; but for Adam there was not found an help meet for him.

21 And the LORD God caused a deep sleep to fall upon Adam, and he slept: and he took one of his ribs, and closed up the flesh instead thereof;

22 And the rib, which the LORD God had taken from man, made he a woman, and brought her unto the man.

23 And Adam said, This is now bone of my bones, and flesh of my flesh: she shall be called Woman, because she was taken out of Man.

24 Therefore shall a man leave his father and his mother, and shall cleave unto his wife: and they shall be one flesh.

25 And they were both naked, the man and his wife, and were not ashamed.

18-20. In the words of Yahweh Himself, **It is not good that the man should be alone; I will make him a help meet for him.** These words relate to the events of verse 22 and following; but the expression **not good** indicates that these events are not a further continuation of chapter 1 and the creative week, but are part of that creative week. When God finished His creation (1:31), He noted that everything was **very good.** Thus, until Eve was created the creative activity of God was not complete. This is the first time in the history of creation that God said, **It is not good.** Man needs a wife who is **a help.** If man is to achieve his objectives in life, he needs the help of his mate in every way. Her position is further defined by the expression, "like him," literally, "as agreeing to him or his counterpart." She is the kind of help man needs, agreeing with him mentally, physically, spiritually; but she is not an inferior being. **The LORD God formed every beast of the field** is to be understood as **The LORD God** had "formed every beast of the field" (cf. ch. 1). The birds and beasts were created before Adam, but Adam's dominion over the animals is seen in verses 19 and 20; for it is the prerogative of a superior to give names to those under him (cf. 1:10 and comments). Thus, **whatsoever Adam called every living creature, that was the name thereof.** God caused all the animals to parade before the man, the crown of His creation; and Adam named the cattle, the fowl of the air, and every beast of the field. This in itself was a tremendous achievement in that there are some 17,000 air-breathing species of animals in existence today. Yet, two things were accomplished as the animals passed by Adam. First, names were given to each of the animals (this implies discerning the character or nature of an object, Isa 9:6); and second, Adam saw with his own eyes that each of the animals of God's creation was subhuman, inferior to him. He, and he alone, had been created in the image of God. He was unique; he was the only one of his **kind.** God was preparing Adam psychologically for his helper.

21-25. Not only did God recognize that man in solitude was **not good** (vs. 18), he also took steps to make the life of man one of joy and fulfillment. **And the LORD God caused a deep sleep to fall upon Adam.** The **deep sleep** (Heb tardēmah) was a divine anesthetic administered by the Great Physician. This sleep is usually produced by a supernatural agency (cf. Gen 15:12; Job 4:13; 33:15). The verb form is used to refer to the complete exhaustion of Jonah (Jon 1:5), thus indicating another agent. The Supernatural Surgeon immediately **took one of his ribs, and closed up the flesh instead thereof.** The Hebrew word for rib (tsēla') is used elsewhere in the Old Testament to mean "side," "wing of a building," and a "panel." There are those who feel it should be translated "side part," possibly to indicate the bisexuality of man and woman. But the same word appears in Akkadian meaning rib. It doubtless includes the surrounding flesh (cf. vs. 23). It was from this rib that God created woman, taken from Adam's side in order that she may labor alongside of him. The absolute unity of the race in its descent from one ancestor is hereby established, a vital doctrine of the Scriptures (cf. Rom 5:18ff), and along with it, the true dignity of womankind is guaranteed: she is not an inferior substance. She is of his bone and his flesh. The unity of the race explains why Eve did not experience spiritual death until Adam ate the fruit in 3:6. Eve was like everyone else, and she died ". . . in Adam . . ." (I Cor 15:22). God then **brought her unto the man.** God performed the first marriage; He sanctified and blessed the first home and the first family. Jesus interpreted this event in Matthew 19:6: "What therefore God hath joined together, let not man put asunder."

When God brought the woman unto Adam, the man said, **This is now bone of my bones, and flesh of my flesh: she shall be called Woman, because she was taken out of Man.** The first part of this verse contains the Hebrew expression that is commonly employed to indicate family kinship (Gen 29:14; Jud 9:2; II Sam 5:1; 19:12-13; I Chr 11:1). The meaning is: formed from the same parents, or from the same family. The source of the bones and the flesh is the same. Thus, this is a metaphorical expression, as though the first man could employ this phrase in the full sense of the words, including their literal connotation: actually, bone of his bones and flesh of his flesh! **She shall be called Woman, because she was taken out of Man** is a play on the words for man and woman, for they have a similar sound in Hebrew. Though they are probably from two different roots, the sounds aptly mark the affinity between the man and the woman. This is missed in a translation ('*īsh* and '*ishah*). Verse 24 gives the goal in marriage, based upon the unity expressed in verses 22 and 23. **Therefore shall a man leave his father and his mother, and shall cleave unto his wife: and they shall be one flesh.** The creation of Adam and Eve teaches us much about the marriage relationship: (1) Marriage was instituted by God (vss. 22-24), not by man, thus God's Word must give us the proper guidelines; (2) marriage was, and is to be, monogamous; God gave Adam only one wife; (3) marriage is to be heterosexual; homosexuality does not have a case in the light of biblical revelation; (4) the husband and wife are to be unified physically and spiritually. The man is to **leave his father and his mother.** This would normally imply leaving them physically and emotionally to become, literally, "glued to his wife." This implies the permanency of marriage; and (5) the husband is to be the head of the wife. The reason is that Adam was created before Eve (cf. I Cor 11:8-9; I Tim 2:13), and Eve was created as a helper for him. The chain exists because God instituted it, not because men are superior.

The first two chapters of Genesis record a great triumph for the LORD God of heaven. In six days He created all that ever was or shall be; He merely spoke the world into existence. All that has thus far happened evokes a note of joy. Suddenly, a note of sadness arises in the third chapter. This sadness is only broken by verse 15, yet that break is the silver lining behind the clouds.

B. The Temptation and Fall. 3:1-24.

3:1. Now the serpent was more subtil than any beast of the field which the LORD God had made. The words **Now the serpent** are placed at the head of the chapter for emphasis. All the stress falls on them. This is a real snake (literally in the Hebrew). He is a creature of God and is described as **more subtil.** The Hebrew word for **subtil** ('*arūm*) sounds like the word for **naked** in 2:25 ('*arūmīm*). To describe a snake in these terms seems to be taking the first step in going behind the scene and letting us know that there is more here than meets the eye. There is to be some connection between nakedness and subtlety. A subtlety is at work such as does not belong to snakes. **And he said unto the woman.** The fact that the serpent speaks constitutes a denial that God has made him (cf. 1:25 being made after his kind). Only man possesses the ability to speak. He probably approached Eve as the New Testament says, "For Adam was first formed, then Eve. And Adam was not deceived, but the woman being deceived was in the transgression" (I Tim 2:13-14). First Peter 3:7 says the woman is the weaker vessel, and II Corinthians 11:3 reports of the serpent beguiling Eve through his subtlety. Hence, this is a revelation of his ". . . subtilty. . . ." With the first words of the serpent it becomes apparent that an enemy of God is speaking; for he says, **Yea, hath God said, Ye shall not eat of every tree of the garden?** The words form a question, which seems designed to cast doubt upon God's goodness and yet, at the same time, seems to imply that if the serpent is misinformed, he is willing to be instructed in the matter (Do you really mean to say God has said you are

CHAPTER 3
NOW the serpent was more subtil than any beast of the field which the LORD God had made. And he said unto the woman, Yea, hath God said, Ye shall not eat of every tree of the garden?

2 And the woman said unto the serpent, We may eat of the fruit of the trees of the garden:
3 But of the fruit of the tree which is in the midst of the garden, God hath said, Ye shall not eat of it, neither shall ye touch it, lest ye die.

4 And the serpent said unto the woman, Ye shall not surely die:
5 For God doth know that in the day ye eat thereof, then your eyes shall be opened, and ye shall be as gods, knowing good and evil.

6 And when the woman saw that the tree was good for food, and that it was pleasant to the eyes, and a tree to be desired to make one wise, she took of the fruit thereof, and did eat, and gave also unto her husband with her; and he did eat.

not to eat from all of them?). He implants the idea that God is unduly strict in not permitting Adam and Eve to eat from all the trees. Another mark of his subtlety is that he has no desire to arrive at the truth. Certainly, the devil is using the snake (Jn 8:44; Rev 12:9; 20:2). Also, the serpent left out the name LORD (Yahweh) in his question, possibly emphasizing the harsh sovereignty of God ('Elōhīm), rather than a loving Redeemer God.

2-3. Instead of turning away, the woman engages in dialogue with the serpent, thereby revealing that she did not really realize that the serpent was her enemy. In her reply she leaves out the word "all" from 2:16, and also the Hebrew phrase "eating thou mayest eat" relating the concept of freely and abundantly. She dismisses it with a mere We may eat. This is an incorrect impression of the truth. Eve's representation of God's command was not accurate, to say the least. She makes the command general, placing it in the plural. God had said, thou shalt not, and she said, Ye shall not. And she adds, neither shall ye touch it. This may not be an adding to God's word as most take it, for in 20:6 and 26:11 the word expresses the taking of a person sexually to be one's own. Thus, it may be translated, "Ye may not eat it, that is, consume it," which would be a common Hebrew way of saying the same thing twice for clarification or emphasis. Lastly, the penalty that God had threatened is stated in general terms, and its forcefulness is weakened. Eve merely says, lest ye die, whereas God had said, thou shalt surely die (2:17). Eve's answers reveal her feeling that God's prohibition had been too stringent and her love for God, and confidence and trust in Him, had begun to waver.

4-5. And the serpent said unto the woman, Ye shall not surely die. Having won the first round, Satan is now in the position of delivering the knockout blow, the direct denial of God's Word. The negative comes first and receives all the emphasis, and Eve must now choose between God and the serpent. There is no halfway station, for Satan is condemning the concept of absolute authority. In verse 5 he impugns the motives of God, For God doth know that in the day ye eat thereof, then your eyes shall be opened, and ye shall be as gods, knowing good and evil. The serpent implies that Eve is confined by her position of trusting God. The word gods is best rendered as God. Satan is not interested in telling the man and the woman that they will attain the plane of divine beings. His point is to oppose the God of goodness. He would make it appear to Adam and Eve that, in reality, God is not good, but jealous. The serpent indicates that the path to knowledge is to bypass God's word.

6. This verse records the tragic story of the fall of mankind. There are four clearly defined steps that Eve took on the pathway to sin. First, when the woman saw that the tree was good for food. Sin begins with the sight of sin (cf. 9:22; Job 31:1). The sight of sin itself is not sin, but that is where the pathway that leads to sin embarks. Thus, as much as is possible, the very sight of sin ought to be avoided. When the woman looked at the tree, she saw that it was a tree to be desired. Her second step on the pathway to sin was desire. Sight alone is no crime; but to desire that which we have innocently seen, if it cannot be ours, is sin (Deut 5:21; Mt 5:28; Jas 1:13-14; I Jn 2:15-17). Eve's third step on the pathway to sin occurred when she took of the fruit thereof, and did eat. She had already sinned by coveting that which was not to be coveted; but she deepened her sin by indulging, by taking that which was not rightfully hers according to the prohibition of God. Desiring the forbidden fruit was covert sin; taking and eating of the fruit was overt and active sin.

Eve had now fallen into sin. She had followed the three inevitable steps that lead to sin: (1) sight; (2) desire; and (3) gratification. It still would have been a great tragedy if these were the only three steps on the pathway to sin, but there is one

7 And the eyes of them both were opened, and they knew that they *were* naked; and they sewed fig leaves together, and made themselves aprons.
8 And they heard the voice of the LORD God walking in the garden in the cool of the day: and Adam and his wife hid themselves from the presence of the LORD God amongst the trees of the garden.

9 And the LORD God called unto Adam, and said unto him, Where *art* thou?
10 And he said, I heard thy voice in the garden, and I was afraid, because I *was* naked; and I hid myself.
11 And he said, Who told thee that thou *wast* naked? Hast thou eaten of the tree, whereof I commanded thee that thou shouldest not eat?
12 And the man said, The woman whom thou gavest *to be* with me, she gave me of the tree, and I did eat.
13 And the LORD God said unto the woman, What *is* this *that* thou hast done? And the woman said, The serpent beguiled me, and I did eat.

more. After Eve saw the forbidden fruit, desired it, and took of it, she **gave also unto her husband with her: and he did eat.** Unfortunately, the final step on the path to sin is the involvement of others in our sin. There is no such thing as private sin; every sin affects someone else. Eve's sin affected Adam; and consequently, Adam's sin affected the entire race. The whole human race sinned in Adam, for ". . . death passed unto all men, for that all have sinned" (Rom 5:12). Our sin always involves others and thus becomes compounded. Other striking examples of these same steps on the pathway to sin can be found in the lives of Achan (Josh 7:21) and David (II Sam 11:1-5, 15, 24). In order not to fall prey to the path of sin, we must stop ourselves short when we discover any of the steps that Eve took, ask the Lord to forgive us for our sins, and reverse our pathway.

7-8. And the eyes of them both were opened reveals the half-truth of the serpent. Now Adam and Eve see good and evil from the standpoint of sinners, from the low level of sin. Their eyes were opened to the fact that they were corrupt and polluted; for they **sewed fig leaves together, and made themselves aprons.** In addition, they sought to hide themselves from God; **and Adam and his wife hid themselves from the presence of the LORD God.** A keen sense of guilt immediately followed the act of sinning, and their intimate fellowship with God was broken. The physical eyes are not spoken of here, but rather the conscience. The knowledge they now have judges everything from a false standpoint; it sees from a perverted position. Previously they were naked (2:25), but they were not ashamed. Actually, what they heard was "the sound or voice of the LORD God traversing the garden as the Spirit of the day." This was a primal *Parousia.* God was coming unto them in judgment for their disobedience. The word **voice** is better rendered *sound* as it appears in theophanies in the Old Testament (cf. Ps 18:13; Jer 25:30; Ezk 1:24ff; Joel 3:16; see the *Westminster Theological Journal,* March, 1978). **The cool of the day** relates to the "Spirit of the day," as **cool** is the Hebrew word for spirit. And the day is a judgment day. No small wonder that as the sound of the **LORD God** was traversing back and forth in the garden seeking out Adam and Eve, they actively **hid themselves** from His presence!

9-13. And the LORD God called unto Adam, and said unto him, Where art thou? Man has broken away from God, but God will not leave him to his lost condition. This is the great marvel of the Scriptures; God does not abandon the creature to his just deserts. In this question God reveals His love; for the purpose of interrogating Adam is to cause him to see where his disobedience has brought him, to contemplate his present status and give an account of why he is in the condition in which he finds himself. **And he said, I heard thy voice in the garden, and I was afraid, because I was naked; and I hid myself.** Here is the voice of the sinner; he is not straightforward, open, and aboveboard. Sin makes man a coward and an evader; it leads him to seek refuge in half-truths, deceit, and evasion. What Adam says is true in part; but he is more concerned with the consequences of his sin than with the heinousness of what he had done. The awareness of his nakedness was more keenly in Adam's mind than the fact that he had broken God's command. Sin causes us to think more of what happens and will happen to us than of the fact that we have disobeyed God. Why should he have been afraid because he was naked (cf. 2:25)? Then God asked another question, **Who told thee that thou wast naked? Hast thou eaten of the tree?** Adam must be brought to the realization that the sin which he had committed was more serious than its consequences. He must have a deeper consciousness of his sin than of its effects. The realization of his nakedness from a sinful perspective was directly related to his eating of the prohibited tree. The straightforward question **Hast thou eaten?**

makes it easy for Adam to answer Yes or No. A simple, honest confession was what God sought. The structure of the twelfth verse is quite interesting, particularly with respect to the first three words (lit., and there said the man, the woman). Adam is shifting the blame to the woman. He mentions her first and, thus, emphasizes her. Adam the leader is now a follower (cf. vs. 6). **The woman whom thou gavest to be with me, she gave me of the tree, and I did eat.** Adam not only shifts the blame to the woman, but also to God. The implication is that if God had not given him the woman, this act would not have taken place. Sin has now divided the family, not only man from God. His confession **I did eat** is to be interpreted in the foregoing light. It is almost a bold challenge. Of course I ate. This woman you gave to me caused me to eat. Like Adam, Eve is also responsible before God; and so He turns to her and asks, **What is this that thou hast done?** Like Adam, Eve has little or no concern over her guilt. Her main object is to shift the blame from herself. She at least acknowledges she had been deceived or **beguiled** as Paul states in II Corinthians 11:3. Again, we have the striking order of statement that appeared also in Adam's words, "And there said the woman, the serpent." She immediately blames the serpent.

14 And the Lord God said unto the serpent, Because thou hast done this, thou *art* cursed above all cattle, and above every beast of the field; upon thy belly shalt thou go, and dust shalt thou eat all the days of thy life:
15 And I will put enmity between thee and the woman, and between thy seed and her seed; it shall bruise thy head, and thou shalt bruise his heel.

14-15. The effects of the Fall reached well beyond the man and woman. Man was appointed to rule over God's creation; and thus, the animals suffered along with man through the Edenic Curse (Jer 12:4; Rom 8:20). But the serpent was cursed **above** or distinct from all cattle and every beast of the field. The Hebrew *mikōl* can be taken as a partitive—"*any* of the beasts of the field"—or as a comparative—"*than* the beasts of the field." Here it must be comparative; the context favors this view also, thus indicating "more than." As a result of man's sin, God said to the serpent, **upon thy belly shalt thou go, and dust shalt thou eat all the days of thy life.** The serpent would crawl upon his belly forevermore, having previously stood erect (Luther), or having been possessed of bone (Josephus), or being capable of standing upright and twining itself round the trees (Lange), or, at the very least, having undergone some external transformation with regard to form (Keil and Delitzsch). It is quite possible, however, that the language of this verse indicates nothing more than the humiliation of the serpent, once exalted as the most subtle beast of the field, to a position in which it is reduced to slithering skillfully through the grass. For it was God who had pronounced the creeping things as good in 1:24-25.

Yet the greater curse upon the serpent is upon that old serpent, the devil. To Satan the Lord God promises, **I will put enmity between thee and the woman, and between thy seed and her seed; it shall bruise thy head, and thou shalt bruise his heel.** Here is the initial messianic prophecy of the Bible. "The traditional Christian interpretation . . . is that it is the first direct expression of the gospel. It recognizes the essential conflict between Satan and the Lord and indicates that this conflict also will involve the people of God and the followers of Satan (cf. Jn 8:44; Acts 13:10; I Jn 3:10). The seed of the woman is a clear reference to the Messiah, the Lord Jesus (cf. Gal 3:16, 19; Rev 12:1-5), who came 'to destroy the works of the devil' (Heb 2:14; I Jn 3:8). The *protevangelium* prophesied that Christ would deliver a death blow to Satan but in so doing would suffer death himself" (Davis, p. 93). The Hebrew word for "seed" is a collective noun in the singular sense. Thus it may refer to only one person or sometimes to many individuals (Gen 22:17 and the culmination of this promise with reference to Christ in Gal 3:16). All of this should be understood in the light of the New Testament's total revelation of the ramifications of this prophecy. Certainly, Adam and Eve were not aware of any of this future revelation.

16 Unto the woman he said, I will

16. Just as the beasts of the field, and most especially the

greatly multiply thy sorrow and thy conception; in sorrow thou shalt bring forth children; and thy desire *shall be* to thy husband, and he shall rule over thee.

serpent, were cursed because of man's sin, so too, the woman received a threefold curse because of sin. Unto her, God said, **I will greatly multiply thy sorrow and thy conception.** Cassuto and others render this as "I will greatly multiply your suffering in general, and more particularly that of your childbearing. Women's pains would exceed that of men and particularly during the period of childbearing" (*Genesis Part One*, p. 165). The second part of the curse on the woman was **thy desire shall be to thy husband.** This phrase has been interpreted in several ways: (1) the common view is that of a sexual desire on the part of the woman for her husband, knowing now there will be more pain in childbearing; (2) some refer to it as a psychological dependence upon the husband, i.e., the woman will be a willing slave; and (3) Calvin says she will desire only what the husband desires. But the rule of the husband is not a result of, or a punishment for, sin, since it was God's intention from the beginning of creation (cf. I Tim 2:13). The clue lies in the Hebrew construction and the parallel usage in 4:7. Rather than translating **thy desire shall be to thy husband,** it should be thy desire shall be "against" thy husband. The preposition *'el* is translated "against" in 4:8, **Cain rose up against Abel his brother and slew him.** The same preposition (*'el*) and noun **desire** (*teshûqah*) appear in 4:7 and are translated **and unto thee shall be his desire.** This clearly implies that the personification of sin has a desire against Cain to destroy him. But God has promised Cain, "but thou shalt rule over him" or "it." Victory could be Cain's if he did that which was right. So, here in verse 16, the woman's desire will be against her husband and his leadership; she will not willingly submit to his rule. The third curse may actually be a promise in disguise; for God has said **he shall rule over thee.** It can be worked out. A parallel promise with the same wording appears in 4:7 with the disjunctive *waw* and the verb "to rule" translated "but you may rule over it." Certainly, we live in a day and age when it is obvious that many women are expressing their desire against their husbands. Paul says for husbands to love their own wives and for the wives to "submit" to their husbands. Why else would it be commanded, if it came naturally? (See Susan Foh's article in *Westminster Theological Journal*, Spring, 1975—amazingly this is a woman's interpretation!)

17-19. Man is condemned to exhausting labor in order to make a living. This is because of God's curse upon the ground. Adam was to work before the Fall (2:15), but now it would be **in the sweat of thy face shalt thou eat bread, till thou return unto the ground.** Years later, Lamech cried out for relief from the curse upon the ground and the difficulty of farming (5:29). Adam was created from the dust of the ground, and **unto dust shalt thou return.** This is not to imply that Adam will go back to the animal kingdom.

17 And unto Adam he said, Because thou hast hearkened unto the voice of thy wife, and hast eaten of the tree, of which I commanded thee, saying, Thou shalt not eat of it: cursed *is* the ground for thy sake; in sorrow shalt thou eat *of* it all the days of thy life;
18 Thorns also and thistles shall it bring forth to thee; and thou shalt eat the herb of the field;
19 In the sweat of thy face shalt thou eat bread, till thou return unto the ground; for out of it wast thou taken: for dust thou *art*, and unto dust shalt thou return.
20 And Adam called his wife's name Eve; because she was the mother of all living.
21 Unto Adam also and to his wife did the Lord God make coats of skins, and clothed them.

20-21. Verse 20 is Adam's response in faith to the revealed Word of God in verses 15 and 16. God had told them that **in the day that thou eatest thereof thou shalt surely die** (2:17), which involved not only a separation from God but, in time, physical death as well. Then God gave them the promise in verses 15-16 that Eve would bear children and continue to live physically. Adam's response to God's promise was to call **his wife's name Eve; because she was the mother of all living.** "Consequently, by the significant nature of the name employed, as well as by the significant way in which the matter is reported at this important juncture, we are to understand that Adam refers to the things implied in the promise of the victory over the devil. In other words, he here gives evidence not only of believing that God spoke the truth but evidence of belief in the salvation which God had promised" (Leupold, p. 177). God responded by providing **coats of skins, and clothed them.** This was His way of demonstrating that fellowship was restored. "While it may be premature to read into this the introduction of animal sacrifice, it certainly illustrated to Adam and Eve, who may even have witnessed the death of these innocent animals, the high cost of their guilt" (Davis, p. 95).

22 ¶And the LORD God said, Behold, the man is become as one of us, to know good and evil: and now, lest he put forth his hand, and take also of the tree of life, and eat, and live for ever:
23 Therefore the LORD God sent him forth from the garden of Eden, to till the ground from whence he was taken.
24 So he drove out the man; and he placed at the east of the garden of Eden Chĕr'u-bĭms̄, and a flaming sword which turned every way, to keep the way of the tree of life.

22-24. Satan's promise in verse 5 was technically true (as revealed in vs. 7 and now in vs. 22). Here they were now like God, fixed in a moral nature; but the terrible thing was that it was fixed in sin, not righteousness. Verse 7 reveals that they were like God, knowing good and evil; but their eyes had been opened to behold all things in the light of their own sinfulness. They knew good, but they were unable to do it; they knew evil, but they were unable to resist it. This is what is called total depravity.

CHAPTER 4

AND Adam knew Eve his wife; and she conceived, and bare Cain, and said, I have gotten a man from the LORD.
2 And she again bare his brother Abel. And Abel was a keeper of sheep, but Cain was a tiller of the ground.
3 And in process of time it came to pass, that Cain brought of the fruit of the ground an offering unto the LORD.
4 And Abel, he also brought of the firstlings of his flock and of the fat thereof. And the LORD had respect unto Abel and to his offering:
5 But unto Cain and to his offering he had not respect. And Cain was very wroth, and his countenance fell.

C. The Two Brothers. 4:1-26.

4:1-5. And Adam knew Eve his wife; and she conceived, and bare Cain, and said, I have gotten a man from the LORD. To know a woman is a common euphemism for sexual union (cf. 19:5; Num 31:17-18, 35; Jud 11:39; 19:22, 25). In Hebrew *qayin* (*Cain*) and *qanītī* (**I have gotten**) form a pun. Cain's name is a play on the words, with the verb meaning "to acquire or get." The last phrase, **from the LORD,** has caused some problems. Luther translated it as "I have the man, the Lord," making *'et* the regular sign of the accusative. This means that Eve was referring to the Deliverer promised in verse 15. The other view would express, I have gotten a man with the help of the Lord, interpreting the preposition as it functions in 49:25; Judges 8:7; Esther 9:29. In this case Eve would be emphasizing God's role in the birth of her child. The *Targum* and LXX favor this second view. **Abel** means breath or vanity, and the question arises as to whether this was a posthumous naming (cf. 4:25c) or a reflection of an earlier experience of the curse's frustration (cf. 5:29; Eccl 1:2ff.).

Much discussion has centered around the offerings of Cain and Abel and why the one was accepted and the other rejected. Were they given in response to a command from God? Many contend that God had commanded Cain and Abel to give offerings, and that He specifically required blood sacrifices. It should be kept in mind that there is no recorded revelation from God to bring a bloody sacrifice, or even a sacrifice. It is most likely that Cain's offering was rejected because of his attitude in offering it. "The term translated 'offering' in this passage, *minha*, is used in the Levitical laws for the bloodless rather than the bloody offering, consisting either of flour and oil or of flour prepared with frankincense (Lev 2:1, 4, 14-15); it is also used in the Old Testament in a broader sense, including both bloodless and bloody offerings. The broader sense is obviously intended here" (Davis, p. 99). There are other indications, too. Neither of the two sacrifices is made for sin. Cain brought **of the fruit of the ground,** whereas Abel **brought of the firstlings of his flock and of the fat thereof.** Also, **firstlings** is from the Hebrew root of *bekōr*, meaning "first-born." This indicates Abel desired to give his best, the first and choicest of his possessions. Cain gave out of formalism (it was time and custom to give), whereas Abel gave the best—pure devout worship. In addition, the individuals are mentioned before there is an acknowledgment of their gifts (note **And the LORD had respect unto Abel and to his offering: But unto Cain and to his offering he had not respect**). The Reader of hearts knew their spiritual standing, which is confirmed by Hebrews 11:4 (cf. Acts 5 and Ananias and Sapphira; I Jn 3:12).

6-8. When Cain learned that God had not accepted his sacrifice, his **countenance** fell. Right behavior results in good feelings and vice versa (cf. 4:7; Ps 31:9-10; 32:3-4; 38:1-8; Jas 1:25). Seeing this, the Lord said, **If thou doest well, shalt thou not be accepted?** (lit., if you do good will [it] not be lifted up?). The "it" may refer to the sacrifice that was not lifted up or accepted. Or it may refer to Cain's countenance, which was just reported to have fallen. The latter is most likely the correct interpretation, even though both are feasible. God has approached Cain in love and has asked him to see the relationship between his present state of anger and depression and to reverse this trend by proper conduct. If not, **sin lieth at the door. And unto thee shall be his desire.** If Cain does not respond correctly by doing that which is ethically good, **sin** is like a lion waiting for the opportunity to devour Cain. But God gives Cain the promise of victory in the statement, **and thou shalt rule over him.** The **and** is better translated "but"; you can have mastery over "it," not **him.** But Cain ignores God; there is no indication of an answer to the seeking and loving Creator's interrogation. So one day out in the field **Cain rose up against Abel his brother, and slew him.** Cain's ultimate nature (I Jn 3:12) was revealed in the course of time as he became angry with God, depressed, sullen, and silent, then bore a hatred for God's people, and ultimately waited for the proper time to murder his righteous brother Abel.

9-12. Just as God had questioned Cain's father in a manner designed to elicit a confession of sin, so too the Lord now says unto Cain, **Where is Abel thy brother?** Cain was evasive and impudent, and he claimed both ignorance and innocence. His ignorance was a lie; his innocence was sarcasm. Both were rejected by God who said, **What hast thou done? the voice of thy brother's blood crieth unto me from the ground.** God's omniscience countered Cain's lies. The results of Cain's sin and unrepentance were twofold: (1) the ground would not yield productively when tilled by Cain; and (2) Cain would be a **fugitive** and a **vagabond** throughout the earth. God had cursed the ground in 3:17, the serpent in 3:14, and now Cain. This was not a damnation of Cain, preventing him from being saved; but he was driven away from his vocation of farming. In essence, he became the symbol of the unregenerate man in his shifting and straying in the earth with no peace or rest. The word for **vagabond** is related to the word **Nod** in vs. 16 where he was eventually to dwell. He would be a homeless wanderer, banished from permanency and consigned to seeking out a living in whatever manner he could.

13-15. Cain immediately objected to the Lord that **My punishment is greater than I can bear.** He has just killed his brother and is blaming God for being too harsh! He even complains that **from thy face shall I be hid.** This had never been his concern previously! And he also became paranoid; for he said, **every one that findeth me shall slay me.** The Bible says, "The wicked flee when no man pursueth: but the righteous are bold as a lion" (Prov 28:1). "The way of the transgressor is hard." **And the Lord said unto him, Therefore whosoever slayeth Cain, vengeance shall be taken on him sevenfold.** Though totally undeserving, Cain did receive mercy from the Lord God who hated the sin, but loved the sinner. Therefore the Lord **set a mark** upon Cain, some special sign (cf. Jud 6:36-40 for Gideon; II Kgs 2:9-12 for Elisha) to assure Cain that no one would kill him. This was not a mark on Cain, nor was it, as Rabbi Joseph asserted, a long horn out of his forehead!

16-22. Cain went out from the presence of the Lord. This is true both physically and spiritually. This portrays the direction of fallen and unsaved humanity: into exile, without God, without hope in the world. What a sad commentary on the

6 And the Lord said unto Cain, Why art thou wroth? and why is thy countenance fallen?
7 If thou doest well, shalt thou not be accepted? and if thou doest not well, sin lieth at the door. And unto thee *shall be* his desire, and thou shalt rule over him.
8 And Cain talked with Abel his brother: and it came to pass, when they were in the field, that Cain rose up against Abel his brother, and slew him.

9 And the Lord said unto Cain, Where *is* Abel thy brother? And he said, I know not: *Am* I my brother's keeper?
10 And he said, What hast thou done? the voice of thy brother's blood crieth unto me from the ground.
11 And now *art* thou cursed from the earth, which hath opened her mouth to receive thy brother's blood from thy hand;
12 When thou tillest the ground, it shall not henceforth yield unto thee her strength; a fugitive and a vagabond shalt thou be in the earth.

13 And Cain said unto the Lord, My punishment *is* greater than I can bear.
14 Behold, thou hast driven me out this day from the face of the earth; and from thy face shall I be hid; and I shall be a fugitive and a vagabond in the earth; and it shall come to pass, *that* every one that findeth me shall slay me.
15 And the Lord said unto him, Therefore whosoever slayeth Cain, vengeance shall be taken on him sevenfold. And the Lord set a mark upon Cain, lest any finding him should kill him.

16 ¶And Cain went out from the presence of the Lord, and dwelt in the land of Nod, on the east of Eden.
17 And Cain knew his wife; and she

conceived, and bare Ē'noch: and he builded a city, and called the name of the city, after the name of his son, Ē'noch.

18 And unto Ē'noch was born Ī'răd: and Ī'răd begat Me-hū'ja-el: and Me-hū'ja-el begat Me-thū'sa-el: and Me-thū'sa-el begat Lā'mech.

19 ¶And Lā'mech took unto him two wives: the name of the one was Adah, and the name of the other Zĭl'lah.

20 And Adah bare Jā'bal: he was the father of such as dwell in tents, and of such as have cattle.

21 And his brother's name was Jū'-bal: he was the father of all such as handle the harp and organ.

22 And Zĭl'lah, she also bare Tū'-bal–cāin, an instructer of every artificer in brass and iron: and the sister of Tū'bal–cāin was Nā'a-mah.

23 And Lā'mech said unto his wives, Adah and Zĭl'lah, Hear my voice; ye wives of Lā'mech, hearken unto my speech: for I have slain a man to my wounding, and a young man to my hurt.

24 If Cain shall be avenged sevenfold, truly Lā'mech seventy and sevenfold.

unsaved. Cain started a new life in a new land and bore a son **Enoch,** meaning "consecration" or "initiation" symbolizing the new beginning for Cain. He could have married one of his sisters, or a niece or grandniece, since there were no mutant genes as there would be today. Leupold indicates the word **builded** is a participle, probably indicating that Cain started the city but never finished it. He probably was attempting a permanent place of residence in defiance of God's statement in verse 12. The mention of cities prepares for the emergence of the kingship (cf. 4:23ff. and the **sons of God** in 6:2ff.), and the naming of the city after the son begins the theme of man's passion to establish his own name in the earth. One of Cain's descendants violated God's clear pattern for marriage by marrying two wives.

A love for the humanities is exhibited early in Cain's descendants. This is not bad in and of itself, yet this must be a commentary on the pursuits of man apart from fellowship with God, as these are the descendants of Cain, whereas the godly are mentioned in chapter 5. **Jubal,** one of Lamech's sons, **was the father of all such as handle the harp and organ.** The **harp** corresponds to what is today called a lyre, and the **organ** is the modern-day "flute." **Father of** is an idiom allowing for remote ancestry. Father-son terminology was even used for the professional relationship of the head of a guild to other members (cf. vss. 20-21). Another son, **Tubalcain,** was described an **an instructor of every artificer in brass and iron.** This bears witness to the highly developed state of man very early in his history. There is evidence that iron goes back to 5000 B.C., which is postdiluvian. (See Jane C. Waldbaum, "The First Archaeological Appearance of Iron and the Transition to the Iron Age," in *The Coming of the Iron Age,* pp. 69-98.)

23-24. These verses express the culmination of centuries of ungodly living among the descendants of Cain. Cain had desired to establish a name for himself (cf. 6:4; 10:9; 11:4); he built a city and named it after his son. His descendants were involved in polygamy as well as purely humanitarian pursuits; and now Lamech had taken the law into his own hands and had killed someone in revenge. "The judicial office degenerated into a vengeful tyranny in this heir of the murderous spirit of the dynasty's founder" (Kline, *The New Bible Commentary,* pp. 86-87). "The song expresses Lamech's overweening pride, his refusal to suffer any hurt without a severalfold and dire revenge. This expression of arrogant self-conceit and disdain for customary retribution is skillfully reinforced by the poet through a clever manipulation of poetic convention" (Gevirtz, *Studies in Ancient Oriental Civilization [SAOC],* 32, p. 25). The poetic conventions include an unusual pairing of *'ish* (man) with *yeled* (boy) instead of the expected *ben-'adam* (son of man; cf. Num 23:19; Prov 8:4; Job 35:8). And why should he boast of killing a mere boy? "Now there is reason to believe that warriors and, more particularly, warleaders and heroes in the ancient world were considerably younger than we are wont to imagine" (Gevirtz, p. 30). Examples include Alexander the Great a military commander at eighteen, Hannibal trained in the art of warfare in his ninth year, Yasmah-Addu set upon throne in childhood, Rameses II "chief of the army" when he was "a boy in the tenth year," and Taharqa (Tirhakah in II Kgs 19:9) who led Nubian forces in his teens. Secondly, the disproportionate parallelism between sevenfold which was God's promise to Cain, and the **seventy and sevenfold** of Lamech's boasting does not fit the normal progression in Hebrew poetry of x in the first stich and the amount of x + 1 in the second. **If Cain shall be avenged sevenfold, truly Lamech seventy and sevenfold** gives witness to the arrogance and defiance of Lamech and his total disregard for the things of God. Thus, wickedness has spread to the top echelons of government; and this sets the background

25 ¶And Adam knew his wife again; and she bare a son, and called his name Seth: For God, *said she,* hath appointed me another seed instead of Abel, whom Cain slew.

26 And to Seth, to him also there was born a son; and he called his name Enos: then began men to call upon the name of the LORD.

CHAPTER 5

THIS *is* the book of the generations of Adam. In the day that God created man, in the likeness of God made he him;

2 Male and female created he them; and blessed them, and called their name Adam, in the day when they were created.

3 ¶And Adam lived an hundred and thirty years, and begat *a son* in his own likeness, after his image; and called his name Seth:

4 And the days of Adam after he had begotten Seth were eight hundred years: and he begat sons and daughters:

5 And all the days that Adam lived were nine hundred and thirty years: and he died.

6 ¶And Seth lived an hundred and five years, and begat Enos:

7 And Seth lived after he begat Enos eight hundred and seven years, and begat sons and daughters:

8 And all the days of Seth were nine hundred and twelve years: and he died.

for why God sends the Flood in chapter 6. There He says **violence** (6:13) fills the earth, which is pictured in the person of Lamech, a ruler, tyrant, and warrior taking law and order into his own hands, fighting against leaders from other countries. He is not picking on young men in the nursery.

25-26. Against this dark picture of man apart from God, there is a brief testimony that God has a remnant who are trusting in him. Adam **knew his wife again; and she bare a son, and called his name Seth.** He is named Seth, meaning the "appointed one." His name is pronounced *shēt;* for God appointed, *shāt,* him, a play on words. Eve is acknowledging here that God has provided a son in the place of the slain Abel. Seth's son, **Enos,** comes from the word for man that means weak or sickly, denoting man's frailty. Thus, this is an indication on the part of God's people that apart from God man's plight is hopeless due to sin. **Then began men to call upon the name of the LORD** is a testimony that the religious worship of the community of faith was organized for their public worship of God together (cf. 4:2ff. which indicates individual worship).

D. Seth and His Descendants. 5:1-32.

5:1-2. This is the book of the generations of Adam. Actually, this closes out the history of Adam that began in chapter 2 and was recorded in relation to his family in the remainder of chapter 2, and then in 3 and 4. Evidently, a **book** was kept of the events which occurred, beginning with 2:5ff.; and this may indicate the written source that Moses used in writing Genesis (Ryrie, p. 14). God **called their name Adam.** This was the generic use of *'adam,* which is contrasted with Adam as a proper name in this same context (note vs. 3).

3-8. And Adam lived a hundred and thirty years, and begat a son in his own likeness, after his image. . . . And the days of Adam after he had begotten Seth were eight hundred years. There is a new feature in the lists found in chapters 5 and 11; and that feature is the inclusion of the number of years A lived before he begat B, as well as the total number of years A lived. The solution to the question concerning the meaning of these numbers was suggested as far back as 1906 by John H. Raven (*Old Testament Introduction,* pp. 134-135). Observing, correctly, that Zilpah was credited with bearing her great grandchildren (Gen 46:18), while Bilhah bore her grandchildren (46:25) and Canaan bore whole nations (10:15-18), Raven allows that the first number in the formula may mean that B literally was born to A, or that B was a distant descendant born to A. If it is the latter case, then "the age of A is his age at the birth of that child from whom B (eventually) descended" (Raven p. 135). Malamat illustrates this telescoping effect of some twenty generations from Levi to Samuel in the genealogy of Heman in I Chr 6:33-38 (18-23 MT).

This verse shows that the sons listed in a genealogy need not be, and often are not, the first-born (or descended therefrom); and the age figure does not need to indicate when the subject first became a father. The begetting **in his own likeness, after his image** (cf. vs. 1 and 1:27) indicates that man, too, reproduces according to his kind (cf. 1:11ff.). The **likeness** is now sinful in contrast to 1:26. **Adam lived . . . nine hundred and thirty years: and he died.** Seth himself lived 912 years; seven of the ten patriarchs listed lived more than 900 years. How are we to understand the extreme longevity? In light of the discovery of other documents in the ancient Near East that represent the lives of monarchs as exceedingly long (the Sumerian king list, for example), many modern scholars have assumed that the ages of the patriarchs in chapter 5 are mythical. Some have attempted to explain these ages by arguing that a year actually means a month, but this reasoning creates more problems than it solves. If the word *year* actually meant month in chapter 5, this would

9 ¶And Enos lived ninety years, and begat Cā-i'nan:

10 And Enos lived after he begat Cā-i'nan eight hundred and fifteen years, and begat sons and daughters:

11 And all the days of Enos were nine hundred and five years: and he died.

12 ¶And Cā-i'nan lived seventy years, and begat Ma-hā'la-le-el:

13 And Cā-i'nan lived after he begat Ma-hā'la-le-el eight hundred and forty years, and begat sons and daughters:

14 And all the days of Cā-i'nan were nine hundred and ten years: and he died.

15 ¶And Ma-hā'la-le-el lived sixty and five years, and begat Jā'red:

16 And Ma-hā'la-le-el lived after he begat Jā'red eight hundred and thirty years, and begat sons and daughters:

17 And all the days of Ma-hā'la-le-el were eight hundred ninety and five years: and he died.

18 ¶And Jā'red lived an hundred sixty and two years, and he begat Ē'noch:

19 And Jā'red lived after he begat Ē'noch eight hundred years, and begat sons and daughters:

20 And all the days of Jā'red were nine hundred sixty and two years: and he died.

21 ¶And Ē'noch lived sixty and five years, and begat Me-thū'se-lah:

22 And Ē'noch walked with God after he begat Me-thū'se-lah three hundred years, and begat sons and daughters:

23 And all the days of Ē'noch were three hundred sixty and five years:

24 And Ē'noch walked with God: and he *was* not; for God took him.

25 ¶And Me-thū'se-lah lived an

28

mean that Seth was only about nine years old when he fathered Enos (cf. vs. 6).

It is impossible to indicate how these patriarchs could have lived so long with clear certainty. Whitcomb and Morris argue that the canopy of waters above the firmament prior to the flood filtered the solar rays and thus caused the sun to have no adverse effects on the longevity of these patriarchs (pp. 404-405). It may also indicate God's intention for man to live forever; but as his sinfulness became so apparent, the span of his life has been drastically shortened.

The last words of verse 5, **and he died,** provide the sad commentary of the effects of sin upon the human race. It demonstrates the reign of death by its insistent refrain (vss. 5b, 8b, etc.).

9-20. The catalogue of Adam's descendants through Seth reads like a geriatrics register. **Enos** lived 905 years, **and he died. Cainan** lived 910 years, **and he died. Mahalaleel** lived 895 years, **and he died. Jared** lived 962 years, **and he died.** Although the life span of each of these descendants of Adam varied to some degree, they all have one thing in common: they all died.

21-24. The "tombstone lane" that makes up chapter 5 is briefly interrupted with the life of **Enoch.** Verse 22 says that **Enoch walked with God.** The verb stem used signifies to walk about or to live, and the preposition denotes intimacy, fellowship. Jude 14-15 records, "And Enoch also, the seventh from Adam, prophesied of these, saying, Behold, the Lord cometh with ten thousands of his saints, To execute judgment upon all, and to convince all that are ungodly among them of all their ungodly deeds which they have ungodly committed, and of all their hard speeches which ungodly sinners have spoken against him." We cannot say for sure, but it is quite likely that Enoch was severely persecuted as he **walked with God;** for the content of his message was very pointed and powerful in his condemnation of evil. His experience evidently involved special revelation received and proclaimed. Then **he was not; for God took him.** God took him; for he ". . . was not found because God had translated him," in order ". . . that he should not see death . . ." (Heb 11:5). The same Hebrew word is used for the translation of Elijah (II Kgs 2:3-5). In other words, he went directly to heaven without dying. His bodily translation into heaven was a sign (during the long prediluvian sway of the curse) that, ultimately, reconciliation with God includes victory over death.

25-32. Methuselah possessed the longest life span of any man

hundred eighty and seven years, and begat Lā'mech:

26 And Me-thū'se-lah lived after he begat Lā'mech seven hundred eighty and two years, and begat sons and daughters:

27 And all the days of Me-thū'se-lah were nine hundred sixty and nine years: and he died.

28 ¶And Lā'mech lived an hundred eighty and two years, and begat a son:

29 And he called his name Noah, saying, This *same* shall comfort us concerning our work and toil of our hands, because of the ground which the LORD hath cursed.

30 And Lā'mech lived after he begat Noah five hundred ninety and five years, and begat sons and daughters:

31 And all the days of Lā'mech were seven hundred seventy and seven years: and he died.

32 ¶And Noah was five hundred years old: and Noah begat Shem, Ham, and Jā'pheth.

CHAPTER 6

AND it came to pass, when men began to multiply on the face of the earth, and daughters were born unto them,

2 That the sons of God saw the daughters of men that they *were* fair; and they took them wives of all which they chose.

3 And the LORD said, My spirit shall not always strive with man, for that he also *is* flesh: yet his days shall be an hundred and twenty years.

4 There were giants in the earth in those days; and also after that, when the sons of God came in unto the daughters of men, and they bare *chil-*

in history. He lived 969 years; but, like those before him, except Enoch, **he died.** Some have falsely interpreted the etymology of his name and have made it a harbinger of the Flood by asserting it means "when he is dead it shall be sent." Pink and others espouse this view; some pragmatically say it makes good preaching. But the word is pointed like a noun, not a verb; and it is a well-established fact that *matū* in Akkadian means "man," and probably the second part means "spear." This last portion is not a verb, **"it shall be sent,"** but is pointed like a noun, "spear" or "dart." Thus, he most likely was a hunter. Stigers says *shelach* may refer to deity, thus "man of God." Maybe he was a law enforcement officer and had a reputation for law and order in a day when violence filled the earth (cf. 6:11). **Lamech,** the son or offspring of Methuselah and not to be confused with the polygamist and arrogant tyrant of Cain's line, lived a mere 777 years, **and he died.** He was noted for his yearning for **comfort . . . concerning our work and toil** due to effects of the curse in 3:17. His oracle of the birth of his son is a word-play, passing over the obvious etymology of the name **Noah,** meaning "rest," for the somewhat similar verb *nacham*, meaning comfort. The allusion to 3:17 may be a sign that he treasured the promise of 3:15. Here is a case, in the very same context as Methuselah, where a birth is the occasion for a prophecy. And the context makes it very clear that it is meant to be interpreted as such! But there is no such indication for Methuselah. Little did Lamech know the role that his son would play in the plan of God.

Noah begat Shem, Ham, and Japheth. Japheth was the oldest (cf. 10:21); **Ham,** the youngest (cf. 9:24). This list demonstrates the pedagogical purposes of the genealogical lists of the Bible. These three sons were brothers, not in the father-son or grandson relationship of the individuals in chapter 5. They are not named in chronological order, either. Shem is mentioned first because it was through him that God's Messiah would come (cf. 11:27 for the same phenomenon). Also, there is a symmetrical structure to these lists (i.e., in chs. 5 and 11; also Mt 1 with three lists of fourteen members each). Each (chs. 5 and 11) contains ten individuals, the tenth in each case having three sons. There is a tenfold scheme of histories in Genesis and a tenfold selective genealogy of Ruth 4:18-22; so the antiquity of the race cannot even approximately be determined from the data of chapters 5 and 11:10ff. The concern of chapter 5 is the continuance of the covenant community through the entire prediluvian age.

This chapter serves at least three ends in the scheme of Genesis: (1) it bears witness to man's value to God; by naming individuals and stages in this early human phase, each is known and remembered; (2) it shows how the line of Seth, "the appointed," led to Noah, "the deliverer"; and (3) it both demonstrates the reign of death by the refrain **and he died** and the standing pledge of death's defeat by the taking of Enoch.

E. Sin and the Flood. 6:1-8:22.

6:1-4. The sons of God saw the daughters of men . . . and they took them wives of all which they chose. The earth's population grew rapidly with the longevity of men. The point of this passage, whichever way we take it, is that a new stage has been reached in the progress of evil. The theme of the rulers, Lamech, etc., in 4:23ff., is resumed. Here, the pinnacle of abominations is reached, provoking divine vengeance. **The sons of God** are identified by some as the sons of Seth, as against those of Cain. Others, including early Jewish writers, take them to mean angels. Most students are familiar with the arguments, pro and con, of these views; so space will be given for the writer's preference, which has not always been presented adequately in other places.

The sons of God may very well be a reference to men like

dren to them, the same *became* mighty men which *were* of old, men of renown.

5 ¶And God saw that the wickedness of man *was* great in the earth, and *that* every imagination of the thoughts of his heart *was* only evil continually.

6 And it repented the LORD that he had made man on the earth, and it grieved him at his heart.

7 And the LORD said, I will destroy man whom I have created from the

Lamech, in 4:23ff., who were the leaders of the day and were very wicked and violent. From a global perspective these would have been city-state or tribal chiefs, kings, sheiks, despots and tyrants. Reasons: (1) *'Elōhīm* in Scripture is used in reference to human leaders in Ex 21:6; Ps 82:1. It is significant that in verse 6 *'Elōhīm* (judges) is synonymous with *benē 'elyōn*. Note, "I said, 'Ye are gods and all of you children (sons) of the Most High!'" So one cannot say that **sons of God** is never used with reference to men in the Old Testament; (2) "son of" is an idiom, meaning to bear the character of someone or something. Thus, the judges in Israel were called **sons of** (*'Elōhīm*) God because they bore His character in judgment among the Israelites; (3) *'Elōhīm* is used in an elative sense in the Old Testament in 23:6; 30:8; Ex 15:15; Jonah 3:3 meaning "mighty, great, or exceeding" (cf. in vs. 4 the **mighty men . . . of renown**); (4) the Aramaic targum Onkelos supports this view with sons of nobles, and so does Symmachus' Greek translation (the sons of the kings or lords); (5) archaeology attests to the fact that a Near Eastern king would consistently be referred to as the son of his god (note: son of Re or Keret as *Krt bn il* = Keret, the son of the god); (6) the offspring in verse 4 are depicted as **mighty men which were of old, men of renown,** i.e., men who made a name for themselves, a reputation. Compare Nimrod, a city founder, called a **mighty one in the earth** in 10:8, and **a mighty hunter before the LORD** in 10:9. Also, at Babel the desire was to **make us a name** (11:4) or a reputation; (7) the context certainly provides a proper hermeneutic for understanding this in the light of the culture and language of the day. City building in 4:17, polygamy in 4:19, tyranny in 4:23-24, along with leaders taking law and order into their own hands for personal benefits, and warfare among the leaders in 4:23-24 are all described. These same sins have been committed since the Flood; but their combination and the widespread general wickedness caused God to judge the earth. Also, verse 3 records that God did **strive with man,** not angels; (8) the Gilgamesh Epic and Sumerian flood stories introduce their flood accounts with allusions to the theme of kingship, centering in cities whose kings had their own sons appointed as kings, much like chapter 4; and (9) the *nepilīm,* in Arabic, means princes born into royal houses.

This view does the most justice to a grammatical, historical, and literal method of interpretation, in addition to the exegetical data; and it contains the fewest problems of all the views. Thus, one would have the **sons of God,** that is **mighty men,** who were warriors and members of the aristocracy, engaged in worldwide violence and warfare.

The Lord God could not tolerate such a situation. Thus, He said, **My spirit shall not always strive with man.** Two interpretations are possible: (1) it is a reference to the Holy Spirit striving, in the sense of judging or executing judgment on mankind for its sinfulness or (2) it is a reference to the fact that the human spirit that God placed in human beings would not always abide. That is, mankind was doomed to death. Man was given 120 years after this warning before the judgment of the Flood actually came. This verse poses a problem for the view that **the sons of God** were angels. So some have opted for a demon possession interpretation, allowing for the Spirit of God to still **strive** with men who are responsible for such an action of possession.

5-8. And God saw invites a bitter contrast with the Creation story of 1:31. Man's evil is presented intensively by the words **every . . . only . . . continually. Imagination** is derived from the potter's verb **formed** used in 2:7 and implies a design or purpose. What an indictment against the hearts of fallen men. So evil had men become by the days of Noah that **it repented the LORD that he had made man on the earth.** The word **repented** does not mean that God made a mistake in His deal-

face of the earth; both man, and beast, and the creeping thing, and the fowls of the air; for it repenteth me that I have made them.

8 But Noah found grace in the eyes of the LORD.

9 ¶These *are* the generations of Noah: Noah was a just man *and* perfect in his generations, *and* Noah walked with God.

10 And Noah begat three sons, Shem, Ham, and Jā'pheth.

11 The earth also was corrupt before God, and the earth was filled with violence.

12 And God looked upon the earth, and, behold, it was corrupt; for all flesh had corrupted his way upon the earth.

13 And God said unto Noah, The end of all flesh is come before me; for the earth is filled with violence through them; and, behold, I will destroy them with the earth.

14 Make thee an ark of gopher wood; rooms shalt thou make in the ark, and shalt pitch it within and without with pitch.

15 And this *is the fashion* which thou shalt make it *of*: The length of the ark *shall be* three hundred cubits, the breadth of it fifty cubits, and the height of it thirty cubits.

16 A window shalt thou make to the ark, and in a cubit shalt thou finish it above; and the door of the ark shalt thou set in the side thereof; *with* lower, second, and third *stories* shalt thou make it.

17 And, behold, I, even I, do bring a flood of waters upon the earth, to destroy all flesh, wherein *is* the breath of life, from under heaven; *and* every thing that *is* in the earth shall die.

18 But with thee will I establish my covenant; and thou shalt come into the ark, thou, and thy sons, and thy wife, and thy sons' wives with thee.

19 And of every living thing of all flesh, two of every *sort* shalt thou bring into the ark, to keep *them* alive with thee; they shall be male and female.

20 Of fowls after their kind, and of

ings with men, but rather indicates a change in divine direction resulting from the actions of man. It is "an anthropopathic" (a human emotion applied to God) description of the pain that is caused to the love of God by the destruction of His creatures (Delitzsch, Vol. 2, p. 225). So evil had man become that God, moved by compassion, decided, **I will destroy man whom I have created from the face of the earth.** There is one footnote, however, to this universal destruction. It is not only a footnote, but the preface to a whole new chapter in the history of mankind. **But Noah found grace in the eyes of the LORD.** In Hebrew **grace** comes from a root meaning "to bend or stoop"; thus, the condescending or unmerited favor of a superior person to an inferior one is implied. This is its first occurrence in Scripture, and it is often used redemptively (Jer 31:2; Zech 12:10). Mankind, the beasts of the field, and the fowl of the air would be destroyed. But God would call out a remnant unto Himself.

9-13. In the closer description of Noah we learn that **Noah was a just man;** and like Enoch, **Noah walked with God. Just** relates to Noah's relationship with God; he was in a right relationship with God. He was also **perfect,** which conveys the idea of maturity or completeness. The phrase **in his generations** conveys the thought that Noah lived this way among his contemporaries who were so wicked that God was going to destroy the world. He of all people knew how to stand alone for God. As God had already determined in His heart, so now He revealed His plan to Noah: **Behold, I will destroy them with the earth.** In a world of physical giants, God sought out a spiritual giant.

14-16. In conversing with Noah, God was quick to explain how He would destroy the inhabitants of the earth and yet save the lives of Noah and his family. **Make thee an ark of gopher wood.** The ark was not a ship, but more of a barge-like vessel. This word appears only here and again in Exodus 2:3, 5, where it describes the small basket into which Moses was placed. It apparently was a flat-bottomed, rectangular barge with no mast or rudder. Noah and his family had no place to go except where God would take them. Gopher wood, or pitch wood, was probably a type of cedar or cyprus. The ark was to be divided into **rooms;** and in order to make it seaworthy, Noah would **pitch it within and without with pitch** (lit., cover it with a covering). Pitch was probably a bitumen or asphalt substance (LXX had Gr *asphaltos;* the Vulgate had Lat *bitum*). The root word is equivalent to our English word "cover."

The dimensions of the ark were **three hundred cubits** by **fifty cubits** by **thirty cubits.** Reckoning a cubit to be eighteen inches in length, this means the ark was approximately 450 feet long, 75 feet wide, and 45 feet high; and these dimensions are exactly those necessary for a barge-like vessel. **A window** was placed at the top of the ark, and **the door of the ark** was placed in its side. Altogether, the ark would contain three stories.

17-22. Again God reiterated His promise **to destroy all flesh . . . and every thing that is in the earth shall die.** Yet, God would remember Noah; therefore, He said, **with thee will I establish my covenant.** The covenant had these conditions placed upon it. First, Noah would be saved only if he, his wife, his sons, and his **sons' wives** would enter the safety of the ark. There would be no shelter or salvation apart from the ark that God commanded Noah to build. In addition, He commanded Noah to take **of every living thing of all flesh . . . male and female** into the ark with him. This included **fowls . . . cattle . . . every creeping thing . . . two of every sort.** God made provision not only for the salvation of eight precious people, but

cattle after their kind, of every creeping thing of the earth after his kind, two of every *sort* shall come unto thee, to keep *them* alive.

21 And take thou unto thee of all food that is eaten, and thou shalt gather *it* to thee; and it shall be for food for thee, and for them.

22 Thus did Noah; according to all that God commanded him, so did he.

CHAPTER 7

AND the LORD said unto Noah, Come thou and all thy house into the ark; for thee have I seen righteous before me in this generation.

2 Of every clean beast thou shalt take to thee by sevens, the male and his female: and of beasts that *are* not clean by two, the male and his female.

3 Of fowls also of the air by sevens, the male and the female; to keep seed alive upon the face of all the earth.

4 For yet seven days, and I will cause it to rain upon the earth forty days and forty nights; and every living substance that I have made will I destroy from off the face of the earth.

5 And Noah did according unto all that the LORD commanded him.

6 And Noah *was* six hundred years old when the flood of waters was upon the earth.

7 And Noah went in, and his sons, and his wife, and his sons' wives with him, into the ark, because of the waters of the flood.

8 Of clean beasts, and of beasts that *are* not clean, and of fowls, and of every thing that creepeth upon the earth,

9 There went in two and two unto Noah into the ark, the male and the female, as God had commanded Noah.

10 And it came to pass after seven days, that the waters of the flood were upon the earth.

11 In the six hundredth year of Noah's life, in the second month, the seventeenth day of the month, the same day were all the fountains of the great deep broken up, and the windows of heaven were opened.

for the continuation of the various species of animals as well. He then advised Noah to lay in store in the ark all the food necessary for his family and the animals.

The last verse of this chapter is most remarkable. Although God has explained that He will destroy all those on the earth, He has not yet explained to Noah how this will be accomplished. He has told Noah to build an ark, but Noah has never seen an ark. He has described the dimensions of this floating vessel to Noah, but has not yet enlightened him as to how it would be set afloat. Nevertheless, in total faith and trust in his God with whom he walks, **Thus did Noah; according to all that God commanded him, so did he.** There is little wonder it is recorded that, "By faith Noah, being warned of God of things not seen as yet, moved with fear, prepared an ark to the saving of his house; by the which he condemned the world, and became heir of the righteousness which is by faith" (Heb 11:7).

7:1-6. And the LORD said unto Noah, Come thou and all thy house into the ark. It is not without significance that this is the first invitation to **come** that God issues in the Bible. To enter the ark is to enter the place of safety and salvation. To be found in Christ is to be found in the place of safety in salvation. Many other calls to **come** will follow. "And the LORD said unto Moses, Come up to me into the mount, and be there: and I will give thee tables of stone . . ." (Ex 24:12). "Come now, and let us reason together, saith the LORD: though your sins be as scarlet, they shall be as white as snow . . ." (Isa 1:18). Jesus Christ said, "Come unto me, all ye that labor and are heavy laden, and I will give you rest" (Mt 11:28). "And Jesus said unto them, Come ye after me, and I will make you to become fishers of men" (Mk 1:17). The final invitation by God is found in Revelation 22:17: "And the Spirit and the bride say, Come. And let him that heareth say, Come. And let him that is athirst come. And whosoever will, let him take the water of life freely."

Noah and his family were invited to come into the ark of safety and salvation and to bring with them **Of every clean beast thou shalt take to thee by sevens, the male and his female: and of beasts that are not clean by two, the male and his female. Of fowls also of the air by sevens, the male and the female.** Here the distinction between clean and unclean relate to sacrifice (cf. 8:20), but later, in Leviticus 11 and Deuteronomy 14, it had to do with eating. **By sevens** (lit., seven seven) most likely means three pairs plus one extra. This is preferred over seven pairs, which would total fourteen in number. The extra animal was to be used for sacrifice after the Flood in 8:20. In verses 9 and 15 all the animals entered the ark **two and two,** but 6:19-20 tells us there were only **two of every sort** which entered. The best translation would be seven by seven and two by two. Again Noah's complete obedience unto the Lord is recorded: **And Noah did according unto all that the LORD commanded him.**

7-10. And Noah went in . . . because of the waters of the flood. . . . And it came to pass after seven days, that the waters of the flood were upon the earth. God allowed an entire week to pass while Noah, his family, and the animals silently waited in the ark. Doubtless, this was done to give the world an opportunity to repent and join those who had found safety (salvation) in God's ark, like the pause before the storm. And yet, Noah's contemporaries continued their lives in revelling and drunkenness, ridicule of the righteous, and reckless disregard to the commandments of God (cf. Lk 17:27).

11-24. God is very much interested in precision, and even the numbers recorded in Scripture are to be taken seriously. In verse 11 God takes note of the exact day on which the Flood began. On that day **were all the fountains of the great deep broken up, and the windows of heaven were opened.** Subter-

12 And the rain was upon the earth forty days and forty nights.

13 In the selfsame day entered Noah, and Shem, and Ham, and Jā′pheth, the sons of Noah, and Noah's wife, and the three wives of his sons with them, into the ark;

14 They, and every beast after his kind, and all the cattle after their kind, and every creeping thing that creepeth upon the earth after his kind, and every fowl after his kind, every bird of every sort.

15 And they went in unto Noah into the ark, two and two of all flesh, wherein is the breath of life.

16 And they that went in, went in male and female of all flesh, as God had commanded him: and the LORD shut him in.

17 And the flood was forty days upon the earth; and the waters increased, and bare up the ark, and it was lift up above the earth.

18 And the waters prevailed, and were increased greatly upon the earth; and the ark went upon the face of the waters.

19 And the waters prevailed exceedingly upon the earth; and all the high hills, that were under the whole heaven, were covered.

20 Fifteen cubits upward did the waters prevail; and the mountains were covered.

21 And all flesh died that moved upon the earth, both of fowl, and of cattle, and of beast, and of every creeping thing that creepeth upon the earth, and every man:

22 All in whose nostrils was the breath of life, of all that was in the dry land, died.

23 And every living substance was destroyed which was upon the face of the ground, both man, and cattle, and the creeping things, and the fowl of the heaven; and they were destroyed from the earth: and Noah only remained alive, and they that were with him in the ark.

24 And the waters prevailed upon the earth an hundred and fifty days.

CHAPTER 8

AND God remembered Noah, and every living thing, and all the cattle that was with him in the ark: and God made a wind to pass over the earth, and the waters assuaged;

2 The fountains also of the deep and the windows of heaven were stopped, and the rain from heaven was restrained;

3 And the waters returned from off the earth continually: and after the end of the hundred and fifty days the waters were abated.

4 And the ark rested in the seventh month, on the seventeenth day of the month, upon the mountains of Ar′a-răt.

5 And the waters decreased continually until the tenth month: in the tenth month, on the first day of the month, were the tops of the mountains seen.

ranean waters, as well as rain, contributed to the Flood. This must be considered a miracle of nature wrought by the hand of God. Simultaneously, it began to rain, continuing for **forty days and forty nights.** At the same time the waters of the ocean (Job 38:16, 30; 41:31; Ps 106:9) and the subterranean reservoirs (Deut 8:7; Job 28:4, 10; Ps 33:7) gushed forth untold tons of water. Although this judgment upon the earth would bring disaster to an unrighteous populace, nonetheless the animals and Noah were safe in the ark; for the LORD **shut him in.** "The 'shutting him' intimated that he had become the special object of divine care and protection, and to those without the season of grace was over (Mt 25:10)" (Jamieson, Fausset, and Brown, *A Commentary Critical, Experimental and Practical on the Old and New Testaments*, p. 22).

Although there are many who assert that the Flood graphically portrayed in these chapters was only a local phenomenon (see Introduction), nonetheless the language of this chapter precludes such a possibility. **And the waters prevailed, and were increased greatly upon the earth** (vs. 18). **And the waters prevailed exceedingly upon the earth; and all the high hills, that were under the whole heaven, were covered** (vs. 19). **And the mountains were covered** (vs. 20). **And all flesh died that moved upon the earth** (vs. 21). **All in whose nostrils was the breath of life . . . died** (vs. 22). **And every living substance was destroyed . . . Noah only remained alive, and they that were with him in the ark** (vs. 23). Finally, **the waters prevailed upon the earth a hundred and fifty days** (vs. 24). Water, which seeks its own level, could not continue to rise for 150 days in a local Mesopotamian valley flood. It is inconceivable that the Great Flood was anything else but a universal judgment of God upon a universally wicked society.

8:1-5. And God remembered Noah. This is not to intimate that during the days of the Flood God had forgotten His righteous servant; the verb remember refers to the special attention or personal care that God gives to His own. The verb is used the same way in reference to Samson (Jud 16:28), Hannah (I Sam 1:11), Abraham, for Lot's benefit (19:29), on behalf of Israel (Ex 2:24), and for the repentant thief on the cross (Lk 23:42). God remembers those who live righteously and express their needs to Him. **The waters assuaged; The fountains also of the deep and the windows of heaven were stopped.** Because of God's loving care for Noah and his family, the rising waters ceased; and abatement began. Just as miraculously as the fountains of the great **deep** were broken up and issued forth incomprehensible amounts of waters, so too, miraculously **the waters returned from off the earth continually.** Psalm 104:6-9 describes the abatement of the waters and tells us that after the ". . . waters stood above the mountains," an obvious reference to the peak flood stage, they ". . . fled . . ." and ". . . hasted away." The expression , "They go up by the mountains; they go down by the valleys . . ." is translated in the ASV as "the mountains rose" and "the valleys sank down." This is a reference to the reconfiguration of the topography of this planet that was caused by the rapid draining of waters into the abyss of the deep. Thus, the mountains and valleys we see today are higher and deeper than those of the antediluvian era. God set them as bounds so that the world would never again be destroyed by a flood.

According to the chronology of these chapters, the floods came when it began to rain and continued for forty days and forty nights. The floors of the oceans cracked open and gushed forth additional volumes of waters so that the flood waters rose for 150 days. When the waters stopped rising and began to assuage, the ark came to rest **upon the mountains of Ararat.** "The name Ararat is identical with the Assyrian Urartu, which, broadly speaking, embraces the territory of Armenia. In three of the four Old Testament passages where the word Ararat occurs, the Septuagint has simply transliterated it (8:4; II Kgs 19:37; Jer 51:27), while in the remaining passage the translators have rendered it with 'Armenia' (Isa 37:38). Since it is believed that the ark rested on the highest peak in the country, it has long been customary to identify the landing-place with Mount Massis (or Agridagh), situated a little northeast of Lake Van and rising to approximately 17,000 feet above sea level" (J. W. Montgomery, *The Quest for Noah's Ark*, p. 40). Yet, it must be remembered that this mountain chain extends for many hundreds of miles; thus, its location is only speculation at best. Some seventy-four days after the ark came to rest, **were the tops of the mountains seen.**

6 ¶And it came to pass at the end of forty days, that Noah opened the window of the ark which he had made:

7 And he sent forth a raven, which went forth to and fro, until the waters were dried up from off the earth.

8 Also he sent forth a dove from him, to see if the waters were abated from off the face of the ground;

9 But the dove found no rest for the sole of her foot, and she returned unto him into the ark, for the waters were on the face of the whole earth: then he put forth his hand, and took her, and pulled her in unto him into the ark.

10 And he stayed yet other seven days; and again he sent forth the dove out of the ark;

11 And the dove came in to him in the evening; and, lo, in her mouth was an olive leaf pluckt off: so Noah knew that the waters were abated from off the earth.

12 And he stayed yet other seven days; and sent forth the dove; which returned not again unto him any more.

13 ¶And it came to pass in the six hundredth and first year, in the first *month,* the first *day* of the month, the waters were dried up from off the earth: and Noah removed the covering of the ark, and looked, and, behold, the face of the ground was dry.

14 And in the second month, on the seven and twentieth day of the month, was the earth dried.

6-12. Another **forty days** elapsed before **Noah opened the window . . . And he sent forth a raven.** This unclean bird was particularly well-suited to discover whether or not the Flood had destroyed all flesh. The raven was a bird of prey and would be able to sustain itself by feeding on carrion (Prov 30:17). But the earth was not yet an inhabitable place, and the raven **went forth to and fro** flying back and forth **until the waters were dried up from off the earth.** Noah also **sent forth a dove,** apparently after seven days (vs. 8), **to see if the waters were abated.** The dove, which naturally inhabits the valleys and not the mountaintops, **found no rest for the sole of her foot, and she returned unto him into the ark.** Seven days later he again sent forth the dove; and when she returned this time, **in her mouth was an olive leaf plucked off.** This was welcome proof to Noah that the waters had sufficiently drained so that the valleys were beginning to be clear. Another seven days passed when he sent forth the dove again, **which returned not again unto him any more.** This proved to Noah that the earth had once again become a friendly and inhabitable environment.

13-14. Again God is greatly interested in details; and He inspires Moses to record the exact day when **Noah removed the covering of the ark,** to view his surroundings, and to discern for himself that **the face of the ground was dry.**

Verse 14 represents the summary note on the chronology of the Flood. There were forty days in which rain fell (7:12), an additional 110 days in which the waters continued to **prevail** (7:24). Seventy-four days elapsed before the tops of the mountains were seen after the waters began their abatement (8:5). It was not until forty days later that Noah sent out the raven (8:6-7), and another seven days before the dove was released for the first time (8:8, 10). Seven more days elapsed before the dove was dispatched the second time (vs. 10), and an additional seven days occurred before the third mission of the dove (vs. 12). This accounts for 285 days since the beginning of the Flood, and another twenty-nine days elapsed before the events recorded in

15 ¶And God spake unto Noah, saying,

16 Go forth of the ark, thou, and thy wife, and thy sons, and thy sons' wives with thee.

17 Bring forth with thee every living thing that *is* with thee, of all flesh, *both* of fowl, and of cattle, and of every creeping thing that creepeth upon the earth; that they may breed abundantly in the earth, and be fruitful, and multiply upon the earth.

18 And Noah went forth, and his sons, and his wife, and his sons' wives with him:

19 Every beast, every creeping thing, and every fowl, *and* whatsoever creepeth upon the earth, after their kinds, went forth out of the ark.

20 ¶And Noah builded an altar unto the LORD; and took of every clean beast, and of every clean fowl, and offered burnt offerings on the altar.

21 And the LORD smelled a sweet savour; and the LORD said in his heart, I will not again curse the ground any more for man's sake; for the imagination of man's heart *is* evil from his youth; neither will I again smite any more every thing living, as I have done.

22 While the earth remaineth, seedtime and harvest, and cold and heat, and summer and winter, and day and night shall not cease.

CHAPTER 9

AND God blessed Noah and his sons, and said unto them, Be fruitful, and multiply, and replenish the earth.

2 And the fear of you and the dread of you shall be upon every beast of the earth, and upon every fowl of the air, upon all that moveth *upon* the earth, and upon all the fishes of the sea; into your hand are they delivered.

3 Every moving thing that liveth shall be meat for you; even as the green herb have I given you all things.

4 But flesh with the life thereof, *which is* the blood thereof, shall ye not eat.

5 And surely your blood of your lives will I require; at the hand of every beast

verse 13. Finally, fifty-seven more days are logged between the removal of the covering of the ark and the date of verse 14. This makes a grand total of 371 days, or more than one year, that the waters of the Great Deluge were upon the face of the earth.

15-19. And God spake unto Noah, saying, Go forth of the ark . . . be fruitful, and multiply upon the earth. The command initially issued to mankind in 1:28 is now reiterated to Noah. Noah would remove all the **fowl . . . cattle, and of every creeping thing** from the ark at the command of God.

20-22. One might think that having spent more than a year at sea, Noah's initial act upon stepping on dry ground would be to bend down and kiss the ground. But Noah was a man who **walked with God** (6:9), and now more than ever he recognized that salvation is of the Lord. Thus, **Noah builded an altar unto the LORD.** Thereupon he sacrificed of every **clean beast** and of every **clean fowl.** So great a salvation demanded a superabundant sacrifice. Perhaps the seventh animal and fowl of each species was sacrificed at this time. **And the LORD smelled a sweet savor.** Sacrifice offered by a righteous man in faith is always acceptable to God. Therefore, **the LORD said in his heart, I will not again curse the ground any more for man's sake.** God was not repealing the curse placed upon the ground as recorded in 3:17, but He was determining in Himself never again to destroy the ground by a universal flood. This determination did not arise as a result of the purity of man's heart. **The imagination of man's heart is evil from his youth;** thus, the problem with man's heart was not solved by the Flood. The eight people who were refuged from cataclysmic judgment by the safety of the ark still retained a sinful nature, and their descendants would still exhibit that nature. Thus, God determined that **While the earth remaineth, seedtime and harvest, and cold and heat, and summer and winter, and day and night shall not cease.** The Great Universal Flood would be the last total disruption of the natural processes of life that the world would see this side of the judgment bar of God. It is only since the Flood that we have a concept of "limited uniformitarianism." "All things" do not "continue as *they were* from the beginning of the creation" as the scoffers asserted in II Pet 3:4.

F. Noah's Later Life and His Descendants. 9:1-10:32.

9:1-7. And God blessed Noah and his sons, and said unto them, Be fruitful, and multiply, and replenish the earth. This is the second time this command has been given to Noah, the third time to mankind in general. God is preparing to establish a covenant with Noah similar to the covenant He established with Adam. This covenant will re-establish man's position before God and His creation. To once again fill the earth restores the relationship that man has to his planet. The **fear . . . and the dread,** which every beast of the earth and every fowl of the air and all the fish of the sea would have toward Noah and his family, re-establish man's dominion over the animal kingdom. This is a time of new beginnings; and thus, God deems it appropriate now to sanction the eating of **meat** as well as the **green herb.** Prior to this time, God had said that **every herb bearing seed . . . and every tree . . . to you it shall be for meat**

will I require it, and at the hand of man;
at the hand of every man's brother will
I require the life of man.

6 Whoso sheddeth man's blood, by
man shall his blood be shed: for in the
image of God made he man.

7 And you, be ye fruitful, and multiply; bring forth abundantly in the
earth, and multiply therein.

8 ¶And God spake unto Noah, and to
his sons with him, saying,

9 And I, behold, I establish my covenant with you, and with your seed after
you;

10 And with every living creature
that *is* with you, of the fowl, of the
cattle, and of every beast of the earth
with you; from all that go out of the ark,
to every beast of the earth.

11 And I will establish my covenant
with you; neither shall all flesh be cut
off any more by the waters of a flood;
neither shall there any more be a flood
to destroy the earth.

12 And God said, This *is* the token of
the covenant which I make between
me and you and every living creature
that *is* with you, for perpetual generations:

13 I do set my bow in the cloud, and it
shall be for a token of a covenant between me and the earth.

14 And it shall come to pass, when I
bring a cloud over the earth, that the
bow shall be seen in the cloud:

15 And I will remember my covenant,
which *is* between me and you and
every living creature of all flesh; and
the waters shall no more become a
flood to destroy all flesh.

16 And the bow shall be in the cloud;
and I will look upon it, that I may
remember the everlasting covenant

(1:29). Although the sinful race undoubtedly violated this prescription many times, it was not until this period of new beginnings that God actually sanctioned the eating of meat. The
Mosaic covenant further imposed limitations on the meats that
Israel could eat, but those limitations were lifted by God Himself for the Christian (Acts 10:11-16; I Tim 4:3-5). The only
restriction given here was that man should not eat of the blood of
the animal.

Verses 5 and 6 record the initiation of the second divinely
established institution. In 2:24 the institution of the family was
established; here the institution of civil government is established. Later, God would establish His church. God has invested
in mankind the right to govern itself; it is one of our inalienable
rights. Those who are set in authority over us are to be a terror
to evil works (Rom 13:3); and those who disobey the God-
ordained powers of human government are liable for punishment because ". . . the minister of God . . . beareth not the
sword in vain: for he is the minister of God, a revenger to
execute wrath upon him that doeth evil" (Rom 13:4). One of the
statutes of the government ". . . sword . . ." that is not borne
in vain is found in 9:6. **Whoso sheddeth man's blood, by man
shall his blood be shed.** This divinely established statute of
capital punishment is nowhere abrogated in Scripture and is as
valid today as it was in the days of Noah.

"Homicide (which in a sense is always fratricide, v. 5) demands a punishment that matches the crime. The justification
for capital punishment, here established, is the nobility of human life, which is made *in the image of God*" (Ryrie, p. 19). It is
not instituted primarily as a deterrent for crime, but as a strong
reminder of the uniqueness of man, created in the image of God.

For the fourth time, God commands to man in general, **be ye
fruitful, and multiply; bring forth abundantly in the earth, and
multiply therein.** The command to **replenish** the earth in verse
1 evidently was not obeyed by Noah's descendants, for the
disobedience occasioned the Babel judgment (cf. 11:4, . . . lest
we be scattered abroad upon the face of the earth).

8-19. As God begins to spell out the terms of the covenant
that He will make with Noah and his descendants, the God of all
mercy makes sure that Noah understands that this covenant also
affects all the animals that were with him in the ark. Basically,
the covenant was this: Never again **shall all flesh be cut off any
more by the waters of a flood.** "It is a fearful thing to fall into
the hands of the living God" (Heb 10:31). This was the lesson of
the Universal Flood. The Flood did not change the character of
mankind, nor did it return him to the position of innocence
which he enjoyed before the Fall. But it was a warning to man
that God will not tolerate sin and whenever man chooses to sin,
divine judgment soon follows. Yet never again will that judgment be in the form of a universal, globe-encircling flood. As a
sign of this covenant God determines: **I do set my bow in the
cloud, and it shall be for a token of a covenant between me
and the earth.** As Yahweh further explains why the rainbow is
so important as a token of the covenant, He says, **And the bow
shall be in the cloud; and I will look upon it, that I may
remember the everlasting covenant between God and every
living creature of all flesh that is upon the earth.** This is
obviously an anthropomorphism, a figure designed to enable
man to identify with God's faultless memory. Calvin notes that it
is introduced to remind man that God is ever-faithful to His
covenant engagements. God needs no prompting of His memory; the rainbow is there to assure us at the end of every
rainstorm that God has held His covenant in remembrance.
Each time we see a rainbow we ought to delight afresh in the
faithfulness of our God (cf. Lam 3:21-23). The word for bow
usually means a weapon. Thus, "the recurring rainbow imposed
on the retreating storm by the shining again of the sun is God's

between God and every living creature of all flesh that *is* upon the earth.

17 And God said unto Noah, This *is* the token of the covenant, which I have established between me and all flesh that *is* upon the earth.

18 ¶And the sons of Noah, that went forth of the ark, were Shem, and Ham, and Jā'pheth: and Ham *is* the father of Canaan.

19 These *are* the three sons of Noah: and of them was the whole earth overspread.

20 ¶And Noah began to be an husbandman, and he planted a vineyard:

21 And he drank of the wine, and was drunken; and he was uncovered within his tent.

22 And Ham, the father of Canaan, saw the nakedness of his father, and told his two brethren without.

23 And Shem and Jā'pheth took a garment, and laid *it* upon both their shoulders, and went backward, and covered the nakedness of their father; and their faces *were* backward, and they saw not their father's nakedness.

24 And Noah awoke from his wine, and knew what his younger son had done unto him.

battle bow laid aside, a token of grace staying the lightning-shafts of wrath" (Kline, *Genesis*, p. 90).

Ham is the father of Canaan. This circumstantial clause serves the function of connecting Canaan with Ham. It is not a mere genealogical note (cf. ch. 10), but to show that Ham, acting as he did, actually revealed himself as the true father of Canaan. The Israelite would immediately reflect upon a number of unfavorable images when he read this clause.

20-24. We do not know how soon after Noah left the ark **he planted a vineyard,** although enough time had to elapse for **Canaan** to be born to Noah's son **Ham** (vss. 18, 22). Perhaps out of necessity, **Noah began to be a husbandman.** The purpose of this expression is simply to identify him as a man of the ground (cf. 46:32, "a man of cattle"; Josh 5:4, "man of war"; II Sam 16:7, "a man of blood"; it may convey the idea that Noah would be considered as the master of the earth, or as Rashi understood it, "the lord of the earth," etc.). The two verbs in this verse are a verbal *hendiadys,* "he proceeded to plant" a vineyard. The verb *wayachel* provides an ominous note as it is used in 10:8 with Nimrod (**he began to be a mighty . . . hunter**) and in 11:6 concerning the activities of Babel (**this they begin to do**). **And he drank of the wine, and was drunken.** This is the first mention of wine in the Bible; but it was not the first occasion of drinking (Mt 24:38), so Noah must have known the effects of drinking. **And he was uncovered within his tent. And Ham, the father of Canaan, saw the nakedness of his father, and told his two brethren without.** The nature of the sin has occasioned much speculation and controversy. We are told Noah "lay uncovered" (*Hith* impf 3ms of *galah*) in his tent after he drank of the wine and became drunk. We are only told that Ham **saw the nakedness of his father,** nothing else. Speiser says, "the specific reference is to the *pudenda;* see the various injunctions in Lev xviii 6ff. The term itself relates to exposure (cf. xlii 9, 12) and does not necessarily imply sexual offenses; cf. ii 25 and Exod xx 26" (p. 61). Cassuto remarks "no evidence can be adduced from the expression, and (Ham) . . . saw the nakedness of his father (vs. 22), which is found elsewhere in the Pentateuch in connection with actual sexual relations (Lev 20:17: *If a man takes his sister, a daughter of his father or a daughter of his mother, and sees her nakedness, and she sees his nakedness; it is a shameful thing*), for of Shem and Japheth is said, in contradistinction to Ham's action: *their faces were turned away,* and they saw not their father's nakedness (vs. 23), from which we may infer, conversely, that Ham's sin consisted of seeing only. Furthermore, the statement (*ibid.*), and covered the nakedness of their father, supports this interpretation: if the covering was an adequate remedy, it follows that the misdemeanour was confined to seeing. And it is the seeing itself, the looking, that is accounted by the refined sensitivity of the Israelite as something disgusting, especially when it is associated, as it is here, with an affront to the dignity of one's father" (*Genesis Part II*, pp. 151-152). Also, the expression *ra'ah 'erwah,* which appears here, is used in Scripture for shameful exposure, mostly of a woman or as a figure of a city in shameful punishment, exposed and defenseless. This is quite different from the idiom used for sexual violation, *galah 'erwah,* "he uncovered the nakedness." This construction appears throughout Leviticus 18 and 20 to describe the sexual conduct of the Canaanites. It should be noted that Noah uncovered himself (the stem is reflexive), instead of it being Ham's responsibility, which would be the likelihood if it were active (Allen P. Ross, "The Curse of Canaan," Part I, *Bibliotheca Sacra,* July-Sept, 1980, pp. 223-241).

37

When Noah awoke from the effect of his wine, he **knew what his younger son had done unto him,** either by special revelation, inquiry, or memory. Literally, the expression for **his younger son** is his son, the little one and may indeed be a reference not to Ham, but to Canaan himself. Origen mentions a tradition that Canaan was the first one to see his grandfather's nakedness and informed his father Ham. Chrysostom held that Canaan was an accomplice to the drunkenness of Noah. What role Canaan played is unsure, but the consequences of that role were devastating. Or it may be that Noah saw in him the evil traits that marked his father Ham. The text has prepared us for this by twice pointing out that Ham was the father of Canaan (Ross, p. 233).

25 And he said, Cursed be Canaan; a servant of servants shall he be unto his brethren.
26 And he said, Blessed be the LORD God of Shem; and Canaan shall be his servant.
27 God shall enlarge Jā'pheth, and he shall dwell in the tents of Shem; and Canaan shall be his servant.

25-27. Once his senses had returned to him, Noah's initial words were, **Cursed be Canaan; a servant of servants shall he be unto his brethren.** The interpretation placed upon this curse by the majority of biblical scholars is wholly unacceptable, for some have even understood this text to vindicate the servitude of the black race. And yet the curse is not on Ham, but upon his son Canaan. The Canaanites lived in Palestine and were a Semitic group of peoples, not black at all. The descendants of Canaan, the Canaanites, largely fulfilled the consequences of this curse when Israel conquered the Promised Land (15:16ff.; Deut 7:1-2) and made them **a servant of servants.** This phrase is a superlative genitive *'ebed 'abadīm* indicating the most abject slavery. As evidence of this, we may point to the next verse, which says, **Blessed be the LORD God of Shem; and Canaan shall be his servant.** That a sharp distinction was to be drawn between paganism and the worship of Yahweh is evident from this curse. But **Japheth** was also blessed by God in that it was promised that **God shall enlarge Japheth** (a play on words as the name Japheth means enlargement). Thus, while Canaan would fall into servitude to the descendants of Shem and Japheth, both Shem and Japheth would be blessed by Yahweh God, Shem by having Yahweh as God, and Japheth by dwelling prosperously in a large portion of the earth, especially in the tents of Shem. This may be a direct result of Japheth's being a partner in covering up Noah.

28 And Noah lived after the flood three hundred and fifty years.
29 And all the days of Noah were nine hundred and fifty years: and he died.

28-29. All the days of Noah were nine hundred and fifty years: and he died. Noah was a man who was **a just man and perfect,** one who **walked with God** (6:9). He was a man of faith (Heb 11:7) who without question did exactly what God commanded him to do (6:22; 7:5). Of the **three hundred and fifty years** that Noah lived after the Flood, there is but one event recorded. Tragically, that event was his drunkenness and nakedness. How important it is that a man ". . . keep himself unspotted from the world" (Jas 1:27), especially after years of faithful service to God. Like the Apostle Paul, we must resolve, ". . . I keep under my body, and bring it into subjection: lest that by any means, when I have preached to others, I myself should be a castaway" (I Cor 9:27). Noah lived faithfully for over 600 years and then fell into sin. We are never beyond temptation and succumbing to it.

CHAPTER 10
NOW these are the generations of the sons of Noah, Shem, Ham, and Jā'pheth: and unto them were sons born after the flood.

10:1. Now these are the generations of the sons of Noah, Shem, Ham, and Japheth. This is the fourth time the term **generations,** better translated histories, has been employed (cf. 2:4; 5:1; 6:9). It most likely ends the section that relates to these individuals, rather than depicting that which follows, just as 2:4 and 5:1 did.

The names which follow are generally referred to as the Table of Nations. Most of these names belong to individuals, some of which were later used to identify entire nations. The chapter is designed to provide a table of the principal races and peoples known to the Israelites. They are arranged in order of seniority, except that the chosen Semite line comes last, according to the usual pattern, even though they are here traced alongside rather

2 The sons of Jā′pheth; Gō′mer, and Mā′gŏg, and Mād′a-ī, and Jā′van, and Tū′bal, and Mē′shĕch, and Tī′ras.

3 And the sons of Gō′mer; Ăsh′kenăz, and Rĭ′phăth, and Tō-gär′mah.

4 And the sons of Jā′van; E-lī′shah, and Tarshish, Kittim, and Dō′da-nĭm.

5 By these were the isles of the Gentiles divided in their lands; every one after his tongue, after their families, in their nations.

6 ¶And the sons of Ham; Cush, and Mĭz′ra-im, and Phut, and Canaan.

7 And the sons of Cush; Sē′ba, and Hăv′i-lah, and Săb′tah, and Rā′a-mah, and Săb′te-chah:and the sons of Rā′amah; Shē′ba, and Dē′dan.

8 And Cush begat Nimrod: he began to be a mighty one in the earth.

9 He was a mighty hunter before the LORD: wherefore it is said, Even as Nimrod the mighty hunter before the LORD.

10 And the beginning of his kingdom was Babel, and E′rĕch, and Ăc′căd, and Căl′nĕh, in the land of Shī′när.

11 Out of that land went forth Asshur, and builded Nĭn′e-veh, and the city Re-hō′bŏth, and Cā′lah,

12 And Rē′sen between Nĭn′e-veh and Cā′lah: the same is a great city.

13 And Mĭz′ra-im begat Lū′dim, and Ăn′a-mĭm, and Le′hā-bĭm, and Năph′tu-hĭm,

than directly to Israel (11:10ff.). The descendants total a conventional seventy, an indication that an exhaustive list is not intended. Apart from obvious exceptions like Nimrod, the sons are collective units genealogically related to the Noachic branch to which they are assigned. Because of early intermarriages, and later marriages between communities, certain groups could trace their lineage to more than one line. Within the three major divisions, subgroupings were distinguishable by the geographical, linguistic, ethnological, and political differences cited in the colophons (vss. 5, 20, 31), (Kline, p. 91).

2-5. The sons of Japheth: **Gomer** is usually identified with the Cimmerians of Greek mythology (cf. Ezk 38:6) and the progenitor of the Indo-European family of nations; **Magog**, originated in "the uttermost parts of the north" (Ezk 38:2, 6; 39:1-2), presumably in the vicinity of the Black Sea in the fifteenth century B.C.; **Madai**, the name used on Assyrian inscriptions for Media, was located west of the Caspian Sea in the ninth century B.C.; **Tubal** and **Meshech**, well known from the prophecies of Ezekiel (cf. Ezk 27:13; 32:26; 38:2; 39:1), are both located in eastern Anatolia, the Muski in northern Mesopotamia; **Tiras** was the ancestor of the Thracians of northern Greece, or perhaps the Etruscans of Italy.

The sons of Gomer: **Ashkenaz** was located southeast of Lake Urmia in the time of Esarhaddon; **Riphath** (I Chr 1:6) and his descendants lived by the Rhebas river, according to Josephus; **Togarmah** was mentioned in Ezekiel 27:14 with Javan, Tubal, and Meshech as well as in Ezekiel 38:6 with Gomer and was generally identified with the western part of Armenia, possibly near Carchemish.

The sons of Javan: **Elishah** probably became the inhabitants of Sicily and Sardinia (cf. Ezk 27:7); **Tarshish** is known as "afar off" (cf. Ps 72:10; Isa 66:19), and sites have ranged from the island of Rhodes to western Anatolia and Sardinia; **Kittim** is usually identified with Kition, the capital of Cyprus (cf. Isa 23:1, 12); **Dodanim** (Rodanim) as in I Chronicles 1:7 and the Septuagint of 10:4 (the letters "r" and "d" in Hebrew were often confused at different times). If "Rodanim" is correct, then Rhodes is the place.

By these were the isles of the Gentiles divided in their lands; every one after his tongue, after their families, in their nations (vs. 5). "Verse 5 is quite important because it seems to imply that the events of 11:1-9 occurred before the 'Gentiles' occupied the coastlands, an implication confirmed by the language of verses 25 and 32. Apparently the judgment at the Tower of Babel occurred during the life of Peleg" (Davis, p. 140).

6-20. And the sons of Ham: **Cush**, Ethiopia (Isa 45:14; Jer 13:23); **Mizraim**, the ordinary Hebrew name for Egypt; **Phut**, the Libyans of North Africa; and **Canaan**, the Canaanite people occupying the land of Phoenicia. These people spoke Semitic languages, not like Ham; so the basis of relation is geographical, not linguistical, i.e., language does not always indicate race.

The sons of Cush: **Seba** and **Havilah** are associated with the inhabitants of Arabia; **Sabtah** is near the western shore of the Persian Gulf. It has been identified as Shabwat, ancient Hadhramaut. **Raamah** was perhaps located on the Persian Gulf in Oman; **Sabtechah** was also on the Persian Gulf; **Sheba** was the principal city of Arabia (I Kgs 10:1); and **Dedan** was located either on the Persian Gulf or bordering Edom (Ezek 25:13; 27:20).

And Cush begat Nimrod: he began to be a mighty one in the earth. Nimrod was one of the most important descendants of Cush; he was a **mighty hunter.** So widely known was the hunting prowess of Nimrod that his name became proverbial for a great hunter: **Wherefore it is said, Even as Nimrod the mighty hunter before the LORD.** Arab traditions record ruins named

14 And Path-rū′sīm, and Căs′lu-hīm, (out of whom came Phĭ-lĭs′tĭm,) and Căph′to-rĭm.

15 ¶And Canaan begat Sī′don his firstborn, and Heth,

16 And the Jĕb′u-sīte, and the Ăm′or-īte, and the Gir′ga-sīte,

17 And the Hī′vīte, and the Ärk′īte, and the Sīn′īte,

18 And the Är′vad-īte, and the Zĕm′a-rīte, and the Hā′math-īte: and afterward were the families of the Canaanites spread abroad.

19 And the border of the Canaanites was from Sī′don, as thou comest to Ge′rär, unto Gä′za; as thou goest, unto Sodom, and Go-mor′rah, and Ăd′mah, and Ze-bō′im, even unto Lā′sha.

20 These are the sons of Ham, after their families, after their tongues, in their countries, and in their nations.

21 ¶Unto Shem also, the father of all the children of Ē′ber, the brother of Jā′pheth the elder, even to him were children born.

22 The children of Shem; Ē′lam, and Asshur, and Är-phăx′ăd, and Lud, and Ä′ram.

23 And the children of Ä′ram; Uz, and Hul, and Gĕ′ther, and Mash.

24 And Är-phăx′ăd begat Sā′lah; and Sā′lah begat Ē′ber.

25 And unto Ē′ber were born two sons: the name of one was Pē′lĕg; for in his days was the earth divided; and his brother's name was Jŏk′tăn.

26 And Jŏk′tăn begat Ăl-mō′dăd, and Shē′leph, and Hā-zar-mā′veth, and Je′rah,

27 And Ha-dō′ram, and Ū′zal, and Dĭk′lah,

28 And Ō′bal, and A-bĭm′a-el, and Shē′ba,

29 And Ō′phir, and Hăv′i-lah, and Jō′-băb: all these were the sons of Jŏk′tăn.

30 And their dwelling was from Mē′-sha, as thou goest unto Sĕ′phar a mount of the east.

31 These are the sons of Shem, after their families, after their tongues, in their lands, after their nations.

32 These are the families of the sons of Noah, after their generations, in their nations: and by these were the na-

after him at Birs-Nimrod, which is Borsippa, and the Nimrud of Calah. His activities centered first in **Shinar** (Babylonia) and included building the Tower of Babel (cf. 11:1-9); then he went to Assyria (cf. Mic 5:6). Stigers believes that since the context deals with men and not animals, his prowess in hunting deals with men; thus, his exploits are of a moral and spiritual nature. Mighty hunter is from *gibōr*, found in 6:4; and his name is derived from *marad*, meaning rebel. His name is **Nimrod** (lit., let us revolt). "Thus he established a thoroughly autocratic, imperialistic, despotic system of tyrannical government (of a kind described in Isa 13, 14), back of which stands Satan in all his rage against God" (*A Commentary on Genesis*, Stigers, p. 125). Certainly, this fits into the context, even with the next chapter (11:1-9) with Babel and the future Babylon of Revelation 17-18. No wonder the phrase **before the LORD** is included; what he did was very significant and gathered the attention of God Himself. God certainly knows what everybody does; but this made a strong impression, just like chapter 6 and the **sons of God.**

The descendants of Canaan: **Sidon,** the famous Phoenician commercial and maritime town on the coast of Syria (I Kgs 5:6; I Chr 22:4); **Heth,** the father of the Hittites (23:3, 5), is problematic here under Canaan. "The text is listing a mixed population in Canaan. And so the term is justified if it describes Hittites who swept south in vast ethnic movements" (Allen P. Ross, "The Table of Nations," *Bibliotheca Sacra* Jan-March, 1981, pp. 27-28); the **Jebusite,** the Canaanite tribe dwelling in Jerusalem and its environs (cf. Josh 15:63; Jud 1:21); the **Amorite,** dwellers on both sides of the Jordan (Josh 10:5); the **Girgasite** (Josh 24:11); the **Hivite,** dwellers in the country about Gibeon (Josh 9:7) and Sichem (34:2); the **Arkite,** inhabitants of Arka, a city of Phoenicia; the **Sinite,** a city near Arka; the **Arvadite,** dwellers of the maritime town, Arvad, some 100 miles north of Sidon (Ezk 27:8, 11); the **Zemarite,** dwellers in Simyra near Arvad; the **Hamathite,** the dwellers in Hamath who, subsequent to the confusion of tongues, were included in the **families of the Canaanites.**

And the border of the Canaanites was from Sidon . . . unto Gaza . . . unto Sodom . . . unto Lasha. This roughly forms a triangle that covers the land of Palestine.

21-32. The children of Shem, **the father of all the children of Eber.** Having dealt with the descendants of Japheth and Ham, the writer now shifts to the descendants of Shem; and the rest of the chapter is devoted to them. The importance of this Semitic line is evidenced from its development not only in verse 21ff. but in 11:10ff. as well. The most important descendant of Shem was Eber. He was the son of Arphaxad (vs. 24) and the father of Peleg and Joktan (vs. 25). Joktan (vss. 26ff.) was the progenitor of many Arab races; and he is dealt with first, thus reserving treatment of Peleg and his descendants, the most important being Abraham, for later in 11:16ff.

The division of the earth in verses 25 and 32 are most likely related to the events of 11:1-9. It does not refer to the splitting apart of the continents, but to the dispersion of peoples at the Tower of Babel. The fact that Peleg's ancestors are not mentioned as being alive at this time (Noah, Shem, etc.) implies that they had long since died. This is another indication that there are gaps in the genealogy of chapter 11. In 11:16-19 there is a considerable lowering of the life span from Eber to Peleg (from 464 to 239), which also suggests both a gap and that Eber may have been a distant ancestor of Peleg. This would also demonstrate why there are gaps in the genealogy.

tions divided in the earth after the flood.

CHAPTER 11

AND the whole earth was of one language, and of one speech.

2 And it came to pass, as they journeyed from the east, that they found a plain in the land of Shī'när; and they dwelt there.

3 And they said one to another, Go to, let us make brick, and burn them throughly. And they had brick for stone, and slime had they for morter.

4 And they said, Go to, let us build us a city and a tower, whose top *may reach* unto heaven; and let us make us a name, lest we be scattered abroad upon the face of the whole earth.

5 And the LORD came down to see the city and the tower, which the children of men builded.

6 And the LORD said, Behold, the people *is* one, and they have all one language; and this they begin to do: and now nothing will be restrained from them, which they have imagined to do.

7 Go to, let us go down, and there confound their language, that they may not understand one another's speech.

8 So the LORD scattered them abroad from thence upon the face of all the earth: and they left off to build the city.

9 Therefore is the name of it called Babel; because the LORD did there confound the language of all the earth: and from thence did the LORD scatter them abroad upon the face of all the earth.

G. The Tower of Babel. 11:1-32.

11:1-4. The whole earth. If **earth** is used in the same way as in 10:32, the linguistic observation applies to a situation not long after the Flood; and this verse bridges a lengthy interval. If it refers to **the land of Shinar,** the perspective of verse 1 is not universal (cf. vs. 9). All the people were of **one language, and of one speech,** most likely indicates that men spoke the same language and dialect. The word for **one speech** may mean "few," but not here; for it is parallel to the singular **one language.** Verse 2 indicates that these early inhabitants traveled actually eastward. In 8:4 Noah and his family landed in Ararat, and the migration would have been southeast and east into the Fertile Crescent. Writing began basically in Sumer, sometime in the fourth millennium B.C. As they journeyed, they dwelt in this plain and determined to stay there **lest we be scattered abroad upon the face of the whole earth.** This expresses an obstinate and defiant spirit, contrary to the clear command of God in 9:1 to **replenish** or fill the earth. Babel was certainly a special judgment on man's embodiment of the ungodly spirit that again characterized human civilization after the Flood. Much as in chapter 4, they decided to build **a city and a tower.** This is the cultural focus of mounting human arrogance. The tower (*migdal*) could be a fortress (Deut 1:28 and 9:1 speak of cities fortified up to heaven). Parallels to the account of the building of Babylon and its temple-tower (cf. the Babylonian epic *Enuma Elish*) suggest that it was a prototype ziggurat, or temple-mound, first found in classical form early in the third millennium B.C. Most likely, due to their defiant attitude it was a fortification with towers for defense; but possibly it was to keep people in (believers who knew they should fill the earth?) as Ryrie suggests. He acknowledges that this tower was not used for worship, but as a rallying point and a symbol of their fame. Their desire to **make us a name** goes back to 4:17, 22ff.; 6:4; 10:9, all focal points of rebellion that led to God's special judgment.

5-9. Man had arrogantly asserted, "Let us make brick . . . let us build us a city . . . let us make us a name" (vss. 3-4). Now God responds, **Let us go down** (cf. 18:2, 21; 19:1). He **came down to see the city and the tower** is not to be taken as His personal presence, as at other times (cf. Ex 19:20; 34:5; Num 11:25; 12:5); but it is an anthropomorphic description of His interposition in the actions of men, "primarily 'judicial cognizance of the actual face,' and then, verse 7, a judicial infliction of punishment" (Davis, p. 149). God came to see the city and the tower **which the children of men builded.** Even though the verb **builded** is in the perfect tense, usually indicating a completed action, it seems as if the Lord came down before the construction was completed. This is due to verse 8, which says that after the judgment these men **left off to build the city.**

The purpose is expressed as **let us go down, and there confound their language, that they may not understand one another's speech;** and so, in verse 9 God **did there confound the language of all the earth: and from thence did the LORD scatter them abroad upon the face of all the earth.** What man would not do willingly, God forced them to do as a result of judgment; and today there are more than 3000 languages and dialects. The result of this confusion was the scattering of mankind. The name Babel is linked with the Hebrew verb *balal* (to confuse). But the ancient Babylonians called the city *Bab-ilu,* meaning gate of God. At any rate, there is a pun of Babel-*balal*. In the Bible this city increasingly came to symbolize the godless society, with its pretensions (ch. 11), persecutions (Dan 3), pleasures, sins, and superstitions (Isa 47:8-13), as well as its riches and eventual doom (Rev 17; 18).

10 ¶These *are* the generations of Shem: Shem *was* an hundred years old, and begat Ăr-phăx'ăd two years after the flood:

11 And Shem lived after he begat Ăr-phăx'ăd five hundred years, and begat sons and daughters.

12 And Ăr-phăx'ăd lived five and thirty years, and begat Sā'lah:

13 And Ăr-phăx'ăd lived after he begat Sā'lah four hundred and three years, and begat sons and daughters.

14 And Sā'lah lived thirty years, and begat Ē'ber:

15 And Sā'lah lived after he begat Ē'ber four hundred and three years, and begat sons and daughters.

16 And Ē'ber lived four and thirty years, and begat Pē'lĕg:

17 And Ē'ber lived after he begat Pē'lĕg four hundred and thirty years, and begat sons and daughters.

18 And Pē'lĕg lived thirty years, and begat Rē'ū:

19 And Pē'lĕg lived after he begat Rē'ū two hundred and nine years, and begat sons and daughters.

20 And Rē'ū lived two and thirty years, and begat Se'rŭg:

21 And Rē'ū lived after he begat Se'rŭg two hundred and seven years, and begat sons and daughters.

22 And Se'rŭg lived thirty years, and begat Nahor:

23 And Se'rŭg lived after he begat Nahor two hundred years, and begat sons and daughters.

24 And Nahor lived nine and twenty years, and begat Te'rah:

25 And Nahor lived after he begat Te'rah an hundred and nineteen years, and begat sons and daughters.

26 And Te'rah lived seventy years, and begat Abram, Nahor, and Hâ'ran.

27 ¶Now these *are* the generations of Te'rah: Te'rah begat Abram, Nahor, and Hâ'ran; and Hâ'ran begat Lot.

28 And Hâ'ran died before his father Te'rah in the land of his nativity, in Ur of the Chăl'deeś.

29 And Abram and Nahor took them wives: the name of Abram's wife *was* Sâ'raī; and the name of Nahor's wife, Mĭl'cah, the daughter of Hâ'ran, the father of Mĭl'cah, and the father of Iś'cah.

30 But Sâ'raī was barren; she *had* no child.

31 And Te'rah took Abram his son, and Lot the son of Hâ'ran his son's son, and Sâ'raī his daughter in law, his son Abram's wife; and they went forth with them from Ur of the Chăl'deeś, to go into the land of Canaan; and they came unto Hâ'ran, and dwelt there.

32 And the days of Te'rah were two hundred and five years: and Te'rah died in Hâ'ran.

10-26. This selective list of ten generations is recorded for the purpose of tracing the ancestry of Abraham. **Shem** is the one who had received a prophetic blessing with messianic import from Noah (9:6). He was selected solely because he was the progenitor of the messianic line (cf. 5:32). The godly line is from Shem through **Terah** and ultimately to **Abram** (vs. 26), who was not the oldest but is listed first due to the emphasis on the messianic line.

Of the names in 10:22ff., only the ancestors of Eber reappear; thereafter, it is Peleg, not Joktan as in 10:25ff. Ten generations are shown, perhaps to match the ten of chapter 5 that deal with Adam to Noah. The growth of nations in chapter 10 makes it quite evident that great intervals lie between them. The life span is steadily contracting from the antediluvian level (an average of 800 years) to, in chapter 11, an average of 200 years. After that Abraham only lived to be 175 and Joseph, 110.

Also, the age of paternity before the Flood ranged from 65 to 187 and averaged 117; after the Flood the ages ranged from 29 to 35, except for Shem's 100, Terah's 70, and Abraham's 100. In the genealogy of chapter 11 the age at death is omitted.

27-32. This portion is a marked contrast to verses 1-9 and its demonstration of human rebellion which ended in divine judgment. Now we have a picture of divine grace, leading to the call of **Abram,** which provided hope and salvation for the nations. We are told **Terah begat Abram, Nahor, and Haran; and Haran begat Lot.** This is the same pattern as 5:32 when the oldest son is not placed first, but the most important son from the messianic viewpoint is first. According to 12:4 Abram was 75 years old when he departed from Haran; and according to verse 32 Terah died when he was 205, which means that Abram was born when his father was 130. So if verse 26 says that Terah **lived seventy years, and begat Abram,** it cannot be that Abram was born when Terah was 70; it must refer to one of the other sons. **Abram** means father of elevation, or exalted father. This signified the honor of his being the progenitor of God's chosen people. Later, in 17:5 his name would be changed to Abraham, which means father of a great number. He was born approximately 2165 B.C. We are told very little about **Terah,** Abraham's father; but according to Joshua 24:2ff, he worshiped heathen gods. His own name, and those of Laban, Sarah, and Milcah, points toward the moon-god as the most prominent pagan deity. Haran was a moon-worship center. **Haran died before his father Terah in the land of his nativity.** Haran literally died in the face of his father, Terah, indicating his father was still alive.

Much discussion has centered around the location of **Ur of the Chaldees.** "Until 1850, 'Ur of the Chaldees' was considered to be Urfa, near Haran, S. Turkey" (Wiseman, in the *Zondervan Pictorial Encyclopedia of the Bible [ZPEB]*, p. 846). But with the excavations at a southern Ur in Sumer, many scholars have opted for this place that has the same name as the biblical reference. In addition, to many at an earlier time, this helped to demonstrate the veracity of the Bible and was a good source for apologetics. But there are some very excellent arguments in favor of the northern Ur view. Namely, southern Ur was basically a Sumerian city; and thus, linguistically, ethnically, socially, politically, and geographically it was very different from a northern Mesopotamian culture. Actually, from the biblical testimony there would be no good reason to pick southern Ur as Abram's homeland if it were not for there being a southern Ur, especially since the northern Ur has not been specifically located (which is really no reason to doubt that it existed). Speiser notes "the mention of Ur of the Chaldeans brings up a problem of a different kind. The ancient and renowned city of Ur is never ascribed expressly, in the many thousands of cuneiform records from that site, to the Chaldean branch of the Aramaean group" (p. 80).

Haran had **died in Ur,** which was described as **the land of his nativity.** The word for **nativity** is *mōledet,* usually rendered birthplace; and there is no reason why it should not be so in this passage. Now, according to Acts 7:2, Abraham was called by God when he was "in Mesopotamia, before he dwelt in Haran" and thus he came ". . . out of the land of the Chaldeans, and dwelt in Haran." Since Haran was older than Abram, we can assume that Abram was raised in the "birthplace" of his brother; for his brother was evidently born there and died there. This must be the same place where Abram received his call from God as Acts 7:2 relates. This is the same as verse 31. In 24:4 Abraham sends his servant to his **country, and to my kindred;** and this is not a southern Ur but in northern Mesopotamia. The word **kindred** is the same as **nativity** of verse 28, *mōladti.* The servant went to Abraham's **country,** to his **kindred** or birthplace. In 24:10 he went to Mesopotamia unto the city of Nahor, possibly named for a brother. Joshua 24:2-3 relates that Terah **dwelt on the other side of the flood,** with **flood** referring to the Euphrates River. But southern Ur was not on the other side of the Euphrates! Deuteronomy 26:5 relates that Jacob was a wandering Aramaean, which would place the homeland in the north and not the south; and Jacob fled from Esau to Paddan-Aram, which was in the north. Also, Laban, Abraham's kinsman, spoke Aramaean (31:47). The word translated **Chaldees** in verse 28 (cf. 22:22) refers to a place in the same geographical area as Aram (Aram-naharaim) in the northern part of Mesopotamia. The archaic form of this word is preserved in this translation. So also in Isaiah 23:13 **Chesed** is placed between Sidon and Chittim before and Tarshish after, and this would indicate a northern locality.

In addition, the personal names of Abram's ancestors indicate that they were well-established in northern Mesopotamia long before Abram came on the scene. In verse 20 **Serug** is also the name of a city located at the confluence of the Barak and Euphrates River valley in the north. Nahor (vs. 23ff.) is also the name of a town in the upper Mesopotamian river basin. Terah (vs. 24ff.) is in the north, and so is Haran. Ur of the Chaldees most likely was a region within or near Haran. Also, Haran would never have been on the trade route from southern Ur to Canaan. There is a tablet from Ebla that reportedly refers to an Ur in Haran. All of this is important if we are to know where Abram lived, for it will help us to understand his culture and way of life and, therefore, to better interpret God's Word.

II. THE PATRIARCHS. 12:1-50:26.
A. Abraham, the Friend of God. 12:1-25:18.
1. His call and migration. 12:1-14:24.

Unlike any other religious literature ever written, the patriarchal narratives in chapters 12-50 are intensely personal accounts

CHAPTER 12

NOW the LORD had said unto Abram,
Get thee out of thy country, and from
thy kindred, and from thy father's
house, unto a land that I will shew thee:
2 And I will make of thee a great nation, and I will bless thee, and make thy
name great; and thou shalt be a blessing:
3 And I will bless them that bless
thee, and curse him that curseth thee:
and in thee shall all families of the earth
be blessed.

4 So Abram departed, as the LORD
had spoken unto him; and Lot went
with him: and Abram *was* seventy and
five years old when he departed out of
Hā'ran.
5 And Abram took Sā'raī his wife,
and Lot his brother's son, and all their
substance that they had gathered, and
the souls that they had gotten in Hā'-
ran; and they went forth to go into the
land of Canaan; and into the land of Canaan they came.
6 ¶And Abram passed through the
land unto the place of Sī'chem, unto the
plain of Mô'reh. And the Canaanite *was*
then in the land.
7 And the LORD appeared unto
Abram, and said, Unto thy seed will I
give this land: and there builded he an
altar unto the LORD, who appeared unto
him.
8 And he removed from thence unto a
mountain on the east of Běth-el, and
pitched his tent, *having* Běth-el on the
west, and Hā'ī on the east: and there he
builded an altar unto the LORD, and
called upon the name of the LORD.
9 And Abram journeyed, going on
still toward the south.

10 ¶And there was a famine in the
land: and Abram went down into Egypt
to sojourn there; for the famine *was*
grievous in the land.
11 And it came to pass, when he was
come near to enter into Egypt, that he
said unto Sā'raī his wife, Behold now, I
know that thou *art* a fair woman to look
upon:
12 Therefore it shall come to pass,
when the Egyptians shall see thee, that
they shall say, This *is* his wife: and they
will kill me, but they will save thee
alive.

of family life in the ancient world. They show us real, human
characters living their lives with all of the problems and successes common to life and dealing with a real, personal God.

Chapter 12 is the pivotal chapter in the whole book; for from
this point on God centers His attention upon one man, Abraham, and his family. Previously, God had dealt with the human
race, but now He turns His attention from a rebellious humanity
recently scattered by the judgment of Babel to this one family
through which the Saviour of the world would ultimately come.

12:1-3. Abram was in Haran in verse 1 (cf. vs. 4) when this
call came. It was originally given to him in **Ur of the Chaldees**
(15:7; Acts 7:2). We must conclude that he did not know where
he was going (to the land of Canaan, vs. 1; Heb 11:8). Thus, his
stay in Haran was not a result of disobedience. The phrase in
11:31 **to go into the land of Canaan** refers then to God's
ultimate purpose for Abram, not His command to him. The first
verse of chapter 12 reveals a threefold sacrifice to be made by
Abram. He was to separate himself: **Get thee out of thy** (1)
country; (2) **kindred;** and (3) **thy father's house.** God would
direct him to a **land.** The men of Babel wanted to make a name
for themselves and failed; but Abram trusted God, and God gave
him a great land!

The sacrifices Abram was to make did not compare to the
blessings he would receive: (1) **a land;** (2) **a seed (a great
nation);** and (3) he would be a **blessing.** Abram's whole life
centered around each of these promises as he was severely tested
in all three areas. When God promised him a great nation, he did
not have a son (cf. 11:30, **But Sarai was barren; she had no
child**).

**4-9. So Abram departed, as the LORD had spoken unto
him.** Once he arrived in the land we are told **the Canaanite was
then in the land.** These were wicked people, and in 15:16ff. and
Deuteronomy 7:1ff. they were later to be destroyed because of
the abominations they practiced. So in the place of God's calling, there were testings that came from his neighbors. In each
place Abram went he **builded an altar unto the LORD, and
called upon the name of the LORD.** He first came to **Sichem**
(Shechem between Mount Ebal and Mount Gerizim) and then
near **Beth-el . . . and Hai** (Ai), which was twenty miles further
south.

10-20. In this place a famine came; and it was in His will.
This was not uncommon in Palestine (cf. 26:1 and 41:56).
Evidently, Abram was not sinning when he **went down into
Egypt**, for God does not say "No" as He did later to Isaac in
26:1-2. But he was sinning when he told Sarai his wife to **say, I
pray thee, thou art my sister: that it may be well with me . . .
and my soul shall live.** This is one of the Bible's remarkable
traits. It reveals the sins of some of its greatest men, even the
man who was called "Abraham my friend" by God (Isa 41:8),
the only person in the Bible referred to by this terminology. It is
startling to see his deception at this particular time, long after he
had believed and answered God's call; but it is even more

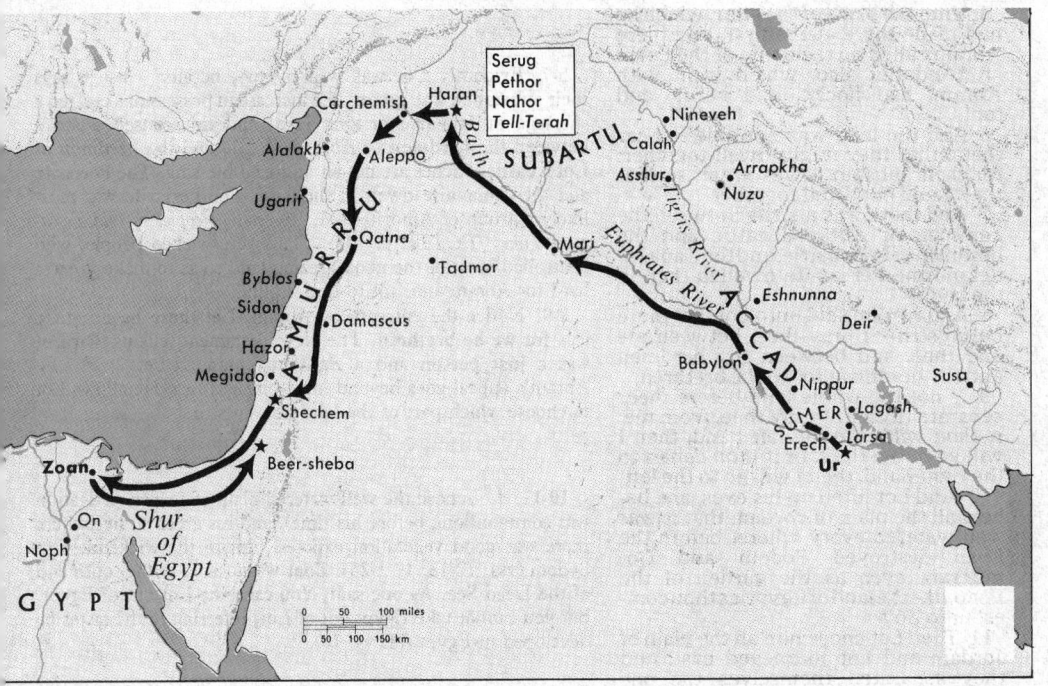

The Tradition of Abraham's Wanderings

13 Say, I pray thee, thou *art* my sister: that it may be well with me for thy sake; and my soul shall live because of thee.

14 ¶And it came to pass, that, when Abram was come into Egypt, the Egyptians beheld the woman that she *was* very fair.

15 The princes also of Pharaoh saw her, and commended her before Pharaoh: and the woman was taken into Pharaoh's house.

16 And he entreated Abram well for her sake: and he had sheep, and oxen, and he asses, and menservants, and maidservants, and she asses, and camels.

17 And the LORD plagued Pharaoh and his house with great plagues because of Sâ′raī Abram's wife.

18 And Pharaoh called Abram, and said, What *is* this *that* thou hast done unto me? why didst thou not tell me that she *was* thy wife?

19 Why saidst thou, She *is* my sister? so I might have taken her to me to wife: now therefore behold thy wife, take *her*, and go thy way.

20 And Pharaoh commanded *his* men concerning him: and they sent him away, and his wife, and all that he had.

CHAPTER 13
AND Abram went up out of Egypt, he, and his wife, and all that he had, and Lot with him, into the south.

2 And Abram *was* very rich in cattle, in silver, and in gold.

3 And he went on his journeys from the south even to Běth-el, unto the place where his tent had been at the beginning, between Běth-el and Hā′ī;

amazing to know that this was his practice from the time he left Ur. Notice 20:13: **And it came to pass, when God caused me to wander from my father's house, that I said unto her, This is thy kindness which thou shalt show unto me; at every place whither we shall come, say of me, He is my brother.** Many Christians would do well to realize salvation does not change all of their old sinful practices. It is true that she was his half-sister; but obviously, his intention was to save his own skin and to deceive others by not revealing they were married. But God knew what Abram had done, and in His sovereignty He **plagued Pharaoh and his house with great plagues because of Sarai Abram's wife.** In His omniscience God disciplined His child. Scheming will not work in the life of God's children. Certainly, Abram was not **a blessing** (vs. 2, **and thou shalt be a blessing**). We will discuss the Nuzi materials and the wife-sister concept in 20:12ff. It is significant to note that God did this—exposed Abram—because of Sarai (note also 20:18). God had patched up the holes in Sarai's umbrella of protection, her husband. She had submitted to her husband by lying, and God had protected her.

13:1-4. Abram **was very rich in cattle, in silver, and in gold.** He seems to have gone to Beth-el to renew his vows on his return. There is no record of how long he was in Egypt, but there is no indication that he ever worshiped the Lord in Egypt either. The phrases **at the beginning** and **at the first** indicate that he needed to make a new start.

4 Unto the place of the altar, which he had made there at the first: and there Abram called on the name of the LORD.

5 ¶And Lot also, which went with Abram, had flocks, and herds, and tents.

6 And the land was not able to bear them, that they might dwell together: for their substance was great, so that they could not dwell together.

7 And there was a strife between the herdmen of Abram's cattle and the herdmen of Lot's cattle: and the Canaanite and the Pĕr′izz-īte dwelled then in the land.

8 And Abram said unto Lot, Let there be no strife, I pray thee, between me and thee, and between my herdmen and thy herdmen; for we be brethren.

9 *Is* not the whole land before thee? separate thyself, I pray thee, from me: if *thou wilt take* the left hand, then I will go to the right; or if *thou depart* to the right hand, then I will go to the left.

10 And Lot lifted up his eyes, and beheld all the plain of Jordan, that it *was* well watered every where, before the LORD destroyed Sodom and Gomŏr′rah, *even* as the garden of the LORD, like the land of Egypt, as thou comest unto Zō′ar.

11 Then Lot chose him all the plain of Jordan; and Lot journeyed east: and they separated themselves the one from the other.

12 Abram dwelled in the land of Canaan, and Lot dwelled in the cities of the plain, and pitched *his* tent toward Sodom.

13 But the men of Sodom *were* wicked and sinners before the LORD exceedingly.

14 ¶And the LORD said unto Abram, after that Lot was separated from him, Lift up now thine eyes, and look from the place where thou art northward, and southward, and eastward, and westward:

15 For all the land which thou seest, to thee will I give it, and to thy seed for ever.

16 And I will make thy seed as the dust of the earth: so that if a man can number the dust of the earth, *then* shall thy seed also be numbered.

17 Arise, walk through the land in the length of it and in the breadth of it; for I will give it unto thee.

18 Then Abram removed *his* tent, and came and dwelt in the plain of Măm′re, which *is* in Hē′bron, and built there an altar unto the LORD.

CHAPTER 14

AND it came to pass in the days of Ăm′raphĕl king of Shī′när, Ā′rī-ŏch king of Ĕl′la-sär, Chĕd-or-lā′ō-mer king of Ē′lam, and Tī′dal king of nations;

2 That these made war with Be′ra king of Sodom, and with Bir′sha king of Go-mŏr′rah, Shī′-năb king of Ăd′mah, and Shĕm-ē′ber king of Ze-boi′im, and the king of Bē′la, which *is* Zō′ar.

3 All these were joined together in the vale of Sĭd′dĭm, which *is* the salt sea.

4 Twelve years they served Chĕd-or-

5-7. Evidently Lot was wealthy too, because verse 6 says **their substance was great.** The increase in possessions created a shortage of available grazing land, and this caused **a strife between the herdmen of Abram's cattle and the herdmen of Lot's cattle.** Riches are not an unmixed blessing. The **Perizzite** and the **Canaanite** dwelt in the land. The **Perizzite** was most likely a group of Amorites (M. Liverani, *Peoples of Old Testament Times [POTT]*, p. 101). They were wicked people, who controlled most of the good grazing land so as to make it extra hard for Abram and Lot to find ground.

8-9. Notice the entreaty by Abram, **Let there be no strife . . . for we be brethren.** The New Testament tells us that Lot was a **just** person and a **righteous man** (II Pet 2:7-8). So Abram's appeal goes beyond mere physical ties. He allows Lot to choose which part of the land he wants first.

10-11. Lot chose the well-watered plain of Jordan (irrigation was common long before his time), and his greed to live where there was good vegetation exposed him to the wickedness of Sodom (vss. 12-13; 19:1-25). **Zoar** was located at the south end of the Dead Sea. As one said, You can take Lot out of Egypt, but you cannot take Egypt out of Lot, referring to the tastes he developed in Egypt (cf. vs. 10).

12-18. God gives the best to those who leave the choice with Him! Lot **dwelled in the cities of the plain, and pitched his tent toward Sodom.** This was the first step downwards. In 14:12 he **dwelt in Sodom** and had to be rescued by Abram; and then in 19:1 he **sat in the gate,** which meant he ruled in the city government. It was only after Lot separated himself from Abram that God called Abram aside. He then received a reaffirmation of God's promise to give the land of Canaan to him and his **seed for ever.** Then Abram **dwelt in the plain of Mamre, which is in Hebron, and built there an altar unto the LORD.** Mamre was an Amorite and an ally of Abram in 14:13.

14:1-12. The exact political situation depicted in this chapter and the particular kings have not yet been identified. Many of the names, however, are recognized as authentic for the early second millennium B.C. Characteristic of that period, too, were coalitions for political power. Yet, it must be recalled that Abraham lived in the third millennium B.C. The name **Amraphel king of Shinar** (cf. 10:10; 11:2 for Shinar), which may indicate Babylon for Shinar and **Amraphel,** was earlier thought to be a reference to Hammurabi; but the final *l* would have to be an error, and the initial *'aleph* a mistake for *'ayin*. Also, Hammurabi lived several centuries later than Abraham. The name **Arioch** is known from both Mari in the eighteenth

lā′ō-mer, and in the thirteenth year they rebelled.

5 And in the fourteenth year came Chĕd-or-lā′ō-mer, and the kings that *were* with him, and smote the Rĕph′a-imŝ in Äsh′te-rŏth Kär-nā′im, and the Zü′zimŝ in Ham, and the Ē′mĭms in Shā′veh Kĭr-ĭ-a-thā′im,

6 And the Hŏ′rītes in their mount Sē′ir, unto Ĕl-pâ′ran, which *is* by the wilderness.

7 And they returned, and came to Ēn-mĭsh′păt, which *is* Kā′desh, and smote all the country of the Am′ă-lek-ītes, and also the Ămorītes, that dwelt in Hăz′e-zŏn-tā′mar.

8 And there went out the king of Sod-om, and the king of Go-mŏr′rah, and the king of Ăd′mah, and the king of Ze-boi′im, and the king of Bē′la (the same *is* Zō′ar;) and they joined battle with them in the vale of Sĭd′dĭm;

9 With Chĕd-or-lā′ō-mer the king of Ē′lam, and with Tī′dal king of nations, and Ăm′ra-phĕl king of Shī′när, and Ā′-rĭ-ŏch king of Ĕl′la-sär; four kings with five.

10 And the vale of Sĭd′dĭm *was full of* slimepits; and the kings of Sodom and Go-mŏr′rah fled, and fell there; and they that remained fled to the mountain.

11 And they took all the goods of Sod-om and Go-mŏr′rah, and all their victuals, and went their way.

12 And they took Lot, Abram's brother's son, who dwelt in Sodom, and his goods, and departed.

13 ¶And there came one that had escaped, and told Abram the Hebrew; for he dwelt in the plain of Măm′re the Ămorīte, brother of Ĕsh′cŏl, and brother of Aner: and these *were* confederate with Abram.

14 And when Abram heard that his brother was taken captive, he armed his trained *servants*, born in his own house, three hundred and eighteen, and pursued *them* unto Dan.

15 And he divided himself against them, he and his servants, by night, and smote them, and pursued them unto Hŏ′bah, which *is* on the left hand of Damascus.

16 And he brought back all the goods, and also brought again his brother Lot, and his goods, and the women also, and the people.

17 ¶And the king of Sodom went out to meet him after his return from the slaughter of Chĕd-or-lā′ō-mer, and of the kings that *were* with him, at the valley of Shā′veh, which *is* the king's dale.

18 And Mĕl-chĭz′e-dĕk king of Salem brought forth bread and wine: and he *was* the priest of the most high God.

19 And he blessed him, and said, Blessed *be* Abram of the most high God, possessor of heaven and earth:

20 And blessed be the most high God,

century B.C. and Nuzi in the fifteenth. Speiser says he was a vassal of Zimri-lim of Mari, a contemporary with Hammurabi. Yet, this would be too late for Abraham. **Chedorlaomer** was king of **Elam,** which is east of Babylonia; and he was the leader of the invaders (cf. vss. 4-5, 9, 17). **Tidal king of nations** identifies him as one of five Hittite kings by which he may be identified, possibly Tudhaliya I.

Fourteen years previous to the time of the incident narrated here, Chedorlaomer had subjugated the plain of Jordan. At this time Abram possibly was still in Haran. Five cities of the plain revolted; and Chedorlaomer, with three allies, marched against them. The reason for their presence is only a guess; but they certainly came a long distance to control this area; so they may have come to control the copper mines south and southwest of the Dead Sea. The Sinaitic Inscriptions reveal that they were worked for centuries. Later, Solomon worked them (Wright, *Biblical Archaeologist*, p. 50ff.).

The course of the invasion seems to have been as follows. They approached from the Damascus area following the King's Highway, a caravan route running from the north southwards to the Gulf of Aqabah (bypassing the cities of the plain), and thence northwest through the Negeb, circling back on the Valley of Siddim. The battle was fought in **the vale of Siddim** near the cities of Sodom and Gomorrah. **Slimepits** were holes from which bitumen had been excavated. The kings of the plain, expecting to use this rough ground as a defense, were rushed into it to their own destruction. It is the capture of Lot that brings this narrative into the inspired record.

13-16. Abram the Hebrew. This is the first use of *'ibri*, and it here serves to identify Abram. It is a noun form of the verb *'abar*, which means to pass over or "through"; so it might reflect the early travels of Abram and his family (11:31), especially since he passed over the Euphrates (the Flood). Peleg's son, Eber, may have been the source of this word. The term is not applied to the Israelites elsewhere in the Bible, except by outsiders (39:14) or for self-identification to foreigners (40:15; 43:32). However, this word should not be equated with the term *Habiru*. Geographically, the *Habiru* were more widespread; chronologically, they were earlier than the Israelites (Abram); and numerically, they far outnumbered them. They were in most cases a pejorative term and not an ethnic one, depicting quite often a low-class type of mercenary soldier or brigand. **Trained servants** is a *hapax legomena* found in the Egyptian Execration texts (nineteenth-eighteenth century B.C.). This term indicates the might of Abram, especially the size and strength of his entourage. The Ebla tablets refer to an *Ebrum*, which was a dynastic title a few centuries before Abram. Perhaps he had some rich and influential relatives from his homeland near northern Ur. He is called a *mighty prince* in 23:6 and thus is recognized by the inhabitants of the land as an influential person, possibly a ruler of a section of the land.

17-20. Returning in victory, Abram received visits from two kings. The first was the king of Sodom, who came to express his gratitude; and the second was Melchizedek, king of Salem, who came to bestow a blessing. **The valley of Shaveh** is the valley of the plain and was situated just north of Salem (Jerusalem). It was called the king's dale, either as a memorial of this incident or from the fact that on this piece of level ground the kings of Judah assembled and exercised their forces. If the latter be the case, and it probably is, we have another example of a later scribal note to identify a place by using its modern name (cf. vss. 2, 6, 7 and the double place names in 5, 7).

which hath delivered thine enemies into thy hand. And he gave him tithes of all.

Who was Melchizedek? Some have depicted him as a theophany (appearance of God Himself). This, however, is unlikely (see J. Borland, *Christ in the Old Testament*, pp. 164-174). His name most probably means my king is just. Several factors indicate this is not a theophany. First, the name Zedek is a dynastic title of Jebusite kings as mentioned in the Amarna letters and in the Bible in Joshua 10:1ff. Adoni-zedek in Joshua 10:1 was not a believer. A wicked king demonstrating God's name is not an accurate guide to spirituality. Second, there is no precedent for theophanies having a permanent place of abode in the Old Testament, and Melchizedek is described as living in Salem. Third, Christ is called a priest **after the order of Melchizedek** in Psalm 110:4, which makes it preposterous to say He was a priest after His own order. Melchizedek was a believer in **the most high God** (Yahweh). This is interesting to note, for there were other believers in addition to our limited account in chapters 12-50 of Abram and his descendants. Abram gave **tithes** (*ma'asēr*), something that is well attested elsewhere. Also, the tenth (*ma'asēr*) is often, but not invariably, used of a sacred payment and compared with the *mekes* used of a levy on war spoils (Num 31:28). In Babylonian texts the tithe (*eširtu, ešrētu*) is used of a levy paid on goods in transit (*miksu*)—and by the end of the first millennium it was used of a tax on field produce, which does not apply here. See CAD, s.v. "eširtu," 4:365 (Wiseman, *Bibliotheca Sacra*, July-Sept, 1977, pp. 235-236). Evidently, it was also a religious practice, even though the Old Testament does not say that God has yet commanded anyone to do so. Actually, Abram only tithed that which he took in the victory, *the tenth of the spoils* in Hebrews 7:4; thus, there is no indication this was a regular practice. By so doing, Abram revealed the superiority of Christ's priesthood according to Hebrews 7:4-10, for Levi was in Abram when Abram tithed. Also, Abram was **blessed** by Melchizedek, indicating his superiority.

21-24. Abram refused to take anything from the **king of Sodom,** so as not to become obligated to him. His refusal demonstrated his total allegiance to the **Lord,** and so he rejected any attempt by the king of Sodom to assume the role of overlord and make him his vassal. Abram took only food for his men and gave his allies the liberty to accept the spoils that were due them.

21 And the king of Sodom said unto Abram, Give me the persons, and take the goods to thyself.

22 And Abram said to the king of Sodom, I have lift up mine hand unto the Lord, the most high God, the possessor of heaven and earth,

23 That I will not *take* from a thread even to a shoelatchet, and that I will not take any thing that *is* thine, lest thou shouldest say, I have made Abram rich:

24 Save only that which the young men have eaten, and the portion of the men which went with me, Aner, Ěsh'-cōl, and Măm're; let them take their portion.

CHAPTER 15

AFTER these things the word of the Lord came unto Abram in a vision, saying, Fear not, Abram: I *am* thy shield, *and* thy exceeding great reward.

2 And Abram said, Lord God, what wilt thou give me, seeing I go childless, and the steward of my house *is* this Ĕ-lī-ĕ'zer of Damascus?

3 And Abram said, Behold, to me thou hast given no seed: and, lo, one born in my house is mine heir.

4 And, behold, the word of the Lord *came* unto him, saying, This shall not be thine heir; but he that shall come forth out of thine own bowels shall be thine heir.

5 And he brought him forth abroad, and said, Look now toward heaven, and tell the stars, if thou be able to number them: and he said unto him, So shall thy seed be.

2. His covenant with God. 15:1-21.

15:1-6. God told Abram to **Fear not;** perhaps he was afraid that the kings would seek retaliation against him for his exploits. Certainly, they were capable of it; for they were dedicated leaders and had come a long way, with much expense, only to be foiled by such a small force as Abram had. But God said, **I am thy shield and thy exceeding great reward.** God would continue to fight for him as He had just demonstrated in chapter 14. And He would continue to **reward** Abram, which was especially significant since Abram had just refused a reward from the king of Sodom. God was his **reward.**

But Abram had no child; his steward, Eliezer, was his **heir.** Cyrus Gordon equated verse 1ff. with the Nuzi text HSS 9 22, which had the word slave; and he contended that this was a parallel. So have most conservative scholars. But there are those (Martin J. Selman "The Social Environment of the Patriarchs," *Tyndale Bulletin* 27, 1976, pp. 114-136 and Kenneth Kitchen, *The Bible In Its World*, pp. 70-71, who has wholeheartedly adopted Selman's position of rejecting the concept that Nuzi was

6 And he believed in the LORD; and he counted it to him for righteousness.

unique as he pointed out invalid parallels, parallels not unique to Nuzi, and others depicting only words or phrases too brief to consider) who believe that the person involved in the HSS 9 22 text was not a slave, as Gordon initially asserted, but an independent, fully responsible person. The term may refer to an official; as such, it designates not status, but a profession. There are six Nuzi tablets cited in which the adopter was himself a slave. It is clear that some of these slaves were men of wealth and authority, and one was even a royal official. If Eliezer was considered an heir, then why didn't he receive an inheritance in 25:5ff.? In cuneiform texts generally, the only way an outsider could inherit was by adoption into the family; thus, it is assumed that Abram had previously adopted Eliezer as son and heir. Yet, in cuneiform texts an adopted son always retained his inheritance claim, even if the adopter subsequently had sons of his own, whereas after the birth of Isaac Eliezer seems to have enjoyed no such right. **Abraham gave all that he had unto Isaac,** and even his concubines' sons received **gifts;** but Eliezer is not even mentioned (25:5-6). The mechanics of an adoption are not present in chapter 15, and most likely he was not adopted at all (cf. Prov 17:2 "A wise servant shall have rule over a son that causeth shame, and shall have part of the inheritance among the brethren"). Abraham may have exerted his *patrias potestas* (cf. Prov 30:23). But in any case, the real adoption of slaves was not confined to Nuzi. There are two examples of such an adoption from the Old Babylonian period and one from the Neo-Babylonian era. And Gordon's initial assertion has been proved to be false; there is no Nuzi text dealing with a childless person adopting his own slave, though there is one at Larsa.

In light of Hebrews 11:8-10, we can be sure that Abram had already experienced saving faith from the time of his original call. Romans 4:6, 22 cite instances of God imputing righteousness into the account of those who are already believers. Verse 22 is a reference to Abraham, and it refers to his believing God's promise that he would have a seed. The fact that he was justified by God fourteen years before he was circumcised is the basis for Paul's argument in Romans 4:9-12 that circumcision is a sign of faith, not a means for obtaining justification. All Abram did in Genesis 15:6 was to confirm, affirm, or say amen to God's promise of verse 5, as Romans 4:22 asserts. The **seed** promise of 12:7 is becoming a reality.

7 And he said unto him, I *am* the LORD that brought thee out of Ur of the Chǎl'-deeṡ, to give thee this land to inherit it.
8 And he said, Lord GOD, whereby shall I know that I shall inherit it?
9 And he said unto him, Take me an heifer of three years old, and a she goat of three years old, and a ram of three years old, and a turtledove, and a young pigeon.
10 And he took unto him all these, and divided them in the midst, and laid each piece one against another: but the birds divided he not.
11 And when the fowls came down upon the carcases, Abram drove them away.
12 And when the sun was going down, a deep sleep fell upon Abram; and, lo, an horror of great darkness fell upon him.
13 And he said unto Abram, Know of a surety that thy seed shall be a stranger in a land *that is* not theirs, and shall serve them; and they shall afflict them four hundred years;
14 And also that nation, whom they shall serve, will I judge: and afterward

7-21. I am the LORD. God's character lies at the basis of any covenant He makes, and it is to this that God refers when He begins with this affirmation of His name. **Whereby shall I know?** Abram is not demanding a sign in order to believe, but rather, after and on account of having believed. It was not doubt that prompted this token, but faith. God gave Abram a sign related to faith; this is the nature of a true sacrament. Ancient covenants were sometimes confirmed by the halving of sacrificial victims and the passing between them of the two parties to the covenant (cf. Mari and Jer 34:18), and Yahweh graciously condescended to confirm His promise to Abram by accommodating Himself to this custom. This paragraph therefore describes the cutting of a covenant between Yahweh and Abram. Note that only one symbol is seen passing between the pieces, namely, the appearance as of a smoking furnace from which torch-like flames shot out. This indicated that Yahweh alone was undertaking the fulfillment of all the conditions attached to the covenant. The covenant of grace is thus not a pact, as between two, but a promise confirmed by covenantal forms. God makes a fourfold revelation: privation, deliverance, peace, and triumph (vss. 13-16). **Four hundred years.** This is a rounded figure, the precise number being 430 (Ex 12:40-41). **Iniquity of the Amorites.** It was this that justified their extermination. **The river of Egypt** (vs. 18). Some take this as the Wadi el Arish (Brook of Egypt), the boundary between Egypt and the

shall they come out with great substance.

15 And thou shalt go to thy fathers in peace; thou shalt be buried in a good old age.

16 But in the fourth generation they shall come hither again: for the iniquity of the Ămorītes *is* not yet full.

17 And it came to pass, that, when the sun went down, and it was dark, behold a smoking furnace, and a burning lamp that passed between those pieces.

18 In the same day the Lord made a covenant with Abram, saying, Unto thy seed have I given this land, from the river of Egypt unto the great river, the river Eū-phrā′tēś:

19 The Kēn′ītes, and the Kĕn′iz-zītes, and the Kād′mon-ītes,

20 And the Hittites, and the Pĕr′iz-zītes, and the Rĕph′a-imś,

21 And the Ămorītes, and the Canaanites, and the Gir′ga-shītes, and the Jĕb′u-sītes.

CHAPTER 16

NOW Sâ′raī Abram's wife bare him no children: and she had an handmaid, an Egyptian, whose name *was* Hā′gär.

2 And Sâ′raī said unto Abram, Behold now, the Lord hath restrained me from bearing: I pray thee, go in unto my maid; it may be that I may obtain children by her. And Abram hearkened to the voice of Sâ′raī.

3 And Sâ′raī Abram's wife took Hā′gär her maid the Egyptian, after Abram had dwelt ten years in the land of Canaan, and gave her to her husband Abram to be his wife.

4 And he went in unto Hā′gär, and she conceived: and when she saw that she had conceived, her mistress was despised in her eyes.

5 And Sâ′raī said unto Abram, My wrong *be* upon thee: I have given my maid into thy bosom; and when she saw that she had conceived, I was despised in her eyes: the Lord judge between me and thee.

6 But Abram said unto Sâ′raī, Behold, thy maid *is* in thy hand; do to her as it pleaseth thee. And when Sâ′raī dealt hardly with her, she fled from her face.

7 ¶And the angel of the Lord found her by a fountain of water in the wilderness, by the fountain in the way to Shur.

8 And he said, Hā′gär, Sâ′raī's maid, whence camest thou? and whither wilt thou go? And she said, I flee from the face of my mistress Sâ′raī.

desert south of Palestine. But Wiseman says it is a wadi located nearer Gaza. Rivers were frequently used to mark boundaries (cf. Josh 1:4; Jud 4:13; I Kings 4:21; see *Bibliotheca Sacra*, July-Sept, 1977, p. 229).

3. The birth of Ishmael. 16:1-17:27.

16:1-6. An Egyptian, whose name was Hagar. Her name means forsake, retire, or emigration, probably indicating her circumstances as an emigrant to Palestine, possibly as a runaway slave. It is significant that the initiative was taken by Sarai, not by Abram. Under the strict laws of monogamy (2:4), the conduct of Abram and Sarai was not permissible; but provision for this kind of arrangement had found a place in the laws of Abram's time. In the early history of Israel and its fathers, many things in the development of the nation were not as emphasized as other things were. **Obtain children by her** (lit., be builded by her), the children being the house. In the ancient Near East a childless couple had several alternatives available. They could adopt a son, the husband could marry a second wife, he could attempt to obtain a son through union with his concubine, or his wife could provide him with a slave girl. These solutions are found in texts from many periods and places, though the only site where all four are known to have been practiced is Nuzi. The last option appears in connection with the barrenness of Sarah, Rachel, and Leah; and it is reminiscent of the Nuzi text HSS 5 67. It should be noted this practice appeared outside of Nuzi as well (Code of Hammurabi 144, 163, and an Old Babylonian contract); in fact, HSS 5 67 is the sole example at Nuzi, thus this practice appears to have been a rarity at Nuzi, but not elsewhere. **Her mistress was despised.** This must mean that in some way Hagar took advantage of the position that Sarai had allowed her to occupy and disregarded the fact that she was still Sarai's maid. Rather unreasonably, Sarai puts the blame for the domestic unhappiness onto Abram, though it was her idea. **Thy maid is in thy hand.** The fact that Sarai had to ask Abram to expel the child suggests that her authority over Ishmael was limited, though this would not need to affect the question whether Ishmael was adopted or not. One would not expect a mother to expel her own child without the husband's authority. **Dealt hardly,** lit., she "humbled, afflicted, or mishandled" her. **She fled.** True to her name.

7-8. The angel of the Lord appears here for the first time in Scripture (cf. 17:1-22; 18:1ff.; 22:11-18; 31:11, 13; 32:30; 48:16; Ex 3:2; 14:19; 23:20; 32:34; 33:2; Josh 5:13-15; Jud 13:21). The context shows that when the **angel** speaks, it is actually Yahweh who is speaking. Since the New Testament indicates that no man has ever seen God the Father (I Tim 6:16), it only seems reasonable that the appearance of the **angel of the Lord** is, in fact, a preincarnate appearance of Christ, the Second Person of the Trinity. Thus, these theophanies were

9 And the angel of the LORD said unto her, Return to thy mistress, and submit thyself under her hands.

10 And the angel of the LORD said unto her, I will multiply thy seed exceedingly, that it shall not be numbered for multitude.

11 And the angel of the LORD said unto her, Behold, thou *art* with child, and shalt bear a son, and shalt call his name Ĭsh′ma-el; because the LORD hath heard thy affliction.

12 And he will be a wild man; his hand *will be* against every man, and every man's hand against him; and he shall dwell in the presence of all his brethren.

13 And she called the name of the LORD that spake unto her, Thou God seest me: for she said, Have I also here looked after him that seeth me?

14 Wherefore the well was called Be′er-la-haï′-roi; behold, *it is* between Kā′desh and Be′rĕd.

15 And Hā′gär bare Abram a son: and Abram called his son's name, which Hā′gär bare, Ĭsh′ma-el.

16 And Abram *was* fourscore and six years old, when Hā′gär bare Ĭsh′ma-el to Abram.

CHAPTER 17

AND when Abram was ninety years old and nine, the LORD appeared to Abram, and said unto him, I *am* the Almighty God; walk before me, and be thou perfect.

2 And I will make my covenant between me and thee, and will multiply thee exceedingly.

3 And Abram fell on his face: and God talked with him, saying,

4 As for me, behold, my covenant *is* with thee, and thou shalt be a father of many nations.

5 Neither shall thy name any more be called Abram, but thy name shall be Abraham; for a father of many nations have I made thee.

6 And I will make thee exceeding fruitful, and I will make nations of thee, and kings shall come out of thee.

7 And I will establish my covenant between me and thee and thy seed after thee in their generations for an everlasting covenant, to be a God unto thee, and to thy seed after thee.

8 And I will give unto thee, and to thy seed after thee, the land wherein thou art a stranger, all the land of Canaan, for an everlasting possession; and I will be their God.

9 ¶And God said unto Abraham, Thou shalt keep my covenant therefore, thou, and thy seed after thee in their generations.

10 This *is* my covenant, which ye shall keep, between me and you and thy seed after thee; Every man child among you shall be circumcised.

11 And ye shall circumcise the flesh

actually Christophanies (temporary visible appearances of Christ). It should also be noted that after the incarnation of Christ as Jesus, there are no more visible appearances of God in Scripture. After His crucifixion, Christ appears in resurrected form. Isaiah 63:9 refers to this angel as the "angel of his presence" in reference to God.

9-16. Return . . . submit. These are always the steps to restored peace and joy. A blessing is given to Hagar, and a promise is made concerning her son. **Ishmael** means "God hears," and his character is to be that of **a wild man** (vs. 12). The wild ass of the Arabian deserts was a noble creature (cf. Job 39:5-8), and was thus a fine symbol of the free-roving life of the Arab. **And he shall dwell in the presence of all his brethren.** This is an idiomatic use of the Hebrew *'al penē* (lit., "upon/against the face of"). More particularly, it means "in defiance/disregard of," as proved by Deuteronomy 21:16 and Genesis 25:18. Thus the idiom and context denote a hostility on the part of Ishmael (and his descendants) against his brethren (Isaac and his descendants and even Ishmael's kin). **Thou God seest me** (Heb *'Ēl Ra′ī*, meaning a God of seeing or a God vision). This means not so much a God who sees as a God who permits Himself to be seen. Hagar's comment is an equally difficult Hebrew phrase to translate and possibly means, Have I even seen God and survived? **Beer-lahai-roi.** Word for word, this name may be translated, "well of the living/seeing," meaning more freely, "well of continuing to live after seeing God." That a man should be allowed to see God and live was a mark of special honor and favor (note Manoah's words, "We shall surely die, because we have seen God" (Jud 13:22; cf. 32:30; Ex 3:6). Thirteen more years passed until God again spoke to Abram.

17:1-8. The Almighty God (Heb *'El Shaddai*) appears to have been something of a new title and, therefore, a new revelation to Abram. His corresponding conduct must be to walk before *'Ēl Shaddai* in uprightness. The name for God presented in this context means, "powerful, mighty," and may be derived from a word for mountain, thus picturing God as the overpowering, almighty One who will provide descendants for Abram when all else fails. Others take it from a root indicating "breasts." Thus, it would indicate "nourishment." **A father of many nations.** The word suggests a din and implies a thronging crowd of nations. The promise points far beyond those who were to be his physical descendants and looks forward to the **families of the earth** that were to be spiritually blessed in him (cf. 12:3). **Abraham.** Abram had meant high father, but he is now to be called Abraham. The longer form suggests, by similarity of sound, the Hebrew for father of a multitude.

9-14. Circumcised. The practice of circumcision was fairly extensively observed in the world of Abraham's time. In its original significance it may have been a kind of religious acknowledgment associated with the powers of human reproduction, but more commonly it seems to have served as a tribal mark; and it is likely that it was in this capacity that God made use of it. For Abraham's family it was to be regarded as **a token of the covenant.** This is one of many instances of God's method

of your foreskin; and it shall be a token of the covenant betwixt me and you.

12 And he that is eight days old shall be circumcised among you, every man child in your generations, he that is born in the house, or bought with money of any stranger, which *is* not of thy seed.

13 He that is born in thy house, and he that is bought with thy money, must needs be circumcised: and my covenant shall be in your flesh for an everlasting covenant.

14 And the uncircumcised man child whose flesh of his foreskin is not circumcised, that soul shall be cut off from his people; he hath broken my covenant.

15 ¶And God said unto Abraham, As for Sâ'raī thy wife, thou shalt not call her name Sâ'raī, but Sarah *shall* her name *be.*

16 And I will bless her, and give thee a son also of her: yea, I will bless her, and she shall be *a mother* of nations; kings of people shall be of her.

17 Then Abraham fell upon his face, and laughed, and said in his heart, Shall *a child* be born unto him that is an hundred years old? and shall Sarah, that is ninety years old, bear?

18 And Abraham said unto God, O that Īsh'ma-el might live before thee!

19 And God said, Sarah thy wife shall bear thee a son indeed; and thou shalt call his name Isaac: and I will establish my covenant with him for an everlasting covenant, *and* with his seed after him.

20 And as for Īsh'ma-el, I have heard thee: Behold, I have blessed him, and will make him fruitful, and will multiply him exceedingly; twelve princes shall he beget, and I will make him a great nation.

21 But my covenant will I establish with Isaac, which Sarah shall bear unto thee at this set time in the next year.

22 And he left off talking with him, and God went up from Abraham.

23 ¶And Abraham took Īsh'ma-el his son, and all that were born in his house, and all that were bought with his money, every male among the men of Abraham's house; and circumcised the flesh of their foreskin in the selfsame day, as God had said unto him.

24 And Abraham *was* ninety years old and nine, when he was circumcised in the flesh of his foreskin.

25 And Īsh'ma-el his son *was* thirteen years old, when he was circumcised in the flesh of his foreskin.

26 In the selfsame day was Abraham circumcised, and Īsh'ma-el his son.

27 And all the men of his house, born in the house, and bought with money of the stranger, were circumcised with him.

of appropriating an already existing practice and dedicating it to His own purpose. Circumcision became a touchstone of later Judaism. It is important not to overlook the difference between the old covenant and the new covenant. Old covenant blessings came by physical descent, of which circumcision was the sign; new covenant blessings are spiritually conveyed and are expressed by a new sign, that which is written in our hearts and lives. **Shall be cut off.** For a Hebrew to refuse circumcision was to excise himself from the covenant community (note Moses and his encounter with the Lord in Ex 4:24ff.).

15-22. Sarai means "my princess," and **Sarah,** "princess." "Perhaps the significance lay only in marking the occasion" (Ryrie, p. 31). **Fell upon his face, and laughed.** Worship and incredulity seem intermixed here. We are under no necessity of making Abraham flawless as the Jewish commentators try to do. He found the promise difficult to believe at first. This is borne out by what he said **in his heart** and by his request to God that the promises might center in Ishmael. The expression **O that Ishmael might live before thee!** indicates Abraham's desire that this son be the heir of the promise and that he adopt him. There is an expression in the Law Code of Hammurabi, "My children" or "My son," indicating a legal adoption formula. If the master had no sons, and a handmaid provided him with a male offspring and sometime subsequent to that he made the previous statement, then the child of the handmaid would inherit his property. But God makes it quite clear; **the son of the bondwoman shall not be heir with the son of the freewoman** (Gal 4:30). That is why in 25:5 **Abraham gave all that he had unto Isaac. But unto the sons of the concubines . . . Abraham gave gifts, and sent them away from Isaac his son.** Isaac was Abraham's **only son** (*yachīd*) whom he **lovest** (22:2). This sets the understanding for the terms "only begotten" and "first-born" in the New Testament. Isaac was not Abraham's only son, or the first son born to him; but he received the first-born status and rank, a position of honor and responsibility. This pattern is clearly depicted in Genesis; Jacob was not the oldest, and yet he was the first-born (so also Ephraim and Manasseh). **Thou shalt call his name Isaac.** Isaac means, "he laughed"; and the name was to serve as a reminder to Abraham of the unlikely means by which he was brought into the world. **My covenant will I establish with Isaac.**

23-27. Abraham **took Ishmael his son, and all that were born in his house, and all that were bought with his money, every male . . . and circumcised** them in obedience to God's Word. He was ninety-nine when he was circumcised, twenty-five years or more after he became a believer. At this early stage the blessing of Abraham was to extend to others, even though they were not physically descended from him. The universal purpose always reveals itself, even in the context of the particularism that was a part of the old covenant.

4. The destruction of Sodom. 18:1-19:38.

Once more a clear revelation concerning the coming birth of Isaac was made, and this time it was made directly to Abraham through a second appearance of the angel of the Lord.

CHAPTER 18

AND the LORD appeared unto him in the plains of Măm′re: and he sat in the tent door in the heat of the day;

2 And he lift up his eyes and looked, and, lo, three men stood by him: and when he saw *them*, he ran to meet them from the tent door, and bowed himself toward the ground,

3 And said, My Lord, if now I have found favour in thy sight, pass not away, I pray thee, from thy servant:

4 Let a little water, I pray you, be fetched, and wash your feet, and rest yourselves under the tree:

5 And I will fetch a morsel of bread, and comfort ye your hearts; after that ye shall pass on: for therefore are ye come to your servant. And they said, So do, as thou hast said.

6 And Abraham hastened into the tent unto Sarah, and said, Make ready quickly three measures of fine meal, knead *it*, and make cakes upon the hearth.

7 And Abraham ran unto the herd, and fetcht a calf tender and good, and gave *it* unto a young man; and he hasted to dress it.

8 And he took butter, and milk, and the calf which he had dressed, and set *it* before them; and he stood by them under the tree, and they did eat.

9 ¶And they said unto him, Where *is* Sarah thy wife? And he said, Behold, in the tent.

10 And he said, I will certainly return unto thee according to the time of life; and, lo, Sarah thy wife shall have a son. And Sarah heard *it* in the tent door, which *was* behind him.

11 Now Abraham and Sarah *were* old *and* well stricken in age; *and* it ceased to be with Sarah after the manner of women.

12 Therefore Sarah laughed within herself, saying, After I am waxed old shall I have pleasure, my lord being old also?

13 And the LORD said unto Abraham, Wherefore did Sarah laugh, saying, Shall I of a surety bear a child, which am old?

14 Is any thing too hard for the LORD? At the time appointed I will return unto thee, according to the time of life, and Sarah shall have a son.

15 Then Sarah denied, saying, I laughed not; for she was afraid. And he said, Nay; but thou didst laugh.

16 ¶And the men rose up from thence, and looked toward Sodom: and Abraham went with them to bring them on the way.

17 And the LORD said, Shall I hide from Abraham that thing which I do;

18 Seeing that Abraham shall surely become a great and mighty nation, and all the nations of the earth shall be blessed in him?

19 For I know him, that he will command his children and his household after him, and they shall keep the way of the LORD, to do justice and judgment; that the LORD may bring upon Abraham that which he hath spoken of him.

20 And the LORD said, Because the

18:1-15. The angel of the Lord was accompanied in this visit by two others, evidently ordinary angels. All three, at first, were simply called **three men** (vs. 2). It is clear that one was truly the angel of the Lord (a Christophany); for He is called LORD (*Yahweh*) in verses 1, 13-14, etc., and He also referred to himself as **I** when speaking in the capacity of God (vss. 17, 26, etc.). The three heavenly visitors approached Abraham as he sat near his tent at Mamre; and he properly offered them rest and refreshment, which they accepted. The food that Abraham prepared was liberal in amount; it included a large quantity of bread and an entire calf for meat, besides butter and milk.

Either during or after the meal, one of the visitors (no doubt, the angel of the Lord) gave the promise that in due time Sarah would truly have a son, apparently repeating the thought of the previous chapter for the sake of emphasis. Though she was inside the tent, Sarah was able to hear the words; and she **laughed within herself** (vs. 12), believing that the words could not be true. Interestingly enough, in chapter 17 it had been Abraham who had laughed. The angel knew she laughed and brought a rebuke, saying **is anything too hard for the LORD?** (vs. 14). Sarah now denied that she had laughed, but this only made her conduct the more reprehensible.

The reason for the laughter of both Abraham and Sarah was most likely that Sarah was past the age of having children (vs. 11; Heb 11:11). Yet, it seems strange that Abraham would have laughed (17:17) at the idea of a 100-year-old man begetting a son, when his own father was 130 at the time of Abraham's birth. Sarah died when he was 137, but he was able to father sons long after that (Gen 25:1-6). No doubt the two reasoned that if God wanted them to have a child, He would have made this possible while Sarah still had the ability to bear children. It is quite clear, however, that God had purposely waited so that, when Isaac should be born, the importance of the birth and the fact that God had been supernaturally responsible for it (being by miracle) would be the more impressed on the parents' minds.

16-22. At this point the three heavenly visitors and Abraham began to walk in the direction of Sodom. As they walked, the angel of the Lord informed Abraham of the impending destruction of Sodom. The rather unusual manner by which the text tells of the angel's action is intended to convey the following thought: God was interested in Abraham as the father of the nation that would inherit all the land, and He wanted Abraham to know why the coming punishment on Sodom was necessary. He did not want Abraham to be confused in thinking that possibly the same thing might happen to all the land he had been promised. Abraham should understand, then, that this punishment was only because of the **cry of Sodom** (cf. vs. 20, cry for punishment due to sin); thus, it was a punishment for that part of the land only, and not all of it. Though the actual term destruction was not used by the angel, the thought was made

cry of Sodom and Go-mŏr'rah is great,
and because their sin is very grievous;
21 I will go down now, and see
whether they have done altogether according to the cry of it, which is come
unto me; and if not, I will know.
22 And the men turned their faces
from thence, and went toward Sodom:
but Abraham stood yet before the
Lord.
23 ¶And Abraham drew near, and
said, Wilt thou also destroy the
righteous with the wicked?
24 Peradventure there be fifty
righteous within the city: wilt thou also
destroy and not spare the place for the
fifty righteous that are therein?
25 That be far from thee to do after
this manner, to slay the righteous with
the wicked: and that the righteous
should be as the wicked, that be far
from thee: Shall not the Judge of all the
earth do right?
26 And the Lord said, If I find in Sodom fifty righteous within the city,
then I will spare all the place for their
sakes.
27 And Abraham answered and said,
Behold now, I have taken upon me to
speak unto the Lord, which am but dust
and ashes:
28 Peradventure there shall lack five
of the fifty righteous: wilt thou destroy
all the city for lack of five? And he said,
If I find there forty and five, I will not
destroy it.
29 And he spake unto him yet again,
and said, Peradventure there shall be
forty found there. And he said, I will
not do it for forty's sake.
30 And he said unto him, Oh let not
the Lord be angry, and I will speak:
Peradventure there shall thirty be
found there. And he said, I will not do
it, if I find thirty there.
31 And he said, Behold now, I have
taken upon me to speak unto the Lord:
Peradventure there shall be twenty
found there. And he said, I will not
destroy it for twenty's sake.
32 And he said, Oh let not the Lord be
angry, and I will speak yet but this
once: Peradventure ten shall be found
there. And he said, I will not destroy it
for ten's sake.
33 And the Lord went his way, as
soon as he had left communing with
Abraham: and Abraham returned unto
his place.

CHAPTER 19

AND there came two angels to Sodom
at even; and Lot sat in the gate of Sodom: and Lot seeing them rose up to
meet them; and he bowed himself with
his face toward the ground;
2 And he said, Behold now, my lords,
turn in, I pray you, into your servant's
house, and tarry all night, and wash
your feet, and ye shall rise up early, and
go on your ways. And they said, Nay;
but we will abide in the street all night.
3 And he pressed upon them greatly;
and they turned in unto him, and entered into his house; and he made them
a feast, and did bake unleavened bread,
and they did eat.

clear enough that Abraham now began an unusual plea for
Sodom's deliverance.

23-33. This plea was given after the two other angels had
continued in their walk toward Sodom, with Abraham and the
angel of the Lord having stopped. Abraham stepped nearer the
angel, in a gesture evidently of deep sincerity, to intercede in
Sodom's behalf. Certainly, his primary interest was in Lot
(which further shows his magnanimous character toward this
undeserving nephew), but no doubt he was also interested in the
preservation of all the people in the city. His intercession was
based on his belief that the presence of a certain number of
righteous people in a city should be enough reason to spare it.
Abraham apparently had noticed the closing words of the
Angel's declaration, which said, in effect, that He was going to
go down now and determine whether the **cry** for punishment
had been serious enough to call for the punishment itself
(vs. 21).

Abraham began with the number **fifty,** asking if this would be
a small enough number of righteous people to make the punishment unnecessary. The Angel replied that it would. Then Abraham reduced the number to forty-five and then forty, finally to
as few as **ten.** Each time His reply was that even as few people as
mentioned would be enough. Abraham did not go to a lower
number than ten, no doubt believing that surely a city where
Lot lived would have at least this many whom God could
consider righteous. Since the city was destroyed, it is clear that
ten righteous people were not found, which means that Abraham's intercession yielded no tangible result.

The implication of the text, however, is that God was pleased
with Abraham's attempt. He made the intercession in full
humility and demonstrated true compassion for others. The fact
that fewer than ten righteous people lived in Sodom, however,
provides a sad commentary on the ineffectiveness of Lot's witness.

19:1-15. The story now concerns the visit of the two ordinary
angels to Lot's home in Sodom. Evening had fallen when they
arrived, and they found **Lot** sitting **in the gate of Sodom.** This
proclaimed him a man of stature in Sodom, possibly a judge (cf.
vs. 9; 34:20). The effect this had on him was amazing, for he
was ". . . vexed with the filthy conversation of the wicked: (For
that righteous man dwelling among them, in seeing and hearing,
vexed his righteous soul from day to day with their unlawful
deeds;)" (see II Pet 2:7-9). Compare his influence with Joseph's
and Daniel's. His alarm in verse 3a indicates that he knew what
would happen to the men if they did not stay with him. **Bring
them out unto us, that we may know them.** What debauchery,
the sin of Sodomy. The law would make it a capital offense,
grouped with incest and bestiality (Lev 18:22; 20:13); and the

4 ¶But before they lay down, the men of the city, *even* the men of Sodom, compassed the house round, both old and young, all the people from every quarter:

5 And they called unto Lot, and said unto him, Where *are* the men which came in to thee this night? bring them out unto us, that we may know them.

6 And Lot went out at the door unto them, and shut the door after him,

7 And said, I pray you, brethren, do not so wickedly.

8 Behold now, I have two daughters which have not known man; let me, I pray you, bring them out unto you, and do ye to them as *is* good in your eyes: only unto these men do nothing; for therefore came they under the shadow of my roof.

9 And they said, Stand back. And they said *again*, This one *fellow* came in to sojourn, and he will needs be a judge: now will we deal worse with thee, than with them. And they pressed sore upon the man, *even* Lot, and came near to break the door.

10 But the men put forth their hand, and pulled Lot into the house to them, and shut to the door.

11 And they smote the men that *were* at the door of the house with blindness, both small and great: so that they wearied themselves to find the door.

12 ¶And the men said unto Lot, Hast thou here any besides? son in law, and thy sons, and thy daughters, and whatsoever thou hast in the city, bring *them* out of this place:

13 For we will destroy this place, because the cry of them is waxen great before the face of the Lord; and the Lord hath sent us to destroy it.

14 And Lot went out, and spake unto his sons in law, which married his daughters, and said, Up, get you out of this place; for the Lord will destroy this city. But he seemed as one that mocked unto his sons in law.

15 ¶And when the morning arose, then the angels hastened Lot, saying, Arise, take thy wife, and thy two daughters, which are here; lest thou be consumed in the iniquity of the city.

16 And while he lingered, the men laid hold upon his hand, and upon the hand of his wife, and upon the hand of his two daughters; the Lord being merciful unto him: and they brought him forth, and set him without the city.

17 And it came to pass, when they had brought them forth abroad, that he said, Escape for thy life; look not behind thee, neither stay thou in all the plain; escape to the mountain, lest thou be consumed.

18 And Lot said unto them, Oh, not so, my Lord:

19 Behold now, thy servant hath found grace in thy sight, and thou hast magnified thy mercy, which thou hast shewed unto me in saving my life; and I cannot escape to the mountain, lest some evil take me, and I die:

20 Behold now, this city *is* near to flee unto, and it *is* a little one: Oh, let me

New Testament is equally appalled at it (Rom 1:26-27; I Cor 6:9; I Tim 1:10). Romans reveals that this is the last stage in a society before it is destroyed. **Behold now, I have two daughters which have not known man** is absolutely an amazing statement, especially on the part of a believer (cf. Jud 19:24). That he would protect two strangers and offer his own flesh and blood is beyond understanding. Doing his best, he has jeopardized his daughters, enraged his townsmen, and finally required rescue by those he was trying to protect. **They smote the men . . . with blindness.** The word **blindness** is found only here and in II Kings 6:18. **But he seemed as one that mocked unto his sons-in-law** indicates that he did not bear a witness in Sodom, and it reflects their own sad condition spiritually.

16-22. The grip of this present evil world is strong, but God's mercy overcame Lot's last-minute procrastination; **And while he lingered, the men laid hold upon his hand.** There is a warning to us to **Remember Lot's wife** (Lk 17:32). What tender mercy of God to gently lead a wayward and backslidden child to safety. **Thou hast magnified thy mercy.** The word **mercy** is *chesed* and indicates the faithfulness of God to those who are in a covenant relationship with Him. It is used 250 times in the Old Testament and is always related to some type of fixed relationship between people that would evaluate an individual's actions in light of being and acting faithful to a prior commitment (cf. 20:13; 21:23; 24:12, 14, 27, 49; 32:10; 39:21; 40:14; 47:29; Ex 34:6; Lam 3:22-23). "Know therefore that the Lord thy God, he is God, the faithful God, which keepeth covenant and mercy" (Deut 7:9). Lot had found **grace;** he had been saved. Therefore, God had also been faithful to him.

escape thither, (*is* it not a little one?) and my soul shall live.

21 And he said unto him, See, I have accepted thee concerning this thing also, that I will not overthrow this city, for the which thou hast spoken.

22 Haste thee, escape thither; for I cannot do any thing till thou be come thither. Therefore the name of the city was called Zō'ar.

23 The sun was risen upon the earth when Lot entered into Zō'ar.

24 Then the LORD rained upon Sodom and upon Go-mŏr'rah brimstone and fire from the LORD out of heaven;

25 And he overthrew those cities, and all the plain, and all the inhabitants of the cities, and that which grew upon the ground.

26 But his wife looked back from behind him, and she became a pillar of salt.

27 And Abraham gat up early in the morning to the place where he stood before the LORD:

28 And he looked toward Sodom and Go-mŏr'rah, and toward all the land of the plain, and beheld, and, lo, the smoke of the country went up as the smoke of a furnace.

29 ¶And it came to pass, when God destroyed the cities of the plain, that God remembered Abraham, and sent Lot out of the midst of the overthrow, when he overthrew the cities in the which Lot dwelt.

30 ¶And Lot went up out of Zō'ar, and dwelt in the mountain, and his two daughters with him; for he feared to dwell in Zō'ar: and he dwelt in a cave, he and his two daughters.

31 And the firstborn said unto the younger, Our father *is* old, and *there is* not a man in the earth to come in unto us after the manner of all the earth:

32 Come, let us make our father drink wine, and we will lie with him, that we may preserve seed of our father.

33 And they made their father drink wine that night: and the firstborn went in, and lay with her father; and he perceived not when she lay down, nor when she arose.

34 And it came to pass on the morrow, that the firstborn said unto the younger, Behold, I lay yesternight with my father: let us make him drink wine this night also; and go thou in, *and* lie with him, that we may preserve seed of our father.

35 And they made their father drink wine that night also: and the younger arose, and lay with him; and he perceived not when she lay down, nor when she arose.

36 Thus were both the daughters of Lot with child by their father.

37 And the firstborn bare a son, and called his name Moab: the same *is* the father of the Moabites unto this day.

38 And the younger, she also bare a son, and called his name Bĕn-ăm'mi: the same *is* the father of the children of Ammon unto this day.

CHAPTER 20

AND Abraham journeyed from thence

23-29. God remembered Abraham, and sent Lot out of the midst of the . . . cities. The word **remember** appears in 8:1 and indicates God's meeting the needs of His people and actively doing something for them. Jesus used the incident of Lot's wife turning to **a pillar of salt** as a warning to others not to look back on the things of this world when He comes (Lk 17:21-33).

30-38. For he feared to dwell in Zoar. The restlessness of fear is classically illustrated by Lot's attitude to Zoar. It was fear that had driven him there (vs. 19ff.); fear drove him out. It had caused him to brush aside the call of God (cf. vss. 17, 21), and now the pledge of God. Possibly, he was afraid because the people thought he was somehow responsible for the destruction, or he may have feared further seismic disturbances. Lot's **cave** is a bitter sequel to the **house** (vs. 3). "The end of choosing to carve out his career was to lose even the custody of his body. His legacy, Moab and Ammon (vs. 37), was destined to provide the worst carnal seduction in the history of Israel (that of Baal-peor, Num 25) and the cruelest religious perversion (that of Molech, Lev 18:21). So much stemmed from a self-regarding choice (13:10ff) and persistence in it" (Kidner, *Genesis*, p. 136).

5. Abraham and Abimelech. 20:1-18.

20:1. Notice how in the life of Abraham quite often after

toward the south country, and dwelled between Kā'desh and Shur, and sojourned in Ge'rär.

2 And Abraham said of Sarah his wife, She *is* my sister: and A-bǐm'e-lěch king of Ge'rär sent, and took Sarah.

3 But God came to A-bǐm'e-lěch in a dream by night, and said to him, Behold, thou *art but* a dead man, for the woman which thou hast taken; for she *is* a man's wife.
4 But A-bǐm'e-lěch had not come near her: and he said, Lord, wilt thou slay also a righteous nation?
5 Said he not unto me, She *is* my sister? and she, even she herself said, He *is* my brother: in the integrity of my heart and innocency of my hands have I done this.
6 And God said unto him in a dream, Yea, I know that thou didst this in the integrity of thy heart; for I also withheld thee from sinning against me: therefore suffered I thee not to touch her.
7 Now therefore restore the man his wife; for he *is* a prophet, and he shall pray for thee, and thou shalt live: and if thou restore *her* not, know thou that thou shalt surely die, thou, and all that *are* thine.
8 Therefore A-bǐm'e-lěch rose early in the morning, and called all his servants, and told all these things in their ears: and the men were sore afraid.
9 Then A-bǐm'e-lěch called Abraham, and said unto him, What hast thou done unto us? and what have I offended thee, that thou hast brought on me and on my kingdom a great sin? thou hast done deeds unto me that ought not to be done.
10 And A-bǐm'e-lěch said unto Abra-

spiritual victories there is a lapse into a life of scheming and sin. This in itself should be a warning to us. Here on the brink of Isaac's birth-story, the very promise is put in jeopardy, traded away for personal safety. If it is to be received, it will have to be a work of God and His grace.

2. She is my sister (note the comments on 15:1ff). Speiser first proposed the wife-sister type of marriage in the ancient world in 1963. He was of the opinion that in certain cases a woman could enjoy a special status of both wife and sister to the same man. The woman's position of sister was bestowed by adoption into sistership (*ana ahatūti*), in addition to her marriage relationship. Verses 1-18; chapters 12:10-20; and 26:6-11 supposedly illustrate this phenomenon. Speiser surmised that *ahatūtu* was characteristic of the upper levels of society at Nuzi.

But it should be noted that the evidence at Nuzi really points in another direction. *Ahatūtu*, like the *martūtu* (daughter) and *kallatūtu* (daughter-in-law), typically involved women who were socially inferior. The evidence from the texts does not support Koschaker's and Speiser's theory. *Ahatūtu* did not create the bond of a sister-wife relationship. The concept of sisterhood adoption was not in any way co-terminous with marriage, nor was it a relationship conferring high status. The *ahatūtu* was similar to the *martūtu* and *kallatūtu* in that it was a business agreement. In general, it included manumitted slaves or lonely, unattached women who needed the protection of a family. It was not practiced in higher levels of Nuzi society, but was basically a lower-class institution. Speiser acknowledged that this supposed concept would have been distasteful to the Hittite king; and there is no *a priori* reason why the Egyptian or Philistine kings should have been any more kindly disposed to the practice, if there was one. In chapter 12 it is emphasized that as soon as the Pharaoh discovered Sarah's true identity as both wife and sister, they were expelled. Kitchen says Speiser's view is "totally irrelevant" (in *BIIW*, p. 70).

3-18. But God came to Abimelech in a dream by night . . . thou art but a dead man. God intervened in chapter 12 under the same conniving circumstances, and He does it again. **For he is a prophet** is surely hard to take. It is an insult, even though it is the truth. Abraham certainly was not acting like a prophet of God, though perhaps he was behaving like the ones in Gerar. **What have I offended thee? . . . thou hast done deeds unto me that ought not to be done.** What preaching by an unsaved man to the prophet of God! Abraham was practicing situational ethics and not trusting in the sovereign power of a living and loving God. After the great victory in chapter 14, God had told him earlier **I am thy shield** (15:1). What a sad testimony to say, **when God caused me to wander from my father's house, that I said unto her, This is thy kindness which thou shalt show unto me; at every place whither we shall come.** And they had certainly been many places over the past twenty-five years since he had trusted in Yahweh. Notice, **kindness** is the same word (*chesed*), translated **mercy** in 19:19, and depicts the faithfulness expected of a woman who had committed her life to her husband in the marriage vows. Because of her oath in marriage, Abraham could expect, even demand, Sarah to be faithful to him. **Behold, he is to thee a covering of the eyes, unto all that are with thee, and with all other.** Literally, "it is a covering for the eyes," which appears to describe a method for diverting or forestalling suspicion. The phrase **thus you have been reproved** conveys the idea "you have been vindicated." Several passages convey the idea of a similar legal or disciplinary connotation (Gen 24:14, 44; 21:25; 31:42; see Speiser, *Genesis*, p. 150). Abimelech's large gift of **a thousand pieces of silver** (no coins existed at this time, so **pieces** is not accurate; everything was weighed) was proof of his high esteem for Abraham and Sarah and would serve to stop any scoffing on the part of her household.

ham. What sawest thou, that thou hast done this thing?

11 And Abraham said, Because I thought, Surely the fear of God *is* not in this place; and they will slay me for my wife's sake.

12 And yet indeed *she is* my sister; she *is* the daughter of my father, but not the daughter of my mother; and she became my wife.

13 And it came to pass, when God caused me to wander from my father's house, that I said unto her, This *is* thy kindness which thou shalt shew unto me; at every place whither we shall come, say of me, He *is* my brother.

14 And A-bĭm'e-lĕch took sheep, and oxen, and menservants, and womenservants, and gave *them* unto Abraham, and restored him Sarah his wife.

15 And A-bĭm'e-lĕch said, Behold, my land *is* before thee: dwell where it pleaseth thee.

16 And unto Sarah he said, Behold, I have given thy brother a thousand *pieces* of silver: behold, he *is* to thee a covering of the eyes, unto all that *are* with thee, and with all *other:* thus she was reproved.

17 So Abraham prayed unto God: and God healed A-bĭm'e-lĕch, and his wife, and his maidservants; and they bare *children.*

18 For the LORD had fast closed up all the wombs of the house of A-bĭm'e-lĕch, because of Sarah Abraham's wife.

CHAPTER 21

AND the LORD visited Sarah as he had said, and the LORD did unto Sarah as he had spoken.

2 For Sarah conceived, and bare Abraham a son in his old age, at the set time of which God had spoken to him.

3 And Abraham called the name of his son that was born unto him, whom Sarah bare to him, Isaac.

4 And Abraham circumcised his son Isaac being eight days old, as God had commanded him.

5 And Abraham was an hundred years old, when his son Isaac was born unto him.

6 And Sarah said, God hath made me to laugh, *so that* all that hear will laugh with me.

7 And she said, Who would have said unto Abraham, that Sarah should have given children suck? for I have born *him* a son in his old age.

8 And the child grew, and was weaned: and Abraham made a great feast the *same* day that Isaac was weaned.

9 ¶And Sarah saw the son of Hā'gär the Egyptian, which she had born unto Abraham, mocking.

10 Wherefore she said unto Abraham, Cast out this bondwoman and her son: for the son of this bondwoman shall not be heir with my son, *even* with Isaac.

11 And the thing was very grievous in Abraham's sight because of his son.

12 And God said unto Abraham, Let it not be grievous in thy sight because of the lad, and because of thy bondwoman; in all that Sarah hath said unto

6. *The birth of Isaac. 21:1-34.*

21:1-7. The matter-of-fact style and the emphasis on what God has **said . . . spoken . . . spoken** (vss. 1, 2) express the quiet precision of His control (cf. 17:21; 18:10, 14 for the promise of God). He called the name of the son **Isaac,** depicting their responses at the announcement that they would have a son (17:17). **Circumcised.** Abraham obeyed the covenant stipulations. **God hath made me to laugh** is the laughter of rejoicing at the blessing of God. God not only rejuvenated Sarah's body so she could bear a child, but also so she could nurse.

8-21. After the birth of Isaac came the expulsion of Ishmael. The discord seemed trivial at first glance (vs. 11), but with time it became a fundamental rift through which the New Testament would expound upon the incompatibility of the natural and the spiritual (Ps 83:5-6; Gal 4:29). The story is the complement of chapter 16, where they had acted on impulse and had been reconciled to live together another fourteen years or more (cf. 17:25). **Mocking** is from the same Hebrew root as **Isaac,** but it is an intensive form of the verb "to laugh." That it is malicious in its intent is demanded by the context and Galatians 4:29 where it says Ishmael who **was born after the flesh persecuted him that was born after the Spirit.** It is used in 19:14, **mocked** and 39:14-17 with the same rendering. **Cast out this bondwoman** is cited in Galatians 4:30 as an inspired demand when Ishmael saw all his hopes for an inheritance shattered due to Isaac's presence. **In Isaac shall thy seed be called** put God's

thee, hearken unto her voice; for in Isaac shall thy seed be called.

13 And also of the son of the bondwoman will I make a nation, because he *is* thy seed.

14 And Abraham rose up early in the morning, and took bread, and a bottle of water, and gave *it* unto Hā′gär, putting *it* on her shoulder, and the child, and sent her away; and she departed, and wandered in the wilderness of Be′er-shē′ba.

15 And the water was spent in the bottle, and she cast the child under one of the shrubs.

16 And she went, and sat her down over against *him* a good way off, as it were a bowshot: for she said, Let me not see the death of the child. And she sat over against *him*, and lift up her voice, and wept.

17 And God heard the voice of the lad; and the angel of God called to Hā′gär out of heaven, and said unto her, What aileth thee, Hā′gär? fear not; for God hath heard the voice of the lad where he *is*.

18 Arise, lift up the lad, and hold him in thine hand; for I will make him a great nation.

19 And God opened her eyes, and she saw a well of water; and she went, and filled the bottle with water, and gave the lad drink.

20 And God was with the lad; and he grew, and dwelt in the wilderness, and became an archer.

21 And he dwelt in the wilderness of Paran: and his mother took him a wife out of the land of Egypt.

22 ¶And it came to pass at that time, that A-bĭm′e-lĕch and Phī′chŏl the chief captain of his host spake unto Abraham, saying, God *is* with thee in all that thou doest:

23 Now therefore swear unto me here by God that thou wilt not deal falsely with me, nor with my son, nor with my son's son: *but* according to the kindness that I have done unto thee, thou shalt do unto me, and to the land wherein thou hast sojourned.

24 And Abraham said, I will swear.

25 And Abraham reproved A-bĭm′e-lĕch because of a well of water, which A-bĭm′e-lĕch's servants had violently taken away.

26 And A-bĭm′e-lĕch said, I wot not who hath done this thing: neither didst thou tell me, neither yet heard I *of it*, but to day.

27 And Abraham took sheep and oxen, and gave them unto A-bĭm′e-lĕch; and both of them made a covenant.

28 And Abraham set seven ewe lambs of the flock by themselves.

29 And A-bĭm′e-lĕch said unto Abraham, What *mean* these seven ewe lambs which thou hast set by themselves?

30 And he said, For *these* seven ewe lambs shalt thou take of my hand, that they may be a witness unto me, that I have digged this well.

31 Wherefore he called that place

choice beyond all doubt. **And Abraham rose up early** is an expression that implies a habit of facing a hard task resolutely as in 22:3.

Hagar's cry was without hope, and it was the lad's voice that brought help. **The angel of God called to Hagar out of heaven** and assured her that Ishmael would survive and God **will make him a great nation.** God watched over him (Lk 2:52), and they lived in the northeast part of the Sinai peninsula.

22-34. This incident takes place some twenty-five miles from Gerar (cf. 20:1) where there was always the possibility of disputes over grazing rights, and it brings out the uncertainties and trials in the life of Abraham. Beer-sheba was the base of operations for both Abraham and Isaac, whereas Jacob was more to the far north and center. **Abimelech** was a dynastic title, not a personal name. He was militarily and politically superior to Abraham, but he evidently recognized God's protection of Abraham and therefore desired a favorable relationship with him. **But according to the kindness that I have done unto thee, thou shalt do unto me.** Again, the word **kindness** is *chesed;* and it is the result of a covenant between these two men, **swear . . . I will swear . . . and both of them made a covenant.** The whole verse (23) speaks very much as Jonathan later spoke to David in I Samuel 20:14-15. **And Abraham reproved Abimelech** indicates that he not only took advantage of the cordial relationship to mention the subject of a well that, unknown to Abimelech, had been seized by his servants; but the Hebrew suggests that Abraham had to make his complaint several times. Perhaps Abimelech was adept at evasion. Isaac had more problems at a later date in chapter 26. Animals were used in ratifying the covenant (cf. 15:9-10). **Beer-sheba** means well of the seven, or of the oath. It probably means seven, and the closeness of the root meaning to swear would not go unnoticed. The seven ewe lambs, **a witness unto me, that I have digged this well,** support this meaning. **Land of the Philistines** has been an item of no small mystery. The real problem is that in the third millennium B.C. there were no people designated by the name of Philistines in Greece. And of course, if we put Abraham in the third millennium (and we do ca. 2165 B.C.), then this most likely is an anachronism. The major Philistine migrations came ca. 1200 B.C. It was this group of people who oppressed Israel so severely

Be'er-she'ba; because there they sware both of them.

32 Thus they made a covenant at Be'er-she'ba: then A-bim'e-lĕch rose up, and Phi'chŏl the chief captain of his host, and they returned into the land of the Philistines.

33 ¶And *Abraham* planted a grove in Be'er-she'ba, and called there on the name of the LORD, the everlasting God.

34 And Abraham sojourned in the Philistines' land many days.

CHAPTER 22

AND it came to pass after these things, that God did tempt Abraham, and said unto him, Abraham: and he said, Behold, *here* I am.

2 And he said, Take now thy son, thine only *son* Isaac, whom thou lovest, and get thee into the land of Mō-rī'ah; and offer him there for a burnt offering upon one of the mountains which I will tell thee of.

3 And Abraham rose up early in the morning, and saddled his ass, and took two of his young men with him, and Isaac his son, and clave the wood for the burnt offering, and rose up, and went unto the place of which God had told him.

4 Then on the third day Abraham lifted up his eyes, and saw the place afar off.

5 And Abraham said unto his young men, Abide ye here with the ass; and I and the lad will go yonder and worship, and come again to you.

6 And Abraham took the wood of the burnt offering, and laid *it* upon Isaac his son; and he took the fire in his hand, and a knife; and they went both of them together.

7 And Isaac spake unto Abraham his father, and said, My father: and he said, Here *am* I, my son. And he said, Behold the fire and the wood: but where *is* the lamb for a burnt offering?

8 And Abraham said, My son, God will provide himself a lamb for a burnt offering: so they went both of them together.

9 And they came to the place which God had told him of; and Abraham built an altar there, and laid the wood in order, and bound Isaac his son, and laid him on the altar upon the wood.

10 And Abraham stretched forth his hand, and took the knife to slay his son.

11 And the angel of the LORD called unto him out of heaven, and said, Abra-

in the days of Samson, Samuel, and Saul (for further information see E. Hindson, *Philistines and the Old Testament*, pp. 93-104; Kitchen, "Philistines," *[POTT]*, pp. 53-78; N. K. Sandars, *The Sea Peoples: Warriors of the Ancient Mediterranean, 1250-1150* B.C.). **The everlasting God** would be "a logical epithet of a Deity called upon to support a formal treaty . . . expected to be valid for all time" (Speiser, p. 159). The name is one of a series, including *El Elyon* (14:18), *El Roi* (16:13), *El Shaddai* (17:1), *El-elohe-Israel* (33:20), *El-Beth-el* (35:7). Each one depicts an aspect of God's self-disclosure.

7. The offering of Isaac. 22:1-24.

22:1. God did tempt Abraham. The word **tempt** is better expressed by proved or tested. God does not tempt anyone with evil (Jas 1:13); but in certain instances He does test, try, or prove us (Jas 1:2; I Pet 1:6-7).

2-8. Take now thy son, thine only son Isaac, whom thou lovest . . . and offer him there for a burnt offering. Obviously, Isaac was not Abraham's only son (cf. Ishmael); but Ishmael never enjoyed the status of son, as Isaac did. The Code of Hammurabi (*Laws* 170-171) shows that a man's offspring by a slave woman were not ordinarily given the rights that belong to the son born of his wife. Only if in the course of his lifetime the father had said to the male offspring of his slave woman (in public and in an official manner), "Thou art my son," would the slave woman's offspring be treated as a real son of the father. If so, then he was counted as an heir; if not, he was given gifts and separated from the household before the inheritance was divided. Isaac remained Abraham's only son in the legal sense; though he had several other offspring (25:1-4), he had only one son in the unique sense, and he gave him his entire inheritance (25:5-6). Isaac was his unique son; and when the New Testament refers to Isaac (Heb 11:17), it calls him his only begotten (*monogenēs*). It is clear that the expression "only begotten" refers to status. Thus, when Christ is referred to as "the only begotten" it is a reference to his status as the unique Son of the Father; it does not signify that he had a beginning (S. Herbert Bess, "The Term 'Son of God' in the Light of Old Testament Idiom," *Grace Journal*, Spring 1965).

Human sacrifice was widely practiced in the ancient Near East in Old Testament times (though not by the godly), yet Jephthah and Abraham would have been acquainted with the practice. God intended to try Abraham's love, to see if he loved God more than his son, and to try his faith in His promise concerning descendants. They had to journey about fifty miles. Abraham's obedience and resoluteness is expressed by **And Abraham rose up early in the morning, and saddled his ass** (cf. 21:14). **And Abraham said unto his young men, Abide ye here with the ass; and I and the lad will go yonder and worship, and come again to you.** This was no empty phrase; it was his full conviction based on **in Isaac shall thy seed be called** (21:12). Hebrews 11:17-19 reveals he was expecting Isaac to be resurrected, thus he would regard him as given back from the dead. Abraham's **God will provide** was to be immortalized in the name of the place in verse 14; **And Abraham called the name of that place Jehovah-jireh** (meaning the Lord will see to it thus He will provide).

9-19. Again the **angel of the LORD** appeared and called unto Abraham and said **now I know that thou fearest God.** He reverenced God more than anyone else since he was willing to offer to God his only unique son. God provided a ram (a picture of the ". . . Lamb of God, which taketh away the sin of the world," Jn 1:29). God then assured Abraham that His covenant with him would be fulfilled; **and as the sand which is upon the sea shore** is like 13:16 and 15:5. **And thy seed shall possess the**

ham, Abraham: and he said, Here *am* I.

12 And he said, Lay not thine hand upon the lad, neither do thou any thing unto him: for now I know that thou fearest God, seeing thou hast not withheld thy son, thine only *son* from me.

13 And Abraham lifted up his eyes, and looked, and behold behind *him* a ram caught in a thicket by his horns: and Abraham went and took the ram, and offered him up for a burnt offering in the stead of his son.

14 And Abraham called the name of that place Je-hō′vah-jī′reh: as it is said *to* this day, In the mount of the LORD it shall be seen.

15 ¶And the angel of the LORD called unto Abraham out of heaven the second time,

16 And said, By myself have I sworn, saith the LORD, for because thou hast done this thing, and hast not withheld thy son, thine only *son*:

17 That in blessing I will bless thee, and in multiplying I will multiply thy seed as the stars of the heaven, and as the sand which *is* upon the sea shore; and thy seed shall possess the gate of his enemies;

18 And in thy seed shall all the nations of the earth be blessed; because thou hast obeyed my voice.

19 So Abraham returned unto his young men, and they rose up and went together to Be′er-shē′ba; and Abraham dwelt at Be′er-shē′ba.

20 ¶And it came to pass after these things, that it was told Abraham, saying, Behold, Mĭl′cah, she hath also born children unto thy brother Nahor;

21 Huz his firstborn, and Buz his brother, and Kĕ-mū′el the father of Ā′ram,

22 And Chē′sĕd, and Hā′zō, and Pĭl′dăsh, and Jĭd′lăph, and Beth-ū′el.

23 And Beth-ū′el begat Rebekah: these eight Mĭl′cah did bear to Nahor, Abraham's brother.

24 And his concubine, whose name *was* Reū′mah, she bare also Tē′bah, and Gā′hăm, and Thā′hăsh, and Mā′achah.

CHAPTER 23

AND Sarah was an hundred and seven and twenty years old: *these were* the years of the life of Sarah.

2 And Sarah died in Kir′jath-är′ba; the same *is* Hēbron in the land of Canaan: and Abraham came to mourn for Sarah, and to weep for her.

3 ¶And Abraham stood up from before his dead, and spake unto the sons of Heth, saying,

4 I *am* a stranger and a sojourner with you: give me a possession of a buryingplace with you, that I may bury my dead out of my sight.

gate of his enemies anticipates the conquest under Joshua, something additional promised (cf. 12:1-3, 15, 17).

20-24. This account of the twelve children of Nahor is most likely introduced at this time to indicate that it may have prompted Abraham's decision in 24:4 to go back to his country and his kindred to seek a wife for Isaac. It may have just confirmed the thought. The significant names are Bethuel and Rebekah. **Uz.** Job lived in the land of Uz. Laban is left out (cf. 24:29), indicating that the center of attention is on Rebekah; and this focus on the Israelite ancestresses continues in chapters 23 and 24.

8. The family burial place. 23:1-20.

23:1. Hebrews 11:13 says, "These all died in faith, not having received the promises . . . confessed that they were strangers and pilgrims on the earth." Abraham had been promised a land, and yet he did not have a place to bury his wife Sarah. By leaving their bones in Canaan, the patriarchs gave their last witness to the promise. Joseph's dying words made this clear, **And Joseph took an oath of the children of Israel, saying, God will surely visit you, and ye shall carry up my bones from hence** (50:25).

2-4. Kirjath-arba was the older name for Hebron (cf. Josh 14:15; Jud 1:10) and means City of Four. In reality, it commemorates a hero of the Anakim (Josh 14:15). Speiser indicates the possibility of a non-Semitic origin of the name, thus supporting a tradition about the **children of Heth** (vs. 5). **Canaan** prepares for the thought thrust upon Abraham by the exigencies of Sarah's burial that he was still **a stranger and a sojourner** in the Promised Land, not its lord, or even a small property owner. A family sepulchre would not be a legal claim to the possession of Canaan, but it would be a prophetic sign. **Give me** does not mean give without payment, as many have interpreted. Abra-

5 And the children of Heth answered Abraham, saying unto him,

6 Hear us, my lord: thou *art* a mighty prince among us: in the choice of our sepulchres bury thy dead; none of us shall withhold from thee his sepulchre, but that thou mayest bury thy dead.

7 And Abraham stood up, and bowed himself to the people of the land, *even* to the children of Heth.

8 And he communed with them, saying, If it be your mind that I should bury my dead out of my sight; hear me, and intreat for me to Ē'phrŏn the son of Zō'här,

9 That he may give me the cave of Măch-pē'läh, which he hath, which *is* in the end of his field; for as much money as it is worth he shall give it me for a possession of a buryingplace amongst you.

10 And Ē'phrŏn dwelt among the children of Heth: and Ē'phrŏn the Hittite answered Abraham in the audience of the children of Heth, *even* of all that went in at the gate of his city, saying,

11 Nay, my lord, hear me: the field give I thee, and the cave that *is* therein, I give it thee; in the presence of the sons of my people give I it thee: bury thy dead.

12 And Abraham bowed down himself before the people of the land.

13 And he spake unto Ē'phrŏn in the audience of the people of the land, saying, But if thou *wilt give it,* I pray thee, hear me: I will give thee money for the field; take *it* of me, and I will bury my dead there.

14 And Ē'phrŏn answered Abraham, saying unto him,

15 My lord, hearken unto me: the land *is worth* four hundred shekels of silver; what *is* that betwixt me and thee? bury therefore thy dead.

16 And Abraham hearkened unto Ē'phrŏn; and Abraham weighed to Ē'phrŏn the silver, which he had named in the audience of the sons of Heth, four hundred shekels of silver, current *money* with the merchant.

17 And the field of Ē'phrŏn, which *was* in Măch-pē'läh, which *was* before Măm're, the field, and the cave which *was* therein, and all the trees that *were* in the field, that *were* in all the borders round about, were made sure

18 Unto Abraham for a possession in the presence of the children of Heth, before all that went in at the gate of his city.

19 And after this, Abraham buried Sarah his wife in the cave of the field of Măch-pē'läh before Măm're: the same *is* Hebron in the land of Canaan.

20 And the field, and the cave that *is* therein, were made sure unto Abraham for a possession of a buryingplace by the sons of Heth.

CHAPTER 24

AND Abraham was old, *and* well strick-

ham, though only a resident alien, was requesting the right to acquire property in perpetuity. In like manner, Ephron did not offer a free gift in verse 11, **the field give I thee.** Note verse 9, **give me the cave of Machpelah . . . for as much money as it is worth he shall give it me for a possession.**

5-20. Children of Heth. It is debatable whether this is a reference to real Hittites or to those who spoke their language. "The negotiations between Abraham and the Hittites have always greatly interested Bible scholars, but only recently, as archaeology has illuminated Hittite law, the interpretation of the passage has undergone drastic change. No longer is it understood as typical oriental haggling for a parcel of land. . . . He asked the Hittites, according to the Authorized Version, to 'give (*natan*) me a possession of a buryingplace,' but *natan* here means 'sell;' the same root in verse 13 means 'pay.' Abraham was asking to buy the cave of Machpelah for an equitable price. Why Ephron refused to sell him only the cave (vs. 11) relates to Hittite law" (Davis, pp. 221-222). Lehmann has observed that Hittite law required the owner of a complete unit of land to continue to perform the king's *ilku* (feudal services). Abraham would avoid transfer of these obligations to himself by purchasing only the cave **which is in the end of his field** (vs. 9). On the other hand, Ephron insisted on selling the entire unit, field and cave, as the conclusion repeatedly notes (vss. 17, 19-20; cf. 49:29ff., especially note vs. 32, **the field and the cave**). Ephron did not want to remain responsible for the feudal services that the owner must render. So Abraham had to purchase **the field and the cave which was therein** (vs. 17). The prominent mention of trees in the final agreement was another characteristic of the Hittite business documents (vs. 17). Since the Hittites were destroyed about 1200 B.C., the liberal critic's assertion of a late date for the composition of Genesis is combated here. It also should motivate the believer to continue to interpret the Scripture in light of the grammatical, historical, and social aspects of the culture into which God gave His revelation. **Mighty prince** (vs. 6). This term is generally translated "prince of God," or "mighty prince." The term *nasi'* (cf. 17:20) designates an official who has been elevated in or by the assembly, hence elected (cf. *Catholic Biblical Quarterly,* 25, 1963, pp. 111-117). Here it is an honorific epithet. The Hittites were acknowledging that God ('*Elōhīm*) had played a mighty part in Abraham's life. This was after Abraham had lived in the area for 62 years (cf. Gen 12:4; 17:17; 23:1). This term is similarly used in early texts of the chiefs of the Midianites (Josh 13:21; Num 25:18) and Shechem (Gen 34:2). The title is later applied to David and Solomon (I Kgs 11:34).

The cave **of the field of Machpelah before Mamre** became the burial spot for Sarah, Abraham, Isaac, Rebekah, Leah, and Jacob (cf. 25:9; 49:31; 50:13). Rachel is a notable exception (cf. 35:19).

9. *The chosen bride for Isaac. 24:1-67.*

24:1-9. This portion gives witness to Abraham's example of

en in age: and the LORD had blessed Abraham in all things.

2 And Abraham said unto his eldest servant of his house, that ruled over all that he had, Put, I pray thee, thy hand under my thigh:

3 And I will make thee swear by the LORD, the God of heaven, and the God of the earth, that thou shalt not take a wife unto my son of the daughters of the Canaanites, among whom I dwell:

4 But thou shalt go unto my country, and to my kindred, and take a wife unto my son Isaac.

5 And the servant said unto him, Peradventure the woman will not be willing to follow me unto this land: must I needs bring thy son again unto the land from whence thou camest?

6 And Abraham said unto him, Beware thou that thou bring not my son thither again.

7 The LORD God of heaven, which took me from my father's house, and from the land of my kindred, and which spake unto me, and that sware unto me, saying, Unto thy seed will I give this land; he shall send his angel before thee, and thou shalt take a wife unto my son from thence.

8 And if the woman will not be willing to follow thee, then thou shalt be clear from this my oath: only bring not my son thither again.

9 And the servant put his hand under the thigh of Abraham his master, and sware to him concerning that matter.

10 ¶And the servant took ten camels of the camels of his master, and departed; for all the goods of his master were in his hand: and he arose, and went to Mĕs-o-po-tā'mĭ-a, unto the city of Nahor.

11 And he made his camels to kneel down without the city by a well of water at the time of the evening, even the time that women go out to draw water.

12 And he said, O LORD God of my master Abraham, I pray thee, send me good speed this day, and shew kindness unto my master Abraham.

13 Behold, I stand here by the well of water; and the daughters of the men of the city come out to draw water:

14 And let it come to pass, that the damsel to whom I shall say, Let down thy pitcher, I pray thee, that I may drink; and she shall say, Drink, and I will give thy camels drink also: let the same be she that thou hast appointed for thy servant Isaac; and thereby shall I know that thou hast shewed kindness unto my master.

15 ¶And it came to pass, before he had done speaking, that, behold, Rebekah came out, who was born to Bethū'el, son of Mĭl'cah, the wife of Nahor, Abraham's brother, with her pitcher upon her shoulder.

16 And the damsel was very fair to look upon, a virgin, neither had any man known her: and she went down to the well, and filled her pitcher, and came up.

17 And the servant ran to meet her, and said, Let me, I pray thee, drink a little water of thy pitcher.

dedication. "With old age and wealth to anchor him to the past or present, he now looked on steadfastly to the next stage of the promise and acted with decision. The story gives living form to the charge 'In all thy ways acknowledge him, and he shall direct thy paths' (Prov 3:6). At this distance from the event, we can see how decisively the courageous obedience of a few individuals over a family matter was to shape the course of history" (Kidner, p. 146). **Well stricken.** This merely implies that he was advanced in age, about 140 years old; he was 100 when Isaac was born (17:17), and Isaac was 40 when he married Rebekah (25:20). **Eldest servant** may have been Eliezer of 15:1ff. He worshiped God (vss. 26ff., 52); he was devoted to Abraham (vss. 12b, 14b, 27); and he was dedicated to finishing the task (vss. 33, 56). If he was Eliezer, then his loyalty in serving the heir who had displaced him is all the greater. **Thigh.** This is a euphemism for the procreative organ. This act "either symbolized that the yet unborn children would avenge any violation of the oath, or solemnized the oath in the name of the God who gave circumcision as the sign of His covenant" (Ryrie, p. 42; cf. 47:29 for the only other instance). **Daughters of the Canaanites.** The command to marry only within God's redeemed community was to be maintained throughout the Old and New Testaments (cf. Deut 7:3-4; I Kgs 11:4; Ezr 9; and Paul's ". . . only in the Lord," I Cor 7:39). The journey back was several hundred miles, and he was not able to take Isaac so the new bride could get to know him first. But Abraham said that God **shall send his angel before** the servant to meet his needs. **The city of Nahor.** It could be a city by this name, as there was one; or it could be the city where Nahor resided (cf. 11:31; 22:20; 27:43). This was the place of Abraham's **kindred,** and it was his **country** (cf. 11:27-28).

10-49. The servant's example of devotion is depicted in these verses. As he sat by a well outside the city of **Nahor,** he prayed that God would **show kindness unto my master.** The word **kindness** is also chesed; he is entreating God to be faithful to His servant Abraham. God had promised Abraham a **seed,** and He had given him one; now Abraham wants to get a bride for the promised seed in accordance with God's standards of separation. So he now asks God to be faithful to His servant Abraham and provide for him. Then, in verses 14, 27, and 49 his testimony is that God did **show** chesed, covenant-faithfulness. There is a wonderful testimony in verse 27. **Blessed be the LORD God of my master Abraham, who hath not left destitute my master of his mercy** (chesed) **and his truth** (promises made): **I being in the way, the LORD led me.** Some people get in the way, and others are in the way so God can lead them.

18 And she said, Drink, my lord: and she hasted, and let down her pitcher upon her hand, and gave him drink.

19 And when she had done giving him drink, she said, I will draw *water* for thy camels also, until they have done drinking.

20 And she hasted, and emptied her pitcher into the trough, and ran again unto the well to draw *water*, and drew for all his camels.

21 And the man wondering at her held his peace, to wit whether the LORD had made his journey prosperous or not.

22 And it came to pass, as the camels had done drinking, that the man took a golden earring of half a shekel weight, and two bracelets for her hands of ten *shekels* weight of gold;

23 And said, Whose daughter *art* thou? tell me, I pray thee: is there room *in* thy father's house for us to lodge in?

24 And she said unto him, I *am* the daughter of Beth-ū'el the son of Mĭl'-cah, which she bare unto Nahor.

25 She said moreover unto him, We have both straw and provender enough, and room to lodge in.

26 And the man bowed down his head, and worshipped the LORD.

27 And he said, Blessed *be* the LORD God of my master Abraham, who hath not left destitute my master of his mercy and his truth: I *being* in the way, the LORD led me to the house of my master's brethren.

28 And the damsel ran, and told *them of* her mother's house these things.

29 ¶And Rebekah had a brother, and his name *was* Lā́ban: and Lā́ban ran out unto the man, unto the well.

30 And it came to pass, when he saw the earring and bracelets upon his sister's hands, and when he heard the words of Rebekah his sister, saying, Thus spake the man unto me; that he came unto the man; and, behold, he stood by the camels at the well.

31 And he said, Come in, thou blessed of the LORD; wherefore standest thou without? for I have prepared the house, and room for the camels.

32 And the man came into the house: and he ungirded his camels, and gave straw and provender for the camels, and water to wash his feet, and the men's feet that *were* with him.

33 And there was set *meat* before him to eat: but he said, I will not eat, until I have told mine errand. And he said, Speak on.

34 And he said, I *am* Abraham's servant.

35 And the LORD hath blessed my master greatly; and he is become great: and he hath given him flocks, and herds, and silver, and gold, and menservants, and maidservants, and camels, and asses.

36 And Sarah my master's wife bare a son to my master when she was old: and unto him hath he given all that he hath.

37 And my master made me swear, saying, Thou shalt not take a wife to my

son of the daughters of the Canaanites, in whose land I dwell:

38 But thou shalt go unto my father's house, and to my kindred, and take a wife unto my son.

39 And I said unto my master, Peradventure the woman will not follow me.

40 And he said unto me, The LORD, before whom I walk, will send his angel with thee, and prosper thy way; and thou shalt take a wife for my son of my kindred, and of my father's house:

41 Then shalt thou be clear from *this* my oath, when thou comest to my kindred; and if they give not thee *one*, thou shalt be clear from my oath.

42 And I came this day unto the well, and said, O LORD God of my master Abraham, if now thou do prosper my way which I go:

43 Behold, I stand by the well of water; and it shall come to pass, that when the virgin cometh forth to draw *water*, and I say to her, Give me, I pray thee, a little water of thy pitcher to drink;

44 And she say to me, Both drink thou, and I will also draw for thy camels: *let* the same *be* the woman whom the LORD hath appointed out for my master's son.

45 And before I had done speaking in mine heart, behold, Rebekah came forth with her pitcher on her shoulder; and she went down unto the well, and drew *water*: and I said unto her, Let me drink, I pray thee.

46 And she made haste, and let down her pitcher from her *shoulder*, and said, Drink, and I will give thy camels drink also: so I drank, and she made the camels drink also.

47 And I asked her, and said, Whose daughter *art* thou? And she said, The daughter of Beth-ū'el, Nahor's son, whom Mil'cah bare unto him: and I put the earring upon her face, and the bracelets upon her hands.

48 And I bowed down my head, and worshipped the LORD, and blessed the LORD God of my master Abraham, which had led me in the right way to take my master's brother's daughter unto his son.

49 And now if ye will deal kindly and truly with my master, tell me: and if not, tell me; that I may turn to the right hand, or to the left.

50 Then Lāban and Beth-ū'el answered and said, The thing proceedeth from the LORD: we cannot speak unto thee bad or good.

51 Behold, Rebekah *is* before thee, take *her*, and go, and let her be thy master's son's wife, as the LORD hath spoken.

52 And it came to pass, that, when Abraham's servant heard their words, he worshipped the LORD, *bowing himself* to the earth.

53 And the servant brought forth jewels of silver, and jewels of gold, and raiment, and gave *them* to Rebekah: he gave also to her brother and to her mother precious things.

54 And they did eat and drink, he and the men that *were* with him, and tarried all night; and they rose up in the

50-67. A further development of Speiser's proposals on patriarchal marriage customs was that he regarded verses 53-61 as containing most of the elements of a Nuzi sistership adoption contract. Out of the five main clauses, four are supposedly identified in this narrative. Yet the most remarkable feature of his reconstruction is that he has omitted any reference to the central purpose of Nuzi sistership adoptions, namely, that the man who adopted a girl as his "sister" could then give her in marriage, and thereby receive the marriage payment from her husband (cf. Nuzi text HSS 19 68, where the girl's real brother who gave her into sistership adoption declared: "I gave my sister A. into sistership to T. son of I., and T. may give her in marriage as he wished and will receive the money from her husband"). Certainly, Abraham's servant did not adopt Rebekah in order to give her to Isaac as a wife. Her statement in verse 58 of **I will go** can hardly refer to her consenting to marriage with Isaac; this had already been agreed upon by her father and

morning, and he said, Send me away unto my master.

55 And her brother and her mother said, Let the damsel abide with us *a few* days, at the least ten; after that she shall go.

56 And he said unto them, Hinder me not, seeing the LORD hath prospered my way; send me away that I may go to my master.

57 And they said, We will call the damsel, and enquire at her mouth.

58 And they called Rebekah, and said unto her, Wilt thou go with this man? And she said, I will go.

59 And they sent away Rebekah their sister, and her nurse, and Abraham's servant, and his men.

60 And they blessed Rebekah, and said unto her, Thou *art* our sister, be thou *the mother* of thousands of millions, and let thy seed possess the gate of those which hate them.

61 ¶And Rebekah arose, and her damsels, and they rode upon the camels, and followed the man: and the servant took Rebekah, and went his way.

62 And Isaac came from the way of the well La-haï'roi; for he dwelt in the south country.

63 And Isaac went out to meditate in the field at the eventide: and he lifted up his eyes, and saw, and, behold, the camels *were* coming.

64 And Rebekah lifted up her eyes, and when she saw Isaac, she lighted off the camel.

65 For she *had* said unto the servant, What man *is* this that walketh in the field to meet us? And the servant *had* said, It *is* my master: therefore she took a vail, and covered herself.

66 And the servant told Isaac all things that he had done.

67 And Isaac brought her into his mother Sarah's tent, and took Rebekah, and she became his wife; and he loved her: and Isaac was comforted after his mother's *death*.

CHAPTER 25

THEN again Abraham took a wife, and her name *was* Ke-tū'rah.

2 And she bare him Zĭm'răn, and Jŏk'shăn, and Mē'dăn, and Mĭd'ĭ-an, and Ĭsh-băk, and Shū'ah.

3 And Jŏk'shăn begat Shē'ba, and Dē'dan. And the sons of Dē'dan were As-shu'rim, and Le-tū'shim, and Lē-ūm'mĭm.

4 And the sons of Mĭd'ĭ-an; Ē'phah, and Ē'pher, and Hā'nŏch, and A-bī'dah, and Ĕl'dā-ah. All these *were* the children of Ke-tū'rah.

5 And Abraham gave all that he had unto Isaac.

6 But unto the sons of the concubines, which Abraham had, Abraham gave gifts, and sent them away from Isaac his son, while he yet lived, eastward, unto the east country.

7 And these *are* the days of the years

brother in verses 50-51, a decision in which she did not participate. The only decision required of Rebekah was whether she would leave for Canaan immediately or delay for a few days (vs. 55).

10. The peoples arising from Abraham. 25:1-18.

Abraham's death is given in the setting of a catalogue of the families that arose from him. Just as in previous cases, the pattern is for those who were to play a little part in the history of salvation to be presented first; then the chief actors come on stage.

25:1-4. The sons of Keturah. At first sight the Hebrew construction indicates that Abraham's marriage to Keturah followed the events just recounted in chapter 24. Some say his vitality points to an earlier date, even though he was to live thirty-five years after Isaac's marriage (vss. 7, 20). The fact she was a concubine (vs. 6; I Chr 1:32), suggests that Sarah was alive when Abraham took her. Many of the names listed have already been identified with Arab tribes, fulfilling God's promise to Abraham that he would be the father of many nations (17:4). **Midian** is the best known name in the list ranging from the head of the Gulf of Aqaba to Moab and even Gilead (cf. Jud 6ff.). **Shuah.** Note the gentilic ". . . Shuhite . . ." in Job 2:11. **Hanoch** is the same name as that of the patriarch Enoch (cf. 4:17; 5:18ff.). **Asshurim** is not to be confused with its namesake, the Assyrians.

5-11. This passage tells of Abraham's will, death, and burial. In verses 5 and 6 we see how the promise **in Isaac shall thy seed be called** guided Abraham's conduct to the very end (see the discussion in chs. 17-22). **Abraham gave all that he had unto Isaac . . . But to the sons of the concubines . . . Abraham gave gifts, and sent them away from Isaac his son.** The dismissal may have occurred at Ishmael's expulsion, or more

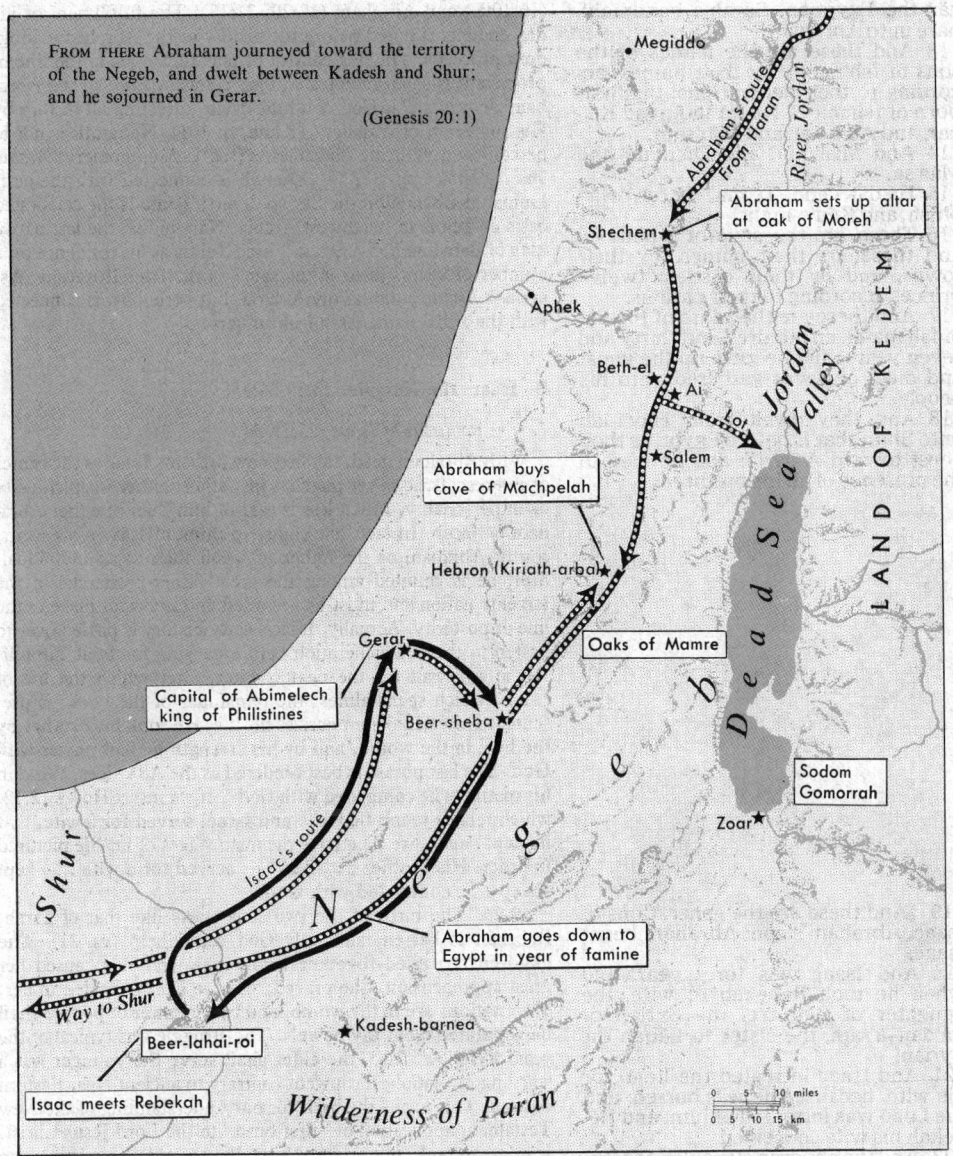

FROM THERE Abraham journeyed toward the territory of the Negeb, and dwelt between Kadesh and Shur; and he sojourned in Gerar.

(Genesis 20:1)

Megiddo

Abraham's route from Haran

River Jordan

Abraham sets up altar at oak of Moreh

Shechem

Aphek

Beth-el

Ai

Lot

Salem

Jordan Sea Valley

Abraham buys cave of Machpelah

Hebron (Kiriath-arba)

Oaks of Mamre

Dead Sea

LAND OF KEDEM

Gerar

Capital of Abimelech king of Philistines

Beer-sheba

Sodom
Gomorrah

Zoar

Negeb

Shur

Isaac's route

Abraham goes down to Egypt in year of famine

Way to Shur

Beer-lahai-roi

Kadesh-barnea

Isaac meets Rebekah

Wilderness of Paran

0   5   10 miles
0 5 10 15 km

Abraham and Isaac in the Land of Canaan

of Abraham's life which he lived, an hundred threescore and fifteen years.

8 Then Abraham gave up the ghost, and died in a good old age, an old man, and full *of years:* and was gathered to his people.

9 And his sons Isaac and Ĭsh'ma-el buried him in the cave of Măch-pē'-läh, in the field of Ē'phrŏn the son of Zō'här the Hittite, which *is* before Măm're;

10 The field which Abraham purchased of the sons of Heth: there was Abraham buried, and Sarah his wife.

11 And it came to pass after the death of Abraham, that God blessed his son Isaac; and Isaac dwelt by the well La-haī'roi.

12 ¶Now these *are* the generations of Ĭsh'ma-el, Abraham's son, whom Hā'-

probably, when Isaac became co-patriarch with Abraham (cf. vs. 5 and 24:62-67). **And was gathered to his people** has been interpreted: (1) as a mere euphemism for death; (2) as a reference to a multiple burial; or (3) as the majority of commentators assert, as a reference to immortality. He was buried by Isaac and Ishmael, which may indicate they had been reconciled.

12-18. This gives the account of the sons of Ishmael. He had been the subject of particular divine promises made to Hagar

gär the Egyptian, Sarah's handmaid, bare unto Abraham:

13 And these are the names of the sons of Ĭsh'ma-el, by their names, according to their generations: the firstborn of Ĭsh'ma-el, Ne-bā'jŏth; and Kē'dar, and Ad'be-el, and Mĭb'săm,

14 And Mĭsh'ma, and Dū'mah, and Măs'sa,

15 Hă'där, and Tē'ma, Jē'tur, Nă'phĭsh, and Kĕd'e-mah:

16 These are the sons of Ĭsh'ma-el, and these are their names, by their towns, and by their castles; twelve princes according to their nations.

17 And these are the years of the life of Ĭsh'ma-el, an hundred and thirty and seven years: and he gave up the ghost and died; and was gathered unto his people.

18 And they dwelt from Hăv'i-lah unto Shur, that is before Egypt, as thou goest toward Assyria: and he died in the presence of all his brethren.

19 ¶And these are the generations of Isaac, Abraham's son: Abraham begat Isaac:

20 And Isaac was forty years old when he took Rebekah to wife, the daughter of Beth-ū'el the Syrian of Pā'dan-â'ram, the sister to Lāban the Syrian.

21 And Isaac intreated the LORD for his wife, because she was barren: and the LORD was intreated of him, and Rebekah his wife conceived.

22 And the children struggled together within her; and she said, If it be so, why am I thus? And she went to enquire of the LORD.

23 And the LORD said unto her, Two nations are in thy womb, and two manner of people shall be separated from thy bowels; and the one people shall be stronger than the other people; and the elder shall serve the younger.

24 And when her days to be delivered were fulfilled, behold, there were twins in her womb.

25 And the first came out red, all over like an hairy garment; and they called his name Esau.

26 And after that came his brother out, and his hand took hold on Esau's heel; and his name was called Jacob: and Isaac was threescore years old when she bare them.

(16:10ff.) and Abraham (17:20; 21:13). The fulfillment of his descendants is noted before the history of the Abrahamic kingdom proceeds. "In this control of mankind outside the line of promise it is again manifested that Yahweh, Lord of the Abrahamic covenant, is God of all the earth, directing all history by His sovereign providence" (Kline, p. 101). **Nebajoth** is not to be confused with the Nabataeans (see J. Montgomery, *Arabia and the Bible*, pp. 31, 54). **Dumah** is connected with the oasis Dumat al-Ghandal in the Syrian desert; **Tema** is the celebrated oasis of Teima in northwest Arabia. Nabonidus, the last native king of Babylon (555-539 B.C.), used Teima as his residence for a number of years. **Jetur** is the same as the later Ituraeans. **Assyria** is Asshur, and hardly Assyria, but perhaps it is connected with the tribal name Asshurim in verse 3.

B. Isaac, the Humble. 25:19-26:35.

1. The twin sons of Isaac. 25:19-34.

With Abraham dead, the text now presents Isaac as the center of interest. Isaac never matches his father, either in spirituality or in personality. Much less is said of him than of either Abraham or Jacob. In fact, one comes to think of Isaac more as the son of Abraham or the father of Jacob than as an individual. Still, he is counted among the great father-patriarchs of the Israelite nation and must be accorded an important place in the line of posterity. Actually, Isaac's early history is passed over to hasten to the new generation before pausing for Isaac himself. His affairs wait for the next chapter, after which the life of Jacob, which spans almost the remainder of the book, is presented. Hosea 12:3 summarizes his life, **He took his brother by the heel in the womb, and by his strength he had power with God.** The last phrase is best rendered as the ASV does, "And in his maturity he contended with God." If we insert Hosea 12:12, which relates **Jacob fled . . . and Israel served for a wife, . . . he kept sheep,** we then have the main stages of his life pictured in order: **His brother . . . fled . . . served for a wife . . . kept sheep . . . contended with God.**

19-26. The birth of the two sons starts like that of Sarah; Rebekah is barren, and only God could help (vs. 21). **The children struggled together within her,** and this caused her great apprehension. She prayed; and the Lord revealed to her, **Two nations are in thy womb, and two manner of people shall be separated from thy bowels.** The struggle was typical of the years to follow. Also, **the elder shall serve the younger** was a startling revelation; for it went contrary to ancient Near Eastern custom. This forms the basis for our understanding of the New Testament application of "first-born" to the Lord Jesus Christ. It refers to rank, not origin. Normally, the eldest son was given preferential treatment. He assumed more responsibility and was rewarded with honor and given two shares in the family inheritance, instead of the single share that each of his younger brothers received. Occasionally, the eldest fell out of favor and was replaced by a younger son, a brother. Notice some examples: Jacob replaced Esau; Ephraim replaced Manasseh in 48:13-20; Joseph replaced Reuben in 49:3-4 (cf. I Chronicles 5:1-2); and Solomon replaced Adonijah in I Kings 1:5-53. Thus, the younger became the "first-born," i.e., he attained to first rank. This term is applied in this sense to the nation of Israel (Ex 4:22).

27 And the boys grew: and Esau was a cunning hunter, a man of the field; and Jacob was a plain man, dwelling in tents.

28 And Isaac loved Esau, because he did eat of his venison: but Rebekah loved Jacob.

29 And Jacob sod pottage: and Esau came from the field, and he was faint:

30 And Esau said to Jacob, Feed me, I pray thee, with that same red pottage; for I am faint: therefore was his name called Edom.

31 And Jacob said, Sell me this day thy birthright.

32 And Esau said, Behold, I am at the point to die: and what profit shall this birthright do to me?

33 And Jacob said, Swear to me this day; and he sware unto him: and he sold his birthright unto Jacob.

34 Then Jacob gave Esau bread and pottage of lentiles; and he did eat and drink, and rose up, and went his way: thus Esau despised his birthright.

CHAPTER 26

AND there was a famine in the land, beside the first famine that was in the days of Abraham. And Isaac went unto A-bĭm'e-lĕch king of the Philistines unto Ge'rär.

2 And the LORD appeared unto him, and said, Go not down into Egypt; dwell in the land which I shall tell thee of:

3 Sojourn in this land, and I will be with thee, and will bless thee; for unto thee, and unto thy seed, I will give all these countries, and I will perform the oath which I sware unto Abraham thy father;

4 And I will make thy seed to multiply as the stars of heaven, and will give unto thy seed all these countries; and in thy seed shall all the nations of the earth be blessed;

5 Because that Abraham obeyed my voice, and kept my charge, my commandments, my statutes, and my laws.

6 ¶ And Isaac dwelt in Ge'rär:

7 And the men of the place asked him of his wife; and he said, She is my sister: for he feared to say, She is my wife; lest, said he, the men of the place should kill me for Rebekah; because she was fair to look upon.

8 And it came to pass, when he had been there a long time, that A-bĭm'e-lĕch king of the Philistines looked out at a window, and saw, and, behold, Isaac was sporting with Rebekah his wife.

9 And A-bĭm'e-lĕch called Isaac, and said, Behold, of a surety she is thy wife: and how saidst thou, She is my sister? And Isaac said unto him, Because I said, Lest I die for her.

10 And A-bĭm'e-lĕch said, What is

27-34. The previous discussion illustrates the statement **and he sold his birthright unto Jacob.** Thus "Esau impetuously forfeited important rights, responsibilities, and honors which were his by birth. He 'despised his birthright;' he considered the responsibilities and honors unimportant, or he was totally uninterested in them. The agreement was solidified by a formal oath (vs. 33)" (Davis, p. 233). A study of the patriarchal narratives indicates that there were two outstanding features associated with birthright, leadership of the clan and the guardianship of the promise. There is nothing in the promise to link it with birthright alone, as it regards the first-born; but the bearer of the promise was always the owner of the birthright as well. This account then sets the tone for the events which follow, not only in the two individuals and their relationships with one another, but as the destinies of two peoples are constructed. One important thing to notice is that **Isaac loved Esau . . . but Rebekah loved Jacob.** The conflict and tragedy that troubled this family ought to provide a practical warning to parents who favor one child over another.

2. Isaac deceives Abimelech. 26:1-11.

The episodes in this chapter follow Abraham's death (cf. vss. 1, 15, 18), "but the earlier of them possibly preceded the birthright exchange (cf. 25:29ff.). Their position between the two supplanting episodes suggests their purpose is to portray the inheritance Jacob coveted" (Kline, p. 101). This is the third account dealing with the "wife-sister" theme (cf. chapter 20 where it was discussed). The two previous situations involved Abraham; now the old adage, "Like father, like son," seems apropos.

26:1-11. There was a famine . . . in the days of Abraham (cf. 12:10). Abraham was not told anything about what he was to do. This time Isaac was told **Go not down into Egypt; dwell in the land which I shall tell thee of.** He had already gone to **Abimelech king of the Philistines unto Gerar.** In times of severe famine in Palestine most people went down to Egypt; it was the normal thing to do. But God forced Isaac to trust in His ability to provide, not to do the natural thing that everybody else would be doing. Abimelech was evidently a Philistine dynastic title (cf. I Sam 21:10-11 and the heading of Ps 34). This probably was not the same Abimelech that Abraham encountered some ninety-seven years earlier. God confirmed the Abrahamic covenant to Isaac; so Isaac **dwelt in Gerar.** Isaac gave the reason why he lied about Rebekah; he said, **the men of the place should kill me.** Abraham had said, **surely the fear of God is not in this place. And they will slay me.** Isaac obeyed God by not going to Egypt, which took faith; but now he was not able to trust God among the heathen. Both men took situations into their own hand when the pressure came. The repetition of these types of situations reveals God's intention of demonstrating to the patriarchs His ability to be **their shield.** All of the early names for God have to do with power, might, and strength; and they are actually disclosures of His very being.

Abimelech saw . . . Isaac was sporting with Rebekah. This is an evidence of sovereign, divine protection. The Hebrew for **sporting** is a play on the name Isaac (*yitschaq*), for it is pronounced (*metsachēq*). The meaning can be "to make sport of" or "to mock" as in 19:14 and 21:9 and Judges 16:25. It shows strong emotion in so doing. It is also used in Exodus 32:6 of sexual immorality. Isaac was probably caressing Rebekah in a way that one would expect of a husband with his wife. God certainly spoke through Abimelech when he said, **What is this thou hast done unto us?**

this thou hast done unto us? one of the people might lightly have lien with thy wife, and thou shouldest have brought guiltiness upon us.

11 And A-bĭm′e-lĕch charged all *his* people, saying, He that toucheth this man or his wife shall surely be put to death.

12 Then Isaac sowed in that land, and received in the same year an hundred-fold: and the LORD blessed him.

13 And the man waxed great, and went forward, and grew until he became very great:

14 For he had possession of flocks, and possession of herds, and great store of servants: and the Philistines envied him.

15 For all the wells which his father's servants had digged in the days of Abraham his father, the Philistines had stopped them, and filled them with earth.

16 And A-bĭm′e-lĕch said unto Isaac, Go from us; for thou art much mightier than we.

17 ¶And Isaac departed thence, and pitched his tent in the valley of Ge′rär, and dwelt there.

18 And Isaac digged again the wells of water, which they had digged in the days of Abraham his father; for the Philistines had stopped them after the death of Abraham: and he called their names after the names by which his father had called them.

19 And Isaac's servants digged in the valley, and found there a well of springing water.

20 And the herdmen of Ge′rär did strive with Isaac's herdmen, saying, The water *is* ours: and he called the name of the well E′sĕk; because they strove with him.

21 And they digged another well, and strove for that also: and he called the name of it Sĭt′nah.

22 And he removed from thence, and digged another well; and for that they strove not: and he called the name of it Re-hō′bŏth; and he said, For now the LORD hath made room for us, and we shall be fruitful in the land.

23 And he went up from thence to Be′er-shē′ba.

24 And the LORD appeared unto him the same night, and said, I *am* the God of Abraham thy father: fear not, for I *am* with thee, and will bless thee, and multiply thy seed for my servant Abraham's sake.

25 And he builded an altar there, and called upon the name of the LORD, and pitched his tent there: and there Isaac's servants digged a well.

26 ¶Then A-bĭm′e-lĕch went to him from Ge′rär, and A-hŭz′zăth one of his friends, and Phī′chŏl the chief captain of his army.

27 And Isaac said unto them, Wherefore come ye to me, seeing ye hate me, and have sent me away from you?

28 And they said, We saw certainly that the LORD was with thee: and we said, Let there be now an oath betwixt us, *even* betwixt us and thee, and let us make a covenant with thee;

3. Isaac's fluctuating fortunes. 26:12-22.

12-17. God blessed Isaac so much that the **Philistines envied him.** This was accomplished in the face of famine and Philistine harassment in filling and stopping up the **wells which his father's servants had digged in the days of Abraham his father.**

18-22. They had asked him to leave, so he did. The encampments at **Esek** (Contention) and **Sitnah** (Enmity) led to the spacious and fruitful place of **Rehoboth** (Plenty of Room). He had many struggles, but we can identify with him and hopefully see how God worked in the life of an average man.

4. The covenant at Beer-sheba. 26:23-35.

23-25. Upon arriving at **Beer-sheba,** God appeared unto him and again confirmed the Abrahamic covenant. So he worshiped there by building an altar.

26-35. This covenant renewed the Abimelech-Abraham covenant of 21:23. It was due to Isaac's initial frankness (vs. 27) and his ability to restrain himself in his conversation that he was able to make peace with honor. The Philistines gave witness that God had abundantly provided for Isaac in fulfillment of His promise to do so if Isaac would not go down to Egypt (cf. vs. 3). **Shebah** can be a reference to: (1) the number seven; (2) satedness or plenty; or (3) oath. Most likely the last one is correct. Here is a case where Isaac was wronged by these men; they had said they had treated him well, but he did not respond in bitterness or retaliation by words or actions. Instead, he let it slide by and

29 That thou wilt do us no hurt, as we have not touched thee, and as we have done unto thee nothing but good, and have sent thee away in peace: thou *art* now the blessed of the LORD.

30 And he made them a feast, and they did eat and drink.

31 And they rose up betimes in the morning, and sware one to another: and Isaac sent them away, and they departed from him in peace.

32 And it came to pass the same day, that Isaac's servants came, and told him concerning the well which they had digged, and said unto him, We have found water.

33 And he called it Shē'bah: therefore the name of the city *is* Be'er-shē'ba unto this day.

34 ¶And Esau was forty years old when he took to wife Judith the daughter of Bē-e'rī the Hittite, and Băsh'e-măth the daughter of Ē'lŏn the Hittite:

35 Which were a grief of mind unto Isaac and to Rebekah.

CHAPTER 27

AND it came to pass, that when Isaac was old, and his eyes were dim, so that he could not see, he called Esau his eldest son, and said unto him, My son: and he said unto him, Behold, *here am* I.

2 And he said, Behold now, I am old, I know not the day of my death:

3 Now therefore take, I pray thee, thy weapons, thy quiver and thy bow, and go out to the field, and take me *some* venison;

4 And make me savoury meat, such as I love, and bring *it* to me, that I may eat; that my soul may bless thee before I die.

5 And Rebekah heard when Isaac spake to Esau his son. And Esau went to the field to hunt *for* venison, *and* to bring *it.*

6 ¶And Rebekah spake unto Jacob her son, saying, Behold, I heard thy father speak unto Esau thy brother, saying,

7 Bring me venison, and make me savoury meat, that I may eat, and bless thee before the LORD before my death.

8 Now therefore, my son, obey my voice according to that which I command thee.

9 Go now to the flock, and fetch me from thence two good kids of the goats; and I will make them savoury meat for thy father, such as he loveth:

10 And thou shalt bring *it* to thy father, that he may eat, and that he may bless thee before his death.

11 And Jacob said to Rebekah his mother, Behold, Esau my brother *is* a hairy man, and I *am* a smooth man:

made peace with those who had wronged him, a good lesson for all.

C. Jacob, the Transformed. 27:1-36:43.

1. Jacob seizes the blessing by deception. 27:1-46.

27:1-4. Behold now, I am old, I know not the day of my death. Isaac was 137 at this time, but he lived for another 43 years (cf. 35:28). In a special study of the background of Isaac's blessing in chapter 27, Speiser argued that this chapter, together with three Nuzi texts, showed that both at Nuzi and among patriarchal clans, a final disposition by the head of a household had solid legal standing and that the eldest son could be appointed to enjoy such a status. There are three problems with this view: (1) none of the Nuzi tablets, or chapter 27, are oral wills; (2) there is no evidence at Nuzi for arbitrary determination of birthright; nor (3) have any of the three Nuzi texts anything to do with paternal blessings, which is the real subject of chapter 27. There is one point of contact concerning the use of oral statements in ancient law. Certain legal safeguards accompanied such statements: the grasping of the hand (48:13) and a kiss (27:26-27; 48:10; Selman, pp. 134-135). **That my soul may bless thee before I die.** Isaac still favored Esau (cf. 25:28). He apparently was ignoring the fact that Esau had bartered his birthright (25:34) and had married heathen women (26:34). This is quite remarkable in light of the pains his father Abraham had taken to get a wife for him (chapter 24).

5-17. Here is the sequel to "Like father, like son": "Like mother, like son." Jacob had objections and he feared that Isaac might curse him; but his mother said **Upon me be thy curse.** So Jacob was to dress like Esau and place a **goodly raiment** upon himself and **skins of the kids of the goats upon his hands, and . . . neck,** and Rebekah skillfully prepared a substitute meal.

12 My father peradventure will feel me, and I shall seem to him as a deceiver; and I shall bring a curse upon me, and not a blessing.

13 And his mother said unto him, Upon me be thy curse, my son: only obey my voice, and go fetch me them.

14 And he went, and fetched, and brought them to his mother: and his mother made savoury meat, such as his father loved.

15 And Rebekah took goodly raiment of her eldest son Esau, which were with her in the house, and put them upon Jacob her younger son:

16 And she put the skins of the kids of the goats upon his hands, and upon the smooth of his neck:

17 And she gave the savoury meat and the bread, which she had prepared, into the hand of her son Jacob.

18 ¶And he came unto his father, and said, My father: and he said, Here am I; who art thou, my son?

19 And Jacob said unto his father, I am Esau thy firstborn; I have done according as thou badest me: arise, I pray thee, sit and eat of my venison, that thy soul may bless me.

20 And Isaac said unto his son, How is it that thou hast found it so quickly, my son? And he said, Because the LORD thy God brought it to me.

21 And Isaac said unto Jacob, Come near, I pray thee, that I may feel thee, my son, whether thou be my very son Esau or not.

22 And Jacob went near unto Isaac his father; and he felt him, and said, The voice is Jacob's voice, but the hands are the hands of Esau.

23 And he discerned him not, because his hands were hairy, as his brother Esau's hands: so he blessed him.

24 And he said, Art thou my very son Esau? And he said, I am.

25 And he said, Bring it near to me, and I will eat of my son's venison, that my soul may bless thee. And he brought it near to him, and he did eat: and he brought him wine, and he drank.

26 And his father Isaac said unto him, Come near now, and kiss me, my son.

27 And he came near, and kissed him: and he smelled the smell of his raiment, and blessed him, and said, See, the smell of my son is as the smell of a field which the LORD hath blessed:

28 Therefore God give thee of the dew of heaven, and the fatness of the earth, and plenty of corn and wine:

29 Let people serve thee, and nations bow down to thee: be lord over thy brethren, and let thy mother's sons bow down to thee: cursed be every one that curseth thee, and blessed be he that blesseth thee.

30 ¶And it came to pass, as soon as Isaac had made an end of blessing Jacob, and Jacob was yet scarce gone out from the presence of Isaac his father, that Esau his brother came in from his hunting.

31 And he also had made savoury meat, and brought it unto his father, and said unto his father, Let my father

18-29. "Jacob had to resort to lying (vss. 19, 24), and Isaac allowed his senses of touch (vs. 22), taste (vs. 25), and smell (vs. 27) to overrule what he heard (vs. 22). The blessing included both benediction (vs. 28) and prediction (vs. 29). The content does not fit exactly with the terminology of previous Abrahamic promise formulations but it does encompass the headship over Isaac's household, **let people serve thee** and 25:23. Other features include paradise land, nationhood with dominion, and mediatorship of divine judgment" (Kline, p. 102).

30-46. Yea, and he shall be blessed. Isaac realized that his blessing was final; it had been administered contrary to his own devices. **For he hath supplanted me.** The root of supplant is 'aqab, meaning "to take by the heel." Esau was distressed and saw the event as a repetition of the birthright exchange, a fulfillment of the birth prophecy, and an explanation for Jacob's name, which forms a pun with "supplanter" and is pronounced, ya'aqōb, ya'qēb. There is another pun with the words for **birthright** (bekōr) and **blessing** (berakah). **Thy dwelling shall be the**

arise, and eat of his son's venison, that thy soul may bless me.

32 And Isaac his father said unto him, Who *art* thou? And he said, I *am* thy son, thy firstborn Esau.

33 And Isaac trembled very exceedingly, and said, Who? where *is* he that hath taken venison, and brought *it* me, and I have eaten of all before thou camest, and have blessed him? yea, *and* he shall be blessed.

34 And when Esau heard the words of his father, he cried with a great and exceeding bitter cry, and said unto his father, Bless me, *even* me also, O my father.

35 And he said, Thy brother came with subtilty, and hath taken away thy blessing.

36 And he said, Is not he rightly named Jacob? for he hath supplanted me these two times: he took away my birthright; and, behold, now he hath taken away my blessing. And he said, Hast thou not reserved a blessing for me?

37 And Isaac answered and said unto Esau, Behold, I have made him thy lord, and all his brethren have I given to him for servants; and with corn and wine have I sustained him: and what shall I do now unto thee, my son?

38 And Esau said unto his father, Hast thou but one blessing, my father? bless me, *even* me also, O my father. And Esau lifted up his voice, and wept.

39 And Isaac his father answered and said unto him, Behold, thy dwelling shall be the fatness of the earth, and of the dew of heaven from above;

40 And by thy sword shalt thou live, and shalt serve thy brother; and it shall come to pass when thou shalt have the dominion, that thou shalt break his yoke from off thy neck.

41 ¶And Esau hated Jacob because of the blessing wherewith his father blessed him: and Esau said in his heart, The days of mourning for my father are at hand; then will I slay my brother Jacob.

42 And these words of Esau her elder son were told to Rebekah: and she sent and called Jacob her younger son, and said unto him, Behold, thy brother Esau, as touching thee, doth comfort himself, *purposing* to kill thee.

43 Now therefore, my son, obey my voice; and arise, flee thou to Lāban my brother to Hā′ran;

44 And tarry with him a few days, until thy brother's fury turn away;

45 Until thy brother's anger turn away from thee, and he forget *that* which thou hast done to him: then I will send, and fetch thee from thence: why should I be deprived also of you both in one day?

46 And Rebekah said to Isaac, I am weary of my life because of the daughters of Heth: if Jacob take a wife of the daughters of Heth, such as these *which are* of the daughters of the land, what good shall my life do me?

CHAPTER 28

AND Isaac called Jacob, and blessed him, and charged him, and said unto

fatness of the earth actually is to be rendered "away from the fatness," (cf. Kline, p. 102; ASV of Ryrie p. 50; and Speiser, p. 210). Edom (Esau) is doomed to privations; yet, his day will come as **it shall come to pass when thou shalt have the dominion, that thou shalt break his yoke from off thy neck.** Esau's descendants (the Edomites) would occupy a territory less fertile than Jacob's (the land of Canaan), note their mountains (cf. Obadiah); but from time to time they would break loose and assert their independence (see II Chr 21:8-10). So **Esau hated Jacob . . . Esau said in his heart . . . then will I slay my brother.** "The sins of all concerned in the business of the blessing began at once to take their toll. To deliver Jacob from Esau's vengeance, Rebekah, expert at scheming, was obliged to deliver her favorite over to her similarly talented brother Laban, and apparently died before it was propitious to recall Jacob (vs. 45; cf. 49:31)" (Kline, p. 102). The **few days** turned into years of frustration for Jacob. **Why should I be deprived also of you both in one day** seems to mean that if Esau were to kill Jacob, then the nearest relative would be obliged to kill the murderer (Esau). Thus, she would lose two sons. **I am weary of my life because of the daughters of Heth.** She again deceived Isaac, and she never saw Jacob again. Jacob certainly had a mother who, though she did not have his name, had a character like his. He learned his carnal nature at home.

2. Jacob is sent to Mesopotamia. 28:1-9.

28:1-5. Thou shalt not take a wife of the daughters of Canaan is like Abraham's desire for Isaac in chapter 24 and was

him, Thou shalt not take a wife of the daughters of Canaan.

2 Arise, go to Pă′dan-â′ram, to the house of Beth-ū′el thy mother's father; and take thee a wife from thence of the daughters of Lāban thy mother's brother.

3 And God Almighty bless thee, and make thee fruitful, and multiply thee, that thou mayest be a multitude of people;

4 And give thee the blessing of Abraham, to thee, and to thy seed with thee; that thou mayest inherit the land wherein thou art a stranger, which God gave unto Abraham.

5 And Isaac sent away Jacob: and he went to Pă′dan-â′ram unto Lāban, son of Beth-shē′ba, the Syrian, the brother of Rebekah, Jacob's and Esau's mother.

6 ¶When Esau saw that Isaac had blessed Jacob, and sent him away to Pă′dan-â′ram, to take him a wife from thence; and that as he blessed him he gave him a charge, saying, Thou shalt not take a wife of the daughters of Canaan;

7 And that Jacob obeyed his father and his mother, and was gone to Pă′dan-â′ram;

8 And Esau seeing that the daughters of Canaan pleased not Isaac his father;

9 Then went Esau unto Ĭsh′ma-el, and took unto the wives which he had Mă′ha-lăth the daughter of Ĭsh′ma-el Abraham's son, the sister of Ne-bā′jŏth, to be his wife.

10 ¶And Jacob went out from Be′er-shē′ba, and went toward Hâ′ran.

11 And he lighted upon a certain place, and tarried there all night, because the sun was set; and he took of the stones of that place, and put *them for* his pillows, and lay down in that place to sleep.

12 And he dreamed, and behold a ladder set up on the earth, and the top of it reached to heaven: and behold the angels of God ascending and descending on it.

13 And, behold, the LORD stood above it, and said, I *am* the LORD God of Abraham thy father, and the God of Isaac: the land whereon thou liest, to thee will I give it, and to thy seed;

14 And thy seed shall be as the dust of the earth, and thou shalt spread abroad to the west, and to the east, and to the north, and to the south: and in thee and in thy seed shall all the families of the earth be blessed.

15 And, behold, I *am* with thee, and will keep thee in all *places* whither thou goest, and will bring thee again into this land; for I will not leave thee, until I have done *that* which I have spoken to thee of.

16 ¶And Jacob awaked out of his sleep, and he said, Surely the LORD is in this place; and I knew *it* not.

17 And he was afraid, and said, How dreadful *is* this place! this *is* none other but the house of God, and this *is* the gate of heaven.

18 And Jacob rose up early in the morning, and took the stone that he

consistent with God's desire and plan. He may also have learned of Esau's intention to kill Jacob. **Padan-aram** was the plain of Aram (in Akkadian **Padan** is road). It was the district near Haran in northwest Mesopotamia where Abraham's brother Nahor had settled. It was Rebekah's homeland, in addition to Abraham's. **God Almighty** (Heb *′Ēl Shaddai*) is similar to chapter 17, where it would take the mighty power of God to provide an offspring for Abraham. Even though Jacob was leaving alone, God would **multiply thee, that thou mayest be a multitude of people.** The land promised to Abraham (cf. 15:18-21) was now guaranteed to Jacob and his descendants.

6-9. An interlude regarding Esau is now inserted. When Esau realized that his parents were grieved at his Hittite marriages (26:35; 28:8) and that, accordingly, they had sent Jacob to Haran to get a wife, he seems to have tried to gain favor with them by marrying a daughter of Ishmael named **Mahalath.** He apparently reasoned that since Ishmael was related through Abraham, this marriage should be pleasing to them. He did not recognize in this, however, that Ishmael had been separated from the house of Abraham by God Himself. His intention may have been good, but he did not really improve his position, either with his parents or with God. The fact that he **went . . . unto Ishmael** meant that he went to Ishmael's family. Ishmael had died fourteen years earlier. There is no record that Esau put away his heathen wives, though.

3. Jacob's dream and vow. 28:10-22.

10-22. Ladder would be better rendered ramp or staircase. It is related to the mound thrown up against a walled city (II Sam 20:15). The streams of messengers **ascending and descending on it** indicate the appropriateness of this rendering. Jesus took this figure of a means of access between heaven and earth as a picture of Himself (Jn 1:51). **The LORD stood above it** makes this no small occasion, for God and His messengers are present. **And, behold, I am with thee . . . keep thee in all places . . . bring thee again into this land.** God lovingly comes to Jacob and confirms to him what Isaac had promised him (cf. 28:3-4). God's promise of His presence was suited to Jacob and his circumstances; in addition, it was His confirmation of the Abrahamic covenant. **Pillar** and **oil** are the symbols normally used for a memorial (cf. Deut 27:2ff.; Isa 19:19) and consecration (Lev 8:10-11). The pillars that were later forbidden were related to Baal worship (Deut 12:3) and objects of worship (Mic 5:13). **Beth-el** means house of God and became the name of nearby Luz. **Then shall the LORD be my God** is actually a part of Jacob's account of what God would do for him. Jacob's own promise begins in verse 22, **I will surely give the tenth.** This was voluntary on Jacob's part; God had not commanded it (cf. 14:20 where Abraham's **tenth** to Melchizedek was also voluntary). It wasn't a requirement until the Law was given to Israel; and then two tithes were to be given, not one as most Christians assume (the annual tithe for the maintenance of the Levites in Lev 27:30; Num 18:21; and one for the Lord's feast in Deut 14:22). It may be that every third year the second tithe was not brought to the sanctuary, but kept at home and used to feed the Levites and the poor according to Deuteronomy 14:28-29. If not, then there was a third tithe every third year. Thus, a consistent Israelite might give 23⅓% annually, plus offerings for sin, etc.

had put *for* his pillows, and set it up *for* a pillar, and poured oil upon the top of it.

19 And he called the name of that place Bĕth-el: but the name of that city *was called* Luz at the first.

20 And Jacob vowed a vow, saying, If God will be with me, and will keep me in this way that I go, and will give me bread to eat, and raiment to put on,

21 So that I come again to my father's house in peace; then shall the LORD be my God:

22 And this stone, which I have set *for* a pillar, shall be God's house: and of all that thou shalt give me I will surely give the tenth unto thee.

CHAPTER 29

THEN Jacob went on his journey, and came into the land of the people of the east.

2 And he looked, and behold a well in the field, and, lo, there *were* three flocks of sheep lying by it; for out of that well they watered the flocks: and a great stone *was* upon the well's mouth.

3 And thither were all the flocks gathered: and they rolled the stone from the well's mouth, and watered the sheep, and put the stone again upon the well's mouth in his place.

4 And Jacob said unto them, My brethren, whence *be* ye? And they said, Of Hâ'ran *are* we.

5 And he said unto them, Know ye Lā'ban the son of Nahor? And they said, We know him.

6 And he said unto them, *Is* he well? And they said, *He is* well: and, behold, Rāchel his daughter cometh with the sheep.

7 And he said, Lo, *it is* yet high day, neither *is it* time that the cattle should be gathered together: water ye the sheep, and go *and* feed *them*.

8 And they said, We cannot, until all the flocks be gathered together, and *till* they roll the stone from the well's mouth; then we water the sheep.

9 ¶And while he yet spake with them, Rāchel came with her father's sheep: for she kept them.

10 And it came to pass, when Jacob saw Rāchel the daughter of Lāban his mother's brother, and the sheep of Lā-ban his mother's brother, that Jacob went near, and rolled the stone from the well's mouth, and watered the flock of Lāban his mother's brother.

11 And Jacob kissed Rāchel, and lifted up his voice, and wept.

12 And Jacob told Rāchel that he *was* her father's brother, and that he *was* Rebekah's son: and she ran and told her father.

13 And it came to pass, when Lāban heard the tidings of Jacob his sister's son, that he ran to meet him, and embraced him, and kissed him, and brought him to his house. And he told Lāban all these things.

14 And Lāban said to him, Surely thou *art* my bone and my flesh. And he abode with him the space of a month.

4. *Jacob and the daughters of Laban.* 29:1-30.

Jacob met his match in Laban. In the providence of God Laban was a divine means of discipline. There were twenty years (31:41) of "drudgery and friction to weather his character; and the reader can reflect that presumably Jacob is not the only person to have needed a Laban in his life:" (Kidner, p. 159). Laban gave Jacob much of his own medicine, but it is to Jacob's credit that even in losing he did not display the negative qualities that Esau expressed.

29:1-14. Into the land of the people of the east is a reference to his being near Haran. **The son of Nahor** as an appellative of **Laban** could be confusing since Laban was actually his grandson (24:15, 29), but **son** was the normal Hebrew way of expressing such a relationship; there was no word for grandson or grandfather. Evidently, in verses 7-8 he was trying to get the men to leave before Rachel arrived. **Jacob kissed Rachel;** kissing was the normal and proper greeting for relatives (vs. 13), especially cousins. But I am sure that Jacob enjoyed being kissing cousins, because it was only a month later that he wanted to marry her (cf. vss. 14, 18). Also, the custom was for the proper person to roll away the stone, as verses 3 and 8 seem to indicate; yet he did not wait. **Surely thou art my bone and my flesh** has been interpreted by some to mean that Laban adopted Jacob as his son (Ryrie, p. 53, after Gordon and Speiser). Chapters 29-31 have probably been the most fertile areas in the Old Testament for those who have sought to find comparisons with the Nuzi documents. Three separate aspects of Jacob's relationship with Laban are thought to be paralleled by Nuzi customs; all are based mostly on one text, Gadd 51. The suggested parallels are: (1) Jacob's adoption by Laban; (2) the classification of Jacob's marriages as *errēbu*-marriages; and (3) the theft of Laban's *teraphīm* as Rachel's attempt to obtain for Jacob either leadership in Laban's family or her father's inheritance. There are several good textual reasons to support the fact that Jacob was not adopted by Laban, in addition to the specific rebuttals to the assertions 2 and 3 above. Those reasons are: (1) in 31:15 the phrase **devoured also our money** could not be used in reference to an *errēbu*-marriage because no bride price is paid in such a marriage, if it exists at all. The father of the bridegroom and bride are the same individual through adoption—there is no bride price in Gadd 51 or HSS 5 67; (2) Laban never called Jacob his son—he used **brother** in 29:15; (3) Jacob never called Laban father—he used **your father** to the wives in 31:5ff. and called Isaac **his father** in 31:18 and 53; and (4) his paternal home was Canaan in 30:25 and 31:13, 18, yet the adoptee and adopter are "Father-Son" in the ancient Near Eastern texts relating to adoption. No tie is expressed with the adoptee's original home. This supposed adoption in Genesis is really a fanciful reconstruction from silence.

Specifically, concerning an *errēbu*-marriage, its existence in the ancient Near East is extremely doubtful. The only possible occurrences are to be found in the use of the verb *erēbu*, meaning to enter, in some Assyrian laws referring to a husband visiting his wife who remained in her father's house, and in an amended reference in the Old Babylonian lexical list called *ana ittišu*. The abstract noun form *errēbūtu* does not actually appear in any cuneiform document. From this slight evidence, the concept has been expanded to include the case in which a young man has been adopted and then given the daughter of the adopter in marriage. But there is a fundamental difference that creates a problem. The case of an adopted son is altogether different from the situation of a visiting husband. In none of the Assyrian laws under discussion can the husband be considered as an adopted son! Though the word *errēbu* does appear in tablets, it is never used of a type of marriage or of a special kind of husband. All references to *errēbu* may be translated in the sense of "usurper" or "intruder." There is no evidence of Jacob only visiting his wives, nor of Laban adopting him in order for him to marry Leah or Rachel. He seems to have had his own household (30:30), and his relationship with Laban could very well be that of an uncle-nephew or employer-employee and nothing else. Both of these were true (Selman, p. 124ff.). The theft of Laban's household gods will be discussed later (31:34).

15-30. Leah was tender-eyed may mean that her eyes were visually weak, or that they just lacked radiance. **That I may go in unto her** is an expression conveying the desire to marry Rachel. **He took Leah his daughter, and brought her to him** was the biggest jolt Jacob had ever received. The deceiver was deceived. He had loved Rachel so much that serving the seven years had only **seemed unto him but a few days** and to find out now that Laban had given Leah to him was most exasperating. **Fulfill her week** indicated that Jacob had to complete the wedding week (cf. Jud 14:17). It would be followed by his marriage to Rachel for which he would have to serve another seven years (vs. 30). **And he loved also Rachel more than Leah.** His parents had had this problem; they had played favorites. This is part of the reason that Jacob was in this dreadful position now. He not only had two wives (bigamy, which was practiced by Cain's descendants, and marrying two sisters concurrently which was later forbidden by Mosaic law in Lev 18:18), but he reaped the many years of agony which this situation produced.

15 ¶And Lāban said unto Jacob, Because thou *art* my brother, shouldest thou therefore serve me for nought? tell me, what *shall* thy wages *be?*

16 And Lāban had two daughters: the name of the elder *was* Leah, and the name of the younger *was* Rāchel.

17 Leah *was* tender eyed; but Rāchel was beautiful and well favoured.

18 And Jacob loved Rāchel; and said, I will serve thee seven years for Rāchel thy younger daughter.

19 And Lāban said, *It is* better that I give her to thee, than that I should give her to another man: abide with me.

20 And Jacob served seven years for Rāchel; and they seemed unto him *but* a few days, for the love he had to her.

21 ¶And Jacob said unto Lāban, Give *me* my wife, for my days are fulfilled, that I may go in unto her.

22 And Lāban gathered together all the men of the place, and made a feast.

23 And it came to pass in the evening, that he took Leah his daughter, and brought her to him; and he went in unto her.

24 And Lāban gave unto his daughter Leah Zīlpah his maid *for* an handmaid.

25 And it came to pass, that in the morning, behold, it *was* Leah: and he said to Lāban, What *is* this thou hast done unto me? did not I serve with thee for Rāchel? wherefore then hast thou beguiled me?

26 And Lāban said, It must not be so done in our country, to give the younger before the firstborn.

27 Fulfil her week, and we will give thee this also for the service which thou shalt serve with me yet seven other years.

28 And Jacob did so, and fulfilled her week: and he gave him Rāchel his daughter to wife also.

29 And Lāban gave to Rāchel his daughter Bīl'hah his handmaid to be her maid.

30 And he went in also unto Rāchel, and he loved also Rāchel more than Leah, and served with him yet seven other years.

31 ¶And when the LORD saw that Leah *was* hated, he opened her womb: but Rāchel *was* barren.

32 And Leah conceived, and bare a son, and she called his name Reuben: for she said, Surely the LORD hath looked upon my affliction; now therefore my husband will love me.

5. Jacob's children. 29:31-30:24.

31-35. And when the LORD saw that Leah was hated, he opened her womb: but Rachel was barren. God supernaturally controlled the birth of children in Jacob's family. The impression is given that all of Jacob's children were born in the first seven years of his marriages, but this is unlikely. Several explanations have been put forth: (1) Clarke suggests that 31:38, 41 indicate two twenty-year periods, but his handling of the

33 And she conceived again, and bare a son; and said, Because the LORD hath heard that I *was* hated, he hath therefore given me this *son* also: and she called his name Simeon.

34 And she conceived again, and bare a son; and said, Now this time will my husband be joined unto me, because I have born him three sons: therefore was his name called Levi.

35 And she conceived again, and bare a son: and she said, Now will I praise the LORD: therefore she called his name Jūdah; and left bearing.

CHAPTER 30

AND when Rāchel saw that she bare Jacob no children, Rāchel envied her sister; and said unto Jacob, Give me children, or else I die.

2 And Jacob's anger was kindled against Rāchel: and he said, *Am* I in God's stead, who hath withheld from thee the fruit of the womb?

3 And she said, Behold my maid Bĭl'-hah, go in unto her; and she shall bear upon my knees, that I may also have children by her.

4 And she gave him Bĭl'hah her handmaid to wife: and Jacob went in unto her.

5 And Bĭl'hah conceived, and bare Jacob a son.

6 And Rāchel said, God hath judged me, and hath also heard my voice, and hath given me a son: therefore called she his name Dan.

7 And Bĭl'hah Rāchel's maid conceived again, and bare Jacob a second son.

8 And Rāchel said, With great wrestlings have I wrestled with my sister, and I have prevailed: and she called his name Năph'ta-lī.

9 When Leah saw that she had left bearing, she took Zilpah her maid, and gave her Jacob to wife.

10 And Zĭlpah Leah's maid bare Jacob a son.

11 And Leah said, A troop cometh: and she called his name Gad.

12 And Zĭlpah Leah's maid bare Jacob a second son.

13 And Leah said, Happy am I, for the daughters will call me blessed: and she called his name Asher.

14 ¶And Reuben went in the days of wheat harvest, and found mandrakes in the field, and brought them unto his mother Leah. Then Rāchel said to Leah, Give me, I pray thee, of thy son's mandrakes.

15 And she said unto her, *Is it* a small matter that thou hast taken my husband? and wouldest thou take away my son's mandrakes also? And Rāchel said, Therefore he shall lie with thee to night for thy son's mandrakes.

16 And Jacob came out of the field in the evening, and Leah went out to meet him, and said, Thou must come in unto me; for surely I have hired thee with my son's mandrakes. And he lay with her that night.

17 And God hearkened unto Leah,

pronoun *zeh* is doubtful; (2) some say the final children were born the last six years of his stay; and (3) still others believe that Dinah was born after Jacob's first seven years. While the text permits this, it does not demand it. Leah had four sons in rapid succession, which indicated her frame of mind. **Reuben** means "See, a son!," indicating Leah's reception of a pledge from God indicating His favor. **Simeon** means "hearing," which reveals that God had heard how much Leah was hated. **Levi** means "attachment," expressing Leah's desire that Jacob would ultimately become attached to her. **Judah** means praise, conveying the thought of not merely the praised one, but the one for whom Jehovah is praised. Evidently, Leah was a godly woman; three of the four names refer to Jehovah.

30:1-3. These events made Rachel angry; she knew only God could remove her sterility (Davis, p. 248). **And she shall bear upon my knees** indicates an adoption rite to some (Kline, p. 103). This is mentioned again in 50:23 (cf. 48:12 where Jacob removed two grandsons prior to their receiving the blessing). But there is no indication of adoption in the patriarchal narratives. It seems better to view this as the welcoming in at birth of a new child. In the Hurrian tales the event is associated with birth, the naming of the child, the welcoming into the family, and the fondling by the parents (Selman, p. 131).

4-13. And she gave him Bilhah her handmaid to wife, the same as Sarah did (16:3). Jacob should have followed his father's example of praying for his wife to bear (25:21), instead of his grandfather's (Abraham). **Dan,** meaning "justice," was born, indicating that God had vindicated or intervened for Rachel. Then **Naphtali,** meaning "wrestling," was born, depicting Rachel's struggles. Then Leah took up the rivalry and gave her handmaid to Jacob; and she bore **Gad,** meaning "troops," and **Asher,** meaning "happy," stating her inner happiness at having another son. Initially, Jacob's frustration had been expressed by **Am I in God's stead, who hath withheld from thee the fruit of the womb** (vs. 2)?

14-24. Mandrakes. This is an herb "of the belladonna family, considered to be aphrodisiac. Bickering and shameless bargaining characterized this bigamous household" (Ryrie, p. 55). It has a yellow fruit the size of a small apple. Peoples of the ancient Near East attributed sensual desire to this plant and thought it would aid conception. It is noteworthy that while Rachel got the mandrakes, Leah received another son! His name was **Issachar,** meaning "reward." **Zebulun** was the sixth son of Leah's, and then **Dinah** was born. She was not the only daughter born to Leah, but her inclusion at this point sets the background for chapter 34. **And God remembered Rachel,** using the same word remember as in 8:1 when God took care of Noah in a supernatural way during the Flood (also Gen 19:29). Her offspring was **Joseph** whose name means either "to take away" or "to add." Either God had removed the reproach of her childlessness or would give her another son. God did give Benjamin much later.

and she conceived, and bare Jacob the fifth son.

18 And Leah said, God hath given me my hire, because I have given my maiden to my husband: and she called his name Ĭs'sa-char.

19 And Leah conceived again, and bare Jacob the sixth son.

20 And Leah said, God hath endued me *with* a good dowry; now will my husband dwell with me, because I have born him six sons: and she called his name Zĕb'u-lun.

21 And afterwards she bare a daughter, and called her name Dinah.

22 ¶And God remembered Rāchel, and God hearkened to her, and opened her womb.

23 And she conceived, and bare a son; and said, God hath taken away my reproach:

24 And she called his name Joseph; and said, The Lord shall add to me another son.

25 ¶And it came to pass, when Rāchel had born Joseph, that Jacob said unto Lāban, Send me away, that I may go unto mine own place, and to my country.

26 Give *me* my wives and my children, for whom I have served thee, and let me go: for thou knowest my service which I have done thee.

27 And Lāban said unto him, I pray thee, if I have found favour in thine eyes, *tarry: for* I have learned by experience that the Lord hath blessed me for thy sake.

28 And he said, Appoint me thy wages, and I will give *it.*

29 And he said unto him, Thou knowest how I have served thee, and how thy cattle was with me.

30 For *it was* little which thou hadst before I *came,* and it is *now* increased unto a multitude; and the Lord hath blessed thee since my coming: and now when shall I provide for mine own house also?

31 And he said, What shall I give thee? And Jacob said, Thou shalt not give me any thing: if thou wilt do this thing for me, I will again feed *and* keep thy flock.

32 I will pass through all thy flock to day, removing from thence all the speckled and spotted cattle, and all the brown cattle among the sheep, and the spotted and speckled among the goats: and *of such* shall be my hire.

33 So shall my righteousness answer for me in time to come, when it shall come for my hire before thy face: every one that *is* not speckled and spotted among the goats, and brown among the sheep, that shall be counted stolen with me.

34 And Lāban said, Behold, I would it might be according to thy word.

35 And he removed that day the he goats that were ringstraked and spotted, and all the she goats that were speckled and spotted, *and* every one that had *some* white in it, and all the brown among the sheep, and gave *them* into the hand of his sons.

36 And he set three days' journey

6. Jacob outwits Laban. 30:25-43.

25-43. After fourteen years of service Jacob wanted to go back to Canaan (vss. 25-26). But God had blessed Laban so much through Jacob that Laban wanted him to stay, expressing his willingness to allow Jacob to set the terms (note this generosity in light of 31:7). Jacob agreed to stay if as his wages he could keep the off-colored and spotted animals that would be born. Evidently, Jacob relied on a superstition that the offspring would be influenced by the fears or expectations of the mother during pregnancy (cf. vss. 37-38). Though this was unscientific, it worked; yet, the results were due to the intervention of God (cf. 31:10-13). The results of his method, however, were not unscientific. Tinkle writes that Laban "had indeed taken the ones which were visibly spotted but the rest were heterozygous for spotting—there were latent genes for that pattern—and spotted kids were the logical result. Breeding tests have shown that spotting is recessive to solid color in goats. Modern genetic studies on dominants and latency have cleared this incident, which at one time seemed to link the Bible with groundless supposition" (Davis, p. 250). Jacob's success was also attributed to selective breeding (vss. 40-42) in addition to divine help (31:10-12).

betwixt himself and Jacob: and Jacob fed the rest of Lāban's flocks.

37 ¶And Jacob took him rods of green poplar, and of the hazel and chesnut tree; and pilled white strakes in them, and made the white appear which *was* in the rods.

38 And he set the rods which he had pilled before the flocks in the gutters in the watering troughs when the flocks came to drink, that they should conceive when they came to drink.

39 And the flocks conceived before the rods, and brought forth cattle ringstraked, speckled, and spotted.

40 And Jacob did separate the lambs, and set the faces of the flocks toward the ringstraked, and all the brown in the flock of Lāban; and he put his own flocks by themselves, and put them not unto Lāban's cattle.

41 And it came to pass, whensoever the stronger cattle did conceive, that Jacob laid the rods before the eyes of the cattle in the gutters, that they might conceive among the rods.

42 But when the cattle were feeble, he put *them* not in: so the feebler were Lāban's, and the stronger Jacob's.

43 And the man increased exceedingly, and had much cattle, and maidservants, and menservants, and camels, and asses.

CHAPTER 31

AND he heard the words of Lāban's sons, saying, Jacob hath taken away all that *was* our father's; and of *that* which *was* our father's hath he gotten all this glory.

2 And Jacob beheld the countenance of Lāban, and, behold, it *was* not toward him as before.

3 And the LORD said unto Jacob, Return unto the land of thy fathers, and to thy kindred; and I will be with thee.

4 And Jacob sent and called Rāchel and Leah to the field unto his flock,

5 And said unto them, I see your father's countenance, that it *is* not toward me as before; but the God of my father hath been with me.

6 And ye know that with all my power I have served your father.

7 And your father hath deceived me, and changed my wages ten times; but God suffered him not to hurt me.

8 If he said thus, The speckled shall be thy wages; then all the cattle bare speckled: and if he said thus, The ringstraked shall be thy hire; then bare all the cattle ringstraked.

9 Thus God hath taken away the cattle of your father, and given *them* to me.

10 And it came to pass at the time that the cattle conceived, that I lifted up mine eyes, and saw in a dream, and, behold, the rams which leaped upon the cattle *were* ringstraked, speckled, and grisled.

11 And the angel of God spake unto me in a dream, *saying,* Jacob: and I said, Here *am* I.

12 And he said, Lift up now thine eyes, and see, all the rams which leap upon the cattle *are* ringstraked,

7. *Jacob's return to Canaan. 31:1-21.*

31:1-18. Laban became openly hostile to Jacob, and so God told Jacob to return to the land of Canaan **and I will be with thee.** His wives agreed that this would be the best; whatever **God hath said unto thee, do.** "Whether they were convinced that this was God's leading or merely the only way to insure receiving any inheritance for themselves and their children (cf. vs. 16) is hard to know" (Ryrie, p. 56). The reference made in verse 13 goes back to 28:16-22.

speckled, and grisled: for I have seen all that Lăban doeth unto thee.

13 I am the God of Bĕth-el, where thou anointedst the pillar, and where thou vowedst a vow unto me: now arise, get thee out from this land, and return unto the land of thy kindred.

14 And Răchel and Leah answered and said unto him, Is there yet any portion or inheritance for us in our father's house?

15 Are we not counted of him strangers? for he hath sold us, and hath quite devoured also our money.

16 For all the riches which God hath taken from our father, that is ours, and our children's: now then, whatsoever God hath said unto thee, do.

17 ¶Then Jacob rose up, and set his sons and his wives upon camels;

18 And he carried away all his cattle, and all his goods which he had gotten, the cattle of his getting, which he had gotten in Pă'dan-â'ram, for to go to Isaac his father in the land of Canaan.

19 And Lăban went to shear his sheep: and Răchel had stolen the images that were her father's.

20 And Jacob stole away unawares to Lăban the Syrian, in that he told him not that he fled.

21 So he fled with all that he had; and he rose up, and passed over the river, and set his face toward the mount Gilead.

19-21. And Rachel had stolen the images that were her father's. Gordon and Speiser first suggested that adoption tablets from Nuzi stipulated that the chief heir should receive the father's gods, and they thus concluded that possession of the gods conveyed some legal advantage with respect to inheritance. Speiser described this event as "perhaps the most outstanding example of an exclusively Hurrian custom which the patriarchal account records, but which becomes incomprehensible later on in Canaanite surroundings" (Biblical and Other Studies, p. 24, n. 40). Yet, it appears rather clear that this is not the case. Further Nuzi texts mentioning household gods have been interpreted; and in nine of the eleven texts, the gods were given as part of an inheritance. In each of these nine texts, heirs who did not receive the gods also participated in the division normally granted to the eldest son. So it is rather plain that the possession of such gods did not represent an automatic claim to an inheritance. The real key to an inheritance was the proper bequeathal, not simply the possession of the gods. This being the case, it is hard to see what advantage Jacob would have secured by his wife's theft. Furthermore, Jacob had a real desire to put as much ground between Laban and himself as he could, which does not betray any great interest on his part in his father-in-law's property. Jacob was probably not Laban's heir; his wealth was gained from wages paid him by Laban (cf. vss. 1-9). Possibly Rachel desired protection on her journey, as cited by Greenberg concerning the Parthians of the late second century B.C. There is a reference to the transportation of gods by fleeing Babylonian troops of the early seventh century B.C. from the annals of Sennacherib. They may have desired to secure divine protection, as well as to protect the gods from being captured. An Akkadian omen text refers to a protective goddess (Sumerian, lama; Akkadian, lamassu), which is well known throughout cuneiform literature and art in its protective function. This same deity is depicted in the art of the lands surrounding Mesopotamia, including Syria, Mitanni, Alalah, Nuzi, Ugarit, and Palestine (A. Spycket, in Revue d'Assyriologie et d'Archéologie orientale (RA) 54, 1960, p. 84; Selman, Published and Unpublished Fifteenth Century B.C. Cuneiform Documents and Their Bearing on the Patriarchal Narratives, pp. 127-128).

8. Laban's pursuit and confrontation. 31:22-42.

22 And it was told Lăban on the third day that Jacob was fled.

23 And he took his brethren with him, and pursued after him seven days'

22-42. "The hand of God is again decisive. On the human level Laban might well have won every business deal (30:25-43) and the present physical encounter as well (vss. 23, 29a). It was only by divine prospering and protection (vs. 24) that Jacob

journey; and they overtook him in the mount Gilead.

24 And God came to Lāban the Syrian in a dream by night, and said unto him, Take heed that thou speak not to Jacob either good or bad.

25 ¶Then Lāban overtook Jacob. Now Jacob had pitched his tent in the mount: and Lāban with his brethren pitched in the mount of Gilead.

26 And Lāban said to Jacob, What hast thou done, that thou hast stolen away unawares to me, and carried

brought anything, even his life, back from exile" (Kidner, p. 165).

God's revelation to Laban (vs. 24) is similar to the warning dream Abimelech had in 20:3ff. Each of the three patriarchs was delivered ingloriously from adverse circumstances.

That which was torn of beasts I brought not unto thee; I bare the loss of it; of my hand didst thou require it, whether stolen by day, or stolen by night (vs. 39). Finkelstein has pointed out that this terminology indicates the relationship between Jacob and Laban was based on an old Babylonian herding contract and not that of adoption (cf. vs. 38ff., "An Old Babylonian Herding Contract and Genesis 31:38f.," *Journal of the*

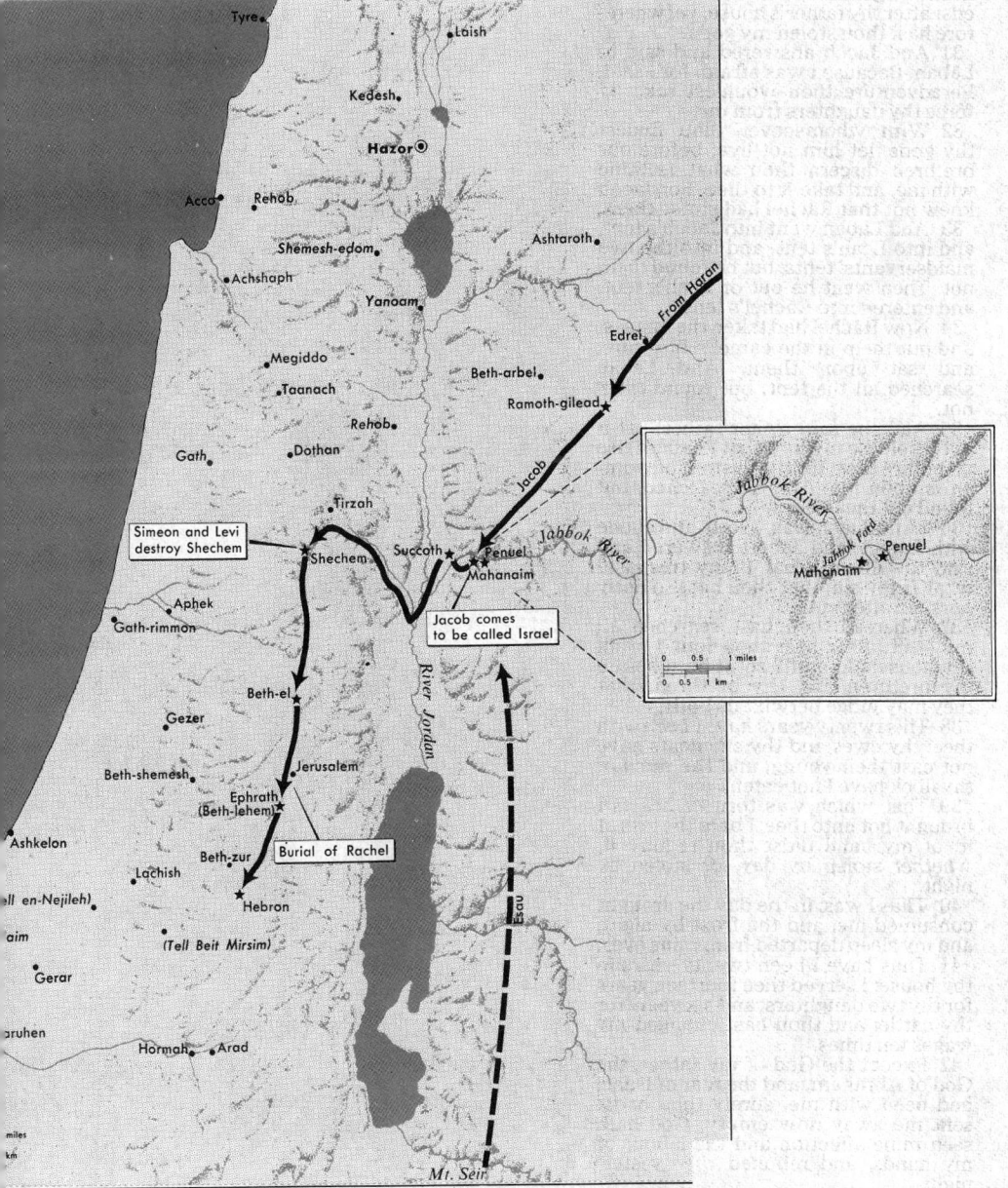

Jacob's Travels in the Land of Canaan

away my daughters, as captives *taken* with the sword?

27 Wherefore didst thou flee away secretly, and steal away from me; and didst not tell me, that I might have sent thee away with mirth, and with songs, with tabret, and with harp?

28 And hast not suffered me to kiss my sons and my daughters? thou hast now done foolishly in *so* doing.

29 It is in the power of my hand to do you hurt: but the God of your father spake unto me yesternight, saying, Take thou heed that thou speak not to Jacob either good or bad.

30 And now, *though* thou wouldest needs be gone, because thou sore longedst after thy father's house, *yet* wherefore hast thou stolen my gods?

31 And Jacob answered and said to Lāban, Because I was afraid: for I said, Peradventure thou wouldest take by force thy daughters from me.

32 With whomsoever thou findest thy gods, let him not live: before our brethren discern thou what *is* thine with me, and take *it* to thee. For Jacob knew not that Rāchel had stolen them.

33 And Laban went into Jacob's tent, and into Leah's tent, and into the two maidservants' tents; but he found *them* not. Then went he out of Leah's tent, and entered into Rāchel's tent.

34 Now Rāchel had taken the images, and put them in the camel's furniture, and sat upon them. And Laban searched all the tent, but found *them* not.

35 And she said to her father, Let it not displease my lord that I cannot rise up before thee; for the custom of women *is* upon me. And he searched, but found not the images.

36 ¶And Jacob was wroth, and chode with Lāban: and Jacob answered and said to Lāban, What *is* my trespass? what *is* my sin, that thou hast so hotly pursued after me?

37 Whereas thou hast searched all my stuff, what hast thou found of all thy household stuff? set *it* here before my brethren and thy brethren, that they may judge betwixt us both.

38 This twenty years *have* I *been* with thee; thy ewes and thy she goats have not cast their young, and the rams of thy flock have I not eaten.

39 That which was torn *of beasts* I brought not unto thee; I bare the loss of it; of my hand didst thou require it, *whether* stolen by day, or stolen by night.

40 *Thus* I was; in the day the drought consumed me, and the frost by night; and my sleep departed from mine eyes.

41 Thus have I been twenty years in thy house; I served thee fourteen years for thy two daughters, and six years for thy cattle: and thou hast changed my wages ten times.

42 Except the God of my father, the God of Abraham, and the fear of Isaac, had been with me, surely thou hadst sent me away now empty. God hath seen mine affliction and the labour of my hands, and rebuked *thee* yesternight.

American Oriental Society [JAOS], 88:1 [January-March, 1968], pp. 30-36). Jacob stresses his liability for animals lost as the prey of wild beasts. This is to be understood as a reproof to Laban, for this goes beyond the prevailing custom of one's accountability, as Speiser even noted (p. 247, citing the Code of Hammurabi). The shepherd is free from liability for animals lost as a result of an epidemic or as prey to lions, upon his declaration of these circumstances in an oath to the owner of the herd (Finkelstein, p. 36).

43 ¶And Lāban answered and said unto Jacob, *These* daughters *are* my daughters, and *these* children *are* my children, and *these* cattle *are* my cattle, and all that thou seest *is* mine: and what can I do this day unto these my daughters, or unto their children which they have born?

44 Now therefore come thou, let us make a covenant, I and thou; and let it be for a witness between me and thee.

45 And Jacob took a stone, and set it up *for* a pillar.

46 And Jacob said unto his brethren, Gather stones; and they took stones, and made an heap: and they did eat there upon the heap.

47 And Lāban called it Jē′gar-sā-ha-dū′tha: but Jacob called it Gǎl′e-ed.

48 And Lāban said, This heap *is* a witness between me and thee this day. Therefore was the name of it called Gǎl′e-ed;

49 And Mizpah; for he said, The LORD watch between me and thee, when we are absent one from another.

50 If thou shalt afflict my daughters, or if thou shalt take *other* wives beside my daughters, no man *is* with us; see, God *is* witness betwixt me and thee.

51 And Lāban said to Jacob, Behold this heap, and behold *this* pillar, which I have cast betwixt me and thee;

52 This heap *be* witness, and *this* pillar *be* witness, that I will not pass over this heap to thee, and that thou shalt not pass over this heap and this pillar unto me, for harm.

53 The God of Abraham, and the God of Nahor, the God of their father, judge betwixt us. And Jacob sware by the fear of his father Isaac.

54 Then Jacob offered sacrifice upon the mount, and called his brethren to eat bread: and they did eat bread, and tarried all night in the mount.

55 And early in the morning Lāban rose up, and kissed his sons and his daughters, and blessed them: and Lāban departed, and returned unto his place.

CHAPTER 32

AND Jacob went on his way, and the angels of God met him.

2 And when Jacob saw them, he said, This *is* God's host: and he called the name of that place Mā-ha-nā′im.

3 And Jacob sent messengers before him to Esau his brother unto the land of Sē′ir, the country of Edom.

4 And he commanded them, saying, Thus shall ye speak unto my lord Esau; Thy servant Jacob saith thus, I have sojourned with Lāban, and stayed there until now:

5 And I have oxen, and asses, flocks, and menservants, and womenservants: and I have sent to tell my lord, that I may find grace in thy sight.

6 ¶And the messengers returned to Jacob, saying, We came to thy brother Esau, and also he cometh to meet thee, and four hundred men with him.

7 Then Jacob was greatly afraid and distressed: and he divided the people

9. The parting covenant. 31:43-55.

43-55. Jacob and Laban made a mutual non-agression pact. "Its features included God as witness (vss. 49, 53), the pillar and cairn (heap) as boundary markers (vs. 52), and a covenant meal to seal the arrangement (vs. 54). Suspicion permeated the entire arrangement (e.g., vs. 50)" (Ryrie, p. 59). **The LORD watch between me and thee, when we are absent one from another** is not meant to convey a benediction, as Christians usually cite it. Rather, it is an imprecation conveying the thought, "May God destroy you if you cross this boundary!" There is no more mention of Laban, and this records the last contact the patriarchs had with their homeland and relatives.

10. Jacob's reconciliation with Esau. 32:1-32.

32:1-24. And Jacob went on his way, and the angels of God met him. This sounds like Abraham's servant who had said **I being in the way, the LORD led me** (24:27). Jacob began in obedience to God's command, and he was met by God's messenger to encourage him. **Mahanaim** was the name given to the place, meaning "double camp," possibly a reference to the two camps or bands of angels, or his camp and the angel's camp. Jacob had remembered Esau's threat (cf. 27:41-42); and thus, he had reason to be **greatly afraid and distressed.** He then prayed, demonstrating humility. He petitioned God based upon His covenant promises of **make thy seed as the sand of the sea.** Prayer based upon God's promises assures answers; God's Word never fails! Jacob spaced his family's groups, after he sent a gift of more than five hundred head of sheep and cattle. They crossed the **Jabbok.** This was a tributary of the Jordan, about twenty-four miles north of the Dead Sea. The name is related to the Hebrew word for wrestled in verse 24, *yabōq* for **Jabbok,** and *yē'abēq* for wrestled. **And there wrestled a man with him,** the man being identified by some as the preincarnate Christ and by others as an angel, a special messenger from God. Davis believes

that *was* with him, and the flocks, and herds, and the camels, into two bands;

8 And said, If Esau come to the one company, and smite it, then the other company which is left shall escape.

9 ¶And Jacob said, O God of my father Abraham, and God of my father Isaac, the LORD which saidst unto me, Return unto thy country, and to thy kindred, and I will deal well with thee:

10 I am not worthy of the least of all the mercies, and of all the truth, which thou hast shewed unto thy servant; for with my staff I passed over this Jordan; and now I am become two bands.

11 Deliver me, I pray thee, from the hand of my brother, from the hand of Esau: for I fear him, lest he will come and smite me, *and* the mother with the children.

12 And thou saidst, I will surely do thee good, and make thy seed as the sand of the sea, which cannot be numbered for multitude.

13 ¶And he lodged there that same night; and took of that which came to his hand a present for Esau his brother;

14 Two hundred she goats, and twenty he goats, two hundred ewes, and twenty rams,

15 Thirty milch camels with their colts, forty kine, and ten bulls, twenty she asses, and ten foals.

16 And he delivered *them* into the hand of his servants, every drove by themselves; and said unto his servants, Pass over before me, and put a space betwixt drove and drove.

17 And he commanded the foremost, saying, When Esau my brother meeteth thee, and asketh thee, saying, Whose *art* thou? and whither goest thou? and whose *are* these before thee?

18 Then thou shalt say, They *be* thy servant Jacob's; it *is* a present sent unto my lord Esau: and, behold, also he *is* behind us.

19 And so commanded he the second, and the third, and all that followed the droves, saying, On this manner shall ye speak unto Esau, when ye find him.

20 And say ye moreover, Behold, thy servant Jacob *is* behind us. For he said, I will appease him with the present that goeth before me, and afterward I will see his face; peradventure he will accept of me.

21 So went the present over before him: and himself lodged that night in the company.

22 And he rose up that night, and took his two wives, and his two womenservants, and his eleven sons, and passed over the ford Jabbok.

23 And he took them, and sent them over the brook, and sent over that he had.

24 ¶And Jacob was left alone; and there wrestled a man with him until the breaking of the day.

25 And when he saw that he prevailed not against him, he touched the hollow of his thigh; and the hollow of Jacob's thigh was out of joint, as he wrestled with him.

26 And he said, Let me go, for the day breaketh. And he said, I will not let thee go, except thou bless me.

Hosea 12:4 indicates the latter position, yet Ryrie cites the same verse to substantiate the former stance. The context seems to favor the angel being the preincarnate Christ (cf. vs. 30).

25-32. Assuming the deity of the messenger, God allowed Himself to be overcome; and Jacob was crippled as his **thigh was out of joint.** Jacob received a blessing, and he called the place **Peniel: for I have seen God face to face, and my life is preserved.** The blessing constituted the changing of his name from Jacob, meaning "heel catcher," "supplanter," or "deceiver," to **Israel,** meaning either "God's fighter" or "may God

27 And he said unto him, What *is* thy name? And he said, Jacob.

28 And he said, Thy name shall be called no more Jacob, but Israel: for as a prince hast thou power with God and with men, and hast prevailed.

29 And Jacob asked *him,* and said, Tell *me,* I pray thee, thy name. And he said, Wherefore *is* it *that* thou dost ask after my name? And he blessed him there.

30 And Jacob called the name of the place Pe-nī′el: for I have seen God face to face, and my life is preserved.

31 And as he passed over Pe-nū′el the sun rose upon him, and he halted upon his thigh.

32 Therefore the children of Israel eat not *of* the sinew which shrank, which *is* upon the hollow of the thigh, unto this day: because he touched the hollow of Jacob's thigh in the sinew that shrank.

CHAPTER 33

AND Jacob lifted up his eyes and looked, and, behold, Esau came, and with him four hundred men. And he divided the children unto Leah, and unto Rāchel, and unto the two handmaids.

2 And he put the handmaids and their children foremost, and Leah and her children after, and Rāchel and Joseph hindermost.

3 And he passed over before them, and bowed himself to the ground seven times, until he came near to his brother.

4 And Esau ran to meet him, and embraced him, and fell on his neck, and kissed him: and they wept.

5 And he lifted up his eyes, and saw the women and the children; and said, Who *are* those with thee? And he said, The children which God hath graciously given thy servant.

6 Then the handmaidens came near, they and their children, and they bowed themselves.

7 And Leah also with her children came near, and bowed themselves: and after came Joseph near and Rāchel, and they bowed themselves.

8 And he said, What *meanest* thou by all this drove which I met? And he said, *These are* to find grace in the sight of my lord.

9 And Esau said, I have enough, my brother; keep that thou hast unto thyself.

10 And Jacob said, Nay, I pray thee, if now I have found grace in thy sight, then receive my present at my hand: for therefore I have seen thy face, as though I had seen the face of God, and thou wast pleased with me.

11 Take, I pray thee, my blessing that is brought to thee; because God hath dealt graciously with me, and because I have enough. And he urged him, and he took *it.*

12 And he said, Let us take our journey, and let us go, and I will go before thee.

13 And he said unto him, My lord knoweth that the children *are* tender, and the flocks and herds with young *are* with me: and if men should overdrive them one day, all the flock will die.

strive (for him)" (Davis, p. 255). The older derivation of prince of God has been largely rejected, as noted by Davis. In his new name, Israel, Jacob's query was already answered (cf. Jud 13:17ff.), as his response shows. This is so since the *'el* in Israel means god.

"The conflict brought to a head the battling and groping of a lifetime, and Jacob's desperate embrace vividly expressed his ambivalent attitude to God, of love and enmity, defiance and dependence. It was against Him, not Esau or Laban, that he had been pitting his strength, as he now discovered; yet the initiative had been God's as it was this night, to chasten his pride and challenge his tenacity. The crippling and the naming show that God's ends were still the same: He would have all of Jacob's will to win, to attain and obtain, yet purged of self-sufficiency and redirected to the proper object of man's love, God himself" (Kidner, p. 169).

11. The meeting with Esau. 33:1-20.

33:1-20. When Jacob saw Esau, he **bowed himself to the ground seven times,** an action reserved as a sign of homage, usually before kings, as the Amarna tablets demonstrate: "To the king, my lord, . . . At the two feet of my lord, the king, seven times and seven times I fall" (*Ancient Near Eastern Texts [ANET]: An Anthology of Texts and Pictures,* p. 272). Many gifts were given by Jacob; initially, Esau would not receive them. They agreed to depart peacefully, Esau to **Seir** (cf. Obadiah) and Jacob to **Succoth,** located east of the Jordan and just north of the **Jabbok** (32:22). The name means "booths." And then he came to **Shalem,** which some take adverbially in the sense of "and then Jacob came safely **to Shechem**" (cf. Kline and ASV). Approximately ten years time may have elapsed in **Succoth** before Jacob went to Shechem. Recognizing that he had returned as a fulfillment of the covenant promise (cf. 28:15), he erected an altar as Abraham had on his arrival (12:7). The name **El-elohe-Israel** indicates that Jacob was confessing, using his new name Israel, that **El** was his God, "a Mighty God is the God of Israel."

14 Let my lord, I pray thee, pass over before his servant: and I will lead on softly, according as the cattle that goeth before me and the children be able to endure, until I come unto my lord unto Sē'ir.

15 And Esau said, Let me now leave with thee *some* of the folk that *are* with me. And he said, What needeth it? let me find grace in the sight of my lord.

16 ¶So Esau returned that day on his way unto Sē'ir.

17 And Jacob journeyed to Sŭc'coth, and built him an house, and made booths for his cattle: therefore the name of the place is called Sŭc'coth.

18 ¶And Jacob came to Shā'lem, a city of Shĕ'chem, which *is* in the land of Canaan, when he came from Pă'dan-â'ram; and pitched his tent before the city.

19 And he bought a parcel of a field, where he had spread his tent, at the hand of the children of Hā'môr, Shĕ'chem's father, for an hundred pieces of money.

20 And he erected there an altar, and called it Ĕl-e-lō'hē-Ĭsrael.

CHAPTER 34

AND Dinah the daughter of Leah, which she bare unto Jacob, went out to see the daughters of the land.

2 And when Shĕ'chem the son of Hā'-môr the Hī'vīte, prince of the country, saw her, he took her, and lay with her, and defiled her.

3 And his soul clave unto Dinah the daughter of Jacob, and he loved the damsel, and spake kindly unto the damsel.

4 And Shĕ'chem spake unto his father Hā'môr, saying, Get me this damsel to wife.

5 And Jacob heard that he had defiled Dinah his daughter: now his sons were with his cattle in the field: and Jacob held his peace until they were come.

6 ¶And Hā'môr the father of Shĕ'-chem went out unto Jacob to commune with him.

7 And the sons of Jacob came out of the field when they heard *it:* and the men were grieved, and they were very wroth, because he had wrought folly in Israel in lying with Jacob's daughter; which thing ought not to be done.

8 And Hā'môr communed with them, saying, The soul of my son Shĕ'chem longeth for your daughter: I pray you give her him to wife.

9 And make ye marriages with us, *and* give your daughters unto us, and take our daughters unto you.

10 And ye shall dwell with us: and the land shall be before you; dwell and trade ye therein, and get you possessions therein.

11 And Shĕ'chem said unto her father and unto her brethren, Let me find grace in your eyes, and what ye shall say unto me I will give.

12 Ask me never so much dowry and gift, and I will give according as ye shall say unto me: but give me the damsel to wife.

13 And the sons of Jacob answered Shĕ'chem and Hā'môr his father de-

12. A massacre at Shechem. 34:1-31.

34:1-31. "Chapter 34 shows the cost of . . . rape, treachery and massacre, a chain of evil that proceeded logically enough from the unequal partnership with the Canaanite community" (Kidner, p. 172). **Dinah** must have been some fourteen years of age (she was born after Leah's sixth son in 30:21, but the intervening chapters 30-33 would have taken at least eight years), and she was not more than five or six when the family left Haran. Joseph was about a year older than Dinah, and he was only seventeen at a later occasion in 37:2.

Even after Dinah had been defiled, Shechem wanted to marry her (vss. 3-4). His father **Hamor** approached Jacob in order to arrange the marriage. This proposal was accepted, provided that Hamor's family submit to circumcision (vs. 15). But this idea was a deception on the part of the sons of Jacob, because they **answered Shechem and Hamor his father deceitfully.** It was also a demeaning of the rite of circumcision. The decision was made in **the gate of their city** that **every male among us be circumcised.** They were circumcised; but on the third day when the men were suffering from fever and inflammation, the brothers of Dinah attacked and killed them (vss. 25-27). They also took **all their wealth . . . little ones, and their wives . . . captive.** Simeon and Levi were the guilty ones, killing all **the males.** Jacob was alarmed and **troubled** at their action; but he did not answer their question, **Should he deal with our sister as with a harlot?**

ceitfully, and said, because he had defiled Dinah their sister:

14 And they said unto them, We cannot do this thing, to give our sister to one that is uncircumcised; for that *were* a reproach unto us:

15 But in this will we consent unto you: If ye will be as we *be*, that every male of you be circumcised;

16 Then will we give our daughters unto you, and we will take your daughters to us, and we will dwell with you, and we will become one people.

17 But if ye will not hearken unto us, to be circumcised; then will we take our daughter, and we will be gone.

18 And their words pleased Hā′môr, and Shĕ′chem Hā′môr's son.

19 And the young man deferred not to do the thing, because he had delight in Jacob's daughter: and he *was* more honourable than all the house of his father.

20 And Hā′môr and Shĕ′chem his son came unto the gate of their city, and communed with the men of their city, saying,

21 These men *are* peaceable with us; therefore let them dwell in the land, and trade therein; for the land, behold, *it is* large enough for them; let us take their daughters to us for wives, and let us give them our daughters.

22 Only herein will the men consent unto us for to dwell with us, to be one people, if every male among us be circumcised, as they *are* circumcised.

23 *Shall* not their cattle and their substance and every beast of theirs *be* ours? only let us consent unto them, and they will dwell with us.

24 And unto Hā′môr and unto Shĕ′chem his son hearkened all that went out of the gate of his city; and every male was circumcised, all that went out of the gate of his city.

25 ¶And it came to pass on the third day, when they were sore, that two of the sons of Jacob, Simeon and Levi, Dinah's brethren, took each man his sword, and came upon the city boldly, and slew all the males.

26 And they slew Hā′môr and Shĕ′chem his son with the edge of the sword, and took Dinah out of Shĕ′chem's house, and went out.

27 The sons of Jacob came upon the slain, and spoiled the city, because they had defiled their sister.

28 They took their sheep, and their oxen, and their asses, and that which *was* in the city, and that which *was* in the field,

29 And all their wealth, and all their little ones, and their wives took they captive, and spoiled even all that *was* in the house.

30 And Jacob said to Simeon and Levi, Ye have troubled me to make me to stink among the inhabitants of the land, among the Canaanites and the Pĕr′iz-zītes: and I *being* few in number, they shall gather themselves together against me, and slay me; and I shall be destroyed, I and my house.

31 And they said, Should he deal with our sister as with an harlot?

CHAPTER 35

AND God said unto Jacob, Arise, go up to Beth-el, and dwell there: and make there an altar unto God, that appeared unto thee when thou fleddest from the face of Esau thy brother.

2 Then Jacob said unto his household, and to all that *were* with him, Put away the strange gods that *are* among you, and be clean, and change your garments:

3 And let us arise, and go up to Bĕth-el; and I will make there an altar unto God, who answered me in the day of my distress, and was with me in the way which I went.

4 And they gave unto Jacob all the strange gods which *were* in their hand, and *all their* earrings which *were* in their ears; and Jacob hid them under the oak which *was* by Shĕ′chem.

5 And they journeyed: and the terror of God was upon the cities that *were* round about them, and they did not pursue after the sons of Jacob.

6 ¶So Jacob came to Luz, which *is* in the land of Canaan, that *is*, Bĕth-el, he and all the people that *were* with him.

7 And he built there an altar, and called the place Ĕl-bĕth-el: because there God appeared unto him, when he fled from the face of his brother.

8 But Dĕborah Rebekah's nurse died, and she was buried beneath Bĕth-el under an oak: and the name of it was called Ăl′lon-băch′uth.

9 ¶And God appeared unto Jacob again, when he came out of Pă′dan-ă′ram, and blessed him.

10 And God said unto him, Thy name *is* Jacob: thy name shall not be called any more Jacob, but Israel shall be thy name: and he called his name Israel.

11 And God said unto him, I *am* God Almighty: be fruitful and multiply; a nation and a company of nations shall be of thee, and kings shall come out of thy loins;

12 And the land which I gave Abraham and Isaac, to thee I will give it, and to thy seed after thee will I give the land.

13 And God went up from him in the place where he talked with him.

14 And Jacob set up a pillar in the place where he talked with him, *even* a pillar of stone: and he poured a drink offering thereon, and he poured oil thereon.

15 And Jacob called the name of the place where God spake with him, Bĕth-el.

16 ¶And they journeyed from Bĕth-el; and there was but a little way to come to Ĕph′rath: and Răchel travailed, and she had hard labour.

17 And it came to pass, when she was in hard labour, that the midwife said unto her, Fear not; thou shalt have this son also.

18 And it came to pass, as her soul was in departing, (for she died) that she called his name Bĕn-ō′nī: but his father called him Benjamin.

19 And Răchel died, and was buried in the way to Ĕph′rath, which *is* Bĕth-lehĕm.

13. To Beth-el again. 35:1-15.

35:1-15. Then **God said unto Jacob, Arise, go up to Beth-el, and dwell there: and make there an altar unto God.** Evidently, Beth-el occupied the same place in Jacob's life that the birth of Isaac did in Abraham's life. For more than twenty years it was a test of his fluctuating disobedience and his hold on the promise. "His return there marks an end and a beginning: a time of parting, in the death of the old retainer Deborah and of the beloved Rachel; and a point of transition, as the promise was reaffirmed, and the family completed by the birth of Benjamin. Jacob was to live on, but the centre of gravity would now shift to his sons" (Kidner, p. 174).

Put away the strange gods that are among you. In the crisis precipitated by the Shechem massacre (34:25ff.), Jacob's divine protector intervened with directions and defense; for **the terror of God was upon the cities . . . and they did not pursue after the sons of Jacob** (vs. 5). He summoned Jacob back to Beth-el, the site of His original covenant revelation to him. This would complete Jacob's vow (cf. 28:20ff.; 31:13). The putting away of the **strange gods** indicates Jacob's desire for an exclusive devotion to his sovereign god, the Suzerain (cf. 31:19; Ex 20:3). The **earrings** probably were amulets with idolatrous significance (Ex 32:2-3). Later, Joshua was to demand the same removal of foreign gods at a covenant renewal (Josh 24:1ff., 23). The altar, **El-beth-el**, gave witness to the Lord's sovereign faithfulness. The renewal was made in verses 9ff. and gave significance to Jacob's renewal of the name of the site (vs. 15; cf. 28:19). God summarized His previous dealings with Jacob, which included the name-blessing, Israel, and the promise of royal nationhood in the land of Abraham (cf. 17:1b, 4ff.; 28:13ff.). The basic elements of treaty-making are present: His title, the stipulations and sanctions, the historical prologue. The stone **pillar** was the customary covenant witness (Josh 24:6ff.).

14. The death of Rachel. 35:16-20.

16-20. They journeyed from Beth-el and were almost to **Ephrath**, another name for **Beth-lehem**, when Rachel gave birth to **Ben-oni**. The name may mean "son of my pain" or "son of my misfortune." The phrase **as her soul was in departing** does not indicate that the **soul** was considered a separate entity from the body, with an existence of its own, but only that the life was departing. Jacob's renaming of his son as **Benjamin**, or "son of my right hand," emphasized the positive aspect of this event. The name appears in the Mari documents and means "son of the south." This indicated their orientation was facing east, thus the south was on their right. Perhaps this indicated Jacob's journey southward. "But 'right hand' is to be taken in its normal sense, accompanied by its propitious overtones of honour (Ps 110:1), skill (Ps 137:5), and soundness (Eccl 10:2)" (Kidner, p. 176).

20 And Jacob set a pillar upon her grave: that *is* the pillar of Răchel's grave unto this day.
21 ¶And Israel journeyed, and spread his tent beyond the tower of Ē'dar.
22 And it came to pass, when Israel dwelt in that land, that Reuben went and lay with Bĭl'hah his father's concubine: and Israel heard *it*. Now the sons of Jacob were twelve:

23 The sons of Leah; Reuben, Jacob's firstborn, and Simeon, and Levi, and Jūdah, and Ĭs'sa-char, and Zĕb'u-lun:
24 The sons of Răchel; Joseph, and Benjamin:
25 And the sons of Bĭl'hah, Răchel's handmaid; Dan, and Năph'ta-lī:
26 And the sons of Zĭlpah, Leah's handmaid; Gad, and Asher: these *are* the sons of Jacob, which were born to him in Pă'dan-â'ram.
27 ¶And Jacob came unto Isaac his father unto Măm're, unto the city of Är'bah, which *is* Hēbron, where Abraham and Isaac sojourned.
28 And the days of Isaac were an hundred and fourscore years.
29 And Isaac gave up the ghost, and died, and was gathered unto his people, *being* old and full of days: and his sons Esau and Jacob buried him.

CHAPTER 36

NOW these *are* the generations of Esau, who *is* Edom.
2 Esau took his wives of the daughters of Canaan; Adah the daughter of Ē'lŏn the Hittite, and A-hŏl-ĭ-bă'mah the daughter of Ā'nah the daughter of Zĭb'e-on the Hī'vīte;
3 And Băsh'e-măth Ĭsh'ma-el's daughter, sister of Ne-bā'jŏth.
4 And Adah bare to Esau Ēl'i-phăz; and Băsh'e-măth bare Reū'el;
5 And A-hŏl-ĭ-bă'mah bare Jē'ŭsh, and Jā-a'lam, and Korah: these *are* the sons of Esau, which were born unto him in the land of Canaan.
6 And Esau took his wives, and his sons, and his daughters, and all the persons of his house, and his cattle, and all his beasts, and all his substance, which he had got in the land of Canaan; and went into the country from the face of his brother Jacob.
7 For their riches were more than that they might dwell together; and the land wherein they were strangers could not bear them because of their cattle.
8 Thus dwelt Esau in mount Sē'ir: Esau *is* Edom.
9 ¶And these *are* the generations of Esau the father of the Edomites in mount Sē'ir:
10 These *are* the names of Esau's sons; Ēl'i-phăz the son of Adah the wife of Esau, Reū'el the son of Băsh'e-măth the wife of Esau.
11 And the sons of Ēl'i-phăz were Tē'-

15. Reuben's unchastity. 35:21-22a.

21-22a. The sin of incest cost Reuben his birthright forever, and he was replaced by Joseph (49:3-4; I Chr 5:1-2), again demonstrating the concept of rank and not origin. The amazingly brief report leaves the shock of this act upon the family to be imagined; it is to be understood in the light of the scathing judgment pronounced by Jacob under divine direction (49:3-4).

16. The twelve sons of Jacob. 35:22b-26.

22b-26. One point of this summary is that the promise or prayer expressed by the name of Jacob's eleventh son (**Joseph**) in 30:24 is now fulfilled by the birth of Benjamin. God added the twelfth son, and this number came to symbolize the whole Israel of God (Rev 21:12, 14). The twelve are listed according to their mothers (vs. 23ff.); and thus they are presented according to legal, rather than chronological, priorities.

17. The death of Isaac 35:27-29.

27-29. Mamre was Hebron, some twenty-two miles south of Jerusalem, named for a noted man of that time (14:13). Isaac was 180 years old when he died (vs. 28). His burial found his sons Jacob and Esau at peace. **Gave up the ghost** means to expire or die and is explained by the next verb **and died. Gathered unto his people** has been discussed in 25:8.

18. The brother of Jacob, Esau, and his descendants. 36:1-43.

This chapter clears the ground for the final portion of the book. The brotherhood of Jacob and Esau, which lived on in the nations of Israel and Edom, is a theme that runs through the whole Old Testament. This chapter gives witness to this kinship, which will later be evident in different contexts, such as diplomacy, law, and national feeling (cf. Num 20:14; Deut 23:7; Ob 10-12).
36:1-8. This section gives us details about Esau and his immediate family; and his wives (vss. 1-3), his sons (vss. 4-5), and his enormous wealth (vss. 6-8) are presented. The passage displays the continuing fulfillment both of God's revealed purpose concerning Esau (cf. 25:23) and of Isaac's inspired blessing on him (cf. 27:39ff.). **For their riches were more than that they might dwell together; and the land . . . could not bear them because of their cattle** sounds like Abraham and Lot (13:6): **And the land was not able to bear them, that they might dwell together: for their substance was great.** So often material blessings are the root of envy, jealousy, and bitterness in families and among friends. What a tragic commentary.

9-43. There is a shift from the family of Esau to the nation of **Edom** in verse 9, and verse 8 gives witness to Esau's move to Mount Seir. The inhabitants of this land were the **Horite**(s); they were the ones the Lord dispossessed before Esau (cf. Deut 2:12, 22) and with whom Esau's descendants intermarried (cf. vs. 2). The reference to **dukes of the sons of Esau** in verse 15 and following is the Hebrew *'alūpē* and has traditionally been rendered chieftains, dukes. The Hebrew is related to thousands,

man, Omar, Zē'phō, and Gā'tam, and Kē'năz.

12 And Tĭm'na was concubine to Ĕl'i-phăz Esau's son; and she bare to Ĕl'i-phăz Ăm'a-lĕk: these *were* the sons of Adah Esau's wife.

13 And these *are* the sons of Reū'el; Nā'hăth, and Ze'rah, Shăm'mah, and Mĭz'zah: these were the sons of Băsh'e-măth Esau's wife.

14 And these were the sons of A-hōl-ĭ-bă'mah, the daughter of Ā'nah the daughter of Zĭb'e-on, Esau's wife: and she bare to Esau Jē'ŭsh, and Jā-a'lam, and Kôrah.

15 ¶These *were* dukes of the sons of Esau: the sons of Ĕl'i-phăz the firstborn *son* of Esau; duke Tē'man, duke Omar, duke Zē'phō, duke Kē'năz,

16 Duke Kôrah, duke Gā'tam, *and* duke Ăm'a-lĕk: these *are* the dukes *that came* of Ĕl'i-phăz in the land of Edom; these *were* the sons of Adah.

17 And these *are* the sons of Reū'el Esau's son; duke Na'hăth, duke Ze'rah, duke Shăm'mah, duke Mĭz'zah: these *are* the dukes *that came* of Reū'el in the land of Edom; these *are* the sons of Băsh'e-măth Esau's wife.

18 And these *are* the sons of A-hōl-ĭ-bă'mah Esau's wife; duke Jē'ŭsh, duke Jā-a'lam, duke Kôrah: these *were* the dukes *that came* of A-hōl-ĭ-bă'mah the daughter of Ā'nah, Esau's wife.

19 These *are* the sons of Esau, who *is* Edom, and these *are* their dukes.

20 ¶These *are* the sons of Sē'ir the Hō'rīte, who inhabited the land; Lō'tăn, and Shō'bal, and Zĭb'e-on, and Ā'nah,

21 And Dĭ'shŏn, and Ē'zer, and Dĭ'shăn: these *are* the dukes of the Hō'rītes, the children of Sē'ir in the land of Edom.

22 And the children of Lō'tăn were Hō'rī and He'mam; and Lō'tăn's sister *was* Tĭm'na.

23 And the children of Shō'bal *were* these; Ăl'van, and Măn'a-hăth, and Ebal, Shē'phō, and Ō'nam.

24 And these *are* the children of Zĭb'e-on; both Ā'jah, and Ā'nah: this *was that* Ā'nah that found the mules in the wilderness, as he fed the asses of Zĭb'e-on his father.

25 And the children of Ā'nah *were* these; Dĭ'shŏn, and A-hōl-ĭ-bă'mah the daughter of Ā'nah.

26 And these *are* the children of Dĭ'shŏn; Hĕm'dăn, and Ĕsh'băn, and Ĭth'răn, and Chē'ran.

27 The children of Ē'zer *are* these; Bĭl'hăn, and Zā'a-văn, and Ā'kăn.

28 The children of Dĭ'shăn *are* these; Uz, and Â'răn.

29 These *are* the dukes *that came* of the Hō'rītes; duke Lō'tăn, duke Shō'bal, duke Zĭb'e-on, duke Ā'nah,

30 Duke Dĭ'shŏn, duke Ē'zer, duke Dĭ'shăn: these *are* the dukes *that came* of Hō'rī, among their dukes in the land of Sē'ir.

31 ¶And these *are* the kings that reigned in the land of Edom, before there reigned any king over the children of Israel.

32 And Bē'la the son of Bē'ôr reigned in Edom: and the name of his city *was* Dĭn'ha-bah.

and most likely in this context it stands for clan, group. The **dukes** was based on the Vulgate. This is confirmed by the supplementary comment **in the land of Edom** in verses 16-17 with 21; individuals would not be so described (Speiser, p. 282).

The **Horite** mentioned in verse 20ff. "can no longer be equated with Hurrians. There is no archaeological or epigraphic trace of the Hurrians anywhere in Edomite territory. Moreover, the Horite personal names recorded in this section are clearly Semitic" (Speiser, p. 283). The name may mean cave-dweller.

The list of Edomite kings in verses 32-39 indicates "an elective, not dynastic, office, the importance of the chiefs appearing in the additional list arranged with special attention of geographical and administrative divisions (vss. 40-43)" (Kline, p. 107).

33 And Bē'la died, and Jō'băb the son
of Ze'rah of Bŏz'rah reigned in his
stead.
34 And Jō'băb died, and Hu'sham of
the land of Tĕm'a-nī reigned in his
stead.
35 And Hu'sham died, and Hā'dăd
the son of Bē'dăd, who smote Mĭd'ĭ-an
in the field of Moab, reigned in his
stead: and the name of his city was
Ā'vĭth.
36 And Hā'dăd died, and Săm'lah of
Măs're-kah reigned in his stead.
37 And Săm'lah died, and Saul of Re-
hō'bŏth by the river reigned in his
stead.
38 And Saul died, and Bā'al-hā'nan
the son of Ăch'bôr reigned in his stead.
39 And Bā'al-hā'nan the son of Ăch'-
bôr died, and Hā'där reigned in his
stead: and the name of his city was Pā'ū;
and his wife's name was Me-hĕt'a-
bĕl, the daughter of Mā'tred, the
daughter of Mĕz'a-hăb.
40 ¶And these are the names of the
dukes that came of Esau, according to
their families, after their places, by
their names: duke Tĭm'nah, duke Āl'vah,
duke Jē'thĕth,
41 Duke A-hōl-ĭ-bă'mah, duke Ē'lah,
duke Pī'nŏn,
42 Duke Kē'năz, duke Tē'man, duke
Mĭb'zär,
43 Duke Măg'dĭ-el, duke Ī'răm: these
be the dukes of Edom, according to
their habitations in the land of their
possession: he is Esau the father of the
Edomites.

CHAPTER 37
AND Jacob dwelt in the land wherein
his father was a stranger, in the land of
Canaan.
2 These are the generations of Jacob.
Joseph, being seventeen years old, was
feeding the flock with his brethren; and
the lad was with the sons of Bĭl'hah,
and with the sons of Zĭlpah, his father's
wives: and Joseph brought unto his
father their evil report.
3 Now Israel loved Joseph more than
all his children, because he was the son
of his old age: and he made him a coat
of many colours.
4 And when his brethren saw that
their father loved him more than all his
brethren, they hated him, and could not
speak peaceably unto him.
5 ¶And Joseph dreamed a dream, and
he told it his brethren: and they hated
him yet the more.
6 And he said unto them, Hear, I pray
you, this dream which I have dreamed:
7 For, behold, we were binding
sheaves in the field, and, lo, my sheaf
arose, and also stood upright; and, behold, your sheaves stood round about,
and made obeisance to my sheaf.
8 And his brethren said to him, Shalt
thou indeed reign over us? or shalt thou
indeed have dominion over us? And
they hated him yet the more for his
dreams, and for his words.
9 And he dreamed yet another
dream, and told it his brethren, and
said, Behold, I have dreamed a dream
more; and, behold, the sun and the

D. Joseph, the True. 37:1-50:26.

"It was God's intention, already revealed to Abraham (15:13-16), to bring the chosen family under foreign domination until 'the iniquity of the Amorites' should be full, and Canaan ripe for possession. So the train of events to lead Israel into Egypt is set in motion through the rivalries and predicaments of the twelve brothers, under the hand of God" (Kidner, p. 179).

1. Joseph sold into slavery. 37:1-36.

Joseph, much like Isaac and Jacob before him, is introduced as a specially chosen member of his family. The fact of divine election is one of the themes of Genesis (cf. Rom 9:11ff.). The account of Joseph's dreams, related at the outset, makes God, not Joseph, the center of the story, its hero. It is a story of divine sovereignty, not human success.

37:1-11. Joseph alienated his family, particularly his brothers. The events of this chapter took place some years before Isaac's death, while Jacob and his family were living near Hebron (cf. vs. 14; 35:27). Being **a lad** is most likely a reference to his being a servant or helper (22:3; Ex 33:11), as his age has already been cited. He was with his ten other brothers, but especially with the four who were sons of secondary wives, **the sons of Bilhah . . . sons of Zilpah.** The early indications of his future preeminence made him the object of jealous hatred, especially among the four sons of the handmaids, who ranked lowest (cf. 30:3-13; 33:2). He brought **their evil report** (vs. 2), which was an evil report in the sense that their actions were evil and he reported this to his father. It is hard to know whether he did this as a tattletale or because his father required him to do it (Lev 5:1). The fact that Jacob **loved Joseph more than all his children** indicates that he had learned nothing from his previous experiences relating to favoritism (25:28). It is recorded that at some time **he made him a coat of many colors.** "The traditional 'coat of many colors,' and the variant 'coat with sleeves' are sheer guesses from the context; nor is there anything remarkable about either colors or sleeves. The phrase *ketōnet pasîm*, occurs aside from this section only in II Sam 13:18ff., where it de- scribes a garment worn by the daughters of kings. Cuneiform inventories may shed light on the garment in question. Among various types of clothing listed there is one called *kitū* (or *kutin- nū*) *pišannu* (cf. JNES 8 1949, p. 177) . . . was a ceremonial robe . . . draped about statues of goddesses, and had various gold ornaments sewed onto it . . . it would be a technical term denoting applique ornaments on costly vests and bodices" (Speiser, pp. 289-290).

The dreams of Joseph, "like those of Abimelech (20:3), Jacob (28:12ff.; 31:11), and Laban (31:24), were divinely inspired, but

moon and the eleven stars made obeisance to me.

10 And he told it to his father, and to his brethren: and his father rebuked him, and said unto him, What is this dream that thou hast dreamed? Shall I and thy mother and thy brethren indeed come to bow down ourselves to thee to the earth?

11 And his brethren envied him; but his father observed the saying.

12 ¶And his brethren went to feed their father's flock in Shĕ'chem.

13 And Israel said unto Joseph, Do not thy brethren feed the flock in Shĕ'chem? come, and I will send thee unto them. And he said to him, Here am I.

14 And he said to him, Go, I pray thee, see whether it be well with thy brethren, and well with the flocks; and bring me word again. So he sent him out of the vale of Hĕbron, and he came to Shĕ'chem.

15 And a certain man found him, and, behold, he was wandering in the field: and the man asked him, saying, What seekest thou?

16 And he said, I seek my brethren: tell me, I pray thee, where they feed their flocks.

17 And the man said, They are departed hence; for I heard them say, Let us go to Dō'than. And Joseph went after his brethren, and found them in Dō'than.

18 ¶And when they saw him afar off, even before he came near unto them, they conspired against him to slay him.

19 And they said one to another, Behold, this dreamer cometh.

20 Come now therefore, and let us slay him, and cast him into some pit, and we will say, Some evil beast hath devoured him: and we shall see what will become of his dreams.

21 And Reuben heard it, and he delivered him out of their hands; and said, Let us not kill him.

22 And Reuben said unto them, Shed no blood, but cast him into this pit that is in the wilderness, and lay no hand upon him; that he might rid him out of their hands, to deliver him to his father again.

23 ¶And it came to pass, when Joseph was come unto his brethren, that they stript Joseph out of his coat, his coat of many colours that was on him;

24 And they took him, and cast him into a pit: and the pit was empty, there was no water in it.

25 And they sat down to eat bread: and they lifted up their eyes and looked, and, behold, a company of Ish'me-el-ītes came from Gilead with their camels bearing spicery and balm and myrrh, going to carry it down to Egypt.

26 And Jūdah said unto his brethren, What profit is it if we slay our brother, and conceal his blood?

27 Come, and let us sell him to the Ish'me-el-ītes, and let not our hand be upon him; for he is our brother and our flesh. And his brethren were content.

28 Then there passed by Mĭd'ĭ-an-ītes merchantmen; and they drew and

unlike them his were filled with symbolism. So were those of the baker, the butler, and Pharaoh" (Davis, p. 264). The meaning of the first dream was obvious to the brothers **and they hated him yet the more.** The second dream involved the subservience of his mother and father too! This referred to Jacob's submission, for he would later come down to Joseph in Egypt. Jacob **rebuked him,** whereas the brothers **envied him.**

12-17. The brothers were shepherding the flock **in Shechem;** and then they went to **Dothan,** which is about twenty miles north of Shechem.

18-36. They saw Joseph **afar off** and plotted to kill him. As the eldest, Reuben felt some responsibility to try and save Joseph (vss. 21-22). The brothers not only hated Joseph as a brother, but the real reason seems to be that they were rebelling "against the matter contained in the dreams, and against the divine power itself . . . who had given the dreams" (Von Rad, p. 348). With murder in their hearts, the brothers could not plead righteous indignation this time (cf. 34:31). They could only conceal it with a cruel lie (vs. 31ff.). The plea for mercy fell on deaf ears (cf. 42:21) until it was baited with the lure of a profit (vs. 26ff.). Thus, Judah's plan "unwittingly thwarted Reuben's (vss. 22, 29ff.) but did save Joseph from death" (Kline, p. 107). This dastardly act did not affect their appetites, and **they sat down to eat bread** (vs. 25). The **Midianites** and the **Ishmaelites** are terms used interchangeably in verse 28, just as in Judges 8:22, 24. The term Ishmaelite may not be an ethnic term, as used here, but is simply a reference to nomadic merchants. **Twenty pieces of silver,** actually shekels (a weight, as coins were not invented until the seventh century B.C.), was probably the average price of a slave. The price varied, due to the circumstances and the slave's age, sex, and condition. Kitchen indicates that in the late third millennium B.C. the average price was ten to fifteen shekels of silver (New Bible Dictionary [NBD], p. 1196).

Jacob, the deceiver in his youth, was now being cruelly deceived (vs. 33); but the Lord he now feared was already overruling events (vs. 36). The very son that Jacob mourned (vs. 34ff.) would yet mourn for Jacob with all Egypt (50:1ff.). Joseph was sold **into Egypt to Potiphar, an officer of Pharaoh's, and captain of the guard.** The majority of scholars place Joseph's arrival in Egypt during the Hyksos period (ca. 1730-1570 B.C.). Davis and Unger put it ca. 1800 B.C. during the Middle Kingdom period, specifically during the reign of Sesostris III (Senusert III, Twelfth Dynasty; see Davis, p. 266). This is most compatible with I Kings 6:1 and Exodus 12:40 which record the sojourn in Egypt as 430 years prior to the 480 years

lifted up Joseph out of the pit, and sold Joseph to the Ĭsh'me-el-ītes for twenty *pieces* of silver: and they brought Joseph into Egypt.

29 ¶And Reuben returned unto the pit; and, behold, Joseph *was* not in the pit; and he rent his clothes.

30 And he returned unto his brethren, and said, The child *is* not; and I, whither shall I go?

31 ¶And they took Joseph's coat, and killed a kid of the goats and dipped the coat in the blood;

32 And they sent the coat of *many* colours, and they brought *it* to their father; and said, This have we found: know now whether it *be* thy son's coat or no.

33 And he knew it, and said, *It is* my son's coat; an evil beast hath devoured him; Joseph is without doubt rent in pieces.

34 And Jacob rent his clothes, and put sackcloth upon his loins, and mourned for his son many days.

35 And all his sons and all his daughters rose up to comfort him; but he refused to be comforted; and he said, For I will go down into the grave unto my son mourning. Thus his father wept for him.

36 And the Mĭd'ĭ-an-ītes sold him into Egypt unto Pŏt'i-phar, an officer of Pharaoh's, *and* captain of the guard.

CHAPTER 38

AND it came to pass at that time, that Jūdah went down from his brethren, and turned in to a certain A-dŭl'lam-īte, whose name *was* Hī'rah.

2 And Jūdah saw there a daughter of a certain Canaanite, whose name *was* Shū'ah; and he took her, and went in unto her.

3 And she conceived, and bare a son; and he called his name Er.

4 And she conceived again, and bare a son; and she called his name Ō'nan.

5 And she yet again conceived, and bare a son; and called his name She'lah: and he was at Chē'zĭb, when she bare him.

6 And Jūdah took a wife for Er his firstborn, whose name *was* Tā'mar.

7 And Er, Jūdah's firstborn, was wicked in the sight of the LORD; and the LORD slew him.

8 And Jūdah said unto Ō'nan, Go in unto thy brother's wife, and marry her, and raise up seed to thy brother.

9 And Ō'nan knew that the seed should not be his; and it came to pass, when he went in unto his brother's wife, that he spilled *it* on the ground, lest that he should give seed to his brother.

10 And the thing which he did displeased the LORD: wherefore he slew him also.

11 Then said Judah to Tā'mar his daughter in law, Remain a widow at thy father's house, till Shē'lah my son be grown: for he said, Lest peradventure he die also, as his brethren *did*. And Tā'mar went and dwelt in her father's house.

which transpired from the Exodus to the fourth year of Solomon's reign when the Temple was erected. **Potiphar** is an Egyptian name meaning, "Whom P'Ra (sun-god) has given." Most authorities would consider Potiphar as an abbreviated form in Hebrew of Potiphera. In Genesis it may well represent a Mosaic modernization of a Middle-Egyptian Didi-ra with the same meaning. He was an "officer of Pharaoh" and "captain of the guard" (vs. 36; 39:1). It followed the same shift of meaning in Hebrew as in Akkadian from official courtier to the more restricted meaning of eunuch. Note, Potiphar was married (39:7). Here, the earlier meaning of official is best. Captain of the bodyguard has been proposed. Vergote prefers butler, in parallel with the baker and cupbearer; however, 40:1-4 favors the usual rendering of **captain of the guard,** as this term also refers to prison keeper (Kitchen, in the *Zondervan Pictorial Encyclopedia of the Bible* [*ZPEB*], p. 823).

2. *Judah and his family succession. 38:1-30.*

Initially, this story seems to be an abrupt interruption of the narrative. It may also seem trivial and unnecessary; yet, as a piece of family history, it is very significant. The information enclosed settles the seniority within the tribe of Judah; it also contributes to the royal genealogy (Mt 1:3; Lk 3:33). "It creates suspense for the reader, with Joseph's future in the balance; it puts the faith and chastity of Joseph, soon to be described, in a context which sets off their rarity; and it fills out the portrait of the effective leader among the ten brothers" (Kidner, p. 187).

38:1-11. Adullamite. It was a Canaanite town situated on the route via Azegah and Soko, halfway between Lachish and Jerusalem. It controlled one of the principal passes into the hill-country of Judah from the northern Shephelah (J. M. Houston, *ZPEB*, p. 65). It might be fifteen miles northwest of Hebron. It was here that Judah married a Canaanite (vs. 2), and that his first-born was slain by the Lord for acting wickedly (vs. 7). From **Shuah** he had three sons, **Er . . . Onan . . . and . . . Shelah. Er** was the first-born who was slain by the Lord. Evidently, he represented the rapid degeneration that had resulted from Shuah's intimate Canaanite alliances (cf. ch. 19). **Er** left no heir; so according to the law of levirate marriage (the marriage of a widow to the brother of her deceased husband), his brother **Onan** was to marry the childless widow and provide a son for Er. This was widely practiced in the ancient Near East and was later incorporated into the Law of Moses (Deut 25:5-10). **And Onan knew that the seed should not be his.** Thus, he forsook his responsibility in favor of his own desires (cf. Ruth 4:6); and God killed him. "The enormity of Onan's sin is in its studied outrage against the family, against his brother's widow and against his own body" (Kidner, p. 188). The death of Judah's two older sons, soon after marrying Tamar, made him hesitant to give his third son. But he promised Tamar that when the boy was old enough, he would give him to her (vs. 11).

12 ¶And in process of time the daughter of Shū'ah Jūdah's wife died; and Jūdah was comforted, and went up unto his sheepshearers to Tĭm'năth, he and his friend Hī'rah the A-dŭl'lam-īte.

13 And it was told Tā'mar, saying, Behold thy father in law goeth up to Tĭm'năth to shear his sheep.

14 And she put her widow's garments off from her, and covered her with a vail, and wrapped herself, and sat in an open place, which is by the way to Tĭm'năth; for she saw that Shē'lah was grown, and she was not given unto him to wife.

15 When Jūdah saw her, he thought her to be an harlot; because she had covered her face.

16 And he turned unto her by the way, and said, Go to, I pray thee, let me come in unto thee; (for he knew not that she was his daughter in law.) And she said, What wilt thou give me, that thou mayest come in unto me?

17 And he said, I will send thee a kid from the flock. And she said, Wilt thou give me a pledge, till thou send it?

18 And he said, What pledge shall I give thee? And she said, Thy signet, and thy bracelets, and thy staff that is in thine hand. And he gave it her, and came in unto her, and she conceived by him.

19 And she arose, and went away, and laid by her vail from her, and put on the garments of her widowhood.

20 And Jūdah sent the kid by the hand of his friend the A-dŭl'lam-īte, to receive his pledge from the woman's hand: but he found her not.

21 Then he asked the men of that place, saying, Where is the harlot, that was openly by the way side? And they said, There was no harlot in this place.

22 And he returned to Jūdah, and said, I cannot find her; and also the men of the place said, that there was no harlot in this place.

23 And Jūdah said, Let her take it to her, lest we be shamed: behold, I sent this kid, and thou hast not found her.

24 ¶And it came to pass about three months after, that it was told Jūdah, saying, Tā'mar thy daughter in law hath played the harlot; and also, behold, she is with child by whoredom. And Jūdah said, Bring her forth, and let her be burnt.

25 When she was brought forth, she sent to her father in law, saying, By the man, whose these are, am I with child: and she said, Discern, I pray thee, whose are these, the signet, and bracelets, and staff.

26 And Jūdah acknowledged them, and said, She hath been more righteous than I; because that I gave her not to Shē'lah my son. And he knew her again no more.

27 ¶And it came to pass in the time of her travail, that, behold, twins were in her womb.

28 And it came to pass, when she travailed, that the one put out his hand: and the midwife took and bound upon his hand a scarlet thread, saying, This came out first.

12-30. For she saw that Shelah was grown, and she was not given unto him to wife. When the time came, Judah failed to make good his promise; so Tamar took matters into her own hands and played the **harlot.** Sheepshearing (vs. 12) was often a time of sexual temptation due to the Canaanite cult, which encouraged ritual fornication as fertility magic. When Judah first saw Tamar, he took her to be a common **harlot** (zōnah vs. 15). But verses 21 and 22 make it clear that she dressed and acted like a Canaanite temple prostitute (haqedēshah). Tamar asked for, and received as pledge of later payment for her services, Judah's **signet,** which was probably a cylinder seal carried on a cord around his neck, **bracelets,** which were cords, and a **staff,** which probably had his identification marks engraved into it.

When Judah was told that Tamar was pregnant because of harlotry (vs. 24), his initial reaction was **let her be burnt** (cf. II Sam 12:5 and David's quick response). This was an unusual punishment (cf. Lev 20:14; 21:9; Deut 22:20-24). He was unable to carry this out when he discovered he was the guilty one! And further, he was forced to admit **She hath been more righteous than I.** He was wrong on two accounts: he had committed adultery with her, and he had not kept his word by refusing to give Tamar his son **Shelah.** Although the hand that appeared first belonged to **Zarah, Pharez,** meaning "breach," was actually born first. He is listed in the genealogy of Christ in Matthew 1:3 (cf. Ruth 4:18ff.). The prenatal struggle, like that of Esau and Jacob in 25:22-26, brings a violent chapter to an end. It also launches the tribe of Judah on its career.

29 And it came to pass, as he drew back his hand, that, behold, his brother came out: and she said, How hast thou broken forth? *this* breach *be* upon thee: therefore his name was called Phā′rĕz.

30 And afterward came out his brother, that had the scarlet thread upon his hand: and his name was called Zā′rah.

CHAPTER 39

AND Joseph was brought down to Egypt; and Pŏt′i-phar, an officer of Pharaoh, captain of the guard, an Egyptian, bought him of the hands of the Ĭsh′me-el-ītes, which had brought him down thither.

2 And the LORD was with Joseph, and he was a prosperous man; and he was in the house of his master the Egyptian.

3 And his master saw that the LORD *was* with him, and that the LORD made all that he did to prosper in his hand.

4 And Joseph found grace in his sight, and he served him: and he made him overseer over his house, and all *that* he had he put into his hand.

5 And it came to pass from the time *that* he had made him overseer in his house, and over all that he had, that the LORD blessed the Egyptian's house for Joseph's sake; and the blessing of the LORD was upon all that he had in the house, and in the field.

6 And he left all that he had in Joseph's hand; and he knew not ought he had, save the bread which he did eat. And Joseph was *a* goodly *person*, and well favoured.

7 ¶And it came to pass after these things, that his master's wife cast her eyes upon Joseph; and she said, Lie with me.

8 But he refused, and said unto his master's wife, Behold, my master wotteth not what *is* with me in the house, and he hath committed all that he hath to my hand;

9 *There is* none greater in this house than I; neither hath he kept back any thing from me but thee, because thou *art* his wife: how then can I do this great wickedness, and sin against God?

10 And it came to pass, as she spake to Joseph day by day, that he hearkened not unto her, to lie by her, *or* to be with her.

11 And it came to pass about this time, that *Joseph* went into the house to do his business; and *there was* none of the men of the house there within.

12 And she caught him by his garment, saying, Lie with me: and he left his garment in her hand, and fled, and got him out.

13 And it came to pass, when she saw that he had left his garment in her hand, and was fled forth,

14 That she called unto the men of her house, and spake unto them, saying, See, he hath brought in an Hebrew unto us to mock us; he came in unto me to lie with me, and I cried with a loud voice:

15 And it came to pass, when he heard that I lifted up my voice and cried, that he left his garment with me, and fled, and got him out.

3. Joseph under test. 39:1-23.

"The symmetry of this chapter, in which the serene opening (vss. 1-6) is matched, point for point, at a new level at the close (vss. 19-23) despite all that intervenes, perfectly expresses God's quiet control and the man of faith's quiet victory. The good seed is buried deeper, still to push upward; the servant, faithful in a little, trains for authority in much" (Kidner, p. 189).

39:1-6. Joseph begins as a trusted slave in the house of **Potiphar.** The key was that **the LORD was with him;** and also note, **his master saw that the LORD was with him, and that the LORD made all that he did to prosper in his hand.** God's guidance in Joseph's life was to prepare for Jacob's household a way out of the dangerous conditions depicted in chapters 37-38. Because of the Lord's blessing Joseph was made **overseer in his house, and over all that he had.** This was a common Egyptian title for Semitic slaves.

7-18. Lie with me were the words of his master's wife. Joseph's reasons for refusing (vss. 8-9) were those that another man might have given for yielding. He was free from supervision, he had made a rapid rise in authority, which had corrupted other stewards (cf. Isa 22:15-25; Lk 16:1ff.), and his realization that only one realm was forbidden to him, were all arguments for his being loyal. He called the proposition **wickedness** and said it was **sin against God.** But she persisted **day by day** (cf. Samson twice in his career in Jud 14:17; 16:16). Evidently, he would not even **be with her.** Joseph's actions are to be contrasted with Reuben's (35:22) and Judah's (38:16). Her first approach involved flattery (vs. 7), then the long enticing (vs. 10), and finally the ambush (vs. 12). Joseph fled, not like a coward, but in the preservation of his honor which the New Testament commands (II Tim 2:22; II Pet 1:4). This is the second time a coat of Joseph is made to lie about him (cf. 37:31ff.).

16 And she laid up his garment by her, until his lord came home.

17 And she spake unto him according to these words, saying, The Hebrew servant, which thou hast brought unto us, came in unto me to mock me:

18 And it came to pass, as I lifted up my voice and cried, that he left his garment with me, and fled out.

19 And it came to pass, when his master heard the words of his wife, which she spake unto him, saying, After this manner did thy servant to me; that his wrath was kindled.

20 And Joseph's master took him, and put him into the prison, a place where the king's prisoners *were* bound: and he was there in the prison.

21 But the LORD was with Joseph, and shewed him mercy, and gave him favour in the sight of the keeper of the prison.

22 And the keeper of the prison committed to Joseph's hand all the prisoners that *were* in the prison; and whatsoever they did there, he was the doer of it.

23 The keeper of the prison looked not to any thing *that was* under his hand; because the LORD was with him, and *that* which he did, the LORD made *it* to prosper.

CHAPTER 40

AND it came to pass after these things, *that* the butler of the king of Egypt and *his* baker had offended their lord the king of Egypt.

2 And Pharaoh was wroth against two *of* his officers, against the chief of the butlers, and against the chief of the bakers.

3 And he put them in ward in the house of the captain of the guard, into the prison, the place where Joseph *was* bound.

4 And the captain of the guard charged Joseph with them, and he served them: and they continued a season in ward.

5 ¶And they dreamed a dream both of them, each man his dream in one night, each man according to the interpretation of his dream, the butler and the baker of the king of Egypt, which *were* bound in the prison.

6 And Joseph came in unto them in the morning, and looked upon them, and, behold, they *were* sad.

7 And he asked Pharaoh's officers that *were* with him in the ward of his lord's house, saying, Wherefore look ye *so* sadly to day?

8 And they said unto him, We have dreamed a dream, and *there is* no interpreter of it. And Joseph said unto them, *Do* not interpretations *belong* to God? tell me *them*, I pray you.

9 And the chief butler told his dream to Joseph, and said to him, In my dream, behold, a vine *was* before me;

10 And in the vine *were* three branches: and it *was* as though it budded, *and* her blossoms shot forth; and the clusters thereof brought forth ripe grapes:

11 And Pharaoh's cup *was* in my

19-23. The woman had other servants of the household seize Joseph on the pretext that he had attacked her (vss. 13-15), and then she lied to her husband (vs. 17). His **master took him, and put him into the prison** (cf. Ps 105:17-18 for the details of his imprisonment). But the exciting thing was that God was still **with Joseph, and showed him mercy** (*chesed*). This is one of the most exciting truths in God's Word. God faithfully demonstrates His loyalty to His people. God had saved Joseph, and now He was being faithful to His covenant with Joseph by giving **him favor in the sight of the keeper of the prison.** Note, when Daniel purposed in his heart **that he would not defile himself with the portion of the king's meat, nor with the wine,** God then granted **favor** (*chesed*) to Daniel **with the prince of the eunuchs** (Dan 1:8). God supernaturally caused this eunuch to like Daniel and show loyalty or faithfulness to him, to allow him to try the new diet for ten days. When we make positive, difficult decisions to live according to God's standards, He will remain faithful to us and meet our needs.

4. Joseph interprets the dreams of the butler and the baker. 40:1-23.

40:1-8. While in prison Joseph met two very influential people, the **butler** and the **baker.** Later, they were called **the chief butler** and **the chief baker** (vss. 9, 16). The translation **butler** is unfortunate. The phrase literally means "cupbearer of the king." Egyptian inscriptions include various titles for those involved in serving wine and beer to the Pharaoh. They **offended their lord the king of Egypt** (vs. 1). The word offend is the Hebrew word for sin. Somehow they sinned against Pharaoh and incurred his anger (vs. 2). **Charged Joseph with them** indicates he was over administrative affairs in the prison, not a superior over high-ranking prisoners (cf. 41:12). The two imprisoned court officials had dreams that perplexed them (vss. 5-7). Joseph's immediate response was, **Do not interpretations belong to God?** (cf. this was the immediate response of his mind in 39:9; 41:16, 51, 52; 45:8).

9-23. Joseph interpreted the cupbearer's dream to mean that he would be restored to his former position (vss. 9-15). Joseph requested of this man that since Joseph met his need, would he now **show kindness** (*chesed*, vs. 14) to Joseph by making **mention of me unto Pharaoh, and bring me out of this house.** Joseph was asking for faithfulness to be demonstrated based on their relationship.

Then the chief baker related his dream to Joseph; but to his alarm, Joseph's interpretation was just the opposite. Joseph's

hand: and I took the grapes, and pressed them into Pharaoh's cup, and I gave the cup into Pharaoh's hand.

12 And Joseph said unto him, This *is* the interpretation of it: The three branches *are* three days:

13 Yet within three days shall Pharaoh lift up thine head, and restore thee unto thy place: and thou shalt deliver Pharaoh's cup into his hand, after the former manner when thou wast his butler.

14 But think on me when it shall be well with thee, and shew kindness, I pray thee, unto me, and make mention of me unto Pharaoh, and bring me out of this house:

15 For indeed I was stolen away out of the land of the Hebrews: and here also have I done nothing that they should put me into the dungeon.

16 When the chief baker saw that the interpretation was good, he said unto Joseph, I also *was* in my dream, and, behold, *I had* three white baskets on my head:

17 And in the uppermost basket *there was* of all manner of bakemeats for Pharaoh; and the birds did eat them out of the basket upon my head.

18 And Joseph answered and said, This *is* the interpretation thereof: The three baskets *are* three days:

19 Yet within three days shall Pharaoh lift up thy head from off thee, and shall hang thee on a tree; and the birds shall eat thy flesh from off thee.

20 ¶And it came to pass the third day, *which was* Pharaoh's birthday, that he made a feast unto all his servants: and he lifted up the head of the chief butler and of the chief baker among his servants.

21 And he restored the chief butler unto his butlership again; and he gave the cup into Pharaoh's hand:

22 But he hanged the chief baker: as Joseph had interpreted to them.

23 Yet did not the chief butler remember Joseph, but forgat him.

CHAPTER 41

AND it came to pass at the end of two full years, that Pharaoh dreamed: and, behold, he stood by the river.

2 And, behold, there came up out of the river seven well favoured kine and fatfleshed; and they fed in a meadow.

3 And, behold, seven other kine came up after them out of the river, ill favoured and leanfleshed; and stood by the *other* kine upon the brink of the river.

4 And the ill favoured and leanfleshed kine did eat up the seven well favoured and fat kine. So Pharaoh awoke.

5 And he slept and dreamed the second time: and, behold, seven ears of corn came up upon one stalk, rank and good.

6 And, behold, seven thin ears and blasted with the east wind sprung up after them.

7 And the seven thin ears devoured the seven rank and full ears. And Pharaoh awoke, and, behold, *it was* a dream.

interpretations both proved valid, and the Pharaoh **lifted up the head of the chief butler and of the chief baker.** Joseph used a key expression, capable of being interpreted in opposite ways, to describe first the cupbearer's pardon and restoration to honor (cf. II Kgs 25:27), then the beheading or hanging of the baker (vs. 19).

5. Joseph interprets Pharaoh's dream. 41:1-57.

41:1-8. Pharaoh dreamed. This providential series of dreams is now concluded. The middle pair in 40:5ff. proved the means for involving Joseph in this third pair (vs. 9ff.), and it was this last pair of dreams that served to fulfill the first pair of 37:5ff. The doubling of the dreams served to signify the certainty of the divine purpose revealed (vs. 32). Two years had passed since the events of chapter 40. Verses 2-7 are supplemented by verses 17-24. The repetition is part of the ancient Near Eastern art of storytelling. **All the magicians of Egypt, and all the wise men thereof . . . but there was none that could interpret them.** The **magicians** were the professional interpreters of dreams who had been trained at special schools (seminaries?).

8 And it came to pass in the morning that his spirit was troubled; and he sent and called for all the magicians of Egypt, and all the wise men thereof: and Pharaoh told them his dream; but *there was* none that could interpret them unto Pharaoh.

9 ¶Then spake the chief butler unto Pharaoh, saying, I do remember my faults this day:

10 Pharaoh was wroth with his servants, and put me in ward in the captain of the guard's house, *both* me and the chief baker:

11 And we dreamed a dream in one night, I and he; we dreamed each man according to the interpretation of his dream.

12 And *there was* there with us a young man, an Hebrew, servant to the captain of the guard; and we told him, and he interpreted to us our dreams; to each man according to his dream he did interpret.

13 And it came to pass, as he interpreted to us, so it was; me he restored unto mine office, and him he hanged.

14 ¶Then Pharaoh sent and called Joseph, and they brought him hastily out of the dungeon: and he shaved *himself,* and changed his raiment, and came in unto Pharaoh.

15 And Pharaoh said unto Joseph, I have dreamed a dream, and *there is* none that can interpret it: and I have heard say of thee, *that* thou canst understand a dream to interpret it.

16 And Joseph answered Pharaoh, saying, *It is* not in me: God shall give Pharaoh an answer of peace.

17 And Pharaoh said unto Joseph, In my dream, behold, I stood upon the bank of the river:

18 And, behold, there came up out of the river seven kine, fatfleshed and well favoured; and they fed in a meadow:

19 And, behold, seven other kine came up after them, poor and very ill favoured and leanfleshed, such as I never saw in all the land of Egypt for badness:

20 And the lean and the ill favoured kine did eat up the first seven fat kine:

21 And when they had eaten them up, it could not be known that they had eaten them; but they *were* still ill favoured, as at the beginning. So I awoke.

22 And I saw in my dream, and, behold, seven ears came up in one stalk, full and good:

23 And, behold, seven ears, withered, thin, *and* blasted with the east wind, sprung up after them:

24 And the thin ears devoured the seven good ears: and I told *this* unto the magicians; but *there was* none that could declare *it* to me.

25 ¶And Joseph said unto Pharaoh, The dream of Pharaoh *is* one: God hath shewed Pharaoh what he *is* about to do.

26 The seven good kine *are* seven years; and the seven good ears *are* seven years: the dream *is* one.

27 And the seven thin and ill favoured kine that came up after them *are* seven years; and the seven empty

9-57. Pharaoh called Joseph; and he said, **It is not in me: God shall give Pharaoh an answer of peace** (cf. vss. 25, 28, 32; Dan 2:27-30). Joseph interpreted the dream, and he advised Pharaoh how to meet the impending disaster (vss. 33-36). Pharaoh was so impressed with Joseph, **a man in whom the spirit of God is,** that he elevated him to a position second only to his own position (vss. 40).

There has been some question as to the exact position Joseph held in the royal court. Some think he was merely an important official with considerable power. Others believe he was a vizier or prime minister. He was set as chief steward over Pharaoh's house (vs. 40); he was in command over **all the land of Egypt** (cf. vss. 41, 43-44, 46, 55; 42:6; 45:8); and he was directly responsible and subordinate only to Pharaoh (vs. 40). Other Asiatics were known to have achieved similar eminence in Egypt's government in the second millennium B.C. Pharaoh made Joseph to ride **in the second chariot** (vs. 43). Thutmose III gave the following charge to his newly appointed vizier: "Look thou to this office of vizier. Be vigilant over everything that is done in it. Behold, it is the support of the entire land. Behold, as to the vizierate, behold, it is not sweet at all, behold, it is bitter as gall. . . ." (*ANET*, p. 213; for previous documentation see Davis, p. 276; Speiser, p. 316; Kline, p. 109).

Pharaoh ordered the Egyptians to **Bow the knee** to Joseph (vs. 43). He gave Joseph an Egyptian name **Zaphnath-paaneah** (vs. 45), the meaning of which is still unclear (with one small change it could mean "Joseph, who is called Ip ankh" *NBD*, p. 1353). He married **Asenath,** "she belongs to Neith," who was the daugher of **Potipherah,** meaning "he whom Ra has given," a **priest of On** (Davis, p. 277). Ra was an important Egyptian deity as early as the Fifth Dynasty. Joseph had spent thirteen years in servitude (cf. vs. 46; 37:2). The climax would not be reached for another nine years (45:6), more than twenty years after the first confrontation with his brothers. Joseph's entrance into the court with his change of name (cf. Dan 1:7) and his marriage to a priest's daughter completed his outward Egyptianization, but he still maintained a bold confession of the God of Israel.

He gathered food according to his plan (vss. 47-49). He had two sons, **Manasseh** and **Ephraim;** his first-born's name means, "one who causes me to forget," indicating all his **toil, and all my father's house.** The reference to his father's house only meant that the hardship brought upon him by his brothers was a thing of the past. Ephraim, meaning "fruitful," signified **God hath caused me to be fruitful in the land of my affliction.** What a sweet, pleasant, and thankful spirit he showed in interpreting the events that had transpired in his life. The fulfillment of Pharaoh's prophetic dreams set the stage for the final scene in the fulfillment of Joseph's own dreams.

ears blasted with the east wind shall be seven years of famine.

28 This *is* the thing which I have spoken unto Pharaoh: What God *is* about to do he sheweth unto Pharaoh.

29 Behold, there come seven years of great plenty throughout all the land of Egypt:

30 And there shall arise after them seven years of famine; and all the plenty shall be forgotten in the land of Egypt; and the famine shall consume the land;

31 And the plenty shall not be known in the land by reason of that famine following; for it *shall be* very grievous.

32 And for that the dream was doubled unto Pharaoh twice; *it is* because the thing *is* established by God, and God will shortly bring it to pass.

33 Now therefore let Pharaoh look out a man discreet and wise, and set him over the land of Egypt.

34 Let Pharaoh do *this*, and let him appoint officers over the land, and take up the fifth part of the land of Egypt in the seven plenteous years.

35 And let them gather all the food of those good years that come, and lay up corn under the hand of Pharaoh, and let them keep food in the cities.

36 And that food shall be for store to the land against the seven years of famine, which shall be in the land of Egypt; that the land perish not through the famine.

37 ¶And the thing was good in the eyes of Pharaoh, and in the eyes of all his servants.

38 And Pharaoh said unto his servants, Can we find *such a one* as this *is*, a man in whom the Spirit of God *is?*

39 And Pharaoh said unto Joseph, Forasmuch as God hath shewed thee all this, *there is* none so discreet and wise as thou *art*:

40 Thou shalt be over my house, and according unto thy word shall all my people be ruled: only in the throne will I be greater than thou.

41 And Pharaoh said unto Joseph, See, I have set thee over all the land of Egypt.

42 And Pharaoh took off his ring from his hand, and put it upon Joseph's hand, and arrayed him in vestures of fine linen, and put a gold chain about his neck;

43 And he made him to ride in the second chariot which he had; and they cried before him, Bow the knee: and he made him *ruler* over all the land of Egypt.

44 And Pharaoh said unto Joseph, I *am* Pharaoh, and without thee shall no man lift up his hand or foot in all the land of Egypt.

45 And Pharaoh called Joseph's name Zăph'năth–pā-a-nē'ah; and he gave him to wife Ăs'e-năth the daughter of Po-tīph'e-rah priest of On. And Joseph went out over *all* the land of Egypt.

46 And Joseph *was* thirty years old when he stood before Pharaoh king of Egypt. And Joseph went out from the

presence of Pharaoh, and went throughout all the land of Egypt.

47 And in the seven plenteous years the earth brought forth by handfuls.

48 And he gathered up all the food of the seven years, which were in the land of Egypt, and laid up the food in the cities: the food of the field, which *was* round about every city, laid he up in the same.

49 And Joseph gathered corn as the sand of the sea, very much, until he left numbering; for *it was* without number.

50 And unto Joseph were born two sons before the years of famine came, which Ãs'e-nãth the daughter of Po-tïph'e-rah priest of On bare unto him.

51 And Joseph called the name of the firstborn Ma-nãs'seh: For God, *said he,* hath made me forget all my toil, and all my father's house.

52 And the name of the second called he Ē'phra-im: For God hath caused me to be fruitful in the land of my affliction.

53 ¶And the seven years of plenteousness, that was in the land of Egypt, were ended.

54 And the seven years of dearth began to come, according as Joseph had said: and the dearth was in all lands; but in all the land of Egypt there was bread.

55 And when all the land of Egypt was famished, the people cried to Pharaoh for bread: and Pharaoh said unto all the Egyptians, Go unto Joseph; what he saith to you, do.

56 And the famine was over all the face of the earth: And Joseph opened all the storehouses, and sold unto the Egyptians; and the famine waxed sore in the land of Egypt.

57 And all countries came into Egypt to Joseph for to buy *corn;* because that the famine was *so* sore in all lands.

CHAPTER 42

NOW when Jacob saw that there was corn in Egypt, Jacob said unto his sons, Why do ye look one upon another?

2 And he said, Behold, I have heard that there is corn in Egypt: get you down thither, and buy for us from thence; that we may live, and not die.

3 ¶And Joseph's ten brethren went down to buy corn in Egypt.

4 But Benjamin, Joseph's brother, Jacob sent not with his brethren; for he said, Lest peradventure mischief befall him.

5 And the sons of Israel came to buy *corn* among those that came: for the famine was in the land of Canaan.

6 And Joseph *was* the governor over the land, *and* he *it was* that sold to all the people of the land: and Joseph's brethren came, and bowed down themselves before him *with* their faces to the earth.

7 And Joseph saw his brethren, and he knew them, but made himself strange unto them, and spake roughly unto them; and he said unto them, Whence come ye? And they said, From the land of Canaan to buy food.

6. *Joseph's brothers in Egypt. 42:1-45:28.*

42:1. When Jacob realized that there were provisions in Egypt for the famine, he asked his sons, **Why do ye look one upon another?** Paraphrased, it means, "Why stand there with your teeth in your mouth? Get going!"

2-5. Jacob wanted only ten of his sons to go to Egypt; he wanted Benjamin to stay home **lest peradventure mischief befall him.** Benjamin was at least twenty years old, so Jacob must have wanted to keep him because he was the only son left of his beloved wife Rachel.

6-17. It is hard to determine Joseph's real motive in testing his brothers. Most scholars have felt that Joseph was not being vindictive, but was engaged merely in official probing and testing. However, Joseph's manner, coupled with the numerous tests through which he put his brothers, gives the distinct impression that he was humbling his previously arrogant brothers (vss. 6-14). The fact that they **bowed down themselves before him** brings to mind the fulfillment of the dreams they had gone to great lengths to thwart (cf. vs. 9; 37:5ff.). Joseph was to test them by demanding that they bring Benjamin down to Egypt. Evidently, he wanted to make sure Benjamin

8 And Joseph knew his brethren, but they knew not him.

9 And Joseph remembered the dreams which he dreamed of them, and said unto them, Ye *are* spies; to see the nakedness of the land ye are come.

10 And they said unto him, Nay, my lord, but to buy food are thy servants come.

11 We *are* all one man's sons; we *are* true *men*, thy servants are no spies.

12 And he said unto them, Nay, but to see the nakedness of the land ye are come.

13 And they said, Thy servants *are* twelve brethren, the sons of one man in the land of Canaan; and, behold, the youngest *is* this day with our father, and one *is* not.

14 And Joseph said unto them, That *is it* that I spake unto you, saying, Ye *are* spies:

15 Hereby ye shall be proved: By the life of Pharaoh ye shall not go forth hence, except your youngest brother come hither.

16 Send one of you, and let him fetch your brother, and ye shall be kept in prison, that your words may be proved, whether *there be any* truth in you: or else by the life of Pharaoh surely ye *are* spies.

17 And he put them all together into ward three days.

18 And Joseph said unto them the third day, This do, and live; *for* I fear God:

19 If ye *be* true *men*, let one of your brethren be bound in the house of your prison: go ye, carry corn for the famine of your houses:

20 But bring your youngest brother unto me; so shall your words be verified, and ye shall not die. And they did so.

21 ¶And they said one to another, We *are* verily guilty concerning our brother, in that we saw the anguish of his soul, when he besought us, and we would not hear; therefore is this distress come upon us.

22 And Reuben answered them, saying, Spake I not unto you, saying, Do not sin against the child; and ye would not hear? therefore, behold, also his blood is required.

23 And they knew not that Joseph understood *them*; for he spake unto them by an interpreter.

24 And he turned himself about from them, and wept; and returned to them again, and communed with them, and took from them Simeon, and bound him before their eyes.

25 ¶Then Joseph commanded to fill their sacks with corn, and to restore every man's money into his sack, and to give them provision for the way: and thus did he unto them.

26 And they laded their asses with the corn, and departed thence.

27 And as one of them opened his sack to give his ass provender in the inn, he espied his money; for, behold, it *was* in his sack's mouth.

28 And he said unto his brethren, My money is restored; and, lo, *it is* even in my sack: and their heart failed *them*,

was still alive, that they had not killed him as they had tried to kill Joseph. He kept them **in prison** for three days, demonstrating his power and insuring their obedience.

18-38. This experience caused the brothers to discuss their guilt concerning Joseph (vss. 21-22), which may have been Joseph's purpose in testing them. Hearing their conversation, he turned from them and **wept.** Certainly, this does not characterize a man of hate. He had their sacks filled with grain and put their money back in the sacks. When they were on their way, one of them discovered his money; **and their heart failed them, and they were afraid saying . . . What is this that God hath done unto us?**

Joseph kept **Simeon** back as a hostage, insuring their return with Benjamin. When they got home, each one found his money in his sack; and **they were afraid.** Evidently, they had not told their father about the one sack with its money; only when in his presence the others opened their sacks, was the cat let out of the bag. Then Reuben, as the eldest son, made an offer that depicted a great sacrifice; **Slay my two sons, if I bring him not to thee.** But this was an ill-timed offer (43:1 indicates the famine got worse and forced Jacob's hand); and also, Jacob did not trust Reuben (vss. 37-38; cf. 49:4). "Such was Jacob's partiality towards Benjamin that he repressed concern to deliver Simeon rather than part with Benjamin under ominous circumstances" (Kline, p. 110).

and they were afraid, saying one to another, What *is* this *that* God hath done unto us?

29 ¶And they came unto Jacob their father unto the land of Canaan, and told him all that befell unto them; saying,

30 The man, *who is* the lord of the land, spake roughly to us, and took us for spies of the country.

31 And we said unto him, We *are* true *men;* we are no spies:

32 We *be* twelve brethren, sons of our father; one *is* not, and the youngest *is* this day with our father in the land of Canaan.

33 And the man, the lord of the country, said unto us, Hereby shall I know that ye *are* true *men;* leave one of your brethren *here* with me, and take *food for* the famine of your households, and be gone:

34 And bring your youngest brother unto me: then shall I know that ye *are* no spies, but *that* ye *are* true *men: so* will I deliver you your brother, and ye shall traffick in the land.

35 And it came to pass as they emptied their sacks, that, behold, every man's bundle of money *was* in his sack: and when *both* they and their father saw the bundles of money, they were afraid.

36 And Jacob their father said unto them, Me have ye bereaved of *my children:* Joseph *is* not, and Simeon *is* not, and ye will take Benjamin *away:* all these things are against me.

37 And Reuben spake unto his father, saying, Slay my two sons, if I bring him not to thee: deliver him into my hand, and I will bring him to thee again.

38 And he said, My son shall not go down with you; for his brother is dead, and he is left alone: if mischief befall him by the way in the which ye go, then shall ye bring down my gray hairs with sorrow to the grave.

CHAPTER 43

AND the famine *was* sore in the land.

2 And it came to pass, when they had eaten up the corn which they had brought out of Egypt, their father said unto them, Go again, buy us a little food.

3 And Judah spake unto him, saying, The man did solemnly protest unto us, saying, Ye shall not see my face, except your brother *be* with you.

4 If thou wilt send our brother with us, we will go down and buy thee food:

5 But if thou wilt not send *him*, we will not go down: for the man said unto us, Ye shall not see my face, except your brother *be* with you.

6 And Israel said, Wherefore dealt ye *so* ill with me, *as* to tell the man whether ye had yet a brother?

7 And they said, The man asked us straitly of our state, and of our kindred, saying, *Is* your father yet alive? have ye *another* brother? and we told him according to the tenor of these words: could we certainly know that he would say, Bring your brother down?

8 And Judah said unto Israel his

This section (43:1-34) records their second visit to Egypt.

43:1-15. Some time within the seven-year period before the famine ended, Jacob asked his sons to return to Egypt; for their supplies had been exhausted (vss. 1-2). Judah said it would be fruitless unless Benjamin went down, also. Jacob then scolded them (vs. 6) for telling the man they had a brother; but Judah guaranteed Benjamin's safe return, and Jacob consented with a final expression of pessimism.

father, Send the lad with me, and we will arise and go; that we may live, and not die, both we, and thou, *and* also our little ones.

9 I will be surety for him; of my hand shalt thou require him: if I bring him not unto thee, and set him before thee, then let me bear the blame for ever:

10 For except we had lingered, surely now we had returned this second time.

11 And their father Israel said unto them, If *it must be* so now, do this; take of the best fruits in the land in your vessels, and carry down the man a present, a little balm, and a little honey, spices, and myrrh, nuts, and almonds:

12 And take double money in your hand; and the money that was brought again in the mouth of your sacks, carry *it* again in your hand; peradventure it *was* an oversight:

13 Take also your brother, and arise, go again unto the man:

14 And God Almighty give you mercy before the man, that he may send away your other brother, and Benjamin. If I be bereaved *of my children,* I am bereaved.

15 ¶And the men took that present, and they took double money in their hand, and Benjamin; and rose up, and went down to Egypt, and stood before Joseph.

16 And when Joseph saw Benjamin with them, he said to the ruler of his house, Bring *these* men home, and slay, and make ready; for *these* men shall dine with me at noon.

17 And the man did as Joseph bade; and the man brought the men into Joseph's house.

18 And the men were afraid, because they were brought into Joseph's house; and they said, Because of the money that was returned in our sacks at the first time are we brought in; that he may seek occasion against us, and fall upon us, and take us for bondmen, and our asses.

19 And they came near to the steward of Joseph's house, and they communed with him at the door of the house,

20 And said, O sir, we came indeed down at the first time to buy food:

21 And it came to pass, when we came to the inn, that we opened our sacks, and, behold, *every* man's money *was* in the mouth of his sack, our money in full weight: and we have brought it again in our hand.

22 And other money have we brought down in our hands to buy food: we cannot tell who put our money in our sacks.

23 And he said, Peace *be* to you, fear not: your God, and the God of your father, hath given you treasure in your sacks: I had your money. And he brought Simeon out unto them.

24 And the man brought the men into Joseph's house, and gave *them* water, and they washed their feet; and he gave their asses provender.

25 And they made ready the present against Joseph came at noon: for they heard that they should eat bread there.

16-34. When Joseph saw Benjamin, he put his plan into operation (vs. 16ff.). **And the men were afraid,** indicating God's working through the circumstances and the money (vss. 21-22). **Fear not: your God . . . hath given you treasure in your sacks** was more true than they realized at this time! They came to eat **and bowed themselves to him to the earth** (cf. 37:8-11, 19-20, and the earlier prophecy). "At the dinner they failed to leap to the one logical explanation of his behavior, with his concern for Jacob (vs. 27), affectionate favoritism for Benjamin (vss. 29-34), and exact knowledge of the interlocking sequence of births of these sons of four mothers (vs. 33)" (Kline, p. 110). The fact that Joseph had the brothers separated from the Egyptians (vs. 32), something which would have been **an abomination unto the Egyptians** if they were not separated, suggests this was a native Egyptian pharaoh. If it was a Hyksos king, he most likely would not have demanded such discrimination. Evidently, the Egyptians had a deep hatred for Asiatic shepherds (cf. 46:34; Ex 8:26). Verse 34 suggests that the brothers were not jealous or resentful toward Benjamin because of the preferential treatment; thus, they seemingly have had a change of heart. But Joseph was to really test them (44:1ff.).

26 And when Joseph came home, they brought him the present which *was* in their hand into the house, and bowed themselves to him to the earth.

27 And he asked them of *their* welfare, and said, *Is* your father well, the old man of whom ye spake? *Is* he yet alive?

28 And they answered, Thy servant our father *is* in good health, he *is* yet alive. And they bowed down their heads, and made obeisance.

29 And he lifted up his eyes, and saw his brother Benjamin, his mother's son, and said, *Is* this your younger brother, of whom ye spake unto me? And he said, God be gracious unto thee, my son.

30 And Joseph made haste; for his bowels did yearn upon his brother: and he sought *where* to weep; and he entered into *his* chamber, and wept there.

31 And he washed his face, and went out, and refrained himself, and said, Set on bread.

32 And they set on for him by himself, and for them by themselves, and for the Egyptians, which did eat with him, by themselves: because the Egyptians might not eat bread with the Hebrews; for that *is* an abomination unto the Egyptians.

33 And they sat before him, the first-born according to his birthright, and the youngest according to his youth: and the men marvelled one at another.

34 And he took *and sent* messes unto them from before him: but Benjamin's mess was five times so much as any of theirs. And they drank, and were merry with him.

CHAPTER 44

AND he commanded the steward of his house, saying, Fill the men's sacks *with* food, as much as they can carry, and put every man's money in his sack's mouth.

2 And put my cup, the silver cup, in the sack's mouth of the youngest, and his corn money. And he did according to the word that Joseph had spoken.

3 As soon as the morning was light, the men were sent away, they and their asses.

4 *And* when they were gone out of the city, *and* not *yet* far off, Joseph said unto his steward, Up, follow after the men; and when thou dost overtake them, say unto them, Wherefore have ye rewarded evil for good?

5 *Is* not this *it* in which my lord drinketh, and whereby indeed he divineth? ye have done evil in so doing.

6 And he overtook them, and he spake unto them these same words.

7 And they said unto him, Wherefore saith my lord these words? God forbid that thy servants should do according to this thing:

8 Behold, the money, which we found in our sacks' mouths, we brought again unto thee out of the land of Canaan: how then should we steal out of thy lord's house silver or gold?

9 With whomsoever of thy servants it

44:1-6. Put every man's money in his sack's mouth. "The purpose of this feature, not subsequently mentioned again, was probably to enflame the brothers' smouldering sense that God was mysteriously dealing with them for their great sin, summoning to repentance (cf. 42:28; 43:23). It would also lend plausibility to a punishment based on communal responsibility, so making Joseph's insistence on isolating Benjamin for punishment more arresting" (Kline, p. 110). Joseph sent his brothers home with the money and with his **silver cup** in Benjamin's sack. He then had his servant pursue them, open the sacks, and require them to return to explain the matter. There was a sacred character attributed to the cup, for he called it a divining cup (cf. vss. 5, 15). This theft may have been punishable by death (cf. 31:32). Divining was fundamentally alien to Israel; God revealed His will explicitly (cf. Num 23:23). Joseph would certainly not have used these means, but he was playing a role and testing his brothers. He wanted to see if they would seize this opportunity to get rid of Benjamin. Would they stand with him? Had their hearts been changed?

7-17. Both let him die, and we also will be my Lord's bondmen indicates the penalty for the crime (cf. 31:32), and their statement would certainly put the pressure upon them. Again, notice the uniqueness of the search as it progressed from the oldest to the youngest, climaxing with Benjamin. **God hath found out the iniquity of thy servants** no doubt has a double meaning. In this instance they were guilty, but also they were convinced that God was judging them for their treatment of Joseph long ago (vs. 16; cf. 42:21-22, 28). Joseph's vague reference to the supernatural by referring to divining may have

be found, both let him die, and we also will be my lord's bondmen.

10 And he said, Now also *let* it *be* according unto your words: he with whom it is found shall be my servant; and ye shall be blameless.

11 Then they speedily took down every man his sack to the ground, and opened every man his sack.

12 And he searched, *and* began at the eldest, and left at the youngest: and the cup was found in Benjamin's sack.

13 Then they rent their clothes, and laded every man his ass, and returned to the city.

14 And Jūdah and his brethren came to Joseph's house; for he *was* yet there: and they fell before him on the ground.

15 And Joseph said unto them, What deed *is* this that ye have done? wot ye not that such a man as I can certainly divine?

16 And Jūdah said, What shall we say unto my lord? what shall we speak? or how shall we clear ourselves? God hath found out the iniquity of thy servants: behold, we *are* my lord's servants, both we, and *he* also with whom the cup is found.

17 And he said, God forbid that I should do so: *but* the man in whose hand the cup is found, he shall be my servant; and as for you, get you up in peace unto your father.

18 ¶Then Jūdah came near unto him, and said, Oh my lord, let thy servant, I pray thee, speak a word in my lord's ears, and let not thine anger burn against thy servant: for thou *art* even as Pharaoh.

19 My lord asked his servants, saying, Have ye a father, or a brother?

20 And we said unto my lord, We have a father, an old man, and a child of his old age, a little one; and his brother is dead, and he alone is left of his mother, and his father loveth him.

21 And thou saidst unto thy servants, Bring him down unto me, that I may set mine eyes upon him.

22 And we said unto my lord, The lad cannot leave his father: for *if* he should leave his father, *his father* would die.

23 And thou saidst unto thy servants, Except your youngest brother come down with you, ye shall see my face no more.

24 And it came to pass when we came up unto thy servant my father, we told him the words of my lord.

25 And our father said, Go again, *and* buy us a little food.

26 And we said, We cannot go down: if our youngest brother be with us, then will we go down: for we may not see the man's face, except our youngest brother *be* with us.

27 And thy servant my father said unto us, Ye know that my wife bare me two *sons:*

28 And the one went out from me, and I said, Surely he is torn in pieces; and I saw him not since:

29 And if ye take this also from me, and mischief befall him, ye shall bring down my gray hairs with sorrow to the grave.

30 Now therefore when I come to thy

alerted them to an omniscient God. Finally, Joseph increased the pressure by allowing them to return to Jacob without Benjamin, ironically telling them to do so in peace.

18-34. Then Judah came near and voiced his plea to Joseph, which was far different to the plea in 37:26-27. "It is possible that Joseph's schemes had been intended to probe his brothers' attitude toward each other and toward their father. He also wanted to test the sincerity of their repentance. Were they willing to break the heart of Jacob again as they had many years ago when they showed him Joseph's bloodstained robe?" (Davis, p. 282). Judah's statement, **let thy servant abide instead of the lad,** indicated that God had changed the hearts of the brothers. His plea reminds one of the servant born to this tribe, the Servant who offered Himself for the transgressions of His people.

servant my father, and the lad *be* not with us; seeing that his life is bound up in the lad's life;

31 It shall come to pass, when he seeth that the lad *is* not *with us*, that he will die: and thy servants shall bring down the gray hairs of thy servant our father with sorrow to the grave.

32 For thy servant became surety for the lad unto my father, saying, If I bring him not unto thee, then I shall bear the blame to my father for ever.

33 Now therefore, I pray thee, let thy servant abide instead of the lad a bondman to my lord; and let the lad go up with his brethren.

34 For how shall I go up to my father, and the lad *be* not with me? lest peradventure I see the evil that shall come on my father.

CHAPTER 45

THEN Joseph could not refrain himself before all them that stood by him; and he cried, Cause every man to go out from me. And there stood no man with him, while Joseph made himself known unto his brethren.

2 And he wept aloud: and the Egyptians and the house of Pharaoh heard.

3 And Joseph said unto his brethren, I *am* Joseph; doth my father yet live? And his brethren could not answer him; for they were troubled at his presence.

4 And Joseph said unto his brethren, Come near to me, I pray you. And they came near. And he said, I *am* Joseph your brother, whom ye sold into Egypt.

5 Now therefore be not grieved, nor angry with yourselves, that ye sold me hither: for God did send me before you to preserve life.

6 For these two years *hath* the famine *been* in the land: and yet *there are* five years, in the which *there shall* neither *be* earing nor harvest.

7 And God sent me before you to preserve you a posterity in the earth, and to save your lives by a great deliverance.

8 So now *it was* not you *that* sent me hither, but God: and he hath made me a father to Pharaoh, and lord of all his house, and a ruler throughout all the land of Egypt.

9 Haste ye, and go up to my father, and say unto him, Thus saith thy son Joseph, God hath made me lord of all Egypt: come down unto me, tarry not:

10 And thou shalt dwell in the land of Goshen, and thou shalt be near unto me, thou, and thy children, and thy children's children, and thy flocks, and thy herds, and all that thou hast:

11 And there will I nourish thee; for yet *there are* five years of famine; lest thou, and thy household, and all that thou hast, come to poverty.

12 And, behold, your eyes see, and the eyes of my brother Benjamin, that *it is* my mouth that speaketh unto you.

13 And ye shall tell my father of all my glory in Egypt, and of all that ye have seen; and ye shall haste and bring down my father hither.

14 And he fell upon his brother Ben-

45:1. This chapter, when Joseph makes himself known to his brothers, is the climax to the story.

2-28. But **his brethren could not answer him; for they were troubled at his presence.** In spite of many assurances, this uneasiness persisted for many years (cf. 50:15). He told them again, **I am Joseph your brother, whom ye sold into Egypt.** But rather than being bitter or resentful, Joseph recognized the sovereignty of God. His brothers had been agents in getting Joseph to Egypt, but God prepared the way: **Now therefore be not grieved, nor angry with yourselves, that ye sold me hither: for God did send me before you to preserve life.** Notice: **God sent me before you to preserve you a posterity in the earth, and to save your lives by a great deliverance** (vs. 7); **And there will I nourish thee** (vs. 11).

"Joseph's intent was not to deny his brothers' guilty responsibility (his whole strategy had aimed at stirring their consciences). But now that a godly sorrow gripped them, Joseph would turn them from remorseful backward looks to thankful appropriation of the future God's mercy had provided (vs. 8ff.)" (Kline, p. 110).

Father to Pharaoh is an expression applied to Egyptian viziers as far back as the third millennium B.C. (Speiser, p. 339). The **land of Goshen** was an Egyptian region (47:6, 27) in the eastern delta area (47:11) and was not far from the court at Memphis (vs. 10). It was in the area around the Wadi Tumilat, a valley that extended for about forty miles. It was highly suitable for cattle (47:4-6), but hated by the Egyptians (46:34); and thus, it provided good seclusion. This isolation would provide for Israel's distinctive cultural preservation under conditions favorable to their growth and unity. God's wonderful care for His people was even extended to the fact **it pleased Pharaoh well** when he heard the news; and he said, **I will give you the good of the land of Egypt, and ye shall eat the fat of the land** (vs. 18).

Joseph admonished his brothers, **See that ye fall not out by the way** (lit., do not quarrel in the way). This was a very realistic word of counsel; for now their hidden sin and crime was bound to come to light before their father, and they could very well end up accusing one another (cf. 42:22 and Reuben's accusations). This would certainly not be an easy task. **I will go** marked the decision by Israel, which shaped the destiny of the nation Israel. The nation "was destined to emerge in a land not theirs, their return to Canaan requiring God's mighty acts in Exodus and conquest that stamped on Israel's possession of the kingdom the character of a sovereign grant from a divine Saviour" (Kline, p. 111).

jamin's neck, and wept; and Benjamin wept upon his neck.

15 Moreover he kissed all his brethren, and wept upon them: and after that his brethren talked with him.

16 ¶And the fame thereof was heard in Pharaoh's house, saying, Joseph's brethren are come: and it pleased Pharaoh well, and his servants.

17 And Pharaoh said unto Joseph, Say unto thy brethren, This do ye; lade your beasts, and go, get you unto the land of Canaan;

18 And take your father and your households, and come unto me: and I will give you the good of the land of Egypt, and ye shall eat the fat of the land.

19 Now thou art commanded, this do ye; take you wagons out of the land of Egypt for your little ones, and for your wives, and bring your father, and come.

20 Also regard not your stuff; for the good of all the land of Egypt is yours.

21 And the children of Israel did so: and Joseph gave them wagons, according to the commandment of Pharaoh, and gave them provision for the way.

22 To all of them he gave each man changes of raiment; but to Benjamin he gave three hundred pieces of silver, and five changes of raiment.

23 And to his father he sent after this manner; ten asses laden with the good things of Egypt, and ten she asses laden with corn and bread and meat for his father by the way.

24 So he sent his brethren away, and they departed: and he said unto them, See that ye fall not out by the way.

25 And they went up out of Egypt, and came into the land of Canaan unto Jacob their father,

26 And told him, saying, Joseph is yet alive, and he is governor over all the land of Egypt. And Jacob's heart fainted, for he believed them not.

27 And they told him all the words of Joseph, which he had said unto them: and when he saw the wagons which Joseph had sent to carry him, the spirit of Jacob their father revived:

28 And Israel said, It is enough; Joseph my son is yet alive: I will go and see him before I die.

CHAPTER 46

AND Israel took his journey with all that he had, and came to Be'er-she'ba, and offered sacrifices unto the God of his father Isaac.

2 And God spake unto Israel in the visions of the night, and said, Jacob, Jacob. And he said, Here am I.

3 And he said, I am God, the God of thy father: fear not to go down into Egypt; for I will there make of thee a great nation:

4 I will go down with thee into Egypt; and I will also surely bring thee up again: and Joseph shall put his hand upon thine eyes.

5 And Jacob rose up from Be'er-she'ba: and the sons of Israel carried Jacob their father, and their

7. Joseph's reunion with his family. 46:1-34.

46:1-7. It may have been that Jacob lived at Hebron a number of years before he journeyed to Egypt (cf. 35:27; 37:14). He stopped at Beer-sheba, and offered sacrifices unto the God of his father Isaac. Both Abraham (21:33) and Isaac (26:25) had erected altars here, and this may have been his motivation for offering sacrifices. Abraham had had a bad experience in Egypt (12:10-20); and Isaac had been forbidden even to go there (26:2), which must have caused Jacob some real anxiety. But God assured Jacob that he need fear not to go down into Egypt; for I will there make of thee a great nation (cf. 15:13ff.; Ps 105:17, 23). The Lord promised to be with Jacob and also surely bring thee up again. One additional fact was that Jacob would die in Egypt as Joseph shall put his hand upon thine eyes, contrasted to the troubled end he had predicted for himself (37:35). Thus, bring thee up again refers to the nation of Israel, not Jacob.

107

little ones, and their wives, in the wagons which Pharaoh had sent to carry him.

6 And they took their cattle, and their goods, which they had gotten in the land of Canaan, and came into Egypt, Jacob, and all his seed with him:

7 His sons, and his sons' sons with him, his daughters, and his sons' daughters, and all his seed brought he with him into Egypt.

8 ¶And these *are* the names of the children of Israel, which came into Egypt, Jacob and his sons: Reuben, Jacob's firstborn.

9 And the sons of Reuben; Hā'nŏch, and Phăl'lū, and Hĕz'ron, and Cär'mī.

10 And the sons of Simeon; Jĕ-mu'el, and Jā'mĭn, and Ō'hăd, and Jā'chin, and Zō'här, and Shā'ul the son of a Canaanitish woman.

11 And the sons of Levi; Ger'shon, Kō'hăth, and Me-râ'rī.

12 And the sons of Judah; Er, and Ō'nan, and Shē'lah, and Phâ'rĕz, and Zâ'rah: but Er and Ō'nan died in the land of Canaan. And the sons of Phâ'rĕz were Hĕz'ron and Hā'mul.

13 And the sons of Ĭs'sa-char; Tō'la, and Phŭ'vah, and Job, and Shĭm'rŏn.

14 And the sons of Zĕb'u-lun; Se'rĕd, and Ē'lŏn, and Jäh'le-el.

15 These *be* the sons of Leah, which she bare unto Jacob in Pă'dan-â'ram, with his daughter Dinah: all the souls of his sons and his daughters *were* thirty and three.

16 And the sons of Gad; Zĭph'ĭ-on, and Hăg'gī, Shū'nī, and Ĕz'bŏn, E'rī, and Ăr'o-dī, and A-rē'lī.

17 And the sons of Asher; Jĭm'nah, and Ĭsh'ū-ah, and Ĭs'ū-ī, and Be-rī'ah, and Se'rah their sister: and the sons of Be-rī'ah; Hē'ber, and Măl'chī-el.

18 These *are* the sons of Zĭl'pah, whom Lāban gave to Leah his daughter, and these she bare unto Jacob, *even* sixteen souls.

19 The sons of Rāchel Jacob's wife; Joseph, and Benjamin.

20 And unto Joseph in the land of Egypt were born Ma-năs'seh and Ē'phra-im, which Ăs'e-năth the daughter of Po-tĭph'e-rah priest of On bare unto him.

21 And the sons of Benjamin *were* Bē'lah, and Bē'cher, and Ăsh'bĕl, Ge'ra, and Nā'a-man, Ē'hī, and Rosh, Mŭp'pĭm, and Hŭp'pĭm, and Ard.

22 These *are* the sons of Rāchel, which were born to Jacob: all the souls *were* fourteen.

23 And the sons of Dan; Hu'shĭm.

24 And the sons of Năph'ta-lī; Jäh'ze-el, and Gū'nī, and Jē'zer, and Shĭl'lem.

25 These *are* the sons of Bĭl'hah, which Lāban gave unto Rāchel his daughter, and she bare these unto Jacob: all the souls *were* seven.

26 All the souls that came with Jacob into Egypt, which came out of his loins, besides Jacob's sons' wives, all the souls *were* threescore and six;

27 And the sons of Joseph, which were born him in Egypt, *were* two souls: all the souls of the house of Jacob, which came into Egypt, *were* threescore and ten.

8-27. The register in verses 8-27 includes essentially those who went down to Egypt at this particular time. Simeon and Joseph and his sons are listed, and they were already there. The phrase **the children of Israel** appears for the first time in reference to the family as a whole. The descendants of Leah and her handmaid, Zilpah, are cited before those of Rachel and Bilhah. Verse 15 totaled the progeny of Leah as thirty-three. This number either included Jacob and Dinah and excluded Er and Onan (who had died in Canaan) or vice versa. The former is most likely. "According to verse 22 Rachel's progeny totaled fourteen, two sons and twelve grandsons. Bilhah's totaled seven, two sons and five grandsons (vs. 25). The grand total was sixty-six (vs. 26), to which Moses added Jacob, Joseph, and Joseph's two sons to make seventy. This agrees with Deuteronomy 10:22 and the Hebrew text of Exodus 1:5. Exodus 1:5 in the Septuagint, however, reads seventy-five, which Stephen apparently quoted in his sermon (Acts 7:14) and which the Dead Sea Scrolls support. The number seventy-five probably includes five later descendants of Joseph" (Davis, p. 288).

28 ¶And he sent Judah before him unto Joseph, to direct his face unto Goshen; and they came into the land of Goshen.

29 And Joseph made ready his chariot, and went up to meet Israel his father, to Goshen, and presented himself unto him; and he fell on his neck, and wept on his neck a good while.

30 And Israel said unto Joseph, Now let me die, since I have seen thy face, because thou *art* yet alive.

31 And Joseph said unto his brethren, and unto his father's house, I will go up, and shew Pharaoh, and say unto him, My brethren, and my father's house, which *were* in the land of Canaan, are come unto me;

32 And the men *are* shepherds, for their trade hath been to feed cattle; and they have brought their flocks, and their herds, and all that they have.

33 And it shall come to pass, when Pharaoh shall call you, and shall say, What *is* your occupation?

34 That ye shall say, Thy servants' trade hath been about cattle from our youth even until now, both we, *and* also our fathers: that ye may dwell in the land of Goshen; for every shepherd *is* an abomination unto the Egyptians.

CHAPTER 47

THEN Joseph came and told Pharaoh, and said, My father and my brethren, and their flocks, and their herds, and all that they have, are come out of the land of Canaan; and, behold, they *are* in the land of Goshen.

2 And he took some of his brethren, *even* five men, and presented them unto Pharaoh.

3 And Pharaoh said unto his brethren, What *is* your occupation? And they said unto Pharaoh, Thy servants *are* shepherds, both we, *and* also our fathers.

4 They said moreover unto Pharaoh, For to sojourn in the land are we come; for thy servants have no pasture for their flocks; for the famine *is* sore in the land of Canaan: now therefore, we pray thee, let thy servants dwell in the land of Goshen.

5 And Pharaoh spake unto Joseph, saying, Thy father and thy brethren are come unto thee:

6 The land of Egypt *is* before thee; in the best of the land make thy father and brethren to dwell; in the land of Goshen let them dwell: and if thou knowest *any* men of activity among them, then make them rulers over my cattle.

7 And Joseph brought in Jacob his father, and set him before Pharaoh: and Jacob blessed Pharaoh.

8 And Pharaoh said unto Jacob, How old *art* thou?

9 And Jacob said unto Pharaoh, The days of the years of my pilgrimage *are* an hundred and thirty years: few and evil have the days of the years of my life been, and have not attained unto the days of the years of the life of my fathers in the days of their pilgrimage.

10 And Jacob blessed Pharaoh, and went out from before Pharaoh.

28-34. When Jacob and Joseph were reunited, Jacob said **now let me die.** He was not expressing the desire to die, but rather that seeing Joseph with his own eyes and knowing that he was well completely satisfied Jacob; nothing else remained as a desire. Joseph prepared his family to emphasize to Pharaoh that **Thy servants' trade hath been about cattle from our youth,** for **every shepherd is an abomination unto the Egyptians.** This also indicates that it was a native Egyptian that Joseph served, for the Hyksos would not have cared for Egyptian customs. Joseph was only trying to put his family into the best light as they came before Pharaoh; there was no deception involved.

8. *Joseph's family in Egypt. 47:1-31.*

47:1-7. Joseph's wise advice in 46:33ff. enabled his brothers to express their desires before Pharaoh and to receive exactly what they wanted. Evidently, Jacob was not intimidated by Pharaoh; and he **blessed Pharaoh** in verses 7 and 10. This is amazing in the light of Hebrews 7:7.

8-10. Jacob was 130 years old when he appeared before Pharaoh (vs. 9) and 147 when he died (vs. 28). Abraham lived until he was 175 and Isaac was 180 years old when he died. Jacob said his days were **few and evil. Evil** did not indicate sinful, but calamitous, constantly confronted by anger, anguish, distress, and tribulation.

11 ¶And Joseph placed his father and his brethren, and gave them a possession in the land of Egypt, in the best of the land, in the land of Răm′e-sēś, as Pharaoh had commanded.

12 And Joseph nourished his father, and his brethren, and all his father's household, with bread, according to *their* families.

13 ¶And *there was* no bread in all the land; for the famine *was* very sore, so that the land of Egypt and *all* the land of Canaan fainted by reason of the famine.

14 And Joseph gathered up all the money that was found in the land of Egypt, and in the land of Canaan, for the corn which they bought: and Joseph brought the money into Pharaoh's house.

15 And when money failed in the land of Egypt, and in the land of Canaan, all the Egyptians came unto Joseph, and said, Give us bread: for why should we die in thy presence? for the money faileth.

16 And Joseph said, Give your cattle; and I will give you for your cattle, if money fail.

17 And they brought their cattle unto Joseph: and Joseph gave them bread *in exchange* for horses, and for the flocks, and for the cattle of the herds, and for the asses: and he fed them with bread for all their cattle for that year.

18 When that year was ended, they came unto him the second year, and said unto him, We will not hide *it* from my lord, how that our money is spent; my lord also hath our herds of cattle; there is not ought left in the sight of my lord, but our bodies, and our lands:

19 Wherefore shall we die before thine eyes, both we and our land? buy us and our land for bread, and we and our land will be servants unto Pharaoh: and give *us* seed, that we may live, and not die, that the land be not desolate.

20 And Joseph bought all the land of Egypt for Pharaoh; for the Egyptians sold every man his field, because the famine prevailed over them: so the land became Pharaoh's.

21 And as for the people, he removed them to cities from *one* end of the borders of Egypt even to the *other* end thereof.

22 Only the land of the priests bought he not; for the priests had a portion *assigned them* of Pharaoh, and did eat their portion which Pharaoh gave them: wherefore they sold not their lands.

23 Then Joseph said unto the people, Behold, I have bought you this day and your land for Pharaoh: lo, *here is* seed for you, and ye shall sow the land.

24 And it shall come to pass in the increase, that ye shall give the fifth *part* unto Pharaoh, and four parts shall be your own, for seed of the field, and for your food, and for them of your households, and for food for your little ones.

25 And they said, Thou hast saved our lives: let us find grace in the sight of my lord, and we will be Pharaoh's servants.

26 And Joseph made it a law over the

11-26. They were to settle in **the land of Rameses.** This has been a problem for interpreters, for the first Rameseside dynasty did not reign until around 1319 B.C. Thus, this expression has been viewed as either an anachronism or a modernization of an older place-name by a later scribe. Harris writes: "Jacob's settlement in Egypt would be before King Rameses on anybody's chronology, and at that time he says he put them in the land of Rameses. Possibly the famous King Rameses chose his name from the land Rameses. Or there could have been another King Rameses. It is also possible that Genesis 47:11 is an anachronism. It may be that some later scribe, finding here a name that nobody knew any more and being very much concerned to have a Bible that even the high school student could understand, inserted this new form of the name. This city of Ra-amses was earlier known as Tanis and, before that, Avaris. It is not impossible that the name Rameses was a name brought up to date in Genesis 47:11" (*Problem Periods in Old Testament History*, p. 11). Davis notes that the contention of many that the name Rameses did not occur earlier than the Nineteenth Dynasty has been refuted. The name clearly is referred to in a burial painting from the reign of Amenhotep III, who was part of the Eighteenth Dynasty. This would precede the reign of Rameses I by at least sixty years. This chapter includes the account of Joseph's severe economic policies that caused the people to sell their **land** to the government. As the famine grew more severe and the people ran out of money, he permitted them to exchange grain for their animals and, at a later stage, their property. It was not very long until Pharaoh owned all the land, except that of the priests (vs. 22). The people still tilled it and kept four-fifths of its produce (vss. 23-24).

land of Egypt unto this day, *that* Pharaoh should have the fifth *part;* except the land of the priests only, *which* became not Pharaoh's.

27 ¶And Israel dwelt in the land of Egypt, in the country of Goshen; and they had possessions therein, and grew, and multiplied exceedingly.

28 And Jacob lived in the land of Egypt seventeen years: so the whole age of Jacob was an hundred forty and seven years.

29 And the time drew nigh that Israel must die: and he called his son Joseph, and said unto him, If now I have found grace in thy sight, put, I pray thee, thy hand under my thigh, and deal kindly and truly with me; bury me not, I pray thee, in Egypt:

30 But I will lie with my fathers, and thou shalt carry me out of Egypt, and bury me in their buryingplace. And he said, I will do as thou hast said.

31 And he said, Swear unto me. And he sware unto him. And Israel bowed himself upon the bed's head.

CHAPTER 48

AND it came to pass after these things, that *one* told Joseph, Behold, thy father *is* sick: and he took with him his two sons, Ma-năs′seh and E′phra-im.

2 And *one* told Jacob, and said, Behold, thy son Joseph cometh unto thee: and Israel strengthened himself, and sat upon the bed.

3 And Jacob said unto Joseph, God Almighty appeared unto me at Luz in the land of Canaan, and blessed me,

4 And said unto me, Behold, I will make thee fruitful, and multiply thee, and I will make of thee a multitude of people; and will give this land to thy seed after thee *for* an everlasting possession.

5 And now thy two sons, E′phra-im and Ma-năs′seh, which were born unto thee in the land of Egypt before I came unto thee into Egypt, *are* mine; as Reuben and Simeon, they shall be mine.

6 And thy issue, which thou begettest after them, shall be thine, *and* shall be called after the name of their brethren in their inheritance.

7 And as for me, when I came from Pă′dan, Răchel died by me in the land of Canaan in the way, when yet *there was* but a little way to come unto Ĕph′rath: and I buried her there in the way of Ĕph′rath; the same *is* Bĕth–lehĕm.

8 And Israel beheld Joseph's sons, and said, Who *are* these?

9 And Joseph said unto his father, They *are* my sons, whom God hath given me in this *place.* And he said, Bring them, I pray thee, unto me, and I will bless them.

10 Now the eyes of Israel were dim

27-29. Deal kindly and truly is an expression that includes the word *chesed,* rendered **kindly.** Jacob appeals to Joseph that if he has found **grace** in his sight, if for some reason he has a unique relationship with Joseph (and he certainly does), then may Joseph be faithful to him and demonstrate it by carrying him **out of Egypt, and bury me in their burying place.** The fact that Joseph put his **hand under my thigh** (referring to Jacob's) was the indication that they entered into an oath, which would require faithfulness to the promises (cf. 24:2-4). Jacob realized that the sojourn in Egypt was temporary and that God would redeem them and return them to the Promised Land.

30-31. "According to verse 31, Israel (Jacob) bowed himself upon the head of his *mtth,* a word which is pointed *mittā* (bed) in the traditional Hebrew text and *matteh* (staff) in the Septuagint. The latter, which is followed by Hebrews 11:21, would be as appropriate as the former since the aged and infirm Jacob could have been leaning on a staff while talking to Joseph. Both versions however, use bed in 48:2" (Davis, p. 292). Speiser is of the opinion that both translations are unacceptable as "in all probability from taking the Heb. stem too literally. The term 'to bow low' need not signify here anything more than a gesture of mute appreciation on the part of a bedridden man on the point of death. The bow or nod would come naturally from the head of the bed" (p. 357).

9. The blessings of Joseph's sons. 48:1-22.

48:1-14. It was this act of Jacob's, out of all the others, that the writer of Hebrews selected as an act of faith (Heb 11:21). "One need not search intensively to discover why. The whole narrative gives unequivocal evidence of Jacob's clear faith in God's covenant promises and his sensitivity to the leadership of the Holy Spirit" (Davis, p. 293). There is a gentle irony in the fact that it was just such an occasion as this one in which Jacob had exercised his guile in his youth (ch. 27). Once more we have an example of the first-born's blessing being given to the younger brother; but in this instance there is no bitterness, resentment, or scheming (cf. Prov 10:22). **They shall be mine** has been taken as a form of adoption on the part of Jacob in relation to **Manasseh and Ephraim.** The purpose may have been to give an inheritance to someone who was not automatically qualified, even though the father already had heirs of his own. But the term **they shall be mine** may mean nothing more than that the grandfather welcomed the two latest additions into the clan of which he was the head. Or, it may mean that the passage was concerned simply with inheritance, as verse 6 indicates. In that case, Jacob was using his paternal authority to enable Joseph's sons to inherit directly from their grandfather, rather than Joseph (Selman, *Published and Unpublished Fifteenth Century B.C. Cuneiform Documents and Their Bearing on the Patriarchal Narratives,* p. 161).

for age, *so that* he could not see. And he brought them near unto him; and he kissed them, and embraced them.

11 And Israel said unto Joseph, I had not thought to see thy face: and, lo, God hath shewed me also thy seed.

12 And Joseph brought them out from between his knees, and he bowed himself with his face to the earth.

13 And Joseph took them both, Ē'phra-im in his right hand toward Israel's left hand, and Ma-nǎs'seh in his left hand toward Israel's right hand, and brought *them* near unto him.

14 And Israel stretched out his right hand, and laid *it* upon Ē'phra-im's head, who *was* the younger, and his left hand upon Ma-nǎs'seh's head, guiding his hands wittingly; for Ma-nǎs'seh *was* the firstborn.

15 ¶And he blessed Joseph, and said, God, before whom my fathers Abraham and Isaac did walk, the God which fed me all my life long unto this day,

16 The Angel which redeemed me from all evil, bless the lads; and let my name be named on them, and the name of my fathers Abraham and Isaac; and let them grow into a multitude in the midst of the earth.

17 And when Joseph saw that his father laid his right hand upon the head of Ē'phra-im, it displeased him: and he held up his father's hand, to remove it from Ē'phra-im's head unto Ma-nǎs'-seh's head.

18 And Joseph said unto his father, Not so, my father: for this *is* the firstborn; put thy right hand upon his head.

19 And his father refused, and said, I know *it*, my son, I know *it;* he also shall become a people, and he also shall be great: but truly his younger brother shall be greater than he, and his seed shall become a multitude of nations.

20 And he blessed them that day, saying, In thee shall Israel bless, saying, God make thee as Ē'phra-im and as Ma-nǎs'seh: and he set Ē'phra-im before Ma-nǎs'seh.

21 And Israel said unto Joseph, Behold, I die: but God shall be with you, and bring you again unto the land of your fathers.

22 Moreover I have given to thee one portion above thy brethren, which I took out of the hand of the Ämorīte with my sword and with my bow.

CHAPTER 49

AND Jacob called unto his sons, and said, Gather yourselves together, that I may tell you *that* which shall befall you in the last days.

15-22. When Jacob blessed Ephraim as the first-born in verse 18, he startled Joseph. Jacob assured Joseph that Manasseh would also be a great nation, and the blessing of Jacob on Ephraim became evident during the time of the judges. By this time it had increased in number and power so that it exercised leadership among the ten northern tribes. Later, the name Ephraim became equal to the name Israel (cf. Isa 7:2; Hos 4:17; 13:1).

The angel which redeemed me from all evil in verse 16 is a reference to Christ Himself pictured as redeeming (*gō'ēl*) him from all calamity (cf. 47:9). This is the first mention of the *gō'ēl* in the Bible, meaning to save or to be a saviour or deliverer (cf. Ex 6:6; Isa 59:20; both of which speak of God as redeeming His people). Leviticus 27:13 and Ruth 4:4 speak of human beings as redeeming property or certain rights of individuals.

The **one portion** in verse 22 is a problem for which Speiser says there is no plausible solution. The Hebrew word for **portion** is *shekem* (lit., shoulder or ridge); thus, some have translated it as mountain slope (cf. Kline and the RSV). But the word also stands for the city of Shechem, which is dominated by the mountain called Mount Gerizim. This area was to fall in Manasseh's territory at the center of the area covered by the two Joseph tribes (cf. Jn 4:5). But there is no record of any conquest of it by Jacob, Joseph, or later by Joshua. Perhaps the property owned by Jacob was taken away by the Amorites after he left the area (cf. 35:4-5), and then some time later he took it back by force. This is not a reference to chapter 34, because Jacob had no hand in the deed and he sharply rebuked his sons. It most likely is not a prophetic perfect, due to the emphatic I do give and the I give being a *perfectum praesens* (G.K. 106i) (Leupold, p. 1158).

10. Jacob's blessing of his sons. 49:1-33.

Apart from Joseph's dying oath in 50:25, this is the last of the great sayings of destiny, the blessings, the curses, the judgments, and the promises that fill the book of Genesis. Jacob concludes his life as other saints who spoke a blessing before their end did: Isaac (ch. 27), Moses (Deut 33), Joshua (Josh 24), and Samuel (I Sam 12). It contains a "rhythmical movement, a beautiful parallelism of members, a profusion of figures, a play upon the names of the sons, other instances of paronomasia, unusual modes of expression, a truly exalted spirit, as well as a heartfelt warmth" (Leupold, p. 1160).

49:1. In the last days introduces the whole prophecy and functions in an important way in the Old Testament. It "refers to Israel's future in dual perspective: the period of their occupation of Canaan, and the time of the coming of Messiah. Sometimes the expression refers to Israel at the end of the Tribulation period (Deut 4:30; Ezk 38:16), sometimes to the history of Gentile nations (Dan 2:28), and sometimes to the present church

2 Gather yourselves together, and hear, ye sons of Jacob; and hearken unto Israel your father.

3 ¶Reuben, thou *art* my firstborn, my might, and the beginning of my strength, the excellency of dignity, and the excellency of power:

4 Unstable as water, thou shalt not excel; because thou wentest up to thy father's bed; then defiledst thou *it:* he went up to my couch.

5 ¶Simeon and Levi *are* brethren; instruments of cruelty *are in* their habitations.

6 O my soul, come not thou into their secret; unto their assembly, mine honour, be not thou united: for in their anger they slew a man, and in their self-will they digged down a wall.

7 Cursed *be* their anger, for *it was* fierce; and their wrath, for it was cruel: I will divide them in Jacob, and scatter them in Israel.

8 ¶Judah, thou *art he* whom thy brethren shall praise: thy hand *shall be* in the neck of thine enemies; thy father's children shall bow down before thee.

9 Jūdah *is* a lion's whelp: from the prey, my son, thou art gone up: he stooped down, he couched as a lion, and as an old lion; who shall rouse him up?

10 The sceptre shall not depart from Jūdah, nor a lawgiver from between his feet, until Shīlōh come; and unto him *shall* the gathering of the people *be.*

11 Binding his foal unto the vine, and his ass's colt unto the choice vine; he washed his garments in wine, and his clothes in the blood of grapes:

12 His eyes *shall be* red with wine, and his teeth white with milk.

13 ¶Zĕb'u-lun shall dwell at the haven of the sea; and he *shall be* for an haven of ships; and his border *shall be* unto Zī'don.

14 ¶Ĭs'sa-char *is* a strong ass couching down between two burdens:

15 And he saw that rest *was* good, and the land that *it was* pleasant; and bowed his shoulder to bear, and became a servant unto tribute.

16 ¶Dan shall judge his people, as one of the tribes of Israel.

17 Dan shall be a serpent by the way, an adder in the path, that biteth the horse heels, so that his rider shall fall backward.

18 I have waited for thy salvation, O Lord.

19 ¶Gad, a troop shall overcome him: but he shall overcome at the last.

20 ¶Out of Asher his bread *shall be* fat, and he shall yield royal dainties.

21 ¶Năph'ta-lī *is* a hind let loose: he giveth goodly words.

22 ¶Joseph *is* a fruitful bough, *even* a fruitful bough by a well; *whose* branches run over the wall:

23 The archers have sorely grieved him, and shot *at him,* and hated him:

24 But his bow abode in strength, and the arms of his hands were made strong by the hands of the mighty *God*

age in its entirety (Heb 1:2) or at its conclusion (II Tim 3:1; Jas 5:3). Jacob's pronouncements in chapter 49 included both prophecy (vs. 1) and blessing (vs. 28)" (Ryrie, p. 86).

2-27. Reuben. Jacob's first-born was a cause both of rejoicing and heartache. He should have received both the birthright (which went to Judah) and the blessing (to Joseph), and he lost them both! His father called him **unstable as water. Unstable** literally means "a boiling over" of water, a vivid metaphor for unstable emotions (cf. Jud 9:4; Zeph 3:4, where the same root depicts pride and frivolity). History gives witness that Reuben never did influence the nation of Israel significantly after his fornication with Bilhah (35:22). No prophet, judge, or hero ever came from this tribe; and when Isaiah lamented for the land east of the Jordan in Isaiah 15, he only mentioned Moab. **Simeon and Levi** (vs. 5) are dealt with together in light of their treachery against the men of Shechem in chapter 34. They are condemned for their **cruelty . . . anger . . .** and **self-will** (vss. 5-6). Jacob's anger expressed at this point is "a moral judgment on a story told earlier without comment" (Kidner, p. 216). **And in their self-will they digged down a wall** is not a correct translation (see Leupold, Ryrie, Speiser, and Brown, Driver and Briggs, *Hebrew and English Lexicon of the Old Testament [BDB],* p. 785). It is, literally, "at their pleasure they lamed oxen." This is supplementary information to 34:27-29; what these two men did not lead away as plunder they destroyed in the fierceness of their anger. They were to be divided and scattered. When Simeon was numbered as a tribe in Numbers 26:14, they were the weakest; and when Moses blessed the tribes, he left them out in Deuteronomy 33:8. Levi received forty-eight cities that were scattered throughout the allotment of the other tribes (Josh 21:1-42). In Exodus 32:26 they were the only tribe that stood for what was right. Simeon was given an inheritance within the inheritance of Judah (Josh 19:1; I Chr 4:39-43). Both of these tribes will enter the messianic kingdom, according to Ezekiel 44 and Revelation 7. **Judah,** meaning "praise," was to be praised by his brothers and to become the leader among the tribes. He had been responsible for the sale of Joseph into slavery; and he had committed fornication against his daughter-in-law, Tamar. The phrase, his **hand shall be in the neck of thine enemies,** was literally fulfilled (Num 2:9; 10:14; Jud 1; 2); his prowess in warfare is a matter of record. The key thought is expressed as **The scepter shall not depart from Judah, nor a lawgiver from between his feet, until Shiloh come; and unto him shall the gathering of the people be. The scepter** was a symbol of royal power. The **lawgiver,** according to Speiser, is a reference to a mace; for etymologically, it is "something pertaining to a legislator or one in authority; and from the context, an analogue of the scepter. When the dignitary was seated, the staff would rest between his feet" (p. 365). Jacob was not saying his rule would end when **Shiloh** came; but on the contrary, "this term denotes the turning-point to which the superiority of Judah will continue, not then to cease, but at that time to be enlarged so as to embrace all the nations" (Bennetch, *The Prophecy of Jacob,* p. 424). **Shiloh** is a cryptic name for Messiah; it is made up of three grammatical parts (sh-l-ōh) meaning him to whom it (the scepter/kingdom) belongs. The *sh* is the relative pronoun, the *l* is the possessive, and the *ōh* is the pronominal suffix (cf. Ezk 21:27). Thus, it is not to be taken as a proper name for Messiah, nor does it refer to the town where the tabernacle was later established; for this would be meaningless prophetically. The phrase **and unto him shall the gathering of the people be** means, literally, "And unto him shall be the obedience of the peoples" (*BDB,* p. 429; Leupold; and ASV). This can only refer to the Messiah. Thus, the reference to a lion in the previous verse (vs. 9) points to that one who is called ". . . the Lion of the tribe of Judah" (Rev 5:5). Verses 11 and

of Jacob; (from thence *is* the shepherd, the stone of Israel:)

25 *Even* by the God of thy father, who shall help thee; and by the Almighty, who shall bless thee with blessings of heaven above, blessings of the deep that lieth under, blessings of the breasts, and of the womb:

26 The blessings of thy father have prevailed above the blessings of my progenitors unto the utmost bound of the everlasting hills: they shall be on the head of Joseph, and on the crown of the head of him that was separate from his brethren.

27 ¶Benjamin shall ravin *as* a wolf: in the morning he shall devour the prey, and at night he shall divide the spoil.

12 describe the millennial prosperity (cf. Isa 11:1-9; Ezk 34:23-31; Amos 9:11-15). **Zebulun shall dwell at the haven of the sea; and he shall be for a haven of ships; and his border shall be unto Zidon.** Literally, it says that Zebulun shall dwell toward the sea. It is clear from Joshua 19:10-16 that this tribe's border never reached the Mediterranean or directly touched Sidon; but she did have contact with sea merchants. It was separated from the Mediterranean by the tribe of Asher and from the Sea of Galilee by the tribe of Naphtali. There was a great caravan route from the east which passed through Zebulun (cf. Deut 33:18-19). **Issachar,** along with Zebulun, Simeon, and Levi, had the same mother. It was predicted that he would be limited to domestic responsibilities. The description of being a **strong ass couching down between two burdens** indicated that the tribe would be more agriculturally and materially minded than politically involved. They received the beautiful tableland of Jezreel, the territory of lower Galilee, which allowed them to produce an abundance of food. They were known as brave warriors and were committed soldiers (Jud 5:14-15, 18). Along with Zebulun, they were industrious by nature as the blessing of Moses makes clear in Deuteronomy 33. **Dan** was to **judge his people,** which according to Deuteronomy 33:7 refers to the whole nation. This was partially fulfilled when Samson judged for twenty years (Jud 16:31). The tribe was unable to conquer its territory; so six hundred families moved north to Laish and encouraged idolatry among the people (Jud 18:17). **Dan shall be a serpent by the way** alludes to their lack of moral commitment and spiritual stability. Dan finds no place among the tribes (Rev 7:4-8). There is little said about the tribe of **Gad,** but Jacob did indicate that it would be constantly attacked and harassed. It was vulnerable to attack because it settled east of the Jordan and needed strong warriors (I Chr 5:18; 12:8). But it was prophesied **he shall overcome at the last. Asher** was to receive the fertile and highly productive land in the lowlands of Carmel, west to the Mediterranean and north to the territory of Tyre (Josh 19:24-31). Moses referred to **Asher** in Deuteronomy 33:24 as the rich produce of the western Galilean hill country and the fact they would be given strength to secure Israel's northern border (Deut 33:25). **Naphtali** is described as **a hind let loose** and as expressing **goodly words.** They would be a free, mountain people; they would breed true and keep their character. Barak apparently came from Naphtali (Jud 4:6); and along with Zebulun, they were recognized for heroism in the great battle with the Canaanite general, Sisera (Jud 5:18). The blessing of **Joseph** was the most eloquent of all. It includes more than Judah's. Joseph is pictured as a **fruitful bough . . . by a well; whose branches run over the wall.** This pictures his depth of character and the breadth of his influence. Perhaps a play on words is intended as the root *parah* (fruitful) appears in **Ephraim** (the fruitful one). From his present glory (vs. 22), verses 23 and 24 give a biography of his past difficult life. But Joseph prevailed due to the **mighty God of Jacob** (lit., from the hands of the Strong One of Jacob). God is strong and is the source of all strength, and He will show Himself strong in behalf of His loved ones. By a second parallel statement Jacob traces back the strength Joseph will display as coming "from where the Shepherd, the Stone of Israel, is." God is pictured as a Shepherd and the Rock of Israel. Joshua, Deborah, and Samuel came from the tribe of Ephraim, and Gideon and Jephthah, from the tribe of Manasseh. Even though there is no reference to a tribe of Joseph, Ephraim and Manasseh, his sons, received an apportionment. Ephraim later became the leader of the northern tribes at the time of the division of the nation following Solomon's reign. **Benjamin** was compared to the **wolf** because of its warlike character as a tribe. Not only would they be successful in war, but they would be cruel (Jud 20-21) as they stood against the other tribes in defense

of their wickedness in Gibeah. They were distinguished as archers and slingers (Jud 20:16; I Chr 8:40; 12:2; II Chr 14:8; 17:17). The judge Ehud, King Saul, and Jonathan were of this tribe. The apostle Paul in the New Testament was also from the tribe of Benjamin.

28-33. I am to be gathered unto my people . . . and was gathered unto his people. Jacob requested that he be buried in the cave that Abraham had purchased from Ephron the Hittite (vss. 29-30), where Abraham, Sarah, Isaac, Rebekah, and Leah (vs. 31) were already buried. He was not only **gathered unto his people** in the cave of Machpelah, but it may be a reference reflecting Jacob's belief that his people, though dead, still exist (cf. vs. 29; 47:30 with vs. 33).

28 ¶All these *are* the twelve tribes of Israel: and this *is it* that their father spake unto them, and blessed them; every one according to his blessing he blessed them.

29 And he charged them, and said unto them, I am to be gathered unto my people: bury me with my fathers in the cave that *is* in the field of Ĕ′phrŏn the Hittite,

30 In the cave that *is* in the field of Măch-pē′läh, which *is* before Măm′re, in the land of Canaan, which Abraham bought with the field of Ĕ′phrŏn the Hittite for a possession of a burying-place.

31 There they buried Abraham and Sarah his wife; there they buried Isaac and Rebekah his wife; and there I buried Leah.

32 The purchase of the field and of the cave that *is* therein *was* from the children of Heth.

33 And when Jacob had made an end of commanding his sons, he gathered up his feet into the bed, and yielded up the ghost, and was gathered unto his people.

CHAPTER 50

AND Joseph fell upon his father's face, and wept upon him, and kissed him.

2 And Joseph commanded his servants the physicians to embalm his father: and the physicians embalmed Israel.

3 And forty days were fulfilled for him; for so are fulfilled the days of those which are embalmed: and the Egyptians mourned for him threescore and ten days.

4 And when the days of his mourning were past, Joseph spake unto the house of Pharaoh, saying, If now I have found grace in your eyes, speak, I pray you, in the ears of Pharaoh, saying,

5 My father made me swear, saying, Lo, I die: in my grave which I have digged for me in the land of Canaan, there shalt thou bury me. Now therefore let me go up, I pray thee, and bury my father, and I will come again.

6 And Pharaoh said, Go up, and bury thy father, according as he made thee swear.

7 ¶And Joseph went up to bury his father: and with him went up all the servants of Pharaoh, the elders of his house, and all the elders of the land of Egypt,

8 And all the house of Joseph, and his brethren, and his father's house: only their little ones, and their flocks, and their herds, they left in the land of Goshen.

9 And there went up with him both chariots and horsemen: and it was a very great company.

10 And they came to the threshing-floor of Ā′tăd, which *is* beyond Jordan, and there they mourned with a great and very sore lamentation: and he

11. Joseph's last days. 50:1-26.

50:1-13. Jacob died at the age of **a hundred forty and seven years** (47:28), and he was **embalmed. Joseph commanded his servants, the physicians** (*harōpe'īm*) to do the work. Since the physicians and the embalmers were two distinct professions, he may have employed the physicians so as to avoid the magic and mysticism of the embalmers and priests (Davis, p. 302; see also his work *Mummies, Men and Madness* for the process of mummification). The **threescore and ten days** of mourning accord with the traditional period for mummification and mourning. The various internal viscera were removed and placed in canopic jars of natron (a mixture of sodium carbonate and sodium bicarbonate), causing rapid dehydration and preventing decomposition of the body. Joseph left with a large company of servants, relatives, and mourners to take Jacob's body back to Canaan. Following a seven-day period of mourning at the threshing floor of **Atad** (named **Abel-mizraim** or mourning of Egypt due to the sorrow expressed by the Egyptians), which is east of the Jordan and north of the Dead Sea, the body was placed in the cave of Machpelah with the other patriarchs.

made a mourning for his father seven
days.
11 And when the inhabitants of the
land, the Canaanites, saw the mourning in the floor of Ā′tăd, they said, This
is a grievous mourning to the Egyptians: wherefore the name of it was
called Ā′bel–mĭz′rā-im, which *is* beyond
Jordan.
12 And his sons did unto him according as he commanded them:
13 For his sons carried him into the
land of Canaan, and buried him in the
cave of the field of Măch-pē′läh, which
Abraham bought with the field for a
possession of a burying place of
Ē′phrŏn the Hittite, before Măm′re.
14 And Joseph returned into Egypt,
he, and his brethren, and all that went
up with him to bury his father, after he
had buried his father.
15 ¶And when Joseph's brethren saw
that their father was dead, they said,
Joseph will peradventure hate us, and
will certainly requite us all the evil
which we did unto him.
16 And they sent a messenger unto
Joseph, saying, Thy father did command before he died, saying,
17 So shall ye say unto Joseph, Forgive, I pray thee now, the trespass of
thy brethren, and their sin; for they did
unto thee evil: and now, we pray thee,
forgive the trespass of the servants of
the God of thy father. And Joseph wept
when they spake unto him.
18 And his brethren also went and
fell down before his face; and they said,
Behold, we *be* thy servants.
19 And Joseph said unto them, Fear
not: for *am* I in the place of God?
20 But as for you, ye thought evil
against me; *but* God meant it unto
good, to bring to pass, as *it is* this day,
to save much people alive.
21 Now therefore fear ye not: I will
nourish you, and your little ones. And
he comforted them, and spake kindly
unto them.
22 ¶And Joseph dwelt in Egypt, he,
and his father's house: and Joseph
lived an hundred and ten years.
23 And Joseph saw Ē′phra-im's children of the third *generation:* the children also of Mā′chĭr the son of Ma-năs′-
seh were brought up upon Joseph's
knees.
24 And Joseph said unto his brethren,
I die: and God will surely visit you, and
bring you out of this land unto the land
which he sware to Abraham, to Isaac,
and to Jacob.
25 And Joseph took an oath of the
children of Israel, saying, God will surely visit you, and ye shall carry up my
bones from hence.
26 So Joseph died, *being* an hundred
and ten years old: and they embalmed
him, and he was put in a coffin in
Egypt.

14-26. Joseph's brothers now feared that he might retaliate
upon them for the evil they did to him earlier. Such was not to
be the case. They had underestimated the genuineness of
Joseph's character and affection. What they meant for **evil**, God
had intended for **good**. This is one of the clearest declarations of
divine providence anywhere in the Bible. "It serves as an important reminder that while the evil of men may appear to be to the
disadvantage of the saints, the purposes and plans of God will
ultimately prevail" (Davis, pp. 303-304).

Eventually, Joseph himself died at the age of 110 years after a
long and successful life. He was buried in Egypt, but made the
Israelites pledge with an **oath** that they would carry his **bones** to
the Promised Land when God visited them to **bring** them **out** of
Egypt (which they did, cf. Ex 13:19; Josh 24:32). Some speculate that the political scene was already beginning to change late
in his life and that it was no longer an easy matter to return to
Canaan. Like his father, he was embalmed and put in a **coffin**
(*'arōn*), which is the same word used for the ark of the covenant
in the Old Testament.

Joseph is included in the hall of fame of Hebrews 11 for his
faith in God's promises to return His people to Canaan. The
very fact that Jacob and Joseph were mummified makes it a
possibility that their bodies may be recovered someday.

Hence, the book of Genesis ends with a solemn reminder of
the curse of sin, which brings death to God's creation. It also
reminds us of our great need of redemption. Only God, the
Creator of life, can give life to His creatures. Only God can
remove the curse of sin and triumph over it through the blood
atonement of His Son, Jesus Christ. Here we are chained by the
curse of earth, but in heaven we have a new and living hope.
Because He lives, we too shall live!

BIBLIOGRAPHY

Barnhouse, D. G. *Genesis*. 2 vols. Grand Rapids: Zondervan, 1971.

Bush, G. *Notes on Genesis*. New York: Ivison, Phinney & Co., 1860.

Calvin, J. *A Commentary on Genesis*. London: Banner of Truth, 1965 reprint; Latin original, 1554.

*Candlish, R. S. *The Book of Genesis*. 2 vols. Edinburgh: Adam & Charles Black, 1868.

Cassuto, V. *A Commentary on the Book of Genesis*. 2 Parts, trans. Israel Abrahams. Jerusalem: The Magnes Press, 1964.

Davies, G. H. Genesis. In *Broadman Bible Commentary*. Nashville: Broadman Press, 1969.

*Davis, J. J. *Paradise to Prison: Studies in Genesis*. Grand Rapids: Baker, 1975.

*Delitzsch, F. *A New Commentary on Genesis*. 2 vols. Edinburgh: T. & T. Clark, 1888.

Hershon, P. I. *Genesis: With a Talmudic Commentary*. London: Samuel Bagster, 1883.

Kevan, E. F. Genesis. In *The New Bible Commentary*. Ed. by F. Davidson. Grand Rapids: Eerdmans, 1953.

Kidner, D. Genesis. In *Tyndale Old Testament Commentaries*. Chicago: InterVarsity Press, 1967.

Kline, Meredith. Genesis. In *The New Bible Commentary*, Revised. Grand Rapids: Eerdmans, 1970.

Lange, J. P. Genesis. In *A Commentary on the Holy Scriptures*. Ed. by J. P. Lange. Grand Rapids: Zondervan, n.d.

*Leupold, H. C. *Exposition of Genesis*. 2 vols. Columbus: Wartburg Press, 1942.

Luther, M. *Commentary on Genesis*. Grand Rapids: Zondervan, 1958.

*Morris, H. M. *The Genesis Record: A Scientific and Devotional Commentary*. Grand Rapids: Baker, 1976.

Murphy, J. B. *The Book of Genesis*. Boston: Estes & Lauriat, 1873.

Pieters, A. *Notes on Genesis*. Grand Rapids: Eerdmans, 1947.

Pink, A. W. *Gleanings in Genesis*. Chicago: Moody Press, 1952.

Schaeffer, F. A. *Genesis in Space and Time*. Downers Grove, Illinois: InterVarsity Press, 1972.

Speiser, E. A. Genesis. In *The Anchor Bible*. New York: Doubleday & Co., 1964.

Stigers, H. G. *A Commentary on Genesis*. Grand Rapids: Zondervan, 1976.

Von Rad, Gerhard. *Genesis*. Revised Ed. Philadelphia: The Westminster Press, 1971.

Whitelaw, T. Genesis. In *The Pulpit Commentary*. Ed. by H. Spence. New York: Funk & Wagnalls, 1888.

Wood, Leon J. *Genesis: A Study Guide*. Grand Rapids: Zondervan, 1975.

Yates, K. M. Genesis. In *The Wycliffe Bible Commentary*. Ed. by C. Pfeiffer and E. Harrison. Chicago: Moody Press, 1962.

EXODUS

INTRODUCTION

Title. In ancient Israel, according to prevalent Near Eastern practice, the title of a book was taken from its opening words; in the case of the second book of Moses they were *we'elleh shemoth*, "Now these are the names of," sometimes shortened simply to "Names." The book begins in verses 1-6 by listing the *names* of the twelve sons of Israel who went down into Egypt to stay a while during a severe famine (Gen 41-46). When Greek-speaking Jews translated this book from Hebrew into Greek (ca. 250 B.C.), they titled it *Exodos*, meaning literally "a way out." This describes the primary movement of chapters 1-14, which culminate in Israel crossing the Red Sea and thus escaping Egyptian bondage. The common designation since that time has been *Exodus* in Latin and later in English as well.

Authorship. Until the rationalism of liberal criticism surfaced in the eighteenth and nineteenth centuries, the almost universally accepted viewpoint throughout history had been that Moses wrote the book of Exodus, as well as the rest of the Pentateuch. Today, few (other than fundamentalist Christians) adhere to this belief, due in large part to the influence of rationalistic higher criticism at many theological institutions. Nevertheless, Exodus clearly states that Moses at various times was commanded to ". . . Write this for a memorial in a book . . ." (Ex 17:14), and ". . . Write thou these words . . ." (Ex 34:27). Exodus 24:4 records that ". . . Moses wrote all the words of the LORD . . . ," and verse 7 declares that ". . . he took the book of the covenant, and read in the audience of the people . . . ." The rest of the Pentateuch bears similar testimony in Numbers 33:1-2 and in Deuteronomy 31:9 and 11, and the remainder of the Old Testament reechoes this again and again (Josh 8:31-32; I Kgs 2:3; II Kgs 14:6 and 21:8; Ezr 6:18; Neh 13:1; Dan 9:11-13; and Mal 4:4). In the New Testament our Lord clearly stated that "Moses . . . wrote" (Jn 5:46-47), and in Mark 7:10 He cites Exodus 20:12 and 21:17 as being from Moses. In addition, Jesus referred to the burning bush incident as being found in ". . . the book of Moses . . ." (Mk 12:26).

The internal testimony of the book of Exodus itself also bears witness to a contemporary author, Moses. There are numerous eyewitness details, as noted carefully by such men as Archer, James, Rawlinson, and others. The text exhibits a thorough knowledge of Egypt and contains numerous words of pure Egyptian origin, as pointed out by F. Albright, Abraham Yahuda, and Gleason Archer (for references, see Archer, *A Survey of Old Testament Introduction*, pp. 102-105). Similarly, of the geographical, seasonal, and plant and animal references are to those types and varieties actively found in Egypt and the Sinai, rather than in Palestine itself (Ex 9:31-32; 25:5; 36:19). This points to an author with Moses' qualifications and life-experience. Furthermore, R. D. Wilson, in his classic *A Scientific Investigation of the Old Testament*, has numerous arguments which support Mosaic authorship based on careful analysis of matters involving text, grammar, and vocabulary. Dr. Wilson was the foremost biblical scholar of his day, being acquainted with more than forty ancient and modern languages. Even though the liberal views of Wellhausian criticism have been answered thoroughly in the past by William H. Green, *The Higher Criticism of the Pentateuch* (1895), Oswald T. Allis, *The Five Books of Moses* (1943), and others, most writers, teachers, seminaries, etc., still cling to forms of this theory and its more advanced counterpart, form criticism. These include such scholarly writers on Exodus as Cassuto, Childs, Clements, Hyatt, Noth, and Rylaarsdam. They all deny that Moses produced the book of Exodus in the fifteenth century B.C. and instead maintain that no formal code of law by Israel existed until many centuries later. This denies what is meant by verbal, plenary inspiration, the inerrancy of the Word of God, the genuineness, authenticity and integrity of the various books, and the truthfulness and trustworthiness of Christ, the apostles and others through the centuries who believed Moses penned Exodus and the Pentateuch.

Date and Place of Writing. From the foregoing remarks it remains to be concluded that Exodus was written by Moses during the wilderness wanderings between the Exodus from Egypt itself and the conquest of Canaan forty years later. The events of the book of Exodus do not go beyond the year spent at Mount Sinai for the construction and erection of the tabernacle, and so it could have been written during that time at Mount Sinai or shortly thereafter. When did the Exodus occur? This is easily ascertained by reading I Kings 6:1. It states that Solomon began to construct the Temple four hundred eighty years after Israel had exited Egypt. The dates given for Solomon's temple construction are variously given as between 1012 B.C. (Ussher) and 958 B.C. (Albright); and most conservative Bible scholars would concur with a date of somewhere near 965 B.C. (Unger gives 961 B.C. and Payne cites 966 B.C.). This would place the date of the Exodus at about 1445 B.C. during the reign of Amenhotep II, who ruled Egypt from approximately 1450 to 1424 B.C. His father, Thutmose III, ruled for fifty-four years prior to ca. 1450, which means that Thutmose III was ruling when Moses killed the Egyptian and was sought to be slain by Pharaoh, as Exodus 2:15 records. This is in accord with Exodus 4:19 which quotes God as saying to Moses ". . . all the men are dead which sought thy life." Thutmose III would have died only recently, having ruled practically the entire forty years Moses spent in the wilderness of Midian. For detailed arguments on the actual date of the Exodus see the remarks on Exodus 12:40-41.

Theme and Purpose. The purpose of the book of Exodus is to continue the record of God's dealings with His people Israel. It is a continuation of the story begun in Genesis. Exodus traces the events from the time Israel entered Egypt as a small group of royally treated guests until they were eventually delivered from the cruel bondage of slavery into which they had been brought by ". . . a new king . . . which knew not Joseph" (Ex 1:8). That is the theme of redemption, or salvation, and is expressed in both the Passover and in the crossing of the Red Sea (Ex 14:13). Other major themes are the making of a covenant between God and Israel (Ex 19:5-8), the accompanying laws which are part of the covenant (Ex 20-24), and the worship of God as expressed through the construction and use of the sacred tent of meeting with its furniture, sacrifices, and ceremonies.

OUTLINE

COMMENTARY

I. THE BONDAGE OF ISRAEL IN EGYPT. 1:1-22.

A. Israel's Past Entrance into Egypt. 1:1-6.

NOW these *are* the names of the children of Israel, which came into Egypt; every man and his household came with Jacob.

2 Reuben, Simeon, Levi, and Jūdah,
3 Is'sa-char, Zĕb'u-lun, and Benjamin,
4 Dan, and Năph'ta-lī, Gad, and Asher.

1:1. Now these are the names of the children of Israel, which came into Egypt. The book of Exodus begins with the very words of Genesis 46:8, where the history of the migration as originally recorded begins. Exodus simply goes back and recalls that initial coming into Egypt.

2-4. Reuben, Simeon, Levi, and Judah were the first four sons of Jacob. Their mother was Leah. Their births, as well as the meanings of their names, are recorded in Genesis 29:31-35. **Issachar** and **Zebulun** are listed next because they also were sons of Leah, though born ninth and tenth in the order of Jacob's twelve sons. **Benjamin** is mentioned after these because he was the son of Rachel, Jacob's favorite wife. **Dan and Naphtali,** the sons of Rachel's handmaid Bilhah, are placed next, followed by **Gad and Asher,** the sons of Zilphah, Leah's handmaid.

5 And all the souls that came out of the loins of Jacob were seventy souls: for Joseph was in Egypt *already*.
6 And Joseph died, and all his brethren, and all that generation.

5-6. Finally **Joseph** is mentioned, because of his prominence in the history and since the story would continue from the point of his relationship with the Pharaoh of Egypt.

B. Israel's Growth and Subsequent Enslavement. 1:7-14.

7 And the children of Israel were fruitful, and increased abundantly, and multiplied, and waxed exceeding mighty; and the land was filled with them.
8 ¶Now there arose up a new king over Egypt, which knew not Joseph.

7. The four words used to describe the numerical growth of the Israelite population indicate a far greater than mere natural multiplication. God's providential blessing was upon Israel's increase.

8. A new king over Egypt, which knew not Joseph. This indicates that the favorable conditions that once prevailed had been superseded by a period of uncertainty and reconsideration. It will be shown (see Ex 12:40-41) that Jacob and his family entered Egypt about 1885 B.C., during the time of the Middle Kingdom under the Twelfth Dynasty (2000-1780 B.C.). It was then that the capitals of that "powerful centralized government" were in Memphis and in the Fayyum, a fertile valley south of Cairo (Steindorff and Seele, *When Egypt Ruled the East,* p. 274). Later, when the government grew weaker and more unstable, Egypt was ruled by foreigners called the Hyksos, from about 1725-1546 B.C. When the Hyksos were expelled, there was a strong reaction against foreigners, including the rapidly growing Israelites. Moses was born about 1525 B.C., approximately twenty years after this changeover, and in the midst of the new "get-tough-with-the-slaves" policy.

9 And he said unto his people, Behold, the people of the children of Israel *are* more and mightier than we:
10 Come on, let us deal wisely with them; lest they multiply, and it come to pass, that, when there falleth out any war, they join also unto our enemies, and fight against us, and *so* get them up out of the land.
11 Therefore they did set over them taskmasters to afflict them with their burdens. And they built for Pharaoh treasure cities, Pī'thom and Rā-ăm'sēś.

9-10. The people of the children of Israel are more and mightier than we declares that Israel was more numerous and powerful than policies for Egyptian security could tolerate. They feared the consequences of a war in which Israel might side with their invaders. This is an understandable threat, since Amenhotep I (1546-25 B.C.) was plagued at that time with wars in both the west and the south.

11. Treasure cities, Pithom and Raamses. Recent critical scholarship generally assumes that Raamses was built by Israel during the reign of Raamses II (1290-1224 B.C.). This was certainly not the case. It is true that Raamses II did build at Tanis, Zoan, or Avaris (other names for Raamses); but even Cassuto notes that archaeology has demonstrated that Pithom and Raamses "were rebuilt" in the time of Raamses II. The name of this city existed long before Raamses II and has even been found on an inscription of the Eighteenth Dynasty (Raamses II, was part of the later Nineteenth Dynasty). See John J. Davis, *Para-*

dise to Prison: Studies in Genesis, p. 291, and Gleason Archer's A Survey of Old Testament Introduction, pp. 227-30.

12 But the more they afflicted them, the more they multiplied and grew. And they were grieved because of the children of Israel.
13 And the Egyptians made the children of Israel to serve with rigour:
14 And they made their lives bitter with hard bondage, in morter, and in brick, and in all manner of service in the field: all their service, wherein they made them serve, was with rigour.
15 ¶And the king of Egypt spake to the Hebrew midwives, of which the name of the one was Shĭph'rah, and the name of the other Pŭ'ah:
16 And he said, When ye do the office of a midwife to the Hebrew women, and see them upon the stools; if it be a son, then ye shall kill him: but if it be a daughter, then she shall live.
17 But the midwives feared God, and did not as the king of Egypt commanded them, but saved the men children alive.

18 And the king of Egypt called for the midwives, and said unto them, Why have ye done this thing, and have saved the men children alive?
19 And the midwives said unto Pharaoh, Because the Hebrew women are not as the Egyptian women; for they are lively, and are delivered ere the midwives come in unto them.
20 Therefore God dealt well with the midwives: and the people multiplied, and waxed very mighty.

21 And it came to pass, because the midwives feared God, that he made them houses.

22 And Pharaoh charged all his people, saying, Every son that is born ye shall cast into the river, and every daughter ye shall save alive.

CHAPTER 2
AND there went a man of the house of Levi, and took to wife a daughter of Levi.
2 And the woman conceived, and bare a son: and when she saw him that he was a goodly child, she hid him three months.

3 And when she could not longer hide him, she took for him an ark of bulrushes, and daubed it with slime and with pitch, and put the child therein; and she laid it in the flags by the river's brink.

12-14. Egypt had enslaved Israel and worked them **with rigor.** Israel was ruthlessly oppressed with a **bitter** and **hard** bondage. God was preparing them to look to Him, because they had no other choice.

C. Israel's Misery Made the Policy of Egypt. 1:15-22.

15-16. Infanticide, the killing of infants, is not a new practice. **Shiphrah** and **Puah,** probably Jewish ladies in charge of a host of other midwives, were commanded to **kill** all male babies of the Hebrews; **but if it be a daughter, then she shall live.** Males were a threat as possible warriors, but women would make acceptable slaves.

17. But the midwives feared God. Because they feared God, they disobeyed the unrighteous law of the king, as later was the case with the three Hebrew children and Daniel (Dan 3 and 6) and Peter and the apostles (Acts 5:29). These midwives **saved the men children alive.**
18-19. When the actions of Shiphrah and Puah were discovered by the king, he inquired, **Why have ye done this thing . . .** ? Fearing for their lives, they lied to the king.

20. Therefore God dealt well with the midwives. Many have mistakenly thought that God approved of the midwives' lies. That is not so. They were blessed for not killing the male babies; and God was not dependent upon their lies to save them, any more than He needed the lies of Rahab to save the spies (Josh 2:1-7). God still hates ". . . a lying tongue . . ." (Prov 6:16-17).
21. Here the reason is definitely stated that **because the midwives feared God,** in spite of their lies, **he made them houses,** i.e., gave them children, families, and descendants.
22. Pharaoh then widened his commandment and **charged all his people** to kill all male babies (of the Hebrews). But God's providence prevented this from being universally carried out. God has promised to bless them that bless Israel, and likewise to curse anyone who curses Israel (Gen 12:3). Both blessing and curse still apply!

II. THE EARLY LIFE AND LATER CALL OF MOSES. 2:1-4:31.

A. Moses' Birth, Hiding, and Early Home Training. 2:1-10.

2:1-2. Moses' parentage on both sides was **of the house of Levi.** This tribe was later chosen to be the priestly tribe. The parents' names are given in Exodus 6:20. Moses' appearance from birth as **a goodly child** indicates a healthy, vigorous condition which his parents took as a sign of his future importance. Thus, his mother **hid him three months,** during which time he would sleep much and cry little.
3-4. Growing older and crying more, Moses had to be taken to a spot out of the hearing of those who might report his existence to Pharaoh. The mother made a small basket (Heb tēbat, used only here and of Noah's ark) of papyrus reeds. This little ark of safety contained Moses and was placed in a spot on the Nile where his older sister, Miriam, watched him.

4 And his sister stood afar off, to wit what would be done to him.

5 ¶And the daughter of Pharaoh came down to wash *herself* at the river; and her maidens walked along by the river's side; and when she saw the ark among the flags, she sent her maid to fetch it.

6 And when she had opened *it*, she saw the child: and, behold, the babe wept. And she had compassion on him, and said, This *is one* of the Hebrews' children.

7 Then said his sister to Pharaoh's daughter, Shall I go and call to thee a nurse of the Hebrew women, that she may nurse the child for thee?

8 And Pharaoh's daughter said to her, Go. And the maid went and called the child's mother.

9 And Pharaoh's daughter said unto her, Take this child away, and nurse it for me, and I will give *thee* thy wages. And the woman took the child, and nursed it.

10 And the child grew, and she brought him unto Pharaoh's daughter, and he became her son. And she called his name Moses: and she said, Because I drew him out of the water.

11 ¶And it came to pass in those days, when Moses was grown, that he went out unto his brethren, and looked on their burdens: and he spied an Egyptian smiting an Hebrew, one of his brethren.

12 And he looked this way and that way, and when he saw that *there was* no man, he slew the Egyptian, and hid him in the sand.

13 And when he went out the second day, behold, two men of the Hebrews strove together: and he said to him that did the wrong, Wherefore smitest thou thy fellow?

14 And he said, Who made thee a prince and a judge over us? intendest thou to kill me, as thou killedst the Egyptian? And Moses feared, and said, Surely this thing is known.

15 Now when Pharaoh heard this thing, he sought to slay Moses. But Moses fled from the face of Pharaoh, and dwelt in the land of Mĭd′ĭ-an: and he sat down by a well.

5-6. God had so guided the circumstances of life that **the daughter of Pharaoh came down to wash** at the very spot where Moses rested in the tiny ark. When she beheld the crying baby boy, **she had compassion on him.** Whether or not the maiden who drew Moses from the water was Hatshepsut we cannot rightly tell, although she was the daughter of Thutmose I, who began his rule in about 1525 B.C., the approximate year of Moses' birth. Or, it may have been Ahmose, the princess from 1546–25 B.C., who became queen upon her brother's death in 1525 B.C.

7-9. Miriam also did not neglect her duty, and at the proper time suggested **a nurse of the Hebrew women.** Pharaoh's daughter had apparently decided to adopt the child as her own, because Miriam hinted that the nurse would **nurse the child for thee.** The plan worked! The child was spared; and, not only that, Moses' mother was paid to take care of her own son!

10. And the child grew. Moses was probably about two years old when his mother weaned him and took him to Pharaoh's daughter (according to their agreement) **and he became her son.** Moses received all the rights, privileges, and education of an Egyptian prince. "The privileges he later renounced (Heb xi. 24) but he never lost the benefits of the education (Acts vii. 22)" (Connell, Exodus in *The New Bible Commentary*, p. 108). Whatever relationship Moses enjoyed with his Hebrew mother, it was apparently sufficient to instill in him a knowledge of the identity of his people and of their God. **She called his name Moses,** an Egyptian word meaning son (Cassuto), and derived from the verb meaning "to produce" or "to draw forth" (Rawlinson). Hebrew has a similar sounding cognate verb that also means "to draw forth"; so there is a possible play on words involved in the naming of Moses, since her adopted son was drawn out of the water.

B. Moses' Homicide and Flight from Egypt. 2:11-15.

11-14. When Moses was grown. Acts 7:23 mentions Moses as being forty years old when he visited **his brethren, and looked on their burdens.**

The sad story of Moses' impatient anger, his murder of an Egyptian, and its discovery are familiar events. Perhaps Moses thought he could help his people by his own power, prestige, and position. He was wrong, and he had time during the next forty years of his life to contemplate his wrong ideas.

15. Moses fled from the face of Pharaoh. Although Hatshepsut ruled from 1504-1482 B.C., she was actually usurping the throne during the early part of the reign of Thutmose III, who continued to reign after her death until 1450 B.C. Moses fled to **the land of Midian** about 1485 B.C. The Midianites, who lived near Mount Sinai, were descendants of Abraham (Gen 25:1-2) and intermarried with Ishmael's line (Gen 37:25, 28; Jud 8:24).

16 Now the priest of Mĭd'ĭ-an had seven daughters: and they came and drew *water*, and filled the troughs to water their father's flock.

17 And the shepherds came and drove them away: but Moses stood up and helped them, and watered their flock.

18 And when they came to Reü'el their father, he said, How *is it that* ye are come so soon to day?

19 And they said, An Egyptian delivered us out of the hand of the shepherds, and also drew *water* enough for us, and watered the flock.

20 And he said unto his daughters, And where *is* he? why *is* it *that* ye have left the man? call him, that he may eat bread.

21 And Moses was content to dwell with the man: and he gave Moses Zĭp-po'rah his daughter.

22 And she bare *him* a son, and he called his name Ger'shom: for he said, I have been a stranger in a strange land.

23 ¶And it came to pass in process of time, that the king of Egypt died: and the children of Israel sighed by reason of the bondage, and they cried, and their cry came up unto God by reason of the bondage.

24 And God heard their groaning, and God remembered his covenant with Abraham, with Isaac, and with Jacob.

25 And God looked upon the children of Israel, and God had respect unto *them*.

CHAPTER 3

NOW Moses kept the flock of Jĕth'rō his father in law, the priest of Mĭd'ĭ-an: and he led the flock to the backside of the desert, and came to the mountain of God, *even* to Hô'rĕb.

2 And the angel of the LORD appeared unto him in a flame of fire out of the midst of a bush: and he looked, and, behold, the bush burned with fire, and the bush *was* not consumed.

3 And Moses said, I will now turn aside, and see this great sight, why the bush is not burnt.

4 And when the LORD saw that he turned aside to see, God called unto him out of the midst of the bush, and said, Moses, Moses. And he said, Here *am* I.

5 And he said, Draw not nigh hither: put off thy shoes from off thy feet, for the place whereon thou standest *is* holy ground.

6 Moreover he said, I *am* the God of thy father, the God of Abraham, the God of Isaac, and the God of Jacob. And Moses hid his face; for he was afraid to look upon God.

C. Moses' Marriage and Sojourn in Midian. 2:16-25.

16-20. Now the priest of Midian had seven daughters. Moses was introduced to **Reuel** (also called Jethro, Ex 3:1) after helping that man's daughters through a dispute at the local well.

21-22. Not long thereafter Moses was married to **Zipporah,** Reuel's daughter, who bore him a son, **Gershom.** They also later had Eliezer (Ex 18:3-4).

23. And it came to pass in process of time, that the king of Egypt died. The biblical narrative wastes no time on the incidents of Moses' forty years in Midian. The concern is with God's people in Egypt. Following our reckoning for the date of the Exodus, the king who died was Thutmose III, who ruled until 1450 B.C.

24-25. God heard their groaning. God is always sympathetic to the plight of His people, and His timing is always perfect. **God remembered his covenant.** The covenant God made with **Abraham, with Isaac, and with Jacob** was an unconditional covenant. Backsliding and sin on the part of Israel notwithstanding, God will fulfill His promises as recorded in Genesis 12:1-3 and repeated again and again (Gen 17:4-8; 26:3-4; 28:1-4). All the land of Canaan has been promised to Israel (Gen 15:18-21); and though they have not yet inherited it all, God will give it to them after the Great Tribulation during the one thousand-year-reign of Christ (see Mic 4:1-8; Jer 23:1-8; Rev 20:1-6).

D. Moses' Call by God at the Burning Bush. 3:1-4:17.

3:1-2. The mountain of God, even to Horeb. Horeb and Sinai are interchangeable terms (Ex 3:1, 12; 19:20). **The angel of the LORD appeared unto him.** This was no mere created angel, but the Messenger of Jehovah, Christ Himself, as is evident from the following context.

3-4. As Moses' attention was drawn by the unconsumed but burning bush, **God called unto him out of the midst of the bush.** The angel (Heb *malakh*) of verse 2 is here identified as God (Heb *Elohim*). God actually appeared in human form to people in the Old Testament numerous times (Gen 12:7; 17:1; 18:1; 32:24-30). This was simply one of the ways in which God chose to reveal Himself.

5. The presence of God sanctified the surrounding ground, and Moses was asked to stay at a distance and to remove his shoes.

6. I am the God of thy father, the God of Abraham. There is no mistaking the plain sense of these words. The revealing person of the Godhead, the Second Person of the Trinity, here appeared to Moses. Moses, consequently, **was afraid to look upon God.**

7 ¶And the Lord said, I have surely seen the affliction of my people which *are* in Egypt, and have heard their cry by reason of their taskmasters; for I know their sorrows;

8 And I am come down to deliver them out of the hand of the Egyptians, and to bring them up out of that land unto a good land and a large, unto a land flowing with milk and honey; unto the place of the Canaanites, and the Hittites, and the Āmorītes, and the Pĕr'-iz-zītes, and the Hī'vītes, and the Jĕb'u-sītes.

9 Now therefore, behold, the cry of the children of Israel is come unto me: and I have also seen the oppression wherewith the Egyptians oppress them.

10 Come now therefore, and I will send thee unto Pharaoh, that thou mayest bring forth my people the children of Israel out of Egypt.

11 ¶And Moses said unto God, Who *am* I, that I should go unto Pharaoh, and that I should bring forth the children of Israel out of Egypt?

12 And he said, Certainly I will be with thee; and this *shall be* a token unto thee, that I have sent thee: When thou hast brought forth the people out of Egypt, ye shall serve God upon this mountain.

13 And Moses said unto God, Behold, *when* I come unto the children of Israel, and shall say unto them, The God of your fathers hath sent me unto you; and they shall say to me, What *is* his name? what shall I say unto them?

14 And God said unto Moses, I AM THAT I AM: and he said, Thus shalt thou say unto the children of Israel, I AM hath sent me unto you.

15 And God said moreover unto Moses, Thus shalt thou say unto the children of Israel, the Lord God of your fathers, the God of Abraham, the God of Isaac, and the God of Jacob, hath sent me unto you: this *is* my name for ever, and this *is* my memorial unto all generations.

16 Go, and gather the elders of Israel together, and say unto them, The Lord God of your fathers, the God of Abraham, of Isaac, and of Jacob, appeared unto me, saying, I have surely visited you, and *seen* that which is done to you in Egypt:

17 And I have said, I will bring you up out of the affliction of Egypt unto the land of the Canaanites, and the Hittites, and the Āmorītes, and the Pĕr'iz-zītes, and the Hī'vītes, and the Jĕb'u-sītes, unto a land flowing with milk and honey.

18 And they shall hearken to thy voice: and thou shalt come, thou and the elders of Israel, unto the king of Egypt, and ye shall say unto him, The Lord God of the Hebrews hath met with us: and now let us go, we beseech thee, three days' journey into the wilderness, that we may sacrifice to the Lord our God.

7-10. God clearly announced His intention of fulfilling His promises to Abraham, Isaac, and Jacob about the land of Palestine. He was fully aware of their plight in Egypt, and the time had now come for their redemption (Gen 15:13-16).

11-12. Who am I, that I should go unto Pharaoh . . . ? Moses had learned humility during his forty-year sojourn in the desert (Num 12:3) and realized the enormity of such a task.

Certainly I will be with thee. God plus one is always a majority. The task seemed impossible, humanly speaking. But with God, all things are possible (Gen 18:14). **This shall be a token . . . that I have sent thee.** As a sign, God assured Moses that he would lead the people back to **serve God upon this mountain.** The sign was to take place after he believed, trusted, and obeyed. Likewise, the sign of the Virgin Birth (Isa 7:14) occurred centuries after it was spoken, but was no less a sign.

13-14. Moses had several questions for God. What name should be given when the people asked him what God's name was. God replied, I AM THAT I AM, using the verb "to be" (Heb *hāyāh*). It means "I am the One who is" and is preferred over "He who causes to be." This is also supported by LXX reading: *egō ei'mi o' ōn*. God expressed the unchanging, eternal, self-existence of His being. He is able to act at will, to keep promises, to redeem Israel. Yet, He is unsearchable (Isa 55:9; 57:15). There is mystery to His existence that none can fathom.

15-17. God further outlined his plan for Moses to approach **the elders of Israel** to inform them of God's plans. Israel was even then divided into twelve distinct tribes, although the Levites would later be separated out as God's possession (Num 1:49; 3:12), while Joseph's two sons Ephraim and Manasseh would each become separate tribes (Num 1:32-35; cf. Gen 48:20-22).

18. And ye shall say unto him. Moses is instructed in precisely what to say to Pharaoh. He is not required to come up with his own line of argumentation; but rather, he is to serve as God's spokesman.

19 And I am sure that the king of Egypt will not let you go, no, not by a mighty hand.

20 And I will stretch out my hand, and smite Egypt with all my wonders which I will do in the midst thereof: and after that he will let you go.

21 And I will give this people favour in the sight of the Egyptians: and it shall come to pass, that, when ye go, ye shall not go empty:

22 But every woman shall borrow of her neighbour, and of her that sojourneth in her house, jewels of silver, and jewels of gold, and raiment: and ye shall put *them* upon your sons, and upon your daughters; and ye shall spoil the Egyptians.

CHAPTER 4

AND Moses answered and said, But, behold, they will not believe me, nor hearken unto my voice: for they will say, The LORD hath not appeared unto thee.

2 And the LORD said unto him, What *is* that in thine hand? And he said, A rod.

3 And he said, Cast it on the ground. And he cast it on the ground, and it became a serpent; and Moses fled from before it.

4 And the LORD said unto Moses, Put forth thine hand, and take it by the tail. And he put forth his hand, and caught it, and it became a rod in his hand:

5 That they may believe that the LORD God of their fathers, the God of Abraham, the God of Isaac, and the God of Jacob, hath appeared unto thee.

6 ¶And the LORD said furthermore unto him, Put now thine hand into thy bosom. And he put his hand into his bosom: and when he took it out, behold, his hand *was* leprous as snow.

7 And he said, Put thine hand into thy bosom again. And he put his hand into his bosom again; and plucked it out of his bosom, and, behold, it was turned again as his *other* flesh.

8 And it shall come to pass, if they will not believe thee, neither hearken to the voice of the first sign, that they will believe the voice of the latter sign.

9 And it shall come to pass, if they will not believe also these two signs, neither hearken unto thy voice, that thou shalt take of the water of the river, and pour *it* upon the dry *land:* and the water which thou takest out of the river shall become blood upon the dry *land.*

10 ¶And Moses said unto the LORD, O my Lord, I *am* not eloquent, neither heretofore, nor since thou hast spoken unto thy servant: but I *am* slow of speech, and of a slow tongue.

11 And the LORD said unto him, Who hath made man's mouth? or who maketh the dumb, or deaf, or the seeing, or the blind? have not I the LORD?

12 Now therefore go, and I will be with thy mouth, and teach thee what thou shalt say.

13 And he said, O my Lord, send, I pray thee, by the hand *of him whom* thou wilt send.

19-20. The king of Egypt will not let you go. God's foreknowledge is revealed to Moses in the matter of Pharaoh's stubbornness, which will eventually be overcome by God smiting Egypt with all His **wonders.**

21-22. Also foretold is the triumphant manner in which the Israelites shall leave Egypt—**ye shall not go empty . . . ye shall spoil the Egyptians.**

4:1-5. Moses feared to do all that God was calling him to do; so he made a series of excuses beginning with **they will not believe me.** God quickly gave him a sign, or miracle, to perform as a proof. He cast his rod **on the ground, and it became a serpent** (cf. Ex 7:8-12).

6-9. As a further sign, God would turn Moses' hand leprous and then restore it again.

A third sign Moses could perform would be to take water from the Egyptians' sacred Nile, pour it out upon the land and have it **become blood upon the dry land** (cf. Ex 7:17-25).

10-12. Moses' second excuse was **I am not eloquent** (lit., a man of words). Having spent forty years in the Midianite wilderness, he could not imagine himself in the role of a prophetic spokesman, properly approaching and addressing the royal court. Note the important value of eloquence in the Middle Kingdom document: "Protests of the Eloquent Peasant," *ANET*, pp. 407-410.

13. In reality, however, Moses did not care to return to Egypt. The task would be extremely dangerous and difficult, so he told God to please send someone else.

14 And the anger of the LORD was kindled against Moses, and he said, *Is* not Aaron the Levite thy brother? I know that he can speak well. And also, behold, he cometh forth to meet thee: and when he seeth thee, he will be glad in his heart.

15 And thou shalt speak unto him, and put words in his mouth: and I will be with thy mouth, and with his mouth, and will teach you what ye shall do.

16 And he shall be thy spokesman unto the people: and he shall be, *even* he shall be to thee instead of a mouth, and thou shalt be to him instead of God.

17 And thou shalt take this rod in thine hand, wherewith thou shalt do signs.

18 ¶And Moses went and returned to Jĕth′rō his father in law, and said unto him, Let me go, I pray thee, and return unto my brethren which be in Egypt, and see whether they be yet alive. And Jĕth′rō said to Moses, Go in peace.

19 And the LORD said unto Moses in Mĭd′ĭ-an, Go, return into Egypt: for all the men are dead which sought thy life.

20 And Moses took his wife and his sons, and set them upon an ass, and he returned to the land of Egypt: and Moses took the rod of God in his hand.

21 And the LORD said unto Moses, When thou goest to return into Egypt, see that thou do all those wonders before Pharaoh, which I have put in thine hand: but I will harden his heart, that he shall not let the people go.

14-17. The anger of the Lord was kindled against Moses. God in essence said, "Moses, you will go! But I will instruct your brother Aaron to speak for you" (cf. Ex 7:1-2). Apparently, however, Moses eventually gained confidence and actually did speak before Pharaoh numerous times (Ex 8:9, 25, 29; 9:29), whereas Aaron rarely spoke!

E. Moses' Return into Egypt to Deliver Israel. 4:18-31.

18. Moses went and returned to Jethro since he could not depart for Egypt without first returning the flock (Ex 3:1), politely obtaining leave to go from his father-in-law, and readying his family for the journey. **See whether they be yet alive** is not meant to imply doubts as to whether his brethren had all died, but is simply an expression of concern. Jethro said, **Go in peace.**

19-20. God next reassured Moses that **all the men are dead which sought thy life** (cf. Mt 2:19-20).

Wife and his sons. Though only one son, Gershom, had been mentioned in the initial account of Moses' marriage to Zipporah (Ex 2:21-22), doubtless Eliezer had also been born during the forty-year stay in Midian (Ex 18:4).

21. But I will harden his heart, that he shall not let the people go. There are eighteen references to the hardening of Pharaoh's heart. Nine times it is attributed to God's actions, first in prophecy (Ex 4:21; 7:3; 14:4), then (in actual occurrence) only after Pharaoh already had hardened his own heart numerous times during the plagues (Ex 9:12; 10:20, 27; 11:10; 14:8), and finally in a summary statement (Ex 10:1). That Pharaoh first of all hardened his own heart, or that his heart grew hard is stated nine times also (Ex 7:13 [as correctly translated in ASV, RSV, NASB, NIV], 7:14, 22; 8:15, 19, 32; 9:7, 34, 35). A moral problem has been supposed here by some who teach that God was responsible for what he did to Pharaoh, and Pharaoh should not have been punished because he had no control over God hardening his heart.

First, it should be carefully noted that Pharaoh first set his own stubborn will against God, and only after that is it recorded that "God hardened" his heart. *Second,* even God's activity in hardening does not need to be interpreted as some direct action (although it could be); it could be accomplished through the circumstances of life, namely the plagues, which Pharaoh repeatedly ignored. *Third,* it was customary in Hebrew thought to attribute all phenomena to God, even the open or barren womb (Gen 29:31; I Sam 1:5) and the accidental killing of a man (Ex 21:13). *Fourth,* this passage has nothing at all to do with the personal salvation of Pharaoh. This is not even contemplated. Pharaoh was already a wicked character, carrying out a cruel policy of killing and enslaving the Hebrews. He had determined to set his own mind and will against God by his own intellectual responses to the circumstances around him. It is also a fact, however, that each response against God's will results in a weakened conscience and lessens the ability of an individual to respond correctly the next time. Pharaoh placed himself in such an obstinate, unretractable position that he willed not to act in any other way. He certainly was not forced into any of his actions, but did all he did willfully and deliberately. For excellent treatments of this problem see Haines, Exodus in *The Wesleyan Bible Commentary* (Vol. I), pp. 183-185; Davis, *Moses and the Gods of Egypt,* pp. 69-71; and Mickelsen, Romans in *The Wycliffe Bible Commentary,* pp. 1211-1212.

22 And thou shalt say unto Pharaoh, Thus saith the LORD, Israel *is* my son, *even* my firstborn:

22. Israel is my son. God has chosen Israel to a special position among the nations. Yet, personal salvation within Israel is a matter of the choice of the heart for each individual.

23 And I say unto thee, Let my son go, that he may serve me: and if thou refuse to let him go, behold, I will slay thy son, *even* thy firstborn.

23. Let my son go. This was to be God's initial demand of Pharaoh through Moses. **If thou refuse . . . I will slay thy son, even thy first-born.** This embryonic prediction was no idle threat or common platitude.

24 ¶And it came to pass by the way in the inn, that the LORD met him, and sought to kill him.
25 Then ZĬp-po′rah took a sharp stone, and cut off the foreskin of her son, and cast *it* at his feet, and said, Surely a bloody husband *art* thou to me.
26 So he let him go: then she said, A bloody husband *thou art,* because of the circumcision.

24-26. The LORD met him and sought to kill him. These verses have troubled critics and devoted interpreters alike. Rylaarsdam, a rationalistic critic, states, "It is of value to us in that it emphasizes the jungle of primitive superstitions out of which the religion of Yahweh was developed," pp. 882-83. Childs nicely summarizes the history of critical interpretation of the passage (*The Book of Exodus: A Critical, Theological Commentary,* pp. 95-101). The plain meaning seems to be that by sudden and shocking means God was reminding Moses that the penalty for uncircumcision was to be ". . . cut off from the people . . ." (Gen 17:14); it was a violation of the Abrahamic covenant. God may have appeared physically before Moses, as in other Christophanies (Gen 17:1-22), or He may have used the means of a severe illness. See the discussion of this matter by Davis, pp. 71-72.

27 ¶And the LORD said to Aaron, Go into the wilderness to meet Moses. And he went, and met him in the mount of God, and kissed him.
28 And Moses told Aaron all the words of the LORD who had sent him, and all the signs which he had commanded him.
29 ¶And Moses and Aaron went and gathered together all the elders of the children of Israel:

27-28. And the Lord said to Aaron. Even as God had plainly revealed His will to Moses, He now made clear to Aaron his part in the divine plan, either by a human form, a voice, or by His Spirit. They met at Mount Sinai before returning together to Egypt.

29. The elders of the children of Israel. These elders (Heb *zaqēn*) may be equivalent to the group of seventy who later ascended Mount Sinai with Moses (Ex 24:9-11) and are not the officers of the children of Israel (Ex 5:6, 10, 14; Heb *shatar*), whom Pharaoh appointed (Ex 5:14).

30 And Aaron spake all the words which the LORD had spoken unto Moses, and did the signs in the sight of the people.

30. And Aaron spake all the words as God had appointed (Ex 4:14-16). **And did the signs** refers to the three miracles of the rod, the leprous hand, and the water turned to blood (Ex 4:1-9).

31 And the people believed: and when they heard that the LORD had visited the children of Israel, and that he had looked upon their affliction, then they bowed their heads and worshipped.

31. And the people believed . . . and worshiped. The elders reverently had been trusting God to hear and answer their prayers and demonstrated their pleasure by humble worship.

III. THE INITIAL CONTEST WITH PHARAOH.
   5:1-7:13.

CHAPTER 5
AND afterward Moses and Aaron went in, and told Pharaoh, Thus saith the LORD God of Israel, Let my people go, that they may hold a feast unto me in the wilderness.
2 And Pharaoh said, Who *is* the LORD, that I should obey his voice to let Israel go? I know not the LORD, neither will I let Israel go.
3 And they said, The God of the Hebrews hath met with us: let us go, we pray thee, three days' journey into the desert, and sacrifice unto the LORD our God; lest he fall upon us with pestilence, or with the sword.
4 And the king of Egypt said unto them, Wherefore do ye, Moses and Aaron, let the people from their works? get you unto your burdens.
5 And Pharaoh said, Behold, the people of the land now *are* many, and

A. Pharaoh Rejects Moses' Initial Demands. 5:1-21.

5:1-2. Thus saith the LORD God of Israel, Let my people go. Moses did just as God had instructed him (Ex 3:18). Pharaoh sarcastically asked, **Who is the LORD. . . ?** He was soon to find out! He also truly said **I know not the Lord** and refused Moses' request. Perhaps he had not even heard of Jehovah.

3. Moses repeated the demand by identifying Jehovah more commonly as **The God of the Hebrews.** It must be remembered that the Egyptians viewed Pharaoh as a god himself, and not merely a representative of the gods.

4-5. The word **let** is an old English word meaning "hinder" in this particular context. Pharaoh was not about to dismiss any slaves.

ye make them rest from their burdens.

6 And Pharaoh commanded the same day the taskmasters of the people, and their officers, saying,

7 Ye shall no more give the people straw to make brick, as heretofore: let them go and gather straw for themselves.

8 And the tale of the bricks, which they did make heretofore, ye shall lay upon them; ye shall not diminish *ought* thereof: for they *be* idle; therefore they cry, saying, Let us go *and* sacrifice to our God.

9 Let there more work be laid upon the men, that they may labour therein; and let them not regard vain words.

10 ¶And the taskmasters of the people went out, and their officers, and they spake to the people, saying, Thus saith Pharaoh, I will not give you straw.

11 Go ye, get you straw where ye can find it: yet not ought of your work shall be diminished.

12 So the people were scattered abroad throughout all the land of Egypt to gather stubble instead of straw.

13 And the taskmasters hasted *them,* saying, Fulfil your works, *your* daily tasks, as when there was straw.

14 And the officers of the children of Israel, which Pharaoh's taskmasters had set over them, were beaten, *and* demanded, Wherefore have ye not fulfilled your task in making brick both yesterday and to day, as heretofore?

15 ¶Then the officers of the children of Israel came and cried unto Pharaoh, saying, Wherefore dealest thou thus with thy servants?

16 There is no straw given unto thy servants, and they say to us, Make brick: and, behold, thy servants *are* beaten; but the fault *is* in thine own people.

17 But he said, Ye *are* idle, *ye are* idle: therefore ye say, Let us go *and* do sacrifice to the LORD.

18 Go therefore now, *and* work; for there shall no straw be given you, yet shall ye deliver the tale of bricks.

19 And the officers of the children of Israel did see *that* they *were* in evil *case,* after it was said, Ye shall not minish *ought* from your bricks of your daily task.

20 ¶And they met Moses and Aaron, who stood in the way, as they came forth from Pharaoh:

21 And they said unto them, The LORD look upon you, and judge; because ye have made our savour to be abhorred in the eyes of Pharaoh, and in the eyes of his servants, to put a sword in their hand to slay us.

22 And Moses returned unto the LORD, and said, Lord, wherefore hast thou *so* evil entreated this people? why *is* it *that* thou hast sent me?

23 For since I came to Pharaoh to speak in thy name, he hath done evil to this people; neither hast thou delivered thy people at all.

CHAPTER 6

THEN the LORD said unto Moses, Now

6-12. Pharaoh's remedy for Moses' **vain words** (vs. 9) was to stop supplying **straw,** while at the same time increasing the number of clay bricks to be produced. Apparently the straw was an essential ingredient in the brick-making process, and the lack of it drove Israel **to gather stubble instead.**

13-16. Since Israel could no longer **fulfill** their **daily tasks,** the Israelite overseers **were beaten.** They replied to Pharaoh that **the fault is in thine own people,** i.e., for not giving them straw as previously had been done.

17-19. Pharaoh no doubt had anticipated this reaction and planned to use it to turn the people against Moses, whom he considered to be a troublemaker. He told the people that they must be **idle,** or lacking work, since they requested time off to **go and do sacrifice to the LORD.** Already Pharaoh had hardened his heart against Israel and the Lord.

20-21. Pharaoh's plan worked. There was contention in the ranks of Israel, and Moses received the blame for Israel's worsened lot. But man's extremity became God's opportunity.

B. Moses Returns to God for Reassurance. 5:22–6:13.

22-23. Moses was greatly discouraged and began: (1) to question his call, **why is it that thou hast sent me?;** and (2) God's inaction, **neither hast thou delivered.** When we are discouraged it is easy to be tempted to question God and wonder about our position in relation to Him. We must trust Him, though, and rest assured that His love works for our ultimate good.

6:1. The LORD said unto Moses. Statements such as this must indicate some type of direct revelation, either by voice or

shalt thou see what I will do to Pharaoh: for with a strong hand shall he let them go, and with a strong hand shall he drive them out of his land.

2 And God spake unto Moses, and said unto him, I *am* the LORD:

3 And I appeared unto Abraham, unto Isaac, and unto Jacob, by *the name of* God Almighty, but by my name JEHOVAH was I not known to them.

4 And I have also established my covenant with them, to give them the land of Canaan, the land of their pilgrimage, wherein they were strangers.

5 And I have also heard the groaning of the children of Israel, whom the Egyptians keep in bondage; and I have remembered my covenant.

6 Wherefore say unto the children of Israel, I *am* the LORD, and I will bring you out from under the burdens of the Egyptians, and I will rid you out of their bondage, and I will redeem you with a stretched out arm, and with great judgments:

7 And I will take you to me for a people, and I will be to you a God: and ye shall know that I *am* the LORD your God, which bringeth you out from under the burdens of the Egyptians.

8 And I will bring you in unto the land, concerning the which I did swear to give it to Abraham, to Isaac, and to Jacob; and I will give it you for an heritage: I *am* the LORD.

9 ¶And Moses spake so unto the children of Israel: but they hearkened not unto Moses for anguish of spirit, and for cruel bondage.

10 And the LORD spake unto Moses, saying,

11 Go in, speak unto Pharaoh king of Egypt, that he let the children of Israel go out of his land.

12 And Moses spake before the LORD, saying, Behold, the children of Israel have not hearkened unto me; how then shall Pharaoh hear me, who *am* of uncircumcised lips?

13 And the LORD spake unto Moses and unto Aaron, and gave them a charge unto the children of Israel, and unto Pharaoh king of Egypt, to bring the children of Israel out of the land of Egypt.

14 ¶These *be* the heads of their fathers' houses: The sons of Reuben the firstborn of Israel; Hā'nŏch, and Păl'lū, Hĕz'ron, and Cär'mī: these *be* the families of Reuben.

15 And the sons of Simeon; Jĕ-mu'el, and Jā'mĭn, and Ō'hăd, and Jā'chin, and Zō'hăr, and Shā'ul the son of a Canaanitish woman: these *are* the families of Simeon.

16 And these *are* the names of the sons of Levi according to their generations; Ger'shon, and Kō'hăth, and Me-rä'rī: and the years of the life of Levi *were* an hundred thirty and seven years.

complete Christophany. God reassured Moses with **Now shalt thou see what I will do to Pharaoh.** God had made no mistakes.

2-4. I am the LORD, or Jehovah. God here announced that the patriarchs Abraham, Isaac, and Jacob had known Him with relation to His mighty greatness indicated by the phrase God Almighty (Heb *El Shaddai*). They had not known the riches of God as **JEHOVAH,** the name now to be associated with God's activity in keeping His **covenant** with Abraham. This is not to say that they did not know the name of Yahweh (thought by many to be the original pronunciation of the name, Jehovah); but they would now come to know the benefits of that name as Israel's covenant-keeping God. See Laird Harris, "The Pronunciation of the Tetragram," in J. Skilton (ed.), *The Law and the Prophets*, pp. 215-225. God's gracious loving-kindness would be manifested to them through a powerful deliverance.

5-8. Moses was to pass on this good news again to the people. It included: (1) redemption for Israel; (2) **great judgments** on Egypt; (3) Israel being God's people; (4) inheritance of **the land** promised to Abraham, Isaac, and Jacob, i.e., the Promised Land.

9. Moses reported these assurances to the people, **but they hearkened not.** Sometimes when no relief is in sight it is difficult to believe things could get any better. But we need to trust God's Word, rather than our feelings or outward appearances.

10-13. Moses received, as it were, a renewed commission from God to demand of Pharaoh the release of Israel **out of his land,** not just three days' journey into the wilderness.

C. The Families of Reuben, Simeon, and Levi. 6:14-27.

14-15. The family groupings with Reuben and Simeon, Israel's two eldest sons, are given here only to introduce the third, Levi, so that the genealogy of Moses and Aaron might be given. They were to be seen as legitimate leaders of Israel.

16-19. The sons of Levi were Gershon, and Kohath, and Merari, who were among the seventy who accompanied Israel into Egypt originally (Gen 46:11, 26-27). **Amram** was one of the sons of **Kohath.**

17 The sons of Ger'shon; Lĭb'nī, and Shĭ'mī, according to their families.

18 And the sons of Kō'hăth; Ăm'răm, and Ĭz'här, and Hē-bron, and Ŭz'zĭ-el: and the years of the life of Kō'hăth *were* an hundred thirty and three years.

19 And the sons of Me-râ'rī; Mä'ha-lī and Mū'shī: these *are* the families of Levi according to their generations.

20 And Ăm'răm took him Jŏch'e-bĕd his father's sister to wife; and she bare him Aaron and Moses: and the years of the life of Ăm'răm *were* an hundred and thirty and seven years.

20. Another **Amram,** who lived several hundred years after the Amram of verse 18, is meant here as the father of Aaron and Moses. That this is the case is seen from: (1) the fact that Israel spent four hundred thirty years in Egypt; and Kohath, the father of the first Amram, was alive at the start of that period; (2) the fact that ten complete generations between Jacob and Joshua are listed in I Chronicles 7:22-27, making merely three between Jacob and Moses virtually impossible; (3) the fact that there were 22,300 male descendants of the original Gershon, Kohath, and Merari at the time of the Exodus (Num 3:22, 28, 34) would have been impossible, since those men had only eight sons born among themselves in that succeeding generation; and (4) the fact that Hebrew genealogies frequently omit some generations for the sake of brevity or other reasons.

21 And the sons of Ĭz'här; Kô'rah, and Nē'phĕg, and Zĭch'rī.

22 And the sons of Ŭz'zĭ-el; Mīsh'a-el, and Ĕl'zā-phăn, and Zĭth'rī.

23 And Aaron took him E-lĭsh'e-ba, daughter of Am-mĭn'a-dăb, sister of Nā-ăsh'on, to wife; and she bare him Nā'dăb, and A-bī'hū, Ĕ-le-ā'zar, and Ĭth'a-mär.

21-23. Aaron married **Elisheba** (LXX Gk Elisabeth) from the tribe of Judah. Her father was the prince of Judah (Num 1:7, 16).

24 And the sons of Kô'rah; Ăs'sir, and Ĕl'kā-nah, and Ă-bī'a-săph: these *are* the families of the Kōr'hītes.

25 And Ĕ-le-ā'zar Aaron's son took him *one* of the daughters of Pū'tĭ-el to wife; and she bare him Phĭn'e-has: these *are* the heads of the fathers of the Lēvītes according to their families.

24-25. Eleazar Aaron's son married, and that produced **Phinehas,** all mentioned here because of their later prominence in Israel (Num 25:6-13).

26 These *are* that Aaron and Moses, to whom the Lord said, Bring out the children of Israel from the land of Egypt according to their armies.

27 These *are* they which spake to Pharaoh king of Egypt, to bring out the children of Israel from Egypt: these *are* that Moses and Aaron.

26-27. The context of these two verses demonstrates that the preceding genealogy was part and parcel of this whole section of Exodus from the first, which the form critics find disturbing.

28 ¶And it came to pass on the day *when* the Lord spake unto Moses in the land of Egypt,

29 That the Lord spake unto Moses, saying, I *am* the Lord: speak thou unto Pharaoh king of Egypt all that I say unto thee.

30 And Moses said before the Lord, Behold, I *am* of uncircumcised lips, and how shall Pharaoh hearken unto me?

D. The Hardening of Pharaoh's Heart. 6:28-7:13.

28-30. These verses go back and pick up the story again from verse 12 where Moses said, **how shall Pharaoh hearken unto me?**

CHAPTER 7

AND the Lord said unto Moses, See, I have made thee a god to Pharaoh: and Aaron thy brother shall be thy prophet.

2 Thou shalt speak all that I command thee: and Aaron thy brother shall speak unto Pharaoh, that he send the children of Israel out of his land.

3 And I will harden Pharaoh's heart, and multiply my signs and my wonders in the land of Egypt.

4 But Pharaoh shall not hearken unto you, that I may lay my hand upon Egypt, and bring forth mine armies, *and* my people the children of Israel,

7:1-2. Made thee a god to Pharaoh means that Moses stands before Pharaoh with divine authority (so ASV, RSV, NASB, NIV). **Aaron . . . shall be thy prophet** indicates he is to be Moses' spokesman. On the prophetic revelation of God to Moses, see Edward J. Young, *My Servants the Prophets,* pp. 38-55.

3-5. I will harden Pharaoh's heart is here predicted again. God would use the circumstances of the ten plagues and Pharaoh's stubborn reactions to them in the hardening process. The hardening would be evident in Pharaoh's refusal to allow Israel to leave Egypt, which would result in the just judgment of God upon Egypt for the hundreds of years of oppressing God's people and seeking to destroy their infant sons. See extended

out of the land of Egypt by great judgments.

5 And the Egyptians shall know that I *am* the LORD, when I stretch forth mine hand upon Egypt, and bring out the children of Israel from among them.

6 And Moses and Aaron did as the LORD commanded them, so did they.

7 And Moses *was* fourscore years old, and Aaron fourscore and three years old, when they spake unto Pharaoh.

8 ¶And the LORD spake unto Moses and unto Aaron, saying,

9 When Pharaoh shall speak unto you, saying, Shew a miracle for you: then thou shalt say unto Aaron, Take thy rod, and cast *it* before Pharaoh, *and* it shall become a serpent.

10 ¶And Moses and Aaron went in unto Pharaoh, and they did so as the LORD had commanded: and Aaron cast down his rod before Pharaoh, and before his servants, and it became a serpent.

11 Then Pharaoh also called the wise men and the sorcerers: now the magicians of Egypt, they also did in like manner with their enchantments.

12 For they cast down every man his rod, and they became serpents: but Aaron's rod swallowed up their rods.

13 And he hardened Pharaoh's heart, that he hearkened not unto them; as the LORD had said.

14 ¶And the LORD said unto Moses, Pharaoh's heart *is* hardened, he refuseth to let the people go.

15 Get thee unto Pharaoh in the morning; lo, he goeth out unto the water; and thou shalt stand by the river's brink against he come; and the rod which was turned to a serpent shalt thou take in thine hand.

16 And thou shalt say unto him, The LORD God of the Hebrews hath sent me unto thee, saying, Let my people go, that they may serve me in the wilderness: and, behold, hitherto thou wouldest not hear.

17 Thus saith the LORD, In this thou shalt know that I *am* the LORD: behold, I will smite with the rod that *is* in mine hand upon the waters which *are* in the river, and they shall be turned to blood.

18 And the fish that *is* in the river shall die, and the river shall stink; and the Egyptians shall lothe to drink of the water of the river.

19 ¶And the LORD spake unto Moses, Say unto Aaron, Take thy rod, and stretch out thine hand upon the waters of Egypt, upon their streams, upon their rivers, and upon their ponds, and upon all their pools of water, that they

comments on Exodus 4:21. God would accomplish this through "signs" (Heb *'otot*); "wonders" (*mopetim*); and "great judgments" (*shepātim gedolīm*).

6-9. Moses was fourscore (that is, eighty) **years old.** Moses lived to one hundred twenty, but noted that man's normal age was seventy, or sometimes eighty (Ps 90:10). "Egyptian records show that service beyond 100 years was not uncommon" (Connell, p. 112).

10. Upon this second encounter with Pharaoh, rather than capitulate through fear, Moses and Aaron trusted and obeyed God. **Aaron cast down his rod . . . and it became a serpent.** Even though some critics refer to this event as the product of "a fanciful imagination" (Rylaarsdam, The Book of Exodus in *The Interpreter's Bible*, p. 895), or simply as Hebrew myth and tradition (Childs, pp. 149-53; Noth, *Exodus: A Commentary*, pp. 71-72), Moses, the eyewitness, presents this as an actual, though temporary, transformation of a wooden stick into a reptile (Heb *tannīn*, rather than Heb *nahāsh* as in Ex 4:3).

11-12. Pharaoh's **wise men and the sorcerers . . . did in like manner with their enchantments.** Jannes and Jambres (II Tim 3:8) apparently used either real snakes that had been stiffened or some of Satan's lying wonders (II Thess 2:9). For details see Rawlinson, The Second Book of Moses called Exodus in *Ellicott's Commentary on the Whole Bible*, pp. 211-12.

13. And he hardened Pharaoh's heart is incorrectly translated and should read, "and Pharaoh's heart was hardened," meaning by the setting of his own will against God (so ASV, RSV, NASB, NIV). See extended comments on Exodus 4:21.

IV. THE PLAGUES AND PASSOVER. 7:14-12:33.

A. The Nine Plagues. 7:14-10:29.

14-16. Moses was to meet Pharaoh **by the river's brink** the next morning with the repeated command **Let my people go.** Pharaoh was soon to discover that to resist God is to be destroyed. The same truth applies today.

17-19. Moses and Aaron were to announce that God would **smite** the sacred river, turning it **to blood,** and thus causing the death of its aquatic contents. This incident is definitely presented in the text as a miracle (Heb *mopet*). Some critical commentators believe this was nothing more than red silt washing downstream from Ethiopia (Cassuto, Clements), but it is disheartening to see the identical naturalistic explanations come from the pen of a conservative scholar like Charles Pfeiffer, *Egypt and the Exodus* (p. 47). Others like Rylaarsdam, Childs, and Noth consider all these accounts to be pure tradition. But the statement in verse 18 that the effects of this plague reached even to the water contained **both in vessels of wood, and in vessels of stone** indicates a supernatural change from water to

131

may become blood; and *that* there may be blood throughout all the land of Egypt, both in *vessels of* wood, and in *vessels of* stone.

20 And Moses and Aaron did so, as the LORD commanded; and he lifted up the rod, and smote the waters that *were* in the river, in the sight of Pharaoh, and in the sight of his servants; and all the waters that *were* in the river were turned to blood.
21 And the fish that *was* in the river died; and the river stank, and the Egyptians could not drink of the water of the river; and there was blood throughout all the land of Egypt.
22 And the magicians of Egypt did so with their enchantments: and Pharaoh's heart was hardened, neither did he hearken unto them; as the LORD had said.
23 And Pharaoh turned and went into his house, neither did he set his heart to this also.
24 And all the Egyptians digged round about the river for water to drink; for they could not drink of the water of the river.
25 And seven days were fulfilled, after that the LORD had smitten the river.

CHAPTER 8

AND the LORD spake unto Moses, Go unto Pharaoh, and say unto him, Thus saith the LORD, Let my people go, that they may serve me.
2 And if thou refuse to let *them* go, behold, I will smite all thy borders with frogs:
3 And the river shall bring forth frogs abundantly, which shall go up and come into thine house, and into thy bedchamber, and upon thy bed, and into the house of thy servants, and upon thy people, and into thine ovens, and into thy kneadingtroughs:
4 And the frogs shall come up both on thee, and upon thy people, and upon all thy servants.
5 ¶And the LORD spake unto Moses, Say unto Aaron, Stretch forth thine hand with thy rod over the streams, over the rivers, and over the ponds, and cause frogs to come up upon the land of Egypt.
6 And Aaron stretched out his hand over the waters of Egypt; and the frogs came up, and covered the land of Egypt.

7 And the magicians did so with their enchantments, and brought up frogs upon the land of Egypt.

8 ¶Then Pharaoh called for Moses and Aaron, and said, Intreat the LORD, that he may take away the frogs from me, and from my people; and I will let the people go, that they may do sacrifice unto the LORD.

blood, even in areas not touched by the natural flow of the river.

Furthermore, the word **blood** (Heb *dam*) occurs over one hundred fifty times in the Pentateuch and is always used of real biological blood, except in two passages (Gen 49:11; Deut 32:14) where it speaks figuratively for the "blood" of the grape. If Moses had simply meant that the Nile would turn "red," he could have used any of several words to signify that color.

20-23. He lifted up the rod, and smote the waters. The miracle was not a gradual change, but a sudden supernatural act. **Magicians . . . their enchantments.** By some trick or sleight of hand Pharaoh's servants performed what appeared to be the same miracle. Thus, Pharaoh had no compelling reason at this point to think that Moses and Aaron were anything more than clever magicians. His stubborn will continued to be **hardened.** On Egyptian magic see K. A. Kitchen, "Magic and Sorcery," *New Bible Dictionary*, p. 769 and B. Mertz, *Red Land, Black Land.*

24-25. God continued to make all Nile water flowing through Egypt to be blood for **seven days,** after which time God probably removed the blood by allowing fresh water above the plague to flow through and cleanse the river. The sudden, not gradual, disappearance of the blood in a single day should have alerted Pharaoh to the miraculous, but his hardened heart took no notice.

8:1-5. Moses and Aaron appeared before Pharaoh the third time to demand **Let my people go,** or else God would **smite all thy borders with frogs.**

6. And the frogs came up, and covered the land of Egypt. God miraculously produced a superabundance of frogs. How, we are not told. It is unusual for frogs to venture too far from a moist environment, but these went everywhere.

7. And the magicians did so, but this time Pharaoh would be disturbed. The plague of blood perhaps did not greatly affect Pharaoh personally as he may have had beverages other than water to drink, but the case of the frogs was different. This plague was directed against the god Hapi and the frog goddess Heqt.

8. I will let the people go, Pharaoh claimed, if only the frogs would be removed.

9 And Moses said unto Pharaoh, Glory over me: when shall I intreat for thee, and for thy servants, and for thy people, to destroy the frogs from thee and thy houses, *that* they may remain in the river only?

10 And he said, To morrow. And he said, *Be it* according to thy word: that thou mayest know that *there is* none like unto the LORD our God.

11 And the frogs shall depart from thee, and from thy houses, and from thy servants, and from thy people; they shall remain in the river only.

12 And Moses and Aaron went out from Pharaoh: and Moses cried unto the LORD because of the frogs which he had brought against Pharaoh.

13 And the LORD did according to the word of Moses; and the frogs died out of the houses, out of the villages, and out of the fields.

14 And they gathered them together upon heaps: and the land stank.

15 But when Pharaoh saw that there was respite, he hardened his heart, and hearkened not unto them; as the LORD had said.

16 ¶And the LORD said unto Moses, Say unto Aaron, Stretch out thy rod, and smite the dust of the land, that it may become lice throughout all the land of Egypt.

17 And they did so; for Aaron stretched out his hand with his rod, and smote the dust of the earth, and it became lice in man, and in beast; all the dust of the land became lice throughout all the land of Egypt.

18 And the magicians did so with their enchantments to bring forth lice, but they could not: so there were lice upon man, and upon beast.

19 Then the magicians said unto Pharaoh, This *is* the finger of God: and Pharaoh's heart was hardened, and he hearkened not unto them; as the LORD had said.

20 ¶And the LORD said unto Moses, Rise up early in the morning, and stand before Pharaoh; lo, he cometh forth to the water; and say unto him, Thus saith the LORD, Let my people go, that they may serve me.

21 Else, if thou wilt not let my people go, behold, I will send swarms *of flies* upon thee, and upon thy servants, and upon thy people, and into thy houses: and the houses of the Egyptians shall be full of swarms *of flies,* and also the ground whereon they *are.*

22 And I will sever in that day the land of Goshen, in which my people dwell, that no swarms *of flies* shall be there; to the end thou mayest know that I *am* the LORD in the midst of the earth.

23 And I will put a division between my people and thy people: to morrow shall this sign be.

24 And the LORD did so; and there came a grievous swarm *of flies* into the house of Pharaoh, and *into* his servants' houses, and into all the land of Egypt: the land was corrupted by reason of the swarm *of flies.*

25 ¶And Pharaoh called for Moses

9-11. Moses asked Pharaoh to set the time for the termination of the frog plague so that Pharaoh would know that it was God who had ended it. **Tomorrow** was the set time.

12-14. Moses cried unto the LORD, that is he prayed for the end of the plague of frogs. As a result **the frogs died.** Imagine the results. It says **the land stank.** Only the greatest of rationalizations by Pharaoh could account for the sudden death of what must have been millions of frogs!

15. Nevertheless, Pharaoh was not true to his word; and instead of releasing Israel (Ex 8:8), **he hardened his heart.**

16-17. The third plague was that of turning **the dust of the land** into **lice,** or gnats (RSV, NASB, NIV). The word lice (Heb *kēn;* LXX *skniphes*) is generally taken to be a type of stinging gnat quite common to the vicinity of marshlands near the Nile.

18-19. Pharaoh's magicians tried to duplicate this miracle, **but they could not.** They announced that **This is the finger of God,** but it did not affect Pharaoh's hardened heart.

20-23. The fourth plague, **swarms of flies** (Heb *'arōb*), Moses announced to Pharaoh with the additional distinction that **the land of Goshen,** the area where Israel lived, would be unaffected by the plague. The LXX renders *kunomuia,* "dog flies." Davis (p. 106) notes that the LXX translators lived in Egypt and may have understood the seriousness of such a plague that could even cause blindness. However, God put a "redemption" (Heb *pedut*), or "division," between His people and the Egyptians.

24. The Egyptians prided themselves on their cleanliness, so they must have felt the land was **corrupted,** or ruined (Heb *shahat*), because of the flies.

25-27. Pharaoh again agreed to let Israel go but sought to compromise their situation by requiring that they **sacrifice . . .**

and for Aaron, and said, Go ye, sacrifice to your God in the land.

26 And Moses said, It is not meet so to do; for we shall sacrifice the abomination of the Egyptians to the LORD our God: lo, shall we sacrifice the abomination of the Egyptians before their eyes, and will they not stone us?

27 We will go three days' journey into the wilderness, and sacrifice to the LORD our God, as he shall command us.

28 And Pharaoh said, I will let you go, that ye may sacrifice to the LORD your God in the wilderness; only ye shall not go very far away: intreat for me.

29 And Moses said, Behold, I go out from thee, and I will intreat the LORD that the swarms of flies may depart from Pharaoh, from his servants, and from his people, to morrow: but let not Pharaoh deal deceitfully any more in not letting the people go to sacrifice to the LORD.

30 And Moses went out from Pharaoh, and intreated the LORD.

31 And the LORD did according to the word of Moses; and he removed the swarms of flies from Pharaoh, from his servants, and from his people; there remained not one.

32 And Pharaoh hardened his heart at this time also, neither would he let the people go.

CHAPTER 9

THEN the LORD said unto Moses, Go in unto Pharaoh, and tell him, Thus saith the LORD God of the Hebrews, Let my people go, that they may serve me.

2 For if thou refuse to let them go, and wilt hold them still,

3 Behold, the hand of the LORD is upon thy cattle which is in the field, upon the horses, upon the asses, upon the camels, upon the oxen, and upon the sheep: there shall be a very grievous murrain.

4 And the LORD shall sever between the cattle of Israel and the cattle of Egypt: and there shall nothing die of all that is the children's of Israel.

5 And the LORD appointed a set time, saying, To morrow the LORD shall do this thing in the land.

6 And the LORD did that thing on the morrow, and all the cattle of Egypt died: but of the cattle of the children of Israel died not one.

7 And Pharaoh sent, and, behold, there was not one of the cattle of the Israelites dead. And the heart of Pharaoh was hardened, and he did not let the people go.

8 ¶And the LORD said unto Moses and unto Aaron, Take to you handfuls of ashes of the furnace, and let Moses sprinkle it toward the heaven in the sight of Pharaoh.

9 And it shall become small dust in all the land of Egypt, and shall be a boil breaking forth with blains upon man, and upon beast, throughout all the land of Egypt.

10 And they took ashes of the furnace, and stood before Pharaoh; and Moses sprinkled it up toward heaven; and it became a boil breaking forth with blains upon man, and upon beast.

in the land. That was not acceptable. God is interested in complete obedience, not in compromise. God was going to remove Israel and perform His promises to Abraham.

28-29. Pharaoh sought another compromise when he saw that the first was rejected. He insisted that though Israel went into **the wilderness,** they should **not go very far away.** But, incomplete obedience is no obedience at all.

30-32. As occurred with the removal of the previous plagues, Pharaoh then refused to allow Israel to leave. Again the text says **Pharaoh hardened his heart** (see comments on Exodus 4:21).

9:1-2. Each plague was conditioned upon Pharaoh's refusal to let Israel go.

3-5. The fifth plague was to affect all manner of **cattle which is in the field,** including camels, sheep, horses, asses, and oxen. **Murrain** (Heb deber) signifies a very deadly disease. There was to be a distinction between Israel and Egypt in this plague, as in the fourth; and a set time was given for the commencement of the disaster so that any Egyptians who believed Moses' message could remove their cattle from **the field.**

6-7. All the cattle of Egypt died refers to all the cattle left in the fields (vs. 3). This plague was a direct affront to the sacred bull, Apis, of the god Ptah and the cow goddess Hathor.

8-10. A boil breaking forth with blains indicates "an inflamed painful boil or abscess, breaking into a running sore" (Johnson, Exodus in *The Wycliffe Bible Commentary*, p. 59). It must have taken place suddenly and universally **upon man, and upon beast.**

11 And the magicians could not stand before Moses because of the boils; for the boil was upon the magicians, and upon all the Egyptians.

12 And the LORD hardened the heart of Pharaoh, and he hearkened not unto them; as the LORD had spoken unto Moses.

13 ¶And the LORD said unto Moses, Rise up early in the morning, and stand before Pharaoh, and say unto him, Thus saith the LORD God of the Hebrews, Let my people go, that they may serve me.

14 For I will at this time send all my plagues upon thine heart, and upon thy servants, and upon thy people; that thou mayest know that there is none like me in all the earth.

15 For now I will stretch out my hand, that I may smite thee and thy people with pestilence; and thou shalt be cut off from the earth.

16 And in very deed for this cause have I raised thee up, for to shew in thee my power; and that my name may be declared throughout all the earth.

17 As yet exaltest thou thyself against my people, that thou wilt not let them go?

18 Behold, to morrow about this time I will cause it to rain a very grievous hail, such as hath not been in Egypt since the foundation thereof even until now.

19 Send therefore now, and gather thy cattle, and all that thou hast in the field; for upon every man and beast which shall be found in the field, and shall not be brought home, the hail shall come down upon them, and they shall die.

20 He that feared the word of the LORD among the servants of Pharaoh made his servants and his cattle flee into the houses:

21 And he that regarded not the word of the LORD left his servants and his cattle in the field.

22 ¶And the LORD said unto Moses, Stretch forth thine hand toward heaven, that there may be hail in all the land of Egypt, upon man, and upon beast, and upon every herb of the field, throughout the land of Egypt.

23 And Moses stretched forth his rod toward heaven: and the LORD sent thunder and hail, and the fire ran along upon the ground; and the LORD rained hail upon the land of Egypt.

24 So there was hail, and fire mingled with the hail, very grievous, such as there was none like it in all the land of Egypt since it became a nation.

25 And the hail smote throughout all the land of Egypt all that was in the field, both man and beast; and the hail smote every herb of the field, and brake every tree of the field.

26 Only in the land of Goshen, where the children of Israel were, was there no hail.

27 ¶And Pharaoh sent, and called for Moses and Aaron, and said unto them, I

11. Ironically, **the magicians** were also overcome with the boils. They had no cure for them or special spell for their removal (cf. Ex 8:19).

12. For the first time the text reads that **the LORD hardened the heart of Pharaoh.** Previously, the text always read either that Pharaoh hardened his own heart, or that his heart grew stubborn.

13-15. The purpose of the plagues was to teach Pharaoh and the Egyptians (and the Israelites as well?), **that there is none like me** (God) **in all the earth.** Not just several natural near disasters, but a complete series of supernatural calamities were to cripple one of the greatest nations on earth.

16-17. Quoted in Romans 9:17, this verse explains the reason why God **raised** up, or more literally preserved, Pharaoh to this point, rather than crushing him earlier and immediately freeing Israel. God's purpose was to allow Pharaoh to experience Jehovah's mighty wonders. As a result, God's character would **be declared throughout all the earth. Exaltest thou thyself** speaks of a unique arrogance on Pharaoh's part directed against God's **people.**

18. A very grievous hail. Rain itself is infrequent in Egypt, and then only along the Mediterranean coast and rarely south of Cairo. Hail would be a very unusual occurrence in Egypt.

19-21. Send . . . and gather thy cattle. God warned all who would heed of the coming danger, just as He does today. Those who heeded were spared; those who **regarded not the word of the LORD,** were sorry.

22-24. The plague was a spectacular display of **thunder and hail, and the fire** mixed with the hail. It easily broke all previous records!

25-26. Egypt was virtually destroyed. All crops (vss. 31-32), plant life, and even trees were broken and smitten down, a preparation for the locusts which soon followed. Israel, however, was completely spared.

27-30. Pharaoh called for Moses and seemed duly humbled as he declared **I have sinned.** He again promised to release the

have sinned this time: the Lord *is* righteous, and I and my people *are* wicked.

28 Intreat the Lord (for *it is* enough) that there be no *more* mighty thunderings and hail; and I will let you go, and ye shall stay no longer.

29 And Moses said unto him, As soon as I am gone out of the city, I will spread abroad my hands unto the Lord; *and* the thunder shall cease, neither shall there be any more hail; that thou mayest know how that the earth *is* the Lord's.

30 But as for thee and thy servants, I know that ye will not yet fear the Lord God.

31 And the flax and the barley was smitten: for the barley *was* in the ear, and the flax *was* bolled.

32 But the wheat and the rie were not smitten: for they *were* not grown up.

33 And Moses went out of the city from Pharaoh, and spread abroad his hands unto the Lord: and the thunders and hail ceased, and the rain was not poured upon the earth.

34 And when Pharaoh saw that the rain and the hail and the thunders were ceased, he sinned yet more, and hardened his heart, he and his servants.

35 And the heart of Pharaoh was hardened, neither would he let the children of Israel go; as the Lord had spoken by Moses.

CHAPTER 10

AND the Lord said unto Moses, Go in unto Pharaoh: for I have hardened his heart, and the heart of his servants, that I might shew these my signs before him:

2 And that thou mayest tell in the ears of thy son, and of thy son's son, what things I have wrought in Egypt, and my signs which I have done among them; that ye may know how that I *am* the Lord.

3 And Moses and Aaron came in unto Pharaoh, and said unto him, Thus saith the Lord God of the Hebrews, How long wilt thou refuse to humble thyself before me? let my people go, that they may serve me.

4 Else, if thou refuse to let my people go, behold, to morrow will I bring the locusts into thy coast:

5 And they shall cover the face of the earth, that one cannot be able to see the earth: and they shall eat the residue of that which is escaped, which remaineth unto you from the hail, and shall eat every tree which groweth for you out of the field:

6 And they shall fill thy houses, and the houses of all thy servants, and the houses of all the Egyptians; which neither thy fathers, nor thy fathers' fathers have seen, since the day that they were upon the earth unto this day. And he turned himself, and went out from Pharaoh.

7 And Pharaoh's servants said unto him, How long shall this man be a snare unto us? let the men go, that they may serve the Lord their God: knowest thou not yet that Egypt is destroyed?

8 And Moses and Aaron were

captive Israelites. Pharaoh was getting a lesson in theology. He was to learn by this tremendous, supernatural display of the powers of the planet that **the earth is the Lord's.**

31-32. These notations about which crops were smitten (flax and barley) perhaps indicate that the time of the year was between January and February. They also tell us that the primary staples for making bread were gone. This plague had humiliated the supposed protective powers of Isis and Seth.

33-35. After God ended **the thunders and hail,** Pharaoh **sinned yet more, and hardened his heart.** This reprieve provided yet another chance to keep the slaves and somehow to get even with Moses. His hardened heart led to great miseries.

10:1-2. Part of the purpose behind the providential hardening of Pharaoh's heart, which was exhibited in his refusal to allow Israel to leave, was that God might continue to demonstrate his **signs.** It would become a lesson to all the world (Josh 2:10-11) and would serve Israel well in the future as a hallmark of God's greatness, power, and loving-kindness toward Israel.

3-7. The eighth plague, that of the locusts, would consume what the hail had left. After Moses and Aaron announced this coming disaster, they left (vs. 6). But Pharaoh's servants persuaded him to reconsider with their forthright question, **knowest thou not yet that Egypt is destroyed?**

8-11. Another compromise was proposed by Pharaoh as he

brought again unto Pharaoh: and he said unto them, Go, serve the LORD your God: *but* who *are* they that shall go?

9 And Moses said, We will go with our young and with our old, with our sons and with our daughters, with our flocks and with our herds will we go; for we *must hold* a feast unto the LORD.

10 And he said unto them, Let the LORD be so with you, as I will let you go, and your little ones: look *to it;* for evil *is* before you.

11 Not so: go now ye *that are* men, and serve the LORD; for that ye did desire. And they were driven out from Pharaoh's presence.

12 ¶And the LORD said unto Moses, Stretch out thine hand over the land of Egypt for the locusts, that they may come up upon the land of Egypt, and eat every herb of the land, *even* all that the hail hath left.

13 And Moses stretched forth his rod over the land of Egypt, and the LORD brought an east wind upon the land all that day, and all *that* night; *and* when it was morning, the east wind brought the locusts.

14 And the locusts went up over all the land of Egypt, and rested in all the coasts of Egypt: very grievous *were they;* before them there were no such locusts as they, neither after them shall be such.

15 For they covered the face of the whole earth, so that the land was darkened; and they did eat every herb of the land, and all the fruit of the trees which the hail had left: and there remained not any green thing in the trees, or in the herbs of the field, through all the land of Egypt.

16 ¶Then Pharaoh called for Moses and Aaron in haste; and he said, I have sinned against the LORD your God, and against you.

17 Now therefore forgive, I pray thee, my sin only this once, and intreat the LORD your God, that he may take away from me this death only.

18 And he went out from Pharaoh, and intreated the LORD.

19 And the LORD turned a mighty strong west wind, which took away the locusts, and cast them into the Red sea; there remained not one locust in all the coasts of Egypt.

20 But the LORD hardened Pharaoh's heart, so that he would not let the children of Israel go.

21 ¶And the LORD said unto Moses, Stretch out thine hand toward heaven, that there may be darkness over the land of Egypt, even darkness *which* may be felt.

22 And Moses stretched forth his hand toward heaven; and there was a thick darkness in all the land of Egypt three days:

23 They saw not one another, neither rose any from his place for three days: but all the children of Israel had light in their dwellings.

24 ¶And Pharaoh called unto Moses, and said, Go ye, serve the LORD; only let

suggested that only **ye that are men** should go and serve the Lord, it being too dangerous for children. But such a move would only insure their return to Egypt.

12-15. After that brief confrontation God brought on the plague of locusts described as **very grievous,** unmatched before in the history of Egypt and to be unsurpassed in its future. One square mile of a locust swarm contains more than 100,000,000 insects and modern swarms have covered as much as 400 square miles.

16-20. After the locusts came Pharaoh admitted, **I have sinned.** It is commendable to recognize one's sins; but in Pharaoh's case he was not sorry for his sin, but only for the results of it, i.e., the locusts which he termed **this death.** Once they were removed, **the LORD hardened Pharaoh's heart** through the surrounding circumstances; and he continued to refuse to allow Israel to go.

21-23. The ninth plague came upon Egypt without warning. It was **a thick darkness** of three days' duration and was so severe that it could be ". . . felt" (vs. 21). This plague struck at the very heart of Egyptian religion, i.e., the deification of the sun as personified by the great gods Re, Amun, Aten, and Horus (the winged Sun disc). Re was to the Egyptians what Yahweh was to the Israelites. He was the ultimate supreme being who sustained all life. The "thick darkness" blotted out his supposed power in the land of Egypt.

24-27. Pharaoh sought yet a fourth compromise (cf. 8:25, 28; 10:10-11), whereby Israel would leave their flocks, herds, and other possessions behind in Egypt while going to **serve the**

your flocks and your herds be stayed: let your little ones also go with you.

25 And Moses said, Thou must give us also sacrifices and burnt offerings, that we may sacrifice unto the LORD our God.

26 Our cattle also shall go with us; there shall not an hoof be left behind; for thereof must we take to serve the LORD our God; and we know not with what we must serve the LORD, until we come thither.

27 ¶But the LORD hardened Pharaoh's heart, and he would not let them go.

28 And Pharaoh said unto him, Get thee from me, take heed to thyself, see my face no more; for in *that* day thou seest my face thou shalt die.

29 And Moses said, Thou hast spoken well, I will see thy face again no more.

CHAPTER 11

AND the LORD said unto Moses, Yet will I bring one plague *more* upon Pharaoh, and upon Egypt; afterwards he will let you go hence: when he shall let *you* go, he shall surely thrust you out hence altogether.

2 Speak now in the ears of the people, and let every man borrow of his neighbour, and every woman of her neighbour, jewels of silver, and jewels of gold.

3 And the LORD gave the people favour in the sight of the Egyptians. Moreover the man Moses *was* very great in the land of Egypt, in the sight of Pharaoh's servants, and in the sight of the people.

4 ¶And Moses said, Thus saith the LORD, About midnight will I go out into the midst of Egypt:

5 And all the firstborn in the land of Egypt shall die, from the firstborn of Pharaoh that sitteth upon his throne, even unto the firstborn of the maidservant that *is* behind the mill; and all the firstborn of beasts.

6 And there shall be a great cry throughout all the land of Egypt, such as there was none like it, nor shall be like it any more.

7 But against any of the children of Israel shall not a dog move his tongue, against man or beast: that ye may know how that the LORD doth put a difference between the Egyptians and Israel.

8 And all these thy servants shall come down unto me, and bow down themselves unto me, saying, Get thee out, and all the people that follow thee: and after that I will go out. And he went out from Pharaoh in a great anger.

9 And the LORD said unto Moses, Pharaoh shall not hearken unto you; that my wonders may be multiplied in the land of Egypt.

10 And Moses and Aaron did all these wonders before Pharaoh: and the LORD hardened Pharaoh's heart, so that he would not let the children of Israel go out of his land.

LORD. But God certainly requires all that we possess, was essentially Moses' reply. There could be no compromise.

28-29. Pharaoh's final words of anger to Moses promised him death if he ever saw his face again. Moses agreed with Pharaoh saying, **Thou hast spoken well,** but then proceeded to inform Pharaoh of the tenth and final judgment that would come upon Egypt.

B. The Passover. 11:1-12:28.

11:1. The drama of the plagues and the contest with Pharaoh were full of suspense for Moses too. He awaited each new revelation from God. God had previously announced to Moses, **I bring one plague more.** Moses probably had no definite idea how many plagues there would be. God also had foretold that **afterwards he will let you go hence.** The various plagues would now reach their climax and accomplish their desired end (cf. Ex 3:19-20).

2-3. The Israelites were also instructed to **borrow . . . jewels of silver, and jewels of gold** from the Egyptians. They were not to go out of Egypt empty after serving as slaves for hundreds of years. They were to receive wages (cf. 3:21-22; 12:35-36).

4-6. Moses continued to inform the people (and Pharaoh as well; verses 1-3 are parenthetic), that Jehovah would go throughout Egypt at **midnight** (apparently several days or weeks later) and slay **all the first-born in the land of Egypt.** This included males and females as well and even involved **all the first-born of beasts.**

7-8. Using a possible hyperbole, Moses said that not even a **dog** should **move his tongue** against Israel as they would be departing. All would be silent. No hand would be raised to prevent their departure, and not even a dog would bark.

9-10. See comments on Exodus 3:19-20, and 4:21.

CHAPTER 12

AND the LORD spake unto Moses and Aaron in the land of Egypt, saying,

2 This month *shall be* unto you the beginning of months: it *shall be* the first month of the year to you.

3 ¶Speak ye unto all the congregation of Israel, saying, In the tenth *day* of this month they shall take to them every man a lamb, according to the house of *their* fathers, a lamb for an house:

4 And if the household be too little for the lamb, let him and his neighbour next unto his house take *it* according to the number of the souls; every man according to his eating shall make your count for the lamb.

5 Your lamb shall be without blemish, a male of the first year: ye shall take *it* out from the sheep, or from the goats:

6 And ye shall keep it up until the fourteenth day of the same month: and the whole assembly of the congregation of Israel shall kill it in the evening.

7 And they shall take of the blood, and strike *it* on the two side posts and on the upper door post of the houses, wherein they shall eat it.

8 And they shall eat the flesh in that night, roast with fire, and unleavened bread; *and* with bitter *herbs* they shall eat it.

9 Eat not of it raw, nor sodden at all with water, but roast *with* fire; his head with his legs, and with the purtenance thereof.

10 And ye shall let nothing of it remain until the morning; and that which remaineth of it until the morning ye shall burn with fire.

11 And thus shall ye eat it; *with* your loins girded, your shoes on your feet, and your staff in your hand; and ye shall eat it in haste: it *is* the LORD's passover.

12 For I will pass through the land of Egypt this night, and will smite all the firstborn in the land of Egypt, both man and beast; and against all the gods of Egypt I will execute judgment: I *am* the LORD.

13 And the blood shall be to you for a token upon the houses where ye *are:* and when I see the blood, I will pass over you, and the plague shall not be upon you to destroy *you,* when I smite the land of Egypt.

14 And this day shall be unto you for a memorial; and ye shall keep it a feast to the LORD throughout your generations; ye shall keep it a feast by an ordinance for ever.

15 ¶Seven days shall ye eat unleavened bread; even the first day ye shall put away leaven out of your houses: for whosoever eateth leavened bread from the first day until the

12:1-2. This month shall be unto you the beginning of months. The Passover was to commence and thereafter commemorate the beginning of the Jewish religious year. It comes in March or April, based on the moon's phases. Thus, the Day of Atonement, which falls on the tenth day of the seventh month (Lev 23:27), comes in October, seven months from Passover.

3-4. The tenth day of this month. Although the Passover was not celebrated until the fourteenth day, **the lamb** had to be observed for four days to make sure it had no blemishes (cf. vss. 5-6). I Corinthians 5:7 says that ". . . Christ our passover is sacrificed for us." The passover lamb typified Christ. Christ also had to be observed for four days in Jerusalem prior to his crucifixion. During those four days He was tested and asked questions, but none could find fault with Him (Mt 21:23-27; 22:15-22; 33-46). **A lamb for a house.** There is a progression of doctrine regarding the sacrificing of a lamb. (1) In Genesis the lamb was slain for the individual (Gen 4:4). (2) In Exodus the lamb was slain for the family (house), (Ex 12:3-4). (3) In Leviticus the lamb was slain for the nation (Lev 16). (4) In the New Testament the Lamb of God was slain for the sin of the world (Jn 1:29).

5-7. To picture the absolute perfection of Christ the lamb had to be **without blemish.** Then, they had to **kill it** and **take of the blood** to apply it to the door as God had specified (on the side and top doorposts). Without the shedding of blood there is no forgiveness of sins (Heb 9:22). Christ has shed His precious blood for our redemption, but it is ineffective until each sinner makes the application personally to his own soul by believing Jesus died, was buried, and rose again for him. Likewise, the Israelite could not be saved from the death angel simply by killing the lamb. **The blood** had to be properly applied.

8-11. Roast with fire. It had to be cooked quickly and could not be boiled. **Unleavened bread** indicates bread made without yeast. There was no time to have the bread rise. Yeast also became a picture of sin, a corrupting influence (Mt 13:33; 16:6; I Cor 5:6-8). **With bitter herbs they shall eat it.** The bitter herbs were to remind them of the bitterness of their hard stay in Egypt as slaves. The lamb was to be fully consumed while they were fully dressed and prepared to depart.

12-13. When I see the blood, I will pass over you. The applied blood was the evidence of an obedient and prepared household. It fulfilled the divine demand for blood atonement and prefigured the blood of Christ shed for our sins.

14-20. Ye shall keep it a feast to the LORD throughout your generations. Although the Passover itself was a one-night occurrence, it was to be part of a yearly one-week celebration. The **first** and **seventh** days were to be sabbaths of rest—**no manner of work shall be done in them.** That seven-day feast period was called the Feast of Unleavened Bread and included Passover and the Feast of First fruits (Lev 23:5-11; Lk 22:1). Later commemorations of this feast are recorded in Joshua 5:10, II Kings 23:22, II Chronicles 35:18, and Ezra 6:19.

seventh day, that soul shall be cut off from Israel.

16 And in the first day *there shall be* an holy convocation, and in the seventh day there shall be an holy convocation to you; no manner of work shall be done in them, save *that* which every man must eat, that only may be done of you.

17 And ye shall observe *the feast of* unleavened bread; for in this selfsame day have I brought your armies out of the land of Egypt: therefore shall ye observe this day in your generations by an ordinance for ever.

18 In the first *month,* on the fourteenth day of the month at even, ye shall eat unleavened bread, until the one and twentieth day of the month at even.

19 Seven days shall there be no leaven found in your houses: for whosoever eateth that which is leavened, even that soul shall be cut off from the congregation of Israel, whether he be a stranger, or born in the land.

20 Ye shall eat nothing leavened; in all your habitations shall ye eat unleavened bread.

21 ¶Then Moses called for all the elders of Israel, and said unto them, Draw out and take you a lamb according to your families, and kill the passover.

22 And ye shall take a bunch of hyssop, and dip *it* in the blood that *is* in the bason, and strike the lintel and the two side posts with the blood that *is* in the bason: and none of you shall go out at the door of his house until the morning.

23 For the Lord will pass through to smite the Egyptians; and when he seeth the blood upon the lintel, and on the two side posts, the Lord will pass over the door, and will not suffer the destroyer to come in unto your houses to smite *you.*

24 And ye shall observe this thing for an ordinance to thee and to thy sons for ever.

25 And it shall come to pass, when ye be come to the land which the Lord will give you, according as he hath promised, that ye shall keep this service.

26 And it shall come to pass, when your children shall say unto you, What mean ye by this service?

27 That ye shall say, It *is* the sacrifice of the Lord's passover, who passed over the houses of the children of Israel in Egypt, when he smote the Egyptians, and delivered our houses. And the people bowed the head and worshipped.

28 And the children of Israel went away, and did as the Lord had commanded Moses and Aaron, so did they.

29 ¶And it came to pass, that at midnight the Lord smote all the firstborn in the land of Egypt, from the firstborn of Pharaoh that sat on his throne unto the firstborn of the captive that *was* in the dungeon; and all the firstborn of cattle.

30 And Pharaoh rose up in the night, he, and all his servants, and all the Egyptians; and there was a great cry in

21-28. Moses called for all the elders of Israel and repeated to them what God had explained to him (Ex 12:1-20). The people were quick to accept Moses' words now, after witnessing the nine terrifying plagues that had come upon the Egyptians. We assume that they were no longer employed as slaves, but were simply waiting for word as to departure time. Leaving was now a foregone conclusion. Verse 27 says, "the people bowed the head and worshiped." They then departed and did as God had commanded them.

C. Death of the First-born. 12:29-33.

29-33. The smiting of **all the first-born in the land of Egypt** was universal. All were affected; no home or stable was immune. It must have created one of the largest mass funerals in the history of the earth. The so-called "moral objections" to this judgment are illegitimate in the face of a Holy God. The Egyptians had deliberately rejected His mighty signs and, thus, were under His wrath. If Amenhotep II was the Pharaoh of the Exodus, his eldest son who died would have been the brother of his successor, Thutmose IV. The primary result was that Pha-

140

Egypt; for *there was* not a house where *there was* not one dead.

31 ¶And he called for Moses and Aaron by night, and said, Rise up, *and* get you forth from among my people, both ye and the children of Israel; and go, serve the LORD, as ye have said.

32 Also take your flocks and your herds, as ye have said, and be gone; and bless me also.

33 And the Egyptians were urgent upon the people, that they might send them out of the land in haste; for they said, We *be* all dead *men.*

34 And the people took their dough before it was leavened, their kneadingtroughs being bound up in their clothes upon their shoulders.

35 And the children of Israel did according to the word of Moses; and they borrowed of the Egyptians jewels of silver, and jewels of gold, and raiment:

36 And the LORD gave the people favour in the sight of the Egyptians, so that they lent unto them *such things as they required.* And they spoiled the Egyptians.

37 ¶And the children of Israel journeyed from Răm'e-sĕs to Sŭc'coth, about six hundred thousand on foot *that were* men, beside children.

38 And a mixed multitude went up also with them; and flocks, and herds, *even* very much cattle.

39 And they baked unleavened cakes of the dough which they brought forth out of Egypt, for it was not leavened; because they were thrust out of Egypt, and could not tarry, neither had they prepared for themselves any victual.

40 ¶Now the sojourning of the children of Israel, who dwelt in Egypt, *was* four hundred and thirty years.

41 And it came to pass at the end of the four hundred and thirty years, even the selfsame day it came to pass, that all the hosts of the LORD went out from the land of Egypt.

42 It *is* a night to be much observed

raoh now readily acceded to all of Moses' previously stated conditions; all Israelites were to leave, including **flocks and herds, as ye have said.** All Egypt joined to help the Israelites to leave quickly before, as the Egyptians expressed it, **We be all dead men.**

V. THE EXODUS AND THE SONG OF MIRIAM. 12:34-15:21.

A. The Journey from Rameses to Succoth. 12:34-51.

34-36. They borrowed of the Egyptians is literally "they asked." And the Egyptians **lent** (lit., gave) the Israelites whatever they needed. There was no borrowing or lending; both knew they would never see each other again.

37. From Rameses to Succoth. The initial direction followed in the Exodus must have been almost directly south, or southeast, from Goshen along the western side of the Red Sea which at that time extended considerably farther north than it does now. **About six hundred thousand . . . men, beside children.** Numbers 1:46 sets the total male population (age twenty and over) at 603,550. The entire group, including women and children, must have surpassed two million. This is not inconceivable, considering the four hundred years they were in Egypt and the blessings of God upon their multiplication (Ex 1:7).

38-39. Mixed multitude. Israel also contained foreign elements (cf. Ex 12:19, "stranger"), who caused trouble along the way (Num 11:4).

40-41. That **four hundred and thirty years** was the number of years from the time Jacob entered Egypt until Israel escaped at the Exodus can be seen from: (1) The clear statement of the Hebrew text in this passage; (2) God's prediction to Abraham that his descendants (seed) would be a stranger in a foreign land, serve the foreigners, and be afflicted by them "four hundred years" (Gen 15:13); (3) The list of eleven generations between Jacob and Joshua in I Chronicles 7:22-27; and (4) The multiplication from seventy to over two million is easiest to reconcile within this time structure.

The date of the Exodus, as mentioned in the Introduction, was approximately 1445 B.C. (1) There is no good reason to discount the accuracy of the years mentioned in I Kings 6:1. Those who ignore or try to explain away that reference usually do so in an attempt to accommodate themselves to the late date theory of the Exodus. (2) The obvious intention of Judges 11:26 is that Israel had dwelt in Heshbon and the surrounding region for at least three hundred years prior to Jephthah who lived at approximately 1100 B.C. (3) The date Paul gives in Acts 13:20 would be impossible to reconcile with a date of ca. 1290 B.C. for the Exodus. See the comments on Exodus 1:11. Also cf. Leon Wood, "Date of the Exodus," in J. B. Payne (ed.), *New Perspectives on the Old Testament,* pp. 66-87, and C. DeWit, *The Date and Route of the Exodus.*

42-45. When thou hast circumcised him. The Passover

unto the LORD for bringing them out from the land of Egypt: this *is* that night of the LORD to be observed of all the children of Israel in their generations.

43 ¶And the LORD said unto Moses and Aaron, This *is* the ordinance of the passover: There shall no stranger eat thereof:

44 But every man's servant that is bought for money, when thou hast circumcised him, then shall he eat thereof.

45 A foreigner and an hired servant shall not eat thereof.

46 In one house shall it be eaten; thou shalt not carry forth ought of the flesh abroad out of the house; neither shall ye break a bone thereof.

47 All the congregation of Israel shall keep it.

48 And when a stranger shall sojourn with thee, and will keep the passover to the LORD, let all his males be circumcised, and then let him come near and keep it; and he shall be as one that is born in the land: for no uncircumcised person shall eat thereof.

49 One law shall be to him that is homeborn, and unto the stranger that sojourneth among you.

50 Thus did all the children of Israel; as the LORD commanded Moses and Aaron, so did they.

51 And it came to pass the selfsame day, *that* the LORD did bring the children of Israel out of the land of Egypt by their armies.

CHAPTER 13

AND the LORD spake unto Moses, saying,

2 Sanctify unto me all the firstborn, whatsoever openeth the womb among the children of Israel, *both* of man and of beast: it *is* mine.

3 ¶And Moses said unto the people, Remember this day, in which ye came out from Egypt, out of the house of bondage; for by strength of hand the LORD brought you out from this *place*: there shall no leavened bread be eaten.

4 This day came ye out in the month Ăbĭb.

5 And it shall be when the LORD shall bring thee into the land of the Canaanites, and the Hittites, and the Ămorites, and the Hīvītes, and the Jeb'usītes, which he sware unto thy fathers to give thee, a land flowing with milk and honey, that thou shalt keep this service in this month.

6 Seven days thou shalt eat unleavened bread, and in the seventh day *shall be* a feast to the LORD.

7 Unleavened bread shall be eaten seven days; and there shall no leavened bread be seen with thee, neither shall there be leaven seen with thee in all thy quarters.

8 And thou shalt shew thy son in that day, saying, This is done because of that *which* the LORD did unto me when I came forth out of Egypt.

9 And it shall be for a sign unto thee upon thine hand, and for a memorial between thine eyes, that the LORD's law may be in thy mouth: for with a strong

could be partaken of by the purchased servants of the Hebrews who had become full Israelites by circumcision. But **a foreigner** or **a hired servant** was not to partake because he had not become joined to Israel.

46-51. Neither shall ye break a bone thereof refers to the Passover lamb and typifies Christ of whom the same could be said when He was crucified (Jn 19:36). **By their armies** (vs. 51) refers to the hosts of multitudes of Israel, not necessarily enlisted fighting men.

B. Parenthesis: Redemption of Israel's First-born. 13:1-16.

13:1-2. Sanctify unto me all the first-born . . . both of man and of beast. Even as God claimed the lives of all first-born human beings and animals in Egypt in the Passover, God placed a similar claim upon Israel. See also verses 11-16.

3-10. These verses reiterate the basic law of the Passover. The feast was to last for seven days; no leaven was to be used; it was to commemorate God's deliverance of Israel from Egypt; and it was to be celebrated every year **in the month Abib** (April).

hand hath the LORD brought thee out of Egypt.

10 Thou shalt therefore keep this ordinance in his season from year to year.

11 ¶And it shall be when the LORD shall bring thee into the land of the Canaanites, as he sware unto thee and to thy fathers, and shall give it thee,

12 That thou shalt set apart unto the LORD all that openeth the matrix, and every firstling that cometh of a beast which thou hast; the males *shall be* the LORD'S.

13 And every firstling of an ass thou shalt redeem with a lamb; and if thou wilt not redeem it, then thou shalt break his neck: and all the firstborn of man among thy children shalt thou redeem.

14 ¶And it shall be when thy son asketh thee in time to come, saying, What *is* this? that thou shalt say unto him, By strength of hand the LORD brought us out from Egypt, from the house of bondage:

15 And it came to pass, when Pharaoh would hardly let us go, that the LORD slew all the firstborn in the land of Egypt, both the firstborn of man, and the firstborn of beast: therefore I sacrifice to the LORD all that openeth the matrix, being males; but all the firstborn of my children I redeem.

16 And it shall be for a token upon thine hand, and for frontlets between thine eyes: for by strength of hand the LORD brought us forth out of Egypt.

17 ¶And it came to pass, when Pharaoh had let the people go, that God led them not *through* the way of the land of the Philistines, although that *was* near; for God said, Lest peradventure the people repent when they see war, and they return to Egypt:

18 But God led the people about, *through* the way of the wilderness of the Red sea: and the children of Israel went up harnessed out of the land of Egypt.

19 And Moses took the bones of Joseph with him: for he had straitly sworn the children of Israel, saying, God will surely visit you; and ye shall carry up my bones away hence with you.

20 ¶And they took their journey from Sŭc'coth, and encamped in Ē'tham, in the edge of the wilderness.

21 And the LORD went before them by

11-16. These verses enlarge on the theme mentioned in verses 1-2. God claimed all first-born Israelites, whether male or female. But instead, he took the Levites who made up approximately the same number as the count of first-borns (Num 3:12-13). The first-born of every animal was offered as a **sacrifice to the LORD.**

C. The Journey to the Edge of the Red Sea. 13:17—14:12.

17. Not through the way . . . of the Philistines. This would have been a short, quick route, but it was filled with danger and the possibility of war.

18. The Red Sea. Some critics have sought to identify the Red Sea (Heb *yam suph*) with a supposed Sea of Reeds; but this is done in an effort to discount the miracles of God's Word, especially the biblical crossing of the Red Sea. The Red Sea is mentioned thirteen times by name in the Pentateuch (Num 21:14 in KJV should not be counted) and twelve times in the rest of the Old Testament. Each time the same Hebrew word is used; and there is no reason to make it refer to any other body of water than the Red Sea, including one or the other of its two gulfs—Suez and Aqaba. Numbers 21:4 indicates that Israel's journey took them from Mount Hor to Edom ". . . by the way of the Red Sea . . . ," clearly one of the gulfs of the Red Sea. The LXX (Gk translation the Jews made of the OT in 250 B.C.) uniformly translates each mention of **Red Sea** (Heb *yam suph*) by the Greek expression *thalassa eruthra,* except where the Hebrew is transliterated once in Judges and where *eschatos* is used once in I Kings. The New Testament confirms the identity also by uniformly speaking of the Red Sea in the same words as the LXX uses to translate the Old Testament references.

19. Moses took the bones of Joseph, as the promise was made to dying Joseph over three hundred fifty years before (Gen 50:24-25) when he repeated the oath of deliverance God had given to Abraham (Gen 15:13-16).

20-22. God's immediate presence was located **in a pillar of a cloud** by day, and in a **pillar of fire** by night. By this visible presence God guided and protected Israel through their marchings in the wilderness.

day in a pillar of a cloud, to lead them the way; and by night in a pillar of fire, to give them light; to go by day and night:

22 He took not away the pillar of the cloud by day, nor the pillar of fire by night, *from* before the people.

CHAPTER 14

AND the LORD spake unto Moses, saying,

2 Speak unto the children of Israel, that they turn and encamp before Pī′-ha-hī′rŏth, between Mĭg′dŏl and the sea, over against Bā′al-zē′phŏn: before it shall ye encamp by the sea.

3 For Pharaoh will say of the children of Israel, They *are* entangled in the land, the wilderness hath shut them in.

4 And I will harden Pharaoh's heart, that he shall follow after them; and I will be honoured upon Pharaoh, and upon all his host; that the Egyptians may know that I *am* the LORD. And they did so.

5 ¶And it was told the king of Egypt that the people fled: and the heart of Pharaoh and of his servants was turned against the people, and they said, Why have we done this, that we have let Israel go from serving us?

6 And he made ready his chariot, and took his people with him:

7 And he took six hundred chosen chariots, and all the chariots of Egypt, and captains over every one of them.

8 And the LORD hardened the heart of Pharaoh king of Egypt, and he pursued after the children of Israel: and the children of Israel went out with an high hand.

9 But the Egyptians pursued after them, all the horses *and* chariots of Pharaoh, and his horsemen, and his army, and overtook them encamping by the sea, beside Pī′-ha-hī′rŏth, before Bā′al-zē′phŏn.

10 ¶And when Pharaoh drew nigh, the children of Israel lifted up their eyes, and, behold, the Egyptians marched after them; and they were sore afraid: and the children of Israel cried out unto the LORD.

11 And they said unto Moses, Because *there were* no graves in Egypt, hast thou taken us away to die in the wilderness? wherefore hast thou dealt thus with us, to carry us forth out of Egypt?

12 *Is* not this the word that we did tell thee in Egypt, saying, Let us alone, that we may serve the Egyptians? For *it had been* better for us to serve the Egyptians, than that we should die in the wilderness.

13 ¶And Moses said unto the people, Fear ye not, stand still, and see the salvation of the LORD, which he will shew to you to day: for the Egyptians whom ye have seen to day, ye shall see them again no more for ever.

14 The LORD shall fight for you, and ye shall hold your peace.

15 ¶And the LORD said unto Moses, Wherefore criest thou unto me? speak unto the children of Israel, that they go forward:

14:1-7. Israel was led by God to **encamp by the sea** in a seemingly defenseless position. This enticed Pharaoh. When Pharaoh and his servants came to realize what it meant that their slaves had departed, they decided to recapture Israel. Their plans, however, were part of God's larger plan to teach the Egyptians to **know that I am the LORD.**

8-10. Israel's camp lay **by the sea, beside Pi-hahiroth, before Baal-zephon.** The exact locations of these sites are completely unknown today. Israel's predicament at Pharaoh's arrival caused them to be **sore afraid.**

11-12. They directed their complaints against Moses and uttered a compromise. **Better for us to serve the Egyptians, than that we should die in the wilderness.**

D. The Crossing of the Red Sea. 14:13-31.

13-15. Moses, by contrast, chose to place his confidence in the powerful working of Almighty God on Israel's behalf. **Stand still, and see the salvation of the LORD.** Israel would be saved, and without even having to fight. What a great God! God instructed Israel to **go forward.**

16 But lift thou up thy rod, and stretch out thine hand over the sea, and divide it: and the children of Israel shall go on dry *ground* through the midst of the sea.

17 And I, behold, I will harden the hearts of the Egyptians, and they shall follow them: and I will get me honour upon Pharaoh, and upon all his host, upon his chariots, and upon his horsemen.

18 And the Egyptians shall know that I *am* the LORD, when I have gotten me honour upon Pharaoh, upon his chariots, and upon his horsemen.

19 ¶And the angel of God, which went before the camp of Israel, removed and went behind them; and the pillar of the cloud went from before their face, and stood behind them:

20 And it came between the camp of the Egyptians and the camp of Israel; and it was a cloud and darkness *to them*, but it gave light by night *to these*: so that the one came not near the other all the night.

21 And Moses stretched out his hand over the sea; and the LORD caused the sea to go *back* by a strong east wind all that night, and made the sea dry *land*, and the waters were divided.

22 And the children of Israel went into the midst of the sea upon the dry *ground*: and the waters *were* a wall unto them on their right hand, and on their left.

23 ¶And the Egyptians pursued, and went in after them to the midst of the sea, *even* all Pharaoh's horses, his chariots, and his horsemen.

24 And it came to pass, that in the morning watch the LORD looked unto the host of the Egyptians through the pillar of fire and of the cloud, and troubled the host of the Egyptians,

25 And took off their chariot wheels, that they drave them heavily: so that the Egyptians said, Let us flee from the face of Israel; for the LORD fighteth for them against the Egyptians.

26 And the LORD said unto Moses, Stretch out thine hand over the sea, that the waters may come again upon the Egyptians, upon their chariots, and upon their horsemen.

27 And Moses stretched forth his hand over the sea, and the sea returned to his strength when the morning appeared; and the Egyptians fled against it; and the LORD overthrew the Egyptians in the midst of the sea.

28 And the waters returned, and covered the chariots, and the horsemen, *and* all the host of Pharaoh that came into the sea after them; there remained not so much as one of them.

29 But the children of Israel walked upon dry *land* in the midst of the sea;

16-21. Parenthetically, Moses related how God revealed to him His plan for crossing the Red Sea on dry ground (vs. 16) and how God intervened between Israel and the Egyptian forces through His messenger in the cloudy pillar (vss. 19-20). The means God used to divide the sea was a supernaturally sent wind (vs. 21).

22. Into the midst of the sea upon the dry ground. That this was a supernatural miracle is seen from the fact that: (1) Israel actually crossed through the Red Sea, not some lowland swamp area (see Ex 13:18); (2) Israel walked on **dry ground;** (3) Israel is described as being in **the midst,** the depths, and the heart of the sea (Ex 15:5, 8), and the New Testament uses the figure of baptism (Gk *baptizo*), i.e., submersion, to describe their movement through the sea to indicate how they went down into it (I Cor 10:1-2), (4) The Egyptian army drowned in the sea, being covered by the depths, and sinking to the bottom (Ex 14:27-28; 15:5). Each of these facts points to a miracle, not just a natural passing through a swampy area.

23-25. The Egyptian pursuit was plagued by God who **troubled the host . . . And took off their chariot wheels.** As a result, they decided to **flee.** God was teaching them who He was.

26-28. At the conclusion of the miraculous parting of the waters, God simply allowed the Red Sea to close down upon the Egyptians in its full **strength.** Rapidly moving water can be a devastating force. The text indicates the destruction of Pharaoh's army and does not necessarily indicate that he himself drowned. There is no reference in Egyptian history to the premature death of a Pharaoh.

29-31. The results of that experience were: (1) salvation from Egypt; (2) destruction of the Egyptian army; (3) Israel's respect,

and the waters *were* a wall unto them on their right hand, and on their left.

30 Thus the LORD saved Israel that day out of the hand of the Egyptians; and Israel saw the Egyptians dead upon the sea shore.

31 And Israel saw that great work which the LORD did upon the Egyptians: and the people feared the LORD, and believed the LORD, and his servant Moses.

CHAPTER 15

THEN sang Moses and the children of Israel this song unto the LORD, and spake, saying, I will sing unto the LORD, for he hath triumphed gloriously: the horse and his rider hath he thrown into the sea.

2 The LORD *is* my strength and song, and he is become my salvation: he *is* my God, and I will prepare him an habitation; my father's God, and I will exalt him.

3 The LORD *is* a man of war: the LORD *is* his name.

4 Pharaoh's chariots and his host hath he cast into the sea: his chosen captains also are drowned in the Red sea.

5 The depths have covered them: they sank into the bottom as a stone.

fear, and trust in God; and (4) Israel's acceptance of Moses as the true spokesman for God. Being baptized in the sea unto Moses signified full allegiance and obedience to God's new leadership in Moses and separation from the old life and authority of Egypt (I Cor 10:1-2).

E. The Song of Praise. 15:1-21.

15:1. Then sang Moses and the children of Israel this song. After the triumph of escape and victory had been enjoyed, it was natural to sing a hymn of praise to God in thanksgiving.

2-6. The theme of this psalm written in Hebrew poetry (parallelistic thought) is God. His character and great works are manifest. **Prepare him a habitation** is better taken as signifying "I will praise Him," parallel with the next expression **I will exalt him.** The character of Hebrew poetry is to repeat each phrase or line in similar words in the next line, or to contrast two thoughts. Most of this poem is in synonymous parallel structure. It is helpful to read this poem in one of the versions that place the phrases in a blank verse type arrangement (as ASV, NASB, NIV).

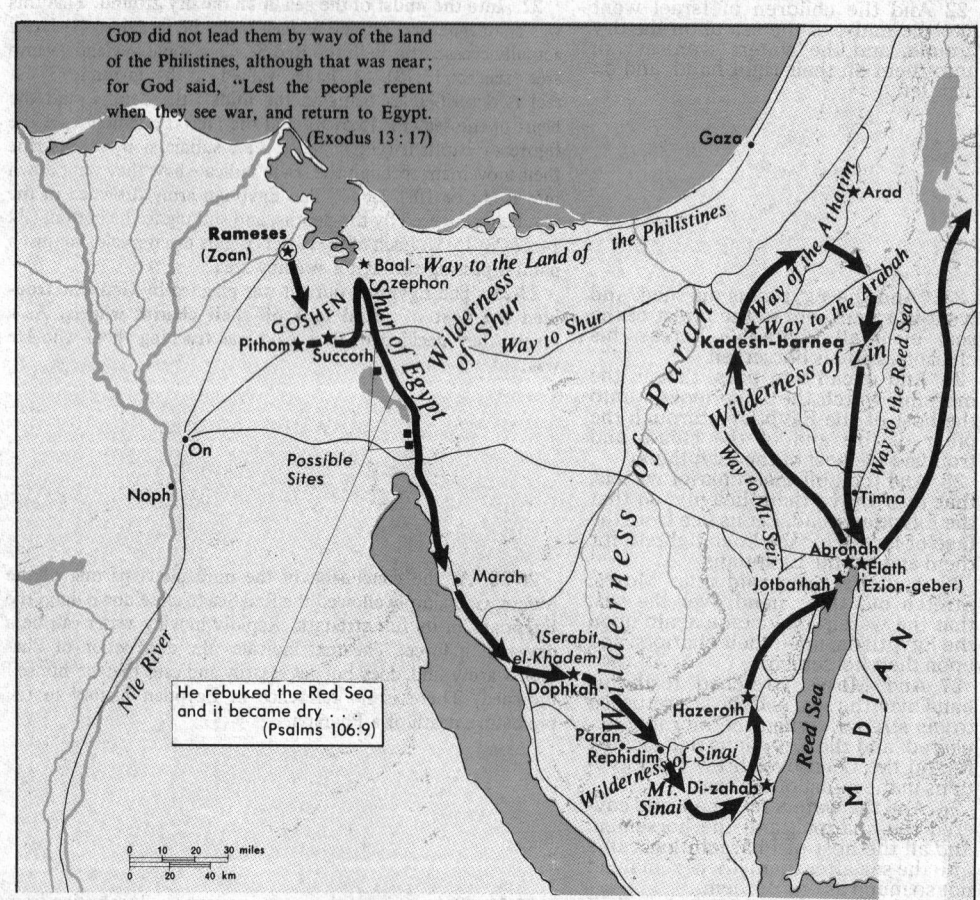

The Exodus And The Route Of The Wandering

6 Thy right hand, O Lord, is become glorious in power: thy right hand, O Lord, hath dashed in pieces the enemy.

7 And in the greatness of thine excellency thou hast overthrown them that rose up against thee: thou sentest forth thy wrath, which consumed them as stubble.

8 And with the blast of thy nostrils the waters were gathered together, the floods stood upright as an heap, and the depths were congealed in the heart of the sea.

9 The enemy said, I will pursue, I will overtake, I will divide the spoil; my lust shall be satisfied upon them; I will draw my sword, my hand shall destroy them.

10 Thou didst blow with thy wind, the sea covered them: they sank as lead in the mighty waters.

11 Who is like unto thee, O Lord, among the gods? who is like thee, glorious in holiness, fearful in praises, doing wonders?

12 Thou stretchedst out thy right hand, the earth swallowed them.

13 Thou in thy mercy hast led forth the people which thou hast redeemed: thou hast guided them in thy strength unto thy holy habitation.

14 The people shall hear, and be afraid: sorrow shall take hold on the inhabitants of Palestina.

15 Then the dukes of Edom shall be amazed; the mighty men of Moab, trembling shall take hold upon them; all the inhabitants of Canaan shall melt away.

16 Fear and dread shall fall upon them; by the greatness of thine arm they shall be as still as a stone; till thy people pass over, O Lord, till the people pass over, which thou hast purchased.

17 Thou shalt bring them in, and plant them in the mountain of thine inheritance, in the place, O Lord, which thou hast made for thee to dwell in, in the Sanctuary, O Lord which thy hands have established.

18 The Lord shall reign for ever and ever.

19 For the horse of Pharaoh went in with his chariots and with his horsemen into the sea, and the Lord brought again the waters of the sea upon them; but the children of Israel went on dry land in the midst of the sea.

20 ¶And Miriam the prophetess, the sister of Aaron, took a timbrel in her hand; and all the women went out after her with timbrels and with dances.

21 And Miriam answered them, Sing ye to the Lord, for he hath triumphed gloriously; the horse and his rider hath he thrown into the sea.

22 ¶So Moses brought Israel from the Red sea, and they went out into the wilderness of Shur; and they went three days in the wilderness, and found no water.

23 ¶And when they came to Mâ'rah, they could not drink of the waters of Mâ'rah, for they were bitter: therefore the name of it was called Mâ'rah.

7-11. Hast overthrown. The Egyptians were completely undone by God. **Blast of thy nostrils.** Of course, God has no bodily parts; but sometimes He is spoken of in this manner to graphically portray elements of truth for us. The practice is called anthropomorphism, (GK *anthropos* and *morphe,* man and form). **Who is like unto thee, O Lord?** God is without equal to an infinite degree, and is **glorious in holiness, fearful** (awesome) **in praises,** who performs awe-inspiring supernatural acts.

12-16. This third and final section (before the epilogue) of the poem turns from God's recent triumph and looks prophetically ahead to the conquest of Canaan. Specifically mentioned as fearing God's power are those of **Palestina** (the Philistines), **Edom** (descendants of Esau), and **Moab** (from Lot, Gen 19:30-38).

17-18. Thou shalt bring them in, and plant them in the mountain of thine inheritance refers to God as a shepherd leading Israel to the new land of mountains and valleys. Israel settled primarily in the hill regions, and the Temple was eventually built in Jerusalem. **The Lord shall reign for ever and ever** is a statement of His eternal kingship. God has always been in control, and He always will be (Ps 103:19; Dan 4:34-35). Man simply needs to realize this!

19-21. The events that led to this great ode of praise to God are recorded in verse 19, while the joy of **Miriam the prophetess** and **all the women** was expressed by their singing and dancing.

VI. THE EVENTS ENROUTE TO MOUNT SINAI.
15:22-18:27.

A. Marah Murmuring and Elim Refreshment. 15:22-27.

22-23. Just after God's special provision of escape and victory the Israelites were tested. They marched for **three days in the wilderness** before finding water, but it was bitter (Heb *marah;* cf. Ruth 1:20).

24 And the people murmured against Moses, saying, What shall we drink?

25 And he cried unto the LORD; and the LORD shewed him a tree, *which* when he had cast into the waters, the waters were made sweet: there he made for them a statute and an ordinance, and there he proved them,

26 And said, If thou wilt diligently hearken to the voice of the LORD thy God, and wilt do that which is right in his sight, and wilt give ear to his commandments, and keep all his statutes, I will put none of these diseases upon thee, which I have brought upon the Egyptians: for I *am* the LORD that healeth thee.

27 ¶And they came to Elim, where *were* twelve wells of water, and threescore and ten palm trees: and they encamped there by the waters.

CHAPTER 16

AND they took their journey from Elim, and all the congregation of the children of Israel came unto the wilderness of Sin, which *is* between Elim and Sī′naī, on the fifteenth day of the second month after their departing out of the land of Egypt.

2 And the whole congregation of the children of Israel murmured against Moses and Aaron in the wilderness:

3 And the children of Israel said unto them, Would to God we had died by the hand of the LORD in the land of Egypt, when we sat by the flesh pots, *and* when we did eat bread to the full; for ye have brought us forth into this wilderness, to kill this whole assembly with hunger.

4 ¶Then said the LORD unto Moses, Behold, I will rain bread from heaven for you; and the people shall go out and gather a certain rate every day, that I may prove them, whether they will walk in my law, or no.

5 And it shall come to pass, that on the sixth day they shall prepare *that* which they bring in; and it shall be twice as much as they gather daily.

6 And Moses and Aaron said unto all the children of Israel, At even, then ye shall know that the LORD hath brought you out from the land of Egypt:

7 And in the morning, then ye shall see the glory of the LORD; for that he heareth your murmurings against the LORD: and what *are* we, that ye murmur against us?

8 And Moses said, *This shall be,* when the LORD shall give you in the evening flesh to eat, and in the morning bread to the full; for that the LORD heareth your murmurings which ye murmur against him: and what *are* we? your murmurings *are* not against us, but against the LORD.

9 And Moses spake unto Aaron, Say unto all the congregation of the children of Israel, Come near before the LORD: for he hath heard your murmurings.

24-26. Instead of trusting God to supply the need, the people **murmured against** their leader **Moses.** Moses sought God's face in prayer and was immediately shown what to do to make the waters sweet. Before moving on, God promised Israel a long-range exemption from the **diseases** of Egypt, conditioned upon the people's continued obedience. There is a lesson to be learned here: it is better to pray rather than complain.

27. They came to Elim. After the trial came the rest at Elim. The incidental mention of the exact number of wells and palm trees is yet another evidence that the author, Moses, was an eyewitness of these experiences. **They encamped there.** The trial at Marah was brief, but God's blessings on the people at Elim were extended. God's loving-kindness toward us is abundant.

B. The Manna Supplied by God. 16:1-36.

16:1-3. Thirty days after their departure from Egypt Israel lacked sufficient food, but instead of trusting they again complained.

4-9. God informed the people of His intention to feed them **flesh** in the evening and **bread** in the morning, and of the double provision on the sixth day, intimating the rest of the Sabbath (vss. 22-29).

10 ¶And it came to pass, as Aaron spake unto the whole congregation of the children of Israel, that they looked toward the wilderness, and, behold, the glory of the LORD appeared in the cloud.

11 And the LORD spake unto Moses, saying,

12 I have heard the murmurings of the children of Israel: speak unto them, saying, At even ye shall eat flesh, and in the morning ye shall be filled with bread; and ye shall know that I am the LORD your God.

13 And it came to pass, that at even the quails came up, and covered the camp: and in the morning the dew lay round about the host.

14 And when the dew that lay was gone up, behold, upon the face of the wilderness there lay a small round thing, as small as the hoar frost on the ground.

15 And when the children of Israel saw it, they said one to another, It is manna: for they wist not what it was. And Moses said unto them, This is the bread which the LORD hath given you to eat.

16 This is the thing which the LORD hath commanded, Gather of it every man according to his eating, an omer for every man, according to the number of your persons; take ye every man for them which are in his tents.

17 And the children of Israel did so, and gathered, some more, some less.

18 And when they did mete it with an omer, he that gathered much had nothing over, and he that gathered little had no lack; they gathered every man according to his eating.

19 And Moses said, Let no man leave of it till the morning.

20 Notwithstanding they hearkened not unto Moses; but some of them left of it until the morning, and it bred worms, and stank: and Moses was wroth with them.

21 And they gathered it every morning, every man according to his eating: and when the sun waxed hot, it melted.

22 ¶And it came to pass, that on the sixth day they gathered twice as much bread, two omers for one man: and all the rulers of the congregation came and told Moses.

23 And he said unto them, This is that which the LORD hath said, To morrow is the rest of the holy sabbath unto the LORD: bake that which ye will bake to day, and seethe that ye will seethe; and that which remaineth over lay up for you to be kept until the morning.

24 And they laid it up till the morning, as Moses bade: and it did not stink, neither was there any worm therein.

25 And Moses said, Eat that to day; for to day is a sabbath unto the LORD: to day ye shall not find it in the field.

26 Six days ye shall gather it; but on the seventh day, which is the sabbath, in it there shall be none.

27 ¶And it came to pass, that there went out some of the people on the seventh day for to gather, and they found none.

28 And the LORD said unto Moses,

10. The glory of the LORD appeared in the cloud. A bright shining magnificence indicative of God's presence was seen by the people in the cloud. It is usually referred to as the Shekinah, from the Hebrew root word for "to dwell" or "abide," since God dwelt with the people.

11-15. Quails came which provided Israel with the best of meat. They knew what **quails** were, but when they saw **a small round thing, as small as the hoar frost,** they said in Hebrew *Manna*, meaning What is it? It came from God, and later Christ claimed to be the true bread of life from heaven (Jn 6:35). When one comes to Christ, he will be fully satisfied!

16-22. They were instructed not to **leave of it till the morning,** but when some did **it bred worms, and stank.** God's provision was to be gathered **every morning.** This should speak to believers to follow this same pattern in spiritual affairs, i.e., feeding on the Word of God early each day.

23-32. God reinstructed His people regarding **the rest of the holy sabbath.** No work was to be done. Everyone was to abide . . . **in his place** (vs. 29). Worship, meditation, and physical rest from a busy week of activity would characterize that day. They worked six days and then rested, according to the divine pattern of the creative week (Gen 2:2-3). Today, Christians rest first (Sunday) and then go forth to serve God with the energy He supplies on that first day.

How long refuse ye to keep my commandments and my laws?

29 See, for that the LORD hath given you the sabbath, therefore he giveth you on the sixth day the bread of two days; abide ye every man in his place, let no man go out of his place on the seventh day.

30 So the people rested on the seventh day.

31 And the house of Israel called the name thereof Manna: and it was like coriander seed, white; and the taste of it was like wafers made with honey.

32 ¶And Moses said, This is the thing which the LORD commandeth, Fill an omer of it to be kept for your generations; that they may see the bread wherewith I have fed you in the wilderness, when I brought you forth from the land of Egypt.

33 And Moses said unto Aaron, Take a pot, and put an omer full of manna therein, and lay it up before the LORD, to be kept for your generations.

34 As the LORD commanded Moses, so Aaron laid it up before the Testimony, to be kept.

35 And the children of Israel did eat manna forty years, until they came to a land inhabited; they did eat manna, until they came unto the borders of the land of Canaan.

36 Now an omer is the tenth part of an ēphah.

CHAPTER 17

AND all the congregation of the children of Israel journeyed from the wilderness of Sin, after their journeys, according to the commandment of the LORD, and pitched in Rĕph'i-dĭm: and there was no water for the people to drink.

2 Wherefore the people did chide with Moses, and said, Give us water that we may drink. And Moses said unto them, Why chide ye with me? wherefore do ye tempt the LORD?

3 And the people thirsted there for water; and the people murmured against Moses, and said, Wherefore is this that thou hast brought us up out of Egypt, to kill us and our children and our cattle with thirst?

4 And Moses cried unto the LORD, saying, What shall I do unto this people? they be almost ready to stone me.

5 And the LORD said unto Moses, Go on before the people, and take with thee of the elders of Israel; and thy rod, wherewith thou smotest the river, take in thine hand, and go.

6 Behold, I will stand before thee there upon the rock in Hô'rĕb; and thou shalt smite the rock, and there shall come water out of it, that the people may drink. And Moses did so in the sight of the elders of Israel.

7 And he called the name of the place Măs'sah, and Mĕr'i-bah, because of the chiding of the children of Israel, and because they tempted the LORD, saying, Is the LORD among us, or not?

8 ¶Then came Ăm'a-lĕk, and fought with Israel in Rĕph'i-dĭm.

9 And Moses said unto Joshua,

33-36. Aaron took a gold **pot, and put an omer full of manna therein** to save perpetually to remind Israel of their murmuring and of God's gracious provision. An **omer** is about three quarts. The pot was placed inside the ark of **the Testimony** (Heb 9:4).

C. The Water from the Smitten Rock. 17:1-7.

17:1-7. At **Rephidim** Israel complained of their lack of water and blamed Moses. In response to God's command, Moses hit the rock; and it gave forth **water.** I Corinthians 10:4 points out that the smitten **rock** represented Christ whose life-giving blood was shed for us. **Massah** means tempting, and **Meribah** means striving.

D. The Amalekites Defeated by Joshua. 17:8-16.

8-13. According to Deuteronomy 25:17, 18, **Amalek** (descendants of Esau) attacked Israel's rear, killing the feeble and the weary. This is the first mention of **Joshua** in Scripture, though

Choose us out men, and go out, fight with Ăm′a-lĕk: to morrow I will stand on the top of the hill with the rod of God in mine hand.

10 So Joshua did as Moses had said to him, and fought with Ăm′a-lĕk: and Moses, Aaron, and Hur went up to the top of the hill.

11 And it came to pass, when Moses held up his hand, that Israel prevailed: and when he let down his hand, Ăm′a-lĕk prevailed.

12 But Moses' hands were heavy; and they took a stone, and put it under him, and he sat thereon; and Aaron and Hur stayed up his hands, the one on the one side, and the other on the other side; and his hands were steady until the going down of the sun.

13 And Joshua discomfited Ăm′a-lĕk and his people with the edge of the sword.

14 And the LORD said unto Moses, Write this for a memorial in a book, and rehearse it in the ears of Joshua: for I will utterly put out the remembrance of Ăm′a-lĕk from under heaven.

15 And Moses built an altar, and called the name of it Je-hō′vah–nĭs′sī:

16 For he said, Because the LORD hath sworn that the LORD will have war with Ăm′a-lĕk from generation to generation.

CHAPTER 18

WHEN Jĕth′rō, the priest of Mĭd′ĭ-an, Moses' father in law, heard of all that God had done for Moses, and for Israel his people, and that the LORD had brought Israel out of Egypt;

2 Then Jĕth′rō, Moses' father in law, took Zĭp-po′rah, Moses' wife, after he had sent her back,

3 And her two sons; of which the name of the one was Ger′shom; for he said, I have been an alien in a strange land:

4 And the name of the other was E-lĭ-ē′zer; for the God of my father, said he, was mine help, and delivered me from the sword of Pharaoh:

5 And Jĕth′rō, Moses' father in law, came with his sons and his wife unto Moses into the wilderness, where he encamped at the mount of God:

6 And he said unto Moses, I thy father in law Jĕth′rō am come unto thee, and thy wife, and her two sons with her.

7 And Moses went out to meet his father in law, and did obeisance, and kissed him; and they asked each other of their welfare; and they came into the tent.

8 And Moses told his father in law all that the LORD had done unto Pharaoh and to the Egyptians for Israel's sake, and all the travail that had come upon them by the way, and how the LORD delivered them.

9 And Jĕth′rō rejoiced for all the goodness which the LORD had done to Israel, whom he had delivered out of the hand of the Egyptians.

10 And Jĕth′rō said, Blessed be the LORD, who hath delivered you out of the hand of the Egyptians, and out of the hand of Pharaoh, who hath delivered

he must have been an important aide to Moses prior to this call for public service. Joshua led Israel to victory as Moses interceded in their behalf in prayer.

14-16. God told Moses to **Write this for a memorial in a book.** This is no doubt a plain reference to the book of Exodus, of which Moses was the author under the guidance of the Holy Spirit. The **altar** of sacrifice built on this occasion was called **Jehovah-Nissi,** meaning Jehovah is my banner.

E. The Judgeship Plan of Jethro Inaugurated. 18:1-27.

18:1-7. Upon returning victoriously from Egypt, Moses' wife and two sons met him near Mount Sinai, along with **Jethro, the priest of Midian, Moses' father-in-law.** After the customary greetings, including **obeisance,** or a respectful bow, they fellowshiped in the tent. Jethro had already heard of God's wonders performed in Egypt, but Moses retold it all.

8-12. Jethro's acknowledgement that **The LORD is greater than all gods** either indicates great respect for Jehovah, or else a full salvation experience. He was a descendant of Abraham through Keturah (Gen 25:1-2).

the people from under the hand of the Egyptians.

11 Now I know that the LORD is greater than all gods: for in the thing wherein they dealt proudly he was above them.

12 And Jĕth'rō, Moses' father in law, took a burnt offering and sacrifices for God: and Aaron came, and all the elders of Israel, to eat bread with Moses' father in law before God.

13 ¶And it came to pass on the morrow, that Moses sat to judge the people: and the people stood by Moses from the morning unto the evening.

14 And when Moses' father in law saw all that he did to the people, he said, What is this thing that thou doest to the people? why sittest thou thyself alone, and all the people stand by thee from morning unto even?

15 And Moses said unto his father in law, Because the people come unto me to enquire of God:

16 When they have a matter, they come unto me; and I judge between one and another, and I do make them know the statutes of God, and his laws.

17 And Moses' father in law said unto him, The thing that thou doest is not good.

18 Thou wilt surely wear away, both thou, and this people that is with thee: for this thing is too heavy for thee; thou art not able to perform it thyself alone.

19 Hearken now unto my voice, I will give thee counsel, and God shall be with thee: Be thou for the people to God-ward, that thou mayest bring the causes unto God:

20 And thou shalt teach them ordinances and laws, and shalt shew them the way wherein they must walk, and the work that they must do.

21 Moreover thou shalt provide out of all the people able men, such as fear God, men of truth, hating covetousness; and place such over them, to be rulers of thousands, and rulers of hundreds, rulers of fifties, and rulers of tens:

22 And let them judge the people at all seasons: and it shall be, that every great matter they shall bring unto thee, but every small matter they shall judge: so shall it be easier for thyself, and they shall bear the burden with thee.

23 If thou shalt do this thing, and God command thee so, then thou shalt be able to endure, and all this people shall also go to their place in peace.

24 So Moses hearkened to the voice of his father in law, and did all that he had said.

25 And Moses chose able men out of all Israel, and made them heads over the people, rulers of thousands, rulers of hundreds, rulers of fifties, and rulers of tens.

26 And they judged the people at all seasons: the hard causes they brought unto Moses, but every small matter they judged themselves.

27 ¶And Moses let his father in law depart; and he went his way into his own land.

13-16. Moses sat to judge the people . . . from the morning unto the evening. This procedure was awkward and time-consuming, yet Moses was the spokesman for God to teach the people God's **statutes . . . and his laws.** However, proper organization and delegation of authority could make the entire process more effective and relieve God's man for more essential duties. Many a pastor and other leaders need to learn what Moses did.

17-23. Jethro suggested a simple, but wise, solution. Moses should: (1) train new leadership to help with the actual judging (vs. 20); (2) choose only capable, God-fearing, qualified men (vs. 21); and (3) personally handle only the more important matters. This suggestion was carefully conditioned upon **If . . . God command thee so.**

24-27. The new leadership training program was approved and put into action, and Jethro departed **into his own land.**

VII. THE COVENANT MADE AT MOUNT SINAI. 19:1-24:18.

A. The Covenant Proposed and the Ten Commandments Given. 19:1-20:26.

19:1-2. It must have been hot in June or July when Israel arrived at Mount Sinai and set up camp. They were to remain there for nearly one year (Num 10:11-12).

CHAPTER 19

IN the third month, when the children of Israel were gone forth out of the land of Egypt, the same day came they *into* the wilderness of Sī'naī.

2 For they were departed from Rĕph'i-dĭm, and were come *to* the desert of Sī'naī, and had pitched in the wilderness; and there Israel camped before the mount.

3 And Moses went up unto God, and the LORD called unto him out of the mountain, saying, Thus shalt thou say to the house of Jacob, and tell the children of Israel;

4 Ye have seen what I did unto the Egyptians, and *how* I bare you on eagles' wings, and brought you unto myself.

5 Now therefore, if ye will obey my voice indeed, and keep my covenant, then ye shall be a peculiar treasure unto me above all people: for all the earth *is* mine:

6 And ye shall be unto me a kingdom of priests, and an holy nation. These *are* the words which thou shalt speak unto the children of Israel.

7 ¶And Moses came and called for the elders of the people, and laid before their faces all these words which the LORD commanded him.

8 And all the people answered together, and said, All that the LORD hath spoken we will do. And Moses returned the words of the people unto the LORD.

9 And the LORD said unto Moses, Lo, I come unto thee in a thick cloud, that the people may hear when I speak with thee, and believe thee for ever. And Moses told the words of the people unto the LORD.

10 ¶And the LORD said unto Moses, Go unto the people, and sanctify them to day and to morrow, and let them wash their clothes,

11 And be ready against the third day: for the third day the LORD will come down in the sight of all the people upon mount Sī'naī.

12 And thou shalt set bounds unto the people round about, saying, Take heed to yourselves, *that* ye go *not* up into the mount, or touch the border of it: whosoever toucheth the mount shall be surely put to death:

13 There shall not an hand touch it, but he shall surely be stoned, or shot through; whether *it be* beast or man, it shall not live: when the trumpet soundeth long, they shall come up to the mount.

14 ¶And Moses went down from the mount unto the people, and sanctified the people; and they washed their clothes.

15 And he said unto the people, Be ready against the third day: come not at *your* wives.

16 ¶And it came to pass on the third day in the morning, that there were thunders and lightnings, and a thick cloud upon the mount, and the voice of

3-8. The key words of the new covenant were **if ye will obey my voice indeed, and keep my covenant.** Only then would God fulfill all the promises for protection and favor. The dispensation of law was clearly based on a conditional covenant. The quotation of parts of verses 5 and 6 in the New Testament (I Pet 2:9; Rev 5:10) is by way of application and in no way indicates that the church has replaced Israel or taken over her promises. See Jeremiah 31:31, where Israel was given a new covenant to replace the broken Sinaitic compact. The church participates only in the salvation aspects of the new covenant. The people quickly affirmed, **All that the LORD hath spoken we will do.** How easy it is to promise something, but so difficult to carry through.

9-13. Moses again climbed the mount to relate to God the people's acceptance of the compact. God in turn gave instructions for the sanctification, or setting apart, of the people prior to the giving of the covenant.

14-19. On the third day, as the people anxiously waited in clean clothes, there came a tremendous **voice of the trumpet** from heaven, accompanied by **thunders and lightnings.** The top of Sinai was ablaze with fire and smoke. God **descended upon it in fire,** and great earthquakes rocked the mountain. God spoke, calling Moses to climb Sinai a third time, while the people below waited petrified.

the trumpet exceeding loud; so that all the people that *was* in the camp trembled.

17 And Moses brought forth the people out of the camp to meet with God; and they stood at the nether part of the mount.

18 And mount Sī′naī was altogether on a smoke, because the LORD descended upon it in fire: and the smoke thereof ascended as the smoke of a furnace, and the whole mount quaked greatly.

19 And when the voice of the trumpet sounded long, and waxed louder and louder, Moses spake, and God answered him by a voice.

20 And the LORD came down upon mount Sī′naī, on the top of the mount: and the LORD called Moses *up* to the top of the mount; and Moses went up.

21 And the LORD said unto Moses, Go down, charge the people, lest they break through unto the LORD to gaze, and many of them perish.

22 And let the priests also, which come near to the LORD, sanctify themselves, lest the LORD break forth upon them.

23 And Moses said unto the LORD, The people cannot come up to mount Sī′naī: for thou chargedst us, saying, Set bounds about the mount, and sanctify it.

24 And the LORD said unto him, Away, get thee down, and thou shalt come up, thou, and Aaron with thee: but let not the priests and the people break through to come up unto the LORD, lest he break forth upon them.

25 So Moses went down unto the people, and spake unto them.

CHAPTER 20
AND God spake all these words, saying,

2 I *am* the LORD thy God, which have brought thee out of the land of Egypt, out of the house of bondage.

3 Thou shalt have no other gods before me.

4 Thou shalt not make unto thee any graven image, or any likeness *of any thing that is* in heaven above, or that *is* in the earth beneath, or that *is* in the water under the earth:

5 Thou shalt not bow down thyself to them, nor serve them: for I the LORD thy God *am* a jealous God, visiting the iniquity of the fathers upon the children unto the third and fourth *generation* of them that hate me;

6 And shewing mercy unto thousands of them that love me, and keep my commandments.

7 Thou shalt not take the name of the LORD thy God in vain; for the LORD will not hold him guiltless that taketh his name in vain.

8 Remember the sabbath day, to keep it holy.

9 Six days shalt thou labour, and do all thy work:

10 But the seventh day *is* the sabbath of the LORD thy God: *in it* thou shalt not do any work, thou, nor thy son, nor thy daughter, thy manservant, nor thy

20-25. God's message was that the people learn to respect God and to reverence Him. He is to be set apart. **Moses went down** and communicated that to the people again.

20:1-3. The Ten Commandments are literally "ten words" (Ex 34:28) and are repeated in Deuteronomy 5:7-20. See the classic exposition of these by the Puritan, Thomas Watson, *The Ten Commandments*. The first commandment stresses God's complete uniqueness. There is no other God, and no false gods are to have a place in our lives.

4-6. The command forbidding **any graven image** specifically demands **thou shalt not bow down thyself to them.** God is spirit and cannot be represented by statues or any likeness. The visitation of **the iniquity of the fathers upon the children** seems to indicate that several generations would be affected by learning and continuing to practice the contaminating sin of idolatry. But some find His **mercy** which is shown **unto thousands.**

7. Taking **the name of the LORD thy God in vain** has to do with using God's holy name for purposes other than worship. Also, Christians ought to shun minced oaths such as the use of Gee, Gosh, and Golly.

8-11. Far from being the most important, as insisted upon by some sects, the fourth commandment is the only commandment not repeated for Christians to observe in the New Testament. The dispensation of the law ended with Christ's death on the cross in which He took away such requirements as holy days, new moon observances and the sabbath day restrictions (Col 2:14-17). Even though believers now normally worship on Sun-

maidservant, nor thy cattle, nor thy stranger that is within thy gates:

11 For in six days the LORD made heaven and earth, the sea, and all that in them is, and rested the seventh day: wherefore the LORD blessed the sabbath day, and hallowed it.

12 ¶Honour thy father and thy mother: that thy days may be long upon the land which the LORD thy God giveth thee.

13 Thou shalt not kill.
14 Thou shalt not commit adultery.

15 Thou shalt not steal.

16 Thou shalt not bear false witness against thy neighbour.

17 Thou shalt not covet thy neighbour's house, thou shalt not covet thy neighbour's wife, nor his manservant, nor his maidservant, nor his ox, nor his ass, nor any thing that is thy neighbour's.

18 ¶And all the people saw the thunderings, and the lightnings, and the noise of the trumpet, and the mountain smoking: and when the people saw it, they removed, and stood afar off.

19 And they said unto Moses, Speak thou with us, and we will hear: but let not God speak with us, lest we die.

20 And Moses said unto the people, Fear not: for God is come to prove you, and that his fear may be before your faces, that ye sin not.

21 And the people stood afar off, and Moses drew near unto the thick darkness where God was.

22 ¶And the LORD said unto Moses, Thus thou shalt say unto the children of Israel, Ye have seen that I have talked with you from heaven.

23 Ye shall not make with me gods of silver, neither shall ye make unto you gods of gold.

24 An altar of earth thou shalt make unto me, and shalt sacrifice thereon thy burnt offerings, and thy peace offerings, thy sheep, and thine oxen: in all places where I record my name I will come unto thee, and I will bless thee.

25 And if thou wilt make me an altar of stone, thou shalt not build it of hewn stone: for if thou lift up thy tool upon it, thou hast polluted it.

26 Neither shalt thou go up by steps unto mine altar, that thy nakedness be not discovered thereon.

CHAPTER 21

NOW these are the judgments which thou shalt set before them.

2 If thou buy an Hebrew servant, six years he shall serve: and in the seventh he shall go out free for nothing.

3 If he came in by himself, he shall go

day, according to the new pattern of the dispensation of grace (I Cor 16:2; Acts 20:7), it is best not to work without an interval of rest as God's original pattern shows. The **Six days** of creation here referred to were literal solar days.

12. Honor thy father and thy mother is an obligation that endures as long as one's parents are alive. They must always be respected and must be obeyed while under their direct authority in the home prior to a young person's marriage (Gen 2:24, i.e., leave his father and his mother). This commandment begins the second table of the law. The first four reveal our duty to God; the final six our proper relations with man.

13-14. Murder and marital infidelity, though seemingly only referring to outward acts, are in actuality based on far higher principles, as Jesus later set forth clearly in the Sermon on the Mount (Mt 5:21-22; 27-28).

15. Thou shalt not steal prohibits taking what does not belong to oneself. This includes small and great items and even relates to the time clock at work, and how honestly one pays his taxes. A Christian ought to report all of his income.

16. Bearing **false witness** is another term for lying. God desires truth in the inward parts, which will be reflected in our outward speech (cf. Ps 51:6; Jer 17:9; Mt 15:19).

17. Thou shalt not covet forbids longing after that which belongs to another, and thus a list is added here. Some churches divide this commandment into two separate ones, while placing the prohibition of graven images inconspicuously under the first commandment.

18-21. The people were so afraid of these proceedings that they requested Moses be God's spokesman, rather than having God speak directly to them.

22-26. An altar of earth, a simple structure, or **of stone** (unhewn), was to be constructed only in those places **where I record my name,** and then only for the purpose of worship by the specified **offerings.** Rather than steps, a ramp was apparently used (cf. vs. 26 with 28:42).

B. Various Personal Judgments. 21:1-23:9.

21:1-3. The personal rights of indentured Hebrew servants are lawfully protected in this section. He was not the perpetual property of his master but would be freed after six years of labor (cf. Lev 25:10; 44-46).

155

out by himself: if he were married, then his wife shall go out with him.

4 If his master have given him a wife, and she have born him sons or daughters; the wife and her children shall be her master's, and he shall go out by himself.

5 And if the servant shall plainly say, I love my master, my wife, and my children; I will not go out free:

6 Then his master shall bring him unto the judges; he shall also bring him to the door, or unto the door post; and his master shall bore his ear through with an aul; and he shall serve him for ever.

7 ¶And if a man sell his daughter to be a maidservant, she shall not go out as the menservants do.

8 If she please not her master, who hath betrothed her to himself, then shall he let her be redeemed: to sell her unto a strange nation he shall have no power, seeing he hath dealt deceitfully with her.

9 And if he have betrothed her unto his son, he shall deal with her after the manner of daughters.

10 If he take him another *wife;* her food, her raiment, and her duty of marriage, shall he not diminish.

11 And if he do not these three unto her, then shall she go out free without money.

12 ¶He that smiteth a man, so that he die, shall be surely put to death.

13 And if a man lie not in wait, but God deliver *him* into his hand; then I will appoint thee a place whither he shall flee.

14 But if a man come presumptuously upon his neighbour, to slay him with guile; thou shalt take him from mine altar, that he may die.

15 And he that smiteth his father, or his mother, shall be surely put to death.

16 ¶And he that stealeth a man, and selleth him, or if he be found in his hand, he shall surely be put to death.

17 ¶And he that curseth his father, or his mother, shall surely be put to death.

18 ¶And if men strive together, and one smite another with a stone, or with *his* fist, and he die not, but keepeth *his* bed:

19 If he rise again, and walk abroad upon his staff, then shall he that smote *him* be quit: only he shall pay *for* the loss of his time, and shall cause *him* to be thoroughly healed.

20 ¶And if a man smite his servant, or his maid, with a rod, and he die under his hand; he shall be surely punished.

21 Notwithstanding, if he continue a day or two, he shall not be punished: for he *is* his money.

22 ¶If men strive, and hurt a woman with child, so that her fruit depart *from* her, and yet no mischief follow: he shall be surely punished, according as the woman's husband will lay upon him; and he shall pay as the judges *determine.*

4-6. If circumstances made him desire to remain with his master, he pledged this by having an **awl,** or sharp, piercing tool, pushed through his **ear** lobe at the **door post** before the **judges.** He thereby signified obedience to that household.

7-11. Rare circumstances of poverty might force a man to sell his daughter into a work or betrothal relationship. Her rights were strictly regarded. She could not be sold to foreigners; she had to be treated like a daughter if betrothed; and she had to be freed if any conditions were not kept.

12. He that smiteth a man, so that he die, shall be surely put to death. To take the life of a murderer is not a violation of "Thou shalt not kill" but is clearly commanded of God. Any nation that refuses to carry out the death penalty is inviting trouble from the Almighty.

13-17. Cities of refuge are implied in verse 13 for cases of accidental manslaughter (see Num 35:13-34). Premeditated killing, the hitting or even cursing of one's parents, and kidnapping were all capital offenses in Israelite society.

18-19. Injuries caused through fighting disputes had to be recompensed, both for **the loss of his time,** and for the treatment obtained for healing.

20-21. If a foreign slave was killed by a master, the judges would set his punishment. But **if he continue a day or two,** before dying, the beating was not considered meant to kill; and the loss of the slave was punishment enough.

22. The case of injury to **a woman with child** was more complicated, especially if **her fruit** (the baby) **depart from her.** The key words to interpret are **yet no mischief follow.** Does it refer to mischief to the baby or only to the mother? From the word order of the sentence, and since no further amplification is given, it would seem that the baby would be in view here. If so, this would strongly teach that abortion is a capital offense (see vs. 23-25).

23-27. If mischief followed the premature delivery of the woman's baby, the offender was to **give life for life,** and on down the line. This *lex talionis*, or law of retaliation, actually limited the amount of retribution that could be sought for any offense. For example, one could not kill a man because he had caused the loss of one's sight. If a man permanently injured a slave, he was to **let him go free** for the loss incurred.

23 And if *any* mischief follow, then thou shalt give life for life,

24 Eye for eye, tooth for tooth, hand for hand, foot for foot,

25 Burning for burning, wound for wound, stripe for stripe.

26 ¶And if a man smite the eye of his servant, or the eye of his maid, that it perish; he shall let him go free for his eye's sake.

27 And if he smite out his manservant's tooth, or his maidservant's tooth; he shall let him go free for his tooth's sake.

28 ¶If an ox gore a man or a woman, that they die: then the ox shall be surely stoned, and his flesh shall not be eaten; but the owner of the ox *shall be* quit.

29 But if the ox were wont to push with his horn in time past, and it hath been testified to his owner, and he hath not kept him in, but that he hath killed a man or a woman; the ox shall be stoned, and his owner also shall be put to death.

30 If there be laid on him a sum of money, then he shall give for the ransom of his life whatsoever is laid upon him.

31 Whether he have gored a son, or have gored a daughter, according to this judgment shall it be done unto him.

32 If the ox shall push a manservant or a maidservant; he shall give unto their master thirty shekels of silver, and the ox shall be stoned.

33 ¶And if a man shall open a pit, or if a man shall dig a pit, and not cover it, and an ox or an ass fall therein;

34 The owner of the pit shall make *it* good, *and* give money unto the owner of them; and the dead *beast* shall be his.

35 ¶And if one man's ox hurt another's, that he die; then they shall sell the live ox, and divide the money of it; and the dead *ox* also they shall divide.

36 Or if it be known that the ox hath used to push in time past, and his owner hath not kept him in; he shall surely pay ox for ox; and the dead shall be his own.

28-36. Personal injuries caused by animals were chargeable to their owners; but if an animal had killed repeatedly, the animal **and his owner also shall be put to death.** Human life was sacred. Injuries to other animals resulted in fining the offending animal's owner, or in his replacing the injured or dead animal.

CHAPTER 22

IF a man shall steal an ox, or a sheep, and kill it, or sell it; he shall restore five oxen for an ox, and four sheep for a sheep.

2 If a thief be found breaking up, and be smitten that he die, *there shall* no blood *be shed* for him.

3 If the sun be risen upon him, *there shall be* blood *shed* for him; *for* he should make full restitution; if he have nothing, then he shall be sold for his theft.

4 If the theft be certainly found in his hand alive, whether it be ox, or ass, or sheep; he shall restore double.

5 ¶If a man shall cause a field or vineyard to be eaten, and shall put in his beast, and shall feed in another man's field; of the best of his own field, and of the best of his own vineyard, shall he make restitution.

6 ¶If fire break out, and catch in thorns, so that the stacks of corn, or the

22:1-4. If a man . . . steal and get caught, he was to pay back four or five times the amount stolen. If he were killed while breaking in at night, his death was excused; but if it were during daylight hours, no bloodshed was allowed or deemed necessary.

5-15. Nearly every verse in this section contains a case preceded by an **If.** The principle established in each was that proper restitution was to be made whenever someone caused loss to another's property.

standing corn, or the field, be consumed *therewith;* he that kindled the fire shall surely make restitution.

7 ¶If a man shall deliver unto his neighbour money or stuff to keep, and it be stolen out of the man's house; if the thief be found, let him pay double.

8 If the thief be not found, then the master of the house shall be brought unto the judges, *to see* whether he have put his hand unto his neighbour's goods.

9 For all manner of trespass, *whether it be* for ox, for ass, for sheep, for raiment, *or* for any manner of lost thing, which *another* challengeth to be his, the cause of both parties shall come before the judges; *and* whom the judges shall condemn, he shall pay double unto his neighbour.

10 If a man deliver unto his neighbour an ass, or an ox, or a sheep, or any beast, to keep; and it die, or be hurt, or driven away, no man seeing *it:*

11 *Then* shall an oath of the Lord be between them both, that he hath not put his hand unto his neighbour's goods; and the owner of it shall accept *thereof,* and he shall not make *it* good.

12 And if it be stolen from him, he shall make restitution unto the owner thereof.

13 If it be torn in pieces, *then* let him bring it *for* witness, *and* he shall not make good that which was torn.

14 ¶And if a man borrow *ought* of his neighbour, and it be hurt, or die, the owner thereof *being* not with it, he shall surely make *it* good.

15 *But* if the owner thereof *be* with it, he shall not make *it* good: if it *be* an hired *thing,* it came for his hire.

16 ¶And if a man entice a maid that is not betrothed, and lie with her, he shall surely endow her to be his wife.

17 If her father utterly refuse to give her unto him, he shall pay money according to the dowry of virgins.

18 ¶Thou shalt not suffer a witch to live.

19 ¶Whosoever lieth with a beast shall surely be put to death.

20 ¶He that sacrificeth unto *any* god, save unto the Lord only, he shall be utterly destroyed.

21 ¶Thou shalt neither vex a stranger, nor oppress him: for ye were strangers in the land of Egypt.

22 Ye shall not afflict any widow, or fatherless child.

23 If thou afflict them in any wise, and they cry at all unto me, I will surely hear their cry;

24 And my wrath shall wax hot, and I will kill you with the sword; and your wives shall be widows, and your children fatherless.

25 ¶If thou lend money to *any of* my people *that is* poor by thee, thou shalt not be to him as an usurer, neither shalt thou lay upon him usury.

16-17. Then, as now, it was possible for a man to **entice a maid . . . and lie with her.** Two results could ensue. Since she, in this case, was not betrothed or engaged, they could become married; or if the father deemed it unwise to have such a rogue as a son-in-law, he might **utterly refuse to give her unto him,** resulting in a heavy payment made by the wicked enticer. This left the woman free to be married later, but she was subject to possible rejection during engagement based on Deuteronomy 24:1.

18. Thou shalt not suffer (allow) **a witch to live.** Witchcraft is no game. God would have all witches exterminated, so great is their degree of wickedness before Him.

19-20. Sexual intercourse with an animal is another sin punishable by **death,** as was worship of any false god.

21-24. God's perpetual concern over the welfare of **any widow, or fatherless child** is abundantly attested in the Scriptures. It is a constant theme (cf. Jas 1:27).

25. Loaning money to the **poor** was not to be accompanied by the charging of interest; it was to be loaned as a favor. Today's modern commercial ventures of loaning and borrowing at interest are not considered in this verse.

26 If thou at all take thy neighbour's raiment to pledge, thou shalt deliver it unto him by that the sun goeth down:

27 For that *is* his covering only, it *is* his raiment for his skin: wherein shall he sleep? and it shall come to pass, when he crieth unto me, that I will hear; for I *am* gracious.

28 ¶Thou shalt not revile the gods, nor curse the ruler of thy people.

29 ¶Thou shalt not delay *to offer* the first of thy ripe fruits, and of thy liquors: the firstborn of thy sons shalt thou give unto me.

30 Likewise shalt thou do with thine oxen, *and* with thy sheep: seven days it shall be with his dam; on the eighth day thou shalt give it me.

31 ¶And ye shall be holy men unto me: neither shall ye eat any flesh *that is* torn of beasts in the field; ye shall cast it to the dogs.

CHAPTER 23
THOU shalt not raise a false report: put not thine hand with the wicked to be an unrighteous witness.

2 Thou shalt not follow a multitude to *do* evil; neither shalt thou speak in a cause to decline after many to wrest *judgment:*

3 Neither shalt thou countenance a poor man in his cause.

4 ¶If thou meet thine enemy's ox or his ass going astray, thou shalt surely bring it back to him again.

5 If thou see the ass of him that hateth thee lying under his burden, and wouldest forbear to help him, thou shalt surely help with him.

6 ¶Thou shalt not wrest the judgment of thy poor in his cause.

7 Keep thee far from a false matter; and the innocent and righteous slay thou not: for I will not justify the wicked.

8 ¶And thou shalt take no gift: for the gift blindeth the wise, and perverteth the words of the righteous.

9 ¶Also thou shalt not oppress a stranger: for ye know the heart of a stranger, seeing ye were strangers in the land of Egypt.

10 And six years thou shalt sow thy land, and shalt gather in the fruits thereof:

11 But the seventh *year* thou shalt let it rest and lie still; that the poor of thy people may eat: and what they leave the beasts of the field shall eat. In like manner thou shalt deal with thy vineyard, *and* with thy oliveyard.

12 Six days thou shalt do thy work, and on the seventh day thou shalt rest: that thine ox and thine ass may rest, and the son of thy handmaid, and the stranger, may be refreshed.

13 And in all *things* that I have said unto you be circumspect: and make no mention of the name of other gods, neither let it be heard out of thy mouth.

14 ¶Three times thou shalt keep a feast unto me in the year.

15 Thou shalt keep the feast of un-

26-27. Against such a loan (vs. 25), one might be prone to take a person's large outer garment as collateral; but since it might be needed to keep the poor man warm at night, it had to be returned by the time **that the sun goeth down.**

28. The gods, nor . . . the ruler of thy people. This verse teaches respect for men in authority. The word "gods" (Heb *elohim*) sometimes refers to human leaders, judges, or those who are mighty.

29-31. In addition, there was to be no **delay** in offering to God what was required (vs. 29-30) and in refraining from using what was forbidden, i.e., **flesh that is torn of beasts,** something unclean.

23:1-2. Bearing a **false report** is here further condemned, as is joining in false group testimony. Mob violence is certainly banned in the prohibition of following **a multitude to do evil.**

3-6. One does not have sympathy for **a poor man** to pervert a genuine judgment against him (vs. 3), nor was hatred of the poor to **wrest the judgment of thy poor,** meaning to cause one to ignore justice due the man (vs. 6). In a practical way, verses 4-5 are the carrying out of the precept ". . . Love thy neighbor as thyself . . ." (Lev 19:18).

7-9. **False** judgments, the taking of a **gift** (as a bribe), and the oppression of **a stranger** are also forbidden. Though common moral precepts, they have been readily violated from generation to generation. God help those who transgress them!

C. Sabbaths and Sacred Feasts. 23:10-19.

10-13. The seventh year thou shalt let it rest. The sabbath of years provided rest for the land and free food for the poor. God supplied a double amount during the sixth year. **On the seventh day thou shalt rest.** The sabbath day provided rest for animals as well as for humans.

14-17. Three times in the year all thy males were required to **appear before the LORD God.** These special feasts were: (1) Unleavened bread (Passover, April); (2) **feast of harvest** (Pente-

leavened bread: (thou shalt eat unleavened bread seven days, as I commanded thee, in the time appointed of
the month Ābīb; for in it thou camest
out from Egypt: and none shall appear
before me empty:)

16 And the feast of harvest, the
firstfruits of thy labours, which thou
hast sown in the field: and the feast of
ingathering, *which is* in the end of the
year, when thou hast gathered in thy
labours out of the field.

17 Three times in the year all thy
males shall appear before the Lord
God.

18 Thou shalt not offer the blood of
my sacrifice with leavened bread;
neither shall the fat of my sacrifice remain until the morning.

19 The first of the firstfruits of thy
land thou shalt bring into the house of
the Lord thy God. Thou shalt not seethe
a kid in his mother's milk.

20 ¶Behold, I send an Angel before
thee, to keep thee in the way, and to
bring thee into the place which I have
prepared.

21 Beware of him, and obey his voice,
provoke him not; for he will not pardon
your transgressions: for my name *is* in
him.

22 But if thou shalt indeed obey his
voice, and do all that I speak; then I will
be an enemy unto thine enemies, and
an adversary unto thine adversaries.

23 For mine Angel shall go before
thee, and bring thee in unto the Amorites, and the Hittites, and the Pĕr'iz-
zītes, and the Canaanites, the Hī'vītes,
and the Jĕb'u-sītes: and I will cut them
off.

24 Thou shalt not bow down to their
gods, nor serve them, nor do after their
works: but thou shalt utterly overthrow
them, and quite break down
their images.

25 And ye shall serve the Lord your
God, and he shall bless thy bread, and
thy water; and I will take sickness
away from the midst of thee.

26 ¶There shall nothing cast their
young, nor be barren, in thy land: the
number of thy days I will fulfil.

27 I will send my fear before thee,
and will destroy all the people to whom
thou shalt come, and I will make all
thine enemies turn their backs unto
thee.

28 And I will send hornets before
thee, which shall drive out the Hī'vīte,
the Canaanite, and the Hittite, from before thee.

29 I will not drive them out from before thee in one year; lest the land become desolate, and the beast of the
field multiply against thee.

30 By little and little I will drive them
out from before thee, until thou be increased, and inherit the land.

31 And I will set thy bounds from the
Red sea even unto the sea of the Philistines, and from the desert unto the river:
for I will deliver the inhabitants of the
land into your hand; and thou shalt
drive them out before thee.

32 Thou shalt make no covenant with
them, nor with their gods.

cost, May); and **(3) feast of ingathering** (Tabernacles, October).
See Deuteronomy 16:1-17 for amplification on each of these
feasts and Leviticus 23 for the complete calendar of Jewish
feasts.

18-19. To **seethe a kid in his mother's milk** was a common
pagan practice of that day. God wanted His people to be different and give Him alone the glory for their harvest.

D. Promise of Canaan Conquest. 23:20-33.

20-23. After reciting what was required of Israel, God indicated what His part of the covenant would be. God said **mine
angel shall go before thee** (vs. 23) and **my name is in him**
(vs. 21). This special Messenger was Christ Himself, the one
who appeared in the burning bush. God also promised to **be an
enemy unto thine enemies,** a near repetition of Genesis 12:3,
"... I will bless them that bless thee, and curse him that
curseth thee."

24-30. For serving the Lord God would **drive them**
(Canaanites) **out from before** Israel.

31. Israel's borders are to extend clear to the Red Sea and
from the eastern deserts to the Mediterranean Sea on the west.

32-33. However, strict adherence to God's covenant was re-

33 They shall not dwell in thy land, lest they make thee sin against me: for if thou serve their gods, it will surely be a snare unto thee.

CHAPTER 24

AND he said unto Moses, Come up unto the Lord, thou, and Aaron, Nā'-dăb, and A-bī'hū, and seventy of the elders of Israel; and worship ye afar off.

2 And Moses alone shall come near the Lord: but they shall not come nigh; neither shall the people go up with him.

3 ¶And Moses came and told the people all the words of the Lord, and all the judgments: and all the people answered with one voice, and said, All the words which the Lord hath said will we do.

4 And Moses wrote all the words of the Lord, and rose up early in the morning, and builded an altar under the hill, and twelve pillars, according to the twelve tribes of Israel.

5 And he sent young men of the children of Israel, which offered burnt offerings, and sacrificed peace offerings of oxen unto the Lord.

6 And Moses took half of the blood, and put it in basons; and half of the blood he sprinkled on the altar.

7 And he took the book of the covenant, and read in the audience of the people: and they said, All that the Lord hath said will we do, and be obedient.

8 And Moses took the blood, and sprinkled it on the people, and said, Behold the blood of the covenant, which the Lord hath made with you concerning all these words.

9 ¶Then went up Moses, and Aaron, Na'dăb, and A-bī'hū, and seventy of the elders of Israel:

10 And they saw the God of Israel: and there was under his feet as it were a paved work of a sapphire stone, and as it were the body of heaven in his clearness.

11 And upon the nobles of the children of Israel he laid not his hand: also they saw God, and did eat and drink.

12 ¶And the Lord said unto Moses, Come up to me into the mount, and be there: and I will give thee tables of stone, and a law, and commandments which I have written; that thou mayest teach them.

13 And Moses rose up, and his minister Joshua: and Moses went up into the mount of God.

14 And he said unto the elders, Tarry ye here for us, until we come again unto you: and, behold, Aaron and Hur are with you: if any man have any matters to do, let him come unto them.

15 ¶And Moses went up into the mount, and a cloud covered the mount.

16 And the glory of the Lord abode upon mount Sī'naī, and the cloud covered it six days: and the seventh day he called unto Moses out of the midst of the cloud.

17 And the sight of the glory of the Lord was like devouring fire on the top of the mount in the eyes of the children of Israel.

18 And Moses went into the midst of the cloud, and gat him up into the

quired; and they were to **make no covenant with the** heathen (cf. Josh 9:14-16).

E. Ratification of the Covenant. 24:1-18.

24:1-8. Moses returned to the people with the written **book of the covenant,** which he read to them (vs. 7). The people agreed to its provisions; then sacrifices were made, and the blood was sprinkled on the people and the altar to signify Israel's acceptance of the covenant.

9-11. A covenant meal followed the sacrifices, participated in by **Moses, and Aaron, Nadab, and Abihu, and seventy of the elders of Israel.** They ascended the mountain before dining. Twice it says **they saw God;** and His feet are mentioned, apparently indicating a Christophany, but accompanied by such glory, splendor, and brightness that the figure was enshrouded in magnificence that primarily shielded Him from their view. **Upon the nobles . . . he laid not his hand** means they were not slain, even though **they saw the God of Israel.**

12-14. Moses was instructed to ascend Mount Sinai now for the fifth time to receive the **tables of stone. Joshua** accompanied Moses, while **Aaron** and **Hur** were left in charge.

15-18. Moses was in the mount forty days and forty nights. It was during this time, just after the ratification of the covenant, that they made the golden calf (cf. Ex 32).

mount: and Moses was in the mount forty days and forty nights.

CHAPTER 25

AND the LORD spake unto Moses, saying,

2 Speak unto the children of Israel, that they bring me an offering: of every man that giveth it willingly with his heart ye shall take my offering.

3 And this *is* the offering which ye shall take of them; gold, and silver, and brass,

4 And blue, and purple, and scarlet, and fine linen, and goats' *hair*,

5 And rams' skins dyed red, and badgers' skins, and shittim wood,

6 Oil for the light, spices for anointing oil, and for sweet incense,

7 Onyx stones, and stones to be set in the ephod, and in the breastplate.

8 And let them make me a sanctuary; that I may dwell among them.

9 According to all that I shew thee, *after* the pattern of the tabernacle, and the pattern of all the instruments thereof, even so shall ye make *it*.

10 ¶And they shall make an ark *of* shittim wood: two cubits and a half *shall be* the length thereof, and a cubit and a half the breadth thereof, and a cubit and a half the height thereof.

11 And thou shalt overlay it with pure gold, within and without shalt thou overlay it, and shalt make upon it a crown of gold round about.

12 And thou shalt cast four rings of gold for it, and put *them* in the four corners thereof; and two rings *shall be* in the one side of it, and two rings in the other side of it.

13 And thou shalt make staves *of* shittim wood, and overlay them with gold.

14 And thou shalt put the staves into the rings by the sides of the ark, that the ark may be borne with them.

15 The staves shall be in the rings of the ark: they shall not be taken from it.

16 And thou shalt put into the ark the testimony which I shall give thee.

17 ¶And thou shalt make a mercy seat *of* pure gold: two cubits and a half *shall be* the length thereof, and a cubit and a half the breadth thereof.

18 And thou shalt make two cherubims *of* gold, *of* beaten work shalt thou make them, in the two ends of the mercy seat.

19 And make one cherub on the one end, and the other cherub on the other end: *even* of the mercy seat shall ye make the cherubims on the two ends thereof.

20 And the cherubims shall stretch forth *their* wings on high, covering the mercy seat with their wings, and their faces *shall look* one to another; toward the mercy seat shall the faces of the cherubims be.

21 And thou shalt put the mercy seat above upon the ark; and in the ark thou

VIII. THE PLANS FOR THE TABERNACLE AND ITS SERVICE. 25:1-31:18.

A. The Offering for the Tabernacle. 25:1-9.

25:1-9. What is meant by a freewill offering is described here. Everyone was to give **willingly with his heart.** The materials enumerated were needed to construct the tabernacle and its furniture for the worship of God. On the spiritual significance of the tabernacle, see S. Wemp, *Teaching from the Tabernacle* and M. Woudstra, "The Tabernacle in Biblical-Theological Perspective," in J. B. Payne (ed.), *New Perspectives on the Old Testament,* pp. 88-103.

B. The Tabernacle Furniture. 25:10-40.

10-11. Make an ark of shittim wood . . . overlay it with pure gold. The most crucial piece was the ark of the covenant, a box about three feet by two feet, which contained the tables of the law (vs. 16) and represented Christ Himself. The wood pictured His humanity, and the gold His deity, unmixed, yet fully united. It was here that God met with Israel and where the atonement for their sins was made each year (Lev 16).

12-16. The staves were rods placed through the golden rings with which the priests would carry the ark. Placed **into the ark** was **the testimony** (stone tablets), the pot of manna (Ex 16:33), and Aaron's rod that budded (Num 17:10; cf. Heb 9:4).

17. The mercy seat was a slightly raised flat platform affixed to the ark (cf. vs. 21). The blood that made the propitiation was sprinkled on it. The Greek word for propitiation (Gr *hilasterion,* see Rom 3:25), is the same word used in the LXX to translate **mercy seat.** Jesus Christ is at once both the blood that is shed for our sins and the mercy seat that bears it up before the Father in heaven.

18-22. Make two cherubim of gold. These creatures, with wings extended over the mercy seat as if to guard it, often appear in connection with God's holiness (Gen 3:24; Ps 80:1; 99:1). **And there I will meet with thee.** The primary purpose of the entire tent and its furnishings was that God should there meet with His people through the anointed representative in the appointed fashion. It was a tent of meeting.

shalt put the testimony that I shall give thee.

22 And there I will meet with thee, and I will commune with thee from above the mercy seat, from between the two cherubims which *are* upon the ark of the testimony, of all *things* which I will give thee in commandment unto the children of Israel.

23 ¶Thou shalt also make a table *of* shittim wood: two cubits *shall be* the length thereof, and a cubit the breadth thereof, and a cubit and a half the height thereof.

24 And thou shalt overlay it with pure gold, and make thereto a crown of gold round about.

25 And thou shalt make unto it a border of an hand breadth round about, and thou shalt make a golden crown to the border thereof round about.

26 And thou shalt make for it four rings of gold, and put the rings in the four corners that *are* on the four feet thereof.

27 Over against the border shall the rings be for places of the staves to bear the table.

28 And thou shalt make the staves *of* shittim wood, and overlay them with gold, that the table may be borne with them.

29 And thou shalt make the dishes thereof, and spoons thereof, and covers thereof, and bowls thereof, to cover withal: *of* pure gold shalt thou make them.

30 And thou shalt set upon the table shewbread before me alway.

31 ¶And thou shalt make a candlestick *of* pure gold: *of* beaten work shall the candlestick be made: his shaft, and his branches, his bowls, his knops, and his flowers, shall be of the same.

32 And six branches shall come out of the sides of it; three branches of the candlestick out of the one side, and three branches of the candlestick out of the other side:

33 Three bowls made like unto almonds, *with* a knop and a flower in one branch; and three bowls made like almonds in the other branch, *with* a knop and a flower: so in the six branches that come out of the candlestick.

34 And in the candlestick *shall be* four bowls made like unto almonds, *with* their knops and their flowers.

35 And *there shall be* a knop under two branches of the same, and a knop under two branches of the same, and a knop under two branches of the same, according to the six branches that proceed out of the candlestick.

36 Their knops and their branches shall be of the same: all it *shall be* one beaten work *of* pure gold.

37 And thou shalt make the seven lamps thereof: and they shall light the lamps thereof, that they may give light over against it.

38 And the tongs thereof, and the snuffdishes thereof, *shall be of* pure gold.

39 *Of* a talent of pure gold shall he make it, with all these vessels.

40 And look that thou make *them* af-

23-30. The **table** of showbread (vs. 30) held the bread of presence. It was about three feet long and two feet wide, constructed of **shittim** (Acacia) **wood,** and overlaid **with pure gold.** It held twelve loaves of bread (Lev 24:5-9) that were to sustain the priests as they ministered within the tabernacle. They picture Christ sustaining believers in their service for Him.

31-32. A seven-branched **candlestick of pure gold** provided the only light within the tent itself, just as Jesus is the light of the world (Jn 8:12; 9:5). The seven lights were not made by candles, but instead seven wicks burned pure olive oil (representing the Holy Spirit) drawn from a common reservoir (Lev 24:1-4).

33-40. The decorations on the **six branches that come out of the candlestick** were **made like unto almonds,** the almond tree being the first to blossom forth in Israel (as early as January) speaking of new life.

ter their pattern, which was shewed thee in the mount.

CHAPTER 26

MOREOVER thou shalt make the tabernacle *with* ten curtains *of* fine twined linen, and blue, and purple, and scarlet: *with* cherubims of cunning work shalt thou make them.

2 The length of one curtain *shall be* eight and twenty cubits, and the breadth of one curtain four cubits: and every one of the curtains shall have one measure.

3 The five curtains shall be coupled together one to another; and *other* five curtains *shall be* coupled one to another.

4 And thou shalt make loops of blue upon the edge of the one curtain from the selvedge in the coupling; and likewise shalt thou make in the uttermost edge of *another* curtain, in the coupling of the second.

5 Fifty loops shalt thou make in the one curtain, and fifty loops shalt thou make in the edge of the curtain that *is* in the coupling of the second; that the loops may take hold one of another.

6 And thou shalt make fifty taches of gold, and couple the curtains together with the taches: and it shall be one tabernacle.

7 ¶And thou shalt make curtains *of* goats' *hair* to be a covering upon the tabernacle: eleven curtains shalt thou make.

8 The length of one curtain *shall be* thirty cubits, and the breadth of one curtain four cubits: and the eleven curtains *shall be* all of one measure.

9 And thou shalt couple five curtains by themselves, and six curtains by themselves, and shalt double the sixth curtain in the forefront of the tabernacle.

10 And thou shalt make fifty loops on the edge of the one curtain that *is* outmost in the coupling, and fifty loops in the edge of the curtain which coupleth the second.

11 And thou shalt make fifty taches of brass, and put the taches into the loops, and couple the tent together, that it may be one.

12 And the remnant that remaineth of the curtains of the tent, the half curtain that remaineth, shall hang over the backside of the tabernacle.

13 And a cubit on the one side, and a cubit on the other side of that which remaineth in the length of the curtains of the tent, it shall hang over the sides of the tabernacle on this side and on that side, to cover it.

14 And thou shalt make a covering for the tent of rams' skins dyed red, and a covering above of badgers' skins.

15 ¶And thou shalt make boards for the tabernacle *of* shittim wood standing up.

16 Ten cubits *shall be* the length of a board, and a cubit and a half *shall be* the breadth of one board.

17 Two tenons *shall there be* in one board, set in order one against another: thus shalt thou make for all the boards of the tabernacle.

C. The Tabernacle Coverings, Altar, and Court. 26:1–27:21.

26:1-6. The tabernacle was inwardly covered with **curtains of fine twined linen,** even-textured, speaking of the perfections of Christ. The embroidered **blue, and purple, and scarlet** may speak of Christ's heavenly origin, royalty, and shed blood to cover our sins. The several **curtains** were fastened together by means of numerous loops, ties, etc.

7-14. Above the fine linen were **curtains of goats' hair,** coupled in like manner. This would provide insulation. A third covering was made of **rams' skins dyed red,** a double picture of death since the rams first had to die, and then their skins were dyed red. The fourth, or outermost, covering was **of badgers' skins,** probably better taken to mean seal, porpoise, or dolphin skins; for waterproofing qualities were needed on top.

15-30. The more substantial framework of the tent consisted of a series of **boards . . . . of shittim wood** standing about fifteen feet high and two feet wide, connected by bars. These boards were overlaid **with gold** (vs. 29) and speak of Christ, i.e., humanity (wood) and deity (gold) united. The boards were supported below on **sockets of silver** (vss. 19, 21, 25), which represent redemption (Ex 30:12-16).

18 And thou shalt make the boards for the tabernacle, twenty boards on the south side southward.

19 And thou shalt make forty sockets of silver under the twenty boards; two sockets under one board for his two tenons, and two sockets under another board for his two tenons.

20 And for the second side of the tabernacle on the north side there shall be twenty boards:

21 And their forty sockets of silver; two sockets under one board, and two sockets under another board.

22 And for the sides of the tabernacle westward thou shalt make six boards.

23 And two boards shalt thou make for the corners of the tabernacle in the two sides.

24 And they shall be coupled together beneath, and they shall be coupled together above the head of it unto one ring: thus shall it be for them both; they shall be for the two corners.

25 And they shall be eight boards, and their sockets of silver, sixteen sockets; two sockets under one board, and two sockets under another board.

26 ¶And thou shalt make bars of shittim wood; five for the boards of the one side of the tabernacle,

27 And five bars for the boards of the other side of the tabernacle, and five bars for the boards of the side of the tabernacle, for the two sides westward.

28 And the middle bar in the midst of the boards shall reach from end to end.

29 And thou shalt overlay the boards with gold, and make their rings of gold for places for the bars: and thou shalt overlay the bars with gold.

30 And thou shalt rear up the tabernacle according to the fashion thereof which was shewed thee in the mount.

31 ¶And thou shalt make a vail of blue, and purple, and scarlet, and fine twined linen of cunning work: with cherubims shall it be made:

32 And thou shalt hang it upon four pillars of shittim wood overlaid with gold: their hooks shall be of gold, upon the four sockets of silver.

33 And thou shalt hang up the vail under the taches, that thou mayest bring in thither within the vail the ark of the testimony: and the vail shall divide unto you between the holy place and the most holy.

34 And thou shalt put the mercy seat upon the ark of the testimony in the most holy place.

35 And thou shalt set the table without the vail, and the candlestick over against the table on the side of the tabernacle toward the south: and thou shalt put the table on the north side.

36 ¶And thou shalt make an hanging for the door of the tent, of blue, and purple, and scarlet, and fine twined linen, wrought with needlework.

37 And thou shalt make for the hanging five pillars of shittim wood, and overlay them with gold, and their hooks shall be of gold: and thou shalt cast five sockets of brass for them.

CHAPTER 27
AND thou shalt make an altar of shit-

31-33. A beautiful veil of . . . fine twined linen, embroidered with cherubim (vs. 31) formed a door that was to divide between the holy place and the most holy (vs. 33). The veil represented Christ's flesh (Heb 10:20), which when broken signified opening the access for us into the most Holy Place, unto God Himself.

34-37. The mercy seat upon the ark was situated inside the veil in the most holy place, a room just over twenty feet square. In the larger room, called the holy place, where the priests ministered daily, they placed the table of shewbread on the right as one would face the veil, and the candlestick on the left. The entire tabernacle pointed west and could only be entered from the one door on the eastern end.

27:1-2. A large altar made of shittim wood covered with

tim wood, five cubits long, and five cubits broad; the altar shall be foursquare: and the height thereof *shall be* three cubits.

2 And thou shalt make the horns of it upon the four corners thereof: his horns shall be of the same: and thou shalt overlay it with brass.

3 And thou shalt make his pans to receive his ashes, and his shovels, and his basons, and his fleshhooks, and his firepans: all the vessels thereof thou shalt make *of* brass.

4 And thou shalt make for it a grate of network *of* brass; and upon the net shalt thou make four brasen rings in the four corners thereof.

5 And thou shalt put it under the compass of the altar beneath, that the net may be even to the midst of the altar.

6 And thou shalt make staves for the altar, staves *of* shittim wood, and overlay them with brass.

7 And the staves shall be put into the rings, and the staves shall be upon the two sides of the altar, to bear it.

8 Hollow with boards shalt thou make it: as it was shewed thee in the mount, so shall they make *it*.

9 ¶And thou shalt make the court of the tabernacle: for the south side southward *there shall be* hangings for the court *of* fine twined linen of an hundred cubits long for one side:

10 And the twenty pillars thereof and their twenty sockets *shall be of* brass; the hooks of the pillars and their fillets *shall be of* silver.

11 And likewise for the north side in length *there shall be* hangings of an hundred *cubits* long, and his twenty pillars and their twenty sockets *of* brass; the hooks of the pillars and their fillets *of* silver.

12 And *for* the breadth of the court on the west side *shall be* hangings of fifty cubits: their pillars ten, and their sockets ten.

13 And the breadth of the court on the east side eastward *shall be* fifty cubits.

14 The hangings of one side *of the gate shall be* fifteen cubits: their pillars three, and their sockets three.

15 And on the other side *shall be* hangings fifteen *cubits:* their pillars three, and their sockets three.

16 And for the gate of the court *shall be* an hanging of twenty cubits, *of* blue, and purple, and scarlet, and fine twined linen, wrought with needlework: *and* their pillars *shall be* four, and their sockets four.

17 All the pillars round about the court *shall be* filleted with silver; their hooks *shall be of* silver, and their sockets *of* brass.

18 The length of the court *shall be* an hundred cubits, and the breadth fifty every where, and the height five cubits *of* fine twined linen, and their sockets *of* brass.

19 All the vessels of the tabernacle in all the service thereof, and all the pins thereof, and all the pins of the court, *shall be of* brass.

20 ¶And thou shalt command the

brass rested outside. It was about seven feet square and nearly five feet high, large enough to burn the sacrifice of bulls, sheep, and other animals. In the Scriptures brass always seems to stand for judgment.

3-8. The brazen altar had **a grate of network of brass** and functioned much like a modern barbecue pit. Various brass **pans . . . shovels,** and other **vessels** were used to remove ashes and maintain the altar.

9-21. The court of the tabernacle was a large open area approximately one hundred fifty by seventy-five feet and surrounded the tent itself. This area was enclosed by a fence of **hangings** (curtains) that were seven and one half feet tall! Inside the enclosure the animals were slaughtered and sacrificed, and the priests carried on their duties.

children of Israel, that they bring thee
pure oil olive beaten for the light, to
cause the lamp to burn always.

21 In the tabernacle of the congregation without the vail, which *is* before
the testimony, Aaron and his sons shall
order it from evening to morning before the LORD: *it shall be* a statute for
ever unto their generations on the behalf of the children of Israel.

CHAPTER 28

AND take thou unto thee Aaron thy
brother, and his sons with him, from
among the children of Israel, that he
may minister unto me in the priest's office, *even* Aaron, Nā′dăb and A-bī′hū,
Ĕ-le-ā′zar and Ĭth′a-mär, Aaron's sons.

2 And thou shalt make holy garments
for Aaron thy brother for glory and for
beauty.

3 And thou shalt speak unto all *that
are* wise hearted, whom I have filled
with the spirit of wisdom, that they
may make Aaron's garments to
consecrate him, that he may minister
unto me in the priest's office.

4 And these *are* the garments which
they shall make; a breastplate, and an
ephod, and a robe, and a broidered
coat, a mitre, and a girdle: and they
shall make holy garments for Aaron
thy brother, and his sons, that he may
minister unto me in the priest's office.

5 And they shall take gold, and blue,
and purple, and scarlet, and fine linen.

6 ¶And they shall make the ephod *of*
gold, *of* blue, and *of* purple, *of* scarlet,
and fine twined linen, with cunning
work.

7 It shall have the two shoulderpieces thereof joined at the two edges
thereof; and *so* it shall be joined together.

8 And the curious girdle of the ephod,
which *is* upon it, shall be of the same,
according to the work thereof; *even of*
gold, *of* blue, and purple, and scarlet,
and fine twined linen.

9 And thou shalt take two onyx
stones, and grave on them the names of
the children of Israel:

10 Six of their names on one stone,
and *the other* six names of the rest on
the other stone, according to their
birth.

11 With the work of an engraver in
stone, *like* the engravings of a signet,
shalt thou engrave the two stones with
the names of the children of Israel:
thou shalt make them to be set in
ouches of gold.

12 And thou shalt put the two stones
upon the shoulders of the ephod *for*
stones of memorial unto the children of
Israel: and Aaron shall bear their
names before the LORD upon his two
shoulders for a memorial.

13 And thou shalt make ouches *of*
gold;

14 And two chains *of* pure gold at the
ends; *of* wreathen work shalt thou
make them, and fasten the wreathen
chains to the ouches.

15 ¶And thou shalt make the breastplate of judgment with cunning work;
after the work of the ephod shalt thou

D. The Priests' Apparel and Consecration. 28:1-29:46.

28:1-8. Aaron . . . and his sons with him were to be fitted in **holy garments** for their priestly work. The costly **garments** listed here are mentioned again in Leviticus 8:7-9. **The ephod** was a beautiful outer garment similar to an apron in the front and back, joined at **the two shoulder pieces** (vs. 7).

9-14. Two onyx stones were to have engraved upon them the names of the twelve **children of Israel** (vs. 9), six on each stone (vs. 10). These were to be worn **upon the shoulders of the ephod for stones of memorial** (vss. 11-12). Aaron bore up the children of Israel **before the LORD. Ouches of gold** mean gold settings in which the engraved stones were placed.

15-21. Attached to the front of the ephod, or outer robe, was **the breastplate of judgment** (vs. 15). It was about eight to ten inches square (vs. 16) and contained four rows of precious

make it; of gold, of blue, and of purple, and of scarlet, and of fine twined linen, shalt thou make it.

16 Foursquare it shall be *being* doubled; a span *shall be* the length thereof, and a span *shall be* the breadth thereof.

17 And thou shalt set in it settings of stones, *even* four rows of stones: *the first* row *shall be* a sardius, a topaz, and a carbuncle: *this shall be* the first row.

18 And the second row *shall be* an emerald, a sapphire, and a diamond.

19 And the third row a ligure, an agate, and an amethyst.

20 And the fourth row a beryl, and an onyx, and a jasper: they shall be set in gold in their inclosings.

21 And the stones shall be with the names of the children of Israel, twelve, according to their names, *like* the engravings of a signet; every one with his name shall they be according to the twelve tribes.

22 And thou shalt make upon the breastplate chains at the ends *of* wreathen work *of* pure gold.

23 And thou shalt make upon the breastplate two rings of gold, and shalt put the two rings on the two ends of the breastplate.

24 And thou shalt put the two wreathen *chains* of gold in the two rings *which are* on the ends of the breastplate.

25 And *the other* two ends of the two wreathen *chains* thou shalt fasten in the two ouches, and put *them* on the shoulderpieces of the ephod before it.

26 And thou shalt make two rings of gold, and thou shalt put them upon the two ends of the breastplate in the border thereof, which *is* in the side of the ephod inward.

27 And two *other* rings of gold thou shalt make, and shalt put them on the two sides of the ephod underneath, toward the forepart thereof, over against the *other* coupling thereof, above the curious girdle of the ephod.

28 And they shall bind the breastplate by the rings thereof unto the rings of the ephod with a lace of blue, that *it* may be above the curious girdle of the ephod, and that the breastplate be not loosed from the ephod.

29 And Aaron shall bear the names of the children of Israel in the breastplate of judgment upon his heart, when he goeth in unto the holy *place*, for a memorial before the LORD continually.

30 ¶And thou shalt put in the breastplate of judgment the Ú'rĭm and the Thŭm'mĭm; and they shall be upon Aaron's heart, when he goeth in before the LORD: and Aaron shall bear the judgment of the children of Israel upon his heart before the LORD continually.

31 ¶And thou shalt make the robe of the ephod all *of* blue.

32 And there shall be an hole in the top of it, in the midst thereof: it shall have a binding of woven work round about the hole of it, as it were the hole of an habergeon, that it be not rent.

33 And *beneath* upon the hem of it thou shalt make pomegranates *of* blue, and *of* purple, and *of* scarlet, round

stones, four to a row (vss. 17-20). Each tribe had its name written on one stone (vs. 21).

22-29. The breastplate was to be affixed securely to the ephod. The purpose of the breastplate was that Aaron would bear up the children of Israel **upon his heart, when he goeth in unto the holy place.** It was to keep Israel **before the LORD continually.**

30. Also attached to **the breastplate of judgment** was **the Urim and the Thummin.** These were apparently connected with the revelation of God's will (Num 27:21; I Sam 28:6), but no one today can be certain exactly how they operated, being just two stones. They were little used after the time of the prophets began with Samuel (cf. Ezr 2:63).

31-35. The high priest's **robe** was adorned with the standard colors of blue, purple, and scarlet; and around the hem this robe had a string of items alternating between **a golden bell and a pomegranate** (vs. 34). Only the high priestly robe had these bells on them. Without them, any ordinary priest seeking to enter **in unto the holy place before the LORD** would certainly die.

about the hem thereof; and bells of gold between them round about.

34 A golden bell and a pomegranate, a golden bell and a pomegranate, upon the hem of the robe round about.

35 And it shall be upon Aaron to minister: and his sound shall be heard when he goeth in unto the holy *place* before the LORD, and when he cometh out, that he die not.

36 ¶And thou shalt make a plate *of* pure gold, and grave upon it, *like* the engravings of a signet, HOLINESS TO THE LORD.

37 And thou shalt put it on a blue lace, that it may be upon the mitre; upon the forefront of the mitre it shall be.

38 And it shall be upon Aaron's forehead, that Aaron may bear the iniquity of the holy things, which the children of Israel shall hallow in all their holy gifts; and it shall be always upon his forehead, that they may be accepted before the LORD.

39 ¶And thou shalt embroider the coat of fine linen, and thou shalt make the mitre *of* fine linen, and thou shalt make the girdle *of* needlework.

40 ¶And for Aaron's sons thou shalt make coats, and thou shalt make for them girdles, and bonnets shalt thou make for them, for glory and for beauty.

41 And thou shalt put them upon Aaron thy brother, and his sons with him; and shalt anoint them, and consecrate them, and sanctify them, that they may minister unto me in the priest's office.

42 And thou shalt make them linen breeches to cover their nakedness; from the loins even unto the thighs they shall reach.

43 And they shall be upon Aaron, and upon his sons, when they come in unto the tabernacle of the congregation, or when they come near unto the altar to minister in the holy *place;* that they bear not iniquity, and die: *it shall be* a statute for ever unto him and his seed after him.

CHAPTER 29

AND this *is* the thing that thou shalt do unto them to hallow them, to minister unto me in the priest's office: Take one young bullock, and two rams without blemish,

2 And unleavened bread, and cakes unleavened tempered with oil, and wafers unleavened anointed with oil: *of* wheaten flour shalt thou make them.

3 And thou shalt put them into one basket, and bring them in the basket, with the bullock and the two rams.

4 And Aaron and his sons thou shalt bring unto the door of the tabernacle of the congregation, and shalt wash them with water.

5 And thou shalt take the garments, and put upon Aaron the coat, and the robe of the ephod, and the ephod, and the breastplate, and gird him with the curious girdle of the ephod:

6 And thou shalt put the mitre upon

36-40. The **mitre,** or headpiece, of the high priest bore a gold engraving that read HOLINESS TO THE LORD. It was a constant reminder of the priest's acceptance before God and of his holy ministry. It should remind all believers of the same. Other garments were also sewn for Aaron and his sons **for glory and for beauty.**

41-43. Finally, Moses was to take Aaron and his sons and **anoint them and consecrate them** (see also Lev 8:1-36). **Linen breeches to cover their nakedness** were undergarments required because of the loose-fitting, skirt-like robes the men wore.

29:1-9. The consecration, or dedication, of **Aaron and his sons** was performed at **the door of the tabernacle.** They were first washed with water, speaking of cleansing. Next, after Aaron was clothed in the new priestly attire, Moses poured the **anointing oil . . . upon his head.** The oil represents the Holy Spirit (Zech 4:3-6). Aaron's four sons were then duly outfitted as well.

his head, and put the holy crown upon the mitre.

7 Then shalt thou take the anointing oil, and pour it upon his head, and anoint him.

8 And thou shalt bring his sons, and put coats upon them.

9 And thou shalt gird them with girdles, Aaron and his sons, and put the bonnets on them: and the priest's office shall be theirs for a perpetual statute: and thou shalt consecrate Aaron and his sons.

10 And thou shalt cause a bullock to be brought before the tabernacle of the congregation: and Aaron and his sons shall put their hands upon the head of the bullock.

11 And thou shalt kill the bullock before the Lord, by the door of the tabernacle of the congregation.

12 And thou shalt take of the blood of the bullock, and put it upon the horns of the altar with thy finger, and pour all the blood beside the bottom of the altar.

13 And thou shalt take all the fat that covereth the inwards, and the caul that is above the liver, and the two kidneys, and the fat that is upon them, and burn them upon the altar.

14 But the flesh of the bullock, and his skin, and his dung, shalt thou burn with fire without the camp: it is a sin offering.

15 ¶Thou shalt also take one ram; and Aaron and his sons shall put their hands upon the head of the ram.

16 And thou shalt slay the ram, and thou shalt take his blood, and sprinkle it round about upon the altar.

17 And thou shalt cut the ram in pieces, and wash the inwards of him, and his legs, and put them unto his pieces, and unto his head.

18 And thou shalt burn the whole ram upon the altar: it is a burnt offering unto the Lord: it is a sweet savour, an offering made by fire unto the Lord.

19 And thou shalt take the other ram; and Aaron and his sons shall put their hands upon the head of the ram.

20 Then shalt thou kill the ram, and take of his blood, and put it upon the tip of the right ear of Aaron, and upon the tip of the right ear of his sons, and upon the thumb of their right hand, and upon the great toe of their right foot, and sprinkle the blood upon the altar round about.

21 And thou shalt take of the blood that is upon the altar, and of the anointing oil, and sprinkle it upon Aaron, and upon his garments, and upon his sons, and upon the garments of his sons with him: and he shall be hallowed, and his garments, and his sons, and his sons' garments with him.

22 Also thou shalt take of the ram the fat and the rump, and the fat that covereth the inwards, and the caul above the liver, and the two kidneys, and the fat that is upon them, and the right shoulder; for it is a ram of consecration:

23 And one loaf of bread, and one cake of oiled bread, and one wafer out

10-18. A bullock, which is a young bull, was then offered as a **sin offering** (vs. 14; cf. Lev 4:1-35), thus atoning for the guilt of sin. Then **one ram** (cf. vs. 1) was slain, had its blood applied to the altar, and became a whole **burnt offering.** The laying of **their hands upon the head of the ram** pictured their identification with the ram, and the fact that the ram would represent them as it was offered.

19-20. The other ram was also slain, but its blood was first placed **upon the tip of the right ear . . . the thumb of their right hand . . . and upon the great toe** of the right foot of Aaron and his sons. This spoke of the sanctification of their ears to hear and obey God's commands, of their hands to be filled with His work, and of their feet to walk in His ways.

21-28. The ram was then waved before the Lord as a heave, or wave, offering, together with unleavened bread (vs. 23; cf. vs. 2). This signified their complete consecration to God.

of the basket of the unleavened bread that *is* before the LORD:

24 And thou shalt put all in the hands of Aaron, and in the hands of his sons; and shalt wave them *for* a wave offering before the LORD.

25 And thou shalt receive them of their hands, and burn *them* upon the altar for a burnt offering, for a sweet savour before the LORD: it *is* an offering made by fire unto the LORD.

26 And thou shalt take the breast of the ram of Aaron's consecration, and wave it *for* a wave offering before the LORD: and it shall be thy part.

27 And thou shalt sanctify the breast of the wave offering, and the shoulder of the heave offering, which is waved, and which is heaved up, of the ram of the consecration, *even* of *that* which *is* for Aaron, and of *that* which is for his sons:

28 And it shall be Aaron's and his sons' by a statute for ever from the children of Israel: for it *is* an heave offering: and it shall be an heave offering from the children of Israel of the sacrifice of their peace offerings, *even* their heave offering unto the LORD.

29 ¶And the holy garments of Aaron shall be his sons' after him, to be anointed therein, and to be consecrated in them.

30 *And* that son that is priest in his stead shall put them on seven days, when he cometh into the tabernacle of the congregation to minister in the holy *place.*

31 ¶And thou shalt take the ram of the consecration, and seethe his flesh in the holy place.

32 And Aaron and his sons shall eat the flesh of the ram, and the bread that *is* in the basket, *by* the door of the tabernacle of the congregation.

33 And they shall eat those things wherewith the atonement was made, to consecrate *and* to sanctify them: but a stranger shall not eat *thereof*, because they *are* holy.

34 And if ought of the flesh of the consecrations, or of the bread, remain unto the morning, then thou shalt burn the remainder with fire: it shall not be eaten, because it *is* holy.

35 And thus shalt thou do unto Aaron, and to his sons, according to all *things* which I have commanded thee: seven days shalt thou consecrate them.

36 And thou shalt offer every day a bullock *for* a sin offering for atonement: and thou shalt cleanse the altar, when thou hast made an atonement for it, and thou shalt anoint it, to sanctify it.

37 Seven days thou shalt make an atonement for the altar, and sanctify it; and it shall be an altar most holy: whatsoever toucheth the altar shall be holy.

38 ¶Now this *is that* which thou shalt offer upon the altar; two lambs of the first year day by day continually.

39 The one lamb thou shalt offer in the morning; and the other lamb thou shalt offer at even:

40 And with the one lamb a tenth deal of flour mingled with the fourth part of

29-37. This consecration process continued for **seven days** (vs. 35). During this same time additional sacrifices were made to consecrate **the altar . . . to sanctify it,** or set it apart for use in God's service. It was **holy** and rendered anything that touched it holy as well.

38-42. Two lambs of the first year day by day continually, one in the morning and the other at evening, was to be the regular daily burnt offering. This offering was to be accompanied by flour, oil, and wine as well.

an hin of beaten oil; and the fourth part of an hin of wine *for* a drink offering.

41 And the other lamb thou shalt offer at even, and shalt do thereto according to the meat offering of the morning, and according to the drink offering thereof, for a sweet savour, an offering made by fire unto the LORD.

42 *This shall be* a continual burnt offering throughout your generations *at* the door of the tabernacle of the congregation before the LORD: where I will meet you, to speak there unto thee.

43 And there I will meet with the children of Israel, and *the tabernacle* shall be sanctified by my glory.

44 And I will sanctify the tabernacle of the congregation, and the altar: I will sanctify also both Aaron and his sons, to minister to me in the priest's office.

45 And I will dwell among the children of Israel, and will be their God.

46 And they shall know that I *am* the LORD their God, that brought them forth out of the land of Egypt, that I may dwell among them: I *am* the LORD their God.

CHAPTER 30

AND thou shalt make an altar to burn incense upon: *of* shittim wood shalt thou make it.

2 A cubit *shall be* the length thereof, and a cubit the breadth thereof; foursquare shall it be: and two cubits *shall be* the height thereof: the horns thereof *shall be* of the same.

3 And thou shalt overlay it with pure gold, the top thereof, and the sides thereof round about, and the horns thereof; and thou shalt make unto it a crown of gold round about.

4 And two golden rings shalt thou make to it under the crown of it, by the two corners thereof, upon the two sides of it shalt thou make *it;* and they shall be for places for the staves to bear it withal.

5 And thou shalt make the staves *of* shittim wood, and overlay them with gold.

6 And thou shalt put it before the vail that *is* by the ark of the testimony, before the mercy seat that *is* over the testimony, where I will meet with thee.

7 And Aaron shall burn thereon sweet incense every morning: when he dresseth the lamps, he shall burn incense upon it.

8 And when Aaron lighteth the lamps at even, he shall burn incense upon it, a perpetual incense before the LORD throughout your generations.

9 Ye shall offer no strange incense thereon, nor burnt sacrifice, nor meat offering; neither shall ye pour drink offering thereon.

10 And Aaron shall make an atonement upon the horns of it once in a year with the blood of the sin offering of atonements: once in the year shall he make atonement upon it throughout your generations: it *is* most holy unto the LORD.

11 ¶And the LORD spake unto Moses, saying,

12 When thou takest the sum of the children of Israel after their number,

43-46. Before Israel could meet with God, all of these sacrifices, consecrations, and anointings had to be completed. God said **I will dwell among the children of Israel, and will be their God** (vs. 45). Since God was holy, everything had to be sanctified, or set apart properly.

E. Guidelines to Tabernacle Worship. 30:1-38.

30:1-6. Another piece of tabernacle furniture was **an altar to burn incense,** meaning frankincense. It was constructed of wood and covered with gold, was about eighteen inches square, and stood about waist high. It was transported by means of golden **staves** placed in its golden **rings.** It was situated just in front of **the veil that is by the ark of the testimony.**

7-10. Incense, picturing the prayers of the saints (Rev 5:8; 8:3-4), was to burn continually upon this altar. The prohibition against offering **strange incense** was violated by Nadab and Abihu in Leviticus 10:1-11, possibly because of a drunken condition. They were slain by God as a result.

11-14. Since Moses was still upon the mountain, **The LORD spake unto Moses.** This was part of the forty days spent between Exodus 24:18 and 32:7. Every person **from twenty years old and above** was required to give **half a shekel** of silver,

then shall they give every man a ransom for his soul unto the LORD, when thou numberest them; that there be no plague among them, when *thou* numberest them.

13 This they shall give, every one that passeth among them that are numbered, half a shekel after the shekel of the sanctuary: (a shekel *is* twenty gerahs:) an half shekel *shall be* the offering of the LORD.

14 Every one that passeth among them that are numbered, from twenty years old and above, shall give an offering unto the LORD.

15 The rich shall not give more, and the poor shall not give less than half a shekel, when *they* give an offering unto the LORD, to make an atonement for your souls.

16 And thou shalt take the atonement money of the children of Israel, and shalt appoint it for the service of the tabernacle of the congregation; that it may be a memorial unto the children of Israel before the LORD, to make an atonement for your souls.

17 ¶And the LORD spake unto Moses, saying,

18 Thou shalt also make a laver *of* brass, and his foot *also of* brass, to wash *withal:* and thou shalt put it between the tabernacle of the congregation and the altar, and thou shalt put water therein.

19 For Aaron and his sons shall wash their hands and their feet thereat:

20 When they go into the tabernacle of the congregation, they shall wash with water, that they die not; or when they come near to the altar to minister, to burn offering made by fire unto the LORD:

21 So they shall wash their hands and their feet, that they die not: and it shall be a statute for ever to them, *even* to him and to his seed throughout their generations.

22 ¶Moreover the LORD spake unto Moses, saying,

23 Take thou also unto thee principal spices, of pure myrrh five hundred *shekels,* and of sweet cinnamon half so much, *even* two hundred and fifty *shekels,* and of sweet calamus two hundred and fifty *shekels,*

24 And of cassia five hundred *shekels,* after the shekel of the sanctuary, and of oil olive an hin:

25 And thou shalt make it an oil of holy ointment, an ointment compound after the art of the apothecary: it shall be an holy anointing oil.

26 And thou shalt anoint the tabernacle of the congregation therewith, and the ark of the testimony,

27 And the table and all his vessels, and the candlestick and his vessels, and the altar of incense,

28 And the altar of burnt offering with all his vessels, and the laver and his foot.

29 And thou shalt sanctify them, that they may be most holy: whatsoever toucheth them shall be holy.

30 And thou shalt anoint Aaron and his sons, and consecrate them, that

termed **a ransom for his soul.** God's continued preservation of Israel was to be thought upon and remembered, **that there be no plague among them** (vs. 12).

15-16. Rich and poor were to give an equal amount. No boasting would be tolerated. All are equally in need of God's provision. **The atonement money** was appointed for **the service of the tabernacle** (cf. 38:25-28), and was used primarily for making the sockets of silver, the foundation of the entire tabernacle.

17-18. Also make a laver of brass. Brass again signified judgment. First came the brazen altar of sacrifice, and then the brazen laver as one approached the tabernacle. Both had to be used, or death would ensue.

19-21. The priests had to **wash their hands and their feet** prior to any ministry. Our initial cleansing also comes first at the altar of sacrifice, through Christ's shed blood; but repeated cleansings are needed daily and are received as we bathe in the Word of God (Jn 15:3) and confess our sins to the Father (I Jn 1:9).

22-25. The official **oil of holy ointment** (vs. 25) was made of **myrrh . . . cinnamon . . . calamus . . . cassia,** carefully mixed with **olive oil.** Today, when elders wish to anoint with oil (Jas 5:14), plain olive oil is used.

26-38. This was used to **anoint the tabernacle . . . the ark,** all its furniture (vss. 27-29), and Aaron and his sons (vs. 30), including all who would follow for **generations** (vs. 31). Attempted duplication of the special oil was strictly forbidden (vss. 32-33).

they may minister unto me in the priest's office.

31 And thou shalt speak unto the children of Israel, saying, This shall be an holy anointing oil unto me throughout your generations.

32 Upon man's flesh shall it not be poured, neither shall ye make *any other* like it, after the composition of it: it *is* holy, *and* it shall be holy unto you.

33 Whosoever compoundeth *any* like it, or whosoever putteth *any* of it upon a stranger, shall even be cut off from his people.

34 ¶And the LORD said unto Moses, Take unto thee sweet spices, stacte, and onycha, and galbanum; *these* sweet spices with pure frankincense: of each shall there be a like *weight:*

35 And thou shalt make it a perfume, a confection after the art of the apothecary, tempered together, pure *and* holy:

36 And thou shalt beat *some* of it very small, and put of it before the testimony in the tabernacle of the congregation, where I will meet with thee: it shall be unto you most holy.

37 And *as for* the perfume which thou shalt make, ye shall not make to yourselves according to the composition thereof: it shall be unto thee holy for the LORD.

38 Whosoever shall make like unto that, to smell thereto, shall even be cut off from his people.

CHAPTER 31

AND the LORD spake unto Moses, saying,

2 See, I have called by name Be-zăl′e-el the son of Ū′rī, the son of Hur, of the tribe of Jūdah:

3 And I have filled him with the spirit of God, in wisdom, and in understanding, and in knowledge, and in all manner of workmanship,

4 To devise cunning works, to work in gold, and in silver, and in brass,

5 And in cutting of stones, to set *them,* and in carving of timber, to work in all manner of workmanship.

6 And I, behold, I have given with him A-hō′lĭ-ăb, the son of A-hĭs′a-măch, of the tribe of Dan: and in the hearts of all that are wise hearted I have put wisdom, that they may make all that I have commanded thee;

7 The tabernacle of the congregation, and the ark of the testimony, and the mercy seat that *is* thereupon, and all the furniture of the tabernacle,

8 And the table and his furniture, and the pure candlestick with all his furniture, and the altar of incense,

9 And the altar of burnt offering with all his furniture, and the laver and his foot,

10 And the cloths of service, and the holy garments for Aaron the priest, and the garments of his sons, to minister in the priest's office,

11 And the anointing oil, and sweet incense for the holy *place:* according to all that I have commanded thee shall they do.

F. The Appointment of Bezaleel and Aholiab. 31:1-11.

31:1-5. Bezaleel is the first man ever spoken of as being **filled . . . with the spirit of God.** His filling was for service—not speaking, but working with his hands. He carefully constructed the tabernacle and its furniture with the help of others, according to the precise instructions of God.

6-11. God gave Bezaleel helpers, including **Aholiab** and others in whom God **put wisdom.** They were to construct all the furniture listed in these verses. It no doubt required long hours of exacting workmanship. God needs many dedicated Spirit-filled workers such as these, not just a few preachers.

12 ¶And the LORD spake unto Moses, saying,

13 Speak thou also unto the children of Israel, saying, Verily my sabbaths ye shall keep: for it *is* a sign between me and you throughout your generations; that *ye* may know that I *am* the LORD that doth sanctify you.

14 Ye shall keep the sabbath therefore; for it *is* holy unto you: every one that defileth it shall surely be put to death: for whosoever doeth *any* work therein, that soul shall be cut off from among his people.

15 Six days may work be done; but in the seventh *is* the sabbath of rest, holy to the LORD: whosoever doeth *any* work in the sabbath day, he shall surely be put to death.

16 Wherefore the children of Israel shall keep the sabbath, to observe the sabbath throughout their generations, *for* a perpetual covenant.

17 It *is* a sign between me and the children of Israel for ever: for *in* six days the LORD made heaven and earth, and on the seventh day he rested, and was refreshed.

18 ¶And he gave unto Moses, when he had made an end of communing with him upon mount Sĭ'naī, two tables of testimony, tables of stone, written with the finger of God.

CHAPTER 32

AND when the people saw that Moses delayed to come down out of the mount, the people gathered themselves together unto Aaron, and said unto him, Up, make us gods, which shall go before us; for *as for* this Moses, the man that brought us up out of the land of Egypt, we wot not what is become of him.

2 And Aaron said unto them, Break off the golden earrings, which *are* in the ears of your wives, of your sons, and of your daughters, and bring *them* unto me.

3 And all the people brake off the golden earrings which *were* in their ears, and brought *them* unto Aaron.

4 And he received *them* at their hand, and fashioned it with a graving tool, after he had made it a molten calf: and they said, These *be* thy gods, O Israel, which brought thee up out of the land of Egypt.

5 And when Aaron saw *it*, he built an altar before it; and Aaron made proclamation, and said, To morrow *is* a feast to the LORD.

6 And they rose up early on the morrow, and offered burnt offerings, and brought peace offerings; and the people sat down to eat and to drink, and rose up to play.

7 ¶And the LORD said unto Moses, Go, get thee down; for thy people, which thou broughtest out of the land of Egypt, have corrupted *themselves:*

8 They have turned aside quickly out

G. The Sabbath Rest Further Enjoined. 31:12-18.

12-14. The keeping of God's **sabbaths** was meant for **the children of Israel.** Anyone who violated the Sabbath was to be **cut off from among his people,** indicating death (cf. vs. 15, Num 15:32-36).

15-17. A perpetual covenant. This was never intended to be binding on the Christian Church, as Paul clearly pointed out in Colossians 2:14-17; and Christian practice was to meet on Sunday, resurrection day, the first day of the week (Acts 20:7; I Cor 16:2).

18. At the conclusion of the forty days and nights of **communing** with God **upon mount Sinai,** God gave Moses **two tables of testimony, tables of stone, written with the finger of God.** This apparently indicates the ten initial commandments.

IX. ISRAEL'S APOSTASY AND MOSES' INTERCESSION. 32:1-35:3.

A. The Worship of the Golden Calf. 32:1-6.

32:1-2. During Moses' delay with God upon the mountain (Ex 24:18-31:18), the people came to **Aaron** and demanded **Up, make us gods.** Aaron seemingly consented, telling the people to **Break off the golden earrings . . . and bring them unto me.** He had no backbone to stand against this blatant treason and idolatry, but instead he became their leader!

3-6. Aaron **received** the gold, **fashioned it** into a **molten calf,** and announced **These be thy gods, O Israel.** Aaron further **built an altar before** the calf and proclaimed a feast day. They offered sacrifices and **sat down to eat and to drink, and rose up to play.** What if Moses had died? Was there no one to stand against this sudden apostasy? No wonder God was so angry with Israel.

B. God's Anger and Moses' Intercession. 32:7-35.

7-10. God announced to **Moses, . . . thy people . . . have corrupted themselves.** Israel is viewed here as Moses' responsibility since he was the mediator of the covenant. God designated Israel as a **stiffnecked people,** the figure coming from a horse or ox that refuses to be turned by the reins. God next suggested the

of the way which I commanded them: they have made them a molten calf, and have worshipped it, and have sacrificed thereunto, and said, These *be* thy gods, O Israel, which have brought thee up out of the land of Egypt.

9 And the LORD said unto Moses, I have seen this people, and, behold, it *is* a stiffnecked people:

10 Now therefore let me alone, that my wrath may wax hot against them, and that I may consume them: and I will make of thee a great nation.

11 And Moses besought the LORD his God, and said, LORD, why doth thy wrath wax hot against thy people, which thou hast brought forth out of the land of Egypt with great power, and with a mighty hand?

12 Wherefore should the Egyptians speak, and say, For mischief did he bring them out, to slay them in the mountains, and to consume them from the face of the earth? Turn from thy fierce wrath, and repent of this evil against thy people.

13 Remember Abraham, Isaac, and Israel, thy servants, to whom thou swearest by thine own self, and saidst unto them, I will multiply your seed as the stars of heaven, and all this land that I have spoken of will I give unto your seed, and they shall inherit *it* for ever.

14 And the LORD repented of the evil which he thought to do unto his people.

15 ¶And Moses turned, and went down from the mount, and the two tables of the testimony *were* in his hand: the tables *were* written on both their sides; on the one side and on the other *were* they written.

16 And the tables *were* the work of God, and the writing *was* the writing of God, graven upon the tables.

17 And when Joshua heard the noise of the people as they shouted, he said unto Moses, *There is* a noise of war in the camp.

18 And he said, *It is* not the voice of *them that* shout for mastery, neither *is it* the voice of *them that* cry for being overcome: *but* the noise of *them that* sing do I hear.

19 ¶And it came to pass, as soon as he came nigh unto the camp, that he saw the calf, and the dancing: and Moses' anger waxed hot, and he cast the tables out of his hands, and brake them beneath the mount.

20 And he took the calf which they had made, and burnt *it* in the fire, and ground *it* to powder, and strawed *it* upon the water, and made the children of Israel drink *of it*.

21 And Moses said unto Aaron, What did this people unto thee, that thou hast brought so great a sin upon them?

22 And Aaron said, Let not the anger of my lord wax hot: thou knowest the people, that they *are set* on mischief.

23 For they said unto me, Make us gods, which shall go before us: for *as*

elimination of Israel and promised Moses **I will make of thee a great nation.** This was a real test of Moses' character, but he responded properly.

11-13. Moses called Israel God's **people, which thou hast brought forth out of the land of Egypt.** He reminded God that His name, character, and power would be called in question by the heathen if they were to consume Israel. He asked God to **Remember Abraham, Isaac, and Israel** with whom He had covenanted to multiply their seed **as the stars of heaven.** Moses stood the test, while Aaron failed miserably.

14. And the LORD repented of the evil. This is an anthropomorphic expression (a description of God using human terminology), to indicate a change in His previously announced plans, due in this case to the intercession of Moses on Israel's behalf. In other cases, when men change their actions, God may change His (Jon 3:10).

15-20. Returning to the camp and viewing the obvious idolatry, Moses angrily **cast the tables out of his hands, and brake them.** The **calf** was **burnt,** ground **to powder,** sprinkled in the water, and drunk by the Israelites, as though internalizing the greatness of their sin.

21-25. Aaron's fear must have been great when Moses questioned him as to his part in the sin, since he had been placed in charge (Ex 24:14), along with Hur. He lied by claiming he had simply cast the gold **into the fire, and there came out this calf** (cf. vss. 2-4). He must have repented, though that is not mentioned here.

21 And the Lord said, Behold, *there is* a place by me, and thou shalt stand upon a rock:

22 And it shall come to pass, while my glory passeth by, that I will put thee in a clift of the rock, and will cover thee with my hand while I pass by:

23 And I will take away mine hand, and thou shalt see my back parts: but my face shall not be seen.

CHAPTER 34

AND the Lord said unto Moses, Hew thee two tables of stone like unto the first: and I will write upon *these* tables the words that were in the first tables, which thou brakest.

2 And be ready in the morning, and come up in the morning unto mount Sī́-naī, and present thyself there to me in the top of the mount.

3 And no man shall come up with thee, neither let any man be seen throughout all the mount; neither let the flocks nor herds feed before that mount.

4 ¶And he hewed two tables of stone like unto the first; and Moses rose up early in the morning, and went up unto mount Sī́naī, as the Lord had commanded him, and took in his hand the two tables of stone.

5 And the Lord descended in the cloud, and stood with him there, and proclaimed the name of the Lord.

6 And the Lord passed by before him, and proclaimed, The Lord, The Lord God, merciful and gracious, longsuffering, and abundant in goodness and truth,

7 Keeping mercy for thousands, forgiving iniquity and transgression and sin, and that will by no means clear *the guilty;* visiting the iniquity of the fathers upon the children, and upon the children's children, unto the third and to the fourth *generation.*

8 And Moses made haste, and bowed his head toward the earth, and worshipped.

9 And he said, If now I have found grace in thy sight, O Lord, let my Lord, I pray thee, go among us; for it *is* a stiff-necked people; and pardon our iniquity and our sin, and take us for thine inheritance.

10 ¶And he said, Behold, I make a covenant: before all thy people I will do marvels, such as have not been done in all the earth, nor in any nation: and all the people among which thou *art* shall see the work of the Lord: for it *is* a terrible thing that I will do with thee.

11 Observe thou that which I command thee this day: behold, I drive out before thee the Amorite, and the Canaanite, and the Hittite, and the Pĕr'iz-zīte, and the Hī'vīte, and the Jĕb'u-sīte.

12 Take heed to thyself, lest thou make a covenant with the inhabitants of the land whither thou goest, lest it be for a snare in the midst of thee:

13 But ye shall destroy their altars, break their images, and cut down their groves:

14 For thou shalt worship no other god: for the Lord, whose name *is* Jealous, *is* a jealous God:

15 Lest thou make a covenant with

34:1-4. These verses form a parenthesis in the midst of the account of the Christophany (appearance of Christ). Moses is to meet God again upon the mountain (vs. 2), alone (vs. 3), and with **two tables of stone like unto the first** (vs. 4). God again would give a copy of the Ten Commandments.

5-7. And the Lord descended . . . and stood (lit., planted Himself), . . . **and . . . passed by before him.** God, the second person of the Trinity, came down and walked before Moses, though shrouded in a glorious brightness such as He had during the transfiguration (Mt 17:2). Moses also learned something of God's attributes especially His **mercy** and forgiveness, as well as His holiness, righteousness, and judgment.

8-9. As a result, Moses **bowed his head toward the earth, and worshipped** before the Lord. God was personally present as He communicated verbally to Moses.

E. God Renews the Covenant. 34:10-35:3.

10. Behold, I make a covenant. The covenant has previously been given, accepted, and ratified by the eating of the covenant meal (Ex 19:3-11). But it had been broken in the golden calf incident. Here God renews the covenant with Israel.

11-17. Observe thou. In driving out the wicked, degenerate people of Canaan, Israel was to watch lest they **make a covenant with the inhabitants of the land** (vs. 12), which they unthinkingly but readily did in Joshua 9:1-17. Great care needed to be taken regarding this, because religious compromise is a downward progression. The questionings of one generation can become the doctrine of the next, and one's dabbling in sin can become another's habitual practice.

the inhabitants of the land, and they go a whoring after their gods, and do sacrifice unto their gods, and *one* call thee, and thou eat of his sacrifice;

16 And thou take of their daughters unto thy sons, and their daughters go a whoring after their gods, and make thy sons go a whoring after their gods.

17 Thou shalt make thee no molten gods.

18 ¶The feast of unleavened bread shalt thou keep. Seven days thou shalt eat unleavened bread, as I commanded thee, in the time of the month Ābīb: for in the month Ābīb thou camest out from Egypt.

19 All that openeth the matrix *is* mine; and every firstling among thy cattle, *whether* ox or sheep, *that is male.*

20 But the firstling of an ass thou shalt redeem with a lamb: and if thou redeem *him* not, then shalt thou break his neck. All the firstborn of thy sons thou shalt redeem. And none shall appear before me empty.

21 ¶Six days thou shalt work, but on the seventh day thou shalt rest: in earing time and in harvest thou shalt rest.

22 ¶And thou shalt observe the feast of weeks, of the firstfruits of wheat harvest, and the feast of ingathering at the year's end.

23 ¶Thrice in the year shall all your menchildren appear before the Lord God, the God of Israel.

24 For I will cast out the nations before thee, and enlarge thy borders: neither shall any man desire thy land, when thou shalt go up to appear before the Lord thy God thrice in the year.

25 Thou shalt not offer the blood of my sacrifice with leaven; neither shall the sacrifice of the feast of the passover be left unto the morning.

26 The first of the firstfruits of thy land thou shalt bring unto the house of the Lord thy God. Thou shalt not seethe a kid in his mother's milk.

27 And the Lord said unto Moses, Write thou these words: for after the tenor of these words I have made a covenant with thee and with Israel.

28 And he was there with the Lord forty days and forty nights; he did neither eat bread, nor drink water. And he wrote upon the tables the words of the covenant, the ten commandments.

29 ¶And it came to pass, when Moses came down from mount Sīʹnaī with the two tables of testimony in Moses' hand, when he came down from the mount, that Moses wist not that the skin of his face shone while he talked with him.

30 And when Aaron and all the children of Israel saw Moses, behold, the skin of his face shone; and they were afraid to come nigh him.

31 And Moses called unto them; and Aaron and all the rulers of the congregation returned unto him: and Moses talked with them.

32 And afterward all the children of Israel came nigh: and he gave them in commandment all that the Lord had spoken with him in mount Sīʹnaī.

18-20. Connected with **The feast of unleavened bread** was the Passover and the death of Egypt's first-born. Israel's first-born therefore belong to the Lord.

21. The Sabbath was to be strictly observed; even **in harvest thou shalt rest.** God is concerned over our physical rest and well-being.

22-26. Here God reiterates the fact that **all** the males of Israel were to **appear before the Lord** three times a year (cf. Ex 23:14-19; Deut 16:16-17). God promised to protect their wives and children while they were gone to worship during these times. **Neither shall any man desire thy land.**

27-28. And the Lord said unto Moses, Write thou these words. Again and again Moses was commanded to write the Book of the Law (Ex 17:14; 24:4). And **Moses wrote upon the tables.** There is no good reason to ascribe this writing of Moses to prophets who lived hundreds of years later or to claim that Moses did not write the entire Pentateuch.

29-35. When Moses came down from mount Sinai . . . the skin of his face shone. Rays of light apparently beamed forth from his face after his prolonged communion with God. As a result of Moses' shining face, the people **were afraid to come nigh him,** so Moses **put a veil on his face** (vs. 33) when talking with men, but removed it when speaking with God.

33 And *till* Moses had done speaking with them, he put a vail on his face.

34 But when Moses went in before the Lord to speak with him, he took the vail off, until he came out. And he came out, and spake unto the children of Israel *that* which he was commanded.

35 And the children of Israel saw the face of Moses, that the skin of Moses' face shone: and Moses put the vail upon his face again, until he went in to speak with him.

CHAPTER 35

AND Moses gathered all the congregation of the children of Israel together, and said unto them, These *are* the words which the Lord hath commanded, that ye should do them.

2 Six days shall work be done, but on the seventh day there shall be to you an holy day, a sabbath of rest to the Lord: whosoever doeth work therein shall be put to death.

3 Ye shall kindle no fire throughout your habitations upon the sabbath day.

4 ¶And Moses spake unto all the congregation of the children of Israel, saying, This *is* the thing which the Lord commanded, saying,

5 Take ye from among you an offering unto the Lord: whosoever *is* of a willing heart, let him bring it, an offering of the Lord; gold, and silver, and brass,

6 And blue, and purple, and scarlet, and fine linen, and goats' *hair*,

7 And rams' skins dyed red, and badgers' skins, and shittim wood,

8 And oil for the light, and spices for anointing oil, and for the sweet incense,

9 And onyx stones, and stones to be set for the ephod, and for the breastplate.

10 And every wise hearted among you shall come, and make all that the Lord hath commanded;

11 The tabernacle, his tent, and his covering, his taches, and his boards, his bars, his pillars, and his sockets,

12 The ark, and the staves thereof, *with* the mercy seat, and the vail of the covering,

13 The table, and his staves, and all his vessels, and the shewbread,

14 The candlestick also for the light, and his furniture, and his lamps, with the oil for the light,

15 And the incense altar, and his staves, and the anointing oil, and the sweet incense, and the hanging for the door at the entering in of the tabernacle,

16 The altar of burnt offering, with his brasen grate, his staves, and all his vessels, the laver and his foot,

17 The hangings of the court, his pillars, and their sockets, and the hanging for the door of the court,

18 The pins of the tabernacle, and the pins of the court, and their cords,

19 The cloths of service, to do service in the holy *place*, the holy garments for

35:1-3. Moses then had to communicate the revelation of Exodus 25:1-31:18 to the people. The golden calf incident had prevented that previously. First to be mentioned was the Sabbath injunction. Violation carried the **death** penalty.

X. THE TABERNACLE BUILT AND DEDICATED. 35:4-40:38.

A. The Abundant Offerings and Willing Workers. 35:4-36:7.

4. Moses began his discourse by saying **This is the thing which the Lord commanded.** He then began to repeat to the people that which God had carefully instructed him earlier on Mount Sinai as recorded in detail in Exodus 25:1-31:18. Now these things are reiterated as the work on the tabernacle is carried out.

5-9. The **offering of the Lord** was to be given by those who possessed **a willing heart.** One who gives out of a feeling of group pressure, or for any other reason, ought not to give at all. They were to bring precious metals (vs. 5), cloths, skins, and lumber (vs. 7), olive oil (vs. 8), and precious stones (vs. 9).

10-19. Wisehearted or skillful men were exhorted to help with the construction of the tabernacle and all its furniture, which were carefully enumerated.

Aaron the priest, and the garments of his sons, to minister in the priest's office.

20 ¶And all the congregation of the children of Israel departed from the presence of Moses.

21 And they came, every one whose heart stirred him up, and every one whom his spirit made willing, and they brought the Lord's offering to the work of the tabernacle of the congregation, and for all his service, and for the holy garments.

22 And they came, both men and women, as many as were willing hearted, and brought bracelets, and earrings, and rings, and tablets, all jewels of gold: and every man that offered offered an offering of gold unto the Lord.

23 And every man, with whom was found blue, and purple, and scarlet, and fine linen, and goats' hair, and red skins of rams, and badgers' skins, brought them.

24 Every one that did offer an offering of silver and brass brought the Lord's offering: and every man, with whom was found shittim wood for any work of the service, brought it.

25 And all the women that were wise hearted did spin with their hands, and brought that which they had spun, both of blue, and of purple, and of scarlet, and of fine linen.

26 And all the women whose heart stirred them up in wisdom spun goats' hair.

27 And the rulers brought onyx stones, and stones to be set, for the ephod, and for the breastplate;

28 And spice, and oil for the light, and for the anointing oil, and for the sweet incense.

29 The children of Israel brought a willing offering unto the Lord, every man and woman, whose heart made them willing to bring for all manner of work, which the Lord had commanded to be made by the hand of Moses.

30 ¶And Moses said unto the children of Israel, See, the Lord hath called by name Be-zăl'e-el the son of Ū'rī, the son of Hur, of the tribe of Jūdah;

31 And he hath filled him with the spirit of God, in wisdom, in understanding, and in knowledge, and in all manner of workmanship;

32 And to devise curious works, to work in gold, and in silver, and in brass,

33 And in the cutting of stones, to set them, and in carving of wood, to make any manner of cunning work.

34 And he hath put in his heart that he may teach, both he, and A-hō'lī-ăb, the son of A-hīs'a-măch, of the tribe of Dan.

35 Them hath he filled with wisdom of heart, to work all manner of work, of the engraver, and of the cunning workman, and of the embroiderer, in blue, and in purple, in scarlet, and in fine linen, and of the weaver, even of them that do any work, and of those that devise cunning work.

CHAPTER 36

THEN wrought Be-zăl'e-el and A-hō'lī-ăb, and every wise hearted man, in

20-21. After hearing the initial list of things that were needed the people **departed . . . And they came** back bringing what they could. Emphasis is again placed upon the willingness of the people to give.

22-29. These verses suggest the sacrificial spirit in which the giving was accomplished. It is noted that **both men and women** helped (vs. 22), and that **every man,** and **Everyone** brought gifts (vss. 23-24). Every person could contribute! **Women** spun (vss. 25-26); and **rulers** gave precious stones, spices, and oil (vss. 27-28). The conclusion was that **The children of Israel brought a willing offering unto the Lord** (vs. 29). Our giving today should emulate that of Israel's on this occasion.

30-35. God specially enabled Bezaleel and Aholiab to do a remarkable work of construction and general overseeing of the physical work. God's work requires different kinds of laborers.

36:1-7. Amazingly enough, Bezaleel and Aholiab soon found that the people were bringing much more than enough for the

182

whom the LORD put wisdom and understanding to know how to work all manner of work for the service of the sanctuary, according to all that the LORD had commanded.

2 And Moses called Be-zăl′e-el and A-hō′lï-ăb, and every wise hearted man, in whose heart the LORD had put wisdom, *even* every one whose heart stirred him up to come unto the work to do it:

3 And they received of Moses all the offering, which the children of Israel had brought for the work of the service of the sanctuary, to make it *withal*. And they brought yet unto him free offerings every morning.

4 ¶And all the wise men, that wrought all the work of the sanctuary, came every man from his work which they made;

5 And they spake unto Moses, saying, The people bring much more than enough for the service of the work, which the LORD commanded to make.

6 And Moses gave commandment, and they caused it to be proclaimed throughout the camp, saying, Let neither man nor woman make any more work for the offering of the sanctuary. So the people were restrained from bringing.

7 For the stuff they had was sufficient for all the work to make it, and too much.

8 ¶And every wise hearted man among them that wrought the work of the tabernacle made ten curtains *of* fine twined linen, and blue, and purple, and scarlet: *with* cherubims of cunning work made he them.

9 The length of one curtain *was* twenty and eight cubits, and the breadth of one curtain four cubits: the curtains *were* all of one size.

10 And he coupled the five curtains one unto another: and *the other* five curtains he coupled one unto another.

11 And he made loops of blue on the edge of one curtain from the selvedge in the coupling: likewise he made in the uttermost side of *another* curtain, in the coupling of the second.

12 Fifty loops made he in one curtain, and fifty loops made he in the edge of the curtain which *was* in the coupling of the second: the loops held one *curtain* to another.

13 And he made fifty taches of gold, and coupled the curtains one unto another with the taches: so it became one tabernacle.

14 ¶And he made curtains *of* goats′ *hair* for the tent over the tabernacle: eleven curtains he made them.

15 The length of one curtain *was* thirty cubits, and four cubits *was* the breadth of one curtain: the eleven curtains *were* of one size.

16 And he coupled five curtains by themselves, and six curtains by themselves.

17 And he made fifty loops upon the uttermost edge of the curtain in the coupling, and fifty loops made he upon the edge of the curtain which coupleth the second.

18 And he made fifty taches *of* brass

service of the work. The people had to be commanded not to bring any more items. What preacher would not like to see his congregation give like Israel did on this occasion!

B. The Construction of the Tabernacle. 36:8-38:31.

8-38. For explanations of the construction of the tabernacle as recounted in these verses, please see the nearly identical earlier portion where the plans were initially given to Moses, i.e., Exodus 26:1-37.

to couple the tent together, that it might be one.

19 ¶And he made a covering for the tent of rams' skins dyed red, and a covering of badgers' skins above that.

20 ¶And he made boards for the tabernacle of shĭttĭm wood, standing up.

21 The length of a board was ten cubits, and the breadth of a board one cubit and a half.

22 One board had two tenons, equally distant one from another: thus did he make for all the boards of the tabernacle.

23 And he made boards for the tabernacle; twenty boards for the south side southward:

24 And forty sockets of silver he made under the twenty boards; two sockets under one board for his two tenons, and two sockets under another board for his two tenons.

25 And for the other side of the tabernacle, which is toward the north corner, he made twenty boards,

26 And their forty sockets of silver; two sockets under one board, and two sockets under another board.

27 And for the sides of the tabernacle westward he made six boards.

28 And two boards made he for the corners of the tabernacle in the two sides.

29 And they were coupled beneath, and coupled together at the head thereof, to one ring: thus he did to both of them in both the corners.

30 And there were eight boards; and their sockets were sixteen sockets of silver, under every board two sockets.

31 ¶And he made bars of shĭttĭm wood; five for the boards of the one side of the tabernacle,

32 And five bars for the boards of the other side of the tabernacle, and five bars for the boards of the tabernacle for the sides westward.

33 And he made the middle bar to shoot through the boards from the one end to the other.

34 And he overlaid the boards with gold, and made their rings of gold to be places for the bars, and overlaid the bars with gold.

35 ¶And he made a vail of blue, and purple, and scarlet, and fine twined linen: with cherubims made he it of cunning work.

36 And he made thereunto four pillars of shĭttĭm wood, and overlaid them with gold: their hooks were of gold; and he cast for them four sockets of silver.

37 ¶And he made an hanging for the tabernacle door of blue, and purple, and scarlet, and fine twined linen, of needlework;

38 And the five pillars of it with their hooks: and he overlaid their chapiters and their fillets with gold: but their five sockets were of brass.

CHAPTER 37

AND Be-zăl'e-el made the ark of shĭttĭm wood: two cubits and a half was the length of it, and a cubit and a half the breadth of it, and a cubit and a half the height of it:

2 And he overlaid it with pure gold

37:1-29. The initial account of the plans for the **ark** (vss. 1-5), **mercy seat** (vss. 6-9), **table** of showbread (vss. 10-16), and the **candlestick** or lampstand (vss. 17-24) are commented on in the treatment of Exodus 25:10-40. **The incense altar** (vss. 25-28) is earlier mentioned in Exodus 30:1-10. **The holy anointing oil** (vs. 29) is fully covered under Exodus 30:23-38.

within and without, and made a crown of gold to it round about.

3 And he cast for it four rings of gold, *to be set* by the four corners of it; even two rings upon the one side of it, and two rings upon the other side of it.

4 And he made staves *of* shĭttĭm wood, and overlaid them with gold.

5 And he put the staves into the rings by the sides of the ark, to bear the ark.

6 ¶And he made the mercy seat *of* pure gold: two cubits and a half *was* the length thereof, and one cubit and a half the breadth thereof.

7 And he made two cherubims *of* gold, beaten out of one piece made he them, on the two ends of the mercy seat;

8 One cherub on the end on this side, and another cherub on the *other* end on that side: out of the mercy seat made he the cherubims on the two ends thereof.

9 And the cherubims spread out *their* wings on high, and covered with their wings over the mercy seat, with their faces one to another; *even* to the mercy seatward were the faces of the cherubims.

10 ¶And he made the table *of* shĭttĭm wood: two cubits *was* the length thereof, and a cubit the breadth thereof, and a cubit and a half the height thereof:

11 And he overlaid it with pure gold, and made thereunto a crown of gold round about.

12 Also he made thereunto a border of an handbreadth round about; and made a crown of gold for the border thereof round about.

13 And he cast for it four rings of gold, and put the rings upon the four corners that *were* in the four feet thereof.

14 Over against the border were the rings, the places for the staves to bear the table.

15 And he made the staves *of* shĭttĭm wood, and overlaid them with gold, to bear the table.

16 And he made the vessels which *were* upon the table, his dishes, and his spoons, and his bowls, and his covers to cover withal, *of* pure gold.

17 ¶And he made the candlestick *of* pure gold: *of* beaten work made he the candlestick; his shaft, and his branch, his bowls, his knops, and his flowers, were of the same:

18 And six branches going out of the sides thereof; three branches of the candlestick out of the one side thereof, and three branches of the candlestick out of the other side thereof:

19 Three bowls made after the fashion of almonds in one branch, a knop and a flower; and three bowls made like almonds in another branch, a knop and a flower: so throughout the six branches going out of the candlestick.

20 And in the candlestick *were* four bowls made like almonds, his knops, and his flowers:

21 And a knop under two branches of the same, and a knop under two branches of the same, and a knop under

two branches of the same, according to the six branches going out of it.

22 Their knops and their branches were of the same: all of it *was* one beaten work *of* pure gold.

23 And he made his seven lamps, and his snuffers, and his snuffdishes, *of* pure gold.

24 *Of* a talent of pure gold made he it, and all the vessels thereof.

25 ¶And he made the incense altar *of* shĭttĭm wood: the length of it *was* a cubit, and the breadth of it a cubit; *it was* foursquare; and two cubits *was* the height of it; the horns thereof were of the same.

26 And he overlaid it with pure gold, *both* the top of it, and the sides thereof round about, and the horns of it: also he made unto it a crown of gold round about.

27 And he made two rings of gold for it under the crown thereof, by the two corners of it, upon the two sides thereof, to be places for the staves to bear it withal.

28 And he made the staves *of* shĭttĭm wood, and overlaid them with gold.

29 ¶And he made the holy anointing oil, and the pure incense of sweet spices, according to the work of the apothecary.

CHAPTER 38

AND he made the altar of burnt offering *of* shĭttĭm wood: five cubits *was* the length thereof, and five cubits the breadth thereof; *it was* foursquare; and three cubits the height thereof.

2 And he made the horns thereof on the four corners of it; the horns thereof were of the same: and he overlaid it with brass.

3 And he made all the vessels of the altar, the pots, and the shovels, and the basons, *and* the fleshhooks, and the firepans: all the vessels thereof made he *of* brass.

4 And he made for the altar a brasen grate of network under the compass thereof beneath unto the midst of it.

5 And he cast four rings for the four ends of the grate of brass, *to be* places for the staves.

6 And he made the staves *of* shĭttĭm wood, and overlaid them with brass.

7 And he put the staves into the rings on the sides of the altar, to bear it withal; he made the altar hollow with boards.

8 ¶And he made the laver *of* brass, and the foot of it *of* brass, of the looking-glasses of *the women* assembling, which assembled *at* the door of the tabernacle of the congregation.

9 ¶And he made the court: on the south side southward the hangings of the court *were of* fine twined linen, an hundred cubits:

10 Their pillars *were* twenty, and their brasen sockets twenty; the hooks of the pillars and their fillets *were of* silver.

11 And for the north side *the hangings were* an hundred cubits, their pillars *were* twenty, and their sockets of brass twenty; the hooks of the pillars and their fillets *of* silver.

38:1-8. Each verse in this section begins with **And he,** referring to Bezaleel. He is here carrying out the commands of God through Moses to construct the **altar of burnt offering** (vss. 1-7) and **the laver of brass.** For their size, purpose, and significance, see the comments on Exodus 27:1-8 and 30:18-21, respectively.

9-20. Bezaleel also constructed **the court** surrounding the tabernacle according to these detailed instructions. Please compare this text with that of Exodus 27:9-19 and note the explanations given upon that section.

12 And for the west side *were* hangings of fifty cubits, their pillars ten, and their sockets ten; the hooks of the pillars and their fillets *of* silver.

13 And for the east side eastward fifty cubits.

14 The hangings of the one side *of the gate were* fifteen cubits; their pillars three, and their sockets three.

15 And for the other side of the court gate, on this hand and that hand, *were* hangings of fifteen cubits; their pillars three, and their sockets three.

16 All the hangings of the court round about *were* of fine twined linen.

17 And the sockets for the pillars *were* of brass; the hooks of the pillars and their fillets *of* silver; and the overlaying of their chapiters *of* silver; and all the pillars of the court *were* filleted with silver.

18 And the hanging for the gate of the court *was* needlework, *of* blue, and purple, and scarlet, and fine twined linen: and twenty cubits *was* the length, and the height in the breadth *was* five cubits, answerable to the hangings of the court.

19 And their pillars *were* four, and their sockets *of* brass four; their hooks *of* silver, and the overlaying of their chapiters and their fillets *of* silver.

20 And all the pins of the tabernacle, and of the court round about, *were of* brass.

21 ¶This is the sum of the tabernacle, *even* of the tabernacle of testimony, as it was counted, according to the commandment of Moses, *for* the service of the Lĕvītes, by the hand of Ĭth′a-mär, son to Aaron the priest.

22 And Be-zăl′e-el the son of Ū′rī, the son of Hur, of the tribe of Jūdah, made all that the Lord commanded Moses.

23 And with him *was* A-hŏ′lĭ-ăb, son of A-hĭs′a-măch, of the tribe of Dan, an engraver, and a cunning workman, and an embroiderer in blue, and in purple, and in scarlet, and fine linen.

24 All the gold that was occupied for the work in all the work of the holy *place*, even the gold of the offering, was twenty and nine talents, and seven hundred and thirty shekels, after the shekel of the sanctuary.

25 And the silver of them that were numbered of the congregation *was* an hundred talents, and a thousand seven hundred and threescore and fifteen shekels, after the shekel of the sanctuary:

26 A bekah for every man, *that is*, half a shekel, after the shekel of the sanctuary, for every one that went to be numbered, from twenty years old and upward, for six hundred thousand and three thousand and five hundred and fifty *men*.

27 And of the hundred talents of silver were cast the sockets of the sanctuary, and the sockets of the vail; an hundred sockets of the hundred talents, a talent for a socket.

28 And of the thousand seven hundred seventy and five *shekels* he made hooks for the pillars, and overlaid their chapiters, and filleted them.

29 And the brass of the offering *was*

21. The sum of the tabernacle . . . was counted . . . by . . . Ithamar, son to Aaron. This must have been quite a task. That Ithamar was a very responsible person can be seen from the work later entrusted to him (Num 4:28, 33; 7:8).

22-23. The tribes of **Judah** and **Dan** were represented in the construction process by the two head artisans, Bezaleel and Aholiab.

24-31. Johnson has figured the amount of gold listed here as "29 talents, 730 shekels, or about 40,940 ounces troy weight" (p. 85). At $500.00 per ounce that would translate into $20,470,000, an enormous sum in that day. The silver, though amounting to only about 141,000 ounces would be valued at about $7,000,000, figuring silver at $50.00 per ounce. But it was one thing to give that much and quite another matter to transform it into carefully crafted pieces of furniture, sockets, hooks, pillars, etc.

seventy talents, and two thousand and four hundred shekels.

30 And therewith he made the sockets to the door of the tabernacle of the congregation, and the brasen altar, and the brasen grate for it, and all the vessels of the altar,

31 And the sockets of the court round about, and the sockets of the court gate, and all the pins of the tabernacle, and all the pins of the court round about.

CHAPTER 39

AND of the blue, and purple, and scarlet, they made cloths of service, to do service in the holy *place*, and made the holy garments for Aaron; as the LORD commanded Moses.

2 And he made the ephod *of* gold, blue, and purple, and scarlet, and fine twined linen.

3 And they did beat the gold into thin plates, and cut *it into* wires, to work *it* in the blue, and in the purple, and in the scarlet, and in the fine linen, *with* cunning work.

4 They made shoulderpieces for it, to couple *it* together: by the two edges was it coupled together.

5 And the curious girdle of his ephod, that *was* upon it, *was* of the same, according to the work thereof; *of* gold, blue, and purple, and scarlet, and fine twined linen; as the LORD commanded Moses.

6 ¶And they wrought onyx stones inclosed in ouches of gold, graven, as signets are graven, with the names of the children of Israel.

7 And he put them on the shoulders of the ephod, *that they should be* stones for a memorial to the children of Israel; as the LORD commanded Moses.

8 ¶And he made the breastplate *of* cunning work, like the work of the ephod; *of* gold, blue, and purple, and scarlet, and fine twined linen.

9 It was foursquare; they made the breastplate double: a span *was* the length thereof, and a span the breadth thereof, *being* doubled.

10 And they set in it four rows of stones: *the first* row *was* a sardius, a topaz, and a carbuncle: this *was* the first row.

11 And the second row, an emerald, a sapphire, and a diamond.

12 And the third row, a ligure, an agate, and an amethyst.

13 And the fourth row, a beryl, an onyx, and a jasper: *they were* inclosed in ouches of gold in their inclosings.

14 And the stones *were* according to the names of the children of Israel, twelve, according to their names, *like* the engravings of a signet, every one with his name, according to the twelve tribes.

15 And they made upon the breastplate chains at the ends, *of* wreathen work *of* pure gold.

16 And they made two ouches *of* gold, and two gold rings; and put the two rings in the two ends of the breastplate.

17 And they put the two wreathen chains of gold in the two rings on the ends of the breastplate.

C. The Sewing of the Priestly Garments. 39:1-31.

39:1-31. Bezaleel and his helpers **made the holy garments for Aaron; as the LORD commanded Moses.** Detailed comments on the materials and symbolic significance of these garments will be found in the treatment of Exodus 28:1-43.

18 And the two ends of the two wreathen chains they fastened in the two ouches, and put them on the shoulderpieces of the ephod, before it.

19 And they made two rings of gold, and put *them* on the two ends of the breastplate, upon the border of it, which *was* on the side of the ephod inward.

20 And they made two *other* golden rings, and put them on the two sides of the ephod underneath, toward the forepart of it, over against the *other* coupling thereof, above the curious girdle of the ephod.

21 And they did bind the breastplate by his rings unto the rings of the ephod with a lace of blue, that it might be above the curious girdle of the ephod, and that the breastplate might not be loosed from the ephod; as the LORD commanded Moses.

22 ¶And he made the robe of the ephod *of* woven work, all *of* blue.

23 And *there was* an hole in the midst of the robe, as the hole of an habergeon, *with* a band round about the hole, that it should not rend.

24 And they made upon the hems of the robe pomegranates *of* blue, and purple, and scarlet, *and* twined *linen*.

25 And they made bells *of* pure gold, and put the bells between the pomegranates upon the hem of the robe, round about between the pomegranates;

26 A bell and a pomegranate, a bell and a pomegranate, round about the hem of the robe to minister *in;* as the LORD commanded Moses.

27 ¶And they made coats *of* fine linen *of* woven work for Aaron, and for his sons,

28 And a mitre *of* fine linen, and goodly bonnets *of* fine linen, and linen breeches *of* fine twined linen,

29 And a girdle *of* fine twined linen, and blue, and purple, and scarlet, *of* needlework; as the LORD commanded Moses.

30 ¶And they made the plate of the holy crown *of* pure gold, and wrote upon it a writing, *like to* the engravings of a signet, HOLINESS TO THE LORD.

31 And they tied unto it a lace of blue, to fasten *it* on high upon the mitre; as the LORD commanded Moses.

32 Thus was all the work of the tabernacle of the tent of the congregation finished: and the children of Israel did according to all that the LORD commanded Moses, so did they.

33 ¶And they brought the tabernacle unto Moses, the tent, and all his furniture, his taches, his boards, his bars, and his pillars, and his sockets,

34 And the covering of rams' skins dyed red, and the covering of badgers' skins, and the vail of the covering,

35 The ark of the testimony, and the staves thereof, and the mercy seat,

36 The table, *and* all the vessels thereof, and the shewbread,

37 The pure candlestick, *with* the lamps thereof, *even with* the lamps to be set in order, and all the vessels thereof, and the oil for light,

D. The Final Erection and Dedication of the Tabernacle. 39:32-40:38.

32. Thus was all the work . . . finished. It must have taken some time to complete this work. After they reached Sinai in June or July, the tabernacle was not erected until the following March or April (Ex 40:12); the Jewish first month is connected with the Passover, (Ex 12:2).

33-41. Just as each item was important in God's service, so no item is omitted from mention in this final summary (one long sentence) of the finished products. Compare Numbers 7:1-89, where each tribe's offering to God is completely enumerated, though all were the same. God is interested in the offerings and the work of each individual, no matter how small it may seem to others.

38 And the golden altar, and the anointing oil, and the sweet incense, and the hanging for the tabernacle door,

39 The brasen altar, and his grate of brass, his staves, and all his vessels, the laver and his foot,

40 The hangings of the court, his pillars, and his sockets, and the hanging for the court gate, his cords, and his pins, and all the vessels of the service of the tabernacle, for the tent of the congregation,

41 The cloths of service to do service in the holy *place*, and the holy garments for Aaron the priest, and his sons' garments, to minister in the priest's office.

42 According to all that the LORD commanded Moses, so the children of Israel made all the work.

43 And Moses did look upon all the work, and, behold, they had done it as the LORD had commanded, even so had they done it: and Moses blessed them.

42-43. Twice it is mentioned in these verses that the work was done **as the LORD had commanded**. . . . We must take care to do things God's way if we would seek His blessing.

CHAPTER 40

AND the LORD spake unto Moses, saying,

2 On the first day of the first month shalt thou set up the tabernacle of the tent of the congregation.

3 And thou shalt put therein the ark of the testimony, and cover the ark with the vail.

4 And thou shalt bring in the table, and set in order the things that are to be set in order upon it; and thou shalt bring in the candlestick, and light the lamps thereof.

5 And thou shalt set the altar of gold for the incense before the ark of the testimony, and put the hanging of the door to the tabernacle.

6 And thou shalt set the altar of the burnt offering before the door of the tabernacle of the tent of the congregation.

7 And thou shalt set the laver between the tent of the congregation and the altar, and shalt put water therein.

8 And thou shalt set up the court round about, and hang up the hanging at the court gate.

40:1-8. Fourteen days prior to the Passover (cf. 40:2 with Num 9:1-5), and almost a year after they left Egypt, **the tabernacle** was erected. **The ark** was specially covered with **the veil,** and the other furniture was set in place inside (vss. 3-5). Outside, **the altar of the burnt offering** was set up, and **the laver** was placed between it and the tabernacle (vss. 6-7). Finally, the courtyard was enclosed (vs. 8).

9 And thou shalt take the anointing oil, and anoint the tabernacle, and all that *is* therein, and shalt hallow it, and all the vessels thereof: and it shall be holy.

10 And thou shalt anoint the altar of the burnt offering, and all his vessels, and sanctify the altar: and it shall be an altar most holy.

11 And thou shalt anoint the laver and his foot, and sanctify it.

9-11. The vessels and altars were then consecrated **most holy** with the anointing oil (cf. Lev 8:10-11).

12 And thou shalt bring Aaron and his sons unto the door of the tabernacle of the congregation, and wash them with water.

13 And thou shalt put upon Aaron the holy garments, and anoint him, and sanctify him; that he may minister unto me in the priest's office.

14 And thou shalt bring his sons, and clothe them with coats:

15 And thou shalt anoint them, as thou didst anoint their father, that they

12-15. Aaron and his sons were then clothed and set apart for holy service. Details regarding their inauguration into service are given in Exodus 29:1-46 and Leviticus 8:11-36.

may minister unto me in the priest's office: for their anointing shall surely be an everlasting priesthood throughout their generations.

16 Thus did Moses: according to all that the LORD commanded him, so did he.

17 ¶And it came to pass in the first month in the second year, on the first day of the month, that the tabernacle was reared up.

18 And Moses reared up the tabernacle, and fastened his sockets, and set up the boards thereof, and put in the bars thereof, and reared up his pillars.

19 And he spread abroad the tent over the tabernacle, and put the covering of the tent above upon it; as the LORD commanded Moses.

20 ¶And he took and put the testimony into the ark, and set the staves on the ark, and put the mercy seat above upon the ark:

21 And he brought the ark into the tabernacle, and set up the vail of the covering, and covered the ark of the testimony; as the LORD commanded Moses.

22 ¶And he put the table in the tent of the congregation, upon the side of the tabernacle northward, without the vail.

23 And he set the bread in order upon it before the LORD; as the LORD had commanded Moses.

24 ¶And he put the candlestick in the tent of the congregation, over against the table, on the side of the tabernacle southward.

25 And he lighted the lamps before the LORD; as the LORD commanded Moses.

26 ¶And he put the golden altar in the tent of the congregation before the vail:

27 And he burnt sweet incense thereon; as the LORD commanded Moses.

28 ¶And he set up the hanging at the door of the tabernacle.

29 And he put the altar of burnt offering by the door of the tabernacle of the tent of the congregation, and offered upon it the burnt offering and the meat offering; as the LORD commanded Moses.

30 ¶And he set the laver between the tent of the congregation and the altar, and put water there, to wash withal.

31 And Moses and Aaron and his sons washed their hands and their feet thereat:

32 When they went into the tent of the congregation, and when they came near unto the altar, they washed; as the LORD commanded Moses.

33 And he reared up the court round about the tabernacle and the altar, and set up the hanging of the court gate. So Moses finished the work.

34 ¶Then a cloud covered the tent of the congregation, and the glory of the LORD filled the tabernacle.

35 And Moses was not able to enter

16-33. Thus did Moses (vs. 16). The work of rearing up the tabernacle is attributed to Moses because he was chief overseer. With 22,000 Levites (Num 3:21-39) to help with the final erection, it was no doubt accomplished in less than a day (cf. Ex 40:1-2, 17). Later, during their travels it was assembled or dismantled on short notice time and again. **So Moses finished the work** (vs. 33). Only then could the people approach God through the sacrificial system (cf. Lev 1-7).

34. As a visible testimony of God's acceptance of their work, God's pillar of **cloud covered the tent of the congregation; and His glory . . . filled the tabernacle.** The pillar of cloud was the visible indication of God's presence among His people. The glory was a bright resplendence of light difficult to look upon (cf. Ex 24:17; Ezk 1:28). Perhaps some of this glory was reflected in Moses' face after being in God's presence earlier (Ex 34:29-35).

35. God was now truly dwelling in the midst of His people,

into the tent of the congregation, because the cloud abode thereon, and the glory of the LORD filled the tabernacle.

36 And when the cloud was taken up from over the tabernacle, the children of Israel went onward in all their journeys:
37 But if the cloud were not taken up, then they journeyed not till the day that it was taken up.
38 For the cloud of the LORD *was* upon the tabernacle by day, and fire was on it by night, in the sight of all the house of Israel, throughout all their journeys.

just as He had promised them (Ex 33:14). That is still His desire today, as our bodies can be transformed into His holy temples by means of the new birth (Jn 14:23; I Cor 6:19-20). In fact, the book of Revelation practically ends on this theme when it says ". . .Behold, the tabernacle of God is with men, and he will dwell with them, and they shall be his people, and God himself shall be with them, and be their God" (Rev 21:3).

36-38. Likewise, **the cloud of the LORD . . . by day, and fire . . . by night** was a constant reminder to Israel of God's presence among them. By it, God led Israel during all their journeys through the wilderness, and apparently into Canaan itself.

BIBLIOGRAPHY

*Bush, George. *Notes, Critical and Practical, on the Book of Exodus*. Chicago: Henry A. Sumner and Company, 1881.

Cassuto, Umberto. *A Commentary on the Book of Exodus*. Trans. by Israel Abrahams. Jerusalem: Magnes Press, 1967.

Childs, Brevard S. *The Book of Exodus: A Critical, Theological Commentary*. Philadelphia: Westminster Press, 1974.

Clements, Ronald E. Exodus. In *The Cambridge Bible Commentary*. Ed. by P. R. Ackroyd, *et al*. Cambridge: University Press, 1972.

Cole, R. Alan. Exodus: An Introduction and Commentary. In *The Tyndale Old Testament Commentaries*. Ed. by D. J. Wiseman. Downers Grove, Illinois: InterVarsity Press, 1973.

Connell, J. Clement. Exodus: *The New Bible Commentary*. 2nd ed. Ed. by F. Davidson, *et al*. Grand Rapids: Eerdmans, 1954.

Cook, Frederick C. and Samuel Clark. Exodus. In *The Bible Commentary*, Vol. I. Ed. by F. C. Cook. New York: Charles Scribner's Sons, n.d.

Cox, Leo G. The Book of Exodus. In *Beacon Bible Commentary*, Vol. I. Ed. by A. F. Harper, *et al*. Kansas City: Beacon Hill Press, 1969.

*Davis, John J. *Moses and the Gods of Egypt: Studies in Exodus*. Grand Rapids: Baker, 1971.

Driver, S. R. *The Book of Exodus*. Cambridge: University Press, 1911.

*Haines, Lee. The Book of Exodus. In *The Wesleyan Bible Commentary*, Vol. I. Ed. by Charles W. Carter. Grand Rapids: Eerdmans, 1967.

Hyatt, J. Philip. Commentary on Exodus. In *New Century Bible*. Ed. by Ronald E. Clements and Matthew Black. London: Oliphants, 1971.

Jamieson, Robert. *A Commentary, Critical, Experimental and Practical on the Old Testament*, Vol. I. Grand Rapids: Eerdmans; reprinted, 1967.

Johnson, Philip C. Exodus. In *The Wycliffe Bible Commentary*. Ed. by Charles F. Pfeiffer and Everett F. Harrison. Chicago: Moody Press, 1962.

Keil, C. F. and Franz Delitzsch. *Biblical Commentary on the Old Testament*, Vols. II and III. Trans. by James Martin. Grand Rapids: Eerdmans; reprinted, n.d.

*Lange, John Peter. Exodus. In *Commentary on the Holy Scriptures*, Vol. II. Ed. by J. P. Lange. Trans. Charles S. Mead. Grand Rapids: Zondervan; reprinted, 1950.

MacRae, Allan A. Book of Exodus. In *The Zondervan Pictorial Encyclopedia of the Bible*, Vol. II. Ed. by Merrill C. Tenney. Grand Rapids: Zondervan, 1975.

*Murphy, James Gracey. *A Critical and Exegetical Commentary on the Book of Exodus*. Andover: Warren F. Draper, 1868.

Noth, Martin. Exodus: A Commentary. In *The Old Testament Library*. Ed. by G. Ernest Wright, *et al*. Trans. by J. S. Bowden. Philadelphia: Westminster Press, 1962.

Pink, Arthur W. *Gleanings in Exodus*. Chicago: Moody Press, n.d.

*Rawlinson, George. The Book of Exodus. In *The Pulpit Commentary*, Vol. I. Ed. by H. D. M. Spence and Joseph S. Exell. Grand Rapids: Eerdmans; reprinted, 1961.

Rylaarsdam, J. Coert. The Book of Exodus. In *The Interpreter's Bible*, Vol. I. Ed. by G. A. Buttrick. New York: Abingdon Press, 1952.

LEVITICUS

INTRODUCTION

Title. The Hebrew title of Leviticus comes from the first words of the Hebrew text *Wayyiqra*, "and he called," referring to God's summoning of Moses to give him further revelation for the Israelites after the setting up of the tabernacle at Mount Sinai (Ex 40). The Greek translation of the Hebrew, called the Septuagint (LXX), titled the book *Levitikon*, which means "pertaining to the Levites." The Latin Vulgate adopted a similar phrase, and hence, our English title of Leviticus. The Levites, however, are only mentioned in chapter 25:32-33, and the book deals primarily with God's laws of sacrifice and sanctification carried out by the priests' families within the tribe of Levi who are mentioned nearly two hundred times.

Authorship. The abundant and clear testimony of the Scriptures is that Moses himself wrote the entire Pentateuch and, hence, Leviticus, its third book. References within the Pentateuch to Moses' writing God's words in a book are found in Exodus 17:14; 34:27; Numbers 33:1-2; and Deuteronomy 31:9 and 11. The rest of the Old Testament writers also testified to Mosaic authorship, beginning with Joshua 8:31-32; I Kings 2:3; II Kings 14:6; and 21:8. Other clear texts are Ezra 6:18; Nehemiah 13:1; Daniel 9:11-13, and Malachi 4:4. In the New Testament the consistent assertion is that Moses wrote the books of the Pentateuch. Jesus said of Moses that ". . . he wrote of me" (Jn 5:46). In John 7:19 Jesus asked the Jews, "Did not Moses give you the law . . .?" Not only our Lord, but the apostles as well inform us that Moses was the actual author of the books of the Law. Peter declares this fact in Acts 3:22, and Paul in Romans 10:5 cites Leviticus 18:5 with the introduction, "For Moses describeth . . . the law. . . ."

Nevertheless, some men will not be persuaded by the clear teaching of the Scriptures and instead prefer new concepts of how the Pentateuch originated. Beginning in 1792 with the French physician Jean Astruc, theories of multiple sources, or documents, have been advanced to explain the writing of the Pentateuch. Letters such as J for Jehovah, E for Elohim, D for Deuteronomy, P for Priestly, meaning the Levites, H for Holiness Code (Lev 17-27), K for Kenite source, and L for Lay source have come into the critics' vocabulary. This became fully developed in nineteenth-century Germany under Graf, Kuenen, Wellhausen, and others. They posited that these various documents were written hundreds of years after the life of Moses and were later forged together by redactors to create our first five books of the Bible. These theories have been thoroughly answered by such men as Oswald T. Allis in *The Five Books of Moses* and Gleason L. Archer, Jr. in *A Survey of Old Testament Introduction*. A more recent aspect of this criticism, called form criticism, would allow that the form of these documents was kept fairly stable through oral transmission until written down long after Moses' time.

These theories are arbitrary and completely subjective. They not only fail to account for the relevant biblical data available, but they go against the parallels of early written records in other Semitic societies related to the Hebrews. For other refutations of these theories as they relate to Leviticus see Roland K. Harrison, *Introduction to the Old Testament*, pp. 591-598, and Bruce K. Waltke, "Leviticus" in vol. 3 of *The Zondervan Pictorial Encyclopedia of the Bible*, pp. 914-916.

Date and Place of Writing. The date of the events of Leviticus can be ascertained by comparing Exodus 40:17 with Numbers 1:1. These instructions must have been given to Moses just after the erection of the tabernacle according to Leviticus 1:1. The tabernacle was set up on the first day of the first month of the second year after leaving Egypt (Ex 40:17), and Aaron and his sons were immediately consecrated during a seven-day ceremony (Lev 8:33), after which time they could offer the first sacrifices (Lev 9:1-2). After that month passed, Moses was commanded to number the people (Num 1:1-2), and just twenty days later Israel began the journey away from Mount Sinai (Num 10:11-13).

If it can be determined when the Exodus occurred, then the date of Leviticus can also be accurately fixed. I Kings 6:1 places the Exodus four hundred eighty years prior to the building of Solomon's temple, which has been generally established at approximately 967-965 B.C. This would establish the date of the Exodus at about 1447-1445 B.C., with the regulations and events of Leviticus occurring just one year later. Documentary and form critics claim that Leviticus came into its final written form sometime after Israel's captivity in the sixth century B.C.

That Mount Sinai is the place where Leviticus transpires is easily seen from Leviticus 7:38; 25:1; 26:46; 27:34. Again, Numbers describes the Israelites' location as being "the wilderness of Sinai." That they are in the wilderness and not yet in the land of Canaan can be discerned from Leviticus 11:5, where mention is made of the "coney," which is native to Sinai and Arabia; from Leviticus 11:16, where the "owl" (ostrich) is named, which is not common in Palestine, but lives only in the desert; and from Leviticus 16:10, where the scapegoat is said to be driven out into the desert (Heb *Midebarah*), a term which according to Gesenius, *Hebrew Lexicon*, p. 449, always refers to the desert of Arabia when it has the definite article, as here.

Purpose. The purpose of Leviticus is to provide legislation to guide a redeemed people in their relationship with a holy God. Sin must be atoned for through the offering of proper sacrifices (chs. 8-

10). Defiling diets, deliveries, and diseases are carefully regulated (chs. 11-15). At the center is the Day of Atonement (ch. 16), when an annual sacrifice was made for the cumulative sin of the people. In addition, the people of God are to be circumspect in their personal, moral, and social living, in contrast to the then currrent practices of the heathen roundabout them (chs. 17-22). The various feasts of Jehovah are also to be convened and practiced according to God's laws. Blessings or curses will accompany either the keeping or the neglect of God's commandments (ch. 26). The final chapter (27) forms an appendix concerning vows to the Lord.

Theme. The primary theme of Leviticus is "holiness." This word occurs eighty-seven times in the book, including a key statement in 11:44. God's demand for holiness in His people is based on His own holy nature, and the same insistence is renewed for us again in the New Testament (Mt 5:48; I Pet 1:15). A corresponding theme is that of "atonement." This word appears forty-five times, and the doctrine is conveniently summarized in 17:11. Holiness must be maintained before God, and holiness can only be attained through a proper atonement. Rightly seen, these concepts, sacrifices, and regulations picture in many ways the person and work of our Saviour, the Lord Jesus Christ.

Text. The Masoretic Hebrew text upon which most English versions are based has been carefully preserved for centuries. One of the oldest of the Dead Sea Scrolls from the first cave contains portions of Leviticus 19-22 in an ancient Hebrew script. It differs little from copies made over a thousand years later by the Jewish Masoretic scholars. This comparison demonstrates a painstakingly accurate transmission of the text.

OUTLINE

COMMENTARY

I. THE APPROACH TO GOD MADE POSSIBLE. 1:1-10:20.

A. The Approach Through Sacrificial Offerings. 1:1-7:38.

The book of Leviticus presents an obvious change, theologically, from that encountered in the book of Exodus. Exodus portrays God's approach to a helpless Israel in Egyptian bondage, while Leviticus presents Israel's approach to God—through His ordered sacrifices, the priesthood, etc. The material found in Leviticus is divinely intended to picture in many ways aspects of the believer's salvation today. Hebrews 9:23 refers to certain

Levitical practices as ". . . patterns of things in the heavens . . . ," and Hebrews 10:1 speaks of the Mosiac ritual as ". . . having a shadow of good things to come. . . ." It must, therefore, be our intention in Leviticus to see not only what God commanded the Israelites to observe, but also how their sacrifices and other practices speak of the person and work of our Saviour, the Lord Jesus Christ.

1. The sweet savor offerings. 1:1-3:17.

a. The whole burnt offering. 1:1-17.

AND the Lord called unto Moses, and spake unto him out of the tabernacle of the congregation, saying,

1.1. And the Lord called unto Moses, and spake unto him out of the tabernacle of the congregation. The Holy of Holies within the tabernacle or tent of meeting was God's place of abode within the midst of His people. From this sacred tent God is said to have spoken audibly with Moses. This terminology occurs repeatedly throughout Leviticus (4:1; 5:14; 6:1, 8, 19, 24; 7:22, 28, etc.) and may indicate God's coming in a human form to communicate with Moses as He explains in Numbers 12:8, where ". . . the similitude of the Lord . . ." is an expression designating what Moses actually saw. For more on the nature of the tabernacle and its furniture see the commentary on Exodus 25:1-28:43. The tabernacle was a tent where God met with His appointed theocratic leaders. It was not a place where Israel gathered for group worship.

2 Speak unto the children of Israel, and say unto them, If any man of you bring an offering unto the Lord, ye shall bring your offering of the cattle, *even* of the herd, and of the flock.

2. The sweet savor offerings were voluntary and were offered to God out of appreciation for what He had done for the individual. The animals had to be selected from **the herd,** that is, from cattle and oxen, or from **the flock,** that is, from sheep and goats. Wild animals could not be used since they already belonged to God (Ps 50:10). What is offered must be the property of the offerer and, hence, cost him something (II Sam 24:24).

3 If his offering *be* a burnt sacrifice of the herd, let him offer a male without blemish: he shall offer it of his own voluntary will at the door of the tabernacle of the congregation before the Lord.
4 And he shall put his hand upon the head of the burnt offering; and it shall be accepted for him to make atonement for him.
5 And he shall kill the bullock before the Lord: and the priests, Aaron's sons, shall bring the blood, and sprinkle the blood round about upon the altar that *is* by the door of the tabernacle of the congregation.

3-5. A burnt sacrifice. This is often called the whole burnt offering, because all of the animal, except its hide, was burned on the altar unto the Lord (Lev 6:22; Deut 33:10; Ps 51:19). Several items should be specifically noted. (1) **A male** was required, speaking of the largest and strongest animal. (2) **Without blemish** indicates the perfection necessary. (3) **Of his own voluntary will** should more accurately be translated "that he may be accepted," as in the ASV and all modern versions. It expresses the purpose of the sacrifice. (4) **Put his hand upon the head** of the offering suggests identifying oneself with the offering. The offering is going to represent the offerer. (5) **Sprinkle the blood.** Care was taken of the blood, and it was applied to the altar, because **it is the blood that maketh an atonement for the soul** (17:11). The life is in the blood.

6 And he shall flay the burnt offering, and cut it into his pieces.
7 And the sons of Aaron the priest shall put fire upon the altar, and lay the wood in order upon the fire:
8 And the priests, Aaron's sons, shall lay the parts, the head, and the fat, in order upon the wood that *is* on the fire which *is* upon the altar:
9 But his inwards and his legs shall he wash in water: and the priest shall burn all on the altar, *to be* a burnt sacrifice, an offering made by fire, of a sweet savour unto the Lord.

6-9. After the young bull was killed and its blood applied, the animal was entirely burned in accordance with God's instructions. This **sweet savor unto the Lord** (vs. 9) pictures Christ in all of His perfections offering Himself entirely to God in our place. Christ's death was voluntary (Jn 10:17-18) and was powerful enough to save sinners completely (Heb 7:25).

10 ¶And if his offering *be* of the flocks, *namely,* of the sheep, or of the goats, for a burnt sacrifice; he shall bring it a male without blemish.
11And he shall kill it on the side of the altar northward before the Lord: and the priests, Aaron's sons, shall sprinkle his blood round about upon the altar.
12 And he shall cut it into his pieces,

10. Rams and he goats could also be used for the whole burnt offering, but the same perfections were required. These animals would not be as expensive as a bullock (young bull).

11-13. The same procedures of killing the animal, sprinkling or applying its blood to the altar, and burning the sacrifice were repeated when either sheep or goats were used; and they picture the same things as before. The reason for cutting up the sacrifice into parts was that it might be consumed more easily by the fire.

with his head and his fat: and the priest shall lay them in order on the wood that *is* on the fire which *is* upon the altar:

13 But he shall wash the inwards and the legs with water: and the priest shall bring *it* all, and burn *it* upon the altar: it *is* a burnt sacrifice, an offering made by fire, of a sweet savour unto the Lord.

14 ¶And if the burnt sacrifice for his offering to the Lord *be* of fowls, then he shall bring his offering of turtledoves, or of young pigeons.

15 And the priest shall bring it unto the altar, and wring off his head, and burn *it* on the altar; and the blood thereof shall be wrung out at the side of the altar:

16 And he shall pluck away his crop with his feathers, and cast it beside the altar on the east part, by the place of the ashes:

17 And he shall cleave it with the wings thereof, *but* shall not divide *it* asunder: and the priest shall burn it upon the altar, upon the wood that *is* upon the fire: it *is* a burnt sacrifice, an offering made by fire, of a sweet savour unto the Lord.

CHAPTER 2

AND when any will offer a meat offering unto the Lord, his offering shall be *of* fine flour; and he shall pour oil upon it, and put frankincense thereon:

2 And he shall bring it to Aaron's sons the priests: and he shall take thereout his handful of the flour thereof, and of the oil thereof, with all the frankincense thereof; and the priest shall burn the memorial of it upon the altar, *to be* an offering made by fire, of a sweet savour unto the Lord:

3 And the remnant of the meat offering *shall be* Aaron's and his sons': *it is* a thing most holy of the offerings of the Lord made by fire.

4 ¶And if thou bring an oblation of a meat offering baken in the oven, *it shall be* unleavened cakes of fine flour mingled with oil, or unleavened wafers anointed with oil.

5 ¶And if thy oblation *be* a meat offering *baken* in a pan, it shall be *of* fine flour unleavened, mingled with oil.

6 Thou shalt part it in pieces, and pour oil thereon: it *is* a meat offering.

7 ¶And if thy oblation *be* a meat offering *baken* in the fryingpan, it shall be made *of* fine flour with oil.

8 And thou shalt bring the meat offering that is made of these things unto the Lord: and when it is presented unto

Later examples of the use of this burnt offering are found in I Samuel 7:9; 13:9; and Psalm 20:3.

14-17. Offering of turtledoves, or of young pigeons. Naturally, some Israelites would be poorer than others and perhaps unable to afford the larger burnt offerings mentioned in verses 3-13. In such cases this offering was accepted on an equal par with the larger, more expensive offerings. God is no respecter of persons (Rom 2:11).

b. The meal offering. 2:1-16.

2:1. A meat offering . . . of fine flour. What is meant by the "meat-offering" in the AV is what is more clearly translated by the words "meal" in ASV, "cereal" in Douay and RSV, or "grain" in NASB. Like the burnt offering, it was brought voluntarily. It was a gift of valuable food—that which is vital to life. **Oil** and **frankincense** were added. The meal offering pictured the finely ground humanity of our Lord in all His perfections. It was offered with a blood sacrifice, even though it is presented separately here (see Num 15:1-16), even as Christ's perfect life is not to be isolated from His sacrificial death. The oil most naturally symbolizes the Holy Spirit's ministry in the life of Christ (Zech 4:3-6), and the frankincense typifies our Lord's prayer life (Rev 8:3-4).

2-3. Part of the offering was burned **upon the altar,** and the **remnant** was eaten by Aaron and his sons. Aaron gained his sustenance from this, which typifies Christ.

4. Oblation. The word here translated "oblation" (Heb *qarban*) is found seventy-eight times in Leviticus and Numbers and occurs only twice elsewhere in the Old Testament and once as "gift" in Mark 7:11. It is the regular word used for offering (vss. 1, 4, 5, 7, 12, 13, etc.) but is sometimes translated "oblation" simply for variety.

5-7. The grain offering could be done in any of three ways: (1) in an **oven** (vs. 4); (2) in a **pan** (vs. 5), meaning a flat object like a cookie sheet; or (3) in a **frying pan** (vs. 7), which speaks of a large cooking pot with a lid on it. This way different textures of the offering could be obtained either for variety or to suit the utensils of the offerer.

8-9. The meal offering would normally be at least **the tenth part of an ephah of fine flour** (6:20), which was between two and three quarts. Only a **handful** (vs. 2) was offered as a memorial of a sweet savor to the Lord.

the priest, he shall bring it unto the altar.

9 And the priest shall take from the meat offering a memorial thereof, and shall burn *it* upon the altar: *it is* an offering made by fire, of a sweet savour unto the LORD.

10 And that which is left of the meat offering *shall be* Aaron's and his sons': *it is* a thing most holy of the offerings of the LORD made by fire.

11 No meat offering, which ye shall bring unto the LORD, shall be made with leaven: for ye shall burn no leaven, nor any honey, in any offering of the LORD made by fire.

12 ¶As for the oblation of the firstfruits, ye shall offer them unto the LORD: but they shall not be burnt on the altar for a sweet savour.

13 And every oblation of thy meat offering shalt thou season with salt; neither shalt thou suffer the salt of the covenant of thy God to be lacking from thy meat offering: with all thine offerings thou shalt offer salt.

14 And if thou offer a meat offering of thy firstfruits unto the LORD, thou shalt offer for the meat offering of thy firstfruits green ears of corn dried by the fire, *even* corn beaten out of full ears.

15 And thou shalt put oil upon it, and lay frankincense thereon: it *is* a meat offering.

16 And the priest shall burn the memorial of it, *part* of the beaten corn thereof, and *part* of the oil thereof, with all the frankincense thereof: *it is* an offering made by fire unto the LORD.

CHAPTER 3

AND if his oblation *be* a sacrifice of peace offering, if he offer *it* of the herd; whether *it be* a male or female, he shall offer it without blemish before the LORD.

2 And he shall lay his hand upon the head of his offering, and kill it *at* the door of the tabernacle of the congregation: and Aaron's sons the priests shall sprinkle the blood upon the altar round about.

3 And he shall offer of the sacrifice of the peace offering an offering made by fire unto the LORD; the fat that covereth the inwards, and all the fat that *is* upon the inwards,

4 And the two kidneys, and the fat that *is* on them, which *is* by the flanks, and the caul above the liver, with the kidneys, it shall he take away.

5 And Aaron's sons shall burn it on the altar upon the burnt sacrifice, which *is* upon the wood that *is* on the fire: *it is* an offering made by fire, of a sweet savour unto the LORD.

6 ¶And if his offering for a sacrifice of peace offering unto the LORD be of the

10. The abundant amount left over became the property of Aaron and the other male members of his family. As it was **most holy,** it had to be eaten in the holy place of the tent of meeting.

11. No leaven, nor any honey were allowed to be mixed with the cereal offering. Leaven no doubt would picture sin, and Christ is without sin. However, the loaves used to celebrate Pentecost in Leviticus 23:17 had to contain leaven, because they pictured the church, which would contain sin (see Mt 13:33 which also speaks of corruption). Honey speaks of natural sweetness, but it can spoil. There was no corruption of any kind in Christ.

12. The first fruits were just barely ripe and would not burn well. Instead, they were to be waved before the Lord (23:10-12), or else **dried by the fire** (vs. 14) prior to offering.

13-16. Season with salt. Salt stands for that which preserves against corruption. Hence, it is a good picture of permanence. God uses this to typify the eternal nature of His covenant with Israel (vs. 13; see also Num 18:19; and II Chron 13:5).

c. The peace offering. 3:1-17.

3:1. A sacrifice of peace offering. The purpose of the peace offering was not to make atonement for sin, but rather to express appreciation and acknowledge with thanksgiving God's matchless and gracious care. It was at once an act of worship and of communion. It was also a voluntary offering; and in this particular case either a male or female animal could be offered, either of the herd (cattle) or of the flock (sheep and goats).

2. Even though no atonement for sin was made through this sacrifice (cf. Lev 1:14; 4:20; 5:16 where atonement was made), the worshiper still must identify himself with the sacrifice by the laying on of his hands. As in the case of the burnt offering, the animal was killed; and its blood was applied to the altar.

3-5. The animal's fat and kidneys were removed and burned on the altar as the Lord's portion. **The fat,** as with cooking today, would burn rapidly and rise quickly to God. Biologically, fat speaks of inward stored energy. This may picture Christ's zeal and devotion, as well as that inward energy He used in accomplishing the Father's will.

6-11. The same procedure was followed for the offering of **a lamb.** It could be male or female, but without blemish, to speak

197

flock; male or female, he shall offer it without blemish.

7 If he offer a lamb for his offering, then shall he offer it before the LORD.

8 And he shall lay his hand upon the head of his offering, and kill it before the tabernacle of the congregation: and Aaron's sons shall sprinkle the blood thereof round about upon the altar.

9 And he shall offer of the sacrifice of the peace offering an offering made by fire unto the LORD; the fat thereof, and the whole rump, it shall he take off hard by the backbone; and the fat that covereth the inwards, and all the fat that is upon the inwards,

10 And the two kidneys, and the fat that is upon them, which is by the flanks, and the caul above the liver, with the kidneys, it shall he take away.

11 And the priest shall burn it upon the altar: it is the food of the offering made by fire unto the LORD.

12 ¶And if his offering be a goat, then he shall offer it before the LORD.

13 And he shall lay his hand upon the head of it, and kill it before the tabernacle of the congregation: and the sons of Aaron shall sprinkle the blood thereof upon the altar round about.

14 And he shall offer thereof his offering, even an offering made by fire unto the LORD; the fat that covereth the inwards, and all the fat that is upon the inwards,

15 And the two kidneys, and the fat that is upon them, which is by the flanks, and the caul above the liver, with the kidneys, it shall he take away.

16 And the priest shall burn them upon the altar: it is the food of the offering made by fire for a sweet savour: all the fat is the LORD's.

17 It shall be a perpetual statute for your generations throughout all your dwellings, that ye eat neither fat nor blood.

CHAPTER 4

AND the LORD spake unto Moses, saying,

2 Speak unto the children of Israel, saying, If a soul shall sin through ignorance against any of the commandments of the LORD concerning things which ought not to be done, and shall do against any of them:

3 If the priest that is anointed do sin according to the sin of the people; then let him bring for his sin, which he hath sinned, a young bullock without blemish unto the LORD for a sin offering.

4 And he shall bring the bullock unto the door of the tabernacle of the congregation before the LORD; and shall

of Christ's perfection. Again, the blood was thrown against the altar, and the fat and the kidneys were burned on the altar as the Lord's portion.

12-15. A goat could also be offered by following the same steps as with cattle and sheep. Since the peace offering was voluntary, either animal could be used.

16-17. All the fat is the LORD's. There remained a portion for the offerer to eat, also. He participated in this sacrifice, just as the priests did with the meal offering, and the sin and trespass offerings. Leviticus 7:15-18 gives some of the regulations governing this feast. More than anything else it pictures the fellowship we enjoy with the Lord on the basis of His sacrifice for us. The offering was brought because of the thankfulness of the grateful worshiper.

2. The non-sweet savor offerings. 4:1-6:7.

While the sweet savor offerings speak of the honor of God, the non-sweet sacrifices emphasize the judgment of God.

a. The sin offering. 4:1-35.

4:1-2. If a soul shall sin through ignorance. The sin offering was not a voluntary sacrifice, as were the three sweet savor oblations. This offering was commanded of all, priests (vss. 3-12), congregation as a whole (vss. 13-21), rulers (vss. 22-26), and common individuals (vss. 27-35). It made atonement for sins done in ignorance, unwittingly, unintentionally, or inadvertently. Compare this with Numbers 15:30-31 and Psalm 51, where the picture is quite different for intentional sins committed knowingly. The sin offering was for the guilt and defilement of the sin nature. It had to do with our natural depravity as the sons of Adam, hence the aspect of sins done in ignorance.

3-6. The priest that is anointed. The priest, though one of the people, stood before God as their spiritual leader. His sin is seen as defiling the tabernacle of God, and therefore, as defiling all the people. His offering must be **a young bullock**. Though his sin may be the same as that of other men, he is more responsible for it by virtue of his position. He must offer the most valuable animal—a bull.

The perfection of the animal (vs. 3), laying on of hands, and the killing of the animal were according to the pattern of the

lay his hand upon the bullock's head, and kill the bullock before the LORD.

5 And the priest that is anointed shall take of the bullock's blood, and bring it to the tabernacle of the congregation:

6 And the priest shall dip his finger in the blood, and sprinkle of the blood seven times before the LORD, before the vail of the sanctuary.

7 And the priest shall put *some* of the blood upon the horns of the altar of sweet incense before the LORD, which *is* in the tabernacle of the congregation; and shall pour all the blood of the bullock at the bottom of the altar of the burnt offering, which *is* at the door of the tabernacle of the congregation.

8 And he shall take off from it all the fat of the bullock for the sin offering; the fat that covereth the inwards, and all the fat that *is* upon the inwards,

9 And the two kidneys, and the fat that *is* upon them, which *is* by the flanks, and the caul above the liver, with the kidneys, it shall he take away,

10 As it was taken off from the bullock of the sacrifice of peace offerings: and the priest shall burn them upon the altar of the burnt offering.

11 And the skin of the bullock, and all his flesh, with his head, and with his legs, and his inwards, and his dung,

12 Even the whole bullock shall he carry forth without the camp unto a clean place, where the ashes are poured out, and burn him on the wood with fire: where the ashes are poured out shall he be burnt.

13 ¶And if the whole congregation of Israel sin through ignorance, and the thing be hid from the eyes of the assembly, and they have done *somewhat against* any of the commandments of the LORD *concerning things* which should not be done, and are guilty;

14 When the sin, which they have sinned against it, is known, then the congregation shall offer a young bullock for the sin, and bring him before the tabernacle of the congregation.

15 And the elders of the congregation shall lay their hands upon the head of the bullock before the LORD: and the bullock shall be killed before the LORD.

16 And the priest that is anointed shall bring of the bullock's blood to the tabernacle of the congregation:

17 And the priest shall dip his finger *in some* of the blood, and sprinkle *it* seven times before the LORD, *even* before the vail.

18 And he shall put *some* of the blood upon the horns of the altar which *is* before the LORD, that *is* in the tabernacle of the congregation, and shall pour out all the blood at the bottom of the altar of the burnt offering, which *is* at the door of the tabernacle of the congregation.

19 And he shall take all his fat from him, and burn *it* upon the altar.

20 And he shall do with the bullock as he did with the bullock for a sin offering, so shall he do with this: and the priest shall make an atonement for them, and it shall be forgiven them.

21 And he shall carry forth the bullock without the camp, and burn him as

other sacrifices. But in this case the blood is sprinkled **seven times before the LORD, before the veil of the sanctuary** (vs. 6). In the other cases it was applied at the altar of burnt offerings out in the courtyard. The priest is seen as also defiling the tabernacle where he has been serving, and it must be cleansed. **Seven times** was a literal seven times, but it speaks symbolically of a complete sprinkling.

7. Blood upon the horns of the altar of sweet incense. This piece of gold tabernacle furniture stood right in front of the entrance to the Holy of Holies. The incense altar speaks of prayer, and it is through asking forgiveness of God in prayer that fellowship is restored (I Jn 1:9). Prayer is ineffectual when sin is in the way. The rest of the blood was taken out to the bronze altar where the animals were actually burned.

8-10. All the fat and the kidneys, including a lobe of the liver, were then burned on the altar, just as with the peace offering.

11-12. The rest of the edible portions of the young bull were then boiled and eaten by the males of the priestly family in the holy part of the tent of meeting (Lev 6:25-29). The remaining skin, head, legs, entrails, etc. were carried outside the camp and deposited along with the ashes. The typology of this practice is noted in Hebrews 13:10-14. Jesus suffered outside the gate. The whole of sin is put away as with the scapegoat on the Day of Atonement.

13. If the whole congregation of Israel sin through ignorance. When the entire Israelite nation sinned in this fashion, their sin likewise defiled the tent of meeting. Thus, the same offering is required; and the identical procedure is followed, as with the sin of an anointed priest.

14-21. As with the offering for the priest, a bullock is presented and killed. Then its blood was applied and offered up in the same way as that given in verses 4-12.

he burned the first bullock: it *is* a sin offering for the congregation.

22 ¶When a ruler hath sinned, and done *somewhat* through ignorance *against* any of the commandments of the Lord his God *concerning things* which should not be done, and is guilty;

23 Or if his sin, wherein he hath sinned, come to his knowledge; he shall bring his offering, a kid of the goats, a male without blemish:

24 And he shall lay his hand upon the head of the goat, and kill it in the place where they kill the burnt offering before the Lord: it *is* a sin offering.

25 And the priest shall take of the blood of the sin offering with his finger, and put *it* upon the horns of the altar of burnt offering, and shall pour out his blood at the bottom of the altar of burnt offering.

26 And he shall burn all his fat upon the altar, as the fat of the sacrifice of peace offerings: and the priest shall make an atonement for him as concerning his sin, and it shall be forgiven him.

27 ¶And if any one of the common people sin through ignorance, while he doeth *somewhat against* any of the commandments of the Lord *concerning things* which ought not to be done, and be guilty;

28 Or if his sin, which he hath sinned, come to his knowledge: then he shall bring his offering, a kid of the goats, a female without blemish, for his sin which he hath sinned.

29 And he shall lay his hand upon the head of the sin offering, and slay the sin offering in the place of the burnt offering.

30 And the priest shall take of the blood thereof with his finger, and put *it* upon the horns of the altar of burnt offering, and shall pour out all the blood thereof at the bottom of the altar.

31 And he shall take away all the fat thereof, as the fat is taken away from off the sacrifice of peace offerings; and the priest shall burn *it* upon the altar for a sweet savour unto the Lord; and the priest shall make an atonement for him, and it shall be forgiven him.

32 And if he bring a lamb for a sin offering, he shall bring it a female without blemish.

33 And he shall lay his hand upon the head of the sin offering, and slay it for a sin offering in the place where they kill the burnt offering.

34 And the priest shall take of the blood of the sin offering with his finger, and put *it* upon the horns of the altar of burnt offering, and shall pour out all the blood thereof at the bottom of the altar:

35 And he shall take away all the fat thereof, as the fat of the lamb is taken away from the sacrifice of the peace offerings; and the priest shall burn them upon the altar, according to the offerings made by fire unto the Lord: and

22. When a ruler hath sinned. A ruler is one placed in civil authority. He is actually ordained of God for such a responsible position and must lead a circumspect life before the people.

23. If his sin . . . come to his knowledge. A priest would almost immediately be aware of his sin, but a civil ruler might not. When he became aware of it, he was required to bring **a kid of the goats, a male.** This was not as large an offering as in the case of a priest, or for cases involving the whole congregation; but it was a male, whereas the common people offered a female (vss. 27-28).

24-25. The ritual involved in his sacrificial offering contained laying on of hands as an act of identification and representation, killing the animal and applying its blood to the **horns of the altar.** These horns were made of brass, as was the entire altar of burnt offerings. Horns signify power. The power to make atonement was in the application of the blood. As with the Passover in Egypt, it was not the killing of the lamb that spared the household, but the application of the blood to the doorposts.

26. After the fat was burned, the priest received his portion. The rest of the animal was disposed according to the instructions in verses 11-12.

27. And if any one of the common people sin through ignorance. The final category enumerated the remainder of the Israelites—the common people.

28-31. A female goat could be offered in this case. It was less expensive than a male, and perhaps it speaks more of passive sin than of active participation. The blood was applied as prescribed in the ruler's sin offering (vss. 25-26).

32-34. It was also possible to offer a female lamb, as specified here. The manner of its offering follows the established pattern.

35. The purpose of all these transactions was **atonement** (Heb *kapar*), a covering over of the sin. The mediation of a priest was always required.

b. The trespass offering. 5:1-6:7.

The trespass offering (vs. 6) is to atone for specific acts of sin

the priest shall make an atonement for his sin that he hath committed, and it shall be forgiven him.

CHAPTER 5

AND if a soul sin, and hear the voice of swearing, and *is* a witness, whether he hath seen or known *of it;* if he do not utter *it*, then he shall bear his iniquity.

2 Or if a soul touch any unclean thing, whether *it be* a carcase of an unclean beast, or a carcase of unclean cattle, or the carcase of unclean creeping things, and *if* it be hidden from him; he also shall be unclean, and guilty.

3 Or if he touch the uncleanness of man, whatsoever uncleanness *it be* that a man shall be defiled withal, and it be hid from him; when he knoweth *of it*, then he shall be guilty.

4 Or if a soul swear, pronouncing with *his* lips to do evil, or to do good, whatsoever *it be* that a man shall pronounce with an oath, and it be hid from him; when he knoweth *of it*, then he shall be guilty in one of these.

5 And it shall be, when he shall be guilty in one of these *things*, that he shall confess that he hath sinned in that *thing*:

6 And he shall bring his trespass offering unto the LORD for his sin which he hath sinned, a female from the flock, a lamb or a kid of the goats, for a sin offering; and the priest shall make an atonement for him concerning his sin.

7 And if he be not able to bring a lamb, then he shall bring for his trespass, which he hath committed, two turtledoves, or two young pigeons, unto the LORD; one for a sin offering, and the other for a burnt offering.

8 And he shall bring them unto the priest, who shall offer *that* which *is* for the sin offering first, and wring off his head from his neck, but shall not divide *it* asunder:

9 And he shall sprinkle of the blood of the sin offering upon the side of the altar; and the rest of the blood shall be wrung out at the bottom of the altar: it *is* a sin offering.

10 And he shall offer the second *for* a burnt offering, according to the manner: and the priest shall make an atonement for him for his sin which he hath sinned, and it shall be forgiven him.

11 But if he be not able to bring two turtledoves, or two young pigeons, then he that sinned shall bring for his offering the tenth part of an ephah of fine flour for a sin offering; he shall put no oil upon it, neither shall he put *any* frankincense thereon: for it *is* a sin offering.

12 Then shall he bring it to the priest, and the priest shall take his handful of it, *even* a memorial thereof, and burn *it* on the altar, according to the offerings made by fire unto the LORD: it *is* a sin offering.

13 And the priest shall make an atonement for him as touching his sin that he hath sinned in one of these, and it shall be forgiven him: and *the rem-*

(vss. 1-5) of which a man is fully aware, whereas the sin offering atoned for the guilt or depravity of sin in general.

5:1. The trespass described in this verse is that of a **witness** who will **not utter it.** When called upon to testify, he refuses to tell what he knows—either to save the innocent or to condemn the guilty. Can there not be an application made here to the Christian's witness?

2-3. Failure to maintain proper ceremonial separation from unclean things, even unknowingly, is another act of sin requiring a trespass offering. Likewise, lack of separation from certain habits, amusements, or other practices can defile a Christian today as well.

4. Failure to keep a vow is another item listed here. It is really a lack of self-control. One ought to fully consider any commitment before agreeing to it. For more on vows see Leviticus 27 and Numbers 30.

5-6. The usual trespass offering was either a female goat, or a lamb. Its purpose was to **make an atonement for him concerning his sin** (vs. 6).

7. If a man was too poor to bring the larger animals of verses 5 and 6, he could substitute two turtledoves or a pair of young pigeons for the offering.

8-10. After the blood was applied to the brazen altar, one of the birds was burned upon the altar in its entirety as a whole burnt offering. This naturally served as the Lord's portion. The remaining bird apparently became the priest's portion.

11-13. But if he be not able. In cases of extreme poverty, a further substitution was allowed. The meal could be offered in place of any animals. The question arises as to how this could satisfy the rule that ". . . without shedding of blood . . ." there is no forgiveness of sin (Heb 9:22). O. T. Allis has suggested that the mingling of the meal on the altar (part was burned, vs. 12) with the other bloody offerings could be seen as meeting this principle, and that the main aspect taught in all these sacrifices—that of vicarious substitution—is perfectly illustrated even in this offering of meal (O. T. Allis, "Leviticus" in *The New Bible Commentary*, p. 140).

nant shall be the priest's, as a meat offering.

14 ¶And the LORD spake unto Moses, saying,

15 If a soul commit a trespass, and sin through ignorance, in the holy things of the LORD; then he shall bring for his trespass unto the LORD a ram without blemish out of the flocks, with thy estimation by shekels of silver, after the shekel of the sanctuary, for a trespass offering:

16 And he shall make amends for the harm that he hath done in the holy thing, and shall add the fifth part thereto, and give it unto the priest: and the priest shall make an atonement for him with the ram of the trespass offering, and it shall be forgiven him.

17 ¶And if a soul sin, and commit any of these things which are forbidden to be done by the commandments of the LORD; though he wist it not, yet is he guilty, and shall bear his iniquity.

18 And he shall bring a ram without blemish out of the flock, with thy estimation, for a trespass offering, unto the priest: and the priest shall make an atonement for him concerning thine ignorance wherein he erred and wist it not, and it shall be forgiven him.

19 It is a trespass offering: he hath certainly trespassed against the LORD.

CHAPTER 6

AND the LORD spake unto Moses, saying,

2 If a soul sin, and commit a trespass against the LORD, and lie unto his neighbour in that which was delivered him to keep, or in fellowship, or in a thing taken away by violence, or hath deceived his neighbour;

3 Or have found that which was lost, and lieth concerning it, and sweareth falsely; in any of all these that a man doeth, sinning therein:

4 Then it shall be, because he hath sinned, and is guilty, that he shall restore that which he took violently away, or the thing which he hath deceitfully gotten, or that which was delivered him to keep, or the lost thing which he found,

5 Or all that about which he hath sworn falsely; he shall even restore it in the principal, and shall add the fifth part more thereto, and give it unto him to whom it appertaineth, in the day of his trespass offering.

6 And he shall bring his trespass offering unto the LORD, a ram without blemish out of the flock, with thy estimation, for a trespass offering, unto the priest:

7 And the priest shall make an atonement for him before the LORD: and it shall be forgiven him for any thing of all that he hath done in trespassing therein.

8 ¶And the LORD spake unto Moses, saying,

9 Command Aaron and his sons, saying, This is the law of the burnt offering: It is the burnt offering, because of the burning upon the altar all night

14-16. A further type of trespass required that restitution be made before a sacrifice was offered for atonement. A trespass **in the holy things of the LORD** would involve failure to give God His proper tithes, offerings, first fruits, first-born, etc. The restitution was to **add the fifth part thereto,** meaning to pay an additional twenty percent penalty besides what was owed, and the offering of the ram. If we were under these laws today, how many Christians would be assessed a twenty percent additional fee for failure to give God His tithes and offerings? When we sin in this regard today, not only do we miss the blessing of obedience, and fail to qualify for His bountiful provision (Lk 6:38); but God will usually take it from us through hardships and other unexpected expenses (Heb 12:5-15).

17-19. A second type of trespass requiring restitution concerned the **things which are forbidden to be done by the commandments of the LORD.** Again, a ram was sacrificed in the usual manner. That restitution was also made can be argued from a comparison of the language used for this offering and that of the sin offering of chapter 4:2, 13, 22, and 27. The only difference must lie in restitution being made in the case of the trespass offering, mention of which is omitted in verse 18 but is implied from verse 16, which treats a similar case within the same section of Scripture.

6:1-3. Sin against one's **neighbor** is also included in this section (6:1-7), which is part of chapter 5 in the Hebrew text (5:20-26). It is still part of the trespass offering. Again, an additional twenty percent restitution had to be made as a reimbursement to the neighbor and as a fine on the offender. As Christians, we should make restitution for past evil acts as far as possible. Where an individual has been wronged, financially or otherwise, restitution should be made privately. We can rejoice that Christ has made an infinite restitution for our iniquities. He "paid it all. All to Him I owe."

4-7. After restitution is made, again **a ram** (vs. 6) is sacrificed. Sin is not a small matter in God's sight. The end result, however, is that **it shall be forgiven him for any thing of all that he hath done in trespassing** (vs. 7). As the psalmist, King David, declared, "Blessed is he whose transgression is forgiven, whose sin is covered" (Ps 32:1).

3. Further instructions about the offerings. 6:8-7:38.

This section deals with some of the details of each of the offerings mentioned in chapters 1-5. They are taken up in order, except that the instructions for the peace offering are placed last.

8. And the LORD spake unto Moses, saying. Moses filled the office of prophet. He received the revelation from God, and spoke it forth to others.

9. Command Aaron and his sons. These instructions are meant for the priests, since they were the ones required to handle the offerings. They needed more specifics on how to offer each sacrifice properly. The priests were to maintain a

LEVITICUS 6:26

unto the morning, and the fire of the altar shall be burning in it.

10 And the priest shall put on his linen garment, and his linen breeches shall he put upon his flesh, and take up the ashes which the fire hath consumed with the burnt offering on the altar, and he shall put them beside the altar.

11 And he shall put off his garments, and put on other garments, and carry forth the ashes without the camp unto a clean place.

12 And the fire upon the altar shall be burning in it; it shall not be put out: and the priest shall burn wood on it every morning, and lay the burnt offering in order upon it; and he shall burn thereon the fat of the peace offerings.

13 The fire shall ever be burning upon the altar; it shall never go out.

14 ¶And this is the law of the meat offering: the sons of Aaron shall offer it before the Lord, before the altar.

15 And he shall take of it his handful, of the flour of the meat offering, and of the oil thereof, and all the frankincense which is upon the meat offering, and shall burn it upon the altar for a sweet savour, even the memorial of it, unto the Lord.

16 And the remainder thereof shall Aaron and his sons eat: with unleavened bread shall it be eaten in the holy place; in the court of the tabernacle of the congregation they shall eat it.

17 It shall not be baken with leaven. I have given it unto them for their portion of my offerings made by fire; it is most holy, as is the sin offering, and as the trespass offering.

18 All the males among the children of Aaron shall eat of it. It shall be a statute for ever in your generations concerning the offerings of the Lord made by fire: every one that toucheth them shall be holy.

19 ¶And the Lord spake unto Moses, saying,

20 This is the offering of Aaron and of his sons, which they shall offer unto the Lord in the day when he is anointed; the tenth part of an ephah of fine flour for a meat offering perpetual, half of it in the morning, and half thereof at night.

21 In a pan it shall be made with oil; and when it is baken, thou shalt bring it in: and the baken pieces of the meat offering shalt thou offer for a sweet savour unto the Lord.

22 And the priest of his sons that is anointed in his stead shall offer it: it is a statute for ever unto the Lord; it shall be wholly burnt.

23 For every meat offering for the priest shall be wholly burnt: it shall not be eaten.

24 ¶And the Lord spake unto Moses, saying,

25 Speak unto Aaron and to his sons, saying, This is the law of the sin offering: In the place where the burnt offering is killed shall the sin offering be killed before the Lord: it is most holy.

26 The priest that offereth it for sin shall eat it: in the holy place shall it be

continual burnt offering on the brazen altar, even at night (see Ex 29:38-42).

10-11. The priests also had to care for the ashes that would accumulate in the altar. Proper attire was required, both for removal and for disposal.

12-13. The fire shall ever be burning upon the altar. The fire was to burn continually as a sign of Israel's devotion to God and as a continual atonement.

14-18. Further regulations for the meal offering are reiterated here. There was a distinction between God's portion, which was burned on the altar, and the priests' portion, which was eaten inside the tabernacle by the male descendants of Aaron. **Everyone that toucheth them shall be holy** (vs. 18) refers not to the offerings making people holy, but that those who do touch the offerings should be in a state of ceremonial cleanliness.

19-23. The particular meal or cereal offering spoken of in these verses was offered of **Aaron and of his sons . . . in the day when he is anointed.** This no doubt refers to the time of the high priest's inauguration, but most commentators also believe it was offered morning and evening as a perpetual oblation. It was burned completely (vss. 22-23), and thus the priests did not partake of it.

24-26. The law of the sin offering is under discussion in verses 24-30. God reaffirms that **it is most holy.** After the fat portions were offered all the rest became the property of the priest who performed the offering ceremony.

eaten, in the court of the tabernacle of the congregation.

27 Whatsoever shall touch the flesh thereof shall be holy: and when there is sprinkled of the blood thereof upon any garment, thou shalt wash that whereon it was sprinkled in the holy place.

28 But the earthen vessel wherein it is sodden shall be broken: and if it be sodden in a brasen pot, it shall be both scoured, and rinsed in water.

29 All the males among the priests shall eat thereof: it *is* most holy.

30 And no sin offering, whereof *any* of the blood is brought into the tabernacle of the congregation to reconcile *withal* in the holy *place*, shall be eaten: it shall be burnt in the fire.

CHAPTER 7

LIKEWISE this *is* the law of the trespass offering: it *is* most holy.

2 In the place where they kill the burnt offering shall they kill the trespass offering: and the blood thereof shall he sprinkle round about upon the altar.

3 And he shall offer of it all the fat thereof; the rump, and the fat that covereth the inwards,

4 And the two kidneys, and the fat that *is* on them, which *is* by the flanks, and the caul *that is* above the liver, with the kidneys, it shall he take away:

5 And the priest shall burn them upon the altar *for* an offering made by fire unto the Lord: it *is* a trespass offering.

6 Every male among the priests shall eat thereof: it shall be eaten in the holy place: it *is* most holy.

7 As the sin offering *is*, so *is* the trespass offering: *there is* one law for them: the priest that maketh atonement therewith shall have *it*.

8 And the priest that offereth any man's burnt offering, *even* the priest shall have to himself the skin of the burnt offering which he hath offered.

9 And all the meat offering that is baken in the oven, and all that is dressed in the fryingpan, and in the pan, shall be the priest's that offereth it.

10 And every meat offering, mingled with oil, and dry, shall all the sons of Aaron have, one *as much* as another.

11 ¶And this *is* the law of the sacrifice of peace offerings, which he shall offer unto the Lord.

12 If he offer it for a thanksgiving, then he shall offer with the sacrifice of thanksgiving unleavened cakes mingled with oil, and unleavened wafers anointed with oil, and cakes mingled with oil, of fine flour, fried.

13 Besides the cakes, he shall offer *for* his offering leavened bread with the sacrifice of thanksgiving of his peace offerings.

14 And of it he shall offer one out of the whole oblation *for* an heave offering unto the Lord, *and* it shall be the priest's that sprinkleth the blood of the peace offerings.

15 And the flesh of the sacrifice of his peace offerings for thanksgiving shall be eaten the same day that it is offered; he shall not leave any of it until the morning.

27-28. It is such a holy sacrifice that anything it touches becomes holy, including the vessel in which the priest boiled (AV "sodden") his portion of the meat. Being holy, the common clay pot must be withdrawn from ordinary use by being broken. A brass pot had to be thoroughly scrubbed and rinsed in water.

29-30. The sin offering of the priest, however, could not be eaten by anyone. Only the qualified **males among the priests** could partake.

7:1-6. The trespass offering is recounted next. The entire ceremony is gone over in detail, including the killing and application of the blood (vs. 2), the portions to be burned before the Lord (vss. 3-5), and the fact that the male priests can partake of the priests' portion (vs. 6). **The rump** (vs. 3) refers to the tail of a flat-tailed sheep, which is usually very extensive and made almost entirely of fat.

7-10. Ample provision is made for the priests in these regulations. Paul's application, when he refers to this passage, is that ". . . the Lord ordained that they which preach the gospel should live of the gospel" (I Cor 9:14).

11-15. The law of the sacrifice of peace offerings (v. 11) fills the rest of chapter 7. Peace offerings could be for thanksgiving (vss. 12-15), or part of a vow, or a freewill offering (vs. 16). With these offerings cakes were also brought, both unleavened (vs. 12) and leavened (vs. 13). The cakes were eaten as part of the fellowship meal, but were not burned upon the altar. The **heave offering** (vs. 14) means it was waved in the air, that is, lifted up to the Lord. The offerer's portion of the thanksgiving oblation had to be eaten the same day it was offered (vs. 15). Naturally, a large animal would make quite a feast and much would go to waste (any left the next day had to be burned) unless the offerer invited friends and neighbors to join him in rejoicing in the blessings of God. This is one of the ways God taught His people to share their blessings.

16 But if the sacrifice of his offering *be* a vow, or a voluntary offering, it shall be eaten the same day that he offereth his sacrifice: and on the morrow also the remainder of it shall be eaten:

17 But the remainder of the flesh of the sacrifice on the third day shall be burnt with fire.

18 And if *any* of the flesh of the sacrifice of his peace offerings be eaten at all on the third day, it shall not be accepted, neither shall it be imputed unto him that offereth it: it shall be an abomination, and the soul that eateth of it shall bear his iniquity.

19 And the flesh that toucheth any unclean *thing* shall not be eaten; it shall be burnt with fire: and as for the flesh, all that be clean shall eat thereof.

20 But the soul that eateth *of* the flesh of the sacrifice of peace offerings, that *pertain* unto the LORD, having his uncleanness upon him, even that soul shall be cut off from his people.

21 Moreover the soul that shall touch any unclean *thing*, *as* the uncleanness of man, or *any* unclean beast, or any abominable unclean *thing*, and eat of the flesh of the sacrifice of peace offerings, which *pertain* unto the LORD, even that soul shall be cut off from his people.

22 ¶And the LORD spake unto Moses, saying,

23 Speak unto the children of Israel, saying, Ye shall eat no manner of fat, of ox, or of sheep, or of goat.

24 And the fat of the beast that dieth of itself, and the fat of that which is torn with beasts, may be used in any other use: but ye shall in no wise eat of it.

25 For whosoever eateth the fat of the beast, of which men offer an offering made by fire unto the LORD, even the soul that eateth *it* shall be cut off from his people.

26 Moreover ye shall eat no manner of blood, *whether it be* of fowl or of beast, in any of your dwellings.

27 Whatsoever soul *it be* that eateth any manner of blood, even that soul shall be cut off from his people.

28 ¶And the LORD spake unto Moses, saying,

29 Speak unto the children of Israel, saying, He that offereth the sacrifice of his peace offerings unto the LORD shall bring his oblation unto the LORD of the sacrifice of his peace offerings.

30 His own hands shall bring the offerings of the LORD made by fire, the fat with the breast, it shall he bring, that the breast may be waved *for* a wave offering before the LORD.

31 And the priest shall burn the fat upon the altar: but the breast shall be Aaron's and his sons'.

32 And the right shoulder shall ye give unto the priest *for* an heave offering of the sacrifices of your peace offerings.

33 He among the sons of Aaron, that offereth the blood of the peace offerings, and the fat, shall have the right shoulder for *his* part.

34 For the wave breast and the heave shoulder have I taken of the children of

16-21. The portion from a vow or freewill type peace offering could be eaten for two days and had to be disposed of after that (vss. 16-18). To eat of these offerings in a state of ceremonial uncleanness was a grave breach of God's law and resulted in being **cut off from his people** (vss. 20-21). That expression most often signifies excommunication or exile from the nation of Israel, though in severe cases where civil laws were also abrogated the death penalty could be involved as in Exodus 31:14.

22-27. God prohibits eating the portions of fat that were normally offered to Him in sacrifice. Even these portions in non-sacrificial animals were not to be eaten. Others areas of fat on the animal were all right to eat (vss. 22-25). The eating of blood was strictly forbidden at all times. Note Acts 15:29, where Christians were also encouraged not to eat blood because it would hinder the winning of Jews to Christ or be an offense to Hebrew Christians.

28-36. The precise pieces of meat given to Aaron and his sons are indicated in these verses. They received the breast after it had been **waved for a wave offering before the LORD** (vs. 30). They also received the right shoulder after it had been lifted up as a **heave offering** to the Lord (vs. 32). Though these pieces are offered to God, God says He has **given them unto Aaron . . . and unto his sons by a statute for ever** (vs. 34).

Israel from off the sacrifices of their peace offerings, and have given them unto Aaron the priest and unto his sons by a statute for ever from among the children of Israel.

35 ¶This *is* the portion of the anointing of Aaron, and of the anointing of his sons, out of the offerings of the LORD made by fire, in the day *when* he presented them to minister unto the LORD in the priest's office;

36 Which the LORD commanded to be given them of the children of Israel, in the day that he anointed them, *by* a statute for ever throughout their generations.

37 This *is* the law of the burnt offering, of the meat offering, and of the sin offering, and of the trespass offering, and of the consecrations, and of the sacrifice of the peace offerings;

38 Which the LORD commanded Moses in mount Sī'naī, in the day that he commanded the children of Israel to offer their oblations unto the LORD, in the wilderness of Sī'naī.

37-38. These verses are a concluding summary of the categories of offerings previously covered. It is noted that these were given at Mount Sinai in the wilderness.

B. The Approach Through Priestly Mediation. 8:1-10:20.

1. The consecration of the priests. 8:1-36.

Naturally, none of the offerings laid out in chapters 1-7 could be offered by a common person. A priest had to mediate between the individual and Almighty God. This is the backdrop for the great high priestly ministry of our Lord Jesus Christ. There is ". . . one mediator between God and men, the man Christ Jesus" (I Tim 2:5). No man can come to God on his own merits. A perfectly qualified priest is needed. Chapters 8-10 speak in many ways of Christ's ministry, but there are also notable dissimilarities. By way of application, some of the work of the high priest pictures what we must do today as believer-priests (Rev 5:9-10).

8:1-5. Take Aaron and his sons with him, and the garments. The detailed description of the priest's clothing is given in Exodus 28 and 29. There Moses is told to assemble Aaron and his sons for consecration. The elements of cleansing, anointing, and sacrifice were to be readied (vs. 2); and all Israel was to be assembled to watch.

CHAPTER 8

AND the LORD spake unto Moses, saying,

2 Take Aaron and his sons with him, and the garments, and the anointing oil, and a bullock for the sin offering, and two rams, and a basket of unleavened bread;

3 And gather thou all the congregation together unto the door of the tabernacle of the congregation.

4 And Moses did as the LORD commanded him; and the assembly was gathered together unto the door of the tabernacle of the congregation.

5 And Moses said unto the congregation, This *is* the thing which the LORD commanded to be done.

6 And Moses brought Aaron and his sons, and washed them with water.

7 And he put upon him the coat, and girded him with the girdle, and clothed him with the robe, and put the ephod upon him, and he girded him with the curious girdle of the ephod, and bound *it* unto him therewith.

8 And he put the breastplate upon him: also he put in the breastplate the Ū'rīm and the Thŭm'mīm.

9 And he put the mitre upon his head;

6. First, they were washed with water, a very definite symbol of cleansing. This would most naturally typify salvation in the order of events which follow.

7. Next, Aaron is clothed with various pieces of material resembling belts, or sashes, and a robe, picturing the New Testament clothing of the believer in the righteousness of Christ (see Rev 7:14 and 19:8).

8. The breastplate was made of beautiful colored linen with gold and held twelve precious stones, including a diamond, a sapphire, an emerald, a jasper, etc. These stones represented the twelve tribes of Israel, and hence the high priest bore Israel up before the Lord as he went about his sacred duties (see Ex 28:15-29). What **the Urim and the Thummim** were precisely, no one really knows today. They were apparently connected in some way with the revelation of God's will (Num 27:21; I Sam 28:6) but basically fell into disuse after the rise of the prophets. They were practically never heard of again after the return from captivity (Ezr 2:63).

9. The mitre upon his head bore the words "HOLINESS TO

also upon the mitre, *even* upon his forefront, did he put the golden plate, the holy crown; as the LORD commanded Moses.

10 And Moses took the anointing oil, and anointed the tabernacle and all that *was* therein, and sanctified them.

11 And he sprinkled thereof upon the altar seven times, and anointed the altar and all his vessels, both the laver and his foot, to sanctify them.

12 And he poured of the anointing oil upon Aaron's head, and anointed him, to sanctify him.

13 And Moses brought Aaron's sons, and put coats upon them, and girded them with girdles, and put bonnets upon them; as the LORD commanded Moses.

14 ¶And he brought the bullock for the sin offering: and Aaron and his sons laid their hands upon the head of the bullock for the sin offering.

15 And he slew *it;* and Moses took the blood, and put *it* upon the horns of the altar round about with his finger, and purified the altar, and poured the blood at the bottom of the altar, and sanctified it, to make reconciliation upon it.

16 And he took all the fat that *was* upon the inwards, and the caul *above* the liver, and the two kidneys, and their fat, and Moses burned *it* upon the altar.

17 But the bullock, and his hide, his flesh, and his dung, he burnt with fire without the camp as the LORD commanded Moses.

18 ¶And he brought the ram for the burnt offering: and Aaron and his sons laid their hands upon the head of the ram.

19 And he killed *it;* and Moses sprinkled the blood upon the altar round about.

20 And he cut the ram into pieces; and Moses burnt the head, and the pieces, and the fat.

21 And he washed the inwards and the legs in water; and Moses burnt the whole ram upon the altar: it *was* a burnt sacrifice for a sweet savour, *and* an offering made by fire unto the LORD; as the LORD commanded Moses.

22 ¶And he brought the other ram, the ram of consecration: and Aaron and his sons laid their hands upon the head of the ram.

23 And he slew *it;* and Moses took of the blood of it, and put *it* upon the tip of Aaron's right ear, and upon the thumb of his right hand, and upon the great toe of his right foot.

24 And he brought Aaron's sons, and Moses put of the blood upon the tip of their right ear, and upon the thumbs of their right hands, and upon the great toes of their right feet: and Moses sprinkled the blood upon the altar round about.

25 And he took the fat, and the rump, and all the fat that *was* upon the inwards, and the caul *above* the liver, and the two kidneys, and their fat, and the right shoulder:

26 And out of the basket of unleavened bread, that *was* before the LORD, he took one unleavened cake, and a cake of oiled bread, and one wa-

THE LORD" (Ex 28:36). It was a constant reminder of the priest's acceptance before the Lord.

10-11. Moses then poured oil (presumably olive oil) on the tabernacle and all its furniture, then sprinkled it on the brazen altar and the laver outside in the courtyard. This action set these objects apart for God's use.

12. Moses then anointed Aaron **to sanctify him,** that is, to set him apart for God's service. Each child of God today is sanctified in this same sense.

13-17. The next act of consecration was the performance of a **sin offering** for Aaron and his sons. Moses sacrificed the young bull precisely according to the regulations given in Leviticus 4:1-35.

18-21. The burnt offering was observed next with the sacrificing of a ram. The same pattern for offering the animal would be followed as prescribed in Leviticus 1:10-13.

22-24. A second ram was then slain as a **ram of consecration.** Its blood was applied to Aaron's right ear, right thumb, and right big toe as an indication that he should hear God's Word, do God's work, and walk in God's ways. Aaron was to be fully consecrated to God, along with his sons.

25-29. The ram of consecration was then cut in the proper manner for burning on the altar, along with unleavened loaves; but before it was placed in the fiery altar, Moses filled Aaron's hands with the pieces which he then waved before the Lord. His hands were to be filled with the service of God, even as ours should be.

fer, and put *them* on the fat, and upon the right shoulder:

27 And he put all upon Aaron's hands, and upon his sons' hands, and waved them *for* a wave offering before the Lord.

28 And Moses took them from off their hands, and burnt *them* on the altar upon the burnt offering: they *were* consecrations for a sweet savour: it *is* an offering made by fire unto the Lord.

29 And Moses took the breast, and waved it *for* a wave offering before the Lord: *for* of the ram of consecration it was Moses' part; as the Lord commanded Moses.

30 And Moses took of the anointing oil, and of the blood which *was* upon the altar, and sprinkled *it* upon Aaron, *and* upon his garments, and upon his sons, and upon his sons' garments with him; and sanctified Aaron, *and* his garments, and his sons, and his sons' garments with him.

31 ¶And Moses said unto Aaron and to his sons, Boil the flesh *at* the door of the tabernacle of the congregation: and there eat it with the bread that *is* in the basket of consecrations, as I commanded, saying, Aaron and his sons shall eat it.

32 And that which remaineth of the flesh and of the bread shall ye burn with fire.

33 And ye shall not go out of the door of the tabernacle of the congregation *in* seven days, until the days of your consecration be at an end: for seven days shall he consecrate you.

34 As he hath done this day, *so* the Lord hath commanded to do, to make an atonement for you.

35 Therefore shall ye abide *at* the door of the tabernacle of the congregation day and night seven days, and keep the charge of the Lord, that ye die not: for so I am commanded.

36 So Aaron and his sons did all things which the Lord commanded by the hand of Moses.

CHAPTER 9

AND it came to pass on the eighth day, *that* Moses called Aaron and his sons, and the elders of Israel;

2 And he said unto Aaron, Take thee a young calf for a sin offering, and a ram for a burnt offering, without blemish, and offer *them* before the Lord.

3 And unto the children of Israel thou shalt speak, saying, Take ye a kid of the goats for a sin offering; and a calf and a lamb, *both* of the first year, without blemish, for a burnt offering;

4 Also a bullock and a ram for peace offerings, to sacrifice before the Lord; and a meat offering mingled with oil: for to day the Lord will appear unto you.

5 ¶And they brought *that* which Moses commanded before the tabernacle of the congregation: and all the congregation drew near and stood before the Lord.

6 And Moses said, This *is* the thing which the Lord commanded that ye

30-32. Aaron and his sons were next sprinkled with anointing oil and with blood. They then partook in the sacrificial meal of the priest's portions of the ram of consecration and some of the unleavened loaves.

33-36. For seven days shall he consecrate you. Seven days probably indicates a perfect consecration, but nonetheless Aaron and his sons were obligated to spend a literal seven days in the tabernacle before going forth to serve. Dedication to God's service is not to be obtained quickly and easily. Aaron and his sons had time to duly contemplate the serious nature of the task with which God was entrusting them. Again, there must be adequate time spent alone with God before one rushes out to serve Him. It was said of Peter and John that ". . . they took knowledge of them, that they had been with Jesus" (Acts 4:13).

2. The ministration of the priests. 9:1-24.

9:1-4. As the priests began their sacred ministry, they must first offer sin and burnt offerings for themselves, and then similar oblations on behalf of the congregation of Israel, represented by their elders.

5-6. Everyone was assembled before **the tabernacle of the congregation** of the Lord, and Moses promised that God and His glory would appear to them (vss. 4, 6). This was fulfilled in verses 23-24.

should do: and the glory of the LORD shall appear unto you.

7 And Moses said unto Aaron, Go unto the altar, and offer thy sin offering, and thy burnt offering, and make an atonement for thyself, and for the people: and offer the offering of the people, and make an atonement for them; as the LORD commanded.

8 ¶Aaron therefore went unto the altar, and slew the calf of the sin offering, which was for himself.

9 And the sons of Aaron brought the blood unto him: and he dipped his finger in the blood, and put it upon the horns of the altar, and poured out the blood at the bottom of the altar:

10 But the fat, and the kidneys, and the caul above the liver of the sin offering, he burnt upon the altar; as the LORD commanded Moses.

11 And the flesh and the hide he burnt with fire without the camp.

12 And he slew the burnt offering; and Aaron's sons presented unto him the blood, which he sprinkled round about upon the altar.

13 And they presented the burnt offering unto him, with the pieces thereof, and the head: and he burnt them upon the altar.

14 And he did wash the inwards and the legs, and burnt them upon the burnt offering on the altar.

15 ¶And he brought the people's offering, and took the goat, which was the sin offering for the people, and slew it, and offered it for sin, as the first.

16 And he brought the burnt offering, and offered it according to the manner.

17 And he brought the meat offering, and took an handful thereof, and burnt it upon the altar, beside the burnt sacrifice of the morning.

18 He slew also the bullock and the ram for a sacrifice of peace offerings, which was for the people: and Aaron's sons presented unto him the blood, which he sprinkled upon the altar round about,

19 And the fat of the bullock and of the ram, the rump, and that which covereth the inwards, and the kidneys, and the caul above the liver:

20 And they put the fat upon the breasts, and he burnt the fat upon the altar:

21 And the breasts and the right shoulder Aaron waved for a wave offering before the LORD; as Moses commanded.

22 And Aaron lifted up his hand toward the people, and blessed them, and came down from offering of the sin offering, and the burnt offering, and peace offerings.

23 And Moses and Aaron went into the tabernacle of the congregation, and came out, and blessed the people: and

7-11. Aaron's sin offering was a **calf** (vs. 8), offered in the prescribed manner, with the remnant taken outside the camp. What a rebuke to the scene that had transpired with the golden calf on a prior occasion (Ex 32)!

12-14. Aaron next sacrificed a ram (vs. 2) as a burnt offering, picturing Christ's complete devotion to the Father, and also what our devotion should be.

15. And he brought the people's offering. Aaron offered a goat as a sin oblation for the children of Israel.

16. This was followed by a burnt offering from the people to demonstrate their appreciation for God's graciousness to them.

17. Next came a meal or grain offering, which was burned on the altar beside the burnt sacrifice, showing its close relationship to the blood offerings.

18-21. Peace offerings followed to complete the thanksgiving of Aaron and the people.

22. Finally, **Aaron** was finished and **lifted up his hand toward the people, and blessed them.** The priest was to give a blessing at the conclusion of his ministration. Contrast this with the speechless Zechariah in Luke 1:22 who had no blessing to impart. But at the conclusion of His earthly ministry, Christ, our great High Priest, ". . . lifted up his hands, and blessed them" (Lk 24:50); and as He was doing so, He ascended back up to heaven (Lk 24:51).

23-24. The glory of the LORD appeared unto all the people. God's glory was the manifest excellence of His divine character, and at times it shone forth in a bright and shining magnificence. Here it was accompanied by a spectacular fiery display which

the glory of the LORD appeared unto all the people.

24 And there came a fire out from before the LORD, and consumed upon the altar the burnt offering and the fat: *which* when all the people saw, they shouted, and fell on their faces.

CHAPTER 10

AND Nādăb and A-bī'hū, the sons of Aaron, took either of them his censer, and put fire therein, and put incense thereon, and offered strange fire before the LORD, which he commanded them not.

2 And there went out fire from the LORD, and devoured them, and they died before the LORD.

3 Then Moses said unto Aaron, This *is it* that the LORD spake, saying, I will be sanctified in them that come nigh me, and before all the people I will be glorified. And Aaron held his peace.

4 And Moses called Mīsh'a-el and Ĕl'zā-phăn, the sons of Ŭz'zī-el the uncle of Aaron, and said unto them, Come near, carry your brethren from before the sanctuary out of the camp.

5 So they went near, and carried them in their coats out of the camp; as Moses had said.

6 And Moses said unto Aaron, and unto Ĕ-le-ā'zar and unto Ĭth'a-mär, his sons, Uncover not your heads, neither rend your clothes; lest ye die, and lest wrath come upon all the people: but let your brethren, the whole house of Israel, bewail the burning which the LORD hath kindled.

7 And ye shall not go out from the door of the tabernacle of the congregation, lest ye die: for the anointing oil of the LORD *is* upon you. And they did according to the word of Moses.

8 ¶And the LORD spake unto Aaron, saying,

9 Do not drink wine nor strong drink, thou, nor thy sons with thee, when ye go into the tabernacle of the congregation, lest ye die: *it shall be* a statute for ever throughout your generations:

10 And that ye may put difference between holy and unholy, and between unclean and clean;

11 And that ye may teach the children of Israel all the statutes which the LORD hath spoken unto them by the hand of Moses.

12 ¶And Moses spake unto Aaron, and unto Ĕ-le-ā'zar and unto Ĭth'a-mär,

consumed the burnt offering on the altar. The people's response was to prostrate themselves before the Lord in worship.

3. The death of Nadab and Abihu. 10:1-20.

10:1. Nadab and Abihu . . . offered strange fire before the LORD. The sin of these two oldest sons of Aaron was severely punished with death. God often judges severely when He is instituting something new and there is an infraction, as with Adam and Eve, violation of the sabbath day (Num 15:32-36), and even the lying of Ananias and Sapphira (Acts 5:1-11). God wanted all to know the seriousness of disobedience and made a graphic example of its results as a warning to others. The sin of Nadab and Abihu may have involved: (1) presuming to do what God had not commanded them; (2) trying to take over the duties of the high priest; (3) vying for supremacy among themselves; and perhaps (4) partial inebriation (cf. vss. 9-10).

2-5. God was neither glorified nor set apart by them in their actions, and they died as a result. How many of us, with all our sin, would still be living if it were not for the grace of God? Their funeral followed, burial being performed by their cousins.

6-7. Anyone who touched a dead body became ceremonially unclean, so Aaron and his two remaining sons were not allowed to come near the dead sons.

8-9. The context is very explicit when it notes that **the LORD spake unto Aaron, saying, Do not drink wine nor strong drink.** Had Nadab and Abihu sinned as a result of being intoxicated? There is a possibility that such was the case. Nevertheless, God will not have His priests drink intoxicating beverages. The same restriction is placed upon God's kings, lest they ". . . forget the law, and pervert the judgment . . ." (Prov 31:4-5). God refers to New Testament believers as kings and priests (see I Pet 2:9; Rev 5:10). Surely we ought to be above reproach at all times in this matter. Social drinking is the allurement of Satan. The only option for a believer who desires to maintain a good testimony is total abstinence, even abstaining ". . . from all appearance of evil" (I Thess 5:22).

10-11. Another reason for this injunction is stated in verse 10. A third reason is given in verse 11.

12-15. And ye shall eat it in the holy place. These verses describe the priests eating their assigned portions of the various offerings, meal, peace, etc., as God had commanded them.

his sons that were left, Take the meat offering that remaineth of the offerings of the LORD made by fire, and eat it without leaven beside the altar: for it *is* most holy:

13 And ye shall eat it in the holy place, because it *is* thy due, and thy sons' due, of the sacrifices of the LORD made by fire: for so I am commanded.

14 And the wave breast and heave shoulder shall ye eat in a clean place; thou, and thy sons, and thy daughters with thee: for *they be* thy due, and thy sons' due, *which* are given out of the sacrifices of peace offerings of the children of Israel.

15 The heave shoulder and the wave breast shall they bring with the offerings made by fire of the fat, to wave *it* *for* a wave offering before the LORD; and it shall be thine, and thy sons' with thee, by a statute for ever; as the LORD hath commanded.

16 ¶And Moses diligently sought the goat of the sin offering, and, behold, it was burnt: and he was angry with É-le-á′zar and Íth′a-mär, the sons of Aaron *which were* left *alive*, saying,

17 Wherefore have ye not eaten the sin offering in the holy place, seeing it *is* most holy, and *God* hath given it you to bear the iniquity of the congregation, to make atonement for them before the LORD?

18 Behold, the blood of it was not brought in within the holy *place:* ye should indeed have eaten it in the holy *place*, as I commanded.

19 And Aaron said unto Moses, Behold, this day have they offered their sin offering and their burnt offering before the LORD; and such things have befallen me: and *if* I had eaten the sin offering to day, should it have been accepted in the sight of the LORD?

20 And when Moses heard *that*, he was content.

CHAPTER 11

AND the LORD spake unto Moses and to Aaron, saying unto them,

2 Speak unto the children of Israel, saying, These *are* the beasts which ye shall eat among all the beasts that *are* on the earth.

3 Whatsoever parteth the hoof, and is clovenfooted, *and* cheweth the cud, among the beasts, that shall ye eat.

4 Nevertheless these shall ye not eat of them that chew the cud, or of them that divide the hoof: as the camel, because he cheweth the cud, but divideth not the hoof; he *is* unclean unto you.

5 And the coney, because he cheweth the cud, but divideth not the hoof; he *is* unclean unto you.

6 And the hare, because he cheweth the cud, but divideth not the hoof; he *is* unclean unto you.

7 And the swine, though he divide the hoof, and be clovenfooted, yet he cheweth not the cud; he *is* unclean to you.

16-20. Another priestly violation appears in these verses when Moses discovered that the priests had not eaten their portion of the people's sin offering (as a token of God's acceptance) and that it had been burned. Aaron's excuse seemed to refer to the tragedies of the day. However, mercy is shown here; no further punishment is exacted.

II. THE ACCESS TO GOD MAINTAINED PROPERLY. 11:1-27:34.

After relating the complete sacrificial system and how it was to be handled by the priests, God next gave instructions of a ceremonial, religious, civil, and moral nature which must be kept to maintain proper communion with God. Breaches of these precepts had to be taken care of by the offering of various sacrifices and by the observance of cleansing rituals.

A. Access Maintained Through Ceremonial Purity. 11:1-15:33.

1. Ceremonial laws regulating diet. 11:1-47.

God was concerned about the health of His people and wanted them to avoid certain contagion and parasitic diseases, so He laid down some guidelines perfectly in accord with modern science. The other cultures of that day based such classifications on magical formulas, while God simply indicated which animals were good to eat and which were not.

11:1-3. These are the beasts which ye shall eat. A principle regarding clean land animals is stated first, i.e., they must have hooves that are split, and they must chew the cud.

4-8. Camels, rock badgers (coney, see Ps 104:18 and Prov 30:26), rabbits, and swine are examples of quadrupeds which do not meet these tests. The rock badgers and rabbits have a motion which looks like a chewing of the cud, but is not. Even to touch one of these unclean animals rendered one unclean until evening (11:25) and required the washing of one's clothes, and sometimes a sin offering.

8 Of their flesh shall ye not eat, and their carcase shall ye not touch; they *are* unclean to you.

9 ¶These shall ye eat of all that *are* in the waters: whatsoever hath fins and scales in the waters, in the seas, and in the rivers, them shall ye eat.

10 And all that have not fins and scales in the seas, and in the rivers, of all that move in the waters, and of any living thing *is* in the waters, they *shall be* an abomination unto you:

11 They shall be even an abomination unto you; ye shall not eat of their flesh, but ye shall have their carcases in abomination.

12 Whatsoever hath no fins nor scales in the waters, that *shall be* an abomination unto you.

13 ¶And these *are they which* ye shall have in abomination among the fowls; they shall not be eaten, they *are* an abomination: the eagle, and the ossifrage, and the ospray,

14 And the vulture, and the kite after his kind;

15 Every raven after his kind;

16 And the owl, and the night hawk, and the cuckow, and the hawk after his kind,

17 And the little owl, and the cormorant, and the great owl,

18 And the swan, and the pelican, and the gier eagle,

19 And the stork, the heron after her kind, and the lapwing, and the bat.

20 All fowls that creep, going upon *all* four, *shall be* an abomination unto you.

21 Yet these may ye eat of every flying creeping thing that goeth upon *all* four, which have legs above their feet, to leap withal upon the earth;

22 *Even* these of them ye may eat; the locust after his kind, and the bald locust after his kind, and the beetle after his kind, and the grasshopper after his kind.

23 But all *other* flying creeping things, which have four feet, *shall be* an abomination unto you.

24 And for these ye shall be unclean: whosoever toucheth the carcase of them shall be unclean until the even.

25 And whosoever beareth *ought* of the carcase of them shall wash his clothes, and be unclean until the even.

26 *The carcases* of every beast which divideth the hoof, and *is* not clovenfooted, nor cheweth the cud, *are* unclean unto you: every one that toucheth them shall be unclean.

27 And whatsoever goeth upon his paws, among all manner of beasts that go on *all* four, those *are* unclean unto you: whoso toucheth their carcase shall be unclean until the even.

28 And he that beareth of the carcase of them shall wash his clothes, and be unclean until the even: they *are* unclean unto you.

29 ¶These also *shall be* unclean unto you among the creeping things that creep upon the earth; the weasel, and the mouse, and the tortoise after his kind,

30 And the ferret, and the chameleon, and the lizard, and the snail, and the mole.

9-12. The category of marine life required fish to have scales. This eliminated catfish, various forms of shell-fish, oysters, clams, lobsters, frogs, squid, etc.

13-19. Listed here are only those among the bird family which may not be eaten. Anyone who studies the habits of these creatures will readily understand that they are primarily birds of prey, carrion eaters, etc. What could be eaten? No doubt doves, pigeons, quail (Num 11:31-32), other smaller birds; and perhaps even chicken and turkey were allowable.

20-23. All fowls that creep. All insects were forbidden except four kinds of locusts that had jumping legs. The phrase **Goeth upon all four** is a common way of saying walking. Insects do have six legs, and Moses was perfectly aware of that.

24-26. Whosoever toucheth the carcase of them shall be unclean until the even. Even touching an unclean animal rendered one ceremonially unclean and required washing his clothes, etc.

27-31. Besides those listed earlier, animals with paws, which would include the dog and cat families (including lions, tigers etc.), and certain reptiles were also unclean.

31 These *are* unclean to you among all that creep: whosoever doth touch them, when they be dead, shall be unclean until the even.

32 And upon whatsoever *any* of them, when they are dead, doth fall, it shall be unclean; whether *it be* any vessel of wood, or raiment, or skin, or sack, whatsoever vessel *it be,* wherein *any* work is done, it must be put into water, and it shall be unclean until the even; so it shall be cleansed.

33 And every earthen vessel, whereinto *any* of them falleth, whatsoever *is* in it shall be unclean; and ye shall break it.

34 Of all meat which may be eaten, *that* on which *such* water cometh shall be unclean: and all drink that may be drunk in every *such* vessel shall be unclean.

35 And every *thing* whereupon *any* part of their carcase falleth shall be unclean; *whether it be* oven, or ranges for pots, they shall be broken down: *for* they *are* unclean, and shall be unclean unto you.

36 Nevertheless a fountain or pit, *wherein there is* plenty of water, shall be clean: but that which toucheth their carcase shall be unclean.

37 And if *any part* of their carcase fall upon any sowing seed which is to be sown, it *shall be* clean.

38 But if *any* water be put upon the seed, and *any part* of their carcase fall thereon, it *shall be* unclean to you.

39 And if any beast, of which ye may eat, die; he that toucheth the carcase thereof shall be unclean until the even.

40 And he that eateth of the carcase of it shall wash his clothes, and be unclean until the even: he also that beareth the carcase of it shall wash his clothes, and be unclean until the even.

41 And every creeping thing that creepeth upon the earth *shall be* an abomination; it shall not be eaten.

42 Whatsoever goeth upon the belly, and whatsoever goeth upon *all* four, or whatsoever hath more feet among all creeping things that creep upon the earth, them ye shall not eat; for they *are* an abomination.

43 Ye shall not make yourselves abominable with any creeping thing that creepeth, neither shall ye make yourselves unclean with them, that ye should be defiled thereby.

44 For I *am* the LORD your God: ye shall therefore sanctify yourselves, and ye shall be holy; for I *am* holy: neither shall ye defile yourselves with any manner of creeping thing that creepeth upon the earth.

45 For I *am* the LORD that bringeth you up out of the land of Egypt, to be your God: ye shall therefore be holy, for I *am* holy.

46 This *is* the law of the beasts, and of the fowl, and of every living creature that moveth in the waters, and of every creature that creepeth upon the earth:

47 To make a difference between the unclean and the clean, and between the

32-40. Contact between any of these creatures and garments, vessels, sacks, etc. made the clothes or vessels unclean; and appropriate action was required.

41-43. Finally, all land reptiles are categorized as unclean. Snake and alligator purses could not be used in Moses' day.

44. Ye shall be holy; for I am holy. This is the key verse of Leviticus. The basis of these laws was grounded in the holiness of God. God's people are to be set apart unto Him. We can now disregard all of these regulations because Christ nailed them to His cross (Col 2:14; cf. I Tim 4:3-5). But we are still today commanded to be a separate people from the world. See Romans 12:1-2; II Corinthians 6:14-7:1; and I John 2:15-17.

45-47. These verses summarize the basic idea of the chapter. God desires our conduct to exhibit His nature, because we are His children.

beast that may be eaten and the beast that may not be eaten.

CHAPTER 12

AND the Lord spake unto Moses, saying,

2 Speak unto the children of Israel, saying, If a woman have conceived seed, and born a man child: then she shall be unclean seven days; according to the days of the separation for her infirmity shall she be unclean.

3 And in the eighth day the flesh of his foreskin shall be circumcised.

4 And she shall then continue in the blood of her purifying three and thirty days; she shall touch no hallowed thing, nor come into the sanctuary, until the days of her purifying be fulfilled.

5 But if she bear a maid child, then she shall be unclean two weeks, as in her separation: and she shall continue in the blood of her purifying threescore and six days.

6 And when the days of her purifying are fulfilled, for a son, or for a daughter, she shall bring a lamb of the first year for a burnt offering, and a young pigeon, or a turtledove, for a sin offering, unto the door of the tabernacle of the congregation, unto the priest:

7 Who shall offer it before the Lord, and make an atonement for her; and she shall be cleansed from the issue of her blood. This *is* the law for her that hath born a male or a female.

8 And if she be not able to bring a lamb, then she shall bring two turtles, or two young pigeons; the one for the burnt offering, and the other for a sin offering: and the priest shall make an atonement for her, and she shall be clean.

CHAPTER 13

AND the Lord spake unto Moses and Aaron, saying,

2 When a man shall have in the skin of his flesh a rising, a scab, or bright spot, and it be in the skin of his flesh *like* the plague of leprosy; then he shall be brought unto Aaron the priest, or unto one of his sons the priests:

3 And the priest shall look on the plague in the skin of the flesh: and when the hair in the plague is turned white, and the plague in sight *be* deeper than the skin of his flesh, it *is* a plague of leprosy: and the priest shall look on him, and pronounce him unclean.

4 If the bright spot *be* white in the skin of his flesh, and in sight *be* not deep-

2. Ceremonial laws regarding delivery of children. 12:1-8.

12:1-2. If a woman have conceived seed, and born a man child: then she shall be unclean. Ceremonial uncleanness adhered to a woman after childbirth and rendered her unfit for any type of sacrificial worship, etc. The reason for this must be related to the fall of man into sin (Gen 3) and the resulting sin nature that is imparted to a child at conception. Even though having children was a joyous experience (Ps 127:3-5; 128:3-4) and in accord with the repeated command to "be fruitful and multiply" (cf. Gen 1:28; 9:7), it was a serious matter to bring into the world a child who bore the depravity of sin (Ps 51:5). It called for extra deliberation of heart and mind.

3. Circumcision was the sign of the Abrahamic covenant (Gen 17:9-14). It was performed on all male babies on **the eighth day**.

4. The mother, however, continued unclean for an additional thirty-three days. She could perform household chores during this time.

5. After a daughter's birth the time of uncleanness was doubled. Perhaps the circumcision of the male child had something to do with the shortened period in that case.

6-7. For purification at the end of the prescribed time, a lamb was offered as a burnt offering first to honor the Lord, and then a pigeon or turtledove was brought for a sin offering, the latter speaking of the sin nature with its original guilt and depravity being remembered and atoned for.

8. And if she be not able to bring a lamb. A poor person was allowed to substitute a young pigeon or turtledove for the lamb of the burnt offering. This is what Mary and Joseph did when presenting Jesus in the Temple on His forty-first day in Luke 2:22-24. The wise men arrived later with the gold after Joseph had secured a "house" (Mt 2:11).

3. Ceremonial laws regarding diseases—Leprosy. 13:1-14:57.

The regulations set forth in these chapters treat the identification of leprosy and other similar skin disorders (ch. 13) and the ritual for its cleansing once cured (ch. 14). The chief point is how such an affliction rendered one unclean ceremonially and caused separation from the rest of Israel. Leprosy may be seen as a type of sin in several ways. (1) It begins inside the body and only becomes outwardly evident later on. (2) It is a filthy disease. (3) It is difficult to cure (though recoveries were made). (4) It began small, but eventuated in death.

13:1-2. A rising, a scab, or bright spot . . . like the plague of leprosy. Various diseases could be included within this general description, though leprosy is the common term used here.

3-8. The procedure was to have a suspected case appear before a priest for examination, and then either be separated from the camp, or return to normal activities depending on the results of the investigation.

er than the skin, and the hair thereof be not turned white; then the priest shall shut up *him that hath* the plague seven days:

5 And the priest shall look on him the seventh day: and, behold, *if* the plague in his sight be at a stay, *and* the plague spread not in the skin; then the priest shall shut him up seven days more:

6 And the priest shall look on him again the seventh day: and, behold, *if* the plague *be* somewhat dark, *and* the plague spread not in the skin, the priest shall pronounce him clean: it *is but* a scab: and he shall wash his clothes, and be clean.

7 But if the scab spread much abroad in the skin, after that he hath been seen of the priest for his cleansing, he shall be seen of the priest again:

8 And *if* the priest see that, behold, the scab spreadeth in the skin, then the priest shall pronounce him unclean: it *is* a leprosy.

9 ¶When the plague of leprosy is in a man, then he shall be brought unto the priest;

10 And the priest shall see *him:* and, behold, *if* the rising *be* white in the skin, and it have turned the hair white, and *there be* quick raw flesh in the rising;

11 It *is* an old leprosy in the skin of his flesh, and the priest shall pronounce him unclean, and shall not shut him up: for he *is* unclean.

12 And if a leprosy break out abroad in the skin, and the leprosy cover all the skin of *him that hath* the plague from his head even to his foot, wheresoever the priest looketh;

13 Then the priest shall consider: and, behold, *if* the leprosy have covered all his flesh, he shall pronounce *him* clean *that hath* the plague: it is all turned white: he *is* clean.

14 But when raw flesh appeareth in him, he shall be unclean.

15 And the priest shall see the raw flesh, and pronounce him to be unclean: *for* the raw flesh *is* unclean: it *is* a leprosy.

16 Or if the raw flesh turn again, and be changed unto white, he shall come unto the priest;

17 And the priest shall see him: and, behold, *if* the plague be turned into white; then the priest shall pronounce *him* clean *that hath* the plague: he *is* clean.

18 ¶The flesh also, in which, *even in* the skin thereof, was a boil, and is healed,

19 And in the place of the boil there be a white rising, or a bright spot, white, and somewhat reddish, and it be shewed to the priest;

20 And if, when the priest seeth it, behold, it *be* in sight lower than the skin, and the hair thereof be turned white; the priest shall pronounce him unclean: it *is* a plague of leprosy broken out of the boil.

21 But if the priest look on it, and, behold, *there be* no white hairs therein, and *if* it *be* not lower than the skin, but *be* somewhat dark; then the priest shall shut him up seven days:

22 And if it spread much abroad in

9-17. These verses deal with diagnosing a case of **an old leprosy** (vs. 11). In some cases what appears to be the disease might cover the entire body (vs. 12) but was not considered leprosy as such unless **raw flesh** (vs. 14) also appeared.

18-28. Differentiation is made between a boil or a burn and leprosy in this section. In order to make this distinction, a second look was always necessitated after **the priest shall shut him up seven days** (vs. 26), a literal week, and also symbolizing a perfect or complete period for observation.

the skin, then the priest shall pronounce him unclean: it *is* a plague.

23 But if the bright spot stay in his place, *and* spread not, it *is* a burning boil; and the priest shall pronounce him clean.

24 ¶Or if there be *any* flesh, in the skin whereof *there is* a hot burning, and the quick *flesh* that burneth have a white bright spot, somewhat reddish, or white;

25 Then the priest shall look upon it: and, behold, *if* the hair in the bright spot be turned white, and it *be in* sight deeper than the skin; it *is* a leprosy broken out of the burning: wherefore the priest shall pronounce him unclean: it *is* the plague of leprosy.

26 But if the priest look on it, and, behold, *there be* no white hair in the bright spot, and it *be* no lower than the *other* skin, but *be* somewhat dark; then the priest shall shut him up seven days:

27 And the priest shall look upon him the seventh day: *and* if it be spread much abroad in the skin, then the priest shall pronounce him unclean: it *is* the plague of leprosy.

28 And if the bright spot stay in his place, *and* spread not in the skin, but it *be* somewhat dark; it *is* a rising of the burning, and the priest shall pronounce him clean: for it *is* an inflammation of the burning.

29 ¶If a man or woman have a plague upon the head or the beard;

30 Then the priest shall see the plague: and, behold, if it *be* in sight deeper than the skin; *and there be* in it a yellow thin hair; then the priest shall pronounce him unclean: it *is* a dry scall, *even* a leprosy upon the head or beard.

31 And if the priest look on the plague of the scall, and, behold, it *be* not in sight deeper than the skin, and *that there is* no black hair in it; then the priest shall shut up *him that hath* the plague of the scall seven days:

32 And in the seventh day the priest shall look on the plague: and, behold, *if* the scall spread not, and there be in it no yellow hair, and the scall *be* not in sight deeper than the skin;

33 He shall be shaven, but the scall shall he not shave; and the priest shall shut up *him that hath* the scall seven days more:

34 And in the seventh day the priest shall look on the scall: and, behold, *if* the scall be not spread in the skin, nor *be* in sight deeper than the skin; then the priest shall pronounce him clean: and he shall wash his clothes, and be clean.

35 But if the scall spread much in the skin after his cleansing;

36 Then the priest shall look on him: and, behold, if the scall be spread in the skin, the priest shall not seek for yellow hair; he *is* unclean.

37 But if the scall be in his sight at a stay, and *that* there is black hair grown up therein; the scall is healed, he *is* clean: and the priest shall pronounce him clean.

38 ¶If a man also or a woman have in

29-44. Cases involving the **plague upon the head or the beard** (vs. 29) are considered in this section. Once again, there are the telltale signs that initially appear (vs. 30), the seven-day period(s) of observation (vss. 31-34), possible spreading or remission, and the final diagnosis (vss. 36, 37, and 44).

the skin of their flesh bright spots, *even* white bright spots;

39 Then the priest shall look: and, behold, *if* the bright spots in the skin of their flesh *be* darkish white; it *is* a freckled spot *that* groweth in the skin; he *is* clean.

40 And the man whose hair is fallen off his head, he *is* bald; *yet is* he clean.

41 And he that hath his hair fallen off from the part of his head toward his face, he *is* forehead bald: *yet is* he clean.

42 And if there be in the bald head, or bald forehead, a white reddish sore; it *is* a leprosy sprung up in his bald head, or his bald forehead.

43 Then the priest shall look upon it: and, behold, *if* the rising of the sore *be* white reddish in his bald head, or in his bald forehead, as the leprosy appeareth in the skin of the flesh;

44 He is a leprous man, he *is* unclean: the priest shall pronounce him utterly unclean; his plague *is* in his head.

45 And the leper in whom the plague *is*, his clothes shall be rent, and his head bare, and he shall put a covering upon his upper lip, and shall cry, Unclean, unclean.

46 All the days wherein the plague *shall be* in him he shall be defiled; he *is* unclean: he shall dwell alone; without the camp *shall* his habitation *be*.

47 ¶The garment also that the plague of leprosy is in, *whether it be* a woollen garment, or a linen garment;

48 Whether *it be* in the warp, or woof; of linen, or of woollen; whether in a skin, or in any thing made of skin;

49 And if the plague be greenish or reddish in the garment, or in the skin, either in the warp, or in the woof, or in any thing of skin; it *is* a plague of leprosy, and shall be shewed unto the priest:

50 And the priest shall look upon the plague, and shut up *it that hath* the plague seven days:

51 And he shall look on the plague on the seventh day: if the plague be spread in the garment, either in the warp, or in the woof, or in a skin, *or* in any work that is made of skin; the plague *is* a fretting leprosy; it *is* unclean.

52 He shall therefore burn that garment, whether warp or woof, in woollen or in linen, or any thing of skin, wherein the plague is: for it *is* a fretting leprosy; it shall be burnt in the fire.

53 And if the priest shall look, and, behold, the plague be not spread in the garment, either in the warp, or in the woof, or in any thing of skin;

54 Then the priest shall command that they wash *the thing* wherein the plague *is*, and he shall shut it up seven days more:

55 And the priest shall look on the plague, after that it is washed: and, behold, *if* the plague have not changed his colour, and the plague be not spread; it *is* unclean; thou shalt burn it in the fire;

45. A man pronounced unclean by the priest then began a terrible separation. His clothes were to be **rent** or torn as a sign of mourning. They would not need to be disposed of since he was unclean himself, and needed to wear something. He was to place an obvious **covering upon his upper lip,** and also call out the words **Unclean, unclean** to anyone that might come near, not to keep them from getting close enough to catch the disease, but to keep them from becoming ceremonially unclean.

46. All the days wherein the plague shall be in him leaves open the possibility of a recovery. Nevertheless, **he shall dwell alone; without the camp.**

47. The garment also. The following verses deal with linen and woolen garments, and skins that have a plague in them, apparently something like mildew.

48. The warp, or woof refers to the weaving of threads in opposite directions. The fault might lie in the one or the other.

49-52. After sufficient inspection and reinspection, if the mildew or infection remained, the garment or skin was to **be burnt in the fire** (vs. 52).

53-59. If after the usual seven days had elapsed and the priest found that **the plague be not spread in the garment** (vs. 53), they would **wash** it and observe it again after seven more days (vs. 54). From that point it was possible for the garment to be pronounced either clean or unclean.

it *is* fret inward, *whether* it *be* bare within or without.

56 And if the priest look, and, behold, the plague *be* somewhat dark after the washing of it; then he shall rend it out of the garment, or out of the skin, or out of the warp, or out of the woof:

57 And if it appear still in the garment, either in the warp, or in the woof, or in any thing of skin; it *is* a spreading *plague:* thou shalt burn that wherein the plague *is* with fire.

58 And the garment, either warp, or woof, or whatsoever thing of skin *it be,* which thou shalt wash, if the plague be departed from them, then it shall be washed the second time, and shall be clean.

59 This *is* the law of the plague of leprosy in a garment of woollen or linen, either in the warp, or woof, or any thing of skins, to pronounce it clean, or to pronounce it unclean.

CHAPTER 14

AND the LORD spake unto Moses, saying,

2 This shall be the law of the leper in the day of his cleansing: He shall be brought unto the priest:

3 And the priest shall go forth out of the camp; and the priest shall look, and, behold, *if* the plague of leprosy be healed in the leper;

4 Then shall the priest command to take for him that is to be cleansed two birds alive *and* clean, and cedar wood, and scarlet, and hyssop:

5 And the priest shall command that one of the birds be killed in an earthen vessel over running water:

6 As for the living bird, he shall take it, and the cedar wood, and the scarlet, and the hyssop, and shall dip them and the living bird in the blood of the bird *that was* killed over the running water:

7 And he shall sprinkle upon him that is to be cleansed from the leprosy seven times, and shall pronounce him clean, and shall let the living bird loose into the open field.

8 And he that is to be cleansed shall wash his clothes, and shave off all his hair, and wash himself in water, that he may be clean: and after that he shall come into the camp, and shall tarry abroad out of his tent seven days.

9 But it shall be on the seventh day, that he shall shave all his hair off his head and his beard and his eyebrows, even all his hair he shall shave off: and he shall wash his clothes, also he shall wash his flesh in water, and he shall be clean.

10 And on the eighth day he shall take two he lambs without blemish, and one ewe lamb of the first year without blemish, and three tenth deals of fine flour *for* a meat offering, mingled with oil, and one log of oil.

11 And the priest that maketh *him* clean shall present the man that is to be made clean, and those things, before the LORD, *at* the door of the tabernacle of the congregation:

12 And the priest shall take one he

14:1-2. Chapter 14 contains **the law of the leper in the day of his cleansing.** The first step was for the man to be seen by the priest.

3. The priest was obligated to go outside the camp to examine the one claiming to be clean of the leprosy.

4. If the leper was found to be clean, two birds were required for the ceremony of cleansing. This pictured in a remarkable way the completed death and resurrection of the Lord Jesus Christ in our behalf.

5-6. One bird was killed and its blood retained in a vessel. The living bird was then dipped into the blood of the dead bird to be identified with it in its death.

7. The former leper was then sprinkled with the blood of the dead bird seven times, as a perfect application of the sacrifice; and the live bird was freed. Thus, resurrection to a new life was pictured as the live bird was released. The man was pronounced **clean.** Resurrection proclaims a justification that is complete (Rom 4:25).

8-9. The cleansed man could then wash his clothes, shave, bathe, and return to the camp. He was to abide in camp for **seven days** before repeating the process.

10-13. The next procedure was to offer a small ram as a trespass offering (vs. 12) along with a cereal or meal offering (one tenth of the three tenths of meal readied in verse 10).

lamb, and offer him for a trespass offering, and the log of oil, and wave
them *for* a wave offering before the
LORD:
13 And he shall slay the lamb in the
place where he shall kill the sin offering
and the burnt offering, in the holy
place: for as the sin offering *is* the
priest's, *so is* the trespass offering: it *is*
most holy:
14 And the priest shall take *some* of
the blood of the trespass offering, and
the priest shall put *it* upon the tip of the
right ear of him that is to be cleansed,
and upon the thumb of his right hand,
and upon the great toe of his right foot:
15 And the priest shall take *some* of
the log of oil, and pour *it* into the palm
of his own left hand:
16 And the priest shall dip his right
finger in the oil that *is* in his left hand,
and shall sprinkle of the oil with his finger seven times before the LORD:
17 And of the rest of the oil that *is* in
his hand shall the priest put upon the
tip of the right ear of him that is to be
cleansed, and upon the thumb of his
right hand, and upon the great toe of
his right foot, upon the blood of the
trespass offering:
18 And the remnant of the oil that *is*
in the priest's hand he shall pour upon
the head of him that is to be cleansed:
and the priest shall make an atonement
for him before the LORD.
19 And the priest shall offer the sin
offering, and make an atonement for
him that is to be cleansed from his uncleanness; and afterward he shall kill
the burnt offering:
20 And the priest shall offer the burnt
offering and the meat offering upon the
altar: and the priest shall make an
atonement for him, and he shall be
clean.
21 And if he *be* poor, and cannot get
so much; then he shall take one lamb
for a trespass offering to be waved, to
make an atonement for him, and one
tenth deal of fine flour mingled with oil
for a meat offering, and a log of oil;
22 And two turtledoves, or two
young pigeons, such as he is able to get;
and the one shall be a sin offering, and
the other a burnt offering.
23 And he shall bring them on the
eighth day for his cleansing unto the
priest, unto the door of the tabernacle
of the congregation, before the LORD.
24 And the priest shall take the lamb
of the trespass offering, and the log of
oil, and the priest shall wave them *for* a
wave offering before the LORD:
25 And he shall kill the lamb of the
trespass offering, and the priest shall
take *some* of the blood of the trespass
offering, and shall put *it* upon the tip of the
right ear of him that is to be cleansed,
and upon the thumb of his right hand,
and upon the great toe of his right foot:
26 And the priest shall pour of the oil
into the palm of his own left hand:
27 And the priest shall sprinkle with
his right finger *some* of the oil that *is* in
his left hand seven times before the
LORD:
28 And the priest shall put of the oil
that *is* in his hand upon the tip of the

14-18. The blood of the trespass offering was then applied to
the right ear . . . thumb and . . . big **toe** of the ex-leper. He was
seven times sprinkled with oil, and then the oil was applied in
the same manner as the blood. The rest of the oil was poured out
on his head.

19-20. The ewe lamb was used for the sin offering, which
came next. The other young ram was made a burnt offering to
complete the ceremony.

21-23. Provision was made for the poor to bring two doves or
young pigeons for the sin and burnt offerings, but a he lamb
still had to be secured for the initial trespass offering.

24-32. The process for restoring the poor to cleanness was the
same as that in verses 10-20, except that certain different animals were allowed for the two final sacrifices.

right ear of him that is to be cleansed, and upon the thumb of his right hand, and upon the great toe of his right foot, upon the place of the blood of the trespass offering:

29 And the rest of the oil that *is* in the priest's hand he shall put upon the head of him that is to be cleansed, to make an atonement for him before the LORD.

30 And he shall offer the one of the turtledoves, or of the young pigeons, such as he can get;

31 *Even* such as he is able to get, the one *for* a sin offering, and the other *for* a burnt offering, with the meat offering: and the priest shall make an atonement for him that is to be cleansed before the LORD.

32 This *is* the law *of him* in whom *is* the plague of leprosy, whose hand is not able to get *that which pertaineth* to his cleansing.

33 ¶And the LORD spake unto Moses and unto Aaron, saying,

34 When ye be come into the land of Canaan, which I give to you for a possession, and I put the plague of leprosy in a house of the land of your possession;

35 And he that owneth the house shall come and tell the priest, saying, It seemeth to me *there is* as it were a plague in the house:

36 Then the priest shall command that they empty the house, before the priest go *into it* to see the plague, that all that *is* in the house be not made unclean: and afterward the priest shall go in to see the house:

37 And he shall look on the plague, and, behold, *if* the plague *be* in the walls of the house with hollow strakes, greenish or reddish, which in sight *are* lower than the wall;

38 Then the priest shall go out of the house to the door of the house, and shut up the house seven days:

39 And the priest shall come again the seventh day, and shall look: and, behold, *if* the plague be spread in the walls of the house;

40 Then the priest shall command that they take away the stones in which the plague *is*, and they shall cast them into an unclean place without the city:

41 And he shall cause the house to be scraped within round about, and they shall pour out the dust that they scrape off without the city into an unclean place:

42 And they shall take other stones, and put *them* in the place of those stones; and he shall take other morter, and shall plaister the house.

43 And if the plague come again, and break out in the house, after that he hath taken away the stones, and after he hath scraped the house, and after it is plaistered;

44 Then the priest shall come and

33. And the LORD spake unto Moses and unto Aaron. Aaron was also a direct recipient of revelation at times (Lev 11:1; 13:1; 15:1) where certain laws directly related to his duties.

34. When ye be come into the land of Canaan. The obvious significance of this statement is that Israel was at that time living in the Sinai Peninsula in tents and had not yet arrived at their promised possession where they would one day dwell in stone houses. This clearly argues against the liberal theory of the dating of the Pentateuch (see Introduction). **The plague of leprosy in a house.** This speaks of mildew, or some rotting influence, in the mortar of the stones.

35-45. If such a condition was found to exist in a dwelling, it was to be examined by a priest after the contents were removed (vss. 36-37), sealed up for seven days before a reexamination (vss. 38-39), and then repaired if the plague had not spread (vss. 40-42), or destroyed if the plague later returned (vss. 43-45).

220

look, and, behold, *if* the plague be spread in the house, it *is* a fretting leprosy in the house: it *is* unclean.

45 And he shall break down the house, the stones of it, and the timber thereof, and all the morter of the house; and he shall carry *them* forth out of the city into an unclean place.

46 Moreover he that goeth into the house all the while that it is shut up shall be unclean until the even.

47 And he that lieth in the house shall wash his clothes; and he that eateth in the house shall wash his clothes.

48 And if the priest shall come in, and look *upon it*, and, behold, the plague hath not spread in the house, after the house was plaistered: then the priest shall pronounce the house clean, because the plague is healed.

49 And he shall take to cleanse the house two birds, and cedar wood, and scarlet, and hyssop:

50 And he shall kill the one of the birds in an earthen vessel over running water:

51 And he shall take the cedar wood, and the hyssop, and the scarlet, and the living bird, and dip them in the blood of the slain bird, and in the running water, and sprinkle the house seven times:

52 And he shall cleanse the house with the blood of the bird, and with the running water, and with the living bird, and with the cedar wood, and with the hyssop, and with the scarlet:

53 But he shall let go the living bird out of the city into the open fields, and make an atonement for the house: and it shall be clean.

54 This *is* the law for all manner of plague of leprosy, and scall,

55 And for the leprosy of a garment, and of a house,

56 And for a rising, and for a scab, and for a bright spot:

57 To teach when *it is* unclean, and when *it is* clean: this *is* the law of leprosy.

CHAPTER 15

AND the LORD spake unto Moses and to Aaron, saying,

2 Speak unto the children of Israel, and say unto them, When any man hath a running issue out of his flesh, *because of* his issue he *is* unclean.

3 And this shall be his uncleanness in his issue: whether his flesh run with his issue, or his flesh be stopped from his issue, it *is* his uncleanness.

4 Every bed, whereon he lieth that hath the issue, is unclean: and every thing, whereon he sitteth, shall be unclean.

5 And whosoever toucheth his bed shall wash his clothes, and bathe *himself* in water, and be unclean until the even.

6 And he that sitteth on *any* thing whereon he sat that hath the issue shall wash his clothes, and bathe *himself* in water, and be unclean until the even.

7 And he that toucheth the flesh of him that hath the issue shall wash his

---

46-47. Any contact with a contaminated house rendered the occupant and its utensils unclean. Ritual washing was required for its cleansing, too.

48-57. The procedure for the cleansing of a **house** was the same as that for the initial admission of a leper back into the camp, i.e., the killing of a bird, sprinkling its blood on the house, dipping the live bird in the other's blood, and releasing it in an open field (cf. vss. 4-7).

4. Ceremonial laws relating to discharges. 15:1-33.

This chapter speaks in a general manner of certain discharges from the body of a man (vss. 1-18) and those of females (vss. 19-33), together with the attaching uncleanness and the ceremonies to be followed for subsequent cleansing.

15:1-2. Moses and Aaron are here informed about what regulations apply **When any man hath a running issue out of his flesh.** Whether this issue was sexual is not stated and should not necessarily be inferred. It could be any of a number of general issues, such as a discharge of blood, pus, or other fluid from a wound, lesion, boil, etc. All would be covered, and any would render a man unclean.

3-6. As long as the condition continued, even if the issue stopped flowing temporarily, he was unclean. In addition, any bed or chair touched by him became unclean, and any person who contacted those items also became unclean until evening, subsequent to a ritual bathing and washing of clothes.

7-12. Naturally, direct contact with the unclean individual caused the uncleanness to spread further, whether to persons (vs. 7), or to objects (vss. 8-9). Even the secondary touch of

clothes, and bathe *himself* in water, and be unclean until the even.

8 And if he that hath the issue spit upon him that is clean; then he shall wash his clothes, and bathe *himself* in water, and be unclean until the even.

9 And what saddle soever he rideth upon that hath the issue shall be unclean.

10 And whosoever toucheth any thing that was under him shall be unclean until the even: and he that beareth *any of* those things shall wash his clothes, and bathe *himself* in water, and be unclean until the even.

11 And whomsoever he toucheth that hath the issue, and hath not rinsed his hands in water, he shall wash his clothes, and bathe *himself* in water, and be unclean until the even.

12 And the vessel of earth, that he toucheth which hath the issue, shall be broken: and every vessel of wood shall be rinsed in water.

13 And when he that hath an issue is cleansed of his issue; then he shall number to himself seven days for his cleansing, and wash his clothes, and bathe his flesh in running water, and shall be clean.

14 And on the eighth day he shall take to him two turtledoves, or two young pigeons, and come before the LORD unto the door of the tabernacle of the congregation, and give them unto the priest:

15 And the priest shall offer them, the one *for* a sin offering, and the other *for* a burnt offering; and the priest shall make an atonement for him before the LORD for his issue.

16 And if any man's seed of copulation go out from him, then he shall wash all his flesh in water, and be unclean until the even.

17 And every garment, and every skin, whereon is the seed of copulation, shall be washed with water, and be unclean until the even.

18 The woman also with whom man shall lie *with* seed of copulation, they shall *both* bathe *themselves* in water, and be unclean until the even.

19 ¶And if a woman have an issue, *and* her issue in her flesh be blood, she shall be put apart seven days: and whosoever toucheth her shall be unclean until the even.

20 And every thing that she lieth upon in her separation shall be unclean: every thing also that she sitteth upon shall be unclean.

21 And whosoever toucheth her bed shall wash his clothes, and bathe *himself* in water, and be unclean until the even.

22 And whosoever toucheth any thing that she sat upon shall wash his clothes, and bathe *himself* in water, and be unclean until the even.

23 And if it *be* on *her* bed, or on any

those objects would render one unclean and require the ritual washing.

13-15. After the **issue** was healed, seven days were counted; and then the ceremonial bathing was performed. The next day two birds were offered to **make an atonement,** one for a sin offering and the other for a burnt offering.

16-17. **Any man's seed of copulation** refers to a seminal discharge, whether voluntary or involuntary. It produced uncleanness until the next sunset; but no offering was required, only the ceremonial washing.

18. Normal husband-wife relations also rendered the couple unclean and required the same bathing. This is why Exodus 19:15 and I Samuel 21:4-5 inquire regarding this. Ceremonial purity was required for certain feasts, etc. This does not mean that the marriage act is impure any more than chapter 12 condemns childbirth. But such is connected with the passing on of a sinful nature in the creation of a new life. See Hebrews 13:4 and I Corinthians 7:3-5 for the normative New Testament teaching on this subject.

19-23. The woman's normal menstrual period is indicated in this section. Seven days is given to cover all normal cases sufficiently, and because of the prominent symbolic use of that number. She passed her uncleanness only to persons she touched or to things upon which she sat or lay. Thus, she was not restricted from performing her normal household duties.

thing whereon she sitteth, when he toucheth it, he shall be unclean until the even.

24 And if any man lie with her at all, and her flowers be upon him, he shall be unclean seven days; and all the bed whereon he lieth shall be unclean.

25 And if a woman have an issue of her blood many days out of the time of her separation, or if it run beyond the time of her separation; all the days of the issue of her uncleanness shall be as the days of her separation: she *shall be* unclean.

26 Every bed whereon she lieth all the days of her issue shall be unto her as the bed of her separation: and whatsoever she sitteth upon shall be unclean, as the uncleanness of her separation.

27 And whosoever toucheth those things shall be unclean, and shall wash his clothes, and bathe *himself* in water, and be unclean until the even.

28 But if she be cleansed of her issue, then she shall number to herself seven days, and after that she shall be clean.

29 And on the eighth day she shall take unto her two turtles, or two young pigeons, and bring them unto the priest, to the door of the tabernacle of the congregation.

30 And the priest shall offer the one *for* a sin offering, and the other *for* a burnt offering; and the priest shall make an atonement for her before the LORD for the issue of her uncleanness.

31 Thus shall ye separate the children of Israel from their uncleanness; that they die not in their uncleanness, when they defile my tabernacle that *is* among them.

32 This *is* the law of him that hath an issue, and *of him* whose seed goeth from him, and is defiled therewith;

33 And of her that is sick of her flowers, and of him that hath an issue, of the man, and of the woman, and of him that lieth with her that is unclean.

CHAPTER 16

AND the LORD spake unto Moses after the death of the two sons of Aaron, when they offered before the LORD, and died;

2 And the LORD said unto Moses, Speak unto Aaron thy brother, that he come not at all times into the holy *place* within the vail before the mercy seat, which *is* upon the ark; that he die not: for I will appear in the cloud upon the mercy seat.

3 Thus shall Aaron come into the holy *place:* with a young bullock for a sin offering, and a ram for a burnt offering.

4 He shall put on the holy linen coat, and he shall have the linen breeches upon his flesh, and shall be girded with a linen girdle, and with the linen mitre shall he be attired: these *are* holy garments; therefore shall he wash his flesh in water, and *so* put them on.

5 And he shall take of the congrega-

24. This verse must refer to a case where the menstrual flow comes on initially and unexpectedly during the marriage act, because Leviticus 20:18 categorically forbids any wilful practice of the marriage act within the **seven days** of uncleanness.

25-30. Unnatural issues from the **woman** are treated next (vss. 25-27). For these the customary sacrifices are required on the eighth day after cleansing (vss. 28-30), but none were offered for her normal monthly issue of blood.

31-33. These verses restate the nature of this chapter. It is to teach and impose a ceremonial uncleanness for certain bodily discharges. These are no longer in force in the New Testament.

B. Access Maintained Through the Day of Atonement. 16:1-34.

The Day of Atonement was the most important single day in the entire Jewish calendar. The Hebrew expression is the well known Yom Kippur. On this day (tenth day of the seventh month, starting from March/April) the nation was reconciled to God once again for another year. Genesis 4 presents a sacrifice for the individual (Abel); Exodus 12 tells of a sacrifice for each family (the Passover lamb); Leviticus 16 relates the sacrifice for the nation; but John 1:29 boldly proclaims Jesus Christ as the Lamb of God who bears away the sin of the world.

16:1. The revelation of chapter 16 follows the death of Nadab and Abihu related in chapter 10. All of the legislation of Leviticus was given in approximately a thirty-day period.

2-4. The high priest, **Aaron,** was never to go beyond the inner veil into the Holy of Holies without bringing blood to sprinkle on the golden mercy seat to atone for sin. In addition Aaron had to be properly attired as specified earlier (See Ex 28 and Lev 8).

5-6. Three animals were needed to make atonement for the

tion of the children of Israel two kids of the goats for a sin offering, and one ram for a burnt offering.

6 And Aaron shall offer his bullock of the sin offering, which *is* for himself, and make an atonement for himself, and for his house.

7 And he shall take the two goats, and present them before the LORD *at* the door of the tabernacle of the congregation.

8 And Aaron shall cast lots upon the two goats; one lot for the LORD, and the other lot for the scapegoat.

9 And Aaron shall bring the goat upon which the LORD's lot fell, and offer him *for* a sin offering.

10 But the goat, on which the lot fell to be the scapegoat, shall be presented alive before the LORD, to make an atonement with him, *and* to let him go for a scapegoat into the wilderness.

11 And Aaron shall bring the bullock of the sin offering, which *is* for himself, and shall make an atonement for himself, and for his house, and shall kill the bullock of the sin offering which *is* for himself:

12 And he shall take a censer full of burning coals of fire from off the altar before the LORD, and his hands full of sweet incense beaten small, and bring *it* within the vail:

13 And he shall put the incense upon the fire before the LORD, that the cloud of the incense may cover the mercy seat that *is* upon the testimony, that he die not:

14 And he shall take of the blood of the bullock, and sprinkle *it* with his finger upon the mercy seat eastward; and before the mercy seat shall he sprinkle of the blood with his finger seven times.

15 Then shall he kill the goat of the sin offering, that *is* for the people, and bring his blood within the vail, and do with that blood as he did with the blood of the bullock, and sprinkle it upon the mercy seat, and before the mercy seat:

16 And he shall make an atonement for the holy *place*, because of the uncleanness of the children of Israel, and because of their transgressions in all their sins: and so shall he do for the tabernacle of the congregation, that remaineth among them in the midst of their uncleanness.

17 And there shall be no man in the tabernacle of the congregation when he goeth in to make an atonement in the holy *place*, until he come out, and have made an atonement for himself, and for his household, and for all the congregation of Israel.

18 And he shall go out unto the altar that *is* before the LORD, and make an atonement for it; and shall take of the blood of the bullock, and of the blood of the goat, and put *it* upon the horns of the altar round about.

19 And he shall sprinkle of the blood upon it with his finger seven times, and cleanse it, and hallow it from the uncleanness of the children of Israel.

people; but before that could begin, Aaron had to make atonement for himself and his family by the sacrifice of a sin offering. He must first be cleansed and accepted before he could intercede for others. In contrast, Hebrews 7:26-27 speaks of Christ, our High Priest, who was ". . . holy, harmless, undefiled, separate from sinners . . . Who needeth not daily, as those high priests, to offer up sacrifice, first for his own sins, and then for the people's . . . ."

7-10. Just as two birds were required for the cleansing of the leper, so **two goats** were needed to bring atonement to the nation. These verses are a preview of the procedure to be followed.

11-14. First, then, Aaron offered a bull for a sin offering for himself and his family (vs. 11). Taking the bullock's **blood** with him, Aaron placed hot coals from the brazen altar into the small portable golden censer, filled his hands with incense, and entered into the sacred presence of God behind the veil, where he stood before the ark of the covenant with its mercy seat. There he filled the room with incense, which speaks of prayer, and also sprinkled the bull's blood on the mercy seat seven times.

15-20. Then Aaron shall . . . **kill the goat of the sin offering** (vs. 15) after casting lots to see which of the two goats would be slain, (vss. 8-9). With that blood Aaron again entered inside the veil and sprinkled this blood on the mercy seat to atone for the holy place, then the same for the tabernacle, and finally for the altar of burnt offerings. The blood was fully applied.

20 ¶And when he hath made an end of reconciling the holy *place,* and the tabernacle of the congregation, and the altar, he shall bring the live goat:

21 And Aaron shall lay both his hands upon the head of the live goat, and confess over him all the iniquities of the children of Israel, and all their transgressions in all their sins, putting them upon the head of the goat, and shall send *him* away by the hand of a fit man into the wilderness:

22 And the goat shall bear upon him all their iniquities unto a land not inhabited: and he shall let go the goat in the wilderness.

23 And Aaron shall come into the tabernacle of the congregation, and shall put off the linen garments, which he put on when he went into the holy *place,* and shall leave them there:

24 And he shall wash his flesh with water in the holy place, and put on his garments, and come forth, and offer his burnt offering, and the burnt offering of the people, and make an atonement for himself, and for the people.

25 And the fat of the sin offering shall he burn upon the altar.

26 And he that let go the goat for the scapegoat shall wash his clothes, and bathe his flesh in water, and afterward come into the camp.

27 And the bullock *for* the sin offering, and the goat *for* the sin offering, whose blood was brought in to make atonement in the holy *place,* shall *one* carry forth without the camp; and they shall burn in the fire their skins, and their flesh, and their dung.

28 And he that burneth them shall wash his clothes, and bathe his flesh in water, and afterward he shall come into the camp.

29 ¶And *this* shall be a statute for ever unto you: *that* in the seventh month, on the tenth *day* of the month, ye shall afflict your souls, and do no work at all, *whether it be* one of your own country, or a stranger that sojourneth among you:

30 For on that day shall *the priest* make an atonement for you, to cleanse you, *that* ye may be clean from all your sins before the LORD.

31 It *shall be* a sabbath of rest unto you, and ye shall afflict your souls, by a statute for ever.

32 And the priest, whom he shall anoint, and whom he shall consecrate to minister in the priest's office in his father's stead, shall make the atonement, and shall put on the linen clothes, *even* the holy garments:

33 And he shall make an atonement for the holy sanctuary, and he shall make an atonement for the tabernacle of the congregation, and for the altar, and he shall make an atonement for the priests, and for all the people of the congregation.

34 And this shall be an everlasting statute unto you, to make an atonement for the children of Israel for all their sins once a year. And he did as the LORD commanded Moses.

21-22. At that point, Aaron placed his hands on the head of the living goat, the scapegoat, confessed the sins of the people on it, **putting them upon the head of the goat,** and then sent the goat away into the wilderness. This symbolism pictures not only Christ's death for our sins in the first goat, but also His bearing away the sins of the world in the second goat.

23-28. Later, after washing and changing clothes, Aaron offered two burnt offerings, one for himself and one for the people. These offerings were disposed of in their prescribed manner.

29-31. The day of atonement was a national day of fasting, and also **a sabbath** during which no work could be done, no matter on what day of the week the seventh day of the tenth month fell.

32-34. This was **an everlasting statute . . . to make an atonement for the children of Israel for all their sins once a year.** Hebrews 9:7 portrays this, while Hebrews 9:12 contrasts this with Christ's work, saying, "Neither by the blood of goats and calves, but by his own blood he entered in once into the holy place, having obtained eternal redemption for us."

CHAPTER 17

AND the LORD spake unto Moses, saying,

2 Speak unto Aaron, and unto his sons, and unto all the children of Israel, and say unto them; This *is* the thing which the LORD hath commanded, saying,

3 What man soever *there be* of the house of Israel, that killeth an ox, or lamb, or goat, in the camp, or that killeth *it* out of the camp,

4 And bringeth it not unto the door of the tabernacle of the congregation, to offer an offering unto the LORD before the tabernacle of the LORD; blood shall be imputed unto that man; he hath shed blood; and that man shall be cut off from among his people:

5 To the end that the children of Israel may bring their sacrifices, which they offer in the open field, even that they may bring them unto the LORD, unto the door of the tabernacle of the congregation, unto the priest, and offer them *for* peace offerings unto the LORD.

6 And the priest shall sprinkle the blood upon the altar of the LORD *at* the door of the tabernacle of the congregation, and burn the fat for a sweet savour unto the LORD.

7 And they shall no more offer their sacrifices unto devils, after whom they have gone a whoring. This shall be a statute for ever unto them throughout their generations.

8 And thou shalt say unto them, Whatsoever man *there be* of the house of Israel, or of the strangers which sojourn among you, that offereth a burnt offering or sacrifice,

9 And bringeth it not unto the door of the tabernacle of the congregation, to offer it unto the LORD; even that man shall be cut off from among his people.

10 ¶And whatsoever man *there be* of the house of Israel, or of the strangers that sojourn among you, that eateth any manner of blood; I will even set my face against that soul that eateth blood, and will cut him off from among his people.

11 For the life of the flesh *is* in the blood: and I have given it to you upon the altar to make an atonement for your souls: for it *is* the blood *that* maketh an atonement for the soul.

12 Therefore I said unto the children of Israel, No soul of you shall eat blood, neither shall any stranger that sojourneth among you eat blood.

13 And whatsoever man *there be* of the children of Israel, or of the strangers that sojourn among you, which hunteth and catcheth any beast or fowl that may be eaten; he shall even pour out the blood thereof, and cover it with dust.

14 For *it is* the life of all flesh; the blood of it *is* for the life thereof: therefore I said unto the children of Israel, Ye shall eat the blood of no manner of flesh: for the life of all flesh *is* the blood

C. Access Maintained Through Properly Regulated Conduct. 17:1-27:34.

1. Laws regulating sacrifice. 17:1-16.

17:1-2. This chapter contains some very solemn commands which are related both to chapter 16 and to the sacrifices of chapters 1-7.

3-4. What man soever. These regulations have universal application. The killing of any animal for food had to be done at the tabernacle where all regular sacrifices were made. A violator would be **cut off from among his people,** a reference either to death (Ex 31:14), or to excommunication.

5-9. There are several reasons for this regulation. Negatively, it prevents **sacrifices unto devils** (vs. 7) out **in the open field** (vs. 5). Israel apparently picked up a good bit of idolatry in Egypt and this had to be ended.

10-14. On the positive side, this law guarded the sanctity of life, which was in the blood. The blood was what God ordained should make the atonement (vs. 11). It was His. Therefore, it must be treated properly. Animals killed by the priests at the tabernacle entrance would have their blood properly drained and poured out, not carelessly eaten.

thereof: whosoever eateth it shall be cut off.

15 And every soul that eateth that which died *of itself*, or that which was torn *with beasts, whether it be* one of your own country, or a stranger, he shall both wash his clothes, and bathe *himself* in water, and be unclean until the even: then shall he be clean.

16 But if he wash *them* not, nor bathe his flesh; then he shall bear his iniquity.

CHAPTER 18

AND the LORD spake unto Moses, saying,

2 Speak unto the children of Israel, and say unto them, I am the LORD your God.

3 After the doings of the land of Egypt, wherein ye dwelt, shall ye not do: and after the doings of the land of Canaan, whither I bring you, shall ye not do: neither shall ye walk in their ordinances.

4 Ye shall do my judgments, and keep mine ordinances, to walk therein: I *am* the LORD your God.

5 Ye shall therefore keep my statutes, and my judgments: which if a man do, he shall live in them: I *am* the LORD.

6 ¶None of you shall approach to any that is near of kin to him, to uncover *their* nakedness: I *am* the LORD.

7 The nakedness of thy father, or the nakedness of thy mother, shalt thou not uncover: she *is* thy mother; thou shalt not uncover her nakedness.

8 The nakedness of thy father's wife shalt thou not uncover: it *is* thy father's nakedness.

9 The nakedness of thy sister, the daughter of thy father, or daughter of thy mother, *whether she be* born at home, or born abroad, *even* their nakedness thou shalt not uncover.

10 The nakedness of thy son's daughter, or of thy daughter's daughter, *even* their nakedness thou shalt not uncover: for theirs *is* thine own nakedness.

11 The nakedness of thy father's wife's daughter, begotten of thy father, she *is* thy sister, thou shalt not uncover her nakedness.

12 Thou shalt not uncover the nakedness of thy father's sister: she *is* thy father's near kinswoman.

13 Thou shalt not uncover the nakedness of thy mother's sister: for she *is* thy mother's near kinswoman.

14 Thou shalt not uncover the naked-

15-16. It was possible that a man might eat of an animal that had died by itself or at the horns of another beast—meaning that the blood would not have been properly cared for. If that were discovered, that man had to undergo the ritual cleansing process.

2. Laws regulating proper moral conduct. 18:1-20:27.

18:1-3. The moral regulations which follow are grounded in God's declaration, **I am the LORD your God** (vs. 2). Israel's conduct is not to be patterned after either the Egyptians or the Canaanites, both of whom had practices not compatible with the nature of a holy God and a people who were to exhibit that likeness as His sons and daughters.

4-5. The solemnity of these verses cannot be overemphasized. These are God's laws and they must be obeyed.

6. What is forbidden here in a summary declaration is **to uncover their nakedness,** referring to those who are **near of kin.** That marriage to one who is near of kin is prohibited is clear from verse 18, where it prohibits taking a sister of one's wife as an additional wife (uncovering her nakedness) while the first one still lives. It is not just illicit sexual relations with near of kin that are forbidden. They are already forbidden with any person other than one's own wife in the seventh commandment (Ex 20:14). The Egyptians frequently married the near of kin mentioned in this chapter, and the Canaanites practiced orgiastic rites with near of kin. God wants His people to be different. It is not certain that any biological or genetic considerations are in view in these laws, even though some feel that barrenness or weak offspring might result from such unions. It seems that moral and social standards are the chief ends of these regulations.

7-8. The nakedness of thy father, or the nakedness of thy mother. What is forbidden is marriage to one's mother, but it shames the honor of the father because of the one flesh relationship he has had with that wife. A stepmother is in view in verse 8.

9-17. Various relationships are covered in these verses, including a half sister or stepsister (vs. 9), granddaughter (vs. 10), half sister or perhaps full sister (vs. 11), aunts (vss. 12-13), wife of a blood uncle (vs. 14), **daughter-in-law** (vs. 15), sister-in-law (vs. 16), and a woman and her daughter or granddaughter (vs. 17).

ness of thy father's brother, thou shalt not approach to his wife: she *is* thine aunt.

15 Thou shalt not uncover the nakedness of thy daughter in law: she *is* thy son's wife; thou shalt not uncover her nakedness.

16 Thou shalt not uncover the nakedness of thy brother's wife: it *is* thy brother's nakedness.

17 Thou shalt not uncover the nakedness of a woman and her daughter, neither shalt thou take her son's daughter, or her daughter's daughter, to uncover her nakedness; *for* they *are* her near kinswomen: it *is* wickedness.

18 Neither shalt thou take a wife to her sister, to vex *her*, to uncover her nakedness, beside the other in her life *time*.

19 Also thou shalt not approach unto a woman to uncover her nakedness, as long as she is put apart for her uncleanness.

20 Moreover thou shalt not lie carnally with thy neighbour's wife, to defile thyself with her.

21 And thou shalt not let any of thy seed pass through *the* fire to Mŏlĕch, neither shalt thou profane the name of thy God: I *am* the LORD.

22 Thou shalt not lie with mankind, as with womankind: it *is* abomination.

23 Neither shalt thou lie with any beast to defile thyself therewith: neither shall any woman stand before a beast to lie down thereto: it *is* confusion.

24 Defile not ye yourselves in any of these things: for in all these the nations are defiled which I cast out before you:

25 And the land is defiled: therefore I do visit the iniquity thereof upon it, and the land itself vomiteth out her inhabitants.

26 Ye shall therefore keep my statutes and my judgments, and shall not commit *any* of these abominations; *neither* any of your own nation, nor any stranger that sojourneth among you:

27 (For all these abominations have the men of the land done, which *were* before you, and the land is defiled;)

28 That the land spue not you out also, when ye defile it, as it spued out the nations that *were* before you.

29 For whosoever shall commit any of these abominations, even the souls that commit *them* shall be cut off from among their people.

30 Therefore shall ye keep mine ordinance, that *ye* commit not *any one* of these abominable customs, which were committed before you, and that ye defile not yourselves therein: I *am* the LORD your God.

CHAPTER 19

AND the LORD spake unto Moses, saying,

18. One could not be married to two sisters at the same time. This forbids divorcing a woman in order to marry her sister. However, when one's wife is no longer living, he may marry his first wife's sister. The probable reason why the regular term for getting married is not used throughout this chapter is that God would not consider these unions to be true marriages. Thus the common terminology is **to uncover her nakedness.**

19. It was improper for a husband and wife to have marriage relations during the wife's seven-day menstrual uncleanness (cf. Lev 15:24). This regulation must also have served to aid the wife during her period of discomfort.

20-21. God repeated again His prohibition of adultery. No Israelite children were to be offered to Molech, an Ammonite god (I Kgs 11:7).

22. Homosexual relations or sodomy are prohibited and called **abomination.** God hates such practices, though He still loves the sinner and wants to see him repent. We as well should have God's view of these matters. See Romans 1:27-28.

23. Bestiality, or mating with an animal, has been and still is practiced in many places around the world. This is termed **confusion,** or perversion.

24-25. The warning is clear. God was casting out the Canaanites, Amorites, and others because the cup of their iniquity was full (Gen 15:16). One day, sad to say, Israel would exceed the wickedness of those they were going to replace (II Kgs 21:11).

26-30. Israel also was responsible for strangers and sojourners. We are, indeed, our brother's keeper. The picture of the land spewing out its inhabitants is that of a person vomiting up that which causes complete nausea and sickness.

19:1-2. **Ye shall be holy: for I the LORD your God am holy.** The various laws that are here given or repeated are based on the

2 Speak unto all the congregation of the children of Israel, and say unto them, Ye shall be holy: for I the Lord your God *am* holy.

3 ¶Ye shall fear every man his mother, and his father, and keep my sabbaths: I *am* the Lord your God.

4 ¶Turn ye not unto idols, nor make to yourselves molten gods: I *am* the Lord your God.

5 ¶And if ye offer a sacrifice of peace offerings unto the Lord, ye shall offer it at your own will.

6 It shall be eaten the same day ye offer it, and on the morrow: and if ought remain until the third day, it shall be burnt in the fire.

7 And if it be eaten at all on the third day, it *is* abominable; it shall not be accepted.

8 Therefore *every one* that eateth it shall bear his iniquity, because he hath profaned the hallowed thing of the Lord: and that soul shall be cut off from among his people.

9 ¶And when ye reap the harvest of your land, thou shalt not wholly reap the corners of thy field, neither shalt thou gather the gleanings of thy harvest.

10 And thou shalt not glean thy vineyard, neither shalt thou gather *every* grape of thy vineyard; thou shalt leave them for the poor and stranger: I *am* the Lord your God.

11 ¶Ye shall not steal, neither deal falsely, neither lie one to another.

12 ¶And ye shall not swear by my name falsely, neither shalt thou profane the name of thy God: I *am* the Lord.

13 ¶Thou shalt not defraud thy neighbour, neither rob *him*: the wages of him that is hired shall not abide with thee all night until the morning.

14 ¶Thou shalt not curse the deaf, nor put a stumbling block before the blind, but shalt fear thy God: I *am* the Lord.

15 ¶Ye shall do no unrighteousness in judgment: thou shalt not respect the person of the poor, nor honour the person of the mighty: *but* in righteousness shalt thou judge thy neighbour.

16 ¶Thou shalt not go up and down *as* a talebearer among thy people: neither shalt thou stand against the blood of thy neighbour: I *am* the Lord.

17 ¶Thou shalt not hate thy brother in thine heart: thou shalt in any wise rebuke thy neighbour, and not suffer sin upon him.

18 ¶Thou shalt not avenge, nor bear any grudge against the children of thy people, but thou shalt love thy neighbour as thyself: I *am* the Lord.

19 ¶Ye shall keep my statutes. Thou shalt not let thy cattle gender with a diverse kind: thou shalt not sow thy field with mingled seed: neither shall a garment mingled of linen and woollen come upon thee.

20 ¶And whosoever lieth carnally with a woman, that *is* a bondmaid, betrothed to an husband, and not at all redeemed, nor freedom given her; she

facts of God's holiness. This concept is stated repeatedly throughout Leviticus (11:44-45; 20:7, 26). Our holiness is to be measured by comparison with **God**.

3-4. Three of the Ten Commandments are mentioned in these two verses, the fifth, fourth, and second. The phrase **I am the Lord your God** is found fifteen times in this chapter, even as it is the initial statement of the Ten Commandments in Exodus 20:2. This is the basis of God's appeal.

5-8. No decay was to be allowed to enter into the peace offering. It all had to be eaten within two days.

9-10. God made provision for the poor by leaving **gleanings** for them. See James 1:27. Kindness should stir us to generosity.

11-12. Three more of the Ten Commandments are reiterated. These forbid stealing, lying, and swearing.

13-18. Many of these provisions seem reechoed in the Sermon on the Mount. God is concerned for the welfare of each individual in society, and we should share the same social concern He had. We should seek not only to provide men with the knowledge of salvation, but we should seek also to promote the principles of economic fairness (vs. 13), respectfulness (vs. 14), justice administered equally to both poor and mighty (vs. 15), truthfulness (vs. 16), and true brotherly love for all men (vss. 16-18). Remember that the parable of the good Samaritan (Lk 10:25-37) was told in answer to the question ". . . who is my neighbor?" (Lk 10:29).

19. The principle of separation is clearly taught in this verse, yet we do not apply it literally today since we are not under the dispensation of law. We do breed mules, plant gardens with various items growing in close proximity, and wear garments that are sixty-five percent polyester and thirty-five percent cotton.

20-22. And whosoever lieth carnally with a woman. The man was considered at fault here and must offer a trespass sacrifice, publicly confessing his guilt. The slave girl, though considered under pressure in this case, was still punished.

shall be scourged; they shall not be put to death, because she was not free.

21 And he shall bring his trespass offering unto the LORD, unto the door of the tabernacle of the congregation, *even* a ram for a trespass offering.

22 And the priest shall make an atonement for him with the ram of the trespass offering before the LORD for his sin which he hath done: and the sin which he hath done shall be forgiven him.

23 ¶And when ye shall come into the land, and shall have planted all manner of trees for food, then ye shall count the fruit thereof as uncircumcised: three years shall it be as uncircumcised unto you: it shall not be eaten of.

24 But in the fourth year all the fruit thereof shall be holy to praise the LORD *withal.*

25 And in the fifth year shall ye eat of the fruit thereof, that it may yield unto you the increase thereof: I *am* the LORD your God.

26 ¶Ye shall not eat *any thing* with the blood: neither shall ye use enchantment, nor observe times.

27 Ye shall not round the corners of your heads, neither shalt thou mar the corners of thy beard.

28 Ye shall not make any cuttings in your flesh for the dead, nor print any marks upon you: I *am* the LORD.

29 ¶Do not prostitute thy daughter, to cause her to be a whore; lest the land fall to whoredom, and the land become full of wickedness.

30 ¶Ye shall keep my sabbaths, and reverence my sanctuary: I *am* the LORD.

31 ¶Regard not them that have familiar spirits, neither seek after wizards, to be defiled by them: I *am* the LORD your God.

32 ¶Thou shalt rise up before the hoary head, and honour the face of the old man, and fear thy God: I *am* the LORD.

33 ¶And if a stranger sojourn with thee in your land, ye shall not vex him.

34 *But* the stranger that dwelleth with you shall be unto you as one born among you, and thou shalt love him as thyself; for ye were strangers in the land of Egypt: I *am* the LORD your God.

35 ¶Ye shall do no unrighteousness in judgment, in meteyard, in weight, or in measure.

36 Just balances, just weights, a just ephah, and a just hin, shall ye have: I *am* the LORD your God, which brought you out of the land of Egypt.

37 Therefore shall ye observe all my statutes, and all my judgments, and do them: I *am* the LORD.

CHAPTER 20

AND the LORD spake unto Moses, saying,

2 Again, thou shalt say to the children of Israel, Whosoever *he be* of the children of Israel, or of the strangers that sojourn in Israel, that giveth *any* of his seed unto Mōlěch; he shall surely be put to death: the people of the land shall stone him with stones.

3 And I will set my face against that

23-25. Fruit and nut trees were dedicated to God for the first four years and not to heathen spirits. The first fruits simply belonged to Him, and He would bless the return following that.

26. Neither shall ye use enchantments, nor observe times. Witchcraft, divination, soothsaying and the like were always punished by death (see Lev 20: 6, 27).

27-29. Ye shall not make any cuttings in your flesh . . . nor print any marks upon you. These practices were of heathen origin and forbidden.

30-31. Ye shall keep my sabbaths . . . neither seek after wizards. Notice the contrast between these two verses.

32-34. Honor the face of the old man. Honoring the aged and befriending strangers is a command that must constantly be impressed upon every new generation.

35-37. God is interested in complete honesty in our business lives. This even includes tax time!

20:1-6. The worship of false gods (vss. 2-5), and demons (vs. 6) was intertwined, and caused the people **to profane my holy name** (vs. 3). Such disgrace had to be dealt with severely.

man, and will cut him off from among his people; because he hath given of his seed unto Mŏlĕch, to defile my sanctuary, and to profane my holy name.

4 And if the people of the land do any ways hide their eyes from the man, when he giveth of his seed unto Mŏlĕch, and kill him not:

5 Then I will set my face against that man, and against his family, and will cut him off, and all that go a whoring after him, to commit whoredom with Mŏlĕch, from among their people.

6 ¶And the soul that turneth after such as have familiar spirits, and after wizards, to go a whoring after them, I will even set my face against that soul, and will cut him off from among his people.

7 Sanctify yourselves therefore, and be ye holy: for I *am* the LORD your God.

8 And ye shall keep my statutes, and do them: I *am* the LORD which sanctify you.

9 ¶For every one that curseth his father or his mother shall be surely put to death: he hath cursed his father or his mother; his blood *shall be* upon him.

10 ¶And the man that committeth adultery with *another* man's wife, *even he* that committeth adultery with his neighbour's wife, the adulterer and the adulteress shall surely be put to death.

11 And the man that lieth with his father's wife hath uncovered his father's nakedness: both of them shall surely be put to death; their blood *shall be* upon them.

12 And if a man lie with his daughter in law, both of them shall surely be put to death: they have wrought confusion; their blood *shall be* upon them.

13 ¶If a man also lie with mankind, as he lieth with a woman, both of them have committed an abomination: they shall surely be put to death; their blood *shall be* upon them.

14 And if a man take a wife and her mother, it *is* wickedness: they shall be burnt with fire, both he and they; that there be no wickedness among you.

15 And if a man lie with a beast, he shall surely be put to death: and ye shall slay the beast.

16 And if a woman approach unto any beast, and lie down thereto, thou shalt kill the woman, and the beast: they shall surely be put to death; their blood *shall be* upon them.

17 And if a man shall take his sister, his father's daughter, or his mother's daughter, and see her nakedness, and she see his nakedness; it *is* a wicked thing; and they shall be cut off in the sight of their people: he hath uncovered his sister's nakedness; he shall bear his iniquity.

18 And if a man shall lie with a woman having her sickness, and shall uncover her nakedness; he hath discovered her fountain, and she hath uncovered the fountain of her blood: and both of them shall be cut off from among their people.

19 And thou shalt not uncover the na-

7-8. The one remedy was for the people to be wholly consecrated to Almighty God and to His righteous statutes.

9. Deliberate, flagrant violation of the fifth commandment brought death. **His blood shall be upon him** indicated that he was fully to blame for his own death.

10-13. Adultery was punishable by death. **Both of them shall surely be put to death.** Neither escaped. Homosexuality is not just another life-style. It is a willful and sinful perversion of God's ordained relationship between the sexes. Participants were not deemed worthy of life.

14. They shall be burnt with fire. Death was by stoning; but the remains were cremated, as with Achan (Josh 7:25).

15-16. If a man lie with a beast. Intercourse between humans and animals was punishable with death for both participants.

17-18. It seems plain that incest with one's sister, as well as deliberate marriage relations during a wife's menstrual period of uncleanness, was also punishable by death. **They shall be cut off in the sight of their people** (see also Lev 15:24).

19-21. Violation of certain marriage restrictions could be

kedness of thy mother's sister, nor of thy father's sister: for he uncovereth his near kin: they shall bear their iniquity.

20 And if a man shall lie with his uncle's wife, he hath uncovered his uncle's nakedness: they shall bear their sin; they shall die childless.

21 And if a man shall take his brother's wife, it *is* an unclean thing: he hath uncovered his brother's nakedness; they shall be childless.

22 ¶Ye shall therefore keep all my statutes, and all my judgments, and do them: that the land, whither I bring you to dwell therein, spue you not out.

23 And ye shall not walk in the manners of the nation, which I cast out before you: for they committed all these things, and therefore I abhorred them.

24 But I have said unto you, Ye shall inherit their land, and I will give it unto you to possess it, a land that floweth with milk and honey: I *am* the LORD your God, which have separated you from *other* people.

25 Ye shall therefore put difference between clean beasts and unclean, and between unclean fowls and clean: and ye shall not make your souls abominable by beast, or by fowl, or by any manner of living thing that creepeth on the ground, which I have separated from you as unclean.

26 And ye shall be holy unto me: for I the LORD *am* holy, and have severed you from *other* people, that ye should be mine.

27 ¶A man also or woman that hath a familiar spirit, or that is a wizard, shall surely be put to death: they shall stone them with stones: their blood *shall be* upon them.

CHAPTER 21

AND the LORD said unto Moses, Speak unto the priests the sons of Aaron, and say unto them, There shall none be defiled for the dead among his people:

2 But for his kin, that is near unto him, *that is,* for his mother, and for his father, and for his son, and for his daughter, and for his brother,

3 And for his sister a virgin, that is nigh unto him, which hath had no husband; for her may he be defiled.

4 *But* he shall not defile himself, *being* a chief man among his people, to profane himself.

5 They shall not make baldness upon their head, neither shall they shave off the corner of their beard, nor make any cuttings in their flesh.

6 They shall be holy unto their God, and not profane the name of their God: for the offerings of the LORD made by fire, *and* the bread of their God, they do offer: therefore they shall be holy.

7 They shall not take a wife *that is* a whore, or profane; neither shall they take a woman put away from her husband: for he *is* holy unto his God.

8 Thou shalt sanctify him therefore; for he offereth the bread of thy God: he shall be holy unto thee: for I the LORD, which sanctify you, *am* holy.

9 And the daughter of any priest, if

punishable by God Himself (vs. 19), or by the people (vs. 20, **shall die childless**), or by childlessness (vs. 21).

22-24. God ends this section with a positive command (vs. 22a), a warning (vs. 22b), a negative injunction coupled with a warning (vs. 23), and a promise (vs. 24).

25-26. On the basis of their spiritual and physical separation from **other people** (vs. 26). Israel is to practice these principles in their daily lives (vs. 25). The undergirding reason is once again repeated, **ye shall be holy unto me: for I the LORD am holy.**

27. One of the most influential defilements was that of witchcraft in its various forms. God concludes this section on proper moral conduct with a final warning against this, coupled with a notice of the death penalty which accompanied violation.

3. Laws regulating proper priestly conduct. 21:1-22:33.

21:1-6. Speak unto the priests (vs. 1). Regulations are here given to the priests. A priest is called **a chief man among his people** (vs. 4); and for this reason, and because he offered God's offerings (vs. 6), he was not to be defiled either by dead bodies, which defile because death is the result of sin (vss. 1-3), or by heathen mourning customs (vs. 5). Yet, God in His mercy allowed several exceptions for the death of one who was near of kin.

7-8. A priest could not marry either a divorced or an immoral woman. He was to be holy because God was. The same is true in the New Testament as well (Lk 16:18).

9. She profaneth her father. The high priest's daughters

she profane herself by playing the whore, she profaneth her father: she shall be burnt with fire.

10 ¶And *he that is* the high priest among his brethren, upon whose head the anointing oil was poured, and that is consecrated to put on the garments, shall not uncover his head, nor rend his clothes;

11 Neither shall he go in to any dead body, nor defile himself for his father, or for his mother;

12 Neither shall he go out of the sanctuary, nor profane the sanctuary of his God; for the crown of the anointing oil of his God *is* upon him: I *am* the LORD.

13 And he shall take a wife in her virginity.

14 A widow, or a divorced woman, or profane, *or* an harlot, these shall he not take: but he shall take a virgin of his own people to wife.

15 Neither shall he profane his seed among his people: for I the LORD do sanctify him.

16 ¶And the LORD spake unto Moses, saying,

17 Speak unto Aaron, saying, Whosoever *he be* of thy seed in their generations that hath *any* blemish, let him not approach to offer the bread of his God.

18 For whatsoever man *he be* that hath a blemish, he shall not approach: a blind man, or a lame, or he that hath a flat nose, or any thing superfluous,

19 Or a man that is brokenfooted, or brokenhanded,

20 Or crookbackt, or a dwarf, or that hath a blemish in his eye, or be scurvy, or scabbed, or hath his stones broken;

21 No man that hath a blemish of the seed of Aaron the priest shall come nigh to offer the offerings of the LORD made by fire: he hath a blemish; he shall not come nigh to offer the bread of his God.

22 He shall eat the bread of his God, *both* of the most holy, and of the holy.

23 Only he shall not go in unto the vail, nor come nigh unto the altar, because he hath a blemish; that he profane not my sanctuaries: for I the LORD do sanctify them.

24 And Moses told *it* unto Aaron, and to his sons, and unto all the children of Israel.

CHAPTER 22

AND the LORD spake unto Moses, saying,

2 Speak unto Aaron and to his sons, that they separate themselves from the holy things of the children of Israel, and that they profane not my holy name *in those things* which they hallow unto me: I *am* the LORD.

3 Say unto them, Whosoever *he be* of all your seed among your generations, that goeth unto the holy things, which the children of Israel hallow unto the LORD, having his uncleanness upon him, that soul shall be cut off from my presence: I *am* the LORD.

4 What man soever of the seed of Aaron *is* a leper, or hath a running issue; he shall not eat of the holy things, until he be clean. And whoso toucheth

must also be above reproach morally or suffer the same consequences as any other woman in Israel.

10-15. The high priest had higher standards placed upon him because of the nature of his office. People usually will not rise higher than their leader, so leaders must walk circumspectly.

16-17. Perfect animals were required for sacrifice. Also, a priest was to be without blemish in order **to offer the bread of his God** (vs. 17).

18. Flat nose speaks of a deformed or mutilated face; **superfluous** speaks of other abnormal bodily parts.

19-24. Various other features (vss. 19-21a) could disqualify one born to the priesthood from actually offering the sacrifices (vs. 21b), but he could eat of the priest's portion (vs. 22).

22:1-3. A priest who had some deformity could still be ceremonially clean, but even a priest without any blemishes was barred from contact with holy things if he were unclean.

4-7. Priests with leprosy were barred from eating the sacrificial offerings until becoming clean again (vs. 4), though most other forms of ceremonial uncleanness lasted only until **the sun is down.** After that time he could partake if properly cleansed.

233

any thing *that is* unclean *by* the dead, or a man whose seed goeth from him;

5 Or whosoever toucheth any creeping thing, whereby he may be made unclean, or a man of whom he may take uncleanness, whatsoever uncleanness he hath;

6 The soul which hath touched any such shall be unclean until even, and shall not eat of the holy things, unless he wash his flesh with water.

7 And when the sun is down, he shall be clean, and shall afterward eat of the holy things; because it *is* his food.

8 That which dieth of itself, or is torn *with beasts,* he shall not eat to defile himself therewith: I *am* the LORD.

9 They shall therefore keep mine ordinance, lest they bear sin for it, and die therefore, if they profane it: I the LORD do sanctify them.

10 There shall no stranger eat *of* the holy thing: a sojourner of the priest, or an hired servant, shall not eat *of* the holy thing.

11 But if the priest buy *any* soul with his money, he shall eat of it, and he that is born in his house: they shall eat of his meat.

12 If the priest's daughter also be *married* unto a stranger, she may not eat of an offering of the holy things.

13 But if the priest's daughter be a widow, or divorced, and have no child, and is returned unto her father's house, as in her youth, she shall eat of her father's meat: but there shall no stranger eat thereof.

14 And if a man eat *of* the holy thing unwittingly, then he shall put the fifth *part* thereof unto it, and shall give *it* unto the priest with the holy thing.

15 And they shall not profane the holy things of the children of Israel, which they offer unto the LORD;

16 Or suffer them to bear the iniquity of trespass, when they eat their holy things: for I the LORD do sanctify them.

17 ¶And the LORD spake unto Moses, saying,

18 Speak unto Aaron, and to his sons, and unto all the children of Israel, and say unto them, Whatsoever *he be* of the house of Israel, or of the strangers in Israel, that will offer his oblation for all his vows, and for all his freewill offerings, which they will offer unto the LORD for a burnt offering;

19 *Ye shall offer* at your own will a male without blemish, of the beeves, of the sheep, or of the goats.

20 *But* whatsoever hath a blemish, *that* shall ye not offer: for it shall not be acceptable for you.

21 And whosoever offereth a sacrifice of peace offerings unto the LORD to accomplish *his* vow, or a freewill offering in beeves or sheep, it shall be perfect to be accepted; there shall be no blemish therein.

22 Blind, or broken, or maimed, or having a wen, or scurvy, or scabbed, ye shall not offer these unto the LORD, nor make an offering by fire of them upon the altar unto the LORD.

23 Either a bullock or a lamb that hath any thing superfluous or lacking

8-9. Uncleanness could be transmitted by touch. God wanted to prevent unclean priests from profaning His altar and its sacrifices.

10-11. No stranger, non-priest, or layman was permitted to partake. An exception was made in the case of a priest's slave who was considered a part of his immediate family.

12-13. A priest's daughter could not partake if married outside the bounds of a priestly family. Later, if she returned home as a childless widow or divorcee, she was allowed to eat of the priestly sacrifices.

14-16. A layman unintentionally might eat of the priest's portion. If so he had to add a **fifth part** to it as a penalty.

17-25. This section goes into greater detail about the precise meaning of offering animals that are **without blemish** (vs. 19). No blind, disabled, maimed, or mutilated animals were accepted. A **wen,** or ulcerous sore, itchy spot (**scurvy**), or scabbed area would also disqualify an offering (vs. 22), as would one whose growth pattern was abnormal (vs. 23) or one that had been castrated in some way, whether intentionally or not (vs. 24).

in his parts, that mayest thou offer *for* a freewill offering; but for a vow it shall not be accepted.

24 Ye shall not offer unto the LORD that which is bruised, or crushed, or broken, or cut; neither shall ye make *any offering thereof* in your land.

25 Neither from a stranger's hand shall ye offer the bread of your God of any of these; because their corruption *is* in them, *and* blemishes *be* in them: they shall not be accepted for you.

26 ¶And the LORD spake unto Moses, saying,

27 When a bullock, or a sheep, or a goat, is brought forth, then it shall be seven days under the dam; and from the eighth day and thenceforth it shall be accepted for an offering made by fire unto the LORD.

28 And *whether it be* cow or ewe, ye shall not kill it and her young both in one day.

29 ¶And when ye will offer a sacrifice of thanksgiving unto the LORD, offer *it* at your own will.

30 On the same day it shall be eaten up; ye shall leave none of it until the morrow: I *am* the LORD.

31 Therefore shall ye keep my commandments, and do them: I *am* the LORD.

32 Neither shall ye profane my holy name; but I will be hallowed among the children of Israel: I *am* the LORD which hallow you,

33 That brought you out of the land of Egypt, to be your God: I *am* the LORD.

CHAPTER 23

AND the LORD spake unto Moses, saying,

2 Speak unto the children of Israel, and say unto them, *Concerning* the feasts of the LORD, which ye shall proclaim *to be* holy convocations, *even* these *are* my feasts.

3 Six days shall work be done: but the seventh day *is* the sabbath of rest, an holy convocation; ye shall do no work *therein*: it *is* the sabbath of the LORD in all your dwellings.

4 ¶These *are* the feasts of the LORD, *even* holy convocations, which ye shall proclaim in their seasons.

5 In the fourteenth *day* of the first month at even *is* the LORD's passover.

6 And on the fifteenth day of the same month *is* the feast of unleavened bread unto the LORD: seven days ye must eat unleavened bread.

7 In the first day ye shall have an holy convocation: ye shall do no servile work therein.

8 But ye shall offer an offering made by fire unto the LORD seven days: in the seventh day *is* an holy convocation: ye shall do no servile work *therein*.

9 ¶And the LORD spake unto Moses, saying,

26-28. The prohibition of killing both parent and offspring in the same day perhaps speaks of the sanctity of the parent-child relationship. It demonstrates a concern for the animals' well-being.

29-30. The thanksgiving peace offering had to be eaten the day it was offered (see Lev 7:15). This would encourage sharing the feast with others.

31-33. All these laws are grounded in the statement **I am the LORD**. God's name is not to be profaned.

4. Laws for observing the Lord's feasts. 23:1-44.

23:1-2. The complete religious calendar of the Jewish year is summarized and regulated in this chapter regarding the seven **feasts of the LORD**. They were **holy convocations**.

3. A weekly holy time was the **sabbath of rest** (Saturday), on which day no servile work was to be done. Each one of the Ten Commandments is repeated for New Testament observance, except this one. Christ's resurrection changed the day for weekly worship to Sunday, the first day of the week (Acts 20:7; I Cor 16:2). They worked and rested at the end of the week, but we rest first and then go forth to serve the Lord on the remaining six days.

4-5. The LORD's passover began on the eve of the fourteenth day of the first month, our March or April. Jewish months were determined by the moon; so it would vary from year to year. The Passover lamb was slain and eaten with bitter herbs and unleavened bread as a memorial of how God passed over the Israelites in Egypt when He saw the blood applied to the doorposts. Christ is our Passover (Ex 12; I Cor 5:7).

6-8. The feast of unleavened bread accompanied the Passover and lasted for seven days. All Jewish men were required to be present at this feast (Deut 16:16); its details are found in Exodus 12:14-20.

9-14. The Feast of **the first fruits of your harvest** occurred most probably on the sixteenth day of that first month, the day

235

10 Speak unto the children of Israel, and say unto them, When ye be come into the land which I give unto you, and shall reap the harvest thereof, then ye shall bring a sheaf of the firstfruits of your harvest unto the priest:

11 And he shall wave the sheaf before the LORD, to be accepted for you: on the morrow after the sabbath the priest shall wave it.

12 And ye shall offer that day when ye wave the sheaf an he lamb without blemish of the first year for a burnt offering unto the LORD.

13 And the meat offering thereof *shall be* two tenth deals of fine flour mingled with oil, an offering made by fire unto the LORD *for* a sweet savour: and the drink offering thereof *shall be* of wine, the fourth *part* of an hin.

14 And ye shall eat neither bread, nor parched corn, nor green ears, until the selfsame day that ye have brought an offering unto your God: it shall be a statute for ever throughout your generations in all your dwellings.

15 ¶And ye shall count unto you from the morrow after the sabbath, from the day that ye brought the sheaf of the wave offering; seven sabbaths shall be complete:

16 Even unto the morrow after the seventh sabbath shall ye number fifty days; and ye shall offer a new meat offering unto the LORD.

17 Ye shall bring out of your habitations two wave loaves of two tenth deals: they shall be of fine flour; they shall be baken with leaven; *they are* the firstfruits unto the LORD.

18 And ye shall offer with the bread seven lambs without blemish of the first year, and one young bullock, and two rams: they shall be *for* a burnt offering unto the LORD, with their meat offering, and their drink offerings, *even* an offering made by fire, of sweet savour unto the LORD.

19 Then ye shall sacrifice one kid of the goats for a sin offering, and two lambs of the first year for a sacrifice of peace offerings.

20 And the priest shall wave them with the bread of the firstfruits *for* a wave offering before the LORD, with the two lambs: they shall be holy to the LORD for the priest.

21 And ye shall proclaim on the selfsame day, *that* it may be an holy convocation unto you: ye shall do no servile work *therein: it shall be* a statute for ever in all your dwellings throughout your generations.

22 ¶And when ye reap the harvest of your land, thou shalt not make clean riddance of the corners of thy field when thou reapest, neither shalt thou gather any gleaning of thy harvest: thou shalt leave them unto the poor, and to the stranger: I *am* the LORD your God.

23 ¶And the LORD spake unto Moses, saying,

24 Speak unto the children of Israel, saying, In the seventh month, in the first *day* of the month, shall ye have a

after the beginning of the feast of unleavened bread. During March or April some grain would be ready for harvest; and it would be plucked, bound together, and waved before the Lord. According to the traditional view of the crucifixion of Christ on Friday the fourteenth, He rose on the sixteenth, a Sunday—the day of the Feast of First Fruits. Christ rose as the first fruits of them that sleep (I Cor 15:23). Just as the first ripe grain was a promise of the rest of the harvest, so also Christ's resurrection assures us of our own as well.

15-16. The feast of Pentecost was also called ". . . the feast of weeks . . ." (Deut 16:16), because it was celebrated seven weeks after the Feast of First Fruits arrived at by counting **fifty days** beginning with the day of first fruits. It would thus occur on the same day of the week as first fruits. All Israelite males were to be in attendance (Deut 16:16).

17. Whereas the sheaf of separate grain was waved on first fruits, the individual grains were united together into one loaf for the Pentecost offering. Many have seen in this a picture of the church as it was initiated on Pentecost as a body of believers.

18-22. Many animals were offered for burnt offerings, along with meal and drink offerings, sin offerings, and peace offerings. It was a holy Sabbath on which no servile work was to be done, though deeds of necessity were allowed. Since this feast accompanied the general time of grain harvest in May, a word is added about leaving the gleanings of the harvest for the poor and the stranger (vs. 22).

23-25. In the first day of the seventh Jewish month came the feast of **trumpets.** It was a day of rest, and its purpose was to awaken Israel to prepare for the events of the rest of the month. The Day of Atonement came ten days later, and the feast of tabernacles occurred on the fifteenth day of the month. God

sabbath, a memorial of blowing of trumpets, an holy convocation.

25 Ye shall do no servile work therein: but ye shall offer an offering made by fire unto the LORD.

26 ¶And the LORD spake unto Moses, saying,

27 Also on the tenth *day* of this seventh month *there shall be* a day of atonement: it shall be an holy convocation unto you; and ye shall afflict your souls, and offer an offering made by fire unto the LORD.

28 And ye shall do no work in that same day: for it *is* a day of atonement, to make an atonement for you before the LORD your God.

29 For whatsoever soul *it be* that shall not be afflicted in that same day, he shall be cut off from among his people.

30 And whatsoever soul *it be* that doeth any work in that same day, the same soul will I destroy from among his people.

31 Ye shall do no manner of work: *it shall be* a statute for ever throughout your generations in all your dwellings.

32 It *shall be* unto you a sabbath of rest, and ye shall afflict your souls: in the ninth *day* of the month at even, from even unto even, shall ye celebrate your sabbath.

33 ¶And the LORD spake unto Moses, saying,

34 Speak unto the children of Israel, saying, The fifteenth day of this seventh month *shall be* the feast of tabernacles *for* seven days unto the LORD.

35 On the first day *shall be* an holy convocation: ye shall do no servile work *therein.*

36 Seven days ye shall offer an offering made by fire unto the LORD: on the eighth day shall be an holy convocation unto you; and ye shall offer an offering made by fire unto the LORD: it *is* a solemn assembly; *and* ye shall do no servile work *therein.*

37 These *are* the feasts of the LORD, which ye shall proclaim *to be* holy convocations, to offer an offering made by fire unto the LORD, a burnt offering, and a meat offering, a sacrifice, and drink offerings, every thing upon his day:

38 Beside the sabbaths of the LORD, and beside your gifts, and beside all your vows, and beside all your freewill offerings, which ye give unto the LORD.

39 Also in the fifteenth day of the seventh month, when ye have gathered in the fruit of the land, ye shall keep a feast unto the LORD seven days: on the first day *shall be* a sabbath, and on the eighth day *shall be* a sabbath.

40 And ye shall take you on the first day the boughs of goodly trees, branches of palm trees, and the boughs of thick trees, and willows of the brook; and ye shall rejoice before the LORD your God seven days.

41 And ye shall keep it a feast unto the LORD seven days in the year. *It shall be* a statute for ever in your genera-

awakens and gathers His people at the end of the long summer; they are to be prepared to move.

26-27. The **day of atonement,** or Yom Kippur, came in the seventh month on the tenth day. It was near the beginning of October and is still celebrated today by Jews around the world. The details of this observance are found in Leviticus 16.

28-32. It was to be a **sabbath of rest** (vs. 32). No work could be done on that day from sundown on the ninth to sundown on the tenth, as Israel reckoned time. Instead, they were to see the work of the high priest.

33-39. **Feast of tabernacles** ran for eight days, from the fifteenth to the twenty-second of the seventh month (October). They were also to observe a Sabbath of rest on the first and last days of this feast, in addition to the regular Saturday Sabbath.

40-44. This feast was to celebrate God's deliverance of the Israelites from Egyptian bondage. To do this they prepared small tabernacles, or **booths,** in which to dwell outdoors. It commemorated their dwelling in booths in the wilderness on the way to the Promised Land. Jesus attended the Feast of Tabernacles in John (see especially Jn 7:2, 37). During the feast they brought water from the pool of Siloam and poured it out to remember how God supplied them with water in the wilderness. Thus, Jesus told men to come to Him and drink (Jn 7:37-39).

tions: ye shall celebrate it in the seventh month.

42 Ye shall dwell in booths seven days; all that are Israelites born shall dwell in booths:

43 That your generations may know that I made the children of Israel to dwell in booths, when I brought them out of the land of Egypt: I am the LORD your God.

44 And Moses declared unto the children of Israel the feasts of the LORD.

CHAPTER 24

AND the LORD spake unto Moses, saying,

2 Command the children of Israel, that they bring unto thee pure oil olive beaten for the light, to cause the lamps to burn continually.

3 Without the vail of the testimony, in the tabernacle of the congregation, shall Aaron order it from the evening unto the morning before the LORD continually: it shall be a statute for ever in your generations.

4 He shall order the lamps upon the pure candlestick before the LORD continually.

5 ¶And thou shalt take fine flour, and bake twelve cakes thereof: two tenth deals shall be in one cake.

6 And thou shalt set them in two rows, six on a row, upon the pure table before the LORD.

7 And thou shalt put pure frankincense upon each row, that it may be on the bread for a memorial, even an offering made by fire unto the LORD.

8 Every sabbath he shall set it in order before the LORD continually, being taken from the children of Israel by an everlasting covenant.

9 And it shall be Aaron's and his sons'; and they shall eat it in the holy place: for it is most holy unto him of the offerings of the LORD made by fire by a perpetual statute.

10 ¶And the son of an Israelitish woman, whose father was an Egyptian, went out among the children of Israel: and this son of the Israelitish woman and a man of Israel strove together in the camp;

11 And the Israelitish woman's son blasphemed the name of the LORD, and cursed. And they brought him unto Moses: (and his mother's name was Shel'ō-mith, the daughter of Dĭb'rī, of the tribe of Dan:)

12 And they put him in ward, that the mind of the LORD might be shewed them.

13 And the LORD spake unto Moses, saying,

14 Bring forth him that hath cursed without the camp; and let all that heard him lay their hands upon his head, and let all the congregation stone him.

15 And thou shalt speak unto the children of Israel, saying, Whosoever curseth his God shall bear his sin.

16 And he that blasphemeth the name of the LORD, he shall surely be put to death, and all the congregation shall

They also lighted the area with torches to commemorate the fiery pillar in the wilderness; but Jesus exclaimed, ". . . I am the light of the world . . ." (Jn 8:12).

5. Laws for tabernacle service. 24:1-9.

24:1-4. Pure oil olive beaten for the light (vs. 2). Olive oil was the fuel of the golden lampstand, the only source of light inside the tabernacle. It was to burn continually. The light itself represents Christ, and the oil stands for the Holy Spirit (Zech 4:2-6; Jn 8:12).

5. Also within the tabernacle was the table of showbread, which held twelve loaves of bread, each one representing one of the tribes of Israel. Each loaf contained **two tenth deals** of **fine flour,** or about six quarts each. That would make about a six pound loaf of bread.

6-7. The loaves were placed in two rows of six, each on the **pure** (gold) **table before the LORD.** Frankincense was placed either on the loaves, or possibly between the rows of bread, for later burning at the altar of incense. These loaves memorialized Israel continually before the Lord.

8-9. Aaron and his sons ate these large loaves each week, and then they were replaced with fresh bread each Saturday.

6. Laws for regulating conduct in the camp. 24:10-23.

10-12. The Israelitish woman's son blasphemed the name of the LORD. This historical interlude describes the serious nature of blasphemy against the Lord. God's name was to be revered and respected. The third commandment forbids taking God's name in vain. The son of Shelomith, a Danite, swore and cursed while in a heated argument. He was apprehended and confined to await sentencing.

13-16. God Himself issued the command for him to be stoned. The witnesses were to **lay their hands upon his head,** signifying that guilt rested solely upon him. His stoning may seem severe to some, but it was just and was certainly a deterrent to others; and it indicates how important God's honor is.

certainly stone him: as well the stranger, as he that is born in the land, when he blasphemeth the name *of the Lord,* shall be put to death.

17 And he that killeth any man shall surely be put to death.

18 And he that killeth a beast shall make it good; beast for beast.

19 And if a man cause a blemish in his neighbour; as he hath done, so shall it be done to him;

20 Breach for breach, eye for eye, tooth for tooth: as he hath caused a blemish in a man, so shall it be done to him *again.*

21 And he that killeth a beast, he shall restore it: and he that killeth a man, he shall be put to death.

22 Ye shall have one manner of law, as well for the stranger, as for one of your own country: for I *am* the Lord your God.

23 ¶And Moses spake to the children of Israel, that they should bring forth him that had cursed out of the camp, and stone him with stones. And the children of Israel did as the Lord commanded Moses.

CHAPTER 25

AND the Lord spake unto Moses in mount Si′naī, saying,

2 Speak unto the children of Israel, and say unto them, When ye come into the land which I give you, then shall the land keep a sabbath unto the Lord.

3 Six years thou shalt sow thy field, and six years thou shalt prune thy vineyard, and gather in the fruit thereof;

4 But in the seventh year shall be a sabbath of rest unto the land, a sabbath for the Lord: thou shalt neither sow thy field, nor prune thy vineyard.

5 That which groweth of its own accord of thy harvest thou shalt not reap, neither gather the grapes of thy vine undressed: *for* it is a year of rest unto the land.

6 And the sabbath of the land shall be meat for you; for thee, and for thy servant, and for thy maid, and for thy hired servant, and for thy stranger that sojourneth with thee,

7 And for thy cattle, and for the beast that *are* in thy land, shall all the increase thereof be meat.

8 ¶And thou shalt number seven sabbaths of years unto thee, seven times seven years; and the space of the seven sabbaths of years shall be unto thee forty and nine years.

9 Then shalt thou cause the trumpet of the jubile to sound on the tenth *day* of the seventh month, in the day of atonement shall ye make the trumpet sound throughout all your land.

10 And ye shall hallow the fiftieth

17. He that killeth any man shall surely be put to death. Capital punishment for first degree murder has been part of God's law since Genesis 9:6. It is repeated here and in the New Testament (Rom 13:4). Jesus submitted to capital punishment in the crucifixion, and Paul acknowledged his willingness to submit to it if guilty (Acts 25:11). Opposition to the principle of capital punishment today is opposition to the revealed will of God.

18-20. The law of retaliation, **as he hath done, so shall it be done to him,** actually restricts and limits cases of retaliation for wrongs committed. If someone put out your eyes, you may desire to kill him; but the punishment is restricted to the putting out of his eyes. It was an exact punishment; it was fair; it was publicly administered; yet in many such cases a just and equitable fine or replacement of damaged property was accomplished.

21-23. Again, capital punishment was required for murder. The same was true for hitting or cursing parents (Ex 21:15, 17), kidnapping (Ex 21:16), violation of the sabbath (Num 15:32-36), blaspheming God's name (Lev 24:16), any type of witchcraft (Lev 20:27), homosexual practices (Lev 20:13), and various types of adultery and incest (Lev 20:10-12).

7. Laws regarding sabbatic years. 25:1-55.

25:1. Again, reference is made to the fact that these laws were given to Moses while the Israelites were still at **mount Sinai.** Moses wrote them down in a book (Ex 24:4). See Introduction.

2. When ye come into the land. This law was for the future, when Israel would dwell in the land of milk and honey. **Then shall the land keep a Sabbath unto the Lord.** Just as God provided a weekly Sabbath for His people, He provided a rest for the land, one year of rest after six years of production.

3-4. During the sabbath year there was to be neither the planting of grain nor the pruning of grape vines. These were the two primary agricultural pursuits of Israel.

5-7. That which grew on its own that year was to be free for all, i.e., rich, poor, stranger, servant, cattle, and beasts. Would there be enough? Yes, plenty. God promised to provide a two years' supply in the harvest of the ordinary sixth year and a three years' supply in the forty-eighth year prior to a double sabbatic (vss. 20-21). Were the people to be idle during the sabbatic year? No. They were to spend some of the time teaching the law of Moses to their children (Deut 31:10-13).

8-10. After the seventh sabbatic year, **the fiftieth year** was to be a jubilee, and they were to **proclaim liberty throughout all the land** (vs. 10) on the Day of Atonement. Possessions of land that had been sold would then revert back to the original owner.

year, and proclaim liberty throughout *all* the land unto all the inhabitants thereof: it shall be a jubile unto you; and ye shall return every man unto his possession, and ye shall return every man unto his family.

11 A jubile shall that fiftieth year be unto you: ye shall not sow, neither reap that which groweth of itself in it, nor gather *the grapes* in it of thy vine undressed.

12 For it *is* the jubile; it shall be holy unto you: ye shall eat the increase thereof out of the field.

13 In the year of this jubile ye shall return every man unto his possession.

14 And if thou sell ought unto thy neighbour, or buyest *ought* of thy neighbour's hand, ye shall not oppress one another:

15 According to the number of years after the jubile thou shalt buy of thy neighbour, *and* according unto the number of years of the fruits he shall sell unto thee:

16 According to the multitude of years thou shalt increase the price thereof, and according to the fewness of years thou shalt diminish the price of it: for *according* to the number *of the years* of the fruits doth he sell unto thee.

17 Ye shall not therefore oppress one another; but thou shalt fear thy God: for I *am* the Lord your God.

18 ¶Wherefore ye shall do my statutes, and keep my judgments, and do them; and ye shall dwell in the land in safety.

19 And the land shall yield her fruit, and ye shall eat your fill, and dwell therein in safety.

20 And if ye shall say, What shall we eat the seventh year? behold, we shall not sow, nor gather in our increase:

21 Then I will command my blessing upon you in the sixth year, and it shall bring forth fruit for three years.

22 And ye shall sow the eighth year, and eat *yet* of old fruit until the ninth year; until her fruits come in ye shall eat *of* the old *store*.

23 ¶The land shall not be sold for ever: for the land *is* mine; for ye *are* strangers and sojourners with me.

24 And in all the land of your possession ye shall grant a redemption for the land.

25 ¶If thy brother be waxen poor, and hath sold away *some* of his possession, and if any of his kin come to redeem it, then shall he redeem that which his brother sold.

26 And if the man have none to redeem it, and himself be able to redeem it:

27 Then let him count the years of the sale thereof, and restore the overplus unto the man to whom he sold it; that he may return unto his possession.

28 But if he be not able to restore *it* to him, then that which is sold shall remain in the hand of him that hath bought it until the year of jubile: and in the jubile it shall go out, and he shall return unto his possession.

29 And if a man sell a dwelling house in a walled city, then he may redeem it

11-16. According to the number of years after the jubilee. Because land would revert back to its original owner in the year of jubilee, it was always priced accordingly when sold!

17-24. God's ample provision for these sabbatic years is reassured in these verses. Obedience is all that God expects. Sadly enough, Israel soon departed from this sabbath-for-the-land observance. Thus, after 490 years of neglect God removed His people to captivity in Babylon in 606 B.C. and allowed the land to take all seventy missed sabbaths at once! Compare Leviticus 26:33-35 and II Chronicles 36:21.

25-28. Land that was sold could be bought back before the year of jubilee; but if it was not, it would automatically return to the original owner during that fiftieth year.

29-31. However, houses inside walled villages, if sold, had to be redeemed within one year; or else they remained the perma-

within a whole year after it is sold; *within* a full year may he redeem it.

30 And if it be not redeemed within the space of a full year, then the house that *is* in the walled city shall be established for ever to him that bought it throughout his generations: it shall not go out in the jubile.

31 But the houses of the villages which have no wall round about them shall be counted as the fields of the country: they may be redeemed, and they shall go out in the jubile.

32 Notwithstanding the cities of the Lēvītes, *and* the houses of the cities of their possession, may the Lēvītes redeem at any time.

33 And if a man purchase of the Lēvītes, then the house that was sold, and the city of his possession, shall go out in *the year of* jubile: for the houses of the cities of the Lēvītes *are* their possession among the children of Israel.

34 But the field of the suburbs of their cities may not be sold; for it *is* their perpetual possession.

35 ¶And if thy brother be waxen poor, and fallen in decay with thee; then thou shalt relieve him: *yea, though he be* a stranger, or a sojourner; that he may live with thee.

36 Take thou no usury of him, or increase: but fear thy God; that thy brother may live with thee.

37 Thou shalt not give him thy money upon usury, nor lend him thy victuals for increase.

38 I *am* the Lord your God, which brought you forth out of the land of Egypt, to give you the land of Canaan, *and* to be your God.

39 ¶And if thy brother *that dwelleth* by thee be waxen poor, and be sold unto thee; thou shalt not compel him to serve as a bondservant:

40 *But* as an hired servant, *and* as a sojourner, he shall be with thee, *and* shall serve thee unto the year of jubile:

41 And *then* shall he depart from thee, *both* he and his children with him, and shall return unto his own family, and unto the possession of his fathers shall he return.

42 For they *are* my servants, which I brought forth out of the land of Egypt: they shall not be sold as bondmen.

43 Thou shalt not rule over him with rigour; but shalt fear thy God.

44 Both thy bondmen, and thy bondmaids, which thou shalt have, *shall be* of the heathen that are round about you; of them shall ye buy bondmen and bondmaids.

45 Moreover of the children of the strangers that do sojourn among you, of them shall ye buy, and of their families that *are* with you, which they begat in your land: and they shall be your possession.

46 And ye shall take them as an inheritance for your children after you, to inherit *them for* a possession; they shall be your bondmen for ever: but over your brethren the children of Israel, ye shall not rule one over another with rigour.

47 ¶And if a sojourner or stranger wax rich by thee, and thy brother *that*

nent possession of the new purchaser. Houses in unwalled villages were treated the same as the land (cf. vss. 25-28).

32-34. The cities of the Levites . . . were forty and eight (Josh 21:41). The Levites' houses and lands were perpetually theirs.

35-38. Loans to the poor could carry no interest rate whatever. God had delivered them from the bondage of Egypt and wanted no bondage placed upon those in need of loans in His land.

39-43. If an Israelite man was poor and desired to sell or indenture himself to provide capital, he was to be treated kindly as a hired servant and released in the year of jubilee, if not before (Ex 21:2-6).

44-46. Israel was permitted to have slaves of the heathen. Their children would also be slaves perpetually. This should be viewed as a form of the just judgment of God upon the wicked and idolatrous practices of the heathen and differs from modern slavery, which was not commanded of God. See Andrew Bonar's *Commentary on Leviticus.*

47-55. He may be redeemed again; one of his brethren may redeem him. The law of the kinsman redeemer taught that a

LEVITICUS 25:48

dwelleth by him wax poor, and sell himself unto the stranger *or* sojourner by thee, or to the stock of the stranger's family:

48 After that he is sold he may be redeemed again; one of his brethren may redeem him:

49 Either his uncle, or his uncle's son, may redeem him, or *any* that is nigh of kin unto him of his family may redeem him; or if he be able, he may redeem himself.

50 And he shall reckon with him that bought him from the year that he was sold to him unto the year of jubile: and the price of his sale shall be according unto the number of years, according to the time of an hired servant shall it be with him.

51 If *there be* yet many years *behind,* according unto them he shall give again the price of his redemption out of the money that he was bought for.

52 And if there remain but few years unto the year of jubile, then he shall count with him, *and* according unto his years shall he give him again the price of his redemption.

53 *And* as a yearly hired servant shall he be with him: *and the other* shall not rule with rigour over him in thy sight.

54 And if he be not redeemed in these *years,* then he shall go out in the year of jubile, *both* he, and his children with him.

55 For unto me the children of Israel *are* servants; they *are* my servants whom I brought forth out of the land of Egypt: I *am* the LORD your God.

CHAPTER 26

YE shall make you no idols nor graven image, neither rear you up a standing image, neither shall ye set up *any* image of stone in your land, to bow down unto it: for I *am* the LORD your God.

2 Ye shall keep my sabbaths, and reverence my sanctuary: I *am* the LORD.

3 ¶If ye walk in my statutes, and keep my commandments, and do them;

4 Then I will give you rain in due season, and the land shall yield her increase, and the trees of the field shall yield their fruit.

5 And your threshing shall reach unto the vintage, and the vintage shall reach unto the sowing time: and ye shall eat your bread to the full, and dwell in your land safely.

6 And I will give peace in the land, and ye shall lie down, and none shall make *you* afraid: and I will rid evil beasts out of the land, neither shall the sword go through your land.

7 And ye shall chase your enemies, and they shall fall before you by the sword.

8 And five of you shall chase an hundred, and an hundred of you shall put ten thousand to flight: and your enemies shall fall before you by the sword.

9 For I will have respect unto you, and make you fruitful, and multiply you, and establish my covenant with you.

10 And ye shall eat old store, and

near kinsman could pay the price to purchase back a kinsman who had been sold (including his land) prior to the year of jubilee. This pictures Christ who became our kinsman (Jn 1:14) and redeemed us from sin. Boaz also performed the duty of a kinsman redeemer for Naomi and her daughter-in-law Ruth (Ruth 2:20; 3:9-13; 4:1-10).

8. Conditions for blessings or curses. 26:1-46.

This chapter forms a fitting conclusion to this book of law. It clearly promises blessing for obedience and chastisement for not keeping God's law. It is one of the great chapters of the Old Testament and is essentially repeated by Moses forty years later in Deuteronomy 28.

26:1-2. God called for His people to repudiate idolatry and to center their worship in His appointed use of the sanctuary with its sacrificial system.

3-13. God promises that If ye walk in my statutes (vs. 3) He will provide proper rainfall and abundant harvests (vss. 4-5), peace in their land and easy victory over all enemies (vss. 6-8), many children (vs. 9), and a perfect relationship with their covenant-keeping God, their redeemer (vss. 9-13).

bring forth the old because of the new.

11 And I will set my tabernacle among you: and my soul shall not abhor you.

12 And I will walk among you, and will be your God, and ye shall be my people.

13 I *am* the LORD your God, which brought you forth out of the land of Egypt, that ye should not be their bondmen; and I have broken the bands of your yoke, and made you go upright.

14 ¶But if ye will not hearken unto me, and will not do all these commandments;

15 And if ye shall despise my statutes, or if your soul abhor my judgments, so that ye will not do all my commandments, *but* that ye break my covenant:

16 I also will do this unto you; I will even appoint over you terror, consumption, and the burning ague, that shall consume the eyes, and cause sorrow of heart: and ye shall sow your seed in vain, for your enemies shall eat it.

17 And I will set my face against you, and ye shall be slain before your enemies: they that hate you shall reign over you; and ye shall flee when none pursueth you.

18 And if ye will not yet for all this hearken unto me, then I will punish you seven times more for your sins.

19 And I will break the pride of your power; and I will make your heaven as iron, and your earth as brass:

20 And your strength shall be spent in vain: for your land shall not yield her increase, neither shall the trees of the land yield their fruits.

21 And if ye walk contrary unto me, and will not hearken unto me; I will bring seven times more plagues upon you according to your sins.

22 I will also send wild beasts among you, which shall rob you of your children, and destroy your cattle, and make you few in number; and your *high* ways shall be desolate.

23 And if ye will not be reformed by me by these things, but will walk contrary unto me;

24 Then will I also walk contrary unto you, and will punish you yet seven times for your sins.

25 And I will bring a sword upon you, that shall avenge the quarrel of *my* covenant: and when ye are gathered together within your cities, I will send the pestilence among you; and ye shall be delivered into the hand of the enemy.

26 *And* when I have broken the staff of your bread, ten women shall bake your bread in one oven, and they shall deliver *you* your bread again by weight: and ye shall eat, and not be satisfied.

27 And if ye will not for all this hearken unto me, but walk contrary unto me;

28 Then I will walk contrary unto you also in fury; and I, even I, will chastise you seven times for your sins.

29 And ye shall eat the flesh of your sons, and the flesh of your daughters shall ye eat.

14-15. But, if Israel **will not hearken unto** God, then calamity unspeakable shall befall them. What follows becomes a history of Israel, because they forsook God, broke His covenant of Mount Sinai, etc. All the major and minor prophets substantiate this on nearly every page.

16-31. I also will do this unto you. God's judgment of a wayward Israel was to take several forms. (1) There would be disease, sorrow, foreign occupation, military defeat, rule by foreigners, and a preoccupation of fear (vss. 16-17). (2) The plagues will be multiplied in intensity, and their efforts at producing will be fruitless (vss. 18-20). (3) The plagues will intensify even more **according to your sins** (vs. 21), and wild beasts (II Kgs 2:23-24) would destroy both cattle and children (vss. 21-22). (4) Continued disobedience would result in death to some by foreign swords, pestilence within population centers, defeat by their enemies, and near starvation (vss. 23-26). (5) Further disobedience, even after all these punishments, would yield starvation so severe that cannibalism would result (II Kgs 6:25, 28-29), large scale death would ensue, and cities would be destroyed (vss. 27-31).

30 And I will destroy your high places, and cut down your images, and cast your carcases upon the carcases of your idols, and my soul shall abhor you.

31 And I will make your cities waste, and bring your sanctuaries unto desolation, and I will not smell the savour of your sweet odours.

32 And I will bring the land into desolation: and your enemies which dwell therein shall be astonished at it.

33 And I will scatter you among the heathen, and will draw out a sword after you: and your land shall be desolate, and your cities waste.

34 Then shall the land enjoy her sabbaths, as long as it lieth desolate, and ye *be* in your enemies' land; *even* then shall the land rest, and enjoy her sabbaths.

35 As long as it lieth desolate it shall rest; because it did not rest in your sabbaths, when ye dwelt upon it.

36 And upon them that are left *alive* of you I will send a faintness into their hearts in the lands of their enemies; and the sound of a shaken leaf shall chase them; and they shall flee, as fleeing from a sword; and they shall fall when none pursueth.

37 And they shall fall one upon another, as it were before a sword, when none pursueth: and ye shall have no power to stand before your enemies.

38 And ye shall perish among the heathen, and the land of your enemies shall eat you up.

39 And they that are left of you shall pine away in their iniquity in your enemies' lands; and also in the iniquities of their fathers shall they pine away with them.

40 If they shall confess their iniquity, and the iniquity of their fathers, with their trespass which they trespassed against me, and that also they have walked contrary unto me;

41 And *that* I also have walked contrary unto them, and have brought them into the land of their enemies; if then their uncircumcised hearts be humbled, and they then accept of the punishment of their iniquity:

42 Then will I remember my covenant with Jacob, and also my covenant with Isaac, and also my covenant with Abraham will I remember; and I will remember the land.

43 The land also shall be left of them, and shall enjoy her sabbaths, while she lieth desolate without them: and they shall accept of the punishment of their iniquity: because, even because they despised my judgments, and because their soul abhorred my statutes.

44 And yet for all that, when they be in the land of their enemies, I will not cast them away, neither will I abhor them, to destroy them utterly, and to break my covenant with them: for I *am* the LORD their God.

45 But I will for their sakes remember the covenant of their ancestors, whom I brought forth out of the land of Egypt in the sight of the heathen, that I might be their God: I *am* the LORD.

46 These *are* the statutes and judgments and laws, which the LORD made

32-39. God's final answer to Israel's disobedience would be to **scatter you among the heathen,** the Gentiles, (vs. 33). He would also send fear among them (vs. 37), and many would perish in foreign lands.

40-42. But **If they shall confess their iniquity** (vs. 40) and really turn back to God in a thoroughly humbled condition, **Then will I remember my covenant with Jacob . . . with Isaac . . . with Abraham.** The Sinai covenant was a covenant of law, do this or else. But the Abrahamic covenant (Gen 12:1-3) was completely of grace and can never be abrogated by God or terminated by the wicked conduct of His people. In God's providence, Israel will yet turn to the Lord when brought low by the Antichrist during the Tribulation period in the future. God will intervene at the Battle of Armageddon and spare His people Israel, the Jews, and establish the long awaited kingdom that Christ promised. See Matthew 19:28; 26:29; Luke 19:11; Acts 1:6-7; and Revelation 20:1-6.

43-46. I will not cast them away. The amazing truth of these verses is confounding to all atheists, skeptics and doubters. God promised that even while they were in their enemies' land, He would not completely destroy them or break His covenant with them. Archaeology has uncovered the remains of the Canaanites, but where are they today? One can travel to the excavated ancient capital of the Hittites and the ruined cities of the Philistines, but they do not exist as a people today. Yet the Jew possesses a distinct identity. All know who the Jews are, no matter what country they reside in or what language they speak. This is truly a remarkable prophecy!

between him and the children of Israel in mount Sĩ'naĩ by the hand of Moses.

CHAPTER 27

AND the LORD spake unto Moses, saying,

2 Speak unto the children of Israel, and say unto them, When a man shall make a singular vow, the persons *shall be* for the LORD by thy estimation.

3 And thy estimation shall be of the male from twenty years old even unto sixty years old, even thy estimation shall be fifty shekels of silver, after the shekel of the sanctuary.

4 And if it *be* a female, then thy estimation shall be thirty shekels.

5 And if *it be* from five years old even unto twenty years old, then thy estimation shall be of the male twenty shekels, and for the female ten shekels.

6 And if *it be* from a month old even unto five years old, then thy estimation shall be of the male five shekels of silver, and for the female thy estimation *shall be* three shekels of silver.

7 And if *it be* from sixty years old and above; if *it be* a male, then thy estimation shall be fifteen shekels, and for the female ten shekels.

8 But if he be poorer than thy estimation, then he shall present himself before the priest, and the priest shall value him; according to his ability that vowed shall the priest value him.

9 And if *it be* a beast, whereof men bring an offering unto the LORD, all that *any man* giveth of such unto the LORD shall be holy.

10 He shall not alter it, nor change it, a good for a bad, or a bad for a good: and if he shall at all change beast for beast, then it and the exchange thereof shall be holy.

11 And if *it be* any unclean beast, of which they do not offer a sacrifce unto the LORD, then he shall present the beast before the priest:

12 And the priest shall value it, whether it be good or bad: as thou valuest it, *who art* the priest, so shall it be.

13 But if he will at all redeem it, then he shall add a fifth *part* thereof unto thy estimation.

14 ¶And when a man shall sanctify his house *to be* holy unto the LORD, then the priest shall estimate it, whether it be good or bad: as the priest shall estimate it, so shall it stand.

15 And if he that sanctified it will redeem his house, then he shall add the fifth *part* of the money of thy estimation unto it, and it shall be his.

16 And if a man shall sanctify unto the LORD *some part* of a field of his possession, then thy estimation shall be according to the seed thereof: an homer of barley seed *shall be valued* at fifty shekels of silver.

17 If he sanctify his field from the year of jubile, according to thy estimation it shall stand.

18 But if he sanctify his field after the jubile, then the priest shall reckon unto him the money according to the years that remain, even unto the year of the

9. *Laws regarding vows and dedications. 27:1-34.*

This final chapter concerns the presentation of non-sacrificial items to God, such as persons (vss. 3-8), animals (vss. 9-13), houses (vss. 14-15), and fields (vss. 16-25).

27:1-2. When a man shall make a singular vow. A final type of dedication, or vow, could relate to non-sacrificial items. When such was the case, a monetary value was donated to God according to the estimation of the priest.

3-7. The principle involved in estimating the value of persons is that the greatest value is placed on males in the prime of life, from ages **twenty** to **sixty**. Thereafter, the value decreases drastically, indicating the decline that comes with age. Females and those under age twenty are also valued accordingly. What this all meant was that the person making this voluntary vow would pay this sum to the Lord within a specified time.

8. Consideration was given to those who were generally of a poorer station in life. The priest could value him lower accordingly.

9-13. An animal, either clean or unclean, could also be dedicated to God. Its value would be estimated, and payment would be made in the same manner.

14-15. And when a man shall sanctify his house. The same law could be applied to a house, which would then be sold and the proceeds given to God. To **redeem** or keep a house voluntarily dedicated in this way meant to pay the price it was worth, plus an additional twenty percent.

16-25. And if a man shall sanctify . . . some part of a field. Dedicated fields were figured as to how much it would cost to plant the field for fifty years, if it were an inherited field. Since it would return to the original family in the year of jubilee, a field that was purchased was valued according to the time remaining until the next jubilee year. Fields could be redeemed or kept by adding twenty percent to the estimation.

245

jubile, and it shall be abated from thy estimation.

19 And if he that sanctified the field will in any wise redeem it, then he shall add the fifth *part* of the money of thy estimation unto it, and it shall be assured to him.

20 And if he will not redeem the field, or if he have sold the field to another man, it shall not be redeemed any more.

21 But the field, when it goeth out in the jubile, shall be holy unto the LORD, as a field devoted; the possession thereof shall be the priest's.

22 And if *a man* sanctify unto the LORD a field which he hath bought, which *is* not of the fields of his possession;

23 Then the priest shall reckon unto him the worth of thy estimation, *even* unto the year of the jubile: and he shall give thine estimation in that day, *as a* holy thing unto the LORD.

24 In the year of the jubile the field shall return unto him of whom it was bought, *even* to him to whom the possession of the land *did belong.*

25 And all thy estimations shall be according to the shekel of the sanctuary: twenty gerahs shall be the shekel.

26 ¶Only the firstling of the beasts, which should be the LORD's firstling, no man shall sanctify it; whether *it be* ox, or sheep: it *is* the LORD's.

27 And if *it be* of an unclean beast, then he shall redeem *it* according to thine estimation, and shall add a fifth *part* of it thereto: or if it be not redeemed, then it shall be sold according to thy estimation.

28 Notwithstanding no devoted thing, that a man shall devote unto the LORD of all that he hath, *both* of man and beast, and of the field of his possession, shall be sold or redeemed: every devoted thing *is* most holy unto the LORD.

29 None devoted, which shall be devoted of men, shall be redeemed; *but* shall surely be put to death.

30 And all the tithe of the land, *whether* of the seed of the land, *or of* the fruit of the tree, *is* the LORD's: it *is* holy unto the LORD.

31 And if a man will at all redeem *ought* of his tithes, he shall add thereto the fifth *part* thereof.

32 And concerning the tithe of the herd, or of the flock, *even* of whatsoever passeth under the rod, the tenth shall be holy unto the LORD.

33 He shall not search whether it be good or bad, neither shall he change it: and if he change it at all, then both it and the change thereof shall be holy; it shall not be redeemed.

34 These *are* the commandments, which the LORD commanded Moses for the children of Israel in mount Sī'naī.

26-27. A notable exception to the dedication of animals concerned all first-born animals, which belonged to God already (Ex 13:2, 12) and would be sacrificed before Him and could then be eaten (Deut 15:19-23). The first-born of all **unclean** animals, such as the ass, had to be redeemed (Ex 13:13).

28-29. Another exception to the redeeming or buying back of dedicated things occurred when God proclaimed special items or individuals as "dedicated," as with Jericho (Josh 6:17-19, "accursed" means under the ban, or devoted to God), Amalek (I Sam 15:3), and others.

30-34. All the tithe of the land also belonged to God and was to be brought to the priests at the tabernacle, and later the Temple (Mal 3:10). Jesus noted that the Pharisees (very strict Jews) tithed even small seeds (Mt 23:23) and of all that they possessed (Lk 18:12). His commendation must be taken as an encouragement to tithe. Christians are to give as God has blessed them. Naturally, it would be good to begin with at least a tithe (ten percent of gross earnings), but it will be difficult for a spiritual believer to legalistically stop there. Giving today should be to and through the local church (Acts 4:34-37; I Cor 16:2;) for the purpose of spreading the gospel of Jesus Christ, the risen Lamb of God.

BIBLIOGRAPHY

*Allis, Oswald T. Leviticus. In *The New Bible Commentary*. 2nd ed. Ed. by F. Davidson, *et al.* Grand Rapids: Eerdmans, 1954.

*Bonar, Andrew A. *A Commentary on Leviticus*. London: Banner of Truth, reprinted, 1966.

*Bush, George. *Notes, Critical and Practical, on the Book of Leviticus*. Boston: Henry A. Young, 1870.

Chapman, A. T. and A. W. Streane. The Book of Leviticus. In *The Cambridge Bible for Schools and Colleges*. Cambridge: University Press, 1914.

Clark, Samuel. The Third Book of Moses Called Leviticus. In *The Bible Commentary*. Ed. by F. C. Cook. New York: Charles Scribner's Sons, n.d.

*Coleman, Robert O. Leviticus. In *The Wycliffe Bible Commentary*. Ed. by C. F. Pfeiffer and E. F. Harrison. Chicago: Moody, 1962.

Erdman, Charles R. *The Book of Leviticus*. Westwood, N.J.: Revell, 1951.

*Gardiner, Frederic. Leviticus. In *Commentary on the Holy Scriptures*. Ed. by J. P. Lange. Grand Rapids: Zondervan; reprinted, n.d.

Genung, George F. The Book of Leviticus. In *An American Commentary on the Old Testament*. Philadelphia: American Baptist Publication Society, 1905.

Gill, John. Leviticus. In *An Exposition of the Old Testament*. Vol. 1. London: Collingridge, 1852.

Ginsburg, C. D. Leviticus. In *Ellicott's Commentary on the Whole Bible*. Vol. I. Ed. by Charles J. Ellicott. Grand Rapids: Zondervan, reprinted, 1970.

Jukes, Andrew. *The Law of the Offerings*. Fincastle, Virginia: Scripture Truth, n.d.

Kellogg, Samuel Henry. The Book of Leviticus. In *The Expositor's Bible*. Vol. I. Ed. by W. Robertson Nicoll. Grand Rapids: Eerdmans, reprinted, 1956.

Keil, Carl Friedrich and Franz Delitzsch. *Biblical Commentary on the Old Testament*. Vol. II. Trans. by James Martin Grand Rapids: Eerdmans, reprinted, n.d.

McGee, J. Vernon. *Learning through Leviticus*. 2 vols. Los Angeles: Thru the Bible, 1964.

Mackintosh, C. H. *Notes on the Book of Leviticus*. New York: Loizeaux Brothers, 1880.

Meyrick, F. The Book of Leviticus. In *The Pulpit Commentary*. Ed. by H. D. M. Spence and Joseph S. Exell. Grand Rapids: Eerdmans, reprinted, 1950.

*Murphy, James Gracey. *A Critical and Exegetical Commentary on the Book of Leviticus*. Andover: Warren F. Draper, 1874.

Pfeiffer, Charles F. *The Book of Leviticus: A Study Manual*. Grand Rapids: Baker, 1957.

Seiss, Joseph Augustus. *The Gospel in Leviticus*. Grand Rapids: Zondervan, reprinted, n.d.

Wenham, Gordon J. The Book of Leviticus. In *The New International Commentary on the Old Testament*. Ed. by R. K. Harrison. Grand Rapids: Eerdmans, 1979.

NUMBERS

INTRODUCTION

The fourth writing of Moses has a fascination of its own. The story that unfolds comes short of victory; however, its message is universal and timeless. It reminds believers of the spiritual warfare in which they are engaged, for Numbers is the book of the service and walk of God's people.

Name. The Septuagint translators assigned the names to the Old Testament books as they now appear in our English version. The Hebrew title for this book means, simply, "in the wilderness" and comes from the original of 1:1. The Greek name "Numbers" was used by the Latin Vulgate and was later adopted in English Bibles as well. Numbers derives its name from the double numbering of the children of Israel (see chs. 1;26). Combining the Hebrew and Greek names, the gist of the book is given: "in the wilderness" and "numberings."

Authorship. The human author of the Pentateuch was Moses. There is internal and external evidence to support this conclusion.

1. Internal evidence. Numbers 33:2a states: "And Moses wrote their goings out according to their journeys by the commandment of the LORD." Here it is expressly stated that Moses wrote the itinerary of the Israelites from Egypt to Moab. If Moses wrote this, without doubt he also wrote the narrative surrounding the wilderness wanderings.

2. External evidence. The book of Joshua is filled with references to Moses. There are several explicit references to the Mosaic authorship of the written Law: "written in the book of the law of Moses" (Josh 8:31; cf. also vss. 32, 34; 23:6); "the word of the LORD by the hand of Moses" (Josh 22:9; cf. also vs. 5).

Like the Old Testament, the New Testament bears witness to the Mosaic authorship of the Law. The words "Moses" and "law" are considered to be equivalent in the New Testament. Christ quotes from the Pentateuch and ascribes it to Moses: "Moses because of the hardness of your hearts suffered you to put away your wives" (Mt 19:8; cf. also Mt 8:4; Mk 1:44; 7:10; 10:5; 12:26; Lk 5:14; 16:31; 20:37. Take special note of Lk 24:27, 44; Jn 5:46-47; 7:19). The remainder of the New Testament is harmonious with Christ's testimony (Acts 3:22; 13:39; 15:5-21; 26:22; 28:23; Rom 10:5, 19; I Cor 9:9; II Cor 3:15; Rev 15:3).

3. Alleged Post Mosaica in Numbers. Numbers 4:3 states the age for the Levites when they commenced their service as thirty years. In 8:24 it states that the Levites service began at age twenty-five. The apparent contradiction has a simple explanation. Chapter 4 relates to the service of the tabernacle until it would be established permanently. Only one duty of the Levites is mentioned. The concluding verses of the chapter (vss. 47-49) give the ages in connection with this service. By contrast, chapter 8 deals with the regular service of the Levites in the tabernacle (see 8:24). Hence there is no contradiction.

In latter times (see I Chr 23:25-27; II Chr 31:17; Ezra 3:8) the regular service of the Levites began at age twenty. If a later date than the writing of Moses is given to the authorship, as the critics would suggest, then they would need to explain why the author did not pattern the Law after the practices extant at that time. Also, what need would there be to give such detailed instructions for carrying the tabernacle years after the event had transpired? Chapter 4 is a further proof of the Mosaic authorship.

It is claimed by the critics that 13:16 records the giving of the name to Joshua, although he already has his name previously (11:28; Ex 17:9; 24:13). This does not detract from the Mosaic authorship. If a later author edited this, a change may have been made. E. J. Young points out: "The verse may be translated, 'These are the names (i.e., the original names) of the men whom Moses sent to spy out the land, and then (after having previously been called Hoshea) Moses called Hoshea the son of Nun, Joshua' " (*Introduction to the Old Testament*, p. 97ff.). The text does not state when the name was changed.

Critics claim that Moses could not have written about ". . . the book of the wars of the LORD . . ." (21:14). It is unnecessary to regard this as the work of a later editor. This verse is reminding the people of what God has done for them, and there was abundant material about God's intervention for such a book to have been written. Also, the critics assume that the book only refers to physical battles.

In 24:7 mention is made of Agag. This is thought by critics to be an anachronism since Agag reigned in the days of Samuel (I Sam 15:8). In addition to the possibility of more than one person by that name, it is likely that Agag was not a proper name here, but rather a descriptive name of Amalekite kings, as Pharoah was of the Egyptians.

Date. The Pentateuch, as it has come down to us, is generally admitted to be a unity. Until the rise of higher criticism in the eighteenth century, the virtually unchallenged view was that the Pentateuch was written by a single writer, that that writer was Moses, and that all the Pentateuch was written ca. 1450 B.C. to 1410 B.C. The critics maintain a later date, as has been noted previously.

Purpose. Numbers resumes the narrative that stopped in Exodus; Leviticus details Israel's legislation. Now that the priestly laws have been revealed, the nation is ready to proceed from Sinai. The itinerary to the plains of Moab is narrated, and it concludes with the instruction for the division of the land.

Numbers is not intended to be a continuous, full narrative. Very little detail is given of the thirty-eight years of wanderings. Emphasis is placed on the significant events, not the extent of time.

Importance. The book of Numbers is referred to many times in the New Testament. The Holy

Spirit called special attention to Numbers in I Corinthians 10:1-12. The words "all these things happened unto them for examples" (I Cor 10:11) is significant. The word here translated as "examples" (Gr *tupos*) means types. A. C. Gaebelein states that the faithless failure of Israel to enter Canaan may well foreshadow, as it certainly illustrates, the failure of the organized Church today to possess the heavenly things in Christ. Numbers is a great book to illustrate the doctrines of the New Testament.

Theme. In Romans 11:22 Paul speaks about "the goodness and severity of God." That, in a capsule,

is the message of Numbers. The severity of God is seen in the death of the old generation in the wilderness; these never entered the Promised Land. The goodness of God is realized in the new generation. God protected, preserved, and provided for these people until they possessed the land. This reminds us of the justice and love of God, which are always in sovereign harmony.

Paul uses this example as a warning against presumption: ". . . let him that thinketh he standeth take heed lest he fall" (I Cor 10:12). A warning is also given of the consequences of unbelief in Hebrews 3:12-19.

OUTLINE

COMMENTARY

I. ISRAEL: AT MOUNT SINAI. 1:1-10:10.

A. Order and Organization. 1:1-4:49.

1. Appointing of the census. 1:1-54.

AND the LORD spake unto Moses in the wilderness of Sī'naī, in the tabernacle of the congregation, on the first *day* of the second month, in the second year after they were come out of the land of Egypt, saying,

1:1. And the LORD spake unto Moses. Before the canon of Scripture was complete, the Lord spoke audibly to reveal truth. Today, God speaks to us through the Bible, as His final revelation. God does not speak audibly in this age. **In the tabernacle of the congregation.** This is where God spoke to Moses "face to face" (Ex 33:11). It is also where the law of the book of Leviticus was given (Lev 1:1). The local church is God's masterpiece in this age for the fulfillment of the Great Commission. **On the first day of the second month, in the second year.** There is a break of just one month between the erecting of the tabernacle, at the

249

2 Take ye the sum of all the congregation of the children of Israel, after their families, by the house of their fathers, with the number of *their* names, every male by their polls;

3 From twenty years old and upward, all that are able to go forth to war in Israel: thou and Aaron shall number them by their armies.

4 And with you there shall be a man of every tribe; every one head of the house of his fathers.

5 ¶And these *are* the names of the men that shall stand with you: of *the tribe of* Reuben; E-lī'zur the son of Shĕd'e-ur.

6 Of Simeon; She-lū'mĭ-el the son of Zū-rĭ-shăd'da-ī.

7 Of Jūdah; Näh'shŏn the son of Am-mĭn'a-dăb.

8 Of Ĭs'sa-char; Ne-thăn'e-el the son of Zū'ar.

9 Of Zĕb'u-lun; E-lī'ab the son of Hē'-lŏn.

10 Of the children of Joseph: of Ē'phra-im; E-lĭsh'a-ma the son of Ăm-mĭ'hŭd: of Ma-năs'seh; Ga-mā'lĭ-el the son of Pe-däh'zur.

11 Of Benjamin; Ab'ĭ-dan the son of Gĭd-e-ō'nĭ.

12 Of Dan; Ā-hĭ-ē'zer the son of Ăm-mĭ-shăd'da-ī.

13 Of Asher; Pā'gĭ-el the son of Ŏc'ran.

14 Of Gad; E-lī'a-săph the son of Deū'el.

15 Of Năph'ta-lī; A-hī'ra the son of Ē'nan.

16 These *were* the renowned of the congregation, princes of the tribes of their fathers, heads of thousands in Israel.

17 ¶And Moses and Aaron took these men which are expressed by *their* names:

18 And they assembled all the congregation together on the first *day* of the second month, and they declared their pedigrees after their families, by the house of their fathers, according to the number of the names, from twenty years old and upward, by their polls.

19 As the LORD commanded Moses, so he numbered them in the wilderness of Sĭ'naī.

20 ¶And the children of Reuben, Israel's eldest son, by their generations, after their families, by the house of their fathers, according to the number of the names, by their polls, every male from twenty years old and upward, all that were able to go forth to war;

21 Those that were numbered of them, *even* of the tribe of Reuben, *were*

end of Exodus, and the start of Numbers. The book of Leviticus comes in this brief space of time. A Hebrew month expresses the idea of a lunation. The commencement of a new month was generally decided by observation of the new moon. It was one year and two weeks since the Exodus from Egypt and ten and a half months since their arrival in Sinai.

2. Take ye the sum. This order was given one month after the tabernacle was set up (cf. Ex 40:2, 17) and is probably the same as the one mentioned in Exodus 30:12 and 38:21. It seems to be the completion of the earlier one. This is concluded on the basis that the figures mentioned in Exodus 38:26 and in Numbers 1:46 are identical (603,550 males from twenty years old and upward). This is the first of three Israelite censuses taken in the Old Testament. (For the others, see ch. 2 and II Sam 24.)

3-17. From twenty years old and upward. It is tragic that of these men, 603,550 in number, 603,548 would later perish in the wilderness (cf. 14:29). The only two men who would later enter Canaan were Joshua and Caleb.

18-45. And they assembled all the congregation together. It is to be noted that this census was to be carried out in a systematic manner. Moses and Aaron were instructed to organize the people in tribes, clans, and families; and a leader was then chosen from each of the twelve tribes who was responsible for the count of his particular tribe. All this serves as an Old Testament example of the Apostle Paul's New Testament command: "Let all things be done decently and in order" (I Cor 14:40). **Of the children of Judah** (vs. 26). This tribe, with 74,600 fighting men, was the largest of the twelve. **Of the children of Joseph** (vs. 32). Here we have the names of the only two grandsons of the patriarch, Jacob, who originally founded one-sixth of the twelve tribes of Israel. Their names were Ephraim and Manasseh. The remaining ten tribes were founded by Jacob's sons. **Of the children of Manasseh** (vs. 34). This group, 32,200 strong, was the smallest of the twelve tribes. It is interesting to note, however, that they would later show the

forty and six thousand and five hundred.

22 ¶Of the children of Simeon, by their generations, after their families, by the house of their fathers, those that were numbered of them, according to the number of the names, by their polls, every male from twenty years old and upward, all that were able to go forth to war;

23 Those that were numbered of them, *even* of the tribe of Simeon, *were* fifty and nine thousand and three hundred.

24 ¶Of the children of Gad, by their generations, after their families, by the house of their fathers, according to the number of the names, from twenty years old and upward, all that were able to go forth to war;

25 Those that were numbered of them, *even* of the tribe of Gad, *were* forty and five thousand six hundred and fifty.

26 ¶Of the children of Jūdah, by their generations, after their families, by the house of their fathers, according to the number of the names, from twenty years old and upward, all that were able to go forth to war;

27 Those that were numbered of them, *even* of the tribe of Jūdah, *were* threescore and fourteen thousand and six hundred.

28 ¶Of the children of Ĭs'sa-char, by their generations, after their families, by the house of their fathers, according to the number of the names, from twenty years old and upward, all that were able to go forth to war;

29 Those that were numbered of them, *even* of the tribe of Ĭs'sa-char, *were* fifty and four thousand and four hundred.

30 ¶Of the children of Zĕb'u-lun, by their generations, after their families, by the house of their fathers, according to the number of the names, from twenty years old and upward, all that were able to go forth to war;

31 Those that were numbered of them, *even* of the tribe of Zĕb'u-lun, *were* fifty and seven thousand and four hundred.

32 ¶Of the children of Joseph, *namely*, of the children of Ē'phra-im, by their generations, after their families, by the house of their fathers, according to the number of the names, from twenty years old and upward, all that were able to go forth to war;

33 Those that were numbered of them, *even* of the tribe of Ē'phra-im, *were* forty thousand and five hundred.

34 ¶Of the children of Ma-năs'seh, by their generations, after their families, by the house of their fathers, according to the number of the names, from twenty years old and upward, all that were able to go forth to war;

35 Those that were numbered of them, *even* of the tribe of Ma-năs'seh, *were* thirty and two thousand and two hundred.

36 ¶Of the children of Benjamin, by their generations, after their families, by the house of their fathers, according to the number of the names, from

largest percentage of growth at the taking of the second census (see 26:34).

twenty years old and upward, all that were able to go forth to war;

37 Those that were numbered of them, *even* of the tribe of Benjamin, *were* thirty and five thousand and four hundred.

38 ¶Of the children of Dan, by their generations, after their families, by the house of their fathers, according to the number of the names, from twenty years old and upward, all that were able to go forth to war;

39 Those that were numbered of them, *even* of the tribe of Dan, *were* threescore and two thousand and seven hundred.

40 ¶Of the children of Asher, by their generations, after their families, by the house of their fathers, according to the number of the names, from twenty years old and upward, all that were able to go forth to war;

41 Those that were numbered of them, *even* of the tribe of Asher, *were* forty and one thousand and five hundred.

42 ¶Of the children of Năph'ta-lī, throughout their generations, after their families, by the house of their fathers, according to the number of the names, from twenty years old and upward, all that were able to go forth to war;

43 Those that were numbered of them, *even* of the tribe of Năph'ta-lī, *were* fifty and three thousand and four hundred.

44 ¶These *are* those that were numbered, which Moses and Aaron numbered, and the princes of Israel, *being* twelve men: each one was for the house of his fathers.

45 So were all those that were numbered of the children of Israel, by the house of their fathers, from twenty years old and upward, all that were able to go forth to war in Israel;

46 Even all they that were numbered were six hundred thousand and three thousand and five hundred and fifty.

46. Six hundred thousand and three thousand and five hundred and fifty. Much speculation has centered around this figure. If taken literally it would strongly suggest a total Israelite population of over two million! The problem, therefore, arises concerning the care and feeding of this multitude for nearly forty years, much of it spent in a desolate and arid desert. For example, it has been estimated that it would require nearly fifty railway cars of manna per day to feed the people. This would not take into account the physical needs of the thousands of animals which accompanied them. The water needs would likewise be immense: some twelve million gallons per day. In fact, the area needed to accommodate this multitude when they camped at night would exceed one hundred square miles!

Some have attempted to solve these problems by a watering down of the text. For example, it is suggested the word translated by the KJV as "thousand" (Heb *'elep*) could as easily be rendered by the word "family" or "clan."

Thus, we would have six hundred and three families with each family contributing perhaps an average of five fighting men each for a total of 3,015 soldiers. Assuming each man was married and had two children, we then would arrive at the figure of some fifteen thousand as the grand total of Israel's camp. But this approach raises far more problems than it solves. Gleason Archer writes: "It is true that there is an *'elep* which means family or clan (I Sam 10:19; Judg 6:15, etc.); but it is very clear from the numeration chapters (chs. 1-4;26) that *'elep* is intended in the sense of 'thousand,' for the smaller unit below this *'elep* is *me'ot*, 'hundreds'' (cf. 1:21, 23, 25, etc.). The most that a "family" could contribute to the national army would be four or five men on the average, and it would be absurd to suppose that 'hundreds' would be mentioned or the next lower numerical unit after an average contingent of five men each.

"Further corroboration is given by the total amount of ransom money—at the rate of half shekel apiece—recorded in Exodus 38:25 as 100 talents, 1775 shekels. Since there were 3000 shekels to the talent, this comes out to exactly 603,550 contributors. It is therefore safe to say that no objective handling of the textual evidence can possibly sustain the thesis that *'elep* in Numbers signifies anything less than a literal thousand" (Gleason Archer, *A Survey of Old Testament Introduction*, pp. 246-247).

47-54. But the Levites . . . were not numbered. The actual number of the Levitical men twenty years and upward is not listed, as is the case of the twelve tribes. However, we are given some idea of the size of this tribe with the information that it had 22,000 male babies one month old and upward (3:39) and 8,580 able-bodied priests from ages thirty to fifty (4:48).

47 ¶But the Lēvītes after the tribe of their fathers were not numbered among them.
48 For the LORD had spoken unto Moses, saying,
49 Only thou shalt not number the tribe of Levi, neither take the sum of them among the children of Israel:
50 But thou shalt appoint the Lēvītes over the tabernacle of testimony, and over all the vessels thereof, and over all things that *belong* to it: they shall bear the tabernacle, and all the vessels thereof; and they shall minister unto it, and shall encamp round about the tabernacle.
51 And when the tabernacle setteth forward, the Lēvītes shall take it down: and when the tabernacle is to be pitched, the Levites shall set it up: and the stranger that cometh nigh shall be put to death.
52 And the children of Israel shall pitch their tents, every man by his own camp, and every man by his own standard, throughout their hosts.
53 But the Lēvītes shall pitch round about the tabernacle of testimony, that there be no wrath upon the congregation of the children of Israel: and the Lēvītes shall keep the charge of the tabernacle of testimony.
54 And the children of Israel did according to all that the LORD commanded Moses, so did they.

CHAPTER 2
AND the LORD spake unto Moses and unto Aaron, saying,

2 Every man of the children of Israel shall pitch by his own standard, with the ensign of their father's house: far off about the tabernacle of the congregation shall they pitch.
3 ¶And on the east side toward the rising of the sun shall they of the standard of the camp of Jūdah pitch throughout their armies: and Näh'shŏn

2. Arrangement of the tribes. 2:1-34.

2:1. And the LORD spake unto Moses. This phrase is found some eighty-five times in the book of Numbers. God was keenly interested in the details concerning the position the tribes assumed during their camp time, their manner of marching, the location of the tabernacle, etc. We see a great emphasis on discipline and order. To understand this, it must be remembered that the people were only a few weeks removed from their enslavement in Egypt. They were totally disorganized as a nation, and they enjoyed no formal administrative background. Thus, the reason for all the detailed orders and discipline, lest anarchy reign.

2-16. The tabernacle of the congregation. This is, literally, "the tent of the meeting," that is, a special place where God Himself would meet with His people (see Ex 25:8).

the son of Am-mĭn′a-dăb *shall be* captain of the children of Jŭdah.

4 And his host, and those that were numbered of them, *were* threescore and fourteen thousand and six hundred.

5 And those that do pitch next unto him *shall be* the tribe of Ĭs′sa-char: and Ne-thăn′e-el the son of Zū′ar *shall be* captain of the children of Ĭs′sa-char.

6 And his host, and those that were numbered thereof, *were* fifty and four thousand and four hundred.

7 *Then* the tribe of Zĕb′u-lun: and E-lī′ab the son of Hē′lŏn *shall be* captain of the children of Zĕb′u-lun.

8 And his host, and those that were numbered thereof, *were* fifty and seven thousand and four hundred.

9 All that were numbered in the camp of Jŭdah *were* an hundred thousand and fourscore thousand and six thousand and four hundred, throughout their armies. These shall first set forth.

10 ¶On the south side *shall be* the standard of the camp of Reuben according to their armies: and the captain of the children of Reuben *shall be* E-lī′zur the son of Shĕd′e-ur.

11 And his host, and those that were numbered thereof, *were* forty and six thousand and five hundred.

12 And those which pitch by him *shall be* the tribe of Simeon: and the captain of the children of Simeon *shall be* She-lū′mī-el the son of Zū-rī-shăd′-da-ī.

13 And his host, and those that were numbered of them, *were* fifty and nine thousand and three hundred.

14 Then the tribe of Gad: and the captain of the sons of Gad *shall be* E-lī′a-săph the son of Reū′el.

15 And his host, and those that were numbered of them, *were* forty and five thousand and six hundred and fifty.

16 All that were numbered in the camp of Reuben *were* an hundred thousand and fifty and one thousand and four hundred and fifty, throughout their armies. And they shall set forth in the second rank.

17 ¶Then the tabernacle of the congregation shall set forward with the camp of the Lēvītes in the midst of the camp: as they encamp, so shall they set forward, every man in his place by their standards.

18 ¶On the west side *shall be* the standard of the camp of Ē′phra-im according to their armies: and the captain of the sons of Ē′phra-im *shall be* E-līsh′a-ma the son of Ăm-mī′hŭd.

19 And his host, and those that were numbered of them, *were* forty thousand and five hundred.

20 And by him *shall be* the tribe of Mă-năs′seh: and the captain of the children of Ma-năs′seh *shall be* Ga-mā′lī-el the son of Pe-däh′zur.

21 And his host, and those that were numbered of them, *were* thirty and two thousand and two hundred.

22 Then the tribe of Benjamin: and the captain of the sons of Benjamin *shall be* Ab′ī-dan the son of Gĭd-e-ō′nī.

23 And his host, and those that were

17-33. The tabernacle . . . in the midst of the camp. The tabernacle was not to play only a part in Israel's national life, but was to occupy the focal place! This is but a foreshadow of God's perfect plan, which reaches its climax as described by John in Scripture's final book: "And I beheld, and, lo, in the midst of the throne and of the four beasts, and in the midst of the elders, stood a Lamb as it had been slain . . ." (Rev 5:6).

numbered of them, *were* thirty and five thousand and four hundred.

24 All that were numbered of the camp of Ē'phra-im *were* an hundred thousand and eight thousand and an hundred, throughout their armies. And they shall go forward in the third rank.

25 ¶The standard of the camp of Dan *shall be* on the north side by their armies: and the captain of the children of Dan *shall be* Ā-hī-ē'zer the son of Ăm-mĭ-shăd'da-ī.

26 And his host, and those that were numbered of them, *were* threescore and two thousand and seven hundred.

27 And those that encamp by him *shall be* the tribe of Asher: and the captain of the children of Asher *shall be* Pā'gĭ-el the son of Ŏc'ran.

28 And his host, and those that were numbered of them, *were* forty and one thousand and five hundred.

29 ¶Then the tribe of Năph'ta-lī: and the captain of the children of Năph'ta-lī *shall be* A-hī'ra the son of Ē'nan.

30 And his host, and those that were numbered of them, *were* fifty and three thousand and four hundred.

31 All they that were numbered in the camp of Dan *were* an hundred thousand and fifty and seven thousand and six hundred. They shall go hindmost with their standards.

32 ¶These *are* those which were numbered of the children of Israel by the house of their fathers: all those that were numbered of the camps throughout their hosts *were* six hundred thousand and three thousand and five hundred and fifty.

33 But the Lēvītes were not numbered among the children of Israel; as the LORD commanded Moses.

34 And the children of Israel did according to all that the LORD commanded Moses: so they pitched by their standards, and so they set forward, every one after their families, according to the house of their fathers.

34. So they pitched by their standards. Harrison writes: "The arrangement of the tribes by their standards in the form of a hollow rectangle around the tabernacle (2:2ff.) is now known to have been a common deployment of encamped forces in the Amarna period" (R. K. Harrison, *Introduction to the Old Testament*, p. 622).

Especially to be noted is the actual arrangement of the various tribes by location. On the east were Issachar, Judah, and Zebulun. On the west were the tribes of Benjamin, Ephraim, and Manasseh. In the north were Asher, Dan, and Naphtali, while the south was occupied by Gad, Reuben, and Simeon. Rabbinical tradition suggests that Judah (leader of the eastern section) carried with it a standard of green because it was on an emerald that the name of Judah was engraved upon the breastplate of the High Priest, and that its emblem was that of a lion because of the prophecy in Genesis 49:9.

Reuben, leader of the southern flank, flew a red standard to commemorate its name written on a sardius stone. Their emblem was that of a human head. The chief tribe of the western side was Ephraim. It displayed a golden flag, for it was upon a golden stone that the name of the tribe was engraved. Ephraim's emblem was a calf, it is said, because Joseph (their founder) was elevated to power in Egypt through a calf vision (see Gen 41:1-32). Finally the color of Dan (northern leader) was red and white, for its stone was the jasper. An eagle was the emblem of this tribe. We are not sure, of course, just how much of this interpretation is based on fact. If it is true, however, it blends in beautifully with the visions of both Ezekiel and John (see Ex 1 and Rev 4).

CHAPTER 3

THESE also *are* the generations of Aaron and Moses in the day *that* the LORD spake with Moses in mount Sī′-naī.

2 And these *are* the names of the sons of Aaron; Nā́dăb the firstborn, and A-bī′hū, Ĕ-le-ā′zar, and Ĭth′a-mär.

3 These *are* the names of the sons of Aaron, the priests which were anointed, whom he consecrated to minister in the priest's office.

4 And Nā́dăb and A-bī′hū died before the LORD, when they offered strange fire before the LORD, in the wilderness of Sī′naī, and they had no children: and Ĕ-le-ā′zar and Ĭth′a-mär ministered in the priest's office in the sight of Aaron their father.

5 ¶And the LORD spake unto Moses, saying,

6 Bring the tribe of Levi near, and present them before Aaron the priest, that they may minister unto him.

7 And they shall keep his charge, and the charge of the whole congregation before the tabernacle of the congregation, to do the service of the tabernacle.

8 And they shall keep all the instruments of the tabernacle of the congregation, and the charge of the children of Israel, to do the service of the tabernacle.

9 And thou shalt give the Lḗvītes unto Aaron and to his sons: they *are* wholly given unto him out of the children of Israel.

10 And thou shalt appoint Aaron and his sons, and they shall wait on their priest's office: and the stranger that cometh nigh shall be put to death.

11 ¶And the LORD spake unto Moses, saying,

12 And I, behold, I have taken the Lḗvītes from among the children of Israel instead of all the firstborn that openeth the matrix among the children of Israel: therefore the Lḗvītes shall be mine;

13 Because all the firstborn *are* mine; *for* on the day that I smote all the firstborn in the land of Egypt I hallowed unto me all the firstborn in Israel, both man and beast: mine shall they be: I *am* the LORD.

14 ¶And the LORD spake unto Moses in the wilderness of Sī′naī, saying,

15 Number the children of Levi after the house of their fathers, by their families: every male from a month old and upward shalt thou number them.

16 And Moses numbered them according to the word of the LORD, as he was commanded.

17 And these were the sons of Levi by their names; Ger′shon, and Kō′hăth, and Me-rā′rī.

18 And these *are* the names of the

256

3. Commission of the Levites. 3:1-4:49.

3:1-11. Nadab . . . Abihu, Eleazar, and Ithamar. Aaron's sons would suffer a fifty percent mortality rate. His eldest two, Nadab and Abihu, had already been struck dead by a divine judgment. The historical context (Lev 10) suggests they may have been drunk at the time. His younger boys, however, would turn out much better. Eleazar would later replace his father, becoming Israel's second High Priest (see 20:25). Ithamar, the youngest, was appointed by God to be in charge of the tabernacle (see 4:28, 33; 7:8).

12-16. I have taken the Levites . . . instead of all the first-born. It would seem that God's original perfect will was to set apart to special service the first-born from all the tribes (Ex 13:1-2), but because of sin God would limit His choice to the tribe of Levi. Part of the reason for this was, undoubtedly, the faithfulness and loyalty of Levi during the terrible sin of the golden calf (see Ex 32:26).

17. Gershon, and Kohath, and Merari. Aaron, Miriam, and Moses were descendants of Levi through his son Kohath (see I Chr 6:1-2; 23:13). The descendants of these three sons are now assigned specific duties concerning the tabernacle. In brief, the Gershonites were responsible for the tent and coverings and the Kohathites for the furniture and vessels, while the Merarites were in charge of the frames, boards, pillars, and sockets.

It must have been inspiring just to witness the harmony of these three highly trained teams as they set up and took down the tabernacle.

18-39. Twenty and two thousand. This is the sum total of

sons of Ger'shon by their families; Lĭb'-nī, and Shĭm'e-ī.

19 And the sons of Kō'hăth by their families; Ăm'răm, and Ĭz'e-här, Hēbron, and Ŭz'zĭ-el.

20 And the sons of Me-râ'rī by their families; Mäh'lī, and Mū'shī. These are the families of the Lēvītes according to the house of their fathers.

21 ¶Of Ger'shon was the family of the Lĭb'nītes, and the family of the Shĭm'-ītes: these are the families of the Ger'shon-ītes.

22 Those that were numbered of them, according to the number of all the males, from a month old and upward, even those that were numbered of them were seven thousand and five hundred.

23 The families of the Ger'shon-ītes shall pitch behind the tabernacle westward.

24 And the chief of the house of the father of the Ger'shon-ītes shall be E-lī'a-săph the son of Lā'el.

25 And the charge of the sons of Ger'shon in the tabernacle of the congregation shall be the tabernacle, and the tent, the covering thereof, and the hanging for the door of the tabernacle of the congregation,

26 And the hangings of the court, and the curtain for the door of the court, which is by the tabernacle, and by the altar round about, and the cords of it for all the service thereof.

27 ¶And of Kō'hăth was the family of the Am'ra-mītes, and the family of the Ĭz'e-här-ītes, and the family of the Hē'bro-nītes, and the family of the Ŭz'zĭ-el-ītes: these are the families of the Kō'hăth-ītes.

28 In the number of all the males, from a month old and upward, were eight thousand and six hundred, keeping the charge of the sanctuary.

29 The families of the sons of Kō'hăth shall pitch on the side of the tabernacle southward.

30 And the chief of the house of the father of the families of the Kō'hăth-ītes shall be E-liz'ā-phăn the son of Ŭz'zĭ-el.

31 And their charge shall be the ark, and the table, and the candlestick, and the altars, and the vessels of the sanctuary wherewith they minister, and the hanging, and all the service thereof.

32 And Ĕ-le-ā'zar the son of Aaron the priest shall be chief over the chief of the Lēvītes, and have the oversight of them that keep the charge of the sanctuary.

33 ¶Of Me-râ'rī was the family of the Mäh'lītes, and the family of the Mū'-shītes: these are the families of Me-râ'-rī.

34 And those that were numbered of them, according to the number of all the males, from a month old and upward, were six thousand and two hundred.

35 And the chief of the house of the father of the families of Me-râ'rī was Zū'rī-el the son of Ăb-i-hā'il: these shall pitch on the side of the tabernacle northward.

the descendants of Levi's three sons. However, a problem arises here; for the number given for the Gershonites is seven thousand five hundred (vs. 22), that of Kohath eight thousand six hundred (vs. 28), and six thousand two hundred from Merari (vs. 34). This adds up to twenty-two thousand three hundred, or three hundred more than stated in verse 39. Ryrie suggests the following: "The addition of one Hebrew letter would change eight thousand, six hundred to eight thousand, three hundred and bring the figures in verses 22, 28, and 34 into agreement with the total in verse 39" (The Ryrie Study Bible, p. 210).

36 And *under* the custody and charge of the sons of Me-râ´rī *shall be* the boards of the tabernacle, and the bars thereof, and the pillars thereof, and the sockets thereof, and all the vessels thereof, and all that serveth thereto.

37 And the pillars of the court round about, and their sockets, and their pins, and their cords.

38 ¶But those that encamp before the tabernacle toward the east, *even* before the tabernacle of the congregation eastward, *shall be* Moses, and Aaron and his sons, keeping the charge of the sanctuary for the charge of the children of Israel; and the stranger that cometh nigh shall be put to death.

39 All that were numbered of the Lē-vītes, which Moses and Aaron numbered at the commandment of the LORD, throughout their families, all the males from a month old and upward, *were* twenty and two thousand.

40 ¶And the LORD said unto Moses, Number all the firstborn of the males of the children of Israel from a month old and upward, and take the number of their names.

41 And thou shalt take the Lēvītes for me (I *am* the LORD) instead of all the firstborn among the children of Israel; and the cattle of the Lēvītes instead of all the firstlings among the cattle of the children of Israel.

42 And Moses numbered, as the LORD commanded him, all the firstborn among the children of Israel.

43 And all the firstborn males by the number of names, from a month old and upward, of those that were numbered of them, were twenty and two thousand two hundred and threescore and thirteen.

44 ¶And the LORD spake unto Moses, saying,

45 Take the Lēvītes instead of all the firstborn among the children of Israel, and the cattle of the Lēvītes instead of their cattle; and the Lēvītes shall be mine: I *am* the LORD.

46 And for those that are to be redeemed of the two hundred and threescore and thirteen of the firstborn of the children of Israel, which are more than the Lēvītes;

47 Thou shalt even take five shekels apiece by the poll, after the shekel of the sanctuary shalt thou take *them:* (the shekel *is* twenty gerahs:)

48 And thou shalt give the money, wherewith the odd number of them is to be redeemed, unto Aaron and to his sons.

49 And Moses took the redemption money of them that were over and above them that were redeemed by the Lēvītes:

50 Of the firstborn of the children of Israel took he the money; a thousand three hundred and threescore and five *shekels,* after the shekel of the sanctuary:

51 And Moses gave the money of them that were redeemed unto Aaron and to his sons, according to the word of the LORD, as the LORD commanded Moses.

40-51. The odd number of them is to be redeemed. Jones writes: "As shown in verse 13, all the first-born belong to the Lord. But since the Levites were now dedicated to the service of the Lord in relation to the tabernacle, they redeem the first-born, that is, they liberate the first-born from their special relationship and responsibility. One Levite is accepted for one of the first-born. Since there were two hundred seventy-three more first-born than Levites, money was given for this number (vss. 46-47). This was in accord with the law in Leviticus 27. This money was given to Aaron and his sons (vs. 51)" (K. Jones, *The Book of Numbers*, p. 23).

CHAPTER 4

AND the Lord spake unto Moses and unto Aaron, saying,

2 Take the sum of the sons of Kō′hăth from among the sons of Levi, after their families, by the house of their fathers,

3 From thirty years old and upward even until fifty years old, all that enter into the host, to do the work in the tabernacle of the congregation.

4 ¶This *shall be* the service of the sons of Kō′hăth in the tabernacle of the congregation, *about* the most holy things:

5 And when the camp setteth forward, Aaron shall come, and his sons, and they shall take down the covering vail, and cover the ark of testimony with it:

6 And shall put thereon the covering of badgers' skins, and shall spread over *it* a cloth wholly of blue, and shall put in the staves thereof.

7 And upon the table of shewbread they shall spread a cloth of blue, and put thereon the dishes, and the spoons, and the bowls, and covers to cover withal: and the continual bread shall be thereon:

8 And they shall spread upon them a cloth of scarlet, and cover the same with a covering of badgers' skins, and shall put in the staves thereof.

9 And they shall take a cloth of blue, and cover the candlestick of the light, and his lamps, and his tongs, and his snuffdishes, and all the oil vessels thereof, wherewith they minister unto it:

10 And they shall put it and all the vessels thereof within a covering of badgers' skins, and shall put *it* upon a bar.

11 And upon the golden altar they shall spread a cloth of blue, and cover it with a covering of badgers' skins, and shall put to the staves thereof:

12 And they shall take all the instruments of ministry, wherewith they minister in the sanctuary, and put *them* in a cloth of blue, and cover them with a covering of badgers' skins, and shall put *them* on a bar:

13 And they shall take away the ashes from the altar, and spread a purple cloth thereon:

14 And they shall put upon it all the vessels thereof, wherewith they minister about it, *even* the censers, the fleshhooks, and the shovels, and the basons, all the vessels of the altar; and they shall spread upon it a covering of badgers' skins, and put to the staves of it.

15 And when Aaron and his sons have made an end of covering the sanctuary, and all the vessels of the sanctuary, as the camp is to set forward; after that, the sons of Kō′hăth shall come to bear *it:* but they shall not touch any holy thing, lest they die. These *things are* the burden of the sons of Kō′hăth in the tabernacle of the congregation.

16 ¶And to the office of Ĕ-le-ā′zar the son of Aaron the priest *pertaineth* the oil for the light, and the sweet incense, and the daily meat offering, and the anointing oil, *and* the oversight of all

4:1-3. From thirty years old. This was the beginning of the Levitical designated age for a priest. In the New Testament Luke records the age of Jesus at His baptism: "And Jesus himself began to be about thirty years of age . . ." (Lk 3:23).

4-14. This shall be the service of the sons of Kohath. Kohath was the second son of Levi, but his descendants are mentioned first here. They were given the most important task in the tabernacle, that of caring for the sacred furniture and vessels. They may have been chosen for this because both Moses and Aaron were Kohathites.

15. Kohath shall come to bear it. The sacred furniture in the tabernacle was to be carried on the shoulders of the Kohathites. Later, heavy wagons drawn by oxen were given to both the Gershonites and Merarites to help them with their labor, but not to the Kohathites (see 7:6-9). Some four centuries later King David would transgress this law with dire consequences when he attempted to bring the Ark of the Covenant into Jerusalem on a cart (see II Sam 6).

16-49. And to . . . Eleazar . . . pertaineth . . . all . . . in the sanctuary. Because of their important duties, the future High Priest of Israel, Eleazar himself was put in charge of the Kohathites. Ithamar, Eleazar's brother, was over the Gershonites and Merarites (vss. 28, 33). The total number of the

259

NUMBERS 4:17

the tabernacle, and of all that therein *is*, in the sanctuary, and in the vessels thereof.

17 ¶And the LORD spake unto Moses and unto Aaron, saying,

18 Cut ye not off the tribe of the families of the families of the Kō′hăth-ītes from among the Lēvītes:

19 But thus do unto them, that they may live, and not die, when they approach unto the most holy things: Aaron and his sons shall go in, and appoint them every one to his service and to his burden:

20 But they shall not go in to see when the holy things are covered, lest they die.

21 ¶And the LORD spake unto Moses, saying,

22 Take also the sum of the sons of Ger′shon, throughout the houses of their fathers, by their families;

23 From thirty years old and upward until fifty years old shalt thou number them; all that enter in to perform the service, to do the work in the tabernacle of the congregation.

24 This *is* the service of the families of the Ger′shon-ītes, to serve, and for burdens:

25 And they shall bear the curtains of the tabernacle, and the tabernacle of the congregation, his covering, and the covering of the badgers' skins that *is* above upon it, and the hanging for the door of the tabernacle of the congregation,

26 And the hangings of the court, and the hanging for the door of the gate of the court, which *is* by the tabernacle and by the altar round about, and their cords, and all the instruments of their service, and all that is made for them: so shall they serve.

27 At the appointment of Aaron and his sons shall be all the service of the sons of the Ger′shon-ītes, in all their burdens, and in all their service: and ye shall appoint unto them in charge all their burdens.

28 This *is* the service of the families of the sons of Ger′shon in the tabernacle of the congregation: and their charge *shall be* under the hand of Ĭth′a-mär the son of Aaron the priest.

29 ¶As for the sons of Me-râ′rī, thou shalt number them after their families, by the house of their fathers;

30 From thirty years old and upward even unto fifty years old shalt thou number them, every one that entereth into the service, to do the work of the tabernacle of the congregation.

31 And this *is* the charge of their burden, according to all their service in the tabernacle of the congregation; the boards of the tabernacle, and the bars thereof, and the pillars thereof, and sockets thereof,

32 And the pillars of the court round about, and their sockets, and their pins, and their cords, with all their instruments, and with all their service: and by name ye shall reckon the instruments of the charge of their burden.

33 This *is* the service of the families of the sons of Me-râ′rī, according to all

Levitical priesthood is given as 8,580 in verse 48. If the estimated Israelite population of that time, some two million, is divided by the number of the priesthood, 8,580, it comes out that each priest was responsible for around two hundred thirty-three people.

260

their service, in the tabernacle of the congregation, under the hand of Ĭth'a-mär the son of Aaron the priest.

34 ¶And Moses and Aaron and the chief of the congregation numbered the sons of the Kō'hăth-ītes after their families, and after the house of their fathers,

35 From thirty years old and upward even unto fifty years old, every one that entereth into the service, for the work in the tabernacle of the congregation:

36 And those that were numbered of them by their families were two thousand seven hundred and fifty.

37 These were they that were numbered of the families of the Kō'hăth-ītes, all that might do service in the tabernacle of the congregation, which Moses and Aaron did number according to the commandment of the Lord by the hand of Moses.

38 ¶And those that were numbered of the sons of Ger'shon, throughout their families, and by the house of their fathers,

39 From thirty years old and upward even unto fifty years old, every one that entereth into the service, for the work in the tabernacle of the congregation,

40 Even those that were numbered of them, throughout their families, by the house of their fathers, were two thousand and six hundred and thirty.

41 These are they that were numbered of the families of the sons of Ger'shon, of all that might do service in the tabernacle of the congregation, whom Moses and Aaron did number according to the commandment of the Lord.

42 ¶And those that were numbered of the families of the sons of Me-râ'rī, throughout their families, by the house of their fathers,

43 From thirty years old and upward even unto fifty years old, every one that entereth into the service, for the work in the tabernacle of the congregation,

44 Even those that were numbered of them after their families, were three thousand and two hundred.

45 These be those that were numbered of the families of the sons of Me-râ'rī, whom Moses and Aaron numbered according to the word of the Lord by the hand of Moses.

46 All those that were numbered of the Lēvītes, whom Moses and Aaron and the chief of Israel numbered, after their families, and after the house of their fathers,

47 From thirty years old and upward even unto fifty years old, every one that came to do the service of the ministry, and the service of the burden in the tabernacle of the congregation,

48 Even those that were numbered of them, were eight thousand and five hundred and fourscore.

49 According to the commandment of the Lord they were numbered by the hand of Moses, every one according to his service, and according to his burden: thus were they numbered of him, as the Lord commanded Moses.

CHAPTER 5

AND the LORD spake unto Moses, saying,

2 Command the children of Israel, that they put out of the camp every leper, and every one that hath an issue, and whosoever is defiled by the dead:

3 Both male and female shall ye put out, without the camp shall ye put them; that they defile not their camps, in the midst whereof I dwell.

4 And the children of Israel did so, and put them out without the camp: as the LORD spake unto Moses, so did the children of Israel.

5 ¶And the LORD spake unto Moses, saying,

6 Speak unto the children of Israel, When a man or woman shall commit any sin that men commit, to do a trespass against the LORD, and that person be guilty;

7 Then they shall confess their sin which they have done: and he shall recompense his trespass with the principal thereof, and add unto it the fifth *part* thereof, and give *it* unto *him* against whom he hath trespassed.

8 But if the man have no kinsman to recompense the trespass unto, let the trespass be recompensed unto the LORD, *even* to the priest; beside the ram of the atonement, whereby an atonement shall be made for him.

9 And every offering of all the holy things of the children of Israel, which they bring unto the priest, shall be his.

10 And every man's hallowed things shall be his: whatsoever any man giveth the priest, it shall be his.

11 ¶And the LORD spake unto Moses, saying,

12 Speak unto the children of Israel, and say unto them, If any man's wife go aside, and commit a trespass against him,

13 And a man lie with her carnally, and it be hid from the eyes of her husband, and be kept close, and she be defiled, and *there be* no witness against her, neither she be taken *with the manner;*

14 And the spirit of jealousy come upon him, and he be jealous of his wife, and she be defiled: or if the spirit of jealousy come upon him, and he be jealous of his wife, and she be not defiled:

15 Then shall the man bring his wife unto the priest, and he shall bring her offering for her, the tenth *part* of an ephah of barley meal; he shall pour no oil upon it, nor put frankincense thereon; for it *is* an offering of jealousy, an offering of memorial, bringing iniquity to remembrance.

16 And the priest shall bring her near, and set her before the LORD:

17 And the priest shall take holy water in an earthen vessel; and of the dust that is in the floor of the tabernacle the priest shall take, and put *it* into the water:

18 And the priest shall set the woman before the LORD, and uncover the wom-

B. Cleansing, Consecration, and Commission. 5:1-10:10.

1. *Purity of the camp. 5:1-31.*

5:1-6. Put out of the camp. In the book of Leviticus the phrase, "Be ye holy, for I am holy," or its equivalent, is found over a dozen times (Lev 11:44-45; 19:2; 20:7, 26). Now, in the book of Numbers this admonition is being put into effect. There were three kinds of individuals who were to be put out of the camp to assure the purity of the people. These were: the leper, the one with a running issue, and one defiled by the dead. Jensen writes: "Apart from any hygienic reasons, the directions for such purging reflect the ways of God in speaking to the Israelites. They thought in terms of the concrete and the visible, and so God continually used the visible, the tangible, and the audible to make clear His message. Here was a threefold reminder that God did not want habitual sinners in the camp.

"The leper was a picture of the awfulness and ugliness of sin; the running issue was a reminder of sin unhealed and taking its toll. Defilement by a dead body was a reminder of the ultimate result of sin, eternal death" (Irving Jensen, *Journey to God's Rest-Land*, p. 33).

7-10. He shall recompense his trespass. A guilty person was not only to restore his victim fully for ill-gotten gains, but was then to add one-fifth to the original theft. In the New Testament, Zaccheus, of course, went far beyond the Levitical law when making his restoration (see Lk 19:8).

11-31. Jones observes: "The situation is that a woman is suspected of adultery, for which sin both the woman and the man involved are to be put to death (Lev 20:10); but in this case there is no proof of the husband's suspicion and jealousy. So there is an unusually detailed description of the test which the woman is to undergo in order to decide her guilt or innocence" (Kenneth Jones, *The Book of Numbers*, p. 26). This may also be regarded as the first example in history of the suspect taking a lie detector test!

an's head, and put the offering of memorial in her hands, which *is* the jealousy offering: and the priest shall have in his hand the bitter water that causeth the curse:

19 And the priest shall charge her by an oath, and say unto the woman, If no man have lain with thee, and if thou hast not gone aside to uncleanness *with another* instead of thy husband, be thou free from this bitter water that causeth the curse:

20 But if thou hast gone aside *to another* instead of thy husband, and if thou be defiled, and some man have lain with thee beside thine husband:

21 Then the priest shall charge the woman with an oath of cursing, and the priest shall say unto the woman, The LORD make thee a curse and an oath among thy people, when the LORD doth make thy thigh to rot, and thy belly to swell;

22 And this water that causeth the curse shall go into thy bowels, to make *thy* belly to swell, and *thy* thigh to rot: And the woman shall say, Amen, amen.

23 And the priest shall write these curses in a book, and he shall blot *them* out with the bitter water:

24 And he shall cause the woman to drink the bitter water that causeth the curse: and the water that causeth the curse shall enter into her, *and become* bitter.

25 Then the priest shall take the jealousy offering out of the woman's hand, and shall wave the offering before the LORD, and offer it upon the altar:

26 And the priest shall take an handful of the offering, *even* the memorial thereof, and burn *it* upon the altar, and afterward shall cause the woman to drink the water.

27 And when he hath made her to drink the water, then it shall come to pass, *that*, if she be defiled, and have done trespass against her husband, that the water that causeth the curse shall enter into her, *and become* bitter, and her belly shall swell, and her thigh shall rot: and the woman shall be a curse among her people.

28 And if the woman be not defiled, but be clean; then she shall be free, and shall conceive seed.

29 This *is* the law of jealousies, when a wife goeth aside *to another* instead of her husband, and is defiled:

30 Or when the spirit of jealousy cometh upon him, and he be jealous over his wife, and shall set the woman before the LORD, and the priest shall execute upon her all this law.

31 Then shall the man be guiltless from iniquity, and this woman shall bear her iniquity.

CHAPTER 6

AND the LORD spake unto Moses, saying,

2 Speak unto the children of Israel, and say unto them, When either man or woman shall separate *themselves* to vow a vow of a Nazarite, to separate *themselves* unto the LORD:

2. Called to separation. 6:1-27.

6:1-2. When either man or woman shall . . . vow a vow of a Nazarite. This is the first mention of a very important Old Testament consecration vow. The word, Nazarite, or Nazirite, is derived from a verb (Heb *Nazar*), meaning "to dedicate." This was a voluntary vow taken for a specific period of time by either a man or woman. There are several well-known biblical Nazarites. Samson is, perhaps, the most famous (Jud 13:5, 7;

263

3 He shall separate *himself* from wine and strong drink, and shall drink no vinegar of wine, or vinegar of strong drink, neither shall he drink any liquor of grapes, nor eat moist grapes, or dried.

4 All the days of his separation shall he eat nothing that is made of the vine tree, from the kernels even to the husk.

5 All the days of the vow of his separation there shall no razor come upon his head: until the days be fulfilled, in the which he separateth *himself* unto the Lord, he shall be holy, *and* shall let the locks of the hair of his head grow.

6 All the days that he separateth *himself* unto the Lord he shall come at no dead body.

7 He shall not make himself unclean for his father, or for his mother, for his brother, or for his sister, when they die: because the consecration of his God *is* upon his head.

8 All the days of his separation he *is* holy unto the Lord.

9 And if any man die very suddenly by him, and he hath defiled the head of his consecration; then he shall shave his head in the day of his cleansing, on the seventh day shall he shave it.

10 And on the eighth day he shall bring two turtles, or two young pigeons, to the priest, to the door of the tabernacle of the congregation:

11 And the priest shall offer the one for a sin offering, and the other for a burnt offering, and make an atonement for him, for that he sinned by the dead, and shall hallow his head that same day.

12 And he shall consecrate unto the Lord the days of his separation, and shall bring a lamb of the first year for a trespass offering: but the days that were before shall be lost, because his separation was defiled.

13 ¶And this *is* the law of the Nazarite, when the days of his separation are fulfilled: he shall be brought unto the door of the tabernacle of the congregation:

14 And he shall offer his offering unto the Lord, one he lamb of the first year without blemish for a burnt offering, and one ewe lamb of the first year without blemish for a sin offering, and one ram without blemish for peace offerings,

15 And a basket of unleavened bread, cakes of fine flour mingled with oil, and wafers of unleavened bread anointed with oil, and their meat offering, and their drink offerings.

16 And the priest shall bring *them* before the Lord, and shall offer his sin offering, and his burnt offering:

17 And he shall offer the ram *for* a

16:17). It would appear the prophet Samuel also became one (I Sam 1:11-28). In the New Testament, John the Baptist immediately comes to mind (Lk 1:15), and also the Apostle Paul (Acts 18:18).

It should be noted here that while Christ was a Nazarene (Mt 2:23), a reference to a citizen of Nazareth, He was not a Nazarite. One of the national sins of Israel, at a later date, was the attempt by the people to force the Nazarites to break their vows (Amos 2:11).

3-6. He shall separate himself from. There were three prohibitions in the Nazarite vow: (1) He was prohibited from drinking any fruit of the vine (vs. 3). Wine was the symbol for joy (Ps 104:15), but the Nazarite was to receive his joy from God alone. (2) He was not to cut his hair (vs. 5). In the New Testament (I Cor 11:14) Paul states that long hair for a man was a shame and disgrace. It may be that by this method the Nazarite male could both understand and demonstrate the reproach of the Lord. (3) He was not to come into contact with a dead body (vs. 6). Physical death, of course, was a direct result of Adam's rebellion against God (Gen 2:17).

7-19. He shall not make himself unclean for his father . . . mother . . . brother, or . . . sister, when they die. The Nazarite vow was so binding that one could not attend the funeral even of a loved family member. Verses 9-12 give instruction on what the Nazarite is to do if he breaks his vow. Verses 13-21 discuss the procedures to be followed by the Nazarite upon completion of his vow.

sacrifice of peace offerings unto the LORD, with the basket of unleavened bread: the priest shall offer also his meat offering, and his drink offering.

18 And the Nazarite shall shave the head of his separation *at* the door of the tabernacle of the congregation, and shall take the hair of the head of his separation, and put *it* in the fire which *is* under the sacrifice of the peace offerings.

19 And the priest shall take the sodden shoulder of the ram, and one unleavened cake out of the basket, and one unleavened wafer, and shall put *them* upon the hands of the Nazarite, after *the hair of* his separation is shaven:

20 And the priest shall wave them *for* a wave offering before the LORD: this *is* holy for the priest, with the wave breast and heave shoulder: and after that the Nazarite may drink wine.

21 This *is* the law of the Nazarite who hath vowed, *and of* his offering unto the LORD for his separation, beside *that* that his hand shall get: according to the vow which he vowed, so he must do after the law of his separation.

22 ¶And the LORD spake unto Moses, saying,

23 Speak unto Aaron and unto his sons, saying, On this wise ye shall bless the children of Israel, saying unto them,

24 The LORD bless thee, and keep thee:

25 The LORD make his face shine upon thee, and be gracious unto thee:

26 The LORD lift up his countenance upon thee, and give thee peace.

27 And they shall put my name upon the children of Israel; and I will bless them.

CHAPTER 7

AND it came to pass on the day that Moses had fully set up the tabernacle, and had anointed it, and sanctified it, and all the instruments thereof, both the altar and all the vessels thereof, and had anointed them, and sanctified them;

2 That the princes of Israel, heads of the house of their fathers, who *were* the princes of the tribes, and were over them that were numbered, offered:

3 And they brought their offering before the LORD, six covered wagons, and twelve oxen; a wagon for two of the princes, and for each one an ox: and they brought them before the tabernacle.

4 And the LORD spake unto Moses, saying,

5 Take *it* of them, that they may be to do the service of the tabernacle of the congregation; and thou shalt give them unto the Lēvītes, to every man according to his service.

6 And Moses took the wagons and the oxen, and gave them unto the Lēvītes.

7 Two wagons and four oxen he gave unto the sons of Ger'shon, according to their service:

8 And four wagons and eight oxen he

20-27. One of Scripture's most beautiful benedictions is found here. This was probably the blessing the people were waiting to hear the priest Zechariah utter (Lk 1:21-22) when he was struck mute by the angel Gabriel.

3. Offerings of twelve tribal leaders. 7:1-89.

7:1-89. On the day that Moses had fully set up the tabernacle. This chapter chronologically belongs after Leviticus 8 and before the book of Numbers. "But it is placed here because it included the bringing of supplies necessary for transporting the tabernacle, which is one of the subjects under consideration in this first part of Numbers. The arrangement of much of Numbers is logical, rather than chronological" (Irving Jensen, p. 27). This is the second longest chapter in the Bible (Ps 119 is the longest).

And they brought their offering before the LORD (vs. 3). The "they" here refers to twelve princes of Israel who brought identical gifts and offerings for the dedication of the altar on twelve successive days. Each prince brought a silver dish weighing approximately four pounds, a two-pound silver bowl, and a golden pan weighing about six ounces. In addition, there was a total of two hundred fifty-two animals, consisting of bullocks, rams, lambs, goats, and oxen. They served as burnt, sin, and peace offerings.

The amazing and wonderful thing about the account of this offering is the way in which it is reported. "It is heart-warming to observe that, although the offerings of the princes were identical, each is separately recorded by inspiration" (*New Scofield Bible*, p. 176).

This fact of God's personal concern is seen also in the New Testament through the widow's mite episode (Lk 21:1-4) and the identical sevenfold message of Christ to His seven churches in Asia Minor (Rev 2-3).

gave unto the sons of Me-râ′rī, according unto their service, under the hand of Ĭth′a-mär the son of Aaron the priest.

9 But unto the sons of Kō′hăth he gave none: because the service of the sanctuary belonging unto them *was that* they should bear upon their shoulders.

10 ¶And the princes offered for dedicating of the altar in the day that it was anointed, even the princes offered their offering before the altar.

11 And the LORD said unto Moses, They shall offer their offering, each prince on his day, for the dedicating of the altar.

12 ¶And he that offered his offering the first day was Näh′shŏn the son of Am-mĭn′a-dăb, of the tribe of Jūdah:

13 And his offering *was* one silver charger, the weight thereof *was* an hundred and thirty *shekels,* one silver bowl of seventy shekels, after the shekel of the sanctuary; both of them *were* full of fine flour mingled with oil for a meat offering:

14 One spoon of ten *shekels* of gold, full of incense:

15 One young bullock, one ram, one lamb of the first year, for a burnt offering:

16 One kid of the goats for a sin offering:

17 And for a sacrifice of peace offerings, two oxen, five rams, five he goats, five lambs of the first year: this *was* the offering of Näh′shŏn the son of Am-mĭn′a-dăb.

18 ¶On the second day Ne-thăn′e-el the son of Zū′ar, prince of Ĭs′sa-char, did offer:

19 He offered *for* his offering one silver charger, the weight whereof *was* an hundred and thirty *shekels,* one silver bowl of seventy shekels, after the shekel of the sanctuary; both of them full of fine flour mingled with oil for a meat offering:

20 One spoon of gold of ten *shekels,* full of incense:

21 One young bullock, one ram, one lamb of the first year, for a burnt offering:

22 One kid of the goats for a sin offering:

23 And for a sacrifice of peace offerings, two oxen, five rams, five he goats, five lambs of the first year: this *was* the offering of Ne-thăn′e-el the son of Zū′ar.

24 ¶On the third day E-lī′ab the son of Hē′lŏn, prince of the children of Zĕb′u-lun, *did offer:*

25 His offering *was* one silver charger, the weight whereof *was* an hundred and thirty *shekels,* one silver bowl of seventy shekels, after the shekel of the sanctuary; both of them full of fine flour mingled with oil for a meat offering:

26 One golden spoon of ten *shekels,* full of incense:

27 One young bullock, one ram, one lamb of the first year, for a burnt offering:

28 One kid of the goats for a sin offering:

29 And for a sacrifice of peace offerings, two oxen, five rams, five he goats, five lambs of the first year: this *was* the offering of E-lī'ab the son of Hē'lŏn.

30 ¶On the fourth day E-lī'zur the son of Shĕd'e-ur, prince of the children of Reuben, *did offer:*

31 His offering *was* one silver charger of the weight of an hundred and thirty *shekels,* one silver bowl of seventy shekels, after the shekel of the sanctuary; both of them full of fine flour mingled with oil for a meat offering:

32 One golden spoon of ten *shekels,* full of incense:

33 One young bullock, one ram, one lamb of the first year, for a burnt offering:

34 One kid of the goats for a sin offering:

35 And for a sacrifice of peace offerings, two oxen, five rams, five he goats, five lambs of the first year: this *was* the offering of E-lī'zur the son of Shĕd'e-ur.

36 ¶On the fifth day She-lū'mī-el the son of Zū-rĭ-shăd'da-ī, prince of the children of Simeon, *did offer:*

37 His offering *was* one silver charger, the weight whereof *was* an hundred and thirty *shekels,* one silver bowl of seventy shekels, after the shekel of the sanctuary; both of them full of fine flour mingled with oil for a meat offering:

38 One golden spoon of ten *shekels,* full of incense:

39 One young bullock, one ram, one lamb of the first year, for a burnt offering:

40 One kid of the goats for a sin offering:

41 And for a sacrifice of peace offerings, two oxen, five rams, five he goats, five lambs of the first year: this *was* the offering of She-lū'mī-el the son of Zū-rĭ-shăd'da-ī.

42 ¶On the sixth day E-lī'a-săph the son of Deū'el, prince of the children of Gad, *offered:*

43 His offering *was* one silver charger of the weight of an hundred and thirty *shekels,* a silver bowl of seventy shekels, after the shekel of the sanctuary; both of them full of fine flour mingled with oil for a meat offering:

44 One golden spoon of ten *shekels,* full of incense:

45 One young bullock, one ram, one lamb of the first year, for a burnt offering:

46 One kid of the goats for a sin offering:

47 And for a sacrifice of peace offerings, two oxen, five rams, five he goats, five lambs of the first year: this *was* the offering of E-lī'a-săph the son of Deū'el.

48 ¶On the seventh day E-līsh'a-ma the son of Ăm-mī'hŭd, prince of the children of Ē'phra-im, *offered:*

49 His offering *was* one silver charger, the weight whereof *was* an hundred and thirty *shekels,* one silver bowl of seventy shekels, after the shekel of the sanctuary; both of them full of fine flour mingled with oil for a meat offering:

50 One golden spoon of ten *shekels,* full of incense:

51 One young bullock, one ram, one lamb of the first year, for a burnt offering:

52 One kid of the goats for a sin offering:

53 And for a sacrifice of peace offerings, two oxen, five rams, five he goats, five lambs of the first year: this *was* the offering of E-līsh'a-ma the son of Ăm-mī'hŭd.

54 ¶On the eighth day *offered* Ga-mā'lī-el the son of Pe-däh'zur, prince of the children of Ma-nās'seh:

55 His offering *was* one silver charger of the weight of an hundred and thirty *shekels,* one silver bowl of seventy shekels, after the shekel of the sanctuary; both of them full of fine flour mingled with oil for a meat offering:

56 One golden spoon of ten *shekels,* full of incense:

57 One young bullock, one ram, one lamb of the first year, for a burnt offering:

58 One kid of the goats for a sin offering:

59 And for a sacrifice of peace offerings, two oxen, five rams, five he goats, five lambs of the first year: this *was* the offering of Ga-mā'lī-el the son of Pe-däh'zur.

60 ¶On the ninth day Ab'ī-dan the son of Gĭd-e-ō'nī, prince of the children of Benjamin, *offered:*

61 His offering *was* one silver charger, the weight whereof *was* an hundred and thirty *shekels,* one silver bowl of seventy shekels, after the shekel of the sanctuary; both of them full of fine flour mingled with oil for a meat offering:

62 One golden spoon of ten *shekels,* full of incense:

63 One young bullock, one ram, one lamb of the first year, for a burnt offering:

64 One kid of the goats for a sin offering:

65 And for a sacrifice of peace offerings, two oxen, five rams, five he goats, five lambs of the first year: this *was* the offering of Ab'ī-dan the son of Gĭd-e-ō'nī.

66 ¶On the tenth day Ā-hī-ē'zer the son of Ăm-mī-shăd'da-ī, prince of the children of Dan, *offered:*

67 His offering *was* one silver charger, the weight whereof *was* an hundred and thirty *shekels,* one silver bowl of seventy shekels, after the shekel of the sanctuary; both of them full of fine flour mingled with oil for a meat offering:

68 One golden spoon of ten *shekels,* full of incense:

69 One young bullock, one ram, one lamb of the first year, for a burnt offering:

70 One kid of the goats for a sin offering:

71 And for a sacrifice of peace offerings, two oxen, five rams, five he goats, five lambs of the first year: this *was* the offering of Ā-hī-ē'zer the son of Ăm-mī-shăd'da-ī.

72 ¶On the eleventh day Pā'gĭ-el the son of Ōc'ran, prince of the children of Asher, *offered:*

73 His offering *was* one silver charger, the weight whereof *was* an hundred and thirty *shekels,* one silver bowl of seventy shekels, after the shekel of the sanctuary; both of them full of fine flour mingled with oil for a meat offering:

74 One golden spoon of ten *shekels,* full of incense:

75 One young bullock, one ram, one lamb of the first year, for a burnt offering:

76 One kid of the goats for a sin offering:

77 And for a sacrifice of peace offerings, two oxen, five rams, five he goats, five lambs of the first year: this *was* the offering of Pā'gĭ-el the son of Ōc'ran.

78 ¶On the twelfth day A-hī'ra the son of Ē'nan, prince of the children of Năph'ta-lī, *offered:*

79 His offering *was* one silver charger, the weight whereof *was* an hundred and thirty *shekels,* one silver bowl of seventy shekels, after the shekel of the sanctuary; both of them full of fine flour mingled with oil for a meat offering:

80 One golden spoon of ten *shekels,* full of incense:

81 One young bullock, one ram, one lamb of the first year, for a burnt offering:

82 One kid of the goats for a sin offering:

83 And for a sacrifice of peace offerings, two oxen, five rams, five he goats, five lambs of the first year: this *was* the offering of A-hī'ra the son of Ē'nan.

84 This *was* the dedication of the altar, in the day when it was anointed, by the princes of Israel: twelve chargers of silver, twelve silver bowls, twelve spoons of gold:

85 Each charger of silver *weighing* an hundred and thirty *shekels,* each bowl seventy: all the silver vessels *weighed* two thousand and four hundred *shekels,* after the shekel of the sanctuary:

86 The golden spoons *were* twelve, full of incense, *weighing* ten *shekels* apiece, after the shekel of the sanctuary: all the gold of the spoons *was* an hundred and twenty *shekels.*

87 All the oxen for the burnt offering *were* twelve bullocks, the rams twelve, the lambs of the first year twelve, with their meat offering: and the kids of the goats for sin offering twelve.

88 And all the oxen for the sacrifice of the peace offerings *were* twenty and four bullocks, the rams sixty, the he goats sixty, the lambs of the first year sixty. This *was* the dedication of the altar, after that it was anointed.

89 And when Moses was gone into the tabernacle of the congregation to speak with him, then he heard the voice of one speaking unto him from off the mercy seat that *was* upon the ark of testimony, from between the two cherubims: and he spake unto him.

CHAPTER 8

AND the LORD spake unto Moses, saying,

2 Speak unto Aaron, and say unto him, When thou lightest the lamps, the seven lamps shall give light over against the candlestick.

3 And Aaron did so; he lighted the lamps thereof over against the candlestick, as the LORD commanded Moses.

4 And this work of the candlestick *was of* beaten gold, unto the shaft thereof, unto the flowers thereof, *was* beaten work: according unto the pattern which the LORD had shewed Moses, so he made the candlestick.

5 ¶And the LORD spake unto Moses, saying,

6 Take the Lēvītes from among the children of Israel, and cleanse them.

7 And thus shalt thou do unto them, to cleanse them: Sprinkle water of purifying upon them, and let them shave all their flesh, and let them wash their clothes, and *so* make themselves clean.

8 Then let them take a young bullock with his meat offering, *even* fine flour mingled with oil, and another young bullock shalt thou take for a sin offering.

9 And thou shalt bring the Lēvītes before the tabernacle of the congregation: and thou shalt gather the whole assembly of the children of Israel together:

10 And thou shalt bring the Lēvītes before the LORD: and the children of Israel shall put their hands upon the Lēvītes:

11 And Aaron shall offer the Lēvītes before the LORD *for* an offering of the children of Israel, that they may execute the service of the LORD.

12 And the Lēvītes shall lay their hands upon the heads of the bullocks: and thou shalt offer the one *for* a sin offering, and the other *for* a burnt offering, unto the LORD, to make an atonement for the Lēvītes.

13 And thou shalt set the Lēvītes before Aaron, and before his sons, and offer them *for* an offering unto the LORD.

14 Thus shalt thou separate the Lēvītes from among the children of Israel: and the Lēvītes shall be mine.

15 And after that shall the Lēvītes go in to do the service of the tabernacle of the congregation: and thou shalt cleanse them, and offer them *for* an offering.

16 For they *are* wholly given unto me from among the children of Israel; instead of such as open every womb, *even instead of* the firstborn of all the children of Israel, have I taken them unto me.

17 For all the firstborn of the children of Israel *are* mine, *both* man and beast: on the day that I smote every firstborn in the land of Egypt I sanctified them for myself.

18 And I have taken the Lēvītes for all the firstborn of the children of Israel.

19 And I have given the Lēvītes *as* a gift to Aaron and to his sons from among the children of Israel, to do the service of the children of Israel in the tabernacle of the congregation, and to

4. Dedication of the Levites. 8:1-26.

8:1-6. When thou lightest the lamps. McGee writes: "This chapter surprises us by beginning with instructions for lighting the lampstand in the Holy Place. At first it seems that the lampstand is out of place—that it belongs back in Exodus where instructions were given for the Tabernacle" (J. V. McGee, *Numbers,* p. 49). But as one reads on into the chapter he sees the account here is appropriate, for the following verses (5-22) record the dedication of the Levites. The spiritual orders here suggest that divine illumination must precede Christian dedication! This passage is somewhat parallel to Leviticus 8 and Numbers 3:5-13.

7-23. And thus shalt thou do unto them. Six things are now to be done in the dedication ceremony of the Levites: (1) They were to be sprinkled with purifying water (vs. 7); (2) all hair was to be shaved from their bodies (vs. 7); (3) their clothes were to be washed and cleansed (vs. 7); (4) a burnt offering, grain offering, and sin offering were to be given (vss. 8, 12); (5) they were to identify themselves with the remaining tribes by the laying on of hands (vss. 10, 17-18); and (6) they were then to be formally offered to God (vs. 21). There are many spiritual applications that can be gleaned from these verses. But the underlying principle seems to be that dedication to God is a very serious and sacred thing. Paul emphasizes this vital element concerning New Testament believers (see Rom 12:1-2).

make an atonement for the children of Israel: that there be no plague among the children of Israel, when the children of Israel come nigh unto the sanctuary.

20 And Moses, and Aaron, and all the congregation of the children of Israel, did to the Lēvītes according unto all that the LORD commanded Moses concerning the Lēvītes, so did the children of Israel unto them.

21 And the Lēvītes were purified, and they washed their clothes; and Aaron offered them *as* an offering before the LORD; and Aaron made an atonement for them to cleanse them.

22 And after that went the Lēvītes in to do their service in the tabernacle of the congregation before Aaron, and before his sons: as the LORD had commanded Moses concerning the Lēvītes, so did they unto them.

23 ¶And the LORD spake unto Moses, saying,

24 This *is it* that *belongeth* unto the Lēvītes: from twenty and five years old and upward they shall go in to wait upon the service of the tabernacle of the congregation:

25 And from the age of fifty years they shall cease waiting upon the service *thereof,* and shall serve no more:

26 But shall minister with their brethren in the tabernacle of the congregation, to keep the charge, and shall do no service. Thus shalt thou do unto the Lēvītes touching their charge.

CHAPTER 9

AND the LORD spake unto Moses in the wilderness of Sī'naī, in the first month of the second year after they were come out of the land of Egypt, saying,

2 Let the children of Israel also keep the passover at his appointed season.

3 In the fourteenth day of this month, at even, ye shall keep it in his appointed season: according to all the rites of it, and according to all the ceremonies thereof, shall ye keep it.

4 And Moses spake unto the children of Israel, that they should keep the passover.

5 And they kept the passover on the fourteenth day of the first month at even in the wilderness of Sī'naī: according to all that the LORD commanded Moses, so did the children of Israel.

6 ¶And there were certain men, who were defiled by the dead body of a man, that they could not keep the passover on that day: and they came before Moses and before Aaron on that day:

7 And those men said unto him, We *are* defiled by the dead body of a man: wherefore are we kept back, that we may not offer an offering of the LORD in his appointed season among the children of Israel?

8 And Moses said unto them, Stand still, and I will hear what the LORD will command concerning you.

9 ¶And the LORD spake unto Moses, saying,

10 Speak unto the children of Israel, saying, If any man of you or of your posterity shall be unclean by reason of

24-26. From twenty and five years old and upward. Jones writes: "It is stated here that the Levites are to serve in the tabernacle from the age of twenty-five to fifty. But in 4:3 it is stated they were not to begin service until thirty. Rabbinic tradition explains this by saying that they served a five-year apprenticeship before thirty. Later on, the age was lowered to twenty (II Chr 31:17; Ezra 3:8), probably because of different circumstances" (Kenneth Jones, p. 31).

5. Passover and leadership. 9:1-10:10.

9:1-7. Keep the passover. The Passover was the first of seven great religious festivals which were to be observed by Israel each year (see Lev 23:5). This feast was first introduced by God and observed by Israel during their final days in Egypt (see Ex 12). The passage here in Numbers 9 records the only instance where Israel observed the Passover during their entire forty-year wilderness wandering. They may have kept it on other occasions, but we are not told about it. The next recorded observance of this feast took place on the western bank of the Jordan (Josh 5:10) in the land of Canaan.

8-12. And Moses said unto them, Stand still, and I will hear what the LORD will command. Moses was faced with a problem at this time concerning what to do with those who desired to observe the Passover but had defiled themselves by touching a corpse. The divine solution was that an extra Passover would be available one month later. The significance of all this was, doubtless, to impress both upon Moses and all believers (see

a dead body, or *be* in a journey afar off, yet he shall keep the passover unto the Lord.

11 The fourteenth day of the second month at even they shall keep it, *and* eat it with unleavened bread and bitter *herbs*.

12 They shall leave none of it unto the morning, nor break any bone of it: according to all the ordinances of the passover they shall keep it.

13 But the man that *is* clean, and is not in a journey, and forbeareth to keep the passover, even the same soul shall be cut off from among his people: because he brought not the offering of the Lord in his appointed season, that man shall bear his sin.

14 And if a stranger shall sojourn among you, and will keep the passover unto the Lord; according to the ordinance of the passover, and according to the manner thereof, so shall he do: ye shall have one ordinance, both for the stranger, and for him that was born in the land.

15 ¶And on the day that the tabernacle was reared up the cloud covered the tabernacle, *namely*, the tent of the testimony: and at even there was upon the tabernacle as it were the appearance of fire, until the morning.

16 So it was alway: the cloud covered it *by day*, and the appearance of fire by night.

17 And when the cloud was taken up from the tabernacle, then after that the children of Israel journeyed: and in the place where the cloud abode, there the children of Israel pitched their tents.

18 At the commandment of the Lord the children of Israel journeyed, and at the commandment of the Lord they pitched: as long as the cloud abode upon the tabernacle they rested in their tents.

19 And when the cloud tarried long upon the tabernacle many days, then the children of Israel kept the charge of the Lord, and journeyed not.

20 And *so* it was, when the cloud was a few days upon the tabernacle; according to the commandment of the Lord they abode in their tents, and according to the commandment of the Lord they journeyed.

21 And *so* it was, when the cloud abode from even unto the morning, and *that* the cloud was taken up in the morning, then they journeyed: whether *it was* by day or by night that the cloud was taken up, they journeyed.

22 Or *whether it were* two days, or a month, or a year, that the cloud tarried upon the tabernacle, remaining thereon, the children of Israel abode in their tents, and journeyed not: but when it was taken up, they journeyed.

23 At the commandment of the Lord they rested in the tents, and at the commandment of the Lord they journeyed: they kept the charge of the Lord, at the commandment of the Lord by the hand of Moses.

CHAPTER 10

AND the Lord spake unto Moses, saying,

I Cor 10:11) that when in doubt, one must turn to the Word of God for an answer!

13-15. The same soul shall be cut off from among his people. There is some question here concerning this phrase. Does it refer to excommunication or death? An argument could be made for either case.

16-21. The cloud . . . by day, and the appearance of fire by night. This cloud was the Shekinah Glory sign of God whereby Israel could enjoy a visible assurance that the people were, indeed, being led by God. At the advent of the Holy Spirit on the Day of Pentecost, this was rendered unnecessary. Paul reminds us: "For we walk by faith, not by sight" (II Cor 5:7). A study of the history of the glory cloud is profitable indeed. The following appearances may be noted: (1) at the Red Sea (Ex 13:21-22); (2) in the tabernacle Holy of Holies (Lev 16:2); (3) in the Temple Holy of Holies (II Chr 5:13); (4) it disappears in Ezekiel's time (Ezk 10); (5) at the birth of Christ (Lk 2:9); (6) on the Mount of Transfiguration (Mt 17:5); and (7) at the Ascension (Acts 1:9-11). Paul refers to this glory cloud as one of the great advantages enjoyed by the nation Israel (see Rom 9:4-5).

22-23. Or a year. The Hebrew word here translated year normally means an extended period of time (cf. Gen 4:3; 24:55; 40:4) that is more than a month. **They kept the charge of the Lord.** This statement is found many times prior to Israel's tragic rebellion at Kadesh-barnea (cf. 14). From that point, it scarcely appears at all.

10:1-10. The trumpets were to be sounded on four specific occasions: (1) To summons (vs. 2). If both trumpets were

2 Make thee two trumpets of silver; of a whole piece shalt thou make them: that thou mayest use them for the calling of the assembly, and for the journeying of the camps.

3 And when they shall blow with them, all the assembly shall assemble themselves to thee at the door of the tabernacle of the congregation.

4 And if they blow *but* with one *trumpet,* then the princes, *which are* heads of the thousands of Israel, shall gather themselves unto thee.

5 When ye blow an alarm, then the camps that lie on the east parts shall go forward.

6 When ye blow an alarm the second time, then the camps that lie on the south side shall take their journey: they shall blow an alarm for their journeys.

7 But when the congregation is to be gathered together, ye shall blow, but ye shall not sound an alarm.

8 And the sons of Aaron, the priests, shall blow with the trumpets; and they shall be to you for an ordinance for ever throughout your generations.

9 And if ye go to war in your land against the enemy that oppresseth you, then ye shall blow an alarm with the trumpets; and ye shall be remembered before the LORD your God, and ye shall be saved from your enemies.

10 Also in the day of your gladness, and in your solemn days, and in the beginnings of your months, ye shall blow with the trumpets over your burnt offerings, and over the sacrifices of your peace offerings; that they may be to you for a memorial before your God: I *am* the LORD your God.

11 ¶And it came to pass on the twentieth *day* of the second month, in the second year, that the cloud was taken up from off the tabernacle of the testimony.

12 And the children of Israel took their journeys out of the wilderness of Sī′naï: and the cloud rested in the wilderness of Paran.

13 And they first took their journey according to the commandment of the LORD by the hand of Moses.

14 ¶In the first *place* went the standard of the camp of the children of Jū-dah according to their armies: and over his host *was* Näh′shŏn the son of Am-mĭn′a-dăb.

15 And over the host of the tribe of the children of Ĭs′sa-char *was* Ne-thăn′e-el the son of Zū′ar.

16 And over the host of the tribe of the children of Zĕb′u-lun *was* E-lī′ab the son of Hē′lŏn.

17 And the tabernacle was taken down; and the sons of Ger′shon and the sons of Me-rä′rī set forward, bearing the tabernacle.

18 And the standard of the camp of Reuben set forward according to their armies: and over his host *was* E-lī′zur the son of Shĕd′e-ur.

19 And over the host of the tribe of the children of Simeon *was* She-lū′mĭ-el the son of Zū-rĭ-shăd′da-ī.

20 And over the host of the tribe of the children of Gad *was* E-lī′a-săph the son of Deū′el.

blown, then the entire congregation was to gather at the tabernacle (vs. 3). If, however, but one trumpet blew, only the heads of the divisions were to appear (vs. 4); (2) to give warning in case of attack (vs. 5); (3) when Israel itself would go to war (vs. 9); and (4) at Israel's appointed feasts (vs. 10). Harrison writes: "Another matter which has a decided bearing upon the antiquity of the sources in Numbers related to the use of long silver trumpets for convening a civil assembly as well as for religious and military purposes (10:1 ff.). Such trumpets were in common use in Egypt during the Amarna Age, and some particularly elegant specimens that were interred with the Pharaoh Tutankhamen (ca. 1330 B.C.) were recovered by Howard Carter in the twentieth century" (R. K. Harrison, p. 623).

II. ISRAEL: FROM SINAI TO KADESH-BARNEA. 10:11-14:45.

A. Moving Forward. 10:11-12:16.

1. Mobilizing for the march. 10:11-32.

11-27. The twentieth day of the second month (vs. 11). The march northward began just eleven days after the census was completed. Israel had been camped at the base of Mount Sinai for approximately eleven months and five days, but now it was time to go forward. As Moses would later write, "The LORD our God spake unto us in Horeb, saying, Ye have dwelt long enough in this mount: Turn you, and take your journey . . . to the land of the Canaanites . . . Behold, I have set the land before you: go in and possess the land which the LORD sware unto your fathers, Abraham, Isaac, and Jacob, to give unto them and to their seed after them" (Deut 1:6-8). **The cloud rested in the wilderness of Paran** (vs. 12). Paran can be identified as that large central wilderness of Sinai.

21 And the Kō'hăth-ītes set forward, bearing the sanctuary: and *the other* did set up the tabernacle against they came.

22 And the standard of the camp of the children of Ē'phra-im set forward according to their armies: and over his host *was* E'lĭsh'a-ma the son of Ăm-mī'hŭd.

23 And over the host of the tribe of the children of Ma-năs'seh *was* Ga-mā'lĭ-el the son of Pe-dăh'zur.

24 And over the host of the tribe of the children of Benjamin *was* Ab'ĭ-dan the son of Gĭd-e-ō'nī.

25 And the standard of the camp of the children of Dan set forward, *which was* the rereward of all the camps throughout their hosts: and over his host *was* Ā-hī-ē'zer the son of Ăm-mĭ-shăd'da-ī.

26 And over the host of the tribe of the children of Asher *was* Pā'gĭ-el the son of Ŏc'ran.

27 And over the host of the tribe of the children of Năph'ta-lī *was* A-hī'ra the son of Ē'nan.

28 Thus *were* the journeyings of the children of Israel according to their armies, when they set forward.

29 ¶And Moses said unto Hō'băb, the son of Ră-gū'el the Mĭd'ĭ-an-īte, Moses' father in law, We are journeying unto the place of which the Lord said, I will give it you: come thou with us, and we will do thee good: for the Lord hath spoken good concerning Israel.

30 And he said unto him, I will not go; but I will depart to mine own land, and to my kindred.

31 And he said, Leave us not, I pray thee; forasmuch as thou knowest how we are to encamp in the wilderness, and thou mayest be to us instead of eyes.

32 And it shall be, if thou go with us, yea, it shall be, that what goodness the Lord shall do unto us, the same will we do unto thee.

33 ¶And they departed from the mount of the Lord three days' journey: and the ark of the covenant of the Lord went before them in the three days' journey, to search out a resting place for them.

34 And the cloud of the Lord *was* upon them by day, when they went out of the camp.

35 And it came to pass, when the ark set forward, that Moses said, Rise up, Lord, and let thine enemies be scattered; and let them that hate thee flee before thee.

36 And when it rested, he said, Return, O Lord, unto the many thousands of Israel.

CHAPTER 11

AND *when* the people complained, it displeased the Lord: and the Lord

28. Thus were the journeyings of the children of Israel. According to 10:11-36, the march consisted of seven basic sections, followed by the mixed multitude. These were: (Section 1) Moses, Aaron, and the Ark (vs. 13); (Section 2) Judah, Issachar, and Zebulun (vss. 14-16); (Section 3) Gershon and Merari (vs. 17); (Section 4) Reuben, Simeon, and Gad (vss. 18-20); (Section 5) Kohathites and sons of Levi (vs. 21); (Section 6) Ephraim, Manasseh, and Benjamin (vss. 22-24); and (Section 7) Dan, Asher, and Naphtali (vss. 25-27).

29-32. And Moses said unto Hobab. At the beginning of the march, Moses attempted to secure the services of his brother-in-law to act as a "wagon-master" guide for the people. It is not certain whether he accepted this offer or not. However, the context of Judges 4:11 would indicate he did not.

2. A murmuring, mixed multitude. 10:33-11:35.

33-36. And the cloud of the Lord was upon them. The distance between Mount Sinai and Kadesh is less than two hundred miles. In 33:16-36 Moses lists some twenty stops between these two places. The Sinai area is dotted with mountains, rugged valleys, and sandy ground; but their journey was never too long or difficult, for **the cloud of the Lord was upon them.**

11:1. When the people complained, it displeased the Lord . . . and his anger was kindled. Apart from the golden calf

heard *it;* and his anger was kindled; and the fire of the LORD burnt among them, and consumed *them that were* in the uttermost parts of the camp.

2 And the people cried unto Moses; and when Moses prayed unto the LORD, the fire was quenched.

3 And he called the name of the place Tăb′e-rah: because the fire of the LORD burnt among them.

4 ¶And the mixt multitude that *was* among them fell a lusting: and the children of Israel also wept again, and said, Who shall give us flesh to eat?

5 We remember the fish, which we did eat in Egypt freely; the cucumbers, and the melons, and the leeks, and the onions, and the garlick:

6 But now our soul *is* dried away: there *is* nothing at all, beside this manna, *before* our eyes.

7 And the manna *was* as coriander seed, and the colour thereof as the colour of bdellium.

8 *And* the people went about, and gathered *it,* and ground *it* in mills, or beat *it* in a mortar, and baked *it* in pans, and made cakes of it: and the taste of it was as the taste of fresh oil.

9 And when the dew fell upon the camp in the night, the manna fell upon it.

10 ¶Then Moses heard the people weep throughout their families, every man in the door of his tent: and the anger of the LORD was kindled greatly; Moses also was displeased.

11 And Moses said unto the LORD, Wherefore hast thou afflicted thy servant? and wherefore have I not found favour in thy sight, that thou layest the burden of all this people upon me?

12 Have I conceived all this people? have I begotten them, that thou shouldest say unto me, Carry them in thy bosom, as a nursing father beareth the sucking child, unto the land which thou swarest unto their fathers?

13 Whence should I have flesh to give unto all this people? for they weep unto me, saying, Give us flesh, that we may eat.

14 I am not able to bear all this people alone, because *it is* too heavy for me.

15 And if thou deal thus with me, kill me, I pray thee, out of hand, if I have found favour in thy sight; and let me not see my wretchedness.

16 ¶And the LORD said unto Moses, Gather unto me seventy men of the elders of Israel, whom thou knowest to be the elders of the people, and officers over them; and bring them unto the tabernacle of the congregation, that they may stand there with thee.

17 And I will come down and talk with thee there: and I will take of the spirit which *is* upon thee, and will put *it* upon them; and they shall bear the burden of the people with thee, that thou bear *it* not thyself alone.

18 And say thou unto the people, Sanctify yourselves against to morrow, and ye shall eat flesh: for ye have wept

punishment in Exodus 32, this marks the first divine judgment against the people. There would be many more after this time.

2-4. The mixed multitude . . . fell a lusting. Barnes says: "The word in the original resembles our 'riff raff' and denotes a mob of people scraped together" (*Barnes Commentary,* Vol. 2, p. 207). Much of Israel's problems would from this point be attributed to this mostly unsaved, partly Egyptian group that leaped on the bandwagon after the mighty Passover miracle in Egypt.

5-15. I am not able to bear all this people alone. The heat, barren country, and hostile crowd were now beginning to get to Moses. Note his complaints (bordering on charges) before God: (1) **Wherefore hast thou afflicted thy servant?** (vs. 11); and (2) **wherefore have I not found favor in thy sight?** (vs. 11).

The despair becomes so severe that Moses demands from God either deliverance or death (see vs. 15). Elijah the prophet would later require a similar thing from God in a moment of despondency (cf. I Kgs 19:4). It is tragic that in his great hour of need Moses did not respond as the Apostle Paul would do when facing an unbearable burden. "And lest I should be exalted above measure through the abundance of the revelations, there was given to me a thorn in the flesh, the messenger of Satan to buffet me, lest I should be exalted above measure. For this thing I besought the Lord thrice, that it might depart from me. And he said unto me, My grace is sufficient for thee: for my strength is made perfect in weakness. Most gladly therefore will I rather glory in my infirmities, that the power of Christ may rest upon me" (II Cor 12:7-9).

16. And the LORD said unto Moses, Gather unto me seventy men. Was this God's perfect or permissive will? Unsuccessful attempts have been made to connect the concept of the seventy elders here with the seventy-member Sanhedrin which would crucify Christ in the New Testament. While it is true that Moses had been allowed by God to appoint some administrative helpers in the past (see Ex 18:13-27), it would seem here in Numbers 11 that the request was granted not so much to glorify God as to accommodate the prophet!

17-24. I will take of the spirit which is upon thee, and will put it upon them. It has been observed that there is now more machinery, but not more power. **Who shall give us flesh to eat?** This continual and carnal cry of the crowd would soon be answered by God, but not in a way the people would expect,

in the ears of the LORD, saying, Who shall give us flesh to eat? for *it was* well with us in Egypt: therefore the LORD will give you flesh, and ye shall eat.

19 Ye shall not eat one day, nor two days, nor five days, neither ten days, nor twenty days;

20 *But* even a whole month, until it come out at your nostrils, and it be loathsome unto you: because that ye have despised the LORD which *is* among you, and have wept before him, saying, Why came we forth out of Egypt?

21 And Moses said, The people, among whom I *am, are* six hundred thousand footmen; and thou hast said, I will give them flesh, that they may eat a whole month.

22 Shall the flocks and the herds be slain for them, to suffice them? or shall all the fish of the sea be gathered together for them, to suffice them?

23 And the LORD said unto Moses, Is the LORD's hand waxed short? thou shalt see now whether my word shall come to pass unto thee or not.

24 ¶And Moses went out, and told the people the words of the LORD, and gathered the seventy men of the elders of the people, and set them round about the tabernacle.

25 And the LORD came down in a cloud, and spake unto him, and took of the spirit that *was* upon him, and gave *it* unto the seventy elders: and it came to pass, *that,* when the spirit rested upon them, they prophesied, and did not cease.

26 But there remained two *of the* men in the camp, the name of the one *was* Ĕl′dăd, and the name of the other Mē′dăd: and the spirit rested upon them; and they *were* of them that were written, but went not out unto the tabernacle: and they prophesied in the camp.

27 And there ran a young man, and told Moses, and said, Ĕl′dăd and Mē′dăd do prophesy in the camp.

28 And Joshua the son of Nun, the servant of Moses, *one* of his young men, answered and said, My lord Moses, forbid them.

29 And Moses said unto him, Enviest thou for my sake? would God that all the LORD's people were prophets, *and* that the LORD would put his spirit upon them!

30 And Moses gat him into the camp, he and the elders of Israel.

31 ¶And there went forth a wind from the LORD, and brought quails from the sea, and let *them* fall by the camp, as it were a day's journey on this side, and as it were a day's journey on the other side, round about the camp, and as it were two cubits *high* upon the face of the earth.

32 And the people stood up all that day, and all *that* night, and all the next day, and they gathered the quails: he that gathered least gathered ten homers: and they spread *them* all abroad for themselves round about the camp.

33 And while the flesh *was* yet between their teeth, ere it was chewed, the

25-28. They prophesied. Does this mean the seventy elders received the gift of prophecy as possessed by Daniel or Isaiah? A more reasonable approach is to interpret this as a forthtelling event, and not that of foretelling. This is to say that these men taught and preached and exhorted with divine authority. **One was Eldad . . . the other Medad.** These two elders continued to prophesy, causing concern in the heart of Joshua, lest the authority of Moses be weakened.

29-35. Would God that all the LORD's people were prophets. Moses' answer here to reassure Joshua also reveals his truly great heart and a soul pure and completely devoid of self-exaltation. **The LORD . . . brought quails from the sea . . . two cubits high upon the face of the earth.** Agnostics throughout the ages have pointed to this verse as proof of a blundering inaccuracy, interpreting it to say the quails were piled up from the earth by the trillions to a height of three feet. But this is not the thrust of the verse at all. It simply states the quail flew about three feet off the ground so that the people could knock them down and kill them easily. **The LORD smote the people.** Verses 33-34 indicate that the plague was a result of the arrogant attitude displayed by the people and not simply of the physical act of eating (cf. also Ps 106:15).

wrath of the LORD was kindled against the people, and the LORD smote the people with a very great plague.

34 And he called the name of that place Kĭb'rŏth-hat-tā'a-vah: because there they buried the people that lusted.

35 *And* the people journeyed from Kĭb'rŏth-hat-tā'a-vah unto Ha-ze'rŏth; and abode at Ha-ze'rŏth.

CHAPTER 12

AND Miriam and Aaron spake against Moses because of the Ē-thĭ-ō'pĭ-an woman whom he had married: for he had married an Ē-thĭ-ō'pĭ-an woman.

2 And they said, Hath the LORD indeed spoken only by Moses? hath he not spoken also by us? And the LORD heard *it.*

3 (Now the man Moses *was* very meek, above all the men which *were* upon the face of the earth.)

4 And the LORD spake suddenly unto Moses, and unto Aaron, and unto Miriam, Come out ye three unto the tabernacle of the congregation. And they three came out.

5 And the LORD came down in the pillar of the cloud, and stood *in* the door of the tabernacle, and called Aaron and Miriam: and they both came forth.

6 And he said, Hear now my words: If there be a prophet among you, *I* the LORD will make myself known unto him in a vision, *and* will speak unto him in a dream.

7 My servant Moses *is* not so, who *is* faithful in all mine house.

8 With him will I speak mouth to mouth, even apparently, and not in dark speeches; and the similitude of the LORD shall he behold: wherefore then were ye not afraid to speak against my servant Moses?

9 And the anger of the LORD was kindled against them; and he departed.

10 And the cloud departed from off the tabernacle; and, behold, Miriam *became* leprous, *white* as snow: and Aaron looked upon Miriam, and, behold, *she was* leprous.

11 And Aaron said unto Moses, Alas, my lord, I beseech thee, lay not the sin upon us, wherein we have done foolishly, and wherein we have sinned.

12 Let her not be as one dead, of whom the flesh is half consumed when he cometh out of his mother's womb.

13 And Moses cried unto the LORD, saying, Heal her now, O God, I beseech thee.

14 ¶And the LORD said unto Moses, If her father had but spit in her face, should she not be ashamed seven days? let her be shut out from the camp seven days, and after that let her be received in *again.*

15 And Miriam was shut out from the camp seven days: and the people journeyed not till Miriam was brought in *again.*

16 And afterward the people removed from Ha-ze'rŏth, and pitched in the wilderness of Paran.

3. Rebellion of leaders. 12:1-16.

12:1-16. And Miriam and Aaron spake against Moses. Moses, of course, had already been criticized by the people. But now Satan succeeds in turning his two closest associates against him. Not only were Miriam and Aaron his sister and brother, but both held the highest spiritual offices. Miriam was a prophetess (Ex 15:20), and Aaron was Israel's High Priest. There is little doubt that Miriam was the ringleader. Several reasons suggest this. A feminine verb is used in 12:1 in the original text. It was Miriam who would receive the most severe judgment from God. Aaron had already shown himself to be less than a tower of strength in times of temptation (cf. Ex 32:21-24).

Their criticism was twofold. (1) Against his wife (vs. 1). It is impossible to be dogmatic here. Is this a reference to Zipporah, his only recorded wife, or does it refer to a new wife? The word **Ethiopian** (Cushite) in verse 1 may indicate it was a new wife. If so, she could have been either a foreigner saved out of Egypt with the Israelites, or a daughter of the Cushites dwelling in Arabia. At any rate, neither marriage would have been wrong, for the prohibition in Exodus 34:16 referred only to the Canaanites. (2) Against his leadership (vs. 2). **Now the man Moses was very meek, above all . . . men . . . of the earth.** Critics have pointed to this, concluding that, if true, it would indicate Moses was not the author of Numbers. Their reasoning is that no one writing under divine inspiration could make such a statement about himself. But just the opposite is true; for if Moses was indeed that meek, he would not presume to make such a claim unless he was inspired by the Holy Spirit to do so. It should also be noted this same author Moses, under inspiration, will later describe his anger and sin (see ch. 20). **Miriam became leprous** (vs. 10). In the Old Testament sin was often punished by God through leprosy (cf. II Kgs 5:20-27; II Chr 26:16-21). **Moses cried unto the LORD, saying, Heal her now, O God** (vs. 13). Miriam thus becomes the first and only recorded Old Testament Israelite ever to be healed of leprosy.

277

CHAPTER 13

AND the Lord spake unto Moses, saying,

2 Send thou men, that they may search the land of Canaan, which I give unto the children of Israel: of every tribe of their fathers shall ye send a man, every one a ruler among them.

3 And Moses by the commandment of the Lord sent them from the wilderness of Paran: all those men *were* heads of the children of Israel.

4 And these *were* their names: of the tribe of Reuben, Shăm-mū′a the son of Zăc′cur.

5 Of the tribe of Simeon, Shā′phat the son of Hô′rī.

6 Of the tribe of Jūdah, Caleb the son of Je-phŭn′neh.

7 Of the tribe of Ĭs′sa-char, Ī′găl the son of Joseph.

8 Of the tribe of Ē′phra-im, Ō-shē′a the son of Nun.

9 Of the tribe of Benjamin, Păl′tī the son of Rā′phŭ.

10 Of the tribe of Zĕb′u-lun, Găd′dĭ-el the son of Sō′dī.

11 Of the tribe of Joseph, *namely,* of the tribe of Ma-năs′seh, Găd′dī the son of Sū′sī.

12 Of the tribe of Dan, Ăm′mĭ-el the son of Ge-măl′lī.

13 Of the tribe of Asher, Sē′thur the son of Michael.

14 Of the tribe of Năph′ta-lī, Năh′bī the son of Vŏph′sī.

15 Of the tribe of Gad, Ge-ū′el the son of Mā′chī.

16 These *are* the names of the men which Moses sent to spy out the land. And Moses called Ō-shē′a the son of Nun Je-hŏsh′u-a.

17 ¶And Moses sent them to spy out the land of Canaan, and said unto them, Get you up this *way* southward, and go up into the mountain:

18 And see the land, what it *is;* and the people that dwelleth therein, whether they *be* strong or weak, few or many;

19 And what the land *is* that they dwell in, whether it *be* good or bad; and what cities *they be* that they dwell in, whether in tents, or in strong holds;

20 And what the land *is,* whether it *be* fat or lean, whether there be wood therein, or not. And be ye of good courage, and bring of the fruit of the land. Now the time *was* the time of the firstripe grapes.

21 So they went up, and searched the land from the wilderness of Zin unto Rē′hŏb, as men come to Hā′măth.

22 And they ascended by the south, and came unto Hēbron; where A-hī′-man, Shē′shaī, and Tăl′maī, the children of Anak, *were.* (Now Hēbron was built seven years before Zō′an in Egypt.)

23 And they came unto the brook of Ĕsh′cŏl, and cut down from thence a branch with one cluster of grapes, and they bare it between two upon a staff; and *they brought* of the pomegranates, and of the figs.

B. Missed Opportunity. 13:1–14:45.

1. Reconnaissance and report. 13:1-33.

13:1-3. Send thou men, that they may search the land of Canaan. In chapter 13 it would seem that this command of God was indicative of His perfect will that Canaan be spied out first, but Moses adds more information as recorded in Deuteronomy 1:19-24 which gives the entire background. "And ye come near unto me every one of you, and said, We will send men before us, and they shall search us out the land, and bring us word again . . ." (Deut 1:22). Thus, it would seem that the original idea for an expedition came from man and not from God.

4-16. And these were their names. The two most important of these twelve scouts were, of course, Caleb (vs. 6) and Joshua (vs. 8). The other ten men would be struck dead by a divine plague in less than eight weeks (see 14:37).

17-19. Get you up . . . into the mountain. This description seemed to cover the entire area of Palestine, from Mount Hermon in the north to Beersheba in the south.

20-24. And be ye of good courage. By these words Moses almost seems to anticipate the doubts and fears which later arise from the hearts of ten of the spies.

24 The place was called the brook Ĕsh′cŏl, because of the cluster of grapes which the children of Israel cut down from thence.

25 And they returned from searching of the land after forty days.

26 ¶And they went and came to Moses, and to Aaron, and to all the congregation of the children of Israel, unto the wilderness of Paran, to Kā′-desh; and brought back word unto them, and unto all the congregation, and shewed them the fruit of the land.

27 And they told him, and said, We came unto the land whither thou sentest us, and surely it floweth with milk and honey; and this *is* the fruit of it.

28 Nevertheless the people *be* strong that dwell in the land, and the cities *are* walled, *and* very great: and moreover we saw the children of Anak there.

29 The Am′ă-lek-ītes dwell in the land of the south: and the Hittites, and the Jĕb′u-sītes, and the Ămorītes, dwell in the mountains: and the Canaanites dwell by the sea, and by the coast of Jordan.

30 And Caleb stilled the people before Moses, and said, Let us go up at once, and possess it; for we are well able to overcome it.

31 But the men that went up with him said, We be not able to go up against the people; for they *are* stronger than we.

32 And they brought up an evil report of the land which they had searched unto the children of Israel, saying, The land, through which we have gone to search it, *is* a land that eateth up the inhabitants thereof; and all the people that we saw in it *are* men of a great stature.

33 And there we saw the giants, the sons of Anak, *which come* of the giants: and we were in our own sight as grasshoppers, and so we were in their sight.

CHAPTER 14

AND all the congregation lifted up their voice, and cried; and the people wept that night.

2 And all the children of Israel murmured against Moses and against Aaron: and the whole congregation said unto them, Would God that we had died in the land of Egypt! or would God we had died in this wilderness!

3 And wherefore hath the Lord brought us unto this land, to fall by the sword, that our wives and our children should be a prey? were it not better for us to return into Egypt?

4 And they said one to another, Let us make a captain, and let us return into Egypt.

5 Then Moses and Aaron fell on their faces before all the assembly of the congregation of the children of Israel.

6 And Joshua the son of Nun, and Caleb the son of Je-phŭn′neh, *which were* of them that searched the land, rent their clothes:

7 And they spake unto all the company of the children of Israel, saying, The land, which we passed through to search it, *is* an exceeding good land.

25-26. And they returned . . . after forty days. Forty in the Bible is, of course, a number associated with testing (cf. Gen 7:4, 12; Ex 24:18; I Sam 17:16; Ps 95:10; Jon 3:4; Mt 4:2).

27-29. Surely it floweth with milk and honey. This was an old expression for a fertile land. **Nevertheless the people be strong . . . and the cities are walled.** These Israelite scouts, having been born and raised in Egyptian captivity, had never seen a walled city. It must have been an unnerving sight, to say the least.

30-33. And Caleb . . . said, Let us go up at once, and possess it: for we are well able to overcome it. This statement should be compared with his overall testimony in Joshua 14:6-12. Caleb is, indeed, one of the truly remarkable men in the Bible.

2. *Decision and discipline. 14:1-45.*

14:1-4. Would God that we had died in . . . Egypt. How soon the people had forgotten the cruel and bitter Egyptian enslavement when they had "sighed by reason of the bondage, and they cried . . ." (Ex 2:23).

Our wives and our children should be a prey. Israel does here what sinners have often done throughout history. In an effort to escape personal responsibility, they hid behind their families, using them as an excuse for their own shabby unbelief.

Let us make a captain, and let us return into Egypt. This probably marks the ultimate in their sin and rebellion. To complain against God is one thing, but to defy both Him and His chosen human leaders is quite another! This tragic failure is amplified by Paul in Hebrews 3:17-19.

5-10. Only rebel not ye against the Lord, neither fear ye the people of the land. What timely and wonderful advice from Joshua! The entire Old Testament record would have been totally different had Israel but heeded these words. **But all the congregation bade stone them with stones.** Not only would Israel not go into the Promised Land, but they would murder anyone who dared to go in. A similar situation is seen in John 11:47-53; 12:10-11.

8 If the LORD delight in us, then he will bring us into this land, and give it us; a land which floweth with milk and honey.

9 Only rebel not ye against the LORD, neither fear ye the people of the land; for they *are* bread for us: their defence is departed from them, and the LORD *is* with us: fear them not.

10 But all the congregation bade stone them with stones. And the glory of the LORD appeared in the tabernacle of the congregation before all the children of Israel.

11 ¶And the LORD said unto Moses, How long will this people provoke me? and how long will it be ere they believe me, for all the signs which I have shewed among them?

12 I will smite them with the pestilence, and disinherit them, and will make of thee a greater nation and mightier than they.

13 And Moses said unto the LORD, Then the Egyptians shall hear *it*, (for thou broughtest up this people in thy might from among them;)

14 And they will tell *it* to the inhabitants of this land: *for* they have heard that thou LORD *art* among this people, that thou LORD art seen face to face, and *that* thy cloud standeth over them, and *that* thou goest before them, by day time in a pillar of a cloud, and in a pillar of fire by night.

15 Now *if* thou shalt kill *all* this people as one man, then the nations which have heard the fame of thee will speak, saying,

16 Because the LORD was not able to bring this people into the land which he sware unto them, therefore he hath slain them in the wilderness.

17 And now, I beseech thee, let the power of my Lord be great, according as thou hast spoken, saying,

18 The LORD *is* longsuffering, and of great mercy, forgiving iniquity and transgression, and by no means clearing *the guilty,* visiting the iniquity of the fathers upon the children unto the third and fourth *generation.*

19 Pardon, I beseech thee, the iniquity of this people according unto the greatness of thy mercy, and as thou hast forgiven this people, from Egypt even until now.

20 And the LORD said, I have pardoned according to thy word:

21 But as truly as I live, all the earth shall be filled with the glory of the LORD.

22 Because all those men which have seen my glory, and my miracles, which I did in Egypt and in the wilderness, and have tempted me now these ten times, and have not hearkened to my voice;

23 Surely they shall not see the land which I sware unto their fathers, neither shall any of them that provoked me see it:

24 But my servant Caleb, because he had another spirit with him, and hath followed me fully, him will I bring into the land whereinto he went; and his seed shall possess it.

25 (Now the Am′ă-lek-ītes and the

11-20. I will smite them. Israel had already once been threatened with divine destruction because of their terrible sin (see Ex 32:10). **And Moses said unto the LORD.** Moses now begins his dialogue with deity. He presents a twofold argument why God should spare sinful Israel: (1) because of God's testimony among the heathen (vss. 13-16); and (2) because of God's former promises to Israel (vss. 17-18). In verse 18 Moses quotes God's own words back to Him, spoken in Exodus 34:6-7. If we, too, desire to remind the Lord of His promises to us, we must first of all know God's Word.

21-24. All the earth shall be filled with the glory of the LORD. In this remarkable statement God declares Israel would, indeed, be pardoned; but their sin demanded severe punishment, and through this judgment His glory would be seen (cf. Ps 76:10). **These ten times.** These ten occasions of rebellion are as follows: (1) At the Red Sea (Ex 14:11-12); (2) at Marah (Ex 15:23-24); (3) in the wilderness of sin (Ex 16:1-3); (4) at Rephidim (Ex 17:1-3); (5) at Sinai (Ex 32:1-6); (6-8) en route to Kadesh (three occasions—11:1-3, 4-9, 31-34); and (9-10) at Kadesh (two occasions—vss. 1-4,10).

25-39. Tomorrow turn you, and get you into the wilder-

Canaanites dwelt in the valley.) To-morrow turn you, and get you into the wilderness by the way of the Red sea.

26 ¶And the LORD spake unto Moses and unto Aaron, saying,

27 How long *shall I bear with* this evil congregation, which murmur against me? I have heard the murmurings of the children of Israel, which they mur-mur against me.

28 Say unto them, *As truly as* I live, saith the LORD, as ye have spoken in mine ears, so will I do to you:

29 Your carcases shall fall in this wil-derness; and all that were numbered of you, according to your whole number, from twenty years old and upward, which have murmured against me,

30 Doubtless ye shall not come into the land, *concerning* which I sware to make you dwell therein, save Caleb the son of Je-phun'neh, and Joshua the son of Nun.

31 But your little ones, which ye said should be a prey, them will I bring in, and they shall know the land which ye have despised.

32 But *as for* you, your carcases, they shall fall in this wilderness.

33 And your children shall wander in the wilderness forty years, and bear your whoredoms, until your carcases be wasted in the wilderness.

34 After the number of the days in which ye searched the land, *even* forty days, each day for a year, shall ye bear your iniquities, *even* forty years, and ye shall know my breach of promise.

35 I the LORD have said, I will surely do it unto all this evil congregation, that are gathered together against me: in this wilderness they shall be con-sumed, and there they shall die.

36 And the men, which Moses sent to search the land, who returned, and made all the congregation to murmur against him, by bringing up a slander upon the land,

37 Even those men that did bring up the evil report upon the land, died by the plague before the LORD.

38 But Joshua the son of Nun, and Caleb the son of Je-phun'neh, *which were* of the men that went to search the land, lived *still.*

39 And Moses told these sayings unto all the children of Israel: and the people mourned greatly.

40 And they rose up early in the morn-ing, and gat them up into the top of the mountain, saying, Lo, we *be here,* and will go up unto the place which the LORD hath promised: for we have sinned.

41 And Moses said, Wherefore now do ye transgress the commandment of the LORD? but it shall not prosper.

42 Go not up, for the LORD *is* not among you; that ye be not smitten be-fore your enemies.

43 For the Am'ă-lek-ītes and the Ca-naanites *are* there before you, and ye shall fall by the sword: because ye are turned away from the LORD, therefore the LORD will not be with you.

44 But they presumed to go up unto the hill top: nevertheless the ark of the

ness. Ryrie writes: "Though the Israelites were at the edge of the Promised Land, they were commanded to turn back into the wilderness where all who were twenty years of age and older would die (except Joshua and Caleb, cf. vss. 29-30) and where they would wander for forty more years (cf. vs. 33)" (*Ryrie Study Bible,* p. 231).

40-45. Lo, we be here, and will go. But it was now too late. Every "what" of God for our lives is usually accompanied by a "when," also. Timing can often determine the difference be-tween obeying and disobeying the will of God.

covenant of the LORD, and Moses, departed not out of the camp.

45 Then the Am'ă-lek-ītes came down, and the Canaanites which dwelt in that hill, and smote them, and discomfited them, *even* unto Hôr'mah.

CHAPTER 15

AND the LORD spake unto Moses, saying,

2 Speak unto the children of Israel, and say unto them, When ye be come into the land of your habitations, which I give unto you,

3 And will make an offering by fire unto the LORD, a burnt offering, or a sacrifice in performing a vow, or in a freewill offering, or in your solemn feasts, to make a sweet savour unto the LORD, of the herd, or of the flock:

4 Then shall he that offereth his offering unto the LORD bring a meat offering of a tenth deal of flour mingled with the fourth *part* of an hin of oil.

5 And the fourth *part* of an hin of wine for a drink offering shalt thou prepare with the burnt offering or sacrifice, for one lamb.

6 Or for a ram, thou shalt prepare *for* a meat offering two tenth deals of flour mingled with the third *part* of an hin of oil.

7 And for a drink offering thou shalt offer the third *part* of an hin of wine, *for* a sweet savour unto the LORD.

8 And when thou preparest a bullock *for* a burnt offering, or *for* a sacrifice in performing a vow, or peace offerings unto the LORD:

9 Then shall he bring with a bullock a meat offering of three tenth deals of flour mingled with half an hin of oil.

10 And thou shalt bring for a drink offering half an hin of wine, *for* an offering made by fire, of a sweet savour unto the LORD.

11 Thus shall it be done for one bullock, or for one ram, or for a lamb, or a kid.

12 According to the number that ye shall prepare, so shall ye do to every one according to their number.

13 All that are born of the country shall do these things after this manner, in offering an offering made by fire, of a sweet savour unto the LORD.

14 And if a stranger sojourn with you, or whosoever *be* among you in your generations, and will offer an offering made by fire, of a sweet savour unto the LORD; as ye do, so he shall do.

15 One ordinance *shall be both* for you of the congregation, and also for the stranger that sojourneth *with you,* an ordinance for ever in your generations: as ye *are,* so shall the stranger be before the LORD.

16 One law and one manner shall be for you, and for the stranger that sojourneth with you.

17 ¶And the LORD spake unto Moses, saying,

18 Speak unto the children of Israel, and say unto them, When ye come into the land whither I bring you,

19 Then it shall be, that, when ye eat of the bread of the land, ye shall offer up an heave offering unto the LORD.

III. ISRAEL: FROM KADESH-BARNEA TO THE EASTERN BANK OF JORDAN. 15:1-36:13.

A. Desert Wanderings. 15:1-19:22.

1. Legislation reaffirmed. 15:1-41.

15:1-13. After the sin at Kadesh, the people needed a reminder of the former commands given at Sinai concerning offerings, lest they conclude they were now no longer in effect. God was still planning to bring the next generation into Canaan. Note His statement: **When ye be come into the land of your habitations, which I give unto you** (vs. 2).

14-29. And if a stranger sojourn with you . . . as ye do, so he shall do. The alien (non-Israelite) person was welcome to worship the God of Abraham alongside the seed of Abraham and to receive His manifold blessings. The heave offerings stressed thanksgiving to God for His providence (vss. 17-21). Verses 22-26 describe those offerings (burnt, meal, sin, drink) which were to be used for unintentional national sins. Verses 27-29 refer to offerings for the purpose of unintentional personal sin.

20 Ye shall offer up a cake of the first of your dough *for* an heave offering: as *ye do* the heave offering of the threshingfloor, so shall ye heave it.

21 Of the first of your dough ye shall give unto the LORD an heave offering in your generations.

22 ¶And if ye have erred, and not observed all these commandments, which the LORD hath spoken unto Moses,

23 *Even* all that the LORD hath commanded you by the hand of Moses, from the day that the LORD commanded *Moses*, and henceforward among your generations;

24 Then it shall be, if *ought* be committed by ignorance without the knowledge of the congregation, that all the congregation shall offer one young bullock for a burnt offering, for a sweet savour unto the LORD, with his meat offering, and his drink offering, according to the manner, and one kid of the goats for a sin offering.

25 And the priest shall make an atonement for all the congregation of the children of Israel, and it shall be forgiven them; for it *is* ignorance: and they shall bring their offering, a sacrifice made by fire unto the LORD, and their sin offering before the LORD, for their ignorance:

26 And it shall be forgiven all the congregation of the children of Israel, and the stranger that sojourneth among them; seeing all the people *were* in ignorance.

27 ¶And if any soul sin through ignorance, then he shall bring a she goat of the first year for a sin offering.

28 And the priest shall make an atonement for the soul that sinneth ignorantly, when he sinneth by ignorance before the LORD, to make an atonement for him; and it shall be forgiven him.

29 Ye shall have one law for him that sinneth through ignorance, *both for* him that is born among the children of Israel, and for the stranger that sojourneth among them.

30 ¶But the soul that doeth *ought* presumptuously, *whether he be* born in the land, or a stranger, the same reproacheth the LORD; and that soul shall be cut off from among his people.

31 Because he hath despised the word of the LORD, and hath broken his commandment, that soul shall utterly be cut off; his iniquity *shall be* upon him.

32 ¶And while the children of Israel were in the wilderness, they found a man that gathered sticks upon the sabbath day.

33 And they that found him gathering sticks brought him unto Moses and Aaron, and unto all the congregation.

34 And they put him in ward, because it was not declared what should be done to him.

35 And the LORD said unto Moses, The man shall be surely put to death: all the congregation shall stone him with stones without the camp.

36 And all the congregation brought him without the camp, and stoned him

30-37. But the soul that doeth . . . presumptuously . . . shall be cut off. For this kind of sin there was no sacrifice; however, God forgives after the sinner repents. **A man that gathered sticks upon the sabbath.** The account here is a vivid example of that kind of presumptuous sin just described. This may seem harsh, but it must be remembered that unrest and rebellion continued to seethe in the hearts of the people at this time. This was even after God had manifested Himself in miracle after miracle. Thus, strictly enforced discipline was absolutely necessary, lest open anarchy take place.

with stones, and he died; as the LORD commanded Moses.

37 ¶And the LORD spake unto Moses, saying,

38 Speak unto the children of Israel, and bid them that they make them fringes in the borders of their garments throughout their generations, and that they put upon the fringe of the borders a ribband of blue:

39 And it shall be unto you for a fringe, that ye may look upon it, and remember all the commandments of the LORD, and do them; and that ye seek not after your own heart and your own eyes, after which ye use to go a whoring:

40 That ye may remember, and do all my commandments, and be holy unto your God.

41 I *am* the LORD your God, which brought you out of the land of Egypt, to be your God: I *am* the LORD your God.

CHAPTER 16

NOW Kôrah, the son of Ĭz'här, the son of Kō'hăth, the son of Levi, and Dā'than and A-bī'ram, the sons of E-lī'ab, and On, the son of Pĕ'lĕth, sons of Reuben, took *men*:

2 And they rose up before Moses, with certain of the children of Israel, two hundred and fifty princes of the assembly, famous in the congregation, men of renown:

3 And they gathered themselves together against Moses and against Aaron, and said unto them, Ye *take* too much upon you, seeing all the congregation *are* holy, every one of them, and the LORD *is* among them: wherefore then lift ye up yourselves above the congregation of the LORD?

4 And when Moses heard *it* he fell upon his face:

5 And he spake unto Kôrah and unto all his company, saying, Even to morrow the LORD will shew who *are* his, and *who is* holy; and will cause *him* to come near unto him: even *him* whom he hath chosen will he cause to come near unto him.

6 This do; Take you censers, Kôrah, and all his company;

7 And put fire therein, and put incense in them before the LORD to morrow: and it shall be *that* the man whom the LORD doth choose, he *shall* be holy: *ye take* too much upon you, ye sons of Levi.

8 And Moses said unto Kôrah, Hear, I pray you, ye sons of Levi:

9 *Seemeth it but* a small thing unto you, that the God of Israel hath separated you from the congregation of Israel, to bring you near to himself to do the service of the tabernacle of the LORD, and to stand before the congregation to minister unto them?

10 And he hath brought thee near *to him*, and all thy brethren the sons of Levi with thee: and seek ye the priesthood also?

11 For which cause *both* thou and all thy company *are* gathered together against the LORD: and what *is* Aaron, that ye murmur against him?

38-41. Bid them that they make them fringes. Jones writes: "As the Christians use the symbols of the cross, the fish, or the yoke, so the Hebrews were given the tassel on their clothing, to remind them of their heritage, and of the commandments of God. Orthodox Jews today still wear the tallith at certain times, though they discontinued wearing fringed garments all the time by the thirteenth century A.D." (Kenneth Jones, p. 51).

2. Leaders challenged. 16:1-50.

16:1-4. Now Korah . . . Dathan and Abiram. This chapter records one of the most critical events that occurred during the wilderness experience. It was in reality a twofold rebellion: (1) a religious revolt, headed by Korah. He was a Levite and Kohathite, as was Moses. His group stood against the exclusive priesthood of Aaron and his sons; and (2) a political revolt, organized by two Reubenites, Dathan and Abiram, against the leadership of Moses.

5-9. And he spake . . . saying . . . the LORD will show who are his. Moses answers his critics wisely here. Paul would later say in reference to Deuteronomy 32:35, "Dearly beloved, avenge not yourselves, but rather give place unto wrath: for it is written, Vengeance is mine; I will repay, saith the Lord" (Rom 12:19).

10-12. Seek ye the priesthood also? The Kohathites (of which Korah was a member) were assigned a very important task of caring for the tabernacle furniture (see 4:1-20). But he apparently coveted the office of the priesthood also, an office limited to Aaron and his sons.

12 ¶And Moses sent to call Dā'than and A-bī'ram, the sons of E-lī'ab: which said, We will not come up:

13 *Is it* a small thing that thou hast brought us up out of a land that floweth with milk and honey, to kill us in the wilderness, except thou make thyself altogether a prince over us?

14 Moreover thou hast not brought us into a land that floweth with milk and honey, or given us inheritance of fields and vineyards: wilt thou put out the eyes of these men? we will not come up.

15 And Moses was very wroth, and said unto the LORD, Respect not thou their offering: I have not taken one ass from them, neither have I hurt one of them.

16 And Moses said unto Kôrah, Be thou and all thy company before the LORD, thou, and they, and Aaron, to morrow:

17 And take every man his censer, and put incense in them, and bring ye before the LORD every man his censer, two hundred and fifty censers; thou also, and Aaron, each *of you* his censer.

18 And they took every man his censer, and put fire in them, and laid incense thereon, and stood in the door of the tabernacle of the congregation with Moses and Aaron.

19 And Kôrah gathered all the congregation against them unto the door of the tabernacle of the congregation: and the glory of the LORD appeared unto all the congregation.

20 And the LORD spake unto Moses and unto Aaron, saying,

21 Separate yourselves from among this congregation, that I may consume them in a moment.

22 And they fell upon their faces, and said, O God, the God of the spirits of all flesh, shall one man sin, and wilt thou be wroth with all the congregation?

23 ¶And the LORD spake unto Moses, saying,

24 Speak unto the congregation, saying, Get you up from about the tabernacle of Kôrah, Dā'than, and A-bī'ram.

25 And Moses rose up and went unto Dā'than and A-bī'ram; and the elders of Israel followed him.

26 And he spake unto the congregation, saying, Depart, I pray you, from the tents of these wicked men, and touch nothing of theirs, lest ye be consumed in all their sins.

27 So they gat up from the tabernacle of Kôrah, Dā'than, and A-bī'ram, on every side: and Dā'than and A-bī'ram came out, and stood in the door of their tents, and their wives, and their sons, and their little children.

28 And Moses said, Hereby ye shall know that the LORD hath sent me to do all these works; for *I have* not *done them* of mine own mind.

29 If these men die the common death of all men, or if they be visited after the visitation of all men; *then the* LORD hath not sent me.

30 But if the LORD make a new thing,

13-18. Thou hast brought us up out of a land that floweth with milk and honey, to kill us. These two troublemakers not only refuse to talk to Moses (vs. 12), but now they slander him with lying accusations. **Take every man his censer.** Here Moses threw out a challenge to Korah, for both men knew only the sons of Aaron were permitted to do this. But if Korah was determined to be a priest, then Moses demanded that he let God make the final decision.

19-28. And Korah gathered all the congregation against them. This indicates the rebels had poisoned the thinking of literally thousands of others. A coup was imminent. **And they fell upon their faces.** In Galatians 6:17 Paul stated that he had borne in his body ". . . the marks of the Lord Jesus." Here, it would seem Moses could testify that he bore the marks of Israel on his face! See also verse 45. Only Moses' and Aaron's intercession on both these occasions saved the entire nation from utter destruction.

29-36. If these men die the common death . . . then the LORD **hath not sent me.** An imprisoned and godly Israelite prophet named Micaiah would, some seven centuries later, utter the same words against wicked King Ahab (see I Kgs 22:28). **But if the** LORD **make a new thing.** No more spectacular or

285

and the earth open her mouth, and swallow them up, with all that *appertain* unto them, and they go down quick into the pit; then ye shall understand that these men have provoked the LORD.

31 ¶And it came to pass, as he had made an end of speaking all these words, that the ground clave asunder that *was* under them.

32 And the earth opened her mouth, and swallowed them up, and their houses, and all the men that *appertained* unto Kôrah, and all *their* goods.

33 They, and all that *appertained* to them, went down alive into the pit, and the earth closed upon them: and they perished from among the congregation.

34 And all Israel that *were* round about them fled at the cry of them: for they said, Lest the earth swallow us up *also*.

35 And there came out a fire from the LORD, and consumed the two hundred and fifty men that offered incense.

36 ¶And the LORD spake unto Moses, saying,

37 Speak unto Ĕ-le-ā′zar the son of Aaron the priest, that he take up the censers out of the burning, and scatter thou the fire yonder; for they are hallowed.

38 The censers of these sinners against their own souls, let them make them broad plates *for* a covering of the altar: for they offered them before the LORD, therefore they are hallowed: and they shall be a sign unto the children of Israel.

39 And Ĕ-le-ā′zar the priest took the brasen censers, wherewith they that were burnt had offered; and they were made broad plates *for* a covering of the altar:

40 *To be* a memorial unto the children of Israel, that no stranger, which *is* not of the seed of Aaron, come near to offer incense before the LORD; that he be not as Kôrah, and as his company: as the LORD said to him by the hand of Moses.

41 ¶But on the morrow all the congregation of the children of Israel murmured against Moses and against Aaron, saying, Ye have killed the people of the LORD.

42 And it came to pass, when the congregation was gathered against Moses and against Aaron, that they looked toward the tabernacle of the congregation: and, behold, the cloud covered it, and the glory of the LORD appeared.

43 And Moses and Aaron came before the tabernacle of the congregation.

44 And the LORD spake unto Moses, saying,

45 Get you up from among this congregation, that I may consume them as in a moment. And they fell upon their faces.

46 And Moses said unto Aaron, Take a censer, and put fire therein from off the altar, and put on incense, and go quickly unto the congregation, and

unlikely prediction could be made as Moses calls for the very earth to open its mouth and swallow up the rebels.

37-40. Speak unto Eleazar . . . that he take up the censers. Israel's next high priest was instructed to gather all the holy censers used illegally by these would-be priests. They were then beaten into metal covering plates for the altar, as a constant reminder of the fearful cost of rebellion.

41-44. Ye have killed the people of the LORD. This statement is possibly the high water mark of brazen and blasphemous insolence on the part of Israel. After witnessing the supernatural, terrifying sight of the ground opening, the dreadful flames belching forth, and hearing the screams of the doomed troublemakers, they now utter pious nonsense and accuse Moses, a mere man, of doing all this.

45-47. I may consume them as in a moment. Again God prepared to destroy the nation, but again Israel was saved by the intercession of Moses. Nevertheless, 14,700 people died in a divine plague before his prayers became effective.

make an atonement for them: for there is wrath gone out from the LORD; the plague is begun.

47 And Aaron took as Moses commanded, and ran into the midst of the congregation; and, behold, the plague was begun among the people: and he put on incense, and made an atonement for the people.

48 And he stood between the dead and the living; and the plague was stayed.

49 Now they that died in the plague were fourteen thousand and seven hundred, beside them that died about the matter of Kôrah.

50 And Aaron returned unto Moses unto the door of the tabernacle of the congregation: and the plague was stayed.

CHAPTER 17

AND the LORD spake unto Moses, saying,

2 Speak unto the children of Israel, and take of every one of them a rod according to the house of *their* fathers, of all their princes according to the house of their fathers twelve rods: write thou every man's name upon his rod.

3 And thou shalt write Aaron's name upon the rod of Levi: for one rod *shall be* for the head of the house of their fathers.

4 And thou shalt lay them up in the tabernacle of the congregation before the testimony, where I will meet with you.

5 And it shall come to pass, *that* the man's rod, whom I shall choose, shall blossom: and I will make to cease from me the murmurings of the children of Israel, whereby they murmur against you.

6 ¶And Moses spake unto the children of Israel, and every one of their princes gave him a rod apiece, for each prince one, according to their fathers' houses, *even* twelve rods: and the rod of Aaron *was* among their rods.

7 And Moses laid up the rods before the LORD in the tabernacle of witness.

8 And it came to pass, that on the morrow Moses went into the tabernacle of witness; and, behold, the rod of Aaron for the house of Levi was budded, and brought forth buds, and bloomed blossoms, and yielded almonds.

9 And Moses brought out all the rods from before the LORD unto all the children of Israel: and they looked, and took every man his rod.

10 ¶And the LORD said unto Moses, Bring Aaron's rod again before the testimony, to be kept for a token against the rebels; and thou shalt quite take away their murmurings from me, that they die not.

11 And Moses did *so*: as the LORD commanded him, so did he.

12 And the children of Israel spake unto Moses, saying, Behold, we die, we perish, we all perish.

13 Whosoever cometh any thing near unto the tabernacle of the LORD shall die: shall we be consumed with dying?

48-50. And he stood between the dead and the living. Here Moses becomes a remarkable type of a New Testament soul-winner (see II Cor 2:15-16). **About the matter of Korah.** Thus ends the account of one of the most infamous troublemakers in biblical history. The author Jude (vs. 11) would later refer to this tragic event.

3. High Priest vindicated. 17:1-13.

17:1-4. And thou shalt write Aaron's name. It has already been observed that Moses and Aaron were faced with both a political and a religious rebellion. In chapter 16 God had vindicated the political leadership of Moses. In this chapter, He will do the same for the religious leadership of Aaron.

5-13. The man's rod, whom I shall choose, shall blossom. Each tribal leader was to put his name upon a wooden rod, including Aaron's name upon the stick representing the tribe of Levi. These were then placed in the tabernacle overnight. The next morning (vs. 8), Aaron's rod had both budded and blossomed, with almonds hanging from it. This episode, of course, lends itself to a spiritual application of Christ's glorious resurrection!

CHAPTER 18

AND the Lord said unto Aaron, Thou and thy sons and thy father's house with thee shall bear the iniquity of the sanctuary: and thou and thy sons with thee shall bear the iniquity of your priesthood.

2 And thy brethren also of the tribe of Levi, the tribe of thy father, bring thou with thee, that they may be joined unto thee, and minister unto thee: but thou and thy sons with thee *shall minister* before the tabernacle of witness.

3 And they shall keep thy charge, and the charge of all the tabernacle: only they shall not come nigh the vessels of the sanctuary and the altar, that neither they, nor ye also, die.

4 And they shall be joined unto thee, and keep the charge of the tabernacle of the congregation, for all the service of the tabernacle: and a stranger shall not come nigh unto you.

5 And ye shall keep the charge of the sanctuary, and the charge of the altar: that there be no wrath any more upon the children of Israel.

6 And I, behold, I have taken your brethren the Lēvītes from among the children of Israel: to you *they are* given *as* a gift for the Lord, to do the service of the tabernacle of the congregation.

7 Therefore thou and thy sons with thee shall keep your priest's office for every thing of the altar, and within the vail; and ye shall serve: I have given your priest's office *unto you as* a service of gift: and the stranger that cometh nigh shall be put to death.

8 ¶And the Lord spake unto Aaron, Behold, I also have given thee the charge of mine heave offerings of all the hallowed things of the children of Israel; unto thee have I given them by reason of the anointing, and to thy sons, by an ordinance for ever.

9 This shall be thine of the most holy things, *reserved* from the fire: every oblation of theirs, every meat offering of theirs, and every sin offering of theirs, and every trespass offering of theirs which they shall render unto me, *shall be* most holy for thee and for thy sons.

10 In the most holy *place* shalt thou eat it; every male shall eat it: it shall be holy unto thee.

11 And this *is* thine; the heave offering of their gift, with all the wave offerings of the children of Israel: I have given them unto thee, and to thy sons and to thy daughters with thee, by a statute for ever: every one that is clean in thy house shall eat of it.

12 All the best of the oil, and all the best of the wine, and of the wheat, the firstfruits of them which they shall of-

4. *Some reassurance to the Levites. 18:1-32.*

The Levites were not to be given any land to possess when Israel would enter Canaan. Their entire lives were to be given in service to the tabernacle and spiritual things. But how would they survive? This chapter simply gives reassurance and some clarification concerning both the responsibilities and privileges afforded to this tribe. In verses 1-25, God speaks to the Levites through Aaron, and in verses 26-32 He talks to them through Moses.

18:1-8. The Lord said unto Aaron, Thou and thy sons . . . shall bear the iniquity of the sanctuary. This meant that the Levites were held accountable for any defilement that might come to them or to the sanctuary (see also Ex 28:38; Lev 22:16). **I also have given thee** (vs. 8). This little phrase seems to be the theme of chapter 18 (see vss. 7, 8, 12, 19, 26). God takes care of His servants.

9-18. Every thing devoted in Israel shall be thine. Jones writes: "The Hebrew word here is *cherem*, which means more than a mere dedication. It was indicative of a way of devoting a thing to God in such a fashion that it would not be redeemed or ever again used for ordinary purposes. The vow was irrevocable. The first-born of all animals belonged to God, but they could be redeemed with a price and used for ordinary purposes. They were *godesh* rather than *cherem*. Both belonged to God, but the first could be redeemed." (Kenneth Jones, p. 55).

fer unto the LORD, them have I given thee.

13 *And* whatsoever is first ripe in the land, which they shall bring unto the LORD, shall be thine; every one that is clean in thine house shall eat *of* it.

14 Every thing devoted in Israel shall be thine.

15 Every thing that openeth the matrix in all flesh, which they bring unto the LORD, *whether it be* of men or beasts, shall be thine: nevertheless the firstborn of man shalt thou surely redeem, and the firstling of unclean beasts shalt thou redeem.

16 And those that are to be redeemed from a month old shalt thou redeem, according to thine estimation, for the money of five shekels, after the shekel of the sanctuary, which *is* twenty gerahs.

17 But the firstling of a cow, or the firstling of a sheep, or the firstling of a goat, thou shalt not redeem; they *are* holy: thou shalt sprinkle their blood upon the altar, and shalt burn their fat *for* an offering made by fire, for a sweet savour unto the LORD.

18 And the flesh of them shall be thine, as the wave breast and as the right shoulder are thine.

19 All the heave offerings of the holy things, which the children of Israel offer unto the LORD, have I given thee, and thy sons and thy daughters with thee, by a statute for ever: it *is* a covenant of salt for ever before the LORD unto thee and to thy seed with thee.

20 ¶And the LORD spake unto Aaron, Thou shalt have no inheritance in their land, neither shalt thou have any part among them: I *am* thy part and thine inheritance among the children of Israel.

21 And, behold, I have given the children of Levi all the tenth in Israel for an inheritance, for their service which they serve, *even* the service of the tabernacle of the congregation.

22 Neither must the children of Israel henceforth come nigh the tabernacle of the congregation, lest they bear sin, and die.

23 But the Lēvītes shall do the service of the tabernacle of the congregation, and they shall bear their iniquity: *it shall be* a statute for ever throughout your generations, that among the children of Israel they have no inheritance.

24 But the tithes of the children of Israel, which they offer *as* an heave offering unto the LORD, I have given to the Lēvītes to inherit: therefore I have said unto them, Among the children of Israel they shall have no inheritance.

25 ¶And the LORD spake unto Moses, saying,

26 Thus speak unto the Lēvītes, and say unto them, When ye take of the children of Israel the tithes which I have given you from them for your inheritance, then ye shall offer up an heave offering of it for the LORD, *even* a tenth *part* of the tithe.

27 And *this* your heave offering shall be reckoned unto you, as though *it were* the corn of the threshingfloor, and as the fulness of the winepress.

19-32. A covenant of salt. This is the second mention of three Old Testament methods whereby covenants could be ratified. The first was by a blood covenant (Gen 15:7-17), and the last by a shoe covenant (Ruth 4:7-9). **I am thy part and thine inheritance.** Of all the gifts of God to the Levites (the services, responsibilities, tithes, and sacrifices of the tabernacle, etc.), this was the grandest of all: He gave Himself!

28 Thus ye also shall offer an heave offering unto the LORD of all your tithes, which ye receive of the children of Israel; and ye shall give thereof the LORD's heave offering to Aaron the priest.

29 Out of all your gifts ye shall offer every heave offering of the LORD, of all the best thereof, *even* the hallowed part thereof out of it.

30 Therefore thou shalt say unto them, When ye have heaved the best thereof from it, then it shall be counted unto the Lēvītes as the increase of the threshingfloor, and as the increase of the winepress.

31 And ye shall eat it in every place, ye and your households: for it *is* your reward for your service in the tabernacle of the congregation.

32 And ye shall bear no sin by reason of it, when ye have heaved from it the best of it: neither shall ye pollute the holy things of the children of Israel, lest ye die.

CHAPTER 19

AND the LORD spake unto Moses and unto Aaron, saying,

2 This *is* the ordinance of the law which the LORD hath commanded, saying, Speak unto the children of Israel, that they bring thee a red heifer without spot, wherein *is* no blemish, *and* upon which never came yoke:

3 And ye shall give her unto Ē-le-ā′zar the priest, that he may bring her forth without the camp, and *one* shall slay her before his face:

4 And Ē-le-ā′zar the priest shall take of her blood with his finger, and sprinkle of her blood directly before the tabernacle of the congregation seven times:

5 And *one* shall burn the heifer in his sight; her skin, and her flesh, and her blood, with her dung, shall he burn:

6 And the priest shall take cedar wood, and hyssop, and scarlet, and cast *it* into the midst of the burning of the heifer.

7 Then the priest shall wash his clothes, and he shall bathe his flesh in water, and afterward he shall come into the camp, and the priest shall be unclean until the even.

8 And he that burneth her shall wash his clothes in water, and bathe his flesh in water, and shall be unclean until the even.

9 And a man *that is* clean shall gather up the ashes of the heifer, and lay *them* up without the camp in a clean place, and it shall be kept for the congregation of the children of Israel for a water of separation: it *is* a purification for sin.

10 And he that gathereth the ashes of the heifer shall wash his clothes, and be unclean until the even: and it shall be unto the children of Israel, and unto the stranger that sojourneth among them, for a statute for ever.

11 ¶He that toucheth the dead body of any man shall be unclean seven days.

12 He shall purify himself with it on the third day, and on the seventh day he shall be clean: but if he purify not him-

5. Cleansing for defilement. 19:1-22.

19:1-10. Laws had already been given whereby a living person coming in contact with a corpse would be considered unclean (disqualified from religious life and service) for a period of seven days. But a crisis had probably now arisen. Due to the recent plague (16:49), no less than 14,700 corpses had come upon the scene. This event alone had, doubtless, contributed to the defilement of tens of thousands of people. What could be done about this? The rite of the **red heifer** was God's answer to this problem.

11-22. He that toucheth the dead body of any man shall be unclean. The cleansing of a defiled Israelite was fourfold: (1) Eleazar was to slaughter an unblemished red heifer outside the camp (vss. 2-3); (2) its blood was to be sprinkled toward the tabernacle seven times (vs. 4); (3) the red heifer was to be burned along with cedar, wood, hyssop, and some scarlet cloth

self the third day, then the seventh day he shall not be clean.

13 Whosoever toucheth the dead body of any man that is dead, and purifieth not himself, defileth the tabernacle of the LORD; and that soul shall be cut off from Israel: because the water of separation was not sprinkled upon him, he shall be unclean; his uncleanness *is* yet upon him.

14 This *is* the law, when a man dieth in a tent: all that come into the tent, and all that *is* in the tent, shall be unclean seven days.

15 And every open vessel, which hath no covering bound upon it, *is* unclean.

16 And whosoever toucheth one that is slain with a sword in the open fields, or a dead body, or a bone of a man, or a grave, shall be unclean seven days.

17 And for an unclean *person* they shall take of the ashes of the burnt heifer of purification for sin, and running water shall be put thereto in a vessel:

18 And a clean person shall take hyssop, and dip *it* in the water, and sprinkle *it* upon the tent, and upon all the vessels, and upon the persons that were there, and upon him that touched a bone, or one slain, or one dead, or a grave:

19 And the clean *person* shall sprinkle upon the unclean on the third day, and on the seventh day: and on the seventh day he shall purify himself, and wash his clothes, and bathe himself in water, and shall be clean at even.

20 But the man that shall be unclean, and shall not purify himself, that soul shall be cut off from among the congregation, because he hath defiled the sanctuary of the LORD: the water of separation hath not been sprinkled upon him; he *is* unclean.

21 And it shall be a perpetual statute unto them, that he that sprinkleth the water of separation shall wash his clothes; and he that toucheth the water of separation shall be unclean until even.

22 And whatsoever the unclean *person* toucheth shall be unclean; and the soul that toucheth *it* shall be unclean until even.

CHAPTER 20

THEN came the children of Israel, *even* the whole congregation, into the desert of Zin in the first month: and the people abode in Kā′desh; and Miriam died there, and was buried there.

2 And there was no water for the congregation: and they gathered themselves together against Moses and against Aaron.

3 And the people chode with Moses, and spake, saying, Would God that we had died when our brethren died before the LORD!

4 And why have ye brought up the congregation of the LORD into this wilderness, that we and our cattle should die there?

5 And wherefore have ye made us to come up out of Egypt, to bring us in unto this evil place? it *is* no place of

material (vss. 5-6); and (4) finally water was to be added to the ashes of the heifer and sprinkled upon the defiled Israelite (vss. 17-19).

B. New Generation. 20:1-22:1.

1. An angry man snared. 20:1-13.

20:1-7. And Miriam died. Miriam must have been over one hundred years of age at her death, for she was at least ten or fifteen years older than Moses (cf. Ex 2:1-10). Almost forty years of wilderness wanderings had now been experienced. The people have made full circle in their travels and are now back at Kadesh. The story here opens up as usual, with Israel conducting its daily slandering session against both God and Moses.

seed, or of figs, or of vines, or of pomegranates; neither *is* there any water to drink.

6 And Moses and Aaron went from the presence of the assembly unto the door of the tabernacle of the congregation, and they fell upon their faces: and the glory of the LORD appeared unto them.

7 ¶And the LORD spake unto Moses, saying,

8 Take the rod, and gather thou the assembly together, thou, and Aaron thy brother, and speak ye unto the rock before their eyes; and it shall give forth his water, and thou shalt bring forth to them water out of the rock: so thou shalt give the congregation and their beasts drink.

9 And Moses took the rod from before the LORD, as he commanded him.

10 And Moses and Aaron gathered the congregation together before the rock, and he said unto them, Hear now, ye rebels; must we fetch you water out of this rock?

11 And Moses lifted up his hand, and with his rod he smote the rock twice: and the water came out abundantly, and the congregation drank, and their beasts *also*.

12 ¶And the LORD spake unto Moses and Aaron, Because ye believed me not, to sanctify me in the eyes of the children of Israel, therefore ye shall not bring this congregation into the land which I have given them.

13 This *is* the water of Měr'i-bah; because the children of Israel strove with the LORD, and he was sanctified in them.

14 ¶And Moses sent messengers from Kā'desh unto the king of Edom, Thus saith thy brother Israel, Thou knowest all the travail that hath befallen us:

15 How our fathers went down into Egypt, and we have dwelt in Egypt a long time; and the Egyptians vexed us, and our fathers:

16 And when we cried unto the LORD, he heard our voice, and sent an angel, and hath brought us forth out of Egypt: and, behold, we *are* in Kā'desh, a city in the uttermost of thy border:

17 Let us pass, I pray thee, through thy country: we will not pass through the fields, or through the vineyards, neither will we drink of the water of the wells: we will go by the king's *high* way, we will not turn to the right hand nor to the left, until we have passed thy borders.

18 And Edom said unto him, Thou shalt not pass by me, lest I come out against thee with the sword.

19 And the children of Israel said unto him, We will go by the high way: and if I and my cattle drink of thy water, then I will pay for it: I will only, without *doing* anything *else*, go through on my feet.

20 And he said, Thou shalt not go through. And Edom came out against him with much people, and with a strong hand.

8-10. Take the rod . . . and speak ye unto the rock. Nearly forty years prior to this, and in another place, God had used a rock to solve Israel's water problems, as He would now instruct Moses to do. But on the first occasion Moses was instructed to strike the rock (Ex 17:6), while here (vs. 8) he was simply to speak to it.

11-13. And Moses . . . smote the rock twice. At this point in his life, Moses, earth's meekest man (12:3), loses control of himself, screams out at the carnal crowd, and disobeys God, not only by hitting the rock, but by smashing it twice. **And the water came out abundantly.** God thus blessed the end, even though He disapproved of the means (cf. also Ezk 36:21-23). The important lesson here is that God is as concerned with the way He performs His will as He is in the actual will itself! **Ye shall not bring this congregation into the land** (vs. 12). But he would be allowed to see it (Deut 27:12-14) before his death, and visit it fourteen centuries after his death (Mt 17:3).

2. The refusal of Edom. 20:14-22.

14-22. Israel wanted to go east from Kadesh through the land of Edom, which included that area south of the Dead Sea. This request was denied, thus forcing Moses and the people to travel over fifty additional miles through a hot, barren, and hostile desert. **And . . . Israel . . . came unto mount Hor** (vs. 22). Mount Hor was located on the Edom border (33:37).

21 Thus Ēdom refused to give Israel passage through his border: wherefore Israel turned away from him.

22 ¶And the children of Israel, even the whole congregation, journeyed from Kā′desh, and came unto mount Hor.

23 And the LORD spake unto Moses and Aaron in mount Hor, by the coast of the land of Ēdom, saying,

24 Aaron shall be gathered unto his people: for he shall not enter into the land which I have given unto the children of Israel, because ye rebelled against my word at the water of Mĕr′i-bah.

25 Take Aaron and Ĕ-le-ā′zar his son, and bring them up unto mount Hor:

26 And strip Aaron of his garments, and put them upon Ĕ-le-ā′zar his son: and Aaron shall be gathered unto his people, and shall die there.

27 And Moses did as the LORD commanded: and they went up into mount Hor in the sight of all the congregation.

28 And Moses stripped Aaron of his garments, and put them upon Ĕ-le-ā′zar his son; and Aaron died there in the top of the mount: and Moses and Ĕ-le-ā′zar came down from the mount.

29 And when all the congregation saw that Aaron was dead, they mourned for Aaron thirty days, even all the house of Israel.

CHAPTER 21

AND when king Ā′răd the Canaanite, which dwelt in the south, heard tell that Israel came by the way of the spies; then he fought against Israel, and took some of them prisoners.

2 And Israel vowed a vow unto the LORD, and said, If thou wilt indeed deliver this people into my hand, then I will utterly destroy their cities.

3 And the LORD hearkened to the voice of Israel, and delivered up the Canaanites; and they utterly destroyed them and their cities: and he called the name of the place Hôr′mah.

4 ¶And they journeyed from mount Hor by the way of the Red sea, to compass the land of Ēdom: and the soul of the people was much discouraged because of the way.

5 And the people spake against God, and against Moses, Wherefore have ye brought us up out of Egypt to die in the wilderness? for there is no bread, neither is there any water; and our soul loatheth this light bread.

6 And the LORD sent fiery serpents among the people, and they bit the people; and much people of Israel died.

7 Therefore the people came to Moses, and said, We have sinned, for we have spoken against the LORD, and against thee; pray unto the LORD, that he take away the serpents from us. And Moses prayed for the people.

8 And the LORD said unto Moses, Make thee a fiery serpent, and set it upon a pole: and it shall come to pass, that every one that is bitten, when he looketh upon it, shall live.

9 And Moses made a serpent of brass, and put it upon a pole, and it came to pass, that if a serpent had bitten any

3. The death of Aaron and appointment of Eleazar. 20:23-29.

23-29. And Aaron died there in the top of the mount. This death, that of the first high priest, would be mourned by the people for thirty days (vs. 29). A glorious change would later, of course, take place with the advent of the believer's great High Priest, Christ Jesus (see Heb 7:23-25). The death of Aaron marks the end of Israel's wanderings. From this point on the nation either marched or halted, but did not wander. It should be noted here that the wilderness experience, but not the wanderings, was originally in the perfect will of God for Israel (Ex 13:17, 18).

4. A serpent problem solved. 21:1-18.

21:1-5. And the LORD hearkened to . . . Israel, and delivered up the Canaanites. The psychological impact of this battle cannot be overemphasized, for it marks Israel's first victory since Kadesh. Their vow of faith to God (vs. 2), instead of the usual daily gripe session, doubtless was the secret of their success.

6-8. The LORD sent fiery serpents among the people. This area (see vs. 4) is known even today for its many venomous reptiles.

9. And Moses made a serpent of brass, and put it upon a pole. Clarke points out, "the word for *brass* or copper comes from the same root with *nachash*, which here signifies a serpent,

man, when he beheld the serpent of brass, he lived.

10 ¶And the children of Israel set forward, and pitched in Ō′bŏth.

11 And they journeyed from Ō′bŏth, and pitched at Ĭj′e-ăb′a-rĭm, in the wilderness which is before Moab, toward the sunrising.

12 ¶From thence they removed, and pitched in the valley of Za′red.

13 From thence they removed, and pitched on the other side of Arnon, which is in the wilderness that cometh out of the coasts of the Ămŏrītes: for Arnon is the border of Moab, between Moab and the Ămŏrītes.

14 Wherefore it is said in the book of the wars of the Lord, What he did in the Red sea, and in the brooks of Arnon,

15 And at the stream of the brooks that goeth down to the dwelling of Ar, and lieth upon the border of Moab.

16 ¶And from thence they went to Beer: that is the well whereof the Lord spake unto Moses, Gather the people together, and I will give them water.

17 Then Israel sang this song, Spring up, O well; sing ye unto it:

18 The princes digged the well, the nobles of the people digged it, by the direction of the lawgiver, with their staves. And from the wilderness they went to Măt′ta-nah:

19 And from Măt′ta-nah to Na-hā′lĭ-el: and from Na-hā′lĭ-el to Bā′mŏth:

20 And from Bā′mŏth in the valley, that is in the country of Moab, to the top of Pĭs′gah, which looketh toward Jesh′ī-mon.

21 ¶And Israel sent messengers unto Sihon king of the Ămŏrītes, saying,

22 Let me pass through thy land: we will not turn into the fields, or into the vineyards; we will not drink of the waters of the well: but we will go along by the king's high way, until we be past thy borders.

23 And Sihon would not suffer Israel to pass through his border: but Sihon gathered all his people together, and went out against Israel into the wilderness: and he came to Jā′hăz, and fought against Israel.

24 And Israel smote him with the edge of the sword, and possessed his land from Arnon unto Jabbok, even unto the children of Ammon: for the border of the children of Ammon was strong.

25 And Israel took all these cities: and Israel dwelt in all the cities of the

probably on account of the *colour;* as most serpents, especially those of the bright spotted kind, have a glistening appearance, and those who have brown or yellow spots appear something like *burnished brass:* but the true meaning of the root cannot be easily ascertained . . ." (*Clarke's Commentary,* Vol. 1, pp. 684-685). Critics have attempted unsuccessfully to compare Moses' action here with the well-known heathen practices of antiquity by which religions ascribed supernatural healing powers to serpents. The most casual reading of the passage here refutes this, making it clear that any healing power came solely from obeying the command of God.

This bronze serpent was later destroyed by King Hezekiah; it had become an object of worship (II Kgs 18:4). In the New Testament this event is used as an illustration of salvation by Jesus (Jn 3:14), and as a warning by Paul the apostle (I Cor 10:9).

10-13. And the children of Israel set forward, and pitched. Especially to be noted are the words **set forward.** Israel is now on the march! Verses 10-20 record their march from Mount Hor, where Aaron was buried, to Mount Pisgah, where Moses would later be buried (Deut 34:1-8).

14-16. The book of the wars of the Lord. This is the first of at least seven non-canonical books of records mentioned in the Old Testament. The others are: the book of Jasher (Josh 10:13); the chronicles of David (I Chr 27:24); the book of Gad (I Chr 29:29); the book of Nathan (I Chr 29:29); the book of the prophet Iddo (II Chr 13:22); and the book of Jehu (II Chr 20:34).

17-18. Then Israel sang this song. It had been a long time, indeed, since the people sang unto the Lord (see Ex 15:1).

5. Advances to the Plains of Moab. 21:19-22:1.

19-26. The top of Pisgah. It was from this elevation that Moses would view Palestine (Deut 34:1). **Let me pass through thy land** (vs. 22). Israel asks of the Amorites the same favor they had once asked of the Edomites (20:17), and received the same negative answer (cf. vs. 23 with 20:18). However, this Israel will not take no for an answer; and they attack and defeat the Amorites (vs. 24). **Unto Jabbok.** This brook had already been the background for a famous Old Testament event (see Gen 32:22).

Ămorītes, in Hěsh'bŏn, and in all the villages thereof.

26 For Hěsh'bŏn *was* the city of Si-hon the king of the Ămorītes, who had fought against the former king of Moab, and taken all his land out of his hand, even unto Arnon.

27 Wherefore they that speak in prov-erbs say, Come into Hěsh'bŏn, let the city of Sihon be built and prepared:

28 For there is a fire gone out of Hěsh'bŏn, a flame from the city of Si-hon: it hath consumed Ar of Moab, *and* the lords of the high places of Arnon.

29 Woe to thee, Moab! thou art un-done, O people of Chě'mŏsh: he hath given his sons that escaped, and his daughters, into captivity unto Sihon king of the Ămorītes.

30 We have shot at them; Hěsh'bŏn is perished even unto Dī'bŏn, and we have laid them waste even unto Nŏ'-phah, which *reacheth* unto Měd'e-ba.

31 ¶Thus Israel dwelt in the land of the Ămorītes.

32 And Moses sent to spy out Jā-ā'zer, and they took the villages thereof, and drove out the Ămorītes that *were* there.

33 ¶And they turned and went up by the way of Bā'shan: and Og the king of Bā'shan went out against them, he, and all his people, to the battle at Ěd're-ī.

34 And the LORD said unto Moses, Fear him not: for I have delivered him into thy hand, and all his people, and his land; and thou shalt do to him as thou didst unto Sihon king of the Ămor-ītes, which dwelt at Hěsh'bŏn.

35 So they smote him, and his sons, and all his people, until there was none left him alive: and they possessed his land.

CHAPTER 22

AND the children of Israel set forward, and pitched in the plains of Moab on this side Jordan *by* Jericho.

2 ¶And Bālăk the son of Zippor saw all that Israel had done to the Amorites.

3 And Moab was sore afraid of the people, because they *were* many: and Moab was distressed because of the children of Israel.

4 And Moab said unto the elders of Mĭd'ī-an, Now shall this company lick up all *that are* round about us, as the ox licketh up the grass of the field. And Bālăk the son of Zippor *was* king of the Moabites at that time.

5 He sent messengers therefore unto Bā'laam the son of Bē'ŏr to Pē'thôr, which *is* by the river of the land of the children of his people, to call him, saying, Behold, there is a people come out from Egypt: behold, they cover the face of the earth, and they abide over against me:

6 Come now therefore, I pray thee, curse me this people; for they *are* too

27-32. Wherefore they that speak in proverbs say. Verses 26 and 27 give the historical facts on which the poem in verses 27-30 is based. The essence of the poem is, "You Amorites have beaten the Moabites, but we Israelites have beaten you."

33-35. Og the king of Bashan. This pagan giant is said to have slept in an iron bed measuring fourteen feet by five feet (Deut 3:11). Og is mentioned a number of times in the Old Testament (see Josh 2:10; I Kgs 4:19; Neh 9:22; Ps 135:11; 136:20; etc.). **Fear him not.** These words must have sounded like heavenly music, indeed, to the Israelites.

22:1. Pitched in the plains of Moab on this side Jordan by Jericho. Here the children of Israel set up their camp.

C. Border Crossing. 22:2-36:13.

1. Problems. 22:2-25:18.

a. Opposition from without. 22:2-24:25.

22:2-4. Balak . . . saw all that Israel had done. This fright-ened pagan king had kept up on Israel's string of victories. He felt his country would be the next victim. Realizing they apparently could not be stopped by armed might, he would try satanic witchcraft of a sort.

5-11. He sent messengers therefore unto Balaam . . . to Pethor. Pethor is commonly identified as Pitru, just south of Carchemish, four hundred miles north of Moab. Verse 5 men-tions for the first time one of the strongest characters in all the Bible—**Balaam.** The more we read about him the less we seem to know. Was he a saved man? How much did he know about the true God? What had he done in the past to earn his reputa-tion as a prophet? Why did God use him at all at this time? **Come now therefore, I pray thee, curse me this people.** Balak

mighty for me: peradventure I shall prevail, *that* we may smite them, and *that* I may drive them out of the land: for I wot that he whom thou blessest *is* blessed, and he whom thou cursest is cursed.

7 And the elders of Moab and the elders of Mĭd′ĭ-an departed with the rewards of divination in their hand; and they came unto Bā′laam, and spake unto him the words of Bālăk.

8 And he said unto them, Lodge here this night, and I will bring you word again, as the LORD shall speak unto me: and the princes of Moab abode with Bā′laam.

9 And God came unto Bā′laam, and said, What men *are* these with thee?

10 And Bā′laam said unto God, Bālăk the son of Zippor, king of Moab, hath sent unto me, *saying,*

11 Behold, *there is* a people come out of Egypt, which covereth the face of the earth: come now, curse me them; peradventure I shall be able to overcome them, and drive them out.

12 And God said unto Bā′laam, Thou shalt not go with them; thou shalt not curse the people: for they *are* blessed.

13 And Bā′laam rose up in the morning, and said unto the princes of Bālăk, Get you into your land: for the LORD refuseth to give me leave to go with you.

14 And the princes of Moab rose up, and they went unto Bālăk, and said, Bā′laam refuseth to come with us.

15 ¶And Bālăk sent yet again princes, more, and more honourable than they.

16 And they came to Bā′laam, and said to him, Thus saith Bālăk the son of Zippor, Let nothing, I pray thee, hinder thee from coming unto me:

17 For I will promote thee unto very great honour, and I will do whatsoever thou sayest unto me: come therefore, I pray thee, curse me this people.

18 And Bā′laam answered and said unto the servants of Bālăk, If Bālăk would give me his house full of silver and gold, I cannot go beyond the word of the LORD my God, to do less or more.

19 Now therefore, I pray you, tarry ye also here this night, that I may know what the LORD will say unto me more.

20 And God came unto Bā′laam at night, and said unto him, If the men come to call thee, rise up, *and* go with them; but yet the word which I shall say unto thee, that shalt thou do.

21 And Bā′laam rose up in the morning, and saddled his ass, and went with the princes of Moab.

22 ¶And God's anger was kindled because he went: and the angel of the LORD stood in the way for an adversary against him. Now he was riding upon his ass, and his two servants *were* with him.

23 And the ass saw the angel of the LORD standing in the way, and his sword drawn in his hand: and the ass turned aside out of the way, and went into the field: and Bā′laam smote the ass, to turn her into the way.

24 But the angel of the LORD stood in a path of the vineyards, a wall *being* on this side, and a wall on that side.

25 And when the ass saw the angel of

296

sends rich rewards to entice Balaam to do his evil work. He was apparently the best prophet money could buy!

12-19. And God said unto Balaam, Thou shalt not go with them. After Balaam has seen the enticing bribes of Balak's messengers, he bids them to stay overnight, hoping God would allow him to go. It was to no avail. **And Balak sent yet again.** Balak was not going to be discouraged. He thought Balaam could be bought if the bribes were greater and more glittering.

20-21. And God came unto Balaam at night, and said . . . rise up, and go with them. After asking the messengers to stay all night, Balaam received the desired permission, but was warned to say only what God wanted him to say.

22-24. And . . . the angel of the LORD stood in the way. Verses 22-32 are, at the same time, some of the most amazing and amusing in the entire Bible. The account tells how the ass upon which Balaam was riding was suddenly confronted by the angel of God standing in the way with drawn sword. Balaam did not see this, but the terrified ass did and began acting in such a manner as to incur the extreme displeasure of Balaam.

25-27. And when the ass saw the angel . . . she . . .

the LORD, she thrust herself unto the wall, and crushed Bā′laam's foot against the wall: and he smote her again.

26 And the angel of the LORD went further, and stood in a narrow place, where *was* no way to turn either to the right hand or to the left.

27 And when the ass saw the angel of the LORD, she fell down under Bā′laam: and Bā′laam's anger was kindled, and he smote the ass with a staff.

28 And the LORD opened the mouth of the ass, and she said unto Bā′laam, What have I done unto thee, that thou hast smitten me these three times?

29 And Bā′laam said unto the ass, Because thou hast mocked me: I would there were a sword in mine hand, for now would I kill thee.

30 And the ass said unto Bā′laam, *Am* not I thine ass, upon which thou hast ridden ever since *I was* thine unto this day? was I ever wont to do so unto thee? And he said, Nay.

31 Then the LORD opened the eyes of Bā′laam, and he saw the angel of the LORD standing in the way, and his sword drawn in his hand: and he bowed down his head, and fell flat on his face.

32 And the angel of the LORD said unto him, Wherefore hast thou smitten thine ass these three times? behold, I went out to withstand thee, because *thy* way is perverse before me:

33 And the ass saw me, and turned from me these three times: unless she had turned from me, surely now also I had slain thee, and saved her alive.

34 And Bā′laam said unto the angel of the LORD, I have sinned; for I knew not that thou stoodest in the way against me: now therefore, if it displease thee, I will get me back again.

35 And the angel of the LORD said unto Bā′laam, Go with the men: but only the word that I shall speak unto thee, that thou shalt speak. So Bā′laam went with the princes of Bā′lăk.

36 ¶And when Bā′lăk heard that Bā′-laam was come, he went out to meet him unto a city of Moab, which *is* in the border of Arnon, which *is* in the utmost coast.

37 And Bā′lăk said unto Bā′laam, Did I not earnestly send unto thee to call thee? wherefore camest thou not unto me? am I not able indeed to promote thee to honour?

38 And Bā′laam said unto Bā′lăk, Lo, I am come unto thee: have I now any power at all to say any thing? the word that God putteth in my mouth, that shall I speak.

39 And Bā′laam went with Bā′lăk, and they came unto Kir′jath-hŭ′zŏth.

40 And Bā′lăk offered oxen and sheep, and sent to Bā′laam, and to the princes that *were* with him.

41 And it came to pass on the morrow, that Bā′lăk took Bā′laam, and brought him up into the high places of Bā′al, that thence he might see the utmost *part* of the people.

CHAPTER 23
AND Bā′laam said unto Bā′lăk, Build

crushed Balaam's foot against the wall. Finally, trapped between two walls (vs. 24), the frightened animal lurched, attempting to avoid the angel standing there. Still unable to see the angel, a furious Balaam begins beating the poor beast of burden with his stick (vs. 27).

28-30. And the LORD opened the mouth of the ass, and she said unto Balaam. This is the second of three biblical instances where a creature from the world of nature speaks: (1) in Genesis 3:1 a serpent speaks; (2) in Numbers 22:28 an ass speaks; and (3) in Revelation 8:13 an eagle (not angel, as translated by KJV) speaks. And Balaam said. The amusing thing here is that apparently Balaam was so furious that he shows no surprise over a speaking animal!

31-36. Then the LORD opened the eyes of Balaam, and he saw the angel of the LORD. The angel here is, probably, a reference to Christ Himself, God's beloved Old Testament servant. And Balaam said . . . I have sinned. On at least eight separate occasions in the Scriptures an individual has been forced to utter these three tragic but true words, "I have sinned." See also: Pharaoh (Ex 9:27; 10:16); Achan (Josh 7:20); Saul (I Sam 26:21); David (II Sam 12:13; 24:10); Job (Job 7:20); Judas (Mt 27:4); and the prodigal son (Lk 15:21). A double tragedy is seen here; for out of eight confessions, it would seem that only three (David, Job, and the prodigal son) really meant it and experienced the forgiveness of God!

37-41. And Balak said . . . Did I not earnestly send unto thee to call thee? Here Balak seems to rebuke Balaam for not coming immediately when he was summoned. But again Balaam warns that he can only speak what God allows him to say (vs. 38).

23:1-10. And Balaam said . . . Build me here seven altars.

me here seven altars, and prepare me here seven oxen and seven rams.

2 And Bā´lăk did as Bā´laam had spoken: and Bā´lăk and Bā´laam offered on *every* altar a bullock and a ram.

3 And Bā´laam said unto Bā´lăk, Stand by thy burnt offering, and I will go: peradventure the LORD will come to meet me: and whatsoever he sheweth me I will tell thee. And he went to an high place.

4 And God met Bā´laam: and he said unto him, I have prepared seven altars, and I have offered upon *every* altar a bullock and a ram.

5 And the LORD put a word in Bā´-laam's mouth, and said, Return unto Bā´lăk, and thus thou shalt speak.

6 And he returned unto him, and, lo, he stood by his burnt sacrifice, he, and all the princes of Moab.

7 And he took up his parable, and said, Bā´lăk the king of Moab hath brought me from Â´ram, out of the mountains of the east, *saying*, Come, curse me Jacob, and come, defy Israel.

8 How shall I curse, whom God hath not cursed? or how shall I defy, *whom* the LORD hath not defied?

9 For from the top of the rocks I see him, and from the hills I behold him: lo, the people shall dwell alone, and shall not be reckoned among the nations.

10 Who can count the dust of Jacob, and the number of the fourth *part* of Israel? Let me die the death of the righteous, and let my last end be like his!

11 And Bā´lăk said unto Bā´laam, What hast thou done unto me? I took thee to curse mine enemies, and, behold, thou hast blessed *them* altogether.

12 And he answered and said, Must I not take heed to speak that which the LORD hath put in my mouth?

13 And Bā´lăk said unto him, Come, I pray thee, with me unto another place, from whence thou mayest see them: thou shalt see but the utmost part of them, and shalt not see them all: and curse me them from thence.

14 ¶And he brought him into the field of Zō´phĭm, to the top of Pĭs´gah, and built seven altars, and offered a bullock and a ram on *every* altar.

15 And he said unto Bā´lăk, Stand here by thy burnt offering, while I meet *the* LORD yonder.

16 And the LORD met Bā´laam, and put a word in his mouth, and said, Go again unto Bā´lăk, and say thus.

17 And when he came to him, behold, he stood by his burnt offering, and the princes of Moab with him. And Bā´lăk said unto him, What hath the LORD spoken?

18 And he took up his parable, and said, Rise up, Bā´lăk, and hear; hearken unto me, thou son of Zippor:

19 God *is* not a man, that he should lie; neither the son of man, that he should repent: hath he said, and shall he not do *it*? or hath he spoken, and shall he not make it good?

20 Behold, I have received *commandment* to bless: and he hath blessed; and I cannot reverse it.

298

The many altar offerings employed here were doubtless a pagan Moabite practice, for their counterpart cannot be found in the Levitical law. In this first prophecy Balaam stresses the impossibility of cursing and denouncing that nation which God Himself had already promised not to curse or denounce. He then utters two predictions: one, that Israel would dwell alone and not be reckoned among the nations (vs. 9); and two, that Israel's seed shall be as the dust of the earth (vs. 10). He concludes by wishing he himself could share in Israel's blessings (vs. 10).

11-30. Balak was both amazed and angered at Balaam's words of blessing instead of cursing. He then suggested (vs. 13) that they go to another hill and try it again. This time they chose the top of Pisgah (vs. 14).

Balaam begins this prophecy with a lecture on the doctrine of God, stressing His truthfulness and immutability (vs. 19). He proceeds by concluding that demonic divination could not penetrate the divine defense which God had placed around the nation that He had brought out of Egypt.

21 He hath not beheld iniquity in Jacob, neither hath he seen perverseness in Israel: the LORD his God *is* with him, and the shout of a king *is* among them.

22 God brought them out of Egypt; he hath as it were the strength of an unicorn.

23 Surely *there is* no enchantment against Jacob, neither *is there* any divination against Israel: according to this time it shall be said of Jacob and of Israel, What hath God wrought!

24 Behold, the people shall rise up as a great lion, and lift up himself as a young lion: he shall not lie down until he eat *of* the prey, and drink the blood of the slain.

25 ¶And Bā'lăk said unto Bā'laam, Neither curse them at all, nor bless them at all.

26 But Bā'laam answered and said unto Bālăk, Told not I thee, saying, All that the LORD speaketh, that I must do?

27 ¶And Bālăk said unto Bā'laam, Come, I pray thee, I will bring thee unto another place; peradventure it will please God that thou mayest curse me them from thence.

28 And Bālăk brought Bā'laam unto the top of Pē'or, that looketh toward Jesh'ĭ-mon.

29 And Bā'laam said unto Bālăk, Build me here seven altars, and prepare me here seven bullocks and seven rams.

30 And Bālăk did as Bā'laam had said, and offered a bullock and a ram on *every* altar.

CHAPTER 24

AND when Bā'laam saw that it pleased the LORD to bless Israel, he went not, as at other times, to seek for enchantments, but he set his face toward the wilderness.

2 And Bā'laam lifted up his eyes, and he saw Israel abiding *in his tents* according to their tribes; and the spirit of God came upon him.

3 And he took up his parable, and said, Bā'laam the son of Bē'ôr hath said, and the man whose eyes are open hath said:

4 He hath said, which heard the words of God, which saw the vision of the Almighty, falling *into a trance,* but having his eyes open:

5 How goodly are thy tents, O Jacob, *and* thy tabernacles, O Israel!

6 As the valleys are they spread forth, as gardens by the river's side, as the trees of lign aloes which the LORD hath planted, *and* as cedar trees beside the waters.

7 He shall pour the water out of his buckets, and his seed *shall be* in many waters, and his king shall be higher than Ăgăg, and his kingdom shall be exalted.

8 God brought him forth out of Egypt; he hath as it were the strength of an unicorn: he shall eat up the nations his enemies, and shall break their bones, and pierce *them* through with his arrows.

9 He couched, he lay down as a lion,

24:1-3. The spirit of God came upon him. This did not necessarily mean, in Old Testament times, that the human instrument which the Holy Spirit visited or used was always a saved individual (see I Sam 16:14; Isa 44:28; 45:1).

4-6. Which heard the words of God, which saw the vision of the Almighty. Like Moses (Ex 33:18-23), Balaam now experiences the glory of God; but unlike Moses, he enjoys no rapport with the God of glory!

7-9. His king . . . and his kingdom shall be exalted. Payne writes: "Israel was to be exalted as a kingdom. It was not simply that Yahweh was their king, as in 23:21, but that they were to have a human monarch. This truth had been implied, indeed, in the forecast of Genesis 49:8-10, that the ruler over Israel would come to reside in Judah; but it is here stated for the first time that the presence of a king is explicitly stated." (J. Barton Payne, *Encyclopedia of Biblical Prophecy,* p. 203). **He shall eat up . . . his enemies** (vs. 8). He concludes this oracle by comparing Israel to a mighty ox and lion who easily tramp over their enemies. A paraphrase is then offered, taken from Genesis 12:3.

and as a great lion: who shall stir him up? Blessed *is* he that blesseth thee, and cursed *is* he that curseth thee.

10 ¶And Bā′lăk's anger was kindled against Bā′laam, and he smote his hands together: and Bālăk said unto Bā′laam, I called thee to curse mine enemies, and, behold, thou hast altogether blessed *them* these three times.

11 Therefore now flee thou to thy place: I thought to promote thee unto great honour; but, lo, the Lord hath kept thee back from honour.

12 And Bā′laam said unto Bālăk, Spake I not also to thy messengers which thou sentest unto me, saying,

13 If Bālăk would give me his house full of silver and gold, I cannot go beyond the commandment of the Lord, to do *either* good or bad of mine own mind; *but* what the Lord saith, that will I speak?

14 And now, behold, I go unto my people: come *therefore, and* I will advertise thee what this people shall do to thy people in the latter days.

15 And he took up his parable, and said, Bā′laam the son of Bĕ′ôr hath said, and the man whose eyes are open hath said:

16 He hath said, which heard the words of God, and knew the knowledge of the most High, *which* saw the vision of the Almighty, falling *into a trance*, but having his eyes open:

17 I shall see him, but not now: I shall behold him, but not nigh: there shall come a Star out of Jacob, and a Sceptre shall rise out of Israel, and shall smite the corners of Moab, and destroy all the children of Sheth.

18 And Ēdom shall be a possession, Sē′ir also shall be a possession for his enemies; and Israel shall do valiantly.

19 Out of Jacob shall come he that shall have dominion, and shall destroy him that remaineth of the city.

20 And when he looked on Ăm′a-lĕk, he took up his parable, and said, Ăm′a-lĕk *was* the first of the nations; but his latter end *shall be* that he perish for ever.

21 And he looked on the Kēn′ītes, and took up his parable, and said, Strong is thy dwellingplace, and thou puttest thy nest in a rock.

22 Nevertheless the Kēn′īte shall be wasted, until Asshur shall carry thee away captive.

23 And he took up his parable, and said, Alas, who shall live when God doeth this!

24 And ships *shall come* from the coast of Chittim, and shall afflict Asshur, and shall afflict Ē′ber, and he also shall perish for ever.

25 And Bā′laam rose up, and went and returned to his place: and Bālăk also went his way.

10-24. Balak is so angry by this time that he claps his hands in frustration and screams out accusations at the embarrassed Balaam, who can only say, "I told you so!" In his final prophecy Balaam discusses both the destruction of God's enemies and the destroyer whom God will use to accomplish this: (1) the destroyed—**Moab, Edom,** the nation of **Amalek,** and the **Kenites;** and (2) the destroyer—**There shall come a Star out of Jacob, and a Scepter shall rise out of Israel** (vs. 17). As Payne notes. "This goes beyond David's victories and finds complete fulfillment only in Jesus, the Messiah's triumph, with its ensuing world dominion, at Armageddon (Rev 16:16; 19:19-21)" (J. Barton Payne, p. 203).

25. And Balaam rose up, and went and returned to his place. This perverted prophet now disappears from the pages of the Bible. He was killed (31:8) when Israel later invaded and defeated the Midianites. In the New Testament, however, he is mentioned by no less than three authors: (1) Peter speaks of the way of Balaam (II Pet 2:15), ". . . who loved the wages of unrighteousness"; (2) Jude (vs. 11) mentions the error of Balaam; and (3) John refers to his doctrine which became a stumbling block to Israel.

b. Opposition from within. 25:1-18.

This chapter is important, for it marks the last rebellion of Israel and final judgment from God during the wilderness experience.

25:1-2. Israel abode in Shittim. This was their final camp, located on the eastern bank of the Jordan (see also Josh 2:1). **And the people began to commit whoredom.** This event demonstrates the subtlety of Satan; for what he could not curse, he would corrupt both by idolatry and immorality. It was Balaam's evil counsel (31:16) which encouraged Moab to do this. John the apostle refers to this sad episode in Revelation 2:14.

3. Baal-peor. Baal was the local heathen god worshiped at Peor. "This was the god of the Moabite mountains who took his name from Mount Peor . . . As the sun-god, Baal was worshiped under two aspects, beneficient and destructive. On the one hand he gave light and warmth to his worshiper; on the other hand the fierce heat of summer destroyed the vegetation he had himself brought into being. Hence human victims were sacrificed to him in order to appease his anger in time of plague or other trouble; the victim being usually the first-born of the sacrificer and being burnt alive" (*International Standard Bible Encyclopedia*, Vol. 1, pp. 345-346). Immorality was a regular part of Baal worship.

4-5. Take all the heads of the people. An angry God demanded the death sentence of all the Israelites who led in this sexual service! This "refers to the punishment of crucifixion, a mode of capital punishment which was adopted by most of the nations of antiquity . . . and was carried out sometimes by driving a stake into the body and so impaling them . . . or other times by fastening them to a stake or nailing them to a cross. In the instance before us, however, the idolaters were not impaled or crucified alive but . . . were first put to death and then impaled upon a stake or fastened to a cross, so that the impaling and crucifixion was only an aggravation of the capital punishment" (Keil and Delitzsch, *Pentateuch*, pp. 204-205).

6-11. And . . . Phinehas . . . took a javelin. To stay a terrible plague that had already spread everywhere, Phinehas executed an especially brazen Israelite man and his Moabite prostitute. When the final body count was in, 24,000 had died. Some have imagined a contradiction here, for in I Corinthians 10:8 Paul gives this number as 23,000. However, the problem is easily resolved if one looks upon Moses' statement (vs. 9) as the total number, while Paul relates those who died in a single day.

12-13. An everlasting priesthood. Because of his faithfulness and fearlessness, God promised Phinehas His **covenant of peace** (vs. 12), and from his family was to come Israel's High Priests. Aaron, Israel's first High Priest, had two priestly sons (two had already died through a divine punishment because of their sin), Eleazar and Ithamar. Phinehas was the son of Eleazar. But for some unknown reason, the High Priesthood was later

---

CHAPTER 25

AND Israel abode in Shĭt'tĭm, and the people began to commit whoredom with the daughters of Moab.

2 And they called the people unto the sacrifices of their gods: and the people did eat, and bowed down to their gods.

3 And Israel joined himself unto Bā'al-pē'ôr: and the anger of the LORD was kindled against Israel.

4 And the LORD said unto Moses, Take all the heads of the people, and hang them up before the LORD against the sun, that the fierce anger of the LORD may be turned away from Israel.

5 And Moses said unto the judges of Israel, Slay ye every one his men that were joined unto Bā'al-pē'ôr.

6 ¶And, behold, one of the children of Israel came and brought unto his brethren a Mĭd'ĭ-an-ĭt-ĭsh woman in the sight of Moses, and in the sight of all the congregation of the children of Israel, who *were* weeping *before* the door of the tabernacle of the congregation.

7 And when Phĭn'e-has, the son of Ē-le-ā'zar, the son of Aaron the priest, saw *it*, he rose up from among the congregation, and took a javelin in his hand;

8 And he went after the man of Israel into the tent, and thrust both of them through, the man of Israel, and the woman through her belly. So the plague was stayed from the children of Israel.

9 And those that died in the plague were twenty and four thousand.

10 ¶And the LORD spake unto Moses, saying,

11 Phĭn'e-has, the son of Ē-le-ā'zar, the son of Aaron the priest, hath turned my wrath away from the children of Israel, while he was zealous for my sake among them, that I consumed not the children of Israel in my jealousy.

12 Wherefore say, Behold, I give unto him my covenant of peace:

13 And he shall have it, and his seed after him, *even* the covenant of an everlasting priesthood; because he was zealous for his God, and made an atonement for the children of Israel.

14 Now the name of the Israelite that was slain, even that was slain with the Mĭd'ĭ-an-ĭt-ĭsh woman, was Zĭmri, the son of Sā'lū, a prince of a chief house among the Simeonites.

15 And the name of the Mĭd'ĭ-an-ĭt-ĭsh woman that was slain was Cŏz'bĭ, the daughter of Zur; he was head over a people, and of a chief house in Mĭd'ĭ-an.

16 ¶And the Lord spake unto Moses, saying,

17 Vex the Mĭd'ĭan-ītes, and smite them:

18 For they vex you with their wiles, wherewith they have beguiled you in the matter of Pē'or, and in the matter of Cŏz'bĭ, the daughter of a prince of Mĭd'ĭ-an, their sister, which was slain in the day of the plague for Pē'or's sake.

CHAPTER 26

AND it came to pass after the plague, that the Lord spake unto Moses and unto Ē-le-ā'zar the son of Aaron the priest, saying,

2 Take the sum of all the congregation of the children of Israel, from twenty years old and upward, throughout their fathers' house, all that are able to go to war in Israel.

3 And Moses and Ē-le-ā'zar the priest spake with them in the plains of Moab by Jordan near Jericho, saying,

4 Take the sum of the people, from twenty years old and upward; as the Lord commanded Moses and the children of Israel, which went forth out of the land of Egypt.

5 ¶Reuben, the eldest son of Israel: the children of Reuben; Hā'nŏch, of whom cometh the family of the Hā'noch-ītes: of Păl'lū, the family of the Păl'lū-ītes:

6 Of Hĕz'ron, the family of the Hĕz'ron-ītes: of Cär'mĭ, the family of the Cär'mītes.

7 These are the families of the Reubenites: and they that were numbered of them were forty and three thousand and seven hundred and thirty.

8 And the sons of Păl'lū; E-lī'ab.

9 And the sons of E-lī'ab; Nĕ-mū'el, and Dā'than, and A-bī'ram. This is that Dā'than and A-bī'ram, which were famous in the congregation, who strove against Moses and against Aaron in the company of Kôrah, when they strove against the Lord:

10 And the earth opened her mouth, and swallowed them up together with Kôrah, when that company died, what time the fire devoured two hundred and fifty men: and they became a sign.

11 Notwithstanding the children of Kôrah died not.

12 ¶The sons of Simeon after their families: of Nĕ-mū'el, the family of the Nĕ-mū'el-ītes: of Jā'mĭn, the family of the Jā'min-ītes: of Jā'chin, the family of the Jā'chin-ītes:

13 Of Ze'rah, the family of the Zär'hītes: of Shā'ul, the family of the Shā'ul-ītes.

switched from Eleazar to Ithamar in the person of Eli (I Sam 1:1-9), a descendant of Ithamar. However, in the days of David it returned to the line promised here through Zadok, a descendant of Eleazar (see I Kgs 1:8).

14-18. Vex the Midianites, and smite them. Both the Moabites and Midianites were involved in Israel's sin.

2. Preparation. 26:1-30:16.

a. Numbering the tribes. 26:1-27:11.

26:1-57. This second census was taken for various reasons. The previous one taken in Numbers 1 was primarily for organizational purposes for the anticipated wilderness journey. But now, forty years had transpired, bringing with it a new generation. Furthermore, the immediate goal was the division of the land they were about to conquer. So, a new census was in order. The total number of adult males shows a net loss of 1,820 from the previous census. During the wandering years some 1,200,000 people had died!

Even though the actual division of the land was done by the casting of lots (vs. 55; Josh 14:2), the numerical size of each tribe was taken into consideration, thus strongly suggesting the hand of God was in the casting itself (cf. Prov 16:33).

14 These *are* the families of the Simeonites, twenty and two thousand and two hundred.

15 ¶The children of Gad after their families: of Zĕ'phŏn, the family of the Zĕ'phon-ītes: of Hăg'gĭ, the family of the Hăg'gītes: of Shū'nī, the family of the Shū'nītes:

16 Of Ŏz'nī, the family of the Ŏz'-nītes: of E'rī, the family of the E'rītes:

17 Of Ä'rŏd, the family of the Ä'ro-dītes: of A-rē'lī, the family of the A-rē'-lītes.

18 These *are* the families of the children of Gad according to those that were numbered of them, forty thousand and five hundred.

19 ¶The sons of Jūdah *were* Er and Ō'nan: and Er and Ō'nan died in the land of Canaan.

20 And the sons of Jūdah after their families were: of Shē'lah, the family of the Shē'lan-ītes: of Phā'rĕz, the family of the Phär'zītes: of Ze'rah, the family of the Zär'hītes.

21 And the sons of Phā'rĕz were: of Hĕz'ron, the family of the Hez'ron-ītes: of Hā'mul, the family of the Hā'mu-lītes.

22 These *are* the families of Jūdah according to those that were numbered of them, threescore and sixteen thousand and five hundred.

23 ¶*Of* the sons of Ĭs'sa-char after their families: of Tō'la, the family of the Tō'la-ītes: of Pū'a, the family of the Pū'nītes:

24 Of Jāsh'ub, the family of the Jāsh'ub-ītes: of Shĭm'rŏn, the family of the Shĭm'ron-ītes.

25 These *are* the families of Ĭs'sa-char according to those that were numbered of them, threescore and four thousand and three hundred.

26 ¶*Of* the sons of Zĕb'u-lun after their families: of Se'rĕd, the family of the Sär'dītes: of E'lŏn, the family of the E'lon-ītes: of Jäh'le-el, the family of the Jäh'le-el-ītes.

27 These *are* the families of the Zĕb'u-lun-ītes according to those that were numbered of them, threescore thousand and five hundred.

28 ¶The sons of Joseph after their families *were* Ma-năs'seh and E'phra-im.

29 Of the sons of Ma-năs'seh: of Mä'chĭr, the family of the Mä'chir-ītes: and Mä'chĭr begat Gilead: of Gilead *come* the family of the Gīleadītes.

30 These *are* the sons of Gilead: *of* Je-ē'zer, the family of the Je-ē'zer-ītes: of Hē'lĕk, the family of the Hē'lek-ītes:

31 And *of* Ăs'rĭ-el, the family of the Ăs'rĭ-el-ītes: and *of* Shē'chem, the family of the Shē'chem-ītes:

32 And *of* She-mī'da, the family of the She-mī'da-ītes: and *of* Hē'pher, the family of the Hē'pher-ītes.

33 And Ze-lō'phe-hăd the son of Hē'pher had no sons, but daughters: and the names of the daughters of Ze-lō'phe-hăd *were* Mäh'lah, and Noah, Hŏg'lah, Mĭl'cah, and Tir'zah.

34 These *are* the families of Ma-năs'-seh, and those that were numbered of them, fifty and two thousand and seven hundred.

35 ¶These *are* the sons of E'phra-im

303

after their families: of Shū´the-lah, the family of the Shū´thal-hītes: of Bē´cher, the family of the Băch´rītes: of Tā´hăn, the family of the Tā´han-ītes.

36 And these *are* the sons of Shū´the-lah: of Ē´răn, the family of the Ē´răn-ītes.

37 These *are* the families of the sons of Ē´phra-im according to those that were numbered of them, thirty and two thousand and five hundred. These *are* the sons of Joseph after their families.

38 ¶The sons of Benjamin after their families: of Bē´la, the family of the Bē´la-ītes: of Ăsh´bĕl, the family of the Ăsh´bel-ītes; of A-hī´ram, the family of the A-hī´ram-ītes:

39 Of Shū´pham, the family of the Shū´pham-ītes: of Hū´pham, the family of the Hū´pham-ītes.

40 And the sons of Bē´la were Ard and Nā´a-man: *of* Ard, the family of the Ărd´ītes: *and* of Nā´a-man, the family of the Nā´a-mītes.

41 These *are* the sons of Benjamin after their families: and they that were numbered of them *were* forty and five thousand and six hundred.

42 ¶These *are* the sons of Dan after their families: of Shū´hăm, the family of the Shū´ham-ītes. These *are* the families of Dan after their families.

43 All the families of the Shū´ham-ītes, according to those that were numbered of them, *were* threescore and four thousand and four hundred.

44 ¶*Of* the children of Asher after their families: of Jĭm´na, the family of the Jĭm´nītes: of Jĕs´ū-ī, the family of the Jĕs´ū-ītes: of Be-rī´ah, the family of the Be-rī´ītes.

45 Of the sons of Be-rī´ah: of Hē´ber, the family of the Hē´ber-ītes: of Măl´chī-el, the family of the Măl´chī-el-ītes.

46 And the name of the daughter of Asher *was* Sarah.

47 These *are* the families of the sons of Asher according to those that were numbered of them; *who were* fifty and three thousand and four hundred.

48 ¶*Of* the sons of Năph´ta-lī after their families: of Jăh´ze-el, the family of the Jăh´ze-el-ītes: of Gū´nī, the family of the Gū´nītes:

49 Of Jē´zer, the family of the Jē´zer-ītes: of Shĭl´lem, the family of the Shĭl´-lem-ītes.

50 These *are* the families of Năph´ta-lī according to their families: and they that were numbered of them *were* forty and five thousand and four hundred.

51 These *were* the numbered of the children of Israel, six hundred thousand and a thousand seven hundred and thirty.

52 ¶And the Lord spake unto Moses, saying,

53 Unto these the land shall be divided for an inheritance according to the number of names.

54 To many thou shalt give the more inheritance, and to few thou shalt give the less inheritance: to every one shall his inheritance be given according to those that were numbered of him.

55 Notwithstanding the land shall be divided by lot: according to the names

of the tribes of their fathers they shall inherit.

56 According to the lot shall the possession thereof be divided between many and few.

57 ¶And these *are* they that were numbered of the Levites after their families: of Ger'shon, the family of the Ger'shon-ītes: of Kō'hăth, the family of the Kō'hăth-ītes: of Me-râ'rī, the family of the Me-râ'rītes.

58 These *are* the families of the Levites: the family of the Lĭb'nītes, the family of the Hē'bro-nītes, the family of the Măh'lītes, the family of the Mū'-shītes, the family of the Kō'rath-ītes. And Kō'hăth begat Ămrăm.

59 And the name of Ămrăm's wife *was* Jōch'e-bĕd, the daughter of Levi, whom *her mother* bare to Levi in Egypt: and she bare unto Ămrăm Aaron and Moses, and Miriam their sister.

60 And unto Aaron was born Nădăb, and A-bī'hū, Ĕ-le-ā'zar, and Ĭth'a-mär.

61 And Nădăb and A-bī'hū died, when they offered strange fire before the LORD.

62 And those that were numbered of them were twenty and three thousand, all males from a month old and upward: for they were not numbered among the children of Israel, because there was no inheritance given them among the children of Israel.

63 ¶These *are* they that were numbered by Moses and Ĕ-le-ā'zar the priest, who numbered the children of Israel in the plains of Moab by Jordan *near* Jericho.

64 But among these there was not a man of them whom Moses and Aaron the priest numbered, when they numbered the children of Israel in the wilderness of Sī'naī.

65 For the LORD had said of them, They shall surely die in the wilderness. And there was not left a man of them, save Caleb the son of Je-phŭn'neh, and Joshua the son of Nun.

CHAPTER 27

THEN came the daughters of Ze-lō'phe-hăd, the son of Hē'pher, the son of Gilead, the son of Mā'chīr, the son of Ma-năs'seh, of the families of Ma-năs'-seh the son of Joseph: and these *are* the names of his daughters: Măh'lah, Noah, and Hŏg'lah, and Mĭl'cah, and Tir'zah.

2 And they stood before Moses, and before Ĕ-le-ā'zar the priest, and before the princes and all the congregation, *by* the door of the tabernacle of the congregation, saying,

3 Our father died in the wilderness, and he was not in the company of them that gathered themselves together against the LORD in the company of Kō-rah; but died in his own sin, and had no sons.

4 Why should the name of our father be done away from among his family, because he hath no son? Give unto us *therefore* a possession among the brethren of our father.

5 And Moses brought their cause before the LORD.

58-65. A comparison of 3:39 and verse 62 shows a one-thousand-man increase of the Levites between the first and second census. A sad note of reminder, however, is attached to this second census (see vss. 64-65).

27:1-11. The legal question described here vividly demonstrates God's impartiality and concern for womanhood. Unlike the pagan religions, which viewed females as mere slaves and sex objects, God looks upon both men and women as ". . . heirs together of the grace of life . . ." (I Pet 3:7). The legal problem was posed by five daughters of a man who had died in the wilderness without any sons. Would these girls receive any land in Canaan? The answer from God was a resounding yes, resulting in a new law of inheritance whereby property could be transferred to daughters as well as sons.

6 ¶And the LORD spake unto Moses, saying,

7 The daughters of Ze-lō′phe-hăd speak right: thou shalt surely give them a possession of an inheritance among their father's brethren; and thou shalt cause the inheritance of their father to pass unto them.

8 And thou shalt speak unto the children of Israel, saying, If a man die, and have no son, then ye shall cause his inheritance to pass unto his daughter.

9 And if he have no daughter, then ye shall give his inheritance unto his brethren.

10 And if he have no brethren, then ye shall give his inheritance unto his father's brethren.

11 And if his father have no brethren, then ye shall give his inheritance unto his kinsman that is next to him of his family, and he shall possess it: and it shall be unto the children of Israel a statute of judgment, as the LORD commanded Moses.

12 ¶And the LORD said unto Moses, Get thee up into this mount Ăb′a-rĭm, and see the land which I have given unto the children of Israel.

13 And when thou hast seen it, thou also shalt be gathered unto thy people, as Aaron thy brother was gathered.

14 For ye rebelled against my commandment in the desert of Zin, in the strife of the congregation, to sanctify me at the water before their eyes: that is the water of Mĕr′i-bah in Kā′desh in the wilderness of Zin.

15 ¶And Moses spake unto the LORD, saying,

16 Let the LORD, the God of the spirits of all flesh, set a man over the congregation,

17 Which may go out before them, and which may go in before them, and which may lead them out, and which may bring them in; that the congregation of the LORD be not as sheep which have no shepherd.

18 ¶And the LORD said unto Moses, Take thee Joshua the son of Nun, a man in whom is the spirit, and lay thine hand upon him;

19 And set him before Ĕ-le-ā′zar the priest, and before all the congregation; and give him a charge in their sight.

20 And thou shalt put some of thine honour upon him, that all the congregation of the children of Israel may be obedient.

21 And he shall stand before Ĕ-le-ā′zar the priest, who shall ask counsel for him after the judgment of Û′rĭm before the LORD: at his word shall they go out, and at his word they shall come in, both he, and all the children of Israel with him, even all the congregation.

22 And Moses did as the LORD commanded him: and he took Joshua, and set him before Ĕ-le-ā′zar the priest, and before all the congregation:

23 And he laid his hands upon him, and gave him a charge, as the LORD commanded by the hand of Moses.

b. A change in commanders. 27:12-23.

12. Get thee up into . . . Mount Abarim. God brings Moses here. **Abarim** was one of the peaks of Mount Nebo, some ten or fifteen miles east of the northern end of the Dead Sea for two purposes: (1) to allow him to view the Promised Land (vs. 12); and (2) to prepare for his successor (vss. 18-21).

13-17. Thou . . . shalt be gathered unto thy people. The old prophet was approaching one hundred twenty years of age, and the time of his departure was at hand. Because of his past sin at Meribah, he would not enter Palestine (vs. 14).

And Moses spake unto the LORD . . . lead them out, and . . . bring them in. This shows that God's plan included the Exodus but was not completed until the conquest of Canaan. These next verses (16-17), perhaps more than any others, reflect the true heart of this grand old lawgiver. Here he asks God to choose a successor, that the **congregation of the LORD be not as sheep which have no shepherd** (vs. 17). Some fourteen centuries later that Great Promised Prophet (Deut 18:15) would display a similar heart concern for mankind (see Mt 9:36).

18-20. Take thee Joshua. No better choice could have been made. He had begun his adult life as a military commander (Ex 17:8-14) and would end it as the wisest of counselors (Josh 23-24). **And set him before . . . all the congregation.** This would eliminate any rumors about a power struggle between Moses and Joshua.

21-23. Eleazar . . . shall ask counsel for him after the judgment of Urim. By this the harmony of both political and religious aspects of Israel's national life would be assured. The Urim is thought to be one of two precious stones (Thummin was the other) placed in the pouch of the breastplate of the high priest (Ex 28:30) to be used (by ways unknown to us today) in determining God's will (see also Lev 8:8; Deut 33:8; I Sam 28:6; Ezr 2:63; Neh 7:65).

CHAPTER 28

AND the LORD spake unto Moses, saying,

2 Command the children of Israel, and say unto them, My offering, *and* my bread for my sacrifices made by fire, *for* a sweet savour unto me, shall ye observe to offer unto me in their due season.

3 And thou shalt say unto them, This *is* the offering made by fire which ye shall offer unto the LORD; two lambs of the first year without spot day by day, *for* a continual burnt offering.

4 The one lamb shalt thou offer in the morning, and the other lamb shalt thou offer at even;

5 And a tenth *part* of an ephah of flour for a meat offering, mingled with the fourth *part* of an hin of beaten oil.

6 *It is* a continual burnt offering, which was ordained in mount Si′naï for a sweet savour, a sacrifice made by fire unto the LORD.

7 And the drink offering thereof *shall be* the fourth *part* of an hin for the one lamb: in the holy *place* shalt thou cause the strong wine to be poured unto the LORD *for* a drink offering.

8 And the other lamb shalt thou offer at even: as the meat offering of the morning, and as the drink offering thereof, thou shalt offer *it*, a sacrifice made by fire, of a sweet savour unto the LORD.

9 ¶And on the sabbath day two lambs of the first year without spot, and two tenth deals of flour *for* a meat offering, mingled with oil, and the drink offering thereof:

10 *This is* the burnt offering of every sabbath, beside the continual burnt offering, and his drink offering.

11 ¶And in the beginnings of your months ye shall offer a burnt offering unto the LORD; two young bullocks, and one ram, seven lambs of the first year without spot;

12 And three tenth deals of flour *for* a meat offering, mingled with oil, for one bullock; and two tenth deals of flour *for* a meat offering, mingled with oil, for one ram;

13 And a several tenth deal of flour mingled with oil *for* a meat offering unto one lamb; *for* a burnt offering of a sweet savour, a sacrifice made by fire unto the LORD.

14 And their drink offerings shall be half an hin of wine unto a bullock, and the third *part* of an hin unto a ram, and a fourth *part* of an hin unto a lamb: this *is* the burnt offering of every month throughout the months of the year.

15 And one kid of the goats for a sin offering unto the LORD shall be offered, beside the continual burnt offering, and his drink offering.

16 ¶And in the fourteenth day of the first month *is* the passover of the LORD.

17 And in the fifteenth day of this month *is* the feast: seven days shall unleavened bread be eaten.

18 In the first day *shall be* an holy convocation; ye shall do no manner of servile work *therein:*

19 But ye shall offer a sacrifice made

28:1–29:40. This chapter is, in a sense, an amplification of Leviticus 23, but it is also unique in that it gives for each festival a specific date and definite quantity for each sacrifice on that date. The only other Old Testament list of specific amounts for special days and festivals is found in Ezekiel 45:18–46:15. This passage has reference to the millennial temple. Note the offerings: (1) Daily Offerings—Each day. **Two lambs . . . day by day** (vss. 3-8); (2) Sabbath Offerings—Each seventh day. **And on the sabbath day two lambs** (vss. 9-10); (3) New Moon Offerings—First day of month. **Two young bullocks, and one ram, seven lambs . . . and one kid of the goats** (vss. 11-15); (4) **Passover—Fourteenth day of the first month.** No animal sacrifice listed here (vs. 16); (5) **Unleavened Bread—Fifteenth day** until the twenty-first day of the first month. **Two young bullocks, and one ram, and seven lambs . . . and one goat** (vss. 17-25); (6) Feast of Weeks—No date given. **Two young bullocks, one ram, seven lambs . . . and one kid of the goats** (vss. 26-31); (7) Feast of Trumpets—**And in the seventh month, on the first day** (29:1-6); (8) Day of Atonement—**On the tenth day of this seventh month.** Same offerings as Feast of Trumpets (vss. 7-11); (9) Feast of Booths—**Fifteenth** to twenty-second days of the **seventh month** (vss. 12-38). Total of one hundred and five lambs, fifteen rams, seventy-one bulls, and eight goats.

c. Offerings and vows. 28:1-30:16.

by fire *for* a burnt offering unto the LORD; two young bullocks, and one ram, and seven lambs of the first year: they shall be unto you without blemish.

20 And their meat offering *shall be of* flour mingled with oil: three tenth deals shall ye offer for a bullock, and two tenth deals for a ram;

21 A several tenth deal shalt thou offer for every lamb, throughout the seven lambs:

22 And one goat *for* a sin offering, to make an atonement for you.

23 Ye shall offer these beside the burnt offering in the morning, which *is* for a continual burnt offering.

24 After this manner ye shall offer daily, throughout the seven days, the meat of the sacrifice made by fire, of a sweet savour unto the LORD: it shall be offered beside the continual burnt offering, and his drink offering.

25 And on the seventh day ye shall have an holy convocation; ye shall do no servile work.

26 ¶Also in the day of the firstfruits, when ye bring a new meat offering unto the LORD, after your weeks *be out,* ye shall have an holy convocation; ye shall do no servile work:

27 But ye shall offer the burnt offering for a sweet savour unto the LORD; two young bullocks, one ram, seven lambs of the first year;

28 And their meat offering of flour mingled with oil, three tenth deals unto one bullock, two tenth deals unto one ram,

29 A several tenth deal unto one lamb, throughout the seven lambs;

30 *And* one kid of the goats, to make an atonement for you.

31 Ye shall offer *them* beside the continual burnt offering, and his meat offering, (they shall be unto you without blemish) and their drink offerings.

CHAPTER 29

AND in the seventh month, on the first *day* of the month, ye shall have an holy convocation; ye shall do no servile work: it is a day of blowing the trumpets unto you.

2 And ye shall offer a burnt offering for a sweet savour unto the LORD; one young bullock, one ram, *and* seven lambs of the first year without blemish:

3 And their meat offering *shall be of* flour mingled with oil, three tenth deals for a bullock, *and* two tenth deals for a ram,

4 And one tenth deal for one lamb, throughout the seven lambs:

5 And one kid of the goats *for* a sin offering, to make an atonement for you:

6 Beside the burnt offering of the month, and his meat offering, and the daily burnt offering, and his meat offering, and their drink offerings, according unto their manner, for a sweet savour, a sacrifice made by fire unto the LORD.

7 ¶And ye shall have on the tenth *day* of this seventh month an holy convocation; and ye shall afflict your souls: ye shall not do any work *therein:*

8 But ye shall offer a burnt offering

unto the LORD *for* a sweet savour; one young bullock, one ram, *and* seven lambs of the first year; they shall be unto you without blemish:

9 And their meat offering *shall be of* flour mingled with oil, three tenth deals to a bullock, *and* two tenth deals to one ram,

10 A several tenth deal for one lamb, throughout the seven lambs:

11 One kid of the goats *for* a sin offering; beside the sin offering of atonement, and the continual burnt offering, and the meat offering of it, and their drink offerings.

12 ¶And on the fifteenth day of the seventh month ye shall have an holy convocation; ye shall do no servile work, and ye shall keep a feast unto the LORD seven days:

13 And ye shall offer a burnt offering, a sacrifice made by fire, of a sweet savour unto the LORD; thirteen young bullocks, two rams, *and* fourteen lambs of the first year; they shall be without blemish:

14 And their meat offering *shall be of* flour mingled with oil, three tenth deals unto every bullock of the thirteen bullocks, two tenth deals to each ram of the two rams,

15 And a several tenth deal to each lamb of the fourteen lambs:

16 And one kid of the goats *for* a sin offering; beside the continual burnt offering, his meat offering, and his drink offering.

17 ¶And on the second day *ye shall offer* twelve young bullocks, two rams, fourteen lambs of the first year without spot:

18 And their meat offering and their drink offerings for the bullocks, for the rams, and for the lambs, *shall be* according to their number, after the manner:

19 And one kid of the goats *for* a sin offering; beside the continual burnt offering, and the meat offering thereof, and their drink offerings.

20 ¶And on the third day eleven bullocks, two rams, fourteen lambs of the first year without blemish;

21 And their meat offering and their drink offerings for the bullocks, for the rams, and for the lambs, *shall be* according to their number, after the manner:

22 And one goat *for* a sin offering; beside the continual burnt offering, and his meat offering, and his drink offering.

23 ¶And on the fourth day ten bullocks, two rams, *and* fourteen lambs of the first year without blemish:

24 Their meat offering and their drink offerings for the bullocks, for the rams, and for the lambs, *shall be* according to their number, after the manner:

25 And one kid of the goats *for* a sin offering; beside the continual burnt offering, his meat offering, and his drink offering.

26 ¶And on the fifth day nine bullocks, two rams, *and* fourteen lambs of the first year without spot:

27 And their meat offering and their drink offerings for the bullocks, for the rams, and for the lambs, *shall be* according to their number, after the manner:

28 And one goat for a sin offering; beside the continual burnt offering, and his meat offering, and his drink offering.

29 ¶And on the sixth day eight bullocks, two rams, and fourteen lambs of the first year without blemish:

30 And their meat offering and their drink offerings for the bullocks, for the rams, and for the lambs, shall be according to their number, after the manner:

31 And one goat for a sin offering; beside the continual burnt offering, his meat offering, and his drink offering.

32 ¶And on the seventh day seven bullocks, two rams, and fourteen lambs of the first year without blemish:

33 And their meat offering and their drink offerings for the bullocks, for the rams, and for the lambs, shall be according to their number, after the manner:

34 And one goat for a sin offering; beside the continual burnt offering, his meat offering, and his drink offering.

35 ¶On the eighth day ye shall have a solemn assembly: ye shall do no servile work therein:

36 But ye shall offer a burnt offering, a sacrifice made by fire, of a sweet savour unto the LORD: one bullock, one ram, seven lambs of the first year without blemish:

37 Their meat offering and their drink offerings for the bullock, for the ram, and for the lambs, shall be according to their number, after the manner:

38 And one goat for a sin offering; beside the continual burnt offering, and his meat offering, and his drink offering.

39 These things ye shall do unto the LORD in your set feasts, beside your vows, and your freewill offerings, for your burnt offerings, and for your meat offerings, and for your drink offerings, and for your peace offerings.

40 And Moses told the children of Israel according to all that the LORD commanded Moses.

CHAPTER 30

AND Moses spake unto the heads of the tribes concerning the children of Israel, saying, This is the thing which the LORD hath commanded.

2 If a man vow a vow unto the LORD, or swear an oath to bind his soul with a bond; he shall not break his word, he shall do according to all that proceedeth out of his mouth.

3 If a woman also vow a vow unto the LORD, and bind herself by a bond, being in her father's house in her youth;

4 And her father hear her vow, and her bond wherewith she hath bound her soul, and her father shall hold his peace at her: then all her vows shall stand, and every bond wherewith she hath bound her soul shall stand.

5 But if her father disallow her in the day that he heareth; not any of her vows, or of her bonds wherewith she hath bound her soul, shall stand: and the LORD shall forgive her, because her father disallowed her.

6 And if she had at all an husband, when she vowed, or uttered ought out

30:1-16. This is the only Old Testament passage dealing with the subject of women's vows in particular. They are referred to in general along with men's vows in Leviticus 27, but not in the detailed sense we read here. Only verse 2 in this chapter deals with the subject of vows of men, and this is only for the purpose of contrast. The contrast is that any and all vows made by a man were unconditional, and he was fully responsible for them; but vows made by a woman were often conditional in nature. There were at least two types of vows which could be invalidated, but only immediately after they were discovered. Those were: (1) the vow of an unmarried daughter living in her father's house which could be invalidated by her father (vss. 3-5); and (2) the vow of a married woman could be invalidated by her husband (vss. 6-8). A widow or a divorced woman, however, was responsible for her own vows (vs. 9).

of her lips, wherewith she bound her soul;

7 And her husband heard *it,* and held his peace at her in the day that he heard *it:* then her vows shall stand, and her bonds wherewith she bound her soul shall stand.

8 But if her husband disallowed her on the day that he heard *it;* then he shall make her vow which she vowed, and that which she uttered with her lips, wherewith she bound her soul, of none effect: and the LORD shall forgive her.

9 But every vow of a widow, and of her that is divorced, wherewith they have bound their souls, shall stand against her.

10 And if she vowed in her husband's house, or bound her soul by a bond with an oath;

11 And her husband heard *it,* and held his peace at her, *and* disallowed her not: then all her vows shall stand, and every bond wherewith she bound her soul shall stand.

12 But if her husband hath utterly made them void on the day he heard *them; then* whatsoever proceeded out of her lips concerning her vows, or concerning the bond of her soul, shall not stand: her husband hath made them void; and the LORD shall forgive her.

13 Every vow, and every binding oath to afflict the soul, her husband may establish it, or her husband may make it void.

14 But if her husband altogether hold his peace at her from day to day; then he establisheth all her vows, or all her bonds, which *are* upon her: he confirmeth them, because he held his peace at her in the day that he heard *them.*

15 But if he shall any ways make them void after that he hath heard *them;* then he shall bear her iniquity.

16 These *are* the statutes, which the LORD commanded Moses, between a man and his wife, between the father and his daughter, *being yet* in her youth in her father's house.

CHAPTER 31

AND the LORD spake unto Moses, saying,

2 Avenge the children of Israel of the Mĭd′ĭ-an-ītes: afterward shalt thou be gathered unto thy people.

3 And Moses spake unto the people, saying, Arm some of yourselves unto the war, and let them go against the Mĭd′ĭ-an-ītes, and avenge the LORD of Mĭd′ĭ-an.

4 Of every tribe a thousand, throughout all the tribes of Israel, shall ye send to the war.

5 So there were delivered out of the thousands of Israel, a thousand of *every* tribe, twelve thousand armed for war.

6 And Moses sent them to the war, a thousand of *every* tribe, them and Phĭn′e-has the son of Ē-le-ā′zar the priest, to the war, with the holy instruments, and the trumpets to blow in his hand.

7 And they warred against the Mĭd′-

3. Transjordan. 31:1-32:42.

a. The destruction of Midian. 31:1-54.

31:1-5. The Midianites were descendants of Abraham through his wife Keturah (Gen 25:2). Some forty years earlier, Moses (a descendant of Abraham through Sarah) had married a Midianite, Zipporah. But in the ensuing years, this tribe had degenerated until they were no different from a dozen other pagan desert people.

6. And Moses sent them to the war, a thousand of every tribe. A great contrast can be seen here as one compares the account here with that described in the Tribulation. In this chapter in the book of Numbers God sends out 12,000 Israelite soldiers to consume their enemies, but in Revelation 7 He will send out 144,000 Israelite preachers to convert their enemies!

7-9. And they slew all the males. This statement is probably

ĭ-an-ītes, as the LORD commanded Moses; and they slew all the males.

8 And they slew the kings of Mĭd'ĭ-an, beside the rest of them that were slain; namely, Ē'vī, and Rē'kem, and Zur, and Hur, and Rē'ba, five kings of Mĭd'ĭ-an: Bā'laam also the son of Bē'ôr they slew with the sword.

9 And the children of Israel took all the women of Mĭd'ĭ-an captives, and their little ones, and took the spoil of all their cattle, and all their flocks, and all their goods.

10 And they burnt all their cities wherein they dwelt, and all their goodly castles, with fire.

11 And they took all the spoil, and all the prey, both of men and of beasts.

12 And they brought the captives, and the prey, and the spoil, unto Moses, and Ĕ-le-ā'zar the priest, and unto the congregation of the children of Israel, unto the camp at the plains of Moab, which are by Jordan near Jericho.

13 ¶And Moses, and Ĕ-le-ā'zar the priest, and all the princes of the congregation, went forth to meet them without the camp.

14 And Moses was wroth with the officers of the host, with the captains over thousands, and captains over hundreds, which came from the battle.

15 And Moses said unto them, Have ye saved all the women alive?

16 Behold, these caused the children of Israel, through the counsel of Bā'laam, to commit trespass against the LORD in the matter of Pē'or, and there was a plague among the congregation of the LORD.

17 Now therefore kill every male among the little ones, and kill every woman that hath known man by lying with him.

18 But all the women children, that have not known a man by lying with him, keep alive for yourselves.

19 And do ye abide without the camp seven days: whosoever hath killed any person, and whosoever hath touched any slain, purify both yourselves and your captives on the third day, and on the seventh day.

20 And purify all your raiment, and all that is made of skins, and all work of goats' hair, and all things made of wood.

21 ¶And Ĕ-le-ā'zar the priest said unto the men of war which went to the battle, This is the ordinance of the law which the LORD commanded Moses;

22 Only the gold, and the silver, the brass, the iron, the tin, and the lead,

23 Every thing that may abide the fire, ye shall make it go through the fire, and it shall be clean: nevertheless it shall be purified with the water of separation: and all that abideth not the fire ye shall make go through the water.

24 And ye shall wash your clothes on the seventh day, and ye shall be clean, and afterward ye shall come into the camp.

25 ¶And the LORD spake unto Moses, saying,

26 Take the sum of the prey that was taken, both of man and of beast, thou,

to be interpreted as all the males living in the battleground area and not the entire Midianite race, for in Gideon's time they are seen back in full force again (see Jud 6:2). **Balaam also . . . they slew with the sword.** It is evident that this materialistic and immoral prophet died unrepentant without seeing his half-hearted prayer answered: **Who can count the dust of Jacob, and the number of the fourth part of Israel? Let me die the death of the righteous and let my last end be like his!** (23:10).

10-18. And they burnt all their cities. The command of God to burn and kill here has bothered many throughout history. But several factors must be kept in mind. First, the order came from the righteous Judge of the earth Himself. He was fully aware of all the circumstances and consequences involved at the time of the command. Second, Israel was fighting for its very survival, and often that meant to kill or be killed. Third, the moral habits of some of these desert people were almost unimaginable in their degeneration.

19-24. After the battle there was need for a twofold purification. First was needed the purification of those Israelite soldiers who had defiled themselves by touching a dead body in battle. Second, the captured enemies' riches were to be cleansed either by fire or water.

25-54. The confiscated wealth from this battle was truly amazing. It included over eight hundred thousand animals and well over one million dollars in gold (approximately six thousand seven hundred ounces, or 16,750 shekels; see vs. 52). But the

and Ĕ-le-ā′zar the priest, and the chief fathers of the congregation:

27 And divide the prey into two parts; between them that took the war upon them, who went out to battle, and between all the congregation:

28 And levy a tribute unto the LORD of the men of war which went out to battle: one soul of five hundred, *both* of the persons, and of the beeves, and of the asses, and of the sheep:

29 Take *it* of their half, and give *it* unto Ĕ-le-ā′zar the priest, *for* an heave offering of the LORD.

30 And of the children of Israel's half, thou shalt take one portion of fifty, of the persons, of the beeves, of the asses, and of the flocks, of all manner of beasts, and give them unto the Lē′vītes, which keep the charge of the tabernacle of the LORD.

31 And Moses and Ĕ-le-ā′zar the priest did as the LORD commanded Moses.

32 And the booty, *being* the rest of the prey which the men of war had caught, was six hundred thousand and seventy thousand and five thousand sheep,

33 And threescore and twelve thousand beeves,

34 And threescore and one thousand asses,

35 And thirty and two thousand persons in all, of women that had not known man by lying with him.

36 And the half, *which was* the portion of them that went out to war, was in number three hundred thousand and seven and thirty thousand and five hundred sheep:

37 And the LORD's tribute of the sheep was six hundred and threescore and fifteen.

38 And the beeves *were* thirty and six thousand; of which the LORD's tribute *was* threescore and twelve.

39 And the asses *were* thirty thousand and five hundred; of which the LORD's tribute *was* threescore and one.

40 And the persons *were* sixteen thousand; of which the LORD's tribute *was* thirty and two persons.

41 And Moses gave the tribute, *which was* the LORD's heave offering, unto Ĕ-le-ā′zar the priest, as the LORD commanded Moses.

42 And of the children of Israel's half, which Moses divided from the men that warred,

43 (Now the half *that pertained unto* the congregation was three hundred thousand and thirty thousand *and* seven thousand and five hundred sheep,

44 And thirty and six thousand beeves,

45 And thirty thousand asses and five hundred,

46 And sixteen thousand persons;)

47 Even of the children of Israel's half, Moses took one portion of fifty, *both* of man and of beast, and gave them unto the Lē′vītes, which kept the charge of the tabernacle of the LORD; as the LORD commanded Moses.

48 ¶And the officers which *were* over thousands of the host, the captains of

soldiers were not to keep for themselves all the booty they had taken, but were to share it equally with those who did not go out to fight (see vss. 26-27). Some four centuries later, David would establish this as a permanent rule of war (see I Sam 30:24-25).

thousands, and captains of hundreds, came near unto Moses:

49 And they said unto Moses, Thy servants have taken the sum of the men of war which *are* under our charge, and there lacketh not one man of us.

50 We have therefore brought an oblation for the Lord, what every man hath gotten, of jewels of gold, chains, and bracelets, rings, earrings, and tablets, to make an atonement for our souls before the Lord.

51 And Moses and Ĕ-le-ā′zar the priest took the gold of them, *even* all wrought jewels.

52 And all the gold of the offering that they offered up to the Lord, of the captains of thousands, and of the captains of hundreds, was sixteen thousand seven hundred and fifty shekels.

53 (*For* the men of war had taken spoil, every man for himself.)

54 And Moses and Ĕ-le-ā′zar the priest took the gold of the captains of thousands and of hundreds, and brought it into the tabernacle of the congregation, *for* a memorial for the children of Israel before the Lord.

CHAPTER 32

NOW the children of Reuben and the children of Gad had a very great multitude of cattle: and when they saw the land of Jā′zer, and the land of Gilead, that, behold, the place *was* a place for cattle;

2 The children of Gad and the children of Reuben came and spake unto Moses, and to Ĕ-le-ā′zar the priest, and unto the princes of the congregation, saying,

3 Ăt′a-rŏth, and Dī′bŏn, and Jā′zer, and Nĭm′rah, and Hĕsh′bŏn, and Ĕ-le-ā′leh, and Shĕ′băm, and Nebo, and Bē′ŏn,

4 *Even* the country which the Lord smote before the congregation of Israel, *is* a land for cattle, and thy servants have cattle:

5 Wherefore, said they, if we have found grace in thy sight, let this land be given unto thy servants for a possession, *and* bring us not over Jordan.

6 ¶And Moses said unto the children of Gad and to the children of Reuben, Shall your brethren go to war, and shall ye sit here?

7 And wherefore discourage ye the heart of the children of Israel from going over into the land which the Lord hath given them?

8 Thus did your fathers, when I sent them from Kā′desh-bär′ne-a to see the land.

9 For when they went up unto the valley of Ĕsh′cōl, and saw the land, they discouraged the heart of the children of Israel, that they should not go into the land which the Lord had given them.

10 And the Lord's anger was kindled the same time, and he sware, saying,

11 Surely none of the men that came up out of Egypt, from twenty years old and upward, shall see the land which I sware unto Abraham, unto Isaac, and unto Jacob; because they have not wholly followed me:

12 Save Caleb the son of Je-phŭn′neh

b. Some worldly warriors. 32:1-42.

32:1-5. Up to this point, all the tribes of Israel had fought together, traveled together, and, all too often, had sinned together. But now this would change somewhat. It began when two of the tribes, Reuben and Gad (half of the tribe of Manasseh would also later be included; see vs. 33) asked permission from Moses to settle on the eastern side of Jordan (an area stretching from the Dead Sea in the south to the Sea of Galilee in the north). There apparently were several reasons for this request, some being obvious, some not. First, the two tribes had acquired much cattle and the area seemed ideal for their herds. Then, inasmuch as both tribes had suffered a decrease in population from the first to the second census (Reuben had lost 2,770, and Gad 5,150, see ch. 26), they may have felt it better to select their own land, rather than have it decided for them by the casting of lots.

6-15. The old lawgiver's thoughts must have immediately gone back to the Kadesh tragedy. He would tolerate none of this again! **And Moses said . . . Shall your brethren go to war, and shall ye sit here?** He reviews for them the rebellion at Kadesh and sternly warns them that their selfish request could trigger another similar revolt.

the Kĕn'ez-īte, and Joshua the son of Nun: for they have wholly followed the LORD.

13 And the LORD's anger was kindled against Israel, and he made them wander in the wilderness forty years, until all the generation, that had done evil in the sight of the LORD, was consumed.

14 And, behold, ye are risen up in your fathers' stead, an increase of sinful men, to augment yet the fierce anger of the LORD toward Israel.

15 For if ye turn away from after him, he will yet again leave them in the wilderness; and ye shall destroy all this people.

16 ¶And they came near unto him, and said, We will build sheepfolds here for our cattle, and cities for our little ones:

17 But we ourselves will go ready armed before the children of Israel, until we have brought them unto their place: and our little ones shall dwell in the fenced cities because of the inhabitants of the land.

18 We will not return unto our houses, until the children of Israel have inherited every man his inheritance.

19 For we will not inherit with them on yonder side Jordan, or forward; because our inheritance is fallen to us on this side Jordan eastward.

20 ¶And Moses said unto them, If ye will do this thing, if ye will go armed before the LORD to war,

21 And will go all of you armed over Jordan before the LORD, until he hath driven out his enemies from before him,

22 And the land be subdued before the LORD: then afterward ye shall return, and be guiltless before the LORD, and before Israel; and this land shall be your possession before the LORD.

23 But if ye will not do so, behold, ye have sinned against the LORD: and be sure your sin will find you out.

24 Build you cities for your little ones, and folds for your sheep; and do that which hath proceeded out of your mouth.

25 And the children of Gad and the children of Reuben spake unto Moses, saying, Thy servants will do as my lord commandeth.

26 Our little ones, our wives, our flocks, and all our cattle, shall be there in the cities of Gilead:

27 But thy servants will pass over, every man armed for war, before the LORD to battle, as my lord saith.

28 So concerning them Moses commanded Ē-le-ā'zar the priest, and Joshua the son of Nun, and the chief fathers of the tribes of the children of Israel:

29 And Moses said unto them, If the children of Gad and the children of Reuben will pass with you over Jordan, every man armed to battle, before the LORD, and the land shall be subdued before you; then ye shall give them the land of Gilead for a possession:

30 But if they will not pass over with you armed, they shall have possessions among you in the land of Canaan.

16-19. The tribes quickly reassure Moses that there was not a rebellious spirit and promise to cross over with the other tribes and do their part in conquering Canaan (vs. 27). It is interesting to note, however, that their original request was to be excused from this (see vs. 5).

20-24. Moses agrees, but urges them to carefully and completely fulfill all their obligations; for, if not, **be sure your sin will find you out** (vs. 23). This statement would haunt the tribes for years to come. First, when Israel did invade and conquer Palestine, a civil war was narrowly averted. This was the result of a misunderstanding among the nine tribes, as well as the two half-tribes concerning this agreement for dividing the eastern land (see Josh 22:10-34). Then, in 732 B.C. the Assyrian invasion of Israel began. The first tribes to be carried into captivity were Reuben, Gad, and the half-tribe of Manasseh (cf. II Kgs 17; I Chr 5:26).

25-42. The tribes concur with Moses' qualifications. Wasting no time, the tribe of Manasseh immediately begins to conquer its staked-out ground by taking Gilead from the Amorites (see vs. 39).

31 And the children of Gad and the children of Reuben answered, saying, As the LORD hath said unto thy servants, so will we do.

32 We will pass over armed before the LORD into the land of Canaan, that the possession of our inheritance on this side Jordan *may be* ours.

33 And Moses gave unto them, *even* to the children of Gad, and to the children of Reuben, and unto half the tribe of Ma-năs'seh the son of Joseph, the kingdom of Sihon king of the Ăm'o-rītes, and the kingdom of Og king of Bā'shan, the land, with the cities thereof in the coasts, *even* the cities of the country round about.

34 ¶And the children of Gad built Dī'-bŏn, and Ăt'a-rŏth, and Ar'ō-er,

35 And Ăt'rŏth, Shō'phăn, and Jā-ā'zer, and Jŏg'be-hah,

36 And Bĕth-nĭm'rah, and Bĕth-hâ'-ran, fenced cities: and folds for sheep.

37 And the children of Reuben built Hĕsh'bŏn, and Ē-le-ā'leh, and Kĭr-jath-ā'ĭm,

38 And Nebo, and Bā'al-mē'ŏn, (their names being changed,) and Shĭb'mah: and gave other names unto the cities which they builded.

39 And the children of Mā'chĭr the son of Ma-năs'seh went to Gilead, and took it, and dispossessed the Amorite which *was* in it.

40 And Moses gave Gilead unto Mā'chĭr the son of Ma-năs'seh; and he dwelt therein.

41 And Jā'ir the son of Ma-năs'seh went and took the small towns thereof, and called them Hā'vŏth-jā'ir.

42 And Nō'bah went and took Kē'-năth, and the villages thereof, and called it Nō'bah, after his own name.

CHAPTER 33

THESE *are* the journeys of the children of Israel, which went forth out of the land of Egypt with their armies under the hand of Moses and Aaron.

2 And Moses wrote their goings out according to their journeys by the commandment of the LORD: and these *are* their journeys according to their goings out.

3 And they departed from Răm'e-sĕś in the first month, on the fifteenth day of the first month; on the morrow after the passover the children of Israel went out with an high hand in the sight of all the Egyptians.

4 For the Egyptians buried all *their* firstborn, which the LORD had smitten among them: upon their gods also the LORD executed judgments.

5 And the children of Israel removed from Răm'e-sĕś, and pitched in Sŭc'-coth.

6 And they departed from Sŭc'coth, and pitched in Ē'tham, which *is* in the edge of the wilderness.

7 And they removed from Ē'tham, and turned again unto Pī'-ha-hī'rŏth, which *is* before Bā'al-zē'phŏn: and they pitched before Mĭg'dŏl.

8 And they departed from before Pī'-ha-hī'rŏth, and passed through the midst of the sea into the wilderness,

4. Recapitulation. 33:1-49.

33:1-49. Moses now summarizes their journey, listing forty stops that were needed between Egypt and their present location. Some of the names must have brought back vivid memories. Earlier places would never have been known or remembered by this younger generation to whom Moses addresses his words. Moses refers only to the places, never the sin attached to some of them. This was, doubtless, to emphasize the fact that the failures of past years were to be put behind them. The immediate future was the all-important issue now.

and went three days' journey in the wilderness of E'tham, and pitched in Mâ'rah.

9 And they removed from Mâ'rah, and came unto Elim: and in Elim *were* twelve fountains of water, and threescore and ten palm trees; and they pitched there.

10 And they removed from Elim, and encamped by the Red sea.

11 And they removed from the Red sea, and encamped in the wilderness of Sin.

12 And they took their journey out of the wilderness of Sin, and encamped in Dŏph'kah.

13 And they departed from Dŏph'kah, and encamped in Ā'lŭsh.

14 And they removed from Ā'lŭsh, and encamped at Rĕph'i-dĭm, where was no water for the people to drink.

15 And they departed from Rĕph'i-dĭm, and pitched in the wilderness of Sī'naī.

16 And they removed from the desert of Sī'naī, and pitched at Kĭb'rŏth-hat-tā'a-vah.

17 And they departed from Kĭb'rŏth-hat-tā'a-vah, and encamped at Ha-ze'-rŏth.

18 And they departed from Ha-ze'-rŏth, and pitched in Rĭth'mah.

19 And they departed from Rĭth'mah, and pitched at Rĭm'mon-pâ'rez.

20 And they departed from Rĭm'mon-pâ'rez, and pitched in Lĭb'nah.

21 And they removed from Lĭb'nah, and pitched at Rĭs'sah.

22 And they journeyed from Rĭs'sah and pitched in Kē-hel'ă-thah.

23 And they went from Kē-hel'ă-thah, and pitched in mount Shā'pher.

24 And they removed from mount Shā'pher, and encamped in Har'ă-dah.

25 And they removed from Har'ă-dah, and pitched in Măk-hē'lŏth.

26 And they removed from Măk-hē'-lŏth, and encamped at Tā'hăth.

27 And they departed from Tā'hăth, and pitched at Tâ'rah.

28 And they removed from Tâ'rah, and pitched in Mĭth'cah.

29 And they went from Mĭth'cah, and pitched in Hăsh-mō'nah.

30 And they departed from Hăsh-mō'nah, and encamped at Mō-sē'rŏth.

31 And they departed from Mō-sē'-rŏth, and pitched in Bĕn-e-jā'a-kan.

32 And they removed from Bĕn-e-jā'a-kan, and encamped at Hôr'-ha-gĭd'găd.

33 And they went from Hôr'-ha-gĭd'-găd, and pitched in Jŏt'ba-thah.

34 And they removed from Jŏt'ba-thah, and encamped at E-brō'nah.

35 And they departed from E-brō'-nah, and encamped at E'zī-on-gā'ber.

36 And they removed from E'zī-on-gā'ber, and pitched in the wilderness of Zin, which *is* Kā'desh.

37 And they removed from Kā'desh, and pitched in mount Hor, in the edge of the land of Edom.

38 And Aaron the priest went up into mount Hor at the commandment of the LORD, and died there, in the fortieth year after the children of Israel were

come out of the land of Egypt, in the first *day* of the fifth month.

39 And Aaron *was* an hundred and twenty and three years old when he died in mount Hor.

40 And king Â'răd the Canaanite, which dwelt in the south in the land of Canaan, heard of the coming of the children of Israel.

41 And they departed from mount Hor, and pitched in Zăl-mŏ'nah.

42 And they departed from Zăl-mŏ'nah, and pitched in Pŭ'nŏn.

43 And they departed from Pŭ'nŏn, and pitched in Ō'bŏth.

44 And they departed from Ō'bŏth, and pitched in Ĭj'e-ăb'a-rĭm, in the border of Moab.

45 And they departed from Ĭ'im, and pitched in Dī'bŏn-găd.

46 And they removed from Di'bŏn-găd, and encamped in Ăl'mon-dĭb-la-thā'im.

47 And they removed from Ăl'mon-dĭb-la-thā'im, and pitched in the mountains of Ăb'a-rĭm, before Nebo.

48 And they departed from the mountains of Ăb'a-rĭm, and pitched in the plains of Moab by Jordan *near* Jericho.

49 And they pitched by Jordan, from Běth-jěs'i-mŏth *even* unto Ā'bel-shĭt'-tĭm in the plains of Moab.

50 ¶And the LORD spake unto Moses in the plains of Moab by Jordan *near* Jericho, saying,

51 Speak unto the children of Israel, and say unto them, When ye are passed over Jordan into the land of Canaan;

52 Then ye shall drive out all the inhabitants of the land from before you, and destroy all their pictures, and destroy all their molten images, and quite pluck down all their high places:

53 And ye shall dispossess *the inhabitants* of the land, and dwell therein: for I have given you the land to possess it.

54 And ye shall divide the land by lot for an inheritance among your families: *and* to the more ye shall give the more inheritance, and to the fewer ye shall give the less inheritance: every man's *inheritance* shall be in the place where his lot falleth; according to the tribes of your fathers ye shall inherit.

55 But if ye will not drive out the inhabitants of the land from before you; then it shall come to pass, that those which ye let remain of them *shall be* pricks in your eyes, and thorns in your sides, and shall vex you in the land wherein ye dwell.

56 Moreover it shall come to pass, *that* I shall do unto you, as I thought to do unto them.

CHAPTER 34

AND the LORD spake unto Moses, saying,

2 Command the children of Israel, and say unto them, When ye come into the land of Canaan; (this *is* the land that shall fall unto you for an inheritance, *even* the land of Canaan with the coasts thereof:)

3 Then your south quarter shall be from the wilderness of Zin along by the

5. Anticipation. 33:50-36:13.

a. A command for the future. 33:50-56.

50-56. On the plains of Moab, opposite Jordan, God gave Israel four commands and a twofold warning. It should be noted in verse 52 that there was no command by God to carry out a mass slaughter of the Canaanites. They were, rather, to drive most of them out of the land.

After these commands there came a warning: **If ye will not drive out the inhabitants** . . . then the following twofold sorrow will be yours: (1) They will become **pricks in your eyes, and thorns in your sides** (vs. 55); and (2) **I shall do unto you, as I thought to do unto them** (vs. 56).

b. Boundaries of the tribes. 34:1-36:13.

34:1-15. God has already given the eastern bank of Jordan to the two and one-half tribes. In this chapter He shows Moses the boundaries of the remainder of Canaan to be distributed among the nine and one-half tribes. This area was possessed by Israel for a brief time during the reigns of David and Solomon.

Your south quarter (vs. 3). This reached from the southern tip of the Dead Sea to the Mediterranean Sea. **The western border** (vs. 6). This is the coastline of the Mediterranean Sea. **Your north border** (vs. 7). This included the area of the Her-

coast of Ēdom, and your south border shall be the outmost coast of the salt sea eastward:

4 And your border shall turn from the south to the ascent of Ă-krăb'bĭm, and pass on to Zin: and the going forth thereof shall be from the south to Kā'desh-bär'ne-a, and shall go on to Hā'zar-ăd'dar, and pass on to Ăz'mon:

5 And the border shall fetch a compass from Ăz'mon unto the river of Egypt, and the goings out of it shall be at the sea.

6 And as for the western border, ye shall even have the great sea for a border: this shall be your west border.

7 And this shall be your north border: from the great sea ye shall point out for you mount Hor:

8 From mount Hor ye shall point out your border unto the entrance of Hā'māth; and the goings forth of the border shall be to Zē'dăd:

9 And the border shall go on to Zĭph'rŏn, and the goings out of it shall be at Hā'zar-ē'nan: this shall be your north border.

10 And ye shall point out your east border from Hā'zar-ē'nan to Shē'pham:

11 And the coast shall go down from Shē'pham to Rĭb'lah, on the east side of Ă'ĭn; and the border shall descend, and shall reach unto the side of the sea of Chĭn'ne-rĕth eastward:

12 And the border shall go down to Jordan, and the goings out of it shall be at the salt sea: this shall be your land with the coasts thereof round about.

13 And Moses commanded the children of Israel, saying, This is the land which ye shall inherit by lot, which the Lord commanded to give unto the nine tribes, and to the half tribe:

14 For the tribe of the children of Reuben according to the house of their fathers, and the tribe of the children of Gad according to the house of their fathers, have received their inheritance; and half the tribe of Ma-năs'seh have received their inheritance:

15 The two tribes and the half tribe have received their inheritance on this side Jordan near Jericho eastward, toward the sunrising.

16 ¶And the Lord spake unto Moses, saying,

17 These are the names of the men which shall divide the land unto you: Ĕle-ā'zar the priest, and Joshua the son of Nun.

18 And ye shall take one prince of every tribe, to divide the land by inheritance.

19 And the names of the men are these: Of the tribe of Jūdah, Caleb the son of Je-phŭn'neh.

20 And of the tribe of the children of Simeon, Shĕ-mū'el the son of Ămmī'hŭd.

21 Of the tribe of Benjamin, E-lī'dăd the son of Chĭs'lŏn.

22 And the prince of the tribe of the children of Dan, Bŭk'kī the son of Jŏg'lī.

23 The prince of the children of Joseph, for the tribe of the children of Manăs'seh, Hăn'nī-el the son of Ephod.

24 And the prince of the tribe of the

mon mountain range. **Your east border** (vs. 10). This is the Jordan Valley from the Sea of Galilee to the Dead Sea.

16-29. These are the names (vs. 17). The land was to be divided by the casting of lots, as supervised by fourteen appointed individuals. These were Eleazar, Joshua, and twelve Israelite leaders, one from each tribe.

children of Ē′phra-im, Kĕ-mū′el the son
of Shĭph′tăn.
25 And the prince of the tribe of the
children of Zĕb′u-lun, Ē-liz′ā-phăn the
son of Pär′nāch.
26 And the prince of the tribe of the
children of Ĭs′sa-char, Păl′tĭ-el the son
of Ăz′zan.
27 And the prince of the tribe of the
children of Asher, A-hī′hŭd the son of
Shel′ō-mī.
28 And the prince of the tribe of the
children of Năph′ta-lī, Pĕd′a-hĕl the
son of Ăm-mī′hŭd.
29 These *are they* whom the Lord
commanded to divide the inheritance
unto the children of Israel in the land of
Canaan.

CHAPTER 35

AND the Lord spake unto Moses in the
plains of Moab by Jordan *near* Jericho,
saying,
2 Command the children of Israel,
that they give unto the Lē′vītes of the
inheritance of their possession cities to
dwell in; and ye shall give *also* unto the
Lē′vītes suburbs for the cities round
about them.
3 And the cities shall they have to
dwell in; and the suburbs of them shall
be for their cattle, and for their goods,
and for all their beasts.
4 And the suburbs of the cities, which
ye shall give unto the Lē′vītes, *shall
reach* from the wall of the city and outward a thousand cubits round about.
5 And ye shall measure from without
the city on the east side two thousand
cubits, and on the south side two thousand cubits, and on the west side two
thousand cubits, and on the north side
two thousand cubits; and the city *shall
be* in the midst: this shall be to them the
suburbs of the cities.
6 And among the cities which ye shall
give unto the Lē′vītes *there shall be* six
cities for refuge, which ye shall appoint
for the manslayer, that he may flee
thither: and to them ye shall add forty
and two cities.
7 *So* all the cities which ye shall give
to the Lē′vītes *shall be* forty and eight
cities: them *shall ye give* with their suburbs.
8 And the cities which ye shall give
shall be of the possession of the children of Israel: from *them that have*
many ye shall give many; but from
them that have few ye shall give few:
every one shall give of his cities unto
the Lē′vītes according to his inheritance which he inheriteth.
9 ¶And the Lord spake unto Moses,
saying,
10 Speak unto the children of Israel,
and say unto them, When ye be come
over Jordan into the land of Canaan;
11 Then ye shall appoint you cities to
be cities of refuge for you; that the
slayer may flee thither, which killeth
any person at unawares.
12 And they shall be unto you cities
for refuge from the avenger; that the
manslayer die not, until he stand before
the congregation in judgment.
13 And of these cities which ye shall
give six cities shall ye have for refuge.
320

35:1-10. Chapter 35 deals with the cities. Verses 1-8 describe
the forty-eight cities of the Levites, while verses 9-34 speak of
cities of refuge. **Command . . . Israel, that they give . . . the
Levites . . . cities to dwell in** (vs. 2). The Levites were to
receive forty-eight cities scattered throughout the other tribes,
with a portion of land attached to each city. Joshua 21 describes
how this was carried out. The basic reason behind this was
probably to insure that their religious influence would be felt
throughout the entire land.

11-14. Then ye shall appoint . . . cities of refuge. There
were six of these cities, three located on the eastern bank of the
Jordan, and three on the western. Jones writes: "It was the
custom in that day for the relatives of a murdered person to
pursue the murderer and kill him in retribution for the crime.
No doubt, many innocent persons were killed in this way, as
they are today in mob action. So Moses gave instruction which
could help assure justice for suspected murderers" (K. Jones,
p. 87).

14 Ye shall give three cities on this side Jordan, and three cities shall ye give in the land of Canaan, which shall be cities of refuge.

15 These six cities shall be a refuge, both for the children of Israel, and for the stranger, and for the sojourner among them; that every one that killeth any person unawares may flee thither.

16 And if he smite him with an instrument of iron, so that he die, he is a murderer: the murderer shall surely be put to death.

17 And if he smite him with throwing a stone, wherewith he may die, and he die, he is a murderer: the murderer shall surely be put to death.

18 Or if he smite him with an hand weapon of wood, wherewith he may die, and he die, he is a murderer: the murderer shall surely be put to death.

19 The revenger of blood himself shall slay the murderer: when he meeteth him, he shall slay him.

20 But if he thrust him of hatred, or hurl at him by laying of wait, that he die;

21 Or in enmity smite him with his hand, that he die: he that smote him shall surely be put to death; for he is a murderer: the revenger of blood shall slay the murderer, when he meeteth him.

22 But if he thrust him suddenly without enmity, or have cast upon him any thing without laying of wait,

23 Or with any stone, wherewith a man may die, seeing him not, and cast it upon him, that he die, and was not his enemy, neither sought his harm:

24 Then the congregation shall judge between the slayer and the revenger of blood according to these judgments:

25 And the congregation shall deliver the slayer out of the hand of the revenger of blood, and the congregation shall restore him to the city of his refuge, whither he was fled: and he shall abide in it unto the death of the high priest, which was anointed with the holy oil.

26 But if the slayer shall at any time come without the border of the city of his refuge, whither he was fled;

27 And the revenger of blood find him without the borders of the city of his refuge, and the revenger of blood kill the slayer; he shall not be guilty of blood:

28 Because he should have remained in the city of his refuge until the death of the high priest: but after the death of the high priest the slayer shall return into the land of his possession.

29 So these things shall be for a statute of judgment unto you throughout your generations in all your dwellings.

30 Whoso killeth any person, the murderer shall be put to death by the mouth of witnesses: but one witness shall not testify against any person to cause him to die.

31 Moreover ye shall take no satisfaction for the life of a murderer, which is guilty of death: but he shall be surely put to death.

32 And ye shall take no satisfaction for him that is fled to the city of his ref-

15-23. These six cities shall be a refuge. The purpose was apparently to protect a suspected murderer until his guilt could be determined. Motive seemed to be the criterion here.

24-34. Then the congregation shall judge between the slayer and the revenger of blood. The Israelite code of justice at this time was, indeed, lofty as compared with their pagan neighbors. **But if the slayer . . . come without the . . . city.** The unintentional slayer of a man was safe as long as he stayed within the city. But if he left, he became fair game for the blood avenger. However, at the death of the high priest (vs. 28) he could leave in safety and return home.

uge, that he should come again to dwell in the land, until the death of the priest.

33 So ye shall not pollute the land wherein ye *are*: for blood it defileth the land: and the land cannot be cleansed of the blood that is shed therein, but by the blood of him that shed it.

34 Defile not therefore the land which ye shall inhabit, wherein I dwell: for I the LORD dwell among the children of Israel.

CHAPTER 36

AND the chief fathers of the families of the children of Gilead, the son of Mā'-chĭr, the son of Ma-năs'seh, of the families of the sons of Joseph, came near, and spake before Moses, and before the princes, the chief fathers of the children of Israel:

2 And they said, The LORD commanded my lord to give the land for an inheritance by lot to the children of Israel: and my lord was commanded by the LORD to give the inheritance of Ze-lō'phe-hăd our brother unto his daughters.

3 And if they be married to any of the sons of the *other* tribes of the children of Israel, then shall their inheritance be taken from the inheritance of our fathers, and shall be put to the inheritance of the tribe whereunto they are received: so shall it be taken from the lot of our inheritance.

4 And when the jubile of the children of Israel shall be, then shall their inheritance be put unto the inheritance of the tribe whereunto they are received: so shall their inheritance be taken away from the inheritance of the tribe of our fathers.

5 And Moses commanded the children of Israel according to the word of the LORD, saying, The tribe of the sons of Joseph hath said well.

6 This *is* the thing which the LORD doth command concerning the daughters of Ze-lō'phe-hăd, saying, Let them marry to whom they think best; only to the family of the tribe of their father shall they marry.

7 So shall not the inheritance of the children of Israel remove from tribe to tribe: for every one of the children of Israel shall keep himself to the inheritance of the tribe of his fathers.

8 And every daughter, that possesseth an inheritance in any tribe of the children of Israel, shall be wife unto one of the family of the tribe of her father, that the children of Israel may enjoy every man the inheritance of his fathers.

9 Neither shall the inheritance remove from *one* tribe to another tribe; but every one of the tribes of the children of Israel shall keep himself to his own inheritance.

10 Even as the LORD commanded Moses, so did the daughters of Ze-lō'phe-hăd:

11 For Mäh'lah, Tir'zah, and Hŏg'lah, and Mĭl'cah, and Noah, the daughters of Ze-lō'phe-hăd, were married unto their father's brothers' sons:

12 *And* they were married into the

36:1-13. And the chief fathers. The heads of the tribes raised the question of the inheritance of women. It was possible that these women would marry men from other tribes. This would mean that the inheritance would pass over to that tribe. The regulation to marry only within the tribe took care of this problem.

The book of Numbers closes with the nation on the eve of entering the land. The last chapter of Deuteronomy takes up the history again, with the death of Moses. The failures of the people make a vivid impression throughout Numbers, but God's faithfulness and patience shines through the dark cloud of Israel's stubbornness and foolishness.

families of the sons of Ma-năs'seh the son of Joseph, and their inheritance remained in the tribe of the family of their father.

13 These *are* the commandments and the judgments, which the LORD commanded by the hand of Moses unto the children of Israel in the plains of Moab by Jordan *near* Jericho.

BIBLIOGRAPHY

*Anderson, C. A. Numbers. In *Old Testament Commentary*. Ed. by H. C. Alleman. Philadelphia: Muhlenberg Press, 1949.

Binns, L. E. Numbers. In *Westminster Commentaries*. London: Methuen & Co., 1927.

Ellicott, C. J. *Bible Commentary for English Readers*. Vol. I. Grand Rapids: Zondervan, n.d.

Gray, G. B. Numbers. In *International Critical Commentary*. Edinburgh: T. & T. Clark, 1912.

Greenstone, J. H. *Numbers with Commentary*. Philadelphia: Jewish Publication Society, 1939.

*Jensen, I. L. *Numbers: Journey to God's Rest-Land*. Chicago: Moody Press, 1964.

Jones, K. E. *The Book of Numbers*. Grand Rapids: Baker, 1972.

*Keil, C. F. and F. Delitzsch. Numbers. In *Commentary on the Old Testament*. Grand Rapids: Eerdmans, reprinted, 1956.

Kerr, D. W. Numbers. In *The Biblical Expositor*. London: Pickering and Inglis, 1960.

Lange, J. P. Numbers. In *A Commentary on the Holy Scriptures*. Grand Rapids: Zondervan, reprinted, 1956.

MacRae, A. A. Numbers. In *The New Bible Commentary*. Grand Rapids: Eerdmans, 1953.

Marsh, J. Book of Numbers. In *The Interpreter's Bible*. Vol. 2. New York: Abingdon Press, 1954.

McNeile, A. H. Numbers. In *The Cambridge Bible for Schools and Colleges*. Cambridge: The University Press, 1911.

*Smick, Elmer. Numbers. In *The Wycliffe Bible Commentary*. Chicago: Moody Press, 1962.

Stevens, Charles H. *Wilderness Journey*. Chicago: Moody Press, 1971.

Watson, R. A. Numbers. In *The Expositor's Bible*. New York: Armstrong & Co., 1903.

DEUTERONOMY

INTRODUCTION

The book of Deuteronomy is different from the other four books in the Pentateuch inasmuch as it contains the fired-up emotions of the prophet who exhorts Israel to remember God's good works and repent from their transgressions. Jesus refers to the five books of the Pentateuch as the Law, thus giving them a unity. Each of the five books is dependent upon the others, and, consequently, the book of Deuteronomy ties them together by building upon what grows out of the previous four books. Genesis contains history and narrative; Exodus begins with narrative and ends with legislation; Leviticus records the giving of the Law; Numbers again contains narrative and history. Deuteronomy is primarily sermonic in character, and its sermons drive home what the Jews should have learned from the first four books. Deuteronomy is a recorded message; this accounts for the differences in style and method of expression found in it.

Name. The book has four Jewish titles. The first is "these be the words . . ." (1:1). It is derived from the first two words of the original (Heb *'ēleh hadbarim*). The second Jewish title is "Fifth," or the fifth part of the Law, Deuteronomy being the fifth book in the Pentateuch. The third Jewish name is "the book of reproofs," because there are so many admonitions in it. The fourth Jewish name is "iteration of the Law." The key verse is Moses' admonition, "Behold, I set before you this day a blessing and a curse; A blessing, if ye obey the commandments of the LORD your God, which I command you this day: And a curse, if ye will not obey the commandments of the LORD your God, but turn aside out of the way which I command you this day, to go after other gods, which ye have not known" (11:26-28). The Septuagint title is *"Deuteronomion,"* which means "second law." Our English version transliterates the Greek; as a result we have Deuteronomy. Therefore, Deuteronomy's title comes from the fourth Jewish name, "iteration of the Law." The title could have come from the phrase ". . . a copy of this Law. . . ." (17:18), where the king sat upon the throne and there was a copy of the Law. (See B. H. Carroll, *An Interpretation of the English Bible: Numbers to Ruth,* p. 65.)

The Law was divided into three distinct parts: first, the Decalogue, or the Ten Commandments, which expressed the moral law of God; second, the civil and criminal law upon which national life was based; and third, the ritual laws which laid the foundation for man's approach to God. Deuteronomy reapplies the first two sections of the Law, but neglects the third section, the ritual law.

The book of Deuteronomy is not a mere repetition and summary of the most important laws and events contained in previous books. Nor is it merely a second copy of the Law intended for the people who did not know the Law. The book of Deuteronomy is an oration by Moses wherein he describes, explains, and seeks to reinforce the most essential contents of the covenant revelation, including its laws, so that the people might understand the spiritual principles of the Law for their well-being.

The people who listened to this sermon were not present when the first law was given. Their fathers had died in the wilderness because of unbelief. Moses gathers them together before God and presents the rules and promises for their lives in the Promised Land.

Moses omits certain things, such as the building of God's house, the service of the priests and Levites, the laws of sacrifice and purification, festivals, and the three annual feasts (Passover, Pentecost, and Tabernacles). On the other hand, he includes certain items not mentioned previously, such as instructions concerning the king whom the people would one day appoint, their relationship to the prophets whom God would raise up, and the rules concerning the wars to be waged with the Canaanites.

In repeating the Law, Moses sums up the essential contents of all the commandments, statutes and obligations which Jehovah had commanded. He exhorts the people to obedience, giving them threats should they disobey and promises should they obey. He attempts to awaken in the hearts of Israel a willing and loving compliance with the laws of God. Toward the end of the book the Palestinian covenant appears, a conditional relationship that God makes with His people: if they keep the Law, they will occupy the land. The keeping of the Sabbath is the symbol that verifies the Palestinian covenant. Even though the land was given unconditionally to Abraham and his seed, Israel was to enter the land under the Palestinian covenant.

Authorship. When the question of who wrote Deuteronomy is raised, the answer is undeniably Moses. Who else would have had the spiritual insight, the legal mentality, and the leadership qualities to write such a book? However, higher criticism denies Mosaic authorship. Vatinger and Koenig claim that it was written under Hezekiah. Ewald, Riehm, and Kautsch indicate that it was written during Manasseh's reign. Wellhausen, Russ, and DeWette believe Deuteronomy was written when Josiah was king. Others claim that it was written after the Babylonian captivity. Obviously, they believe that the prophecies of Deuteronomy were written after their fulfillment, so as to explain away the supernatural character of the manuscript. In contrast, the Mosaic authorship of the book has been defended by Archer, Allis, Aalders, Cassuto, Harrison, Kline, Keil and Delitzsch, Manley, Segal, Unger, and Young.

Jesus Christ quoted from Deuteronomy three

times in answering the temptations of Satan (6:13, 16; 8:3; cf. Mt 4:4, 7, 10; Lk 4:4, 8, 12). Christ placed His trustworthiness and impeccability on the line by equating Deuteronomy with Scripture. When Jesus was tempted to disobey God, He quoted from the book of obedience. Jesus personified the book of Deuteronomy; He was obedient unto death. Jesus quoted Deuteronomy 24:1-4 when speaking to the Pharisees (Mk 10:4), noting that Moses gave the commandment and thereby claiming Mosaic authorship. In Mark 12:19, Jesus quotes from Deuteronomy 25:5, again attributing Mosaic authorship to this book.

Luke, the author of Acts, also attests to Mosaic authorship in Acts 3:22 and 7:37, when he quotes from Deuteronomy 18:15, 18. Paul also followed the same format in Romans 10:19, attributing Mosaic authorship to Deuteronomy 32:21. Therefore, the entire thrust of the New Testament supports the Mosaic authorship of Deuteronomy.

Time of Writing. Deuteronomy covers a period of thirty-seven days. The book begins, "And it came to pass in the fortieth year . . ." (1:3). This is the fortieth year after Israel left Egypt. More specifically, the book begins, "in the eleventh month, on the first day of the month, . . . Moses spake unto the children of Israel. . . ." There are seventy days between this reference and Joshua 4:19, because Israel crossed the Jordan on the tenth day of the new year, an interval of two months plus ten days, or seventy days. Deuteronomy ends with Israel spending thirty days mourning the death of Moses

(34:8). Hence, by subtracting the period of mourning from the time of entrance into the land, we find that the book of Deuteronomy covers a period of forty days. But we must also subtract the time between Joshua 1:11 and 3:2, the three days that the children of Israel waited to enter the land. Hence, the events of the book of Deuteronomy cover thirty-seven days. During this time there were seven sermons, as well as some narrative recorded.

The action begins on the east side of the Jordan River. Israel is viewing the Promised Land. They had first arrived at this location thirty-eight years earlier. Israel had progressed as far as the edge of the Promised Land, to a place called Kadesh-barnea in the southern part of what is now called Judaea. Because of Israel's rebellion and refusal to enter the land, they had wandered for thirty-eight years. As Deuteronomy opens, Israel is ready to enter the Promised Land; but the Jordan River separates them from their westward conquest.

Before they invade the land, a successor to Moses must be installed. For forty years, Moses had been their deliverer. Actually, if time is measured from when he took Israel's side and killed the Egyptian taskmaster, he had been their deliverer for eighty years. Moses is to die before Israel enters the Promised Land. But Moses is still the leader, and he wants to renew Israel's pledge to God before he dies. Therefore, the book of Deuteronomy is his message to Israel so that they may more fully understand their covenant obligations before God.

OUTLINE

COMMENTARY

I. INTRODUCTION. 1:1-5.

THESE *be* the words which Moses spake unto all Israel on this side Jordan in the wilderness, in the plain over against the Red *sea*, between Paran, and Tō'phel, and Lā'ban, and Ha-ze'-rŏth, and Dĭz'a-hăb.

2 (*There are* eleven days' *journey* from Hō'rĕb by the way of mount Sē'ir unto Kā'desh-bär'ne-a.)

3 And it came to pass in the fortieth year, in the eleventh month, on the first *day* of the month, *that* Moses spake unto the children of Israel, according unto all that the LORD had given him in commandment unto them;

4 After he had slain Sihon the king of the Ăm'o-rītes, which dwelt in Hĕsh'-bŏn, and Og the king of Bā'shan, which dwelt at Ăs'ta-rŏth in Ĕd're-ī:

5 On this side Jordan, in the land of Moab, began Moses to declare this law, saying,

1:1-4. The very first phrase in the book, **These be the words which Moses spake,** gives an insight into what is to follow. Deuteronomy is a book of sermons. Israel is gathered on the east bank of Jordan, ready to enter the Promised Land. It had taken them thirty-eight years to get there since their rebellion at Kadesh-barnea. Verse 2 indicates that the journey would normally have taken eleven days. But they had wandered in the wilderness, led by a cloud during the day and by a pillar of fire at night. Now Israel is physically ready to enter the land, but Moses realizes that they must also be ready spiritually. The time of year is the Jewish eleventh month, or March according to our calendar.

5. Verse 5 sets the stage for the first sermon by Moses. He was undertaking to expound the Law. He had given many other sermons, but none was as important as this message. If this sermon failed, the people would not properly occupy the land, if they were allowed to enter at all.

II. RETROSPECT: A VIEW OF ISRAEL'S WANDERINGS. 1:6-4:43.

In this section, Moses reminds the people of their problems and victories during their time of wandering in the wilderness. His emphasis is on the past deliverances of God, but he also reminds the people that God will continue to fight for them in the future.

A. Israel at Sinai. 1:6-18.

6. Moses begins by using the word **our,** reminding them that Jehovah is on their side. This also presupposes that the people will receive the Palestinian covenant presented later in the book. He uses the term **Horeb,** which is a mountain range, rather than Sinai, which is one peak. The hearers knew that Israel was too large to gather in front of one mountain. **Ye have dwelt long enough in this mount** is a rhetorical call to national repentance. No mention is made of the cloud or of the trumpets, the usual means by which God spoke to Israel. This was an unusual call.

6 The LORD our God spake unto us in Hō'rĕb, saying, Ye have dwelt long enough in this mount:

7. Every word in this verse reveals a loving God who will guide them specifically according to His divine purpose, according to His promise to Abraham (Gen 15:18; 17:8).

7 Turn you, and take your journey, and go to the mount of the Ăm'o-rītes, and unto all *the places* nigh thereunto, in the plain, in the hills, and in the vale, and in the south, and by the sea side, to the land of the Canaanites, and unto Lebanon, unto the great river, the river Eū-phrā'tĕs.

8 Behold, I have set the land before you: go in and possess the land which the LORD sware unto your fathers, Abraham, Isaac, and Jacob, to give unto them and to their seed after them.

8. Moses emphasizes **set.** God had put the Promised Land there originally; now it is at the disposal of Israel. He had promised to give the land to Abraham and his descendants. ". . . Unto thy seed will I give this land . . ." (Gen 12:7). Since God keeps His promises, Israel will now enter the land, but this verse also foreshadows Israel's return to the land in the Millennium.

9 ¶And I spake unto you at that time, saying, I am not able to bear you myself alone:

9. I spake unto you. There is no contradiction here with Exodus 18:17 and what follows, where Jethro is the speaker. Jethro had only advised; Moses put the advice into effect. **I am not able to bear you** was not complaining on Moses' part, but a recognition of his failure and inability.

10 The LORD your God hath multiplied you, and, behold, ye *are* this day as the stars of heaven for multitude.

11 (The LORD God of your fathers

10-11. If Moses feels guilty for his last statement, here he puts the burden of pastoral care back on God; **The LORD your God hath multiplied you.** When Moses says that Israel is **as the stars of heaven,** he is reminding them that God has fulfilled His

make you a thousand times so many more as ye *are*, and bless you, as he hath promised you!)

12 How can I myself alone bear your cumbrance, and your burden, and your strife?

13 Take you wise men, and understanding, and known among your tribes, and I will make them rulers over you.

14 And ye answered me, and said, The thing which thou hast spoken *is* good *for us* to do.

15 So I took the chief of your tribes, wise men, and known, and made them heads over you, captains over thousands, and captains over hundreds, and captains over fifties, and captains over tens, and officers among your tribes.

16 And I charged your judges at that time, saying, Hear *the causes* between your brethren, and judge righteously between *every* man and his brother, and the stranger *that is* with him.

17 Ye shall not respect persons in judgment; *but* ye shall hear the small as well as the great; ye shall not be afraid of the face of man; for the judgment *is* God's: and the cause that is too hard for you, bring *it* unto me, and I will hear it.

18 And I commanded you at that time all the things which ye should do.

19 ¶And when we departed from Hō′-rĕb, we went through all that great and terrible wilderness, which ye saw by the way of the mountain of the Ăm′o-rītes, as the LORD our God commanded us; and we came to Kā′desh-bär′ne-a.

20 And I said unto you, Ye are come unto the mountain of the Ăm′o-rītes, which the LORD our God doth give unto us.

21 Behold, the LORD thy God hath set the land before thee: go up *and* possess *it*, as the LORD God of thy fathers hath said unto thee; fear not, neither be discouraged.

22 ¶And ye came near unto me every one of you, and said, We will send men before us, and they shall search us out the land, and bring us word again by what way we must go up, and into what cities we shall come.

23 And the saying pleased me well: and I took twelve men of you, one of a tribe:

24 And they turned and went up into the mountain, and came unto the valley of Ĕsh′cōl, and searched it out.

25 And they took of the fruit of the land in their hands, and brought *it* down unto us, and brought us word again, and said, *It is* a good land which the LORD our God doth give us.

26 Notwithstanding ye would not go up, but rebelled against the commandment of the LORD your God:

27 And ye murmured in your tents, and said, Because the LORD hated us, he hath brought us forth out of the land of Egypt, to deliver us into the hand of the Ăm′o-rītes, to destroy us.

28 Whither shall we go up? our brethren have discouraged our heart, saying, The people *is* greater and taller than we; the cities *are* great and walled

promise to Abraham (Gen 15:5). The phrase **make you a thousand times so many more as ye are** points back to Genesis 12:2, showing that God had blessed Israel both physically and spiritually.

12-15. The responsibilities of decision and judging were too vast for Moses. The congregation is instructed to nominate wise and respected men according to tribes. Moses would appoint them as judges over the nation (Ex 18:21 ff.).

16-18. The elders are instructed to **Hear the causes between your brethren,** specifically, to listen to both sides of the dispute. He reminds them to **judge righteously.** The basis was that **the judgment is God's,** i.e., they were God's representatives and sat in the Lord's place before men, hence the expression ". . . bring the causes unto God" (Ex 18:19). The more difficult cases were to be brought before Moses for judgment (Ex 18:26).

B. Israel at Kadesh-barnea. 1:19-46.

19-21. Moses describes the trip from Horeb to the Promised Land. He reminds them that their fathers' fathers came to Kadesh-barnea, which was the entrance to **the mountain of the Amorites, which the LORD our God doth give unto us.** The condition was that Israel was to **go up and possess it.**

22-25. Moses mentions the spies next. The people had asked for the spies; it had not been Moses' idea (although he approved), nor had it been God's idea. When Jehovah heard their request, He approved; and the spies were sent to search out the Promised Land. Moses gives a partial summary of the report of the spies, noting the good aspects of the land.

26-28. Moses describes Israel's rebellion first by describing their murmuring in the tents (Num 14:2), and second, by referring to their outward rebellion (Num 14:4). He reminds Israel of their ingratitude with the phrase **the LORD hated us,** when in fact God's greatest blessing was in delivering them from Egypt. When Israel said **Whither shall we go up?,** it was because of a lack of faith in God. Israel was afraid of their enemies; and their description of their cities as **walled up to heaven,** literally "towering up into the heaven," is a rhetorical description of their impression of the size of the enemies' towns.

up to heaven; and moreover we have seen the sons of the Anakims there.

29 Then I said unto you, Dread not, neither be afraid of them.

30 The LORD your God which goeth before you, he shall fight for you, according to all that he did for you in Egypt before your eyes;

31 And in the wilderness, where thou hast seen how that the LORD thy God bare thee, as a man doth bear his son, in all the way that ye went, until ye came into this place.

32 Yet in this thing ye did not believe the LORD your God,

33 Who went in the way before you, to search you out a place to pitch your tents in, in fire by night, to shew you by what way ye should go, and in a cloud by day.

34 And the LORD heard the voice of your words, and was wroth, and sware, saying,

35 Surely there shall not one of these men of this evil generation see that good land, which I sware to give unto your fathers,

36 Save Caleb the son of Je-phŭn'-neh; he shall see it, and to him will I give the land that he hath trodden upon, and to his children, because he hath wholly followed the LORD.

37 Also the LORD was angry with me for your sakes, saying, Thou also shalt not go in thither.

38 But Joshua the son of Nun, which standeth before thee, he shall go in thither: encourage him: for he shall cause Israel to inherit it.

39 Moreover your little ones, which ye said should be a prey, and your children, which in that day had no knowledge between good and evil, they shall go in thither, and unto them will I give it, and they shall possess it.

40 But as for you, turn you, and take your journey into the wilderness by the way of the Red sea.

41 Then ye answered and said unto me, We have sinned against the LORD, we will go up and fight, according to all that the LORD our God commanded us. And when ye had girded on every man his weapons of war, ye were ready to go up into the hill.

42 And the LORD said unto me, Say unto them, Go not up, neither fight; for I am not among you; lest ye be smitten before your enemies.

43 So I spake unto you; and ye would not hear, but rebelled against the commandment of the LORD, and went presumptuously up into the hill.

44 And the Ăm'o-rītes, which dwelt in that mountain, came out against you, and chased you, as bees do, and destroyed you in Sē'ir, even unto Hôr'-mah.

45 And ye returned and wept before the LORD; but the LORD would not hearken to your voice, nor give ear unto you.

46 So ye abode in Kā'desh many days, according unto the days that ye abode there.

29-35. When Moses had exhorted the people to **Dread not** (vs. 29), it was meant as a challenge to their faith. Trust in God does not hide the difficulties; it demonstrates faith in God who will help in overcoming impossible situations. One basis for the challenge was God's past act, which **he did for you in Egypt.** The second basis for God's help was that He **bare thee, as a man doth bear his son,** which shows the gracious nature of God. The phrase **ye did not believe** is a participle showing that unbelief was not a permanent condition. God's Presence accompanied them in pillars of cloud and fire to both guide and protect them. The justice of God is revealed in the phrase **the LORD . . . was wroth;** but even in God's anger He remembered His covenant, for God cannot deny His promise. These events were not only intended to teach Israel their past history, but to challenge them to holiness.

36-38. The three leaders of Israel, Moses, Joshua, and Caleb, are mentioned in this paragraph. Joshua and Caleb are mentioned as positive examples because of their obedience. Moses testifies to his sin but explains that his errors were for their sakes. The lapse by Moses is now used as a sermon illustration to strengthen the faith of Israel and to point them to full obedience. **Joshua . . . which standeth before thee** indicates that Joshua was visible to the congregation as Moses preached. **Encourage him** is Moses' way of telling Israel that Joshua will be the next leader. His future is defined by the words, **he shall cause Israel to inherit it,** which involved Joshua's conquering, dividing, and settling of the Promised Land.

39-46. Those who were innocent of rebellion **had no knowledge between good and evil.** God had told them that they should **Go not up, neither fight; for I am not among you.** The people rebelled, in that they fought the Amorites in spite of God's warnings and were defeated. An apparent repentance is seen in the words **ye returned and wept before the LORD,** but it was a fleshly repentance; they were sorry because they had been defeated, not because they had disobeyed. As a result, **the LORD would not hearken to your voice.**

CHAPTER 2

THEN we turned, and took our journey into the wilderness by the way of the Red sea, as the Lord spake unto me: and we compassed mount Sē′ir many days.

2 And the Lord spake unto me, saying,

3 Ye have compassed this mountain long enough: turn you northward.

4 And command thou the people, saying, Ye *are* to pass through the coast of your brethren the children of Esau, which dwell in Sē′ir; and they shall be afraid of you: take ye good heed unto yourselves therefore:

5 Meddle not with them; for I will not give you of their land, no, not so much as a foot breadth; because I have given mount Sē′ir unto Esau *for* a possession.

6 Ye shall buy meat of them for money, that ye may eat; and ye shall also buy water of them for money, that ye may drink.

7 For the Lord thy God hath blessed thee in all the works of thy hand: he knoweth thy walking through this great wilderness: these forty years the Lord thy God *hath been* with thee; thou hast lacked nothing.

8 And when we passed by from our brethren the children of Esau, which dwelt in Sē′ir, through the way of the plain from Ē′lāth, and from Ē′zĭ-on-gā′ber, we turned and passed by the way of the wilderness of Moab.

9 And the Lord said unto me, Distress not the Moabites, neither contend with them in battle: for I will not give thee of their land *for* a possession; because I have given Ar unto the children of Lot *for* a possession.

10 The Ē′mĭms dwelt therein in times past, a people great, and many, and tall, as the Anakims;

11 Which also were accounted giants, as the Anakims; but the Moabites call them Ē′mĭms.

12 The Hō′rĭms also dwelt in Sē′ir beforetime; but the children of Esau succeeded them, when they had destroyed them from before them, and dwelt in their stead; as Israel did unto the land of his possession, which the Lord gave unto them.

13 Now rise up, *said I,* and get you over the brook Ze′red. And we went over the brook Ze′red.

14 And the space in which we came from Kā′desh-bär′ne-a, until we were come over the brook Ze′red, *was* thirty and eight years; until all the generation of the men of war were wasted out from among the host, as the Lord sware unto them.

15 For indeed the hand of the Lord was against them, to destroy them from among the host, until they were consumed.

16 ¶So it came to pass, when all the men of war were consumed and dead from among the people,

17 That the Lord spake unto me, saying,

18 Thou art to pass over through Ar, the coast of Moab, this day:

19 And *when* thou comest nigh over

C. Israel's Journey from Kadesh to Moab. 2:1-3:29.

2:1-7. Chapter 1 ends with the second person **you,** but chapter 2 begins with the first person **we turned** (see A. C. Gaebelein, *The Annotated Bible,* Vol. 1, p. 385). Here Moses identifies with those in rebellion. In his dejection he does not remember the time it took to pass Mount Seir but says only that it was **many days.** Those who were faithful identified with those who were under the judgment of God. This is true obedience and humility.

A tender picture of the Lord's graciousness is seen in the phrase **thou hast lacked nothing.** The people who had insulted God and had not trusted Him lacked nothing, for the Lord had given them food, clothing, and protection. The Lord knew their path in the great wilderness, and for forty years He had taken care of them.

8-14. Moses traces the history of Israel and her travels through the nations. God gave a divine injunction not to attack Edom, Moab, or Ammon; for Israel might have coveted their land and settled down outside of the Promised Land. These people were blood relatives of Israel; and Jehovah would not allow Israel to attack them, for He had given Mount Seir to Esau as a possession (Gen 32:3; 36:6-8).

The command **Now rise up** was given after the thirty-eight years in the wilderness. It must have been a tremendous encouragement to journey with a purpose after having wandered for so long. The main purpose during the thirty-eight years was to allow unfaithful Israel to die. This is described as **wasted out.**

15-23. Although Ammon and Moab had harrassed Israel, God would not give Israel their land. **I have given it unto the children of Lot for a possession.** God always keeps His promises, so Israel had to obey the command of God and bypass these nations. Their obedience was a lesson in faith.

A race of giants is mentioned as living in these territories. **Zamzummin** means "to murmur and meditate," which implies demon worship and communication with spirits. These enemies had not died a natural death. **The Lord destroyed them.**

against the children of Ammon, distress them not, nor meddle with them: for I will not give thee of the land of the children of Ammon *any* possession; because I have given it unto the children of Lot *for* a possession.

20 (That also was accounted a land of giants: giants dwelt therein in old time; and the Ammonites call them Zăm-zŭm'mĭmś;

21 A people great, and many, and tall, as the Anakims; but the LORD destroyed them before them; and they succeeded them, and dwelt in their stead:

22 As he did to the children of Esau, which dwelt in Sē'ir, when he destroyed the Hō'rīms from before them; and they succeeded them, and dwelt in their stead even unto this day:

23 And the Ā'vīms which dwelt in Ha-ze'rīm, *even* unto Āz'zah, the Căph'to-rīms, which came forth out of Căph'tôr, destroyed them, and dwelt in their stead.)

24 ¶Rise ye up, take your journey, and pass over the river Arnon: behold, I have given into thine hand Sihon the Ăm'o-rīte, king of Hĕsh'bŏn, and his land: begin to possess *it*, and contend with him in battle.

25 This day will I begin to put the dread of thee and the fear of thee upon the nations *that are* under the whole heaven, who shall hear report of thee, and shall tremble, and be in anguish because of thee.

26 ¶And I sent messengers out of the wilderness of Kĕd'e-mŏth unto Sihon king of Hĕsh'bŏn with words of peace, saying,

27 Let me pass through thy land: I will go along by the high way, I will neither turn unto the right hand nor to the left.

28 Thou shalt sell me meat for money, that I may eat; and give me water for money, that I may drink: only I will pass through on my feet;

29 (As the children of Esau which dwell in Sē'ir, and the Moabites which dwell in Ar, did unto me;) until I shall pass over Jordan into the land which the LORD our God giveth us.

30 But Sihon king of Hĕsh'bŏn would not let us pass by him: for the LORD thy God hardened his spirit, and made his heart obstinate, that he might deliver him into thy hand, as *appeareth* this day.

31 And the LORD said unto me, Behold, I have begun to give Sihon and his land before thee: begin to possess, that thou mayest inherit his land.

32 Then Sihon came out against us, he and all his people, to fight at Jā'hăz.

33 And the LORD our God delivered him before us; and we smote him, and his sons, and all his people.

34 And we took all his cities at that time, and utterly destroyed the men, and the women, and the little ones, of every city, we left none to remain:

35 Only the cattle we took for a prey unto ourselves, and the spoil of the cities which we took.

36 From Ar'ŏ-er, which *is* by the brink of the river of Arnon, and *from* the city that *is* by the river, even unto

24-37. Whereas Israel had been commanded not to fight the tribes of Edom, Moab, and Ammon (vss. 9, 19), the situation changed with Sihon, the Amorite. Moses sent messengers to Sihon, King of Heshbon, with **words of peace.** Sihon rejected the proposal and was hostile toward Israel. The divine foreknowledge of the hardness of Sihon is not an indication that God destroyed his free will. God saw the circumstances and told Israel to completely destroy Sihon and his people. The campaign against Sihon began when God had said **I begin to put the dread of thee and the fear of thee upon the nations. Under the whole heaven** is a hyperbole referring to all nations who received the report of Israel's journeyings.

Gilead, there was not one city too strong for us: the LORD our God delivered all unto us:

37 Only unto the land of the children of Ammon thou camest not, *nor* unto any place of the river Jabbok, nor unto the cities in the mountains, nor unto whatsoever the LORD our God forbad us.

CHAPTER 3

THEN we turned, and went up the way to Bā'shan: and Og the king of Bā'shan came out against us, he and all his people, to battle at Ĕd're-ī.

2 And the LORD said unto me, Fear him not: for I will deliver him, and all his people, and his land, into thy hand; and thou shalt do unto him as thou didst unto Sihon king of the Ăm'o-rītes, which dwelt at Hĕsh'bŏn.

3 So the LORD our God delivered into our hands Og also, the king of Bā'shan, and all his people: and we smote him until none was left to him remaining.

4 And we took all his cities at that time, there was not a city which we took not from them, threescore cities, all the region of Är'gŏb, the kingdom of Og in Bā'shan.

5 All these cities *were* fenced with high walls, gates, and bars; beside unwalled towns a great many.

6 And we utterly destroyed them, as we did unto Sihon king of Hĕsh'bŏn, utterly destroying the men, women, and children, of every city.

7 But all the cattle, and the spoil of the cities, we took for a prey to ourselves.

8 And we took at that time out of the hand of the two kings of the Ăm'o-rītes the land that *was* on this side Jordan, from the river of Arnon unto mount Hermon;

9 (*Which* Hermon the Si-dō'ni-ans call Sĭr'i-on; and the Ăm'o-rītes call it She'nir;)

10 All the cities of the plain, and all Gilead, and all Bā'shan, unto Săl'chah and Ĕd're-ī, cities of the kingdom of Og in Bā'shan.

11 For only Og king of Bā'shan remained of the remnant of giants; behold, his bedstead *was* a bedstead of iron; *is* it not in Răb'bath of the children of Ammon? nine cubits *was* the length thereof, and four cubits the breadth of it, after the cubit of a man.

12 And this land, *which* we possessed at that time, from Är'o-er, which *is* by the river Arnon, and half mount Gilead, and the cities thereof, gave I unto the Reubenites and to the Găd'ītes.

13 And the rest of Gilead, and all Bā'shan, *being* the kingdom of Og, gave I unto the half tribe of Ma-năs'seh; all the region of Är'gŏb, with all Bā'shan, which was called the land of giants.

14 Jā'ir the son of Ma-năs'seh took all the country of Är'gŏb unto the coasts of Gĕsh'u-rī and Mā-ăch'a-thī; and called them after his own name Bā'shan–hā'-vŏth-jāir, unto this day.

15 And I gave Gilead unto Mā'chĭr.

16 And unto the Reubenites and unto the Găd'ītes I gave from Gilead even

3:1-2. Israel had advanced to the Jordan River after defeating Sihon. There they had met the powerful Amorite king, Og. He had conquered the northern half of Gilead and all of Bashan. God had encouraged Israel to **Fear him not,** because they would defeat Og as they had defeated Sihon.

3-7. Bashan, Og's capital, got its name from the surrounding soil. The word **Bashan** means "soft and level." Archaeological research has proven the existence of strong, fortified cities in that territory. Moses reminds Israel that they had **gates and bars** and that **we utterly destroyed them.** He is challenging Israel to go across Jordan and conquer cities, just as they had done in the past.

8-10. Mount Hermon is mentioned because it is the northern boundary of Israel's inheritance. Moses also identifies it by the Sidonian name of **Sirion,** "the high or eminent," and by the **Amorite** name of **Shenir.**

11. The giants lived in Bashan even in Abraham's day (Gen 14:5) and were called "Rephaim." King Og's bed is mentioned by Moses. It was twelve feet long and six feet wide. This does not mean Og was that tall, because warriors normally had beds constructed which were somewhat longer than their stature. But he was a giant, and Moses mentions the size of his bed to illustrate the great victory which the Lord had given them.

12-20. In this section, Moses reviews the distribution of the conquered land. Two and one-half tribes were to receive their inheritance on the east side of Jordan, the Reubenites, the Gadites, and half of the tribe of Manesseh (repeated in Josh 13:15-20, 24-28). Moses uses the phrase **gave I** to reinforce his leadership. **Unto this day** does not imply the date of writing, but speaks of their permanence (Josh 13:13). Moses did not intend to repeat the historical details of the distribution, including the sixty towns. Rather, he was persuading Israel to follow the Lord.

Moses reminds the two and one-half tribes of their responsibility to cross Jordan and help conquer the Promised Land. The wives, children, and cattle were allowed to remain with their possessions.

unto the river Arnon half the valley, and the border even unto the river Jabbok, *which is* the border of the children of Ammon;

17 The plain also, and Jordan, and the coast *thereof*, from Chĭn′ne-rĕth even unto the sea of the plain, *even* the salt sea, under Ăsh′dŏth-pĭs′gah eastward.

18 ¶And I commanded you at that time, saying, The LORD your God hath given you this land to possess it: ye shall pass over armed before your brethren the children of Israel, all *that are* meet for the war.

19 But your wives, and your little ones, and your cattle, (*for* I know that ye have much cattle,) shall abide in your cities which I have given you;

20 Until the LORD have given rest unto your brethren, as well as unto you, and *until* they also possess the land which the LORD your God hath given them beyond Jordan: and *then* shall ye return every man unto his possession, which I have given you.

21 ¶And I commanded Joshua at that time, saying, Thine eyes have seen all that the LORD your God hath done unto these two kings: so shall the LORD do unto all the kingdoms whither thou passest.

22 Ye shall not fear them: for the LORD your God he shall fight for you.

23 ¶And I besought the LORD at that time, saying,

24 O Lord GOD, thou hast begun to shew thy servant thy greatness, and thy mighty hand: for what God *is there* in heaven or in earth, that can do according to thy works, and according to thy might?

25 I pray thee, let me go over, and see the good land that *is* beyond Jordan, that goodly mountain, and Lebanon.

26 But the LORD was wroth with me for your sakes, and would not hear me: and the LORD said unto me, Let it suffice thee; speak no more unto me of this matter.

27 Get thee up into the top of Pĭs′gah, and lift up thine eyes westward, and northward, and southward, and eastward, and behold *it* with thine eyes: for thou shalt not go over this Jordan.

28 But charge Joshua, and encourage him, and strengthen him: for he shall go over before this people, and he shall cause them to inherit the land which thou shalt see.

29 So we abode in the valley over against Bĕth-pē′ôr.

CHAPTER 4

NOW therefore hearken, O Israel, unto the statutes and unto the judgments, which I teach you, for to do *them*, that ye may live, and go in and possess the land which the LORD God of your fathers giveth you.

2 Ye shall not add unto the word which I command you, neither shall ye diminish *ought* from it, that ye may keep the commandments of the LORD your God which I command you.

21-22. Moses challenges his successor to vigilance; Joshua is reminded of what he observed, that is, the victories wrought by God. **So shall the LORD do** was the promise to Joshua when he was finally to enter the Promised Land. The word **he** after **the LORD your God** is emphatic. It adds force to the thought that God would fight for them.

23-29. Moses had asked God for permission to enter into the Promised Land, but God could not break His vow. This prayer was not mentioned in the historical account, but it must have come before he prayed for a successor (Num 27:16). Moses asked permission to go over and was denied, but God did show the land to him (Deut 34:1). Moses reminds the congregation that he could not enter because of his sin (Num 20:12; 27:14). The events mentioned in verse 27 actually occur in chapter 34, which shows that Moses must have written some or all of Deuteronomy on Mount Pisgah.

The commission of Joshua to take Moses' place comes from God, i.e., **charge Joshua.** Joshua was a reluctant leader, so God told Moses to **encourage him, and strengthen him.**

D. Israel on the Plains of Moab. 4:1-43.

1. A sermon on obedience. 4:1-40.

4:1-2. With the phrase **Now therefore,** Moses passes from Israel's past and emphasizes the present. Israel is to keep the statutes and judgments. The statutes related to the moral law, and the judgments related to the social law. He tells the nation to **hearken** and **do them,** which is repeating the theme of Deuteronomy, "hear and obey." His promise that **ye may live** does not speak of eternal life, but of a lengthy stay in the land.

Israel was not to delete from or add to the Law. Even Christ did not do that; He came to fulfill the Law (Mt 5:17). **Do them, that ye may live.** God's offer of life to the Jews under the Law was a genuine offer. However, no one was saved by obedience to God's commands, "For as many as are of the works of the law are under the curse: for it is written, Cursed is everyone that continueth not in all things which are written in the book of the law to do them" (Gal 3:10). Men were unable to keep the law completely. Only by God's grace, received through faith by obedience to the sacrifice which God had instituted, did men escape God's condemnation. Because, "Christ hath redeemed us from the curse of the law, being made a curse for us . . ." (Gal 3:13).

3 Your eyes have seen what the LORD did because of Bā′al-pē′ôr: for all the men that followed Bā′al-pē′ôr, the LORD thy God hath destroyed them from among you.

4 But ye that did cleave unto the LORD your God are alive every one of you this day.

5 Behold, I have taught you statutes and judgments, even as the LORD my God commanded me, that ye should do so in the land whither ye go to possess it.

6 Keep therefore and do them; for this is your wisdom and your understanding in the sight of the nations, which shall hear all these statutes, and say, Surely this great nation is a wise and understanding people.

7 For what nation is there so great, who hath God so nigh unto them, as the LORD our God is in all things that we call upon him for?

8 And what nation is there so great, that hath statutes and judgments so righteous as all this law, which I set before you this day?

9 Only take heed to thyself, and keep thy soul diligently, lest thou forget the things which thine eyes have seen, and lest they depart from thy heart all the days of thy life: but teach them thy sons, and thy sons' sons;

10 Specially the day that thou stoodest before the LORD thy God in Hō′rĕb, when the LORD said unto me, Gather me the people together, and I will make them hear my words, that they may learn to fear me all the days that they shall live upon the earth, and that they may teach their children.

11 And ye came near and stood under the mountain; and the mountain burned with fire unto the midst of heaven, with darkness, clouds, and thick darkness.

12 And the LORD spake unto you out of the midst of the fire: ye heard the voice of the words, but saw no similitude; only ye heard a voice.

13 And he declared unto you his covenant, which he commanded you to perform, even ten commandments; and he wrote them upon two tables of stone.

14 ¶And the LORD commanded me at that time to teach you statutes and judgments, that ye might do them in the land whither ye go over to possess it.

15 Take ye therefore good heed unto yourselves; for ye saw no manner of similitude on the day that the LORD spake unto you in Hō′rĕb out of the midst of the fire:

16 Lest ye corrupt yourselves, and make you a graven image, the similitude of any figure, the likeness of male or female,

3-9. The phrase **Your eyes have seen** could be translated, "your eyes the seeing," which means that they actually witnessed the destruction of those who followed Baal-peor. They were alive, which was a forceful illustration of Moses' message. Yet, in the midst of a warning of judgment Moses reminds them of the grace of God. God was near them and heard their prayer.

Three times in this chapter (vss. 9, 15, 23) they are warned to **take heed.**

10-11. The day is a reference to God's giving Israel the Ten Commandments at Mount Sinai. First, God directed Moses to assemble the people before the mountain, so that when they saw the smoke and lightning, they would fear God. Second, they were to come near the mountain, which burned with fire, literally "even the heart of heaven," an awesome picture of the mighty God. The further description of **darkness, clouds, and thick darkness** speaks of the smoking mountain.

12-19. Ye heard the voice of the words, but saw no similitude reinforces the doctrine of God. No person has seen God, for God is spirit (Jn 1:18; 4:24). The only Word of God that has been seen is Jesus who became flesh (Jn 1:1; I Jn 1:1-3).

Israel had received the Ten Commandments (lit., ten words) on two tablets of stone. Here Moses reminds them that they did not see God. This became the basis for warning them about idols. Since they did not know what God looked like, they could not fashion a likeness to Him (lit., form a sculpture). The terrible rebellion of idolatry is twofold. First, God makes man in His image, and man rejects God and makes an idol in his image. Second, man assumes that since God makes a creature to look like Himself, man can pretend to be God and make idols in his own likeness. Israel is also prohibited from worshiping the sun, moon, stars, or anything else (vs. 19).

17 The likeness of any beast that *is* on the earth, the likeness of any winged fowl that flieth in the air,

18 The likeness of any thing that creepeth on the ground, the likeness of any fish that *is* in the waters beneath the earth:

19 And lest thou lift up thine eyes unto heaven, and when thou seest the sun, and the moon, and the stars, *even* all the host of heaven, shouldest be driven to worship them, and serve them, which the LORD thy God hath divided unto all nations under the whole heaven.

20 But the LORD hath taken you, and brought you forth out of the iron furnace, *even* out of Egypt, to be unto him a people of inheritance, as *ye are* this day.

21 Furthermore the LORD was angry with me for your sakes, and sware that I should not go over Jordan, and that I should not go in unto that good land, which the LORD thy God giveth thee *for* an inheritance:

22 But I must die in this land, I must not go over Jordan: but ye shall go over, and possess that good land.

23 Take heed unto yourselves, lest ye forget the covenant of the LORD your God, which he made with you, and make you a graven image, *or* the likeness of any *thing*, which the LORD thy God hath forbidden thee.

24 For the LORD thy God *is* a consuming fire, *even* a jealous God.

25 ¶When thou shalt beget children, and children's children, and ye shall have remained long in the land, and shall corrupt *yourselves*, and make a graven image, *or* the likeness of any *thing*, and shall do evil in the sight of the LORD thy God, to provoke him to anger:

26 I call heaven and earth to witness against you this day, that ye shall soon utterly perish from off the land whereunto ye go over Jordan to possess it; ye shall not prolong *your* days upon it, but shall utterly be destroyed.

27 And the LORD shall scatter you among the nations, and ye shall be left few in number among the heathen, whither the LORD shall lead you.

28 And there ye shall serve gods, the work of men's hands, wood and stone, which neither see, nor hear, nor eat, nor smell.

29 But if from thence thou shalt seek the LORD thy God, thou shalt find *him*, if thou seek him with all thy heart and with all thy soul.

30 When thou art in tribulation, and all these things are come upon thee, *even* in the latter days, if thou turn to the LORD thy God, and shalt be obedient unto his voice;

31 (For the LORD thy God *is* a merciful God;) he will not forsake thee, neither destroy thee, nor forget the covenant of thy fathers which he sware unto them.

32 For ask now of the days that are past, which were before thee, since the day that God created man upon the earth, and *ask* from the one side of

20-25. Moses reminds Israel of punishment in this section by recalling how they suffered in the iron furnace of Egypt. They were a people of inheritance. To reinforce God's punishment if they should sin, Moses tells them of his punishment, **I should not go in unto that good land.** Because of this he describes God as a consuming fire.

26-29. I call heaven and earth to witness against you this day is in the accusative case, which means to give a witness against a person under oath. Heaven and earth are personified, not as the instruments of judgment if they disobey, but as witnesses that God had warned His people against idols. **Not prolong your days** meant that the Lord would scatter them as He had promised. **Ye shall serve gods** is a pitiful description of God's people. When Israel rejected the God of revelation, they also gave up the God of reason and worshiped idols.

Moses has given a prophetic glimpse of Israel's coming ruin because of idolatry. Now he prophetically lays the foundation for national repentance; one day all Israel will be saved (Rom 11:25-27). The condition for future restoration is with **all thy heart.** Paul also calls the Jews to turn their hearts to God (II Cor 3:15-16).

30-31. The latter days is usually a reference to the coming Tribulation, called the time of Jacob's Trouble. When Israel repents, **he will not forsake thee, neither destroy thee.** Moses invites them to **ask** of God. This is a new concept of prayer (Jn 14:14; 16:24).

32-35. Moses reminds Israel that nothing had been heard like it, a reference to God's seeking a captive people, and to the miracles at Sinai. The omnipotent God revealed Himself in three ways in Egypt: first, by signs and wonders (Ex 7:3), second, by

heaven unto the other, whether there hath been *any such thing* as this great thing *is*, or hath been heard like it?

33 Did *ever* people hear the voice of God speaking out of the midst of the fire, as thou hast heard, and live?

34 Or hath God assayed to go *and* take him a nation from the midst of *another* nation, by temptations, by signs, and by wonders, and by war, and by a mighty hand, and by a stretched out arm, and by great terrors, according to all that the LORD your God did for you in Egypt before your eyes?

35 Unto thee it was shewed, that thou mightest know that the LORD he *is* God; *there is* none else beside him.

36 Out of heaven he made thee to hear his voice, that he might instruct thee: and upon earth he shewed thee his great fire; and thou heardest his words out of the midst of the fire.

37 And because he loved thy fathers, therefore he chose their seed after them, and brought thee out in his sight with his mighty power out of Egypt;

38 To drive out nations from before thee greater and mightier than thou *art*, to bring thee in, to give thee their land *for* an inheritance, as *it is* this day.

39 Know therefore this day, and consider *it* in thine heart, that the LORD he *is* God in heaven above, and upon the earth beneath: *there is* none else.

40 Thou shalt keep therefore his statutes, and his commandments, which I command thee this day, that it may go well with thee, and with thy children after thee, and that thou mayest prolong *thy* days upon the earth, which the LORD thy God giveth thee, for ever.

41 ¶Then Moses severed three cities on this side Jordan toward the sunrising;

42 That the slayer might flee thither, which should kill his neighbour unawares, and hated him not in times past; and that fleeing unto one of these cities he might live:

43 *Namely*, Bĕ′zer in the wilderness, in the plain country, of the Reubenites; and Rā′mŏth in Gilead, of the Găd′ītes; and Gŏ′lan in Bā′shan, of the Ma-năs′-sītes.

44 ¶And this *is* the law which Moses set before the children of Israel:

45 These *are* the testimonies, and the statutes, and the judgments, which Moses spake unto the children of Israel, after they came forth out of Egypt,

46 On this side Jordan, in the valley over against Bĕth-pē′ôr, in the land of Sihon king of the Ăm′o-rītes, who dwelt at Hĕsh′bŏn, whom Moses and

conflict (Ex 14:14), and third, by great terror (Ex 12:30-36). Each of these was an agent to lead Israel to magnify the Lord.

36. These miracles were performed to **instruct thee**. This is not a reference to imparting knowledge; it means "to discipline." God wanted Israel under a holy discipline.

37-39. He loved thy fathers does not refer to the preceding thought. The clause is independent, to convince the hearers to be faithful to Abraham, whom Moses had in mind when he said **thy fathers. In his sight** is literally "by his face." God did not use an angel to direct Israel out of Egypt (Ex 33:2); Israel was directed by His own Presence (Ex 33:14-15).

40. Moses surveys how God drove out the nations before Israel and how He will give them the land. If they keep God's commandments, they will dwell in the land **for ever**, literally, "all time for the future."

2. The cities of refuge. 4:41-43.

41-43. Moses introduces a new subject, the three cities of refuge, between his first and second message. They are discussed here because Israel must know that the land belongs to Jehovah, that she would possess the two Amorite kingdoms on the other side of Jordan, and that the people were required to obey the Law. Yet, in the midst of duty, there is forgiveness for those who fail. The cities of refuge stand as citadels of grace in the land of the Law.

III. REHEARSAL OF ISRAEL'S LAW. 4:44-26:19.

This address is the longest in Deuteronomy and begins with a repetition of the Ten Commandments. It includes an explanation of the legal requirements of the Law, that Israel was to strive after righteousness and love the Lord with all her heart (6:5). The message of Moses deals specifically with obedience in the land.

A. Commands Regarding God. 4:44-12:32.

1. The Law as reflected in the Ten Commandments. 4:44-5:33.

44-49. This section begins with a title, **this is the law.** This speaks of the Torah, which every present-day Jew recognizes. Earlier Moses had given a full description of its **testimonies, and . . . statutes, and . . . judgments,** which included every part of the Law. The phrase **after they came forth out of Egypt** is better rendered "on their coming out." God spoke during the march before they reached the Promised Land. The phrase **in the land of Sihon** meant that Israel was standing on land which they had conquered as they listened to Moses. That was the basis upon which God would give them the rest of the Promised Land. The phrase **toward the sunrising** was spoken by faith.

335

the children of Israel smote, after they were come forth out of Egypt:

47 And they possessed his land, and the land of Og king of Bā'shan, two kings of the Ăm'o-rītes, which were on this side Jordan toward the sunrising;

48 From Ar'ō-er, which is by the bank of the river Arnon, even unto mount Sion, which is Hermon,

49 And all the plain on this side Jordan eastward, even unto the sea of the plain, under the springs of Pĭs'gah.

CHAPTER 5

AND Moses called all Israel, and said unto them, Hear, O Israel, the statutes and judgments which I speak in your ears this day, that ye may learn them, and keep, and do them.

2 The LORD our God made a covenant with us in Hō'rĕb.

3 The LORD made not this covenant with our fathers, but with us, even us, who are all of us here alive this day.

4 The LORD talked with you face to face in the mount out of the midst of the fire,

5 (I stood between the LORD and you at that time, to shew you the word of the LORD: for ye were afraid by reason of the fire, and went not up into the mount;) saying,

6 ¶I am the LORD thy God, which brought thee out of the land of Egypt, from the house of bondage.

7 Thou shalt have none other gods before me.

8 Thou shalt not make thee any graven image, or any likeness of any thing that is in heaven above, or that is in the earth beneath, or that is in the waters beneath the earth:

9 Thou shalt not bow down thyself unto them, nor serve them: for I the LORD thy God am a jealous God, visiting the iniquity of the fathers upon the children unto the third and fourth generation of them that hate me,

10 And shewing mercy unto thousands of them that love me and keep my commandments.

11 Thou shalt not take the name of the LORD thy God in vain: for the LORD will not hold him guiltless that taketh his name in vain.

12 Keep the sabbath day to sanctify it, as the LORD thy God hath commanded thee.

13 Six days thou shalt labour, and do all thy work:

14 But the seventh day is the sabbath of the LORD thy God: in it thou shalt not do any work, thou, nor thy son, nor thy daughter, nor thy manservant, nor thy maidservant, nor thine ox, nor thine ass, nor any of thy cattle, nor thy stranger that is within thy gates; that thy manservant and thy maidservant may rest as well as thou.

15 And remember that thou wast a servant in the land of Egypt, and that the LORD thy God brought thee out thence through a mighty hand and by a stretched out arm: therefore the LORD thy God commanded thee to keep the sabbath day.

16 ¶Honour thy father and thy mother, as the LORD thy God hath com-

Moses spoke as though Israel already occupied the land and had to look back east over Jordan where the sun arose.

5:1-5. Moses repeats the four key words of Deuteronomy when he calls Israel together. These words are **Hear** (Heb shama', used over thirty times), **learn** (Heb lamad, seven times), **keep** (Heb shamar, thirty-nine times), and **do** (Heb casah, almost one hundred times). What the Lord demanded of Israel then is still required of His people today. The only difference is that today we are empowered by the Holy Spirit to please the Lord and forgiven by grace when we sin. **The LORD made not this covenant with our fathers** is a reference to the Patriarchs, not to the unfaithful who fell in the wilderness. To emphasize this point, Moses added **even us.** The Lord had talked face-to-face with Israel (Ex 33:11), as one person stands close to another for conversation. It does not mean that Israel saw God's face. Moses adds his role as mediator; he stood between the people and God.

6-22. The ten covenant words are repeated (see Exodus 20:3-17 for full explanation) with some variations, specifically applying the Ten Commandments to Israel as they prepared themselves to enter the Promised Land.

When God first gave the Ten Commandments, He said Israel should keep the Sabbath day because He had rested on the seventh day of creation (Ex 20:11), but here the exhortation is **remember that thou wast a servant in the land of Egypt . . . therefore the LORD thy God commanded thee to keep the sabbath day.**

Moses concludes his repetition of the Ten Commandments by describing what happened after God first gave them to Israel. Three phenomena are noted: fire, clouds, and a great voice (vs. 22). The adverbial form of the latter signifies the loud volume of sound, not the authority of God.

manded thee; that thy days may be prolonged, and that it may go well with thee, in the land which the LORD thy God giveth thee.

17 Thou shalt not kill.

18 Neither shalt thou commit adultery.

19 Neither shalt thou steal.

20 Neither shalt thou bear false witness against thy neighbour.

21 Neither shalt thou desire thy neighbour's wife, neither shalt thou covet thy neighbour's house, his field, or his manservant, or his maidservant, his ox, or his ass, or any *thing* that *is* thy neighbour's.

22 ¶These words the LORD spake unto all your assembly in the mount out of the midst of the fire, of the cloud, and of the thick darkness, with a great voice: and he added no more. And he wrote them in two tables of stone, and delivered them unto me.

23 And it came to pass, when ye heard the voice out of the midst of the darkness, (for the mountain did burn with fire,) that ye came near unto me, *even* all the heads of your tribes, and your elders;

24 And ye said, Behold, the LORD our God hath shewed us his glory and his greatness, and we have heard his voice out of the midst of the fire: we have seen this day that God doth talk with man, and he liveth.

25 Now therefore why should we die? for this great fire will consume us: if we hear the voice of the LORD our God any more, then we shall die.

26 For who *is there of* all flesh, that hath heard the voice of the living God speaking out of the midst of the fire, as we *have*, and lived?

27 Go thou near, and hear all that the LORD our God shall say: and speak thou unto us all that the LORD our God shall speak unto thee; and we will hear *it*, and do *it*.

28 And the LORD heard the voice of your words, when ye spake unto me; and the LORD said unto me, I have heard the voice of the words of this people, which they have spoken unto thee: they have well said all that they have spoken.

29 O that there were such an heart in them, that they would fear me, and keep all my commandments always, that it might be well with them, and with their children for ever!

30 Go say to them, Get you into your tents again.

31 But as for thee, stand thou here by me, and I will speak unto thee all the commandments, and the statutes, and the judgments, which thou shalt teach them, that they may do *them* in the land which I give them to possess it.

32 Ye shall observe to do therefore as the LORD your God hath commanded you: ye shall not turn aside to the right hand or to the left.

33 Ye shall walk in all the ways which the LORD your God hath commanded you, that ye may live, and *that it may be* well with you, and *that* ye may prolong *your* days in the land which ye shall possess.

23-33. Moses reminds his hearers that Israel feared God's judgment, so God appointed a mediator. The Lord knows the heart of Israel and yearns for someone who will obey. Again, this chapter, as many others in Deuteronomy, ends with a demand for obedience.

CHAPTER 6

NOW these *are* the commandments, the statutes, and the judgments, which the LORD your God commanded to teach you, that ye might do *them* in the land whither ye go to possess it:

2 That thou mightest fear the LORD thy God, to keep all his statutes and his commandments, which I command thee, thou, and thy son, and thy son's son, all the days of thy life; and that thy days may be prolonged.

3 ¶Hear therefore, O Israel, and observe to do *it*; that it may be well with thee, and that ye may increase mightily, as the LORD God of thy fathers hath promised thee, in the land that floweth with milk and honey.

4 Hear, O Israel: The LORD our God *is* one LORD:

5 And thou shalt love the LORD thy God with all thine heart, and with all thy soul, and with all thy might.

6 And these words, which I command thee this day, shall be in thine heart:

7 And thou shalt teach them diligently unto thy children, and shalt talk of them when thou sittest in thine house, and when thou walkest by the way, and when thou liest down, and when thou risest up.

8 And thou shalt bind them for a sign upon thine hand, and they shall be as frontlets between thine eyes.

9 And thou shalt write them upon the posts of thy house, and on thy gates.

10 And it shall be, when the LORD thy God shall have brought thee into the land which he sware unto thy fathers, to Abraham, to Isaac, and to Jacob, to give thee great and goodly cities, which thou buildedst not,

11 And houses full of all good *things*, which thou filledst not, and wells digged, which thou diggedst not, vineyards and olive trees, which thou plantedst not; when thou shalt have eaten and be full;

12 *Then* beware lest thou forget the LORD, which brought thee forth out of the land of Egypt, from the house of bondage.

13 Thou shalt fear the LORD thy God, and serve him, and shalt swear by his name.

14 Ye shall not go after other gods, of the gods of the people which *are* round about you;

15 (For the LORD thy God *is* a jealous God among you) lest the anger of the LORD thy God be kindled against thee, and destroy thee from off the face of the earth.

16 ¶Ye shall not tempt the LORD your God, as ye tempted *him* in Măs′sah.

2. The command to love. 6:1-25.

6:1-3. Moses again exhorts Israel to obey the statutes and judgments of the Lord (4:1; 5:1). There are four reasons why the Law had this preeminence: (1) by heeding the Law, Israel would live; (2) keeping the Law warded off God's displeasure; (3) Israel would be respected as a wise people by other nations by obeying God's laws; (4) the Law of God was unique for its high spiritual quality. The phrase **Hear therefore, O Israel** parallels "teach" in verse 1 and is equated with learning.

4-5. These verses are called the *Shema*, after the word **Hear** (Heb *shama'*). Even though some have tried to deny the Trinity because of this verse, the word **one** (Heb *'echad*), means "compound unity." The phrase **one LORD** means God has one name; it is also a testimony against polytheism. Both the unity and the trinity of the Godhead are taught in the Old Testament (Gen 1:26-27; Ps 2:7; Isa 48:16).

Love is the motive behind man's relationship to God. The personal pronoun **thy God** points out the correct object of love. The heart is mentioned first because it is the seat of the intellect (Mk 2:6), emotion (Jn 14:1), and volition, or will (II Cor 9:7; Rom 6:17). Christ calls this "the first and great commandment" (Mt 22:38) and uses it to summarize the first four commandments. God has no higher commandment than love.

6-9. These verses are still carried out literally by many orthodox Jews as they write verses on parchment and place them in little boxes that they bind with strips of leather to their foreheads and upon their hands. Also, they nail them near the doorways of their homes. The intent of this passage is that the Word of God should be hidden in a person's heart and should constantly be a source of devotion and obedience to the Lord. The main thrust was that they should teach their children the Word of God. Verse 7 has become the foundation for the Christian school movement, where the core of the curriculum is the Word of God.

10-19. Gratitude is the least remembered of all virtues, and the Israelites were exposed to the danger of forgetfulness as they entered Canaan. They would enjoy houses, gardens, and wells for which they had not worked, so Moses suggests a formula for remembering God. **Fear** is the first step in not forgetting God, and service is the second. The third step is swearing by his name. This does not merely refer to a solemn oath in court, but rather to an assertive fact whereby a person dedicates his life to live for God. The reference to not tempting the Lord was quoted by Jesus Christ when tempted by Satan in the wilderness. Satan knew that Christ was obedient to the Father and tried to make Him act selfishly.

17 Ye shall diligently keep the commandments of the LORD your God, and his testimonies, and his statutes, which he hath commanded thee.

18 And thou shalt do *that which is* right and good in the sight of the LORD: that it may be well with thee, and that thou mayest go in and possess the good land which the LORD sware unto thy fathers,

19 To cast out all thine enemies from before thee, as the LORD hath spoken.

20 ¶*And* when thy son asketh thee in time to come, saying, What *mean* the testimonies, and the statutes, and the judgments, which the LORD our God hath commanded you?

21 Then thou shalt say unto thy son, We were Pharaoh's bondmen in Egypt; and the LORD brought us out of Egypt with a mighty hand:

22 And the LORD shewed signs and wonders, great and sore, upon Egypt, upon Pharaoh, and upon all his household, before our eyes:

23 And he brought us out from thence, that he might bring us in, to give us the land which he sware unto our fathers.

24 And the LORD commanded us to do all these statutes, to fear the LORD our God, for our good always, that he might preserve us alive, as *it is* at this day.

25 And it shall be our righteousness, if we observe to do all these commandments before the LORD our God, as he hath commanded us.

CHAPTER 7

WHEN the LORD thy God shall bring thee into the land whither thou goest to possess it, and hath cast out many nations before thee, the Hittites, and the Gir'ga-shītes, and the Ăm'o-rītes, and the Canaanites, and the Pĕr'iz-zītes, and the Hī'vītes, and the Jĕb'u-sītes, seven nations greater and mightier than thou;

2 And when the LORD thy God shall deliver them before thee; thou shalt smite them, *and* utterly destroy them; thou shalt make no covenant with them, nor shew mercy unto them:

3 Neither shalt thou make marriages with them; thy daughter thou shalt not give unto his son, nor his daughter shalt thou take unto thy son.

4 For they will turn away thy son from following me, that they may serve other gods: so will the anger of the LORD be kindled against you, and destroy thee suddenly.

5 But thus shall ye deal with them; ye shall destroy their altars, and break down their images, and cut down their groves, and burn their graven images with fire.

6 For thou *art* an holy people unto the LORD thy God: the LORD thy God hath chosen thee to be a special people unto himself, above all people that *are* upon the face of the earth.

7 The LORD did not set his love upon you, nor choose you, because ye were more in number than any people; for ye *were* the fewest of all people:

8 But because the LORD loved you,

20-25. The basis for the education of the young is redemption; their children were to be instructed in the method by which God brought Israel out of Egypt. The reference to **wonders, great and sore** is to the Egyptian plagues, which produced fear in the ungodly as well as in Israel. Moses uses the phrase **it shall be our righteousness,** which implies that their righteousness will come from observing the Law with a willing spirit, not with an empty obedience. Moses adds the phrase **before the LORD our God** which refers back to a heart attitude of love (vs. 5).

3. The command to destroy the Canaanites. 7:1-26.

7:1-9. As Israel has been warned against idolatry, now Moses exhorts them to beware of tolerating Canaanites in the land, because the presence of the heathen nation would tempt them to idolatry. He lists the nations that are greater and mightier than Israel, noting that they must be destroyed. Israel could make no covenant with them, nor could they marry their young. God tells Israel to completely destroy the remains of idolatry after the heathen nations are eliminated. Israel was a better people, not because of who they were, but because they were holy unto the Lord. God elevated them by choosing them. God's motive for choosing Israel was love, and the Lord wanted reciprocity; Israel should love God.

339

and because he would keep the oath which he had sworn unto your fathers, hath the LORD brought you out with a mighty hand, and redeemed you out of the house of bondmen, from the hand of Pharaoh king of Egypt.

9 Know therefore that the LORD thy God, he *is* God, the faithful God, which keepeth covenant and mercy with them that love him and keep his commandments to a thousand generations;

10 And repayeth them that hate him to their face, to destroy them: he will not be slack to him that hateth him, he will repay him to his face.

11 Thou shalt therefore keep the commandments, and the statutes, and the judgments, which I command thee this day, to do them.

12 Wherefore it shall come to pass, if ye hearken to these judgments, and keep, and do them, that the LORD thy God shall keep unto thee the covenant and the mercy which he sware unto thy fathers:

13 And he will love thee, and bless thee, and multiply thee: he will also bless the fruit of thy womb, and the fruit of thy land, thy corn, and thy wine, and thine oil, the increase of thy kine, and the flocks of thy sheep, in the land which he sware unto thy fathers to give thee.

14 Thou shalt be blessed above all people: there shall not be male or female barren among you, or among your cattle.

15 And the LORD will take away from thee all sickness, and will put none of the evil diseases of Egypt, which thou knowest, upon thee; but will lay them upon all *them* that hate thee.

16 And thou shalt consume all the people which the LORD thy God shall deliver thee; thine eye shall have no pity upon them: neither shalt thou serve their gods; for that *will be* a snare unto thee.

17 If thou shalt say in thine heart, These nations *are* more than I; how can I dispossess them?

18 Thou shalt not be afraid of them: *but* shalt well remember what the LORD thy God did unto Pharaoh, and unto all Egypt;

19 The great temptations which thine eyes saw, and the signs, and the wonders, and the mighty hand, and the stretched out arm, whereby the LORD thy God brought thee out: so shall the LORD thy God do unto all the people of whom thou art afraid.

20 Moreover the LORD thy God will send the hornet among them, until they that are left, and hide themselves from thee, be destroyed.

21 Thou shalt not be affrighted at them: for the LORD thy God *is* among you, a mighty God and terrible.

22 And the LORD thy God will put out those nations before thee by little and little: thou mayest not consume them at once, lest the beasts of the field increase upon thee.

23 But the LORD thy God shall deliver them unto thee, and shall destroy them

10-17. God does not delay judgment on those that hate Him. **Destroy** means to cause them to perish. Israel would be blessed by observing the commandments of God. The phrase **hearken to these judgments** literally means the "demand of right." The Law, which was an expression of the nature of God, demands obedience. When Israel kept the Law, they would receive the blessings of the fruit of the body (children), the fruit of the field (crops), and the fruit of cattle (sheep and other animals). Also, Israel would be preserved from diseases, especially the malignancies that might have come from Egypt. Later, God would use diseases to bring Israel's enemies to defeat. With this in mind, Moses emphasized again the command to blot out the Canaanites.

18-26. Moses reminds his hearers of the numerous ways by which God would defeat their enemies. God had promised to drive out the nations gradually (Ex 23:30). Here is an insight into the protective care of the Lord. The enemy would be driven out slowly so that wild beasts would not take over the land. Israel was commanded to burn the idols of the Canaanites lest they become a temptation. An idol is an image made by man, whereas man is made in the image of God. God hates idols for two reasons: first, because man makes himself God by following the same role as God in creation; and second, because the idol becomes a substitute for God.

with a mighty destruction, until they be destroyed.

24 And he shall deliver their kings into thine hand, and thou shalt destroy their name from under heaven: there shall no man be able to stand before thee, until thou have destroyed them.

25 The graven images of their gods shall ye burn with fire: thou shalt not desire the silver or gold *that is* on them, nor take *it* unto thee, lest thou be snared therin: for it *is* an abomination to the Lord thy God.

26 Neither shalt thou bring an abomination into thine house, lest thou be a cursed thing like it: *but* thou shalt utterly detest it, and thou shalt utterly abhor it; for it *is* a cursed thing.

CHAPTER 8

ALL the commandments which I command thee this day shall ye observe to do, that ye may live, and mulitply, and go in and possess the land which the Lord sware unto your fathers.

2 And thou shalt remember all the way which the Lord thy God led thee these forty years in the wilderness, to humble thee, *and* to prove thee, to know what *was* in thine heart, whether thou wouldest keep his commandments, or no.

3 And he humbled thee, and suffered thee to hunger, and fed thee with manna, which thou knewest not, neither did thy fathers know; that he might make thee know that man doth not live by bread only, but by every *word* that proceedeth out of the mouth of the Lord doth man live.

4 Thy raiment waxed not old upon thee, neither did thy foot swell, these forty years.

5 Thou shalt also consider in thine heart, that, as a man chasteneth his son, *so* the Lord thy God chasteneth thee.

6 Therefore thou shalt keep the commandments of the Lord thy God, to walk in his ways, and to fear him.

7 For the Lord thy God bringeth thee into a good land, a land of brooks of water, of fountains and depths that spring out of valleys and hills;

8 A land of wheat, and barley, and vines, and fig trees, and pomegranates; a land of oil olive, and honey;

9 A land wherein thou shalt eat bread without scarceness, thou shalt not lack any *thing* in it; a land whose stones *are* iron, and out of whose hills thou mayest dig brass.

10 When thou hast eaten and art full, then thou shalt bless the Lord thy God for the good land which he hath given thee.

11 Beware that thou forget not the Lord thy God, in not keeping his commandments, and his judgments, and his statutes, which I command thee this day:

12 Lest *when* thou hast eaten and art full, and hast built goodly houses, and dwelt *therein*;

13 And *when* thy herds and thy flocks multiply, and thy silver and thy gold is

4. Remembering God's past work. 8:1-10:11.

8:1-6. Moses introduces another threat, namely, that Israel would forget God and become proud of her attainments. Therefore, the people are reminded of the forty years spent in the wilderness because: (1) they had learned humility; (2) God had proved their faithfulness; and (3) God had revealed what was in their hearts. God had fed them manna, a food that was unknown to them. The phrase **every word that proceedeth out of the mouth of the Lord** is more than just a reference to Scripture; it refers to the entire will of God that preserves the life of man. God had protected them by not allowing their clothes to wear out, nor their feet to become tender. God was educating Israel as His sons. **As a man chasteneth his son** means to educate a son by negative discipline. God intended the entire wilderness wandering as an education for Israel.

7-20. To educate the people in the goodness of God, Moses exhorts them to obedience, based on the fact that God gave them a good land with plenty of water (vs. 7), good fertility (vs. 8), and mineral prosperity (vs. 9). But Israel is warned not to forget the lessons of the past when they come into prosperity. There was danger in wealth and ease. Their children might turn from God because they would not appreciate the good things of life. Therefore, God reminds them of the noxious and fatal things of the wilderness, such as serpents, no water, and hard rocks. He also reminds them that during their wanderings He had fed them (vs. 16) and taken care of them (vs. 17). The basis of Moses' exhortation was that God **giveth thee power to get wealth;** therefore do not disobey Him. The phrase **as it is this day** means that the establishment of God's covenant of Palestine had already commenced.

multiplied, and all that thou hast is multiplied;

14 Then thine heart be lifted up, and thou forget the LORD thy God, which brought thee forth out of the land of Egypt, from the house of bondage;

15 Who led thee through that great and terrible wilderness, *wherein were* fiery serpents, and scorpions, and drought, where *there was* no water; who brought thee forth water out of the rock of flint;

16 Who fed thee in the wilderness with manna, which thy fathers knew not, that he might humble thee, and that he might prove thee, to do thee good at thy latter end;

17 And thou say in thine heart, My power and the might of *mine* hand hath gotten me this wealth.

18 But thou shalt remember the LORD thy God: for *it is* he that giveth thee power to get wealth, that he may establish his covenant which he sware unto thy fathers, as *it is* this day.

19 And it shall be, if thou do at all forget the LORD thy God, and walk after other gods, and serve them, and worship them, I testify against you this day that ye shall surely perish.

20 As the nations which the LORD destroyeth before your face, so shall ye perish; because ye would not be obedient unto the voice of the LORD your God.

CHAPTER 9

HEAR, O Israel: Thou *art* to pass over Jordan this day, to go in to possess nations greater and mightier than thyself, cities great and fenced up to heaven,

2 A people great and tall, the children of the Anakims, whom thou knowest, and *of whom* thou hast heard *say*, Who can stand before the children of Anak!

3 Understand therefore this day, that the LORD thy God *is* he which goeth over before thee; *as* a consuming fire he shall destroy them, and he shall bring them down before thy face: so shalt thou drive them out, and destroy them quickly, as the LORD hath said unto thee.

4 Speak not thou in thine heart, after that the LORD thy God hath cast them out from before thee, saying, For my righteousness the LORD hath brought me in to possess this land: but for the wickedness of these nations the LORD doth drive them out from before thee.

5 Not for thy righteousness, or for the uprightness of thine heart, dost thou go to possess their land: but for the wickedness of these nations the LORD thy God doth drive them out from before thee, and that he may perform the word which the LORD sware unto thy fathers, Abraham, Isaac, and Jacob.

6 Understand therefore, that the LORD thy God giveth thee not this good land to possess it for thy righteousness; for thou *art* a stiffnecked people.

7 ¶Remember, *and* forget not, how thou provokedst the LORD thy God to wrath in the wilderness: from the day that thou didst depart out of the land of Egypt, until ye came unto this place, ye have been rebellious against the LORD.

9:1-3. In this chapter Moses turns his attention to two more of Israel's problems, i.e., pride and self-righteousness. Instead of receiving the blessings of the Promised Land as unmerited gifts of grace, Israel felt they deserved the land. The reason is not given; perhaps it was because they felt it was promised to them, or because of some good work they had done. The reference to **this day** is an indication that the time was at hand to possess the Promised Land. Their enemies were superior in size and strength, and they dwelt in cities; yet the Lord promised to destroy them. The phrase **Thou art to pass** is an imperative; Israel was commanded to enter the land. The twofold repetition of destroy indicates a complete destruction.

4-6. God sees conceit in Israel as indicated by the phrase **For my righteousness.** Moses reminds Israel that it is not for her righteousness, but because of their wickedness, that the nations are to be destroyed. God is to give them the land, not because of their righteousness, but because of His promise to the Patriarchs. Therefore, the occupation of the Promised Land was due to the free grace of God, not to any merit on Israel's part. This is a picture of salvation which comes by grace through faith (Eph 2:8-9).

7-11. This section begins with the exhortation **Remember.** God is reminding Israel of her rebellion. This statement reduces her self-righteousness. Israel's rebellion began from the day **that thou didst depart.** Even before the children of Israel went through the Red Sea, they began rebelling against God. Hence the tragedy of rebellion is not in the act, but in the attitude of the

8 Also in Hŏ'rĕb ye provoked the LORD to wrath, so that the LORD was angry with you to have destroyed you.

9 When I was gone up into the mount to receive the tables of stone, *even* the tables of the covenant which the LORD made with you, then I abode in the mount forty days and forty nights, I neither did eat bread nor drink water.

10 And the LORD delivered unto me two tables of stone written with the finger of God; and on them *was written* according to all the words, which the LORD spake with you in the mount out of the midst of the fire in the day of the assembly.

11 And it came to pass at the end of forty days and forty nights, *that* the LORD gave me the two tables of stone, *even* the tables of the covenant.

12 And the LORD said unto me, Arise, get thee down quickly from hence; for thy people which thou hast brought forth out of Egypt have corrupted *themselves*; they are quickly turned aside out of the way which I commanded them; they have made them a molten image.

13 Furthermore the LORD spake unto me, saying, I have seen this people, and, behold, it *is* a stiffnecked people:

14 Let me alone, that I may destroy them, and blot out their name from under heaven: and I will make of thee a nation mightier and greater than they.

15 So I turned and came down from the mount, and the mount burned with fire: and the two tables of the covenant *were* in my two hands.

16 And I looked, and, behold, ye had sinned against the LORD your God, *and* had made you a molten calf: ye had turned aside quickly out of the way which the LORD had commanded you.

17 And I took the two tables, and cast them out of my two hands, and brake them before your eyes.

18 And I fell down before the LORD, as at the first, forty days and forty nights: I did neither eat bread, nor drink water, because of all your sins which ye sinned, in doing wickedly in the sight of the LORD, to provoke him to anger.

19 For I was afraid of the anger and hot displeasure, wherewith the LORD was wroth against you to destroy you. But the LORD hearkened unto me at that time also.

20 And the LORD was very angry with Aaron to have destroyed him: and I prayed for Aaron also the same time.

21 And I took your sin, the calf which ye had made, and burnt it with fire, and stamped it, *and* ground *it* very small, *even* until it was as small as dust: and I cast the dust thereof into the brook that descended out of the mount.

22 And at Tăb'e-rah, and at Măs'sah, and at Kĭb'rŏth-hat-tā'a-vah, ye provoked the LORD to wrath.

23 Likewise when the LORD sent you from Kā'desh-bär'ne-a, saying, Go up and possess the land which I have given you; then ye rebelled against the commandment of the LORD your God, and ye believed him not, nor hearkened to his voice.

heart. They began rebelling the day they left their Egyptian captors. Also, while at Mount Horeb receiving the Ten Commandments, Israel had openly sinned against God. Moses reminds them that he spent forty days and nights fasting. The number forty symbolizes judgment. (The Law judges sin but never saves the sinner.)

12-21. While Moses was praying, God told him to **get . . . down quickly** to perform a twofold responsibility: first, to stop the apostasy of making the golden calf; and second, to divert by intercession the divine execution of the people by God. Moses reminds his hearers that when he came down from the mountain, he broke the two tablets of the Ten Commandments because the people had sinned (vss. 15-17). Then he reminds them that he had interceded before God. In the two phrases **ye had turned aside** and **because of all your sins** Moses identifies the guilt of the present congregation with their fathers who had sinned, again condemning their self-righteousness. He identifies Aaron as one who was to have been destroyed because of disobedience. Even though Aaron was not yet a high priest, he was condemned because he had been one of the leaders of Israel. The details of how they had to get rid of the golden calf are not coincidental. Moses wants to remind them of their rebellion.

22-24. In verses 22-24 Moses gives a list of other occasions when Israel had rebelled against God. The list is not arranged chronologically, but begins with the smaller offenses and progresses to the more serious rebellion.

24 Ye have been rebellious against the LORD from the day that I knew you.

25 Thus I fell down before the LORD forty days and forty nights, as I fell down *at the first*; because the LORD had said he would destroy you.

26 I prayed therefore unto the LORD, and said, O Lord GOD, destroy not thy people and thine inheritance, which thou hast redeemed through thy greatness, which thou hast brought forth out of Egypt with a mighty hand.

27 Remember thy servants, Abraham, Isaac, and Jacob; look not unto the stubbornness of this people, nor to their wickedness, nor to their sin:

28 Lest the land whence thou broughtest us out say, Because the LORD was not able to bring them into the land which he promised them, and because he hated them, he hath brought them out to slay them in the wilderness.

29 Yet they *are* thy people and thine inheritance, which thou broughtest out by thy mighty power and by thy stretched out arm.

CHAPTER 10

AT that time the LORD said unto me, Hew thee two tables of stone like unto the first, and come up unto me into the mount, and make thee an ark of wood.

2 And I will write on the tables the words that were in the first tables which thou brakest, and thou shalt put them in the ark.

3 And I made an ark *of* shittim wood, and hewed two tables of stone like unto the first, and went up into the mount, having the two tables in mine hand.

4 And he wrote on the tables, according to the first writing, the ten commandments, which the LORD spake unto you in the mount out of the midst of the fire in the day of the assembly: and the LORD gave them unto me.

5 And I turned myself and came down from the mount, and put the tables in the ark which I had made; and there they be, as the LORD commanded me.

6 ¶And the children of Israel took their journey from Bē-ē'rŏth of the children of Jā'a-kăn to Mō-sē'ra: there Aaron died, and there he was buried; and Ē-le-ā'zar his son ministered in the priest's office in his stead.

7 From thence they journeyed unto Gŭd'gō-dah; and from Gŭd'gō-dah to Jŏt'băth, a land of rivers of waters.

8 ¶At that time the LORD separated the tribe of Levi, to bear the ark of the covenant of the LORD, to stand before the LORD to minister unto him, and to bless in his name, unto this day.

9 Wherefore Levi hath no part nor inheritance with his brethren; the LORD *is* his inheritance, according as the LORD thy God promised him.

10 ¶And I stayed in the mount, according to the first time, forty days and forty nights; and the LORD hearkened unto me at that time also, *and* the LORD would not destroy thee.

11 And the LORD said unto me, Arise, take *thy* journey before the people, that

25-29. Moses identifies the people as belonging to God, not to him, **thy people and thine inheritance.** Israel was not Moses' nation; they belonged to God. He prayed for God to deliver them because the honor of God in the sight of the other nations would have been tarnished if they had been destroyed. Moses also reminds God that He cannot destroy the people because of the promises that He had made to Abraham, Isaac, and Jacob.

10:1-7. Moses reminds his hearers of the success of his intercession. The phrase **At that time** refers to the second reception of the Law, when Moses hewed out new tablets himself. His reference to putting the Ten Commandments in the ark does not refer to a chronological sequence of events; the ark was not constructed until the tabernacle was made. When Moses hewed out the two tablets, God had already given him the blueprint for the ark of the covenant. Instead, Moses is referring to their ultimate resting place.

The reference to the Ten Commandments, according to the first writing, was proof that God had restored the covenant with Israel (vs. 4). When Moses broke the commandments after Israel had made a golden calf, that symbolically broke their covenant relationship. Putting the Ten Commandments in the ark in the midst of the people symbolically showed that Israel accepted their part of the covenant and would obey the commandments.

8-11. God had forgiven Aaron and had conferred the priesthood upon him. The phrase **At that time** is a reference to the death of Aaron. His son Eleazar was then invested with the high priesthood in Aaron's stead. This reference to his death and Eleazar's appointment spoke symbolically to Israel. Their fathers had sinned and now, as sons, they were to carry out the commands of God. The reference to Moses' intercession showed that the High Priest had been maintained by Moses' prayer.

The reference to the appointment of the tribe of Levi for priestly service carried with it a spiritual inheritance. They could not own property (18:1-2); they were to be sustained by the gifts that the people brought to the place of worship. When God tells them to **Arise, take thy journey before the people** (vs. 11), He was speaking in terms of priority. The Levites were

they may go in and possess the land, which I sware unto their fathers to give unto them.

12 ¶And now, Israel, what doth the LORD thy God require of thee, but to fear the LORD thy God, to walk in all his ways, and to love him, and to serve the LORD thy God with all thy heart and with all thy soul,

13 To keep the commandments of the LORD, and his statutes, which I command thee this day for thy good?

14 Behold, the heaven and the heaven of heavens *is* the LORD's thy God, the earth *also*, with all that therein *is*.

15 Only the LORD had a delight in thy fathers to love them, and he chose their seed after them, *even* you above all people, as *it is* this day.

16 Circumcise therefore the foreskin of your heart, and be no more stiffnecked.

17 For the LORD your God *is* God of gods, and Lord of lords, a great God, a mighty, and a terrible, which regardeth not persons, nor taketh reward:

18 He doth execute the judgment of the fatherless and widow, and loveth the stranger, in giving him food and raiment.

19 Love ye therefore the stranger: for ye were strangers in the land of Egypt.

20 Thou shalt fear the LORD thy God; him shalt thou serve, and to him shalt thou cleave, and swear by his name.

21 He *is* thy praise, and he *is* thy God, that hath done for thee these great and terrible things, which thine eyes have seen.

22 Thy fathers went down into Egypt with threescore and ten persons; and now the LORD thy God hath made thee as the stars of heaven for multitude.

CHAPTER 11

THEREFORE thou shalt love the LORD thy God, and keep his charge, and his statutes, and his judgments, and his commandments, alway.

2 And know ye this day: for *I speak* not with your children which have not known, and which have not seen the chastisement of the LORD your God, his greatness, his mighty hand, and his stretched out arm,

3 And his miracles, and his acts, which he did in the midst of Egypt unto Pharaoh the king of Egypt, and unto all his land;

4 And what he did unto the army of Egypt, unto their horses, and to their chariots; how he made the water of the Red sea to overflow them as they pursued after you, and *how* the LORD hath destroyed them unto this day;

5 And what he did unto you in the wilderness, until ye came into this place;

6 And what he did unto Dā'than and A-bī'ram, the sons of E-lī'ab, the son of Reuben: how the earth opened her mouth, and swallowed them up, and their households, and their tents, and

to carry the ark upon their shoulders before Israel. More than being a spiritual example, they led the procession and went before the people in the wilderness. Finally, when the tabernacle was set up, they stood before the Lord to serve Him (18:5; 21:5).

5. The call to dedication. 10:12-11:32.

12-17. God would not tolerate self-righteousness. He gave Israel three commands of fear, love, and obedience to counteract their self-conceit. These commands are hard for the natural man to fulfill because his heart is deceitful and rebellious. Fear is the first command and begins with man's knowledge of his unholiness in the presence of a righteous God. Biblical love is built on grace; and only when a man realizes that he is a sinner, can he love God because of redemption. The final step is obedience, which is **for thy good.** The *Shema* (6:4-5) exhorted Israel only to love; Moses now adds fear and obedience because of the sovereignty of God. To accomplish this, God calls for them to **Circumcise . . . the foreskin of your heart.** Every Jew understood circumcision of the flesh; it was the sign of the Abrahamic covenant and the basis of becoming a Jew. Now God speaks of spiritual matters. They were told to become "Jews of the heart." The phrase **God of gods and Lord of lords** shows the absolute exclusiveness of God. There is no other God, and all idols are false.

18-21. The Lord is concerned about defenseless orphans and widows because of His loving care, so he instructs Israel to look after them. The basis for Israel's providing for sojourners was the fact that they once were sojourners. **He is thy praise** means, literally, "He is the song of praise," an exhortation to strong expressions of praise because the Lord gives songs in the heart.

22. Israel consisted of seventy souls when they went into Egypt. God had foretold that in Egypt Israel would be made a great nation (Gen 15:13-14), and now they were an innumerable host. God was beginning to fulfill the prophecy that they would become as the stars of heaven.

11:1-5. In this chapter, Moses again ties obedience to love. That is why many refer to this book as the "gospel of Deuteronomy." Israel had previously been told to keep God's statutes, judgments, and commandments; now Moses adds the phrase **his charge,** which refers to the exhortations in the book of Deuteronomy. He reminds his hearers that they had **not seen the chastisement of the LORD.** They had been children in the wilderness and had not experienced the plagues that came upon Egypt, even though they had seen the miracles in the wilderness. His hearers were forty to sixty years old; all the others had died. Therefore, Moses reminds them of God's miracle in overthrowing Pharaoh and his army in the Red Sea. The phrase **overflow them** is literally "over whose face he made the waters of the Red Sea to flow." Here Moses reminds them that their enemies had been drowned.

6. Moses also reminds his hearers of the rebellion of Korah (Num 16). However, Korah's name is not mentioned, only the names of his followers, Dathan and Abiram. Moses might be considering the sons who were present and listening to his message; they had not been swallowed up with their families,

all the substance that *was* in their possession, in the midst of all Israel:

7 But your eyes have seen all the great acts of the LORD which he did.

8 Therefore shall ye keep all the commandments which I command you this day, that ye may be strong, and go in and possess the land, whither ye go to possess it;

9 And that ye may prolong *your* days in the land, which the LORD sware unto your fathers to give unto them and to their seed, a land that floweth with milk and honey.

10 ¶For the land, whither thou goest in to possess it, *is* not as the land of Egypt, from whence ye came out, where thou sowedst thy seed, and wateredst *it* with thy foot, as a garden of herbs:

11 But the land, whither ye go to possess it, *is* a land of hills and valleys, *and* drinketh water of the rain of heaven:

12 A land which the LORD thy God careth for: the eyes of the LORD thy God *are* always upon it, from the beginning of the year even unto the end of the year.

13 ¶And it shall come to pass, if ye shall hearken diligently unto my commandments which I command you this day, to love the LORD your God, and to serve him with all your heart and with all your soul,

14 That I will give *you* the rain of your land in his due season, the first rain and the latter rain, that thou mayest gather in thy corn, and thy wine, and thine oil.

15 And I will send grass in thy fields for thy cattle, that thou mayest eat and be full.

16 Take heed to yourselves, that your heart be not deceived, and ye turn aside, and serve other gods, and worship them;

17 And *then* the LORD's wrath be kindled against you, and he shut up the heaven, that there be no rain, and that the land yield not her fruit; and *lest* ye perish quickly from off the good land which the LORD giveth you.

18 ¶Therefore shall ye lay up these my words in your heart and in your soul, and bind them for a sign upon your hand, that they may be as frontlets between your eyes.

19 And ye shall teach them your children, speaking of them when thou sittest in thine house, and when thou walkest by the way, when thou liest down, and when thou risest up.

20 And thou shalt write them upon the door posts of thine house, and upon thy gates:

21 That your days may be multiplied, and the days of your children, in the land which the LORD sware unto your fathers to give them, as the days of heaven upon the earth.

22 ¶For if ye shall diligently keep all these commandments which I command you, to do them, to love the LORD your God, to walk in all his ways, and to cleave unto him;

23 Then will the LORD drive out all these nations from before you, and ye

even though all their possessions had been lost in the earthquake.

7-12. The miracles in the wilderness were educational in nature, so that Israel might see and learn. Therefore, Israel is exhorted to obedience. However, Moses adds a new reason for obedience. When they enter the Promised Land, it will be a land of fertility ordered by the hand of God. They will drink the water of the rain of heaven. In comparison, they had come from Egypt, which was irrigated by the flooding of the Nile or by man. There was not enough rain in Egypt. **Wateredst it with thy foot** refers to the large pumping wheels worked by foot to draw water from the Nile for the gardens. Israel was reminded that God would give them water from heaven to water the Promised Land; so they should not sin against God, since He could shut up heaven. Finally, Moses reminds Israel that God had picked out this spot for them from the beginning of time. They should live in dependence upon the Lord who loved them.

13-17. Moses continues describing the land which Israel would inherit if they obeyed and served the Lord with all of their heart and soul (see 6:5). The early rain would fall from the middle of October through January, to prepare the ground for seeds. The latter rain would fall in March and April and cause germination, so that the crops would grow. There is a false theory that the latter rain means a spiritual revival or a special outpouring of the Holy Spirit that will come in this time, or right before the coming of Christ. There is no foundation in the Word of God for such a "spiritualizing" of this verse. Moses is referring to God's blessing upon the Promised Land; the reference is to grass in the field and the growing of crops. God provided these rains so that Israel might not serve other gods. However, if Israel rebelled, God threatened that there would be no rain and they would perish from the land.

18-21. So that Israel might continue to obey God, they were told to make sure that the Word of God was bound upon their hand, placed between their eyes, and taught to their children at all times of the day (vss. 18-19; cf. also 6:6-9). When Israel obeyed God, the land would be theirs **as the days of heaven upon the earth.** This meant as long as heaven continued upon the earth. This is the basis by which Israel will one day occupy the land during the Kingdom Age. The promise of the land continues forever. The boundaries of the Promised Land are from the desert (Arabia on the south) to Lebanon (on the north), and from the river Euphrates (on the east) to the Mediterranean Sea (on the west).

22-29. Moses sets before Israel a blessing and a curse. He explains these by a reference to two mountains, Mount Gerizim, the mountain of blessing, and Mount Ebal, the mountain of cursing. These mountains are located in the middle of the Promised Land and face each other across a valley approximately sixteen hundred feet wide. Later, Israel will stand and read blessings from Mount Gerizim, and others will repeat

shall possess greater nations and mightier than yourselves.

24 Every place whereon the soles of your feet shall tread shall be yours: from the wilderness and Lebanon, from the river, the river Eū-phrā'tēs, even unto the uttermost sea shall your coast be.

25 There shall no man be able to stand before you: for the LORD your God shall lay the fear of you and the dread of you upon all the land that ye shall tread upon, as he hath said unto you.

26 ¶Behold, I set before you this day a blessing and a curse;

27 A blessing, if ye obey the commandments of the LORD your God, which I command you this day:

28 And a curse, if ye will not obey the commandments of the LORD your God, but turn aside out of the way which I command you this day, to go after other gods, which ye have not known.

29 And it shall come to pass, when the LORD thy God hath brought thee in unto the land whither thou goest to possess it, that thou shalt put the blessing upon mount Gĕr'i-zĭm, and the curse upon mount Ebal.

30 Are they not on the other side Jordan, by the way where the sun goeth down, in the land of the Canaanites, which dwell in the champaign over against Gilgal, beside the plains of Mô'reh?

31 For ye shall pass over Jordan to go in to possess the land which the LORD your God giveth you, and ye shall possess it, and dwell therein.

32 And ye shall observe to do all the statutes and judgments which I set before you this day.

CHAPTER 12

THESE are the statutes and judgments, which ye shall observe to do in the land, which the LORD God of thy fathers giveth thee to possess it, all the days that ye live upon the earth.

2 Ye shall utterly destroy all the places, wherein the nations which ye shall possess served their gods, upon the high mountains, and upon the hills, and under every green tree:

3 And ye shall overthrow their altars, and break their pillars, and burn their groves with fire; and ye shall hew down the graven images of their gods, and destroy the names of them out of that place.

4 Ye shall not do so unto the LORD your God.

5 But unto the place which the LORD your God shall choose out of all your tribes to put his name there, even unto his habitation shall ye seek, and thither thou shalt come:

curses from Mount Ebal. This symbolic reading of the blessings and cursings will remind Israel that they are to obey the Word of the Lord if they want to receive His blessings. If they disobey, God will send curses upon them.

30-32. The phrase **by the way where the sun goeth down** is a reference to the other side of the river. Moses was showing Israel how to find the mountains of blessing and cursing. Even by giving them directions, Moses is building their anticipation of occupying the land. He tells them that they are on the other side of Jordan, which kindles their desire to go over into the Promised Land.

6. *The command concerning a central place of worship. 12:1-32.*

12:1-5. The main emphasis in this chapter is on the place where Israel should worship. The promises and commands of this chapter were to be carried out in the land, and on six occasions (vss. 5, 11, 14, 18, 21, and 26) God demands that Israel worship in a specific geographical place. Many see the local church in this chapter. The church, however, was not established until the New Testament (Mt 16:18). But, just as God had a place for public worship in the Old Testament, so He also has a place for corporate worship in the New Testament. In the Old Testament the place was central; in the New Testament it is local. In the Old Testament there were four qualifications for the place of worship: first, God's name was there (vs. 11); second, His presence was there (vs. 11); third, the symbols of redemption, such as the burnt offerings and sacrifices, were there; fourth, the Levite was ministering at the place. In the New Testament, God's place for assembly is His church. The name of the Lord is there (I Cor 1:2; I Thess 1:1); Christ's presence is there (Col 1:24); the symbols of redemption, which are the ordinances of baptism and the Lord's table, are there; and God has given to it His gifted men (Eph 4:11-12).

In the Old Testament God's presence originally resided in the tabernacle, where He manifested Himself to Israel. When Israel first entered the land, God chose to manifest Himself (Ex 20:23-24) in Shiloh (Josh 18:1). Later He told David to build a sanctuary on the site of the threshing floor of Araunah (II Sam 24:18; I Chr 21:18). This was ultimately the site of Solomon's temple in Jerusalem.

The sanctity of God's place is seen in verses 1-4, because they were commanded to destroy all of **the places** where the foreign gods were worshiped. The heathen worshiped idols everywhere, on high mountains, under green trees, and wherever else they chose. Specifically, Israel was commanded to destroy the altars, break the pillars, and burn the trees with fire. God wanted all remnants of idolatry blotted out because He understood the temptation these would become to His people. Notice that the word **place** (vs. 3) referred to the heathen gods. The heathens had a place for gods on every hillside. In contrast, God had one place where He manifested Himself.

The problem with worship was not geography, but rebellion. Man wanted to worship God when and where he chose, which is a rebellion that continues today. Man does not want to submit to God's laws and worship according to God's ways. The Lord has given certain directions, and we must follow them. Even today, "not every place" is acceptable for corporate worship. According to the New Testament, our "place" is not the tabernacle or Temple, but rather the local church, where one must be baptized in the name of the Father, the Son, and the Holy Spirit as a testimony to his identification with Jesus Christ (Mt 28:19-20) and use his gifts to serve Him.

The phrase **thither thou shalt come** is more than a suggestion; it is a command that every Israelite come to the designated place (vs. 18). The Patriarchs worshiped God in many places. For example, Abraham offered sacrifices to God in his travels. But Abraham was a Patriarch with the responsibility of the spiritual oversight of his people. That included acting as priest, prophet, and king. He led his group of people in the worship of God. Israel was in a new dispensation with a new priesthood. Therefore, each person was to go to God's designated place and worship according to the plans laid down by God.

6-11. Moses gives a list of things that are to be brought to "the place." These included burnt offerings, sacrifices, tithes, heave offerings, vows, and free-will offerings. An Israelite could not pay his tithe in just any place; it had to be brought to God's place. Some of the animal sacrifices and food crops were to be eaten with the Levite in worship to God. They were not to eat the tithe offering at any place, or else they would be guilty of man-made religion. This is expressed in the phrase **every man whatsoever is right in his own eyes** (vs. 8). Moses is not warning them of open idolatry, but of worshiping in a disobedient manner.

Israel was to bring all of their offerings to God at His chosen place. The phrase **all your choice vows** means "the result of your vows," or the equivalent of fulfilling their promise to God.

6 And thither ye shall bring your burnt offerings, and your sacrifices, and your tithes, and heave offerings of your hand, and your vows, and your freewill offerings, and the firstlings of your herds and of your flocks:

7 And there ye shall eat before the LORD your God, and ye shall rejoice in all that ye put your hand unto, ye and your households, wherein the LORD thy God hath blessed thee.

8 Ye shall not do after all *the things* that we do here this day, every man whatsoever *is* right in his own eyes.

9 For ye are not as yet come to the rest and to the inheritance, which the LORD your God giveth you.

10 But *when* ye go over Jordan, and dwell in the land which the LORD your God giveth you to inherit, and *when* he giveth you rest from all your enemies round about, so that ye dwell in safety;

11 Then there shall be a place which the LORD your God shall choose to cause his name to dwell there; thither shall ye bring all that I command you; your burnt offerings, and your sacrifices, your tithes, and the heave offering of your hand, and all your choice vows which ye vow unto the LORD:

12 And ye shall rejoice before the LORD your God, ye, and your sons, and your daughters, and your menservants, and your maidservants, and the Levite that *is* within your gates; forasmuch as he hath no part nor inheritance with you.

13 Take heed to thyself that thou offer not thy burnt offerings in every place that thou seest:

14 But in the place which the LORD

12-14. The phrase **rejoice before the LORD** applies to the celebration of the Feast of Tabernacles at the end of harvest (Lev 23:39-43) when Israel brought its offerings to God and ate sacrificial meals. The Levite and the people sat down to have a feast together. **The Levite** is a reference to the priest who made the sacrifice for each family. Just as today most Christians have a minister who preaches, teaches, and ministers to the congregation; so each Jew in the Old Testament had a specific Levite through whom he brought his tithe to God and who sacrificed for him. **The Levite that is within your gates** was a frequent

shall choose in one of thy tribes, there thou shalt offer thy burnt offerings, and there thou shalt do all that I command thee.

15 Notwithstanding thou mayest kill and eat flesh in all thy gates, whatsoever thy soul lusteth after, according to the blessing of the LORD thy God which he hath given thee: the unclean and the clean may eat thereof, as of the roebuck, and as of the hart.

16 Only ye shall not eat the blood; ye shall pour it upon the earth as water.

17 ¶Thou mayest not eat within thy gates the tithe of thy corn, or of thy wine, or of thy oil, or the firstlings of thy herds or of thy flock, nor any of thy vows which thou vowest, nor thy freewill offerings, or heave offering of thine hand:

18 But thou must eat them before the LORD thy God in the place which the LORD thy God shall choose, thou, and thy son, and thy daughter, and thy manservant, and thy maidservant, and the Levite that is within thy gates: and thou shalt rejoice before the LORD thy God in all that thou puttest thine hands unto.

19 Take heed to thyself that thou forsake not the Levite as long as thou livest upon the earth.

20 ¶When the LORD thy God shall enlarge thy border, as he hath promised thee, and thou shalt say, I will eat flesh, because thy soul longeth to eat flesh; thou mayest eat flesh, whatsoever thy soul lusteth after.

21 If the place which the LORD thy God hath chosen to put his name there be too far from thee, then thou shalt kill of thy herd and of thy flock, which the LORD hath given thee, as I have commanded thee, and thou shalt eat in thy gates whatsoever thy soul lusteth after.

22 Even as the roebuck and the hart is eaten, so thou shalt eat them: the unclean and the clean shall eat of them alike.

23 Only be sure that thou eat not the blood: for the blood is the life; and thou mayest not eat the life with the flesh.

24 Thou shalt not eat it; thou shalt pour it upon the earth as water.

25 Thou shalt not eat it; that it may go well with thee, and with thy children after thee, when thou shalt do that which is right in the sight of the LORD.

26 Only thy holy things which thou hast, and thy vows, thou shalt take, and go unto the place which the LORD shall choose:

27 And thou shalt offer thy burnt offerings, the flesh and the blood, upon the altar of the LORD thy God: and the blood of thy sacrifices shall be poured

description of a person's priest, although he seldom visited in the homes of the people. Extra corn, animals, and food that were brought to the tabernacle, and later the Temple, were given to each person's Levite. He had no way of making a living, since God had instructed that he should receive no part or inheritance in the land (18:1). Therefore, he depended on the gifts of the people to whom he ministered for his livelihood. The food that he did not eat at the sacrificial meal was stored for later use. The spiritual prosperity of Israel could be tied to these storehouses (Mal 3:10). When Israel stopped paying their tithes, the priest suffered; and the storehouses became empty. When the storehouses were full, it was an indication of the spiritual health of Israel.

15-28. In verses 15-17 the Israelites are reminded that they could eat food at home and enjoy feasting as long as they did not touch or eat blood upon the earth (vs. 24), as it was against the Lord's commandment to eat it. They were not, however, permitted to eat tithed food at home; it had to be brought to the Lord's house.

Today, the tithe is to be gathered by the local church. Although some argue against storehouse tithing, its foundation is found in the Old Testament. Just as God's people were commanded to bring the tithe to God's appointed place in the Old Testament, so God's people must bring the tithe to the assembly in the New Testament. In both testaments the tithe must be brought to the place where: (1) God's name is located; (2) God's presence is located; (3) the symbols of redemption are administered; and (4) God's man is ministering.

out upon the altar of the LORD thy God, and thou shalt eat the flesh.

28 Observe and hear all these words which I command thee, that it may go well with thee, and with thy children after thee for ever, when thou doest *that which is* good and right in the sight of the LORD thy God.

29 ¶When the LORD thy God shall cut off the nations from before thee, whither thou goest to possess them, and thou succeedest them, and dwellest in their land;

30 Take heed to thyself that thou be not snared by following them, after that they be destroyed from before thee; and that thou enquire not after their gods, saying, How did these nations serve their gods? even so will I do likewise.

31 Thou shalt not do so unto the LORD thy God: for every abomination to the LORD, which he hateth, have they done unto their gods; for even their sons and their daughters they have burnt in the fire to their gods.

32 What thing soever I command you, observe to do it: thou shalt not add thereto, nor diminish from it.

CHAPTER 13

IF there arise among you a prophet, or a dreamer of dreams, and giveth thee a sign or a wonder,

2 And the sign or the wonder come to pass, whereof he spake unto thee, saying, Let us go after other gods, which thou hast not known, and let us serve them;

3 Thou shalt not hearken unto the words of that prophet, or that dreamer of dreams: for the LORD your God proveth you, to know whether ye love the LORD your God with all your heart and with all your soul.

4 Ye shall walk after the LORD your God, and fear him, and keep his commandments, and obey his voice, and ye shall serve him, and cleave unto him.

5 And that prophet, or that dreamer of dreams, shall be put to death; because he hath spoken to turn *you* away from the LORD your God, which brought you out of the land of Egypt, and redeemed you out of the house of bondage, to thrust thee out of the way which the LORD thy God commanded thee to walk in. So shalt thou put the evil away from the midst of thee.

6 ¶If thy brother, the son of thy mother, or thy son, or thy daughter, or the wife of thy bosom, or thy friend, which *is* as thine own soul, entice thee secretly, saying, Let us go and serve

350

29-32. Many Israelites made spontaneous vows to God, perhaps impulsively. They were also to be paid at God's place and were called the vow offerings. The chapter ends where it began, with Israel being warned against returning to Canaanite idolatry (vss. 2, 29-31). Just as the Canaanites were destroyed because of their idolatry, Israel is warned that it could be destroyed. The Canaanites had burned their sons and daughters in the fire to the gods; the Lord calls this an abomination. Not only should Israel obey these commands; but Moses adds **nor diminish from it,** which meant that Israel should not lose its desire to obey the Lord.

B. Commands Concerning False Prophets. 13:1-18.

13:1-2. Moses warns Israel against two sins in this chapter. First, he warns them against the false prophet who would lead them away from the Lord; and second, he warns them against the danger of idols if they do not eliminate them from the cities that they occupy.

3-4. The false prophet is called a **dreamer of dreams.** Inasmuch as God spoke to Israel by dreams, the pseudo-prophet sought to imitate the real communication of God (cf. Gen 37:5; Dan 2:47). Also, God spoke through signs and wonders (Ex 4:21; Num 12:6) to authenticate the messenger and his message. However, a false prophet could also perform signs and wonders. As a result of his false message, the people would follow after him saying, **Let us go after other gods** (vs. 2). Even the Antichrist will be accompanied by miracles and signs (II Thess 2:9). Moses warns Israel not to hearken to these false messengers. God would use them to prove Israel as a test of their love, once again referring back to the *Shema* (6:4-5). Israel was not to regard miracles as the highest test or proof of certainty from God. Moses had given them the commandments that were the authority of God. The people were to test the prophet by his acceptance of the Law. Even miracles did not give one authority to break the Law. Jesus came performing miracles, but did not break the Law. Rather, He fulfilled it (Mt 5:17). Israel had already received the Word of God, and it had been confirmed by signs and miracles at Mount Sinai. Now they were to obey it.

5-12. Israel was commanded to **put to death** the false prophet. **So shalt thou put the evil away from the midst of thee** is repeated eight or more times in Deuteronomy (17:7, 12; 19:19; 21:21; 22:21, 22, 24; 24:7) and literally means "to burn out in order to clear out." Israel was commanded to put to death the false prophets who preached apostasy. This command was enjoined upon all the community, and not upon individuals. **Evil** here is a reference to the wicked thing. God hates idolatry, or anything else that replaces obedience to Him. Israel is charged not to tolerate the false prophet, nor to hide him in the village. If the false prophet **entice thee secretly** (this is the first time the word entice is used in the Old Testament), they were not to keep the temptation concealed. The person who heard the

other gods, which thou hast not known, thou, nor thy fathers;

7 *Namely*, of the gods of the people which *are* round about you, nigh unto thee, or far off from thee, from the *one* end of the earth even unto the *other* end of the earth;

8 Thou shalt not consent unto him, nor hearken unto him; neither shall thine eye pity him, neither shalt thou spare, neither shalt thou conceal him:

9 But thou shalt surely kill him; thine hand shall be first upon him to put him to death, and afterwards the hand of all the people.

10 And thou shalt stone him with stones, that he die; because he hath sought to thrust thee away from the LORD thy God, which brought thee out of the land of Egypt, from the house of bondage.

11 And all Israel shall hear, and fear, and shall do no more any such wickedness as this is among you.

12 ¶If thou shalt hear *say* in one of thy cities, which the LORD thy God hath given thee to dwell there, saying,

13 *Certain* men, the children of Bě'li-al, are gone out from among you, and have withdrawn the inhabitants of their city, saying, Let us go and serve other gods, which ye have not known;

14 Then shalt thou enquire, and make search, and ask diligently, and, behold, *if it be* truth, *and* the thing certain, *that* such abomination is wrought among you;

15 Thou shalt surely smite the inhabitants of that city with the edge of the sword, destroying it utterly, and all that *is* therein, and the cattle thereof, with the edge of the sword.

16 And thou shalt gather all the spoil of it into the midst of the street thereof, and shalt burn with fire the city, and all the spoil thereof every whit, for the LORD thy God: and it shall be an heap for ever; it shall not be built again.

17 And there shall cleave nought of the cursed thing to thine hand: that the LORD may turn from the fierceness of his anger, and shew thee mercy, and have compassion upon thee, and multiply thee, as he hath sworn unto thy fathers;

18 When thou shalt hearken to the voice of the LORD thy God, to keep all his commandments which I command thee this day, to do *that which is* right in the eyes of the LORD thy God.

CHAPTER 14

YE *are* the children of the LORD your God: ye shall not cut yourselves, nor make any baldness between your eyes for the dead.

2 For thou *art* an holy people unto the LORD thy God, and the LORD hath chosen thee to be a peculiar people unto himself, above all the nations that *are* upon the earth.

3 ¶Thou shalt not eat any abominable thing.

false prophet was to witness against him and to cast the first stone (17:7). The result was stoning to death.

13-18. Moses instructs the people on how to deal with a town that is led into idolatry. This is the first occurrence of the word **Belial** (Heb *belia'l*) in the Old Testament. It denotes all that is wicked and implies an instigator of uncleanness. When a town was accused of worshiping idols, Israel was to judge the case. The word **diligently** means to thoroughly investigate. If the reports were true, Moses instructs them to **destroy . . . it utterly** with the edge of the sword. They could not take spoil or keep any of the treasures of the city. The entire city was to be destroyed with fire. This would remove from Israel the temptation to listen to a false charge against the village so that outsiders could plunder it. The phrase **every whit, for the LORD thy God** actually means "As a whole offering for the Lord" (Lev 6:23). In essence, the whole village becomes an offering sanctified to God. The phrase **it shall be a heap for ever** signifies that the town was to be an eternal hill. Everytime outsiders saw the hill, they would be reminded of God's judgment on idolatry. This is what happened to Achan and his family (Josh 7:24-26) when he kept some of the spoil of Jericho.

C. Commands Concerning Food. 14:1-21.

14:1-2. In this chapter, Moses deals with foods, prescribing which were acceptable and which were prohibited to Israel. The basis of their dietary laws is found in the first verse. **Ye are the children of the LORD.** God's people were to reflect Him even in their diet. Moses also notes that they should not disfigure their bodies as the heathen do. Israel was called **a holy people unto the LORD . . . a peculiar people.** Their divine kinship was based upon election and calling, because God had chosen Israel from among the nations of the earth. Because of the free love of God, Israel should have obeyed the commands of God, even those pertaining to food.

3-21. The Israelites could not eat anything that was abominable. But before Moses reminds them of specific prohibitions, he tells them what they can eat, i.e., animals that part the hoof

351

4 These *are* the beasts which ye shall eat: the ox, the sheep, and the goat,

5 The hart, and the roebuck, and the fallow deer, and the wild goat, and the pygarg, and the wild ox, and the chamois.

6 And every beast that parteth the hoof, and cleaveth the cleft into two claws, *and* cheweth the cud among the beasts, that ye shall eat.

7 Nevertheless these ye shall not eat of them that chew the cud, or of them that divide the cloven hoof; *as* the camel, and the hare, and the coney: for they chew the cud, but divide not the hoof; *therefore* they *are* unclean unto you.

8 And the swine, because it divideth the hoof, yet cheweth not the cud, it *is* unclean unto you: ye shall not eat of their flesh, nor touch their dead carcase.

9 ¶These ye shall eat of all that *are* in the waters: all that have fins and scales shall ye eat:

10 And whatsoever hath not fins and scales ye may not eat; it *is* unclean unto you.

11 ¶*Of* all clean birds ye shall eat.

12 But these *are they* of which ye shall not eat: the eagle, and the ossifrage, and the ospray,

13 And the glede, and the kite, and the vulture after his kind,

14 And every raven after his kind,

15 And the owl, and the night hawk, and the cuckow, and the hawk after his kind,

16 The little owl, and the great owl, and the swan,

17 And the pelican, and the gier eagle, and the cormorant,

18 And the stork, and the heron after her kind, and the lapwing, and the bat.

19 And every creeping thing that flieth *is* unclean unto you: they shall not be eaten.

20 *But of* all clean fowls ye may eat.

21 ¶Ye shall not eat *of* any thing that dieth of itself: thou shalt give it unto the stranger that *is* in thy gates, that he may eat it; or thou mayest sell it unto an alien: for thou *art* an holy people unto the LORD thy God. Thou shalt not seethe a kid in his mother's milk.

22 Thou shalt truly tithe all the increase of thy seed, that the field bringeth forth year by year.

23 And thou shalt eat before the LORD thy God, in the place which he shall choose to place his name there, the tithe of thy corn, of thy wine, and of thine oil, and the firstlings of thy herds and of thy flocks; that thou mayest learn to fear the LORD thy God always.

24 And if the way be too long for thee, so that thou art not able to carry it; *or* if the place be too far from thee, which the LORD thy God shall choose to set his name there, when the LORD thy God hath blessed thee:

25 Then shalt thou turn *it* into money, and bind up the money in thine hand, and shalt go unto the place which the LORD thy God shall choose:

26 And thou shalt bestow that money for whatsoever thy soul lusteth after,

and chew the cud. Then, Moses mentions the animals that they should not eat, i.e., those that either chew the cud or divide the hoof (but not both), such as the camel, the hare, the coney, and the hog. There are reasons why God set these types of animals apart as not to be eaten: some were considered unclean in the minds of the people of that day, some were scavenger animals, the meat of some would spoil quickly, causing disease, and other reasons known only to God.

Later, when God's strategy shifted from a group of people (Israel) living in a certain location (the Promised Land) to individual Christians living throughout the world (the Age of Grace), God cleansed all the animals and made them edible. When Peter was told, "Rise, Peter; kill, and eat" (Acts 10:13), God not only was cleansing the animals, but symbolically was commanding the gospel to be preached to the Gentiles who had been separated from God. During the time of Moses, however, Israel manifested their separation as children of God by abstaining from certain meats. Moses lists the animals and birds by name (vss. 12-19). All but the glede were previously mentioned in Leviticus but not in Numbers. These are probably animals that Israel had learned of during their forty years in the wilderness. Lest Israel think this was a "narrow law," they should have remembered that for forty years they had eaten only manna. The dietary laws are no longer applicable today but are still symbolic to the Christian, who should not feed upon the filth of this world, but upon Jesus Christ, the Bread of Life.

Additional dietary laws included the prohibition that Israel could not eat anything that had died, i.e., was not killed. The reason for this was that a communicable disease might have caused the animal's death.

D. Commands Concerning Tithes. 14:22-29.

22-25. In this section, Moses continues to discuss eating but applies his remarks specifically to the feasts unto the Lord. He repeats the fact that festive meals were to be eaten at the chosen place. It was there that God had located His name, where God's presence dwelt, where the symbols of redemption were operative, and where the Levite ministered (see comments on ch. 12). However, God did make provision for those who would have a long distance to travel for the feast. These Israelites were allowed to sell their tithe-products and take the money to **the place** that God had chosen for them. Once they arrived, they could buy cattle, sheep, or grain for a heave offering or a thank offering. Then the farmer could make his appropriate offering before God. During Jesus' ministry He cleansed the Temple of the moneychangers (Jn 2:14-16). These moneychangers were not doing the wrong thing; they were providing a service in keeping with Deuteronomy 14:25-26. Their sin was in changing the money in the Temple, rather than conducting their business in the stalls in the city.

26-27. The phrase **lusteth after** does not mean an evil lusting, but rather a normal desire. They were told they could buy what

for oxen, or for sheep, or for wine, or for strong drink, or for whatsoever thy soul desireth: and thou shalt eat there before the LORD thy God, and thou shalt rejoice, thou, and thine household.

27 And the Levite that *is* within thy gates; thou shalt not forsake him; for he hath no part nor inheritance with thee.

28 ¶At the end of three years thou shalt bring forth all the tithe of thine increase the same year, and shalt lay *it* up within thy gates:

29 And the Levite, (because he hath no part nor inheritance with thee,) and the stranger, and the fatherless, and the widow, which *are* within thy gates, shall come, and shall eat and be satisfied; that the LORD thy God may bless thee in all the work of thine hand which thou doest.

CHAPTER 15
AT the end of *every* seven years thou shalt make a release.

2 And this *is* the manner of the release: Every creditor that lendeth *ought* unto his neighbour shall release *it;* he shall not exact *it* of his neighbour, or of his brother; because it is called the LORD's release.

3 Of a foreigner thou mayest exact *it again:* but *that* which is thine with thy brother thine hand shall release;

4 Save when there shall be no poor among you; for the LORD shall greatly bless thee in the land which the LORD thy God giveth thee *for* an inheritance to possess it:

5 Only if thou carefully hearken unto the voice of the LORD thy God, to observe to do all these commandments which I command thee this day.

6 For the LORD thy God blesseth thee, as he promised thee: and thou shalt lend unto many nations, but thou shalt not borrow; and thou shalt reign over many nations, but they shall not reign over thee.

7 ¶If there be among you a poor man of one of thy brethren within any of thy gates in thy land which the LORD thy God giveth thee, thou shalt not harden thine heart, nor shut thine hand from thy poor brother:

8 But thou shalt open thine hand wide unto him, and shalt surely lend him sufficient for his need, *in that* which he wanteth.

9 Beware that there be not a thought in thy wicked heart, saying, The seventh year, the year of release, is at hand; and thine eye be evil against thy poor brother, and thou givest him nought; and he cry unto the LORD against thee, and it be sin unto thee.

10 Thou shalt surely give him, and

they desired and take the animal into the temple for a sacrificial feast to the Lord. Hence, they should not feel guilty when they chose an animal that was appealing to the eye. Also, the Levite was to eat the meal with them because he had no inheritance of property (18:1-2).

28-29. Every three years an Israelite was allowed to have a sacrificial feast at home without going to the appointed place. This became known as "the third tithe," or "the poor tithe." He was instructed to invite the Levite, the stranger, the widow, and the orphan to this feast. Because of their generosity in giving to the poor, the Israelites were promised that **the LORD thy God may bless thee.**

E. Commands Concerning the Sabbatical Year. 15:1-23.

15:1-2. Here Moses gives the regulations regarding the year of release (every seventh year). Israelites were not to be pressed to pay their debts during this year. The phrase **At the end** is included because debts were not paid until the crops were gathered and the farmer had made his profit. Then he could pay his debts. However, the seventh year was different. The word **release** meant literally, "to let lie down" or to "let go." This does not signify a remission of the debt, or that debtors were to be released from all claims against them. It meant simply that the time of payment was extended for one year. The phrase **he shall not exact it** meant "thou shalt not press thy neighbor." At the end of seven years all of the debts that had been contracted were extended for another year. The debts were forgiven in the year of jubilee (every fiftieth year). This was seven sabbatical years plus one (Lev 25:10).

3. The Israelites were allowed to press foreigners among them for their loans; but they were not allowed to press their brethren, remembering that once they had been in bondage in Egypt.

4-6. The phrase **Save when there shall be no poor among you** seems to be inconsistent with verse 11, which states, **For the poor shall never cease.** Actually, in verse 4 it means "die from neglect." The Israelites could kill off the poor by demanding their loans or by not giving charity to them in the prescribed manner. God promised He would bless those who gave charity to the poor. The basis of charity was **the LORD thy God giveth thee.** Beyond this, Israel was promised that she would lend to many nations and rule over them. Perhaps this is a prophecy about the future financial expertise of the Jews in that those who borrow are servants to those who lend (Prov 22:7).

7-11. But some of the crafty Israelites might be reluctant to lend money to the needy immediately before the year of release. They are warned not to have **a thought in thy wicked heart,** which meant "a word in thy heart of worthlessness." They were commanded to give to the needy, so that **thine heart shall not be grieved,** which means that their heart would not become evil. Since there will always be poor people, Israel was commanded to open its hand to them.

thine heart shall not be grieved when thou givest unto him: because that for this thing the Lord thy God shall bless thee in all thy works, and in all that thou puttest thine hand unto.

11 For the poor shall never cease out of the land: therefore I command thee, saying, Thou shalt open thine hand wide unto thy brother, to thy poor, and to thy needy, in thy land.

12 ¶And if thy brother, an Hebrew man, or an Hebrew woman, be sold unto thee, and serve thee six years; then in the seventh year thou shalt let him go free from thee.

13 And when thou sendest him out free from thee, thou shalt not let him go away empty:

14 Thou shalt furnish him liberally out of thy flock, and out of thy floor, and out of thy winepress: of that wherewith the Lord thy God hath blessed thee thou shalt give unto him.

15 And thou shalt remember that thou wast a bondman in the land of Egypt, and the Lord thy God redeemed thee: therefore I command thee this thing to day.

16 And it shall be, if he say unto thee, I will not go away from thee; because he loveth thee and thine house, because he is well with thee;

17 Then thou shalt take an aul, and thrust it through his ear unto the door, and he shall be thy servant for ever. And also unto thy maidservant thou shalt do likewise.

18 It shall not seem hard unto thee, when thou sendest him away free from thee; for he hath been worth a double hired servant to thee, in serving thee six years: and the Lord thy God shall bless thee in all that thou doest.

19 ¶All the firstling males that come of thy herd and of thy flock thou shalt sanctify unto the Lord thy God: thou shalt do no work with the firstling of thy bullock, nor shear the firstling of thy sheep.

20 Thou shalt eat it before the Lord thy God year by year in the place which the Lord shall choose, thou and thy household.

21 And if there be any blemish therein, as if it be lame, or blind, or have any ill blemish, thou shalt not sacrifice it unto the Lord thy God.

22 Thou shalt eat it within thy gates: the unclean and the clean person shall eat it alike, as the roebuck, and as the hart.

23 Only thou shalt not eat the blood thereof; thou shalt pour it upon the ground as water.

CHAPTER 16

OBSERVE the month of A'bĭb, and keep the passover unto the Lord thy God: for in the month of A'bĭb the Lord thy God brought thee forth out of Egypt by night.

2 Thou shalt therefore sacrifice the passover unto the Lord thy God, of the flock and the herd, in the place which the Lord shall choose to place his name there.

3 Thou shalt eat no leavened bread

12-17. Moses teaches Israel the principles of the Hebrew bondslave and the conditions for setting him free. After the slave had served seven years, he was to be free. This seventh year was not the same as the sabbatical year, but was the seventh year from the beginning of the slave's bondage. When a slave was released, he was not to be sent away empty. His owner was commanded to **furnish him liberally,** which could be translated literally, "Thou shalt put upon his neck from thy flock and of thy grain." The basis of Israel's giving to their bondmen was that they had received much from their masters when they left Egypt. In verse 17 the maidservant is added to the list. This category was not originally mentioned in Exodus 21:5-6.

18. When the slave went out, it was noted that **he hath been worth a double hired servant.** This meant that he was worth double the wages of a day laborer. When freed he did not deserve twice as much reward; but if the master had hired someone, he would have had to pay twice what it had cost to have a slave in the house.

19-23. In the final section of the chapter Moses reminds Israel that the first-born of the flock was to be sacrificed to the Lord in remembrance of their deliverance out of Egypt (Ex 13:2, 12). The night the death angel came through the land, he took the first-born. Israel was to offer the first-born year by year; hence, their obedience became the basis for the future blessing of God upon their flocks.

F. Commands Concerning Festivals. 16:1-17.

Israel was commanded to appear before Jehovah at His appointed place three times a year (vs. 16) to celebrate the Feast of the Passover (vss. 2-8), the Feast of Pentecost (also called the Feast of Weeks) (vss. 9-12), and the Feast of Tabernacles (vss. 13-25). These were the primary feasts; attendance at the Feast of Trumpets and the Day of Atonement was not obligatory.

16:1-3. Abib (Heb 'abib) means "green ears." The first month of the year came in the spring, when the land turned green. Moses had in mind a broader meaning than that of the Passover. Usually, Passover was on one day, and the only sacrifice involved was the paschal lamb. Here, Moses instructs the people to celebrate for seven days. They were to eat more than the paschal lamb; they were to eat **of the flock and the herd.** Obviously, they would not eat an ox on the day of Passover. During the other six days they ate the different sacrifices. Also, during this time Israel could eat no leavened bread. There are

with it; seven days shalt thou eat unleavened bread therewith, *even* the bread of affliction; for thou camest forth out of the land of Egypt in haste: that thou mayest remember the day when thou camest forth out of the land of Egypt all the days of thy life.

4 And there shall be no leavened bread seen with thee in all thy coast seven days; neither shall there *any thing* of the flesh, which thou sacrificedst the first day at even, remain all night until the morning.

5 Thou mayest not sacrifice the passover within any of thy gates, which the LORD thy God giveth thee:

6 But at the place which the LORD thy God shall choose to place his name in, there thou shalt sacrifice the passover at even, at the going down of the sun, at the season that thou camest forth out of Egypt.

7 And thou shalt roast and eat *it* in the place which the LORD thy God shall choose: and thou shalt turn in the morning, and go unto thy tents.

8 Six days thou shalt eat unleavened bread: and on the seventh day *shall be* a solemn assembly to the LORD thy God: thou shalt do no work *therein*.

9 ¶Seven weeks shalt thou number unto thee: begin to number the seven weeks from *such time as* thou beginnest *to put* the sickle to the corn.

10 And thou shalt keep the feast of weeks unto the LORD thy God with a tribute of a freewill offering of thine hand, which thou shalt give *unto the* LORD *thy God,* according as the LORD thy God hath blessed thee:

11 And thou shalt rejoice before the LORD thy God, thou, and thy son, and thy daughter, and thy manservant, and thy maidservant, and the Levite that *is* within thy gates, and the stranger, and the fatherless, and the widow, that *are* among you, in the place which the LORD thy God hath chosen to place his name there.

12 And thou shalt remember that thou wast a bondman in Egypt: and thou shalt observe and do these statutes.

13 ¶Thou shalt observe the feast of tabernacles seven days, after that thou hast gathered in thy corn and thy wine:

14 And thou shalt rejoice in thy feast, thou, and thy son, and thy daughter, and thy manservant, and thy maidservant, and the Levite, the stranger, and the fatherless, and the widow, that *are* within thy gates.

15 Seven days shalt thou keep a solemn feast unto the LORD thy God in the place which the LORD shall choose: because the LORD thy God shall bless thee in all thine increase, and in all the works of thine hands, therefore thou shalt surely rejoice.

16 ¶Three times in a year shall all thy males appear before the LORD thy God in the place which he shall choose; in the feast of unleavened bread, and in the feast of weeks, and in the feast of tabernacles: and they shall not appear before the LORD empty:

17 Every man *shall give* as he is able,

two reasons for abstinence from leaven: first, to remind Israel that they had left Egypt in haste and were unable to leaven their dough; and second, because leaven in the dough is the result of fermentation or putrefaction, and hence, a symbol of evil.

4-8. Moses repeats two points of law regarding the Passover: first, that no leaven could be seen in the land during this time; and second, that none of the flesh of the paschal lamb could be left over until the following morning. Moses also reminds Israel that the Passover must be sacrificed **at the place,** which meant that every Jew had to travel to the central place of worship. Immediately after celebrating the Passover, they were to **turn in the morning, and go unto thy tents,** which meant they were allowed to go home.

9-17. The Feast of Pentecost was held fifty days after Passover (Lev 23:15-16); here Moses reminds them that the interval is seven weeks **as thou beginnest to put the sickle to the corn.** For this feast, Moses tells Israel to include all of the strangers, servants, widows, orphans, and Levites.

The third feast mentioned in this chapter is Tabernacles, celebrated in the seventh month. Israel kept this feast by living in booths or tents (Lev 23:34-43). Not all of the details for celebrating this feast are included here; Moses simply is giving a reminder to Israel that they have an obligation to observe the Feast of Tabernacles.

Every male was obligated to attend these three feasts at God's chosen place every year. The Passover was best attended, Tabernacles had the second highest attendance record, and Pentecost had the fewest number of attendees. Apparently, some Jews of the Old Testament did not take the command to assemble themselves any more seriously than some Christians do in this dispensation.

according to the blessing of the Lord thy God which he hath given thee.

18 ¶Judges and officers shalt thou make thee in all thy gates, which the Lord thy God giveth thee, throughout thy tribes: and they shall judge the people with just judgment.

19 Thou shalt not wrest judgment; thou shalt not respect persons, neither take a gift: for a gift doth blind the eyes of the wise, and pervert the words of the righteous.

20 That which is altogether just shalt thou follow, that thou mayest live, and inherit the land which the Lord thy God giveth thee.

21 Thou shalt not plant thee a grove of any trees near unto the altar of the Lord thy God, which thou shalt make thee.

22 Neither shalt thou set thee up *any* image; which the Lord thy God hateth.

CHAPTER 17

THOU shalt not sacrifice unto the Lord thy God *any* bullock, or sheep, wherein is blemish, *or* any evilfavouredness: for that *is* an abomination unto the Lord thy God.

2 ¶If there be found among you, within any of thy gates which the Lord thy God giveth thee, man or woman, that hath wrought wickedness in the sight of the Lord thy God, in transgressing his covenant,

3 And hath gone and served other gods, and worshipped them, either the sun, or moon, or any of the host of heaven, which I have not commanded;

4 And it be told thee, and thou hast heard *of it*, and enquired diligently, and, behold, *it be* true, *and* the thing certain, *that* such abomination is wrought in Israel:

5 Then shalt thou bring forth that man or that woman, which have committed that wicked thing, unto thy gates, *even* that man or that woman, and shalt stone them with stones, till they die.

6 At the mouth of two witnesses, or three witnesses, shall he that is worthy of death be put to death; *but* at the mouth of one witness he shall not be put to death.

7 The hands of the witnesses shall be first upon him to put him to death, and afterward the hands of all the people. So thou shalt put the evil away from among you.

8 ¶If there arise a matter too hard for thee in judgment, between blood and blood, between plea and plea, and between stroke and stroke, *being* matters of controversy within thy gates: then shalt thou arise, and get thee up into the place which the Lord thy God shall choose;

9 And thou shalt come unto the priests the Lēvītes, and unto the judge that shall be in those days, and enquire;

G. Commands Concerning Leaders. 16:18-18:22.

18-22. Moses has just finished reminding Israel of their religious obligations; he now gives them rules for civil order. First, he commands the appointment of judges and other officials in every town. Second, he establishes a higher judicial court for more difficult cases. Third, he establishes the foundation for the future selection of a king. Just as Israel was to manifest their spiritual character in their worship of God, so they were also to manifest their holiness by proper civil relationships. In these verses, the nation as a whole is addressed and is obligated to appoint judges and officials. Note that a popular majority vote was unknown under Mosaic law. Apparently, the leaders were appointed by their age, wisdom, and leadership within the community. Also, Moses does not lay down a rule about the number of judges in each place, because the number of judges would depend upon the number of inhabitants. In the midst of setting up legal requirements for judges, Moses comes back to the theme of idolatry. Israel was not to plant a grove of trees, a symbol of heathen worship, nor were they to **set . . . up any image,** which meant they were not to establish a pillar to be used in idol worship.

17:1-7. Israel was not allowed to sacrifice an animal with a blemish. This was symbolic of Christ, the lamb without spot or blemish who would bear the sins of the world.

Before Moses continues to discuss the judges, he reminds the people of a difficulty, i.e., judging idolatry. Those that were guilty of transgressing the covenant of God by worshiping idols were to be brought to the city gate, usually a large open space where judgment was made and where the elders met in council (vs. 5). The ones who were guilty of worshiping idols were to be stoned, but there had to be two or more witnesses before they could be put to death. According to the Torah, the witnesses were to be the first to lift up their hands against the criminal to stone him, thereby attesting to the truth of their statements. **So thou shalt put the evil away.**

8. When Moses first set up judges at Sinai, the people brought to him the cases that were too difficult for them to decide. After his death, there would be no one to take his place. Therefore, Moses established a high court that was to be located at the central place of worship. The local judges were to bring their difficult cases there. The phrase **too hard for thee in judgment** referred to a matter too incomprehensible to understand. Therefore, judges were set up at **the place.** This superior court was not a court of appeal, for it did not review a local court's verdict. The superior court only took cases which the lower court referred to them.

9-13. **The priests and Levites** were assigned to teach the Law regarding difficult decisions. These Levites were to interpret the Law; and the judges were to inquire of them. The direct

and they shall shew thee the sentence of judgment:

10 And thou shalt do according to the sentence, which they of that place which the LORD shall choose shall shew thee; and thou shalt observe to do according to all that they inform thee:

11 According to the sentence of the law which they shall teach thee, and according to the judgment which they shall tell thee, thou shalt do: thou shalt not decline from the sentence which they shall shew thee, *to* the right hand, nor *to* the left.

12 And the man that will do presumptuously, and will not hearken unto the priest that standeth to minister there before the LORD thy God, or unto the judge, even that man shall die: and thou shalt put away the evil from Israel.

13 And all the people shall hear, and fear, and do no more presumptuously.

14 ¶When thou art come unto the land which the LORD thy God giveth thee, and shalt possess it, and shalt dwell therein, and shalt say, I will set a king over me, like as all the nations that *are* about me;

15 Thou shalt in any wise set *him* king over thee, whom the LORD thy God shall choose: *one* from among thy brethren shalt thou set king over thee: thou mayest not set a stranger over thee, which *is* not thy brother.

16 But he shall not multiply horses to himself, nor cause the people to return to Egypt, to the end that he should multiply horses: forasmuch as the LORD hath said unto you, Ye shall henceforth return no more that way.

17 Neither shall he multiply wives to himself, that his heart turn not away: neither shall he greatly multiply to himself silver and gold.

18 And it shall be, when he sitteth upon the throne of his kingdom, that he shall write him a copy of this law in a book out of *that which is* before the priests the Lēvītes:

19 And it shall be with him, and he shall read therein all the days of his life: that he may learn to fear the LORD his God, to keep all the words of this law and these statutes, to do them:

20 That his heart be not lifted up above his brethren, and that he turn not aside from the commandment, *to* the right hand, or *to* the left: to the end that he may prolong *his* days in his kingdom, he, and his children, in the midst of Israel.

CHAPTER 18

THE priests the Lēvītes, *and* all the tribe of Levi, shall have no part nor inheritance with Israel: they shall eat the offerings of the LORD made by fire, and his inheritance.

2 Therefore shall they have no inheritance among their brethren: the LORD *is* their inheritance, as he hath said unto them.

3 ¶And this shall be the priest's due from the people, from them that offer a sacrifice, whether *it be* ox or sheep; and they shall give unto the priest the

result of inquiry is revealed in the phrase **shall show thee.** The judges, then, were to do **according to all that they inform thee,** which is, literally, "according to the sound of the word." The judges were to make decisions according to the Torah, as taught by the Levites assigned to them. Israel was thus commanded not to act presumptuously, but to **hearken unto the priest** (see E. W. Bullinger, *The Companion Bible,* p. 263).

14-20. The rules regarding the future kings were next. Israel was allowed to have a king, if they so desired. Therefore, God gave certain rules for establishing a king over His people. First, an earthly king was not to oppose the theocracy, i.e., the direct rule of the Lord over His people. Second, God did not command them to establish a monarchy, He only permitted them to have a king. Third, God said He would appoint, or set up, a king. The monarchy would not come by popular vote. Fourth, the king could not be a foreigner but had to be from among the brethren. Fifth, he could not multiply horses, lest Israel be tempted to return to the ease of Egypt by horseback. Sixth, the king could not multiply wives, lest they turn his heart away from the Lord. Solomon transgressed both of these last commandments by multiplying both horses and women (I Kgs 10:25-26; 11:1). Finally, the king was to possess a copy of the Law and **read therein all the days of his life. He shall write** does not mean that he had to copy the Law, but that he should have it written for his benefit. The object was for him to **keep all the words of this law . . . to do them.**

18:1-4. When God divided the Promised Land among the twelve tribes, the tribe of Levi did not receive a geographical inheritance. They were set apart to serve the Lord. The priests were not to make a living by working with their hands; their employment was to **stand . . . before the LORD** (vs. 7). In order to provide for their needs, the priests received food from the offerings and sacrifices that were brought to the Lord. Not all of the sacrifices were completely consumed by fire. The phrase **made by fire** meant "belonging to the firings," the place in the brazen altar where the fire consumed the sacrifice. The Levites could eat certain portions of the meat that was brought as a sacrifice. This was more than an offering to the priest; it was the

shoulder, and the two cheeks, and the maw.

4 The firstfruit *also* of thy corn, of thy wine, and of thine oil, and the first of the fleece of thy sheep, shalt thou give him.

5 For the LORD thy God hath chosen him out of all thy tribes, to stand to minister in the name of the LORD, him and his sons for ever.

6 ¶And if a Levite come from any of thy gates out of all Israel, where he sojourned, and come with all the desire of his mind unto the place which the LORD shall choose;

7 Then he shall minister in the name of the LORD his God, as all his brethren the Lēvītes *do*, which stand there before the LORD.

8 They shall have like portions to eat, beside that which cometh of the sale of his patrimony.

9 ¶When thou art come into the land which the LORD thy God giveth thee, thou shalt not learn to do after the abominations of those nations.

10 There shall not be found among you *any one* that maketh his son or his daughter to pass through the fire, *or* that useth divination, *or* an observer of times, or an enchanter, or a witch,

11 Or a charmer, or a consulter with familiar spirits, or a wizard, or a necromancer.

12 For all that do these things *are* an abomination unto the LORD: and because of these abominations the LORD thy God doth drive them out from before thee.

13 Thou shalt be perfect with the LORD thy God.

14 For these nations, which thou shalt possess, hearkened unto observers of times, and unto diviners: but as for thee, the LORD thy God hath not suffered thee so *to do.*

15 ¶The LORD thy God will raise up unto thee a Prophet from the midst of thee, of thy brethren, like unto me; unto him ye shall hearken;

16 According to all that thou desiredst of the LORD thy God in Hô′rĕb in the day of the assembly, saying, Let me not hear again the voice of the LORD my God, neither let me see this great fire any more, that I die not.

17 And the LORD said unto me, They have well *spoken that* which they have spoken.

18 I will raise them up a Prophet from among their brethren, like unto thee, and will put my words in his mouth; and he shall speak unto them all that I shall command him.

priest's due. Specifically, the Lord said of the animals that the priest should have **the shoulder, and the two cheeks, and the maw.** This meant that the priest was able to take for his own needs the shoulders and the stomach of each animal. The question is, did this involve every slaughter of every animal made by the Israelites? Obviously, the Levites did not receive something when a family slaughtered for its own use. Also, not all Israelite families could get the meat to the priest because of distance. In addition, it would involve much more than a tithe to the Lord. Finally, the word **sacrifice** indicates that which was offered at the designated place. Therefore, the priests only received part of the ritual sacrifices.

5-8. The priests were willing to stand and minister in the name of the Lord. When they obeyed God and served Him with a willing heart, the people brought their sacrifices; and the priests prospered with food. When the priests became hardhearted, Israel did not respond; and the priests went hungry. Also, the priests were allowed to visit in the homes of Israelites who did not live near God's chosen place of worship. When a priest visited in a home, he was to expect **all the desire of his mind,** which means that he was to be given the food that he requested.

This section ends with the phrase **cometh of the sale of his patrimony.** Literally, this referred to that which was sold with the fathers. When a son sold part of the inheritance of his father (presuming the father had died), he could not exclude giving to the priest what should be sacrificed to the Lord. This is similar to Leviticus 25:33-34, which forbids the sale of pasture ground belonging to the Levites.

9-14. In this section Moses uses the contrast between the false prophet and the prophet of God to communicate his message. He identifies the false prophet by grouping together different synonyms for false prophets: divination, observer of times, enchanter, witch, charmer, consulter with familiar spirits, wizard, and necromancer. All of these were an abomination to the Lord; and because of these practices, God drove the Canaanites out of the land.

15-19. In contrast, Moses promises the people that God will raise up a prophet from among them **like unto me.** The fact that the prophet was to come from Israel was a comfort to the people. Moses admonishes them that **unto him ye shall hearken.** Next, he repeats the promise because God had put His words in the prophet's mouth. The phrase **like unto me** identified the coming prophet with the role of intercessor and deliverer. In verse 16 Moses reminds the people of how they came to Mount Horeb in fear for their lives. They pleaded that they should not see God and die, and God was pleased with their words. He promised them a prophet who would mediate between God and man; this was a prophetic reference to Jesus Christ who fulfilled the prophecy of Moses. Philip told Nathanael, "We have found him, of whom Moses in the law, and the prophets, did write . . ." (Jn 1:45). Again, Jesus said, ". . . had ye believed Moses, ye would have believed me . . ." (Jn 5:46).

19 And it shall come to pass, *that* whosoever will not hearken unto my words which he shall speak in my name, I will require *it* of him.

20 But the prophet, which shall presume to speak a word in my name, which I have not commanded him to speak, or that shall speak in the name of other gods, even that prophet shall die.

21 And if thou say in thine heart, How shall we know the word which the LORD hath not spoken?

22 When a prophet speaketh in the name of the LORD, if the thing follow not, nor come to pass, that *is* the thing which the LORD hath not spoken, *but* the prophet hath spoken it presumptuously: thou shalt not be afraid of him.

CHAPTER 19

WHEN the LORD thy God hath cut off the nations, whose land the LORD thy God giveth thee, and thou succeedest them, and dwellest in their cities, and in their houses;

2 Thou shalt separate three cities for thee in the midst of thy land, which the LORD thy God giveth thee to possess it.

3 Thou shalt prepare thee a way, and divide the coasts of thy land, which the LORD thy God giveth thee to inherit, into three parts, that every slayer may flee thither.

4 ¶And this *is* the case of the slayer, which shall flee thither, that he may live: Whoso killeth his neighbour ignorantly, whom he hated not in time past;

5 As when a man goeth into the wood with his neighbour to hew wood, and his hand fetcheth a stroke with the axe to cut down the tree, and the head slippeth from the helve, and lighteth upon his neighbour, that he die; he shall flee unto one of those cities, and live:

6 Lest the avenger of the blood pursue the slayer, while his heart is hot, and overtake him, because the way is long, and slay him; whereas he *was* not worthy of death, inasmuch as he hated him not in time past.

7 Wherefore I command thee, saying, Thou shalt separate three cities for thee.

8 And if the LORD thy God enlarge thy coast, as he hath sworn unto thy fathers, and give thee all the land which he promised to give unto thy fathers;

9 If thou shalt keep all these commandments to do them, which I command thee this day, to love the LORD thy God, and to walk ever in his ways; then shalt thou add three cities more for thee, beside these three:

10 That innocent blood be not shed in thy land, which the LORD thy God giveth thee *for* an inheritance, and *so* blood be upon thee.

11 ¶But if any man hate his neighbour, and lie in wait for him, and rise up against him, and smite him mortally that he die, and fleeth into one of these cities:

12 Then the elders of his city shall send and fetch him thence, and deliver him into the hand of the avenger of blood, that he may die.

13 Thine eye shall not pity him, but

20-22. The next part of this chapter deals with the false prophets. He **shall presume to speak a word.** Since God did not command the false prophet to speak that word, the people were to test his prophecy; and if his prediction did not **come to pass,** the people were to: (1) know that he had not spoken in the name of the Lord; (2) know that he had spoken presumptuously; (3) not be afraid of him; and (4) know that **that prophet shall die.**

H. Commands Concerning Human Relationships. 19:1-26:19.

19:1-13. The laws concerning the cities of refuge were intended to save the life of the manslayer (Num 35:9-34), described by the phrase, **Whoso killeth his neighbor ignorantly,** which meant that he was not guilty of premeditated murder. Moses gives an illustration of two men who were cutting wood when an ax head slipped and accidently killed one of them. The survivor was to flee to the nearest city of refuge for safety. The phrase **the avenger** is a reference to the kinsman avenger, a close relative of the dead person who was to avenge the slaying of his relative. The purpose of the cities of refuge was to prevent the entire nation from suffering purposeless executions. This is explained in the phrase **so blood be upon thee** (vs. 10). However, the man who intentionally murdered someone could not find refuge in one of these cities. The elders of the city of refuge were to deliver the murderer to the avenger of blood so that the capital offense could be punished.

thou shalt put away *the guilt of* innocent blood from Israel, that it may go well with thee.

14 ¶Thou shalt not remove thy neighbour's landmark, which they of old time have set in thine inheritance, which thou shalt inherit in the land that the LORD thy God giveth thee to possess it.

15 ¶One witness shall not rise up against a man for any iniquity, or for any sin, in any sin that he sinneth: at the mouth of two witnesses, or at the mouth of three witnesses, shall the matter be established.

16 If a false witness rise up against any man to testify against him *that which is* wrong;

17 Then both the men, between whom the controversy *is*, shall stand before the LORD, before the priests and the judges, which shall be in those days;

18 And the judges shall make diligent inquisition: and, behold, *if* the witness *be* a false witness, *and* hath testified falsely against his brother;

19 Then shall ye do unto him, as he had thought to have done unto his brother: so shalt thou put the evil away from among you.

20 And those which remain shall hear, and fear, and shall henceforth commit no more any such evil among you.

21 And thine eye shall not pity; *but* life *shall go* for life, eye for eye, tooth for tooth, hand for hand, foot for foot.

CHAPTER 20

WHEN thou goest out to battle against thine enemies, and seest horses, and chariots, *and* a people more than thou, be not afraid of them: for the LORD thy God *is* with thee, which brought thee up out of the land of Egypt.

2 And it shall be, when ye are come nigh unto the battle, that the priest shall approach and speak unto the people,

3 And shall say unto them, Hear, O Israel, ye approach this day unto battle against your enemies: let not your hearts faint, fear not, and do not tremble, neither be ye terrified because of them;

4 For the LORD your God *is* he that goeth with you, to fight for you against your enemies, to save you.

5 ¶And the officers shall speak unto the people, saying, What man *is there* that hath built a new house, and hath not dedicated it? let him go and return to his house, lest he die in the battle, and another man dedicate it.

6 And what man *is he* that hath planted a vineyard, and hath not *yet* eaten of it? let him *also* go and return unto his house, lest he die in the battle, and another man eat of it.

7 And what man *is there* that hath betrothed a wife, and hath not taken her? let him go and return unto his house, lest he die in the battle, and another man take her.

8 And the officers shall speak further

14. In this verse Moses deals with the crime of removing the landmarks. Since the land was an inheritance from God, anyone who tried to steal land by moving the boundary markers was actually committing a crime against God. Landmarks were important to God because a man's property consisted of his life and his inheritance for the future.

15-21. Moses lays down rules for dealing with false witnesses. He stipulates that there must be at least two or three witnesses before a decision could be made legally. If the testimony of only one witness was accepted, he could be wrong and cause his brother irreparable harm. This is called being a false witness. When hearing a matter, the judges were to make **diligent inquisition**, which meant that they were to investigate the case thoroughly so as to determine if the testimony was false. It is to be noted that the witnesses were to **stand before the LORD,** which was symbolically carried out when they stood before the priests and the judges. Hence, the false witness would stand in the presence of the Lord and in the sanctuary when he testified under oath. If the judges determined that a witness had lied, he was to suffer the punishment that the defendant would have suffered had his testimony been true. As an illustration, in a trial involving capital punishment, the false witness would have his life taken.

20:1-9. Moses gives instructions regarding military service. The army was to put their trust in the Lord, even if they saw that the enemy had horses, chariots, and more troops. Moses reminds Israel that the Lord would give them victory. Before the army went into battle, the priest was to exhort the soldiers. In modern terminology, these were the chaplains who spoke to the men before they faced possible death. Phinehas was a priest who had accompanied Israel into battle (Num 31:6). These priests were called the "anointed of the battle." They gave the army a threefold assurance: (1) the Lord goeth with you; (2) He will fight for you; and (3) He will save you. Victory by Israel was dependent upon their obedience to God.

The **officers** (Heb *shatar*) had certain duties, such as keeping geological tables, appointing men to battle, and releasing others from battle. These **officers** had four standards by which a man could be excused from battle: (1) any man who had built a new house and had not consecrated it; (2) any man who had planted a new vineyard and had not eaten of its fruit; and (3) any man who was betrothed to a wife and had not married her. These men were excused so that they might not die before they enjoyed the fruit of their labors. The fourth criterion had to do with fearfulness and cowardice. Such a man might cause other soldiers to retreat from a battle. When Gideon faced the Midianites, he told the fearful to return from battle (Jud 7:3). Twenty-two thousand left Gideon because they were afraid of defeat. His example proved the practicality of Moses' command.

After the officers had eliminated those who should not go to battle, their duty was to appoint captains to lead the troops (vs. 9).

unto the people, and they shall say, What man *is there that is* fearful and fainthearted? let him go and return unto his house, lest his brethren's heart faint as well as his heart.

9 And it shall be, when the officers have made an end of speaking unto the people, that they shall make captains of the armies to lead the people.

10 ¶When thou comest nigh unto a city to fight against it, then proclaim peace unto it.

11 And it shall be, if it make thee answer of peace, and open unto thee, then it shall be, *that* all the people *that is* found therein shall be tributaries unto thee, and they shall serve thee.

12 And if it will make no peace with thee, but will make war against thee, then thou shalt besiege it:

13 And when the LORD thy God hath delivered it into thine hands, thou shalt smite every male thereof with the edge of the sword:

14 But the women, and the little ones, and the cattle, and all that is in the city, *even* all the spoil thereof, shalt thou take unto thyself; and thou shalt eat the spoil of thine enemies, which the LORD thy God hath given thee.

15 Thus shalt thou do unto all the cities *which are* very far off from thee, which *are* not of the cities of these nations.

16 But of the cities of these people, which the LORD thy God doth give thee *for* an inheritance, thou shalt save alive nothing that breatheth:

17 But thou shalt utterly destroy them; namely, the Hittites, and the Ăm′o-rītes, the Canaanites, and the Pĕr′iz-zītes, the Hī′vītes, and the Jĕb′u-sītes; as the LORD thy God hath commanded thee:

18 That they teach you not to do after all their abominations, which they have done unto their gods; so should ye sin against the LORD your God.

19 ¶When thou shalt besiege a city a long time, in making war against it to take it, thou shalt not destroy the trees thereof by forcing an axe against them: for thou mayest eat of them, and thou shalt not cut them down (for the tree of the field *is* man's *life*) to employ *them* in the siege:

20 Only the trees which thou knowest that they *be* not trees for meat, thou shalt destroy and cut them down; and thou shalt build bulwarks against the city that maketh war with thee, until it be subdued.

CHAPTER 21

IF *one* be found slain in the land which the LORD thy God giveth thee to possess it, lying in the field, *and* it be not known who hath slain him:

2 Then thy elders and thy judges shall come forth, and they shall measure unto the cities which *are* round about him that is slain:

3 And it shall be, *that* the city which *is* next unto the slain man, even the elders of that city shall take an heifer, which hath not been wrought with, *and* which hath not drawn in the yoke;

4 And the elders of that city shall

10-13. Moses gives instructions concerning battle. When Israel attacked a city, they were to call for it to surrender, i.e., **proclaim peace unto it.** A city would signify its surrender by the phrase **open unto thee,** which meant open the gates. Israel was to collect tribute from that city and make it subservient.

14-18. The cities that would not surrender were to be completely destroyed with the edge of the sword, including all of the men of war. But they were to save the women, children and cattle as spoil. Israel was to accept the surrender of cities that were **very far off** (vs. 15), but not cities in the Promised Land. God instructed that the six nations who lived there were to be destroyed. Idolatry was the sin of these nations and would be a constant temptation to Israel.

19-20. Rules concerning the cutting down of trees were important to survival. The phrase **the tree of the field is man's life** was the basis for these rules. It meant that man lives off the fruit of the trees, and his life is bound to them; therefore, trees were not to be destroyed during a siege. The phrase **forcing an axe against them** is a Hebrew idiom meaning "to cut down." However, some trees that could be cut down for battle were those that did not produce fruit. They could be used to make bulwarks and siege towers.

21:1-9. Moses explains how a town is to judge a murder committed by an unknown person. When they found a corpse, the elders and judges were to measure the distance from the body to the closest city. That city then became responsible for that crime. According to Israelite law, the burden of guilt rested upon that town. The elders were to take a heifer (young cow) that had never been worked in **a rough valley,** i.e., one which had not been used to raise crops in the fields. Also, there had to be a brook of constantly flowing water running through the valley. There the elders would break the animal's neck, i.e., **strike off the heifer's neck.** This punishment of the animal was symbolic of what should have happened to the murderer. The

bring down the heifer unto a rough valley, which is neither eared nor sown, and shall strike off the heifer's neck there in the valley:

5 And the priests the sons of Levi shall come near; for them the LORD thy God hath chosen to minister unto him, and to bless in the name of the LORD; and by their word shall every controversy and every stroke be *tried:*

6 And all the elders of that city, *that are* next unto the slain *man*, shall wash their hands over the heifer that is beheaded in the valley:

7 And they shall answer and say, Our hands have not shed this blood, neither have our eyes seen *it*.

8 Be merciful, O LORD, unto thy people Israel, whom thou hast redeemed, and lay not innocent blood unto thy people of Israel's charge. And the blood shall be forgiven them.

9 So shalt thou put away the *guilt of* innocent blood from among you, when thou shalt do *that which is* right in the sight of the LORD.

10 ¶When thou goest forth to war against thine enemies, and the LORD thy God hath delivered them into thine hands, and thou hast taken them captive,

11 And seest among the captives a beautiful woman, and hast a desire unto her, that thou wouldest have her to thy wife;

12 Then thou shalt bring her home to thine house; and she shall shave her head, and pare her nails;

13 And she shall put the raiment of her captivity from off her, and shall remain in thine house, and bewail her father and her mother a full month: and after that thou shalt go in unto her, and be her husband, and she shall be thy wife.

14 And it shall be, if thou have no delight in her, then thou shalt let her go whither she will; but thou shalt not sell her at all for money, thou shalt not make merchandise of her, because thou hast humbled her.

15 ¶If a man have two wives, one beloved, and another hated, and they have born him children, *both* the beloved and the hated; and *if* the firstborn son be hers that was hated:

16 Then it shall be, when he maketh his sons to inherit *that* which he hath, *that* he may not make the son of the beloved firstborn before the son of the hated, *which is indeed* the firstborn:

17 But he shall acknowledge the son of the hated *for* the firstborn, by giving him a double portion of all that he hath: for he *is* the beginning of his strength; the right of the firstborn *is* his.

18 ¶If a man have a stubborn and rebellious son, which will not obey the voice of his father, or the voice of his mother, and *that*, when they have chastened him, will not hearken unto them:

19 Then shall his father and his mother lay hold on him, and bring him out unto the elders of his city, and unto the gate of his place;

20 And they shall say unto the elders of his city, This our son *is* stubborn and

valley was chosen so that the blood of the animal would not spoil the crops and so that the flowing water would wash it away. Even though the Levites were involved in the ceremony, it was not an expiatory sacrifice because there was no slaughtering in the ceremonial manner and no sprinkling of blood. Afterward, the elders of the town were to wash their hands over the slain heifer to symbolically cleanse themselves from any suspicion of guilt on behalf of the inhabitants of the town. Implied in this action is the thought that no one should take vengeance on the entire town.

10-14. Moses tells Israel how to treat a wife who was taken from among the prisoners of war. If an Israelite saw a woman captive and wanted her to be his wife, he was to separate her for thirty days as a sign of cleansing (Lev 14:8; Num 8:7). The captive woman had to put aside her raiment of captivity, symbolic of passing out of the state of slavery. Then she had to shave her head and cut her nails, customary signs of purification. During this time she was to bewail her father and mother for a month. This action gave her opportunity to forget her natural affection for her people and for her father's house. Bringing her into an Israelite house gave her the rights of a daughter of Israel (Ex 21:7). If at that time her Israelite husband found no delight in her, he could let her go; but he could not sell her as a slave.

15-17. Moses recognizes the rights of the first-born. If a man had two wives, of whom he hated one and loved the other, he could not give preference to the son of the one he loved over the natural inheritance of the son of the one he hated. Regardless of which mother was involved, the father had to regard the firstborn for what he was, the rightful heir, worthy of a double portion. Note the phrase **beginning of his strength,** which means the first child of his youth.

18-21. The punishment of an incorrigible son seems severe on the surface, but an examination of the text reveals the severity of the boy's problem. First, the elders of the city were to hear the case at the city gate, which was the seat of town authority; public affairs were discussed there (22:15; 25:7). When the parents accused their son of being stubborn and rebellious, such a charge was almost proof in itself. The heart of a loving father and mother could not be brought to such a point unless their child's sin was a fact. But the guilt of the boy was more than just disobedience. Note the text: **he is a glutton, and a drunkard.**

rebellious, he will not obey our voice; *he is* a glutton, and a drunkard.
21 And all the men of his city shall stone him with stones, that he die: so shalt thou put evil away from among you; and all Israel shall hear, and fear.

22 ¶And if a man have committed a sin worthy of death, and he be to be put to death, and thou hang him on a tree:
23 His body shall not remain all night upon the tree, but thou shalt in any wise bury him that day; (for he that is hanged *is* accursed of God;) that thy land be not defiled, which the LORD thy God giveth thee *for* an inheritance.

CHAPTER 22
THOU shalt not see thy brother's ox or his sheep go astray, and hide thyself from them: thou shalt in any case bring them again unto thy brother.
2 And if thy brother *be* not nigh unto thee, or if thou know him not, then thou shalt bring it unto thine own house, and it shall be with thee until thy brother seek after it, and thou shalt restore it to him again.
3 In like manner shalt thou do with his ass; and so shalt thou do with his raiment; and with all lost things of thy brother's, which he hath lost, and thou hast found, shalt thou do likewise: thou mayest not hide thyself.
4 ¶Thou shalt not see thy brother's ass or his ox fall down by the way, and hide thyself from them: thou shalt surely help him to lift *them* up again.
5 ¶The woman shall not wear that which pertaineth unto a man, neither shall a man put on a woman's garment: for all that do so *are* abomination unto the LORD thy God.
6 ¶If a bird's nest chance to be before thee in the way in any tree, or on the ground, *whether they be* young ones, or eggs, and the dam sitting upon the young, or upon the eggs, thou shalt not take the dam with the young:
7 *But* thou shalt in any wise let the dam go, and take the young to thee; that it may be well with thee, and *that* thou mayest prolong *thy* days.
8 ¶When thou buildest a new house, then thou shalt make a battlement for thy roof, that thou bring not blood upon thine house, if any man fall from thence.
9 ¶Thou shalt not sow thy vineyard with divers seeds: lest the fruit of thy seed which thou hast sown, and the fruit of thy vineyard, be defiled.
10 ¶Thou shalt not plow with an ox and an ass together.
11 ¶Thou shalt not wear a garment of divers sorts, *as* of woollen and linen together.
12 ¶Thou shalt make thee fringes upon the four quarters of thy vesture, wherewith thou coverest *thyself.*
13 ¶If any man take a wife, and go in unto her, and hate her,

This charge showed that the son was unmanageable and incorrigible. The punishment was stoning to death by the men of the town, not by the father and mother. The basis of such severe punishment was the idea that if a man would not obey his parents, he would not obey God, nor was he likely to obey civil authority. Punishing the incorrigible son was punishing crime in its embryonic form.

22-23. For certain crimes, men were hanged upon a tree until they were dead, i.e., were crucified. Such a man was **accursed of God**, reminding us that, "Christ hath redeemed us from the curse of the law, being made a curse for us . . . ." (Gal 3:13). Also, one who was thus executed had to be taken from the tree the same day that he died. Joseph and Nicodemus, who requested the body of Jesus (Jn 19:38-40), were not only expressing their love for Christ, they were fulfilling Old Testament law. Historically, there is no record of a man having been executed by crucifixion in the Old Testament. Stoning was the usual method of execution. However, God prophetically included this portion of Scripture so that Christ might die on a cross to fulfill prophecy, not a bone of Him being broken (cf. Jn 19:36).

22:1-12. This chapter deals with the duties of a man toward his neighbor. Israel was to recognize the sanctity of private property. Therefore, every man had to help preserve that which belonged to his neighbor. As an illustration, Moses commanded that a man was to care for stray animals (vss. 2, 4).

Verse 5 has caused divisions and confusion among sincere Christian brethren. Some have used this verse to maintain that women should not wear slacks. The word **pertaineth unto** (Heb *keli*) in the original language is used elsewhere not only of clothes, but also of decorations or utensils used by the opposite sex. The intent of this law was to maintain the distinction between the sexes. Today, it would apply to any unisex clothing that would cloud the distinction between men and women. The New Testament recognizes such a distinction (I Cor 11:3) and maintains that long hair on women was a sign of that distinction (I Cor 11:6-14). During the days of Moses, garments (Heb *simlah*) worn by men and women were very similar (robes), so this command was designed to keep a woman from appearing as a man for purposes of licentiousness (to deceive the man). The major difference between male and female robes was their decoration or ornamentation, and not their cut. The principle taught by this passage is that the proper distinction between men and women in all cultures should be maintained. The passage does not teach against slacks *per se* (or hats, shoes, gloves, etc.—all worn by both sexes), but against men or women wearing any item specifically ornamented for the opposite sex (e.g., a man wearing female slacks, lipstick, etc.). The wearing of slacks by ladies today is not an attempt to deceive men, although some may be immodest and improper in certain situations. The final criteria are that women look like females, that they are modest (I Tim 2:9-10), and that their outward appearance reflects their inner character (I Pet 3:3).

The Lord recognizes the affection of parents for their young. This is reflected by a law that commanded men to help animals protect their young (vss. 6-7). This also applied to the building of houses. Since roofs were flat, each new home was to have a balustrade to protect people from falling off accidentally. Finally, (vss. 9-11), God prohibits mixing together the things that were separated in His creation.

13-21. Moses honors the laws of chastity in marriage on the basis that marriage must be founded upon faithfulness and

363

14 And give occasions of speech against her, and bring up an evil name upon her, and say, I took this woman, and when I came to her, I found her not a maid:

15 Then shall the father of the damsel, and her mother, take and bring forth *the tokens of* the damsel's virginity unto the elders of the city in the gate:

16 And the damsel's father shall say unto the elders, I gave my daughter unto this man to wife, and he hateth her;

17 And, lo, he hath given occasions of speech *against her*, saying, I found not thy daughter a maid; and yet these *are the tokens of* my daughter's virginity. And they shall spread the cloth before the elders of the city.

18 And the elders of that city shall take that man and chastise him;

19 And they shall amerce him in an hundred *shekels* of silver, and give *them* unto the father of the damsel, because he hath brought up an evil name upon a virgin of Israel: and she shall be his wife; he may not put her away all his days.

20 But if this thing be true, *and the tokens of* virginity be not found for the damsel:

21 Then they shall bring out the damsel to the door of her father's house, and the men of her city shall stone her with stones that she die: because she hath wrought folly in Israel, to play the whore in her father's house: so shalt thou put evil away from among you.

22 ¶If a man be found lying with a woman married to an husband, then they shall both of them die, *both* the man that lay with the woman, and the woman: so shalt thou put away evil from Israel.

23 If a damsel *that is* a virgin be betrothed unto an husband, and a man find her in the city, and lie with her;

24 Then ye shall bring them both out unto the gate of that city, and ye shall stone them with stones that they die; the damsel, because she cried not, *being* in the city; and the man, because he hath humbled his neighbour's wife: so thou shalt put away evil from among you.

25 ¶But if a man find a betrothed damsel in the field, and the man force her, and lie with her: then the man only that lay with her shall die:

26 But unto the damsel thou shalt do nothing; *there is* in the damsel no sin worthy of death: for as when a man riseth against his neighbour, and slayeth him, even so *is* this matter:

27 For he found her in the field, *and* the betrothed damsel cried, and *there was* none to save her.

28 ¶If a man find a damsel *that is* a virgin, which is not betrothed, and lay hold on her, and lie with her, and they be found;

29 Then the man that lay with her shall give unto the damsel's father fifty *shekels* of silver, and she shall be his wife; because he hath humbled her, he may not put her away all his days.

purity. To illustrate, he uses the case of a man who marries a woman and after gratifying his carnality tries to get rid of her by accusing her of not being a virgin (vss. 13-21). As a result, the husband gives the wife an evil name. The father and mother were to bring **tokens of the damsel's virginity** to the elders of the city for a public hearing. These tokens were the blood-spotted bed clothes taken directly from the marriage bed. These were sufficient proof of her virginity and established her premarital chastity. The elders were to accept such proof. Their judgment on the husband was to be threefold. First, they were to **chastise him,** which meant they were to administer forty stripes with the whip for his lying. Second, they were to impose a fine of one hundred shekels of silver which he was to pay to the father of the young girl. Third, the elders were to deprive the man of his divorce rights. On the other hand, if the tokens of her virginity were not found, she was to be led to the door of her father's house and there stoned by the men of the city for her unfaithfulness. The execution was administered at **the door of her father's house** because she had been wrong **to play the whore** there.

22-25. Moses gives instructions concerning rape and the seduction of a virgin. He deals with three issues. First, if a betrothed virgin allowed a man who was not her fiancé to have intercourse with her within the city, they were both to be taken out of town and stoned to death. Even if she was raped, she was guilty because she had not cried out for help. In this instance, God placed betrothal on a par with marriage. Hence, when the virgin Mary was betrothed to Joseph, it was a union as sacred and permanent as marriage.

26-27. On the other hand, if a man met a betrothed girl in a field and raped her, this was not a death-sin for her. She could not call for and receive help in the open field.

28-30. The third case involves a man's finding a virgin who is not betrothed and having intercourse with her. The man was forced to pay the girl's father fifty shekels of silver, and also forced to marry the girl whom he had humbled. The Scripture adds that he was not able to divorce her later.

The last verse in the chapter prohibits incest. The word **skirt** is a figure of speech for a father's nakedness.

30 ¶A man shall not take his father's wife, nor discover his father's skirt.

CHAPTER 23

HE that is wounded in the stones, or hath his privy member cut off, shall not enter into the congregation of the Lord.

2 A bastard shall not enter into the congregation of the Lord; even to his tenth generation shall he not enter into the congregation of the Lord.

3 An Ammonite or Moabite shall not enter into the congregation of the Lord; even to their tenth generation shall they not enter into the congregation of the Lord for ever:

4 Because they met you not with bread and with water in the way, when ye came forth out of Egypt; and because they hired against thee Bā'laam the son of Bē'ôr of Pē'thôr of Mĕs-o-po-tā'mĭ-a, to curse thee.

5 Nevertheless the Lord thy God would not hearken unto Bā'laam; but the Lord thy God turned the curse into a blessing unto thee, because the Lord thy God loved thee.

6 Thou shalt not seek their peace nor their prosperity all thy days for ever.

7 Thou shalt not abhor an Edomite; for he is thy brother: thou shalt not abhor an Egyptian; because thou wast a stranger in his land.

8 The children that are begotten of them shall enter into the congregation of the Lord in their third generation.

9 ¶When the host goeth forth against thine enemies, then keep thee from every wicked thing.

10 If there be among you any man, that is not clean by reason of uncleanness that chanceth him by night, then shall he go abroad out of the camp, he shall not come within the camp:

11 But it shall be, when evening cometh on, he shall wash himself with water: and when the sun is down, he shall come into the camp again.

12 Thou shalt have a place also without the camp, whither thou shalt go forth abroad:

13 And thou shalt have a paddle upon thy weapon; and it shall be, when thou wilt ease thyself abroad, thou shalt dig therewith, and shalt turn back and cover that which cometh from thee:

14 For the Lord thy God walketh in the midst of thy camp, to deliver thee, and to give up thine enemies before thee; therefore shall thy camp be holy: that he see no unclean thing in thee, and turn away from thee.

15 ¶Thou shalt not deliver unto his master the servant which is escaped from his master unto thee:

16 He shall dwell with thee, even among you, in that place which he shall choose in one of thy gates, where it

23:1-2. Moses explains the qualifications of citizenship in Israel. A man who was mutilated in his sexual members, literally "wounded by crushing," could not be an Israelite. This excluded him from holding an office in the congregation, from marrying an Israelite woman, and from admission to the covenant of fellowship. He was mutilated in the nature of man, as created by God. He could not have an heir; so he could not share in the inheritance of Israel.

Also, the child begotten out of wedlock or incest was illegitimate and unworthy of Israelite citizenship for ten generations. This does not mean, as some mistakenly think, that an illegitimate person cannot be saved or be used greatly by God. His mercy and grace through Christ are sufficient for all.

3-8. Some see the word **for ever** as complete exclusion. However, Ruth, the Moabitess (Ruth 1:1), was married to Boaz (a Jew); and she was received into full Israelite covenant relationship. Ruth became an heir of the promise and was also in the line of the Messiah. She was in the eleventh generation from Moab, who was born out of an act of incest (Gen 19:30-38). Also, note that David was listed as the tenth generation descendant of Pharez (cf. Gen 38; Ruth 4). The Ammonites and Moabites were also excluded because of their treatment of Israel when Israel came out of Egypt, for they had hired Baalam to curse God's people.

9-14. The people were commanded to stay pure in the camp. Moses told them to keep from **every wicked thing,** which is a reference to excrement. They were not to defile their camp by any type of uncleanness, so that when Jehovah walked through the camp, He would not see any unclean thing and so turn away from Israel. If a man became unclean by chance during the night, he was to go out of the camp during the day and not return until the following evening. The Bible commands him to wash with water. The soldiers were to carry a shovel, i.e., paddle, to dig a hole for their demands of nature. There was nothing shameful in the excrement itself; the attitude of a person toward uncleanness determined his purity.

15-18. Slaves who escaped from a foreign country and sought refuge in Israel were allowed to dwell in the land. On the other hand, male and female prostitutes of Israelite descent were not tolerated. This command also excluded foreign prostitutes. Specifically, the use of prostitutes was prohibited as an act of worship in the house of the Lord. The phrase **the price of a dog**

liketh him best: thou shalt not oppress him.

17 ¶There shall be no whore of the daughters of Israel, nor a sodomite of the sons of Israel.

18 Thou shalt not bring the hire of a whore, or the price of a dog, into the house of the LORD thy God for any vow: for even both these *are* abomination unto the LORD thy God.

19 ¶Thou shalt not lend upon usury to thy brother; usury of money, usury of victuals, usury of any thing that is lent upon usury:

20 Unto a stranger thou mayest lend upon usury; but unto thy brother thou shalt not lend upon usury: that the LORD thy God may bless thee in all that thou settest thine hand to in the land whither thou goest to possess it.

21 ¶When thou shalt vow a vow unto the LORD thy God, thou shalt not slack to pay it: for the LORD thy God will surely require it of thee; and it would be sin in thee.

22 But if thou shalt forbear to vow, it shall be no sin in thee.

23 That which is gone out of thy lips thou shalt keep and perform; *even* a freewill offering, according as thou hast vowed unto the LORD thy God, which thou hast promised with thy mouth.

24 ¶When thou comest into thy neighbour's vineyard, then thou mayest eat grapes thy fill at thine own pleasure; but thou shalt not put *any* in thy vessel.

25 When thou comest into the standing corn of thy neighbour, then thou mayest pluck the ears with thine hand; but thou shalt not move a sickle unto thy neighbour's standing corn.

CHAPTER 24

WHEN a man hath taken a wife, and married her, and it come to pass that she find no favour in his eyes, because he hath found some uncleanness in her: then let him write her a bill of divorcement, and give *it* in her hand, and send her out of his house.

2 And when she is departed out of his house, she may go and be another man's *wife*.

3 And *if* the latter husband hate her, and write her a bill of divorcement, and giveth *it* in her hand, and sendeth her out of his house; or if the latter husband die, which took her *to be* his wife;

4 Her former husband, which sent her away, may not take her again to be his wife, after that she is defiled; for that *is* abomination before the LORD: and thou shalt not cause the land to sin, which the LORD thy God giveth thee *for* an inheritance.

5 ¶When a man hath taken a new wife, he shall not go out to war, neither shall he be charged with any business: *but* he shall be free at home one year, and shall cheer up his wife which he hath taken.

does not refer to the sale price of a dog, but to the dog-like manner in which a man debased himself when he fulfilled his lust with a prostitute.

19-24. Moses gives summary laws for Israel and the land in this section. Israel was not to take interest (usury) from lending to their brothers; but when they lent to strangers, they could collect interest. This is one of the ways by which God would bless them and by which they would prosper financially. When a man vowed a vow and added the Lord's name to that vow, he was required to pay it. This is probably a reference to borrowing money and vowing to repay it. However, men did not have to give the vow when borrowing money; they needed only to keep their word.

25. The illustration of walking through a neighbor's field and eating his fruit is a sign of grace and neighborliness. A man could not put a sickle to his neighbor's corn, nor could he put anything in a container. He could only pick that which he could eat immediately. When Jesus went through the corn fields, He plucked the ears of corn, rubbed out the grain, and ate the food (Mt 12:1; Lk 6:1).

24:1-5. This section contains two laws concerning the relationship of a man to his wife. The first concerns divorce. The custom of giving letters of divorce was probably adopted by the Israelites from the Egyptians because they had a practice of writing out contracts in relationship to every area of life. Jesus noted that Moses did not abolish the tradition "because of the hardness of [the people's] hearts" (Mt 19:8). The basis for a divorce occurred when a man's wife did not find favor in his sight because he **found some uncleanness in her.** The word uncleanness (Heb '*arwah*) means "shame" or "disgrace." Its interpretation has been disputed among the rabbis. If the uncleanness was adultery, it would be punished by death (Ex 20:14; Lev 20:10; Deut 22:22). Because its meaning was unclear, the Pharisees tempted Jesus by asking, "Is it lawful for a man to put away his wife for every cause?" (Mt 19:3). It is thought that the meaning was attached to nakedness, disgrace, or some other action having to do with sexual uncleanness which would bring shame upon the family, but was short of adultery.

If a woman was divorced and married another man, she could not return and marry her first husband. There are two reasons: first, a reunion would lower the dignity of the woman, inasmuch as she would appear to be like property, to be disposed of and reclaimed; second, the physical union of marriage made man and wife "one flesh" (Gen 2:24). When that union was broken by another, adultery was committed. Jesus supports this interpretation when He says, "whosoever shall marry her that is divorced committeth adultery" (Mt 5:32). Even if she remarried her former husband, adultery was committed because the original union was broken.

The importance of marriage is reinforced by Moses when he commands that the newly married man was not required to perform military service for a whole year (vs. 5). Also, the bridegroom could not be required to be away from the home for business. God recognized the importance of a good adjustment in marriage, so the man was to remain home with his wife during their first year of marriage.

6-9. Moses gives various prohibitions regarding life. A creditor could not take the upper millstone as security for a debt, because the entire mill would be useless. The family would then be unable to prepare daily food for the house. Moses also repeats the law against man stealing (Ex 21:16). Then he notes that Israel shall obey the priests' teaching concerning leprosy. The phrase **Take heed** does not mean to be on guard against coming in physical contact with leprosy. Rather, it meant to be on spiritual guard, i.e., to obey the teachings of the priest. Disobedience brought punishment, which could be leprosy. The Vulgate would be translated, "Watch diligently, that thou do not incur the plague of leprosy."

6 ¶No man shall take the nether or the upper millstone to pledge: for he taketh *a man's* life to pledge.

7 ¶If a man be found stealing any of his brethren of the children of Israel, and maketh merchandise of him, or selleth him; then that thief shall die; and thou shalt put evil away from among you.

8 ¶Take heed in the plague of leprosy, that thou observe diligently, and do according to all that the priests the Lēvītes shall teach you: as I commanded them, *so* ye shall observe to do.

9 Remember what the Lord thy God did unto Miriam by the way, after that ye were come forth out of Egypt.

10 ¶When thou dost lend thy brother any thing, thou shalt not go into his house to fetch his pledge.

11 Thou shalt stand abroad, and the man to whom thou dost lend shall bring out the pledge abroad unto thee.

12 And if the man *be* poor, thou shalt not sleep with his pledge:

13 In any case thou shalt deliver him the pledge again when the sun goeth down, that he may sleep in his own raiment, and bless thee: and it shall be righteousness unto thee before the Lord thy God.

14 ¶Thou shalt not oppress an hired servant *that is* poor and needy, *whether he be* of thy brethren, or of thy strangers that *are* in thy land within thy gates:

15 At his day thou shalt give *him* his hire, neither shall the sun go down upon it; for he *is* poor, and setteth his heart upon it: lest he cry against thee unto the Lord: and it be sin unto thee.

16 ¶The fathers shall not be put to death for the children, neither shall the children be put to death for the fathers: every man shall be put to death for his own sin.

17 ¶Thou shalt not pervert the judgment of the stranger, *nor* of the fatherless; nor take a widow's raiment to pledge:

18 But thou shalt remember that thou wast a bondman in Egypt, and the Lord thy God redeemed thee thence: therefore I command thee to do this thing.

19 ¶When thou cuttest down thine harvest in thy field, and hast forgot a sheaf in the field, thou shalt not go again to fetch it: it shall be for the stranger, for the fatherless, and for the widow: that the Lord thy God may bless thee in all the work of thine hands.

20 When thou beatest thine olive tree, thou shalt not go over the boughs again: it shall be for the stranger, for the fatherless, and for the widow.

21 When thou gatherest the grapes of thy vineyard, thou shalt not glean *it*

10-15. Moses gives commandments against oppressing the poor. It was against the Torah to go into the house of a poor man and collect a debt. The phrase **stand abroad** meant that the borrower was to bring the money to the home of the creditor. That the rich man was not to sleep with his pledge meant that the poor often had nothing to secure a loan but his upper garment or topcoat. Therefore, Moses says to return the topcoat in the evening so that the poor may sleep in warmth. Also, the rich could not withhold the wages of the poor to collect a debt, in our society called garnisheeing his wages. The Lord noticed that the poor **setteth his heart upon it.** Literally, this meant, "he lifts up his soul" or "he needs his money to live."

16-18. Moses prohibits further injustices, such as taking the life of the son for the crime of his father or vice versa. The Lord teaches that everyone shall be punished for his own crime, underscoring the necessity of personal responsibility.

19-22. Moses told the people how to harvest their crops. Once the laborers had gone through a field, they could not return to pick up the gleanings (Lev 19:10). God provided for the poor by allowing them to follow the reapers and pick up what was left of the scattered grain. They also could go through the vineyards to pick up the leftover grapes. God respected their dignity and gave them work to make a living. Later, Ruth went through the fields picking up the gleanings of the grain (Ruth 1:22).

afterward: it shall be for the stranger, for the fatherless, and for the widow.

22 And thou shalt remember that thou wast a bondman in the land of Egypt: therefore I command thee to do this thing.

CHAPTER 25

IF there be a controversy between men, and they come unto judgment, that the judges may judge them; then they shall justify the righteous, and condemn the wicked.

2 And it shall be, if the wicked man be worthy to be beaten, that the judge shall cause him to lie down, and to be beaten before his face, according to his fault, by a certain number.

3 Forty stripes he may give him, and not exceed: lest, if he should exceed, and beat him above these with many stripes, then thy brother should seem vile unto thee.

4 ¶Thou shalt not muzzle the ox when he treadeth out the corn.

5 ¶If brethren dwell together, and one of them die, and have no child, the wife of the dead shall not marry without unto a stranger: her husband's brother shall go in unto her, and take her to him to wife, and perform the duty of an husband's brother unto her.

6 And it shall be, that the firstborn which she beareth shall succeed in the name of his brother which is dead, that his name be not put out of Israel.

7 And if the man like not to take his brother's wife, then let his brother's wife go up to the gate unto the elders, and say, My husband's brother refuseth to raise up unto his brother a name in Israel, he will not perform the duty of my husband's brother.

8 Then the elders of his city shall call him, and speak unto him: and if he stand to it, and say, I like not to take her;

9 Then shall his brother's wife come unto him in the presence of the elders, and loose his shoe from off his foot, and spit in his face, and shall answer and say, So shall it be done unto that man that will not build up his brother's house.

10 And his name shall be called in Israel, The house of him that hath his shoe loosed.

11 ¶When men strive together one with another, and the wife of the one draweth near for to deliver her husband out of the hand of him that smiteth him, and putteth forth her hand, and taketh him by the secrets:

12 Then thou shalt cut off her hand, thine eye shall not pity her.

13 ¶Thou shalt not have in thy bag divers weights, a great and a small.

25:1-4. Moses recognizes the authority of corporal punishment. The judges of the different towns could pronounce a man "guilty" (Ex 22:8). For those not counted worthy of death, the punishment was beating. The phrase **wicked man be worthy** means "son of stripes" and identifies a man liable to be punished. He was to be beaten forty times with the whip, the number forty symbolizing judgment. However, the Law indicated that the guilty could not receive more than forty stripes; so the Jews gave a man forty lashes less one. Paul was beaten by the Jews five times after this manner (II Cor 11:24).

In verse 4 Moses commands that the ox be not muzzled when he is working. This applied to all animals, not merely the ox. The Apostle Paul applied the principle of the toiling ox to the serving minister (I Tim 5:18), showing that the laborer is worthy of his reward.

5-6. Moses commands that a surviving brother was to marry his brother's widow. This is called the law of the kinsman-redeemer. This law was an ancient tradition (Gen 38:8-11), and Moses recognized its value and included it in the Torah. A brother-in-law was requested to marry his brother's widow to carry on the inheritance in Israel. The spiritual and physical heritage was given to Abraham and his seed (Gen 12:1-3). Therefore, it was necessary to produce children to carry on the promise of God. Hence, the family would preserve its name and spiritual heritage by having a son who would perpetuate the family line. Israel sometimes applied this law to the childless couple, or at other times to the situation of a couple who had only a daughter. This law has its greatest human application in the story of Ruth, the Moabitess. After the death of her Israelite husband, Ruth married another Israelite named Boaz, her deceased husband's closest kinsman. When he applied this law and raised up a son by Ruth, he perpetuated the line of the Messiah (Ruth 4:17-22; cf. Mt 1, esp. vs. 5).

7-10. If a man refused to become the kinsman-redeemer, the widow was to bring him before the town magistrates at the city gate. She was to loose his shoe from off his foot, symbolic of the exchange of property. By tradition, a person walked over his property to assert his ownership. Therefore, exchanging shoes was symbolic of exchanging property. When the man refused to raise up his brother's kin, she took his shoe, which was symbolic of his losing the inheritance. He was thus deprived of a position which he ought to have had via receiving the inheritance of the deceased brother. The phrase **spit in his face** merely meant to spit on the ground before his eyes. That was a disgrace to him in the eyes of the elders, because he had repudiated the inheritance of Israel.

11-16. In this section Moses gives definite regulations concerning business life in Israel. The phrase **divers weights, a great and a small** is literally "stone and stone." A person often had two stones in his bag for weighing, a large one for buying and a small one for selling. Hence, that person was deceitful and covetous. **A perfect and just weight** spoke of a man's honor. Such a man would lengthen his stay in the land.

14 Thou shalt not have in thine house divers measures, a great and a small.

15 *But* thou shalt have a perfect and just weight, a perfect and just measure shalt thou have: that thy days may be lengthened in the land which the LORD thy God giveth thee.

16 For all that do such things, *and* all that do unrighteously, *are* an abomination unto the LORD thy God.

17 ¶Remember what Ăm′a-lĕk did unto thee by the way, when ye were come forth out of Egypt;

18 How he met thee by the way, and smote the hindmost of thee, *even* all *that* *were* feeble behind thee, when thou *wast* faint and weary; and he feared not God.

19 Therefore it shall be, when the LORD thy God hath given thee rest from all thine enemies round about, in the land which the LORD thy God giveth thee *for* an inheritance to possess it, *that* thou shalt blot out the remembrance of Ăm′a-lĕk from under heaven; thou shalt not forget *it*.

CHAPTER 26

AND it shall be, when thou *art* come in unto the land which the LORD thy God giveth thee *for* an inheritance, and possessest it, and dwellest therein;

2 That thou shalt take of the first of all the fruit of the earth, which thou shalt bring of thy land that the LORD thy God giveth thee, and shalt put *it* in a basket, and shalt go unto the place which the LORD thy God shall choose to place his name there.

3 And thou shalt go unto the priest that shall be in those days, and say unto him, I profess this day unto the LORD thy God, that I am come unto the country which the LORD sware unto our fathers for to give us.

4 And the priest shall take the basket out of thine hand, and set it down before the altar of the LORD thy God.

5 And thou shalt speak and say before the LORD thy God, A Syrian ready to perish *was* my father, and he went down into Egypt, and sojourned there with a few, and became there a nation, great, mighty, and populous:

6 And the Egyptians evil entreated us, and afflicted us, and laid upon us hard bondage:

7 And when we cried unto the LORD God of our fathers, the LORD heard our voice, and looked on our affliction, and our labour, and our oppression:

8 And the LORD brought us forth out of Egypt with a mighty hand, and with an outstretched arm, and with great terribleness, and with signs, and with wonders:

9 And he hath brought us into this place, and hath given us this land, *even* a land that floweth with milk and honey.

10 And now, behold, I have brought the firstfruits of the land, which thou, O LORD, hast given me. And thou shalt set

17-19. God commands Israel not to forget Amalek. This nation had attacked the weary, the aged, and the children when Israel passed through its borders. God abhorred this despicable act and commanded Israel to completely blot out Amalek. Egypt typifies the world that God's people were to flee. Amalek typifies the flesh that hinders God's people from leaving the world. Baalam had prophesied that when the sceptre would rise out of Israel (referring to the coming of Christ), He would have complete dominion (Num 24:20). Then Amalek will perish forever. In this way the Bible promises that when we receive our glorified bodies, we will no longer have difficulties with the flesh.

26:1-2. Moses commands the people to bring the first fruits of the ground and present them to the Lord at the place of worship as a symbol that they had finally conquered the land. Some scholars believe that this was a command to be followed only once. However, the first fruits were offered yearly on the day after Passover (Lev 23:10-11).

3-4. The first of the fruits were presented to the Lord in a basket made of wicker (vss. 2-4). The priest was not the high priest, but one who attended to the sacrifice of the altar and who received the sacrificial gifts. When Israel made the statement **I profess this day unto the LORD** it was a confession of faith in God. The fruit was a tangible proof that Israel had occupied the land as they had been commanded. Also, the fruit was a practical confession that they were indebted to God for the gift of the land. As a prayer of thanksgiving, Israel recognized that her existence was based on the grace of God and manifested in a miraculous redemption out of Egypt.

5-11. The phrase **A Syrian ready to perish was my father** means "an Aramaen was my father"; this reference was to Jacob. The word **perish** meant "in danger of being destroyed." The danger was not spiritual temptation, but the prospect of extinction. Although Abraham was the leader of a large tribe of at least three hundred eighteen armed men (Gen 14:14), Jacob had only seventy souls with him when he went to Egypt (Gen 46:27). The reference is to Jacob rather than Abraham, because Jacob was the father of the sons who led the twelve tribes. Also, the nation derived its name Israel from him. Jacob is called an Aramaean because of his long stay in Syria (Gen 29-31) and because his two wives and most of his children came from there. When an Israelite appeared before God and called himself an Aramaean, it was a confession of his worthlessness and a testimony that he depended upon the grace of God.

The phrase **now behold** (vs. 10) signifies that the person made his confession before he brought the basket to God. Then Moses commanded **thou shalt set it before the LORD** (vs. 10), meaning that after the confession the basket was to be set before the Lord.

it before the LORD thy God, and worship before the LORD thy God:

11 And thou shalt rejoice in every good *thing* which the LORD thy God hath given unto thee, and unto thine house, thou, and the Levite, and the stranger that *is* among you.

12 ¶When thou hast made an end of tithing all the tithes of thine increase the third year, *which is* the year of tithing, and hast given *it* unto the Levite, the stranger, the fatherless, and the widow, that they may eat within thy gates, and be filled;

13 Then thou shalt say before the LORD thy God, I have brought away the hallowed things out of *mine* house, and also have given them unto the Levite, and unto the stranger, to the fatherless, and to the widow, according to all thy commandments which thou hast commanded me: I have not transgressed thy commandments, neither have I forgotten *them:*

14 I have not eaten thereof in my mourning, neither have I taken away *ought* thereof for *any* unclean *use,* nor given *ought* thereof for the dead: but I have hearkened to the voice of the LORD my God, *and* have done according to all that thou hast commanded me.

15 Look down from thy holy habitation, from heaven, and bless thy people Israel, and the land which thou hast given us, as thou swarest unto our fathers, a land that floweth with milk and honey.

16 ¶This day the LORD thy God hath commanded thee to do these statutes and judgments: thou shalt therefore keep and do them with all thine heart, and with all thy soul.

17 Thou hast avouched the LORD this day to be thy God, and to walk in his ways, and to keep his statutes, and his commandments, and his judgments, and to hearken unto his voice:

18 And the LORD hath avouched thee this day to be his peculiar people, as he hath promised thee, and that *thou* shouldest keep all his commandments;

19 And to make thee high above all nations which he hath made, in praise, and in name, and in honour; and that thou mayest be an holy people unto the LORD thy God, as he hath spoken.

CHAPTER 27

AND Moses with the elders of Israel commanded the people, saying, Keep all the commandments which I command you this day.

2 And it shall be on the day when ye shall pass over Jordan unto the land which the LORD thy God giveth thee, that thou shalt set thee up great stones, and plaister them with plaister:

3 And thou shalt write upon them all the words of this law, when thou art passed over, that thou mayest go in unto the land which the LORD thy God giveth thee, a land that floweth with

370

12-15. Moses commands Israel to deliver the tithe to the sanctuary, or to the place of corporate worship. He uses the phrase **tithing all the tithes,** which means "paying all the tithes that are commanded." After the tithes were paid, a person could **say before the LORD thy God** a prayer that an Israelite could make at any place. He was not necessarily confined to praying in the sanctuary. He could invoke the blessing of God on his endeavor because he had obeyed God and had sanctified his house. The phrase **the hallowed things** is a reference to the tithe. It was called holy. A person was to cleanse his house by delivering everything out of it that was tithe, i.e., every tenth head of cattle born, a tenth of the crops, a tenth of the profit, etc. Moses reminds them not to eat the tithe. They could not even use it to send as provision to the house of a friend who was mourning a death. Some have mistakenly interpreted this verse as meaning that Moses was prohibiting Israel from putting money or provisions into a grave along with the corpse as the Egyptians did.

16-19. Moses ends this discourse by demanding a public confession by Israel. Israel **avouched** that they accepted the Lord as their God and that they promised to walk in His ways. After the people did this, the Lord **avouched** that Israel was His peculiar people. They would be God's praise, honor, and glory. In the New Testament Christians are reminded that they are a peculiar people: ". . . ye should shew forth the praises of him who hath called you out of darkness into his marvelous light" (I Pet 2:9). Therefore, the sanctification of Israel is similar to the sanctification of Christians in the New Testament.

IV. RENEWAL OF ISRAEL'S COVENANT. 27:1-30:20.

In this section, renewal of the covenant that was given at Horeb is promised when Israel occupies Canaan and fulfills the law of the Lord. The commandments in this chapter are to be specifically carried out in the Land of Promise. Up until this time, the sermons by Moses in Deuteronomy had centered on the second giving of the Law, or the repetition of the Torah. This section is different because it does not deal with repetition of the Law already given, but with the future application of the Law.

A. Reminder of Blessings and Curses. 27:1-28:68.

27:1-10. This chapter begins with Moses and the elders giving commandments to Israel. Beginning with verse 9, the giving of commandments continues with the priests and Levites. Israel is commanded to keep the Law. In order to do this they were commanded to set up large stones on Mount Ebal, which was the mount of cursings. (Since the Law carried a curse, it is to be expected that the Law was to be written on the mount of cursings.) Moses does not tell the people how many large stones to set up, but he prescribes that they were to be plastered with a coating of lime or gypsum. This was similar to the custom in Egypt where they covered their walls and buildings with lime, then painted them with figures and heiroglyphics. The tempor-

milk and honey; as the LORD God of thy fathers hath promised thee.

4 Therefore it shall be when ye be gone over Jordan, *that* ye shall set up these stones, which I command you this day, in mount Ebal, and thou shalt plaister them with plaister.

5 And there shalt thou build an altar unto the LORD thy God, an altar of stones: thou shalt not lift up *any* iron *tool* upon them.

6 Thou shalt build the altar of the LORD thy God of whole stones: and thou shalt offer burnt offerings thereon unto the LORD thy God:

7 And thou shalt offer peace offerings, and shalt eat there, and rejoice before the LORD thy God.

8 And thou shalt write upon the stones all the words of this law very plainly.

9 ¶And Moses and the priests the Lēvītes spake unto all Israel, saying, Take heed, and hearken, O Israel; this day thou art become the people of the LORD thy God.

10 Thou shalt therefore obey the voice of the LORD thy God, and do his commandments and his statutes, which I command thee this day.

11 ¶And Moses charged the people the same day, saying,

12 These shall stand upon mount Gĕr'i-zīm to bless the people, when ye are come over Jordan; Simeon, and Levi, and Judah, and Ĭs'sa-char, and Joseph, and Benjamin:

13 And these shall stand upon mount Ebal to curse; Reuben, Gad, and Asher, and Zĕb'u-lun, Dan, and Năph'ta-lī.

14 ¶And the Lēvītes shall speak, and say unto all the men of Israel with a loud voice,

15 Cursed *be* the man that maketh *any* graven or molten image, an abomination unto the LORD, the work of the hands of the craftsman, and putteth *it* in *a* secret *place*. And all the people shall answer and say, Amen.

16 Cursed *be* he that setteth light by his father or his mother. And all the people shall say, Amen.

17 Cursed *be* he that removeth his neighbour's landmark. And all the people shall say, Amen.

ary coating of lime indicated that the writing of the laws on these large stones was not for posterity, but was to be done as a public announcement. They were told to write the laws **very plainly.**

There must have been a large number of stones because Moses was commanded to write **all the words of this law.** The phrase **this law** could be interpreted to mean "write the entire book of Deuteronomy." Others believe it means that they were to write the six hundred thirteen different commandments contained in the Pentateuch. Again, others believe that they were to select the most significant laws and write them as a symbol for the whole Law.

After they had written on the stones, God commanded them to **build an altar unto the LORD,** and to construct it with stones. These were not to be the same stones upon which they had written the Law, because the stones that were used for sacrifice were to be unhewn stones (Ex 20:22-25). The picture of the Law and the sacrifice together shows the relationship between law and grace. The Law brought a curse upon man because it revealed his sinfulness (Gal 3:13), but the altar was a symbol of the forgiveness grounded in the mercy of God. By connecting the sacrificial ceremony with the Law, Israel was given a practical demonstration of how it could settle the tension between perfection and redemption.

11-14. Moses divided the twelve tribes into two groups. Six tribes were to station themselves on the side of Mount Gerizim and face the valley. The other six tribes were likewise to station themselves on the side of Mount Ebal. The Levites were to stand in the midst of the valley (approximately 1600 feet across). The Levites were to read the curses in unison. Judging from the context, this must have made a great noise. In response to the readings, **all the people shall say, Amen** (vs. 26). Those who responded with an **Amen** were more than just the elders from each of the tribes (note the word **all**). The entire nation of Israel was involved in one loud praise service to God.

The six tribes on Mount Gerizim, the mount of blessings, were Simeon, Levi, Judah, Issachar, Joseph, and Benjamin (vs. 12). These were chosen to read the blessings because they sprang from the two accepted wives of Jacob, Leah and Rachel. On Mount Ebal, the mount of cursings, were situated Reuben, along with Gad and Asher, the two sons of Leah's maid Zilpah, and Zebulun, along with Dan and Napthali, the two sons of Rachel's maid, Bilhah (vs. 13). It was only natural that the blessing should be assigned to the tribes that came from Jacob's proper wives, since those sons occupied a higher position in the inheritance. But in order to secure the division into sixes, it was necessary that two of the eight sons of the proper wives should be associated with those who announced the curses. This distinction fell to Reuben, because he forfeited his rights through incest (Gen 49:4), and Zebulun, the youngest son of Leah.

The Levites who stationed themselves in the valley represented more than just the priests; they included the teachers and the guardians of the Law, as well as those who carried the ark of the covenant (Josh 8:30).

15-26. There are twelve curses listed in this section, and the Levites were to read them aloud. The curses applied to every breach of the Law, referring to sins and transgressions already mentioned by Moses in Deuteronomy. The one thing they all had in common was that these sins could easily be concealed from judicial authorities. What the eyes of the community leaders could not see, God asked all Israel (vs. 26) to testify to publicly. Hence, they would be convicted of their secret transgressions of the Law.

18 Cursed *be* he that maketh the blind to wander out of the way. And all the people shall say, Amen.

19 Cursed *be* he that perverteth the judgment of the stranger, fatherless, and widow. And all the people shall say, Amen.

20 Cursed *be* he that lieth with his father's wife; because he uncovereth his father's skirt. And all the people shall say, Amen.

21 Cursed *be* he that lieth with any manner of beast. And all the people shall say, Amen.

22 Cursed *be* he that lieth with his sister, the daughter of his father, or the daughter of his mother. And all the people shall say, Amen.

23 Cursed *be* he that lieth with his mother in law. And all the people shall say, Amen.

24 Cursed *be* he that smiteth his neighbour secretly. And all the people shall say, Amen.

25 Cursed *be* he that taketh reward to slay an innocent person. And all the people shall say, Amen.

26 Cursed *be* he that confirmeth not *all* the words of this law to do them. And all the people shall say, Amen.

CHAPTER 28

AND it shall come to pass, if thou shalt hearken diligently unto the voice of the LORD thy God, to observe *and* to do all his commandments which I command thee this day, that the LORD thy God will set thee on high above all nations of the earth:

2 And all these blessings shall come on thee, and overtake thee, if thou shalt hearken unto the voice of the LORD thy God.

3 Blessed *shalt* thou *be* in the city, and blessed *shalt* thou *be* in the field.

4 Blessed *shall be* the fruit of thy body, and the fruit of thy ground, and the fruit of thy cattle, the increase of thy kine, and the flocks of thy sheep.

5 Blessed *shall be* thy basket and thy store.

6 Blessed *shalt* thou *be* when thou comest in, and blessed *shalt* thou *be* when thou goest out.

7 The LORD shall cause thine enemies that rise up against thee to be smitten before thy face: they shall come out against thee one way, and flee before thee seven ways.

8 The LORD shall command the blessing upon thee in thy storehouses, and in all that thou settest thine hand unto; and he shall bless thee in the land which the LORD thy God giveth thee.

9 The LORD shall establish thee an holy people unto himself, as he hath sworn unto thee, if thou shalt keep the commandments of the LORD thy God, and walk in his ways.

10 And all people of the earth shall see that thou art called by the name of the LORD; and they shall be afraid of thee.

11 And the LORD shall make thee plenteous in goods, in the fruit of thy body, and in the fruit of thy cattle, and in the fruit of thy ground, in the land

28:1-14. This is one of the most solemn chapters in the Bible. An entire nation is given an opportunity to serve the Lord and enjoy the blessings of one of the most prosperous lands available. At the same time, the nation is warned that if it disobeys God, it will be completely decimated as a national entity by the judgment of Almighty God. Orthodox Jews read the entire Pentateuch each year in their synagogues. When they come to this chapter, the Rabbi reads it in a subdued voice. Even the Jew recognizes the sad and sorrowful history that came upon the nation which was heir to such wonderful promises. Here, approximately four thousand years ago, Moses predicted that the nation Israel would be scattered throughout the earth, that their people would endure suffering and tribulation, and yet that the individual Jew would not be annihilated. The fulfillment of these prophecies supports the supernatural origin of Deuteronomy. Today's Christian should read this chapter in reverence, realizing that ". . . if God spared not the natural branches, take heed lest He also spare not thee" (Rom 11:21).

The chapter begins with a condition, **if,** which implies the possibility of Israel's failure. The Bible teaches the responsibility of individuals; and this verse teaches the responsibility of the nation, which is the sum total of its individuals. Should Israel keep the commandments of the Lord, God promises to **set thee on high** (vs. 1).

The word **blessed** is repeated six times in this section to reflect the blessings of God in all areas of life (vss. 3-8). The Lord had called Israel a **holy people** (vs. 9) when He established the nation (Ex 19:6) and had based His promise on His sworn oath to the fathers (vs. 11), which was made to Abraham and Jacob. The phrase **the LORD shall make thee plenteous in goods** is, literally, "super abundance will the Lord give thee for good." The fact that God would make Israel the head and not the tail is self-interpretive. No other nation has ever had such an opportunity for self-advancement, self-prosperity, and self-expansion; if only they had obeyed God.

which the LORD sware unto thy fathers to give thee.

12 The LORD shall open unto thee his good treasure, the heaven to give the rain unto thy land in his season, and to bless all the work of thine hand: and thou shalt lend unto many nations, and thou shalt not borrow.

13 And the LORD shall make thee the head, and not the tail; and thou shalt be above only, and thou shalt not be beneath; if that thou hearken unto the commandments of the LORD thy God, which I command thee this day, to observe and to do them:

14 And thou shalt not go aside from any of the words which I command thee this day, to the right hand, or to the left, to go after other gods to serve them.

15 ¶But it shall come to pass, if thou wilt not hearken unto the voice of the LORD thy God, to observe to do all his commandments and his statutes which I command thee this day; that all these curses shall come upon thee, and overtake thee:

16 Cursed shalt thou be in the city, and cursed shalt thou be in the field.

17 Cursed shall be thy basket and thy store.

18 Cursed shall be the fruit of thy body, and the fruit of thy land, the increase of thy kine, and the flocks of thy sheep.

19 Cursed shalt thou be when thou comest in, and cursed shalt thou be when thou goest out.

20 The LORD shall send upon thee cursing, vexation, and rebuke, in all that thou settest thine hand unto for to do, until thou be destroyed, and until thou perish quickly; because of the wickedness of thy doings, whereby thou hast forsaken me.

21 The LORD shall make the pestilence cleave unto thee, until he have consumed thee from off the land, whither thou goest to possess it.

22 The LORD shall smite thee with a consumption, and with a fever, and with an inflammation, and with an extreme burning, and with the sword, and with blasting, and with mildew; and they shall pursue thee until thou perish.

23 And thy heaven that is over thy head shall be brass, and the earth that is under thee shall be iron.

24 The LORD shall make the rain of thy land powder and dust: from heaven shall it come down upon thee, until thou be destroyed.

25 The LORD shall cause thee to be smitten before thine enemies: thou shalt go out one way against them, and flee seven ways before them: and shalt be removed into all the kingdoms of the earth.

26 And thy carcase shall be meat unto all fowls of the air, and unto the beasts of the earth, and no man shall fray them away.

27 The LORD will smite thee with the botch of Egypt, and with the emerods, and with the scab, and with the itch, whereof thou canst not be healed.

28 The LORD shall smite thee with

15-22. The other side of the promise of blessing is the curse pronounced on Israel for disobedience. Just as there was a sixfold blessing, Moses repeats a sixfold curse (vss. 16-20). Each of the curses is the antithesis of a blessing and promises the punishment of God for disobedience. God promised a threefold judgment: **cursing, vexation, and rebuke.** The three words are synonymous, which reflects Hebrew parallelism. Out of these curses comes the promise of the sevenfold judgment of God (vss. 21-22). The number seven speaks of the complete work of God. Also, the judgments become progressively more severe toward the end of the list.

23-26. Added to the seven judgments was the threat of a terrible drought (vss. 23-24), and the fact that Israel would be defeated in battle (vss. 25-26). Being defeated in battle is the opposite of the blessing promised in verse 7.

27-35. God continues to multiply judgment by adding four incurable diseases. The **botch of Egypt** is ulcers, a particular form of leprosy. Emerods are hemmorroids, boils, or tumors. The scab and the itch were medical words for several forms of skin disease found in Syria and Egypt. Added to these judg-

madness, and blindness, and astonishment of heart:

29 And thou shalt grope at noonday, as the blind gropeth in darkness, and thou shalt not prosper in thy ways: and thou shalt be only oppressed and spoiled evermore, and no man shall save *thee*.

30 Thou shalt betroth a wife, and another man shall lie with her: thou shalt build an house, and thou shalt not dwell therein: thou shalt plant a vineyard, and shalt not gather the grapes thereof.

31 Thine ox *shall be* slain before thine eyes, and thou shalt not eat thereof: thine ass *shall be* violently taken away from before thy face, and shall not be restored to thee: thy sheep *shall be* given unto thine enemies, and thou shalt have none to rescue *them*.

32 Thy sons and thy daughters *shall be* given unto another people, and thine eyes shall look, and fail *with longing* for them all the day long: and *there shall be* no might in thine hand.

33 The fruit of thy land, and all thy labours, shall a nation which thou knowest not eat up; and thou shalt be only oppressed and crushed alway:

34 So that thou shalt be mad for the sight of thine eyes which thou shalt see.

35 The LORD shall smite thee in the knees, and in the legs, with a sore botch that cannot be healed, from the sole of thy foot unto the top of thy head.

36 The LORD shall bring thee, and thy king which thou shalt set over thee, unto a nation which neither thou nor thy fathers have known; and there shalt thou serve other gods, wood and stone.

37 And thou shalt become an astonishment, a proverb, and a byword, among all nations whither the LORD shall lead thee.

38 Thou shalt carry much seed out into the field, and shalt gather *but* little in; for the locust shall consume it.

39 Thou shalt plant vineyards, and dress *them*, but shalt neither drink *of* the wine, nor gather *the grapes;* for the worms shall eat them.

40 Thou shalt have olive trees throughout all thy coasts, but thou shalt not anoint *thyself* with the oil; for thine olive shall cast *his fruit*.

41 Thou shall beget sons and daughters, but thou shalt not enjoy them; for they shall go into captivity.

42 All thy trees and fruit of thy land shall the locust consume.

43 The stranger that *is* within thee shall get up above thee very high; and thou shalt come down very low.

44 He shall lend to thee, and thou shalt not lend to him: he shall be the head, and thou shalt be the tail.

45 Moreover all these curses shall come upon thee, and shall pursue thee, and overtake thee, till thou be destroyed; because thou hearkenedst not unto the voice of the LORD thy God, to keep his commandments and his statutes which he commanded thee:

46 And they shall be upon thee for a sign and for a wonder, and upon thy seed for ever.

47 Because thou servedst not the

ments were three problems: idiocy, blindness, and confusion of the mind (vs. 28). Next, God promised to take away their wives, houses, vineyards, and animals of burden (vss. 30-33). Lest Israel think these to be natural calamities, Moses adds the words, **The LORD shall smite thee.** As noted earlier, the **botch** was leprosy. God had excluded anyone from fellowship with Him who had leprosy; it was a sign of sin. Therefore, Israel would be spiritually exiled because of their sin.

The prediction that God would make the Jews a proverb has been fulfilled. The term "Jew" is one of the most emotion-packed words used to describe any group of people. To call some people a Jew is the same as cursing them. These people who became a curse are the same people on which God chose to place His blessing.

36-48. The judgment of God is compounded in this chapter, so that should they be guilty of disobedience, Israel would be cursed. They would lose their possessions, their children would go into captivity, and the insects would destroy their vegetation. The purpose of these curses is explained as a **sign** or **wonder.** The technical phrase for sign always spoke of a divine work that pointed to the credibility of God's message. Hence, the purpose of the judgments upon Israel was to show the certainty of God's promises.

LORD thy God with joyfulness, and with gladness of heart, for the abundance of all *things*;

48 Therefore shalt thou serve thine enemies which the LORD shall send against thee, in hunger, and in thirst, and in nakedness, and in want of all *things*: and he shall put a yoke of iron upon thy neck, until he have destroyed thee.

49 The LORD shall bring a nation against thee from far, from the end of the earth, *as swift* as the eagle flieth; a nation whose tongue thou shalt not understand;

50 A nation of fierce countenance, which shall not regard the person of the old, nor shew favour to the young:

51 And he shall eat the fruit of thy cattle, and the fruit of thy land, until thou be destroyed: which *also* shall not leave thee *either* corn, wine, or oil, *or* the increase of thy kine, or flocks of thy sheep, until he have destroyed thee.

52 And he shall besiege thee in all thy gates, until thy high and fenced walls come down, wherein thou trustedst, throughout all thy land: and he shall besiege thee in all thy gates throughout all thy land, which the LORD thy God hath given thee.

53 And thou shalt eat the fruit of thine own body, the flesh of thy sons and of thy daughters, which the LORD thy God hath given thee, in the siege, and in the straitness, wherewith thine enemies shall distress thee:

54 *So that* the man *that is* tender among you, and very delicate, his eye shall be evil toward his brother, and toward the wife of his bosom, and toward the remnant of his children which he shall leave:

55 So that he will not give to any of them of the flesh of his children whom he shall eat: because he hath nothing left him in the siege, and in the straitness, wherewith thine enemies shall distress thee in all thy gates.

56 The tender and delicate woman among you, which would not adventure to set the sole of her foot upon the ground for delicateness and tenderness, her eye shall be evil toward the husband of her bosom, and toward her son, and toward her daughter,

57 And toward her young one that cometh out from between her feet, and toward her children which she shall bear: for she shall eat them for want of all *things* secretly in the siege and straitness, wherewith thine enemy shall distress thee in thy gates.

58 If thou wilt not observe to do all the words of this law that are written in this book, that thou mayest fear this glorious and fearful name, THE LORD THY GOD;

59 Then the LORD will make thy plagues wonderful, and the plagues of thy seed, *even* great plagues, and of long continuance, and sore sicknesses, and of long continuance.

60 Moreover he will bring upon thee all the diseases of Egypt, which thou wast afraid of; and they shall cleave unto thee.

49-59. The nation that comes from afar to judge Israel is pictured as an eagle. This is a picture of the Roman Empire, which defeated the Jews and brought them into subjection. The eagle was the symbol of Rome, and since the Jews did not understand Latin, they fulfilled the promise **whose tongue thou shalt not understand.** The severity of the Romans is seen in that they would slaughter the young and old, purge the land, and destroy the walled cities. Obedience is the key to blessing, so Moses commands Israel to observe the **words of this law that are written in this book** (vs. 58). **This book** refers to the entire book of Deuteronomy, specifically to the commands given in the renewal of the covenant (chs. 28-30).

60-62. Even though God has pronounced many judgments in this section, He continues to compound them by adding the phrases **all the diseases of Egypt** and **every sickness, and every plague.** These are direct references to the plagues of Egypt. The

61 Also every sickness, and every plague, which *is* not written in the book of this law, them will the LORD bring upon thee, until thou be destroyed.

62 And ye shall be left few in number, whereas ye were as the stars of heaven for multitude; because thou wouldest not obey the voice of the LORD thy God.

63 And it shall come to pass, *that* as the LORD rejoiced over you to do you good, and to multiply you; so the LORD will rejoice over you to destroy you, and to bring you to nought; and ye shall be plucked from off the land whither thou goest to possess it.

64 And the LORD shall scatter thee among all people, from the one end of the earth even unto the other; and there thou shalt serve other gods, which neither thou nor thy fathers have known, *even* wood and stone.

65 And among these nations shalt thou find no ease, neither shall the sole of thy foot have rest: but the LORD shall give thee there a trembling heart, and failing of eyes, and sorrow of mind:

66 And thy life shall hang in doubt before thee; and thou shalt fear day and night, and shalt have none assurance of thy life:

67 In the morning thou shalt say, Would God it were even! and at even thou shalt say, Would God it were morning! for the fear of thine heart wherewith thou shalt fear, and for the sight of thine eyes which thou shalt see.

68 And the LORD shall bring thee into Egypt again with ships, by the way whereof I spake unto thee, Thou shalt see it no more again: and there ye shall be sold unto your enemies for bondmen and bondwomen, and no man shall buy *you.*

CHAPTER 29

THESE *are* the words of the covenant, which the LORD commanded Moses to make with the children of Israel in the land of Moab, beside the covenant which he made with them in Hô′rĕb.

2 ¶And Moses called unto all Israel, and said unto them, Ye have seen all that the LORD did before your eyes in the land of Egypt unto Pharaoh, and unto all his servants, and unto all his land;

3 The great temptations which thine eyes have seen, the signs, and those great miracles:

4 Yet the LORD hath not given you an heart to perceive, and eyes to see, and ears to hear, unto this day.

5 And I have led you forty years in the wilderness: your clothes are not waxen old upon you, and thy shoe is not waxen old upon thy foot.

6 Ye have not eaten bread, neither have ye drunk wine or strong drink: that ye might know that I *am* the LORD your God.

7 And when ye came unto this place,

implication is obvious; as God judged Egypt by ten plagues because they rejected His commands, so God will judge Israel with the same plagues for the same reason.

63. As the Lord rejoiced in the prospect of blessing Israel, the Scriptures promise that **the LORD will rejoice over you to destroy you.** This does not mean that God delights in causing suffering, but that God must judge according to His nature and every sin must be punished. Because Israel despised God's goodness and longsuffering, God had to punish her.

64-68. The mention of scattering among the people of the earth has a twofold reference. First, it speaks of the Babylonian captivity when Israel was led captive out of the land; and second, it speaks of the ultimate scattering of Israel throughout the entire earth after A.D. 70, when Titus destroyed Jerusalem. The predicted anti-Semitism is seen in the phrase **shalt thou find no ease.** As a result, Israel would have a **trembling heart,** which refers to fear, **failing of eyes,** which refers to the light of life going out, and **sorrow of mind,** which is literally despair of soul. During this time Israel's life **shall hang in doubt** before them, which literally means that their life is to be hung by a thin thread before their eyes. This thread might be torn down at any moment (see Keil and Delitzsch, *Biblical Commentary on the Old Testament,* Vol. 3, p. 445).

B. The Palestinian Covenant. 29:1-30:20.

29:1. This is the conclusion of God's renewal of the covenant. The phrase **which the LORD commanded** is written in the past tense, showing that Moses is coming to the conclusion of his sermon. The phrase **the words of the covenant** refers to Moses' addresses, or messages, concerning God's covenant. The geographical location is in Moab, across the Jordan River from the Promised Land; but Moses is referring to the original covenant that was made at Mount Horeb. What was declared at Mount Horeb is now being renewed as the people prepare to enter the land.

2-9. Moses called unto all Israel is literally an invitation to enter the covenant with God. The word **all** indicates that the entire nation is being asked to ratify God's covenant, not just the elders or the heads of the tribes. Moses once again unfolds the Lord's past dealings with them in Egypt. Yet, in spite of the signs and miracles, **The LORD hath not given you a heart to perceive.** Perhaps the people did not understand because they had not requested wisdom (Jas 1:5). As a result, they did not have an understanding heart. The real problem, however, was that they had hardened their hearts. Their blindness was predictive of a judicial blindness that was to come upon all Israel. Isaiah predicted that the Lord would shut their eyes and stop up their ears, lest they should understand the words of the Lord (Isa 6:9-10). The judicial blindness of Israel was repeated with Jesus (Mt 13:14-15) when the nation rejected the Messiah who came to them. Paul quoted this reference in Isaiah when talking about the final rejection of his message by the leaders of Israel shortly before they were dispersed by Titus in A.D. 70 (Acts 28:25-28).

Sihon the king of Hĕsh'bŏn, and Og the king of Bā'shan, came out against us unto battle, and we smote them:

8 And we took their land, and gave it for an inheritance unto the Reubenites, and to the Gadites, and to the half tribe of Ma-năs'seh.

9 Keep therefore the words of this covenant, and do them, that ye may prosper in all that ye do.

10 ¶Ye stand this day all of you before the LORD your God; your captains of your tribes, your elders, and your officers, *with* all the men of Israel,

11 Your little ones, your wives, and thy stranger that *is* in thy camp, from the hewer of thy wood unto the drawer of thy water:

12 That thou shouldest enter into covenant with the LORD thy God, and into his oath, which the LORD thy God maketh with thee this day:

13 That he may establish thee to day for a people unto himself, and *that* he may be unto thee a God, as he hath said unto thee, and as he hath sworn unto thy fathers, to Abraham, to Isaac, and to Jacob.

14 Neither with you only do I make this covenant and this oath;

15 But with *him* that standeth here with us this day before the LORD our God, and also with *him* that *is* not here with us this day:

16 (For ye know how we have dwelt in the land of Egypt; and how we came through the nations which ye passed by;

17 And ye have seen their abominations, and their idols, wood and stone, silver and gold, which *were* among them:)

18 Lest there should be among you man, or woman, or family, or tribe, whose heart turneth away this day from the LORD our God, to go *and* serve the gods of these nations; lest there should be among you a root that beareth gall and wormwood;

19 And it come to pass, when he heareth the words of this curse, that he bless himself in his heart, saying, I shall have peace, though I walk in the imagination of mine heart, to add drunkenness to thirst:

20 The LORD will not spare him, but then the anger of the LORD and his jealousy shall smoke against that man, and all the curses that are written in this book shall lie upon him, and the LORD shall blot out his name from under heaven.

21 And the LORD shall separate him unto evil out of all the tribes of Israel, according to all the curses of the covenant that are written in this book of the law:

22 So that the generation to come of your children that shall rise up after you, and the stranger that shall come from a far land, shall say, when they see the plagues of that land, and the sicknesses which the LORD hath laid upon it;

23 *And that* the whole land thereof *is* brimstone, and salt, *and* burning, *that* it is not sown, nor beareth, nor any grass groweth therein, like the overthrow of

10-15. The phrase **Ye stand this day** is a reference to the fact that they were actually standing to hear his sermon. The words **this day** are literally "today," so that without exception, the heads of the tribes, the elders, the officers, and all the men of Israel were given the opportunity to respond affirmatively to God. But it was not the men only who were present, but also the wives, children, strangers, and even the lowest servants. They were all included in the covenant. The phrase **shouldest enter into covenant with the LORD** meant that they were challenged to completely accept God's provisions. If Israel had done that, they would have been **a people unto himself.** Those who stood before Moses had an awesome responsibility. Their decision would obligate future generations; so Moses reminds them, **Neither with you only do I make this covenant.** Every Hebrew born in future generations would suffer the consequences of what they did.

16-18. Moses repeats the evil results that would fall upon Israel for their apostasy and breaching of the covenant. Again, they were warned against turning away, **lest there should be among you a root that beareth gall and wormwood.** This is a striking illustration of the destructiveness of worshiping idols, because these were usually carved from a root. **Wormwood** was not, strictly speaking, a poisonous plant, but was extremely bitter. Those who turned Israel away from Jehovah would make the nation bitter.

19. Moses also warns against self-deception. He uses the phrase **he bless himself in his heart,** which meant that a person would congratulate himself, or become proud. This person would feel peaceful, but actually would have hardened his heart.

20-26. Moses repeats a proverb of that day, **to add drunkenness to thirst** (vs. 19) which literally means "to sweep away that which is saturated with the thirsty." It meant that the Lord would destroy all, both those who had drunk the poison of rebellion and those who were thirsting for the Lord. God will not spare in His judgment; the Lord **shall smoke against that man,** which literally meant that God's judgment was about to break forth in fire.

Sodom, and Go-mŏr′rah, Ăd′mah, and Ze-bō′im, which the LORD overthrew in his anger, and in his wrath:

24 Even all nations shall say, Wherefore hath the LORD done thus unto this land? what *meaneth* the heat of this great anger?

25 Then men shall say, Because they have forsaken the covenant of the LORD God of their fathers, which he made with them when he brought them forth out of the land of Egypt:

26 For they went and served other gods, and worshipped them, gods whom they knew not, and *whom* he had not given unto them:

27 And the anger of the LORD was kindled against this land, to bring upon it all the curses that are written in this book:

28 And the LORD rooted them out of their land in anger, and in wrath, and in great indignation, and cast them into another land, as *it is* this day.

29 The secret *things belong* unto the LORD our God: but those *things which are* revealed *belong* unto us and to our children for ever, that *we* may do all the words of this law.

CHAPTER 30

AND it shall come to pass, when all these things are come upon thee, the blessing and the curse, which I have set before thee, and thou shalt call *them* to mind among all the nations, whither the LORD thy God hath driven thee,

2 And shalt return unto the LORD thy God, and shalt obey his voice according to all that I command thee this day, thou and thy children, with all thine heart, and with all thy soul;

3 That then the LORD thy God will turn thy captivity, and have compassion upon thee, and will return and gather thee from all the nations, whither the LORD thy God hath scattered thee.

4 If *any* of thine be driven out unto the outmost *parts* of heaven, from thence will the LORD thy God gather thee, and from thence will he fetch thee:

5 And the LORD thy God will bring thee into the land which thy fathers possessed, and thou shalt possess it; and he will do thee good, and multiply thee above thy fathers.

6 And the LORD thy God will circumcise thine heart, and the heart of thy seed, to love the LORD thy God with all thine heart, and with all thy soul, that thou mayest live.

7 And the LORD thy God will put all these curses upon thine enemies, and on them that hate thee, which persecuted thee.

8 And thou shalt return and obey the voice of the LORD, and do all his commandments which I command thee this day.

27-28. Moses goes on to describe the response of visitors and tourists to the Promised Land in coming days. They would see the land's desolation and barrenness and would wonder how the Israelites could have ever called it a land flowing with milk and honey. The reason why the land would become barren was that **the anger of the LORD was kindled against this land, to bring upon it all the curses that are written in this book.** God would root Israel out of the land, as a farmer roots out thistles and weeds, and disperse them among the nations.

29. It may be difficult for someone who does not know the Lord to understand how God could punish His children so severely. But Moses explains that **The secret things belong unto the LORD our God.** Whereas most people use the term **secret** as an interpretation of the unexplainable blessings of God, it actually refers to the hidden causes which motivate God to punish His people.

30:1-2. The actual Palestinian covenant is given in this chapter, including the conditions under which Israel was to enter the Promised Land. Ultimately, because Israel did not keep their part of the covenant, God took them out of the land. Yet here, God makes certain promises that He will return Israel to the land in the future and fulfill His eternal covenant with Abraham. Verse 1 predicts that when Israel is in captivity, they will remember the blessings and the cursings of the Palestinian covenant. The phrase **call them to mind** means that Israel would recognize the obligations of the Palestinian covenant and **return unto the LORD,** which speaks of national repentance. The depth of their repentance was measured by the phrase **with all thine heart, and with all thy soul.**

3-7. The promise that **the LORD thy God will turn thy captivity** actually refers to the bringing back of the prisoners. At another place, "the captivity of Jacob's tents" (Jer 30:18) is synonymous with having mercy on his dwelling place. God will bring Israel back into their land where they will possess it once again. This is the promise of Ezekiel 36:24, i.e., that the Lord will bring them from the nations and gather them again into the Promised Land. God promised the land to Abraham (Gen 15:18). Therefore, God must fulfill that promise in the future. But Israel will not be brought back in unbelief. **The LORD thy God will circumcise thine heart** means that Israel would believe. Paul states that ". . . all Israel shall be saved . . ." (Rom 11:26). This is a picture of the national salvation of Israel. When this happens, they will ultimately fulfill the command of the *Shema* to love the Lord their God with all their heart (vs. 6; cf. 6:5).

8-10. Moses repeats the promise that Israel **shalt return** and that they will **obey the voice of the LORD.** This will happen in the Millennium, when Christ shall rule the world with a rod of iron. Just as the Lord came walking in the garden looking for fellowship

378

9 And the LORD thy God will make thee plenteous in every work of thine hand, in the fruit of thy body, and in the fruit of thy cattle, and in the fruit of thy land, for good: for the LORD will again rejoice over thee for good, as he rejoiced over thy fathers:

10 If thou shalt hearken unto the voice of the LORD thy God, to keep his commandments and his statutes which are written in this book of the law, *and* if thou turn unto the LORD thy God with all thine heart, and with all thy soul.

11 ¶For this commandment which I command thee this day, it *is* not hidden from thee, neither *is* it far off.

12 It *is* not in heaven, that thou shouldest say, Who shall go up for us to heaven, and bring it unto us, that we may hear it, and do it?

13 Neither *is* it beyond the sea, that thou shouldest say, Who shall go over the sea for us, and bring it unto us, that we may hear it, and do it?

14 But the word *is* very nigh unto thee, in thy mouth, and in thy heart, that thou mayest do it.

15 ¶See, I have set before thee this day life and good, and death and evil;

16 In that I command thee this day to love the LORD thy God, to walk in his ways, and to keep his commandments and his statutes and his judgments, that thou mayest live and multiply: and the LORD thy God shall bless thee in the land whither thou goest to possess it.

17 But if thine heart turn away, so that thou wilt not hear, but shalt be drawn away, and worship other gods, and serve them;

18 I denounce unto you this day, that ye shall surely perish, *and that* ye shall not prolong *your* days upon the land, whither thou passest over Jordan to go to possess it.

19 I call heaven and earth to record this day against you, *that* I have set before you life and death, blessing and cursing: therefore choose life, that both thou and thy seed may live:

20 That thou mayest love the LORD thy God, *and* that thou mayest obey his voice, and that thou mayest cleave unto him: for he *is* thy life, and the length of thy days: that thou mayest dwell in the land which the LORD sware unto thy fathers, to Abraham, to Isaac, and to Jacob, to give them.

CHAPTER 31

AND Moses went and spake these words unto all Israel.

2 And he said unto them, I *am* an hundred and twenty years old this day; I can no more go out and come in: also the LORD hath said unto me, Thou shalt not go over this Jordan.

3 The LORD thy God, he will go over before thee, *and* he will destroy these nations from before thee, and thou shalt possess them: *and* Joshua, he shall go over before thee, as the LORD hath said.

4 And the LORD shall do unto them as he did to Sihon and to Og, kings of the Āmorītes, and unto the land of them, whom he destroyed.

with Adam (Gen 3:8), in that day Israel will manifest fellowship with God by obeying His voice.

Some say the return predicted by Moses was fulfilled when a remnant of the Jews came back from Babylon. This is incorrect; for neither were the people scattered in all of the nations, nor did the remnant go back believing.

11-14. The promise that Israel would return to the land might have come as a shock to the hearers that day. But Moses reminded them that Israel's return **is not hidden from thee,** which meant that it was "not too wonderful to grasp nor too unintelligible to comprehend." Moses goes on in this verse to explain that **neither is it far off,** which meant it was not beyond God's reach; He would be able to perform His promises. The promise was very near to them, i.e., **in thy mouth, and in thy heart, that thou mayest do it.** This expression may be a prediction that because of the preaching of the gospel the Jews would believe, become converted, and return to the land in faith.

15-20. Moses sets before them the greatest commandment, which was to love God, and also points out that they should continue loving God in the future. Love is still the essential principle in fulfilling the commandments (6:4-5).

V. CONCLUSION. 31:1-34:12.

A. Moses' Final Charge. 31:1-30.

31:1-6. After Moses concluded his sermons in the book of Deuteronomy, he moved, apparently from the podium or the spot where he was addressing Israel. The content of this chapter is completely different from all that has gone before. Previously, he has been preaching the Law to Israel. Now he gives personal material that involves his retirement and death. Moses reminds them that he is a hundred and twenty years old. His eye was still as sharp as a young man's, and his mind was quick (34:7). Yet he says **I can no more go out and come in,** which meant that he could no longer lead the nation because the Lord had forbidden him to cross over Jordan and go into Canaan (Num 20:12). Moses promises that the presence of God will go with Israel and that **he will go over before thee.** Moses promises that God will destroy the nations and help Israel to possess the land. Because of the promise of God, Israel was exhorted to be of good courage

5 And the LORD shall give them up before your face, that ye may do unto them according unto all the commandments which I have commanded you.

6 Be strong and of a good courage, fear not, nor be afraid of them: for the LORD thy God, he *it is* that doth go with thee; he will not fail thee, nor forsake thee.

7 ¶And Moses called unto Joshua, and said unto him in the sight of all Israel, Be strong and of a good courage: for thou must go with this people unto the land which the LORD hath sworn unto their fathers to give them; and thou shalt cause them to inherit it.

8 And the LORD, he *it is* that doth go before thee; he will be with thee, he will not fail thee, neither forsake thee: fear not, neither be dismayed.

9 ¶And Moses wrote this law, and delivered it unto the priests the sons of Levi, which bare the ark of the covenant of the LORD, and unto all the elders of Israel.

10 And Moses commanded them, saying, At the end of *every* seven years, in the solemnity of the year of release, in the feast of tabernacles,

11 When all Israel is come to appear before the LORD thy God in the place which he shall choose, thou shalt read this law before all Israel in their hearing.

12 Gather the people together, men, and women, and children, and thy stranger that *is* within thy gates, that they may hear, and that they may learn, and fear the LORD your God, and observe to do all the words of this law:

13 And *that* their children, which have not known *any thing*, may hear, and learn to fear the LORD your God, as long as ye live in the land whither ye go over Jordan to possess it.

14 ¶And the LORD said unto Moses, Behold, thy days approach that thou must die: call Joshua, and present yourselves in the tabernacle of the congregation, that I may give him a charge. And Moses and Joshua went, and presented themselves in the tabernacle of the congregation.

15 And the LORD appeared in the tabernacle in a pillar of a cloud: and the pillar of the cloud stood over the door of the tabernacle.

16 ¶And the LORD said unto Moses, Behold, thou shalt sleep with thy fathers; and this people will rise up, and go a whoring after the gods of the strangers of the land, whither they go *to be* among them, and will forsake me, and break my covenant which I have made with them.

17 Then my anger shall be kindled against them in that day, and I will forsake them, and I will hide my face from them, and they shall be devoured, and many evils and troubles shall befall them; so that they will say in that day,

and to be fearless. The power of the victorious life is in God; and if a person allows God to work through him, he has the promise that **he will not fail thee, nor forsake thee.**

7-9. Moses called Joshua to the place where he was standing, so that they both stood in the presence of all Israel. Joshua was given a personal challenge to be courageous, then was given the leadership responsibility with the words **thou shalt cause them to inherit it.** The phrase **Moses wrote this law** should be sufficient evidence for any Bible scholar as to who wrote the Pentateuch. Also, Jesus gave His personal endorsement to Mosaic authorship in Matthew 19:7-8.

10-13. Next, Moses handed over the Law to the priest and to all the elders of Israel. This symbolic act shows that he was giving them the assignment of teaching the Law and the responsibility of causing all Israel to obey it. The command that they should **read this law** was to be fulfilled every seven years at the Feast of Tabernacles. Specifically, the priests were to read the entire book of Deuteronomy in the month of October when everyone assembled at the designated place of corporate worship. They were to gather together all of the people for the reading of the word, including men, women, children, and strangers living among them. What Israel did at the Feast of Tabernacles continues today in the church. Many authorities have used verse 12 as the basis for Sunday school, i.e., the reaching, teaching, winning arm of the church. The first task of Sunday school is to **Gather the people together,** which is reaching them for Christ. The second step is to teach them the Word of God as implied in the phrase **that they may hear, and . . . learn.** Teaching begins with hearing and concludes with learning. The third element of Sunday school is reflected in the phrase **fear the LORD,** Old Testament terminology for salvation. Hence, what was important for Israel in the Old Testament remains imperative for the church of today.

14-22. God told Moses that his death was imminent, so Moses and Joshua were called to the tabernacle. God's statement **that I may give him a charge** is the official appointment of Joshua to the office of leading the people. God appears in the tabernacle in a pillar of cloud. But before the Lord appoints Joshua, He reiterates His hatred of anyone who would go **whoring after** [strange] **gods.** God was angry at the thought that His people would one day seek other gods. To keep Israel pure, the Lord commanded them to **write ye this song for you, and teach it the children of Israel.** Even though it is primarily the song of Moses (ch. 32), Joshua was in the presence of God when the commandment was given to write the song. The fact that God used a song to communicate His message shows the impact of music. When the people once learned the words, they would sing it during their daily activities. Thus, the song could be transmitted from generation to generation. By singing, people would be warned against idolatry. Even though the command was given to both Moses and Joshua, **Moses therefore wrote this song the same day.**

Are not these evils come upon us, because our God is not among us?

18 And I will surely hide my face in that day for all the evils which they shall have wrought, in that they are turned unto other gods.

19 Now therefore write ye this song for you, and teach it the children of Israel: put it in their mouths, that this song may be a witness for me against the children of Israel.

20 For when I shall have brought them into the land which I sware unto their fathers, that floweth with milk and honey; and they shall have eaten and filled themselves, and waxen fat; then will they turn unto other gods, and serve them, and provoke me, and break my covenant.

21 And it shall come to pass, when many evils and troubles are befallen them, that this song shall testify against them as a witness; for it shall not be forgotten out of the mouths of their seed: for I know their imagination which they go about, even now, before I have brought them into the land which I sware.

22 Moses therefore wrote this song the same day, and taught it the children of Israel.

23 And he gave Joshua the son of Nun a charge, and said, Be strong and of a good courage: for thou shalt bring the children of Israel into the land which I sware unto them: and I will be with thee.

24 ¶And it came to pass, when Moses had made an end of writing the words of this law in a book, until they were finished,

25 That Moses commanded the Lēvītes, which bare the ark of the covenant of the LORD, saying,

26 Take this book of the law, and put it in the side of the ark of the covenant of the LORD your God, that it may be there for a witness against thee.

27 For I know thy rebellion, and thy stiff neck: behold, while I am yet alive with you this day, ye have been rebellious against the LORD; and how much more after my death?

28 Gather unto me all the elders of your tribes, and your officers, that I may speak these words in their ears, and call heaven and earth to record against them.

29 For I know that after my death ye will utterly corrupt yourselves, and turn aside from the way which I have commanded you; and evil will befall you in the latter days; because ye will do evil in the sight of the LORD, to provoke him to anger through the work of your hands.

30 And Moses spake in the ears of all the congregation of Israel the words of this song, until they were ended.

CHAPTER 32

GIVE ear, O ye heavens, and I will speak; and hear, O earth, the words of my mouth.

2 My doctrine shall drop as the rain,

23-26. The final charge that appointed Joshua to the office as the leader of Israel is given in verse 23. When Moses finished writing the book of the Law, he gave it to the Levites to place in the ark of the covenant. These were not ordinary Levites, but were those who were entrusted with the care and transportation of the ark of the Lord (Num 4:4ff.). The tables of the Law were kept in the ark (Ex 25:16; 40:20), along with this book of the Law that was written by the very hand of Moses.

27-30. Moses realized the disobedient nature of the people (vss. 27-30); so he asked for a gathering of all of the elders and officers, so that he could give them one final warning against rebellion. His message is recorded in the song that God had asked him to write (ch. 32).

B. The Song of Moses. 32:1-43.

Chapter 32 is the song that the Lord commanded Moses to write (31:19). It tells of the faithfulness of God. He will surely bless His people; but when they reject His love, He will just as surely punish them in His anger. Because of its poetic nature, the people would be reminded of the practical consequences of doctrine every time they sang this song. The song has several characteristics: (1) it has an abundance of pictures, metaphors, and poetic expressions that show the feelings of God; (2) it is a witness against the disobedient nation that has been blessed far above all the other nations of the earth; and (3) the song is a prophetic anticipation of the future judgments. At the time of writing, it was unlikely that such a song would ever be fulfilled, inasmuch as it was written when Israel was at the zenith of their obedience.

32:1-7. Here Moses asks heaven and earth to listen to the words of the song, first, in honor of its Creator, and second, because heaven and earth would be affected by the judgment which God would pour out upon faithless Israel. Moses ascribes

my speech shall distil as the dew, as the small rain upon the tender herb, and as the showers upon the grass:

3 Because I will publish the name of the LORD: ascribe ye greatness unto our God.

4 *He is* the Rock, his work *is* perfect: for all his ways *are* judgment: a God of truth and without iniquity, just and right *is* he.

5 They have corrupted themselves, their spot *is* not *the spot* of his children: *they are* a perverse and crooked generation.

6 Do ye thus requite the LORD, O foolish people and unwise? *is* not he thy father *that* hath bought thee? hath he not made thee, and established thee?

7 Remember the days of old, consider the years of many generations: ask thy father, and he will shew thee; thy elders, and they will tell thee.

8 When the Most High divided to the nations their inheritance, when he separated the sons of Adam, he set the bounds of the people according to the number of the children of Israel.

9 For the LORD's portion *is* his people; Jacob *is* the lot of his inheritance.

10 He found him in a desert land, and in the waste howling wilderness; he led him about, he instructed him, he kept him as the apple of his eye.

11 As an eagle stirreth up her nest, fluttereth over her young, spreadeth abroad her wings, taketh them, beareth them on her wings:

12 *So* the LORD alone did lead him, and *there was* no strange god with him.

13 He made him ride on the high places of the earth, that he might eat the increase of the fields; and he made him to suck honey out of the rock, and oil out of the flinty rock;

14 Butter of kine, and milk of sheep, with fat of lambs, and rams of the breed of Bā′shan, and goats, with the fat of kidneys of wheat; and thou didst drink the pure blood of the grape.

15 But Jĕsh′u-run waxed fat, and kicked: thou art waxen fat, thou art grown thick, thou art covered *with fat-ness;* then he forsook God *which* made him, and lightly esteemed the Rock of his salvation.

16 They provoked him to jealousy with strange *gods,* with abominations provoked they him to anger.

17 They sacrificed unto devils, not to God; to gods whom they knew not, to new *gods that* came newly up, whom your fathers feared not.

18 Of the Rock *that* begat thee thou art unmindful, and hast forgotten God that formed thee.

19 And when the LORD saw *it,* he abhorred *them,* because of the provoking of his sons, and of his daughters.

20 And he said, I will hide my face from them, I will see what their end

greatness to God, and yet he wants heaven and earth to join him in his praise. By calling God a rock, Moses is pointing out the unchangeable nature of God, that He is a defense for His people and a refuge in trouble. He is a God of faithfulness, reminding us of the old hymn, "Great Is Thy Faithfulness." When the people are reminded of their sin, it is not referring to a future sin, but pointing back to their rebellion in the wilderness. In making reference to their **spot,** Moses is referring to their moral stain. Because of their rebellion, though they were still the children of the Lord, they were stained with disobedience. Lest Israel forget its sin, they are told to **ask thy father.**

8-12. The song refers the singers back to pre-Abrahamic times to the tower of Babel. At that time the Lord **separated the sons of Adam** and **set the bounds of the people.** He did this by sovereignly confounding the speech of the people. The purpose for placing nations within boundaries is **according to the number of the children of Israel.** God foreknew that Israel would one day inhabit the Promised Land, so He set all other nations in their places around the earth. But God reserved the Promised Land for Israel. Yet, lest Israel think too highly of themselves, God reminds them that they are His portion. Israel is represented as a man who is lost in a horrible desert, in danger of perishing; yet the Lord finds him there. The phrase **howling wilderness** refers to the desert where the wild animals howl. There the Lord kept Israel **as the apple of his eye,** a figure of speech implying most careful preservation. The Lord teaches Israel about His protection by using the picture of an eagle teaching its young to fly. The eagle protects them from injury by watchful guidance. The phrase **beareth them on her wings** speaks of the eagle soaring over its young, using its powerful wings to protect the little ones from harm.

13-14. The song repeats how God had blessed Israel and prospered them in the wilderness. The phrase **high places** means "to cause to drive over the high places of the earth," a figurative expression of victorious subjection. When Israel is pictured as sucking honey out of the rock and oil out of the flint rock, that is a picture of God's blessing in a barren place.

15-17. Israel is here called **Jeshurun,** the righteous nation. When Moses composes the song, Israel is not even in the Promised Land, much less set up as a social order. This is a prophetic sarcasm intended to challenge them to godliness. The phrase **provoked him to jealousy** means that they excited God to jealousy, a technical phrase having to do with the breaking of a marriage contract. Israel did this by sacrificing to devils, **not to God.** The phrase actually means "not God." They sacrificed to something that was not God. Because of that, the people are later called **not a people** (vs. 21).

18-21. In this section we have a striking incidence of inspiration. The song predicts the coming judgment on Israel because of their apostasy. God saw Israel's sin and abhorred it, which means He rejected their idol worship. There were two results of this rejection: first, God would hide His face, i.e., withdraw His favor from Israel; and second, He would chasten them according to His promises. Israel had worshiped **not God;** therefore, God calls them **not a people. Not God** meant a god who could not

shall be: for they are a very froward generation, children in whom is no faith.

21 They have moved me to jealousy with that which is not God; they have provoked me to anger with their vanities: and I will move them to jealousy with those which are not a people; I will provoke them to anger with a foolish nation.

22 For a fire is kindled in mine anger, and shall burn unto the lowest hell, and shall consume the earth with her increase, and set on fire the foundations of the mountains.

23 I will heap mischiefs upon them; I will spend mine arrows upon them.

24 They shall be burnt with hunger, and devoured with burning heat, and with bitter destruction: I will also send the teeth of beasts upon them, with the poison of serpents of the dust.

25 The sword without, and terror within, shall destroy both the young man and the virgin, the suckling also with the man of gray hairs.

26 I said, I would scatter them into corners, I would make the remembrance of them to cease from among men:

27 Were it not that I feared the wrath of the enemy, lest their adversaries should behave themselves strangely, and lest they should say, Our hand is high, and the LORD hath not done all this.

28 For they are a nation void of counsel, neither is there any understanding in them.

29 O that they were wise, that they understood this, that they would consider their latter end!

30 How should one chase a thousand, and two put ten thousand to flight, except their Rock had sold them, and the LORD had shut them up?

31 For their rock is not as our Rock, even our enemies themselves being judges.

32 For their vine is of the vine of Sodom, and of the fields of Go-mŏr'rah: their grapes are grapes of gall, their clusters are bitter:

33 Their wine is the poison of dragons, and the cruel venom of asps.

34 Is not this laid up in store with me, and sealed up among my treasures?

35 To me belongeth vengeance, and recompence; their foot shall slide in due time: for the day of their calamity is at hand, and the things that shall come upon them make haste.

36 For the LORD shall judge his people, and repent himself for his servants, when he seeth that their power is gone, and there is none shut up, or left.

37 And he shall say, Where are their gods, their rock in whom they trusted,

38 Which did eat the fat of their sacrifices, and drank the wine of their drink offerings? let them rise up and help you, and be your protection.

39 See now that I, even I, am he, and there is no god with me: I kill, and I make alive; I wound, and I heal: neither is there any that can deliver out of my hand.

take care of his people, and therefore does not deserve to be worshiped. And not a people refers to a nation that has refused God's laws and customs as a way of life (see Keil and Delitzsch, p. 479).

22-28. God tells of His burning wrath and jealousy, which will result in judgment upon His people. He will use hunger, pestilence, plague, wild beasts, poisonous serpents, and war to carry out this destruction. The phrase I would scatter them into corners literally means, "I will blow them away." God will take the wind and blow them to the four corners of the earth, removing them from the place that He had given them.

29-31. The song makes the request O that they were wise, which implies that Israel was not wise. If Israel had been wise, they could have easily conquered all of their foes in the power of God (Lev 26:7-8). The Lord was truly their rock. In this verse Moses allows the heathen to decide if Israel was wise. Their rock is a reference to a few stones that were set up and worshiped as idols. Those on the outside would have realized that Israel had everything going for them but had turned back on the way of wisdom.

32-35. The phrase their vine is of the vine of Sodom meant that Israel was like a vine that gives snake poison, the poison of a snake whose bite meant immediate death. But the death came from God who said To me belongeth vengeance. The emphasis is that God was going to punish Israel. When Moses predicts that their foot shall slide, he is saying that the shaking of the foot is the beginning of a fall. God would not delay in punishing Israel, because they refused to stand on a firm foundation.

36-39. When God began to judge the people, He asked where [is] . . . their rock? as if to say, "Where is the idol that they trusted for deliverance?" The problem was that their support and power were gone. When all of the rotten props of Israel were eliminated, the nation crashed in ruin. As a result, God says, Let them rise up and help you, an obvious sarcasm.

40 For I lift up my hand to heaven, and say, I live for ever.

41 If I whet my glittering sword, and mine hand take hold on judgment; I will render vengeance to mine enemies, and will reward them that hate me.

42 I will make mine arrows drunk with blood, and my sword shall devour flesh; *and that* with the blood of the slain and of the captives, from the beginning of revenges upon the enemy.

43 Rejoice, O ye nations, *with* his people: for he will avenge the blood of his servants, and will render vengeance to his adversaries, and will be merciful unto his land, *and* to his people.

44 ¶And Moses came and spake all the words of this song in the ears of the people, he, and Hō-shē'a the son of Nun.

45 And Moses made an end of speaking all these words to all Israel:

46 And he said unto them, Set your hearts unto all the words which I testify among you this day, which ye shall command your children to observe to do, all the words of this law.

47 For it *is* not a vain thing for you; because it *is* your life: and through this thing ye shall prolong *your* days in the land, whither ye go over Jordan to possess it.

48 ¶And the LORD spake unto Moses that selfsame day, saying,

49 Get thee up into this mountain Ăb'a-rīm, *unto* mount Nebo, which *is* in the land of Moab, that *is* over against Jericho; and behold the land of Canaan, which I give unto the children of Israel for a possession:

50 And die in the mount whither thou goest up, and be gathered unto thy people; as Aaron thy brother died in mount Hor, and was gathered unto his people:

51 Because ye trespassed against me among the children of Israel at the waters of Mĕr'ibah-Kā'desh, in the wilderness of Zin; because ye sanctified me not in the midst of the children of Israel.

52 Yet thou shalt see the land before *thee;* but thou shalt not go thither unto the land which I give the children of Israel.

CHAPTER 33

AND this *is* the blessing, wherewith Moses the man of God blessed the children of Israel before his death.

2 And he said, The LORD came from Sĭ'naī, and rose up from Sē'ir unto them; he shined forth from mount Paran, and he came with ten thousands of saints: from his right hand *went* a fiery law for them.

3 Yea, he loved the people; all his saints *are* in thy hand: and they sat

40-43. The judgment of God is again seen in verses 40-42. To lift up one's hand to heaven was the gesture of a person taking an oath to God. Inasmuch as it is a reference to God, this is God swearing by Himself: for He can swear by no greater than Himself (Isa 45:23; Jer 22:5; Heb 6:17). He promises that He will judge Israel. The poetic language about the Lord sharpening His flashing sword speaks of a man getting ready for battle. A warrior would boast that his arrows would drink blood; hence, the Lord saying **drunk with blood** shows that God will take vengeance in a mighty way.

C. The Testament of Moses. 32:44-33:29.

44-52. The Mosaic authorship of the song is repeated, and Joshua is included as the coauthor (see Samuel Schultz, *Deuteronomy, The Gospel of Love*, p. 117). God had given both men the command to write the song (31:14, 19). **That selfsame day** refers to the day when Moses introduced the song to the children of Israel. At that time the Lord repeated to Moses the fact that he was soon to die. To anyone but a Christian, the words **And die in the mount** must seem like an awesome judgment. But to Moses, his future was in the hands of God. God reminds him that his trespass was an awful sin for a leader, yet God is gracious to him. Moses was told that he would **see the land** that God was about to give to Israel.

Some have questioned the authorship of the rest of Deuteronomy, inasmuch as Moses deposited the Law in the ark of the covenant at this point in time. However, the style and language of the remainder of the book complement the earlier portions. Therefore, there is no reason to suggest a different author. Although the book of Deuteronomy was symbolically placed in the ark of the covenant, part of what goes on in the rest of the book (31:27-34:12) could have been written by Moses before the book was permanently placed into the ark; or, parts could have been written later by Moses and added to the portions already in the ark.

33:1. Some of this chapter describes Moses and his death; so a second author has been attributed to this section. However, this would not mean that the chapter is not inspired by God. The author distinguishes Moses as **the man of God,** a quality that Moses would not ascribe to himself since he was the meekest man on the face of the earth (Num 12:3). This title was usually given to a prophet (I Sam 9:6; I Kgs 12:22; 13:14), a man who had direct revelation from God. While it is possible Moses wrote this in advance, it is most likely that someone else wrote the conclusion of this chapter (perhaps, Joshua).

2-5. The three clauses **The LORD came from Sinai . . . from Seir. . . . from Mount Paran** are not references to different manifestations of God, but to His one appearance at Mount Sinai. Moses gave them the Law, and the people received it as the Word of God. The Lord is called **king in Jeshurun,** which literally means, "the King in righteous nations." God intended that Israel would be a righteous nation because He expected

down at thy feet; *every one* shall receive of thy words.

4 Moses commanded us a law, *even* the inheritance of the congregation of Jacob.

5 And he was king in Jĕsh'u-run, when the heads of the people *and* the tribes of Israel were gathered together.

6 ¶Let Reuben live, and not die; and let *not* his men be few.

7 ¶And this *is the blessing* of Judah: and he said, Hear, LORD, the voice of Judah, and bring him unto his people: let his hands be sufficient for him; and be thou an help *to him* from his enemies.

8 ¶And of Levi he said, *Let* thy Thŭm'mĭm and thy Û'rĭm *be* with thy holy one, whom thou didst prove at Măs'sah, *and with* whom thou didst strive at the waters of Mĕr'i-bah;

9 Who said unto his father and to his mother, I have not seen him; neither did he acknowledge his brethren, nor knew his own children: for they have observed thy word, and kept thy covenant.

10 They shall teach Jacob thy judgments, and Israel thy law: they shall put incense before thee, and whole burnt sacrifice upon thine altar.

11 Bless, LORD, his substance, and accept the work of his hands: smite through the loins of them that rise against him, and of them that hate him, that they rise not again.

12 ¶And of Benjamin he said, The beloved of the LORD shall dwell in safety by him; *and the* LORD shall cover him all the day long, and he shall dwell between his shoulders.

13 ¶And of Joseph he said, Blessed of the LORD *be* his land, for the precious things of heaven, for the dew, and for the deep that coucheth beneath,

14 And for the precious fruits *brought forth* by the sun, and for the precious things put forth by the moon,

15 And for the chief things of the an-

them to obey the Word of God; hence, they were to be a glorious manifestation of His righteousness.

The content of the blessings that Moses pronounces on the tribes is different from those that Jacob gave (Gen 49). Jacob foresaw the entire history of each son; Moses describes only those blessings that they will enjoy as they obey the Lord. The twelve sons of Jacob are not listed according to the order of their birth, nor according to the distribution of their tribal inheritance in the Promised Land, nor according to their placement around the tabernacle in the wilderness. Reuben is mentioned first; he was the eldest son of Jacob. Simeon, the next son, is omitted; and Judah, to whom Jacob gave the birthright that was taken from Reuben, is mentioned next. After Judah comes Levi, the priestly tribe, Benjamin and Joseph (the sons of Rachel), and Zebulun and Issachar (the last two sons of Leah). The last to be mentioned are the sons of the maids: Gad, the first son of Zilpah; Dan and Naphtali, the sons of Bilhah; and finally Asher, the second son of Zilpah. It is interesting to note the blessing promised to each.

6. Reuben. The right of the first-born was withheld from Reuben (Gen 49:3-4), but Moses promises that he will prosper. The phrase **let not his men be few** means that his descendants would continue in existence and would not be small in number.

Simeon is passed over entirely and not mentioned by Moses. In Jacob's blessing (Gen 49:7) his posterity was to be scattered in Israel and was to lose its identity as a tribe. As a result, the Simeonites received a number of towns within the territory of Judah as their inheritance.

7. Judah. Jacob had promised that the sceptre would not depart from Judah (Gen 49:10), which meant that the Messiah would come through this tribe. To this blessing Moses adds, **bring him unto his people: let his hands be sufficient for him.** Judah was given the responsibility of championing his brothers in the wars of Israel against the nations. In turn, God would prosper all of the tribes because of his courage.

8-11. Levi. Moses says of him: **Let thy Thummim and thy Urim be with thy holy one,** which literally means, "thy right and thy light is to this godly man." The Urim and Thummim were worn by the High Priest on his breastplate. God had given His people the right to have light. Here, the words are reversed in reference to Levi. This signified that they had to defend the "right of the Lord" to all of the people. The phrase **thy holy one** is not a reference to Aaron, who sinned, but to **Levi,** the tribal father. God blessed all of the people because of the faithfulness of Levi.

12. Benjamin. His name means "beloved of the Lord." He first was beloved of his father (Gen 35:18; 44:20) and later became beloved of the Lord in this blessing by Moses. The prediction that Benjamin would **dwell between his shoulders** is equivalent of being carried on the back. It is a figure of a father carrying his son, the relationship that Benjamin had with God.

13-17. Joseph. Jacob had had great desires for Joseph; he had given him a coat of many colors, which had exalted him above his brethren. Moses also has great desires for this tribe. He gives them the greatest possible abundance of earthly blessings, which include the prosperity of a good life. Note the repeated use of the word **precious** in reference to Joseph. The two sons of Joseph, Ephraim and Manasseh, are mentioned and given blessings. Ephraim had been born second but was raised

cient mountains, and for the precious things of the lasting hills,

16 And for the precious things of the earth and fulness thereof, and *for* the good will of him that dwelt in the bush: let *the blessing* come upon the head of Joseph, and upon the top of the head of him *that was* separated from his brethren.

17 His glory *is like* the firstling of his bullock, and his horns *are like* the horns of unicorns: with them he shall push the people together to the ends of the earth: and they *are* the ten thousands of Ē'phra-im, and they *are* the thousands of Ma-năs'seh.

18 ¶And of Zĕb'u-lun he said, Rejoice, Zĕb'u-lun, in thy going out; and, Ĭs'sa-char, in thy tents.

19 They shall call the people unto the mountain; there they shall offer sacrifices of righteousness: for they shall suck *of* the abundance of the seas, and *of* treasures hid in the sand.

20 ¶And of Gad he said, Blessed *be* he that enlargeth Gad: he dwelleth as a lion, and teareth the arm with the crown of the head.

21 And he provided the first part for himself, because there, *in* a portion of the lawgiver, *was* he seated; and he came with the heads of the people, he executed the justice of the LORD, and his judgments with Israel.

22 ¶And of Dan he said, Dan *is* a lion's whelp: he shall leap from Bā'shan.

23 ¶And of Năph'ta-lī he said, O Năph'ta-lī, satisfied with favour, and full with the blessing of the LORD: possess thou the west and the south.

24 ¶And of Asher he said, *Let* Asher *be* blessed with children; let him be acceptable to his brethren, and let him dip his foot in oil.

25 Thy shoes *shall be* iron and brass; and as thy days, *so shall* thy strength *be.*

26 ¶ *There is* none like unto the God of Jĕsh'u-run, *who* rideth upon the heaven in thy help, and in his excellency on the sky.

27 The eternal God *is thy* refuge, and underneath *are* the everlasting arms: and he shall thrust out the enemy from before thee; and shall say, Destroy *them.*

28 Israel then shall dwell in safety alone: the fountain of Jacob *shall be* upon a land of corn and wine; also his heavens shall drop down dew.

29 Happy *art* thou, O Israel: who *is* like unto thee, O people saved by the LORD, the shield of thy help, and who *is* the sword of thy excellency! and thine enemies shall be found liars unto thee; and thou shalt tread upon their high places.

to the level of first-born by Jacob (Gen 48:8-20). Moses recognizes this priority and assigns to Ephraim a more numerous growth.

18-19. Zebulun. This tribe was blessed in **going out,** which refers to enterprise and labor. Later, the Zebulunites excelled in shipping, trade, and commerce, which fulfilled this prophecy made by Moses.

Issachar. He was blessed **in thy tents,** which speaks of the comfortable enjoyment of life. Taken together, Zebulun and Issachar had the joint blessings of labor and rest. They would enjoy the prosperity of God, both at home and abroad.

20-21. Gad. Moses praises God for enlarging Gad, implying an unlimited space for development. Gad is likened to a lioness, a fierce beast that was unchallenged in the area where she dwelt. As a lioness must capture its food and lodging, so Gad would have to conquer that which they desired. The reference to Gad's choosing the first fruit territory, i.e., **the first part,** relates to Gad's obtaining land beyond Jordan from Moses. The tribe's initiative in being the first to request land predated this reference to its geographical expansion, but confirmed Moses' prediction concerning them.

22. Dan. When Jacob blessed Dan, he compared him to a serpent that bit a horse's feet so that the rider fell backward (Gen 49:17). Now Moses compares the tribe to a young lion which suddenly springs from its ambush to make an attack. He is making reference to the impetuous nature of the Danites and to the fact that they were quick to follow their inclinations.

23. Naphtali. Moses gives this tribe a blessing that is extremely general in nature, so it is difficult to interpret its meaning in the light of ensuing history.

24-25. Asher. The name Asher meant "prosperous," and the tribe justly bore its name. Moses blessed it with earthly goods. Even the expression **dip his foot in oil** meant prosperity. Also, the phrase **as thy days, so shall thy strength be** meant technically, "let thine old age be as thy youth."

26-29. After Moses blesses the twelve tribes, he once again refers to **the God of Jeshurun,** reminding them that the Lord is the King of righteous nations. The fact that the Lord rides upon heaven is a picture of His omnipotence. When Moses says that **The eternal God is thy refuge,** he is speaking to a people who are houseless. They had been dwelling in tents for forty years, and he reminds them that God has been their house. The expression **everlasting arms** refers to those arms whose strength is never exhausted.

CHAPTER 34

AND Moses went up from the plains of Moab unto the mountain of Nebo, to the top of Pĭs'gah, that is over against Jericho. And the LORD shewed him all the land of Gilead, unto Dan,

2 And all Năph'ta-lī, and the land of É'phra-im, and Ma-năs'seh, and all the land of Judah, unto the utmost sea,

3 And the south, and the plain of the valley of Jericho, the city of palm trees, unto Zō'ar.

4 And the LORD said unto him, This is the land which I sware unto Abraham, unto Isaac, and unto Jacob, saying, I will give it unto thy seed: I have caused thee to see it with thine eyes, but thou shalt not go over thither.

5 ¶So Moses the servant of the LORD died there in the land of Moab, according to the word of the LORD.

6 And he buried him in a valley in the land of Moab, over against Bĕth-pĕ'ôr: but no man knoweth of his sepulchre unto this day.

7 ¶And Moses was an hundred and twenty years old when he died: his eye was not dim, nor his natural force abated.

8 ¶And the children of Israel wept for Moses in the plains of Moab thirty days: so the days of weeping and mourning for Moses were ended.

9 ¶And Joshua the son of Nun was full of the spirit of wisdom; for Moses had laid his hands upon him: and the children of Israel hearkened unto him, and did as the LORD commanded Moses.

10 ¶And there arose not a prophet since in Israel like unto Moses, whom the LORD knew face to face,

11 In all the signs and the wonders, which the LORD sent him to do in the land of Egypt to Pharaoh, and to all his servants, and to all his land,

12 And in all that mighty hand, and in all the great terror which Moses shewed in the sight of all Israel.

D. The Death of Moses. 34:1-12.

34:1-4. After blessing the tribes, Moses climbs Mount Nebo, going to the peak of Pisgah. **The LORD showed him all the land.** Moses could not enter the Promised Land because of his sin, but God gave him a life-fulfilling vision. This was not a psychic vision; he saw it with his physical eyes. From the peak of Pisgah he was able to see the whole of Napthali, the land of Ephraim and Manasseh, the whole of Judah, and even the Mediterranean Sea. Looking to the north, he could see the Jordan Valley and the city of Jericho with all of its palm trees. What a joy it must have been for Moses to look out over the dream of a lifetime. One can only imagine the peace that must have filled the heart of this servant when he finally saw that which God had promised.

5-8. Moses died **according to the word of the LORD,** which has been interpreted by the rabbis to mean that "he died by the kiss of the Lord." This is because the literal meaning of the verse is, "he died at the mouth of the Lord." God buried him in a valley (vs. 6). The structure of this sentence implies that Moses was the only man to be buried by the hand of God. The phrase **buried him in a valley** does not mean that God brought Moses down into the Jordan Valley and buried him. There was evidently some small crevice or valley at the top of the mountain. He was buried there. No one knows his burial place, which is a blessing to the memory of Moses. Perhaps some might have made his sepulcher a place of superstitious or even idolatrous reverence. Moses would have abhorred that thought, because he fought idolatry all of his life.

God was preparing the circumstances so that He could bring Moses back to the Mount of Transfiguration (Mt 17:3-4). Even though Moses did not enter the Promised Land in his lifetime, on the Mount of Transfiguration he stood in the Promised Land with Elijah and Jesus in the presence of three of the disciples. Knowing this fact, the devil had tried to confiscate the body of Moses (Jude 9); but Michael, the archangel, fought with him because God had future use for Moses' body. During the Tribulation Period two witnesses will minister in earthly Jerusalem (Rev 11:3-12). One witness will shut up heaven so that it will not rain (Elijah?), while the other witness will turn water into blood and bring plagues on the earth (Moses?). Even though God buried him in Moab, Moses, the servant of the Lord, was not finished with his service for God.

9-12. Joshua had become the leader when Moses laid his hands upon him and the people listened to him. However, Joshua was not like Moses. As a matter of fact, no one has ever been like Moses. **There arose not a prophet since in Israel like unto Moses.** Obviously, Moses was the redeemer and deliverer of Israel. By his wisdom and leadership he had brought a group of slaves into the Promised Land. No one else could have accomplished what he accomplished. Also, there was no one else like him because of the Mosaic law and the covenant that he gave to Israel. No prophet could ever arise in Israel like unto Moses, because no prophet could ever give the Law to Israel that he gave. Moses would be the outstanding leader of Israel until a person with a greater law than the Mosaic law entered the scene. And that is what happened when Jesus Christ came to fulfill the Law that was given by Moses. Jesus was the founder and mediator of a new and better covenant (Heb 8:6; 9:15; 12:24).

The phrase **whom the LORD knew face to face** means that God knew him by divine knowledge because He had carefully observed his life, had manifested Himself to Moses, and had endued him with His Spirit. God had known him **face to face** and "mouth to mouth" (Num 12:8). God knew Moses in signs and wonders that he did by the mighty hand of the Lord, **which Moses showed in the sight of all Israel.**

BIBLIOGRAPHY

Barclay, Robert A. *The Lawgivers: Leviticus and Deuteronomy*. London: Lutterworth, 1964.

Carroll, B. H. *An Interpretation of the English Bible: Numbers to Ruth*. Ed. by J. B. Cranfil. Grand Rapids: Baker, 1976 reprint of 1948 ed.

Diver, S. R. *A Critical and Exegetical Commentary on Deuteronomy*. New York: Charles Scribner's Sons, 1895.

Francisco, Clyde G. *The Book of Deuteronomy*. Grand Rapids: Baker, 1964.

Gaebelein, A. C. *The Annotated Bible*. Vol. 1. Wheaton, Ill.: VanKampen Press, 1913.

*Harrison, R. K. Deuteronomy. In *The New Bible Commentary Revised*. Ed. by D. Guthrie and J. A. Motyer. Grand Rapids: Eerdmans, 1970.

*Keil, C. F. and F. Delitzsch, *Biblical Commentary on the Old Testament*. Vol. 3. Trans. by J. Martin. Grand Rapids: Eerdmans, 1949.

*Kline, Meredith. Deuteronomy. In *The Wycliffe Bible Commentary*. Ed. by C. H. Pfeiffer and E. H. Harrison. Chicago: Moody Press, 1962.

_____. *Treaty of the Great King: The Covenant Structure of Deuteronomy*. Grand Rapids: Eerdmans, 1963.

*Manley, G. T. *The Book of the Law*. London: Tyndale Press, 1957.

_____. Deuteronomy. In *The New Bible Commentary*. Ed. by J. Davidson. Grand Rapids: Eerdmans, 1953.

Reider, J. *Deuteronomy*. Philadelphia: Jewish Publication Society of America, 1937.

Schroeder, F. W. Deuteronomy. In *Commentary on the Holy Scriptures*. Ed. by J. P. Lange. Grand Rapids: Zondervan, reprinted, n.d.

Schultz, Samuel J. *Deuteronomy: The Gospel of Love*. Chicago: Moody Press, 1971.

Thompson, J. A. Deuteronomy. In *Tyndale Old Testament Commentaries*. Ed. by D. J. Wiseman. London: InterVarsity Press, 1974.

Wright, G. E. The Book of Deuteronomy. In *The Interpreter's Bible*. New York: Abingdon Press, 1953.

JOSHUA

INTRODUCTION

Title. The first book of the Prophets, the second division of the Old Testament canon, is named after Joshua, the chief character of the book. In the Hebrew language the name "Joshua" has four principal forms: *yehoshua* (Deut 3:21); *yeshoshua* (Josh 1:1, et al); *hoshea* (Deut 32:44); and *yeshua* (Neh 8:17). The very name Joshua, the Hebrew form of Jesus, means "Jehovah is salvation."

Authorship. According to the rationalist critics of the Wellhausen school, the book of Joshua is not a literary unit composed by a single author. These negative critics have attempted to include Joshua with the five books of the Pentateuch, calling the whole collection the Hexateuch. But the Samaritans, who accepted only the Pentateuch as canon, did not accept Joshua, even though there is prominent mention of Shechem in Ephraim, the chief hero of the book is the Ephraimite general (Joshua the son of Nun), and the whole tone of the book would have made wonderful nationalistic propaganda for the Samaritans. In fact, Scripture knows nothing of a so-called Hexateuch. The Pentateuch is distinct (Josh 1:7-8; II Chr 34:14; cf. Christ's own testimony, Lk 24:44). While Joshua forms a sequel to the law of Moses (Josh 24:26), nevertheless it is distinct from it.

The higher critics of modern biblical criticism have maintained that the basic material in Joshua has come from two sources thought to be J (ca. 950-850) and E (ca. 750), with considerable editorial work done by a supposed Deuteronomic school D (ca. 550). Later redaction was said to have been done by a Priestly school P (ca. 400), which made major insertions in chapters 13-21. For an excellent refutation of this approach see G. E. Wright, *The Old Testament Against Its Environment.*

But the documentary hypothesis which engenders this fragmented compilation of the book is greatly undermined by the evident unity displayed in the book. The Wellhausen school has built its critical approach on the faulty preconception that the religion of the Hebrews underwent a drastic evolutionary development, a position which cannot be proved nor seriously maintained by God-honoring scholars. For an account of the rise of higher criticism as embodied in the documentary hypothesis and the utter failure of this hypothesis, see chapters 6-13 of *A Survey of Old Testament Introduction* by Gleason L. Archer, Jr.

It is therefore maintained that Joshua is the primary author of the book which bears his name. Some references are in the first person plural (e.g., 5:1, 6), and intimate biographical details are given that only Joshua may have known. Joshua 24:26 clearly indicated that the Israelite general "wrote these words in the book of the law of God, and took a great stone, and set it up there under an oak, that was by the sanctuary of the LORD."

On the other hand, it is evident that portions of the book cannot have been written by Joshua. Not only do we have notification of Joshua's decease (24:29-30), but also there is the record of events which took place after Joshua's death. Some of the most notable are: the conquest of Hebron by Caleb (Josh 15:13b-14; cf. Jud 1:1, 10, 20), or Debir by Othniel (Josh 15:15-19; cf. Jud 1:11-15), and of Leshem by the Danites (Josh 19:47; cf. Jud 18:7, 14). There is a Jewish tradition that Eleazar added the account of Joshua's death and that Phinehas added the account of Eleazar's death.

Date. Since Joshua was the primary author and an eyewitness to many of the events described (Josh 5:1, 6), and since Rahab was still alive (Josh 6:25), the date of the book must be placed shortly before and after Joshua's death. The book must be pre-Solomonic (Josh 16:10; cf. I Kgs 9:16) and pre-Davidic (Josh 15:63; cf. II Sam 5:5-9). As the Philistines were not a menace to Israel in Joshua's day, the book must have been written prior to the Philistine invasion of Palestine shortly after 1200 B.C. Moreover, according to Joshua 13:4-6 and 19:28, Sidon was the most important city of Phoenicia, thus indicating the period of the twelfth century B.C., after which Tyre attained the domination in Phoenicia.

It is most likely that the concluding verses of Joshua were written during the early judgeship of Othniel (ca. 1370-1330).

An Ephraimite, the son of Nun (I Ch 7:22-27), Joshua was born in Egypt, the land of bondage. Two months after Israel's exodus he is mentioned as the commander of Israel's forces which successfully repulsed an Amalekite attack at Rephidim (Ex 17:9). God's future plans for Joshua are seen in Exodus 17:14 where "the LORD said unto Moses, Write this for a memorial in a book, and rehearse it in the ears of (not Israel, but) Joshua: for I will utterly put out the remembrance of Amalek from under heaven."

The next time we encounter Joshua is on Mount Sinai where Joshua is said to be the "minister" (Heb *mesharēt*) of Moses (Ex 24:13). Upon returning from the mountain and hearing the mischievous music of the idolatrous Israelites, Joshua wrongly interpreted the sounds as the noise of war in the camp (Ex 32:17-18). Joshua is then seen with Moses in the tabernacle (Ex 33:11) learning about the glory of God. Later, he is found seeking to quiet two prophets because Moses had not sanctioned them to speak (Num 11:28).

In Numbers 13 Joshua's preparation for leadership takes a giant step at the hand of Eleazar and/or his son Phinehas, also inspired of God. On the biblical evidence for the date of Joshua and the conquest see Leon Wood, *A Survey of Israel's History,* pp. 168-202.

Purpose. Joshua is a multi-purpose book. It continues the history of Israel begun in the Pentateuch, recording how God brought His theocratic nation from the wilderness into the Promised Land. In addition, the book demonstrates the faithfulness of God to His covenants in settling the tribes into their promised homeland (Josh 11:23; 21:43-45). Joshua presents a glimpse of God's holiness in His judgment on the wicked Canaanites. The book also serves to show how Joshua completely trusted Jehovah and performed all the duties entrusted to him. The entrance into the land illustrates the Christian experience of maturity, victory, and blessing (Eph 1:3; 2:6; 6:12), which makes the book a special blessing to New Testament believers. He was one of the twelve spies sent on the reconnaissance mission into the Promised Land. Caleb and he, convinced of divine enablement, brought back a positive, but minority, report on Israel's ability to possess the land; but the Israelites did not share their aggressive eagerness.

On the plain of Moab, when Joshua and Caleb alone represented the original Israelites numbered at the foot of Sinai, Joshua had been sufficiently prepared so as to warrant his public ordination (Num 27:18-23). The decision conceived in eternity was now made public: God had been training Joshua to receive the mantle of leadership from Moses. In Moses' farewell address he encouraged Joshua to "Be strong and of a good courage" for the Lord would carry His people over the river to possess the land of their inheritance (Deut 31:2-8).

Joshua, probably now in his nineties, did not come quickly to the leadership of Israel. "Lay hands suddenly on no man . . ." (I Tim 5:22) is forcefully depicted in the selection and preparation of Joshua as Israel's leader. Israel's new leader had been appointed by God, not chosen by the people. Joshua was empowered by the Holy Spirit (Num 27:18) with possession of unusual faith and exhibited tremendous courage. He did not seek leadership; but, when confronted by the Holy God, he could not refuse it. There are two major incidents in the book of Joshua which have created much discussion.

The Extermination of the Canaanites. With the capture of Jericho and Ai, the Israelite forces were commanded to completely exterminate the heathen inhabitants. Critics of the Bible have raised the question of the ethical propriety of such tactics. Was is just of God to allow the utter annihilation of the Canaanites? How can a God of love have permitted Israel to follow this extermination policy? Several things must be kept in mind.

First, we must remember that the responsibility for this extreme punishment cannot be laid at the feet of Israel. It was God Himself, rather than the Hebrews, who commanded the extermination of the Canaanites. The Israelite armies were but following the orders of their commander-in-chief as he received his orders directly from God.

Second, the Holy God always avenges the righteous and punishes the wicked. For example, divine punishment arising from divine wrath lay at the root of the Flood which swept away all but eight souls in the days of Noah. Another time God's punishment was evidenced in the pestilences which

plagued Egypt. Still other times such punishment was witnessed in a burned city, a ravishing earthquake, and a howling gale. Once "the Assyrian" was the rod of God's wrath to cut off nations, though he did not know he was being the instrument of God's wrath (Isa 10:5-7). But always God's punishment was directed toward the ungodly, the unrighteous. The righteous may experience divine chastening, but never divine wrath (Rom 8:1; I Thess 5:9).

Third, the Canaanites were singled out for extermination because of their excessive wickedness. Not only were they idolaters, but they were guilty of sexual practices and sacrificial practices which the heathen themselves regarded with abhorrence. The Ras Shamra tablets have brought to light the excesses of the most degenerate forms of polytheism and sexual impurity that were commonplace among the Canaanites. Their depravity and gross idolatry is also recorded in Leviticus 18:3-28. They engaged in religious prostitution (cf. the abomination of Baal-peor in Numbers 25); they practiced child sacrifice; and they incorporated the baser elements of all the foreign cults surrounding them. Theirs was not simple wickedness; it was a life-style based on wickedness. In order to punish such a life-style and to keep Israel pure from similar degeneration, the Canaanites had to be exterminated.

Fourth, God hates sin. He has always hated sin. His hatred for sin does not mitigate His love for the sinner. Yet, nevertheless, in order to be a Holy God (the chief attribute of God's character), He cannot tolerate blatant sin. It is correct to say that God is a God of love. But it is folly to believe that this love will prevent Him from maintaining His holiness. It may be difficult for us to accept the divine command for the complete extermination of a people, but then our hatred for sin doesn't even approximate the divine hatred for sin. As a people today we do not shun the presence of sin and abhor evil as the ancient Jews did. We are far more enlightened and far less pious. The generation of Israel under Joshua was the most pious one in all their history. They received their daily provision from God; they received their direction from God; and they had entered the Promised Land by the hand of God. They burned Achan and his family because of sin with the same holy zeal that they went after the Canaanites. Twentieth-century man does not seem to share that same zeal for holiness and piety, and we are quick to question God's judgment of the Israelites for their obedience to God's righteous command.

Joshua's Long Day. Perhaps the most hotly contested miracle recorded in Scripture is Joshua's long day. In conquering the Promised Land, Joshua and the Israelite forces had to come to the aid of the Gibeonites who were being besieged by an Amorite league of kings. During the course of this battle supernatural aid was sought, giving Israel a smashing victory. That aid was the elongation of a day at the request of Joshua that the sun stand still.

It has been argued that if the earth stopped its rotation for twenty-four hours, inconceivable events would follow: earthquakes would gouge the surface of the earth, oceans would overflow their shores, perhaps even stars would plummet to the earth. Catastrophe after catastrophe has been suggested. But even those who accept the omnipotence of God disagree on the interpretation of this miracle.

Some say that the language here is but poetic. They say that Joshua did not actually ask for a miracle, but in poetical language he was simply appealing for divine strength and enablement. He did not actually expect the sun to stand still, but he was just musing, "Oh, if the sun would only stand still . . ." This explanation hardly does justice to the text.

Others suggest that the Hebrew text does not demand that we understand the planet to have stopped suddenly in its rotation. Translating Joshua 10:13 as "the sun did not hasten to set for an entire day," it is held that a retardation of the sun's movement caused the rotation of the earth to take forty-eight hours rather than the usual twenty-four. But such an interpretation hardly silences the criticism of inevitable catastrophe.

Still others, notably Dr. E. W. Maunders of Greenwich and Dr. Robert Dick Wilson of Princeton University, interpret Joshua's prayer to be a call for the sun to cease issuing its radiant heat. The petition for the sun's rays to stop beating on the heads of Israel's armies would thus enable Israel to fight in more favorable conditions. See R. D. Wilson, "What Does 'The Sun Stood Still' Mean?" *Princeton Theological Review*, XVI (1918) pp. 46-47. But what about the Amorites? Does not the sun shine on all men alike? In fact, verse 13 unquestionably favors a prolongation of the day, not an alleviation of the sunlight.

Even Keil and Delitzsch, in the *Biblical Commentary on the Old Testament*, hold that the prolongation of the day was a psychological phenomenon rather than a physical one, that Joshua and Israel accomplished in that one day what ordinarily would have taken two days. They interpret the scene as a miraculous effort on the part of Israel's troops, but such an interpretation sorely falls short of dealing with the question of the prolonged day. It unwarrantedly shifts the miracle from God's heavens to God's armies.

Hugh J. Blair, in the *New Bible Commentary*, advances a rather unique interpretation. Blair suggests that Joshua's prayer was lifted to God in the early morning, since the moon was in the west and the sun was in the east. The hailstorm which ensued was God's way of prolonging the darkness and thus enabling a surprise attack by the Israelites after their all-night march. But this would be a prolonged night and not a prolonged day and again does not call for the sun to stand still, but simply to be slow in showing itself due to the driving hailstorm.

There is one final interpretation, of course, and that is that the sun actually stood still. This would allow Joshua's forces, who had gained the upper hand, to continue the battle and gain a complete victory. We need not be concerned with the miraculous nature of this act, or with the possible catastrophes which might result. A God who is powerful enough to stop the sun in its tracks is powerful enough to prevent any attending catastrophes. Why should the critics accept the miraculous nature of Israel's crossing the Red Sea, of the daily provision of manna, or of the entrance into the Promised Land and not the miraculous nature of the sun standing still? Those who are not ready to receive the miraculous nature of any of these miracles are not ready to receive the blessings of the book of Joshua. We must become accustomed to seeing the miracles of God if we are to enter our own Promised Land of blessing and maturity.

OUTLINE

COMMENTARY

I. ENTRANCE INTO THE PROMISED LAND. 1:1-5:12.

A. Joshua's Divine Commission. 1:1-9.

NOW after the death of Moses the servant of the LORD it came to pass, that the LORD spake unto Joshua the son of Nun, Moses' minister, saying,

1:1. Moses, as the chosen leader of God, had been the great emancipator of Israel. He had led them from Egyptian bondage to the very brink of the Promised Land. The eulogy issued upon his death, recorded in the last verses of Deuteronomy, includes the remarks, "And there arose not a prophet since in Israel like unto Moses, whom the LORD knew face to face" (Deut 34:10). But the great man was dead, and the book of Joshua begins almost matter-of-factly with the statement **Now after the death of Moses . . . the LORD spake unto Joshua.** This is a stark reminder that no servant of God, however large or small, is indispensable. The Lord's workers may die, but His work moves on.

A distinction must be drawn in this first verse of the book between **Moses the servant** and Joshua, **Moses' minister.** The word translated servant (Heb *'ebed*) is applied to the heavens and the earth (Ps 119:91), to the angels (Job 4:18), to the Jewish people (Ex 19:5), to the prophets (Jer 7:25), to Zerubbabel (Hag 2:23), and even, as the appointed minister of God's wrath, to Nebuchadnezzar (Jer 25:9). It is an expression used either to describe one who piously worships the Lord (Lev 25:42, 55; Isa 41:8; 43:10) or one who has been given a special commission by the Lord (Gen 26:24; II Sam 3:18; II Chr 32:16). Moses was both a pious worshiper of the Lord and His servant commissioned to lead the Israelites out of Egypt.

But once the great hero of Israel was dead, the Lord spake unto Joshua the son of Nun in his stead. This book gives evidence of a series of such revelations (Josh 3:7; 4:1, 15; 5:2, 9; 6:2, etc.). That Joshua was Moses' minister (Heb *mesharēt*) means more than that he was Moses' *aide-de-camp*. This word is generally used of service in the house of God and applied to Aaron and his sons (Ex 28:43, 39:41, etc.), Samuel (I Sam 2:11;

2 Moses my servant is dead; now therefore arise, go over this Jordan, thou, and all this people, unto the land which I do give to them, *even* to the children of Israel.

3 Every place that the sole of your foot shall tread upon, that have I given unto you, as I said unto Moses.

4 From the wilderness and this Lebanon even unto the great river, the river Eū-phrā'tēs, all the land of the Hittites, and unto the great sea toward the going down of the sun, shall be your coast.

5 There shall not any man be able to stand before thee all the days of thy life: as I was with Moses, *so* I will be with thee: I will not fail thee, nor forsake thee.

6 Be strong and of a good courage: for unto this people shalt thou divide for an inheritance the land, which I sware unto their fathers to give them.

7 Only be thou strong and very courageous, that thou mayest observe to do according to all the law, which Moses my servant commanded thee: turn not from it *to* the right hand or *to* the left, that thou mayest prosper whithersoever thou goest.

8 This book of the law shall not depart out of thy mouth; but thou shalt meditate therein day and night, that thou mayest observe to do according to all that is written therein: for then thou shalt make thy way prosperous, and then thou shalt have good success.

9 Have not I commanded thee? Be strong and of a good courage; be not afraid, neither be thou dismayed: for the LORD thy God *is* with thee whithersoever thou goest.

3:1, etc.), and the priests and Levites (I Chr 6:32; 16:4; Ezk 14:5; Joel 1:9, etc.). When the word does not refer to one performing a religious function, it generally refers to one performing a military function (cf. Ex 24:13, Num 27:18-23; Deut 1:38; 31:23). Joshua had performed both.

2-4. Now therefore arise, go over this Jordan. This is the first mention of the Jordan in the book of Joshua, which more frequently than any other book of the Bible (seventy times) refers to the Jordan River. Springing from the foothills of the Lebanon mountains, the Jordan flows into the Sea of Galilee, which is approximately seven hundred feet below sea level. From there its seventy-mile journey to the Dead Sea, approximately 1300 feet below sea level, actually covers two hundred miles because of its serpentine curves. This descent in elevation from the Sea of Galilee to the Dead Sea gives rise to the name Jordan (Heb *yardēn*), which means "descender."

Although Moses could not enter the Promised Land, Joshua must. Armed with God's commitment, **Every place that the sole of your foot shall tread upon, that have I given unto you, as I said unto Moses.** These words are a quotation, almost word for word, from Deuteronomy 11:24. The original promise was made in Genesis 12:1-7 (cf. Gen 13:14-17; 15:18; 17:8). The conquest of the land was intended by God to be complete. The boundaries of the Promised Land are specifically delineated as **From the wilderness and this Lebanon even unto the great river, the river Euphrates, all the land of the Hittites, and unto the Great Sea.** From the Lebanon mountains in the North to the Euphrates River in the Northeast, all the way to the coast of the Mediterranean Sea (the Great Sea), was to be the possession of Abraham's descendants. This is encompassed in the phrase, **all the land of the Hittites,** which is taken to mean the land of Canaan in general (I Kgs 10:29; II Kgs 7:6; Ezk 16:3), but extending far beyond that border and including Syria, Moab, Ammon, Bashan, and parts of Arabia.

5-7. I will not fail thee, nor forsake thee. Be strong and of a good courage: . . . Only be thou strong and very courageous, that thou mayest observe to do according to all the law. The Lord God knew it was necessary to also provide divine encouragement to Joshua at his commissioning. Jehovah is the God of all encouragement (II Cor 1:3-4). His promise to Joshua is that He will never fail His servant. The verb (Heb *rapah*) literally means "I will not be weak towards thee." God will not relax His divine enablement now that Moses is dead. The repetition of the command to be strong indicates that God is interested not only in the spiritual character of His servants, but in their physical actions as well. Armed with divine power, Joshua is encouraged that he will be successful in all that he undertakes for the Lord. Personal courage and complete obedience to God's will are always two of the main ingredients in success for the believer.

8-9. This book of the law. If our dating of the book of Joshua is accurate (see Introduction), then it must be admitted that a **book of the law** already existed as a recognized authority given by the revelation of God (cf. Ex 17:14; 24:4, 7; Deut 31:9, 11, 24, 26). The critical and erroneous assumption that Scripture, especially Deuteronomy and other books of the Pentateuch, were passed on by oral tradition until the seventh and eighth centuries B.C. and then later redacted to their present form cannot be seriously held in light of this verse. The secret of success for the servant of the Lord in any generation is always the same, i.e., that the Scriptures **shall not depart out of thy mouth; but thou shalt meditate therein day and night, that thou mayest observe to do according to all that is written therein.** Accompanying the command to encouragement is also the command to speak of the Scriptures daily and, more than that, to meditate upon them. Simply memorizing or quoting

Scripture is not enough; meditation involves mature reflection on the Word of God, and it is the basis for spiritual growth (cf. Ps 1:1-3; 63:6; 119:15, 97; 143:5).

Be not afraid, neither be dismayed: for the LORD thy God is with thee whithersoever thou goest. The special promise of the Lord God to His servants in the Old Testament (cf. Deut 31:6-8) is clearly the same promise which Christ gave to His servants in the New Testament (Mt 28:19-20; Jn 20:21-23). Any believer who is immersed in the Book is bound to be encouraged.

B. Joshua Organizes Israel for Crossing the Jordan. 1:10-18.

10 ¶Then Joshua commanded the officers of the people, saying,

11 Pass through the host, and command the people, saying, Prepare you victuals; for within three days ye shall pass over this Jordan, to go in to possess the land, which the LORD your God giveth you to possess it.

10-11. Then Joshua commanded the officers . . . Pass through the host, and command the people. In order to successfully cross the Jordan River and secure the Promised Land, Israel had to be organized into a coordinated company. Thus, Joshua issues the call to preparation and commands that his officers relay that call to the people. The officers and the people (Heb *shōtĕrē ha'am*) literally means "scribes." It is difficult to determine exactly what their office was. Some believe that they were genealogists, others that they were secretaries or recorders. When the equivalent word is translated in Acts 19:35 as "town clerk," *grammateus* is used. Given Joshua's context, it seems most likely that these officers were the scribes of the military role and were commanded to muster the people.

The phrase **within three days ye shall pass over this Jordan** has caused much controversy. In 2:22 the spies are said to spend three days in the mountains before returning to Joshua. And in 3:2 we are told that after three days **the officers went through the host.** It is most likely that these events were happening simultaneously, and thus it is not necessary to assume a chronological difficulty or an elongation of the period of waiting to conquer the land.

12 ¶And to the Reubenites, and to the Gadites, and to half the tribe of Manăs'seh, spake Joshua, saying,

13 Remember the word which Moses the servant of the LORD commanded you, saying, The LORD your God hath given you rest, and hath given you this land.

14 Your wives, your little ones, and your cattle, shall remain in the land which Moses gave you on this side Jordan; but ye shall pass before your brethren armed, all the mighty men of valour, and help them;

15 Until the LORD have given your brethren rest, as *he hath given* you, and they also have possessed the land which the LORD your God giveth them: then ye shall return unto the land of your possession, and enjoy it, which Moses the LORD's servant gave you on this side Jordan toward the sunrising.

12-15. And to the Reubenites, and to the Gadites, and to half the tribe of Manasseh. In the special instructions given to these two and a half tribes we see a remarkable example of the inspiration of Scripture. With the mention of their cattle in verse 14 we are reminded that these tribes desired an inheritance on the other side of the Jordan because they were particularly rich in cattle. From elsewhere in Scripture we learn that this area was also particularly well-suited for cattle. Indeed, the bulls of Bashan (Ps 22:12; Ezk 39:18) and the pasture fields of Bashan (Jer 50:19; Mic 7:14) are almost legendary. Mesha, king of Moab, was a "sheepmaster" (II Kgs 3:4) and paid his tribute to Israel in sheep. This quiet correspondence of the facts is nevertheless a boisterous vote of assurance for inspiration.

Reuben, Gad, and half the tribe of Manasseh are here reminded of their military responsibility to the rest of Israel. Earlier, Moses had given them permission to receive an inheritance in the land of Jordan that bore the name Mishor, or "level land," as contrasted with the rocky region on the other side of the Jordan. But they were only permitted to settle there after they had fulfilled their military responsibility with regard to the conquest of Canaan (Num 32). This obligation would only be fulfilled when **The LORD your God hath given you rest, and hath given you this land,** literally, when the Lord God caused them to rest (cf. Heb 3:11-18; 4:1-11).

16 ¶And they answered Joshua, saying, All that thou commandest us we will do, and whithersoever thou sendest us, we will go.

17 According as we hearkened unto Moses in all things, so will we hearken unto thee: only the LORD thy God be with thee, as he was with Moses.

16-18. All that thou commandest us we will do, . . . only be strong and of a good courage. There was immediate and enthusiastic agreement reconfirmed to Joshua as it had been to Moses. Whereas once the tribes of Reuben, Gad, and Manasseh would follow to the death their leader Moses, now they encouraged Joshua in a similar manner by promising to adhere to their agreements with Moses.

18 Whosoever *he be* that doth rebel against thy commandment, and will not hearken unto thy words in all that thou commandest him, he shall be put to death: only be strong and of a good courage.

CHAPTER 2

AND Joshua the son of Nun sent out of Shĭt'tĭm two men to spy secretly, saying, Go view the land, even Jericho. And they went, and came into an harlot's house, named Rahab, and lodged there.

2 And it was told the king of Jericho, saying, Behold, there came men in hither to night of the children of Israel to search out the country.

3 And the king of Jericho sent unto Rahab, saying, Bring forth the men that are come to thee, which are entered into thine house: for they be come to search out all the country.

4 And the woman took the two men, and hid them, and said thus, There came men unto me, but I wist not whence they *were:*

5 And it came to pass *about the time* of shutting of the gate, when it was dark, that the men went out: whither the men went I wot not: pursue after them quickly; for ye shall overtake them.

6 But she had brought them up to the roof of the house, and hid them with the stalks of flax, which she had laid in order upon the roof.

7 And the men pursued after them the way to Jordan unto the fords: and as soon as they which pursued after them were gone out, they shut the gate.

C. Joshua Sends Spies to Jericho. 2:1-24.

2:1-3. And Joshua the son of Nun sent out of Shittim two men to spy secretly. The expression **out of Shittim** is literally "from the Valley of Acacias." This place, elsewhere called Abel-Shittim (cf. Num 33:49), is where Israel had sojourned prior to entering the land. The word "Abel" means "meadow" and signifies a large, grassy plain replete with acacia trees. This name apparently survived in the time of Josephus, the first-century A.D. Jewish historian, in the name Abila, a site which, according to Josephus, lay seven miles east of the Jordan River (*Antiq.* 8,i; v,i,i).

Joshua's action of sending spies into the land should not be interpreted as a lack of trust in God's promise to deliver the land into Israel's hand. Rather, Joshua was a keen army general and had participated in an earlier crucial mission from Kadesh-barnea as a spy (Num 13-14). Israel must not march blindly into the Promised Land, and thus their general engaged in a secret intelligence-gathering mission. "He had learned by experience that spy reports should be brought to the leaders only, for the people did not have sufficient orientation or experience to properly evaluate such a report. Because of the proximity of the tribes of Israel to Jericho, it was necessary that this spy mission be carried out with as little commotion as possible" (John J. Davis, *Conquest and Crisis*, p. 33).

And they went, and came into a harlot's house, named Rahab, and lodged there. Throughout the centuries, Christian commentators have attempted to explain away this seemingly inappropriate action on behalf of Israel's spies. Many scholars, like Josephus (*Antiq.* V:8:2,7), refer to Rahab simply as an "innkeeper." But in light of Joshua's description of her as a harlot (Heb *zōnah*) and corresponding references in the New Testament (Gr *pornē*) in Hebrews 11:31 and James 2:25, such an interpretation cannot be maintained. Rahab doubtless was an innkeeper, and her establishment no doubt was a café as well as an inn; but she was clearly a harlot as well. There is no hint whatsoever of immorality, however, in the spies' seeking shelter at Rahab's house. Undoubtedly, the café would have been the most likely place to hear the common talk of the town and the least likely place where those who were obviously strangers would be recognized. It was the right tactical move on their part. Unfortunately, the two men were quickly recognized; and the king of Jericho was apprised of their presence. Soldiers were quickly dispatched to Rahab's house to inquire as to the presence of the Israelite spies.

4-7. She had brought them up to the roof of the house, and hid them with the stalks of flax. Rahab had apparently already discerned that these men were spies from the armies of Israel. She could have simply asked them to leave; but there were stirrings in her heart, seeds of faith in the God of Israel, which could not be ignored. Thus, she chose to hide the men instead. She took them up to the flat roof of her Oriental home, a place commonly used for drying corn and other grains (cf. I Sam 9:25-26; II Sam 11:2; 16:22). There she hid them, literally each one in a different place, among the stalks of flax (a plant from which the fibers of the bark in the ancient Orient were drawn, twisted, and bleached to make linen).

Upon the arrival of the soldiers and the question to Rahab where the two spies had gone, Rahab replied, **There came men unto me, but I wist not whence they were: And it came to pass about the time of the shutting of the gate, when it was dark, that the men went out: whither the men went I wot not.** This clever deception did serve to spare the lives of the two spies, but it has clouded the question of doing evil so that good may come. Was Rahab's lie justified? Many present theologians tend to justify this lie by saying that she did what was right in that situation. But such "situational ethics" lead to the justification of the end for the means. Rahab's lie was wrong; but there is not a single note of condemnation in the narrative of Joshua; and it may be unwise for any commentator to piously do that which the eyewitnesses failed to do.

However, several observations should be made. First, Rahab was a pagan woman living in a pagan society. The degree of ethical consciousness displayed by the early Phoenicians and Canaanites was very low indeed. No doubt Rahab was absolutely unaware that telling this lie was a sin. She was humanly no more concerned over this falsehood than she was over her own occupation. Secondly, nowhere do we find a reference that either the spies, or later Joshua, ever condoned this lie. A lie by any other name, even if it is little and white, is nevertheless a lie. The spies did not ask Rahab to lie for them, nor did they commend her for this action. Thirdly, although there appears to be seedlike faith in Rahab, nevertheless there is no clear reference to her faith in the true God of Israel until after the lie was told. The deception, which was almost matter-of-factly and routinely carried out, was not at all ethically troublesome to Rahab before her confession of faith in Jehovah. One can only assume that the situation would have been different after that confession.

8-11. I know that the LORD hath given you the land. What a strange utterance coming from this quarter! Some thirty-eight years earlier Joshua and Caleb had uttered words almost identical to these (Josh 2:24), and no one believed them. Now these words are uttered by an inhabitant of that land because she did believe. Rahab had heard **how the LORD dried up the water of the Red Sea . . . and what ye did unto the two kings of the Amorites, that were on the other side Jordan, Sihon and Og, whom ye utterly destroyed.** The news of God's conquests through Israel had preceded their arrival to the banks of the Jordan. So awesome were the victories of Israel that Rahab admitted **our hearts did melt, neither did there remain any more courage in any man, because of you.** The harlot reasoned that Canaan, and most particularly her city of Jericho, would be the next to fall in the way of mighty Israel. But that reasoning did not win her favor with God. It was her faith and her confession of that faith which pleased God because she said **for the LORD your God, he is God in heaven above, and in earth beneath.** We need not scrutinize this confession for repentance or for personal acceptance of Jehovah, for they are both implicit in her statement. Rahab the pagan believed God, and He counted it unto her for righteousness.

Abraham, in his day, also believed God; and it was counted unto him for righteousness. Like Abraham, she had believed out of a cultural background of paganism; and the language of faith is undoubtedly different from that expressed out of a Christian culture, but the faith is nevertheless the same. The writer of Hebrews makes it clear, "By faith the harlot Rahab perished not with them that believed not, when she had received the spies with peace" (Heb 11:31). Her lying past had not been condoned by God; it was simply forgiven by Him, as has our past. As one of the three women mentioned by name in the genealogy of Christ (Mt), Rahab (Gr *Rachab*) takes her rightful place as one who had faith in God and was treated as if she were righteous.

12-14. Swear unto me by the LORD . . . that ye will also show kindness unto my father's house. Having exercised belief in Jehovah, Rahab's first concern is for her family. She asks the spies to show kindness to the house of her father, to **save alive my father, and my mother, and my brethren, and my**

8 ¶And before they were laid down, she came up unto them upon the roof;

9 And she said unto the men, I know that the LORD hath given you the land, and that your terror is fallen upon us, and that all the inhabitants of the land faint because of you.

10 For we have heard how the LORD dried up the water of the Red sea for you, when ye came out of Egypt; and what ye did unto the two kings of the Amorites, that *were* on the other side Jordan, Sihon and Og, whom ye utterly destroyed.

11 And as soon as we had heard *these things*, our hearts did melt, neither did there remain any more courage in any man, because of you: for the LORD your God, he *is* God in heaven above, and in earth beneath.

12 Now therefore, I pray you, swear unto me by the LORD, since I have shewed you kindness, that ye will also shew kindness unto my father's house, and give me a true token:

13 And *that* ye will save alive my father, and my mother, and my brethren, and my sisters, and all that they have, and deliver our lives from death.

14 And the men answered her, Our life for yours, if ye utter not this our business. And it shall be, when the LORD hath given us the land, that we will deal kindly and truly with thee.

15 Then she let them down by a cord through the window: for her house *was* upon the town wall, and she dwelt upon the wall.

16 And she said unto them, Get you to the mountain, lest the pursuers meet you; and hide yourselves there three days, until the pursuers be returned: and afterward may ye go your way.

17 And the men said unto her, We *will be* blameless of this thine oath which thou hast made us swear.

18 Behold, *when* we come into the land, thou shalt bind this line of scarlet thread in the window which thou didst let us down by: and thou shalt bring thy father, and thy mother, and thy brethren, and all thy father's household, home unto thee.

19 And it shall be, *that* whosoever shall go out of the doors of thy house into the street, his blood *shall be* upon his head, and we *will be* guiltless: and whosoever shall be with thee in the house, his blood *shall be* on our head, if *any* hand be upon him.

20 And if thou utter this our business, then we will be quit of thine oath which thou hast made us to swear.

21 And she said, According unto your words, so *be* it. And she sent them away, and they departed: and she bound the scarlet line in the window.

22 And they went, and came unto the mountain, and abode there three days, until the pursuers were returned: and the pursuers sought *them* throughout all the way, but found *them* not.

23 So the two men returned, and descended from the mountain, and passed over, and came to Joshua the son of Nun, and told him all *things* that befell them:

24 And they said unto Joshua, Truly the LORD hath delivered into our hands all the land; for even all the inhabitants of the country do faint because of us.

CHAPTER 3

AND Joshua rose early in the morning; and they removed from Shĭt'tĭm, and came to Jordan, he and all the children of Israel, and lodged there before they passed over.

2 And it came to pass after three days, that the officers went through the host;

sisters. There is no mention of husband or children because as a harlot she would have none. But now as a believer, her interest is entirely directed toward the salvation of her family. The spies agreed, covenanting **Our life for yours.** The condition upon which their lives were spared became the eventual salvation of Rahab's family.

15-16. Then she let them down by a cord through the window. Rahab's house was located upon the wall, not at all an uncommon feature in Oriental cities even today. The men were permitted to escape by being lowered from her window to the ground outside the wall. The distance from her window to the ground need not be great, for the conversation continued after the men had lowered themselves. To the spies Rahab said, **Get you to the mountain.** Although it does not mention a specific mountain to which the spies would flee, the Jebel Kuruntul mountain range to the west would have been the only mountains in sight. Although the opposite direction from their camp, the advice to flee to this mountain was quickly accepted by the spies. The mountain is honeycombed with hundreds of caves, and they could have easily hidden for three days in one of those caves. Also, since it is the opposite direction, the armies of the king of Jericho would not naturally be looking for the spies on that side of the city of Jericho. Rahab was a cunning woman, indeed.

17-21. Behold, when we come into the land, thou shalt bind this line of scarlet thread in the window . . . and whosoever shall be with thee in the house, his blood shall be on our head, if any hand be upon him. The scarlet thread, which actually was more of a rope, has from the start of Christendom been interpreted as symbolic of the blood of Christ. Clement of Rome in his epistle to the Corinthians, chapter 12; Justin Martyr in his *Dialogue With Trypho*, paragraph 111; Irenaeus' *Against Heresies*, iv. 37; and Origin's *Homily* II on Joshua are all examples of this interpretation of the crimson cord. Because this rope clearly marked Rahab's house, there is a clear parallel here to the Passover in ancient Egypt. Death came to everyone but those whose houses were marked by the blood. Death came to every person of Jericho but the one house marked by the crimson cord. Also, the house of Rahab is very similar in nature to the ark, in that safety and shelter are found only in God's place of salvation. For the Christian that place is at the foot of the cross in the death, burial, and resurrection of the Lord Jesus Christ. He is our crimson cord, our ark of safety.

22-24. So the two men returned . . . and came to Joshua . . . And they said unto Joshua, Truly the LORD hath delivered into our hands all the land. After a waiting period of three days, the two spies had returned to their commanding general. The report that was brought to Joshua was very similar to the report which one day he had brought to Moses. But now the circumstances were different. Israel was ready to obey the Lord and would occupy her inheritance.

D. Joshua Leads the Israelites Across the Jordan. 3:1-5:1.

3:1-4. And Joshua rose early in the morning. A vital lesson for every servant of the Lord to learn is that God does things early in the morning. The Scriptures are replete with the marvelous activity of God "early in the morning." It was early in the morning that Abraham rose up with his son Isaac to go to Mount Moriah and test the faith of Abraham (Gen 22:3). It was early in the morning that Joshua's predecessor was commanded to stand

3 And they commanded the people, saying, When ye see the ark of the covenant of the LORD your God, and the priests the Lēvītes bearing it, then ye shall remove from your place, and go after it.

4 Yet there shall be a space between you and it, about two thousand cubits by measure: come not near unto it, that ' may know the way by which ye ṟust go: for ye have not passed *this* way heretofore.

5 And Joshua said unto the people, Sanctify yourselves: for to morrow the LORD will do wonders among you.

6 And Joshua spake unto the priests, saying, Take up the ark of the covenant, and pass over before the people. And they took up the ark of the covenant, and went before the people.

7 ¶And the LORD said unto Joshua, This day will I begin to magnify thee in the sight of all Israel, that they may know that, as I was with Moses, *so* I will be with thee.

8 And thou shalt command the priests that bear the ark of the covenant, saying, When ye are come to the brink of the water of Jordan, ye shall stand still in Jordan.

9 ¶And Joshua said unto the children of Israel, Come hither, and hear the words of the LORD your God.

10 And Joshua said, Hereby ye shall know that the living God *is* among you, and *that* he will without fail drive out from before you the Canaanites, and the Hittites, and the Hī'vītes, and the Pĕr'iz-zītes, and the Gir'ga-shītes, and the Ămŏrītes, and the Jĕb'u-sītes.

11 Behold, the ark of the covenant of the Lord of all the earth passeth over before you into Jordan.

12 Now therefore take you twelve men out of the tribes of Israel, out of every tribe a man.

13 And it shall come to pass, as soon as the soles of the feet of the priests that bear the ark of the LORD, the Lord of all the earth, shall rest in the waters of Jordan, *that* the waters of Jordan shall be cut off *from* the waters that come down from above; and they shall stand upon an heap.

before Pharaoh and say ". . . Let my people go . . ." (Ex 8:20). It was early in the morning that young David left for the battlefield the day he defeated the Philistine giant Goliath (I Sam 17:20). And it was early in the morning that the women went to the tomb of Jesus and found Him risen from the dead (Mk 16:2, 9). Apparently, the morning after the spies returned with their report Joshua, too, rose early and removed the people from their camp at Abel-Shittim to the very edge of the river Jordan.

Again, the officers passed through the people informing them that the ark of the covenant, borne by the priests, would precede them as they crossed the river. We must distinguish between the religious use of the ark here and its superstitious use in I Samuel 4:3-4. The ark represented the presence of God; and as they crossed the river, it was God who led the way. But in respect to the holiness of God, the people were commanded to leave **a space between you and it, about two thousand cubits by measure** (vs. 4). This distance of about three thousand feet was to be maintained as sacred space circling the ark. No one was to violate that space. There is something exciting in the words **ye have not passed this way heretofore.** The new generation of Israel was embarking on the adventure of her life. For a thorough discussion on the biblical and historical significance of the ark see M. Woudstra, *The Ark of the Covenant from Conquest to Kingship.*

5-6. Sanctify yourselves: for tomorrow the Lord will do wonders among you. The people are not commanded to prepare their weapons, draw their swords, or polish their shields. Instead, they are to prepare their hearts. The sanctification mentioned here was not ceremonial, but spiritual. They were to prepare themselves to see the mighty hand of God moving among them in a way heretofore unknown. For a people who had seen God's hand leading them miraculously all along the way, this was a tremendous promise.

7-8. And the LORD said unto Joshua, This day will I begin to magnify thee in the sight of all Israel, that they may know that, as I was with Moses, so I will be with thee. It is never easy to replace a great man of God. In fact, it is impossible. Only God can replace His man, and Moses had now been replaced by Joshua. That which God was about to do through Joshua would supersede anything which He had done through Moses. Thus encouraged, Joshua was commanded to tell the priests to bear the ark of the covenant to the brink of the water.

9-13. Joshua communicated to the people that which he had received from the Lord God. **And Joshua said, Hereby ye shall know that the living God is among you.** Yet another proof that Jehovah is God was to be seen in the miraculous crossing of the river and the capturing of the land. God would drive out the inhabitants of the land. These inhabitants included **the Canaanites,** descendants of Canaan, the son of Ham (Gen 9:18). As their name signifies, they were the inhabitants of the lowlands of Palestine, the less mountainous portions by the sea (Num 13:29; Josh 5:1) and by the side of Jordan (Num 13:29). **The Hittites** were the principal tribe in Palestine at this time. They were descendants of Heth (Gen 10:15). **The Hivites** were a tribe not enumerated in the nations of Canaan (Gen 15:19-21), but they were listed among Canaan's descendants in Genesis 10:17 and I Chronicles 1:15. Shechem, the prince, also of the city with the same name, was a Hivite (Gen 34:2). **The Perizzites,** whose name signifies those who dwell in the open (Deut 3:5; I Sam 6:18), are much less known than the preceding tribes named. **The Girgashites,** which are not mentioned elsewhere in Scripture save in Joshua 24:11, Genesis 15:21, and Deuteronomy 7:1, were undoubtedly a very small tribe. The most powerful of the Canaanite peoples (Amos 2:9 were **the Amorites.** They inhabited the mountains (Num 13:29; Josh 11:3), as well as the country from the Arnon to the Jabbok Rivers, which they wrested from the Moabites (Num 21:13, 24, 26). They dwelt in Transjordan until they were dispossessed by Moses. Finally, **the Jebusites** possessed the central highlands around Jerusalem, which was their major city. They maintained possession of this area until David's time (II Sam 5:6-8). On the various Canaanite peoples see A. R. Millard, "The Canaanites," in *People of Old Testament Times*, pp. 29-52.

The LORD of all the earth, shall rest in the waters of Jordan. Continuing to describe to the people what they were about to see, Joshua encourages them that a miracle is about to take place before their very eyes. The Lord will be in the midst of the waters of the flooded Jordan, and He shall divide the waters as their forefathers had seen Him divide the waters of the Red Sea.

14 ¶And it came to pass, when the people removed from their tents, to pass over Jordan, and the priests bearing the ark of the covenant before the people;
15 And as they that bare the ark were come unto Jordan, and the feet of the priests that bare the ark were dipped in the brim of the water, (for Jordan overfloweth all his banks all the time of harvest,)
16 That the waters which came down from above stood and rose up upon an heap very far from the city Adam, that is beside Zăr′e-tăn: and those that came down toward the sea of the plain, even the salt sea, failed, and were cut off: and the people passed over right against Jericho.
17 And the priests that bare the ark of the covenant of the LORD stood firm on dry ground in the midst of Jordan, and all the Israelites passed over on dry ground, until all the people were passed clean over Jordan.

14-17. For Jordan overfloweth all his banks all the time of harvest. The time of harvest mentioned here is the barley harvest, which took place about the tenth day of Nisan. This was some six or seven weeks earlier than the wheat harvest, which occurred about Pentecost (Ex 34:22). It is important to make this distinction because by the time of the wheat harvest the flooded waters of the Jordan had returned to their normal levels. At the earlier barley harvest, however, the waters are usually sixteen to twenty feet above flood stage. The flooding is caused by the melting snows on Mount Hermon, the waters of which rush down to the headwaters of the Jordan, formerly through Lake Huleh (now drained by the Israeli government) into the Sea of Galilee and out the southern end of Galilee via ". . . the swelling of Jordan" (Jer 12:5; 49:19; 50:44). Such overflow of water drives the wild beasts from the banks to higher ground (I Chr 12:15).

And the feet of the priests that bare the ark were dipped into the brim of the water . . . That the waters which came down from above stood and rose up upon a heap (vss. 15-16). It took great courage and tremendous faith in God for the priests to step into the rushing torrent of the flooded Jordan. But as long as they stood on the eastern bank, no Israelite would be able to cross the river. The priests had to "get their feet wet" before their task could be accomplished.

As soon as the priests were in the water, the waters of Jordan began to back up into a heap. This event occurred at the city of Adam, that is beside Zaretan. The location of Adam is marked by the present site of Damieh, some sixteen miles north of Jericho. Since Jericho is a few miles north of the Dead Sea, the area in which the water was completely removed from the bed of the Jordan would cover approximately twenty miles. The neighboring city of Zaretan is identified with Tell es-Sa'idiyeh, approximately twelve miles north of Adam.

Some have claimed that this event is just too miraculous to believe and have dismissed it as an embellishment of the truth. But no scholar wishing to honor the Word of God could hold such a position. After listing all the data compiled during his surface excavations at Zaretan, the late archaeologist Nelson Glueck declared, "The actual archaeological facts agree completely with the conclusions to be derived from a careful examination of Joshua 3:16. This verse was meant to be taken literally, to the effect that the Jordan River was dammed up from Adamah as far as Zaretan, enabling the Israelites to freely and easily cross on dry land to the west side of the Jordan" (Nelson Glueck, *The River Jordan*, p. 157).

Others have suggested that God used natural means to dam the waters of the Jordan. Earthquakes are frequent in this area, and the occasions of natural calamities obstructing the flow of the Jordan are a matter of record. The earliest occurrence on record dates from A.D. December 8, 1267, when a mound of dirt toppled from the West Bank into the river and prevented the flow of the water for some sixteen hours. A similar incident occurred in 1906. The most recent such incident happened in 1927. "On this last occasion the high West Bank immediately below the ford collapsed, carrying with it the roadway . . . and just below, a section of the cliff, which here rises to a height of one hundred fifty feet, fell bodily across the river and completely dammed it, so that no water flowed down the river bed for twenty-one and a half hours. Meanwhile, the waters gradually filled up the plain around Tell El Damieh, and eventually found their way back to the riverbed where the temporary barrage was in turn destroyed, and normal conditions were gradually resumed. During this time, it is asserted by several living witnesses that they crossed and recrossed the bed of the river freely on foot" (John Garstang, *Joshua, Judges*, p. 137). God may use any means He desires. The use of an earthquake in no way lessens the miraculous nature of the crossing of Israel, for the timing of this event would have to be a miracle. Nevertheless, this explanation does not satisfactorily deal with the fact that all the wadis and other streams which feed the Jordan before it empties into the Dead Sea were stopped as well.

Perhaps we may best explain this miracle by assuming that it was a supernatural event, a miracle with no explanatory strings attached. After all, on two subsequent occasions the waters of the Jordan were also parted to permit passage with no necessity of an earthquake (cf. II Kgs 2:8, 14). Such miracles do not need explanation; they need eyes of faith that believe.

And all the Israelites passed over on dry ground, until all the people were passed clean over Jordan (vs. 17). This summary statement gives witness to the completeness of God's assistance on behalf of Israel. Whereas a few days earlier it would have appeared impossible for anyone to safely cross the torrents of the Jordan, now all Israel had crossed. All had crossed safely because **the priests that bare the ark of the covenant of the LORD stood firm on dry ground in the midst of Jordan.** True faith always produces works. The priests stepped into the muddy Jordan on faith, and the people accomplished the work of entering into the Promised Land.

4:1-3. The LORD spake unto Joshua, saying, . . . Take you hence out of the midst of Jordan . . . twelve stones, and ye shall carry them over with you. By now Joshua had learned never to question the command of the Lord. When the command came to choose twelve men, one man from each tribe, and have each man carry a stone from the bed of the Jordan to the western bank, Joshua made no hesitation. The commemoration of events by setting up huge stones was by no means peculiar to the Jews (cf. the British Stonehenge, many Central and South American Indian antiquities, etc.). This in no way means, as Harrelson implies, that since the Hebrew word *gilgal* means "circle," a cult center was established in which the twelve stones were arranged in a circle (see W. Harrelson, *Interpreting the Old Testament.*) The Jewish people often used piles of stones as a means of commemoration (cf. Gen 28:18; 35:14; I Sam 7:12).

4-7. In giving the command that the Lord had given him to the twelve men, Joshua also included an explanation as to why they were erecting this stone memorial. **That this may be a sign among you, that when your children ask their fathers in time to come, saying, What mean ye by these stones? Then ye shall answer them.** The stones were designed to be a perpetual memorial to the miraculous event of the crossing of the Jordan. Subsequent generations would produce children who, when passing by the stone memorial, would inquisitively ask their fathers what these stones meant. At that point the fathers could relay to their children **That the waters of Jordan were cut off before the ark of the covenant of the LORD; when it passed over Jordan, the waters of Jordan were cut off: and these stones shall be for a memorial unto the children of Israel for ever.**

CHAPTER 4

AND it came to pass, when all the people were clean passed over Jordan, that the LORD spake unto Joshua, saying,

2 Take you twelve men out of the people, out of every tribe a man,

3 And command ye them, saying, Take you hence out of the midst of Jordan, out of the place where the priests' feet stood firm, twelve stones, and ye shall carry them over with you, and leave them in the lodging place, where ye shall lodge this night.

4 Then Joshua called the twelve men, whom he had prepared of the children of Israel, out of every tribe a man:

5 And Joshua said unto them, Pass over before the ark of the LORD your God into the midst of Jordan, and take you up every man of you a stone upon his shoulder, according unto the number of the tribes of the children of Israel:

6 That this may be a sign among you, *that* when your children ask *their* fathers in time to come, saying, What mean ye by these stones?

7 Then ye shall answer them, That the waters of Jordan were cut off before the ark of the covenant of the

LORD; when it passed over Jordan, the waters of Jordan were cut off: and these stones shall be for a memorial unto the children of Israel for ever.

8 And the children of Israel did so as Joshua commanded, and took up twelve stones out of the midst of Jordan, as the LORD spake unto Joshua, according to the number of the tribes of the children of Israel, and carried them over with them unto the place where they lodged, and laid them down there.

9 And Joshua set up twelve stones in the midst of Jordan, in the place where the feet of the priests which bare the ark of the covenant stood: and they are there unto this day.

10 ¶For the priests which bare the ark stood in the midst of Jordan, until everything was finished that the LORD commanded Joshua to speak unto the people, according to all that Moses commanded Joshua: and the people hasted and passed over.

11 And it came to pass, when all the people were clean passed over, that the ark of the LORD passed over, and the priests, in the presence of the people.

12 And the children of Reuben, and the children of Gad, and half the tribe of Ma-năs′seh, passed over armed before the children of Israel, as Moses spake unto them:

13 About forty thousand prepared for war passed over before the LORD unto battle, to the plains of Jericho.

14 ¶On that day the LORD magnified Joshua in the sight of all Israel; and they feared him, as they feared Moses, all the days of his life.

15 ¶And the LORD spake unto Joshua, saying,

16 Command the priests that bear the ark of the testimony, that they come up out of Jordan.

17 Joshua therefore commanded the priests, saying, Come ye up out of Jordan.

18 And it came to pass, when the priests that bare the ark of the covenant of the LORD were come up out of the midst of Jordan, and the soles of the priests' feet were lifted up unto the dry land, that the waters of Jordan returned unto their place, and flowed over all his banks, as they did before.

19 ¶And the people came up out of Jordan on the tenth day of the first month, and encamped in Gilgal, in the east border of Jericho.

20 And those twelve stones, which they took out of Jordan, did Joshua pitch in Gilgal.

8-10. Not only did the twelve men comply with the command of the Lord in carrying out the stones to the place where they lodged, but in addition to that, **Joshua set up twelve stones in the midst of Jordan.** A second memorial was established on the bed of the river itself. This memorial could not be seen, save by God; but all Israel knew it would be there forever.

11-14. About forty thousand prepared for war passed over before the LORD unto battle, to the plains of Jericho (vs. 13). These words refer to forty thousand trained fighting men from the tribes of Reuben, Gad, and half the tribe of Manasseh. Numbers 26:7, 18, and 34 give the total potential fighting force of these tribes as about 110,580 men. Apparently, only forty thousand of these soldiers crossed over the Jordan in order to allow the strong guard to remain behind and defend those tribes on the east of the river. Nevertheless, they were living up to their pledge to God to defend the land and their brethren until all Israel could dwell safely in the land.

On that day the LORD magnified Joshua in the sight of all Israel; and they feared him, as they feared Moses, all the days of his life. Earlier, in Joshua 1:5, God had privately assured Joshua that He would be with Israel's new commander as He had been with Moses, Israel's former commander. That private assurance, tenaciously guarded in the heart of Joshua, now gives way to public attestation of the hand of God upon Joshua's life.

15-18. The final step in the crossing of the Jordan was to remove the priests who were bearing the ark of the covenant from the bed of the river. Therefore, Joshua commanded the priests saying, **Come ye up out of Jordan.** When the priests, who in great faith had obeyed Joshua's command to set foot into the waters of Jordan, removed themselves from that river **and the soles of the priests' feet were lifted up unto the dry land, that the waters of Jordan returned unto their place, and flowed over all his banks, as they did before.** The original language is a bit more picturesque than this. When the priests stepped into the water and the waters rolled back in a heap, they were left standing in the muddy bed of the river. On all sides of them the bed had been beaten to hard clay by the pounding of millions of feet as the Israelites crossed the Jordan. All the time the priests, bearing the ark of the covenant, were standing in one spot. When Joshua describes the soles of the priests being "lifted up" (Heb *nataq*) unto the dry land, he literally says that they "were plucked up" out of the soft adhesive of the riverbed. Immediately, the mighty Jordan thundered back into its natural course and even overflowed its banks to the same extent it had prior to this miraculous crossing.

19-24. And the people came up out of Jordan on the tenth day of the first month, and encamped in Gilgal, in the east border of Jericho. The notation that Israel exited the Jordan on the tenth day of the month is important, for in 5:10 mention is made of Israel keeping her first Passover in the Promised Land. Since this occurs always on the fourteenth day of the first

21 And he spake unto the children of Israel, saying, When your children shall ask their fathers in time to come, saying, What *mean* these stones?

22 Then ye shall let your children know, saying, Israel came over this Jordan on dry land.

23 For the LORD your God dried up the waters of Jordan from before you, until ye were passed over, as the LORD your God did to the Red sea, which he dried up from before us, until we were gone over:

24 That all the people of the earth might know the hand of the LORD, that it *is* mighty: that ye might fear the LORD your God for ever.

CHAPTER 5

AND it came to pass, when all the kings of the Āmorītes, which *were* on the side of Jordan westward, and all the kings of the Canaanites, which *were* by the sea, heard that the LORD had dried up the waters of Jordan from before the children of Israel, until we were passed over, that their heart melted, neither was there spirit in them any more, because of the children of Israel.

2 ¶At that time the LORD said unto Joshua, Make thee sharp knives, and circumcise again the children of Israel the second time.

3 And Joshua made him sharp knives, and circumcised the children of Israel at the hill of the foreskins.

4 And this *is* the cause why Joshua did circumcise: All the people that came out of Egypt, *that were* males, *even* all the men of war, died in the wilderness by the way, after they came out of Egypt.

5 Now all the people that came out were circumcised: but all the people *that were* born in the wilderness by the way as they came forth out of Egypt, *them* they had not circumcised.

6 For the children of Israel walked forty years in the wilderness, till all the people *that were* men of war, which came out of Egypt, were consumed, because they obeyed not the voice of the LORD: unto whom the LORD sware that he would not shew them the land, which the LORD sware unto their fathers that he would give us, a land that floweth with milk and honey.

7 And their children, *whom* he raised up in their stead, them Joshua circumcised: for they were uncircumcised, because they had not circumcised them by the way.

8 And it came to pass, when they had done circumcising all the people, that they abode in their places in the camp, till they were whole.

9 And the LORD said unto Joshua, This day have I rolled away the

month, there was just enough time for the events which occur between the tenth and fourteenth day to transpire. Here again, the accuracy of the account is seen.

The encampment at Gilgal was located perhaps five miles from the bank of the river and several miles from the city of Jericho itself. It was here that the twelve-stone monument was erected for the children to remember forever the miraculous crossing of the Jordan. But this was not the only reason why the monument was erected. It was placed in Gilgal that **The earth might know the hand of the LORD, that it is mighty: that ye might fear the LORD your God for ever.** It was the Lord God's intent that this memorial would not only serve to remind the Israelites of His mighty hand, but all peoples of the world as well. It is His desire that all men and women come to the experience of Rahab to claim that, **the LORD your God, he is God in heaven above, and in earth beneath** (2:11).

5:1. Their heart melted, neither was their spirit in them any more, because of the children of Israel. A large portion of the territory of the Amorites had already been conquered (cf. 3:10). Thus Joshua is careful to observe that the kings of the Amorites who were yet to be conquered were westward (literally, seaward) from the Jordan. These kings, and those of the Canaanites, were now in utter terror because of the miraculous provision of the Lord on behalf of Israel. This is a clear fulfillment of the promise given in Exodus 23:27 and also confirms the evaluation of Rahab (2:11). The Lord God had prepared the inhabitants of the land for the conquest by Israel. Fanciful, indeed, is Martin Noth's contention that the Hebrew tribes merely infiltrated peacefully into the settled land and gradually became sedentary (see M. Noth, *The History of Israel*).

E. Joshua Renews Circumcision and Observes the Passover at Gilgal. 5:2-12.

2-8. And Joshua made him sharp knives, and circumcised the children of Israel at the hill of the foreskins. Ordinarily, such a ceremony as circumcision would be injudicious, having just entered a foreign land in preparation for battle. Why did Joshua risk this ceremony now? At the hill of the foreskins, the name given to the mound upon which the circumcision took place, **all the people that were born in the wilderness by the way as they came forth out of Egypt** were circumcised because they had not heretofore undergone this covenant-sign surgical procedure (see J. A. Soggin, *Joshua*, pp. 69-70). Those men of war who came out of Egypt had now all died during the period of the forty years of wandering in the wilderness. But now the Lord God had led Israel into the land of her father, **a land that floweth with milk and honey.**

This is the standard expression in the Pentateuch to express the great fertility of the land of Canaan. Milk and honey are found mainly in a land rich in grass and flowers, both of which were plentiful in Canaan (cf. Isa 7:15, 22). The milk from cows, sheep, and goats (Deut 32:14) was a mainstay of the ancient Hebrew diet. Honey, especially that from wild bees, was also found in large quantities (Jud 14:8; I Sam 14:26; Mt 3:4). It was in this beautiful land that the communal circumcision took place, and **when they had done circumcising all the people, that they abode in their places in the camp, till they were whole.** For several days, physically and religiously, Israel would be unable to engage in combat. But God had already prepared for that situation by melting the hearts of the inhabitants of the land.

9-11. And the LORD said unto Joshua, This day have I rolled away the reproach of Egypt from off you. The inter-

reproach of Egypt from off you. Wherefore the name of the place is called Gilgal unto this day.

10 ¶And the children of Israel encamped in Gilgal, and kept the passover on the fourteenth day of the month at even in the plains of Jericho.

11 And they did eat of the old corn of the land on the morrow after the passover, unleavened cakes, and parched *corn* in the selfsame day.

12 ¶And the manna ceased on the morrow after they had eaten of the old corn of the land; neither had the children of Israel manna any more; but they did eat of the fruit of the land of Canaan that year.

13 ¶And it came to pass, when Joshua was by Jericho, that he lifted up his eyes and looked, and, behold, there stood a man over against him with his sword drawn in his hand: and Joshua went unto him, and said unto him, *Art* thou for us, or for our adversaries?

14 And he said, Nay; but *as* captain of the host of the LORD am I now come. And Joshua fell on his face to the earth, and did worship, and said unto him, What saith my lord unto his servant?

15 And the captain of the LORD's host said unto Joshua, Loose thy shoe from off thy foot; for the place whereon thou standest *is* holy. And Joshua did so.

pretations of this phrase are many and varied. Perhaps it means the reproach which comes from the Egyptians, or else the reproach of having sojourned in Egypt. It is likely that the reproach is simply the degradation of God's people having to live under pagan bondage. But all that is now gone, and at Gilgal Israel **kept the Passover on the fourteenth day of the month at even in the plains of Jericho.** Keeping the Passover, like circumcising people, was an act of obedience to the Lord. Most would not prepare for battle in this way; most do not enter battle dependent upon the Lord for victory. Hence, **the old corn,** the main food of the land, **unleavened cakes** made from the corn, and **parched corn,** that is ears roasted in the fire, were all eaten for the first time in forty years.

12. And the manna ceased on the morrow. That which could not be cultivated but only could be received from the Lord, that which had been their sustenance throughout their wilderness wanderings, was now to disappear forever. **But they did eat of the fruit of the land of Canaan that year.**

II. CONQUEST OF THE PROMISED LAND. 5:13-12:24.

A. Joshua and the Captain of the Lord's Host. 5:13-6:5.

13-15. There are times when each of us must get alone with God in a special way. Usually those times come just before a big decision in our lives. Joshua went to a hill overlooking Jericho and began to contemplate the conquest of that great fortress city. As he was there alone communing with God and planning strategy, **he lifted up his eyes and looked, and, behold, there stood a man over against him with his sword drawn in his hand.** The expression **he lifted up his eyes** is usually, though not always, indicative of an unexpected or marvelous sight (cf. Gen 18:2; 22:13; Num 24:2; I Sam 6:13; I Chr 21:16). What Joshua saw obviously caught him off guard. He did not immediately recognize the man. Since the man had his sword drawn, Joshua could only surmise that he was prepared for battle and thus asked, **Art thou for us, or for our adversaries?**

The answer this man gave must have been as startling to Joshua as his very presence. **And he said, Nay; but as captain of the host of the LORD am I now come.** The **host of the LORD** must refer to the angels of God (Gen 32:2; I Kgs 22:19; Ps 103:20-21; 148:2; Lk 2:13). But who is this stranger, the captain of the Lord's host? Jewish interpretation differs on this point. Maimonides does not regard this appearance as a real one. Most Jewish scholars, however, believe the captain of the Lord's host was an angel of God and go so far as to declare his identity to be that of Michael, the archangel. In proof of this they advance Daniel 12:1 which says that, ". . . at that time shall Michael stand up, the great prince which standeth for the children of thy people. . . ." But such an interpretation is unacceptable. A much sounder view is expressed by Origen in his *Sixth Homily* on the book of Joshua when he states, "Joshua knew not only that he was of God, but that he was God. For he would not have worshiped, had he not recognized him to be God. For who else is the Captain of the Lord's host but our Lord Jesus Christ?" (see also James Borland, *Christ in the Old Testament*).

It is interesting to see the parallel between this appearance of the Lord to Joshua and an earlier one to Moses. As the Lord appeared to Moses in a special way to prepare him for leadership (Ex 3:2), now the Lord appears to Joshua in the same manner (5:13-15). "Observe how well God suits the revelation of Himself unto His saints according to their circumstances and needs: to Abraham in his tent He appeared as a Traveler (Gen 18:1-3); to Moses at the backside of the desert in a bush (Ex 3:1-2); to Joshua at the beginning of his campaign as 'a Man of war' (cf. Ex 15:3)" (Arthur W. Pink, *Gleanings in Joshua*, p. 141).

Loose thy shoe from off thy foot; for the place whereon

403

CHAPTER 6

NOW Jericho was straitly shut up because of the children of Israel: none went out, and none came in.

2 And the LORD said unto Joshua, See, I have given into thine hand Jericho, and the king thereof, and the mighty men of valour.

3 And ye shall compass the city, all ye men of war, and go round about the city once. Thus shalt thou do six days.
4 And seven priests shall bear before the ark seven trumpets of rams' horns: and the seventh day ye shall compass the city seven times, and the priests shall blow with the trumpets.
5 And it shall come to pass, that when they make a long blast with the ram's horn, and when ye hear the sound of the trumpet, all the people shall shout with a great shout; and the wall of the city shall fall down flat, and the people shall ascend up every man straight before him.

thou standest is holy. Another interesting parallel to Moses was the command of God for Joshua to remove his sandals from off his feet. This was identical to the situation of Moses (cf. Ex 3:5) when he encountered the Lord God personally. As the Lord had been with Moses, He promised to be with Joshua. As the Lord had appeared unto Moses, He has now appeared unto Joshua. The preparations for conquest are now complete.

6:1. Now Jericho was straitly shut up because of the children of Israel: none went out, and none came in. Jericho appears to have been the principal stronghold of the Canaanites. It was a frontier town and the key city in a string of fortresses protecting the eastern frontier. Its capture was indispensable before progress could be made by Israel in conquering and occupying the land. Joshua knew that he must take Jericho or forfeit his leadership and the inheritance of Israel. Thus, this parenthetical verse is included in the Lord's conversation with Joshua in order to enhance the necessity of the Lord God's leadership of Israel in battle against the Canaanites.

2. And the LORD said unto Joshua, See, I have given into thine hand Jericho, and the king thereof, and the mighty men of valor. The expression **I have given** (Heb natan) is an exclamation of prophetic certainty. Joshua had not yet fought the battle of Jericho; but the Lord appeared to him to say, **I have given into thine hand Jericho.** This is not the first time God has announced certainty before the fact. When Abraham was ninety years old and his wife Sarah had as yet borne him no sons, God said to him, ". . . for a father of many nations have I made thee" (Gen 17:5). This can be done because we can count God's "wills" as God's "haves." God is above time, and that which is yet future for us is present for Him. What was for Joshua yet to happen in the capturing of Jericho, was for God already an accomplished fact.

3-5. It was the English hymnist William Cowper who said, "God moves in a mysterious way, His wonders to perform." God's mysterious method for the conquest of Jericho was now revealed to Joshua. **And ye shall compass the city, all ye men of war, and go round about the city once. Thus shalt thou do six days.** It is not necessary to assume that all the people of Israel marched around Jericho, just the men of war. This march, however, was more than a military one; it was a religious march. **And seven priests shall bear before the ark seven trumpets of rams' horns.** The prominent place given to the priests and the ark indicate that God was at the center of the march. Six days the men of war and the priests were to encircle the city in silence. On the seventh day the priests shall blow with the trumpets. **And it shall come to pass, that when they make a long blast with the ram's horn, and when ye hear the sound of the trumpet, all the people shall shout with a great shout.** Six days of a single cycle around the city would give way on the seventh day to seven such cycles. At that point the priests would blow upon the rams' horns (literally, the horns of jubilee) and the people would shout in one tremendous shout. The result of this mysterious plan? **And the wall of the city shall fall down flat, and the people shall ascend up every man straight before him.** God promised victory to Joshua. He promised that the walls of the great city would fall down flat (literally, underneath it). The walls would give way at their very foundations so that every man of Israel could march into the city from the location he occupied outside the city.

Joshua was not a newcomer to the battle scene. As Moses' minister, he had been trained well in military technique. He was a proven leader in battle. As a military strategist, he had to know that God's mysterious method for taking Jericho was, to say the least, unusual. Had the plan been left up to Joshua, he would undoubtedly have drawn his battle lines, brought up his flanks, perhaps created a diversionary tactic, and used conventional warfare to attack Jericho. But the plan of attack was not left up to Joshua; it was a divine plan. On ancient military tactics see Yigael Yadin, *The Art of Warfare in Biblical Times* and Chaim Herzog and Mordechai Gichon, *Battles of the Bible*, pp. 25-30.

B. Israel's Central Campaign. 6:6-8:35.

1. Conquest of Jericho. 6:6-27.

6-11. Without a moment's hesitation **Joshua the son of Nun called the priests, and said unto them. . . .** The exact orders that were given to Joshua by the captain of the Lord's host were now disseminated among the people. The march was organized as follows. Initially, soldiers would begin, followed by priests with rams' horns. In the center was located the ark of the covenant, the physical representation of God among Israel. Next, **the rearward came after the ark, the priests going on.** The **rearward** is a strange expression meaning rear guard (Num 10:25; Isa 52:12; 58:8). Calvin translated it *quis cogebat agmen;* the LXX renders it *ho loipos ochlos;* the Vulgate prefers *vulgus reliquum;* and Luther translates it *der Haufe.* Literally, it means "the gathering together," and suggests a body of troops that collects stragglers and brings up the rear, completing the marching force.

6 ¶And Joshua the son of Nun called the priests, and said unto them, Take up the ark of the covenant, and let seven priests bear seven trumpets of rams' horns before the ark of the LORD.
7 And he said unto the people, Pass on, and compass the city, and let him that is armed pass on before the ark of the LORD.
8 ¶And it came to pass, when Joshua had spoken unto the people, that the seven priests bearing the seven trumpets of rams' horns passed on before the LORD, and blew with the trumpets: and the ark of the covenant of the LORD followed them.
9 And the armed men went before the priests that blew with the trumpets, and the rereward came after the ark, *the priests* going on, and blowing with the trumpets.
10 And Joshua had commanded the people, saying, Ye shall not shout, nor make any noise with your voice, neither shall *any* word proceed out of your mouth, until the day I bid you shout; then shall ye shout.
11 So the ark of the LORD compassed the city, going about *it* once: and they came into the camp, and lodged in the camp.
12 ¶And Joshua rose early in the morning, and the priests took up the ark of the LORD.
13 And seven priests bearing seven trumpets of rams' horns before the ark of the LORD went on continually, and blew with the trumpets: and the armed men went before them; but the rereward came after the ark of the LORD, *the priests* going on, and blowing with the trumpets.
14 And the second day they compassed the city once, and returned into the camp: so they did six days.
15 And it came to pass on the seventh day, that they rose early about the dawning of the day, and compassed the city after the same manner seven times: only on that day they compassed the city seven times.
16 And it came to pass at the seventh time, when the priests blew with the trumpets, Joshua said unto the people, Shout; for the LORD hath given you the city.

12-13. And Joshua rose early in the morning following the instructions of the Lord exactly. Israel's commander was eager to practice those military tactics and religious ceremonial guidelines that he had received from the captain of the Lord's hosts. Thus, the work of the first day accomplished, the Israelite forces marched around the city once and returned to Gilgal without incident.

14-16. And the second day they compassed the city once, and returned into the camp: so they did six days. When the Israelites appeared outside of the walls of Jericho on that first day, the hearts of the inhabitants of Jericho must have melted even more. The silence of their march was deafening to their ears. Psychologically, Israel had won a great battle. The king of Jericho must have been terrified at Israel's battle plan. Day after day he could see them out there, but when would they attack? The second and third days of march must have caused similar but lessened fear. Whereas the first day was evidenced in silence both outside the walls and inside the walls, by the third day a few sarcastic remarks must have been uttered toward the Israelites. Days four and five undoubtedly saw those of Jericho openly ridicule Israel for her unconventional tactics. By day six, the noise of derisive laughter must have arisen from the fortified city. The mocking and ridicule would have been similar to that heaped on Nehemiah by Sanballat and Tobiah (Neh 4:1-3). The human heart takes great delight in ridiculing the people of God. But the march continued unabated. **And it came to pass at the seventh time, when the priests blew with the trumpets, Joshua said unto the people, Shout; for the LORD hath given you the city.**

405

17 And the city shall be accursed, *even* it, and all that *are* therein, to the LORD: only Rahab the harlot shall live, she and all that *are* with her in the house, because she hid the messengers that we sent.

18 And ye, in any wise keep *yourselves* from the accursed thing, lest ye make *yourselves* accursed, when ye take of the accursed thing, and make the camp of Israel a curse, and trouble it.

19 But all the silver, and gold, and vessels of brass and iron, *are* consecrated unto the LORD: they shall come into the treasury of the LORD.

20 So the people shouted when *the priests* blew with the trumpets: and it came to pass, when the people heard the sound of the trumpet, and the people shouted with a great shout, that the wall fell down flat, so that the people went up into the city, every man straight before him, and they took the city.

21 And they utterly destroyed all that *was* in the city, both man and woman, young and old, and ox, and sheep, and ass, with the edge of the sword.

17-19. And the city shall be accursed, even it, and all that are therein, to the LORD. . . . And ye, in any wise keep yourselves from the accursed thing. Verses 17-19 are parenthetical, giving additional instructions to Israel about the capture of the city. Jericho and all that was therein was accursed unto God; and Israel was strictly commanded not to take anything from the city, else they would be accursed and would **make the camp of Israel a curse, and trouble it.** The only exception to this rule was **all the silver, and gold, and vessels of brass and iron, are consecrated unto the LORD: they shall come into the treasury of the LORD.**

The Hebrew word translated "accursed" (Heb *chērem*) means to "ban" or "devote." It may also mean to "seclude," as from society. This term was both applied to capital punishment (Lev 27:29) and to offerings given to God (Ezk 44:29; Num 18:14). It is used of the "utter destruction" of the enemies of God (Isa 34:5; Deut 7:26; 20:17). The original meaning of the word appears to have been "to shut up." Hence, it meant "a net." A derivative of the word is the Eastern word *harem*, meaning the enclosed apartment reserved for the women of the family. Thus, it comes to mean that which is devoted for a special purpose or a particular person. Israel was not to take anything from the city of Jericho, for it had been banned by God; and its destruction was devoted as a monument to the omnipotence of Jehovah, the God of Israel. For further reference see Gerhard von Reed, *Der Heilige Krieg im Alten Israel*, p. 110, and Roland de Vaux, *Ancient Israel*, pp. 258-267.

20-21. As per their instructions, **the people shouted when the priests blew with the trumpets . . . the wall fell down flat, . . . and they took the city.** It was at this time that the Israelites utterly destroyed the city of Jericho, killing all present, men, women, children, and animals, in response to God's command. For the divine justification for this action see the Introduction.

God's mysterious methods are not always understandable to us. But God does not ask us to understand them; rather, He asks us to obey them. Israel at the fall of Jericho is a good example of this truth. Although God's methods were mysterious, nevertheless Israel trusted them explicitly (vs. 6); followed them exactly (vss. 8-13); employed them enthusiastically (vss. 9, 14-15); continued them expectantly (vs. 15); and accomplished them entirely (vs. 20). God's work, done in God's way, always has God's blessing.

Liberal scholars have for years downplayed the validity of this account of Jericho's flattened walls, especially in the light of the archaeological findings at that site. One example of such a critic is the Jewish scholar H. H. Ben-Sasson who writes, "The findings at Jericho also conflict with the biblical version of its fall. More recent archaeological investigations have proved that its famed walls, the focus of the biblical story, belonged to the Middle Bronze Age, that is, to the first half of the second millennium, and not to the days of the Israelite conquest. Yet, for all this, the narrative fundamentally is no mere fiction. In the fourteenth and perhaps even in the early thirteenth centuries, a relatively meager and open settlement existed at Jericho, and in all likelihood it was this settlement that suffered destruction at the hands of the Israelites. The biblical folk-tradition of the collapse of its walls may have derived from the visible remnants of the once-mighty defences" (H. H. Ben-Sasson, *A History of the Jewish People*, pp. 52-53).

What exactly is the archaeological evidence found at Jericho? Excavations at Jericho (Tell es-Sultan) were first carried on from 1907 to 1909 by the German Oriental Society under the direction of Ernst Sellin and Carl Watzinger, who outlined the city wall and determined the size of the ancient city. John Garstang directed a British School of Archaeology expedition which excavated the site from 1930-1936 and completed the outline of the history of the mound which the Germans had begun. Garstang gave special attention to City D, which he identified as the one destroyed by Joshua. He located flattened walls amid the ruins with traces of intense fire, reddened masses of brick, cracked stones, charred timbers and ashes. His identification of these walls as the walls of Joshua's time immediately drew wide acceptance.

A third expedition jointly sponsored by the British School of Archaeology and the American Schools of Oriental Research was conducted from 1952 to 1958 under the leadership of Miss Kathleen Kenyon, then director of the British School. Her significant excavations have called into question Garstang's dating of the Jericho walls and found them to be remains from the Early Bronze Age, a thousand years before Joshua's time. Kenyon's work uncovered no Late Bronze (1500-1200 B.C.) walls at all.

Do these more recent discoveries disprove the biblical account? Does this mean that archaeology contradicts the Bible? Not in the least! The tell of Jericho is an eight-acre site, and the excavations of Sellin, Garstang, and Kenyon have not exhausted this site by any means. "Even Jericho, one of the most fully excavated sites in Palestine, could still keep a large expedition busy for many years. In fact, Miss Kenyon had planned her excavations so that substantial portions of the tell will remain available for future excavations when archaeological methodology has been improved and new techniques and analyses developed and refined" (Paul A. Lapp, "Palestine: Known But Mostly Unknown," *Biblical Archaeologist*, XXVI, Dec., 1963, pp. 124-125). No confirmed discovery of archaeology has ever contradicted the Bible, and Jericho will not be the first. Additional excavations may well produce the fabled walls of Joshua's day; but if they do not, the biblical account still must be maintained as accurate. For a discussion of suggestions made to correlate the biblical record of Jericho with the archaeological data see Edwin Yamauchi, *The Stones and The Scriptures*, p. 58.

22 But Joshua had said unto the two men that had spied out the country, Go into the harlot's house, and bring out thence the woman, and all that she hath, as ye sware unto her.
23 And the young men that were spies went in, and brought out Rahab, and her father, and her mother, and her brethren, and all that she had; and they brought out all her kindred, and left them without the camp of Israel.
24 And they burnt the city with fire, and all that was therein: only the silver, and the gold, and the vessels of brass and of iron, they put into the treasury of the house of the LORD.
25 And Joshua saved Rahab the harlot alive, and her father's household, and all that she had; and she dwelleth in Israel even unto this day; because she hid the messengers, which Joshua sent to spy out Jericho.

26 ¶And Joshua adjured them at that time, saying, Cursed be the man before the LORD, that riseth up and buildeth this city Jericho: he shall lay the foundation thereof in his firstborn, and in his youngest son shall he set up the gates of it.
27 So the LORD was with Joshua; and his fame was noised throughout all the country.

22-25. But Joshua had said unto the two men that had spied out the country, Go into the harlot's house, and bring out thence the woman, and all that she hath, as ye sware unto her. This account of Rahab is a remarkable example of God's grace in the Old Testament. She had been a harlot. She had told a lie. Nevertheless, she had given evidence of true faith in God by having "received the spies with peace" (Heb 11:31; cf. Josh 6:17, 25). Thus, while the city was being destroyed around her, God preserved her and her family in the midst of that destruction. The preservation of Rahab's house must have been part of the miracle since it was upon the city wall (cf. Heb 11:30-31). This is not to indicate that there is any validity to the superstition that Rahab's house remained intact, but that Rahab's family remained intact through the destruction of the city. God is not interested in houses; He is interested in people. **And Joshua saved Rahab the harlot alive, and her father's household, and all that she had; and she dwelleth in Israel even unto this day.**

26-27. Finally, Joshua made the people swear an oath saying, **Cursed be the man before the LORD, that riseth up and buildeth this city Jericho: he shall lay the foundation thereof in his first-born, and in his youngest son shall he set up the gates of it.** The object of this solemn vow was to preserve Jericho as a spot devoted to God forever (cf. vs. 17ff.). This curse involved the refortification of Jericho, not simply its future inhabitation. The words "foundation" and "gates" (vs. 26) refer to the establishment of a fortified wall around the city. This is evident from Judges 1:16; 3:13 (cf. Deut 34:3). It is obvious that the city of Jericho was reinhabited for a short time after its destruction. The first attempt, however, to refortify the city is recorded in I Kings 16:34. In the reign of King Ahab, a reckless man by the name of Hiel attempted to rebuild the walls of Jericho and in so doing lost two of his sons in the fulfillment of this curse (cf. Josephus, *Antiq.* V. i. 8). Some commentators actually interpret the passage in I Kings 16 to indicate that Hiel's eldest son died when the foundation was laid; the rest of his sons (except the youngest) died during the refortification of the city; and the youngest was killed when the gates were erected. This, however, is reading more into the text than it states.

So the Lord was with Joshua; and his fame was noised throughout all the country. Undoubtedly, the purpose of God's mysterious method for seizing Jericho was designed to test Israel's obedience to the will of God. More than that, it must have been arranged to strike even greater fear in the hearts of the enemy when the walls "came tumbling down." But perhaps the greatest purpose in the taking of Jericho by these mysterious methods was to reaffirm Israel's faith in Joshua's leadership. It is now firmly entrenched in Israel's mind that Jehovah, who had been with Moses, was now with Joshua in the same relationship.

2. *The campaign against Ai. 7:1-5.*

7:1. But the children of Israel committed a trespass in the accursed thing. The verbal form of the noun, translated trespass (Heb *ma'al*), originally signified "to cover" as a garment. Hence, the noun came to mean a deceitful act or a misappropriation of property considered to be sacred (cf. Lev 5:15). It is significant that this very word rendered in the LXX (*enosphisanto*) is used by Luke in regard to the transgression of Ananias and Sapphira (Acts 5:2). The one guilty of taking the accursed thing was Achan, called Achar in I Chronicles 2:7. He had "troubled" Israel (6:18; 7:25); and thus the valley in which his punishment was enacted obtained the name Achor, meaning "trouble." Although it was Achan who took the accursed thing, **the anger of the Lord was kindled against the children of Israel.** As Paul regards the Corinthian church to have been polluted by the presence of one single offender (I Cor 5:2, 6, 7), so all of Israel is polluted by the offense of one named Achan.

2-5. And Joshua sent men from Jericho to Ai . . . saying, Go up and view the country. The city Ai is always written in Hebrew with a definite article (Heb *ha'ay*, meaning "the heap" or "the ruin"). The city lay east of Beth-el and the altar which Abraham built (Gen 12:8), adjacent to Bethaven (Josh 7:2) and north of Michmash (Isa 10:28). It is identified with modern Et-Tell. See Joseph A. Callaway, "The 1961 Ai (et-Tell) Excavations," *Bulletin of the American Schools of Oriental Research,* CLXXVII (April, 1965) also "New Evidence on the Conquest of 'Ai,'" *Journal of Biblical Literature,* LXXXVII (1968).

As had become Israel's custom, Joshua sent spies from Jericho to ascertain the strength of Ai. The party followed the ancient causeway from Beth-el to the Jordan as far as Michmash, from which they ascended the Great Wadi west of Ai. This put them within a quarter-mile of the city without ever having come into its sight. Ai was a small town; but because of its strategic location, it had to be taken by the forces of Israel. The report of the spies was an accurate one, advising, **Let not all the people go up; but let about two or three thousand men go up and smite Ai.**

Thus, Joshua sent a force of about three thousand men, but the Israelites were quickly routed. **And the men of Ai smote of them about thirty and six men.** The Israelite forces must have been in shock. Their hearts melted, not because of cowardice, but because the strong hand of the Lord, upon which they relied, had apparently been removed from them. It is indeed ironic that the description which usually was used of the Canaanites in relationship to the melting of the heart has now been used of the Israelites (cf. 2:11 with 5:1).

CHAPTER 7

BUT the children of Israel committed a trespass in the accursed thing: for Aʹchăn, the son of Cärʹmĭ, the son of Zăbʹdĭ, the son of Zeʹrah, of the tribe of Judah, took of the accursed thing: and the anger of the Lord was kindled against the children of Israel.

2 And Joshua sent men from Jericho to AʹĪ, which *is* beside Bĕth-āʹven, on the east side of Bĕth-el, and spake unto them, saying, Go up and view the country. And the men went up and viewed Aʹī.

3 And they returned to Joshua, and said unto him, Let not all the people go up; but let about two or three thousand men go up and smite Aʹī; *and* make not all the people to labour thither; for they *are but* few.

4 So there went up thither of the people about three thousand men: and they fled before the men of Aʹī.

5 And the men of Aʹī smote of them about thirty and six men: for they chased them *from* before the gate *even* unto Shĕbʹa-rĭm, and smote them in the going down: wherefore the hearts of the people melted, and became as water.

6 ¶And Joshua rent his clothes, and fell to the earth upon his face before the ark of the Lord until the eventide, he and the elders of Israel, and put dust upon their heads.

7 And Joshua said, Alas, O Lord God, wherefore hast thou at all brought this people over Jordan, to deliver us into the hand of the Amorites, to destroy us? would to God we had been content, and dwelt on the other side Jordan!

8 O Lord, what shall I say, when Israel turneth their backs before their enemies!

9 For the Canaanites and all the inhabitants of the land shall hear of it, and shall environ us round, and cut off our name from the earth: and what wilt thou do unto thy great name?

10 ¶And the Lord said unto Joshua, Get thee up; wherefore liest thou thus upon thy face?

11 Israel hath sinned, and they have also transgressed my covenant which I commanded them: for they have even taken of the accursed thing, and have also stolen, and dissembled also, and they have put it even among their own stuff.

12 Therefore the children of Israel could not stand before their enemies, but turned their backs before their enemies, because they were accursed: neither will I be with you any more, except ye destroy the accursed from among you.

13 Up, sanctify the people, and say, Sanctify yourselves against to morrow: for thus saith the Lord God of Israel, There is an accursed thing in the midst of thee, O Israel: thou canst not stand before thine enemies, until ye take away the accursed thing from among you.

14 In the morning therefore ye shall be brought according to your tribes: and it shall be, that the tribe which the Lord taketh shall come according to the families thereof; and the family which the Lord shall take shall come by households; and the household which the Lord shall take shall come man by man.

15 And it shall be, that he that is taken with the accursed thing shall be burnt with fire, he and all that he hath: because he hath transgressed the covenant of the Lord, and because he hath wrought folly in Israel.

16 ¶So Joshua rose up early in the morning, and brought Israel by their tribes; and the tribe of Judah was taken:

17 And he brought the family of Judah; and he took the family of the Zär′hītes: and he brought the family of the Zär′hītes man by man; and Zăb′dī was taken:

18 And he brought his household man by man; and Ā′chăn, the son of Căr′mī, the son of Zăb′dī, the son of Ze′rah, of the tribe of Jūdah, was taken.

3. The sin and punishment of Achan. 7:6-26.

6. And Joshua rent his clothes . . . he and the elders of Israel, and put dust upon their heads. Upon hearing of the defeat of his forces, Joshua demonstrated his deep sorrow and humiliation in the usual Israelite manner (cf. Gen 37:29, 34; 44:13). The practice of putting dust on one's head to show humiliation is well attested (cf. I Sam 4:12; II Sam 1:2; 13:31; Job 2:12; Lam 2:10). This was also a customary practice among the Greeks as witnessed by Homer's *Iliad*, XVIII.

7-9. And Joshua said, Alas, O Lord God . . . what shall I say, when Israel turneth their backs before their enemies! After the initial shock of Israel's defeat at Ai, Joshua immediately turned his face toward the Lord. His concern was not so much that the men of Ai had evened his record of victories and defeats, but that **the Canaanites and all the inhabitants of the land shall hear of it, and shall environ us round, and cut off our name from the earth: and what wilt thou do unto thy great name?** Joshua was familiar with this argument. It was invariably the argument of Moses (cf. Ex 32:12; Num 14:13-16; Deut 9:28; 32:26-27). How could God allow His name to be maligned, as it obviously would be with Israel's defeat?

10-15. The response to Joshua's question was that God did not expect a lengthy lamentation over those lost at the battle of Ai, but rather expected Joshua to **Get thee up** and pursue the battle again. What a tremendous lesson for any Christian who experiences defeat. God was fully aware of what had happened. **Israel hath sinned . . . for they have even taken of the accursed thing . . . and they have put it even among their own stuff.** God was not looking for excuses, nor a sociological assessment of what caused Israel to sin. God was interested in repentance, confession of sin, and restoration to fellowship. He was fully aware that Israel **turned their backs before their enemies, because they were accursed.** There was no hiding the problem. If something were not done, the divine response would be devastating: **neither will I be with you any more, except ye destroy the accursed from among you.**

The call to sanctify the people is reminiscent of Joshua 3:5. God never moves in unclean vessels. If Israel is to be used of God, she must be purged of her sin. The method of determining the sinner was ingenious. In the morning all Israel would be assembled by tribe, by family, by household, and man by man. The genealogies of the children of Israel were very strictly kept, as the books of Chronicles, Ezra, and Nehemiah indicate. With God's guidance, it would be a relatively easy task for the sinner in the camp to be determined. God always deals severely with sin because sin is severe. Just as He dealt harshly with the Canaanite inhabitants of Jericho because of their sin, He now deals equally so with an Israelite of Gilgal because of his sin. The divine command was **he that is taken with the accursed thing shall be burnt with fire, he and all that he hath.**

16-19. So Joshua rose up early in the morning. The task was not pleasant, but it was a necessary one. As has been Joshua's practice, he rose early in the morning to begin the survey of Israel. Tribe by tribe Israel was brought before him. The tribe of **Judah** was taken, and of that tribe the family of **Zarhites.** Of this family man by man, Zabdi was taken, **and Achan, the son of Carmi, the son of Zabdi, the son of Zerah, of the tribe of Judah was taken.**

What follows is a tender and passionate scene. **And Joshua said unto Achan, My son, give, I pray thee, glory to the Lord God of Israel, and make confession unto him.** Israel's leader is

19 And Joshua said unto Ā'chăn, My son, give, I pray thee, glory to the LORD God of Israel, and make confession unto him; and tell me now what thou hast done; hide *it* not from me.

20 And Ā'chăn answered Joshua, and said, Indeed I have sinned against the LORD God of Israel, and thus and thus have I done:

21 When I saw among the spoils a goodly Babylonish garment, and two hundred shekels of silver, and a wedge of gold of fifty shekels weight, then I coveted them, and took them; and, behold, they *are* hid in the earth in the midst of my tent, and the silver under it.

22 So Joshua sent messengers, and they ran unto the tent; and, behold, *it was* hid in his tent, and the silver under it.

23 And they took them out of the midst of the tent, and brought them unto Joshua, and unto all the children of Israel, and laid them out before the LORD.

24 And Joshua, and all Israel with him, took Ā'chăn the son of Ze'rah, and the silver, and the garment, and the wedge of gold, and his sons, and his daughters, and his oxen, and his asses, and his sheep, and his tent, and all that he had: and they brought them unto the valley of Ā'chôr.

25 And Joshua said, Why hast thou troubled us? the LORD shall trouble thee this day. And all Israel stoned him with stones, and burned them with fire, after they had stoned them with stones.

26 And they raised over him a great heap of stones unto this day. So the

410

not being hypocritical here; he genuinely is touched by the necessity of Achan's confession. God's glory will only be reflected back to Him when the life of God's servant is cleared of guilt.

20-21. Summarizing his trespass, Achan said, **When I saw among the spoils a goodly Babylonish garment . . . then I coveted them, and took them; and, behold, they are hid in the earth in the midst of my tent.** Knowing full well that he was not permitted to take the beautiful mantle of Shinar which he discovered at Jericho, nor the silver and gold which he had confiscated, Achan deliberately sinned against God and took this booty back to his house to hide beneath his tent. In essence, Achan had made the same mistake Moses did when ". . . he slew the Egyptian, and hid him in the sand" (Ex 2:12). Neither of them understood that you cannot successfully hide sin from God. Psalm 69:5 reminds us, "O God, thou knowest my foolishness; and my sins are not hid from thee." See also Mark 4:21-23.

The path to sin is now a well-established one. As Achan (1) **saw among the spoils a goodly Babylonish garment,** and (2) **coveted them,** and (3) **took them,** he followed exactly the same path that Eve did ". . . when the woman 'saw' that the tree was good for food, and that it was pleasant to the eyes, and a tree to be 'desired' (coveted) to make one wise, she 'took' of the fruit thereof, and did eat, and gave also unto her husband with her: and he did eat" (Gen 3:6). The similar pathway was used by David, as recorded in II Samuel 11:2-4, when one evening upon the roof of the king's house he "'saw' a woman washing herself . . . 'sent and inquired' after the woman . . . and 'took her'" (emphasis added). These and other examples illustrate the unbroken pathway to sin. Sin begins with innocent sight, degenerates into lustful desire or covetousness, and falls from there into participation. But the pathway to sin does not end here, as each example shows. The fourth step to sin is always involvement of others. Eve gave the forbidden fruit to Adam and he too partook of it. David's sin with Bathsheba involved her husband as well, for David sent Uriah the Hittite to the head of the battle in order to be killed (II Sam 11:6, 17). And Achan's personal sin in taking of the accursed thing brought about the deaths of thirty-six innocent Israelite soldiers. Perhaps the most terrifying thing about sin is that there is no such thing as private sin. All sin affects others; the personal sin of Achan kindled the anger of God against Israel. The personal sin of believers always affects the church at large. Every sin involves society; and since each of us makes up society, every sin affects us.

22-24. Upon hearing Achan's confession, Joshua sent messengers to his tent and removed all the accursed spoils of war **and laid them out before the LORD.** The offering to the Lord was the easy part; the punishment of Achan and his family was more difficult. **And Joshua, and all Israel with him, took Achan the son of Zerah, . . . and all that he had: and they brought them unto the valley of Achor.** Here Achan and his family, who apparently had participated in hiding the spoils of war, were to be severely punished for their sin. For a full discussion on the severity of this punishment, see John Calvin, *Commentaries on the Book of Joshua,* pp. 116-118. Also see, H. W. Robinson, *Corporate Personality in Ancient Israel,* where he demonstrates that the concept of a single person representing an entire group was so common that it was not considered unfair in the Hebrew mind for a family to suffer because of its father's sins (cf. II Sam 21:1-14).

25-26. Because they had troubled Israel, **all Israel stoned him with stones, and burned them with fire, after they had stoned them with stones.** God could not allow unconfessed sin to exist in the camp of Israel. He could not use unclean vessels. The Holy God can never associate Himself with that which is unholy. But once sin was dealt with **the LORD turned from the**

LORD turned from the fierceness of his anger. Wherefore the name of that place was called, The valley of Ā'chôr, unto this day.

CHAPTER 8

AND the LORD said unto Joshua, Fear not, neither be thou dismayed: take all the people of war with thee, and arise, go up to Ā'ī: see, I have given into thy hand the king of Ā'ī, and his people, and his city, and his land:

2 And thou shalt do to Ā'ī and her king as thou didst unto Jericho and her king: only the spoil thereof, and the cattle thereof, shall ye take for a prey unto yourselves: lay thee an ambush for the city behind it.

3 ¶So Joshua arose, and all the people of war, to go up against Ā'ī: and Joshua chose out thirty thousand mighty men of valour, and sent them away by night.

4 And he commanded them, saying, Behold, ye shall lie in wait against the city, *even* behind the city: go not very far from the city, but be ye all ready:

5 And I, and all the people that *are* with me, will approach unto the city: and it shall come to pass, when they come out against us, as at the first, that we will flee before them,

6 (For they will come out after us) till we have drawn them from the city; for they will say, They flee before us, as at the first: therefore we will flee before them.

7 Then ye shall rise up from the ambush, and seize upon the city: for the LORD your God will deliver it into your hand.

8 And it shall be, when ye have taken the city, *that* ye shall set the city on fire: according to the commandment of the LORD shall ye do. See, I have commanded you.

9 Joshua therefore sent them forth: and they went to lie in ambush, and abode between Běth–el and Ā'ī, on the west side of Ā'ī: but Joshua lodged that night among the people.

10 And Joshua rose up early in the morning, and numbered the people, and went up, he and the elders of Israel, before the people to Ā'ī.

11 And all the people, *even the people* of war that *were* with him, went up, and drew nigh, and came before the city, and pitched on the north side of Ā'ī: now *there was* a valley between them and Ā'ī.

12 And he took about five thousand men, and set them to lie in ambush between Běth–el and Ā'ī, on the west side of the city.

13 And when they had set the people, *even* all the host that *was* on the north of the city, and their liers in wait on the west of the city, Joshua went that night into the midst of the valley.

14 And it came to pass, when the king of Ā'ī saw *it*, that they hasted and rose up early, and the men of the city went out against Israel to battle, he and all

fierceness of his anger. From that day until now, the place where Achan was stoned has been called **the valley of Achor.** All who would live righteously before the Lord must be very careful to avoid sin. Gross errors tend to stigmatize those who otherwise have unblemished or near unblemished records (e.g., Thomas, Judas, Achan, et. al). Living righteously consistently is the only acceptable life-style.

4. The campaign against Ai completed. 8:1-35.

8:1-2. Fear not, neither be thou dismayed . . . see, I have given into thy hand the king of Ai. It was now necessary to inspire new courage in Joshua and the people. Therefore, God again prophetically pronounces that the city of Ai, its king, people, and land, have already been delivered into Joshua's hand. All the man of God must do is claim it.

3-9. Joshua chose out thirty thousand mighty men of valor . . . saying, Behold, ye shall lie in wait against the city, even behind the city. The tactical maneuvers which were employed to capture Ai were brilliant. Joshua was commanded to select thirty thousand men and send them away by night to make the thirteen-mile journey to Ai, stealthily position themselves on the west side of the city, and wait there in ambush. The ambush (Heb *'ōrēb*), literally "a lier in wait," would remain in position until, on the next day, Joshua would draw up the main army of Israel on the north side of Ai (vs. 11). When light would dawn and the inhabitants of Ai would discover Israel amassing her forces on the north, like William the Conqueror at Hastings, Joshua would reverse the movement of his forces feigning flight. **Then ye shall rise up from the ambush, and seize upon the city.** When the inhabitants of Ai were drawn into the field of battle, the thirty-thousand-man ambush would be free to move uninhibitedly into Ai.

10-13. And Joshua rose up early in the morning . . . and pitched on the north side of Ai. With the main forces in place, Joshua now **took about five thousand men and set them to lie in ambush between Beth-el and Ai.** This additional ambush was deployed as a defensive measure in order to keep the armies of Beth-el from entering the battle and preventing the thirty thousand troops on the west side of the city from taking Ai.

14-17. And Joshua and all Israel made as if they were beaten before them. Once the king of Ai sent his troops into the valley after Joshua, the captain of Israel then deployed his maneuver in order to gain the victory. Commentator Matthew

411

his people, at a time appointed, before the plain; but he wist not that *there were* liers in ambush against him behind the city.

15 And Joshua and all Israel made as if they were beaten before them, and fled by the way of the wilderness.

16 And all the people that *were* in Āī were called together to pursue after them: and they pursued after Joshua, and were drawn away from the city.

17 And there was not a man left in Āī or Bĕth-el, that went not out after Israel: and they left the city open, and pursued after Israel.

18 And the LORD said unto Joshua, Stretch out the spear that *is* in thy hand toward Āī; for I will give it into thine hand. And Joshua stretched out the spear that *he had* in his hand toward the city.

19 And the ambush arose quickly out of their place, and they ran as soon as he had stretched out his hand: and they entered into the city, and took it, and hasted and set the city on fire.

20 And when the men of Āī looked behind them, they saw, and, behold, the smoke of the city ascended up to heaven, and they had no power to flee this way or that way: and the people that fled to the wilderness turned back upon the pursuers.

21 And when Joshua and all Israel saw that the ambush had taken the city, and that the smoke of the city ascended, then they turned again, and slew the men of Āī.

22 And the other issued out of the city against them; so they were in the midst of Israel, some on this side, and some on that side: and they smote them, so that they let none of them remain or escape.

23 And the king of Āī they took alive, and brought him to Joshua.

24 And it came to pass, when Israel had made an end of slaying all the inhabitants of Āī in the field, in the wilderness wherein they chased them, and when they were all fallen on the edge of the sword, until they were consumed, that all the Israelites returned unto Āī, and smote it with the edge of the sword.

25 And *so* it was, *that* all that fell that day, both of men and women, *were* twelve thousand, *even* all the men of Āī.

26 For Joshua drew not his hand back, wherewith he stretched out the spear, until he had utterly destroyed all the inhabitants of Āī.

27 Only the cattle and the spoil of that city Israel took for a prey unto themselves, according unto the word of the LORD which he commanded Joshua.

28 And Joshua burnt Āī, and made it an heap for ever, *even* a desolation unto this day.

29 And the king of Āī he hanged on a tree until eventide: and as soon as the sun was down, Joshua commanded that they should take his carcase down from the tree, and cast it at the entering of the gate of the city, and raise thereon

Henry notes a correlation between this movement and Christ. "Joshua conquered by yielding. So our Lord Jesus Christ, when He bowed His head and gave up the Ghost, seemed as if death had triumphed over Him; but in His resurrection He rallied again, and gave the powers of darkness a total defeat." **And there was not a man left in Ai or Beth-el.** It is not entirely discernible why Beth-el is here included (in fact these words are not in the LXX); Beth-el and Ai must have been in league with one another. Regardless, the plan of God worked perfectly.

18-23. And the LORD said unto Joshua, Stretch out the spear that is in thy hand toward Ai; for I will give it into thine hand. This spear was probably a long, slender lance that Joshua would use to direct the armies of Israel. When the men of Ai saw the smoke rising from their defeated city, **they had no power to flee this way or that way.** They had been delivered into the hand of Israel by the hand of God. Thus, the Israelites **slew the men of Ai . . . so that they let none of them . . . escape. And the king of Ai they took alive.** Israel's victory was complete, much unlike their previous attempt to conquer the mighty men of Ai.

24-27. And so it was, that all that fell that day, both of men and women, were twelve thousand. The righteous hand of God had fallen on this adulterous city. Every inhabitant of Ai was slain, **Only the cattle and the spoil of that city Israel took for a prey unto themselves.** This was done as commanded by the Lord in verse 2.

28-29. And Joshua burnt Ai, and made it a heap for ever, even a desolation unto this day. This verse is especially significant in the fact that Ai is always written with the definite article in the Hebrew (Heb *ha'ay*) and means "the heap" or "the ruin." Characteristically, **the king of Ai he hanged on a tree until eventide.** This may well mean that he was placed on a tree after his death (see Deut 21:22-23). "We find here a remarkable coincidence with the precept in Deuteronomy 21:23. The fact

a great heap of stones, *that remaineth* unto this day.

30 ¶Then Joshua built an altar unto the LORD God of Israel in mount Ebal,
31 As Moses the servant of the LORD commanded the children of Israel, as it is written in the book of the law of Moses, an altar of whole stones, over which no man hath lift up *any* iron: and they offered thereon burnt offerings unto the LORD, and sacrificed peace offerings.
32 And he wrote there upon the stones a copy of the law of Moses, which he wrote in the presence of the children of Israel.

33 And all Israel, and their elders, and officers, and their judges, stood on this side the ark and on that side before the priests the Levites, which bare the ark of the covenant of the LORD, as well the stranger, as he that was born among them; half of them over against mount Gĕr′i-zĭm, and half of them over against mount Ebal; as Moses the servant of the LORD had commanded before, that they should bless the people of Israel.
34 And afterward he read all the words of the law, the blessings and cursings, according to all that is written in the book of the law.
35 There was not a word of all that Moses commanded, which Joshua read not before all the congregation of Israel, with the women, and the little ones, and the strangers that were conversant among them.

CHAPTER 9

AND it came to pass, when all the kings which *were* on this side Jordan, in the hills, and in the valleys, and in all the coasts of the great sea over against Lebanon, the Hittite, and the Ā′mor-īte, the Canaanite, the Pĕr′iz-zīte, the Hī′-vīte, and the Jĕb′u-sīte, heard *thereof;*
2 That they gathered themselves together, to fight with Joshua and with Israel, with one accord.

3 ¶And when the inhabitants of Gĭb-eon heard what Joshua had done unto Jericho and to Ā′ī,

that no notice is here taken of that passage is conclusive against its having been inserted with a view to that precept in later times, and this affords a strong presumption against the Elohist and Jehovist theory" (J. J. Lias, Joshua, in the *Pulpit Commentary,* p. 134).

30-32. Then Joshua built an altar unto the LORD God of Israel in Mount Ebal . . . And he wrote there upon the stones a copy of the law of Moses. From the city of Ai Israel moved to the base of Mount Ebal in the central section of Canaan. Mount Ebal rises to a height of 3,077 feet above sea level (1,402 feet above the valley) and is just north of Mount Gerizim, which rises 2,849 feet above sea level. Here Joshua built an altar unto the Lord God in thankfulness for the defeat of Jericho and Ai. Here, too, he inscribed in stone a copy of the law of Moses.

Many liberal scholars have judged this passage an interpolation. They have unjustly concluded that Deuteronomy was not written by Moses, but was a late revision of the law of Moses by Ezra. But here is distinct proof that the book of Joshua was written after the book of Deuteronomy, for Deuteronomy is quoted as "the book of the law of Moses" (cf. Deut 31:9, 24, 26). Liberal scholars have attempted to overcome this weighty evidence by indicating that this portion of Joshua was later added to the rest of the writing. But such a revision of God's Word is both unsubstantiated and unacceptable.

33-35. And all Israel . . . stood on this side the ark and on that side. Israel gathered in the narrow valley between Mount Ebal and Mount Gerizim to pronounce the blessings and cursings as they had been commanded by Moses (see Deut 27:12). No doubt certain representatives from each of the tribes stood on the mountains, half on Mount Gerizim and the other half on Mount Ebal; and the majority of the people crowded at the base of the mountains to hear the pronouncement of the blessings and cursings. Topographically, these mountains form a natural amphitheater that made it acoustically possible for all Israel to hear every word that was spoken.

And afterward he read all the words of the law. This was a significant occasion for Israel. She had just won a great victory, but now she must recognize that the victory was hers because of her covenant with Jehovah. In sight of all the congregation of Israel, including women and children and those strangers who had attached themselves to Israel, the Law was read aloud. Such a practice was an integral part of Israel's life and worship in many periods of her history (see Ex 24:4, 7; II Kgs 23:2; Neh 8).

C. Israel's Southern Campaign 9:1-10:43.

1. The deceit of the Gibeonites. 9:1-15.

9:1-2. They gathered themselves together, to fight with Joshua and with Israel, with one accord. Threatened by the advance of Israel and the power of her God, the kings of the Amorite city-states, who controlled the southern portion of Canaan, desperately formed a coalition in order to survive the onslaught of Israel. The peoples mentioned, with the exception of the Girgashites, are the ones enumerated in 3:10. **With one accord** literally means "with one mouth," according to the Hebrew, referring not only to their opinions but to their common expression of those opinions. It is interesting that the phrase "with one accord" occurs so frequently in the early chapters of Acts with reference to the church. We cannot help but wonder what the result would be if believers in this century attacked the devil and his forces with the same unity of purpose that the devil and his forces attack believers.

3-6. The inhabitants of Gibeon . . . did work wilily. The Hivite inhabitants of one town of Canaan, Gibeon (see J. B. Pritchard, *Gibeon, Where the Sun Stood Still*), declined to join

413

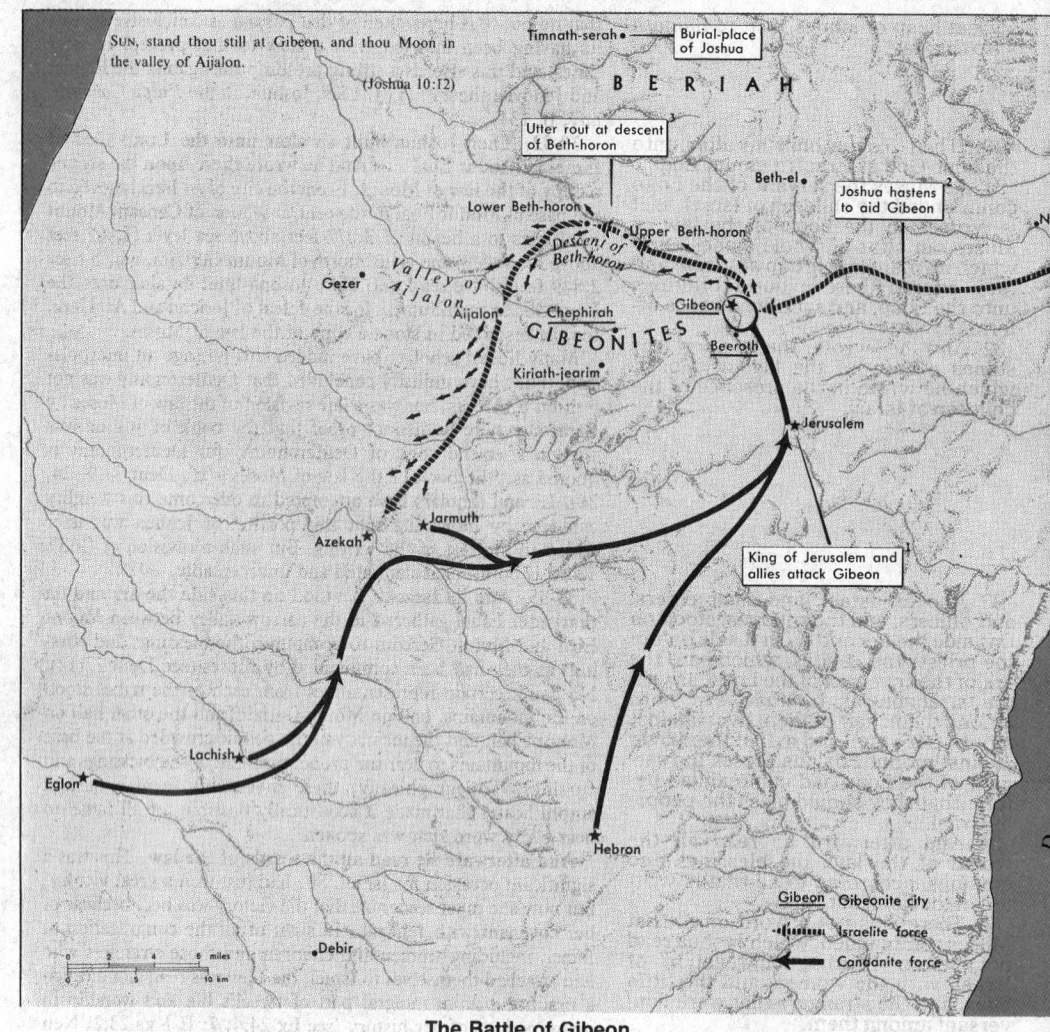

Sun, stand thou still at Gibeon, and thou Moon in the valley of Aijalon.

(Joshua 10:12)

B E R I A H

Timnath-serah •

Burial-place of Joshua

Utter rout at descent of Beth-horon

Beth-el •

Joshua hastens to aid Gibeon

Lower Beth-horon

Upper Beth-horon

Descent of Beth-horon

Gezer •

Valley of Aijalon

Aijalon •

Chephirah •

Gibeon ☆

GIBEONITES

Beeroth •

Kiriath-jearim •

Jerusalem ☆

King of Jerusalem and allies attack Gibeon

Jarmuth ★

Azekah ★

Lachish ★

Eglon ★

Hebron •

Gibeon — Gibeonite city
⫘⫘⫘ Israelite force
⬅ Canaanite force

Debir •

0 2 4 6 miles
0   5   10 km

The Battle of Gibeon

4 They did work wilily, and went and made as if they had been ambassadors, and took old sacks upon their asses, and wine bottles, old, and rent, and bound up;
5 And old shoes and clouted upon their feet, and old garments upon them; and all the bread of their provision was dry *and* mouldy.
6 And they went to Joshua unto the camp at Gilgal, and said unto him, and to the men of Israel, We be come from a far country: now therefore make ye a league with us.

7 And the men of Israel said unto the Hi'vites, Peradventure ye dwell among us; and how shall we make a league with you?

the Canaanite league against Israel in preference for a mutual defense treaty with Israel. But Deuteronomy 7:1-2 and 20:10-15 clearly did not permit Israel to make treaties with the seven Canaanite nations living in proximity to them. Thus, the Gibeonites **made as if they had been ambassadors, and took old sacks upon their asses, and wine bottles, old, and rent, and bound up; And old shoes and clouted upon their feet, and old garments upon them; and all the bread of their provision was dry and moldy.**

Israel was the recipient of a crafty plan to deceive her. Worn-out bags of sackcloth were placed on the backs of asses; worn-out and torn wineskins were presented; worn-out shoes (lit., things tied on; i.e., sandals) which were clouted (i.e., patched) and old garments were worn; and bread that was dry and moldy (lit., marked with points, i.e., mildewed) was taken as provision. All of this was done to convince Joshua and the Israelites that they had come from a far country, that it would be permissible for Israel to enter into a league with them.

7-10. When questioned as to the possibility that the Gibeonites dwelt near Israel, they answered Joshua saying, **We are thy servants.** This phrase was a common one in the east as a token of respect (e.g., Gen 32:4, 18; 50:18; II Kgs 10:5; 16:7).

8 And they said unto Joshua, We *are* thy servants. And Joshua said unto them, Who *are* ye? and from whence come ye?

9 And they said unto him, From a very far country thy servants are come because of the name of the LORD thy God: for we have heard the fame of him, and all that he did in Egypt,

10 And all that he did to the two kings of the Āmorītes, that *were* beyond Jordan, to Sihon king of Hĕsh'bŏn, and to Og king of Bā'shan, which *was* at Ăsh'ta-rŏth.

11 Wherefore our elders and all the inhabitants of our country spake to us, saying, Take victuals with you for the journey, and go to meet them, and say unto them, We *are* your servants: therefore now make ye a league with us.

12 This our bread we took hot *for* our provision out of our houses on the day we came forth to go unto you; but now, behold, it is dry, and it is mouldy:

13 And these bottles of wine, which we filled, *were* new; and, behold, they be rent: and these our garments and our shoes are become old by reason of the very long journey.

14 And the men took of their victuals, and asked not *counsel* at the mouth of the LORD.

15 And Joshua made peace with them, and made a league with them, to let them live: and the princes of the congregation sware unto them.

16 ¶And it came to pass at the end of three days after they had made a league with them, that they heard that they *were* their neighbours, and *that* they dwelt among them.

17 And the children of Israel journeyed, and came unto their cities on the third day. Now their cities *were* Gĭb'eon, and Che-phī'rah, and Bē-ē'rŏth, and Kir'jath-jē'a-rĭm.

18 And the children of Israel smote them not, because the princes of the congregation had sworn unto them by the LORD God of Israel. And all the congregation murmured against the princes.

19 But all the princes said unto all the congregation, We have sworn unto them by the LORD God of Israel: now therefore we may not touch them.

20 This we will do to them; we will even let them live, lest wrath be upon us, because of the oath which we sware unto them.

21 And the princes said unto them, Let them live; but let them be hewers of wood and drawers of water unto all the congregation; as the princes had promised them.

22 ¶And Joshua called for them, and he spake unto them, saying, Wherefore have ye beguiled us, saying, We *are* very far from you; when ye dwell among us?

23 Now therefore ye *are* cursed, and there shall none of you be freed from being bondmen, and hewers of wood

They were not asking to become the slaves of Israel, but for Israel to enter a mutual pact with them.

To convince Joshua of their interest and desperate need to make a league with Israel, the Gibeonites said, **From a very far country thy servants are come because of the name of the LORD thy God.** They heard what God did for Israel in Egypt and to the two kings of the Amorites beyond the Jordan, Sihon and Og. **Ashtaroth** has been identified with the Assyrian *Ishtar* and appears as Astaratu in the Karnak list of cities captured by Thutmose III. It is last mentioned in Jewish history as having been conquered by Judas Maccabaeus (*I Macc VI*).

11-13. The deception worked well. The Gibeonites claimed that their elders had instructed them to make a league with Israel and that they had taken bread hot from the oven on the day they left. It was now dry and moldy. Also, they said their bottles of wine (lit., "skins of wine," glass bottles were not known at this age) were filled at the beginning of their journey, but were now worn and useless. Everything contributed to a convincing story.

14-15. And the men took of their victuals, and asked not counsel at the mouth of the LORD. Joshua made peace with the Gibeonites on the basis of circumstantial evidence. Even in those things which are most obvious it is not wise to implicitly trust our own judgment. Joshua and the congregation had been deceived; and the notation, **and asked not counsel at the mouth of the LORD,** all too graphically explains why they fell into this error.

2. The servanthood of the Gibeonites. 9:16-27.

16-21. The Gibeonites' deception was soon discovered by Israel. Immediately, the princes of Israel made a three-day march to the cities of the Gibeonites. These cities are noted as **Gibeon**, identified with El-Jib, **Chephirah**, on a spur five miles west of Gibeon, dominating the Wadi Qatneh, **Beeroth**, three miles to the northeast of Gibeon, identified today as El-Bireh, and **Kirjath-jearim**, south of Chephirah and chiefly known for the twenty-year sojourn of the ark there (I Sam 7:2).

It is significant that, although the princes of Israel murmured against their deception, nevertheless, they decided to honor the covenant made with the Gibeonites **lest wrath be upon us, because of the oath which we sware unto them.** Although many contend that this oath was obtained by fraud and thus the Israelites could declare it *ab initio*, null and void, Israel chose not to break the league; for "the violation of an oath is a sin of the first magnitude, for it is a breach of the third commandment, a taking of God's name in vain, which He will not hold guiltless. As Leviticus 19:12 informs us, to commit perjury in the name of God is an act of profanity. From such awful considerations it follows that an oath is to be feared (Eccl 9:2), and that once made it is binding (Num 30:3), a solemn example of which is seen in the case of Jephthah (Jud 11:29-31)" (Pink, p. 256).

22-27. Although their oath with the Gibeonites was not broken, nevertheless such deception had to be punished. **And Joshua made them that day hewers of wood and drawers of water for the congregation, and for the altar of the LORD . . . in the place which he should choose.** The Gibeonites were to be employed forever in servile work. But the phrase about **the altar of the LORD,** and especially the use of the imperfect tense,

and drawers of water for the house of my God.

24 And they answered Joshua, and said, Because it was certainly told thy servants, how that the LORD thy God commanded his servant Moses to give you all the land, and to destroy all the inhabitants of the land from before you, therefore we were sore afraid of our lives because of you, and have done this thing.

25 And now, behold, we are in thine hand: as it seemeth good and right unto thee to do unto us, do.

26 And so did he unto them, and delivered them out of the hand of the children of Israel, that they slew them not.

27 And Joshua made them that day hewers of wood and drawers of water for the congregation, and for the altar of the LORD, even unto this day, in the place which he should choose.

CHAPTER 10

NOW it came to pass, when A-dŏ′nĭ-zĕ′dĕc king of Jerusalem had heard how Joshua had taken Ā′ī, and had utterly destroyed it; as he had done to Jericho and her king, so he had done to Ā′ī and her king; and how the inhabitants of Gĭ́beon had made peace with Israel, and were among them;

2 That they feared greatly, because Gibeon was a great city, as one of the royal cities, and because it was greater than Ā′ī, and all the men thereof were mighty.

3 Wherefore A-dŏ′nĭ-zĕ′dĕc king of Jerusalem sent unto Hō′hăm king of Hēbron, and unto Pī′ram king of Jär′mŭth, and unto Ja-phī′a king of Lā′chĭsh, and unto Dĕ′bir king of Ĕg′lŏn, saying,

4 Come up unto me, and help me, that we may smite Gĭ́beon: for it hath made peace with Joshua and with the children of Israel.

5 Therefore the five kings of the Āmor-ītes, the king of Jerusalem, the king of Hēbron, the king of Jär′mŭth, the king of Lā′chĭsh, the king of Ĕg′lŏn, gathered themselves together, and went up, they and all their hosts, and encamped before Gĭ́beon, and made war against it.

6 ¶And the men of Gĭ́beon sent unto Joshua to the camp to Gilgal, saying, Slack not thy hand from thy servants; come up to us quickly, and save us, and help us: for all the kings of the Āmor-ītes that dwell in the mountains are gathered together against us.

7 So Joshua ascended from Gilgal, he, and all the people of war with him, and all the mighty men of valour.

8 ¶And the LORD said unto Joshua, Fear them not: for I have delivered them into thine hand; there shall not a man of them stand before thee.

9 Joshua therefore came unto them suddenly, and went up from Gilgal all night.

10 And the LORD discomfited them before Israel, and slew them with a great slaughter at Gĭ́beon, and chased

clearly implies that Solomon's temple was not yet built. This strongly witnesses against any theory of a late writing of the book of Joshua. The ark of God, and the tabernacle which contained it, had not yet found a permanent resting place.

3. The defeat of the Amorites. 10:1-28.

10:1-2. They feared greatly, because Gibeon was a great city. Adonizedek, king of Jerusalem, upon hearing of the destruction of Ai and Jericho, and the recently instituted peace between Gibeon and Israel, viewed the Gibeonite league as a dangerous trend in southern Canaan. He discerned that opposition against the Israelites was wearing down when such a great city as Gibeon, a royal city, one that was greater than Ai, established a league with Israel. Something had to be done.

3-5. The Jerusalemite king summoned other kings whose positions were threatened by Gibeon's association with Israel. As we might expect, Adonizedek stood at the head of this Amorite league. Next came **Hebron,** a city of great importance from a very early period (Gen 23:2; 35:27) and her king **Hoham. Piram king of Jarmuth** was also summoned. Jarmuth is also mentioned in chapter 15:35 and in Nehemiah 11:29. It has been identified with Yarmuk. **Japhia, king of Lachish,** a city in the Shephelah or lowlands of Judah, and **Debir, king of Eglon,** the modern Ajlan, not far from Lachish, were summoned saying, **Come up unto me, and help me, that we may smite Gibeon.** Since most of these kings were in the lowlands, the expression **come up** is accurate coming from the mouth of the king of Jerusalem in the hills of Judea. Adonizedek does not propose to attack Israel directly, but to attack Gibeon and punish her for her league with Israel.

6-11. Immediately upon hearing of the Amorite encroachment around Gibeon **Joshua ascended from Gilgal, he, and all the people of war with him, and all the mighty men of valor.** By employing an all-night forced march, the armies of Israel quickly ascended the twenty-five miles of Gilgal to Gibeon. **And the LORD discomfited them before Israel, and slew them with a great slaughter at Gibeon.** The original meaning of the word "discomfited" is to throw into confusion or to rout. Some have stated concern at the expression in this verse **the way that goeth up to Beth-horon** and the expression in the next verse **were in the going down to Beth-horon.** There is no inconsistency here in that there were two towns named Beth-horon, upper Beth-horon and lower Beth-horon. The former town led to a difficult pass from Gibeon called the "ascent" to Beth-horon. Between the two towns was a rocky path that was so rugged that steps had been cut into the rock to facilitate the **going down to Beth-horon** mentioned in verse 11 (see I Macc 3:16-24). **Azekah** (15:35; cf. I Sam 17:1) and **Makkedah,** one of the lowland cities

them along the way that goeth up to Bĕth–hô´ron, and smote them to A–zē´kah, and unto Mak–kē´dah.

11 And it came to pass, as they fled from before Israel, *and* were in the going down to Bĕth–hô´ron, that the LORD cast down great stones from heaven upon them unto A-zē´kah, and they died: *they were* more which died with hailstones than *they* whom the children of Israel slew with the sword.

12 ¶Then spake Joshua to the LORD in the day when the LORD delivered up the Amorites before the children of Israel, and he said in the sight of Israel, Sun, stand thou still upon Gĭbeon; and thou, Moon, in the valley of Ăj´a-lŏn.

13 And the sun stood still, and the moon stayed, until the people had avenged themselves upon their enemies. *Is* not this written in the book of Jă´sher? So the sun stood still in the midst of heaven, and hasted not to go down about a whole day.

14 And there was no day like that before it or after it, that the LORD hearkened unto the voice of a man: for the LORD fought for Israel.

15 ¶And Joshua returned, and all Israel with him, unto the camp to Gilgal.

16 But these five kings fled, and hid themselves in a cave at Mak-kē´dah.

17 And it was told Joshua, saying, The five kings are found hid in a cave at Mak-kē´dah.

18 And Joshua said, Roll great stones upon the mouth of the cave, and set men by it for to keep them:

19 And stay ye not, *but* pursue after your enemies, and smite the hindmost of them; suffer them not to enter into

of Judah (15:41), are both mentioned to geographically establish how far the Israelites pursued the Amorite league.

The LORD cast down great stones from heaven upon them unto Azekah, and they died: they were more which died with hailstones than they whom the children of Israel slew with the sword. A great storm of hailstones began to rain down upon the Amorites. Unlike anything they had previously seen, the great stones began to take their toll upon God's enemy. We dare not underestimate the destructive power of these hailstones. On May 1, 1888, during a hailstorm in Moradad, India, two hundred fifty lives were lost. Many more were lost at the battle of Ajalon. Likewise, these hailstones were noted to be **great stones.** The largest American hailstone ever recorded was seventeen inches in circumference, with a weight of one and one-half pounds. These stones could have been as large, or even larger. At any rate, their destruction was devastating.

The great hailstorm was conclusive proof, both to the Israelites and to the Amorites, that Israel's victory was from the hand of Jehovah and was not due to the power of men. James Kelso remarks, "The crossing of the Jordan at high flood and the cyclonic hailstorm at Ajalon are of special theological significance; for Baal was the great Canaanite storm god who was supposed to control the rain, the hail, the snow and the floods of Palestine. These episodes proved that Baal was as powerless before Yahweh in Palestine as he had been in the episode of the plagues of Egypt" (James L. Kelso, *Archaeology and Our Old Testament Contemporaries*, p. 53).

12-14. Then spake Joshua to the LORD . . . So the sun stood still. A favorite passage of biblical critics and scoffers, the theme is later found under almost the identical circumstances in Greek literature. Agamemnon prayed to Zeus not to let the sun go down before the Achaeans were victorious (*Iliad*, II, 412ff.). No single explanation of this phenomenon is entirely satisfactory (see Introduction for various explanations). Better than a natural explanation is what may be learned from the passage. To be noted here are Joshua's intrepid faith in God in the midst of an impossible situation and Jehovah's complete and utter providence over His creation. "Here, as in many other passages, we are taught that the Lord God has a superintendence over all the creatures of His hand. He sends forth His imperious commands not only unto angels and men (Dan 4:34), but to the birds of the air (I Kgs 17:4) and to the wild beasts (Dan 6:22), yea, to inanimate things . . . The host of heaven, as well as the inhabitants of the earth, are entirely at His disposal. The whole source of nature moves or stands still at the mere will of its Maker" (Pink, p. 282).

The book of Jasher is believed by many to be "the book of the wars of the LORD" mentioned in Numbers 21:14. It is also referred to in II Samuel 1:18 and apparently was a national epic recording the warlike exploits and notable battles of the Israelites. Joshua's reference to its historicity, coupled with the fact that it recorded the event of the sun standing still during Joshua's lifetime, enhance the validity of this great miracle.

15-20. But these five kings fled, and hid themselves in a cave at Makkedah. Joshua now completes the "mopping up" operation of southern Palestine. In the terror of battle, Adonizedek, Hoham, Piram, Japhia, and Debir (the five who fought against the Gibeonites) banded together and hid in a cave. There were numerous caves in Palestine (see Gen 19:30; Jud 20:47; I Sam 22:1; 24:3; etc.), but the cave which these kings entered provided no protection. Joshua entombed them therein by rolling a **great stone** over the mouth of the cave while the Israelites pursued and defeated their armies.

their cities: for the LORD your God hath delivered them into your hand.

20 And it came to pass, when Joshua and the children of Israel had made an end of slaying them with a very great slaughter, till they were consumed, that the rest *which* remained of them entered into fenced cities.

21 And all the people returned to the camp to Joshua at Mak-kē'dah in peace: none moved his tongue against any of the children of Israel.

22 Then said Joshua, Open the mouth of the cave, and bring out those five kings unto me out of the cave.

23 And they did so, and brought forth those five kings unto him out of the cave, the king of Jerusalem, the king of Hēbron, the king of Jär'mŭth, the king of Lā'chĭsh, *and* the king of Ĕg'lŏn.

24 And it came to pass, when they brought out those kings unto Joshua, that Joshua called for all the men of Israel, and said unto the captains of the men of war which went with him, Come near, put your feet upon the necks of these kings. And they came near, and put their feet upon the necks of them.

25 And Joshua said unto them, Fear not, nor be dismayed, be strong and of good courage: for thus shall the LORD do to all your enemies against whom ye fight.

26 And afterward Joshua smote them, and slew them, and hanged them on five trees: and they were hanging upon the trees until the evening.

27 And it came to pass at the time of the going down of the sun, *that* Joshua commanded, and they took them down off the trees, and cast them into the cave wherein they had been hid, and laid great stones in the cave's mouth, *which remain* until this very day.

28 ¶And that day Joshua took Mak-kē'dah, and smote it with the edge of the sword, and the king thereof he utterly destroyed, them, and all the souls that *were* therein; he let none remain: and he did to the king of Mak-kē'dah as he did unto the king of Jericho.

29 Then Joshua passed from Mak-kē'dah, and all Israel with him, unto Lĭb'nah, and fought against Lĭb'nah:

30 And the LORD delivered it also, and the king thereof, into the hand of Israel; and he smote it with the edge of the sword, and all the souls that *were* therein; he let none remain in it; but did unto the king thereof as he did unto the king of Jericho.

31 ¶And Joshua passed from Lĭb'nah, and all Israel with him, unto Lā'-chĭsh, and encamped against it, and fought against it:

32 And the LORD delivered Lā'chĭsh into the hand of Israel, which took it on the second day, and smote it with the edge of the sword, and all the souls that *were* therein, according to all that he had done to Lĭb'nah.

33 ¶Then Hō'răm king of Gē'zer came up to help Lā'chĭsh; and Joshua smote him and his people, until he had left him none remaining.

34 ¶And from Lā'chĭsh Joshua

21-28. Upon returning to the cave, Joshua commanded that the pagan kings be brought forth and told his men, **put your feet upon the necks of these kings.** This was a well-known Oriental symbol of victory and superiority, as Assyrian and Egyptian monuments attest. But Joshua's command was more of encouragement than conceit (see vs. 25). This was also true of the act of hanging kings on trees after slaying them. Israel must know that Jehovah was with them, and they would continue to be victorious as they continued to rely on Him. The complete annihilation of Makkedah provided immediate substantiation.

4. The destruction of the southern alliance. 10:29-43.

29-39. No indication of time is given for the rest of the chapter, but the implication is that the rest of southern Canaan fell in weeks, perhaps days, from this point. **Libnah, Lachish, Gezer, Eglon, Hebron, and Debir** all fell to the Israelites. The geographical and topographical accuracy of the text is attested by the statement **And Joshua went up from Eglon . . . unto Hebron,** since Hebron is situated on the hills of Judah while Eglon is down in the plain of the Philistines.

passed unto Ĕg'lŏn, and all Israel with him; and they encamped against it, and fought against it:

35 And they took it on that day, and smote it with the edge of the sword, and all the souls that *were* therein he utterly destroyed that day, according to all that he had done to Lā'chĭsh.

36 And Joshua went up from Ĕg'lŏn, and all Israel with him, unto Hḗbron; and they fought against it:

37 And they took it, and smote it with the edge of the sword, and the king thereof, and all the cities thereof, and all the souls that *were* therein; he left none remaining, according to all that he had done to Ĕg'lŏn; but destroyed it

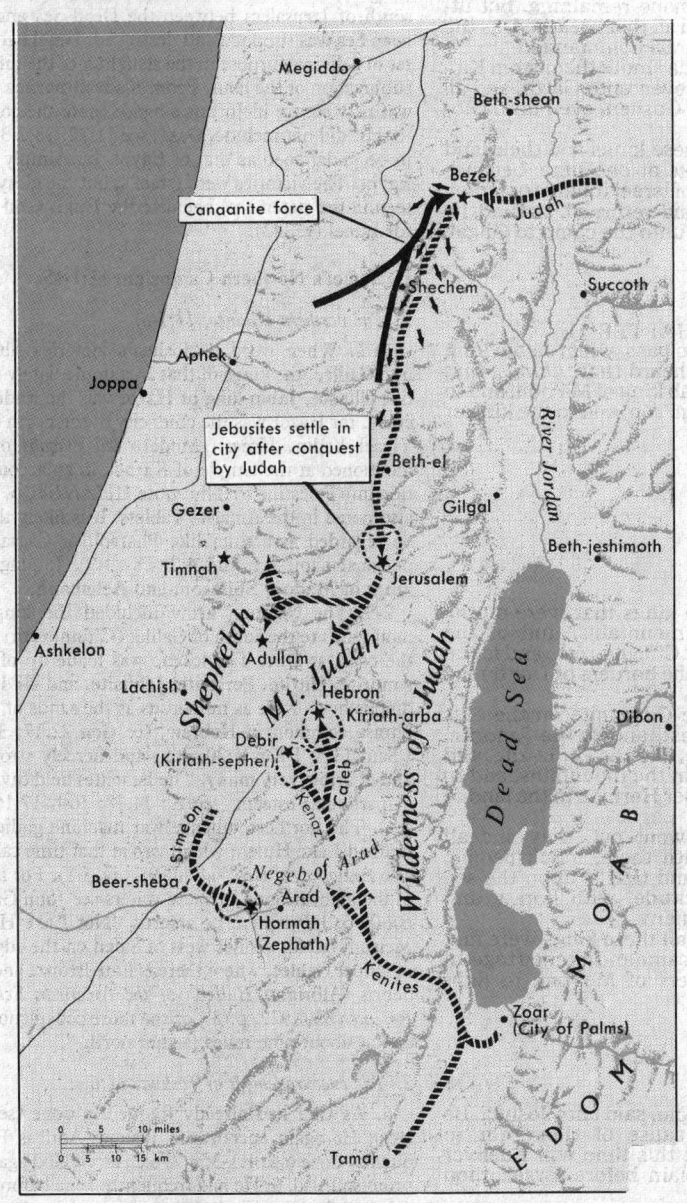

The Invasion of Judah and the Southern Tribes

utterly, and all the souls that *were* therein.

38 ¶And Joshua returned, and all Israel with him, to Dē'bir; and fought against it:

39 And he took it, and the king thereof, and all the cities thereof; and they smote them with the edge of the sword, and utterly destroyed all the souls that *were* therein; he left none remaining: as he had done to Hēbron, so he did to Dē'bir, and to the king thereof; as he had done also to Līb'nah, and to her king.

40 ¶So Joshua smote all the country of the hills, and of the south, and of the vale, and of the springs, and all their kings: he left none remaining, but utterly destroyed all that breathed, as the LORD God of Israel commanded.

41 And Joshua smote them from Kā'desh-bär'ne-a even unto Gā'za, and all the country of Goshen, even unto Gīb-eon.

42 And all these kings and their land did Joshua take at one time, because the LORD God of Israel fought for Israel.

43 And Joshua returned, and all Israel with him, unto the camp to Gilgal.

CHAPTER 11

AND it came to pass, when Jā'bin king of Hā'zôr had heard *those things*, that he sent to Jō'băb king of Mā'dŏn, and to the king of Shǐm'rŏn, and to the king of Ăch'shăph,

2 And to the kings that *were* on the north of the mountains, and of the plains south of Chǐn'ne-rŏth, and in the valley, and in the borders of Dor on the west,

3 *And to* the Canaanite on the east and on the west, and *to* the Āmorīte, and the Hittite, and the Pěr'iz-zīte, and the Jěb'u-sīte in the mountains, and *to* the Hī'vīte under Hermon in the land of Mǐz'peh.

4 And they went out, they and all their hosts with them, much people, even as the sand that *is* upon the sea shore in multitude, with horses and chariots very many.

5 And when all these kings were met together, they came and pitched together at the waters of Me'rom, to fight against Israel.

6 ¶And the LORD said unto Joshua, Be not afraid because of them: for to morrow about this time will I deliver them up all slain before Israel: thou

40-43. The expanse of Joshua's victories is now surveyed. **Joshua smote all the country of the hills, and of the south** (Negev), **and of the vale** (Shephelah) . . . **all** of the hill country south of Jerusalem between the Dead Sea and the Mediterranean Sea was subdued and destroyed. Israel had been the minister of a divine purpose in the slaughter of the inhabitants and the subjugation of the land. **From Kadesh-barnea even unto Gaza** was now secure in Joshua's hands (note the conquest extended to, but did not include, Gaza, see 11:22; 13:2-3). **Goshen** is not to be understood as that of Egypt, but simply the land toward Egypt. The victories were Israel's, but the glory was God's, as is seen in the statement, **because the LORD God of Israel fought for Israel** (vs. 42).

D. Israel's Northern Campaign. 11:1-15.

1. The northern alliance. 11:1-5.

11:1. When word of Joshua's victories filtered northward into Galilee, the kings of that area immediately formed a protective alliance. **Jabin king of Hazor** was the leader of the confederacy, for Hazor was the chief city of the north (see vs. 10; also, Yigael Yadin, *Hazor*). Modern *tell waqqās* or *el-queda*, it is mentioned at the temple of Karnak in an account of an expedition into Palestine by Thutmose III (*ANET*, p. 243). The city is also noted in the Amarna Tablets. It is likely that **Jabin** should be regarded as a title, like Pharaoh or Caesar, rather than a personal name (cf. Jud 4:2; Ps 83:9). Joining Jabin were the kings of **Madon, Shimron,** and **Achshaph.**

2-5. The coalition army included the kings north of the mountains to the south of Galilee (**Chinneroth**) and westward to the coast at **Dor.** The league was made up of the **Canaanite, Amorite, Hittite, Perizzite, Jebusite,** and **Hivite.** The multitudinous hosts were as numerous as the sands of the sea (a poetic phrase common in Hebrew, see Gen 22:17; 32:19; Jud 7:12; I Sam 13:5; I Kgs 4:20; etc.) and fiercely strong, **with horses and chariots very many.** The Israelites held cavalry and chariots in particular esteem (see Ex 14:18; Josh 17:16, 18; Jud 1:19; 4:3). The northern alliance war machine gathered by the now drained Lake Huleh, which was at that time called **Merom** (see also *Antiq.* v. 1; *Bell Jud* iii. 9.7; iv. i.1). For an alternate view of the identification of these waters see John Gray, *The Century Bible*, p. 119, where he asserts, "Not Lake Huleh, but either Meirun, ca. four miles west of Safed on the edge of the plateau of Upper Galilee, where there is Late Bronze and Early Iron Age debris (Albright, *Bulletin of the American Schools of Oriental Research* 35, 1929, p. 8), or the more conspicuous tell of Marun er-Ras about nine miles farther north."

2. The encouragement of Joshua. 11:6.

6. As God had already frequently done (see 1:6-7, 9; 8:1; etc.), He again encouraged Joshua. And as He had also frequently done (see 1:1-3; 3:7; 6:2; etc.), God again gave Joshua a promise. Also, as He had frequently done before (see 3:8, 12-13; 6:3-4; 8:2; etc.), God again gave a plan of attack to Joshua.

shalt hough their horses, and burn their chariots with fire.

7 So Joshua came, and all the people of war with him, against them by the waters of Me'rom suddenly; and they fell upon them.

8 And the LORD delivered them into the hand of Israel, who smote them, and chased them unto great Zi'don, and unto Mis're-phŏth-mā'im, and unto the valley of Mĭz'peh eastward; and they smote them, until they left them none remaining.

9 And Joshua did unto them as the LORD bade him: he houghed their horses, and burnt their chariots with fire.

10 ¶And Joshua at that time turned back, and took Hā'zôr, and smote the king thereof with the sword: for Hā'zôr beforetime was the head of all those kingdoms.

11 And they smote all the souls that were therein with the edge of the sword, utterly destroying them: there was not any left to breathe: and he burnt Hā'zôr with fire.

12 And all the cities of those kings, and all the kings of them, did Joshua take, and smote them with the edge of the sword, and he utterly destroyed them, as Moses the servant of the LORD commanded.

13 But as for the cities that stood still in their strength, Israel burned none of them, save Hā'zôr only; that did Joshua burn.

14 And all the spoil of these cities, and the cattle the children of Israel took for a prey unto themselves; but every man they smote with the edge of the sword, until they had destroyed them, neither left they any to breathe.

15 As the LORD commanded Moses his servant, so did Moses command Joshua, and so did Joshua; he left nothing undone of all that the LORD commanded Moses.

16 So Joshua took all that land, the hills, and all the south country, and all the land of Goshen, and the valley, and the plain, and the mountain of Israel, and the valley of the same;

God's encouragement was **Be not afraid.** His promise was **for tomorrow about this time will I deliver them up all slain before Israel.** His plan was to **hough their horses, and burn their chariots.**

To **hough their horses** means to hamstring them. The word is *neurokopein* in the LXX. A horse is hamstrung when the sinews behind the hoof or hock are severed, thus rendering the horse useless. Given the larger picture of war, this was not a cruel act, but was probably done to prevent the Israelites from amassing a large chariot force from the spoils of war (see Deut 17:16; Ps 20:7; Isa 31:1). God would be their only trust.

3. The destruction of Hazor. 11:7-14.

7-9. So Joshua came . . . against them . . . suddenly. No doubt swooping down from the mountain passes, the armies of Israel employed their usual swift and surprise attack. Quickly, as He had promised, the Lord delivered the northern alliance into Joshua's hand, who chased them unto **great Zidon.** Zidon is called "great" to indicate its importance. Such designation argues strongly for the early date of Joshua. From the time of David to Alexander the Great, Tyre outstripped her rival as the great city of Phoenicia, in spite of Nebuchadnezzar's conquest (Ezk 26-27).

Misrephoth-main, meaning "burnings of waters," probably denotes either salt pits or hot springs. Joshua did all that the Lord had commanded him to do.

10-14. Joshua at that time turned back, and took Hazor. Having pursued the enemy all the way to the sea, Joshua now returned to destroy the capital of the confederacy. So complete was the destruction of Hazor that nothing that breathed was left. Joshua burned the city, something he did not do to the cities **that stood still in their strength.** This implies cities that were "heaped up," or built high mounds for defense and strength, like the castles along the Rhine.

4. The commands completed. 11:15.

15. This verse gives witness to Joshua's simple faith in God and his implicit obedience to God's commands. Some of those commands were given to Moses; nevertheless, Joshua carried out the commands as if they were his own. Joshua was a soldier and as such had learned to obey every command without question. He had learned to assume the responsibility for those commands given to his superiors, and thus Joshua **left nothing undone of all that the LORD commanded Moses.**

E. Summary of Israel's Conquests. 11:16-12:24.

1. Areas conquered by Israel. 11:16-23.

16. The conquests of Israel included the **hills,** the highlands of Judah north and south of Jerusalem, the **south country,** the Negev or dry country of the south, **Goshen,** that area which leads to Egypt, the **valley** or Shephelah, which was a piedmont area stretching from Gaza northward to Joppa, and the **plain,** or Arabah. Both mountains and valleys were captured by Israel.

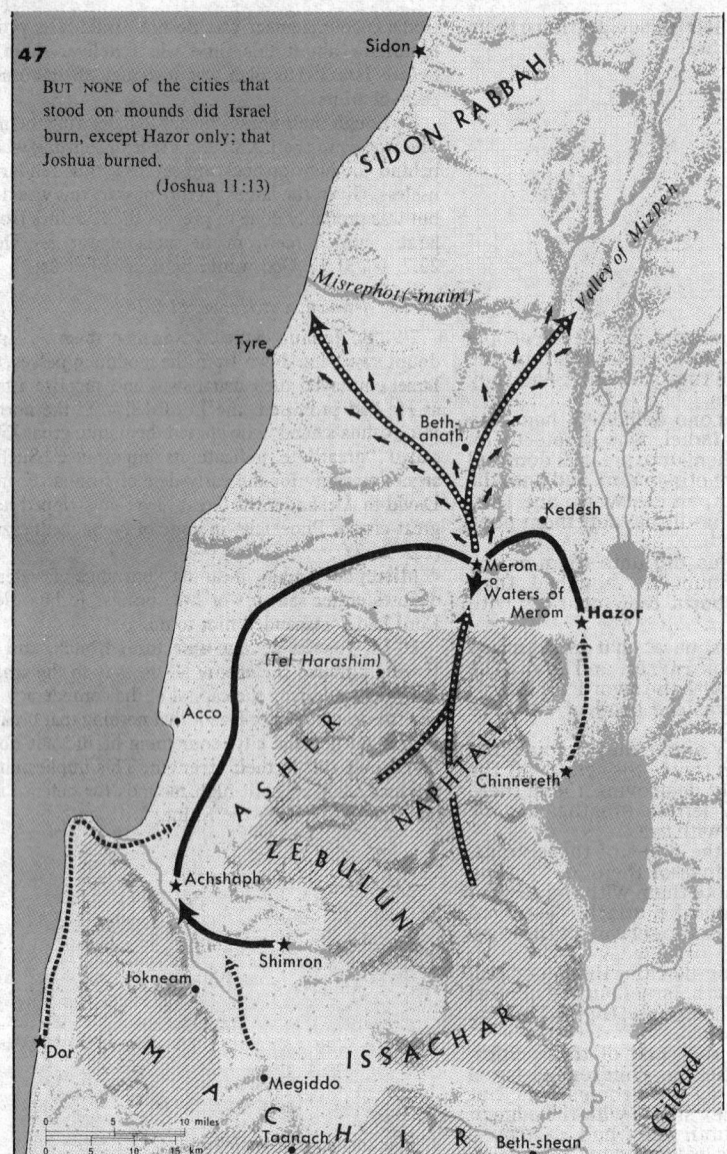

47

BUT NONE of the cities that stood on mounds did Israel burn, except Hazor only; that Joshua burned.

(Joshua 11:13)

The Battle of the Waters of Merom

17 *Even* from the mount Hā′lăk, that goeth up to Sē′ir, even unto Bā′al–gad in the valley of Lebanon under mount Hermon: and all their kings he took, and smote them, and slew them.

The Arabah is "generally any part of the geographical rift which extends from the Sea of Kinnereth (Galilee) down the course of the Jordan River to 'the Sea of the Arabah' (the Dead Sea) and beyond to the Gulf of Aqabah. . . . 'The Arabah' is sometimes used in the Old Testament to refer more specifically to that portion of the rift below the Dead Sea" (J. Maxwell Miller and Gene M. Tucker, *The Book of Joshua*, p. 186).

17. The northern areas subdued by Israel extend to **mount Halak,** the "smooth mountain that goes up to **Seir,**" the mountainous region well-known in the territory of Esau (Gen 32:3). To distinguish even further the far-reaching northern conquests is added the description **even unto Baal-gad** in the Lebanon valley at the base of **mount Hermon.** Baal-gad has been variously interpreted as Baalbek in Lebanon, Heliopolis in Syria, or Caesarea-Philippi in Israel. The exact identification of Baal-gad,

18 Joshua made war a long time with all those kings.

19 There was not a city that made peace with the children of Israel, save the Hī′vītes the inhabitants of Gĭbeon: all *other* they took in battle.

20 For it was of the LORD to harden their hearts, that they should come against Israel in battle, that he might destroy them utterly, *and* that they might have no favour, but that he might destroy them, as the LORD commanded Moses.

21 ¶And at that time came Joshua, and cut off the Anakims from the mountains, from Hēbron, from Dē′bir, from Anăb, and from all the mountains of Judah, and from all the mountains of Israel: Joshua destroyed them utterly with their cities.

22 There was none of the Anakims left in the land of the children of Israel: only in Gā′za, in Gath, and in Ăsh′dŏd, there remained.

23 So Joshua took the whole land, according to all that the LORD said unto Moses; and Joshua gave it for an inheritance unto Israel according to their divisions by their tribes. And the land rested from war.

CHAPTER 12

NOW these *are* the kings of the land, which the children of Israel smote, and possessed their land on the other side Jordan toward the rising of the sun, from the river Arnon unto mount Hermon, and all the plain on the east:

2 Sihon king of the Ămorītes, who dwelt in Hĕsh′bŏn, *and* ruled from Ar′ō-er, which *is* upon the bank of the river Arnon, and from the middle of the river, and from half Gilead, even unto the river Jabbok, *which is* the border of the children of Ammon;

3 And from the plain to the sea of Chĭn′ne-rŏth on the east, and unto the sea of the plain, *even* the salt sea on the east, the way to Bĕth–jĕsh′i-mŏth; and from the south, under Ăsh′dŏth–pĭs′gah:

4 And the coast of Og king of Bā′shan, *which was* of the remnant of the giants, that dwelt at Ăsh′ta-rŏth and at Ĕd′re-ī,

5 And reigned in mount Hermon, and in Săl′cah, and in all Bā′shan, unto the border of the Gĕsh′u-rītes, and the Mā-ăch′a-thītes, and half Gilead, the border of Sihon king of Hĕsh′bŏn.

6 Them did Moses the servant of the LORD and the children of Israel smite: and Moses the servant of the LORD gave it *for* a possession unto the Reubenites, and the Gădītes, and the half tribe of Ma-năs′seh.

7 ¶And these *are* the kings of the country which Joshua and the children of Israel smote on this side Jordan on

which means "the lord of fortune," is tenuous; but Caesarea-Philippi is most likely.

18-20. So great was the hatred for Jehovah and His people that only the Hivites made peace with Israel. All the rest made war and lost. Once again Joshua explains that even this was in the plan of God: **For it was of the LORD to harden their hearts, that they should come against Israel in battle.** Thus, the Lord God could utterly destroy the paganism that would have destroyed His people (see Introduction).

21-22. The Anakim. Literally, "the long-necked" men, these were the gigantic children of Anak (Num 13:28, 33; Josh 15:13-14). Their long-necked character may be the derivation of the German *nacken* and the English *neck*. The Hebrew word is used of the chains around camels' necks (Jud 8:26) and even of a necklace (Song 4:9). The children of Anak were subdued from the mountains and cut off from **Hebron,** from **Debir,** and from **Anab,** a town about ten miles southwest of Hebron. The only places the Anakim retained were **Gaza, Gath,** and **Ashdod** (see I Sam 17:4; II Sam 21:18-22; I Chr 20:4-8). It may be that the later Philistine "giant" of Gath was actually a descendant of the Anakim.

23. So Joshua took the whole land. The word "whole" (Heb *kal*) is meant to imply that he had established an unquestioned military presence in the land, and not that he had subdued every nook and cranny of the land. The remaining inhabitants would be expatriated by degrees. This was in the divine plan (see Jud 2:20-23). With the tremendous conquests of Joshua in the South and in the North, **the land rested from war.**

2. Kings conquered by Moses. 12:1-6.

12:1-3. Chapter 12 summarizes the victories God gave Israel both east and west of the Jordan River. Verses 1-6 list the conquests of Sihon and Og by Moses. The **Arnon** ("swift stream") flows into the Dead Sea from the east at about the center latitude of the sea. The river **Jabbok,** the present Wadi Zerka, flows from the east into the Jordan River, approximately midway between the **Sea of Chinneroth** (Sea of Galilee) and the **Salt Sea** (Dead Sea). **Ashdoth-pisgah** refers to the slopes of Pisgah, the northernmost point of the Abarim mountain range, which is east of the Dead Sea. Mount Nebo, from which Moses viewed the Promised Land, is its chief peak.

4-6. On **Ashtaroth** see 9:10. **Edrei,** "strong city," was one of many fortified cities of **Bashan.** The **Geshurites** hailed from the northeast corner of Bashan, adjacent to Syria. The territory of the **Maachathites** adjoined that of the Geshurites. All of this territory of Transjordan was presented as an inheritance to the **Reubenites, and the Gadites, and the half tribe of Manasseh.**

3. Kings conquered by Joshua. 12:7-24.

7-8. The summary of the kings defeated by the Israelites under Joshua now begins. Again the territory captured is given before the king list begins. That territory encompasses the

the west, from Bā'al–gǎd in the valley of Lebanon even unto the mount Hā'lǎk, that goeth up to Sē'ir; which Joshua gave unto the tribes of Israel *for* a possession according to their divisions;

8 In the mountains, and in the valleys, and in the plains, and in the springs, and in the wilderness, and in the south country; the Hittites, the Ā'morites, and the Canaanites, the Pēr'izzītes, the Hī'vītes, and the Jēb'u-sītes:

9 The king of Jericho, one; the king of Ā'ī, which *is* beside Bēth-el, one;

10 The king of Jerusalem, one; the king of Hēbron, one;

11 The king of Jär'mǔth, one; the king of Lā'chǐsh, one;

12 The king of Ěg'lŏn, one; the king of Gē'zer, one;

13 The king of Dē'bir, one; the king of Gē'der, one;

14 The king of Hôr'mah, one; the king of Ā'rǎd, one;

15 The king of Lǐb'nah, one; the king of Adǔllam, one;

16 The king of Mak-kē'dah, one; the king of Bēth-el, one;

17 The king of Tǎp'pū-ah, one; the king of Hē'pher, one;

18 The king of Ā'phěk, one; the king of Lǎ-shâr'on, one;

19 The king of Mā'dǒn, one; the king of Hā'zôr, one;

20 The king of Shǐm'rǒn-me'rǒn, one; the king of Ǎch'shǎph, one;

21 The king of Tā'a-nǎch, one; the king of Me-gǐd'dō, one;

22 The king of Kē'děsh, one; the king of Jǒk'ne-am of Carmel, one;

23 The king of Dor in the coast of Dor, one; the king of the nations of Gilgal, one;

24 The king of Tir'zah, one: all the kings thirty and one.

CHAPTER 13

NOW Joshua was old *and* stricken in years; and the LORD said unto him, Thou art old *and* stricken in years, and there remaineth yet very much land to be possessed.

2 This *is* the land that yet remaineth: all the borders of the Philistines, and all Gēsh'u-rī;

3 From Sī'hôr, which *is* before Egypt, even unto the borders of Ěkron northward, *which* is counted to the Canaanite: five lords of the Philistines; the Gā'zath-ītes, and the Ǎsh'dŏth-ītes, the Ěsh'ka-lon-ītes, the Gǐt'tītes, and the Ěkronītes; also the Ā'vītes:

4 From the south, all the land of the
424

whole of Canaan. It also was taken from the major ethnic nationalities.

9-24. Thirty-one cities with their kings are listed as having been taken by Joshua. Beginning with **Jericho,** other cities captured were **Hormah** and **Arad** (vs. 14), both Negev cities near the Edomite border, **Tappuah,** (vs. 17), a city near Sachoh, northwest of Samaria (I Kgs 4:10), **Lasharon** (vs. 18), the same as Sharon or Hasharon (Isa 33:9) in the plain of Sharon, **Madon** (vs. 19), near the Sea of Galilee, **Achshaph** (vs. 20), in the territory of Asher on the Mediterranean Sea, **Jokneam of Carmel** (vs. 22), on the southern slopes of Mount Carmel, and **Tirzah** (vs. 24), mentioned in I Kings as the residence of the kings of Israel for a time (14:17; 15:21, 33: 16:6; 9-10).

The most remarkable aspect of the list of conquered kings is the diversity of locations from which these kings reigned. All that territory had now been delivered into the hands of Israel, and most of it had been expunged of pagan practices. The land was truly ready for an inheritance.

III. APPORTIONMENT OF THE PROMISED LAND. 13:1-22:34.

A. The Apportionment of Transjordan. 13:1-33.

1. Survey of the apportioned land. 13:1-14.

13:1. Thou art old and stricken in years, and there remaineth yet very much land to be possessed. These words of the Lord to Joshua speak a timeless truth. Joshua was now of advanced age, and he had brought Israel well along the road to the blessing promised to them by Jacob (Gen 49) and by Moses (Deut 33). Yet, it was now Israel's responsibility to "possess" her possession, to colonize her designated territories. What was true of Israel is also true of the Christian church today. We have been around many years as an organized body of believers, but there is still much land to be possessed for the Lord Jesus. The Apostle Paul may have had this thought in mind when he chided, "Awake to righteousness, and sin not; for some have not the knowledge of God: I speak this to your shame" (I Cor 15:34).

2-3. The portions of the land which yet remained to be subdued extended across Canaan from the Philistine league in the southwest to the territory of the Geshurites in northeast Bashan. **Sihor,** which means "the black river," has been identified with the Nile; for both the Greeks and Romans knew the Nile by that title. But the phrase **which is before Egypt** would seem to preclude the Nile, as it is more centrally located in Egypt. It is more likely a reference to the Wadi el Arish which is called the "River of Egypt" (see Gen 15:18; Num 34:5, I Kgs 8:65; Isa 27:12). In these latter passages the Hebrew word *nahal* or winter torrent is used (hardly a word applicable to the Nile). From this wadi northward the cities of the Philistines had yet to be subdued.

4-6. Joshua continues to describe the land from which the

Canaanites, and Mē-â′rah that *is* beside the Si-dō′ni-anś, unto Ā′phĕk, to the borders of the Ămorītes:

5 And the land of the Gĭb′lītes, and all Lebanon, toward the sunrising, from Bā′al-găd under mount Hermon unto the entering into Hā′măth.

6 All the inhabitants of the hill country from Lebanon unto Mĭs′re-phŏth-mā′im, *and* all the Si-dō′ni-anś, them will I drive out from before the children of Israel: only divide thou it by lot unto the Israelites for an inheritance, as I have commanded thee.

7 Now therefore divide this land for an inheritance unto the nine tribes, and the half tribe of Ma-năs′seh,

8 With whom the Reubenites and the Găditēs have received their inheritance, which Moses gave them, beyond Jordan eastward, *even* as Moses the servant of the LORD gave them;

9 From Ar′ō-er, that *is* upon the bank of the river Arnon, and the city that *is* in the midst of the river, and all the plain of Mĕd′e-ba unto Dī′bŏn;

10 And all the cities of Sihon king of the Ămorītes, which reigned in Hĕsh′-bŏn, unto the border of the children of Ammon;

11 And Gilead, and the border of the Gĕsh′u-rītes and Mā-ăch′a-thītes, and all mount Hermon, and all Bā′shan unto Săl′cah;

12 All the kingdom of Og in Bā′shan, which reigned in Ăsh′ta-rŏth and in Ĕd′re-ī, who remained of the remnant of the giants: for these did Moses smite, and cast them out.

13 Nevertheless the children of Israel expelled not the Gĕsh′u-rītes, nor the Mā-ăch′a-thītes: but the Gĕsh′u-rītes and the Mā-ăch′a-thītes dwell among the Israelites until this day.

14 Only unto the tribe of Levi he gave none inheritance; the sacrifices of the LORD God of Israel made by fire *are* their inheritance, as he said unto them.

15 ¶And Moses gave unto the tribe of the children of Reuben *inheritance* according to their families.

16 And their coast was from Ar′ō-er, that *is* on the bank of the river Arnon, and the city that *is* in the midst of the river, and all the plain by Mĕd′e-ba;

17 Hĕsh′bŏn, and all her cities that *are* in the plain; Dī′bŏn, and Bā′-mŏth-bā′al, and Bĕth-bā′al-me′ŏn,

18 And Ja-hā′za, and Kĕd′e-mŏth, and Mĕph′a-ăth,

19 And Kĭr-jath-ā′īm, and Sĭb′mah, and Zā′reth-shā′har in the mount of the valley,

20 And Bĕth-pē′ôr, and Ăsh′-dŏth-pĭs′gah, and Bĕth-jĕsh′i-mŏth,

21 And all the cities of the plain, and all the kingdom of Sihon king of the Amorites, which reigned in Hĕsh′bŏn, whom Moses smote with the princes of Mĭd′ī-an, Ē′vī, and Rĕ′kem, and Zur, and Hur, and Rĕ′ba, *which were* dukes of Sihon, dwelling in the country.

22 ¶Bā′laam also the son of Bĕ′ôr, the soothsayer, did the children of Israel slay with the sword among them that were slain by them.

23 And the border of the children of

Lord would drive out the inhabitants, including the land of the **Canaanites, and Mearah** ("cave"). This is probably to be identified with the village of Mogheiriyeh, north of Sidon, which is called "the village of the cave." Also unsubdued was the **entering into Hamath,** a frequent way of referring to the northern border of Israel (I Kgs 8:65; II Kgs 14:25). Even though these areas were not yet secured from the inhabitants of the land, they should nevertheless be apportioned to the Israelites because God had promised to drive out the inhabitants; and what God promises He performs.

7-8. Thus, the command comes to divide the land among the nine and one-half tribes, for the **Reubenites and Gadites** have already received their inheritance from the Transjordan land taken by Moses. See G. E. Wright and F. M. Cross, Jr., "The Boundary and Province Lists of the Kingdom of Judah," *JBL* LXXV (1956).

9-13. This Transjordan land is comprised of the kingdoms of Sihon and Og, from the **plain of Medeba unto Dibon** (see Num 21:30; Isa 15:2). Now called Dhiban, it was here that the Moabite Stone, which mentions the occupation of Medeba by Israel's king Omri, until his overthrow by the Moabite king Mesha, was found in 1868. From these cities in the South, to **Gilead . . . and all Bashan** in the North, were drawn the inheritances of the two and one-half tribes.

14. Only unto the tribe of Levi he gave none inheritance. See Numbers 18:20-24 where this original command is recorded.

2. Portion to the Reubenites. 13:15-23.

15-23. Specifically, the inheritance given to the Reubenites included **Aroer** (12:2), **Heshbon** (modern Hisban), **Bamoth-baal,** "the high places of Baal," **Shibmah** (see Num 32:38), close by Heshbon, and **Zareth-shahar** meaning "splendor of the dawn," located on the Dead Sea. In short, the tribe of Reuben received all the cities of the southern plain that once belonged to **Sihon king of the Amorites.** This included the land once possessed by **Balaam . . . the soothsayer,** or diviner, who pretended to be able to tell future events (see Num 22-24).

Reuben was Jordan, and the border *thereof.* This *was* the inheritance of the children of Reuben after their families, the cities and the villages thereof.

24 ¶And Moses gave *inheritance* unto the tribe of Gad, *even* unto the children of Gad according to their families.

25 And their coast was Jā′zer, and all the cities of Gilead, and half the land of the children of Ammon, unto Ar′ō-er that *is* before Răb′bah;

26 And from Hěsh′bŏn unto Rā-math–mĭz′peh, and Bět′o-nĭm; and from Mā-ha-nā′im unto the border of Dě′bir;

27 And in the valley, Běth–a′râm, and Běth–nĭm′rah, and Sŭc′coth, and Zā′phŏn, the rest of the kingdom of Si-hon king of Hěsh′bŏn, Jordan and *his* border, *even* unto the edge of the sea of Chĭn′ne-rěth on the other side Jordan eastward.

28 This *is* the inheritance of the children of Gad after their families, the cities, and their villages.

29 ¶And Moses gave *inheritance* unto the half tribe of Ma-năs′seh: and *this* was *the possession* of the half tribe of the children of Ma-năs′seh by their families.

30 And their coast was from Mā-ha-nā′im, all Bā′shan, all the kingdom of Og king of Bā′shan, and all the towns of Jā′ir, which *are* in Bā′shan, threescore cities;

31 And half Gilead, and Ăsh′ta-rŏth, and Ĕd′re-ī, cities of the kingdom of Og in Bā′shan, *were pertaining* unto the children of Mā′chĭr the son of Ma′năs′-seh, *even* to the one half of the children of Mā′chĭr by their families.

32 These *are the countries* which Moses did distribute for inheritance in the plains of Moab, on the other side Jordan, by Jericho, eastward.

33 But unto the tribe of Levi Moses gave not *any* inheritance: the LORD God of Israel *was* their inheritance, as he said unto them.

CHAPTER 14

AND these *are the countries* which the children of Israel inherited in the land of Canaan, which Ē-le-ā′zar the priest, and Joshua the son of Nun, and the heads of the fathers of the tribes of the children of Israel, distributed for inheritance to them.

2 By lot *was* their inheritance, as the LORD commanded by the hand of Moses, for the nine tribes, and *for* the half tribe.

3 For Moses had given the inheritance of two tribes and an half tribe on the other side Jordan: but unto the Lĕ′vītes he gave none inheritance among them.

4 For the children of Joseph were two tribes, Ma-năs′seh and Ē′phra-im: therefore they gave no part unto the Lĕ-vītes in the land, save cities to dwell *in,* with their suburbs for their cattle and for their substance.

5 As the LORD commanded Moses, so the children of Israel did, and they divided the land.

6 ¶Then the children of Jŭdah came unto Joshua in Gilgal: and Caleb the son of Je-phŭn′neh the Kĕn′ez-īte said

426

3. *Portion to the Gadites. 13:24-28.*

24-28. Moses gave to the tribe of Gad **all the cities of Gilead** (Deut 3:12) from the border of **Jazer . . . unto Aroer that is before Rabbah.** This is obviously a different Aroer from that mentioned in verse 9. Also included is the area between **Heshbon** and the border of **Debir,** specifically **Succoth** ("booths"), where Jacob rested after meeting with Esau (Gen 33:17). The western boundary was the Jordan River.

4. *Portion to the half tribe of Manasseh. 13:29-33.*

29-33. To half the tribe of Manasseh went **all the kingdom of Og** and all the towns of **Jair** (lit., Havoth-jair, as in Num 32:41 and Deut 3:14). The number of these towns is sixty. Also, to the children of **Machir,** the son of Manasseh, went one-half of **Gilead** (see further 17:5-6).

Thus was the allotment made by Moses **in the plains of Moab** east of Jericho, in Transjordan. What was promised before the conquest of the land would now be fulfilled completely.

B. The Apportionment of Canaan. 14:1-19:51.

1. *Portion to Caleb. 14:1-15.*

14:1-5. By lot was their inheritance, as the LORD commanded. In a show of national unity **Eleazar the priest, and Joshua** (the heads of church and state, so to speak) began the task of apportioning the land. The inheritance was determined by **lot** (Heb *gōral,* meaning a small pebble) but was in no way done by mere caprice. Lots were frequently used to determine the will of God (see the choice of Saul as king, I Sam 10:19-21; and choice of Matthias as apostle, Acts 1:26) because they assured that no personal ambition or external pressure would decide the outcome. The sovereignty of God alone would prevail, and they would trust that "The lot is cast into the lap; but the whole disposing thereof is of the LORD" (Prov 16:33).

6-12. Caleb, the son of Jephunneh the Kenezite was the one-time spy partner of Joshua (cf. Num 13:26-33). These two godly men brought back the unpopular, yet proper, report that

unto him, Thou knowest the thing that the LORD said unto Moses the man of God concerning me and thee in Kā′-desh–bär′ne-a.

7 Forty years old *was* I when Moses the servant of the LORD sent me from Kā′desh–bär′ne-a to espy out the land; and I brought him word again as *it was* in mine heart.

8 Nevertheless my brethren that went up with me made the heart of the people melt: but I wholly followed the LORD my God.

9 And Moses sware on that day, saying, Surely the land whereon thy feet have trodden shall be thine inheritance, and thy children's for ever, because thou hast wholly followed the LORD my God.

10 And now, behold, the LORD hath kept me alive, as he said, these forty and five years, even since the LORD spake this word unto Moses, while *the children of* Israel wandered in the wilderness: and now, lo, I *am* this day fourscore and five years old.

11 As yet I *am as* strong this day as *I was* in the day that Moses sent me: as my strength *was* then, even so *is* my strength now, for war, both to go out, and to come in.

12 Now therefore give me this mountain, whereof the LORD spake in that day; for thou heardest in that day how the Anakims *were* there, and *that* the cities *were* great *and* fenced: if so be the LORD *will be* with me, then I shall be able to drive them out, as the LORD said.

13 And Joshua blessed him, and gave unto Caleb the son of Je-phŭn′neh Hē-bron for an inheritance.

14 Hēbron therefore became the inheritance of Caleb the son of Je-phŭn′-neh the Kĕn′ez-īte unto this day, because that he wholly followed the LORD God of Israel.

15 And the name of Hēbron before *was* Kir′jath–är′ba; *which Ar′ba was* a great man among the Anakims. And the land had rest from war.

CHAPTER 15

THIS then was the lot of the tribe of the children of Jūdah by their families; *even* to the border of Ēdom the wilderness of Zin southward *was* the uttermost part of the south coast.

2 And their south border was from the shore of the salt sea, from the bay that looketh southward:

3 And it went out to the south side to Mā-al′eh-ă-cräb′bĭm, and passed along to Zin, and ascended up on the south side unto Kā′desh–bär′ne-a, and passed along to Hēz′ron, and went up to Ā′där, and fetched a compass to Kär′ka-a:

4 From *thence* it passed toward Āz′mon, and went out unto the river of Egypt; and the goings out of that coast were at the sea: this shall be your south coast.

5 And the east border *was* the salt sea, *even* unto the end of Jordan. And *their* border in the north quarter *was* from the bay of the sea at the uttermost part of Jordan:

Israel should invade the Promised Land immediately from **Kadesh-barnea.** Because of Caleb's faithfulness to the Lord, Moses swore that day saying, **Surely the land whereon thy feet have trodden shall be thine inheritance;** and now, forty-five years later, the day had come. Even though Caleb was eighty-five years old, he was yet as strong and capable of being a soldier as on the day this promise was made. He could boldly claim his inheritance, saying **give me this mountain.**

Caleb's statements give a definite clue to the time lapse in the conquest of the land. If forty-five years had passed since Caleb received the promise of an inheritance (vs. 10) and that promise was given to him thirty-eight years before the crossing of the Jordan (cf. Num 14:24), then the actual time of the conquest was approximately seven years. Josephus apparently rounds this number off to five years (*Antiq.* V:1:19). For further discussion see Keil and Delitzsch, pp. 149-150.

13-15. And Joshua blessed him, and gave unto Caleb . . . . Hebron for an inheritance. The importance of Hebron as an inheritance cannot be minimized. It was at one time known as **Kirjath** ("the city of") **-arba,** named after Arba, a giant of the **Anakim.** But, more importantly, it was the burial site of the Patriarchs: Abraham (Gen 25:7-10; cf. 23:19), Isaac (Gen 35:27-29), and Jacob (Gen 50:12-13). The tradition of the rabbis, followed by the Vulgate and Wycliffe translations, makes a **great man** (lit., "the greatest man") to be Adam, adding his name to the list buried at Hebron. Thus, it can easily be seen why Caleb would request this village as his inheritance.

2. Portion to Judah. 15:1-63.

15:1-12. The first twelve verses of this chapter define the boundaries of Judah's inheritance. The description begins with the **wilderness of Zin** (not to be confused with the wilderness of Sin, see Ex 16:1; cf. Num 34:11, 36) on the south at the border of Moab, **from the bay** (Heb *lashōn,* lit., the "tongue") of the **Salt Sea** (Dead Sea) at the peninsula that cuts off the lower end of the sea from the upper end. From here the boundary winds southward toward "the ascent of Acrabbim" (the literal rendering of **Maaleh-acrabbim** is "the rise of the scorpion," a creature found in abundance in this area) and continues southwest toward **Kadesh-barnea** and deflects in the direction of **Karkaa.** Here it turns westward toward **the river of Egypt** (Wadi el Arish) and to the sea. This was the southern and western border.

The eastern border begins where the Jordan River empties into the Dead Sea, continues to **Beth-hogla** (vs. 6), meaning "the house of the partridge," north of "the house of Arabah," i.e., **Beth-arabah,** to **the stone of Bohan the son of Reuben,** west of Beth-arabah. Ascending from the **valley of Achor** past **Debir** (not the Debir of ch. 10) the boundary reached the waters of **En-shemesh,** near Bethany, which empty into the water source of Jerusalem, **En-rogel** (where Jonathan and Ahimaaz

6 And the border went up to
Bĕth-hŏg′la, and passed along by the
north of Bĕth-ăr′a-bah; and the border
went up to the stone of Bō′hăn the son
of Reuben:

7 And the border went up toward
Dē′bir from the valley of Ā′chŏr, and so
northward, looking toward Gilgal, that
is before the going up to A-dŭm′mĭm,
which is on the south side of the river:
and the border passed toward the waters of Ĕn-shĕ′-mesh, and the goings
out thereof were at Ĕn-rō′gel:

8 And the border went up by the valley of the son of Hĭn′nom unto the
south side of the Jĕb′u-sīte; the same is
Jerusalem: and the border went up to
the top of the mountain that lieth before the valley of Hĭn′nom westward,
which is at the end of the valley of the
giants northward:

9 And the border was drawn from the
top of the hill unto the fountain of the
water of Nĕph′tō-ah, and went out to
the cities of mount Ē′phron; and the
border was drawn to Bā′al-ah, which is
Kir′jath-jĕ′a-rĭm:

10 And the border compassed from
Bā′al-ah westward unto mount Sē′ir,
and passed along unto the side of
mount Jĕ′a-rĭm, which is Chĕs′a-lŏn, on
the north side, and went down to
Bĕth-shĕ′mesh, and passed on to Tĭm′-
nah:

11 And the border went out unto the
side of Ekron northward: and the border was drawn to Shĭ′crŏn, and passed
along to mount Bā′al-ah, and went out
unto Jăb′ne-el: and the goings out of
the border were at the sea.

12 And the west border was to the
great sea, and the coast thereof. This is
the coast of the children of Jūdah round
about according to their families.

13 ¶And unto Caleb the son of Je-
phŭn′neh he gave a part among the
children of Jūdah, according to the
commandment of the LORD to Joshua,
even the city of Ārba the father of
Anak, which city is Hēbron.

14 And Caleb drove thence the three
sons of Anak, Shĕ′shaī, and A-hī′man,
and Tăl′maī, the children of Anak.

15 And he went up thence to the
inhabitants of Dē′bir: and the name of
Dē′bir before was Kir′jath-sē′pher.

16 And Caleb said, He that smiteth
Kir′jath-sē′pher, and taketh it, to him
will I give Āch′sah my daughter to wife.

17 And Oth′nī-el the son of Kĕ′năz,
the brother of Caleb, took it: and he
gave him Āch′sah his daughter to wife.

18 And it came to pass, as she came
unto him, that she moved him to ask of
her father a field: and she lighted off
her ass; and Caleb said unto her, What
wouldest thou?

19 Who answered, Give me a blessing; for thou hast given me a south
land; give me also springs of water.
And he gave her the upper springs, and
the nether springs.

20 This is the inheritance of the tribe
of the children of Jūdah according to
their families.

21 ¶And the uttermost cities of the
tribe of the children of Jūdah toward

gained news from David). From here the border went up the
valley of Hinnom, south of Jerusalem, where Israelite children
would one day be sacrificed to Chemish or Molech (II Kgs 16:3;
II Chr 2:3; Jer 7:31-32; 19:2, 4). Around the south of Jerusalem
(this city was itself the inheritance of Benjamin) toward Kirjath-
jearim, west of Jerusalem, the boundary again deflected at
Baalah westward toward mount Seir, not the dwelling place of
Esau (Gen 32:3) but a mountain range running southwest from
Kirjath-jearim, toward Beth-shemesh, "the house of the sun,"
and Timnah, also called Timnath (Jud 14:1-6) and Timnatha
(14:43). At Ekron, the Philistine city, the territory of Judah
turned northward to Jabneel and ended at the Great Sea
(Mediterranean), which was the west border.

13-19. Verse 13 repeats the information given in chapter 14.
In verses 14 and 15 it is recorded that Caleb drove from his
inheritance the children of Anak and continued to Debir,
formerly called Kirjath-sepher. Upon reaching this town, Caleb
issued a challenge to anyone who could conquer Kirjath-sepher.
The prize was to be the hand of his daughter Achsah in marriage. Possibly to Caleb's surprise, Othniel, a brave and capable
warrior (Jud 3:9), and also the nephew of Caleb, captured the
town and received Achsah in marriage. The new bride met her
father in a field, alighted from her donkey, and pleaded, Give
me a blessing. The blessing was more than a dowry, for Caleb
had already given Othniel and Achsah land. But the land was in
the south (Heb negeb, the Negev), and it was barren of water.
Her real request was, give me also springs of water. A reasonable request. Her father responded by giving the couple several
springs at various levels in Debir. "Your Father knoweth what
things ye have need of, before ye ask him" (Mt 6:8).

20-62. The rest of the inheritance of the tribe of Judah is
described with reference to geographical location: (1) The
Negev, including thirty-six cities (the rendering twenty and
nine goes back to the LXX, but the number is thirty-six); (2) the
Shephelah, consisting of three groups of cities of fourteen or

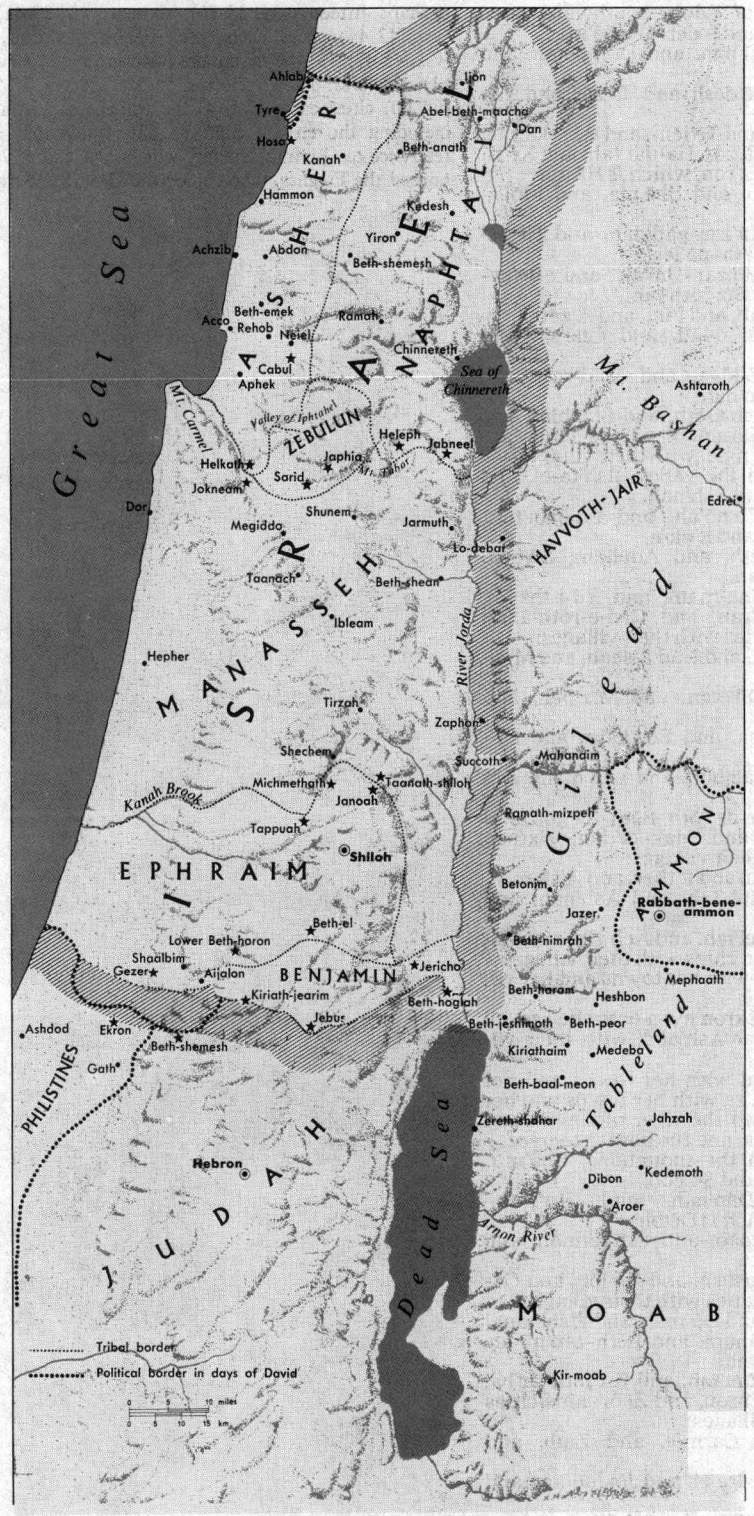

The Borders of the Tribal Territories

the coast of Ēdom southward were Kăb′ze-el, and Ē′der, and Jā′gur,

22 And Kĭ′nah, and Dī-mō′nah, and Ăd′a-dah,

23 And Kē′dĕsh, and Hā′zôr, and Ĭth′năn,

24 Ziph, and Tē′lĕm, and Bē′a-lŏth,

25 And Hā′zôr, Ha-dăt′tah, and Kē′rĭ-ŏth, *and* Hĕz′ron, which *is* Hā′zôr,

26 Ā′măm, and Shē′ma, and Mŏl′a-dah,

27 And Hā′zar-găd′dah, and Hĕsh′-mŏn, and Bĕth–pā′let,

28 And Hā′zar-shū′al, and Be′er-shē′ba, and Bĭz-jŏth′jah,

29 Bā′al-ah, and Ī′im, and Ā′zem,

30 And Ĕl′tō-lăd, and Chē′sil, and Hôr′mah,

31 And Ziklag, and Măd-măn′nah, and Săn-săn′nah.

32 And Leb′ā-ŏth, and Shĭl′hĭm, and Ā′ĭn, and Rimmon: all the cities *are* twenty and nine, with their villages.

33 *And* in the valley, Ĕsh′ta-ol, and Zō′rē-ah, and Ăsh′nah,

34 And Za′nō′ah, and Ĕn-găn′nĭm, Tăp′pū-ah, and Ē′nam,

35 Jär′mūth, and Adŭllam, Sō′cōh, and A-zē′kah,

36 And Sha-rā′im, and Ăd-i-thā′im, and Ge-de′rah, and Ged-e-roth-ā′ĭm; fourteen cities with their villages:

37 Zē′nan, and Had′ă-shah, and Mĭg′-dal–găd,

38 And Dĭl′e-an, and Mĭz′peh, and Jŏk′the-el,

39 Lā′chĭsh, and Bŏz′kăth, and Ĕg′-lŏn,

40 And Căb′bon, and Läh′măm, and Kĭth′lĭsh,

41 And Ge-de′rŏth, Bĕth–dā′gon, and Nā′a-mah, and Mak-kē′dah; sixteen cities with their villages:

42 Lĭb′nah, and Ē′ther, and Ā′shan,

43 And Jĭph′tah, and Ăsh′nah, and Nĕ′zĭb,

44 And Keī′lah, and Ăch′zĭb, and Ma-rē′shah; nine cities with their villages:

45 Ēkron, with her towns and her villages:

46 From Ēkron even unto the sea, all that *lay* near Ăsh′dŏd, with their villages:

47 Ăsh′dŏd with her towns and her villages, Gā′za with her towns and her villages, unto the river of Egypt, and the great sea, and the border *thereof:*

48 And in the mountains, Shā′mir, and Jăt′tir, and Sō′cōh,

49 And Dăn′nah, and Kir′jath-săn′nah, which *is* Dē′bir,

50 And Anăb, and Ēsh′te-mōh, and Ā′nĭm,

51 And Goshen, and Hō′lŏn, and Gī′-lōh; eleven cities with their villages:

52 Arab, and Dū′mah, and Ē′she-an,

53 And Jānum, and Bĕth-tăp′pū-ah, and A-phē′kah,

54 And Hŭm′tah, and Kir′jath–är′ba, which *is* Hĕbron, and Zī′ôr; nine cities with their villages:

55 Mā′on, Carmel, and Ziph, and Jŭt′tah,

56 And Jĕz′re-el, and Jŏk′de-am, and Za-nō′ah,

57 Cain, Gĭb′e-ah, and Tĭm′nah; ten cities with their villages:

58 Hăl′hŭl, Bĕth′–zûr, and Gē′dôr,

perhaps fifteen (vss. 33-36), sixteen (vss. 32-41), and nine (vss. 42-44) cities each, plus **Ekron, Ashdod,** and **Gaza** (vss. 45-47); (3) the mountains, five groups of eleven (vss. 48-51), nine (vss. 51-54), ten (vss. 55-57), six (vss. 58-59), and two (vs. 60) cities each; and (4) the wilderness, listing six cities, including the **city of Salt** (vs. 62), which may be an early reference to Qumran, the city which later and at various times housed the Essenes, who copied the Dead Sea Scrolls.

59 And Mā'a-răth, and Bĕth-ā'nŏth, and Ĕl'te-kŏn; six cities with their villages:

60 Kir'jath-bā'al, which *is* Kir'jath-jĕ'a-rĭm, and Răb'bah; two cities with their villages:

61 In the wilderness, Bĕth-ăr'a-bah, Mĭd'din, and Sec'ā-cah,

62 And Nĭb'shăn, and the city of Salt, and Ĕn-gĕ'dĭ; six cities with their villages.

63 ¶As for the Jĕb'u-sītes the inhabitants of Jerusalem, the children of Jūdah could not drive them out: but the Jĕb'u-sītes dwell with the children of Jūdah at Jerusalem unto this day.

63. As for . . . the inhabitants of Jerusalem, the children of Judah could not drive them out. Apparently, according to Judges 1:8, 21 and II Samuel 5:6, the Israelites set fire to the lower city of Jerusalem, but the Jebusites maintained the stronghold of Zion. The strategic location of Jerusalem (described by the psalmist as "beautiful for situation," Ps 48:2) made it difficult to conquer. **Unto this day** is striking evidence that this book was written prior to David, who conquered the Jebusite city and made it Israel's capital (II Sam 5:6-10).

3. Portion to Ephraim. 16:1-10.

16:1-4. The portion of the inheritance which fell to the children of Joseph was bounded by the **Jordan** River on the east, northward through the hill country of **mount Beth-el** to the borders of the **Archi**, or the Archite (II Sam 15:32; 16:16; I Chr 27:33), and **Japhleti**, or the Japhlethite. Then the boundary followed the sea southward to the area of **Beth-horon** and **Gezer**. Essentially, the portion of Ephraim and one-half tribe of Manasseh was bounded by the sea on the west, the Jordan on the east, the territories of Dan and Benjamin on the south and the Jezreel Valley on the north.

CHAPTER 16

AND the lot of the children of Joseph fell from Jordan by Jericho, unto the water of Jericho on the east, to the wilderness that goeth up from Jericho throughout mount Bĕth-el,

2 And goeth out from Bĕth-el to Luz, and passeth along unto the borders of Ăr'chī to Ăt'a-rŏth,

3 And goeth down westward to the coast of Jăph-le'tī, unto the coast of Bĕth-hô'ron the nether, and to Gē'zer; and the goings out thereof are at the sea.

4 So the children of Joseph, Ma-năs'-seh and Ē'phra-im, took their inheritance.

5 ¶And the border of the children of Ē'phra-im according to their families was *thus:* even the border of their inheritance on the east side was Ăt'-a-rŏth-ăd'dar, unto Bĕth-hô'ron the upper;

6 And the border went out toward the sea to Mĭch'me-thah on the north side; and the border went about eastward unto Tā'a-năth-shī'lŏh, and passed by it on the east to Ja-nō'hah;

7 And it went down from Ja-nō'hah to Ăt'a-rŏth, and to Nā'a-răth, and came to Jericho, and went out at Jordan.

8 The border went out from Tăp'pū-ah westward unto the river Kā'nah; and the goings out thereof were at the sea. This *is* the inheritance of the tribe of the children of Ē'phra-im by their families.

9 And the separate cities for the children of Ē'phra-im *were* among the inheritance of the children of Ma-năs'-seh, all the cities with their villages.

10 And they drave not out the Canaanites that dwelt in Gē'zer: but the Canaanites dwell among the Ē'phra-im-ītes unto this day, and serve under tribute.

5-9. Particularly, **the border of the children of Ephraim** is most difficult to follow. It runs from **Ataroth-addar** toward **Beth-horon on the upper** westward to **Michmethah** on the Mediterranean. From there the boundary went eastward, or deflected eastward, unto **Taanath-shiloh** and down from **Ataroth**, skirting **Jericho** to the Jordan River. The border between the territories of Ephraim and Manasseh was the **river Kanah**. A few cities were assigned to Ephraim, but were actually in the territory of Manasseh.

10. And they drove not out the Canaanites but caused them to **serve under tribute.** Perhaps tired of war, the Ephraimites lost heart in ridding **Gezer** of the pagans. In fact, Gezer did not come under full Israelite control until the time of Solomon (I Kgs 9:16). Ephraim took the current "easy way out" of collecting **tribute** from the Canaanites, but the easy way is rarely the right way. This action came back to haunt them.

4. Portion to Manasseh. 17:1-18.

17:1-11. The boundaries of Manasseh's western land ran thus. **Asher** is not the tribe of Asher but a town, Yasir, north of Nablus in present-day Israel. From here the border proceeded

CHAPTER 17

THERE was also a lot for the tribe of Ma-năs'seh; for he *was* the firstborn of Joseph; *to wit,* for Mā'chĭr the firstborn of Ma-năs'seh, the father of Gilead: because he was a man of war, therefore he had Gilead and Bā'shan.

2 There was also *a lot* for the rest of the children of Ma-năs'seh by their families; for the children of Ă-bĭ-ē'zer, and for the children of Hē'lĕk, and for the children of Ăs'rĭ-el, and for the children of Shĕ'chem, and for the children of Hē'pher, and for the children of She-mi'da: these *were* the male children of Ma-năs'seh the son of Joseph by their families.

3 ¶But Ze-lō'phe-hăd, the son of Hē'pher, the son of Gilead, the son of Mā'chĭr, the son of Ma-năs'seh, had no sons, but daughters: and these *are* the names of his daughters, Măh'lah, and Noah, Hŏg'lah, Mĭl'cah, and Tir'zah.

4 And they came near before Ē-le-ā'-zar the priest, and before Joshua the son of Nun, and before the princes, saying, The LORD commanded Moses to give us an inheritance among our brethren. Therefore according to the commandment of the LORD he gave them an inheritance among the brethren of their father.

5 And there fell ten portions to Ma-năs'seh, beside the land of Gilead and Bā'shan, which *were* on the other side Jordan;

6 Because the daughters of Ma-năs'seh had an inheritance among his sons: and the rest of Ma-năs'seh's sons had the land of Gilead.

7 ¶And the coast of Ma-năs'seh was from Asher to Mĭch'me-thah, that *lieth* before Shĕ'chem; and the border went along on the right hand unto the inhabitants of Ĕn-tăp'pū-ah.

8 *Now* Ma-năs'seh had the land of Tăp'pū-ah: but Tăp'pū-ah on the border of Ma-năs'seh *belonged* to the children of Ē'phra-im;

9 And the coast descended unto the river Kā'nah, southward of the river: these cities of Ē'phra-im *are* among the cities of Ma-năs'seh: the coast of Ma-năs'seh also *was* on the north side of the river, and the outgoings of it were at the sea:

10 Southward *it was* Ē'phra-im's, and northward *it was* Ma-năs'seh's, and the sea is his border; and they met together in Asher on the north, and in Ĭs'sa-char on the east.

11 And Ma-năs'seh had in Ĭs'sa-char and in Asher Bĕth–shĕ'an and her towns, and Ĭb'le-am and her towns, and the inhabitants of Dor and her towns, and the inhabitants of Ĕn–dôr and her towns, and the inhabitants of Tā'a-năch and her towns, and the inhabitants of Me-gĭd'dō and her towns, *even* three countries.

12 Yet the children of Ma-năs'seh could not drive out *the inhabitants of* those cities; but the Canaanites would dwell in that land.

13 Yet it came to pass, when the children of Israel were waxen strong, that they put the Canaanites to tribute, but did not utterly drive them out.

14 ¶And the children of Joseph spake unto Joshua, saying, Why hast thou given me *but* one lot and one portion to

to **Michmethah** near **Shechem,** now known as Nablus, and to the land of **Tappuah** (see 12:17), from which it descended to the river **Kanah,** the boundary between Ephraim and Manasseh. South of the river was Ephraim's territory; north was Manasseh's. Also included in Manasseh's territory were the famous towns of Issachar and Asher known as **Beth-shean** (a "noble city," according to Eusebius and Jerome), **Ibleam** (near Megiddo, see II Kgs 9:27), **Dor** (on the Mediterranean coast), **En-dor** (see I Sam 28:7-20), **Taanach,** and **Megiddo** (frequently mentioned together, see 12:21; Jud 1:27; 5:19), which were fortified guardians of the *Via Maris*.

12-13. The same tragic mistake made by the Ephraimites (see 16:10) is now recorded of the Manassites. They opted wrongly to force the peoples of their land into forced labor rather than **drive out the inhabitants of those cities.**

14-18. Seeing I am a great people. Upon receiving their inheritance, the descendants of Joseph complained that it was not enough. The Ephraimites were notorious complainers (see

inherit, seeing I *am* a great people, forasmuch as the LORD hath blessed me hitherto?

15 And Joshua answered them, If thou *be* a great people, *then* get thee up to the wood *country*, and cut down for thyself there in the land of the Pĕr'izzītes and of the giants, if mount E'phra-im be too narrow for thee.

16 And the children of Joseph said, The hill is not enough for us: and all the Canaanites that dwell in the land of the valley have chariots of iron, *both they* who *are* of Bĕth-shē'an and her towns, and *they* who *are* of the valley of Jĕz're-el.

17 And Joshua spake unto the house of Joseph, *even* to E'phra-im and to Ma-nă̆s'seh, saying, Thou *art* a great people, and hast great power: thou shalt not have one lot *only:*

18 But the mountain shall be thine; for it *is* a wood, and thou shalt cut it down: and the outgoings of it shall be thine: for thou shalt drive out the Canaanites, though they have iron chariots, *and* though they *be* strong.

CHAPTER 18

AND the whole congregation of the children of Israel assembled together at Shī'lōh, and set up the tabernacle of the congregation there. And the land was subdued before them.

2 And there remained among the children of Israel seven tribes, which had not yet received their inheritance.

3 And Joshua said unto the children of Israel, How long *are* ye slack to go to possess the land, which the LORD God of your fathers hath given you?

4 Give out from among you three men for *each* tribe: and I will send them, and they shall rise, and go through the land, and describe it according to the inheritance of them; and they shall come *again* to me.

5 And they shall divide it into seven parts: Jūdah shall abide in their coast on the south, and the house of Joseph shall abide in their coasts on the north.

6 Ye shall therefore describe the land *into* seven parts, and bring *the description* hither to me, that I may cast lots for you here before the LORD our God.

7 But the Lēvītes have no part among you; for the priesthood of the LORD *is* their inheritance: and Gad, and Reuben, and half the tribe of Ma-nă̆s'seh, have received their inheritance beyond Jordan on the east, which Moses the servant of the LORD gave them.

8 ¶And the men arose, and went away: and Joshua charged them that went to describe the land, saying, Go and walk through the land, and describe it, and come again to me, that I may here cast lots for you before the LORD in Shī'lōh.

9 And the men went and passed through the land, and described it by cities into seven parts in a book, and

also Jud 8:1-3; 12:1-6). At the census of Numbers 1 the tribe of Joseph outnumbered all but the tribe of Judah. At the census taken in the plains of Moab (Num 26) they outnumbered all the other tribes. Joshua chided them not to complain, but to **get thee up to the wood country, and cut down . . . if mount Ephraim be too narrow for thee.** Joshua's sarcasm was directed at those who wanted their inheritance simply handed to them, those who would not work for it. Their complaint that the Canaanites who dwell in the valley have **chariots of iron** apparently fell on deaf ears. Joshua simply encouraged them that they indeed were a great people and would not just have one portion **But the mountain shall be thine.** All they had to do was clear the forest and **drive out the Canaanites.**

5. Portion to the rest commanded. 18:1-10.

18:1. And the whole congregation . . . assembled together at Shiloh. The text does not tell who called for this assembly, but the whole congregation (LXX, *sunagoge*) closed ranks in a show of national and religious unity at the tabernacle. This is similar to the "of one accord" expressions in Acts (2:1, 46, etc.) where the church assembled in a spirit of unity. Having moved the administrative affairs of Israel to Shiloh, this town was to become the center of Israelite political and religious life for the next three hundred years.

2-10. Now Joshua accuses the Israelites, and rightly so, of being **slack to go to possess the land.** How frequently God's people give up just before victory. To prod Israel into possessing her inheritance, Joshua commanded that a twenty-one-man task force be formed, **three men for each tribe,** and that these men bring back a written report in seven parts indicating a fair distribution of the remaining land among the remaining tribes. Then, in order to decide which tribe would be awarded which portion of land, **Joshua cast lots for them in Shiloh before the LORD.**

came *again* to Joshua to the host at Shī′lōh.

10 And Joshua cast lots for them in Shī′lōh before the LORD: and there Joshua divided the land unto the children of Israel according to their divisions.

11 ¶And the lot of the tribe of the children of Benjamin came up according to their families: and the coast of their lot came forth between the children of Jū́dah and the children of Joseph.

12 And their border on the north side was from Jordan; and the border went up to the side of Jericho on the north side, and went up through the mountains westward; and the goings out thereof were at the wilderness of Bĕth-ā′ven.

13 And the border went over from thence toward Luz, to the side of Luz, which *is* Bĕth-el, southward; and the border descended to Ăt′a-rŏth-ā′dar, near the hill that *lieth* on the south side of the nether Bĕth-hō′ron.

14 And the border was drawn *thence,* and compassed the corner of the sea southward, from the hill that *lieth* before Bĕth-hō′ron southward; and the goings out thereof were at Kir′jath-bā′al, which *is* Kir′jath-jē′a-rĭm, a city of the children of Judah: this *was* the west quarter.

15 And the south quarter *was* from the end of Kir′jath-jē′a-rĭm, and the border went out on the west, and went out to the well of waters of Nĕph′tō-ah:

16 And the border came down to the end of the mountain that *lieth* before the valley of the son of Hĭn′nom, *and* which *is* in the valley of the giants on the north, and descended to the valley of Hĭn′nom, to the side of Jĕ-bu′sī on the south, and descended to Ĕn-rō′gel,

17 And was drawn from the north, and went forth to Ĕn-shĕ′mesh, and went forth toward Gel′ī-lōth, which *is* over against the going up of A-dŭm′mĭm, and descended to the stone of Bō′hăn the son of Reuben,

18 And passed along toward the side over against Ăr′a-bah northward, and went down unto Ăr′a-bah:

19 And the border passed along to the side of Bĕth-hŏg′lah northward: and the outgoings of the border were at the north bay of the salt sea at the south end of Jordan: this *was* the south coast.

20 And Jordan was the border of it on the east side. This *was* the inheritance of the children of Benjamin, by the coasts thereof round about, according to their families.

21 Now the cities of the tribe of the children of Benjamin according to their families were Jericho, and Bĕth-hŏg′lah, and the valley of Kē′zĭz,

22 And Bĕth-ăr′a-bah, and Zĕm-a-rā′im, and Bĕth-el,

23 And Ā′vĭm, and Pâ′rah, and Ŏph′rah,

24 And Chĕ′phar-hā-ăm′mo-naī, and Ŏph′nī, and Gā′ba; twelve cities with their villages:

25 Gĭbeon, and Rā′mah, and Bē-ĕ′rŏth,

6. Portion to Benjamin. 18:11-28.

11-20. The portion of land inherited by the tribe of Benjamin was not large; but since it was centrally located, it was very important. It encompasses the land between Ephraim and Judah. The northeast corner of the inheritance was at the Jordan, and it proceeded west above Jericho through the **wilderness of Beth-aven to Beth-el.** From here it descended to Lower **Beth-horon** and south to **Kirjath-jearim,** retreating to the Valley of Hinnom and along the **Arabah** north of **Beth-hoglah** to the northern tip of the **Salt Sea.**

21-28. Two groups of major cities (twelve and fourteen cities respectively) are listed as included in Benjamin's territory. The most notable are: **Jericho, Beth-el, Ramah** (dwelling place of Samuel, I Sam 1:1), **Mizpeh,** and, most importantly, **Jebusi, which is Jerusalem.**

26 And Mĭz′peh, and Che-phī′rah, and Mō′zah,

27 And Rē′kem, and Ĭr′pe-el, and Tăr′a-lah,

28 And Zē′lah, Ē′lĕph, and Jē-bu′sī, which is Jerusalem, Gĭb′e-ath, and Kĭr′-jăth; fourteen cities with their villages. This is the inheritance of the children of Benjamin according to their families.

CHAPTER 19

AND the second lot came forth to Simeon, even for the tribe of the children of Simeon according to their families: and their inheritance was within the inheritance of the children of Jūdah.

2 And they had in their inheritance Be′er-shē′ba, and Shē′ba, and Mōl′a-dah,

3 And Hā′zar-shū′al, and Bā′lah, and Ā′zem,

4 And Ĕl′tō-lăd, and Bĕth-ul, and Hôr′mah,

5 And Ziklag, and Bĕth-mär′ca-bôth, and Hā′zar-sū′sah,

6 And Bĕth-leb′ā-ŏth, and Sha-rū′hen; thirteen cities and their villages:

7 A′ĭn, Rĕm′mon, and Ē′ther, and Ā′shan; four cities and their villages:

8 And all the villages that were round about these cities to Bā′al-ăth-bē′er, Rǎ′math of the south. This is the inheritance of the tribe of the children of Simeon according to their families.

9 Out of the portion of the children of Jūdah was the inheritance of the children of Simeon: for the part of the children of Jūdah was too much for them: therefore the children of Simeon had their inheritance within the inheritance of them.

10 ¶And the third lot came up for the children of Zĕb′u-lun according to their families: and the border of their inheritance was unto Sā′rĭd:

11 And their border went up toward the sea, and Mär′a-lah, and reached to Dăb′ba-shĕth, and reached to the river that is before Jŏk′ne-am;

12 And turned from Sâ′rĭd eastward toward the sunrising unto the border of Chĭs′lŏth-tā′bor, and then goeth out to Dăb′e-räth, and goeth up to Ja-phī′a,

13 And from thence passeth on along on the east to Gĭt′tah-hē′pher, to Ĭt′tah-kā′zĭn, and goeth out to Rĕm′-mon-mĕth′ō-är to Nē′ah;

14 And the border compasseth it on the north side to Hăn′na-thŏn: and the outgoings thereof are in the valley of Jĭph′thah-ĕl:

15 And Kăt′tăth, and Na-hăl′lal, and Shĭm′rŏn, and Ĭd′a-lah, and Bĕth-lehĕm: twelve cities with their villages.

16 This is the inheritance of the children of Zĕb′u-lun according to their families, these cities with their villages.

17 ¶And the fourth lot came out to Ĭs′sa-char, for the children of Ĭs′sa-char according to their families.

18 And their border was toward Jĕz′-re-el, and Che-sūl′lŏth, and Shū′nem,

19 And Hăph-rā′im, and Shī′hŏn, and An-ā-ha′răth,

20 And Răb′bĭth, and Kīsh′ī-on, and Abĕz,

7. Portion to Simeon. 19:1-9.

19:1-9. Since Simeon had no definite portion alloted to it and since it was the smallest tribe at the last census (Num 26:14), perhaps a fulfillment of Jacob's prophecy (Gen 44:5-7), her **inheritance was within the inheritance of the children of Judah.** Two groups of cities were part of this inheritance, including **Beer-sheba** "the well of the oath," an important town from Genesis 21:31 onward, **Hazar-shual** "hamlet of jackals," **Ziklag,** and **Ramath of the south** (cf. I Sam 30:27).

8. Portion to Zebulun. 19:10-16.

10-16. The third lot went to the descendants of Zebulun; and truly they would say with David, "The lines are fallen unto me in pleasant places; yea, I have a goodly heritage" (Ps 16:6). It is speculated that **Sarid** was the middle point of Zebulun territory which stretched east and west from it. The border toward the west **reached to the river that is before Jokneam** (probably the river Kishon which is near Jokneam, see 12:22, at the foot of Mount Carmel). The border toward the east reached **Chisloth-tabor,** "the flanks of Tabor," at the very edge of Mount Tabor and then went east to **Gittah-hepher,** the birthplace of the prophet Jonah (II Kgs 14:25), toward **Remmon-methoar** and **Neah,** compassing or "skirting" it on the north to the **valley of Jiphthah-el.**

Included in Zebulun's inheritance was **Beth-lehem,** the "house of bread," not to be confused with the birthplace of Christ. This Beth-lehem is located just west of Nazareth. Thus, it was of the utmost importance that Micah, in his prophecy of the birthplace of the Messiah, made specific reference to Beth-lehem Ephratah (Mic 5:2) as being "among the thousands of Judah." How remarkably accurate indeed are the prophecies of God's Word!

9. Portion to Issachar. 19:17-23.

17-23. Like Benjamin, the portion given to Issachar was small, but important. The eastern border was at the Jordan, including **Beth-shemesh** (not the same as the town in Judah's territory, 15:10) and Mount **Tabor.** But the major area of Issachar's inheritance was **Jezreel.** Without doubt, this is the most famous valley in the world. Later known as the Plain of Esdraelon (cf. Judith 1:8; 6:2; II Macc 12:49), the Jezreel Valley is today the "breadbasket of Israel," being the most fertile valley in the Middle East. But it has not always been so.

21 And Rĕ′meth, and Ĕn-găn′nĭm, and Ĕn-hăd′dah, and Bĕth-păz′zez;

22 And the coast reacheth to Tā′bor, and Shā-haz′ī-mah, and Bĕth-shĕ′mesh; and the outgoings of their border were at Jordan: sixteen cities with their villages.

23 This *is* the inheritance of the tribe of the children of Ĭs′sa-char according to their families, the cities and their villages.

24 ¶And the fifth lot came out for the tribe of the children of Asher according to their families.

25 And their border was Hĕl′kăth, and Hā′lī, and Bĕ′ten, and Ăch′shăph,

26 And A-lăm′me-lĕch, and Ā′măd, and Mĭsh′e-al; and reacheth to Carmel westward, and to Shī′hôr-lĭb′nath;

27 And turneth toward the sunrising to Bĕth-dā′gon, and reacheth to Zĕb′u-lun, and to the valley of Jĭph′thah-ĕl toward the north side of Bĕth-e′mĕk, and Nĕ-ī′el, and goeth out to Cā′bul on the left hand,

28 And Hēbron, and Rĕ′hŏb, and Hăm′mon, and Kā′nah, *even* unto great Zī′don;

29 And *then* the coast turneth to Rā′mah, and to the strong city Tyre; and the coast turneth to Hō′sah; and the outgoings thereof are at the sea from the coast to Ăch′zĭb:

30 Ŭm′mah also, and Ā′phĕk, and Rĕ′hŏb: twenty and two cities with their villages.

31 This *is* the inheritance of the tribe of the children of Asher according to their families, these cities with their villages.

32 ¶The sixth lot came out to the children of Năph′ta-lī, *even* for the children of Năph′ta-lī according to their families.

33 And their coast was from Hĕ′lĕph, from Ăl′lon to Zā-a-năn′nĭm, and Ăd′a-mi, Nĕ′kĕb, and Jăb′ne-el, unto Lăk′-kum; and the outgoings thereof were at Jordan:

34 And *then* the coast turneth westward to Ăz′nŏth-tā′bor, and goeth out from thence to Hŭk′kŏk, and reacheth to Zĕb′u-lun on the south side, and reacheth to Asher on the west side, and to Jūdah upon Jordan toward the sunrising.

35 And the fenced cities *are* Zĭd′dĭm, Zer, and Hăm′măth, Răk′kath, and Chĭn′ne-rĕth,

36 And Ăd′a-mah, and Rā′mah, and Hā′zôr,

37 And Kĕ′dĕsh, and Ĕd′re-ī, and Ĕn-hā′zôr,

38 And Ī′ron, and Mĭg′dal-ĕl, Hō′rĕm, and Bĕth-ā′nath, and Bĕth-shĕ′mesh; nineteen cities with their villages.

39 This *is* the inheritance of the tribe of the children of Năph′ta-lī according to their families, the cities and their villages.

Both Thutmose III and Ramses II invaded Syria via this valley. Gideon overthrew the Midianites here. It has been the site of conflict involving armies under the leadership of Saul, Deborah, Barak, Ahab, Jehu, Josiah, Omri, Azariah, Holofernes and Judith, Vespasian, Saladin, and Napoleon. It was the scene of bitter fighting in the 1948 War of Independence and the June of 1967 "Six-Day War" for modern Israel. But most importantly, it will be the scene of the last great battle of history; for this valley is ". . . called in the Hebrew tongue Armageddon" (Rev 16:16). It is here that ". . . the King of kings, and Lord of lords" (I Tim 6:15) shall ride forth in battle against the nations ". . . and he shall rule them with a rod of iron . . ." (Rev 19:15).

10. Portion to Asher. 19:24-31.

24-31. Asher was allotted a long, narrow strip of territory between Naphtali and the Mediterranean Sea. The difficulty in tracing her boundaries stems from the fact that they are established, not by natural or topographical features, but by the relative position of its principal cities. The southwestern border began at the sea below **Carmel** and progressed **toward the sunrising to Beth-dagon,** finally reaching the territory of Zebulun. Going north past **great Zidon**, the boundary turned westward toward **the strong city of Tyre,** meaning a fortified city, "not the insular Tyre, but the town of Tyre, which was on the mainland, . . . situated by the seacoast, in a beautiful plain" (Keil and Delitzsch, p. 201), ending at the sea again. This mention of "Great" Sidon reinforces the antiquity of the book (see note on 11:8). Twenty-two major cities and their villages were included in this territory.

11. Portion to Naphtali. 19:32-39.

32-39. Generally, the portion which fell to the descendants of Naphtali was located in the extreme north between the Jordan River and the territory of Asher. The border was from **Heleph** through **Lakum** unto the Jordan on the east. Here the territory turned westward to **Aznoth-tabor,** southwest of the Sea of Galilee, until it reached the border of Zebulun on the south and Asher on the west. Thus, Naphtali was bounded by Asher on the west, Zebulun and Issachar on the south, and the Jordan on the east. The northern boundary is not clearly defined. The fortified cities include **Chinnereth** (on the Sea of Galilee which at that time bore the name Sea of Chinnereth), **Hazor,** (see 11:1-10), **Kedesh** (home of Barak, Jud 4:6), **Migdal-el** (Magdala of the New Testament), and **Beth-shemesh** (a common name derived from the worship of the sun, and not the Beth-shemesh of Judah or Issachar).

12. Portion to Dan. 19:40-48.

40 ¶*And* the seventh lot came out for the tribe of the children of Dan according to their families.

41 And the coast of their inheritance was Zō'rah, and Ĕsh'ta-ol, and Ĭr-shĕ'mesh,

42 And Shā-al-ăb'bin, and Ăj'a-lŏn, and Jĕth'lah,

43 And Ē'lŏn, and Thĭm'na-thah, and Ĕkron,

44 And Ĕl'te-keh, and Gĭb'be-thŏn, and Bā'al-ăth,

45 And Jehud, and Bĕn'e-be'răk, and Găth-rĭm'mon,

46 And Mē-jär'kŏn, and Răk'kŏn, with the border before Jā'phō.

47 And the coast of the children of Dan went out *too little* for them: therefore the children of Dan went up to fight against Lē'shem, and took it, and smote it with the edge of the sword, and possessed it, and dwelt therein, and called Lē'shem, Dan, after the name of Dan their father.

48 This *is* the inheritance of the tribe of the children of Dan according to their families, these cities with their villages.

49 ¶When they had made an end of dividing the land for inheritance by their coasts, the children of Israel gave an inheritance to Joshua the son of Nun among them:

50 According to the word of the Lord they gave him the city which he asked, *even* Tĭm'năth-se'rah in mount Ē'phra-im: and he built the city, and dwelt therein.

51 These *are* the inheritances, which Ĕ-le-ā'zar the priest, and Joshua the son of Nun, and the heads of the fathers of the tribes of the children of Israel, divided for an inheritance by lot in Shī'-lōh before the Lord, at the door of the tabernacle of the congregation. So they made an end of dividing the country.

CHAPTER 20

THE Lord also spake unto Joshua, saying,

2 Speak to the children of Israel, saying, Appoint out for you cities of refuge, whereof I spake unto you by the hand of Moses:

3 That the slayer that killeth *any* person unawares *and* unwittingly may flee thither: and they shall be your refuge from the avenger of blood.

4 And when he that doth flee unto one of those cities shall stand at the entering of the gate of the city, and shall declare his cause in the ears of the elders of that city, they shall take him into the city unto them, and give him a

12. Portion to Dan. 19:40-48.

40-48. The seventh lot fell to the tribe of Dan. The cities of **Zorah** and **Eshtaol** were on the border between Judah and Dan, Judah being to the south. **Ajalon** was where the sun was commanded to stand still (cf. 10:12). **Ekron** was one of the five Philistine cities. The border closed on the sea at **Japho** (called Joppa in II Chron 2:16; Ezr 3:7; in Jon, and in the New Testament), modern Jaffa.

And the coast . . . of Dan went out too little for them. This is a difficult passage to interpret. "Went out too little" has been interpreted to mean that the territory of Dan was too small for their number, 64,400 at the last census (see Num 26:43). Others have interpreted the expression to mean that the territory of Dan expanded, "went out," far beyond that originally assigned to them by the taking of **Leshem.** But Judges 1:34 indicates the probable cause for the expansion of the Danite border when it says, "And the Amorites forced the children of Dan into the mountain: for they would not suffer them to come down to the valley." At least a part of the tribe of Dan left, or were driven out of, their original territory, migrated north to fight against Leshem (Laish), and took it. The full account is given in Judges 18. The city was then renamed **Dan** after their ancestor.

13. Portion to Joshua. 19:49-51.

49-51. Only after Joshua had seen to the welfare of his people did he receive an inheritance for himself. This is a mark of a truly great leader. Joshua's choice of an inheritance was the city of **Timnath-serah,** not to be confused with the Timnath of the territory of Dan (see vs. 43). Called Thamna by Josephus and the LXX, it has been identified today with Tibneh, a city of some size in the Old Testament. It was located in the mountainous region of Ephraim. Here Joshua **built the city, and dwelt in it.**

With this proclamation **Eleazar the priest** and **Joshua,** whom God had told Moses to appoint to the task to dividing the land (Num 34:17-29), finished the task given them in **Shiloh** at the door of the tabernacle. Another plateau in the life of Israel had been reached. For an extensive account of the occupation of the land, see Yohanan Aharoni, *The Land of the Bible*, pp. 174-253; George C. Mendenhall, "The Hebrew Conquest of Palestine," *The Biblical Archaeologist*, XXV, No. 3, (Sept., 1962); and Y. Kaufman, *The Biblical Account of the Conquest of Palestine*.

C. The Apportionment of the Cities of Refuge. 20:1-9.

1. The purpose of the cities. 20:1-6.

20:1-2. Appoint out for you cities of refuge. The Lord God now commands Joshua to fulfill that which He spoke to Moses, i.e., to establish the cities of refuge. The concept for these cities of shelter was expressed to Moses in Exodus 21:13; Numbers 35:6ff.; and Deuteronomy 19:2. Moses actually appointed the cities east of the Jordan in Deuteronomy 4:41-43. The reference to Moses here gives veiled testimony that Joshua was acquainted with the Pentateuch, perhaps as a corpus, since the words quoted are from Numbers and Deuteronomy. Also, these books were recognized to be **by the hand of Moses.**

3-6. The purpose of the cities of refuge (Heb *miqlat,* meaning "to contract" or "receive") was to provide a shelter for any who **killeth any person unawares and unwittingly.** The Old Testament makes a clear distinction between premeditated murder and unintentional manslaughter (cf. Num 35:16-18; Deut 19:5). When a premeditated murder was committed, the penalty must be paid. The **avenger of blood** (Heb *goēl hadam*) was literally a "redeemer" who bought back the honor of the family by slaying the murderer (Deut 19:12). But he who took the life of another

437

place, that he may dwell among them.

5 And if the avenger of blood pursue after him, then they shall not deliver the slayer up into his hand; because he smote his neighbour unwittingly, and hated him not beforetime.

6 And he shall dwell in that city, until he stand before the congregation for judgment, *and* until the death of the high priest that shall be in those days: then shall the slayer return, and come unto his own city, and unto his own house, unto the city from whence he fled.

7 ¶And they appointed Kĕ′dĕsh in Galilee in mount Năph′ta-lī, and Shĕ′-chem in mount Ē′phra-im, and Kĭr′-jath-är′ba, which *is* Hĕbron, in the mountain of Jūdah.

8 And on the other side Jordan by Jericho eastward, they assigned Bē′zer in the wilderness upon the plain out of the tribe of Reuben, and Rā′mŏth in Gilead out of the tribe of Gad, and Gō′lan in Bā′shan out of the tribe of Ma-năs′-seh.

9 These were the cities appointed for all the children of Israel, and for the stranger that sojourneth among them, that whosoever killeth *any* person at unawares might flee thither, and not die by the hand of the avenger of blood, until he stood before the congregation.

CHAPTER 21

THEN came near the heads of the fathers of the Lēvītes unto Ĕ-le-ā′zar the priest, and unto Joshua the son of Nun, and unto the heads of the fathers of the tribes of the children of Israel;

2 And they spake unto them at Shī′-lōh in the land of Canaan, saying, The LORD commanded by the hand of Moses to give us cities to dwell in, with the suburbs thereof for our cattle.

3 And the children of Israel gave unto the Lēvītes out of their inheritance, at the commandment of the LORD, these cities and their suburbs.

4 And the lot came out for the families of the Kō′hăth-ītes: and the children of Aaron the priest, *which were* of the Lēvītes, had by lot out of the tribe of Jūdah, and out of the tribe of Simeon, and out of the tribe of Benjamin, thirteen cities.

5 And the rest of the children of Kō′hăth *had* by lot out of the families of the tribe of Ē′phra-im, and out of the tribe of Dan, and out of the half tribe of Ma-năs′seh, ten cities.

6 And the children of Ger′shon *had* by lot out of the families of the tribe of

accidentally would present himself at the **entering** or gate of one of the cities of refuge (where all legal business was transacted, see Ruth 4:1; II Sam 15:2) and plead his cause to the elders of the city and thus would find shelter in the city. Later, he had to stand trial before the **congregation** of the town nearest the scene of the slaying. If deemed innocent, he was returned to the shelter of the city of refuge until the death of the current high priest (presumably enough time for the wrath of the family of the slain to be abated).

For the sinner, to be found in the city of refuge was to be found in the only place of salvation. The correspondence between these cities and the Lord Jesus is striking. The Apostle Paul, after rehearsing his pedigree and privileges in the Jew's religion (Phil 3:4-6), counted them all but loss for the excellency of the knowledge of Christ Jesus and the joy to ". . . be found in him . . ." (Phil 3:9). Also, the writer of Hebrews alludes to God as the only one to whom we ". . . have fled for refuge to lay hold upon the hope set before us" (Heb 6:18). Christ Jesus is the refuge for the sinner; and thus, He calls to all and says, "Come unto me, all ye that labor and are heavy laden, and I will give you rest" (Mt 11:28).

2. *The naming of the cities. 20:7-9.*

7-9. The cities appointed (Heb *qadash*, lit., "sanctified," Luther translated it *heiligten*) were six in number. **Kedesh in Galilee** (Heb *galil*). This is the first place in the Bible where Galilee is applied to a region. **Shechem** was one of the oldest cities in Palestine (Gen 12:6; 37:14; I Kgs 12:1, etc.). It is situated about thirty miles north of Jerusalem in the hill country of Manasseh (Josh 17:7). **Hebron** was the dwelling place of Abraham (Gen 13:18; 23:2), a part of the inheritance of Caleb (see especially the note on 14:13-15), and was the city from which David ruled until Jerusalem was captured (II Sam 5:1-10). Each of these cities was on the west side of the Jordan.

On the east side were **Bezer** (Deut 4:43; I Chr 6:78) and **Ramoth in Gilead** (Deut 4:43). Note that not only were these cities on both sides of the Jordan (three on each side), but they were also equally distributed throughout the upper, middle, and lower sections of the land. Each were Levitical cities as well.

D. The Apportionment of the Levitical Cities. 21:1-45.

1. *The portion out of each tribe. 21:1-12.*

21:1-3. Eleazar, the priest, and unto Joshua. The descendants of Levi were not given a specific inheritance, but were scattered throughout Israel (see Gen 49:7) so they may teach the law to the tribes and exert spiritual influence on them (cf. 13:33; 14:3; 18:7; Deut 18:1-2). When the heads of the Levites appeared before Eleazar and Joshua at Shiloh, they reminded them that the Lord had commanded Moses (Num 35) to give them **cities** to dwell in and **suburbs** (Heb *migrash*, lit., "pasture lands").

4-12. Again, the **lot** was used to apportion the cities. This referred the matter entirely to God. **Kohath** received cities in the territories of Ephraim, Dan, and Manasseh: ten cities in all. **Gershon** received the tribes of Issachar, Asher, Naphtali, and Manasseh east of the Jordan: thirteen cities. **Merari** received cities in the territories of Reuben, Gad, and Zebulun: twelve cities. Again, the sons of **Kohath** received of the tribes of Judah and Simeon including **the city of Arba** (ancient Kirjath-arba), which is **Hebron,** but the pasture fields and villages belonged to **Caleb** (see note on 14:13-15).

"The method followed by Israel in selecting the Levitical cities appears to have been something like this. First, the court,

Ĭs'sa-char, and out of the tribe of Asher, and out of the tribe of Năph'ta-lĭ, and out of the half tribe of Ma-năs'seh in Bā'shan, thirteen cities.

7 The children of Me-râ'rī by their families *had* out of the tribe of Reuben, and out of the tribe of Gad, and out of the tribe of Zĕb'u-lun, twelve cities.

8 And the children of Israel gave by lot unto the Lēvītes these cities with their suburbs, as the LORD commanded by the hand of Moses.

9 ¶And they gave out of the tribe of the children of Jūdah, and out of the tribe of the children of Simeon, these cities which are *here* mentioned by name,

10 Which the children of Aaron, *being* of the families of the Kō'hăth-ītes, *who were* of the children of Levi, had: for theirs was the first lot.

11 And they gave them the city of Är'ba the father of Anak, which *city is* Hēbron, in the hill *country* of Jūdah, with the suburbs thereof round about it.

12 But the fields of the city, and the villages thereof, gave they to Caleb the son of Je-phŭn'neh for his possession.

13 Thus they gave to the children of Aaron the priest Hēbron with her suburbs, *to be* a city of refuge for the slayer; and Lĭb'nah with her suburbs,

14 And Jăt'tir with her suburbs, and Ĕsh-te-mō'a with her suburbs,

15 And Hō'lŏn with her suburbs, and Dē'bir with her suburbs,

16 And Ä'ĭn with her suburbs, and Jŭt'tah with her suburbs, *and* Bĕth-shĕmesh with her suburbs; nine cities out of those two tribes.

17 And out of the tribe of Benjamin, Gĭbeon with her suburbs, Gē'ba with her suburbs,

18 Än'a-thŏth with her suburbs, and Äl'mon with her suburbs; four cities.

19 All the cities of the children of Aaron, the priests, *were* thirteen cities with their suburbs.

20 ¶And the families of the children of Kō'hăth, the Lēvītes which remained of the children of Kō'hăth, even they had the cities of their lot out of the tribe of Ē'phra-im.

21 For they gave them Shĕ'chem with her suburbs in mount Ē'phra-im, *to be* a city of refuge for the slayer; and Gē'zer with her suburbs,

22 And Kĭb'zā-im with her suburbs, and Bĕth-hō'ron with her suburbs; four cities.

23 And out of the tribe of Dan, Ĕl'te-keh with her suburbs, Gĭb'be-thŏn with her suburbs,

24 Āij'a-lŏn with her suburbs, Găth-rĭm'mon with her suburbs; four cities.

25 And out of the half tribe of Ma-năs'seh, Tā'năch with her suburbs, and Găth-rĭm'mon with her suburbs; two cities.

26 All the cities *were* ten with their suburbs for the families of the children of Kō'hăth that remained.

27 ¶And unto the children of Ger'shon, of the families of the Lē'vītes, out of the *other* half tribe of Ma-năs'seh

after duly considering the size of its inheritance, appointed how many cities should be taken out of each tribe. Then the 'fathers of the tribes' agreed among themselves which cities were most suitable. After that had been settled, the forty-eight cities were divided into four groups, for the four branches of the Levitical tribe. Lots were cast to determine the distribution of them. The sons of Levi were Gershom, Kohath, Merari. From Kohath descended Moses, Aaron and Miriam (I Chr 6:1-3). The 'children of Aaron' (Josh 21:4) were not only Levites, but priests too, whose more immediate work was to serve at the altar. It should be duly noted that though this was the least numerous of the four branches, yet, in keeping with the prominence of the priesthood throughout the book of Joshua, 'the first lot' (vs. 10) was for the children of Aaron, and thus was honour placed again upon this Divine institution. It is further to be observed that more cities were assigned unto them than to any other branch of Levi" (Pink, p. 394).

2. The cities of Kohath. 21:13-26.

13-19. The major cities assigned by lot to the sons of Kohath included **Hebron** (see above), **Libnah** (II Kgs 8:22), **Holon** (15:51; cf. I Chr 6:58), **Debir, Ain** (or Asham, see 15:42; I Chr 6:59), and **Beth-shemesh** out of the territories of Judah and Simeon. From Benjamin they received **Gibeon, Geba, Anathoth** (the birthplace of Jeremiah, Jer 1:1), and **Almon.** These were the cities of the priests of Aaron who were the descendants of Kohath.

20-26. The cities of the Levites of Aaron came from the tribe of Ephraim, including **Shechem, Gezer** (Jud 1:29), **Kibzaim,** and **Beth-horon,** four cities in all. Also four cities came from the tribe of Dan, **Eltekeh, Gibbethon, Aijalon,** and **Gath-rimmon,** and two cities from the western tribe of Manasseh, **Tanach** (cf. **Taanach** in 12:21), and **Gath-rimmon.** The second reference to **Gath-rimmon** (vs. 25) is probably due to scribal error in recopying the city mentioned in verse 24. First Chronicles 6:70 preserves the intended rendering as Bileam (cf. **Ibleam** 17:11). Ten cities in all were designated for the Levites of Aaron who were the descendants of Kohath.

3. The cities of Gershon. 21:27-33.

27-33. To the families of Gershon, out of the territory of the half tribe of Manasseh in Bashan were given **Golan** and **Beesh-terah** (perhaps Og's city of Ashtaroth, see 12:4 and I Chr 6:71).

they gave Gō'lan in Bā'shan with her suburbs, *to be* a city of refuge for the slayer; and Bē-ĕsh'-te-rah with her suburbs; two cities.

28 And out of the tribe of Ĭs'sa-char, Kĭ'shŏn with her suburbs, Dăb'a-reh with her suburbs,

29 Jär'mŭth with her suburbs, Ĕn-găn'nĭm with her suburbs; four cities.

30 And out of the tribe of Asher, Mĭ'-shal with her suburbs, Ăbdŏn with her suburbs,

31 Hĕl'kăth with her suburbs, and Rĕ'hŏb with her suburbs; four cities.

32 And out of the tribe of Năph'ta-lī, Kĕ'dĕsh in Galilee with her suburbs, *to be* a city of refuge for the slayer; and Hăm'moth-dôr with her suburbs, and Kär'tăn with her suburbs; three cities.

33 All the cities of the Ger'shon-ītes according to their families *were* thirteen cities with their suburbs.

34 ¶And unto the families of the children of Me-râ'rī, the rest of the Lĕvītes, out of the tribe of Zĕb'u-lun, Jŏk'ne-am with her suburbs, and Kär'tah with her suburbs,

35 Dĭm'nah with her suburbs, Nā'ha-lăl with her suburbs; four cities.

36 And out of the tribe of Reuben, Bĕ'zer with her suburbs, and Ja-hā'zah with her suburbs,

37 Kĕd'e-mŏth with her suburbs, and Mĕph'a-ăth with her suburbs; four cities.

38 And out of the tribe of Gad, Rā'-mŏth in Gilead with her suburbs, *to be* a city of refuge for the slayer; and Mā'ha-nā'im with her suburbs,

39 Hĕsh'bŏn with her suburbs, Jā'zer with her suburbs; four cities in all.

40 So all the cities for the children of Me-râ'rī by their families, which were remaining of the families of the Lĕvītes, were *by* their lot twelve cities.

41 All the cities of the Lĕvītes within the possession of the children of Israel *were* forty and eight cities with their suburbs.

42 These cities were every one with their suburbs round about them: thus *were* all these cities.

43 ¶And the LORD gave unto Israel all the land which he sware to give unto their fathers; and they possessed it, and dwelt therein.

44 And the LORD gave them rest round about, according to all that he sware unto their fathers: and there stood not a man of all their enemies before them; the LORD delivered all their enemies into their hand.

45 There failed not ought of any good thing which the LORD had spoken unto the house of Israel; all came to pass.

CHAPTER 22
THEN Joshua called the Reubenites,

From Issachar they were alloted four cities, including **Kishon** and **Jarmuth**. From the territory of Asher came four cities and three from Naphtali with **Kedesh in Galilee** (see 20:7) being notable. In all, thirteen cities were set apart unto the Gershonites.

4. The cities of Merari. 21:34-42.

34-42. To the descendants of this son of Levi were apportioned cities from the territories of Zebulun, Reuben, and Gad, four cities from each tribe. Although the cities mentioned from Reuben (vss. 36-37) have a note appended to them that they are not recorded in the true Jewish tradition (the Masora), nevertheless they are found in the LXX and all other ancient versions. In addition, they are necessary to make the total number of cities forty-eight. Major cities of **Merari** are **Jokneam, Bezer, Ramoth in Gilead** (see 20:8), **Mahanaim** (13:26; see also II Sam 17:22-24), and **Heshbon.**

5. The promise of God. 21:43-45.

43-45. And the LORD gave unto Israel all the land which he sware to give. . . . This had been an oft-repeated promise (cf. Gen 12:7; 26:3-4; 28:4,13-14; etc.). Once they entered into their inheritance **the LORD gave them rest.** A reference to this passage occurs in the Epistle to the Hebrews, where the writer draws the analogy between the Israelites and the Christian when he says, "There remaineth therefore a rest to the people of God. For he that is entered into his rest, he also hath ceased from his own works, as God did from his. Let us labor therefore to enter into that rest . . ." (Heb 4:9-11). Like the Israelites passing through the wilderness and the kingdoms of Sihon and Og, the Christian is but a stranger and a pilgrim in this life, laboring and seeking the rest from his labors which only comes when he reaches his home and his inheritance (see Phil 3:20-21; I Pet 1:3-4).

E. The Dismissal of the Transjordan Tribes. 22:1-34.

1. The blessing of Joshua. 22:1-9.

22:1. Joshua called. After the initial conquest of the land, the allotment of the territories, and the establishment of the

and the Gādītes, and the half tribe of Ma-năs′seh,

2 And said unto them, Ye have kept all that Moses the servant of the LORD commanded you, and have obeyed my voice in all that I commanded you:
3 Ye have not left your brethren these many days unto this day, but have kept the charge of the commandment of the LORD your God.

4 And now the LORD your God hath given rest unto your brethren, as he promised them: therefore now return ye, and get you unto your tents, *and* unto the land of your possession, which Moses the servant of the LORD gave you on the other side Jordan.

5 But take diligent heed to do the commandment and the law, which Moses the servant of the LORD charged you, to love the LORD your God, and to walk in all his ways, and to keep his commandments, and to cleave unto him, and to serve him with all your heart and with all your soul.

6 So Joshua blessed them, and sent them away: and they went unto their tents.
7 ¶Now to the *one* half of the tribe of Ma-năs′seh Moses had given *possession* in Bā′shan: but unto the *other* half thereof gave Joshua among their brethren on this side Jordan westward. And when Joshua sent them away also unto their tents, then he blessed them,
8 And he spake unto them, saying, Return with much riches unto your tents, and with very much cattle, with silver, and with gold, and with brass, and with iron, and with very much raiment: divide the spoil of your enemies with your brethren.
9 And the children of Reuben and the children of Gad and the half tribe of Ma-năs′seh returned, and departed from the children of Israel out of Shī′-

refuge and Levitical cities, Joshua summoned the tribes of Reuben, Gad, and the half tribe of Manasseh to Shiloh. His purpose in doing so is clearly stated in verse 6, **So Joshua blessed them, and sent them away.** Joshua's blessing consisted of three aspects: (1) to commend them on their faithful and valiant service to the other tribes (vss 2-3); (2) to commission them to return to the land of their inheritance (vs. 4); and (3) to charge them concerning their continued responsibilities to the Lord God (vs. 5).

2-3. Ye have kept . . . and have obeyed. Moses originally promised these two and one-half tribes permission to settle east of the Jordan River, provided they assisted their brethren in the conquest of Canaan (Num 32:1-42). This they had done. Not only so, but they also obeyed the commands of Joshua subsequent to Moses' death. They deserved commendation, having stayed in the thick of the battle these **many days** (lit., "great many days," indicating a prolonged and difficult period of time). They had fought a good fight, finished the course, and kept the faith (II Tim 4:7).

4. Now return ye. Having publicly thanked these tribes, Joshua now commissions them to return to **the land of your possession.** Since the Lord God had given rest (the LXX has *katepause,* the same word used in Heb 4:8) unto their brethren, these tribes were released from further military commitments. Their possession was **on the other side** of the Jordan. They are now free to possess their possession.

5. But take diligent heed. Although their military commitments were ended, their spiritual commitments would never end. The writer employs six infinitives to emphasize the seriousness of Joshua's charge. The passage is a series of quotations from the book of Deuteronomy (6:5; 10:12; 11:13-22; 30:6, 16, 20; etc.). The tribes are: (1) **To do** (perform) all the commandments of the law (Deut 6:1); (2) **to love** the Lord always (Deut 6:5). But love is an emotion which is not contained but expressed. Jesus taught, "If ye love me, keep my commandments" (Jn 14:15). As a Christian you are not obligated to believe someone who claims to love the Lord Jesus if you don't see in that person a willingness to obey the Lord's commands. These tribes could only truly say they "loved" God when they were willing to express that love in obedience; (3) **to walk** in the Lord God's commandments. Remember how frequently Paul challenged the believer to ". . . walk worthy of the vocation wherewith ye are called" (Eph 4:1; see also Col 1:10; I Thess 2:12); (4) **to keep** the commandments of the Lord (see Deut 6:2); (5) **to cleave** unto Him heartily (the Hebrew is to cleave "into" Him as a branch unto a vine [Jn 15] and as the believer is "rooted and grounded" in the love of Christ, Eph 3:17); and (6) **to serve** the Lord with all your heart and soul (I Sam 12:24).

6-9. Having been commended, commissioned, and charged, the one-half tribe of Manasseh began to return to Bashan. Especially blessed as this tribe was with riches, they were to divide their spoils among the needier brethren. Thus, **Reuben, Gad,** and half of **Manasseh** departed from the assembly of Shiloh.

lōh, which *is* in the land of Canaan, to go unto the country of Gilead, to the land of their possession, whereof they were possessed, according to the word of the LORD by the hand of Moses.

10 ¶And when they came unto the borders of Jordan, that *are* in the land of Canaan, the children of Reuben and the children of Gad and the half tribe of Ma-năs′seh built there an altar by Jordan, a great altar to see to.

11 ¶And the children of Israel heard say, Behold, the children of Reuben and the children of Gad and the half tribe of Ma-năs′seh have built an altar over against the land of Canaan, in the borders of Jordan, at the passage of the children of Israel.

12 And when the children of Israel heard *of it*, the whole congregation of the children of Israel gathered themselves together at Shī′lŏh, to go up to war against them.

13 And the children of Israel sent unto the children of Reuben, and to the children of Gad, and to the half tribe of Ma-năs′seh, into the land of Gilead, Phĭn′e-has the son of Ĕ-le-ā′zar the priest,

14 And with him ten princes, of each chief house a prince throughout all the tribes of Israel; and each one *was* an head of the house of their fathers among the thousands of Israel.

15 And they came unto the children of Reuben, and to the children of Gad, and to the half tribe of Ma-năs′seh, unto the land of Gilead, and they spake with them, saying,

16 Thus saith the whole congregation of the LORD, What trespass *is* this that ye have committed against the God of Israel, to turn away this day from following the LORD, in that ye have builded you an altar, that ye might rebel this day against the LORD?

17 *Is* the iniquity of Pē′or too little for us, from which we are not cleansed until this day, although there was a plague in the congregation of the LORD,

18 But that ye must turn away this day from following the LORD? and it will be, *seeing* ye rebel to day against the LORD, that to morrow he will be wroth with the whole congregation of Israel.

19 Notwithstanding, if the land of your possession *be* unclean, *then* pass ye over unto the land of the possession of the LORD, wherein the LORD's tabernacle dwelleth, and take possession among us: but rebel not against the LORD, nor rebel against us, in building you an altar beside the altar of the LORD our God.

20 Did not Ā′chăn the son of Ze′rah commit a trespass in the accursed thing, and wrath fell on all the congregation of Israel? and that man perished not alone in his iniquity.

21 ¶Then the children of Reuben and the children of Gad and the half tribe of

2. The misunderstanding of the altar. 22:10-20.

10-12. No sooner had the two and one-half tribes arrived at the banks of the Jordan than they erected **a great altar to see,** large and visible in all directions. When this came to the attention of the other tribes, **the whole congregation . . . gathered . . . at Shiloh, to go up to war. . . . The children of Israel** had assumed that their brethren erected the great altar for an evil intent. Most commentators hold that the tribes were concerned that Reuben, Gad, and Manasseh had thought to establish a center of worship to rival Shiloh. This, however, is unlikely because the altar was too close to Shiloh and too distant from the Transjordan tribes to effect such a purpose. It is more likely that the Israelites assumed the two and one-half tribes were attempting to separate themselves totally and finally from their brethren. If the western tribes found themselves in battle, they should no longer rely on the eastern tribes to fight for them, to finish the task of driving the heathen out of Canaan. As will be seen, whatever they assumed was incorrect.

13-15. When cooler heads prevailed, **Phinehas,** the son of Eleazar the priest, led a group of the heads of each family on a fact-finding mission to the two and one-half tribes. This august group would surely emphasize the seriousness of the situation; and Phinehas was the ideal person to head up the mission, for he represented the high priest and had been zealous in purifying the nation Israel when she fell prey to sin with Baal-peor (Num 25).

16-19. John J. Davis summarizes the charges against the eastern tribes as falling into three categories. "In verses 16 ff., the charge against the two and one-half tribes takes the form of three kinds of sin. In verse 16, reference is made to a trespass (Heb *ma'al*). The word for trespass as used in this verse is the same one employed in 7:1, in connection with the sin of Achan. The sin of the two and one-half tribes was also likened to the 'iniquity of Peor' (vs. 17). The iniquity of Peor had as an essential element idolatry and open disobedience to God's will with regard to worship (cf. Num 25). Finally, their sin is described as an act of rebellion (vs. 18-19)" (Davis, pp. 85-86).

20. If the eastern tribes did intend to rebel against Israel and have defiled their inheritance by their intention, they must repent and forsake their inheritance for the good of all Israel. **Achan** is elicited as an example of the sin of one affecting all. Israel could not chance that again.

3. The explanation of the tribes. 22:21-29.

21-23. The LORD God of gods. The repetition of the phrase is a favorite Hebrew form of emphasis. But more, employing the

Ma-năs′seh answered, and said unto the heads of the thousands of Israel,

22 The LORD God of gods, the LORD God of gods, he knoweth, and Israel he shall know; if *it be* in rebellion, or if in transgression against the LORD, (save us not this day,)

23 That we have built us an altar to turn from following the LORD, or if to offer thereon burnt offering or meat offering, or if to offer peace offerings thereon, let the LORD himself require *it;*

24 And if we have not *rather* done it for fear of *this* thing, saying, In time to come your children might speak unto our children, saying, What have ye to do with the LORD God of Israel?

25 For the LORD hath made Jordan a border between us and you, ye children of Reuben and children of Gad; ye have no part in the LORD: so shall your children make our children cease from fearing the LORD.

26 Therefore we said, Let us now prepare to build us an altar, not for burnt offering, nor for sacrifice:

27 But *that* it *may be* a witness between us and you, and our generations after us, that we might do the service of the LORD before him with our burnt offerings, and with our sacrifices, and with our peace offerings; that your children may not say to our children in time to come, Ye have no part in the LORD.

28 Therefore said we, that it shall be, when they should *so* say to us or to our generations in time to come, that we may say *again,* Behold the pattern of the altar of the LORD, which our fathers made, not for burnt offerings, nor for sacrifices; but *is* a witness between us and you.

29 God forbid that we should rebel against the LORD, and turn this day from following the LORD, to build an altar for burnt offerings, for meat offerings, or for sacrifices, beside the altar of the LORD our God that *is* before his tabernacle.

30 ¶And when Phĭn′e-has the priest, and the princes of the congregation and heads of the thousands of Israel which *were* with him, heard the words that the children of Reuben and the children of Gad and the children of Ma-năs′seh spake, it pleased them.

31 And Phĭn′e-has the son of Ĕ-le-ā′zar the priest said unto the children of Reuben, and to the children of Gad, and to the children of Ma-năs′seh, This day we perceive that the LORD *is* among us, because ye have not committed this trespass against the LORD: now ye have delivered the children of Israel out of the hand of the LORD.

32 And Phĭn′e-has the son of Ĕ-le-ā′zar the priest, and the princes, returned from the children of Reuben, and from the children of Gad, out of the land of Gilead, unto the land of Canaan, to the children of Israel, and brought them word again.

33 And the thing pleased the children of Israel; and the children of Israel blessed God, and did not intend to go up against them in battle, to destroy

three names of God together, El, Elohim, and Jehovah (or Yahweh), each twice repeated, expresses the great horror with which the two and one-half tribes learned of the assumptions made by their brethren. If their intent was to rebel against Israel, they should not be saved from God's wrath. No, there was another explanation for building the altar.

24-29. The purpose of the altar is stated as thus: **Your children might speak unto our children, saying, What have ye to do with the LORD God of Israel?** The Jordan Valley was a vast and formidable barrier between the eastern and western tribes. The two and one-half tribes feared that in the years to come succeeding generations of children from the West Bank would taunt their children claiming they were not a part of the people of God. The altar was a facsimile (Heb *tabnīt* "pattern" in vs. 28) of the one at Shiloh and was built to **be a witness** between the eastern and western tribes of their bond in Yahweh, physically and spiritually. It was built on the western side of Jordan so "their" altar would be a part of Israel's land, much like a man puts a ring on his wife's hand instead of his own to show the bond between them. **God forbid that we should rebel against the LORD.** The two and one-half tribes find this assumption just as appalling as many assumptions the Apostle Paul encountered when he repeated this favorite expression of abhorrence, "God forbid" (see Rom 3:4, 6; 6:2, 15; 7:7, 13; 9:14; 11:1, 11).

4. The acceptance of the explanation. 22:30-34.

30-34. And when Phinehas . . . and the princes . . . heard the words . . . it pleased them. Phinehas' zealous piety was real; he did not delight in fighting among the brethren. He knew that brotherly love "rejoiceth not in iniquity, but rejoiceth in the truth" (I Cor 13:6). This is an attitude many Christian brethren would do well to foster. Phinehas and the princes were satisfied with the explanation and with the eastern tribes' purity of motive, and returned to Canaan thanking God that they had not entered a bloody conflict which would have certainly meant the extermination of the two and one-half tribes.

The fact that the account ends happily does not excuse the eastern tribes from erecting a presumptuous altar. Building altars was a violation of God's design for centralized worship in Israel, as is evidenced by the action of Jeroboam after the secession of the ten northern tribes later in Israel's history (see I Kgs 12:25-33). God's plan was for every Israelite male to appear before the Lord three times a year at the tabernacle (Ex 23:17). Whether the eastern tribes intended to violate this plan or not, the erection of a needless altar without divine command authority should not have been undertaken. It would have been much better for them to "Abstain from all appearance of evil" (I Thess 5:22).

the land wherein the children of Reuben and Gad dwelt.

34 And the children of Reuben and the children of Gad called the altar *Ed:* for it *shall be* a witness between us that the Lord *is* God.

CHAPTER 23

AND it came to pass a long time after that the Lord had given rest unto Israel from all their enemies round about, that Joshua waxed old *and* stricken in age.

2 And Joshua called for all Israel, *and* for their elders, and for their heads, and for their judges, and for their officers, and said unto them, I am old *and* stricken in age:

3 And ye have seen all that the Lord your God hath done unto all these nations because of you; for the Lord your God *is* he that hath fought for you.

4 Behold, I have divided unto you by lot these nations that remain, to be an inheritance for your tribes, from Jordan, with all the nations that I have cut off, even unto the great sea westward.

5 And the Lord your God, he shall expel them from before you, and drive them from out of your sight; and ye shall possess their land, as the Lord your God hath promised unto you.

6 Be ye therefore very courageous to keep and to do all that is written in the book of the law of Moses, that ye turn not aside therefrom *to* the right hand or *to* the left;

7 That ye come not among these nations, these that remain among you; neither make mention of the name of their gods, nor cause to swear *by them,* neither serve them, nor bow yourselves unto them:

8 But cleave unto the Lord your God, as ye have done unto this day.

9 For the Lord hath driven out from before you great nations and strong: but *as for* you, no man hath been able to stand before you unto this day.

10 One man of you shall chase a thousand: for the Lord your God, he *it is* that fighteth for you, as he hath promised you.

11 Take good heed therefore unto yourselves, that ye love the Lord your God.

12 Else if ye do in any wise go back, and cleave unto the remnant of these nations, *even* these that remain among you, and shall make marriages with them, and go in unto them, and they to you:

13 Know for a certainty that the Lord your God will no more drive out *any of* these nations from before you; but they shall be snares and traps unto you, and scourges in your sides, and thorns in your eyes, until ye perish from off this good land which the Lord your God hath given you.

14 And, behold, this day I *am* going the way of all the earth: and ye know in

IV. JOSHUA'S FAREWELL AND DEATH. 23:1—24:33.

A. Joshua's Farewell Call to Israel. 23:1-16.

1. The call to assemble. 23:1-2.

23:1-2. Joshua waxed old. Joshua 24:29 indicates that the great warrior of Israel died at age one hundred and ten years. He could not have been much less than that on this occasion. Because of his advanced age, Joshua felt a need to call Israel to a convocation and say farewell to his beloved people. **All Israel** was present through their representatives, the **elders, heads, judges,** and **officers** (see 24:1). The stage was now set for Joshua's final address.

2. The call to remembrance. 23:3-4.

3-4. The Lord your God is he that hath fought for you. Joshua never failed to reflect the glory for Israel's great victories toward the Lord God. He takes frequent opportunity to remind Israel that it was Jehovah who drove the enemy out of the land. Not only must they remember who the agent of their deliverance was, but the extent of that deliverance. The inheritance divided among the tribes extended **from Jordan . . . unto the Great Sea.** From east to west, the Promised Land was now the inheritance of Israel. They must not forget to be grateful.

3. The call to courage. 23:5-10.

5-10. The land was secured, but the inhabitants were not one hundred percent subdued. The remaining conquest would be gradual; but if Israel obeyed that which was written in **the book of the law of Moses,** the conquest would be complete. It was now time to "buckle down," be **very courageous,** and take the remaining territory. This they could do if the other nations did not mingle with Israel and if Israel would not **make mention, cause to swear, serve,** or **bow** to the heathen gods. This would take courage, for **One man of you shall chase a thousand** (a quotation from the song of Moses, Deut 32:20). But they would be courageous if they would only remember that it is **the Lord your God . . . that fighteth for you,** and He has promised victory.

4. The call to separation. 23:11-16.

11-13. Joshua cautions the elders of Israel to be separate from the nations around them and unto God. Double separation (both negative and positive) is always God's program. Separation from evil arises out of **love** for the Lord God. If they truly loved the Lord, they would not **cleave unto the remnant of these nations,** nor would they **make marriages with them** (the most intimate relation possible and thus the greatest threat to purity). The history of Israel proves their love to be weak indeed. Such relationships are said to be **snares and traps** to catch them unawares, **scourges** (translated *helous,* "nails" in the LXX) in their sides and **thorns** in their eyes. There is not a much more graphic way to describe the danger of intermarriage with the heathen (see the New Testament counterpart in II Corinthians 6:14).

14-16. This day Joshua knows the day of his departure is at hand. He must caution the elders of Israel that if they transgress

all your hearts and in all your souls, that not one thing hath failed of all the good things which the LORD your God spake concerning you; all are come to pass unto you, *and* not one thing hath failed thereof.

15 Therefore it shall come to pass, *that* as all good things are come upon you, which the LORD your God promised you; so shall the LORD bring upon you all evil things, until he have destroyed you from off this good land which the LORD your God hath given you.

16 When ye have transgressed the covenant of the LORD your God, which he commanded you, and have gone and served other gods, and bowed yourselves to them; then shall the anger of the LORD be kindled against you, and ye shall perish quickly from off the good land which he hath given unto you.

CHAPTER 24

AND Joshua gathered all the tribes of Israel to Shĕ'chem, and called for the elders of Israel, and for their heads, and for their judges, and for their officers; and they presented themselves before God.

2 And Joshua said unto all the people, Thus saith the LORD God of Israel, Your fathers dwelt on the other side of the flood in old time, *even* Te'rah, the father of Abraham, and the father of Nā'chôr: and they served other gods.

3 And I took your father Abraham from the other side of the flood, and led him throughout all the land of Canaan, and multiplied his seed, and gave him Isaac.

4 And I gave unto Isaac Jacob and Esau: and I gave unto Esau mount Sē'ir, to possess it; but Jacob and his children went down into Egypt.

5 I sent Moses also and Aaron, and I plagued Egypt, according to that which I did among them: and afterward I brought you out.

6 And I brought your fathers out of Egypt: and ye came unto the sea; and the Egyptians pursued after your fathers with chariots and horsemen unto the Red sea.

7 And when they cried unto the LORD, he put darkness between you and the Egyptians, and brought the sea upon them, and covered them; and your eyes have seen what I have done in Egypt: and ye dwelt in the wilderness a long season.

8 And I brought you into the land of the Āmorītes, which dwelt on the other

the **covenant of the LORD your God** that the Sovereign will withhold the good promised Israel and **bring upon you all evil things** to destroy them, yet not utterly (see Rom 11). The history books of the nations reveal that since Israel did transgress God's law, she suffered mercilessly at the hands of the heathen (cf. the Babylonian captivity, Antiochus Epiphanes, the Roman general, Titus, the persecutions of the Middle Ages, the Spanish Inquisition, the ghettos of Warsaw, and the crematoriums at Auschwitz and Dachau). Separation is a necessary part of purity; and when Israel refused to pay the price of separation, she had to pay the penalty.

B. Joshua's Farewell Covenant with Israel. 24:1-28.

1. Review of Israel's history. 24:1-13.

24:1. Joshua gathered all the tribes of Israel to Shechem. The Septuagint (LXX) and Arabic versions read Shiloh instead of Shechem. Since most of the other events in the latter chapters of this book take place in Shiloh, and since the Israelites gathered to present **themselves before God** (the tabernacle was in Shiloh), it seems natural enough to accept this variation from our text. However, we must resist the temptation to do so. Shechem is the natural place for this covenant ceremony, for it was the scene of God's first covenant with Abraham (Gen 12:6-7) and the formal renewal of the Genesis 35:2-4 covenant. Here, too, Joshua and the people pronounced the blessings and cursings which were then inscribed on Mount Gerizim and Mount Ebal. This would have been the best place in the Promised Land to address **all the tribes of Israel,** because of the natural amphitheater made by the acoustical phenomenon of the facing mountains. And too, it was Mizpeh and Shechem (not Shiloh) which were the fixed meeting places for a gathering of the tribes (see Jud 10:17; 11:11; 20:1; I Sam 7:5).

2-8. Your fathers dwelt. The grand review of Israel's history began with Abraham's father, **Terah,** and the service of **other gods.** The presence of the teraphim in the household of Laban amply illustrates this truth (Gen 31:19, 30). Abraham was taken by God from the other side of the **flood,** i.e. the Euphrates River, and led to **Canaan,** where **Isaac, Jacob,** and **Esau** were subsequently born. When the descendants of Jacob went down into Egypt, God called upon **Moses** to bring them through the **Red Sea** unto the land of the **Amorites** (see 12:1-6; Num 21:21-34; Deut 2:31-36; 3:1-17).

side Jordan; and they fought with you: and I gave them into your hand, that ye might possess their land; and I destroyed them from before you.

9 Then Bā´lăk the son of Zippor, king of Moab, arose and warred against Israel, and sent and called Bā´laam the son of Bē´ôr to curse you:

10 But I would not hearken unto Bā´laam; therefore he blessed you still: so I delivered you out of his hand.

11 And ye went over Jordan, and came unto Jericho: and the men of Jericho fought against you, the Ămorītes, and the Pĕr´iz-zītes, and the Canaanites, and the Hittites, and the Gir´ga-shītes, the Hī´vītes, and the Jĕb´u-sītes; and I delivered them into your hand.

12 And I sent the hornet before you, which drave them out from before you, even the two kings of the Ămorītes; but not with thy sword, nor with thy bow.

13 And I have given you a land for which ye did not labour, and cities which ye built not, and ye dwell in them; of the vineyards and oliveyards which ye planted not do ye eat.

14 ¶Now therefore fear the Lord, and serve him in sincerity and in truth: and put away the gods which your fathers served on the other side of the flood, and in Egypt; and serve ye the Lord.

15 And if it seem evil unto you to serve the Lord, choose you this day whom ye will serve; whether the gods which your fathers served that were on the other side of the flood, or the gods of the Ămorītes, in whose land ye dwell: but as for me and my house, we will serve the Lord.

16 And the people answered and said, God forbid that we should forsake the Lord, to serve other gods;

17 For the Lord our God, he it is that brought us up and our fathers out of the land of Egypt, from the house of bondage, and which did those great signs in our sight, and preserved us in all the way wherein we went, and among all the people through whom we passed:

18 And the Lord drave out from before us all the people, even the Ămorītes which dwelt in the land: therefore will we also serve the Lord; for he is our God.

19 And Joshua said unto the people, Ye cannot serve the Lord: for he is an holy God; he is a jealous God; he will

9-12. Then Balak . . . arose and warred against Israel. "The meaning of fought is 'opposed' since there is no record of a military attack by Balak, although such was his intention (cf. Num 22:6-11). The weapon he decided to use was Balaam's power to curse, as the verse goes on to relate" (A. Cohen, *Joshua*, p. 145). **Balak** would have fought against Israel, but God superintended through **Balaam** to bless Israel and deliver them so that they might cross the **Jordan.** In preparation for this event, God sent **the hornet** before the Israelites. The "hornet" has been variously explained by serious Bible students. They may be understood as literal, stinging creatures, or as creatures which were sent as a plague into Canaan to prepare the way for the children of Israel. Archaeologist John Garstang (who became renowned for his excavation of Jericho) believed the "hornet" to be a reference to Egyptian armies that defeated the peoples of Canaan shortly before the conquest (see *Joshua-Judges*, p. 259). But there is no historical evidence that such an invasion actually took place. Besides, the "hornet" was yet a future phenomenon at the eve of the conquest (Deut 7:20). A more likely interpretation is that the "hornet" was a poetic way of describing the terror which struck the hearts of those in Canaan when they heard of the rapid fall of Sihon and Og (2:11; 6:1; see also Ex 23:27-30; Deut 2:25; 7:20).

13. God had given to Israel a **land** for which she did not labor and **cities** which she did not build. She reaped the benefits of **vineyards** and **oliveyards,** which she did not plant. Such unmerited grace called for a commitment of service on the part of Israel.

2. The covenant of the heart. 24:14-24.

14-15. Amid the call for Israel to **fear** (give reverence to) **the Lord, and serve him in sincerity,** Joshua concedes that some of the Israelites may still be wavering in their commitment to the Lord, like some Christians in this century. Therefore, he joins other outstanding biblical personages who exhort and call for a crisis-commitment. Elijah exhorted the Israelites on Mount Carmel, "How long halt ye between two opinions? if the Lord be God, follow him . . ." (I Kgs 18:21). Paul exhorted "If ye then be risen with Christ, seek those things which are above . . ." (Col 3:1). Hosea prophesied that, speaking of God, Ephraim would one day say, "What have I to do any more with idols? I have heard him, and observed him" (Hos 14:8). Here, Joshua exhorts, **And if it seem evil unto you to serve the Lord, choose you this day whom ye will serve.** We can almost see the centenarian as he stands proudly and defiantly and declares **but as for me and my house, we will serve the Lord.**

16-21. Upon receiving such a challenge, the people immediately responded **God forbid that we should forsake the Lord, to serve other gods.** It was Jehovah who brought them from Egyptian bondage and into the land. No one can seriously doubt their sincerity at this point. They made a heart commitment to serve the Lord God. But Joshua somewhat cramped their commitment when he said, **Ye cannot serve the Lord.** Why? Because Yahweh (Jehovah) is a **jealous God** who will not share the adoration with others that is due Him alone. Saint Augustine sees in Joshua's statement an early understanding of the Pauline doctrine that self-righteousness does not win justification (Rom 3:20). Perhaps so, but Israel deepens her determination to make a heart covenant to serve God repeating, **but we will serve the Lord.**

not forgive your transgressions nor your sins.

20 If ye forsake the Lord, and serve strange gods, then he will turn and do you hurt, and consume you, after that he hath done you good.

21 And the people said unto Joshua, Nay; but we will serve the Lord.

22 And Joshua said unto the people, Ye *are* witnesses against yourselves that ye have chosen you the Lord, to serve him. And they said, *We are* witnesses.

23 Now therefore put away, *said he,* the strange gods which *are* among you, and incline your heart unto the Lord God of Israel.

24 And the people said unto Joshua, The Lord our God will we serve, and his voice will we obey.

25 So Joshua made a covenant with the people that day, and set them a statute and an ordinance in She′chem.

26 And Joshua wrote these words in the book of the law of God, and took a great stone, and set it up there under an oak, that *was* by the sanctuary of the Lord.

27 And Joshua said unto all the people, Behold, this stone shall be a witness unto us; for it hath heard all the words of the Lord which he spake unto us: it shall be therefore a witness unto you, lest ye deny your God.

28 So Joshua let the people depart, every man unto his inheritance.

29 ¶And it came to pass after these things, that Joshua the son of Nun, the servant of the Lord, died, *being* an hundred and ten years old.

30 And they buried him in the border of his inheritance in Tĭm′năth-se′rah, which *is* in mount Ē′phra-im, on the north side of the hill of Gā′ash.

31 And Israel served the Lord all the days of Joshua, and all the days of the elders that overlived Joshua, and which had known all the works of the Lord, that he had done for Israel.

32 ¶And the bones of Joseph, which the children of Israel brought up out of Egypt, buried they in She′chem, in a parcel of ground which Jacob bought of the sons of Hā′môr the father of She′chem for an hundred pieces of silver: and it became the inheritance of the children of Joseph.

33 ¶And Ē-le-ā′zar the son of Aaron died; and they buried him in a hill *that pertained to* Phĭn′e-has his son, which was given him in mount Ē′phra-im.

22-24. Joshua comes back at them one more time, reminding them that both they and he are witnesses to their heart covenant with God. Again, the third time, they repeat, **the Lord our God will we serve, and his voice will we obey.** This triple affirmation is reminiscent of many Christians who rededicate their lives to the Lord over and over again, but who have never made a real heart covenant with their Lord in the first place. It is also reminiscent of Jesus' triple inquiry of Peter and Peter's persistent claim of love for the Lord (Jn 21:15-19).

3. The covenant of stone. 24:25-28.

25-28. Convinced that Israel would little note nor long remember what she had affirmed at his farewell address, Joshua **set them a statute and an ordinance in Shechem.** This time it was in stone that Joshua made a covenant (Heb *berīt*, lit., "cut a covenant," a common Hebrew, Greek, and Latin expression for the formation of a covenant which was accompanied by a sacrifice cut into pieces and offered to the deity). The practice of chiseling a covenant in stone (like the tablets of the Mosaic law) was common in the ancient Near East. Joshua set the great covenant stone under an oak as a **witness unto us** of what Israel had covenanted, **lest ye deny your God.** With these precautions taken against idolatry, Joshua permitted the people to depart to their homes.

C. Joshua's Death and Related Events. 24:29-33.

1. Joshua's death and burial. 24:29-31.

29-31. Joshua the son of Nun, the servant of the Lord, died. Here is the double reference; the first the usual designation to distinguish the identity of Joshua with relation to his father, the second to distinguish the identity of Joshua with relation to his Lord. One can have no better epitaph than "the servant of the Lord." The old warrior was buried within his inheritance in **Timnath-serah** (see note on 19:50). The value of Joshua's personal influence on the Israelite nation is seen in the statement, **And Israel served the Lord all the days of Joshua,** and even the days of his close associates, the elders, who were greatly influenced by him and outlived this man of God. Truly great will be his reward.

2. Joseph's burial. 24:32.

32. The bones of Joseph (see Gen 50:24-25; Ex 13:19). The respect given Joseph is again seen in the scrupulous fulfillment of his request to be buried in **Shechem.** Accordingly, his bones were brought from Egypt in the Exodus and were laid to rest in the **parcel of ground** (lit., "portion of the field," see Gen 33:19) which Jacob bought from Hamor.

3. Eleazar's death and burial. 24:33.

33. To close out the triple conclusion to the conquest of Promised Land, the death and burial of **Eleazar** (see Ex 6:23; 28:1; Josh 14:1) is recorded. He was buried in a **hill** that belonged to his son **Phinehas.**

With the passing of Joshua and Eleazar, an era in Israel's history comes to a close. But also with the deaths of these stalwart servants of Jehovah, the children passed into a much darker period of history.

BIBLIOGRAPHY

Blaike, W. G. Joshua. In *The Expositor's Bible*. Ed. by W. R. Nicholl. Grand Rapids: Eerdmans, 1947.

Blair, H. J. Joshua. In *The New Bible Commentary*. Ed. by F. Davidson. Grand Rapids: Eerdmans, 1953.

Bright, John. Joshua. In *The Interpreter's Bible*. Ed. by G. Buttrick. Nashville: Abingdon, 1953.

*Davis, John J. *Conquest and Crisis: Studies in Joshua, Judges and Ruth*. Grand Rapids: Baker, 1969.

Fay, F. R. Joshua. In *Commentary on the Holy Scriptures*. Ed. by J. P. Lange. Grand Rapids: Zondervan, n.d.

Friederberg, S. *Joshua: An Annotated Hebrew Text*. London: Heinemann, 1913.

*Garstang, J. *Joshua-Judges*. New York: Richard Smith, 1931.

Jamieson, R. Joshua. In *A Commentary Critical and Explanatory on the Old and New Testaments*. Ed. by Jamieson, Fausset, and Brown. Grand Rapids: Eerdmans, n.d.

Kaufman, Yehezkel, *The Biblical Account of the Conquest of Palestine*. Jerusalem: Magnes Press, 1935.

————. *The Book of Joshua with Commentary and Introduction*. Jerusalem: Magnes Press, 1959.

*Keil, C. F. Joshua. In *Biblical Commentary on the Old Testament*. Ed. by Keil and Delitzsch. Grand Rapids: Eerdmans, reprinted, 1950.

*Lias, J. J. Joshua. In *The Pulpit Commentary*. Ed. by Spence and Exell. Grand Rapids: Eerdmans, reprinted, 1950.

Lloyd, John. *The Book of Joshua*. London: Hodder & Stoughton, 1886.

Maclear, G. F. The Book of Joshua. In *Cambridge Bible for Schools and Colleges*. Cambridge: University Press, 1894.

Pink, A. W. *Gleanings in Joshua*. Chicago: Moody Press, 1964.

Rea, John. Joshua. In *The Wycliffe Bible Commentary*. Ed. by Pfeiffer and Harrison. Chicago: Moody Press, 1962.

*Schaeffer, F. A. *Joshua and the Flow of Biblical History*. Downers Grove, Ill.: InterVarsity Press, 1976.

Scroggie, W. G. *The Land and Life of Rest*. Glasgow: Pickering and Inglis, 1950.

Smith, T. *The History of Joshua*. Edinburgh: William Oliphant, 1870.

Waller, C. H. Joshua. In *A Bible Commentary for English Readers*. Ed. by Ellicot. London: Cassel & Co., n.d.

JUDGES

INTRODUCTION

Title. The book of Judges derives its title from the Latin *Liber Judicum*. The Hebrew title is *shōpetīm*. The biblical judges were actually heroes, or deliverers, more than they were legal arbiters. They were raised up and empowered by the Lord specifically to execute the judgment of God on behalf of the people of Israel. It is interesting to note that only God Himself is described as the Judge (*shōpēt*) in 11:27. The verbal form (judged) is used of the activity of the various deliverers. Thus, recognizing the sovereignty of God over the affairs of His people, the author makes it clear that it is He who judges Israel for her sin; it is He who raises up oppressors against her; and it is He who raises up judges to deliver her from oppression.

Theme. The recurring theme of the book of Judges is spiritual apostasy. Several cycles of compromise-apostasy-oppression-repentance-deliverance occur throughout the book. In many ways Judges is the opposite of Joshua. Under Joshua's leadership, Israel strictly obeyed the commands of the Law and won constant victories. By contrast, during the time of the judges Israel forsook the Law and compromised with her enemies, and toleration of and coexistence with the enemy replaced their desire for total victory. The victorious conquest was followed by an incomplete settlement of the conquered territory, and the lack of clearly defined leadership led to confusion as "every man did that which was right in his own eyes" (17:6). This confusion was reflected in the moral and spiritual weakness of Israel during this time. The people had sinned against their covenant with God by disobeying the command to totally drive out the Canaanites (cf. Ex 23:31-33; Num 33:51-56; Deut 7:1-5). They intermarried with the people of the land (3:6) and adopted pagan worship of Baal and Ashtaroth (2:13). Soon they were committing numerous violations of the Mosaic law, including the recognition of improper priests and private worship sanctuaries. The moral code of the people of that day was so low that lying, stealing, adultery, and murder were often condoned.

Authorship. The books of Judges and Ruth originally formed one document in the Hebrew Bible. They deal with events following Joshua's death (ca. 1380 B.C.) and continue until the reference to David in Ruth 4:17, 22, but they were written from a prophetic viewpoint following the days of the judges (cf. 17:6; 18:1; 19:1; 21:25, "In those days there was no king in Israel") and prior to David's conquest of Jerusalem, since it was still held by the Jebusites according to the author in 1:21. While the author is not indicated by the text, Jewish tradition has always ascribed it to Samuel the prophet, and rightly so, since he was the major spiritual figure of the time of the judges.

The liberal-critical view which would attribute the authorship of this book to a Deuteronomistic recension based on mythological hero sagas must be rejected in light of the many historical details which may only be attributed to the time of the judges themselves. For a detailed discussion of the authorship questions related to the book of Judges, see R. K. Harrison, *Introduction to the Old Testament*, pp. 680-694. For a criticism of the "Deuteronomistic" composition of both Joshua and Judges, see Y. Kaufmann, *The Biblical Account of the Conquest of Palestine*, who states that "the Former Prophets are not a Deuteronomistic historical work."

Chronology. If Samuel the prophet was the author of Judges, its composition would date from ca. 1050-1000 B.C. The chronological material in the book has been subject to a great deal of discussion and widely variant dating. British evangelical scholarship (e.g., Bruce and Cundall) has tended to follow the late date for the Exodus and, therefore, dates Othniel at 1200 B.C., while conservative American scholars (Pfeiffer, Ryrie, Wood) date him at ca. 1350 B.C. The latter approach takes the biblical data regarding these dates seriously. In Judges 11:26 Jephthah referred to a period of three hundred years between the conquest and his own time, which correlates with the figures supplied in the text by subtracting the eighteen-year Ammonite oppression with which he was contemporary.

The total number of years mentioned in Judges is four hundred ten. However, a simple adding up of numbers may not be the key to the chronology of this period; for there may have been overlapping judgeships, functioning at the same time, but in different locations. The text itself does not make it clear whether Jephthah, Ibzan, Elon, and Abdon, for example, succeeded each other or were contemporaries. Many commentators believe that the twenty years of Samson's judgeship should be included within the Philistine oppression, which was finally broken by Samuel at Ebenezer (I Sam 7). If the period of the judges began as early as 1381 B.C. (Geisler, *A Popular Survey of the Old Testament*, p. 106) and ended as late as King Saul in 1043 B.C., that would only account for three hundred thirty-eight years. Therefore, there must have been overlapping judgeships and oppressions, so that, while part of the land was under oppression, another part might be in a state of deliverance.

Jephthah's reference (11:26) to three hundred years from Joshua (1405 B.C.) to himself (1105 B.C.) coincides with the statement in I Kings 6:1 regarding four hundred eighty years from the Exodus (1445 B.C.) to the fourth year of Solomon's reign (931 B.C.). Even Cundall (p. 33) admits the biblical data supports the early date for the Exodus, but he rejects it in favor of so-called critical objections.

The following chart is a suggested compilation of the chronology of the period of the Judges.

EXODUS & WILDERNESS JOURNEY: 1445-1405 B.C.
CONQUEST & SETTLEMENT: 1405-1381 B.C.

CYCLE	ENEMY	PERIOD OF SERVITUDE	JUDGE	PERIOD OF REST
FIRST 3:7-11	Mesopotamia	8 years (1381-1373 B.C.)	Othniel	40 years (1373-1334 B.C.)
SECOND 3:12-31	Moab	18 years (1334-1316 B.C.)	Ehud (Shamgar)	80 years (1316-1237 B.C.)
THIRD 4:1-5:31	Canaanites	20 years (1257-1237 B.C.)	Deborah and Barak	40 years (1237-1198 B.C.)
FOURTH 6:1-8:32	Midianites	7 years (1198-1191 B.C.)	Gideon	40 years (1191-1151 B.C.)
FIFTH 8:33-10:5	Usurpation of Abimelech	3 years (1151-1149 B.C.)	Tola Jair	45 years (1149-1105 B.C.)
SIXTH 10:6-12:15	Ammonites (in east)	18 years (1105-1087 B.C.)	Jephthah Ibzan Elon Abdon	31 years (1087-1058 B.C.)
SEVENTH 13:1-16:31	Philistines (in west)	40 years (1087-1047 B.C.)	Samson	20 years (1069-1049 B.C.)

JUDGESHIP OF ELI: 1107-1067 B.C.
JUDGESHIP OF SAMUEL: 1067-1020 B.C.
LENGTH OF SAUL'S REIGN: 1043-1011 B.C.

Style. The book of Judges follows a thematic scheme, rather than a purely chronological format. For example, chapters 17-21 form an appendix to the previous accounts. While they fit an earlier period of time, these chapters were placed at the end of the book because their content does not fit the thematic scheme of apostasy-judgment-deliverance which is so predominantly obvious in chapters 3-16. This inspired book of Scripture contains both prose and poetry, historical records and eyewitness accounts, military sagas and personal stories. It reveals the grace of the Lord in His continual covenant mercies to Israel as He continues to restore His erring people. Throughout the book the author makes several references to historical and geographical details which he personally substantiates. There can be no doubt that the apologetic style of the author was intended to verify the historicity of these accounts.

Historical Background. The events recorded in the book of Judges occurred during one of the most turbulent and transitional times in the history of the ancient Near East. In Egypt the confusion of the Amarna Period had allowed Joshua a free hand in the conquest and settlement of Canaan. Assuming the early date for the Exodus, the first judges were contemporary with the powerful Pharaohs of the Nineteenth Dynasty, while the later judges would have been contemporary with the period of confusion which followed. Meanwhile, to the north, the Kingdom of Mitanni fell to the Hittites in ca. 1370 B.C. Further west, the great Minoan

and Mycenean empires also collapsed; and a period of mass migrations (people movements) followed, ultimately bringing the Bronze Age culture to an end and introducing the Iron Age. The Israelite disadvantage in regard to iron weapons and chariots is mentioned several times throughout the book of Judges.

In Palestine itself (which derived its name from the Philistines) the Canaanites had gained a strong foothold since the days of Abraham, and many walled fortresses dotted the land. Even after Joshua's devastating conquest, the Canaanites seem to have been able to quickly rebuild their major fortresses (Jericho and Hazor). However, McKenzie, *The World of the Judges* (p. 38), notes that the manner in which these cities fell so easily indicates that their defense was not equal to the offense. The loose structure of the Canaanite politic caused the various city-states to be at war with each other almost constantly. In addition, both the Canaanites and Israelites were pressured by the invading Sea Peoples (Philistines) who gained firm control of the coastal area. To the south and east, the nomadic tribes had begun to settle into the Transjordanian Kingdoms of Moab, Ammon, and Edom. This discordant milieu is the setting of the book of Judges. Thus, God had ample sources to draw upon as a means to discipline the sins of Israel. However, it must be remembered that the sovereign hand of God, and not just political chaos, ruled over the events of men during this time.

OUTLINE

I. Reason for the Judges. 1:1-2:23.
  A. Political Problems in the Days of the Judges. 1:1-36.
    1. Conquest and settlement of Canaan. 1:1-26.
    2. Catalogue of unoccupied territory. 1:27-36.
  B. Religious Apostasy in the Days of the Judges. 2:1-23.
    1. Rebuke by the angel of the Lord. 2:1-3.
    2. Repentance of the people. 2:4-5.
    3. Retrospect: Joshua's victories. 2:6-10.
    4. Re-evaluation: Cycles of apostasy, oppression, repentance, and deliverance. 2:11-23.
II. Rule of the Judges. 3:1-16:31.
  A. First Cycle: Othniel versus Cushan-rishathaim. 3:1-11.
    1. Servitude to Mesopotamia—eight years. 3:1-8.
    2. Salvation by Othniel—forty years. 3:9-11.
  B. Second Cycle: Ehud versus Eglon. 3:12-31.
    1. Servitude to Moab, Ammon, and Amalek—eighteen years. 3:12-14.
    2. Salvation by Ehud—eighty years. 3:15-30.
    3. Shamgar delivers Israel from the Philistines. 3:31.
  C. Third Cycle: Deborah and Barak versus Jabin and Sisera. 4:1-5:31.
    1. Servitude to the Canaanites—twenty years. 4:1-3.
    2. Salvation by Deborah and Barak—forty years. 4:4-24.

3. Victory song of Deborah and Barak. 5:1-31.
  D. Fourth Cycle: Gideon versus Midianites. 6:1-8:35.
    1. Servitude to the Midianites—seven years. 6:1-10.
    2. Salvation by Gideon—forty years. 6:11-8:35.
  E. Fifth Cycle: Israel versus Abimelech. 9:1-10:5.
    1. Servitude to Abimelech—three years. 9:1-57.
    2. Salvation by Tola and Jair—forty-five years. 10:1-5.
  F. Sixth Cycle: Jephthah versus the Ammonites. 10:6-12:15.
    1. Servitude to the Ammonites—eighteen years. 10:6-18.
    2. Salvation by Jephthah, Ibzan, Elon, Abdon—thirty-one years. 11:1-12:13.
  G. Seventh Cycle: Samson versus Philistines. 13:1-16:31.
    1. Servitude to the Philistines—forty years. 13:1-25.
    2. Salvation by Samson—twenty years. 14:1-16:31.
III. Ruin of the Judges. 17:1-21:25.
  A. Idolatry of Micah and the Danites. 17:1-18:31.
  B. Immorality of the Gibeonites and Benjamites. 19:1-21:25.

COMMENTARY

I. REASON FOR THE JUDGES. 1:1-2:23.

A. Political Problems in the Days of the Judges. 1:1-36.

1. Conquest and settlement of Canaan. 1:1-26.

NOW after the death of Joshua it came to pass, that the children of Israel asked the LORD, saying, Who shall go up for us against the Canaanites first, to fight against them?

2 And the LORD said, Jūdah shall go up: behold, I have delivered the land into his hand.

3 And Jūdah said unto Simeon his brother, Come up with me into my lot, that we may fight against the Canaanites; and I likewise will go with thee into thy lot. So Simeon went with him.

4 And Jūdah went up; and the LORD delivered the Canaanites and the Pĕr'-iz-zītes into their hand: and they slew of them in Bē'zĕk ten thousand men.

5 And they found A-dō'nī-bē'zĕk in Bē'zĕk: and they fought against him, and they slew the Canaanites and the Pĕr'iz-zītes.

6 But A-dō'nī-bē'zĕk fled; and they

1:1-8. The transition from Moses' leadership to that of Joshua is one of the most encouraging events in all of Scripture. However, no strong central ruler took over after the **death of Joshua** (in ca. 1390-1380 B.C.). Whereas the book of Joshua represents the apex of victory for the Israelite tribes; the book of Judges, by contrast, presents the tragic defeat that was the result of compromise with their enemies. Joshua is a picture of the potential of total victory that is available to every child of God, while Judges is a picture of potential defeat which will be experienced every time one fails to totally drive out the enemy. The literary format of Judges is remarkably similar to that of Joshua, in spite of the fact that one book deals almost exclusively with victory, whereas the other deals almost continually with defeat. Israel is now pictured as settled in the land by the tribal allotments that had been apportioned to them by Joshua. While the initial conquest was lightning-quick and decisive, the settlement of the tribal territories was slow and cumbersome. Many pockets of resistance remained; and in time the Israelites settled on a policy of coexistence, rather than total conquest.

The contrast between Joshua and Judges presents a parallel

451

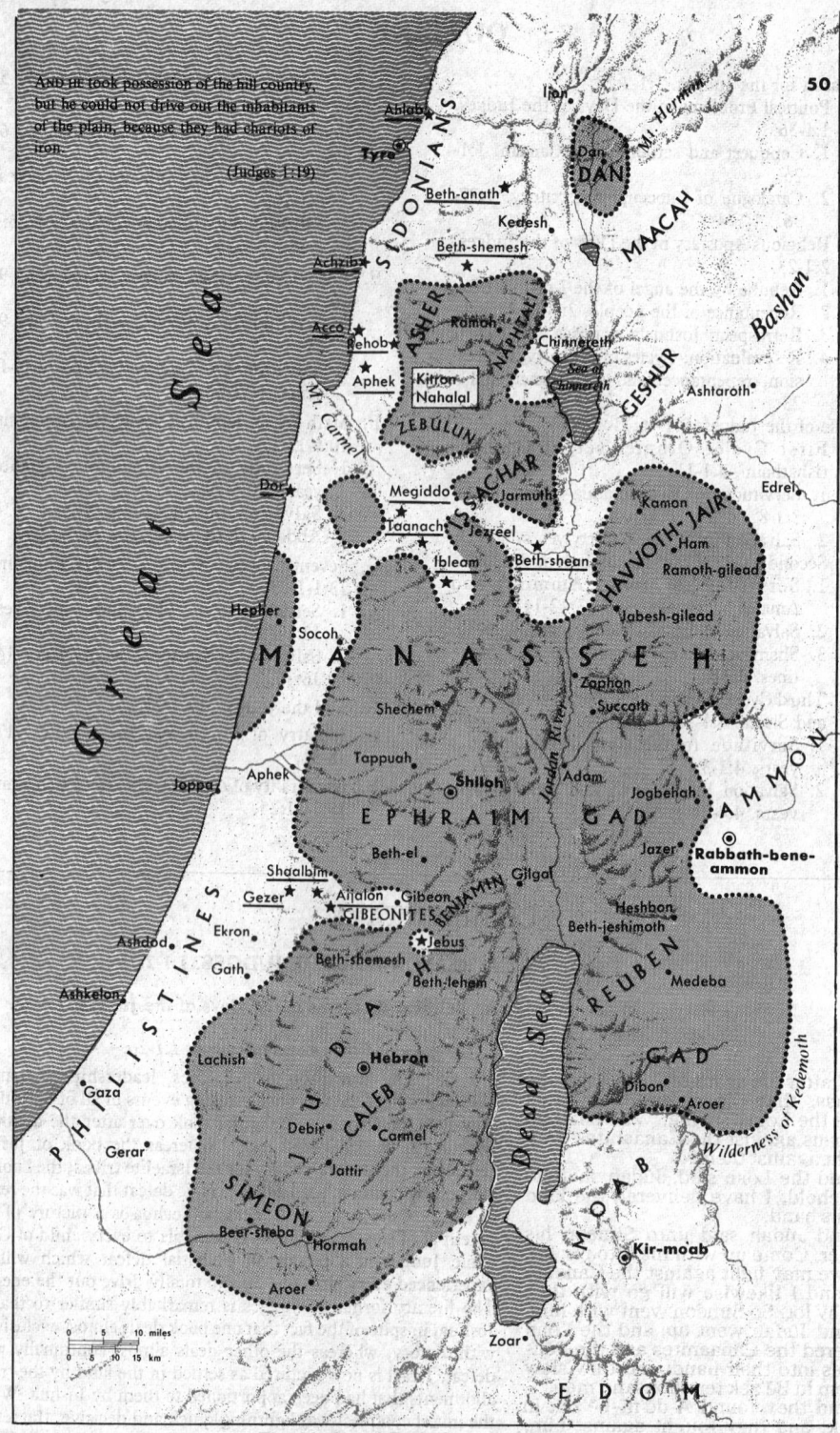

AND HE took possession of the hill country, but he could not drive out the inhabitants of the plain, because they had chariots of iron.

(Judges 1:19)

The Limits of Early Israelite Control

pursued after him, and caught him, and cut off his thumbs and his great toes.

7 And A-dō̆′nī–bē′zĕk said,Threescore and ten kings, having their thumbs and their great toes cut off, gathered *their meat* under my table: as I have done, so God hath requited me. And they brought him to Jerusalem, and there he died.

8 ¶Now the children of Jū̆dah had fought against Jerusalem, and had taken it, and smitten it with the edge of the sword, and set the city on fire.

between the unconditional and conditional covenant agreements of God. God had unconditionally guaranteed the land to Abraham and his descendants (Gen 15). However, under Moses, He had established a conditional covenant to determine whether or not they would be blessed in the land they were to possess (Deut 28). The Bible makes it clear that man can do nothing to earn his own salvation; but it is also equally clear that in order to enjoy the salvation that has been given to him as a free gift, he must become obedient to the lordship of Christ. Faith, not obedience, determines one's salvation. Obedience determines the degree of blessing to be enjoyed by the saved person. There is, therefore, no real contradiction then between Joshua and Judges. The victory reported so decisively in Joshua was a reality for the Israelites. However, their subsequent compromise of coexistence with their enemies led to their losing much of the land which they had initially acquired.

The resistance came from their perennial enemies, the **Canaanites.** The term Canaanites is generally used as a designation for all the aboriginal tribal inhabitants of the Levant (i.e., Palestine). Sometimes a distinction is made between the Canaanites and the Amorites (for a thorough discussion of these peoples see A. R. Millard, "The Canaanites," and M. Liverani, "The Amorites," in *Peoples of Old Testament Times,* and also E. Anati, *Palestine Before the Hebrews).* The Canaanites were a loosely confederated settlement of various city-states and did not represent a strong unified central government. The Perizzites, Jebusites, and Amorites are generally considered to be related to one another. The Canaanites had already developed their own religious beliefs and practices by this time. Their religion was essentially that of a nature cult based on a pantheon of gods led by El and Baal.

Judah and **Simeon,** who were tribal blood brothers, allied themselves to go to war against the Canaanites and the Perizzites of whom they slew ten thousand men in **Bezek.** The tribe of Simeon was not assigned a specific territory of its own and was allowed to settle within the portion assigned to Judah (cf. Josh 19:9). Thus, the two tribes became virtually inseparable. The location of Bezek is unknown (possibly Khirbet Bezqa near Gezer) and the meaning of the name of its king **Adoni-bezek** means "lord of Bezek." He is not to be confused with Adoni-zedek of Joshua 10. Adoni-zedek was previously the king of Jerusalem and was the leader of the southern confederation of Canaanite cities against the Gibeonites. Adoni-bezek, by contrast, was defeated at Bezek and brought to Jerusalem afterwards. The passage indicates that Adoni-bezek had conquered seventy kings, whom he brought under his submission by **having their thumbs and their great toes cut off.** This may seem strange to the modern reader, but was very significant in the ancient Near East. Physical mutilation disqualified a person from religious or political office (cf. Lev 21:16-24). It was also used to render a person militarily impotent. By having his thumb cut off he could no longer handle a weapon effectively. That the defeated kings **gathered their meat under my table** indicates that they became vassal servants of the overlord and were allowed to remain alive. In a similar fashion, Adoni-bezek was allowed to remain at Jerusalem until he died.

Afterwards, the tribe of Judah **fought against Jerusalem . . . and set the city on fire.** The site of Jerusalem is one of the oldest cities in the world. Its original occupation was on the Hill of Ophel, south of the area where the Temple would later stand. It is referred to as the city of Salem in Genesis 14:18. It is mentioned in the Tell Mardikh Tablets found at Ebla and in the Tell El-Amarna Tablets as "Urusalim," one of the most important Canaanite city-states. It is also mentioned in Egyptian texts as early as 1900 B.C. (for a discussion of this important city and its archaeological remains see M. Avi-Yonah, *Jerusalem* and

C. Pfeiffer, *Jerusalem Through The Ages*). The fact that this passage states that the children of Judah conquered Jerusalem, whereas Joshua 15:63 states that they had not done it "unto this day," would indicate the antiquity of the date of the book of Joshua. In the Joshua reference the Jebusites are referred to as controlling the city. Some have suggested that the tribe of Judah conquered the city itself, but not the stronghold of the Jebusite tower. Judges 19:10 ff., also indicates that the Jebusites were again in control of the city, which was not permanently conquered and settled by the Israelites until the time of David (cf. I Chr 11:4-9).

9 And afterward the children of Jūdah went down to fight against the Canaanites, that dwelt in the mountain, and in the south, and in the valley.

10 And Judah went against the Canaanites that dwelt in Hēbron: (now the name of Hēbron before *was* Kĭr′jath-är′ba:) and they slew Shē′shaī, and A-hī′man, and Tăl′maī.

11 And from thence he went against the inhabitants of Dē′bir: and the name of Dē′bir before *was* Kĭr′jath-sē′pher:

12 And Caleb said, He that smiteth Kir′jath-sē′pher, and taketh it, to him will I give Ăch′sah my daughter to wife.

13 And Ŏth′nī-el the son of Kē′năz, Caleb's younger brother, took it: and he gave him Ăch′sah his daughter to wife.

14 And it came to pass, when she came *to him*, that she moved him to ask of her father a field: and she lighted from off *her* ass; and Caleb said unto her, What wilt thou?

15 And she said unto him, Give me a blessing: for thou hast given me a south land; give me also springs of water. And Caleb gave her the upper springs and the nether springs.

16 ¶And the children of the Kēn′īte, Moses' father in law, went up out of the city of palm trees with the children of Jūdah into the wilderness of Jūdah, which *lieth* in the south of Ā′răd; and they went and dwelt among the people.

17 And Jūdah went with Simeon his brother, and they slew the Canaanites that inhabited Zē′phăth, and utterly destroyed it. And the name of the city was called Hôr′mah.

18 Also Jūdah took Gā′za with the coast thereof, and Ăs′ke-lŏn with the coast thereof, and Ĕk-ron with the coast thereof.

19 And the LORD was with Jūdah; and he drave out *the inhabitants of* the mountain; but could not drive out the inhabitants of the valley, because they had chariots of iron.

20 And they gave Hēbron unto Caleb, as Moses said: and he expelled thence the three sons of Anak.

21 ¶And the children of Benjamin did not drive out the Jĕb′u-sītes that inhabited Jerusalem; but the Jĕb′u-sītes dwell with the children of Benjamin in Jerusalem unto this day.

9-15. The tribe of Judah, under the leadership of **Caleb,** conquered **Hebron,** which became the early Judean capital. It was located about twenty miles south of Jerusalem in the highest mountains of Judah. The patriarchal burial ground was located there (Gen 23). It had been assigned earlier to Caleb (Num 14:24) in anticipation of his subsequent conquest, which is also related in Joshua 15. It was previously called **Kirjath-arba,** meaning "fourfold city" or "tetrapolis." It was the home of the giant-like Anakim. The names of **Sheshai . . . Ahiman . . . Talmai** are of Aramaean origin. Next, Caleb turned his attention to the city of **Debir,** which was formerly known as **Kirjath-sepher** ("city of books" or "scribes"). Cundall (p. 55) suggests Caleb's interest in this area may have come from his original assignment as a spy to reconnoiter this territory. Debir was eleven miles southwest of Hebron and has been identified in archaeological excavations as Tell Beit Mirsim (cf. W. F. Albright, "Debir," in *Archaeology And Old Testament Study*, pp. 207-222). Caleb promised to give his daughter **Achsah** to be the wife of the man who would take the city. His nephew **Othniel,** who would later become the first judge, accepted the challenge and conquered the city. The bravery of Othniel and the leadership of the tribe of Judah appears again in the invasion described in chapter 3. His wife's request for the **springs of water** (Heb *gulōt-mayim*) was extremely important since they were in a very arid region near the Negev. Discoveries in this area have revealed many water shafts, or wells, that could provide adequate water for those living in the area.

16-21. The reference to the **Kenite** refers to the nomadic people who later settled among the Amalekites. The Kenites are also associated with the Midianites (Ex 18), indicating their constantly nomadic condition. They were related to the Israelites through Moses' marriage to Zipporah (Ex 2:21). As a rule, they remained in favorable relationship with the Israelites until even as late as the time of David. In Judges 4 the Israelite defender, Jael, is married to Heber the Kenite. The **city of palm trees** commonly refers to Jericho, though this has been questioned by some (cf. Cundall, p. 56). Most Hebrew scholars suggest that the phrase **dwelt among the people** be amended to read "dwelt among Amalek." **Arad** is normally identified with Tell 'Arad, seventeen miles south of Hebron. The remainder of this section describes the conquest by the tribes of Judah and Simeon over Zephath, which was renamed **Hormah,** meaning "devotion to destruction." Next, they conquered **Gaza . . . Askelon . . . Ekron,** which later formed part of the Philistine pentapolis, though at this time, prior to the arrival of the main body of Philistines in this area, they were still under Canaanite control. Verse 19 indicates that Judah was able to conquer the hill country but **could not drive out the inhabitants of the valley** where the use of their **chariots of iron** neutralized the Israelite attack. It would be many years until the Israelites acquired a knowledge of ironworking, giving the Canaanites a superior advantage in this skill which they had learned from the Hittites (cf. A. Goetz "Hittite and Anatolian Studies," in *The Bible and the Ancient Near East*, pp. 421-438). Verse 21 notes that the **children of Benjamin** were not able to drive out the

Jebusites who inhabited Jerusalem. Since Benjamin and Judah formed a common tribal border near Jerusalem, it is not unusual for this reference to include the Benjamites. The text also notes that the Jebusites still held the city "unto this day" (i.e., the time of the author of the book). Thus, the initial victory of the men of Judah against Jerusalem was already lost, and the city reverted back to Jebusite control. It would never permanently come under Israelite conquest until it was taken by David and Joab (II Sam 5:6-9).

22 ¶And the house of Joseph, they also went up against Bĕth-el: and the Lord *was* with them.

23 And the house of Joseph sent to descry Bĕth-el. (Now the name of the city before *was* Luz.)

24 And the spies saw a man come forth out of the city, and they said unto him, Shew us, we pray thee, the entrance into the city, and we will shew thee mercy.

25 And when he shewed them the entrance into the city, they smote the city with the edge of the sword; but they let go the man and all his family.

26 And the man went into the land of the Hittites, and built a city, and called the name thereof Luz: which *is* the name thereof unto this day.

22-26. The house of Joseph refers to the tribes of Ephraim and Manasseh. **Beth-el** was twelve miles north of Jerusalem. Beth-el means "house of God," a name given to it by Jacob in Genesis 28:19, where it is also noted that its original name was **Luz.** Beth-el remained a very important city in and throughout biblical history. Originally, it was evidently a strong Canaanite cult-center. It later became a prominent city in Israel; and finally, it lapsed into a center of idolatry. They captured a man of the city who showed them the entrance so that they were able to conquer it completely. In return, they let the man and his family escape **into the land of the Hittites,** i.e., northern Syria (as opposed to the great Hittite Empire which was located in Asia Minor). The escapee from the Canaanite city of Luz established a new and unknown city by the same name in the area beyond the Orontes River in the territory which was under Hittite control. Bruce (p. 240) suggests that this man may have been himself an immigrant Hittite who had settled in the hill country of Judah.

2. Catalogue of unoccupied territory. 1:27-36.

27-36. This chapter ends with the sad note of incomplete settlement of the land by the various Israelite tribes. It is not legitimate to call this an incomplete conquest, since the book of Joshua makes it clear that the land was totally under Israelite control in Joshua's time, in accord with the promise of God. What it refers to is the fact that, having received their tribal allotments, the various tribes were unable or unwilling to bring their territory under total settlement so that the enemy could not filter back into their territory. Thus, **Manasseh** was unable to control **Beth-shean . . . Taanach . . . Dor . . . Ibleam . . . Megiddo.** These cities formed a line of Canaanite resistance across the plain of Esdraelon, separating the central tribes from the northern tribes. These particular cities were, for the most part, under Egyptian occupied control during this time and would, therefore, present stronger resistance to the Israelites (cf. G. E. Wright, *Biblical Archaeology,* pp. 53-55). Rather than totally driving out the Canaanites, Israel put them **to tribute,** meaning that they subjugated them to the status of taxpaying vassals. Next, it is stated that **Ephraim** did not drive the Canaanites out of **Gezer.** The city was later under Philistine control and was not fully conquered by the Israelites until ca. 950 B.C. (I Kgs 9:16).

27 ¶Neither did Ma-năs′seh drive out *the inhabitants of* Bĕth-shĕ′an and her towns, nor Tā′a-năch and her towns, nor the inhabitants of Dor and her towns, nor the inhabitants of Ĭb′le-am and her towns, nor the inhabitants of Me-gĭd′dō and her towns: but the Canaanites would dwell in that land.

28 And it came to pass, when Israel was strong, that they put the Canaanites to tribute, and did not utterly drive them out.

29 Neither did Ē′phra-im drive out the Canaanites that dwelt in Gē′zer; but the Canaanites dwelt in Gē′zer among them.

30 Neither did Zĕb′u-lun drive out the inhabitants of Kĭt′rŏn, nor the inhabitants of Nā′ha-lŏl; but the Canaanites dwelt among them, and became tributaries.

31 Neither did Asher drive out the inhabitants of Ăc′chō, nor the inhabitants of Zī′don, nor of Äh′lăb, nor of Ăch′zĭb, nor of Hĕl′bah, nor of Ā′phĭk, nor of Rē′hŏb:

32 But the Asherites dwelt among the Canaanites, the inhabitants of the land: for they did not drive them out.

33 Neither did Năph′ta-lī drive out the inhabitants of Bĕth-shĕ′mesh, nor the inhabitants of Bĕth-ā′nāth; but he dwelt among the Canaanites, the inhabitants of the land: nevertheless the inhabitants of Bĕth-shĕ′mesh and of Bĕth-ā′nāth became tributaries unto them.

34 And the Ămorītes forced the children of Dan into the mountain: for they would not suffer them to come down to the valley:

35 But the Ămorītes would dwell in mount Hē′res in Āij′a-lŏn, and in Shā-

The cities mentioned in Zebulon have never been positively identified. Next, it is noted that Asher was unable to drive out the inhabitants of **Accho** (also known as Acre, north of Mount Carmel)—Zidon (the famous, the powerful Phoenician city on the Mediterranean coast)—**Ahlab** (unknown)—Achzib (about ten miles north of Accho)—**Helbah** (Mahalliba, northeast of Tyre)—**Aphik** (Tell Kurdaneh, south of Accho)—**Rehob** (Tell Berweh). Even in the time of David and Solomon the Israelites never conquered Phoenicia, but were able to maintain friendly relationships with them. It is most likely that it was from them that they borrowed the concept of the alphabet. Next, we are told that the tribe of **Naphtali** was unable to control **Beth-shemesh** and **Beth-anath.** Beth-shemesh means "house of the sun" and Beth-anath, "house of anath"; they both were centers of Canaanite worship. Finally, the chapter ends with the tragic

ăl'bĭm: yet the hand of the house of Joseph prevailed, so that they became tributaries.

36 And the coast of the Ămorītes *was* from the going up to Ă-krăb'bĭm, from the rock, and upward.

CHAPTER 2

AND an angel of the LORD came up from Gilgal to Bō'chĭm, and said, I made you to go up out of Egypt, and have brought you unto the land which I sware unto your fathers; and I said, I will never break my covenant with you.

2 And ye shall make no league with the inhabitants of this land; ye shall throw down their altars: but ye have not obeyed my voice: why have ye done this?

3 Wherefore I also said, I will not drive them out from before you; but they shall be *as thorns* in your sides, and their gods shall be a snare unto you.

4 And it came to pass, when the angel of the LORD spake these words unto all the children of Israel, that the people lifted up their voice, and wept.

statement that the **Amorites forced the children of Dan into the mountain** (hill country) and would not even allow them to come down into the valley. Thus, the Danites were driven into the hills for protection and safety, and they rarely made excursions from them. Eventually, they were unable to control any of their territory and were forced to migrate far to the north (ch. 18). It is also interesting to note that Samson, the strongest man, came from Dan, the weakest tribe! The **Amorites** were considered "westerners" by the Akkadians. They were Semitic desert invaders who arrived in Palestine ca. 2000 B.C. The Canaanite dialect became a local derivation of the Amorite dialect; and most of the cultural development of the Canaanites was undoubtedly borrowed from the Amorites, who were the previous settlers of the Fertile Crescent. From their capital at Mari at one time they controlled extensive territory in the northern Mesopotamian Valley.

B. Religious Apostasy in the Days of the Judges. 2:1-23.

1. Rebuke by the angel of the Lord. 2:1-3.

2:1-3. The confusion and incomplete victory that ends chapter 1 serves as general introduction to the events of the second chapter. The great victories of the past under the leadership of Joshua and the elders who served with him were nullified by subsequent periods of compromise, in which the covenant was neglected, idolatry was tolerated, and intermarriage with the Canaanites became commonplace. It is under these circumstances that the **angel of the LORD** came to deliver God's message to them. Bruce, in the *New Bible Commentary* (p. 240), notes that: "The angel of Yahweh is the expression widely used in the Old Testament to denote Yahweh Himself in His manifestation to men." Theologically, such appearances of God in human form are called a "theophany." By such a manifestation, God had appeared unto Adam, Abraham, Hagar, Moses, Joshua, etc. On the significance of Theophanies (or "Christophanies," appearances of the preincarnate Christ) see E. Hengstenberg, *Christology of the Old Testament* and J. Borland, *Christ in the Old Testament*.

He came up from **Gilgal,** where the main military camp had been located during the time of the conquest, to **Bochim** (lit., weepers), whose exact location is unknown. It was somewhere between Beth-el and Shiloh, about twenty miles from the Dead Sea. The LXX has "Bethel." As the Angel speaks His message, it is actually the message of God Himself! He reminded them that He had brought them out of Egypt into the land that He had promised their fathers, reaffirming that He would never break His **covenant** with them. They, in turn, were to **make no league** (covenant) with the inhabitants of the land. For the terms of this covenant see Exodus 23:23; 34:12; Deuteronomy 7:2ff; 12:3. The Lord went on to remind them that they had **not obeyed my voice** and asked them why they had done this. Assuming an insufficient explanation, He then told them that He would **not drive . . . out** all of their enemies as He had originally promised since they had not kept their covenant with Him. Instead, He would allow them to remain as **thorns in your sides,** and their **gods** would be a **snare** unto them. Since Israel had compromised her loyalty to God by her idolatry, she had forfeited the privileges of the original covenant promises. The words of the **angel of the LORD** anticipate then the history of the judges which follows.

2. Repentance of the people. 2:4-5.

4-5. The message was one of such severe judgment that the people of Israel lifted up their voice and wept and thus **called the name of that place Bochim** ("weepers") and **sacrificed** unto the Lord. The Bible clearly indicates that significant place

456

5 And they called the name of that place Bŏ'chĭm: and they sacrificed there unto the LORD.

6 ¶And when Joshua had let the people go, the children of Israel went every man unto his inheritance to possess the land.

7 And the people served the LORD all the days of Joshua, and all the days of the elders that outlived Joshua, who had seen all the great works of the LORD, that he did for Israel.

8 And Joshua the son of Nun, the servant of the LORD, died, *being* an hundred and ten years old.

9 And they buried him in the border of his inheritance in Tĭm'năth-he'reŝ, in the mount of Ē'phra-im, on the north side of the hill Gā'ash.

10 And also all that generation were gathered unto their fathers: and there arose another generation after them, which knew not the LORD, nor yet the works which he had done for Israel.

11 ¶And the children of Israel did evil in the sight of the LORD, and served Bā'al-ĭm:

12 And they forsook the LORD God of their fathers, which brought them out of the land of Egypt, and followed other gods, of the gods of the people that *were* round about them, and bowed themselves unto them, and provoked the LORD to anger.

13 And they forsook the LORD, and served Bā'al and Ăsh'ta-rŏth.

14 And the anger of the LORD was hot against Israel, and he delivered them into the hands of spoilers that spoiled them, and he sold them into the hands of their enemies round about, so that they could not any longer stand before their enemies.

15 Whithersoever they went out, the hand of the LORD was against them for evil, as the LORD had said, and as the LORD had sworn unto them: and they were greatly distressed.

names were associated with historical events. The use of place names in the Bible is not merely aetiological tradition, as many critical scholars have assumed (see the discussion by Kitchen, *Ancient Orient and Old Testament*, pp. 19-64, where he criticizes the overuse of this concept by Alt and Noth).

3. Retrospect: Joshua's victories. 2:6-10.

6-10. Under Joshua, the initial phase of the conquest was totally successful. However, after the land was divided among the tribes, it was necessary for them to occupy the territory assigned to them in order to maintain it. The text now goes back and refers to the transition from the time of Joshua until the period of the judges. There is a very clear correlation between the end of the book of Joshua and the beginning of the book of Judges; this is typical of inspired narrative. The statement that **the people served the LORD all the days of Joshua** clearly indicates the success of his leadership and makes the subsequent failure of the new generation of Israelites all the greater sin by contrast. **The elders that outlived Joshua** were those who had served with him and had observed the **great works of the LORD**. The miraculous intervention of God on behalf of the people in the days of Moses and Joshua was now past history. After Joshua's death at the age of one hundred ten and the death of **all that generation**, there arose **another generation . . . which knew not the LORD**. This new generation had forgotten the intervention of Jehovah on behalf of their forefathers and neglected the covenant mercies of God toward them. The apostasy of the new generation set the pattern for subsequent periods of apostasy, restoration, and renewed apostasy.

4. Re-evaluation: Cycles of apostasy, oppression, repentance, and deliverance. 2:11-23.

11-13. The statement that they **served Baalim** (vs. 11) indicates that they worshiped localized Baal deities, thus the plural form *īm* is used. Baal was a fertility god. He was looked upon as the chief vegetation god of the Canaanites and was thought to bring productivity to crops, animals, and men. He was also associated with the occurrences of weather and was usually depicted in Canaanite carvings as holding a lightning bolt in his hand. Thus, he is also called the "god of fire," indicating the significance of Elijah's challenge to the prophets of Baal (I Kgs 18). The Hebrew word *ba'al* means "master," or "lord." When the Israelites settled in Canaan, they soon discovered the local Baal deities were looked upon as the individual lords of the land. Thus, by worshiping him they were forsaking the lordship of their God for the lordship of Baal! The text also refers to their serving **other gods . . . of the people** among whom they lived. As they forsook the Lord, **they . . . served Baal and Ashtaroth.** The Hebrew ending *ōt* is also a plural ending, indicating they worshiped localized Ashtar deities. These were multi-breasted female fertility deities, whose worship often included bizzare sexual practices. The Babylonian form of this deity was Ishtar, and the Roman form was Easter (whose fertility signs, interestingly, were a rabbit and an egg).

14-15. Since idolatry was regarded as a breach of covenant with the God of Israel, His anger was expressed against them by allowing them to be **delivered . . . into the hands of spoilers** (1:1, enemies). Because of the Israelites' tendency to turn to Baal worship in times of peace, God kept the pressure on them by allowing invasions of their enemies so that they were **greatly distressed.** Since their worship of Yahweh was the unifying factor among the Israelite tribes, the apostasy into Baal worship also tended to decentralize the strength of the nation. Their neglect of the covenant which bound them to the Lord, and also bound them together, caused them to present a divided front to their enemy invaders.

16 ¶Nevertheless the LORD raised up judges, which delivered them out of the hand of those that spoiled them.

17 And yet they would not hearken unto their judges, but they went a whoring after other gods, and bowed themselves unto them: they turned quickly out of the way which their fathers walked in, obeying the commandments of the LORD; *but* they did not so.

18 And when the LORD raised them up judges, then the LORD was with the judge, and delivered them out of the hand of their enemies all the days of the judge: for it repented the LORD because of their groanings by reason of them that oppressed them and vexed them.

19 And it came to pass, when the judge was dead, *that* they returned, and corrupted *themselves* more than their fahers, in following other gods to serve them, and to bow down unto them; they ceased not from their own doings, nor from their stubborn way.

20 ¶And the anger of the LORD was hot against Israel; and he said, Because that this people hath transgressed my covenant which I commanded their fathers, and have not hearkened unto my voice;

21 I also will not henceforth drive out any from before them of the nations which Joshua left when he died:

22 That through them I may prove Israel, whether they will keep the way of the LORD to walk therein, as their fathers did keep *it*, or not.

23 Therefore the LORD left those nations, without driving them out hastily; neither delivered he them into the hand of Joshua.

16-23. When the people repented and turned again to the Lord, He **raised up judges** who delivered them out of the hand of their enemies and led them back to fidelity to the Law and to their covenant with the Lord. The Hebrew word for "judge" is *shōpēt*, meaning "ruler," rather than magistrate, and is the source of the noun *mishpat*, meaning "judgment" or "justice." Its cognates are found in Akkadian, Phoenician, Aramaic, and even Punic (cf. A. Harris, *A Grammar of the Phoenician Language*, p. 153). The basic concept of the word has to do with a verdict given by a judge and is descriptive of every phase of the judge's work. Therefore, the noun *mishpat* means the judgment given by the *shōpēt* and, thus, may indicate justice, ordinance, or codified law (*tōrah*) given by God Himself, since Yahweh is the God of *mishpat* (Gen 18:25). Real judgment and justice cannot be separated from Him who is the basis of all ethical righteousness (cf. N. Snaith, *The Distinctive Ideas of the Old Testament*, pp. 74-77). Thus, to the Hebrew mind God's justice (*mishpat*) was not a mere idea, but an activated principle in time and history. It was manifested in real and observable events because the real God acted with vindicating righteousness upon His people. When Israel repented and sought the Lord, He raised up "judges" to accomplish His act of deliverance for Israel. Thus, the English title "judge" may often be misleading since it conveys the idea of acting mainly in the legal realm of arbitrating disputes, whereas, the biblical judges were primarily "saviors" or "deliverers" from their enemies (cf. G. Vos, *Biblical Theology*, pp. 270-75).

Actually, the noun *shōpēt* is not used to describe the men themselves, though the verb "judged" is used of the action of Othniel (3:10), Deborah (4:4), Tola (10:2), Jair (10:3), Jephthah (12:7), Ibzan (12:8), Elon (12:11), Abdon (12:13), and Samson (15:20). Their main duty was the act of "judging" by which they delivered Israel from oppression. As Cundall, in the *Tyndale Old Testament Commentary* (p. 15), has shown, the actual "Judge" in Israel was the Lord Himself; for He only is called the *shōpēt!* The individual judges were called by divine appointment and brought to prominence in the role of a deliverer through whom God administered His justice by empowerment with His Spirit (3:10). Perhaps later they settled as civil leaders as well, since the years of each one's "judgeship" are recorded after the initial deliverance of the people from oppression.

The cycle of apostasy, repentance, re-apostasy which follows in the historical narrative is here explained by way of introduction. After deliverance by a particular judge, the people **would not hearken** unto their leadership, but would return to **whoring after other gods,** indicating that apostasy was looked upon as a form of spiritual adultery and infidelity. Sadly, we are told **they turned quickly out of the way** of the Lord and the leadership of the judge.

Verse 18 indicates that the Lord was with them throughout the period of the judge's leadership and "delivered them out of the hand of their enemies." **All the days of the judge.** The statement that it **repented the LORD** because of their cry unto Him as a result of the subsequent oppression does not mean that God changed His mind about the need for allowing the oppression, but rather that He felt "sorrow" or "grief" for their agony. In other words, the author is merely indicating that God was not pleased with having to discipline His people in such a way, but that it was necessary lest they continue in greater sinfulness. Since God's covenant with Israel was conceived of in the terms of a marriage, spiritual adultery was all the more serious. It was an attempt on the part of Israel to break her vows to Yahweh, her spiritual husband.

As a result of continued apostasies, **the anger of the LORD** was expressed against them by His decision that He would **not henceforth drive out** the enemy nations which remained in the land. Thus, Israel would not lose the land that God had promised to her, but neither would the Canaanites be totally dispossessed. The statement **that through them I may prove Israel** means that Israel's failure to drive out the Canaanites was God's means for chastening His people for their idolatry and apostasy. It would also become a means by which He would test their future faithfulness to Him in keeping **the way of the LORD.** Therefore, certain Canaanite tribes and other nations were left among them.

The relationship of this chapter to the statements in the book of Joshua that they had won a total and resounding victory over their enemies need not be seen as a contradiction, since Joshua 23:7 makes it clear that there were "nations that remain among you" with whom they were not to marry nor associate with their gods. The correlation of the two books makes it clear that the victory of Joshua was sudden and instantaneous and brought the land under the control of the Israelites. However, conquest was one thing and settlement another. In order to maintain supreme control of the land it would now be necessary for the Israelites to continually drive out their enemies from any encroachment into the territory that God had given them.

The spiritual theme at this point is rather obvious: the victory given by God must be maintained by its recipients. The pattern of Joshua-Judges serves as an excellent illustration of the conflicts of the Christian life. In Christ we have been guaranteed total victorious possession of "the land." The inheritance of our salvation is assured; however, we must maintain our personal relationship to God by continually driving out our "enemies." Therefore, separated and dedicated Christian living is necessary to maintain the victory which has been assured to us.

II. RULE OF THE JUDGES. 3:1-16:31.

A. First Cycle: Othniel versus Cushan-rishathaim. 3:1-11.

1. Servitude to Mesopotamia—eight years. 3:1-8.

3:1-4. The third chapter provides a list of the people whom the generation of the judges were unable to dislodge from the land. The statement that some of them had not known **the wars of Canaan** (i.e., the conquest battles led by Joshua) is related to the explanation that the nations were also left behind to teach subsequent generations of Israelites the art of warfare (cf. Ex 23:29; Deut 7:22). The **five lords of the Philistines** refers to the leaders (Heb *seren*) of the five-city pentapolis of Ashdod, Ashkelon, Ekron, Gath, and Gaza, which formed the centralized Philistine government. The Philistines were descendants of the Greek and Aegean "Sea Peoples" who had migrated into Israel as early as the time of Abraham (Gen 20; 26), but did not move into the area en masse until about 1200 B.C. (see E. Hindson *The Philistines and the Old Testament*).

The reference to **all the Canaanites** refers to the variously amalgamated tribes which were especially strong in the Valley of Esdraelon and who would still hold the Jebusite fortress at Jerusalem until the time of David. **Sidonians** refers to the inhabitants of the Phoenician city-state of Sidon, to the north on the Mediterranean coast. The **Hivites that dwelt in mount Lebanon** refers to the Horites, or Hurrians, who established the kingdom of Mitanni in upper Mesopotamia in about 1500 B.C. From there, they spread southward into Canaan during the fifteenth and fourteenth centuries B.C. The records of the Nuzi Tablets found in this area give clear indication that many of the patriarchal customs were of Horite origin. At this time they occupied four cities northwest of Jerusalem forming the Gibeonite confederacy (Josh 9:7).

Mount Baal-hermon was later known simply as Mount Hermon and is the more easterly range parallel to Lebanon, running

CHAPTER 3

NOW these *are* the nations which the LORD left, to prove Israel by them, *even* as many *of Israel* as had not known all the wars of Canaan;

2 Only that the generations of the children of Israel might know, to teach them war, at the least such as before knew nothing thereof;

3 *Namely,* five lords of the Philistines, and all the Canaanites, and the Si-dō′ni-anṡ, and the Hī′vītes that dwelt in mount Lebanon, from mount Bā′al-her′mon unto the entering in of Hā′māth.

4 And they were to prove Israel by them, to know whether they would hearken unto the commandments of the LORD, which he commanded their fathers by the hand of Moses.

5 ¶And the children of Israel dwelt among the Canaanites, Hittites, and Amorites, and Pĕr′iz-zites, and Hī′vites, and Jĕb′u-sītes:

6 And they took their daughters to be their wives, and gave their daughters to their sons, and served their gods.

7 And the children of Israel did evil in the sight of the LORD, and forgat the LORD their God, and served Bā′al-ĭm and the groves.

8 Therefore the anger of the LORD was hot against Israel, and he sold them into the hand of Chū′shăn–rĭsh-a-thā′im king of Mĕs-o-po-tā′mĭ-a: and the children of Israel served Chū′-shăn–rĭsh-a-thā′im eight years.

southwest from Damascus. It may be identical with Baal-Gad, the northern limit of Joshua's conquest. **Hamath** was on the Orontes River, about 150 miles north of Dan. Pfeiffer (p. 239) notes: "The word translated 'entering in' (*lebō*) may conceal the name of a town, *Lebo of Hamath*, identified with modern Lebweh in the Bequa's Valley, which separates the Lebanon Mountains from the Anti-Lebanon ranges. This was Hivite territory during the period of the judges."

5-8. The reference to the **Canaanites, Hittites, . . . Amorites, . . . Perizzites, . . . Hivites, and Jebusites** names the confederated Canaanite tribes and their allies which stood in opposition to Israel's possession of the land. It must be remembered at this time that all of these people were seminomadic and that, even though cities had been established in the land, no single group seems to have had clear possession of them. The term "Canaanites" is used as a general designation of all of the inhabitants of the land at the time of the Israelite conquest. The distinction between them and the "Amorites" is made regarding those tribes who dwelt in the mountains (cf. Num 13:29). The Perizzites and the Jebusites were aboriginal groups of Canaanites. Jebusites in particular were known for their possession of the stronghold at Jerusalem.

The Hittites, by contrast, were an Indo-European people who established a great empire in Asia Minor during the period from 1800-1200 B.C. On the significance of Hittite archaeological discoveries and their bearing upon patriarchal customs, and especially the significance of suzerainty treaties, see O. R. Gurney *The Hittites* and P. K. Hitti, *History of Syria*. The serious sin of the Israelites was that they both intermarried with their ungodly neighbors and **served their gods.** In doing so, they forsook **the LORD their God, and served Baalim and the groves,** meaning the worship centers of the pagan gods. The RV reads "Asheroth" in place of "groves." *'Ashērōt* is a rare plural of *'ashērah*, the Canaanite goddess who is named in the Ras Shamra Tablets as the consort of the god El. It is also possible that *'ashtarōt* is to be read here as the normal plural for Ashtar, the consort of Baal, since the normal plural of *'ashērah* is *'ashērīm.*

The War of Ehud

- Israelite force
- Moabites

2. Salvation by Othniel—forty years. 3:9-11.

9 And when the children of Israel cried unto the LORD, the LORD raised up a deliverer to the children of Israel, who delivered them, *even* Ŏth′nĭ-el the son of Kĕ′năz, Caleb's younger brother.
10 And the Spirit of the LORD came upon him, and he judged Israel, and went out to war: and the LORD delivered Chŭ′shăn–rĭsh-a-thā′im king of Mĕs-o-po-tā′mĭ-a into his hand; and his hand prevailed against Chŭ′shăn–rĭsh-a-thā′im.
11 And the land had rest forty years. And Ŏth′nĭ-el the son of Kĕ′năz died.

9-11. The first oppressor is called **Chushan-rishathaim king of Mesopotamia,** who oppressed the Israelites for **eight years.** The name of the oppressor literally means "the doubly wicked Cushan" and may have been an epithet used by his enemies. Cundall (p. 73) prefers the emendation *Cūshan rō'sh Tēman,* meaning "Cushan, Chief of Teman." Teman was a town in northern Edom (an area which bordered on Judah) from which Othniel came as the deliverer. However, there is extensive linguistic evidence to support the possibility of a northern invasion. Cush was the father of Nimrod, who established the Babylonian civilization, which was later overrun by the Kassites. A cognate Kassite name of a woman, Kashsharishat, helps confirm the possibility of such a name being of genuine Aramaean-Babylonian origin. The name **Mesopotamia** in Hebrew is *Aram-naharayim,* referring to the area of northeastern Syria extending from the Orontes River to the Euphrates and covering part of modern Iraq (cf. D. J. Wiseman, "Mesopotamia," in *New Bible Dictionary,* p. 811, and M. Unger, *Israel and the Aramaeans of Damascus*). Since extensive military campaigns were carried on throughout the Levant as early as the time of Sargon of Akkad (ca. 2400 B.C.), it is entirely possible that an otherwise unknown king, perhaps of Hittite origin, attacked the Israelites in the land of Canaan and was eventually defeated and expelled. The modern designation of the term Mesopotamia for the land between the Tigris and Euphrates Rivers (ancient Babylon) was not commonly used until the fourth century B.C.

Repentance on the part of the Israelites brought an end to the eight-year oppression when **the LORD raised up a deliverer . . . Othniel,** already referred to in chapter 1. Here, he is introduced as a "savior" who delivers his people from the oppression of Cushan. The source of his power is clearly indicated in the statement that the **spirit of the LORD came upon him.** This charismatic endowment of the power of the Spirit caused him to "judge" Israel, go out to war, and deliver the people from their enemy (vs. 10). The invading king was **delivered . . . into his hand,** indicating that he was put to death by Othniel. The result of the victory was that **the land had rest forty years,** indicating that it was free from foreign interference during the rest of Othniel's generation.

B. Second Cycle: Ehud versus Eglon. 3:12-31.

1. Servitude to Moab, Ammon, and Amalek—eighteen years. 3:12-14.

12 ¶And the children of Israel did evil again in the sight of the LORD: and the LORD strengthened Ĕg′lŏn the king of Moab against Israel, because they had done evil in the sight of the LORD.
13 And he gathered unto him the children of Ammon and Ăm′a-lĕk, and went and smote Israel, and possessed the city of palm trees.
14 So the children of Israel served Ĕg′lŏn the king of Moab eighteen years.

12-14. The second oppression was the result of an invasion led by **Eglon the king of Moab.** After the death of Othniel, there was another time of backsliding and idolatry among the Israelites. Therefore, God raised up another enemy nation as an instrument of judgment on His people. Moab is the land east of the Dead Sea, lying between the Arnon and the Zered Rivers. The Moabites, like the other Transjordanian kingdoms, had been previously nomadic peoples. Eglon was able to gather a confederacy of men of **Moab, Ammon and Amalek** in order to defeat the Israelites. The Ammonites were closely allied to the Moabites throughout their history, and the nomadic Amalekites had been bitter foes of Israel since the battle at Rephaim. These amalgamated tribes had harassed Israel considerably during the wilderness journey and remained a constant threat to them during the early settlement period as well. (For detailed discussion of their Bronze Age settlement of the area and their archaeological remains see N. Glueck, *The Other Side of the Jordan.*)

The Transjordanian confederacy followed the same route that Israel had taken earlier and captured the **city of palm trees,** i.e., Jericho. The city previously destroyed by Joshua occupied such

461

a strategic position that apparently another city was built on the site a short time after its destruction. Archaeological remains show that Jericho was actually built, destroyed, and rebuilt several times (on the problems of dating the archaeological levels at Jericho see K. Kenyon "Jericho," in *Archaeology and Old Testament Study* and E. Smick, *Archaeology of the Jordan Valley*).

2. Salvation by Ehud—eighty years. 3:15-30.

15-18. To counteract the eighteen-year oppression brought on by Eglon, God raised up a **deliverer, Ehud . . . a Benjamite, a man lefthanded.** The term "lefthanded" comes from the Hebrew *'iṭēr yad-yemīnō*, meaning "bound of his right hand." The Benjamites apparently were known for being **lefthanded** (20:16) and even ambidextrous (I Chr 12:2). In a clever move, Ehud was selected to bring a **present** (the tribute money) demanded of Israel by the Moabite king. In actuality, the tribute was probably paid in the form of agricultural produce or a series of gifts, demanding a number of porters (vs. 18) to carry it all. Bruce (p. 242) suggests that the gift was taken to Jericho, which was being used as a temporary headquarters within Israel by the Moabite king, rather than to Kir Haresheth, the capital of Moab. Davis (*Conquest and Crisis*, p. 107) dates the Moabite conquest from about 1335 B.C., including their infiltration into the Jordan Valley. Ehud, who perhaps had had this dubious responsibility previously, decided to use it as an opportunity to assassinate the Moabite king. In order to carry out the assassination attempt, Ehud made a **dagger** which was a **cubit length** (vs. 16). The Hebrew word *gōmed*, for **cubit**, is used no other place in the entire Old Testament. It refers to a short cubit, i.e., the distance between the elbow and knuckles of a closed fist; therefore, it was about twelve to fourteen inches long. Hiding the dagger under his robe, Ehud brought the tribute caravan to Eglon, who is described as a **very fat man** (indicating the need for the length of the dagger). After the official presentation of the tribute, Ehud dismissed the entourage and requested a private audience with the king himself.

19. The reference in verse 19 that he **turned again from the quarries that were by Gilgal** has caused considerable confusion. The Hebrew word translated **quarries** (Heb *pesīlīm*) is usually translated "sculptured stones" (RSV) or "graven images" (LXX, RV mg). They are mentioned again in verse 26, where they are an important landmark. The latter reference seems to indicate that when he had passed them he was safe from the Moabites. Thus, it has been suggested that they marked the limits of the Moabite territory and would be similar to boundary stones. Cundall (p. 77) prefers the idea that they were the actual stones set up earlier by Joshua to commemorate the miraculous crossing of the Jordan and, thus, were a well-known landmark.

Having dismissed his retinue, Ehud turned back to seek a private audience with Eglon. The implication of this move was to reinforce the concept of the secrecy of his mission. Perhaps Eglon thought that Ehud had come to deliver a message of the nature of that which a spy would bring, or perhaps he thought Ehud was prepared to bring a special bribe to him personally in addition to the tribute. The fact that the king responded to his secret errand with the statement **Keep silence** (Heb *has*, an onomatopoetic word, similar to hush) further suggests that he expected something of a personal nature that he did not want the others to know about; thus, he sent them out.

20-22. Verse 20 notes that Eglon was sitting in a **summer parlor** (Heb *'aliyah*), referring to the latticed upper room in one corner of the roof. It was the coolest room in the house and was especially popular during the summer heat. Waiting until they were alone, Ehud announced that he had **a message from God** (Heb *'Elōhīm*) for Eglon and jumped out of his seat, grabbing the dagger with his left hand from his right thigh as he ran, and

15 But when the children of Israel cried unto the LORD, the LORD raised them up a deliverer, Ē'hŭd the son of Ge'ra, a Benjamite, a man left-handed: and by him the children of Israel sent a present unto Ĕg'lŏn the king of Moab.
16 But Ē'hŭd made him a dagger which had two edges, of a cubit length; and he did gird it under his raiment upon his right thigh.
17 And he brought the present unto Ĕg'lŏn king of Moab: and Ĕg'lŏn was a very fat man.
18 And when he had made an end to offer the present, he sent away the people that bare the present.

19 But he himself turned again from the quarries that were by Gilgal, and said, I have a secret errand unto thee, O king: who said, Keep silence. And all that stood by him went out from him.

20 And Ē'hŭd came unto him; and he was sitting in a summer parlour, which he had for himself alone. And Ē'hŭd said, I have a message from God unto thee. And he arose out of his seat.
21 And Ē'hŭd put forth his left hand, and took the dagger from his right thigh, and thrust it into his belly:

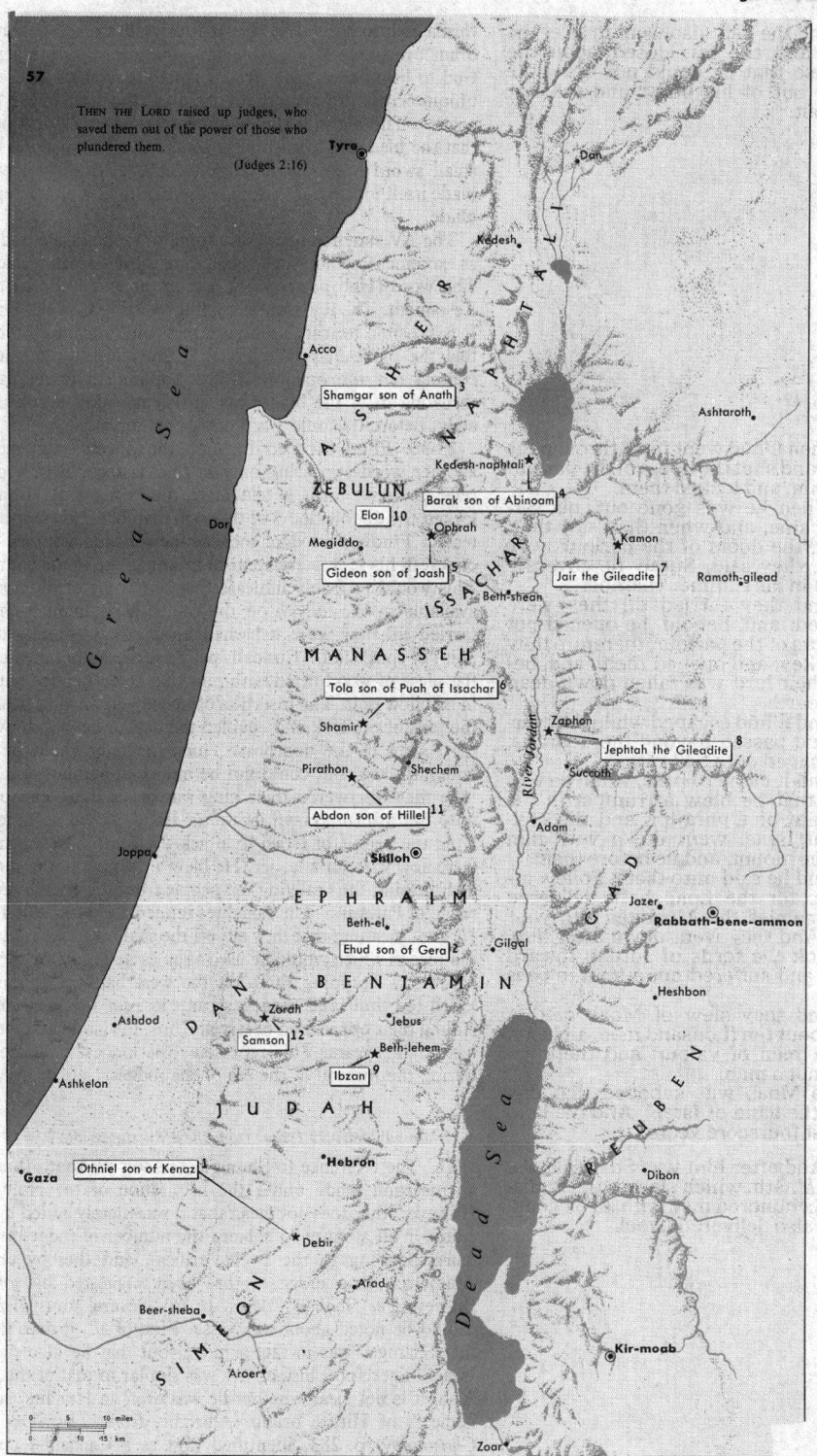

57

THEN THE LORD raised up judges, who
saved them out of the power of those who
plundered them.

(Judges 2:16)

Tyre•

Great Sea

•Dan

Kedesh•

A
S
H
E
R

N
A
P
H
T
A
L
I

•Acco

Ashtaroth•

Shamgar son of Anath 3

ZEBULUN

Kedesh-naphtali★

Barak son of Abinoam 4

Elon 10

Dor•

Megiddo•

•Ophrah

Kamon•

I
S
S
A
C
H
A
R

Gideon son of Joash 5

Beth-shean•

Jair the Gileadite 7

Ramoth-gilead•

MANASSEH

Tola son of Puah of Issachar 6

Shamir★

Zaphon•

Pirathon•

Shechem•

Jephtah the Gileadite 8

River Jordan

Succoth•

Abdon son of Hillel 11

Adam•

Joppa•

Shiloh◎

E P H R A I M

Jazer•

Rabbath-bene-ammon◎

Beth-el•

Gilgal•

Ehud son of Gera 2

G
A
D

D
A
N

B E N J A M I N

Heshbon•

•Ashdod

Zorah★

•Jebus

Samson 12

•Beth-lehem

Ibzan 9

•Ashkelon

J U D A H

Othniel son of Kenaz 1

•Hebron

Dead Sea

R
E
U
B
E
N

•Dibon

•Gaza

★Debir

S
I
M
E
O
N

•Arad

Beer-sheba•

Aroer★

Kir-moab◎

0   5   10 miles
0   5 10 15 km

Zoar•

The Judges According to their Tribes

463

22 And the haft also went in after the blade; and the fat closed upon the blade, so that he could not draw the dagger out of his belly; and the dirt came out.

23 Then Ē'hŭd went forth through the porch, and shut the doors of the parlour upon him, and locked them.
24 When he was gone out, his servants came; and when they saw that, behold, the doors of the parlour were locked, they said, Surely he covereth his feet in his summer chamber.
25 And they tarried till they were ashamed: and, behold, he opened not the doors of the parlour; therefore they took a key, and opened them: and, behold, their lord was fallen down dead on the earth.
26 And Ē'hŭd escaped while they tarried, and passed beyond the quarries, and escaped unto Sē'i-răth.
27 And it came to pass, when he was come, that he blew a trumpet in the mountain of Ē'phra-im, and the children of Israel went down with him from the mount, and he before them.
28 And he said unto them, Follow after me: for the LORD hath delivered your enemies the Moabites into your hand. And they went down after him, and took the fords of Jordan toward Moab, and suffered not a man to pass over.
29 And they slew of Moab at that time about ten thousand men, all lusty, and all men of valour; and there escaped not a man.
30 So Moab was subdued that day under the hand of Israel. And the land had rest fourscore years.

31 ¶And after him was Shăm'găr the son of Ā'năth, which slew of the Philistines six hundred men with an ox goad: and he also delivered Israel.

thrust it into his belly. The narrative has all the elements of drama: the secrecy of the meeting, the sovereign intervention of God to bring about the circumstances for deliverance, and the unique cross-draw method of Ehud the lefthanded dagger-sticker. The blow to the abdomen was so quick and powerful that the blade went in entirely, **haft** and all (indicating that the small sword had no crosspiece), and the handle followed the blade itself into Eglon's stomach so that the **fat closed upon the blade.**

The AV statement that **dirt came out,** should be understood as excrement, which such a wound to the abdomen would cause. The word (Heb *parshedōnah*) occurs nowhere else in the Old Testament. The RV margin reading "vestibule" is not plausible. It is possible to translate the term as an "opening," indicating that the blade may have gone all the way through the body, coming out the opening at the bottom. In either case, the thrusting in of the blade was sufficient to kill Eglon immediately, before he could warn any of his servants.

23-30. Ehud escaped through the **porch** (Heb *misderōn*), another word appearing only in this passage. It may possibly refer to some form of elaborate roof colonnade. Ehud then locked the double doors of the roof-chamber and escaped undetected. Finding the door locked, the servants assumed that he **covereth his feet,** a euphemism meaning "go to the bathroom." This would probably indicate that some sort of plumbing was available in the *'aliyah* on the roof. The statement that they **tarried till they were ashamed** means they "waited until the point of confusion." Cundall (p. 78) suggests that the key was a flat piece of wood fitted with pins that corresponded with holes in a hollow bolt. The insertion of this key in the bolt pushed out the pins of the lock and enabled the bolt to be withdrawn from the socket in the doorpost. Thus, the door could be locked without a key, but could not be unlocked without one. By the time they discovered their king was dead, **Ehud escaped . . . unto Seirath** (unknown location). Ehud wasted no time in rallying the people of Israel to attack the confused Moabites who were now without a leader. He blew a trumpet in **the mountain of Ephraim,** thus rallying the people from the central mountain range of Palestine. The Israelites immediately **took the fords of Jordan,** meaning that they cut off the shallow water fords across the Jordan which would be used as an escape route by the fleeing Moabites. Trapping them on the west bank of Jordan, they killed **ten thousand men,** a serious loss for the Moabites, thus ending their oppression of Israel. Thus, the land had **rest** for the next eighty years. This represents the longest period of peace during the turmoil of the era of the judges.

3. Shamgar delivers Israel from the Philistines. 3:31.

31. The reference to **Shamgar the son of Anath** is certainly an insertion made under the inspiration of the Holy Spirit. However, this does not mean that it was merely added by a later editor in an attempt to balance the number of judges at twelve (corresponding to the twelve tribes), and thereby eliminate Abimelech as a judge, as has been suggested by some (cf. Burney, *The Book of Judges*, p. 76). Several unusual features should be noted about this verse. First of all, it does not state that Shamgar was in fact a judge, but that **he also delivered Israel.** Therefore, his activity was similar to that of the judges. Also, it is not clear whether he was even an Israelite, since his name is of Hittite origin (Albright, *From The Stone Age to Christianity*, p. 283, identified him as a Canaanite chieftain; Garstang, *Joshua-Judges*, p. 287, has identified him with Ben Anath, a Syrian sea captain, allied with Ramses II). It is more likely that Cundall (p. 80) is correct in identifying the **son of Anath** as a reference to Beth-anath in Galilee, which would better explain the reference to him in the song of Deborah (5:6) which recounts the victory of the northern tribes. Anath was a Canaanite goddess whose worship centers were prevalent at that time.

The characteristic features of the general narration of the book are absent in this passage. Israel's sin that leads to judgment is not mentioned, and there is no reference to a Philistine oppression of any specified duration. Rather, the reference seems to be to a rising Philistine menace caused by the continuing infiltration of Philistines into the area. This infiltration had begun as early as the time of Abraham and continued until it reached its apex at the time of Samson. It is possible that Shamgar was not really a judge, since Ehud was the major judge at that time. It should also be noted that he is later mentioned in connection with the woman Jael, who was also not a judge, but somewhat of a local heroine.

Shamgar's weapon was an **ox goad,** a long-handled, pointed stick tipped with metal and used to prod animals. Its length was normally about ten feet, and it was useful as a weapon in times of emergency. The Philistines later became famous for disarming their enemies, and it should be noted that Shamgar may have had no other weapon available to him. With it, he slew **six hundred men,** which may represent the sum of a lifetime of combat, rather than a single incident. Despite his unknown origin and humble weapon, he was used of God to spare the Israelites. That his exploits were well known is indicated by the reference to him in Deborah's song. There is no substantial reason for the fanciful exaggerations that have often been given to explain away the historicity of this event (e.g., MacKenzie, pp. 125-126; who believes the incident was inserted at this point to give a reason for the reference to him later in chapter 5). Most liberal commentators look on Shamgar as an insertion by the so-called Deuteronomic historian, believing the book of Judges actually to have been written during the Assyrian period in Israel. This view has been successfully discounted by Y. Kaufmann, *The Biblical Account of the Conquest of Palestine,* where he shows that Judges 2-3 presents a very unfavorable and unidealistic picture of Israel's history during this early period, which is not the so-called Deuteronomistic viewpoint at all. The details of these chapters must be viewed as very ancient and true to Israel's history.

C. Third Cycle: Deborah and Barak versus Jabin and Sisera. 4:1-5:31.

1. Servitude to the Canaanites—twenty years. 4:1-3.

4:1-3. After the death of Ehud the eighty-year period of rest came to an end, and the Israelites again sinned against God. The Scripture says that the LORD **sold them into the hand of Jabin king of Canaan,** whose headquarters were at **Hazor.** The name **Jabin** was probably a dynastic title, rather than a personal name. According to Joshua 11, the Israelites earlier had conquered the city of Hazor and killed "Jabin," the king of that city a century before. Several such names appear in the Bible and are prevalent in these early accounts. Notice that the personal name of Pharaoh is never given. Other such name-titles include Abimelech of the Philistines. This is similar to the usage of the personal name Caesar as a throne name for the subsequent rulers of the Roman Empire. Most scholars assume that Hazor was rebuilt after the destruction by Joshua and again occupied a place of prominence at this time. However, Kitchen (*Ancient Orient and Old Testament,* p. 68) suggests that the destruction by fire under Joshua was the final destruction of the city and that Jabin was merely from that area and, therefore, associated with it since no emphasis is actually placed on the city of Hazor itself. Jabin's main source of strength came from his general **Sisera** from **Harosheth**

CHAPTER 4

AND the children of Israel again did evil in the sight of the LORD, when Ē'hŭd was dead.

2 And the LORD sold them into the hand of Jā'bin king of Canaan, that reigned in Hā'zôr; the captain of whose host *was* Sĭs'e-ra, which dwelt in Ha-rŏ'shĕth of the Gentiles.

3 And the children of Israel cried unto the LORD: for he had nine hundred chariots of iron; and twenty years he mightily oppressed the children of Israel.

of the Gentiles. Sisera's name has been identified as possibly Hittite, or even Egyptian, by those who see him as an official in the Megiddo district, which was under strong Egyptian influence (Bruce, p. 223). Pfeiffer (p. 241) notes that Sisera's home, *charōshet hagōyim*, is usually identified with modern Tell-amar, located at the place where the Kishon River passes through a narrow gorge to enter the Plain of Acre, about ten miles northwest of Megiddo. For details on the archaeological excavation at Hazor see Y. Yadin *Hazor*. The oppression by Jabin and Sisera lasted for **twenty years** because of the superior military strength of the Canaanites. Verse 3 claims that Sisera had **nine hundred chariots of iron.** This number is rarely questioned since Thutmose III captured eight hundred twenty-four chariots among the spoils of the Battle of Meggido (James B. Pritchard, *Ancient Near Eastern Texts*, p. 237). This gave Sisera, the military leader of the combined armies, a source of complete dominance until a situation arose in which chariots could not be used.

2. Salvation by Deborah and Barak—forty years. 4:4-24.

4-5. To counter this time of oppression, God raised up a unique female leader, **Deborah, a prophetess,** who is called the wife of Lapidoth, of whom nothing else is known. She not only held the position of prophetess, but also the text says that she **judged Israel at that time.** The context makes it clear that she was a well-respected leader in Israel. Her place of residence was located between **Ramah** and **Beth-el** in Mount Ephraim, putting her in the south of Ephraim, about fifty miles from the scene of the battle. For the most part, prior to the incident where she rallies the tribes together and assists **Barak** in leading them to victory, her position seems to be that of a non-military judge.

6-9. The fact that she was a woman has caused questions as to why she occupied the position of a judge. A thorough reading of chapters 4 and 5 makes it clear that women played the predominant roles in this entire incident, and their significance is a reflection on the weakness of male leadership in Israel at that time. The entire book of Judges shows us a behind-the-scenes exposé of the spiritual decline and weakness that was then prevalent in Israel. Nothing in the Mosaic law directly prohibited women from taking a place of responsibility that was normally the place of men; and the principle seems clear that when a man was not on the scene to deliver the people, God chose to use a woman. However, this incident cannot be taken as a justification for contradicting the pastoral qualifications listed in the New Testament Epistles. One should always remember that Old Testament procedures do not necessarily justify New Testament policies. That pastors of churches should be men, not women, is made clear by such passages as I Timothy 3 and I Corinthians 14; and there are no records of women pastors in the New Testament. However, there are extensive references to the important place and activity of women in the New Testament congregations.

It is also interesting to note that Deborah did not lead this military reprisal herself, but chose **Barak** to serve as the commander of the tribe. He was an inhabitant of **Kedesh-naphtali**, near Hazor. As God's spokesman, Deborah tells him that he is to take **ten thousand men** toward **mount Tabor**, and that God said He would **draw unto thee . . . Sisera . . . and . . . deliver him into thine hand.** The brave Barak responded that he would not go unless Deborah would go with him! She replied that she would be willing to go; but the battle would not be in his honor, for **the LORD shall sell Sisera into the hand of a woman.** Again, there can be no doubt that this passage is intended to indicate the weakness of male leadership at that time.

10-17. Barak appealed to the two northern tribes of **Zebulun** and **Naphtali** to meet the Canaanite encroachment into that area. Verse 11 reminds the reader that **Heber the Kenite** had

4 ¶And Dĕb′o-rah, a prophetess, the wife of Lăp′i-dŏth, she judged Israel at that time.
5 And she dwelt under the palm tree of Dĕb′o-rah between Rā′mah and Bĕth-el in mount Ē′phra-im: and the children of Israel came up to her for judgment.

6 And she sent and called Bâ′rak the son of A-bĭn′o-am out of Kĕ′dĕsh-nȧph′ta-lī, and said unto him, Hath not the LORD God of Israel commanded, *saying*, Go and draw toward mount Tā′bor, and take with thee ten thousand men of the children of Nȧph′ta-lī and of the children of Zĕb′u-lun?
7 And I will draw unto thee to the river Kī′shŏn Sĭs′e-ra, the captain of Jā′bin's army, with his chariots and his multitude; and I will deliver him into thine hand.
8 And Bâ′rak said unto her, If thou wilt go with me, then I will go: but if thou wilt not go with me, *then* I will not go.
9 And she said, I will surely go with thee: notwithstanding the journey that thou takest shall not be for thine honour; for the LORD shall sell Sĭs′e-ra into the hand of a woman. And Dĕb′o-rah arose, and went with Bâ′rak to Kĕ′dĕsh.

10 And Bâ′rak called Zĕb′u-lun and Nȧph′ta-lī to Kĕ′dĕsh; and he went up

with ten thousand men at his feet: and Dĕb'o-rah went up with him.

11 Now Hē'ber the Kĕn'īte, *which was* of the children of Hō'băb the father in law of Moses, had severed himself from the Kĕn'ītes, and pitched his tent unto the plain of Zā-a-nā'im, which *is* by Kĕ'dĕsh.

12 And they shewed Sīs'e-ra that Bâ'rak the son of A-bĭn'ō-am was gone up to mount Tā'bor.

13 And Sīs'e-ra gathered together all his chariots, *even* nine hundred chariots of iron, and all the people that *were* with him, from Ha-rō'shĕth of the Gentiles unto the river of Kī'shŏn.

14 And Dĕb'o-rah said unto Bâ'rak, Up; for this *is* the day in which the LORD hath delivered Sīs'e-ra into thine hand: is not the LORD gone out before thee? So Bâ'rak went down from mount Tā'bor, and ten thousand men after him.

15 And the LORD discomfited Sīs'e-ra, and all *his* chariots, and all *his* host, with the edge of the sword before Bâ'rak; so that Sīs'e-ra lighted down off *his* chariot, and fled away on his feet.

16 But Bâ'rak pursued after the chariots, and after the host, unto Ha-rō'shĕth of the Gentiles: and all the host of Sīs'e-ra fell upon the edge of the sword; *and* there was not a man left.

17 Howbeit Sīs'e-ra fled away on his feet to the tent of Jā'el the wife of Hē'ber the Kĕn'īte: for *there was* peace between Jā'bin the king of Hā'zōr and the house of Hē'ber the Kĕn'īte.

18 And Jā'el went out to meet Sīs'e-ra, and said unto him, Turn in, my lord, turn in to me; fear not. And when he had turned in unto her into the tent, she covered him with a mantle.

19 And he said unto her, Give me, I pray thee, a little water to drink; for I am thirsty. And she opened a bottle of milk, and gave him drink, and covered him.

20 Again he said unto her, Stand in the door of the tent, and it shall be, when any man doth come and enquire of thee, and say, Is there any man here? that thou shalt say, No.

21 Then Jā'el Hē'ber's wife took a nail of the tent, and took an hammer in her hand, and went softly unto him, and smote the nail into his temples, and fastened it into the ground: for he was fast asleep and weary. So he died.

22 And, behold, as Bâ'rak pursued Sīs'e-ra, Jā'el came out to meet him, and said unto him, Come, and I will shew thee the man whom thou seekest. And when he came into her *tent*, behold, Sīs'e-ra lay dead, and the nail *was* in his temples.

separated himself from the main body of his tribe and had settled near Kedesh. The Kenites were first encountered by Moses while he was in the Midianite desert and appear several times in the early history of Israel. In the meantime, Sisera gathered his army and his nine hundred chariots and came from Harosheth to the bank of the Kishon River. Barak, in turn, took his 10,000 men and went out to meet him. **Is not the LORD gone out before thee?** (vs. 14) is Deborah's reminder of God's promise. In the explanation of the ensuing victory, it is assumed by the author that the reader understands what happened. However, it is necessary to notice the explanation of this incident in Deborah's song in 5:21 where it is said **the river of Kishon swept them away.** The passage here states that the Lord **discomfited Sisera** and all his chariots, so that they had to flee on foot.

The context seems to make it clear that as the two armies engaged in battle, they were caught in a flash flood brought about by a severe rainstorm. The AV translation **discomfited** does not fully convey the intensity of the Hebrew verb *hamam* (routed or destroyed). The 10,000 Israelites, who were lightly armed and highly mobile, engaged in the combat with the cavalry and chariots of Sisera which were caught in the sudden flooding of the swollen river to such a degree that the chariots became mired in the mud, and the drivers were forced to flee on foot. The normally dry wadi was now filled with water, immobilizing the chariots, and giving the advantage to the ground troops. It is interesting to note that this same situation was repeated when Napoleon defeated the Turkish army at the Battle of Mount Tabor on April 16, 1799; hundreds of fleeing Turkish troops were swept away and drowned. Thus, the story clearly indicates the direct intervention of God, who inspired the prediction of Deborah and sent the storm just in time to defeat Israel's enemies.

In the battle that followed, the Israelites pursued the fleeing army all the way back to Harosheth and annihilated the entire force. In the meantime, however, **Sisera fled away** on foot and came to the tent of Heber the Kenite (thus explaining the significance of the earlier reference in vs. 11). It was there that he met Heber's wife Jael, from whom he sought refuge. Verse 17 notes that there was peace between Jabin and Heber at that time, and this made an ideal place for the defeated king's general to hide himself.

18-24. The text offers no explanation as to why Jael turned against Sisera. Perhaps, as a sense of duty to defend God's people, or perhaps because she disagreed with the Kenite-Canaanite coalition. Obviously, Sisera would have been soaking wet from the rainstorm; and she covered him with a mantle (Heb *semîkah*) and offered him a **bottle of milk** (i.e., a "skin of milk" RSV). The skins of animals were often used to store milk, which in turn could be easily churned to produce curds (note 5:25 where **butter** is best rendered as curd). This drink, similar to liquid yogurt, is still commonly used by modern-day Arabs.

Instead of protecting him, Jael quickly murdered the sleeping Sisera. Taking the **nail of the tent** (tent peg or stake) and a **hammer** (wooden mallet), she quietly approached her unsuspecting guest and literally nailed him to the tent floor, driving the tent peg into his temples and through his head. The explanation, **So he died,** is hardly necessary! Therefore, when Barak arrived in pursuit of Sisera, he found that he was already dead and that the honor of his capture had gone to a woman, just as Deborah had prophesied. Pfeiffer (p. 243) notes that no attempt is made in the text to justify Jael's action. She is looked upon as a heroine who delivers the enemy into the hands of the Israelites. Throughout the scene, God is acting in history while actually controlling history. He allows the heathen to chasten His people and then in turn raises up deliverers to save them. The victory

23 So God subdued on that day Jā′bin the king of Canaan before the children of Israel.

24 And the hand of the children of Israel prospered, and prevailed against Jā′bin the king of Canaan, until they had destroyed Jā′bin king of Canaan.

CHAPTER 5

THEN sang Dĕb′o-rah and Bā′rak the son of A-bĭn′ō-am on that day, saying,

2 Praise ye the LORD for the avenging of Israel, when the people willingly offered themselves.

3 Hear, O ye kings; give ear, O ye princes; I, even I, will sing unto the LORD; I will sing praise to the LORD God of Israel.

4 LORD, when thou wentest out of Sē′ir, when thou marchedst out of the field of Ēdom, the earth trembled, and the heavens dropped, the clouds also dropped water.

5 The mountains melted from before the LORD, even that Sī′naī from before the LORD God of Israel.

6 In the days of Shăm′gär the son of Ā′năth, in the days of Jā′el, the highways were unoccupied, and the travellers walked through byways.

7 The inhabitants of the villages ceased, they ceased in Israel, until that I Dĕb′o-rah arose, that I arose a mother in Israel.

8 They chose new gods; then was war in the gates: was there a shield or spear seen among forty thousand in Israel?

9 My heart is toward the governors of Israel, that offered themselves willingly among the people. Bless ye the LORD.

10 Speak, ye that ride on white asses, ye that sit in judgment, and walk by the way.

11 They that are delivered from the noise of archers in the places of drawing water, there shall they rehearse the righteous acts of the LORD, even the righteous acts toward the inhabitants of his villages in Israel: then shall the people of the LORD go down to the gates.

led to the complete demise of Jabin and brought peace and prosperity to Israel for about forty years (5:31).

3. Victory song of Deborah and Barak. 5:1-31.

5:1-7. Then sang Deborah and Barak a song of victory, similar to many that are preserved in Scripture to commemorate the intervention of God on behalf of His people. The song is one of **praise** unto the Lord for His deliverance and recounts the oppression under the Canaanites, the mustering of the tribes, the Battle of Kishon, and the death of Sisera. In essence the song of chapter 5 repeats in poetic form the narrative of chapter 4. Nearly all commentators agree that this ode of triumph is contemporary with the events it describes. Even in its translated form it retains a spirit of excitement and gives the reader the experience of being an eyewitness to its events. The authorship of the poem is attributed to Deborah and Barak themselves and should be accepted as such. The fact that they are referred to in both the first and the third person throughout the poem is typical in ancient Near Eastern texts. This poetic song contains both the rhythm and parallelism of typical Hebrew poetry (e.g., **Hear, O ye kings; give ear, O ye princes**). The poetic form of the song is somewhat obscure in the AV and is generally more effective in the new translations.

The poem begins by acknowledging the power of Jehovah as He marches from Mount **Seir** in **Edom** leading His people from Sinai to the Promised Land. Then the song bewails the condition of foreign domination of the land, which caused the highways to be unoccupied in the days of **Shamgar** and **Jael**. The reference to both of them together should not seem as unusual as is often remarked by commentators. They were both relatively unknown and probably non-Israelite deliverers who aided Israel at a time when she was virtually unable to help herself. The statement that **the highways were unoccupied** implies that at that time the major trade routes were controlled by the Philistines and the Canaanites, and that the Israelites were forced to travel the **byways** (NASB, roundabout ways). The phrase, **the inhabitants of the villages** (vs. 7), has been variously translated as "peasantry" (NASB), "village life" (NIV), and "champions" (NEB). The latter is to be preferred, for it makes the context more clear: "Champions there were none, none left in Israel, until I Deborah arose."

8-10. The troubles which Israel encountered had been brought on because they **chose new gods,** an act of rebellion against the Lord. This statement was mistranslated by the Peshitta and the Vulgate as "God chose something new." This turning to idols for help brought nothing but war and defeat. So severe was the situation in Israel, that verse 8 implies that they were virtually unarmed. The rhetorical question: **was there a shield or spear seen among forty thousand in Israel?** implies the answer, "No." Thus, Deborah and Barak were all the more thrilled that the people had so **willingly** volunteered themselves for such a dangerous mission. This may seem difficult for some to comprehend, but the same statement is repeated in I Samuel 13:22, where even in the days of Saul they were still virtually unarmed. Hence, the statement that they needed to **teach them war** (3:2).

11-16. The purpose of the song is to call the people to **rehearse the righteous acts of the LORD** (vs. 11). The song regards all the tribes of Israel as worshipers of the Lord and bound to one another by their covenant with Him. The word **rehearse** (Heb tanah, to chant) is an Aramaism, conveying the sense of singing responsively. Without a doubt, this victory song of Deborah and Barak was sung in Israel for years to come. Keil

12 Awake, awake, Dĕb'o-rah: awake, awake, utter a song: arise, Bâ'rak, and lead thy captivity captive, thou son of A-bĭn'ō-am.
13 Then he made him that remaineth have dominion over the nobles among the people: the LORD made me have dominion over the mighty.
14 Out of Ē'phra-im *was there* a root of them against Ăm'a-lĕk; after thee, Benjamin, among thy people; out of Mā'chĭr came down governors, and out of Zĕb'u-lun they that handle the pen of the writer.
15 And the princes of Ĭs'sa-char *were* with Dĕb'o-rah; even Ĭs'sa-char, and also Bâ'rak: he was sent on foot into the valley. For the divisions of Reuben *there were* great thoughts of heart.
16 Why abodest thou among the sheepfolds, to hear the bleatings of the flocks? For the divisions of Reuben *there were* great searchings of heart.
17 Gilead abode beyond Jordan: and why did Dan remain in ships? Asher continued on the sea shore, and abode in his breaches.
18 Zĕb'u-lun and Năph'ta-lī *were* a people *that* jeoparded their lives unto the death in the high places of the field.

19 The kings came *and* fought, then fought the kings of Canaan in Ta'a-năch by the waters of Me-gĭd'dō; they took no gain of money.
20 They fought from heaven; the stars in their courses fought against Sĭs'e-ra.
21 The river of Kī'shŏn swept them away, that ancient river, the river Kī'shŏn. O my soul, thou hast trodden down strength.
22 Then were the horsehoofs broken by the means of the pransings, the pransings of their mighty ones.

23 Curse ye Me'rŏz, said the angel of the LORD, curse ye bitterly the inhabitants thereof; because they came not to the help of the LORD, to the help of the LORD against the mighty.
24 Blessed above women shall Jā'el the wife of Hē'ber the Kĕn'īte be, blessed shall she be above women in the tent.
25 He asked water, *and* she gave *him*

and Delitzsch, (*Biblical Commentary on the Old Testament*, p. 135) view this as a scene of victory in which the warriors are returning home from the battle singing the song of victory to the women at the wells. The call to **awake** and **rise** introduces Deborah and Barak, the singers of the song, as the subjects of the song as well. To **lead thy captivity captive** (Heb *shabah*) means to "lead away captives" as the fruit of victory. Note that this phrase is repeated in Psalm 68:18 and is quoted in Ephesians 4:8 as predictive of Christ who also "led captivity captive" (i.e., led multitudes of captives to freedom).

17-18. The middle of the song praises the tribes who came to aid Deborah and Barak and taunts those who did not. **Gilead abode beyond Jordan** refers to the two and one-half tribes which settled east of the Jordan and were not involved in this battle. Dan, Asher, and Reuben are also chided for their non-participation. The reference to **Dan** remaining **in ships** (vs. 17) has raised some questions as to its meaning. Evidently, this incident took place before the Danite migration northward as described in chapter 18. Therefore, at this time they were undoubtedly under a great deal of pressure from the Canaanites and the Philistines (Sea Peoples), by whom they were eventually defeated and driven from their tribal territory. The reference seems to indicate the unsettled nature of their situation at that time. The far-fetched explanation that they migrated by sea to Europe, as proposed by Anglo-Israelites, is certainly contradictory to the explanation of their migration to the northernmost part of Israel itself. In contrast to the indifference of many of the tribes, **Zebulun and Naphtali were a people that jeoparded their lives unto the death.**

19-22. The poem concludes with the song of victory and the lament of Sisera's mother, which is intended to interpose the reverse of the expected outcome of the battle. In other words, instead of Israelite women weeping for their sons and husbands, the Canaanite women, who undoubtedly expected victory, would now be shocked by the results of the battle. **Taanach by the waters of Megiddo** refers to **Taanach**, five miles southeast of **Megiddo**, commanding one of the main passes to the Plain of Esdraelon. **The waters of Megiddo** are the Kishon River and its tributaries. The intervention of **heaven** is poetically phrased as the **stars in their courses** which fought against Sisera. Jehovah is viewed here as controlling the process of nature itself, a common Israelite belief throughout the Old Testament era. The key statement in the entire song is found in verse 21, where it is said that the **river of Kishon swept them away.** This explains the nature of the defeat of the Canaanites, described in the previous chapter, where they fled from their chariots on foot and were virtually annihilated by the Israelites.

23-31. Then, in typical Near Eastern style, a blessing and a curse are contrasted. Bruce (p. 244) assumes that **Meroz** received the **curse** because of failing some previous obligation. He identifies it with Khirbet Marus, about seven and one-half miles south of Kedesh-naphtali. The beatitude **Blessed above women shall Jael . . . be** (vs. 24) recognizes the true heroine of the story. The descriptiveness of the poem makes it clear that she deliberately deceived Sisera into thinking he was in a place of safety, when in reality he had fallen into the hands of his real

milk; she brought forth butter in a lordly dish.

26 She put her hand to the nail, and her right hand to the workmen's hammer; and with the hammer she smote Sĭs′e-ra, she smote off his head, when she had pierced and stricken through his temples.

27 At her feet he bowed, he fell, he lay down: at her feet he bowed, he fell: where he bowed, there he fell down dead.

28 The mother of Sĭs′e-ra looked out at a window, and cried through the lattice, Why is his chariot *so* long in coming? why tarry the wheels of his chariots?

29 Her wise ladies answered her, yea, she returned answer to herself,

30 Have they not sped? have they *not* divided the prey; to every man a damsel *or* two; to Sĭs′e-ra a prey of divers colours, a prey of divers colours of needlework, of divers colours of needlework on both sides, *meet* for the necks of *them that take* the spoil?

31 So let all thine enemies perish, O Lord: but *let* them that love him *be* as the sun when he goeth forth in his might. And the land had rest forty years.

CHAPTER 6

AND the children of Israel did evil in the sight of the Lord: and the Lord delivered them into the hand of Mĭd′ī-an seven years.

2 And the hand of Mĭd′ī-an prevailed against Israel: *and* because of the Mĭd′-ī-an-ītes the children of Israel made them the dens which *are* in the mountains, and caves, and strong holds.

3 And *so* it was, when Israel had sown, that the Mĭd′ī-an-ītes came up, and the Am′ă-lek-ītes, and the children of the east, even they came up against them;

4 And they encamped against them, and destroyed the increase of the earth, till thou come unto Gā′za, and left no sustenance for Israel, neither sheep, nor ox, nor ass.

5 For they came up with their cattle and their tents, and they came as grasshoppers for multitude; *for* both they and their camels were without number: and they entered into the land to destroy it.

6 And Israel was greatly impoverished because of the Mĭd′ī-an-ītes; and the children of Israel cried unto the Lord.

7 ¶And it came to pass, when the children of Israel cried unto the Lord because of the Mĭd′ī-an-ītes,

8 That the Lord sent a prophet unto the children of Israel, which said unto them, Thus saith the Lord God of Israel, I brought you up from Egypt, and brought you forth out of the house of bondage;

enemy. Wood, in *Distressing Days of the Judges* (p. 198), unnecessarily tries to explain this away. The NASB translates verse 25: "He asked for water and she gave him milk; in a magnificent bowl she brought him curds." This is followed by the description of her deliberately nailing him to the floor, with the explanation in verse 27 that "Between her feet he bowed, he fell; he lay; between her feet, he fell; where he bowed, there he fell dead." The statement that she **smote off his head** should be translated "crushed his head" (Heb *machaq*, meaning "to crush"). The song ends with a conjectured soliloquy by Sisera's mother wondering why he has not returned from battle. Then, the poem of victory suddenly breaks off with the statement **So let all thine enemies perish, O Lord,** and is reminiscent of the imprecatory psalms, where blessing is prayed down on the followers of Jehovah and judgment is desired upon His enemies. The chapter ends with the statement that, following this decisive victory over the Canaanites, the land had rest for forty years.

D. Fourth Cycle: Gideon versus Midianites. 6:1-8:35.

1. Servitude to the Midianites—seven years. 6:1-10.

6:1-6. Again, the cycle of victory-apostasy-punishment-deliverance is repeated. This time the oppressors are the people of **Midian,** and the oppression lasts for **seven years.** Wood (p. 202) dates this oppression as beginning ca. 1169 B.C. This oppression was so severe that it caused the Israelites to hide in the **mountains, and caves.** It was now more than a century since Joshua had conquered the land, and the Midianite oppression was almost the conquest in reverse! The Midianites were desert nomads who had learned to domesticate camels and were now using them for the purpose of long-distance raids into more settled areas. Midian was south of Edom, near the Gulf of Aqaba. The oppression headed by the Midianites was also aided by the **Amalekites** and the **children of the east,** nomadic groups from the Syrian desert. The statement that their **camels were without number** is the first documentation of extensive use of camels in a military campaign, giving the Midianite-Arab alliance a tremendous advantage against the Israelites.

The extent of their infiltration and invasions reached into the tribal areas of the north and also penetrated as far south as **Gaza** in the territory of the Philistines. The final battle took place in the Valley of Jezreel (vs. 33) and drove the Midianites completely out of Israelite territory. The statements that they **destroyed the increase of the earth. . . . And Israel was greatly impoverished** would imply that these were probably annual raids which were made on the agricultural produce of the Israelites. They literally rushed in like **grasshoppers** (i.e., locusts) covering the land and devouring everything in their path. It is no wonder then that the children of Israel prayed for deliverance from this invading desert horde. (On the Midianites and Amalekites see R. K. Harrison, *Old Testament Times*, pp. 180ff.)

7-10. As a result of their prayer, **the Lord sent a prophet unto . . . them** to announce God's message to the people. He reminded them that God had delivered them from the **Egyptians** and other oppressors, urging them to **fear not the gods of the Amorites.** However, the oppression is viewed by the writer of Judges as the means of God's disciplining His people for idolatry because they have **not obeyed** His voice. There can be no doubt that the prophet was reminding them that they did not deserve

9 And I delivered you out of the hand of the Egyptians, and out of the hand of all that oppressed you, and drave them out from before you, and gave you their land;

10 And I said unto you, I *am* the LORD your God; fear not the gods of the Ămorītes, in whose land ye dwell: but ye have not obeyed my voice.

11 ¶And there came an angel of the LORD, and sat under an oak which *was* in Ŏph'rah, that *pertained* unto Jŏ'ăsh the Ă'bĭ-ĕz'rīte: and his son Gideon threshed wheat by the winepress, to hide *it* from the Mĭd'ī-an-ītes.

deliverance because of their repeated relapses into idolatry. He did not say, however, that there would be no such deliverance.

2. Salvation by Gideon—forty years. 6:11-8:35.

11. While the Israelites awaited further answer from God, the **angel of the LORD** sat under a tree watching **Gideon** threshing wheat! The introduction to the story of Gideon and his deliverance is vital in understanding the true significance of this incident. The irony that is often so obvious in the book of Judges again plays a significant part in the story. The **angel of the LORD** is none other than Christ Himself. Virtually all commentators agree that this was a "theophany," that is, an appearance of God in human form as the angel of Yahweh. See note on 2:1.

The angel sat under an **oak** tree (or terebinth, Heb '*ēlah*). The location of **Ophrah** is uncertain; but the fact that Gideon's father is referred to as Joash **the Abiezrite** would indicate that they were part of the sub-tribe of Abiezer, belonging to the western part of Manasseh, near the border of Ephraim. It was here that **Gideon threshed wheat by the winepress** (better translated "in the winepress," RV, RSV, NASB, NIV). In other words, he was literally beating out the grain inside a winepress in order to **hide it from the Midianites,** fearing they would steal it if he were caught. Thus, in this opening scene we find Gideon afraid and hiding from the enemy.

12 And the angel of the LORD ap-

12-13. While it cannot be denied that Gideon became a man

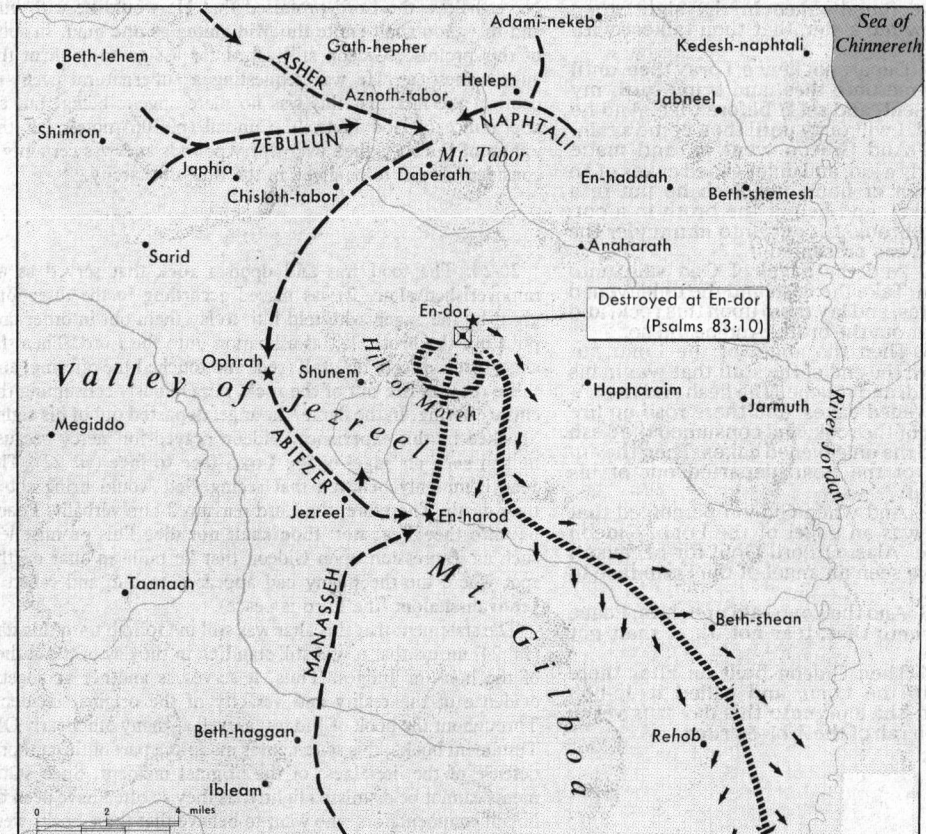

The War of Gideon

peared unto him, and said unto him, The Lord *is* with thee, thou mighty man of valour.

13 And Gideon said unto him, Oh my Lord, if the Lord be with us, why then is all this befallen us? and where *be* all his miracles which our fathers told us of, saying, Did not the Lord bring us up from Egypt? but now the Lord hath forsaken us, and delivered us into the hands of the Mĭd′ĭ-an-ītes.

14 And the Lord looked upon him, and said, Go in this thy might, and thou shalt save Israel from the hand of the Mĭd′ĭ-an-ītes: have not I sent thee?

15 And he said unto him, Oh my Lord, wherewith shall I save Israel? behold, my family *is* poor in Ma-năs′seh, and I *am* the least in my father's house.

16 And the Lord said unto him, Surely I will be with thee, and thou shalt smite the Mĭd′ĭ-an-ītes as one man.

17 And he said unto him, If now I have found grace in thy sight, then shew me a sign that thou talkest with me.

18 Depart not hence, I pray thee, until I come unto thee, and bring forth my present, and set *it* before thee. And he said, I will tarry until thou come again.

19 And Gideon went in, and made ready a kid, and unleavened cakes of an ephah of flour: the flesh he put in a basket, and he put the broth in a pot, and brought *it* out unto him under the oak, and presented *it*.

20 And the angel of God said unto him, Take the flesh and the unleavened cakes, and lay *them* upon this rock, and pour out the broth. And he did so.

21 Then the angel of the Lord put forth the end of the staff that *was* in his hand, and touched the flesh and the unleavened cakes; and there rose up fire out of the rock, and consumed the flesh and the unleavened cakes. Then the angel of the Lord departed out of his sight.

22 And when Gideon perceived that he *was* an angel of the Lord, Gideon said, Alas, O Lord God! for because I have seen an angel of the Lord face to face.

23 And the Lord said unto him, Peace *be* unto thee; fear not: thou shalt not die.

24 Then Gideon built an altar there unto the Lord, and called it Je-hō′-vah-shā′lom: unto this day it *is* yet in Ŏph′rah of the Ā′bī-ĕz′rītes.

of great faith who led his people to victory, it should also be noted that the idea of fear runs like a red thread throughout the story of Gideon's life (cf. vss. 11, 22, 27; 7:3, 10; 8:20). Gideon started out being afraid of the Midianites; he doubted the promise of the angel of the Lord; he constantly asked for signs and fleeces; he was afraid to throw down the altar of Baal, so he did it by night; he sent home the fearful in his army but, nevertheless, ended up with an army of cowards and ultimately discovered that the enemy was more afraid of him than he was of them; and, finally, he scared the Midianites into a fear so great that they destroyed themselves! A careful reading of the text will reveal that this is not at all a far-fetched explanation. Even the words that the angel spoke to Gideon calling him **thou mighty man of valor** are received by Gideon as if they were a joke. He reminded the angel that if the Lord was with them **why then is all this befallen us?** It must be remembered that this was a new generation who had not seen the miracles of the past. Unfortunately, it is very easy to question the genuineness of a miracle when one has not seen it for himself.

14-19. Verse 14 states the **Lord looked upon him,** indicating that the **angel of the Lord** who spoke to him was the **Lord** Himself! He reminded Gideon that **thou shalt save Israel,** that is, he would be the next judge-deliverer. However, Gideon immediately began to make excuses for himself. He objected that his family in Manasseh was poor, and that he was **least in my father's house** (i.e., he was the youngest son of his family, and they were an insignificant family from a militarily impoverished tribe). In essence, he was saying that he was not qualified for this task, neither was his family, and neither was his tribe. Nevertheless, the Lord promised that He would be with him and that **thou shalt smite the Midianites as one man.** In spite of this promise, Gideon still asked for a **sign** to confirm the angel's message. He was requesting a supernatural event to confirm the fact that this was no mere angelic being, but an appearance of God Himself! Cundall (p. 106) notes that the **ephah of flour** weighed over thirty pounds and was certainly a considerable gift to be given in the time of scarcity.

20-24. The food was laid upon a **rock** that served as an impoverished altar. It was placed according to the directions given by the angel, who told him to lay them out in order and **pour out the broth** . . . as a libation unto the Lord. Then the angel reached forth his **staff** (rod) and touched the offering; and **there rose up fire out of the rock,** miraculously consuming the entire offering. In the flame, the angel **departed out of his sight.** Shocked by this experience, Gideon prayed for mercy because he had **seen an angel of the Lord face to face** (vs. 22). The Jews commonly believed that seeing God would bring about their death. Therefore, the Lord reassured him verbally: **Peace be unto thee; fear not: thou shalt not die.** This promise left such an impression upon Gideon that he built an altar on the spot where the theophany had appeared to him and called it **Jehovah-shalom** (the Lord is peace).

The statement that this altar was still in Ophrah **unto this day** (vs. 24) means that it was still standing in the day of the author of the book of Judges. Thus, it serves as another apologetic evidence of the reality and veracity of the original incident. Throughout the book of Judges, as well as many other early Old Testament books, this statement is made as a part of the author's defense of the literalness of the original incident. Such statements cannot be dismissed lightly, as they so often have been by liberal commentators who want to believe that these books were written much later than the events which they describe. For a discussion of this, see O. T. Allis, *The Old Testament: Its Claims* and Its Critics; J. Bright, *The Authority of the Old Testament;* P. Fairbairn, "The Historical Element in God's Revelation," in *Classical Evangelical Essays in Old Testament Interpretation,* pp. 67-86.

25 ¶And it came to pass the same night, that the LORD said unto him, Take thy father's young bullock, even the second bullock of seven years old, and throw down the altar of Bā'al that thy father hath, and cut down the grove that *is* by it:

26 And build an altar unto the LORD thy God upon the top of this rock, in the ordered place, and take the second bullock, and offer a burnt sacrifice with the wood of the grove which thou shalt cut down.

27 Then Gideon took ten men of his servants, and did as the LORD had said unto him: and *so* it was, because he feared his father's household, and the men of the city, that he could not do *it* by day, that he did *it* by night.

28 ¶And when the men of the city arose early in the morning, behold, the altar of Bā'al was cast down, and the grove was cut down that *was* by it, and the second bullock was offered upon the altar that *was* built.

29 And they said one to another, Who hath done this thing? And when they enquired and asked, they said, Gideon the son of Jō'ăsh hath done this thing.

30 Then the men of the city said unto Jō'ăsh, Bring out thy son, that he may die: because he hath cast down the altar of Bā'al, and because he hath cut down the grove that *was* by it.

31 And Jō'ăsh said unto all that stood against him, Will ye plead for Bā'al? will ye save him? he that will plead for him, let him be put to death whilst *it is* yet morning: if he *be* a god, let him plead for himself, because *one* hath cast down his altar.

32 Therefore on that day he called him Je-rŭb'ba-al, saying, Let Bā'al plead against him, because he hath thrown down his altar.

25-32. Having convinced Gideon of His power, God now instructed him to sacrifice his father's **young bullock** unto the Lord Jehovah. In addition, he was to **throw down the altar of Baal** that belonged to his father. This incident reveals the strange and inconsistent situation that prevailed in Israel. Though they claimed to worship the Lord, they had mixed the true religion of Yahweh with the cultic religion of the Canaanites. Gideon's father's name, Joash, means Yahweh has given. Yet, he was apparently a priest of Baal, since he maintained a Baal altar as well as **the grove** (probably a mistranslation of Asherah, the Canaanite female deity). This situation gives us a glimpse into the terrible spiritual condition of the people of Israel just one century after entering the Promised Land. They were not only willing to compromise with pagan religion, but now their own religion had become totally confused with it. Gideon was ordered by God to tear down both the altar to Baal and the pillar of Asherah and to replace it with an altar **unto the LORD thy God . . . in the ordered place,** i.e., with stones laid in due order.

In order to accomplish this task, Gideon took **ten men of his servants,** indicating that he was a man of some position and, perhaps, wealth. Working together, they obeyed the command **by night** because he feared the reprisal of the people of the community. This would indicate that his father was the custodian of the Baal cult-center serving the entire town, and that the majority of the people resorted there for worship. Thus, when the people awoke the next morning, **behold, the altar of Baal was cast down . . . the grove was cut down . . . the second bullock was offered** upon the altar of the Lord. The entire incident is quite significant in contrast to Canaanite religious practices, in which the god El was characterized by the sacred bull as the head of the Canaanite pantheon (see W. F. Albright, "The Role of the Canaanites in the History of Civilization," in *The Bible and the Ancient Near East*).

Another interesting contrast is the fact that the number seven was considered unlucky by the Canaanites, whereas it was virtually a sacred number to the Israelites. Thus, offering the second bullock of seven years old to Yahweh was a deliberate denial of the power of Baal and was an assertion of the victory of Yahweh over Baal. Naturally, the people were extremely upset when they discovered what had happened. The bullock had been offered, the Asherah pole had been cut up and used for the wood to burn the sacrifice, and the altar itself had been destroyed. In its place stood an altar to the Lord God of Israel. When they inquired as to who had done this thing, they were told, **Gideon the son of Joash.** Thereupon, the men came to his father and demanded that Gideon be put to death for what he had dared to do. However, his father, taking note of his son's unusual (and perhaps unexpected) act of bravery, defended his son by asking the townspeople if they would **plead for Baal.**

By asking **will ye save him,** he was implying that Baal, if he were really a god, should be capable of saving himself. "If Baal cannot save himself, how do you expect him to save you?" is the real implication of Joash's reply. The passage makes it clear that Joash was convicted and challenged by his son's action; and, therefore, he **called him Jerubbaal,** meaning "let Baal plead." The idea is that Baal ought to be able to plead for himself, and that the men of the city were not capable of pleading on behalf of a god. The fact that Baal had been unable to stop Gideon's action implies that his father no longer believed that he was a god. One must view the incident from the context of the people themselves. An Israelite man had compromised with Baal worship and somehow had convinced the community to follow him. Now, that same man was questioning the authenticity of such worship and was defending the action of his son.

Compound names with Baal were not uncommon, though the Hebrew word *bōshet* (shame) was often substituted for the name Baal (e.g., Ish-baal was amended to Ishbosheth, and Merib-baal to Mephibosheth). The fact that Gideon was not put to death by the men of the city must mean that his father successfully defended him and turned the city to rally behind this surprising new leader. The total context of the story indicates that his father was stunned by such action on the part of his son (who had been previously known for his cowardice).

33-40. In the meantime, the Midianite-Amalekite-Arab alliance moved into the area with renewed aggression and pitched their tents in the **valley of Jezreel,** extending from Mount Carmel to the Jordan Valley. This was often a major battleground, for it cut into the heart of Palestine. In response to this challenge, **the spirit of the Lord came upon Gideon;** and he rallied the men of Abiezer, his hometown, and the men of **Asher . . . Zebulun . . . Naphtali** joined with them. It must be assumed that Gideon was empowered by the Holy Spirit, as were the other judges. However, the Hebrew word *labash* (to clothe) is used here, rather than *hayah* (was upon). For an excellent discussion of the work of the Holy Spirit in Old Testament times see L. Wood, *The Holy Spirit in the Old Testament,* including his chart on the usage of Hebrew verbs with the activity of the Spirit (pp. 130-131).

In spite of all that had happened, Gideon still revealed his personal hesitation in the incident involving the **fleece of wool** (vs. 37). His question as to whether or not God would save Israel by his hand implies that he was still afraid to fully trust God's promise. Thus, he prayed that the fleece would be wet and the ground would be dry. Then he reversed the condition, asking that the ground be wet and the fleece be dry. As an encouragement to the fearful leader, God answered his request.

This has often raised the question of the use of fleeces. The context of the entire story indicates that the fleece incident would have been unnecessary if Gideon had fully trusted the Lord. There is nothing in the New Testament to indicate that Christian believers ought to use signs and circumstances in attempting to discern the will of God (e.g., if it rains today I will know that I am not to go to church). Such a dependence on signs is the exact opposite of a clear exercise of true faith. God wants us to believe His Word and clearly act thereupon.

33 ¶Then all the Mĭd′ĭ-an-ĭtes and the Am′ă-lek-ĭtes and the children of the east were gathered together, and went over, and pitched in the valley of Jĕz′re-el.

34 But the Spirit of the Lord came upon Gideon, and he blew a trumpet; and Ă′bĭ-ē′zer was gathered after him.

35 And he sent messengers throughout all Ma-năs′seh; who also was gathered after him: and he sent messengers unto Asher, and unto Zĕb′u-lun, and unto Năph′ta-lĭ; and they came up to meet them.

36 ¶And Gideon said unto God, If thou wilt save Israel by mine hand, as thou hast said,

37 Behold, I will put a fleece of wool in the floor; *and* if the dew be on the fleece only, and *it be* dry upon all the earth *beside,* then shall I know that thou wilt save Israel by mine hand, as thou hast said.

38 And it was so: for he rose up early on the morrow, and thrust the fleece together, and wringed the dew out of the fleece, a bowl full of water.

39 And Gideon said unto God, Let not thine anger be hot against me, and I will speak but this once: let me prove, I pray thee, but this once with the fleece; let it now be dry only upon the fleece, and upon all the ground let there be dew.

40 And God did so that night: for it was dry upon the fleece only, and there was dew on all the ground.

CHAPTER 7

THEN Je-rŭb′ba-al, who *is* Gideon, and all the people that *were* with him, rose up early, and pitched beside the well of Hâ′rŏd: so that the host of the Mĭd′ĭ-an-ĭtes were on the north side of them, by the hill of Mô′reh, in the valley.

2 And the Lord said unto Gideon, The people that *are* with thee *are* too many for me to give the Mĭd′ĭ-an-ĭtes into their hands, lest Israel vaunt themselves against me, saying, Mine own hand hath saved me.

3 Now therefore go to, proclaim in the ears of the people, saying, Whosoever *is* fearful and afraid, let him return and depart early from mount Gilead. And there returned of the people twenty and two thousand; and there remained ten thousand.

4 And the Lord said unto Gideon, The people *are* yet *too* many; bring them down unto the water, and I will try them for thee there: and it shall be, *that* of whom I say unto thee, This shall go

7:1-8. The famous story of Gideon's three hundred men follows in these verses. He is told by God that he has too many men with him in order to bring about the kind of victory God intends. Therefore, the total number will have to be cut down. The details of the story are significant, in that Gideon and his men encamped **beside the well of Harod** (spring of trembling), perhaps Ain Jalud near the foot of Mount Gilboa. The Midianites were across the valley to the north, by the **hill of Moreh,** some four miles away. Thus, the scene is set for the famous incident that follows.

Fearful and trembling, Gideon, who must obey at night under cover of darkness and be constantly reassured by signs and fleeces, now arrives at the well of trembling. On his behalf it should be remembered that he had never led an army and that the vast majority of his soldiers were untrained and inexperienced. However, God's main reason for cutting down the size of the army was **lest Israel vaunt themselves against me,** by assuming that they had won the victory through their own strength. Thus, the Lord told Gideon that **The people . . . are too many for me.**

The process of elimination may seem strange, until one

with thee, the same shall go with thee; and of whomsoever I say unto thee, This shall not go with thee, the same shall not go.

5 So he brought down the people unto the water: and the LORD said unto Gideon, Every one that lappeth of the water with his tongue, as a dog lappeth, him shalt thou set by himself; likewise every one that boweth down upon his knees to drink.

6 And the number of them that lapped, *putting* their hand to their mouth, were three hundred men: but all the rest of the people bowed down upon their knees to drink water.

7 And the LORD said unto Gideon, By the three hundred men that lapped will I save you, and deliver the Mĭd′ĭ-an-ītes into thine hand: and let all the *other* people go every man unto his place.

8 So the people took victuals in their hand, and their trumpets: and he sent all *the rest of* Israel every man unto his tent, and retained those three hundred men: and the host of Mĭd′ĭ-an was beneath him in the valley.

9 ¶And it came to pass the same night, that the LORD said unto him, Arise, get thee down unto the host; for I have delivered it into thine hand.

10 But if thou fear to go down, go thou with Phū′rah thy servant down to the host:

11 And thou shalt hear what they say; and afterward shall thine hands be strengthened to go down unto the host. Then went he down with Phū′rah his servant unto the outside of the armed men that *were* in the host.

12 And the Mĭd′ĭ-an-ītes and the Am′ă-lek-ītes and all the children of the east lay along in the valley like grasshoppers for multitude; and their camels *were* without number, as the sand by the sea side for multitude.

13 And when Gideon was come, be-

understands what was actually happening. First, he asked **whosoever is fearful and afraid** to return home; and twenty-two thousand left, leaving only ten thousand men. Anyone who has ever been in battle will honestly admit that he was afraid. Therefore, it would not be improper to suggest that those who went home were the wisest and the most honest of the entire group. Of the ten thousand that remained, there were still **too many.** Gideon, therefore, was instructed to bring them **down unto the water** where God would **try them** (vs. 4). There are two basic views on the water trial. Most commentators assume that those who **lapped** were those who drank water while crouching or standing, lapping it from their cupped hands and readily watching for the enemy. However, ancient Jewish interpretation, as reflected by Josephus (*Antiquities* V; 6:3), prefers to interpret the passage in a directly opposite manner. The men selected by Gideon who lapped water out of their hands and were looking about were, in reality, the ones who were the most afraid of all! While the correct interpretation may never be totally settled, the details and context of the story give it great credibility.

Gideon is first discovered by the angel of the Lord while he is hiding and threshing grain inside a winepress. The angel, almost with a sense of humor, called him a **mighty man of valor** (6:12); and Gideon acted as if he must be talking about someone else! He was reluctant to believe the angel was real, or that the message was true, and only obeyed the command to tear down the altar at night because he feared his father and the other men. Now he arrives at the Valley of Jezreel to confront the Midianites with thirty-two thousand men, as opposed to their one hundred thirty-five thousand (8:10). He asked those who were afraid to leave, and the majority of the army left. He then took the army to drink; and those that got down on their knees and drank right out of the spring were set aside, and those who, in fear, lapped the water were kept to follow him. While most Christian commentators have not followed the old Jewish viewpoint, it does have much to commend itself and certainly brings out the theme of irony that runs throughout the book. Since the enemy was encamped more than four miles distant, it hardly seems necessary that the **men that lapped** needed to be looking about in order to be prepared for battle at any moment. Rather, it seems more likely that these were the men who were afraid of fear itself. When given the opportunity to go home, they were too afraid to leave! When given an opportunity for a refreshing drink, they lapped it up in fear. Now God promised **by the three hundred men that lapped will I save you.** By now, even Gideon was too afraid to leave, and he continued to follow God's orders. Therefore, nearly another ten thousand men were sent away, and only three hundred remained to help Gideon defeat the Midianites.

9-14. Gideon must have been completely in shock by now; and in order to prepare him to win the battle that would follow, God brought about an unusual set of circumstances. He ordered Gideon to **get thee down unto the host** and spy on the Midianite encampment. This is followed by the statement **if thou fear to go down** (vs. 10) take **Phurah thy servant** with you. The fact that he went down **with Phurah** (vs. 11) indicates that indeed he was afraid to go alone! There can be no doubt that the element of fear is deliberately woven throughout the entire story by the narrator. Even Phurah's name means foliage, indicating that Gideon was hiding behind his armorbearer! The significance of the spying incident was the dream that he heard and its suggested interpretation.

Having observed the **multitude** of the enemy's encampment, Gideon must have become more fearful than ever until he overheard the guards talking to each other. The first said that he had dreamed about a **cake of barley bread,** which tumbled into the host of Midian and knocked over his tent (vs. 13). Unable to

hold, *there was* a man that told a dream unto his fellow, and said, Behold, I dreamed a dream, and, lo, a cake of barley bread tumbled into the host of Mĭd′ĭ-an, and came unto a tent, and smote it that it fell, and overturned it, that the tent lay along.

14 And his fellow answered and said, This *is* nothing else save the sword of Gideon the son of Jŏ′ăsh, a man of Israel: *for* into his hand hath God delivered Mĭd′ĭ-an, and all the host.

15 ¶And it was *so*, when Gideon heard the telling of the dream, and the interpretation thereof, that he worshipped, and returned into the host of Israel, and said, Arise; for the LORD hath delivered into your hand the host of Mĭd′ĭ-an.

16 And he divided the three hundred men *into* three companies, and he put a trumpet in every man's hand, with empty pitchers, and lamps within the pitchers.

17 And he said unto them, Look on me, and do likewise: and, behold, when I come to the outside of the camp, it shall be *that*, as I do, so shall ye do.

18 When I blow with a trumpet, I and all that *are* with me, then blow ye the trumpets also on every side of all the camp, and say, The sword of the LORD, and of Gideon.

19 ¶So Gideon, and the hundred men that *were* with him, came unto the outside of the camp in the beginning of the middle watch; and they had but newly set the watch: and they blew the trumpets, and brake the pitchers that *were* in their hands.

20 And the three companies blew the trumpets, and brake the pitchers, and held the lamps in their left hands, and the trumpets in their right hands to blow *withal:* and they cried, The sword of the LORD, and of Gideon.

21 And they stood every man in his place round about the camp: and all the host ran, and cried, and fled.

22 And the three hundred blew the trumpets, and the LORD set every man's sword against his fellow, even throughout all the host: and the host fled to Bĕth–shĭt′tah in Zĕr′e-răth, *and* to the border of Ā′bel–mĕ-hō′lah, unto Tăb′bath.

23 And the men of Israel gathered themselves together out of Năph′ta-lī, and out of Asher, and out of all Ma-năs′seh, and pursued after the Mĭd′ĭ-an-ītes.

24 And Gideon sent messengers throughout all mount Ē′phra-im, saying, Come down against the Mĭd′ĭ-an-ītes, and take before them the waters unto Bĕth–bâ′rah and Jordan. Then all the men of Ē′phra-im gathered themselves together, and took the waters unto Bĕth–bâ′rah and Jordan.

25 And they took two princes of the Mĭd′ĭ-an-ītes, Ō′reb and Zē′eb; and they slew Ō′reb upon the rock Ō′reb, and Zē′eb they slew at the winepress of Zē′eb, and pursued Mĭd′ĭ-an, and brought the heads of Ō′reb and Zē′eb to Gideon on the other side Jordan.

understand the meaning of the dream, he asked his friend for a suggested interpretation, to which his friend replied, **This is nothing else save the sword of Gideon . . . for into his hand hath God delivered Midian, and all the host.** Nothing will encourage a coward more than discovering that his enemy is afraid of him. The significance of the dream was to convince Gideon (the barley thresher) that the Midianites were more afraid of him than he was of them! Thus, God would use an encouraged coward to frighten the enemy away!

15-25. The discovery of his enemy's fear gave Gideon renewed courage, and upon hearing the **interpretation . . . he worshiped** God for giving him this renewed assurance of victory. With revived confidence he came back and rallied the host of Israel, **Arise; for the LORD hath delivered into your hand the host of Midian.** Instead of a direct assault, however, Gideon **divided the three hundred men into three companies** so that they might surround the enemy. Pfeiffer (p. 248) is certainly correct in referring to this as psychological warfare. The army was divided into three companies of one hundred each, and they were to carry **trumpets** (Heb *shōparōt*, rams' horns) and **empty pitchers** containing **lamps** (i.e., torches). They were to conceal the torches within the open-topped pitchers until the last possible minute, when they would break the pitchers, wave the torches, and blow the trumpets, giving the enemy the impression that a great host was coming down upon them.

Several factors regarding ancient Near Eastern warfare should be noted when interpreting this incident. As a normal custom in those days, armies rarely fought at night (notice I Sam 17 where the two armies re-engaged each other day after day but did not fight at night). When an army did engage in battle at night, only a minority of men carried torches in order to light up the battlefield. In addition, only a certain number of men would carry and blow trumpets during the conflict. Therefore, when the Midianites awoke to the sight of three hundred torches and the sound of three hundred trumpets blaring at them from every conceivable direction, they could only assume that thousands upon thousands were attacking them (on Near Eastern methods of warfare, see Y. Yadin, *The Art of Warfare in Biblical Lands*).

The noisy assault began at midnight during the **middle watch.** The sound of the horns would signal the call to battle, and the breaking of the pitchers would simulate the clash of arms. The awaking Midianites assumed that the battle had already begun and that they were outnumbered. The battle cry, **The sword of the LORD, and of Gideon,** would strike fear in the minds of the confused Midianites and their allies. Since the invaders were a combination of at least three different language dialects, they began to attack one another in the confusion of the night. Thus, the **LORD set every man's sword against his fellow.** The enemy literally put itself to rout by attacking one another.

The Israelites subsequently pursued **after the Midianites** (vs. 23) and called upon the men of Ephraim to help them. They cut off the escape routes leading toward the Jordan River at **Beth-barah,** near the Wadi Fara'a. The Israelite army captured **Oreb** (raven) and **Zeeb** (wolf) and brought their heads as trophies of victory back to Gideon on the other side of the Jordan (i.e., Transjordan). Bruce (p. 246) notes that these events were actual history, not merely aetiological explanations, since they are also recounted in Isaiah 9:4; 10:26.

CHAPTER 8

AND the men of Ē'phra-im said unto him, Why hast thou served us thus, that thou calledst us not, when thou wentest to fight with the Mĭd'ĭ-an-ītes? And they did chide with him sharply.

2 And he said unto them, What have I done now in comparison of you? Is not the gleaning of the grapes of Ē'phra-im better than the vintage of Ā'bĭ-ē'zer?

3 God hath delivered into your hands the princes of Mĭd'ĭ-an, Ō'reb and Zē'eb: and what was I able to do in comparison of you? Then their anger was abated toward him, when he had said that.

4 ¶And Gideon came to Jordan, and passed over, he, and the three hundred men that were with him, faint, yet pursuing them.

5 And he said unto the men of Sŭc'coth, Give, I pray you, loaves of bread unto the people that follow me; for they be faint, and I am pursuing after Zē'bah and Zăl-mŭn'na, kings of Mĭd'-ĭ-an.

6 And the princes of Sŭc'coth said, Are the hands of Zē'bah and Zăl-mŭn'na now in thine hand, that we should give bread unto thine army?

7 And Gideon said, Therefore when the LORD hath delivered Zē'bah and Zăl-mŭn'na into mine hand, then I will tear your flesh with the thorns of the wilderness and with briers.

8 And he went up thence to Pe-nū'el, and spake unto them likewise: and the men of Pe-nū'el answered him as the men of Sŭc'coth had answered him.

9 And he spake also unto the men of Pe-nū'el, saying, When I come again in peace, I will break down this tower.

10 ¶Now Zē'bah and Zăl-mŭn'na were in Kär'kôr, and their hosts with them, about fifteen thousand men, all that were left of all the hosts of the children of the east: for there fell an hundred and twenty thousand men that drew sword.

11 ¶And Gideon went up by the way of them that dwelt in tents on the east of Nō'bah and Jŏg'be-hah, and smote the host: for the host was secure.

12 And when Zē'bah and Zăl-mŭn'na fled, he pursued after them, and took the two kings of Mĭd'ĭ-an, Zē'bah and Zăl-mŭn'na, and discomfited all the host.

13 ¶And Gideon the son of Jō'ăsh returned from battle before the sun was up,

14 And caught a young man of the men of Sŭc'coth, and enquired of him: and he described unto him the princes of Sŭc'coth, and the elders thereof, even threescore and seventeen men.

15 And he came unto the men of Sŭc'coth, and said, Behold Zē'bah and Zăl-mŭn'na, with whom ye did upbraid me, saying, Are the hands of Zē'bah and Zăl-mŭn'na now in thine hand, that we should give bread unto thy men that are weary?

16 And he took the elders of the city, and thorns of the wilderness and briers, and with them he taught the men of Sŭc'coth.

8:1-3. This chapter opens with the unbelievable complaint of the Ephraimites that they had been left out of this potential victory (a problem which would recur in the time of Jephthah in chapter 12). The fact that they **did chide with him sharply** indicates their selfish attitude toward the victory and helps explain why God used such unusual means to bring it about. The Ephraimites wanted to take credit for the whole thing; therefore, it is no wonder that God chose an unlikely leader to gather a minute force to win such an unusual battle. Gideon, now a hero, was able to calm the critical reaction of the Ephraimites by reminding them that they were not under the oppression of the Midianites as severely as the people of Abiezer, his hometown. Thus, he appeased their anger and avoided an unnecessary conflict with one of Israel's strongest tribes.

4-9. In the meantime Gideon and his three hundred men continued **pursuing after Zebah and Zalmunna, kings of Midian.** About to **faint,** his men arrived at the city of **Succoth,** east of the Jordan. Famished and faint, Gideon asked for **loaves of bread** to strengthen his impoverished army; and they refused to help him, with the taunt that he had not yet actually captured the kings of Midian. Gideon replied that he would return and **tear your flesh with the thorns.** The verb **tear** (actually to thresh) is constructed with a double accusative and is used in a figurative sense meaning "to punish severely" (Keil and Delitzsch, p. 352). The nature of the threat was made clear later when Gideon returned to "thresh" their flesh with thorns as one would thresh corn or grain. The refusal of the men of **Succoth** and **Penuel** to help him was typical of the divided attitude of the Israelites at that time. Since no central power existed, the various cities and territories were a law unto themselves. When the men of Penuel also refused to help him, Gideon threatened to return and **break down this tower** (vs. 9).

10-21. Zebah and Zalmunna, the kings of the Midianites, had escaped to **Karkor** (site unknown) with about **fifteen thousand men.** This was all that was left of the invasion force since the text indicates that one hundred twenty thousand of them were slain in the initial skirmish. They apparently assumed they were in safety at this unknown desert hideout. The location of **Nobah** and **Jogbehah** can be located at Jubeihat, fifteen miles southeast of Penuel. Gideon and his men surprised the Midianite encampment and captured the two kings (vs. 18). In addition, he terrified or **discomfited** (Heb *charad*) **all the host.** Upon his return, Gideon dealt with the men of Succoth and Penuel. The phrase **before the sun was up** uses the rare word *cheres*, and many have suggested the translation should read "from the ascent from Heres."

While returning, Gideon caught **a young man . . . of Succoth** who **described** (Heb wrote or registered) for him seventy-seven of the elders of the city. It was previously assumed in liberal scholarship that people could not write well at this time, but all scholarship now recognizes that such an objection was made out of ignorance. Alphabetic writing was already common at this time. A pottery sherd found at Isbet Sartah is inscribed with the oldest extant Hebrew alphabet known at this time (cf. A. Demsky and M. Kockavi, "An Alphabet from the Days of the Judges," in *Biblical Archaeology Review*, IV. 3, 1978, pp. 23-31). Therefore, it is most likely that he wrote these names on a piece of pottery so that Gideon would know with whom to deal when he captured the city.

Upon his return, he took the elders of the city, according to the list, and, using the thorns, **he taught** (Heb *yada*) **the men of Succoth.** This Hebrew verb may be translated "caused to

17 And he beat down the tower of Penū'el, and slew the men of the city.

18 ¶Then said he unto Zē'bah and Zǎl'mǔn'na, What manner of men were they whom ye slew at Tā'bor? And they answered, As thou art, so were they; each one resembled the children of a king.

19 And he said, They were my brethren, even the sons of my mother: as the LORD liveth, if ye had saved them alive, I would not slay you.

20 And he said unto Jē'ther his firstborn, Up, and slay them. But the youth drew not his sword: for he feared, because he was yet a youth.

21 Then Zē'bah and Zǎl'mǔn'na said, Rise thou, and fall upon us: for as the man is, so is his strength. And Gideon arose, and slew Zē'bah and Zǎl'mǔn'na, and took away the ornaments that were on their camels' necks.

22 ¶Then the men of Israel said unto Gideon, Rule thou over us, both thou, and thy son, and thy son's son also: for thou hast delivered us from the hand of Mǐd'ǐ-an.

23 And Gideon said unto them, I will not rule over you, neither shall my son rule over you: the LORD shall rule over you.

24 And Gideon said unto them, I would desire a request of you, that ye would give me every man the earrings of his prey. (For they had golden earrings, because they were Ish'ma-el-ītes.)

25 And they answered, We will willingly give them. And they spread a garment, and did cast therein every man the earrings of his prey.

26 And the weight of the golden earrings that he requested shekels of gold; beside ornaments, and collars, and purple raiment that was on the kings of Mǐd'ǐ-an, and beside the chains that were about their camels' necks.

27 And Gideon made an ephod thereof, and put it in his city, even in Ŏph'rah: and all Israel went thither a whoring after it: which thing became a snare unto Gideon, and to his house.

know" or "made submissive." Evidently, he wrapped them in thorns and briars and threshed them as he had threatened earlier. He treated the men at Penuel even more severely, in that he destroyed the tower and slew the men of the city (vs. 17). Having dealt with these rebellious cities, he then turned his attention to the Midianite kings, Zebah and Zalmunna, and asked them What manner of men . . . ye slew at Tabor? Bruce (p. 246) assumes that Gideon's brothers were slain in 6:33 when the Midianites invaded Jezreel. Gideon's reply that they were my brethren, even the sons of my mother indicates that his full brothers had been killed at some time earlier by these Midianites. It is possible that Bruce is wrong and that they were killed much earlier by these Midianites. This would explain why Gideon, the youngest son, was hiding in the winepress threshing grain in the first place.

Their reply that they . . . resembled the children of a king was a form of arrogant flattery. Therefore, the duty of blood revenge rested upon Gideon (cf. Deut 19:6), and he ordered Jether his first-born to slay them. However, he could not; for he feared. Gideon's son seems as fearful as his father once was. With an arrogant and haughty challenge, the Midianite kings retorted, Rise thou, and fall upon us: for as the man is, so is his strength. They were challenging Gideon to prove that he was not a coward like his son. Therefore, Gideon arose and slew them immediately. Having killed them, he also took the ornaments that were on their camels' necks, i.e., their crescent, or moon-shaped ornaments (Heb saharōn). These were amulets to bring good luck in battle and may indicate that the Midianites were moon worshipers (cf. also Isa 3:18).

22-27. As a result of this stunning victory, the men of Israel urged Gideon to Rule thou over us. For the first time the tribes begin to desire a king and a central government. However, Gideon refused the offer because he believed that the LORD shall rule over you. Israel was a theocracy that recognized God as her sovereign. Gideon refused for himself and his sons to hold such a position. Many more years would pass before God would authorize a true king in Israel. However, the desire for centralized leadership to replace the loosely confederated tribal amphictyony had already been initiated.

The historian very carefully weaves the story of Gideon into that of Abimelech, his usurper son who illegitimately attempted to make himself king of Israel. Having refused the kingdom, Gideon requested instead that they give him the earrings of his prey, which they had taken from the fallen Ishmaelites (used interchangeably here for Midianites; cf. Gen 37:25, 36, where the same groups are interchangeably referred to in the narrative about Joseph). Both Ishmael, by Hagar, and Midian, by Keturah, were sons of Abraham; and their descendants became closely allied. The men willingly responded and spread a garment upon which each man cast the earrings of his prey.

The weight of the golden earrings was one thousand seven hundred shekels of gold (about seventy pounds), from which Gideon for some unexplained reason made an ephod. The nature of this ephod is uncertain. The name was given to part of the attire of the high priest (Ex 28:4); and on occasion it was consulted as a source of divine guidance, by using the urim and thummim stones which were upon it. Whatever Gideon's reason for making the ephod, the end result was that all Israel went thither a whoring after it so that it became a snare unto Gideon, and to his house (v. 27). It is possible that Gideon meant no harm by his actions and was equally shocked by the unfortunate result. Some commentators suggest that he actually made an idol clothed with the ephod, but this seems highly unlikely. Instead of giving glory to God for His miraculous deliverance, the people began worshiping the prey of that deliverance. The

28 ¶Thus was Mĭd'ian subdued before the children of Israel, so that they lifted up their heads no more. And the country was in quietness forty years in the days of Gideon.

29 And Je-rŭb'ba-al the son of Jŏ'ash went and dwelt in his own house.

30 And Gideon had threescore and ten sons of his body begotten: for he had many wives.

31 And his concubine that was in Shĕ'chem, she also bare him a son, whose name he called A-bĭm'e-lĕch.

32 And Gideon the son of Jŏ'ash died in a good old age, and was buried in the sepulchre of Jŏ'ash his father, in Ŏph'rah of the Ă'bĭ-ĕz'rītes.

33 And it came to pass, as soon as Gideon was dead, that the children of Israel turned again, and went a whoring after Bā'al-Ĭm, and made Bā'al-bĕ'rīth their god.

34 And the children of Israel remembered not the LORD their God, who had delivered them out of the hands of all their enemies on every side:

35 Neither shewed they kindness to the house of Je-rŭb'ba-al, namely, Gideon, according to all the goodness which he had shewed unto Israel.

CHAPTER 9

AND A'bĭm'e-lĕch the son of Je-rŭb'ba-al went to Shĕ'-chem unto his mother's brethren, and communed with them, and with all the family of the house of his mother's father, saying,

2 Speak, I pray you, in the ears of all the men of Shĕ'chem, Whether is better for you, either that all the sons of Je-rŭb'ba-al, which are threescore and ten persons, reign over you, or that one reign over you? remember also that I am your bone and your flesh.

3 And his mother's brethren spake of him in the ears of all the men of Shĕ'-chem all these words: and their hearts inclined to follow A-bĭm'e-lĕch; for they said, He is our brother.

4 And they gave him threescore and ten pieces of silver out of the house of Bā'al-bĕ'rīth, wherewith A-bĭm'e-lĕch hired vain and light persons, which followed him.

5 And he went unto his father's house at Ŏph'rah, and slew his brethren the sons of Je-rŭb'ba-al, being threescore and ten persons, upon one stone: notwithstanding yet Jŏ'tham the youngest son of Je-rŭb'ba-al was left; for he hid himself.

6 And all the men of Shĕ'chem gathered together, and all the house of Mĭl'lō, and went, and made A-bĭm'e-lĕch king, by the plain of the pillar that was in Shĕ'chem.

fact that it became a **snare unto Gideon** would imply that he was not happy with this result.

28-35. The text is choppy at this point, and several ideas are quickly inserted. The author notes a forty-year period of rest **in the days of Gideon.** This would indicate that he lived some forty years after this incident, during which Israel was at peace. This is followed by the statement that Gideon had **threescore and ten sons . . . many wives.** In addition, he had a **concubine** who lived at **Shechem,** and by whom he fathered **Abimelech.** The statement that Gideon died in a **good old age** (vs. 32) indicates that he lived a peaceful life in semi-retirement until his death. However, as soon as he died, **the children of Israel turned again . . . after Baalim.**

The following story indicates that since Abimelech is never referred to as a legitimate judge, there may well have been overlapping time periods between the judges of Israel. Instead of being faithful to the Lord who had delivered them, the Israelites not only wanted to worship Gideon's ephod, but were now returning to the worship of the local Baal gods immediately after his death. The constant emphasis on fidelity to the Lord, which brings deliverance until the death of the judge, would seem to indicate that each leader's judgeship was marked by a time of spiritual revival and renewed dedication to the Lord God of Israel. Tragically, however, the death of each judge was always followed by an increased period of idolatry and paganism. This relapse into apostasy was especially severe in that the people made **Baal-berith their God.** Berīt is the Hebrew word for covenant. Their original covenant was with the Lord Jehovah, and this new act of rebellion caused them actually to recognize Baal as their new lord of the covenant!

E. Fifth Cycle: Israel versus Abimelech. 9:1-10:5.

1. Servitude to Abimelech—three years. 9:1-57.

9:1-6. The story of **Abimelech** is one of the most tragic incidents in Israel's history. It also reveals, as do the later family narratives of David and Solomon, the tragedy that so often follows multiple marriages. Abimelech is identifed as the **son of Jerubbaal,** rather than using the more acceptable name of Gideon. Nowhere is Abimelech called a judge: rather, he is a usurper attempting to be a **king** (vs. 6). As the son of a concubine, he was considered to be part of his mother's family. In the ancient East such women usually remained with their own clan and were visited by their husbands from time to time. Thus, the son of a concubine had a closer relationship to his mother's family than to his father's. This explains why Abimelech **went to Shechem** to appeal to his mother's family for the backing that would be needed to overpower Gideon's other sons who were apparently vying for rulership, although this is not clearly stated in the text.

It is possible that only Abimelech was interested in being the next ruler. Evidently, his mother's relatives spoke on his behalf and convinced the rest of the leaders of Shechem that they should **follow Abimelech.** Therefore, they gave him seventy pieces of silver from the house of **Baal-berith.** Ancient temples were often the source of great amounts of wealth; and while this is not a large amount, it was sufficient for Abimelech to hire **vain and light persons** (scoundrels). Shechem was an unusual city throughout Bible history (cf. G. E. Wright, "Shechem," in *AOTS*, pp. 355-370). Jacob's sons had been there, and under Joshua it was both a Levitical city and a city of refuge. It was there that Joshua gathered all Israel before his death and reminded them of their covenant relationship to God. In a sense, the Abimelech incident is the low point in the book of Judges, for it represents the exact opposite of victory under Joshua's leadership.

Urged on by the men of Shechem, Abimelech went back to Ophrah and **slew his brethren the sons of Jerubbaal . . . upon one stone,** suggesting a formal execution rather than a defeat in battle. The number **threescore and ten** (seventy) is rounded off as a whole number. The implied usage of the numbers seems to indicate that Gideon had seventy sons, plus Abimelech, and that the latter used seventy pieces of silver to hire enough men to kill each of the seventy sons. **Notwithstanding yet Jotham the youngest son . . . hid himself.** Somehow, unexplained by the text, Jotham was able to escape and became the only living descendant of Gideon. What a tragic end for the family of a man so mightily used of God, to have his family destroyed in such a vicious manner. Then the Shechemites gathered together with the **house of Millo** (i.e., Beth-millo, house of the fortress). Together they **made Abimelech king.**

Davis (p. 118) states: "It is doubtful that the reign of Abimelech gained recognition anywhere else than in the Shechem area, and even this was shortlived." Therefore, Abimelech is usually not counted as an actual king over all Israel, nor does the text state that he exercised the Spirit-given position of a judge. He must be looked upon as a usurper king. **By the plain of the pillar** is better translated terebinth or oak. There is a significant connection of this incident with biblical history. Jacob had buried the teraphim (idols) of his family under an oak at Shechem (Gen 35:4), and Joshua set up a pillar as a witness to the covenant between God and Israel at the same location (Josh 24:26). Cundall (p. 127) observes: "It is of interest to note that Rehoboam went to Shechem, following the death of Solomon, to secure the acclamation of the Israelites, though the city itself was in ruins at that time (I Kgs 12)."

7-13. The "Parable of the Trees," which was told by Jotham to the people of Shechem, is one of the unique literary pieces of the Old Testament. For a discussion on the interpretation of such parables, see F. R. Norden, *Parables of the Old Testament.* In the manner of a prophet, Jotham stood upon Mount Gerizim and **lifted up his voice, and cried, . . . Hearken unto me, ye men of Shechem.** The form of the "Parable of the Trees" is rhythmic and symbolic. It definitely reflects an antimonarchic attitude. Pfeiffer (p. 250) notes: "A triangular rock platform projects from the side of Gerizim, which forms a natural pulpit overlooking Shechem." The usage of this parable makes it clear that parables were common Oriental methods of teaching in the Near East long before the time of Jesus.

The subjects of the parable are all **trees,** which is interesting in relation to Abimelech's later felling of trees to be used as battering rams (vs. 48). First, the trees went to the **olive tree** to request it to become king over them, but it refused. Olive groves are plentiful around the area of Shechem, and the olive tree is one of the most valuable to the people of the Near East. The **fig tree** was the next to be requested to **reign over us.** It was the most common fruit tree of Palestine, but it also refused. Third, the trees requested **the vine** to reign over them; and it also refused. **Which cheereth God** (Heb *'elōhīm*) and **man** may be rendered gods. It is possible that Jotham is using this reference in the sense of a religious libation poured out to the gods in sacrifice. Such a practice was common among pagans in the ancient Near East. This does not mean that Jotham necessarily believed in this practice himself, nor should it be taken to mean that God Himself could actually be encouraged by the use of wine. It should be remembered that the parable has a poetic format and should not be taken literally (e.g., the trees did not actually talk to one another).

14-21. Finally, the trees came to the **bramble** (thornbush which clung to the rocks of that area). The bramble was of no practical value whatever. It was not only worthless as timber, but a menace to both the farms and the forests of that area.

7 And when they told *it* to Jŏ′tham, he went and stood in the top of mount Gĕr′i-zĭm, and lifted up his voice, and cried, and said unto them, Hearken unto me, ye men of Shĕ′chem, that God may hearken unto you.

8 The trees went forth *on a time* to anoint a king over them; and they said unto the olive tree, Reign thou over us.

9 But the olive tree said unto them, Should I leave my fatness, wherewith by me they honour God and man, and go to be promoted over the trees?

10 And the trees said to the fig tree, Come thou, *and* reign over us.

11 But the fig tree said unto them, Should I forsake my sweetness, and my good fruit, and go to be promoted over the trees?

12 Then said the trees unto the vine, Come thou, *and* reign over us.

13 And the vine said unto them, Should I leave my wine, which cheereth God and man, and go to be promoted over the trees?

14 Then said all the trees unto the bramble, Come thou, *and* reign over us.

15 And the bramble said unto the trees, If in truth ye anoint me king over

you, *then* come *and* put your trust in my shadow: and if not, let fire come out of the bramble, and devour the cedars of Lebanon.

16 Now therefore, if ye have done truly and sincerely, in that ye have made A-bĭm′e-lĕch king, and if ye have dealt well with Je-rŭb′ba-al and his house, and have done unto him according to the deserving of his hands;

17 (For my father fought for you, and adventured his life far, and delivered you out of the hand of Mĭd′ĭ-an:

18 And ye are risen up against my father's house this day, and have slain his sons, threescore and ten persons, upon one stone, and have made A-bĭm′e-lĕch, the son of his maidservant, king over the men of Shĕ′chem, because he *is* your brother;)

19 If ye then have dealt truly and sincerely with Je-rŭb′ba-al and with his house this day, *then* rejoice ye in A-bĭm′e-lĕch, and let him also rejoice in you:

20 But if not, let fire come out from A-bĭm′e-lĕch, and devour the men of Shĕ′chem, and the house of Mĭl′lō; and let fire come out from the men of Shĕ′-chem, and from the house of Mĭl′lō, and devour A-bĭm′e-lĕch.

21 And Jō′tham ran away, and fled, and went to Beer, and dwelt there, for fear of A-bĭm′e-lĕch his brother.

22 ¶When A-bĭm′e-lĕch had reigned three years over Israel,

23 Then God sent an evil spirit between A-bĭm′e-lĕch and the men of Shĕ′chem; and the men of Shĕ′chem dealt treacherously with A-bĭm′e-lĕch:

24 That the cruelty *done* to the threescore and ten sons of Je-rŭb′ba-al might come, and their blood be laid upon A-bĭm′e-lĕch their brother, which slew them; and upon the men of Shĕ′-chem, which aided him in the killing of his brethren.

25 And the men of Shĕ′chem set liers in wait for him in the top of the mountains, and they robbed all that came along that way by them: and it was told A-bĭm′e-lĕch.

26 And Gā′al the son of Ē′bĕd came with his brethren, and went over to Shĕ′chem: and the men of Shĕ′chem put their confidence in him.

27 And they went out into the fields, and gathered their vineyards, and trode *the* grapes, and made merry, and went into the house of their god, and did eat and drink, and cursed A-bĭm′e-lĕch.

28 And Gā′al the son of Ē′bĕd said, Who *is* A-bĭm′e-lĕch, and who *is* Shĕ′-chem, that we should serve him? *is* not *he* the son of Je-rŭb′ba-al? and Zē′bul his officer? serve the men of Hā′môr the father of Shĕ′chem: for why should we serve him?

29 And would to God this people

Therefore, the request to **put your trust in my shadow** (vs. 15) was ridiculous indeed. The point of the parable is well taken, for in it the most worthless of all trees becomes the king of trees! However, the attitude of such a worthless thing was selfish to begin with. The bramble clings close to the ground and casts no shadow whatever in which to trust.

The ultimate point of the parable is that Abimelech (the bramble king) could offer no real security to the men of Shechem and, in fact he would ultimately become the source of their destruction. The threat to **devour the cedars of Lebanon** was certainly a realistic threat. Fires in that area were spurred on by the quickly burning dried brambles and often burned completely out of control during the summer heat. Moore (p. 249) correctly observes that, "Those who made the thorn king over them put themselves in this dilemma: If they were true to him, they enjoyed his protection, which was a mockery; if they were false to him, he would be their ruin." To make sure that the parable was correctly interpreted, Jotham offered the interpretation himself. He reminded the people of Shechem that his father had fought for and defended them; and now they had turned upon his family and slew his seventy sons, making Abimelech, the **son of his maidservant** (Heb '*amah* means slave-concubine), to be the king. It is interesting to note that he also refers to his seventy brothers as being slain upon **one stone** and that Abimelech was eventually killed by a millstone (vs. 53)!

Again, the theme of irony runs throughout the book of Judges, interwoven into virtually every one of these stories. Jotham concluded by stating that if they had done **truly and sincerely** with Gideon's family, then they deserved to rejoice; but if not, he pronounced the curse upon them. He prayed, **let fire come out from Abimelech, and devour the men of Shechem;** and then he added to that curse one on Abimelech as well. Having delivered the parable, Jotham ran for his life and fled to **Beer** (the well, possibly El-Bireh between Shechem and Jerusalem).

22-32. Treachery begets treachery, and it was not long until there were problems between Abimelech and the Shechemites. The statements that **Abimelech . . . reigned three years over Israel** should not be taken to mean that he was actually king over all the tribes of Israel. His authority seems to have extended only over the western portion of Manasseh, including Arumah and Thebez. The Hebrew word (Heb *sarar*) is better translated governed, rather than reigned. Abimelech was actually little more than a local chieftain, or city king, controlling a limited area. However, it is also true that he was the only person in Israel claiming to be a king. The meaning of his name is itself a claim to rulership, for '*Abimelek* means my father is king. In the corporate personality viewpoint of the Near Eastern peoples, to claim that your father was king was equally to claim yourself to be king (cf. H. W. Robinson, *Corporate Personality In Ancient Israel*).

The ensuing conflict is viewed by the writer of Judges as resulting because **God sent an evil spirit between Abimelech and the men of Shechem.** Such a statement is not uncommon in the Old Testament (cf. I Sam 16:14; 18:10; 19:9). The spirit of animosity that developed between them is viewed here as a result of God working in human history. That evil spirits can be commanded by God, and His giving them permission to work their evil desires is as old as the story of the book of Job.

The immediate crisis was precipitated by bands of armed Shechemites ambushing the trade routes, thus depriving Abimelech of the revenues that could be collected by taxing the caravans passing through his territory. In other words, the activity of the Shechemites was bad for business. This rebellion against Abimelech was led by **Gaal the son of Ebed,** of whom little is known. Most commentators have assumed that he was

481

were under my hand! then would I remove A-bĭm′e-lĕch. And he said to A-bĭm′e-lĕch, Increase thine army, and come out.

30 ¶And when Zē′bul the ruler of the city heard the words of Gā′al the son of Ē′bĕd, his anger was kindled.

31 And he sent messengers unto A-bĭm′e-lĕch privily, saying, Behold, Gā′al the son of Ē′bĕd and his brethren be come to Shē′chem; and, behold, they fortify the city against thee.

32 Now therefore up by night, thou and the people that *is* with thee, and lie in wait in the field:

33 And it shall be, *that* in the morning, as soon as the sun is up, thou shalt rise early, and set upon the city: and, behold, *when* he and the people that *is* with him come out against thee, then mayest thou do to them as thou shalt find occasion.

34 ¶And A-bĭm′e-lĕch rose up, and all the people that *were* with him, by night, and they laid wait against Shē′-chem in four companies.

35 And Gā′al the son of Ē′bĕd went out, and stood in the entering of the gate of the city: and A-bĭm′e-lĕch rose up, and the people that *were* with him, from lying in wait.

36 And when Gā′al saw the people, he said to Zē′bul, Behold, there come people down from the top of the mountains. And Zē′bul said unto him, Thou seest the shadow of the mountains as *if* they *were* men.

37 And Gā′al spake again and said, See there come people down by the middle of the land, and another company come along by the plain of Mē-ŏn′e-nĭm.

38 Then said Zē′bul unto him, Where *is* now thy mouth, wherewith thou saidst, Who *is* A-bĭm′e-lĕch, that we should serve him? *is* not this the people that thou hast despised? go out, I pray now, and fight with them.

39 And Gā′al went out before the men of Shē′chem, and fought with A-bĭm′e-lĕch.

40 And A-bĭm′e-lĕch chased him, and he fled before him, and many were overthrown *and* wounded, *even* unto the entering of the gate.

41 And A-bĭm′e-lĕch dwelt at A-rŭ′-

probably a Canaanite since he urged the people to **serve the men of Hamor the father of Shechem** (cf. Gen 33:19 where Jacob had dealings with these original Canaanite settlers at Shechem). He was actually calling for a return to Canaanite control and the expulsion of the Israelite opportunist, Abimelech.

The reference to the gathering of grapes and merry-making in **the house of their god** where they **cursed Abimelech** is almost certainly a reference to the new year's festival, the chief religious ceremony in the Canaanite cult-religion. It was associated with the collection of the summer fruits and was held at the end of the summer harvest. Taking advantage of Abimelech's absence, Gaal challenged the people to remember the parentage of Abimelech through his father Jerubbaal, rather than referring to his mother, the Shechemite. All of this action took place in the temple of Baal-berith, lord of the treaty, and Albright (*Archaeology and the Religion of Israel*, p. 113) suggests that the expression "sons of Hamor" is equivalent to "sons of the treaty."

In the context of the passage, it would appear that Abimelech was actually residing at **Arumah** (vs. 41) and that **Zebul** was his commanding officer (lieutenant governor) in charge of **Shechem**. Angered by this talk of insurrection, Zebul **sent messengers unto Abimelech privily** warning him of the incipient rebellion. Some have suggested that the text be emended to read "at Arumah" rather than **privily** (privately). The entire scene is one of drunken depravity. The arrogant Gaal literally challenges the absent Abimelech to come and fight him. **Fortify** (incite) **the city** to revolution. Zebul advised Abimelech to come that night and set an ambush for the city, which would be inactive the next morning. In this way Zebul performed the duty of an espionage agent within the city, serving as a fifth column against Gaal.

33-45. Dividing his invasion force into four companies, Abimelech began to move toward the city. Spotting the moves of the ambush, Gaal remarked to Zebul that **there come people down from the top of the mountains,** to which Zebul remarked that his eyes were playing tricks on him and that it was only the **shadow of the mountains. Plain of Meonenim** may be translated tree of the diviners and may refer to the terebinth mentioned earlier. The taunt, **Where is now thy mouth . . . ?** , was intended to force Gaal into a direct conflict with Abimelech. In the battle that followed Gaal's forces were decisively defeated and put to flight by Abimelech, who apparently returned to Arumah, leaving Zebul to **thrust out Gaal and his brethren.** In an act of vengeance against those who had dared to rebel against his leadership, Abimelech returned and destroyed the city of Shechem. The people **went out into the field,** either for the purpose of farming or possibly as a marauding band, and were caught again in an ambush by Abimelech who **rushed forward** and took the gate of the city, cutting off the retreat of the people. At the end of the day the angry Abimelech **slew the people . . . and beat down the city, and sowed it with salt** (vs. 45). Abimelech fully intended to make the city a virtual desert. However, it was later rebuilt and fortified by Jeroboam (I Kgs 12:25).

mah: and Zē'bul thrust out Gā'al and his brethren, that they should not dwell in Shē'chem.

42 And it came to pass on the morrow, that the people went out into the field; and they told A-bĭm'e-lĕch.

43 And he took the people, and divided them into three companies, and laid wait in the field, and looked, and, behold, the people *were* come forth out of the city; and he rose up against them, and smote them.

44 And A-bĭm'e-lĕch, and the company that *was* with him, rushed forward, and stood in the entering of the gate of the city: and the two *other* companies ran upon all *the people* that *were* in the fields, and slew them.

45 And A-bĭm'e-lĕch fought against the city all that day; and he took the city, and slew the people that *was* therein, and beat down the city, and sowed it with salt.

46 ¶And when all the men of the tower of Shē'chem heard *that*, they entered into an hold of the house of the god Be'rĭth.

47 And it was told A-bĭm'e-lĕch, that all the men of the tower of Shē'chem were gathered together.

48 And A-bĭm'e-lĕch gat him up to mount Zăl'mon, he and all the people that *were* with him; and A-bĭm'e-lĕch took an axe in his hand, and cut down a bough from the trees, and took it, and laid *it* on his shoulder, and said unto the people that *were* with him, What ye have seen me do, make haste, *and* do as I *have done.*

49 And all the people likewise cut down every man his bough, and followed A-bĭm'e-lĕch, and put *them* to the hold, and set the hold on fire upon them; so that all the men of the tower of Shē'chem died also, about a thousand men and women.

50 ¶Then went A-bĭm'e-lĕch to Thē'bez, and encamped against Thē'bez, and took it.

51 But there was a strong tower within the city, and thither fled all the men and women, and all they of the city, and shut *it* to them, and gat them up to the top of the tower.

52 And A-bĭm'e-lĕch came unto the tower, and fought against it, and went hard unto the door of the tower to burn it with fire.

53 And a certain woman cast a piece of a millstone upon A-bĭm'e-lĕch's head, and all to brake his skull.

54 Then he called hastily unto the young man his armourbearer, and said unto him, Draw thy sword, and slay me, that men say not of me, A woman slew him. And his young man thrust him through, and he died.

55 And when the men of Israel saw that A-bĭm'e-lĕch was dead, they departed every man unto his place.

56 ¶Thus God rendered the wickedness of A-bĭm'e-lĕch, which he did unto his father, in slaying his seventy brethren:

57 And all the evil of the men of Shē'chem did God render upon their

46-57. The tale of Abimelech's vengeance ends with the interesting story of the use of trees as battering rams. The men of the city who remained alive fled to the **tower of Shechem . . . into a hold of the house of the god Berith.** Since Shechem was a walled city, this would indicate that they fled to the temple of Baal-berith for refuge. Ancient walled cities were never considered totally conquered until the stronghold, or **tower,** was taken. In order to accomplish this, Abimelech took his men into the forest to cut down branches **from the trees.** It is obvious that he intended to burn down the temple and the tower with the branches which would serve as kindling. However, the fact that he laid it on his shoulder would also seem to indicate that his **boughs** were used as battering rams first and kindling second. Thus, the parable of Jotham came true. The bramble-king of the trees now brings his tree boughs as battering-rams to knock down the stronghold of the tower of Shechem and to set it on fire, killing about one thousand men and women.

In a similar move he then turned against **Thebez,** where there was also a **strong tower** to which the people fled. Leading his own forces, Abimelech **went hard unto the door of the tower,** again implying the use of the same technique. Only this time an unnamed **woman** threw a **piece of a millstone** down onto **Abimelech's head . . . to brake his skull.** The **piece of a millstone** (Heb *pelach rekeb*) means upper millstone, referring to the upper movable part of a millstone, which could easily be handled by a woman, and yet would serve as an effective weapon when hurled from the height of a tower. This portion of the millstone was generally about eighteen inches in diameter and two or three inches thick, weighing as much as twenty to thirty pounds. It undoubtedly fractured Abimelech's skull. Since death at the hands of a woman was considered to be an utter disgrace for a warrior, he urged his **armor-bearer** to kill him by thrusting him through with his sword. It is interesting to note that a century later, Israel's other questionable first king, Saul, also died in a disgraceful manner at Mount Gilboa just a few miles away! The reference to the **men of Israel** implies that the Israelites supported Abimelech, whereas the Canaanites were in rebellion against him, thus indicating that the entire incident was a Canaanite rebellion against Israelite encroachment and control.

The chapter concludes with the author's observation **God rendered** (requited) **the wickedness of Abimelech. . . . And all the evil of the men of Shechem,** noting that the **curse of Jotham** had come upon them. Throughout Old Testament history, it is obvious that the biblical writers saw the hand of God in every situation of life and death. Their astute theocentric view of

heads: and upon them came the curse of Jō′tham the son of Je′rŭb′ba-al.

CHAPTER 10

AND after A-bĭm′e-lĕch there arose to defend Israel Tō′la the son of Pū′ah, the sone of Dodo, a man of Ĭs′sa-char; and he dwelt in Shā′mir in mount Ē′phra-im.

2 And he judged Israel twenty and three years, and died, and was buried in Shā′mir.

3 ¶And after him arose Jā′ir, a Gilead-ite, and judged Israel twenty and two years.

4 And he had thirty sons that rode on thirty ass colts, and they had thirty cities, which are called Hă′vŏth-jā′ir unto this day, which are in the land of Gilead.

5 And Jā′ir died, and was buried in Cā′mon.

6 ¶And the children of Israel did evil again in the sight of the LORD, and served Bā′al-ĭm, and Ăsh′ta-rŏth, and the gods of Syria, and the gods of Zī′-don, and the gods of Moab, and the gods of the children of Ammon, and the gods of the Philistines, and forsook the LORD, and served not him.

7 And the anger of the LORD was hot against Israel, and he sold them into the hands of the Philistines, and into the hands of the children of Ammon.

8 And that year they vexed and op-pressed the children of Israel: eighteen years, all the children of Israel that were on the other side Jordan in the land of the Ămorītes, which is in Gil-ead.

9 Moreover the children of Ammon passed over Jordan to fight also against Jūdah, and against Benjamin, and against the house of Ē′phra-im; so that Israel was sore distressed.

life led to the intense wisdom which characterized Israel's great leaders and thinkers. The poetic Psalms and Proverbs would become the greatest expression of practical wisdom in the ancient world because Israel's great men saw that God Himself was actually sovereignly in control of the affairs of men.

2. Salvation by Tola and Jair—forty-five years. 10:1-5.

10:1-2. Tola the son of Puah was one of the lesser known judges of this time. **Tola** was a tribal name (see Gen 46:13). **Dodo** means beloved and is of the same derivation as David. No mighty deeds are recorded of these lesser known judges. How-ever, that does not mean that they did not accomplish any such deeds. Bruce (p. 248) suggests that they were merely judicial arbitrators. Wood (p. 264) prefers to see them as military lead-ers who held the office of judge (Heb *shapat*) at a time when no military activity was necessary. Tola is described as being of the tribe of **Issachar,** but actually dwelling in **mount Ephraim.** This would place him near the previous judgeship of Deborah (4:5). While the exact location of **Shamir** remains unidentified, it has been suggested by some that it should be identified with the later Samaria (Aharoni, *Macmillan Atlas,* map 82). His twenty-three-year judgeship was the longest of any of the minor judges. The text notes that he **arose to defend Israel.** Thus, his mis-sion, like that of the other judges, was to save or deliver Israel.

3-5. Tola was followed by **Jair, a Gileadite.** This would seem to place his judgeship in the area east of the Jordan. The fact that he was buried in **Camon** would also suggest that it was the city of his residence as well. Aharoni locates this city about twelve miles southeast of the Sea of Galilee. He judged Israel for twenty-two years, one less than Tola. The years of their judgeships may well have overlapped, since they served on opposite sides of the Jordan. He is one of the three minor judges who is said to have had a large family, suggesting his influence in the community. His **thirty sons** probably served as administra-tive assistants. The **thirty cities** over which they ruled are called **Havoth-jair.** The term Havoth was originally applied to Be-douin tent settlements and later came to be applied to small villages. Thus, each of Jair's sons was associated with the Gileadite village that bore the name of their father. Jair and Jephthah are the only judges to serve on the east side of the Jordan.

F. Sixth Cycle: Jephthah versus the Ammonites. 10:6-12:15.

1. Servitude to the Ammonites—eighteen years. 10:6-18.

6-9. These relatively peaceful judgeships were followed by a Philistine-Ammonite oppression that lasted for eighteen years. The Philistines invaded the Israelite territory on the west of the Jordan, while the Ammonites overran the Israelite territory in Transjordan. By this period the Ammonites and Moabites had apparently organized themselves into a kingdom in an attempt to defend themselves and from which to launch a more success-ful invasion of Israel. The immediate cause of this oppression was the idolatry of the Israelites, who **forsook the LORD** and served **Baalim** and **Ashtaroth.** This recurring temptation con-tinued as a major struggle for the Israelites for several centuries. Notice again that the endings (Heb *īm* and *ōt*) are plurals. Baal and Ashtar were the main god and goddess of the Canaanites, while the **gods of Syria** were Hadad and Rimmon. The **gods of Zidon** were also identified with Baal and Ashtar; the **gods of Moab** included Chemosh; and the **gods of . . . Ammon** in-cluded Molech; and the **gods of the Philistines** were Dagon and Baal-Zebub. Davis (p. 120) notes that the spiritual trend in Israel at this time was not merely a matter of syncretism, but often involved the total abandonment of the worship of Jehovah in favor of the gods of the nations.

The text seems to indicate clearly that the oppression of the Philistines and the Ammonites took place contemporary to the judgeships of Jephthah and Samson. The literary arrangement in the book of Judges serves as an introduction to those two accounts as well. It would appear that for eighteen years the Ammonites oppressed the Israelites who settled in Gilead. After that they **passed over Jordan** to attack **Judah . . . Benjamin . . . Ephraim** as well. By worshiping Baal, the Israelites had broken their covenant with Jehovah; and, until they truly repented, could no longer expect His blessing.

10 ¶And the children of Israel cried unto the LORD, saying, We have sinned against thee, both because we have forsaken our God, and also served Bā′al-ĭm.

11 And the LORD said unto the children of Israel, *Did* not *I deliver you* from the Egyptians, and from the Āmor-ītes, from the children of Ammon, and from the Philistines?

12 The Zĭ-dō′nĭ-ans also, and the Am′ă-lek-ītes, and the Mā′on-ītes, did oppress you; and ye cried to me, and I delivered you out of their hand.

13 Yet ye have forsaken me, and served other gods: wherefore I will deliver you no more.

14 Go and cry unto the gods which ye have chosen; let them deliver you in the time of your tribulation.

15 And the children of Israel said unto the LORD, We have sinned: do thou unto us whatsoever seemeth good unto thee; deliver us only, we pray thee, this day.

16 And they put away the strange gods from among them, and served the LORD: and his soul was grieved for the misery of Israel.

17 Then the children of Ammon were gathered together, and encamped in Gilead. And the children of Israel assembled themselves together, and encamped in Mĭz′peh.

18 And the people *and* princes of Gilead said one to another, What man *is* he that will begin to fight against the children of Ammon? he shall be head over all the inhabitants of Gilead.

10-18. Repenting of their idolatry, **the children of Israel cried unto the LORD,** acknowledging that they had **forsaken . . . God.** Undoubtedly through the mouth of a prophet, **the LORD said . . . Did not I deliver you from the Egyptians . . . the Amorites . . . the children of Ammon . . . the Philistines? The Zidonians . . . the Amalekites, and the Maonites, did oppress you . . . and I delivered you out of their hand.** There is no other reference to a Zidonian oppression; therefore, most commentators have associated this with the invasion of Jabin in Judges 4 (see Pfeiffer, p. 253). The reference to the **Maonites** is translated "Midianites" in the LXX and may refer to Ma'an near Petra in the Midianite territory. The severity of their sins is indicated by the response of the Lord that **I will deliver you no more** (vs. 13). God further tells them to **go and cry unto the gods which ye have chosen** (vs. 14). Certainly, the Lord Himself did not want His children to become permanent pagans; rather, He, through His spokesman, was emphasizing the seriousness of their idolatry and apostasy. The implication of the statement is to the effect that a god who cannot deliver you is not worth your worship. The response of the Israelites shows genuine confession on their part. They acknowledged that **We have sinned** (vs. 15) and placed themselves at the mercy of God. Furthermore, **they put away the strange gods . . . and served the LORD.** A true act of repentance is more than a verbal plea, and it will result in a definite change of action. Any discussion of the theological concept of repentance in the New Testament must be grounded in an understanding of the concept of repentance in the Old Testament. In preparation for the ensuing encounter, the Ammonite army **encamped in Gilead,** while the Israelites encamped in **Mizpeh.** Mizpeh means watchtower and may be identical with the Mizpeh where Jacob and Laban piled the stones of witness between them. It may also be identified with Ramath-Mizpeh and Ramoth-Gilead (Deut 4:43; Josh 13:26; I Kgs 4:13).

2. Salvation by Jephthah, Ibzan, Elon, Abdon—thirty-one years. 11:1-12:13.

CHAPTER 11

NOW Jĕph′thah the Gileadite was a mighty man of valour, and he *was* the son of an harlot: and Gilead begat Jĕph′thah.

2 And Gilead's wife bare him sons; and his wife's sons grew up, and they thrust out Jĕph′thah, and said unto him, Thou shalt not inherit in our father's house; for thou *art* the son of a strange woman.

3 Then Jĕph′thah fled from his brethren, and dwelt in the land of Tob: and there were gathered vain men to Jĕph′thah, and went out with him.

11:1-3. Jephthah the Gileadite (the name perhaps means God opens the womb). He was the son of a Gileadite named Gilead, probably from the ancestor Gilead, the grandson of Manasseh (Num 26:29). Since he was both **the son of a harlot** and a half-Canaanite he was accorded an inferior status within the family. Like Abimelech, he was not acknowledged as a full member of his father's clan. Thus, the legitimate sons of Gilead called Jephthah the **son of a strange woman** and drove him from his home. Disinherited by his half brothers, he moved northeastward into the **land of Tob,** east of Transjordanian Manasseh in the vicinity of the Yarmuk River. Wood (p. 33) suggests that Jephthah may have gone as far as Tob to get away from the Ammonite intrusion. It was here that he gathered around him a group of **vain men** (Heb *rēq*), meaning empty or reckless ones. Most commentators see them as a band of discontents who allied with Jephthah, in contrast with the more respectable members of society. Wood may be overly complimentary in suggesting that they were merely empty of em-

4 ¶And it came to pass in process of time, that the children of Ammon made war against Israel.

5 And it was so, that when the children of Ammon made war against Israel, the elders of Gilead went to fetch Jĕph'thah out of the land of Tob:

6 And they said unto Jĕph'thah, Come, and be our captain, that we may fight with the children of Ammon.

7 And Jĕph'thah said unto the elders of Gilead, Did not ye hate me, and expel me out of my father's house? and why are ye come unto me now when ye are in distress?

8 And the elders of Gilead said unto Jĕph'thah, Therefore we turn again to thee now, that thou mayest go with us, and fight against the children of Ammon, and be our head over all the inhabitants of Gilead.

9 And Jĕph'thah said unto the elders of Gilead, If ye bring me home again to fight against the children of Ammon, and the LORD deliver them before me, shall I be your head?

10 And the elders of Gilead said unto Jĕph'thah, The LORD be witness between us, if we do not so according to thy words.

11 Then Jĕph'thah went with the elders of Gilead, and the people made him head and captain over them: and Jĕph'thah uttered all his words before the LORD in Mĭz'peh.

12 ¶And Jĕph'thah sent messengers unto the king of the children of Ammon, saying, What hast thou to do with me, that thou art come against me to fight in my land?

13 And the king of the children of Ammon answered unto the messengers of Jĕph'thah, Because Israel took away my land, when they came up out of Egypt, from Arnon even unto Jabbok, and unto Jordan: now therefore restore those *lands* again peaceably.

14 And Jĕph'thah sent messengers again unto the king of the children of Ammon:

15 And said unto him, Thus saith Jĕph'thah, Israel took not away the land of Moab, nor the land of the children of Ammon:

16 But when Israel came up from Egypt, and walked through the wilderness unto the Red sea, and came to Kā'-desh;

17 Then Israel sent messengers unto the king of Ēdom, saying, Let me, I pray thee, pass through thy land: but the king of Ēdom would not hearken *thereto.* And in like manner they sent unto the king of Moab: but he would not *consent:* and Israel abode in Kā'-desh.

18 Then they went along through the wilderness, and compassed the land of Edom, and the land of Moab, and came by the east side of the land of Moab, and pitched on the other side of Arnon, but came not within the border of Moab: for Arnon *was* the border of Moab.

ployment. Nevertheless, he was able to gather a band of outcasts similar to that which David would gather in his time of exile.

4-11. The subsequent Ammonite invasion caused the **elders of Gilead** to turn to Jephthah for help. Their request that he **come, and be our captain** would imply that his reputation as a leader was now widespread. An indication of the spiritual laxity of the times may be seen in their willing acknowledgment of their improper treatment of Jephthah, despite their subsequent request for his help. In other words, when he challenged them as to why they had thrown him out, their response basically was, "We don't care; we want you to be our leader now." In order to gain his help, they promised that he could be **head** over Gilead. Receiving assurance from the delegation that his sovereignty would be recognized by the Gileadites, Jephthah accepted the offered position; and the choice was approved by the people. The statement that **Jephthah uttered all his words before the LORD in Mizpeh** would indicate that he was indeed a godly man in spite of his illegitimate birth. The relationship between Jephthah and the people here must certainly be seen as a solemn ceremony in which he takes the judgeship over Gilead.

12-28. There could be no doubt that Jephthah is looked upon in the narrative as a powerful and confident leader. Instead of attacking the enemy, he expressed his confidence by initiating a series of negotiations with them. Though unsuccessful, he had given them an opportunity to avoid the forthcoming battle. These negotiations are interesting in light of the happenings between Israel and the Arabs today. The debate was over who possessed the territory in question, territory bounded on the north by the Jabbok River and on the south by the Arnon River and extending westward to the Jordan. At one time this had been the kingdom of Sihon, who had taken it from Moab (Num 21:26). Therefore, Jephthah reminded them that the Moabites had just as legitimate a claim to the land as they did, but they had not made such a claim in nearly three hundred years (vs. 20). He further reminded them of the fact that Israel had not taken away either the territory of Moab or the children of **Ammon** when **Israel came up from Egypt** (vs. 16). Further, he reminded them that the Israelites, under Moses, had bypassed both Edom and Moab after their refusal to let them cross their land and were willing to do the same for Sihon when he attacked them. The result of the invasion by Sihon was that **the LORD God of Israel delivered Sihon . . . into the hand of Israel** (vs. 21). Like many times in Israel's history, she had actually gained territory by being invaded by her enemies!

The interesting statement to note is Jephthah's claim that the **God of Israel hath dispossessed the Amorites** from the land. The theological and historical view of the Old Testament biblical writers is that God was ultimately the true Owner of the land. As the legitimate Landlord, He had the right to give the land to whomever He chose. Israel made no apology for believing that He had chosen them to possess it. This belief is still at the heart and core of orthodox Judaism. Jephthah's challenge that they should **possess that which Chemosh** their god had given them does not prove that he believed Chemosh to be a real deity as

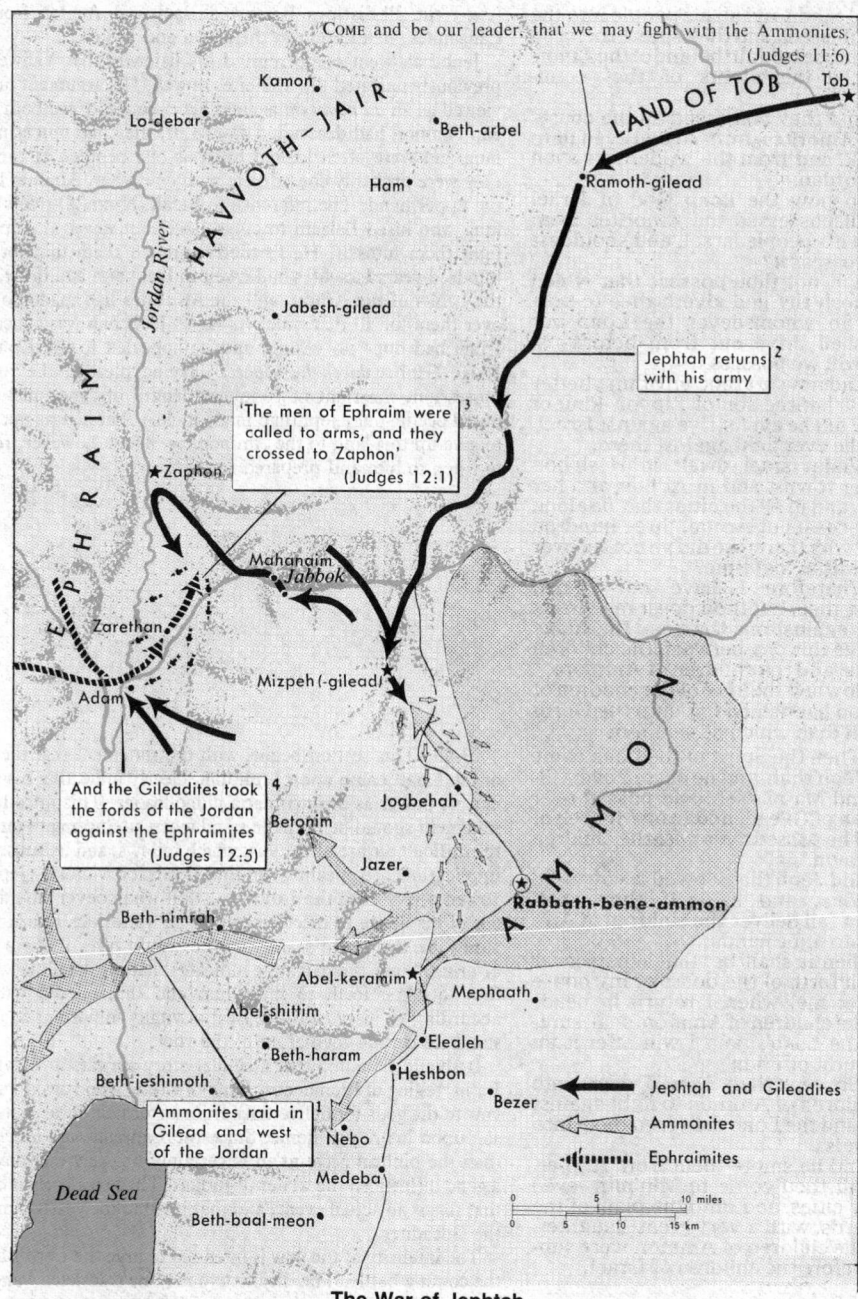

COME and be our leader, that we may fight with the Ammonites.
(Judges 11:6)

'The men of Ephraim were called to arms, and they crossed to Zaphon' (Judges 12:1)

Jephtah returns with his army [2]

And the Gileadites took the fords of the Jordan against the Ephraimites (Judges 12:5) [4]

Ammonites raid in Gilead and west of the Jordan [1]

— Jephtah and Gileadites

⟸ Ammonites

-⟨⟨⟨⟨⟨⟨ Ephraimites

0   5   10 miles
0   5   10   15 km

The War of Jephtah

19 And Israel sent messengers unto Sihon king of the Ämorītes, the king of Hĕsh′bŏn; and Israel said unto him, Let us pass, we pray thee, through thy land into my place.

20 But Sihon trusted not Israel to pass through his coast: but Sihon gathered all his people together, and pitched in Jä′hăz, and fought against Israel.

21 And the LORD God of Israel de-

some have tried to suggest (e.g., J. McKenzie, p. 147). It is obvious from the context that Jephtah believed in Jehovah as the only true God (for agreement, see Albright, *Religion of Israel*, pp. 117ff.). This is the only reference in the Old Testament to Chemosh as a deity of the Ammonites, since he is normally identified as a Moabite god. Otherwise, Milcom is normally recognized as the main Ammonite deity. This may also suggest that the Ammonites controlled most of the Moabite territory at this time and had even appropriated the Moabite deity, a practice that was often followed in the ancient Near East

livered Sihon and all his people into the
hand of Israel, and they smote them: so
Israel possessed all the land of the Ămorītes, the inhabitants of that country.

22 And they possessed all the coasts
of the Ămorītes, from Arnon even unto
Jabbok, and from the wilderness even
unto Jordan.

23 So now the LORD God of Israel
hath dispossessed the Ămorītes from
before his people Israel, and shouldest
thou possess it?

24 Wilt not thou possess that which
Chĕ'mŏsh thy god giveth thee to possess? So whomsoever the LORD our
God shall drive out from before us,
them will we possess.

25 And now *art* thou any thing better
than Bā'lăk the son of Zippor, king of
Moab? did he ever strive against Israel,
or did he ever fight against them,

26 While Israel dwelt in Hĕsh'bŏn
and her towns, and in Ar'ō-er and her
towns, and in all the cities that *be* along
by the coasts of Arnon, three hundred
years? why therefore did ye not recover
them within that time?

27 Wherefore I have not sinned
against thee, but thou doest me wrong
to war against me: the LORD the Judge
be judge this day between the children
of Israel and the children of Ammon.

28 Howbeit the king of the children of
Ammon hearkened not unto the words
of Jĕph'thah which he sent him.

29 ¶Then the Spirit of the LORD came
upon Jĕph'thah, and he passed over Gilead, and Ma-năs'seh, and passed over
Mĭz'peh of Gilead, and from Mĭz'peh of
Gilead he passed over *unto* the children
of Ammon.

30 And Jĕph'thah vowed a vow unto
the LORD, and said, If thou shalt
without fail deliver the children of Ammon into mine hands,

31 Then it shall be, that whatsoever
cometh forth of the doors of my house
to meet me, when I return in peace
from the children of Ammon, shall surely be the LORD's, and I will offer it up
for a burnt offering.

32 ¶So Jĕph'thah passed over unto
the children of Ammon to fight against
them; and the LORD delivered them into
his hands.

33 And he smote them from Ar'ō-er,
even till thou come to Mĭn'nĭth, *even*
twenty cities, and unto the plain of the
vineyards, with a very great slaughter.
Thus the children of Ammon were subdued before the children of Israel.

(e.g., the Philistines borrowed Baal and Ashtar from the
Canaanites, in addition to their own god Dagon).

Jephthah went on to remind his listeners that Yahweh had
previously defeated the Moabites as well. His argument must be
viewed as an *ad hominem* against his enemies. Since both Moab
and Ammon had descended from Lot, they had much in common and were often looked upon as one people. At this time
they were probably confederate with one other, Ammon having
the upper hand. The reference to **Balak** (Num 22) refers to the
king who hired Balaam to curse Israel but never attempted to
fight them himself. He further reminded them that for three
hundred years Israelites had dwelt in **Heshbon** and in **Aroer** on
the banks of the Arnon, and the Moabites had made no claim
over them for all that time. As far as Jephthah was concerned,
Israel had done no wrong; and he appealed to **the LORD the
Judge** (Heb *yahweh hashōphēt*). Having pleaded the right of
possession, the right of conquest, length of time, and undisputed occupation, Jephthah made it clear that he was not about
to give up this land to the Ammonites. They, however, refused
to listen to him and prepared for battle.

29-33. This section begins with the statement that the **spirit
of the LORD came upon Jephthah,** clearly indicating his supernatural power as a charismatic judge-leader. This introductory
statement should be borne in mind when attempting to interpret
the difficult nature of the vow which follows, and its subsequent
implications. Appealing to the Lord for victory, Jephthah
vowed a vow unto the LORD . . . that whatsoever would come
out of his house to meet him upon his victorious return would
surely be the LORD's and that he would offer it **for a burnt
offering.** Since the narrative indicates that his daughter was the
first to come forth to meet him and that he **did with her
according to his vow** (vs. 39), it is vitally important to understand for certain the nature of the vow.

It should be noted that a similar story appears in Servius, in
Latin, telling of Idomeneus, King of Crete, who vowed a similar
vow to the gods for deliverance from a storm and was met by his
son upon his return home. Since the Latin story is much later
than the biblical account, it is certainly unlikely that any such
legend influenced the writer of Judges. The text clearly indicates
that this is an actual event, and that it led to the yearly lament of
the Gileadites.

The intensity of the vow is intended to urge the Lord's help in
the coming battle. The disjunctive may be translated "and," or
as "or." However, commentators disagree extensively on this
matter. One possible interpretation would be that the vow indicates that "whatever" comes to meet him shall belong to the
Lord and be offered as a burnt offering; or "whoever" comes
out shall "belong to the Lord," rather then be sacrificed. Therefore, if an animal were to meet him, coming forth from his house
(which was certainly a possibility in those times), it would be
offered as a sacrifice unto God. On the other hand, if a person
were to meet him, that person would be given to the Lord's
service (i.e., the tabernacle at Shiloh). The words **whatsoever
cometh forth** are usually translated "he that goeth out," implying that he expected a person to be the object of the vow

rather than an animal. To say the least, this has become one of the most debated issues of interpretation in the Bible. Early commentators, such as Josephus, Augustine, and Eusebius, interpreted the vow to mean that he literally offered his daughter as a human sacrifice. There was little historical support for the contrary view, until Rabbi David Kimchi in the Middle Ages put forth the view that he merely dedicated his daughter to the service of the sanctuary of Jehovah in a lifelong virginity. Luther, with some hesitation, accepted the idea that she was literally put to death, as do many modern commentators (cf. F. F. Bruce, J. J. Davis, J. B. Payne, C. Pfeiffer, J. Rea, G. A. Cooke, A. E. Cundall). In contrast, many commentators have argued just as strongly for the position that his daughter was not actually made a human sacrifice (see G. Archer, P. Cassel, Keil and Delitzsch, and L. Wood). In the battle which followed Jephthah won a decisive victory over the Ammonites in which he **smote them from Aroer . . . to Minnith** (vs. 33). This Aroer apparently is not the town on the Arnon River, but another of the same name east of Rabbath-Ammon (cf. Josh 13:25). The **plain of the vineyards** is actually the place name 'Abel-keramim.

34-40. Upon returning to **Mizpeh . . . his daughter came out to meet him** in a celebration of dancing with timbrels. The text notes that she was his **only child;** and when he saw her, immediately he **rent his clothes** because of the vow that he had made. He could not renege on the vow, for several factors should be noted. (1) Jephthah was the son of a common heathen prostitute (Heb *zōnah*) and spent a great deal of time among the Canaanites; (2) The term **burnt offering** (Heb *'ōlah*) always conveys the idea of a burnt sacrifice. Other kings in later times are referred to in the Old Testament as practicing child sacrifice, e.g., the king of Moab (II Kgs 3:26), Ahaz (II Chr 28:3), Manasseh (II Kgs 21:6); and (3) The fact that Jephthah slaughtered forty-two thousand Israelites in Judges 12, would indicate that he was certainly capable of something as severe as sacrificing his own daughter.

On the other side of the issue, there are a number of other serious matters to consider as well: (1) Jephthah is listed in Hebrews 11 as a man of faith; therefore, we certainly have to see him as a man of God; (2) The statement of the vow comes right after the statement that **the spirit of the LORD came upon Jephthah;** and (3) His lengthy exhortation, based upon Old Testament law and history, would indicate that he was too well acquainted with the Law to be unaware of the restriction against human sacrifice.

The irony of this incident is that Jephthah, who had just defeated the child-sacrificing Ammonites, would now have to sacrifice his daughter as a result of the vow he had taken! He was shocked when she came forth from the house to meet him, instead of a servant or perhaps even an animal. **Alas, my daughter!** he cried, **for I have opened my mouth unto the LORD, and I cannot go back.** Thus, it is clear that the vow was binding upon him; and even though she was his own daughter, he could not change the vow. However, her response hardly sounds like someone who is facing impending death when she states: **do to me according to that which hath proceeded out of thy mouth.** It is possible that she was willing to die for the victory that her father had wrought, which victory she accredited to the LORD who **hath taken vengeance for thee of thine enemies.** Her request was that he give her **two months** to go up and down the mountains of that area and **bewail my virginity.** Wood (p. 290) strongly argues that she was not actually put to death, thus ending any possibility of producing children. But rather, that she was being devoted to God in perpetual celibacy as a permanent virgin servant at the house of God in Shiloh. He argues that the two-month bewailing period would have been useless if she

34 ¶And Jĕph'thah came to Mĭz'peh unto his house, and, behold, his daughter came out to meet him with timbrels and with dances: and she *was* his only child; beside her he had neither son nor daughter.

35 And it came to pass, when he saw her, that he rent his clothes, and said, Alas, my daughter! thou hast brought me very low, and thou art one of them that trouble me: for I have opened my mouth unto the LORD, and I cannot go back.

36 And she said unto him, My father, *if* thou hast opened thy mouth unto the LORD, do to me according to that which hath proceeded out of thy mouth; forasmuch as the LORD hath taken vengeance for thee of thine enemies, *even* of the children of Ammon.

37 And she said unto her father, Let this thing be done for me: let me alone two months, that I may go up and down upon the mountains, and bewail my virginity, I and my fellows.

38 And he said, Go. And he sent her away *for* two months: and she went with her companions, and bewailed her virginity upon the mountains.

39 And it came to pass at the end of two months, that she returned unto her father, who did with her *according* to his vow which he had vowed: and she knew no man. And it was a custom in Israel,

40 *That* the daughters of Israel went yearly to lament the daughter of Jĕph'thah the Gileadite four days in a year.

were merely being put to death and that such restrictions against human sacrifice in Israelite law would have brought tremendous protest and reprisal from the religious leaders of the community. To hold a death threat over her for two more months would have been even more severe.

After she and her friends finished this period of bereavement, he **did with her according to his vow.** The text does not actually say that he put her to death, but that he completed the requirement of the vow. The interpretation of what happens here depends essentially upon one's interpretation of the vow in verse 31. Most commentators spend a great deal of time on the fact that they **went yearly to lament** (Heb *tanah*), which is best translated "to recount" (Brown, Driver, Briggs, *Lexicon*, p. 1072). It is often argued that the recounting was a commemoration of her death, rather than a celebration of her dedication. However, very few have commented on the statement in verse 39, **And it was a custom in Israel.** Since there is no mention elsewhere in the Old Testament of such a practice, it must have been confined to the region of Gilead and, as Cundall notes (p. 149), the imperfect verb suggests that the custom was still practiced in the time of the editor. It seems difficult to believe that the people of Israel would have made a regular custom out of the practice of lamenting a girl sinfully put to death by her father, as opposed to lamenting her perpetual virginity. In either case, the line of Jephthah was cut off forever, so that in the midst of triumph there was a serious note of tragedy.

Whether she was actually put to death or dedicated to temple service will probably never be fully decided without further light on the text. That women did serve at the tabernacle, is well established by the use of the Hebrew *tsaba'*, translated assembled, actually meaning served (Ex 38:8; I Sam 2:22). Had his daughter known that she was going to become a perpetual temple virgin and that she was headed to a lifetime of service, it would seem to make more sense that she and her friends would **bewail** that situation, rather than go through the agony of prolonging her impending death.

Cundall's comment (p. 148) that interpretive attempts which view her as being placed in permanent service, rather than actually being sacrificed, are "well-meaning but misguided," is certainly an overstatement in light of the lack of clear evidence from within the text itself. That many early commentators interpreted the passage to mean that she was literally sacrificed does not in itself prove that they were correct, since many ancient Hebrew customs (such as temple service) were not as well known to earlier interpreters as they are now. The statement that **she knew no man** (vs. 39) would seem to indicate that her virginity would be perpetuated as a result of the vow, either by death or by dedication. In either case, the seriousness of the rash vow taken by Jephthah had a consequence that was severe enough to bring great grief to him. Even had he potentially intended to sacrifice someone other than his daughter, such a vow was an unnecessary and extreme expression on his part. However, it cannot be denied that God honored the vow. One might sincerely question, though, whether or not He would have given the victory knowing it would cost the girl's life. A casual reading of the text would seem to imply that her father put her to death; however, a careful comparison of the character of God and His dealings with Israel, and the character of Jephthah, would seem to prefer the idea that she was given in permanent dedication to the Lord's service. As such, she would never have married and would have remained a virgin forever, unable to perpetuate the line of her father.

12:1-7. The men of Ephraim again showed their despicable attitude by contending with Jephthah that he neglected calling them to the battle in which he had so convincingly defeated the

CHAPTER 12

AND the men of É'phra-im gathered themselves together, and went northward, and said unto Jĕph'thah, Wherefore passedst thou over to fight against the children of Ammon, and didst not call us to go with thee? we will burn thine house upon thee with fire.

2 And Jĕph'thah said unto them, I and my people were at great strife with the children of Ammon; and when I called you, ye delivered me not out of their hands.

3 And when I saw that ye delivered *me* not, I put my life in my hands, and passed over against the children of Ammon, and the LORD delivered them into my hand: wherefore then are ye come up unto me this day, to fight against me?

4 The Jĕph'thah gathered together all the men of Gilead, and fought with Ē'phra-im: and the men of Gilead smote Ē'phra-im, because they said, Ye Gileadites *are* fugitives of Ē'phra-im among the Ē'phra-im-ītes, *and* among the Ma-nǎs'sītes.

5 And the Gileadites took the passages of Jordan before the Ē'phra-im-ītes: and it was *so,* that when those Ē'phra-im-ītes which were escaped said, Let me go over; that the men of Gilead said unto him, *Art* thou an Ē'phra-im-īte? If he said, Nay;

6 Then said they unto him, Say now Shĭb'bo-leth: and he said Sĭb'bo-leth: for he could not frame to pronounce *it* right. Then they took him, and slew him at the passages of Jordan: and there fell at that time of the Ē'phra-im-ītes forty and two thousand.

7 And Jĕph'thah judged Israel six years. Then died Jĕph'thah the Gileadite, and was buried in *one of* the cities of Gilead.

8 ¶And after him Ĭb'zăn of Bĕth-lehĕm judged Israel.

9 And he had thirty sons, and thirty daughters, *whom* he sent abroad, and took in thirty daughters from abroad for his sons. And he judged Israel seven years.

10 Then died Ĭb'zăn, and was buried at Bĕth-lehĕm.

11 ¶And after him Ē'lŏn, a Zĕb'u-lon-īte, judged Israel; and he judged Israel ten years.

12 And Ē'lŏn the Zĕb'u-lon-īte died, and was buried in Āij'a-lŏn in the country of Zĕb'u-lun.

13 ¶And after him Āb'dŏn the son of Hĭl'lel, a Pīr'a-thŏn-īte, judged Israel.

14 And he had forty sons and thirty nephews, that rode on threescore and ten ass colts: and he judged Israel eight years.

15 And Āb'dŏn the son of Hĭl'lel the Pīr'a-thŏn-īte died, and was buried in Pīr'a-thŏn in the land of Ē'phra-im, in the mount of the Am'ā-lek-ītes.

Ammonites. They had earlier resented the same action on the part of Gideon (ch. 8). It seems obvious in the text that they were not really interested in fighting on the side of a losing cause, and only after the victories did they show regret, in that they were not part of the victory celebration. They assembled together and crossed the Jordan, going toward Zaphon (AV, northward). In a hostile spirit they demanded that Jephthah make condolence to them. They threatened to **burn** him with **fire,** placing their actions on the same level as the Philistine threat against Samson's in-laws in chapter 14. Jephthah made it clear that he had called them, and they had failed to respond to his call. With the same logic that he had confronted the Ammonites, he now refutes the Ephraimites, reminding them that **I put my life in my hands.** In other words, he had risked his life to save the Israelites; and now these ungrateful Ephraimite-Israelites were complaining about it, forgetting to recognize that the Lord had delivered the enemy into his hand.

The taunt of the Ephraimites against the **Gileadites** claiming that they were **fugitives** implies that they looked upon the Transjordanian tribes as deserters. Instead of reprimanding Jephthah and the Gileadites, the Ephraimites were severely defeated as the Gileadites seized the fords of the Jordan in order to prevent their escape. Forty-two thousand of them were put to death; and those escaping who were caught, were ordered to **Say now Shibboleth** (Heb for an ear of grain). This word was chosen as password because it contained a consonant which the Ephraimites could not pronounce. Instead, they pronounced the word **Sibboleth.** Pfeiffer (p. 255) notes that "the existence of distinct dialects of Hebrew during the period of the Judges is consistent with the concept of tribal, rather than national, consciousness that appears throughout the book." Bruce (p. 251) notes that this linguistic test shows that the Ephraimite dialect followed the Arabic influence in which *s* took the place of *sh.* This pronunciation test would be very similar to the efforts of northern and southern soldiers during the Civil War in the United States to discover one another by certain words. This section ends abruptly with the statement that he **judged Israel six years,** died, **and was buried in one of the cities of Gilead.** Some manuscripts of the LXX read "in his city, Mizpeh of Gilead."

8-15. The chapter ends with the brief statement of three minor judges, Ibzan, Elon, and Abdon, about whom very little is known other than their location and the length of their judgeship. They may have been contemporary with Jephthah or followed him in succession. **Ibzan of Beth-lehem** probably refers to Beth-lehem in Judah, though some have suggested Bethlehem in Zebulun. The marriage of his **thirty sons** was apparently for the purpose of political alliances to strengthen his influence over a significant part of the country. In all, he judged Israel **seven years** (vs. 9). The phrase **And after him** would indicate that **Elon** followed Ibzan chronologically and judged Israel for **ten years** (vs. 11). After his death he was buried in **Aijalon,** the consonants of which match the vocalized reading of Elon's name. Its exact location is unknown and may have been interchangeable with the reading of Elon's name, or with the name Elon itself.

He was succeeded by **Abdon the son of Hillel.** This judge is referred to as a **Pirathonite,** meaning a resident of Pirathon in Ephraim, near Shechem. He had **forty sons and thirty nephews** (literally, grandsons). All of them rode on **ass colts,** indicating a distinction of high-ranking authority. His judgeship lasted **eight years;** and he was buried in the **mount of the Amalekites,** indicating an Amalekite occupation of the hill country of Ephraim at that time. The lesser judges are not referred to in light of unusual events caused by the empowerment of the Holy Spirit. This does not mean that the Holy Spirit was not available to them, but that we simply have no record of it. We also have no record of whether they engaged in any military battles, or if they were merely local civil magistrates of some sort. This section of the book of Judges ends with the brief recounting of the five minor judges, plus the controversial Jephthah. It is followed by the amazing exploits and tragic demise of Samson.

G. Seventh Cycle: Samson versus Philistines. 13:1-16:31.

1. Servitude to the Philistines—forty years. 13:1-25.

13:1. The Philistines oppressed Israel for **forty years.** They did not play a major part in the book of Judges until this time. Nearly a century earlier they had been repelled by Shamgar (3:31). The invasion of these Sea Peoples continued for nearly two centuries. The bulk of the Philistines arrived in Canaan during the first half of the twelfth century, and by Samson's time they were well settled and prepared to assume the role of aggressors. In the meantime, they had been repelled by Ramses III of Egypt and had settled on the Palestinian coast, while Israel held the mountain area. They established lords as the rulers of their five-city Pentapolis (Gaza, Ashkelon, Ashdod, Ekron, and Gath) and began to push eastward into the Shephelah border and foothills of Judah. At this point they came into direct contact with Israel, and God raised up Samson to **begin to deliver** (vs. 5) Israel from the Philistines.

The **children of Israel did evil again** against God, which resulted in His delivering them into the hands of the Philistines for forty years. This was the longest oppression that Israel experienced during the time of the judges. Wood (p. 304) places the beginning of this oppression at about 1095 B.C. making it contemporary with the Ammonite uprising, and ending about 1055 B.C. with Samuel's victory at Mizpeh, which was followed shortly by the inauguration of Saul as king in ca. 1050 B.C.

These Aegean intruders were far superior to the Hebrews and Canaanites in culture and military craft. Their city-state government, ruled over by the lords of the Pentapolis, provided a strong central power against the loosely organized tribal government of the Hebrews. The Philistine monopoly on the use of iron also kept the Israelites in subjection (cf. I Sam 13:19-22). The Israelites were not permitted to make iron swords or spears, and Saul's army later is said to have been devoid of such weapons. Therefore, it is not unlikely during this period that Israelite warriors used such strange weapons (Shamgar's ox-goad, Samson's jawbone, and David's sling).

Despite the Philistines' prowess, they soon combined their religious practices with those of the Canaanites, whom they had conquered on the coast. The religio-cultural diffusion that followed enabled the Philistines to adjust to their surroundings while retaining much of their Aegean origin. By the time of Samson (early eleventh century B.C.) this process was well established, and the military confederacy was also entrenched. The Philistine penetration reached its peak in their victory at the disastrous Battle of Aphek, when Israel was badly defeated some twenty years before the Battle of Mizpeh (I Sam 7:2). Aphek was located about twenty-five miles north of Ekron, their northernmost city; and from this point the Philistines were able to penetrate Israelite territory all the way to Shiloh, where they destroyed the tabernacle.

2-7. Samson was born into the family of **Manoah** of the city of **Zorah** and the tribe of the **Danites.** Cundall (p. 154) notes that the Philistine pressure on the Amorites led to a corresponding pressure on the Israelites, which in turn forced the migration of the Danites to the extreme north (ch. 18). He suggests that Samson and his family were probably some of the remnant of the Danites that still remained in their original tribal area, about fourteen miles west of Jerusalem. Zorah was a small border town

---

CHAPTER 13

AND the children of Israel did evil again in the sight of the LORD; and the LORD delivered them into the hand of the Philistines forty years.

2 ¶And there was a certain man of Zôʹrah, of the family of the Danites, whose name was Ma-nōʹah; and his wife was barren, and bare not.

3 And the angel of the LORD appeared unto the woman, and said unto her, Behold now, thou art barren, and bearest not: but thou shalt conceive, and bear a son.

492

4 Now therefore beware, I pray thee, and drink not wine nor strong drink, and eat not any unclean *thing:*

5 For, lo, thou shalt conceive, and bear a son; and no razor shall come on his head: for the child shall be a Nazarite unto God from the womb: and he shall begin to deliver Israel out of the hand of the Philistines.

6 ¶Then the woman came and told her husband, saying, A man of God came unto me, and his countenance *was* like the countenance of an angel of God, very terrible: but I asked him not whence he *was,* neither told he me his name:

7 But he said unto me, Behold, thou shalt conceive, and bear a son; and now drink no wine nor strong drink, neither eat any unclean *thing:* for the child shall be a Nazarite to God from the womb to the day of his death.

8 ¶Then Ma-nō'ah intreated the LORD, and said, O my Lord, let the man of God which thou didst send come again unto us, and teach us what we shall do unto the child that shall be born.

9 And God hearkened to the voice of Ma-nō'ah; and the angel of God came again unto the woman as she sat in the field: but Ma-nō'ah her husband *was* not with her.

10 And the woman made haste, and ran, and shewed her husband, and said unto him, Behold, the man hath appeared unto me, that came unto me the *other* day.

11 And Ma-nō'ah arose, and went af-

in the eastern Shephelah, on the border between Dan and Judah. However, it was also on the ever-shifting border between Israel and Philistia and brought Samson into early contact with his people's enemies. It lay on the northern rim overlooking the Valley of Sorek, which was later the scene of most of Samson's exploits. Immediately across the valley was the major city of Beth-shemesh, which was under strong Philistine influence. It was here that Samson spent the major part of his life. His recorded exploits generally place him between Zorah, on the high ridge, and the Philistine town of Timnath (or Timnah) down in the valley.

The **angel of the LORD** appeared to Samson's parents and announced his birth in a formula similar to that found in Isaiah 7:14. The angel explained that the promised son was to become a **Nazarite unto God** from birth. The spelling "Nazirite" is to be preferred over the AV reading **Nazarite**, since the term derives from a word (Heb *nazir*) meaning to be separated or consecrated. The stipulations of the Nazirite vow found in Numbers 6 are parallel to the restrictions placed on Samson's mother in vss. 4-5. The three stipulations were: (1) not to drink **wine nor strong drink** (i.e., drink made from grain, rather than from grapes); (2) not to eat any unclean **thing** or touch any dead body; and (3) not to cut his hair during the period of the vow. The restrictions given to the mother are obviously intended only for the time of her pregnancy while she would be carrying the child. Afterward, they would apply to the child himself. The Nazirite vow becomes the theological focal point of the story of Samson and gives it its meaning and purpose.

Two important facts should be observed. First, the strength of Samson is clearly said to lie ultimately not in the length of his hair, but in the fact that he was moved by the **spirit of the LORD** (13:25; 14:6, 19; 15:14). Secondly, the events of Samson's life clearly show that he broke each of the three stipulations of the Nazirite vow and thus lost his power (14:8-10; 16:19). Those who have attempted to interpret the Samson narrative apart from the significance of this vow have clearly missed the entire point of the story (cf. McKenzie, p. 151).

The ordinary Nazirite vow was entered voluntarily for a temporary period, and thus the restrictions for the vow were also temporary. However, in Samson's life the vow was neither voluntary nor temporary and placed him in a unique category of his own. The purpose of this special son was that he was to **begin to deliver** Israel from the Philistine oppression. This was extremely important in light of the fact that Israel had lapsed into a complacent coexistence with the Philistines, who were now infiltrating through trade and intermarriage. Israel's uniqueness as the people of God eventually would have been lost entirely had it not been for Samson's resistance to the Philistines. He engaged in a one-man war against the Philistines, with surprisingly little support from his own countrymen. The excitement of Manoah's wife seems to have caused her to confuse the identity of the **angel,** whom she refers to as **A man of God** (vs. 6).

8-23. Manoah **entreated the LORD** for a second visit by the **man of God** in order to more clearly explain the promise which had been given. The **angel of God** appeared again to the woman, but her **husband was not with her.** This time, a little more composed, she ran to get him; and they returned to the place where the angel was. The angel reminded the couple of the seriousness of the vow that was to be kept by her during her pregnancy and then by the son throughout his life. Manoah's offer of fellowship and a meal is typical in light of the Near Eastern concept of friendship and hospitality. Since he **knew not** that his visitor was the **angel of the LORD,** this cannot be seen as an attempt to sacrifice to the **man of God,** whom he probably took to be a prophet. The father-to-be then requested the name of his unusual guest that he might honor his prophecy when it

ter his wife, and came to the man, and said unto him, *Art* thou the man that spakest unto the woman? And he said, I *am.*

12 And Ma-nō'ah said, Now let thy words come to pass. How shall we order the child, and *how* shall we do unto him?

13 And the angel of the Lord said unto Ma-nō'ah, Of all that I said unto the woman let her beware.

14 She may not eat of any *thing* that cometh of the vine, neither let her drink wine or strong drink, nor eat any unclean *thing:* all that I commanded her let her observe.

15 ¶And Ma-nō'ah said unto the angel of the Lord, I pray thee, let us detain thee, until we shall have made ready a kid for thee.

16 And the angel of the Lord said unto Ma-nō'ah, Though thou detain me, I will not eat of thy bread: and if thou wilt offer a burnt offering, thou must offer it unto the Lord. For Ma-nō'ah knew not that he *was* an angel of the Lord.

17 And Ma-nō'ah said unto the angel of the Lord, What *is* thy name, that when thy sayings come to pass we may do thee honour?

18 And the angel of the Lord said unto him, Why askest thou thus after my name, seeing it *is* secret?

19 So Ma-nō'ah took a kid with a meat offering, and offered *it* upon a rock unto the Lord: and *the angel* did wonderously; and Ma-nō'ah and his wife looked on.

20 For it came to pass, when the flame went up toward heaven from off the altar, that the angel of the Lord ascended in the flame of the altar. And Ma-nō'ah and his wife looked on *it,* and fell on their faces to the ground.

21 But the angel of the Lord did no more appear to Ma-nō'ah and to his wife. Then Ma-nō'ah knew that he *was* an angel of the Lord.

22 And Ma-nō'ah said unto his wife, We shall surely die, because we have seen God.

23 But his wife said unto him, If the Lord were pleased to kill us, he would not have received a burnt offering and a meat offering at our hands, neither would he have shewed us all these *things,* nor would as at this time have told us *such things* as these.

24 ¶And the woman bare a son, and called his name Samson: and the child grew, and the Lord blessed him.

25 And the Spirit of the Lord began to move him at times in the camp of Dan between Zō'rah and Ėsh'ta-ol,

came to pass. However the angel replied that **my name . . . is secret** (vs. 18). This does not fully translate the meaning of the adjective (Heb *pil'ī*) meaning wonderful or ineffable (cf. Isaiah 9:6). Keil and Delitzsch (p. 407) note that the word is not the proper name of the angel of the Lord, but expresses the character of His name and denotes the peculiarity of His nature as well. Thus, it is to be understood in the absolute sense as a predicate belonging to deity, absolutely and supremely wonderful.

In response to the offering, the angel **did wondrously, and ascended in the flame** of the burnt offering. The couple's sacrifice of a kid was accompanied by a **meat offering** (Heb *minchah,* meaning meal or cereal offering as in Lev 2). The miraculous disappearance of the angel caused Manoah to realize who He was (vs. 21). The divinely-authenticating sign was necessary to convince them in the months, and even years, ahead of the unique nature and purpose of the vow. Since the angel had refused to eat a meal and would only allow the offering to be made **unto the Lord** (vs. 16), which He then accepted, it must indicate the legitimate conclusion of Manoah: **we have seen God.** There can be no doubt that the text indicates that the appearance of the angel was a theophany (an anthropomorphic appearance of God). In the Old Testament God frequently appeared in this manner to His people in order to communicate with them and reveal the truth to them. Cundall (p. 158) is correct when he notes, "As the centuries passed such appearances became less frequent, for communion and communication became increasingly inward and spiritual." As the process continued to unfold and climax in the revelation of God to man in the person of His Son, such appearances were no longer needed.

24-25. Just as the angel of the Lord predicted, the woman **bare a son** whom she named **Samson** (Heb *shimshōn,* which seems to be derived from the word *shemesh,* or sun). This is also supported by the fact that Zorah was opposite the town of Beth-shemesh (house of the sun) and was probably originally of Canaanite derivation since it occurs in the Ugaritic texts of the fourteenth-fifteenth century B.C. Samson's birth and early childhood are clearly stated to have been **blessed** of the Lord. Thus, God is involved from the very beginning of his life in the exploits that will follow, and apparently even during his youth the **spirit of the Lord began to move him at times.** Like the other judges, he received this charismatic anointing for the task to which he was called. In Samson's case this meant spectacular human strength to wage a one-man campaign against the Philistines. This initial activity is said to have happened in the **camp**

of Dan, which probably implies a temporary habitation or displaced person's camp, since the tribe of Dan had given up its tribal territory. It seems incredible that Israel's strongest man came from her weakest tribe, showing us again that God does have a sense of humor!

2. *Salvation by Samson—twenty years. 14:1-16:31.*

14:1-4. The events in Samson's life fall in two categories: (1) those prior to the incident at Gaza; and (2) those afterwards. However, the narrative divides itself in relation to the three women in Samson's life: the girl at Timnath, the prostitute at Gaza, and Delilah of the Valley of Sorek. From the start it becomes obvious that a love for women is his weakness. His mighty deeds proved that the God of the Israelites was still alive and powerful and capable of helping His people. But Samson's personal actions "not only bear the stamp of adventure, foolhardiness, and willfulness, but they are almost all associated with love affairs" (Keil and Delitzsch, p. 399). They also note that his personal weakness reflected the natural character of the nation itself to continually fraternize with the heathen. His frivolous attitude toward his vow of separation led to the insufficiency of his judgeship to procure a lasting supremacy for Israel over her foes. What he did accomplish by his manifestation of supernatural power was to show Israel the possibility of deliverance.

The first woman in Samson's life was the girl from **Timnath,** a Philistine town only four miles down the valley from Zorah. Despite Philistine domination of the Israelites at that time, Samson was free to stroll through the valley. At Timnath he met the first of his lovers. The proximity of the Danites to the foreigners probably weakened the attitude of separation among the younger generation of Israelites; for Samson had no hesitation about marrying the girl, even though he was breaking the Mosiac law regarding mixed marriages (Ex 34:16; Deut 7:3).

It was unusual for Hebrew children to disobey their parents' wishes; yet, Samson dismissed their displeasure with his choice of the girl by demanding that they **get her for me** because **she pleaseth me.** His poor and impatient choice is reflected by the fact that the marriage was to be a somewhat less than desirable situation. She is described by the common word **woman** and is not designated as a virgin or maiden. Delilah (16:4) is called by the same term. R. DeVaux, *Ancient Israel* (p. 43), and McKenzie (p. 153) suggest that this was "beena" marriage in which the woman remained in her father's house, while her husband visited her with gifts and presents. His parents rightly opposed the marriage, but the author's comment (vs. 4) indicates that God was able to use this human mistake to gain an **occasion** against the Philistines. Looking back over the events, the writer, possibly Samuel, could make this observation.

5-7. Samson then traveled down the valley with his parents to Timnath to contract the marriage. Evidently he became separated from his parents and at that time a **young lion roared against him.** Moved **mightily** by the spirit of the Lord, he rent the lion in half. The text notes that he had no weapon in his hand, possibly due to Philistine disarmament. It should be observed that the **spirit of the LORD** gave Samson unusual strength at the time of crisis.

8-9. Sometime after talking with the girl at Timnath, Samson returned alone to the **carcase** of the lion to find that a swarm of bees had made **honey** in the dehydrated body. By eating the honey, Samson deliberately broke one aspect of his Nazirite vow; for he was not to touch a corpse. This is the reason he did not tell his parents the source of this gift he made to them.

CHAPTER 14

AND Samson went down to Tĭm'năth, and saw a woman in Tĭm'năth of the daughters of the Philistines.

2 And he came up, and told his father and his mother, and said, I have seen a woman in Tĭm'năth of the daughters of the Philistines: now therefore get her for me to wife.

3 Then his father and his mother said unto him, *Is there* never a woman among the daughters of thy brethren, or among all my people, that thou goest to take a wife of the uncircumcised Philistines? And Samson said unto his father, Get her for me; for she pleaseth me well.

4 But his father and his mother knew not that it *was* of the LORD, that he sought an occasion against the Philistines: for at that time the Philistines had dominion over Israel.

5 Then went Samson down, and his father and his mother, to Tĭm'năth, and came to the vineyards of Tĭm'năth: and, behold, a young lion roared against him.

6 And the Spirit of the LORD came mightily upon him, and he rent him as he would have rent a kid, and *he had* nothing in his hand: but he told not his father or his mother what he had done.

7 And he went down, and talked with the woman; and she pleased Samson well.

8 ¶And after a time he returned to take her, and he turned aside to see the carcase of the lion: and, behold, *there was* a swarm of bees and honey in the carcase of the lion.

9 And he took thereof in his hands,

and went on eating, and came to his
father and mother, and he gave them,
and they did eat: but he told not them
that he had taken the honey out of the
carcase of the lion.

10 ¶So his father went down unto the
woman: and Samson made there a
feast; for so used the young men to do.

11 And it came to pass, when they
saw him, that they brought thirty companions to be with him.

12 And Samson said unto them, I will
now put forth a riddle unto you: if ye
can certainly declare it me within the
seven days of the feast, and find it out,
then I will give you thirty sheets and
thirty change of garments:

13 But if ye cannot declare it me, then
shall ye give me thirty sheets and thirty
change of garments. And they said
unto him, Put forth thy riddle, that we
may hear it.

14 And he said unto them, Out of the
eater came forth meat, and out of the
strong came forth sweetness. And they
could not in three days expound the
riddle.

15 And it came to pass on the seventh
day, that they said unto Samson's wife,
Entice thy husband, that he may declare
unto us the riddle, lest we burn
thee and thy father's house with fire:
have ye called us to take that we have?
is it not so?

16 And Samson's wife wept before
him, and said, Thou dost but hate me,
and lovest me not: thou hast put forth a
riddle unto the children of my people,
and hast not told it me. And he said
unto her, Behold, I have not told it my
father nor my mother, and shall I tell it
thee?

17 And she wept before him the
seven days, while their feast lasted:
and it came to pass on the seventh day,
that he told her, because she lay sore
upon him: and she told the riddle to the
children of her people.

18 And the men of the city said unto
him on the seventh day before the sun
went down, What is sweeter than
honey? and what is stronger than a
lion? And he said unto them, If ye had
not plowed with my heifer, ye had not
found out my riddle.

19 And the Spirit of the LORD came

10-11. It was not long until the second part of the vow was
also broken; for verse 10 states that Samson made a **feast** at the
wedding according to Philistine custom, and probably under
some pressure from the girl's family and friends. Feast (Heb
mishteh) may refer to a meal as in Genesis 19:3, or a drinking
feast (see Davis, p. 136). There is abundant evidence that the
Philistines were given to drinking and carousing. Several beer
mugs used for barley beer were found at Tell Abu Hureira
(Gerar?), jugs and chalices were found at Tell el-Far'ah and Tell
en-Nasbeh. Albright (*Archaeology of Palestine*, p. 115) suggests
that the extensive production of mugs and wine craters gives
ample evidence of the Philistines' excessive drinking.

It is also strange that this wedding feast was at the bride's
house, rather than the home of the groom. Perhaps Samson's
marriage feast was not held in his home because his parents
would not sanction the marriage. The length of the feast was
seven days, at the end of which the marriage was actually
consummated. In this case **thirty companions** (sons of the
bridechamber) were selected as a bodyguard (vs. 11) against any
who might attempt to plunder the wedding party. Evidently, the
girl's parents chose the bodyguard because Samson had not
brought any friends with him.

12-14. During the opening festivities Samson proposed a **riddle** to the thirty Philistines to exalt his wisdom. Such procedure
was common to the Near East and also to ancient Greece.
Because of the Philistines' Aegean origin, Samson may have
wanted to vindicate himself before them on their own level. The
secret of the riddle related to the lion in which he had found the
honey. **Out of the eater came forth meat, and out of the strong
came forth sweetness** (vs. 14).

15-17. Unable to discern the meaning of Samson's riddle, the
Philistines turned to threatening the girl to find out the secret
for them. Their threat was to **burn** her family's **house** with them
in it. So she wept before Samson to persuade him to tell her the
answer. Here the text is a bit ambiguous. Verse 15 states they
came to his wife on the seventh day to threaten her, but verses
16-17 indicate that she wept and begged him for the answer for
seven days. Some have suggested that out of curiosity she
begged to know the answer and did not really become urgent
until the last day. However, Cassel (p. 200) seems to be more
correct when he suggests that verse 15 be translated: "and they
had said," indicating that they came to the girl at the first day of
the feast when the riddle was put forth and she was not able to
discover the answer until the last day. The Philistine men had
told her to **Entice** (Heb *patah*, fool or trick) her husband, and
only her constant recourse to tears moved him to reveal the
answer to the riddle. Her claim that he must hate her (v. 16)
implies that she used a racial argument to cause him to give in to
her demand.

18-20. Almost immediately, the Philistines announced to
Samson, **What is sweeter than honey? And what is stronger
than a lion?** In bitter reply, he said: **If ye had not plowed with
my heifer, ye had not found out my riddle.** Thereby, he clearly
indicated that he was aware of the source of their information.
The blunder should have forewarned him of one similar, but far
worse, that was yet to come. The debt he now owed was sub-

upon him, and he went down to Ash'ke-lŏn, and slew thirty men of them, and took their spoil, and gave change of garments unto them which expounded the riddle. And his anger was kindled, and he went up to his father's house.

20 But Samson's wife was *given* to his companion, whom he had used as his friend.

CHAPTER 15

BUT it came to pass within a while after, in the time of wheat harvest, that Samson visited his wife with a kid; and he said, I will go in to my wife into the chamber. But her father would not suffer him to go in.

2 And her father said, I verily thought that thou hadst utterly hated her; therefore I gave her to thy companion: *is* not her younger sister fairer than she? take her, I pray thee, instead of her.

3 ¶ And Samson said concerning them, Now shall I be more blameless than the Philistines, though I do them a displeasure.

4 And Samson went and caught three hundred foxes, and took firebrands, and turned tail to tail, and put a firebrand in the midst between two tails.

5 And when he had set the brands on fire, he let *them* go into the standing corn of the Philistines, and burnt up both the shocks, and also the standing corn, with the vineyards *and* olives.

6 Then the Philistines said, Who hath done this? And they answered, Samson, the son in law of the Tĭm'nĭte, because he had taken his wife, and given her to his companion. And the Philistines came up, and burnt her and her father with fire.

stantial. The **sheets** (vs. 13) were fine linen festival garments, such as those worn to the wedding. Enraged by the events that had transpired, he left the wedding to secure payment for the thirty garments, which he obviously did not possess himself. He went to Ashkelon, twenty miles away on the coast and one of the main cities of the Philistine Pentapolis. It lay in a rich, fertile, and densely populated area. The Philistines took the city from Judah in the twelfth century B.C. and from there subjugated the tribe of Dan and pushed them into the Judaean hills. This could give good reason why Samson, a Danite, would choose Ashkelon as the site of his wrath. Cundall also suggests that its distance from Timnath, and Samson's yet unknown fame, would have made it unlikely that the Ashkelonites would be able to trace him back to the events at the remote outpost of Timnath.

The author notes that the **spirit of the LORD came upon him** to enable Samson to accomplish the feat of slaying thirty Philistines and using their garments in payment of the answered riddle. Thus, Yahweh found **an occasion against the Philistines** (vs. 4) who had dealt treacherously with Samson. However, in the meantime the Philistine girl's father was disgraced by Samson's rude departure and instead gave the girl to the **companion** (best man) of Samson! Samson must have returned to deliver the garments and in anger went on back to Zorah unaware of what had transpired. This marriage was apparently a temporary arrangement; Samson did not intend to live with the girl permanently, but, rather, to visit her upon occasion.

15:1-2. At the time of the wheat harvest Samson returned to visit his wife at Timnath. The time was probably during late May or early June, and his anger was now satisfied. He brought the gift of a **kid** (young goat) as the probable offering prescribed by the marriage in which the wife remained in her parents' home. Thus, Samson visited her in the same way one would visit a prostitute (cf. Gen 38:15-17). Upon his return he discovered that his bride had been given to his best man. In response, the girl's father offered her younger sister to Samson in an admission that he had acted too hastily. It was the Philistines who had initially aggravated the entire situation by threatening his wife, and Samson retaliated against all the Philistines in the region by burning their entire wheat crop. In doing this he turned his personal wrong into an exploit of national importance against the enemies of his people.

3-6. Until this time Samson had been too free in his association with the Philistines. The disastrous events of his attempted marriage to one of their women turned his attitude against them in such a way that Yahweh could now use him to **begin to deliver** (13:5) Israel from the Philistines. At this point in the narrative one can see a definite break in Samson's relations with the Philistines lasting for several years. Samson was ready to make war, but he had no soldiers at his disposal. Instead, he turned to the beasts of the field as his confederates. He captured three hundred **foxes**, or jackals (Heb *shū'al*), tied them tail-to-tail in pairs, lit their tails as torches, and sent them wildly scattering through the almost ready-to-harvest grain of the Philistines. Such an act constituted national aggression and made Samson the chief enemy of the Philistines. The burning of the enemies' crops was always a common method of war in the ancient Near East. It meant total loss to the enemy, and in an agrarian culture this was a serious matter!

The reference to **shocks** (vs. 5) indicates that the grain was already being harvested and stacked in sheaves. The fire spread from the shocks to the standing grain and then to the olive trees. Samson's identity was no secret to the Philistines, but they blamed the unwise action of his father-in-law for Samson's retaliation upon them. It is interesting that they did not try to harm Samson, who was evidently still in the area (cf. vs. 7). Instead, they burned the girl and her father **with fire**. They probably burned their house with them in it, the very fate she had tried to avert by exposing Samson's riddle! Whatever one may think of Samson's so-called cruelty to the jackals, no one may deny the greater cruelty of the Philistines.

The moral implications of the story are very important. First, Samson was wrong in desiring to marry a woman of the enemies of his people, and all sorts of terrible repercussions came from his uncontrolled lust. Despite his error, Samson came to see the enemy in the proper light; and God could use him to begin Israel's deliverance. Secondly, the girl should have gone immediately to Samson about the Philistines' threats, instead of using trickery to persuade him to divulge the answer to the riddle. The very fate she sought to escape, thereby, ultimately came upon her. Thirdly, every aspect of the narrative indicates that the father-in-law acted in haste by giving the bride to the best man.

7 ¶And Samson said unto them, Though ye have done this, yet will I be avenged of you, and after that I will cease.

8 And he smote them hip and thigh with a great slaughter: and he went down and dwelt in the top of the rock Ēʹtam.

9 ¶Then the Philistines went up, and pitched in Jūdah, and spread themselves in Lēʹhī.

10 And the men of Jūdah said, Why are ye come up against us? And they answered, To bind Samson are we come up, to do to him as he hath done to us.

11 Then three thousand men of Jūdah went to the top of the rock Ēʹtam, and said to Samson, Knowest thou not that the Philistines are rulers over us? what is this that thou hast done unto us? And he said unto them, As they did unto me, so have I done unto them.

12 And they said unto him, We are come down to bind thee, that we may deliver thee into the hand of the Philistines. And Samson said unto them, Swear unto me, that ye will not fall upon me yourselves.

13 And they spake unto him, saying, No; but we will bind thee fast, and deliver thee into their hand: but surely we will not kill thee. And they bound him with two new cords, and brought him up from the rock.

14 ¶And when he came unto Lēʹhī, the Philistines shouted against him: and the Spirit of the Lᴏʀᴅ came mightily upon him, and the cords that were upon his arms became as flax that was burnt with fire, and his bands loosed from off his hands.

15 And he found a new jawbone of an ass, and put forth his hand, and took it, and slew a thousand men therewith.

16 And Samson said, With the jawbone of an ass, heaps upon heaps, with

7-8. In reaction to the Philistines' cruel murder of the girl and her father, Samson turned upon them. His words to them (vs. 7) implies that the cowardly Philistines sought to pacify Samson by their act of cruelty and he announced that he would not **cease** (rest) until he had taken vengeance upon them. He then turned on those who had burned the girl and her father and smote them **hip and thigh** (a slang term meaning he beat them piece by piece).

9-11. Realizing the danger he was now in, Samson fled to a cave in **the top of the rock Etam** (vs. 8), which was probably located in the cliffs above Timnath. The Philistines dispatched a reconnaissance force to capture the Hebrew renegade, and they brought soldiers to encamp against Judah in whose territory Samson was hiding. The narrative gives thorough evidence of the timid attitude of the Hebrews to the Philistine menace, for the men of Judah criticized Samson for his acts: **Knowest thou not that the Philistines are rulers over us? what is this that thou hast done unto us?** Thus, the one-man army found no support, even from among his own people. Fearing the threat of war, they begged Samson to leave them and the Philistines alone. This reveals the cowardly attitude among the Hebrews of Samson's day. It also indicates the powerful control and influence of the Philistines over Judah and the failure of the Jews to trust their God. The Philistine encroachment was an ever-threatening menace in those days. Therefore, it is clear why Israel needed a deliverer. The subtle Philistine approach would soon have permanently dominated Israel and threatened the life of the nation (see Albright, *The Biblical Period from Abraham to Ezra*, pp. 35-38).

12-13. The scene is probably to be set like this: the Philistines camped in the valley before the face of the cliff in which the cave was cut. Similar to many Judaean caves, it had to be entered by descending from the top of the cliff and swinging into the mouth of the cave. Evidently, the Judaeans came to the top of the hill and called down to Samson to surrender. When they promised not to attempt to slay him, he permitted them to bring him up, bind him, and take him to the Philistines.

14-17. When they came to Lehi, the Philistines **shouted** against him. **Lehi** means jawbone and is used proleptically by the author in anticipation of the event about to happen and from which the name was derived. The shouts of triumph by the Philistines brought the manifestation of the **Spirit of the Lᴏʀᴅ** upon Samson, moving him again with unusual physical strength. He snapped the ropes that bound him, seized the jawbone of a freshly slain ass, and engaged the Philistines with it. Because of his unarmed condition, any weapon was a welcome find. The jawbone was evidently one of a recently perished ass whose bones had been picked clean by the vultures, for the

the jaw of an ass have I slain a thousand men.

17 And it came to pass, when he had made an end of speaking, that he cast away the jawbone out of his hand, and called that place Rā′math-lē′hī.

18 ¶And he was sore athirst, and called on the LORD, and said, Thou hast given this great deliverance into the hand of thy servant: and now shall I die for thirst, and fall into the hand of the uncircumcised?

19 But God clave an hollow place that was in the jaw, and there came water thereout; and when he had drunk, his spirit came again, and he revived: wherefore he called the name thereof Ĕn-hăk′ko-re, which is in Lē′hī unto this day.

20 And he judged Israel in the days of the Philistines twenty years.

CHAPTER 16
THEN went Samson to Gā′za, and saw there an harlot, and went in unto her.

2 And it was told the Gā′zītes, saying, Samson is come hither. And they compassed him in, and laid wait for him all night in the gate of the city, and were quiet all the night, saying, In the morning, when it is day, we shall kill him.

3 And Samson lay till midnight, and

jawbone was "fresh" and not brittle. Thus, it was not easily broken. Again, we see the Hebrews using the most unusual of weapons because of the Philistine monopoly on iron and their policy of disarmament. God would assure all observers that He was able to give victory to His people over all opposing advantages.

Using this unusual weapon, Samson slew a **thousand** Philistines and put the rest to panic and flight. The number, one thousand, may be a round number for a great host. No details are given of the battle. The reference to **heaps** may imply that he slew the thousand in several encounters as he pursued the fleeing army. Samson responded to his victory in a play on the words **ass** (Heb *chamōr*) and **heap** (Heb *chamōr*) which are identical. The idea of the poetic expression was that the red ass's jawbone was used to beat the Philistines bloody red, or perhaps to make donkeys of them (see NIV).

18-19. The pursuit of the Philistines left Samson exhausted with thirst, which is easily explained by the season of the year. The weather was usually hot during the wheat harvest (vs. 1). The overwrought warrior had much to fear, for he stood alone in his conflict with the enemy. It is possible that the three thousand men of Judah aided Samson; but since there is no mention of this in the text, it is unlikely. The entire passage gives adequate evidence of the apathetic attitude of the men of Judah. They were not ashamed to drag their bound hero into the enemy's hands. They were not moved when the Philistines shouted against Samson; and even worse, they apparently made no intervention to aid Samson in the conflict. Their faith in God was so weak that they feared to trust Him even under these circumstances. As great as the triumph of Samson was, the failure of Israel was even greater. Samson was fully conscious that he was fighting for the Lord when he referred to himself as the Lord's **servant** (vs. 18), and yet the so-called people of God gave him no aid. It should be noted that the above incident reveals that Samson's strength was an abnormal human strength and not the magical power of a superman. After the conflict he was completely exhausted. Through this experience God was trying to teach him his need to rely upon the Lord alone and not upon his own strength and ability. Apparently he did not learn this lesson very well. Even in his victory there was a note of defeat: the jawbone of a dead animal was unclean according to the Law!

20. Chronologically, the events of his life divide between the end of chapter 15 and the beginning of chapter 16. The fifteenth chapter concludes with the note that Samson judged Israel **in the days of the Philistines** for **twenty years.** The Philistine oppression lasted forty years, but during the major part of Samson's judgeship it appears that he was able to maintain relative peace between Israel and the Philistines. There is undoubtedly a great time lapse between chapters 15 and 16. We may suppose that following the humiliating defeats inflicted by Samson's single-handed efforts, the Philistines no longer attempted to confront him; and their penetration of the Judaean hill country was temporarily halted. Israel probably enjoyed relative peace and security during these years as a result of the partial **deliverance** accomplished by Samson who remained among his people during these years as a judge. He either remained in the vicinity of Zorah or possibly lived in Hebron, the unofficial capital of those days.

16:1-3. Samson's early passion for the woman of Timnath was overcome by his zeal for the Lord. Equipped by God with every necessary potential to be a great leader in Israel, he continued to squander his greatest opportunities to serve the Lord. He who could strangle a lion and kill a thousand men single-handedly, could not conquer his own passion and lust. Samson's fall began with a trip to the Philistine city of Gaza, which was southernmost of the Philistine Pentapolis. This

arose at midnight, and took the doors of the gate of the city, and the two posts, and went away with them, bar and all, and put *them* upon his shoulders, and carried them up to the top of an hill that *is* before Hēbron.

ancient city was probably originally inhabited by the Avvim who were later driven out by the Caphtorim (proto-Philistines). It then passed from Amorite to Hyksos to Canaanite control, and finally the Hebrews lost it to the Philistines. Tell el-Ajjul has been identified as the most likely site of ancient Gaza. Excavations there in the 1930s by Sir Flinders Petrie revealed substantial amounts of Philistine pottery.

How it is that the Israelite hero is able to wander casually into this major Philistine city is uncertain. Two things are certain though: he was an unwelcome guest (vs. 2), and his intentions were not the best. Probably due to an overt sense of pride in his own strength, he ventured into the territory of Philistia and came to Gaza. It is unlikely that he went there for the purpose of visiting the prostitute, for he did not see her until after he had arrived (vs. 1). One of the great lessons of the spiritual life has always been that one must take heed when he thinks he is standing sure, lest he fall (I Cor 10:12). Thus, Samson's pride brought him to Gaza, and in the weakness of that pride he saw there a **harlot** (Heb *zōnah*) and lusted for her in his heart.

As an alien visitor, Samson would not have been welcome to remain overnight in the city, except at a place such as the house of a prostitute, which was always open to strangers. Those women basically were female innkeepers; yet, prostitution was still very much their regular business. Cassel (p. 212) goes to great lengths to vindicate Samson's coming to the Gazite prostitute under these circumstances, but his explanation is more ingenious than satisfactory. Every detail of the narrative indicates that his intentions were of the worst sort. Having seen the *harlot* (Heb *zōnah*), Samson **went in unto her** (vs. 1). This Hebrew euphemism almost always means that he entered her chamber for the purpose of sexual intercourse. Also, notice that he **lay till midnight.** If he intended to merely lodge for the evening in this house, why did he arise at midnight to leave? It seems more likely that he went to her house for the single purpose of engaging the woman sexually and then leaving when he was finished.

Even at this low point of Samson's life, God was ready to deliver him from the Philistines. When the men of Gaza found out that Samson was in their city, they came to the gate of the city to wait out the night and ambush him in the morning. Many have questioned how Samson could have carried off the gate while they were there. In verse 2 we find that the Gazites laid in wait for him all night and slept by the gate, supposing to take him in the morning when he left the city. Thus, the phrase **they . . . were quiet all the night** indicates that they lapsed into careless repose and fell asleep. Arriving at midnight, Samson took them by surprise and carried away the entire gate in which they were trusting so greatly. In ancient times the gates of walled cities were locked at night, and the Gazites probably imagined that Samson could not get out until the gate was opened in the morning, at which time they would be ready for him.

Taking the doors of the gate, the two posts, bar and all, he broke it loose from the wall and carried it away to the top of a hill that was **before Hebron.** Hebron was the chief center of the tribe of Judah in those days and may have been Samson's residence during his judgeship. However, Hebron was nearly thirty-eight miles from Gaza, a straight uphill climb from the coastal plain to 3,300 feet above sea level on the crest of the mountains of Judah: an extraordinary feat for any man! The details of the text are not really clear; for it is possible that it may mean that Samson carried the gate to the foothills that are before Hebron, or that he carried it to the top of a hill near Gaza towards Hebron. However, the plain meaning of the text seems to be that he actually carried the gate to Hebron. Consider these factors: (1) once having taken the gate of Gaza as his trophy, it would have been more likely that he would want to keep it in mockery of the Philistines; (2) for the gate of Gaza to lie before the Israelite city of Hebron would have marked a sign of triumph over the powerful Philistines; (3) a man who could attack an entire army without a weapon (vss. 2, 12) could surely carry the gate of Gaza, however heavy it might have been, up to the summit of Hebron.

Despite this triumph, Samson's weakness for Philistine women had again been aroused and would lead to his humiliation. The beauty and voluptuousness of these women of Greek descent proved more than he could handle, and the Hebrew hero that sent fear into the hearts of the Philistine warriors would be conquered by a woman.

4 ¶And it came to pass afterward, that he loved a woman in the valley of Sô'rĕk, whose name was De-lī'lah,

4. Delilah is a woman of some mystery in the Old Testament, for no one can be certain who she was. The simple statement (vs. 4) of the text says she was a **woman in the valley of Sorek.** Most commentators have assumed she was a Philistine, though she is not definitely specified as such. Living in the Valley of Sorek, where both peoples freely mingled, indicates she could have been either Philistine or Hebrew. However, Samson definitely had a passion for Philistine women; and it seems unlikely that the five lords of the Philistines would venture into Hebrew territory to bribe an Israelite girl. Though her name is Semitic in form, the Philistines often borrowed names from the Semitic peoples about them. Whoever this girl was, she was the instrument of Samson's great downfall.

God will not permit His own children to continue indulging in sin without soon receiving its stinging results. Twice before, Samson's passion had led him into the place of danger. This was to be the last. The escape at Gaza had taught the mighty warrior nothing about God's patience to deliver his erring soul. That Delilah was a professional prostitute seems obvious from the context, and her residence in the Valley of Sorek placed her near the hometown of Samson at Zorah.

5 And the lords of the Philistines came up unto her, and said unto her, Entice him, and see wherein his great strength lieth, and by what means we may prevail against him, that we may bind him to afflict him: and we will give thee every one of us eleven hundred pieces of silver.

5. Almost immediately the **lords of the Philistines** came to bribe Delilah into discovering the secret of Samson's strength. It is most likely that the men who visited her were the five lords of the Pentapolis. They each offered to give her 1,100 pieces of silver, which would have amounted to 5,500 pieces of silver for betraying Samson into their hands. They evidently recognized Samson to be no giant or "superman," and because of this they rightly assumed his abnormal strength came from another source. However, they wrongly thought it to be from some external magical charm or amulet. Such superstitious gimmicks were frequently worn by the Philistines themselves when they went into battle (II Sam 5:21); they carried their idols with them on their battle campaigns intending these portable images ('atsabîm) to serve as good luck amulets. However, Samson's strength was the result of the moving of the spirit of the Lord upon him; and this was related to the provisions of his Nazirite vow.

6 And De-lī'lah said to Samson, Tell me, I pray thee, wherein thy great strength lieth, and wherewith thou mightest be bound to afflict thee.

6. Delilah immediately set out with ruthless efficiency to procure the "secret" from Samson. Moved by the desire to satisfy his own lustful passion, Samson became blinded to the motives behind her continuous questions. It should be noted that her repeated attempts to find the answer indicate that he was in the habit of visiting her regularly; so she could continually pursue the matter. One should not overlook the brutal cleverness of Delilah. With the heartlessness of a professional prostitute, she used her trade to lull Samson into sleeping passivity. The full context shows that she could read him clearly. She had known that he was lying to her the first three times she had asked him, and she knew when he was finally telling her the truth (vs. 18).

7 And Samson said unto her, If they bind me with seven green withs that were never dried, then shall I be weak, and be as another man.

7-9. Delilah's pleading to know the source of his strength brought equally jesting remarks from Samson in their deadly lovers' game. The first suggestion he gave her was to bind him with **seven green withes** (fresh bowstrings in the RSV). Now

501

8 Then the lords of the Philistines brought up to her seven green withs which had not been dried, and she bound him with them.

9 Now *there were* men lying in wait, abiding with her in the chamber. And she said unto him, The Philistines *be* upon thee, Samson. And he brake the withs, as a thread of tow is broken when it toucheth the fire. So his strength was not known.

10 And De-lī′lah said unto Samson, Behold, thou hast mocked me, and told me lies: now tell me, I pray thee, wherewith thou mightest be bound.

11 And he said unto her, If they bind me fast with new ropes that never were occupied, then shall I be weak, and be as another man.

12 De-lī′lah therefore took new ropes, and bound him therewith, and said unto him, The Philistines *be* upon thee, Samson. And *there were* liers in wait abiding in the chamber. And he brake them from off his arms like a thread.

13 And De-lī′lah said unto Samson, Hitherto thou hast mocked me, and told me lies: tell me wherewith thou mightest be bound. And he said unto her, If thou weavest the seven locks of my head with the web.

14 And she fastened *it* with the pin, and said unto him, The Philistines *be* upon thee, Samson. And he awaked out of his sleep, and went away with the pin of the beam, and with the web.

15 ¶And she said unto him, How canst thou say, I love thee, when thine heart *is* not with me? thou hast mocked me these three times, and hast not told me wherein thy great strength *lieth.*

16 And it came to pass, when she pressed him daily with her words, and urged him, *so* that his soul was vexed unto death;

17 That he told her all his heart, and said unto her, There hath not come a razor upon mine head; for I *have been* a Nazarite unto God from my mother's womb: if I be shaven, then my strength will go from me, and I shall become weak, and be like any *other* man.

18 And when De-lī′lah saw that he had told her all his heart, she sent and called for the lords of the Philistines, saying, Come up this once, for he hath shewed me all his heart. Then the lords of the Philistines came up unto her, and brought money in their hand.

19 And she made him sleep upon her knees; and she called for a man, and she caused him to shave off the seven locks of his head; and she began to afflict him, and his strength went from him.

20 And she said, The Philistines *be* upon thee, Samson. And he awoke out of his sleep, and said, I will go out as at other times before, and shake myself. And he wist not that the LORD was departed from him.

the reader should carefully notice the details of the text. After this disclosure, the lords of the Philistines brought her the bowstrings to try on Samson. They also left men to lie in wait to ambush Samson once the secret was discovered. Upon her next opportunity, Delilah bound the sleeping Samson and called **The Philistines be upon thee,** and, awaking from his sleep, he immediately snapped the bowstrings (vs. 9). The text does not say that the liers-in-wait actually came upon him, but only that she screamed **The Philistines be upon thee.** Had these men rushed into the room three times after Samson's disclosure of the secret, he would surely have been suspicious of Delilah's treachery. This writer believes they never actually engaged him the first three times.

10-14. The second playful suggestion by Samson was to bind him with **new ropes,** which had failed to hold him years earlier (15:13). Again, Delilah tied him up and cried out in pretense of attack to expose his life. Attempt number three brought Samson perilously close to the truth when he told her to pin his hair into the mechanism of a weaver's loom. The loom in her house was probably vertical and the two posts were fixed in the ground and fastened by a crossbeam from which the warp threads were suspended. Apparently she wove Samson's long hair into the warp and pinned it in the web so that it resembled a piece of cloth. Upon her screaming again, Samson awoke and jerked his head pulling the hair out of the loom, pin and all!

15-20. From this point, Delilah, who had willingly played games with Samson's halfhearted replies, began to put the pressure on him. **Thou hast mocked me these three times. . . . How canst thou say, I love thee, when thine heart is not with me?** (vs. 15). One can easily imagine her tears flowing freely to reinforce her plea to the evermore tenderhearted Samson! Her nagging became so incessant that **she pressed him daily with her words, and urged him, so that his soul was vexed unto death** (vs. 16). She literally nagged him to death. What man could stand up under such an attack? This became the turning point. He then revealed all his heart to her concerning the Nazirite vow and, presumably, the fact that the uncut hair was the only remaining sign of his consecration to Yahweh.

Verse 18 is the key to understanding the entire account: **And when Delilah saw that he had told her all his heart, she sent and called for the lords of the Philistines, saying, Come up this once, for he hath showed me all his heart.** The prostitute could read his emotions clearly, and she now knew he was no longer jesting with her and had surely emptied his heart to her in foolish trust. Therefore, she called the lords themselves to come up this one time to take him and also to bring the money with them; for she was convinced that Samson had revealed the truth to her. Poor unsuspecting Samson! His disregard for his consecration to the Lord would now lead to the removal of the last sign of the Nazirite vow and render him useless to the Lord's service.

It is a poor understanding of the theology of this account to declare that Samson thought his strength lay in his uncut hair alone. Every mention of his physical prowess is accompanied by the remark that the spirit of the Lord came upon him to move him to such great physical strength. The importance of the uncut hair was that it was one of the signs of the vow; in fact, it was the only one of the three signs that was outwardly observable. He himself stated to Delilah that a haircut would break the vow and render him powerless because physical strength was the particular gift he had from God as a result of his consecration to Him. His loss of strength afterwards was clearly attributed to the departure of the Spirit from him (vs. 20).

It is most likely that Delilah used sexual intercourse to induce heavy sleep upon the mighty Samson, and he slept through the haircut. Delilah, greedy for the great reward of silver, sat calmly, conscious of the awful fate to which she was delivering her lover. The utter heartless cruelty of Delilah, so typical of a prostitute, is revealed in the phrase **and she began to afflict him** (vs. 19). Delilah herself beat Samson back to consciousness as she called in mocking tones, **The Philistines be upon thee, Samson.** In reality, the only Philistine attacking him was Delilah herself! When he awoke, Samson doubtless leaped up, supposing this to be another gag whereby she had somehow bound him, and said, **I will go out as at other times before, and shake myself.** The brief note at the end of verse 20 has to be one of the saddest comments in all Scripture: **And he wist not that the LORD was departed from him.** The special manifestation of the spirit of Yahweh as the fulfillment of the Nazirite vow was now gone, for the last stipulation of Samson's consecration had been broken. The self-sufficient warrior thought he could still exert his strength and did not immediately perceive that it was gone.

21-22. God had patiently dealt with Samson after he touched the dead lion and drank wine at the feast; but now, as the outward sign of Samson's Nazirite vow disappeared, His patience turned to judgment, and Samson was utterly powerless without the help of the Lord. The lords of the Philistines rushed into Delilah's chamber for the first time and took Samson, put out his eyes, and then bound him with **fetters of brass** (Heb *nechōshet*). The dual form may suggest he was bound hand and foot, or that he was bound doubly secure.

The Philistines brought Samson to Gaza in this state of utter humiliation. The very city whose gate he had recently carried away now welcomed its blind captive. Samson's future potential was now annulled. His uncontrolled lust had placed him in a condition where God could no longer use him to battle the Philistines hand to hand, for he was blind. He had disqualified himself by his selfish sin.

The Philistines allowed him to live and chained him to the grinding mill where he ground out the grain by hand. This was the most tedious and lowest form of slave labor and was usually the work of women slaves (cf. 9:53). It is very unlikely that he ground at an ox or ass mill, for his strength was no longer abnormal; and such large, animal-powered mills did not even exist until the fifth century B.C. Thus, the Philistines brought Samson to the depth of utter humiliation. In the now hollowed sockets of his eyes he carried the mark of his shame and unfaithfulness as God's servant. Although his hair is said to have begun to grow again, he was not in prison very long before the Philistines brought him forth to celebrate their victory. There is also no evidence that the growing of his hair caused him to receive any strength, until after he called upon the Lord (vs. 28).

23-24. The Philistines credited their new acquisition to their god **Dagon** as a victory over Yahweh of the Hebrews. So the lords of the Pentapolis gathered at Gaza for a great feast to praise their god. Dagon was the Semitic grain deity whom the Philistines had borrowed from the Canaanites. Earlier commentators thought Dagon to be a fish deity (Heb *dag*, "fish"), but recent Semitic studies have shown Dagon to be derived from the Hebrew word *dagan* (grain). For a discussion of this, see "Dagon," *New Bible Dictionary*, pp. 287-288. Therefore, he

21 But the Philistines took him, and put out his eyes, and brought him down to Gā′za, and bound him with fetters of brass; and he did grind in the prison house.

22 Howbeit the hair of his head began to grow again after he was shaven.

23 Then the lords of the Philistines gathered them together for to offer a great sacrifice unto Dā′gŏn their god, and to rejoice: for they said, Our god hath delivered Samson our enemy into our hand.

24 And when the people saw him, they praised their god: for they said, Our god hath delivered into our hands

our enemy, and the destroyer of our country, which slew many of us.

25 And it came to pass, when their hearts were merry, that they said, Call for Samson, that he may make us sport. And they called for Samson out of the prison house; and he made them sport: and they set him between the pillars.
26 And Samson said unto the lad that held him by the hand, Suffer me that I may feel the pillars whereupon the house standeth, that I may lean upon them.
27 Now the house was full of men and women; and all the lords of the Philistines were there; and there were upon the roof about three thousand men and women, that beheld while Samson made sport.

28 And Samson called unto the LORD, and said, O Lord GOD, remember me, I pray thee, and strengthen me, I pray thee, only this once, O God, that I may be at once avenged of the Philistines for my two eyes.
29 And Samson took hold of the two middle pillars upon which the house stood, and on which it was borne up, of the one with his right hand, and of the other with his left.
30 And Samson said, Let me die with the Philistines. And he bowed himself with all his might; and the house fell upon the lords, and upon all the people that were therein. So the dead which he slew at his death were more than they which he slew in his life.

31 Then his brethren and all the house of his father came down, and took him, and brought him up, and buried him between Zô'rah and Ĕsh'ta-ol in the buryingplace of Ma-nō'ah his

was probably part of the fertility pantheon of the Canaanites. In Ugaritic literature he appears as the father of Baal. **Dagon** appears in name forms as early as the third millennium B.C. It is interesting to note the Philistines believed that by grinding out the grain, Samson was acknowledging the supremacy of their god, Dagon, over him!

25-26. The Philistines' great mistake was in thinking that their god had delivered Samson into their hands (vs. 23). Yahweh could not permit this illusion. He had delivered His faithless servant into their hands, but He would yet find one more occasion against the Philistines because of Samson. At the peak of the revelry at the feast to Dagon, they called for Samson to **make us sport**, or entertain them. Every Philistine could dare mock and curse the helpless blind hero who was made to put on a performance for the crowd.

27. The **house** was probably the pillared temple of Dagon. The lords and rulers were in the covered section below, while the crowd of guests was upon the roof (vs. 27) watching Samson in the courtyard below. Cundall (p. 180) notes that the great host of people upon the roof may have made the whole structure unstable. After the performance, Samson was chained to the **pillars** just under the edge of the roof, being led by a young boy. The details of the temple's structure are unknown, as is the matter of exactly how pulling out two pillars could collapse the whole structure. Such pillars, though, were common to Philistine temples built around courtyards. A recent discovery of a Philistine temple at Tell Qas in 1972 revealed that the structure was made of sun-dried mudbricks laid as stone foundations, with a central hall whose roof was supported by two wooden pillars set on round stone bases, proving that the Bible writer knew his facts. See "Samson and the House of Dagon," *Bible and Spade*, 3.2 (1974), p. 5.

28-30. The humiliating consequences of Samson's sin must certainly have caused him to do some serious thinking and had probably moved him to repentance. The very fact that he prayed to the Lord gives some evidence of spirituality. This is the only recorded prayer of Samson that we have in Scripture. Despite the sixfold use of the personal pronoun, the prayer was a sincere request to God to allow Samson to do the only thing that he now could do in his state of blindness. He called upon God using three different titles, Adonai, Yahweh, Elohim. Samson asked the lad who guided him to place him at the central pillars. After his prayer, he took hold of the two middle pillars, bowed himself forward, sliding the pillars off their stone bases, and brought death to a great host of the Philistines, especially those under the roof (vs. 30). How many were killed is not specified, except that the number was more than he had previously killed during his lifetime.

Dr. Cassel (p. 224) must be given credit here for an ingenious observation. He asks the question, "Who furnished the report of the last hours of the hero's life?" If this is no mere folk legend, how were the details reported? Cassel observed that the **lad** (Heb na'ar) who led the blind Samson by the hand (vs. 26) was probably a Hebrew slave, for surely they would have feared to let a Philistine boy near the Hebrew rogue. The boy may even have been Samson's attendant, who willingly stayed with him in the prison. Knowing what he was about to do, it is unlikely that Samson would have let the boy die with him. The lad could have reported the events of the feast and Samson's prayer when he escaped to his home.

31. After Samson died with the Philistines in the collapse of the temple of Dagon at Gaza, his fellow-countrymen came to bury his dead body. This is the first hint of any action on their part. Perhaps this was their first glimpse of the need to stand up for Yahweh against the enemy. This time of catastrophe and

father. And he judged Israel twenty years.

CHAPTER 17

AND there was a man of mount Ē′phraim, whose name *was* Mī′cah.

2 And he said unto his mother, The eleven hundred *shekels* of silver that were taken from thee, about which thou cursedst, and spakest of also in mine ears, behold, the silver *is* with me; I took it. And his mother said, Blessed *be thou* of the LORD, my son.

3 And when he had restored the eleven hundred *shekels* of silver to his mother, his mother said, I had wholly dedicated the silver unto the LORD from my hand for my son, to make a graven image and a molten image: now therefore I will restore it unto thee.

4 Yet he restored the money unto his mother; and his mother took two hundred *shekels* of silver, and gave them to the founder, who made thereof a graven image and a molten image: and they were in the house of Mī′cah.

5 And the man Mī′cah had an house of gods, and made an ephod, and teraphim, and consecrated one of his sons, who became his priest.

death was one of mitigated hatred on the part of both bereaved groups. The Philistines evidently made no attempt to refuse Samson a proper burial in his family tomb, though they were not so kind to Saul in later times (I Sam 31:9-10). Samson's father, Manoah, was probably deceased by this time; for he is not said to have come himself. The reference to Samson's **brethren** must be to his tribal countrymen since he was an only child. They buried Samson in the hill country overlooking the Valley of Sorek, the very scene of his greatest triumphs and his greatest failures!

The biblical writers do not hesitate to record valid history that includes both the victories and defeats of its heroes, and no attempt is made to conceal the moral impurities of Samson. Thus, Garstang (p. 341) concluded that there is no reason to doubt the original authenticity of Joshua-Judges. Samson's spiritual failures are not condoned by the text; rather, they are the means of his downfall. He is a tragic picture of a man of God fully equipped to serve the Lord, but whose service is rendered ineffective by his passion and lust.

III. RUIN OF THE JUDGES. 17:1-21:25.

A. Idolatry of Micah and the Danites. 17:1-18:31.

17:1-5. The last five chapters of the book of Judges formulate the appendix and supplement the author's history of the period of the judges. Virtually all commentators agree that these chapters are out of sequence with the chronology of the rest of the book and actually occurred during the early period of the judges. Pfeiffer (p. 261) notes that rabbinic commentators placed the story of Micah in the time of Othniel. These appendices do not contain any references to great leaders or national oppressions. However, they are of great interest in the study of the history of Israel; for they reveal the condition of Israelite spiritual life during the time of the judges. While God was raising up unusual leaders from time to time to deliver the people from bondage, these incidents clearly indicate that the general quality of Israel's spiritual life was extremely low during that entire period. Davis (p. 143) notes that these chapters deal with the subject of spiritual apostasy as it affected both individual families and the nation as a whole. Since this narrative follows the story of Samson, who was of the tribe of Dan, this section seems to have been placed here in logical, rather than chronological, order.

Micah had stolen **eleven hundred shekels of silver** from his wealthy mother. While the eleven hundred pieces of silver correlate with the amount paid to Delilah by each of the lords of the Philistines, it is highly unlikely that she is the mother of this incident. In Hebrew Micah's name means "who is like Jehovah." Cassel (p. 228) notes that such names were usually only given in homes where Jehovah was at least outwardly recognized. His mother, then, pronounced a serious curse (probably in the name of Jehovah) on the one who had taken the money. Fearing the power of his mother's curse, Micah confessed that he was the one who had taken the silver. Ancient peoples greatly feared the power of a parental curse (cf. Sirach 3:9). His mother's strange response was **Blessed be thou of the LORD, my son.** Literally "Out of the same mouth proceedeth blessing and cursing" (Jas 3:10). Apparently, she feared the silver had been taken by someone from whom she would never be able to recover it; and she was relieved to discover that her own son had it.

This parental relationship serves as an illustration of the permissive spiritual condition that was prevalent in Israel at that time. Micah **restored** the silver to his mother, who claimed that she had **dedicated the silver unto the LORD.** However, her concept of dedication certainly was not in accordance with the

Mosaic law since she had decided to make a **graven image** with it! She then took only **two hundred** pieces of silver and gave it to her son for the purpose of having the idol made. The details of the story are not sufficient enough to help us understand why these things happened the way they did. Perhaps she felt guilty about the manner in which she had acquired the large sum of money, and therefore her son felt justified in taking it. She, in turn, was relieved to discover that he still had it; and it is possible that she claimed to have dedicated it to Jehovah merely as a justification for having the money in the first place! It seems unusual that she only gave a small portion of it to her son, if in fact she had really dedicated the money to the Lord for the purpose of making the image. Nevertheless, the image was made of carved wood, overlaid with silver, with the detail-work being done by a **founder** (or silversmith). Micah then set the idol in a shrine, which the AV calls a **house of gods.** Cundall (p. 183) rightly questions the legitimacy and sincerity of both her behavior and his. Micah also made an **ephod and teraphim,** which served as additional idols or representations thereof.

6. The recurring statement **In those days there was no king in Israel, but every man did that which was right in his own eyes** appears throughout this section of the book of Judges (cf. 18:1; 19:1; 21:25) and is intended to explain the moral relativism of the times. Rather than follow the law of God, man had become a law unto himself. In this incident we see people who claim to know the Lord and to be dedicated unto Jehovah lying, stealing, conniving, and justifying their own behavior. Davis (p. 143 ff.) notes three characteristics of spiritual apostasy in this story: religious syncretism, moral relativism, and extreme materialism. Wood (p. 147 ff.) notes several sins that openly occurred in this account: (1) The failure and apostasy of the Danites; (2) the making of graven images; (3) unauthorized priests serving for hire; (4) establishment of private worship sanctuaries; (5) the movement of the Levites from their assigned cities; and (6) the justification of stealing.

6 In those days *there was* no king in Israel, *but* every man did *that which was* right in his own eyes.

7-13. An unnamed young man, a **Levite** from the town of **Beth-lehem-judah** (of the **family of Judah**), wandered northward into Mount Ephraim, where he came upon Micah. Discovering that he was unemployed and away from his normal responsibilities, Micah hired him to be their private family **priest.** The Levites, according to the law of Moses, were assigned specific cities in which to live and serve. Since Bethlehem is not listed as a Levitical city (cf. Num 35:1-8; Josh 21:1-41), it is questionable what he was doing there in the first place. The statement that he could not **find a place** would seem to suggest that he was an opportunist looking for the best situation that would satisfy him. Thus, he accepted Micah's offer of **ten shekels of silver by the year.**

7 ¶And there was a young man out of Bĕth-lehĕm-jūdah of the family of Jū-dah, who *was* a Levite, and he sojourned there.
8 And the man departed out of the city from Bĕth-lehĕm-jūdah to sojourn where he could find *a place:* and he came to mount Ē′phra-im to the house of Mī′cah, as he journeyed.
9 And Mī′cah said unto him, Whence comest thou? And he said unto him, I *am* a Levite of Bĕth-lehĕm-jūdah, and I go to sojourn where I may find *a place.*
10 And Mī′cah said unto him, Dwell with me, and be unto me a father and a priest, and I will give thee ten *shekels* of silver by the year, and a suit of apparel, and thy victuals. So the Levite went in.
11 And the Levite was content to dwell with the man; and the young man was unto him as one of his sons.
12 And Mī′cah consecrated the Levite; and the young man became his priest, and was in the house of Mī′cah.
13 Then said Mī′cah, Now know I that the LORD will do me good, seeing I have a Levite to *my* priest.

Micah then **consecrated the Levite** (vs. 12), which he had no business doing. He then naively assumed that **the LORD will do me good,** since he had a Levite for a priest! It is obvious that Micah's motivation was based on superstition, not faith in God's revelation. Thus, we may conclude that the average Israelite, even a religious Israelite, was basically ignorant of the true content of the Law. It is difficult to imagine that a Levite would be content to accept such a position in spite of what he knew of the prohibitions in the Law regarding idolatry. Thus, the sin of the Levite contributed to the deepening of Micah's apostasy.

CHAPTER 18
IN those days *there was* no king in Israel: and in those days the tribe of the Danites sought them an inheritance to dwell in; for unto that day *all their* inheritance had not fallen unto them among the tribes of Israel.

18:1-6. This chapter begins by noting again that there was **no king in Israel,** reminding us that much of the spiritual and political confusion of this time was due to a lack of unified leadership in the nation. There can be no doubt that these appendices were intended to bridge the gap and pave the way from the time of the judges to that of the monarchy which would

2 And the children of Dan sent of their family five men from their coasts, men of valour, from Zô'rah, and from Ĕsh'ta-ol, to spy out the land, and to search it; and they said unto them, Go, search the land: who when they came to mount E'phra-im, to the house of Mī'cah, they lodged there.

3 When they *were* by the house of Mī'cah, they knew the voice of the young man the Levite: and they turned in thither, and said unto him, Who brought thee hither? and what makest thou in this *place?* and what hast thou here?

4 And he said unto them, Thus and thus dealeth Mī'cah with me, and hath hired me, and I am his priest.

5 And they said unto him, Ask counsel, we pray thee, of God, that we may know whether our way which we go shall be prosperous.

6 And the priest said unto them, Go in peace: before the LORD *is* your way wherein ye go.

7 ¶Then the five men departed, and came to Lā'ish, and saw the people that

be introduced in I Samuel. According to Numbers 26:43, the tribe of Dan had sixty-four thousand men. However, they were still unable to occupy the territory that was allotted to them because of the oppression of the Amorites and the Philistines. It should be remembered that the Samson narrative also relates to the tribe of Dan. Samson, the strongest man, came from Dan, the weakest tribe! The difficulties in the conquest and settlement of the land had caused a lack of precision regarding intertribal boundaries. The reference to the **camp of Dan** (13:25) indicates the unsettled situation of this tribe. In desperation, the Danites decided to seek a more secure location. Joshua 19:47 also refers to this migration and must be considered an editorial addition to that book in order to clarify a point.

The sending of **five men . . . to spy out the land** was a common Israelite tactic. In the process of their search they came to Mount Ephraim to the **house of Micah,** where they lodged. Upon their arrival they recognized the Levite, apparently from a previous contact with him, and questioned how he had gotten there. The fact that he had become a hireling did not seem to bother them at all, and they urged him to **Ask counsel . . . of God** that they might know what to do. Apparently, they assumed that the Levite could serve as a fortune-teller by use of his ephod. His encouraging report led them to believe that the expedition could expect the blessing of the Lord. His favorable reply had important consequences for subsequent events.

7-13. The northward journey of the spies would take them about one hundred miles from their original starting point in an

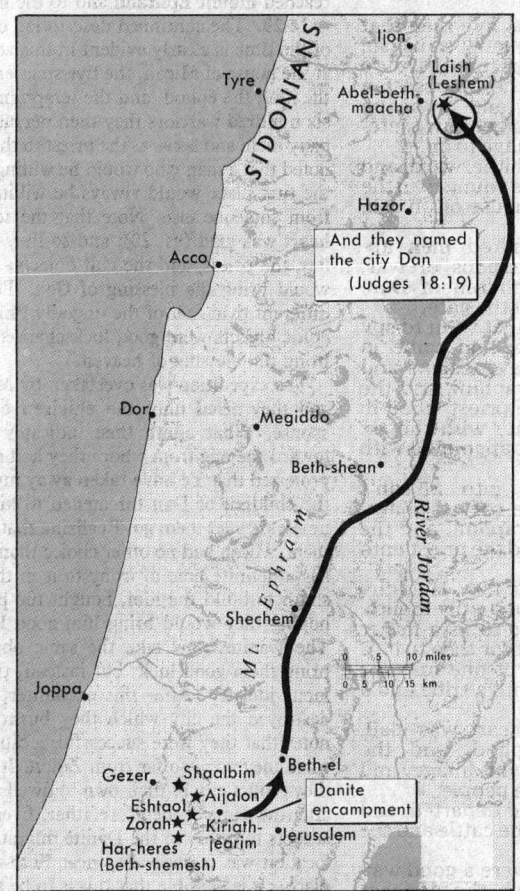

The Migration of the Tribe of Dan

were therein, how they dwelt careless, after the manner of the Zī-dō'nī-ans, quiet and secure; and *there was* no magistrate in the land, that might put *them* to shame in *any* thing; and they *were* far from the Zī-dō'nī-ans, and had no business with *any* man.

8 And they came unto their brethren to Zô'rah and Ĕsh'ta-ol: and their brethren said unto them, What *say* ye?

9 And they said, Arise, that we may go up against them: for we have seen the land, and, behold, it *is* very good: and *are* ye still? be not slothful to go, *and* to enter to possess the land.

10 When ye go, ye shall come unto a people secure, and to a large land: for God hath given it into your hands; a place where *there is* no want of any thing that *is* in the earth.

11 ¶And there went from thence of the family of the Danites, out of Zô'rah and out of Ĕsh'ta-ol, six hundred men appointed with weapons of war.

12 And they went up, and pitched in Kir'jath-jē'a-rĭm, in Judah: wherefore they called that place Mā'ha-neh–dăn unto this day: behold, *it is* behind Kir'-jath-jē'a-rĭm.

13 And they passed thence unto mount Ē'phra-im, and came unto the house of Mī'cah.

14 Then answered the five men that went to spy out the country of Lā'ĭsh, and said unto their brethren, Do ye know that there is in these houses an ephod, and teraphim, and a graven image, and a molten image? now therefore consider what ye have to do.

15 And they turned thitherward, and came to the house of the young man the Levite, *even* unto the house of Mī'cah, and saluted him.

16 And the six hundred men appointed with their weapons of war, which *were* of the children of Dan, stood by the entering of the gate.

17 And the five men that went to spy out the land went up, *and* came in thither, *and* took the graven image, and the ephod, and the teraphim, and the molten image: and the priest stood in the entering of the gate with the six hundred men *that were* appointed with weapons of war.

18 And these went into Mī'cah's house, and fetched the carved image, the ephod, and the teraphim, and the molten image. Then said the priest unto them, What do ye?

19 And they said unto him, Hold thy peace, lay thine hand upon thy mouth, and go with us, and be to us a father and a priest: *is it* better for thee to be a priest unto the house of one man, or that thou be a priest unto a tribe and a family in Israel?

20 And the priest's heart was glad, and he took the ephod, and the teraphim, and the graven image, and went in the midst of the people.

21 So they turned and departed, and put the little ones and the cattle and the carriage before them.

22 ¶And when they were a good way from the house of Mī'cah, the men that

attempt to find a new settlement. They wandered beyond the region occupied by the Israelites into a small, fertile valley populated by people of Phoenician origin (Zidonians). The original name of the area was **Laish,** and it is referred to as Leshem in Joshua 19:47 and appears as Lus in the Egyptian texts of the nineteenth century B.C. It has been identified by archaeologists as Tell el-Qadi, being about half a mile in diameter. The text notes that they were dwelling there **careless . . . quiet and secure,** meaning at peace and ease. However, the spies found that the city had no strong central government and that it was far removed from the Phoenicians of Zidon itself. It was cut off from Syria by Mount Hermon and from Phoenicia by the Lebanon range.

The statement that they had **no business with any man** means they had no treaties with neighboring peoples to protect them in the event of an attack. Thus, it was an ideal place for the battle-weary Danites to conquer. Upon returning to **Zorah and Eshtaol,** where the Danite camp was, the spies encouraged them to go and capture Laish. Therefore, **six hundred men** were sent out as a warrior party to take the city (vs. 11). The context clearly indicates that their wives, children, and possessions went with them. On their journey they stopped at **Kirjath-jearim** (city of forests). This location was just three hours from Eshtaol, and the Danite encampment nearby was called **Mahaneh-dan** (the camp of Dan). The fact that the author says it was called that **unto this day** indicates that the location bore the same name in the day, or time, of the author. From there the expedition reached **mount Ephraim** and to the **house of Micah.**

14-29. The continued description of the spiritual wickedness of the time is clearly evident in this account. Upon their arrival at the house of Micah, the five spies entered the shrine and stole the idol, the ephod, and the teraphim. With the support of the six hundred warriors they then persuaded the Levite to accompany them and serve as the priest to the entire tribe. It should be noted that a man who would be willing to hire his services out in the first place would always be willing to accept a better offer from someone else. Note that the text says that **the priest's heart was glad** (vs. 20); and so they departed with their families, the priest, and the cult objects, assuming that all of these would bring the blessing of God. Their attitude is not much different than that of the ungodly Philistines who assumed that cultic objects were good luck charms that would automatically bring the blessing of heaven.

The expedition was overtaken by Micah's neighbors (vs. 22), and they **cried unto the children of Dan.** The Danites' response, **What aileth thee** indicates their despicable attitude toward the one from whom they had stolen these things. Micah protested that **Ye have taken away my gods which I made,** and the children of Dan threatened to kill him and his household unless they let them go. Realizing that he was inadequate to stop them, Micah had no other choice than to let them go. The story has a definite note of irony to it in that Micah paid the silversmith to build the idol, bought the priest and the cult objects hoping they would bring him good luck, and then lost them. The Danites now take the same objects, assuming they will bring them good luck; but instead, the tribe turns to blasphemous idolatry. After this encounter, they came to Laish and destroyed the city which they **burnt . . . with fire.** The text notes that they were successful because there was **no deliverer** since they were so far from Zidon. It was on that location that they built a city of their own to dwell in, which they called **Dan** after the name of their forefather. Even McKenzie (p. 160) fully accepts the story of the Danite migration as being historical. Its location was in the valley near **Beth-rehob** (house of the open place). It is possible that this is to be associated with the Rehob of Numbers 13:21, the most northerly city observed by the

were in the houses near to Mī′cah′s house were gathered together, and overtook the children of Dan.

23 And they cried unto the children of Dan. And they turned their faces, and said unto Mī′cah, What aileth thee, that thou comest with such a company?

24 And he said, Ye have taken away my gods which I made, and the priest, and ye are gone away: and what have I more? and what *is* this *that* ye say unto me, What aileth thee?

25 And the children of Dan said unto him, Let not thy voice be heard among us, lest angry fellows run upon thee, and thou lose thy life, with the lives of thy household.

26 And the children of Dan went their way: and when Mī′cah saw that they *were* too strong for him, he turned and went back unto his house.

27 And they took the things which Mī′cah had made, and the priest which he had, and came unto Lā′ish, unto a people *that were* at quiet and secure: and they smote them with the edge of the sword, and burnt the city with fire.

28 And *there was* no deliverer, because it *was* far from Zī′don, and they had no business with *any* man; and it was in the valley that *lieth* by Bĕth-rē′hŏb. And they built a city, and dwelt therein.

29 And they called the name of the city Dan, after the name of Dan their father, who was born unto Israel: howbeit the name of the city *was* Lā′ish at the first.

30 And the children of Dan set up the graven image: and Jonathan, the son of Ger′shom, the son of Ma-năs′seh, he and his sons were priests to the tribe of Dan until the day of the captivity of the land.

31 And they set them up Mī′cah′s graven image, which he made, all the time that the house of God was in Shī′-lōh.

twelve spies. Since this site is also called "Dan" in Judges 5:17, it is possible that the events in this chapter occurred before the war with Sisera.

30-31. In addition to building a city of their own, the Danites set up a sanctuary and installed **Jonathan, the son of Gershom** as their priest. Also, **Micah's graven image** was worshiped by them during the entire time that the **house of God was in Shiloh,** referring to the location of the tabernacle during the period of the judges. In other words, the Danites had their own private sanctuary and did not recognize the location of God's true sanctuary at Shiloh. The reading, **the son of Manasseh,** is due to a scribal emendation introduced into the Hebrew text. The Hebrew consonants *msh* are the same for the name of Moses (the true father of Gershom, Ex 2:21-22) and for Manasseh. All commentators agree that original reference was to Moses, but observe that the ancient scribes removed his name because of its associations with idolatry. In reality, Moses was not responsible for the idolatry in which Jonathan participated. It is also interesting that the alteration of the name to that of Manasseh corresponds with the wicked king of Judah (II Kgs 21:1-2). It is also important to observe that Dan was one of the two cult sanctuaries set up by Jeroboam I in his attempt to counteract the temple worship center at Jerusalem. Cundall (p. 191) suggests that the golden calf, or bull, which he set up may have been modeled after the molten image of Micah. Jeroboam's cult centers at Dan and Beth-el were opposed by the true priests of Judah throughout Israel's history.

The reference to the **day of the captivity** may refer either to the ultimate northern deportation by Tiglath-pileser of Assyria, or, more likely, to the time of the Philistines' overthrow of Shiloh. Throughout its history, Dan was known as a center of idolatry and became a symbol of the apostate tribe of Israel. Thus, it is not named in Revelation 7 as one of the twelve tribes of the future kingdom. In the list that appears in the Apocalypse, the tribe of Levi appears in the inheritance in the place of Dan, and the tribe of Ephraim is referred to as the tribe of

Joseph. Thus, in the irony of history, the tribe of Dan, which stole the Levite and the image from an Ephraimite, is replaced in the list of God's people by those very tribes. It is not improper to suggest that the tribe of Dan is a type of Judas Iscariot, the apostate disciple. It is certainly interesting to note that while we also normally speak of twelve apostles, in reality there were thirteen. Judas, the apostate disciple, corresponds to Dan, the apostate tribe, both of whom lose their true inheritance in the kingdom of God.

B. Immorality of the Gibeonites and Benjamites.
   19:1-21:25.

19:1-9. This chapter also begins with the note that there was **no king in Israel,** referring to the lack of authority that prevailed in the nation at the time. This narrative also centers on **a certain Levite** from **Ephraim** who was married to a **concubine** from **Beth-lehem-judah.** Thus, the similarities between the two stories should be observed. The time of the incident would appear to be early in the period of the judges, since Phinehas, the grandson of Aaron, is mentioned in 20:28 and the tribal league is still functioning by combined action. There is no mention of the Philistines, who would have suppressed such action during the latter part of the judges' period. Cundall (p. 193) correctly observed that the reference **from Dan even to Beer-sheba** (20:1) was probably added later by an editor to explain the entirety of the land. The concubine **played the whore** (vs. 2), i.e., was sexually unfaithful to her husband, and returned to her father. While this section of the book of Judges centers on the resulting civil war between the tribe of Benjamin and the other tribes of Israel, it also reveals the moral laxity of this period throughout Israel.

After **four whole months** the Levite returned to Beth-lehem to recover the concubine. Concubinage, though certainly not an ideal union, was nevertheless recognized as a legal marriage. When the Levite arrived at the girl's house, her father **rejoiced to meet him** and persuaded him to remain for four days. However, her father seemed reluctant to let her go and persuaded the Levite to remain most of the **fifth day.** He remained until **afternoon,** and her father again attempted to get him to stay another night. Perhaps fearing that he would never be able to leave with the girl, the Levite refused to stay, took the girl and departed late in the day.

CHAPTER 19

AND it came to pass in those days, when *there was* no king in Israel, that there was a certain Levite sojourning on the side of mount Ē'phra-im, who took to him a concubine out of Bĕth-lehĕm-jūdah.

2 And his concubine played the whore against him, and went away from him unto her father's house to Bĕth-lehĕm-jūdah, and was there four whole months.

3 And her husband arose, and went after her, to speak friendly unto her, *and* to bring her again, having his servant with him, and a couple of asses: and she brought him into her father's house: and when the father of the damsel saw him, he rejoiced to meet him.

4 And his father in law, the damsel's father, retained him; and he abode with him three days: so they did eat and drink, and lodged there.

5 And it came to pass on the fourth day, when they arose early in the morning, that he rose up to depart: and the damsel's father said unto his son in law, Comfort thine heart with a morsel of bread, and afterward go your way.

6 And they sat down, and did eat and drink both of them together: for the damsel's father had said unto the man, Be content, I pray thee, and tarry all night, and let thine heart be merry.

7 And when the man rose up to depart, his father in law urged him: therefore he lodged there again.

8 And he arose early in the morning on the fifth day to depart: and the damsel's father said, Comfort thine heart, I pray thee. And they tarried until afternoon, and they did eat both of them.

9 And when the man rose up to depart, he, and his concubine, and his servant, his father in law, the damsel's father, said unto him, Behold, now the day draweth toward evening, I pray you tarry all night: behold, the day groweth to an end, lodge here, that thine heart may be merry; and to morrow get you early on your way, that thou mayest go home.

10 But the man would not tarry that night, but he rose up and departed, and came over against Jē'bus, which *is* Jerusalem; and *there were* with him two asses saddled, his concubine also *was* with him.

11 *And* when they *were* by Jē'bus, the day was far spent; and the servant said unto his master, Come, I pray thee, and let us turn in into this city of the Jĕb'u-sītes, and lodge in it.

12 And his master said unto him, We

10-21. Beth-lehem was about six miles south of ancient Jerusalem; and Gibeah, their destination, was about five miles north of the town. Preferring to reside in an Israelite city, they probably passed on beyond Jerusalem because, at this time, it was still under Jebusite control. Thus, the inhospitality of the Gibeonites was all the more hideous. By sunset, the Levite, with his wife and servant, arrived at **Gibeah, which belongeth to Benjamin.** They had made only about a ten-mile journey that afternoon, indicating that their departure could not have been much earlier than 3:00 P.M.: **Ramah,** mentioned as an alternate stop, was yet two miles further north. However, the little group

will not turn aside hither into the city of a stranger, that *is* not of the children of Israel; we will pass over to Gĭb′e-ah.

13 And he said unto his servant, Come, and let us draw near to one of these places to lodge all night, in Gĭb′e-ah, or in Rā′mah.

14 And they passed on and went their way; and the sun went down upon them *when they were* by Gĭb′e-ah, which *belongeth* to Benjamin.

15 And they turned aside thither, to go in *and* to lodge in Gĭb′e-ah: and when he went in, he sat him down in a street of the city: for *there was* no man that took them into his house to lodging.

16 ¶And, behold, there came an old man from his work out of the field at even, which *was* also of mount E′phra-im; and he sojourned in Gĭb′e-ah: but the men of the place *were* Benjamites.

17 And when he had lifted up his eyes, he saw a wayfaring man in the street of the city: and the old man said, Whither goest thou? and whence comest thou?

18 And he said unto him, We *are* passing from Bĕth–lehĕm–jūdah toward the side of mount E′phra-im; from thence *am* I: and I went to Bĕth–lehĕm–jūdah, but I *am* now going to the house of the Lord; and there *is* no man that receiveth me to house.

19 Yet there is both straw and provender for our asses; and there is bread and wine also for me, and for thy handmaid, and for the young man *which is* with thy servants: *there is* no want of any thing.

20 And the old man said, Peace *be* with thee; howsoever *let* all thy wants *lie* upon me; only lodge not in the street.

21 So he brought him into his house, and gave provender unto the asses: and they washed their feet, and did eat and drink.

22 ¶Now as they were making their hearts merry, behold, the men of the city, certain sons of Bĕ′lĭ-al, beset the house round about, *and* beat at the door, and spake to the master of the house, saying, Bring forth the man that came into thine house, that we may know him.

23 And the man, the master of the house, went out unto them, and said unto them, Nay, my brethren, *nay,* I pray you, do not *so* wickedly; seeing that this man is come into mine house, do not this folly.

24 Behold, *here is* my daughter a maiden, and his concubine; them I will bring out now, and humble ye them, and do with them what seemeth good unto you: but unto this man do not so vile a thing.

25 But the men would not hearken to him: so the man took his concubine, and brought her forth unto them; and they knew her, and abused her all the night until the morning: and when the day began to spring, they let her go.

26 Then came the woman in the dawning of the day, and fell down at the

found no place to lodge in Gibeah, the city that would become the birthplace and subsequent capital of Saul (I Sam 10:26).

The failure to offer hospitality was a breach of etiquette rarely found in the ancient East, where it was considered a sacred duty. Instead of being received by the Benjamites of the city, the group was offered lodging by another Ephraimite, also a stranger in the city (vs. 16). The reference to their going to the **house of the Lord** may mean that they planned to stop off at Shiloh on their return to Mount Ephraim; or it may have merely been a ploy to gain the desired hospitality, since they would appear to be on a journey of religious purpose. The story is similar to that of Lot and his two angelic visitors at Sodom. The man met them in the street and urged them not to lodge. Instead, he brought them into his house where they were attacked by the men of the city, who desired a homosexual relationship with them.

22-30. The men of the city surrounded (beset) the house and beat on the door, demanding that the man be brought out that they might **know him,** implying intimate sexual relationship. That their desire was for homosexual sin is indicated by the host's response, **Do not so wickedly.** The men of the city are referred to as **sons of Belial,** meaning worthless or ungodly. Psalm 18:4-5 clearly implies a relationship between Belial and Sheol; thus, the term was idiomatic for "sons of hell." In desperation, the host offered his daughter and the concubine in place of his guest. There can be no doubt in the comparison between this incident and that of Genesis 19 that homosexuality was considered the worst possible sin of sexual violation. That the Levite and his host would sexually offer the women to the men in place of a homosexual relationship was certainly not a godly choice. Either sexual sin is equally wrong; however, the reaction of these spiritually impoverished people shows that even in a time when sexual immorality was prevalent, homosexuality was still regarded as the worst possible form of sexual abuse!

Verse 25 indicates that the Levite himself **brought her forth unto them** and surrendered the concubine to their immoral sexual desires in an attempt to protect himself. The statement that follows is one of the most tragic in all of Scripture. The text says **they knew her, and abused her all the night,** meaning that she was sexually assaulted the entire night by the men of the

door of the man's house where her lord *was*, till it was light.

27 And her lord rose up in the morning, and opened the doors of the house, and went out to go his way: and, behold, the woman his concubine was fallen down *at* the door of the house, and her hands *were* upon the threshold.

28 And he said unto her, Up, and let us be going. But none answered. Then the man took her *up* upon an ass, and the man rose up, and gat him unto his place.

29 ¶And when he was come into his house, he took a knife, and laid hold on his concubine, and divided her, *together* with her bones, into twelve pieces, and sent her into all the coasts of Israel.

30 And it was so, that all that saw it said, There was no such deed done nor seen from the day that the children of Israel came up out of the land of Egypt unto this day: consider of it, take advice, and speak *your minds*.

CHAPTER 20

THEN all the children of Israel went out, and the congregation was gathered together as one man, from Dan even to Be'er–shē'ba, with the land of Gilead, unto the LORD in Mĭz'peh.

2 And the chief of all the people, *even* of all the tribes of Israel, presented themselves in the assembly of the people of God, four hundred thousand footmen that drew sword.

3 (Now the children of Benjamin heard that the children of Israel were gone up to Mĭz'peh.) Then said the children of Israel, Tell *us*, how was this wickedness?

4 And the Levite, the husband of the woman that was slain, answered and said, I came into Gĭb'e-ah that *belongeth* to Benjamin, I and my concubine, to lodge.

5 And the men of Gĭb'e-ah rose against me, and beset the house round about upon me by night, *and* thought to have slain me: and my concubine have they forced, that she is dead.

6 And I took my concubine, and cut her in pieces, and sent her throughout all the country of the inheritance of Israel: for they have committed lewdness and folly in Israel.

7 Behold, ye *are* all children of Israel: give here your advice and counsel.

8 ¶And all the people arose as one man, saying, We will not any *of us* go to

city. This abuse was kept up until morning, when they let her go. She returned, undoubtedly with a great deal of difficulty, **and fell down at the door of the man's house.** The next statement is equally as shocking as the abuse that had taken place; for verse 27 says **and her lord rose up in the morning,** implying that he had slept that evening while she was undergoing such a terrible fate.

The wickedness of the men of the city was matched by the inconsideration of her husband, who gave her away and slept calmly all evening, expecting her to be ready to depart with him the next morning. Instead, he discovered her lying dead upon the threshold of the house. The statement, **But none answered** (vs. 28), indicates that she was unable to answer because she was dead. Only then was the Levite outraged, and he loaded her dead body onto one of the animals and continued his journey. It was not until he arrived at home that he **took a knife . . . and divided her . . . into twelve pieces.** This method for rallying a nation was normally done by dismembering animals (see I Sam 11, where Saul divided a yoke of oxen in order to rally the twelve tribes of Israel together). The verb "to divide" refers to a ritual dissection (cf. Ex 29:17; Lev 1:6). The Levite sent the twelve pieces of her body to the twelve tribes of Israel in an effort to rally the nation out of its lethargy and to a willingness to acknowledge its responsibility.

Davis (p. 149) states, "This act on the part of the Levite was designed to get action, and it worked." It must be assumed that the tribe of Benjamin was included in the summons, but refused, thus identifying themselves with the action of the men of Gibeah. The shock of seeing the girl's dismembered body and undoubtedly hearing the story of this undeniable outrage against the law of God caused Israel to consider this the greatest atrocity of the nation's early history. It brought a tremendous reprisal. **Consider of it, take advice, and speak your minds.** The verbs which close the chapter are perfects of consequence, expressing the results which the Levite expected from this action (see Keil and Delitzsch, p. 446).

20:1-8. According to the text, **four hundred thousand footmen** responded to this challenge. It should be noted that this was the only incident in all of the time of the judges when the entire nation, and all the tribes, rallied in a concerted effort for any reason. In later times only a few tribes would rally to support one another; and by the time of Samson, which closes the period of the judges, he was able to rally no one to support his cause. The phrase **from Dan even to Beer-sheba** does not likely indicate that this event took place chronologically after the capture of Laish by the Danites, but was probably inserted in the final editing of the book to clarify the extent of Israel's territory and the extensive nature of the response of the people to this challenge. In ancient times **Mizpeh** was the central assembly point of the tribes (cf. I Sam 7:5). It is usually identified today with Tell-en-nasbeh, about eight miles north of Jerusalem.

Some have questioned the size of the number of the Israelite force of four hundred thousand, since only forty thousand were involved in the conquest of Jericho (cf. J. W. Wenham, "The Large Numbers of the Old Testament," in *Tyndale Bulletin*, 18, 1967, pp. 24ff.; and R. E. Clark, "The Large Numbers of the Old Testament" in *JTVI*, 87, 1955, pp. 82-92). While the word which is translated thousand (Heb *'elep*) may refer to family units, that alone does not eliminate the possibility that there really were four hundred thousand men at Mizpeh. The severe nature of such an atrocity, in a nation that considered itself to be a theocracy, would have brought the greatest possible response at this point. The fact that so many men showed up in response to the Levite's call does not mean that these men were a normally standing army, but rather, that every man who was ca-

his tent, neither will we any *of us* turn into his house.

9 But now this *shall be* the thing which we will do to Gĭb′e-ah; *we will go up* by lot against it;
10 And we will take ten men of an hundred throughout all the tribes of Israel, and an hundred of a thousand, and a thousand out of ten thousand, to fetch victual for the people, that they may do, when they come to Gĭb′e-ah of Benjamin, according to all the folly that they have wrought in Israel.
11 So all the men of Israel were gathered against the city, knit together as one man.
12 ¶And the tribes of Israel sent men through all the tribe of Benjamin, saying, What wickedness *is* this that is done among you?
13 Now therefore deliver *us* the men, the children of Bē′lĭ-al, which *are* in Gĭb′e-ah, that we may put them to death, and put away evil from Israel. But the children of Benjamin would not hearken to the voice of their brethren the children of Israel:
14 But the children of Benjamin gathered themselves together out of the cities unto Gĭb′e-ah, to go out to battle against the children of Israel.
15 And the children of Benjamin were numbered at that time out of the cities twenty and six thousand men that drew sword, beside the inhabitants of Gĭb′e-ah, which were numbered seven hundred chosen men.
16 Among all this people *there were* seven hundred chosen men lefthanded; every one could sling stones at an hair breadth, and not miss.
17 And the men of Israel, beside Benjamin, were numbered four hundred thousand men that drew sword: all these *were* men of war.
18 ¶And the children of Israel arose, and went up to the house of God, and asked counsel of God, and said, Which of us shall go up first to the battle against the children of Benjamin? An the LORD said, Jûdah *shall go up* first.
19 And the children of Israel rose up in the morning, and encamped against Gĭb′e-ah.
20 And the men of Israel went out to battle against Benjamin; and the men of Israel put themselves in array to fight against them at Gĭb′e-ah.
21 And the children of Benjamin came forth out of Gĭb′e-ah, and destroyed down to the ground of the Israelites that day twenty and two thousand men.
22 And the people the men of Israel encouraged themselves, and set their battle again in array in the place where they put themselves in array the first day.
23 (And the children of Israel went up

pable of holding a sword arrived in angry retaliation for the hideous nature of the deed that had been done. The report of the Levite (vss. 4-6) certainly recounted the awful deed that had been done, in that the rape of his concubine had brought about her death; and undoubtedly a homosexual assault on him would have done the same. However, it is also important to note that his account of the incident leaves himself blameless, whereas, the inspired historian's account makes it clear that he was not blameless in his actions.

9-25. Instead of taking the entire army, a **lot** was cast to determine to take one tenth of the men of the tribes against the city of Gibeah for the **folly** (wantonness or impiety) which they had committed in Israel. Noth (p. 105) regards the phrase **folly that they have wrought in Israel** as a technical term signifying a violation of the divine law. The other tribes of Israel sent a warning to the **tribe of Benjamin** to **put away evil from Israel** by delivering to them the Gibeonites who had committed this crime. However, the men of Benjamin prepared themselves for war and went out to battle against the children of Israel (vs. 14). Instead of responding to this wickedness with an act of justice, the Benjamites attempted to defend the wicked men of Gibeah. This further serves to help us understand the ungodly conditions that prevailed at that time. Pfeiffer (p. 263) notes that the term to **put away evil** in Jewish liturgy meant the complete removal of leaven on the eve of the Passover. Thus, the Israelites desired to extirpate evil from the corporateness of the nation by punishing the offenders with death.

The Benjamites mustered a force of twenty-six thousand men, plus seven hundred men who were inhabitants of Gibeah. **Among all this people there were seven hundred chosen men lefthanded** who **could sling stones.** Surprisingly, the outnumbered Benjamites were able to win the first two bloody battles, but they were decisively devastated in the third encounter. The hilly terrain in the vicinity of Gibeah favored a defensive force, rather than an attacking force. Great numbers of men were of limited value, since they could not be deployed effectively. The men of Israel went to the **house of God,** the rendering of Beth-el (RV, RSV), located about five miles from Mizpeh. Surprisingly, the Benjamites inflicted heavy casualties on the Israelite confederacy and killed twenty-two thousand men in the first engagement. The second engagement of the armies resulted in another defeat in which eighteen thousand men of Israel were slain. Though they had consulted the Lord up until this point, their failure would now drive them back to God in deep humility. Cundall states (p. 202), "To the tears of the day before were now added the discipline of fasting and offering of sacrifices, all of which suggest the sense of urgency with which they now sought the Lord."

and wept before the LORD until even, and asked counsel of the LORD, saying, Shall I go up again to battle against the children of Benjamin my brother? And the LORD said, Go up against him.)

24 And the children of Israel came near against the children of Benjamin the second day.

25 And Benjamin went forth against them out of Gĭb'e-ah the second day, and destroyed down to the ground of the children of Israel again eighteen thousand men; all these drew the sword.

26 ¶Then all the children of Israel, and all the people, went up, and came unto the house of God, and wept, and sat there before the LORD, and fasted that day until even, and offered burnt offerngs and peace offerings before the LORD.

27 And the children of Israel enquired of the LORD, (for the ark of the covenant of God was there in those days,

28 And Phĭn'e-has, the son of Ē-le-ā'zar, the son of Aaron, stood before it in those days,) saying, Shall I yet again go out to battle against the children of Benjamin my brother, or shall I cease? And the LORD said, Go up; for to morrow I will deliver them into thine hand.

29 ¶And Israel set liers in wait round about Gĭb'e-ah.

30 And the children of Israel went up against the children of Benjamin on the third day, and put themselves in array against Gĭb'e-ah, as at other times.

31 And the children of Benjamin went out against the people, and were drawn away from the city; and they began to smite of the people, and kill, as at other times, in the highways, of which one goeth up to the house of God, and the other to Gĭb'e-ah in the field, about thirty men of Israel.

32 And the children of Benjamin said, They are smitten down before us, as at the first. But the children of Israel said, Let us flee, and draw them from the city unto the highways.

33 And all the men of Israel rose up out of their place, and put themselves in array at Bā'al-tā'mar: and the liers in wait of Israel came forth out of their places, even out of the meadows of Gĭb'e-ah.

34 And there came against Gĭb'e-ah ten thousand chosen men out of all Israel, and the battle was sore: but they knew not that evil was near them.

35 And the LORD smote Benjamin before Israel: and the children of Israel destroyed of the Benjamites that day twenty and five thousand and an hundred men: all these drew the sword.

36 So the children of Benjamin saw that they were smitten: for the men of Israel gave place to the Benjamites, because they trusted unto the liers in wait which they had set beside Gĭb'e-ah.

37 And the liers in wait hasted, and rushed upon Gĭb'e-ah; and the liers in wait drew themselves along, and smote all the city with the edge of the sword.

26-48. Commentators differ on the location of the house of God (vs. 31) during this period. Joshua 18:10 and I Samuel 1:3 indicate that the ark of the covenant was at Shiloh. This does not, however, mean that it remained at Shiloh from the time of Joshua until the time of Eli. It is possible that the ark was moved from Shiloh to Beth-el and back to Shiloh again. Nevertheless, there is nothing in the text itself to indicate that there is any reason to be concerned about erroneous information. One of two things seems obvious. Either they returned to Beth-el where the ark was at that time in order to inquire of the Lord, or this time they went to Shiloh to the ark of the Lord in order to be sure of receiving the right information. The chronology of the passage is further complicated by the statement that **Phinehas,** the son of Eleazar, the son of Aaron, was the priest in those days. Phinehas was one of Israel's great heroes. As a young man, he had been commended by the Lord for his action at Shittim (Num 25); and he had taken a prominent role in the campaign against Midian (Num 31) and against the supposed apostasy of the eastern tribes (Josh 22). Thus, it is possible that this is the same Phinehas, who would now have been quite elderly.

This time God promised victory to Israel if they would go up against the Benjamites. In this engagement Israel used the same strategy that had been successfully employed by Joshua at Ai. They drew the Benjamites out of Gibeah to fight an Israelite army, which pretended to retreat, drawing the men away from the city. The Israelites then reformed at Baal-Tamar (unknown location) and the **liers in wait** came out from their ambush and attacked the city of Gibeah. The Israelites took the city and set it on fire. Seeing the smoke, the other Israelites stopped their pretended retreat, turned upon the Benjamites, and killed eighteen thousand of them. Verse 44 indicates that eighteen thousand men were killed by the ambush, five thousand more were killed in retreat, and two thousand more at **Gidom** (vs. 45). Therefore, a total of twenty-five thousand men that drew the sword were killed in all (compare the rounded figure in vs. 46 with the twenty-five thousand one hundred of vs. 45). The slaughter was so unbelievably extensive that only 600 men of Benjamin remained; and they fled unto the rock **Rimmon** where they remained for four months (vs. 47). These were the only Benjamites to escape.

In the meantime, the enraged Israelite army turned on all the cities of Benjamin and slaughtered the women and children until none remained (21:16). Wood (p. 151) correctly comments that the slaughter was entirely unreasonable. The enraged Israelites had obviously overreacted to the situation. They were undoubtedly upset by the atrocity on the concubine that led to the initial skirmish, and then they were even more enraged by the heavy losses that had been inflicted on them by the Benjamites. However, when the slaughter was finished, they finally realized that they had virtually annihilated one of the tribes of God's people.

38 Now there was an appointed sign between the men of Israel and the liers in wait, that they should make a great flame with smoke rise up out of the city.

39 And when the men of Israel retired in the battle, Benjamin began to smite *and* kill of the men of Israel about thirty persons: for they said, Surely they are smitten down before us, as *in* the first battle.

40 But when the flame began to arise up out of the city with a pillar of smoke, the Benjamites looked behind them, and, behold, the flame of the city ascended up to heaven.

41 And when the men of Israel turned again, the men of Benjamin were amazed: for they saw that evil was come upon them.

42 Therefore they turned *their backs* before the men of Israel unto the way of the wilderness; but the battle overtook them; and them which *came* out of the cities they destroyed in the midst of them.

43 *Thus* they inclosed the Benjamites round about, *and* chased them, *and* trode them down with ease over against Gīb'e-ah toward the sunrising.

44 And there fell of Benjamin eighteen thousand men; all these *were* men of valour.

45 And they turned and fled toward the wilderness unto the rock of Rimmon: and they gleaned of them in the highways five thousand men: and pursued hard after them unto Gī'dom, and slew two thousand men of them.

46 So that all which fell that day of Benjamin were twenty and five thousand men that drew the sword; all these *were* men of valour.

47 But six hundred men turned and fled to the wilderness unto the rock Rimmon, and abode in the rock Rimmon four months.

48 And the men of Israel turned again upon the children of Benjamin, and smote them with the edge of the sword, as well the men of *every* city, as the beast, and all that came to hand: also they set on fire all the cities that they came to.

CHAPTER 21

NOW the men of Israel had sworn in Mīz'peh, saying, There shall not any of us give his daughter unto Benjamin to wife.

2 And the people came to the house of God, and abode there till even before God, and lifted up their voices, and wept sore;

3 And said, O LORD God of Israel, why is this come to pass in Israel, that there should be to day one tribe lacking in Israel?

4 And it came to pass on the morrow, that the people rose early, and built there an altar, and offered burnt offerings and peace offerings.

5 And the children of Israel said, Who *is there* among all the tribes of Israel that came not up with the congregation unto the LORD? For they had made a great oath concerning him that came

21:1-15. The tribe of Benjamin was now in danger of extinction. There were six hundred men remaining, but they had no wives and no children. The Israelites, in anger, had vowed never to give their daughters in marriage to the tribe of Benjamin. However, the extensive slaughter that had resulted from this civil war was so serious that the people came **before God, and lifted up their voices, and wept sore** (vs. 2). When the anger and emotion of battle had passed, the Israelites realized what had happened to them. The amphictyonic league of twelve tribes who were supposed to be the people of God had so degenerated spiritually from the time of their enormous victories under Joshua that they were now in danger of annihilating one another. The spiritual decline of this period was paralleled by a political decline that had weakened the very foundation of the theocracy. If we are correct in assuming that this incident occurred early during the time of the judges, it is no wonder that Israel was so easily overrun by her enemies throughout that period. The enormity of this slaughter must have certainly weakened Israel for many generations to come.

515

not up to the LORD to Mĭz'peh, saying, He shall surely be put to death.

6 And the children of Israel repented them for Benjamin their brother, and said, There is one tribe cut off from Israel this day.

7 How shall we do for wives for them that remain, seeing we have sworn by the LORD that we will not give them of our daughters to wives?

8 ¶And they said, What one *is there* of the tribes of Israel that came not up to Mĭz'peh to the LORD? And, behold, there came none to the camp from Jā'-besh–gĭl'e-ad to the assembly.

9 For the people were numbered, and, behold, *there were* none of the inhabitants of Jā'besh–gĭl'e-ad there.

10 And the congregation sent thither twelve thousand men of the valiantest, and commanded them, saying, Go and smite the inhabitants of Jā'besh–gĭl'e-ad with the edge of the sword, with the women and the children.

11 And this *is* the thing that ye shall do, Ye shall utterly destroy every male, and every woman that hath lain by man.

12 And they found among the inhabitants of Jā'besh–gĭl'e-ad four hundred young virgins, that had known no man by lying with any male: and they brought them unto the camp to Shī'lōh, which *is* in the land of Canaan.

13 And the whole congregation sent *some* to speak to the children of Benjamin that *were* in the rock Rimmon, and to call peaceably unto them.

14 And Benjamin came again at that time; and they gave them wives which they had saved alive of the women of Jā'besh–gĭl'e-ad: and yet so they sufficed them not.

15 And the people repented them for Benjamin, because that the LORD had made a breach in the tribes of Israel.

16 ¶Then the elders of the congregation said, How shall we do for wives for them that remain, seeing the women are destroyed out of Benjamin?

17 And they said, There must be an inheritance for them that be escaped of Benjamin, that a tribe be not destroyed out of Israel.

18 Howbeit we may not give them wives of our daughters: for the children of Israel have sworn, saying, Cursed *be* he that giveth a wife to Benjamin.

19 Then they said, Behold, *there is* a feast of the LORD in Shī'lōh yearly *in a place* which *is* on the north side of Běth-el, on the east side of the highway that goeth up from Běth-el to Shě'chem, and on the south of Le-bō'nah.

20 Therefore they commanded the children of Benjamin, saying, Go and lie in wait in the vineyards;

21 And see, and, behold, if the daughters of Shī'lōh come out to dance in dances, then come ye out of the vineyards, and catch you every man his wife of the daughters of Shī'lōh, and go to the land of Benjamin.

22 And it shall be, when their fathers or their brethren come unto us to complain, that we will say unto them, Be favourable unto them for our sakes:

In the meantime, **the children of Israel repented** (vs. 6) for what they had done to the Benjamites, fearing that the tribe had been **cut off** permanently. Notice the sincerity and severity of oath-taking, in that they would not go against what they had **sworn by the LORD**. Finally, it was determined that no one had rallied to this battle from the city of **Jabesh-gilead**. In their anger, they had also sworn that anyone who did not respond to the call to assembly would be put to death. This would certainly explain why such a large number (four hundred thousand) responded to the call!

Now, to make things even worse, the army commanded **twelve thousand men** to smite the inhabitants of Jabesh-gilead (vs. 10). The Gileadites were descended from Manasseh, the grandson of Rachel, and thus, were related to the descendants of Benjamin, her son. Throughout Israel's history, there was always a close link between the tribe of Benjamin and Jabesh-gilead (cf. I Sam 11). The Israelite army attacked the city and killed all the men, the married women, and the children, sparing only **four hundred young virgins** (vs. 12). These girls were brought to the camp at Shiloh; and it was decided that they would be offered as wives to the six hundred men of Benjamin, who were still hiding in the Rock of Rimmon. Thus, peace was made between the Benjamites and the Israelites, and they returned to take the women of Jabesh-gilead. However, there were not enough of them for every man to have his own wife.

16-25. In order to solve the problem of the inequity of only four hundred women being available to marry the six hundred Benjamites, the **elders of the congregation** decided that there must be an **inheritance** for the Benjamites that a tribe **be not destroyed out of Israel**. Still under the ban of the curse, by which they had determined not to give their own wives to the Benjamites, it was decided that they would capture two hundred **daughters of Shiloh** when they came out to **dance in dances** at the **feast of the LORD**. It should be noted that Shiloh is referred to here as being **in the land of Canaan** (vs. 12).

Cundall (p. 210) correctly observes that the reference to Shiloh need not cause the unnecessary alarm that it has to many commentators. It is obvious that at this time, it was not the location of the tabernacle. A careful reading of the entire books of Joshua, Judges, and I Samuel seems to indicate that while the tabernacle was originally located at Shiloh, it was apparently moved to Beth-el and later was permanently moved back to Shiloh, where it was eventually destroyed by the Philistines. The reference to the **feast of the Lord** is to be taken as a local ceremony, rather than one clearly attributed to the Mosiac law. In other words, this seems to have been a time of great confusion and religious mixing. While Shiloh had been totally under the control of the Israelites (see Josh 18), it is now referred to as being in the **land of Canaan**. Therefore, it is most certain that Israelites were still living there and that the worship of Yahweh was still recognized there; yet it was under the influence and control of the Canaanites.

because we reserved not to each man his wife in the war: for ye did not give unto them at this time, *that* ye should be guilty.

23 And the children of Benjamin did so, and took *them* wives, according to their number, of them that danced, whom they caught: and they went and returned unto their inheritance, and repaired the cities, and dwelt in them.

24 And the children of Israel departed thence at that time, every man to his tribe and to his family, and they went out from thence every man to his inheritance.

25 In those days *there was* no king in Israel: every man did *that which was* right in his own eyes.

The shift of the scene of these events to the area of **Rimmon**, where the Benjamites were hiding, would make Shiloh a more likely choice for the subsequent kidnapping. Archaeological excavations have identified Shiloh as Seilun, about ten miles northeast of Beth-el. It was here at this Canaanite enclave within Israel that a pilgrimage or feast (Heb *chag*) would be the scene of the kidnapping at the time of the vintage harvest. Therefore, the two hundred remaining men of Benjamin rushed out of the vineyard and grabbed the women **whom they caught** and took them back to their cities which they then repaired and dwelt in (vs. 23). The statement in verse 24 indicates that after this incident the men of Israel went back to their own inheritance.

While it is overlooked in most commentaries, the term **inheritance** (Heb *nachalah*) seems to be crucial to the understanding of the appendices. In the first section, the Danites gave up their inheritance and by ungodly means took another. In this account, the Benjamites nearly lost their inheritance at the hands of their own brothers. The recurring theme, then, in the book of Judges has to do with Israel's inheritance, which she is in danger of losing because of her violation of God's law. In the law of Moses, the inheritance was apportioned by God Himself and then determined by lot under the leadership of Joshua. However, after the total victory under Joshua, Israel had now fallen into spiritual decline and was, therefore, in danger of losing her inheritance. The theological concept underlying the proper understanding of the book of Judges is that the land belonged to Jehovah and that He had the right to apportion it to the people as He chose. The subsequent invasion of Israel's enemies, the resulting oppressions, and the threatened annihilation which culminated in the activities of the Philistines, were also God's means of challenging Israel's inheritance. Just because He had given her the land did not mean that she had an unconditional right to its blessings if she chose to live in rebellion to His laws.

The entire sweep of the Old Testament seems to make it clear that God's unconditional covenant with Abraham (Gen 15) guaranteed the land to Israel, but the conditional covenant (Deut 28) determined whether or not Israel would be allowed to remain there in blessing determined by her obedience to God's law. Therefore, under the leadership of Joshua the standard of the Law was maintained without compromise, and the blessing of the Lord was abundant. However, in the time of the judges religious and spiritual compromise and deterioration were so prevalent that the blessing was removed and Israel found herself temporarily under the curse of God. The roller-coaster effect that resulted meant that Israel, because of her disobedience, was unable to maintain a high level of stability throughout the times of the judges, Eli, Samuel, and Saul. Not until the time of David, and the centralizing of the nation under his leadership, would Israel again enjoy the abundant blessing of God.

Thus, the concluding statement of the book reiterates the self-justified form of situation ethics that was prevalent in Israel at that time. **In those days there was no king in Israel: every man did that which was right in his own eyes** (vs. 25). In other words, the book closes with the reflection by the author on the absence of strong leadership and the lack of spiritual discernment that had led to the near total disintegration of Israel's uniqueness as a nation. The tragic comment of the inspired historian who wrote the book of Judges notes that a nation unified under Moses, and miraculously victorious under Joshua, had now fallen into sin, defeat, and disunity. Thus, the book of Judges gives us a picture of the tragic results of sinful compromise with an ungodly world. Fortunately, the appendix of the book of Ruth indicates that God was still at work among His people, even during this dark hour. A ray of hope was about to dawn through which God's man would come to rule His people.

BIBLIOGRAPHY

Bruce, F. F. Judges. In *New Bible Commentary*. Ed. by F. Davidson. Grand Rapids: Eerdmans, 1954.

Burney, C. F. *The Book of Judges*. 2nd ed. London: Rivingtons, 1930.

*Cassel, Paul. Judges. In *Commentary on the Holy Scriptures*. Ed. by J. P. Lange. Grand Rapids: Zondervan, reprinted, 1871.

Cohen, A. Joshua and Judges. In the *Soncino Bible*. London: Soncino Press, 1950.

Cooke, G. A. The Book of Judges. In *The Cambridge Bible*. Cambridge: The University Press, 1913.

*Cundall, A. E. Judges. In the *Tyndale Old Testament Commentary*. Downers Grove: InterVarsity Press, 1968.

*Davis, J. J. *Conquest and Crisis: Studies in Joshua, Judges, and Ruth*. Grand Rapids: Baker, 1969.

Douglas, G. *The Book of Judges*. Edinburgh: T. & T. Clark, 1881.

Garstang, J. *Joshua-Judges*. London: Constable and Co., 1931.

*Keil, C. F. and F. Delitzsch. Joshua, Judges and Ruth. In *Biblical Commentary on the Old Testament*. Vol. IV. Grand Rapids: Eerdmans, reprinted, 1950.

McKenzie, J. *The World of the Judges*. Englewood Cliffs, N.J.: Prentice Hall, 1966.

Moore, G. F. A Critical and Exegetical Commentary on Judges. In *International Critical Commentary*. New York: Charles Scribner's Sons, 1901.

Myers, J. M. The Book of Judges. In *The Interpreter's Bible*. Vol. 2. New York: Abingdon, 1953.

Pfeiffer, C. F. Judges. In *Wycliffe Bible Commentary*. Chicago: Moody Press, 1961.

Rideout, S. *Lectures on the Books of Judges and Ruth*. New York: Loizeaux Brothers, 1958.

Simpson, C. A. *Composition of the Book of Judges*. Oxford: Blackwell, 1957.

Thatcher, G. W. Judges and Ruth. In *The Century Bible*. London: Caxton, 1904.

Watson, R. A. Judges and Ruth. In *The Expositor's Bible*. New York: Armstrong & Sons, 1899.

*Wood, L. *Distressing Days of the Judges*. Grand Rapids: Zondervan, 1975.

RUTH

INTRODUCTION

Title. The name of the book comes from its heroine, Ruth the Moabitess. Her name is derived from the Hebrew word meaning "friendship." Like the book of Esther, it is named after the woman who is its principal character and in whose life the providence of God is dramatically shown. In spite of her humble origin, Ruth plays a very important part in the historical development of the Old Testament, as the great-grandmother of King David (4:18) and an ancestress in the line of Jesus Christ (Mt 1:5). Keil and Delitzsch (p. 466) state: "The genealogical proof of the descent of David from Perez through Boaz and the Moabitess Ruth forms not only the end, but the starting-point, of the history contained in the book" (*Biblical Commentary on the Old Testament*).

Date and Authorship. Scholars have dated the book of Ruth from the time of Samuel (Talmud, *Baba Bathra*) all the way down to the third century B.C. Morris (p. 229) observes that most scholars prefer a late date for the authorship of Ruth; then he proceeds to discredit their conclusions in favor of the early date (*Tyndale Old Testament Commentaries*). Conservative scholars generally agree that the book was written during the reign of David.

E. J. Young (*Introduction to the Old Testament*, p. 358) notes that the absence of Solomon and later Judaean kings in the genealogy definitely indicates that the book was written no later than the time of David. MacDonald (p. 258) notes that Samuel may have been the author, though there is nothing in the text itself to verify this (*New Bible Commentary*). He also observes that Samuel would have been quite young at best during the time when these events took place. If Samuel were the author of the book of Judges, then it would better stand to reason that he probably was also the author of the book of Ruth. It is interesting to note that Josephus states that Ruth lived during the days of Eli (*Antiq.* vs. 9, 1). However, Salmon, the husband of Rahab, is stated to be the father of Boaz; and this would point to a much earlier time, the period of the judges, placing the events of the book closer to the time of Gideon.

Many have assumed that the inclusion of the Davidic genealogy at the end of the book proves that it was not written prior to the time of David. However, this is not necessarily so; for the genealogy could have been added by another inspired writer at a later time. The relationship of Ruth to the book of Judges is noted in the very first verse. Josephus' reference to twenty-two books of the Old Testament canon seems to indicate that Ruth was originally considered an appendix to the book of Judges, as Lamentations to Jeremiah. Thus, Ruth serves as a contrast to the tragic conditions that prevailed during the period of the judges.

There can be no doubt that Ruth serves as a "bridge" from the book of Judges to the books of Samuel. It provides a behind-the-scenes account of how the people lived. As great nations and leaders rose and fell, life among the common people continued at a normal pace. The agrarian culture, the labor of the land, rural customs, love, marriage, family, and simple faith in God are all depicted as vital ingredients of this story.

The argument for a later date of the book of Ruth is based on two major considerations: (1) Aramaisms which are characteristic of late Hebrew; and (2) the inclusion of Ruth in the Hebrew Bible in the "Writings" (*Kethubīm*) and among the five "scrolls" (*Megillōth*). The argument based on Aramaisms is weak at best for several reasons: (1) Aramaic-type words are now known from the middle Babylonian period dating as far back as 1400 B.C. and parallel to the time of the judges (cf. D. J. Wiseman, "Studies in Aramaic Lexicography," *Journal of the American Oriental Society*, 82, pp. 290-299). (2) The book contains many archaic forms of Hebrew morphology which are difficult to explain if the document is to be dated in or near the post-Exilic period. In addition, the literary and linguistic style of Ruth is far more like that of Judges and Samuel, rather than that of later historical books such as Ezra or Chronicles. (3) The alleged Aramaisms are found only in the speech of the characters, not in the author's narrative. Thus, rustic rural people talk in a rustic dialect of their own, reflecting the genuine antiquity of the story. The context also indicates that the author explains and updates many of the previous customs which were no longer in vogue. Many of these customs are paralleled in the Nuzi tablets which date from ca. 1500 B.C. and further substantiate the early date for the book's composition. (4) The marriage of a Jew to a Moabite girl would certainly fit better with the chaotic conditions of the period of the judges rather than the severe separatism of the post-Exilic period of Ezra-Nehemiah, when marriages to foreigners were strictly prohibited. Cassel (in J. P. Lange, *Commentary on the Holy Scriptures*, p. 34) points out that the positive kindness shown to foreigners fits best with the reign of David, who commended his own parents to the king of Moab in a time of crisis (I Sam 22:3). It should also be noted that the office of the "kinsman" (Heb *gō'ēl*) is very early and certainly does not fit well with the late date view on the authorship of the book.

Morris correctly observes that the change in style and expression from the narrative of the author to the speeches of the characters probably betrays an underlying poetic original, though the present story is in the form of prose (Ruth, in *Tyndale Old Testament Commentaries*, p. 242). While on the whole the book is written in classical Hebrew, there can be no doubt that it contains some very unusual forms. The book's later inclusion in the *Megillōth*, along with Esther, Song of Solomon,

Ecclesiastes, and Lamentations, also recognizes its poetic-like form. Also it should be noted that the story takes place in four definite scenes, which may indicate four distinct acts of an original poetic play: Act one: in Moab; Act two: in the fields of Beth-lehem; Act three: at the threshing floor of Boaz; Act four: in the city gate. Thus, the inspired author has given us a four-act romantic drama which conveys the original conversations of the characters and the primitive cultural customs of the original historic incident. This love-poem, similar to that of the Song of Solomon, is expressed as a historic narrative similar to the story of Esther. Each of these should be viewed as literal and historic accounts traced by the literary genius of their authors and under the revelation and guidance of the Holy Spirit.

The inclusion of the book of Ruth in the five scrolls which were read in the synagogues on five special occasions during the year, therefore, seems to be a matter of liturgical, rather than historical development. Their order placed Ruth in the second position, where it was related to the feast later known as Pentecost, the second of five special Jewish festivals. The theological significance of this positioning is clear in Christian theological interpretation. Since the book of Ruth presents a practical picture of the Kinsman-Redeemer and his marriage to the bride whom he has redeemed, the Christian significance of Pentecost becomes obvious! Christ is now the Redeemer who has come to purchase His bride, and on the Day of Pentecost the church begins! As Boaz would come forth from Beth-lehem to take a Gentile bride, so Jesus would

also come forth from Beth-lehem and take His gentile bride; i.e., the church!

Theme and Purpose. The story of Ruth is a beautiful pastoral story. The main character, Ruth, is one of the key women of the Bible. The *PRACTICAL* purpose of the book is to teach the providence of God in blessing His children (even in finding the right mate). The story reveals the love of God toward women, as well as men, and makes it clear that God has a special and unique purpose for the family. The *THEOLOGICAL* purpose of the book is to teach the biblical concept of redemption. The Kinsman-Redeemer serves as a picture of the person and work of Christ on behalf of His bride. The *gō'ēl* could redeem a widow, an orphan, or a slave. In order to meet the qualifications of the *levirate* and *gō'ēl* he had to be: (1) related to the individual; (2) free; (3) able to pay the price of redemption; (4) willing to pay the price; (5) prepared to marry the widow. In a very similar sense, Christ became our kinsman after the flesh through taking on a human nature by which He became related to us. He was free from the sin which had bound us. His shed blood was the price of our redemption; and He alone, by His sinless life, was able to pay the price. In the Garden of Gethsemane He made it clear that He was willing to pay that price, and the result of His redemption was His marriage to the church, His bride. The *HISTORICAL* purpose of the book was to trace the ancestry of King David and to verify that ten generations had passed since the illegitimate conception of Pharez. In contrast to the book of Judges, the book of Ruth gives us a glimpse of genuine piety among the true followers of Jehovah.

OUTLINE

COMMENTARY

I. LOVE'S RESOLVE: GOD'S DEALING. (SCENE: MOAB). 1:1-22.

A. Departure of Elimelech. 1:1-5.

NOW it came to pass in the days when the judges ruled, that there was a famine in the land. And a certain man of Bĕth–lĕhĕm–jūdah went to sojourn in the country of Moab, he, and his wife, and his two sons.

1:1. The book opens with the definite statement that the events recorded therein took place in **the days when the judges ruled** (RV, "judged"). This would place the events between the fourteenth and eleventh centuries B.C. On the background of the judges see the commentary on Judges. No explanation is given to the cause of the **famine.** However, the turbulent conditions of the period of the judges would certainly give adequate explanation for such an occurrence. **Beth-lehem-judah** is so designated to distinguish it from other cities of the same name. It was from this town, the same place where David and Jesus would later be born, that the family around whom the story centers originates. Because of the desperation wrought by the famine, the husband decided to take his wife and two sons into the **country of Moab,** or "the field (Heb *sadeh*) of Moab." The reference may be to the rich pasture land of the rolling plateau south of the Arnon River, or it may possibly refer to the unsettled condition of Moab as a predominantly rural country at that time. Moab was the son of Lot by an incestuous relation between him and his daughter (Gen 19:36). Throughout Israel's history the Moabites often antagonized the Israelites.

2-3. The decision to leave their native Judah and emigrate to Moab was made by **Elimelech** ("my God is King"). Thus the story seems to view him as a believer who disobeys God by forsaking his inheritance within the land of Israel, and thus accounting for the tragic consequences which followed. Naomi's name means "pleasant," and their sons' names interestingly were **Mahlon** ("puny") and **Chilion** ("pining"). Thus, their early deaths seem to be attributed to lifelong physical weaknesses. The term **Ephrathites** refers to the ancient name of Beth-lehem ("house of bread"), as noted in Genesis 35:19. Since the total time of their residence in Moab is designated as **about ten years** (vs. 4), including the marriage and death of Naomi's sons, it seems almost certain that Elimelech died soon after their arrival.

4-5. The two sons **took them wives of the women of Moab,** probably indicating that they contracted marriages on their own initiative. Nothing in the passage indicates Naomi's involvement in arranging for these marriages; however, her close personal relationship to the girls afterwards indicates definite intimate involvement with them. Jewish commentators unanimously view this passage as a silent protest against intermarriage. Although the law did not directly prohibit marriage to a Moabite, there was a prohibition against admitting Moabites into the congregation of Israel and the offspring of a marriage with a Moabite was not to be admitted to the congregation until the tenth generation (cf. Deut 23:3), indicating the purpose of the ten generations genealogy which closes the book. Certainly the entire incident is typical of the spiritual compromise of the Israelites during the period of the judges. **Orpah** (perhaps derived from Heb *'orep*) apparently means "stiff-necked," while Ruth means "friendship." As the tragedy unfolded, Mahlon and Chilion also died; and Naomi was left alone with her two daughters-in-law.

B. Despair of Naomi. 1:6-13.

6-8. After ten years of tragedy, Naomi decided to **return** to her own country where she had now heard that **the Lord had visited his people,** probably indicating a time of deliverance under one of the judges (most likely Gideon). The spiritual significance of the story cannot be overlooked as the drama unfolds. A man who knows better leaves his inheritance among the people of God to dwell in safety with his enemies. There he dies. Eventually, his two sons marry gentile wives and both of the sons die also. Now the scene centers on the tragic lives of these three women. It almost unfolds like an ancient Near Eastern soap opera. In desperation, Naomi urges her daughters-in-law to **Go, return each to her mother's house,** rather than return with her to the **land of Judah.**

9-10. The invocation in the name of the **Lord** (Jehovah) would indicate that His name was at least familiar in some sense to the girls. Naomi's desire that they find **rest** (Heb *menûchah,*

---

2 And the name of the man *was* E-lĭm'e-lĕch, and the name of his wife Naomi, and the name of his two sons Mäh'lon and Chĭl'ĭ-on, Ĕph'rath-ītes of Bĕth-lehĕm-jūdah. And they came into the country of Moab, and continued there.

3 And E-lĭm'e-lĕch Naomi's husband died; and she was left, and her two sons.

4 And they took them wives of the women of Moab; the name of the one *was* Ôr'pah, and the name of the other Ruth: and they dwelled there about ten years.

5 And Mäh'lon and Chĭl'ĭ-on died also both of them; and the woman was left of her two sons and her husband.

6 ¶Then she arose with her daughters in law, that she might return from the country of Moab: for she had heard in the country of Moab how that the Lord had visited his people in giving them bread.

7 Wherefore she went forth out of the place where she was, and her two daughters in law with her; and they went on the way to return unto the land of Judah.

8 And Naomi said unto her two daughters in law, Go, return each to her mother's house: the Lord deal kindly with you, as ye have dealt with the dead, and with me.

9 The Lord grant you that ye may find rest, each *of you* in the house of her husband. Then she kissed them; and they lifted up their voice, and wept.

10 And they said unto her, Surely we will return with thee unto thy people.

11 And Naomi said, Turn again, my daughters: why will ye go with me? *are* there yet *any more* sons in my womb, that they may be your husbands?

12 Turn again, my daughters, go *your way;* for I am too old to have an husband. If I should say, I have hope, *if* I should have an husband also to night, and should also bear sons;

13 Would ye tarry for them till they were grown? would ye stay for them from having husbands? nay, my daughters; for it grieveth me much for your sakes that the hand of the LORD is gone out against me.

14 And they lifted up their voice, and wept again: and Ôr'pah kissed her mother in law; but Ruth clave unto her.

15 And she said, Behold, thy sister in law is gone back unto her people, and unto her gods: return thou after thy sister in law.

16 And Ruth said, Intreat me not to leave thee, *or* to return from following after thee: for whither thou goest, I will go; and where thou lodgest, I will lodge: thy people *shall be* my people, and thy God my God:

17 Where thou diest, will I die, and there will I be buried: the LORD do so to me, and more also, *if ought* but death part thee and me.

18 When she saw that she was stedfastly minded to go with her, then she left speaking unto her.

meaning "place of rest") indicates that she hoped they would find a better situation than she could provide for them. The very personal details of this account indicate that these women were able to communicate in a bilingual manner and that they shared a similar concept of God. The reference to the **house of her husband** cannot refer to Naomi's sons and must be taken to mean that she genuinely hoped that they would have the opportunity of remarriage, and that she hoped that the second marriage would be more blessed than the first.

11-13. Initially they insisted on returning with her, but Naomi's reminder that there were not **any more sons . . . that they may be your husbands** evidently caused Orpah to decide to return. Naomi's statement is an indication of the concept of the Israelite law of levirate marriage which required a man to marry the widow of his deceased brother and to raise a family in memory of his brother's name (Deut 25:5; Mt 22:23-28). There can be no doubt that the girls understood the implication of this concept. For an excellent and thorough discussion of the concept see D. A. Leggett, *The Levirate and Goel Institutions in the Old Testament,* where he distinguishes between the legal stipulations of the levirate institution in Deuteronomy 25 and the practical application of this law in the story of Ruth. Naomi further explained the extremity of their plight by reminding the girls that even if she were to remarry immediately and bear a son, they would never wait for him to be fully grown to marry their brother's widows. Therefore, she concluded that it would be better for them to return to their own families, since she sensed that the **hand of the LORD** was against her. There can be no doubt that Naomi viewed her tragic experiences as an act of God's judgment upon her family.

C. Decision of Ruth. 1:14-22.

14-18. As the drama further unfolds we find that these three women **wept again.** The touching personal details of the story reveal the genuineness and reality of the account. As they stood there crying, **Orpah kissed** Naomi goodbye and left her, but **Ruth clave unto her,** i.e., she literally clung to her mother-in-law. Naomi reminded her that her sister-in-law had **gone back unto her people** and also unto **her gods** and she further bid her do the same! This was certainly the lowest point of Naomi's spiritual life and serves as a fitting climax to the weakness that was so obvious in her family. MacDonald observes that "the worship of Jehovah made no abiding impression on Orpah and Naomi clearly knew it, whereas Jehovah was deliberately invoked by Ruth indicating her choice of the God of Israel" (Ruth, in the *New Bible Commentary,* p. 259). Ruth's vow not to leave Naomi was in itself a confession of her faith in the God of Israel. **Entreat me not to leave thee** means "do not insist that I return." Ruth promised Naomi that wherever she went and wherever she lodged she would also go and that **thy people shall be my people, and thy God my God.** Thereby, Ruth clearly proclaimed her desire to become a follower of the Lord and of the people of Israel.

While these words are often quoted out of context by Christian couples in wedding ceremonies, they are not totally inappropriate at such a time. This verse is probably the strongest expression of personal commitment by one human being to another found anywhere in Scripture. It certainly reveals the genuine spiritual decision and the character of Ruth's determination to do that which was right. Her correct decision would lead to untold blessing in the future! Finally, Naomi sensed Ruth's sincere determination to return with her to Beth-lehem and gave up her attempt to dissuade her. Pfeiffer notes that it was a testimony to the influence of her mother-in-law that Ruth was willing to entrust herself to the God whom she worshiped (Ruth in the *Wycliffe Bible Commentary,* p. 269).

19 ¶So they two went until they came to Běth-lehěm. And it came to pass, when they were come to Běth-lehěm, that all the city was moved about them, and they said, *Is* this Naomi?
20 And she said unto them, Call me not Naomi, call me Mâ'ra: for the Almighty hath dealt very bitterly with me.
21 I went out full, and the LORD hath brought me home again empty: why *then* call ye me Naomi, seeing the LORD hath testified against me, and the Almighty hath afflicted me?
22 So Naomi returned, and Ruth the Moabitess, her daughter in law, with her, which returned out of the country of Moab: and they came to Běth-lehěm in the beginning of barley harvest.

CHAPTER 2
AND Naomi had a kinsman of her husband's, a mighty man of wealth, of the family of E-lǐm'e-lěch; and his name *was* Bō'ăz.
2 And Ruth the Moabitess said unto Naomi, Let me now go to the field, and glean ears of corn after *him* in whose sight I shall find grace. And she said unto her, Go, my daughter.
3 And she went, and came, and gleaned in the field after the reapers: and her hap was to light on a part of the field *belonging* unto Bō'ăz, who *was* of the kindred of E-lǐm'e-lěch.

19-22. Upon their return to Beth-lehem (a journey of about fifty or sixty miles), they were welcomed by the people of the city, who questioned: **Is this Naomi?** To which she responded: **Call me not Naomi, call me Mara.** The meaning of Naomi is pleasant, whereas Mara means bitter. In other words, Naomi was asking that they not call her a name which was no longer true of her personal experiences. This clearly indicates the interchangeable use of names in the ancient Near East based upon one's life-changing experiences. Naomi's statement that the **LORD hath testified against me** reveals again that she interpreted her bitter experiences in Moab as God's punishment for forsaking the family's inheritance in the community of Israel. The chapter ends with the note that they returned to Beth-lehem **in the beginning of barley harvest,** that is, at the time of the spring harvest in April. Thus, the majority of the events in this book actually cover only a matter of a few weeks.

II. LOVE'S RESPONSE: RUTH'S DETERMINATION. (SCENE: FIELDS OF BETH-LEHEM). 2:1-23.

A. Destiny of Meeting Boaz. 2:1-14.

2:1-3. From this point on the story centers around Boaz, the "friend" (Heb *mōyda'*) and "kinsman" (Heb *gō'ēl*) of the family of Elimelech. The designation **a mighty man of wealth** (Heb *chayil*) may be rendered "mighty man of valour" but more appropriately indicates a "man of property or fame." The fact that he was related to the **family of Elimelech** indicates the basis of his kinsmanship to Naomi through her marriage. The term **family** probably denotes a larger group of relatives, similar to a clan. There can be no doubt that in the context Boaz appears as a powerful landowner who becomes the potential hero of the drama because of his position and relationship to the widow Ruth. In reality, to the Hebrew mind, the story actually centers on the descendancy of the family's seed more than it does on the plight of Ruth herself, though the two are certainly interrelated. Thus, the story has a double plot related to the perpetuity of the family line as it affects both Naomi and Ruth.

The significance of the *gō'ēl* (Kinsman-Redeemer) is central to the entire book. Leggett (p. 292ff.) traces the origin of the concept of the *gō'ēl* to that of a trustee of Yahweh's possession of the land. Thus, he could act to recover property lost to the family (Lev 25:25; Jer 32:7) or to emancipate a fellow family member whose economic plight had necessitated selling himself into slavery (Lev 25:48-49). During the period of the judges the possession of the *gō'ēl* appears to have been one of care and protection of the childless widow and the possibility of voluntary exercise of a Levirate. Thus, the **kinsman** was acting as the agent of Yahweh by demonstrating his covenant loyalty to the purpose of God among His people. Leggett (p. 298) observes: "In the actions of Boaz as *Goel* we see foreshadowed the saving work of Jesus Christ, his later descendant. As Boaz had the right of redemption and yet clearly was under no obligation to intervene on Ruth's behalf, so it is with Christ." Therefore, the concept of redemption, which is essential to the understanding of the work of Christ, is clearly illustrated by the example of Boaz in this account.

Ruth is referred to as **the Moabitess** five times in this book. As a daughter of her people's enemies she was definitely considered a Gentile. Both her character and that of Boaz immediately rise to the surface of the drama. Realizing their plight, Ruth took the initiative to volunteer to go to the fields to **glean.**

"Gleaning" was an activity of the poorest of the people who would follow reapers in the fields and pick up the scraps that remained. Gleaning was a right guaranteed to the poor (Lev 19:9) and to widows (Deut 24:19). Nevertheless, she hoped to **find grace** from a landowner who would allow her to glean in his field. This probably indicates that, typical of the time of the judges, not all Israelites were devout adherents of the Law. As the reapers passed through the fields harvesting the crop by hand, some small amounts of scraps would be left behind for the gleaners to gather for themselves.

Now comes the interesting turn of events in the story as it was her **hap** to enter the field which belonged to Boaz. From a human standpoint she coincidentally happened upon the right field by chance. However, the story makes it clear that in the divine providence of God she was led to exactly the right place at the right time.

4 ¶And, behold, Bō′ăz came from Bĕth–lehĕm, and said unto the reapers, The LORD be with you. And they answered him, The LORD bless thee.

5 Then said Bō′ăz unto his servant that was set over the reapers, Whose damsel is this?

6 And the servant that was set over the reapers answered and said, It is the Moabitish damsel that came back with Naomi out of the country of Moab:

7 And she said, I pray you, let me glean and gather after the reapers among the sheaves: so she came, and hath continued even from the morning until now, that she tarried a little in the house.

4-7. Morris (p. 270) observes that the field referred to in this account was probably a common place whose ownership was shared by many people. Therefore the Hebrew text indicates that she came to the **part of the field belonging unto Boaz** (vs. 3). While she was gleaning there **Boaz came from Bethlehem** to oversee the day's activities. The interjection, **behold,** calls the reader's attention to the vivid intrusion of the hero and may be translated "then, look . . ." (Berkeley). This would fit with the concept of viewing the book as a four-part drama. The employer-employee relationship in the passage is outstanding as Boaz pronounces a blessing on the workers and they in turn pronounce a blessing on him. Upon his arrival he immediately noticed this gentile girl, asking: **Whose damsel is this?** There appears to be a definite play on words here as Boaz addresses his **servant,** inquiring about the **damsel** (servant-girl). The question **whose . . . is** is similar to that which Saul asked about David (I Sam 17:55), meaning that he was inquiring as to her legal right to be there in relation to which family she was from. Pfeiffer (p. 269) takes the phrase, **It is the Moabitish damsel,** to be a derogatory response, meaning: "It is that foreigner who came back with Naomi from Moab!" The servant then explained to Boaz why he allowed her to remain in the field and recounted her industrious effort, noting that she **tarried a little in the house,** indicating that she had worked hard and spent only a limited amount of time for rest and refreshment in the hut erected in the field.

8 Then said Bō′ăz unto Ruth, Hearest thou not, my daughter? Go not to glean in another field, neither go from hence, but abide here fast by my maidens:

9 Let thine eyes be on the field that they do reap, and go thou after them: have I not charged the young men that they shall not touch thee? and when thou art athirst, go unto the vessels, and drink of that which the young men have drawn.

10 Then she fell on her face, and bowed herself to the ground, and said unto him, Why have I found grace in thine eyes, that thou shouldest take knowledge of me, seeing I am a stranger?

11 And Bō′ăz answered and said unto her, It hath fully been shewed me, all that thou hast done unto thy mother in law since the death of thine husband: and how thou hast left thy father and thy mother, and the land of thy nativity, and art come unto a people which thou knewest not heretofore.

12 The LORD recompense thy work, and a full reward be given thee of the LORD God of Israel, under whose wings thou art come to trust.

13 Then she said, Let me find favour in thy sight, my lord; for that thou hast comforted me, and for that thou hast spoken friendly unto thine handmaid,

8-14. Willing to fulfill his responsibility as the family gō′ēl, Boaz encouraged her to **abide here fast,** i.e., close by his own **maidens** (the girls for whose provision he was also responsible). The wealthy landowner went on to explain that she would be protected while in his field and that he had **charged the young men** not to touch her. He further noted that when she was thirsty she was to **go unto the vessels, and drink.** In other words, he was taking pity upon the plight of a poor foreign girl. She had every reason to believe that he might reject her but had every hope that he would accept her. The flow of the narrative seems to imply love-at-first-sight. While the final outcome is held in abeyance, the hope of the reader is that he will fall in love with the stranger, marry her, and redeem her from her plight of childless widowhood. Thus, not only is Boaz a type of Christ, the bridegroom from Beth-lehem, but Ruth is a type of the church, the undeserving gentile bride, who had nothing with which to commend herself to her master.

Ruth's personal humility and godliness as a foreigner who had come to trust in the God of Israel was itself a retort at the unspiritual condition which prevailed among the Israelites at that time! Her question, **Why have I found grace in thine eyes?** focuses our attention upon the ultimate intention of God and begins to unveil His universal love for all people. Boaz indicated that he was willing to show every kindness to Ruth because of the kindness that she had shown to her mother-in-law. The term **kindness** (Heb chesed) indicates the personal expression of godliness on the part of one servant of the Lord to another. Wright (Old Testament and Theology, p. 75) notes that it is the eternal loving-kindness of God expressed in His eternal covenant on

though I be not like unto one of thine handmaidens.

14 And Bō′ăz said unto her, At mealtime come thou hither, and eat of the bread, and dip thy morsel in the vinegar. And she sat beside the reapers: and he reached her parched *corn*, and she did eat, and was sufficed, and left.

15 And when she was risen up to glean, Bō′ăz commanded his young men, saying, Let her glean even among the sheaves, and reproach her not:

16 And let fall also *some* of the handfuls of purpose for her, and leave *them*, that she may glean *them*, and rebuke her not.

17 So she gleaned in the field until even, and beat out that she had gleaned: and it was about an ephah of barley.

18 ¶And she took *it* up, and went into the city: and her mother in law saw what she had gleaned: and she brought forth, and gave to her that she had reserved after she was sufficed.

19 And her mother in law said unto her, Where hast thou gleaned to day? and where wroughtest thou? blessed be he that did take knowledge of thee. And she shewed her mother in law with whom she had wrought, and said, The man's name with whom I wrought to day *is* Bō′ăz.

20 And Naomi said unto her daughter in law, Blessed *be* he of the LORD, who hath not left off his kindness to the living and to the dead. And Naomi said unto her, The man *is* near of kin unto us, one of our next kinsmen.

21 And Ruth the Moabitess said, He said unto me also, Thou shalt keep fast by my young men, until they have ended all my harvest.

22 And Naomi said unto Ruth her daughter in law, *It is* good, my daughter, that thou go out with his maidens, that they meet thee not in any other field.

23 So she kept fast by the maidens of Bō′ăz to glean unto the end of barley harvest and of wheat harvest; and dwelt with her mother in law.

behalf of the poor and needy among His people. See also Snaith's discussion of the covenant-love of God in *Distinctive Ideas of the Old Testament*, pp. 94-130. It is also possible that Boaz encouraged Ruth to remain in his field where he might keep an eye on her not only for the purpose of protection, but possibly because of a personal interest in her. The impression is definitely given that he has set his heart upon her from the beginning. Boaz also recognized that she had become a believer in Yahweh **the LORD God of Israel, under whose wings** she had **come to trust** and was now a participant (at least to some degree) in the blessings of the covenant community. Pfeiffer (p. 270) observes: "Ruth had found a place of refuge in Israel's God." Perhaps because of her poverty, her gentile nationality, or her heathen background, she considered his kindness to the others as understandable; but his kindness to her was pure grace!

B. Definite provision for Ruth. 2:15-23.

15-17. Not only had she been impressed with him, but he was now impressed with her! Therefore, Boaz commanded his servants, **Let her glean even among the sheaves,** meaning that she could now harvest the unpicked crop for herself. The Law gave the gleaners the right to follow the reapers, but grace would give her the right to share in his possession! Furthermore, they were to drop **handfuls of purpose** for her. We would say "handfuls on purpose" meaning that they were to literally drop handfuls of grain for her to glean. Thus, the kinsman's provision was more than adequate. One must imagine himself to be in Ruth's position in order to appreciate the significance of the story at this point. A childless, widowed foreign girl returns to her mother-in-law's homeland and chooses a field, happening to meet the one man who can change her future and her fate. Not only is the encounter of their meeting a pleasant one, but she immediately becomes the object of his special grace. What a beautiful picture of the love of Christ and His provision for His bride!

18-23. The average receipt of a gleaner was only enough to support a family for one day, and, therefore, the process had to be repeated constantly. However, Ruth returned home with an **ephah of barley** (approximately three pecks) which would have been enough to support them for about five days. Naomi was certainly surprised by such a large amount and was even more thrilled to discover that Ruth had already met Boaz. Her blessing to the Lord indicated that He had extended His **kindness to the living and to the dead.** This is the only reference in the Old Testament to this attitude and action (Heb *chesed*) being extended toward the dead; and in this sole instance it refers to the memory of her husband and sons. Her excitement was due to one simple fact: **The man is near of kin** (Heb *qarōb*) **unto us, one of our next kinsmen.** *Qarōb* indicates "near" in time or place. Morris (p. 281) is undoubtedly correct when he observes that Naomi already had in mind the possibility of the way the events might eventually to turn out. In other words, it was more than she could have hoped for in one day. Ruth, her Moabite daughter-in-law, had met the one man that could redeem them both! He could potentially marry Ruth and produce children, thus preserving the seed of Naomi's husband and her son. She further recognized that Boaz was not only **near of kin**, but that he was also one of their **next kinsman**, meaning that he was one of the closest relatives of Elimelech in the line of redemption. The line of relationship included brothers, then uncles, then male cousins. The responsibility of the kinsman was to ensure that property remained within the family and, therefore, the obligation rested upon him to marry the widow of a fellow family member who had died childless. Pleased by the results that had already transpired, Ruth was encouraged to keep **fast by the maidens of Boaz** until the end of the wheat and barley harvest.

CHAPTER 3

THEN Naomi her mother in law said unto her, My daughter, shall I not seek rest for thee, that it may be well with thee?

2 And now *is* not Bō'ăz of our kindred, with whose maidens thou wast? Behold, he winnoweth barley to night in the threshingfloor.

The meaning of *gō'ēl* is derived from the verb (Heb *ga'al*) meaning "to redeem." Thus, the *gō'ēl* was the redeemer or the one who had the right to redeem. MacDonald (p. 260) notes a progressive awareness of Boaz' potential relationship from a *mōyda'* (vs. 1, "kinsman"); to a *mishpachah* (vs. 3, "kindred"); to a *qarōb* (vs. 20, "near of kin"); to that of a *gō'ēl* (Kinsman-Redeemer)!

III. LOVE'S REQUEST: BOAZ' DECISION. (SCENE: THRESHING FLOOR). 3:1-18.

A. Desire to Marry. 3:1-11.

3:1-2. The events in the third chapter revolve around both the levirate and *gō'ēl* institution of ancient Israel. Naomi assumes the part of Ruth's mother in taking the initiative to arrange for a possible marriage. MacDonald (p. 260) is perhaps correct when he notes that she herself had the prior claim on Boaz and was willing to abandon this claim in favor of Ruth. Thus, her plan would reveal to Boaz that her choice had fallen upon him and that she had waived her own right in order to secure the marriage of Ruth. Every detail of the story expresses an element of genuine love on the part of each character.

Keil and Delitzsch (p. 481) note that an Israelite family received its property by lot as a permanent inheritance from the Lord. Whenever one was obliged to sell his inheritance on the account of poverty, it was the duty of the nearest relative to redeem it. If it could not be redeemed it would come back to the family at the next Year of Jubilee. In essence, no actual sale took place, but simply a sale of the yearly produce until the Year of Jubilee. They suggest that Elimelech had possessed a portion at Beth-lehem, which Naomi later sold in poverty. As a relative of Elimelech, Boaz was the potential redeemer, whom Naomi hoped would fulfill the duty of redemption, not only ransoming the purchased field, but marrying her daughter-in-law Ruth (widow of the rightful heir of the landed possession of Elimelech). Urged on by the hope of Boaz' earlier kindness to Ruth, Naomi suggested a confrontation to bring the situation to the point of a decision.

The term **rest** here seems to be equivalent to marriage, indicating that if Ruth were to marry Boaz she could cease from her labors as a poor gleaner in the fields. She reminded Ruth that Boaz was **our kindred** (i.e., kinsman) and therefore was in a position to potentially redeem her from her widowhood. There was evidently a night breeze that would enable him to **winnoweth** the grain at the **threshing floor,** which was usually located at a central place in the harvest area of the field. The process of winnowing involved throwing the whole grain in the air and allowing the wind to carry away the chaff. This antiquated and time-consuming method would certainly have exhausted him. It was often customary for the landowner to oversee this process in order to ensure honest handling of the crop (cf. "Farming," in *Eerdman's Family Encyclopedia of the Bible,* pp. 227-229).

3 Wash thyself therefore, and anoint thee, and put thy raiment upon thee, and get thee down to the floor: *but* make not thyself known unto the man, until he shall have done eating and drinking.

4 And it shall be, when he lieth down, that thou shalt mark the place where he shall lie, and thou shalt go in, and uncover his feet, and lay thee down; and he will tell thee what thou shalt do.

5 And she said unto her, All that thou sayest unto me I will do.

3-5. Naomi's advice to Ruth is as good today as it was then. She instructed her to **wash** herself, **anoint** herself, and to change her **raiment** and finally to **get . . . down to the floor.** In other words, she was advising her to clean and beautify herself and to go and propose to Boaz. On the basis of this incident we certainly cannot say that the Bible is against women proposing marriage to men. While there are few examples of this in the Scripture, it certainly worked on this occasion! When she arrived at the threshing floor she was not to reveal herself to Boaz until he had fallen asleep. The term **uncover his feet** refers to a recognized and morally acceptable, though primitive, custom in which the girl would slightly pull back the edge of the man's robe and then request him to spread the robe (lit., wing) over her. The implication of this meant that she was proposing marriage to him and asking that she be taken into his family as his wife, and thus, come under his protection. The Targum recognized this as a claim to espousal (cf. Ezk 16:8; Deut 22:30). Every indication in the story certainly emphasizes that there was nothing immodest or questionable about this practice, since the character of both Ruth and Boaz is above reproach throughout the entire account.

6 ¶And she went down unto the floor, and did according to all that her mother in law bade her.
7 And when Bō'ăz had eaten and drunk, and his heart was merry, he went to lie down at the end of the heap of corn: and she came softly, and uncovered his feet, and laid her down.
8 ¶And it came to pass at midnight, that the man was afraid, and turned himself: and, behold, a woman lay at his feet.
9 And he said, Who art thou? And she answered, I am Ruth thine handmaid: spread therefore thy skirt over thine handmaid; for thou art a near kinsman.
10 And he said, Blessed be thou of the LORD, my daughter: for thou hast shewed more kindness in the latter end than at the beginning, inasmuch as thou followedst not young men, whether poor or rich.
11 And now, my daughter, fear not; I will do to thee all that thou requirest: for all the city of my people doth know that thou art a virtuous woman.

12 And now it is true that I am thy near kinsman: howbeit there is a kinsman nearer than I.
13 Tarry this night, and it shall be in the morning, that if he will perform unto thee the part of a kinsman, well; let him do the kinsman's part: but if he will not do the part of a kinsman to thee, then will I do the part of a kinsman to thee, as the LORD liveth: lie down until the morning.

14 ¶And she lay at his feet until the morning: and she rose up before one could know another. And he said, Let it not be known that a woman came into the floor.
15 Also he said, Bring the vail that thou hast upon thee, and hold it. And when she held it, he measured six measures of barley, and laid it on her: and she went into the city.
16 And when she came to her mother in law, she said, Who art thou, my daughter? And she told her all that the man had done to her.

6-11. In complete obedience to her mother-in-law's instruction, she went immediately to the threshing floor and waited until Boaz fell asleep at the end of a pile of grain, having finished his evening meal. The scene lends itself to the height of dramatic portrayal. As the unsuspecting Boaz slept, Ruth quietly slipped in, uncovered his feet, lay down and waited. There is definitely an implication of humor in the story as Boaz suddenly awoke **at midnight,** startled and **afraid.** It is not difficult to imagine Boaz' shock at awakening in the middle of the night to discover that someone was lying at his feet. Thus, the text merely states **behold, a woman lay at his feet.** The startled Boaz cried out: **Who art thou?** To which the girl simply answered: **I am Ruth thy handmaid.** Then followed the proposal of marriage: **spread therefore thy skirt over thine handmaid; for thou art a near kinsman.** There could be no doubt that she was requesting him to fulfill the part of the gō'ēl to her. The entire incident indicates that she had come to the end of her mourning and was ready to consider the possibility of remarriage.

Scripture is very clear that while remarriage may not always be the will of God in every case of widowhood, it is certainly permissible for widows to remarry with the blessing of God. In fact, Ruth's second marriage turned out far better than her first one. The response of Boaz is equally and pleasantly humorous: **Blessed be thou of the LORD, my daughter.** The account makes it clear that Boaz was considerably older than Ruth. He was extremely impressed that she was willing to accept him in spite of the difference in their ages. Not only was Boaz in a position to redeem her but his response indicated that he was willing to redeem her. **I will do to thee all that thou requirest,** meaning that he had accepted the proposal. His decision was based on one significant fact, and that was that all of his people knew that she was a **virtuous woman.** Such virtue is certainly not impugned in any way by this curious Oriental custom of which we know very little in western society today.

B. Decision Delayed. 3:12-18.

12-13. However, as in all true dramas, there is an element of suspense which enters the story. Boaz recognized that while he was a **near kinsman,** there was a **kinsman nearer** than himself. This probably indicates that Boaz was a nephew of Elimelech, whereas the other man was perhaps a brother. He went on to urge her to remain there at the threshing floor for the evening until he could confront the kinsman about his responsibility and opportunity. If he were not willing to perform the right of gō'ēl, then Boaz promised Ruth that he would fulfill the obligation of the gō'ēl to her.

14-18. Some have questioned why she **lay at his feet until the morning** and then left secretly with a load of **six measures of barley.** However, the explanation seems rather obvious. Since Boaz was impressed with her virtue, he certainly would have been reluctant to send her back alone in the middle of the night, or even to escort her himself. It is highly unlikely that they were there all alone. Evidently, he felt that there was less question about her remaining there until early morning than attempting the return during the night. In most ancient cities only women of ill repute were ever out alone at night.

In the morning she returned to Naomi with the six measures of barley in her **veil** (apron or mantle). She arrived home in a

17 And she said, These six *measures* of barley gave he me; for he said to me, Go not empty unto thy mother in law.

18 Then said she, Sit still, my daughter, until thou know how the matter will fall: for the man will not be in rest, until he have finished the thing this day.

CHAPTER 4

THEN went Bō′ăz up to the gate, and sat him down there: and, behold, the kinsman of whom Bō′ăz spake came by; unto whom he said, Ho, such a one! turn aside, sit down here. And he turned aside, and sat down.

2 And he took ten men of the elders of the city, and said, Sit ye down here. And they sat down.

3 And he said unto the kinsman, Na-omi, that is come again out of the country of Moab, selleth a parcel of land, which *was* our brother E-lĭm′e-lĕch′s:

4 And I thought to advertise thee, saying, Buy *it* before the inhabitants, and before the elders of my people. If thou wilt redeem *it*, redeem *it*: but if thou wilt not redeem *it*, *then* tell me, that I may know: for *there is* none to redeem *it* beside thee; and I *am* after thee. And he said, I will redeem *it*.

5 Then said Bō′ăz, What day thou buyest the field of the hand of Naomi, thou must buy *it* also of Ruth the Moab-itess, the wife of the dead, to raise up the name of the dead upon his inheri-tance.

6 And the kinsman said, I cannot re-deem *it* for myself, lest I mar mine own inheritance: redeem thou my right to thyself; for I cannot redeem *it*.

7 Now this *was the manner* in former time in Israel concerning redeeming and concerning changing, for to con-firm all things; a man plucked off his shoe, and gave *it* to his neighbour: and this *was* a testimony in Israel.

state of great excitement, which was certainly understandable in light of Boaz' response to her proposal. Thus, Naomi had to remind her to **Sit still, my daughter.** In other words, she was reminding her to relax and calm down **until thou know how the matter will fall,** meaning wait until you see what happens or how it works out. The wise mother-in-law's observation of human nature and the character of men in general caused her to remark that Boaz would not be in **rest, until he have finished the thing this day.** There was no doubt in Naomi's mind that Boaz was as interested in Ruth as she was interested in him. Therefore, she assumed that he would go to whatever lengths were necessary to assure himself the opportunity of marriage to Ruth.

IV. LOVE'S REWARD: FAMILY'S DESTINY. (SCENE: CITY OF BETH-LEHEM). 4:1-22.

A. Dealing with the Kinsman 4:1-12.

4:1. In the morning Boaz went immediately **up to the gate** of Beth-lehem, indicating that the threshing floor was below the city, which sat on a hill. In ancient Palestinian cities there was usually no large open courtyard or plaza. Therefore, the gate area, which was similar to a shaded tunnel, served as a common meeting place, as well as the preeminent place for legal transac-tions. See L. Köhler, "Justice in the Gate" in *Hebrew Man*.

2-3. The narrative in this chapter indicates Boaz' intimate knowledge with the affairs of the town of Bethlehem, of which he must have been one of its leading citizens. As he waited in the gate, the other kinsman came by, turned aside, and sat down. Boaz then took **ten men of the elders of the city** to serve as official witnesses to the transaction which he was about to propose. The number ten was significant to the Jews as a quorum necessary for a synagogue gathering and for the mar-riage benediction. From the most ancient times it represented an official gathering of those in authority. Boaz proceeded to tell the kinsman that **Naomi . . . selleth a parcel of land.** The form of the Hebrew verb is in the perfect tense and normally de-scribes completed action. MacDonald (p. 261) is of the opinion that she had already sold the land upon her return, and now it had to be redeemed from the purchaser. By contrast, Morris (p. 299) views the verb form as a "perfect of certain," indicating that Naomi is imminently about to sell the property, which either of them may buy. He notes that in vs. 5 the sale is still viewed as future. The **parcel of land** is undoubtedly Elimelech's share of the common field.

4-8. Boaz proceeded to indicate that it was his desire to **advertise** ("uncover thy ear," RSV) meaning that he wanted to know the intention of the other kinsman. **If thou wilt redeem it.** Since the nearer kinsman was in the line of succession, Boaz was required to give him first right to the obligation of the *gō'ēl.* However, he very cleverly mentioned only the field and not the girl. The other kinsman responded **I will redeem it,** indicating that his intention was to pay the price for the family possession. However, Boaz proceeded to remind him that in the day that he bought the field of Naomi, he would also have to buy it of **Ruth the Moabitess, the wife of the dead.** By the nature of the transaction the kinsman would never actually own the land itself, but would actually hold it in trust for the son of Ruth in order to **raise up the name of the dead.** By cleverly presenting the matter the way that he did, Boaz confronted the other kinsman with a dual responsibility involving a great expenditure which he was not willing to make. Cassel (p. 47) suggests that he was unwilling to marry her simply because she was a Moabitess. But this is not clear. H. Bess (*Systems of Land Tenure in Ancient Israel,* p. 78) best explains: "He must have reasoned in order to buy Naomi's land he would have to invest a part of the value of

528

8 Therefore the kinsman said unto Bŏ′ăz, Buy it for thee. So he drew off his shoe.

9 ¶And Bŏ′ăz said unto the elders, and unto all the people, Ye are witnesses this day, that I have bought all that was E-lĭm′e-lĕch′s, and all that was Chĭl′ĭ-on′s̆ and Măh′lon′s, of the hand of Naomi.
10 Moreover Ruth the Moabitess, the wife of Măh′lon, have I purchased to be my wife, to raise up the name of the dead upon his inheritance, that the name of the dead be not cut off from among his brethren, and from the gate of his place: ye are witnesses this day.
11 And all the people that were in the gate, and the elders, said, We are witnesses. The LORD make the woman that is come into thine house like Răchel and like Leah, which two did build the house of Israel: and do thou worthily in Ĕph′ra-tăh, and be famous in Bĕth-lehĕm:

12 And let thy house be like the house of Phă′rĕz, whom Tă′mar bare unto Jū-dah, of the seed which the LORD shall give thee of this young woman.

13 ¶So Bŏ′ăz took Ruth, and she was his wife: and when he went in unto her, the LORD gave her conception, and she bare a son.
14 And the women said unto Naomi, Blessed be the LORD, which hath not left thee this day without a kinsman, that his name may be famous in Israel.
15 And he shall be unto thee a restorer of thy life, and a nourisher of thine old age: for thy daughter in law, which loveth thee, which is better to thee than seven sons, hath born him.
16 And Naomi took the child, and laid it in her bosom, and became nurse unto it.
17 And the women her neighbours gave it a name, saying, There is a son born to Naomi; and they called his

his own estate, or inheritance. . . . He seemed willing to redeem Naomi's property if it should not hurt him personally, or if he might possibly gain from it, but he could not accept the responsibility if it should eventuate in a diminution of his own resources and a consequent injustice of his own heir."

9-11. With the other kinsman's official rejection of the offer, Boaz was now free to perform the duty of the Kinsman-Redeemer. Therefore, Boaz clearly indicated that he was willing to buy **all that was Elimelech's . . . Chilion's and Mahlon's** possession which Naomi now held in trust, perhaps as a provision of her husband's will. Boaz further clarified his intentions by announcing **Ruth . . . have I purchased to be my wife.** The reference to "purchase" here is that of the concept of "redeeming." He also announced that he was willing to **raise up the name of the dead upon his inheritance.** This meant that he was willing to perpetuate the line of Elimelech and Mahlon which had been temporarily cut off by their deaths. Therefore, his son by Ruth would be considered as fulfilling the extension of their seed and would guarantee their possession remaining in Israel. The people responded so positively that they not only verified the transaction, but pronounced a benediction on Ruth, hoping that she would be **like Rachel and like Leah,** who were the wives of Jacob, and the legal mothers of the twelve tribes of Israel. The conclusion of the benediction is even more significant: **do thou worthily in Ephratah, and be famous in Beth-lehem.** Certainly they were to become famous in Beth-lehem! This couple would become the great-grandparents of David of Beth-lehem, who would eventually become Israel's greatest king. He in turn would be the forefather of the predicted Messiah, Jesus Christ Himself!

12. While the story is a personal account of a family's real experiences under the providential care of God, it is also the historical link with the past. In essence, the very Davidic line of Christ was threatened during the chaotic period of the judges; and God Himself had overruled to preserve "the seed of the woman" which would ultimately bring forth Him who was to crush the head of the serpent! It is also interesting to note the reference in the benediction to **Tamar** who was also a gentile (Canaanite) girl and was also in the line of Christ's ancestors. There can be no doubt that the inclusion of both Ruth and Tamar is intended to remind us of the ultimate desire of God to extend His grace unto all people. The relationship between Boaz and Ruth becomes a beautiful picture of the love of Christ for his gentile bride—the church. He loves her with pure grace and undeserved favor. She has nothing whereby to commend herself to him; and yet, because of His loving-kindness (Heb chesed), He extends to her the opportunity of redemption.

B. David's Genealogical Line. 4:13-22.

13-22. Sometime after their marriage Ruth and Boaz gave birth to a son, and the **women** became so excited about this blessed event that they virtually attributed it to Naomi! They praised the Lord for the provision of the kinsman whose name would be **famous in Israel.** The reference to Naomi's becoming a **nurse** to the child indicates her special oversight regarding his care. It does not refer to her actually feeding the child, which would have been an impossibility at her age. It is also possible that this process was symbolic of an adoption since the **neighbors** named the child, rather than the father, and proclaimed: **There is a son born to Naomi.** The intertwining of the relationships here is actually nothing more than an intimate picture of the blessing of the child to each member of the family. The child makes it clear that Boaz has a son, that Ruth, the widow, is now the mother of new life, and that Naomi who lost both her husband and her sons is now a grandmother! The child's name **Obed** means worshiper (as in "Obadiah"). The name is derived

name Ō'bed: he *is* the father of Jesse, the father of David.

18 ¶Now these *are* the generations of Phā'rĕz: Phā'rĕz begat Hĕz'ron,

19 And Hĕz'ron begat Ram, and Ram begat Am-mĭn'a-dăb,

20 And Am-mĭn'a-dăb begat Näh'shŏn, and Näh'shŏn begat Săl'mon,

21 And Săl'mon begat Bō'ăz, and Bō'ăz begat Ō'bed,

22 And Ō'bed begat Jesse, and Jesse begat David.

from the Hebrew word *'ebed*, meaning servant. The concept of the name indicates that he would be a true servant and worshiper of Jehovah whose providential oversight had made his birth possible in the first place. As in the story of Esther, the sovereign and providential care of God is constantly woven into the theme of the story, which has become one of the great spiritual classics of all time.

The book ends with a ten-generation genealogy of the **generations of Pharez**. Since he was the illegitimate son of Judah and Tamar (cf. Gen 38), the Law required that ten generations passed before one of his descendants could serve in the leadership of the congregation of Israel (cf. Deut 23:2). It is obvious that this genealogical listing is intended to confirm that at least that many generations had passed by the time of **David. Pharez** was the son of Judah; **Amminadab** was the father-in-law of Aaron; **Nahshon** was his son and served as the head of the house of Judah at the time of the Exodus; **Salmon** is a form of Salma and occurs in I Chr 2:51 as ". . . the father of Beth-lehem. . . ." It is interesting to note that Mahlon is not mentioned at all in the genealogy and is replaced by Boaz. Obed is succeeded by **Jesse** and his son **David,** with no other reference to David's brothers. While the genealogy may be somewhat compressed, since it covers a period of many hundreds of years, it is, nevertheless, obviously intended as an important part of the book.

The drama of redemption which unfolds in the book of Ruth is one of the most beautiful stories in all of ancient literature. This tiny book alone provides us with the clearest insights we have into the personal family details of a devout Hebrew family of the pre-monarchial period. It stands as a refreshing contrast to the chaotic and the disheartening ending of the book of Judges. In this dramatic portrayal of the meeting and marriage of the great-grandparents of David we see the true heart of God, Who is always interested in the personal details of the lives of His children. As in the account of Abraham's servant seeking a bride for his master's son (Gen 20:4), we discover that the will of God certainly extends to the matter of finding one's life's partner. This reminds the reader that God is interested in every detail of his personal life, and the will of God is never brought about by panic or manipulation. Nothing really happens by chance in the life of the believer, for even what appear to be circumstantial quirks of history are really under the sovereign control of the Lord of history—Jesus Christ! The book of Ruth also provides us with the clearest portrayal in the Old Testament of the concept of redemption and certainly provides the contextual biblical understanding of the activity of Christ as the Redeemer of the church, which becomes his gentile bride. In the sovereignty of God over human history, Boaz becomes a perfect type or illustration of Christ, Who would also come forth from Beth-lehem and go out into the fields of harvest and call unto Himself a gentile bride, to whom He would extend all the love that grace could give to redeem and endue her with all the rights and privileges of heirship that she might bring forth His "seed." One day we shall rejoice, ". . . for the marriage of the Lamb is come, and his wife hath made herself ready" (Rev 19:7). On that glorious day her redemption shall be complete!

BIBLIOGRAPHY

Cassel, Paul. Ruth. In *Commentary on the Holy Scriptures*. Ed. by J. P. Lang. Grand Rapids: Zondervan, reprint of 1871 ed.

Cooke, G. A. The Book of Ruth. In *The Cambridge Bible*. Cambridge: The University Press, 1913.

Davis, J. J. *Conquest and Crisis: Studies in Joshua, Judges and Ruth*. Grand Rapids: Baker, 1969.

Gray, J. Joshua, Judges, Ruth. In *The Century Bible*. London: Oxford, 1967.

Herbert, A. S. Ruth. In *Peake's Commentary on the Bible*. Ed. by M. Black and H. H. Rowley. London: Blackwells, 1962.

*Keil, C. F. and F. Delitzsch. Joshua, Judges and Ruth. In *Biblical Commentary on the Old Testament*. Vol. 4. Grand Rapids: Eerdmans, reprinted, 1950.

Kennedy, J. H. Ruth. In *Broadman's Bible Commentary*. Nashville: Broadman Press, 1972.

Lattey, C. *The Book of Ruth*. London: Longmans, 1935.

Learoyd, W. Ruth. In *A New Commentary on Holy Scripture*. Ed. by C. Gore, et. al. London: S.P.C.K., 1937.

*Leggett, D. *The Levirate and Goel Institutions in the Old Testament with Special Attention to the Book of Ruth*. Cherry Hill, N.J.: Mack Publishing Co., 1974.

MacDonald, A. Ruth. In the *New Bible Commentary*. Ed. by F. Davidson. Grand Rapids: Eerdmans, 1954.

*Morris, L. Ruth. In the *Tyndale Old Testament Commentaries*. Downers Grove: InterVarsity Press, 1968.

Myers, J. *The Linguistic and Literary Form of the Book of Ruth*. Leiden: E. J. Brill, 1955.

Pfeiffer, C. F. Ruth. In the *Wycliffe Bible Commentary*. Chicago: Moody Press, 1962.

Rideout, S. *Lectures on the Books of Judges and Ruth*. New York: Loizeaux Brothers, 1958.

Rossell, W. *Handbook of Ruth*. Fort Worth: Southwestern Baptist Theological Seminary, 1955.

Slotki, J. J. *The Five Megilloth*. London: Soncino Press, 1946.

Thatcher, G. W. Judges and Ruth. In *The Century Bible*. London: Caxton, 1904.

Watson, R. A. Judges and Ruth. In *The Expositor's Bible*. New York: Armstrong & Sons, 1899.

Wright, C. H. *The Book of Ruth in Hebrew*. Williams & Norgate, 1864.

I AND II SAMUEL

INTRODUCTION

Name and Canonical Significance. Traditionally, the three major divisions of the Hebrew Old Testament are: The Law, The Prophets, and The Writings. I and II Samuel, together with Joshua, Judges, and I and II Kings, comprised the section called the Former Prophets, which served as a history of God's providential dealings with His people. The two books of I and II Samuel were originally one book which was first divided into two by the Septuagint. The name of this historical book does not come from its author but from the first prominent person in the history of the monarchy, Samuel the Prophet. The first seven chapters are essentially about Samuel and his career; and therefore, in the Hebrew way of thinking, it made a good name for the book. Another example of naming a book by whatever comes first is Genesis, which was named "In-the-Beginning," after the first word in Hebrew. The meaning of Samuel's name would seem to be "God answered." Of the two possible meanings (Heb *Shemuel*), this is the one which makes most sense in the context where the name is given (see I Sam 1:19-20).

Purpose. The purpose of these books is more than historical; for they are not merely a collection of stories about religion and politics in Israel during the period. Nor are these books pure biographies of Samuel, Saul, and David. The writer has selected certain facts of history along with various experiences from the lives of these men in order to reveal the acts of God in the providential accomplishment of salvation for His people. This revelation was written down by the inspiration of the Spirit of God, so that when the writer had finished his task the product was neither history nor biography, but the Word of the Living God. All the Bible aims toward the revelation of God in Christ, and this unit is no exception. It also has a deeper, underlying, messianic significance. It portrays God acting in history to prepare a people for Himself, and to bring salvation to them through His ultimate, anointed King, Jesus Christ.

In studying I and II Samuel, the real message is to be found by recalling that God had called Israel into a special relationship with Himself. God was their real King, and He would always deliver them; the people were never able to solve their own problems or make their own choices. These books, like the others of the Old Testament, were written as temporal illustrations of the ultimate salvation God brings to us in Christ.

Authorship and Date. The book is anonymous; we simply do not know who wrote it. We may know for sure that if I and II Samuel is a unit written by one person, as it appears, then Samuel the prophet could not have been the author, since many of the events recorded took place after his death. The writer, whoever he may have been, obviously lived some time after the events recorded (see II Sam 18:18), and shows the use of many written records and sources in his composition of the book. The use of court records is assumed for II Samuel 9-20. I Chronicles 29:29 mentions the chronicles of Samuel (along with other writings of Nathan and Gad); these had specifically to do with David and could have been part of the author's sources.

Neither is the date of writing known. General inferences are made on the basis of internal evidence; the *terminus a quo* would seem to be the death of Solomon, since the divided monarchy is alluded to in I Samuel 27:6, while the *terminus ad quem* may be the Fall of Samaria, since the writer would surely have mentioned such a significant event if it had occurred. Some scholars date the book even later, but there appears no compelling evidence for this.

Historical Background. Samuel was born prior to 1100 B.C. during the Philistine oppression. The last of God's chosen deliverers (called Judges) was Samson; he had been a judge for twenty years (Jud 15:20) and was credited with the marvelous deliverance of the people of God from the Philistines during his lifetime. Samson's final revenge upon the Philistines was accomplished by the power of the Holy Spirit and resulted in the death of more of the oppressors than he had killed during his lifetime. It was toward the end of this long period of the judges that Samuel was born. It was, as can be seen from the apparent spiritual degradation of I Samuel 2:12-26, a time when every man did what was ". . . right in his own eyes" (Jud 17:6; 21:25). Morals were almost completely lacking. It seems that Samuel was born for the task of transitioning God's rule among His people from judges to kings who would rule in His name.

Samuel was, in fact, a judge himself (I Sam 7:3-11), and it is interesting to note that part of his judgeship was contemporary with that of Samson. Even Samuel's sons were judges in a technical sense by appointment (I Sam 8:1-3), but not in a spiritual sense. Samuel was more than a judge; he was preeminently a prophet. He did not deliver the people physically, as the other judges had, but spiritually. He prepared God's people for receiving David, the king of God's choice, and ultimately the Son of David, Jesus Christ. Humanly speaking, Samuel single-handedly delivered the nation from complete extinction. There was little unity left during the period of the judges, and the cycles of sin, oppression, repentance, and deliverance were tightening into a deadly spin to destruction. It was Samuel who stopped the spin and brought them back to unity as a nation. Samuel was God's man of the hour; he functioned as judge, prophet, priest, and king, and brought the people through this time of transition.

New Testament Use. Luke, John, Mark, Paul, and the writer of the book of Hebrews quote or allude to I and II Samuel. It is interesting that of the eighteen references to these books in the New Testament, almost all emphasize God's accomplished salvation through Jesus Christ as the Messiah. Not one reference is used to establish or even rehearse a historical fact or an event from the lives of Samuel, Saul, or David. The inspired New Testament writers undoubtedly viewed the whole Old Testament as salvation history, and their references would remind us to emphasize whatever is christocentric in our interpretation of this material.

OUTLINE
I SAMUEL

I. The Saving Acts of God Through Samuel. 1:1-7:17.
  A. The Birth of Samuel and Hannah's Song of Deliverance. 1:1-2:10.
  B. Samuel's Ministry in the Temple. 2:11-3:21.
  C. The Capture of the Ark of God. 4:1-6:21.
  D. The Return of the Ark. 7:1-17.
II. God's Providence Toward His People Under Saul. 8:1-15:35.
  A. The Request for a King. 8:1-22.
  B. Saul Anointed and Vindicated. 9:1-11:15.
  C. Samuel's Call for Faith. 12:1-25.

  D. Deliverance from the Philistines. 13:1-14:52.
  E. God's Rejection of Saul as King for His People. 15:1-35.
III. God Anoints David and Leads Him to the Throne. 16:1-31:13.
  A. David Is Anointed by Samuel. 16:1-23.
  B. God's Deliverance through David's Fight with Goliath. 17:1-58.
  C. Saul's Rage and God's Help for David. 18:1-20:42.
  D. David's Wilderness Wanderings. 21:1-30:31.
  E. Saul's Death on Mount Gilboa. 31:1-13.

COMMENTARY

I. THE SAVING ACTS OF GOD THROUGH SAMUEL. 1:1-7:17.

A. The Birth of Samuel and Hannah's Song of Deliverance. 1:1-2:10.

NOW there was a certain man of Rămath-ā'im-zō'phĭm, of mount Ē'phra-im, and his name *was* Ĕl'kā-nah, the son of Jer'ō-hăm, the son of E-lī'hū, the son of Tō'hū, the son of Zuph, an Ĕph'rath-īte:

1:1. Now there was a certain man of Ramathaim-zophim. Only an outline of the barest essentials concerning the circumstances of Samuel's background is given by the writer here since this is a book about what God is doing, rather than a mere biography. Samuel's father was from **Ramathaim** (meaning "twin peaks"), probably the modern Beit Rima west of Shiloh, or less likely, the Ramah five miles north of Jerusalem. Samuel also lived here (7:17), and was buried here (25:1). **Elkanah** was an **Ephrathite**, which simply derives from the fact that he lived in the tribal territory of Ephraim and traced his ancestry back to **Zuph.**

2 And he had two wives; the name of the one *was* Hannah, and the name of the other Pe-nĭn'nah: and Pe-nĭn'nah had children, but Hannah had no children.

2. And he had two wives. This is a statement of fact, and no moral judgment is given here. Polygamy is not justified simply because it was practiced by biblical characters any more than other sins are. If anything, the mention of polygamy darkens an already bleak picture of the background for the birth of Hannah's special child. Hebrew names such as these have the meanings chosen by the original inventors of the names (note parallels in nicknames given today: Tiny, Smiley, Happy, etc). **Elkanah** (vs. 1) means "God-chosen," **Hannah** means "Grace," and **Peninnah** means "Pearl."

3 And this man went up out of his city yearly to worship and to sacrifice unto the LORD of hosts in Shī'lōh. And the two sons of Eli, Hŏph'nī and Phĭn'e-has, the priests of the LORD, *were* there.
4 And when the time was that Ĕl'kā-nah offered, he gave to Pe-nĭn'nah his wife, and to all her sons and her daughters, portions:
5 But unto Hannah he gave a worthy portion; for he loved Hannah: but the LORD had shut up her womb.
6 And her adversary also provoked

3-8. Went up . . . yearly. The idiom and the tense of the verb in Hebrew emphasize the continual faithfulness of Elkanah in **worship** (Heb *shachah*) and in keeping the requirements of the sacrificial laws of God. He went to the holy place at **Shiloh** and fulfilled the outward requirements of the law; but the text emphasizes that in spite of the fact that worship was in general completely corrupt (implied by the mention here of the notorious **Hophni and Phinehas**), Elkanah persistently and faithfully lived righteously and worshiped God from the heart.

But unto Hannah he gave a worthy portion. The traditional Hebrew text appears to be incomplete here; **worthy** (Heb *'apayim*) cannot be derived from the Hebrew text. The NIV

533

her sore, for to make her fret, because the LORD had shut up her womb.

7 And as he did so year by year, when she went up to the house of the LORD, so she provoked her; therefore she wept, and did not eat.

8 Then said El'kā-nah her husband to her, Hannah, why weepest thou? and why eatest thou not? and why is thy heart grieved? am not I better to thee than ten sons?

9 ¶So Hannah rose up after they had eaten in Shī'lōh, and after they had drunk. Now Eli the priest sat upon a seat by a post of the temple of the LORD.

10 And she was in bitterness of soul, and prayed unto the LORD, and wept sore.

11 And she vowed a vow, and said, O LORD of hosts, if thou wilt indeed look on the affliction of thine handmaid, and remember me, and not forget thine handmaid, but wilt give unto thine handmaid a man child, then I will give him unto the LORD all the days of his life, and there shall no razor come upon his head.

12 ¶And it came to pass, as she continued praying before the LORD, that Eli marked her mouth.

13 Now Hannah, she spake in her heart; only her lips moved, but her voice was not heard: therefore Eli thought she had been drunken.

14 And Eli said unto her, How long wilt thou be drunken? put away thy wine from thee.

15 And Hannah answered and said, No, my lord, I am a woman of a sorrowful spirit: I have drunk neither wine nor strong drink, but have poured out my soul before the LORD.

16 Count not thine handmaid for a daughter of Bē'lī-al: for out of the abundance of my complaint and grief have I spoken hitherto.

17 Then Eli answered and said, Go in peace: and the God of Israel grant thee thy petition that thou hast asked of him.

18 And she said, Let thine handmaid find grace in thy sight. So the woman went her way, and did eat, and her countenance was no more sad.

19 ¶And they rose up in the morning early, and worshipped before the LORD, and returned, and came to their house

534

follows the conjectured meaning given in the KJV; an older text seems to be preserved in the Septuagint, which is followed in the majority of the recent translations. A better translation of verse 5 would be: "Although he loved Hannah, he would give Hannah only one portion because the Lord had closed her womb." This also fits better into the theme of the context, since the writer is contrasting the misery and destitution of Hannah before the birth of Samuel with the joy that came afterward. God plants the seeds of praise in the soil of adversity (cf. Hannah's Song, especially 2:5).

Added to the implied social stigma of receiving only one part of the sacrifice is the incessant irritation of the rival wife, Peninnah, who **provoked her sore.** The Hebrew cognate accusative here emphasizes the severe anxiety and depression caused by the nagging rival. Because he loved her so much, Elkanah tried often to console Hannah when, in her depression, she continually cried and would not eat. He said, **am not I better to thee than ten sons?** Ten was a number of completion and fulfillment. Ten sons would have been the perfect family, all any woman could ask.

9-11. Hannah's despair drove her closer to the Lord; in her misery she trusted in God's true grace. Her prayer was accompanied by the vow that if God would give her a son, she would dedicate him to Yahweh as a Nazarite for the rest of his life. **Eli the priest** was the aged guardian of the sanctuary at Shiloh. **The temple of the LORD.** The word **temple** (Heb hēkal) had the connotation of a large or impressive royal room, palace, or temple. It is used of palaces of pagan kings as well as the Temple in Jerusalem and the tabernacle. **She vowed a vow.** We would say "made a vow." The literal translation comes from the cognate accusative in Hebrew. **Then I will give him unto the LORD all the days of his life.** If she knew about the levitical retirement age of fifty, then she was extending her vow beyond that; at least the language shows complete surrender of the child for levitical service. See Numbers 3:11-13 on the substitution of the Levites for the first-born. Hannah vowed further that the child for which she was asking would be a Nazarite (see Num 6:1-4), thus making her vow even more intense and promising a more complete degree of separation from sin and special dedication to God for special service. Samson had been a Nazarite.

12-18. And Eli said unto her, How long wilt thou be drunken? Overindulgence in the use of wine at the worship feasts must have been quite common at this time, since Eli was so quick to jump to the conclusion that Hannah was drunk. The incident also shows that completely silent prayer was not yet common at this time. Hannah's prayer was intense, completely spiritual, and inward; she was not merely performing an outward ceremony. **Daughter of Belial** is an idiom meaning "very wicked"; the same idiom is used to sum up all the wickedness of the sons of Eli in 2:12-17. Eli accepts the explanation of Hannah and blesses her (vs. 17) so that she is able to go back and finish the meal. Hannah's faith in God is obvious from the fact that she **was no more sad.**

19-20. And they rose up in the morning early, and worshiped before the LORD, and returned. Their worship was completed in the same way it had been done so many times

to Rā'mah: and Ěl'kā-nah knew Hannah his wife; and the LORD remembered her.

20 Wherefore it came to pass, when the time was come about after Hannah had conceived, that she bare a son, and called his name Samuel, *saying*, Because I have asked him of the LORD.

21 And the man Ěl'kā-nah, and all his house, went up to offer unto the LORD the yearly sacrifice, and his vow.

22 But Hannah went not up; for she said unto her husband, *I will not go up* until the child be weaned, and *then* I will bring him, that he may appear before the LORD, and there abide for ever.

23 And Ěl'kā-nah her husband said unto her, Do what seemeth thee good; tarry until thou have weaned him; only the LORD establish his word. So the woman abode, and gave her son suck until she weaned him.

24 ¶And when she had weaned him, she took him up with her, with three bullocks, and one ephah of flour, and a bottle of wine, and brought him unto the house of the LORD in Shī'lōh: and the child *was* young.

25 And they slew a bullock, and brought the child to Eli.

26 And she said, Oh my lord, *as* thy soul liveth, my lord, I *am* the woman that stood by thee here, praying unto the LORD.

27 For this child I prayed; and the LORD hath given me my petition which I asked of him:

28 Therefore also I have lent him to the LORD; as long as he liveth he shall be lent to the LORD. And he worshipped the LORD there.

CHAPTER 2

AND Hannah prayed, and said, My heart rejoiceth in the LORD, mine horn is exalted in the LORD: my mouth is enlarged over mine enemies; because I rejoice in thy salvation.

2 *There is* none holy as the LORD: for *there is* none beside thee: neither *is there* any rock like our God.

before, and they returned to their home and lived as they had before. But this time it was different, for **the LORD remembered her.** The birth of this child was not chance, but the deliberate action of God as He responded to Hannah's faith in order to accomplish His own will for His people. **Called his name Samuel.** The meaning of the name (Heb *Shemū'ēl*) has two possible interpretations. It would seem, however, that although there is no direct linguistic connection, Hannah's remark, **Because I have asked him of the LORD,** would somehow explain the reason for the name. Obviously, **asked** (Heb *sha'al*) does not come from the same linguistic root as **Samuel,** but because she "asked," she was "heard by God," which can be connected to the root "hear" (Heb *shama'*) and the name **Samuel.** It seems logical, then, that she called him "Heard by God," (meaning thereby, "God has heard my prayer, and has answered my request") and gave the explanation that the choice was because she had **asked him of the LORD.** The other possible derivation from "name" (Heb *shēm*) with the meaning "Name of God," fits well enough linguistically, but does not seem to fit the context too well, especially since the personal name Yahweh is not part of the name. Compare the same name in the active form "Ishmael," meaning, "God hears," if the first of the two possibilities is correct.

21-28. And the man Elkanah, and all his house, went up to offer unto the LORD the yearly sacrifice. Each seasonal visit by Elkanah was his persistent and continuing response to his own vow to the Lord; he went up to offer his vow (Heb *neder*), meaning the animal he had promised to sacrifice to the Lord. **But Hannah went not up** until the child was **weaned.** The age for weaning in Palestine in this era was two or three years, so that a period of at least this long is implied, during which Hannah did not accompany her husband on his yearly family pilgrimages. **That he may appear before the LORD, and there abide for ever.** Hannah was under no delusions and had no intention of anything but faithfully fulfilling her vow and promise to God. She considered herself a servant of the Lord whom God had chosen to bring this special child into the world; he was destined to live and remain in God's service. After she had weaned the child, in fulfillment of her vow to God and in accordance to her promise to her husband, **she took him up with her, with three bullocks.** The more recent translations here follow the Septuagint rather than the traditional Hebrew text and translate, "with a three-year-old bull." This translation is certainly supported by verse 25 which reads, "Then they killed the bull," (singular, with the definite article in Hebrew, meaning the one they had brought for this purpose). The Septuagint shows that there were several aspects of the worship ceremonies when Samuel was dedicated. The father is active in leading the family in the regular yearly sacrifices; he takes part with Hannah in the sacrifice of the bull; and Samuel himself participates (**he worshiped the LORD there,** vs. 28). The whole family participated. **He shall be lent** (Heb *sha'al*) gives the misleading idea that the Lord is just borrowing Samuel and Hannah may take him back eventually. The word is a passive participle meaning "asked for," and an accurate and faithful translation would bring out the meaning that God's providence had demanded Samuel's lifetime service and brought him to this complete "dedication." The NIV has, "For his whole life he will be given over to the LORD."

2:1-2. Hannah's poetic song of praise for her deliverance and exaltation is alluded to at least four times by Luke in the Magnificat of Mary and the Benedictus of Zechariah. The redemptive theme of God acting to provide the salvation of His people finds parallel expression in both the dedication of the child Samuel and the events surrounding the birth of Jesus Christ (including the birth of John the Baptist as the one who

535

would prepare for the coming kingdom of Christ). This outlook on history as the history of salvation is in fact common to the whole Bible. The song must be understood not merely as a record of the words of Hannah's praise, although it is that primarily, but also as the revealed Word of God; for it is also a prophecy that is the inspiration for an evolving prophetic hope finally realized in Jesus Christ. **My heart rejoiceth in the LORD.** In Luke 1:46, the Magnificat begins: "My soul doth magnify the Lord." **Mine horn is exalted in the LORD.** The word **horn** (Heb *qeren*) is symbolic of strength; this may be a metaphor of a wild animal with head and horns held high in triumph and pride, or it may parallel the joy in the preceding line as inner strength. The corresponding line in the Magnificat reads: "My spirit hath rejoiced. . . ."

I rejoice in thy salvation. Again, **salvation** is paralleled by "God my Savior" in the Magnificat. The salvation is, of course, primarily physical and temporal deliverance from the barrenness and depression Hannah had before Samuel was born; but it has a secondary, spiritual and eternal interpretation as God's ultimate deliverance of His people from sin through Jesus Christ. **There is none holy as the LORD.** Holy (Heb *qadōsh*) refers to the distinctive glory of God; He dwells in unapproachable light (I Tim 6:16). The next thought is parallel, **there is none besides thee, neither is there any rock.** The metaphor of God as a **rock** (Heb *tsūr*) is a significant biblical concept related to salvation (see Deut 32:4,15; Ps 18:2; etc.); the significance is that God is a place of refuge and deliverance for His people.

3-7. **Talk no more so exceeding proudly,** refers to Hannah's former rival, but beyond that to all the enemies of God and His people. God is aware of all subtle plans and will defeat them. Furthermore, **by him actions are weighed.** The precise translation of this last clause is uncertain, although the general meaning is the same throughout the passage. The Septuagint reads, "God carefully prepares all his affairs." **They that were full . . . they that were hungry.** Again the tables are turned because God makes all the difference, and those who are on His side will always win. Luke 1:52-53 alludes to this pattern: God has exalted the desolate and filled the hungry with good things. Great emphasis is placed upon the providence of God; He kills or brings to life. He sends poverty or wealth and is, in fact, in control of all things.

8. **He raiseth up the poor out of the dust.** These same words and thoughts are repeated as classic in Psalm 113:7-9; it is God who is in control, and it is He who does these things whenever they happen. Here the primary reference is to Hannah, and she praises God for her exaltation; but whenever such reverses in life occur it is the work of God.

9-10. **He will keep the feet of his saints.** The Hebrew word denotes those who love and are faithful to God as His people; God will watch over them and protect them. Those who oppose Him will, on the other hand, be cut off, or **broken to pieces.** God will **judge them.** It is important to note that God will **exalt the horn of his anointed.** The **horn,** or strength (see vs. 1), of God's King is exalted. The word **anointed** (Heb *mashīach*) became very important during this period as the designation for the Lord's chosen king. It was used of Saul, then more distinctively of David as the divine choice. Ultimately pointed to Jesus Christ. This is the first use of the word in the Bible with reference to kings (it had been used of anointed priests). It is probably used in a general or ideal sense in this passage, but it should be kept in mind that the idea of the "anointed" one is a major theological motif of the period. The predictive element in Hannah's song is most apparent in this word, and it is obvious from Luke's quotation of this verse (Lk 1:69) that he regards the song as predictive prophecy finding its ultimate fulfillment in

3 Talk no more so exceeding proudly; let *not* arrogancy come out of your mouth: for the LORD *is* a God of knowledge, and by him actions are weighed.

4 The bows of the mighty men *are* broken, and they that stumbled are girded with strength.

5 *They that were* full have hired out themselves for bread; and *they that were* hungry ceased: so that the barren hath born seven; and she that hath many children is waxed feeble.

6 The LORD killeth, and maketh alive: he bringeth down to the grave, and bringeth up.

7 The LORD maketh poor, and maketh rich: he bringeth low, and lifteth up.

8 He raiseth up the poor out of the dust, *and* lifteth up the beggar from the dunghill, to set *them* among princes, and to make them inherit the throne of glory: for the pillars of the earth *are* the LORD's, and he hath set the world upon them.

9 He will keep the feet of his saints, and the wicked shall be silent in darkness; for by strength shall no man prevail.

10 The adversaries of the LORD shall be broken to pieces; out of heaven shall he thunder upon them: the LORD shall judge the ends of the earth; and he shall give strength unto his king, and exalt the horn of his anointed.

Jesus Christ, God's King in the line of David, God's Servant who finally accomplishes salvation for His people. It would seem impossible to overstress the predictive and messianic motif introduced here by the use of this word, since Luke plays upon so many of the parallels in the birth narratives of Samuel and Jesus (Lk 1:46-48; 1:53; 1:69; 2:52) and since the very word "Christ" is the Greek or New Testament equivalent to this Hebrew word which is transliterated into English as "Messiah."

B. Samuel's Ministry in the Temple. 2:11-3:21.

11. The child did minister (Heb *sharat*) denotes a special or technical ministry; we would call it a full-time ministry. The Septuagint uses the Greek equivalent, and both Hebrew and Greek words are used primarily throughout the Bible for the ministry of priests, Levites, and apostolic men. The Hebrew construction of the word here (paraphrastic participle) stresses the constant and progressive nature of Samuel's ministry from the very beginning as a real servant of the Lord.

12-17. Now the sons of Eli were sons of Belial. This is an idiom used to characterize the extremely base character of the sons of Eli. To this is added the dictum that **they knew not the LORD.** Even though they were outwardly acting as servants of the Lord, they did not in reality know and serve Him. The worship ceremony was so empty and degraded that open selfishness and greed altered the rules of the offerings. The sons of Eli took all of the offerings they could get, and instead of taking the allotted pieces after the prescribed offering to the Lord had been made, they selected the best cuts first. The worshipers were forced to comply. **The sin of the young men was very great before the LORD.**

11 ¶And Ĕl′kā-nah went to Rā′mah to his house. And the child did minister unto the LORD before Eli the priest.

12 Now the sons of Eli *were* sons of Bē′lĭ-al; they knew not the LORD.
13 And the priest's custom with the people *was, that,* when any man offered sacrifice, the priest's servant came, while the flesh was in seething, with a fleshhook of three teeth in his hand;
14 And he struck *it* into the pan, or kettle, or caldron, or pot; all that the fleshhook brought up the priest took for himself. So they did in Shī′lōh unto all the Israelites that came thither.
15 Also before they burnt the fat, the priest's servant came, and said to the man that sacrificed, Give flesh to roast for the priest; for he will not have sodden flesh of thee, but raw.
16 And if any man said unto him, Let them not fail to burn the fat presently, and *then* take *as much* as thy soul desireth; then he would answer him, *Nay;* but thou shalt give *it me* now: and if not, I will take *it* by force.
17 Wherefore the sin of the young men was very great before the LORD: for men abhorred the offering of the LORD.

18-21. But Samuel ministered (cf. vs. 11). There is a deliberate contrast between the pure and dedicated ministry of Samuel, who was a mere child (Heb *na'ar*) and the perfunctory, selfish work of Eli's sons. **Girded with a linen ephod** (Heb *'ēpōd*). The **ephod** was a sort of bib, or symbolic vest, patterned after the more elaborate prototype of the ephod of the high priest, but made of plain white cloth. The word **girded** is also a technical term for the symbolic tying on of the ephod. Even the **little coat** which Samuel's mother brought resembled clothing worn by the high priest so that throughout the passage the dedication and pure service in a special, sacred calling are stressed. **And the child Samuel grew before the LORD.** Luke considers this typical of Christ in His allusion (Lk 2:52) to I Samuel 2:21, 26, and 3:1.

18 ¶But Samuel ministered before the LORD, *being* a child, girded with a linen ephod.
19 Moreover his mother made him a little coat, and brought *it* to him from year to year, when she came up with her husband to offer the yearly sacrifice.
20 And Eli blessed Ĕl′kā-nah and his wife, and said, The LORD give thee seed of this woman for the loan which is lent to the LORD. And they went unto their own home.
21 And the LORD visited Hannah, so that she conceived, and bare three sons and two daughters. And the child Samuel grew before the LORD.

22-23. How they lay with the women that assembled at the door of the tabernacle of the congregation. This is obviously intended to show the incredible degeneration of the worship of Jehovah in Israel. Whether this is cultic prostitution, as was practiced in other Canaanite religions, or simply fornication is academic and relatively unimportant. The point is that the depth of this willful, flagrant, and unforgivable sin was appalling. We know that the women had a legitimate and recognized appointment to serve the Lord here (exactly the same Hebrew words are used in Ex 38:8), and we know that the blame here is

22 ¶Now Eli was very old, and heard all that his sons did unto all Israel; and how they lay with the women that assembled at the door of the tabernacle of the congregation.
23 And he said unto them, Why do ye such things? for I hear of your evil dealings by all this people.

24 Nay, my sons; for *it is* no good report that I hear: ye make the LORD's people to transgress.

25 If one man sin against another, the judge shall judge him: but if a man sin against the LORD, who shall intreat for him? Notwithstanding they hearkened not unto the voice of their father, because the LORD would slay them.

26 And the child Samuel grew on, and was in favour both with the LORD, and also with men.

27 ¶And there came a man of God unto Eli, and said unto him, Thus saith the LORD, Did I plainly appear unto the house of thy father, when they were in Egypt in Pharaoh's house?

28 And did I choose him out of all the tribes of Israel *to be* my priest, to offer upon mine altar, to burn incense, to wear an ephod before me? and did I give unto the house of thy father all the offerings made by fire of the children of Israel?

29 Wherefore kick ye at my sacrifice and at mine offering, which I have commanded *in my* habitation; and honourest thy sons above me, to make yourselves fat with the chiefest of all the offerings of Israel my people?

30 Wherefore the LORD God of Israel saith, I said indeed *that* thy house, and the house of thy father, should walk before me for ever: but now the LORD saith, Be it far from me; for them that honour me I will honour, and they that despise me shall be lightly esteemed.

31 Behold, the days come, that I will cut off thine arm, and the arm of thy father's house, that there shall not be an old man in thine house.

32 And thou shalt see an enemy *in my* habitation, in all *the wealth* which *God* shall give Israel: and there shall not be an old man in thine house for ever.

33 And the man of thine, *whom* I shall not cut off from mine altar, *shall be* to consume thine eyes, and to grieve thine heart: and all the increase of thine house shall die in the flower of their age.

34 And this *shall be* a sign unto thee, that shall come upon thy two sons, on Hŏph'nī and Phĭn'e-has; in one day they shall die both of them.

35 And I will raise me up a faithful priest, *that* shall do according to *that* which *is* in mine heart and in my mind: and I will build him a sure house; and he shall walk before mine anointed for ever.

36 And it shall come to pass, *that* every one that is left in thine house shall come *and* crouch to him for a piece of silver and a morsel of bread, and shall say, Put me, I pray thee, into

upon the sons of Eli who had perverted themselves and made it all but impossible for those who wanted to worship the Lord to do so.

24. Ye make the LORD's people to transgress. Sin is all the more serious if it hinders others from worshiping or believing. "Whosoever shall offend one of these little ones that believe in me, it is better for him that a millstone were hanged about his neck, and he were cast into the sea" (Mk 9:42).

25-26. Who shall entreat for him? These words show the willful and unforgivable nature of their sin. These men have gone beyond the point of no return; they have hardened their hearts against the Lord, and God's judgment is certain and inescapable. Eli's toothless rebuke was too late (3:13 implies that he should have exercised more discipline when they were younger). His sons had already gone too far, and God had determined to judge them and work through Samuel to bring about His will. **Samuel . . . was in favor both with the LORD, and also with men.** The opposite was true of the sons of Eli. This line is considered typical of Christ, the ultimate Priest, according to the quotation in Luke 2:52.

27-30. A man of God. That he is a prophet with a message of warning and judgment from the Lord is immediately apparent. Samuel must also serve as a prophet and deliver the same message (3:1-4:1). **Thy father** shows that Eli is a descendant of Aaron and was therefore chosen **to offer . . . to wear an ephod** and to perform the other functions of the priests. The honor and privilege of the office have now been rejected. **Wherefore kick ye . . . ?** This is an idiom and should not be translated literally; it means, rather, to hold in disrespect. The NIV has correctly translated the idiom "Why do you scorn my sacrifice?" Hebrews 10:29 (RSV) uses the very same idiom with reference to the ultimate divine sacrifice, "How much worse punishment do you think will be deserved by the man who has spurned the Son of God . . . ?" **But now the LORD saith,** a higher divine law supersedes the conditional promise, **them that honor me I will honor.**

31-34. Judgment must now come upon the whole priestly line; the death of **Hophni and Phinehas** is symbolic of that judgment.

35-36. I will raise me up a faithful priest. This prophecy shows that the priesthood did not die with Eli. God is always acting to deliver His people, to bring them back to Himself. A new start is made. Historically, after the death of Eli the priestly functions were taken over by Samuel himself, and only gradually was confidence restored to the office. This must be considered an immediate and partial fulfillment of the promise. However, **he shall walk before mine anointed for ever,** does not fit the facts for Samuel himself or for his sons. Zadok also, who replaced Abiathar (I Kgs 2:27), must be considered as a

one of the priests' offices, that I may eat a piece of bread.

CHAPTER 3

AND the child Samuel ministered unto the LORD before Eli. And the word of the LORD was precious in those days; *there was* no open vision.

2 And it came to pass at that time, when Eli *was* laid down in his place, and his eyes began to wax dim, *that* he could not see;
3 And ere the lamp of God went out in the temple of the LORD, where the ark of God *was*, and Samuel was laid down *to sleep*;

4 That the LORD called Samuel: and he answered, Here *am* I.
5 And he ran unto Eli, and said, Here *am* I; for thou calledst me. And he said, I called not; lie down again. And he went and lay down.
6 And the LORD called yet again, Samuel. And Samuel arose and went to Eli, and said, Here *am* I; for thou didst call me. And he answered, I called not, my son; lie down again.
7 Now Samuel did not yet know the LORD, neither was the word of the LORD yet revealed unto him.
8 And the LORD called Samuel again the third time. And he arose and went

partial fulfillment of this prophecy. He was established and walked before Solomon who was the anointed of the Lord. Zadok's descendants are named as those who minister to the Lord in Ezekiel's restored Temple (40:46) before the anointed Son of David. However, both Samuel and Zadok, according to most commentators, should be considered only partial fulfillments of the prophecy. Jesus Christ Himself is the final and ultimate fulfillment of the **faithful priest**; He is the true and eternal High Priest who offers Himself as the only sacrifice which can ever completely atone for sin and bring us eternally back to God. It may seem inconsistent by our standards of literature and logic to see Christ as the final fulfillment of both the **faithful priest** and the **anointed** King, but we have no right to impose our standards upon this ancient Book. This kind of predictive prophecy was accepted and proper in its day. Furthermore, the New Testament writers have made clear their interpretations of these prophecies as fulfilled in Christ. The whole warning and announcement should be viewed, not from the side of gloom and doom, but from the side of victory and hope for the people of God as he works to accomplish their salvation.

3:1. The child Samuel ministered, (see 2:11). Again, the Hebrew construction indicates a continued or faithful ministry; one translation has, ". . . the boy Samuel was ministering to the LORD . . ." (RSV). **The word of the LORD was precious.** The word **precious** (Heb *yaqar*) should rather be understood in its sense of "rare." This translation is confirmed by the next clause which is parallel, **there was no open vision,** but which must also be clarified by the translation, "there were not many visions." This last clause could also mean that visions, even when they did occur, were not being adequately explained to the people. At any rate, the dark circumstances of the period reflected in the immorality of Eli's sons and their judgment, together with the lack of guidance from God by way of visions, must have made the people of Israel ready to recognize Samuel as God's prophet and spokesman.

2-3. And ere the lamp of God went out. The lamp was filled with just enough oil to burn through the night; the implication is that the time of this divine revelation was deep in the night, perhaps near dawn. The **lamp** was, of course, the seven-branched candelabrum called the "menorah." **In the temple of the LORD.** The **temple** (Heb *hēkal*) refers to a building and no longer the original tent or "tabernacle" of the congregation. The **temple** here had doors which Samuel had to open (vs. 15). The (NIV) text reads, "Samuel was lying down in the temple of the LORD, where the ark of God was." **Where the ark of God was.** The point that Samuel was near the ark is probably made to emphasize the significance and genuineness of this revelation; in Exodus 25:22 God had promised to meet and commune with Moses from above the mercy seat, which was the lid or cover of the ark.

4-9. The LORD called Samuel. Some Old Testament revelation came in dreams, but this is not a dream; Samuel was awake and active. Neither is it a vision, since Yahweh is heard, not seen. **Now Samuel did not yet know the Lord.** This means to explain why God had to speak three times, i.e., Samuel was not used to participating in visions. This does not mean that, as we might say today, "Samuel was not a Christian yet." It is obvious that he was more devout than all others; he was simply unfamiliar with the procedure of revelation, as the next clause also states. **Speak, LORD; for thy servant heareth.** The progressive action of the verb is better translated, "Your servant is listening." The advice of Eli was essential; without this receptive attitude there could be no revelation from God, and this had been the heart of the problem in the days of the judges. Samuel

to Eli, and said, Here *am* I; for thou didst call me. And Eli perceived that the LORD had called the child.

9 Therefore Eli said unto Samuel, Go, lie down: and it shall be, if he call thee, that thou shalt say, Speak, LORD; for thy servant heareth. So Samuel went and lay down in his place.

10 And the LORD came, and stood, and called as at other times, Samuel, Samuel. Then Samuel answered, Speak; for thy servant heareth.

11 ¶And the LORD said to Samuel, Behold, I will do a thing in Israel, at which both the ears of every one that heareth it shall tingle.

12 In that day I will perform against Eli all *things* which I have spoken concerning his house: when I begin, I will also make an end.

13 For I have told him that I will judge his house for ever for the iniquity which he knoweth; because his sons made themselves vile, and he restrained them not.

14 And therefore I have sworn unto the house of Eli, that the iniquity of Eli's house shall not be purged with sacrifice nor offering for ever.

15 ¶And Samuel lay until the morning, and opened the doors of the house of the LORD. And Samuel feared to shew Eli the vision.

16 Then Eli called Samuel, and said, Samuel, my son. And he answered, Here *am* I.

17 And he said, What *is* the thing that *the* LORD hath said unto thee? I pray thee hide *it* not from me: God do so to thee, and more also, if thou hide *any* thing from me of all the things that he said unto thee.

18 And Samuel told him every whit, and hid nothing from him. And he said, It *is* the LORD: let him do what seemeth him good.

19 And Samuel grew, and the LORD was with him, and did let none of his words fall to the ground.

20 And all Israel from Dan even to Be′er-shē′ba knew that Samuel *was* established *to be* a prophet of the LORD.

21 And the LORD appeared again in Shī′lōh: for the LORD revealed himself to Samuel in Shī′lōh by the word of the LORD.

CHAPTER 4

AND the word of Samuel came to all Israel. Now Israel went out against the Philistines to battle, and pitched beside Ĕb′en-ē′zer: and the Philistines pitched in Ā′phĕk.

2 And the Philistines put themselves in array against Israel: and when they joined battle, Israel was smitten before the Philistines: and they slew of the army in the field about four thousand men.

3 ¶And when the people were come into the camp, the elders of Israel said, Wherefore hath the LORD smitten us to day before the Philistines? Let us fetch the ark of the covenant of the LORD out of Shī′lōh unto us, that, when it cometh among us, it may save us out of the hand of our enemies.

4 So the people sent to Shī′lōh, that

was to be that chosen servant of the Lord who would receive and proclaim messages from God.

10-18. The dreadful content of this specific message is so shocking that it would cause the ears to **tingle.** The idiom would be equivalent to ours of hair standing up on the neck, or making one's flesh to crawl; it is used also in II Kings 21:12, and Jeremiah 19:3 of the fall of Jerusalem. Here it refers to the events which comprise the fall of Shiloh. **He restrained them not.** Whatever discipline Eli had exercised upon his sons, it must have been too little, too late. This message to Samuel is not really different from the one delivered by the unnamed prophet in chapter 2.

19-21. Samuel was by this revelation established and made known as a prophet. **The LORD was with him, and did let none of his words fall to the ground.** The meaning is that none of his prophecies went unfulfilled. **All Israel from Dan even to Beersheba.** This is an expression which emphasizes the recognition of the people from the extreme north to the extreme south; all knew and accepted Samuel as **a prophet of the LORD.**

C. The Capture of the Ark of God. 4:1-6:21.

4:1-4. Now Israel went out against the Philistines. There may be a line of introduction missing from the Hebrew text; the Septuagint has, "It happens that during this time, the Philistine federation was at war with Israel." The Philistines came from Caphtor (Deut 2:23; Jer 47:4-5; Amos 9:7;), which is believed to be Crete; they are mentioned in the stele of Rameses III. Although the date of arrival in Palestine is uncertain, they seem to have been present at the time of the Exodus (13:17; etc.). At any rate, they were well established in the land at this time and were organized into a federation with five centers: Ashdod, Ekron, Ashkelon, Gaza, and Gath. (see Edward E. Hindson, *Philistines and the Old Testament*). In this particular battle, Israel was **pitched beside Ebenezer,** referring to the army camp. **Ebenezer** was near Mizpah if it is the same place named in 7:12. The Philistines, on the other hand, were camped in **Aphek,** the site of which is unknown. **Israel was smitten.** In the encounter Israel was defeated and lost four thousand men. The **elders**

they might bring from thence the ark of the covenant of the LORD of hosts, which dwelleth *between* the cherubims: and the two sons of Eli, Hŏph'nī and Phĭn'e-has, *were* there with the ark of the covenant of God.

5 And when the ark of the covenant of the LORD came into the camp, all Israel shouted with a great shout, so that the earth rang again.

6 And when the Philistines heard the noise of the shout, they said, What *meaneth* the noise of this great shout in the camp of the Hebrews? And they understood that the ark of the LORD was come into the camp.

7 And the Philistines were afraid, for they said, God is come into the camp. And they said, Woe unto us! for there hath not been such a thing heretofore.

8 Woe unto us! who shall deliver us out of the hand of these mighty Gods? these *are* the Gods that smote the Egyptians with all the plagues in the wilderness.

9 Be strong, and quit yourselves like men, O ye Philistines, that ye be not servants unto the Hebrews, as they have been to you: quit yourselves like men, and fight.

10 ¶And the Philistines fought, and Israel was smitten, and they fled every man into his tent: and there was a very great slaughter; for there fell of Israel thirty thousand footmen.

11 And the ark of God was taken; and the two sons of Eli, Hŏph'nī and Phĭn'e-has, were slain.

12 ¶And there ran a man of Benjamin out of the army, and came to Shī'lŏh the same day with his clothes rent, and with earth upon his head.

13 And when he came, lo, Eli sat upon a seat by the wayside watching: for his heart trembled for the ark of God. And when the man came into the city, and told *it*, all the city cried out.

14 And when Eli heard the noise of the crying, he said, What *meaneth* the noise of this tumult? And the man came in hastily, and told Eli.

15 Now Eli was ninety and eight years old; and his eyes were dim, that he could not see.

16 And the man said unto Eli, I *am* he that came out of the army, and I fled to day out of the army. And he said, What is there done, my son?

17 And the messenger answered and said, Israel is fled before the Philistines, and there hath been also a great slaughter among the people, and thy two sons also, Hŏph'nī and Phĭn'e-has, are dead, and the ark of God is taken.

18 And it came to pass, when he made mention of the ark of God, that he fell from off the seat backward by the side of the gate, and his neck brake, and he died: for he was an old man, and heavy. And he had judged Israel forty years.

19 ¶And his daughter in law, Phĭn'e-has' wife, was with child, *near* to be delivered: and when she heard the tidings that the ark of God was taken, and that her father in law and her husband were

understood this as a sign from the Lord, but unfortunately believed that if they took the **ark** closer to the fighting, God's presence would save them. Evidently they did not understand that the ark was merely a symbol of God's presence.

5-7. All Israel shouted. This shout appears to have all but frightened the Philistines into retreat. Humanly speaking, this gave the Israelites a tactical advantage at this point. They were, however, trusting in the outward form of their religion rather than in God's real supernatural power.

8-11. Who shall deliver us out of the hand of these mighty Gods? The Philistines are the real believers in this situation; they know what God can do and tremble before Him. Nevertheless, the Philistines encourage themselves to hope against hope and fight valiantly to defeat Israel. Neither side is aware that God is working behind the scenes to accomplish His will. **Thirty thousand.** This number seems very large; but such large losses have been recorded by other historians, and it must be remembered that this was an international war as the instrument of God's judgment upon Israel for idolatry and sin (see Ps 78:56-64). **The ark of God was taken; and the two sons of Eli, Hophni and Phinehas, were slain.** This is the fulfillment of the two prophetic messages of the man of God in chapter 2, and of Samuel in chapter 3 and is the real reason for Israel's defeat in the battle.

12-18. A man of Benjamin out of the army. His presence supports the idea of a very large army from the whole nation, rather than a small tribal force. Thus, the loss of thirty thousand is not incredible. **With his clothes rent.** The tearing of one's clothes and throwing dirt upon one's head were customary ways of showing sorrow and grief. This was a great national tragedy. **Eli sat upon a seat by the wayside watching.** The word order here follows the Hebrew literally (using the *Qere* for "beside"); the apparent difficulty of the man getting by Eli may be partially explained by the Septuagint reading, "Eli sat on his bench beside the gate watching the road." Also, Eli was nearly blind and probably did not see the messenger pass. Eli surely would have expected bad news, and this was no doubt the reason for his position beside the gate. He now heard the moaning and called for an explanation, **What meaneth the noise of this tumult?** The man had to explain who he was and where he had just come from because Eli's **eyes were dim, that he could not see.** It is interesting that it was at the **mention of the ark of God** that Eli collapsed and died. This was the key in God's judgment against the nation; the ark symbolized God's presence with His people. The writer stresses that not even the death of Eli's sons was as great a disaster to him as the loss of the ark.

19-22. The great national tragedy is also highlighted in the account of the death of **Phinehas' wife,** who also survived the news of her husband's death only long enough to name the child she delivered in death with an epitaph for the nation, **Ichabod.** The name means, "No Glory." It is explained in both verses 21 and 22 that the proposition, **The glory is departed from Israel,**

dead, she bowed herself and travailed; for her pains came upon her.

20 And about the time of her death the women that stood by her said unto her, Fear not; for thou hast born a son. But she answered not, neither did she regard it.

21 And she named the child Ĭ'-cha-bŏd, saying, The glory is departed from Israel: because the ark of God was taken, and because of her father in law and her husband.

22 And she said, The glory is departed from Israel: for the ark of God is taken.

CHAPTER 5

AND the Philistines took the ark of God, and brought it from Ĕb'en-ē'zer unto Ăsh'dŏd.

2 When the Philistines took the ark of God, they brought it into the house of Dā'gŏn, and set it by Dā'gŏn.

3 ¶And when they of Ăsh'dŏd arose early on the morrow, behold, Dā'gŏn was fallen upon his face to the earth before the ark of the LORD. And they took Dā'gŏn, and set him in his place again.

4 And when they arose early on the morrow morning, behold, Dā'gŏn was fallen upon his face to the ground before the ark of the LORD; and the head of Dā'gŏn and both the palms of his hands were cut off upon the threshold; only the stump of Dā'gŏn was left to him.

5 Therefore neither the priests of Dā'-gŏn, nor any that come into Da'gŏn's house, tread on the threshold of Dā'gŏn in Ăsh'dŏd unto this day.

6 ¶But the hand of the LORD was heavy upon them of Ăsh'dŏd, and he destroyed

has reference primarily to the loss of the ark and the sad reality symbolized in the loss, namely that God was no longer with His people, but had been separated from them by their sins.

5:1-5. The Philistines took the ark of God, and brought it from Ebenezer unto Ashdod. The Septuagint uses the name "Azotus," which is mentioned in Acts 8:40. It was located about thirty miles west of Jerusalem near the sea, and was one of the five cities of the Philistines. **Brought it into the house of Dagon.** The repetition in both the Hebrew and Greek texts of verse 2, as well as the accusative of direction towards in verse 1, may hint that the temple of the Philistine god was outside the city of Ashdod. **Dagon** is now known to be the god of agriculture; the name derives from the word for "corn" or "grain" (Heb dagan). The ark was placed in front of the Philistine god, and in the morning it was discovered that **Dagon was fallen upon his face to the earth before the ark of the LORD.** In Hebrew a vivid progressive action participle is used, as if the god was caught in the process of bowing down before the ark. The Septuagint has, "They found Dagon flat on his face before the ark." The pagan god is helpless and must be set back up in place; and the next morning he is again flat on his face before the ark, this time smashed by the fall into several pieces.

6-7. The hand of the LORD was heavy upon them. The ark was not a mere trophy of victory, it was the symbol of the

The Wanderings of the Ark of the Covenant

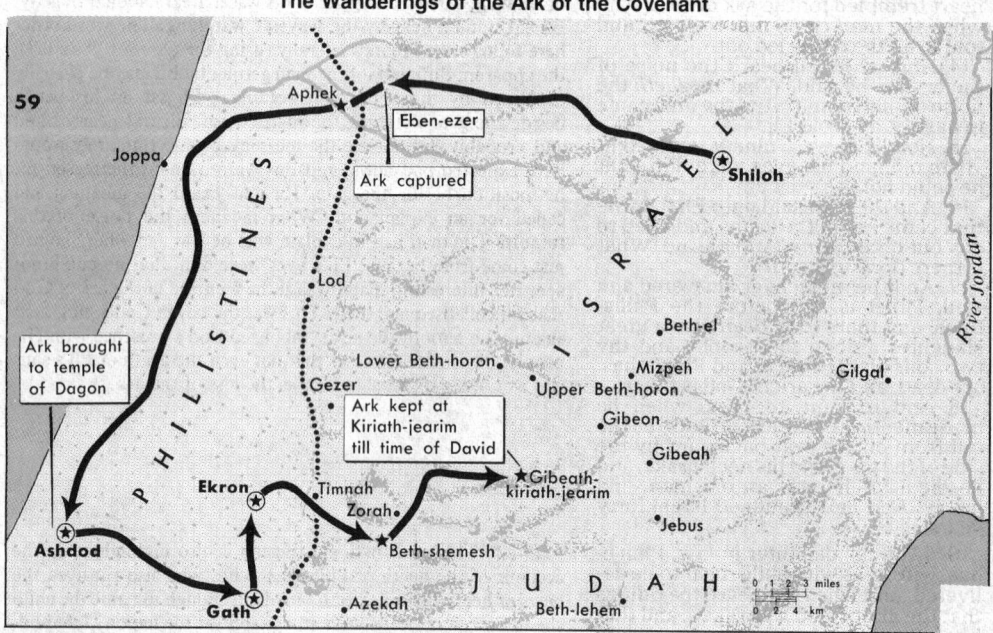

← Route of the Ark

them, and smote them with emerods, *even* Ăsh'dŏd and the coasts thereof.

7 And when the men of Ăsh'dŏd saw that *it was* so, they said, The ark of the God of Israel shall not abide with us: for his hand is sore upon us, and upon Dā'gŏn our god.

8 They sent therefore and gathered all the lords of the Philistines unto them, and said, What shall we do with the ark of the God of Israel? And they answered, Let the ark of the God of Israel be carried about unto Gath. And they carried the ark of the God of Israel about *thither.*

9 And it was *so,* that, after they had carried it about, the hand of the LORD was against the city with a very great destruction: and he smote the men of the city, both small and great, and they had emerods in their secret parts.

10 ¶Therefore they sent the ark of God to Ĕkron. And it came to pass, as the ark of God came to Ĕkron, that the Ĕkronītes cried out, saying, They have brought about the ark of the God of Israel to us, to slay us and our people.

11 So they sent and gathered together all the lords of the Philistines, and said, Send away the ark of the God of Israel, and let it go again to his own place, that it slay us not, and our people: for there was a deadly destruction throughout all the city; the hand of God was very heavy there.

12 And the men that died not were smitten with the emerods: and the cry of the city went up to heaven.

CHAPTER 6

AND the ark of the LORD was in the country of the Philistines seven months.

2 And the Philistines called for the priests and the diviners, saying, What shall we do to the ark of the LORD? tell us wherewith we shall send it to his place.

3 And they said, If ye send away the ark of the God of Israel, send it not empty; but in any wise return him a trespass offering: then ye shall be healed, and it shall be known to you why his hand is not removed from you.

4 Then said they, What *shall be* the trespass offering which we shall return to him? They answered, Five golden emerods, and five golden mice, *according to* the number of the lords of the Philistines: for one plague *was* on you all, and on your lords.

5 Wherefore ye shall make images of your emerods, and images of your mice that mar the land; and ye shall give glory unto the God of Israel: peradventure he will lighten his hand from off you, and from off your gods, and from off your land.

6 Wherefore then do ye harden your

presence of the true God who is sovereign over all. The **hand** of the **LORD** shows that it is God Himself who is responsible for this punitive action. **He destroyed them** (Heb *shamēm*) which, with the following clause, means simply, "He afflicted them with a plague." **With emerods** (Heb *'opēl*). The word is used for boils, abscesses, swellings, and even a hill; here the plague seems to be the bubonic plague rather than hemorrhoids. Part of the Hebrew text seems to be missing, and the Septuagint contains further information here about boils or swellings in the belly and about an outbreak of mice or rats associated with the plague (cf. 5:9; 6:1). The incidents with the ark in the temple of Dagon, and now the plague, made it very obvious that the **hand** of the Lord was punishing them.

8-9. The lords (Heb *seren*) **of the Philistines** were the five princes or rulers of the five Philistine cities; the word is a technical term not used in other connections. The decision of the council was that the ark should be **carried about unto Gath**, another of the Philistine cities. When the ark came to Gath, however, so did the punishing presence of God, and **the hand of the LORD was against the city with a very great destruction.** The last clause of the verse, **they had emerods in their secret parts,** is an apparent conflation of the texts from both Hebrew and Greek; a literal translation of the Hebrew MT is found in the RSV, "tumors broke out upon them."

10-12. Next the **ark** was sent to **Ekron,** the third Philistine city, but the **Ekronites** requested it be sent back **to his own place** even before it arrived. Nevertheless, many died in Ekron as well; for the plague followed the ark.

6:1-16. The Philistines called for the priests and the diviners (Heb *qasam*), fortunetellers, who had a great deal of influence in all ancient cultures. The advice was to send the ark out with a **trespass offering** (Heb *'asham*). This is the word used for sin offering in the Old Testament, but it is closely related to the whole idea of ransom money or the process of redemption. There was the belief in most ancient religions that money could be paid to avoid divine punishment. This very word is used in Isaiah 53:10 for the offering of the life of the Servant of Jehovah which God would give to redeem His people, and Jesus quoted the passage (Mk 10:45) using the corresponding Greek word for ransom to refer to the giving of His own life for us as a sin offering. The offering was to be **Five golden emerods, and five golden mice.** The images were symbolic of the plague; the idea was that God would know exactly what the ransom money was for and would then heal them of the plague. **Wherefore then do ye harden your hearts, as the Egyptians . . . ?** This is another indication that they knew the facts of history and respected the Hebrews and their God. God was in all His actions revealing Himself to the Philistines and others outside of Israel.

Two milch kine. Natural instinct would cause the cows to follow their calves which were to be led back to the farm just as the cows were turned loose. If the cows went on toward **Bethshemesh**, the nearest Israelite town, contrary to their natural instincts to follow their calves, then the Philistines reasoned that

hearts, as the Egyptians and Pharaoh hardened their hearts? when he had wrought wonderfully among them, did they not let the people go, and they departed?

7 Now therefore make a new cart, and take two milch kine, on which there hath come no yoke, and tie the kine to the cart, and bring their calves home from them:

8 And take the ark of the Lord, and lay it upon the cart; and put the jewels of gold, which ye return him for a trespass offering, in a coffer by the side thereof; and send it away, that it may go.

9 And see, if it goeth up by the way of his own coast to Bĕth-shĕmesh, then he hath done us this great evil: but if not, then we shall know that it is not his hand that smote us; it was a chance that happened to us.

10 ¶And the men did so; and took two milch kine, and tied them to the cart, and shut up their calves at home:

11 And they laid the ark of the Lord upon the cart, and the coffer with the mice of gold and the images of their emerods.

12 And the kine took the straight way to the way of Bĕth-shĕmesh, and went along the highway, lowing as they went, and turned not aside to the right hand or to the left; and the lords of the Philistines went after them unto the border of Bĕth-shĕmesh.

13 And they of Bĕth-shĕmesh were reaping their wheat harvest in the valley: and they lifted up their eyes, and saw the ark, and rejoiced to see it.

14 And the cart came into the field of Joshua, a Bĕth-shĕmite, and stood there, where there was a great stone: and they clave the wood of the cart, and offered the kine a burnt offering unto the Lord.

15 And the Levites took down the ark of the Lord, and the coffer that was with it, wherein the jewels of gold were, and put them on the great stone: and the men of Bĕth-shĕmesh offered burnt offerings and sacrificed sacrifices the same day unto the Lord.

16 And when the five lords of the Philistines had seen it, they returned to Ĕkron the same day.

17 And these are the golden emerods which the Philistines returned for a trespass offering unto the Lord; for Ăsh'dŏd one, for Gā'za one, for Ăs'ke-lŏn one, for Gath one, for Ĕkron one;

18 And the golden mice, according to the number of all the cities of the Philistines belonging to the five lords, both of fenced cities, and of country villages, even unto the great stone of Abel, whereon they set down the ark of the Lord: which stone remaineth unto this day in the field of Joshua, the Bĕth-shĕmite.

19 ¶And he smote the men of Bĕth-shĕmesh, because they had looked into the ark of the Lord, even he smote of the people fifty thousand and threescore and ten men: and the people lamented, because the Lord had smitten many of the people with a great slaughter.

they could be sure that God had brought the plague upon them. Otherwise it was a chance, a mere coincidence of events. The cows, of course, went straight to Beth-shemesh. The Israelites offered the kine a burnt offering unto the Lord. The whole point of this early part of Samuel is to show God judging His people and leading them back to Himself; these sacrifices, and the coming of the Levites to perform this sacred task, are the beginning of the restoration of order after the calamity of defeat and the destruction of Shiloh as a worship center.

17-21. Some of the men of Beth-shemesh were also killed by the plague. The text of verse 19 has been corrected in most of the newer translations and should read "But God struck down some of the men of Beth-shemesh, putting seventy of them to death because they had looked into the ark of the Lord." The ark was to impress the people with the holiness of God. Looking at it, or into it, for mere curiosity was not permitted. Who is able to stand before this holy Lord God? The lesson of Numbers 4:20 is thus crystal clear to the people of the city as they begin to make the decision as to where the ark is to be taken. Kirjath-jearim. The ancient name of the town was Baale of Judah (II Sam 6:2); it was located ten miles west of Jerusalem on the road to Lydda, according to Eusebius. The site is near the modern village of Abu Ghosh.

20 And the men of Bĕth–shĕmesh said, Who is able to stand before this holy LORD God? and to whom shall he go up from us?

21 And they sent messengers to the inhabitants of Kir′jath–jĕ′a-rĭm, saying, The Philistines have brought again the ark of the LORD; come ye down, *and* fetch it up to you.

CHAPTER 7

AND the men of Kir′jath–jĕ′a-rĭm came, and fetched up the ark of the LORD, and brought it into the house of A-bĭn′a-dăb in the hill, and sanctified Ē-le-ā′zar his son to keep the ark of the LORD.

2 And it came to pass, while the ark abode in Kir′jath–jĕ′a-rĭm, that the time was long; for it was twenty years: and all the house of Israel lamented after the LORD.

3 ¶ And Samuel spake unto all the house of Israel, saying, If ye do return unto the LORD with all your hearts, *then* put away the strange gods and Ăsh′ta-rŏth from among you, and prepare your hearts unto the LORD, and serve him only: and he will deliver you out of the hand of the Philistines.

4 Then the children of Israel did put away Bā′al-ĭm and Ăsh′ta-rŏth, and served the LORD only.

5 And Samuel said, Gather all Israel to Mĭz′peh, and I will pray for you unto the LORD.

6 And they gathered together to Mĭz′-peh, and drew water, and poured *it* out before the LORD, and fasted on that day, and said there, We have sinned against the LORD. And Samuel judged the children of Israel in Mĭz′peh.

7 And when the Philistines heard that the children of Israel were gathered together to Mĭz′peh, the lords of the Philistines went up against Israel. And when the children of Israel heard *it*, they were afraid of the Philistines.

8 And the children of Israel said to Samuel, Cease not to cry unto the LORD our God for us, that he will save us out of the hand of the Philistines.

9 And Samuel took a sucking lamb, and offered *it for* a burnt offering wholly unto the LORD: and Samuel cried unto the LORD for Israel; and the LORD heard him.

10 And as Samuel was offering up the burnt offering, the Philistines drew near to battle against Israel: but the LORD thundered with a great thunder on that day upon the Philistines, and

D. The Return of the Ark. 7:1-17.

7:1-2. The ark was at **Kirjath-jearim** for twenty years during this period of slow national revival. **Eleazar** was consecrated **to keep the ark of the LORD.** Abinadab, the father of Eleazar, was quite probably a Levite, which would be the reason for bringing the ark to his house. Eleazar is now, for all practical purposes, the priest. It must be remembered that time and a gradual restoration were required because of the deep moral depression prior to the death of Eli and the destruction of Shiloh. Samuel is, of course, the real leader during this time of revival.

3-4. If ye do return unto the LORD. Samuel is the one who is recognized as a prophet of the Lord during this time. He no doubt performed the functions of a priest, military leader, judge, and king as well; but his main task in life is expressed here. He is to bring the people back to the Lord. His work is revival and the unification of the people under God's chosen ruler. He speaks as a prophet when he tells them to **put away the strange gods and Ashtaroth.** The people had backslidden into idolatry. The **Ashtaroth** (a Hebrew plural form) were statues of an almost universal goddess of sex and fertility. **Prepare your hearts unto the Lord, and serve him only.** The true God was not like any of the other deities; He was spiritual and supernatural. He wanted His people to worship Him from the heart, but they had been influenced by the outward and visible form of Canaanite religion. Also, since God was the one true God, He could not allow syncretism into Israel. They must serve Him alone. **Then the children of Israel did put away Baalim.** Baal was the chief Canaanite god, the son of Dagon, and the god of agriculture. The word is in the plural because of the many statues of Baal which had been set up in various places.

5-7. Mizpeh. This is an important site which is still called Nebi Samwil; it is located just north of Jerusalem. Samuel later announced Saul as king at Mizpeh, in accordance with the people's demands (10:17-24). **Drew water, and poured it out before the LORD.** The pouring out of water as a libation or symbol of worship is not prescribed in the Bible as accepted symbol of worship, but neither is it forbidden. Here it seems to be pleasing to the Lord as an outward sign of the repentance that was in their heart. ". . . the LORD looketh on the heart" (I Sam 16:7). **And Samuel judged the children of Israel.** Perhaps, since this refers to this specific act of revival, a better translation would be, "And so Samuel functioned as a judge on this occasion in Mizpeh." The Philistines heard about the convocation and determined to squelch a budding revolution by attacking the Israelites.

8-11. Cease not to cry unto the LORD our God for us, that he will save us. This is exactly the response that the Lord wants. His people must look to Him as the only source of deliverance. The salvation here is purely physical deliverance from the Philistines, but it is typical of spiritual salvation; and both the word **save** (Heb *yasha‘*), and the concept of salvation are very prominent in this book. The name "Joshua" in the Old Testament and the name "Jesus" in the New Testament come from this word and mean "Jehovah is salvation." When we cry out to the Lord to save us from our sins, He will also deliver us.

Samuel did what the people asked and offered a **lamb . . . for a burnt offering;** and the Lord accepted the sacrifice, answered the prayer for deliverance, and again saved His people.

discomfited them; and they were smitten before Israel.

11 And the men of Israel went out of Mĭz'peh, and pursued the Philistines, and smote them, until *they came* under Bĕth-cär.

12 Then Samuel took a stone, and set *it* between Mĭz'peh and Shen, and called the name of it Ĕb'en-ē'zer, saying, Hitherto hath the LORD helped us.

13 So the Philistines were subdued, and they came no more into the coast of Israel: and the hand of the LORD was against the Philistines all the days of Samuel.

14 And the cities which the Philistines had taken from Israel were restored to Israel, from Ĕkron even unto Gath; and the coasts thereof did Israel deliver out of the hands of the Philistines. And there was peace between Israel and the Ămorītes.

15 ¶And Samuel judged Israel all the days of his life.

16 And he went from year to year in circuit to Bĕth-el, and Gilgal, and Mĭz'peh, and judged Israel in all those places.

17 And his return *was* to Rā'mah; for there *was* his house; and there he judged Israel; and there he built an altar unto the LORD.

CHAPTER 8

AND it came to pass, when Samuel was old, that he made his sons judges over Israel.

2 Now the name of his firstborn was Jō'el; and the name of his second, Ā-bī'ah: *they were* judges in Be'er-shē'ba.

3 And his sons walked not in his ways, but turned aside after lucre, and took bribes, and perverted judgment.

4 Then all the elders of Israel gathered themselves together, and came to Samuel unto Rā'mah,

5 And said unto him, Behold, thou art old, and thy sons walk not in thy ways: now make us a king to judge us like all the nations.

6 ¶But the thing displeased Samuel, when they said, Give us a king to judge us. And Samuel prayed unto the LORD.

7 And the LORD said unto Samuel, Hearken unto the voice of the people in all that they say unto thee: for they have not rejected thee, but they have rejected me, that I should not reign over them.

8 According to all the works which they have done since the day that I brought them up out of Egypt even unto this day, wherewith they have forsaken me, and served other gods, so do they also unto thee.

12-14. Ebenezer means "stone of help" and the significance of the memorial was to acknowledge that it was only by the help of the Lord that the victory had been accomplished. The thunder of the Lord had thrown the Philistines into confusion and started them into disorganized retreat, so all Israel had to do was pursue. The Philistines were decisively defeated and **came no more into the coast of Israel.**

15-17. Samuel . . . went from year to year in circuit. Samuel seems to have effected a national revival and reeducated the people in the laws of the Lord almost single-handedly. He played the part of judge, priest, Levite, and ruler, as well as prophet. He traveled the circuit from Ramah, his home, to Bethel, Gilgal, and Mizpeh. The **altar** at Ramah, although it was in violation of the technical points of the law (Deut 12:5, 13), was permitted because of the need for revival and unification of the nation. It was better than having no sacrifices at all.

II. GOD'S PROVIDENCE TOWARD HIS PEOPLE UNDER SAUL. 8:1-15:35.

A. The Request for a King. 8:1-22.

8:1-3. He made his sons judges over Israel. Samuel trained many young men in his school of the prophets, but he would have been most proud and happy to have his sons assist him and eventually take over as judges and leaders. His own sons, however, were probably his greatest disappointment and shame. **His sons walked not in his ways, but turned aside after lucre.** Samuel, of all people, should have learned from his experience in bringing God's message of judgment to Eli (especially 3:13) and should have given proper training and restraint to his children. But now the sons of the best of the judges had **perverted judgment.**

4-5. The providence of God appears behind these events, but the people are first moved to request a king by the moral failures of Samuel's sons. The request comes to Samuel since he is the real leader of the people. **Make us a king to judge us like all the nations.** The whole system of judges was to deliver the people from oppression by their enemies, and their rule was now recognized as deficient and of merely temporary value. The Israelite nation had God Himself as its King and Ruler; they were in essence now rebelling against God, although the people who made the request did not think of it in these terms.

6-10. Samuel prayed unto the Lord. No doubt, he felt some personal injury because of the request, since he had served so selflessly for his whole life; but Samuel's prayer to the Lord is mainly a function of his prophetic office. He knows that in this matter also he must seek the face of the Lord, listen for God's Word, and then proclaim it to the people. The decision is not his but the Lord's. **They have rejected me, that I should not reign over them.** God was the King who reigned (Heb *malak*) over them, and the people not only rejected (Heb *ma'as*, "scorn," "belittle"; Septuagint has "make light of") God, but they have, in rejecting Samuel, rejected God's rule through Samuel (Hebrew infinitive construct). **Hearken unto their voice: howbeit yet protest solemnly.** Samuel is to give the people what they

9 Now therefore hearken unto their voice: howbeit yet protest solemnly unto them, and shew them the manner of the king that shall reign over them.

10 ¶And Samuel told all the words of the Lord unto the people that asked of him a king.

11 And he said, This will be the manner of the king that shall reign over you: He will take your sons, and appoint *them* for himself, for his chariots, and *to be* his horsemen; and *some* shall run before his chariots.

12 And he will appoint him captains over thousands, and captains over fifties; and *will set them* to ear his ground, and to reap his harvest, and to make his instruments of war, and instruments of his chariots.

13 And he will take your daughters *to be* confectionaries, and *to be* cooks, and *to be* bakers.

14 And he will take your fields, and your vineyards, and your oliveyards, *even* the best *of them*, and give *them* to his servants.

15 And he will take the tenth of your seed, and of your vineyards, and give to his officers, and to his servants.

16 And he will take your menservants, and your maidservants, and your goodliest young men, and your asses, and put *them* to his work.

17 He will take the tenth of your sheep: and ye shall be his servants.

18 And ye shall cry out in that day because of your king which ye shall have chosen you; and the Lord will not hear you in that day.

19 ¶Nevertheless the people refused to obey the voice of Samuel; and they said, Nay; but we will have a king over us;

20 That we also may be like all the nations; and that our king may judge us, and go out before us, and fight our battles.

21 And Samuel heard all the words of the people, and he rehearsed them in the ears of the Lord.

22 And the Lord said to Samuel, Hearken unto their voice, and make them a king. And Samuel said unto the men of Israel, Go ye every man unto his city.

CHAPTER 9

NOW there was a man of Benjamin, whose name *was* Kish, the son of A'bï'-el, the son of Ze'rôr, the son of Be-chô'-răth, the son of A-phï'ah, a Benjamite, a mighty man of power.

2 And he had a son, whose name *was* Saul, a choice young man, and a goodly: and *there was* not among the children of Israel a goodlier person than he: from his shoulders and upward *he was* higher than any of the people.

3 And the asses of Kish Saul's father were lost. And Kish said to Saul his son, Take now one of the servants with thee, and arise, go seek the asses.

4 And he passed through mount Ē'phra-im, and passed through the land of Shal'ï-sha, but they found *them* not: then they passed through the land of Shā'lïm, and *there they were* not: and

have asked for. The Lord knows they would not have it any other way.

11-22. Samuel proceeds to tell them what kind of a king they are going to get. He would have glory, guards, and grandeur. But someone would have to pay for all of this; the bottom line was **ye shall be his servants.** Samuel also made it very clear that this king would be their choice and not the Lord's choice. The people were determined in their desire, however; and Samuel went back to the Lord in prayer with the report of the people's determination. The word of the Lord came back a third time, and the matter was settled. **Hearken unto their voice.** It only remained for Samuel to administer and execute the demand of the people which had been allowed by the Lord for providential reasons.

B. Saul Anointed and Vindicated. 9:1-11:15.

9:1-2. There was a man of Benjamin. This pedigree is given to show that Saul came from a proper and prestigious family; and from outward, physical appearances, no better choice could be made. Saul was **goodly,** and **from his shoulders and upward he was higher than any of the people.** The point made by the biblical author is that Saul is a promising choice from a human perspective, but God's permissive will is active behind the scenes.

3-6. And the asses of Kish. The translation of the NIV is less offensive, "Now the donkeys belonging to Saul's father Kish were lost." The lost donkeys become the occasion for the meeting between Samuel and Saul, but the writer makes it clear that even the straying of the donkeys is a part of providence and the plan of salvation. It is no coincidence that Saul is unable to find the donkeys and decides to give up, nor is it mere chance that Saul's servant happens to remember that **there is in this**

547

he passed through the land of the Benjamites, but they found *them* not.

5 *And* when they were come to the land of Zuph, Saul said to his servant that *was* with him, Come, and let us return; lest my father leave *caring* for the asses, and take thought for us.

6 And he said unto him, Behold now, *there is* in this city a man of God, and *he is* an honourable man; all that he saith cometh surely to pass: now let us go thither; peradventure he can shew us our way that we should go.

7 Then said Saul to his servant, But, behold, *if* we go, what shall we bring the man? for the bread is spent in our vessels, and *there is* not a present to bring to the man of God: what have we?

8 And the servant answered Saul again, and said, Behold, I have here at hand the fourth part of a shekel of silver: *that* will I give to the man of God, to tell us our way.

9 (Beforetime in Israel, when a man went to enquire of God, thus he spake, Come, and let us go to the seer: for *he that is* now *called* a Prophet was beforetime called a Seer.)

10 Then said Saul to his servant, Well said; come, let us go. So they went unto the city where the man of God *was.*

11 ¶*And* as they went up the hill to the city, they found young maidens going out to draw water, and said unto them, Is the seer here?

12 And they answered them, and said, He is; behold, *he is* before you: make haste now, for he came to day to the city; for *there is* a sacrifice of the people to day in the high place:

13 As soon as ye be come into the city, ye shall straightway find him, before he go up to the high place to eat: for the people will not eat until he come, because he doth bless the sacrifice; *and* afterwards they eat that be bidden. Now therefore get you up; for about this time ye shall find him.

14 And they went up into the city: *and* when they were come into the city, behold, Samuel came out against them, for to go up to the high place.

15 ¶Now the LORD had told Samuel in his ear a day before Saul came, saying,

16 To morrow about this time I will send thee a man out of the land of Benjamin, and thou shalt anoint him *to be* captain over my people Israel, that he may save my people out of the hand of the Philistines: for I have looked upon my people, because their cry is come unto me.

city (probably Ramah, since Samuel lived there) **a man of God.** Samuel has the reputation of being honorable; but, more importantly, **all that he saith cometh surely to pass.** The word **surely** comes from the emphasis or certainty expressed in the Hebrew text by the infinitive absolute used before the verb of the same stem (Heb *bōʼ*). This emphasis upon what he says coming true is missed in some of the more recent translations; it is very important in this passage since the writer is establishing Samuel's authority as a prophet. According to Deuteronomy 18:15-22, there would be false prophets as well as true prophets; and one need not obey these. Samuel is a true prophet, and his words and authority in anointing Saul are to be respected.

7-10. When Saul decides to go to Samuel, even the quartershekel which the servant happens to have with him is providential. The comment, **he that is now called a Prophet was beforetime called a Seer,** shows that although Samuel is called here a "man of God," he is legitimately also a **Prophet** (Heb *nabiʼ*) or **Seer** (Heb *rōʼeh*). The three terms are synonymous and show that Samuel has the authority to speak the Word of God.

11-16. A sacrifice of the people today in the high place. Usually the term **high place** refers to the Canaanite centers of idolatrous worship, but here it denotes the place of prayer and sacrifice. The celebration may have been planned especially for the anointing of Saul, at least, many of the aspects of it were. **I will send,** shows the element of providence. **Thou shalt anoint him to be captain over my people Israel, that he may save my people. Anoint** (Heb *mashach*) was at first used of the priests (Ex 28:41) as a part of their ordination ceremonies to show that God had chosen them and consecrated them for His service. Holy objects like the tabernacle, laver, and altar, had also been anointed. Saul is the first anointed king and as such is typical of the true choice of God for the king of His people, namely David (16:1-13), as well as God's ultimate King, Jesus Christ.

The biblical theme of the anointed king begins, in one sense at least, at this point in the narrative. After this "anointed man" is always the man whom God has chosen to be king over His people and to save them from some evil. This Hebrew word, in fact, became such a distinctive name for God's chosen king that it was eventually transliterated into Greek and then into English (see Dan 9:25-26; John 1:41; 4:25) as "Messiah." Whenever this word was translated into Greek (rather than transliterated), the word "anointed man" (Gr *christos*) was used, so that it also became a theological technical term which in turn was transliterated into English as "Christ." We now know that these terms are synonymous and that the Greek term for "anointed man" has become a part of the name "Jesus Christ" to signify that he is God's ultimate King.

Captain (Heb *nagîd*) would be better translated "leader," and is also used often in the Old Testament with messianic motifs. It did not, however, maintain the same importance in the New Testament as the "anointed one" motif. **My people** shows the special favor God grants to His people, Israel. In the New Testament the same special love comes to those who believe in Jesus Christ as God's promised Messiah. **That he may save my people.** Salvation or deliverance is the reason for anointing Saul as king. The word **save** (Heb *yashaʻ*) also becomes an important and key theological term in the Bible. In this passage it is primarily a physical and literal deliverance from the Philistines

17 And when Samuel saw Saul, the LORD said unto him, Behold the man whom I spake to thee of! this same shall reign over my people.

18 Then Saul drew near to Samuel in the gate, and said, Tell me, I pray thee, where the seer's house *is.*

19 And Samuel answered Saul, and said, I *am* the seer: go up before me unto the high place; for ye shall eat with me to day, and to morrow I will let thee go, and will tell thee all that *is* in thine heart.

20 And as for thine asses that were lost three days ago, set not thy mind on them; for they are found. And on whom *is* all the desire of Israel? *Is it* not on thee, and on all thy father's house?

21 And Saul answered and said, *Am* not I a Benjamite, of the smallest of the tribes of Israel? and my family the least of all the families of the tribe of Benjamin? wherefore then speakest thou so to me?

22 And Samuel took Saul and his servant, and brought them into the parlour, and made them sit in the chiefest place among them that were bidden, which *were* about thirty persons.

23 And Samuel said unto the cook, Bring the portion which I gave thee, of which I said unto thee, Set it by thee.

24 And the cook took up the shoulder, and *that* which *was* upon it, and set *it* before Saul. And Samuel said, Behold that which is left! set *it* before thee, *and* eat: for unto this time hath it been kept for thee since I said, I have invited the people. So Saul did eat with Samuel that day.

25 ¶And when they were come down from the high place into the city, *Samuel* communed with Saul upon the top of the house.

26 And they arose early: and it came to pass about the spring of the day, that Samuel called Saul to the top of the house, saying, Up, that I may send thee away. And Saul arose, and they went out both of them, he and Samuel, abroad.

27 *And* as they were going down to the end of the city, Samuel said to Saul, Bid the servant pass on before us, (and he passed on,) but stand thou still a while, that I may shew thee the word of God.

CHAPTER 10

THEN Samuel took a vial of oil, and poured *it* upon his head, and kissed him, and said, *Is it* not because the LORD hath anointed thee *to be* captain over his inheritance?

2 When thou art departed from me to day, then thou shalt find two men by Răchel's sepulchre in the border of Benjamin at Zĕl'zah; and they will say unto thee, The asses which thou wentest to seek are found: and, lo, thy

that is in view, but even this literal salvation is typical of spiritual salvation which comes through the ultimate Saviour Jesus Christ who saves us from our sins. It is interesting to note that the name Jesus derives in part from this same Hebrew word and means, "Jehovah will save." Note the similar phraseology in connection with the name of Jesus in Matthew 1:21.

17-27. God had told Samuel all about Saul; the possibility of supernatural communication to the prophet is assumed throughout the books. Saul has been chosen to **reign** (Heb *'atsar*), which usually has the meaning of "restrain" or "hold back" and may also carry some of that meaning here. The word has apparently no messianic meanings, and a different word is used in 10:1. Samuel identifies himself as the **seer,** and instructs Saul to precede him to the **high place** with the promise of solving all his problems. God knows all about the donkeys, and the **desire** of Israel (their lust for a king) is now upon Saul. Saul's display of humility draws no response from Samuel who proceeds with the well-organized celebration for the anointing of Saul. **That I may show thee the word of God.** The Septuagint has, "Stay and listen to the word of God."

10:1-5. Samuel took a vial of oil, formerly used for anointing the priests and holy objects, and **poured it upon his head.** This was not magical, but symbolic; and Samuel gives three signs, or prophecies, to authenticate the anointing: two men will confirm that the donkeys have been found as well as the concern of Kish for Saul, the three men who will give Saul two loaves of bread, and the meeting of the prophets at the Hill of God.

father hath left the care of the asses, and sorroweth for you, saying, What shall I do for my son?

3 Then shalt thou go on forward from thence, and thou shalt come to the plain of Tā′bor, and there shall meet thee three men going up to God to Bĕth-el, one carrying three kids, and another carrying three loaves of bread, and another carrying a bottle of wine:

4 And they will salute thee, and give thee two *loaves* of bread; which thou shalt receive of their hands.

5 After that thou shalt come to the hill of God, where *is* the garrison of the Philistines: and it shall come to pass, when thou art come thither to the city, that thou shalt meet a company of prophets coming down from the high place with a psaltery, and a tabret, and a pipe, and a harp, before them; and they shall prophesy:

6 And the Spirit of the LORD will come upon thee, and thou shalt prophesy with them, and shalt be turned into another man.

7 And let it be, when these signs are come unto thee, *that* thou do as occasion serve thee; for God *is* with thee.

8 And thou shalt go down before me to Gilgal; and, behold, I will come down unto thee, to offer burnt offerings, *and* to sacrifice sacrifices of peace offerings: seven days shalt thou tarry, till I come to thee, and shew thee what thou shalt do.

9 ¶And it was *so*, that when he had turned his back to go from Samuel, God gave him another heart: and all those signs came to pass that day.

10 And when they came thither to the hill, behold, a company of prophets met him; and the Spirit of God came upon him, and he prophesied among them.

11 And it came to pass, when all that knew him beforetime saw that, behold, he prophesied among the prophets, then the people said one to another, What *is* this *that* is come unto the son of Kish? *Is* Saul also among the prophets?

12 And one of the same place answered and said, But who *is* their father? Therefore it became a proverb, *Is* Saul also among the prophets?

13 And when he had made an end of prophesying, he came to the high place.

14 ¶And Saul's uncle said unto him and to his servant, Whither went ye? And he said, To seek the asses: and when we saw that *they were* no where, we came to Samuel.

15 And Saul's uncle said, Tell me, I pray thee, what Samuel said unto you.

16 And Saul said unto his uncle, He told us plainly that the asses were found. But of the matter of the kingdom, whereof Samuel spake, he told him not.

17 ¶And Samuel called the people together unto the LORD to Mĭz′peh;

18 And said unto the children of Israel, Thus saith the LORD God of

6. The spirit of the LORD will come upon thee, and thou shalt prophesy with them. The group of prophets who met Saul as they came down from Gibeah prophesied and may have been the human instruments used by God to encourage Saul and give him the new-man strength to become God's anointed king. At any rate, it was at this point that the **spirit** of God came upon him to empower and transform him.

7-9. God is with thee. This is not regeneration in the Christian sense, but rather it is God empowering the man He has chosen to do His work. **God gave him another heart.** This means that his former lack of courage and dedication was gone, and in its place was the desire to do great things for God. It was this inner drive which enabled Saul to be used by God for the deliverance of his people from the Philistines.

10-16. The spirit of God came upon him, and he prophesied among them. This one act of prophecy on the part of Saul served two purposes: it gave Saul confidence in himself since he could see that what Samuel said was true; and secondly, it became proverbial among the people, so that they could trust Saul as their king and know that God had in fact chosen him. **But of the matter of the kingdom, whereof Samuel spake, he told him not.** From this statement, and verse 22, it appears that Saul did not yet have an abundance of self-confidence.

17-18. It is important to recognize the motif of salvation for God's people running through even this account of the coronation of Saul. This is the public declaration of Saul as king; his anointing had been a more or less private affair (9:27; 10:1). The

Israel, I brought up Israel out of Egypt, and delivered you out of the hand of the Egyptians, and out of the hand of all kingdoms, *and* of them that oppressed you:

19 And ye have this day rejected your God, who himself saved you out of all your adversities and your tribulations; and ye have said unto him, *Nay,* but set a king over us. Now therefore present yourselves before the LORD by your tribes, and by your thousands.
20 And when Samuel had caused all the tribes of Israel to come near, the tribe of Benjamin was taken.
21 When he had caused the tribe of Benjamin to come near by their families, the family of Mă′trī was taken, and Saul the son of Kish was taken: and when they sought him, he could not be found.
22 Therefore they enquired of the LORD further, if the man should yet come thither. And the LORD answered, Behold, he hath hid himself among the stuff.
23 And they ran and fetched him thence: and when he stood among the people, he was higher than any of the people from his shoulders and upward.
24 And Samuel said to all the people, See ye him whom the LORD hath chosen, that *there is* none like him among all the people? And all the people shouted, and said, God save the king.

25 Then Samuel told the people the manner of the kingdom, and wrote *it* in a book, and laid *it* up before the LORD. And Samuel sent all the people away, every man to his house.

26 And Saul also went home to Gĭb′e-ah; and there went with him a band of men, whose hearts God had touched.
27 But the children of Bē′lĭ-al said, How shall this man save us? And they despised him, and brought him no presents. But he held his peace.

CHAPTER 11
THEN Nā̆hăsh the Ammonite came up, and encamped against Jā′besh-gĭl′e-ad: and all the men of Jā′besh said unto Nā̆hăsh, Make a covenant with us, and we will serve thee.
2 And Nā̆hăsh the Ammonite answered them, On this *condition* will I make *a covenant* with you, that I may

public gathering is at **Mizpeh,** where once before (7:5-11) victory over the Philistines had been accomplished through Samuel's prayer and dependence upon the Lord. **Delivered you out of the hand of the Egyptians.** Samuel, by recounting these historical deliverances, is reminding the people that God alone is their salvation; it is He who has delivered them from all their enemies.

19-21. Ye have this day rejected your God. The choice of Saul was a mistake in that he was a king like other nations had; the choice was, in that sense, the choice of the people. On the other hand, once the people had made the request to have a human king, rather than looking to God alone, the selection of Saul was determined by divine providence in the interest of both the physical salvation of the people from the Philistines and the ultimate spiritual salvation through Jesus Christ. Samuel reminds the people of these things publicly before the formal selection is made by lot.

22-24. The LORD answered, Behold, he hath hid himself among the stuff. There were various ways in which God revealed Himself and His will in the Old Testament. This was certainly not a dream, vision, or prophetic trance, and probably was not the audible voice of God. It is reasonable to surmise something like picking out black or white stones from a hat or, more probably, from the pockets of the priestly vest called the ephod. This device is called the Urim and Thummim and was used by the high priest to discover the will of God. Its use here is suggested by the phrase **enquired of the LORD.**

Some scholars have rejected this whole account because of the apparent difficulties of Saul being chosen by lot (without being present) and yet hidden (but too tall to hide). With the Urim and Thummim device, however, Saul could easily have been chosen without being present. The information about where he was hiding could also have been gained through questions with yes or no answers.

25. Then Samuel told the people the manner of the kingdom, and wrote it in a book. The **manner** (Heb *mishpat*) indicates more specifically the details of administration and is translated "regulations" by the NIV. The **kingdom** refers to the new kind of government (monarchy, but Israel's monarch was to be different from all other kings and was in effect a prime minister under God) which had been chosen by the people and effected providentially by God. This document was doubtless in the form of a scroll and would have been stored at Mizpeh, the new center of worship after the destruction of Shiloh. After the session was complete, Samuel dismissed the people.

26-27. Saul went to Gibeah, and certain men **whose hearts God had touched** immediately associated themselves with him, presumably for the positions of power which would be available in the kingdom. The touching of their hearts does not refer to spiritual revival, but to courage and strength which came from God and enabled Saul and his army to accomplish God's will in the deliverance of His people. There were, of course, some who disbelieved and refused to put their trust in Saul. They showed their mistrust by withholding the usual offerings of **presents** (Heb *minchah*).

11:1-5. Here the writer gives an account of the confirmation of Saul as king. The occasion is the rescue of Jabesh-gilead from the threatening Ammonites. **Nahash the Ammonite** besieged the city with his bedouin army and refused to accept surrender except under the gory condition stated in verse 2. The **elders** of the city asked for **seven days' respite,** during which time they would look for someone **to save** them. Note the prominence

thrust out all your right eyes, and lay it *for* a reproach upon all Israel.

3 And the elders of Jā′besh said unto him, Give us seven days' respite, that we may send messengers unto all the coasts of Israel: and then, if *there be* no man to save us, we will come out to thee.

4 ¶Then came the messengers to Gĭb′e-ah of Saul, and told the tidings in the ears of the people: and all the people lifted up their voices, and wept.

5 And, behold, Saul came after the herd out of the field; and Saul said, What *aileth* the people that they weep?

throughout the narrative of the theme of salvation, or deliverance. When the messengers came to Gibeah looking for their human saviour, they found Saul who had been anointed before this as king.

The Salvation of Jabesh-Gilead

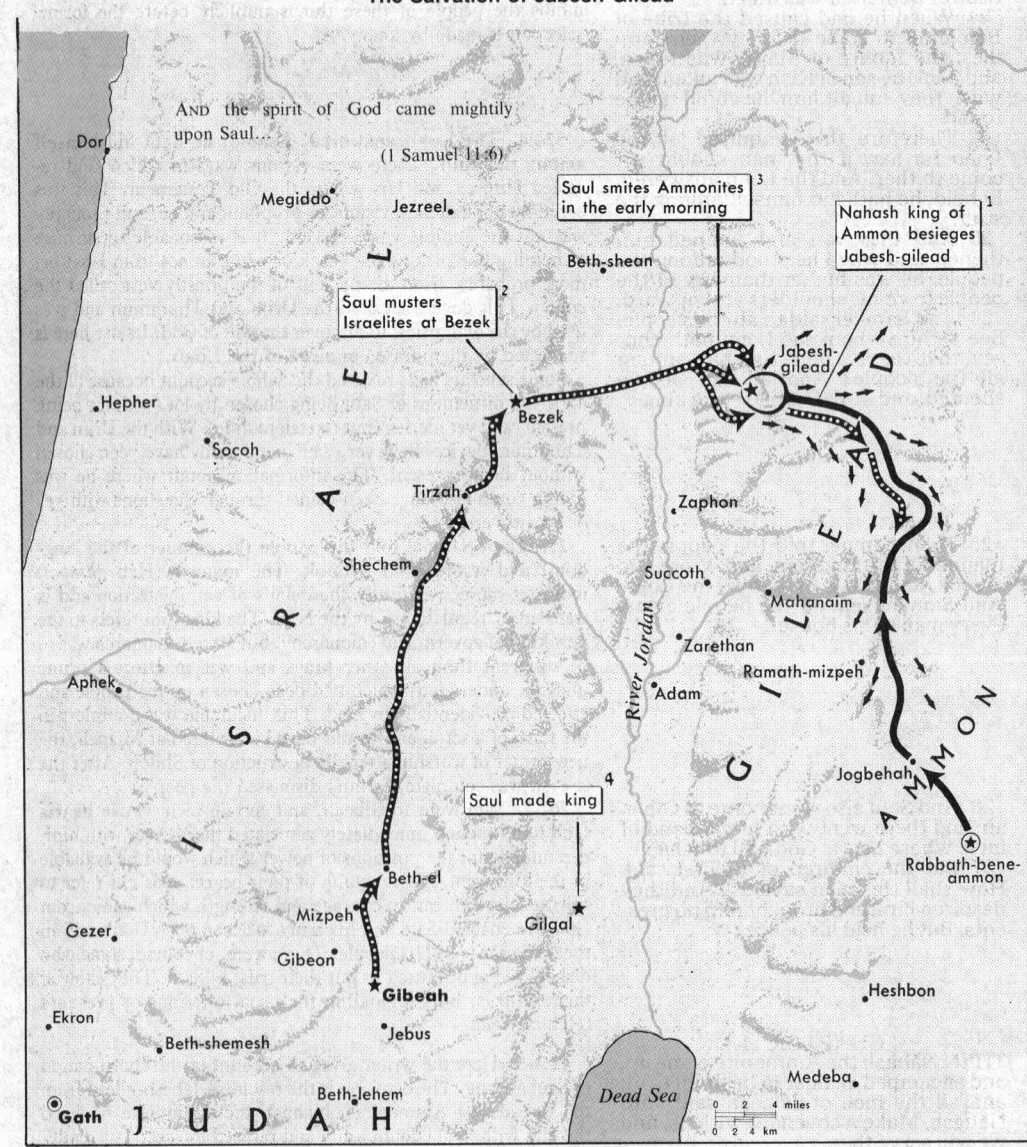

AND the spirit of God came mightily upon Saul...

(1 Samuel 11:6)

Saul smites Ammonites in the early morning [3]

Nahash king of Ammon besieges Jabesh-gilead [1]

Saul musters Israelites at Bezek [2]

Saul made king [4]

Israel
Ammon

And they told him the tidings of the men of Jā'besh.

6 And the Spirit of God came upon Saul when he heard those tidings, and his anger was kindled greatly.

7 And he took a yoke of oxen, and hewed them in pieces, and sent *them* throughout all the coasts of Israel by the hands of messengers, saying, Whosoever cometh not forth after Saul and after Samuel, so shall it be done unto his oxen. And the fear of the LORD fell on the people, and they came out with one consent.

8 And when he numbered them in Bē'zĕk, the children of Israel were three hundred thousand, and the men of Jūdah thirty thousand.

9 And they said unto the messengers that came, Thus shall ye say unto the men of Jā'besh-gĭl'e-ad, To morrow, by *that time* the sun be hot, ye shall have help. And the messengers came and shewed *it* to the men of Jā'besh; and they were glad.

10 Therefore the men of Jā'besh said, To morrow we will come out unto you, and ye shall do with us all that seemeth good unto you.

11 And it was *so* on the morrow, that Saul put the people in three companies; and they came into the midst of the host in the morning watch, and slew the Ammonites until the heat of the day: and it came to pass, that they which remained were scattered, so that two of them were not left together.

12 ¶And the people said unto Samuel, Who *is* he that said, Shall Saul reign over us? bring the men, that we may put them to death.

13 And Saul said, There shall not a man be put to death this day: for to day the LORD hath wrought salvation in Israel.

14 ¶Then said Samuel to the people, Come, and let us go to Gilgal, and renew the kingdom there.

15 And all the people went to Gilgal; and there they made Saul king before the LORD in Gilgal; and there they sacrificed sacrifices of peace offerings before the LORD; and there Saul and all the men of Israel rejoiced greatly.

CHAPTER 12

AND Samuel said unto all Israel, Behold, I have hearkened unto your voice in all that ye said unto me, and have made a king over you.

2 And now, behold, the king walketh before you: and I am old and grayheaded; and, behold, my sons *are* with you: and I have walked before you from my childhood unto this day.

3 Behold, here I *am:* witness against me before the LORD, and before his anointed: whose ox have I taken? or whose ass have I taken? or whom have I defrauded? whom have I oppressed? or of whose hand have I received *any* bribe to blind mine eyes therewith? and I will restore it to you.

4 And they said, Thou hast not defrauded us, nor oppressed us, neither hast thou taken ought of any man's hand.

5 And he said unto them, The LORD *is*

6-11. The spirit of God came upon Saul. Once more the point is made that God has chosen Saul and empowered him to deliver the people. Saul's righteous indignation and strength in the firm and shocking call to unity were engendered by the Spirit of God for the deliverance of the people of Jabesh-gilead. **Ye shall have help** (Heb *teshū'ah*). A better translation would be, "You shall have deliverance." The cognate word is used in verse 3, and the same word is used again in verse 13. Saul unified the whole national army, put them in **three companies,** and defeated the Ammonites. This great victory through the campaign of Saul confirmed the trust of the people in their new king and made possible the subsequent victories.

12-15. Bring the men. The lives of the unbelievers who had before insulted both God and Saul were now in jeopardy. Saul was merciful on this day, however, the reason being that God had accomplished **salvation in Israel.** This again shows the thread of salvation running through the fabric of these historical narratives. **They made Saul king before the LORD in Gilgal.** This is not a contradictory account, but simply the confirmation of the choice of Saul as king and the celebration of his initial success and wider acceptance.

C. Samuel's Call for Faith. 12:1-25.

12:1-5. In retiring from his office as judge, Samuel reviews his own accomplishments and faith, especially in the matter of the unification of Israel under the first anointed king. Samuel promises here to continue to intercede for the people and provide prophetic guidance. He calls upon them to fear the Lord and serve Him alone as they are being made into His very own people. **Made a king over you.** Samuel had not simply listened to the people's demand but had taken the matter to the Lord; and, after receiving God's approval and direction, he had anointed Saul. The choice was made by the people; and, humanly speaking, Saul was their king. **The king walketh before you.** There was no longer any need for Samuel's leadership as a judge. **Before the LORD, and before his anointed.** This phrase is repeated in verse 5, and shows the intended relationship of the king to the Lord Himself. God was to be the real King and Ruler over His people. He was to accomplish His will for them and bring them salvation through His anointed king.

witness against you, and his anointed *is* witness this day, that ye have not found ought in my hand. And they answered, *He is* witness.

6 ¶And Samuel said unto the people, *It is* the LORD that advanced Moses and Aaron, and that brought your fathers up out of the land of Egypt.

7 Now therefore stand still, that I may reason with you before the LORD of all the righteous acts of the LORD, which he did to you and to your fathers.

8 When Jacob was come into Egypt, and your fathers cried unto the LORD, then the LORD sent Moses and Aaron, which brought forth your fathers out of Egypt, and made them dwell in this place.

9 And when they forgat the LORD their God, he sold them into the hand of Sĭs'e-ra, captain of the host of Hā'zôr, and into the hand of the Philistines, and into the hand of the king of Moab, and they fought against them.

10 And they cried unto the LORD, and said, We have sinned, because we have forsaken the LORD, and have served Bā'al-ĭm and Ăsh'ta-rŏth: but now deliver us out of the hand of our enemies, and we will serve thee.

11 And the LORD sent Je-rŭb'ba-al, and Bē'dăn, and Jĕph'thah, and Samuel, and delivered you out of the hand of your enemies on every side, and ye dwelled safe.

12 And when ye saw that Nāhăsh the king of the children of Ammon came against you, ye said unto me, Nay; but a king shall reign over us: when the LORD your God *was* your king.

13 Now therefore behold the king whom ye have chosen, *and* whom ye have desired! and, behold, the LORD hath set a king over you.

14 If ye will fear the LORD, and serve him, and obey his voice, and not rebel against the commandment of the LORD, then shall both ye and also the king that reigneth over you continue following the LORD your God:

15 But if ye will not obey the voice of the LORD, but rebel against the commandment of the LORD, then shall the hand of the LORD be against you, as *it was* against your fathers.

16 Now therefore stand and see this great thing, which the LORD will do before your eyes.

17 *Is it* not wheat harvest to day? I will call unto the LORD, and he shall send thunder and rain; that ye may perceive and see that your wickedness *is* great, which ye have done in the sight of the LORD, in asking you a king.

18 So Samuel called unto the LORD; and the LORD sent thunder and rain that day: and all the people greatly feared the LORD and Samuel.

19 And all the people said unto Samuel, Pray for thy servants unto the LORD thy God, that we die not: for we

6-9. Brought your fathers up out of the land of Egypt. Samuel reminds the people of the way in which God accomplished salvation through His chosen leaders in the past in order to encourage them to trust Him to do it now. **That I may reason with you** is reminiscent of Isaiah 1:18. **Righteous acts.** These are the saving acts of God, His work in history to accomplish the salvation of His people. **And when they forgat the LORD their God.** Forgetting God does not mean that they merely forgot how He had delivered them, but that they ceased to actively worship and serve Him. The cycle of sin, judgment upon sin, crying out for forgiveness, and salvation is the plot of the Bible.

10-11. The example of backsliding given here is from the period of the judges. **We have sinned, because we have forsaken the LORD, and have served Baalim and Ashtaroth** is their cry of repentance. **Deliver us** (Heb *natsal*) is another salvation word meaning to "snatch away," or "rescue from danger at the last moment." The Septuagint translated it with the same word that is used for spiritual rescue in Galatians 1:4, "that he might rescue us from this present evil age." **Bedan.** The Septuagint and all current Bible translations read "Barak." Samuel himself is included among the deliverers or judges who were sent by God to rescue His people and bring them to security and worship of Him. Note again the emphasis upon the salvation theme.

12-18. Now, once again, the cycle has been started. There has been sin and judgment by God at the hands of their enemies (**Nahash**). Now they have their king; and if they will continue to **fear the LORD, and serve him, and obey his voice,** then the Lord will continue to bless them. If the people rebel and sin again, then the cycle will be repeated. To confirm Samuel's call to faithfulness as the word of the Lord, there is a miracle of thunder and rain. Miracles were performed by Jesus for the same reason: to confirm His claim to messiahship as the Word of God. See also the reason for apostolic miracles in Hebrews 2:3-4.

19-25. Pray for thy servants. The people now truly repent for their sins and for their demand of a king, and God responds through Samuel with mercy. **Fear not . . . but serve the LORD with all your heart.** This is the primary requirement for the

have added unto all our sins *this* evil, to ask us a king.

20 And Samuel said unto the people, Fear not: ye have done all this wickedness: yet turn not aside from following the LORD, but serve the LORD with all your heart;

21 And turn ye not aside: for *then should ye go* after vain *things*, which cannot profit nor deliver; for they *are* vain.

22 For the LORD will not forsake his people for his great name's sake: because it hath pleased the LORD to make you his people.

23 Moreover as for me, God forbid that I should sin against the LORD in ceasing to pray for you: but I will teach you the good and the right way:

24 Only fear the LORD, and serve him in truth with all your heart: for consider how great *things* he hath done for you.

25 But if ye shall still do wickedly, ye shall be consumed, both ye and your king.

CHAPTER 13

SAUL reigned one year; and when he had reigned two years over Israel,

2 Saul chose him three thousand *men* of Israel; *whereof* two thousand were with Saul in Mĭch′măsh and in mount Běth–el, and a thousand were with Jonathan in Gĭb′e–ah of Benjamin: and the rest of the people he sent every man to his tent.

3 And Jonathan smote the garrison of the Philistines that *was* in Gē′ba, and the Philistines heard *of it*. And Saul blew the trumpet throughout all the land, saying, Let the Hebrews hear.

4 And all Israel heard say *that* Saul had smitten a garrison of the Philistines, and *that* Israel also was had in abomination with the Philistines. And the people were called together after Saul to Gilgal.

5 And the Philistines gathered themselves together to fight with Israel, thirty thousand chariots, and six thousand horsemen, and people as the sand which *is* on the sea shore in multitude: and they came up, and pitched in Mĭch′măsh, eastward from Běth–ā′ven,

6 When the men of Israel saw that they were in a strait, (for the people were distressed,) then the people did hide themselves in caves, and in thickets, and in rocks, and in high places, and in pits.

7 And *some of* the Hebrews went over Jordan to the land of Gad and Gilead. As for Saul, he *was* yet in Gilgal, and all the people followed him trembling.

8 And he tarried seven days, according to the set time that Samuel *had appointed*: but Samuel came not to Gilgal; and the people were scattered from him.

blessing of the Lord. **Vain things** refer to false gods which are not able to deliver or save as God Himself does. **It hath pleased the LORD to make you his people.** This shows the election of Israel as God's special people. The word used here (Heb *'am*) corresponds to the New Testament word (Gr *laos*) which is used so often to show the sustained relationship of the church to God as His people (see the *Liberty Commentary on the New Testament,* I Peter 2:9). The Septuagint has, "The Lord has graciously taken you to himself as his people." It is in this light that Samuel pledges to pray for the people of the Lord and promises the continued prophetic function of teaching them **the good and right way.**

D. Deliverance from the Philistines. 13:1-14:52.

13:1. The Hebrew text is fragmentary. At the time the Septuagint was translated it was either in the same condition or nonexistent, since it is omitted there. Almost every new translation has a different computed number of years for the age of Saul at the beginning of his reign and the length of the reign. It is perhaps best to leave blanks in the translation, "Saul was . . . years old when he began to reign; and he reigned . . . . and two years over Israel."

2-7. Saul organized and commanded an army of three thousand men, with two thousand stationed in **Michmash** to the north of Jerusalem, and a thousand with Jonathan **in Gibeah of Benjamin.** Jonathan with his army **smote the garrison of the Philistines.** This was as important as the first battle of the war then formally declared **throughout all the land.** The people then joined the regular army at Gilgal and waited with great anxiety for Samuel, growing more and more fearful of the vastly superior army of the Philistines.

8-15. Saul waited the seven days for Samuel to come and offer sacrifice as **Samuel had appointed** (see 10:8). When Samuel did not arrive, Saul took it upon himself to offer the **burnt offering.** No sooner had he finished than Samuel came. **What hast thou done?** Saul rationalized that there was no time to wait longer and

9 And Saul said, Bring hither a burnt offering to me, and peace offerings. And he offered the burnt offering.

10 And it came to pass, that as soon as he had made an end of offering the burnt offering, behold, Samuel came; and Saul went out to meet him, that he might salute him.

11 And Samuel said, What hast thou done? And Saul said, Because I saw that the people were scattered from me, and *that* thou camest not within the days appointed, and *that* the Philistines gathered themselves together at Mĭch'măsh;

12 Therefore said I, The Philistines will come down now upon me to Gilgal, and I have not made supplication unto the LORD: I forced myself therefore, and offered a burnt offering.

13 And Samuel said to Saul, Thou hast done foolishly: thou hast not kept the commandment of the LORD thy God, which he commanded thee: for now would the LORD have established thy kingdom upon Israel for ever.

14 But now thy kingdom shall not continue: the LORD hath sought him a man after his own heart, and the LORD hath commanded him *to be* captain over his people, because thou hast not kept *that* which the LORD commanded thee.

15 And Samuel arose, and gat him up from Gilgal unto Gĭb'e-ah of Benjamin. And Saul numbered the people *that were* present with him, about six hundred men.

16 And Saul, and Jonathan his son, and the people *that were* present with them, abode in Gĭb'e-ah of Benjamin: but the Philistines encamped in Mĭch'-măsh.

17 ¶And the spoilers came out of the camp of the Philistines in three companies: one company turned unto the way *that leadeth to* Ŏph'rah, unto the land of Shū'al:

18 And another company turned the way *to* Bĕth-hō'ron: and another company turned *to* the way of the border that looketh to the valley of Ze-bō'im toward the wilderness.

19 ¶Now there was no smith found throughout all the land of Israel: for the Philistines said, Lest the Hebrews make *them* swords or spears:

20 But all the Israelites went down to the Philistines, to sharpen every man his share, and his coulter, and his axe, and his mattock.

21 Yet they had a file for the mattocks, and for the coulters, and for the forks, and for the axes, and to sharpen the goads.

22 So it came to pass in the day of battle, that there was neither sword nor spear found in the hand of any of the people that *were* with Saul and Jonathan: but with Saul and with Jonathan his son was there found.

23 And the garrison of the Philistines went out to the passage of Mĭch'măsh.

CHAPTER 14

NOW it came to pass upon a day, that Jonathan the son of Saul said unto the young man that bare his armour,

that a sacrifice had to be made (11-12). **Thou hast not kept the commandment of the LORD.** This was Saul's sin: disobedience. His disobedience was a sin against God, for Samuel was the prophet of God and spoke the Word of God. **Now would the LORD have established thy kingdom upon Israel for ever.** It was not that God had made a bad choice; God had known about Saul's wilful and selfish heart before he was selected. The sin and responsibility were Saul's; God did not make him sin. God did, however, allow the sin for purposes that would lead eventually to the salvation of His people. **Thy kingdom shall not continue.** It was not that one mistake had caused the loss of the kingdom for Saul's descendants, either. Saul had a rebellious heart, and he was not inclined to the will of God. God was able to use Saul when empowered by the Spirit to accomplish the immediate physical deliverance of Israel, but God had already revealed to Samuel that he sought a **man after his own heart.**

16-23. Raiders came against Israel from the Philistines, and Saul was now down to six hundred men. The Israelites were at a disadvantage, too, because they were not as technically advanced in the use of iron. Nevertheless, both sides were preparing for battle at Michmash (16-23).

14:1-5. Jonathan the son of Saul was the cause of a major victory because of his faith in God. He and his armor-bearer crossed behind the enemy lines without the knowledge of Saul,

Come, and let us go over to the Philistines' garrison, that *is* on the other side. But he told not his father.

2 And Saul tarried in the uttermost part of Gĭb'e-ah under a pomegranate tree which *is* in Mĭg'rŏn: and the people that *were* with him *were* about six hundred men;

3 And A-hī'ah, the son of A-hī'tŭb, Ĭ'-cha-bŏd's brother, the son of Phĭn'e-has, the son of Eli, the Lord's priest in Shī'lōh, wearing an ephod. And the people knew not that Jonathan was gone.

4 ¶And between the passages, by which Jonathan sought to go over unto the Philistines' garrison, *there was* a sharp rock on the one side, and a sharp rock on the other side: and the name of the one *was* Bō'zez, and the name of the other Sĕ'neh.

5 The forefront of the one *was* situate northward over against Mĭch'măsh, and the other southward over against Gĭb'e-ah,

6 And Jonathan said to the young man that bare his armour, Come, and let us go over unto the garrison of these uncircumcised: it may be that the Lord will work for us: for *there is* no restraint to the Lord to save by many or by few.

7 And his armourbearer said unto him, Do all that *is* in thine heart: turn thee; behold, I *am* with thee according to thy heart.

8 Then said Jonathan, Behold, we will pass over unto *these* men, and we will discover ourselves unto them.

9 If they say thus unto us, Tarry until we come to you; then we will stand still in our place, and will not go up unto them.

10 But if they say thus, Come up unto us; then we will go up: for the Lord hath delivered them into our hand: and this *shall be* a sign unto us.

11 And both of them discovered themselves unto the garrison of the Philistines: and the Philistines said, Behold, the Hebrews come forth out of the holes where they had hid themselves.

12 And the men of the garrison answered Jonathan and his armourbearer, and said, Come up to us, and we will shew you a thing. And Jonathan said unto his armourbearer, Come up after me: for the Lord hath delivered them into the hand of Israel.

13 And Jonathan climbed up upon his hands and upon his feet, and his armourbearer after him: and they fell before Jonathan; and his armourbearer slew after him.

14 And that first slaughter, which Jonathan and his armourbearer made, was about twenty men, within as it were an half acre of land, *which* a yoke of oxen might plow.

15 ¶And there was trembling in the host, in the field, and among all the people: the garrison, and the spoilers, they also trembled, and the earth quaked: so it was a very great trembling.

16 And the watchmen of Saul in

who remained at Migron with his small army of six hundred (vs. 2). The priest **Ahiah** remained with Saul. The **ephod** is mentioned to show that this outward means of learning the will of God was with Saul, although God was actually communicating with Jonathan in another way. Ahiah is evidently the same person as Ahimelech (a synonymous name in Hebrew) who was later killed by Saul for helping David (22:16-18).

6-9. There is no restraint to the Lord to save by many or by few. This truly remarkable faith of Jonathan is based upon his knowledge that God was a saving God. He knew that God would save His people, for He had done it in the past. This same kind of faith in God as being able to save is required of anyone who would be spiritually saved today (cf. Heb 11:6).

10-15. The Lord hath delivered them. Here, the same English word, **delivered,** is a different Hebrew word with exactly the opposite meaning to the one treated above. Here it means delivered up for destruction. Jonathan depended by faith upon this **sign** to know the will of God; and God honored it because Saul was not using the other available means for learning the will of God, the ephod, and had disobeyed God's prophet Samuel. Only about **twenty men** were killed by Jonathan and his armorbearer, but it was such a surprise that confusion developed, resulting in panic and disorderly retreat with the loss of many more men by the Philistines.

16-17. The watchmen of Saul in Gibeah. Saul and the army

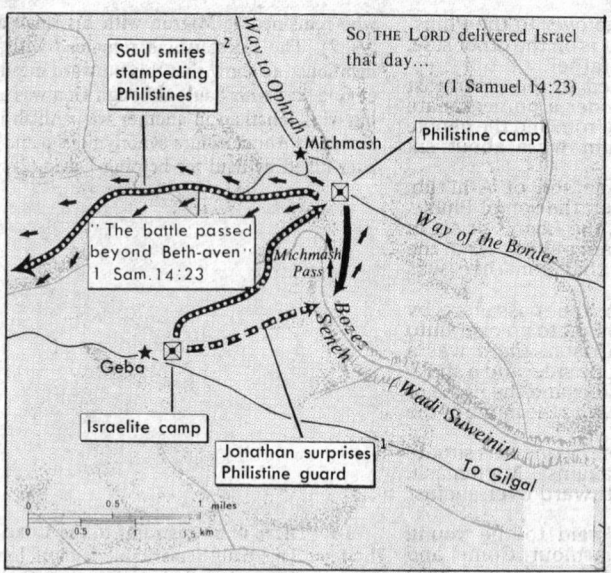

So THE LORD delivered Israel that day...

(1 Samuel 14:23)

Saul smites stampeding Philistines

Michmash

Philistine camp

Way to Ophrah

Way of the Border

"The battle passed beyond Beth-aven" 1 Sam.14:23

Michmash Pass

Bozez Seneh

Geba

Israelite camp

Jonathan surprises Philistine guard

(Wadi Suweinit)

To Gilgal

The Battle of Michmash

Gīb'e-ah of Benjamin looked; and, behold, the multitude melted away, and they went on beating down *one another.*

17 ¶Then said Saul unto the people that *were* with him, Number now, and see who is gone from us. And when they had numbered, behold, Jonathan and his armourbearer *were* not *there.*

18 And Saul said unto A-hī'ah, Bring hither the ark of God. For the ark of God was at that time with the children of Israel.

19 ¶And it came to pass, while Saul talked unto the priest, that the noise that *was* in the host of the Philistines went on and increased: and Saul said unto the priest, Withdraw thine hand.

20 And Saul and all the people that *were* with him assembled themselves, and they came to the battle: and, behold, every man's sword was against his fellow, *and there was* a very great discomfiture.

21 Moreover the Hebrews *that* were with the Philistines before that time, which went up with them into the camp *from the country* round about, even they also *turned* to be with the Israelites that *were* with Saul and Jonathan.

22 Likewise all the men of Israel which had hid themselves in mount Ē'phra-im, *when* they heard that the Philistines fled, even they also followed hard after them in the battle.

23 So the LORD saved Israel that day: and the battle passed over unto Bĕth-ā'ven.

24 ¶And the men of Israel were distressed that day: for Saul had adjured the people, saying, Cursed *be* the man that eateth *any* food until evening, that I may be avenged on mine enemies. So none of the people tasted *any* food.

25 And all *they* of the land came to a

had not known of Jonathan's venture, but now they observed the rapid retreat of the Philistines, which from a distance looked as if the enemy **melted away.** When Saul found out that **Jonathan and his armor-bearer were not there,** he surmised what was happening and was forced to make a decision whether or not to go to battle.

18-23. Bring hither the ark. The Septuagint does not mention the ark but has "bring the ephod." The ephod was present with Saul in the camp (14:3), but it is highly unlikely that the ark was. Furthermore, it was not the ark but the ephod that was used to enquire concerning the will of the Lord; and still further, the statement in verse 19 **Withdraw thine hand** refers to the priest taking his hand out of the ephod pocket with the answer from the Lord. Evidently a yes answer was received on the question of going to battle, or else Saul was too impatient to wait for the answer. At any rate, the Israelites began to pursue the retreating Philistines who were killing each other in the confusion. **So the LORD saved** (Heb *yasha‘*) **Israel.** God had again accomplished His will in delivering the people from their enemies.

24-35. Saul's oath caused the people to sin even in their victory. **Cursed.** Since the people were forbidden to eat all day, even though they discovered honey, they did not eat it (except for Jonathan). **Did eat them with the blood.** When the time of the oath was expired, the people were so hungry that they violated the law of God (Lev 17:10-14). This is not the only instance in the Bible where man's law was kept and God's law

wood; and there was honey upon the ground.

26 And when the people were come into the wood, behold, the honey dropped; but no man put his hand to his mouth: for the people feared the oath.

27 But Jonathan heard not when his father charged the people with the oath: wherefore he put forth the end of the rod that *was* in his hand, and dipped it in an honeycomb, and put his hand to his mouth; and his eyes were enlightened.

28 Then answered one of the people, and said, Thy father straitly charged the people with an oath, saying, Cursed *be* the man that eateth *any* food this day. And the people were faint.

29 Then said Jonathan, My father hath troubled the land: see, I pray you, how mine eyes have been enlightened, because I tasted a little of this honey.

30 How much more, if haply the people had eaten freely to day of the spoil of their enemies which they found? for had there not been now a much greater slaughter among the Philistines?

31 And they smote the Philistines that day from Mĭch′măsh to Āij′a-lŏn: and the people were very faint.

32 And the people flew upon the spoil, and took sheep, and oxen, and calves, and slew *them* on the ground: and the people did eat *them* with the blood.

33 Then they told Saul, saying, Behold, the people sin against the Lord, in that they eat with the blood. And he said, Ye have transgressed: roll a great stone unto me this day.

34 And Saul said, Disperse yourselves among the people, and say unto them, Bring me hither every man his ox, and every man his sheep, and slay *them* here, and eat; and sin not against the Lord in eating with the blood. And all the people brought every man his ox with him that night, and slew *them* there.

35 And Saul built an altar unto the Lord: the same was the first altar that he built unto the Lord.

36 ¶And Saul said, Let us go down after the Philistines by night, and spoil them until the morning light, and let us not leave a man of them. And they said, Do whatsoever seemeth good unto thee. Then said the priest, Let us draw near hither unto God.

37 And Saul asked counsel of God, Shall I go down after the Philistines? wilt thou deliver them into the hand of Israel? But he answered him not that day.

38 And Saul said, Draw ye near hither, all the chief of the people: and know and see wherein this sin hath been this day.

39 For, *as* the Lord liveth, which saveth Israel, though it be in Jonathan my son, he shall surely die. But *there was* not a man among all the people *that* answered him.

40 Then said he unto all Israel, Be ye on one side, and I and Jonathan my son will be on the other side. And the peo-

violated. **Roll a great stone.** This made provision for the people so that they did not sin further against the Lord. **Saul built an altar unto the Lord.** This may have been more political than religious, but Saul did build other altars, a fact implied in the statement that this **was the first.**

36-46. Jonathan was condemned for eating, although he did not know of Saul's oath and had to be delivered by the people. **Saul asked counsel of God.** He should have done this earlier; now God would give him no answer at all. **Sin.** It was correctly surmised that there must be some sin which caused God to refuse to give answer by the oracle. The sin was in reality Saul's, but he was too dense to recognize it. **Give a perfect lot.** It should be noted that the Septuagint reads, "If the sin is in me or my son Jonathan, respond with Urim (probably meaning yes); if your people Israel have sinned, respond with Thummim (probably meaning no)." The sin was, of course, found to be in either Saul or Jonathan. Saul immediately suspected Jonathan, rather than himself, and was willing to let him die. At this point the Septuagint text implies that some other form of casting lots was used at the insistence of Saul, and Jonathan was chosen by the people as being the guilty party. **Shall Jonathan die, who hath wrought this great salvation . . . ?** Although the people were willing to acknowledge that he had committed this petty sin, they were not willing to let him die for it. **So the people rescued Jonathan.** The word **rescued** (Heb *padah*) is a common word for "redeem," or "ransom" in the Old Testament, and implies

559

ple said unto Saul, Do what seemeth good unto thee.

41 Therefore Saul said unto the LORD God of Israel, Give a perfect *lot*. And Saul and Jonathan were taken: but the people escaped.

42 And Saul said, Cast *lots* between me and Jonathan my son. And Jonathan was taken.

43 Then Saul said to Jonathan, Tell me what thou hast done. And Jonathan told him, and said, I did but taste a little honey with the end of the rod that *was* in mine hand, *and,* lo, I must die.

44 And Saul answered, God do so and more also: for thou shalt surely die, Jonathan.

45 And the people said unto Saul, Shall Jonathan die, who hath wrought this great salvation in Israel? God forbid: *as* the LORD liveth, there shall not one hair of his head fall to the ground; for he hath wrought with God this day. So the people rescued Jonathan, that he died not.

46 Then Saul went up from following the Philistines: and the Philistines went to their own place.

47 ¶So Saul took the kingdom over Israel, and fought against all his enemies on every side, against Moab, and against the children of Ammon, and against Ēdom, and against the kings of Zōbah, and against the Philistines: and whithersoever he turned himself, he vexed *them.*

48 And he gathered an host, and smote the Am'ă-lek-ītes, and delivered Israel out of the hands of them that spoiled them.

49 ¶Now the sons of Saul were Jonathan, and Ĭsh'ū-ī, and Měl'chī-shū'a: and the names of his two daughters *were these;* the name of the firstborn Me'răb, and the name of the younger Mī'chal:

50 And the name of Saul's wife *was* A-hĭn'ō-am, the daughter of A-hĭm'ā-az: and the name of the captain of his host *was* Abner, the son of Ner, Saul's uncle.

51 And Kish *was* the father of Saul; and Ner the father of Abner *was* the son of Ā'bĭ-el.

52 And there was sore war against the Philistines all the days of Saul: and when Saul saw any strong man, or any valiant man, he took him unto him.

CHAPTER 15

SAMUEL also said unto Saul, The LORD sent me to anoint thee *to be* king over his people, over Israel: now therefore hearken thou unto the voice of the words of the LORD.

2 Thus saith the LORD of hosts, I remember *that* which Am'a-lěk did to Israel, how he laid *wait* for him in the way, when he came up from Egypt.

3 Now go and smite Ăm'a-lěk, and utterly destroy all that they have, and spare them not; but slay both man and woman, infant and suckling, ox and sheep, camel and ass.

4 And Saul gathered the people together, and numbered them in Tel'ā-im, two hundred thousand footmen, and ten thousand men of Judah.

usually the payment of ransom money. Some versions translate this as "ransom."

47-52. This was not all that Saul accomplished as Israel's first king. He had unified the people and was a valiant warrior. **Fought against all his enemies on every side.** Some of his conquests are listed here. **Delivered Israel.** This again shows one of the main contributions of Saul. He at least accomplished physical deliverance.

E. God's Rejection of Saul as King for His People. 15:1-35.

15:1-10. Saul is again given specific commands through the prophet Samuel, and even though Saul is still accomplishing God's will in the deliverance of the people, he is being tested to prove his disobedience (cf. 13:13). **Smite Amalek, and utterly destroy all.** This was not carried out to the letter, but reasoned away by Saul. There is no way that the command could have been misunderstood by Saul, since the word used here (Heb *charam*) is very intensive and is used for what is completely dedicated to the Lord. The same word is used in verses 8, 9, 15, 18, 20, and 21. **Saul smote the Amalekites,** in partial obedience to the command of God, but spared Agag the king and the best of the spoil.

5 And Saul came to a city of Ăm′a-lĕk, and laid wait in the valley.

6 ¶And Saul said unto the Kēn′ītes, Go, depart, get you down from among the Am′ă-lek-ītes, lest I destroy you with them: for ye shewed kindness to all the children of Israel, when they came up out of Egypt. So the Kēn′ītes departed from among the Am′ă-lek-ītes.

7 And Saul smote the Am′ă-lek-ītes from Hăv′i-lah *until* thou comest to Shur, that *is* over against Egypt.

8 And he took Agăg the king of the Am′ă-lek-ītes alive, and utterly destroyed all the people with the edge of the sword.

9 But Saul and the people spared Agăg, and the best of the sheep, and of the oxen, and of the fatlings, and the lambs, and all *that was* good, and would not utterly destroy them: but every thing *that was* vile and refuse, that they destroyed utterly.

10 ¶Then came the word of the LORD unto Samuel, saying,

11 It repenteth me that I have set up Saul *to be* king: for he is turned back from following me, and hath not performed my commandments. And it grieved Samuel; and he cried unto the LORD all night.

12 And when Samuel rose early to meet Saul in the morning, it was told Samuel, saying, Saul came to Carmel, and, behold, he set him up a place, and is gone about, and passed on, and gone down to Gilgal.

13 And Samuel came to Saul: and Saul said unto him, Blessed *be* thou of the LORD: I have performed the commandment of the LORD.

14 And Samuel said, What *meaneth* then this bleating of the sheep in mine ears, and the lowing of the oxen which I hear?

15 And Saul said, They have brought them from the Am′ă-lek-ītes: for the people spared the best of the sheep and of the oxen, to sacrifice unto the LORD thy God; and the rest we have utterly destroyed.

16 Then Samuel said unto Saul, Stay, and I will tell thee what the LORD hath said to me this night. And he said unto him, Say on.

17 And Samuel said, When thou *wast* little in thine own sight, *wast* thou not made the head of the tribes of Israel, and the LORD anointed thee king over Israel?

18 And the LORD sent thee on a journey, and said, Go and utterly destroy the sinners the Am′ă-lek-ītes, and fight against them until they be consumed.

19 Wherefore then didst thou not obey the voice of the LORD, but didst fly upon the spoil, and didst evil in the sight of the LORD?

20 And Saul said unto Samuel, Yea, I have obeyed the voice of the LORD, and have gone the way which the LORD sent me, and have brought Agăg the king of Ăm′a-lĕk, and have utterly destroyed the Am′ă-lek-ītes.

21 But the people took of the spoil, sheep and oxen, the chief of the things

11-12. It repenteth me that I have set up Saul to be king. This is the revelation that came to Samuel from the Lord. The word **repenteth** (Heb *nacham*) in the Old Testament does not correspond to the New Testament word for repentance. In the New Testament repentance is a technical religious word associated with conversion. In the Old Testament the word is used mainly with God as the subject and simply denotes a change in His administration. God's overall plan was the same (salvation), but a change in human instrumentality is required here.

13-21. I have performed the commandment. Even if Samuel had not been a prophet, he might have suspected disobedience on hearing such a greeting as this. **What meaneth then this bleating . . . ?** Saul tries to rationalize his sin as necessary for a religious offering to the Lord. Saul tries again and again to bluff or shift the blame, but he is unable to avoid the cutting prophetic rebuke.

which should have been utterly destroyed, to sacrifice unto the LORD thy God in Gilgal.

22 And Samuel said, Hath the LORD *as great* delight in burnt offerings and sacrifices, as in obeying the voice of the LORD? Behold, to obey *is* better than sacrifice, *and* to hearken than the fat of rams.

23 For rebellion *is as* the sin of witchcraft, and stubbornness *is as* iniquity and idolatry. Because thou hast rejected the word of the LORD, he hath also rejected thee from *being* king.

24 And Saul said unto Samuel, I have sinned: for I have transgressed the commandment of the LORD, and thy words: because I feared the people, and obeyed their voice.

25 Now therefore, I pray thee, pardon my sin, and turn again with me, that I may worship the LORD.

26 And Samuel said unto Saul, I will not return with thee: for thou hast rejected the word of the LORD, and the LORD hath rejected thee from being king over Israel.

27 And as Samuel turned about to go away, he laid hold upon the skirt of his mantle, and it rent.

28 And Samuel said unto him, The LORD hath rent the kingdom of Israel from thee this day, and hath given it to a neighbour of thine, *that is* better than thou.

29 And also the Strength of Israel will not lie nor repent: for he *is* not a man, that he should repent.

30 Then he said, I have sinned: *yet* honour me now, I pray thee, before the elders of my people, and before Israel, and turn again with me, that I may worship the LORD thy God.

31 So Samuel turned again after Saul; and Saul worshipped the LORD.

32 ¶Then said Samuel, Bring ye hither to me Agag the king of the Am′ă-lek-ītes. And Agag came unto him delicately. And Agag said, Surely the bitterness of death is past.

33 And Samuel said, As thy sword hath made women childless, so shall thy mother be childless among women. And Samuel hewed Agag in pieces before the LORD in Gilgal.

34 ¶Then Samuel went to Rā′mah; and Saul went up to his house to Gĭb′e-ah of Saul.

35 And Samuel came no more to see Saul until the day of his death: nevertheless Samuel mourned for Saul: and the LORD repented that he had made Saul king over Israel.

CHAPTER 16

AND the LORD said unto Samuel, How long wilt thou mourn for Saul, seeing I have rejected him from reigning

22. To obey is better than sacrifice, and to hearken than the fat of rams. Both members of the parallelism have the same meaning ("hearken" means obeying in the Old Testament). Obedience is basic to biblical religion. Legalistic fulfillment of the letter of the law can never take the place of intending from the heart to do the will of God. In Isaiah 1:10-13 Judah is rebuked by the prophet for outward conformity to the law without obedience from the heart, "Hear the word of the Lord . . . ." This is why Jesus so often denounced the Pharisees, they were near with their lips but often not with their heart. To ". . . love the LORD thy God with all thy heart . . ." is more important than ". . . all whole burnt offerings and sacrifices" (Mk 12:30-33).

23-25. Rebellion. Failure to give complete obedience is rebellion, and this is as bad as witchcraft or idolatry. **I have sinned.** That this is not true repentance is understood by Saul's continued attempt to shift the blame to **the people.** Saul claims to have feared and obeyed the people, but he should have feared and obeyed God instead. **Pardon.** If Saul's repentance had been genuine and his request for pardon sincere, God would have granted forgiveness. But they were not, and Saul had shown again that he had rejected the will of God for his own will.

26-31. The LORD hath rejected thee from being king over Israel. God's patience had ended with this man who had hardened his heart in disobedience. The accidental tearing of Samuel's mantle provides a parting symbolism of God's tearing away the kingdom. **Before the elders.** Saul was less concerned about the prophecy (which he evidently did not believe), than about his public image.

32-35. Agag came unto him delicately. "Agag came to him confidently." The Hebrew word may indicate either "cheerfully," or as the Septuagint reads, "trembling." Samuel himself had to see that God's command was carried out by executing Agag. **Mourned for Saul.** This probably means that Samuel lamented the fact that although Saul had been anointed, he failed and was rejected by God.

III. GOD ANOINTS DAVID AND LEADS HIM TO THE THRONE. 16:1-31:13.

A. David Is Anointed by Samuel. 16:1-23.

16:1-6. Fill thine horn with oil. Anointing was only symbolic of God's choice. Only one king had been anointed in Israel, but the significance had already been established with the anointing

over Israel? fill thine horn with oil, and go, I will send thee to Jesse the Běth-lehěmīte: for I have provided me a king among his sons.

2 And Samuel said, How can I go? if Saul hear *it*, he will kill me. And the LORD said, Take an heifer with thee, and say, I am come to sacrifice to the LORD.

3 And call Jesse to the sacrifice, and I will shew thee what thou shalt do: and thou shalt anoint unto me *him* whom I name unto thee.

4 And Samuel did that which the LORD spake, and came to Běth-lehěm. And the elders of the town trembled at his coming, and said, Comest thou peaceably?

5 And he said, Peaceably: I am come to sacrifice unto the LORD: sanctify yourselves, and come with me to the sacrifice. And he sanctified Jesse and his sons, and called them to the sacrifice.

6 And it came to pass, when they were come, that he looked on E-lī'ab, and said, Surely the LORD's anointed *is* before him.

7 But the LORD said unto Samuel, Look not on his countenance, or on the height of his stature; because I have refused him: for *the LORD seeth* not as man seeth; for man looketh on the outward appearance, but the LORD looketh on the heart.

8 Then Jesse called A-bǐn'a-dăb, and made him pass before Samuel. And he said, Neither hath the LORD chosen this.

9 Then Jesse made Shăm'mah to pass by. And he said, Neither hath the LORD chosen this.

10 Again, Jesse made seven of his sons to pass before Samuel. And Samuel said unto Jesse, The LORD hath not chosen these.

11 And Samuel said unto Jesse, Are here all *thy* children? And he said, There remaineth yet the youngest, and, behold, he keepeth the sheep. And Samuel said unto Jesse, Send and fetch him: for we will not sit down till he come hither.

12 And he sent, and brought him in. Now he *was* ruddy, *and* withal of a beautiful countenance, and goodly to look to. And the LORD said, Arise, anoint him: for this *is* he.

13 Then Samuel took the horn of oil, and anointed him in the midst of his brethren: and the Spirit of the LORD came upon David from that day forward. So Samuel rose up, and went to Rā'mah.

14 ¶But the Spirit of the LORD departed from Saul, and an evil spirit from the LORD troubled him.

15 And Saul's servants said unto him,

of the priests and the holy things for ministry to the Lord. The king was now to be God's servant; God had rejected Saul because he was self-serving. **I will send thee to Jesse.** God had already made the choice. **Say, I am come to sacrifice.** Samuel's primary purpose in going to Beth-lehem was to anoint David, but if that had been known to Saul, the prophet's life would have been in jeopardy. Samuel did come to sacrifice, but it was necessary to conceal his ultimate purpose. **Thou shalt anoint unto me him whom I name.** The final revelation as to which one of the sons of Jesse would be anointed would come at the last possible moment.

7-10. Samuel was looking for another Saul, mature and obviously a kingly sort. He supposed immediately that it was Eliab. **Look not on his countenance.** His outward appearance was not to be considered at all in making the choice. **The LORD seeth not as man seeth; for man looketh on the outward appearance, but the LORD looketh on the heart.** The principle is found throughout the Bible; but even Samuel had to be reminded of it here, and the choice must be all of God. "My thoughts are not your thoughts," Isaiah 55:8. **Neither hath the LORD chosen this.** This same negative revelation came to Samuel as he viewed each of the sons of Jesse, and it became very obvious that the anointed one would indeed be God's chosen one.

11-13. He keepeth the sheep. Even the fact that David was a shepherd was to be typical of the Great Shepherd, Jesus Christ. **Anointed him.** All the same things that Samuel had spoken to Saul at his anointing (10:1) were no doubt spoken, or at least surely implied here in the action. He was anointed as king over God's people; he would reign and save them from their enemies; he was to be the leader or prince over God's heritage; and he was typical of that future King who would also come as God's chosen One to accomplish our salvation: Jesus Christ, the Son of David.

Until his death, Saul is respected by David as the Lord's anointed; afterward David is the Lord's anointed. David's descendants are also anointed, but Jesus Christ as the Son of David is the ultimate Anointed One who is chosen of God to take away our sins and bring us true and eternal salvation. **The spirit of the LORD came upon David from that day forward.** This is the guiding, protecting, empowering, and success-producing work of the Spirit of God with reference to David as the chosen king. The word **came** (Heb *tsalach*) means, literally, "to be in good condition, strong, efficient." From this point on the Spirit of God assures the success of David as the anointed one. This coming of the Spirit upon David is typical of the coming of the Spirit upon Jesus at his baptism.

14-23. While David was being prepared for office, Saul was being punished by the Lord. The evil spirit was evidently a mental affliction next to insanity. Since Saul was unable to function with this spiritual malady, it was necessary to hire a musician for symptomatic treatment; this was a recognized

Behold now, an evil spirit from God troubleth thee.

16 Let our lord now command thy servants, *which are* before thee, to seek out a man, *who is* a cunning player on an harp: and it shall come to pass, when the evil spirit from God is upon thee, that he shall play with his hand, and thou shalt be well.

17 And Saul said unto his servants, Provide me now a man that can play well, and bring *him* to me.

18 Then answered one of the servants, and said, Behold, I have seen a son of Jesse the Bĕth–lĕhĕmīte, *that is* cunning in playing, and a mighty valiant man, and a man of war, and prudent in matters, and a comely person, and the LORD *is* with him.

19 ¶Wherefore Saul sent messengers unto Jesse, and said, Send me David thy son, which *is* with the sheep.

20 And Jesse took an ass *laden* with bread, and a bottle of wine, and a kid, and sent *them* by David his son unto Saul.

21 And David came to Saul, and stood before him: and he loved him greatly; and he became his armourbearer.

22 And Saul sent to Jesse, saying, Let David, I pray thee, stand before me; for he hath found favour in my sight.

23 And it came to pass, when the *evil* spirit from God was upon Saul, that David took an harp, and played with his hand: so Saul was refreshed, and was well, and the evil spirit departed from him.

CHAPTER 17

NOW the Philistines gathered together their armies to battle, and were gathered together at Shō'chōh, which *belongeth* to Judah, and pitched between Shō'chōh and A-zē'kah, in Ē'phes–dăm'mĭm,

2 And Saul and the men of Israel were gathered together, and pitched by the valley of Ē'lah, and set the battle in array against the Philistines.

3 And the Philistines stood on a mountain on the one side, and Israel stood on a mountain on the other side: and *there was* a valley between them.

4 And there went out a champion out of the camp of the Philistines, named Golīath, of Gath, whose height *was* six cubits and a span.

5 And *he had* an helmet of brass upon his head, and he *was* armed with a coat of mail; and the weight of the coat *was* five thousand shekels of brass.

6 And *he had* greaves of brass upon his legs, and a target of brass between his soulders.

7 And the staff of his spear *was* like a weaver's beam; and his spear's head *weighed* six hundred shekels of iron: and one bearing a shield went before him.

8 And he stood and cried unto the armies of Israel, and said unto them, Why are ye come out to set *your* battle in array? *am* not I a Philistine, and ye servants to Saul? choose you a man for you, and let him come down to me.

9 If he be able to fight with me, and to

method of treatment and was apparently at least partially effective. David was prepared for this work, and one of Saul's servants knew about David. **Became his armor-bearer.** This probably did not happen at this time. David must have come to play for Saul for a short time, and when Saul recovered, David returned to Beth-lehem. Later, David killed Goliath and then became more closely associated with Saul. The writer of Samuel did not necessarily list events chronologically; his purpose was not mere history, but salvation-history.

B. God's Deliverance through David's Fight with Goliath. 17:1-58.

17:1-4. This battle would have been several years after the battle of Michmash (ch. 14). Again there was a threatening situation, a need for God to deliver His people. **The valley of Elah.** This was a wide valley fifteen miles southwest of Jerusalem. **Champion** (a Greek concept). His **height was six cubits and a span,** which makes him about nine feet and nine inches tall. He was a descendant of a race of giants, the Anakim, who had been wiped out by Joshua during the conquest of the land. Joshua 11:22 states that the only Anakim left were in Gaza, Ashdod, and Gath.

5-11. His armor was all of bronze. **Coat of mail.** This was a long vest made of overlapping bronze plates. His **spear's head** was made of iron which could easily pierce the bronze mail of his enemies. **Choose you a man for you.** It was possible in ancient times to decide the outcome of a battle on the basis of this kind of contest. **They were dismayed, and greatly afraid.** They had no match for this well-armed giant; it was an impossible situation, humanly speaking.

kill me, then will we be your servants: but if I prevail against him, and kill him, then shall ye be our servants, and serve us.

10 And the Philistine said, I defy the armies of Israel this day; give me a man, that we may fight together.

11 When Saul and all Israel heard those words of the Philistine, they were dismayed, and greatly afraid.

12 ¶Now David *was* the son of that Ĕph'rath-īte of Bĕth–lehĕm–jūdah, whose name *was* Jesse; and he had eight sons: and the man went among men *for* an old man in the days of Saul.

13 And the three eldest sons of Jesse went *and* followed Saul to the battle: and the names of his three sons that went to the battle *were* E-lī'ab the first-born, and next unto him A-bĭn'a-dăb, and the third Shăm'mah.

14 And David *was* the youngest: and the three eldest followed Saul.

15 But David went and returned from Saul to feed his father's sheep at Bĕth–lehĕm.

16 And the Philistine drew near morning and evening, and presented himself forty days.

17 And Jesse said unto David his son, Take now for thy brethren an ephah of this parched *corn,* and these ten loaves, and run to the camp to thy brethren;

18 And carry these ten cheeses unto the captain of *their* thousand, and look how thy brethren fare, and take their pledge.

19 Now Saul, and they, and all the men of Israel, *were* in the valley of Ē'lah, fighting with the Philistines.

20 And David rose up early in the morning, and left the sheep with a keeper, and took, and went, as Jesse had commanded him; and he came to the trench, as the host was going forth to the fight, and shouted for the battle.

21 For Israel and the Philistines had put the battle in array, army against army.

22 And David left his carriage in the hand of the keeper of the carriage, and ran into the army, and came and saluted his brethren.

23 And as he talked with them, behold, there came up the champion, the Philistine of Gath, Goliath by name, out of the armies of the Philistines, and spake according to the same words: and David heard *them.*

24 And all the men of Israel, when they saw the man, fled from him, and were sore afraid.

25 And the men of Israel said, Have ye seen this man that is come up? surely to defy Israel is he come up: and it shall be, *that* the man who killeth him, the king will enrich him with great riches, and will give him his daughter, and make his father's house free in Israel.

26 And David spake to the men that stood by him, saying, What shall be done to the man that killeth this Philistine, and taketh away the reproach from Israel? for who *is* this uncircumcised Philistine, that he should defy the armies of the living God?

27 And the people answered him af-

12-27. David is again introduced as the son of Jesse. These events are not intended to follow chronologically, but to show that God had prepared David for this occasion as His chosen deliverer. **David went and returned from Saul.** David had been with Saul to play his harp but had since returned to Beth-lehem. He had the task of taking food to his brothers who were in Saul's army, and so heard the challenge of the Philistine Goliath. **That he should defy the armies of the living God.** David had great faith in God and believed that as long as the people trusted in God there was no enemy they could not conquer.

I SAMUEL 17:28

ter this manner, saying, So shall it be done to the man that killeth him.

28 And E-lī'ab his eldest brother heard when he spake unto the men; and E-lī'ab's anger was kindled against David, and he said, Why camest thou down hither? and with whom hast thou left those few sheep in the wilderness? I know thy pride, and the naughtiness of thine heart; for thou art come down that thou mightest see the battle.

29 And David said, What have I now done? Is there not a cause?

30 And he turned from him toward another, and spake after the same manner: and the people answered him again after the former manner.

31 And when the words were heard which David spake, they rehearsed them before Saul: and he sent for him.

32 ¶And David said to Saul, Let no man's heart fail because of him; thy servant will go and fight with this Philistine.

33 And Saul said to David, Thou art not able to go against this Philistine to fight with him: for thou art but a youth, and he a man of war from his youth.

34 And David said unto Saul, Thy servant kept his father's sheep, and there came a lion, and a bear, and took a lamb out of the flock:

35 And I went out after him, and smote him, and delivered it out of his mouth: and when he arose against me, I caught him by his beard, and smote him, and slew him.

36 Thy servant slew both the lion and the bear: and this uncircumcised Philistine shall be as one of them, seeing he hath defied the armies of the living God.

37 David said moreover, The LORD that delivered me out of the paw of the lion, and out of the paw of the bear, he will deliver me out of the hand of this Philistine. And Saul said unto David, Go, and the LORD be with thee.

38 ¶And Saul armed David with his armour, and he put an helmet of brass upon his head; also he armed him with a coat of mail.

39 And David girded his sword upon his armour, and he assayed to go; for he had not proved it. And David said unto Saul, I cannot go with these; for I have not proved them. And David put them off him.

40 And he took his staff in his hand, and chose him five smooth stones out of the brook, and put them in a shepherd's bag which he had, even in a scrip; and his sling was in his hand: and he drew near to the Philistine.

41 And the Philistine came on and drew near unto David; and the man that bare the shield went before him.

42 And when the Philistine looked about, and saw David, he disdained him: for he was but a youth, and ruddy, and of a fair countenance.

43 And the Philistine said unto David, Am I a dog, that thou comest to me with staves? And the Philistine cursed David by his gods.

44 And the Philistine said to David, Come to me, and I will give thy flesh

28-33. Eliab's anger was kindled. David was being put down by his brother who may have been genuinely concerned for his safety or may have been moved by jealousy. Eliab belittles David's age, his task, the number of sheep in his care and questions his reason for coming. **Is there not a cause?** A better translation of this idiom might be, "There is nothing wrong with asking, is there?" At any rate, Eliab does not seem to be able to stop him from asking; and David makes thorough enquiry into the matter. His inquisitiveness even came to the attention of Saul himself, who sent for him. David tries to encourage faith in Saul, **Let no man's heart fail,** and offers to defeat the giant himself, with God on his side that is. **Thou art but a youth.** The NIV has, "You are only a boy." This is a bit sarcastic, but David and Saul are not on the same wave length. David is not thinking of going in his own strength! Nevertheless, he answers a fool according to his folly.

34-46. There came a lion, and a bear. These were ferocious animals, feared by grown and experienced men, but David had faced them time and again. **Delivered** (Heb natsal) means "rescue, save," the same word used when God delivered His people from danger. Since David had rescued sheep from his father's flock with the help of God, he could see no difficulty in rescuing Israel, the sheep of God's flock through the same trust in God. Since Goliath had **defied the armies of the living God,** he did not stand a chance. **He will deliver me.** David trusted in God alone to rescue him (same Hebrew word as in verse 35). **Saul armed David with his armor.** Since Saul was himself a large man, David must have been close to the same size. David does not say that he cannot wear the armor because it is too big, but rather because he is unaccustomed to it. And so, armed with **sling** and **stones,** David and God went out to fight the Philistine and his armor-bearer.

566

unto the fowls of the air, and to the beasts of the field.

45 Then said David to the Philistine, Thou comest to me with a sword, and with a spear, and with a shield: but I come to thee in the name of the LORD of hosts, the God of the armies of Israel, whom thou hast defied.

46 This day will the LORD deliver thee into mine hand; and I will smite thee, and take thine head from thee; and I will give the carcases of the host of the Philistines this day unto the fowls of the air, and to the wild beasts of the earth; that all the earth may know that there is a God in Israel.

47 And all this assembly shall know that the LORD saveth not with sword and spear: for the battle is the LORD's, and he will give you into our hands.

48 And it came to pass, when the Philistine arose, and came and drew nigh to meet David, that David hasted, and ran toward the army to meet the Philistine.

49 And David put his hand in his bag, and took thence a stone, and slang it, and smote the Philistine in his forehead, that the stone sunk into his forehead; and he fell upon his face to the earth.

50 So David prevailed over the Philistine with a sling and with a stone, and smote the Philistine, and slew him; but there was no sword in the hand of David.

51 Therefore David ran, and stood upon the Philistine, and took his sword, and drew it out of the sheath thereof, and slew him, and cut off his head therewith. And when the Philistines saw their champion was dead, they fled.

52 And the men of Israel and of Jūdah arose, and shouted, and pursued the Philistines, until thou come to the valley, and to the gates of Ĕkron. And the wounded of the Philistines fell down by the way to Shā-a-rā'im, even unto Gath, and unto Ĕkron.

53 And the children of Israel returned from chasing after the Philistines, and they spoiled their tents.

54 And David took the head of the Philistine, and brought it to Jerusalem; but he put his armour in his tent.

55 ¶And when Saul saw David go forth against the Philistine, he said unto Abner, the captain of the host, Abner, whose son is this youth? And Abner said, As thy soul liveth, O king, I cannot tell.

56 And the king said, Enquire thou whose son the stripling is.

57 And as David returned from the slaughter of the Philistine, Abner took him, and brought him before Saul with the head of the Philistine in his hand.

58 And Saul said to him, Whose son art thou, thou young man? And David answered, I am the son of thy servant Jesse the Bĕth–lehĕmīte.

CHAPTER 18

AND it came to pass, when he had made an end of speaking unto Saul, that the soul of Jonathan was knit with the soul of David, and Jonathan loved him as his own soul.

47-51. All the mockery and fierceness of the man could not shake the confidence and faith of David. He knew that the faith of the whole army of Israel would rally when they saw the giant fall down dead. **The LORD saveth not with sword and spear: for the battle is the LORD's.** Again, it is emphasized that God is a saving-God. **Saveth** (Heb *yasha'*) means to "save, help, or come to the aid of." It is to be contrasted with the Hebrew word for "deliver" found in verses 35 and 37 (Heb *natsal*), as well as with the word for "deliver" found in verse 46 (Heb *sagar*) which means "to close up or abandon to." The action emphasized by the verb is progressive, so that the meaning is God's help is never (in any of His saving acts) merely a sword or spear. God's help to man is always supernatural and beyond human possibility. David's faith in God's certain help is expressed here with the same word used in Jonathan's statement in 14:6.

52-58. The men of Israel and of Judah. They are unified in their faith. So they were victorious over the Philistines and had been saved from what looked like certain destruction.

C. Saul's Rage and God's Help for David. 18:1-20:42.

18:1-16. Jonathan loved him. The mutual brotherly love and admiration of these men was obviously based upon their common faith in God. They were both heroic warriors, but their bravery was based in the knowledge that God will always aid and save His people in a supernatural way (cf. 14:6; 17:47). The

2 And Saul took him that day, and would let him go no more home to his father's house.

3 Then Jonathan and David made a covenant, because he loved him as his own soul.

4 And Jonathan stripped himself of the robe that *was* upon him, and gave it to David, and his garments, even to his sword, and to his bow, and to his girdle.

5 ¶And David went out whithersoever Saul sent him, *and* behaved himself wisely: and Saul set him over the men of war, and he was accepted in the sight of all the people, and also in the sight of Saul's servants.

6 ¶And it came to pass as they came, when David was returned from the slaughter of the Philistine, that the women came out of all cities of Israel, singing and dancing, to meet king Saul, with tabrets, with joy, and with instruments of musick.

7 And the women answered one *another* as they played, and said, Saul hath slain his thousands, and David his ten thousands.

8 And Saul was very wroth, and the saying displeased him; and he said, They have ascribed unto David ten thousands, and to me they have ascribed *but* thousands: and *what* can he have more but the kingdom?

9 And Saul eyed David from that day and forward.

10 ¶And it came to pass on the morrow, that the evil spirit from God came upon Saul, and he prophesied in the midst of the house: and David played with his hand, as at other times: and *there was* a javelin in Saul's hand.

11 And Saul cast the javelin; for he said, I will smite David even to the wall *with it.* And David avoided out of his presence twice.

12 ¶And Saul was afraid of David, because the LORD was with him, and was departed from Saul.

13 Therefore Saul removed him from him, and made him his captain over a thousand; and he went out and came in before the people.

14 And David behaved himself wisely in all his ways; and the LORD *was* with him.

15 Wherefore when Saul saw that he behaved himself very wisely, he was afraid of him.

16 But all Israel and Jūdah loved David, because he went out and came in before them.

17 ¶And Saul said to David, Behold my elder daughter Me′răb, her will I give thee to wife: only be thou valiant for me, and fight the LORD's battles. For Saul said, Let not mine hand be upon him, but let the hand of the Philistines be upon him.

18 And David said unto Saul, Who *am* I? and what *is* my life, *or* my father's family in Israel, that I should be son in law to the king?

19 But it came to pass at the time when Me′răb Saul's daughter should have been given to David, that she was given unto Ā′drĭ-el the Me-hōl′ath-īte to wife.

20 And Mī′chal Saul's daughter loved

robe (vs. 4) and gifts were given as symbolic expressions. **Saul hath slain his thousands, and David his ten thousands.** When David's heroic acts began to be praised in this way by the public, Saul became jealous and hateful. **Saul eyed David from that day and forward.** This seems to mean that he watched him very closely and continuously (Hebrew participle), perhaps waiting for the opportunity of verse 11. David twice evaded these insane attempts on his life. **Afraid.** Actually, threatened by his presence. Saul hoped David's bravery would eventually kill him, and so promoted him to **captain over a thousand.** In verse 14 and 15 **wisely** (Heb *sakal*) should probably be translated "was successful." The last preposition should then relate as cause; because **the LORD was with him.** This makes the verse fulfill the expectations of 16:13, since it is the Spirit who makes him to prosper.

17-30. To further obligate David in hopes of death in the line of duty, Saul promised to make David his son-in-law with the exhortation: **only be thou valiant for me, and fight the LORD's battles.** When **Merab,** Saul's older daughter, was married to another, David was given **Michal** instead. The purpose was the same; **that she may be a snare to him.** In order to convince David, and overcome his modesty, he was counseled that the only **dowry** (a customary Oriental payment of money or valuable gift to the father of the bride) would be a **hundred foreskins of the Philistines.** David paid double the number, and was completely unharmed. **More afraid.** The more successful David became, the more threatened Saul felt; every time Saul sent David into a dangerous situation it brought David ever closer to the kingship.

David: and they told Saul, and the thing pleased him.

21 And Saul said, I will give him her, that she may be a snare to him, and that the hand of the Philistines may be against him. Wherefore Saul said to David, Thou shalt this day be my son in law in *the one of* the twain.

22 And Saul commanded his servants, *saying*, Commune with David secretly, and say, Behold, the king hath delight in thee, and all his servants love thee: now therefore be the king's son in law.

23 And Saul's servants spake those words in the ears of David. And David said, Seemeth it to you a light *thing* to be a king's son in law, seeing that I *am* a poor man, and lightly esteemed?

24 And the servants of Saul told him, saying, On this manner spake David.

25 And Saul said, Thus shall ye say to David, The king desireth not any dowry, but an hundred foreskins of the Philistines, to be avenged of the king's enemies. But Saul thought to make David fall by the hand of the Philistines.

26 And when his servants told David these words, it pleased David well to be the king's son in law: and the days were not expired.

27 Wherefore David arose and went, he and his men, and slew of the Philistines two hundred men; and David brought their foreskins, and they gave them in full tale to the king, that he might be the king's son in law. And Saul gave him Mī′chal his daughter to wife.

28 And Saul saw and knew that the LORD *was* with David, and *that* Mī′chal Saul's daughter loved him.

29 And Saul was yet the more afraid of David; and Saul became David's enemy continually.

30 Then the princes of the Philistines went forth: and it came to pass, after they went forth, *that* David behaved himself more wisely than all the servants of Saul; so that his name was much set by.

CHAPTER 19

AND Saul spake to Jonathan his son, and to all his servants, that they should kill David.

2 But Jonathan Saul's son delighted much in David: and Jonathan told David, saying, Saul my father seeketh to kill thee: now therefore, I pray thee, take heed to thyself until the morning, and abide in a secret *place*, and hide thyself:

3 And I will go out and stand beside my father in the field where thou *art*, and I will commune with my father of thee; and what I see, that I will tell thee.

4 And Jonathan spake good of David unto Saul his father, and said unto him, Let not the king sin against his servant, against David; because he hath not sinned against thee, and because his works *have been* to thee-ward very good:

5 For he did put his life in his hand, and slew the Philistine, and the LORD wrought a great salvation for all Israel: thou sawest *it*, and didst rejoice: where-

19:1-12. That they should kill David. In his insanity, Saul now openly sought help in getting rid of David. Jonathan was able to appease Saul, however, and to convince David to return. **Was in his presence, as in times past.** Again David forgave Saul, respected him, and fought for him as before. **Javelin.** Once more David was able to evade. **Michal let David down through a window.** It is assumed that the house was on a wall, so that David escaped the watching messengers of Saul who intended to kill him in the morning.

fore then wilt thou sin against innocent blood, to slay David without a cause?

6 And Saul hearkened unto the voice of Jonathan: and Saul sware, As the LORD liveth, he shall not be slain.

7 And Jonathan called David, and Jonathan shewed him all those things. And Jonathan brought David to Saul, and he was in his presence, as in times past.

8 ¶And there was war again: and David went out, and fought with the Philistines, and slew them with a great slaughter; and they fled from him.

9 And the evil spirit from the LORD was upon Saul, as he sat in his house with his javelin in his hand: and David played with his hand.

10 And Saul sought to smite David even to the wall with the javelin; but he slipped away out of Saul's presence, and he smote the javelin into the wall: and David fled, and escaped that night.

11 Saul also sent messengers unto David's house, to watch him, and to slay him in the morning: and Mī′chal David's wife told him, saying, If thou save not thy life to night, to morrow thou shalt be slain.

12 So Mī′chal let David down through a window: and he went, and fled, and escaped.

13 And Mī′chal took an image, and laid it in the bed, and put a pillow of goats' hair for his bolster, and covered it with a cloth.

14 And when Saul sent messengers to take David, she said, He is sick.

15 And Saul sent the messengers again to see David, saying, Bring him up to me in the bed, that I may slay him.

16 And when the messengers were come in, behold, there was an image in the bed, with a pillow of goats' hair for his bolster.

17 And Saul said unto Mī′chal, Why hast thou deceived me so, and sent away mine enemy, that he is escaped? And Mī′chal answered Saul, He said unto me, Let me go; why should I kill thee?

18 ¶So David fled, and escaped, and came to Samuel to Rā′mah, and told him all that Saul had done to him. And he and Samuel went and dwelt in Nā′ioth.

19 And it was told Saul, saying, Behold, David is at Nā′ioth in Rā′mah.

20 And Saul sent messengers to take David: and when they saw the company of the prophets prophesying, and Samuel standing as appointed over them, the Spirit of God was upon the messengers of Saul, and they also prophesied.

21 And when it was told Saul, he sent other messengers, and they prophesied likewise. And Saul sent messengers again the third time, and they prophesied also.

22 Then went he also to Rā′mah, and came to a great well that is in Sē′chu: and he asked and said, Where are Samuel and David? And one said, Behold, they be at Nā′ioth in Rā′mah.

23 And he went thither to Nā′ioth in Rā′mah: and the Spirit of God was

13-24. Image (Heb terapîm) means literally, "the vanishing ones," and is a synonym for idols which according to the Hebrew religion were nothing at all. In spite of the commandment, the Hebrews did often have idols in their houses (Gen 31:19). It seems a bit strange, however, that the idol should be life-size; and perhaps we should take the word figuratively as meaning a representation of a human form of her own contrivance. At any rate, it fooled those who had come to kill David. Naioth means literally, "dwellings," and may have originally indicated the quarters of the men in the school of the prophets. Here, God supernaturally delivered David from the attempts of Saul by causing all the messengers to turn into prophets. Even Saul himself fell under the control of the Spirit and prophesied when he reached the place.

upon him also, and he went on, and prophesied, until he came to Nā′iŏth in Rā′mah.

24 And he stripped off his clothes also, and prophesied before Samuel in like manner, and lay down naked all that day and all that night. Wherefore they say, *Is* Saul also among the prophets?

CHAPTER 20

AND David fled from Nā′iŏth in Rā′mah, and came and said before Jonathan, What have I done? what *is* mine iniquity? and what *is* my sin before thy father, that he seeketh my life?

2 And he said unto him, God forbid; thou shalt not die: behold, my father will do nothing either great or small, but that he will shew it me: and why should my father hide this thing from me? it *is* not *so.*

3 And David sware moreover, and said, Thy father certainly knoweth that I have found grace in thine eyes; and he saith, Let not Jonathan know this, lest he be grieved: but truly *as* the LORD liveth, and *as* thy soul liveth, *there is* but a step between me and death.

4 Then said Jonathan unto David, Whatsoever thy soul desireth, I will even do *it* for thee.

5 And David said unto Jonathan, Behold, to morrow *is* the new moon, and I should not fail to sit with the king at meat: but let me go, that I may hide myself in the field unto the third *day* at even.

6 If thy father at all miss me, then say, David earnestly asked *leave* of me that he might run to Bĕth–lehĕm his city: for *there is* a yearly sacrifice there for all the family.

7 If he say thus, *It is* well; thy servant shall have peace: but if he be very wroth, *then* be sure that evil is determined by him.

8 Therefore thou shalt deal kindly with thy servant; for thou hast brought thy servant into a covenant of the LORD with thee: notwithstanding, if there be in me iniquity, slay me thyself; for why shouldest thou bring me to thy father?

9 And Jonathan said, Far be it from thee: for if I knew certainly that evil were determined by my father to come upon thee, then would not I tell it thee?

10 Then said David to Jonathan, Who shall tell me? or what *if* thy father answer thee roughly?

11 And Jonathan said unto David, Come, and let us go out into the field. And they went out both of them into the field.

12 And Jonathan said unto David, O LORD God of Israel, when I have sounded my father about to morrow any time, *or* the third *day,* and, behold, *if there be* good toward David, and I then send not unto thee, and shew it thee;

13 The LORD do so and much more to Jonathan: but if it please my father *to do* thee evil, then I will shew it thee, and send thee away, that thou mayest go in peace: and the LORD be with thee, as he hath been with my father.

14 And thou shalt not only while yet I

20:1-14. After leaving Naioth in Ramah, David returned to Jonathan his closest friend (also his brother-in-law) for help and advice. **What is my sin before thy father, that he seeketh my life?** It was very obvious that Saul was trying to kill David, but Jonathan was not yet convinced. **There is but a step between me and death.** Several times a sidestep from where Saul had aimed his javelin was all that had kept David alive. **New moon.** The first day of the lunar month was a religious holiday with a festival meal. This scheme was devised by David to fully convince Jonathan of the danger. If Saul became angry because of David's absence, there would be no more doubt.

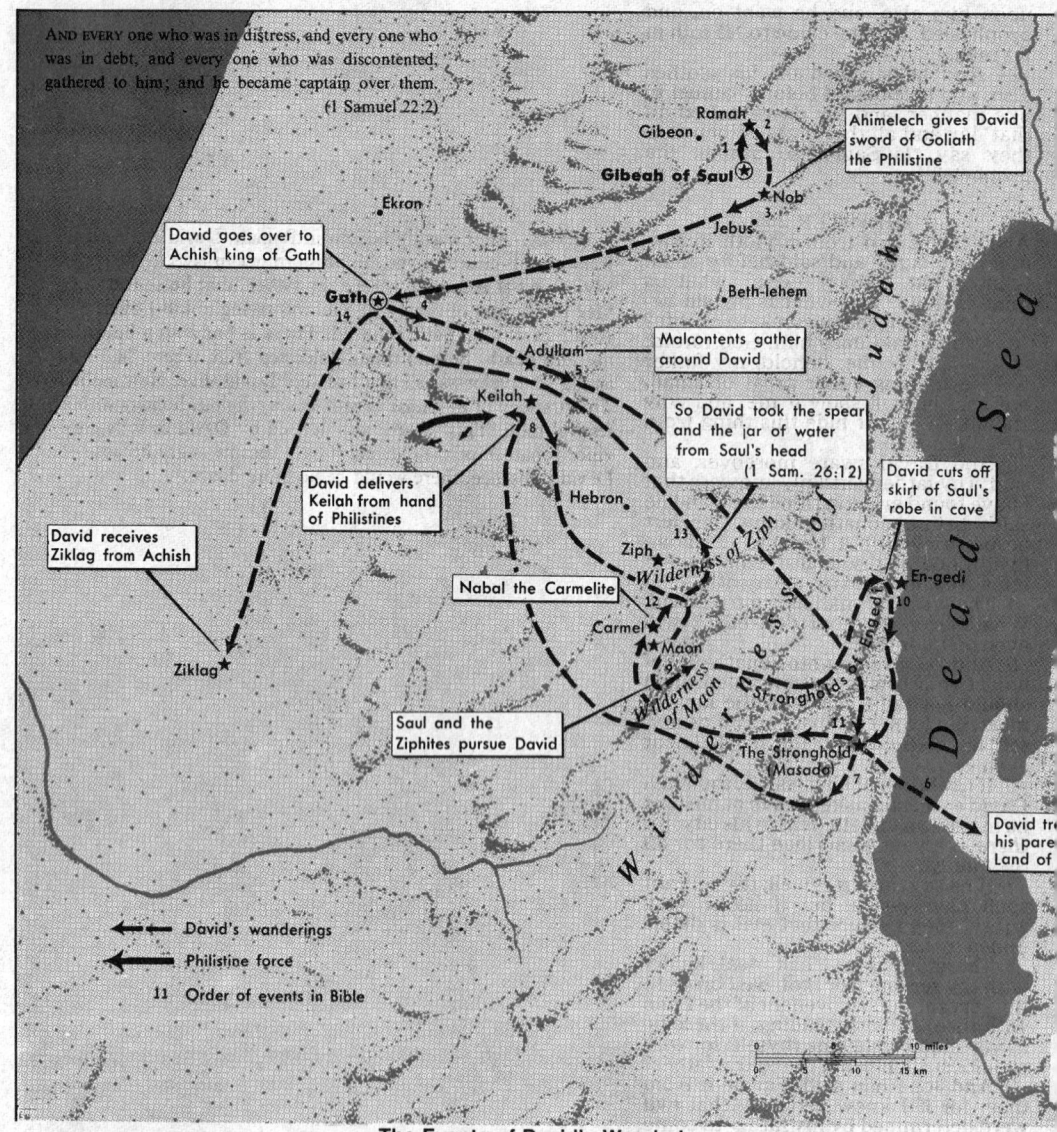

AND EVERY one who was in distress, and every one who was in debt, and every one who was discontented, gathered to him; and he became captain over them. (1 Samuel 22:2)

Ahimelech gives David sword of Goliath the Philistine

David goes over to Achish king of Gath

Malcontents gather around David

So David took the spear and the jar of water from Saul's head (1 Sam. 26:12)

David cuts off skirt of Saul's robe in cave

David delivers Keilah from hand of Philistines

David receives Ziklag from Achish

Nabal the Carmelite

Saul and the Ziphites pursue David

David tr his pare Land of

← David's wanderings

← Philistine force

11 Order of events in Bible

The Events of David's Wanderings

live shew me the kindness of the LORD, that I die not:

15 But *also* thou shalt not cut off thy kindness from my house for ever: no, not when the LORD hath cut off the enemies of David every one from the face of the earth.

16 So Jonathan made *a covenant* with the house of David, *saying,* Let the LORD even require *it* at the hand of David's enemies.

17 And Jonathan caused David to swear again, because he loved him: for he loved him as he loved his own soul.

18 Then Jonathan said to David, To morrow *is* the new moon: and thou shalt be missed, because thy seat will be empty.

19 And *when* thou hast stayed three days, *then* thou shalt go down quickly,

15-18. Thou shalt not cut off thy kindness from my house. Jonathan apparently knew that David would become king and that the families of previous kings were often destroyed when a new king took office. He was asking for mercy when David would come to the throne. This kindness was later fulfilled when David provided for Mephibosheth (II Sam 9).

19-29. Ezel. The stone was perhaps named "stone of departure" later as a memorial of the event and place where the two

and come to the place where thou didst hide thyself when the business was *in hand*, and shalt remain by the stone Ē'zel.

20 And I will shoot three arrows on the side *thereof*, as though I shot at a mark.

21 And, behold, I will send a lad, *saying*, Go, find out the arrows. If I expressly say unto the lad, Behold, the arrows *are* on this side of thee, take them; then come thou: for *there is* peace to thee, and no hurt; *as* the Lord liveth.

22 But if I say thus unto the young man, Behold, the arrows *are* beyond thee; go thy way: for the Lord hath sent thee away.

23 And *as touching* the matter which thou and I have spoken of, behold, the Lord *be* between thee and me for ever.

24 ¶So David hid himself in the field: and when the new moon was come, the king sat him down to eat meat.

25 And the king sat upon his seat, as at other times, *even* upon a seat by the wall: and Jonathan arose, and Abner sat by Saul's side, and David's place was empty.

26 Nevertheless Saul spake not any thing that day: for he thought, Something hath befallen him, he *is* not clean; surely he *is* not clean.

27 And it came to pass on the morrow, *which was* the second *day* of the month, that David's place was empty: and Saul said unto Jonathan his son, Wherefore cometh not the son of Jesse to meat, neither yesterday, nor to day?

28 And Jonathan answered Saul, David earnestly asked *leave* of me *to go* to Bēth-lehĕm:

29 And he said, Let me go, I pray thee; for our family hath a sacrifice in the city; and my brother, he hath commanded me *to be there*: and now, if I have found favour in thine eyes, let me get away, I pray thee, and see my brethren. Therefore he cometh not unto the king's table.

30 Then Saul's anger was kindled against Jonathan, and he said unto him, Thou son of the perverse rebellious *woman*, do not I know that thou hast chosen the son of Jesse to thine own confusion, and unto the confusion of thy mother's nakedness?

31 For as long as the son of Jesse liveth upon the ground, thou shalt not be established, nor thy kingdom. Wherefore now send and fetch him unto me, for he shall surely die.

32 And Jonathan answered Saul his father, and said unto him, Wherefore shall he be slain? what hath he done?

33 And Saul cast a javelin at him to smite him: whereby Jonathan knew that it was determined of his father to slay David.

34 So Jonathan arose from the table in fierce anger, and did eat no meat the second day of the month: for he was grieved for David, because his father had done him shame.

35 ¶And it came to pass in the morning, that Jonathan went out into the

separated. **On this side.** This was to be the sign of peace; David would then return with Jonathan. **The arrows are beyond thee.** This was the agreed signal. If spies were present, David would be warned to escape and save himself from any planned evil. **The Lord be between thee and me for ever.** This was a solemn oath intended to seal their agreement (cf. Gen 31:53).

30-42. It happened exactly as David had predicted; Saul became violently angry when David did not show. **Son of the perverse rebellious woman.** In that day this was an extremely vulgar expletive. **Is not the arrow beyond thee?** This was the signal that had been agreed upon, and David would know that he must flee. Jonathan made the signal most clear and then sent the boy away. Since there was no one else in sight, he also said his goodbyes.

field at the time appointed with David,
and a little lad with him.

36 And he said unto his lad, Run, find
out now the arrows which I shoot. *And*
as the lad ran, he shot an arrow beyond
him.

37 And when the lad was come to the
place of the arrow which Jonathan had
shot, Jonathan cried after the lad, and
said, *Is* not the arrow beyond thee?

38 And Jonathan cried after the lad,
Make speed, haste, stay not. And Jonathan's lad gathered up the arrows,
and came to his master.

39 But the lad knew not any thing:
only Jonathan and David knew the
matter.

40 And Jonathan gave his artillery
unto his lad, and said unto him, Go,
carry *them* to the city.

41 ¶*And* as soon as the lad was gone,
David arose out of *a place* toward the
south, and fell on his face to the
ground, and bowed himself three
times: and they kissed one another, and
wept one with another, until David exceeded.

42 And Jonathan said to David, Go in
peace, forasmuch as we have sworn
both of us in the name of the LORD,
saying, The LORD be between me and
thee, and between my seed and thy
seed for ever. And he arose and departed: and Jonathan went into the
city.

CHAPTER 21

THEN came David to Nob to A-hĭm′e-
lĕch the priest: and A-hĭm′e-lĕch was
afraid at the meeting of David, and said
unto him, Why *art* thou alone, and no
man with thee?

2 And David said unto A-hĭm′e-lĕch
the priest, The king hath commanded
me a business, and hath said unto me,
Let no man know any thing of the business whereabout I send thee, and what
I have commanded thee: and I have appointed *my* servants to such and such a
place.

3 Now therefore what is under thine
hand? give *me* five *loaves of* bread in
mine hand, or what there is present.

4 And the priest answered David, and
said, *There is* no common bread under
mine hand, but there is hallowed bread;
if the young men have kept themselves
at least from women.

5 And David answered the priest, and
said unto him, Of a truth women *have
been* kept from us about these three
days, since I came out, and the vessels
of the young men are holy, and *the
bread is* in a manner common, yea,
though it were sanctified this day in the
vessel.

6 So the priest gave him hallowed
bread: for there was no bread there but
the shewbread, that was taken from
before the LORD, to put hot bread in the
day when it was taken away.

7 Now a certain man of the servants
of Saul *was* there that day, detained before the LORD; and his name *was* Dō′eg,
and Edomite, the chiefest of the herdmen that *belonged* to Saul.

8 And David said unto A-hĭm′e-lĕch,
And is there not here under thine hand
spear or sword? for I have neither

D. David's Wilderness Wanderings. 21:1-30:31.

21:1-6. **Nob** was within sight of Jerusalem and was the location of the tabernacle at this time. David had come because he
was hungry and needed help. To answer the suspicions of the
priest, David lied and said that Saul had sent him on a mission.
No common bread (Heb *chōl*) means bread that could be eaten
by anyone, having no religious significance. The only bread
available was the holy bread, the **showbread** (vs. 6). This could
legally be eaten only by the priest. Ahimelech was willing to give
the holy bread if he could be assured it would not be eaten by
those who were ceremonially unclean. Jesus refers to this occasion to show that it is the moral spirit of biblical laws that is most
important, not the legalistic letter of the law (cf. Mk 2:25-26,
etc.). **Showbread** was considered holy because it was dedicated
to the Lord.

7-9. Doeg, an Edomite. A proselyte who worked for Saul
and who gained the dubious distinction of being the only person
willing to carry out the cold-blooded killing of the priests and
massacre of the whole city of Nob (22:17-19). David was also
able to "borrow" the sword of Goliath, which had been kept as a
memorial at the tabernacle, by telling the priest that **the king's
business required haste** and he was unable to bring his own.

brought my sword nor my weapons with me, because the king's business required haste.

9 And the priest said, The sword of Goliath the Philistine, whom thou slewest in the valley of Ē'lah, behold, it *is here* wrapped in a cloth behind the ephod: if thou wilt take that, take *it:* for *there is* no other save that here. And David said, *There is* none like that; give it me.

10 ¶And David arose, and fled that day for fear of Saul, and went to Ā'chĭsh the king of Gath.

11 And the servants of Ā'chĭsh said unto him, *Is* not this David the king of the land? did they not sing one to another of him in dances, saying, Saul hath slain his thousands, and David his ten thousands?

12 And David laid up these words in his heart, and was sore afraid of Ā'chĭsh the king of Gath.

13 And he changed his behavior before them, and feigned himself mad in their hands, and scrabbled on the doors of the gate, and let his spittle fall down upon his beard.

14 Then said Ā'chĭsh unto his servants, Lo, ye see the man is mad: wherefore *then* have ye brought him to me?

15 Have I need of mad men, that ye have brought this *fellow* to play the mad man in my presence? shall this *fellow* come into my house?

CHAPTER 22

DAVID therefore departed thence, and escaped to the cave A-dŭl'lam: and when his brethren and all his father's house heard *it,* they went down thither to him.

2 And every one *that was* in distress, and every one that *was* in debt, and every one *that was* discontented, gathered themselves unto him; and he became a captain over them: and there were with him about four hundred men.

3 ¶And David went thence to Mĭz'peh of Moab: and he said unto the king of Moab, Let my father and my mother, I pray thee, come forth, *and be* with you, till I know what God will do for me.

4 And he brought them before the king of Moab: and they dwelt with him all the while that David was in the hold.

5 ¶And the prophet Gad said unto David, Abide not in the hold; depart, and get thee into the land of Jūdah. Then David departed, and came into the forest of Hā'rĕth.

6 ¶When Saul heard that David was discovered, and the men that *were* with him, (now Saul abode in Gĭb'e-ah under a tree in Rā'mah, having his spear in his hand, and all his servants *were* standing about him;)

7 Then Saul said unto his servants that stood about him, Hear now, ye Benjamites; will the son of Jesse give every one of you fields and vineyards, *and* make you all captains of thousands, and captains of hundreds;

8 That all of you have conspired against me, and *there is* none that sheweth me that my son hath made a

10-15. Achish, the Philistine king of Gath, knew who David was and had heard the reports of his fame and heroism. **Feigned himself mad.** David pretended to have gone insane by making marks on the doors of the gate and letting the spittle run down in **his beard** (no man in his right mind would violate his beard in that day).

22:1-7. The cave of Adullam. Some believe the cave was located in the area of the valley of Elah. There are in that place several large caves which may have housed the relatives, friends, and soldiers of David during this time. Others believe it was located near Beth-lehem. **Mizpeh of Moab** was the next location of David's camp. Here David committed his father and mother to the king of Moab for safekeeping. This place is called (vss. 4-5) **the hold** (Heb *metsūdah*), or more specifically, "the stronghold." From this place David went back to Judah, to **the forest of Hareth** at the direction of the prophet **Gad** who was evidently a long-time spiritual guardian and prophet to David (II Sam 24:11).

8-13. All of you have conspired against me. Saul was paranoid; because he could not break through the providential protection to satisfy his jealous revenge in killing David, he imag-

league with the son of Jesse, and *there is* none of you that is sorry for me, or sheweth unto me that my son hath stirred up my servant against me, to lie in wait, as at this day?

9 ¶Then answered Dō'eg the Edomite, which was set over the servants of Saul, and said, I saw the son of Jesse coming to Nob, to A-hĭm'e-lĕch the son of A-hī'tŭb.

10 And he enquired of the LORD for him and gave him victuals, and gave him the sword of Golīath the Philistine.

11 ¶Then the king sent to call A-hĭm'e-lĕch the priest, the son of A-hī'-tŭb, and all his father's house, the priests that *were* in Nob: and they came all of them to the king.

12 And Saul said, Here now, thou son of A-hī'tŭb. And he answered, Here I *am*, my lord.

13 And Saul said unto him, Why have ye conspired against me, thou and the son of Jesse, in that thou hast given him bread, and a sword, and hast enquired of God for him, that he should rise against me, to lie in wait, as at this day?

14 Then A-hĭm'e-lĕch answered the king, and said, And who *is so* faithful among all thy servants as David, which is the king's son in law, and goeth at thy bidding, and is honourable in thine house?

15 Did I then begin to enquire of God for him? be it far from me: let not the king impute *any* thing unto his servant, *nor* to all the house of my father: for thy servant knew nothing of all this, less or more.

16 And the king said, Thou shalt surely die, A-hĭm'e-lĕch, thou, and all thy father's house.

17 And the king said unto the footmen that stood about him, Turn, and slay the priests of the LORD; because their hand also *is* with David, and because they knew when he fled, and did not shew it to me. But the servants of the king would not put forth their hand to fall upon the priests of the LORD.

18 And the king said to Dō'eg, Turn thou, and fall upon the priests. And Dō'eg the Edomite turned, and he fell upon the priests, and slew on that day fourscore and five persons that did wear a linen ephod.

19 And Nob, the city of the priests, smote he with the edge of the sword, both men and women, children and sucklings, and oxen, and asses, and sheep, with the edge of the sword.

20 ¶And one of the sons of A-hĭm'e-lĕch the son of A-hī'tŭb, named Ă-bī'a-thar, escaped, and fled after David.

21 And Ă-bī'a-thar shewed David that Saul had slain the LORD's priests.

22 And David said unto Ă-bī'a-thar, I knew *it* that day, when Dō'eg the Edomite *was* there, that he would surely tell Saul: I have occasioned the *death* of all the persons of thy father's house.

23 Abide thou with me, fear not: for he that seeketh my life seeketh thy life: but with me thou *shalt be* in safeguard.

CHAPTER 23

THEN they told David, saying, Behold,

ined that even his loyal followers from his own tribe were against him. **Doeg the Edomite** had by this time been advanced over the servants of Saul and had a place of some authority. **I saw the son of Jesse.** Doeg testified against David and the priests who aided him. **Inquired of the LORD for him** implies that **Ahimelech** used the ephod and the Urim and Thummim to determine the will of God for David. The charges against Ahimelech were that he had **conspired** with David against Saul, that he had **given him bread,** and had **inquired of God for him.** But what was the priest for?

14-23. Who is so faithful? Obviously Ahimelech had done nothing at all that could be in any way construed against him. **Footmen.** These men could see the insanity of Saul; they knew it would be morally wrong to kill these priests. Only **Doeg the Edomite** was low enough, or perhaps ambitious enough, to carry out this terrible massacre. He murdered eighty-five priests who **did wear** (Heb *nasa'*), which means literally to "lift up," the **linen ephod.** This last expression seems to be the origin of the current designation of clergymen as "men of the cloth." Beyond the utter disregard of the sanctity of those who had been called to holy service, the massacre extended to the whole city of **Nob** where the tabernacle stood. It is as if Saul and his henchman, Doeg, were possessed by Satan and were attempting to destroy entirely the worship of Yahweh from the nation of Israel. Fortunately, at least one of the priests escaped. **Abiathar** was able somehow also to secure and remove the ephod (23:6) with the Urim and Thummim and bring them to David.

23:1-8. Keilah. An Israelite border town in the Shephelah

the Philistines fight against Keī′lah, and they rob the threshingfloors.

2 Therefore David enquired of the LORD, saying, Shall I go and smite these Philistines? And the LORD said unto David, Go, and smite the Philistines, and save Keī′lah.

3 And David's men said unto him, Behold, we be afraid here in Jūdah: how much more then if we come to Keī′lah against the armies of the Philistines?

4 Then David enquired of the LORD yet again. And the LORD answered him and said, Arise, go down to Keī′lah; for I will deliver the Philistines into thine hand.

5 So David and his men went to Keī′-lah, and fought with the Philistines, and brought away their cattle, and smote them with a great slaughter. So David saved the inhabitants of Keī′lah.

6 And it came to pass, when Ă-bī′a-thar the son of A-hīm′e-lĕch fled to David to Keī′lah, *that* he came down *with* an ephod in his hand.

7 ¶And it was told Saul that David was come to Keī′lah. And Saul said, God hath delivered him into mine hand; for he is shut in, by entering into a town that hath gates and bars.

8 And Saul called all the people together to war, to go down to Keī′lah, to besiege David and his men.

9 And David knew that Saul secretly practised mischief against him; and he said to Ă-bī′a-thar the priest, Bring hither the ephod.

10 Then said David, O LORD God of Israel, thy servant hath certainly heard that Saul seeketh to come to Keī′lah, to destroy the city for my sake.

11 Will the men of Keī′lah deliver me up into his hand? will Saul come down, as thy servant hath heard? O LORD God of Israel, I beseech thee, tell thy servant. And the LORD said, He will come down.

12 Then said David, Will the men of Keī′lah deliver me and my men into the hand of Saul? And the LORD said, They will deliver *thee* up.

13 Then David and his men, *which were* about six hundred, arose and departed out of Keī′lah, and went whithersoever they could go. And it was told Saul that David was escaped from Keī′lah; and he forbare to go forth.

14 And David abode in the wilderness in strong holds, and remained in a mountain in the wilderness of Ziph. And Saul sought him every day, but God delivered him not into his hand.

15 And David saw that Saul was come out to seek his life: and David *was* in the wilderness of Ziph in a wood.

16 ¶And Jonathan Saul's son arose, and went to David into the wood, and strengthened his hand in God.

17 And he said unto him, Fear not: for the hand of Saul my father shall not find thee; and thou shalt be king over Israel, and I shall be next unto thee; and that also Saul my father knoweth.

18 And they two made a covenant before the LORD: and David abode in the wood, and Jonathan went to his house.

which was being systematically robbed of its grain by the Philistines. **David inquired of the LORD,** and was commissioned to attack the Philistines and **save** (Heb *yasha‛*) **Keilah.** Again we see that God's chosen king has the function of saving or delivering God's people, a typical theme that finds its ultimate antitype in Christ. **David inquired of the Lord yet again.** A double-check on the will of God in order to give confidence to David's men. **So David saved.** He was able to be victorious and deliver God's people because God had chosen and enabled him to do it. **God hath delivered.** This is actually the translation of the Septuagint text rather than the Hebrew text. The Hebrew text does imply **delivered,** but more precisely places the emphasis upon "denunciation." Saul imagines that God has now "rejected" David and in the process has therefore allowed David to be outwitted.

9-17. Bring hither the ephod. Abiathar had brought the ephod with him and was thus able to make these enquiries to discover the will of God. **Will . . . Keilah deliver** (Heb *sagar*), means literally, "abandon, or surrender to." All these questions could easily be answered by the Lord through the priest and the Urim and Thummim. From the Lord's answers David determined that he would leave the city and move to the open country. **Wilderness of Ziph.** David lived here in the woods near Hebron, and Jonathan came to strengthen and encourage him. Both David and Jonathan, as well as Saul, knew that David would be **king over Israel.**

18-29. Covenant. This is not a covenant of the Lord, but a solemn agreement between the two men made in the presence and name of the Lord to make it more binding upon both of

19 ¶Then came up the Zĭph′ītes to Saul to Gĭb′e-ah, saying, Doth not David hide himself with us in strong holds in the wood, in the hill of Hachĭ′-lah, which *is* on the south of Jeshĭ′-mon?

20 Now therefore, O king, come down according to all the desire of thy soul to come down; and our part *shall be* to deliver him into the king's hand.

21 And Saul said, Blessed *be* ye of the LORD; for ye have compassion on me.

22 Go, I pray you, prepare yet, and know and see his place where his haunt is, *and* who hath seen him there: for it is told me *that* he dealeth very subtilly.

23 See therefore, and take knowledge of all the lurking places where he hideth himself, and come ye again to me with the certainty, and I will go with you: and it shall come to pass, if he be in the land, that I will search him out throughout all the thousands of Jūdah.

24 And they arose, and went to Ziph before Saul: but David and his men *were* in the wilderness of Mā′on, in the plain on the south of Jeshĭ′-mon.

25 Saul also and his men went to seek *him.* And they told David: wherefore he came down into a rock, and abode in the wilderness of Mā′on. And when Saul heard *that,* he pursued after David in the wilderness of Mā′on.

26 And Saul went on this side of the mountain, and David and his men on that side of the mountain: and David made haste to get away for fear of Saul; for Saul and his men compassed David and his men round about to take them.

27 ¶But there came a messenger unto Saul, saying, Haste thee, and come; for the Philistines have invaded the land.

28 Wherefore Saul returned from pursuing after David, and went against the Philistines: therefore they called that place Sē′la-ham′māh-le′kŏth.

29 ¶And David went up from thence, and dwelt in strong holds at Ĕn-gĕ′dī.

CHAPTER 24

AND it came to pass, when Saul was returned from following the Philistines, that it was told him, saying, Behold, David *is* in the wilderness of Ĕn-gĕ′dī.

2 Then Saul took three thousand chosen men out of all Israel, and went to seek David and his men upon the rocks of the wild goats.

3 And he came to the sheepcotes by the way, where *was* a cave; and Saul went in to cover his feet: and David and his men remained in the sides of the cave.

4 And the men of David said unto him, Behold the day of which the LORD said unto thee, Behold, I will deliver thine enemy into thine hand, that thou mayest do to him as it shall seem good unto thee. Then David arose, and cut off the skirt of Saul's robe privily.

5 And it came to pass afterward, that David's heart smote him, because he had cut off Saul's skirt.

6 And he said unto his men, The LORD forbid that I should do this thing unto my master, the LORD's anointed, to stretch forth mine hand against him, seeing he *is* the anointed of the LORD.

7 So David stayed his servants with

them. **The Ziphites** betrayed David's presence to Saul and promised to **deliver** (*sagar,* vs. 11) him. Saul did pursue David, with the help of the Ziphites, but had to call off the search because of a new Philistine invasion. **Sela-hammah-lekoth** is a transliteration of the Hebrew words meaning either "rock of division," alluding to the rocks which divided Saul from David, or "rock of smoothness," perhaps alluding to David's escape. From here, David went to **En-gedi,** a natural rock fortress overlooking the Dead Sea. The name means "spring of a goat," perhaps because it would take a goat to get to it.

24:1-19. Three thousand chosen men. After Saul had chased out the Philistine raiding party, he returned to the pursuit of David near En-gedi with an army of three thousand. **To cover his feet.** A Hebrew euphemism for the English, "to go to the bathroom." Saul probably left his robe at the entrance or mouth of the cave, or somewhere within easy access to David and his men who were **in the sides of the cave. The LORD's anointed.** David had such profound respect for the office to which Saul had been anointed and chosen by the Lord, even though he knew that it was temporary and that he would himself succeed Saul, that he would not lift his hand to harm the king. **Bowed himself.** Out of reverence for Saul as the Lord's anointed one. **The LORD judge between me and thee.** David leaves the entire matter in the hands of the Lord; he will not take vengeance himself.

these words, and suffered them not to rise against Saul. But Saul rose up out of the cave, and went on *his* way.

8 ¶David also arose afterward, and went out of the cave, and cried after Saul, saying, My lord the king. And when Saul looked behind him, David stooped with his face to the earth, and bowed himself.

9 And David said to Saul, Wherefore hearest thou men's words, saying, Behold, David seeketh thy hurt?

10 Behold, this day thine eyes have seen how that the LORD had delivered thee to day into mine hand in the cave: and *some* bade *me* kill thee: but *mine eye* spared thee; and I said, I will not put forth mine hand against my lord; for he *is* the LORD's anointed.

11 Moreover, my father, see, yea, see the skirt of thy robe in my hand: for in that I cut off the skirt of thy robe, and killed thee not, know thou and see that *there is* neither evil nor transgression in mine hand, and I have not sinned against thee; yet thou huntest my soul to take it.

12 The LORD judge between me and thee, and the LORD avenge me of thee: but mine hand shall not be upon thee.

13 As saith the proverb of the ancients, Wickedness proceedeth from the wicked: but mine hand shall not be upon thee.

14 After whom is the king of Israel come out? after whom dost thou pursue? after a dead dog, after a flea.

15 The LORD therefore be judge, and judge between me and thee, and see, and plead my cause, and deliver me out of thine hand.

16 ¶And it came to pass, when David had made an end of speaking these words unto Saul, that Saul said, *Is* this thy voice, my son David? And Saul lifted up his voice, and wept.

17 And he said to David, Thou *art* more righteous than I: for thou hast rewarded me good, whereas I have rewarded thee evil.

18 And thou hast shewed this day how that thou hast dealt well with me: forasmuch as when the LORD had delivered me into thine hand, thou killedst me not.

19 For if a man find his enemy, will he let him go well away? wherefore the LORD reward thee good for that thou hast done unto me this day.

20 And now, behold, I know well that thou shalt surely be king, and that the kingdom of Israel shall be established in thine hand.

21 Swear now therefore unto me by the LORD, that thou wilt not cut off my seed after me, and that thou wilt not destroy my name out of my father's house.

22 And David sware unto Saul. And Saul went home; but David and his men gat them up unto the hold.

CHAPTER 25

AND Samuel died; and all the Israelites were gathered together, and lamented him, and buried him in his house at Rā'-

20-22. Saul openly acknowledges the Lord's choice and blessing upon David, **Thou shalt surely be king.** The statement is emphatic (Hebrew infinitive absolute before the cognate verb), showing that Saul understands fully the truth that he has been rejected and David established as king. **Swear now.** Saul goes so far as to plead for the lives of his family (since it was common for a victor to kill the family of his predecessor when he came to power).

25:1. Samuel died. Since Samuel was such an important person in the political and spiritual history of the nation, **all the Israelites . . . lamented him,** and he was buried with all possible formal honors in **Ramah,** where he had been born. **Paran.**

579

mah. And David arose, and went down to the wilderness of Paran.

2 And *there was* a man in Mā'on, whose possessions *were* in Carmel; and the man *was* very great, and he had three thousand sheep, and a thousand goats: and he was shearing his sheep in Carmel.

3 Now the name of the man *was* Nā'bal; and the name of his wife Āb'i-gāil: and *she was* a woman of good understanding, and of a beautiful countenance: but the man *was* churlish and evil in his doings; and he *was* of the house of Caleb.

4 And David heard in the wilderness that Nā'bal did shear his sheep.

5 And David sent out ten young men, and David said unto the young men, Get you up to Carmel, and go to Nā'bal, and greet him in my name:

6 And thus shall ye say to him that liveth *in prosperity*, Peace *be* both to thee, and peace *be* to thine house, and peace *be* unto all that thou hast.

7 And now I have heard that thou hast shearers: now thy shepherds which were with us, we hurt them not, neither was there ought missing unto them, all the while they were in Carmel.

8 Ask thy young men, and they will shew thee. Wherefore let the young men find favour in thine eyes: for we come in a good day: give, I pray thee, whatsoever cometh to thine hand unto thy servants, and to thy son David.

9 And when David's young men came, they spake to Nā'bal according to all those words in the name of David, and ceased.

10 And Nā'bal answered David's servants, and said, Who *is* David? and who *is* the son of Jesse? there be many servants now a days that break away every man from his master.

11 Shall I then take my bread, and my water, and my flesh that I have killed for my shearers, and give *it* unto men, whom I know not whence they *be*?

12 So David's young men turned their way, and went again, and came and told him all those sayings.

13 And David said unto his men, Gird ye on every man his sword. And they girded on every man his sword; and David also girded on his sword: and there went up after David about four hundred men; and two hundred abode by the stuff.

14 ¶ But one of the young men told Āb'i-gāil, Nā'bal's wife, saying, Behold, David sent messengers out of the wilderness to salute our master; and he railed on them.

15 But the men *were* very good unto us, and we were not hurt, neither missed we any thing, as long as we were conversant with them, when we were in the fields:

16 They were a wall unto us both by night and day, all the while we were with them keeping the sheep.

17 Now therefore know and consider what thou wilt do; for evil is determined against our master, and against all his household: for he *is such* a son of

The Septuagint reads "Maon," which appears to be supported by the context.

2-17. Carmel. This is not the same location as Elijah's Mount Carmel. **The name of the man was Nabal,** which means literally "a fool," and accurately describes his character as presented in this passage. **Churlish** (Heb *qashah*), meaning "hard to deal with," is the first of the two adjectives which summarize his actions. On the basis of the kindness and protection of David's men toward the shepherds of Nabal, a simple request was made. **Give . . . unto thy servants.** Common courtesy would have provided these basic supplies without having to ask. It was customary. **Who is David?** Nabal refused to recognize David as the Lord's anointed.

Bē'lĭ-al, that *a man* cannot speak to him.

18 Then Ăb'i-gāil made haste, and took two hundred loaves, and two bottles of wine, and five sheep ready dressed, and five measures of parched *corn,* and an hundred clusters of raisins, and two hundred cakes of figs, and laid *them* on asses.

19 And she said unto her servants, Go on before me; behold, I come after you. But she told not her husband Nā'bal.

20 And it was *so, as* she rode on the ass, that she came down by the covert of the hill, and, behold, David and his men came down against her; and she met them.

21 Now David had said, Surely in vain have I kept all that this *fellow* hath in the wilderness, so that nothing was missed of all that *pertained* unto him: and he hath requited me evil for good.

22 So and more also do God unto the enemies of David, if I leave of all that *pertain* to him by the morning light any that pisseth against the wall.

23 And when Ăb'i-gāil saw David, she hasted, and lighted off the ass, and fell before David on her face, and bowed herself to the ground,

24 And fell at his feet, and said, Upon me, my lord, *upon me let this* iniquity *be:* and let thine handmaid, I pray thee, speak in thine audience, and hear the words of thine handmaid.

25 Let not my lord, I pray thee, regard this man of Bē'lĭ-al, *even* Nā'bal: for as his name *is,* so *is* he; Nā'bal *is* his name, and folly *is* with him: but I thine handmaid saw not the young men of my lord, whom thou didst send.

26 Now therefore, my lord, *as* the LORD liveth, and *as* thy soul liveth, seeing the LORD hath withholden thee from coming to *shed* blood, and from avenging thyself with thine own hand, now let thine enemies, and they that seek evil to my lord, be as Nā'bal.

27 And now this blessing which thine handmaid hath brought unto my lord, let it even be given unto the young men that follow my lord.

28 I pray thee, forgive the trespass of thine handmaid: for the LORD will certainly make my lord a sure house; because my lord fighteth the battles of the LORD, and evil hath not been found in thee *all* thy days.

29 Yet a man is risen to pursue thee, and to seek thy soul: but the soul of my lord shall be bound in the bundle of life with the LORD thy God; and the souls of thine enemies, them shall he sling out, *as out* of the middle of a sling.

30 And it shall come to pass, when the LORD shall have done to my lord according to all the good that he hath spoken concerning thee, and shall have appointed thee ruler over Israel;

31 That this shall be no grief unto thee, nor offence of heart unto my lord, either that thou hast shed blood causeless, or that my lord hath avenged himself: but when the LORD shall have dealt well with my lord, then remember thine handmaid.

32 ¶And David said to Ăb'i-gāil,

18-41. Abigail made haste. Only the superior wisdom and quick thinking of Nabal's wife saved David from avenging himself upon the whole household of Nabal, and thus killing innocent persons. When Abigail's explanations and apologies were given, David's fierce anger dissipated and he realized the seriousness of the mistake he was about to make. **The LORD** (Yahweh, the personal, covenant name of God used by His people, also translated Jehovah in some versions) **will certainly** (emphasis using the infinitive absolute before the cognate verb) **make my lord** ("master," a title which shows respect like "mister") **a sure house.** With this statement, Abigail reveals a complete understanding of the Lord's choice and anointing of David to be king over Israel, and the promise of a "son of David" to rule after him. **Appointed thee ruler** (Heb *nagid*). This again acknowledges the direct command of God that David is God's choice as leader of his people. Only a fool (like Nabal) could have failed to see this at the time. The relative clause which appears at the end of verse 34 (and vs. 22) is now vulgar and has been translated into current, idiomatic English in all twentieth-century versions. Nabal was too drunk to care that night; but when he heard what had happened, **his heart died within him.** It was probably a stroke, but surely was the judgment of God. The incident shows, in typical form, the seriousness of rejecting God's chosen king.

Blessed *be* the LORD God of Israel, which sent thee this day to meet me:

33 And blessed *be* thy advice, and blessed *be* thou, which hast kept me this day from coming to *shed* blood, and from avenging myself with mine own hand.

34 For in very deed, *as* the LORD God of Israel liveth, which hath kept me back from hurting thee, except thou hadst hasted and come to meet me, surely there had not been left unto Nā'-bal by the morning light any that pisseth against the wall.

35 So David received of her hand *that* which she had brought him, and said unto her, Go up in peace to thine house; see, I have hearkened to thy voice, and have accepted thy person.

36 ¶ And Āb'i-gāil came to Nā'bal; and, behold, he held a feast in his house, like the feast of a king; and Nā'-bal's heart *was* merry within him, for he *was* very drunken: wherefore she told him nothing, less or more, until the morning light.

37 But it came to pass in the morning, when the wine was gone out of Nā'bal, and his wife had told him these things, that his heart died within him, and he became *as* a stone.

38 And it came to pass about ten days *after*, that the LORD smote Nā'bal, that he died.

39 And when David heard that Nā'bal was dead, he said, Blessed *be* the LORD, that hath pleaded the cause of my reproach from the hand of Nā'bal, and hath kept his servant from evil: for the LORD hath returned the wickedness of Nā'bal upon his own head. And David sent and communed with Āb'i-gāil, to take her to him to wife.

40 And when the servants of David were come to Āb'i-gāil to Carmel, they spake unto her, saying, David sent us unto thee, to take thee to him to wife.

41 And she arose, and bowed herself on *her* face to the earth, and said, Behold, *let* thine handmaid *be* a servant to wash the feet of the servants of my lord.

42 And Āb'i-gāil hasted, and arose, and rode upon an ass, with five damsels of hers that went after her; and she went after the messengers of David, and became his wife.

43 David also took A-hin'ō-am of Jĕz're-el; and they were also both of them his wives.

44 But Saul had given Mī'chal his daughter, David's wife, to Phăl'tī the son of Lā'ish, which *was* of Găl'līm.

CHAPTER 26

AND the Zīph'ītes came unto Saul to Gib'e-ah, saying, Doth not David hide himself in the hill of Hach'ī-lah, *which is* before Jesh'-ī-mon?

2 Then Saul arose, and went down to the wilderness of Ziph, having three thousand chosen men of Israel with him, to seek David in the wilderness of Ziph.

3 And Saul pitched in the hill of Hach'ī-lah, *which is* before Jesh'-ī-mon, by the way. But David abode in the wilderness, and he saw that Saul came after him into the wilderness.

42-44. Abigail . . . became his wife. David simply assumed the rights of Oriental kings to marry with a word any woman he chose. He **also took Ahinoam;** when he reigned in Hebron he had six wives (I Chr 3:1-3).

26:1-15. The Ziphites. They had betrayed David before (23:19) with very similar consequences (cf. 24:6, 10; 26:11, 14-16). **Jeshimon** is between Hebron and the Dead Sea. David's spies were aware of Saul's presence in the area and the location of his camp, so that **David and Abishai** were able to catch **Saul . . . sleeping within the trench** (i.e., the camp). **God hath delivered** (Heb *sagar*, "abandoned") **thine enemy.** The fact that they were able to get to Saul without waking Abner and the others who would surely be on guard is attributed to God's supernatural help (see vs. 12). David still had such high respect for the office of the chosen king that he would not allow Abishai to kill Saul. **Who can stretch forth his hand against the LORD's**

4 David therefore sent out spies, and understood that Saul was come in very deed.

5 ¶And David arose, and came to the place where Saul had pitched: and David beheld the place where Saul lay, and Abner the son of Ner, the captain of his host: and Saul lay in the trench, and the people pitched round about him.

6 Then answered David and said to A-hĭm′e-lĕch the Hittite, and to A-bĭ′shaĭ the son of Zer-ŭ-i′ah, brother to Jō′ăb, saying, Who will go down with me to Saul to the camp? And A-bĭ′shaĭ said, I will go down with thee.

7 So David and A-bĭ′shaĭ came to the people by night: and, behold, Saul lay sleeping within the trench, and his spear stuck in the ground at his bolster: but Abner and the people lay round about him.

8 Then said A-bĭ′shaĭ to David, God hath delivered thine enemy into thine hand this day: now therefore let me smite him, I pray thee, with the spear even to the earth at once, and I will not *smite* him the second time.

9 And David said to A-bĭ′shaĭ, Destroy him not: for who can stretch forth his hand against the Lord's anointed, and be guiltless?

10 David said furthermore, *As* the Lord liveth, the Lord shall smite him; or his day shall come to die; or he shall descend into battle, and perish.

11 The Lord forbid that I should stretch forth mine hand against the Lord's anointed: but, I pray thee, take thou now the spear that *is* at his bolster, and the cruse of water, and let us go.

12 So David took the spear and the cruse of water from Saul's bolster; and they gat them away, and no man saw *it,* nor knew *it,* neither awaked: for they *were* all asleep; because a deep sleep from the Lord was fallen upon them.

13 ¶Then David went over to the other side, and stood on the top of an hill afar off; a great space *being* between them:

14 And David cried to the people, and to Abner the son of Ner, saying, Answerest thou not, Abner? Then Abner answered and said, Who *art* thou *that* criest to the king?

15 And David said to Abner, *Art* not thou a *valiant* man? and who *is* like to thee in Israel? wherefore then hast thou not kept thy lord the king? for there came one of the people in to destroy the king thy lord.

16 This thing *is* not good that thou hast done. *As* the Lord liveth, ye *are* worthy to die, because ye have not kept your master, the Lord's anointed. And now see where the king's spear *is,* and the cruse of water that *was* at his bolster.

17 And Saul knew David's voice, and said, *Is* this thy voice, my son David? And David said, *It is* my voice, my lord, O king.

18 And he said, Wherefore doth my lord thus pursue after his servant? for what have I done? or what evil *is* in mine hand?

anointed? As far as David is concerned, God has made the choice to put Saul in office; and God Himself must remove him.

16-18. Ye are worthy to die. The guard (Heb masc., pl., personal pronoun) have failed in their sworn responsibility to protect the king, and therefore they all deserve death. **The king's spear . . . the cruse of water.** David had removed these to make obvious the fact that he intended no harm to Saul.

19 Now therefore, I pray thee, let my lord the king hear the words of his servant. If the LORD have stirred thee up against me, let him accept an offering: but if *they be* the children of men, cursed *be* they before the LORD: for they have driven me out this day from abiding in the inheritance of the LORD, saying, Go, serve other gods.

20 Now therefore, let not my blood fall to the earth before the face of the LORD: for the king of Israel is come out to seek a flea, as when one doth hunt a partridge in the mountains.

21 ¶Then said Saul, I have sinned: return, my son David: for I will no more do thee harm, because my soul was precious in thine eyes this day: behold, I have played the fool, and have erred exceedingly.

22 And David answered and said, Behold the king's spear! and let one of the young men come over and fetch it.

23 The LORD render to every man his righteousness and his faithfulness: for the LORD delivered thee into *my* hand to day, but I would not stretch forth mine hand against the LORD's anointed.

24 And, behold, as thy life was much set by this day in mine eyes, so let my life be much set by in the eyes of the LORD, and let him deliver me out of all tribulation.

25 Then Saul said to David, Blessed *be* thou, my son David: thou shalt both do great *things*, and also shalt still prevail. So David went on his way, and Saul returned to his place.

CHAPTER 27

AND David said in his heart, I shall now perish one day by the hand of Saul: *there is* nothing better for me than that I should speedily escape into the land of the Philistines; and Saul shall despair of me, to seek me any more in any coast of Israel: so shall I escape out of his hand.

2 And David arose, and he passed over with the six hundred men that *were* with him unto Ā'chĭsh, the son of Mā'och, king of Gath.

3 And David dwelt with Ā'chĭsh at Gath, he and his men, every man with his household, *even* David with his two wives, A-hĭn'ō-am the Jĕz're-el-ĭt-ess, and Ăb'i-gāil the Carmelitess, Nā'bal's wife.

4 And it was told Saul that David was fled to Gath: and he sought no more again for him.

5 ¶And David said unto Ā'chĭsh, If I have now found grace in thine eyes, let them give me a place in some town in the country, that I may dwell there: for why should thy servant dwell in the royal city with thee?

6 Then Ā'chĭsh gave him Ziklag that day: wherefore Ziklag pertaineth unto the kings of Jūdah unto this day.

7 And the time that David dwelt in

19-20. Let him accept an offering (Heb *minchah*). If there was some unknown sin in David for which Saul was pursuing him, David was willing to confess it and offer the sacrifice for forgiveness. David was demonstrating the fact that there was no justification for Saul to kill him, even if there were real charges against him. It was obviously not the will of God that David was being hunted. **Inheritance of the LORD.** The word **inheritance** (Heb *nachelah*) is an important and developing theological technical term in the Old Testament. It refers to the people of God as His special and prized possession. The word is used only three times in the books of Samuel, each time with the meaning of the people of God (see I Sam 10:1). The same theme finds continuity in the New Testament. **Go, serve other gods.** To drive someone out from among the people of God and thus hinder him from worshiping God was an unthinkably cruel offense in the Old Testament, as well as in the New Testament (see Mk 9:42). A person who would do this (Saul) was saying, in effect, **Go, serve other gods.**

21-25. I have sinned . . . I have played the fool. As true as the confession is, it is either not sincere, or else it is not very permanent; for David was forced to find refuge in a pagan land and culture (27:1).

27:1-7. So shall I escape out of his hand. David was simply waiting in faith for God to accomplish His will. He had no lapse of faith but went to **the land of the Philistines** to get away from Saul's continued pursuit. **David dwelt with Achish at Gath.** Through a series of diplomatic lies, David was able to act as the agent of God in raiding the enemies of the people of the Lord and still remain safe from Saul by persuading the Philistine king **Achish** that his raids were against Israel. **Why should thy servant dwell in the royal city . . . ?** Achish trusted David enough to allow him to live in his own country village of **Ziklag**. From this base David was able to make his raids. All this was in the providence of God, and **David dwelt in the country of the Philistines . . . a full year and four months.**

the country of the Philistines was a full year and four months.

8 ¶And David and his men went up, and invaded the Gĕsh'u-rītes, and the Gĕz'rītes, and the Am'ă-lek-ītes: for those *nations were* of old the inhabitants of the land, as thou goest to Shur, even unto the land of Egypt.

9 And David smote the land, and left neither man nor woman alive, and took away the sheep, and the oxen, and the asses, and the camels, and the apparel, and returned, and came to Ā'chĭsh.

10 And Ā'chĭsh said, Whither have ye made a road to day? And David said, Against the south of Jūdah, and against the south of the Je-răh'me-el-ītes, and against the south of the Kĕn'ītes.

11 And David saved neither man nor woman alive, to bring *tidings* to Gath, saying, Lest they should tell on us, saying, So did David, and so *will be* his manner all the while he dwelleth in the country of the Philistines.

12 And Ā'chĭsh believed David, saying, He hath made his people Israel utterly to abhor him; therefore he shall be my servant for ever.

CHAPTER 28

AND it came to pass in those days, that the Philistines gathered their armies together for warfare, to fight with Israel. And Ā'chĭsh said unto David, Know thou assuredly, that thou shalt go out with me to battle, thou and thy men.

2 And David said to Ā'chĭsh, Surely thou shalt know what thy servant can do. And Ā'chĭsh said to David, Therefore will I make thee keeper of mine head for ever.

3 ¶Now Samuel was dead, and all Israel had lamented him, and buried him in Rā'mah, even in his own city. And Saul had put away those that had familiar spirits, and the wizards, out of the land.

4 And the Philistines gathered themselves together, and came and pitched in Shū'nem: and Saul gathered all Israel together, and they pitched in Gĭl-bō'a.

5 And when Saul saw the host of the Philistines, he was afraid, and his heart greatly trembled.

6 And when Saul enquired of the LORD, the LORD answered him not, neither by dreams, nor by U'rĭm, nor by prophets.

7 Then said Saul unto his servants, Seek me a woman that hath a familiar spirit, that I may go to her, and enquire of her. And his servants said to him, Behold, *there is* a woman that hath a familiar spirit at Ĕn-dôr.

8 And Saul disguised himself, and put on other raiment, and he went, and two men with him, and they came to the woman by night: and he said, I pray thee, divine unto me by the familiar spirit, and bring me *him* up, whom I shall name unto thee.

9 And the woman said unto him, Behold, thou knowest what Saul hath done, how he hath cut off those that have familiar spirits, and the wizards, out of the land: wherefore then layest

8-12. Geshurites, and the Gezrites, and the Amalekites. These were all enemies of the people of God, so that David was even now acting as the king and delivering them. **David saved.** Literally, "David did not allow a man or woman to live." David was being obedient to the Lord in this utter destruction. It was the exact opposite of the disobedience of Saul which cost him the kingdom (see I Sam 15:17-23).

28:1-5. Thou shalt go out with me to battle. We do not know what would have happened in the event David had gone with **Achish,** since the other Philistines would not allow it (see 29:1-11). **Familiar spirits.** These were the spiritist mediums of the day. They claimed the ability to communicate with the dead. This was forbidden to the Israelites (Lev 20:27). If any of them ever accomplished anything supernaturally, it would have been by the power of Satan rather than by God's power. **His heart greatly trembled.** Saul had known for some time that he had been rejected and forsaken by God. He was at least intermittently insane.

6-10. When Saul inquired (Heb *sha'al*). This is the common word for "question," or "ask," and is also the word used for asking the will of God through the **Urim** and Thummim (cf. Lev 8:8; I Sam 23:2,4). It is different from the word **inquire** in verse 7. Saul was abandoned by God to his own insane wickedness. There was no way to find God's will other than these which he had tried: **By dreams . . . by Urim . . . and by prophets. Inquire** (Heb *darash*) denotes a more intensive "seeking after," and is thus distinguished from the word in verse 6. Saul was now at the point of desperation. I Chronicles 10:13-14 mentions this desperate consultation of the medium rather than seeking God as one of the reasons why God killed him. But his stubbornness was habitual and chronic.

585

thou a snare for my life, to cause me to die?

10 And Saul sware to her by the LORD, saying, As the LORD liveth, there shall no punishment happen to thee for this thing.

11 Then said the woman, Whom shall I bring up unto thee? And he said, Bring me up Samuel.

12 And when the woman saw Samuel, she cried with a loud voice: and the woman spake to Saul, saying, Why hast thou deceived me? for thou art Saul.

13 And the king said unto her, Be not afraid: for what sawest thou? And the woman said unto Saul, I saw gods ascending out of the earth.

14 And he said unto her, What form is he of? And she said, An old man cometh up; and he is covered with a mantle. And Saul perceived that it was Samuel, and he stooped with his face to the ground, and bowed himself.

15 And Samuel said to Saul, Why hast thou disquieted me, to bring me up? And Saul answered, I am sore distressed; for the Philistines make war against me, and God is departed from me, and answereth me no more, neither by prophets, nor by dreams: therefore I have called thee, that thou mayest make known unto me what I shall do.

16 Then said Samuel, Wherefore then dost thou ask of me, seeing the LORD is departed from thee, and is become thine enemy?

17 And the LORD hath done to him, as he spake by me: for the LORD hath rent the kingdom out of thine hand, and given it to thy neighbour, even to David:

18 Because thou obeyedst not the voice of the LORD, nor executedst his fierce wrath upon Ăm'a-lĕk, therefore hath the LORD done this thing unto thee this day.

19 Moreover the LORD will also deliver Israel with thee into the hand of the Philistines: and to morrow shalt thou and thy sons be with me: the LORD also shall deliver the host of Israel into the hand of the Philistines.

20 Then Saul fell straightway all along on the earth, and was sore afraid, because of the words of Samuel: and there was no strength in him; for he had eaten no bread all the day, nor all the night.

21 ¶And the woman came unto Saul, and saw that he was sore troubled, and said unto him, Behold, thine handmaid hath obeyed thy voice, and I have put my life in my hand, and have hearkened unto thy words which thou spakest unto me.

22 Now therefore, I pray thee, hearken thou also unto the voice of thine handmaid, and let me set a morsel of bread before thee; and eat, that thou mayest have strength, when thou goest on thy way.

23 But he refused, and said, I will not eat. But his servants, together with the woman, compelled him; and he hearkened unto their voice. So he arose from the earth, and sat upon the bed.

24 And the woman had a fat calf in the house; and she hasted, and killed it,

11-16. Bring me up Samuel. If the medium had not by this time seen through his thin disguise, she might have guessed Saul's identity now. Who else would want to talk to Samuel? **I saw gods ascending out of the earth. Gods** (Heb 'elōhīm) is the same word and form used for the true God, but in this context means, "a ghost" or "spirit." Her description is purposely vague, and **Saul perceived that it was Samuel. And Samuel said.** It is, of course, the medium telling Saul what Samuel's ghost is saying. We cannot believe that God would need to communicate with Saul by means of this pagan practice which He had condemned. Furthermore, God had already refused to reveal His will through the legitimate and normal means (vs. 6). If Samuel could have spoken to Saul from his grave, he would have said things very much like this. The information given by the medium was all common knowledge among the people of the land and even among the Philistines.

17-25. The LORD hath rent the kingdom out of thine hand. Even Saul himself had acknowledged this several times. **Thou obeyedst not.** This incident had been the climax of a stubborn and disobedient heart (I Sam 15:23). It would not have taken a prophet to predict the outcome of the imminent and massive Philistine offensive already in progress. Even the young Amalekite who told David of the death of Saul (II Sam 1:13) knew all the details of the relationship between Saul and David. The spiritist woman was right about Saul and his sons; everyone knew they were doomed. Her prediction about the army was a bit more gloomy than proved to be true in the actual battle: **The LORD also shall deliver** (Heb nathan) **the host of Israel into the hand of the Philistines.** Israel lost the battle, but not the war. It was really only a very short time before David began to reunite the people and deliver them completely from their enemies.

and took flour, and kneaded *it*, and did bake unleavened bread thereof.

25 And she brought *it* before Saul, and before his servants; and they did eat. Then they rose up, and went away that night.

CHAPTER 29

NOW the Philistines gathered together all their armies to Ā'phĕk: and the Israelites pitched by a fountain which *is* in Jĕz're-el.

2 And the lords of the Philistines passed on by hundreds, and by thousands: but David and his men passed on in the rereward with Ā'chĭsh.

3 Then said the princes of the Philistines, What *do* these Hebrews *here*? And Ā'chĭsh said unto the princes of the Philistines, *Is* not this David, the servant of Saul the king of Israel, which hath been with me these days, or these years, and I have found no fault in him since he fell *unto me* unto this day?

4 And the princes of the Philistines were wroth with him; and the princes of the Philistines said unto him, Make this fellow return, that he may go again to his place which thou hast appointed him, and let him not go down with us to battle, lest in the battle he be an adversary to us: for wherewith should he reconcile himself unto his master? *should it* not *be* with the heads of these men?

5 *Is* not this David, of whom they sang one to another in dances, saying, Saul slew his thousands, and David his ten thousands?

6 ¶Then Ā'chĭsh called David, and said unto him, Surely, *as* the LORD liveth, thou hast been upright, and thy going out and thy coming in with me in the host *is* good in my sight: for I have not found evil in thee since the day of thy coming unto me unto this day: nevertheless the lords favour thee not.

7 Wherefore now return, and go in peace, that thou displease not the lords of the Philistines.

8 And David said unto Ā'chĭsh, But what have I done? and what hast thou found in thy servant so long as I have been with thee unto this day, that I may not go fight against the enemies of my lord the king?

9 And Ā'chĭsh answered and said to David, I know that thou *art* good in my sight, as an angel of God: notwithstanding the princes of the Philistines have said, He shall not go up with us to the battle.

10 Wherefore now rise up early in the morning with thy master's servants that are come with thee: and as soon as ye be up early in the morning, and have light, depart.

11 So David and his men rose up early to depart in the morning, to return into the land of the Philistines. And the Philistines went up to Jĕz're-el.

CHAPTER 30

AND it came to pass, when David and his men were come to Ziklag on the third day, that the Am'ă-lek-ītes had invaded the south, and Ziklag, and smitten Ziklag, and burned it with fire;

2 And had taken the women captives, that *were* therein: they slew not any,

29:1-11. What do these Hebrews here? Because of the suspicions of the rest of the Philistines, David was not able to join them as Achish had hoped. This also was within the providence of God. **As the LORD liveth.** This is perhaps transferred into Israelite idiom by the writer, since we would not expect to find a Philistine swearing by Yahweh. It at least makes clear that Achish trusted David completely. **Angel of God.** Perhaps this also has a more general meaning, "messenger of the gods," since it comes from unbelieving lips.

30:1-10. It was only by God's providence that David was available to save the women and children of his own village, **Ziklag,** who had been captured by the **Amalekites** while David was away. The steps of a righteous man are ordered of the Lord. **David encouraged himself in the LORD his God.** At this point he did not know how close he was to the kingship. He was alone,

either great or small, but carried *them* away, and went on their way.

3 So David and his men came to the city, and, behold, *it was* burned with fire; and their wives, and their sons, and their daughters, were taken captives.

4 Then David and the people that *were* with him lifted up their voice and wept, until they had no more power to weep.

5 And David's two wives were taken captives, A-hǐn'ō-am the Jěz're-el-īt-ess, and Ăb'i-gāil the wife of Nā'bal the Carmelite.

6 And David was greatly distressed; for the people spake of stoning him, because the soul of all the people was grieved, every man for his sons and for his daughters: but David encouraged himself in the LORD his God.

7 And David said to Ā-bī'a-thar the priest, A-hǐm'e-lěch's son, I pray thee, bring me hither the ephod. And Ā-bī'a-thar brought thither the ephod to David.

8 And David enquired at the LORD, saying, Shall I pursue after this troop? shall I overtake them? And he answered him, Pursue: for thou shalt surely overtake *them,* and without fail recover *all.*

9 So David went, he and the six hundred men that *were* with him, and came to the brook Bē'sôr, where those that were left behind stayed.

10 But David pursued, he and four hundred men: for two hundred abode behind, which were so faint that they could not go over the brook Bē'sôr.

11 ¶And they found an Egyptian in the field, and brought him to David, and gave him bread, and he did eat; and they made him drink water;

12 And they gave him a piece of a cake of figs, and two clusters of raisins: and when he had eaten, his spirit came again to him: for he had eaten no bread, nor drunk *any* water, three days and three nights.

13 And David said unto him, To whom *belongest* thou? and whence *art* thou? And he said, I *am* a young man of Egypt, servant to an Am'ă-lek-īte; and my master left me, because three days agone I fell sick.

14 We made an invasion *upon* the south of the Chěr'e-thītes, and upon *the coast* which *belongeth* to Jūdah, and upon the south of Caleb; and we burned Ziklag with fire.

15 And David said to him, Canst thou bring me down to this company? And he said, Swear unto me by God, that thou wilt neither kill me, nor deliver me into the hands of my master, and I will bring thee down to this company.

16 And when he had brought him down, behold, *they were* spread abroad upon all the earth, eating and drinking, and dancing, because of all the great spoil that they had taken out of the land of the Philistines, and out of the land of Jūdah.

17 And David smote them from the twilight even unto the evening of the next day: and there escaped not a man

driven from the people of God and hunted by Saul; and now he had lost everything in the raid, including his wives. He found his comfort still in the Lord. **Bring me hither the ephod.** In this deep depression David did not lose his faith in the Lord; but he looked immediately to God to learn His will. **And he answered him.** Presumably by Urim and Thummim again.

11-25. They found an Egyptian. He turned out to be a slave of one of the Amalekites who had raided Ziklag, and he was able to lead them to the Amalekite camp. **And David smote them.** Although outnumbered, David had the element of surprise; and, more importantly, God was on his side. **David recovered** (Heb *natsal,* connotes "snatched from the jaws of destruction in the nick of time.") **All that the Amalekites had carried away.** There were no losses at all, but instead gains because of the spoil. **We will not give them aught.** These vain men would not have shared what they felt they had gained by their own strength in battle. David knew, however, that it was the LORD who had **given,** and **preserved** (Heb *shamar,* "watch over"), and accomplished the victory. Those who had stayed **by the stuff** were God's people, too, and deserved an equal part.

of them, save four hundred young men, which rode upon camels, and fled.

18 And David recovered all that the Am'ă-lek-ītes had carried away: and David rescued his two wives.

19 And there was nothing lacking to them, neither small nor great, neither sons nor daughters, neither spoil, nor any *thing* that they had taken to them: David recovered all.

20 And David took all the flocks and the herds, *which* they drave before those *other* cattle, and said, This *is* David's spoil.

21 ¶And David came to the two hundred men, which were so faint that they could not follow David, whom they had made also to abide at the brook Bē'sôr: and they went forth to meet David, and to meet the people that *were* with him: and when David came near to the people, he saluted them.

22 Then answered all the wicked men and *men* of Bē'lĭ-al, of those that went with David, and said, Because they went not with us, we will not give them *ought* of the spoil that we have recovered, save to every man his wife and his children, that they may lead *them* away, and depart.

23 Then said David, Ye shall not do so, my brethren, with that which the LORD hath given us, who hath preserved us, and delivered the company that came against us into our hand.

24 For who will hearken unto you in this matter? but as his part *is* that goeth down to the battle, so *shall* his part *be* that tarrieth by the stuff: they shall part alike.

25 And it was *so* from that day forward, that he made it a statute and an ordinance for Israel unto this day.

26 ¶And when David came to Ziklag, he sent of the spoil unto the elders of Jūdah, *even* to his friends, saying, Behold a present for you of the spoil of the enemies of the LORD;

27 To *them* which *were* in Bĕth-el, and to *them* which *were* in south Rā'mŏth, and to *them* which *were* in Jăt'tir,

28 And to *them* which *were* in Ar'ō-er, and to *them* which *were* in Sĭph'-mŏth, and to *them* which *were* in Ĕsh-te-mō'a,

29 And to *them* which *were* in Rā'-chăl, and to *them* which *were* in the cities of the Je-răh'me-el-ītes, and to *them* which *were* in the cities of the Kēn'-ītes,

30 And to *them* which *were* in Hôr'-mah, and to *them* which *were* in Chôr-ā'shan, and to *them* which *were* in Ā'thăch,

31 And to *them* which *were* in Hē-bron, and to all the places where David himself and his men were wont to haunt.

CHAPTER 31

NOW the Philistines fought against Israel: and the men of Israel fled from before the Philistines, and fell down slain in mount Gĭl-bō'a.

2 And the Philistines followed hard upon Saul and upon his sons; and the

---

26-31. David acknowledged the victory that the Lord had given, and sent shares of the spoil to all the places where he had been helped during his flight from Saul. This would surely have helped to reunite the people under David as the new king.

E. Saul's Death on Mount Gilboa. 31:1-13.

31:1-8. The men of Israel fled. This chapter continues with the story of chapter 29 and is parallel also with I Chronicles 10:1-12. The battle was lost, and the Israelites were forced to retreat. **Slew Jonathan.** The sons of Saul, as successors to the throne, would be prime targets. **The battle went sore against Saul, and the archers hit him.** Literally "found him," but the

Philistines slew Jonathan, and A-bĭn'a-dăb, and Mĕl'chĭ-shū'a, Saul's sons.

3 And the battle went sore against Saul, and the archers hit him; and he was sore wounded of the archers.

4 Then said Saul unto his armour-bearer, Draw thy sword, and thrust me through therewith; lest these uncir-cumcised come and thrust me through, and abuse me. But his armourbearer would not; for he was sore afraid. There-fore Saul took a sword, and fell upon it.

5 And when his armourbearer saw that Saul was dead, he fell likewise upon his sword, and died with him.

6 So Saul died, and his three sons, and his armourbearer, and all his men, that same day together.

7 ¶And when the men of Israel that were on the other side of the valley, and they that were on the other side Jordan, saw that the men of Israel fled, and that Saul and his sons were dead, they for-sook the cities, and fled; and the Philis-tines came and dwelt in them.

8 ¶And it came to pass on the morrow, when the Philistines came to strip the slain, that they found Saul and his three sons fallen in mount Gĭl-bō'a.

9 And they cut off his head, and stripped off his armour, and sent into the land of the Philistines round about, to publish it in the house of their idols, and among the people.

10 And they put his armour in the house of Ăsh'ta-rŏth: and they fastened his body to the wall of Bĕth'-shăn.

11 And when the inhabitants of Jā'-besh-gĭl'e-ad heard of that which the Philistines had done to Saul;

12 All the valiant men arose, and went all night, and took the body of Saul and the bodies of his sons from the wall of Bĕth'-shăn, and came to Jā'-besh, and burnt them there.

13 And they took their bones, and buried them under a tree at Jā'besh, and fasted seven days.

implication is the same. **Sore wounded.** The Septuagint locates the wound as being in the soft part of the body below the breast bone and above the navel (Gr *hypochondrion*), a mortal wound. **Thrust me through.** This, he thought, would be better than falling into the hand of the Philistines. **Fell upon it.** When the **Armor-bearer would not,** Saul killed himself. The same facts are related in I Chronicles 10, while II Samuel 1:6-10 states that Saul was killed by an Amalekite. Either Saul was not successful in his suicide attempt, or else the Amalekite lied to David about his part in Saul's death. More important is the fact itself, that Saul was dead. He was rejected from being king over God's people, forsaken by God, and thus destroyed in battle because God's protecting hand was withdrawn.

9-11. They cut off his head. This may have been done in retaliation for what David had done to their hero Goliath. The head was used as a token of victory along with the armor. **Fastened his body to the wall of Beth-shan.** It is probably an ironic coincidence that the Greek name for **Beth-shan** later became Scythopolis, which meant either "city of the Scythians," or, because of the extreme cruelty and barbarism (they scalped or cut off the heads of their enemies) of the Scythians, "city of barbarism." The name may have been a pun like "Sin City." At any rate, this display of the bodies of Saul and his sons is about as barbaric an act as can be imagined.

12-13. Valiant men . . . burnt them. These men of **Jabesh** were especially indebted to Saul because he had begun his successful military career by delivering them from Nahash the Ammonite (I Sam 11:1-13). The distance to **Jabesh** from **Beth-shan** is twenty miles.

(see page 636 for Bibliography to I and II Samuel)

OUTLINE
II SAMUEL

COMMENTARY

I. GOD'S RULE THROUGH DAVID AS THE CHOSEN KING. 1:1-10:19.

II Samuel is not a different book from I Samuel in the same sense that II Corinthians is different from I Corinthians. The division was made long after Samuel was written by the translators of the Septuagint. The significance, authorship and date, historical background, etc., are the same as for I Samuel; and the content simply continues with the history of God's dealing with His people in the time of David.

A. The News of the Death of Saul. 1:1-27.

1:1-9. A man came out of the camp from Saul. No doubt this Amalekite thought he would be well treated by David since he brought news of the death of David's enemy. He was mistaken. He claimed to have killed Saul, the anointed King, and was killed for news he thought would bring him great reward. **Saul and Jonathan his son are dead.** The Amalekite must have discovered the body of Saul shortly after he had died, and then started out immediately for Ziklag to tell David. **Leaned upon his spear.** This report does not seem to mean that Saul was just casually leaning and had not been wounded, since according to verse 10 he had been so mortally wounded that it did not appear that he would live anyway. Neither does the information about **chariots and horsemen** necessarily contradict the account given in I Samuel 31:3 that the archers had found Saul. It could have referred to mounted archers.

NOW it came to pass after the death of Saul, when David was returned from the slaughter of the Am'ă-lek-ītes, and David had abode two days in Ziklag;

2 It came even to pass on the third day, that, behold, a man came out of the camp from Saul with his clothes rent, and earth upon his head: and *so* it was, when he came to David, that he fell to the earth, and did obeisance.

3 And David said unto him, From whence comest thou? And he said unto him, Out of the camp of Israel am I escaped.

4 And David said unto him, How went the matter? I pray thee, tell me. And he answered, That the people are fled from the battle, and many of the people also are fallen and dead; and Saul and Jonathan his son are dead also.

5 And David said unto the young man that told him, How knowest thou that Saul and Jonathan his son be dead?

6 And the young man that told him said, As I happened by chance upon mount Gĭl-bō'a, behold, Saul leaned upon his spear; and, lo, the chariots and horsemen followed hard after him.

7 And when he looked behind him, he saw me, and called unto me. And I answered, Here *am* I.

8 And he said unto me, Who *art* thou? And I answered, I *am* an Am'ă-lek-īte.

9 He said unto me again, Stand, I pray thee, upon me, and slay me: for

591

anguish is come upon me, because my life *is* yet whole in me.

10 So I stood upon him, and slew him, because I was sure that he could not live after that he was fallen: and I took the crown that *was* upon his head, and the bracelet that *was* on his arm, and have brought them hither unto my lord.

11 Then David took hold on his clothes, and rent them; and likewise all the men that *were* with him:

12 And they mourned, and wept, and fasted until even, for Saul, and for Jonathan his son, and for the people of the LORD, and for the house of Israel; because they were fallen by the sword.

13 ¶And David said unto the young man that told him, Whence *art* thou? And he answered, I *am* the son of a stranger, an Am′ă-lek-īte.

14 And David said unto him, How wast thou not afraid to stretch forth thine hand to destroy the LORD's anointed?

15 And David called one of the young men, and said, Go near, *and* fall upon him. And he smote him that he died.

16 And David said unto him, Thy blood *be* upon thy head; for thy mouth hath testified against thee, saying, I have slain the LORD's anointed.

17 ¶And David lamented with this lamentation over Saul and over Jonathan his son:

18 (Also he bade them teach the children of Jūdah *the use of* the bow: behold, *it is* written in the book of Jā′-sher.)

19 The beauty of Israel is slain upon thy high places: how are the mighty fallen!

20 Tell *it* not in Gath, publish *it* not in the streets of Ăs′ke-lŏn; lest the daughters of the Philistines rejoice, lest the daughters of the uncircumcised triumph.

21 Ye mountains of Gĭl-bō′a, *let there be* no dew, neither *let there be* rain, upon you, nor fields of offerings: for there the shield of the mighty is vilely cast away, the shield of Saul, *as though he had* not *been* anointed with oil.

22 From the blood of the slain, from the fat of the mighty, the bow of Jonathan turned not back, and the sword of Saul returned not empty.

23 Saul and Jonathan *were* lovely and pleasant in their lives, and in their death they were not divided: they were swifter than eagles, they were stronger than lions.

24 Ye daughters of Israel, weep over Saul, who clothed you in scarlet, with

10. So I stood upon him, and slew him. This is the only part of the story that does not square with I Samuel 31:4 and I Chronicles 10:4, which state that Saul killed himself. It is possible that the Amalekite came along just in time to finish what Saul had attempted, but it is more likely that the man lied about how Saul died in order to make the story more plausible and have a better chance at whatever reward David would give when he heard that his only rival to the throne was dead. **The crown . . . and the bracelet** (armlet) were brought to prove that it was really Saul that had fallen in the battle.

11-12. David took hold on his clothes, and rent them. This was the first reaction to show mourning and sorrow for a great calamity or someone's death, especially the death of a relative or loved one. This was not at all the reaction expected. David and his men **mourned, and wept, and fasted** for all those who had been killed in battle, and **for Saul.**

13-17. Stranger (Heb *gēr*) is a technical term for a "sojourner," a person living in a new land without all the rights and cultural backgrounds of a native citizen. The man should have known the seriousness of harming the **LORD's anointed.** David had a profound respect for Saul and would never have harmed him because he had been chosen by the Lord. The phrase was an important and developing theological term which eventually came into English as "Messiah," and "Christ." Note its repeated use, especially in the books of Samuel. (See 5:3 for a list of its uses in Samuel.) Although David had several opportunities to kill Saul, he had not done it because of the office. **Fall upon him.** By claiming to killing The LORD's anointed the Amalekite had lied himself into a death sentence.

18. Teach the children of Judah the use of the bow. The words **the use of** are added to the Hebrew text, which reads simply, **teach the children of Judah the bow.** The title of the whole elegy, or lamentation poem, was, the **bow** (Heb *qeshet*); and it was this lamentation poem that was to be taught to the people of Judah. The Septuagint has only, "Teach it to the people of Judah." **The book of Jasher** is the writer's source for the elegy of the bow; it is mentioned in Joshua 10:13 and should perhaps be translated "The Book of the Righteous," as it is in the Septuagint.

19-27. The beauty of Israel refers poetically to Saul and Jonathan as glorious heroes who were the means of salvation from the Philistines. **Mighty** also alludes to them and the others lost in the war. **Gath** and **Askelon** (vs. 20) were two of the Philistine cities, and the elegy would deny them the opportunity to rejoice in the death of Saul. Mount **Gilboa** is called upon to produce no grain in mute memorial to this solemn event. **The bow of Jonathan . . . and the sword of Saul** were the main subjects of lament, aside from the men themselves. The weapons are mourned because they were used for the salvation and deliverance of the people from their enemies. **My brother Jonathan.** David loved Jonathan as a brother; he would have given his own life for him if he could have. **Thy love.** The genitive could also be objective. This passage shows David's profound love for Jonathan, a love akin to that of brother for brother of comrades in arms. **How are the mighty fallen.** This line divides the stanzas of the elegy and expresses its chief lamentation.

other delights, who put on ornaments of gold upon your apparel.

25 How are the mighty fallen in the midst of the battle! O Jonathan, *thou wast* slain in thine high places.

26 I am distressed for thee, my brother Jonathan: very pleasant hast thou been unto me: thy love to me was wonderful, passing the love of women.

27 How are the mighty fallen, and the weapons of war perished!

CHAPTER 2

AND it came to pass after this, that David enquired of the LORD, saying, Shall I go up into any of the cities of Jūdah? And the LORD said unto him, Go up. And David said, Whither shall I go up? And he said, Unto Hēbron.

2 So David went up thither, and his two wives also, A-hīn′ō-am the Jĕz′re-el-īt-ess, and Ăb′i-gāil Nā′bal′s wife the Carmelite.

3 And his men that *were* with him did David bring up, every man with his household: and they dwelt in the cities of Hēbron.

4 And the men of Jūdah came, and there they anointed David king over the house of Jūdah. And they told David, saying, *That* the men of Jā′-besh-gĭl′e-ad *were they* that buried Saul.

5 ¶And David sent messengers unto the men of Jā′besh-gĭl′e-ad, and said unto them, Blessed *be* ye of the LORD, that ye have shewed this kindness unto your lord, *even* unto Saul, and have buried him.

6 And now the LORD shew kindness and truth unto you: and I also will require you this kindness, because ye have done this thing.

7 Therefore now let your hands be strengthened, and be ye valiant: for your master Saul is dead, and also the house of Jūdah have anointed me king over them.

8 ¶But Abner the son of Ner, captain of Saul's host, took Ĭsh-bō′sheth the son of Saul, and brought him over to Mā-ha-nā′im;

9 And made him king over Gilead, and over the Ăsh′ur-ītes, and over Jĕz′-re-el, and over Ē′phra-im, and over Benjamin, and over all Israel.

10 Ĭsh-bō′sheth Saul's son *was* forty years old when he began to reign over Israel, and reigned two years. But the house of Jūdah followed David.

11 And the time that David was king in Hēbron over the house of Jūdah was seven years and six months.

12 ¶And Abner the son of Ner, and the servants of Ĭsh-bō′sheth the son of Saul, went out from Mā-ha-nā′im to Gĭb′-e-on.

13 And Jō′ăb the son of Zer-ū-i′ah, and the servants of David, went out, and met together by the pool of Gĭb′-e-on: and they sat down, the one on the one side of the pool, and the other on the other side of the pool.

14 And Abner said to Jō′ăb, Let the young men now arise, and play before us. And Jō′ăb said, Let them arise.

15 Then there arose and went over by

B. David's Anointing and the War with Abner. 2:1-32.

2:1-3. David inquired of the LORD. David, and nearly everyone else in the land, including Israel's enemies, knew that David would now be king. The priest was with David in Ziklag, and it was now important to determine the will of God before any action was taken. The move to **Hebron** was thus divinely sanctioned.

4. They anointed (Heb *mashach*) **David king over the house of Judah.** His own tribe was the first to acknowledge publicly and openly the earlier private anointing of David by the prophet Samuel (I Sam 10:1). Hebron was already an important city for the leadership of Judah, and it would be an opportunity for the other tribes to align themselves with David.

5-7. The men of Jabesh-gilead had cremated and buried Saul; David now sends to thank them for that kindness, but also to ask them to join him and the people of Judah in order to present a united front to the common enemies of Israel. The call for political unity under God is phrased, **let your hands be strengthened, and be ye valiant.** David refers also to the confirmation of God's choice by **the house of Judah,** who had **anointed** him as **king.**

8-11. Abner knew about David's anointing; and from his close association with Saul as the captain of his army, he should have known as Saul did that David would be king. He chose **Ish-bosheth,** however, another son of **Saul,** to establish as king. **Made him king . . . over all Israel.** This shows that as the leader of the army Abner maintained a considerable amount of political power as well.

12-17. Gibeon is five miles northwest of Jerusalem and is now known as El Jib. **Met together by the pool of Gibeon.** The purpose of the meeting is not revealed, and no one knows exactly what kind of a game **Abner** suggested; but the challenge was accepted, and the result was a mutual massacre.

number twelve of Benjamin, which *pertained* to Ĭsh–bō′sheth the son of Saul, and twelve of the servants of David.

16 And they caught every one his fellow by the head, and *thrust* his sword in his fellow's side; so they fell down together: wherefore that place was called Hĕl′kăth–hăz′zu–rĭm, which *is* in Gĭb′e-on.

17 And there was a very sore battle that day; and Abner was beaten, and the men of Israel, before the servants of David.

18 ¶And there were three sons of Zer-ū-i′ah there, Jō′ăb, and A-bī′shaī, and Ā′sa-hĕl: and Ā′sa-hĕl *was as* light of foot as a wild roe.

19 And Ā′sa-hĕl pursued after Abner; and in going he turned not to the right hand nor to the left from following Abner.

20 Then Abner looked behind him, and said, *Art* thou Ā′sa-hĕl? And he answered, I *am*.

21 And Abner said to him, Turn thee aside to thy right hand or to thy left, and lay thee hold on one of the young men, and take thee his armour. But Ā′sa-hĕl would not turn aside from following of him.

22 And Abner said again to Ā′sa-hĕl, Turn thee aside from following me: wherefore should I smite thee to the ground? how then should I hold up my face to Jō′ăb thy brother?

23 Howbeit he refused to turn aside: wherefore Abner with the hinder end of the spear smote him under the fifth *rib*, that the spear came out behind him; and he fell down there, and died in the same place: and it came to pass, *that* as many as came to the place where Ā′sa-hĕl fell down and died stood still.

24 Jō′ăb also and A-bī′shaī pursued after Abner: and the sun went down when they were come to the hill of Ăm′-mah, that *lieth* before Gī′ah by the way of the wilderness of Gĭbeon.

25 ¶And the children of Benjamin gathered themselves together after Abner, and became one troop, and stood on the top of an hill.

26 Then Abner called to Jō′ăb, and said, Shall the sword devour for ever? knowest thou not that it will be bitterness in the latter end? how long shall it be then, ere thou bid the people return from following their brethren?

27 And Jō′ăb said, *As* God liveth, unless thou hadst spoken, surely then in the morning the people had gone up every one from following his brother.

28 So Jō′ăb blew a trumpet, and all the people stood still, and pursued after Israel no more, neither fought they any more.

29 And Abner and his men walked all that night through the plain, and passed over Jordan, and went through all Bĭth′rŏn, and they came to Mā-ha-nā′im.

30 And Jō′ăb returned from following Abner: and when he had gathered all the people together, there lacked of David's servants nineteen men and Ā′sa-hĕl.

18-23. Asahel pursued after Abner, who tried to get **Asahel** to desist and, when he would not, drove the handle or shaft of his spear through him and killed him.

24-32. Joab . . . and Abishai continued in pursuit of **Abner** on into the night unsuccessfully. Abner was finally able to convince Joab to call off the chase. In the battle, Abner lost three-hundred sixty men, while Joab lost only twenty.

31 But the servants of David had smitten of Benjamin, and of Abner's men, *so that* three hundred and three-score men died.

32 ¶And they took up Ă'sa-hĕl, and buried him in the sepulchre of his father, which *was in* Bĕth-lĕhĕm. And Jŏ'ăb and his men went all night, and they came to Hēbron at break of day.

CHAPTER 3

NOW there was long war between the house of Saul and the house of David: but David waxed stronger and stronger, and the house of Saul waxed weaker and weaker.

2 ¶And unto David were sons born in Hēbron: and his firstborn was Ăm'nŏn, of A-hĭn'ō-am the Jĕz're-el-ĭt-ess;

3 And his second, Chĭl'e-ăb, of Ăb'i-gāil the wife of Nā'bal the Carmelite; and the third, Ăb'sa-lom the son of Mā'a-cah the daughter of Tăl'maī king of Gĕ'shur;

4 And the fourth, Ăd-o-nī'jah the son of Hăg'gĭth; and the fifth, Shĕph-a-tī'ah the son of Ăb'ī-tal;

5 And the sixth, Ĭth're-am, by Ĕg'lah David's wife. These were born to David in Hēbron.

6 ¶And it came to pass, while there was war between the house of Saul and the house of David, that Abner made himself strong for the house of Saul.

7 And Saul had a concubine, whose name *was* Rĭz'pah, the daughter of Ā-ī'ah: and *Ish–bo'sheth* said to Abner, Wherefore hast thou gone in unto my father's concubine?

8 Then was Abner very wroth for the words of Ĭsh-bō'sheth, and said, *Am* I a dog's head, which against Jūdah do shew kindness this day unto the house of Saul thy father, to his brethren, and to his friends, and have not delivered thee into the hand of David, that thou chargest me to day with a fault concerning this woman?

9 So do God to Abner, and more also, except, as the LORD hath sworn to David, even so I do to him;

10 To translate the kingdom from the house of Saul, and to set up the throne of David over Israel and over Jūdah, from Dan even to Be'er-shē'ba.

11 And he could not answer Abner a word again, because he feared him.

12 ¶And Abner sent messengers to David on his behalf, saying, Whose *is* the land? saying *also*, Make thy league with me, and, behold, my hand *shall be* with thee, to bring about all Israel unto thee.

13 And he said, Well; I will make a league with thee: but one thing I require of thee, that is, Thou shalt not see my face, except thou first bring Mī'chal Saul's daughter, when thou comest to see my face.

14 And David sent messengers to Ĭsh-bō'sheth Saul's son, saying, Deliver *me* my wife Mī'chal, which I espoused to me for an hundred foreskins of the Philistines.

15 And Ĭsh-bō'sheth sent, and took her from *her* husband, *even* from Phăl'-tĭ-el the son of Lā'ĭsh.

C. The Murder of Abner. 3:1-39.

3:1. There was long war; it was actually between David and Abner, or Judah and the other tribes (Israel) who had not yet accepted David as king. **David waxed stronger and stronger.** More and more of the people were in support of David, although Ish-bosheth was their king.

2-6. Six sons were born to David by six different wives while he ruled in **Hebron.**

7-17. Then was Abner very wroth. When Abner was rebuked for going in to Saul's concubine by the man whom he had set up as king, Abner became very angry. It was this minor incident that finally made him change his mind and become a supporter of David. **To set up the throne of David over Israel.** He now allows himself to believe what he has known all along, that God had chosen David. The plans for reunification are sent to David who approves on the condition that **Michal Saul's daughter** be brought to David. **David sent messengers to Ish-bosheth** who was now and from the beginning a mere figurehead more than a real king. Michal was taken from her **husband,** who followed **weeping behind her to Bahurim.**

16 And her husband went with her along weeping behind her to Ba-hū′rĭm. Then said Abner unto him, Go, return. And he returned.

17 ¶And Abner had communication with the elders of Israel, saying, Ye sought for David in times past to be king over you:

18 Now then do it: for the LORD hath spoken of David, saying, By the hand of my servant David I will save my people Israel out of the hand of the Philistines, and out of the hand of all their enemies.

19 And Abner also spake in the ears of Benjamin: and Abner went also to speak in the ears of David in Hēbron all that seemed good to Israel, and that seemed good to the whole house of Benjamin.

20 So Abner came to David to Hē-bron, and twenty men with him. And David made Abner and the men that were with him a feast.

21 And Abner said unto David, I will arise and go, and will gather all Israel unto my lord the king, that they may make a league with thee, and that thou mayest reign over all that thine heart desireth. And David sent Abner away; and he went in peace.

22 ¶And, behold, the servants of David and Jō′ăb came from pursuing a troop, and brought in a great spoil with them: but Abner was not with David in Hēbron; for he had sent him away, and he was gone in peace.

23 When Jō′ăb and all the host that was with him were come, they told Jō′ăb, saying, Abner the son of Ner came to the king, and he hath sent him away, and he is gone in peace.

24 Then Jō′ăb came to the king, and said, What hast thou done? behold, Abner came unto thee; why is it that thou hast sent him away, and he is quite gone?

25 Thou knowest Abner the son of Ner, that he came to deceive thee, and to know thy going out and thy coming in, and to know all that thou doest.

26 And when Jō′ăb was come out from David, he sent messengers after Abner, which brought him again from the well of Sī′rah: but David knew it not.

27 And when Abner was returned to Hēbron, Jō′ăb took him aside in the gate to speak with him quietly, and smote him there under the fifth rib, that he died, for the blood of Ā′sa-hĕl his brother.

28 ¶And afterward when David heard it, he said, I and my kingdom are guiltless before the LORD for ever from the blood of Abner the son of Ner:

29 Let it rest on the head of Jō′ăb, and on all his father's house; and let there not fail from the house of Jō′ăb one that hath an issue, or that is a leper, or that leaneth on a staff, or that falleth on the sword, or that lacketh bread.

30 So Jō′ăb and A-bī′shaī his brother slew Abner, because he had slain their brother Ā′sa-hĕl at Gĭbeon in the battle.

31 ¶And David said to Jō′ăb, and to all the people that were with him, Rend

18-19. By the hand of my servant David I will save my people Israel. David is the man after God's own heart (I Sam 13:14; Acts 13:22). He is called **my servant** (Heb 'ebed), a word which becomes very important as a technical term for the "Servant of Yahweh" of whom David is the type. This again is part of the developing theology of salvation in the Old Testament. Even here God is working out the redemptive groundwork for the final salvation of His people in Jesus Christ. The words **servant, save** (Heb yasha'), and **people**, are in this verse already to be considered technical terms. Note that the verse speaks of salvation of God's people from **all their enemies.**

20-39. So Abner came to David to Hebron. Here peace was effected, unity accomplished, and Abner forgiven. **He went in peace.** The fact that he had gone in peace is repeated in the next two verses, to show that it was not revenge on David's part. **Joab . . . brought him again . . . but David knew it not.** It is very important to the writer to show that it was not David's revenge that killed Abner. **Joab . . . smote him . . . that he died.** It is mentioned here several times that it was Joab, and not David or his kingdom, who was to blame. **David himself followed the bier.** Every verse stresses the lamentation and sorrow of the king over Abner; all the people lamented, and David fasted. **The people took notice of it.** A very important political atmosphere was being created. David wanted to leave the punishment for the murder up to the Lord; **the LORD shall reward the doer of evil according to his wickedness.**

II SAMUEL 4:7

your clothes, and gird you with sackcloth, and mourn before Abner. And king David *himself* followed the bier.

32 And they buried Abner in Hēbron: and the king lifted up his voice, and wept at the grave of Abner; and all the people wept.

33 And the king lamented over Abner, and said, Died Abner as a fool dieth?

34 Thy hands *were* not bound, nor thy feet put into fetters: as a man falleth before wicked men, *so* fellest thou. And all the people wept again over him.

35 And when all the people came to cause David to eat meat while it was yet day, David sware, saying, So do God to me, and more also, if I taste bread, or ought else, till the sun be down.

36 And all the people took notice *of it,* and it pleased them: as whatsoever the king did pleased all the people.

37 For all the people and all Israel understood that day that it was not of the king to slay Abner the son of Ner.

38 And the king said unto his servants, Know ye not that there is a prince and a great man fallen this day in Israel?

39 And I *am* this day weak, though anointed king; and these men the sons of Zer-ū-i'ah *be* too hard for me: the LORD shall reward the doer of evil according to his wickedness.

CHAPTER 4

AND when Saul's son heard that Abner was dead in Hēbron, his hands were feeble, and all the Israelites were troubled.

2 And Saul's son had two men *that were* captains of bands: the name of the one *was* Bā'a-nah, and the name of the other Rē'chāb, the sons of Rimmon a Bē-ē'rŏth-īte, of the children of Benjamin: (for Bē-ē'rŏth also was reckoned to Benjamin:

3 And the Bē-ē'rŏth-ītes fled to Gĭt'ta-im, and were sojourners there until this day.)

4 And Jonathan, Saul's son, had a son *that was* lame of *his* feet. He was five years old when the tidings came of Saul and Jonathan out of Jĕz're-el, and his nurse took him up, and fled: and it came to pass, as she made haste to flee, that he fell, and became lame. And his name *was* Me-phĭb'o-shĕth.

5 ¶And the sons of Rimmon the Bē-ē'rŏth-īte, Rē'chāb and Bā'a-nah, went, and came about the heat of the day to the house of Ĭsh-bō'sheth, who lay on a bed at noon.

6 And they came thither into the midst of the house, *as though* they would have fetched wheat; and they smote him under the fifth *rib*: and Rē'chāb and Bā'a-nah his brother escaped.

7 For when they came into the house, he lay on his bed in his bedchamber, and they smote him, and slew him, and beheaded him, and took his head, and

D. The Murder of Ish-bosheth. 4:1-12.

4:1. David's slow, methodical, and deliberate moves toward establishing his kingdom within the framework of the law of God and precisely in the will of God were wearing down Ish-bosheth. When he heard that **Abner was dead in Hebron** he fell into complete despair. **The Israelites,** that is those who had not joined Judah in recognizing David, **were troubled.**

2-3. Just as Abner had finally come around to see that David was the true king of Israel, so Ish-bosheth's **two . . . captains** saw that unless they changed sides very soon, they would be on the losing side. They conspired to kill their king and join David.

4. Mephibosheth. This verse is inserted to show that once Ish-bosheth had been removed, there were no others with a legitimate claim to Saul's throne; there would be no competition at all for David.

5-9. Rechab and Baanah . . . came . . . at noon, during the siesta, when everyone was asleep. **They brought the head of Ish-bosheth unto David,** thinking that they would be welcomed and praised for removing the last obstacle to the unity of all Israel. **Who hath redeemed my soul out of all adversity.** This is the reason David is called a king after God's heart, one who pleases him. David understands that God is working behind the scenes to accomplish His own will with His people. David is quite willing to wait, to be patient as long as he must; because it is God who is directing his steps. **Redeemed** (Heb *padah*) means to buy back something that has been given up or sold out. This becomes an extremely important theological term in both the Old Testament and the New Testament. The Bible is in one

597

gat them away through the plain all night.

8 And they brought the head of Ĭsh-bō′sheth unto David to Hēbron, and said to the king, Behold, the head of Ĭsh-bō′sheth the son of Saul thine enemy, which sought thy life; and the LORD hath avenged my lord the king this day of Saul, and of his seed.

9 ¶And David answered Rē′chăb and Bā′a-nah his brother, the sons of Rimmon the Bē-ē′rŏth-īte, and said unto them, As the LORD liveth, who hath redeemed my soul out of all adversity,

10 When one told me, saying, Behold, Saul is dead, thinking to have brought good tidings, I took hold of him, and slew him in Ziklag, who thought that I would have given him a reward for his tidings:

11 How much more, when wicked men have slain a righteous person in his own house upon his bed? shall I not therefore now require his blood of your hand, and take you away from the earth?

12 And David commanded his young men, and they slew them, and cut off their hands and their feet, and hanged them up over the pool in Hēbron. But they took the head of Ĭsh-bō′sheth, and buried it in the sepulchre of Abner in Hēbron.

CHAPTER 5

THEN came all the tribes of Israel to David unto Hēbron, and spake, saying, Behold, we are thy bone and thy flesh.

2 Also in time past, when Saul was king over us, thou wast he that leddest out and broughtest in Israel: and the LORD said to thee, Thou shalt feed my people Israel, and thou shalt be a captain over Israel.

3 So all the elders of Israel came to the king to Hēbron; and king David made a league with them in Hēbron before the LORD: and they anointed David king over Israel.

4 David was thirty years old when he began to reign, and he reigned forty years.

5 In Hēbron he reigned over Jūdah seven years and six months: and in Jerusalem he reigned thirty and three years over all Israel and Jūdah.

6 ¶And the king and his men went to Jerusalem unto the Jĕb′u-sītes, the inhabitants of the land: which spake unto David, saying, Except thou take away the blind and the lame, thou shalt not come in hither: thinking, David cannot come in hither.

7 Nevertheless David took the strong hold of Zion: the same is the city of David.

8 And David said on that day, Whosoever getteth up to the gutter,

sense a history of redemption. In the New Testament it is the death of Jesus Christ upon the cross that is the price for buying us back from the certain condemnation and destruction of our sins. The term is important in this Old Testament text because it shows that God is always working to accomplish the redemption of His people.

He has always **Redeemed** David because David was His anointed and chosen king. David was chosen, not only to bring immediate physical salvation to the people of God, but to provide the line that would bring the Son of David, the ultimate Anointed One, who would accomplish spiritual and eternal redemption. The word is used in the same sense in this verse as in I Samuel 14:45 where Jonathan was ransomed from destruction at the hands of Saul. It is also used in the sense of redemption of the people as a whole in II Samuel 7:23.

10-12. When one told me. David recounts how this deed is reminiscent of the Amalekite who lied about having killed Saul, who had been more of a real threat to David. That man had been killed. Now the situation is a case of cold-blooded murder and not a battlefield maneuver. **Shall I not . . . take you away from the earth?** This is a euphemism for "kill." David believes that he is simply applying the law of God: capital punishment (Gen 9:6). This is the law of God and must be carried out.

E. David Established as King of All Israel. 5:1-10:19.

5:1-5. Then came all the tribes of Israel to David unto Hebron. Now that there were no others to succeed or claim the throne of Saul, the nation was to be united under David. **Leddest out.** David was experienced as a leader even while Saul was still king. **Thou shalt feed my people Israel, and thou shalt be a captain over Israel.** Feed (Heb ra'ah) means, literally, to feed and tend a flock of sheep. The figurative application is to God's **people,** the flock of God, so that this becomes a technical term for "shepherding God's flock." **Captain** (Heb nagīd) is also a technical term especially for Saul and David as "leaders" over Israel, the people of God. This is also typical of Jesus Christ, the Messiah Prince (see Daniel 9:25, where the words are used together to refer to the coming King). **David made a league with them. League** (Heb berīt) is the word regularly translated "covenant." It is an agreement solemnized in the presence of the Lord. **They anointed David king over Israel.** This is the third time David has been **anointed** (Heb mashach), first, by Samuel, then by the people of Judah, and now by the rest of the tribes. Note the development of the theology of this word in I Sam 2:10, 35; 9:16; 10:1; 12:3, 5; 15:1, 17; 16:3, 12, 13; 24:6, 10; 26:9, 11,16, 23; II Sam 1:14, 16, 21; 2:4, 7; 3:39; 5:3, 17; 12:7; 19:10, 21; 22:51; 23:1. The word corresponds to the English words "Messiah" and "Christ."

6-10. The Jebusites. These were Canaanites still in possession of Jebus, or Jerusalem, at the time of David. They refused to surrender because of their superior fortification. **The blind and the lame** are mentioned because the defense was considered so effective that the city could be defended by cripples without need for strong soldiers. A better translation might be, "You will not come in here, but the blind and the lame will ward you off." David was able to conquer Jerusalem, but he did it by discovering and attacking their weakest point, **the gutter** (Heb tsinōr). The meaning of this word was unknown until the early part of this century when Warren discovered a shaft forty feet

and smiteth the Jĕb'u-sītes, and the lame and the blind, *that are* hated of David's soul, *he shall be chief and captain.* Wherefore they said, The blind and the lame shall not come into the house.

9 So David dwelt in the fort, and called it the city of David. And David built round about from Mĭl'lō and inward.

10 And David went on, and grew great, and the LORD God of hosts *was* with him.

11 ¶And Hiram king of Tyre sent messengers to David, and cedar trees, and carpenters, and masons: and they built David an house.

12 And David perceived that the LORD had established him king over Israel, and that he had exalted his kingdom for his people Israel's sake.

13 ¶And David took *him* more concubines and wives out of Jerusalem, after he was come from Hēbron: and there were yet sons and daughters born to David.

14 And these *be* the names of those that were born unto him in Jerusalem; Shăm-mū'ah, and Shō'băb, and Nā'-than, and Sŏlomon,

15 Ĭb'här also and Ĕl-i-shū'a, and Nĕ'phĕg, and Ja-phī'a,

16 And E-līsh'a-ma, and E-lī'a-da, and E-lĭph'a-lĕt.

17 ¶But when the Philistines heard that they had anointed David king over Israel, all the Philistines came up to seek David; and David heard *of it*, and went down to the hold.

18 The Philistines also came and spread themselves in the valley of Rĕph'a-im.

19 And David enquired of the LORD, saying, Shall I go up to the Philistines? wilt thou deliver them into mine hand? And the LORD said unto David, Go up: for I will doubtless deliver the Philistines into thine hand.

20 And David came to Bā'al-per'a-zĭm, and David smote them there, and said, the LORD hath broken forth upon mine enemies before me, as the breach of waters. Therefore he called the name of that place Bā'al-per'a-zĭm.

21 And there they left their images, and David and his men burned them.

22 ¶And the Philistines came up yet again, and spread themselves in the valley of Rĕph'a-im.

23 And when David enquired of the LORD, he said, Thou shalt not go up; *but* fetch a compass behind them, and come upon them over against the mulberry trees.

24 And let it be, when thou hearest the sound of a going in the tops of the mulberry trees, that then thou shalt bestir thyself: for then shall the LORD go out before thee, to smite the host of the Philistines.

25 And David did so, as the LORD had commanded him; and smote the Philistines from Gĕ'ba until thou come to Gā'zer.

deep connecting to a water tunnel that led outside the walls to a water supply used in siege.

City of David was for a time the designation of this captured and strategic fortress of Jerusalem. **From Millo and inward.** Millo is not an English word, but simply a transliteration of a Hebrew word. The word means "the fill" and probably referred to a fill for defense purposes, like a huge casemate wall. **The LORD God of hosts was with him.** The writer is making the point that once God's king was in power and God was helping him, he began to be accepted and successful as well as expand his kingdom.

11-16. David perceived that the LORD had established him king over Israel, and that he had exalted his kingdom for his people Israel's sake. Both the establishment and choice, as well as the exaltation, had been for the sake of God's **people. More concubines and wives out of Jerusalem.** David was a polygamist; the Bible does not approve of this, but the matter of the general salvation of the people of God was more important at this point.

17-19. When the Philistines heard of the new king's successes, they again took the offensive. **David . . . went down to the hold** (Heb *metsūdah*); the place was probably Adullam. The word **hold** means a fortress or a place that is difficult to get to and was used of the cave of Adullam in I Samuel 22:4. **Inquired of the LORD.** Both here and in verse 23 David shows his complete dependence upon the will of the Lord which he probably learned through the priest and the Urim and Thummim. The device is not mentioned, but it was the approved and regular way of learning God's will in that time. God was in control and promised to **deliver the Philistines** into David's hand without fail (Hebrew infinitive absolute before the cognate verb for emphasis). David was victorious precisely because he believed and fully trusted these promises of God.

20-25. The LORD hath broken forth (Heb *parats*). This word pictures the power of God as the force of water breaking the dam and sweeping away everything in its path. It is used three times in this verse. **Baal-perazim** is the same Hebrew word, but transliterated. It would mean "Master of breakings," if translated, and has reference to God's power of destruction against the Philistines here. **When thou hearest the sound of a going in the tops of the mulberry trees.** The sound was not that of wind rustling the leaves, but, as all modern translations have, "the sound of marching." The Hebrew word means the rhythmic beat of marching troops, the mixed sound of tramping feet and clinking armor. The troops David was to hear were the invisible hosts of Almighty God. **As the LORD had commanded.** This was the secret of David's success. He **smote the Philistines** as God had promised. **Gazer** should read "Gezer."

CHAPTER 6

AGAIN, David gathered together all *the* chosen *men* of Israel, thirty thousand.

2 And David arose, and went with all the people that *were* with him from Bā′-al-e of Jŭdah, to bring up from thence the ark of God, whose name is called by the name of the LORD of hosts that dwelleth *between* the cherubims.

3 And they set the ark of God upon a new cart, and brought it out of the house of A-bĭn′a-dăb that *was* in Gĭb′e-ah: and Ŭz′zah and A-hĭ′o, the sons of A-bĭn′a-dăb, drave the new cart.

4 And they brought it out of the house of A-bĭn′a-dăb which *was* at Gĭb′e-ah, accompanying the ark of God: and A-hĭ′o went before the ark.

5 And David and all the house of Israel played before the LORD on all manner of *instruments made of* fir wood, even on harps, and on psalteries, and on timbrels, and on cornets, and on cymbals.

6 And when they came to Nā′chŏn′s threshingfloor, Ŭz′zah put forth *his hand* to the ark of God, and took hold of it; for the oxen shook *it.*

7 And the anger of the LORD was kindled against Ŭz′zah; and God smote him there for *his* error; and there he died by the ark of God.

8 And David was displeased, because the LORD had made a breach upon Ŭz′-zah: and he called the name of the place Pe′rĕz-ūz′zah to this day.

9 And David was afraid of the LORD that day, and said, How shall the ark of the LORD come to me?

10 So David would not remove the ark of the LORD unto him into the city of David: but David carried it aside into the house of Ō′bed-ē′dom the Gĭt′tīte.

11 And the ark of the LORD continued in the house of Ō′bed-ē′dom the Gĭt′tīte three months: and the LORD blessed Ō′bed-ē′dom, and all his household.

12 ¶And it was told king David, saying, The LORD hath blessed the house of Ō′bed-ē′dom, and all that *pertaineth* unto him, because of the ark of God. So David went and brought up the ark of God from the house of Ō′bed-ē′dom into the city of David with gladness.

13 And it was *so,* that when they that bare the ark of the LORD had gone six paces, he sacrificed oxen and fatlings.

14 And David danced before the LORD with all *his* might; and David *was* girded with a linen ephod.

15 So David and all the house of Israel brought up the ark of the LORD with shouting, and with the sound of the trumpet.

16 And as the ark of the LORD came into the city of David, Mī′chal Saul's

6:1-5. Baale of Judah. The name means "Lords of Judah" and perhaps signified the elders of Judah. In I Samuel 7:2 the place is called Kirjath-jearim. The location is about ten miles west of Jerusalem near the present-day Abu-Ghosh. **And they brought** the ark **out of the house of Abinadab** to take it to Jerusalem. The ark had been there for over seventy years, probably all but forgotten.

6-7. Nachon's threshing floor. I Chronicles 13:9 gives the place a different name (perhaps a name given after the event), but there is no contradiction. **Uzzah put forth his hand to the ark of God, and took hold of it** (see I Chr 13:10). His action was intended to steady the ark. **The anger of the LORD was kindled against Uzzah.** The severe judgment of God here appears to be altogether unwarranted and undeserved. The ark was a sacred symbol of the presence of God, and the Israelites had become careless and indifferent to its deep religious meaning for them. They had carried it into battle like a fetish but had ignored it for two generations. It was very important for them to be made aware of its significance and of the holiness of God again. Uzzah's act was innocent and of good intention, but it was without proper regard for the awesome and holy presence of Yahweh represented by the ark.

8-11. Breach (Heb *parats*) is the same word used to describe God's powerful destruction of the Philistines (5:20). The word appears three times in this verse and graphically portrays the terrible destroying power of God. In great fear David named **the place Perez-uzzah.** This is again the transliteration of the Hebrew words. **Three months.** So effective was this terrible demonstration of the power of God that David allowed this period of time for the wrath of God to diminish.

12-19. David . . . brought up the ark of God . . . into the city of David. This time much more care and preparation were given to the handling of the ark. A sacrifice was made after the ark had been moved **six paces. David danced before the LORD.** The dance was ceremonial, an expression of joy and happiness in the worship of the LORD. **Michal . . . despised.** This was probably because she was still bitter about being taken back from Phaltiel (II Sam 3:16); she found something to criticize because of her motivating resentment. **In the midst of the tabernacle.** Most translations have "tent." This was not the tabernacle proper, which was still at Gibeon (I Chr 16:39), but a special tent David prepared for the ark.

daughter looked through a window, and saw king David leaping and dancing before the LORD; and she despised him in her heart.

17 ¶And they brought in the ark of the LORD, and set it in his place, in the midst of the tabernacle that David had pitched for it: and David offered burnt offerings and peace offerings before the LORD.

18 And as soon as David had made an end of offering burnt offerings and peace offerings, he blessed the people in the name of the LORD of hosts.

19 And he dealt among all the people, *even* among the whole multitude of Israel, as well to the women as men, to every one a cake of bread, and a good piece *of flesh,* and a flagon *of wine.* So all the people departed every one to his house.

20 ¶Then David returned to bless his household. And Mī'chal the daughter of Saul came out to meet David, and said, How glorious was the king of Israel to day, who uncovered himself to day in the eyes of the handmaids of his servants, as one of the vain fellows shamelessly uncovereth himself!

21 And David said unto Mī'chal, *It was* before the LORD, which chose me before thy father, and before all his house, to appoint me ruler over the people of the LORD, over Israel: therefore will I play before the LORD.

22 And I will yet be more vile than thus, and will be base in mine own sight: and of the maidservants which thou hast spoken of, of them shall I be had in honour.

23 Therefore Mī'chal the daughter of Saul had no child unto the day of her death.

CHAPTER 7

AND it came to pass, when the king sat in his house, and the LORD had given him rest round about from all his enemies;

2 That the king said unto Nāthan the prophet, See now, I dwell in an house of cedar, but the ark of God dwelleth within curtains.

3 And Nāthan said to the king, Go, do all that *is* in thine heart; for the LORD *is* with thee.

4 ¶And it came to pass that night, that the word of the LORD came unto Nāthan, saying,

5 Go and tell my servant David, Thus saith the LORD, Shalt thou build me an house for me to dwell in?

6 Whereas I have not dwelt in *any* house since the time that I brought up the children of Israel out of Egypt, even to this day, but have walked in a tent and in a tabernacle.

7 In all *the places* wherein I have walked with all the children of Israel spake I a word with any of the tribes of Israel, whom I commanded to feed my people Israel, saying, Why build ye not me an house of cedar?

8 Now therefore so shalt thou say unto my servant David, Thus saith the LORD of hosts, I took thee from the sheepcote, from following the sheep, to be ruler over my people, over Israel:

20-23. David may have worn little clothing during the dance and procession, perhaps only the linen ephod; and this may have evoked the criticism of **Michal. Michal . . . had no child unto the day of her death.** This was a severe punishment and humiliation for her. In biblical times children were considered the assurance of God's blessing and the joy of life.

7:1-3. The LORD had given him rest (Heb *nûach*). The form of the verb in the original emphasizes that God has delivered him from his enemies and has caused him to live in peace. **Nathan.** David was very careful to do nothing without consulting the Lord through priest or prophet. Nathan was an important link here in communicating the will of God and plays an important role elsewhere as well (cf. II Sam 12:1; I Kgs 1:10, 22, 34; II Chr 9:29). **The LORD is with thee.** Apparently Nathan gave his approval because he saw nothing wrong with the idea until the Lord revealed His will in a dream.

4-9. The word of the LORD came unto Nathan. The same expression recurs frequently in the prophets; it denotes the primary means of revelation to the prophets. This means of communicating the will of God seems to be distinct in some way from dreams (although this word came at night and perhaps similarly to a dream; cf. I Sam 3:1-4:1), visions, and the Urim and Thummim of the priests. **My servant David** is an extremely honorable title; it indicated God's special choice. Later, this became a title applied to the nation as a whole and then to Jesus Christ as the ultimate Servant of the Lord. **My servant David** is repeated and further explained in **to be ruler** (Heb *nāgîd*), which is another technical term of that time. Note the other significant and recurring theological term, **my people . . . Israel,** which corresponds in the figure here to **sheep.** David was still a shepherd but was now over the flock of God.

9 And I was with thee whithersoever thou wentest, and have cut off all thine enemies out of thy sight, and have made thee a great name, like unto the name of the great *men* that *are* in the earth.

10 Moreover I will appoint a place for my people Israel, and will plant them, that they may dwell in a place of their own, and move no more; neither shall the children of wickedness afflict them any more, as beforetime,

11 And as since the time that I commanded judges *to be* over my people Israel, and have caused thee to rest from all thine enemies. Also the LORD telleth thee that he will make thee an house.

12 And when thy days be fulfilled, and thou shalt sleep with thy fathers, I will set up thy seed after thee, which shall proceed out of thy bowels, and I will establish his kingdom.

13 He shall build an house for my name, and I will stablish the throne of his kingdom for ever.

14 I will be his father, and he shall be my son. If he commit iniquity, I will chasten him with the rod of men, and with the stripes of the children of men:

15 But my mercy shall not depart away from him, as I took *it* from Saul, whom I put away before thee.

16 And thine house and thy kingdom shall be established for ever before thee: thy throne shall be established for ever.

17 According to all these words, and according to all this vision, so did Nathan speak unto David.

18 ¶Then went king David in, and sat before the LORD, and he said, Who *am* I, O Lord GOD? and what *is* my house, that thou hast brought me hitherto?

19 And this was yet a small thing in thy sight, O Lord GOD; but thou hast spoken also of thy servant's house for a great while to come. And *is* this the manner of man, O Lord GOD?

20 And what can David say more unto thee? for thou, Lord GOD, knowest thy servant.

21 For thy word's sake, and according to thine own heart, hast thou done all these great things, to make thy servant know *them*.

10-12. I will appoint (Heb *sîm*) **a place for my people Israel.** This part of the Davidic covenant promises a land for God's people, and thus Palestine was called the Promised Land. The same promises were given in the Abrahamic covenant (cf. Gen 17:8). It is interesting that a similar promise is made to New Testament believers in Christ the Son of David in John 14:2, ". . . I go to prepare a place for you." **The LORD telleth thee that he will make thee a house.** Verse 5 should be read with verse 11. Far better than David building a house (literal) for God, God will build a house (spiritual, that is descendants, seed) for David. **I will set up thy seed** (Heb *zera'*) has primary reference here to Solomon and secondary, typical reference to Jesus Christ. The secondary, or prophetic, reference to Christ likewise extends to **I will establish his kingdom.**

13-15. He shall build a house for my name. Again, the primary reference in this chapter is to Solomon and his building of the Temple as a literal building dedicated to God. The word "house" is used as a figurative term for the people of God in both the Old Testament and the New Testament. Christians today are the "house" of God, built and ruled over by Jesus Christ the Son of David (cf. I Pet 2:5 and Heb 3:3-6). There is also a double fulfillment of the words, **I will be his father, and he shall be my son.** The immediate and primary reference is to God's blessing upon and direction of Solomon in his building of the Temple and his rule over the people of God. But the writer of the book of Hebrews quotes this verse as being fulfilled in Jesus Christ, who is the Son of God in the highest sense. There is in fact another (third) fulfillment, for it is quoted also in II Corinthians, 6:18 as referring to believers who are in a lesser sense "sons" of God.

16-17. The house, kingdom, and **throne** are to endure **for ever.** The word translated **for ever** (Heb *'ōlam*) may mean in some contexts "for a long time," and as far as this applies to Solomon and the immediate literal descendants of David, this would be the interpretation. But in other contexts the word connotes *ad infinitum* and corresponds to the Greek idiom translated "for ever" in the New Testament. It is this eternal sense of the word that applies to the **throne** of David as assumed by Jesus Christ. This last aspect of the Davidic covenant is both alluded to and infallibly interpreted in Luke 1:32-33. From the high frequency of New Testament quotations to this passage, it is obvious that it is very important to biblical theology and messianic prophecy. This word of God through Nathan is in fact the matrix of the whole "Son of David" apocalyptic expectation, which found its fulfillment in Jesus Christ and was such an indispensable element in the gospel of the apostolic preachers like Paul.

18-22. Who am I . . . and what is my house . . . ? Obviously, David did not regard this prophetic word as negative in any sense. It stopped David from building a literal house or temple for God, but the positive way to look at it (and the biblical way) is that God had promised to establish and save the spiritual house of God's people through David. David naturally felt and expressed his humble unworthiness of such a magnanimous prophecy and promise. **A great while to come.** This shows that David is unaware of the full christological and eternal implications, although he submits wholeheartedly to the will of God.

22 Wherefore thou art great, O LORD God: for *there is* none like thee, neither *is there any* God beside thee, according to all that we have heard with our ears.

23 And what one nation in the earth *is* like thy people, *even* like Israel, whom God went to redeem for a people to himself, and to make him a name, and to do for you great things and terrible, for thy land, before thy people, which thou redeemedst to thee from Egypt, *from* the nations and their gods?

24 For thou hast confirmed to thyself thy people Israel *to be* a people unto thee for ever: and thou, LORD, art become their God.

25 And now, O LORD God, the word that thou hast spoken concerning thy servant, and concerning his house, establish *it* for ever, and do as thou hast said.

26 And let thy name be magnified for ever, saying, The LORD of hosts *is* the God over Israel: and let the house of thy servant David be established before thee.

27 For thou, O LORD of hosts, God of Israel, hast revealed to thy servant, saying, I will build thee an house: therefore hath thy servant found in his heart to pray this prayer unto thee.

28 And now, O Lord GOD, thou *art* that God, and thy words be true, and thou hast promised this goodness unto thy servant:

29 Therefore now let it please thee to bless the house of thy servant, that it may continue for ever before thee: for thou, O Lord GOD, hast spoken *it:* and with thy blessing let the house of thy servant be blessed for ever.

CHAPTER 8

AND after this it came to pass, that David smote the Philistines, and subdued them: and David took Mĕ'thĕg–ăm'-mah out of the hand of the Philistines.

2 And he smote Moab, and measured them with a line, casting them down to the ground; even with two lines measured he to put to death, and with one full line to keep alive. And *so* the Moabites became David's servants, *and* brought gifts.

3 ¶David smote also Hăd-ad-ē'zer, the son of Rĕ'hŏb, king of Zōbah, as he went to recover his border at the river Eū-phrā'tēs.

4 And David took from him a thousand *chariots,* and seven hundred horsemen, and twenty thousand footmen: and David houghed all the chariot *horses,* but reserved of them *for* an hundred chariots.

5 And when the Syrians of Damascus came to succour Hăd-ad-ē'zer king of Zōbah, David slew of the Syrians two and twenty thousand men.

6 Then David put garrisons in Syria of Damascus: and the Syrians became servants to David, *and* brought gifts. And the LORD preserved David whithersoever he went.

7 And David took the shields of gold that were on the servants of Hăd-ad-ē'zer, and brought them to Jerusalem.

8 And from Bē'tah, and from Ber'ō-

23-29. Thy people. David shows keen insight into the theology of the **people** of God and God's redemptive love toward His **people.** The word **redeem** (Heb *padah*) is used in this verse twice and is also an important technical term that recurs wherever the salvational-historical acts of God toward His people are narrated. Here, in David's prayer of worship, note the emphasis on salvation. David is God's king, God's servant, who is used by God to save God's people for God's own glory. Each of these terms has also a prophetic and typical, forward-pointing aspect that may be demonstrated by New Testament usage.

8:1-4. David smote the Philistines. From the very beginning of the "anointed one" concept with Saul, the chosen king was also *ipso facto* the "savior" of God's people. David here defeats **the Philistines,** and thus saves the people from their greatest enemies (cf. I Chr 18:1). The people of **Moab** were once friendly to David (I Sam 22:3-4), but they had become the enemies of God's people and must be subdued. **Measured them with a line.** David spared from death one third of the enemy; those to be spared were determined by making them lie down on the ground and measuring them off with a length of cord. The first and second lengths were put to death, while the third length was allowed to live. **Hadadezer.** That David should conquer the Syrians shows the extent and greatness of his power. Other details of the battle are given in I Samuel 10:15-19. **David houghed all the chariot horses.** He hamstrung all but a hundred of the chariot horses.

5-18. Toi king of Hamath, when he heard of David's power and victories, especially over Hadadezer, took the opportunity to side with David and thus contributed to the wealth of Israel. **David gat him a name.** He became famous for his victories so that the Edomites became subject to him. Syrians should read instead "Edomites," as in the modern versions that follow the Septuagint. The success of David's kingdom and reign under God is summarized in the words **executed judgment and justice unto all his people.** The facts of verse 17 are given also in I Chronicles 18:16, except for the erroneous spelling of **Ahimelech,** which appears there as Abimelech. The Septuagint has Ahimelech in both places. It appears, however, that the

AND WHEN all the kings who were servants of Hadadezer saw that they had been defeated by Israel, they made peace with Israel, and became subject to them.

(2 Samuel 10: 19)

HAMATH

Cun

Gebal

Lebo-hamath

(Beirut)

ARAM-ZOBAH

Berothah

Sidon

BETH-REHOB

ARAM - DAMASCUS

Damascus

Tyre

Dan

Kedesh

MAACAH

Acco

Chinnereth

GESHUR

Ashtaroth

Aphek

Kenath

I S R A E L

Dor

Megiddo

Beth-shean

Ramoth-gilead

Tob

Salecah

Hepher

Wadi Mart

Shechem

Mahanaim

Joppa

Beth-el

River Jordan

AMMON

Rabbath-bene-ammon

Ashdod

Ekron

Jerusalem

Medeba

Ashkelon

Gath

PHILISTINES

Gaza

Hebron

King's Highway

Aroer

Raphia

Gerar

J U D A H

Sharuhen

Beer-sheba

Kir-moab

Brook of Egypt

Zoar

M O A B

Tamar

Bozrah

Kadesh-barnea

E D O M

Teman

Great Sea

	Judah and Israel
	Conquered kingdom
	Sphere of influence
····	Border of David's empire
····	Interior border

Elath

0   10   20 miles
0 10 20 30 km

The Kingdom in David's Days

thaī, cities of Hăd-ad-ē′zer, king David took exceeding much brass.

9 ¶When Tō′ī king of Hā′măth heard that David had smitten all the host of Hăd-ad-ē′zer,

10 Then Tō′ī sent Joram his son unto king David, to salute him, and to bless him, because he had fought against Hăd-ad-ē′zer, and smitten him: for Hăd-ad-ē′zer had wars with Tō′ī. And *Joram* brought with him vessels of silver, and vessels of gold, and vessels of brass:

11 Which also king David did dedicate unto the LORD, with the silver and gold that he had dedicated of all nations which he subdued;

12 Of Syria, and of Moab, and of the children of Ammon, and of the Philistines, and of Ăm′a-lĕk, and of the spoil of Hăd-ad-ē′zer, son of Rē′hŏb, king of Zōbah.

13 And David gat *him* a name when he returned from smiting of the Syrians in the valley of salt, *being* eighteen thousand *men.*

14 ¶And he put garrisons in Ēdom; throughout all Ēdom put he garrisons, and all they of Ēdom became David's servants. And the LORD preserved David whithersoever he went.

15 And David reigned over all Israel; and David executed judgment and justice unto all his people.

16 And Jō′ăb the son of Zer-ū-ī′ah *was* over the host; and Je-hŏsh′a-phăt the son of A-hī′lud *was* recorder;

17 And Zā′dŏk the son of A-hī′tŭb, and A-hĭm′e-lĕch the son of Ă-bī′a-thar, *were* the priests; and Se-ra-ī′ah *was* the scribe;

18 And Be-nā′iah the son of Je-hoi′a-da *was over* both the Chĕr′e-thītes and the Pĕl′e-thītes; and David's sons were chief rulers.

CHAPTER 9

AND David said, Is there yet any that is left of the house of Saul, that I may shew him kindness for Jonathan's sake?

2 And *there was* of the house of Saul a servant whose name *was* Zī′ba. And when they had called him unto David, the king said unto him, Art thou Zī′ba? And he said, Thy servant *is* he.

3 And the king said, *Is* there not yet any of the house of Saul, that I may shew the kindness of God unto him? And Zī′ba said unto the king, Jonathan hath yet a son, *which is* lame on *his* feet.

4 And the king said unto him, Where *is* he? And Zī′ba said unto the king, Behold, he *is* in the house of Mā′chīr, the son of Ăm′mī-el, in Lō-dē′bar.

5 Then king David sent, and fetched him out of the house of Mā′chīr, the son of Ăm′mī-el, from Lō-dē′bar.

6 Now when Me-phĭb′o-shĕth, the son of Jonathan, the son of Saul, was come unto David, he fell on his face, and did reverence. And David said, Mephĭb′o-shĕth. And he answered, Behold thy servant!

7 ¶And David said unto him, Fear not: for I will surely shew thee kindness for Jonathan thy father's sake, and will

order of the two names **Ahimelech** and **Abiathar** should be reversed to read, "Abiathar the son of Ahimelech." This reading is supported by some text traditions and is in agreement with I Samuel 22:20.

9:1-6. Show him kindness. The word **kindness** (Heb *chesed*) would be better translated "love." The same word is frequently used of God's undeserved love and care to us as His people, as in Psalm 32:10 where this word is contrasted with the woes and pains of the wicked. In showing love to Jonathan's son, David is portrayed at his best. David has not forgotten his oath to Jonathan (I Sam 20:42). Since God has been so good to him, he wants to show love to the descendants of Jonathan. This was unusual; the custom was for the new king to kill or banish the relatives of a former king. **Lame on his feet.** When Mephibosheth was five years old, he had been maimed (see II Sam 4:4) so that he was lame the rest of his life.

7-13. David said unto him, Fear not. He would have natural cause to fear, being summoned to the king, especially David who had killed the Amalekite who announced Saul's death

restore thee all the land of Saul thy father; and thou shalt eat bread at my table continually.

8 And he bowed himself, and said, What *is* thy servant, that thou shouldest look upon such a dead dog as I *am?*

9 ¶Then the king called to Zī′ba, Saul's servant, and said unto him, I have given unto thy master's son all that pertained to Saul and to all his house.

10 Thou therefore, and thy sons, and thy servants, shall till the land for him, and thou shalt bring in *the fruits,* that thy master's son may have food to eat: but Me-phĭb′o-shĕth thy master's son shall eat bread alway at my table. Now Zī′ba had fifteen sons and twenty servants.

11 Then said Zī′ba unto the king, According to all that my lord the king hath commanded his servant, so shall thy servant do. As for Me-phĭb′o-shĕth, *said the king,* he shall eat at my table, as one of the king's sons.

12 And Me-phĭb′o-shĕth had a young son, whose name *was* Mī′cha. And all that dwelt in the house of Zī′ba *were* servants unto Me-phĭb′o-shĕth.

13 So Me-phĭb′o-shĕth dwelt in Jerusalem: for he did eat continually at the king's table; and was lame on both his feet.

CHAPTER 10

AND it came to pass after this, that the king of the children of Ammon died, and Hā′nun his son reigned in his stead.

2 Then said David, I will shew kindness unto Hā′nun the son of Nā′hăsh, as his father shewed kindness unto me. And David sent to comfort him by the hand of his servants for his father. And David's servants came into the land of the children of Ammon.

3 And the princes of the children of Ammon said unto Hā′nun their lord, Thinkest thou that David doth honour thy father, that he hath sent comforters unto thee? hath not David *rather* sent his servants unto thee to search the city, and to spy it out, and to overthrow it?

4 Wherefore Hā′nun took David's servants, and shaved off the one half of their beards, and cut off their garments in the middle, *even* to their buttocks, and sent them away.

5 When they told *it* unto David, he sent to meet them, because the men were greatly ashamed: and the king said, Tarry at Jericho until your beards be grown, and *then* return.

6 ¶And when the children of Ammon saw that they stank before David, the children of Ammon sent and hired the Syrians of Bĕth-rē′hŏb, and the Syrians of Zō′ba, twenty thousand footmen, and of king Mā′a-cah a thousand men, and of Ĭsh′-tŏb twelve thousand men.

7 And when David heard of *it,* he sent Jō′ăb, and all the host of the mighty men.

8 And the children of Ammon came out, and put the battle in array at the entering in of the gate: and the Syrians

(II Sam 1:15), and Rechab and Baanah (II Sam 4:12). David not only showed mercy to Mephibosheth but actually made him rich with the inheritance of Saul. This kind of undeserved love and blessing showered upon him is illustrative of the love of God to His people. **In Jerusalem. Mephibosheth** was thus entertained in the royal palace all the rest of his life.

10:1-5. The king of the children of Ammon died. This was Nahash, the enemy out of whose hand Saul had first delivered Jabesh-gilead (I Sam 11:1). He must have somehow helped David when they were mutual enemies of Saul. **David** again shows his magnanimous spirit by determining to be kind and gracious to **Hanun. David sent to comfort him by the hand of his servants.** David is beginning to stay at home; some attribute his subsequent sins to allowing himself to be idle. **Thinkest thou that David doth honor thy father . . . ?** It was incredible that one should love his enemies. Hanun could not believe that David had come in peace and genuine sympathy. **Shaved off the one half of their beards.** This was one of the most humiliating things he could have done. Even today the Orientals would consider this an unthinkable indignity. It would be like shaving a woman's head. **Tarry at Jericho until your beards be grown.** This was the only remedy; time heals all things.

6-19. Hired the Syrians. Once the indignity had been performed, there was no way out. It was certain that David would now punish the Ammonites more than ever, so they had to hire mercenaries. David had no choice but to send his men into battle. Joab's strategy and the help of **Abishai his brother,** together with their faith in the Lord, gave them an advantage over evidently superior numbers. When the Syrians gave up in retreat, the Ammonites shut themselves up in the city. Both David and Hadarezer must have come to join their armies for the showdown. **David slew the men of seven hundred chariots.** This number is more plausible than the seven thousand of I Chronicles 19:18. It was at this time that **Hadarezer** surren-

of Zō'ba, and of Rē'hŏb, and Ĭsh'-tŏb, and Mā'a-cah, *were* by themselves in the field.

9 When Jō'ăb saw that the front of the battle was against him before and behind, he chose of all the choice *men* of Israel, and put *them* in array against the Syrians:

10 And the rest of the people he delivered into the hand of A-bī'shaī his brother, that he might put *them* in array against the children of Ammon.

11 And he said, If the Syrians be too strong for me, then thou shalt help me: but if the children of Ammon be too strong for thee, then I will come and help thee.

12 Be of good courage, and let us play the men for our people, and for the cities of our God: and the LORD do that which seemeth him good.

13 And Jō'ăb drew nigh, and the people that *were* with him, unto the battle against the Syrians: and they fled before him.

14 And when the children of Ammon saw that the Syrians were fled, then fled they also before A-bī'shaī, and entered into the city. So Jō'ăb returned from the children of Ammon, and came to Jerusalem.

15 ¶And when the Syrians saw that they were smitten before Israel, they gathered themselves together.

16 And Hād-ar-ē'zer sent, and brought out the Syrians that *were* beyond the river: and they came to Hē'-lam; and Shō'băch the captain of the host of Hād-ar-ē'zer *went* before them.

17 And when it was told David, he gathered all Israel together, and passed over Jordan, and came to Hē'lam. And the Syrians set themselves in array against David, and fought with him.

18 And the Syrians fled before Israel; and David slew *the men of* seven hundred chariots of the Syrians, and forty thousand horsemen, and smote Shō'băch the captain of their host, who died there.

19 And when all the kings *that were* servants to Hād-ar-ē'zer saw that they were smitten before Israel, they made peace with Israel, and served them. So the Syrians feared to help the children of Ammon any more.

CHAPTER 11

AND it came to pass, after the year was expired, at the time when kings go forth *to battle,* that David sent Jō'ăb, and his servants with him, and all Israel; and they destroyed the children of Ammon, and besieged Răb'bah. But David tarried still at Jerusalem.

2 ¶And it came to pass in an eveningtide, that David arose from off his bed, and walked upon the roof of the king's house: and from the roof he saw a woman washing herself; and the woman *was* very beautiful to look upon.

3 And David sent and enquired after the woman. And *one* said, *Is* not this Băth'-shē-ba, the daughter of E-lī'am, the wife of Ū-rī'ah the Hittite?

dered and **made peace with Israel** and became subject to the expanding kingdom of David.

II. GOD'S PATIENCE WITH DAVID AND HIS SINS. 11:1-18:33.

A. David and Bathsheba. 11:1-12:31.

11:1. The army of David had the Ammonites trapped in **Rabbah,** which is the modern city of Amman. **David** himself remained in **Jerusalem.** This fact is presented by the writer as the mistake that made David susceptible to the sin of adultery. Far from trying to hide the sins of its heroes, the Bible presents the facts as they are so that we may learn from these examples how to live in a manner pleasing to the Lord.

2-5. David . . . saw a woman washing herself. Some commentators have suggested that Bathsheba had an ulterior motive in bathing where she could be seen by the king. Whether or not this is true is unimportant to the biblical writer: the sin is David's, and the lessons to be learned center on him, his fall and his forgiveness. **Inquired after the woman.** The word **inquired** (Heb *darash*) might also be translated "sought after" and could then indicate the beginning of lust on David's part. **One said.** The Hebrew is elliptical, literally, "and he said," meaning

4 And David sent messengers, and took her; and she came in unto him, and he lay with her; for she was purified from her uncleanness: and she returned unto her house.

5 And the woman conceived, and sent and told David, and said, I *am* with child.

6 And David sent to Jō′ăb, *saying,* Send me Ū-rī′ah the Hittite. And Jō′ăb sent Ū-rī′ah to David.

7 And when Ū-rī′ah was come unto him, David demanded *of him* how Jō′ăb did, and how the people did, and how the war prospered.

8 And David said to Ū-rī′ah, Go down to thy house, and wash thy feet. And Ū-rī′ah departed out of the king's house, and there followed him a mess *of meat* from the king.

9 But Ū-rī′ah slept at the door of the king's house with all the servants of his lord, and went not down to his house.

10 And when they had told David, saying, Ū-rī′ah went not down unto his house, David said unto Ū-rī′ah, Camest thou not from *thy* journey? why *then* didst thou not go down unto thine house?

11 And Ū-rī′ah said unto David, The ark, and Israel, and Jūdah, abide in tents; and my lord Jō′ăb, and the servants of my lord, are encamped in the open fields; shall I then go into mine house, to eat and to drink, and to lie with my wife? *as* thou livest, and *as* thy soul liveth, I will not do this thing.

12 And David said to Ū-rī′ah, Tarry here to day also, and tomorrow I will let thee depart. So Ū-rī′ah abode in Jerusalem that day, and the morrow.

13 And when David had called him, he did eat and drink before him; and he made him drunk: and at even he went out to lie on his bed with the servants of his lord, but went not down to his house.

14 ¶And it came to pass in the morning, that David wrote a letter to Jō′ăb, and sent *it* by the hand of Ū-rī′ah.

15 And he wrote in the letter, saying, Set ye Ū-rī′ah in the forefront of the hottest battle, and retire ye from him, that he may be smitten, and die.

16 And it came to pass, when Jō′ăb observed the city, that he assigned Ū-rī′ah unto a place where he knew that valiant men *were.*

17 And the men of the city went out, and fought with Jō′ăb: and there fell *some* of the people of the servants of David; and Ū-rī′ah the Hittite died also.

18 ¶Then Jō′ăb sent and told David all the things concerning the war;

19 And charged the messenger, saying, When thou hast made an end of telling the matters of the war unto the king,

20 And if so be that the king's wrath arise, and he say unto thee, Wherefore approached ye so nigh unto the city

probably the person David sent after Bathsheba, or possibly David himself. **Uriah** means, "Yahweh is my Light." Although he was of **Hittite** background, his name indicates that he was a worshiper of God. **And David sent messengers, and took her . . . and he lay with her.** But this was against the laws of God; and David was sinning against God, even though acting in an acceptable manner according to society. The principle of James 1:15 is in progress, "Then when lust hath conceived, it bringeth forth sin; and sin, when it is finished, bringeth forth death." **I am with child.** That David knew he was violating the laws of God is obvious from the fact that it must be kept secret.

6-13. Send me Uriah the Hittite. He supposed at first that he could make it look as if the child had been Uriah's. **Uriah slept at the door of the king's house with all the servants.** This first attempt to cover the sin was foiled by the faithfulness and loyalty of Uriah. **I will not do this thing.** David must have been cut to the heart by this splendid dedication of the one against whom he had sinned. **Made him drunk.** Even intoxicated by drink, Uriah would not go home to sleep with his wife.

14-25. Set ye Uriah in the forefront of the hottest battle, and retire ye from him, that he may be smitten, and die. The intent of murder is so obvious it is incredible; who could believe this of the king "the LORD hath sought after his own heart" (I Sam 13:14). That this is admitted is testimony of the truthfulness and trustworthiness of the Bible in all its content. David could have been presented in a much better light by simply omitting a few verses. **The sword devoureth one as well as another** (vs. 25). This is of course a true statement, but it is here a lie of rationalization; and it is clearly recognized as a sin.

when ye did fight? knew ye not that they would shoot from the wall?

21 Who smote A-bǐm′e-lĕch the son of Je-rŭb′be-shĕth? did not a woman cast a piece of a millstone upon him from the wall, that he died in Thē′bez? why went ye nigh the wall? then say thou, Thy servant Ū-rī′ah the Hittite is dead also.

22 ¶So the messenger went, and came and shewed David all that Jō′ăb had sent him for.

23 And the messenger said unto David, Surely the men prevailed against us, and came out unto us into the field, and we were upon them even unto the entering of the gate.

24 And the shooters shot from off the wall upon thy servants; and *some* of the king's servants be dead, and thy servant Ū-rī′ah the Hittite is dead also.

25 Then David said unto the messenger, Thus shalt thou say unto Jō′ăb, Let not this thing displease thee, for the sword devoureth one as well as another: make thy battle more strong against the city, and overthrow it: and encourage thou him.

26 ¶And when the wife of Ū-rī′ah heard that Ū-rī′ah her husband was dead, she mourned for her husband.

27 And when the mourning was past, David sent and fetched her to his house, and she became his wife, and bare him a son. But the thing that David had done displeased the LORD.

CHAPTER 12

AND the LORD sent Nāthan unto David. And he came unto him, and said unto him, There were two men in one city; the one rich, and the other poor.

2 The rich *man* had exceeding many flocks and herds:

3 But the poor *man* had nothing, save one little ewe lamb, which he had bought and nourished up: and it grew up together with him, and with his children; it did eat of his own meat, and drank of his own cup, and lay in his bosom, and was unto him as a daughter.

4 And there came a traveller unto the rich man, and he spared to take of his own flock and of his own herd, to dress for the wayfaring man that was come unto him; but took the poor man's lamb, and dressed it for the man that was come to him.

5 And David's anger was greatly kindled against the man; and he said to Nāthan, *As* the LORD liveth, the man that hath done this *thing* shall surely die:

6 And he shall restore the lamb fourfold, because he did this thing, and because he had no pity.

7 ¶And Nāthan said to David, Thou *art* the man. Thus saith the LORD God of Israel, I anointed thee king over Israel, and I delivered thee out of the hand of Saul;

8 And I gave thee thy master's house, and thy master's wives into thy bosom, and gave thee the house of Israel and of Jūdah; and if *that had been* too little, I would moreover have given unto thee such and such things.

26-27. She became his wife, and bare him a son. God was patient with David in that He did not punish him immediately and severely for his sin. This whole story is an illustration of how God deals with His people in patience and love to help them to live in a way pleasing to Him. **The thing David had done displeased the LORD.** There was to be no mistake; God did not approve of the sin. He was merely being merciful and patient.

12:1-6. The LORD sent Nathan to David. God has allowed David time to discover the misery of living with unconfessed sin, so that he would be ready to repent. **One little ewe lamb.** The terminology is intended to describe the lamb as so wholesomely beautiful and vulnerable as to engender pity in the hardest of hearts. The lamb was a family pet, almost like a child to the poor man. The rich man had all that he needed, and there was no need at all to exploit the poor man. **There came a traveler.** This, in the allegorical interpretation of the prophetic message, would be the lust of David. If David had wanted merely to satisfy the traveler, he could have taken from his own flock; he already had many wives. The point is that there was no justification from any point of view for the sin. The intended judgment was evoked from David's tender heart: **The man that has done this thing shall surely die.** Not only restoration fourfold according to the law (Ex 22:1), but death; this was the judgment from David's own lips.

7-8. Thou art the man. Nathan simply makes the application. The situation presented was an allegory so clear and lucid that David immediately perceived the interpretation with very little explanation necessary. Rebuke seems to have been the primary function of a prophet, and here Nathan performs his task with wonderful success. After all God had given David; how could he do this thing? **I anointed thee** (Heb *mashach*). The highest honor that could be paid to a man was that of being God's chosen king. God had **delivered** (Heb *natsal*, meaning to rescue from certain destruction) David in order that he in turn

9 Wherefore hast thou despised the commandment of the Lord, to do evil in his sight? thou hast killed Ū-rī′ah the Hittite with the sword, and hast taken his wife *to be* thy wife, and hast slain him with the sword of the children of Ammon.

10 Now therefore the sword shall never depart from thine house; because thou hast despised me, and hast taken the wife of Ū-rī′ah the Hittite to be thy wife.

11 Thus saith the Lord, Behold, I will raise up evil against thee out of thine own house, and I will take thy wives before thine eyes, and give *them* unto thy neighbour, and he shall lie with thy wives in the sight of this sun.

12 For thou didst *it* secretly: but I will do this thing before all Israel, and before the sun.

13 And David said unto Nā′than, I have sinned against the Lord. And Nā′than said unto David, The Lord also hath put away thy sin; thou shalt not die.

14 Howbeit, because by this deed thou hast given great occasion to the enemies of the Lord to blaspheme, the child also *that is* born unto thee shall surely die.

15 ¶And Nā′than departed unto his house. And the Lord struck the child that Ū-rī′ah′s wife bare unto David, and it was very sick.

16 David therefore besought God for the child; and David fasted, and went in, and lay all night upon the earth.

17 And the elders of his house arose, *and went* to him, to raise him up from the earth: but he would not, neither did he eat bread with them.

18 And it came to pass on the seventh day, that the child died. And the servants of David feared to tell him that the child was dead: for they said, Behold, while the child was yet alive, we spake unto him, and he would not hearken unto our voice: how will he then vex himself, if we tell him that the child is dead?

19 But when David saw that his servants whispered, David perceived that the child was dead: therefore David said unto his servants, Is the child dead? And they said, He is dead.

20 Then David arose from the earth, and washed, and anointed *himself*, and changed his apparel, and came into the house of the Lord, and worshipped: then he came to his own house; and when he required, they set bread before him, and he did eat.

21 Then said his servants unto him, What thing *is* this that thou hast done? thou didst fast and weep for the child, *while it was* alive; but when the child was dead, thou didst rise and eat bread.

22 And he said, While the child was yet alive, I fasted and wept: for I said, Who can tell *whether* God will be gracious to me, that the child may live?

23 But now he is dead, wherefore should I fast? can I bring him back

might deliver God's people. David could have had anything his heart desired and yet he betrayed the trust put in him and sinned.

9-15. Despised the commandment. David was guilty of both murder and adultery. **The sword shall never depart from thine house.** The problems and troubles of David's later reign were all a part of his punishment. **I will raise up evil against thee out of thine own house.** This was because of the nature of the sin and the effects of that sin upon his own family. **I have sinned.** David sees it all very quickly, and his repentance is sincere. See Psalm 51 for his inner feelings leading to repentance. **Thou shalt not die.** Even though by his own judgment David was worthy of death, God had revealed to Nathan His mercy. God forgave his sin as soon as he repented. **The child . . . shall surely die.** The sin was forgiven, but there would be the necessary fourfold restitution according to the law (Ex 22:1); and the death of the child would be the first installment in the punishment. **The Lord struck the child.** As soon as the child became sick, it was recognized that the sickness was the punishment for David's sin.

16-23. David therefore besought God for the child. Although he had been told the child would die for his sin, he still hoped in the mercy of God and prayed to that end. **The servants of David feared to tell him that the child was dead.** If he had so fanatically fasted for the whole period that the child was sick, what would he do when he learned that there was no more hope? But David could guess from their concerned whispering that the child was dead; and when this was confirmed, David was willing to release the child into the hands of God. David explained his seemingly strange action to the servants. His fasting could not now bring the dead child back; there would be no point in continuing to **fast. I shall go to him, but he shall not return to me.** Here David expresses his firm belief in immortality; the child was with God, having crossed from this life to the next, and David knew that someday he would die and see his child again.

again? I shall go to him, but he shall not return to me.

24 ¶And David comforted Băth'-shē-ba his wife, and went in unto her, and lay with her: and she bare a son, and he called his name Sŏlomon: and the LORD loved him.

25 And he sent by the hand of Nāthan the prophet; and he called his name Jĕd-i-dī'ah, because of the LORD.

26 ¶And Jŏ'ăb fought against Răb'-bah of the children of Ammon, and took the royal city.

27 And Jŏ'ăb sent messengers to David, and said, I have fought against Răb'bah, and have taken the city of waters.

28 Now therefore gather the rest of the people together, and encamp against the city, and take it: lest I take the city, and it be called after my name.

29 And David gathered all the people together, and went to Răb'bah, and fought against it, and took it.

30 And he took their king's crown from off his head, the weight whereof was a talent of gold with the precious stones: and it was set on David's head. And he brought forth the spoil of the city in great abundance.

31 And he brought forth the people that were therein, and put them under saws, and under harrows of iron, and under axes of iron, and made them pass through the brick-kiln: and thus did he unto all the cities of the children of Ammon. So David and all the people returned unto Jerusalem.

CHAPTER 13

AND it came to pass after this, that Ăb'sa-lom the son of David had a fair sister, whose name was Tā'mar; and Ămnŏn the son of David loved her.

2 And Ămnŏn was so vexed, that he fell sick for his sister Tā'mar; for she was a virgin; and Ămnŏn thought it hard for him to do anything to her.

3 But Ămnŏn had a friend, whose name was Jŏn'a-dăb, the son of Shĭm'e-ah David's brother: and Jŏn'a-dăb was a very subtil man.

4 And he said unto him, Why art thou, being the king's son, lean from day to day? wilt thou not tell me? And Ămnŏn said unto him, I love Tā'mar, my brother Ăb'sa-lom's sister.

5 And Jŏn'a-dăb said unto him, Lay thee down on thy bed, and make thyself sick: and when thy father cometh to see thee, say unto him, I pray thee, let my sister Tā'mar come, and give me meat, and dress the meat in my sight, that I may see it, and eat it at her hand.

6 So Ămnŏn lay down, and made himself sick: and when the king was come to see him, Ămnŏn said unto the king, I pray thee, let Tā'mar my sister come, and make me a couple of cakes in my sight, that I may eat at her hand.

7 Then David sent home to Tā'mar, saying, Go now to thy brother Ămnŏn's house, and dress him meat.

8 So Tā'mar went to her brother Ăm-

24-25. She bare him a son . . . Solomon. The name means "peace" and was probably given with reference to the inner peace that David and Bathsheba could have before God now that the sin had been confessed. **The LORD loved him.** This shows the approval of God upon this child. **He sent** refers to God's commissioning **Nathan** to give assurance to David with the divinely given name **Jedidiah,** which means, in current idiom, "God's little lover." The word from which the name was derived (Heb dōd) is from babytalk, and was assumed to express love. David's own name may be from the same word.

26-31. The royal city. The Septuagint calls this "The city of the kingdoms." The name probably alludes to Amman as a leading city among many Ammonite villages in the area. Heshbon (a few miles southwest) was referred to many times in the Bible before this as "Heshbon and all its villages." **City of waters** was another name for Amman. Heshbon was also famous for its beautiful pools of water, which have been recently excavated (cf. Song 7:4). **David . . . fought against it, and took it.** The battle had already been won, but David was able to be there in person when the city was taken so that the fame would be his. **Put them under saws.** David was a violent and austere warrior for the Lord, but the implication of various forms of sadistic torture given in this translation is not in keeping with his character. The Hebrew text here and in the parallel passage in I Chronicles 20:3 may be satisfactorily translated as work or labor with saws.

B. Amnon and Tamar. 13:1–14:33.

13:1-12. After this. These words mean to imply only the general period of time after the Ammonite war. The purpose is not to give a strict chronological history, but to show the results and punishments of David's great sin. **Amnon** was the eldest son of David by Ahinoam the Jezreelite (II Sam 3:2). **His sister** (stepsister) was a **virgin,** and for this reason either carefully chaperoned or otherwise kept from him and his lust. **Jonadab,** Amnon's friend, was **subtil** and suggested a trick to get Tamar alone. Amnon then pretended to be **sick** and asked that David send **Tamar** with **a couple of cakes** (Heb lebibah). Neither this word nor the cognate verb are found anywhere except 13:6, 8, 10. It is related to the word for "heart," but the exact meaning is unknown. It is hardly likely that they were "heart-shaped" in our modern sense of "valentine cookies," since David and the other relatives would not have approved. It is possible and more likely that they were made especially for sick people to cheer them up, or give "heart."

nŏn's house; and he was laid down. And she took flour, and kneaded *it,* and made cakes in his sight, and did bake the cakes.

9 And she took a pan, and poured *them* out before him; but he refused to eat. And Ămnŏn said, Have out all men from me. And they went out every man from him.

10 And Ămnŏn said unto Tă'mar, Bring the meat into the chamber, that I may eat of thine hand. And Tă'mar took the cakes which she had made, and brought *them* into the chamber to Ămnŏn her brother.

11 And when she had brought *them* unto him to eat, he took hold of her, and said unto her, Come lie with me, my sister.

12 And she answered him, Nay, my brother, do not force me: for no such thing ought to be done in Israel: do not thou this folly.

13 And I, whither shall I cause my shame to go? and as for thee, thou shalt be as one of the fools in Israel. Now therefore, I pray thee, speak unto the king; for he will not withhold me from thee.

14 Howbeit he would not hearken unto her voice: but, being stronger than she, forced her, and lay with her.

15 ¶Then Ămnŏn hated her exceedingly; so that the hatred wherewith he hated her *was* greater than the love wherewith he had loved her. And Ămnŏn said unto her, Arise, be gone.

16 And she said unto him, *There is* no cause: this evil in sending me away *is* greater than the other that thou didst unto me. But he would not hearken unto her.

17 Then he called his servant that ministered unto him, and said, Put now this *woman* out from me, and bolt the door after her.

18 And *she had* a garment of divers colours upon her: for with such robes were the king's daughters *that were* virgins apparelled. Then his servant brought her out, and bolted the door after her.

19 ¶And Tă'mar put ashes on her head, and rent her garment of divers colours that *was* on her, and laid her hand on her head, and went on crying.

20 And Ăb'sa-lom her brother said unto her, Hath Ămnŏn thy brother been with thee? but hold now thy peace, my sister: he *is* thy brother; regard not this thing. So Tă'mar remained desolate in her brother Ăb'sa-lom's house.

21 ¶But when king David heard of all these things, he was very wroth.

22 And Ăb'sa-lom spake unto his brother Ămnŏn neither good nor bad: for Ăb'sa-lom hated Ămnŏn, because he had forced his sister Tă'mar.

23 ¶And it came to pass after two full years, that Ăb'sa-lom had sheepshearers in Bă'al-hă'zôr, which *is* beside Ē'phra-im: and Ăb'sa-lom invited all the king's sons.

24 And Ăb'sa-lom came to the king, and said, Behold now, thy servant hath sheepshearers; let the king, I beseech thee, and his servants go with thy servant.

13-19. Speak unto the king. Tamar begs that Amnon ask for her hand in marriage. This probably would have been permitted, even though it was strictly forbidden by the law (Lev 18:9). Afterward, he **hated her exceedingly.** Great emphasis is placed upon the root word **hate,** which appears four times in the original, showing that the **love** which he had felt before was pure, unbridled, sexual lust. The **garment of divers colors.** The exact nature of this special garment cannot be certainly determined; it may have been rather an ankle-length robe with sleeves.

20-33. Tamar remained desolate in her brother Absalom's house. The meaning is that she was kept out of circulation because of this unfortunate seduction by Amnon. Because of all this, Absalom simply waited his chance to get even. **Absalom invited all the king's sons.** The festival at **Baal-hazor** was set up as a trap for Amnon. It was probably surmised that the king himself would not come. **When Amnon's heart is merry with wine.** The plot was determined and prearranged so that Amnon would be murdered as soon as he was drunk enough. After the murder there was pandemonium as **every man gat him up upon his mule, and fled.**

Tidings came to David, perhaps intentionally exaggerated so as to soften the blow, that **all** of his **sons** had been murdered by Absalom. Then **Jonadab,** whose scheme had helped to bring all this about, revealed the "good news" that this was planned vengeance and **Amnon only** had been murdered by **Absalom.**

25 And the king said to Ăb′sa-lom, Nay, my son, let us not all now go, lest we be chargeable unto thee. And he pressed him: howbeit he would not go, but blessed him.

26 Then said Ăb′sa-lom, If not, I pray thee, let my brother Ămnŏn go with us. And the king said unto him, Why should he go with thee?

27 But Ăb′sa-lom pressed him, that he let Ămnŏn and all the king's sons go with him.

28 ¶Now Ăb′sa-lom had commanded his servants, saying, Mark ye now when Ămnŏn's heart is merry with wine, and when I say unto you, Smite Ămnŏn; then kill him, fear not: have not I commanded you? be courageous, and be valiant.

29 And the servants of Ăb′sa-lom did unto Ămnŏn as Ăb′sa-lom had commanded. Then all the king's sons arose, and every man gat him up upon his mule, and fled.

30 ¶And it came to pass, while they were in the way, that tidings came to David, saying, Ăb′sa-lom hath slain all the king's sons, and there is not one of them left.

31 Then the king arose, and tare his garments, and lay on the earth; and all his servants stood by with their clothes rent.

32 And Jŏn′a-dăb, the son of Shĭm′e-ah David's brother, answered and said, Let not my lord suppose that they have slain all the young men the king's sons; for Ămnŏn only is dead: for by the appointment of Ăb′sa-lom this hath been determined from the day that he forced his sister Tă′mar.

33 Now therefore let not my lord the king take the thing to his heart, to think that all the king's sons are dead: for Ămnŏn only is dead.

34 But Ăb′sa-lom fled. And the young man that kept the watch lifted up his eyes, and looked, and, behold, there came much people by the way of the hill side behind him.

35 And Jŏn′a-dăb said unto the king, Behold, the king's sons come: as thy servant said, so it is.

36 And it came to pass, as soon as he had made an end of speaking, that, behold, the king's sons came, and lifted up their voice and wept: and the king also and all his servants wept very sore.

37 ¶But Ăb′sa-lom fled, and went to Tăl′maī, the son of Ăm-mī′hŭd, king of Gĕ′shur. And David mourned for his son every day.

38 So Ăb′sa-lom fled, and went to Gĕ′shur, and was there three years.

39 And the soul of king David longed to go forth unto Ăb′sa-lom: for he was comforted concerning Ămnŏn, seeing he was dead.

CHAPTER 14

NOW Jŏ′ăb the son of Zer-ū-i′ah perceived that the king's heart was toward Ăb′sa-lom.

2 And Jŏ′ăb sent to Te-kō′ah, and fetched thence a wise woman, and said unto her, I pray thee, feign thyself to be a mourner, and put on now mourning

34-39. Absalom fled. Since this was a deliberate murder, he could not find refuge in any of the cities of Israel. **King of Geshur.** This was his grandfather on his mother's side. **Absalom . . . was there three years.** David was aware that this was punishment in part for his own sin, and it took him this long to get over his grief.

14:1-11. Joab . . . perceived that the king's heart was toward Absalom. This may mean either that David longed to see **Absalom,** or the opposite passion, that he still was angry with him. The latter interpretation seems more in line with the fact that David would not allow his son to come into his presence when he finally did return. **Joab** hoped to maintain the favor of

613

II SAMUEL 14:3

apparel, and anoint not thyself with oil, but be as a woman that had a long time mourned for the dead:

3 And come to the king, and speak on this manner unto him. So Jō′áb put the words in her mouth.

4 ¶And when the woman of Te-kō′ah spake to the king, she fell on her face to the ground, and did obeisance, and said, Help, O king.

5 And the king said unto her, What aileth thee? And she answered, I *am* indeed a widow woman, and mine husband is dead.

6 And thy handmaid had two sons, and they two strove together in the field, and *there was* none to part them, but the one smote the other, and slew him.

7 And, behold, the whole family is risen against thine handmaid, and they said, Deliver him that smote his brother, that we may kill him, for the life of his brother whom he slew; and we will destroy the heir also: and so they shall quench my coal which is left, and shall not leave to my husband *neither* name nor remainder upon the earth.

8 And the king said unto the woman, Go to thine house, and I will give charge concerning thee.

9 And the woman of Te-kō′ah said unto the king, My lord, O king, the iniquity *be* on me, and on my father's house: and the king and his throne *be* guiltless.

10 And the king said, Whosoever saith *ought* unto thee, bring him to me, and he shall not touch thee any more.

11 Then said she, I pray thee, let the king remember the Lord thy God, that thou wouldest not suffer the revengers of blood to destroy any more, lest they destroy my son. And he said, *As* the Lord liveth, there shall not one hair of thy son fall to the earth.

12 Then the woman said, Let thine handmaid, I pray thee, speak *one* word unto my lord the king. And he said, Say on.

13 And the woman said, Wherefore then hast thou thought such a thing against the people of God? for the king doth speak this thing as one which is faulty, in that the king doth not fetch home again his banished.

14 For we must needs die, and *are* as water spilt on the ground, which cannot be gathered up again; neither doth God respect *any* person: yet doth he devise means, that his banished be not expelled from him.

15 Now therefore that I am come to speak of this thing unto my lord the king, *it is* because the people have made me afraid: and thy handmaid said, I will now speak unto the king; it may be that the king will perform the request of his handmaid.

16 For the king will hear, to deliver his handmaid out of the hand of the man *that would* destroy me and my son together out of the inheritance of God.

17 Then thine handmaid said, The word of my lord the king shall now be comfortable: for as an angel of God, so *is* my lord the king to discern good and

David and at the same time obligate Absalom to him. **Fetched thence a wise woman.** She was an artist of deceit, perhaps someone Joab had known from his hometown. **Joab put the words in her mouth.** The scheme was his; she was simply paid to play the part. The story about brother killing brother was perhaps immediately suspect to David, but he quickly reacted with a merciful judgment in the matter. Two wrongs do not make a right; it would not do to kill the heir of the departed Israelite and thus cut off his inheritance among God's people. **There shall not one hair of thy son fall to the earth.** He was now protected by the royal decree of the king.

12-17. Let thine handmaid . . . speak one word. The meaning is in our idiom, "By the way. . . ." The application of the whole scheme is now made crystal clear. **Wherefore then hast thou thought such a thing against the people of God?** The word **thought** (Heb *chashab*) usually means "plan against." The refusal to show the same kind of mercy to Absalom was conduct unbecoming a ruler over God's people. David was contradicting himself. **Neither doth God respect any person.** The most accurate translations have, "God will not take away the life of a person." The idea is that God is a pardoning God; and although punishment (like being temporarily banished) is sometimes necessary, He will forgive the penitent and allow him a place among His people. The exact intent of the writer is unclear in this text, but there may also have been some reference to David's own complicated sin with Bathsheba. **As an angel of God.** A diplomatic spoonful of honey to make the medicine taste good.

614

bad: therefore the Lord thy God will be with thee.

18 Then the king answered and said unto the woman, Hide not from me, I pray thee, the thing that I shall ask thee. And the woman said, Let my lord the king now speak.

19 And the king said, Is not the hand of Jŏ'ăb with thee in all this? And the woman answered and said, As thy soul liveth, my lord the king, none can turn to the right hand or to the left from ought that my lord the king hath spoken: for thy servant Jŏ'ăb, he bade me, and he put all these words in the mouth of thine handmaid:

20 To fetch about this form of speech hath thy servant Jŏ'ăb done this thing: and my lord is wise, according to the wisdom of an angel of God, to know all things that are in the earth.

21 ¶And the king said unto Jŏ'ăb, Behold now, I have done this thing: go therefore, bring the young man Ăb'sa-lom again.

22 And Jŏ'ăb fell to the ground on his face, and bowed himself, and thanked the king: and Jŏ'ăb said, To day thy servant knoweth that I have found grace in thy sight, my lord, O king, in that the king hath fulfilled the request of his servant.

23 So Jŏ'ăb arose and went to Gĕ'-shur, and brought Ăb'sa-lom to Jerusalem.

24 And the king said, Let him turn to his own house, and let him not see my face. So Ăb'sa-lom returned to his own house, and saw not the king's face.

25 ¶But in all Israel there was none to be so much praised as Ăb'sa-lom for his beauty: from the sole of his foot even to the crown of his head there was no blemish in him.

26 And when he polled his head, (for it was at every year's end that he polled it: because the hair was heavy on him, therefore he polled it:) he weighed the hair of his head at two hundred shekels after the king's weight.

27 And unto Ăb'sa-lom there were born three sons, and one daughter, whose name was Tā'mar: she was a woman of a fair countenance.

28 ¶So Ăb'sa-lom dwelt two full years in Jerusalem, and saw not the king's face.

29 Therefore Ăb'sa-lom sent for Jŏ'ăb, to have sent him to the king; but he would not come to him: and when he sent again the second time, he would not come.

30 Therefore he said unto his servants, See, Jŏ'ăb's field is near mine, and he hath barley there; go and set it on fire. And Ăb'sa-lom's servants set the field on fire.

31 Then Jŏ'ăb arose, and came to Ăb'sa-lom unto his house, and said unto him, Wherefore have thy servants set my field on fire?

32 And Ăb'sa-lom answered Jŏ'ăb, Behold, I sent unto thee, saying, Come hither, that I may send thee to the king, to say, Wherefore am I come from Gĕ'shur? it had been good for me to have been there still: now therefore let

18-24. Now David recognizes the hand of Joab in this whole scheme. **Is not the hand of Joab with thee in all this?** It can hardly be denied at this point, but at least the object has been fulfilled. **Bring the young man Absalom again.** This was what Joab was after. **Absalom** was allowed to return to Jerusalem again, but he was still kept from the household of David itself.

25-33. None to be so much praised as Absalom for his beauty. But God had reminded Samuel that ". . . man looketh on the outward appearance, but the Lord looketh on the heart" (I Sam 16:7).

Two hundred shekels would be either six pounds, or three and one-half pounds, depending on which standard was used. **Two full years in Jerusalem, and saw not the king's face.** This makes five years (three years in Geshur) since Absalom had murdered Amnon. **Set the field on fire.** This was simply a way of getting the attention of Joab. Absalom wanted very badly to be restored to the favor of the king, but not for any sentimental reasons. He was already planning his rebellion.

me see the king's face; and if there be *any* iniquity in me, let him kill me.

33 So Jō'ăb came to the king, and told him: and when he had called for Ăb'sa-lom, he came to the king, and bowed himself on his face to the ground before the king: and the king kissed Ăb'sa-lom.

CHAPTER 15

AND it came to pass after this, that Ăb'sa-lom prepared him chariots and horses, and fifty men to run before him.

2 And Ăb'sa-lom rose up early, and stood beside the way of the gate: and it was *so,* that when any man that had a controversy came to the king for judgment, then Ăb'sa-lom called unto him, and said, Of what city *art* thou? And he said, Thy servant *is* of one of the tribes of Israel.

3 And Ăb'sa-lom said unto him, See, thy matters *are* good and right; but *there is* no man *deputed* of the king to hear thee.

4 Ăb'sa-lom said moreover, Oh that I were made judge in the land, that every man which hath any suit or cause might come unto me, and I would do him justice!

5 And it was *so,* that when any man came nigh *to him* to do him obeisance, he put forth his hand, and took him, and kissed him.

6 And on this manner did Ăb'sa-lom to all Israel that came to the king for judgment: so Ăb'sa-lom stole the hearts of the men of Israel.

7 ¶And it came to pass after forty years, that Ăb'sa-lom said unto the king, I pray thee, let me go and pay my vow, which I have vowed unto the LORD, in Hēbron.

8 For thy servant vowed a vow while I abode at Gĕ'shur in Syria, saying, If the LORD shall bring me again indeed to Jerusalem, then I will serve the LORD.

9 And the king said unto him, Go in peace. So he arose, and went to Hē-bron.

10 ¶But Ăb'sa-lom sent spies throughout all the tribes of Israel, saying, As soon as ye hear the sound of the trumpet, then ye shall say, Ăb'sa-lom reigneth in Hēbron.

11 And with Ăb'sa-lom went two hundred men out of Jerusalem, *that were* called; and they went in their simplicity, and they knew not any thing.

12 And Ăb'sa-lom sent for A-hĭth'o-phĕl the Gī'lo-nīte, David's counsellor, from his city, *even* from Gī'lōh, while he offered sacrifices. And the conspiracy was strong; for the people increased continually with Ăb'sa-lom.

13 ¶And there came a messenger to David, saying, The hearts of the men of Israel are after Ăb'sa-lom.

14 And David said unto all his servants that *were* with him at Jerusalem, Arise, and let us flee; for we shall not *else* escape from Ăb'sa-lom: make speed to depart, lest he overtake us suddenly, and bring evil upon us, and

C. The Rebellion of Absalom. 15:1-18:33.

15:1-6. Fifty men to run before him. Absalom was one of the most clever of ancient politicians. In this way he was able to impress the people with his authority and dignity. **Stood beside the way of the gate.** His was a handshaking campaign; he talked with people about their problems and agreed with them, only lamenting that he did not have the power to do anything. **There is no man deputed of the king to hear thee.** It was, Absalom implied, a "taxation without representation" issue. **I would do him justice!** Political promises! **So Absalom stole the hearts of the men of Israel** (vs. 6). This was a deliberate attempt to establish a base of support throughout the country and undermine the confidence of the people in David.

7-12. Forty years. The Septuagint and all other versions read "four years." It was a long-range plan at that, and in no way could the reading "forty" be made to harmonize. **Then I will serve the LORD.** The word **serve** (Heb *'abad*) was already a technical term for the king as the "servant of Yahweh," and this was a veiled claim to the throne. **Hebron** was the place of his birth, and he was able to find avid supporters there. **Ahithophel** was the grandfather of Bathsheba. He may have sided with Absalom because of the great sin of David and Bathsheba and his resulting loss of confidence in the king.

13-18. The hearts of the men of Israel are after Absalom. The long campaign had paid off, and now that it was too late, even David's closest attendants realized exactly what had happened. **Arise, and let us flee.** David was able to assess the situation quickly and with good judgment make the necessary decision to escape. His concern was not only for his own safety but for the city, lest Absalom **smite the city with the edge of the sword. The Gittites** were the **six hundred** men who had been with him at Ziklag, whose wives and children David had saved.

smite the city with the edge of the sword.

15 And the king's servants said unto the king, Behold, thy servants *are ready to do* whatsoever my lord the king shall appoint.

16 And the king went forth, and all his household after him. And the king left ten women, *which were* concubines, to keep the house.

17 And the king went forth, and all the people after him, and tarried in a place that was far off.

18 And all his servants passed on beside him; and all the Chĕr'e-thītes, and all the Pĕl'e-thītes, and all the Gĭt'tītes, six hundred men which came after him from Gath, passed on before the king.

19 ¶Then said the king to Ĭt'ta-ī the Gĭt'tīte, Wherefore goest thou also with us? return to thy place, and abide with the king: for thou *art* a stranger, and also an exile.

20 Whereas thou camest *but* yesterday, should I this day make thee go up and down with us? seeing I go whither I may, return thou, and take back thy brethren: mercy and truth *be* with thee.

21 And Ĭt'ta-ī answered the king, and said, *As* the LORD liveth, and *as* my lord the king liveth, surely in what place my lord the king shall be, whether in death or life, even there also will thy servant be.

22 And David said to Ĭt'ta-ī, Go and pass over. And Ĭt'ta-ī the Gĭt'tīte passed over, and all his men, and all the little ones that *were* with him.

23 And all the country wept with a loud voice, and all the people passed over: the king also himself passed over the brook Kidron, and all the people passed over, toward the way of the wilderness.

24 ¶And lo Zā'dŏk also, and all the Lēvītes *were* with him, bearing the ark of the covenant of God: and they set down the ark of God; and Ā-bī'a-thar went up, until all the people had done passing out of the city.

25 And the king said unto Zā'dŏk, Carry back the ark of God into the city: if I shall find favour in the eyes of the LORD, he will bring me again, and shew me *both* it, and his habitation:

26 But if he thus say, I have no delight in thee; behold, *here am* I, let him do to me as seemeth good unto him.

27 The king said also unto Zā'dŏk the priest, *Art not* thou a seer? return into the city in peace, and your two sons with you, A-hĭm'ă-az thy son, and Jonathan the son of Ā-bī'a-thar.

28 See, I will tarry in the plain of the wilderness, until there come word from you to certify me.

29 Zā'dŏk therefore and Ā-bī'a-thar carried the ark of God again to Jerusalem: and they tarried there.

30 ¶And David went up by the ascent of *mount* Olivet, and wept as he went up, and had his head covered, and he went barefoot: and all the people that *was* with him covered every man his head, and they went up, weeping as they went up.

31 And *one* told David, saying, A-hĭth'o-phĕl *is* among the conspirators

They had remained faithful ever since and were a sort of honor guard to him.

19-23. Ittai the Gittite must have been one of the great heroes of the group. He expresses deep loyalty to David. **Mercy and truth be with you.** David tried to persuade Ittai to go back rather than wander in the wilderness with him. The parting blessing is more adequately translated, "May the Lord show steadfast love and faithfulness to you." The reply of **Ittai** is expressed in poetic beauty in this verse. It should be compared with the similar, determined faithfulness of Ruth (Ruth 1:16-17). **And all the country wept.** It was a tragedy for the heart of the nation, and all those who were faithful to David, as they **passed over the brook Kidron** toward the wilderness east of Jerusalem.

24-37. Zadok . . . and all the Levites . . . bearing the ark of the covenant of God. Evidently this was done without David's knowledge or else he changed his mind and decided that the priests and the ark would better serve him and the people of God in Jerusalem. **Abiathar went up** could also be translated "Abiathar offered sacrifices." **I will tarry in the plain of the wilderness.** The reading **plain** was caused by a scribal error of transposing two letters in the Hebrew word. It should be the "fords of the wilderness," or the place where one crosses the Jordan in the wilderness. So Zadok the priest took the ark back into the city where he and Abiathar would await further developments. **David went up by the ascent of mount Olivet, and wept as he went up.** At the summit of the Mount of Olives, David prayed and committed the matter to the LORD. The plan was that **Hushai the Archite** would return and pretend loyalty to Absalom while actually functioning as a spy for David. Any essential information was to be relayed by **Ahimaaz** and **Jonathan.**

with Ăb'sa-lom. And David said, O
LORD, I pray thee, turn the counsel of A-
hĭth'o-phĕl into foolishness.

32 ¶And it came to pass, that when
David was come to the top of the
mount, where he worshipped God, behold, Hu'shaī the Ăr'chīte came to meet
him with his coat rent, and earth upon
his head:

33 Unto whom David said, If thou
passest on with me, then thou shalt be a
burden unto me:

34 But if thou return to the city, and
say unto Ăb'sa-lom, I will be thy servant, O king; as I have been thy father's
servant hitherto, so will I now also be
thy servant: then mayest thou for me
defeat the counsel of A-hĭth'o-phĕl.

35 And hast thou not there with thee
Zā'dŏk and Ā-bī'a-thar the priests?
therefore it shall be, that what thing soever thou shalt hear out of the king's
house, thou shalt tell it to Zā'dŏk and
Ā-bī'a-thar the priests.

36 Behold, they have there with them
their two sons, A-hĭm'ă-az Zā'dŏk's
son, and Jonathan Ā-bī'a-thar's son;
and by them ye shall send unto me
every thing that ye can hear.

37 So Hu'shaī David's friend came
into the city, and Ăb'sa-lom came into
Jerusalem.

CHAPTER 16

AND when David was a little past the
top of the hill, behold, Zī'ba the servant
of Me-phĭb'o-shĕth met him, with a
couple of asses saddled, and upon them
two hundred loaves of bread, and an
hundred bunches of raisins, and an
hundred of summer fruits, and a bottle
of wine.

2 And the king said unto Zī'ba, What
meanest thou by these? And Zī'ba said,
The asses be for the king's household to
ride on; and the bread and summer
fruit for the young men to eat; and the
wine, that such as be faint in the wilderness may drink.

3 And the king said, And where is thy
master's son? And Zī'ba said unto the
king, Behold, he abideth at Jerusalem:
for he said, To day shall the house of
Israel restore me the kingdom of my
father.

4 Then said the king to Zī'ba, Behold,
thine are all that pertained unto Me-
phĭb'o-shĕth. And Zī'ba said, I humbly
beseech thee that I may find grace in
thy sight, my lord, O king.

5 ¶And when king David came to Ba-
hū'rĭm, behold, thence came out a man
of the family of the house of Saul,
whose name was Shĭm'e-ī, the son of
Ge'ra: he came forth, and cursed still as
he came.

6 And he cast stones at David, and at
all the servants of king David: and all
the people and all the mighty men were
on his right hand and on his left.

7 And thus said Shĭm'e-ī when he
cursed, Come out, come out, thou
bloody man, and thou man of Bē'lĭ-al:

8 The LORD hath returned upon thee
all the blood of the house of Saul, in
whose stead thou hast reigned; and the
LORD hath delivered the kingdom into
the hand of Ăb'sa-lom thy son: and, be-

16:1-4. Ziba the servant of Mephibosheth brought generous
supplies to David with the lie that his master still aspired to the
throne. David was unable to see through his fabrication at the
time. **All** the property and inheritance of **Mephibosheth** were
now transferred to **Ziba.**

5-14. Shimei . . . a man of the family of the house of Saul
met them somewhere on the road to the Jordan and began to
heap insults and curses upon David.

Come out is really "Get out, get out. . . ." **Bloody man** is
really an unjust charge, since David had not attained his kingdom from Saul by means of bloodshed, nor had he taken
vengeance in the usual manner after he was in power. He had
instead returned good for evil and demonstrated love for the
surviving members of Saul's house. **Abishai** wanted to **take off
his head,** but David was content to leave the matter in the hands
of the Lord. Perhaps God had told Shimei to **curse David.**
David was willing to accept this as a part of the judgment for his
sin.

hold, thou *art taken* in thy mischief, because thou *art* a bloody man.

9 ¶Then said A-bī'shaī the son of Zer-ū-i'ah unto the king, Why should this dead dog curse my lord the king? let me go over, I pray thee, and take off his head.

10 And the king said, What have I to do with you, ye sons of Zer-ū-i'ah? so let him curse, because the LORD hath said unto him, Curse David. Who shall then say, Wherefore hast thou done so?

11 And David said to A-bī'shaī, and to all his servants, Behold, my son, which came forth of my bowels, seeketh my life: how much more now *may this* Benjamite *do it?* let him alone, and let him curse; for the LORD hath bidden him.

12 It may be that the LORD will look on mine affliction, and that the LORD will requite me good for his cursing this day.

13 And as David and his men went by the way, Shĭm'e-ī went along on the hill's side over against him, and cursed as he went, and threw stones at him, and cast dust.

14 And the king, and all the people that *were* with him, came weary, and refreshed themselves there.

15 ¶And Ăb'sa-lom, and all the people the men of Israel, came to Jerusalem, and A-hĭth'o-phĕl with him.

16 And it came to pass, when Hu'shaī the Ăr'chīte, David's friend, was come unto Ăb'sa-lom, that Hu'shaī said unto Ăb'sa-lom, God save the king, God save the king.

17 And Ăb'sa-lom said to Hu'shaī, *Is* this thy kindness to thy friend? why wentest thou not with thy friend?

18 And Hu'shaī said unto Ăb'sa-lom, Nay; but whom the LORD, and this people, and all the men of Israel, choose, his will I be, and with him will I abide.

19 And again, whom should I serve? *should I* not *serve* in the presence of his son? as I have served in thy father's presence, so will I be in thy presence.

20 ¶Then said Ăb'sa-lom to A-hĭth'o-phĕl, Give counsel among you what we shall do.

21 And A-hĭth'o-phĕl said unto Ăb'sa-lom, Go in unto thy father's concubines, which he hath left to keep the house; and all Israel shall hear that thou art abhorred of thy father: then shall the hands of all that *are* with thee be strong.

22 So they spread Ăb'sa-lom a tent upon the top of the house; and Ăb'sa-lom went in unto his father's concubines in the sight of all Israel.

23 And the counsel of A-hĭth'o-phĕl, which he counselled in those days, *was* as if a man had enquired at the oracle of God: so *was* all the counsel of A-hĭth'o-phĕl both with David and with Ăb'sa-lom.

CHAPTER 17

MOREOVER A-hĭth'o-phĕl said unto Ăb'sa-lom, Let me now choose out twelve thousand men, and I will arise and pursue after David this night:

2 And I will come upon him while he

15-23. Ahithophel was Absalom's chief counselor now; he had also served David. **God save the King.** The word **God** is not found in the original text; more literally and less offensive to the name of God would be, "Long live the king!" **Hushai** gave this greeting in order to suggest his loyalty to Absalom. It was received with some suspicion. **Hushai** continued his diplomatic deceit with the convincing words, **whom the LORD, and this people . . . choose, his will I be.** The first counsel of Ahithophel was, **Go in unto thy father's concubines.** This was, of course, the greatest possible insult to David, as well as a sort of formal and public display of the takeover of the kingdom. This was done as a sign that Absalom was the new king (see I Kgs 2:22).

17:1-4. Ahithophel was actually a very wise and able military counselor as can be seen here. The plan was to strike while David and his men were in retreat and exhausted. The people would be without a leader once David was killed and would theoretically return to Absalom.

is weary and weak handed, and will make him afraid: and all the people that *are* with him shall flee; and I will smite the king only:

3 And I will bring back all the people unto thee: the man whom thou seekest *is* as if all returned: *so* all the people shall be in peace.

4 And the saying pleased Ăb′sa-lom well, and all the elders of Israel.

5 Then said Ăb′sa-lom, Call now Hu′shaĭ the Ăr′chĭte also, and let us hear likewise what he saith.

6 And when Hu′shaĭ was come to Ăb′sa-lom, Ăb′sa-lom spake unto him, saying, A-hĭth′o-phĕl hath spoken after this manner: shall we do *after* his saying? if not; speak thou.

7 And Hu′shaĭ said unto Ăb′sa-lom, The counsel that A-hĭth′o-phĕl hath given *is* not good at this time.

8 For, said Hu′shaĭ, thou knowest thy father and his men, that they *be* mighty men, and they *be* chafed in their minds, as a bear robbed of her whelps in the field: and thy father *is* a man of war, and will not lodge with the people.

9 Behold, he is hid now in some pit, or in some *other* place: and it will come to pass, when some of them be overthrown at the first, that whosoever heareth it will say, There is a slaughter among the people that follow Ăb′sa-lom.

10 And he also *that is* valiant, whose heart *is* as the heart of a lion, shall utterly melt: for all Israel knoweth that thy father *is* a mighty man, and *they* which *be* with him *are* valiant men.

11 Therefore I counsel that all Israel be generally gathered unto thee, from Dan even to Be′er-shē′ba, as the sand that *is* by the sea for multitude; and that thou go to battle in thine own person.

12 So shall we come upon him in some place where he shall be found, and we will light upon him as the dew falleth on the ground: and of him and of all the men that *are* with him there shall not be left so much as one.

13 Moreover, if he be gotten into a city, then shall all Israel bring ropes to that city, and we will draw it into the river, until there be not one small stone found there.

14 And Ăb′sa-lom and all the men of Israel said, The counsel of Hu′shaĭ the Ăr′chĭte *is* better than the counsel of A-hĭth′o-phĕl. For the LORD had appointed to defeat the good counsel of A-hĭth′o-phĕl, to the intent that the LORD might bring evil upon Ăb′sa-lom.

15 ¶Then said Hu′shaĭ unto Zā′dŏk and to Ă-bī′a-thar the priests, Thus and thus did A-hĭth′o-phĕl counsel Ăb′sa-lom and the elders of Israel; and thus and thus have I counselled.

16 Now therefore send quickly, and tell David, saying, Lodge not this night in the plains of the wilderness, but speedily pass over; lest the king be swallowed up, and all the people that *are* with him.

17 Now Jonathan and A-hĭm′ă-az stayed by Ĕn-rō′gel; for they might not be seen to come into the city: and a

5-14. Hushai the Archite now gives the opposite counsel to what **Ahithophel** has given. **The counsel that Ahithophel hath given is not good at this time.** He does not mean that it will be good counsel at another time, but that this time, in contrast to all the other times that Ahithophel has given counsel, it simply is not good at all. Hushai had a better idea. **As a bear robbed of her whelps in the field.** Hushai's argument runs thus: David and his men are competent and experienced soldiers; and since they have just been driven out, they will be determined to die rather than surrender. It could be difficult to find David; and if there were a preliminary struggle and David was not immediately killed, any loss of morale among Absalom's troops might be disastrous. **All Israel be generally gathered unto thee . . . as the sand that is by the sea for multitude.** This would of course take some time and, although it sounded good to Absalom, was God's way of delivering David. **For the LORD had appointed.** In the providence of God David would be protected by the Lord even though betrayed by his former counselor and military adviser.

15-23. Zadok and . . . Abiathar now passed this information on to **Jonathan and Ahimaaz,** who in turn took it to David. **En-rogel** is a spring near the southern end of the Kidron Valley, not far from the present city of Jerusalem. A careful system of intelligence had been worked out whereby the **wench** (Heb *shipchah,* with the definite article), a female servant, brought the information to the well while pretending to draw water, and the young men ran on with it. Evidently there were a number of David's supporters left; for even when the **lad saw them** and they were being pursued, they found shelter in **Bahurim.** Meanwhile, **Ahithophel,** unable to face life any longer since his advice had been ignored, committed suicide.

wench went and told them; and they went and told king David.

18 Nevertheless a lad saw them, and told Ăb'sa-lom: but they went both of them away quickly, and came to a man's house in Ba-hū'rĭm, which had a well in his court; whither they went down.

19 And the woman took and spread a covering over the well's mouth, and spread ground corn thereon; and the thing was not known.

20 And when Ăb'sa-lom's servants came to the woman to the house, they said, Where is A-hĭm'ă-az and Jona-than? And the woman said unto them, They be gone over the brook of water. And when they had sought and could not find them, they returned to Jerusalem.

21 And it came to pass, after they were departed, that they came up out of the well, and went and told David, and said unto David, Arise, and pass quickly over the water: for thus hath A-hĭth'o-phĕl counselled against you.

22 Then David arose, and all the people that were with him, and they passed over Jordan: by the morning light there lacked not one of them that was not gone over Jordan.

23 ¶And when A-hĭth'o-phĕl saw that his counsel was not followed, he saddled his ass, and arose, and gat him home to his house, to his city, and put his household in order, and hanged himself, and died, and was buried in the sepulchre of his father.

24 Then David came to Mă-ha-nā'im. And Ăb'sa-lom passed over Jordan, he and all the men of Israel with him.

25 And Ăb'sa-lom made Am'ă-sa captain of the host instead of Jō'ăb: which Am'ă-sa was a man's son, whose name was Ĭth'ra an Israelite, that went in to Ăb'i-gāil the daughter of Nā'hăsh, sister to Zer-ū-i'ah Jō'ăb's mother.

26 So Israel and Ăb'sa-lom pitched in the land of Gilead.

27 ¶And it came to pass, when David was come to Mă-ha-nā'im, that Shō'bī the son of Nā'hăsh of Răb'bah of the children of Ammon, and Mā'chĭr the son of Ăm'mĭ-el of Lō-dē'bar, and Bär-zĭl'la-ī the Gileadite of Rō-ge'lĭm,

28 Brought beds, and basons, and earthen vessels, and wheat, and barley, and flour, and parched corn, and beans, and lentiles, and parched pulse,

29 And honey, and butter, and sheep, and cheese of kine, for David, and for the people that were with him, to eat: for they said, The people is hungry, and weary, and thirsty, in the wilderness.

CHAPTER 18

AND David numbered the people that were with him, and set captains of thousands and captains of hundreds over them.

2 And David sent forth a third part of the people under the hand of Jō'ăb, and a third part under the hand of A-bī'shaī the son of Zer-ū-i'ah, Jō'ăb's brother, and a third part under the hand of Ĭt'ta-ī the Gĭt'tīte, And the king said unto the

24-29. David then set up his camp at **Mahanaim.** The Hebrew word means "dual camps." The place was so named by Jacob in Genesis 32:2 because an additional army or camp of God's supernatural angels met him there. Here David was again assisted by three generous supporters, **Shobi . . . Machir . . . and Barzillai,** who provided supplies for the entire camp. These men were thus serving the Lord by being kind and helpful to David.

18:1-8. And David numbered (Heb *paqad*); a better translation would be "mustered." David sent out his army under the three leaders Joab, Abishai, and Ittai. David himself stayed in the city at the request of the people. **Thou art worth ten thousand of us.** David, as the king, was the one they were after; and even if Absalom's men could kill thousands, they would still be after one man: David. **Deal gently for my sake with the young man, even with Absalom.** Absalom was still David's son, and David was still concerned for his well-being. **There was there a great slaughter that day of twenty thousand men.**

people, I will surely go forth with you myself also.

3 But the people answered, Thou shalt not go forth: for if we flee away, they will not care for us; neither if half of us die, will they care for us: but now *thou art* worth ten thousand of us: therefore now *it is* better that thou succour us out of the city.

4 And the king said unto them, What seemeth you best I will do. And the king stood by the gate side, and all the people came out by hundreds and by thousands.

5 And the king commanded Jō'ăb and A-bĭ'shaī and Ĭt'ta-ī, saying, *Deal* gently for my sake with the young man, *even* with Ăb'sa-lom. And all the people heard when the king gave all the captains charge concerning Ăb'sa-lom.

6 ¶So the people went out into the field against Israel: and the battle was in the wood of Ē'phra-im;

7 Where the people of Israel were slain before the servants of David, and there was there a great slaughter that day of twenty thousand *men*.

8 For the battle was there scattered over the face of all the country: and the wood devoured more people that day than the sword devoured.

9 ¶And Ăb'sa-lom met the servants of David. And Ăb'sa-lom rode upon a mule, and the mule went under the thick boughs of a great oak, and his head caught hold of the oak, and he was taken up between the heaven and the earth; and the mule that *was* under him went away.

10 And a certain man saw *it*, and told Jō'ăb, and said, Behold, I saw Ăb'sa-lom hanged in an oak.

11 And Jō'ăb said unto the man that told him, And, behold, thou sawest *him*, and why didst thou not smite him there to the ground? and I would have given thee ten *shekels* of silver, and a girdle.

12 And the man said unto Jō'ăb, Though I should receive a thousand *shekels* of silver in mine hand, *yet* would I not put forth mine hand against the king's son: for in our hearing the king charged thee and A-bĭ'shaī and Ĭt'ta-ī, saying, Beware that none *touch* the young man Ăb'sa-lom.

13 Otherwise I should have wrought falsehood against mine own life: for there is no matter hid from the king, and thou thyself wouldest have set thyself against *me*.

14 Then said Jō'ăb, I may not tarry thus with thee. And he took three darts in his hand, and thrust them through the heart of Ăb'sa-lom, while he *was* yet alive in the midst of the oak.

15 And ten young men that bare Jō'ăb's armour compassed about and smote Ăb'sa-lom, and slew him.

16 And Jō'ăb blew the trumpet, and the people returned from pursuing after Israel: for Jō'ăb held back the people.

17 And they took Ăb'sa-lom, and cast him into a great pit in the wood, and laid a very great heap of stones upon him: and all Israel fled every one to his tent.

Because all of David's men were faithful to him, Absalom's army was full of men who were inexperienced in battle. **The wood devoured more,** that is, a great number of people were killed in trying to escape through the tangled brush of the woods. Absalom himself was killed in this way.

9-18. The death of **Absalom,** although it might appear to the casual reader to be accidental, is presented by the writer of Samuel as the wrath and vengeance of God. God does not depend on even the superior military strategy of David's men; He is able to use a **mule** and an **oak** (literally, "terebinth"). The oak caught **Absalom** by the head and held him, while the **mule** passed on. It remained only for Joab to execute him. **And they took Absalom, and cast him into a great pit in the wood.** This was the unceremonious burial place of **Absalom. Absalom in his lifetime had taken and reared up for himself a pillar** as a memorial burial place so that all would remember his greatness and his name, but in his death he was humiliated and robbed of the glory he had planned.

18 ¶Now Ăb'sa-lom in his lifetime had taken and reared up for himself a pillar, which *is* in the king's dale: for he said, I have no son to keep my name in remembrance: and he called the pillar after his own name: and it is called unto this day, Ăb'sa-lom's place.

19 ¶Then said A-hĭm'ă-az the son of Zā'dŏk, Let me now run, and bear the king tidings, how that the LORD hath avenged him of his enemies.

20 And Jō'ăb said unto him, Thou shalt not bear tidings this day, but thou shalt bear tidings another day: but this day thou shalt bear no tidings, because the king's son is dead.

21 Then said Jō'ăb to Cū'shī, Go tell the king what thou hast seen. And Cū'shī bowed himself unto Jō'ăb, and ran.

22 Then said A-hĭm'ă-az the son of Zā'dŏk yet again to Jō'ăb, But howsoever, let me, I pray thee, also run after Cū'shī. And Jō'ăb said, Wherefore wilt thou run, my son, seeing that thou hast no tidings ready?

23 But howsoever, *said he,* let me run. And he said unto him, Run. Then A-hĭm'ă-az ran by the way of the plain, and overran Cū'shī.

24 And David sat between the two gates: and the watchman went up to the roof over the gate unto the wall, and lifted up his eyes, and looked, and behold a man running alone.

25 And the watchman cried, and told the king. And the king said, If he *be* alone, *there is* tidings in his mouth. And he came apace, and drew near.

26 And the watchman saw another man running: and the watchman called unto the porter, and said, Behold *another* man running alone. And the king said, He also bringeth tidings.

27 And the watchman said, Me thinketh the running of the foremost is like the running of A-hĭm'ă-az the son of Zā'dŏk. And the king said, He *is* a good man, and cometh with good tidings.

28 And A-hĭm'ă-az called, and said unto the king, All is well. And he fell down to the earth upon his face before the king, and said, Blessed *be* the LORD thy God, which hath delivered up the men that lifted up their hand against my lord the king.

29 And the king said, Is the young man Ăb'sa-lom safe? And A-hĭm'ă-az answered, When Jō'ăb sent the king's servant, and *me* thy servant, I saw a great tumult, but I knew not what *it* was.

30 And the king said *unto him,* Turn aside, *and* stand here. And he turned aside, and stood still.

31 And, behold, Cū'shī came; and Cū'shī said, Tidings, my lord the king: for the LORD hath avenged thee this day of all them that rose up against thee.

32 And the king said unto Cū'shī, *Is* the young man Ăb'sa-lom safe? And Cū'shī answered, The enemies of my lord the king, and all that rise up against thee to do *thee* hurt, be as *that* young man *is.*

33 ¶And the king was much moved, and went up to the chamber over the gate, and wept: and as he went, thus he said, O my son Ăb'sa-lom, my son, my

19-28. The LORD hath avenged him (Heb *shapat,* "judged") **of his enemies.** The meaning is that David had been proven as the Lord's anointed king, and the usurper had been put down. It is more than deliverance from danger, or even mere victory. **Joab** assigned the unpleasant task of telling the king about Absalom to **Cushi** (literally, a Cushite slave). **Ahimaaz** outran the slave by taking a longer but more level route. **All is well.** This is one word in the original, "Peace!" (Heb *shalôm*). The same greeting is used in Israel to this day. **Ahimaaz** was a priest, and his news is interpreted by his theology; the news is good because God has **delivered** (Heb *sagar,* "close, abandon to") **up the men.** The idea is that God had been the real agent in closing David's hand upon his enemies. In the report of **Ahimaaz,** all the praise was to go to the Lord.

29-33. Is the young man Absalom safe? There is a play upon the word "peace" here. The Hebrew word was introduced with the greeting of Ahimaaz, and now David uses the same word. "Is there peace to the young man Absalom?" To understand the pathos of the question, one must know that the same word "peace" is a part of the name of Absalom. David repeats the same question to the Cushite slave in exactly the same words, with the same play upon the word "peace," even though the Cushite did not use the word in his greeting. **O my son Absalom, my son, my son Absalom!** David's cry comes from a truly broken heart. He realizes that this is part of the judgment of God for his own sin, and his parental love would have preferred his own death to that of his son.

son Ăb'sa-lom! would God I had died for thee, O Ăb'sa-lom, my son, my son!

CHAPTER 19

AND it was told Jŏ'ăb, Behold, the king weepeth and mourneth for Ăb'sa-lom.

2 And the victory that day was *turned* into mourning unto all the people: for the people heard say that day how the king was grieved for his son.

3 And the people gat them by stealth that day into the city, as people being ashamed steal away when they flee in battle.

4 But the king covered his face, and the king cried with a loud voice, O my son Ăb'sa-lom, O Ăb'sa-lom, my son, my son!

5 And Jŏ'ăb came into the house to the king, and said, Thou hast shamed this day the faces of all thy servants, which this day have saved thy life, and the lives of thy sons and of thy daughters, and the lives of thy wives, and the lives of thy concubines;

6 In that thou lovest thine enemies, and hatest thy friends. For thou hast declared this day, that thou regardest neither princes nor servants: for this day I perceive, that if Ăb'sa-lom had lived, and all we had died this day, then it had pleased thee well.

7 Now therefore arise, go forth, and speak comfortably unto thy servants: for I swear by the Lord, if thou go not forth, there will not tarry one with thee this night: and that will be worse unto thee than all the evil that befell thee from thy youth until now.

8 Then the king arose, and sat in the gate. And they told unto all the people, saying, Behold, the king doth sit in the gate. And all the people came before the king: for Israel had fled every man to his tent.

9 ¶And all the people were at strife throughout all the tribes of Israel, saying, The king saved us out of the hand of our enemies, and he delivered us out of the hand of the Philistines; and now he is fled out of the land for Ăb'sa-lom.

10 And Ăb'sa-lom, whom we anointed over us, is dead in battle. Now therefore why speak ye not a word of bringing the king back?

11 ¶And king David sent to Zā'dŏk and to Ā-bī'a-thar the priests, saying, Speak unto the elders of Jūdah, saying, Why are ye the last to bring the king back to his house? seeing the speech of all Israel is come to the king, *even* to his house.

12 Ye *are* my brethren, ye *are* my bones and my flesh: wherefore then are ye the last to bring back the king?

13 And say ye to Am'ā-sa, *Art* thou not of my bone, and of my flesh? God do so to me, and more also, if thou be not captain of the host before me continually in the room of Jŏ'ăb.

14 And he bowed the heart of all the men of Jūdah, even as *the heart of* one man; so that they sent *this word* unto the king, Return thou, and all thy servants.

III. GOD'S RESTORATION OF DAVID TO POWER.
19:1-24:25.

A. David's Return to Jerusalem and His Kingdom.
19:1-20:26.

19:1-8. The king weepeth and mourneth for Absalom. David's deep grief was not shared by **Joab** who was more politically minded. **Victory that day was turned into mourning.** This should have been a time of great joy since God had delivered His people once again. The people were sympathetic to David and his personal loss, however, and did not dare to celebrate the victory. **Thou lovest thine enemies, and hatest thy friends.** This was not true; but at the moment David's love for his son was being expressed in grief, and the love he had for his friends was not visible. Compare the saying of Jesus, "If any man come to me, and hate not his father . . . he cannot be my disciple" (Lk 14:26). David's grief for Absalom was so intense that it seemed as if he did not appreciate the victory, and so for the sake of political strategy he was urged to sit in the gate. **All the people came before the king.** The people here are those who had remained loyal to David; all the others **fled.**

9-15. The king saved us out of the hand of our enemies, and he delivered us out of the hand of the Philistines. Again redemptive language is used. The first word **saved** (Heb *natsal*), means to "rescue from danger just in time"; the second, **delivered** (Heb *malat*), is a more general word and not as significant. David had been anointed by God for the purpose of saving the people and had been successful in accomplishing it, and the people now realized that he was absent. **Why speak ye not a word of bringing the king back?** It was Israel (not Judah), or the rest of the tribes, which first realized the mistake and moved for restoring David to power. **Why are ye the last to bring the king back to his house?** It should be remembered that a great number of the people of Judah would have been with David; the rest would have been reluctant because they had supported Absalom more avidly than the other tribes. **Return thou.** Once David had sent the message, it quickly convinced the people of Judah; and the vote was unanimous. David came back to the royal city, and Jerusalem again became the city of David.

15 So the king returned, and came to Jordan. And Jūdah came to Gilgal, to go to meet the king, to conduct the king over Jordan.

16 ¶And Shĭm′e-ī the son of Ge′ra, a Benjamite, which *was* of Ba-hū′rĭm, hasted and came down with the men of Jūdah to meet king David.

17 And *there were* a thousand men of Benjamin with him, and Zī′ba the servant of the house of Saul, and his fifteen sons and his twenty servants with him; and they went over Jordan before the king.

18 And there went over a ferry boat to carry over the king's household, and to do what he thought good. And Shĭm′e-ī the son of Ge′ra fell down before the king, as he was come over Jordan;

19 And said unto the king, Let not my lord impute iniquity unto me, neither do thou remember that which thy servant did perversely the day that my lord the king went out of Jerusalem, that the king should take it to his heart.

20 For thy servant doth know that I have sinned: therefore, behold, I am come the first this day of all the house of Joseph to go down to meet my lord the king.

21 But A-bī′shaī the son of Zer-ū-i′ah answered and said, Shall not Shĭm′e-ī be put to death for this, because he cursed the LORD's anointed?

22 And David said, What have I to do with you, ye sons of Zer-ū-i′ah, that ye should this day be adversaries unto me? shall there any man be put to death this day in Israel? for do not I know that I *am* this day king over Israel?

23 Therefore the king said unto Shĭm′e-ī, Thou shalt not die. And the king sware unto him.

24 ¶And Me-phĭb′o-shĕth the son of Saul came down to meet the king, and had neither dressed his feet, nor trimmed his beard, nor washed his clothes, from the day the king departed until the day he came *again* in peace.

25 And it came to pass, when he was come to Jerusalem to meet the king, that the king said unto him, Wherefore wentest not thou with me, Me-phĭb′o-shĕth?

26 And he answered, My lord, O king, my servant deceived me: for thy servant said, I will saddle me an ass, that I may ride thereon, and go to the king; because thy servant *is* lame.

27 And he hath slandered thy servant unto my lord the king; but my lord the king *is* as an angel of God: do therefore *what is* good in thine eyes.

28 For all *of* my father's house were but dead men before my lord the king: yet didst thou set thy servant among them that did eat at thine own table. What right therefore have I yet to cry any more unto the king?

29 And the king said unto him, Why speakest thou any more of thy matters? I have said, Thou and Zī′ba divide the land.

30 And Me-phĭb′o-shĕth said unto the king, Yea, let him take all, forasmuch as my lord the king is come again in peace unto his own house.

16-43. Shimei . . . came down with the men of Judah to meet king David. The reason **Shimei** rushed down to the Jordan was obviously to try to save his own neck. His repentance seems shallow and can hardly be genuine, but David accepted it and promised that he would not be killed. **Mephibosheth the son of Saul came down to meet the king.** He explained that he would have gone out of Jerusalem with David but had been tricked by Ziba his servant. David did not seem to know how to decide the case, but preferred to have the property divided between Mephibosheth and Ziba equally. **Barzillai the Gileadite** also came to escort David over the **Jordan.** His kindnesses in supporting the kingdom at **Mahanaim** were greatly appreciated by David who offered to repay them in Jerusalem. Barzillai preferred to return to his native home for the remaining years of his life so he might die near **the grave** of his parents.

31 ¶And Bär-zĭl'la-ī the Gīleadīte
came down from Rō-ge'lĭm, and went
over Jordan with the king, to conduct
him over Jordan.

32 Now Bär-zĭl'la-ī was a very aged
man, *even* fourscore years old: and he
had provided the king of sustenance
while he lay at Mā-ha-nā'im; for he *was*
a very great man.

33 And the king said unto Bär-zĭl'la-ī,
Come thou over with me, and I will
feed thee with me in Jerusalem.

34 And Bär-zĭl'la-ī said unto the king,
How long have I to live, that I should go
up with the king unto Jerusalem?

35 I *am* this day fourscore years old:
and can I discern between good and
evil? can thy servant taste what I eat or
what I drink? can I hear any more the
voice of singing men and singing wom-
en? wherefore then should thy servant be yet a burden unto my lord the
king?

36 Thy servant will go a little way
over Jordan with the king: and why
should the king recompense it me with
such a reward?

37 Let thy servant, I pray thee, turn
back again, that I may die in mine own
city, *and be buried* by the grave of my
father and of my mother. But behold
thy servant Chĭm'hăm; let him go over
with my lord the king; and do to him
what shall seem good unto thee.

38 And the king answered, Chĭm'-
hăm shall go over with me, and I will
do to him that which shall seem good
unto thee: and whatsoever thou shalt
require of me, *that* will I do for thee.

39 And all the people went over Jordan. And when the king was come
over, the king kissed Bär-zĭl'la-ī, and
blessed him; and he returned unto his
own place.

40 Then the king went on to Gilgal,
and Chĭm'hăm went on with him: and
all the people of Jūdah conducted the
king, and also half the people of Israel.

41 ¶And, behold, all the men of Israel
came to the king, and said unto the
king, Why have our brethren the men
of Jūdah stolen thee away, and have
brought the king, and his household,
and all David's men with him, over Jordan?

42 And all the men of Jūdah answered the men of Israel, Because the
king *is* near of kin to us: wherefore then
be ye angry for this matter? have we
eaten at all of the king's *cost?* or hath he
given us any gift?

43 And the men of Israel answered
the men of Jūdah, and said, We have
ten parts in the king, and we have also
more *right* in David than ye: why then
did ye despise us, that our advice
should not be first had in bringing back
our king? And the words of the men of
Jūdah were fiercer than the words of
the men of Israel.

CHAPTER 20

AND there happened to be there a man
of Bē'lī-al, whose name *was* Shē'ba, the
son of Bĭch'rī, a Benjamite: and he blew
a trumpet, and said, We have no part in
David, neither have we inheritance in

20:1-3. Another who came to meet David was **a man of
Belial.** The expression means, literally, "a worthless person."
Sheba . . . blew a trumpet. This was a means of getting the
public attention, and the purpose here was to establish himself
as the leader of a revolution. This is the first open revolt of the

the son of Jesse: every man to his tents, O Israel.

2 So every man of Israel went up from after David, *and* followed Shē'ba the son of Bĭch'rĭ: but the men of Jūdah clave unto their king, from Jordan even to Jerusalem.

3 ¶And David came to his house at Jerusalem; and the king took the ten women *his* concubines, whom he had left to keep the house, and put them in ward, and fed them, but went not in unto them. So they were shut up unto the day of their death, living in widowhood.

4 ¶Then said the king to Am'ā-sa, Assemble me the men of Jūdah within three days, and be thou here present.

5 So Am'ā-sa went to assemble *the men of* Jūdah: but he tarried longer than the set time which he had appointed him.

6 And David said to A-bī'shaī, Now shall Shē'ba the son of Bĭch'rĭ do us more harm than *did* Āb'sa-lom: take thou thy lord's servants, and pursue after him, lest he get him fenced cities, and escape us.

7 And there went out after him Jō'āb's men, and the Chĕr'e-thītes, and the Pĕl'e-thītes, and all the mighty men: and they went out of Jerusalem, to pursue after Shē'ba the son of Bĭch'rĭ.

8 When they *were* at the great stone which *is* in Gĭbeon, Am'ā-sa went before them. And Jō'āb's garment that he had put on was girded unto him, and upon it a girdle *with* a sword fastened upon his loins in the sheath thereof; and as he went forth it fell out.

9 And Jō'āb said to Am'ā-sa, *Art* thou in health, my brother? And Jō'āb took Am'ā-sa by the beard with the right hand to kiss him.

10 But Am'ā-sa took no heed to the sword that *was* in Jō'āb's hand: so he smote him therewith in the fifth *rib*, and shed out his bowels to the ground, and struck him not again; and he died. So Jō'āb and A-bī'shaī his brother pursued after Shē'ba the son of Bĭch'rĭ.

11 And one of Jō'āb's men stood by him, and said, He that favoureth Jō'āb, and he that *is* for David, *let him go* after Jō'āb.

12 And Am'ā-sa wallowed in blood in the midst of the highway. And when the man saw that all the people stood still, he removed Am'ā-sa out of the highway into the field, and cast a cloth upon him, when he saw that every one that came by him stood still.

13 When he was removed out of the highway, all the people went on after Jō'āb, to pursue after Shē'ba the son of Bĭch'rĭ.

14 ¶And he went through all the tribes of Israel unto Abel, and to Bĕth-mā'a-chah, and all the Bē'rītes: and they were gathered together, and went also after him.

15 And they came and besieged him in Abel of Bĕth-mā'a-chah, and they cast up a bank against the city, and it stood in the trench: and all the people that *were* with Jō'āb battered the wall, to throw it down.

16 ¶Then cried a wise woman out of

tribes of **Israel** from **Judah,** which went on up to Jerusalem with David.

4-13. David asked **Amasa** to **Assemble . . . the men of Judah** and prepare for putting down the revolt of Sheba within a certain time. When that time had expired, Amasa did not show; and **Abishai** was sent instead with all the men of the army including Joab. When the group came to Gibeon, they met Amasa; and Joab took the opportunity to murder the mistrusted successor to his position. They left **Amasa** to wallow in his own **blood in the midst of the highway** and went on in pursuit of Sheba.

14-26. Sheba did finally enter into a walled city at **Abel . . . Beth-maachah.** This city was located in the extreme northern part of Israel near Dan. Here **Joab** attempted to batter down the wall. During the siege a woman of wisdom bargained with Joab for the preservation of the city. Joab spared the city for **the head of Sheba.** Once **Sheba** had been killed, the siege was called off; and the army went back **to Jerusalem.** A list of David's officers is given in verses 23-26.

the city, Hear, hear; say, I pray you, unto Jō′ăb, Come near hither, that I may speak with thee.

17 And when he was come near unto her, the woman said, Art thou Jō′ăb? And he answered, I am he. Then she said unto him, Hear the words of thine handmaid. And he answered, I do hear.

18 Then she spake, saying, They were wont to speak in old time, saying, They shall surely ask counsel at Abel: and so they ended the matter.

19 I am one of them that are peaceable and faithful in Israel: thou seekest to destroy a city and a mother in Israel: why wilt thou swallow up the inheritance of the LORD?

20 And Jō′ăb answered and said, Far be it, far be it from me, that I should swallow up or destroy.

21 The matter is not so: but a man of mount Ē′phra-im, Shē′ba the son of Bĭch′rĭ by name, hath lifted up his hand against the king, even against David: deliver him only, and I will depart from the city. And the woman said unto Jō′ăb, Behold, his head shall be thrown to thee over the wall.

22 Then the woman went unto all the people in her wisdom. And they cut off the head of Shē′ba the son of Bĭch′rĭ, and cast it out to Jō′ăb. And he blew a trumpet, and they retired from the city, every man to his tent. And Jō′ăb returned to Jerusalem unto the king.

23 ¶Now Jō′ăb was over all the host of Israel: and Be-nā′iah the son of Je-hoi′a-da was over the Chĕr′e-thītes and over the Pĕl′e-thītes:

24 And Ă-dō′ram was over the tribute: and Je-hŏsh′a-phăt the son of A-hī′lud was recorder:

25 And Shē′va was scribe: and Zā′-dŏk and Ă-bī′a-thar were the priests:

26 And Īra also the Jā′ir-īte was a chief ruler about David.

CHAPTER 21

THEN there was a famine in the days of David three years, year after year; and David enquired of the LORD. And the LORD answered, It is for Saul, and for his bloody house, because he slew the Gĭb′e-o-nītes.

2 And the king called the Gĭb′e-o-nītes, and said unto them; (now the Gĭb′e-o-nītes were not of the children of Israel, but of the remnant of the Ămor-ītes; and the children of Israel had sworn unto them: and Saul sought to slay them in his zeal to the children of Israel and Jūdah.)

3 Wherefore David said unto the Gĭb′e-o-nītes, What shall I do for you? and wherewith shall I make the atonement, that ye may bless the inheritance of the LORD?

4 And the Gĭb′e-o-nītes said unto him, We will have no silver nor gold of Saul, nor of his house; neither for us shalt thou kill any man in Israel. And he said, What ye shall say, that will I do for you.

5 And they answered the king, The man that consumed us, and that devised against us that we should be de-

B. The Later Years of David's Rule. 21:1-24:25.

21:1-5. Then there was a famine in the days of David. There is no indication of the time of the **famine**; the events of these last chapters do not necessarily follow chronologically. **David inquired of the LORD.** He was searching for the reason for the three years of famine. The reply indicated that Saul had killed the Gibeonites and thus broken the treaty. **What shall I do for you?** This is not something to be done at the demand of the Gibeonites, rather because God has shown His displeasure. **That ye may bless the inheritance of the LORD.** The **inheritance** (Heb nachelah) is a significant theological term referring to the people of the Lord in both the Old and New Testaments.

stroyed from remaining in any of the coasts of Israel,

6 Let seven men of his sons be delivered unto us, and we will hang them up unto the LORD in Gĭb′e-ah of Saul, *whom* the LORD did choose. And the king said, I will give *them*.

7 But the king spared Me-phĭb′o-shĕth, the son of Jonathan the son of Saul, because of the LORD's oath that *was* between them, between David and Jonathan the son of Saul.

8 But the king took the two sons of Rĭz′pah the daughter of Ă-ī′ah, whom she bare unto Saul, Ăr-mō′nī and Me-phĭb′o-shĕth; and the five sons of Mī′-chal the daughter of Saul, whom she brought up for Ā′drĭ-el the son of Bär-zĭl′la-ī the Me-hōl′ath-īte:

9 And he delivered them into the hands of the Gĭb′e-o-nītes and they hanged them in the hill before the LORD: and they fell *all* seven together, and were put to death in the days of harvest, in the first *days*, in the beginning of barley harvest.

10 ¶And Rĭz′pah the daughter of Ă-ī′ah took sackcloth, and spread it for her upon the rock, from the beginning of harvest until water dropped upon them out of heaven, and suffered neither the birds of the air to rest on them by day, nor the beasts of the field by night.

11 And it was told David what Rĭz′-pah the daughter of Ă-ī′ah, the concubine of Saul, had done.

12 And David went and took the bones of Saul and the bones of Jonathan his son from the men of Jă′-besh-gĭl′e-ad, which had stolen them from the street of Bĕth′-shăn, where the Philistines had hanged them, when the Philistines had slain Saul in Gĭl-bō′a:

13 And he brought up from thence the bones of Saul and the bones of Jonathan his son; and they gathered the bones of them that were hanged.

14 And the bones of Saul and Jonathan his son buried they in the country of Benjamin in Zē′lah, in the sepulchre of Kish his father: and they performed all that the king commanded. And after that God was intreated for the land.

15 ¶Moreover the Philistines had yet war again with Israel; and David went down, and his servants with him, and fought against the Philistines: and David waxed faint.

16 And Ĭsh′bĭ-bē′nŏb, which *was* of the sons of the giant, the weight of whose spear *weighed* three hundred *shekels* of brass in weight, he being girded with a new *sword*, thought to have slain David.

17 But A-bĭ′shaī the son of Zer-ū-i′ah succoured him, and smote the Philistine, and killed him. Then the men of David sware unto him, saying, Thou shalt go no more out with us to battle, that thou quench not the light of Israel.

18 And it came to pass after this, that there was again a battle with the Philistines at Gob: then Sĭb′be-chaī the Hu′shath-īte slew Saph, which *was* of the sons of the giant.

6-9. Seven men of his sons. These descendants of Saul were to be destroyed by the Gibeonites and were thus the ransom for the deliverance of the whole nation of Israel from the famine. **Whom the LORD did choose.** There is uncertainty in the Hebrew text, but the AV reading is supported by the Septuagint. One conjecture reads (with one different letter which looks almost identical), "that we may hang them up . . . on the mountain of the LORD." The meaning of the AV is that the seven men who were to die would be chosen by the Lord. At any rate, David decided to give the men up to the Gibeonites. **The king spared Mephibosheth.** This was to show love to the memory of **Jonathan. Hanged them in the hill before the LORD.** This supports the conjecture in verse 6, since the words would then correspond exactly.

10-14. The kindness of **Rizpah** toward the seven dead victims evidently stirred David's heart for Saul and Jonathan. He **took the bones of Saul and . . . Jonathan** and buried them along with the bodies of the seven in Saul's father's burial place. **God was entreated for the land.** The word **entreated** (Heb *'atar*) refers to prayer in the sense of supplications made to the Lord after His demands have been met. Again in this passage we are taught that obedience must come before prayer, and prayer without obedience is mere hypocrisy.

15-22. The list of heroic deeds must have a common source which preserved the records of encounters with freak Philistine giants. All these who were killed by the heroes were **of the sons of the giant** (Heb *rapah*), which may be a proper name for a common ancestor of a race of giants (cf. Gen 6:4; Num 13:33; Deut 9:2; Josh 15:13). **Elhanan . . . slew the brother of Goliath the Gittite.** Neither the Hebrew text nor the Septuagint translation of it has the addition of **the brother of** which is found in the AV. The harmonization of this text with I Chronicles 20:5 is necessary, however, unless there were two Goliaths of Gath, one killed by David and the other by Elhanan.

19 And there was again a battle in Gob with the Philistines, where Ĕl-hā′-nan the son of Jā-ar′e-ôr′e-ğĭm, a Bĕth-lehĕmīte, slew *the brother of* Go-lī′ath the Gĭt′tīte, the staff of whose spear *was* like a weaver's beam.

20 And there was yet a battle in Gath, where was a man of *great* stature, that had on every hand six fingers, and on every foot six toes, four and twenty in number; and he also was born to the giant.

21 And when he defied Israel, Jona-than the son of Shĭm′e-ah the brother of David slew him.

22 These four were born to the giant in Gath, and fell by the hand of David, and by the hand of his servants.

CHAPTER 22

AND David spake unto the LORD the words of this song in the day *that* the LORD had delivered him out of the hand of all his enemies, and out of the hand of Saul:

2 And he said, The LORD *is* my rock, and my fortress, and my deliverer;

3 The God of my rock; in him will I trust: *he is* my shield, and the horn of my salvation, my high tower, and my refuge, my saviour; thou savest me from violence.

4 I will call on the LORD, *who is* worthy to be praised: so shall I be saved from mine enemies.

5 When the waves of death com-passed me, the floods of ungodly men made me afraid;

6 The sorrows of hell compassed me about; the snares of death prevented me;

7 In my distress I called upon the LORD, and cried to my God: and he did hear my voice out of his temple, and my cry *did enter* into his ears.

8 Then the earth shook and trembled; the foundations of heaven moved and shook, because he was wroth.

9 There went up a smoke out of his nostrils, and fire out of his mouth de-voured: coals were kindled by it.

10 He bowed the heavens also, and came down; and darkness *was* under his feet.

11 And he rode upon a cherub, and did fly: and he was seen upon the wings of the wind.

12 And he made darkness pavilions round about him, dark waters, *and* thick clouds of the skies.

13 Through the brightness before him were coals of fire kindled.

14 The LORD thundered from heaven, and the most High uttered his voice.

15 And he sent out arrows, and scat-tered them; lightning, and discomfited them.

16 And the channels of the sea ap-peared, the foundations of the world were discovered, at the rebuking of the LORD, at the blast of the breath of his nostrils.

17 He sent from above, he took me; he drew me out of many waters;

18 He delivered me from my strong enemy, *and* from them that hated me: for they were too strong for me.

19 They prevented me in the day of

22:1-51. David spake unto the LORD the words of this song. This psalm was written by David early in his reign. It occurs also in the biblical book of Psalms (Ps 18) with only very minor variations. It is indeed a **song,** and it is addressed to the LORD his God in worship and praise for deliverance (Heb *natsal,* "rescue") from **Saul,** his most evil personal enemy, as well as the enemies of the Lord's people. The word **delivered** is used three times in the chapter (22;1, 18, 49) and expresses the theme that Yahweh was always there to rescue David just when he most needed the help. The vivid pictures of protection and deliverance from danger are drawn mainly from David's life in the wilderness. God is like a **fortress** (vs. 2), a **rock** (vs. 3) and a **shield** (vs. 3), etc.

My rock; in him will I trust (vs. 3). This clause is quoted in Hebrews 2:13 as coming from the mouth of Jesus Christ, that greater Son of David. Christ Himself, like David, put Himself completely in the hands of God in order to accomplish the salvation of God's people. The writer of Hebrews quotes from the Septuagint version of the Old Testament and uses the same Greek words.

Besides deliverance, **salvation** (Heb *yesha‘*) is another synonym expressing the major theme of the psalm. It occurs twice as a verb (vss. 3, 28), and three times as a noun (vss. 3, 36, 47). **I will give thanks unto thee, O LORD, among the heathen** (vs. 50). Paul the Apostle quotes this verse in Romans 15:9 as applying to the work of Christ in accomplishing the salvation of the Gentiles. Paul also uses the words of the Septuagint transla-tion of the Old Testament for his quotation and once again confirms the fact that David is looked upon as a type of Christ. **His anointed** (vs. 51). The primary reference here is to David, who had been chosen and established as God's king. There is, however, a secondary and typical reference to Jesus Christ as the eternal descendant of David who is elsewhere called the Beloved One, the Anointed One, and God's chosen King.

my calamity: but the LORD was my stay.

20 He brought me forth also into a large place: he delivered me, because he delighted in me.

21 The LORD rewarded me according to my righteousness: according to the cleanness of my hands hath he recompensed me.

22 For I have kept the ways of the LORD, and have not wickedly departed from my God.

23 For all his judgments were before me: and as for his statutes, I did not depart from them.

24 I was also upright before him, and have kept myself from mine iniquity.

25 Therefore the LORD hath recompensed me according to my righteousness; according to my cleanness in his eye sight.

26 With the merciful thou wilt shew thyself merciful, and with the upright man thou wilt shew thyself upright.

27 With the pure thou wilt shew thyself pure; and with the froward thou wilt shew thyself unsavoury.

28 And the afflicted people thou wilt save: but thine eyes are upon the haughty, that thou mayest bring them down.

29 For thou art my lamp, O LORD; and the LORD will lighten my darkness.

30 For by thee I have run through a troop: by my God have I leaped over a wall.

31 As for God, his way is perfect; the word of the LORD is tried: he is a buckler to all them that trust in him.

32 For who is God, save the LORD? and who is a rock, save our God?

33 God is my strength and power: and he maketh my way perfect.

34 He maketh my feet like hinds' feet: and setteth me upon my high places.

35 He teacheth my hands to war; so that a bow of steel is broken by mine arms.

36 Thou hast also given me the shield of thy salvation: and thy gentleness hath made me great.

37 Thou hast enlarged my steps under me; so that my feet did not slip.

38 I have pursued mine enemies, and destroyed them; and turned not again until I had consumed them.

39 And I have consumed them, and wounded them, that they could not arise: yea, they are fallen under my feet.

40 For thou hast girded me with strength to battle: them that rose up against me hast thou subdued under me.

41 Thou hast also given me the necks of mine enemies, that I might destroy them that hate me.

42 They looked, but there was none to save; even unto the LORD, but he answered them not.

43 Then did I beat them as small as the dust of the earth, I did stamp them as the mire of the street, and did spread them abroad.

44 Thou also hast delivered me from the strivings of my people, thou hast kept me to be head of the heathen: a

people *which* I knew not shall serve me.

45 Strangers shall submit themselves unto me: as soon as they hear, they shall be obedient unto me.

46 Strangers shall fade away, and they shall be afraid out of their close places.

47 The LORD liveth; and blessed *be* my rock; and exalted be the God of the rock of my salvation.

48 It *is* God that avengeth me, and that bringeth down the people under me,

49 And that bringeth me forth from mine enemies: thou also hast lifted me up on high above them that rose up against me: thou hast delivered me from the violent man.

50 Therefore I will give thanks unto thee, O LORD, among the heathen, and I will sing praises unto thy name.

51 *He is* the tower of salvation for his king: and sheweth mercy to his anointed, unto David, and to his seed for evermore.

CHAPTER 23

NOW these *be* the last words of David. David the son of Jesse said, and the man *who was* raised up on high, the anointed of the God of Jacob, and the sweet psalmist of Israel, said,

2 The Spirit of the LORD spake by me, and his word *was* in my tongue.

3 The God of Israel said, the Rock of Israel spake to me, He that ruleth over men *must be* just, ruling in the fear of God.

4 And *he shall be* as the light of the morning, *when* the sun riseth, *even* a morning without clouds; *as* the tender grass *springing* out of the earth by clear shining after rain.

5 Although my house *be* not so with God; yet he hath made with me an everlasting covenant, ordered in all *things*, and sure: for *this is* all my salvation, and all *my* desire, although he make *it* not to grow.

6 But *the sons* of Bĕ'lĭ-al *shall be* all of them as thorns thrust away, because they cannot be taken with hands:

7 But the man *that* shall touch them must be fenced with iron and the staff of a spear; and they shall be utterly burned with fire in the *same* place.

8 ¶These *be* the names of the mighty men whom David had: The Tăch'mo-nīte that sat in the seat, chief among the captains; the same *was* Ăd'ĭ-nō the Ĕz'-nīte: *he lift up his spear* against eight hundred, whom he slew at one time.

9 And after him *was* Ĕ-le-ā'zar the son of Dodo the A-hō'hīte, *one* of the three mighty men with David, when they defied the Philistines *that* were there gathered together to battle, and the men of Israel were gone away:

10 He arose, and smote the Philistines until his hand was weary, and his hand clave unto the sword: and the LORD wrought a great victory that day; and the people returned after him only to spoil.

11 And after him *was* Shăm'mah the son of Ăg'ee the Hă'ra-rīte. And the Philistines were gathered together into

23:1-7. Now these be the last words of David. These may be the last literary or poetic words of David, but the exact significance of **last words** is unknown. **David the son of Jesse said.** The word **said** (Heb *ne'um*, "utterance") is always used with inspired sayings of the prophets and implies here the importance and inspiration of the following song. The anointed again refers to David as the true chosen king. **The Spirit of the LORD spake by me, and his word was in my tongue.** This provides double emphasis upon the inspired character of the song and David's prophetic insight. God's king (and here there is also reference to the future house of David and to Christ as the coming King) **must be just, ruling in the fear of God** (vs. 3) **Although my house be not so with God** (vs. 5). David realized that he had not been perfect, but he fully trusted in God to provide whatever is needed in the future to give rise to a righteous king. **An everlasting covenant.** This is David's hope for the future of his house; it is the ground of his prophetic insight into the future. The covenant is expressed in II Samuel 7:8-16 and in the ultimate sense refers to the Son of David expectation fulfilled in Jesus Christ.

8-39. Records of the heroic deeds of David's most valiant men are listed in these verses. A very similar list is given in I Chronicles 11:11-41. Verse 8 should be made to correspond to I Chronicles 11:11. Two groups of three men with their mighty deeds mentioned appear in the first part of the record. The second part is simply a list of thirty men who were part of the legion of honor. Joab's heroic deeds were probably not mentioned because he was general or leader of the army. Two names appear to be missing from the total of thirty-seven.

a troop, where was a piece of ground full of lentiles: and the people fled from the Philistines.

12 But he stood in the midst of the ground, and defended it, and slew the Philistines: and the LORD wrought a great victory.

13 And three of the thirty chief went down, and came to David in the harvest time unto the cave of Adŭllam: and the troop of the Philistines pitched in the valley of Rĕph'a-im.

14 And David was then in an hold, and the garrison of the Philistines was then in Bĕth-lehĕm.

15 And David longed, and said, Oh that one would give me drink of the water of the well of Bĕth-lehĕm, which is by the gate!

16 And the three mighty men brake through the host of the Philistines, and drew water out of the well of Bĕth-lehĕm, that was by the gate, and took it, and brought it to David: nevertheless he would not drink thereof, but poured it out unto the LORD.

17 And he said, Be it far from me, O LORD, that I should do this: is not this the blood of the men that went in jeopardy of their lives? therefore he would not drink it. These things did these three mighty men.

18 And A-bī'shaī, the brother of Jō'-ăb, the son of Zer-ū-i'ah, was chief among three. And he lifted up his spear against three hundred, and slew them, and had the name among three.

19 Was he not most honourable of three? therefore he was their captain: howbeit he attained not unto the first three.

20 And Be-nā'iah the son of Je-hoi'a-da, the son of a valiant man, of Kăb'ze-el, who had done many acts, he slew two lionlike men of Moab: he went down also and slew a lion in the midst of a pit in time of snow:

21 And he slew an Egyptian, a goodly man: and the Egyptian had a spear in his hand; but he went down to him with a staff, and plucked the spear out of the Egyptian's hand, and slew him with his own spear.

22 These things did Be-nā'iah the son of Je-hoi'a-da, and had the name among three mighty men.

23 He was more honourable than the thirty, but he attained not to the first three. And David set him over his guard.

24 Ā'sa-hĕl the brother of Jō'ăb was one of the thirty; Ĕl-hā'nan the son of Dodo of Bĕth-lehĕm,

25 Shăm'mah the Hâ'rod-īte, E-lī'ka the Hâ'rod-īte,

26 Hĕ'lĕz the Păl'tīte, Ira the son of Ĭk'kesh the Te-kō'īte,

27 Ā-bi-ĕ'zer the Ăn'e-thŏth-īte, Me-bŭn'naī the Hu'shath-īte,

28 Zăl'mon the A-hō'hīte, Mā-har'a-ī the Ne-tōph'a-thīte,

29 Hĕ'lĕb the son of Bā'a-nah, a Ne-tōph'a-thīte, Ĭt'ta-ī the son of Rī'baī out of Gĭb'e-ah of the children of Benjamin,

30 Be-nā'iah the Pĭr'a-thŏn-īte, Hĭd'-da-ī of the brooks of Gā'ash,

31 Ā'bī-ăl'bon the Är'bath-īte, Ăz'ma-vĕth the Bär-hū'mīte,

32 E-lī′ah-ba the Shā-ăl′bo-nīte, of the sons of Jā′shen, Jonathan,

33 Shăm′mah the Hâ′ra-rīte, A-hī′am the son of Shâ′rär the Hâ′ra-rīte,

34 E-līph′e-lĕt the son of A-hăs′ba-ī, the son of the Mā-ăch′a-thīte, E-lī′am the son of A-hīth′o-phĕl the Gī′lo-nīte,

35 Hĕz′ra-ī the Carmelite, Pā′a-raī the Är′bīte,

36 ī′găl the son of Nāthan of Zōbah, Bā′nī the Gădīte,

37 Zē′lĕk the Ammonite, Nā′ha-rī the Bē-ē′rŏth-īte, armourbearer to Jō′ăb the son of Zer-ū-i′ah,

38 īra an īth′rīte, Gâ′rĕb an īth′rīte,

39 Ū-rī′ah the Hittite: thirty and seven in all.

CHAPTER 24

AND again the anger of the LORD was kindled against Israel, and he moved David against them to say, Go, number Israel and Judah.

2 For the king said to Jō′ăb the captain of the host, which was with him, Go now through all the tribes of Israel, from Dan even to Be′er-shē′ba, and number ye the people, that I may know the number of the people.

3 And Jō′ăb said unto the king, Now the LORD thy God add unto the people, how many soever they be, an hundredfold, and that the eyes of my lord the king may see it: but why doth my lord the king delight in this thing?

4 Notwithstanding the king's word prevailed against Jō′ăb, and against the captains of the host. And Jō′ăb and the captains of the host went out from the presence of the king, to number the people of Israel.

5 And they passed over Jordan, and pitched in Ar′ō-er, on the right side of the city that lieth in the midst of the river of Gad, and toward Jā′zer:

6 Then they came to Gilead, and to the land of Tăh′tīm–hŏd′shī; and they came to Dăn–jā′an, and about to Zī′don,

7 And came to the strong hold of Tyre, and to all the cities of the Hī′vītes, and of the Canaanites: and they went out to the south of Jūdah, even to Be′er-shē′ba.

8 So when they had gone through all the land, they came to Jerusalem at the end of nine months and twenty days.

9 And Jō′ăb gave up the sum of the number of the people unto the king: and there were in Israel eight hundred thousand valiant men that drew the sword; and the men of Jūdah were five hundred thousand men.

10 ¶And David's heart smote him after that he had numbered the people. And David said unto the LORD, I have sinned greatly in that I have done: and now, I beseech thee, O LORD, take away the iniquity of thy servant; for I have done very foolishly.

11 For when David was up in the morning, the word of the LORD came unto the prophet Gad, David's seer, saying,

24:1-2. The anger of the LORD was kindled against Israel. The wrath of God at this time was probably not in response to any specific sin, but to another general deterioration of worship in Israel. **He moved David against them to say, Go, number Israel and Judah.** In I Chronicles 21:1 we learn that it was Satan who rose up against Israel and incited David to take the census. From this we should probably assume that God allowed Satan to tempt David into this sin for the purpose of punishing the people. The numbering, or counting, of the people is accepted by David as his own personal sin; it was wrong because it was done in pride and self-glory.

3-8. Why doth my lord the king delight in this thing? On this occasion **Joab** seems to have more spiritual insight than David. He knows that the Lord would give victory no matter how outnumbered Israel's troops were. The census was taken nevertheless because it was the king's command. They counted the fighting men from one end of the land to the other.

9. There were in Israel eight hundred thousand valiant men . . . and the men of Judah were five hundred thousand. These numbers were somewhat different, according to I Chronicles 21:5. This need not imply that one text is wrong, since there may have been elements included in one total that were not included in the other.

10-14. I have sinned greatly. David's repentance was genuine, and he immediately confessed his sin. **The word of the LORD came unto the prophet Gad.** The prophet probably had given some rebuke to David since that was one of the main functions of a prophet in this period. The way in which God revealed Himself to the prophets is unknown, but the same biblical formula is given consistently: **the word of the LORD came.** David was given a choice of punishments that were designed to bring the people back to God. **Let us now fall into the hand of the LORD; for his mercies are great.** David knew

12 Go and say unto David, Thus saith the LORD, I offer thee three *things;* choose thee one of them, that I may *do it* unto thee.

13 So Gad came to David, and told him, and said unto him, Shall seven years of famine come unto thee in thy land? or wilt thou flee three months before thine enemies, while they pursue thee? or that there be three days' pestilence in thy land? now advise, and see what answer I shall return to him that sent me.

14 And David said unto Gad, I am in a great strait: let us fall now into the hand of the LORD; for his mercies *are* great: and let me not fall into the hand of man.

15 ¶So the LORD sent a pestilence upon Israel from the morning even to the time appointed: and there died of the people from Dan even to Be′er-shē′ba seventy thousand men.

16 And when the angel stretched out his hand upon Jerusalem to destroy it, the LORD repented him of the evil, and said to the angel that destroyed the people, It is enough: stay now thine hand. And the angel of the LORD was by the threshingplace of A-rau′nah the Jĕb′u-sīte.

17 And David spake unto the LORD when he saw the angel that smote the people, and said, Lo, I have sinned, and I have done wickedly: but these sheep, what have they done? let thine hand, I pray thee, be against me, and against my father's house.

18 ¶And Gad came that day to David, and said unto him, Go up, rear an altar unto the LORD in the threshingfloor of A-rau′nah the Jĕb′u-sīte.

19 And David, according to the saying of Gad, went up as the LORD commanded.

20 And A-rau′nah looked, and saw the king and his servants coming on toward him: and A-rau′nah went out, and bowed himself before the king on his face upon the ground.

21 And A-rau′nah said, Wherefore is my lord the king come to his servant? And David said, To buy the threshingfloor of thee, to build an altar unto the LORD, that the plague may be stayed from the people.

22 And A-rau′nah said unto David, Let my lord the king take and offer up what *seemeth* good unto him: behold, *here be* oxen for burnt sacrifice, and threshing instruments and *other* instruments of the oxen for wood.

23 All these *things* did A-rau′nah, *as a* king, give unto the king. And A-rau′nah said unto the king, The LORD thy God accept thee.

24 And the king said unto A-rau′nah, Nay; but I will surely buy *it* of thee at a price: neither will I offer burnt offerings unto the LORD my God of that which doth cost me nothing. So David bought the threshingfloor and the oxen for fifty shekels of silver.

25 And David built there an altar unto the LORD, and offered burnt offerings and peace offerings. So the LORD was intreated for the land, and the plague was stayed from Israel.

that he had sinned and the sin must be punished, but he also knew that God is a pardoning and merciful God.

15-17. The LORD sent a pestilence. The exact nature of this plague is unknown; but it was deadly and happened very quickly, resulting in seventy thousand deaths throughout the land. **The angel.** The identity of this particular messenger of God is specified only to the extent that he is the one **that destroyed the people.** In this verse he is also called **the angel of the LORD,** a phrase which often marks a theophany in the Old Testament. That this angel was visible to David is certain from I Chronicles 21:16, and verse 17 here. He saw the angel standing between heaven and earth with a drawn sword. This visible sign would have made it obvious that the plague was a definite punishment from God, and not just a coincidence of nature. **I have sinned . . . but these sheep.** David refers to himself and the people in metaphor; he is the shepherd, and the people are the **sheep.** The same figure is used of Christ and the church in the New Testament.

18-25. Rear an altar unto the LORD. The purpose was to worship with burnt offerings and offerings of supplication in order to turn away the wrath of God and plead His pardon. **The threshing floor of Araunah the Jebusite** was on Mount Moriah in Jerusalem. This later became the site of the Temple (at the time of this sacrifice the tabernacle was at Gibeon) in accordance with the command of God in I Chronicles 22:1. **All these things did Araunah, as a king, give unto the king.** Araunah was not a king, but rather, one of the ancient Jebusite inhabitants of the city of Jerusalem. A better translation would be, "all this, O king, Araunah gives to the king." **Neither will I offer burnt offerings unto the LORD my God of that which doth cost me nothing.** David would not accept the generosity of Araunah; it would not then have been an offering by David. David's statement has expressed the biblical principle that God puts a higher value on sacrificial offerings than on their monetary value. **So the LORD was entreated.** After the sacrifices on the newly constructed altar God answered the supplications and stopped the destruction of the **plague.**

BIBLIOGRAPHY

Black, Matthew and H. H. Rowley, eds. *Peake's Commentary on the Bible*. London: Thomas Nelson and Sons, Ltd., 1962.

Buttrick, George Arthur, et al., eds. *The Interpreter's Dictionary of the Bible*. 4 vols. New York: Abingdon Press, 1962.

. Caird, George B. The First and Second Books of Samuel: Introduction and Exegesis. In *The Interpreter's Bible*. Vol. 2. New York: Abingdon Press, 1953.

Deane, W. J. *Samuel and Saul: Their Lives and Times*. New York: Fleming H. Revell Co., n.d.

Driver, S. R. *Notes on the Hebrew Text and the Topography of the Books of Samuel*. Oxford: Oxford University Press, 1913.

Goldman, S. *Samuel*. London: The Soncino Press, 1951.

Hertzberg, Hans Wilhelm. I and II Samuel. Trans. by J. S. Bowden. In *The Old Testament Library*. Philadelphia: The Westminster Press, 1964.

Keil, C. F., and F. Delitzsch. *Samuel*. Edinburgh: T. & T. Clark, 1872.

Kirkpatrick, A. F. I, II Samuel. In *The Cambridge Bible for Schools and Colleges*. Cambridge: The University Press, 1930.

McKane, William. I and II Samuel. In *Torch Bible Commentaries*. London: SCM Press, Ltd., 1963.

Rust, Eric C. Judges, Ruth and Samuel. In *The Laymen's Bible Commentary*. Richmond: John Knox Press, 1961.

Smith, Henry Preserved. A Critical and Exegetical Commentary on the Books of Samuel. In *The International Critical Commentary*. Edinburgh: T. & T. Clark, 1899.

Smith, H. P. Samuel. In *International Critical Commentary*. Edinburgh: T. & T. Clark, 1899.

I AND II KINGS

INTRODUCTION

Title. These books are appropriately designated since they are a record of the reigns of the kings of Judah and Israel from the time of Solomon until the fall of the Jewish monarchy and destruction of Jerusalem in 586 B.C. The title *Kings* is a literal translation of the Hebrew (Heb *melek*), and these books appear in the Hebrew division of the Bible known as the "Former Prophets."

Like the books of Samuel, the books of Kings originally appeared in one volume. The division into two books in the middle of the reign of Ahaziah is artificial and seems to have no special significance, other than being near the middle and, hence, a convenient dividing place. The division into two books was first made in the Septuagint, the Greek translation of the Old Testament, which divided Samuel and Kings into four scrolls entitled "Kingdoms." Therefore, while our I and II Samuel are styled "Kingdoms" I and II in the Septuagint, our I and II Kings correspond to "Kingdoms" III and IV.

Date of writing. The date of writing and authorship cannot be determined with absolute certainty. It is evident that the final chapter of II Kings could not have been written prior to 561 B.C.; for it was in that approximate year that the Babylonian king Evil-merodach released the exiled Jewish king, Jehoiachin, from prison and awarded him royal honors. Since there is no mention of the return of some of the Jews to Jerusalem in 536 B.C., it is probable that the books were completed some time between 561 B.C. and 536 B.C.

Authorship. The name of the author is not recorded. The Jewish Talmud (*Baba Bathra* 15A) states that Jeremiah wrote Kings, in addition to Jeremiah and Lamentations. This tradition is appealing to some scholars. "Since the author speaks from a consistently prophetic standpoint and is a man of great literary ability, it is possible that Jeremiah may have composed everything except the final chapter" (Archer, *A Survey of Old Testament Introduction*, p. 277). Keil, *Commentary on the Book of the Kings* (p. 11), notes the similarity in the language of Jeremiah and Kings and believes it is impossible for Jeremiah to have written Kings for two reasons: (1) Jeremiah's last days were spent in Egypt (Jer 43); and (2) he would have been at least eighty-six years old in 561 B.C. if he had been only twenty years old at the beginning of his ministry in the thirteenth year of Josiah (Jer 1:2), sixty-six years earlier.

It is best to assume that while the author may not have been Jeremiah, he was probably a contemporary of his. He was a man of God who was concerned that his people did not obey the law of God. In all probability he was a Babylonian captive because the elevation of the prisoner Jehoiachin would have been of significance primarily to the Babylonian captives.

It has been suggested that the author drew upon earlier written documents, especially if he were writing some time after 561 B.C. about events that happened as early as 971 B.C. (Solomon's inauguration); for he cites at least three specific non-canonical prophetic books. For the reign of Solomon, he quotes the ". . . Book of the Acts of Solomon" (I Kgs 11:41); for the kings of the northern kingdom, he quotes the "Book of the Chronicles of the Kings of Israel" eighteen times (e.g., I Kgs 14:19); and for the kings of the southern kingdom, he quotes the "Book of the Chronicles of Judah" fifteen times (e.g., I Kgs 14:29).

It appears that certain kings had in their service one who bore the title, recorder (Heb *mazkir*, lit., remembrancer). It is likely that his function was to keep an official record for the king (cf. II Sam 8:16; I Kgs 4:3; II Kgs 18:18; II Chr 34:8). Parallel accounts in II Chronicles (e.g., cf. I Kgs 11:41 and II Chr 9:29) cite the following writers: Nathan the prophet, Ahijah the Shilonite, and Iddo the seer. Other writers cited separately are Shemaiah the prophet (II Chr 12:5), Isaiah the prophet (II Chr 26:22; 32:32), and Jehu the seer (cf. II Chr 19:2; 20:34).

Although the writer quotes freely from non-inspired prophetic works, he does not serve only as a compiler. It would be a serious error to assume that his work was merely a collection of extracts, even if he were directed to them by the Holy Spirit. Rather, his references to statements in non-inspired works constitute divine approval of the truth of the facts the author of Kings uses. His inspiration is from above, not from divine direction to earthly sources.

Style and Structure. The author draws upon his sources to present a consistently careful chronology of all the important events (cf. 6:1; 7:1; 11:42) and judges the conduct of the kings according to the standard of the Mosaic law (cf. 2:3; II Kgs 10:31; 14:6).

Most notable are the similar phrases in each of the royal biographies. There is an opening and a closing formula for each reign, the opening formula being more complete for the kings of Judah than for the kings of Israel. For the kings of Israel the opening formula states: (1) the synchronization of the accession with the regnal year of Judah's kingdom; (2) the length of the reign; and (3) the writer's judgment of the reign. For the kings of Judah we find an additional two items: (4) the king's age at his accession; and (5) his mother's name.

In the closing formula three items are to be noted: (1) a reference to the source material for additional information; (2) a notice of the king's death and burial; and (3) the name of his successor.

Purpose. These books are closely related to the books of Samuel with which they are numbered in the Septuagint. Kings carries on the history of the theocracy until its end in the Babylonian exile. The history is more than an objective political history; it is spiritual. "The dominant purpose of the narra-

I KINGS

tives is religious instruction. The historical records are but the vehicle of moral and spiritual truths which are conveyed to the reader" (Slotki, *Kings: Hebrew Text and English Translation with Introduction and Commentary*, p. xi). Consistently, obedience to the law of Moses is commended; and idolatry and image worship, sins which, persisted in, ultimately led to exile, were condemned.

The lives and actions of the kings are judged without partiality. All of the kings of Israel were evil; and they are condemned because of their continuance in the sin of Jeroboam the son of Nebat ". . . who made Israel to sin" (14:16). The kings of Judah were appraised by their fidelity to Jehovah. They either did that which was right in the sight of the Lord, or they did not. Even all the good kings, except two, were stigmatized by their acceptance of the high places. Only Hezekiah and Josiah received the supreme praise: "And he did that which was right in the sight of the LORD, according to all that David his father did" (II Kgs 18:3; cf. 22:2).

The prominence given to the ministry of the prophets Elijah and Elisha of Israel and the mention of great prophets such as Isaiah and Jeremiah in Judah are indicative of the prophetic standpoint of the author. God's people failed to keep His covenant and refused to heed the warnings of His prophets. Therefore, it is clear that the Exile is a divine punishment.

Chronology. A challenge to be faced by any serious student of Kings is the problem of chronology. For the period of the divided monarchy the author uses a careful, but simplistic, system of cross-reference between the kings of Israel and Judah. For example, a king of Judah's reign is cited as beginning in a given year in the reign of the kings of Israel and vice versa. Despite this simple chronology, difficult problems emerge.

One problem is seen in the totals of the regnal years. The period from one fixed point in the history of Israel and Judah to another fixed in their common history does not produce the same total of years. For example, Jeroboam (Israel) and Rehoboam (Judah) began their reigns in the same year. Likewise, Jehoram (Israel) and Ahaziah (Judah) met their deaths in the same year. Instead of agreeing, the total number of years of the reigns of Israel and of Judah during this period show ninety-eight years for Israel and ninety-five years for Judah. Similarly, Jehu (Israel) and Athaliah (Judah) ascended the throne the same year. The fall of Samaria occurred in the ninth year of Hoshea's (Israel) reign, which coincided with the sixth year of Hezekiah's (Judah) reign. Again, instead of the total years agreeing, 143 years have elapsed for Israel and 166 years have elapsed for Judah.

The problem involves at least three factors:

1. Determining the accession year of the king. Two systems were employed. The first was the Ascension, or Post-dating, method in which the reign was calculated as beginning on the first day of the following year. The second was the Non-ascension, or Antedating, method in which the reign was calculated as beginning on the day of the king's accession.

2. Determining the calendar year employed. The Jews employed two years in their calendar, the religious and the civil. The religious year began in the month Nisan (March-April), and the civil year began in the month Tishri (September-October).

3. Determining coregencies. Some kings associated their sons with them on the throne during their final years of reigning. In the case of a coregency, the regnal years were usually counted from the beginning of the coregency.

It is difficult to fix absolute dates, but Assyrian chronology has been helpful. Each year the Assyrians appointed an official to be an eponym, and his name was given to his year in office. Lists of their names were kept, and special events were noted. If any one year can be fixed by our reckoning, then the whole series can also be fixed. In the year of the eponym Bur-Sagale an eclipse of the sun occurred on June 15, 763 B.C. Thus, a whole series of years and events from 892-648 B.C., with material reaching back to 911 B.C., is fixed. Coinciding events in Jewish and Assyrian history aid in the fixing of biblical dates.

For further study of chronology, the reader is referred to Thiele, *The Mysterious Numbers of the Hebrew Kings* and Kitchen and Mitchell, "Chronology of the Old Testament" in *The New Bible Dictionary*, pp. 212-223.

OUTLINE
I KINGS

I. The United Kingdom. 1:1-11:43.
   A. Solomon's Selection and Ascension to David's Throne. 1:1-2:46.
     1. Adonijah's unsuccessful bid for the throne. 1:1-53.
     2. David's final words and death. 2:1-12.
     3. Solomon's purge of ungodly political aspirants. 2:13-46.
   B. Solomon's Glorious Beginning as King. 3:1-4:34.
     1. His marriage alliance with Egypt. 3:1-2.
     2. His sacrifice at Gibeon. 3:3-15.
     3. His wisdom demonstrated. 3:16-28.
     4. His officials and administrative districts. 4:1-19.
     5. His tribute and provisions. 4:20-28.
     6. His wisdom summarized. 4:29-34.
   C. Solomon's Building Projects. 5:1-9:28.
     1. The building preparations. 5:1-18.
     2. The building of the Temple. 6:1-38.
     3. The building of Solomon's house. 7:1-8.
     4. The building materials. 7:9-12.
     5. The building artisan. 7:13-14.
     6. The building furnishings. 7:15-51.

COMMENTARY

I. THE UNITED KINGDOM. 1:1-11:43.

A. Solomon's Selection and Ascension to David's Throne. 1:1-2:46.

1. Adonijah's unsuccessful bid for the throne. 1:1-53.

The first two chapters of I Kings are a continuation of David's reign as begun and recorded in II Samuel. They serve as a transition from his reign to the glorious reign of Solomon.

1:1-4. David was old. Comparing II Samuel 5:4, David was approaching the end of his seventieth year. **Stricken** is not a reference to senility, but to old age (lit., he came into days). He could not get warm even when covered with **clothes,** i.e., bed-clothes.

His servants recommended warming the chilled king by a vigorous and healthy body. A young virgin, a Shunammite, **Abishag,** was selected to render this service. Shunen was a town (probably modern Solem) in the territory of Issachar in the Plain of Esdraelon, north of Jezreel and Mount Gilboa. Abishag served as David's constant companion and personal nurse, but he **knew her not.** While she was considered a concubine of David (cf. 2:13-25; II Sam 3:6-7), she did not serve as an ordinary concubine. Her relationship to the king was not for sexual purposes.

5-10. Since no precedence had been set in Israel for succession to the throne, on the grounds of primogeniture Adonijah made his bid for the throne. Three reasons are given for his behavior and claim to succession: (1) he was a spoiled child because **his father had not displeased him at any time;** (2) he was attractive, **very goodly,** probably similar to his brother Absalom (cf. II Sam 14:25); and (3) he was next in order as heir because he was born **after Absalom.** He was David's fourth son

NOW king David was old *and* stricken in years; and they covered him with clothes, but he gat no heat.

2 Wherefore his servants said unto him, Let there be sought for my lord the king a young virgin: and let her stand before the king, and let her cherish him, and let her lie in thy bosom, that my lord the king may get heat.

3 So they sought for a fair damsel throughout all the coasts of Israel, and found Ăb'i-shăg a Shū'nam-mīte, and brought her to the king.

4 And the damsel *was* very fair, and cherished the king, and ministered to him: but the king knew her not.

5 ¶Then Ăd-o-nī'jah the son of Hăg'gĭth exalted himself, saying, I will be king: and he prepared him chariots and horsemen, and fifty men to run before him.

6 And his father had not displeased him at any time in saying, Why hast thou done so? and he also *was* a very

goodly *man;* and *his mother* bare him after Ăb′sa-lom.

7 And he conferred with Jō′ăb the son of Zer-ū-i′ah, and with Ă-bī′a-thar the priest: and they following Ăd-o-nī′jah helped *him.*

8 But Zā′dŏk the priest, and Be-nā′iah the son of Je-hoi′a-da, and Nāthan the prophet, and Shĭm′e-ī, and Rē′ī, and the mighty men which *belonged* to David, were not with Ăd-o-nī′jah.

9 And Ăd-o-nī′jah slew sheep and oxen and fat cattle by the stone of Zō′he-lĕth, *is* by Ĕn-rō′gel, and called all his brethren the king's sons, and all the men of Jūdah the king's servants:

10 But Nāthan the prophet, and Be-nā′iah, and the mighty men, and Sŏlomon his brother, he called not.

11 ¶Wherefore Nāthan spake unto Băth′-shē-ba the mother of Sŏlomon, saying, Hast thou not heard that Ăd-o-nī′jah the son of Hăg′gĭth doth reign, and David our lord knoweth *it* not?

12 Now therefore come, let me, I pray thee, give thee counsel, that thou mayest save thine own life, and the life of thy son Sŏlomon.

13 Go and get thee in unto king David, and say unto him, Didst not thou, my lord, O king, swear unto thine handmaid, saying, Assuredly Sŏlomon thy son shall reign after me, and he shall sit upon my throne? why then doth Ăd-o-nī′jah reign?

14 Behold, while thou yet talkest there with the king, I also will come in after thee, and confirm thy words.

15 ¶And Băth′-shē-ba went in unto the king into the chamber: and the king was very old; and Ăb′i-shăg the Shū′nam-mīte ministered unto the king.

16 And Băth′-shē-ba bowed, and did obeisance unto the king. And the king said, What wouldest thou?

17 And she said unto him, My lord, thou swarest by the LORD thy God unto thine handmaid, *saying,* Assuredly Sŏlomon thy son shall reign after me, and he shall sit upon my throne.

18 And now, behold, Ăd-o-nī′jah reigneth; and now, my lord the king, thou knowest *it* not:

19 And he hath slain oxen and fat cattle and sheep in abundance, and hath called all the sons of the king, and Ă-bī′a-thar the priest, and Jō′ăb the captain of the host: but Sŏlomon thy servant hath he not called.

20 And thou, my lord, O king, the eyes of all Israel *are* upon thee, that thou shouldest tell them who shall sit on the throne of my lord the king after him.

21 Otherwise it shall come to pass, when my lord the king shall sleep with his fathers, that I and my son Sŏlomon shall be counted offenders.

22 ¶And, lo, while she yet talked with the king, Nāthan the prophet also came in.

(cf. II Sam 3:3-5). Amnon, the first son, was killed by Absalom's order; Absalom, the third son, was killed by Joab; and Chileab, the second son, may have died at an early age since he is never mentioned again.

Adonijah's move was supported by **Joab** (he was the son of **Zeruiah,** David's sister, I Chr 2:16), thus David's nephew and Adonijah's cousin, the famous and loyal captain of David's army, and **Abiathar,** one of the two chief priests serving at that time.

Zadok, the other priest, **Benaiah,** the one apparently second-in-command to Joab (II Sam 20:23), **Nathan,** the prophet (II Sam 7:1ff; 12:1ff.), and two lesser known men, **Shimei** and **Rei,** remained faithful to David.

Adonijah's self-coronation was solemnized by the slaughtering (sacrificing) of animals at the **stone of Zoheleth,** i.e., the serpent's stone, near **En-rogel,** i.e., the fuller's fountain, south of Jerusalem in the Kidron Valley. It is known today as Job's well. Many, including his younger brothers, were invited to the ceremony; but Nathan and Benaiah, David's faithful men, were excluded. **Solomon his brother, he called not.** Adonijah was aware that his brother was his rival for the throne.

11-12. That David knew nothing of Adonijah's plans is indicated by Nathan's intervention on behalf of **Bath-sheba** and **Solomon.** Had Adonijah been successful in ascending the throne, the lives of the dethroned king, legitimate successor, all relatives, and rivals would become endangered (cf. 15:29; II Kgs 10:6, 13-14). Therefore, Nathan urged Bath-sheba, **save thine own life, and the life of thy son Solomon.**

13-14. Nathan counseled Bath-sheba to remind David of his promise concerning Solomon. When David had promised Bath-sheba that Solomon would succeed him on the throne is uncertain, but presumably it occurred after the Davidic Covenant was made (II Sam 7:12-17). That Nathan was aware of the promise may support the opinion that both Adonijah and Joab were also aware of the promise and were trying to force the king's hand. Once Adonijah was crowned, perhaps David would cancel his promise to Bath-sheba.

15-20. Bath-sheba followed Nathan's counsel and was admitted to David's **chamber,** i.e., his sick room, where he was being ministered to by Abishag (1:2-4). **Adonijah reigneth** (vs. 18). He had already proclaimed himself king; and unless David intervened, he would retain the kingship. All the eyes of Israel were upon David that he **shouldest tell them who shall sit on the throne** (vs. 20). "Only when the dead King's wishes were unknown could the eldest son claim the right of succession. Bath-sheba suggests an immediate proclamation in favour of Solomon" (Slotki, *Kings,* p. 5).

21-27. She and Solomon would be **offenders** (Heb *chata*′) i.e., sinners, in a political, not moral, sense; and the consequences would be severe subsequent to David's death. **While she yet talked,** Nathan appeared as planned (vs. 14). Confirmation from a second source would lend credibility to Bath-sheba's report (vss. 23-27).

23 And they told the king, saying, Behold Nāthan the prophet. And when he was come in before the king, he bowed himself before the king with his face to the ground.

24 And Nāthan said, My lord, O king, hast thou said, Ăd-o-nī'jah shall reign after me, and he shall sit upon my throne?

25 For he is gone down this day, and hath slain oxen and fat cattle and sheep in abundance, and hath called all the king's sons, and the captains of the host, and Ă-bī'a-thar the priest; and, behold, they eat and drink before him, and say, God save king Ăd-o-nī'jah.

26 But me, even me thy servant, and Zā'dŏk the priest, and Be-nā'iah the son of Je-hoi'a-da, and thy servant Sŏlo-mon, hath he not called.

27 Is this thing done by my lord the king, and thou hast not shewed it unto thy servant, who should sit on the throne of my lord the king after him?

28 ¶Then king David answered and said, Call me Băth'-shē-ba. And she came into the king's presence, and stood before the king.

29 And the king sware, and said, As the LORD liveth, that hath redeemed my soul out of all distress,

30 Even as I sware unto thee by the LORD God of Israel, saying, Assuredly Sŏlomon thy son shall reign after me, and he shall sit upon my throne in my stead; even so will I certainly do this day.

31 Then Băth'-shē-ba bowed with her face to the earth, and did reverence to the king, and said, Let my lord king David live for ever.

32 ¶And king David said, Call me Zā'-dŏk the priest, and Nāthan the prophet, and Be-nā'iah the son of Je-hoi'a-da. And they came before the king.

33 The king also said unto them, Take with you the servants of your lord, and cause Sŏlomon my son to ride upon mine own mule, and bring him down to Gī'hŏn:

34 And let Zā'dŏk the priest and Nāthan the prophet anoint him there king over Israel: and blow ye with the trumpet, and say, God save king Sŏlomon.

35 Then ye shall come up after him, that he may come and sit upon my throne; for he shall be king in my stead: and I have appointed him to be ruler over Israel and over Jūdah.

36 And Be-nā'iah the son of Je-hoi'a-da answered the king, and said, Amen: the LORD God of my lord the king say so too.

37 As the LORD hath been with my lord the king, even so be he with Sŏlomon, and make his throne greater than the throne of my lord king David.

38 So Zā'dŏk the priest, and Nāthan the prophet, and Be-nā'iah the son of Je-hoi'a-da, and the Chĕr'e-thītes, and the Pĕl'e-thītes, went down, and caused Sŏlomon to ride upon king David's mule, and brought him to Gī'hŏn.

39 And Zā'dŏk the priest took an horn of oil out of the tabernacle, and

28-31. Call me Bath-sheba. When Nathan had entered the chamber, she had retired from the room according to Oriental etiquette. David assured her that he would make good his promise concerning Solomon. **Even so will I certainly do this day.**

32. "The quick and firm resolution of David shows how strong he was yet in mind and will, notwithstanding all his bodily weaknesses" (Bahr, *The Books of the Kings*, p. 24). David's loyalists, Nathan, Zadok, and Benaiah, were instructed concerning the anointing of Solomon.

33. Solomon was to ride David's **mule.** Commoners rode asses, but only a king could ride the king's mule. **Gihon** was a spring west of Jerusalem. Years later Hezekiah cut a conduit from this spring to the Pool of Siloam (II Chr 32:30).

34-38. David expressly gave the order for Solomon's anointing, thus instituting a temporary coregency. The men, quick to carry out David's orders, were aided by the **Cherethites** and the **Pelethites.** Information concerning these peoples is limited, but they appear to have been personal bodyguards under the leadership of Benaiah (II Sam 8:18; 20:23, I Chr 18:17). Through the rebellions of Absalom (II Sam 15:18) and Sheba (II Sam 20:7) they remained faithful to David, and here they aided in the anointing of his son, Solomon. They are never mentioned again.

39-41. Upon anointing Solomon, **they blew the trumpet** to alert the people (cf. vs. 20) that the king's choice had been

anointed Sŏlomon. And they blew the
trumpet; and all the people said, God
save king Sŏlomon.

40 And all the people came up after
him, and the people piped with pipes,
and rejoiced with great joy, so that the
earth rent with the sound of them.

41 ¶And Ăd-o-nī′jah and all the
guests that *were* with him heard *it* as
they had made an end of eating. And
when Jŏ′ăb heard the sound of the
trumpet, he said, Wherefore *is* this
noise of the city being in an uproar?

42 And while he yet spake, behold,
Jonathan the son of Ă-bī′a-thar the
priest came; and Ăd-o-nī′jah said unto
him, Come in; for thou *art* a valiant
man, and bringest good tidings.

43 And Jonathan answered and said
to Ăd-o-nī′jah, Verily our lord king David hath made Sŏlomon king.

44 And the king hath sent with him
Zā′dŏk the priest, and Nāthan the
prophet, and Be-nā′iah the son of Je-
hoi′a-da, and the Chĕr′e-thītes, and the
Pĕl′e-thītes, and they have caused him
to ride upon the king's mule:

45 And Zā′dŏk the priest and Nāthan
the prophet have anointed him king in
Gī′hŏn: and they are come up from
thence rejoicing, so that the city rang
again. This *is* the noise that ye have
heard.

46 And also Sŏlomon sitteth on the
throne of the kingdom.

47 And moreover the king's servants
came to bless our lord king David,
saying, God make the name of Sŏlomon better than thy name, and make
his throne greater than thy throne. And
the king bowed himself upon the bed.

48 And also thus said the king,
Blessed *be* the LORD God of Israel,
which hath given *one* to sit on my
throne this day, mine eyes even seeing
it.

49 And all the guests that *were* with
Ăd-o-nī′jah were afraid, and rose up,
and went every man his way.

50 And Ăd-o-nī′jah feared because of
Sŏlomon, and arose, and went, and
caught hold on the horns of the altar.

51 And it was told Sŏlomon, saying,
Behold, Ăd-o-nī′jah feareth king Sŏlomon: for, lo, he hath caught hold on the
horns of the altar, saying, Let king Sŏlomon swear unto me today that he will
not slay his servant with the sword.

52 And Sŏlomon said, If he will shew
himself a worthy man, there shall not
an hair of him fall to the earth: but if
wickedness shall be found in him, he
shall die.

53 So king Sŏlomon sent, and they
brought him down from the altar. And
he came and bowed himself to king Sŏlomon: and Sŏlomon said unto him, Go
to thine house.

CHAPTER 2

NOW the days of David drew nigh that
he should die; and he charged Sŏlomon
his son, saying,

anointed. The noise of the excitement at Gihon reached Adonijah's coronation celebration, still in progress at En-rogel (vs. 9).
Joab, the experienced warrior, was the first to hear the trumpet
and sense trouble.

42-46. Jonathan the son of Abiathar (note his responsibility
on behalf of David during Absalom's rebellion in II Sam 17:17-
21) was probably left behind in Jerusalem to observe the happenings there and to report any developments. **Solomon sitteth
upon the throne of the kingdom,** and with David's approval
and support (vs. 46).

47-48. In worship and gratitude to God, David **bowed himself upon the bed** (cf. Gen 47:31). His "response is to bless God,
i.e., to thank Him, on the realization of the promise of dynastic
succession" (Gray, *I and II Kings,* p. 94).

49. Adonijah's friends showed their fickleness by deserting
him in panic, leaving him sorely distressed.

50. In fear he went and **caught hold on the horns of the
altar.** Among all nations the altar was a place of asylum for
criminals deserving of death, but in Israel it was intended originally for unintentional manslaughter (Ex 21:14). "By grasping
the horns of the altar, the culprit placed himself under the
protection of the saving and helping grace of God, which wipes
away sin, and therefore abolishes punishment" (Keil, p. 25).

51-53. Solomon granted Adonijah a conditional pardon on
the basis of good behavior and his relinquishing any further
claims on the throne.

2. David's final words and death. 2:1-12.

According to I Chronicles 23:1 and 29:20-25 Solomon was
anointed as king a second time before his father, David, died.
The first anointing was rather impromptu because of the circumstances, but the second was more formal before all the
people.

2:1-2. How much time elapsed in the co-regency can not be
determined. **I go the way of all the earth,** i.e., the way of death
(cf. Josh 23:14). David's last charge, **be thou strong therefore,**

2 I go the way of all the earth: be thou strong therefore, and shew thyself a man;

3 And keep the charge of the LORD thy God, to walk in his ways, to keep his statutes, and his commandments, and his judgments, and his testimonies, as it is written in the law of Moses, that thou mayest prosper in all that thou doest, and whithersoever thou turnest thyself:

4 That the LORD may continue his word which he spake concerning me, saying, If thy children take heed to their way, to walk before me in truth with all their heart and with all their soul, there shall not fail thee (said he) a man on the throne of Israel.

5 Moreover thou knowest also what Jŏ′ăb the son of Zer-ŭ-i′ah did to me, *and* what he did to the two captains of the hosts of Israel, unto Abner the son of Ner, and unto Am′ă-sa the son of Jĕ′ther, whom he slew, and shed the blood of war in peace, and put the blood of war upon his girdle that *was* about his loins, and in his shoes that *were* on his feet.

6 Do therefore according to thy wisdom, and let not his hoar head go down to the grave in peace.

7 But shew kindness unto the sons of Bär-zĭl′la-ĭ the Gĭleadĭte, and let them be of those that eat at thy table: for so they came to me when I fled because of Ăb′sa-lom thy brother.

8 And, behold, *thou hast* with thee Shĭm′e-ĭ the son of Ge′ra, a Benjamite of Ba-hŭ′rĭm, which cursed me with a grievous curse in the day when I went to Mă-ha-nă′im: but he came down to meet me at Jordan, and I sware to him by the LORD, saying, I will not put thee to death with the sword.

9 Now therefore hold him not guiltless: for thou *art* a wise man, and knowest what thou oughtest to do unto him; but his hoar head bring thou down to the grave with blood.

10 ¶So David slept with his fathers, and was buried in the city of David.

11 And the days that David reigned over Israel *were* forty years: seven years reigned he in Hĕbron, and thirty and three years reigned he in Jerusalem.

12 ¶Then sat Sŏlomon upon the throne of David his father; and his kingdom was established greatly.

13 ¶And Ăd-o-nĭ′jah the son of Hăg′gĭth came to Băth′-shē-ba the mother of Sŏlomon. And she said, Comest thou peaceably? And he said, Peaceably.

14 He said moreover, I have somewhat to say unto thee. And she said, Say on.

15 And he said, Thou knowest that the kingdom was mine, and *that* all Israel set their faces on me, that I should reign: howbeit the kingdom is turned about, and is become my brother's: for it was his from the LORD.

16 And now I ask one petition of thee, deny me not. And she said unto him, Say on.

17 And he said, Speak, I pray thee, unto Sŏlomon the king, (for he will not

reechoes the sentiment of Moses' parting exhortation to Joshua (Deut 31:23).

3-4. The key to David's successes was his obedience to the Word of God. Solomon was admonished to prosper (cf. Josh 1:8) by keeping the **charge of the LORD.** Gray shows a distinction in the terms used: **His statutes** (Heb *chuqah,* lit., things engraved); **his commandments** (Heb *mitswah,* "direct orders in the form 'thou shalt . . .' or 'thou shalt not' as opposed to casuistic laws"); **his judgments** (Heb *mishpat,* "decisions which are accumulated as legal precedents"); and **his testimonies** (Heb *'ēdūt*) meaning "solemn charges" in which God is called upon as a witness (p. 97). While these distinctions need not be pressed here, the totality of the Law is definitely stressed.

5-6. Liberal scholarship falsely criticizes David for blackening his record upon his deathbed by taking vengeance upon Joab and Shimei. He is accused of being superstitious about bloodguilt and the power of a curse (cf. Dentan, *The First and Second Books of Kings,* p. 21). However, the murders of Joab must be noted. He had murdered **Abner,** Saul and Ishbosheth's captain, in revenge and jealousy (cf. II Sam 2:22-23; 3:12-27). He had killed Absalom against David's wishes (II Sam 18:5, 14), and had supported Adonijah's attempt to seize the throne (1:7). David was not taking vengeance so much as he was dealing with Joab's wickedness.

7. Barzillai was to be given preferential treatment because he had demonstrated his faithfulness by supplying food for David when he fled Absalom (II Sam 17:27-29).

8-9. Shimei had violated Exodus 22:28, "Thou shalt not . . . curse the ruler of thy people," when he had cursed David as he fled Jerusalem (II Sam 16:5-8). Some believe David now ordered Shimei's death because of superstition, suggesting that he feared the curse and believed that the curse could be removed if the one who uttered the curse was removed. However, Scripture clearly indicates that Shimei had bitterly rebelled against God in rejecting David (God's anointed) in favor of Saul, whom God had publicly rejected.

10-12. David died and was buried in the **city of David,** i.e., Jerusalem, the Jebusite stronghold he had conquered and fortified for his capital (II Sam 5:6-9). He had reigned a total of forty years, seven in Hebron and thirty-three in Jerusalem (ca. 1011-971 B.C.).

3. Solomon's purge of ungodly political aspirants. 2:13-46.

13-16. Comest thou peaceably? i.e., on friendly terms? Bath-sheba appeared to be alarmed at this unexpected visit by Adonijah. **The kingdom was mine** (vs. 15). By right of primogeniture, it was his. In his estimation, all the eyes of Israel were focused on him and ready to support him (cf. 1:6 and II Sam 15:6). Is it from sincerity or expediency that he admitted divine intervention in placing Solomon on the throne?

17. His request to Solomon through Bath-sheba was **give me Abishag . . . to wife.** This may have been an innocent request of

say thee nay,) that he give me Ăb′i-shăg the Shū′nam-mīte to wife.

18 And Băth′-shē-ba said, Well; I will speak for thee unto the king.

19 ¶Băth′-shē-ba therefore went unto king Sŏlomon, to speak unto him for Ăd-o-nī′jah. And the king rose up to meet her, and bowed himself unto her, and sat down on his throne, and caused a seat to be set for the king's mother; and she sat on his right hand.
20 Then she said, I desire one small petition of thee; I pray thee, say me not nay. And the king said unto her, Ask on, my mother: for I will not say thee nay.
21 And she said, Let Ăb′i-shăg the Shū′nam-mīte be given to Ăd-o-nī′jah thy brother to wife.
22 And king Sŏlomon answered and said unto his mother, And why dost thou ask Ăb′i-shăg the Shū′nam-mīte for Ăd-o-nī′jah? ask for him the kingdom also; for he is mine elder brother; even for him, and for Ă-bī′a-thar the priest, and for Jō′ăb the son of Zer-ū-i′ah.
23 Then king Sŏlomon sware by the LORD, saying, God do so to me, and more also, if Ăd-o-nī′jah have not spoken this word against his own life.
24 Now therefore, as the LORD liveth, which hath established me, and set me on the throne of David my father, and who hath made me an house, as he promised, Ăd-o-nī′jah shall be put to death this day.
25 And king Sŏlomon sent by the hand of Be-nā′iah the son of Je-hoi′a-da; and he fell upon him that he died.

26 ¶And unto Ă-bī′a-thar the priest said the king, Get thee to Ăn′a-thŏth, unto thine own fields; for thou art worthy of death: but I will not at this time put thee to death, because thou barest the ark of the Lord GOD before David my father, and because thou hast been afflicted in all wherein my father was afflicted.
27 So Sŏlomon thrust out Ă-bī′a-thar from being priest unto the LORD; that he might fulfil the word of the LORD, which he spake concerning the house of Eli in Shī′lŏh.

28 ¶Then tidings came to Jō′ăb: for Jō′ăb had turned after Ăd-o-nī′jah, though he turned not after Ăb′sa-lom, And Jō′ăb fled unto the tabernacle of the LORD, and caught hold on the horns of the altar.
29 And it was told king Sŏlomon that Jō′ăb was fled unto the tabernacle of the LORD; and, behold, he is by the altar.

romance; but it was a suspicious one, an indirect claim to the throne. "In the ancient East, after a king died, or his kingdom passed from him, the harem fell to the new ruler. On the other hand, also, he who took to himself the king's wives, was regarded as having taken to himself the rights of the king. The claim to the possession of the women of the harem was understood to mean the claim to the throne" (Bahr, p. 35).

18. Did Bath-sheba naively agree to make the request? Ellison (p. 303) suggests "that she inwardly rejoiced at the possibility of removing the last threat to her son."

19-21. She was seated **on his right hand.** The seat of highest distinction was given to the queen-mother. Solomon states, **ask on . . . I will not say thee nay.** Little did he realize that his mother would ask something he could not grant.

22. Solomon recognized immediately the intentions of Adonijah. **Ask for him the kingdom also** (cf. II Sam 3:6; 16:21-22). **Abiathar** and **Joab** are listed because both had supported Adonijah and Solomon saw them as part of the scheme. Their participation provided Solomon reason to take action against them, also.

23-24. Solomon had pardoned Adonijah in the past on the condition of good behavior. Adonijah had now forfeited his chance to live.

25. Benaiah, who had been loyal to David (cf. 1:8; II Sam 20:23) and had been made captain in Joab's place in Solomon's reign (cf. 2:35; 4:4), was issued the order to execute Adonijah for conspiracy.

26. Abiathar, the priest who had supported Adonijah, was demoted and sent home to **Anathoth,** a little city of the tribe of Benjamin about three miles north of Jerusalem. Later, it was the home of the prophet Jeremiah (Jer 1:1).

27. That he might fulfill the word of the LORD. Two high priests had been ministering concurrently. One, Zadok, traced his lineage to Aaron's third son, Eleazar (I Chr 24:3); and the other, Abiathar, traced his lineage through Eli (I Sam 1:3) to Aaron's fourth son, Ithamar (cf. I Sam 14:3; 22:20; I Chr 24:3). From millennial passages (Ezk 44:15; 48:11) it appears that Zadok (the line of Eleazar) was God's choice for high priest. Solomon's action carried out God's promise of punishment upon the house of Eli (I Sam 2:31-36).

28-29. Joab anticipated the consequences of following also after Adonijah and took asylum at the horns of the altar (cf. comment on 1:50). Benaiah was ordered to **fall upon him,** i.e., execute him.

Then Sŏlomon sent Be-nā′iah the son of Je-hoi′a-da, saying, Go, fall upon him.

30 And Be-nā′iah came to the tabernacle of the LORD, and said unto him, Thus saith the king, Come forth. And he said, Nay; but I will die here. And Be-nā′iah brought the king word again, saying, Thus said Jŏ′ăb, and thus he answered me.

31 And the king said unto him, Do as he hath said, and fall upon him, and bury him; that thou mayest take away the innocent blood, which Jŏ′ăb shed, from me, and from the house of my father.

32 And the LORD shall return his blood upon his own head, who fell upon two men more righteous and better than he, and slew them with the sword, my father David not knowing thereof, to wit, Abner the son of Ner, captain of the host of Israel, and Am′ā-sa the son of Jĕ′ther, captain of the host of Jūdah.

33 Their blood shall therefore return upon the head of Jŏ′ăb, and upon the head of his seed for ever: but upon David, and upon his seed, and upon his house, and upon his throne, shall there be peace for ever from the LORD.

34 So Be-nā′iah the son of Je-hoi′a-da went up, and fell upon him, and slew him: and he was buried in his own house in the wilderness.

35 ¶And the king put Re-nā′iah the son of Je-hoi′a-da in his room over the host: and Zā′dŏk the priest did the king put in the room of Ā-bī′a-thar.

36 ¶And the king sent and called for Shĭm′e-ī, and said unto him, Build thee an house in Jerusalem, and dwell there, and go not forth thence any whither.

37 For it shall be, that on the day thou goest out, and passest over the brook Kidron, thou shalt know for certain that thou shalt surely die: thy blood shall be upon thine own head.

38 And Shĭm′e-ī said unto the king, The saying is good: as my lord the king hath said, so will thy servant do. And Shĭm′e-ī dwelt in Jerusalem many days.

39 And it came to pass at the end of three years, that two of the servants of Shĭm′e-ī ran away unto Ā′chĭsh son of Mā′a-chah king of Gath. And they told Shĭm′e-ī, saying, Behold, thy servants be in Gath.

40 And Shĭm′e-ī arose, and saddled his ass, and went to Gath to Ā′chĭsh to seek his servants: and Shĭm′e-ī went, and brought his servants from Gath.

41 And it was told Sŏlomon that Shĭm′e-ī had gone from Jerusalem to Gath, and was come again.

42 And the king sent and called for Shĭm′e-ī, and said unto him, Did I not make thee to swear by the LORD, and protested unto thee, saying, Know for a certain, on the day thou goest out, and walkest abroad any whither, that thou shalt surely die? and thou saidst unto me, The word that I have heard is good.

43 Why then hast thou not kept the oath of the LORD, and the commandment that I have charged thee with?

44 The king said moreover to Shĭm′-e-ī, Thou knowest all the wickedness

30-35. Benaiah was reverent and consequently reluctant to shed blood in the holy place. Therefore he called, **Come forth.** Joab was wanted for his many crimes. His death sentence was justified because of his previous murders. According to the Law, there was no asylum for premeditated manslaughter (Ex 21:14). Therefore, his request was granted (vs. 30); and he was slain at the altar. **He was buried.** Joab was shown the dignity of receiving a decent burial.

36-38. Solomon saw one last political threat in Shimei. Therefore, Solomon stipulated that he build a house in Jerusalem and reside there where he could be kept under surveillance. He was therefore cut off from his hometown, Bahurim (II Sam 16:5), and his tribe of Benjamin. Note that Sheba, a Benjamite, had rebelled against David (II Sam 20:1-22). The arrangement seemed good to Shimei.

39-40. Three years later Shimei pursued his runaway servants to **Achish** king of **Gath,** a Philistine city. This is possibly the same Achish that befriended David when he was an exile from Saul (I Sam 27:2).

41-46. It was told Solomon. Shimei's every move was monitored. He had broken his oath, a crime for which there was no excuse. As Keil (p. 37) noted, "If Shimei had wished to remain faithful to his oath, he might have informed the king of the flight of his slaves, have entreated the king that they be brought back, and have awaited his decision." **And the kingdom was established.** All potential political rivals had been eliminated.

which thine heart is privy to, that thou didst to David my father: therefore the LORD shall return thy wickedness upon thine own head;

45 And king Sŏlomon *shall be* blessed, and the throne of David shall be established before the LORD for ever.

46 So the king commanded Be-nā'iah the son of Je-hoi'a-da; which went out, and fell upon him, that he died. And the kingdom was established in the hand of Sŏlomon.

CHAPTER 3

AND Sŏlomon made affinity with Pharaoh king of Egypt, and took Pharaoh's daughter, and brought her into the city of David, until he had made an end of building his own house, and the house of the LORD, and the wall of Jerusalem round about.

2 Only the people sacrificed in high places, because there was no house built unto the name of the LORD, until those days.

3 And Sŏlomon loved the LORD, walking in the statutes of David his father: only he sacrificed and burnt incense in high places.

4 And the king went to Gĭbeon to sacrifice there; for that *was* the great high place: a thousand burnt offerings did Sŏlomon offer upon that altar.

5 ¶In Gĭbeon the LORD appeared to Sŏlomon in a dream by night: and God said, Ask what I shall give thee.

6 And Sŏlomon said, Thou hast shewed unto thy servant David my father great mercy, according as he walked before thee in truth, and in righteousness, and in uprightness of heart with thee; and thou hast kept for him this great kindness, that thou hast given him a son to sit on his throne, as *it is* this day.

7 And now, O LORD my God, thou hast made thy servant king instead of David my father: and I *am* but a little child: I know not *how* to go out or come in.

8 And thy servant *is* in the midst of thy people which thou hast chosen, a great people, that cannot be numbered nor counted for multitude.

9 Give therefore thy servant an understanding heart to judge thy people, that I may discern between good and bad: for who is able to judge this thy so great a people?

10 And the speech pleased the LORD, that Sŏlomon had asked this thing.

11 And God said unto him, Because thou hast asked this thing, and hast not

B. Solomon's Glorious Beginning as King. 3:1—4:34.

1. *His marriage alliance with Egypt. 3:1-2.*

3:1-2. Solomon's marriage to Pharaoh's daughter was clearly a diplomatic alliance; **Pharaoh** is a title, not a proper name. He is probably to be identified as Psusennes II, the last Pharaoh of the weak Twenty-first Dynasty. The Amarna Tablets indicate that in the Eighteenth Dynasty no daughter of a Pharaoh married foreigners, so the marriage is significant. Egypt was weak and recognized Solomon's strength and superiority at that time. Note in 9:16 that she was given an impressive dowry, the city of Gezer. Because of the dowry, some have identified the Pharaoh as Sheshonk (biblical Shishak, 14:25), the first Pharaoh of the Twenty-second Dynasty, since he was more aggressive.

There is a hint that the Temple was not yet constructed in that the people **sacrificed in the high places** (Heb *bamah*). This was the Canaanite name for elevated platforms on which their cultic objects were placed and worshiped. In the early years of Solomon's reign, Israel apparently worshiped Jehovah on similar elevations.

2. *His sacrifice at Gibeon. 3:3-15.*

3-4. Solomon began his reign in the steps of his father, in love and obedience to the Lord. He went to **Gibeon to sacrifice there.** According to II Chronicles 1:3-6, the tabernacle and the brazen altar resided in Gibeon, modern El-Jib, which is about six miles northwest of Jerusalem. Presumably the tabernacle was moved there from Shiloh soon after the battle with the Philistines at Aphek (I Sam 4:1-11) when the ark was captured for a time. The ark, however, resided in Jerusalem in a tent that David had constructed for it there (II Sam 6:12-17).

5-8. The LORD appeared . . . in a dream. To receive divine revelation by means of a dream was not uncommon (cf. I Sam 28:15; Job 33:14-16). **I . . . a little child** (vs. 7). Rabbinic tradition has Solomon ascending the throne at age twelve; Josephus (*Antiq.* VIII. 7.8) says he was fourteen (Slotki, p. 24). However, he must have been nearly twenty years old (old enough to have children) because after a reign of forty years, his son Rehoboam took the throne at the age of forty-one, making him a year old when his father began to reign (cf. 11:42; 14:21).

The expression is probably a reference to humility and inexperience. Saul, who stood head and shoulders over everyone else (I Sam 10:23), was small in his own eyes when he began to reign (I Sam 15:17). Compare also Jeremiah 1:6.

9. Give . . . an understanding heart (lit., a hearing heart). This can be understood in two ways: (1) hearing the voice of God and following its lead in obedience; or (2) having the patience to hear a case and understand it fully. Both qualities are needed in making good judgments.

10-14. The attitude and request of Solomon **pleased the LORD** (lit., it was good in the eyes of the Lord) because in a time of opportunity he had not sought personal gain and acclaim, but something far more practical, wisdom. As a reward, riches and

asked for thyself long life; neither hast asked riches for thyself, nor hast asked the life of thine enemies; but hast asked for thyself understanding to discern judgment;

12 Behold, I have done according to thy words: lo, I have given thee a wise and an understanding heart; so that there was none like thee before thee, neither after thee shall any arise like unto thee.

13 And I have also given thee that which thou hast not asked, both riches, and honour: so that there shall not be any among the kings like unto thee all thy days.

14 And if thou wilt walk in my ways, to keep my statutes and my commandments, as thy father David did walk, then I will lengthen thy days.

15 And Sŏlomon awoke; and, behold, *it was* a dream. And he came to Jerusalem, and stood before the ark of the covenant of the LORD, and offered up burnt offerings, and offered peace offerings, and made a feast to all his servants.

16 ¶Then came there two women, *that were* harlots, unto the king, and stood before him.

17 And the one woman said, O my lord, I and this woman dwell in one house; and I was delivered of a child with her in the house.

18 And it came to pass the third day after that I was delivered, that this woman was delivered also: and we *were* together; *there was* no stranger with us in the house, save we two in the house.

19 And this woman's child died in the night; because she overlaid it.

20 And she arose at midnight, and took my son from beside me, while thine handmaid slept, and laid it in her bosom, and laid her dead child in my bosom.

21 And when I rose in the morning to give my child suck, behold, it was dead: but when I had considered it in the morning, behold, it was not my son, which I did bear.

22 And the other woman said, Nay; but the living *is* my son, and the dead *is* thy son. And this said, No; but the dead *is* thy son, and the living *is* my son. Thus they spake before the king.

23 Then said the king, The one saith, This *is* my son that liveth, and thy son *is* the dead: and the other saith, Nay; but thy son *is* the dead, and my son *is* the living.

24 And the king said, Bring me a sword. And they brought a sword before the king.

25 And the king said, Divide the living child in two, and give half to the one, and half to the other.

26 Then spake the woman whose the living child *was* unto the king, for her bowels yearned upon her son, and she said, O my lord, give her the living child, and in no wise slay it. But the other said, Let it be neither mine nor thine, *but* divide *it.*

27 Then the king answered and said, Give her the living child, and in no wise slay it: she *is* the mother thereof.

28 And all Israel heard of the judg-

honor would also be his. If he were faithful to God's commands, then he would **lengthen** his days. This promise was never fully realized (11:42) because of his apostasy later in life.

15. Solomon returned to Jerusalem to the **ark of the covenant,** which was housed in the tent erected by David (II Sam 6:17).

3. His wisdom demonstrated. 3:16-28.

16-22. Solomon's wisdom was quickly put to a test as two **harlots** came to him. Both women had a baby; both had slept with their baby; one mother had inadvertently smothered hers and exchanged the babies, her dead one for the living one, while the other mother slept. Now both women claimed the living baby. As Ellison has noted, "The fact that two such women had access to the king's court shows that it was really open to all and explains why Solomon felt the prospect of his judicial functions to be such a burden" (p. 305).

23-28. When Solomon feigned to divide the living baby between the women, the true mother's **bowels yearned** for her son. According to ancient Hebrew thought, the bowels (Heb *racham*) (or womb), were the seat of the emotions. In compassion for her baby, she preferred to lose her suit and suffer the loss of her child, rather than allow him to be killed; so Solomon awarded her the custody of her child.

Keil summarizes, "This judicial decision convinced all the people that Solomon was endowed with divine wisdom for the administration of justice" (p. 43).

ment which the king had judged; and they feared the king: for they saw that the wisdom of God *was* in him, to do judgment.

CHAPTER 4

SO king Sŏlomon was king over all Israel.

2 And these *were* the princes which he had; Ăz-a-rī′ah the son of Zā′dŏk the priest,

3 Ĕl-i-hô′reph and A-hī′ah, the sons of Shī′sha, scribes; Je-hŏsh′a-phăt the son of A-hī′lud, the recorder.

4 And Be-nā′iah the son of Je-hoi′a-da *was* over the host: and Zā′dŏk and Ă-bī′a-thar *were* the priests:

5 And Ăz-a-rī′ah the son of Nāthan *was* over the officers: and Zā′bŭd the son of Nāthan *was* principal officer, *and* the king's friend:

6 And A-hī′shär *was* over the household: and Ăd-o-nī′ram the son of Ăb′da *was* over the tribute.

7 ¶And Sŏlomon had twelve officers over all Israel, which provided victuals for the king and his household: each man his month in a year made provision.

8 And these *are* their names: The son of Hur, in mount Ē′phra-im:

9 The son of Dē′kar, in Mā′kăz, and in Shā-ăl′bĭm, and Bĕth-shĕ′mesh, and Ē′lon-bĕth-hā′nan:

10 The son of Hē′sed, in Ar′ŭ-bŏth; to him *pertained* Sō′chŏh, and all the land of Hē′pher:

11 The son of A-bĭn′a-dăb, in all the region of Dor; which had Tā′phăth the daughter of Sŏlomon to wife:

12 Bā′a-na the son of A-hī′lud; *to him pertained* Tā-a-năch and Me-gĭd′dŏ, and all Bĕth-shĕ′an, which *is* by Zăr′tanah beneath Jĕz′re-el, from Bĕth-shĕ′-an to Ā′bel-mĕ-hō′lah, *even* unto *the place that is* beyond Jŏk′ne-am:

13 The son of Gĕ′ber, in Rä′moth-gĭl′e-ad; to him *pertained* the towns of Jā′ir the son of Ma-năs′seh, which *are* in Gilead; to him *also pertained* the region of

4. His officials and administrative districts. 4:1-19.

4:1-6. These were the princes. These princes (Heb *sar*) are not members of the royal family, but high-ranking officials. One does well to compare this list of officials with that of David's (II Sam 20:23-26); for the service of some of David's officials drew Solomon's attention, and he retained them in his administration. It will be noted also that Solomon found a need to enlarge his staff.

David employed one scribe, but Solomon had need of three: **Elihoreph, Ahiah,** and Zadok the priest's son **Azariah. Jehoshaphat** was retained. He served as the recorder (Heb *mazkir* remembrancer), "whose duty it was to record events as they occurred and who probably was responsible for the official archives of the realm" (Davis, p. 177). **Benaiah** not only was retained, but he was promoted to captain of the host. **Zadok** and **Abiathar** were the priests. One need not think that Abiathar remained on as priest in a lesser capacity following his demotion (2:26-27). Rather, this list was compiled before Abiathar was removed from office. Thus, his name appears here.

If **Nathan** is the same person as the prophet (1:8ff.), then apparently Solomon rewarded his faithfulness by employing two of his sons: **Azariah,** who was over the officers (v. 7), and **Zabud,** the principal officer and the **king's friend,** possibly one who was a confidential advisor to the king (cf. II Sam 15:37; 16:16).

Ahishar was over the affairs of the palace. **Adoniram** is probably the **Adoram** (12:18) of David's administration since he served in the same capacity, over the **tribute** (Heb *mas*), the corvee, or tax, or forced labor. He met his death attempting to collect "tribute" in the reign of Rehoboam (12:18). One need not believe, as Gray does, that one man's ministry could not have spanned three kings' reigns. He may have been employed late in David's reign (note that in an earlier official list, II Sam 8:15-18, Adoram's name is omitted) and served through Solomon's reign to the first year of Rehoboam's reign.

7. Solomon appointed **twelve officers** over twelve regions to provide the royal court with provisions on a monthly basis. **Israel** is regarded as separate from Judah (cf. vs. 20) by the royal administration because the twelve districts did not coincide with the original tribal allotments and apparently did not include Judah (Aharoni and Avi-Yonah, *The Macmillan Bible Atlas*, p. 72-73). This evident favoritism to his tribe, Judah, would certainly provide a reason for discontent with Solomon's rule.

8-19. The officers and districts are enumerated; but specific boundaries are not given, just principal cities. The districts are: (1) Ephraim (vs. 8); (2) Dan's original allotment (vs. 9); (3) the coastal region around Hepher (vs. 10); (4) the coastal region around Dor (vs. 11); (5) the Plain of Esdraelon (vs. 12); (6) Manasseh east of the Jordan River (vs. 13); (7) the region allotted to Reuben and Gad (vs. 14); (8) Naphtali (vs. 15); (9) Asher (vs. 16); (10) Issachar (vs. 17); (11) Benjamin (vs. 18); and (12) Gilead, the area touching the southern border of the sixth district (vs. 19).

Är'gŏb, which *is* in Bā'shan, threescore great cities with walls and brasen bars:

14 A-hĭn'a-dăb the son of Ĭd'dō *had* Mā-ha-nā'im:

15 A-hĭm'ă-az *was* in Năph'ta-lī; he also took Bās'măth the daughter of Sŏl'omon to wife:

16 Bā'a-nah the son of Hu'shaī *was* in Asher and in Ā'lŏth:

17 Je-hŏsh'a-phăt the son of Par'ū-ah, in Ĭs'sa-char:

18 Shĭm'e-ī the son of Ē'lah, in Benjamin:

19 Gē'ber the son of Ū'rī *was* in the country of Gilead, *in* the country of Sihon king of the Ămo͞rītes, and of Og king of Bā'shan; and *he was* the only officer which *was* in the land.

20 ¶Jūdah and Israel *were* many, as the sand which *is* by the sea in multitude, eating and drinking, and making merry.

21 And Sŏlomon reigned over all kingdoms from the river unto the land of the Philistines, and unto the border of Egypt: they brought presents, and served Sŏlomon all the days of his life.

22 ¶And Sŏlomon's provision for one day was thirty measures of fine flour, and threescore measures of meal,

23 Ten fat oxen, and twenty oxen out of the pastures, and an hundred sheep, beside harts, and roebucks, and fallow-deer, and fatted fowl.

24 For he had dominion over all *the region* on this side the river, from Tĭph'-sah even to Ăz'zah, over all the kings on this side the river: and he had peace on all sides round about him.

25 And Jūdah and Israel dwelt safely, every man under his vine and under his fig tree, from Dan even to Be'er-shē'ba, all the days of Sŏlomon.

26 ¶And Sŏlomon had forty thousand stalls of horses for his chariots, and twelve thousand horsemen.

27 And those officers provided victual for king Sŏlomon, and for all that came unto king Sŏlomon's table, every man in his month: they lacked nothing.

28 Barley also and straw for the horses and dromedaries brought they unto the place where *the officers* were, every man according to his charge.

29 ¶And God gave Sŏlomon wisdom and understanding exceeding much, and largeness of heart, even as the sand that *is* on the sea shore.

30 And Sŏlomon's wisdom excelled the wisdom of all the children of the east country, and all the wisdom of Egypt.

31 For he was wiser than all men; than Ethan the Ĕz'ra-hīte, and Hē'măn, and Chăl'cŏl, and Där'da, the sons of Mā'hŏl: and his fame was in all nations round about.

32 And he spake three thousand proverbs: and his songs were a thousand and five.

33 And he spake of trees, from the cedar tree that *is* in Lebanon even unto the hyssop that springeth out of the wall: he spake also of beasts, and of fowl, and of creeping things, and of fishes.

34 And there came of all people to

5. His tribute and provisions. 4:20-28.

20-21. Solomon's control extended over all the kingdoms from the **river** to the **border of Egypt.** Comparing Genesis 15:18, the **river** is probably the Euphrates River; and the **border of Egypt** is the River of Egypt (Wadi el-Arish). These kingdoms served Solomon by bringing him **presents,** i.e., tribute (Heb *minchah*).

22-23. Measures (Heb *kŏr*) were roughly equivalent to eleven bushels each.

24-25. His dominion extended from **Tiphsah,** i.e., Thapsacus, to **Azzah,** i.e., Gaza. **Every man under his vine . . . fig tree** denotes the peace, security, and contentment enjoyed from **Dan,** the northernmost city, to **Beer-sheba,** the southernmost city.

26-28. Forty thousand is evidently an error in copying because a parallel passage, II Chronicles 9:25, indicates that Solomon had four thousand stalls of horses, a more suitable number. The **officers** are listed in verses 7-19. **Dromedaries** should be rendered "swift steeds" (ASV).

6. His wisdom summarized. 4:29-34.

29-31. God gave Solomon **largeness of heart,** which indicates a broad and comprehensive understanding. Solomon's wisdom was unexcelled. **The children of the east country** may be a reference to people of Mesopotamia, but it more likely refers to the Arabians. The identity of the four wisemen is unknown. The four names appear as descendants of Judah in I Chronicles 2:6, and two of the men, **Ethan** and **Heman,** appear in the superscriptions of Psalms 88 and 89.

32-34. Solomon spoke **three thousand proverbs.** Undoubtedly, many of these proverbs appear in the book of Proverbs. Unfortunately, most of his songs have been lost. Solomon was able to use details of nature to teach moral lessons.

hear the wisdom of Sŏlomon, from all kings of the earth, which had heard of his wisdom.

CHAPTER 5

AND Hiram king of Tyre sent his servants unto Sŏlomon; for he had heard that they had anointed him king in the room of his father: for Hiram was ever a lover of David.

2 And Sŏlomon sent to Hiram, saying,

3 Thou knowest how that David my father could not build an house unto the name of the LORD his God for the wars which were about him on every side, until the LORD put them under the soles of his feet.

4 But now the LORD my God hath given me rest on every side, *so that there is* neither adversary nor evil occurrent.

5 And, behold, I purpose to build an house unto the name of the LORD my God, as the LORD spake unto David my father, saying, Thy son, whom I will set upon thy throne in thy room, he shall build an house unto my name.

6 Now therefore command thou that they hew me cedar trees out of Lebanon; and my servants shall be with thy servants; and unto thee will I give hire for thy servants according to all that thou shalt appoint: for thou knowest that *there is* not among us any that can skill to hew timber like unto the Si-dŏ'nianś.

7 ¶And it came to pass, when Hiram heard the words of Sŏlomon, that he rejoiced greatly, and said, Blessed *be* the LORD this day, which hath given unto David a wise son over this great people.

8 And Hiram sent to Sŏlomon, saying, I have considered the things which thou sentest to me for: *and* I will do all thy desire concerning timber of cedar, and concerning timber of fir.

9 My servants shall bring *them* down from Lebanon unto the sea: and I will convey them by sea in floats unto the place that thou shalt appoint me, and will cause them to be discharged there, and thou shalt receive *them:* and thou shalt accomplish my desire, in giving food for my household.

10 So Hiram gave Sŏlomon cedar trees and fir trees *according to* all his desire.

11 And Sŏlomon gave Hiram twenty thousand measures of wheat *for* food to his household, and twenty measures of pure oil: thus gave Sŏlomon to Hiram year by year.

12 And the LORD gave Sŏlomon wisdom, as he promised him: and there was peace between Hiram and Sŏlomon; and they two made a league together.

13 ¶And king Sŏlomon raised a levy out of all Israel; and the levy was thirty thousand men.

C. Solomon's Building Projects. 5:1-9:28.

1. The building preparations. 5:1-18.

5:1. Hiram (Huram in Chr) was the king of the great Phoenician city of Tyre who had enjoyed friendly relationships and trade agreements with David (II Sam 5:11). Upon hearing of Solomon's anointing, he sent his congratulations and greetings.

2-3. In II Samuel 7:2 David desired to build a house for God, but God had denied him that privilege because he had been a man of war (cf. I Chr 22:8; 28:2). However, David had been promised that his son Solomon would be permitted to carry out this desire (I Chr 22:9-10). David had not remained idle. He had begun purchasing building materials from Tyre and stocked them until Solomon was ready to use them. So Hiram was well aware of David's unfulfilled intentions.

4-5. Solomon was now king; he was at peace; therefore, he was now ready to carry out his father's wishes.

6. Hew me cedar trees. A fuller account of Solomon's request is found in II Chronicles 2:7-10. Solomon would send his servants to provide the crude, unskilled labor to help Hiram's skilled servants, for no Israelite could hew wood like the **Sidonians,** i.e., Phoenicians.

7-11. Hiram was eager to oblige. He promised to have the timbers, cedar and fir, i.e., cypress, cut from Lebanon, transported down to the **sea,** i.e., the Mediterranean, made into rafts, and floated down to an appointed place. According to II Chronicles 2:16, this **place** was Joppa (the port of Jaffa), the nearest port to Jerusalem. There they would be broken up and transported overland to the construction site in Jerusalem.

In addition to paying the hire of Hiram's servants (vs. 6), Solomon paid for the timbers with large quantities of food from Israel. Ellison suggests that II Chronicles 2:10 ". . . probably gives the total annual amount, Kings mentioning the higher quality food reserved by Hiram for his court" (p. 306). This payment **year by year** evidently continued until the completion of Solomon's building program.

12. There was peace between Hiram and Solomon because they made a treaty. Their friendship was strained somewhat when Hiram was dissatisfied with his payment of a few cities (9:10-13), but the relationship was evidently mended as they cooperated later in naval operations (9:26-27).

13. Solomon raised a levy (Heb *mas*), i.e., a tax of forced labor. Solomon is apparently the first Israelite king to impose such a tax upon his people. David had imposed a similar requirement upon the "strangers," i.e., foreigners, who resided in the land (I Chr 22:2). Solomon's action was the very thing of which the prophet Samuel had warned Israel when they clamored for a king (I Sam 8:16).

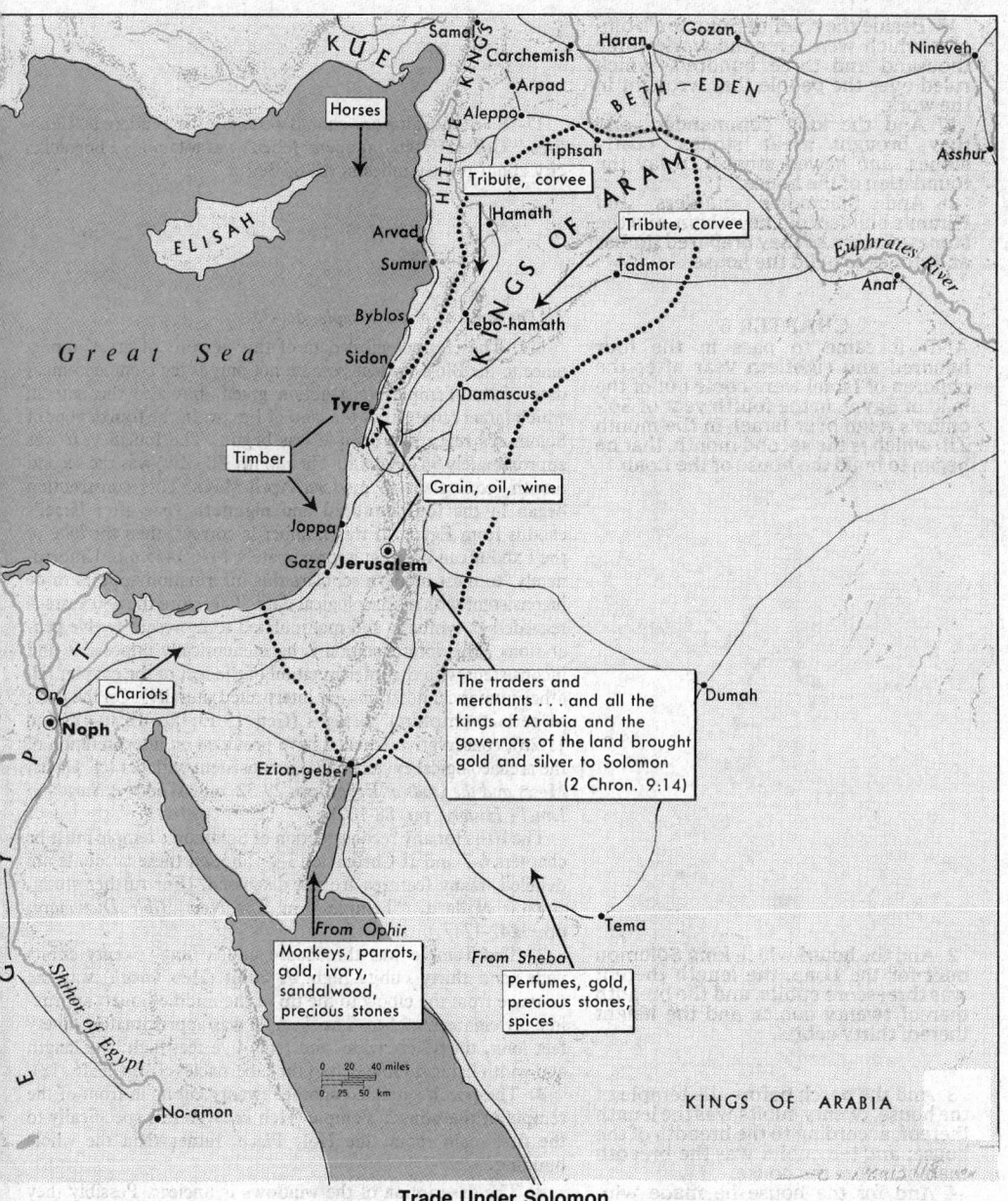

Trade Under Solomon

If **All Israel** is to be interpreted as it was in 4:7, then it is possible that Judah was favored and excluded from the levy while the ten northern tribes supplied 30,000 men for hard labor.

14 And he sent them to Lebanon, ten thousand a month by courses: a month they were in Lebanon, *and* two months at home: and Ăd-o-nĭ'ram *was* over the levy.

15 And Sŏlomon had threescore and ten thousand that bare burdens, and fourscore thousand hewers in the mountains;

14. To avoid widespread discontent, the men were divided into three labor gangs of 10,000 men. The gangs were alternated monthly, one month in Lebanon and two months at home. "This amounted to a 33 and ⅓ per cent tax on the time and earning capacity of the men involved" (Bentan, p. 30).

All served under the supervision of **Adoniram**.

15-16. In addition to the levy were 70,000 that **bare burdens**, i.e., the porters, and 80,000 stone **hewers** in the mountains, probably Palestinian limestone hills. Over these workmen were 3,300 officers.

16 Beside the chief of Sŏlomon's officers which *were* over the work, three thousand and three hundred, which ruled over the people that wrought in the work.

17 And the king commanded, and they brought great stones, costly stones, *and* hewed stones, to lay the foundation of the house.

18 And Sŏlomon's builders and Hiram's builders did hew *them,* and the stonesquarers: so they prepared timber and stones to build the house.

CHAPTER 6

AND it came to pass in the four hundred and eightieth year after the children of Israel were come out of the land of Egypt, in the fourth year of Sŏlomon's reign over Israel, in the month Zif, which *is* the second month, that he began to build the house of the Lord.

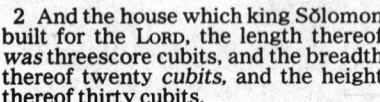

2 And the house which king Sŏlomon built for the Lord, the length thereof *was* threescore cubits, and the breadth thereof twenty *cubits,* and the height thereof thirty cubits.

3 And the porch before the temple of the house, twenty cubits *was* the length thereof, according to the breadth of the house; *and* ten cubits *was* the breadth thereof before the house.

4 And for the house he made windows of narrow lights.

5 And against the wall of the house he built chambers round about, *against* the walls of the house round about, *both* of the temple and of the oracle: and he made chambers round about:

6 The nethermost chamber *was* five cubits broad, and the middle *was* six cubits broad, and the third *was* seven cubits broad: for without in the wall of the house he made narrowed rests round about, that *the beams* should not be fastened in the walls of the house.

17-18. Stonesquarers should probably be rendered "Gebalites." Gebal (Byblus, modern Jebeil) was a famous Phoenician city about twenty miles north of Beirut.

2. *The building of the Temple. 6:1-38.*

6:1. The chronological data of this verse is of great importance to the Bible student because not only is the commencement date of the Temple construction given, but also the date in which Israel came out of the land of Egypt. In the **fourth year** of Solomon's reign the Temple was begun. The fourth year was approximately 967/966 B.C. The month **Zif** (Ziv) was the second month (equivalent to modern April-May). This construction began in the **four hundred and eightieth year** after Israel's exodus from Egypt. If this number is correct, then the date of the Exodus can be set at approximately 1446/1445 B.C. Unfortunately, to most modern scholars this information appears to be inconsistent with archaeological data. Therefore the 480 years is regarded as symbolic and manipulated to represent twelve generations. This interpretation is hermeneutically impossible and inconsistent with the interpretation of the rest of the chapter (all other numerical notations are interpreted literally). On the basis of certain scriptural passages (Gen 15:13; Ex 12:40-41; Jud 11:26), conservative scholars have provided an interpretation of the archaeological evidence that is consistent with 6:1 (cf. Davis, *Moses and the Gods of Egypt,* pp. 29-32, and Wood, *A Survey of Israel's History,* pp. 88-109).

The basis for any reconstruction of Solomon's temple must be chapters 6-7 and II Chronicles 3-4. Though these accounts are detailed, many features are not discussed. (For further study, consult Millard, "Temple," in *The New Bible Dictionary,* pp. 1242-1247.)

2. The Temple was **threescore** cubits long, **twenty** cubits wide, and **thirty** cubits high. A **cubit** (Heb *'amah*) was the distance from the elbow to the tip of the middle finger, approximately eighteen inches. The Temple was approximately ninety feet long, thirty feet wide, and forty-five feet high, the length and width being double that of the tabernacle (cf. Ex 26:16, 18).

3. The **porch** extended another twenty cubits in front of the **temple of the house. Temple** (Heb *hēkal*) refers specifically to the first main room, the Holy Place, rather than the whole building.

4. The description of the **windows** is unclear. Possibly they were framed with immovable lattice-work. Their purpose was both to provide circulation of air and to tone down the bright rays of light.

5-6. Around three sides of the house were built three stories of **chambers.** The width of the bottom story (five cubits) was successively increased by one cubit on each of the other two stories. So that no holes would be bored in the temple walls for the beams that formed the ceilings of the lower stories and the floors of the upper ones, the thickness of the wall was successively reduced by one cubit in the second and third stories. It was on these **narrowed rests** that the beams were placed. Such a description gives some indication of the thickness of the walls at their bases.

The chambers "doubtless housed various stores and vestments, provided accommodation, maybe, for the priests in course, and sheltered the offerings of money and goods made by the worshippers" (Millard, p. 1245).

7-8. The stones were so well prepared at the quarry that no tools for dressing them were required on the building site. The chambers were entered by a door on the first floor. Access to the three upper floors was by a spiral staircase.

7 And the house, when it was in building, was built of stone made ready before it was brought thither: so that there was neither hammer nor axe *nor* any tool of iron heard in the house, while it was in building.

8 The door for the middle chamber *was* in the right side of the house: and they went up with winding stairs into the middle *chamber,* and out of the middle into the third.

9 So he built the house, and finished it; and covered the house with beams and boards of cedar.

10 And *then* he built chambers against all the house, five cubits high: and they rested on the house with timber of cedar.

11 ¶And the word of the LORD came to Solomon, saying,

12 *Concerning* this house which thou art in building, if thou wilt walk in my statutes, and execute my judgments, and keep all my commandments to walk in them; then will I perform my word with thee, which I spake unto David thy father:

13 And I will dwell among the children of Israel, and will not forsake my people Israel.

14 So Solomon built the house, and finished it.

15 And he built the walls of the house within with boards of cedar, both the floor of the house, and the walls of the ceiling: *and* he covered *them* on the inside with wood, and covered the floor of the house with planks of fir.

16 And he built twenty cubits on the sides of the house, both the floor and the walls with boards of cedar: he even built *them* for it within, *even* for the oracle, *even* for the most holy *place.*

17 And the house, that *is,* the temple before it, was forty cubits *long.*

18 And the cedar of the house within *was* carved with knops and open flowers: all *was* cedar; there was no stone seen.

19 And the oracle he prepared in the house within, to set there the ark of the covenant of the LORD.

20 And the oracle in the forepart *was* twenty cubits in length, and twenty cubits in breadth, and twenty cubits in the height thereof: and he overlaid it with pure gold; and *so* covered the altar *which was* of cedar.

21 So Solomon overlaid the house within with pure gold: and he made a partition by the chains of gold before the oracle; and he overlaid it with gold.

22 And the whole house he overlaid with gold, until he had finished all the house: also the whole altar that *was* by the oracle he overlaid with gold.

23 ¶And within the oracle he made two cherubims *of* olive tree, *each* ten cubits high.

24 And five cubits *was* the one wing of the cherub, and five cubits the other wing of the cherub: from the uttermost part of the one wing unto the uttermost part of the other *were* ten cubits.

9-15. The task of building was a great undertaking, perhaps greater than Solomon had anticipated. Therefore, during the progress of building he received divine encouragement. In view of 3:5; 9:2; and 11:9, this was probably not a direct revelation of Jehovah, but a strengthening through an unnamed prophet. God's promise (vs. 13) is reminiscent of the one that He made to Moses in Exodus 25:8.

16-18. The stone walls and the ceiling of the house were all totally panelled with boards of cedar and overlaid with gold. The cedar was decorated with carvings of **knobs** (gourds) and **open flowers.** According to II Chronicles 3:6, the walls were adorned also with jewels.

19-21. The house was divided into two large rooms. The **temple** (vs. 3) was the first main hall, and the **oracle** (Heb *debĭr*), or the **hinder parts** (7:25), were the second and inner rooms. This room, a perfect cube of twenty cubits, was also known as **the most holy place** (vs. 16).

22. Since there are striking similarities between this house and the tabernacle, the **altar that was by the oracle** may be an allusion to the altar of incense that stood before the inner curtain that divided the Most Holy Place from the Holy Place in the tabernacle (cf. Ex 30:1-6).

23-30. An added feature to the Most Holy Place was the presence of two cherubim. These are not to be confused with the two cherubim that stood over the mercy seat of the ark of the covenant, which would eventually be housed in this room.

25 And the other cherub *was* ten cubits: both the cherubims *were* of one measure and one size.

26 The height of the one cherub *was* ten cubits, and so *was* it of the other cherub.

27 And he set the cherubims within the inner house: and they stretched forth the wings of the cherubims, so that the wing of the one touched the *one* wall, and the wing of the other cherub touched the other wall; and their wings touched one another in the midst of the house.

28 And he overlaid the cherubims with gold.

29 And he carved all the walls of the house round about with carved figures of cherubims and palm trees and open flowers, within and without.

30 And the floor of the house he overlaid with gold, within and without.

31 ¶And for the entering of the oracle he made doors *of* olive tree: the lintel *and* side posts *were* a fifth part *of the wall.*

32 The two doors also *were of* olive tree; and he carved upon them carvings of cherubims and palm trees and open flowers, and overlaid *them* with gold, and spread gold upon the cherubims, and upon the palm trees.

33 So also made he for the door of the temple posts *of* olive tree, a fourth part *of the wall.*

34 And the two doors *were of* fir tree: the two leaves of the one door *were* folding, and the two leaves of the other door *were* folding.

35 And he carved *thereon* cherubims and palm trees and open flowers: and covered *them* with gold fitted upon the carved work.

36 And he built the inner court with three rows of hewed stone, and a row of cedar beams.

37 ¶In the fourth year was the foundation of the house of the Lord laid, in the month Zif:

38 And in the eleventh year, in the month Bul, which *is* the eighth month, was the house finished throughout all the parts thereof, and according to all the fashion of it. So was he seven years in building it.

CHAPTER 7

BUT Sŏlomon was building his own house thirteen years, and he finished all his house.

31-35. The outer doors leading into the **temple** were similar in construction, but were larger and made of cypress wood. Of the outer walls, they were a **fourth part,** i.e., one quarter of the wall, five cubits.

36. Three rows of hewed stone, and a row of cedar beams is not an indication of the height of the wall, but a description of the type of construction. Note the same proportion of stone and wood in Ezra 6:4. "This feature seems to be exactly paralleled at Ras Shamra in Syria, and several other sites have a comparable technique in using wood with brick or stone" (Wright, *Biblical Archaeology*, p. 140). The layer of wood was evidently a bonding agent between every three courses of stones.

Archaeologists have noted that Solomon's temple parallels a Phoenician temple. Though the basic design of the two rooms, the Holy Place and the Most Holy Place, parallels the tabernacle, it is not surprising to see Phoenician parallels in construction and ornamentation, for Solomon had employed skilled Phoenician craftsmen to direct this building project.

37-38. During Solomon's eleventh year of reign, in the eighth month, **Bul,** the Temple was completed. **Seven years** is a round number, for the actual time of construction was seven and one half years.

3. The building of Solomon's house. 7:1-8.

7:1. Several reasons may be offered as to why the building of his house took twice as long as that of the Temple: (1) extensive preparations had not been made for his palace; (2) the palace was larger than the Temple; and (3) he had accelerated the construction on the Temple, but let construction of his residence be delayed.

2 ¶He built also the house of the forest of Lebanon; the length thereof *was* an hundred cubits, and the breadth thereof fifty cubits, and the height thereof thirty cubits, upon four rows of cedar pillars, with cedar beams upon the pillars.

3 And *it was* covered with cedar above upon the beams, that *lay* on forty five pillars, fifteen *in* a row.

4 And *there were* windows *in* three rows, and light *was* against light *in* three ranks.

5 And all the doors and posts *were* square, with the windows: and light *was* against light *in* three ranks.

6 ¶And he made a porch of pillars; the length thereof *was* fifty cubits, and the breadth thereof thirty cubits: and the porch *was* before them: and the *other* pillars and the thick beam *were* before them.

7 Then he made a porch for the throne where he might judge, *even* the porch of judgment: and *it was* covered with cedar from one side of the floor to the other.

8 And his house where he dwelt *had* another court within the porch, *which* was of the like work. Sŏlomon made also an house for Pharaoh's daughter, whom he had taken *to* wife, like unto this porch.

9 All these *were of* costly stones, according to the measures of hewed stones, sawed with saws, within and without, even from the foundation unto the coping, and *so* on the outside toward the great court.

10 And the foundation *was of* costly stones, even great stones, stones of ten cubits, and stones of eight cubits.

11 And above *were* costly stones, after the measures of hewed stones, and cedars.

12 And the great court round about *was* with three rows of hewed stones, and a row of cedar beams, both for the inner court of the house of the LORD, and for the porch of the house.

13 ¶And king Sŏlomon sent and fetched Hiram out of Tyre.

14 He *was* a widow's son of the tribe of Năph′ta-lī, and his father *was* a man of Tyre, a worker in brass: and he was filled with wisdom, and understanding, and cunning to work all works in brass. And he came to king Sŏlomon, and wrought all his work.

15 For he cast two pillars of brass, of eighteen cubits high apiece: and a line of twelve cubits did compass either of them about.

16 And he made two chapiters *of* molten brass, to set upon the tops of the pillars: the height of the one chapiter *was* five cubits, and the height of the other chapiter *was* five cubits:

17 *And* nets of checker work, and wreaths of chain work, for the chapiters which *were* upon the top of the pillars; seven for the one chapiter, and seven for the other chapiter.

18 And he made the pillars, and two

2-5. The house of the forest of Lebanon is to be identified with the building of verse 1 and also of verse 8 (cf. 9:10). It was not built in a forest, nor in Lebanon. It may have received its name from its four rows of cedar pillars. This large area (one hundred by fifty cubits) of the house may have served as the armory (cf. 10:17; Isa 22:8).

6-7. Adjacent was the **porch** (hall) of **pillars,** which may have served as a waiting room for those with lawsuits before they were admitted into the next-mentioned room, and the **porch** (hall) of **judgment,** the throne room of the king.

8. After describing the public quarters of the palace, the private quarters, Solomon's royal residence and the harem quarters (e.g., the **house for Pharaoh's daughter**), are noted without description.

4. The building materials. 7:9-12.

9-12. The buildings (Temple and palace) were constructed of expensive and carefully surfaced stones. Even the foundation was constructed of the choicest stones, the standard measurement being ten cubits and eight cubits. Gray cites the large hewn blocks of the lower courses of the Wailing Wall from Herod's construction as being of comparable size. One measures sixteen and a half feet by thirteen feet (p. 170).

5. The building artisan. 7:13-14.

13-14. This **Hiram** is not the king of Tyre (5:1). His father was a Tyrian, but his mother was from the tribe of Naphtali. According to II Chronicles 2:14, she was from the tribe of Dan, an apparent contradiction. One tribe may have been her tribal lineage, the other her place of birth or residence. Or as Keil has suggested, she may have been of one tribe and have married into another in a previous marriage (p. 96). The description of his skill is similar to that of Bezaleel in Exodus 31:1-5.

6. The building furnishings. 7:15-51.

15-22. Positioned on the porch of the Temple were two enormous free-standing pillars. Both stood twenty-seven feet high, were eighteen feet in circumference, and had a **Chapiter** (capital) that was seven and one-half feet in height. The capital was elaborately ornamented with nets of checker-work, wreaths of chain-work, pomegranates, and a border of lily-work. On the extreme top was a bowl (vs. 41). It is possible that the two pillars served as giant lampstands (Unger, *Archaeology of the Old Testament*, p. 231).

On one pillar was the name **Jachin** (i.e., he shall establish), and on the other was the name **Boaz** (i.e., in him is strength). These names were probably the first words of an inscription on them. "The 'Jachin' formula may have been, 'Yahweh will

rows round about upon the one network, to cover the chapiters that *were* upon the top, with pomegranates: and so did he for the other chapiter.

19 And the chapiters that *were* upon the top of the pillars *were* of lily work in the porch, four cubits.

20 And the chapiters upon the two pillars *had pomegranates* also above, over against the belly which *was* by the network: and the pomegranates *were* two hundred in rows round about upon the other chapiter.

21 And he set up the pillars in the porch of the temple: and he set up the right pillar, and called the name thereof Jā'chin: and he set up the left pillar, and called the name thereof Bō'ăz.

22 And upon the top of the pillars *was* lily work: so was the work of the pillars finished.

23 ¶And he made a molten sea, ten cubits from the one brim to the other: *it was* round all about, and his height *was* five cubits: and a line of thirty cubits did compass it round about.

24 And under the brim of it round about *there were* knops compassing it, ten in a cubit, compassing the sea round about: the knops *were* cast in two rows, when it was cast.

25 It stood upon twelve oxen, three looking toward the north, and three looking toward the west, and three looking toward the south, and three looking toward the east: and the sea *was set* above upon them, and all their hinder parts *were* inward.

26 And it *was* an hand breadth thick, and the brim thereof was wrought like the brim of a cup, with flowers of lilies: it contained two thousand baths.

27 ¶And he made ten bases of brass; four cubits *was* the length of one base, and four cubits the breadth thereof, and three cubits the height of it.

28 And the work of the bases *was* on this *manner:* they had borders, and the borders *were* between the ledges:

29 And on the borders that *were* between the ledges *were* lions, oxen, and cherubims: and upon the ledges *there was* a base above: and beneath the lions and oxen *were* certain additions made of thin work.

30 And every base had four brasen wheels, and plates of brass: and the four corners thereof had undersetters: under the laver *were* undersetters molten, at the side of every addition.

31 And the mouth of it within the chapiter and above *was* a cubit: but the mouth thereof *was* round *after* the work of the base, a cubit and an half: and also upon the mouth of it *were* gravings with their borders, foursquare, not round.

32 And under the borders *were* four wheels; and the axletrees of the wheels *were joined* to the base: and the height of a wheel *was* a cubit and half a cubit.

33 And the work of the wheels *was* like the work of a chariot wheel: their axletrees, and their naves, and their felloes, and their spokes, *were* all molten.

34 And *there were* four undersetters to the four corners of one base: *and* the

establish (Heb *yakīn*) thy throne forever, or the like; and the 'Boaz' oracle may have run, 'In Yahweh is the king's strength', or something like that" (Unger, p. 231).

23-26. The **molten sea** was a huge bowl, fifteen feet in diameter and seven and one-half feet high. It was mounted upon four groups of three brass oxen facing the four directions of the compass. This **sea** took the place of the laver of the tabernacle (Ex 30:18-21). One need not suspect that the sea had to do with Canaanite mythology; it was so named because of its size.

27-39. Ten portable lavers were also constructed. Small basins were mounted on bases, which in turn were mounted on wheels for mobility. These carriage-like bases were decorated with ornamental cherubim, lions, and oxen.

undersetters *were* of the very base it-self.

35 And in the top of the base *was there* a round compass of half a cubit high: and on the top of the base the ledges thereof and the borders thereof *were* of the same.

36 For on the plates of the ledges thereof, and on the borders thereof, he graved cherubims, lions, and palm trees, according to the proportion of every one, and additions round about.

37 After this *manner* he made the ten bases: all of them had one casting, one measure, *and* one size.

38 Then made he ten lavers of brass: one laver contained forty baths: *and* every laver was four cubits: *and* upon every one of the ten bases one laver.

39 And he put five bases on the right side of the house, and five on the left side of the house: and he set the sea on the right side of the house eastward over against the south.

40 ¶And Hiram made the lavers, and the shovels, and the basons. So Hiram made an end of doing all the work that he made king Sŏlomon for the house of the LORD:

41 The two pillars, and the *two* bowls of the chapiters that *were* on the top of the two pillars; and the two networks, to cover the two bowls of the chapiters which *were* upon the top of the pillars;

42 And four hundred pomegranates for the two networks, *even* two rows of pomegranates for one network, to cover the two bowls of the chapiters that *were* upon the pillars;

43 And the ten bases, and ten lavers on the bases;

44 And one sea, and twelve oxen under the sea;

45 And the pots, and the shovels, and the basons: and all these vessels, which Hiram made to king Sŏlomon for the house of the LORD, *were of* bright brass.

46 In the plain of Jordan did the king cast them, in the clay ground between Sŭc'coth and Zär'thăn,

47 And Sŏlomon left all the vessels *unweighed,* because they were exceeding many: neither was the weight of the brass found out.

48 And Sŏlomon made all the vessels that *pertained* unto the house of the LORD: the altar of gold, and the table of gold, whereupon the shewbread *was,*

49 And the candlesticks of pure gold, five on the right *side,* and five on the left, before the oracle, with the flowers, and the lamps, and the tongs of gold,

50 And the bowls, and the snuffers, and the basons, and the spoons, and the censers of pure gold; and the hinges *of* gold, *both* for the doors of the inner house, the most holy *place, and* for the doors of the house, *to wit,* of the temple.

51 So was ended all the work that king Sŏlomon made for the house of the LORD. And Sŏlomon brought in the things which David his father had dedicated; *even* the silver, and the gold, and the vessels, did he put among the treasures of the house of the LORD.

40-47. All the intricate temple furnishings are enumerated. Of special interest is verse 46. The work of Hiram was not engraving, but casting. Large molds were dug in the clay, and the molten brass was poured into them.

48-51. The tabernacle was lighted by a single seven-lamp candlestick (Ex 25:31-40). The Holy Place of the Temple was lighted by ten candlesticks, five on each side.

CHAPTER 8

THEN Sŏlomon assembled the elders of Israel, and all the heads of the tribes, the chief of the fathers of the children of Israel, unto king Sŏlomon in Jerusalem, that they might bring up the ark of the covenant of the LORD out of the city of David, which is Zion.

2 And all the men of Israel assembled themselves unto king Sŏlomon at the feast in the month Ēth′a-nĭm, which is the seventh month.

3 And all the elders of Israel came, and the priests took up the ark.

4 And they brought up the ark of the LORD, and the tabernacle of the congregation, and all the holy vessels that were in the tabernacle, even those did the priests and the Levites bring up.

5 And king Sŏlomon, and all the congregation of Israel, that were assembled unto him, were with him before the ark, sacrificing sheep and oxen, that could not be told nor numbered for multitude.

6 And the priests brought in the ark of the covenant of the LORD unto his place, into the oracle of the house, to the most holy place, even under the wings of the cherubims.

7 For the cherubims spread forth their two wings over the place of the ark, and the cherubims covered the ark and the staves thereof above.

8 And they drew out the staves, that the ends of the staves were seen out in the holy place before the oracle, and they were not seen without: and there they are unto this day.

9 There was nothing in the ark save the two tables of stone, which Moses put there at Hŏ′rĕb, when the LORD made a covenant with the children of Israel, when they came out of the land of Egypt.

10 And it came to pass, when the priests were come out of the holy place, that the cloud filled the house of the LORD,

11 So that the priests could not stand to minister because of the cloud: for the glory of the LORD had filled the house of the LORD.

12 ¶Then spake Sŏlomon, The LORD said that he would dwell in the thick darkness.

13 I have surely built thee an house to dwell in, a settled place for thee to abide in for ever.

14 And the king turned his face about, and blessed all the congregation of Israel: (and all the congregation of Israel stood;)

15 And he said, Blessed be the LORD God of Israel, which spake with his mouth unto David my father, and hath with his hand fulfilled it, saying,

16 Since the day that I brought forth my people Israel out of Egypt, I chose no city out of all the tribes of Israel to build an house, that my name might be

7. *The building dedication. 8:1-9:9.*

8:1-2. Solomon summoned the representatives of Israel to Jerusalem to join the celebration in placing the ark in the new Temple. The time chosen was **the feast** of the seventh month, **Ethanim.** This feast was the Feast of Tabernacles which began on the fifteenth day and continued for seven days (cf. Lev 23:34).

According to 6:38, the Temple was completed in the eighth month. In light of 7:51 it is doubtful that Solomon would have placed the ark in the Temple one month before its completion (in the seventh month). Solomon probably waited until the next year to dedicate the Temple. If 9:1-10 indicates a strict chronological sequence, it is not impossible that the dedication of the Temple did not occur until thirteen years later when both the Lord's and the king's houses were completed.

3-5. The **priests** were careful to transport the ark. (Recount the events of II Sam 6:3-7.) The **ark** was brought from the tent that David had prepared for it in Jerusalem (II Sam 6:17), and the **tabernacle** and its **holy vessels** were brought up from Gibeon (II Chr 1:3).

6-8. The ark was transported to the **most holy place** and placed between the two cherubim (6:23-27) whose outstretched wings overshadowed the ark.

9. There was nothing in the ark save the two tablets of stone. It is pointless to speculate what happened to the other items (pot of manna and Aaron's rod) listed in Hebrews 9:4.

10-11. The cloud, symbolizing the glorious presence of God, filled the house. The description of the event is reminiscent of that in Exodus 40:34-35.

12-13. After seeing a demonstration of God's presence, he reflected on an earlier promise of God's presence made to Moses (Lev 16:2). He must have been thinking of the Davidic covenant (II Sam 7:13) when he said, **I have surely built thee a house.** In contrast to the temporary nature of the tabernacle, this dwelling place would be permanent, **a settled place.**

14-21. In the audience of all his people Solomon praised God for His faithfulness to David in two respects: David's heart's desire to build a house for God had been accomplished, and David's son was sitting on the throne.

therein; but I chose David to be over my people Israel.

17 And it was in the heart of David my father to build an house for the name of the LORD God of Israel.

18 And the LORD said unto David my father, Whereas it was in thine heart to build an house unto my name, thou didst well that it was in thine heart.

19 Nevertheless thou shalt not build the house; but thy son that shall come forth out of thy loins, he shall build the house unto my name.

20 And the LORD hath performed his word that he spake, and I am risen up in the room of David my father, and sit on the throne of Israel, as the LORD promised, and have built an house for the name of the LORD God of Israel.

21 And I have set there a place for the ark, wherein *is* the covenant of the LORD, which he made with our fathers, when he brought them out of the land of Egypt.

22 ¶And Solomon stood before the altar of the LORD in the presence of all the congregation of Israel, and spread forth his hands toward heaven:

23 And he said, LORD God of Israel, *there is* no God like thee, in heaven above, or on earth beneath, who keepest covenant and mercy with thy servants that walk before thee with all their heart:

24 Who hast kept with thy servant David my father that thou promisedst him: thou spakest also with thy mouth, and hast fulfilled *it* with thine hand, as *it is* this day.

25 Therefore now, LORD God of Israel, keep with thy servant David my father that thou promisedst him, saying, There shall not fail thee a man in my sight to sit on the throne of Israel; so that thy children take heed to their way, that they walk before me as thou hast walked before me.

26 And now, O God of Israel, let thy word, I pray thee, be verified, which thou spakest unto thy servant David my father.

27 But will God indeed dwell on the earth? behold, the heaven and heaven of heavens cannot contain thee; how much less this house that I have builded?

28 Yet have thou respect unto the prayer of thy servant, and to his supplication, O LORD my God, to hearken unto the cry and to the prayer, which thy servant prayeth before thee to day:

29 That thine eyes may be open toward this house night and day, *even* toward the place of which thou hast said, My name shall be there: that thou mayest hearken unto the prayer which thy servant shall make toward this place.

30 And hearken thou to the supplication of thy servant, and of thy people

22. The **altar** was the brazen altar of burnt offerings in the court beyond the laver. There is no mention of this altar being constructed in Kings, although its existence is presupposed here and in 8:64. (For construction of an altar, see II Chr 4:1.) It is possible that the brazen altar of the tabernacle was used (cf. 8:4). Second Chronicles 6:13 has Solomon erecting a scaffold, i.e., a platform, upon which he stood while addressing the people.

In Solomon's prayer he enumerated many conditions and circumstances in which Israel might be found, and he petitioned God on the basis of each one.

23-26. Solomon requested a general fulfillment of God's covenant to David in the future as He had in the past.

27-30. Concerning the Temple, he prayed that God, from His dwelling place in heaven, would always keep His eyes turned to this place of worship and prayer. There is no theological contradiction in verses 12-13 and 27. The Temple would only serve as a point of contact for communion between Israel and her omnipresent and transcendent God.

Israel, when they shall pray toward this place: and hear thou in heaven thy dwelling place: and when thou hearest, forgive.

31 ¶If any man trespass against his neighbour, and an oath be laid upon him to cause him to swear, and the oath come before thine altar in this house:

32 Then hear thou in heaven, and do, and judge thy servants, condemning the wicked, to bring his way upon his head; and justifying the righteous, to give him according to his righteousness.

33 ¶When thy people Israel be smitten down before the enemy, because they have sinned against thee, and shall turn again to thee, and confess thy name, and pray, and make supplication unto thee in this house:

34 Then hear thou in heaven, and forgive the sin of thy people Israel, and bring them again unto the land which thou gavest unto their fathers.

35 ¶When heaven is shut up, and there is no rain, because they have sinned against thee; if they pray toward this place, and confess thy name, and turn from their sin, when thou afflictest them:

36 Then hear thou in heaven, and forgive the sin of thy servants, and of thy people Israel, that thou teach them the good way wherein they should walk, and give rain upon thy land, which thou hast given to thy people for an inheritance.

37 ¶If there be in the land famine, if there be pestilence, blasting, mildew, locust, or if there be caterpiller; if their enemy besiege them in the land of their cities; whatsoever plague, whatsoever sickness there be;

38 What prayer and supplication soever be made by any man, or by all thy people Israel, which shall know every man the plague of his own heart, and spread forth his hands toward this house:

39 Then hear thou in heaven thy dwelling place, and forgive, and do, and give to every man according to his ways, whose heart thou knowest; (for thou, even thou only, knowest the hearts of all the children of men;)

40 That they may fear thee all the days that they live in the land which thou gavest unto our fathers.

41 ¶Moreover concerning a stranger, that is not of thy people Israel, but cometh out of a far country for thy name's sake;

42 (For they shall hear of thy great name, and of thy strong hand, and of thy stretched out arm;) when he shall come and pray toward this house;

43 Hear thou in heaven thy dwelling place, and do according to all that the stranger calleth to thee for: that all people of the earth may know thy name, to fear thee, as do thy people Israel; and that they may know that this house, which I have builded, is called by thy name.

44 ¶If thy people go out to battle against their enemy, whithersoever thou shalt send them, and shall pray

31-32. Solomon prayed that God would deal righteously with the one who had sinned against Him.

33-40. When his people repented, he asked that God would be quick to forgive and would remove the drought and calamities that were so common to Israel.

41-43. Solomon prayed for the **stranger,** i.e., the foreigner. The Temple was to be a worship site for all God-fearing foreigners, just as Moses had allowed foreigners to bring their offerings to the tabernacle (Num 15:14).

44-53. Solomon asked that when prayers of God's people were directed to the Temple and when they were away from Jerusalem, whether in battle or captivity, they might be heard.

unto the LORD toward the city which thou hast chosen, and *toward* the house that I have built for thy name:

45 Then hear thou in heaven their prayer and their supplication, and maintain their cause.

46 If they sin against thee, (for *there is* no man that sinneth not,) and thou be angry with them, and deliver them to the enemy, so that they carry them away captives unto the land of the enemy, far or near;

47 *Yet* if they shall bethink themselves in the land whither they were carried captives, and repent, and make supplication unto thee in the land of them that carried them captives, saying, We have sinned, and have done perversely, we have committed wickedness;

48 And *so* return unto thee with all their heart, and with all their soul, in the land of their enemies, which led them away captive, and pray unto thee toward their land, which thou gavest unto their fathers, the city which thou hast chosen, and the house which I have built for thy name:

49 Then hear thou their prayer and their supplication in heaven thy dwelling place, and maintain their cause,

50 And forgive thy people that have sinned against thee, and all their transgressions wherein they have transgressed against thee, and give them compassion before them who carried them captive, that they may have compassion on them:

51 For they *be* thy people, and thine inheritance, which thou broughtest forth out of Egypt, from the midst of the furnace of iron:

52 That thine eyes may be open unto the supplication of thy servant, and unto the supplication of thy people Israel, to hearken unto them in all that they call for unto thee.

53 For thou didst separate them from among all the people of the earth, *to be* thine inheritance, as thou spakest by the hand of Moses thy servant, when thou broughtest our fathers out of Egypt, O Lord GOD.

54 ¶And it was *so*, that when Sŏlomon had made an end of praying all this prayer and supplication unto the LORD, he arose from before the altar of the LORD, from kneeling on his knees with his hands spread up to heaven.

55 And he stood, and blessed all the congregation of Israel with a loud voice, saying,

56 Blessed *be* the LORD, that hath given rest unto his people Israel, according to all that he promised: there hath not failed one word of all his good promise, which he promised by the hand of Moses his servant.

57 The LORD our God be with us, as he was with our fathers: let him not leave us, nor forsake us:

58 That he may incline our hearts unto him, to walk in all his ways, and to keep his commandments, and his statutes, and his judgments, which he commanded our fathers.

59 And let these my words, wherewith I have made supplication before the

54-61. Solomon closed his dedicatory prayer with a benediction. Second Chronicles 7:1ff. omits this benediction, but it includes the account of fire falling from heaven and igniting his burnt offering.

LORD, be nigh unto the LORD our God day and night, that he maintain the cause of his servant, and the cause of his people Israel at all times, as the matter shall require:

60 That all the people of the earth may know that the LORD *is* God, *and that there is* none else.

61 Let your heart therefore be perfect with the LORD our God, to walk in his statutes, and to keep his commandments, as at this day.

62 ¶And the king, and all Israel with him, offered sacrifice before the LORD.

63 And Sŏlomon offered a sacrifice of peace offerings, which he offered unto the LORD, two and twenty thousand oxen, and an hundred and twenty thousand sheep. So the king and all the children of Israel dedicated the house of the LORD.

64 The same day did the king hallow the middle of the court that *was* before the house of the LORD: for there he offered burnt offerings, and meat offerings, and the fat of the peace offerings: because the brasen altar that *was* before the LORD *was* too little to receive the burnt offerings, and meat offerings, and the fat of the peace offerings.

65 ¶And at that time Sŏlomon held a feast, and all Israel with him, a great congregation, from the entering in of Hä´măth unto the river of Egypt, before the LORD our God, seven days and seven days, *even* fourteen days.

66 On the eighth day he sent the people away: and they blessed the king, and went unto their tents joyful and glad of heart for all the goodness that the LORD had done for David his servant, and for Israel his people.

CHAPTER 9

AND it came to pass, when Sŏlomon had finished the building of the house of the LORD, and the king's house, and all Sŏlomon's desire which he was pleased to do,

2 That the LORD appeared to Sŏlomon the second time, as he had appeared unto him at Gĭbeon.

3 And the LORD said unto him, I have heard thy prayer and thy supplication, that thou hast made before me: I have hallowed this house, which thou hast built, to put my name there for ever; and mine eyes and mine heart shall be there perpetually.

4 And if thou wilt walk before me, as David thy father walked, in integrity of heart, and in uprightness, to do according to all that I have commanded thee, *and* wilt keep my statutes and my judgments:

5 Then I will establish the throne of thy kingdom upon Israel for ever, as I promised to David thy father, saying, There shall not fail thee a man upon the throne of Israel.

6 *But* if ye shall at all turn from following me, ye or your children, and will not keep my commandments *and* my

62-63. Solomon and the people dedicated the house of the Lord with **peace offerings.** The number of animals slaughtered was very large (22,000 oxen and 120,000 sheep); but it is realistic when one considers the number of Israelites gathered there, the number of days, and the nature of the offering. The fat and certain parts of the offering were burnt, but most of the animal was eaten by the one offering it (cf. Lev 3).

64. The brazen altar . . . was too little to hold all the offerings (**burnt, peace,** and **meat,** i.e., meal); so Solomon utilized the floor of the Temple court.

65. All Israel from the **entering in of Hamath,** an extremely northern city on the Orontes River (this may be in reference to the opening from the south into the valley between the two Lebanon ranges), and the **river of Egypt,** i.e., Wadi el-Arish, was present.

Seven days and seven days, even fourteen days indicates that prior to the seven days of the Feast of Tabernacles, Solomon and Israel celebrated a feast dedication for the Temple, a total of fourteen days.

66. In accordance with Leviticus 23:36, the Feast of Tabernacles culminated after seven days; and on the **eighth day** Solomon sent the people to their homes.

9:1-2. Following the completion of the Temple and its dedication, Solomon was certain to be elated. "It was therefore opportune that God should again exhort the king that the success of his reign and the welfare of the people would depend upon loyalty to the Divine law" (Slotki, p. 69). **The LORD appeared . . . the second time.** The first time was at Gibeon (3:5-15).

3-5. Thy prayer and thy supplication. Contextually, this seems to refer to the petitions of Solomon's dedicatory prayer in 8:22-53. **If thou wilt walk . . . as David thy father walked.** In spite of David's serious shortcomings, he was held up by God as a godly example and moral standard for the kings that were to follow him.

6-9. David sinned, but he never served other gods as Solomon would (11:5). A warning is needed, but it will go unheeded in Solomon's later years. The context of these verses parallels

statutes which I have set before you, but go and serve other gods, and worship them:

7 Then will I cut off Israel out of the land which I have given them; and this house, which I have hallowed for my name, will I cast out of my sight; and Israel shall be a proverb and a byword among all people:

8 And at this house, *which* is high, every one that passeth by it shall be astonished, and shall hiss; and they shall say, Why hath the LORD done thus unto this land, and to this house?

9 And they shall answer, Because they forsook the LORD their God, who brought forth their fathers out of the land of Egypt, and have taken hold upon other gods, and have worshipped them, and served them: therefore hath the LORD brought upon them all this evil.

10 ¶And it came to pass at the end of twenty years, when Sŏlomon had built the two houses, the house of the LORD, and the king's house,

11 (*Now* Hiram the king of Tyre had furnished Sŏlomon with cedar trees and fir trees, and with gold, according to all his desire,) that then king Sŏlomon gave Hiram twenty cities in the land of Galilee.

12 And Hiram came out from Tyre to see the cities which Sŏlomon had given him; and they pleased him not.

13 And he said, What cities *are* these which thou hast given me, my brother? And he called them the land of Câ'bul unto this day.

14 And Hiram sent to the king sixscore talents of gold.

15 ¶And this *is* the reason of the levy which king Sŏlomon raised; for to build the house of the LORD, and his own house, and Mĭl'lō, and the wall of Jerusalem, and Hā'zôr, and Me-gĭd'dō, and Gē'zer.

16 *For* Pharaoh king of Egypt had gone up, and taken Gē'zer, and burnt it with fire, and slain the Canaanites that dwelt in the city, and given it *for* a present unto his daughter, Sŏlomon's wife.

17 And Sŏlomon built Gē'zer, and Bĕth-hô'ron the nether,

18 And Bā'al-ăth, and Tăd'môr in the wilderness, in the land,

19 And all the cities of store that Sŏlomon had, and cities for his chariots, and cities for his horsemen, and that which Sŏlomon desired to build in Jerusalem, and in Lebanon, and in all the land of his dominion.

20 *And* all the people *that were* left of the Ămorītes, Hittites, Pĕr'iz-zītes, Hī'-vītes, and Jĕb'u-sītes, which *were* not of the children of Israel,

21 Their children that were left after them in the land, whom the children of Israel also were not able utterly to destroy, upon those did Sŏlomon levy a tribute of bondservice unto this day.

22 But of the children of Israel did Sŏlomon make no bondmen: but they *were* men of war, and his servants, and his princes, and his captains, and rulers of his chariots, and his horsemen.

23 These *were* the chief of the officers

very closely the words of Moses in Deuteronomy 28:36-37 and 29:24ff.

7. The building projects summarized. 9:10-28.

10-14. Twenty years includes seven years of building the Temple (6:38) and thirteen years building his own house (7:1). In 5:11 Solomon sent wheat and oil to Hiram as annual payment for cedar and fir. Perhaps the **twenty cities** given to Hiram were payment for the gold here mentioned, or simply a gift for completing the two houses (vs. 10). Hiram was displeased with these unnamed cities (villages) and called them **Cabul**, which may mean "as nothing," because they were inferior. Second Chronicles 8:2 may suggest that Solomon and Hiram swapped cities, or that Hiram returned the cities Solomon had given to him.

15-19. The **levy** of 5:14 did not serve to build only the Temple and the palace, but also to build (i.e., rebuild) special projects: **Millo** (from the verb to fill), probably a part of the wall of Jerusalem that was weak and needed to be filled in; **Hazor,** the old Canaanite city (cf. Josh 11:1-15); **Megiddo,** a city archaeology has shown to be an excellent example of one of Solomon's cities for horses; and **Gezer,** the dowry of his Egyptian wife (3:1).

20-25. There is no contradiction here with 5:13. In addition to the levy of Israelites, there were those remnant Canaanite peoples remaining in the land whom Solomon subjected to slavery. No Israelite was reduced to slavery. Those who did not serve in the levy served in the army.

that *were* over Sŏlomon's work, five hundred and fifty, which bare rule over the people that wrought in the work.

24 ¶But Pharaoh's daughter came up out of the city of David unto her house which *Solomon* had built for her: then did he build Mĭl'lō.

25 ¶And three times in a year did Sŏlomon offer burnt offerings and peace offerings upon the altar which he built unto the Lord, and he burnt incense upon the altar that *was* before the Lord. So he finished the house.

26 ¶And king Sŏlomon made a navy of ships in Ē'zĭ-on-gē'ber, which *is* beside Ē'lŏth, on the shore of the Red sea, in the land of Ē'dom.

27 And Hiram sent in the navy his servants, shipmen that had knowledge of the sea, with the servants of Sŏlomon.

28 And they came to Ō'phir, and fetched from thence gold, four hundred and twenty talents, and brought *it* to king Sŏlomon.

CHAPTER 10

AND when the queen of Shēba heard of the fame of Sŏlomon concerning the name of the Lord, she came to prove him with hard questions.

2 And she came to Jerusalem with a very great train, with camels that bare spices, and very much gold, and precious stones: and when she was come to Sŏlomon, she communed with him of all that was in her heart.

3 And Sŏlomon told her all her questions: there was not *any* thing hid from the king, which he told her not.

4 And when the queen of Shēba had seen all Sŏlomon's wisdom, and the house that he had built,

5 And the meat of his table, and the sitting of his servants, and the attendance of his ministers, and their apparel, and his cupbearers, and his ascent by which he went up unto the house of the Lord; there was no more spirit in her.

6 And she said to the king, It was a true report that I heard in mine own land of thy acts and of thy wisdom.

7 Howbeit I believed not the words, until I came, and mine eyes had seen *it:* and, behold, the half was not told me: thy wisdom and prosperity exceedeth the fame which I heard.

8 Happy *are* thy men, happy *are* these thy servants, which stand continually before thee, *and* that hear thy wisdom.

9 Blessed be the Lord thy God, which delighted in thee, to set thee on the throne of Israel: because the Lord loved Israel for ever, therefore made he thee king, to do judgment and justice.

26-28. Ezion-geber, located on the northern tip of the Red Sea, proved to be an ideal location for Solomon's port. Archaeologists have found the remains of copper mines and a very sophisticated smelting operation here. With the help of Hiram's navy and crewmen, Solomon had a very thriving commercial fleet at sea (cf. note on 10:22).

Ophir, possibly located in southwestern Arabia or in India, was seemingly known for its high quality gold (cf. Job 22:24; Ps 45:9; Isa 13:12).

D. Solomon's Glory and Wealth. 10:1-29.

1. Queen of Sheba's visit to Solomon. 10:1-13.

10:1. Solomon's wisdom was unexcelled and of widespread fame (4:29-31). A visit from an unnamed Sabaean queen of Sheba was the result of her hearing of Solomon's fame **concerning the name of the Lord.** The wisdom of Solomon was divine, belonging to and acquired through the Lord.

Her primary purpose was to test Solomon's wisdom with **hard questions** (Heb *chīdah*), i.e., riddles or enigmatic sayings (cf. Jud 14:13). She may have been interested also in negotiating a trade-agreement with Solomon since he was already purchasing gold from nearby Ophir (9:28). **Sheba** was located in southwestern Arabia, modern Yemen.

2. In accordance with diplomatic protocol, she was accompanied by a **great train,** i.e., her retinue (". . . a very great company . . ." II Chr 9:1), and expensive gifts. She tested Solomon with all the riddles she had prepared, **all that was in her heart.**

3-5. Not only did Solomon exhibit his wisdom by solving all her riddles, he also openly displayed the luxuries of his kingdom: the **house,** i.e., his palace, the **sitting of his servants,** i.e., the officials who ate with him; the **ministers,** i.e., those who waited on his tables, and **his ascent . . . unto the house of the Lord.** This may refer to the stairway to the Temple or his royal procession to the Temple. After her guided tour, the queen was at a loss for words.

6-8. She openly confessed that not only were the reports of Solomon's wisdom and glory true, but that what she had just observed far exceeded any of those reports.

9. Her statement, **Blessed be the Lord thy God,** may give a hint of possible salvation; but the statement itself does not have to be taken as a confession of her becoming a proselyte to the Hebrew faith. As Bahr (p. 54) has noted, polytheism is not exclusivistic. It is not inconsistent for a polytheist to recognize

10 And she gave the king an hundred and twenty talents of gold, and of spices very great store, and precious stones: there came no more such abundance of spices as these which the queen of Shēba gave to king Sŏlomon.

11 And the navy also of Hiram, that brought gold from Ō'phir, brought in from Ō'phir great plenty of almug trees, and precious stones.

12 And the king made of the almug trees pillars for the house of the LORD, and for the king's house, harps also and psalteries for singers: there came no such almug trees, nor were seen unto this day.

13 And king Sŏlomon gave unto the queen of Shēba all her desire, whatsoever she asked, beside *that* which Sŏlomon gave her of his royal bounty. So she turned and went to her own country, she and her servants.

14 ¶Now the weight of gold that came to Sŏlomon in one year was six hundred threescore and six talents of gold,

15 Beside *that he had* of the merchantmen, and of the traffick of the spice merchants, and of all the kings of Arabia, and of the governors of the country.

16 ¶And king Sŏlomon made two hundred targets *of* beaten gold: six hundred *shekels* of gold went to one target.

17 And *he made* three hundred shields *of* beaten gold; three pound of gold went to one shield: and the king put them in the house of the forest of Lebanon.

18 ¶Moreover the king made a great throne of ivory, and overlaid it with the best gold.

19 The throne had six steps, and the top of the throne *was* round behind: and *there were* stays on either side on the place of the seat, and two lions stood beside the stays.

20 And twelve lions stood there on the one side and on the other upon the six steps: there was not the like made in any kingdom.

21 And all king Sŏlomon's drinking vessels *were of* gold, and all the vessels of the house of the forest of Lebanon *were of* pure gold; none *were of* silver: it was nothing accounted of in the days of Sŏlomon.

22 For the king had at sea a navy of Thär'shĭsh with the navy of Hiram: once in three years came the navy of Thär'shĭsh, bringing gold, and silver, ivory, and apes, and peacocks.

23 So king Sŏlomon exceeded all the kings of the earth for riches and for wisdom.

24 ¶And all the earth sought to Sŏlomon, to hear his wisdom, which God had put in his heart.

25 And they brought every man his present, vessels of silver, and vessels of gold, and garments, and armour, and spices, horses, and mules, a rate year by year.

26 ¶And Sŏlomon gathered together

the deity of another nation without rejecting its own specific national gods.

10-13. The queen gave Solomon a generous gift, but he reciprocated by giving to her **all her desire** and much more (vs. 13). These verses are parenthetical. The subject-matter was alluded to by the costly gifts of the queen.

2. Solomon's trade and riches. 10:14-29.

14-15. Solomon's revenue for one year was 666 talents of gold, not to mention that which was brought to him by merchants and the kings of Arabia.

16-17. Solomon made two sizes of shields from beaten gold. The larger ones, **targets,** probably covered the whole body. Both sets were hung in the armory room of his palace (cf. note on 7:2).

18-20. Solomon made a spectacular throne of ivory overlaid with gold for himself. The throne was ascended by way of six steps, flanked on both sides by twelve lions, six on each side. Two lions stood by the **stays,** i.e., arm rests, on each side of the seat.

21-22. Due to the abundance of gold available to Solomon, silver was virtually worthless. **Tharshish** (Tarshish) has been generally identified with Tartessus of Spain. However, Albright has suggested that the word Tarshish is connected with mining or smelting. Therefore, any mineral-producing land might be called Tarshish. Scholars have concluded that Solomon's **navy of Tharshish** did not necessarily sail to Spain. Rather, the name signified a specialized refinery fleet of ships sailing primarily to colonial mines and bringing smelted metal home.

23-25. Solomon's wisdom and riches so exceeded that of the other kings of his time that his fame attracted many visitors such as the queen of Sheba. Each visitor brought his present to Solomon.

26-29. In Deuteronomy 17:16 Moses had instructed that no

chariots and horsemen: and he had a thousand and four hundred chariots, and twelve thousand horsemen, whom he bestowed in the cities for chariots, and with the king at Jerusalem.

27 And the king made silver *to be* in Jerusalem as stones, and cedars made he *to be* as the sycomore trees that *are* in the vale, for abundance.

28 ¶And Sŏlomon had horses brought out of Egypt, and linen yarn: the king's merchants received the linen yarn at a price.

29 And a chariot came up and went out of Egypt for six hundred *shekels* of silver, and an horse for an hundred and fifty: and so for all the kings of the Hittites, and for the kings of Syria, did they bring *them* out by their means.

CHAPTER 11

BUT king Sŏlomon loved many strange women, together with the daughter of Pharaoh, women of the Moabites, Ammonites, Edomites, Zī-dō′nī-ans, *and* Hittites:

2 Of the nations *concerning* which the LORD said unto the children of Israel, Ye shall not go in to them, neither shall they come in unto you: *for* surely they will turn away your heart after their gods: Sŏlomon clave unto these in love.

3 And he had seven hundred wives, princesses, and three hundred concubines: and his wives turned away his heart.

4 For it came to pass, when Sŏlomon was old, *that* his wives turned away his heart after other gods: and his heart was not perfect with the LORD his God, as *was* the heart of David his father.

5 For Sŏlomon went after Ăsh′to-rĕth the goddess of the Zī-dō′nī-ans, and after Mĭl′com the abomination of the Ammonites.

6 And Sŏlomon did evil in the sight of the LORD, and went not fully after the LORD, as *did* David his father.

7 Then did Sŏlomon build an high place for Chĕ′mŏsh, the abomination of Moab, in the hill that *is* before Jerusalem, and for Mō′lĕch, the abomination of the children of Ammon.

8 And likewise did he for all his strange wives, which burnt incense and sacrificed unto their gods.

9 ¶And the LORD was angry with Sŏlomon, because his heart was turned from the LORD God of Israel, which had appeared unto him twice,

10 And had commanded him concerning this thing, that he should not go after other gods: but he kept not that which the LORD commanded.

11 Wherefore the LORD said unto Sŏlomon, Forasmuch as this is done of

king of Israel was ever to accumulate horses to himself or to return to Egypt for the purchase of horses. Solomon ignored both of these instructions, for he was a horse trader.

Verse 28 is inaccurate as it stands in the AV. **Linen yarn** (Heb *miqweh*) should rather be, "from Kue," or Cilicia. Solomon was purchasing horses from Egypt and Cilicia. While many of the purchases were for his own armies, Solomon may well have been the middleman in commercial transactions with other nations.

E. Solomon's Apostasy and Resultant Troubles. 11:1-43.

1. Polygamy and foreign wives. 11:1-13.

11:1. Solomon's marriage to Pharaoh's daughter (3:1) was not the beginning of his polygamous household. He must have married Naamah, an Ammonitess, a couple of years before he was made king; for his son Rehoboam was forty-one when Solomon died after reigning forty years (cf. 11:42; 14:21).

From the number of wives he had (vs. 3), it is doubtful that Solomon loved women only of the **Moabites** and **Hittites**.

2. His marriages were in direct disobedience to the clear commands of God. He had already ignored Moses' instructions concerning amassing horses and gold (Deut 17:16-17), and now he violated a third instruction about not multiplying wives. God's prohibition had theological purpose, to prevent His people becoming involved with foreign gods.

3. He had **seven hundred wives . . . three hundred concubines.** The size of his harem is not necessarily indicative of lust since most of these marriages were probably political unions. A common and effective way of confirming a treaty was for one king to give his daughter to another king for a wife. What king would offend his father-in-law by breaking his commitment to a treaty?

4. International marriages involved foreign deities, and foreign wives brought their gods with them. Just as predicted (vs. 2), his wives diverted his attention from Jehovah to their gods.

5-6. He went after **Ashtoreth** (the Hebrew name for the Phoenician Ashtarte and Babylonian Ishtar), the consort of Baal, who was the goddess of fertility, and **Milcom,** commonly known as Molech, the god of the Ammonites, to which children were offered as human sacrifices (cf. II Kgs 23:10).

7-8. After Solomon became accustomed to these gods, they found public acceptance when he built high places for **Chemosh** and **Molech,** and for all the gods of his foreign wives. These shrines were stationed on the **hill** (possibly the Mount of Olives) **that is before Jerusalem,** the city where Solomon had built the house for Jehovah. In spite of subsequent reformations of Asa and Hezekiah, these high places were permitted to stand approximately three hundred years until the reign of Josiah (II Kgs 23:13-15).

9-13. Jehovah had already appeared to Solomon twice (cf. 3:5-14; 9:2-9), but Solomon was living contrary to God's commandments. Therefore, a division of the kingdom is forecast. **I will surely rend the kingdom from thee.** In deference to David, the kingdom would not be divided in Solomon's day; and to remain faithful to the Davidic covenant, Solomon's son, Rehoboam, would be permitted to rule over one tribe, Judah.

REHOBOAM went to Shechem, for all Israel had come to Shechem to make him king.

(1 Kings 12:1)

Royal sanctuary

Sidon

Damascus

Tyre

Dan

Royal sanctuary

ARAM–DAMASCUS

Hazor

GESHUR

Acco

Ashtaroth

Dor

Megiddo

Ramoth-gilead

Coronation of
Jeroboam over
Israel

I S R A E L

Shechem

Penuel

Zeredah

AMMON

Joppa

Beth-el

Royal sanctuary

Rabbath-bene-ammon

Gibbethon

Gezer

Gath

Jerusalem

Gaza

Hebron

Dibon

Raphia

J U D A H

Beer-sheba

Arad

M O A B

Kir-moab

Great Sea

PHILISTINES

Tamar

Bozrah

Kadesh-barnea

E G Y P T

Teman

E D O M

Elath

0   10   20 miles
0 10 20 30 km

The Division of the Kingdom

thee, and thou hast not kept my covenant and my statutes, which I have commanded thee, I will surely rend the kingdom from thee, and will give it to thy servant.

12 Notwithstanding in thy days I will not do it for David thy father's sake: *but* I will rend it out of the hand of thy son.

13 Howbeit I will not rend away all the kingdom; *but* will give one tribe to thy son for David my servant's sake, and for Jerusalem's sake which I have chosen.

14 ¶And the Lord stirred up an adversary unto Sŏlomon, Hä'dăd the Edomite: he *was* of the king's seed in Ēdom.

15 For it came to pass, when David was in Ēdom, and Jŏ'ăb the captain of the host was gone up to bury the slain, after he had smitten every male in Ēdom;

16 (For six months did Jŏ'ăb remain there with all Israel, until he had cut off every male in Ēdom:)

17 That Hä'dăd fled, he and certain Edomites of his father's servants with him, to go into Egypt; Hä'dăd *being* yet a little child.

18 And they arose out of Mĭd'ĭ-an, and came to Paran: and they took men with them out of Paran, and they came to Egypt, unto Pharaoh king of Egypt; which gave him an house, and appointed him victuals, and gave him land.

19 And Hä'dăd found great favour in the sight of Pharaoh, so that he gave him to wife the sister of his own wife, the sister of Täh'pen-ēś the queen.

20 And the sister of Täh'pen-ēś bare him Ge-nŭ'băth his son, whom Täh'pen-ēś weaned in Pharaoh's house: and Ge-nŭ'băth was in Pharaoh's household among the sons of Pharaoh.

21 And when Hä'dăd heard in Egypt that David slept with his fathers, and that Jŏ'ăb the captain of the host was dead, Hä'dăd said to Pharaoh, Let me depart, that I may go to mine own country.

22 Then Pharaoh said unto him, But what hast thou lacked with me, that, behold, thou seekest to go to thine own country? And he answered, Nothing: howbeit let me go in any wise.

23 ¶And God stirred him up *another* adversary, Rē'zon the son of E-lĭ'a-dah, which fled from his lord Hăd-ad-ē'zer king of Zōbah;

24 And he gathered men unto him, and became captain over a band, when David slew them *of Zōbah*: and they went to Damascus, and dwelt therein, and reigned in Damascus.

25 And he was an adversary to Israel all the days of Sŏlomon, beside the mischief that Hä'dăd *did:* and he abhorred Israel, and reigned over Syria.

26 ¶And Jĕr-o-bō'am the son of Nē'băt, an Ēph'rath-īte of Zĕr'e-da, Sŏlomon's servant, whose mother's name

2. Hadad of Edom. 11:14-22.

14. Earlier, Solomon had told Hiram that he had **neither adversary nor evil occurrent** (5:4). Now the Lord raised up an adversary for Solomon, **Hadad,** an Edomite from the royal family.

15-20. Hadad had survived the campaign of David into Edomite territory (II Sam 8:13-14), and Joab's six-month purge of the males. While yet a lad he had escaped with his father's servants to Egypt where the Pharaoh had befriended him. He so won the favor of Pharaoh that he was awarded Pharaoh's sister-in-law **Tahpenes** for a wife. The son she bore was reared in Pharaoh's household.

21-22. Upon hearing of David's and Joab's deaths, he desired to return home to Edom. How he served as an adversary is not told. Perhaps he carried on guerrilla attacks against the garrisons David had erected there (II Sam 8:13). The success of his attacks must have been somewhat limited since there is no indication that shipments of goods from the port city, Ezion-geber, through Edomite territory was hindered in Solomon's day.

3. Rezon of Damascus. 11:23-25.

23-25. Another adversary was **Rezon,** who had been an ally of the Syrian king of Zobah, **Hadadezer,** but had deserted him when he was needed most (cf. II Sam 8:12). Whereupon, he had organized his own marauding band. He went to Damascus, took it, and reigned there on one of the major trade routes to the east. Hadad to the south and Rezon to the north were constant thorns in Solomon's side, although there is no evidence of open warfare.

4. Jeroboam son of Nebat. 11:26-40.

26. A third adversary was Solomon's own servant, **Jeroboam the son of Nebat,** son of a widow, **Zeruah,** from the little village of **Zereda** in Ephraim. **He lifted up his hand against the king,** i.e., he rebelled. Scripture does not state what form this rebel-

was Ze-rū′ah, a widow woman, even he lifted up *his* hand against the king.

27 And this *was* the cause that he lifted up *his* hand against the king: Sŏlomon built Mĭl′lō, *and* repaired the breaches of the city of David his father.

28 And the man Jĕr-o-bō′am *was* a mighty man of valour: and Sŏlomon seeing the young man that he was industrious, he made him ruler over all the charge of the house of Joseph.

29 And it came to pass at that time when Jĕr-o-bō′am went out of Jerusalem, that the prophet A-hī′jah the Shī′lo-nīte found him in the way; and he had clad himself with a new garment; and they two *were* alone in the field:

30 And A-hī′jah caught the new garment that *was* on him, and rent it *in* twelve pieces:

31 And he said to Jĕr-o-bō′am, Take thee ten pieces: for thus saith the Lord, the God of Israel, Behold, I will rend the kingdom out of the hand of Sŏlomon, and will give ten tribes to thee:

32 (But he shall have one tribe for my servant David's sake, and for Jerusalem's sake, the city which I have chosen out of all the tribes of Israel:)

33 Because that they have forsaken me, and have worshipped Ăsh′to-rĕth the goddess of the Zī-dō′nĭ-ans, Chē′mŏsh the god of the Moabites, and Mĭl′com the god of the children of Ammon, and have not walked in my ways, to do *that which is* right in mine eyes, and *to keep* my statutes and my judgments, as *did* David his father.

34 Howbeit I will not take the whole kingdom out of his hand: but I will make him prince all the days of his life for David my servant's sake, whom I chose, because he kept my commandments and my statutes:

35 But I will take the kingdom out of his son's hand, and will give it unto thee, *even* ten tribes.

36 And unto his son will I give one tribe, that David my servant may have a light alway before me in Jerusalem, the city which I have chosen me to put my name there.

37 And I will take thee, and thou shalt reign according to all that thy soul desireth, and shalt be king over Israel.

38 And it shall be, if thou wilt hearken unto all that I command thee, and wilt walk in my ways, and do *that is* right in my sight, to keep my statutes and my commandments, as David my servant did; that I will be with thee, and build thee a sure house, as I built for David, and will give Israel unto thee.

39 And I will for this afflict the seed of David, but not for ever.

40 Sŏlomon sought therefore to kill Jĕr-o-bō′am. And Jĕr-o-bō′am arose, and fled into Egypt, unto Shī′shăk king of Egypt, and was in Egypt until the death of Sŏlomon.

lion took, but verses 27-39 serve as a background (**the cause,** vs. 27) for the revolt.

27-28. When Solomon was involved with his building projects such as **Millo** (9:15), Jeroboam had proved himself invaluable. He had the qualities of leadership ability and ambition (**he was industrious,** lit., a doer of work), therefore he was placed over the **charge of the house of Joseph,** i.e., over the tribes of Ephraim (his own tribe) and Manasseh. **Charge** is literally burden, the compulsory labor spoken of in 5:13 and 9:15. Jeroboam was well aware of the burden of human taxation under Solomon.

29-32. Ahijah, a prophet from Shiloh, is introduced to the story. Ahijah met Jeroboam alone and tore his new mantle into twelve pieces (cf. I Sam 15:27). Ten pieces were given to Jeroboam. This symbolic act was prophetic of the fact that the kingdom would be divided, with Jeroboam receiving ten tribes while the Davidic line would retain only one. (This one tribe, Judah, evidently included the tribe of Simeon, which had been absorbed into Judah years before).

33. It is significant that even though Jeroboam is advised that the reason for the rending of much of the kingdom from Solomon's hand is idolatry (11:5-8), it will be Jeroboam who will make his ten northern tribes, Israel, to sin by introducing idolatry.

34-39. To be faithful to the Davidic covenant, God retains one tribe for the Davidic line to rule over. The promise of blessing for obedience that was given to Jeroboam is similar to that given to Solomon (cf. 3:14 and 9:4-5).

40. Because of his sympathy for those subjected to the burden of forced labor (vs. 28) and God's promise to be king of Israel, Jeroboam evidently made his bid for the throne and rebelled (vs. 26). Solomon's reaction was to attempt to kill Jeroboam in order to save the throne for his own son, Rehoboam. Jeroboam had to flee to Egypt, where he found political asylum with **Shishak,** founder of the Twenty-second Dynasty of Egypt, until the death of Solomon.

41 ¶And the rest of the acts of Solomon, and all that he did, and his wisdom, are they not written in the book of the acts of Solomon?

42 And the time that Solomon reigned in Jerusalem over all Israel was forty years.

43 And Solomon slept with his fathers, and was buried in the city of David his father: and Rē-ho-bō′am his son reigned in his stead.

CHAPTER 12

AND Rē-ho-bō′am went to Shĕ′chem: for all Israel were come to Shĕ′chem to make him king.

2 And it came to pass, when Jĕr-o-bō′am the son of Nē′băt, who was yet in Egypt, heard of it, (for he was fled from the presence of king Solomon, and Jĕr-o-bō′am dwelt in Egypt;)

3 That they sent and called him. And Jĕr-o-bō′am and all the congregation of Israel came, and spake unto Rē-ho-bō′am, saying,

4 Thy father made our yoke grievous: now therefore make thou the grievous service of thy father, and his heavy yoke which he put upon us, lighter, and we will serve thee.

5 And he said unto them, Depart yet for three days, then come again to me. And the people departed.

6 ¶And king Rē-ho-bō′am consulted with the old men, that stood before Solomon his father while he yet lived, and said, How do ye advise that I may answer this people?

7 And they spake unto him, saying, If thou wilt be a servant unto this people this day, and wilt serve them, and answer them, and speak good words to them, then they will be thy servants for ever.

8 But he forsook the counsel of the old men, which they had given him, and consulted with the young men that were grown up with him, and which stood before him:

9 And he said unto them, What counsel give ye that we may answer this people, who have spoken to me, saying, Make the yoke which thy father did put upon us lighter?

10 And the young men that were grown up with him spake unto him, saying, Thus shalt thou speak unto this people that spake unto thee, saying, Thy father made our yoke heavy, but make thou it lighter unto us; thus shalt thou say unto them, My little finger shall be thicker than my father's loins.

11 And now whereas my father did lade you with a heavy yoke, I will add to your yoke: my father hath chastised you with whips, but I will chastise you with scorpions.

12 ¶So Jĕr-o-bō′am and all the people came to Rē-ho-bō′am the third day, as

5. The death of Solomon. 11:41-43.

41. Other details of Solomon's life and reign were recorded in the **Book of the Acts of Solomon,** a chronicle that was kept (cf. II Chr 9:29) but is not extant today (see Introduction).

42-43. The time of his reign was forty years, approximately 971-931 B.C. He was buried in the **city of David,** i.e., Jerusalem.

II. THE DIVIDED KINGDOM. 12:1-22:53.

A. The Division. 12:1-24.

1. Israel's request for lower taxes. 12:1-15.

12:1. Rehoboam went to Shechem to be made king there. Shechem was a city in Ephraim at the base of Mount Gerizim and Ebal. The reason this site was selected is not given, but it may be that **all Israel,** i.e., the northern tribes (cf. note on 5:13), had joined Jeroboam in his revolt (11:26) and would not have come to Jerusalem for the occasion. Therefore, he went into hostile surroundings hoping to win their sympathy and rally their support.

2-3. Jeroboam was still in exile in Egypt when Solomon died. He was called home by the northern tribes to be present at Shechem when Rehoboam arrived. In all probability, Jeroboam was the spokesman on behalf of his people. No one else could have represented them better, for he had been involved in the forced labor program and knew the grievances of the people (cf. 11:28).

4-5. The request was simple. Make the **heavy yoke . . . lighter.** Though the labor requirements had shown favoritism to Judah, there is no reason to doubt the word of these tribes. They would have served him.

From what follows it appears that Rehoboam's verdict was already determined, even though he took **three days** to consider the request.

6-7. He consulted with the old men. These old men had served as counselors to Solomon and had had ample opportunity to witness the schism that was developing among the tribes and would ultimately divide them if necessary precautions were not taken. Therefore, they advised Rehoboam to **speak good words to them,** i.e., tell them what they want to hear, that their request had been granted.

8-11. Rejecting the advice of the old men, Rehoboam turned to the younger men that **stood before him,** i.e., who grew up with him, his peers. They were probably status seekers who appealed to the king's ego. Their advice was to make the yoke heavier. Rehoboam could thus enjoy the same standard of living as his father.

The expression **My little finger . . . my father's loins** is a metaphor of contrast that is plainly explained in the next verse. The **yoke** (vs. 4) would become much more severe and would be accompanied with **whips** and **scorpions.** A whip was a plain, single leather strap; and a scorpion was a whip of many strands to which were attached metal knobs.

12-15. On the appointed day the king announced his decision to deny their request. **The cause was from the LORD.** The

the king had appointed, saying, Come to me again the third day.

13 And the king answered the people roughly, and forsook the old men's counsel that they gave him·

14 And spake to them after the counsel of the young men, saying, My father made your yoke heavy, and I will add to your yoke: my father *also* chastised you with whips, but I will chastise you with scorpions.

15 Wherefore the king hearkened not unto the people; for the cause was from the LORD, that he might perform his saying, which the LORD spake by A-hī'-jah the Shī'lo-nīte unto Jĕr-o-bō'am the son of Nĕ'băt.

16 ¶So when all Israel saw that the king hearkened not unto them, the people answered the king, saying, What portion have we in David? neither *have we* inheritance in the son of Jesse: to your tents, O Israel: now see to thine own house, David. So Israel departed unto their tents.

17 But *as for* the children of Israel which dwelt in the cities of Jūdah, Rē-ho-bō'am reigned over them.

18 Then king Rē-ho-bō'am sent Ă-dō'ram, who *was* over the tribute; and all Israel stoned him with stones, that he died. Therefore king Rē-ho-bō'am made speed to get him up to his chariot, to flee to Jerusalem.

19 So Israel rebelled against the house of David unto this day.

20 ¶And it came to pass, when all Israel heard that Jĕr-o-bō'am was come again, that they sent and called him unto the congregation, and made him king over all Israel: there was none that followed the house of David, but the tribe of Jūdah only.

21 ¶And when Rē-ho-bō'am was come to Jerusalem, he assembled all the house of Jūdah, with the tribe of Benjamin, an hundred and fourscore thousand chosen men, which were warriors, to fight against the house of Israel, to bring the kingdom again to Rē-ho-bō'am the son of Sōlomon.

22 But the word of God came unto Shem-a-i'ah the man of God, saying,

23 Speak unto Rē-ho-bō'am, the son of Sōlomon, king of Jūdah, and unto all the house of Jūdah and Benjamin, and to the remnant of the people, saying,

24 Thus saith the LORD, Ye shall not go up, nor fight against your brethren the children of Israel: return every man to his house; for this thing is from me. They hearkened therefore to the word of the LORD, and returned to depart, according to the word of the LORD.

25 ¶Then Jĕr-o-bō'am built Shĕ'chem in mount Ē'phra-im, and dwelt therein; and went out from thence, and built Pe-nŭ'el.

26 ¶And Jĕr-o-bō'am said in his heart, Now shall the kingdom return to the house of David:

27 If this people go up to do sacrifice in the house of the LORD at Jerusalem, then shall the heart of this people turn

sovereign God of history was directing the events of this rebellion to accomplish His purpose and fulfill the word prophesied by Ahijah (11:31ff.).

2. Results of a denied request. 12:16-24.

16. The response of the people to this denial was essentially that of Sheba (II Sam 20:1). **What portion have we in David?** With these words they rejected their former hero, the founder of the reigning dynasty.

To your tents. This does not mean to arms or prepare for battle, but go home. The expression is reminiscent of nomadic days when Israel did reside in tents.

17-19. The Jews in the southern province of Judah remained loyal to Rehoboam. Rehoboam did not seem to understand the gravity of the situation. In sheer folly he sent Adoram (cf. note on 4:6), one who would be a most vivid reminder of the reason for rebellion (he was **over the tribute**), either to quell the disturbance or to enroll more laborers. Israel's response was to stone Adoram. Rehoboam quickly fled to the safety of Jerusalem, for the rebellion was to be permanent.

20-24. Jeroboam was unquestionably the logical choice for leadership and was promptly crowned king of the northern ten tribes. It was not unnatural for Rehoboam to attempt to regain control over the northern tribes. The reference to **Benjamin** may appear contradictory to verse 20. It is doubtful that very many warriors would have been from Benjamin at this time. Benjamin historically aligned itself with the northern tribes and gradually returned under Rehoboam's control (cf. Wood, p. 303).

Before Rehoboam was able to engage in warfare, godly Shemaiah delivered a message from God. Rehoboam was not to go against Israel because **this thing is from me** (cf. vs. 15). Thus civil war was averted.

B. Jeroboam of Israel. 12:25-14:20.

1. Jeroboam's idolatrous religious policies. 12:25-33.

25. Jeroboam's first course of action was to fortify Shechem to serve as his capital. Later, he did the same at Penuel across the Jordan. Perhaps this occurred at the time of Shishak's invasion, ca. 924 B.C. (14:25).

26-27. Jeroboam knew that a religiously unified people was a politically unified people. According to the Law, three times a year all Israel was to make the pilgrimage to Jerusalem to worship God (Ex 23:17; Lev 23). If the northern tribes were permitted to return annually to Jerusalem, their loyalty might turn from Jeroboam once again to Rehoboam. To prevent this

again unto their lord, *even* unto Rē-ho-bō′am king of Jūdah, and they shall kill me, and go again to Rē-ho-bō′am king of Jūdah.

28 Whereupon the king took counsel, and made two calves *of* gold, and said unto them, It is too much for you to go up to Jerusalem: behold thy gods, O Israel, which brought thee up out of the land of Egypt.

possibility, he employed the tactics outlined in verses 28-33 (cf. Whitcomb, *Solomon to the Exile*, p. 23).

28. He changed the symbols of worship. The ark of God dwelled between the cherubim. Jeroboam fashioned **two calves of gold** and said, **behold thy gods . . .** , in reference to Aaron's text (Ex 32:4).

Two viewpoints are promoted concerning these calves. First, the calves were not meant to be idols of worship, but merely a visible throne upon which the invisible God, Jehovah, stood. Canaanite influence is seen, for some of the Canaanites imagined that Baal was standing upon a bull that signified strength and fertility. Second, the calves indicate Egyptian influence, for the sacred bull was worshiped in Egypt as a symbol of the goddess Hathor. Possibly Jeroboam became acquainted with this cult when he fled to Egypt in Solomon's reign (11:40) and was now inclined to setting up calf-worship from what he had observed there (Free, pp. 180-181).

29 And he set the one in Bĕth-el, and the other put he in Dan.
30 And this thing became a sin: for the people went *to worship* before the one, *even* unto Dan.

29-30. He changed the centers of worship. To discourage attendance at Jerusalem for worship, he appointed **Dan** and **Beth-el** as sites of worship and appealed to convenience (vs. 29). **Dan** had been an idolatrous worship center for many years. **Beth-el** was significant because God had spoken to Jacob there in a dream (Gen 28:11-19; 35:7).

31 And he made an house of high places, and made priests of the lowest of the people, which were not of the sons of Levi.

31. He changed the priesthood. It was no longer restricted to the Levites; but according to II Chronicles 13:9, anyone who could consecrate himself with a bullock and seven rams qualified to be a priest. Consequently, the Levitical priests migrated south to Judah *en masse*, thus strengthening the kingdom of Rehoboam (II Chr 11:13-19).

32 And Jĕr-o-bō′am ordained a feast in the eighth month, on the fifteenth day of the month, like unto the feast that *is* in Jūdah, and he offered upon the altar. So did he in Bĕth-el, sacrificing unto the calves that he had made: and he placed in Bĕth-el the priests of the high places which he had made.
33 So he offered upon the altar which he had made in Bĕth-el the fifteenth day of the month, *even* in the month which he had devised of his own heart; and ordained a feast unto the children of Israel: and he offered upon the altar, and burnt incense.

32-33. He changed the scheduled feasts. All the Jews were to celebrate the Day of Atonement on the fifteenth day of the seventh month and the Feast of Tabernacles on the following seven days. Jeroboam scheduled a comparable feast on the fifteenth day, but one month later. Undoubtedly, his celebration was more elaborate and attractive so as to be climactic in comparison to the festivities at Jerusalem. Consequently, in a few years the feasts at Jerusalem would cease to be attractive; and there would be no more pilgrimages to worship there.

CHAPTER 13
AND, behold, there came a man of God out of Jūdah by the word of the LORD unto Bĕth-el: and Jĕr-o-bō′am stood by the altar to burn incense.
2 And he cried against the altar in the word of the LORD, and said, O altar, altar, thus saith the LORD; Behold, a child shall be born unto the house of David, Jō-sī′ah by name; and upon thee shall he offer the priests of the high places that burn incense upon thee, and men's bones shall be burnt upon thee.

2. The man of God from Judah. 13:1-32.

13:1-2. Jeroboam led Israel into gross idolatry (cf. his reputation in 14:16); but God graciously sent an unnamed prophet out of Judah to denounce the altar at Beth-el, thus issuing a warning to Jeroboam who was caught in the act of burning incense there.

The prophet announced that **Josiah,** a son of David (a king from Judah), would someday burn the bones of Jeroboam's ungodly priests on that very altar. This prophecy is remarkable in that it specifically names Josiah three hundred years before the actual event (II Kgs 23:15-20). Such miraculous predictions are a unique feature of Old Testament prophetic Scripture (cf. Isa 44, where Cyrus is so named). Modern scholarship that denies the prophetic element in Scripture falsely insists that the mention of Josiah is a *vaticinium post eventum* (prophecy after the event) or a later gloss (Gray, p. 296).

3 And he gave a sign the same day, saying, This *is* the sign which the LORD hath spoken; Behold, the altar shall be rent, and the ashes that *are* upon it shall be poured out.
4 ¶And it came to pass, when king Jĕr-o-bō′am heard the saying of the man of God, which had cried against

3-6. He gave a sign, a present happening, that would confirm the prediction as authentic. **The altar shall be rent.** Wanting to hush the prophet, Jeroboam attempted to seize him, but failed. One is wrong to attempt to explain away this miracle by suggesting natural causes, e.g., cold water was spilled on the hot stones of the altar and they split open (Gray, p. 296). Jeroboam recognized the event as a miracle and the prophet as an obvious

the altar in Běth-el, that he put forth his hand from the altar, saying, Lay hold on him. And his hand, which he put forth against him, dried up, so that he could not pull it in again to him.

5 The altar also was rent, and the ashes poured out from the altar, according to the sign which the man of God had given by the word of the LORD.

6 And the king answered and said unto the man of God, Intreat now the face of the LORD thy God, and pray for me, that my hand may be restored me again. And the man of God besought the LORD, and the king's hand was restored him again, and became as *it was* before.

7 ¶And the king said unto the man of God, Come home with me, and refresh thyself, and I will give thee a reward.

8 And the man of God said unto the king, If thou wilt give me half thine house, I will not go in with thee, neither will I eat bread nor drink water in this place:

9 For so was it charged me by the word of the LORD, saying, Eat no bread, nor drink water, nor turn again by the same way that thou camest.

10 So he went another way, and returned not by the way that he came to Běth-el.

11 ¶Now there dwelt an old prophet in Běth-el; and his sons came and told him all the works that the man of God had done that day in Běth-el: the words which he had spoken unto the king, them they told also to their father.

12 And their father said unto them, What way went he? For his sons had seen what way the man of God went, which came from Jūdah.

13 And he said unto his sons, Saddle me the ass. So they saddled him the ass: and he rode thereon,

14 And went after the man of God, and found him sitting under an oak: and he said unto him, *Art* thou the man of God that camest from Jūdah? And he said, I *am*.

15 Then he said unto him, Come home with me, and eat bread.

16 And he said, I may not return with thee, nor go in with thee: neither will I eat bread nor drink water with thee in this place:

17 For it was said to me by the word of the LORD, Thou shalt eat no bread nor drink water there, nor turn again to go by the way that thou camest.

18 He said unto him, I *am* a prophet also as thou *art;* and an angel spake unto me by the word of the LORD, saying, Bring him back with thee into thine house, that he may eat bread and drink water. *But* he lied unto him.

19 So he went back with him, and did eat bread in his house, and drank water.

20 ¶And it came to pass, as they sat at the table, that the word of the LORD came unto the prophet that brought him back:

man of God; and he requested another miracle, which was granted—that his hand be restored.

7-10. Jeroboam's invitation for the prophet was not motivated by repentance. He may have hoped the prophet would soften his denouncement, or possibly he intended to bribe him to remain in his service. The man of God refused because of the divine instructions, **Eat no bread, nor drink water.** "Such social intercourse might well have created the impression in the minds of the people that the judgment pronounced by the prophet had either been averted or at least mitigated" (Gates, I Kings, *Wycliffe Bible Commentary*, p. 325). **Nor turn again by the same way.** This would eliminate the possibility of forming any social acquaintance or being waylaid by those who saw him arrive at Beth-el.

11. Now there dwelt an old prophet in Beth-el. Josephus describes him as a wicked man, a false prophet whom Jeroboam held in high regard (*Antiq*. VIII, IX). If he was a true prophet of Jehovah, one questions his remaining in Israel in the midst of Jeroboam's idolatry and his sons' presence at the site of calf worship. His action in subsequent verses demonstrates his spiritual compromise.

12-17. The old prophet pursued the man of God and found him resting under an oak. One wonders if the man of God would have been found had he been more diligent in his retreat from Beth-el and had not stopped. Jeroboam's invitation was repeated by the old prophet, but once again it was refused on the basis of divine prohibition.

18-19. I am a prophet . . . an angel spake unto me. It may be significant that he did not claim a communication directly from God. However, even yet **he lied.** Why he deceived the man of God is a matter of speculation. The old prophet was successful where Jeroboam had been unsuccessful, for the man accepted the invitation to eat.

20-22. During the course of the meal the **word of the LORD** truly came to the old prophet, a message of judgment upon the man of God for his disobedience to the clear command of God. If the old prophet were indeed a false prophet, one need not doubt

21 And he cried unto the man of God that came from Jūdah, saying, Thus saith the LORD, Forasmuch as thou hast disobeyed the mouth of the LORD, and hast not kept the commandment which the LORD thy God commanded thee,
22 But camest back, and hast eaten bread and drunk water in the place, of the which the LORD did say to thee, Eat no bread, and drink no water; thy carcase shall not come unto the sepulchre of thy fathers.
23 ¶And it came to pass, after he had eaten bread, and after he had drunk, that he saddled for him the ass, to wit, for the prophet whom he had brought back.
24 And when he was gone, a lion met him by the way, and slew him: and his carcase was cast in the way, and the ass stood by it, the lion also stood by the carcase.
25 And, behold, men passed by, and saw the carcase cast in the way, and the lion standing by the carcase: and they came and told it in the city where the old prophet dwelt.
26 ¶And when the prophet that brought him back from the way heard thereof, he said, It is the man of God, who was disobedient unto the word of the LORD: therefore the LORD hath delivered him unto the lion, which hath torn him, and slain him, according to the word of the LORD, which he spake unto him.
27 And he spake to his sons, saying, Saddle me the ass. And they saddled him.
28 And he went and found his carcase cast in the way, and the ass and the lion standing by the carcase: the lion had not eaten the carcase, nor torn the ass.
29 And the prophet took up the carcase of the man of God, and laid it upon the ass, and brought it back: and the old prophet came to the city, to mourn and to bury him.
30 And he laid his carcase in his own grave; and they mourned over him, saying, Alas, my brother!
31 And it came to pass, after he had buried him, that he spake to his sons, saying, When I am dead, then bury me in the sepulchre wherein the man of God is buried; lay my bones beside his bones:
32 For the saying which he cried by the word of the LORD against the altar in Bĕth-el, and against all the houses of the high places which are in the cities of Sa-mâ'rĭ-a, shall surely come to pass.

33 ¶After this thing Jĕr-o-bō'am returned not from his evil way, but made again of the lowest of the people priests of the high places: whosoever would, he consecrated him, and he became one of the priests of the high places.
34 And this thing became sin unto the house of Jĕr-o-bō'am, even to cut it off, and to destroy it from off the face of the earth.

CHAPTER 14

AT that time A-bī'jah the son of Jĕr-o-bō'am fell sick.

674

that God could speak through him (cf. Num 22:28-30 where God caused even an ass to speak).

Thy carcase shall not come unto the sepulchre of thy fathers. He would be judged by death before he returned to Judah and would thus be buried in Israel. One may be tempted to feel sympathetic for the man who was judged severely by God after being deceived by a prophet of God. However, the man of God clearly understood God's initial prohibition and should have known also that God never contradicts His own word.

23-28. The judgment recorded here is a fulfillment of the old prophet's prediction, showing that he had indeed spoken the word of the Lord. The scene evidences a supernatural judgment. It is unnatural for an ass to remain in the company of a lion (vs. 24), and it was also unnatural for a lion not to devour the human carcass or the ass. All the details point not to an accidental death, but to divine judgment.

29-30. After giving the man of God an honorable burial, the old prophet cried, **Alas, my brother!** This may merely have been an established form of lament used over the dead (cf. Jer 22:18), or he may have been expressing genuine grief because he had contributed to the death of this man.

31-32. The old man was careful to instruct his sons to bury him in the same grave as the man of God. This was done in anticipation of the prediction concerning Josiah (cf. vs. 2 and II Kgs 23:17-18). He wanted to be associated with the man of God and not have his bones desecrated with those of the evil priests.

The reference to the **cities of Samaria** is anachronistic in terms of the time and setting of the story (not until Ahab's reign, when he built Samaria, did the north acquire the name, Samaria), but it was not anachronistic to the time of writing.

3. Failure to repent, denunciation, and death. 13:33-14:20.

33-34. Jeroboam was not deterred. He ignored the warnings and signs and continued in the religious course he had set for Israel in 12:28-33. Therefore, because of his persistence in sin, his house was doomed for destruction without becoming a dynasty.

14:1. At that time, i.e., soon after Jeroboam's first prophetic warning, **Abijah** became ill.

2 And Jĕr-o-bō′am said to his wife, Arise, I pray thee, and disguise thyself, that thou be not known to be the wife of Jĕr-o-bō′am; and get thee to Shī′lōh: behold, there is A-hī′jah the prophet, which told me that I should be king over this people.

3 And take with thee ten loaves, and cracknels, and a cruse of honey, and go to him: he shall tell thee what shall become of the child.

4 And Jĕr-o-bō′am's wife did so, and arose, and went to Shī′lōh, and came to the house of A-hī′jah. But A-hī′jah could not see; for his eyes were set by reason of his age.

5 ¶And the LORD said unto A-hī′jah, Behold, the wife of Jĕr-o-bō′am cometh to ask a thing of thee for her son; for he is sick: thus and thus shalt thou say unto her: for it shall be, when she cometh in, that she shall feign herself to be another woman.

6 And it was so, when A-hī′jah heard the sound of her feet, as she came in at the door, that he said, Come in, thou wife of Jĕr-o-bō′am; why feignest thou thyself to be another? for I am sent to thee with heavy tidings.

7 Go, tell Jĕr-o-bō′am, Thus saith the LORD God of Israel, Forasmuch as I exalted thee from among the people, and made thee prince over my people Israel,

8 And rent the kingdom away from the house of David, and gave it thee: and yet thou hast not been as my servant David, who kept my commandments, and who followed me with all his heart, to do that only which was right in mine eyes;

9 But hast done evil above all that were before thee: for thou hast gone and made thee other gods, and molten images, to provoke me to anger, and hast cast me behind thy back:

10 Therefore, behold, I will bring evil upon the house of Jĕr-o-bō′am, and will cut off from Jĕr-o-bō′am him that pisseth against the wall, and him that is shut up and left in Israel, and will take away the remnant of the house of Jĕr-o-bō′am, as a man taketh away dung, till it be all gone.

11 Him that dieth of Jĕr-o-bō′am in the city shall the dogs eat; and him that dieth in the field shall the fowls of the air eat: for the LORD hath spoken it.

12 Arise thou therefore, get thee to thine own house: and when thy feet enter into the city, the child shall die.

13 And all Israel shall mourn for him, and bury him: for he only of Jĕr-o-bō′am shall come to the grave, because in him there is found some good thing toward the LORD God of Israel in the house of Jĕr-o-bō′am.

14 Moreover the LORD shall raise him up a king over Israel, who shall cut off the house of Jĕr-o-bō′am that day: but what? even now.

15 For the LORD shall smite Israel, as a reed is shaken in the water, and he shall root up Israel out of this good land, which he gave to their fathers, and shall scatter them beyond the riv-

2-3. To inquire of the Lord concerning his son's welfare, Jeroboam sent his wife to **Ahijah**, who appears at the beginning and the end of the Jeroboam narrative. No indication is given of any communication in the meantime. In fact, Jeroboam's instruction to his wife to **disguise thyself** seems to indicate Ahijah had broken off from Jeroboam because of his religious policies. He feared that if she were recognized by the prophet, he would deliver a condemning message to the king. In keeping with custom (cf. I Sam 9:7-8; II Kgs 5:15; 8:8), she took the prophet a gift of the simple food of a commoner, not of royalty. **Cracknels** may be bread or cake that had become dry and crumby.

4-6. Old age may have impaired the prophet's vision, but his spiritual sight remained keen and his ears were tuned to the Lord. Jeroboam was pagan, indeed, in his theology to think that he could deceive the omniscient God. Blind Ahijah promptly identified the unseen and disguised wife of Jeroboam, rebuked her for her deception, and greeted her with **heavy tidings**, i.e., a message of doom and judgment.

7-9. Go, tell Jeroboam. Jeroboam was reminded that he was divinely chosen and appointed to reign over Israel. **But hast done evil above all that were before thee.** This does not refer only to united Israel's kings, who had preceded Jeroboam, but also to earlier rulers (e.g., the judges). Jeroboam had made for himself **gods,** i.e., golden calves; but these were nothing more than **molten images.**

10-11. In graphic and uninhibited language the male children of the house of Jeroboam are described. Their doom is certain. **Dogs** were not pets in the ancient Near East, but scavengers of the city street. Their counterparts of the open country were **fowls,** i.e., vultures. To be refused burial and allowed to be devoured by these scavengers was a disgrace.

12-15. Abijah would die as soon as his mother returned home. He alone would be granted a decent burial. "So horrible was the judgment awaiting the royal family (I Kings 14:10-11) that to avoid it by dying in bed would be a great blessing!" (Whitcomb, p. 26). The king of Israel who would cut off the house of Jeroboam was Baasha (15:27-30).

er, because they have made their groves, provoking the LORD to anger.

16 And he shall give Israel up because of the sins of Jĕr-o-bŏ'am, who did sin, and who made Israel to sin.

17 ¶And Jĕr-o-bŏ'am's wife arose, and departed, and came to Tir'zah: and when she came to the threshold of the door, the child died;

18 And they buried him; and all Israel mourned for him, according to the word of the LORD, which he spake by the hand of his servant A-hī'jah the prophet.

19 And the rest of the acts of Jĕr-o-bŏ'am, how he warred, and how he reigned, behold, they are written in the book of the chronicles of the kings of Israel.

20 And the days which Jĕr-o-bŏ'am reigned were two and twenty years: and he slept with his fathers, and Nā'-dăb his son reigned in his stead.

21 ¶And Rē-ho-bŏ'am the son of Sŏl-omon reigned in Jūdah. Rē-ho-bŏ'am was forty and one years old when he began to reign, and he reigned seventeen years in Jerusalem, the city which the LORD did choose out of all the tribes of Israel, to put his name there. And his mother's name was Nā'a-mah an Ammonitess.

22 And Jūdah did evil in the sight of the LORD, and they provoked him to jealousy with their sins which they had committed, above all that their fathers had done.

23 For they also built them high places, and images, and groves, on every high hill, and under every green tree.

24 And there were also sodomites in the land: and they did according to all the abominations of the nations which the LORD cast out before the children of Israel.

25 ¶And it came to pass in the fifth year of king Rē-ho-bŏ'am, that Shī'-shăk king of Egypt came up against Jerusalem:

26 And he took away the treasures of the house of the LORD, and the treasures of the king's house; he even took away all: and he took away all the shields of gold which Sŏlomon had made.

27 And king Rē-ho-bŏ'am made in their stead brasen shields, and committed them unto the hands of the chief of the guard, which kept the door of the king's house.

28 And it was so, when the king went into the house of the LORD, that the guard bare them, and brought them back into the guard chamber.

16. Jeroboam . . . who made Israel to sin. What an epithet by which to be remembered in the royal chronicles and the pages of Scripture (at least twenty times). Whereas the fidelity of David was the standard for measuring the spiritual qualities of Judah's kings, the sin of Jeroboam was the standard for measuring the depths of Israel's sinning kings.

17-18. Jeroboam's wife returned to **Tirzah,** and her son died and was buried according to Ahijah's prophetic word. **Tirzah,** located about six miles north of Shechem, was apparently Jeroboam's third, and final, capital (cf. 12:25).

19. The Book of the Chronicles of the Kings of Israel, no longer extant, was the fuller and official annal of the northern kings, a source the biblical writer undoubtedly consulted (see Introduction).

20. For a more complete account of events leading to Jeroboam's death, see II Chronicles 13:2-20. Jeroboam reigned twenty-two years, approximately 931-910 B.C.; and Nadab inherited the throne for a short reign (cf. 15:25ff.).

C. Judah's Kings: Rehoboam, Abijam, and Asa. 14:21-15:24.

1. Rehoboam. 14:21-31.

21. The historical scene now shifts to the southern kingdom, Judah. Rehoboam **reigned seventeen years** (ca. 931-913 B.C.). His mother, **Naamath,** was an **Ammonitess** who worshiped the god Molech (11:1, 7); and in all likelihood he worshiped this god also. Comparing his age (forty-one years) and the length of his father's reign (forty years, 11:42), it becomes apparent that Solomon had engaged in foreign marriages prior to his becoming king.

22-24. Judah did evil by building: (1) **high places,** i.e., elevations for cultic shrines; (2) **images** (Heb matsēbah, lit., pillars), i.e., standing stones that represented the presence of the male god, Baal; and (3) **groves** (Heb 'ashērîm, lit., Asherim, which is the plural form of Asherah, the goddess who was the consort of Baal). Asherim were posts or trees carved to symbolize this goddess.

There were also sodomites (Heb qadēsh, lit., a consecrated one). These Sodomites were male prostitutes who had devoted themselves to the sexual rituals of heathen worship. Israel had failed miserably in ridding the land of the Canaanites and their religious practices. Now, even the southern kingdom was deeply involved in religious syncretism.

25-28. The glory of Solomon's state was short-lived, because in the fifth year of Rehoboam, his son, the treasures of the Temple and the golden shields he had made were all confiscated by Shishak (Sheshonk I) of Egypt (for an expanded account, see II Chr 12). Shishak thought very highly of this particular campaign, and on the walls of the temple of Karnak in Upper Egypt he had a picture carved of himself smiting the Asiatics (Wright, p. 148). Also included in the carving was an inscription listing the names of cities conquered by him and showing that his campaign extended into Israel also. A fragment of a stele of Shishak has been found at Megiddo (Aharoni and Avi-Yonah, p. 77).

29 ¶Now the rest of the acts of Rĕ-ho-bō'am, and all that he did, are they not written in the book of the chronicles of the kings of Jūdah?

30 And there was war between Rĕ-ho-bō'am and Jĕr-o-bō'am all their days.

31 And Rĕ-ho-bō'am slept with his fathers, and was buried with his fathers in the city of David. And his mother's name was Nā'a-mah an Ammonitess. And A-bī'jam his son reigned in his stead.

CHAPTER 15

NOW in the eighteenth year of king Jĕr-o-bō'am the son of Nĕ'băt reigned A-bī'jam over Jūdah.

2 Three years reigned he in Jerusalem. And his mother's name was Mā'a-chah, the daughter of A-bĭsh'a-lom,

3 And he walked in all the sins of his father, which he had done before him: and his heart was not perfect with the LORD his God, as the heart of David his father.

4 Nevertheless for David's sake did the LORD his God give him a lamp in Jerusalem, to set up his son after him, and to establish Jerusalem.

5 Because David did that which was right in the eyes of the LORD, and turned not aside from any thing that he commanded him all the days of his life, save only in the matter of Ū-rī'ah the Hittite.

6 And there was war between Rĕ-ho-bō'am and Jĕr-o-bō'am all the days of his life.

7 Now the rest of the acts of A-bī'jam, and all that he did, are they not written in the book of the chronicles of the kings of Jūdah? And there was war between A-bī'jam and Jĕr-o-bō'am.

8 And A-bī'jam slept with his fathers; and they buried him in the city of David: and Āsa his son reigned in his stead.

9 ¶And in the twentieth year of Jĕr-o-bō'am king of Israel reigned Āsa over Jūdah.

10 And forty and one years reigned he in Jerusalem. And his mother's name was Mā'a-chah, the daughter of A-bĭsh'a-lom,

11 And Āsa did that which was right in the eyes of the LORD, as did David his father.

12 And he took away the sodomites out of the land, and removed all the idols that his fathers had made.

13 And also Mā'a-chah his mother, even her he removed from being queen, because she had made an idol in a grove; and Āsa destroyed her idol, and burnt it by the brook Kidron.

14 But the high places were not removed: nevertheless Āsa's heart was perfect with the LORD all his days.

15 And he brought in the things which his father had dedicated, and the things which himself had dedicated,

29-31. The Chronicles of the Kings of Judah were official annals of the southern kingdom that are no longer extant (cf. II Chr 12:15 and see Introduction). However, they were not compiled by the Holy Spirit and were never accepted as inspired Scripture. The war between Rehoboam and Jeroboam was not an open warfare. That was forbidden by God (12:24). In all likelihood there were minor conflicts and threats involving the territory of Benjamin since both kings would have wanted to control that area as a buffer zone (Wood, p. 339).

2. Abijam. 15:1-8.

15:1. Rehoboam was followed by his son **Abijam**. The name indicates Canaanite influence, "My father is Yam" (Yam was a Canaanite sea-god). His Hebrew name, Abijah ("My father is Yah," i.e., Jehovah), is used in II Chronicles 13.

2-7. He was not Rehoboam's oldest son, but the son of his favorite wife, Maachah (II Chr 11:18-22), the daughter of Abishalom (a longer spelling of the name Absalom).

Daughter may mean granddaughter. According to II Samuel 14:27, Absalom had only one daughter, Tamar. She probably married Uriel of Gibeah and gave birth to Maachah (Michaiah, cf. II Chr 13:2).

Abijam's reign was for only three years (ca. 913-911 B.C.); but it was only because of the grace of God that he ruled that long, for he was wicked like his father. In faithfulness to David who had been a righteous king, God maintained a Davidic **lamp in Jerusalem.**

8. Abijam also shared hostilities with Jeroboam, which resulted in one major open conflict where God demonstrably fought for Judah (cf. II Chr 13:1-20).

3. Asa. 15:9-24.

9-11. Asa, the son of Abijam, enjoyed a lengthy reign of forty-one years (ca. 911-870 B.C.). **His mother's name was Maachah** (cf. vs. 2). Mother here obviously means grandmother. It is refreshing to see the grace of God touch the life of one who had been reared in a wicked environment and establish him as a righteous king. He did that which was **right in the eyes of the LORD.**

12-15. Asa initiated a reform, actually, more of a revival, that was seriously enforced and by which the people ". . . sought him with their whole desire . . ." (cf. II Chr 15:13-15). The reform began with his family, for he not only removed the Sodomites and the idols from the land, he also demoted his grandmother Maachah from her honored position as **queen**, i.e., queen mother, because she had made **an idol in a grove**, i.e., an abominable image for an Asherah, the Canaanite mother-goddess. Asa cut down this image and burned it in the Kidron Valley. This valley became the regular place for reforming kings to destroy idolatrous objects.

To say that Asa's **heart was perfect** does not mean that he

677

into the house of the LORD, silver, and gold, and vessels.

16 ¶And there was war between Āsa and Bā′a-sha king of Israel all their days.

17 And Bā′a-sha king of Israel went up against Jūdah, and built Rā′mah, that he might not suffer any to go out or come in to Āsa king of Jūdah.

18 Then Āsa took all the silver and the gold *that were* left in the treasures of the house of the LORD, and the treasures of the king's house, and delivered them into the hand of his servants: and king Āsa sent them to Bĕn-hā′dăd, the son of Tăb′rĭ-mon, the son of Hĕ′zĭ-ŏn, king of Syria, that dwelt at Damascus, saying,

19 *There is* a league between me and thee, *and* between my father and thy father: behold, I have sent unto thee a present of silver and gold; come and break thy league with Bā′a-sha king of Israel, that he may depart from me.

20 So Bĕn-hā′dăd hearkened unto king Āsa, and sent the captains of the hosts which he had against the cities of Israel, and smote Ī′jŏn, and Dan, and Ā′bel-bĕth-mā′a-chah, and all Cĭn′ne-rŏth, with all the land of Năph′ta-lī.

21 And it came to pass, when Bā′a-sha heard *thereof,* that he left off building of Rā′mah, and dwelt in Tir′zah.

22 Then king Āsa made a proclamation throughout all Jūdah; none *was* exempted: and they took away the stones of Rā′mah, and the timber thereof, wherewith Bā′a-sha had builded; and king Āsa built with them Gĕ′ba of Benjamin, and Miz′pah.

23 The rest of all the acts of Āsa, and all his might, and all that he did, and the cities which he built, *are* they not written in the book of the chronicles of the kings of Jūdah? Nevertheless in the time of his old age he was diseased in his feet.

24 And Āsa slept with his fathers, and was buried with his fathers in the city of David his father: and Je-hŏsh′a-phăt his son reigned in his stead.

25 ¶And Nā′dăb the son of Jĕr-o-bō′am began to reign over Israel in the second year of Āsa king of Jūdah, and reigned over Israel two years.

26 And he did evil in the sight of the LORD, and walked in the way of his father, and in his sin wherewith he made Israel to sin.

27 ¶And Bā′a-sha the son of A-hī′jah, of the house of Ĭs′sa-char, conspired against him; and Bā′a-sha smote him at Gĭb′be-thŏn, which *belonged* to the Philistines; for Nā′dăb and all Israel laid siege to Gĭb′be-thŏn.

28 Even in the third year of Āsa king of Jūdah did Bā′a-sha slay him, and reigned in his stead.

29 And it came to pass, when he reigned, *that* he smote all the house of

was sinless (cf. his attitude during his latter days, II Chr 16:10-12), but he was one who trusted God.

16-17. During Asa's reign there was a change of dynasties in Israel (15:27ff.). **Baasha** was king. Baasha **built Ramah,** i.e., fortified the city, which was only four or five miles north of Jerusalem. This was his response to Asa's reform, as well as his attempt to contain it. Many from the tribes of Benjamin, Manasseh, Ephraim, and Simeon were being touched by the southern revival and were leaving Israel to join Asa at Jerusalem (II Chr 15:9-10). Baasha was therefore closing the border crossing and threatening the security of Judah.

18-19. In panic, Asa forgot the power of Jehovah that had delivered him from the Ethiopians earlier (cf. II Chr 12:8-15). He took what was left in the Temple after Shishak's invasion (14:26) to buy protection from Ben-hadad, king of the Syrians at Damascus. **Break thy league with Baasha.** This shows what an opportunist the fickle Syrian king was. He made and kept treaties with the latest and highest bidder.

20. Ben-hadad obliged and invaded Israel from the north, taking those southern cities in the Sea of Galilee area.

21. Baasha was forced to leave his southern border and return to his capital at Tirzah.

22. Meanwhile, Asa enlisted all of Judah to destroy methodically the fortification at Ramah, and he used the ruins to build his own fortifications nearby at **Geba** (about two miles east) and **Mizpah** (about three miles north).

23-24. During the final days of his life he incurred a serious foot disease (II Chr 16:12). This may have necessitated the co-regency of his godly son Jehoshaphat, who was to follow him to the throne.

D. Israel's Kings: Nadab, Baasha, Elah, and Zimri. 15:25-16:20.

The biblical historian must turn once again to the kings of Israel because during the forty-one-year reign of Asa, eight kings (or usurpers) of the North came and went.

1. The short evil reign of Nadab. 15:25-26.

25-26. This section begins where 14:20 ended, with the accession of Nadab, who reigned only two years (ca. 910-909 B.C.). His short reign was characterized by the same sins as his father.

2. The conspiracy and evil of Baasha. 15:27-34.

27-28. Judah had only one dynastic family in its history, David's. Israel to the north, however, had eight different dynasties (if one considers Zimri's seven-day reign a dynasty). **Baasha,** a conspirator, became the head of the second dynasty when he killed Nadab at **Gibbethon.** Gibbethon was a Levitical city (Josh 21:23) controlled by the Philistines, and Nadab was attempting to reclaim it.

29-34. After Nadab's assassination, the whole royal family was destroyed, and no one was left to avenge Nadab's blood. All

Jĕr-o-bō'am; he left not to Jĕr-o-bō'am any that breathed, until he had destroyed him, according unto the saying of the LORD, which he spake by his servant A-hī'jah the Shī'lo-nīte:

30 Because of the sins of Jĕr-o-bō'am which he sinned, and which he made Israel sin, by his provocation wherewith he provoked the LORD God of Israel to anger.

31 ¶Now the rest of the acts of Na'-dăb, and all that he did, are they not written in the book of the chronicles of the kings of Israel?

32 And there was war between Āsa and Bā'a-sha king of Israel all their days.

33 ¶In the third year of Āsa king of Jūdah began Bā'a-sha the son of A-hī'-jah to reign over all Israel in Tir'zah, twenty and four years.

34 And he did evil in the sight of the LORD, and walked in the way of Jĕr-o-bō'am, and in his sin wherewith he made Israel to sin.

CHAPTER 16

THEN the word of the LORD came to Jehu the son of Ha-nā'nī against Bā'a-sha, saying,

2 Forasmuch as I exalted thee out of the dust, and made thee prince over my people Israel; and thou hast walked in the way of Jĕr-o-bō'am, and hast made my people Israel to sin, to provoke me to anger with their sins;

3 Behold, I will take away the posterity of Bā'a-sha, and the posterity of his house; and will make thy house like the house of Jĕr-o-bō'am the son of Nē'băt.

4 Him that dieth of Bā'a-sha in the city shall the dogs eat; and him that dieth of his in the fields shall the fowls of the air eat.

5 Now the rest of the acts of Bā'a-sha, and what he did, and his might are they not written in the book of the chronicles of the kings of Israel?

6 So Bā'a-sha slept with his fathers, and was buried in Tir'zah: and Ē'lah his son reigned in his stead.

7 And also by the hand of the prophet Jehu the son of Ha-nā'nī came the word of the LORD against Bā'a-sha, and against his house, even for all the evil that he did in the sight of the LORD, in provoking him to anger with the work of his hands, in being like the house of Jĕr-o-bō'am; and because he killed him.

8 ¶In the twenty and sixth year of Āsa king of Jūdah began Ē'lah the son of Bā'a-sha to reign over Israel in Tir'zah, two years.

9 And his servant Zimri, captain of half his chariots, conspired against him, as he was in Tir'zah, drinking himself

of this was in fulfillment of God's judgment upon **Jeroboam,** who **made Israel sin** (vs. 30; cf. 14:10-14). Unfortunately, destroying Jeroboam's family did not destroy the seed of sin he had sown, for the successive dynasties followed in his idolatrous ways. Even Baasha, who was an instrument of God for judging Jeroboam's house (although not by command, cf. 16:7), was not a servant of God; for he followed in the sinful steps of Jeroboam. He reigned for twenty-four years at Tirzah (ca. 909-886 B.C.).

3. The death of Baasha. 16:1-7.

16:1. It is impossible to determine at what point in Baasha's rule **Jehu the son of Hanani** pronounced this judgment upon the king. Even if this occurred near the beginning of Baasha's reign, then Jehu was of necessity a very young man; for, unless there was a later prophet of the same name and father, his ministry possibly spanned some fifty years until after the death of Ahab (cf. II Chr 19:2). However if his prophecy was spoken shortly before its fulfillment, his ministry may have spanned approximately thirty-five years. This prophet was also a historian whose work was included "in the Book of the Kings of Israel" (II Chr 20:34).

2-4. Baasha was of lowly origin, **out of the dust;** but God had made him king. However, his continuance in the same sin as Jeroboam was going to terminate by the same judgment Jeroboam's family experienced. Baasha's posterity would be completely destroyed and similarly devoured by the scavengers.

5-7. The word of the Lord against Baasha came for two reasons: he had perpetuated Jeroboam's sin and **because he killed him.** He had arbitrarily made himself a fulfiller of prophecy (14:11). "The very fact that Baasha continued Jeroboam's sin and caused the illegal worship to be perpetuated, showed clearly enough that in exterminating the family of Jeroboam he did not act under divine direction, but simply pursued his own selfish ends" (Keil, p. 224).

4. The reign of Elah and the conspiracy of Zimri. 16:8-14.

8-10. Baasha's weak son Elah replaced him on the throne for two years (ca. 886-885 B.C.); but while he was drunk, he was killed by his servant Zimri in the house of the probable co-conspirator, Arza. Zimri immediately declared himself the new king.

self drunk in the house of Är'za steward of *his* house in Tir'zah.

10 And Zimri went in and smote him, and killed him, in the twenty and seventh year of Āsa king of Jūdah, and reigned in his stead.

11 ¶And it came to pass, when he began to reign, as soon as he sat on his throne, *that* he slew all the house of Bā'a-sha: he left him not one that pisseth against a wall, neither of his kinsfolks, nor of his friends.

12 Thus did Zimri destroy all the house of Bā'a-sha, according to the word of the LORD, which he spake against Bā'a-sha by Jehu the prophet,

13 For all the sins of Bā'a-sha, and the sins of Ē'lah his son, by which they sinned, and by which they made Israel to sin, in provoking the LORD God of Israel to anger with their vanities.

14 Now the rest of the acts of Ē'lah, and all that he did, *are* they not written in the book of the chronicles of the kings of Israel?

15 ¶In the twenty and seventh year of Āsa king of Jūdah did Zimri reign seven days in Tir'zah. And the people *were* encamped against Gĭb'be-thŏn, which *belonged* to the Philistines.

16 And the people *that were* encamped heard say, Zimri hath conspired, and hath also slain the king: wherefore all Israel made Omri, the captain of the host, king over Israel that day in the camp.

17 And Omri went up from Gĭb'be-thŏn, and all Israel with him, and they besieged Tir'zah.

18 And it came to pass, when Zimri saw that the city was taken, that he went into the palace of the king's house, and burnt the king's house over him with fire, and died.

19 For his sins which he sinned in doing evil in the sight of the LORD, in walking in the way of Jĕr-o-bō'am, and in his sin which he did, to make Israel to sin.

20 Now the rest of the acts of Zimri, and his treason that he wrought, *are* they not written in the book of the chronicles of the kings of Israel?

21 ¶Then were the people of Israel divided into two parts: half of the people followed Tĭb'nī the son of Gī'năth, to make him king; and half followed Omri.

22 But the people that followed Omri prevailed against the people that followed Tĭb'nī the son of Gī'năth: so Tĭb'nī died, and Omri reigned.

23 ¶In the thirty and first year of Āsa king of Jūdah began Omri to reign over Israel, twelve years: six years reigned he in Tir'zah.

24 And he bought the hill Sa-mâ'rĭ-a of Shē'mer for two talents of silver, and built on the hill, and called the name of the city which he built, after the name of Shē'mer, owner of the hill, Sa-mâ'rĭ-a.

25 ¶But Omri wrought evil in the eyes of the LORD, and did worse than all that *were* before him.

26 For he walked in all the way of Jĕr-

11-14. Zimri was very thorough in his extermination of Baasha's household. Not only did he kill all the male descendants, but he also killed all **his kinfolks** (Heb *gō'ēl*, i.e., his redeemers) who would be obligated to avenge the murder, and **his friends,** i.e., those who would be opposed to Zimri the usurper.

5. The seven-day reign of Zimri. 16:15-20.

15-18. Zimri was a busy man as an exterminator, and his reign allowed him only seven days to accomplish his purposes. He apparently did not have the support of the people; for when word of the conspiracy and massacre reached Gibbethon, where Israel's army was besieging the Philistines, Omri, the captain, promptly left Gibbethon and returned to Tirzah to besiege it. Sensing that his cause was lost and his doom was inevitable, Zimri withdrew to his palace and committed suicide by burning his house over him.

19-20. His major crimes were: repeating the sins of Jeroboam and **treason,** i.e., conspiracy and murder.

E. The Period of the Omride Dynasty: Omri, Ahab, and Ahaziah. 16:21-22:53.

1. The dynasty is established. 16:21-34.

21-22. Although Omri had been named king (vs. 16), he was not automatically the undisputed king. For approximately five years (cf. vss. 15 and 23) the North was divided in its support of two contenders, Omri and Tibni. When **Tibni died,** Omri became the undisputed ruler.

23. Omri reigned **twelve years** (ca. 885-879 B.C.), but he was sole ruler over Israel for only about seven years (cf. vss. 15, 23, 29).

24. As founder of a new dynasty, he purchased a hill from Shemer, built a new city (his new capital), and called it Samaria, the modern Sebustieh. This was a wise move; for Samaria was located strategically close to the major trade route, the *Via Maris*, and on a three-hundred-foot-high hill that was virtually impregnable, except by siege.

25-26. Omri carried on in the tradition of Jeroboam's sin, only to a greater extent than his predecessors.

o-bŏ'am the son of Nĕ'băt, and in his sin wherewith he made Israel to sin, to provoke the LORD God of Israel to anger with their vanities.

27 Now the rest of the acts of Omri which he did, and his might that he shewed, are they not written in the book of the chronicles of the kings of Israel?

28 So Omri slept with his fathers, and was buried in Sa'mâ'rĭ-a: and Ahab his son reigned in his stead.

29 ¶And in the thirty and eighth year of Āsa king of Jūdah began Ahab the son of Omri to reign over Israel: and Ahab the son of Omri reigned over Israel in Sa'mâ'rĭ-a twenty and two years.

30 And Ahab the son of Omri did evil in the sight of the LORD above all that were before him.

31 And it came to pass, as if it had been a light thing for him to walk in the sins of Jĕr-o-bŏ'am the son of Nĕ'băt, that he took to wife Jĕz'e-bel the daughter of Ĕth-bā'al king of the Zī-dŏ'-nĭ-ans, and went and served Bā'al, and worshipped him.

32 And he reared up an altar for Bā'al in the house of Bā'al, which he had built in Sa'mâ'rĭ-a.

33 And Ahab made a grove; and Ahab did more to provoke the LORD God of Israel to anger than all the kings of Israel that were before him.

34 ¶In his days did Hī'el the Bethelite build Jericho: he laid the foundation thereof in A-bī'ram his firstborn, and set up the gates thereof in his youngest son Sĕ'gŭb, according to the word of the LORD, which he spake by Joshua the son of Nun.

CHAPTER 17
AND E-lī'jah the Tĭsh'bīte, who was of the inhabitants of Gilead, said unto Ahab, As the LORD God of Israel liveth, before whom I stand, there shall not be dew nor rain these years, but according to my word.

2 And the word of the LORD came unto him, saying,

3 Get thee hence, and turn thee eastward, and hide thyself by the brook Chĕ'rĭth, that is before Jordan.

4 And it shall be, that thou shalt drink of the brook; and I have commanded the ravens to feed thee there.

27. **His might that he showed.** Omri's strength and prominence were noted in extrabiblical sources. In his inscription Mesha stated Omri had conquered Moab (cf. Thomas, *Documents from Old Testament Times*, pp. 195-198). Also, Assyria referred to Israel as "the Land of Omri" or "the House of Omri" (Wright, p. 151).

28-33. Omri's son, Ahab, reigned for twenty-two years (ca. 874-853 B.C.). This extremely wicked king is probably best remembered for his infamous wife **Jezebel,** the daughter of the Zidonian (Phoenician) king **Ethbaal.** The marriage was undoubtedly political, but the far-reaching results were religious. Due to Jezebel's influence, Ahab served **Baal,** more specifically, Baal-Melkarth, the principal deity of Tyre. Ahab showed international courtesy to his new wife by building an altar and a house for Baal, along with a grove (the Asherah). Then he joined her in worship. He had the distinction of being Israel's most wicked king (vs. 33).

34. Ahab himself may have encouraged **Hiel** to **build,** i.e., repair and fortify, **Jericho.** In the process, however, the curse of Joshua was fulfilled (Josh 6:26); and Hiel lost two sons by divine judgment.

2. The ministry of Elijah. 17:1-19:21.

a. The prediction of drought. 17:1-7.

Elijah arrived providentially on the historical scene as a shining light, its rays piercing the darkness of wicked Ahab's reign. Ahab had so totally committed himself to Baalism that Elijah and his successor, Elisha, never addressed themselves to the idolatry of Dan and Beth-el, but devoted their whole ministries to denouncing Baalism. Their ministries involved a new outburst of miracles such as had not been seen since the Exodus and conquest. All indications point to the fact that truly "Israel once again stood at the crossroads of destiny" (Ellison, p. 315).

17:1-2. Elijah the Tishbite. Information concerning the background of this prophet is scanty. His name means "Yah is El" or "Jehovah is God." He was a resident of Tishbe in Gilead across the Jordan.

He appeared unannounced before Ahab to deliver a divine pronouncement. **Before whom I stand** identifies Elijah as God's servant (cf. 10:8). To a land such as Palestine that was dependent upon its rainfall, the prediction of Elijah that there would be no **dew or rain these years** was indeed serious, for the result would be a disastrous famine. God was obviously challenging the power of Jezebel's god, Baal-Melkarth, the god of storms and good crops.

3-7. The **brook Cherith** was a tributary of the Jordan on the eastern side, perhaps the Wadi Qilt south of Jericho. God arranged for provisions to be flown in to Elijah by ravens, birds that were unclean and could not be eaten (Lev 11:15). Twice a day he received a meal of bread and meat (cf. the manna and quail of the wilderness experience, Ex 16:8). When the brook

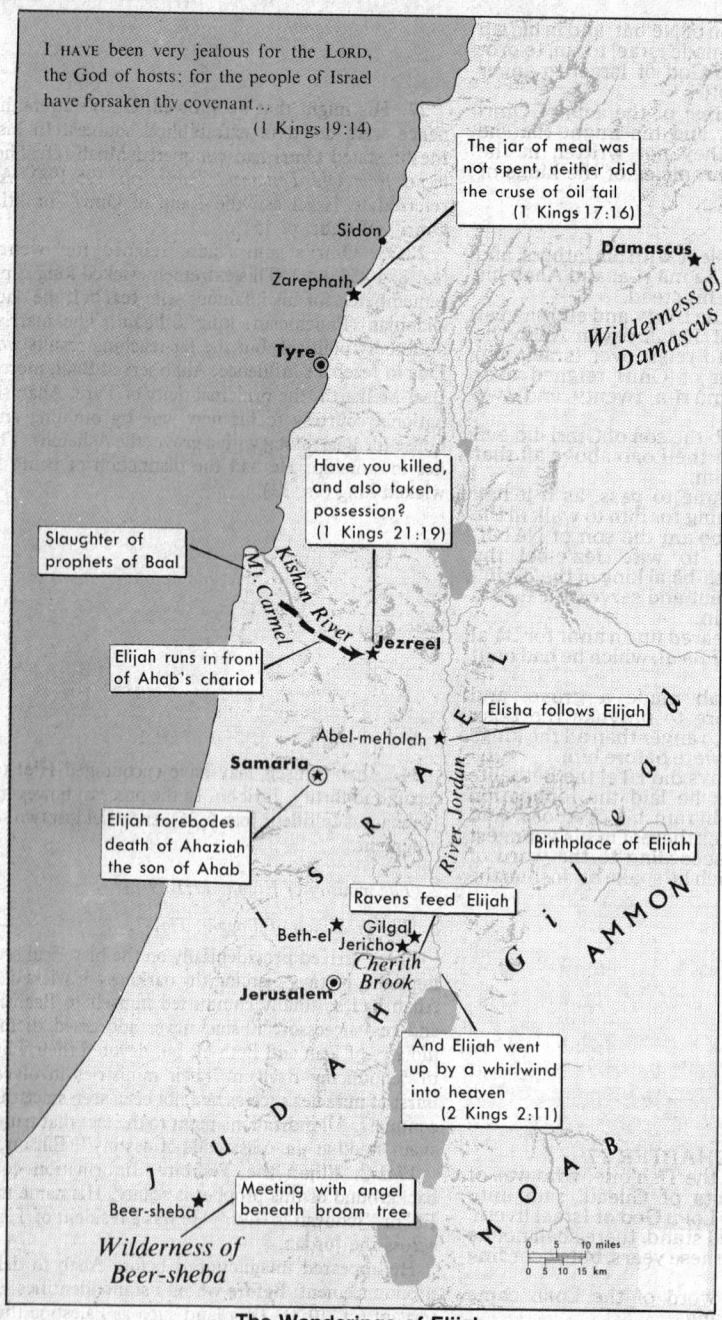

I HAVE been very jealous for the LORD, the God of hosts: for the people of Israel have forsaken thy covenant...
(1 Kings 19:14)

The jar of meal was not spent, neither did the cruse of oil fail
(1 Kings 17:16)

Sidon

Damascus

Zarephath

Wilderness of Damascus

Tyre

Have you killed, and also taken possession?
(1 Kings 21:19)

Slaughter of prophets of Baal

Mt. Carmel

Kishon River

Jezreel

Elijah runs in front of Ahab's chariot

Elisha follows Elijah

Abel-meholah

River Jordan

Samaria

Gilead

Birthplace of Elijah

Elijah forebodes death of Ahaziah the son of Ahab

I S R A E L

AMMON

Ravens feed Elijah

Beth-el   Gilgal
            Jericho
            Cherith
            Brook

Jerusalem

And Elijah went up by a whirlwind into heaven
(2 Kings 2:11)

J U D A H

M O A B

Beer-sheba

Meeting with angel beneath broom tree

Wilderness of Beer-sheba

0   5   10 miles
0 5 10 15 km

The Wanderings of Elijah

5 So he went and did according unto the word of the LORD: for he went and dwelt by the brook Chĕ′rĭth, that *is* before Jordan.

6 And the ravens brought him bread and flesh in the morning, and bread and flesh in the evening; and he drank of the brook.

7 And it came to pass after a while, that the brook dried up, because there had been no rain in the land.

dried up, God closed the miracle supply of food, only to provide it in a new locality.

8 ¶And the word of the LORD came unto him, saying,

9 Arise, get thee to Zăr'e-phăth, which *belongeth* to Zī'don, and dwell there: behold, I have commanded a widow woman there to sustain thee.

10 So he arose and went to Zăr'e-phăth. And when he came to the gate of the city, behold, the widow woman *was* there gathering of sticks: and he called to her, and said, Fetch me, I pray thee, a little water in a vessel, that I may drink.

11 And as she was going to fetch *it*, he called to her, and said, Bring me, I pray thee, a morsel of bread in thine hand.

12 And she said, *As* the LORD thy God liveth, I have not a cake, but an handful of meal in a barrel, and a little oil in a cruse: and, behold, I *am* gathering two sticks, that I may go in and dress it for me and my son, that we may eat it, and die.

13 And E-lī'jah said unto her, Fear not; go *and* do as thou hast said: but make me thereof a little cake first, and bring *it* unto me, and after make for thee and for thy son.

14 For thus saith the LORD God of Israel, The barrel of meal shall not waste, neither shall the cruse of oil fail, until the day *that* the LORD sendeth rain upon the earth.

15 And she went and did according to the saying of E-lī'jah: and she, and he, and her house, did eat *many* days.

16 *And* the barrel of meal wasted not, neither did the cruse of oil fail, according to the word of the LORD, which he spake by E-lī'jah.

17 ¶And it came to pass after these things, *that* the son of the woman, the mistress of the house, fell sick; and his sickness was so sore, that there was no breath left in him.

18 And she said unto E-lī'jah, What have I to do with thee, O thou man of God? art thou come unto me to call my sin to remembrance, and to slay my son?

19 And he said unto her, Give me thy son. And he took him out of her bosom, and carried him up into a loft, where he abode, and laid him upon his own bed.

20 And he cried unto the LORD, and said, O LORD my God, hast thou also brought evil upon the widow with whom I sojourn, by slaying her son?

21 And he stretched himself upon the child three times, and cried unto the LORD, and said, O LORD my God, I pray thee, let this child's soul come into him again.

22 And the LORD heard the voice of E-lī'jah; and the soul of the child came into him again, and he revived.

23 And E-lī'jah took the child, and brought him down out of the chamber into the house, and delivered him unto his mother: and E-lī'jah said, See, thy son liveth.

24 And the woman said to E-lī'jah, Now by this I know that thou *art* a man of God, *and* that the word of the LORD in thy mouth *is* truth.

b. The first miracle at Zarephath. 17:8-16.

8-9. Elijah was sent to the Phoenician coastal town, **Zarephath,** situated midway between Tyre and Sidon. It is interesting to note that God hid Elijah in Jezebel's homeland, where Ahab never thought to search for him (cf. 18:10).

10-15. The widow to whom Elijah was sent is not identified as either Phoenician or Israelite; but she was apparently a worshiper of Jehovah since she verified her statements by Elijah's God, and not one of the native Phoenician gods.

She was a poor lady who was preparing one final meal before the famine claimed her and her only son's lives. She was subjected to a severe test of faith when Elijah requested a meal and promised subsequent provisions, but her demonstration of faith was tremendous.

16. The continual supply of meal and oil was truly a miracle and should not be explained away by saying that "the generosity of the widow touched the conscience of her better-provided neighbors" (Gray, p. 340).

c. The second miracle at Zarephath. 17:17-24.

17. The widow faced further testing when her only son became ill. It is not specifically stated that he died, but verses 20-21 obviously support that conclusion.

18. She was haunted by the superstition that the presence of a man of God in her house had drawn God's attention to her sin that in the past had gone unnoticed. Now she was receiving retribution for her sins in the death of her son.

19-23. Carrying the boy to his room, Elijah **stretched himself upon the child three times,** evidently a symbolic action that his own health and vitality might be transferred to the boy as he prayed, **let this child's soul** (lit., life) **come into him again.** The prayer was answered, and the Lord restored the boy's life.

24. This second miracle increased the woman's faith, and she was further convinced that Elijah was truly **a man of God.**

CHAPTER 18

AND it came to pass *after* many days, that the word of the LORD came to E-lī'jah in the third year, saying, Go, shew thyself unto Ahab; and I will send rain upon the earth.

2 And E-lī'jah went to shew himself unto Ahab. And *there was* a sore famine in Sa-mâ'rĭ-a.

3 And Ahab called Ō-ba-dī'ah, which *was* the governor of *his* house. (Now Ō-ba-dī'ah feared the LORD greatly:

4 For it was *so,* when Jĕz'e-bel cut off the prophets of the LORD, that Ō-ba-dī'ah took an hundred prophets, and hid them by fifty in a cave, and fed them with bread and water.)

5 And Ahab said unto Ō-ba-dī'ah, Go into the land, unto all fountains of water, and unto all brooks: peradventure we may find grass to save the horses and mules alive, that we lose not all the beasts.

6 So they divided the land between them to pass throughout it: Ahab went one way by himself, and Ō-ba-dī'ah went another way by himself.

7 ¶And as Ō'ba-dī'ah was in the way, behold, E-lī'jah met him: and he knew him, and fell on his face, and said, *Art* thou that my lord E-lī'jah?

8 And he answered him, I *am:* go, tell thy lord, Behold, E-lī'jah *is here.*

9 And he said, What have I sinned, that thou wouldest deliver thy servant into the hand of Ahab, to slay me?

10 *As* the LORD thy God liveth, there is no nation or kingdom, whither my lord hath not sent to seek thee: and when they said, *He is* not *there;* he took an oath of the kingdom and nation, that they found thee not.

11 And now thou sayest, Go, tell thy lord, Behold, E-lī'jah *is here.*

12 And it shall come to pass, *as soon as* I am gone from thee, that the Spirit of the LORD shall carry thee whither I know not; and *so* when I come and tell Ahab, and he cannot find thee, he shall slay me: but I thy servant fear the LORD from my youth.

13 Was it not told my lord what I did when Jĕz'e-bel slew the prophets of the LORD, how I hid an hundred men of the LORD's prophets by fifty in a cave, and fed them with bread and water?

14 And now thou sayest, Go, tell thy lord, Behold, E-lī'jah *is here:* and he shall slay me.

15 And E-lī'jah said, *As* the LORD of hosts liveth, before whom I stand, I will surely shew myself unto him to day.

16 So Ō-ba-dī'ah went to meet Ahab, and told him: and Ahab went to meet E-lī'jah.

17 ¶And it came to pass, when Ahab saw E-lī'jah, that Ahab said unto him, *Art* thou he that troubleth Israel?

18 And he answered, I have not troubled Israel; but thou, and thy father's house, in that ye have forsaken the commandments of the LORD, and thou hast followed Bā'al-ĭm.

19 Now therefore send, *and* gather to

d. The meeting with Ahab. 18:1-16.

18:1-2. In the third year, i.e., the third year of famine, Elijah returned from Zarephath to appear before Ahab in what was an uncontested, but classic, showdown between God and the Baals. Three is a round number; Luke 4:25 and James 5:17 give the exact length of the famine as three years and six months.

3a. The writer introduces Obadiah, the governor (lit., who was over) of Ahab's house, through whom Elijah will make his appointment to meet Ahab. The name means servant of Jehovah.

3b-4. A parenthetical note describes the character of Obadiah. He feared Jehovah to the extent that he had risked his own life to protect true prophets of God from the hand of Jezebel, who was committed to exterminating the worship of Jehovah and promoting Baalism. The **hundred prophets** may be the same as the **sons of the prophets** in II Kings 2:3-4.

5-6. The effects of the drought were so extreme that Ahab feared he would lose his beasts, primarily the horses and mules that were crucial to his military. Therefore, he and Obadiah divided the land and combed it in search of forage.

7-16. Obadiah was understandably reluctant to announce to Ahab that Elijah was back on the scene. Ahab had thoroughly searched all the surrounding nations (except Phoenicia!) for Elijah (vs. 10) and had been unsuccessful. Ahab's growing, vehement wrath for the prophet might be directed upon Obadiah if Elijah, as was his reputation, should suddenly disappear and not show for the arranged meeting.

e. The contest on Mount Carmel. 18:17-46.

17-18. Art thou he that troubleth Israel? Ahab was mistaken in attributing the lack of rain to Elijah's powers. He failed to see the judging hand of God. Ahab himself was the troublemaker because he had **forsaken the commandments of the LORD and . . . followed Baalim.**

19-20. After three and one-half years of famine, those of

me all Israel unto mount Carmel, and the prophets of Bā′al four hundred and fifty, and the prophets of the groves four hundred, which eat at Jĕz′e-bel's table.

20 So Ahab sent unto all the children of Israel, and gathered the prophets together unto mount Carmel.

21 ¶And E-lī′jah came unto all the people, and said, How long halt ye between two opinions? if the LORD be God, follow him: but if Bā′al, then follow him. And the people answered him not a word.

22 Then said E-lī′jah unto the people, I, even I only, remain a prophet of the LORD; but Bā′al's prophets are four hundred and fifty men.

23 Let them therefore give us two bullocks; and let them choose one bullock for themselves, and cut it in pieces, and lay it on wood, and put no fire under: and I will dress the other bullock, and lay it on wood, and put no fire under:

24 And call ye on the name of your gods, and I will call on the name of the LORD: and the God that answereth by fire, let him be God. And all the people answered and said, It is well spoken.

25 And E-lī′jah said unto the prophets of Bā′al, Choose you one bullock for yourselves, and dress it first; for ye are many; and call on the name of your gods, but put no fire under.

26 And they took the bullock which was given them, and they dressed it, and called on the name of Bā′al from morning even until noon, saying, O Bā′al, hear us. But there was no voice, nor any that answered. And they leaped upon the altar which was made.

27 And it came to pass at noon, that E-lī′jah mocked them, and said, Cry aloud: for he is a god; either he is talking, or he is pursuing, or he is in a journey, or peradventure he sleepeth, and must be awaked.

28 And they cried aloud, and cut themselves after their manner with knives and lancets, till the blood gushed out upon them.

29 And it came to pass, when midday was past, and they prophesied until the time of the offering of the evening sacrifice, that there was neither voice, nor any to answer, nor any that regarded.

30 And E-lī′jah said unto all the people, Come near unto me. And all the people came near unto him. And he repaired the altar of the LORD that was broken down.

31 And E-lī′jah took twelve stones, according to the number of the tribes of the sons of Jacob, unto whom the word of the LORD came, saying, Israel shall be thy name:

32 And with the stones he built an al-

Israel who had given themselves to Baalism should have had serious doubts about the abilities of Baal, the fertility god, to answer prayer and send the necessary rain so badly needed for good crops.

Now Ahab was invited with all Israel to Mount Carmel, where Elijah would publicly demonstrate the inability of Baal and the futility of worshiping him. Mount Carmel was chosen for Baal's contest with Jehovah. If Baal were truly a god, he should have a decided advantage on this coastal site near Phoenicia. Also invited were Baal's four hundred fifty prophets and Asherah's (rendered "groves" in AV) four hundred prophets, all of which were supported by Jezebel. With all these prophets nearby, Baal had no excuse for failure. Moreover, there would be eight hundred fifty official witnesses if Baal failed. The prophets of Asherah, however, failed to appear (cf. vs. 22).

21. How long halt ye between two opinions? is reminiscent of Joshua's challenge, ". . . choose you this day whom ye will serve . . ." (Josh 24:15). Baalism would accommodate other gods, but Jehovah demanded total and uncompromising loyalty and worship.

22. For all practical purposes, Elijah (I only) stood alone as God's spokesman because the hundred prophets hidden away by Obadiah (vs. 4) were inactive.

23-25. An agreement was made that the deity that responded in sending fire upon a slaughtered bullock would be unequivocally declared the true God. To prevent any complaints or excuses of an unfair advantage, Elijah allowed the prophets of Baal to select the bullock of their choice.

26-27. When their prayers went unanswered, at noon Elijah began to taunt Baal's prophets in sarcastic terms that fit only man, not deity. Cry aloud, i.e. speak up so he can hear you, for you say he is a god. Perhaps he is talking, or musing, i.e., thinking the matter over, or he is pursuing, or gone aside, a euphemism for relieving himself, or he is in a journey (contrast our God whose presence we cannot escape, Ps 139:7-10), or he sleepeth, . . . (the God that kept Israel neither slumbered nor slept, Ps 121:3-4).

28-29. Hoping to arouse Baal's attention and pity, the prophets submitted themselves to self-torture by slashing themselves with knives and lances. In spite of the fact that they prophesied, i.e., they raved and worked themselves into a frenzy, Baal still had not responded by evening.

30-31. Elijah invited the exhausted and bloodied prophets of Baal to direct their attention to the altar of Jehovah. He repaired the altar of the LORD . . . by taking twelve stones. The united monarchy of David and Solomon was broken, and the worship of Jehovah had been broken by the infiltration of idolatry; so Elijah's action to repair the broken altar with twelve stones was symbolic. But it was also an implicit condemnation of the existence of a separate northern nation and her idolatry.

32-35. Elijah's preparation of his sacrifice was most unusual,

685

tar in the name of the LORD: and he made a trench about the altar, as great as would contain two measures of seed.

33 And he put the wood in order, and cut the bullock in pieces, and laid *him* on the wood, and said, Fill four barrels with water, and pour *it* on the burnt sacrifice, and on the wood.

34 And he said, Do *it* the second time. And they did *it* the second time. And he said, Do *it* the third time. And they did *it* the third time.

35 And the water ran round about the altar; and he filled the trench also with water.

36 And it came to pass at *the time of* the offering of the *evening* sacrifice, that E-lī′jah the prophet came near, and said, LORD God of Abraham, Isaac, and of Israel, let it be known this day that thou *art* God in Israel, and *that* I *am* thy servant, and *that* I have done all these things at thy word.

37 Hear me, O LORD, hear me, that this people may know that thou *art* the LORD God, and *that* thou hast turned their heart back again.

38 Then the fire of the LORD fell, and consumed the burnt sacrifice, and the wood, and the stones, and the dust, and licked up the water that *was* in the trench.

39 And when all the people saw *it*, they fell on their faces: and they said, The LORD, he *is* the God; the LORD, he *is* the God.

40 And E-lī′jah said unto them, Take the prophets of Bā′al; let not one of them escape. And they took them: and E-lī′jah brought them down to the brook Kī′shŏn, and slew them there.

41 ¶And E-lī′jah said unto Ahab, Get thee up, eat and drink; for *there is* a sound of abundance of rain.

42 So Ahab went up to eat and to drink. And E-lī′jah went up to the top of Carmel; and he cast himself down upon the earth, and put his face between his knees,

43 And said to his servant, Go up now, look toward the sea. And he went up, and looked, and said, *There is* nothing. And he said, Go again seven times.

44 And it came to pass at the seventh time, that he said, Behold, there ariseth a little cloud out of the sea, like a man's hand. And he said, Go up, say unto Ahab, Prepare *thy chariot*, and get thee down, that the rain stop thee not.

45 And it came to pass in the mean while, that the heaven was black with clouds and wind, and there was a great rain. And Ahab rode, and went to Jĕz′re-el.

46 And the hand of the LORD was on E-lī′jah; and he girded up his loins, and ran before Ahab to the entrance of Jĕz′re-el.

CHAPTER 19

AND Ahab told Jĕz′e-bel all that E-lī′jah had done, and withal how he had slain all the prophets with the sword.

2 Then Jĕz′e-bel sent a messenger unto E-lī′jah, saying, So let the gods do *to me*, and more also, if I make not thy life as the life of one of them by to morrow about this time.

but it made God's answer to prayer even more spectacular and convincing.

36-38. In response to Elijah's request for Jehovah to show Himself to be God, **the fire of the LORD fell.** Israel should have remembered from past history that Jehovah had an established reputation for responding with fire (cf. Gen 19:24; Lev 10:2; II Chr 7:1). The manner in which the whole altar was consumed prohibits any notion that this fire was merely lightning that preceded an ensuing rainstorm.

39. The demonstration of divine visitation was so overwhelming that the people could only exclaim in reverential awe, **The LORD, he is the God; the LORD, he is the God.**

40. The action taken against the prophets of Baal was not to avenge the murder of the prophets (vs. 4), but it was in direct obedience to God's command to put to death a false prophet (Deut 13:1-5).

41-46. Jehovah was about to make one more display of His deity by doing what Baal, the storm god, could not do—sending the rain He had shut off three and one-half years previously.

Ahab was encouraged to strengthen himself with food before the heavy rain came. From the top of Mount Carmel Elijah prayed. **He cast himself down** while his servant watched the horizon over the Mediterranean Sea. When a rain cloud was sighted, so distant that it appeared no larger than a man's hand, Ahab was warned to return to Jezreel (the site of his second palace where Jezebel was waiting for a report on the success of her prophets). Then, amid a torrential rain the vindicated prophet humbled himself to be Ahab's forerunner.

f. Elijah's failure and renewal. 19:1-21.

19:1-3. Any hopes for a change in Jezebel's attitude and nature were quickly shattered. Jezebel promptly responded with her intent to kill the prophet.

And when he saw (LXX and other versions read "he was afraid"), he fled to **Beer-sheba,** the southernmost city of Judah, out of the range of Jezebel's vindictive pursuits.

At a time when prospects for a nationwide spiritual revival

3 And when he saw *that*, he arose, and went for his life, and came to Be'er-shē'ba, which *belongeth* to Jūdah, and left his servant there.

4 ¶But he himself went a day's journey into the wilderness, and came and sat down under a juniper tree: and he requested for himself that he might die; and said, It is enough; now, O LORD, take away my life; for I *am* not better than my fathers.

5 And as he lay and slept under a juniper tree, behold, then an angel touched him, and said unto him, Arise *and* eat.

6 And he looked, and, behold, *there was* a cake baken on the coals, and a cruse of water at his head. And he did eat and drink, and laid him down again.

7 And the angel of the LORD came again the second time, and touched him, and said, Arise *and* eat; because the journey *is* too great for thee.

8 And he arose, and did eat and drink, and went in the strength of that meat forty days and forty nights unto Hô'rĕb the mount of God.

9 ¶And he came thither unto a cave, and lodged there; and, behold, the word of the LORD *came* to him, and he said unto him, What doest thou here, E-lī'jah?

10 And he said, I have been very jealous for the LORD God of hosts: for the children of Israel have forsaken thy covenant, thrown down thine altars, and slain thy prophets with the sword; and I, *even* I only, am left; and they seek my life, to take it away.

11 And he said, Go forth, and stand upon the mount before the LORD. And, behold, the LORD passed by, and a great and strong wind rent the mountains, and brake in pieces the rocks before the LORD: *but* the LORD *was* not in the wind: and after the wind an earthquake; *but* the LORD *was* not in the earthquake:

12 And after the earthquake a fire; *but* the LORD *was* not in the fire: and after the fire a still small voice.

13 And it was *so*, when E-lī'jah heard *it*, that he wrapped his face in his mantle, and went out, and stood in the entering in of the cave. And, behold, there came a voice unto him, and said, What doest thou here, E-lī'jah?

14 And he said, I have been very jealous for the LORD God of hosts: because the children of Israel have forsaken thy covenant, thrown down thine altars, and slain thy prophets with the sword; and I, *even* I only, am left; and they seek my life, to take it away.

15 And the LORD said unto him, Go, return on thy way to the wilderness of Damascus: and when thou comest, anoint Hāz'a-el *to be* king over Syria:

16 And Jehu the son of Nĭm'shī shalt thou anoint *to be* king over Israel: and E-lī'sha the son of Shā'phat of Ā'bel-mĕ-hō'lah shalt thou anoint *to be* prophet in thy room.

were the greatest, the prophet himself spoiled them by fleeing in discouragement and abandoning the nation without spiritual leadership. Instead, he sought only to protect himself.

4. Another **day's journey** may have taken him as far as the wilderness of Paran. **Under a juniper tree,** or broom tree (a desert shrub that may reach a height of twelve feet), and in deep depression, he requested that he might die.

5-7. Instead, he was strengthened by sleep and food prepared by a heavenly messenger. That **the journey is too great** is indicative that Elijah's intention was to press on further south.

8. Horeb, or Sinai, was the mountain where God first appeared to Moses and later gave the Ten Commandments (Ex 3:1, 12; 19:3, 18, 20). The distance from Beer-sheba to Horeb is about two hundred miles. For Elijah to spend forty days and nights en route, he must have been in utter despair.

9. Tradition says that the **cave** where Elijah lodged was none other than the cleft of the rock where God sent Moses when His glory passed by (Ex 33:22).

What doest thou here, Elijah? This is a leading question, asked both to allow Elijah to state his case and for God to rebuke him gently.

10. I only, am left. Elijah had quickly forgotten that many had declared, **The LORD, he is the God,** and had aided in the slaying of Baal's prophets (18:39-40).

Elijah was totally committed to the holiness of God. He desired that God should exercise His vengeance on all idolators as he had done to Baal's prophets at Mount Carmel. Therefore, he pleaded against Israel (cf. Rom 11:2-4).

11-14. The series of phenomenal acts of nature were significant. God "will indeed display His punishing, destroying might to His despisers and enemies, but His own true and innermost essence is grace, rescuing, preserving, and quickening love, and though the people have broken the covenant of grace, yet He maintains this covenant, and remains faithful and gracious as He promised" (Bahr, p. 220).

In the midst of the demonstration Elijah **wrapped his face in his mantle.** Compare the action of Moses in the presence of Jehovah (Ex 3:6).

15-17. Judgment upon Israel would be by the hands of three men. First, Elijah was told to anoint **Hazael** king over Syria, Israel's enemy on her northern border (cf. II Kgs 8:13-15). Second, he was to anoint **Jehu,** a captain in Ahab's army, as king over Israel (cf. II Kgs 9:1-10). Third, he was to anoint **Elisha** as his prophetic successor.

17 And it shall come to pass, *that* him that escapeth the sword of Hăz′a-el shall Jehu slay: and him that escapeth from the sword of Jehu shall E-lī′sha slay.

18 Yet I have left *me* seven thousand in Israel, all the knees which have not bowed unto Bā′al, and every mouth which hath not kissed him.

19 ¶So he departed thence, and found E-lī′sha the son of Shā′phat, who *was* plowing *with* twelve yoke *of* oxen before him, and he with the twelfth: and E-lī′jah passed by him, and cast his mantle upon him.

20 And he left the oxen, and ran after E-lī′jah, and said, Let me, I pray thee, kiss my father and my mother, and *then* I will follow thee. And he said unto him, Go back again: for what have I done to thee?

21 And he returned back from him, and took a yoke of oxen, and slew them, and boiled their flesh with the instruments of the oxen, and gave unto the people, and they did eat. Then he arose, and went after E-lī′jah, and ministered unto him.

CHAPTER 20

AND Bĕn–hă′dăd the king of Syria gathered all his host together: and *there were* thirty and two kings with him, and horses, and chariots: and he went up and besieged Sa-mâ′rī-a, and warred against it.

2 And he sent messengers to Ahab king of Israel into the city, and said unto him, Thus saith Bĕn–hă′dăd,

3 Thy silver and thy gold *is* mine; thy wives also and thy children, *even* the goodliest, *are* mine.

4 And the king of Israel answered and said, My lord, O king, according to thy saying, I *am* thine, and all that I have.

5 And the messengers came again, and said, Thus speaketh Bĕn–hă′dăd, saying, Although I have sent unto thee, saying, Thou shalt deliver me thy silver, and thy gold, and thy wives, and thy children;

6 Yet I will send my servants unto thee to morrow about this time, and they shall search thine house, and the houses of thy servants; and it shall be, *that* whatsoever is pleasant in thine eyes, they shall put *it* in their hand, and take *it* away.

7 Then the king of Israel called all the elders of the land, and said, Mark, I pray you, and see how this *man* seeketh mischief: for he sent unto me for my wives, and for my children, and for my silver, and for my gold; and I denied him not.

8 And all the elders and all the people said unto him, Hearken not *unto him*, nor consent.

9 Wherefore he said unto the messengers of Bĕn–hă′dăd, Tell my lord the king, All that thou didst send for to thy servant at the first I will do: but this thing I may not do. And the messengers departed, and brought him word again.

10 And Bĕn–hă′dăd sent unto him, and said, The gods do so unto me, and more also, if the dust of Sa-mâ′rī-a shall suf-

18. For encouragement, Elijah was reminded that the spiritual situation in Israel was seven thousand times better then he had thought.

19-21. Elijah was renewed, and he obeyed immediately. Scripture omits recording an account of the anointing of Hazael and Jehu. Elisha was apparently from a wealthy family (twelve yoke of oxen); but when Elijah threw the mantle upon him, he understood the symbolic action, recognized his call, and asked permission to make that call known to his family and friends by a farewell feast. Whereupon, he assumed his new role as a prophet-in-training.

3. Ahab's wars with Syria. 20:1-43.

20:1-2. Ben-hadad. Opinions differ as to whether or not this is the same Ben-hadad of 15:18ff. With Assyria strengthening herself, Ben-hadad saw an invasion impending; so he headed up an Aramaean alliance with thirty-two vassal kings. To strengthen himself on the northern border, he decided to eliminate any threat on his southern border.

3. Thy silver . . . is mine. . . . Ben-hadad's demands may indicate that Ahab was already a vassal or, with the siege of Samaria, was being persuaded to become one.

4-6. Ahab quickly agreed, and Ben-hadad arrogantly increased his demands. His servants would search the city for everything of value.

7-9. Ahab, a wicked king, was not necessarily a weak king. He called together the elders for counsel. **Mark** (lit., know, i.e., be informed) what Ben-hadad is demanding. All agreed that Ahab should not comply with the demands. It was one thing to surrender royal possessions (the first demand), but quite another to surrender the city (the second demand).

10. Ben-hadad boasted that Samaria would be so utterly destroyed by his great army that the city would be carried away as **handfuls** of dust (cf. Hushai's boast in II Sam 17:13).

fice for handfuls for all the people that follow me.

11 And the king of Israel answered and said, Tell *him*, Let not him that girdeth on *his harness* boast himself as he that putteth it off.

12 And it came to pass, when *Ben-ha'dad* heard this message, as he *was* drinking, he and the kings in the pavilions, that he said unto his servants, Set *yourselves in array*. And they set *themselves in array* against the city.

13 ¶And, behold, there came a prophet unto Ahab king of Israel, saying, Thus saith the LORD, Hast thou seen all this great multitude? behold, I will deliver it into thine hand this day; and thou shalt know that I *am* the LORD.

14 And Ahab said, By whom? And he said, Thus saith the LORD, *Even* by the young men of the princes of the provinces. Then he said, Who shall order the battle? And he answered, Thou.

15 Then he numbered the young men of the princes of the provinces, and they were two hundred and thirty two: and after them he numbered all the people, *even* all the children of Israel, *being* seven thousand.

16 And they went out at noon. But Bĕn-hā'dăd *was* drinking himself drunk in the pavilions, he and the kings, the thirty and two kings that helped him.

17 And the young men of the princes of the provinces went out first; and Bĕn-hā'dăd sent out, and they told him, saying, There are men come out of Sa-mā'rĭ-a.

18 And he said, Whether they be come out for peace, take them alive; or whether they be come out for war, take them alive.

19 So these young men of the princes of the provinces came out of the city, and the army which followed them.

20 And they slew every one his man: and the Syrians fled; and Israel pursued them: and Bĕn-hā'dăd the king of Syria escaped on an horse with the horsemen.

21 And the king of Israel went out, and smote the horses and chariots, and slew the Syrians with a great slaughter.

22 ¶And the prophet came to the king of Israel, and said unto him, Go, strengthen thyself, and mark, and see what thou doest: for at the return of the year the king of Syria will come up against thee.

23 And the servants of the king of Syria said unto him, Their gods *are* gods of the hills; therefore they were stronger than we; but let us fight against them in the plain, and surely we shall be stronger than they.

24 And do this thing, Take the kings away, every man out of his place, and put captains in their rooms:

25 And number thee an army, like the army that thou hast lost, horse for horse, and chariot for chariot: and we will fight against them in the plain, *and* surely we shall be stronger than they. And he hearkened unto their voice, and did so.

26 And it came to pass at the return of the year, that Bĕn-hā'dăd numbered

11. Ahab's response, **Let not him that girdeth . . . as he that putteth it off** was a proverbial saying, comparable to "Don't count your chickens before they are hatched."

12. Ben-hadad, drinking in his **pavilions** (Heb *sukah*), i.e., booths (cf. Lev 23:42; Neh 8:14-17), was probably drunk when he gave the order, **Set.** perhaps a reference to the battering rams used to smash the city walls.

13-15. An unnamed prophet (Josephus says it was Micaiah, *Antiq.* VII. XIV) delivered Jehovah's promise of victory over the Syrians and ordered Ahab to go out in battle, even though his total number of available men was only seven thousand.

16-21. At noon, when the overconfident Ben-hadad was relaxing and drunk from a premature victory celebration, the 232 princes of Israel went out of the city. Arrogantly, Ben-hadad ordered them to be taken alive, but the army and Ahab had also come out of the city for battle. With the Lord fighting against them, the Syrians fled, but not before they had lost horses, chariots, and men in **a great slaughter.**

22-26. While Ahab was being warned that Syria would return a second time, Ben-hadad was being ill-advised on the basis of theological error. The Syrians thought Jehovah was a god of the hills and would be ineffective in the plains. Therefore, plans were made, and they came out to fight with Israel at Aphek. Since there were five different Apheks, the site of this battle cannot be determined with certainty; but the locality just east of the Sea of Chinnereth (or Galilee in the New Testament) is most likely.

the Syrians, and went up to Ā'phĕk, to fight against Israel.

27 And the children of Israel were numbered, and were all present, and went against them: and the children of Israel pitched before them like two little flocks of kids; but the Syrians filled the country.

28 ¶And there came a man of God, and spake unto the king of Israel, and said, Thus saith the LORD, Because the Syrians have said, The LORD is God of the hills, but he is not God of the valleys, therefore will I deliver all this great multitude into thine hand, and ye shall know that I am the LORD.

29 And they pitched one over against the other seven days. And so it was, that in the seventh day the battle was joined: and the children of Israel slew of the Syrians an hundred thousand footmen in one day.

30 But the rest fled to Ā'phĕk, into the city; and there a wall fell upon twenty and seven thousand of the men that were left. And Bĕn-hā'dăd fled, and came into the city, into an inner chamber.

31 ¶And his servants said unto him, Behold now, we have heard that the kings of the house of Israel are merciful kings: let us, I pray thee, put sackcloth on our loins, and ropes upon our heads, and go out to the king of Israel: peradventure he will save thy life.

32 So they girded sackcloth on their loins, and put ropes on their heads, and came to the king of Israel, and said, Thy servant Bĕn-hā'dăd saith, I pray thee, let me live. And he said, Is he yet alive? he is my brother.

33 Now the men did diligently observe whether any thing would come from him, and did hastily catch it: and they said, Thy brother Bĕn-hā'dăd. Then he said, Go ye, bring him. Then Bĕn-hā'dăd came forth to him; and he caused him to come up into the chariot.

34 And Ben-ha'dad said unto him, The cities, which my father took from thy father, I will restore; and thou shalt make streets for thee in Damascus, as my father made in Sa-mâ'rī-a. Then said Ahab, I will send thee away with this covenant. So he made a covenant with him, and sent him away.

35 ¶And a certain man of the sons of the prophets said unto his neighbour in the word of the LORD, Smite me, I pray thee. And the man refused to smite him.

36 Then said he unto him, Because thou hast not obeyed the voice of the LORD, behold, as soon as thou art departed from me, a lion shall slay thee. And as soon as he was departed from him, a lion found him, and slew him.

37 Then he found another man, and said, Smite me, I pray thee. And the man smote him, so that in smiting he wounded him.

38 So the prophet departed, and waited for the king by the way, and disguised himself with ashes upon his face.

39 And as the king passed by, he cried unto the king: and he said, Thy servant went out into the midst of the

27-28. Again, Israel was severely outnumbered by the Syrians; so victory had to come from Jehovah, who was about to demonstrate in a most vivid way that He was not restricted to the hills as the Syrians had surmised. The sovereign God of all creation was fighting for Israel.

29-30. When they finally engaged in battle on the seventh day, the Syrians faced the proverbial "out of the frying pan and into the fire" experience. They lost 100,000 men; and the rest (27,000) rushed to find safety inside the city of Aphek, only to have a wall fall on them. Scripture does not state whether the wall collapsed by divine miracle, or by Israel's battering ram.

31-34. Israel had a reputation for being **merciful** (Heb chesed), i.e., being loyal to a covenant. Donning clothes of mourning and humiliation (**sackcloth . . . ropes**), Ben-hadad's servants appealed to Ahab's sympathy (cf. Josh 9:3-15), stating Ben-hadad's offer to be a vassal (**Thy servant**). Ahab's response, **my brother** (a parity covenantal term), indicated his intention to be lenient. Ben-hadad promised the return of Israel's cities taken years before and the use of special **streets** for commercial trading within Damascus. So Ahab **made a covenant with him.**

Ahab's motive was to use Syria as buffer in the event of an invasion from Shalmaneser III (859-824 B.C.) of Assyria.

35-36. Ahab's action called for divine reprimand. It was not his prerogative to dictate terms of peace for a victory Jehovah had won. An unnamed man from the **sons of the prophets,** i.e., the guild of prophets, received both revelation for Ahab and the method for conveying the revelation to the king. The **neighbor** who failed to cooperate with the divine method was killed by a lion.

37-38. Another man cooperated and injured the prophet, who **disguised himself with ashes upon his face,** perhaps this could be better translated, "with a headband (or bandage) over his eyes."

39-41. By pretending to be a wounded soldier, the prophet induced Ahab to judge his own case. **So shall thy judgment be: thyself hast decided it** (cf. Nathan and David, II Sam 12:1-7).

battle; and, behold, a man turned aside, and brought a man unto me, and said, Keep this man: if by any means he be missing, then shall thy life be for his life, or else thou shalt pay a talent of silver.

40 And as thy servant was busy here and there, he was gone. And the king of Israel said unto him, So *shall* thy judgment *be;* thyself hast decided *it.*

41 And he hasted, and took the ashes away from his face; and the king of Israel discerned him that he *was* of the prophets.

42 And he said unto him, Thus saith the Lord, Because thou hast let go out of *thy* hand a man whom I appointed to utter destruction, therefore thy life shall go for his life, and thy people for his people.

43 And the king of Israel went to his house heavy and displeased, and came to Sa-mâ'rǐ-a.

CHAPTER 21

AND it came to pass after these things, *that* Nā'bŏth the Jĕz're-el-īte had a vineyard, which *was* in Jĕz're-el, hard by the palace of Ahab king of Sa-mâ'rǐ-a.

2 And Ahab spake unto Nā'bŏth, saying, Give me thy vineyard, that I may have it for a garden of herbs, because it *is* near unto my house: and I will give thee for it a better vineyard than it; *or,* if it seem good to thee, I will give thee the worth of it in money.

3 And Nā'bŏth said to Ahab, The Lord forbid it me, that I should give the inheritance of my fathers unto thee.

4 And Ahab came into his house heavy and displeased because of the word which Nā'bŏth the Jĕz're-el-īte had spoken to him: for he had said, I will not give thee the inheritance of my fathers. And he laid him down upon his bed, and turned away his face, and would eat no bread.

5 ¶But Jĕz'e-bel his wife came to him, and said unto him, Why is thy spirit so sad, that thou eatest no bread?

6 And he said unto her, Because I spake unto Nā'bŏth the Jĕz're-el-īte, and said unto him, Give me thy vineyard for money; or else, if it please thee, I will give thee *another* vineyard for it: and he answered, I will not give thee my vineyard.

7 And Jĕz'e-bel his wife said unto him, Dost thou now govern the kingdom of Israel? arise, *and* eat bread, and let thine heart be merry: I will give thee the vineyard of Nā'bŏth the Jĕz're-el-īte.

8 So she wrote letters in Ahab's name, and sealed *them* with his seal, and sent the letters unto the elders and to the nobles that *were* in his city, dwelling with Nā'bŏth.

9 And she wrote in the letters, saying, Proclaim a fast, and set Nā'bŏth on high among the people:

10 And set two men, sons of Bē'lǐ-al, before him, to bear witness against him, saying, Thou didst blaspheme God and the king. And *then* carry him out, and stone him, that he may die.

42-43. Ahab was doomed, now that he had allowed Ben-hadad to live (cf. Saul and Agag, I Sam 15). Ahab's motive for sparing Ben-hadad revealed a lack of trust in Jehovah to exercise His power against Assyria as He had done against Syria.

4. Naboth's vineyard. 21:1-29.

21:1-2. Naboth, a resident of Jezreel where Ahab had his resort palace, **had a vineyard . . . hard by,** i.e., adjoining the royal property. Ahab, wishing to make it a vegetable garden, offered to trade vineyards or purchase it outright with cash.

3. On the basis of Mosaic law, Naboth refused the offer. According to Leviticus 25:23ff., the land was not to be sold; for it belonged to God. The Israelites were mere tenants by courtesy of God (cf. also the relation of the family to the land, Num 27:8-11).

4. If Ahab understood Naboth's reason for refusal, he certainly could not relate it to Jezebel without facing ridicule.

5-7. Upon finding the reason for Ahab's childish sulking, Jezebel asked with dripping sarcasm, **dost thou now govern the kingdom of Israel?** She remembered her Phoenician background where kings acted with absolute sovereignty. What the king wanted, he got. Therefore, she promised her husband his desire.

8-10. Jezebel, the evil genius behind the throne, displayed her diabolical nature by immediate action. **She wrote letters in Ahab's name . . . with his seal,** all the evidence of authentic royal authorization.

Proclaim a fast. A day of humiliation was needed for some sin committed either against the king or God. **Set Naboth on high,** or at the head, in a place of honor. Two worthless men, **sons of Belial,** were selected to testify falsely against Naboth in a case of blaspheming God. Two was the prescribed number of witnesses for such criminal cases (Deut 17:6; 19:15), and blasphemy was a crime deserving of death by stoning (Lev 24:16).

691

11 And the men of his city, *even* the elders and the nobles who were the inhabitants in his city, did as Jĕz'e-bel had sent unto them, *and* as it *was* written in the letters which she had sent unto them.

12 They proclaimed a fast, and set Nă'bŏth on high among the people.

13 And there came in two men, children of Bĕ'lī-al, and sat before him: and the men of Bĕ'lī-al witnessed against him, *even* against Nă'bŏth, in the presence of the people, saying, Nă'bŏth did blaspheme God and the king. Then they carried him forth out of the city, and stoned him with stones, that he died.

14 Then they sent to Jĕz'e-bel, saying, Nă'bŏth is stoned, and is dead.

15 ¶And it came to pass, when Jĕz'e-bel heard that Nă'bŏth was stoned, and was dead, that Jĕz'e-bel said to Ahab, Arise, take possession of the vineyard of Nă'bŏth the Jĕz're-el-īte, which he refused to give thee for money: for Nă'bŏth is not alive, but dead.

16 And it came to pass, when Ahab heard that Nă'bŏth was dead, that Ahab rose up to go down to the vineyard of Nă'bŏth the Jĕz're-el-īte, to take possession of it.

17 ¶And the word of the Lord came to E-lī'jah the Tĭsh'bīte, saying,

18 Arise, go down to meet Ahab king of Israel, which *is* in Sa-mâ'rĭ-a: behold, *he is* in the vineyard of Nă'bŏth, whither he is gone down to possess it.

19 And thou shalt speak unto him, saying, Thus saith the Lord, Hast thou killed, and also taken possession? And thou shalt speak unto him, saying, Thus saith the Lord, In the place where dogs licked the blood of Nă'bŏth shall dogs lick thy blood, even thine.

20 And Ahab said to E-lī'jah, Hast thou found me, O mine enemy? And he answered, I have found *thee:* because thou hast sold thyself to work evil in the sight of the Lord.

21 Behold, I will bring evil upon thee, and will take away thy posterity, and will cut off from Ahab him that pisseth against the wall, and him that is shut up and left in Israel,

22 And will make thine house like the house of Jĕr-o-bō'am the son of Nĕ'băt, and like the house of Bā'a-sha the son of A-hī'jah, for the provocation wherewith thou hast provoked *me* to anger, and made Israel to sin.

23 And of Jĕz'e-bel also spake the Lord, saying, The dogs shall eat Jĕz'e-bel by the wall of Jĕz're-el.

24 Him that dieth of Ahab in the city the dogs shall eat; and him that dieth in the field shall the fowls of the air eat.

25 But there was none like unto Ahab, which did sell himself to work wickedness in the sight of the Lord, whom Jĕz'e-bel his wife stirred up.

26 And he did very abominably in following idols, according to all *things* as did the Amorites, whom the Lord cast out before the children of Israel.

27 And it came to pass, when Ahab heard those words, that he rent his clothes, and put sackcloth upon his

11-14. Jezebel's instructions were executed precisely. **They . . . stoned him . . . he died.** Second Kings 9:26 indicates that Naboth's sons were murdered also. This action eliminated any descendants from claiming the property.

15-16. "Either the property of slain criminals was forfeited to the crown, or this is an illegal confiscation of property by the king" (Matheney, I Kings, in *The Broadman Bible Commentary*, p. 220).

17-18. While Jezebel was instructing Ahab to claim Naboth's vineyard, God was also instructing Elijah to meet Ahab there.

19. In the place should be understood as "because of." Ahab did not die in Naboth's vineyard at Jezreel, but because of Naboth's blood being licked up by dogs on account of Jezebel's and Ahab's sin, his blood would be licked up by dogs in Samaria (22:37-38).

20. Hast thou found me, O mine enemy? (cf. 18:17). Elijah appeared at the most inopportune times for Ahab. Probably they had not faced each other since their parting in 18:46. Ahab knew that Elijah never came to commend him, but to condemn him.

21-24. Ahab was the third northern king to hear the curse of annihilation placed on his male offspring (cf. Jeroboam, 14:10-14, and Baasha, 16:3-4). This was not accomplished until Jehu's purge in II Kings 9:4-10:17.

25-26. The reason that Jezebel was specifically named, along with Ahab's sons, in the curse (vs. 23) was her influence on Ahab for evil. She **stirred up**, incited, and prompted wicked Ahab to act even more wickedly.

27-29. Upon hearing Elijah's pronouncement, Ahab outwardly demonstrated his remorse by donning clothes of mourning and **went softly** (NASB "went about despondently"). This repentance was sincere only in that he turned temporarily from

neither with small nor great, save only with the king of Israel.

32 And it came to pass, when the captains of the chariots saw Je-hŏsh′a-phăt, that they said, Surely it is the king of Israel. And they turned aside to fight against him: and Je-hŏsh′a-phăt cried out.

33 And it came to pass, when the captains of the chariots perceived that it was not the king of Israel, that they turned back from pursuing him.

34 ¶And a certain man drew a bow at a venture, and smote the king of Israel between the joints of the harness: wherefore he said unto the driver of his chariot, Turn thine hand, and carry me out of the host; for I am wounded.

35 And the battle increased that day: and the king was stayed up in his chariot against the Syrians, and died at even: and the blood ran out of the wound into the midst of the chariot.

36 And there went a proclamation throughout the host about the going down of the sun, saying, Every man to his city, and every man to his own country.

37 So the king died, and was brought to Sa-mâ′rǐ-a; and they buried the king in Sa-mâ′rǐ-a.

38 And one washed the chariot in the pool of Sa-mâ′rǐ-a; and the dogs licked up his blood; and they washed his armour; according unto the word of the LORD which he spake.

39 Now the rest of the acts of Ahab, and all that he did, and the ivory house which he made, and all the cities that he built, are they not written in the book of the chronicles of the kings of Israel?

40 So Ahab slept with his fathers; and Ā-ha-zī′ah his son reigned in his stead.

41 ¶And Je-hŏsh′a-phăt the son of Āsa began to reign over Jūdah in the fourth year of Ahab king of Israel.

42 Je-hŏsh′a-phăt was thirty and five years old when he began to reign; and he reigned twenty and five years in Jerusalem. And his mother's name was A-zū′bah the daughter of Shĭl′hī.

43 And he walked in all the ways of Āsa his father; he turned not aside from it, doing that which was right in the eyes of the LORD: nevertheless the high places were not taken away; for the people offered and burnt incense yet in the high places.

44 And Je-hŏsh′a-phăt made peace with the king of Israel.

45 Now the rest of the acts of Je-hŏsh′a-phăt, and his might that he shewed, and how he warred, are they not written in the book of the chronicles of the kings of Jūdah?

46 And the remnant of the sodomites, which remained in the days of his father Āsa, he took out of the land.

47 There was then no king in Edom: a deputy was king.

48 Je-hŏsh′a-phăt made ships of Thär′shĭsh to go to Ō′phir for gold: but

34-36. One archer took a random shot (**at a venture**), i.e., he did not know at whom he was aiming, and his arrow found its predetermined target, a crack in Ahab's armor. Ahab, seriously wounded, retreated from active involvement in the battle, but remained propped up in his chariot, where he slowly bled to death.

Suffering defeat, the Israelite army retreated, the men returning to their own respective cities and countries (Israel and Judah).

37-38. Although Ahab received a burial in his capital, dogs licked up his blood (21:19). **And they washed his armor.** A further indignity to Ahab was the washing of his chariot in the pool where the harlots bathed themselves.

39-40. Ahab's palace, **the ivory house,** was appropriately named; for not only was it constructed of white marble, which gave it the appearance of ivory, its furniture and walls were decorated with ivory plaques and panels.

6. Jehoshaphat of Judah. 22:41-50.

The introduction of Jehoshaphat's reign at this point is virtually parenthetical; for, beginning with verse 51, attention is again directed to the Omride dynasty, and the writer concentrates on the northern kingdom until the end of Jehu's reign (II Kgs 10:36).

41-47. Jehoshaphat reigned twenty-five years (ca. 873-848 B.C.). Though his relationship with Ahab somewhat clouded his image, he was characterized as a good king, doing **right in the eyes of the LORD.** For a fuller account of Jehoshaphat's life, read II Chronicles 17:1-21:1.

48-49. Jehoshaphat wanted to restore the navy developed by Solomon (9:26-28; 10:22), but the ships were broken. He re-

they went not; for the ships were broken at Ē'zĭ-on-gē'ber.

49 Then said Ă-ha-zī'ah the son of Ahab unto Je-hŏsh'a-phăt, Let my servants go with thy servants in the ships. But Je-hŏsh'a-phăt would not.

50 ¶And Je-hŏsh'a-phăt slept with his fathers, and was buried with his fathers in the city of David his father: and Je-hŏ'ram his son reigned in his stead.

51 ¶Ă-ha-zī'ah the son of Ahab began to reign over Israel in Sa-mâ'rĭ-a the seventeenth year of Je-hŏsh'a-phăt king of Jūdah, and reigned two years over Israel.

52 And he did evil in the sight of the LORD, and walked in the way of his father, and in the way of his mother, and in the way of Jĕr-o-bō'am the son of Nē'băt, who made Israel to sin:

53 For he served Bā'al, and worshipped him, and provoked to anger the LORD God of Israel, according to all that his father had done.

fused an offer from Ahaziah, Ahab's son, to help man the ships (probably because of the rebuke he received from Jehu after he fought with Ahab against Syria, II Chr 19:1-4). Later he reversed his decision and accepted the offer (II Chr 20:35-37).

50. Upon Jehoshaphat's death, his son Jehoram (or Joram) reigned. He will be introduced again in II Kings 8:16.

7. Ahaziah of Israel. 22:51-53.

51-53. Ahaziah had a short reign of two years (ca. 853-852 B.C.) that came to a tragic end. His reign was long enough to demonstrate the same extreme wickedness of his father.

(see page 748 for Bibliography to I and II Kings)

OUTLINE
II KINGS

D. Recurring Apostasy and the Destruction of Jerusalem. 23:36-25:21.
1. The reign of Jehoiakim. 23:36-24:7.
2. The reign of Jehoiachin. 24:8-16.

3. The reign of Zedekiah and destruction of Jerusalem. 24:17-25:21.
E. The Assassination of Gedaliah and Elevation of Jehoiachin. 25:22-30.

COMMENTARY

I. THE DIVIDED KINGDOM. 1:1-17:41

A. The Period of the Omride Dynasty: Ahaziah and Jehoram. 1:1-8:29.

1. Ahaziah and his confrontation with Elijah. 1:1-18.

THEN Moab rebelled against Israel after the death of Ahab.

1:1. This parenthetical note concerning **Moab** is confirmed by the Moabite Stone, an inscription by the Moabite king, Mesha (Thomas, pp. 195-198).

2 And Ā-ha-zī'ah fell down through a lattice in his upper chamber that *was* in Sa-mā'rī-a, and was sick: and he sent messengers, and said unto them, Go, enquire of Bā'al-zē'bŭb the god of Ekron whether I shall recover of this disease.

2. Ahaziah was **sick,** i.e., severely injured, when he fell through the lattice-work that surrounded his balcony, or second story terrace. **Go inquire of Baal-zebub,** the local god of **Ekron,** the northernmost and closest of Philistia's chief cities. Baal-zebub means, Lord of Flies, a god associated with flies, the bearers of disease. This name appears to be one of Jewish ridicule; for according to Ugaritic texts, the real name was Baal-zebul (a name supported in the Greek NT, Mt 10:25; 12:24; Mk 3:22; Lk 11:15), who was worshiped as the god of life and health (Gray, p. 413).

3 But the angel of the LORD said to E-lī'jah the Tīsh'bīte, Arise, go up to meet the messengers of the king of Sa-mā'rī-a, and say unto them, *Is it* not because *there is* not a God in Israel, *that* ye go to enquire of Bā'al-zē'bŭb the god of Ekron?
4 Now therefore thus saith the LORD, Thou shalt not come down from that bed on which thou art gone up, but shalt surely die. And E-lī'jah departed.
5 ¶And when the messengers turned back unto him, he said unto them, Why are ye now turned back?
6 And they said unto him, There came a man up to meet us, and said unto us, Go, turn again unto the king that sent you, and say unto him, Thus saith the LORD, *Is it* not because *there is* not a God in Israel, *that* thou sendest to enquire of Bā'al-zē'bŭb the god of Ekron? therefore thou shalt not come down from that bed on which thou art gone up, but shalt surely die.
7 And he said unto them, What manner of man *was he* which came up to meet you, and told you these words?
8 And they answered him, He *was* an hairy man, and girt with a girdle of leather about his loins. And he said, It *is* E-lī'jah the Tīsh'bīte.

9 Then the king sent unto him a captain of fifty with his fifty. And he went up to him: and, behold, he sat on the top of an hill. And he spake unto him, Thou man of God, the king hath said, Come down.
10 And E-lī'jah answered and said to the captain of fifty, If I *be* a man of God,

3-4. The angel of the LORD was none other than Jehovah Himself (cf. Gen 22:15-16; Num 22:22-35; Jud 2:1-5; 6:21-23). He is often thought to be the Second Person of the Trinity in a preincarnate form. **Elijah departed** to carry out his mission.

5-7. The messengers' quick return meant the mission was unaccomplished. **What manner of man was he . . . ?** The nature of this message prompted recollections of his father's encounters with Elijah.

8. He was a hairy man (lit., a master, owner of hair). "He wore a garment of haircloth" (RSV) may be an accurate meaning, but there is also the possibility that Elijah was simply hairy or possessed long hair, having taken the vow of the Nazarite (Num 6:5), though Scripture is silent on this point. Note a similar description of John the Baptizer (Mk 1:6).

9-10. Feeling insulted by Elijah, who had challenged his royal command, Ahaziah ordered Elijah to be seized. The captain in charge of this mission spoke derisively, emphasizing his own commission over the prophet's commission, **the king hath said.** Elijah did not act in self-defense, but demonstrated the superiority of his authority as the messenger of God by casting down fire to consume the captain and his fifty men.

697

then let fire come down from heaven, and consume thee and thy fifty. And there came down fire from heaven, and consumed him and his fifty.

11 Again also he sent unto him another captain of fifty with his fifty. And he answered and said unto him, O man of God, thus hath the king said, Come down quickly.

12 And E-lī′jah answered and said unto them, If I be a man of God, let fire come down from heaven, and consume thee and thy fifty. And the fire of God came down from heaven, and consumed him and his fifty.

13 And he sent again a captain of the third fifty with his fifty. And the third captain of fifty went up, and came and fell on his knees before E-lī′jah, and besought him, and said unto him, O man of God, I pray thee, let my life, and the life of these fifty thy servants, be precious in thy sight.

14 Behold, there came fire down from heaven, and burnt up the two captains of the former fifties with their fifties: therefore let my life now be precious in thy sight.

15 And the angel of the LORD said unto E-lī′jah, Go down with him: be not afraid of him. And he arose, and went down with him unto the king.

16 And he said unto him, Thus saith the LORD, Forasmuch as thou hast sent messengers to enquire of Bā′al-zē′bŭb the God of Ēkron, is it not because there is no God in Israel to enquire of his word? therefore thou shalt not come down off that bed on which thou art gone up, but shalt surely die.

17 ¶So he died according to the word of the LORD which E-lī′jah had spoken. And Je-hō′ram reigned in his stead in the second year of Je-hō′ram the son of Je-hŏsh′a-phăt king of Jūdah; because he had no son.

18 Now the rest of the acts of Ā-ha-zī′ah which he did, are they not written in the book of the chronicles of the kings of Israel?

CHAPTER 2

AND it came to pass, when the LORD would take up E-lī′jah into heaven by a whirlwind, that E-lī′jah went with E-lī′sha from Gilgal.

2 And E-lī′jah said unto E-lī′sha, Tarry here, I pray thee; for the LORD hath sent me to Bĕth-el. And E-lī′sha said unto him, As the LORD liveth, and as thy soul liveth, I will not leave thee. So they went down to Bĕth-el.

3 And the sons of the prophets that were at Bĕth-el came forth to E-lī′sha, and said unto him, Knowest thou that the LORD will take away thy master from thy head to day? And he said, Yea, I know it; hold ye your peace.

11-14. Undaunted, Ahaziah sacrificed another captain and his fifty. This captain was even more insolent, ordering Elijah to come **quickly.** The third captain approached Elijah respectfully and in humility. Knowing full well what happened to the other captain, he pleaded for his life.

15-16. This time Elijah is instructed to accompany the captain back to Ahaziah. **And he** (Elijah) **said unto him** (Ahaziah). The message of doom remained unchanged (vss. 3-4, 6).

17-18. What Ahaziah's intentions were for calling Elijah, or what his reaction to Elijah's message was, are not given. **He died according to the word of the LORD,** perhaps immediately, before he could take action against Elijah. Having no son, Ahaziah left the throne to his brother **Jehoram.**

2. Elijah's translation and anointing of Elisha. 2:1-25.

2:1-2. The writer introduces this section by telling in advance (vs. 11) in what manner Elijah will leave—**by a whirlwind.** The narrative indicates that Elijah was aware of his imminent departure, probably by revelation; and he had informed both Elisha and the sons of the prophets, or they had had separate prophetic premonitions. **Elisha** was still accompanying Elijah (cf. I Kgs 19:21). **Gilgal,** its location uncertain, is not to be identified as the Gilgal where Joshua had his base of operations (Josh 4:19); for Elijah left this site and **went down to Beth-el.**

Tarry here. As Elijah was about to visit two schools of prophets for the last time, three times he told Elisha to tarry. Each time Elisha was characterized by his persistence to be with Elijah, thus passing the test of faithfulness and showing himself to be a suitable successor to Elijah.

3. Sons of the prophets were men associated together in a guild or school to be trained as prophets. They are mentioned as such in the time of Elijah and Elisha and may have been under their leadership, although the school may have originated with Samuel (I Sam 19:20).

Beth-el, the site of cultic calf-worship (I Kgs 12:28-29) was a strange location for a theological school. The prophets obviously were not too effective. **Yea, I know it; hold ye your peace.** In

4 And E-lī′jah said unto him, E-lī′sha, tarry here, I pray thee; for the LORD hath sent me to Jericho. And he said, As the LORD liveth, and as thy soul liveth, I will not leave thee. So they came to Jericho.

5 And the sons of the prophets that were at Jericho came to E-lī′sha, and said unto him, Knowest thou that the LORD will take away thy master from thy head to day? And he answered, Yea, I know it: hold ye your peace.

6 And E-lī′jah said unto him, Tarry, I pray thee, here; for the LORD hath sent me to Jordan. And he said, As the LORD liveth, and as thy soul liveth, I will not leave thee. And they two went on.

7 And fifty men of the sons of the prophets went, and stood to view afar off: and they two stood by Jordan.

8 And E-lī′jah took his mantle, and wrapped it together, and smote the waters, and they were divided hither and thither, so that they two went over on dry ground.

9 ¶And it came to pass, when they were gone over, that E-lī′jah said unto E-lī′sha, Ask what I shall do for thee, before I be taken away from thee. And E-lī′sha said, I pray thee, let a double portion of thy spirit be upon me.

10 And he said, Thou hast asked a hard thing: nevertheless, if thou see me when I am taken from thee, it shall be so unto thee; but if not, it shall not be so.

11 And it came to pass, as they still went on, and talked, that, behold, there appeared a chariot of fire, and horses of fire, and parted them both asunder; and E-lī′jah went up by a whirlwind into heaven.

12 And E-lī′sha saw it, and he cried, My father, my father, the chariot of Israel, and the horsemen thereof. And he saw him no more: and he took hold of his own clothes, and rent them in two pieces.

13 He took up also the mantle of E-lī′jah that fell from him, and went back, and stood by the bank of Jordan;

14 And he took the mantle of E-lī′jah that fell from him, and smote the waters, and said, Where is the LORD God of E-lī′jah? and when he also had smitten the waters, they parted hither and thither: and E-lī′sha went over.

15 And when the sons of the prophets which were to view at Jericho saw him, they said, The spirit of E-lī′jah doth rest on E-lī′sha. And they came to meet him, and bowed themselves to the ground before him.

16 And they said unto him, Behold now, there be with thy servants fifty strong men; let them go, we pray thee, and seek thy master: lest peradventure the Spirit of the LORD hath taken him up, and cast him upon some mountain, or into some valley. And he said, Ye shall not send.

17 And when they urged him till he

essence, Elisha was saying, "Yes, I'm aware that Elijah is leaving. Don't distract me with your curiosity."

4-8. At **Jericho** was another school, where the events at Beth-el were repeated identically. Elijah was called to **Jordan.** Fifty student-prophets, sensing that something extraordinary was about to happen to Elijah, followed him. Some five hundred and fifty years earlier the Jordan had miraculously offered a similar dry passage to the Israelites (Josh 3:14-17).

9-10. Elisha's final request from Elijah was **a double portion of thy spirit.** The double portion was by Hebrew law the share of the oldest son (Deut 21:17). Elisha was not attempting to excel Elijah; he wanted to be a worthy successor in the prophetic ministry.

If thou see me. . . . This may simply mean if Elisha were to witness the event or, as Stigers (p. 342) suggests, "If Elisha would have the courage to face Elijah's translation, and the spiritual understanding to know the meaning of the older man's going, he would be the successor."

11. Elijah did not ride into heaven in a chariot of fire. Note that the fiery chariot and horses first isolated Elijah from Elisha, and then the **whirlwind** snatched him up. Scripture never discusses what happened to Elijah en route to heaven.

12-13. My father . . . the chariot . . . the horsemen. King Joash uttered these identical words as Elisha lay dying (13:14). In respect and devotion, Elisha called Elijah his spiritual father. The war chariot and horsemen were sought after by Israel's kings for national security measures, but to Elisha these were a symbolical representation of the strong defense that Elijah had been through his prophetic ministry to Israel. Israel had rejected her true defense, Jehovah, in turning to idolatry. In sorrow over personal loss of his companion, Elisha tore his clothing.

14-15. Where is the LORD God of Elijah? Elisha was not seeking information, but confirmation. Had the divine power exemplified in Elijah's ministry been transferred to him? **The spirit of Elijah doth rest on Elisha.** What a compliment to be recognized immediately as a man of God!

16-18. The fifty prophets who had possibly witnessed the translation from a distance, or were informed of it by Elisha, either doubted or did not understand the permanence of Elijah's departure. Therefore, they searched futilely for three days to see where God might have dropped him.

was ashamed, he said, Send. They sent therefore fifty men; and they sought three days, but found him not.

18 And when they came again to him, (for he tarried at Jericho,) he said unto them, Did I not say unto you, Go not?

19 ¶And the men of the city said unto E-lī´sha, Behold, I pray thee, the situation of this city is pleasant, as my lord seeth: but the water is naught, and the ground barren.

20 And he said, Bring me a new cruse, and put salt therein. And they brought it to him.

21 And he went forth unto the spring of the waters, and cast the salt in there, and said, Thus saith the LORD, I have healed these waters; there shall not be from thence any more death or barren land.

22 So the waters were healed unto this day, according to the saying of E-lī´sha which he spake.

23 ¶And he went up from thence unto Běth-el: and as he was going up by the way, there came forth little children out of the city, and mocked him and said unto him, Go up, thou bald head; go up, thou bald head.

24 And he turned back, and looked on them, and cursed them in the name of the LORD. And there came forth two she bears out of the wood, and tare forty and two children of them.

25 And he went from thence to mount Carmel, and from thence he returned to Sa-mā´rī-a.

CHAPTER 3

NOW Je-hō´ram the son of Ahab began to reign over Israel in Sa-mā´rī-a the eighteenth year of Je-hŏsh´a-phăt king of Jūdah, and reigned twelve years.

2 And he wrought evil in the sight of the LORD; but not like his father, and like his mother: for he put away the image of Bā´al that his father had made.

3 Nevertheless he cleaved unto the sins of Jěr-o-bō´am the son of Ně´băt, which made Israel to sin; he departed not therefrom.

4 ¶And Mē´sha king of Moab was a sheepmaster, and rendered unto the king of Israel an hundred thousand lambs, and an hundred thousand rams, with the wool.

5 But it came to pass, when Ahab was dead, that the king of Moab rebelled against the king of Israel.

6 ¶And king Je-hō´ram went out of Sa-mā´rī-a the same time, and numbered all Israel.

7 And he went and sent to Je-hŏsh´a-

19-22. Two miracles promptly confirm Elisha's prophetic succession. At Jericho the men complained, **the water is naught** (lit., bad). Taking **salt,** a cleansing and preserving agent, in a new **cruse,** he sprinkled it on the contaminated spring; and the **waters were healed,** i.e., purified (cf. Moses at Marah, Ex 15:23-25). Ellison (p. 319) sees this first miracle as also a symbolic action: "The water of Israel's religion had become corrupt and disease bringing. If Elisha were listened to, he could heal it."

23-25. At **Beth-el** he was approached by **little children.** Thanks to this rendering, **little children,** the story has been grossly misunderstood or misrepresented. Honeycutt (p. 233) incorrectly stresses the smallness of these children and the immorality of Elisha's action. He states that "no interpreter would defend this as a pattern of moral action or as a reflection of divine judgment." The Hebrew ne῾arim qetanim can legitimately be translated "young lads" (NASB). Solomon was called a "little child" when he took the throne (see note on I Kgs 3:7). These then were no innocent children, but a band of rowdy teenagers.

These irresponsible young men were taunting Elisha. **Go up** is a mockery of Elijah's translation. They may have refused to believe the report concerning Elijah, or perhaps they were wishing to be rid of Elisha by a similar experience. A **bald head** was thought to be a disgrace in the East, but this taunt may have been contrasting Elisha's baldness with Elijah's abundance of hair (see note 1:8). Regardless, it was an insult to God's appointed prophet; so Elisha cursed them in the name of Jehovah, and they were torn by bears. Note Moses' warning against apostasy in Leviticus 26:21-22. Ellison (p. 319) comments, "It can only have been the result of the teaching of the lads' parents, who in the conception of the time were the chief sufferers from the punishment."

3. Jehoram and the Moabite war. 3:1-27.

3:1-3. Comparing 1:17, it is evident that Jehoshaphat and his son Jehoram (Ahab also had a son Jehoram) were coreigning in Judah at this time. His reign was evil, but not to the degree of his father. Baal was temporarily set aside, but Jeroboam's calf-worship remained. However, with Ahab's descendant on the throne, Baalism could flourish again at any moment.

4-5. Mesha . . . rendered, i.e., paid tribute, sheep and wool to the king of Israel. This would have been Ahab, for Moab rebelled following his death (see note on 1:1).

6-7. To recover this last source of tribute, Jehoram prepared for battle against Moab, recruiting the services of the southern king Jehoshaphat as Ahab had done. Jehoshaphat's response was almost identical (I Kgs 22:4). He had quickly forgotten the

phăt the king of Jūdah, saying, The king of Moab hath rebelled against me: wilt thou go with me against Moab to battle? And he said, I will go up: I *am* as thou *art*, my people as thy people, *and* my horses as thy horses.

8 And he said, Which way shall we go up? And he answered, The way through the wilderness of Ēdom.

9 So the king of Israel went, and the king of Jūdah, and the king of Ēdom: and they fetched a compass of seven days' journey: and there was no water for the host, and for the cattle that followed them.

10 And the king of Israel said, Alas! that the LORD hath called these three kings together, to deliver them into the hand of Moab!

11 But Je-hŏsh´a-phăt said, *Is there* not here a prophet of the LORD, that we may enquire of the LORD by him? And one of the king of Israel's servants answered and said, Here *is* E-lī´sha the son of Shā´phat, which poured water on the hands of E-lī´jah.

12 And Je-hŏsh´a-phăt said, The word of the LORD is with him. So the king of Israel and Je-hŏsh´a-phăt and the king of Ēdom went down to him.

13 And E-lī´sha said unto the king of Israel, What have I to do with thee? get thee to the prophets of thy father, and to the prophets of thy mother. And the king of Israel said unto him, Nay: for the LORD hath called these three kings together, to deliver them into the hand of Moab.

14 And E-lī´sha said, *As* the LORD of hosts liveth, before whom I stand, surely, were it not that I regard the presence of Je-hŏsh´a-phăt the king of Jūdah, I would not look toward thee, nor see thee.

15 But now bring me a minstrel. And it came to pass, when the minstrel played, that the hand of the LORD came upon him.

16 And he said, Thus saith the LORD, Make this valley full of ditches.

17 For thus saith the LORD, Ye shall not see wind, neither shall ye see rain; yet that valley shall be filled with water, that ye may drink, both ye, and your cattle, and your beasts.

18 And this is *but* a light thing in the sight of the LORD: he will deliver the Moabites also into your hand.

19 And ye shall smite every fenced city, and every choice city, and shall fell every good tree, and stop all wells of water, and mar every good piece of land with stones.

20 And it came to pass in the morning, when the meat offering was offered, that, behold, there came water by the way of Ēdom, and the country was filled with water.

21 ¶And when all the Moabites heard that the kings were come up to fight against them, they gathered all that were able to put on armour, and upward, and stood in the border.

22 And they rose up early in the morning, and the sun shone upon the water,

rebuke he had received from Jehu for assisting Ahab under similar circumstances (II Chr 19:1-4).

8. That Jehoram wanted to attack Moab from the south **through the wilderness of Edom** indicates that Mesha had fortified strongholds that would have prevented a direct attack from the north.

9-10. The king of Edom (cf. I Kgs 22:47) would have been a vassal to Jehoshaphat. By alliance he would have been obligated to assist Jehoshaphat in this campaign, although the Edomites had their own revengeful reasons for fighting Moab (cf. II Chr 20:23 where Mount Seir refers to Edom).

They fetched a compass, i.e., their travel was in a circular fashion. When they could find no water, wicked Jehoram was quick to blame Jehovah.

11-12. When Jehoshaphat requested a prophet, Elisha, who apparently was present on this expedition apart from any of the three kings' knowledge, was brought forward. That this campaign occurred shortly after Elijah's translation is possible, since Elisha is still identified as Elijah's servant—he **poured water on the hands of Elijah.**

13-14. Elisha addressed Jehoram. **What have I to do with thee?** (i.e., "What do you, an idol worshiper, and I, a prophet of Jehovah, have in common?"). It was only for the sake of Jehoshaphat, who was out of place with Jehoram, that Elisha sought divine instruction.

15. The **minstrel** was not called for magical purposes. Music soothes the troubled mind (cf. I Sam 16:23) and Elisha needed to be calmed mentally in order that he might concentrate spiritually on God.

16-18. The instruction was to make ditches which God would fill apart from a local rainstorm. To God this miracle was so insignificant (**a light thing**) that He would use it also to **deliver the Moabites** over to them.

19-20. God commanded a thorough destruction of cities, trees, wells, and fields. The trenches were filled with water that came **by the way of Edom.** This suggests that God sent rain to Edom, unknown to either Moab or the Israelites; and the water flowed to the prepared and waiting ditches.

21-23. The Moabites prepared to withstand an invasion. Seeing the valley, which should have been dry, full of water, with the rising sun's rays giving it a reddish tint, they suspected a fallout among their enemies and imagined that the water was blood.

and the Moabites saw the water on the other side *as* red as blood:

23 And they said, This *is* blood: the kings are surely slain, and they have smitten one another: now therefore, Moab, to the spoil.

24 And when they came to the camp of Israel, the Israelites rose up and smote the Moabites, so that they fled before them: but they went forward smiting the Moabites, even in *their* country.

25 And they beat down the cities, and on every good piece of land cast every man his stone, and filled it; and they stopped all the wells of water, and felled all the good trees: only in Kĭr-hăr′a-sĕth left they the stones thereof; howbeit the slingers went about *it*, and smote it.

26 ¶And when the king of Moab saw that the battle was too sore for him, he took with him seven hundred men that drew swords, to break through *even* unto the king of Edom: but they could not.

27 Then he took his eldest son that should have reigned in his stead, and offered him *for* a burnt offering upon the wall. And there was great indignation against Israel: and they departed from him, and returned to *their own* land.

CHAPTER 4

NOW there cried a certain woman of the wives of the sons of the prophets unto E-lī′sha, saying, Thy servant my husband is dead; and thou knowest that thy servant did fear the LORD: and the creditor is come to take unto him my two sons to be bondmen.

2 And E-lī′sha said unto her, What shall I do for thee? tell me, what hast thou in the house? And she said, Thine handmaid hath not any thing in the house, save a pot of oil.

3 Then he said, Go, borrow thee vessels abroad of all thy neighbours, *even* empty vessels; borrow not a few.

4 And when thou art come in, thou shalt shut the door upon thee and upon thy sons, and shalt pour out into all those vessels, and thou shalt set aside that which is full.

5 So she went from him, and shut the door upon her and upon her sons, who brought *the vessels* to her; and she poured out.

6 And it came to pass, when the vessels were full, that she said unto her son, Bring me yet a vessel. And he said unto her, *There is* not a vessel more. And the oil stayed.

7 Then she came and told the man of God. And he said, Go, sell the oil, and pay thy debt, and live thou and thy children of the rest.

8 ¶And it fell on a day, that E-lī′sha

24-25. They rushed carelessly into the enemy camp to collect spoil. The Israelites, however, rose up and smote Moab as God had directed (vs. 19). Only one city, Kirharaseth, was left.

26. Mesha made an attempt to defeat the Israelites by breaking **through even unto the king of Edom.** Various interpretations are offered for this action: (1) Mesha saw Edom as the weak link in this invading confederacy; (2) in revenge he wanted to kill his neighboring king for joining the confederacy; or (3) Aram (Syria) is often confused with Edom in the Hebrew text. Mesha hoped to break through the Israelite lines with his seven hundred swordsmen to seek help from Syria.

27. Mesha's final effort was to sacrifice his own son, the crown prince, to his god Chemosh in order to gain his favor. The Israelites, superstitious and idolatrous as they were, were so frightened at the prospect of what Moab's god, Chemosh, might do in response to this horrible sacrifice, they returned to their own land.

The events of this war should have convinced Israel why she should turn from her idolatry, but the lessons went unheeded.

4. The miracles of Elisha. 4:1-6:7.

a. Multiplying the widow's oil. 4:1-7.

4:1. The sons of the prophets were not celibates. They had wives, children, and social obligations. With her husband dead, the lady had no means to pay her debts. Mosaic law allowed one to voluntarily and temporarily sell himself to pay his debts (cf. Ex 21:7; Lev 25:39; Neh 5:5), but here the creditor was taking the sons.

2-3. She was so poor her last possession was a **pot of oil. Go, borrow thee vessels.** It may have been embarrassing to borrow, but the increase of her oil was to be proportionate to her faith and obedience.

4-7. Shut the door. This miracle was to be private. Not even the prophet was present, so the miracle could not be attributed to sleight of hand, but only to the power of God. Selling the increase of oil, she was able to pay her debt, save her sons, and live off what was left.

b. Raising the Shunammite's son to life. 4:8-37.

8. Shunem (modern Solem) lay near Jezreel, about fifteen

hold, the mountain *was* full of horses and chariots of fire round about E-lī′-sha.

18 And when they came down to him, E-lī′sha prayed unto the LORD, and said, Smite this people, I pray thee, with blindness. And he smote them with blindness according to the word of E-lī′sha.

19 And E-lī′sha said unto them, This *is* not the way, neither *is* this the city: follow me, and I will bring you to the man whom ye seek. But he led them to Sa-mā′rī-a.

20 And it came to pass, when they were come into Sā-mā′rī-a, that E-lī′sha said, LORD, open the eyes of these *men,* that they may see. And the LORD opened their eyes, and they saw; and, behold, *they were* in the midst of Sā-mā′rī-a.

21 And the king of Israel said unto E-lī′sha, when he saw them, My father, shall I smite *them?* shall I smite *them?*

22 And he answered, Thou shalt not smite *them:* wouldest thou smite those whom thou hast taken captive with thy sword and with thy bow? set bread and water before them, that they may eat and drink, and go to their master.

23 And he prepared great provision for them: and when they had eaten and drunk, he sent them away, and they went to their master. So the bands of Syria came no more into the land of Israel.

24 ¶And it came to pass after this, that Bĕn-hă′dăd king of Syria gathered all his host, and went up, and besieged Sā-mā′rī-a.

25 And there was a great famine in Sā-mā′rī-a: and, behold, they besieged it, until an ass's head was *sold* for fourscore *pieces* of silver, and the fourth part of a cab of dove's dung for five *pieces* of silver.

26 ¶And as the king of Israel was passing by upon the wall, there cried a woman unto him, saying, Help, my lord, O king.

27 And he said, If the LORD do not help thee, whence shall I help thee? out of the barnfloor, or out of the winepress?

28 And the king said unto her, What aileth thee? And she answered, This woman said unto me, Give thy son, that we may eat him to day, and we will eat my son to morrow.

29 So we boiled my son, and did eat him: and I said unto her on the next day, Give thy son, that we may eat him: and she hath hid her son.

30 And it came to pass, when the king heard the words of the woman, that he rent his clothes; and he passed by upon the wall, and the people looked, and, behold, *he had* sackcloth within upon his flesh.

31 Then he said, God do so and more also to me, if the head of E-lī′sha the son of Shā′phat shall stand on him this day.

32 But E-lī′sha sat in his house, and the elders sat with him; and *the king* sent a man from before him: but ere the

18-20. Meanwhile, according to Elisha's prayer, the Syrians were smitten with temporary **blindness** (cf. Gen 19:11). Unbeknown to the Syrians because of their blindness, they were guided by the man they were sent to capture into the capital of the enemy. There their eyes were opened. Undoubtedly they were already surrounded by Israel's baffled king and army.

21-23. Since these were the Lord's prisoners, not Israel's, and had not been taken in battle, the Syrians were given the most unusual treatment; they were fed and released to return to Syria. They were evidently impressed with God's mercy and His unusual protection of Israel, for they ceased raiding Israel for a time.

b. The Syrian siege of Samaria. 6:24-7:20.

24. Ben-hadad had intentions of making this his final invasion. He thought he could conquer Israel once and for all by inflicting a siege on Samaria.

25. The siege resulted in unbelievable famine and desperate circumstances. An **ass's head,** which normally would not have been eaten, was being sold for the exorbitant price of eighty shekels of silver. A **cab** (about one-fourth pint) **of dove's dung** sold for five shekels of silver. This excrement was probably used for fuel, not for food.

26-29. Even mothers were reduced to savage cannibals, and one mother appealed to the king to enforce a contract whereby she could eat a friend's son (cf. Moses' warning in Lev 26:29 and Deut 28:53).

30-31. The king was so shocked and horrified with conditions in Samaria that he vented his own anxieties and frustrations on Elisha, swearing to behead him.

32. Son of a murderer may be interpreted one of two ways: (1) Taken as a Hebrew idiom, it means he was a murderer; or (2) taken literally, it means his father (Ahab) was a murderer.

messenger came to him, he said to the elders, See ye how this son of a murderer hath sent to take away mine head? look, when the messenger cometh, shut the door, and hold him fast at the door: is not the sound of his master's feet behind him?

33 And while he yet talked with them, behold, the messenger came down unto him: and he said, Behold, this evil is of the LORD; what should I wait for the LORD any longer?

CHAPTER 7

THEN E-lī'sha said, Hear ye the word of the LORD; Thus saith the LORD, To morrow about this time shall a measure of fine flour be sold for a shekel, and two measures of barley for a shekel, in the gate of Sā-mā'rī-a.

2 Then a lord on whose hand the king leaned answered the man of God, and said, Behold, if the LORD would make windows in heaven, might this thing be? And he said, Behold, thou shalt see it with thine eyes, but shalt not eat thereof.

3 ¶And there were four leprous men at the entering in of the gate: and they said one to another, Why sit we here until we die?

4 If we say, We will enter into the city, then the famine is in the city, and we shall die there: and if we sit still here, we die also. Now therefore come, and let us fall unto the host of the Syrians: if they save us alive, we shall live; and if they kill us, we shall but die.

5 And they rose up in the twilight, to go unto the camp of the Syrians: and when they were come to the uttermost part of the camp of Syria, behold, there was no man there.

6 For the Lord had made the host of the Syrians to hear a noise of chariots, and a noise of horses, even the noise of a great host: and they said one to another, Lo, the king of Israel hath hired against us the kings of the Hittites, and the kings of the Egyptians, to come upon us.

7 Wherefore they arose and fled in the twilight, and left their tents, and their horses, and their asses, even the camp as it was, and fled for their life.

8 And when these lepers came to the uttermost part of the camp, they went into one tent, and did eat and drink, and carried thence silver, and gold, and raiment, and went and hid it; and came again, and entered into another tent, and carried thence also, and went and hid it.

9 Then they said one to another, We do not well: this day is a day of good tidings, and we hold our peace: if we tarry till the morning light, some mischief will come upon us: now therefore come, that we may go and tell the king's household.

10 So they came and called unto the porter of the city: and they told them, saying, We came to the camp of the Syrians, and, behold, there was no man there, neither voice of man, but horses tied, and asses tied, and the tents as they were.

11 And he called the porters; and

Shut the door. The doors were barred to prevent the executioner from entering because Elisha knew the king had changed his mind and was coming to reverse his order of execution.

33. And he said. This is the king speaking. Upon his arrival the door was opened to him and Elisha addressed him (cf. 7:2). **Behold this evil is of the LORD.** The king recognized that Elisha was not to blame. The Lord was judging Samaria (cf. Amos 3:6).

7:1. Tomorrow the siege would be lifted and the famine ended. **A measure** (Heb se'ah) was approximately equivalent to a bushel. Grain would be sold **in the gate,** the marketplace of the city.

2. A lord (lit., the third man), i.e., a royal official, showed his lack of faith when he doubted Elisha's word. Therefore his fate would be to witness the miracle, but not participate in it.

3-5. Only those behind the walls of Samaria were starving. The Syrians, encamped around the city, were living off the land and had plenty to eat.

Four lepers, outcasts of the city who by virtue of their disease were destined to die, decided to risk entering the Syrian camp to beg for food. The evil consequences could be no worse than the death to which they were already doomed.

6-7. In the silence of Samaria's night, God had miraculously created a great noise of horses and chariots in the ears of the Syrians causing them to believe that the **Hittites** from the north and the **Egyptians** from the south had converged upon Samaria to aid the Israelite king. In a panic, their only recourse was to flee, leaving everything behind.

8-11. For a short while the hungry lepers fared sumptuously until their consciences reminded them of the starvation within the city. Therefore, in fear of divine punishment for withholding such **good tidings,** they promptly reported their discovery to the city.

they told it to the king's house within.

12 ¶And the king arose in the night, and said unto his servants, I will now shew you what the Syrians have done to us. They know that we be hungry; therefore are they gone out of the camp to hide themselves in the field, saying, When they come out of the city, we shall catch them alive, and get into the city.

13 And one of his servants answered and said, Let some take, I pray thee, five of the horses that remain, which are left in the city, (behold, they are as all the multitude of Israel that are left in it: behold, I say, they are even as all the multitude of the Israelites that are consumed:) and let us send and see.

14 They took therefore two chariot horses; and the king sent after the host of the Syrians, saying, Go and see.

15 And they went after them unto Jordan: and, lo, all the way was full of garments and vessels, which the Syrians had cast away in their haste. And the messengers returned, and told the king.

16 And the people went out, and spoiled the tents of the Syrians. So a measure of fine flour was sold for a shekel, and two measures of barley for a shekel, according to the word of the LORD.

17 ¶And the king appointed the lord on whose hand he leaned to have the charge of the gate: and the people trode upon him in the gate, and he died, as the man of God had said, who spake when the king came down to him.

18 And it came to pass as the man of God had spoken to the king, saying, Two measures of barley for a shekel, and a measure of fine flour for a shekel, shall be to morrow about this time in the gate of Să-mā′rī-a:

19 And that lord answered the man of God, and said, Now, behold, if the LORD should make windows in heaven, might such a thing be? And he said, Behold, thou shalt see it with thine eyes, but shalt not eat thereof.

20 And so it fell out unto him: for the people trode upon him in the gate, and he died.

CHAPTER 8

THEN spake E-lī′sha unto the woman, whose son he had restored to life, saying, Arise, and go thou and thine household, and sojourn wheresoever thou canst sojourn: for the LORD hath called for a famine; and it shall also come upon the land seven years.

2 And the woman arose, and did after the saying of the man of God: and she went with her household, and sojourned in the land of the Philistines seven years.

3 And it came to pass at the seven years' end, that the woman returned out of the land of the Philistines: and she went forth to cry unto the king for her house and for her land.

4 And the king talked with Ge-hā′zī the servant of the man of God, saying, Tell me, I pray thee, all the great things that E-lī′sha hath done.

12-14. The king suspected a ruse to draw Israel out of the city for an ambush. Therefore, several brave men were sent on a reconnaissance mission to search out the whereabouts of the Syrians.

15-16. They were convinced that the Syrians were truly departed when they found **the way,** i.e., their route back to Syria, strewn with **garments and vessels** that they had discarded or lost in their hasty withdrawal. The city then emptied to feed on the spoil of the Syrian camp.

17-20. The king's official (vs. 2) was appointed to control the crowd as it rushed from the city. He witnessed the miracle and the excitement it created, but he never participated in eating; for he was trampled by the crowd he could not control, and he died.

c. The Shunammite woman's property restored. 8:1-6.

8:1-2. The narrative returns to the Shunammite woman (4:8-37). In the face of an impending seven-year famine, Elisha had warned her to move temporarily for the duration of the famine. She had moved to the **land of the Philistines** (i.e., South Palestinian coast), the nearest land unaffected by the famine.

3-6. When she returned to her land, it was occupied by strangers, possibly relatives; or perhaps it had been turned over to the crown. Evidently her husband was dead (cf. 4:14); so she pled her own case before the king, who providentially was engaged at the time in listening to the accomplishments of Elisha, more precisely, the raising to life of this woman's son. Her association with the prophet influenced the king to return her property (see note on 4:12-13).

5 And it came to pass, as he was telling the king how he had restored a dead body to life, that, behold, the woman, whose son he had restored to life, cried to the king for her house and for her land. And Ge-hā'zī said, My lord, O king, this *is* the woman, and this *is* her son, whom E-lī'sha restored to life.

6 And when the king asked the woman, she told him. So the king appointed unto her a certain officer, saying, Restore all that *was* hers, and all the fruits of the field since the day that she left the land, even until now.

7 ¶And E-lī'sha came to Damascus; and Běn-hā'dăd the king of Syria was sick; and it was told him, saying, The man of God is come hither.

8 And the king said unto Hăz'a-el, Take a present in thine hand, and go, meet the man of God, and enquire of the LORD by him, saying, Shall I recover of this disease?

9 So Hăz'a-el went to meet him, and took a present with him, even of every good thing of Damascus, forty camels' burden, and came and stood before him, and said, Thy son Běn-hā'dăd king of Syria hath sent me to thee, saying, Shall I recover of this disease?

10 And E-lī'sha said unto him, Go, say unto him, Thou mayest certainly recover: howbeit the LORD hath shewed me that he shall surely die.

11 And he settled his countenance stedfastly, until he was ashamed: and the man of God wept.

12 And Hăz'a-el said, Why weepeth my lord? And he answered, Because I know the evil that thou wilt do unto the children of Israel: their strong holds wilt thou set on fire, and their young men wilt thou slay with the sword, and wilt dash their children, and rip up their women with child.

13 And Hăz'a-el said, But what, *is* thy servant a dog, that he should do this great thing? And E-lī'sha answered, The LORD hath shewed me that thou *shalt be* king over Syria.

14 So he departed from E-lī'sha, and came to his master; who said to him, What said E-lī'sha to thee? And he answered, He told me *that* thou shouldest surely recover.

15 And it came to pass on the morrow, that he took a thick cloth, and dipped *it* in water, and spread *it* on his face, so that he died: and Hăz'a-el reigned in his stead.

16 ¶And in the fifth year of Joram the son of Ahab king of Israel, Je-hŏsh'a-phăt *being* then king of Jūdah, Je-hŏ'-ram the son of Je-hŏsh'a-phăt king of Jūdah began to reign.

17 Thirty and two years old was he when he began to reign; and he reigned eight years in Jerusalem.

18 And he walked in the way of the kings of Israel, as did the house of Ahab: for the daughter of Ahab was his wife: and he did evil in the sight of the LORD.

19 Yet the LORD would not destroy Jūdah for David his servant's sake, as

d. Hazael's conspiracy in Syria. 8:7-15.

7-9. The purpose of Elisha's visit to Damascus is not told, but his reputation had preceded him (cf. Naaman's healing, 5:1-19). Ben-hadad was sick and was concerned that he might not recover, and he sent a large gift to Elisha to find out.

10. Thou mayest certainly recover: howbeit . . . he shall surely die can be interpreted two ways: (1) Ben-hadad's illness is not fatal, but he will die (by the hand of Hazael); or (2) tell Ben-hadad he will live (as you already intend to do), but the Lord says he will die.

11-13. Elisha looked at Hazael with such a fixed stare that Hazael was embarrassed; but Elisha began to weep because in a vision he saw the atrocities Hazael would commit (10:32, cf. Amos 1:3), although he denied he was capable of such cruelty.

Thou shalt be king. Certainly Hazael knew of this, for Elijah had had orders to anoint him (see note on I Kgs 19:15-17).

14-15. Hazael returned and lied to Ben-hadad concerning his health; then he smothered him with a wet cloth. **Hazael reigned in his stead.** That he was a usurper and not of royal blood is confirmed by an inscription of Shalmaneser III which reads, "Hazael, son of nobody, seized the throne" (Free, p. 188).

e. The reigns of Jehoram and Ahaziah of Judah. 8:16-27.

16-19. Upon the death of Jehoshaphat, Jehoram became sole king (see note on 3:1). He reigned eight years as sole ruler (ca. 848-841 B.C.). The far-reaching impact of the alliance between Ahab and Jehoshaphat (see note on I Kgs 22:4) is now seen; for Jehoram did not walk in the godly ways of his father, but was influenced by his wife to walk in the ways of his father-in-law, Ahab.

he promised him to give him alway a light, *and* to his children.

20 ¶In his days Ēdom revolted from under the hand of Jūdah, and made a king over themselves.

21 So Joram went over to Zā'ir, and all the chariots with him: and he rose by night, and smote the Edomites which compassed him about, and the captains of the chariots: and the people fled into their tents.

22 Yet Ēdom revolted from under the hand of Jūdah unto this day. Then Lĭb'-nah revolted at the same time.

23 And the rest of the acts of Joram, and all that he did, *are* they not written in the book of the chronicles of the kings of Jūdah?

24 And Joram slept with his fathers, and was buried with his fathers in the city of David: and Ā-ha-zī'ah his son reigned in his stead.

25 ¶In the twelfth year of Joram the son of Ahab king of Israel did Ā-ha-zī'ah the son of Je-hō'ram king of Jūdah begin to reign.

26 Two and twenty years old *was* Ā-ha-zī'ah when he began to reign; and he reigned one year in Jerusalem. And his mother's name *was* Ăth-a-lī'ah, the daughter of Omri king of Israel.

27 And he walked in the way of the house of Ahab, and did evil in the sight of the LORD, as *did* the house of Ahab: for he *was* the son in law of the house of Ahab.

28 ¶And he went with Joram the son of Ahab to the war against Hăz'a-el king of Syria in Rǎ'moth–gĭl'e-ad; and the Syrians wounded Joram.

29 And king Joram went back to be healed in Jĕz're-el of the wounds which the Syrians had given him at Rǎ'mah, when he fought against Hăz'a-el king of Syria. And Ā-ha-zī'ah the son of Je-hō'ram king of Jūdah went down to see Joram the son of Ahab in Jĕz're-el, because he was sick.

CHAPTER 9

AND E-lī'sha the prophet called one of the children of the prophets, and said unto him, Gird up thy loins, and take this box of oil in thine hand, and go to Rǎ'moth–gĭl'e-ad:

2 And when thou comest thither, look out there Jehu the son of Je'-hōsh'a-phăt the son of Nĭm'shī, and go in, and make him arise up from among his brethren, and carry him to an inner chamber;

3 Then take the box of oil, and pour *it* on his head, and say, Thus saith the LORD, I have anointed thee king over Israel. Then open the door, and flee, and tarry not.

4 So the young man, *even* the young man the prophet, went to Rǎ'moth–gĭl'e-ad.

5 And when he came, behold, the captains of the host *were* sitting; and he said, I have an errand to thee, O captain. And Jehu said, Unto which of all us? And he said, To thee, O captain.

6 And he arose, and went into the house; and he poured the oil on his head, and said unto him, Thus saith the LORD God of Israel, I have anointed

20-24. Edom . . . made a king (see note on 3:9-10). Jehoram's unsuccessful attempt to squelch the revolt almost cost him his army. Edom's revolt evidently encouraged **Libnah,** a city in the lowlands near Philistia, to successfully follow suit. A more complete account of Jehoram is found in II Chronicles 21:1-20.

25-27. Jehoram's son, Ahaziah, reigned only one year. With Athaliah, the daughter (i.e., granddaughter) of Omri, for his mother, he was certain to follow in the steps of Ahab, as his father did.

f. Hazael and Joram at Ramoth-gilead. 8:28-29.

28-29. In a concerted effort he joined **Joram** (alternate spelling for Jehoram) of Israel (his uncle) to regain Israel's city, **Ramoth-gilead** (cf. similar attempt in I Kgs 22:4ff.). Joram was wounded and returned to Jezreel (see note on I Kgs 21:1) to recuperate.

B. The Revolt of Jehu and the Purge of Baalism. 9:1-10:36.

1. Jehu anointed King of Israel. 9:1-13.

9:1-4. While Joram was convalescing and Ahaziah was visiting him, Elisha sent one of the younger prophets to anoint **Jehu the son of Jehoshaphat** (not to be confused with Jehoshaphat of Judah).

5-6. To thee, O captain. Jehu must have been chief of the captains. Going into the **house** (Israel must have regained Ramoth-gilead, cf. vs. 13) for privacy, the prophet anointed Jehu king of Israel. If Elijah did indeed carry out his commission (I Kgs 19:16), then this was Jehu's second anointing; and he had become the head of Israel's new dynasty.

thee king over the people of the LORD, *even* over Israel.

7 And thou shalt smite the house of Ahab thy master, that I may avenge the blood of my servants the prophets, and the blood of all the servants of the LORD, at the hand of Jĕz'e-bel.

8 For the whole house of Ahab shall perish: and I will cut off from Ahab him that pisseth against the wall, and him that is shut up and left in Israel:

9 And I will make the house of Ahab like the house of Jĕr-o-bō'am the son of Nĕ'băt, and like the house of Bā'a-sha the son of A-hī'jah:

10 And the dogs shall eat Jĕz'e-bel in the portion of Jĕz're-el, and *there shall be* none to bury *her*. And he opened the door, and fled.

11 ¶Then Jehu came forth to the servants of his lord: and *one* said unto him, *Is* all well? wherefore came this mad *fellow* to thee? And he said unto them, Ye know the man, and his communication.

12 And they said, *It is* false; tell us now. And he said, Thus and thus spake he to me, saying, Thus saith the LORD, I have anointed thee king over Israel.

13 Then they hasted, and took every man his garment, and put *it* under him on the top of the stairs, and blew with trumpets, saying, Jehu is king.

14 So Jehu the son of Je-hŏsh'a-phăt the son of Nĭm'shī conspired against Joram. (Now Joram had kept Rā'-moth-gĭl'e-ad, he and all Israel, because of Hăz'a-el king of Syria.)

15 But king Joram was returned to be healed in Jĕz're-el of the wounds which the Syrians had given him, when he fought with Hăz'a-el king of Syria.) And Jehu said, If it be your minds, *then* let none go forth *nor* escape out of the city to go to tell *it* in Jĕz're-el.

16 So Jehu rode in a chariot, and went to Jĕz're-el; for Joram lay there. And Ā-ha-zī'ah king of Jūdah was come down to see Joram.

17 And there stood a watchman on the tower in Jĕz're-el, and he spied the company of Jehu as he came, and said, I see a company. And Joram said, Take an horseman, and send to meet them, and let him say, *Is it* peace?

18 So there went one on horseback to meet him, and said, Thus saith the king, *Is it* peace? And Jehu said, What hast thou to do with peace? turn thee behind me. And the watchman told, saying, The messenger came to them, but he cometh not again.

19 Then he sent out a second on horseback, which came to them, and said, Thus saith the king, *Is it* peace? And Jehu answered, What hast thou to do with peace? turn thee behind me.

20 And the watchman told, saying, He came even unto them, and cometh not again: and the driving *is* like the driving of Jehu the son of Nĭm'shī; for he driveth furiously.

21 And Joram said, Make ready. And his chariot was made ready. And Joram king of Israel and Ā-ha-zī'ah king of Jūdah went out, each in his chariot, and they went out against Jehu, and

7-10. Jehu's inaugural commission was to carry out a fulfillment of God's predicted judgment on the house of Ahab (I Kgs 21:21-24).

11-13. This mad fellow is an anti-prophetical description. Jehu tried to conceal the prophet's purpose. The tone of his voice and the oil dripping from his head showed he was suppressing the truth. Therefore, he told the truth and was immediately crowned as the new king. **Jehu is king** (cf. the impromptu coronations of Absalom, II Sam 15:10, and Solomon, I Kgs 1:39). "The captains were deeply moved by the prophetic message, or Jehu's popularity was greater than their loyalty to the king" (Slotki, p. 217).

2. Murder of Joram, Ahaziah, and Jezebel. 9:14-37.

14-15. Joram had kept, i.e., guarded, Ramoth-gilead, indicating he had taken the city when he was wounded and had left Jehu and the captains in command. In the absence of both Joram and Ahaziah, Jehu quickly conspired with other captains. **Let none go forth.** If the captains were truly supporting him, it was vitally important that word of the revolt did not precede Jehu back to Jezreel.

16-20. Jehu and **A company** with him rode swiftly to Jezreel, where Joram was anxiously awaiting word concerning the affairs at Ramoth-gilead. Jehu must have been spotted a great distance away to allow two different horsemen to leave the city to meet him before he was properly identified by his notorious driving.

21. Noting that Jehu would not address the two horsemen, Joram supposed Jehu's message was of such importance that he went out with Ahaziah to meet Jehu (providentially at Naboth's property).

met him in the portion of Nā'bŏth the Jĕz're-el-īte.

22 And it came to pass, when Joram saw Jehu, that he said, Is it peace, Jehu? And he answered, What peace, so long as the whoredoms of thy mother Jĕz'e-bel and her witchcrafts are so many?

23 And Joram turned his hands, and fled, and said to Ā-ha-zī'ah, There is treachery, O Ā-ha-zī'ah.

24 And Jehu drew a bow with his full strength, and smote Je-hô'ram between his arms, and the arrow went out at his heart, and he sunk down in his chariot.

25 Then said Jehu to Bĭd'kär his captain, Take up, and cast him in the portion of the field of Nā'bŏth the Jĕz're-el-īte: for remember how that, when I and thou rode together after Ahab his father, the LORD laid this burden upon him;

26 Surely I have seen yesterday the blood of Nā'bŏth, and the blood of his sons, saith the LORD; and I will requite thee in this plat, saith the LORD. Now therefore take and cast him into the plat of ground, according to the word of the LORD.

27 ¶But when Ā-ha-zī'ah the king of Jūdah saw this, he fled by the way of the garden house. And Jehu followed after him, and said, Smite him also in the chariot. And they did so at the going up to Gur, which is by Ĭb'le-am. And he fled to Me-gĭd'dō, and died there.

28 And his servants carried him in a chariot to Jerusalem, and buried him in his sepulchre with his fathers in the city of David.

29 And in the eleventh year of Joram the son of Ahab began Ā-ha-zī'ah to reign over Jūdah.

30 ¶And when Jehu was come to Jĕz're-el, Jĕz'e-bel heard of it; and she painted her face, and tired her head, and looked out at a window.

31 And as Jehu entered in at the gate, she said, Had Zimri peace, who slew his master?

32 And he lifted up his face to the window, and said, Who is on my side? who? And there looked out to him two or three eunuchs.

33 And he said, Throw her down. So they threw her down: and some of her blood was sprinkled on the wall, and on the horses: and he trode her under foot.

34 And when he was come in, he did eat and drink, and said, Go, see now this cursed woman, and bury her: for she is a king's daughter.

35 And they went to bury her: but they found no more of her than the skull, and the feet, and the palms of her hands.

36 Wherefore they came again, and told him. And he said, This is the word of the LORD, which he spake by his servant E-lī'jah the Tĭsh'bīte, saying, In the portion of Jĕz're-el shall dogs eat the flesh of Jĕz'e-bel:

22. Is it peace? Jehu played upon the word **peace** when he asked, Is all well (at Ramoth-gilead, or in general)? How could there be peace for the people of God as long as the **whoredoms** (harlotries, i.e., the ritual prostitution) and **witchcrafts** (sorceries, i.e., seductive arts) were allowed to remain in the land?

23-26. There is treachery. Joram now recognized the revolt. Before he could escape, Jehu remembered the Lord's burden against Ahab (I Kgs 21:19). A **burden** is a divine judgment that the offender must bear.

27-29. Ahaziah fled for his life, but was mortally wounded near **Ibleam**, about five miles south of Jezreel; and he died at **Megiddo.** There are three possible reasons why Jehu also killed Ahaziah: (1) He was an ally of Joram; (2) he was a grandson of Ahab, and as his descendant God's judgment was upon him also; and (3) as a nephew of Joram, if all of Ahab's children were killed, Ahaziah would be the nearest kinsman and blood avenger.

30. Returning to Jezreel, Jehu initiated one of the most thorough cleanup campaigns in history. **Jezebel heard** of Joram's death and Jehu's return to Jezreel. She **painted her face** (lit., eyes) and fixed her hair, showing composure as she prepared for her death, which she knew was imminent.

31. Had Zimri peace, who slew his master? would be better rendered, "Is it well, Zimri, your master's murderer?" (NASB). She reminded Jehu of Zimri who had a short seven-day reign after he had murdered Baasha (I Kgs 16:9-10).

32-37. Jezebel was thrown from a window and Jehu trampled her with his horses. Jehu's cold, calloused indifference to the death of Jezebel resulted in the fulfillment of another aspect of Elijah's prophecy (I Kgs 21:23-24); when the dogs had finished eating and dismembering Jezebel, there was not enough of her corpse remaining to make a positive identification, **This is Jezebel.**

37 And the carcase of Jĕz′e-bel shall
be as dung upon the face of the field in
the portion of Jĕz′re-el; so that they
shall not say, This is Jĕz′e-bel.

CHAPTER 10

AND Ahab had seventy sons in Sa-mâ′-
rĭ-a. And Jehu wrote letters, and sent to
Sa-mâ′rĭ-a, unto the rulers of Jĕz′re-el,
to the elders, and to them that brought
up Ahab's children, saying,

2 Now as soon as this letter cometh to
you, seeing your master's sons are with
you, and there are with you chariots
and horses, a fenced city also, and armour;
3 Look even out the best and meetest
of your master's sons, and set him on
his father's throne, and fight for your
master's house.
4 But they were exceedingly afraid,
and said, Behold, two kings stood not
before him: how then shall we stand?
5 And he that was over the house,
and he that was over the city, the elders
also, and the bringers up of the children, sent to Jehu, saying, We are thy
servants, and will do all that thou shalt
bid us; we will not make any king: do
thou that which is good in thine eyes.
6 Then he wrote a letter the second
time to them, saying, If ye be mine, and
if ye will hearken unto my voice, take
ye the heads of the men your master's
sons, and come to me to Jĕz′re-el by to
morrow this time. Now the king's sons,
being seventy persons, were with the
great men of the city, which brought
them up.
7 And it came to pass, when the letter
came to them, that they took the king's
sons, and slew seventy persons, and
put their heads in baskets, and sent him
them to Jĕz′re-el.
8 And there came a messenger, and
told him, saying, They have brought
the heads of the king's sons. And he
said, Lay ye them in two heaps at the
entering in of the gate until the morning.
9 And it came to pass in the morning,
that he went out, and stood, and said to
all the people, Ye be righteous: behold,
I conspired against my master, and
slew him: but who slew all these?
10 Know now that there shall fall
unto the earth nothing of the word of
the LORD, which the LORD spake concerning the house of Ahab: for the LORD
hath done that which he spake by his
servant E-lī′jah.
11 So Jehu slew all that remained of
the house of Ahab in Jĕz′re-el, and all
his great men, and his kinsfolks, and
his priests, until he left him none remaining.
12 ¶And he arose and departed, and
came to Sa-mâ′rĭ-a. And as he was at
the shearing house in the way,
13 Jehu met with the brethren of Ā-
ha-zī′ah king of Jūdah, and said, Who
are ye? And they answered, We are the
brethren of Ā-ha-zī′ah; and we go down
to salute the children of the king and
the children of the queen.
14 And he said, Take them alive. And

3. Divinely commanded executions. 10:1-14.

10:1. The **seventy sons** included grandsons. The **rulers of Jezreel** were probably in Samaria to discuss the latest developments and implications of Jehu's revolt, especially as it con-
cerned the house of Ahab and those associated with the family,
especially **them that brought up Ahab's children,** i.e., their
guardians.
2-5. Two letters were sent to Samaria. The first invited
Ahab's sons to select a king from them and to fight against Jehu
in a contest to determine the right to the throne. Ahab's descendants realized that they were no match for Jehu, so they surrendered their destiny to Jehu's terms.

6-8. Jehu's second letter contained his terms. The rulers and
guardians in Samaria were to deliver the seventy sons' heads to
Jezreel by the next day. The terms were promptly met. Whitcomb suggests that Jehu, using a ploy of the Assyrians, stacked
the heads at the gate to discourage any counter-revolution
(p. 85).

9-12. **Ye be righteous,** i.e., you are innocent of these deaths.
He admitted to executing Joram, but the answer to the question
who slew all of these should be explained that he had nothing to
do with their deaths. God was judging them according to Elijah's prediction (vs. 10).

13-14. **Brethren of Ahaziah** must mean relatives (cf.
II Chr 21:17; 22:8) who were en route to visit their royal
cousins, children of the queen, i.e., the queen mother Jezebel.
They were evidently oblivious to the revolution in progress.

they took them alive, and slew them at the pit of the shearing house, *even* two and forty men; neither left he any of them.

15 ¶And when he was departed thence, he lighted on Je-hŏn′a-dăb the son of Rē′chăb *coming* to meet him: and he saluted him, and said to him, Is thine heart right, as my heart *is* with thy heart? And Je-hŏn′a-dăb answered, It is. If it be, give *me* thine hand. And he gave *him* his hand; and he took him up to him into the chariot.

16 And he said, Come with me, and see my zeal for the LORD. So they made him ride in his chariot.

17 And when he came to Sa-mâ′rĭ-a, he slew all that remained unto Ahab in Sa-mâ′rĭ-a, till he had destroyed him, according to the saying of the LORD, which he spake to E-lī′jah.

18 ¶And Jehu gathered all the people together, and said unto them, Ahab served Bā′al a little; *but* Jehu shall serve him much.

19 Now therefore call unto me all the prophets of Bā′al, all his servants, and all his priests; let none be wanting: for I have a great sacrifice *to do* to Bā′al; whosoever shall be wanting, he shall not live. But Jehu did *it* in subtilty, to the intent that he might destroy the worshippers of Bā′al.

20 And Jehu said, Proclaim a solemn assembly for Bā′al. And they proclaimed *it.*

21 And Jehu sent through all Israel: and all the worshippers of Bā′al came, so that there was not a man left that came not. And they came into the house of Bā′al; and the house of Bā′al was full from one end to another.

22 And he said unto him that *was* over the vestry, Bring forth vestments for all the worshippers of Bā′al. And he brought them forth vestments.

23 And Jehu went, and Je-hŏn′a-dăb the son of Rē′chăb, into the house of Bā′al, and said unto the worshippers of Bā′al, Search, and look that there be here with you none of the servants of the LORD, but the worshippers of Bā′al only.

24 And when they went in to offer sacrifices and burnt offerings, Jehu appointed fourscore men without, and said, *If* any of the men whom I have brought into your hands escape, *he that* letteth him go, his life *shall be* for the life of him.

25 And it came to pass, as soon as he had made an end of offering the burnt offering, that Jehu said to the guard and to the captains, Go in, *and* slay them; let none come forth. And they smote them with the edge of the sword; and the guard and the captains cast *them* out, and went to the city of the house of Bā′al.

26 And they brought forth the images out of the house of Bā′al, and burned them.

27 And they brake down the image of Bā′al, and brake down the house of Bā′al, and made it a draught house unto this day.

4. Purge of Baalism. 10:15-28.

15-16. Jehonadab, according to Jeremiah 35:6, was the founder of the Rechabites, a strict sect known for their simple life. This group of Kenite extraction (I Chr 2:55) was zealous for Jehovah, and Jehu saw in Jehonadab a sympathetic ally. **Is thine heart right . . . ?** This question means: Are we in agreement?

17-21. Returning to Samaria, Jehu executed any person associated with Ahab. **Jehu shall serve him** (Baal) **much.** This lie alleviated any suspicions that might have arisen when **all the prophets of Baal** and Baal's worshipers were invited to the house of Baal to be led in worship by the new king.

22-25. Assisted by Jehonadab, Jehu issued **vestments,** i.e., garments for worshiping Baal, to all Baal's followers to prevent any **servants of the LORD** from entering the building. Eight men were selected to prevent any escape from the building when the massacre began. After he feigned giving a burnt offering, the signal was given to slaughter the adherents of Baalism.

26-28. Jehu was thorough in his destruction of Baalism, not relaxing his efforts until the images of Baal were burned and the house of Baal was broken down and made a latrine.

28 Thus Jehu destroyed Bā'al out of Israel.

29 Howbeit *from* the sins of Jěr-o-bō'am the son of Nē'băt, who made Israel to sin, Jehu departed not from after them, *to wit*, the golden calves that *were* in Běth-el, and that *were* in Dan.

30 And the LORD said unto Jehu, Because thou hast done well in executing *that which is* right in mine eyes, *and* hast done unto the house of Ahab according to all that *was* in mine heart, thy children of the fourth *generation* shall sit on the throne of Israel.

31 But Jehu took no heed to walk in the law of the LORD God of Israel with all his heart: for he departed not from the sins of Jěr-o-bō'am, which made Israel to sin.

32 ¶In those days the LORD began to cut Israel short: and Hăz'a-el smote them in all the coasts of Israel;

33 From Jordan eastward, all the land of Gilead, the Gădītes, and the Reubenites, and the Ma-năs'sītes, from Ar'ŏ-er, which *is* by the river Arnon, even Gilead and Bā'shan.

34 Now the rest of the acts of Jehu, and all that he did, and all his might, *are* they not written in the book of the chronicles of the kings of Israel?

35 And Jehu slept with his fathers: and they buried him in Sa-mâ'rī-a. And Je-hō'a-hăz his son reigned in his stead.

36 And the time that Jehu reigned over Israel in Sa-mâ'rī-a *was* twenty and eight years.

CHAPTER 11

AND when Ăth-a-lī'ah the mother of Ā-ha-zī'ah saw that her son was dead, she arose and destroyed all the seed royal.

2 But Je-hōsh'e-ba, the daughter of king Joram, sister of Ā-ha-zī'ah, took Jō'ăsh the son of Ā-ha-zī'ah, and stole him from among the king's sons *which were* slain; and they hid him, *even* him and his nurse, in the bedchamber from Ăth-a-lī'ah, so that he was not slain.

3 And he was with her hid in the house of the LORD six years. And Ăth-a-lī'ah did reign over the land.

4 ¶And the seventh year Je-hoi'a-da sent and fetched the rulers over hundreds, with the captains and the guard, and brought them to him into the house of the LORD, and made a covenant with them, and took an oath of them in the house of the LORD, and shewed them the king's son.

5 And he commanded them, saying, This *is* the thing that ye shall do; A third part of you that enter in on the sabbath shall even be keepers of the watch of the king's house;

6 And a third part *shall be* at the gate of Sur; and a third part at the gate behind the guard: so shall ye keep the watch of the house, that it be not broken down.

7 And two parts of all you that go forth on the sabbath, even they shall keep the watch of the house of the LORD about the king.

8 And ye shall compass the king round about, every man with his weapons in his hand: and he that cometh

5. Evaluation of Jehu's reign. 10:29-36.

29-31. Unfortunately, Jehu was obviously more of an instrument for the Lord than he was a servant; for though he eliminated Baalism from Israel, he still remained an idolater, loyal to the calf cult of Jeroboam.

He had faithfully executed God's commission to destroy the house of Ahab, but he had been so ruthless that even "the blood of Jezreel" would be avenged upon Jehu's house (cf. Hos 1:4).

32-34. The LORD began to cut Israel short, i.e., by removing the Transjordan territory from her by Hazael who attacked her **coasts,** i.e., borders, as far south as **Aroer** east of the Dead Sea.

35-36. Following a twenty-eight-year reign (ca. 841-814 B.C.), Jehu's son Jehoahaz began to reign.

C. Judah's Rulers: Athaliah and Joash. 11:1-12:21.

1. Athaliah. 11:1-16.

11:1. Athaliah (cf. 8:18, 26) destroyed all royal descendants so that she would be the sole remaining legal claimant to the throne.

2-3. Note how God providentially intervened. Ahaziah's sister, **Jehosheba** (she may have had a different mother), who, according to II Chronicles 22:11, was married to the godly priest, Jehoiada (vs. 4), showed concern for her nephew **Joash** (alternate spelling is **Jehoash,** vs. 21) and hid him. Joash could have been no more than one year old at the time (cf. vss. 3, 21) and was probably the easiest child to hide (cf. the hiding of Moses, Ex 2:2ff.).

4. After six years of Athaliah's reign (she was the only woman to rule on the throne of either Israel or Judah), in the **seventh year** of Joash, Jehoiada made a covenant (to ensure their assistance in dethroning Athaliah) with the king's bodyguards (II Chr 23:1-3 includes the Levites and heads of families) and disclosed to them the king's son, Joash.

5-8. Jehoiada chose a most opportune time for presenting the boy king, at the changing of the Temple guard when the most protection would be present with the least disturbance. "One third of those who came on duty on the Sabbath were to be divided into three parts: one band was to stand guard at the king's house—the palace; another was to guard the palace exit—the gate Sur; and the third was to guard the approach and the gate to the king's house. The two thirds released on the Sabbath were to guard the Temple and Joash with closed ranks" (Stigers, p. 351) and were to kill any who broke through the ranks.

within the ranges, let him be slain: and be ye with the king as he goeth out and as he cometh in.

9 And the captains over the hundreds did according to all *things* that Je-hoi′a-da the priest commanded: and they took every man his men that were to come in on the sabbath, with them that should go out on the sabbath, and came to Je-hoi′a-da the priest.

10 And to the captains over hundreds did the priest give king David's spears and shields, that *were* in the temple of the LORD.

11 And the guard stood, every man with his weapons in his hand, round about the king, from the right corner of the temple to the left corner of the temple, *along* by the altar and the temple.

12 And he brought forth the king's son, and put the crown upon him, and *gave him* the testimony; and they made him king, and anointed him; and they clapped their hands, and said, God save the king.

13 ¶And when Ăth-a-lī′ah heard the noise of the guard *and* of the people, she came to the people into the temple of the LORD.

14 And when she looked, behold, the king stood by a pillar, as the manner *was*, and the princes and the trumpeters by the king, and all the people of the land rejoiced, and blew with trumpets: and Ăth-a-lī′ah rent her clothes, and cried, Treason, Treason.

15 But Je-hoi′a-da the priest commanded the captains of the hundreds, the officers of the host, and said unto them, Have her forth without the ranges: and him that followeth her kill with the sword. For the priest had said, Let her not be slain in the house of the LORD.

16 And they laid hands on her; and she went by the way by the which the horses came into the king's house: and there was she slain.

17 ¶And Je-hoi′a-da made a covenant between the LORD and the king and the people, that they should be the LORD's people; between the king also and the people.

18 And all the people of the land went into the house of Bā′al, and brake it down; his altars and his images brake they in pieces thoroughly, and slew Măt′tan the priest of Bā′al before the altars. And the priest appointed officers over the house of the LORD.

19 And he took the rulers over hundreds, and the captains, and the guard, and all the people of the land; and they brought down the king from the house of the LORD, and came by the way of the gate of the guard to the king's house. And he sat on the throne of the kings.

20 And all the people of the land rejoiced, and the city was in quiet: and they slew Ăth-a-lī′ah with the sword *beside* the king's house.

21 Seven years old *was* Je-hō′ăsh when he began to reign.

9-11. Jehoiada's well-laid plans were carefully followed, and Joash was closely guarded by men heavily armed with former King David's armor.

12. Joash was crowned and given the **testimony**. In Exodus 16:34 and 25:21 the **testimony** is the Mosaic law. Jehoiada, the spiritual leader, was careful to incorporate the spiritual aspect into Joash's coronation by making it possible for the young king to follow Moses' instruction to know the law of God (Deut 17:18-19). Would that today's leaders, instead of taking an oath of office over the Bible, would vow to obey the Word of God while they were in office.

13. Athaliah heard. The strange commotion of changing the guard aroused her curiosity.

14. She could only cry **Treason, treason.** If all the royal offspring were dead, as she thought, then she had the only legitimate right to the throne. No doubt she was remembering the murderous revolt in Israel just six years before that had annihilated her father's house.

15-16. Have her forth without the ranges, i.e., bring her out between the ranks of guards under escort. She could not escape, nor could anyone rescue her. She was killed outside the Temple area near the horse gate.

2. Joash. 11:17-12:21.

17-18. Jehoiada should not be underrated as the spiritual force and counselor for the young king (cf. 12:2). Until Joash was mature, Jehoiada was really the power behind the throne, while Joash was a figurehead.

He mediated a covenant between Joash and Judah and Jehovah, then concentrated all his energy to destroying Baalism.

19-20. Joash was placed on the throne as the legitimate king.

21. Joash began to reign. Due to Jehu's purge of the house of Ahab and jealous murder among the descendants of

CHAPTER 12

IN the seventh year of Jehu Je-hō'ăsh began to reign; and forty years reigned he in Jerusalem. And his mother's name was Zĭb'ĭ-ah of Be'er-shē'ba.

2 And Je-hō'ăsh did *that which was* right in the sight of the LORD all his days wherein Je-hoi'a-da the priest instructed him.

3 But the high places were not taken away: the people still sacrificed and burnt incense in the high places.

4 ¶And Je-hō'ăsh said to the priests, All the money of the dedicated things that is brought into the house of the LORD, *even* the money of every one that passeth *the account,* the money that every man is set at, *and* all the money that cometh into any man's heart to bring into the house of the LORD,

5 Let the priests take *it* to them, every man of his acquaintance: and let them repair the breaches of the house, wheresoever any breach shall be found.

6 But it was *so, that* in the three and twentieth year of king Je-hō'ăsh the priests had not repaired the breaches of the house.

7 Then king Je-hō'ăsh called for Je-hoi'a-da the priest, and the *other* priests, and said unto them, Why repair ye not the breaches of the house? now therefore receive no *more* money of your acquaintance, but deliver it for the breaches of the house.

8 And the priests consented to receive no *more* money of the people, neither to repair the breaches of the house.

9 But Je-hoi'a-da the priest took a chest, and bored a hole in the lid of it, and set it beside the altar, on the right side as one cometh into the house of the LORD: and the priests that kept the door put therein all the money *that was* brought into the house of the LORD.

10 And it was *so,* when they saw that *there was* much money in the chest, that the king's scribe and the high priest came up, and they put up in bags, and told the money that was found in the house of the LORD.

11 And they gave the money, being told, into the hands of them that did the work, that had the oversight of the house of the LORD: and they laid it out to the carpenters and builders, that wrought upon the house of the LORD,

12 And to masons, and hewers of stone, and to buy timber and hewed stone to repair the breaches of the house of the LORD, and for all that was laid out for the house to repair *it.*

13 Howbeit there were not made for the house of the LORD bowls of silver, snuffers, basons, trumpets, any vessels of gold, or vessels of silver, of the money *that was* brought into the house of the LORD:

14 But they gave that to the work-

Jehoshaphat, Joash was the last living relative of Ahab and the last descendant of David. But God was faithful to His covenant with David (II Sam 7:16), and He maintained a **light** (8:19) in Jerusalem (I Kgs 11:36).

12:1-3. Jehoash (or Joash) had a lengthy reign of forty years (ca. 835-796 B.C.). The writer intimates that Joash would turn away from the Lord in later life (cf. II Chr 24:2, 15-22).

4-5. All the money is a general statement for the specified revenues which follow, **the money of every one that passeth,** "current money" (NASB), may refer to the yearly half-shekel contributed by every Israelite over the age of twenty (Ex 30:13-14), or it may mean simply the money that was weighed out in everyday business (Israel did not yet have coined money). **The money that every man is set at,** i.e., the monetary payment based upon an individual's personal assessment (Lev 27:2ff.). **All the money . . . any man's heart,** i.e., a free will offering to the Lord. These revenues were to be collected by the priests and used for repairing the damage that Athaliah had done to the Temple (II Chr 24:7).

6-7. The year of Joash's order is not given, but in the twenty-third year the work had not been carried out. No explanation for the failure was given.

8-9. No accusation of misappropriation of funds was made, but Joash's first arrangement had not worked. Therefore, the priests were relieved of their fund-collecting responsibilities, and Joash ordered Jehoiada (II Chr 24:8) to build a collection box to receive the money. It was set **beside the altar.** Second Chronicles 24:8 says it was placed without the gate; so perhaps two locations were used on a trial basis to determine which was the most accessible.

10-12. When the box was full, the money was taken and distributed to the workmen repairing the Temple.

13-15. Initially, all the funds were used for repairing the Temple proper, not for replacing gold and silver utensils in the Temple. Later, however, when the Temple was finished, the rest of the money was applied to vessels for the Temple (II Chr 24:14).

men, and repaired therewith the house of the LORD.

15 Moreover they reckoned not with the men, into whose hand they delivered the money to be bestowed on workmen: for they dealt faithfully.

16 The trespass money and sin money was not brought into the house of the LORD: it was the priests'.

17 ¶Then Hăz′a-el king of Syria went up, and fought against Gath, and took it: and Hăz′a-el set his face to go up to Jerusalem.

18 And Je-hō′ăsh king of Jūdah took all the hallowed things that Je-hŏsh′a-phăt, and Je-hō′ram, and Ā-ha-zī′ah, his fathers, kings of Jūdah, had dedicated, and his own hallowed things, and all the gold *that was* found in the treasures of the house of the LORD, and in the king's house, and sent *it* to Hăz′a-el king of Syria: and he went away from Jerusalem.

19 ¶And the rest of the acts of Jō′ăsh, and all that he did, *are* they not written in the book of the chronicles of the kings of Jūdah?

20 And his servants arose, and made a conspiracy, and slew Jō′ăsh in the house of Mĭl′lō, which goeth down to Sĭl′la.

21 For Jōz′a-chär the son of Shĭm′e-ăth, and Je-hōz′a-băd the son of Shō′mer, his servants, smote him, and he died; and they buried him with his fathers in the city of David: and Ăm-a-zī′ah his son reigned in his stead.

CHAPTER 13

IN the three and twentieth year of Jō′ăsh the son of Ā-ha-zī′ah king of Jūdah Je-hō′a-hăz the son of Jehu began to reign over Israel in Sa-mâ′rĭ-a, *and reigned* seventeen years.

2 And he did *that which was* evil in the sight of the LORD, and followed the sins of Jĕr-o-bō′am the son of Nē′băt, which made Israel to sin; he departed not therefrom.

3 And the anger of the LORD was kindled against Israel, and he delivered them into the hand of Hăz′a-el king of Syria, and into the hand of Bĕn-hā′dăd the son of Hăz′a-el, all *their* days.

4 And Je-hō′a-hăz besought the LORD, and the LORD hearkened unto him: for he saw the oppression of Israel, because the king of Syria oppressed them.

5 (And the LORD gave Israel a saviour, so that they went out from under the hand of the Syrians: and the children of Israel dwelt in their tents, as beforetime.

6 Nevertheless they departed not from the sins of the house of Jĕr-o-bō′am, who made Israel sin, *but* walked therein: and there remained the grove also in Sa-mâ′rĭ-a.)

7 Neither did he leave of the people to Je-hō′a-hăz but fifty horsemen, and ten chariots, and ten thousand footmen;

16. The trespass money . . . was the priests'. According to the Mosaic law (Num 5:7-10), the trespass offering included restitution for the debt (according to the assessment of the priest), plus an additional payment equal to one-fifth the value. If the person to whom the payment was due had died, then payment was made to the priest. Joash allowed the priest to retain the funds from these offerings.

17-18. Hazael, the energetic Syrian king (10:32-33), invaded Philistia, took **Gath,** and then set his sights on Jerusalem. After first suffering defeat (II Chr 24:24), Joash followed the precedent of Asa (I Kgs 15:18) and paid tribute to Hazael.

19-21. Joash, who had such a promising future under the tutorship of Jehoiada, fell far short of the expectations of his people. His own servants conspired against him and killed him because he had ordered the death of the prophet Zechariah the son of Jehoiada (II Chr 24:21-25). He was buried in **the city of David** (Jerusalem), but not in the sepulchre of the kings (II Chr 24:25).

D. Israel's Kings: Jehoahaz and Jehoash. 13:1-25.

1. Jehoahaz. 13:1-9.

13:1-3. Jehu's son, **Jehoahaz,** reigned seventeen years (ca. 814-798 B.C.). He duplicated his father's religious policies by supporting Jeroboam's calf cult. Because of this sin, the Lord subjected Israel to invasions and harrassment by two Syrian kings, Hazael and his son Ben-hadad.

4-5. Because Jehoahaz sought the Lord in his oppression, an unidentified **savior** was sent. This may have been an Assyrian king (Adadnirari II), who might have diverted Syria's attention from Israel to defend itself from Assyria; it may have been a military force that won a victory against Syria; it may be a reference to Jehoahaz's son, Joash, who was successful against the Syrians (13:25); or it may have been Jeroboam II (14:27).

6-9. Jehoahaz's seeking the Lord (vs. 4) did not involve repentance, for he and Israel continued in their sin. In 853 B.C., at the battle at Qarqar, Ahab had two thousand chariots in his army. Israel's chariot force had dwindled to an insignificant **ten chariots** in Jehoahaz's day.

for the king of Syria had destroyed them, and had made them like the dust by threshing.

8 ¶Now the rest of the acts of Je-hō'a-hăz, and all that he did, and his might, *are* they not written in the book of the chronicles of the kings of Israel?

9 And Je-hō'a-hăz slept with his fathers; and they buried him in Sa-mâ'rĭ-a: and Jō'ăsh his son reigned in his stead.

10 ¶In the thirty and seventh year of Jō'ăsh king of Jūdah began Je-hō'ăsh the son of Je-hō'a-hăz to reign over Israel in Sa-mâ'rĭ-a, *and reigned* sixteen years.

11 And he did *that which was* evil in the sight of the LORD; he departed not from all the sins of Jĕr-o-bō'am the son of Nĕ'băt, who made Israel sin: *but he* walked therein.

12 And the rest of the acts of Jō'ăsh, and all that he did, and his might wherewith he fought against Ăm-a-zī'ah king of Jūdah, *are* they not written in the book of the chronicles of the kings of Israel?

13 And Jō'ăsh slept with his fathers; and Jĕr-o-bō'am sat upon his throne: and Jō'ăsh was buried in Sa-mâ'rĭ-a with the kings of Israel.

14 ¶Now E-lī'sha was fallen sick of his sickness whereof he died. And Jō'-ăsh the king of Israel came down unto him, and wept over his face, and said, O my father, my father, the chariot of Israel, and the horsemen thereof.

15 And E-lī'sha said unto him, Take bow and arrows. And he took unto him bow and arrows.

16 And he said to the king of Israel, Put thine hand upon the bow. And he put his hand *upon it:* and E-lī'sha put his hands upon the king's hands.

17 And he said, Open the window eastward. And he opened *it.* Then E-lī'sha said, Shoot. And he shot. And he said, The arrow of the LORD's deliverance, and the arrow of deliverance from Syria: for thou shalt smite the Syrians in Ā'phĕk, till thou have consumed *them.*

18 And he said, Take the arrows. And he took *them.* And he said unto the king of Israel, Smite upon the ground. And he smote thrice, and stayed.

19 And the man of God was wroth with him, and said, Thou shouldest have smitten five or six times; then hadst thou smitten Syria till thou hadst consumed *it:* whereas now thou shalt smite Syria *but* thrice.

20 ¶And E-lī'sha died, and they buried him. And the bands of the Moabites invaded the land at the coming in of the year.

21 And it came to pass, as they were burying a man, that, behold, they spied a band *of men;* and they cast the man into the sepulchre of E-lī'sha: and when the man was let down, and touched the bones of E-lī'sha, he revived, and stood up on his feet.

22 ¶But Hăz'a-el king of Syria oppressed Israel all the days of Je-hō'a-hăz.

23 And the LORD was gracious unto

2. *Jehoash. 13:10-25.*

10-13. Jehoahaz's son, Jehoash (also called Joash, but not to be confused with Judah's king Joash who reigned at the same time) reigned sixteen years (ca. 798-782 B.C.). He was another religious carbon-copy of his father and grandfather. **He fought against Amaziah** (see notes on 14:8-16).

14. Elisha was fallen sick. He had faithfully served the Lord some forty-five to fifty-five years (through the reigns of Joram, Jehu, Jehoahaz, and Jehoash). Since he was near death, Jehoahaz paid him a final visit. **My father** (see note on 2:12). Though Jehoahaz had not followed after Jehovah, he still regretted losing the prophet of Jehovah, his only point of contact with God in time of emergency.

15-16. Take bow and arrows, Joash's means of defense. On his deathbed Elisha had Joash enact his final prophecy.

17. Open the window eastward, the direction of Transjordan, where Syria had occupied land belonging to Israel (10:32-33). The **arrow** symbolized Jehovah's deliverance from Syria. The Syrians were to be consumed at **Aphek** (contrast Ahab's treatment of the Syrians at Aphek, I Kgs 20:26-34.)

18-19. Striking the ground symbolized smiting Syria. **Five or six times** represented total victory over Syria, whereas three times represented partial victory. Elisha's anger over Joash's action seems to indicate that Joash understood what was being symbolized, but deliberately chose not to comply with God's plans. With Assyria gaining in strength, Joash, like Ahab (see notes on I Kgs 20:31-34), did not want Syria destroyed altogether.

20-21. Following Elisha's death and burial, Israel was invaded by a band of Moabites. On one occasion some Israelites were burying a man when they spotted a band of Moabites. In fear of the Moabites, they abandoned their plans to dig a grave for the man and hurriedly placed his corpse in Elisha's sepulchre. The man returned to life when he came in contact with the prophet's bones. In his life and death, fourteen miracles are attributed to Elisha (twice as many as attributed to Elijah).

22-24. These verses summarize and relate the events of verses 3-4.

them, and had compassion on them, and had respect unto them, because of his covenant with Abraham, Isaac, and Jacob, and would not destroy them, neither cast he them from his presence as yet.

24 So Hăz'a-el king of Syria died; and Běn-hā'dăd his son reigned in his stead.

25 And Je-hō'ăsh the son of Je-hō'a-hăz took again out of the hand of Běn-hā'dăd the son of Hăz'a-el the cities, which he had taken out of the hand of Je-hō'a-hăz his father by war. Three times did Jō'ăsh beat him, and recovered the cities of Israel.

CHAPTER 14

IN the second year of Jō'ăsh son of Je-hō'a-hăz king of Israel reigned Ăm-a-zī'ah the son of Jō'ăsh king of Jūdah.

2 He was twenty and five years old when he began to reign, and reigned twenty and nine years in Jerusalem. And his mother's name was Je-hō-ad'-dan of Jerusalem.

3 And he did that which was right in the sight of the LORD, yet not like David his father: he did according to all things as Jō'ăsh his father did.

4 Howbeit the high places were not taken away: as yet the people did sacrifice and burnt incense on the high places.

5 ¶And it came to pass, as soon as the kingdom was confirmed in his hand, that he slew his servants which had slain the king his father.

6 But the children of the murderers he slew not: according unto that which is written in the book of the law of Moses, wherein the LORD commanded, saying, The fathers shall not be put to death for the children, nor the children be put to death for the fathers; but every man shall be put to death for his own sin.

7 He slew of Ĕdom in the valley of salt ten thousand, and took Sē'lah by war, and called the name of it Jŏk'the-el unto this day.

8 ¶Then Ăm-a-zī'ah sent messengers to Je-hō'ăsh, the son of Je-hō'a-hăz son of Jehu, king of Israel, saying, Come, let us look one another in the face.

9 And Je-hō'ăsh the king of Israel sent to Ăm-a-zī'ah king of Jūdah, saying, The thistle that was in Lebanon sent to the cedar that was in Lebanon, saying, Give thy daughter to my son to wife: and there passed by a wild beast that was in Lebanon, and trode down the thistle.

10 Thou hast indeed smitten Ĕdom, and thine heart hath lifted thee up: glory of this, and tarry at home: for why shouldest thou meddle to thy hurt, that thou shouldest fall, even thou, and Jūdah with thee?

11 But Ăm-a-zī'ah would not hear. Therefore Je-hō'ăsh king of Israel went up; and he and Ăm-a-zī'ah king of Jūdah looked one another in the face at Běth-shĕ'mesh, which belongeth to Jūdah.

25. Joash was able to regain the territory his father had lost to Syria. Three times (cf. vs. 18-19) he was successful.

E. Judah's Kings: Amaziah and Azariah. 14:1-22.

1. Amaziah. 14:1-20.

Beginning with this period, there is an abundance of complex chronological problems. For a thorough discussion see Thiele, *The Mysterious Numbers of the Hebrew Kings* (p. 76ff.).

14:1-2. Judah's king following Joash was **Amaziah,** who reigned twenty-nine years (ca. 796-767 B.C.).

3-5. He served the Lord, but not with the same fervor as **David his father,** i.e., his ancestor. One of his first actions was to punish his father's conspirators, Jozachar and Jehozabad (12:21).

6-7. The children . . . he slew not, intimating that Israel may have ignored this Mosaic command (Deut 24:16) and had followed the custom of killing the conspirator's children, also. He regained control of Edom, which had been lost by a revolt under Jehoram (8:20-22). The **valley of salt** is a depression just below the Dead Sea. **Selah** (lit., rock or cliff) may be a reference to the Nabatean capital of Petra, the city carved out of the rocky cliffs. For a more complete account of this victory see II Chronicles 25:5-16.

8. This action is anticipated in 13:12. After defeating Edom and receiving foolish advice (II Chr 25:17), Amaziah arrogantly challenged Israel to battle. **Come, let us look one another in the face** was an invitation to war, not to get acquainted.

9-10. Jehoash had also just been successful in battle (13:25). He responded by means of the "thistle fable" (cf. the fable in Jud 9:8-15). Amaziah was the thistle, Jehoash the cedar. In essence, Jehoash was saying that to fight him Amaziah would be fighting out of his league, all because of his pride (**thine heart hath lifted thee**).

11-14. Amaziah was so confident of victory that he attacked Jehoash on his own territory at **Beth-shemesh,** about fifteen miles west of Jerusalem. Judah was soundly defeated by Israel. Amaziah himself was temporarily taken captive; the wall of Jerusalem was broken; the palace and Temple were spoiled; and Jehoash returned to Samaria with hostages (lit., sons of the

12 And Jūdah was put to the worse before Israel; and they fled every man to their tents.

13 And Je-hō'ăsh king of Israel took Ăm-a-zī'ah king of Jūdah, the son of Je-hō'ăsh the son of Ā-ha-zī'ah, at Bĕth-shĕ'mesh, and came to Jerusalem, and brake down the wall of Jerusalem from the gate of Ē'phra-im unto the corner gate, four hundred cubits.

14 And he took all the gold and silver, and all the vessels that were found in the house of the LORD, and in the treasures of the king's house, and hostages, and returned to Sa-mā'rī-a.

15 ¶Now the rest of the acts of Je-hō'ăsh which he did, and his might, and how he fought with Ăm-a-zī'ah king of Jūdah, are they not written in the book of the chronicles of the kings of Israel?

16 And Je-hō'ăsh slept with his fathers, and was buried in Sa-mā'rī-a with the kings of Israel; and Jĕr-o-bō'am his son reigned in his stead.

17 ¶And Ăm-a-zī'ah the son of Jō'ăsh king of Jūdah lived after the death of Je-hō'ăsh son of Je-hō'a-hăz king of Israel fifteen years.

18 And the rest of the acts of Ăm-a-zī'ah, are they not written in the book of the chronicles of the kings of Jūdah?

19 Now they made a conspiracy against him in Jerusalem: and he fled to Lā'chĭsh; but they sent after him to Lā'chĭsh, and slew him there.

20 And they brought him on horses: and he was buried at Jerusalem with his fathers in the city of David.

21 ¶And all the people of Jūdah took Ăz-a-rī'ah, which was sixteen years old, and made him king instead of his father Ăm-a-zī'ah.

22 He built Ē'lăth, and restored it to Jūdah, after that the king slept with his fathers.

23 ¶In the fifteenth year of Ăm-a-zī'ah the son of Jō'ăsh king of Jūdah Jĕr-o-bō'am the son of Jō'ăsh king of Israel began to reign in Sa-mā'rī-a, and reigned forty and one years.

24 And he did that which was evil in the sight of the LORD: he departed not from all the sins of Jĕr-o-bō'am the son of Nĕ'băt, who made Israel to sin.

25 He restored the coast of Israel from the entering of Hā'măth unto the sea of the plain, according to the word of the LORD God of Israel, which he spake by the hand of his servant Jonah, the son of A-mĭt'ta-ī, the prophet, which was of Găth-hē'pher.

26 For the LORD saw the affliction of Israel, that it was very bitter: for there was not any shut up, nor any left, nor any helper for Israel.

27 And the LORD said not that he would blot out the name of Israel from under heaven: but he saved them by the hand of Jĕr-o-bō'am the son of Jō'ăsh.

28 ¶Now the rest of the acts of Jĕr-o-bō'am, and all that he did, and his might, how he warred, and how he recovered Damascus, and Hā'măth, which belonged to Jūdah, for Israel, are they not written in the book of the chronicles of the kings of Israel?

29 And Jĕr-o-bō'am slept with his

pledges), indicating that Amaziah was probably subjected to serving Jehoash.

15-16. These verses are repetitive of 13:12-13.

17-20. Amaziah was the second king of Judah to die by conspiracy (cf. 12:20); but in contrast to the events in Israel, Judah always installed the son of the slain king as the new king. This **conspiracy** may have been the result of growing dissatisfaction with Amaziah after his senseless war with Jehoash. He fled to **Lachish,** an important stronghold thirty-five miles southwest of Jerusalem, and was killed there. He was permitted a royal burial in Jerusalem.

2. Azariah. 14:21-22.

21-22. Azariah took the throne at age sixteen. It is probable that he was elevated to the throne as a co-ruler as early as the fifteenth year of Amaziah (cf. vs. 23; 15:1, 8). He rebuilt Solomon's important Red Sea naval base (cf. I Kgs 9:26; 22:48).

F. Israel's King, Jeroboam II. 14:23-29.

23-25 Jeroboam (Jeroboam II) was the last strong king of Israel, reigning forty-one years (ca. 793-753 B.C.). Defeating the Syrians, he restored the Davidic borders north of Damascus as far as **Hamath,** as he was instructed by God through the prophet **Jonah,** the prophet of the book that bears his name. Is it possible that Jeroboam II was commanded to be aggressive soon after Jonah's mission to Nineveh, while the Assyrians there were still repentant and would not have been a threat?

The prophets Amos and Hosea both prophesied during this time (Amos 1:1; Hos 1:1).

26-29. The LORD saw the affliction of Israel, i.e., He purposed to relieve Israel's distress (cf. Ex 2:25; 3:7). **He saved them** from the oppression of the Syrians, but the books of Hosea and Amos depict the moral and religious character of Israel that stemmed from the prosperity of this time.

fathers, *even* with the kings of Israel; and Zăch-a-rī′ah his son reigned in his stead.

CHAPTER 15

IN the twenty and seventh year of Jĕr-o-bō′am king of Israel began Ăz-a-rī′ah son of Ăm-a-zī′ah king of Jūdah to reign.

2 Sixteen years old was he when he began to reign, and he reigned two and fifty years in Jerusalem. And his mother's name *was* Jĕch-o-lī′ah of Jerusalem.

3 And he did *that which was* right in the sight of the LORD, according to all that his father Ăm-a-zī′ah had done;

4 Save that the high places were not removed: the people sacrificed and burnt incense still on the high places.

5 ¶And the LORD smote the king, so that he was a leper unto the day of his death, and dwelt in a several house. And Jō′tham the king's son *was* over the house, judging the people of the land.

6 And the rest of the acts of Ăz-a-rī′ah, and all that he did, *are* they not written in the book of the chronicles of the kings of Jūdah?

7 So Ăz-a-rī′ah slept with his fathers; and they buried him with his fathers in the city of David: and Jō′tham his son reigned in his stead.

8 ¶In the thirty and eighth year of Ăz-a-rī′ah king of Jūdah did Zăch-a-rī′ah the son of Jĕr-o-bō′am reign over Israel in Sa-mâ′rĭ-a six months.

9 And he did *that which was* evil in the sight of the LORD, as his fathers had done: he departed not from the sins of Jĕr-o-bō′am the son of Nē′băt, who made Israel to sin.

10 And Shăl′lum the son of Jā′besh conspired against him, and smote him before the people, and slew him, and reigned in his stead.

11 And the rest of the acts of Zăch-a-rī′ah, behold, they *are* written in the book of the chronicles of the kings of Israel.

12 This *was* the word of the LORD which he spake unto Jehu, saying, Thy sons shall sit on the throne of Israel unto the fourth *generation*. And so it came to pass.

13 ¶Shăl′lum the son of Jā′besh began to reign in the nine and thirtieth year of Uz-zī′ah king of Jūdah; and he reigned a full month in Sa-mâ′rĭ-a.

14 For Mĕn′a-hĕm the son of Gā′dī went up from Tir′zah, and came to Sa-mâ′rĭ-a, and smote Shăl′lum the son of Jā′besh in Sa-mâ′rĭ-a, and slew him, and reigned in his stead.

15 And the rest of the acts of Shăl′lum, and his conspiracy which he made, behold, they *are* written in the book of the chronicles of the kings of Israel.

16 Then Mĕn′a-hĕm smote Tĭph′sah, and all that *were* therein, and the coasts thereof from Tir′zah: because they opened not *to him*, therefore he smote *it*; *and* all the women therein that were with child he ripped up.

17 ¶In the nine and thirtieth year of

G. Judah's King, Azariah. 15:1-7.

15:1-4. Azariah (an alternate spelling is **Uzziah**, vs. 13) reigned fifty-two years (ca. 790-739 B.C.). The first twenty-three years were probably as a co-regent with his father (see note on 14:21).

5-7. The LORD smote the king, with incurable leprosy (for background, his pride and usurpation of the priestly responsibility, see II Chr 26:16-19). He retained his office as king, but his son **Jotham** was elevated to co-reign with him during his last eleven years. He was more or less a figurehead, while Jotham undertook the royal duties.

H. Israel's Kings: Zachariah, Shallum, Menahem, Pekahiah, and Pekah. 15:8-31.

1. Zachariah. 15:8-12.

8-9. The period that follows is one of political turmoil. The son of Jeroboam II, **Zachariah,** reigned only six months and was evil, like all his predecessors.

10-12. He was killed publicly by **Shallum,** but there is no indication that the people called for retribution. Jehu had been promised a son on the throne after him for four generations (10:30). That promise was now fulfilled.

2. Shallum. 15:13-16.

13. The murderous Shallum reigned for only one month. Only Zimri had a shorter reign (I Kgs 16:15).

14-15. Menahem retaliated by slaying Shallum. Scripture implies what Josephus (*Antiq.* IX: XI:1) affirms, that Menaham was a general at Tirzah under Zachariah. Stiger's observation may be correct. "Menahem's action was based on the facts that the Israelite kingdom was a military monarchy, that Shallum was a usurper, and that when the Jehu line died out, the throne would go to the commander in chief of the army" (p. 359).

16. Encountering apparent opposition at **Tiphsah** (location is unknown), he employed the tactics of the Syrians and the Ammonites, ripping open the pregnant women (8:12; Amos 1:13). Such cruelty would have demoralized any opposition.

3. Menahem. 15:17-22.

17-18. This evil king reigned ten years (ca. 752-742 B.C.).

Ăz-a-rī′ah king of Jūdah began Mĕn′a-hĕm the son of Gā′dī to reign over Israel, *and reigned* ten years in Sa-mâ′-rī-a.

18 And he did *that which was* evil in the sight of the LORD: he departed not all his days from the sins of Jĕr-o-bō′am the son of Nē′băt, who made Israel to sin.

19 *And* Pul the king of Assyria came against the land: and Mĕn′a-hĕm gave Pul a thousand talents of silver, that his hand might be with him to confirm the kingdom in his hand.

20 And Mĕn′a-hĕm exacted the money of Israel, *even* of all the mighty men of wealth, of each man fifty shekels of silver, to give to the king of Assyria. So the king of Assyria turned back, and stayed not there in the land.

21 ¶And the rest of the acts of Mĕn′a-hĕm, and all that he did, *are* they not written in the book of the chronicles of the kings of Israel?

22 And Mĕn′a-hĕm slept with his fathers; and Pĕk-a-hī′ah his son reigned in his stead.

23 ¶In the fiftieth year of Ăz-a-rī′ah king of Jūdah Pĕk-a-hī′ah the son of Mĕn′a-hĕm began to reign over Israel in Sa-mâ′rī-a, *and reigned* two years.

24 And he did *that which was* evil in the sight of the LORD: he departed not from the sins of Jĕr-o-bō′am the son of Nē′băt, who made Israel to sin.

25 But Pē′kah the son of Rĕm-a-lī′ah, a captain of his, conspired against him, and smote him in Sa-mâ′rī-a, in the palace of the king's house, with Är′gŏb and Â-rī′eh, and with him fifty men of the Gileadites: and he killed him, and reigned in his room.

26 And the rest of the acts of Pĕk-a-hī′ah, and all that he did, behold, they *are* written in the book of the chronicles of the kings of Israel.

27 ¶In the two and fiftieth year of Ăz-a-rī′ah king of Jūdah Pē′kah the son of Rĕm-a-lī′ah began to reign over Israel in Sa-mâ′rī-a, *and reigned* twenty years.

28 And he did *that which was* evil in the sight of the LORD: he departed not from the sins of Jĕr-o-bō′am the son of Nē′băt, who made Israel to sin.

29 In the days of Pē′kah king of Israel came Tĭg′lăth-pĭ-lē′ser king of Assyria, and took ī′jŏn, and Ā′bel-bĕth-mā′a-chah, and Ja-nō′ah, and Kē′dĕsh, and Hā′zŏr, and Gilead, and Galilee, all the land of Năph′ta-lī, and carried them captive to Assyria.

30 And Hō-shē′a the son of Ē′lah made a conspiracy against Pē′kah the son of Rĕm-a-lī′ah, and smote him, and slew him, and reigned in his stead, in the twentieth year of Jō′tham the son of Uz-zī′ah.

31 And the rest of the acts of Pē′kah, and all that he did, behold, they *are* written in the book of the chronicles of the kings of Israel.

19. **Pul** is Tiglath-pileser III of Assyria. **Pul,** or **Pulu,** was his real name and the one he retained in Babylon; but he assumed the name Tiglath-pileser upon coming to power in Assyria in 745 B.C. In 743 B.C. he came against Menahem and exacted payment of a thousand talents of silver from him for the privilege of remaining on the throne. Thus, Menahem became a vassal of Assyria.

20-22. To raise money for the tribute, Menahem had to exact a tax from 60,000 of Israel's wealthier men. Tiglath-pileser's account of this reads: "As for Menahem, I overwhelmed him like a snowstorm and he . . . . fled like a bird, alone, and bowed to my feet. I returned him to his place and imposed tribute upon him, to wit: gold, silver, linen garments with multicolored trimmings. . ." (Pritchard, *Ancient Near Eastern Texts,* p. 283).

4. Pekahiah. 15:23-26.

23-26. **Pekahiah,** Menahem's son, reigned two years (ca. 742-740 B.C.) before being killed in a conspiracy by his captain, **Pekah.**

5. Pekah. 15:27-31.

27-28. **Pekah** became sole ruler of this time. It is said that he reigned twenty years. The known dates of Menahem's payment to Tiglath-pileser (743 B.C.) and the fall of Samaria (722 B.C.) make this twenty-year reign impossible, unless, as seems the case, he began ruling as a rival the same year Menahem began to reign. Or as Ellison (p. 325) suggests, Pekah had been the power behind the throne of Menahem and Pekahiah. Therefore, when he came to the throne he counted his reign as beginning with Menahem's accession as though he had co-reigned. His reign extended from about 752 to 732 B.C.

29. For the reason behind this invasion, see 16:5ff. Around 733 B.C. the cities of northern Israel, north and west of the Sea of Galilee, were taken; and the people were carried captive to Assyria in the first of two deportations.

30-31. His reign ended with his death at the hand of another conspirator, **Hoshea.**

I. Judah's Kings: Jotham and Ahaz. 15:32-16:20.

1. Jotham. 15:32-38.

32 ¶In the second year of Pē′kah the son of Rĕm-a-lī′ah king of Israel began Jŏ′tham the son of Uz-zī′ah king of Jū-dah to reign.

33 Five and twenty years old was he when he began to reign, and he reigned sixteen years in Jerusalem. And his mother's name *was* Je-rū′sha, the daughter of Zā′dŏk.

34 And he did *that which was* right in the sight of the LORD: he did according to all that his father Uz-zī′ah had done.

35 Howbeit the high places were not removed: the people sacrificed and burned incense still in the high places. He built the higher gate of the house of the LORD.

36 ¶Now the rest of the acts of Jŏ′-tham, and all that he did, *are* they not written in the book of the chronicles of the kings of Jūdah?

37 In those days the LORD began to send against Jūdah Rē′zīn the king of Syria, and Pē′kah the son of Rĕm-a-lī′ah.

38 And Jŏ′tham slept with his fathers, and was buried with his fathers in the city of David his father: and Ahaz his son reigned in his stead.

CHAPTER 16

IN the seventeenth year of Pē′kah the son of Rĕm-a-lī′ah Ahaz the son of Jŏ′-tham king of Jūdah began to reign.

2 Twenty years old *was* Ahaz when he began to reign, and reigned sixteen years in Jerusalem, and did not *that which was* right in the sight of the LORD his God, like David his father.

3 But he walked in the way of the kings of Israel, yea, and made his son to pass through the fire, according to the abominations of the heathen, whom the LORD cast out from before the children of Israel.

4 And he sacrificed and burnt incense in the high places, and on the hills, and under every green tree.

5 ¶Then Rē′zīn king of Syria and Pē′kah son of Rĕm-a-lī′ah king of Israel came up to Jerusalem to war: and they besieged Ahaz, but could not overcome *him*.

6 At that time Rē′zīn king of Syria recovered Ē′lăth to Syria, and drave the Jews from Ē′lăth: and the Syrians came to Ē′lăth, and dwelt there unto this day.

7 So Ahaz sent messengers to Tĭg′lăth-pĭ-lē′ser king of Assyria, saying, I *am* thy servant and thy son: come up, and save me out of the hand of the king of Syria, and out of the hand of the king of Israel, which rise up against me.

8 And Ahaz took the silver and gold that was found in the house of the LORD, and in the treasures of the king's house, and sent *it for* a present to the king of Assyria.

9 And the king of Assyria hearkened unto him: for the king of Assyria went up against Damascus, and took it, and carried *the people of* it captive to Kir, and slew Rē′zīn.

10 ¶And king Ahaz went to Damas-cus to meet Tĭg′lăth-pĭ-lē′ser king of

32-36. The godly **son of Uzziah** (Azariah), **Jotham**, is cred-ited here for sixteen years of reigning, the period of his co-regency with his father and his sole reign (ca. 750-735 B.C.), but not the years of his co-regency with his son, Ahaz (ca. 735-751 B.C.). For a fuller account of Jotham, see II Chronicles 27.

37-38. In the days of his co-regency with Ahaz, Rezin of Syria and Pekah of Israel had banded together in an anti-Assyrian confederacy. Judah refused to join the confederacy; therefore, she came under attack from the two northern kings.

2. Ahaz. 16:1-20.

16:1-2. Ahaz, son of Jotham, reigned in Jerusalem as sole ruler for sixteen years (ca. 731-715 B.C.).

3-4. He was a shocking contrast to his immediate predeces-sors, ranking with Judah's wicked kings, Jehoram, Manasseh, Jehoiakim, and Zedekiah. He even offered his own son as a sacrifice to the god Molech (cf. II Chr 28:3; Lev 18:21).

5-6. Came up to Jerusalem to war. For a more complete account see II Chronicles 28:5ff. (120,000 were slain, and 200,000 were taken captive). Further loss was suffered when **Elath** (cf. 14:22) was taken and controlled by the Syrians.

7-8. Ahaz sent messengers to Tiglath-pileser. The coalition to the north, Rezin and Pekah, had threatened to remove Ahaz from the throne and replace him with a puppet king of their choice (cf. Isa 7:6). Thoroughly frightened, he appealed to Assyria for help. To pay for this assistance, gold was taken from the Temple.

9. Assyria obliged, invading Syria (**Damascus**), killing Rezin, and taking captives. With Israel's buffer state defeated, she became an easy victim for Assyria. In 734 B.C. she, too, was invaded (see note on 15:29).

10. Ahaz went to Damascus to meet Tiglath-pileser to per-sonally thank the Assyrian for relief. He saw **an altar.** It is likely

Asyria, and saw an altar that *was* at Damascus: and king Ahaz sent to Ū-rī′-jah the priest the fashion of the altar, and the pattern of it, according to all the workmanship thereof.

11 And Ū-rī′jah the priest built an altar according to all that king Ahaz had sent from Damascus: so Ū-rī′jah the priest made *it* against king Ahaz came from Damascus.

12 And when the king was come from Damascus, the king saw the altar: and the king approached to the altar, and offered thereon.

13 And he burnt his burnt offering and his meat offering, and poured his drink offering, and sprinkled the blood of his peace offerings, upon the altar.

14 And he brought also the brasen altar, which *was* before the LORD, from the forefront of the house, from between the altar and the house of the LORD, and put it on the north side of the altar.

15 And king Ahaz commanded Ū-rī′-jah the priest, saying, Upon the great altar burn the morning burnt offering, and the evening meat offering, and the king's burnt sacrifice, and his meat offering, with the burnt offering of all the people of the land, and their meat offering, and their drink offerings; and sprinkle upon it all the blood of the burnt offering, and all the blood of the sacrifice: and the brasen altar shall be for me to enquire *by.*

16 Thus did Ū-rī′jah the priest, according to all that king Ahaz commanded.

17 ¶And king Ahaz cut off the borders of the bases, and removed the laver from off them; and took down the sea from off the brasen oxen that *were* under it, and put it upon a pavement of stones.

18 And the covert for the sabbath that they had built in the house, and the king's entry without, turned he from the house of the LORD for the king of Assyria.

19 ¶Now the rest of the acts of Ahaz which he did, *are* they not written in the book of the chronicles of the kings of Jūdah?

20 And Ahaz slept with his fathers, and was buried with his fathers in the city of David: and Hĕz-e-kī′ah his son reigned in his stead.

CHAPTER 17

IN the twelfth year of Ahaz king of Jū-dah began Hō-shē′a the son of Ē′lah to reign in Sa-mâ′rī-a over Israel nine years.

2 And he did *that which was* evil in the sight of the LORD, but not as the kings of Israel that were before him.

3 Against him came up Shăl-man-ē′ser king of Assyria; and Hō-shē′a became his servant, and gave him presents.

4 And the king of Assyria found conspiracy in Hō-shē′a: for he had sent messengers to So king of Egypt, and

that this was an Assyrian altar, not one of the Syrians who had been defeated. (However, Amaziah worshiped the gods of the people he had just defeated, cf. II Chr 25:14.)

11-12. Urijah the priest built a replica of the Assyrian altar by the time Ahaz returned from Damascus.

13-16. At Ahaz's command the brazen altar that Solomon had built was moved to the north side of the court. Its new purpose was to be used by Ahaz **to enquire by,** possibly meaning he would use that altar to practice the custom of divining by looking at the entrails of animals. The new altar, known as the **great altar** probably because of its size, took the place of the brazen altar and had two functions: (1) It stood at a prominent place as a symbol of allegiance to Assyria; and (2) it was used syncretistically for worship—offering all the prescribed sacrifices to Jehovah, on a pagan altar from Assyria.

17. He also pillaged the Temple by stripping the furnishings of valuable ornamentation. He **cut off the borders of the bases,** i.e., he dismantled the portable lavers constructed by Solomon (see note on I Kgs 7:27-39). The **brazen oxen** were confiscated for their metal; and the large laver, **the sea,** was placed on a cheap substitute, i.e., on stones.

18. He also altered the structure of the Temple, removing the king's entry. All was done **for the king of Assyria,** i.e., because of Tiglath-pileser III. "Ahaz, fearing the cupidity of the Assyrian king, took the precaution of removing the costly articles and ornamental structures from their exposed positions so that the Assyrian agents might not see them and demand that they be handed to their king" (Slotki, p. 262).

19-20. Fortunately for Judah, Ahaz was replaced by a godly son, **Hezekiah.**

J. The Fall of Samaria. 17:1-41.

17:1-2. The last king to reign in Israel was **Hoshea,** who gained the throne by conspiracy (15:30). Tiglath-pileser took credit for placing Hoshea on the throne; so apparently he was pro-Assyrian at the first. He was an evil king, but he did not rank with his predecessors. He reigned nine years (ca. 732-722 B.C.) until Samaria fell to Assyria.

3-4. Tiglath-pileser III died in 727 B.C., and his son **Shalmaneser** (V) became the king of Assyria to which Hoshea gave **presents,** i.e., tribute.

After six years of paying tribute, Hoshea sought help from Egypt against Assyria and failed to pay tribute. He had learned that once one became a vassal of Assyria, he was always a vassal. Shalmaneser had Hoshea imprisoned.

brought no present to the king of Assyria, as *he had done* year by year: therefore the king of Assyria shut him up, and bound him in prison.

5 Then the king of Assyria came up throughout all the land, and went up to Sa-mâ'rĭ-a, and besieged it three years.

6 In the ninth year of Hō-shē'a the king of Assyria took Sa-mâ'rĭ-a, and carried Israel away into Assyria, and placed them in Hā'lah and in Hā'bôr *by* the river of Gō'zăn, and in the cities of the Medes.

7 For *so* it was, that the children of Israel had sinned against the Lᴏʀᴅ their God, which had brought them up out of the land of Egypt, from under the hand of Pharaoh king of Egypt, and had feared other gods,

8 And walked in the statutes of the heathen, whom the Lᴏʀᴅ cast out from before the children of Israel, and of the kings of Israel, which they had made.

9 And the children of Israel did secretly *those* things that *were* not right against the Lᴏʀᴅ their God, and they built them high places in all their cities, from the tower of the watchmen to the fenced city.

10 And they set them up images and groves in every high hill, and under every green tree:

11 And there they burnt incense in all the high places, as *did* the heathen whom the Lᴏʀᴅ carried away before them; and wrought wicked things to provoke the Lᴏʀᴅ to anger:

12 For they served idols, whereof the Lᴏʀᴅ had said unto them, Ye shall not do this thing.

13 Yet the Lᴏʀᴅ testified against Israel, and against Jūdah, by all the prophets, *and by* all the seers, saying, Turn ye from your evil ways, and keep my commandments *and* my statutes, according to all the law which I commanded your fathers, and which I sent to you by my servants the prophets.

14 Notwithstanding they would not hear, but hardened their necks, like to the neck of their fathers, that did not believe in the Lᴏʀᴅ their God.

15 And they rejected his statutes, and his covenant that he made with their fathers, and his testimonies which he testified against them; and they followed vanity, and became vain, and went after the heathen that *were* round about them, *concerning* whom the Lᴏʀᴅ had charged them, that they should not do like them.

16 And they left all the commandments of the Lᴏʀᴅ their God, and made

5. While Israel was without a functioning king, the Assyrians came through the land, apparently taking the smaller cities until they reached Samaria. Samaria was held in siege for three years.

6. In 722 B.C. the Assyrians took Samaria, and Israel fell permanently. **The king of Assyria** is identified by most historians as Sargon II. Shalmaneser V died, and Sargon II succeeded him in the same year Samaria fell. Sargon II claims credit for taking Samaria (Thomas, pp. 59-60), but there is a strong case that in his later years he assumed credit that was due Shalmaneser V (cf. Free, pp. 199-200). So Shalmaneser V was the king who captured Samaria; and when he died, Sargon II carried out the deportation of 27,290 Israelites (by his count) to **Assyria,** i.e., the territory under Assyrian control. **Halah** is in the region of Nineveh. **Habor** refers to the region around the Habor River, a northern tributary of the Euphrates River. **Gozan** was probably north of Habor. **The cities of the Medes** refers to the most easternly part of the Assyrian empire.

Verses 7-23 not only review Israel's history, but also lists the many reasons why Israel deserved the judgment she received.

7. **Israel had sinned against the Lᴏʀᴅ.** Samaria did not fall to Assyria because God was helpless to rescue Israel. The Exodus from Egypt was proof of that.

8. Israel's sin fell into two related categories: (1) **Statutes of the heathen,** i.e., the religious ways of the Canaanites; and (2) **of the kings of Israel,** i.e., the idolatry supported by her kings, namely worship of the golden calves (cf. vs. 16).

9-12. The Israelites had practiced idolatry everywhere in flagrant obedience to the clear command, **Ye shall not do this thing.**

13-15. God graciously had sent prophets repeatedly to warn Israel to turn from her idolatries and return to God, but they refused to respond. Instead, they rejected **his statutes, and his covenant** with them in willing rebellion.

16-17. The extent of Israel's paganism is detailed. **Two calves,** i.e., the two gods erected by Jeroboam at Dan and

729

them molten images, *even* two calves, and made a grove, and worshipped all the host of heaven, and served Bā'al.

17 And they caused their sons and their daughters to pass through the fire, and used divination and enchantments, and sold themselves to do evil in the sight of the LORD, to provoke him to anger.

18 Therefore the LORD was very angry with Israel, and removed them out of his sight: there was none left but the tribe of Jūdah only.

19 Also Jūdah kept not the commandments of the LORD their God, but walked in the statutes of Israel which they made.

20 And the LORD rejected all the seed of Israel, and afflicted them, and delivered them into the hand of spoilers, until he had cast them out of his sight.

21 For he rent Israel from the house of David; and they made Jĕr-o-bō'am the son of Nĕ'băt king: and Jĕr-o-bō'am drave Israel from following the LORD, and made them sin a great sin.

22 For the children of Israel walked in all the sins of Jĕr-o-bō'am which he did; they departed not from them;

23 Until the LORD removed Israel out of his sight, as he had said by all his servants the prophets. So was Israel carried away out of their own land to Assyria unto this day.

24 ¶And the king of Assyria brought *men* from Babylon, and from Cū'thah, and from Ā'va, and from Hā'măth, and from Sĕph-ar-vā'im, and placed *them* in the cities of Sa-mâ'rĭ-a instead of the children of Israel: and they possessed Sa-mâ'rĭ-a, and dwelt in the cities thereof.

25 And *so* it was at the beginning of their dwelling there, *that* they feared not the LORD: therefore the LORD sent lions among them, which slew *some* of them.

26 Wherefore they spake to the king of Assyria, saying, The nations which thou hast removed, and placed in the cities of Sa-mâ'rĭ-a, know not the manner of the God of the land: therefore he hath sent lions among them, and, behold, they slay them, because they know not the manner of the God of the land.

27 Then the king of Assyria commanded, saying, Carry thither one of the priests whom ye brought from thence; and let them go and dwell there, and let him teach them the manner of the God of the land.

28 Then one of the priests whom they had carried away from Sa-mâ'rĭ-a came and dwelt in Bĕth-el, and taught them how they should fear the LORD.

29 Howbeit every nation made gods of their own, and put *them* in the houses of the high places which the Sa-mâr'i-tans had made, every nation in their cities wherein they dwelt.

30 And the men of Babylon made Sŭc'coth-bē'nŏth, and the men of Cuth made Nēr'găl, and the men of Hā'măth made Ash'ī-ma.

31 And the Ā'vītes made Nĭb'hăz and Tär'tăk, and the Sĕph'ar-vītes burnt

Beth-el (I Kgs 12:28-29); **A grove,** i.e., an Asherah; the **host of heaven,** probably the stellar deities of Assyria (cf. Moses' explicit prohibition in Deut 4:14-19); **Baal,** the worship of which reached its height during the reign of Ahab and Jezebel; **pass through the fire,** probably a reference to child sacrifice to the god Molech (cf. Lev 18:21; Deut 18:10); **divination and enchantments,** i.e., practices of magic and the occult (cf. Deut 18:10-12). To summarize, they **sold themselves to do evil.**

18-22. Judah alone was left, but she needed to take heed. She was guilty of the same sin as Israel, only to a lesser degree. Therefore, similar judgment was inevitable for Judah if she did not repent.

23-24. Following this lengthy review of Israel's sin, the writer repeats Israel's judgment, deportation (cf. vs. 6). Isaiah (Isa 7:8) told Ahaz in 735 B.C. that the deportation process would last sixty-five years (until 669 B.C.). Therefore, the last Assyrian king involved in the deportation was Esar-haddon (cf. Ezr 4:2). Israel's territory was repopulated in a reverse deportation of foreigners from **Cuthah,** a city north of **Babylon,** and from **Ava, Hamath,** and **Sepharvaim,** all possibly Syrian cities.

25-26. The new settlers did not fare well in the land. They recognized the **lions** as judgment from Jehovah; so they requested that a priest teach them **the manner of the . . . land,** i.e., the local religion.

27-28. The Assyrian king obliged by returning an Israelite priest (one certain to be contaminated with calf-worship!) to teach them to fear Jehovah.

29-33. The term **Samaritans** refers to the Israelites who had inhabited the land. Later, the Samaritans came to be known as a mongrel race, Jews and those who had been transplanted in their district. It was these people with whom the southern Jews had no dealing (Jn 4:9).

Jehovah was worshiped merely as another god. All the transplanted peoples still worshiped their local deities.

their children in fire to A-drăm′me-lĕch and A-năm′me-lĕch, the gods of Sĕph-ar-vā′im.

32 So they feared the LORD, and made unto themselves of the lowest of them priests of the high places, which sacrificed for them in the houses of the high places.

33 They feared the LORD, and served their own gods, after the manner of the nations whom they carried away from thence.

34 Unto this day they do after the former manners: they fear not the LORD, neither do they after their statutes, or after their ordinances, or after the law and commandment which the LORD commanded the children of Jacob, whom he named Israel;

35 With whom the LORD had made a covenant, and charged them, saying, Ye shall not fear other gods, nor bow yourselves to them, nor serve them, nor sacrifice to them:

36 But the LORD, who brought you up out of the land of Egypt with great power and a stretched out arm, him shall ye fear, and him shall ye worship, and to him shall ye do sacrifice.

37 And the statutes, and the ordinances, and the law, and the commandment, which he wrote for you, ye shall observe to do for evermore; and ye shall not fear other gods.

38 And the covenant that I have made with you ye shall not forget; neither shall ye fear other gods.

39 But the LORD your God ye shall fear; and he shall deliver you out of the hand of all your enemies.

40 Howbeit they did not hearken, but they did after their former manner.

41 So these nations feared the LORD, and served their graven images, both their children, and their children's children: as did their fathers, so do they unto this day.

CHAPTER 18

NOW it came to pass in the third year of Hŏ-shē′a son of Ē′lah king of Israel, that Hĕz-e-kī′ah the son of Ahaz king of Jūdah began to reign.

2 Twenty and five years old was he when he began to reign; and he reigned twenty and nine years in Jerusalem. His mother's name also was Ā′bī, the daughter of Zăch-a-rī′ah.

3 And he did that which was right in the sight of the LORD, according to all that David his father did.

4 He removed the high places, and brake the images, and cut down the groves, and brake in pieces the brasen serpent that Moses had made: for unto those days the children of Israel did burn incense to it: and he called it Ne-hūsh′tan.

5 He trusted in the LORD God of Israel; so that after him was none like him among all the kings of Jūdah, nor any that were before him.

6 For he clave to the LORD, and departed not from following him, but kept his commandments, which the LORD commanded Moses.

7 And the LORD was with him; and he

34-41. Unto this day, i.e., the day of the writing of Kings, even after the fall and deportation, the Jews continued in their syncretistic religious ways.

II. THE REMAINING KINGDOM. 18:1-25:30

A. The Reign of Hezekiah. 18:1-20:21.

1. His reformation. 18:1-12.

18:1-3. The three chapters devoted to godly **Hezekiah** show how important his reign was. He reigned as sole ruler for twenty-nine years (ca. 715-686 B.C.). If he came to the throne in the third year of Hoshea, he evidently was a co-regent with his father Ahaz (cf. Stigers, 357ff.).

4. He promoted a large scale revival (see II Chr 29:3-31:21 for an expanded account). Almost seven hundred years after Moses had erected the **brazen serpent** for Israel to see (Num 21:8-9), this object was still superstitiously reverenced and even worshiped. Hezekiah reduced this object of veneration to scrap metal and called it **Nehushtan,** i.e., a piece of brass.

5-6. Of all the other godly kings of Judah, none ranked with Hezekiah.

7-8. Ahaz had become a vassal of Assyria (16:7-8), but Heze-

prospered whithersoever he went forth: and he rebelled against the king of Assyria, and served him not.

8 He smote the Philistines, *even* unto Gā′za, and the borders thereof, from the tower of the watchmen to the fenced city.

9 And it came to pass in the fourth year of king Hĕz-e-kī′ah, which *was* the seventh year of Hō-shē′a son of Ē′lah king of Israel, *that* Shăl-man-ē′-ṡer king of Assyria came up against Sa-mâ′rĭ-a, and besieged it.

10 And at the end of three years they took it: *even* in the sixth year of Hĕz-e-kī′ah, that *is* the ninth year of Hō-shē′a king of Israel, Sa-mâ′rĭ-a was taken.

11 And the king of Assyria did carry away Israel unto Assyria, and put them in Hā′lah and in Hā′bôr *by* the river of Gō′zän, and in the cities of the Medes:

12 Because they obeyed not the voice of the LORD their God, but transgressed his covenant, *and* all that Moses the servant of the LORD commanded, and would not hear *them*, nor do *them*.

13 ¶Now in the fourteenth year of king Hĕz-e-kī′ah did Sen-năch′e-rĭb king of Assyria come up against all the fenced cities of Jūdah, and took them.

14 And Hĕz-e-kī′ah king of Jūdah sent to the king of Assyria to Lā′chĭsh, saying, I have offended; return from me: that which thou puttest on me will I bear. And the king of Assyria appointed unto Hĕz-e-kī′ah king of Jūdah three hundred talents of silver and thirty talents of gold.

15 And Hĕz-e-kī′ah gave *him* all the silver that was found in the house of the LORD, and in the treasures of the king's house.

16 At that time did Hĕz-e-kī′ah cut off *the* gold *from* the doors of the temple of the LORD, and *from* the pillars which Hĕz-e-kī′ah king of Jūdah had overlaid, and gave it to the king of Assyria.

17 And the king of Assyria sent Tartan and Răb′-sa-rĭs and Răb′-sha-keh from Lā′chĭsh to king Hĕz-e-kī′ah with a great host against Jerusalem. And they went up and came to Jerusalem. And when they were come up, they came and stood by the conduit of the upper pool, which *is* in the highway of the fuller's field.

18 And when they had called to the king, there came out to them E-lī′a-kĭm the son of Hĭl-kī′ah, which *was* over the household, and Shĕb′na the scribe, and Jō′ah the son of Ā′säph the recorder.

19 And Răb′-sha-keh said unto them, Speak ye now to Hĕz-e-kī′ah, Thus saith the great king, the king of Assyria, What confidence *is* this wherein thou trustest?

20 Thou sayest, (but *they are but* vain words,) *I have* counsel and strength for the war. Now on whom dost thou trust, that thou rebellest against me?

21 Now, behold, thou trustest upon the staff of this bruised reed, *even* upon Egypt, on which if a man lean, it will go into his hand, and pierce it: so *is*

kiah **rebelled** and broke with Assyria. He was able to do this because Sargon II was preoccupied with affairs on Assyria's eastern borders.

9-12. These verses are a review of the events of II Kings 17, synchronizing Hezekiah's reign with those events.

2. His crisis with Assyria. 18:13-19:37.

13. Second Kings 18:13-20:21 is paralleled in Isaiah 36-39. In 705 B.C. **Sennacherib** became king of Assyria. When Assyria was consolidated under his rule, he invaded Judah to enforce Ahaz's commitment to Assyria that Hezekiah had broken (vs. 7).

14. Sennacherib's campaign in 701 B.C. brought him to **Lachish,** only about thirty miles southwest of Jerusalem. Hezekiah quickly admitted his guilt in breaking with Assyria and offered to pay whatever Sennacherib asked.

15-18. Hezekiah had to strip the Temple of its gold to meet Sennacherib's demands. While still at Lachish, he sent three top officials and an army against Jerusalem. **Tartan** is equivalent to commander-in-chief; **Rab-saris** means chief eunuch (cf. Potiphar, Gen 37:36); and **Rab-shakeh** means chief of the officers. These three Assyrians stood **by the conduit** (cf. Isa 7:3) to address Hezekiah's representatives **Eliakim, Shebna,** and **Joah** (for their offices, see note on I Kgs 4:1-6).

19-20. Rab-shakeh delivered Sennacherib's message, so that all those on the walls could hear (cf. vs. 26). **What confidence is this . . . ?** Assyria tried to weaken Hezekiah's defenses by frightening and demoralizing the general populace.

21. Within the walls of Jerusalem there was a pro-Egypt party that wanted to get aid from Egypt. Isaiah warned against such a move (Isa 30:2-7). Sennacherib stressed that Egypt was totally unreliable and too weak to be of any assistance.

Pharaoh king of Egypt unto all that trust on him.

22 But if ye say unto me, We trust in the LORD our God: is not that he, whose high places and whose altars Hĕz-e-kī'-ah hath taken away, and hath said to Jūdah and Jerusalem, Ye shall worship before this altar in Jerusalem?

23 Now therefore, I pray thee, give pledges to my lord the king of Assyria, and I will deliver thee two thousand horses, if thou be able on thy part to set riders upon them.

24 How then wilt thou turn away the face of one captain of the least of my master's servants, and put thy trust on Egypt for chariots and for horsemen?

25 Am I now come up without the LORD against this place to destroy it? The LORD said to me, Go up against this land, and destroy it.

26 Then said E-lī'a-kĭm the son of Hĭl-kī'ah, and Shĕb'na and Jō'ah, unto Rāb'-sha-keh, Speak, I pray thee, to thy servants in the Syrian language; for we understand it: and talk not with us in the Jews' language in the ears of the people that are on the wall.

27 But Rāb'-sha-keh said unto them, Hath my master sent me to thy master, and to thee, to speak these words? hath he not sent me to the men which sit on the wall, that they may eat their own dung, and drink their own piss with you?

28 ¶Then Rāb'-sha-keh stood and cried with a loud voice in the Jews' language, and spake, saying, Hear the word of the great king, the king of As-syria:

29 Thus saith the king, Let not Hĕz-e-kī'ah deceive you: for he shall not be able to deliver you out of his hand:

30 Neither let Hĕz-e-kī'ah make you trust in the LORD, saying, The LORD will surely deliver us, and this city shall not be delivered into the hand of the king of Assyria.

31 Hearken not to Hĕz-e-kī'ah: for thus saith the king of Assyria, Make an agreement with me by a present, and come out to me, and then eat ye every man of his own vine, and every one of his fig tree, and drink ye every one the waters of his cistern:

32 Until I come and take you away to a land like your own land, a land of corn and wine, a land of bread and vineyards, a land of oil olive and of honey, that ye may live, and not die: and hearken not unto Hĕz-e-kī'ah, when he persuadeth you, saying, The LORD will deliver us.

33 Hath any of the gods of the nations delivered at all his land out of the hand of the king of Assyria?

34 Where are the gods of Hā'măth, and of Är'păd? where are the gods of Sĕph-ar-vā'im, Hĕ'na, and Ī'vah? have they delivered Sa-mâ'rĭ-a out of mine hand?

35 Who are they among all the gods of the countries, that have delivered their country out of mine hand, that the LORD should deliver Jerusalem out of mine hand?

36 But the people held their peace,

22. Whose altars Hezekiah hath taken away. Sennacherib completely misinterpreted Hezekiah's revival (vs. 4). Why would God help the king who so sacrilegiously destroyed all the **altars** of worship?

23-24. Sennacherib had such a large army, he could spare **two thousand horses** that he would give to Hezekiah, if he could find enough men to ride them. Who needed Egypt's chariots?

25. The LORD said to me, Go . . . destroy it. He claimed he was on a divine mission. This may have been mere pretense; or he may have been aware of one of Isaiah's sermons, "O Assyrian, the rod of mine anger. . ." (Isa 10:5).

26. Hezekiah's servants requested that Rab-shakeh speak in the **Syrian language,** i.e., Aramaic, the commercial and diplomatic language of the day. They did not want the Jews on the city walls to understand his persuasive speech.

27. That they may eat . . . ? Refusal to surrender would result in a terrible famine (cf. famine conditions in Samaria, 6:24-29).

28-30. Rab-shakeh addressed those on the wall in the **Jews' language,** i.e., Hebrew, warning them of their king's deception.

31-32. Come out to me, i.e., surrender, and eat off the land. **Until I come.** Then he would take them to a good land just like theirs, even providing the transportation. However, the Assyrians had a bad reputation for leading their "guests" away on a leash with hooks through their noses.

33-35. Where are the gods . . . ? In Sennacherib's estimation he had demonstrated that the gods that protected cities greater than Jerusalem were ineffective against him. What god could possibly save Jerusalem?

36-37. The people remained silent, not betraying their un-

and answered him not a word: for the king's commandment was, saying, Answer him not.

37 Then came E-lī′a-kĭm the son of Hĭl-kī′ah, which *was* over the household, and Shĕb′na the scribe, and Jō′ah the son of Ā′săph the recorder, to Hĕz-e-kī′ah with *their* clothes rent, and told him the words of Răb′-sha-keh.

CHAPTER 19

AND it came to pass, when king Hĕz-e-kī′ah heard *it*, that he rent his clothes, and covered himself with sackcloth, and went into the house of the LORD.

2 And he sent E-lī′a-kĭm, which *was* over the household, and Shĕb′na the scribe, and the elders of the priests, covered with sackcloth, to Isaiah the prophet the son of Amoz.

3 And they said unto him, Thus saith Hĕz-e-kī′ah, This day *is* a day of trouble, and of rebuke, and blasphemy: for the children are come to the birth, and *there is* not strength to bring forth.

4 It may be the LORD thy God will hear all the words of Răb′-sha-keh, whom the king of Assyria his master hath sent to reproach the living God; and will reprove the words which the LORD thy God hath heard: wherefore lift up *thy* prayer for the remnant that are left.

5 So the servants of king Hĕz-e-kī′ah came to Isaiah.

6 ¶And Isaiah said unto them, Thus shall ye say to your master, Thus saith the LORD, Be not afraid of the words which thou hast heard, with which the servants of the king of Assyria have blasphemed me.

7 Behold, I will send a blast upon him, and he shall hear a rumour, and shall return to his own land; and I will cause him to fall by the sword in his own land.

8 ¶So Răb′-sha-keh returned, and found the king of Assyria warring against Lĭb′nah: for he had heard that he was departed from Lā′chĭsh.

9 And when he heard say of Tir′hā-kah king of Ē-thĭ-ō′pĭ-a, Behold, he is come out to fight against thee: he sent messengers again unto Hĕz-e-kī′ah, saying,

10 Thus shall ye speak to Hĕz-e-kī′ah king of Judah, saying, Let not thy God in whom thou trustest deceive thee, saying, Jerusalem shall not be delivered into the hand of the king of Assyria.

11 Behold, thou hast heard what the kings of Assyria have done to all lands, by destroying them utterly: and shalt thou be delivered?

12 Have the gods of the nations delivered them which my fathers have destroyed; as Gō′zăn, and Hâ′ran, and Rē′zĕph, and the children of Eden which *were* in The-lā′sar?

13 Where *is* the king of Hā′măth, and the king of Är′păd, and the king of the city of Sĕph-ar-vā′im, of Hē′na, and Ī′vah?

14 ¶And Hĕz-e-kī′ah received the letter of the hand of the messengers, and read it: and Hĕz-e-kī′ah went up into the house of the LORD, and spread it before the LORD.

easiness; and Hezekiah's servants rent their clothes, horrified at Sennacherib's demands, his insults to Hezekiah, and his blasphemies against Jehovah.

19:1. Hezekiah **rent his clothes . . . sackcloth.** Hezekiah presented himself to the Lord in humility and penitence.

2. This is the first mention of **Isaiah,** although his ministry began years before during the reign of Uzziah (Isa 1:1). Hezekiah consulted him, hoping for an encouraging word from the Lord.

3. The people were completely demoralized. It was to them a "day of distress, rebuke, and rejection" (NASB).

4-5. Hezekiah suggested that perhaps the Lord would rebuke Assyria for her blasphemy and scorn, and perhaps Isaiah would pray for the remaining Israelites.

6-7. Be not afraid. Isaiah's answer is one of comfort. Sennacherib would return to his land in fear and die there. Verse 8 is not the fulfillment of Isaiah's prophecy.

8. Rab-shakeh temporarily left Jerusalem to join his king in battle at Libnah, about six miles north of Lachish (see note on 18:14).

9-10. Tirhakah was the Ethiopian pharaoh Taharqa of Egypt's Twenty-fifth Dynasty. He was probably only a commander at this time, but he was made a king later. Rumors were that he was coming up against Sennacherib. Rab-shakeh warned Hezekiah by letter not to get his hopes up, thinking that Egypt would aid him.

11-13. No god had been able to stand in Sennacherib's way. Hezekiah should not be deceived by his god (cf. 18:33-35).

14-19. Hezekiah **spread it** (the letter) **before the LORD.** His prayer included four points: (1) He recognized God's sovereignty, **thou art the God** (vs. 15), and that He had complete authority over what He had created; (2) the pagan Sennacherib had defied the living and sovereign God (vs. 16); (3) Sennach-

15 And Hĕz-e-kī′ah prayed before the LORD, and said, O LORD God of Israel, which dwellest *between* the cherubims, thou art the God, *even* thou alone, of all the kingdoms of the earth; thou hast made heaven and earth.

16 LORD, bow down thine ear, and hear: open, LORD, thine eyes, and see: and hear the words of Sen-năch′e-rĭb, which hath sent him to reproach the living God.

17 Of a truth, LORD, the kings of Assyria have destroyed the nations and their lands,

18 And have cast their gods into the fire: for they *were* no gods, but the work of men's hands, wood and stone: therefore they have destroyed them.

19 Now therefore, O LORD our God, I beseech thee, save thou us out of his hand, that all the kingdoms of the earth may know that thou *art* the LORD God, *even* thou only.

20 ¶Then Isaiah the son of Amoz sent to Hĕz-e-kī′ah, saying, Thus saith the LORD God of Israel, *That* which thou hast prayed to me against Sen-năch′e-rĭb king of Assyria I have heard.

21 This *is* the word that the LORD hath spoken concerning him; The virgin the daughter of Zion hath despised thee, *and* laughed thee to scorn; the daughter of Jerusalem hath shaken her head at thee.

22 Whom hast thou reproached and blasphemed? and against whom hast thou exalted *thy* voice, and lifted up thine eyes on high? *even* against the Holy *One* of Israel.

23 By thy messengers thou hast reproached the Lord, and hast said, With the multitude of my chariots I am come up to the height of the mountains, to the sides of Lebanon, and will cut down the tall cedar trees thereof, *and* the choice fir trees thereof: and I will enter into the lodgings of his borders, *and into* the forest of his Carmel.

24 I have digged and drunk strange waters, and with the sole of my feet have I dried up all the rivers of besieged places.

25 Hast thou not heard long ago *how* I have done it, *and* of ancient times that I have formed it? now have I brought it to pass, that thou shouldest be to lay waste fenced cities *into* ruinous heaps.

26 Therefore their inhabitants were of small power, they were dismayed and confounded; they were *as* the grass of the field, and *as* the green herb, *as* the grass on the house tops, and *as corn* blasted before it be grown up.

27 But I know thy abode, and thy going out, and thy coming in, and thy rage against me.

28 Because thy rage against me and thy tumult is come up into mine ears, therefore I will put my hook in thy nose, and my bridle in thy lips, and I will turn thee back by the way by which thou camest.

29 And this *shall be* a sign unto thee, Ye shall eat this year such things as grow of themselves, and in the second year that which springeth of the same; and in the third year sow ye, and reap,

erib had indeed destroyed other nations and other gods, **for they were no gods** (vss. 17-18)—Sennacherib's claims (18:33-35; 19:11-13) only proved that pagan gods were not gods; and (4) he requested that God save His people and show the world that Jehovah was the only God.

20. Thus saith the LORD. God had heard Hezekiah's prayer, and His answer is recorded in verses 21-34. Verses 21-28 are directed to Sennacherib.

21. The virgin the daughter is Jerusalem. She had not been violated nor conquered since the days of David. To shake the head is a gesture of decision (cf. Ps 22:7).

22. Sennacherib had not mocked or reviled Jerusalem or Hezekiah, but the **Holy One of Israel.**

23-24. Expressions are used metaphorically here to depict Sennacherib's boasts of easy victories and successful achievements.

25. I have done it. Sennacherib had claimed personal credit for his successes, but he had been a mere instrument in the hand of God—**I brought it to pass.**

26. Therefore . . . or small power. Sennacherib's accomplishments were not to be attributed to his strength or other nations' weaknesses, but to God who had ordained them to fall.

27-28. I know. The omniscient God knew every movement of Sennacherib. God knew all about Sennacherib's **rage,** i.e., his blasphemy against God and his **tumult,** i.e., his arrogance. **I will put my hook in thy nose.** Sennacherib had planned to lead the Jews shamefully back to Assyria (see note on 18:31-32), but he himself would return shamefully, led by the God he had reviled.

29-31. These verses pertain to the remnant and their crops. Sennacherib had devastated their crops for that year. The following year they would eat **things as grow of themselves,** which may indicate a sabbatical year (cf. Lev 25). By the third year they would return to a normal agricultural cycle.

and plant vineyards, and eat the fruits thereof.

30 And the remnant that is escaped of the house of Jūdah shall yet again take root downward, and bear fruit upward.

31 For out of Jerusalem shall go forth a remnant, and they that escape out of mount Zion: the zeal of the LORD *of hosts* shall do this.

32 Therefore thus saith the LORD concerning the king of Assyria, He shall not come into this city, nor shoot an arrow there, nor come before it with shield, nor cast a bank against it.

33 By the way that he came, by the same shall he return, and shall not come into this city, saith the LORD.

34 For I will defend this city, to save it, for mine own sake, and for my servant David's sake.

35 ¶And it came to pass that night, that the angel of the LORD went out, and smote in the camp of the Assyrians an hundred fourscore and five thousand: and when they arose early in the morning, behold, they *were* all dead corpses.

36 So Sen-năch'e-rĭb king of Assyria departed, and went and returned, and dwelt at Nĭn'e-veh.

37 And it came to pass, as he was worshipping in the house of Nĭs'rŏch his god, that A-drăm'me-lĕch and Sha-rē'zer his sons smote him with the sword: and they escaped into the land of Är-mē'nĭa. And Ē'sar-hăd'don his son reigned in his stead.

CHAPTER 20

IN those days was Hĕz-e-kī'ah sick unto death. And the prophet Isaiah the son of Amoz came to him, and said unto him, Thus saith the LORD, Set thine house in order; for thou shalt die, and not live.

2 Then he turned his face to the wall, and prayed unto the LORD, saying,

3 I beseech thee, O LORD, remember now how I have walked before thee in truth and with a perfect heart, and have done *that which is* good in thy sight. And Hĕz-e-kī'ah wept sore.

4 And it came to pass, afore Isaiah was gone out into the middle court, that the word of the LORD came to him, saying,

5 Turn again, and tell Hĕz-e-kī'ah the captain of my people, Thus saith the LORD, the God of David thy father, I have heard thy prayer, I have seen thy tears: behold, I will heal thee: on the third day thou shalt go up unto the house of the LORD.

6 And I will add unto thy days fifteen years; and I will deliver thee and this city out of the hand of the king of Assyr-

32-34. Here is absolute proof that Assyria would not harm Jerusalem, for not so much as one **arrow** would be shot in the city. God would **defend this city.**

35. The angel of the LORD (see note on 1:3) killed 185,000 Assyrians that very night. The Greek historian, Herodotus, records the tradition that mice ate the Assyrians' bowstrings and leather shield handles. Many modern scholars, therefore, attribute the death of the Assyrians to the bubonic plague, but this is doubtful. It was clearly the miraculous judgment of God, regardless of the way He caused the deaths.

36. Sennacherib returned to Nineveh. In an inscription he says he defeated other Palestinian cities; but concerning Hezekiah and Jerusalem he could only say, "As for himself, like a bird in a cage in his royal city Jerusalem, I shut (him) up." As Free has noted, actually, Hezekiah was reposing quite safe in his "cage".

37. Twenty years later (681 B.C.) he was killed by his own two sons (cf. vs. 7) while he was worshiping his god.

3. His illness. 20:1-21.

20:1. In those days. It is probable that the events of this chapter occurred before Sennacherib's invasion (cf. Whitcomb, pp. 125-126). It is unlikely that Hezekiah would show his Babylonian visitors all **his precious things** (vs. 13) if he had just given them to Sennacherib for tribute. Also, II Chronicles 32:25-26 indicates that after Hezekiah was healed, he became proud; and divine wrath (judgment from Sennacherib) was upon him.

Thou shalt die. The reason is not given, but verse 5 shows the pronouncement to be conditional.

2-3. Remember. . . . Hezekiah was quick to pray as he appealed to his faithful performance. **A perfect heart** does not mean he was perfect, but he served God wholeheartedly. **Hezekiah wept sore.** Isaiah 38:10-20 expresses the anguish of his soul at this time, for he did not want to die before completing his moral reform.

4. God's answer was equally prompt, **afore Isaiah was gone out.**

5-6. This message was easier to deliver than the last one (vs. 1), **I will heal thee . . . I will add fifteen years.**

ia; and I will defend this city for mine own sake, and for my servant David's sake.

7 And Isaiah said, Take a lump of figs. And they took and laid *it* on the boil, and he recovered.

8 ¶And Hĕz-e-kī'ah said unto Isaiah, What *shall be* the sign that the LORD will heal me, and that I shall go up into the house of the LORD the third day?

9 And Isaiah said, This sign shalt thou have of the LORD, that the LORD will do the thing that he hath spoken: shall the shadow go forward ten degrees, or go back ten degrees?

10 And Hĕz-e-kī'ah answered, It is a light thing for the shadow to go down ten degrees: nay, but let the shadow return backward ten degrees.

11 And Isaiah the prophet cried unto the LORD: and he brought the shadow ten degrees backward, by which it had gone down in the dial of Ahaz.

12 ¶At that time Be-rō'dăch–băl'a-dan, the son of Băl'a-dan, king of Babylon, sent letters and a present unto Hĕz-e-kī'ah: for he had heard that Hĕz-e-kī'ah had been sick.

13 And Hĕz-e-kī'ah hearkened unto them, and shewed them all the house of his precious things, the silver, and the gold, and the spices, and the precious ointment, and *all* the house of his armour, and all that was found in his treasures: there was nothing in his house, nor in all his dominion, that Hĕz-e-kī'ah shewed them not.

14 ¶Then came Isaiah the prophet unto king Hĕz-e-kī'ah, and said unto him, What said these men? and from whence came they unto thee? And Hĕz-e-kī'ah said, They are come from a far country, *even* from Babylon.

15 And he said, What have they seen in thine house? And Hĕz-e-kī'ah answered, All *the things* that *are* in mine house have they seen: there is nothing among my treasures that I have not shewed them.

16 And Isaiah said unto Hĕz-e-kī'ah, Hear the word of the LORD.

17 Behold, the days come, that all that *is* in thine house, and that which thy fathers have laid up in store unto this day, shall be carried into Babylon: nothing shall be left, saith the LORD.

18 And of thy sons that shall issue from thee, which thou shalt beget, shall they take away; and they shall be eunuchs in the palace of the king of Babylon.

7. The **lump of figs,** a poultice, was the medication of that day for boils. **He recovered.** This recovery is either local (i.e., for the boil only), and the rest of the body remained weak; or it was total, and it followed the sign given in verses 8-11.

8. Hezekiah requested a **sign,** some extraordinary event to confirm the spoken promise that he would be healed.

9-10. Hezekiah had a choice of signs, i.e., the lengthening or shortening of the sun's shadow. He chose what he thought to be the most difficult.

11. The **dial** (lit. steps) was not the traditional sun dial. Perhaps this phrase should be rendered, "And he brought the shadow on the stairway back ten steps by which it had gone down . . ." (NASB). This was obviously caused by the miraculous intervention of God.

Opinion differs widely over the nature of this miracle. Although it may have been a universal phenomenon, some have suggested that it was a local prolongation of light in Judah. Comparing the account in II Chronicles 32, Hezekiah was promised a "sign" (Heb *mōpēt,* II Chr 32:24), but later the Babylonian ambassadors inquired of the "wonder (Heb *mōpēt)* that was done in the land" (II Chr 32:31). If this is taken to mean Judah, it would be a local phenomenon. If "in the land" (Heb *ba'erets)* is understood as "in the earth," it would indicate a worldwide miracle. Neither interpretation reduces the miraculous nature of the phenomenon.

12-13. **Berodach-baladan** should read Merodach-baladan (cf. Isa 39:1), the Babylonian king Marduk-apla-iddina. He sent ambassadors, supposedly to congratulate Hezekiah on his recovery and to inquire of the miracle (II Chr 32:31); but most historians believe his real purpose was to induce him to rebel against the Assyrians.

14-15. Possibly because of God's promise of defense (vs. 6), Hezekiah's self-confidence led him to show all his treasures to the Babylonians.

16-18. The Babylonians to whom Hezekiah carelessly had exposed everything would someday return to claim for themselves Judah's possessions and people, including the king's sons.

19 Then said Hĕz-e-kī′ah unto Isaiah, Good *is* the word of the LORD which thou hast spoken. And he said, *Is it* not *good,* if peace and truth be in my days?

20 ¶And the rest of the acts of Hĕz-e-kī′ah, and all his might, and how he made a pool, and a conduit, and brought water into the city, *are* they not written in the book of the chronicles of the kings of Jūdah?

21 And Hĕz-e-kī′ah slept with his fathers: and Ma-năs′seh his son reigned in his stead.

CHAPTER 21

MA-NĂS′SEH *was* twelve years old when he began to reign, and reigned fifty and five years in Jerusalem. And his mother's name *was* Hĕph′zī-bah.

2 And he did *that which was* evil in the sight of the LORD, after the abominations of the heathen, whom the LORD cast out before the children of Israel.

3 For he built up again the high places which Hĕz-e-kī′ah his father had destroyed; and he reared up altars for Bā′al, and made a grove, as did Ahab king of Israel; and worshipped all the host of heaven, and served them.

4 And he built altars in the house of the LORD, of which the LORD said, In Jerusalem will I put my name.

5 And he built altars for all the host of heaven in the two courts of the house of the LORD.

6 And he made his son pass through the fire, and observed times, and used enchantments, and dealt with familiar spirits and wizards: he wrought much wickedness in the sight of the LORD, to provoke *him* to anger.

7 And he set a graven image of the grove that he had made in the house, of which the LORD said to David, and to Solomon his son, In this house, and in Jerusalem, which I have chosen out of all tribes of Israel, will I put my name for ever:

8 Neither will I make the feet of Israel move any more out of the land which I gave their fathers; only if they will observe to do according to all that I have commanded them, and according to all the law that my servant Moses commanded them.

9 But they hearkened not: and Ma-năs′seh seduced them to do more evil than did the nations whom the LORD destroyed before the children of Israel.

10 ¶And the LORD spake by his servants the prophets, saying,

11 Because Ma-năs′seh king of Jūdah hath done these abominations, *and* hath done wickedly above all that the Amorītes did, which *were* before him, and hath made Jūdah also to sin with his idols:

12 Therefore thus saith the LORD God of Israel, Behold, I *am* bringing *such* evil upon Jerusalem and Jūdah, that whosoever heareth of it, both his ears shall tingle.

13 And I will stretch over Jerusalem the line of Sa-mâ′rī-a, and the plummet of the house of Ahab: and I will wipe

19-21. Hezekiah's response can be interpreted one of two ways: (1) He was glad judgment would not fall on him personally, unconcerned for those upon whom the judgment would come; or (2) he was admitting God's justice in the sentence, but was recognizing God's mercy in postponing the judgment, allowing time for his descendants to avert it by their loyalty to God. (For Hezekiah's construction of the **conduit,** see II Chr 32:3-4, 30.)

B. The Apostasy of Manasseh and Amon. 21:1-26.

1. Manasseh. 21:1-18.

21:1. Hezekiah's twelve-year-old son, **Manasseh,** reigned for fifty-five years (ca. 695-642 B.C.), the longest reign of any Jewish king. Since it is impossible to fit his reign into the period remaining until the fall of Jerusalem (586 B.C.), he probably was a co-regent with his father for about ten years.

2. The years of co-regency had little spiritual impact on Manasseh, for he was the most wicked king of Judah.

3-5. This "Ahab of Judah" sponsored a movement to undo his father's reformation. In open defiance of Jehovah, he restored the worship of **Baal,** Asherah (**grove**), and astral deities (**the host of heaven**), even erecting altars for them in the Temple.

6-8. Pass through the fire. Manasseh sacrificed his own son to the Ammonite god Molech (cf. 3:27). From Psalm 106:36-37 we learn the connection of Molech worship to demonism. **Enchantments . . . familiar spirits and wizards** all pertain to an outburst of demon-energized occultism supported by the king in defiance of clear Mosaic prohibitions (Deut 18:10-12) and God's promise of His presence in Jerusalem (I Kgs 9:3).

9-11. Thanks to Manasseh, Judah became more heathen than the peoples the Israelites had destroyed under the leadership of Moses and Joshua.

12-13. Both his ears shall tingle, i.e., the news of Jerusalem's punishment would make one's ears hurt as a sharp discordant note does. **The line . . . and the plummet,** i.e., the measuring line and the plumb line, two standards of the builder, are used here metaphorically as standards of judgment to come upon Jerusalem as it had come upon Samaria. **Turning it** (the dish) **upside down** is another metaphor depicting the depopulation of Judah (cf. Jer 51:34).

Jerusalem as *a man* wipeth a dish, wiping *it*, and turning *it* upside down.

14 And I will forsake the remnant of mine inheritance, and deliver them into the hand of their enemies; and they shall become a prey and a spoil to all their enemies;

15 Because they have done *that which was* evil in my sight, and have provoked me to anger, since the day their fathers came forth out of Egypt, even unto this day.

16 Moreover Ma-năs'seh shed innocent blood very much, till he had filled Jerusalem from one end to another; beside his sin wherewith he made Jūdah to sin, in doing *that which was* evil in the sight of the Lord.

17 ¶Now the rest of the acts of Ma-năs'seh, and all that he did, and his sin that he sinned, *are* they not written in the book of the chronicles of the kings of Jūdah?

18 And Ma-năs'seh slept with his fathers, and was buried in the garden of his own house, in the garden of Ŭz'za: and Ämon his son reigned in his stead.

19 ¶Ämon *was* twenty and two years old when he began to reign, and he reigned two years in Jerusalem. And his mother's name *was* Me-shŭl'le-mĕth, the daughter of Hâ'rūz of Jŏt'-bah.

20 And he did *that which was* evil in the sight of the Lord, as his father Ma-năs'seh did.

21 And he walked in all the way that his father walked in, and served the idols that his father served, and worshipped them:

22 And he forsook the Lord God of his fathers, and walked not in the way of the Lord.

23 And the servants of Ämon conspired against him, and slew the king in his own house.

24 And the people of the land slew all them that had conspired against king Ämon; and the people of the land made Jō-sī'ah his son king in his stead.

25 Now the rest of the acts of Ämon which he did, *are* they not written in the book of the chronicles of the kings of Jūdah?

26 And he was buried in his sepulchre in the garden of Ŭz'za: and Jō-sī'ah his son reigned in his stead.

CHAPTER 22

JŌ-SĪ'AH *was* eight years old when he began to reign, and he reigned thirty and one years in Jerusalem. And his mother's name *was* Je-dī'dah, the daughter of Ăd-a-ī'ah of Bŏs'căth.

2 And he did *that which was* right in the sight of the Lord, and walked in all the way of David his father, and turned not aside to the right hand or to the left.

3 ¶And it came to pass in the eighteenth year of king Jō-sī'ah, *that* the king sent Shā'phan the son of Ăz-a-lī'ah, the son of Me-shŭl'lam, the scribe, to the house of the Lord, saying,

4 Go up to Hĭl-kī'ah the high priest, that he may sum the silver which is brought into the house of the Lord,

14-15. The **remnant** is the remaining tribe, Judah.

16. He shed **innocent blood,** probably those who opposed his religious policies. According to Jewish tradition, the prophet Isaiah was sawn asunder by him (cf. Heb 11:37).

17-18. Manasseh's captivity, humbling, and repentance, all which occurred late in his reign (II Chr 33:11-19), are not mentioned here, evidently because they left no lasting impression.

2. Amon. 21:19-26.

19-20. Manasseh's son, **Amon,** had a short, evil reign of only two years (ca. 642-640 B.C.).

21-22. That Manasseh's wickedness, and not his life after repentance, influenced his son is observable in Amon's embrace of idolatry.

23-26. Though a reason is not given, Amon, like Joash (12:20-21), died at the hands of his servants. That the conspiracy was not a popular overthrow of his policies is seen by **the people of the land,** i.e., the general population, slaying the assassins and setting Amon's son, Josiah, on the throne.

C. The Reign and Reformation of Josiah. 22:1-23:35.

1. Repairing the Temple and finding the Book of the Law. 22:1-20.

22:1-2. **Josiah** reigned thirty-one years (ca. 640-609 B.C.). Due to his young age (eight years), undoubtedly he was under the guardianship of the elders or the priests for a time (see note on Joash, 11:17-18). Like Hezekiah, more space is given in this book to his reign (nearly two chapters), showing the importance of it.

And he did that which was right. According to II Chronicles 34:3-7, he began seeking the Lord at age sixteen, his eighth year, and began his religious reformation in his twelfth year.

3-7. Six years later, his eighteenth (622 B.C.), Josiah called for the repair of the Temple. Since Joash had repaired the Temple (12:4ff.), there was ample occasion for deterioration (cf. the evil reigns of Ahaz and Manesseh, and Hezekiah's stripping the Temple of valuables to pay tribute).

Hilkiah was to **sum the silver,** i.e., take the silver that had been collected up to that point and make an accurate account of

which the keepers of the door have gathered of the people:

5 And let them deliver it into the hand of the doers of the work, that have the oversight of the house of the LORD: and let them give it to the doers of the work which *is* in the house of the LORD, to repair the breaches of the house,

6 Unto carpenters, and builders, and masons, and to buy timber and hewn stone to repair the house.

7 Howbeit there was no reckoning made with them of the money that was delivered into their hand, because they dealt faithfully.

8 ¶And Hĭl-kī′ah the high priest said unto Shā′phan the scribe, I have found the book of the law in the house of the LORD. And Hĭl-kī′ah gave the book to Shā′phan, and he read it.

9 And Shā′phan the scribe came to the king, and brought the king word again, and said, Thy servants have gathered the money that was found in the house, and have delivered it into the hand of them that do the work, that have the oversight of the house of the LORD.

10 And Shā′phan the scribe shewed the king, saying, Hĭl-kī′ah the priest hath delivered me a book. And Shā′-phan read it before the king.

11 And it came to pass, when the king had heard the words of the book of the law, that he rent his clothes.

12 And the king commanded Hĭl-kī′-ah the priest, and A-hī′kam the son of Shā′phan, and Ăch′bôr the son of Mĭ-chā′iah, and Shā′phan the scribe, and Aşāhiah a servant of the king's, saying,

13 Go ye, enquire of the LORD for me, and for the people, and for all Jūdah, concerning the words of this book that is found: for great *is* the wrath of the LORD that is kindled against us, because our fathers have not hearkened unto the words of this book, to do according unto all that which is written concerning us.

14 So Hĭl-kī′ah the priest, and A-hī′kam, and Ăch′bôr, and Shā′phan, and Aşāhiah, went unto Hŭl′dah the prophetess, the wife of Shăl′lum the son of Tĭk′vah, the son of Här′hăs, keeper of the wardrobe; (now she dwelt in Jerusalem in the college;) and they communed with her.

15 And she said unto them, Thus saith the LORD God of Israel, Tell ye the man that sent you to me,

16 Thus saith the LORD, Behold, I will bring evil upon this place, and upon the inhabitants thereof, *even* all the words of the book which the king of Jūdah hath read:

17 Because they have forsaken me, and have burned incense unto other gods, that they might provoke me to anger with all the works of their hands; therefore my wrath shall be kindled against this place, and shall not be quenched.

the sum of it. His instructions for repairing the Temple were similar to those of Joash.

8-10. The book of the law is the Mosiac law. It cannot be determined whether this book contained the whole Pentateuch, or just Deuteronomy as most modern scholars maintain (the former is preferable). Regardless, in light of the reaction to its reading (vs. 11), Shaphon the scribe must have opened it to a section on God's judgment (cf. Lev 26; Deut 28).

Where the book was found is not stated. Slotki (p. 299) suggests that it was under the silver in the collection chest. Free (p. 215) offers the possibility of its being placed in the cornerstone by Solomon at the time of construction.

Unfortunately, the consensus of liberal scholarship maintains that this book of the Law has no connection with Moses, but was a forgery written just prior to 622 B.C. and used as a basis for Josiah's reformation. This book, having undergone a series of editorial changes between 622 B.C. and about 400 B.C., is what we know today as Deuteronomy. The internal biblical evidence does not support this idea at all. Instead, there are clear statements concerning God's speaking to Moses (Deut 1:1; 5:1; 10:1; 27:1; 29:1; 31:1) and Moses' writing the book (Deut 31:24-26).

11-13. When Josiah heard the Law read, **he rent his clothes,** horrified at his people's neglect of divine commandments and their impending judgment as a result. **Go ye, inquire of the LORD,** i.e., consult a prophet concerning the divine warning to find out if any hope remained for Judah.

14. Jeremiah (Jer 1:1-2) and possibly Zephaniah (Zeph 1:1) were both prophesying at this time, but evidently **Huldah the prophetess** was either better known or closest at hand. She lived in Jerusalem **in the college** (Heb *mishneh*), better translated "in the second quarter," i.e., the second district of the city. She may have been an aunt of Jeremiah (cf. Jer 32:7).

15-17. Huldah's word was not good. The people were too deeply entrenched in apostasy. Therefore, God's wrath had been **kindled;** and it would **not be quenched.**

18 But to the king of Jūdah which sent you to enquire of the Lord, thus shall ye say to him, Thus saith the Lord God of Israel, *As touching* the words which thou hast heard;

19 Because thine heart was tender, and thou hast humbled thyself before the Lord, when thou heardest what I spake against this place, and against the inhabitants thereof, that they should become a desolation and a curse, and hast rent thy clothes, and wept before me; I also have heard *thee*, saith the Lord.

20 Behold therefore, I will gather thee unto thy fathers, and thou shalt be gathered into thy grave in peace; and thine eyes shall not see all the evil which I will bring upon this place. And they brought the king word again.

CHAPTER 23

AND the king sent, and they gathered unto him all the elders of Jūdah and of Jerusalem.

2 And the king went up into the house of the Lord, and all the men of Jūdah and all the inhabitants of Jerusalem with him, and the priests, and the prophets, and all the people, both small and great: and he read in their ears all the words of the book of the covenant which was found in the house of the Lord.

3 And the king stood by a pillar, and made a covenant before the Lord, to walk after the Lord, and to keep his commandments and his testimonies and his statutes with all *their* heart and all *their* soul, to perform the words of this covenant that were written in this book. And all the people stood to the covenant.

4 And the king commanded Hĭl-kī′ah the high priest, and the priests of the second order, and the keepers of the door, to bring forth out of the temple of the Lord all the vessels that were made for Bā′al, and for the grove, and for all the host of heaven: and he burned them without Jerusalem in the fields of Kidron, and carried the ashes of them unto Bĕth-el.

5 And he put down the idolatrous priests, whom the kings of Jūdah had ordained to burn incense in the high places in the cities of Jūdah, and in the places round about Jerusalem; them also that burned incense unto Bā′al, to the sun, and to the moon, and to the planets, and to all the host of heaven.

6 And he brought out the grove from the house of the Lord, without Jerusalem, unto the brook Kidron, and burned it at the brook Kidron, and stamped *it* small to powder, and cast the powder thereof upon the graves of the children of the people.

7 And he brake down the houses of the sodomites, that *were* by the house of the Lord, where the women wove hangings for the grove.

8 And he brought all the priests out of the cities of Jūdah, and defiled the high places where the priests had burned incense, from Gē′ba to Be′er-shē′ba, and brake down the high places of the gates that *were* in the entering in of the gate

18-20. However, because Josiah's **heart was tender,** i.e., he was receptive to the newly found Law, he would be spared this judgment.

Thou shalt be gathered into thy grave in peace. Josiah died in battle (23:29), but he died in a state of peace and fellowship with God as a godly king (cf. Isa 57:21).

2. Instituting reforms. 23:1-28.

It should be noted that Josiah began his purge of idolatry in his twelfth year (II Chr 34:3), and in his eighteenth year (22:3) the purge took on new intensity after the book of the Law had been found. It should be noted also that Josiah's purge was far more extensive than that of Hezekiah.

23:1-2. Although Huldah's prophecy (22:16-17) offered no hope, Josiah devoted himself to eradicating idolatry from Judah. To guarantee any degree of success, Josiah needed the support and assistance of Judah's leadership. Therefore, he called the elders, priests, and prophets to Jerusalem.

3. To address his people, **the king stood by a pillar** (cf. 11:14). This must have been an official location from which a king made his authoritative declarations. The king **made a covenant** (lit., the covenant). The definite article may note especially that this covenant was a direct confirmation of the words **that were written in this book.**

4. The priests of the second order were those of second rank to the high priest.

Verses 4-25 consist of Josiah's actions of reform. All the **vessels** used for idolatrous purposes were removed from the Temple and burned.

5. He put down (lit., caused to cease) the idolatrous priests who burned incense to Baal and various astral deities. **Planets** (lit., constellations) may refer to the signs of the zodiac.

6. He removed the **grove,** i.e., the Asherah, from the Temple (cf. 21:3).

7. The Sodomites were male Baal-cult prostitutes. The **hangings** which the women wove may have been robes for the ritual prostitutes, or they may have been woven curtains behind which the obscene rituals were practiced.

8-9. The **high places,** i.e., the local places of worship, were defiled; and the priests were brought to Jerusalem, where they were allowed to eat priestly food (for sustenance) but were not permitted to perform any priestly tasks.

of Joshua the governor of the city, which were on a man's left hand at the gate of the city.

9 Nevertheless the priests of the high places came not up to the altar of the Lord in Jerusalem, but they did eat of the unleavened bread among their brethren.

10 And he defiled Tō'pheth, which is in the valley of the children of Hĭn'nom, that no man might make his son or his daughter to pass through the fire to Mō'lĕch.

11 And he took away the horses that the kings of Jūdah had given to the sun, at the entering in of the house of the Lord, by the chamber of Nā'-than-mĕ'lech the chamberlain, which was in the suburbs, and burned the chariots of the sun with fire.

12 And the altars that were on the top of the upper chamber of Ahaz, which the kings of Jūdah had made, and the altars which Ma-năs'seh had made in the two courts of the house of the Lord, did the king beat down, and brake them down from thence, and cast the dust of them into the brook Kidron.

13 And the high places that were before Jerusalem, which were on the right hand of the mount of corruption, which Sŏlomon the king of Israel had builded for Ăsh'to-rĕth the abomination of the Zī-dō'nī-ans, and for Chē'-mŏsh the abomination of the Moabites, and for Mĭl'com the abomination of the children of Ammon, did the king defile.

14 And he brake in pieces the images, and cut down the groves, and filled their places with the bones of men.

15 ¶Moreover the altar that was at Bĕth-el, and the high place which Jĕr-o-bŏ'am the son of Nē'băt, who made Israel to sin, had made, both that altar and the high place he brake down, and burned the high place, and stamped it small to powder, and burned the grove.

16 And as Jō-sī'ah turned himself, he spied the sepulchres that were there in the mount, and sent, and took the bones out of the sepulchres, and burned them upon the altar, and polluted it, according to the word of the Lord which the man of God proclaimed, who proclaimed these words.

17 Then he said, What title is that that I see? And the men of the city told him, It is the sepulchre of the man of God, which came from Jūdah, and proclaimed these things that thou hast done against the altar of Bĕth-el.

18 And he said, Let him alone; let no man move his bones. So they let his bones alone, with the bones of the prophet that came out of Sa-mā'rī-a.

19 And all the houses also of the high places that were in the cities of Sa-mā'-rī-a, which the kings of Israel had made to provoke the Lord to anger, Jō-sī'ah took away, and did to them according to all the acts that he had done in Bĕth-el.

20 And he slew all the priests of the high places that were there upon the altars, and burned men's bones upon them, and returned to Jerusalem.

21 ¶And the king commanded all the people, saying, Keep the passover unto

10-11. Topheth was a large fireplace where children were burned as sacrifices to the Ammonite god Molech. **Horses** were removed and **chariots** that had been dedicated to the use of the sun god were burned.

12. The altars **on the top of the upper chamber of Ahaz** were those situated on the top of his house for worshiping the hosts of heaven, astral deities. For Manasseh's altars, see 21:4.

13-14. The altars Solomon had erected over three hundred years earlier for the gods of his wives had survived Hezekiah's reform. (See note on I Kgs 11:7-8.)

15-16. In fulfillment of prophecy (I Kgs 13:2ff.), Josiah broke the altar at Beth-el, exhumed the bones from nearby sepulchres, and burned them upon the altar.

17-18. What title (i.e., grave marker) **is that I see?** The man of God was venerated, and his bones went untouched. **The prophet . . . of Samaria.** (See note regarding his request in I Kings 13:31-32.)

19-20. Not limiting his reform to Judah, Josiah extended it to **the cities of Samaria,** destroying high places and slaying pagan priests.

21-23. For Josiah's commemoration of the Passover, see notes on the more complete account in II Chronicles 35:1-19.

which Sŏlomon king of Israel had made in the temple of the LORD, as the LORD had said.

14 And he carried away all Jerusalem, and all the princes, and all the mighty men of valour, *even* ten thousand captives, and all the craftsmen and smiths: none remained, save the poorest sort of the people of the land.

15 And he carried away Je-hoi′a-chĭn to Babylon, and the king's mother, and the king's wives, and his officers, and the mighty of the land, *those* carried he into captivity from Jerusalem to Babylon.

16 And all the men of might, *even* seven thousand, and craftsmen and smiths a thousand, all *that were* strong *and* apt for war, even them the king of Babylon brought captive to Babylon.

17 And the king of Babylon made Măt-ta-nī′ah his father's brother king in his stead, and changed his name to Zĕd-e-kī′ah.

18 ¶Zĕd-e-kī′ah *was* twenty and one years old when he began to reign, and he reigned eleven years in Jerusalem. And his mother's name *was* Ha-mū′tal, the daughter of Jĕr-e-mī′ah of Lĭb′nah.

19 And he did *that which was* evil in the sight of the LORD, according to all that Je-hoi′a-kĭm had done.

20 For through the anger of the LORD it came to pass in Jerusalem and Jūdah, until he had cast them out from his presence, that Zĕd-e-kī′ah rebelled against the king of Babylon.

CHAPTER 25

AND it came to pass in the ninth year of his reign, in the tenth month, in the tenth *day* of the month, *that* Nĕb-u-chad-nĕz′zar king of Babylon came, he, and all his host, against Jerusalem, and pitched against it; and they built forts against it round about.

2 And the city was besieged unto the eleventh year of king Zĕd-e-kī′ah.

3 And on the ninth *day* of the *fourth* month the famine prevailed in the city, and there was no bread for the people of the land.

4 And the city was broken up, and all the men of war fled by night by the way of the gate between two walls, which *is* by the king's garden: (now the Chăl′-deĕs *were* against the city round about:) and *the king* went the way toward the plain.

5 And the army of the Chăl′deĕs pursued after the king, and overtook him in the plains of Jericho: and all his army were scattered from him.

6 So they took the king, and brought him up to the king of Babylon to Rĭb′-lah; and they gave judgment upon him.

7 And they slew the sons of Zĕd-e-kī′-ah before his eyes, and put out the eyes of Zĕd-e-kī′ah, and bound him with fetters of brass, and carried him to Babylon.

8 ¶And in the fifth month, on the seventh *day* of the month, which *is* the nineteenth year of king Nĕb-u-chad-nĕz′zar king of Babylon, came Nĕb′u-zar-ă′dan, captain of the guard, a ser-

3. The reign of Zedekiah and destruction of Jerusalem. 24:17-25:21.

17. Mattaniah (Zedekiah), Josiah's son and Jehoiakim's brother, was placed on the throne by Nebuchadnezzar.

18-19. Zedekiah had an evil eleven-year reign (ca. 597-587 B.C.). Though he ruled as king, Zedekiah was never recognized as king by Ezekiel (who dated his ministry in terms of Jehoiachin's reign) or by God (Jer 22:30), for the last legitimate king, Jehoiachin, was still alive, though in captivity.

20. Through the anger of the LORD Zedekiah participated in a rebellion against Babylon that would consequently lead to disaster.

25:1. Nebuchadnezzar besieged Jerusalem in Zedekiah's ninth year . . . tenth month . . . tenth day, i.e., January 15, 588 B.C. For Judah's experiences during the siege, see Jeremiah 37-38.

2-3. The siege of Jerusalem lasted until the **eleventh year . . . ninth day . . . fourth month,** i.e., July 18, 586 B.C. (cf. Jer 39:1-2).

4. The city was broken up, i.e., the walls were breached. With his **men of war** having fled, Zedekiah also attempted to flee to **the plain** (lit., the Arabah), probably referring here to the Jordan Valley.

5-6. His likely intention was to cross Jordan at a ford near Jericho, for he was captured **in the plains of Jericho** and taken to **Riblah** (in Syria) to stand before Nebuchadnezzar.

7. The last thing Zedekiah was permitted to see before he was blinded and taken to Babylon was the death of his sons. There were no claimants left to the throne.

8-10. The fifth month . . . seventh day (same year), i.e., August 15, 586 B.C., **Nebuzaradan, captain of the guard** sacked Jerusalem, burning both the Temple and palace and breaking down the city walls (cf. 23:27).

vant of the king of Babylon, unto Jerusalem:

9 And he burnt the house of the LORD, and the king's house, and all the houses of Jerusalem, and every great *man's* house burnt he with fire.

10 And all the army of the Chăl'dees, that *were with* the captain of the guard, brake down the walls of Jerusalem round about.

11 Now the rest of the people *that were* left in the city, and the fugitives that fell away to the king of Babylon, with the remnant of the multitude, did Něb'u-zar-ā'dan the captain of the guard carry away.

12 But the captain of the guard left of the poor of the land *to be* vinedressers and husbandmen.

13 And the pillars of brass that *were* in the house of the LORD, and the bases, and the brasen sea that *was* in the house of the LORD, did the Chăl'dees break in pieces, and carried the brass of them to Babylon.

14 And the pots, and the shovels, and the snuffers, and the spoons, and all the vessels of brass wherewith they ministered, took they away.

15 And the firepans, and the bowls, *and* such things as *were* of gold, *in* gold, and of silver, *in* silver, the captain of the guard took away.

16 The two pillars, one sea, and the bases which Sŏlomon had made for the house of the LORD; the brass of all these vessels was without weight.

17 The height of the one pillar *was* eighteen cubits, and the chapiter upon it *was* brass: and the height of the chapiter three cubits; and the wreathen work, and pomegranates upon the chapiter round about, all of brass: and like unto these had the second pillar with wreathen work.

18 ¶And the captain of the guard took Se-ra-ī'ah the chief priest, and Zěph-a-nī'ah the second priest, and the three keepers of the door:

19 And out of the city he took an officer that was set over the men of war, and five men of them that were in the king's presence, which were found in the city, and the principal scribe of the host, which mustered the people of the land, and threescore men of the people of the land *that were* found in the city:

20 And Něb'u-zar-ā'dan captain of the guard took these, and brought them to the king of Babylon to Rĭb'lah:

21 And the king of Babylon smote them, and slew them at Rĭb'lah in the land of Hā'măth. So Jūdah was carried away out of their land.

22 ¶And *as for* the people that remained in the land of Jūdah, whom Něb-u-chad-něz'zar king of Babylon had left, even over them he made Gěd-a-lī'ah the son of A-hī'kam, the son of Shā'phan, ruler.

23 And when all the captains of the armies, they and their men, heard that the king of Babylon had made Gěd-a-lī'ah governor, there came to Gěd-a-lī'ah to Miz'pah, even Ĭsh'ma-el the son of Něth-a-nī'ah, and Jŏ-hā'nan the son of

11-12. This was the third and final deportation. Only the poor were left to till the land.

13-17. Anything pertaining to the Temple, whether it was a part of the structure or a furnishing, that was made of gold, silver, or brass, was taken as spoil. Truly, the glory of the Lord had departed the Temple (cf. Ezekiel's vision, Ezk 8-11).

18-21. The leading citizens of the city, who had probably been leaders in resisting Nebuchadnezzar, were also led to Riblah, where Nebuchadnezzar had them executed. The event of these verses probably occurred simultaneously to that of verse 7 (cf. Jer 52:10).

E. The Assassination of Gedaliah and Elevation of Jehoiachin. 25:22-30.

22. Gedaliah was Nebuchadnezzar's appointed governor to remain in the land (note his friendship with Jeremiah, Jer 39:14).

23-24. Gedaliah settled at **Mizpah,** where he was accompanied by Jeremiah (Jer 40:6). Upon Gedaliah's appointment, the remaining captains gathered to him. From Gedaliah's statement of encouragement (vs. 24), one is led to believe these men were pro-Egypt and were advising Gedaliah to migrate to Egypt. One was plotting Gedaliah's death (cf. Jer 40:7-16).

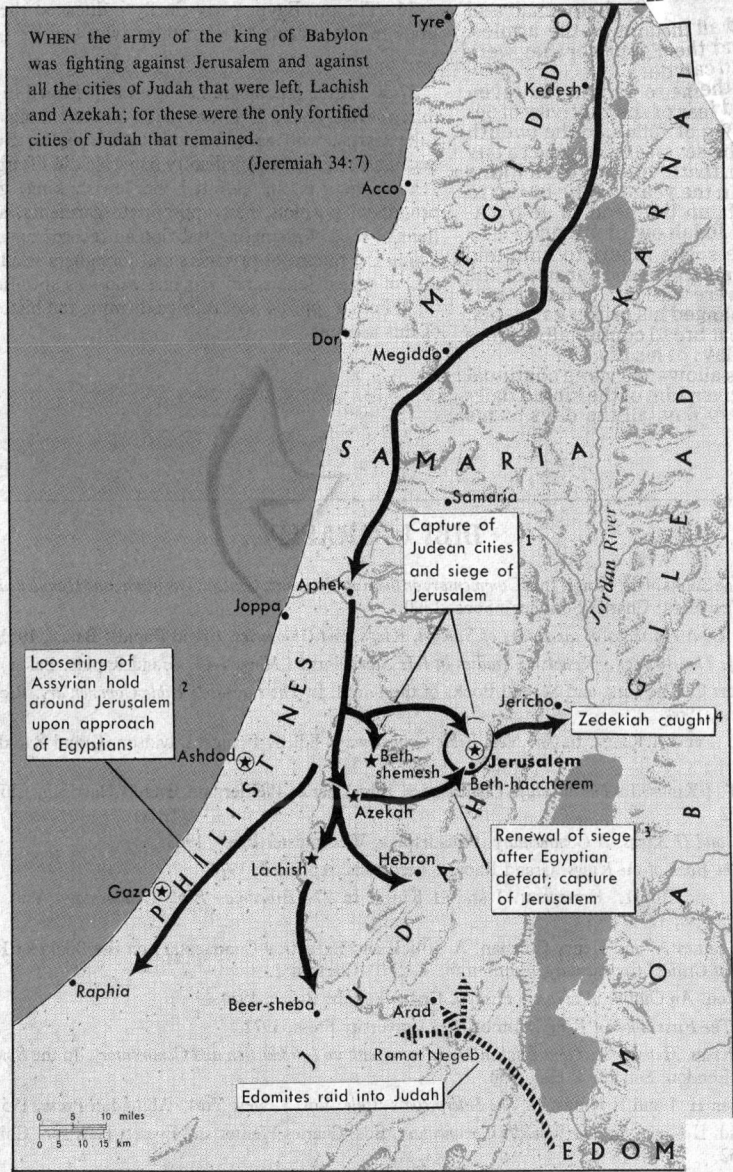

WHEN the army of the king of Babylon was fighting against Jerusalem and against all the cities of Judah that were left, Lachish and Azekah; for these were the only fortified cities of Judah that remained.

(Jeremiah 34:7)

Capture of Judean cities and siege of Jerusalem

Loosening of Assyrian hold around Jerusalem upon approach of Egyptians

Zedekiah caught

Renewal of siege after Egyptian defeat; capture of Jerusalem

Edomites raid into Judah

The Campaign of Nebuchadnezzar Against Judah

Ca-rē′ah, and Se-ra-ī′ah the son of Tăn′-hū-meth the Ne-tōph′a-thīte, and Jā-ăz-a-nī′ah the son of a Mā-ăch′a-thīte, they and their men.

24 And Gĕd-a-lī′ah sware to them, and to their men, and said unto them, Fear not to be the servants of the Chăl′-deeś: dwell in the land, and serve the king of Babylon; and it shall be well with you.

25 But it came to pass in the seventh month, that Ĭsh′ma-el the son of Nĕth-a-nī′ah, the son of E-lĭsh′a-ma, of the seed royal, came, and ten men with him, and smote Gĕd-a-lī′ah, that he died, and the Jews and the Chăl′deeś that were with him at Miz′pah.

25. Ishmael succeeded in assassinating Gedaliah and stirring up turmoil (cf. Jer 41).

eople, both small and
26 And all captains of the armies,
great, and t to Egypt: for they were
arose, and hal'dees.
afraid of t came to pass in the seven
27 And year of the captivity of Je-
and thir king of Jūdah, in the twelfth
hoi'a-ch the seven and twentieth *day*
month nth, *that* Ē'vil–mĕ-ro'dăch king
of the lon in the year that he began to
of B did lift up the head of Je-hoi'a-
reig king of Jūdah out of prison;
ch And he spake kindly to him, and
t his throne above the throne of the
kings that *were* with him in Babylon;
29 And changed his prison garments:
and he did eat bread continually before
him all the days of his life.
30 And his allowance *was* a continual
allowance given him of the king, a daily
rate for every day, all the days of his
life.

26. The pro-Egypt party finally influenced the Jews to migrate to Egypt against Jeremiah's advice (Jer 42:1-43:7).

27-30. After Jehoiachin had been imprisoned in captivity for
thirty-seven years, **Evil-merodach** became king of Babylon.
Like Cyrus, who gave freedom to the exiles, Evil-merodach
began his reign on a conciliatory note. He **did lift up the head of
Jehoiachin**, i.e., he elevated the Jewish king, giving him a
prominent position, new appropriate garments, and daily rations of food. Fascinating Babylonian records have been found
listing the rations of prisoners and foreigners residing in Babylon, of which Jehoiachin was one who was specifically named,
(cf. Thomas, pp. 84-86), thus confirming the historical validity
of this account.

BIBLIOGRAPHY

Bahr, Karl. The Books of the Kings. In *A Commentary on the Holy Scripture: Critical, Doctrinal, and Homiletical*. Ed. by J. P.
Lange. New York: Charles Scribner's Sons, 1890.

Crockett, W. D. *A Harmony of the Books of Samuel, Kings, and Chronicles*. Grand Rapids: Baker, 1951.

*Davis, John J. *The Birth of a Kingdom: Studies in I-II Samuel and I Kings 1-11*. Grand Rapids: Baker, 1970.

Dentan, Robert C. The First and Second Books of the Kings. In *The Layman's Bible Commentary*. Richmond: John
Knox Press, 1964.

*Ellison, H. L. I and II Kings. In *The New Bible Commentary*. Ed. by Francis Davidson. Grand Rapids: Eerdmans,
1953.

Gates, John T. I Kings. In *The Wycliffe Commentary*. Eds. Charles Pfeiffer and Everett Harrison. Chicago: Moody
Press, 1962.

Gray, John. *I and II Kings: A Commentary*. Philadelphia: Westminster Press, 1963.

*Keil, C. F. *The Book of the Kings*. Grand Rapids: Eerdmans, reprinted, 1970.

Matheney, M. and Roy L. Honeycott. I and II Kings. In *The Broadman Bible Commentary*. Vol. 3. Nashville:
Broadman Press, 1970.

Montgomery, James A. and Henry Gehman. A Critical and Exegetical Commentary on the Books of Kings. In *The
International Critical Commentary*. Edinburgh: T. & T. Clark, n.d.

Payne, J. Barton. *An Outline of Hebrew History*. Grand Rapids: Baker, 1954.

Robinson, J. *The First Book of Kings*. Cambridge: University Press, 1972.

Slotki, I. W. *Kings: Hebrew Text and English Translation with an Introduction and Commentary*. In the *Soncino Books of
the Bible*. London: Soncino Press, 1950.

Snaith, Norman H. I and II Kings. In *The Interpreter's Bible*. Vol. 3. New York: Abingdon Press, 1954.

Stigers, Harold. II Kings. In *The Wycliffe Commentary*. Eds. Charles Pfeiffer and Everett Harrison. Chicago: Moody
Press, 1962.

Thiele, Edwin R. *The Mysterious Numbers of the Hebrew Kings*. Grand Rapids: Eerdmans, 1965.

Whitcomb, John C. *Chart of Old Testament Kings and Prophets*. Chicago: Moody Press, 1962.

*Whitcomb, John C. *Solomon to the Exile: Studies in Kings and Chronicles*. Grand Rapids: Baker, 1971.

Wood, Leon. *A Survey of Israel's History*. Grand Rapids: Zondervan, 1970.

I AND II CHRONICLES

INTRODUCTION

Title. Like the books of Samuel and Kings, the books of Chronicles originally appeared in the Hebrew Bible as one volume bearing the name *dibrē hayamīm*, "the words of the days," or more freely, "the events of the times." From I Chronicles 27:1-14 it is seen that the term has the sense of annals. The one volume was separated into two at a convenient place (between the reigns of David and Solomon) by the Alexandrian translators of the Septuagint and was called *Paraleipomenōn prōton* and *deuteron*. The term *paraleipomenōn* means "omissions" or "things left out," i.e., historical items of importance that were not included in the books of Samuel and Kings, especially as they involve Judah. The Latin title, *Paralipomenon*, merely a transliteration of the Greek word, was used in the Vulgate, although Jerome preferred the word *Chronicon*, meaning "Chronicles," which fits better these accounts. English versions have followed Jerome's preference, and thus we have I and II Chronicles.

Position in the canon. In the Latin and English versions the books of Chronicles follow immediately after Samuel and Kings and before Ezra and Nehemiah. This arrangement is due to the influence of the Septuagint whose translators, believing the Chronicles to be "omitted things," placed these books after Kings, the principal records of the kings, as supplementary material.

In the Hebrew Bible, however, Chronicles is placed in the third division known as the "Writings" (Heb *Kethubīm* or Gr *Hagiographa*). Some manuscripts placed Chronicles at the beginning of this division, but in the majority of Hebrew manuscripts and according to Talmudic tradition, Chronicles was the last book of this division (Slotki, *Chronicles: Hebrew Text and English Translation with an Introduction and Commentary*, p. xi). It is apparent that this arrangement was the one used in Christ's day, for in Luke 11:51 He referred to the first and last named martyrs in relation to the Hebrew canon, "Abel" (Gen 4:8) and "Zechariah" (II Chr 24:20-21).

Authorship. Since the Chronicles do not state when or by whom they were written, the name of the Chronicler will probably remain unknown to us. The Jewish Talmud (*Baba Bathra* 15a) states that "Ezra wrote the genealogy of Chronicles unto himself." Young understands the words "unto himself" possibly to mean that "Ezra continued the history down to his own time" (E. J. Young, *Introduction to the Old Testament*, p. 389).

Ezra the scribe, and of priestly extraction (Ezra 7:1-6), was one in every respect qualified to accomplish this task under divine guidance. As Archer has noted, the writer of Chronicles was concerned with giving "to the Jews of the Second Commonwealth the true spiritual foundations of their theocracy as the covenant people of Jehovah"; and Ezra, the leader of spiritual and moral revival of the Second Commonwealth, would have not only the incentive to produce such a work, but he probably would be most likely to have access to the records and reference works for writing Chronicles (Gleason Archer, *A Survey of Old Testament Introduction*, pp. 390-391).

Also, most scholars recognize the many similarities in Ezra and Chronicles. Both have frequent lists and genealogies, stress priestly ritual, and show high regard for the law of Moses.

Of special note are the concluding verses of II Chronicles and the opening verses of Ezra. These may point to common authorship; although, if Young (p. 389) is correct, the opening verses of Ezra were written after II Chronicles 36:22-23 and are expansions of it.

Date. It can be said with certainty that II Chronicles 36:22-23 precludes any possibility of being written before 538 B.C., the year Cyrus made his decree allowing Jews to return from exile. A proper understanding of I Chronicles 3:19-21 supports the same conclusion. The genealogy of Jehoiachin is traced through Zerubbabel and ends with Pelatiah and Jeshaiah about 500 B.C. Four unrelated names follow in verse 21, and then the genealogy of Shecaniah is traced. If, as seems probable, Shecaniah were born in approximately the same period as Jehoiachin, then the four additional generations would again bring us to approximately 500 B.C. This date, then, seems to be the earliest possible date of writing.

Scholars usually note also that the language of Chronicles indicates that it comes from the approximate period of Ezra. Therefore most conservative scholars date Chronicles in the second half of the fifth century B.C., between 450 and 425.

Sources. Over half the material of Chronicles finds its parallel in other books of the Old Testament (cf. the genealogies of chs. 1-9 with Gen, Ex, Num, and Josh). In historical sections the Chronicles follow Samuel and Kings very closely, though at times altering the arrangement of the materials.

There are definite references to historical writings: the "Book of the Kings of Israel and Judah" (I Chr 9:1; II Chr 27:7; 35:27; 36:8); the "Book of the Kings of Judah and Israel" (II Chr 16:11; 25:26; 32:32); the "Book of the Kings of Israel" (II Chr 20:34); the "Words (Heb *dibrē*) of the Kings of Israel" (II Chr 33:18); and the "story (Heb *midrash*) of the Book of the Kings" (II Chr 24:27). The first four titles are probably the same book, and it is possible that the fifth is only another variant designation. Young conjectures, "The author of Kings quotes the annals of the kingdoms as two separate works, but evidently the history had been worked up into one volume or book which lay before the Chronicler and which he could designate Midrash" (p. 393).

Other writers cited by the Chronicles are known prophetic persons: Samuel the seer and Gad the seer (I Chr 29:29); Nathan the prophet (I Chr 29:29; 11 Chr 9:29); Iddo the seer (II Chr 9:29; 12:15; or Iddo the prophet, 13:22); Shemaiah the prophet (II Chr 12:15); Jehu the son of Hanani (II Chr 20:34); Hozai (II Chr 33:19, rendered "the seers" in AV); Isaiah the prophet, the son of Amoz (II Chr 26:22; 32:32); and Ahijah the Shilonite (II Chr 9:29).

Purpose. By comparing Samuel and Kings with Chronicles, it is apparent that the Chronicler proposed not only to write history, but also to teach doctrinal and moral truth. In 458 B.C. Ezra had returned from Babylon to Jerusalem, where he had been instrumental in restoring temple worship (Ezr 7:19-28; 8:32-36) and eliminating the mixed marriages (Jews with pagans) that had occurred (Ezr 10:9-10). Chronicles, a post-exile writing, built upon the foundation of Ezra's revival and was written for the benefit of the post-exilic Jewish community that needed to know or be reminded of how it came into existence, that it was truly a continuation of the pre-exilic kingdom. The Chronicler showed that "the true glory of the Hebrew nation was found in its covenant relationship to God, as safeguarded by the prescribed forms of worship in the Temple and administered by the divinely ordained priesthood under the protection of the divinely authorized dynasty of David" (Archer, p. 389).

The Chronicler's omissions in the historical narrative show his concern for the Davidic line. Therefore, King Saul is mentioned only in passing; and the rebellious northern kingdom, not of the faithful or Davidic line, is mentioned only where its history concerns the southern kingdom. Many details of the kings are omitted (e.g., David's sin with Bathsheba, Absalom's rebellion, Adonijah's usurpation of the throne, etc.). Even the history of Elijah and Elisha and their ministry in the northern kingdom is omitted.

On the other hand, prominence is given to the genealogical lists showing Israel's heritage and her connection to the Patriarchs. The Chronicler gives a fuller account of those things that relate to the priestly worship. Emphasis is placed upon the ark,

the Temple, the devotion of Judah's kings to temple worship, the Levites, and the temple singers. Therefore, Chronicles furnishes history from the priestly standpoint, from the death of Saul to the decree of Cyrus, where the book of Ezra continues the history.

Historical reliability. If Chronicles were read by itself, it would give an unbalanced picture of Israelite history; however, it is apparent that the Chronicler was not writing a complete history, but presumed his readers' knowledge of the books of Samuel and Kings. It is unfortunate that most modern scholars reject the history as untrustworthy, for Chronicles is viewed in the same light as parts of the Pentateuch (the so-called Priestly code). To them, much of the history was manufactured to show God's hand in history.

Historically, Jewish rabbis, while not doubting Chronicles' place in the canon, have doubted the reliability of some passages that seemingly contradict parallel passages in Samuel and Kings (Slotki, p. xii). Two areas of objection that are most often noted are variations in spelling and numbers.

While the original text was correct, certain variant spellings by copyists in transmitting the text resulted in similar Hebrew letters being mistaken for each other, e.g., the letter *dalet* (d) and *resh* (r) (cf. "Dodanim," Gen 10:4 with "Rodanim," I Chr 1:7 in some manuscripts).

Concerning numbers, there are occasions where Chronicles has larger numbers in its statistics than its parallel account in Samuel or Kings (e.g., cf. II Sam 24:9 and I Chr 21:5). Other times, the number in Chronicles is smaller than the parallel passages (e.g., cf. I Kgs 4:26 and II Chr 9:25). Since some discrepancies are so obvious, there must be some explanation; for certainly the Chronicler would not have deliberately tried to make his records appear ridiculous. Precisely what system of numerical notation was used in ancient times is difficult to determine (several theories exist); but again, it seems probable that most numerical discrepancies can be attributed to variant transmission. Archer has stated, "It is safe to say that all the so-called discrepancies that have been alleged are capable of resolution either by textual criticism or by contextual exegeses." For a more thorough treatment on the problem of apparent discrepancies, the reader is encouraged to see Archer (pp. 392-395) and Young (pp. 394-400).

OUTLINE
I CHRONICLES

COMMENTARY

I. GENEALOGIES. 1:1-9:44.

A. Genealogies From Adam to the Patriarchs. 1:1-2:2.

Beginning with Adam and tracing his genealogy through Abraham to Jacob and Esau, the Chronicler's purpose is to show the place of God's people, Israel, in history. Special attention is devoted to the tribe of Judah and the Davidic line, as well as the descendants of Levi. Many of the names are taken from canonical books, especially Genesis; and often variant spellings of names appear.

1:1-4. The names of these four verses cover the history of Genesis 1-9 and are an abbreviated form of Genesis 5:1-32. The slight variations of spellings are the result of the Authorized Version's translators more accurately transliterating the names here than in Genesis 5. No mention is made of Cain or Abel, for the Chronicler was interested only in the direct line to the chosen people. The genealogy concludes with the three sons of **Noah,** not three successive generations after him.

5-7. Of Noah's sons, the genealogy of Shem receives central attention. Therefore, it is placed last for emphasis. **The sons of Japheth.** Verses 5-23 are taken from the table of nations in Genesis 10 (see notes there for identification of these nations). Except for several variations of spelling, this section parallels Genesis 10:2-5.

8-16. The sons of Ham. These descendants are described in greater detail. Some names are commented upon (cf. vs. 10), but these comments are reproduced from the parallel and expanded passage in Genesis 10:6-20.

ADAM, Sheth, Ē'nŏsh,
2 Ke'nan, Ma-hă'la-le-el, Je'rĕd,
3 Hĕ'nŏch, Me-thū'se-lah, Lā'mech,
4 Noah, Shem, Ham, and Jā'pheth.

5 ¶The sons of Jā'pheth; Gō'mer, and Mā'gŏg, and Mād'a-ī, and Jā'van, and Tū'bal, and Mĕ'shĕch, and Tī'ras.
6 And the sons of Gō'mer; Ăsh'che-năz, and Rī'phăth, and Tō-gär'mah.
7 And the sons of Jā'van; E-lī'shah, and Tär'shīsh, Kīt'tīm, and Dō'da-nīm.
8 ¶The sons of Ham; Cush, and Mīz'ra-im, Put, and Canaan.
9 And the sons of Cush; Sē'ba, and Hăv'i-lah, and Săb'ta, and Rā'a-mah, and Săb'te-cha. And the sons of Rā'a-mah; Shē'ba, and Dē'dan.
10 And Cush begat Nimrod: he began to be mighty upon the earth.
11 And Mīz'ra-im begat Lū'dim, and Ăn'a-mīm, and Le'hā-bīm, and Năph'-tu-hīm,
12 And Path-rū'sīm, and Căs'lu-hīm, (of whom came the Philistines,) and Căph'tho-rīm.
13 And Canaan begat Zī'don his first-born, and Heth,
14 The Jĕb'u-sīte also, and the Ămor-īte, and the Gir'ga-shīte,

751

15 And the Hī'vīte, and the Ärk'īte, and the Sīn'īte,

16 And the Är'vad-īte, and the Zĕm'a-rīte, and the Hā'math-īte.

17 ¶The sons of Shem; Ē'lam, and Asshur, and Är-phăx'ăd, and Lud and Ā'ram, and Uz, and Hul, and Gē'ther, and Mē'shĕch.

18 And Är-phăx'ăd begat Shē'lah, and Shē'lah begat Ē'ber.

19 And unto Ē'ber were born two sons: the name of the one was Pē'lĕg; because in his days the earth was divided: and his brother's name was Jŏk'-tăn.

20 And Jŏk'tăn begat Äl-mō'dăd, and Shē'leph, and Hā'zar-mā'veth, and Je'rah,

21 Ha-dō'ram also, and Ū'zal, and Dĭk'lah,

22 And Ebal, and A-bĭm'a-el, and Shē'ba,

23 And Ō'phir, and Hăv'i-lah, and Jō'-băb. All these were the sons of Jŏk'tăn.

24 ¶Shem, Är-phăx'ăd, Shē'lah,

25 Ēb'er, Pē'lĕg, Rē'ū,

26 Se'rŭg, Nahor, Te'rah,

27 Abram; the same is Abraham.

28 The sons of Abraham; Isaac, and Ĭsh'ma-el.

29 ¶These are their generations: The firstborn of Ĭsh'ma-el, Ne-bā'iŏth; then Kē'dar, and Ăd'be-el, and Mĭb'săm,

30 Mĭsh'ma, and Dū'mah, Măs'sa, Hā'dăd, and Tē'ma,

31 Jē'tur, Nā'phĭsh, and Kĕd'e-mah. These are the sons of Ĭsh'ma-el.

32 ¶Now the sons of Ke-tū'rah, Abraham's concubine: she bare Zĭm'răn, and Jŏk'shăn, and Mē'dăn, and Mĭd'ī-an, and Ĭsh'băk, and Shū'ah. And the sons of Jŏk'shăn; Shē'ba, and Dē'dan.

33 And the sons of Mĭd'ī-an; Ē'phah, and Ē'pher, and Hē'nŏch, and A-bī'da, and Ĕl'dă-ah. All these are the sons of Ke-tū'rah.

34 And Abraham begat Isaac. The sons of Isaac; Esau and Israel.

35 ¶The sons of Esau; Ĕl'i-phăz, Reū'-el, and Jē'ush, and Jā-a'lam, and Kôrah.

36 The sons of Ĕl'i-phăz; Tē'man, and Ōmär, Zē'phī, and Gā'tam, Kē'năz, and Tĭm'na, and Ăm'a-lĕk.

37 The sons of Reū'el; Nāhăth, Ze'rah, Shăm'mah, and Mĭz'zah.

38 And the sons of Sē'ir; Lō'tăn, and Shō'bal, and Zĭb'e-on, and Ā'nah, and Dĭ'shŏn, and Ē'zar, and Dī'shăn.

39 And the sons of Lō'tăn; Hō'rī, and Hō'măm: and Tĭm'na was Lō'tăn's sister.

40 The sons of Shō'bal; Ă-lī'an, and Măn'a-hăth, and Ebal, Shē'phī, and Ō'nam, and the sons of Zĭb'e-on; Ă-ī'ah, and Ā'nah.

41 The sons of Ā'nah; Dī'shŏn. And the sons of Dī'shŏn; Ăm-răm, and Ĕsh'-băn, and Ĭth'răn, and Chē'ran.

42 The sons of Ē'zer; Bĭl'hăn, and Zā'-van, and Jā'kan. The sons of Dī'shăn; Uz, and Ā'răn.

43 ¶Now these are the kings that reigned in the land of Ēdom before any king reigned over the children of Israel; Bē'la the son of Bē'ôr: and the name of his city was Dĭn'ha-bah.

44 And when Bē'la was dead, Jō'băb

17-27. The sons of Shem. The parallel passage is Genesis 10:22-29. Verses 17a-24a are omitted in LXX. In the days of **Peleg** the **earth was divided,** a reference to Babel and the dispersion of the nations (Gen 11:1-9). Verses 17-27 are summarized by tracing Shem's genealogy through **Arphaxad** to **Abraham,** the father of God's covenant people (cf. Gen 11:12-26).

28-33. The sons of Abraham. The line of **Ishmael,** Abraham's first son by Hagar (Gen 16), is given first (Gen 25:12-15), then the sons born to Abraham by **Keturah** after Sarah's death (Gen 24:67-25:4); but attention is focused on Isaac, the son of promise.

34-54. The sons of Isaac. Since the sons of Israel (i.e., Jacob, Gen 32:28) are central to the Chronicler's purpose of establishing the lineage of a covenant people, **The sons of Esau** are listed first. Verses 34-42 have a fuller parallel in Genesis 36:10-28. There, Esau's sons are listed according to his wives Adah and Aholibamah. **Timna** (vs. 36), according to Genesis 36:12, was not the son of **Eliphaz,** but his concubine who gave birth to **Amalek. Seir,** originally a place-name for a mountain east of the Jordan, is here and in Genesis 36:20 a reference to the Horite inhabitants of the area to be occupied by Esau's descendants. At times Seir is used synonymously for the inhabitants of Edom.

Verses 43-54 are almost verbatim of Genesis 36:31-43. **Hadad** (vs. 51) is Hadar in Genesis 36:39. He **died also** (a line not found in Gen) probably indicates he was still alive in Moses' day.

the son of Ze′rah of Bŏz′rah reigned in his stead.

45 And when Jō′băb was dead, Hu′sham of the land of the Tē′man-ītes reigned in his stead.

46 And when Hu′sham was dead, Hă′dăd the son of Bĕ′dăd, which smote Mĭd′ĭ-an in the field of Moab, reigned in his stead: and the name of his city was Ă′vĭth.

47 And when Hă′dăd was dead, Săm′lah of Măs′re-kah reigned in his stead.

48 And when Săm′lah was dead, Shā′-ul of Re-hō′bŏth by the river reigned in his stead.

49 And when Shā′ul was dead, Bā′al-hă′nan the son of Ăch′bôr reigned in his stead.

50 And when Bā′al-hă′nan was dead, Hă′dăd reigned in his stead: and the name of his city was Pā′ī; and his wife's name was Me-hĕt′a-bĕl, the daughter of Mā′tred, the daughter of Mĕz′a-hăb.

51 Hă′dăd died also. And the dukes of Ēdom were; duke Tīm′nah, duke Ā-lī′ah, duke Jĕ′thĕth,

52 Duke A-hōl-ĭ-bă′mah, duke Ē′lah, duke Pī′nŏn,

53 Duke Kĕ′năz, duke Tē′man, duke Mĭb′zär,

54 Duke Măg′dī-el, duke Ī′răm. These are the dukes of Ēdom.

CHAPTER 2

THESE are the sons of Israel; Reuben, Simeon, Levi, and Jūdah, Ĭs′sa-char, and Zĕb′u-lun,

2 Dan, Joseph, and Benjamin, Năph′ta-lī, Gad, and Asher.

3 ¶The sons of Jūdah; Er, and Ō′nan, and Shē′lah: which three were born unto him of the daughter of Shū′a the Canaanitess. And Er, the firstborn of Jūdah, was evil in the sight of the LORD; and he slew him.

4 And Tā′mar his daughter in law bore him Phā′rĕz and Ze′rah. All the sons of Jūdah were five.

5 The sons of Phā′rĕz; Hĕz′ron, and Hă′mul.

6 And the sons of Ze′rah; Zimri, and Ē′than, and Hē′măn, and Căl′cŏl, and Dâ′ra: five of them in all.

7 And the sons of Cär′mī; Ā′chär, the troubler of Israel, who transgressed in the thing accursed.

8 And the sons of Ē′than; Ăz-a-rī′ah.

9 The sons also of Hĕz′ron, that were born unto him; Je-räh′me-el, and Ram, and Che-lū′baī.

10 And Ram begat Am-mĭn′a-dăb; and Am-mĭn′a-dăb begat Näh′shŏn, prince of the children of Jūdah;

11 And Näh′shŏn begat Săl′ma, and Săl′ma begat Bō′ăz,

12 And Bō′ăz begat Ō′bed, and Ō′bed begat Jesse,

13 And Jesse begat his firstborn E-lī′ab, and A-bĭn′a-dăb the second, and Shĭm′ma the third,

2:1-2. The sons of Israel. The strange order of these twelve sons is peculiar to this section. Leah's sons are placed first; Rachel's sons are placed between Zebulun and Dan, Bilhah's sons; and last are Zilpah's sons. In the chapters to follow, the tribes of Zebulun and Dan are not enumerated; but Joseph is counted as two in Ephraim and Manasseh.

B. Genealogies of Judah. 2:3-4:23.

1. Descendants of Hezron. 2:3-55.

3-12. Verses 3-4 are a condensed account of Genesis 38. **Pharez.** See Genesis 46:12. **Zimri** is Zabdi in Joshua 7:1. Zerah's remaining four sons may be the Ezrahites of I Kings 4:31. **Carmi** is the son of **Zimri** (the reader's knowledge of Josh 7:1 is assumed). **Achar** (Achan) may be an intentional play on the Hebrew words (*'achar* which means to trouble, cf. Josh 7:25). Of the three sons of **Hezron, Ram,** the ancestor of David is placed first. **Chelubai** is Caleb in verse 18. Verses 10-12 have their parallel in Ruth 4:19-22.

13-17. For the first three of Jesse's sons, see I Samuel 16:6, 8-9. **David the seventh.** According to I Samuel 16:10-11, David was the eighth son. One of Jesse's sons may have died young, or

14 Ne-thăn′e-el the fourth, Răd′da-ī the fifth,

15 Ō′zem the sixth, David the seventh:

16 Whose sisters were Zer-ū-i′ah, and Ăb′i-gāil. And the sons of Zer-ū-i′ah; A-bī′shaī, and Jō′ăb, and Ă′sa-hĕl, three.

17 And Ăb′i-gāil bare Am′ā-sa: and the father of Am′ā-sa was Jē′ther the Ĭsh′me-el-īte.

18 ¶And Caleb the son of Hĕz′ron begat children of A-zū′bah his wife, and of Jĕ′rī-ŏth: her sons are these; Jē′sher, and Shō′băb, and Ardon.

19 And when A-zū′bah was dead, Caleb took unto him Ĕph′rath, which bare him Hur.

20 And Hur begat Ū′rī, and Ū′rī begat Be-zăl′e-el.

21 And afterward Hĕz′ron went in to the daughter of Mā′chĭr the father of Gilead, whom he married when he was threescore years old; and she bare him Sē′gŭb.

22 And Sē′gŭb begat Jā′ir, who had three and twenty cities in the land of Gilead.

23 And he took Gē′shur, and Â′ram, with the towns of Jā′ir, from them, with Kē′năth, and the towns thereof, even threescore cities. All these belonged to the sons of Mā′chĭr the father of Gilead.

24 And after that Hĕz′ron was dead in Cā′leb–ĕph′ra-täh, then Ă-bī′ah Hĕz′-ron′s wife bare him Ashur the father of Te-kō′a.

25 ¶And the sons of Je-räh′me-el the firstborn of Hĕz′ron were, Ram the firstborn, and Bū′nah, and Ō′ren, and Ō′zem, and A-hī′jah.

26 Je-räh′me-el had also another wife, whose name was Ăt′a-rah; she was the mother of Ō′nam.

27 And the sons of Ram the firstborn of Je-räh′me-el were, Mā′ăz, and Jā′-mĭn, and Ē′ker.

28 And the sons of Ō′nam were, Shăm′ma-ī, and Jā′da. And the sons of Shăm′ma-ī; Nădăb, and Ab′ī-shur.

29 And the name of the wife of Ab′ī-shur was Ăb-i-hā′il, and she bare him Ăh′băn, and Mō′lĭd.

30 And the sons of Nădăb; Sē′lĕd, and Ăp′pa-im: but Sē′lĕd died without children.

31 And the sons of Ăp′pa-im; Ĭ′shī. And the sons of Ĭ′shī; Shē′shan. And the children of Shē′shan; Äh′laī.

32 And the sons of Jā′da the brother of Shăm′ma-ī; Jē′ther, and Jonathan: and Jē′ther died without children.

33 And the sons of Jonathan; Pē′lĕth, and Zā′za. These were the sons of Je-räh′me-el.

34 ¶Now Shē′shan had no sons, but daughters. And Shē′shan had a servant, an Egyptian, whose name was Jär′ha.

35 And Shē′shan gave his daughter to Jär′ha his servant to wife; and she bare him Ăt′taī.

36 And Ăt′taī begat Nāthan, and Nā-than begat Zā′băd,

37 And Zā′băd begat Ĕph′lăl, and Ĕph′lăl begat Ō′bed.

38 And Ō′bed begat Jehu, and Jehu begat Ăz-a-rī′ah,

perhaps his name was dropped because he was childless. David's **sisters** were half sisters, the daughters of Nahash (II Sam 17:25). The three sons of **Zeruiah** served as leaders in David's army (II Sam 2:18). **Amasa** served Absalom in his rebellion (II Sam 17:25).

18-24. Caleb's descendants and the ancestors of **Bezaleel**, Moses' artisan for constructing the tabernacle (Ex 31:2), are given. **Machir** was the only son of Manasseh (Gen 50:23; Num 26:29). The twenty-three cities of **Jair** were given to Manasseh by Moses (Num 32:39-41; Deut 3:14). For **he took Geshur, and Aram,** read "But Geshur and Aram took the towns of Jair" (NASB).

25-33. The sons of Jerahmeel. The Jerahmeelites were a little-known clan that lived in the territory south of Judah (I Sam 27:10).

34-41. These verses are supplementary to verses 25-33, beginning with **Sheshan** (vs. 31) and tracing the line to **Elishama**. While verses 31 and 34 appear to be contradictory, **Ahlai** (vs. 31) may have been a grandson by one of Sheshan's daughters, or the daughter that was given to Sheshan's servant to wife (vs. 34).

39 And Ăz-a-rī'ah begat Hē'lĕz, and Hē'lĕz begat Ĕ-le'ā-sah,
40 And Ĕ-le'ā-sah begat SĪ-sam'a-ī, and SĪ-sam'a-ī begat Shăl'lum,
41 And Shăl'lum begat Jĕk-a-mī'ah, and Jĕk-a-mī'ah begat E-līsh'a-ma.
42 ¶Now the sons of Caleb the brother of Je-răh'me-el were, Mē'sha his firstborn, which was the father of Ziph; and the sons of Ma-rē'shah the father of Hēbron.
43 And the sons of Hēbron: Kôrah, and Tăp'pū-ah, and Rē'kem, and Shē'ma.
44 And Shē'ma begat Raham, the father of Jôr'kŏ-am: and Rē'kem begat Shăm'ma-ī.
45 And the son of Shăm'ma-ī was Mā'on: and Mā'on was the father of Bĕth'-zûr.
46 And Ē'phah, Caleb's concubine, bare Hā'ran, and Mō'za, and Gā'zez: and Hā'ran begat Gā'zez.
47 And the sons of Jăh'da-ī; Rē'gem, and Jō'tham, and Gē'sham, and Pē'let, and Ē'phah, and Shā'aph.
48 Mā'a-chah, Caleb's concubine, bare Shē'ber, and Tir'hă-nah.
49 She bare also Shā'aph the father of Măd-măn'nah, Shē'va the father of Măch'bē-nah, and the father of Gĭb'e-a: and the daughter of Caleb was Ăch'sa.
50 ¶These were the sons of Caleb the son of Hur, the firstborn of Ēph'ra-täh; Shō'bal the father of Kir'jath-jē'a-rĭm,
51 Săl'ma the father of Bĕth-lehĕm, Hā'rĕph the father of Bĕth-gā'der.
52 And Shō'bal the father of Kir'-jath-jē'a-rĭm had sons; Har'ō-eh, and half of the Mă-na'hĕth-ītes.
53 And the families of Kir'jath-jē'a-rĭm; the Ĭth'rītes, and the Pū'hītes, and the Shū'math-ītes, and the Mīsh'ra-ītes; of them came the Zâ're-ath-ītes, and the Ĕsh'ta-ul-ītes.
54 The sons of Săl'ma; Bĕth-lehĕm, and the Ne-tōph'a-thītes, Ăt'a-rŏth, the house of Jō'ăb, and half of the Mă-na'-hĕth-ītes, and the Zō'rītes.
55 And the families of the scribes which dwelt at Jā'bez; the Tī'rath-ītes, the Shĭm'e-ath-ītes, and Sū'chath-ītes. These are the Kēn'ītes that came of Hē'măth, the father of the house of Rē'chăb.

CHAPTER 3

NOW these were the sons of David, which were born unto him in Hēbron; the firstborn Ăm'nŏn, of A-hĭn'ō-am the Jĕz're-el-ĭt-ess; the second Daniel, of Ăb'i-gāil the Carmelitess:
2 The third, Ăb'sa-lom the son of Mā'a-chah the daughter of Tăl'maī king of Gē'shur; the fourth, Ăd-o-nī'jah the son of Hăg'gĭth:
3 The fifth, Shĕph-a-tī'ah of Ăb-ī-tal: the sixth, Ĭth're-am by Ĕg'lah his wife.
4 These six were born unto him in Hēbron; and there he reigned seven years and six months: and in Jerusalem he reigned thirty and three years.
5 And these were born unto him in Je-rusalem; Shĭm'e-a, and Shō'băb, and Nāthan, and Solomon, four, of Băth'-shū-a the daughter of Ăm'mī-el:
6 Ĭb'hăr also, and E-līsh'a-ma, and E-lĭph'e-lĕt,

42-49. These verses are supplementary to verses 18-24. **Brother of Jerahmeel** identifies this Caleb with the Caleb of verses 9 and 18; however, the reference to Caleb's daughter **Achsah** (vs. 49) is problematic since Joshua's associate, Caleb the son of Jephunneh (Josh 15:16; Jud 1:12; I Chr 4:15), had a daughter named Achsah. Keil suggests that Caleb (the son of Hezron) had a descendant, Caleb, the son of Jephunneh, whose immediate daughter was Achsah. Here "daughter" loosely means that Achsah was a distant descendant of the first Caleb (C. F. Keil, *The Books of the Chronicles*, p. 73). A preferable view is that there were two Calebs, and each had a daughter named Achsah (Slotki, p. 15).

50-55. **Ephratah** is Ephrath of verse 19, making this **Caleb** the same also. Therefore, verse 50 should read, "These were the sons of Caleb. The sons of Hur, . . ." (NASB). Not all these names are persons. **Kirjath-jearim . . . Beth-lehem . . . Beth-gader** are cities that were "fathered," i.e., founded or colonized, by Caleb's sons. **Rechab** (vs. 55) was the father of Jehonadab (see notes on II Kgs 10:15 ff.).

2. Descendants of David. 3:1-24.

The line of Judah was traced as far as David in 2:12. Now the Chronicler focuses attention on this principal character and traces his lineage down to the second generation of Zerubbabel.

3:1-4. These six sons were born to David by six different wives while he was king at Hebron (cf. II Sam 2:1-4; 5:4-5). This section corresponds to II Samuel 3:2-5, except for the second son, **Daniel,** which appears as Chileab there.

5-9. This section contains David's sons born at Jerusalem and largely corresponds to II Samuel 5:14-16 and I Chronicles 14:4-7, with a few variations. **Nathan** was the son through which the Davidic line is traced in Luke 3:23-31. **Bath-shua** is Bath-sheba (II Sam 11:3). **Elishama** and **Eliphelet** are probably Elishua and Elpalet (I Chr 14:5), otherwise there were two sets of sons with

7 And Nō′gah, and Nē′phĕg, and Ja-phī′a,

8 And E-lĭsh′a-ma, and E-lī′a-da, and E-lĭph′e-lĕt, nine.

9 *These were* all the sons of David, beside the sons of the concubines, and Tā′mar their sister.

10 ¶And Solomon's son *was* Rē-ho-bō′am, Ā-bī′a his son, Ā′sa his son, Je-hŏsh′a-phăt his son,

11 Joram his son, Ā-ha-zī′ah his son, Jō′ăsh his son,

12 Ăm-a-zī′ah his son, Ăz-a-rī′ah his son, Jō′tham his son,

13 Ahaz his son, Hĕz-e-kī′ah his son, Ma-năs′seh his son,

14 Āmon his son, Jō-sī′ah his son.

15 And the sons of Jō-sī′ah *were*, the firstborn Jō-hā′nan, the second Je-hoi′a-kĭm, the third Zĕd-e-kī′ah, the fourth Shăl′lum.

16 And the sons of Je-hoi′a-kĭm: Jĕc-o-nī′ah his son, Zĕd-e-kī′ah his son.

17 ¶And the sons of Jĕc-o-nī′ah; Ăs′-sir, Sa-lā′thĭ-el his son,

18 Măl-chī′ram also, and Pe-dā′iah, and She-nă′zar, Jĕc-a-mī′ah, Hŏsh′a-ma, and Nĕd-a-bī′ah.

19 And the sons of Pe-dā′iah *were*, Ze-rŭb′ba-bel, and Shĭm′e-ī: and the sons of Ze-rŭb′ba-bel; Me-shŭl′lam, and Hăn-a-nī′ah, and Shel′ō-mĭth their sister:

20 And Ha-shū′bah, and Ō′hĕl, and Bĕr-e-chī′ah, and Hăs-a-dī′ah, Jū′-shab-hē′sĕd, five.

21 And the sons of Hăn-a-nī′ah; Pĕl-a-tī′ah, and Je-sā′iah: the sons of Reph-ā-i′ah, the sons of Arnan, the sons of Ō-ba-dī′ah, the sons of Shĕch-a-nī′ah.

22 And the sons of Shĕch-a-nī′ah; Shem-ā-i′ah: and the sons of Shem-ā-i′ah; Hăt′tŭsh, and Ĭg′e-al, and Ba-rī′ah, and Nĕ-a-rī′ah, and Shā′phat, six.

23 And the sons of Nĕ′a-rī′ah; Ĕ-lĭ-ō-ē′na-ī, and Hĕz-e-kī′ah, and Ăz′ri-kam, three.

24 And the sons of Ĕ-lĭ-ō-ē′na-ī *were*, Hŏd-ā-i′ah, and E-lī′a-shĭb, and Pel-ā-i′ah, and Ăk′kŭb, and Jō-hā′nan, and Dal-ā-i′ah, and An-ā′nī, seven.

CHAPTER 4

THE sons of Jūdah; Phă′rĕz, Hĕz′ron, and Cär′mĭ, and Hur, and Shō′bal.

2 And Rē-ā-i′ah the son of Shō′bal be-gat Jā′hăth; and Jā′hăth begat A-hū′ma-ī, and Lā′hăd. These *are* the fam-ilies of the Zō′rath-ītes.

3 And these *were of* the father of Ē′tam; Jĕz′re-el, and Ĭsh′ma, and Ĭd′-băsh: and the name of their sister *was* Hăz′e-lĕl-pō′nī.

4 And Pe-nū′el the father of Gē′dôr, and Ē′zer the father of Hu′shah. These *are* the sons of Hur, the firstborn of Ĕph′ra-täh, the father of Bĕth-lehĕm.

5 ¶And Ashur the father of Te-kō′a had two wives, Hĕ′lah and Nā′a-rah.

6 And Nā′a-rah bare him A-hŭ′zam, and Hē′pher, and Tĕm′e-nī, and Hā-a-hăsh′ta-rī. These *were* the sons of Nā′a-rah.

7 And the sons of Hĕ′lah *were*, Ze′-reth, and Je-zō′ar, and Ĕth′nan.

8 And Coz begat Ā′nŭb, and Zō-

identical names. **Elpalet** and **Nogah** are omitted in II Samuel 5:15. **Tamar** was David's daughter who was raped by her brother Amnon (II Sam 13).

10-16. This section traces the Davidic lineage from Solomon to the captivity in the reign of Zedekiah. **Abia** is also rendered Abijam in I Kings and Abijah elsewhere in Chronicles. **Azariah** is Uzziah in II Kings 15:13, 32, 34, and in the prophets (cf. Isa 6:1). **Johanan** (vs. 15) is otherwise unknown. **Shallum** is also known as Jehoahaz (cf. II Kgs 23:31; II Chr 36:1; Jer 22:11). **Jeconiah** is Jehoiachin (II Kgs 24:6ff.) or Coniah (Jer 22:24). **Zedekiah** was actually the uncle of Jeconiah and a **son** only in the sense of a successor to the throne.

17-24. This section lists the Davidic descendants through the exile. **The sons of Jeconiah** is not a contradiction of Jeremiah 22:28-30. Jeconiah was not denied children, but reigning children. **Assir** should probably be rendered "prisoner," not as a name. Thus, it would read "Jeconiah, the prisoner" (NASB). **Zerubbabel** is here listed as the son of **Pedaiah,** but in other places he is listed as the son of **Salathiel,** or Shealtiel (cf. Ezr 3:2, 8; 5:2; Neh 12:1; Hag 1:12, 14; 2:2, 23; Mt 1:12). It is possible that Salathiel died early and Pedaiah married his widow and raised up children for Salatiel in accordance with the rules of levirate marriage (cf. Deut 25:5-10). The other names are not mentioned in the genealogy of Jesus (Mt 1:1-16). The four names, **Rephaiah, Arnan, Obadiah,** and **Shechaniah,** are prob-lematic because their connection with the preceding names is uncertain (cf. H. L. Ellison, I Chronicles, in *The New Bible Commentary,* p. 343). The lineage of Shechaniah is traced through four generations.

3. *Other descendants of Judah. 4:1-23.*

Fragmentary and supplementary genealogies of the tribe of Judah follow, but their connection to one another is often diffi-cult to determine.

4:1-4. The sons of Judah. The names that follow appear to be descendants, not brothers. **Carmi** probably should be Caleb (cf. 2:19, 50). **Reaiah** is Haroeh in 2:52. **Zorathites** is probably Zareathites of 2:53, a reference to a geographical location of Zorah (Jud 13:2). These verses concerning the **sons of Hur** supplement 2:19, 50. Many of these names and those which follow (vss. 3:12) are not genealogical, but are geographical (see note on 2:50-55).

5-10. This is supplementary information on the families of **Ashur,** a son of Caleb (2:24). **Coz, Jabez** (vs. 8, 9), **Chelub** (vs. 11), **Kenaz** (vs. 13), **Meonothai** (vs. 14), **Jehaleleel** (vs. 16), **Ezra** (vs. 17), **Hodiah** (vs. 19) **Shimon** and **Ishi** (vs. 20), are all heads of genealogies which seemingly have no connection one with another. **Jabez,** a place name in 2:55, is a personal name here (lit., he giveth pain). This note on Jabez emphasizes that God answers the prayer of faith, for Jabez was able to triumph over his name.

bĕ′bah, and the families of A-hâr′hĕl the son of Hâ′rum.

9 ¶And Jā′bez was more honourable than his brethren: and his mother called his name Jā′bez, saying, Because I bare him with sorrow.

10 And Jā′bez called on the God of Israel, saying, Oh that thou wouldest bless me indeed, and enlarge my coast, and that thine hand might be with me, and that thou wouldest keep me from evil, that it may not grieve me! And God granted him that which he requested.

11 ¶And Chē′lŭb the brother of Shū′ah begat Mē′hir, which was the father of Ĕsh′ton.

12 And Ĕsh′ton begat Bĕth-rā′pha, and Pa-sē′ah, and Te-hĭn′nah the father of Ĭr-nā′hăsh. These are the men of Rē′-chăh.

13 And the sons of Kē′năz; Ŏth′nĭ-el, and Se-ra-ī′ah: and the sons of Ŏth′nĭ-el; Hā′thăth.

14 And Mē-ŏn′o-thaī begat Ŏph′rah: and Se-ra-ī′ah begat Jō′ăb, the father of the valley of Chär′a-shĭm; for they were craftsmen.

15 And the sons of Caleb the son of Je-phŭn′neh; Ī′rū, Ē′lah, and Nā′am: and the sons of Ē′lah, even Kē′năz.

16 And the sons of Jē′ha-lē′le-el; Ziph, and Zī′phah, Tĭr′ī-a, and A-sâ′rē-el.

17 And the sons of Ezra were, Jē′ther, and Me′rĕd, and Ē′pher, and Jāl′ŏn: and she bare Miriam, and Shăm′ma-ī, and Ĭsh′bah the father of Ĕsh-te-mō′a.

18 And his wife Jē-hu-dī′jah bare Je′rĕd the father of Gē′dôr, and Hē′ber the father of Sō′chō, and Je-kū′thĭ-el the father of Za-nō′ah. And these are the sons of Bĭth′ī-ah the daughter of Pharaoh, which Me′rĕd took.

19 And the sons of his wife Hō-dī′ah the sister of Naham, the father of Keī′-lah the Gär′mīte, and Ĕsh-te-mō′a the Mā-ăch′a-thīte.

20 And the sons of Shī′mon were, Ăm′nŏn, and Rĭn′nah, Bĕn-hā′nan, and Tī′lon. And the sons of ĭ′shī were, Zō′-hĕth, and Bĕn-zō′hĕth.

21 ¶The sons of Shē′lah the son of Jū-dah were, Er the father of Lē′cah, and Lā′a-dah the father of Ma-rē′shah, and the families of the house of them that wrought fine linen, of the house of Ăsh-bē′a,

22 And Jō′kĭm, and the men of Chō-zē′ba, and Jō′ăsh, and Sâ′raph, who had the dominion in Moab, and Jash′ū-bī-lē′hĕm. And these are ancient things.

23 These were the potters, and those that dwelt among plants and hedges: there they dwelt with the king for his work.

24 ¶The sons of Simeon were, Nĕ-mū′el, and Jā′mĭn, Jâ′rĭb, Ze′rah, and Shā′ul:

25 Shăl′lum his son, Mĭb′săm his son, Mĭsh′ma his son.

26 And the sons of Mĭsh′ma; Hā-mu′ĕl his son, Zăc′chur his son, Shĭm′-e-ī his son.

27 And Shĭm′e-ī had sixteen sons and six daughters; but his brethren had not many children, neither did all their fam-

11-23. Sons of Kenaz, i.e., the Kenizzite (cf. Gen 15:19; 36:42). **Othniel,** the first judge of Israel, was the nephew of Caleb (Josh 15:17; Jud 3:9). **Caleb the son of Jephunneh,** not the Caleb of 2:19, 42, 50, but the associate of Joshua who was also a Kenizzite (Josh 14:14). Apparently, part of this one family from the Edomites (cf. Gen 36:31, 42; I Chr 1:35, 53) joined the tribe of Judah (by adoption? cf. J. Barton Payne, I Chronicles, in The Wycliffe Bible Commentary, p. 372). In verse 17 the antecedent for **she bare** is lacking and may be Bithiah of verse 18. **His wife Jehudijah** is better rendered "his Jewish wife" (NASB). **His wife Hodiah** is better rendered "the wife of Hodiah" (NASB). **The sons of Shelah** are supplementary to 2:3. **Plants and hedges are** probably place names Nataim (modern Kh. en-Nuweiti) and Gederah (possibly Tell el-Judeideh).

C. Genealogies of Simeon, Reuben, and Gad. 4:24-5:17.

24-27. This list of **the sons of Simeon,** while very brief, extends the genealogy found in parallel passages (Gen 46:10; Ex 6:15; Num 26:12-14). **Their family** (vs. 27), i.e., the Simeonites, always remained a small tribe.

ily multiply, like to the children of Jūdah.

28 And they dwelt at Be′er-shē′ba, and Mŏl′a-dah, and Hā′zar-shū′al,

29 And at Bĭl′hah, and at Ē′zem, and at Tō′lăd,

30 And at Beth-ū′el, and at Hôr′mah, and at Ziklag,

31 And at Bĕth-mär′ca-bôth. and Hā′-zar-sū′sĭm, and at Bĕth-bir′e-ī, and at Shā′a-rā′im. These *were* their cities unto the reign of David.

32 And their villages *were*, Ē′tam, and Ā′ĭn, Rimmon, and Tō′chen, and Ā′shan, five cities:

33 And all their villages that *were* round about the same cities, unto Bā′al. These *were* their habitations, and their genealogy.

34 And Me-shō′băb, and Jăm-lĕch, and Jŏ′shah the son of Ăm-a-zī′ah,

35 And Jō′el, and Jehu the son of Jŏs-i-bī′ah, the son of Se-ra-ī′ah, the son of Ā′sĭ-el,

36 And Ĕ-lĭ-ō-ē′na-ī, and Jā-ak′ō-bah, and Jĕsh-o-hā′iah, and Aś-ā′iah, and Ā′-dĭ-el, and Jesim′ĭ-el, and Be-nā′iah,

37 And Zī′za the son of Shī′phī, the son of Āl′lon, the son of Je-dā′iah, the son of Shĭm′rī, the son of Shem-ā-i′ah;

38 These mentioned by *their* names *were* princes in their families: and the house of their fathers increased great-ly.

39 ¶And they went to the entrance of Gĕ′dôr, *even* unto the east side of the valley, to seek pasture for their flocks.

40 And they found fat pasture and good, and the land *was* wide, and quiet, and peaceable; for *they* of Ham had dwelt there of old.

41 And these written by name came in the days of Hĕz-e-kī′ah king of Jū-dah, and smote their tents, and the habitations that were found there, and destroyed them utterly unto this day, and dwelt in their rooms: because *there was* pasture there for their flocks.

42 And some of them, *even* of the sons of Simeon, five hundred men, went to mount Sē′ir, having for their captains Pĕl-a-tī′ah, and Nē′a-rī′ah, and Reph-ā-i′ah, and Ŭz′zĭ-el, the sons of I′shī.

43 And they smote the rest of the Am′ā-lek-ītes that were escaped, and dwelt there unto this day.

CHAPTER 5

NOW the sons of Reuben the firstborn of Israel, (for he *was* the firstborn; but, forasmuch as he defiled his father's bed, his birthright was given unto the sons of Joseph the son of Israel: and the genealogy is not to be reckoned after the birthright.

2 For Jūdah prevailed above his brethren, and of him *came* the chief ruler; but the birthright *was* Joseph's:)

3 The sons, *I say*, of Reuben the firstborn of Israel *were*, Hā′nŏch, and Păl′-lū, Hĕz′ron, and Cär′mī.

4 The sons of Jō′el; Shem-ā-i′ah his son, Gog his son, Shĭm′e-ī his son,

5 Mī′cah his son, Rē-ā-ī′a his son, Bā′al his son,

6 Bē-ē′rah his son, whom Tĭl′găth-pĭl-nē′ser king of Assyria carried away

28-38. This list of cities and villages, occupied by Simeon, is similar to that in Joshua 19:2-8, with spelling variants. These sites indicate that although Simeon occupied land originally given to Judah (Josh 19:9) and apparently was absorbed into Judah, she never completely lost her identity in Judah. **Beer-sheba** (vs. 28) was a southernmost city (from Dan to Beer-sheba). **Ziklag** (vs. 30), a Philistine city in David's day (I Sam 27:7), was claimed by Simeon. The listed names in verses 34-38 are not found elsewhere.

39-43. The families of these princes increased to the extent that it was necessary for them to migrate to **Gedor**, an unidenti-fied site, probably south of Judah. **Ham** is probably a Canaanite tribe. **These written by name** (vs. 41), i.e., those enumerated in verses 34-38. **The Amalekites that were escaped** (vs. 43) were those who remained following the exterminating attempts of Saul (I Sam 14:48; 15:3, 8) and David (II Sam 8:12).

5:1-2. Reuben was in fact the **first-born of Israel** (Gen 29:32). When the priesthood was given to Levi, the double portion (Deut 21:17) of the **birthright** went to Joseph; and his two sons, Ephraim and Manasseh, were recognized as distinct tribes. Reuben **defiled his father's bed** in his incest with Bilhah (Gen 35:22; 49:4). **Judah prevailed**, as predicted (Gen 49:8, 9) and fulfilled in the **chief ruler**, i.e., King David (II Sam 5:3).

3-10. Reuben's four sons are the same as given elsewhere (Gen 46:9; Ex 6:14; Num 26:5-7). The connection of **Joel** to Reuben is not stated. For the Assyrian **Tilgath-pilneser** (Tiglath-pileser III, 745-727 B.C.), see II Kings 15:29. Reuben's **war with the Hagarites,** an Arab tribe descended from Hagar, is elaborated on in verses 18-22.

captive: he *was* prince of the Reubenites.

7 And his brethren by their families, when the genealogy of their generations was reckoned, *were* the chief, Jeĭ'el, and Zĕch-a-rī'ah,

8 And Bē'la the son of Ā'zăz, the son of Shē'ma, the son of Jō'el, who dwelt in Ar'ŏ-er, even unto Nebo and Bā'al-mē'on:

9 And eastward he inhabited unto the entering in of the wilderness from the river Eū-phrā'tēs: because their cattle were multiplied in the land of Gilead.

10 And in the days of Saul they made war with the Hă'gar-ītes, who fell by their hand: and they dwelt in their tents throughout all the east *land* of Gilead.

11 ¶And the children of Gad dwelt over against them, in the land of Bā'-shan unto Săl'cah:

12 Jō'el the chief, and Shā'pham the next, and Jā-a'naī, and Shā'phat in Bā'shan.

13 And their brethren of the house of their fathers *were,* Michael, and Me-shŭl'lam, and Shē'ba, and Jō'raī, and Jā'chan, and Zī'a, and Hē'ber, seven.

14 These *are* the children of Ăb-i-hā'il the son of Hū'rī, the son of Ja-rō'ah, the son of Gilead, the son of Michael, the son of Je-shĭsh'a-ī, the son of Jäh'dō, the son of Buz;

15 Ā'hī the son of Ăb'dī-el, the son of Gū'nī, chief of the house of their fathers.

16 And they dwelt in Gilead in Bā'-shan, and in her towns, and in all the suburbs of Shâr'on, upon their borders.

17 All these were reckoned by genealogies in the days of Jō'tham king of Jūdah, and in the days of Jĕr-o-bō'am king of Israel.

18 ¶The sons of Reuben, and the Găd'-ītes, and half the tribe of Ma-năs'seh, of valiant men, men able to bear buckler and sword, and to shoot with bow, and skilful in war, *were* four and forty thousand seven hundred and threescore, that went out to the war.

19 And they made war with the Hă'-gar-ītes, with Jē'tur, and Nē'phĭsh, and Nō'dăb,

20 And they were helped against them, and the Hă'gar-ītes were delivered into their hand, and all that *were* with them: for they cried to God in the battle, and he was intreated of them; because they put their trust in him.

21 And they took away their cattle; of their camels fifty thousand, and of sheep two hundred and fifty thousand, and of asses two thousand, and of men an hundred thousand.

22 For there fell down many slain, because the war *was* of God. And they dwelt in their steads until the captivity.

23 ¶And the children of the half tribe of Ma-năs'seh dwelt in the land: they increased from Bā'shan unto Bā'al-her-mon and Sē'nir, and unto mount Hermon.

24 And these *were* the heads of the house of their fathers, even E'pher, and I'shī, and E-lī'el, and Ăz'rī-el, and Jĕr-e-mī'ah, and Hŏd-a-vī'ah, and Jäh'dī-el, mighty men of valour, famous men,

11-17. Gad dwelt over against them, i.e., to the north of Reuben. It is not stated how **Joel** and the following chiefs were connected with the sons of Gad because this material is unparalleled and not included in Gad's genealogies elsewhere (Gen 46:16; Num 26:15-18). **Gilead** and the **suburbs,** better rendered "pasturelands," of **Sharon** were occupied by the Gadites. This was the official list in the days of **Jotham** (cf. II Kgs 15:32 ff.; II Chr 27:1-9) and **Jeroboam** (cf. II Kgs 14:23-29).

D. Genealogies of Reuben, Gad, and Half of Manasseh. 5:18-26.

18-22. The time of this battle is not stated. Compare the number of **valiant men** with the number of eligible men (Num 26:7, 18, 34) and those who assisted Joshua in the conquest (Jos 4:13). The **Hagarites** (see vs. 10) were assisted by the related peoples of **Jetur, and Nephish, and Nodab** who were apparently descendants of Hagar's son Ishmael (Gen 25:15). All credit for success was attributed to God. These tribes occupied the land they acquired until the **captivity,** i.e., the Exile (vs. 26).

23-26. This eastern half of the tribe of Manasseh occupied the land north of Gad. The **famous men** listed here were celebrated family heads, but their connection with the descendants of Manasseh listed elsewhere is not indicated (Num 26:28-34; II Chr 7:14-20). The idolatry of these tribes resulted in divine punishment by exile. **Pul** and **Tilgath-pilneser** (Tiglath-pileser III) were the same person. Pul was his real name, which he retained in Babylon; but he assumed the name Tiglath-pileser III in Assyria. Therefore, a better rendering is "Pul,

and heads of the house of their fathers.

25 ¶And they transgressed against the God of their fathers, and went a whoring after the gods of the people of the land, whom God destroyed before them.

26 And the God of Israel stirred up the spirit of Pul king of Assyria, and the spirit of Tĭl′găth–pĭl–ně′ser king of Assyria, and he carried them away, even the Reubenites, and the Găd′ītes, and the half tribe of Ma-năs′seh, and brought them unto Hā′lah, and Hā′bôr, and Hā′ra, and to the river Gō′zăn, unto this day.

CHAPTER 6

THE sons of Levi; Ger′shon, Kō′hăth, and Me-râ′rī.

2 And the sons of Kō′hăth; Ăm′răm, Ĭz′hăr, and Hē′bron, and Ŭz′zĭ-el.

3 And the children of Ăm′răm; Aaron, and Moses, and Miriam. The sons also of Aaron; Nā′dăb, and A-bī′hū, Ĕ-le-ā′zar, and Ĭth′a-mär.

4 Ĕ-le-ā′zar begat Phĭn′e-has, Phĭn′e-has begat A-bĭsh′ū-a,

5 And A-bĭsh′ū-a begat Bŭk′kī, and Bŭk′kī begat Ŭz′zi,

6 And Ŭz′zi begat Zĕr-a-hī′ah, and Zĕr-a-hī′ah begat Me-rā′ioth,

7 Me-rā′ioth begat Ăm-a-rī′ah, and Ăm-a-rī′ah begat A-hī′tŭb,

8 And A-hī′tŭb begat Zā′dŏk, and Zā′dŏk begat A-hĭm′ă-az,

9 And A-hĭm′ă-az begat Ăz-a-rī′ah, and Ăz-a-rī′ah begat Jō-hā′nan,

10 And Jō-hā′nan begat Ăz-a-rī′ah, (he *it is* that executed the priest's office in the temple that Solomon built in Jerusalem:)

11 And Ăz-a-rī′ah begat Ăm-a-rī′ah, and Ăm-a-rī′ah begat A-hī′tŭb,

12 And A-hī′tŭb begat Zā′dŏk, and Zā′dŏk begat Shăl′lum,

13 And Shăl′lum begat Hĭl-kī′ah, and Hĭl-kī′ah begat Ăz-a-rī′ah,

14 And Ăz-a-rī′ah begat Se-ra-ī′ah, and Se-ra-ī′ah begat Je-hōz′a-dăk,

15 And Je-hōz′a-dăk went *into captivity,* when the LORD carried away Jū′dah and Jerusalem by the hand of Nĕb-u-chad-nĕz′zar.

16 ¶The sons of Levi; Ger′shom, Kō′hăth, and Me-râ′rī.

17 And these *be* the names of the sons of Ger′shom; Lĭb′nī, and Shĭm′e-ī.

18 And the sons of Kō′hăth *were,* Ăm′răm, and Ĭz′hăr, and Hē′bron, and Ŭz′zĭ-el.

19 The sons of Me-râ′rī; Măh′lī, and Mū′shī. And these *are* the families of the Lē′vītes according to their fathers.

20 Of Ger′shom; Lĭb′nī his son, Jā′hăth his son, Zimmah his son,

21 Jō′ah his son, Ĭd′dō his son, Ze′rah his son, Jē-ăt′e-raī his son.

22 The sons of Kō′hăth; Am-mĭn′a-dăb his son, Kō′rah his son, Ăs′sir his son,

23 Ĕl′kă-nah his son, and E-bī′a-săph his son, and Ăs′sir his son,

24 Tā′hăth his son, Ŭ′rĭ-el his son, Uz-zī′ah his son, and Shā′ul his son.

25 And the sons of Ĕl′kă-nah; A-mās′a-ī, and A-hī′moth.

26 *As for* Ĕl′kă-nah: the sons of Ĕl′kă-

king of Assyria, even the spirit of Tilgath-pilneser" (NASB). The date of this event was ca. 733 B.C. (II Kgs 15:29).

E. Genealogies of Levi. 6:1-81.

1. Descendants of Aaron. 6:1-15.

6:1-15. The information of this chapter is repeated and expanded in chapters 23-25. **Nadab, and Abihu** were killed for defiantly offering "strange fire" (Lev 10:1, 2).

The names that follow are successive Aaronic priests through his son **Eleazar** to the Babylonian captivity. The **Ithamar** line of priests (Eli-Abiathar) are omitted. Other known priests are also omitted: e.g., Meraioth (I Chr 9:11), Jehoiada (II Chr 22:11), Urijah (II Kgs 16:10). **Zadok** was the first priest under kings David (II Sam 20:25) and Solomon (I Kgs 4:4). Special attention to the temple ministry of **Azariah** may be a reference to the incident described in II Chronicles 26:17ff. **Hilkiah** was the priest who discovered the Book of the Law in 622 B.C. which initiated Josiah's reform (II Kgs 22:8; II Chr 34:14f.). **Jehozadak** (variant spelling is Jozadak, Ezr 3:2) was taken captive in 586 B.C. at the fall of Jerusalem. His son Joshua returned from exile to Jerusalem as his successor (Ezr 3:2, 8; 5:2; Hag 1:1).

2. Descendants of other Levites. 6:16-30.

16-21. This list of the sons of **Gershom** (Gershon, 6:1), **Kohath,** and **Merari** corresponds to Exodus 6:16-19. Many of the names in verses 20-21 appear as the ancestors to Asaph in verses 39-43.

22-30. **The sons of Kohath** are clearly a reverse order of the ancestors of Heman (vss. 33-38). A parallel arrangement of the two lists indicate certain variations and omissions. **Amminadab** is another name for Izhar (cf. vss. 18, 38). **Korah** was swallowed by the earth for rebellion (cf. Num 16:1, 32). **Zophai, Nahath,** and **Eliab** (vs. 26ff.) correspond respectively to **Zuph, Toah,** and **Eliel** (vs. 34ff.). **Elkanah** (vs. 27) is the husband of Hannah and father of Samuel (I Sam 1:1-2). Samuel had two sons (I Sam 8:2). The first-born, Joel (vs. 33), is omitted in verse 28. **Vashni**

nah; Zō'phaī his son, and Nā'hăth his son,

27 E-lī'ab his son, Jer'ō-hăm his son, Ĕl'kă-nah his son.

28 And the sons of Samuel; the first-born Vāsh'nī, and A-bī'ah.

29 The sons of Me-râ'rī; Māh'lī, Lĭb'nī his son, Shĭm'e-ī his son, Ŭz'za his son,

30 Shĭm'e-a his son, Hăg-gī'ah his son, Aṣ-ā'iah his son.

31 And these *are they* whom David set over the service of song in the house of the Lord, after that the ark had rest.

32 And they ministered before the dwelling place of the tabernacle of the congregation with singing, until Solomon had built the house of the Lord in Jerusalem: and *then* they waited on their office according to their order.

33 And these *are* they that waited with their children. Of the sons of the Kō'hăth-ītes: Hē'man a singer, the son of Jō'el the son of Shĕ-mū'el,

34 The son of Ĕl'kă-nah, the son of Jer'ō-hăm, the son of E-lī'el, the son of Tō'ah,

35 The son of Zuph, the son of Ĕl'kă-nah, the son of Mā'hăth, the son of A-măs'a-î,

36 The son of Ĕl'kă-nah, the son of Jō'el, the son of Ăz-a-rī'ah, the son of Zĕph-a-nī'ah,

37 The son of Tā'hăth, the son of Ăs'-sir, the son of E-bī'a-săph, the son of Kō'rah,

38 The son of Ĭz'här, the son of Kō'hăth, the son of Levi, the son of Israel.

39 And his brother Ā'săph, who stood on his right hand, *even* Ā'săph the son of Bĕr-a-chī'ah, the son of Shĭm'e-a,

40 The son of Michael, the son of Bā'a-sĕ'iah, the son of Măl-chī'ah,

41 The son of Ĕth'nī, the son of Ze'rah, the son of Ăd-a-ī'ah,

42 The son of Ē'than, the son of Zim-mah, the son of Shĭm'e-ī,

43 The son of Jā'hăth, the son of Ger'shom, the son of Levi.

44 And their brethren the sons of Me-râ'rī *stood* on the left hand: Ē'than the son of Kĭsh'ī, the son of Ăb'dī, the son of Măl'luch,

45 The son of Hăsh-a-bī'ah, the son of Ăm-a-zī'ah, the son of Hĭl-kī'ah,

46 The son of Ăm'zī, the son of Bā'nī, the son of Shā'mer,

47 The son of Māh'lī, the son of Mū'-shī, the son of Me-râ'rī, the son of Levi.

48 Their brethren also the Lĕ'vītes *were* appointed unto all manner of service of the tabernacle of the house of God.

49 ¶But Aaron and his sons offered upon the altar of the burnt offering, and on the altar of incense, *and were appointed* for all the work of the *place* most holy, and to make an atonement for Israel, according to all that Moses the servant of God had commanded.

50 And these *are* the sons of Aaron; Ĕ-le-ā'zar his son, Phĭn'e-has his son, A-bĭsh'ū-a his son,

51 Bŭk'kī his son, Ŭz'zi his son, Zĕr-a-hī'ah his son,

52 Me-râ'ioth his son, Ăm-a-rī'ah his son, A-hī'tŭb his son,

53 Zā'dŏk his son, A-hĭm'ă-az his son.

54 ¶Now these *are* their dwelling

is not an alternate name, but should be rendered "and the second."

3. Ancestry of David's Levitical singers. 6:31-48.

31-32. **After that the ark had rest** from its excursion through Philistine territory (cf. I Sam 5:1-7:2), it permanently resided at Jerusalem (II Sam 6:2-17). **Tabernacle of the congregation** is literally the tabernacle of the tent of meeting, probably a reference to the tent where David deposited the ark (II Sam 6:17). The three men who follow, Heman, Asaph, and Ethan, and their children, representing the families of Levi's three sons, assisted in worship with their singing.

33-48. The ancestry of the Kohathite, **Heman,** is given here (see notes on 22-30). The ancestry of the Gershonite, **Asaph,** is given in verses 39-43. **Brother** is used in a wide sense as relative. Verses 44-49 record the ancestry of the Merarite, **Ethan,** traced through Merari's second son, Mushi (6:19).

4. Duties of the Aaronic priests. 6:49-53.

49-53. The Aaronic priests performed their functions at the **altar of the burnt offering** (the brazen altar in the tabernacle court), **altar of incense** (the golden altar in the Holy Place), and the mercy seat in the **place most holy** to make **atonement** (Lev 16) The names in verses 50-53 parallel verses 4-8.

5. Cities of the Levites. 6:54-81.

This section finds its essential parallel in Joshua 21, with some rearrangement in order, abridgment, and spelling variations.

54-60. Listed are the cities of Aaron's family. For **dwelling**

places throughout their castles in their coasts, of the sons of Aaron, of the families of the Kō'hăth-ītes: for theirs was the lot.

55 And they gave them Hē'bron in the land of Jū'dah, and the suburbs thereof round about it.

56 But the fields of the city, and the villages thereof, they gave to Caleb the son of Je-phŭn'neh.

57 And to the sons of Aaron they gave the cities of Jū'dah, *namely*, Hē'-bron, *the city* of refuge, and Lĭb'nah with her suburbs, and Jăt'tir, and Ĕsh-te-mō'a, with their suburbs,

58 And Hī'len with her suburbs, Dĕ'bir with her suburbs,

59 And A'shan with her suburbs, and Bĕth-shĕ'mesh with her suburbs:

60 And out of the tribe of Benjamin; Gē'ba with her suburbs, and Āl'e-meth with her suburbs, and Ăn'a-thōth with her suburbs. All their cities throughout their families *were* thirteen cities.

61 And unto the sons of Kō'hăth, *which were* left of the family of that tribe, *were cities given* out of the half tribe, *namely, out of* the half *tribe* of Ma-năs'seh, by lot, ten cities.

62 And to the sons of Ger'shom throughout their families out of the tribe of Ĭs'sa-char, and out of the tribe of Asher, and out of the tribe of Năph'-ta-lī, and out of the tribe of Ma-năs'-seh in Bā'shan, thirteen cities.

63 Unto the sons of Me-râ'rī *were given* by lot, throughout their families, out of the tribe of Reuben, and out of the tribe of Gad, and out of the tribe of Zĕb'u-lun, twelve cities.

64 And the children of Israel gave to the Lē'vītes *these* cities with their suburbs.

65 And they gave by lot out of the tribe of the children of Jū'dah, and out of the tribe of the children of Simeon, and out of the tribe of the children of Benjamin, these cities, which are called by *their* names.

66 And *the residue* of the families of the sons of Kō'hăth had cities of their coasts out of the tribe of Ē'phra-im.

67 And they gave unto them, *of* the cities of refuge, Shĕ'chem in mount Ē'phra-im with her suburbs; *they gave* also Gē'zer with her suburbs,

68 And Jŏk'me-am with her suburbs, and Bĕth-hô'ron with her suburbs,

69 And Āij'a-lŏn with her suburbs, and Găth-rĭm'mon with her suburbs:

70 And out of the half tribe of Ma-năs'seh; Aner with her suburbs, and Bĭl'e-am with her suburbs, for the family of the remnant of the sons of Kō'-hăth.

71 Unto the sons of Ger'shom *were given* out of the family of the half tribe of Ma-năs'seh, Gō'lan in Bā'shan with her suburbs, and Ăsh'ta-rŏth with her suburbs:

72 And out of the tribe of Ĭs'sa-char; Kē'dĕsh with her suburbs, Dăb'e-răth with her suburbs,

73 And Rā'mŏth with her suburbs, and Ā'nem with her suburbs:

74 And out of the tribe of Asher; Mā'shal with her suburbs, and Ăb'dŏn with her suburbs,

places . . . castles . . . coasts, read "settlements according to their camps within their borders" (NASB). **Hebron** was originally given to and claimed by **Caleb** (Jud 1:20; Josh 14:6-15). Only eleven of the **thirteen cities** are named (cf. Josh 21:4; 13-19).

61-81. Listed are the cities of Levi's three sons. Of the **ten cities** of the Kohathites (vs. 61), eight are found in verses 66-70 (cf. Josh 21:5, 20-26). The **thirteen cities** of the Gershonites (vs. 62) are found in verses 71-76 (cf. Josh 21:6, 27-33). Of the **twelve cities** of the Merarites (vs. 63), ten are found in verses 77-81 (cf. Josh 21:7, 34-40). Therefore, forty-two of the forty-eight cities of Joshua 21 are repeated here.

75 And Hū'kŏk with her suburbs, and Rĕ'hŏb with her suburbs:

76 And out of the tribe of Năph'ta-lī; Kĕ'dĕsh in Galilee with her suburbs, and Hăm'mon with her suburbs, and Kĭr-jath-ā'ĭm with her suburbs.

77 Unto the rest of the children of Me-râ'rī were given out of the tribe of Zĕb'u-lun, Rimmon with her suburbs, Tā'bor with her suburbs:

78 And on the other side Jordan by Jericho, on the east side of Jordan, were given them out of the tribe of Reuben, Bĕ'zer in the wilderness with her suburbs, and Jăh'zah with her suburbs,

79 Kĕd'e-mŏth also with her suburbs, and Mĕph'a-ăth with her suburbs:

80 And out of the tribe of Gad; Rā'mŏth in Gilead with her suburbs, and Mā'ha-nā'im with her suburbs,

81 And Hĕsh'bŏn with her suburbs, and Jā'zer with her suburbs.

CHAPTER 7

NOW the sons of Ĭs'sa-char were, Tō'la, and Pū'ah, Jāsh'ub, and Shĭm'rŏm, four.

2 And the sons of Tō'la; Ūz'zi, and Reph-ā-i'ah, and Je'rī-el, and Jăh'ma-ī, and Jĭb'săm, and Shĕ-mū'el, heads of their father's house, to wit, of Tō'la: they were valiant men of might in their generations; whose number was in the days of David two and twenty thousand and six hundred.

3 And the sons of Ūz'zi; Ĭz-ra-hī'ah: and the sons of Ĭz-ra-hī'ah; Michael, and Ō-ba-dī'ah, and Jō'el, Ĭ-shī'ah, five: all of them chief men.

4 And with them, by their generations, after the house of their fathers, were bands of soldiers for war, six and thirty thousand men: for they had many wives and sons.

5 And their brethren among all the families of Ĭs'sa-char were valiant men of might, reckoned in all by their genealogies fourscore and seven thousand.

6 ¶The sons of Benjamin; Bĕ'la, and Bĕ'cher, and Je-dī'a-el, three.

7 And the sons of Bĕ'la; Ēz'bŏn, and Ūz'zi, Ūz'zĭ-el, and Jĕr'ī-mŏth, and Ī'rī, five; heads of the house of their fathers, mighty men of valour; and were reckoned by their genealogies twenty and two thousand and thirty and four.

8 And the sons of Bĕ'cher; Ze-mī'ra, and Jō'ăsh, and Ē-lī-ē'zer, and Ē-lī-ō-ē'na-ī, and Omri, and Jĕr'ī-mŏth, and Ā-bī'ah, and Ăn'a-thŏth, and Ăl'a-meth. All these are the sons of Bĕ'cher.

9 And the number of them, after their genealogy by their generations, heads of the house of their fathers, mighty men of valour, was twenty thousand and two hundred.

10 The sons also of Je-dī'a-el; Bĭl'hăn: and the sons of Bĭl'hăn; Jĕ'ush, and Benjamin, and Ē'hŭd, and Che-nā'a-nah, and Zĕ'than, and Thär'shĭsh, and A-hĭsh'a-här.

11 All these the sons of Je-dī'a-el, by the heads of their fathers, mighty men of valour, were seventeen thousand and two hundred soldiers, fit to go out for war and battle.

12 Shŭp'pĭm also, and Hŭp'pĭm, the

F. Genealogies of Issachar-Asher. 7:1-40.

7:1. The sons of Issachar are those names found elsewhere (Gen 46:13; Num 26:23-25) with two variant spellings (**Puah** for Phuva and **Jashub** for Job).

2-5. These descendants of **Tola** do not occur elsewhere. Their total **in the days of David** may hint at the census taken by Joab (I Chr 21).

6-12. The list of the **sons of Benjamin** differs from Genesis 46:21 and Numbers 26:38-41 because of omission and variant spellings. **Jediael** may be the Ashbel in Genesis. These descendants of Benjamin's first three sons occur only here.

Verse 12 is difficult to explain. If **Ir** is Benjamin's wife, then **Shuppim** and **Huppim** are Muppim (Gen 46:21) and Hupham (Num 26:39); and **Aher** may be either Ehi (Gen 46:21) or Ahiram (Num 26:38) (James G. Murphy, *The Book of Chronicles*, p. 37). Another explanation is that **Ir** is Iri (vs. 7).

children of Ir, *and* Hu'shĭm, the sons of
Ā'her.

13 ¶The sons of Năph'ta-lĭ; Jäh'zĭ-el,
and Gū'nĭ, and Jĕ'zer, and Shăl'lum, the
sons of Bĭl'hah.

14 ¶The sons of Ma-năs'seh; Ăsh'rĭ-
el, whom she bare: (*but* his concubine
the Ā'ram-ĭt-ess bare Mā'chĭr the
father of Gilead:

15 And Mā'chĭr took to wife *the sister*
of Hŭp'pĭm and Shŭp'pĭm, whose sister's name *was* Mā'a-chah;) and the
name of the second *was* Ze-lō'phe-hăd:
and Ze-lō'phe-hăd had daughters.

16 And Mā'a-chah the wife of Mā'chĭr
bare a son, and she called his name Pe'-
rĕsh; and the name of his brother *was*
She'rĕsh; and his sons *were* Ū'lam and
Rā'kĕm.

17 And the sons of Ū'lam; Bĕ'dăn.
These *were* the sons of Gilead, the son
of Mā'chĭr, the son of Ma-năs'seh.

18 And his sister Hăm-mŏl'e-kĕth
bare Ĭ'shŏd, and Ă-bĭ-ē'zer, and Mā-hā'-
läh.

19 And the sons of She-mĭ'dah were,
A-hĭ'an, and Shĕ'chem, and Lĭk'hĭ, and
A'nĭ-am.

20 ¶And the sons of Ē'phra-im;
Shū'the-lah, and Be'rĕd his son, and
Tā'hăth his son, and Ĕl'a-dah his son,
and Tā'hăth his son,

21 And Zā'băd his son, and Shū'the-
lah his son, and Ē'zer, and Ē'le-ad,
whom the men of Gath *that were* born
in *that* land slew, because they came
down to take away their cattle.

22 And Ē'phra-im their father
mourned many days, and his brethren
came to comfort him.

23 ¶And when he went in to his wife,
she conceived, and bare a son, and he
called his name Be-rī'ah, because it
went evil with his house.

24 (And his daughter *was* Shĕ'rah,
who built Bĕth-hō'ron the nether, and
the upper, and Ŭz'zen-shĕ'rah.)

25 And Rĕ'phah *was* his son, also
Rĕ'shĕph, and Tē'lah his son, and
Tā'hăn his son,

26 Lā'a-dan his son, Ăm-mī'hŭd his
son, E-lĭsh'a-ma his son,

27 Non his son, Je-hŏsh'u-ah his son.

28 ¶And their possessions and habitations *were*, Bĕth-el and the towns
thereof, and eastward Nā'a-răn, and
westward Gĕ'zer, with the towns thereof; Shĕ'chem also and the towns
thereof, unto Gā'za and the towns
thereof:

29 And by the borders of the children
of Ma-năs'seh, Bĕth-shē'an and her
towns, Tā'a-năch and her towns, Me-
gĭd'dō and her towns, Dor and her
towns. In these dwelt the children of
Joseph the son of Israel.

30 ¶The sons of Asher; Ĭm'nah, and
Ĭs'ū-ah, and Ĭsh'ū-ai, and Be-rī'ah, and
Se'rah their sister.

31 And the sons of Be-rī'ah; Hē'ber,
and Măl'chĭ-el, who *is* the father of Bir'-
zā-vĭth.

32 And Hē'ber begat Jăph'let, and
Shō'mer, and Hō'tham, and Shū'a their
sister.

13-14. The genealogies of **Naphtali** are the same grandsons of **Bilhah**, Rachel's maid (Gen 30:1-8) that occur elsewhere (Gen 46:24; Num 26:48-51) except with slight spelling variations. The **sons of Manasseh** appear to be those in Transjordan. The arrangement of names is fragmentary and supplementary to those found in Numbers 26:29-34. **Ashriel** was actually a great-grandson through **Machir** and **Gilead**. The antecedent to **she bare** is his Aramean concubine.

15-19. Machir's wife, **Maachah,** was the sister of Huppim and Shuppim (vs. 12). **The second,** i.e., the second "son" of mention (Ashriel was the first) was **Zelophehad,** the son of Hepher, who had only daughters (cf. Num 27:1-11; 36:1-12). **Hammoleketh** was Machir's sister. **Shemida** was another great-grandson of Manasseh through Machir and Gilead (Num 26:32).

20-29. The first four **sons of Ephraim** are those found in Numbers 26:35-37 with variant spellings. The last three were killed in an attempted cattle-stealing raid. **Beriah** is a play on the Hebrew *bera'ah*, "in evil". The names that follow are the ancestors of **Jehoshua** (Joshua), Moses' successor. The description of Ephraim's territory included **Gaza.** This site is too far south from Ephraim and should possibly be rendered Ayyah (NASB).

30-40. Of the genealogies of **Asher,** with the exception of **Birzavith,** which is thought to be a town, all the names are found in earlier lists (Gen 46:17; Num 26:44-47). These latter names are unattested elsewhere. **Shamer** (vs. 34) and **Helem** (vs. 35) are probably **Shomer** and **Hotham** (vs. 32). **Jether** (vs. 38) is possibly **Ithran** (vs. 37).

33 And the sons of Jăph′let; Pā′săch, and Bĭm′hăl, and Ăsh′văth. These *are* the children of Jăph′let.

34 And the sons of Shā′mer; Ā′hī, and Rōh′gah, Je-hub′bah, and Ā′ram,

35 And the sons of his brother Hē′lĕm; Zō′phah, and Ĭm′na, and Shē′lesh, and Ā′mal.

36 The sons of Zō′phah; Sū′ah, and Hăr′ne-pher, and Shū′al, and Be′rī, and Ĭm′rah,

37 Bē′zer, and Hod, and Shăm′ma, and Shĭl′shah, and Ĭth′răn, and Be-ē′ra.

38 And the sons of Jē′ther; Je-phŭn′neh, and Pĭs′pah, and Â′ra.

39 And the sons of Ŭl′la; Ā′rah, and Hăn′ī-el, and Re-zī′a.

40 All these *were* the children of Asher, heads of *their* father's house, choice *and* mighty men of valour, chief of the princes. And the number throughout the genealogy of them that were apt to the war *and* to battle *was* twenty and six thousand men.

CHAPTER 8

NOW Benjamin begat Bē′la his firstborn, Ăsh′bĕl the second, and A-hâr′ah the third,

2 Nō′hah the fourth, and Rā′pha the fifth.

3 And the sons of Bē′la were, Ăd′där, and Ge′ra, and A-bī′hŭd,

4 And A-bĭsh′ū-a, and Nā′a-man, and A-hō′ah,

5 And Ge′ra, and She-phū′phan, and Hū′ram.

6 And these *are* the sons of Ē′hŭd: these are the heads of the fathers of the inhabitants of Gē′ba, and they removed them to Măn′a-hăth:

7 And Nā′a-man, and A-hī′ah, and Ge′ra, he removed them, and begat Ŭz′za, and A-hī′hŭd.

8 And Shā-ha-rā′im begat *children* in the country of Moab, after he had sent them away; Hu′shĭm and Bā′a-ra *were* his wives.

9 And he begat of Hō′dĕsh his wife, Jō′băb, and Zĭb′ī-a, and Mē′sha, and Măl′chăm,

10 And Jē′ŭz, and Sha-chī′a, and Mir′ma. These *were* his sons, heads of the fathers.

11 And of Hu′shĭm he begat Ab′ī-tŭb, and Ĕl′pā-al.

12 The sons of Ĕl′pā-al; Ē′ber, and Mĭ′shăm, and Shā′med, who built Ō′nō, and Lod, with the towns thereof:

13 Be-rī′ah also, and Shē′ma, who *were* heads of the fathers of the inhabitants of Āij′a-lŏn, who drove away the inhabitants of Gath:

14 And A-hī′o, Shā′shăk, and Jĕr′e-mŏth,

15 And Zĕb-a-dī′ah, and Â′răd and Ā′der,

16 And Michael, and Ĭs′pah, and Jō′ha, the sons of Be-rī′ah;

17 And Zĕb-a-dī′ah, and Me-shŭl′lam, and Hez′e-kī, and Hē′ber,

18 Ĭsh′me-raī also, and Jez-lī′ah, and Jō′băb, the sons of Ĕl′pā-al;

19 And Jakim, and Zĭch′rī, and Zăb′dī,

20 And Ĕ-lī-ē′na-ī, and Zĭl′thaī, and E-lī′el,

G. Genealogies of Benjamin and Saul's House. 8:1-40.

A second Benjamin genealogy is given, and more details are enumerated than for any other tribe except Judah and Levi. The purpose of the Chronicler was to trace the ancestry of Israel's first king, Saul. Also, many Benjamites helped comprise the postexilic Jewish community at Jerusalem (Neh 11:4, 7, 31, 36).

8:1-5. The names found here vary from previous lists (Gen 46:21; Num 26:38-41). Even the I Chronicles 7:6-12 list offers many divergences. Murphy's (p. 41) suggestion that this Benjamin is not Jacob's son, but his grandson who was born to Bilhan (7:10), lacks support.

6-13. The connection of the names of this section with those of Benjamin's immediate descendants in the previous section is not stated. These names appear only here. The identity of **Ehud** (vs. 6) is uncertain. The spelling of his name here (Heb *'echūd*) is different than that of 7:10 (Heb *'ehūd*), the son of Bilhan. The Benjamite judge (Jud 3:15) had the name found in 7:10, but he was the son of Gera. The details of Ehud's sons' captivity (vs. 7) are unclear. **Shaharaim . . . sent . . . away,** i.e., divorced two of his wives (vs. 8) after they had borne him children (cf. vs. 11). A dating for the events of verses 12-13 is uncertain.

14-28. These dwelt in Jerusalem (vs. 28). This refers to those named in verses 14-27. Since Jerusalem lay just within the original boundary of Benjamin's tribal territory, one should expect to find a large Benjamite population there during the monarchial period (cf. Neh 11).

21 And Ăd-a-ī′ah, and Bĕr-a-ī′ah, and Shĭm′răth, the sons of Shĭm′hī;

22 And Ĭsh′păn, and Hē′ber, and E-lī′el,

23 And Ăbdŏn, and Zĭch′rī, and Hā′-nan,

24 And Hăn-a-nī′ah, and Ē′lam, and Ăn-tō-thī′jah,

25 And Ĭph-e-dē′iah, and Pe-nū′el, the sons of Shā′shăk;

26 And Shăm-she-ra′ī, and Shē-ha-rī′ah, and Ăth-a-lī′ah,

27 And Jâr-e-sī′ah, and E-lī′ah, and Zĭch′rī, the sons of Jer′ō-hăm.

28 These *were* heads of the fathers, by their generations, chief *men*. These dwelt in Jerusalem.

29 And at Gibeon dwelt the father of Gibeon; whose wife's name *was* Mā′a-chah:

30 And his firstborn son Ăbdŏn, and Zur, and Kish, and Bā′al, and Nā′dăb,

31 And Gē′dôr, and A-hī′o, and Zā′-cher,

32 And Mĭk′lŏth begat Shĭm′e-ah. And these also dwelt with their brethren in Jerusalem, over against them.

33 ¶And Ner begat Kish, and Kish begat Saul, and Saul begat Jonathan, and Măl′chī-shu′a, and A-bĭn′a-dăb, and Ĕsh-bā′al.

34 And the son of Jonathan *was* Mĕr′-ib-bā′al; andMĕr′ib-bā′al begat Mī′cah.

35 And the sons of Mī′cah *were*, Pī′thŏn, and Mē′lêch, and Tâ′re-a, and Ahaz.

36 And Ahaz begat Je-hō′a-dah; and Je-hō′a-dah begat Ăl′e-meth, and Ăz′ma-vĕth, and Zimri; and Zimri begat Mō′za.

37 And Mō′za begat Bĭn′e-a: Râ′pha *was* his son, Ĕ-le′ă-sah his son, Ā′zel his son:

38 And Ā′zel had six sons, whose names *are* these, Ăz′ri-kam, Bōch′e-rū, and Ĭsh′ma-el, and Shē-a-rī′ah, and Ō-ba-dī′ah, and Hā′nan. All these *were* the sons of Ā′zel.

39 And the sons of Ĕ′shĕk his brother *were*, Ū′lam his firstborn, Jē′hŭsh the second, and E-lĭph′e-lĕt the third.

40 And the sons of Ū′lam were mighty men of valour, archers, and had many sons, and sons' sons, an hundred and fifty. All these *are* of the sons of Benjamin.

CHAPTER 9

SO all Israel were reckoned by genealogies; and, behold, they *were* written in the book of the kings of Israel and Jū′dah, *who* were carried away to Babylon for their transgression.

2 ¶Now the first inhabitants that dwelt in their possessions in their cities *were*, the Israelites, the priests, Lē′-vītes, and the Nĕth′i-nĭmś.

3 And in Jerusalem dwelt of the

29-40. The father of Gibeon is identified as Jehiel in 9:35 (or Abiel in I Sam 9:1; 14:51), but his connection with the preceding Benjamite is not stated. He was the great-grandfather of Saul.

Ner, Jehiel's fifth son and the important link to Kish, is omitted in verse 30, but included in 9:36. **Abinadab** is thought by some to be the same as Ishui in I Samuel 14:49; but it seems more likely that Abinadab was omitted there (cf. I Sam 31:2), and Ishui is Ishbosheth or **Eshbaal. Eshbaal** (man of baal) was probably his actual name; but because of shameful associations with the Canaanite god Baal, the name Ishbosheth (man of shame) was substituted. Saul may not have had the god Baal in mind when he named his son, since *ba'al* simply means "master" (Payne, p. 374).

In like manner, **Merib-baal** (vs. 34), which means Baal contends, is called Mephibosheth, possibly meaning scatterer of shame, in II Samuel 4:4.

H. Inhabitants of Jerusalem. 9:1-44.

9:1. This is actually a summary of all of the preceding genealogies, rather than an introduction to the following section. **All Israel** includes Judah. **The book of the Kings** is probably the annals that are no longer extant.

2. This verse is often thought to introduce a section parallel to the post-exilic list found in Nehemiah 11:3ff.; but apart from the initial groups that are found here (Israelites, priests, etc.) and the similarity of arrangement, the names of the two lists do not correspond very closely. Therefore, it is best to understand **first inhabitants,** not in the sense of principal or "chief" inhabitants (Neh 11:3), but as the inhabitants before the captivity. **Their possessions** were their land allotments. **Israelites** (lit., Israel) probably refers to all non-Levites. **Nethinim** (cf. Ezr 2:43; 8:20) is literally "given ones." They probably were non-Israelite temple servants who traced their ancestry to the Gibeonites (Josh 9:16-27).

3-6. Of those who lived **in Jerusalem,** the families of

children of Jŭ′dah, and of the children of Benjamin, and of the children of Ē′phra-im, and Ma-năs′seh;

4 Ū′tha-ī the son of Ăm-mī′hŭd, the son of Omri, the son of Ĭm′rī, the son of Bā′nī, of the children of Phâ′rĕz the son of Jŭ′dah.

5 And of the Shī′lo-nītes; Aṡ-ā′iah the firstborn, and his sons.

6 And of the sons of Ze′rah; Je-ū′el, and their brethren, six hundred and ninety.

7 And of the sons of Benjamin; Săl′lū the son of Me-shŭl′lam, the son of Hŏd-a-vī′ah, the son of Hăs-e-nū′ah,

8 And Ĭb-nē′iah the son of Jer′ō-hăm, and Ē′lah the son of Ūz′zi, the son of Mĭch′rī, and Me-shŭl′lam the son of Sheph-a-thi′ah, the son of Re-ū′el, the son of Ĭb-nī′jah;

9 And their brethren, according to their generations, nine hundred and fifty and six. All these men *were* chief of the fathers in the house of their fathers.

10 ¶And of the priests; Je-dā′iah, and Je-hoi′a-rīb, and Jā′chin,

11 And Ăz-a-rī′ah the son of Hīl-kī′ah, the son of Me-shŭl′lam, the son of Zā′dŏk, the son of Me-rā′ioth, the son of A-hī′tŭb, the ruler of the house of God;

12 And Ăd-a-ī′ah the son of Jer′ō-hăm, the son of Păsh′ur, the son of Măl-chī′jah, and Mā-ăs′ī-aī the son of Ā′dī-el, the son of Jäh′ze-rah, the son of Me-shŭl′lam, the son of Me-shĭl′le-mĭth, the son of Ĭm′mer;

13 And their brethren, heads of the house of their fathers, a thousand and seven hundred and threescore; very able men for the work of the service of the house of God.

14 ¶And of the Lē′vītes; Shem-ā-i′ah the son of Hăs′shub, the son of Ăz′ri-kam, the son of Hăsh-a-bī′ah, of the sons of Me-rā′rī;

15 And Băk-băk′kar, He′rĕsh, and Gā′lăl, and Măt-ta-nī′ah the son of Mī′cah, the son of Zĭch′rī, the son of Ā′săph;

16 And Ō-ba-dī′ah the son of Shem-ā-i′ah, the son of Gā′lăl, the son of Jed′ū-thun, and Bĕr-e-chī′ah the son of Ā′sa, the son of Ĕl′kā-nah, that dwelt in the villages of the Ne-tōph′a-thītes.

17 And the porters *were*, Shăl′lum, and Ăk′kŭb, and Tăl′mon, and A-hī′man, and their brethren: Shăl′lum *was* the chief;

18 Who hitherto *waited* in the king′s gate eastward: they *were* porters in the companies of the children of Levi.

19 And Shăl′lum the son of Kô′re, the son of E-bī′a-săph, the son of Kô′rah, and his brethren, of the house of his father, the Kô′rah-ītes, *were* over the work of the service, keepers of the gates of the tabernacle: and their fathers, *being* over the host of the Lord, *were* keepers of the entry.

20 And Phĭn′e-has the son of Ē-le-ā′zar was the ruler over them in time past, *and* the Lord *was* with him.

21 *And* Zĕch-a-rī′ah the son of Me-shĕl-e-mī′ah *was* porter of the door of the tabernacle of the congregation.

22 All these which were chosen to be porters in the gates *were* two hundred

Ephraim and Manasseh, though mentioned here, supply no names in the following lists. The Shilonites are probably descendants of Shelah (Num 26:20). Thus, the three sons of Judah (Pharez, vs. 4, and Zerah, vs. 6) are represented here.

7-16. These sons of Benjamin can not be traced to the genealogy in chapter 8. Jedaiah, Jehoiarib, and Jachin are only three of the twenty-four priestly courses established by David (I Chr 24:7, 17). Adaiah and Maasiai are descendants of Malchijah and Immer, respectively, of the priestly courses (I Chr 24:9, 14). The villages of the Netophathites are thought to have been located near Beth-lehem. Two of David's mighty men came from here (II Sam 23:28-29), and some of the exiles returned here (Ezr 2:22).

17-19. Other Levites were porters, i.e., gatekeepers, of whom Shallum was chief. The men of his particular company had guarded the eastern gate, through which the king entered hitherto, i.e., from the time of their appointment by David (vs. 22). Shallum (spelled Meshelemiah in vs. 21; cf. 26:14) traced his ancestry to Korah, who rebelled in the wilderness (Num 16:1, 32). Korah was destroyed, but his family continued (Num 26:11) and was important to the Kohathites (cf. 6:22 where the Kohath line is traced through Korah).

20-25. Phinehas was Aaron's grandson who succeeded his father Eleazar as priest (Josh 24:33). The house of the tabernacle refers, not to Moses' tabernacle, but to the tent erected by David to house the ark of the covenant (15:1; II Sam 6:17) before the Temple was constructed.

and twelve. These were reckoned by their genealogy in their villages, whom David and Samuel the seer did ordain in their set office.

23 So they and their children *had* the oversight of the gates of the house of the LORD, *namely*, the house of the tabernacle, by wards.

24 In four quarters were the porters, toward the east, west, north, and south.

25 And their brethren, *which were* in their villages, *were* to come after seven days from time to time with them.

26 For these Lē′vītes, the four chief porters, were in *their* set office, and were over the chambers and treasuries of the house of God.

27 And they lodged round about the house of God, because the charge *was* upon them, and the opening thereof every morning *pertained* to them.

28 And *certain* of them had the charge of the ministering vessels, that they should bring them in and out by tale.

29 *Some* of them also *were* appointed to oversee the vessels, and all the instruments of the sanctuary, and the fine flour, and the wine, and the oil, and the frankincense, and the spices.

30 And *some* of the sons of the priests made the ointment of the spices.

31 And Măt-ti-thī′ah, *one* of the Lē′vītes, who *was* the firstborn of Shăl′lum the Kō′rah-īte, had the set office over the things that were made in the pans.

32 And *other* of their brethren, of the sons of the Kō′hăth-ītes, *were* over the shewbread, to prepare *it* every sabbath.

33 And these *are* the singers, chief of the fathers of the Lē′vītes, *who remaining* in the chambers *were* free: for they were employed in *that* work day and night.

34 These chief fathers of the Lē′vītes *were* chief throughout their generations; these dwelt at Jerusalem.

35 ¶And in Gibeon dwelt the father of Gibeon, Je-hī′el, whose wife's name *was* Mā′a-chah:

36 And his firstborn son Ăb′dŏn, then Zur, and Kish, and Bā′al, and Ner, and Nā′dăb,

37 And Gē′dôr, and A-hī′o, and Zĕch-a-rī′ah, and Mĭk′lŏth.

38 And Mĭk′lŏth begat Shim′e-am. And they also dwelt with their brethren at Jerusalem, over against their brethren.

39 And Ner begat Kish; and Kish begat Saul; and Saul begat Jonathan, and Măl′chī-shu′a, and A-bĭn′a-dăb, and Ĕsh-bā′al.

40 And the son of Jonathan *was* Mĕr′-ib-bā′al: and Mĕr′ib-bā′al begat Mī′cah.

41 And the sons of Mī′cah *were*, Pī′-thŏn, and Mē′lĕch, and Täh′re-a, *and* Ahaz.

42 And Ahaz begat Jâ′rah; and Jâ′rah begat Ăl′e-meth, and Ăz′ma-vĕth, and Zimri; and Zimri begat Mō′za;

43 And Mō′za begat Bĭn′e-a; and Reph-ā-ī′ah his son, Ĕ-le′ā-sah his son, Ā′zel his son.

26-34. Other responsibilities of the Levites are now enumerated. The **chambers** of the **house of God** (cf. I Kgs 6:10) were those rooms where the tithes and sacred vessels were kept (cf. II Chr 31:11-12; Neh 13:4-9). Determining the antecedent for **these** in verse 33 is difficult; the names found in verses 15ff. are possibilities.

35-44. These verses are repetitions of 8:33-40. Here they serve as an introduction to the death of Saul (ch. 10) and the fall of his house from the throne of Israel.

44 And Ā′zel had six sons, whose names are these, Ăz′ri-kam, Bŏch′e-rū, and Ĭsh′ma-el, and Shē′a-rī-ah, and Ō-ba-dī′ah, and Hā′nan: these were the sons of Ā′zel.

CHAPTER 10

NOW the Philistines fought against Israel; and the men of Israel fled from before the Philistines, and fell down slain in mount Gĭl-bō′a.

2 And the Philistines followed hard after Saul, and after his sons; and the Philistines slew Jonathan, and A-bĭn′a-dăb, and Mal′chi–shu′a, the sons of Saul.

3 And the battle went sore against Saul, and the archers hit him, and he was wounded of the archers.

4 Then said Saul to his armourbearer, Draw thy sword, and thrust me through therewith; lest these uncircumcised come and abuse me. But his armourbearer would not; for he was sore afraid. So Saul took a sword, and fell upon it.

5 And when his armourbearer saw that Saul was dead, he fell likewise on the sword, and died.

6 So Saul died, and his three sons, and all his house died together.

7 And when all the men of Israel that were in the valley saw that they fled, and that Saul and his sons were dead, then they forsook their cities, and fled: and the Philistines came and dwelt in them.

8 ¶And it came to pass on the morrow, when the Philistines came to strip the slain, that they found Saul and his sons fallen in mount Gĭl-bō′a.

9 And when they had stripped him, they took his head, and his armour, and sent into the land of the Philistines round about, to carry tidings unto their idols, and to the people.

10 And they put his armour in the house of their gods, and fastened his head in the temple of Dā′gŏn.

11 ¶And when all Jā′besh-gĭl′e-ad heard all that the Philistines had done to Saul,

12 They arose, all the valiant men, and took away the body of Saul, and the bodies of his sons, and brought them to Jā′besh, and buried their bones under the oak in Jā′besh, and fasted seven days.

13 ¶So Saul died for his transgression which he committed against the LORD, even against the word of the LORD, which he kept not, and also for asking counsel of one that had a familiar spirit, to enquire of it;

14 And enquired not of the LORD: therefore he slew him, and turned the kingdom unto David the son of Jesse.

CHAPTER 11

THEN all Israel gathered themselves to David unto Hē′bron, saying, Behold, we are thy bone and thy flesh.

2 And moreover in time past, even when Saul was king, thou wast he that leddest out and broughtest in Israel: and the LORD thy God said unto thee, Thou shalt feed my people Israel, and

II. THE REIGN OF DAVID. 10:1-29:30.

A. The Death of Saul. 10:1-14.

10:1-12. As background to David's ascent to the throne, this chapter is devoted to the death of Saul and the destruction of his sons at the hands of the Philistines. Verses 1-12 are practically identical to I Samuel 31:1-13 (see Samuel commentary). The major variation occurs in verses 11-12. Samuel records that the Philistines fastened his body to the wall of Beth-shan. Here his head, apart from the body, was fastened to the house of Dagon. Samuel also adds that his bones were burned before being buried.

13-14. These verses have no parallel in I Samuel 31. The Chronicler presumes his readers' acquaintance with Saul's life of failure as recorded in I Samuel. For his transgression . . . against the word of the LORD, see I Sam 13:8-13; 15:3, 19. Also, he had consulted a familiar spirit (cf. I Sam 28:7ff.).

B. David's Coronation and Capture of Jerusalem. 11:1-9.

11:1-9. David's seven-and-one-half year reign at Hebron (II Sam 2-4) is overlooked by the Chronicler, and attention immediately focuses on the new king of a united monarchy. Except for one omission, the reference to David's age and his years as king of Hebron (II Sam 5:4-5), and two small additions, this account of David's call and anointing and his securing Jerusalem for his capital is practically identical to II Samuel 5:1-10 (see Samuel commentary).

769

thou shalt be ruler over my people Israel.

3 Therefore came all the elders of Israel to the king to Hĕ′bron; and David made a covenant with them in Hĕ′bron before the Lord; and they anointed David king over Israel, according to the word of the Lord by Samuel.

4 ¶And David and all Israel went to Jerusalem, which is Jĕ′bus; where the Jĕb′u-sītes were, the inhabitants of the land.

5 And the inhabitants of Jĕ′bus said to David, Thou shalt not come hither. Nevertheless David took the castle of Zion, which is the city of David.

6 And David said, Whosoever smiteth the Jĕb′u-sītes first shall be chief and captain. So Jō′ăb the son of Zer-ū-i′ah went first up, and was chief.

7 And David dwelt in the castle; therefore they called it the city of David.

8 And he built the city round about, even from Mĭl′lō round about: and Jō′ăb repaired the rest of the city.

9 So David waxed greater and greater: for the Lord of hosts was with him.

10 ¶These also are the chief of the mighty men whom David had, who strengthened themselves with him in his kingdom, and with all Israel, to make him king, according to the word of the Lord concerning Israel.

11 And this is the number of the mighty men whom David had; Ja-shō′be-am, an Hăch′mō-nīte, the chief of the captains: he lifted up his spear against three hundred slain by him at one time.

12 And after him was Ĕ-le-ā′zar the son of Dodo, the A-hō′hīte, who was one of the three mighties.

13 He was with David at Păs-dăm′-mĭm, and there the Philistines where gathered together to battle, where was a parcel of ground full of barley; and the people fled from before the Philistines.

14 And they set themselves in the midst of that parcel, and delivered it, and slew the Philistines; and the Lord saved them by a great deliverance.

15 Now three of the thirty captains went down to the rock to David, into the cave of A-dŭl′lam; and the host of the Philistines encamped in the valley of Rĕph′a-im.

16 And David was then in the hold, and the Philistines' garrison was then at Bĕth-lĕhĕm.

17 And David longed, and said, Oh that one would give me drink of the water of the well of Bĕth-lĕhĕm, that is at the gate!

18 And the three brake through the host of the Philistines, and drew water out of the well of Bĕth-lĕhĕm, that was

Joab . . . was chief (vs. 6). In response to David's challenge and promise of position, David's nephew (**Zeruiah** was David's half sister, cf. II Sam 17:25) was the first to enter the Jebusite city of Jerusalem in order to take it (II Sam 5:8). As a reward he was made captain of the army. Joab had been David's captain at Hebron, and now he won the right to be over the army of all Israel.

Millo (from the verb "to fill") was probably a part of the wall that was weak and needed to be "filled in." Joab's activity in repairing the city is peculiar to the Chronicler's account.

C. David's Mighty Men. 11:10-12:40.

10. The account of Joab's heroic deed is followed by an extensive list of other **mighty men** of David and their heroic accomplishments. Most of the list (vss. 11-41a) is a close parallel to II Samuel 23:8-39, though there are some variations.

Verse 10 is peculiar to Chronicles and may indicate why the Chronicler chose to place this list at the beginning of David's reign and not at the end as it appears in II Samuel. These men **strengthened themselves with him in his kingdom, and with all Israel.** . . . While it is not necessary to believe that these men had performed all their heroic feats before David became king, probably many had accompanied him in exile, had been supportive of him in his rise to the throne of Judah and had helped secure recognition of his kingship over all Israel.

11-41a. For discussion on these verses, see the II Samuel commentary on the parallel passage (23:8-39).

by the gate, and took *it*, and brought *it* to David: but David would not drink *of* it, but poured it out to the LORD,

19 And said, My God forbid it me, that I should do this thing: shall I drink the blood of these men that have put their lives in jeopardy? for with *the jeopardy of* their lives they brought it. Therefore he would not drink it. These things did these three mightiest.

20 And A-bī'shaī the brother of Jō'ăb, he was chief of the three: for lifting up his spear against three hundred, he slew *them*, and had a name among the three.

21 Of the three, he was more honourable than the two; for he was their captain: howbeit he attained not to the *first* three.

22 Be-nā'iah the son of Je-hoi'a-da, the son of a valiant man of Kăb'ze-el, who had done many acts; he slew two lionlike men of Moab: also he went down and slew a lion in a pit in a snowy day.

23 And he slew an Egyptian, a man of *great* stature, five cubits high; and in the Egyptian's hand *was* a spear like a weaver's beam; and he went down to him with a staff, and plucked the spear out of the Egyptian's hand, and slew him with his own spear.

24 These *things* did Be-nā'iah the son of Je-hoi'a-da, and had the name among the three mighties.

25 Behold, he was honourable among the thirty, but attained not to the *first* three: and David set him over his guard.

26 Also the valiant men of the armies *were*, Ă'sa-hĕl the brother of Jō'ăb, Ĕl-hā'nan the son of Dodo of Bĕth'-lehĕm,

27 Shăm'mŏth the Hă'ro-rīte, Hē'lĕz the Pĕl'o-nīte,

28 Ī'ra the son of Ĭk'kesh the Te-kō'ite, Ă'bī-e'zer the Ăn'toth-īte,

29 Sĭb'be-caī the Hu'shath-īte, Ī'laī the A-hō'hīte,

30 Mā-har'a-ī the Ne-tōph'a-thīte, Hē'lĕd the son of Bā'a-nah the Netōph'a-thīte,

31 Ĭth'a-ī the son of Rī'baī of Gĭb'e-ah, *that pertained* to the children of Benjamin, Be-nā'iah the Pĭr'a-thŏn-īte,

32 Hū'raī of the brooks of Gā'ash, Ă'bī-el the Ăr'bath-īte,

33 Ăz'ma-vĕth the Ba'hā'rūm-īte, E-lī'ah-ba the Shā-ăl'bo-nīte,

34 The sons of Hā'shĕm the Gī'zonīte, Jonathan the son of Shā'ge the Hā'ra-rīte,

35 A-hī'am the son of Sa'car the Hā'ra-rīte, El-ī'phal the son of Ur,

36 Hē'pher the Me-chē'rath-īte, A-hī'jah the Pĕl'o-nīte,

37 Hĕz'rō the Carmelite, Nā'a-raī the son of Ĕz'ba-ī,

38 Jō'el the brother of Nā'than, Mĭb'här the son of Hăg'ge-rī,

39 Zē'lĕk the Ammonite, Nā-har'a-ī the Be'roth-īte, the armourbearer of Jō'ăb the son of Zer-ū-ī'ah,

40 Ī'ra the ĭth'rīte, Gâ'rĕb the ĭth'rīte,

41 Ū-rī'ah the Hittite, Zā'băd the son of Äh'laī,

42 Ăd'i-na the son of Shī'za the Reu-

41b-47. Beginning with **Zabad**, sixteen names appear as supplemental to II Samuel 23 and do not appear elsewhere. No explanation is given, but perhaps these were added when some of the original members died.

benite, a captain of the Reubenites, and thirty with him,

43 Hā'nan the son of Mā'a-chah, and Jŏsh'a-phăt the Mĭth'nīte,

44 Uz-zī'a the Ăsh'te-răth-īte, Shā'ma and Je-hī'el the sons of Hō'than the Ar'ō-er-īte,

45 Je-dī'a-el the son of Shĭm'rī, and Jō'ha his brother, the Tī'zīte,

46 E-lī'el the Mā'ha-vīte, and Jĕr'i-baī, and Jŏsh-a-vī'ah, the sons of Ĕl'nā-am, and ĭth'mah the Moabite,

47 E-lī'el, and Ō'bed, and Jā'sĭ-el the Me-sō'ba-īte.

CHAPTER 12

NOW these *are* they that came to David to Ziklag, while he yet kept himself close because of Saul the son of Kish: and they *were* among the mighty men, helpers of the war.

2 *They were* armed with bows, and could use both the right hand and the left in *hurling* stones and *shooting* arrows out of a bow, *even* of Saul's brethren of Benjamin.

3 The chief *was* Ā-hī'e-zer, then Jō'ăsh, the sons of She-mā'ah the Gĭb'e-ath-īte; and Jĕ'zi-el, and Pē'let, the sons of Ăz'ma-vĕth; and Bĕr'a-chah, and Jehu the An'toth-ite,

4 And Ĭs-mā-i'ah the Gĭb'e-o-nīte, a mighty man among the thirty, and over the thirty; and Jĕr-e-mī'ah, and Ja-hā'-ziel, and Jō-hā'nan, and Jŏs'a-băd the Gĕd'e-rath-īte,

5 E-lū'za-ī, and Jĕr'ī-mŏth, and Bē-a-lī'ah, and Shĕm-a-rī'ah, and Shĕph-a-tī'ah the Har'ū-phīte,

6 Ĕl'kā-nah, and Je-sī'ah, and A-zar'e-el, and Jō-ē'zer, and Ja-shō'be-am, the Kŏr'hītes,

7 And Jō-ē'lah, and Zĕb-a-dī'ah, the sons of Jer'ō-hăm of Gĕ'dôr.

8 And of the Găd'ītes there separated themselves unto David into the hold to the wilderness men of might, *and* men of war *fit* for the battle, that could handle shield and buckler, whose faces *were like* the faces of lions, and *were* as swift as the roes upon the mountains;

9 Ē'zer the first, Ō-ba-dī'ah the second, E-lī'ab the third,

10 Mĭsh-măn'nah the fourth, Jĕr-e-mī'ah the fifth,

11 Ăt'taī the sixth, E-lī'el the seventh,

12 Jō-hā'nan the eighth, Ĕl'zā-băd the ninth,

13 Jĕr-e-mī'ah the tenth, Măch'bă-naī the eleventh.

14 These *were* of the sons of Gad, captains of the host: one of the least *was* over an hundred, and the greatest over a thousand.

15 These *are* they that went over Jordan in the first month, when it had overflown all his banks; and they put to flight all *them* of the valleys, *both* toward the east, and toward the west.

16 And there came of the children of Benjamin and Jū'dah to the hold unto David.

17 And David went out to meet them, and answered and said unto them, If ye

12:1. Chapter 12 is supplementary to Samuel. It contains a list of those who joined David in his exile from Saul, as well as a list of those tribes who made him king of united Israel. **Ziklag** was the city on Judah's border that had fallen to the Philistines. Achish, king of Gath, gave the city to David for his residence while he was an exile from Saul (cf. background in I Sam 27:1-7).

2-7. Among the **mighty men** (vs. 1) who came to assist him were **Saul's brethren of Benjamin.** The injustice of his reign had fostered discontent among Saul's own tribe, so that many deserted him and took refuge with David (cf. Saul's distrust in Benjamin, I Sam 22:7-8).

8-15. The defection of these **Gadites,** a Transjordan tribe, precedes chronologically that of the Benjamites above since David had not yet fled to Ziklag. Identification of **the hold** is uncertain. It may be a reference to the cave of Adullam (I Sam 22:1), but the strongholds of En-gedi would have been more convenient for contact and seem more likely. So dedicated were these men to David's cause that they crossed the Jordan (vs. 15) at flood time (cf. Josh 3:15).

16-17. David's suspicions were aroused because of four previous occasions of betrayal: by Doeg the Edomite (I Sam 22: 9ff); by the residents of Keilah (I Sam 23:1-12); and twice by the residents of Ziph (I Sam 23:19ff.; 26:1ff.).

be come peaceably unto me to help me, mine heart shall be knit unto you: but if *ye be come* to betray me to mine enemies, seeing *there is* no wrong in mine hands, the God of our fathers look thereon, and rebuke *it*.

18 Then the spirit came upon A-măs´a-ī, *who was* chief of the captains, *and he said*, Thine *are* we, David, and on thy side, thou son of Jesse: peace, peace *be* unto thee, and peace *be* to thine helpers; for thy God helpeth thee. Then David received them and made them captains of the band.

19 And there fell *some* of Ma-năs´seh to David, when he came with the Philistines against Saul to battle: but they helped them not: for the lords of the Philistines upon advisement sent him away, saying, He will fall to his master Saul to *the jeopardy of* our heads.

20 As he went to Ziklag, there fell to him of Ma-năs´seh, Ăd´nah, and Jŏz´a-băd, and Je-dī´a-el, and Michael, and Jŏz´a-băd, and E-lī´hū, and Zĭl´thaī, captains of the thousands that *were* of Ma-năs´seh.

21 And they helped David against the band *of the rovers* for they *were* all mighty men of valour, and were captains in the host.

22 For at *that* time day by day there came to David to help him, until *it was* a great host, like the host of God.

23 ¶And these *are* the numbers of the bands *that were* ready armed to the war, *and* came to David to Hē´bron, to turn the kingdom of Saul to him, according to the word of the LORD.

24 The children of Jū´dah that bare shield and spear *were* six thousand and eight hundred, ready armed to the war.

25 Of the children of Simeon, mighty men of valour for the war, seven thousand and one hundred.

26 Of the children of Levi four thousand and six hundred.

27 And Je-hoi´a-da *was* the leader of the Aăr´o-nītes, and with him *were* three thousand and seven hundred;

28 And Zā´dŏk, a young man mighty of valour, and of his father's house twenty and two captains.

29 And of the children of Benjamin, the kindred of Saul, three thousand: for hitherto the greatest part of them had kept the ward of the house of Saul.

30 And of the children of Ē´phra-im twenty thousand and eight hundred, mighty men of valour, famous throughout the house of their fathers.

31 And of the half tribe of Ma-năs´seh eighteen thousand, which were expressed by name, to come and make David king.

32 And of the children of Ĭs´sa-char, which *were* men that had understanding of the times, to know what Israel ought to do; the heads of them *were* two hundred; and all their brethren *were* at their commandment.

33 Of Zĕb´u-lun, such as went forth to battle, expert in war, with all instruments of war, fifty thousand, which could keep rank: *they were* not of double heart.

34 And of Năph´ta-lī a thousand cap-

18. The spirit came upon Amasai (lit., the Spirit clothed Himself with Amasai, cf. Jud 6:34; II Chr 24:20), and he pledged his allegiance to David. If Amasai is the same as Amasa (II Sam 17:25), it seems ironic that he would desert David and support Absalom's rebellion.

19-22. The defection of these captains of Manasseh must have occurred just prior to Israel's battle with the Philistines at Gilboa (for background see I Sam 29). The Philistine lords mistrusted David, and he was sent back to Ziklag. Enroute he would have passed through the territory of Manasseh where he was undoubtedly joined by these seven captains.

Beginning with his stay at Ziklag and continuing through his seven and one-half years at Hebron, David's strength continued to increase (cf. II Sam 3:1).

23-38. This account, which is peculiar to Chronicles, is an enlargement of the event described in II Samuel 5:1-3 (cf. I Chr 11:1-3). Here those tribes that came to Hebron to make David king over a once-again united monarchy are enumerated. Every tribe was represented, including the Levites and both halves (east and west of Jordan) of Manasseh. The special mention of **Zadok** (vs. 28) may refer to the Levite who was one of David's priests (II Sam 20:25). The decision to make David king was one of total unity. **All these men of war . . . came with a perfect heart.**

tains, and with them with shield and spear thirty and seven thousand.

35 And of the Danites expert in war twenty and eight thousand and six hundred.

36 And of Asher, such as went forth to battle, expert in war, forty thousand.

37 And on the other side of Jordan, of the Reubenites, and the Găd'ītes, and of the half tribe of Ma-năs'seh, with all manner of instruments of war for the battle, an hundred and twenty thousand.

38 All these men of war, that could keep rank, came with a perfect heart to Hē'bron, to make David king over all Israel and all the rest also of Israel were of one heart to make David king.

39 And there they were with David three days, eating and drinking: for their brethren had prepared for them.

40 Moreover they that were nigh them, even unto Ĭs'sa-char and Zĕb'u-lun and Năph'ta-lī, brought bread on asses, and on camels, and on mules, and on oxen, and meat, meal, cakes of figs, and bunches of raisins, and wine, and oil, and oxen, and sheep abundantly: for there was joy in Israel.

CHAPTER 13

AND David consulted with the captains of thousands and hundreds, and with every leader.

2 And David said unto all the congregation of Israel, If it seem good unto you, and that it be of the LORD our God, let us send abroad unto our brethren every where, that are left in all the land of Israel, and with them also to the priests and Lē'vītes which are in their cities and suburbs, that they may gather themselves unto us:

3 And let us bring again the ark of our God to us: for we enquired not at it in the days of Saul.

4 And all the congregation said that they would do so: for the thing was right in the eyes of all the people.

5 So David gathered all Israel together, from Shī'hôr of Egypt even unto the entering of Hē'măth, to bring the ark of God from Kir'jath-jē'a-rīm.

6 And David went up, and all Israel, to Bā'al-ah, that is, to Kir'jath-jē'a-rīm, which belonged to Jū'dah, to bring up thence the ark of God the LORD, that dwelleth between the cherubims, whose name is called on it.

7 And they carried the ark of God in a new cart out of the house of A-bĭn'a-dăb: and Ŭz'za and A-hī'o drave the cart.

8 And David and all Israel played before God with all their might, and with singing, and with harps, and with psalteries, and with timbrels, and with cymbals, and with trumpets.

9 ¶And when they came unto the threshingfloor of Chī'don, Ŭz'za put

39-40. The coronation of the new king was celebrated by three joyous days of festive eating and drinking.

D. David and the Ark. 13:1-16:43.

1. His first attempt to transfer the ark to Jerusalem. 13:1-14.

The events of this chapter do not immediately follow chapter 12 chronologically, but occur some time after his capture of Jerusalem for his capital (11:1-9). Here, the decision is reached to make Jerusalem the religious center, as well as the political center. The parallel account appears in II Samuel 6:1-11.

13:1-2. The first four verses are peculiar to Chronicles. **David consulted** his captains and leaders (implied in I Sam 6:1).

All Israel was to be invited to Jerusalem to join in a project he wished to initiate if it met his advisors' approval. **Brethren . . . left in all the land** alludes to the desolation in the land caused by the Philistines.

3-4. Bring again the ark. For the account of the ark's capture at Ebenezer, its travels between Philistine cities, and its coming to reside at Kirjath-jearim, see I Samuel 5:1-7:2. It had remained at Kirjath-jearim for approximately seventy years (cf. Leon Wood's computation of the time in A Survey of Israel's History, p. 235). **We inquired not at it in the days of Saul.** Saul did in fact on one occasion request that the ark be brought to him, but there is no record that this command was obeyed or that he inquired of the Lord when it arrived.

5-14. The intention of David and Israel was commendable, but the method chosen to remove the ark from the house of Abinadab was not according to God's prescribed directions for transporting the ark (cf. its construction, Ex 25:14-15, and its transporters, Num 4:4-15; 7:9). Therefore, Uzza's misfortune occurred; and the ark was temporarily transferred to the house of Obed-edom.

These verses have an almost verbatim correspondence to II Samuel 6:1-11 (see Samuel commentary for a more complete discussion).

forth his hand to hold the ark; for the oxen stumbled.

10 And the anger of the Lord was kindled against Ŭz′za, and he smote him, because he put his hand to the ark: and there he died before God.

11 And David was displeased, because the Lord had made a breach upon Ŭz′za: wherefore that place is called Pe′rĕz–ŭz′za to this day.

12 And David was afraid of God that day, saying, How shall I bring the ark of God *home* to me?

13 So David brought not the ark *home* to himself to the city of David, but carried it aside into the house of Ō′bed–ē′dom the Gĭt′tīte.

14 And the ark of God remained with the family of Ō′bed–ē′dom in his house three months. And the Lord blessed the house of Ō′bed–ē′dom, and all that he had.

CHAPTER 14

NOW Hiram king of Tyre sent messengers to David, and timber of cedars, with masons and carpenters, to build him an house.

2 And David perceived that the Lord had confirmed him king over Israel, for his kingdom was lifted up on high, because of his people Israel.

3 ¶ And David took more wives at Jerusalem: and David begat more sons and daughters.

4 Now these *are* the names of *his* children which he had in Jerusalem; Shăm–mū′a, and Shō′băb, Nā′than, and Sŏl′o–mon,

5 And Ĭb′här, and Ĕl-i-shū′a, and Ĕl′pă-let.

6 And Nō′gah, and Nē′phĕg, and Ja-phī′a,

7 And E-lĭsh′a-ma, and Bē-el-ī′a-da, and E-lĭph′a-lĕt.

8 ¶ And when the Philistines heard that David was anointed king over all Israel, all the Philistines went up to seek David. And David heard *of it*, and went out against them.

9 And the Philistines came and spread themselves in the valley of Rĕph′a-im.

10 And David enquired of God, saying, Shall I go up against the Philistines? And wilt thou deliver them into mine hand? And the Lord said unto him, Go up; for I will deliver them into thine hand.

11 So they came up to Bā′al–per′a-zĭm; and David smote them there. Then David said, God hath broken in upon mine enemies by mine hand like the breaking forth of waters: therefore they called the name of that place Bā′al–per′a-zĭm.

12 And when they had left their gods there, David gave a commandment, and they were burned with fire.

13 And the Philistines yet again spread themselves abroad in the valley.

14 Therefore David enquired again of God; and God said unto him, Go not up after them; turn away from them, and come upon them over against the mulberry trees.

15 And it shall be, when thou shalt hear a sound of going in the tops of the mulberry trees, *that* then thou shalt go

2. His family and independence from the Philistines. 14:1-17.

That the Chronicler's arrangement of his data differs from Samuel's is quite evident, for in Samuel this information precedes David's attempt to bring the ark to Jerusalem (II Sam 5:11-25).

14:1-7. Verses 1-2 parallel II Samuel 5:11-12 (see Samuel commentary). (On verses 3-7 see notes on 3:5-9—for parallel in II Sam 5:13-16, see Samuel commentary).

8-16. David's two early encounters in verses 8-12 and 13-16, whereby independence from the Philistines was won, find their parallel in II Samuel 5:17-25 (see Samuel commentary).

out to battle: for God is gone forth before thee to smite the host of the Philistines.

16 David therefore did as God commanded him: and they smote the host of the Philistines from Gĭb'e-on even to Gā'zer.

17 And the fame of David went out into all lands; and the LORD brought the fear of him upon all nations.

CHAPTER 15

AND *David* made him houses in the city of David, and prepared a place for the ark of God, and pitched for it a tent.

2 Then David said, None ought to carry the ark of God but the Lē'vītes: for them hath the LORD chosen to carry the ark of God, and to minister unto him for ever.

3 And David gathered all Israel together to Jerusalem, to bring up the ark of the LORD unto his place, which he had prepared for it.

4 And David assembled the children of Aaron, and the Lē'vītes:

5 Of the sons of Kō'hăth; Ū'rĭ-el the chief, and his brethren an hundred and twenty:

6 Of the sons of Me-râ'rī; Aś-ā'iah the chief, and his brethren two hundred and twenty:

7 Of the sons of Ger'shom; Jō'el the chief, and his brethren an hundred and thirty:

8 Of the sons of Ĕ-lĭz'ā-phan; Shem-ā-i'ah the chief, and his brethren two hundred:

9 Of the sons of Hē'bron; E-lī'el the chief, and his brethren fourscore:

10 Of the sons of Ŭz'zĭ-el; Am-mĭn'a-dăb the chief, and his brethren an hundred and twelve:

11 And David called for Zā'dŏk and Ā-bī'a-thar the priests, and for the Lē'vītes, for Ū'rĭ-el, Aś-ā'iah, and Jō'el, Shem-ā-i'ah, and E-lī'el, and Am-mĭn'a-dăb,

12 And said unto them, Ye *are* the chief of the fathers of the Lē'vītes: sanctify yourselves, *both* ye and your brethren, that ye may bring up the ark of the LORD God of Israel unto *the place that* I have prepared for it.

13 For because ye *did it* not at the first, the LORD our God made a breach upon us, for that we sought him not after the due order.

14 So the priests and the Lē'vītes

17. The fame of David went out. This is not to be interpreted as an exaggeration by the Chronicler to merely glorify David. David's victory over the Philistines was significant; for now he was fully established as king, and Israel was recognized as a force with which to be reckoned. **The LORD brought the fear . . . upon all nations.** His fame may have spread to all countries, or this may refer primarily to all the nations on his borders.

3. Preparations for moving the ark. 15:1-24.

The story of bringing the ark up to Jerusalem, which was begun in chapter 13, is taken up again. Obed-edom had been enjoying blessing from the Lord the three months the ark was stored in his house (13:14), obviously indicating that God had not been opposed to the moving of the ark, but rather the manner in which it had been moved. David's carefully prepared second attempt to move the ark is peculiar to Chronicles.

15:1. He prepared a place . . . pitched for it (the ark) **a tent.** This was not the Mosaic tabernacle, for it was located at Gibeon (II Chr 1:3). No explanation is given as to why the tabernacle was at Gibeon, how it got there, or why David erected another tent instead of bringing the Mosaic tabernacle to Jerusalem.

2-3. David may have chosen to move the ark on a new cart the first time (13:7) because it was the method successfully employed by the Philistines, who were ignorant of God's revelation (I Sam 6:7ff.). David learned through Uzza's death that God's blessing only follows obedience to specific revelation (Num 4:4-15; 7:9). This time, therefore, David limited the transporting of the ark to **None . . . but the Levites.**

4-10. At David's summons eight hundred and sixty-two Levites from six different families assembled (the three regular families of Kohath, Merari, and Gershom, and three other families that evidently gained the prestige to be named independently).

11-16. The Aaronic priests are addressed. **Zadok,** representing the line of Eleazar, and **Abiathar,** representing the line of Ithamar, were both priests at this time. Both priests and Levites were told to **sanctify yourselves,** i.e., a ceremonial sanctification by washing the body and clothing and avoiding defilement (Ex 19:10, 14, 15; Lev 11:44). Following a proper preparation, the Levites followed the prescribed manner of transporting the ark.

sanctified themselves to bring up the ark of the LORD God of Israel.

15 And the children of the Lĕ′vītes bare the ark of God upon their shoulders with the staves thereon, as Moses commanded according to the word of the LORD.

16 And David spake to the chief of the Lĕ′vītes to appoint their brethren *to be* the singers with instruments of musick, psalteries and harps and cymbals, sounding, by lifting up the voice with joy.

17 So the Lĕ′vītes appointed Hĕ′man the son of Jō′el; and of his brethren, Ā′sǎph the son of Bĕr-e-chī′ah; and of the sons of Me-râ′rī their brethren, Ē′than the son of Kū-shā′iah;

18 And with them their brethren of the second *degree*, Zĕch-a-rī′ah, Ben, and Jā-a′zī-el, and She-mĭr′a-mŏth, and Je-hī′el, and Ŭn′nī, E-lī′ab, and Be-nā′iah, and Mā-a-sē′iah, and Mǎt-ti-thī′ah, and E-lĭph′e-leh, and Mĭk-nē′iah, and Ō′bed-ē′dom, and Je-ī′el, the porters.

19 So the singers, Hĕ′mǎn, Ā′sǎph, and Ē′than, *were appointed* to sound with cymbals of brass;

20 And Zĕch-a-rī′ah, and Ā′zĭ-el, and She-mĭr′a-mŏth, and Je-hī′el, and Ŭn′nī, and E-lī′ab, and Mā-a-sē′iah, and Be-nā′iah, with psalteries on Ăl′a-mŏth;

21 And Mǎt-ti-thī′ah, and E-lĭph′e-leh, and Mĭk-nē′iah, and Ō′bed-ē′dom, and Je-ī′el, and Ăz-a-zī′ah, with harps on the Shem′i-nith to excel.

22 And Chĕn-a-nī′ah, chief of the Lĕ′vītes, *was* for song: he instructed about the song, because he *was* skilful.

23 And Bĕr-e-chī′ah and Ĕl′kâ-nah *were* doorkeepers for the ark.

24 And Shĕb-a-nī′ah, and Je-hŏsh′a-phǎt, and Ne-thăn′e-el, and A-mǎs′a-ī, and Zĕch-a-rī′ah, and Be-nā′iah, and Ĕ-lī-ē′zer, the priests, did blow with the trumpets before the ark of God: and Ō′bed-ē′dom and Je-hī′ah *were* doorkeepers for the ark.

25 ¶So David, and the elders of Israel, and the captains over thousands, went to bring up the ark of the covenant of the LORD out of the house of Ō′bed-ē′dom with joy.

26 And it came to pass, when God helped the Lĕ′vītes that bare the ark of the covenant of the LORD, that they offered seven bullocks and seven rams.

27 And David *was* clothed with a robe of fine linen, and all the Lĕ′vītes that bare the ark, and the singers, and Chĕn-a-nī′ah the master of the song with the singers: David also *had* upon him an ephod of linen.

28 Thus all Israel brought up the ark of the covenant of the LORD with shouting, and with sound of the cornet, and with trumpets, and with cymbals, making a noise with psalteries and harps.

29 And it came to pass, *as* the ark of the covenant of the LORD came to the city of David, that Mī′chal the daughter of Saul looking out at a window saw king David dancing and playing: and she despised him in her heart.

17-19. Heman (cf. 6:33), **Asaph** (cf. 6:39), and **Ethan** (cf. 6:44), representing the three families of the Levites, were singers who also played cymbals (vs. 19) and were evidently musicians of the first degree. Those musicians of verse 18 were **second degree,** i.e., of lesser rank. The name **Ben** does not appear in verse 20, nor in 16:5. It should probably be translated "son of," the name of Zechariah's father evidently having been lost in transmission.

20. The three men of verse 17 played the cymbals. Those listed here were a second group who played the psaltery. **Alamoth** is the plural of the Hebrew *'almah,* which means maidens. Since young women with their treble voices did not sing in the Levitical choirs, this is probably a reference to high-pitched tones.

21-24. The third group played the harps. **On the Sheminith** means, literally, upon the eighth, possibly an octave below. Therefore, the psalteries played the higher notes, while the harps played the lower ones. The fourth musical group consisted of seven priests who blew the trumpet and preceded the ark. There were two sets of **doorkeepers.** The first two (vs. 23) possibly led the procession and opened the doors, while the other two listed here closed the doors.

4. Bringing the ark to Jerusalem. 15:25-16:6.

25-26. David, his civil administrators, and his military leaders accompanied the ark to Jerusalem; but it was carried by the Levites. **Seven bullocks . . . rams** seem to be in conflict with the offering in II Samuel 6:13. Two possible explanations remove the apparent contradictions. The offering in Samuel occurred at the beginning of the procession, the offering here occurred after the ark was moved; or David's offering is recorded in Samuel, and the Levites' offering is recorded here.

27-29. In addition to his **robe of fine linen,** David wore also **an ephod of linen,** a short tunic or apron worn around the waist. A linen ephod was regular attire for the priest and often was a distinguishing mark of identification (cf. I Sam 22:18). The joy of the occasion was not shared by **Michal,** David's wife (see II Sam 6:14, 20ff. for a fuller account).

CHAPTER 16

SO they brought the ark of God, and set it in the midst of the tent that David had pitched for it: and they offered burnt sacrifices and peace offerings before God.

2 And when David had made an end of offering the burnt offerings and the peace offerings, he blessed the people in the name of the LORD.

3 And he dealt to every one of Israel, both man and woman, to every one a loaf of bread, and a good piece of flesh, and a flagon *of wine*.

4 ¶And he appointed *certain* of the Lē'vītes to minister before the ark of the LORD, and to record, and to thank and praise the LORD God of Israel;

5 Ā'săph the chief, and next to him Zĕch-a-rī'ah, Je-ī'el, and She-mīr'a-mŏth, and Je-hī'el, and Măt-ti-thī'ah, and E-lī'ab, and Be-nā'iah, and Ō'bed–ē'dom: and Je-ī'el with psalteries and with harps; but Ā'săph made a sound with cymbals;

6 Be-nā'iah also and Ja-hā'zi-el the priests with trumpets continually before the ark of the covenant of God.

7 ¶Then on that day David delivered first *this psalm* to thank the LORD into the hand of Ā'săph and his brethren.

8 Give thanks unto the LORD, call upon his name, make known his deeds among the people.

9 Sing unto him, sing psalms unto him, talk ye of all his wondrous works.

10 Glory ye in his holy name: let the heart of them rejoice that seek the LORD.

11 Seek the LORD and his strength, seek his face continually.

12 Remember his marvellous works that he hath done, his wonders, and the judgments of his mouth;

13 O ye seed of Israel his servant, ye children of Jacob, his chosen ones.

14 He *is* the LORD our God; his judgments *are* in all the earth.

15 Be ye mindful always of his covenant; the word *which* he commanded to a thousand generations;

16 *Even of the covenant* which he made with Abraham, and of his oath unto Isaac;

17 And hath confirmed the same to Jacob for a law, *and* to Israel *for* an everlasting covenant,

18 Saying, Unto thee will I give the land of Canaan, the lot of your inheritance:

19 When ye were but few, even a few, and strangers in it.

20 And *when* they went from nation to nation, and from *one* kingdom to another people;

21 He suffered no man to do them wrong: yea, he reproved kings for their sakes,

22 *Saying*, Touch not mine anointed, and do my prophets no harm.

23 Sing unto the LORD, all the earth;

16:1-3. Once the ark was safely deposited within the tent David had erected for it, **burnt offerings** were dedicated to God and **peace offerings** provided a sacrificial meal for the people. The last of the foods listed in verse 3 probably should not read a **flagon of wine,** but a cake of raisins or a sweet cake.

4-6. David's appointment of **Levites to minister** was upon divine order (cf. II Chr 29:25). **To record** (Heb *zakar*) literally means here to make mention, to commemorate, or possibly, to celebrate. These names are taken from the list that occurred earlier (15:20-21). Those who were omitted from this list may have served at Gibeon (cf. vss. 38-42).

5. His psalm of thanks. 16:7-36.

7. The words **this psalm** (AV) do not appear in the Hebrew text. Therefore, this section of psalms, verses 8-36, is not explicitly stated to be of Davidic authorship, neither here nor in the book of Psalms. **David delivered first** can properly be rendered ". . . David first assigned Asaph and his relatives to give thanks to the LORD" (NASB).

8-22. This section is an extensive quotation of the first fifteen verses from the historical Psalm 105 (see Psalms commentary for treatment of these verses within their context).

23-33. The thirteen verses of Psalm 96 are quoted here with a few minor omissions: 1a, 2a, 10a, and 13b (see Psalms commen-

shew forth from day to day his salvation.

24 Declare his glory among the heathen: his marvellous works among all nations.

25 For great is the LORD, and greatly to be praised: he also is to be feared above all gods.

26 For all the gods of the people are idols: but the LORD made the heavens.

27 Glory and honour are in his presence; strength and gladness are in his place.

28 Give unto the LORD, ye kindreds of the people, give unto the LORD glory and strength.

29 Give unto the LORD the glory due unto his name: bring an offering, and come before him: worship the LORD in the beauty of holiness.

30 Fear before him, all the earth: the world also shall be stable, that it be not moved.

31 Let the heavens be glad, and let the earth rejoice: and let men say among the nations, The LORD reigneth.

32 Let the sea roar, and the fulness thereof: let the fields rejoice, and all that is therein.

33 Then shall the trees of the wood sing out at the presence of the LORD, because he cometh to judge the earth.

34 O give thanks unto the LORD; for he is good; for his mercy endureth for ever.

35 And say ye, Save us, O God of our salvation, and gather us together, and deliver us from the heathen, that we may give thanks to thy holy name, and glory in thy praise.

36 Blessed be the LORD God of Israel for ever and ever. And all the people said, Amen, and praised the LORD.

37 ¶So he left there before the ark of the covenant of the LORD Ā′săph and his brethren, to minister before the ark continually, as every day's work required:

38 And Ō′bed-ē′dom with their brethren, threescore and eight; Ō′bed-ē′dom also the son of Jed′ū-thun and Hō′sah to be porters:

39 And Zā′dŏk the priest, and his brethren the priests, before the tabernacle of the LORD in the high place that was at Gĭb′e-on,

40 To offer burnt offerings unto the LORD upon the altar of the burnt offering continually morning and evening, and to do according to all that is written in the law of the LORD, which he commanded Israel;

41 And with them Hē′man and Jed′ū-thun, and the rest that were chosen, who were expressed by name, to give thanks to the LORD, because his mercy endureth for ever;

42 And with them Hē′man and Jed′ū-thun with trumpets and cymbals for those that should make a sound, and with musical instruments of God. And the sons of Jed′ū-thun were porters.

43 And all the people departed every man to his house: and David returned to bless his house.

CHAPTER 17

NOW it came to pass, as David sat in

tary for treatment of this psalm in its context of the other psalms).

34. This expression of praise is common in the Psalms. It is identical to Psalm 107:1 (cf. also Ps 106:1).

35-36. Because of the similarities, these verses appear to be an enlarged variation of Psalm 106:47-48.

6. Levitical appointments at Jerusalem and Gibeon. 16:37-43.

37-43. David appointed the Levite singer **Asaph** (15:19; 16:7) to remain in Jerusalem to minister in song before the ark with his brothers and assistants. **Zadok the priest**, however, was appointed to serve in Gibeon, where the Mosaic tabernacle and altar were located. He was to offer the burnt offerings in accordance with the Mosaic law. To lead in the singing were the other two leading Levite singers, **Heman and Jeduthun** (also known as Ethan, cf. 15:19).

E. David's Line Established. 17:1-20:8.

1. God's covenant with David concerning His house. 17:1-27.

17:1-27. This chapter dealing with David's ambition to build

his house, that David said to Nā′than the prophet, Lo, I dwell in an house of cedars, but the ark of the covenant of the LORD *remaineth* under curtains.

2 Then Nā′than said unto David, Do all that *is* in thine heart; for God *is* with thee.

3 ¶And it came to pass the same night, that the word of God came to Nā′than, saying,

4 Go and tell David my servant, Thus saith the LORD, Thou shalt not build me an house to dwell in:

5 For I have not dwelt in an house since the day that I brought up Israel unto this day; but have gone from tent to tent, and from *one* tabernacle *to an-other*.

6 Wheresoever I have walked with all Israel, spake I a word to any of the judges of Israel, whom I commanded to feed my people, saying, Why have ye not built me an house of cedars?

7 Now therefore thus shalt thou say unto my servant David, Thus saith the LORD of hosts, I took thee from the sheepcote, *even* from following the sheep, that thou shouldest be ruler over my people Israel:

8 And I have been with thee withersoever thou hast walked, and have cut off all thine enemies from before thee, and have made thee a name like the name of the great men that *are* in the earth.

9 Also I will ordain a place for my people Israel, and will plant them, and they shall dwell in their place, and shall be moved no more; neither shall the children of wickedness waste them any more, as at the beginning,

10 And since the time that I commanded judges *to be* over my people Israel. Moreover I will subdue all thine enemies. Furthermore I tell thee that the LORD will build thee an house.

11 And it shall come to pass, when thy days be expired that thou must go *to be* with thy fathers, that I will raise up thy seed after thee, which shall be of thy sons; and I will establish his kingdom.

12 He shall build me an house, and I will stablish his throne for ever.

13 I will be his father, and he shall be my son: and I will not take my mercy away from him, as I took *it* from *him* that was before thee:

14 But I will settle him in mine house and in my kingdom for ever: and his throne shall be established for evermore.

15 According to all these words, and according to all this vision, so did Nā′-than speak unto David.

16 ¶And David the king came and sat before the LORD, and said, Who *am* I, O LORD God, and what *is* mine house, that thou hast brought me hitherto?

17 And *yet* this was a small thing in thine eyes, O God; for thou hast *also* spoken of thy servant's house for a great while to come, and hast regarded me according to the estate of a man of high degree, O LORD God.

18 What can David *speak* more to thee for the honour of thy servant? for thou knowest thy servant.

a house for the Lord, the Lord's response and promise concerning David's house, and David's gratitude and thanksgiving for the promise is virtually identical to II Samuel 7:1-29. Therefore, for discussion of details of this section, see the Samuel commentary.

19 O Lord, for thy servant's sake, and according to thine own heart, hast thou done all this greatness, in making known all *these* great things.

20 O Lord, *there is* none like thee, neither *is there any* God beside thee, according to all that we have heard with our ears.

21 And what one nation in the earth *is* like thy people Israel, whom God went to redeem *to be* his own people, to make thee a name of greatness and terribleness, by driving out nations from before thy people, whom thou hast redeemed out of Egypt?

22 For thy people Israel didst thou make thine own people for ever; and thou, Lord, becamest their God.

23 Therefore now, Lord, let the thing that thou hast spoken concerning thy servant and concerning his house be established for ever, and do as thou hast said.

24 Let it even be established, that thy name may be magnified for ever, saying, The Lord of hosts *is* the God of Israel, *even* a God to Israel: and *let* the house of David thy servant *be* established before thee.

25 For thou, O my God, hast told thy servant that thou wilt build him an house: therefore thy servant hath found *in his heart* to pray before thee.

26 And now, Lord, thou art God, and hast promised this goodness unto thy servant:

27 Now therefore let it please thee to bless the house of thy servant, that it may be before thee for ever: for thou blessest, O Lord, and *it shall be* blessed for ever.

CHAPTER 18

NOW after this it came to pass, that David smote the Philistines, and subdued them, and took Gath and her towns out of the hand of the Philistines.

2 And he smote Moab; and the Moabites became David's servants, *and* brought gifts.

3 ¶And David smote Hăd-ar-ē'zer king of Zō'bah unto Hā'măth, as he went to stablish his dominion by the river Eū-phrā'tēs.

4 And David took from him a thousand chariots, and seven thousand horsemen, and twenty thousand footmen: David also houghed all the chariot *horses*, but reserved of them an hundred chariots.

5 And when the Syrians of Damascus came to help Hăd-ar-ē'zer king of Zō'bah, David slew of the Syrians two and twenty thousand men.

6 Then David put *garrisons* in Syria–damascus; and the Syrians became David's servants, *and* brought gifts. Thus the Lord preserved David whithersoever he went.

7 And David took the shields of gold that were on the servants of Hăd-ar-ē'zer, and brought them to Jerusalem.

8 Likewise from Tĭb'hăth, and from Chun, cities of Hăd-ar-ē'zer, brought David very much brass, wherewith Sŏlomon made the brasen sea, and the pillars, and the vessels of brass.

9 ¶Now when Tō'ū king of Hā'măth

2. Summary of David's wars and officers. 18:1-20:8.

18:1-7. This summary of David's wars with the Philistines (vs. 1), Moab (vs. 2), the Syrians (vss. 3-11), and Edom (vss. 12-13) closely corresponds to II Samuel 8, with a few variations and minor additions (for discussion of details, see II Sam 8:1-18).

8-12. Tibhath is Betah and **Chun** is Berothai in II Samuel 8:8. **Wherewith Solomon . . . brazen sea, . . . pillars, . . . vessels of brass** is all peculiar to Chronicles. **Hadoram** is Joram in II Samuel 8:10. **Moreover, Abishai . . . Zeruiah** is peculiar to Chronicles. Samuel attributes the slaughter to David himself (cf. the title of Ps 60, where credit is attributed to Joab). The

heard how David had smitten all the host of Hăd-ar-ē′zer king of Zō′bah;

10 He sent Ha′dŏ′ram his son to king David, to enquire of his welfare, and to congratulate him, because he had fought against Hăd-ar-ē′zer, and smitten him; (for Hăd-ar-ē′zer had war with Tō′ū;) and *with him* all manner of vessels of gold and silver and brass.

11 Them also king David dedicated unto the LORD, with the silver and the gold that he brought from all *these* nations; from Ē′dom, and from Moab, and from the children of Ammon, and from the Philistines, and from Ăm′a-lĕk.

12 Moreover, A-bī′shaī the son of Zer-ū-i′ah slew of the Edomites in the valley of salt eighteen thousand.

13 And he put garrisons in Ē′dom; and all the Edomites became David's servants. Thus the LORD preserved David whithersoever he went.

14 ¶So David reigned over all Israel, and executed judgment and justice among all his people.

15 And Jō′ăb the son of Zer-ū-i′ah *was* over the host; and Je-hŏsh′a-phăt the son of A-hī′lud, recorder.

16 And Zā′dŏk the son of A-hī′tŭb, and A-bĭm′e-lĕch the son of Ă-bī′a-thar, *were* the priests; and Shăv′sha was scribe;

17 And Be-nā′iah the son of Je-hoi′a-da *was* over the Chĕr′e-thītes and the Pĕl′e-thītes; and the sons of David *were* chief about the king.

CHAPTER 19

NOW it came to pass after this, that Nā′hăsh the king of the children of Ammon died, and his son reigned in his stead.

2 And David said, I will shew kindness unto Hā′nun the son of Nā′hăsh, because his father shewed kindness to me. And David sent messengers to comfort him concerning his father. So the servants of David came into the land of the children of Ammon to Hā′nun, to comfort him.

3 But the princes of the children of Ammon said to Hā′nun, Thinkest thou that David doth honour thy father, that he hath sent comforters unto thee? are not his servants come unto thee for to search, and to overthrow, and to spy out the land?

4 Wherefore Hā′nun took David's servants, and shaved them, and cut off their garments in the midst hard by their buttocks, and sent them away.

5 Then there went *certain*, and told David how the men were served. And he sent to meet them: for the men were greatly ashamed. And the king said, Tarry at Jericho until your beards be grown, and *then* return.

6 ¶And when the children of Ammon saw that they had made themselves odious to David, Hā′nun and the children of Ammon sent a thousand talents of silver to hire them chariots and horsemen out of Mĕs-o-po-tā′mĭ-a and out of Sȳr′ĭ-a-mā′a-chăh, and out of Zō′bah.

7 So they hired thirty and two thousand chariots, and the king of Mā′a-

reference to **Edomites** is correct here, but Syrians (Aramaeans) is evidently a transcriptional mistake in II Samuel 8:13 (where the Hebrew letter "r" *resh* was substituted for the letter "d" *dalet*).

13-17. Abimelech is Ahimelech elsewhere (II Sam 8:17). **The son of Abiathar.** Abiathar had both a father and a son by the name of Ahimelech (cf. 24:3, 6). In accordance with I Samuel 22:20 and II Samuel 20:25, it seems possible that in early transcription an inversion occurred. This line probably should read, "Abiathar the son of Abimelech," since Abiathar, not Ahimelech, was one of the priests in David's time. **Shavsha** is Seraiah (II Sam 8:17).

19:1-19. The events of this chapter, the insulting of David's ambassadors by the Ammonites (vss. 1-5), Israel's victory over the Ammonites under Joab's leadership (vss. 6-15), and Israel's campaign against the Syrians (vss. 16-19), are almost identical to those recorded in II Samuel 10:1-19, with the exception of a few variations to be noted below (for discussion of the details, see Samuel commentary).

The Ammonites hired **thirty and two thousand chariots** (vs. 7), a number not given in Samuel. However, Samuel gives the total number of accompanying footmen as thirty-three thousand.

For the **seven thousand . . . chariots** (vs. 18) here, II Samuel has only seven hundred. Instead of **forty thousand footmen,** II Samuel has forty thousand horsemen. Apparently, the Hebrew text has been corrupted in the process of transcription, but it is not a simple matter to determine which reading, that of II Samuel or I Chronicles, is probably the most preferred.

chah and his people; who came and pitched before Měd'e-ba. And the children of Ammon gathered themselves together from their cities, and came to battle.

8 And when David heard *of it*, he sent Jō'ăb, and all the host of the mighty men.

9 And the children of Ammon came out, and put the battle in array before the gate of the city: and the kings that were come *were* by themselves in the field.

10 Now when Jō'ăb saw that the battle was set against him before and behind, he chose out of all the choice of Israel, and put *them* in array against the Syrians.

11 And the rest of the people he delivered unto the hand of A-bī'shaī his brother, and they set *themselves* in array against the children of Ammon.

12 And he said, If the Syrians be too strong for me, then thou shalt help me: but if the children of Ammon be too strong for thee, then I will help thee.

13 Be of good courage, and let us behave ourselves valiantly for our people, and for the cities of our God: and let the LORD do *that which is* good in his sight.

14 So Jō'ăb and the people that *were* with him drew nigh before the Syrians unto the battle; and they fled before him.

15 And when the children of Ammon saw that the Syrians were fled, they likewise fled before A-bī'shaī his brother, and entered into the city. Then Jō'ăb came to Jerusalem.

16 ¶And when the Syrians saw that they were put to the worse before Israel, they sent messengers, and drew forth the Syrians that *were* beyond the river: and Shō'phăch the captain of the host of Hăd-ar-ē'zer *went* before them.

17 And it was told David; and he gathered all Israel, and passed over Jordan, and came upon them, and set *the battle* in array against them. So when David had put the battle in array against the Syrians, they fought with him.

18 But the Syrians fled before Israel; and David slew of the Syrians seven thousand *men which fought in* chariots, and forty thousand footmen, and killed Shō'phăch the captain of the host.

19 And when the servants of Hăd-ar-ē'zer saw that they were put to the worse before Israel, they made peace with David, and became his servants: neither would the Syrians help the children of Ammon any more.

CHAPTER 20

AND it came to pass, that after the year was expired, at the time that kings go out *to battle*, Jō'ăb led forth the power of the army, and wasted the country of the children of Ammon, and came and besieged Răb'bah. But David tarried at Jerusalem. And Jō'ăb smote Răb'bah, and destroyed it.

20:1. This verse corresponds very closely to II Samuel 11:1. Following the line **But David tarried at Jerusalem,** II Samuel includes the account of David's sin with Bath-sheba, his murder of her husband, Uriah the Hittite, his confrontation by Nathan, and the results of his sin (II Sam 11:2-12:25). This material is not omitted to whitewash David, but it was not within the Chronicler's purpose to include it (see Introduction).

And Joab smote Rabbah. This final phrase corresponds to II Samuel 12:26, with the next three verses in II Samuel omitted here.

2 And David took the crown of their king from off his head, and found it to weigh a talent of gold, and *there were* precious stones in it; and it was set upon David's head: and he brought also exceeding much spoil out of the city.

3 And he brought out the people that were in it, and cut *them* with saws, and with harrows of iron, and with axes. Even so dealt David with all the cities of the children of Ammon. And David and all the people returned to Jerusalem.

4 ¶And it came to pass after this, that there arose war at Gē′zer with the Philistines; at which time Sĭb′be-chaī the Hu′shath-īte slew Sĭp′paī, *that was* of the children of the giant: and they were subdued.

5 And there was war again with the Philistines; and Ĕl-hā′nan the son of Jā′ir slew Lăh′mī the brother of Goliath the Gĭt′tīte, whose spear staff *was* like a weaver's beam.

6 And yet again there was war at Gath, where was a man of *great* stature, whose fingers and toes *were* four and twenty, six *on each hand,* and six *on each foot* and he also was the son of the giant.

7 But when he defied Israel, Jonathan the son of Shĭm′e-a David's brother slew him.

8 These were born unto the giant in Gath; and they fell by the hand of David, and by the hand of his servants.

CHAPTER 21

AND Satan stood up against Israel, and provoked David to number Israel.

2 And David said to Jō′ăb and to the rulers of the people, Go, number Israel from Be′er-shē′ba even to Dan; and bring the number of them to me, that I may know *it.*

3 And Jō′ăb answered, The LORD make his people an hundred times so many more as they *be:* but, my lord the king, *are* they not all my lord's servants? why then doth my lord require this thing? why will he be a cause of trespass to Israel?

4 Nevertheless the king's word prevailed against Jō′ăb. Wherefore Jō′ăb departed, and went throughout all Israel, and came to Jerusalem.

5 And Jō′ăb gave the sum of the number of the people unto David. And all they of Israel were a thousand thousand and an hundred thousand men that drew sword: and Judah *was* four hundred threescore and ten thousand men that drew sword.

6 But Levi and Benjamin counted he not among them: for the king's word was abominable to Jō′ăb.

7 And God was displeased with this thing; therefore he smote Israel.

8 And David said unto God, I have sinned greatly, because I have done this thing: but now, I beseech thee, do away the iniquity of thy servant; for I have done very foolishly.

9 ¶And the LORD spake unto Gad, David's seer, saying,

10 Go and tell David, saying, Thus saith the LORD, I offer thee three *things:*

2-3. These verses correspond to a fuller account in II Samuel 12:30-31 (for discussion, see Samuel commentary).

4-8. Of the four campaigns against the Philistines listed in II Samuel, the Chronicler mentions only the last three in this section, which corresponds to II Samuel 21:18-22 (for discussion see Samuel commentary). **Jair** is "Jaare-oregim, a Bethlehemite" in II Samuel 21:19. **Lahmi the brother of** is peculiar to I Chronicles—the victim of Jair appears to be the brother of Goliath in II Samuel.

F. David's Preparations for Building the Temple. 21:1-22:19.

1. The census—occasion for selecting the Temple site. 21:1-22:1.

This section is regarded as introductory to David's Temple building preparation. It was his sin of taking the census recorded here which resulted in his buying a parcel of land on which to build an altar to seek pardon for his sin. This purchased land later became the site for the Temple. This chapter has its direct parallel in II Samuel 24; but there are several additions, omissions, and variations. For discussion on this section see Samuel commentary, for only divergences from Samuel will be noted here.

21:1-3. Satan literally means adversary, but it was no mere adversary who prompted David to number the people. Here Satan is the personal name of the devil, the prince of evil who stands in opposition to God. In II Samuel David's act is attributed to God's prompting. The two accounts are not contradictory, but complementary. God was the ultimate cause in that He was bringing punishment upon Israel (cf. context in II Samuel where this census follows several rebellions against David which had gained Israel's support). Satan, though evil, is a created angel of God who has only as much power as God has entrusted him (cf. Job 1:6-12; 2:1-6). Here, Satan is God's minister, an instrument of God's purposes.

4. This verse is expanded considerably in II Samuel 24:5-8, outlining Joab's route of travel and noting the time involved (nine months and twenty days).

5-11. There is considerable divergence in the two accounts concerning the totals of Joab's census. Here, the figures for Israel and Judah respectively are 1,100,000 and 470,000. II Samuel 24:9 records 800,000 for Israel and 500,000 for Judah. Various explanations have been offered, but none are entirely satisfactory. For a number of possible solutions and further discussion of the problem, see A. M. Renwick, I and II Samuel, in *The New Bible Commentary,* p. 292, and John J. Davis, *Biblical Numerology,* pp. 79ff.

choose thee one of them, that I may do *it* unto thee.

11 So Gad came to David, and said unto him, Thus saith the LORD, Choose thee

12 Either three years' famine; or three months to be destroyed before thy foes, while that the sword of thine enemies overtaketh *thee;* or else three days the sword of the LORD, even the pestilence, in the land, and the angel of the LORD destroying throughout all the coasts of Israel. Now therefore advise thyself what word I shall bring again to him that sent me.

13 And David said unto Gad, I am in a great strait: let me fall now into the hand of the LORD; for very great *are* his mercies: but let me not fall into the hand of man.

14 ¶So the LORD sent pestilence upon Israel: and there fell of Israel seventy thousand men.

15 And God sent an angel unto Jerusalem to destroy it: and as he was destroying, the LORD beheld, and he repented him of the evil, and said to the angel that destroyed, It is enough, stay now thine hand. And the angel of the LORD stood by the threshingfloor of Ôr′nan the Jēb′u-sīte.

16 And David lifted up his eyes, and saw the angel of the LORD stand between the earth and the heaven, having a drawn sword in his hand stretched out over Jerusalem. Then David and the elders *of Israel, who were* clothed in sackcloth, fell upon their faces.

17 And David said unto God, *Is it* not I *that* commanded the people to be numbered? even I it is that have sinned and done evil indeed; but *as for these* sheep, what have they done? let thine hand, I pray thee, O LORD my God, be on me, and on my father's house; but not on thy people, that they should be plagued.

18 ¶Then the angel of the LORD commanded Gad to say to David, that David should go up, and set up an altar unto the LORD in the threshingfloor of Ôr′nan the Jēb′u-sīte.

19 And David went up at the saying of Gad, which he spake in the name of the LORD.

20 And Ôr′nan turned back, and saw the angel; and his four sons with him hid themselves. Now Ôr′nan was threshing wheat.

21 And as David came to Ôr′nan, Ôr′nan looked and saw David, and went out of the threshingfloor, and bowed himself to David with *his* face to the ground.

22 Then David said to Ôr′nan, Grant me the place of *this* threshingfloor, that I may build an altar therein unto the LORD: thou shalt grant it me for the full price: that the plague may be stayed from the people.

23 And Ôr′nan said unto David, Take *it* to thee, and let my lord the king do *that which is* good in his eyes: lo, I give *thee* the oxen *also* for burnt offerings, and the threshing instruments for wood, and the wheat for the meat offering; I give it all.

24 And king David said to Ôr′nan,

12-14. Three years' famine appears as seven years in II Samuel 24:13. Three years is to be preferred, as it has the support of the Septuagint in II Samuel.

15-20. Ornan the Jebusite is Araunah the Jebusite in II Samuel. Verse 20 is peculiar to Chronicles. No mention of Ornan's son is made in II Samuel.

21-27. There is no discrepancy between these verses and II Samuel 24:24. II Samuel records the price of the threshing floor (fifty shekels of silver); and here the Chronicler gives the price for the place, i.e., the threshing floor and surrounding area (six hundred shekels of gold). God's answering **from heaven by fire** is reminiscent of God's answering Elijah on Mount Carmel (I Kgs 18:38). II Samuel 24:25 summarizes verse 25 thus; ". . . and the plague was stayed. . . ." Here the parallel with II Samuel ends.

Nay; but I will verily buy it for the full price: for I will not take *that* which *is* thine for the LORD, nor offer burnt offerings without cost.

25 So David gave to Ôr'nan for the place six hundred shekels of gold by weight.

26 And David built there an altar unto the LORD, and offered burnt offerings and peace offerings, and called upon the LORD; and he answered him from heaven by fire upon the altar of burnt offering.

27 And the LORD commanded the angel; and he put up his sword again into the sheath thereof.

28 ¶At that time when David saw that the LORD had answered him in the threshingfloor of Ôr'nan the Jĕb'u-sīte, then he sacrificed there.

29 For the tabernacle of the LORD, which Moses made in the wilderness, and the altar of the burnt offering, *were* at that season in the high place at Gĭb'e-on.

30 But David could not go before it to enquire of God: for he was afraid because of the sword of the angel of the LORD.

CHAPTER 22

THEN David said, This *is* the house of the LORD God, and this *is* the altar of the burnt offering for Israel.

2 And David commanded to gather together the strangers that *were* in the land of Israel; and he set masons to hew wrought stones to build the house of God.

3 And David prepared iron in abundance for the nails for the doors of the gates, and for the joinings; and brass in abundance without weight;

4 Also cedar trees in abundance: for the Zĭd-ō'nĭ-ans and they of Tyre brought much cedar wood to David.

5 And David said, Sŏlomon my son *is* young and tender, and the house *that is* to be builded for the LORD *must be* exceeding magnifical, of fame and of glory throughout all countries: I will *therefore* now make preparation for it. So David prepared abundantly before his death.

6 ¶Then he called for Sŏlomon his son, and charged him to build an house for the LORD God of Israel.

7 And David said to Sŏlomon, My son, as for me, it was in my mind to build an house unto the name of the LORD my God:

8 But the word of the LORD came to me, saying, Thou hast shed blood abundantly, and hast made great wars: thou shalt not build an house unto my name, because thou hast shed much blood upon the earth in my sight.

9 Behold, a son shall be born to thee, who shall be a man of rest; and I will give him rest from all his enemies round about: for his name shall be Sŏlo-

28. Verses 28ff.-22:1 serve as a connecting link between the preceding narrative and the preparations to build the Temple in chapter 22. Seeing that God had answered him at the threshing floor site, **then he sacrificed there,** i.e., David continued to sacrifice there from that time on.

29-30. These verses are a parenthetical explanation of why David sacrificed at the threshing floor. David's fear of the **sword of the angel of the LORD** and a direct divine command through Gad (vs. 18) had prevented him from going to the tabernacle at Gibeon. He took this as a divine sign to sacrifice at the threshing floor thereafter.

22:1. This is the house of the LORD God. David is referring to the site of Ornan's threshing floor, where the house of God will be built. Compare the site for Solomon's building the Temple (II Chr 3:1).

2. Collecting materials and instructing Solomon. 22:2-19.

2-4. David's preparations involved **strangers** (Heb *ger*), i.e., resident aliens or tolerated sojourners, those who were remnants of Canaan's old inhabitants. Solomon's building projects involved both Israelites (I Kgs 5:13) and strangers (I Kgs 9:20-21). **Masons** were stonecutters. **Zidonians,** i.e., the Phoenicians. David undoubtedly purchased the cedar wood through Hiram, king of Tyre, and had also prepared the way for Solomon's dealing with the Phoenicians (I Kgs 5:2ff.; II Chr 2:3ff.).

5-7. Solomon . . . is young and tender. Solomon's age at this time cannot be determined with any certainty, though he was probably not too much younger than when he became sole ruler (see note on I Kgs 3:7).

The time of David's charge to Solomon can be fixed with more certainty. Apparently, a basis for Adonijah's attempt to usurp David's throne (I Kgs 1:5ff.) was that David's successor had been unnamed. Here, Solomon is addressed as the commonly known successor to the throne. So it appears that the events of this chapter and the rest of the book occur after Solomon has had his impromptu anointing (I Kgs 1:39ff.). This charge is not to be identified with the one in I Kings 2:1ff.

8. The word of the LORD came to me, i.e., by the prophet Nathan (II Sam 7:4ff.; I Chr 7:4ff.), although there is no written account elsewhere of the following **Thou hast shed blood . . . made great wars.** Solomon alluded to this fact when he addressed Hiram (I Kgs 5:3).

9-11. These verses parallel somewhat 17:11-13 (cf. II Sam 7:12-14). **His name shall be Solomon** (Heb *Shelōmōh*), i.e., peaceful. Not only is there a play on words contrasting David, the man of war, but also "the idea of peace means more than the

mon, and I will give peace and quietness unto Israel in his days.

10 He shall build an house for my name; and he shall be my son, and I will be his father; and I will establish the throne of his kingdom over Israel for ever.

11 Now, my son, the LORD be with thee; and prosper thou, and build the house of the LORD thy God, as he hath said of thee.

12 Only the LORD give thee wisdom and understanding, and give thee charge concerning Israel, that thou mayest keep the law of the LORD thy God.

13 Then shalt thou prosper, if thou takest heed to fulfil the statutes and judgments which the LORD charged Moses with concerning Israel: be strong, and of good courage; dread not, nor be dismayed.

14 Now, behold, in my trouble I have prepared for the house of the LORD an hundred thousand talents of gold, and a thousand thousand talents of silver; and of brass and iron without weight; for it is in abundance: timber also and stone have I prepared; and thou mayest add thereto.

15 Moreover there are workmen with thee in abundance, hewers and workers of stone and timber, and all manner of cunning men for every manner of work.

16 Of the gold, the silver, and the brass, and the iron, there is no number. Arise therefore, and be doing, and the LORD be with thee.

17 ¶David also commanded all the princes of Israel to help Sŏlomon his son, saying,

18 Is not the LORD your God with you? and hath he not given you rest on every side? for he hath given the inhabitants of the land into mine hand; and the land is subdued before the LORD, and before his people.

19 Now set your heart and your soul to seek the LORD your God; arise therefore, and build ye the sanctuary of the LORD God, to bring the ark of the covenant of the LORD, and the holy vessels of God, into the house that is to be built to the name of the LORD.

CHAPTER 23

SO when David was old and full of days, he made Sŏlomon his son king over Israel.

2 ¶And he gathered together all the princes of Israel, with the priests and the Lē´vītes.

3 Now the Lē´vītes were numbered from the age of thirty years and upward: and their number by their polls, man by man, was thirty and eight thousand.

4 Of which, twenty and four thousand were to set forward the work of the house of the LORD; and six thousand were officers and judges:

5 Moreover four thousand were porters; and four thousand praised the LORD with the instruments which I made, said David to praise therewith.

6 And David divided them into

mere absence of war—what is implied is the whole idea of the community's being blessed by God and its consequent prosperity" (R. J. Coggins, The First and Second Books of the Chronicles, p. 115).

12-13. The LORD give thee wisdom and understanding. Perhaps David's fatherly concern in this charge came to mind when Solomon made his request for ". . . an understanding heart . . ." (I Kgs 3:9) and ". . . wisdom and knowledge . . ." (II Chr 1:10). Verse 13 is reminiscent of God's charge to Joshua (Josh 1:7).

14-16. David's **trouble** might be interpreted as afflictions, i.e., of war, poverty, or great pain. In spite of his trouble, he had successfully amassed extraordinary wealth and supplies for the construction of the Temple. Solomon was without excuse if he failed to carry out the project his father had initiated.

17-19. When David's private charge to Solomon was ended, he addressed the **princes of Israel,** i.e., the tribal leaders, civil and military officials, to encourage their full support of the young Solomon as he endeavored to build the Temple in fulfillment of David's ambition.

G. David's Organization of Religious, Military, and Civil Leaders. 23:1-27:34.

1. Divisions of the Levites. 23:1-32.

23:1-2. David was old. This is an allusion to I Kings 1:1-2. David was about seventy years of age (see note on I Kgs 1:1). **He made Solomon his son king.** The details of Solomon's succession to the throne (I Kgs 1:11-40) are omitted.

3-5. The total number of Levites **from the age of thirty years and upward,** presumably to age fifty (cf. Num 4:3), was thirty-eight thousand. These were divided into four groups: (1) twenty-four thousand **to set forward the work of the house of the LORD,** i.e., the priests and their assistants (these are treated in further detail in ch. 24); (2) six thousand **officers and judges** (cf. 26:29-32); (3) four thousand **porters,** i.e., gatekeepers (cf. 26:1-28); and (4) four thousand who **praised the LORD,** i.e., the singers (cf. 25:1-31).

6-11. The three traditional families of the Levites were di-

787

courses among the sons of Levi, *namely*, Gerʹshon, Kōʹhăth, and Me-râʹrī.

7 ¶Of the Gerʹshon-ītes *were*, Lāʹa-dan, and Shĭmʹe-ī.

8 The sons of Lāʹa-dan; the chief *was* Je-hīʹel, and Zēʹtham, and Jōʹel, three.

9 The sons of Shĭmʹe-ī; Shelʹô-mĭth, and Hăʹzī-el, and Hâʹran, three. These *were* the chief of the fathers of Lāʹa-dan.

10 And the sons of Shĭmʹe-ī *were*, Jāʹhăth, Zĭʹna, and Jěʹŭsh, and Be-rīʹah. These four *were* the sons of Shĭmʹe-ī.

11 And Jāʹhăth was the chief, and Zĭʹzah the second: but Jěʹŭsh and Be-rīʹah had not many sons; therefore they were in one reckoning, according to *their* father's house.

12 ¶The sons of Kōʹhăth; Ămʹrăm, Ĭzʹhär, Hēʹbron, and Ŭzʹzī-el, four.

13 The sons of Ămʹrăm; Aaron and Moses: and Aaron was separated, that he should sanctify the most holy things, he and his sons for ever, to burn incense before the LORD, to minister unto him, and to bless in his name for ever.

14 Now *concerning* Moses the man of God, his sons were named of the tribe of Levi.

15 The sons of Moses *were*, Gerʹshom, and Ĕ-lī-ēʹzer.

16 Of the sons of Gerʹshom, Shěbʹū-el *was* the chief.

17 And the sons of Ĕ-lī-ēʹzer *were*, Rē-ha-bīʹah the chief. And Ĕ-lī-ēʹzer had none other sons; but the sons of Rē-ha-bīʹah were very many.

18 Of the sons of Ĭzʹhär; Shelʹō-mĭth the chief.

19 Of the sons of Hēʹbron; Je-rīʹah the first, Ăm-a-rīʹah the second, Ja-hăʹzi-el the third, and Jěk-a-mēʹam the fourth.

20 Of the sons of Ŭzʹzī-el; Mīʹcah the first, and Je-sīʹah the second.

21 ¶The sons of Me-râʹrī; Mähʹlī, and Mūʹshī. The sons of Mähʹlī; Ĕ-le-âʹzar, and Kish.

22 And Ĕ-le-âʹzar died, and had no sons, but daughters: and their brethren the sons of Kish took them.

23 The sons of Mūʹshī; Mähʹlī, and Ĕʹder, and Jěrʹe-mŏth, three.

24 ¶These *were* the sons of Levi after the house of their fathers; *even* the chief of the fathers, as they were counted by number of names by their polls, that did the work for the service of the house of the LORD, from the age of twenty years and upward.

25 For David said, The LORD God of Israel hath given rest unto his people, that they may dwell in Jerusalem for ever:

26 And also unto the Lēʹvītes; they shall no *more* carry the tabernacle, nor any vessels of it for the service thereof.

27 For by the last words of David the Lēʹvītes *were* numbered from twenty years old and above:

28 Because their office *was* to wait on the sons of Aaron for the service of the house of the LORD, in the courts, and in the chambers, and in the purifying of all holy things, and in the work of the service of the house of God;

29 Both for the shewbread, and for

vided into **courses** (lit., divisions). The courses of the **Gershonites** are listed. **Laadan** is elsewhere Libni (cf. 6:17). **Zina** (vs. 10) is **Zizah** (vs. 11). Because of their smallness, the families of **Jeush** and **Beriah** were considered one, making the total of courses for the Gershonites nine.

12-20. The courses of the Kohathites are listed next. Aaron's two sons that made up the priesthood (ch. 24) are omitted. From Moses' descendants there were two courses; from **Izhar,** one; from **Hebron,** four; and from **Uzziel,** two, making a total of nine courses from the Kohathites.

21-23. The courses of the Merarites are also listed. **Mahli's** son, **Eleazar,** had no sons. Therefore, he was not awarded a course. The total of courses from the Merarites was four, making the total of courses among the Levites twenty-two.

24-27. Here, the age of Levites is from **twenty years and upward** (cf. vs. 3). Perhaps the two ages should be viewed as corresponding to the two ages in Numbers 4:3 and 8:24, where the younger age of twenty-five seemed to be one of enlistment for the Levite; and after a five-year apprenticeship and time of maturing, he carried out full duties at age thirty. Another possible explanation is that David lowered the minimum age. Once worship was centralized at Jerusalem in the Temple, the work would be easier; for there would be no more need to transport the tabernacle (vs. 26), but there would be a need for a greater number of Levites to maintain the ritual of the Temple.

28-32. The role of the Levites was subsidiary to the priests, for they were **to wait on the sons of Aaron,** i.e., a role of assistance. **Meat offering** is better rendered meal or grain offering (cf. Lev 2:1-16; 6:14-18). **That which is fried,** is better rendered ". . . what is well-mixed . . ." (NASB). **And to offer all burnt sacrifices.** This phrase is governed by **to stand** of verse

the fine flour for meat offering, and for the unleavened cakes, and for *that which is baked in* the pan, and for that which is fried, and for all manner of measure and size;

30 And to stand every morning to thank and praise the LORD, and likewise at even;

31 And to offer all burnt sacrifices unto the LORD in the sabbaths, in the new moons, and on the set feasts, by number, according to the order commanded unto them, continually before the LORD:

32 And that they should keep the charge of the tabernacle of the congregation, and the charge of the holy place, and the charge of the sons of Aaron their brethren, in the service of the house of the LORD.

CHAPTER 24

NOW *these are* the divisions of the sons of Aaron. The sons of Aaron; Nā′dăb, and A-bī′hū, Ĕ-le-ā′zar, and Ĭth′a-mär.

2 But Nā′dăb and A-bī′hū died before their father, and had no children: therefore Ĕ-le-ā′zar and Ĭth′a-mär executed the priest's office.

3 And David distributed them, both Zā′dŏk of the sons of Ĕ-le-ā′zar, and A-hĭm′e-lĕch of the sons of Ĭth′a-mär, according to their offices in their service.

4 And there were more chief men found of the sons of Ĕ-le-ā′zar than of the sons of Ĭth′a-mär; and *thus* were they divided. Among the sons of Ĕ-le-ā′zar *there were* sixteen chief men of the house of *their* fathers, and eight among the sons of Ĭth′a-mär according to the house of their fathers.

5 Thus were they divided by lot, one sort with another; for the governors of the sanctuary, and governors *of the house* of God, were of the sons of Ĕ-le-ā′zar, and of the sons of Ĭth′a-mär.

6 And Shem-ā-i′ah the son of Ne-thăn′e-el the scribe, *one* of the Lē′vītes, wrote them before the king, and the princes, and Zā′dŏk the priest, and A-hĭm′e-lĕch the son of Ă-bī′a-thar, and *before* the chief of the fathers of the priests and Lē′vītes: one principal household being taken for Ĕ-le-ā′zar, and *one* taken for Ĭth′a-mär.

7 Now the first lot came forth to Je-hoi′a-rĭb, the second to Je-dā′iah,

8 The third to Hâ′rĭm, the fourth to Sē-ô′rĭm,

9 The fifth to Măl-chī′jah, the sixth to Mĭj′a-mĭn,

10 The seventh to Hăk′kŏz, the eighth to A-bī′jah,

11 The ninth to Jĕsh′u-ah, the tenth to Shĕc-a-nī′ah,

12 The eleventh to E-lī′a-shĭb, the twelfth to Jā′kĭm,

13 The thirteenth to Hŭp′pah, the fourteenth to Je-shĕb′e-ăb,

14 The fifteenth to Bĭl′gah, the sixteenth to Ĭm′mer,

15 The seventeenth to Hē′zir, the eighteenth to Āph′sĕs,

16 The nineteenth to Pĕth-a-hī′ah, the twentieth to Je-hĕz′e-kĕl,

17 The one and twentieth to Jā′chin, the two and twentieth to Gā′mul,

30 and should read literally "to stand . . . at every offering of burnt offerings," i.e., the Levites did not officiate at the altar, but assisted the priests with the sacrifices. The **tabernacle** was still at Gibeon (cf. 16:39; II Chr 1:3).

2. Division of priests and their assistants. 24:1-31.

24:1-3. The sons of Aaron. This is not a genealogy of Aaron (cf. 6:3-15). For the death of **Nadab and Abihu,** see Leviticus 10:1-2. They **had no children** (cf. Num 3:4); so only the descendants of **Eleazar** and **Ithamar** are to be divided into courses of service. From the line of **Ithamar** came **Ahimelech,** the son of **Abiathar,** the same Ahimelech of verse 6; but his mention here is difficult to explain since it is Abiathar who is usually elsewhere serving alongside Zadok (II Sam 15:35; 17:15; 20:25; I Kgs 4:4; I Chr 15:11).

4-6. Due to the greater number of **chief men** among the sons of Eleazar, David assigned sixteen courses to Eleazar's line and eight courses to Ithamar's line. **Shemaiah** wrote the names of the heads of the divisions as they were drawn by lot (vs. 5). The drawn names were taken alternately for Eleazar and Ithamar, with Eleazar receiving the last eight names. Alternately, he received two names for every one Ithamar received.

7-19. The twenty-four heads of the courses of priests are listed in the order that they were determined by lot. According to the order in which the twenty-four courses of priests were drawn, they served in the house of the Lord on a rotating basis under the direction of the high priests, Zadok and Ahimelech.

18 The three and twentieth to Dĕl-a-ī'ah, the four and twentieth to Mā-a-zī'ah.

19 These *were* the orderings of them in their service to come into the house of the LORD, according to their manner, under Aaron their father, as the LORD God of Israel had commanded him.

20 ¶And the rest of the sons of Levi *were these:* Of the sons of Ăm'răm; Shū'ba-el: of the sons of Shū'ba-el; Jĕh-dē'iah.

21 Concerning Rē-ha-bī'ah: of the sons of Rē-ha-bī'ah, the first *was* Ĭs-shī'ah.

22 Of the ĭz'har-ĭtes; Shĕl'ō-mŏth: of the sons of Shĕl'ō-mŏth; Jā'ăth.

23 And the sons *of Hē'bron;* Je-rī'ah the first, Ăm-a-rī'ah the second, Ja-hā'zi-el the third, Jĕk-a-mē'am the fourth.

24 *Of* the sons of Ŭz'zĭ-el; Mī'chah: of the sons of Mī'chah; Shā'mir.

25 The brother of Mī'chah *was* Ĭs-shī'ah: of the sons of Ĭs-shī'ah; Zĕch-a-rī'ah.

26 The sons of Me-râ'rī *were* Mäh'lī and Mū'shī: the sons of Jā'a-zī'ah; Bē'nō.

27 The sons of Me-râ'rī by Jā-a-zī'ah; Bē'nō, and Shō'hăm, and Zăc'cur, and Ĭb'rī.

28 Of Mäh'lī *came* Ĕ-le-ā'zar, who had no sons.

29 Concerning Kish: the son of Kish *was* Je-rähʹme-el.

30 The sons also of Mū'shī; Mäh'lī, and Ē'der, and Jĕr'ĭ-mŏth. These *were* the sons of the Lē'vītes after the house of their fathers.

31 These likewise cast lots over against their brethren the sons of Aaron in the presence of David the king, and Zā'dŏk, and A-hĭm'e-lĕch, and the chief of the fathers of the priests and Lē'vītes, even the principal fathers over against their younger brethren.

CHAPTER 25

MOREOVER David and the captains of the host separated to the service of the sons of Ā'săph, and of Hē'măn, and of Jed'ū-thun, who should prophesy with harps, with psalteries, and with cymbals: and the number of the workmen according to their service was:

2 Of the sons of Ā'săph; Zăc'cur, and Joseph, and Nĕth-a-nī'ah, and Ăs-a-rē'-lah, the sons of Ā'săph under the hands of Ā'săph, which prophesied according to the order of the king.

3 Of Jed'ū-thun: the sons of Jed'ū-thun; Gĕd-a-lī'ah, and Ze'rī, and Je-shā'-iah, Hăsh-a-bī'ah, and Măt-ti-thī'ah, six, under the hands of their father Jed'ū-thun, who prophesied with a harp, to give thanks and to praise the LORD.

4 Of Hē'man: the sons of Hē'man: Buk-kī'ah, Măt-ta-nī'ah, Ŭz'zī-el,

20-31. The rest of the sons of Levi here listed appear to be a supplementary group whose relation to the other list is not stated explicitly. However, they apparently made up the rest of the twenty-four thousand who worked in the house of the Lord (23:4) and served as assistants to the priests.

It is difficult to organize the names as they appear here into twenty-four courses to correspond to the courses of the priests (cf. two different attempts by Payne, p. 387, and Murphy, p. 79). The names of the Kohathites (vss. 20-26) contain those found in 23:20-25, with a few names from an additional generation added. The Merarites (vss. 27-30) have an additional son, **Jaaziah** with his sons (cf. 23:21-23); and strangely the Gershonites (23:6-11) are omitted altogether.

These Levites were also arranged by lot, evidently to match the courses of their **brethren**, i.e., their relatives, the priests.

3. Divisions of musicians. 25:1-31.

25:1. Captains of the host elsewhere refers to military commanders (cf. II Sam 2:8; I Chr 19:16; 27:3), but it is questionable that they should appoint Levitical singers; so here the term applies to those chiefs who presided over the order of worship. They **separated,** i.e., set apart or appointed, the sons of **Asaph, Heman,** and **Jeduthun** (Ethan, 6:44), representatives of the Gershonites, Kohathites, and Merarites respectively (cf. 6:33-47). They were to **prophesy.** In this context prophesy means to praise (cf. Wood, *The Holy Spirit in the Old Testament,* pp. 111, 148 for discussion of prophesying). All was done according to divine command through His prophets, Gad and Nathan (II Chr 29:25).

2-4. Asarelah is Jesharelah (vs. 14). **Zeri** is Izri (vs. 11). Only five sons of **Jeduthun** are listed, not **six.** Shemei (vs. 17), who is not listed as a son (vss. 2-5), probably belongs here after **Jeshaiah,** as it appears in the Septuagint, thus making a total of six sons. **Uzziel** is Azareel (vs. 18); **Shebuel** is Shubael (vs. 20); and **Jerimoth** is Jeremoth (vs. 22). Beginning with **Hananiah,** many scholars see a reconstruction of the following nine names to be possibly a prayer of Heman's (e.g., cf. Jacob M. Myers, *I Chronicles,* pp. 172 ff., Payne, p. 387).

Shĕb'ū-el, and Jĕr'ī-mŏth, Hăn-a-nī'ah, Ha-nā'nī, E-lī'a-thah,Gid-dăl'tī, and Rō-măm'tī-ē̄zer, Jŏsh-bek'ā-shah, Măl'-lothī, Hō'thir, and Ma-hă'zī-ŏth:

5 All these were the sons of Hē'man the king's seer in the words of God, to lift up the horn. And God gave to Hē'-man fourteen sons and three daughters.

6 All these were under the hands of their father for song in the house of the LORD, with cymbals, psalteries, and harps, for the service of the house of God, according to the king's order to A'sǎph, Jed'ū-thun, and Hē'man.

7 So the number of them, with their brethren that were instructed in the songs of the LORD, even all that were cunning, was two hundred fourscore and eight.

8 ¶And they cast lots, ward against ward, as well the small as the great, the teacher as the scholar.

9 Now the first lot came forth for A'sǎph to Joseph: the second to Gĕd-a-lī'ah, who with his brethren and sons were twelve:

10 The third to Zăc'cur, he, his sons, and his brethren, were twelve:

11 The fourth to Ĭz'rī, he, his sons, and his brethren, were twelve:

12 The fifth to Nĕth-a-nī'ah, he, his sons, and his brethren, were twelve:

13 The sixth to Buk-kī'ah, he, his sons, and his brethren, were twelve:

14 The seventh to Jĕ-shar'ē-lah, he, his sons, and his brethren, were twelve:

15 The eighth to Je-shā'iah, he, his sons, and his brethren, were twelve:

16 The ninth to Măt-ta-nī'ah, he, his sons, and his brethren, were twelve:

17 The tenth to Shĭm'e-ī, he, his sons, and his brethren, were twelve:

18 The eleventh to Ă-zar'e-el, he, his sons, and his brethren, were twelve:

19 The twelfth to Hăsh-a-bī'ah, he, his sons, and his brethren, were twelve:

20 The thirteenth to Shū'ba-el, he, his sons, and his brethren, were twelve:

21 The fourteenth to Măt-ti-thī'ah, he, his sons, and his brethren, were twelve:

22 The fifteenth to Jĕr'e-mŏth, he, his sons, and his brethren, were twelve:

23 The sixteenth to Hăn-a-nī'ah, he, his sons, and his brethren, were twelve:

24 The seventeenth to Jŏsh-bek'a-shah, he, his sons, and his brethren, were twelve:

25 The eighteenth to Ha-nā'nī, he, his sons, and his brethren, were twelve:

26 The nineteenth to Măl'lo-thī, he, his sons, and his brethren, were twelve:

27 The twentieth to E-lī'a-thah, he, his sons, and his brethren, were twelve:

28 The one and twentieth to Hō'thir, he, his sons, and his brethren, were twelve:

29 The two and twentieth to Gid-dăl'-tī, he, his sons, and his brethren, were twelve:

30 The three and twentieth to Ma-hă'-zī-ŏth, he, his sons, and his brethren, were twelve:

5-6. The king's seer is a title given to Jeduthun (II Chr 35:15) and Gad (II Chr 21:9). Asaph is called "the seer" in II Chronicles 29:30. In the words of God refers to those matters pertaining to God. To lift up the horn usually means to heighten one's power (cf. Ps 89:17; 92:10; 148:14; Lam 2:17). Thus, Heman was exalted in that he was blessed with many children who were involved in the things (words) of the Lord.

7-8. The number of those who were instructed . . . cunning, i.e., trained and skilled in music, was two hundred and eighty-eight. This is the total of twenty-four courses, plus eleven Levites per course (vss. 9-31). Lots were again cast to determine the order in which the courses would serve. The teacher . . . scholar refers to the master musician, as opposed to the apprentice or the unskilled. Apparently, all two hundred and eighty-eight were skilled, but the remaining Levites of the four thousand musicians (23:5) were unskilled.

9-31. The twenty-four courses of musicians are listed in the order in which they were selected to serve.

31 The four and twentieth to Rō-măm′tǐ-ē′zer, *he*, his sons, and his brethren, *were* twelve.

CHAPTER 26

CONCERNING the divisions of the porters: Of the Kôr′hĭtes *was* Me-shĕl-e-mī′ah the son of Kô′re, of the sons of A′săph.

2 And the sons of Me-shĕl-e-mī′ah *were*, Zĕch-a-rī′ah the firstborn, Je-dī′a-el the second, Zĕb-a-dī′ah the third, Jăth′nǐ-el the fourth,

3 Ē′lam the fifth, Je-hō-hā′nan the sixth, Ē-lǐ-ō-ē′na-ī the seventh.

4 Moreover the sons of Ō′bed-ē′dom *were*, Shem-ā-i′ah the firstborn, Je-hōz′a-băd the second, Jō′ah the third, and Sā′cär the fourth, and Ne-thăn′e-el the fifth,

5 Ăm′mǐ-el the sixth, Ĭs′sa-char the seventh, Pē-ŭl′thaī the eighth: for God blessed him.

6 Also unto Shem-ā-i′ah his son were sons born, that ruled throughout the house of their father: for they *were* mighty men of valour.

7 The sons of Shem-ā-i′ah; Ŏth′nǐ, and Rĕ′pha-el and Ō′bed, Ĕl′zā-băd, whose brethren *were* strong men, E-lī′hū, and Sĕm-a-chī′ah.

8 All these of the sons of Ō′bed-ē′dom: they and their sons and their brethren, able men for strength for the service, *were* threescore and two of Ō′bed-ē′dom.

9 And Me-shĕl-e-mī′ah had sons and brethren, strong men, eighteen.

10 Also Hō′sah, of the children of Me-rā′rī, had sons; Sĭm′rī the chief, (for *though* he was not the firstborn, yet his father made him the chief;)

11 Hĭl-kī′ah the second, Tĕb-a-lī′ah the third, Zĕch-a-rī′ah the fourth: all the sons and brethren of Hō′sah *were* thirteen.

12 Among these *were* the divisions of the porters, *even* among the chief men, *having* wards one against another, to minister in the house of the LORD.

13 ¶And they cast lots, as well the small as the great, according to the house of their fathers, for every gate.

14 And the lot eastward fell to Shĕl-e-mī′ah. Then for Zĕch-a-rī′ah his son, a wise counsellor, they cast lots; and his lot came out northward.

15 To Ō′bed-ē′dom southward; and to his sons the house of A-sŭp′pǐm.

16 To Shŭp′pǐm and Hō′sah *the lot came forth* westward, with the gate Shăl′le-chĕth, by the causeway of the going up, ward against ward.

17 Eastward *were* six Lē′vītes, northward four a day, southward four a day, and toward A-sŭp′pǐm two *and* two.

18 At Pär′bar westward, four at the causeway, *and* two at Pär′bar.

4. Divisions of porters, treasury guardians, officers, and judges. 26:1-32.

26:1-3. The **porters**, i.e., the doorkeepers, were probably responsible for guarding Temple property and restricting entrance into the Temple by those unqualified to enter. Those listed here are from the Kohathites and the Merarites (vs. 10). The **Korhites** were descendants of Korah the Kohathite who rebelled against Moses (Num 16:1ff). **Meshelemiah** is Shelemiah (vs. 14) and Shallum (9:19). **Asaph** is not the musician, but Ebiasaph (cf. 9:19).

4-5. The connection of **Obed-edom** to Meshelemiah is not stated. He was the Levite who had the opportunity to care for the ark after the tragic death of **Uzza** (13:10) in moving the ark to Jerusalem (13:13). He later assisted in moving the ark (16:5) and was appointed by David to be a porter at the tent of the ark in Jerusalem (16:38). **God blessed him** with many descendants (cf. 13:14). According to verse 8 he had sixty-two sons and grandsons.

6-11. Shemaiah is the only son of Obed-edom to have his sons named. **Hosah**, a Merarite, was an associate of Obed-edom's (cf. 16:38).

12. How **the divisions of the porters** were determined is not clear. While there are apparently twenty-four names mentioned if Shemaiah, as represented by his sons, is omitted, there is no suggestion that there were twenty-four courses. Comparing 16:38, there were initially sixty-eight porters; but verses 8, 9, and 11 suggest that the number had increased to ninety-three. Compare this number with a later (ca. 586 B.C.) count of two hundred and twelve porters (9:29). The ninety-three mentioned here were apparently chief porters over the remaining four thousand (23:5).

13-19. They cast lots, not for the time of service as before, but for the place of service. The **house of Asuppim** is literally the house of the gatherings, i.e., the storehouse (NASB). The **gate Shallecheth** appears only here in the Bible, and its location has not been determined. **Parbar**, possibly related to the Hebrew word *parwarīm*, translated "suburbs" in II Kings 23:11, occurs only here and may mean "colonnade" (NEB), or an open chamber. Verses 17 and 18 give a total of twenty-four porters on duty at a time.

19 These *are* the divisions of the porters among the sons of Kô're, and among the sons of Me-râ'rī.

20 ¶And of the Lē'vītes, A-hī'jah *was* over the treasures of the house of God, and over the treasures of the dedicated things.

21 *As concerning* the sons of Lā'adan; the sons of the Ger'shon-īte Lā'adan, chief fathers, *even* of Lā'a-dan the Ger'shon-īte, *were* Je-hī'e-lī.

22 The sons of Je-hī'e-lī; Zē'tham, and Jō'el his brother, *which were* over the treasures of the house of the Lord.

23 Of the Ăm'ra-mītes, *and* the Īz'har-ītes, the Hē'bron-ītes, *and* the Ŭz'zī-el-ītes:

24 And Shĕb'ū-el the son of Ger'shom, the son of Moses, *was* ruler of the treasures.

25 And his brethren by Ĕ-lī-ē'zer; Rē-ha-bī'ah his son, and Je-shā'iah his son, and Joram his son, and Zīch'rī his son, and Shel'ō-mīth his son.

26 Which Shel'ō-mīth and his brethren *were* over all the treasures of the dedicated things, which David the king, and the chief fathers, the captains over thousands and hundreds, and the captains of the host, had dedicated.

27 Out of the spoils won in battles did they dedicate to maintain the house of the Lord.

28 And all that Samuel the seer, and Saul the son of Kish, and Abner the son of Ner, and Jō'ăb the son of Zer-ū-i'ah, had dedicated; *and* whosoever had dedicated *any thing, it was* under the hand of Shel'ō-mīth, and of his brethren.

29 ¶Of the Īz'har-ītes, Chĕn-a-nī'ah and his sons *were* for the outward business over Israel, for officers and judges.

30 *And* of the Hē'bro-nītes, Hăsh-a-bī'ah and his brethren, men of valour, a thousand and seven hundred, *were* officers among them of Israel on this side Jordan westward in all the business of the Lord, and in the service of the king.

31 Among the Hē'bro-nītes *was* Je-rī'jah the chief, *even* among the Hē'bro-nītes, according to the generations of his fathers. In the fortieth year of the reign of David they were sought for, and there were found among them mighty men of valour at Jā'zer of Gilead.

32 And his brethren, men of valour, *were* two thousand and seven hundred chief fathers, whom king David made rulers over the Reubenites, the Găd'ītes, and the half tribe of Ma-năs'seh, for every matter pertaining to God, and affairs of the king.

CHAPTER 27

NOW the children of Israel after their number, *to wit,* the chief fathers and captains of thousands and hundreds, and their officers that served the king in any matter of the courses, which came in and went out month by month throughout all the months of the year, of every course *were* twenty and four thousand.

2 Over the first course for the first month *was* Ja-shō'be-am the son of

20-28. **Ahijah** is otherwise unknown, and his connection to the Levites cannot be determined. The name is probably not a proper noun, but should be rendered "brothers" as it appears in the Septuagint. It would thus read "And the Levites, their relatives . . ." (NASB), the relatives being the named descendants of Laadon (vss. 21-22) and of Moses' sons Gershom and Eliezer (vss. 24-28).

These men were over the **treasures.** In 9:26 the keeping of the treasures had become a responsibility of the porters, but here it seems to be a separate duty. **Shelomith** (vs. 26) had the responsibility of guarding those valuables taken as spoil in battle and dedicated to the Lord (cf. II Sam 8:10-11; I Chr 18:11; II Chr 5:1).

29-32. Another group of Levites was the **officers and judges** who were over the **outward business,** i.e., they held administrative positions. Murphy suggests the judges administered the law and the officers collected the revenue (p. 84).

Only two families of the Gershonites (vss. 21, 23) are mentioned, the **Izharites** (vs. 29) and the **Hebronites** (vs. 30); and they provided four thousand and four hundred of the six thousand designated in 23:4. One thousand and seven hundred served on the western side of the Jordan (vs. 30), while two thousand and seven hundred served on the eastern side (vs. 32). The time of this appointment was David's last year of reign, his **fortieth** (vs. 31, cf. 29:27).

5. *Divisions of military and civil leaders. 27:1-34.*

27:1. David's military organization was comprised of twelve army corps of twenty-four thousand men who served on a rotating basis. It **came in and went out month by month,** i.e., each corps came on duty, served for one month out of the year, and then was relieved by another corps.

2-3. Over each **course,** or corps, was a captain. Each was a distinguished military person; each was listed among David's

Zăb'dĭ-el: and in his course were twenty and four thousand.

3 Of the children of Pe'rĕz was the chief of all the captains of the host for the first month.

4 And over the course of the second month was Dō'da-ī an A-hō'hīte, and of his course was Mĭk'lōth also the ruler: in his course likewise were twenty and four thousand.

5 The third captain of the host for the third month was Be-nā'iah the son of Je-hoi'a-da, a chief priest: and in his course were twenty and four thousand.

6 This is that Be-nā'iah, who was mighty among the thirty, and above the thirty: and in his course was Am-mĭz'a-băd his son.

7 The fourth captain for the fourth month was Ä'sa-hĕl the brother of Jō'ăb, and Zĕb-a-dī'ah his son after him: and in his course were twenty and four thousand.

8 The fifth captain for the fifth month was Shăm'hŭth the Ĭz'ra-hīte: and in his course were twenty and four thousand.

9 The sixth captain for the sixth month was Ī'ra the son of Ĭk'kesh the Te-kō'īte: and in his course were twenty and four thousand.

10 The seventh captain for the seventh month was Hē'lĕz the Pĕl'o-nīte, of the children of Ē'phra-im: and in his course were twenty and four thousand.

11 The eighth captain for the eighth month was Sĭb'be-caī the Hu'shath-īte, of the Zär'hītes: and in his course were twenty and four thousand.

12 The ninth captain for the ninth month was A-bī-ē'zer the Ăn-e-tŏth'īte, of the Benjamites: and in his course were twenty and four thousand.

13 The tenth captain for the tenth month was Mā-har'a-ī the Ne-tōph'a-thīte, of the Zär'hītes: and in his course were twenty and four thousand.

14 The eleventh captain for the eleventh month was Be-nā'iah the Pīr'a-thŏn-īte, of the children of Ē'phra-im: and in his course were twenty and four thousand.

15 The twelfth captain for the twelfth month was Hĕl'da-ī the Ne-tōph'a-thīte, of Ŏth'nī-el: and in his course were twenty and four thousand.

16 ¶Furthermore over the tribes of Israel: the ruler of the Reubenites was Ĕ-lī-ē'zer the son of Zĭch'rī: of the Simeonites, Shĕph-a-tī'ah the son of Mā'a-chah:

17 Of the Lē'vītes, Hăsh-a-bī'ah the son of Kē-mū'el: of the Aär'ŏ-nītes, Zā'-dŏk:

18 Of Jū'dah, E-lī'hū, one of the brethren of David: of Ĭs'sa-char, Omri the son of Michael:

19 Of Zĕb'u-lun, Ĭsh-mā-i'ah the son of Ō-ba-dī'ah: of Năph'ta-lī, Jĕr'ĭ-mŏth the son of Ăz'rī-el:

20 Of the children of Ē'phra-im, Hō-shē'a the son of Ăz-a-zī'ah: of the half tribe of Ma-năs'seh, Jō'el the son of Pe-dā'iah:

21 Of the half tribe of Ma-năs'seh in Gilead, Ĭd'dō the son of Zĕch-a-rī'ah: of Benjamin, Jā-ā'sĭ-el the son of Abner:

22 Of Dan, Ă-zar'e-el the son of

mighty men in chapter 11 (primarily vss. 26-31) as either one of "the three" or "the thirty." **Jashobeam** was the outstanding figure who ranked first (chief of the captains, 11:11) among David's three most notable heroes.

4-15. Dodai, Dodo in 11:12, 26, was also one of "the three." **Benaiah** almost ranked with "the three" (11:22-25). He was the son of **Jehoiada, a chief priest,** (cf. 12:27). This was a strange role for the son of a priest, especially if his service as an executioner is noted (cf. I Kgs 2:25, 29, 34, 46). The reference to **Asahel,** who was killed when David was still king in Hebron (II Sam 2:18-23), "implies that this division was of long standing, though perhaps in a less developed form" (Ellison, p. 352). Asahel and the following captains all belonged to "the thirty." **Shamhuth** is Shammoth in 11:27. **Heldai** is Heled in 11:30.

16-22. In contrast to the military organization and leadership, the civil and tribal leaders are now listed. The arrangement of the tribes as it appears here is peculiar to Chronicles in that both the Levites and the Levite, Aaron, are listed as tribes (vs. 17); both halves of Manasseh are listed; and the tribes of Gad and Asher are curiously excluded with no apparent explanation. **Elihu** is presumably a variant spelling for David's brother Eliab (I Sam 16:6) and appears as such in the Septuagint.

Jer'ō-hăm. These were the princes of the tribes of Israel.

23 ¶But David took not the number of them from twenty years old and under: because the LORD had said he would increase Israel like to the stars of the heavens.

24 Jō'ăb the son of Zer-ū-i'ah began to number, but he finished not, because there fell wrath for it against Israel; neither was the number put in the account of the chronicles of king David.

25 ¶And over the king's treasures was Ăz'ma-věth the son of Ā'dī-el: and over the storehouses in the fields, in the cities, and in the villages, and in the castles, was Je-hŏn'a-than the son of Uz-zī'ah:

26 And over them that did the work of the field for tillage of the ground was Ĕz'rī the son of Chē'lŭb:

27 And over the vineyards was Shĭm'e-ī the Rā'math-īte: over the increase of the vineyards for the wine cellars was Zăb'dī the Shĭph'mĭte:

28 And over the olive trees and the sycomore trees that were in the low plains was Bā'al-hā'nan the Gēd'e-rīte: and over the cellars of oil was Jō'ăsh:

29 And over the herds that fed in Shăr'on was Shĭt'ra-ī the Shăr'on-īte: and over the herds that were in the valleys was Shā'phat the son of Ăd'la-ī:

30 Over the camels also was Ō'bĭl the Ĭsh'ma-el-īte: and over the asses was Jĕh-dē'iah the Me-rŏn'o-thīte:

31 And over the flocks was Jā'zĭz the Hă'ger-īte. All these were the rulers of the substance which was king David's.

32 Also Jonathan David's uncle was a counsellor, a wise man, and a scribe: and Je-hī'el the son of Hăch'mō-nī was with the king's sons:

33 And A-hĭth'o-phĕl was the king's counsellor: and Hu'shaī the Ăr'chīte was the king's companion:

34 And after A-hĭth'o-phĕl was Jehoi'a-da the son of Be-nă'iah, and Ā-bī'a-thar: and the general of the king's army was Jō'ăb.

CHAPTER 28

AND David assembled all the princes of Israel, the princes of the tribes, and the captains of the companies that ministered to the king by course, and the captains over the thousands, and captains over the hundreds, and the stewards over all the substance and possession of the king, and of his sons, with the officers, and with the mighty men, and with all the valiant men, unto Jerusalem.

2 Then David the king stood up upon his feet, and said, Hear me, my brethren, and my people: As for me, I had in mine heart to build an house of rest for the ark of the covenant of the LORD, and for the footstool of our God, and had made ready for the building:

23-24. These verses refer to David's census in 21:1ff. In keeping with Numbers 1:3, David did not number those **from twenty years old and under,** i.e., those too young for military service. **He finished not** the numbering (cf. 21:6). A number was recorded (see discussion on 21:5); but it was not recorded in **the Chronicles of king David,** annals that are no longer extant.

25-31. The names of twelve administrators over crown property follow. Obviously, every area of David's royal possessions was carefully supervised.

32-34. The personal counselors that appear are supplementary to other references to his royal staff (cf. II Sam 20:23-26 and I Chr 18:15-17). David's uncle **Jonathan,** due to his age alone, would have been a wise counselor. **Jehiel** is responsible for the king's sons' upbringing and education. For **Ahithophel** and **Hushai,** see II Samuel 15:12, 34-37; 16:16, ff. For **the king's companion,** see note on "the king's friend" (I Kgs 4:5). After Ahithophel's suicide (II Sam 17:23), he was succeeded by **Jehoiada. Abiathar** is presumably the priest (cf. I Sam 22:20; II Sam 20:25).

H. David's Final Words and Death. 28:1-29:30.

This final section of I Chronicles continues the narrative that was broken in 23:1 for the inclusion of organizational information concerning David's religious, military, and civil leaders.

28:1. For the public presentation of Solomon as his successor, **David assembled all the princes of Israel . . . unto Jerusalem.** The princes of Israel were enumerated in chapter 27. Reference to the priests is strangely omitted here (cf. 23:2).

2. My brethren. Not only were the people gathered there his subjects, they were his kin. David related what Israel must have already known, that he had his heart set on a **house of rest,** i.e., a permanent residence for the **ark of the covenant** and for **the footstool of our God,** i.e., the mercy seat (vs. 11) above the ark between the cherubim where the Lord met His people (Ex 25:19-22). This was the focal point of Israel's worship (cf. Ps 132:7). Israel would have known of David's desire because he **had made ready for the building** (cf. 22:2ff.).

3 But God said unto me, Thou shalt not build an house for my name, because thou *hast been* a man of war, and hast shed blood.

4 Howbeit the LORD God of Israel chose me before all the house of my father to be king over Israel for ever: for he hath chosen Jŭ'dah *to be* the ruler; and of the house of Jŭ'dah, the house of my father; and among the sons of my father he liked me to make *me* king over all Israel:

5 And of all my sons, (for the LORD hath given me many sons,) he hath chosen Sŏlomon my son to sit upon the throne of the kingdom of the LORD over Israel.

6 And he said unto me, Sŏlomon thy son, he shall build my house and my courts: for I have chosen him *to be* my son, and I will be his father.

7 Moreover I will establish his kingdom for ever, if he be constant to do my commandments and my judgments, as at this day.

8 Now therefore in the sight of all Israel the congregation of the LORD, and in the audience of our God, keep and seek for all the commandments of the LORD your God: that ye may possess this good land, and leave *it* for an inheritance for your children after you for ever.

9 ¶And thou, Sŏlomon my son, know thou the God of thy father, and serve him with a perfect heart and with a willing mind: for the LORD searcheth all hearts, and understandeth all the imaginations of the thoughts: if thou seek him, he will be found of thee: but if thou forsake him, he will cast thee off for ever.

10 Take heed now; for the LORD hath chosen thee to build an house for the sanctuary: be strong, and do *it*.

11 ¶Then David gave to Sŏlomon his son the pattern of the porch, and of the houses thereof, and of the treasuries thereof, and of the upper chambers thereof, and of the inner parlours thereof, and of the place of the mercy seat,

12 And the pattern of all that he had by the spirit, of the courts of the house of the LORD, and of all the chambers round about, of the treasuries of the house of God, and of the treasuries of the dedicated things:

13 Also for the courses of the priests and the Levites, and for all the work of the service of the house of the LORD, and for all the vessels of service in the house of the LORD.

14 *He gave* of gold by weight for *things* of gold, for all instruments of all manner of service; *silver also* for all instruments of silver by weight, for all instruments of every kind of service:

15 Even the weight for the candlesticks of gold, and for their lamps of gold, by weight for every candlestick, and for the lamps thereof: and for the candlesticks of silver by weight, *both* for the candlestick, and *also* for the lamps thereof, according to the use of every candlestick.

16 And by weight *he gave* gold for the tables of shewbread, for every table;

3-4. However, David now made public the reason why he was unable to build the Temple (he had privately told Solomon earlier in 22:7-8). God had chosen David **to be king over Israel for ever,** a reference to the Davidic covenant (17:11-14; II Sam 7:12-16), which would ultimately culminate in Christ's millennial reign.

5-7. Now David, God's chosen king, presented God's chosen successor. **He hath chosen Solomon.** Though there is no direct statement of God's selection, II Samuel 12:24-25 hints at God's choice. Solomon was God's man, not only to reign, but also to build the Temple (cf. 22:9-11).

8-10. Before he publicly charged Solomon, David charged the gathered assembly, **keep and seek . . . the commandments of the LORD your God.** This would be the test and security of Israel. The fatherly admonition that is given to Solomon, though it does not entirely correspond to the private charge in I Kings 2:1ff., parallels that charge in spirit. The charge is resumed in verse 20.

11-18. Although Solomon is remembered as the Temple builder, the **pattern,** (Heb *tabnīt*), i.e., the plans for the Temple, was a divine blueprint that was given to David by revelation, just as the plans for the tabernacle had been revealed to Moses (Ex 25:9, 40). The information recorded here shows how inclusive the details of the pattern received by David were, listing not only the different items of furnishings, but also noting their weight and composition of gold or silver.

and *likewise* silver for the tables of silver:

17 Also pure gold for the fleshhooks, and the bowls, and the cups: and for the golden basons *he gave gold* by weight for every bason; and *likewise silver* by weight for every bason of silver:

18 And for the altar of incense refined gold by weight; and gold for the pattern of the chariot of the cherubims, that spread out *their wings,* and covered the ark of the covenant of the LORD.

19 All *this, said David,* the LORD made me understand in writing by *his* hand upon me, *even* all the works of this pattern.

19. The pattern was more than oral communication. It consisted of written specifications that evidently were handed over to Solomon in this public ceremony (vs. 11). **The LORD made me understand.** The pattern was not of David's invention, but by divine revelation; for he experienced the Lord's hand upon him. Myers understands **writing** to mean "a written document, possibly even a model of some kind" (*I Chronicles*, p. 190). Evidently, then, where the Temple plans were modified and different from the tabernacle, all was by divine design.

20-21. David's final admonition to Solomon is reminiscent of God's encouraging word to Joshua (Josh 1:7, 9).

20 And David said to Sŏlomon his son, Be strong and of good courage, and do *it:* fear not, nor be dismayed: for the LORD God, *even* my God, *will be* with thee; he will not fail thee, nor forsake thee, until thou hast finished all the work for the service of the house of the LORD.

21 And, behold, the courses of the priests and the Lĕ'vītes, *even they shall be with thee* for all the service of the house of God: and *there shall be* with thee for all manner of workmanship every willing skilful man, for any manner of service: also the princes and all the people *will be* wholly at thy commandment.

CHAPTER 29

FURTHERMORE David the king said unto all the congregation, Sŏlomon my son, whom alone God hath chosen, *is* yet young and tender, and the work *is* great: for the palace *is* not for man, but for the LORD God.

2 Now I have prepared with all my might for the house of my God the gold for *things to be made* of gold, and the silver for *things* of silver, and the brass for *things* of brass, the iron for *things* of iron, and wood for *things* of wood; onyx stones, and *stones* to be set, glistering stones, and of divers colours, and all manner of precious stones, and marble stones in abundance.

3 Moreover, because I have set my affection to the house of my God, I have of mine own proper good, of gold and silver, *which* I have given to the house of my God, over and above all that I have prepared for the holy house,

4 *Even* three thousand talents of gold, of the gold of Ō'phir, and seven thousand talents of refined silver, to overlay the walls of the houses *withal:*

5 The gold for *things* of gold, and the silver for *things* of silver, and for all manner of work *to be made* by the hands of artificers. And who *then* is willing to consecrate his service this day unto the LORD?

6 ¶Then the chief of the fathers and princes of the tribes of Israel, and the

29:1-2. Once again David addressed the gathered assembly. In concern for his son, he appealed to them for assistance and support for Solomon because he was **young and tender,** i.e., lacking in experience in what God had chosen him to do (concerning his age, see note on I Kgs 3:7). The Temple was to be a **palace** for the **LORD God,** the King of kings. Therefore, David appealed for liberal offerings to assist in the building of a house that was worthy of God. Attention is called to the resources for building that he has stocked for Solomon's use (cf. 22:2-5).

3-5. David did not ask of his subjects what he himself was not willing to do. He donated an enormous private gift from his own fortune. On the basis of his example, he asked for a similar response on their part. **To consecrate his service** is literally "to fill his hand," a technical expression used for induction into the priestly office (cf. Ex 28:41; 32:29; II Chr 13:9; 29:31). Here, David asked the assembly who would be as equally devoted as the priests.

6-7. Sparked by the generosity of the king, the leaders of Israel responded by matching his spirit of giving. Their willing-

captains of thousands and of hundreds, with the rulers of the king's work, offered willingly,

7 And gave for the service of the house of God of gold five thousand talents and ten thousand drams, and of silver ten thousand talents, and of brass eighteen thousand talents, and one hundred thousand talents of iron.

8 And they with whom *precious* stones were found gave *them* to the treasure of the house of the Lord, by the hand of Je-hi'el the Ger'shon-ite.

9 Then the people rejoiced, for that they offered willingly, because with perfect heart they offered willingly to the Lord: and David the king also rejoiced with great joy.

10 ¶Wherefore David blessed the Lord before all the congregation: and David said, Blessed *be* thou, Lord God of Israel our father, for ever and ever.

11 Thine, O Lord, *is* the greatness, and the power, and the glory, and the victory, and the majesty: for all *that is* in the heaven and in the earth *is thine;* thine *is* the kingdom, O Lord, and thou art exalted as head above all.

12 Both riches and honour *come* of thee, and thou reignest over all; and in thine hand *is* power and might; and in thine hand *it is* to make great, and to give strength unto all.

13 Now therefore, our God, we thank thee, and praise thy glorious name.

14 But who *am* I, and what *is* my people, that we should be able to offer so willingly after this sort? for all things *come* of thee, and of thine own have we given thee.

15 For we *are* strangers before thee, and sojourners, as *were* all our fathers: our days on the earth *are* as a shadow, and *there is* none abiding.

16 O Lord our God, all this store that we have prepared to build thee an house for thine holy name *cometh* of thine hand, and *is* all thine own.

17 I know also, my God, that thou triest the heart, and hast pleasure in uprightness. As for me, in the uprightness of mine heart I have willingly offered all these things: and now have I seen with joy thy people, which are present here, to offer willingly unto thee.

18 O Lord God of Abraham, Isaac, and of Israel, our fathers, keep this for ever in the imagination of the thoughts of the heart of thy people, and prepare their heart unto thee:

19 And give unto Sŏlomon my son a perfect heart, to keep thy commandments, and thy testimonies, and thy statutes, and to do all *these things,* and to build the palace, *for* the which I have made provision.

20 ¶And David said to all the congregation, Now bless the Lord your God. And all the congregation blessed the Lord God of their fathers, and bowed down their heads, and worshipped the Lord, and the king.

21 And they sacrificed sacrifices unto the Lord, and offered burnt offerings unto the Lord, on the morrow after

ness (cf. vs. 9) is reminiscent of Israel's giving for the tabernacle in Exodus 36:3-7. **Drams** (daric in NASB) were Persian gold coins, possibly named for Darius I (520-486 B.C.), and therefore anachronistic to David's era, but not necessarily to the time of writing by the Chronicler. He used the daric, the current unit of exchange, to evaluate the offering of Israel's leaders.

8-14. The offering was given to **Jehiel** (cf. 26:21), a guardian of the treasure, for safe-keeping. Overwhelmed by the willingness of the people to give, David spontaneously lifted a prayer of blessing and thanksgiving to God. Jehovah is addressed as the sovereign God who is the source of all blessings (cf. Rev 5:12-13). The understanding of David needs to be that of every believer. **All things come of thee.** All that David or anyone ever gives to God is merely returning to Him what was originally His.

15-19. We are strangers . . . sojourners. Israel was dependent upon the care and protection of God, just as an alien is dependent upon the good will of the ruler of the land in which he finds himself. **Thou triest the heart.** David knew that the true measure of Israel's giving was not the amount that they gave, but the willingness with which they gave. **Keep this for ever in the imagination . . . of the heart.** David prayed that his people might never lose the generosity and devotion that they now exhibited.

20. Closing his prayer, David asked the assembly to **bless the Lord your God.** The word bless (Heb *barak*) originally meant to bend the knee. Therefore, Israel did homage. They **worshiped the Lord . . . king. Worshiped** (Heb *shachah,* i.e., lit, to prostrate oneself.) Israel did not worship her king, but did obeisance to God and the king.

21-22. In addition to the **burnt offerings,** sacrifices or peace offerings, whereby the people feasted, were in abundance. Solomon was made king **the second time.** The anointing in 23:1

ter that day, *even* a thousand bullocks, a thousand rams, *and* a thousand lambs, with their drink offerings, and sacrifices in abundance for all Israel:

22 And did eat and drink before the LORD on that day with great gladness. And they made Sŏlomon the son of David king the second time, and anointed *him* unto the LORD *to be* the chief governor, and Zā′dŏk *to be* priest.

23 Then Sŏlomon sat on the throne of the LORD as king instead of David his father, and prospered; and all Israel obeyed him.

24 And all the princes, and the mighty men, and all the sons likewise of king David, submitted themselves unto Sŏlomon the king.

25 And the LORD magnified Sŏlomon exceedingly in the sight of all Israel, and bestowed upon him *such* royal majesty as had not been on any king before him in Israel.

26 ¶Thus David the son of Jesse reigned over all Israel.

27 And the time that he reigned over Israel *was* forty years; seven years reigned he in Hēbron, and thirty and three *years* reigned he in Jerusalem.

28 And he died in a good old age, full of days, riches, and honour: and Sŏlomon his son reigned in his stead.

29 Now the acts of David the king, first and last, behold, they *are* written in the book of Samuel the seer, and in the book of Nāthan the prophet, and in the book of Gad the seer,

30 With all his reign and his might, and the times that went over him, and over Israel, and over all the kingdoms of the countries.

refers to this same occasion. The first anointing was the impromptu event which hastily occurred to counteract Adonijah's attempt to usurp the throne (I Kgs 1:32-40). The first anointing had been valid, but his second anointing was a public confirmation.

Zadok was also confirmed as solitary high priest because Abiathar had disqualified himself by his participation in Adonijah's plots (cf. I Kgs 1:7) and was to be later deposed as priest (I Kgs 2:26-27).

23-28. When Solomon took the throne, **all Israel obeyed him,** including **all the sons likewise of king David.** The Chronicler undoubtedly has in mind the usurper, Adonijah (cf. I Kgs 1:5, 50-53). For length of David's reign see parallel passages (II Sam 5:4-5; I Kgs 2:11). **A good old age, full of days.** David was seventy years old (II Sam 5:4), the full time of life (Ps 90:10).

29-30. The **acts of David** as recorded by **Nathan the Prophet** and **Gad the Seer** are no longer extant.

(see page 858 for Bibliography to I and II Chronicles)

OUTLINE
II CHRONICLES

COMMENTARY

I. THE REIGN OF SOLOMON. 1:1-9:31.

Beginning with the reign of Solomon, the parallels between II Chronicles and I and II Kings abound. In fact, the history of Judah by the Chronicler corresponds so closely to the books of Kings, he appears to have rewritten Judah's history, abridging the Kings' account at times and supplementing Kings at other times. As was noted in the Introduction, the Chronicler omits all references to Israel, the northern kingdom, except as its history affects Judah, the southern kingdom.

A. His Prayer and Divine Confirmation as King. 1:1-17.

1:1-2. The first six verses are essentially peculiar to II Chronicles. This verse, however, reiterates I Chronicles 29:25.

AND Solomon the son of David was strengthened in his kingdom, and the LORD his God was with him, and magnified him exceedingly.

2 Then Solomon spake unto all Israel, to the captains of thousands and of hundreds, and to the judges, and to every governor in all Israel, the chief of the fathers.

3 So Solomon, and all the congregation with him, went to the high place that was at Gibeon; for there was the tabernacle of the congregation of God, which Moses the servant of the LORD had made in the wilderness.

4 But the ark of God had David brought up from Kir'jath-je'a-rim to the place which David had prepared for it: for he had pitched a tent for it at Jerusalem.

3-4. Gibeon, about seven miles northwest of Jerusalem, was the small city that was the home of the Mosaic tabernacle. From the time of Joshua (Josh 18:1) until the time of Eli (I Sam 4:3ff.), the tabernacle resided at Shiloh. With Israel's defeat by the Philistines and consequent loss of the ark of the covenant (I Sam 4:10-11), the ark and the tabernacle became separated, the ark finally coming to reside in Kirjath-jearim until David had it brought to Jerusalem. The tabernacle, however, was apparently moved temporarily to Nob (cf. David's encounter with the priesthood there, I Sam 21:1ff.) and finally came to reside at Gibeon. Neither Samuel, the writer of Kings, nor the Chronicler indicate precisely what precipitated the moving of the tabernacle. Neither are we told why David did not have the ark rejoin the tabernacle, even if it meant moving the tabernacle to Jerusalem.

5 Moreover the brasen altar, that Be-zal'e-el the son of U'ri, the son of Hur, had made, he put before the tabernacle of the LORD: and Solomon and the congregation sought unto it.

6 And Solomon went up thither to the brasen altar before the LORD, which was at the tabernacle of the congregation, and offered a thousand burnt offerings upon it.

5-6. The Mosaic **brazen altar,** upon which the burnt offerings were offered, was still positioned before the tabernacle. Solomon's action in going to Gibeon to offer burnt offerings there indicates that this was still the official place of worship, even though the ark was in Jerusalem.

7 ¶In that night did God appear unto Solomon, and said unto him, Ask what I shall give thee.

8 And Solomon said unto God, Thou hast shewed great mercy unto David my father, and hast made me to reign in his stead.

9 Now, O LORD God, let thy promise unto David my father be established: for thou hast made me king over a people like the dust of the earth in multitude.

10 Give me now wisdom and knowledge, that I may go out and come in before this people: for who can judge this thy people, that is so great?

11 And God said to Solomon, Because this was in thine heart, and thou hast not asked riches, wealth, or honour, nor the life of thine enemies, neither yet hast asked long life; but hast asked wisdom and knowledge for thyself, that thou mayest judge my people, over whom I have made thee king:

7-13. In that night did God appear unto Solomon. In the parallel account in I Kings this appearance is in the form of a dream. The Chronicler abridges somewhat the details of Solomon's confirmation as they appear in I Kings 3:5-15 (for a fuller discussion of this section, see notes in Kings commentary).

12 Wisdom and knowledge *is* granted unto thee; and I will give thee riches, and wealth, and honour, such as none of the kings have had that *have been* before thee, neither shall there any after thee have the like.

13 ¶Then Sŏlomon came *from his journey* to the high place that *was* at Gĭbeon to Jerusalem, from before the tabernacle of the congregation, and reigned over Israel.

14 And Sŏlomon gathered chariots and horsemen: and he had a thousand and four hundred chariots, and twelve thousand horsemen, which he placed in the chariot cities, and with the king at Jerusalem.

15 And the king made silver and gold at Jerusalem *as plenteous* as stones, and cedar trees made he as the sycomore trees that *are* in the vale for abundance.

16 And Sŏlomon had horses brought out of Egypt, and linen yarn: the king's merchants received the linen yarn at a price.

17 And they fetched up, and brought forth out of Egypt a chariot for six hundred *shekels* of silver, and an horse for an hundred and fifty: and so brought they out *horses* for all the kings of the Hittites, and for the kings of Syria, by their means.

CHAPTER 2

AND Sŏlomon determined to build an house for the name of the LORD, and an house for his kingdom.

2 And Sŏlomon told out threescore and ten thousand men to bear burdens, and fourscore thousand to hew in the mountain, and three thousand and six hundred to oversee them.

3 ¶And Sŏlomon sent to Hū′ram the king of Tyre, saying, As thou didst deal with David my father, and didst send him cedars to build him an house to dwell therein, *even so deal with me.*

4 Behold, I build an house to the name of the LORD my God, to dedicate *it* to him, *and* to burn before him sweet incense, and for the continual shewbread, and for the burnt offerings morning and evening, on the sabbaths, and on the new moons, and on the solemn feasts of the LORD our God. This *is an ordinance* for ever to Israel.

5 And the house which I build *is* great: for great *is* our God above all gods.

6 But who is able to build him an house, seeing the heaven and heaven of heavens cannot contain him? who *am* I then, that I should build him an house, save only to burn sacrifice before him?

7 Send me now therefore a man cunning to work in gold, and in silver, and in brass, and in iron, and in purple, and crimson, and blue, and that can skill to grave with the cunning men that *are* with me in Jūdah and in Jerusalem, whom David my father did provide.

8 Send me also cedar trees, fir trees, and algum trees, out of Lebanon: for I know that thy servants can skill to cut timber in Lebanon; and, behold, my servants *shall be* with thy servants,

9 Even to prepare me timber in abun-

14-17. This description of Solomon's wealth, though out of sequence with the I Kings narrative, is virtually identical to I Kings 10:26-29 (for discussion, see notes in Kings commentary; cf. also II Chr 9:13-20).

B. His Building of the Temple. 2:1-4:22.

1. Correspondence and preparation. 2:1-18.

2:1-2. Solomon told, i.e., he counted out, a total number of one hundred and fifty-three thousand "strangers" (vss. 17-18), i.e., aliens to do labor (cf. notes on I Kgs 5:13-18). The Chronicler's total of overseers exceeds the number in I Kings by three hundred. Also, the Chronicler does not mention the thirty thousand Israelites under Adoniram's supervision who were taxed with forced labor.

3-4. Huram is the name used by the Chronicler for Hiram in I Kings. The following correspondence with Huram parallels I Kings 5:3-6 (see I Kings commentary). Though Solomon's explanation of David's inability to build the Temple is omitted, the letter is given here in an expanded form.

5-6. The same theological consideration of God's omnipresence and transcendence is included in this letter, as appears in Solomon's dedicatory prayer in 6:18. In a rare occurrence an Israelite king gives witness to a heathen of the greatness and supremacy of his God, the true God.

7-10. Solomon's request for an artisan is peculiar to II Chronicles, although I Kings 7:13ff. records his receiving one. Solomon's promise of payment in food is peculiar to II Chronicles.

dance: for the house which I am about to build *shall be* wonderful great.

10 And, behold, I will give to thy servants, the hewers that cut timber, twenty thousand measures of beaten wheat, and twenty thousand measures of barley, and twenty thousand baths of wine, and twenty thousand baths of oil.

11 ¶Then Hū′ram the king of Tyre answered in writing, which he sent to Sŏlomon, Because the Lord hath loved his people, he hath made thee king over them.

12 Hū′ram said moreover, Blessed *be* the Lord God of Israel, that made heaven and earth, who hath given to David the king a wise son, endued with prudence and understanding, that might build an house for the Lord, and an house for his kingdom.

13 And now I have sent a cunning man, endued with understanding, of Hū′ram my father's,

14 The son of a woman of the daughters of Dan, and his father *was* a man of Tyre, skilful to work in gold, and in silver, in brass, in iron, in stone, and in timber, in purple, in blue, and in fine linen, and in crimson; also to grave any manner of graving, and to find out every device which shall be put to him, with thy cunning men, and with the cunning men of my lord David thy father.

15 Now therefore the wheat, and the barley, the oil, and the wine, which my lord hath spoken of, let him send unto his servants:

16 And we will cut wood out of Lebanon, as much as thou shalt need: and we will bring it to thee in floats by sea to Jŏppa; and thou shalt carry it up to Jerusalem.

17 ¶And Sŏlomon numbered all the strangers that *were* in the land of Israel, after the numbering wherewith David his father had numbered them; and they were found an hundred and fifty thousand and three thousand and six hundred.

18 And he set threescore and ten thousand of them *to be* bearers of burdens, and fourscore thousand *to be* hewers in the mountain, and three thousand and six hundred overseers to set the people a work.

CHAPTER 3

THEN Sŏlomon began to build the house of the Lord at Jerusalem in mount Mŏ-rī′ah, where *the Lord* appeared unto David his father, in the place that David had prepared in the threshingfloor of Ŏr′nan the Jĕb′u-sīte.

2 And he began to build in the second *day* of the second month, in the fourth year of his reign.

3 ¶Now these *are* the things wherein Sŏlomon was instructed for the building of the house of God. The length by cubits after the first measure *was* threescore cubits, and the breadth twenty cubits.

11-18. Huram's return correspondence is again expanded somewhat here, but it parallels I Kings 5:7-9 (see I Kings commentary). King Huram was quick to send an artisan bearing the same name, Huram, to Solomon (for discussion of his lineage see notes on I Kgs 7:13-14). **My father's** (Heb *'abî*) may be part of a variant spelling of Huram's name (Huram-abi), or it may be interpreted as "my counselor" or "my chief craftsman." Huram's role as artisan corresponds to that of Bezaleel in Exodus 31:1-5.

2. Construction of the Temple and all its furnishings. 3:1-4:22.

The Chronicler's account of the Temple construction corresponds to I Kings 6:1-7:51. However, his record is often abbreviated, though there are additions which will be noted (for a fuller discussion of the Temple construction, see notes in I Kings commentary).

3:1. The Chronicler is more specific here than I Kings is. Solomon began to build **at Jerusalem in mount Moriah.** The name only appears elsewhere in Genesis 22:2, where Abraham was instructed to offer his son Isaac as a sacrifice on one of the mountains of Moriah. The Temple was to be built on the very site where God had demonstrated His presence to David by igniting his burnt offering with fire from heaven (I Chr 21:26), **in the threshing floor of Ornan the Jebusite.**

2-9. For commencement date (vs. 2), see notes on I Kings 6:1. The opening phrase, **Now these are the things wherein Solomon was instructed,** would be better rendered, "Now these are the foundations which Solomon laid" (NASB). **The greater house** is synonymous to the Temple (*hēkal*), the main room located between the porch and the "oracle" (*debîr*), or the "Holy Place" (cf. notes on I Kgs 6:3, 19-20). The **gold of Parvaim** was apparently high quality gold, possibly taken from a

4 And the porch that *was* in the front *of the house,* the length *of it was* according to the breadth of the house, twenty cubits, and the height *was* an hundred and twenty: and he overlaid it within with pure gold.

5 And the greater house he cieled with fir tree, which he overlaid with fine gold, and set thereon palm trees and chains.

6 And he garnished the house with precious stones for beauty: and the gold *was* gold of Pär-vā'im.

7 He overlaid also the house, the beams, the posts, and the walls thereof, and the doors thereof, with gold; and graved cherubims on the walls.

8 And he made the most holy house, the length whereof *was* according to the breadth of the house, twenty cubits, and the breadth thereof twenty cubits: and he overlaid it with fine gold, *amounting* to six hundred talents.

9 And the weight of the nails *was* fifty shekels of gold. And he overlaid the upper chambers with gold.

10 And in the most holy house he made two cherubims of image work, and overlaid them with gold.

11 And the wings of the cherubims *were* twenty cubits long: one wing *of the one cherub was* five cubits, reaching·to the wall of the house: and the other wing *was likewise* five cubits, reaching to the wing of the other cherub.

12 And *one* wing of the other cherub *was* five cubits, reaching to the wall of the house: and the other wing *was* five cubits *also,* joining to the wing of the other cherub.

13 The wings of these cherubims spread themselves forth twenty cubits: and they stood on their feet, and their faces *were* inward.

14 And he made the vail *of* blue, and purple, and crimson, and fine linen, and wrought cherubims thereon.

15 Also he made before the house two pillars of thirty and five cubits high, and the chapiter that *was* on the top of each of them *was* five cubits.

16 And he made chains, *as* in the oracle, and put *them* on the heads of the pillars; and made an hundred pomegranates, and put *them* on the chains.

17 And he reared up the pillars before the temple, one on the right hand, and the other on the left; and called the name of that on the right hand Jā'chin, and the name of that on the left Bō'ăz.

CHAPTER 4

MOREOVER he made an altar of brass, twenty cubits the length thereof, and twenty cubits the breadth thereof, and ten cubits the height thereof.

mine identified with Sak el-Farwin or with Farma, both located in the Yemen (Slotki, p. 168).

10-16. These cherubim, though located in the **most holy house,** are not to be confused with the cherubim above the ark of the covenant (cf. 5:7-8). The twenty-cubit wingspan of the two cherubim extended from wall to wall (vss. 3, 9-13) in this sacred room. The **veil** is not mentioned in I Kings. Presumably, it hung between the Holy Place and the Most Holy Place, thus corresponding to the veil in the Mosaic tabernacle (cf. Ex 26:31ff.).

17. For discussion on the names **Jachin** and **Boaz,** see note on I Kings 7:21.

4:1. Construction of the **altar of brass** is not mentioned in I Kings and is not listed in the summary of furnishings in this chapter (vss. 11-18). This has led some scholars (cf. Clyde Francisco, I-II Chronicles. In *The Broadman Bible Commentary,* p. 366) to believe that perhaps originally Solomon had transferred the brazen altar from the tabernacle to the Temple; but due to an increase of sacrifices in Jerusalem (cf. I Kgs 8:64), a new and larger altar was constructed. The Mosaic altar's dimensions were five cubits by five cubits by three cubits high. This altar was twenty cubits by twenty cubits (the width of the Temple) by ten cubits high and was placed in the courtyard before the Temple (cf. II Kgs 16:14). The height of this altar

2 ¶Also he made a molten sea of ten cubits from brim to brim, round in compass, and five cubits the height thereof; and a line of thirty cubits did compass it round about.

3 And under it *was* the similitude of oxen, which did compass it round about: ten in a cubit, compassing the sea round about. Two rows of oxen *were* cast, when it was cast.

4 It stood upon twelve oxen, three looking toward the north, and three looking toward the west, and three looking toward the south, and three looking toward the east: and the sea *was* set above upon them, and all their hinder parts *were* inward.

5 And the thickness of it *was* an handbreadth, and the brim of it like the work of the brim of a cup, with flowers of lilies; *and* it received and held three thousand baths.

6 ¶He made also ten lavers, and put five on the right hand, and five on the left, to wash in them: such things as they offered for the burnt offering they washed in them; but the sea *was* for the priests to wash in.

7 And he made ten candlesticks of gold according to their form, and set *them* in the temple, five on the right hand, and five on the left.

8 He made also ten tables, and placed *them* in the temple, five on the right side, and five on the left. And he made an hundred basons of gold.

9 ¶Furthermore he made the court of the priests, and the great court, and doors for the court, and overlaid the doors of them with brass.

10 And he set the sea on the right side of the east end, over against the south.

11 ¶And Hū'ram made the pots, and the shovels, and the basons. And Hū'ram finished the work that he was to make for king Sŏlomon for the house of God;

12 *To wit,* the two pillars, and the pommels, and the chapiters *which were* on the top of the two pillars, and the two wreaths to cover the two pommels of the chapiters which *were* on the top of the pillars;

13 And four hundred pomegranates on the two wreaths; two rows of pomegranates on each wreath, to cover the two pommels of the chapiters which *were* upon the pillars.

14 He made also bases, and lavers made he upon the bases;

15 One sea, and twelve oxen under it.

16 The pots also, and the shovels, and the fleshhooks, and all their instruments, did Hū'ram his father make to king Sŏlomon for the house of the Lord of bright brass.

17 In the plain of Jordan did the king cast them, in the clay ground between Sŭc'coth and Zĕ-red'ā-thah.

18 Thus Sŏlomon made all these vessels in great abundance: for the weight of the brass could not be found out.

19 ¶And Sŏlomon made all the vessels that *were* for the house of God, the

would have necessitated some form of ascent to it, either an incline or steps.

2-6. For the *molten sea*, see remarks on I Kings 7:23-26.

7-8. The construction of **ten candlesticks**, i.e., lampstands, is peculiar to II Chronicles, although they are listed in the summary of furnishings with a more precise location, in the room "before the oracle," in I Kings 7:49. The Mosaic tabernacle had only one candlestick (Ex 25:31ff.). The candlesticks were probably placed on the **ten tables,** which are not mentioned in I Kings.

9. The **court of the priests** was an inner court into which only the priests had access. **The great court** was the outer court where all the Israelites could gather as an assembly.

10-22. These final verses provide a summarizing inventory of the articles made by Huram. For a brief comment on the casting of brass in the **clay ground** (vs. 17), see the virtually identical passage in I Kings 7:40-51.

golden altar also, and the tables whereon the shewbread *was set;*

20 Moreover the candlesticks with their lamps, that they should burn after the manner before the oracle, of pure gold;

21 And the flowers, and the lamps, and the tongs, *made he of* gold, *and* that perfect gold;

22 And the snuffers, and the basons, and the spoons, and the censers, *of* pure gold: and the entry of the house, the inner doors thereof for the most holy *place,* and the doors of the house of the temple, *were of* gold.

CHAPTER 5

THUS all the work that Sŏlomon made for the house of the LORD was finished: and Sŏlomon brought in *all* the things that David his father had dedicated; and the silver, and the gold, and all the instruments, put he among the treasures of the house of God.

2 ¶Then Sŏlomon assembled the elders of Israel, and all the heads of the tribes, the chief of the fathers of the children of Israel, unto Jerusalem, to bring up the ark of the covenant of the LORD out of the city of David, which *is* Zion.

3 Wherefore all the men of Israel assembled themselves unto the king in the feast which *was* in the seventh month.

4 And all the elders of Israel came; and the Lē'vītes took up the ark.

5 And they brought up the ark, and the tabernacle of the congregation, and all the holy vessels that *were* in the tabernacle, these did the priests *and* the Lē'vītes bring up.

6 Also king Sŏlomon, and all the congregation of Israel that were assembled unto him before the ark, sacrificed sheep and oxen, which could not be told nor numbered for multitude.

7 And the priests brought in the ark of the covenant of the LORD unto his place, to the oracle of the house, into the most holy *place, even* under the wings of the cherubims:

8 For the cherubims spread forth *their* wings over the place of the ark, and the cherubims covered the ark and the staves thereof above.

9 And they drew out the staves *of the ark,* that the ends of the staves were seen from the ark before the oracle; but they were not seen without. And there it is unto this day.

10 *There was* nothing in the ark save the two tables which Moses put *therein* at Hŏ'rĕb, when the LORD made *a covenant* with the children of Israel, when they came out of Egypt.

11 ¶And it came to pass, when the priests were come out of the holy *place:* (for all the priests *that were* present were sanctified, *and* did not *then* wait by course;

12 Also the Lē'vītes *which were* the singers, all of them of Ā'săph, of Hē'mǎn, of Jĕd'ū-thun, with their sons and their brethren, *being* arrayed in white linen, having cymbals and psalteries and harps, stood at the east end of the altar, and with them an hundred and

C. His Dedication of the Temple. 5:1-7:22.

1. The installation of the ark of the covenant. 5:1-14.

5:1-10. Upon completion of the Temple, Solomon had all the elders of Israel and tribal leaders assemble at Jerusalem for a great ceremonial occasion, the transferring of the ark from its temporary tent in Jerusalem (cf. I Chr 16:1) to its permanent location within the "oracle of the house" (vs. 7), i.e., the Most Holy Place. The first eleven verses have been commented upon in the parallel passage, I Kings 8:1-10.

11-12. Beginning with the second half of verse 11, the remainder of the chapter has no parallel in I Kings. **All the priests that were present.** This solemn occasion was of such importance that all twenty-four courses (cf. I Chr 24) were present without any regard for the normal rotation of priests that would follow later. Likewise, all the **Levites . . . the singers** i.e., all twenty-four courses (I Chr 25), were present and singing, while one hundred and twenty priests were **sounding the trumpets** (cf. Num 10:8).

twenty priests sounding with trumpets:)

13 It came even to pass, as the trumpeters and singers *were* as one, to make one sound to be heard in praising and thanking the LORD; and when they lifted up *their* voice with the trumpets and cymbals and instruments of musick, and praised the LORD, *saying,* For *he is* good; for his mercy *endureth* for ever: that *then* the house was filled with a cloud, *even* the house of the LORD;

14 So that the priests could not stand to minister by reason of the cloud: for the glory of the LORD had filled the house of God.

CHAPTER 6

THEN said Sŏlomon, The LORD hath said that he would dwell in the thick darkness.

2 But I have built an house of habitation for thee, and a place for thy dwelling for ever.

3 And the king turned his face, and blessed the whole congregation of Israel: and all the congregation of Israel stood.

4 And he said, Blessed *be* the LORD God of Israel, who hath with his hands fulfilled *that* which he spake with his mouth to my father David, saying,

5 Since the day that I brought forth my people out of the land of Egypt I chose no city among all the tribes of Israel to build an house in, that my name might be there; neither chose I any man to be a ruler over my people Israel:

6 But I have chosen Jerusalem, that my name might be there; and have chosen David to be over my people Israel.

7 Now it was in the heart of David my father to build an house for the name of the LORD God of Israel.

8 But the LORD said to David my father, Forasmuch as it was in thine heart to build an house for my name, thou didst well in that it was in thine heart:

9 Notwithstanding thou shalt not build the house; but thy son which shall come forth out of thy loins, he shall build the house for my name.

10 The LORD therefore hath performed his word that he hath spoken: for I am risen up in the room of David my father, and am set on the throne of Israel, as the LORD promised, and have built the house for the name of the LORD God of Israel.

11 And in it have I put the ark, wherein *is* the covenant of the LORD, that he made with the children of Israel.

12 ¶And he stood before the altar of the LORD in the presence of all the congregation of Israel, and spread forth his hands:

13 For Sŏlomon had made a brasen scaffold of five cubits long, and five cubits broad, and three cubits high, and had set it in the midst of the court: and upon it he stood, and kneeled down upon his knees before all the congrega-

13-14. While their praise was ascending, the glory of the Lord descended and **filled the house of God** in a manner reminiscent of the event in Exodus 40:34-35.

2. The dedicatory prayer. 6:1-42.

6:1-11. Having recognized the presence of the Lord in the audience of all Israel, Solomon gave a brief testimony to the faithfulness of God before offering his prayer of dedication (see notes on parallel passage in I Kgs 8:12-21). **I have chosen Jerusalem.** I Kings states that God had chosen a city for His name, but the Chronicler specifically names it.

12-42. This lengthy section is given wholly to Solomon's prayer of dedication. With the exception of verse 13, an additional note concerning a **Brazen scaffold,** i.e., a platform, from which Solomon addressed the people and offered his dedicatory prayer, verses 12-39 are drawn almost verbatim from I Kings 8:22-50a (see I Kings commentary for notes on this prayer). The Chronicler omits a portion of the prayer (cf. I Kgs 8:50b-53) but adds a conclusion that is peculiar to II Chronicles, but corresponding to Psalm 132:8-10. Payne (p. 396) suggests that Solomon was quoting words his father may have written for an

tion of Israel, and spread forth his hands toward heaven,

14 And said, O LORD God of Israel, *there is* no God like thee in the heaven, nor in the earth; which keepest covenant, and *shewest* mercy unto thy servants, that walk before thee with all their hearts:

15 Thou which hast kept with thy servant David my father that which thou hast promised him; and spakest with thy mouth, and hast fulfilled *it* with thine hand, as *it is* this day.

16 Now therefore, O LORD God of Israel, keep with thy servant David my father that which thou hast promised him, saying, There shall not fail thee a man in my sight to sit upon the throne of Israel; yet so that thy children take heed to their way to walk in my law, as thou hast walked before me.

17 Now then, O LORD God of Israel, let thy word be verified, which thou hast spoken unto thy servant David.

18 But will God in very deed dwell with men on the earth? behold, heaven and the heaven of heavens cannot contain thee; how much less this house which I have built!

19 Have respect therefore to the prayer of thy servant, and to his supplication, O LORD my God, to hearken unto the cry and the prayer which thy servant prayeth before thee:

20 That thine eyes may be open upon this house day and night, upon the place whereof thou hast said that thou wouldest put thy name there; to hearken unto the prayer which thy servant prayeth toward this place.

21 Hearken therefore unto the supplications of thy servant, and of thy people Israel, which they shall make toward this place: hear thou from thy dwelling place, *even* from heaven; and when thou hearest, forgive.

22 ¶If a man sin against his neighbour, and an oath be laid upon him to make him swear, and the oath come before thine altar in this house;

23 Then hear thou from heaven, and do, and judge thy servants, by requiting the wicked, by recompensing his way upon his own head; and by justifying the righteous, by giving him according to his righteousness.

24 ¶And if thy people Israel be put to the worse before the enemy, because they have sinned against thee; and shall return and confess thy name, and pray and make supplication before thee in this house;

25 Then hear thou from the heavens, and forgive the sin of thy people Israel, and bring them again unto the land which thou gavest to them and to their fathers.

26 ¶When the heaven is shut up, and there is no rain, because they have sinned against thee; *yet* if they pray toward this place, and confess thy name, and turn from their sin, when thou dost afflict them;

27 Then hear thou from heaven, and forgive the sin of thy servants, and of thy people Israel, when thou hast taught them the good way, wherein they should walk; and send rain upon

analogous occasion—installing the ark in the tent in Jerusalem (cf. I Chr 16).

807

thy land, which thou hast given unto thy people for an inheritance.

28 ¶If there be dearth in the land, if there be pestilence, if there be blasting, or mildew, locusts, or caterpillers; if their enemies besiege them in the cities of their land; whatsoever sore or whatsoever sickness *there be:*

29 *Then* what prayer *or* what supplication soever shall be made of any man, or of all thy people Israel, when every one shall know his own sore and his own grief, and shall spread forth his hands in this house:

30 Then hear thou from heaven thy dwelling place, and forgive, and render unto every man according unto all his ways, whose heart thou knowest; (for thou only knowest the hearts of the children of men:)

31 That they may fear thee, to walk in thy ways, so long as they live in the land which thou gavest unto our fathers.

32 ¶Moreover concerning the stranger, which is not of thy people Israel, but is come from a far country for thy great name's sake, and thy mighty hand, and thy stretched out arm; if they come and pray in this house;

33 Then hear thou from the heavens, *even* from thy dwelling place, and do according to all that the stranger calleth to thee for; that all people of the earth may know thy name, and fear thee, as *doth* thy people Israel, and may know that this house which I have built is called by thy name.

34 ¶If thy people go out to war against their enemies by the way that thou shalt send them, and they pray unto thee toward this city which thou hast chosen, and the house which I have built for thy name;

35 Then hear thou from the heavens their prayer and their supplication, and maintain their cause.

36 ¶If they sin against thee, (for *there is* no man which sinneth not,) and thou be angry with them, and deliver them over before *their* enemies, and they carry them away captives unto a land far off or near;

37 Yet *if* they bethink themselves in the land whither they are carried captive, and turn and pray unto thee in the land of their captivity, saying, We have sinned, we have done amiss, and have dealt wickedly;

38 If they return to thee with all their heart and with all their soul in the land of their captivity, whither they have carried them captives, and pray toward their land, which thou gavest unto their fathers, and *toward* the city which thou hast chosen, and toward the house which I have built for thy name:

39 Then hear thou from the heavens, *even* from thy dwelling place, their prayer and their supplications, and maintain their cause, and forgive thy people which have sinned against thee.

40 Now, my God, let, I beseech thee, thine eyes be open, and *let* thine ears *be* attent unto the prayer *that is made* in this place.

41 Now therefore arise, O Lᴏʀᴅ God,

into thy resting place, thou, and the ark of thy strength: let thy priests, O Lord God, be clothed with salvation, and let thy saints rejoice in goodness.

42 O Lord God, turn not away the face of thine anointed: remember the mercies of David thy servant.

CHAPTER 7

NOW when Sŏlomon had made an end of praying, the fire came down from heaven, and consumed the burnt offering and the sacrifices; and the glory of the Lord filled the house.

2 And the priests could not enter into the house of the Lord, because the glory of the Lord had filled the Lord's house.

3 And when all the children of Israel saw how the fire came down, and the glory of the Lord upon the house, they bowed themselves with their faces to the ground upon the pavement, and worshipped, and praised the Lord, saying, For he is good; for his mercy endureth for ever.

4 ¶Then the king and all the people offered sacrifices before the Lord.

5 And king Sŏlomon offered a sacrifice of twenty and two thousand oxen, and an hundred and twenty thousand sheep: so the king and all the people dedicated the house of God.

6 And the priests waited on their offices: the Lē′vītes also with instruments of musick of the Lord, which David the king had made to praise the Lord, because his mercy endureth for ever, when David praised by their ministry; and the priests sounded trumpets before them, and all Israel stood.

7 Moreover Sŏlomon hallowed the middle of the court that was before the house of the Lord: for there he offered burnt offerings, and the fat of the peace offerings, because the brasen altar which Solomon had made was not able to receive the burnt offerings, and the meat offerings, and the fat.

8 ¶Also at the same time Sŏlomon kept the feast seven days, and all Israel with him, a very great congregation, from the entering in of Hā′măth unto the river of Egypt.

9 And in the eighth day they made a solemn assembly: for they kept the dedication of the altar seven days, and the feast seven days.

10 And on the three and twentieth day of the seventh month he sent the people away into their tents, glad and merry in heart for the goodness that the Lord had shewed unto David, and to Sŏlomon, and to Israel his people.

11 Thus Sŏlomon finished the house of the Lord, and the king's house: and all that came into Sŏlomon's heart to make in the house of the Lord, and in his own house, he prosperously effected.

12 ¶And the Lord appeared to Sŏlomon by night, and said unto him, I have heard thy prayer, and have chosen this place to myself for an house of sacrifice.

13 If I shut up heaven that there be no rain, or if I command the locusts to de-

3. *The sacrifices and the divine response. 7:1-22.*

7:1-3. The conclusion of Solomon's prayer was climaxed when **fire came down from heaven,** an immediate divine response. God's acceptance is reminiscent of three other occasions: (1) Leviticus 9:24, the inaugural sacrifice at the Mosaic tabernacle; (2) I Chronicles 21:26, David's sacrifice on Mount Moriah; and (3) I Kings 18:38, Elijah's prayer in the contest on Mount Carmel.

The glory of the Lord so filled the Temple **the priests could not enter** (cf. 5:13-14). Compare the experience of Moses following the completion of the tabernacle's construction (Ex 40:34-35.)

4-7. The king . . . offered sacrifices. This account of the dedication feast and subsequent Feast of Tabernacles (vss. 4-11) is paralleled in I Kings 8:62-66 (see notes).

8. Solomon kept the feast (i.e., the Feast of Tabernacles, vs. 9) **seven days.** This feast was observed immediately subsequent to the dedication of the altar (vs. 9).

9-11. The days are a little difficult to reconcile with I Kings 8:65-66. The dedication week occurred in the seventh month (5:3), ending on the fourteenth day in order for the week of the Feast of Tabernacles (days fifteen to twenty-one, cf. Lev 23:33-36) to be completed in fourteen days (cf. I Kgs 8:65, ". . . seven days and seven days, even fourteen days"), on the twenty-first of the month. Apparently, at the end of the **eighth day** of the feast (cf. Lev 23:36), the twenty-second day of the month, the people were released to go home (I Kgs 8:66). On the **three and twentieth day** the people returned **into their tents.**

12-22. And the Lord appeared to Solomon. The words of the Lord in His divine response to Solomon's prayer (6:14-42) on this second appearance (cf. 1:7-12) are essentially those already commented on in I Kings 9:2-9.

The Chronicler has an additional note (vss. 14-16) that is omitted in I Kings. **If my people . . . then will I.** Israel belonged to God. She was the only nation upon which His name

vour the land, or if I send pestilence among my people;

14 If my people, which are called by my name, shall humble themselves, and pray, and seek my face, and turn from their wicked ways; then will I hear from heaven, and will forgive their sin, and will heal their land.

15 Now mine eyes shall be open, and mine ears attent unto the prayer *that is made* in this place.

16 For now have I chosen and sanctified this house, that my name may be there for ever: and mine eyes and mine heart shall be there perpetually.

17 And as for thee, if thou wilt walk before me, as David thy father walked, and do according to all that I have commanded thee, and shalt observe my statutes and my judgments;

18 Then will I stablish the throne of thy kingdom, according as I have covenanted with David thy father, saying, There shall not fail thee a man *to be* ruler in Israel.

19 But if ye turn away, and forsake my statutes and my commandments, which I have set before you, and shall go and serve other gods, and worship them;

20 Then will I pluck them up by the roots out of my land which I have given them; and this house, which I have sanctified for my name, will I cast out of my sight, and will make it *to be* a proverb and a byword among all nations.

21 And this house, which is high, shall be an astonishment to every one that passeth by it; so that he shall say, Why hath the Lord done thus unto this land, and unto this house?

22 And it shall be answered, Because they forsook the Lord God of their fathers, which brought them forth out of the land of Egypt, and laid hold on other gods, and worshipped them, and served them: therefore hath he brought all this evil upon them.

CHAPTER 8

AND it came to pass at the end of twenty years, wherein Sŏlomon had built the house of the Lord, and his own house,

2 That the cities which Hū′ram had restored to Sŏlomon, Sŏlomon built them, and caused the children of Israel to dwell there.

3 And Sŏlomon went to Hā′măth-zō′bah, and prevailed against it.

4 And he built Tăd′môr in the wilderness, and all the store cities, which he built in Hā′măth.

5 Also he built Bĕth-hô′ron the upper, and Bĕth-hô′ron the nether, fenced cities, with walls, gates, and bars;

6 And Bā′al-ăth, and all the store cities that Sŏlomon had, and all the chariot cities, and the cities of the horsemen, and all that Sŏlomon desired to build in Jerusalem, and in Lebanon, and throughout all the land of his dominion.

7 ¶As for all the people *that were* left of the Hittites, and the Amorītes, and

had been called. Therefore, His requirement for national blessing was their seeking His face in true repentance (**turn from their wicked ways**). Only then could He remove their guilt and restore them to usefulness.

D. His Glorious Kingdom. 8:1-9:31.

1. His achievements as king. 8:1-18.

8:1-3. Twenty years was the time spent in building **the house of the Lord, and his own house,** seven years for the Temple and thirteen for his palace (cf. I Kgs 6:38-7:1). For details of the construction of Solomon's house that are omitted in II Chronicles, see I Kings 7:1-8. **The cities . . . restored to Solomon.** The cities Solomon gave to Huram did not meet his approval (I Kgs 9:11-13), so they were returned to Solomon. Solomon's action against **Hamath-zobah** was probably retaliation for breaking a voluntary peace agreement that was made with David (cf. II Sam 8:9ff; I Chr 18:9 ff.).

4-11. With the exception of a few variations, this section parallels I Kings 9:18-25. **My wife shall not dwell in the house of David** (vs. 11). Though the Chronicler does not record Solomon's marriage to Pharaoh's daughter (cf. I Kgs 3:1), the context indicates his statement was made with reference to her. Even though Solomon was not obedient to God's command forbidding the marrying of foreign wives, his spiritual sensitivity still led him to remove this idolatrous wife from close proximity to the **places** that **are holy** (cf. Payne, p. 398).

the Pĕr'iz-zītes, and the Hī'vītes, and the Jĕb'u-sītes, which *were* not of Israel,

8 *But* of their children, who were left after them in the land, whom the children of Israel consumed not, them did Sŏlomon make to pay tribute until this day.

9 But of the children of Israel did Sŏlomon make no servants for his work; but they *were* men of war, and chief of his captains, and captains of his chariots and horsemen.

10 And these *were* the chief of king Sŏlomon's officers, *even* two hundred and fifty, that bare rule over the people.

11 ¶And Sŏlomon brought up the daughter of Pharaoh out of the city of David unto the house that he had built for her: for he said, My wife shall not dwell in the house of David king of Israel, because *the places are* holy, whereunto the ark of the LORD hath come.

12 ¶Then Sŏlomon offered burnt offerings unto the LORD on the altar of the LORD, which he had built before the porch,

13 Even after a certain rate every day, offering according to the commandment of Moses, on the sabbaths, and on the new moons, and on the solemn feasts, three times in the year, *even* in the feast of unleavened bread, and in the feast of weeks, and in the feast of tabernacles.

14 And he appointed, according to the order of David his father, the courses of the priests to their service, and the Lē'vītes to their charges, to praise and minister before the priests, as the duty of every day required: the porters also by their courses at every gate: for so had David the man of God commanded.

15 And they departed not from the commandment of the king unto the priests and Lē'vītes concerning any matter, or concerning the treasures.

16 Now all the work of Sŏlomon was prepared unto the day of the foundation of the house of the LORD, and until it was finished. *So* the house of the LORD was perfected.

17 ¶Then went Sŏlomon to Ē'zĭon-gē'ber, and to Ē'lōth, at the sea side in the land of Ēdom.

18 And Hū'ram sent him by the hands of his servants ships, and servants that had knowledge of the sea; and they went with the servants of Sŏlomon to Ō'phir, and took thence four hundred and fifty talents of gold, and brought *them* to king Sŏlomon.

CHAPTER 9

AND when the queen of Shēba heard of the fame of Sŏlomon, she came to prove Sŏlomon with hard questions at Jerusalem, with a very great company, and camels that bare spices, and gold in abundance, and precious stones: and when she was come to Sŏlomon, she communed with him of all that was in her heart.

2 And Sŏlomon told her all her questions: and there was nothing hid from Sŏlomon which he told her not.

12-16. Then Solomon offered burnt offerings. These verses expand considerably I Kings 9:25, indicating the place of Solomon's worship, the frequency of that worship, and his employment of the courses of priests (cf. I Chr 24) as David had prescribed.

Now all the work of Solomon was prepared . . . the house of the LORD was perfected (vs. 16). This verse is best understood as a summary of Solomon's Temple construction. It is fitting here because Solomon's worship at Jerusalem was impossible apart from a completed Temple. The following rendering makes clearer this summary statement. "Thus all the work of Solomon was carried out from the day of the foundation of the house of the LORD, and until it was finished. So the house of the LORD was completed" (NASB).

17-18. For **Ezion-geber** and **Ophir,** see notes on I Kings 9:26-28.

2. *His wisdom and wealth. 9:1-31.*

9:1-12. When the queen of Sheba heard . . . she came. This account of the Queen of Sheba's visit to Solomon is virtually identical to I Kings 10:1-13 (see discussion in I Kgs commentary).

3 And when the queen of Shēba had seen the wisdom of Sŏlomon, and the house that he had built,

4 And the meat of his table, and the sitting of his servants, and the attendance of his ministers, and their apparel; his cupbearers also, and their apparel; and his ascent by which he went up into the house of the Lord; there was no more spirit in her.

5 And she said to the king, *It was* a true report which I heard in mine own land of thine acts, and of thy wisdom:

6 Howbeit I believed not their words, until I came, and mine eyes had seen *it*: and, behold, the one half of the greatness of thy wisdom was not told me: *for* thou exceedest the fame that I heard.

7 Happy *are* thy men, and happy *are* these thy servants, which stand continually before thee, and hear thy wisdom.

8 Blessed be the Lord thy God, which delighted in thee to set thee on his throne, *to be* king for the Lord thy God: because thy God loved Israel, to establish them for ever, therefore made he thee king over them, to do judgment and justice.

9 And she gave the king an hundred and twenty talents of gold, and of spices great abundance, and precious stones: neither was there any such spice as the queen of Shēba gave king Sŏlomon.

10 And the servants also of Hū'ram, and the servants of Sŏlomon, which brought gold from Ō'phir, brought algum trees and precious stones.

11 And the king made *of* the algum trees terraces to the house of the Lord, and to the king's palace, and harps and psalteries for singers: and there were none such seen before in the land of Jū-dah.

12 And king Sŏlomon gave to the queen of Shēba all her desire, whatsoever she asked, beside *that* which she had brought unto the king. So she turned, and went away to her own land, she and her servants.

13 ¶Now the weight of gold that came to Sŏlomon in one year was six hundred and three score and six talents of gold;

14 Beside *that which* chapmen and merchants brought. And all the kings of Arabia and governors of the country brought gold and silver to Sŏlomon.

15 ¶And king Sŏlomon made two hundred targets of beaten gold: six hundred *shekels* of beaten gold went to one target.

16 And three hundred shields *made he of* beaten gold: three hundred *shekels* of gold went to one shield. And the king put them in the house of the forest of Lebanon.

17 ¶Moreover the king made a great throne of ivory, and overlaid it with pure gold.

18 And *there were* six steps to the throne, with a footstool of gold, *which were* fastened to the throne, and stays on each side of the sitting place, and two lions standing by the stays:

19 And twelve lions stood there on the one side and on the other upon the

13-28. The following summary of Solomon's trade and wealth is an expansion of 1:14-17, and corresponds very closely with I Kings 10:14-29, already commented upon.

In verse 21 **the king's ships went to Tarshish** (see note on I Kgs 10:22). A literal rendering of "to Tarshish" is "goers of Tarshish" (Heb *holkōt tarshīsh*). Few scholars believe that Solomon's Phoenician-manned ships (cf. 8:18) circumnavigated Africa to reach Spain on the Mediterranean Sea. Solomon's ships were ocean-going ships like those which sailed to Tarshish; but the cargoes brought back were not Mediterranean products, but products purchased down the Red Sea from Africa and possibly as far east as India.

six steps. There was not the like made in any kingdom.

20 ¶And all the drinking vessels of king Sŏlomon *were of* gold, and all the vessels of the house of the forest of Lebanon *were of* pure gold: none *were of* silver; it was *not* any thing accounted of in the days of Sŏlomon.

21 For the king's ships went to Tärshish with the servants of Hū'ram: every three years once came the ships of Tärshish bringing gold, and silver, ivory, and apes, and peacocks.

22 And king Sŏlomon passed all the kings of the earth in riches and wisdom.

23 ¶And all the kings of the earth sought the presence of Sŏlomon, to hear his wisdom, that God had put in his heart.

24 And they brought every man his present, vessels of silver, and vessels of gold, and raiment, harness, and spices, horses, and mules, a rate year by year.

25 ¶And Sŏlomon had four thousand stalls for horses and chariots, and twelve thousand horsemen; whom he bestowed in the chariot cities, and with the king at Jerusalem.

26 ¶And he reigned over all the kings from the river even unto the land of the Philistines, and to the border of Egypt.

27 And the king made silver in Jerusalem as stones, and cedar trees made he as the sycomore trees that *are* in the low plains in abundance.

28 And they brought unto Sŏlomon horses out of Egypt, and out of all lands.

29 ¶Now the rest of the acts of Sŏlomon, first and last, *are* they not written in the book of Nāthan the prophet, and in the prophecy of A-hī'jah the Shī'lonīte, and in the visions of Ĭd'dō the seer against Jĕr-o-bō'am the son of Nĕ'băt?

30 And Sŏlomon reigned in Jerusalem over all Israel forty years.

31 And Sŏlomon slept with his fathers, and he was buried in the city of David his father: and Rē-ho-bō'am his son reigned in his stead.

CHAPTER 10

AND Rē-ho-bō'am went to Shĕ'chem: for to Shĕ'chem were all Israel come to make him king.

2 And it came to pass, when Jĕr-obō'am the son of Nĕ'băt, who *was* in Egypt, whither he had fled from the presence of Sŏlomon the king, heard *it*, that Jĕr-o-bō'am returned out of Egypt.

3 And they sent and called him. So Jĕr-o-bō'am and all Israel came and spake to Rē'ho-bō'am, saying,

4 Thy father made our yoke grievous:

29-31. As the Chronicler had done with the reign of David, so he omits an account of Solomon's idolatry and problems (cf. I Kgs 11:1-40) and summarizes his reign (cf. I Kgs 11:41-43). The Chronicler cites **the book of Nathan . . . , the prophecy of Ahijah . . . , and . . . the visions of Iddo,** whereas the writer of I Kings refers to the "Book of the Acts of Solomon."

II. THE KINGS OF JUDAH. 10:1-36:23.

The fourth division of the Chronicles extends from the division of the kingdom in 931 B.C. to the decree of Cyrus in 538 B.C. allowing the exiles to return from Babylon to Jerusalem. Much of the remaining chapters corresponds to the history of Judah appearing in I and II Kings and needs not be repeated here. Comments will be reserved for important variations and additions to Judah's political and religious history by the Chronicler. As previously noted, references to the apostate northern kingdom, Israel, are intentionally omitted, except where Israel's history involves that of Judah.

A. Rehoboam. 10:1-12:16.

1. Division of the monarchy. 10:1-19.

10:1-19. This chapter, covering Israel's request to the new king, Rehoboam (vss. 1-5), the counsel he received (vss. 6-11), his foolish decision and answer (vss. 12-15), and the resultant revolt of the northern tribes (vss. 16-19), corresponds verse by verse to I Kings 12:1-19 (see I Kings commentary). It appears that the Chronicler intentionally omitted any mention of Jeroboam who was made king over Israel (cf. I Kgs 12:20).

now therefore ease thou somewhat the grievous servitude of thy father, and his heavy yoke that he put upon us, and we will serve thee.

5 And he said unto them, Come again unto me after three days. And the people departed.

6 ¶ And king Rē-ho-bō'am took counsel with the old men that had stood before Sŏlomon his father while he yet lived, saying, What counsel give ye *me* to return answer to this people?

7 And they spake unto him, saying, If thou be kind to this people, and please them, and speak good words to them, they will be thy servants for ever.

8 But he forsook the counsel which the old men gave him, and took counsel with the young men that were brought up with him, that stood before him.

9 And he said unto them, What advice give ye that we may return answer to this people, which have spoken to me, saying, Ease somewhat the yoke that thy father did put upon us?

10 And the young men that were brought up with him spake unto him, saying, Thus shalt thou answer the people that spake unto thee, saying, Thy father made our yoke heavy, but make thou *it* somewhat lighter for us; thus shalt thou say unto them, My little *finger* shall be thicker than my father's loins.

11 For whereas my father put a heavy yoke upon you, I will put more to your yoke: my father chastised you with whips, but I *will chastise you* with scorpions.

12 ¶ So Jĕr-o-bo'am and all the people came to Rē-ho-bō'am on the third day, as the king bade, saying, Come again to me on the third day.

13 And the king answered them roughly; and king Rē-ho-bō'am forsook the counsel of the old men,

14 And answered them after the advice of the young men, saying, My father made your yoke heavy, but I will add thereto: my father chastised you with whips, but I *will chastise you* with scorpions.

15 So the king hearkened not unto the people: for the cause was of God, that the LORD might perform his word, which he spake by the hand of A-hī'jah the Shī'lo-nīte to Jĕr-o-bō'am the son of Nē'băt.

16 And when all Israel *saw* that the king would not hearken unto them, the people answered the king, saying, What portion have we in David? and *we have* none inheritance in the son of Jesse: every man to your tents, O Israel: *and* now, David, see to thine own house. So all Israel went to their tents.

17 But *as for* the children of Israel that dwelt in the cities of Jūdah, Rē-ho-bō'am reigned over them.

18 Then king Rē-ho-bō'am sent Ha-dō'ram that *was* over the tribute; and the children of Israel stoned him with stones, that he died. But king Rē-ho-bō'am made speed to get him up to *his* chariot, to flee to Jerusalem.

19 And Israel rebelled against the house of David unto this day.

six steps. There was not the like made in any kingdom.

20 ¶ And all the drinking vessels of king Solomon were of gold, and all the vessels of the house of the forest of Lebanon were of pure gold: none were of silver; it was not any thing accounted of in the days of Solomon.

21 For the king's ships went to Tarshish with the servants of Huram: every three years once came the ships of Tarshish bringing gold, and silver, ivory, and apes, and peacocks.

22 And king Solomon passed all the kings of the earth in riches and wisdom.

23 And all the kings of the earth sought the presence of Solomon, to hear his wisdom, that God had put in his heart.

24 And they brought every man his present, vessels of silver, and vessels of gold, and raiment, harness, and spices, horses, and mules, a rate year by year.

25 ¶ And Solomon had four thousand stalls for horses and chariots, and twelve thousand horsemen; whom he bestowed in the chariot cities, and with the king at Jerusalem.

26 And he reigned over all the kings from the river even unto the land of the Philistines, and to the border of Egypt.

27 And the king made silver in Jerusalem as stones, and cedar trees made he as the sycomore trees that are in the low plains in abundance.

28 And they brought unto Solomon horses out of Egypt, and out of all lands.

29 ¶ Now the rest of the acts of Solomon, first and last, are they not written in the book of Nathan the prophet, and in the prophecy of A-hī'jah the Shī'lo-nīte, and in the visions of Iddo the seer against Jĕr-o-bō'am the son of Nē'băt?

30 And Solomon reigned in Jerusalem over all Israel forty years.

31 And Solomon slept with his fathers, and he was buried in the city of David his father: and Rē-ho-bō'am his son reigned in his stead.

CHAPTER 10

AND Rē-ho-bō'am went to Shē'chem: for to Shē'chem were all Israel come to make him king.

2 And it came to pass, when Jĕr-o-bō'am the son of Nē'băt, who was in Egypt, whither he had fled from the presence of Solomon the king, heard *it*, that Jĕr-o-bō'am returned out of Egypt.

3 And they sent and called him. So Jĕr-o-bō'am and all Israel came and spake to Rē-ho-bō'am, saying,

4 Thy father made our yoke grievous:

CHAPTER 11

AND when Rē-ho-bō'am was come to Jerusalem, he gathered of the house of Jūdah and Benjamin an hundred and fourscore thousand chosen *men*, which were warriors, to fight against Israel, that he might bring the kingdom again to Rē-ho-bō'am.

2 But the word of the LORD came to Shem-ā-i'ah the man of God, saying,

3 Speak unto Rē-ho-bō'am the son of Sŏlomon, king of Jūdah, and to all Israel in Jūdah and Benjamin, saying,

4 Thus saith the LORD, Ye shall not go up, nor fight against your brethren: return every man to his house: for this thing is done of me. And they obeyed the words of the LORD, and returned from going against Jĕr-o-bō'am.

5 And Rē-ho-bō'am dwelt in Jerusalem, and built cities for defence in Jūdah.

6 He built even Bĕth-lehĕm, and Ē'tam, and Te-kō'a,

7 And Bĕth'-zūr, and Shō'cō, and Adullam,

8 And Gath, and Ma-rē'shah, and Ziph,

9 And Ăd-o-rā'im, and Lā'chĭsh, and A-zē'kah,

10 And Zô'rah, and Āij'a-lŏn, and Hēbron, which *are* in Jūdah and in Benjamin fenced cities.

11 And he fortified the strong holds, and put captains in them, and store of victual, and of oil and wine.

12 And in every several city *he* put shields and spears, and made them exceeding strong, having Jūdah and Benjamin on his side.

13 And the priests and the Lēvītes that *were* in all Israel resorted to him out of all their coasts.

14 For the Lēvītes left their suburbs and their possession, and came to Jūdah and Jerusalem: for Jĕr-o-bō'am and his sons had cast them off from executing the priest's office unto the LORD:

15 And he ordained him priests for the high places, and for the devils, and for the calves which he had made.

16 And after them out of all the tribes of Israel such as set their hearts to seek the LORD God of Israel came to Jerusalem, to sacrifice unto the LORD God of their fathers.

17 So they strengthened the kingdom of Jūdah, and made Rē-ho-bō'am the son of Sŏlomon strong, three years: for three years they walked in the way of David and Sŏlomon.

18 ¶And Rē-ho-bō'am took him Mā'ha-lăth the daughter of Jĕr'ĭ-mŏth the son of David to wife, *and* Ăb-i-hā'il the daughter of E-lī'ab the son of Jesse;

19 Which bare him children; Jē'ŭsh, and Shĕm-a-rī'ah, and Zā'hăm.

20 And after her he took Mā'a-chah the daughter of Ăb'sa-lom; which bare

2. *Conflicts with the northern kingdom and immigration of northern religious loyalists. 11:1-17.*

11:1-4. Ye shall not go up, nor fight against your brethren. Only by this divine directive was civil war averted (for comments on parallel passage, see I Kgs 12:21-24).

5-12. He built cities for defense in Judah. Since these cities were in existence before Rehoboam's time, "built" has the meaning of "rebuilt" or "fortified." Rehoboam's purpose was not to defend Judah from Israel to the north or to keep in subjection the people of Judah, but to protect his small kingdom from an invasion from Egypt (cf. 12:2ff.). All of the listed **strongholds** were southern cities that comprised a fortification line blocking all roads leading into Judah (cf. Yohanan Aharoni and Michael Avi-Yonah, *The Macmillan Bible Atlas*, p. 119).

13-14. The priests and the Levites . . . resorted to him, i.e., Rehoboam. The Chronicler has omitted the background to this action. The northern king, Jeroboam, had changed the symbols of worship, the center of worship, the priesthood, and the scheduled feasts (cf. I Kgs 12:25-33). With the institution of all these changes, the priests and Levites had two options: (1) forsake Jehovah and serve Jeroboam's golden calves; or (2) migrate to Judah where Jehovah was worshiped. They chose the latter.

15. He ordained him priests. This was a new priesthood for **the high places** (cf. 13:9). **Devils** (Heb *se'îrîm*), often translated "satyrs" and thought to be hairy, animal-like demons, may be he-goats, which were used in conjunction with the **calves**, i.e., the golden calves at Dan and Beth-el.

16-17. The religious migration was not limited to the Levites, but included loyalists of all the tribes of Israel who desired to remain true to Jehovah. Israel's loss was Judah's gain because the migration of the pious ones **strengthened the kingdom of Judah** for Rehoboam, but unfortunately they too apparently apostatized after **three years.**

3. *His royal family and apostasy. 11:18-12:1.*

18-23. Any reference to the royal family is omitted in I Kings. **Mahalath,** apparently his first wife, had as her parents **Jerimoth,** an otherwise unnamed son of David, and **Abihail,** the daughter of David's brother, **Eliab.** His favorite wife, however, was **Maachah the daughter of Absalom.** She was apparently a granddaughter; for according to II Samuel 14:27, Absalom had only one daughter named Tamar who evidently married Uriel (cf. 13:2). **Abijah the son of Maachah** is Abijam in I Kings. **He**

him A-bī′jah, and Āt′taī, and Zī′za, and Shel′ō-mĭth.

21 And Rē-ho-bō′am loved Mā′a-chah the daughter of Āb′sa-lom above all his wives and his concubines: (for he took eighteen wives, and threescore concubines; and begat twenty and eight sons, and threescore daughters.)

22 And Rē-ho-bō′am made A-bī′jah the son of Mā′a-chah the chief, *to be* ruler among his brethren: for *he thought* to make him king.

23 And he dealt wisely, and dispersed of all his children throughout all the countries of Jūdah and Benjamin, unto every fenced city: and he gave them victual in abundance. And he desired many wives.

CHAPTER 12

AND it came to pass, when Rē-ho-bō′am had established the kingdom, and had strengthened himself, he forsook the law of the LORD, and all Israel with him.

2 And it came to pass, *that* in the fifth year of king Rē-ho-bō′am Shī′shăk king of Egypt came up against Jerusalem, because they had transgressed against the LORD,

3 With twelve hundred chariots, and threescore thousand horsemen: and the people *were* without number that came with him out of Egypt; the Lū′-bĭms, the Sŭk′kĭ-ĭms, and the Ē-thī-ō′pĭ-ans.

4 And he took the fenced cities which *pertained* to Jūdah, and came to Jerusalem.

5 Then came Shem-ā-i′ah the prophet to Rē-ho-bō′am, and *to* the princes of Jūdah, that were gathered together to Jerusalem because of Shī′shăk, and said unto them, Thus saith the LORD, Ye have forsaken me, and therefore have I also left you in the hand of Shī′shăk.

6 Whereupon the princes of Israel and the king humbled themselves; and they said, The LORD *is* righteous.

7 And when the LORD saw that they humbled themselves, the word of the LORD came to Shem-ā-i′ah, saying, They have humbled themselves; *therefore* I will not destroy them, but I will grant them some deliverance; and my wrath shall not be poured out upon Jerusalem by the hand of Shī′shăk.

8 Nevertheless they shall be his servants; that they may know my service, and the service of the kingdoms of the countries.

9 So Shī′shăk king of Egypt came up against Jerusalem, and took away the treasures of the house of the LORD, and the treasures of the king's house; he took all: he carried away also the

dealt wisely in dispersing his sons throughout the country as his agents to maintain a firm grip on the people in the remote parts of his kingdom.

12:1. When his kingdom was established, however, **he forsook the law of the LORD, and all Israel with him.** Details of his apostasy, which consequently led to divine punishment at the hand of the Egyptian Pharaoh, are omitted here; but they are given in an expanded parallel passage, I Kings 14:21-24.

4. Invasion of Shishak I and death of Rehoboam. 12:2-16.

2. In the fifth year (ca. 526 B.C.) . . . **Shishak** (Sheshonk I) of Egypt's Twenty-first Dynasty came against Jerusalem. On the walls of the temple of Karnak in Upper Egypt he had carved a picture of himself smiting the Asiatics. The carving listed cities he had encountered, indicating that his campaign extended beyond Judah (as recorded in II Chr) into Israel (G. E. Wright, *Biblical Archaeology,* p. 148), reaching as far north as Megiddo where his stele has been found (Aharoni and Avi-Yonah, p. 77). This invasion was divinely (cf. vs. 5) initiated because Judah **had transgressed against the LORD** (cf. God's method of chastising Israel during the period of the judges, Jud 3:8, 12).

3. Aiding the Egyptians were the **Lubim,** i.e., Libyans, **Sukkim** ("Troglodytes" in LXX), a people not positively identified, but possibly foreign mercenaries, and the **Ethiopians.**

4-11. God used Shishak to bring Judah to repentance (cf. the cycle of sin, oppression, repentance, and deliverance as historically repeated and recorded in the book of Judges). **Shishak . . . took away the treasures of the house of the LORD.** The glory of the kingdom that had been Solomon's had already begun to fade, symbolized by the stripping of the Temple and palace of their golden articles, which were replaced by bronze articles.

shields of gold which Sŏlomon had made.

10 Instead of which king Rē-ho-bō'am made shields of brass, and committed *them* to the hands of the chief of the guard, that kept the entrance of the king's house.

11 And when the king entered into the house of the LORD, the guard came and fetched them, and brought them again into the guard chamber.

12 And when he humbled himself, the wrath of the LORD turned from him, that he would not destroy *him* altogether: and also in Jŭ'dah things went well.

13 ¶So king Rē-ho-bō'am strengthened himself in Jerusalem, and reigned: for Rē-ho-bō'am *was* one and forty years old when he began to reign, and he reigned seventeen years in Jerusalem, the city which the LORD had chosen out of all the tribes of Israel, to put his name there. And his mother's name *was* Nā'a-mah an Ammonitess.

14 And he did evil, because he prepared not his heart to seek the LORD.

15 Now the acts of Rē-ho-bō'am, first and last, *are* they not written in the book of Shem-ā-i'ah the prophet, and of Id'dō the seer concerning genealogies? And *there were* wars between Rē-ho-bō'am and Jĕr-o-bō'am continually.

16 And Rē-ho-bō'am slept with his fathers, and was buried in the city of David: and A-bī'jah his son reigned in his stead.

CHAPTER 13

NOW in the eighteenth year of king Jĕr-o-bō'am began A-bī'jah to reign over Jŭdah.

2 He reigned three years in Jerusalem. His mother's name also *was* Mī-chā'iah the daughter of Ū'rĭ-el of Gĭb'e-ah. And there was war between A-bī'jah and Jĕr-o-bō'am.

3 And A-bī'jah set the battle in array with an army of valiant men of war, *even* four hundred thousand chosen men: Jĕr-o-bō'am also set the battle in array against him with eight hundred thousand chosen men, *being* mighty men of valour.

4 ¶And A-bī'jah stood up upon mount Zĕm-a-rā'im, which *is* in mount E'phra-im, and said, Hear me, thou Jĕr-o-bō'am, and all Israel;

5 Ought ye not to know that the LORD God of Israel gave the kingdom over Israel to David for ever, *even* to him and to his sons by a covenant of salt?

6 Yet Jĕr-o-bō'am the son of Nē'băt, the servant of Sŏlomon the son of David, is risen up, and hath rebelled against his lord.

7 And there are gathered unto him vain men, the children of Bē'lĭ-al, and have strengthened themselves against Rē-ho-bō'am the son of Sŏlomon, when Rē-ho-bō'am was young and tenderhearted, and could not withstand them.

8 And now ye think to withstand the

12-16. In Judah things went well. A literal rendering is "in Judah were good things." In spite of Judah's spiritual lapses, in contrast to the northern kingdom, there were still those who remained faithful. **Rehoboam strengthened himself** following Shishak's invasion (cf. 11:5-12; 12:1). His reign was seventeen years (ca. 931-913 B.C.). The concluding remarks concerning the **acts of Rehoboam** parallel I Kings 14:29-31.

B. Abijah and Asa. 13:1-16:14.

13:1-2. Abijah is Abijam in I Kings (see note on name in I Kgs 15:1). His reign was for only **three years** (ca. 913-911 B.C.). **Michaiah** is Maachah in I Kings (cf. notes on I Kgs 15:2 and II Chr 11:20).

3. Abijah set the battle in array. What incited the conflict is not stated. In the case of Rehoboam the Lord had prohibited war with Israel; but here He did not interfere, possibly because Jeroboam's flagrant idolatry deserved judgment.

Abijah was greatly outnumbered, two to one. Though the numbers are very large, the word **thousand** need not be changed to mean "units." Liberal critics are prone to accept this interpretation (cf. the military potential recorded in Joab's census for David, I Chr 21:5).

4-6. Mount Zemaraim is located in the territory of Benjamin, just a few miles southwest of **Beth-el** (cf. vs. 19). Abijah's address is surprising. I Kings 15:3 portrays him (Abijam) as wicked (". . . his heart was not perfect with the LORD, . . ."); but the Chronicler shows that he was capable of occasional acts of faith, even though his life was generally characterized by disobedience to the will of God. **A covenant of salt** is descriptive of a permanent covenant (cf. Lev 2:13, Num 18:19) since salt is a preservative.

7. Jeroboam's kingdom was extremely rotten, built upon the **children of Belial,** i.e., worthless, base men. **When Rehoboam was young and tenderhearted** is a reference to his immaturity and lack of experience, not his age (cf. 12:13).

8-10. Abijah (Abijam) rightly ridiculed the **golden calves** (cf.

kingdom of the LORD in the hand of the sons of David; and ye *be* a great multitude, and *there are* with you golden calves, which Jĕr-o-bō'am made you for gods.

9 Have ye not cast out the priests of the LORD, the sons of Aaron, and the Lē'vītes, and have made you priests after the manner of the nations of *other* lands? so that whosoever cometh to consecrate himself with a young bullock and seven rams, *the same* may be a priest of *them that are* no gods.

10 But as for us, the LORD *is* our God, and we have not forsaken him; and the priests, which minister unto the LORD, *are* the sons of Aaron, and the Lē'vītes *wait* upon *their* business:

11 And they burn unto the LORD every morning and every evening burnt sacrifices and sweet incense: the shewbread also *set they in order* upon the pure table; and the candlestick of gold with the lamps thereof, to burn every evening: for we keep the charge of the LORD our God; but ye have forsaken him.

12 And, behold, God himself *is* with us for *our* captain, and his priests with sounding trumpets to cry alarm against you. O children of Israel, fight ye not against the LORD God of your fathers; for ye shall not prosper.

13 ¶But Jĕr-o-bō'am caused an ambushment to come about behind them: so they were before Jūdah, and the ambushment *was* behind them.

14 And when Jūdah looked back, behold, the battle *was* before and behind: and they cried unto the LORD, and the priests sounded with the trumpets.

15 Then the men of Jūdah gave a shout: and as the men of Jūdah shouted, it came to pass, that God smote Jĕr-o-bō'am and all Israel before A-bī'jah and Jūdah.

16 And the children of Israel fled before Jūdah: and God delivered them into their hand.

17 And A-bī'jah and his people slew them with a great slaughter: so there fell down slain of Israel five hundred thousand chosen men.

18 Thus the children of Israel were brought under at that time, and the children of Jūdah prevailed, because they relied upon the LORD God of their fathers.

19 And A-bī'jah pursued after Jĕr-o-bō'am, and took cities from him, Bĕth-el with the towns thereof, and Jĕsh'a-nah with the towns thereof, and Ē'phra-in with the towns thereof.

20 Neither did Jĕr-o-bō'am recover strength again in the days of A-bī'jah: and the LORD struck him, and he died.

21 ¶But A-bī'jah waxed mighty, and married fourteen wives, and begat twenty and two sons, and sixteen daughters.

22 And the rest of the acts of A-bī'jah, and his ways, and his sayings, *are* written in the story of the prophet Ĭd'dō.

CHAPTER 14

SO A-bī'jah slept with his fathers, and they buried him in the city of David:

818

I Kgs 12:28-29), the objects of worship for Jeroboam's man-made religion. **Have ye not cast out the priests of the LORD . . . ?** Compare the religious migration of priests and Levites in 11:13-15 because of Jeroboam's religious folly. He had staffed the sacred offices with any non-Levite who could meet one stipulation—payment of a **bullock and seven rams.**

The Lord is our God. In contrast to Israel, Judah still served Jehovah, though Abijam's allegiance was only token (cf. I Kgs 15:3).

11. In addition to the legitimate Aaronic priesthood, Judah possessed the original Mosaic articles, such as the **showbread . . . upon the pure table; and the candlestick** (Solomon's temple had ten candesticks, 4:7).

12-19. **God himself is with us for our captain** (cf. Josh 5:14-15, the captain of the Lord's host). **Priests with sounding trumpets to cry alarm** were God's appointed pledges that He would remember them in war (cf. Num 10:9). Jeroboam was unimpressed. Encircling Abijah, he attacked from the front and the rear. **God smote Jeroboam . . . God delivered them . . . Abijah . . . slew them.** Whether God delivered Judah supernaturally through divine intervention or providentially through Abijah's army is not indicated.

20-22. **The LORD struck him,** i.e., Jeroboam. The details of his death, though scanty, are given only here, unless his death was precipitated by his son's death (cf. I Kgs 14:1-20). The Chronicler once again cites the **prophet Iddo** (cf. 9:29). **Story** (cf. 24:27) is literally "commentary" (Heb *midrash*).

14:1-2. **Asa his son reigned.** His was a lengthy reign of forty-one years (I Kgs 15:10). On account of his father's victory

and Āsa his son reigned in his stead. In his days the land was quiet ten years.

2 And Āsa did *that which was good* and right in the eyes of the LORD his God:

3 For he took away the altars of the strange *gods*, and the high places, and brake down the images, and cut down the groves:

4 And commanded Jūdah to seek the LORD God of their fathers, and to do the law and the commandment.

5 Also he took away out of all the cities of Jūdah the high places and the images: and the kingdom was quiet before him.

6 ¶And he built fenced cities in Jūdah: for the land had rest, and he had no war in those years; because the LORD had given him rest.

7 Therefore he said unto Jūdah, Let us build these cities, and make about *them* walls, and towers, gates, and bars, *while* the land *is* yet before us; because we have sought the LORD our God, we have sought *him*, and he hath given us rest on every side. So they built and prospered.

8 And Āsa had an army *of men* that bare targets and spears, out of Jūdah three hundred thousand; and out of Benjamin, that bare shields and drew bows, two hundred and fourscore thousand: all these *were* mighty men of valour.

9 ¶And there came out against them Ze′rah the E̅-thĭ-ō′pĭ-an with an host of a thousand thousand, and three hundred chariots; and came unto Ma-rē′shah.

10 Then Āsa went out against him, and they set the battle in array in the valley of Zĕph′a-thah at Ma-rē′shah.

11 And Āsa cried unto the LORD his God, and said, LORD, *it is* nothing with thee to help, whether with many, or with them that have no power: help us, O LORD our God; for we rest on thee, and in thy name we go against this multitude. O LORD, thou *art* our God; let not man prevail against thee.

12 So the LORD smote the E̅-thĭ-ō′pĭ-ans before Āsa, and before Jūdah; and the E̅-thĭ-ō′pĭ-ans fled.

13 And Āsa and the people that *were* with him pursued them unto Ge′rär: and the E̅-thĭ-ō′pĭ-ans were overthrown, that they could not recover themselves; for they were destroyed before the LORD, and before his host; and they carried away very much spoil.

14 And they smote all the cities round about Ge′rär; for the fear of the LORD came upon them: and they spoiled all the cities; for there was exceeding much spoil in them.

15 They smote also the tents of cattle, and carried away sheep and camels in abundance, and returned to Jerusalem.

over Jeroboam (13:3-20) and his own religious reforms, **the land was quiet ten years**, i.e., at peace (note the words **quiet**, vss. 1, 5, and **rest**, vss. 6, 7). **Asa did . . . good and right.** For one reared in a wicked environment to be established as a righteous king is a demonstration of the grace of God.

3-5. Details of his reform are enumerated. **High places** (Heb *bamah*) were elevated platforms upon which cultic objects were placed and worshiped. Coggins mistakenly asserts that "this statement is in flat contradiction of I Kings 15:14" (p. 201). The apparent contradiction can be reconciled in one of two ways: (1) Chronicles records Asa's personal act to remove the high places, while Kings implies the people's persistence in resorting to them; or (2) the Kings's notation is really a reference to Asa's inability to destroy the high places in the northern kingdom when his reformation crossed the border into Israel (cf. 15:17). The **images**, literally "pillars" (Heb *matsebah*), were free standing stones symbolizing a deity and regarded as sacred. The **groves** (Heb *'asherah*) were carved poles or trees to symbolize the goddess Asherah, the consort of Baal. Images would be better rendered "incense altars" (NASB).

6-8. Asa's building and fortifying cities parallels Rehoboam's efforts in 11:5-12. **Because we have sought the LORD our God.** Asa correctly recognized that Judah's best defense was the Lord (cf. Isa 26:1; Zech 2:5).

9-10. Zerah has usually been identified as Osorkon I, a pharaoh of the Twenty-second Dynasty of Egypt. **The Ethiopian** is literally "the Cushite", possibly referring to one of the Arabian descendants of the ancestor Cush (Gen 10:7). His invasion parallels that of Shishak I against Rehoboam, although the results were wonderfully different. **Mareshah** was one of the southern cities Rehoboam had fortified (11:8).

11. Asa's prayer is a remarkable display of faith. **It is nothing with thee to help . . . with many . . . with them that have no power.** He knew he was outnumbered approximately two to one (vss. 8-9); but more importantly, he knew that God's victories did not depend upon the number or strength of men (cf. Jonathan's similar statement in I Sam 14:6).

12-15. The LORD smote the Ethiopians. Details are omitted (cf. note on 13:15-17). **Gerar** was a Philistine city south of Gaza. Asa's faith was rewarded by the victory and the spoils, taken apparently from Philistine cities.

CHAPTER 15

AND the Spirit of God came upon Ăz-a-rī'ah the son of Ō'ded:

2 And he went out to meet Āsa, and said unto him, Hear ye me, Āsa, and all Jūdah and Benjamin; The LORD *is* with you, while ye be with him; and if ye seek him, he will be found of you; but if ye forsake him, he will forsake you.

3 Now for a long season Israel *hath been* without the true God, and without a teaching priest, and without law.

4 But when they in their trouble did turn unto the LORD God of Israel, and sought him, he was found of them.

5 And in those times *there was* no peace to him that went out, nor to him that came in, but great vexations *were* upon all the inhabitants of the countries.

6 And nation was destroyed of nation, and city of city: for God did vex them with all adversity.

7 Be ye strong therefore, and let not your hands be weak: for your work shall be rewarded.

8 ¶And when Āsa heard these words, and the prophecy of Ō'ded the prophet, he took courage, and put away the abominable idols out of all the land of Jūdah and Benjamin, and out of the cities which he had taken from mount Ē'phra-im, and renewed the altar of the LORD, that *was* before the porch of the LORD.

9 And he gathered all Jūdah and Benjamin, and the strangers with them out of Ē'phra-im and Ma-năs'seh, and out of Simeon: for they fell to him out of Israel in abundance, when they saw that the LORD his God *was* with him.

10 So they gathered themselves together at Jerusalem in the third month, in the fifteenth year of the reign of Āsa.

11 And they offered unto the LORD the same time, of the spoil *which* they had brought, seven hundred oxen and seven thousand sheep.

12 And they entered into a covenant to seek the LORD God of their fathers with all their heart and with all their soul;

13 That whosoever would not seek the LORD God of Israel should be put to death, whether small or great, whether man or woman.

14 And they sware unto the LORD with a loud voice, and with shouting, and with trumpets, and with cornets.

15 And all Jūdah rejoiced at the oath: for they had sworn with all their heart, and sought him with their whole desire; and he was found of them: and the LORD gave them rest round about.

16 ¶And also concerning Mă'a-chah the mother of Āsa the king, he removed her from *being* queen, because she had

15:1-2. Azariah the son of Oded is not mentioned elsewhere. **He went out to meet Asa,** apparently as Asa was returning from victory over Zerah (14:9-15).

3. Israel hath been without the true God. The verb, which must be supplied, is better rendered "was" (NASB). Instead of referring to the northern kingdom, Israel, verses 3-6 appear to be a reference to the nation of Israel during the period of the judges when ". . . every man did that which was right in his own eyes" (Jud 17:6; 21:25).

A teaching priest. One of the most important responsibilities of the priests was to teach the Law (cf. Lev 10:11; Deut 33:10).

4-6. In their trouble Israel would then seek the Lord, and He would deliver them (cf. the sin-oppression-repentance-deliverance cycle in Jud 2:14-19).

7. Be ye strong therefore. In view of his present reforms (14:3-5) and dependence upon the Lord (14:11), and Israel's failures in the past, Asa is encouraged to remain firm in his loyalty to God and to continue his reform because **your work shall be rewarded.**

8. Oded the prophet is undoubtedly the person of verse one (both the LXX and Syriac have included Azariah here). **Abominable idols** is literally "detestable things" (one Hebrew word, *shiqûts*), which included anything associated with idolatry (cf. Asa's treatment of sodomites in I Kgs 15:12). He **renewed the altar,** implying that some form of desecration had occurred.

9. The revival was not limited to Judah, for a notable number from the tribes of **Ephraim, Manasseh,** and **Simeon** joined Asa **when they saw that the LORD his God was with him.** This influx of believers from the north alarmed Baasha and caused him to take preventive action (16:1).

10-12. They gathered themselves . . . third month, probably a reference to the Feast of Weeks, one of the three required pilgrimage feasts (cf. Ex 23:14-17; Lev 23:15-21; Deut 16:9-12). Comparing the **ten years** of 14:1 with **the fifteenth,** the year of Zerah's invasion, it is apparent that gaps exist in the chronology.

13-15. Whosoever would not seek the LORD . . . should be put to death. Asa's method of enforcing his reform was in line with Moses' command in Deuteronomy 17:2-6. Undoubtedly, there were those who were reformed as a matter of expediency.

16-18. Maachah was the mother of Abijah and thus the grand-**mother** of Asa (cf. I Kgs 15:2, 10). She was removed from her influential position as **queen**-mother because of her

made an idol in a grove: and Āsa cut down her idol, and stamped *it*, and burnt *it* at the brook Kidron.

17 But the high places were not taken away out of Israel: nevertheless the heart of Āsa was perfect all his days.

18 And he brought into the house of God the things that his father had dedicated, and that he himself had dedicated, silver, and gold, and vessels.

19 And there was no *more* war unto the five and thirtieth year of the reign of Āsa.

CHAPTER 16

IN the six and thirtieth year of the reign of Āsa Bā′a-sha king of Israel came up against Jū′dah, and built Rā′mah, to the intent that he might let none go out or come in to Āsa king of Jū′dah.

2 Then Āsa brought out silver and gold out of the treasures of the house of the LORD and of the king's house, and sent to Bĕn–hā′dăd king of Syria, that dwelt at Damascus, saying,

3 *There is* a league between me and thee, as *there was* between my father and thy father: behold, I have sent thee silver and gold; go, break thy league with Bā′a-sha king of Israel, that he may depart from me.

4 And Bĕn–hā′dăd hearkened unto king Āsa, and sent the captains of his armies against the cities of Israel; and they smote Ī′jŏn, and Dan, and Ā′bel–mā′ĭm, and all the store cities of Năph′ta-lī.

5 And it came to pass, when Bā′a-sha heard *it*, that he left off building of Rā′-mah, and let his work cease.

6 Then Āsa the king took all Jū′dah; and they carried away the stones of Rā′mah, and the timber thereof, wherewith Bā′a-sha was building; and he built therewith Gē′ba and Mizpah.

7 ¶And at that time Ha-nā′nī the seer came to Āsa king of Jū′dah, and said unto him, Because thou hast relied on the king of Syria, and not relied on the LORD thy God, therefore is the host of the king of Syria escaped out of thine hand.

8 Were not the Ē-thī-ō′pĭ-ans and the Lū′bĭms a huge host, with very many chariots and horsemen? yet, because thou didst rely on the LORD, he delivered them into thine hand.

9 For the eyes of the LORD run to and fro throughout the whole earth, to shew himself strong in the behalf of *them* whose heart *is* perfect toward him. Herein thou hast done foolishly: therefore from henceforth thou shalt have wars.

idol in a grove, literally "an abominable image for Asherah." For **the high places**, see note on 14:3.

19. And there was no more war unto the five and thirtieth year. The word "more" is lacking in Hebrew. According to verse 10, Zerah's invasion occurred in Asa's fifteenth year. "The Chronicler must be measuring these years from the division of the kingdom in 931 B.C., for the 15th year of Asa's own reign was also the 35th year of the divided kingdom. Such an interpretation . . . actually solves two chronological problems of considerable importance. First it eliminates the anomaly of Baasha waiting twenty-one years to block the southern flow of his citizens (II Chron 15:9; 16:1). Second, and more important, it eliminates the absurdity of Baasha invading Judah nine years after he had died! (cf. I Kgs 15:33)" (John Whitcomb, *Solomon to the Exile*, p. 33, cf. also Edwin J. Thiele, *The Mysterious Numbers of the Hebrew Kings*, pp. 59f).

16:1. In the six and thirtieth year, i.e., since the division of the kingdom in 931 B.C. and corresponding to Asa's sixteenth year (cf. note on 15:19). Baasha **built**, i.e., fortified, **Ramah**, a city just four or five miles north of Jerusalem with the intention of preventing pious northern Jews from joining Asa (I Kgs 15:17).

2-6. For Asa's panic-stricken, God-abandoning action, see comments on parallel passage in I Kings 15:18-22.

7-9. Hanani the seer (the father of Jehu in I Kgs 16:1) was sent to Asa with a severe four-point rebuke: (1) **Syria escaped.** If he had trusted God, he not only could have defeated Israel, but Syria as well; (2) **the LORD, he delivered them.** He had already seen God destroy the **Ethiopians** and **Lubim** (vs. 8); (3) **The eyes of the LORD run to and fro** (vs. 9). The Lord eagerly watches for an opportunity to help those who trust Him; and (4) **shalt have wars.** This was the result of Asa's foolish and deliberate sin in not trusting God.

10 Then Āsa was wroth with the seer, and put him in a prison house; for *he was* in a rage with him because of this *thing*. And Āsa oppressed *some* of the people the same time.

11 ¶And, behold, the acts of Āsa, first and last, lo, they *are* written in the book of the kings of Jū'dah and Israel.

12 And Āsa in the thirty and ninth year of his reign was diseased in his feet, until his disease *was* exceeding *great*: yet in his disease he sought not to the Lord, but to the physicians.

13 And Āsa slept with his fathers, and died in the one and fortieth year of his reign.

14 And they buried him in his own sepulchres, which he had made for himself in the city of David, and laid him in the bed which was filled with sweet odours and divers kinds *of spices* prepared by the apothecaries' art: and they made a very great burning for him.

CHAPTER 17

AND Je-hŏsh'a-phăt his son reigned in his stead, and strengthened himself against Israel.

2 And he placed forces in all the fenced cities of Jū'dah, and set garrisons in the land of Jū'dah, and in the cities of Ē'phra-im, which Āsa his father had taken.

3 And the Lord was with Je-hŏsh'a-phăt, because he walked in the first ways of his father David, and sought not unto Bā'al-ĭm;

4 But sought to the Lord God of his father, and walked in his commandments, and not after the doings of Israel.

5 Therefore the Lord stablished the kingdom in his hand; and all Jū'dah brought to Je-hŏsh'a-phăt presents; and he had riches and honour in abundance.

6 And his heart was lifted up in the ways of the Lord: moreover he took away the high places and groves out of Jū'dah.

7 ¶Also in the third year of his reign he sent to his princes, *even* to Bĕn-hā'il, and to Ō-ba-dī'ah, and to Zĕch-a-rī'ah, and to Ne-thăn'-e-el, and to Mī-chā'iah, to teach in the cities of Jū'dah.

8 And with them *he* sent Lēvītes, *even* Shem-ā-i'ah, and Nĕth-a-nī'ah, and Zĕb-a-dī'ah, and Ā'sa-hĕl, and She-mīr'a-mŏth, and Je-hŏn'a-than, and Ăd-o-nī'jah, and Tō-bī'jah, and Tŏb'-ăd-o-nī'jah, Lēvītes; and with them E-līsh'a-ma and Je-hō'ram, priests.

9 And they taught in Jū'dah, and *had* the book of the law of the Lord with them, and went about throughout all the cities of Jū'dah, and taught the people.

10 ¶And the fear of the Lord fell upon all the kingdoms of the lands that *were* round about Jū'dah, so that they made no war against Je-hŏsh'a-phăt.

11 Also *some* of the Philistines brought Je-hŏsh'a-phăt presents, and tribute silver; and the Arabians brought him flocks, seven thousand and seven hundred rams, and seven thousand and seven hundred he goats.

10-11. Instead of being repentant, **Asa was wroth. Hanani** (vs. 7) was submitted to a form of torture, being placed in a **prison house** (lit., house of stocks). He also **oppressed some of the people,** possibly those who sought the prophet's release.

12-13. The thirty and ninth year (cf. vs. 13). During the last three years of his reign and life he suffered from a severe foot disease. He is not necessarily condemned for consulting the **physicians,** unless they resorted to magic. The Chronicler is amazed, though, that Asa was so hardened that **he sought not to the Lord,** even when seriously ill.

14. They made a very great burning for him. This is not a reference to cremation, but to the burning of spices in honor of a worthy king (cf. Jer 34:5).

C. Jehoshaphat. 17:1-20:37.

1. His faithfulness and prosperity. 17:1-19.

17:1-4. Jehoshaphat . . . strengthened himself against Israel, i.e., the northern kingdom. This was done by placing **forces,** i.e., troops, in the cities and setting **garrisons,** i.e., military posts, throughout Judah and in the cities his father had taken in Ephraim. **He walked in the first ways of his father David.** The Septuagint omits that reference to David. Regardless of which text is preferred (Heb or LXX), the Chronicler is admitting that the latter ways of David (or Asa) were less than exemplary. **The doings of Israel** included the idolatrous worship of the golden calves at Dan and Beth-el.

5-6. His heart was lifted up. Usually, the verb is used negatively (cf. 26:16; 32:25; Ezk 28:2, 5, 17); but here he took pride, not in his **riches and honor** (vs. 5), but **in the ways of the Lord.** For **high places and groves,** see 14:3.

7-11. He sent to his princes, even to Ben-hail. The verse would be better rendered if the preposition **to** were omitted as follows: "he sent his princes Ben-hail, and Obadiah. . . ." Jehoshaphat was in effect initiating the first itinerate Bible-teaching team to be sponsored by royalty. These laymen accompanied certain **Levites** and **priests** to teach **the book of the law,** i.e., the books of Moses, in Judah (cf. note on priestly responsibility, 15:3). As a reward, God honored him with peace and such prestige that the Philistines and Arabians brought him tribute.

12 ¶And Je-hŏsh′a-phăt waxed great exceedingly; and he built in Jŭ′dah castles, and cities of store.

13 And he had much business in the cities of Jŭ′dah: and the men of war, mighty men of valour, were in Jerusalem.

14 And these are the numbers of them according to the house of their fathers: Of Jŭ′dah, the captains of thousands; Ăd′nah the chief, and with him mighty men of valour three hundred thousand.

15 And next to him was Je-hō-hā′nan the captain, and with him two hundred and fourscore thousand.

16 And next him was Ăm-a-sī′ah the son of Zĭch′rī, who willingly offered himself unto the Lord; and with him two hundred thousand mighty men of valour.

17 And of Benjamin; E-lī′a-da a mighty man of valour, and with him armed men with bow and shield two hundred thousand.

18 And next him was Je-hōz′a-băd, and with him an hundred and fourscore thousand ready prepared for the war.

19 These waited on the king, beside those whom the king put in the fenced cities throughout all Jŭ′dah.

CHAPTER 18

NOW Je-hŏsh′a-phăt had riches and honour in abundance, and joined affinity with Ahab.

2 And after certain years he went down to Ahab to Sa-mā′rĭ-a. And Ahab killed sheep and oxen for him in abundance, and for the people that he had with him, and persuaded him to go up with him to Rā′moth–gĭl′e-ad.

3 And Ahab king of Israel said unto Je-hŏsh′a-phăt king of Jŭ′dah, Wilt thou go with me to Rā′moth–gĭl′e-ad? And he answered him, I am as thou art, and my people as thy people; and we will be with thee in the war.

4 ¶And Je-hŏsh′a-phăt said unto the king of Israel, Enquire, I pray thee, at the word of the Lord to day.

5 Therefore the king of Israel gathered together of prophets four hundred men, and said unto them, Shall we go to Rā′moth–gĭl′e-ad to battle, or shall I forbear? And they said, Go up; for God will deliver it into the king's hand.

6 ¶But Je-hŏsh′a-phăt said, Is there not here a prophet of the Lord besides, that we might enquire of him?

7 And the king of Israel said unto Je-hŏsh′a-phăt, There is yet one man, by whom we may enquire of the Lord: but I hate him; for he never prophesied good unto me, but always evil: the same is Mī-cā′iah the son of Ĭm′la. And Je-hŏsh′a-phăt said, Let not the king say so.

8 And the king of Israel called for one of his officers, and said, Fetch quickly Mī-cā′iah the son of Ĭm′la.

9 And the king of Israel and Je-hŏsh′a-phăt king of Jŭ′dah sat either of

12-19. That **Jehoshaphat waxed great exceedingly** is evidenced by his cities and men of war. Within the tribe of Judah he had three armies, one of 300,000 men (vs. 14), another 240,000 (vs. 15), and another 200,000 men (vs. 16), making a total of 780,000 men. Within Benjamin he had two armies, one of 200,000 men (vs. 17) and another of 180,000 men (vs. 18), making a total of 380,000. The grand total was an enormous army of 1,160,000 men.

2. His alliance with Ahab. 18:1-19:4.

18:1. When Jehoshaphat acquired his **riches and honor,** he also became careless in his diplomatic relations and **joined affinity with Ahab.** This alliance was evidently clinched by the marriage of his son Jehoram to Ahab's daughter, Athaliah (21:6).

2-34. This alliance led to Jehoshaphat's involvement in battle as an ally of wicked Ahab of Israel against Syria (for details of these vss., see previous discussion on the virtually identical passage in I Kgs 22:1-38).

them on his throne, clothed in *their* robes, and they sat in a void place at the entering in of the gate of Sa-mā′rĭ-a; and all the prophets prophesied before them.

10 And Zĕd-e-kī′ah the son of Che-nā′a-nah had made him horns of iron, and said, Thus saith the Lord, With these thou shalt push Syria until they be consumed.

11 And all the prophets prophesied so, saying, Go up to Rā′moth–gĭl′e-ad, and prosper: for the Lord shall deliver *it* into the hand of the king.

12 And the messenger that went to call Mĭ-cā′iah spake to him, saying, Behold, the words of the prophets *declare* good to the king with one assent; let thy word therefore, I pray thee, be like one of theirs, and speak thou good.

13 And Mĭ-cā′iah said, *As* the Lord liveth, even what my God saith, that will I speak.

14 And when he was come to the king, the king said unto him, Mĭ-cā′iah, shall we go to Rā′moth–gĭl′e-ad to battle, or shall I forbear? And he said, Go ye up, and prosper, and they shall be delivered into your hand.

15 And the king said to him, How many times shall I adjure thee that thou say nothing but the truth to me in the name of the Lord?

16 Then he said, I did see all Israel scattered upon the mountains, as sheep that have no shepherd: and the Lord said, These have no master; let them return *therefore* every man to his house in peace.

17 And the king of Israel said to Je-hŏsh′a-phăt, Did I not tell thee *that* he would not prophesy good unto me, but evil?

18 Again he said, Therefore hear the word of the Lord; I saw the Lord sitting upon his throne, and all the host of heaven standing on his right hand and *on* his left.

19 And the Lord said, Who shall entice Ahab king of Israel, that he may go up and fall at Rā′moth–gĭl′e-ad? And one spake saying after this manner, and another saying after that manner.

20 Then there came out a spirit, and stood before the Lord, and said, I will entice him. And the Lord said unto him, Wherewith?

21 And he said, I will go out, and be a lying spirit in the mouth of all his prophets. And *the* Lord said, Thou shalt entice *him*, and thou shalt also prevail: go out, and do *even* so.

22 Now therefore, behold, the Lord hath put a lying spirit in the mouth of these thy prophets, and the Lord hath spoken evil against thee.

23 ¶Then Zĕd-e-kī′ah the son of Che-nā′a-nah came near, and smote Mĭ-cā′iah upon the cheek, and said, Which way went the Spirit of the Lord from me to speak unto thee?

24 And Mĭ-cā′iah said, Behold, thou shalt see on that day when thou shalt go into an inner chamber to hide thyself.

25 Then the king of Israel said, Take ye Mĭ-cā′iah, and carry him back to

Ămon the governor of the city, and to Jŏ'ăsh the king's son;

26 And say, Thus saith the king, Put this *fellow* in the prison, and feed him with bread of affliction and with water of affliction, until I return in peace.

27 And Mĭ-cā'iah said, If thou certainly return in peace, *then* hath not the LORD spoken by me. And he said, Hearken, all ye people.

28 So the king of Israel and Je-hŏsh'a-phăt the king of Jū'dah went up to Rā'moth-gĭl'e-ad.

29 And the king of Israel said unto Je-hŏsh'a-phăt, I will disguise myself, and will go to the battle; but put thou on thy robes. So the king of Israel disguised himself; and they went to the battle.

30 Now the king of Syria had commanded the captains of the chariots that *were* with him, saying, Fight ye not with small or great, save only with the king of Israel.

31 And it came to pass, when the captains of the chariots saw Je-hŏsh'a-phăt, that they said, It *is* the king of Israel. Therefore they compassed about him to fight: but Je-hŏsh'a-phăt cried out, and the LORD helped him; and God moved them *to depart* from him.

32 For it came to pass, that, when the captains of the chariots perceived that it was not the king of Israel, they turned back again from pursuing him.

33 And a *certain* man drew a bow at a venture, and smote the king of Israel between the joints of the harness: therefore he said to his chariot man, Turn thine hand, that thou mayest carry me out of the host; for I am wounded.

34 And the battle increased that day: howbeit the king of Israel stayed *himself* up in *his* chariot against the Syrians until the even: and about the time of the sun going down he died.

CHAPTER 19

AND Je-hŏsh'a-phăt the king of Jū'dah returned to his house in peace to Jerusalem.

2 And Jehu the son of Ha-nā'nĭ the seer went out to meet him, and said to king Je-hŏsh'a-phăt, Shouldest thou help the ungodly, and love them that hate the LORD? therefore *is* wrath upon thee from before the LORD.

3 Nevertheless there are good things found in thee, in that thou hast taken away the groves out of the land, and hast prepared thine heart to seek God.

4 And Je-hŏsh'a-phăt dwelt at Jerusalem: and he went out again through the people from Be'er-shē'ba to mount Ē'phra-im, and brought them back unto the LORD God of their fathers.

5 And he set judges in the land throughout all the fenced cities of Jū'dah, city by city,

6 And said to the judges, Take heed what ye do: for ye judge not for man, but for the LORD, who *is* with you in the judgment.

7 Wherefore now let the fear of the LORD be upon you; take heed and do *it:* for *there is* no iniquity with the LORD our God, nor respect of persons, nor taking of gifts.

8 Moreover in Jerusalem did Je-

19:1-4. Jehoshaphat returned **in peace,** i.e., safely, from his involvement with Ahab against the Syrians (18:2-34). **Jehu the son of Hanani** had delivered the sober news to Baasha that his dynasty would end (cf. note on I Kgs 16:1). Jehu first rebuked Jehoshaphat for helping the **ungodly,** i.e., Ahab, and loving **them that hate the LORD,** i.e., the people of Israel. The **wrath . . . from before the LORD** may be a reference to the Ammonite invasion in 20:1ff. Jehu then commended the king for the **good things,** i.e., his past reforms (17:4-9). **Beer-sheba** (cf. I Chr 21:2) and **mount Ephraim** (17:2) were the southern and northern limits of his realm.

3. His judicial reforms. 19:5-11.

5-7. He initiated new reforms within the judicial system. If his appointed judges were mindful of a most important principle that ultimately they were not judging **for man, but for the LORD** (vs. 6), there would be no **respect of persons,** i.e., impartiality, **nor taking of gifts,** i.e., bribery for a favorable court decision (vs. 7).

8-9. Centrally located, **Jerusalem** served as the site of the

hŏsh'a-phăt set of the Lē'vītes, and *of* the priests, and of the chief of the fathers of Israel, for the judgment of the LORD, and for controversies, when they returned to Jerusalem.

9 And he charged them, saying, Thus shall ye do in the fear of the LORD, faithfully, and with a perfect heart.

10 And what cause soever shall come to you of your brethren that dwell in their cities, between blood and blood, between law and commandment, statutes and judgments, ye shall even warn them that they trespass not against the LORD, and *so* wrath come upon you, and upon your brethren: this do, and ye shall not trespass.

11 And, behold, Ăm-a-rī'ah the chief priest *is* over you in all matters of the LORD; and Zĕb-a-dī'ah the son of Ĭsh'ma-el, the ruler of the house of Jū'dah, for all the king's matters: also the Lē'vītes *shall be* officers before you. Deal courageously, and the LORD shall be with the good.

CHAPTER 20

IT came to pass after this also, *that* the children of Moab, and the children of Ammon, and with them *other* beside the Ammonites, came against Je-hŏsh'a-phăt to battle.

2 Then there came some that told Je-hŏsh'a-phăt, saying, There cometh a great multitude against thee from beyond the sea on this side Syria; and, behold, they *be* in Hăz'a-zŏn-tā'mar, which *is* Ěn-gě'dī.

3 And Je-hŏsh'a-phăt feared, and set himself to seek the LORD, and proclaimed a fast throughout all Jū'dah.

4 And Jū'dah gathered themselves together, to ask *help* of the LORD: even out of all the cities of Jū'dah they came to seek the LORD.

5 ¶And Je-hŏsh'a-phăt stood in the congregation of Jū'dah and Jerusalem, in the house of the LORD, before the new court,

6 And said, O LORD God of our fathers, *art* not thou God in heaven? and rulest *not* thou over all the kingdoms of the heathen? and in thine hand *is there not* power and might, so that none is able to withstand thee?

7 *Art* not thou our God, *who* didst drive out the inhabitants of this land before thy people Israel, and gavest it to the seed of Abraham thy friend for ever?

8 And they dwelt therein, and have built thee a sanctuary therein for thy name, saying,

9 If, *when* evil cometh upon us, *as* the sword, judgment, or pestilence, or famine, we stand before this house, and in thy presence, (for thy name *is* in this house,) and cry unto thee in our affliction, then thou wilt hear and help.

10 And now, behold, the children of Ammon and Moab and mount Sē'ir, whom thou wouldest not let Israel invade, when they came out of the land of Egypt, but they turned from them, and destroyed them not;

11 Behold, *I say, how* they reward us, to come to cast us out of thy posses-

final court of appeals for **the judgment of the LORD,** i.e., religious cases, and for **controversies,** i.e., civil cases.

10-11. Between blood and blood indicated cases of bloodshed where premeditated murder or involuntary manslaughter must be decided. The name **Amariah** appears in I Chronicles 5:11, but **Zebadiah** is otherwise unknown.

4. The Ammonite-Moabite attack and summary of his reign. 20:1-37.

20:1-4. Other beside the Ammonites is a difficult Hebrew phrase which is probably more accurately rendered in the Septuagint as "and some of the Meunim," people from Ma'an, a city south of the Dead Sea or from Arabia. **From beyond the sea,** i.e., the Dead Sea, **on this side Syria.** Syria (Heb *'aram*) should probably read "Edom" (Heb *'edōm*) in light of Mount Seir in verse 10 (cf. discussion on identical problem in I Chr 18:12). The invading multitude reached **En-gedi,** a site on the east side of the Dead Sea where Saul had pursued David (I Sam 24:1). In spite of his large army (cf. 17:14-18), **Jehoshaphat feared** because of Jehu's warning of God's wrath (19:2).

5-13. Jehoshaphat stood and led his people, Judah, in prayer to God in the face of an attack by the enemy. **The new court** is a reference to the outer court that was apparently renovated, or an innovation since the time of Solomon. On the basis of his sound theology and a personal knowledge of God's sovereignty and omnipotence (vs. 6), His faithfulness to Israel and Abraham (vs. 7), and His promise to hear His people in their affliction (vs. 8-9), Jehoshaphat described Judah's plight to God. Three nations **whom thou wouldest not let Israel invade** (cf. Deut 2:4ff., 9ff., 19ff. for God's prohibition concerning disturbing **mount Seir,** i.e., "Esau" or Edom, **Moab,** and **Ammon,** all distant relatives of Israel) were about to dispossess Judah from her God-given land (vss. 10-11). Demonstrating their utter dependence upon the Lord (vs. 12), the people of Judah stood in His presence awaiting His answer (vs. 13).

sion, which thou hast given us to inherit.

12 O our God, wilt thou not judge them? for we have no might against this great company that cometh against us; neither know we what to do: but our eyes *are* upon thee.

13 And all Jū'dah stood before the LORD, with their little ones, their wives, and their children.

14 Then upon Ja-hā'zi-el the son of Zěch-a-rī'ah, the son of Be-nā'iah, the son of Je-ī'el, the son of Măt-ta-nī'ah, a Levite of the sons of Ā'săph, came the Spirit of the LORD in the midst of the congregation;

15 And he said, Hearken ye, all Jū'dah, and ye inhabitants of Jerusalem, and thou king Je-hŏsh'a-phăt, Thus saith the LORD unto you, Be not afraid nor dismayed by reason of this great multitude; for the battle *is* not yours, but God's.

16 To morrow go ye down against them: behold, they come up by the cliff of Ziz; and ye shall find them at the end of the brook, before the wilderness of Jer'ū-el.

17 Ye shall not *need* to fight in this *battle:* set yourselves, stand ye *still,* and see the salvation of the LORD with you, O Jū'dah and Jerusalem: fear not, nor be dismayed; to morrow go out against them: for the LORD *will be* with you.

18 And Je-hŏsh'a-phăt bowed his head with *his* face to the ground: and all Jū'dah and the inhabitants of Jerusalem fell before the LORD, worshipping the LORD.

19 And the Lē'vītes, of the children of the Kō'hăth-ītes, and of the children of the Kŏr'hītes, stood up to praise the LORD God of Israel with a loud voice on high.

20 ¶And they rose early in the morning, and went forth into the wilderness of Te-kō'a: and as they went forth, Je-hŏsh'a-phăt stood and said, Hear me, O Jū'dah, and ye inhabitants of Jerusalem; Believe in the LORD your God, so shall ye be established; believe his prophets, so shall ye prosper.

21 And when he had consulted with the people, he appointed singers unto the LORD, and that should praise the beauty of holiness, as they went out before the army, and to say, Praise the LORD; for his mercy *endureth* for ever.

22 ¶And when they began to sing and to praise, the LORD set ambushments against the children of Ammon, Moab, and mount Sē'ir, which were come against Jū'dah; and they were smitten.

23 For the children of Ammon and Moab stood up against the inhabitants of mount Sē'ir, utterly to slay and destroy *them:* and when they had made an end of the inhabitants of Sē'ir, every one helped to destroy another.

24 And when Jū'dah came toward the watch tower in the wilderness, they looked unto the multitude, and, behold, they *were* dead bodies fallen to the earth, and none escaped.

25 And when Je-hŏsh'a-phăt and his people came to take away the spoil of them, they found among them in abun-

14-19. God's response through **Jahaziel** (his genealogy is traced to Asaph of I Chr 25:2) was assuring. **The battle is not yours, but God's** (cf. David's words to the Philistine, Goliath, I Sam 17:47). The **cliff,** i.e., ascent, **of Ziz** led inland to the northwest of En-gedi. **Set yourselves, stand ye still, and see the salvation of the LORD** (cf. Moses' words at the parting of the Red Sea, Ex 14:13). As Jehoshaphat responded appropriately, bowing and **worshiping the LORD,** certain ones of the **Kohathites** and **Korhites** stood to praise Him.

20-25. Judah approached the battle with the king's reminder, **Believe in the LORD your God,** ringing in their ears and praise for the Lord issuing from their lips. **The LORD set ambushments** (lit., liers in wait). Whether the Lord employed supernatural agents or surprised the enemy by an unexpected attack by the inhabitants of the area, is not clear. What is clear is that the Lord inflicted the enemy nations with panic and turned them on each other, and **every one helped to destroy another** (cf. similar circumstance under Gideon's leadership, Jud 7:21-22). **And when Judah came toward,** i.e., when they arrived on the scene, they were too late for the battle, but right on time **to take away the spoil of them.**

dance both riches with the dead bodies, and precious jewels, which they stripped off for themselves, more than they could carry away: and they were three days in gathering of the spoil, it was so much.

26 And on the fourth day they assembled themselves in the valley of Bĕr'a-chah; for there they blessed the LORD: therefore the name of the same place was called, The valley of Bĕr'a-chah, unto this day.

27 Then they returned, every man of Jū'dah and Jerusalem, and Je-hŏsh'a-phăt in the forefront of them, to go again to Jerusalem with joy; for the LORD had made them to rejoice over their enemies.

28 And they came to Jerusalem with psalteries and harps and trumpets unto the house of the LORD.

29 And the fear of God was on all the kingdoms of *those* countries, when they had heard that the LORD fought against the enemies of Israel.

30 So the realm of Je-hŏsh'a-phăt was quiet: for his God gave him rest round about.

31 ¶And Je-hŏsh'a-phăt reigned over Jū'dah: *he was* thirty and five years old when he began to reign, and he reigned twenty and five years in Jerusalem. And his mother's name *was* A-zū'bah the daughter of Shĭl'hī.

32 And he walked in the way of Āsa his father, and departed not from it, doing *that which was* right in the sight of the LORD.

33 Howbeit the high places were not taken away: for as yet the people had not prepared their hearts unto the God of their fathers.

34 Now the rest of the acts of Je-hŏsh'a-phăt, first and last, behold, they *are* written in the book of Jehu the son of Ha-nā'nī, who *is* mentioned in the book of the kings of Israel.

35 ¶And after this did Je-hŏsh'a-phăt king of Jū'dah join himself with Ā-ha-zī'ah king of Israel, who did very wickedly:

36 And he joined himself with him to make ships to go to Tärshĭsh: and they made the ships in Ē'zĭ-on-gā'ber.

37 Then Ē-lĭ-ē'zer the son of Dō'da-vah of Ma-rē'shah prophesied against Je-hŏsh'a-phăt, saying, Because thou hast joined thyself with Ā-ha-zī'ah, the LORD hath broken thy works. And the ships were broken, that they were not able to go to Tärshĭsh.

CHAPTER 21

NOW Je-hŏsh'a-phăt slept with his fathers, and was buried with his fathers in the city of David. And Je-hō'ram his son reigned in his stead.

2 And he had brethren the sons of Je-hŏsh'a-phăt, Āz-a-rī'ah, and Je-hī'el, and Zĕch-a-rī'ah, and Āz-a-rī'ah, and Michael, and Shĕph-a-tī'ah: all these *were* the sons of Je-hŏsh'a-phăt king of Israel.

3 And their father gave them great gifts of silver, and of gold, and of precious things, with fenced cities in Jū'dah: but the kingdom gave he to Je-hō'ram; because he *was* the firstborn.

26-30. After three days of collecting spoil, Judah returned to Jerusalem rejoicing in God's victory, news which could not be suppressed, but was spread abroad to neighboring countries.

31-34. These summarizing verses parallel I Kings 22:41-45. **The high places were not taken away.** Though Jehoshaphat officially removed the high places (cf. 17:6), the people apparently persisted in resorting to them.

35-37. After this did Jehoshaphat . . . join . . . Ahaziah. Prior to this event, Ahaziah, the wicked son of Ahab, had offered to assist Jehoshaphat with his fleet (cf. I Kgs 22:48-49); but Jehoshaphat had refused the offer because he had just received a scathing rebuke from Jehu (19:1-2) for his alliance with Ahab. Now he accepts that assistance (for **Tarshish,** see note on 9:21). Through **Eliezer,** who is otherwise unknown, Jehoshaphat was made mindful of God's displeasure of such alliances; for his **ships were broken** (by divine judgment), **that they were not able to go to Tarshish.**

D. Jehoram and Ahaziah. 21:1-22:9.

21:1-10. With the exception of verses 2-4 and the last phrase of verse 10, this section is virtually identical to I Kings 22:50 and II Kings 8:16-22 (see comments on these passages).

To strengthen himself, Jehoram **slew all his brethren . . . and . . . princes of Israel** (vs. 4). This action supposes that his ambition and jealousy led him to eliminate all who might be political rivals or opponents to his religious policies (cf. vs. 13). **Israel** is used here (also in vs. 2) as a general reference to the northern kingdom.

4 Now when Je-hô′ram was risen up to the kingdom of his father, he strengthened himself, and slew all his brethren with the sword, and *divers* also of the princes of Israel.

5 ¶Je-hô′ram *was* thirty and two years old when he began to reign, and he reigned eight years in Jerusalem.

6 And he walked in the way of the kings of Israel, like as did the house of Ahab: for he had the daughter of Ahab to wife: and he wrought *that which was* evil in the eyes of the LORD.

7 Howbeit the LORD would not destroy the house of David, because of the covenant that he had made with David, and as he promised to give a light to him and to his sons for ever.

8 ¶In his days the Edomites revolted from under the dominion of Jū′dah, and made themselves a king.

9 Then Je-hô′ram went forth with his princes, and all his chariots with him: and he rose up by night, and smote the Edomites which compassed him in, and the captains of the chariots.

10 So the Edomites revolted from under the hand of Jū′dah unto this day. The same time *also* did Lĭb′nah revolt from under his hand; because he had forsaken the LORD God of his fathers.

11 Moreover he made high places in the mountains of Jū′dah, and caused the inhabitants of Jerusalem to commit fornication, and compelled Jū′dah *thereto.*

12 ¶And there came a writing to him from E-lī′jah the prophet, saying, Thus saith the LORD God of David thy father, Because thou hast not walked in the ways of Je-hŏsh′a-phăt thy father, nor in the ways of Āsa king of Jū′dah,

13 But hast walked in the way of the kings of Israel, and hast made Jū′dah and the inhabitants of Jerusalem to go a whoring, like to the whoredoms of the house of Ahab, and also hast slain thy brethren of thy father's house, *which were* better than thyself:

14 Behold, with a great plague will the LORD smite thy people, and thy children, and thy wives, and all thy goods:

15 And thou *shalt have* great sickness by disease of thy bowels, until thy bowels fall out by reason of the sickness day by day.

16 ¶Moreover the LORD stirred up against Je-hô′ram the spirit of the Philistines, and of the Arabians, that *were* near the Ē-thī-ō′pī-ans:

17 And they came up into Jū′dah, and brake into it, and carried away all the substance that was found in the king's house, and his sons also, and his wives; so that there was never a son left him, save Je-hō′a-hăz, the youngest of his sons.

18 And after all this the LORD smote him in his bowels with an incurable disease.

19 And it came to pass, that in process of time, after the end of two years, his bowels fell out by reason of his sickness: so he died of sore diseases. And his people made no burning for him, like the burning of his fathers.

20 Thirty and two years old was he

11. Jehoram attempted to undo his father's reform by building **high places** and by compelling Judah to **commit fornication,** i.e., with reference to going after false gods.

12-15. A writing . . . **from Elijah** proves interesting. If the chronology of II Kings 2 and 3 is followed, Elijah was translated and replaced by Elisha before Jehoshaphat had died, leaving Jehoram as sole ruler. It is not impossible that the influence of his wicked grandfather Ahab and mother Athaliah was so evident in his life-style before he began to reign that the prophet had written the message prior to his translation to be delivered later.

16-17. Kings does not mention this raid. The **Philistines** and **Arabians** had paid tribute to Jehoshaphat (17:11) (on the **Ethiopians,** Cushites, see 14:9). **The substance . . . in the King's** house was taken. That Jerusalem was taken, or even invaded, is not suggested; so the **king's house** was probably a royal residence outside Jerusalem. **Jehoahaz,** also known as Ahaziah and meaning "Jehovah has taken," was the sole son left to Jehoram following the raid.

18-20. The prophecy of Elijah (vs. 15) is fulfilled. His **incurable disease** pertaining to **his bowels** may have been some form of dysentery. They **made no burning for him** (cf. 16:14), neither did they give him an honorable burial **in the sepulchers of the kings.**

when he began to reign, and he reigned in Jerusalem eight years, and departed without being desired. Howbeit they buried him in the city of David, but not in the sepulchres of the kings.

CHAPTER 22

AND the inhabitants of Jerusalem made Ā-ha-zī′ah his youngest son king in his stead: for the band of men that came with the Arabians to the camp had slain all the eldest. So Ā-ha-zī′ah the son of Je-hō′ram king of Jū′dah reigned.

2 Forty and two years old *was* Ā-ha-zī′ah when he began to reign, and he reigned one year in Jerusalem. His mother's name also *was* Āth-a-lī′ah, the daughter of Omri.

3 He also walked in the ways of the house of Ahab: for his mother was his counsellor to do wickedly.

4 Wherefore he did evil in the sight of the LORD like the house of Ahab: for they were his counsellors after the death of his father to his destruction.

5 He walked also after their counsel, and went with Je-hō′ram the son of Ahab king of Israel to war against Hāz′a-el king of Syria at Rǎ′moth–gǐl′e-ad: and the Syrians smote Joram.

6 And he returned to be healed in Jěz′re-el because of the wounds which were given him at Rā′mah, when he fought with Hāz′a-el king of Syria. And Ǎz-a-rī′ah the son of Je-hō′ram king of Jū′dah went down to see Je-hō′ram the son of Ahab at Jěz′re-el, because he was sick.

7 And the destruction of Ā-ha-zī′ah was of God by coming to Joram: for when he was come, he went out with Je-hō′ram against Jehu the son of Nǐmshī, whom the LORD had anointed to cut off the house of Ahab.

8 And it came to pass, that, when Jehu was executing judgment upon the house of Ahab, and found the princes of Jū′dah, and the sons of the brethren of Ā-ha-zī′ah, that ministered to Ā-ha-zī′ah, he slew them.

9 And he sought Ā-ha-zī′ah: and they caught him, (for he was hid in Sa-mā′-rǐ-a,) and brought him to Jehu: and when they had slain him, they buried him: Because, said they, he *is* the son of Je-hŏsh′a-phǎt, who sought the LORD with all his heart. So the house of Ā-ha-zī′ah had no power to keep still the kingdom.

10 ¶But when Ǎth-a-lī′ah the mother of Ā-ha-zī′ah saw that her son was dead, she arose and destroyed all the seed royal of the house of Jū′dah.

11 But Jē-hō-shǎb′e-ath, the daughter of the king, took Jō′ăsh the son of Ā-ha-zī′ah, and stole him from among the king's sons that were slain, and put him and his nurse in a bedchamber. So Jē-hō-shǎb′e-ath, the daughter of king Je-hō′ram, the wife of Je-hoi′a-da the priest, (for she was the

22:1-6. Jehoram's **youngest son** Ahaziah was made king because the older sons had all been killed by the raiding **band of men** (21:16-17). His age of **forty and two years** is impossible in light of 21:20. It is probably a scribal mistake for twenty-two years (cf. II Kgs 8:26). **Azariah** (occurring only here in vs. 6) is evidently a scribal misspelling of Ahaziah appearing throughout the chapter. For additional notes on verses 1-6, see parallel passage in II Kings 8:25-29.

7-8. Ahaziah's destruction **was of God,** for He had anointed Jehu **to cut off the house of Ahab** (cf. Jehu's anointing and instructions in II Kgs 9:6-10). **The sons of the brethren** were actual sons born to Ahaziah's older brothers before they were slain (cf. 21:17 and 22:1) or **sons** is used loosely of his relatives.

9. Many scholars believe this account of Ahaziah's death to be irreconcilable with the account in II Kings 8:27-28. There are difficulties, but a harmony is not impossible. Upon witnessing the murder of his uncle Joram by Jehu, Ahaziah had fled to Samaria, where he hid until found by Jehu's men. They **brought him to Jehu** who fatally wounded him near Ibleam. He was able to flee once again, this time to Megiddo, where he died. He was brought back to Jerusalem to be buried with the other kings (cf. Payne, p. 408).

E. Joash. 22:10-24:27.

1. Athaliah's interim reign and demise. 22:10-23:21.

10-12. For details of Joash's life being providentially spared while his grandmother, the wicked daughter of Ahab and Jezebel, temporarily reigned, see notes on II Kings 11:1-3. The account of Jehoiada's presenting Joash, the crown prince, to Judah and the death of Athaliah coincides almost identically with II Kings 11:4-20. Two exceptions are verses 1-3 and 18-19.

sister of Ā-ha-zī′ah,) hid him from Ăth-a-lī′ah, so that she slew him not.

12 And he was with them hid in the house of God six years: and Ăth-a-lī′ah reigned over the land.

CHAPTER 23

AND in the seventh year Je-hoi′a-da strengthened himself, and took the captains of hundreds, Ăz-a-rī′ah the son of Jer′ō-hăm, and Ĭsh′ma-el the son of Je-hō-hā′nan, and Ăz-a-rī′ah the son of Ō′bed, and Mā-a-sē′iah the son of Ăd-a-ī′ah, and E-lĭsh′a-phăt the son of Zĭch′rī, into covenant with him.

2 And they went about in Jū′dah, and gathered the Lē′vītes out of all the cities of Jū′dah, and the chief of the fathers of Israel, and they came to Jerusalem.

3 And all the congregation made a covenant with the king in the house of God. And he said unto them, Behold, the king's son shall reign, as the LORD hath said of the sons of David.

4 This is the thing that ye shall do; A third part of you entering on the sabbath, of the priests and of the Lē′vītes, shall be porters of the doors;

5 And a third part shall be at the king's house; and a third part at the gate of the foundation: and all the people shall be in the courts of the house of the LORD.

6 But let none come into the house of the LORD, save the priests, and they that minister of the Lē′vītes; they shall go in, for they are holy: but all the people shall keep the watch of the LORD.

7 And the Lē′vītes shall compass the king round about, every man with his weapons in his hand; and whosoever else cometh into the house, he shall be put to death: but be ye with the king when he cometh in, and when he goeth out.

8 So the Lē′vītes and all Jū′dah did according to all things that Je-hoi′a-da the priest had commanded, and took every man his men that were to come in on the sabbath, with them that were to go out on the sabbath: for Je-hoi′a-da the priest dismissed not the courses.

9 Moreover Je-hoi′a-da the priest delivered to the captains of hundreds spears, and bucklers, and shields, that had been king David's, which were in the house of God.

10 And he set all the people, every man having his weapon in his hand, from the right side of the temple to the left side of the temple, along by the altar and the temple, by the king round about.

11 Then they brought out the king's son, and put upon him the crown, and gave him the testimony, and made him king. And Je-hoi′a-da and his sons anointed him, and said, God save the king.

12 ¶Now when Ăth-a-lī′ah heard the noise of the people running and praising the king, she came to the people into the house of the LORD:

13 And she looked, and, behold, the king stood at his pillar at the entering in, and the princes and the trumpets by the king: and all the people of the land

23:1-17. The Chronicler specifically names the **captains of hundreds** Jehoiada the priest commissioned to gather secretly the **Levites** of Judah to Jerusalem to covenant together to make Joash king.

rejoiced, and sounded with trumpets, also the singers with instruments of musick, and such as taught to sing praise. Then Ăth-a-lī′ah rent her clothes, and said, Treason, Treason.

14 Then Je-hoi′a-da the priest brought out the captains of hundreds that were set over the host, and said unto them, Have her forth of the ranges: and whoso followeth her, let him be slain with the sword. For the priest said, Slay her not in the house of the Lord.

15 So they laid hands on her; and when she was come to the entering of the horse gate by the king's house, they slew her there.

16 ¶And Je-hoi′a-da made a covenant between him, and between all the people, and between the king, that they should be the Lord's people.

17 Then all the people went to the house of Bā′al, and brake it down, and brake his altars and his images in pieces, and slew Măt′tan the priest of Bā′al before the altars.

18 Also Je-hoi′a-da appointed the offices of the house of the Lord by the hand of the priests the Lē′vītes, whom David had distributed in the house of the Lord, to offer the burnt offerings of the Lord, as *it is* written in the law of Moses, with rejoicing and with singing, *as it was ordained* by David.

19 And he set the porters at the gates of the house of the Lord, that none *which was* unclean in any thing should enter in.

20 And he took the captains of hundreds, and the nobles, and the governors of the people, and all the people of the land, and brought down the king from the house of the Lord: and they came through the high gate into the king's house, and set the king upon the throne of the kingdom.

21 And all the people of the land rejoiced: and the city was quiet, after that they had slain Ăth-a-lī′ah with the sword.

CHAPTER 24

JŌ′ĂSH *was* seven years old when he began to reign, and he reigned forty years in Jerusalem. His mother's name also *was* Zĭb′ĭ-ah of Be′er-shē′ba.

2 And Jō′ăsh did *that which was* right in the sight of the Lord all the days of Je-hoi′a-da the priest.

3 And Je-hoi′a-da took for him two wives; and he begat sons and daughters.

4 ¶And it came to pass after this, *that* Jō′ăsh was minded to repair the house of the Lord.

5 And he gathered together the priests and the Lē′vītes, and said to them, Go out unto the cities of Jū′dah, and gather of all Israel money to repair the house of your God from year to year, and see that ye hasten the matter. Howbeit the Lē′vītes hastened *it* not.

6 And the king called for Je-hoi′a-da the chief, and said unto him, Why hast thou not required of the Lē′vītes to bring in out of Jū′dah and out of Jerusalem the collection, *according to the commandment* of Moses the servant of

18-21. In covenanting with Judah to be the Lord's people (vs. 16), not only was the house of Baal destroyed, but **Jehoiada appointed the offices of the house of the Lord**, implying that the worship of Jehovah was being restored in place of Baal worship.

2. The repair of the Temple. 24:1-14.

The Chronicler's account of Joash's repairing the Temple parallels II Kings 12:1-15 (see notes there), with several variations to be noted here.

24:1-4. An additional note to Joash's biographical sketch concerns **Jehoiada**, the priest who served as Joash's parent and legal guardian, taking **two wives** for the young king.

5. The Chronicler records Joash's instructing the Levites to **Go out unto the cities of Judah, and gather . . . money**, whereas in II Kings he addressed the priests, instructing them to collect money from those who came to the Temple. The accounts are not contradictory, but supplementary.

6-12. The Chronicler explains the reason for repairing the Temple. **The sons of Athaliah . . . had broken up** (better rendered broken into, Heb *parats*) **the house of God.** In addition to their vandalism, they had stolen **dedicated things**, possibly the golden and silver vessels (cf. vs. 14), to use them in the worship of Baal.

the LORD, and of the congregation of Israel, for the tabernacle of witness?

7 For the sons of Āth-a-lī'ah, that wicked woman, had broken up the house of God; and also all the dedicated things of the house of the LORD did they bestow upon Bā'al-ĭm.

8 And at the king's commandment they made a chest, and set it without at the gate of the house of the LORD.

9 And they made a proclamation through Jū'dah and Jerusalem, to bring in to the LORD the collection that Moses the servant of God laid upon Israel in the wilderness.

10 And all the princes and all the people rejoiced, and brought in, and cast into the chest, until they had made an end.

11 Now it came to pass, that at what time the chest was brought unto the king's office by the hand of the Lē'vītes, and when they saw that there was much money, the king's scribe and the high priest's officer came and emptied the chest, and took it, and carried it to his place again. Thus they did day by day, and gathered money in abundance.

12 And the king and Je-hoi'a-da gave it to such as did the work of the service of the house of the LORD, and hired masons and carpenters to repair the house of the LORD, and also such as wrought iron and brass to mend the house of the LORD.

13 So the workmen wrought, and the work was perfected by them, and they set the house of God in his state, and strengthened it.

14 And when they had finished it, they brought the rest of the money before the king and Je-hoi'a-da, whereof were made vessels for the house of the LORD, even vessels to minister, and to offer withal, and spoons, and vessels of gold and silver. And they offered burnt offerings in the house of the LORD continually all the days of Je-hoi'a-da.

15 ¶But Je-hoi'a-da waxed old, and was full of days when he died; an hundred and thirty years old was he when he died.

16 And they buried him in the city of David among the kings, because he had done good in Israel, both toward God, and toward his house.

17 Now after the death of Je-hoi'a-da came the princes of Jū'dah, and made obeisance to the king. Then the king hearkened unto them.

18 And they left the house of the LORD God of their fathers, and served groves and idols: and wrath came upon Jū'dah and Jerusalem for this their trespass.

19 Yet he sent prophets to them, to bring them again unto the LORD; and they testified against them: but they would not give ear.

20 And the Spirit of God came upon Zěch-a-rī'ah the son of Je-hoi'a-da the priest, which stood above the people, and said unto them, Thus saith God, Why transgress ye the commandments of the LORD, that ye cannot prosper? be-

13-14. The reference to making **spoons, and vessels of gold and silver** need not be taken as contradictory to II Kings 12:13, ". . . there were not made . . . vessels of gold, or vessels of silver. . . ." The explanation given in the Talmud (*K'thuboth* 106b) is simple enough. "Chronicles refers to a time when there was a surplus which could be used for the provision of vessels, and the account in Kings to a time when there was no surplus" (Slotki, p. 272).

3. His apostasy and death. 24:15-27.

15-16. Jehoiada, the priest, **because he had done good in Israel,** received a burial among the kings of Judah, an honor that was not granted to King Joash (vs. 25).

17-19. The princes . . . made obeisance, evidently a move to flatter the king. **The king hearkened unto them.** The nature of their request is inferred in their action in verse 18. They received royal permission to revert to their old ways, to serve **groves and idols.** The antecedent to **he sent prophets** is **the LORD God.**

20. The spirit of God came upon Zechariah (lit., clothed Zechariah). **Zechariah** was a cousin of Joash (cf. 22:11; II Kgs 11:2).

cause ye have forsaken the LORD, he hath also forsaken you.

21 And they conspired against him, and stoned him with stones at the commandment of the king in the court of the house of the LORD.

22 Thus Jō′ash the king remembered not the kindness which Je-hoi′a-da his father had done to him, but slew his son. And when he died, he said, The LORD look upon it, and require it.

23 ¶And it came to pass at the end of the year, that the host of Syria came up against him: and they came to Jū′dah and Jerusalem, and destroyed all the princes of the people from among the people, and sent all the spoil of them unto the king of Damascus.

24 For the army of the Syrians came with a small company of men, and the LORD delivered a very great host into their hand, because they had forsaken the LORD God of their fathers. So they executed judgment against Jō′ash.

25 And when they were departed from him, (for they left him in great diseases,) his own servants conspired against him for the blood of the sons of Je-hoi′a-da the priest, and slew him on his bed, and he died: and they buried him in the city of David, but they buried him not in the sepulchres of the kings.

26 And these are they that conspired against him; Zā′băd the son of Shĭm′e-āth an Ammonitess, and Je-hŏz′a-băd the son of Shĭm′rĭth a Moabitess.

27 Now concerning his sons, and the greatness of the burdens laid upon him, and the repairing of the house of God, behold, they are written in the story of the book of the kings. And Ăm-a-zī′ah his son reigned in his stead.

CHAPTER 25

ĂM-A-ZĪ′AH was twenty and five years old when he began to reign, and he reigned twenty and nine years in Jerusalem. And his mother's name was Je-hō-ad′dan of Jerusalem.

2 And he did that which was right in the sight of the LORD, but not with a perfect heart.

3 Now it came to pass, when the kingdom was established to him, that he slew his servants that had killed the king his father.

4 But he slew not their children, but did as it is written in the law in the book of Moses, where the LORD commanded, saying, The fathers shall not die for the children, neither shall the children die for the fathers, but every man shall die for his own sin.

5 ¶Moreover Ăm-a-zī′ah gathered Jū′dah together, and made them captains over thousands, and captains over hundreds, according to the houses of their fathers, throughout all Jū′dah and Benjamin: and he numbered them from twenty years old and above, and found them three hundred thousand choice men, able to go forth to war, that could handle spear and shield.

6 He hired also an hundred thousand

21-22. They conspired . . . and stoned him, i.e., Joash's idolatrous peers, the princes, killed Zechariah at the command of the king, probably on the basis of some trumped-up charge (cf. the case of Naboth in I Kgs 21:8-13). **Joash . . . remembered not the kindness of Jehoiada.** Joash owed his life, his throne, and past spiritual successes to his uncle; but that was all disregarded in the murder of his cousin. Jesus referred to Zechariah's murder as the last martyrdom of the Old Testament, thus indicating that in His time Chronicles appeared as the last book of the Hebrew Canon.

23-27. The host of Syria came up against him (for a supplementary account, see II Kgs 12:17-21). The **king of Damascus** was Hazael (II Kgs 12:17). As instruments for the Lord, **they** (the Syrians) **executed judgment against Joash.** While weakened from his **great diseases,** i.e., sickness or suffering caused by wounds, probably inflicted by the Syrians, he was killed in a conspiracy by two of his servants, **Zabad** and **Jehozabad** (cf. 25:3).

F. Amaziah-Ahaz. 25:1-28:27.

25:1-4. See comments on parallel passage (II Kgs 14:1-6) concerning Amaziah's accession to the throne.

5. Amaziah had only **three hundred thousand choice men** in his army, a marked decrease since the time of Asa (14:8) and Jehoshaphat (17:14-18), indicating, perhaps, Judah's disastrous defeat in the days of Joash (24:24).

6-10. Because of his military deficiencies, Amaziah hired **A hundred thousand** mercenaries from the northern tribe,

mighty men of valour out of Israel for an hundred talents of silver.

7 But there came a man of God to him, saying, O king, let not the army of Israel go with thee; for the LORD *is* not with Israel, *to wit, with* all the children of Ē′phra-im.

8 But if thou wilt go, do *it*, be strong for the battle: God shall make thee fall before the enemy: for God hath power to help, and to cast down.

9 And Ăm-a-zī′ah said to the man of God, But what shall we do for the hundred talents which I have given to the army of Israel? And the man of God answered, The LORD is able to give thee much more than this.

10 Then Ăm-a-zī′ah separated them, *to wit,* the army that was come to him out of Ē′phra-im, to go home again: wherefore their anger was greatly kindled against Jū′dah, and they returned home in great anger.

11 And Ăm-a-zī′ah strengthened himself, and led forth his people, and went to the valley of salt, and smote of the children of Sē′ir ten thousand.

12 And *other* ten thousand *left* alive did the children of Jū′dah carry away captive, and brought them unto the top of the rock, and cast them down from the top of the rock, that they all were broken in pieces.

13 But the soldiers of the army which Ăm-a-zī′ah sent back, that they should not go with him to battle, fell upon the cities of Jū′dah, from Sa-mā′rĭ-a even unto Bĕth-hō′ron, and smote three thousand of them, and took much spoil.

14 ¶Now it came to pass, after that Ăm-a-zī′ah was come from the slaughter of the Edomites, that he brought the gods of the children of Sē′ir, and set them up *to be* his gods, and bowed down himself before them, and burned incense unto them.

15 Wherefore the anger of the LORD was kindled against Ăm-a-zī′ah, and he sent unto him a prophet, which said unto him, Why hast thou sought after the gods of the people, which could not deliver their own people out of thine hand?

16 And it came to pass, as he talked with him, that *the* king said unto him, Art thou made of the king's counsel? forbear; why shouldest thou be smitten? Then the prophet forbare, and said, I know that God hath determined to destroy thee, because thou hast done this, and hast not hearkened unto my counsel.

17 ¶Then Ăm-a-zi′ah king of Jū′dah took advice, and sent to Jō′ăsh, the son of Je-hō′a-hăz, the son of Jehu, king of Israel, saying, Come, let us see one another in the face.

18 And Jō′ăsh king of Israel sent to Ăm-a-zī′ah king of Jū′dah, saying, The thistle that *was* in Lebanon sent to the cedar that *was* in Lebanon, saying, Give thy daughter to my son to wife: and there passed by a wild beast that *was* in Lebanon, and trode down the thistle.

19 Thou sayest, Lo, thou hast smitten the Edomites; and thine heart lifteth thee up to boast: abide now at home;

Ephraim. However, an unidentified **man of God** instructed him to send the mercenaries home; for God could not bless Amaziah with them present since they were from Israel and the LORD was **not with Israel.** Though he had already paid the mercenaries and had risked the possibility of humiliating Ephraim, who might seek retaliation, he obeyed the word of the Lord.

11-13. The **valley of salt** is probably the valley south of the Dead Sea. **Seir** is a synonym of Edom. For **the rock,** see note on "Selah" in II Kings 14:7. The mercenaries of Ephraim did retaliate. Instead of returning directly home, they attacked the cities of Judah, killing three thousand men.

14-16. He brought the gods . . . of Seir . . . to be his gods. Amaziah's action was unsurpassably senseless. His own defeat of Edom had proved these gods powerless to save even their own worshipers. Therefore, Amaziah stood condemned by the unnamed prophet.

17-28. For a discussion of Amaziah's senseless pride leading him into a battle with Joash of Israel and a summary of Amaziah's reign, see comments already given on the parallel passage in II Kings 14:8-20.

why shouldest thou meddle to *thine* hurt, that thou shouldest fall, *even* thou, and Jū'dah with thee?

20 But Ăm-a-zī'ah would not hear: for it *came* of God, that he might deliver them into the hand *of their enemies,* because they sought after the gods of Edom.

21 So Jō'ash the king of Israel went up; and they saw one another in the face, *both* he and Ăm-a-zī'ah king of Jū'dah, at Bĕth-shē'mesh, which *belongeth* to Jū'dah.

22 And Jū'dah was put to the worse before Israel, and they fled every man to his tent.

23 And Jō'ash the king of Israel took Ăm-a-zī'ah king of Jū'dah, the son of Jō'ash, the son of Je-hō'a-hăz, at Bĕth-shē'mesh, and brought him to Jerusalem, and brake down the wall of Jerusalem from the gate of Ē'phra-im to the corner gate, four hundred cubits.

24 And *he took* all the gold and the silver, and all the vessels that were found in the house of God with Ō'bed-ē'dom, and the treasures of the king's house, the hostages also, and returned to Sa-mâ'rĭ-a.

25 ¶And Ăm-a-zī'ah the son of Jō'ash king of Jū'dah lived after the death of Jō'ash son of Je-hō'a-hăz king of Israel fifteen years.

26 Now the rest of the acts of Ăm-a-zī'ah, first and last, behold, *are* they not written in the book of the kings of Jū'dah and Israel?

27 Now after the time that Ăm-a-zī'ah did turn away from following the LORD they made a conspiracy against him in Jerusalem; and he fled to Lā'chĭsh: but they sent to Lā'chĭsh after him, and slew him there.

28 And they brought him upon horses, and buried him with his fathers in the city of Jū'dah.

CHAPTER 26

THEN all the people of Jū'dah took Uz-zī'ah, who *was* sixteen years old, and made him king in the room of his father Ăm-a-zī'ah.

2 He built Ē'lŏth, and restored it to Jū'dah, after that the king slept with his fathers.

3 Sixteen years old *was* Uz-zī'ah when he began to reign, and he reigned fifty and two years in Jerusalem. His mother's name also *was* Jĕc-o-lī'ah of Jerusalem.

4 And he did *that which was* right in the sight of the LORD, according to all that his father Ăm-a-zī'ah did.

5 And he sought God in the days of Zĕch-a-rī'ah, who had understanding in the visions of God: and as long as he sought the LORD, God made him to prosper.

6 And he went forth and warred against the Philistines, and brake down the wall of Gath, and the wall of Jăb'neh, and the wall of Ăsh'dŏd, and built cities about Ăsh'dod, and among the Philistines.

7 And God helped him against the Philistines, and against the Arabians that dwelt in Gûr-bā'al, and the Me-hū'nĭmś.

26:1-5. Uzziah is Azariah in II Kings, and in I Chronicles 3:12 (for notes on his accession, see II Kings 15:1-7). All that is known of **Zechariah** is stated here. He is not to be confused with the book that bears his name. **As long as he sought the LORD, God made him to prosper.** Uzziah's reign is unfortunately similar to those of Asa, Joash, and Amaziah. All had good beginnings; but when they became preoccupied with their success and prosperity, instead of giving God the glory, they sinned against Him.

6-8. The years in which Uzziah's reign coincided with Jeroboam II of Israel (ca. 790-750 B.C.) were opportune ones because while Jeroboam II was preoccupied with defeating the Syrians and restoring his borders, Uzziah was free to extend his borders westward into Philistine territory. For the **Mehunim,** see note on 20:1. The **gifts** Uzziah received and the spread of **his name** are reminiscent of the days of Jehoshaphat (17:10-11).

8 And the Ammonites gave gifts to Uz-zī′ah: and his name spread abroad *even* to the entering in of Egypt; for he strengthened *himself* exceedingly.

9 Moreover Uz-zī′ah built towers in Jerusalem at the corner gate, and at the valley gate, and at the turning *of the wall*, and fortified them.

10 Also he built towers in the desert, and digged many wells: for he had much cattle, both in the low country, and in the plains: husbandmen *also*, and vine dressers in the mountains, and in Carmel: for he loved husbandry.

11 ¶Moreover Uz-zī′ah had a host of fighting men, that went out to war by bands, according to the number of their account by the hand of Je-ī′el the scribe and Mā′a-sē′iah the ruler, under the hand of Hăn-a-nī′ah, *one* of the king's captains.

12 The whole number of the chief of the fathers of the mighty men of valour *were* two thousand and six hundred.

13 And under their hand *was* an army, three hundred thousand and seven thousand and five hundred, that made war with mighty power, to help the king against the enemy.

14 And Uz-zī′ah prepared for them throughout all the host shields, and spears, and helmets, and habergeons, and bows, and slings *to cast* stones.

15 And he made in Jerusalem engines, invented by cunning men, to be on the towers and upon the bulwarks, to shoot arrows and great stones withal. And his name spread far abroad; for he was marvellously helped, till he was strong.

16 ¶But when he was strong, his heart was lifted up to *his* destruction: for he transgressed against the LORD his God, and went into the temple of the LORD to burn incense upon the altar of incense.

17 And Ăz-a-rī′ah the priest went in after him, and with him fourscore priests of the LORD, *that were* valiant men:

18 And they withstood Uz-zī′ah the king and said unto him, It appertaineth not unto thee, Uz-zī′ah, to burn incense unto the LORD, but to the priests the sons of Aaron, that are consecrated to burn incense: go out of the sanctuary; for thou hast trespassed; neither *shall it be* for thine honour from the LORD God.

19 Then Uz-zī′ah was wroth, and *had* a censer in his hand to burn incense: and while he was wroth with the priests, the leprosy even rose up in his forehead before the priests in the house of the LORD, from beside the incense altar.

20 And Ăz-a-rī′ah the chief priest, and all the priests, looked upon him, and, behold, he *was* leprous in his forehead, and they thrust him out from thence; yea, himself hasted also to go out, because the LORD had smitten him.

21 And Uz-zī′ah the king was a leper unto the day of his death, and dwelt in a several house, *being* a leper; for he was cut off from the house of the LORD: and

9-11. Uzziah provided for his cattle by building **towers** to defend them from raiding Bedouins. He **digged many wells** (lit., hewed out many cisterns) for the collecting and storage of rain. **Carmel** should probably be rendered "fruitful field."

12-15. Compared to the armies of past kings, Uzziah's was not large, but well equipped. **Habergeons** might be rendered "coats of mail." The **engines** were war machines used for launching arrows and stones, the latest in military equipment. **He was marvelously helped,** i.e., by God (cf. vss. 5, 7).

16. His heart was lifted up. Pride in his strength led to further sin, burning **incense upon the altar of incense** in the Temple, a function reserved exclusively for the priests (cf. vs. 18; Ex 30:7-8). He was apparently dissatisfied with his role as mere king and desired to be a divine king, similar to contemporary pagan priest-kings; but God had reserved that unique position for the Lord Jesus Christ, our Priest-King (cf. Whitcomb, p. 107).

17-21. Azariah the priest (not mentioned elsewhere) and eighty other priests restrained and condemned the king, succeeding only in infuriating him. Whereupon, he was smitten with leprosy (cf. Miriam's divine punishment, Num 12:1ff.). **A leper unto the day of his death,** he lived in a **several house,** i.e., a separate house, somewhat quarantined according to the Law (Lev 13:45-46). Uzziah remained a royal figurehead, but his son **Jotham** was elevated to carry out the royal duties as coregent his last eleven years (II Kgs 15:5).

Jŏ'tham his son *was* over the king's house, judging the people of the land.

22 ¶Now the rest of the acts of Uz-zī'ah, first and last, did Isaiah the prophet, the son of Amoz, write.

23 So Uz-zī'ah slept with his fathers, and they buried him with his fathers in the field of the burial which *belonged* to the kings; for they said, He *is* a leper: and Jŏ'tham his son reigned in his stead.

CHAPTER 27

JŎ'THAM *was* twenty and five years old when he began to reign, and he reigned sixteen years in Jerusalem. His mother's name also *was* Je-rū'shah, the daughter of Zā'dŏk.

2 And he did *that which was* right in the sight of the LORD, according to all that his father Uz-zī'ah did: howbeit he entered not into the temple of the LORD. And the people did yet corruptly.

3 He built the high gate of the house of the LORD, and on the wall of Ō'phĕl he built much.

4 Moreover he built cities in the mountains of Jū'dah, and in the forests he built castles and towers.

5 He fought also with the king of the Ammonites, and prevailed against them. And the children of Ammon gave him the same year an hundred talents of silver, and ten thousand measures of wheat, and ten thousand of barley. So much did the children of Ammon pay unto him, both the second year, and the third.

6 So Jŏ'tham became mighty, because he prepared his ways before the LORD his God.

7 ¶Now the rest of the acts of Jŏ'-tham, and all his wars, and his ways, lo, they *are* written in the book of the kings of Israel and Jū'dah.

8 He was five and twenty years old when he began to reign, and reigned sixteen years in Jerusalem.

9 And Jŏ'tham slept with his fathers, and they buried him in the city of David: and Ahaz his son reigned in his stead.

CHAPTER 28

AHAZ *was* twenty years old when he began to reign, and he reigned sixteen years in Jerusalem: but he did not *that which was* right in the sight of the LORD, like David his father:

2 For he walked in the ways of the kings of Israel, and made also molten images for Bā'al-ĭm.

3 Moreover he burnt incense in the valley of the son of Hĭn'nom, and burnt his children in the fire, after the abominations of the heathen whom the LORD had cast out before the children of Israel.

4 He sacrificed also and burnt incense in the high places, and on the hills, and under every green tree.

5 Wherefore the LORD his God delivered him into the hand of the king of Syria; and they smote him, and carried away a great multitude of them captives, and brought *them* to Damascus. And he was also delivered into the hand of the king of Israel, who smote him with a great slaughter.

22-23. Isaiah was the writing prophet of the book bearing his name (cf. Isa 6:1). Even in Uzziah's death the stigma of his leprosy remained; and he was deprived the privilege of burial in the **sepulchers of the kings** (21:20).

27:1-2. Jotham . . . reigned sixteen years in Jerusalem (for notes on his accession and coregency with Uzziah, see II Kgs 15:32-33). **He did . . . right,** as his father had done at the first, imitating his virtues, not his faults. **He entered not into the temple.** This point is stressed, indicating that Jotham continued in divine favor in contrast to his father who had forfeited it by his presumptuous action (26:16).

3-4. He built (i.e., rebuilt or restored) **the high gate** situated on the north side of the Temple (cf. 23:20). **Ophel** (lit., mound or hill) was a spur on the hill south of the Temple and the northern part of David's original city (cf. 33:14). The **castles and towers** were for defense.

5-6. Apparently, the Ammonites had rebelled and had ceased paying tribute (cf. 26:8). Therefore, Jotham fought the Ammonites, bringing them once again under subjection and causing them to pay tribute in silver and grain for at least three years. His success is credited to his obedience to his God.

7-9. All his wars include his wars with the Ammonites, Pekah of Israel and Rezin of Syria (cf. notes on summary of Jotham's reign in II Kgs 15:36-38).

28:1-4. Ahaz . . . reigned sixteen years in Jerusalem. For notes on the accession and a general summary of this wicked king who was characteristic of the worst of Israel's kings, see parallel passage in II Kings 16:4. **The valley of the son of Hinnom.** The Hebrew name for this site is, more precisely, *Gē'-ben-hinōm* which was later shortened to Gē'-hinōm, from which Gehenna, the New Testament word for eternal punishment, is derived.

5-8. These verses are supplementary to II Kings 16:5 and Isaiah 7-8. As punishment for his wickedness, God allowed Ahaz to be subjected to Pekah of Israel and Rezin of Syria who apparently wished for him to join their move to resist Assyria. When Ahaz refused, Judah was invaded but not overcome, though Pekah killed **A hundred and twenty thousand in one day.** Ahaz's own son, **Maaseiah,** and **Elkanah that was next to**

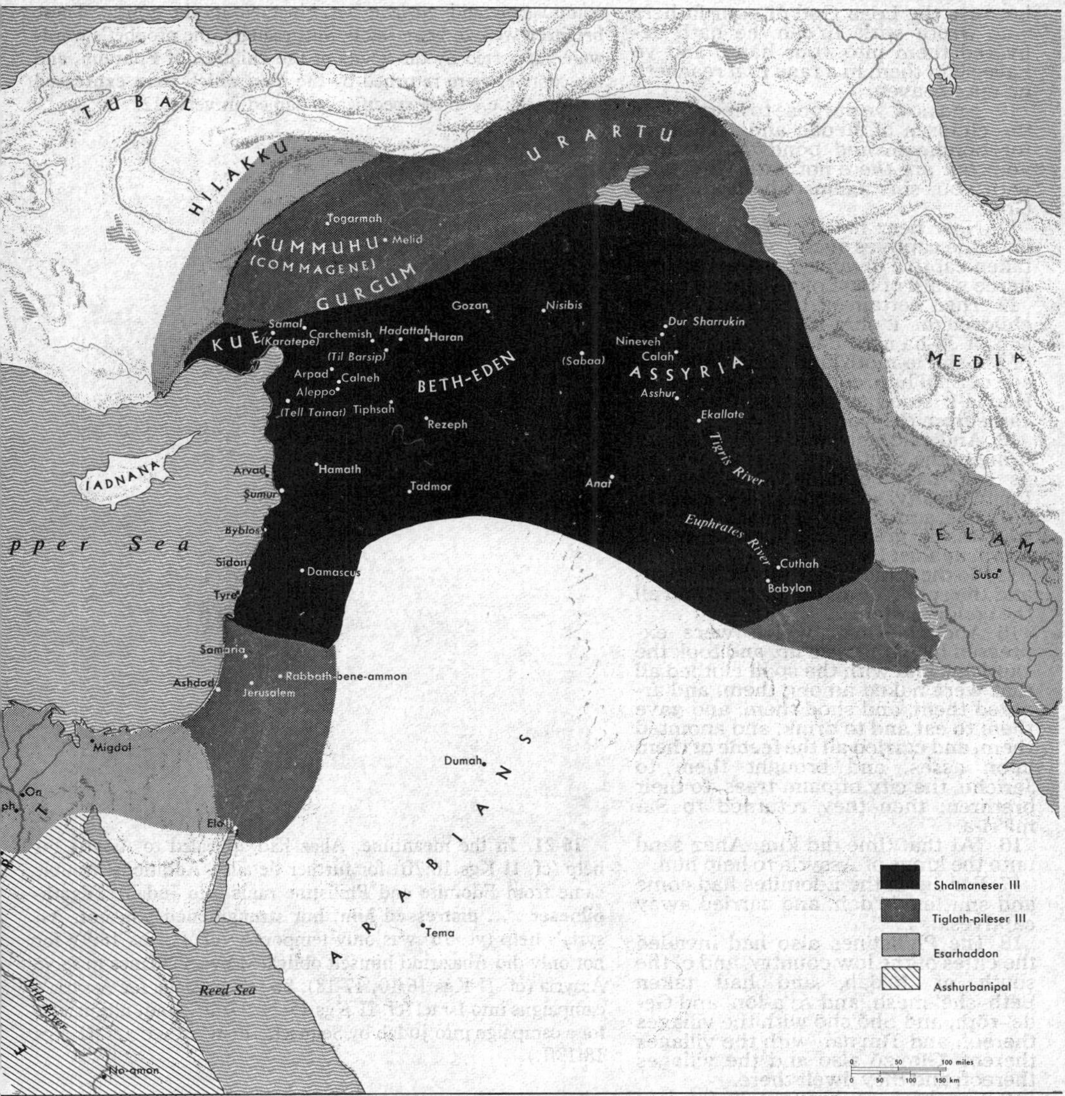
TUBAL
HILAKKU
URARTU
Togarmah
KUMMUHU
(COMMAGENE)
Melid
GURGUM
Gozan
Nisibis
Dur Sharrukin
Samal
KUE
(Karatepe)
Carchemish
Hadattah
Haran
(Til Barsip)
Nineveh
Calah
(Sabaa)
MEDIA
Arpad
Calneh
Aleppo
BETH-EDEN
ASSYRIA
Asshur
(Tell Tainat)
Tiphsah
Rezeph
Ekallate
Tigris River
IADNANA
Arvad
Hamath
Şumur
Tadmor
Anat
Euphrates River
Byblos
ELAM
pper Sea
Sidon
Damascus
Cuthah
Susa
Babylon
Tyre
Samaria
Rabbath-bene-ammon
Ashdod
Jerusalem
Migdol
ARABIANS
Dumah
On
Elath
Tema
Reed Sea
Nile River
No-amon
Shalmaneser III
Tiglath-pileser III
Esarhaddon
Asshurbanipal
0 50 100 miles
0 50 100 150 km

The Rise of the Kingdom of Assyria

6 For Pē'kah the son of Rĕm-a-lī'ah
slew in Jū'dah an hundred and twenty
thousand in one day, *which were* all valiant men; because they had forsaken
the LORD God of their fathers.
7 And Zĭch'rī, a mighty man of Ē-
phra'im, slew Mā'a-sē'iah the king's
son, and Ăz'ri-kam the governor of the
house, and Ĕl'kā-nah *that was* next to
the king.
8 And the children of Israel carried
away captive of their brethren two
hundred thousand, women, sons, and
daughters, and took also away much
spoil from them, and brought the spoil
to Sa-mâ'rĭ-a.
9 But a prophet of the LORD was
there, whose name *was* O'ded: and he
went out before the host that came to
Sa-mâ'rĭ-a, and said unto them, Behold,

the king, i.e., second in authority, was killed. Also **two hundred thousand** were taken captive.

9-15. Oded, the prophet in Samaria who is otherwise unknown, met Pekah's army returning with captives from Judah to deliver a message from God. Israel had been an instrument of God to punish sinning Judah. Now she dared not go beyond His

because the LORD God of your fathers was wroth with Jū'dah, he hath delivered them into your hand, and ye have slain them in a rage *that* reacheth up unto heaven.

10 And now ye purpose to keep under the children of Jū'dah and Jerusalem for bondmen, and bondwomen unto you: *but are there* not with you, even with you, sins against the LORD your God?

11 Now hear me therefore, and deliver the captives again, which ye have taken captive of your brethren: for the fierce wrath of the LORD *is* upon you.

12 Then certain of the heads of the children of Ē'phra-im, Ăz-a-rī'ah the son of Jo-ha'nan, Ber-e-chi'ah the son of Me-shĭl'le-mŏth, and Jē'hĭz-kī'ah the son of Shăl'lum, and Am'ā-sa the son of Hăd'la-ī, stood up against them that came from the war,

13 And said unto them, Ye shall not bring in the captives hither: for whereas we have offended against the LORD *already,* ye intend to add *more* to our sins and to our trespass: for our trespass is great, and *there is* fierce wrath against Israel.

14 So the armed men left the captives and the spoil before the princes and all the congregation.

15 And the men which were expressed by name rose up, and took the captives, and with the spoil clothed all that were naked among them, and arrayed them, and shod them, and gave them to eat and to drink, and anointed them, and carried all the feeble of them upon asses, and brought them to Jericho, the city of palm trees, to their brethren: then they returned to Samâ'rī-a.

16 ¶At that time did king Ahaz send unto the kings of Assyria to help him.

17 For again the Edomites had come and smitten Jū'dah, and carried away captives.

18 The Philistines also had invaded the cities of the low country, and of the south of Jū'dah, and had taken Bĕth-shĕ'-mesh, and Ăj'a-lŏn, and Ge-de'-rŏth, and Shō'chō with the villages thereof, and Tĭm'nah with the villages thereof, Gĭm'zō also and the villages thereof: and they dwelt there.

19 For the LORD brought Jū'dah low because of Ahaz king of Israel; for he made Jū'dah naked, and transgressed sore against the LORD.

20 And Tĭl'găth-pĭl-nē'ser king of Assyria came unto him, and distressed him, but strengthened him not.

21 For Ahaz took away a portion *out* of the house of the LORD, and *out* of the house of the king, and of the princes, and gave *it* unto the king of Assyria: but he helped him not.

22 And in the time of his distress did he trespass yet more against the LORD: this *is that* king Ahaz.

23 For he sacrificed unto the gods of Damascus, which smote him: and he said, Because the gods of the kings of Syria help them, *therefore* will I sacrifice to them, that they may help me. But they were the ruin of him, and of all Israel.

commission and enslave her kinsmen in the south. These **brethren** were to be released. Surprisingly, the prophet's words were supported by the **heads of the children of Ephraim,** and the captives were returned by **the men which were expressed by name,** i.e., those specifically named in verse 12.

16-21. In the meantime, Ahaz had appealed to Assyria for help (cf. II Kgs 16:7ff. for further details). Additional trouble came from Edomite and Philistine raids into Judah. **Tilgath-pilneser . . . distressed him, but strengthened him not.** Assyria's **help** (vs. 16) was only temporary (cf. II Kgs 16:9); for not only did Ahaz find himself obligated by an alliance to serve Assyria (cf. II Kgs 16:10, 17-18), he set the stage for Assyria's campaigns into Israel (cf. II Kgs 15:29; 17:6ff.) and, ultimately, for a campaign into Judah by Sennacherib in 701 B.C. (cf. II Kgs 18:13ff.).

22-25. These verses appear to be parenthetical, summarizing Ahaz's religious activities. **His distress** did not bring him to repentance, but in hardness of heart he sinned further against the Lord. **He sacrificed unto the gods of Damascus.** This probably refers to the time when he was under attack by the Syrians and was not in connection with II Kings 16:10 (see note *ad loc*). He pillaged the **vessels of the house of God** (cf. 29:19; II Kgs 16:17-18). He also **shut up the doors of the house of the LORD.** In view of his action in II Kings 16:10-16, he may not

24 And Ahaz gathered together the vessels of the house of God, and cut in pieces the vessels of the house of God, and shut up the doors of the house of the LORD, and he made him altars in every corner of Jerusalem.

25 And in every several city of Jū′dah he made high places to burn incense unto other gods, and provoked to anger the LORD God of his fathers.

26 ¶Now the rest of his acts and of all his ways, first and last, behold, they are written in the book of the kings of Jū′-dah and Israel.

27 And Ahaz slept with his fathers, and they buried him in the city, even in Jerusalem: but they brought him not into the sepulchres of the kings of Israel: and Hĕz-e-kī′ah his son reigned in his stead.

CHAPTER 29

HĔZ-E-KĪ′AH began to reign when he was five and twenty years old, and he reigned nine and twenty years in Jerusalem. And his mother's name was A-bī′jah, the daughter of Zĕch-a-rī′ah.

2 And he did that which was right in the sight of the LORD, according to all that David his father had done.

3 ¶He in the first year of his reign, in the first month, opened the doors of the house of the LORD, and repaired them.

4 And he brought in the priests and the Lē′vītes, and gathered them together into the east street,

5 And said unto them, Hear me, ye Lē′vītes, sanctify now yourselves, and sanctify the house of the LORD God of your fathers, and carry forth the filthiness out of the holy place.

6 For our fathers have trespassed, and done that which was evil in the eyes of the LORD our God, and have forsaken him, and have turned away their faces from the habitation of the LORD, and turned their backs.

7 Also they have shut up the doors of the porch, and put out the lamps, and have not burned incense nor offered burnt offerings in the holy place unto the God of Israel.

8 Wherefore the wrath of the LORD was upon Jū′dah and Jerusalem, and he hath delivered them to trouble, to astonishment, and to hissing, as ye see with your eyes.

9 For, lo, our fathers have fallen by the sword, and our sons and our daughters and our wives are in captivity for this.

10 Now it is in mine heart to make a covenant with the LORD God of Israel, that his fierce wrath may turn away from us.

11 My sons, be not now negligent: for the LORD hath chosen you to stand before him, to serve him, and that ye should minister unto him, and burn incense.

12 ¶Then the Lē′vītes arose, Mā′hăth the son of A-măs′a-ī, and Jō′el the son of Ăz-a-rī′ah; and of the sons of the Kō′hăth-ītes: and of the sons of Me-râ′rī, Kish the son of Ăb′dī, and Ăz-a-rī′ah the son

have shut the door by command, necessarily, but his syncretistic worship led to the neglect of true worship and the actual abandonment of the Temple because of the rival altar there.

26-27. Ahaz was so utterly characterized by wickedness that in death he was not awarded a royal burial in the **sepulchers of the kings of Israel.**

G. Hezekiah. 29:1-32:33.

1. The great revival. 29:1-36.

29:1-2. On Hezekiah's accession and biographical summary, compare II Kings 18:1-3. His righteous reign, in contrast to his father's extremely wicked one, is testimony to the grace of God in his life.

3-4. While Kings concentrates primarily on the political struggles of Hezekiah, Chronicles deals primarily on the positive aspects of his religious reforms. **The first year . . . first month** indicates that he immediately endeavored to re-establish the true worship of Jehovah. **He . . . opened the doors** (cf. vs. 7; 28:24). The **east street** was the open space to the east of the tabernacle.

5-11. Hezekiah, sounding more like a prophet than a king, instructed the priests and Levites in the action they were to take to initiate the necessary reform. **Carry forth the filthiness** (Heb *nidah*), i.e., impurity, refers primarily to the accumulation of debris within the Temple; but it may also refer to the pollution of the sacred place due to the idolatry practiced there. **The wrath of the LORD was upon Judah** alludes to the war with Syria and Ephraim (28:5-6) and the resultant demanding alliance with Assyria (28:16). Though Ephraim had returned her captives (28:15), Judah's other enemies (28:5, 8, 17) had not followed suit; and some of Judah's population were still **in captivity.**

12-19. All three clans (**Kohathites, Merari,** and **Gershonites**) of the Levites had representatives overseeing the cleansing of the Temple, as well as sons of **Asaph, Heman,** and **Jeduthun,** the heads of the temple singers (cf. I Chr 25). Only the **priests** entered the Temple to bring out **all the uncleanness**

of Je-hăl′e-lel: and of the Ger′shon-ītes; Jŏ′ah the son of Zimmah, and Eden the son of Jŏ′ah:

13 And of the sons of Ĕ-liz′ă-phan; Shĭm′rī, and Je-ī′el: and of the sons of Ā′săph; Zĕch-a-rī′ah, and Măt-ta-nī′ah:

14 And of the sons of Hē′măn; Je-hī′el, and Shĭm′e-ī: and of the sons of Jed′ū-thun; Shem-a-i′ah, and Ŭz′zī-el.

15 And they gathered their brethren, and sanctified themselves, and came, according to the commandment of the king, by the words of the LORD, to cleanse the house of the LORD.

16 And the priests went into the inner part of the house of the LORD, to cleanse it, and brought out all the uncleanness that they found in the temple of the LORD into the court of the house of the LORD. And the Lē′vītes took it, to carry it out abroad into the brook Kidron.

17 Now they began on the first day of the first month to sanctify, and on the eighth day of the month came they to the porch of the LORD: so they sanctified the house of the LORD in eight days; and in the sixteenth day of the first month they made an end.

18 Then they went in to Hĕz-e-kī′ah the king, and said, We have cleansed all the house of the LORD, and the altar of burnt offering, with all the vessels thereof, and the shewbread table, with all the vessels thereof.

19 Moreover all the vessels, which king Ahaz in his reign did cast away in his transgression, have we prepared and sanctified, and, behold, they are before the altar of the LORD.

20 ¶Then Hĕz-e-kī′ah the king rose early, and gathered the rulers of the city, and went up to the house of the LORD.

21 And they brought seven bullocks, and seven rams, and seven lambs, and seven he goats, for a sin offering for the kingdom, and for the sanctuary, and for Jū′dah. And he commanded the priests the sons of Aaron to offer them on the altar of the LORD.

22 So they killed the bullocks, and the priests received the blood, and sprinkled it on the altar: likewise, when they had killed the rams, they sprinkled the blood upon the altar: they killed also the lambs, and they sprinkled the blood upon the altar.

23 And they brought forth the he goats for the sin offering before the king and the congregation; and they laid their hands upon them:

24 And the priests killed them, and they made reconciliation with their blood upon the altar, to make an atonement for all Israel: for the king commanded that the burnt offering and the sin offering should be made for all Israel.

25 And he set the Lē′vītes in the house of the LORD with cymbals, with psalteries, and with harps, according to the commandment of David, and of Gad the king's seer, and Nā′than the prophet: for so was the commandment of the LORD by his prophets.

26 And the Lē′vītes stood with the instruments of David, and the priests with the trumpets.

(cf. vs. 5), while the **Levites** carried it to **the brook Kidron,** a stream east of Jerusalem (cf. 15:16). The **first day** to the **eighth day** was the period for clearing the Temple of debris; on the **sixteenth day** they ceased the period of cleansing the Temple. When the vessels discarded by Ahaz (cf. 28:24; II Kgs 16:17) had been made ready, the Levites and priests reported to Hezekiah.

20-22. The remainder of the chapter concerns the appropriate sacrifices that were offered. **A sin offering** (cf. Lev 4) was made for **the kingdom,** probably a reference to the royal household, **the sanctuary,** i.e., the Temple, and **Judah,** the southern kingdom.

23-24. They laid their hands upon them, i.e., on the **he goats,** denoting the animals as the typical substitute for themselves (cf. 4:1-5:13). In addition to the sin offering, the **burnt offering** (cf. Lev 1:3-17; 6:8-13) was offered. Both offerings were for **all Israel** (cf. Lev 4:13). Since Samaria, the capital of the northern kingdom, had already fallen to Assyria in 722 B.C., the reference to **Israel** may reflect Hezekiah's anticipation of drawing the remnant people of the north into his revival (cf. 30:1ff.).

25-29. The temple musicians, which appeared to be a Davidic institution in I Chronicles 25, are rightly shown here to be divinely instituted through the commandment of two of God's prophets, **Gad** (cf. I Sam 22:5) and **Nathan** (II Sam 12:1).

27 And Hĕz-e-kī′ah commanded to offer the burnt offering upon the altar. And when the burnt offering began, the song of the Lord began *also* with the trumpets, and with the instruments *ordained* by David king of Israel.

28 And all the congregation worshipped, and the singers sang, and the trumpeters sounded: *and* all *this continued* until the burnt offering was finished.

29 And when they had made an end of offering, the king and all that were present with him bowed themselves, and worshipped.

30 Moreover Hĕz-e-kī′ah the king and the princes commanded the Lē′vītes to sing praise unto the Lord with the words of David, and of Ā′sȧph the seer. And they sang praises with gladness, and they bowed their heads and worshipped.

31 Then Hĕz-e-kī′ah answered and said, Now ye have consecrated yourselves unto the Lord, come near and bring sacrifices and thank offerings into the house of the Lord. And the congregation brought in sacrifices and thank offerings; and as many as were of a free heart burnt offerings.

32 And the number of the burnt offerings, which the congregation brought, was threescore and ten bullocks, an hundred rams, *and* two hundred lambs: all these *were* for a burnt offering to the Lord.

33 And the consecrated things *were* six hundred oxen and three thousand sheep.

34 But the priests were too few, so that they could not flay all the burnt offerings: wherefore their brethren the Lē′vītes did help them, till the work was ended, and until the *other* priests had sanctified themselves: for the Lē′vītes *were* more upright in heart to sanctify themselves than the priests.

35 And also the burnt offerings *were* in abundance, with the fat of the peace offerings, and the drink offerings for *every* burnt offering. So the service of the house of the Lord was set in order.

36 And Hĕz-e-kī′ah rejoiced, and all the people, that God had prepared the people: for the thing was *done* suddenly.

CHAPTER 30

AND Hĕz-e-kī′ah sent to all Israel and Jū′dah, and wrote letters also to Ē′phra-im and Ma-năs′seh, that they should come to the house of the Lord at Jerusalem, to keep the passover unto the Lord God of Israel.

2 For the king had taken counsel, and his princes, and all the congregation in Jerusalem, to keep the passover in the second month.

3 For they could not keep it at that time, because the priests had not sanctified themselves sufficiently, neither had the people gathered themselves together to Jerusalem.

4 And the thing pleased the king and all the congregation.

5 So they established a decree to make proclamation throughout all

30-33. The Levites sang **praise . . . with the words of David, and of Asaph,** indicating the Psalms were being collected and used in the worship of Jehovah. Participation in worship was enthusiastic. **As many as were of a free heart burnt offerings,** i.e., the people responded willingly and spontaneously.

34-36. The priests were too few. Originally, it had been the worshiper's responsibility to ". . . flay the burnt offering . . ." (Lev 1:5-6). The priests, who had assumed the responsibility, were too few, probably because Urijah, the priest, had cooperated with Ahaz (cf. II Kgs 16:10-16) and had undoubtedly drawn many additional priests, who were now reluctant to assist Hezekiah, into idolatry.

2. Observance of the Passover. 30:1-31:1.

30:1. Hezekiah saw the time as a golden opportunity to reunite the tribes in a religious revival, especially since Samaria had fallen to the Assyrians (cf. II Kgs 17:6) and her deported king, Hoshea, would be no threat to such an attempt. **Ephraim** and **Manasseh,** two major tribes in the north, received special attention in the invitation.

2-4. The Passover was to be observed in the first month (Ex 12); but here it was observed **in the second month,** a delay of one month as prescribed by Mosaic law (Num 9:10-11) for such extenuating circumstances. Those circumstances mentioned here are: (1) **The priests had not sanctified themselves sufficiently;** and (2) the people had not yet arrived at Jerusalem.

5. The invitation was extended to all Israelites **from Beersheba even to Dan,** the traditional boundaries of Israel. **They**

843

Israel, from Be'er-she'ba even to Dan, that they should come to keep the passover unto the LORD God of Israel at Jerusalem: for they had not done *it* of a long *time in such sort* as it was written.

6 So the posts went with the letters from the king and his princes throughout all Israel and Jū'dah, and according to the commandment of the king, saying, Ye children of Israel, turn again unto the LORD God of Abraham, Isaac, and Israel, and he will return to the remnant of you, that are escaped out of the hand of the kings of Assyria.

7 And be not ye like your fathers, and like your brethren, which trespassed against the LORD God of their fathers, *who* therefore gave them up to desolation, as ye see.

8 Now be ye not stiffnecked, as your fathers *were, but* yield yourselves unto the LORD, and enter into his sanctuary, which he hath sanctified for ever: and serve the LORD your God, that the fierceness of his wrath may turn away from you.

9 For if ye turn again unto the LORD, your brethren and your children *shall find* compassion before them that lead them captive, so that they shall come again into this land: for the LORD your God *is* gracious and merciful, and will not turn away *his* face from you, if ye return unto him.

10 So the posts passed from city to city through the country of Ē'phra-im and Ma-năs'seh even unto Zĕb'u-lun: but they laughed them to scorn, and mocked them.

11 Nevertheless divers of Asher and Ma-năs'seh and of Zĕb'u-lun humbled themselves, and came to Jerusalem.

12 Also in Jū'dah the hand of God was to give them one heart to do the commandment of the king and of the princes, by the word of the LORD.

13 ¶And there assembled at Jerusalem much people to keep the feast of unleavened bread in the second month, a very great congregation.

14 And they arose and took away the altars that *were* in Jerusalem, and all the altars for incense took they away, and cast *them* into the brook Kidron.

15 Then they killed the passover on the fourteenth *day* of the second month: and the priests and the Lē'vītes were ashamed, and sanctified themselves, and brought in the burnt offerings into the house of the LORD.

16 And they stood in their place after their manner, according to the law of Moses the man of God: the priests sprinkled the blood, *which they received* of the hand of the Lē'vītes.

17 For *there were* many in the congregation that were not sanctified: therefore the Lē'vītes had the charge of the killing of the passovers for every one *that was* not clean, to sanctify *them* unto the LORD.

18 For a multitude of the people, *even* many of Ē'phra-im, and Ma-năs'seh, Ĭs'sa-char, and Zĕb'u-lun, had not cleansed themselves, yet did they eat the passover otherwise than it was written. But Hĕz-e-kī'ah prayed for

had not done it (kept the Passover) **of a long time,** or "in great numbers" (NASB). With the division of the monarchy in 931 B.C., the northern tribes no longer worshiped in Jerusalem; and of the southern tribes, probably only the pious minority actually kept the Passover.

6-9. The posts (lit., the runners) i.e., the couriers, went **throughout all Israel and Judah** carrying Hezekiah's message, which was more characteristic of a prophet than a king. Addressing the **remnant** who had escaped Assyrian captivity, he warns them to avoid the sins of their fathers and **be ye not stiffnecked,** a Mosaic expression (cf. Deut 9:6; 10:16) descriptive of stubborn disobedience.

10-12. The northern tribes of Asher, Naphtali, and Dan probably had been subdued, first by Syria, and then by Assyria, leaving **Zebulun** the extreme northern point at this time. Though many made mockery of Hezekiah's plea, many from the north responded.

13-16. As the priests had cleansed the Temple, the people cleansed the city of idolatrous altars in like manner. **They killed the passover,** which historically looked back to deliverance from Egypt (Ex 12:27) and prophetically and typically looked ahead to Christ, the substitutionary Lamb of God (I Cor 5:7). The **priests and Levites were ashamed** because the people were more responsive and zealous than they were. By their failure to sanctify themselves, they were responsible for the one month delay of the Passover.

17-20. Since many people had not sanctified themselves, the Levites were made responsible for killing the Passover lambs, a responsibility of the individual worshiper (cf. Ex 12:6). Those who were not cleansed were primarily people from the northern tribes who had responded immediately to Hezekiah's invitation and had not had time to prepare themselves. Their presence at Jerusalem was evidence enough that their hearts were right before God. Thus, Hezekiah prayed, **The good LORD pardon every one.**

them, saying, The good LORD pardon every one

19 *That* prepareth his heart to seek God, the LORD God of his fathers, though *he be* not *cleansed* according to the purification of the sanctuary.

20 And the LORD hearkened to Hĕz-e-kī′ah, and healed the people.

21 And the children of Israel that were present at Jerusalem, kept the feast of unleavened bread seven days with great gladness: and the Lē′vītes and the priests praised the LORD day by day, *singing* with loud instruments unto the LORD.

22 And Hĕz-e-kī′ah spake comfortably unto all the Lē′vītes that taught the good knowledge of the LORD: and they did eat throughout the feast seven days, offering peace offerings, and making confession to the LORD God of their fathers.

23 And the whole assembly took counsel to keep other seven days: and they kept *other* seven days with gladness.

24 For Hĕz-e-kī′ah king of Jū′dah did give to the congregation a thousand bullocks and seven thousand sheep; and the princes gave to the congregation a thousand bullocks and ten thousand sheep: and a great number of priests sanctified themselves.

25 And all the congregation of Jū′dah, with the priests and the Lē′vītes, and all the congregation that came out of Israel, and the strangers that came out of the land of Israel, and that dwelt in Jū′dah, rejoiced.

26 So there was great joy in Jerusalem: for since the time of Sŏl′o-mon the son of David king of Israel *there was* not the like in Jerusalem.

27 Then the priests the Lē′vītes arose and blessed the people: and their voice was heard, and their prayer came *up* to his holy dwelling place, *even* unto heaven.

CHAPTER 31

NOW when all this was finished, all Israel that were present went out to the cities of Jū′dah, and brake the images in pieces, and cut down the groves, and threw down the high places and the altars out of all Jū′dah and Benjamin, in Ē′phra-im also and Ma-năs′seh, until they had utterly destroyed them all. Then all the children of Israel returned, every man to his possession, into their own cities.

2 ¶And Hĕz-e-kī′ah appointed the courses of the priests and the Lē′vītes after their courses, every man according to his service, the priests and Lē′vītes for burnt offerings and for peace offerings, to minister, and to give thanks, and to praise in the gates of the tents of the LORD.

3 *He appointed* also the king's portion of his substance for the burnt offerings, *to wit,* for the morning and evening burnt offerings, and the burnt offerings for the sabbaths, and for the new moons, and for the set feasts, as *it is* written in the law of the LORD.

4 Moreover he commanded the peo-

21-24. The feast of unleavened bread. This feast commenced on the fourteenth day, the day of the Passover feast, and continued through the twenty-first day (Ex 12:15-19). Responses of revival were so great that the assembly agreed to extend the feast another week.

25-27. The revival affected not only people of Judah and Israel, but also **strangers,** i.e., proselytes (cf. Ex 12:48). Certainly, such a spirit of unity in worship of Jehovah brought joy to Jerusalem comparable only to the dedication of the Temple (I Kgs 8:65).

31:1. Hezekiah's reformation had a definite negative aspect—the removal of idolatry from the land. For note on **groves** and **high places,** see 14:3 (cf. also II Kgs 18:4). The reformation reached into **Ephraim** and **Manasseh** to the north; but since it was supported by a minority (cf. 30:10-11), it need not be supposed Hezekiah made a clean sweep of the idols there.

3. Reorganization of the priests and Levites. 31:2-21.

2-4. Hezekiah appointed the courses of the priests. This is actually a reorganization of what David had established (cf. I Chr 24-25). **The king's portion.** Hezekiah was not exempt; but as instructed by the Law, he contributed to the offerings (cf. Num 28-29) and the feasts (cf. Lev 23). **The portion of the priests and the Levites,** was the first fruits (cf. Ex 23:19) and tithes (Num 18:21) which they were to receive from the other tribes so that they might devote themselves to the **law of the LORD** (cf. the problem in Neh 13:10).

ple that dwelt in Jerusalem to give the portion of the priests and the Lē'vītes, that they might be encouraged in the law of the LORD.

5 And as soon as the commandment came abroad, the children of Israel brought in abundance the firstfruits of corn, wine, and oil, and honey, and of all the increase of the field; and the tithe of all *things* brought they in abundantly.

6 And *concerning* the children of Israel and Jū'dah, that dwelt in the cities of Jū'dah, they also brought in the tithe of oxen and sheep, and the tithe of holy things which were consecrated unto the LORD their God, and laid *them* by heaps.

7 In the third month they began to lay the foundation of the heaps, and finished *them* in the seventh month.

8 And when Hĕz-e-kī'ah and the princes came and saw the heaps, they blessed the LORD, and his people Israel.

9 Then Hĕz-e-kī'ah questioned with the priests and the Lē'vītes concerning the heaps.

10 And Ăz-a-rī'ah the chief priest of the house of Zā'dŏk answered him, and said, Since *the people* began to bring the offerings into the house of the LORD, we have had enough to eat, and have left plenty: for the LORD hath blessed his people; and that which is left *is* this great store.

11 ¶Then Hĕz-e-kī'ah commanded to prepare chambers in the house of the LORD; and they prepared *them*,

12 And brought in the offerings and the tithes and the dedicated *things* faithfully: over which Cŏn-o-nī'ah the Lē'vīte *was* ruler, and Shĭm'e-ī his brother *was* the next.

13 And Je-hī'el, and Ăz-a-zī'ah, and Na'hăth, and A'sa-hĕl, and Jĕr'ĭ-mŏth, and Jōz'a-băd, and E-lī'el, and Ĭs-ma-chī'ah, and Ma'hath, and Be-nā'iah, *were* overseers under the hand of Cŏn-o-nī'ah and Shĭm'e-ī his brother, at the commandment of Hĕz-e-kī'ah the king, and Ăz-a-rī'ah the ruler of the house of God.

14 And Kō're the son of Ĭm'nah the Lē'vīte, the porter toward the east, *was* over the freewill offerings of God, to distribute the oblations of the LORD, and the most holy things.

15 And next him *were* Eden, and Mĭn'i-a-mĭn, and Jĕsh'u-a, and Shem-ā-i'ah, Ăm-a-rī'ah, and Shĕc-a-nī'ah, in the cities of the priests, in *their* set office, to give to their brethren by courses, as well to the great as to the small:

16 Beside their genealogy of males, from three years old and upward, *even* unto every one that entereth into the house of the LORD, his daily portion for their service in their charges according to their courses;

17 Both to the genealogy of the priests by the house of their fathers, and the Lē'vītes from twenty years old and upward, in their charges by their courses;

18 And to the genealogy of all their little ones, their wives, and their sons, and their daughters, through all the

5-10. The immediate and generous response of the people in their giving was staggering; and by the surprise of the priests, it is evident that supporting the priests had long gone unpracticed. The **third month** was the month of the Feast of Weeks, or Pentecost, when grain harvest was completed (Ex 23:16; Lev 23:11); and the **seventh month** was the month of the Feast of Tabernacles or Ingatherings (Ex 23:16; Lev 23:34ff.).

11-19. Prepare chambers in the house of the LORD. These storage chambers that had been built in the Temple by Solomon (I Kgs 6:5ff.) evidently needed repair. **Cononiah** and his brother-assistant, **Shimei,** were over ten porter-treasures (cf. I Chr 26:20, 26) who were responsible for collecting the offerings and tithes, while **Kore** assumed responsibility for distributing the **most holy things,** i.e., the portions of offerings to be eaten by the priests. Subordinate to Kore were assistants who distributed to the thirteen **cities of the priests** (cf. Josh 21:9-19). **From three years old and upward** evidently indicates the age priests and Levites began receiving public support from the offerings. Children younger than three years were probably not considered weaned. (for the **Levites from twenty years old and upward,** see note on I Chr 23:24).

congregation: for in their set office they sanctified themselves in holiness:

19 Also of the sons of Aaron the priests, *which were* in the fields of the suburbs of their cities, in every several city, the men that were expressed by name, to give portions to all the males among the priests, and to all that were reckoned by genealogies among the Lĕ'vītes.

20 And thus did Hĕz-e-kī'ah throughout all Jū'dah, and wrought *that which was* good and right and truth before the LORD his God.

21 And in every work that he began in the service of the house of God, and in the law, and in the commandments, to seek his God, he did *it* with all his heart, and prospered.

CHAPTER 32

AFTER these things, and the establishment thereof, Sen-năch'e-rīb king of Assyria came, and entered into Jū'dah, and encamped against the fenced cities, and thought to win them for himself.

2 And when Hĕz-e-kī'ah saw that Sen-năch'e-rīb was come, and that he was purposed to fight against Jerusalem,

3 He took counsel with his princes and his mighty men to stop the waters of the fountains which *were* without the city: and they did help him.

4 So there was gathered much people together, who stopped all the fountains, and the brook that ran through the midst of the land, saying, Why should the kings of Assyria come, and find much water?

5 Also he strengthened himself, and built up all the wall that was broken, and raised *it* up to the towers, and another wall without, and repaired Mĭl'lō *in* the city of David, and made darts and shields in abundance.

6 And he set captains of war over the people, and gathered them together to him in the street of the gate of the city, and spake comfortably to them, saying,

7 Be strong and courageous, be not afraid nor dismayed for the king of Assyria, nor for all the multitude that *is* with him: for *there be* more with us than with him:

8 With him *is* an arm of flesh; but with us *is* the LORD our God to help us, and to fight our battles. And the people rested themselves upon the words of Hĕz-e-kī'ah king of Jū'dah.

9 ¶After this did Sen-năch'e-rīb king of Assyria send his servants to Jerusalem, (but he *himself laid siege* against Lā'chĭsh, and all his power with him,) unto Hĕz-e-kī'ah king of Jū'dah, and unto all Jū'dah that *were* at Jerusalem, saying,

10 Thus saith Sen-năch'e-rīb king of Assyria, Whereon do ye trust, that ye abide in the siege in Jerusalem?

11 Doth not Hĕz-e-kī'ah persuade you to give over yourselves to die by famine and by thirst, saying, The LORD our God shall deliver us out of the hand of the king of Assyria?

12 Hath not the same Hĕz-e-kī'ah

20-21. In summary of Hezekiah's reformation, he did that which was **good . . . before the Lord his God.** He was zealously committed to the Law and to his God. Therefore, he **prospered** (cf. the promise to Joshua, Josh 1:7-8).

4. Sennacherib's invasion, Hezekiah's illness and death. 32:1-33.

This chapter is an abbreviated account of the events recorded in II Kings 18:13-20:21. Portions which are peculiar to II Chronicles and supplementary to II Kings will be noted.

32:1. After these things, i.e., events of the preceding chapters which are described as **the establishment** (lit., the faithfulness), the Assyrian Sennacherib invaded Judah (cf. II Kgs 18:13ff. for notes on historical setting).

2-5. In view of Sennacherib's invasion, Hezekiah took immediate defensive measures, actions that were condemned by the prophet Isaiah (Isa 22:9-11). **He was purposed to fight** means, literally, "his face (was) for war." **To stop the waters of the fountains.** Hezekiah reasoned that he would not contribute to Sennacherib's siege of Jerusalem by providing an adequate supply of water, so the water sources were stopped, including the **brook that ran.** This was probably Gihon (cf. vs. 30; II Kgs 20:20). To provide water for Jerusalem, Hezekiah had an eighteen-hundred-foot-long conduit cut underground in the rock, from the spring of Gihon outside the city walls to the Pool of Siloam within the city walls. Thus, the spring could be covered over, but still supply water to Jerusalem. He also **built up all the wall** of the city **and repaired Millo** (cf. note on I Chr 11:8).

6-8. At the **street of the gate,** i.e., a broad place (cf. 29:4), Hezekiah **spake comfortably,** i.e., encouragingly. **With us is the LORD our God to help us.** The truth of this fact gave Hezekiah confidence in the face of attack by the "arm of flesh" Assyrian, Sennacherib.

9-19. For discussion on Sennacherib's threats to the besieged Hezekiah, see notes on the expanded account in II Kings 18:13-19:37.

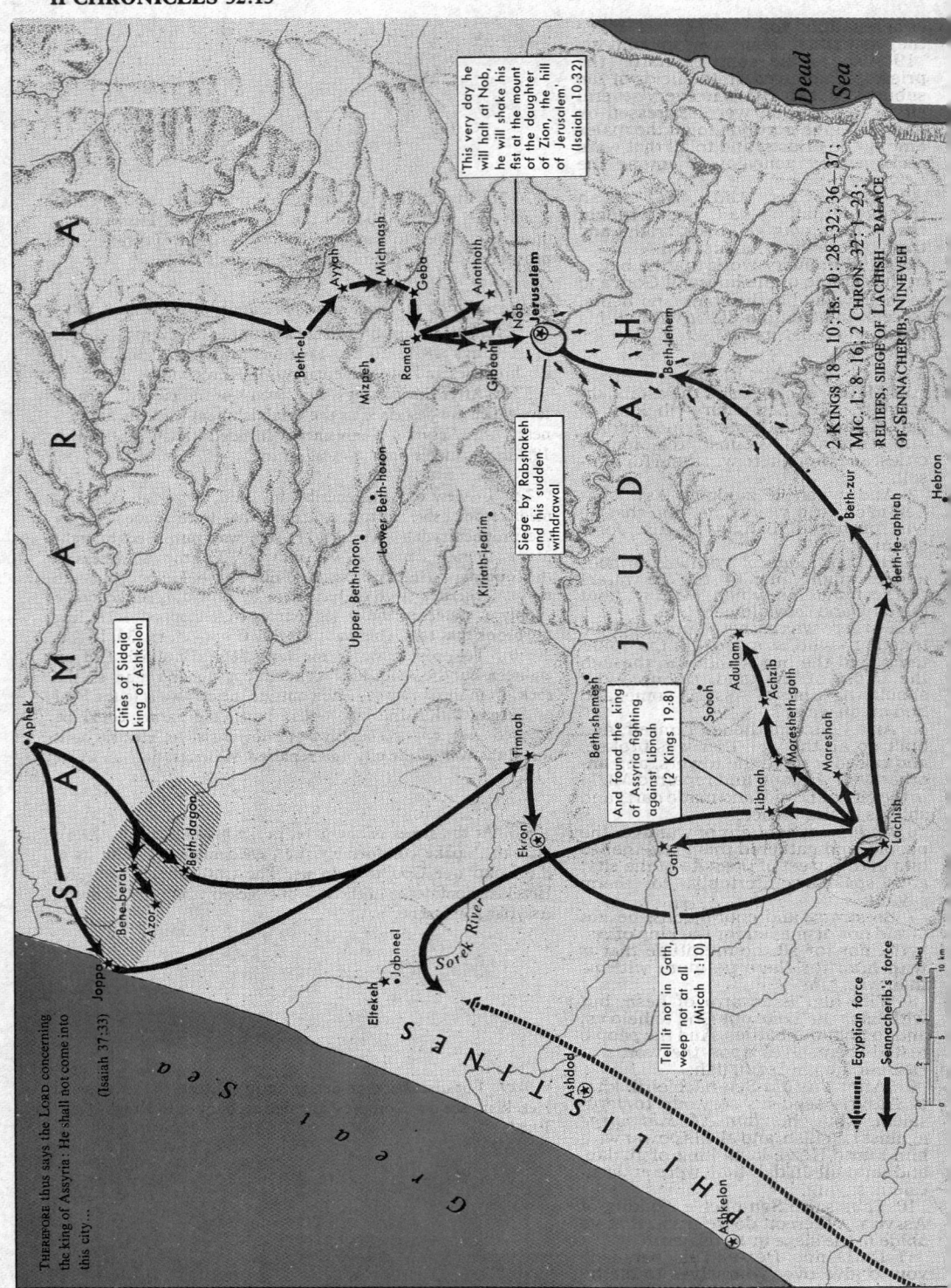

Dead Sea

This very day he will halt at Nob, he will shake his fist at the mount of the daughter of Zion, the hill of Jerusalem (Isaiah 10:32)

2 KINGS 18 — 10; IS. 10:28-32; 36 — 37;
MIC. 1: 8 — 16; 2 CHRON. 32: 1 — 23;
RELIEFS, SIEGE OF LACHISH — PALACE
OF SENNACHERIB, NINEVEH

Siege by Rabshakeh and his sudden withdrawal

Cities of Sidqia king of Ashkelon

And found the king of Assyria fighting against Libnah (2 Kings 19:8)

Tell it not in Gath, weep not at all (Micah 1:10)

THEREFORE thus says the LORD concerning the king of Assyria: He shall not come into this city ...

(Isaiah 37:33)

Great Sea

Egyptian force

Sennacherib's force

Sennacherib's Campaign in Philistia and Judah

taken away his high places and his altars, and commanded Jū′dah and Jerusalem, saying, Ye shall worship before one altar, and burn incense upon it?

13 Know ye not what I and my fathers have done unto all the people of *other* lands? were the gods of the nations of those lands any ways able to deliver their lands out of mine hand?

14 Who *was there* among all the gods of those nations that my fathers utterly destroyed, that could deliver his people out of mine hand, that your God should be able to deliver you out of mine hand?

15 Now therefore let not Hĕz-e-kī′ah deceive you, nor persuade you on this manner, neither yet believe him: for no god of any nation or kingdom was able to deliver his people out of mine hand, and out of the hand of my fathers: how much less shall your God deliver you out of mine hand?

16 And his servants spake yet *more* against the LORD God, and against his servant Hĕz-e-kī′ah.

17 He wrote also letters to rail on the LORD God of Israel, and to speak against him, saying, As the gods of the nations of *other* lands have not delivered their people out of mine hand, so shall not the God of Hĕz-e-kī′ah deliver his people out of mine hand.

18 Then they cried with a loud voice in the Jews' speech unto the people of Jerusalem that *were* on the wall, to affright them, and to trouble them; that they might take the city.

19 And they spake against the God of Jerusalem, as against the gods of the people of the earth, *which were* the work of the hands of man.

20 And for this *cause* Hĕz-e-kī′ah the king, and the prophet Isaiah the son of Amoz, prayed and cried to heaven.

21 And the LORD sent an angel, which cut off all the mighty men of valour, and the leaders and captains in the camp of the king of Assyria. So he returned with shame of face to his own land. And when he was come into the house of his god, they that came forth of his own bowels slew him there with the sword.

22 Thus the LORD saved Hĕz-e-kī′ah and the inhabitants of Jerusalem from the hand of Sen-năch′e-rīb the king of Assyria, and from the hand of all *other*, and guided them on every side.

23 And many brought gifts unto the LORD to Jerusalem, and presents to Hĕz-e-kī′ah king of Judah: so that he was magnified in the sight of all nations from thenceforth.

24 ¶In those days Hĕz-e-kī′ah was sick to the death, and prayed unto the LORD: and he spake unto him, and he gave him a sign.

25 But Hĕz-e-kī′ah rendered not again according to the benefit *done* unto him; for his heart was lifted up: therefore there was wrath upon him, and upon Jū′dah and Jerusalem.

26 Notwithstanding Hĕz-e-kī′ah humbled himself for the pride of his heart, *both* he and the inhabitants of Je-

20. Hezekiah . . . and the prophet Isaiah . . . prayed. Although Isaiah had condemned Hezekiah's actions (Isa 38:1), he had been consulted by the king (II Kgs 19:5ff.); and here he joined him in prayer. Though his words are not given, he may have shared the words of Hezekiah (II Kgs 19:14-19).

21-23. God answered Hezekiah by word through Isaiah the prophet (II Kgs 19:20-34) before He answered by action upon the Assyrians (see notes on God's course of action and Sennacherib's demise in II Kgs 19:35-37).

24-26. Hezekiah was sick. For his illness see notes on expanded account in II Kings 20:1-11. **His heart was lifted up.** His recovery from his fatal illness caused him to be proud and act foolishly, and he recklessly showed Babylonian ambassadors Judah's possessions (vs. 31; II Kgs 20:12-19). **There was wrath upon him** is probably a reference to Sennacherib's invasion (cf. note on time of Hezekiah's illness, II Kgs 20:1).

rusalem, so that the wrath of the LORD came not upon them in the days of Hĕz-e-kī'ah.

27 ¶And Hĕz-e-kī'ah had exceeding much riches and honour: and he made himself treasuries for silver, and for gold, and for precious stones, and for spices, and for shields, and for all manner of pleasant jewels;

28 Storehouses also for the increase of corn, and wine, and oil; and stalls for all manner of beasts, and cotes for flocks.

29 Moreover he provided him cities, and possessions of flocks and herds in abundance: for God had given him substance very much.

30 This same Hĕz-e-kī'ah also stopped the upper watercourse of Gī'hŏn, and brought it straight down to the west side of the city of David. And Hĕz-e-kī'ah prospered in all his works.

31 Howbeit in *the business of* the ambassadors of the princes of Babylon, who sent unto him to enquire of the wonder that was *done* in the land, God left him, to try him, that he might know all *that was* in his heart.

32 ¶Now the rest of the acts of Hĕz-e-kī'ah, and his goodness, behold, they *are* written in the vision of Isaiah the prophet, the son of Amoz, *and* in the book of the kings of Jū'dah and Israel.

33 And Hĕz-e-kī'ah slept with his fathers, and they buried him in the chiefest of the sepulchres of the sons of David: and all Judah and the inhabitants of Jerusalem did him honour at his death. And Ma-năs'seh his son reigned in his stead.

CHAPTER 33

MA-NĂS'SEH *was* twelve years old when he began to reign, and he reigned fifty and five years in Jerusalem:

2 But did *that which was* evil in the sight of the LORD, like unto the abominations of the heathen, whom the LORD had cast out before the children of Israel.

3 For he built again the high places which Hĕz-e-kī'ah his father had broken down, and he reared up altars for Bā'al-ĭm, and made groves, and worshipped all the host of heaven, and served them.

4 Also he built altars in the house of the LORD, whereof the LORD had said, In Jerusalem shall my name be for ever.

5 And he built altars for all the host of heaven in the two courts of the house of the LORD.

6 And he caused his children to pass through the fire in the valley of the son of Hĭn'nom: also he observed times, and used enchantments, and used witchcraft, and dealt with a familiar spirit, and with wizards: he wrought much evil in the sight of the LORD, to provoke him to anger.

7 And he set a carved image, the idol which he had made, in the house of God, of which God had said to David and to Sŏl'o-mon his son, In this house, and in Jerusalem, which I have chosen before all the tribes of Israel, will I put my name for ever:

8 Neither will I any more remove the

27-30. Hezekiah's accumulation of wealth is summarized, and the Chronicler is careful to give rightful credit. **God had given him substance very much** (for the **watercourse of Gihon**, see vss. 3-4).

31. For a fuller account of the Babylonian visit to Hezekiah and Isaiah's condemnation of Hezekiah's action, see II Kings 20:12-19.

32-33. For the **acts of Hezekiah . . . in the vision of Isaiah,** see Isaiah 36-39. In contrast to his wicked father (28:27), not only did he receive a royal burial, but one of highest honor, **in the chiefest** (i.e., uppermost) **of the sepulchers.**

H. Manasseh-Zedekiah. 33:1-36:21.

33:1-10. For the sin of this most wicked and longest reigning of Judah's kings, see notes on the virtually identical passage in II Kings 21:1-20.

foot of Israel from out of the land which I have appointed for your fathers; so that they will take heed to do all that I have commanded them, according to the whole law and the statutes and the ordinances by the hand of Moses.

9 So Ma-năs'seh made Jū'dah and the inhabitants of Jerusalem to err, *and* to do worse than the heathen, whom the LORD had destroyed before the children of Israel.

10 ¶And the LORD spake to Ma-năs'-seh, and to his people: but they would not hearken.

11 Wherefore the LORD brought upon them the captains of the host of the king of Assyria, which took Ma-năs'seh among the thorns, and bound him with fetters, and carried him to Babylon.

12 And when he was in affliction, he besought the LORD his God, and humbled himself greatly before the God of his fathers,

13 And prayed unto him: and he was intreated of him, and heard his supplication, and brought him again to Jerusalem into his kingdom. Then Ma-năs'seh knew that the LORD he *was* God.

14 ¶Now after this he built a wall without the city of David, on the west side of Gī'hŏn, in the valley, even to the entering in at the fish gate, and compassed about Ō'phĕl, and raised it up a very great height, and put captains of war in all the fenced cities of Jū'dah.

15 And he took away the strange gods, and the idol out of the house of the LORD, and all the altars that he had built in the mount of the house of the LORD, and in Jerusalem, and cast *them* out of the city.

16 And he repaired the altar of the LORD, and sacrificed thereon peace offerings and thank offerings and commanded Jū'dah to serve the LORD God of Israel.

17 Nevertheless the people did sacrifice still in the high places, *yet* unto the LORD their God only.

18 ¶Now the rest of the acts of Ma-năs'seh, and his prayer unto his God, and the words of the seers that spake to him in the name of the LORD God of Israel, behold, they *are written* in the book of the kings of Israel.

19 His prayer also, and *how God* was intreated of him, and all his sins, and his trespass, and the places wherein he built high places, and set up groves and graven images, before he was humbled: behold, they *are* written among the sayings of the seers.

20 So Ma-năs'seh slept with his fathers, and they buried him in his own house: and Ā'mon his son reigned in his stead.

21 ¶Ă'mon *was* two and twenty years old when he began to reign, and reigned two years in Jerusalem.

22 But he did *that which was* evil in the sight of the LORD, as did Ma-năs'seh his father: for Ă'mon sacrificed unto all

11-13. This account of Manasseh's humbling does not appear in II Kings, nor in any other known extrabiblical source. **The king of Assyria** was probably either Esarhaddon (681-669 B.C.) or his son Ashurbanipal (669-633). Both claimed Manasseh as a tributary in their records. In favor of Ashurbanipal is the revolt, led by Babylon, of the southern Mediterranean states between the years of 652-647 B.C. which he had to put down. Manasseh might have been a participant in the revolt. In favor of Esarhaddon is the fact he forcibly made Manasseh a tributary, and the methods he employed in taking captives seems to be described here. He possibly forced Manasseh to pay to help support his rebuilding of Babylon. **Thorns** (Heb *chach*) should be rendered "hooks," a reference to the cruel practice of leading prisoners with hooks piercing their nostrils. Driven to his knees by **affliction,** he **humbled himself greatly before the God of his fathers.** That it was genuine repentance is evidenced by his works that followed after he was released.

14-17. He took away the strange gods . . . repaired the altar of the LORD. How much of Manasseh's reign remained after his repentance is not told, but it is evident that the trends he had set were not easily reversed; for **the people did sacrifice still in the high places.** Unfortunately, it was his wickedness, not his life of repentance, that would be emulated by his people, and even his own son Amon.

18-20. In summary, it is unfortunate that his reign was so clouded by wickedness that even the Chronicler remembered Manasseh more for his sin than for his repentance and the good he performed subsequently.

21-25. The reign of **Amon** was a compact carbon copy of his father's pagan rule, lacking in no detail, except for a repentant humbling as his father had experienced (vs. 23) (for notes on his reign, see parallel passage in II Kings 21:19-26).

the carved images which Ma-năs′seh his father had made, and served them;

23 And humbled not himself before the LORD, as Ma-năs′seh his father had humbled himself; but Ā′mon trespassed more and more.

24 And his servants conspired against him, and slew him in his own house.

25 But the people of the land slew all them that had conspired against king Ā′mon; and the people of the land made Jō-sī′ah his son king in his stead.

CHAPTER 34

JŌ-SĪ′AH *was* eight years old when he began to reign, and he reigned in Jerusalem one and thirty years.

2 And he did *that which was* right in the sight of the LORD, and walked in the ways of David his father, and declined *neither* to the right hand, nor to the left.

3 For in the eighth year of his reign, while he was yet young, he began to seek after the God of David his father: and in the twelfth year he began to purge Jū′dah and Jerusalem from the high places, and the groves, and the carved images, and the molten images.

4 And they brake down the altars of Bā′al-ĭm in his presence; and the images, that *were* on high above them, he cut down; and the groves, and the carved images, and the molten images, he brake in pieces, and made dust of *them*, and strowed *it* upon the graves of them that had sacrificed unto them.

5 And he burnt the bones of the priests upon their altars, and cleansed Jū′dah and Jerusalem.

6 And *so did he* in the cities of Ma-năs′seh, and Ē′phra-im, and Simeon, even unto Năph′ta-lī, with their mattocks round about.

7 And when he had broken down the altars and the groves, and had beaten the graven images into powder, and cut down all the idols throughout all the land of Israel, he returned to Jerusalem.

8 ¶Now in the eighteenth year of his reign, when he had purged the land, and the house, he sent Shā′phan the son of Ăz-a-lī′ah, and Mā-a-sē′iah the governor of the city, and Jō′ah the son of Jō′a-hăz the recorder, to repair the house of the LORD his God.

9 And when they came to Hĭl-kī′ah the high priest, they delivered the money that was brought into the house of God, which the Lē′vītes that kept the doors had gathered of the hand of Ma-năs′seh and Ē′phra-im, and of all the remnant of Israel, and of all Jū′dah and Benjamin; and they returned to Jerusalem.

10 And they put *it* in the hand of the workmen that had the oversight of the house of the LORD, and they gave it to the workmen that wrought in the house of the LORD, to repair and amend the house:

11 Even to the artificers and builders

34:1-2. For introduction to **Josiah** and an evaluation of his character, see notes on corresponding verses in II Kings 22:1-2.

3. In the eighth year of his reign (age sixteen) . . . **he began to seek after . . . God.** Josiah undoubtedly had begun his reign under the guardianship of the elders or the priest because of his young age. From this time until his **twelfth year** (age twenty), his religious instruction created within him the desire to restore the worship of God. Therefore, **he began to purge Judah,** spending six years on this endeavor (cf. vs. 8). The efforts of this initial reform are omitted in II Kings, but the Chronicler largely omits the more intensive reform that followed the discovery of the Law which II Kings covers in some detail.

4-7. For Josiah's attempt to rid the land of idolatry, see notes on Asa's action in 14:3-5. **He burnt the bones of the priests . . . and cleansed Judah and Jerusalem.** He later moved north to Beth-el and repeated the procedure (cf. note on II Kgs 23:15-16). He apparently exercised military control over the remnant of the northern tribe; for he enforced his reform as far north as **Naphtali,** showing his reform to be even more extreme than Hezekiah's (cf. 31:1).

8-13. In the eighteenth year (age twenty-six) Josiah directed his attention to the repair of the Temple. The account here is supplementary to II Kings 22:3-7. II Kings emphasizes Josiah's instruction to collect money for repairing the Temple, while II Chronicles emphasizes the implementation of those instructions.

gave they *it*, to buy hewn stone, and timber for couplings, and to floor the houses which the kings of Jū′dah had destroyed.

12 And the men did the work faithfully: and the overseers of them *were* Jā′hăth and Ō-ba-dī′ah, the Lē′vītes, of the sons of Me-rā′rī; and Zĕch-a-rī′ah and Me-shŭl′lam, of the sons of the Kō′hăth-ītes, to set *it* forward; and *other of* the Lē′vītes, all that could skill of instruments of musick.

13 Also *they were* over the bearers of burdens, and *were* overseers of all that wrought the work in any manner of service: and of the Lē′vītes *there were* scribes, and officers, and porters.

14 ¶And when they brought out the money that was brought into the house of the LORD, Hĭl-kī′ah the priest found a book of the law of the LORD *given* by Moses.

15 And Hĭl-kī′ah answered and said to Shā′phan the scribe, I have found the book of the law in the house of the LORD. And Hĭl-kī′ah delivered the book to Shā′phan.

16 And Shā′phan carried the book to the king, and brought the king word back again, saying, All that was committed to thy servants, they do *it*.

17 And they have gathered together the money that was found in the house of the LORD, and have delivered it into the hand of the overseers, and to the hand of the workmen.

18 Then Shā′phan the scribe told the king, saying, Hĭl-kī′ah the priest hath given me a book. And Shā′phan read it before the king.

19 And it came to pass, when the king had heard the words of the law, that he rent his clothes.

20 And the king commanded Hĭl-kī′-ah, and A-hī′kam the son of Shā′phan, and Ăb′dŏn the son of Mī′cah, and Shā′phan the scribe, and Aṡ-ā′iah a servant of the king's, saying,

21 Go, enquire of the LORD for me, and for them that are left in Israel and in Jū′dah, concerning the words of the book that is found: for great *is* the wrath of the LORD that is poured out upon us, because our fathers have not kept the word of the LORD, to do after all that is written in this book.

22 And Hĭl-kī′ah, and *they* that the king *had* appointed, went to Hŭl′dah the prophetess, the wife of Shăl′lum the son of Tĭk′vath, the son of Hăs′rah, keeper of the wardrobe; (now she dwelt in Jerusalem in the college:) and they spake to her to that *effect*.

23 And she answered them, Thus saith the LORD God of Israel, Tell ye the man that sent you to me,

24 Thus saith the LORD, Behold, I will bring evil upon this place, and upon the inhabitants thereof, *even* all the curses that are written in the book which they have read before the king of Jū′dah:

25 Because they have forsaken me, and have burned incense unto other gods, that they might provoke me to anger with all the works of their hands; therefore my wrath shall be poured out upon this place, and shall not be quenched.

14-28. For Hilkiah's discovery of the Law and Huldah's prophecy, see notes on the virtually identical passage in II Kings 22:8-20.

26 And as for the king of Jū'dah, who sent you to enquire of the LORD, so shall ye say unto him, Thus saith the LORD God of Israel *concerning* the words which thou hast heard;

27 Because thine heart was tender, and thou didst humble thyself before God, when thou heardest his words against this place, and against the inhabitants thereof, and humbledst thyself before me, and didst rend thy clothes, and weep before me; I have even heard *thee* also, saith the LORD.

28 Behold, I will gather thee to thy fathers, and thou shalt be gathered to thy grave in peace, neither shall thine eyes see all the evil that I will bring upon this place, and upon the inhabitants of the same. So they brought the king word again.

29 ¶Then the king sent and gathered together all the elders of Jū'dah and Jerusalem.

30 And the king went up into the house of the LORD, and all the men of Jū'dah, and the inhabitants of Jerusalem, and the priests, and the Lē'vītes, and all the people, great and small: and he read in their ears all the words of the book of the covenant that was found in the house of the LORD.

31 And the king stood in his place, and made a covenant before the LORD, to walk after the LORD, and to keep his commandments, and his testimonies, and his statutes, with all his heart, and with all his soul, to perform the words of the covenant which are written in this book.

32 And he caused all that were present in Jerusalem and Benjamin to stand *to it.* And the inhabitants of Jerusalem did according to the covenant of God, the God of their fathers.

33 And Jō-sī'ah took away all the abominations out of all the countries that *pertained* to the children of Israel, and made all that were present in Israel to serve, *even* to serve the LORD their God. *And* all his days they departed not from following the LORD, the God of their fathers.

CHAPTER 35

MOREOVER Jō-sī'ah kept a passover unto the LORD in Jerusalem: and they killed the passover on the fourteenth *day* of the first month.

2 And he set the priests in their charges, and encouraged them to the service of the house of the LORD,

3 And said unto the Levites that taught all Israel, which were holy unto the LORD, Put the holy ark in the house which Sŏl'o-mon the son of David king of Israel did build; *it shall* not *be* a burden upon *your* shoulders: serve now the LORD your God, and his people Israel,

4 And prepare *yourselves* by the houses of your fathers, after your courses, according to the writing of David king of Israel, and according to the writing of Sŏl'o-mon his son.

5 And stand in the holy *place* accord-

29-32. For Josiah's commitment **to perform the words of the covenant,** see notes on II Kings 23:1-3. Here, **Benjamin** is included in those present for the occasion.

33. Josiah took away all the abominations out of all the countries (for elaboration of the details of these additional efforts cf. vss. 3-7 and see II Kgs 23:4-20, 24).

35:1. In the same year he repaired the Temple (34:8), **Josiah kept a passover** (cf. 35:19) on the prescribed date, on **the fourteenth day of the first month** (cf Ex 12:6). Hezekiah had to delay its observance one month (30:15). This observance certainly was confirmation of his obedience to the newly found Law.

2-6. He set the priests in their charges, i.e., he assigned them to their respective duties as prescribed in I Chronicles 23:32 and **encouraged them,** i.e., he prodded them into action. **Put the holy ark in the house.** Apparently, the ark had been removed, possibly for one of two reasons: (1) It had been removed from the Most Holy Place during the reign of one of the preceding wicked kings, either by a king himself of by the priests to protect it from the king by hiding it; or (2) it had been removed while the Temple was being repaired. **Stand . . . according to the divisions.** A section of the Levites was to assist each division of **the people,** i.e., the lay Israelites.

ing to the divisions of the families of the fathers of your brethren the people, and *after* the division of the families of the Lē′vītes.

6 So kill the passover, and sanctify yourselves, and prepare your brethren, that *they* may do according to the word of the Lord by the hand of Moses.

7 And Jō-sī′ah gave to the people, of the flock, lambs and kids, all for the passover offerings, for all that were present, to the number of thirty thousand, and three thousand bullocks: these *were* of the king's substance.

8 And his princes gave willingly unto the people, to the priests, and to the Lē′vītes: Hĭl-kī′ah and Zĕch-a-rī′ah and Je-hī′el, rulers of the house of God, gave unto the priests for the passover offerings two thousand and six hundred *small cattle*, and three hundred oxen.

9 Cŏn-a-nī′ah also, and Shem-ā-i′ah and Ne-thăn′e-el, his brethren, and Hăsh-a-bī′ah and Je-ī′el and Jōz′a-băd, chief of the Lē′vītes, gave unto the Lē′vītes for passover offerings five thousand *small cattle*, and five hundred oxen.

10 So the service was prepared, and the priests stood in their place, and the Lē′vītes in their courses, according to the king's commandment.

11 And they killed the passover, and the priests sprinkled *the blood* from their hands, and the Lē′vītes flayed *them*.

12 And they removed the burnt offerings, that they might give according to the divisions of the families of the people, to offer unto the Lord, as *it is* written in the book of Moses. And so *did they* with the oxen.

13 And they roasted the passover with fire according to the ordinance: but the *other* holy *offerings* sod they in pots, and in caldrons, and in pans, and divided *them* speedily among all the people.

14 And afterward they made ready for themselves, and for the priests: because the priests the sons of Aaron *were busied* in offering of burnt offerings and the fat until night; therefore the Lē′vītes prepared for themselves, and for the priests the sons of Aaron.

15 And the singers the sons of Ā′sāph *were* in their place, according to the commandment of David, and Ā′sāph, and Hē′măn, and Jed′ū-thun the king's seer; and the porters *waited* at every gate; they might not depart from their service; for their brethren the Lē′vītes prepared for them.

16 So all the service of the Lord was prepared the same day, to keep the passover, and to offer burnt offerings upon the altar of the Lord, according to the commandment of king Jō-sī′ah.

17 And the children of Israel that were present kept the passover at that time, and the feast of unleavened bread seven days.

18 And there was no passover like to that kept in Israel from the days of Samuel the prophet; neither did all the kings of Israel keep such a passover as Jō-sī′ah kept, and the priests, and the

7-9. Josiah and his princes provided the people with thirty thousand lambs for the **passover offerings** and **three thousand bullocks** for peace offerings.

10-14. They killed the passover as prescribed by the Law (cf. Ex 12:6-10). The actual Passover sacrifice and the peace offerings in the following week of the Feast of Unleavened Bread have been amalgamated in verse 12. The Passover was to be roasted, not boiled (Ex 12:9); but the peace offerings **sod they in pots,** i.e., boiled, not on the Passover night, but on the subsequent days of the feast.

15-19. The singers (cf. I Chr 25). . . , **according to the commandment of David** (cf. 29:25), . . . **and the porters** (I Chr 26) were all at their stations ready to serve in the festivities of the occasion. **There was no passover like to that kept in Israel from the days of Samuel,** i.e., ". . . from the days of the judges . . ." (II Kgs 23:22). Even Hezekiah's great Passover did not compare because it was delayed one month (30:15). Some of its participants had not prepared themselves (30:17-18), and not as many lambs were slain (cf. the seventeen thousand sheep in Hezekiah's day, 30:24, to the thirty thousand lambs in Josiah's day, vs. 7).

Lē'vītes, and all Jū'dah and Israel that were present, and the inhabitants of Jerusalem.

19 In the eighteenth year of the reign of Jō-sī'ah was this passover kept.

20 ¶After all this, when Jō-sī'ah had prepared the temple, Nĕ'chō king of Egypt came up to fight against Cär'che-mĭsh by Eū-phrā'tēs: and Jō-sī'ah went out against him.

21 But he sent ambassadors to him, saying, What have I to do with thee, thou king of Jū'dah? *I come* not against thee this day, but against the house wherewith I have war: for God commanded me to make haste: forbear thee from *meddling with* God, who *is* with me, that he destroy thee not.

22 Nevertheless Jō-sī'ah would not turn his face from him, but disguised himself, that he might fight with him, and hearkened not unto the words of Nĕ'chō from the mouth of God, and came to fight in the valley of Me-gĭd'dō.

23 And the archers shot at king Jō-sī'ah; and the king said to his servants, Have me away; for I am sore wounded.

24 His servants therefore took him out of that chariot, and put him in the second chariot that he had; and they brought him to Jerusalem, and he died, and was buried in *one of* the sepulchres of his fathers. And all Jū'dah and Jerusalem mourned for Jō-sī'ah.

25 And Jĕr-e-mī'ah lamented for Jō-sī'ah: and all the singing men and the singing women spake of Jō-sī'ah in their lamentations to this day, and made them an ordinance in Israel: and, behold, they *are* written in the lamentations.

26 Now the rest of the acts of Jō-sī'ah, and his goodness, according to *that which was* written in the law of the LORD,

27 And his deeds, first and last, behold, they *are* written in the book of the kings of Israel and Jū'dah.

CHAPTER 36

THEN the people of the land took Je-hō'a-hăz the son of Jō-sī'ah, and made him king in his father's stead in Jerusalem.

2 Je-hō'a-hăz *was* twenty and three years old when he began to reign, and he reigned three months in Jerusalem.

3 And the king of Egypt put him down at Jerusalem, and condemned the land in an hundred talents of silver and a talent of gold.

4 And the king of Egypt made E-lī'a-kĭm his brother king over Jū'dah and Jerusalem, and turned his name to Je-hoi'a-kĭm. And Nĕ'chō took Je-hō'a-hăz his brother, and carried him to Egypt.

5 ¶Je-hoi'a-kĭm *was* twenty and five years old when he began to reign, and he reigned eleven years in Jerusalem: and he did *that which was* evil in the sight of the LORD his God.

6 Against him came up Nĕb-u-chad-

20. In 612 B.C. the Assyrian capital, Nineveh, had fallen to the Babylonians. Now, in 609 B.C. Egypt was going to the aid of her ally, Assyria (see note on "went up against" the king of Assyria, II Kgs 23:29) at **Carchemish by Euphrates** because it was advantageous to her to have a weak Assyria as a buffer against the Babylonians. Josiah saw Egypt's potential power as a threat to his newly gained independence, so **Josiah went out against him,** i.e., Necho of Egypt.

21-24a. God commanded me to make haste. Necho warned Josiah not to interfere, for to do so would be to interfere with God's command. Necho's statement cannot be dismissed as diplomatic propaganda, for the Chronicler condemns Josiah for rejecting a divine prophecy, i.e., **the words of Necho from the mouth of God.** Necho was not a prophet, but a pagan king who served momentarily as spokesman for God (note another pagan king directly addressed by God, Gen 20:3-7). Further evidence of the validity of Necho's statement is Josiah's death.

24b-25. All Judah and Jerusalem mourned for Josiah. Josiah's death came as a shattering blow to Judah's hopes for independence. One named mourner was **Jeremiah,** the prophet of the book bearing his name. **The lamentations** are not to be confused with the book of Lamentations.

26-27. Though Josiah's action, leading to his death, is criticized, this summary statement concerning Josiah is indeed favorable.

36:1-4. For the three-month reign of Josiah's third son, **Jehoahaz,** see comments on II Kings 23:31-34.

5. For the eleven-year reign of Jehoahaz's brother, **Jehoiakim,** see notes on the fuller account in II Kings 23:34-24:7.

6. The Chronicler adds a supplementary note to the II Kings account. After a victory over Necho of Egypt in a rematch at

nĕz′zar king of Babylon, and bound him in fetters, to carry him to Babylon.

7 Nĕb-u-chad-nĕz′zar also carried of the vessels of the house of the Lord to Babylon, and put them in his temple at Babylon.

8 Now the rest of the acts of Je-hoi′a-kĭm, and his abominations which he did, and that which was found in him, behold, they *are* written in the book of the kings of Israel and Jū′dah: and Je-hoi′a-chĭn his son reigned in his stead.

9 ¶Je-hoi′a-chĭn *was* eight years old when he began to reign, and he reigned three months and ten days in Jerusalem: and he did *that which was* evil in the sight of the Lord.

10 And when the year was expired, king Nĕb-u-chad-nĕz′zar sent, and brought him to Babylon, with the goodly vessels of the house of the Lord, and made Zĕd-e-kī′ah his brother king over Jū′dah and Jerusalem.

11 Zĕd-e-kī′ah *was* one and twenty years old when he began to reign, and reigned eleven years in Jerusalem.

12 And he did *that which was* evil in the sight of the Lord his God, *and* humbled not himself before Jĕr-e-mī′ah the prophet *speaking* from the mouth of the Lord.

13 And he also rebelled against king Nĕb-u-chad-nĕz′zar, who had made him swear by God: but he stiffened his neck, and hardened his heart from turning unto the Lord God of Israel.

14 Moreover all the chief of the priests, and the people, transgressed very much after all the abominations of the heathen; and polluted the house of the Lord which he had hallowed in Jerusalem.

15 And the Lord God of their fathers sent to them by his messengers, rising up betimes, and sending; because he had compassion on his people, and on his dwelling place:

16 But they mocked the messengers of God, and despised his words, and misused his prophets, until the wrath of the Lord arose against his people, till *there was* no remedy.

17 Therefore he brought upon them the king of the Chăl′dees, who slew their young men with the sword in the house of their sanctuary, and had no compassion upon young man or maiden, old man, or him that stooped for age: he gave *them* all into his hand.

18 And all the vessels of the house of God, great and small, and the treasures of the house of the Lord, and the treasures of the king, and of his princes; all *these* he brought to Babylon.

19 And they burnt the house of God, and brake down the wall of Jerusalem, and burnt all the palaces thereof with fire, and destroyed all the goodly vessels thereof.

20 And them that had escaped from

Carchemish in 605 B.C., **Nebuchadnezzar king of Babylon came** south to Jerusalem and **bound him,** i.e., Jehoiakim, **in fetters, to carry him to Babylon;** but his plans were altered. Nebuchadnezzar, the **king of Babylon,** was actually the crown prince and coregent with his father Nabopolassar. While at Jerusalem, Nebuchadnezzar received word of his father's death; and he was called home to Babylon for immediate coronation as sole king.

7-8. Nebuchadnezzar also carried of the vessels of the house of the Lord to be kept in his temple at Babylon (cf. Ezr 1:7). In addition, Daniel 1:1-3 records the seizing and deporting of some captives, thus marking 605 B.C. as the beginning of the seventy-year Babylonian captivity.

9-10. For the tragic three-month reign of **Jehoiachin,** see notes on fuller account in II Kings 24:8-16.

11. For the eleven-year evil reign of **Zedekiah** and the resultant destruction of Jerusalem, see notes on the more extensively detailed account in II Kings 24:18-25:21 (details peculiar to II Chronicles are noted here).

12. He . . . humbled not himself before Jeremiah the prophet (cf. Jer 37-38). This is the Chronicler's second reference to Jeremiah (cf. 35:25) who was not named in II Kings.

13-16. The core of the spiritual leadership, **the chief of the priests,** was extremely corrupt. They **polluted the house of the Lord.** Compare the corruption witnessed by Ezekiel that was occurring in the Temple (Ezk 8). **They mocked the messengers of God** instead of repenting (cf. Jer 26:20ff; 32:2ff.; 37:15ff.; 38:6). **There was no remedy.** God could no longer exercise mercy, but He had to take drastic measures of judgment upon His people who persisted in sin.

17-21. To fulfil the word of the Lord by . . . Jeremiah (cf. Jer 25:12). **Until the land had enjoyed her sabbaths.** The people would remain in captivity until the land had been compensated for the years dating from the beginning of the monarchy when the sabbatical years had not been observed as prescribed by the Law (cf. Lev 25:1-7; 26:34-35).

the sword carried he away to Babylon;
where they were servants to him and
his sons until the reign of the kingdom
of Persia:
21 To fulfil the word of the LORD by
the mouth of Jĕr-e-mī'ah, until the
land had enjoyed her sabbaths: *for* as
long as she lay desolate she kept sabbath, to fulfil threescore and ten years.
22 ¶Now in the first year of Cyrus
king of Persia, that the word of the
LORD *spoken* by the mouth of Jĕr-e-
mī'ah might be accomplished, the LORD
stirred up the spirit of Cyrus king of
Persia, that he made a proclamation
throughout all his kingdom, and *put it*
also in writing, saying,
23 Thus saith Cyrus king of Persia,
All the kingdoms of the earth hath the
LORD God of heaven given me; and he
hath charged me to build him an house
in Jerusalem, which *is* in Jū'dah. Who
is there among you of all his people?
The LORD his God *be* with him, and let
him go up.

22-23. These final verses are virtually identical to the introductory verses of Ezra (for comments, see Ezra Commentary).

BIBLIOGRAPHY

Coggins, R. J. *The First and Second Books of the Chronicles*. Cambridge: University Press, 1976.

Crockett, William Day. *A Harmony of the Books of Samuel, Kings and Chronicles*. Grand Rapids: Baker, 1951.

Curtis, Edward L., and Albert A. Madsen. A Critical and Exegetical Commentary on the Books of Chronicles. In *The International Critical Commentary*. Edinburgh: T. & T. Clark, reprinted, 1965.

Ellison, H. L. I and II Chronicles. In *The New Bible Commentary*. Ed. by Francis Davidson. Grand Rapids: Eerdmans, 1953.

Francisco, Clyde T. I-II Chronicles. In *The Broadman Bible Commentary*. Vol. 3. Nashville: Broadman Press, 1970.

*Keil, C. F. *The Books of the Chronicles*. Grand Rapids: Eerdmans, reprinted, 1971.

Murphy, James G. *The Books of the Chronicles*. Minneapolis: James and Kloch, reprinted, 1976.

Myers, Jacob M. I Chronicles. In *The Anchor Bible*. Garden City, New York: Doubleday, 1965.

*Payne, J. Barton. I and II Chronicles. In *The Wycliffe Bible Commentary*. Eds. Charles Pfeiffer and Everett Harrison. Chicago: Moody Press, 1962.

Slotki, I. W. Chronicles: Hebrew Text and English Translation With an Introduction and Commentary. In the *Soncino Books of the Bible*. London: Soncino Press, 1952.

*Whitcomb, John C. *Solomon to the Exile: Studies in Kings and Chronicles*. Winona Lake, Ind.: BMH Books, 1971.

EZRA

INTRODUCTION

The Hebrew Old Testament (Massoretic Text) considered the books of Ezra and Nehemiah to be one volume containing the continuous story of the return of the remnant, the rebuilding of the Temple and the rebuilding of the walls. However, the repetition of Ezra 2 in Nehemiah 7 indicates that the two books were originally separate compositions. In the LXX, Ezra and Nehemiah were called Esdros B, to distinguish them from the apocryphal Esdros A.

Authorship. Ezra himself wrote the book which bears his name (the personal pronoun appears throughout the latter chapters). He undoubtedly utilized several sources in compiling this book, including the proclamation of Cyrus (1:1-4), census and other lists (2:1-62; 8:1-14; 10:18-43), official documents and letters in Aramaic (4:7-6:18; 7:12-26), and the Ezra memoirs (principally 7:27; 8:1-34).

Critical scholarship rejects Ezra's authorship of the book, arguing that it was written at a much later time. However, conservative scholars since Robert Dick Wilson have argued that the Hebrew of Ezra resembles that of Daniel, Haggai, and Chronicles much more than that of Ecclesiasticus (ca. 180 B.C.). John Whitcomb (*The Wycliffe Bible Commentary,* p. 423) also notes that the Aramaic sections of Ezra are very similar to the language of

the fifth century B.C. Elephantine papyri, thus, substantiating the authenticity of the book. For a thorough discussion of authorship questions, see R. K. Harrison, *Introduction to the Old Testament,* p. 1143 ff.

Date. While some scholars have suggested that Ezra was written in the third century B.C., this view is incompatible with the biblical evidence. Ezra arrived in Jerusalem in 457 B.C. and Nehemiah in 445 B.C. This conclusion is based on the assumption that the Artaxerxes mentioned in 7:1 is Artaxerxes I (Longimanus) and not Artaxerxes II (Mnemon). Gleason Archer, *A Survey of Old Testament Introduction,* pp. 396-399, notes that this view best accords with the Elephantine papyri, which refer to Johanan the high priest and Sanballat the governor of Samaria. Johanan was a grandson of Eliashib (Neh 3:1, 20) and was a contemporary of Nehemiah. Archer notes: "It therefore follows that when the Biblical record speaks of Nehemiah going to Jerusalem in the twentieth year of Artaxerxes (Neh 1:1) and again in his thirty-second year (Neh 13:6), the reference must be to Artaxerxes I (yielding the dates 445 B.C. and 433 B.C. respectively) rather than the reign of Artaxerxes II, which would result in the dates 384 B.C. and 372 B.C. respectively—far too late for the high priesthood of Johanan."

OUTLINE

COMMENTARY

I. THE RETURN OF ZERUBBABEL. 1:1-2:70.

A. The Proclamation of Cyrus. 1:1-4.

NOW in the first year of Cyrus king of Persia, that the word of the LORD by the mouth of Jĕr-e-mī′ah might be fulfilled, the LORD stirred up the spirit of Cyrus king of Persia, that he made a proclamation throughout all his kingdom, and *put it* also in writing, saying,

1:1. Now in the first year of Cyrus king of Persia. This introductory phrase ties the events of Ezra to the end of II Chronicles (II Chr 36:22-23). Cyrus began his reign over the Babylonian Empire in 536 B.C. This date is compatible with Jeremiah's prophecy of the seventy-year captivity. **Word of the LORD by the mouth of Jeremiah might be fulfilled.** The reference here is to Jeremiah 25:11-14 and Jeremiah 29:10. Jeremiah prophesies a period of captivity for Judah. He gives the captors,

Babylon, and the length of the captivity, seventy years. This captivity began under Nebuchadnezzar when he carried away Daniel and other youths to Babylon (Dan 1:1-2) in the fourth year of the reign of Jehoiakim (606 B.C.). Seventy years from 606 B.C. would be the first year of the reign of Cyrus over the Babylonian Empire, thus fulfilling Jeremiah's prophecy exactly. **The LORD stirred up the spirit of Cyrus.** The heart of the king is in the Lord's hand (Prov 21:1). God uses heathen kings and potentates to accomplish His will. Even Satan is the unwilling messenger of God. **Made a proclamation.** The concept here is that he sends heralds throughout the kingdom to proclaim his edict.

2 Thus saith Cyrus king of Persia, The LORD God of heaven hath given me all the kingdoms of the earth; and he hath charged me to build him an house at Jerusalem, which *is* in Jū′dah.

2. The decree of Cyrus was not limited to the Jewish people. It included all the residents of the empire. **The LORD God of heaven hath given me.** Cyrus refers to Jehovah. Some commentators have asserted that the author of Ezra added Jehovah's name to the edict since Cyrus was a heathen king. However, it is more logical to ascertain that Cyrus did have high respect and honor for Jehovah. Daniel held a high position in the kingdom of Darius the Mede, who was the father-in-law of Cyrus; and consequently, Cyrus was familiar with Jehovah and His teachings (Keil and Delitzsch, *Biblical Commentary on the Old Testament*, pp. 23-24).

3 Who *is there* among you of all his people? his God be with him, and let him go up to Jerusalem, which *is* in Jū′dah, and build the house of the LORD God of Israel, (he *is* the God,) which *is* in Jerusalem.
4 And whosoever remaineth in any place where he sojourneth, let the men of his place help him with silver, and with gold, and with goods, and with beasts, beside the freewill offering for the house of God that *is* in Jerusalem.

3-4. The first part of the decree deals with the Jews and is twofold. First, he gives the Jews permission to return to Jerusalem; and second, he grants them the right to rebuild the Temple in Jerusalem. The second major part of the decree deals with the heathen in the empire. **Whosoever remaineth in any place.** This does not refer only to the Jews who stay behind. It refers to the entire community, Jews and Gentiles, who will remain and will not return to Jerusalem. Apparently, they were to support the immigrants with both gifts and a **freewill offering. Goods.** This could refer to tents, food, or clothing. The gifts were to aid the Jews in their personal needs; the **offering** was for the **house of God** (cf. vss. 7-8).

B. The Preparations for the Return. 1:5-11.

5 ¶Then rose up the chief of the fathers of Jū′dah and Benjamin, and the priests, and the Lē′vītes, with all *them* whose spirit God had raised, to go up to build the house of the LORD which *is* in Jerusalem.

5. All them whose spirit God had raised. The decree to return was given to all the Jews. However, only those whom God had touched responded and answered the call. Returning to Palestine was a step of faith. The land was desolate and occupied with heathen nations. Those who returned would leave the security of Babylon. They were launching out into the unknown, but they went with a vision, **to build the house of the LORD.** People with a vision can always accomplish the impossible. They can overcome dangers, hostility, and opposition and emerge victorious.

6 And all they that *were* about them strengthened their hands with vessels of silver, with gold, with goods, and with beasts, and with precious things, beside all *that* was willingly offered.

6. All they that were about them. The people who lived around the immigrants responded to the king's command. This included both the Jews who had decided to remain in Babylon and the Gentile community. **Strengthened.** The verb used here means to grasp by the hand, i.e., to assist.

7 ¶Also Cyrus the king brought forth the vessels of the house of the LORD, which Nĕb-u-chad-nĕz′zar had brought forth out of Jerusalem, and had put them in the house of his gods;
8 Even those did Cyrus king of Persia bring forth by the hand of Mĭth′re-dăth the treasurer, and numbered them unto Shĕsh-băz-zar, the prince of Jū′dah.

7-8. Cyrus sets the example for his kingdom by returning the Temple vessels. These vessels had been taken by Nebuchadnezzar and placed in his heathen temple (II Chr 36:7; Dan 1:2). The vessels were given to **Sheshbazzar, the prince of Judah,** the leader of the returning Jews. The name Sheshbazzar is probably the Chaldean name for Zerubbabel (2:2; 3:2, 8; 4:3). Zerubbabel was appointed by Cyrus as the governor of the Jewish settlement in Palestine (5:14). Zerubbabel probably obtained his Chaldean name from Cyrus, and it is likely to assume that he had a position of authority in Cyrus' kingdom.

9 And this *is* the number of them: thirty chargers of gold, a thousand chargers of silver, nine and twenty knives,

9-11. The author lists the number and kinds of vessels given to Zerubbabel. Two lists are given: one detailed and another general. A problem emerges in that the two lists are not in agreement. Note the explanation in verse 11. There were thirty

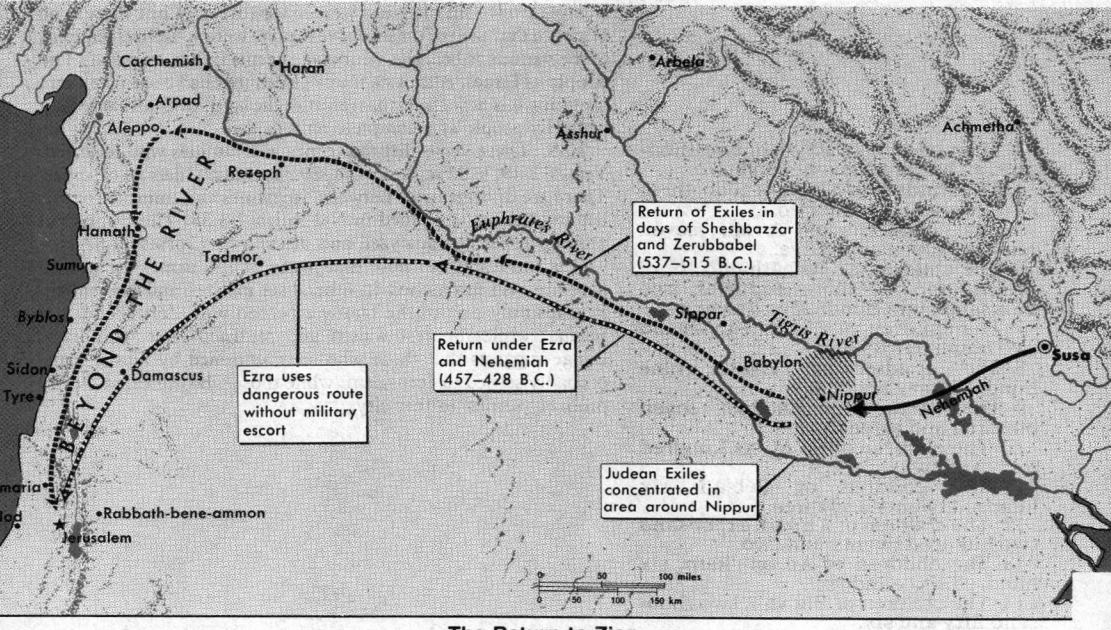

The Return to Zion

10 Thirty basons of gold, silver basons of a second *sort* four hundred and ten, *and* other vessels a thousand.

11 All the vessels of gold and of silver *were* five thousand and four hundred. All *these* did Shĕsh-băz'zar bring up with *them of* the captivity that were brought up from Babylon unto Jerusalem.

CHAPTER 2

NOW these *are* the children of the province that went up out of the captivity, of those which had been carried away, whom Nĕb-u-chad-nĕz'zar the king of Babylon had carried away unto Babylon, and came again unto Jerusalem and Jū'dah, every one unto his city;

2 Which came with Ze-rŭb'ba-bel: Jĕsh'u-a, Nĕ-he-mĭ'ah, Se-ra-ī'ah, Rē-el-a-ī'ah, Môr'de-caī, Bĭl-shăn, Mĭz'pär, Bĭg'va-ī, Rē'hum, Bā'a-nah. The number of the men of the people of Israel:

gold and 1000 silver **chargers.** According to the Talmud, these were probably vessels for collecting the blood of animals. Twenty-nine **knives.** It is uncertain as to whether these were actual knives, or basins used for sacrifice. The word used here could refer to "sacrificial dishes serving for the pouring out of the blood of the sacrifice" (Lange, *Commentary on the Holy Scriptures*, p. 24). Thirty **basins.** These were goblets with covers. The total number of vessels listed is 2,499. The total given in verse 11 is 5,400, more than twice the number given in verses 9 and 10. Some have suggested that this is due to a scribal error in copying the text. Perhaps there were 2000 silver cups rather than 1000. This would bring the total to 5,499 and would be compatible with verse 11. Others have appropriately suggested that the 2,499 refers only to the important vessels while 5,400 refers to all the vessels. **Brought up.** Whenever Jerusalem is mentioned, one always speaks of going **up.** Even though the journey may be southward, it is always referred to as going up. This is due to the fact that Jerusalem was the center of worship for Jews, and that it is situated on hills, so that travel is upward.

C. The People Who Returned. 2:1-70.

2:1. Children of the province. This refers to the **province** over which the governor of Jerusalem was to reign. **Every one unto his city.** This does not mean that they returned to the original city of their ancestors, for those Jews who returned occupied only a small part of the southern kingdom. They returned to a city that became their own.

2. Which came with Zerubbabel. Zerubbabel was the undisputed leader of this group of returning Jews and was the officially appointed governor of the new settlement. **Jeshua.** He was the "first priest of the new community" (Lange, p. 30). Apart from Zerubbabel and Jeshua, nine other leaders are mentioned by name. The similar list in Nehemiah gives an additional person (Nahamani), and this would give a total of twelve leaders (Neh 7:7). These leaders were representative of the twelve original tribes. It is interesting to note that at the dedication of the

Temple twelve sin offerings were made (6:17). While there is no evidence that each of these twelve leaders were actual descendants of the various tribes, the symbolism seems rather apparent. **The people of Israel.** Although it was Judah that had been taken into captivity, it is now Israel that resettles the land. God is now dealing with His people as a complete nation.

3-35. These verses list the names and families who returned. Verses 3-19 list families, and 20-35 contain names of cities. There are discrepancies between the names and numbers of this list and the list contained in Nehemiah 7:8-38. These apparent differences will be analyzed and discussed in verses 64-67.

It is interesting to note that many of the names mentioned here are also mentioned in other lists in Ezra and Nehemiah. Perhaps only part of the family returned with Zerubbabel and Jeshua, while the rest waited and returned later with Ezra. Lange suggests that those who are mentioned by family name probably settled in Jerusalem, while those who are listed by city probably settled in that city.

3 The children of Pâ'rŏsh, two thousand an hundred seventy and two.
4 The children of Shĕph-a-tī'ah, three hundred seventy and two.
5 The children of A'rah, seven hundred seventy and five.
6 The children of Pâ'hăth-mō'ăb, of the children of Jĕsh'u-a and Jō'ăb, two thousand eight hundred and twelve.
7 The children of E'lam, a thousand two hundred fifty and four.
8 The children of Zăt'tū, nine hundred forty and five.
9 The children of Zăc'ca-ī, seven hundred and threescore.
10 The children of Bā'nī, six hundred forty and two.
11 The children of Bĕb'a-ī, six hundred twenty and three.
12 The children of Āz'găd, a thousand two hundred twenty and two.
13 The children of Ăd-on-ī'kam, six hundred sixty and six.
14 The children of Bĭg'va-ī, two thousand fifty and six.
15 The children of A'din, four hundred fifty and four.
16 The children of A'ter of Hĕz-e-kī'-ah, ninety and eight.
17 The children of Bē'zaī, three hundred twenty and three.
18 The children of Jō'rah, an hundred and twelve.
19 The children of Hā'shum, two hundred twenty and three.
20 The children of Gĭb'băr, ninety and five.
21 The children of Bĕth-le-hĕm, an hundred twenty and three.
22 The men of Ne-tō'phah, fifty and six.
23 The men of Ăn'a-thŏth, an hundred twenty and eight.
24 The children of Āz-ma-vĕth, forty and two.
25 The children of Kir'jath-â'rĭm, Che-phī'rah, and Bē-ē'rŏth, seven hundred and forty and three.
26 The children of Rā'mah and Gā'ba, six hundred twenty and one.
27 The men of Mĭch'măs, an hundred twenty and two.
28 The men of Bĕth-el and A'ī, two hundred twenty and three.
29 The children of Nebo, fifty and two.
30 The children of Măg'bĭsh, an hundred fifty and six.
31 The children of the other E'lam, a thousand two hundred fifty and four.
32 The children of Hā'rĭm, three hundred and twenty.
33 The children of Lod, Hā'dĭd, and Ō'nō, seven hundred twenty and five.
34 The children of Jericho, three hundred forty and five.
35 The children of Se-nā'ah, three thousand and six hundred and thirty.

36 ¶The priests: the children of Je-dā'-iah, of the house of Jěsh'u-a, nine hundred seventy and three.
37 The children of Ĭm'mer, a thousand fifty and two.
38 The children of Păsh'ur, a thousand two hundred forty and seven.
39 The children of Hā'rĭm, a thousand and seventeen.
40 ¶The Lē'vītes: the children of Jěsh'u-a and Kăd'mĭ-el, of the children of Hŏd-a-vī'ah, seventy and four.
41 ¶The singers: the children of Ā'săph, an hundred twenty and eight.
42 ¶The children of the porters: the children of Shăl'lum, the children of Ā'ter, the children of Tăl'mon, the children of Ăk'kŭb, the children of Hăt'ĭ-ta, the children of Shō'ba-ī, in all an hundred thirty and nine.
43 ¶The Něth'ĭ-nĭmś: the children of Zī'ha, the children of Ha-sū'pha, the children of Tăb'ba-ŏth,
44 The children of Ke'rŏs, the children of Sī'a-ha, the children of Pā'don.
45 The children of Lěb'a-nah, the children of Hăg'a-bah, the children of Ăk'kŭb.
46 The children of Hā'găb, the children of Shăl'ma-ī, the children of Hā'nan,
47 The children of Gĭd'del, the children of Gā'här, the children of Rē-ā-i'ah,
48 The children of Rē'zĭn, the children of Ne-kō'da, the children of Găz'zam,
49 The children of Ŭz'za, the children of Pa-sē'ah, the children of Bē'śaī,
50 The children of Ās'nah, the children of Me-hū'nĭm, the children of Ne-phū'sĭm,
51 The children of Băk'bŭk, the children of Ha-kū'pha, the children of Här'hŭr,
52 The children of Băz'luth, the children of Me-hī'da, the children of Här'sha,
53 The children of Bär'kŏs, the children of Sīs'e-ra, the children of Thā'mah,
54 The children of Ne-zī'ah, the children of Hat'ĭ-pha.
55 The children of Solomon's servants: the children of Sō'ta-ī, the children of Sŏph'e-rěth, the children of Pe-rū'da,
56 The children of Jā-a'lah, the children of Där'kŏn, the children of Gĭd'del,
57 The children of Shěph-a-tī'ah, the children of Hăt'til, the children of Pŏch'e-rěth of Ze-bā'im, the children of Ā'mī.
58 All the Něth'ĭ-nĭmś, and the children of Solomon's servants, were three hundred ninety and two.
59 And these were they which went up from Těl-mē'lah, Těl-här'sa, Cherub, Ăd'dan, and Ĭm'mer: but they could not shew their father's house, and their seed, whether they were of Israel.
60 The children of Děl-a-ī'ah, the children of Tō-bī'ah, the children of Ne-kō'da, six hundred fifty and two.

36-39. The list of priests is divided into four classes. These names agree with the classes of priests mentioned in I Chronicles 24:7-18 and is identical with the list in Nehemiah 7:39-42.

40-58. This portion of the list includes the Levites and Solomon's servants. There are three classes of Levites mentioned. First, the Levites who assisted the priests in performing their duties. These were the Levites in the technical sense. Second, the singers are listed, and third, the doorkeepers. The **Nethinim.** Thirty-five families of the **Nethinim** are mentioned. These families are listed along with ten families of Solomon's servants. Both the Nethinim and Solomon's servants were prisoners of war who performed the duties of servants.

59-60. They could not show their father's house. These were people who could not prove from which family their ancestors descended **and their seed.** Some could not even prove their Jewish origin. Although they were permitted to return to Jerusalem, they were never granted the right of citizenship. Their names do not appear in the lists in 10:25-45 and Nehemiah 10:15-28. These lists enumerate those who settled the new colony.

61 And of the children of the priests: the children of Ha-bā'iah, the children of Koz, the children of Bär-zĭl'la-ī; which took a wife of the daughters of Bär-zĭl'la-ī the Gĭl'e-ad-īte, and was called after their name:

62 These sought their register *among* those that were reckoned by genealogy, but they were not found: therefore were they, as polluted, put from the priesthood.

63 And the Tir'shā-tha said unto them, that they should not eat of the most holy things, till there stood up a priest with Ū'rĭm and with Thŭm'mĭm.

64 ¶The whole congregation together *was* forty and two thousand three hundred *and* threescore,

65 Beside their servants and their maids, of whom *there were* seven thousand three hundred thirty and seven: and *there were* among them two hundred singing men and singing women.

66 Their horses *were* seven hundred thirty and six; their mules, two hundred forty and five;

67 Their camels, four hundred thirty and five; *their* asses, six thousand seven hundred and twenty.

68 ¶And *some* of the chief of the fathers, when they came to the house of the LORD which *is* at Jerusalem, offered freely for the house of God to set it up in his place:

69 They gave after their ability unto the treasure of the work threescore and one thousand drams of gold, and five thousand pound of silver, and one hundred priests' garments.

70 So the priests, and the Lē'vītes, and *some* of the people, and the singers, and the porters, and the Nĕth'i-

61-63. These verses contain a list of priests who could not prove their right of priesthood. **As polluted.** This is a pregnant term. Because they could not prove their priesthood, they were excluded from such service. **Till there stood up a priest with Urim and with Thummim.** A decision would be made by the Urim and Thummim as to whether these priests could serve in the new Temple. However, there is no evidence to support the belief that this decision was ever made. "On the contrary, the unanimous testimony of the Rabbis, that after the Babylonian exile God no longer manifested His will by the Urim and Thummim, this kind of divine revelation being reckoned by them among the five things which were wanting in the second temple" (Keil, pp. 44-45).

64-67. The writer now concludes the list by giving the sum total of those who returned along with their servants, maids, and beasts of burden. The total of the people is 42,360. This total is identical to Nehemiah 7:60-69. However, the total of the individual lists in both books do not add up to 42,360. Neither do they agree with each other. Consider the following diagram (Keil, p. 45).

	EZRA	NEHEMIAH
Men of Israel	24,144	25,406
Priests	4,289	4,289
Levites	341	360
Nethinim & servants of Solomon	392	392
Those who could not prove the Israelitish origin	652	642
	29,818	31,089

Since the sum total of 42,300 occurs in both Ezra and Nehemiah, it is proper to assume that this is the correct total. Therefore, the discrepancy must be in the listing of the individual totals.

Several possible solutions have been propagated by different commentators. Some think that the individual lists include only Jews and Benjamites, while the total includes the other ten tribes. Others think that the individual lists include those over twenty years old with the total number including those over twelve years old. Keil (p. 45) concludes that "these differences are undoubtedly owing to mere clerical errors, and attempts to reconcile them in other ways cannot be justified."

The reconciliation of these discrepancies is a synthesis of two views. First, the sum total includes people not listed in the individual lists. Second, the differences between Ezra and Nehemiah are attributed to scribal mistakes in copying the manuscripts. On the other hand, their means of calculation may have been obvious to them in their culture, whereas it is difficult for us to calculate it by our standards. **Two hundred singing men and singing women.** These were hired servants who sang at various feasts and important occasions and were probably not of Jewish origin.

68-70. Offered freely. Many of the heads of households gave offerings for the Temple to rebuild it (**set it up in his place**). **They gave after their ability.** This refers to gifts given over and above the tithe, not gifts given under the ability to tithe. This is God's standard for giving. The amount of the gift is not as important as the proportion of the gift in accordance with the individual's ability to give (cf. I Cor 9:6-15). They gave 61,000 darius of gold, five hundred mina of silver, and one hundred priest's garments. **Dwelt in their cities.** The people were settled in the land. The author does not mention the condition of the land or the cities. He simply concludes that they **dwelt in their cities.**

nĭmś, dwelt in their cities, and all Israel in their cities.

CHAPTER 3

AND when the seventh month was come, and the children of Israel *were* in the cities, the people gathered themselves together as one man to Jerusalem.

2 Then stood up Jĕsh'u-a the son of Jŏz'a-dăk, and his brethren the priests, and Ze-rŭb'ba-bel the son of Shē-ăl'tĭ-el, and his brethren, and builded the altar of the God of Israel, to offer burnt offerings thereon, as *it is* written in the law of Moses the man of God.

3 And they set the altar upon his bases; for fear *was* upon them because of the people of those countries: and they offered burnt offerings thereon unto the Lord, *even* burnt offerings morning and evening.

4 They kept also the feast of tabernacles, as *it is* written, and *offered* the daily burnt offerings by number, according to the custom, as the duty of every day required;

5 And afterward *offered* the continual burnt offering, both of the new moons, and of all the set feasts of the Lord that were consecrated, and of every one that willingly offered a freewill offering unto the Lord.

6 From the first day of the seventh month began they to offer burnt offerings unto the Lord. But the foundation of the temple of the Lord was not *yet* laid.

7 They gave money also unto the masons, and to the carpenters; and meat, and drink, and oil, unto them of Zī'don, and to them of Tyre, to bring cedar trees from Lebanon to the sea of Jŏp'pa, according to the grant that they had of Cyrus king of Persia.

8 ¶Now in the second year of their coming unto the house of God at Jerusalem, in the second month, began Ze-rŭb'ba-bel the son of Shē-ăl'tĭ-el, and Jĕsh'u-a the son of Jŏz'a-dăk, and the remnant of their brethren the priests and the Lē'vītes, and all they that were come out of the captivity unto Jerusalem; and appointed the Lē'vītes, from twenty years old and upward, to set forward the work of the house of the Lord.

9 Then stood Jĕsh'u-a *with* his sons and his brethren, Kăd'mĭ-el and his sons, the sons of Jū'dah, together, to set forward the workmen in the house of God: the sons of Hĕn'a-dăd, *with* their sons and their brethren the Lē'vītes.

10 And when the builders laid the foundation of the temple of the Lord, they set the priests in their apparel with

II. THE BUILDING OF THE TEMPLE. 3:1-6:22.

A. The Restoration of Worship. 3:1-13.

3:1. And when the seventh month was come. Although the year is not mentioned, it is implied that this was the seventh month of their first year in Jerusalem. This is substantiated by the opening statement of verse 8, **As one man.** The idea was that they gathered in unity for the same purpose. Unity is one of the basic foundations for accomplishing a work for God (Phil 2:1-4). Lack of unity is one of the hindrances to revival in the twentieth-century church.

2. Great enthusiasm prevailed as the people re-established the sacrificial worship of God. Apparently, work had been done on the altar prior to the seventh month, for the sacrifices actually began on the first day of the seventh month (vs. 6).

3. And they set the altar upon his bases. The word **bases** should be in the singular, not the plural. The idea is that they built the altar on its former base, utilizing the foundation of the original altar. **Fear was upon them.** The people were fearful of the surrounding heathen nations. Their restoration of worship was motivated by a desire for protection from God, and the offerings are now restored.

4. Feast of tabernacles. Beyond the daily sacrifices, the people observed special occasions. **By number.** According to Keil this means "the burnt offerings commanded for several days of this festival, viz. on the first day thirteen oxen, on the second twelve, etc., compare Numbers 29:13-34" (Keil, p. 51).

5. And afterward. After the Feast of Tabernacles the priests observed the **new moons** and **set feasts . . . and of every one that willingly offered a freewill offering unto the Lord.** These offerings could be offered at any time. However, they were usually brought on special feast days.

6. Verses 6-7 are transitional in the story of the rebuilding of the Temple. The sacrificial worship has been established; now the people begin the task of rebuilding the Temple. The people had great zeal and enthusiasm for the worship of God. **But the foundation of the temple of the Lord was not yet laid.** This is the transitional phrase. The people were anxious to complete this task.

7-8. They gave money. Preparations are made to begin this new task. Wood is received from Lebanon. **Now in the second year.** This is the second year of their return to Jerusalem. **Appointed the Levites.** The Levites were given the responsibility to oversee the rebuilding of the Temple. **All they that were come out of the captivity.** Again, the writer emphasizes the complete unity of the group (vs. 1). This task of rebuilding was something in which every person was involved. It was a team effort.

9. The Levites assume this responsibility. Three classes of Levites are mentioned: Jeshua and his family, Kadmiel and his family, and Henadad and his family. The writer is careful to give us many details concerning the rebuilding. We can conclude that this task was accomplished in an orderly fashion. Good organization and administration were the key to efficient work.

10-11. When the builders laid the foundation. The laying of the foundation was accompanied by festivity and singing. The priests were dressed in **their apparel with trumpets,** and the

trumpets, and the Lē'vītes the sons of Ā'săph with cymbals, to praise the LORD, after the ordinance of David king of Israel.

11 And they sang together by course in praising and giving thanks unto the LORD; because *he is* good, for his mercy *endureth* for ever toward Israel. And all the people shouted with a great shout, when they praised the LORD, because the foundation of the house of the LORD was laid.

12 But many of the priests and Lē'vītes and chief of the fathers, *who were* ancient men, that had seen the first house, when the foundation of this house was laid before their eyes, wept with a loud voice; and many shouted aloud for joy:

13 So that the people could not discern the noise of the shout of joy from the noise of the weeping of the people: for the people shouted with a loud shout, and the noise was heard afar off.

CHAPTER 4

NOW when the adversaries of Jū'dah and Benjamin heard that the children of the captivity builded the temple unto the LORD God of Israel;

2 Then they came to Ze-rŭb'ba-bel, and to the chief of the fathers, and said unto them, Let us build with you: for we seek your God, as ye *do;* and we do sacrifice unto him since the days of Ē'sar–hăd'don king of Assur, which brought us up hither.

3 But Ze-rŭb'ba-bel, and Jĕsh'u-a, and the rest of the chief of the fathers of Israel, said unto them, Ye have nothing to do with us to build an house unto our God; but we ourselves together will build unto the LORD God of Israel, as king Cyrus the king of Persia hath commanded us.

4 Then the people of the land weakened the hands of the people of Jū'dah, and troubled them in building,

5 And hired counsellors against them, to frustrate their purpose, all the days of Cyrus king of Persia, even until the reign of Darius king of Persia.

6 And in the reign of A-haś-ū-ē'rus, in the beginning of his reign, wrote they *unto him* an accusation against the inhabitants of Jū'dah and Jerusalem.

7 And in the days of Är-ta-xer'xēś wrote Bīsh'lam, Mĭth're-dăth, Tă'be-el, and the rest of their companions, unto Är-ta-xer'xēś king of Persia; and the writing of the letter *was* written in the Syrian tongue, and interpreted in the Syrian tongue.

8 Rĕ'hum the chancellor and Shĭm'shaï the scribe wrote a letter against Jerusalem to Är-ta-xer'xēś the king in this sort:

Levites **with cymbals,** to **praise the LORD. They sang together.** They undoubtedly sang many of the psalms. This was probably a responsive type of singing. One group would sing "Praise the Lord for He is good," and then the other group would answer "For His mercy endureth forever." **Shouted with a great shout.** The enthusiasm of the people could not be contained. They were uninhibited in their praise for God.

12-13. There was sorrow mingled with joy. **Ancient men.** Those who were old and who had seen the original Temple **wept with a loud voice.** Their tears came probably because the new Temple would not attain the glory and beauty of the original Temple. This was a time of deep emotional expression. Many were joyous, while those who had seen the glory of Solomon's Temple experienced sorrow. Both groups expressed their emotions. **The noise was heard afar off.**

B. The Opposition Encountered. 4:1-24.

4:1-3. Adversaries of Judah and Benjamin. These people were adversaries from before the return of the people. Their opposition goes all the way back to the time of the southern kingdom. These enemies want to help in the rebuilding. They legitimize their right to build by claiming **we seek your God, as ye do; and we do sacrifice unto him since the days of Esarhaddon.** Their claim sounds legitimate. However, the only place of true sacrifice was Jerusalem. These people were sacrificing on other altars and were not true worshipers of God. They had settled in cities of Samaria and were the beginning of the Samaritan nation (II Kgs 17:24).

Ye have nothing to do with us to build. The leaders of the new colony were emphatic in their reply to the Samaritans. The idea is that they had nothing in common with the Samaritans. The Samaritans wanted to include Jehovah with their other gods, but Zerubbabel and Jeshua were building a home **unto our God.** They thus imply that their God was not the god of the Samaritans. They identify clearly who their God is: **the LORD God of Israel.** The worship of the true God is not something we add to what we already have. It must be the worship of Him alone. When we accept Him, "old things are passed away, behold all things are become new."

4-5. Angered by the refusal of Zerubbabel and Jeshua, the Samaritans now seek to stop the building of the Temple. They **weakened the hands of the people . . . and troubled them in building.** They probably threatened the people with physical force and thus made them fearful (**weakened**). **And hired counselors.** Apparently, they hired consultants who appeared in the Persian court to misrepresent the Jewish community. They did this for a total of fourteen years.

6-7. The Samaritans vented their hostility by sending letters to Ahasuerus and Artaxerxes. The letter to Artaxerxes is outlined in this passage and was written by three Samaritans, Bishlam, Mithredath, and Tabeel.

8-10. Rehum and **Shimshai** were probably high officials in the Persian court. They wrote the letter in behalf of Bishlam, Mithredath, and Tabeel. Note the various peoples mentioned.

9 Then *wrote* Rē'hum the chancellor, and Shĭm'shaī the scribe, and the rest of their companions; the Dī'na-ītes, the A-phär'sath-chītes, the Tär'pel-ītes, the A-phär'sītes, the Är'che-vītes, the Babylonians, the Sū'san-chītes, the De-hā'-vītes, *and* the Ē'lam-ītes,

10 And the rest of the nations whom the great and noble Ăs-năp'per brought over, and set in the cities of Sa-mâ'ri-a, and the rest *that are* on this side the river, and at such a time.

11 This *is* the copy of the letter that they sent unto him, *even* unto Är-ta-xĕr'xĕś the king; Thy servants the men on this side the river, and at such a time.

12 Be it known unto the king, that the Jews which came up from thee to us are come unto Jerusalem, building the rebellious and the bad city, and have set up the walls *thereof*, and joined the foundations.

13 Be it known now unto the king, that, if this city be builded, and the walls set up *again, then* will they not pay toll, tribute, and custom, and *so* thou shalt endamage the revenue of the kings.

14 Now because we have maintenance from the *king's* palace, and it was not meet for us to see the king's dishonour, therefore have we sent and certified the king;

15 That search may be made in the book of the records of thy fathers: so shalt thou find in the book of the records, and know that this city *is* a rebellious city, and hurtful unto kings and provinces, and that they have moved sedition within the same of old time: for which cause was this city destroyed.

16 We certify the king that, if this city be builded *again*, and the walls thereof set up, by this means thou shalt have no portion on this side the river.

17 ¶Then sent the king an answer unto Rē'hum the chancellor, and *to* Shĭm'shaī the scribe, and *to* the rest of their companions that dwell in Sa-mâ'ri-a, and *unto* the rest beyond the river, Peace, and at such a time.

18 The letter which ye sent unto us hath been plainly read before me.

19 And I commanded, and search hath been made, and it is found that this city of old time hath made insurrection against kings, and *that* rebellion and sedition have been made therein.

20 There have been mighty kings also over Jerusalem, which have ruled over all *countries* beyond the river; and toll, tribute, and custom, was paid unto them.

21 Give ye now commandment to cause these men to cease, and that this city be not builded, until *another* commandment shall be given from me.

22 Take heed now that ye fail not to do this: why should damage grow to the hurt of the kings?

23 ¶Now when the copy of king Är-ta-xĕr'xĕś' letter *was* read before Rē'hum, and Shĭm'shaī the scribe, and their companions, they went up in

The idea was to impress on the Persian king the vast number of different peoples who were opposed to the Jewish settlement.

11-12. Thy servants the men on this side the river. The Samaritans introduced the letter by pledging their allegiance to the king. They were implying that the Jews were not true servants of the king. The letter begins by describing the condition of Jerusalem. **Have set up the walls thereof, and joined the foundations.** This was clear exaggeration. Nehemiah later found the walls in terrible condition. The Samaritans knew that the king would likely be upset by a walled city. Consequently, they lied to prejudice their cause.

13-14. The argument is that if the walls are completed, it will hurt the cause of the king. He will lose **toll, tribute, and custom.** These three distinct taxes are mentioned again in verse 20 and 7:24. They varied from highway tolls to individual taxes. **Now because we have maintenance from the king's palace.** This literally states "because we eat the salt of the palace." This is a figurative expression that speaks of being in the king's pay. It means that because they were obligated to the king, they deemed it necessary to inform him about the rebellious Jews.

15-16. They want the king to review the history of Jerusalem. It was customary for ancient kings to keep careful records of their reign. These records were passed on to the next generation. **For which cause was this city destroyed.** This refers to the time when Nebuchadnezzar destroyed Jerusalem and took Judah into captivity. **Thou shalt have no portion on this side the river.** The Samaritan argument is that if the Jews are permitted to rebuild Jerusalem, then the king would not have control over that section of his empire. The river mentioned is the Euphrates.

17-20. Then sent the king an answer. The word **answer** could be translated as edict or sentence. The king responds with a royal decree. The king has read the history of Jerusalem and continues the rebellion that has been characteristic of Jerusalem. **Ruled over all countries beyond the river.** Again, this refers to all the land west of the Euphrates. **Mighty kings.** This probably refers to David and Solomon, whose kingdoms were vast.

21-24. Give ye now commandment. The king acts. He commands that work on the city be stopped. **That ye fail not.** The king tells the Samaritans not to make a mistake in fulfilling his command. The chapter concludes by giving the result of this royal command. The Samaritans utilize force in performing the king's desire. **Then ceased the work of the house of God.** It is interesting to note the deception of the Samaritans. They accused the Jews of rebuilding Jerusalem. Orders were given not to build the city. However, it was not work on the city that stopped, but rather on the Temple.

haste to Jerusalem unto the Jews, and made them to cease by force and power.

24 Then ceased the work of the house of God which *is* at Jerusalem. So it ceased unto the second year of the reign of Darius king of Persia.

CHAPTER 5

THEN the prophets, Hăg'ga-ī the prophet, and Zĕch-a-rī'ah the son of Ĭd'dō, prophesied unto the Jews that *were* in Jŭ'dah and Jerusalem in the name of the God of Israel, *even* unto them.

2 Then rose up Ze-rŭb'ba-bel the son of Shĕ-ăl'tĭ-el, and Jĕsh'u-a the son of Jŏz'a-dăk, and began to build the house of God which *is* at Jerusalem: and with them *were* the prophets of God helping them.

3 ¶At the same time came to them Tăt'na-ī, governor on this side the river, and Shĕ'thär-bŏz'na-ī and their companions, and said thus unto them, Who hath commanded you to build this house, and to make up this wall?

4 Then said we unto them after this manner, What are the names of the men that make this building?

5 But the eye of their God was upon the elders of the Jews, that they could not cause them to cease, till the matter came to Darius: and then they returned answer by letter concerning this *matter*.

6 ¶The copy of the letter that Tăt'na-ī, governor on this side the river, and Shĕ'thär-bŏz'na-ī and his companions the A-phär'sach-ītes, which *were* on this side the river, sent unto Darius the king:

7 They sent a letter unto him, wherein was written thus; Unto Darius the king, all peace.

8 Be it known unto the king, that we went into the province of Judea, to the house of the great God, which is builded with great stones, and timber is laid in the walls, and this work goeth fast on, and prospereth in their hands.

9 Then asked we those elders, *and* said unto them thus, Who commanded you to build this house, and to make up these walls?

10 We asked their names also, to certify thee, that we might write the names of the men that *were* the chief of them.

11 And thus they returned us answer,

C. The Resumption of the Building. 5:1-5.

5:1. Then the prophets. During this time when the Temple building had ceased, Haggai and Zechariah encouraged the people. Many of the people were involved in building their own homes, and some had lost interest in the Temple. The messages of the prophets were probably messages of encouragement and reminders of their obligation to finish God's house. Notice, they prophesied to those in **Judah and Jerusalem** about the **God of Israel.** The God they served was God of the entire Jewish population.

2-3. Began to build. The people had been reminded by the prophets that God wanted the Temple built. They responded by obeying the prophet's message. **Tatnai,** governor of the west of the Euphrates, **Shethar-boznai,** and their **companions** visit Jerusalem to inspect the progress of the building. They demand to know **Who hath commanded** the Jews **to build this house, and to make up this wall?**

4-5. Then said we. The answer given in this verse does not correspond in any way with the question asked by Tatnai. The text could be translated as "then said they to them," thus making this question the second question asked by Tatnai (Lange, p. 58). Tatnai wanted to know who authorized the building and who was involved in the building. **But the eye of their God was upon the elders of the Jews.** Tatnai and his companions did not make the Jews stop building. Rather, he permitted them to continue until he received official word from the king. This act of kindness is attributed to the providence of God. He molds and directs all the circumstances and incidents of life (cf. Rom 8:20).

D. The Letter to Darius. 5:6-17.

6-7. After inspecting the situation at Jerusalem, Tatnai sends a letter to the king. **All peace.** The writer of the letter begins by wishing Darius and his kingdom **peace.**

8. Be it known unto the king. This letter begins with the same statement as the letter in 4:12. This latest report is not as prejudiced as the report given by the Samaritans. **The great God.** It is unlikely that these heathen men had respect for Jehovah. They use His name simply to identify Him from other heathen gods. **Timber is laid in the walls.** This refers to both wall partitions as well as scaffolding utilized in placing the **great stones. This work goeth fast on.** The Jews were working with great zeal. **And prospereth.** The rebuilding of the Temple was being completed with great haste.

9-10. The questions of verses 3 and 4 are repeated.

11. And thus they returned us answer. The answers that

saying, We are the servants of the God of heaven and earth, and build the house that was builded these many years ago, which a great king of Israel builded and set up.

12 But after that our fathers had provoked the God of heaven unto wrath, he gave them into the hand of Něb-u-chad-něz′zar the king of Babylon, the Chăl-dē′an, who destroyed this house, and carried the people away into Babylon.

13 But in the first year of Cyrus the king of Babylon *the same* king Cyrus made a decree to build this house of God.

14 And the vessels also of gold and silver of the house of God, which Něb-u-chad-něz′zar took out of the temple that *was* in Jerusalem, and brought them into the temple of Babylon, those did Cyrus the king take out of the temple of Babylon, and they were delivered unto *one,* whose name *was* Shěsh-băz′zar, whom he had made governor;

15 And said unto him, Take these vessels, go, carry them into the temple that *is* in Jerusalem, and let the house of God be builded in his place.

16 Then came the same Shěsh-băz′-zar, *and* laid the foundation of the house of God which *is* in Jerusalem: and since that time even until now hath it been in building, and *yet* it is not finished.

17 Now therefore, if *it seem* good to the king, let there be search made in the king's treasure house, which *is* there at Babylon, whether it be *so,* that a decree was made of Cyrus the king to build this house of God at Jerusalem, and let the king send his pleasure to us concerning this matter.

CHAPTER 6

THEN Darius the king made a decree, and search was made in the house of the rolls, where the treasures were laid up in Babylon.

2 And there was found at Ăch′me-tha, in the palace that *is* in the province of the Medes, a roll, and therein *was* a record thus written:

3 In the first year of Cyrus the king *the same* Cyrus the king made a decree *concerning* the house of God at Jerusalem, Let the house be builded, the place where they offered sacrifices, and let the foundations thereof be strongly laid; the height thereof threescore cubits, *and* the breadth thereof threescore cubits;

4 *With* three rows of great stones, and a row of new timber: and let the expenses be given out of the king's house:

5 And also let the golden and silver vessels of the house of God, which Něb-u-chad-něz′zar took forth out of the temple which *is* at Jerusalem, and brought unto Babylon, be restored, and brought again unto the temple which *is*

were omitted earlier in the narrative are now given in this letter to Darius. **We are the servants of the God of heaven and earth.** They identify the authority by which they build. He is God of both heaven and earth. **A great king.** This refers to Solomon. They do not mention him by name, for their emphasis is that the God of heaven and earth made Solomon a great king.

12-15. Our fathers had provoked the God. The reason the Temple was destroyed was the sin of the people. For more information on the decree of Cyrus, read 1:1-4. For more information on verses 14 and 15 consult 1:7-8.

16-17. Since that time even until now hath it been in building. Nothing is mentioned about the Samaritan letter and the resulting halt in construction. The impression is given that their construction has continued since the original decree of Cyrus. Tatnai asks for a search to be made to determine whether or not Cyrus made a decree permitting the Temple to be rebuilt.

E. The Decree of Cyrus Confirmed. 6:1-12.

6:1-2. Then Darius the king made a decree. These words connect the events of chapter 6 with those of chapter 5. Darius commands that the records be searched to determine if Cyrus had made a decree permitting the rebuilding of the Temple at Jerusalem. **Where the treasures were laid up.** Apparently, the valuable treasures were stored in the same place as the historical documents. **And there was found at Achmetha.** The document they sought was not at Babylon. Probably all of Cyrus' documents were at this fortress in Achmetha.

3-5. These verses contain the content of the document they found. Contained in this document was the authorization to build. **Let the house be builded.** The **height** and **breadth** were both to be sixty cubits. Solomon's Temple was only thirty cubits high and twenty cubits broad. These instructions to rebuild authorized a much larger facility. Cyrus wanted to rebuild a bigger and more impressive facility than the one which was destroyed.

Let the expenses be given out of the king's house. Cyrus not only permitted the rebuilding, but he was willing to underwrite the expenses of the project. **Also let the golden and silver vessels.** The vessels were crucial to the re-establishing of the sacrifices and proper worship of Jehovah.

at Jerusalem, *every one* to his place, and place *them* in the house of God.

6 Now *therefore* Tăt´na-ī, governor beyond the river, Shē´thär–bōz´na-ī, and your companions the A-phär´sach-ītes, which *are* beyond the river, be ye far from thence:

7 Let the work of this house of God alone; let the governor of the Jews and the elders of the Jews build this house of God in his place.

8 Moreover I make a decree what ye shall do to the elders of these Jews for the building of this house of God: that of the king's goods, *even* of the tribute beyond the river, forthwith expenses be given unto these men, that they be not hindered.

9 And that which they have need of, both young bullocks, and rams, and lambs, for the burnt offerings of the God of heaven, wheat, salt, wine, and oil, according to the appointment of the priests which *are* at Jerusalem, let it be given them day by day without fail:

10 That they may offer sacrifices of sweet savours unto the God of heaven, and pray for the life of the king, and of his sons.

11 Also I have made a decree, that whosoever shall alter this word, let timber be pulled down from his house, and being set up, let him be hanged thereon; and let his house be made a dunghill for this.

12 And the God that hath caused his name to dwell there destroy all kings and people, that shall put to their hand to alter *and* to destroy this house of God which *is* at Jerusalem. I Darius have made a decree; let it be done with speed.

13 ¶Then Tăt´na-ī, governor on this side the river, Shē´thär–bōz´na-ī, and their companions, according to that which Darius the king had sent, so they did speedily.

14 And the elders of the Jews builded, and they prospered through the prophesying of Hăg´ga-ī the prophet and Zĕch-a-rī´ah the son of Ĭd´dō. And they builded, and finished *it*, according to the commandment of the God of Israel, and according to the commandment of Cyrus, and Darius, and Är-ta-xer´xēs king of Persia.

15 And this house was finished on the third day of the month Ā´där, which was in the sixth year of the reign of Darius the king.

16 ¶And the children of Israel, the priests, and the Lē´vītes and the rest of the children of the captivity, kept the dedication of this house of God with joy,

17 And offered at the dedication of this house of God an hundred bullocks, two hundred rams, four hundred lambs; and for a sin offering for all Israel, twelve he goats, according to the number of the tribes of Israel.

18 And they set the priests in their divisions, and the Lē´vītes in their courses, for the service of God, which *is* at Jerusalem; as it is written in the book of Moses.

6-8. Now therefore, Tatnai. Verses 6-12 contain Darius' response, and he even goes beyond the decree of Cyrus in assisting the Jewish settlement in their building project. **Be ye far from thence.** This warns Tatnai not to interfere with the building of the Temple. **Let the work of this house of God alone.** They were not to hinder the work project in any way. **Moreover I make a decree what ye shall do to the elders.** First, they were not to hinder the work. Now, Darius gives them instructions as to what they were to do to help the work. They were to give money from **tribute** (taxes) to the Jews in order to finance their expenses.

9-10. Darius goes one step further in his decree. **And that which they have need of.** Darius wanted the Jews provided with animals and supplies so they could perform their worship completely. Darius also had ulterior motives in helping the Jews re-establish their worship. **And pray for the life of the king, and of his sons.** Cyrus had recognized the authority of the Jewish God (1:2). Now Darius recognizes the authority of this God and seeks His blessing.

11-12. Whosoever shall alter this word. Darius decrees that anyone who disobeys will be **hanged.** The idea was that the person would be nailed to a piece of wood. This kind of crucifixion was customary among the Assyrians. Darius invokes God's wrath on anyone who interferes with the Temple. **Let it be done with speed.** The decree concludes with the king's desire for prompt obedience to his orders.

F. The Temple Completed. 6:13-22.

13. The response of Tatnai is recorded. **So they did speedily.** Since Darius had made a decree, Tatnai and his friends moved with haste to perform the king's command.

14-15. They prospered through the prophesying of Haggai the prophet and Zechariah the son of Iddo. Note the close relationship between physical prosperity and spiritual prosperity. They were able to build. They also received spiritual nourishment along with their building program. **They . . . finished it, according to the commandment of the God of Israel.** God's command precedes and supersedes the commandments of both Cyrus and Darius. The writer reminds us that in all the events of the rebuilding God was at work. He utilized heathen kings to accomplish His will. However, all that had happened was in His control. The Temple was finished on the **third day of the month Adar.** This month was the last month of the year.

16-17. The Temple is dedicated **with joy.** This was indeed a festive occasion. The task which they had set out to do was complete. They had faced adversity but God had overruled and now the Temple was complete. They offered **a hundred bullocks, two hundred rams, four hundred lambs** as sacrifices. They also offered **twelve he goats** as **a sin offering for all Israel.** Although it was the southern tribes (Judah) who were taken into captivity, permitted to return, and rebuild, they were conscious of the fact that Israel was a nation of twelve tribes.

18. The priests and Levites were organized according to their responsibilities, and a schedule was established for the continuing worship of God. They followed the **book of Moses.**

19 ¶And the children of the captivity kept the passover upon the fourteenth *day* of the first month.

20 For the priests and the Lē'vītes were purified together, all of them *were* pure, and killed the passover for all the children of the captivity, and for their brethren the priests, and for themselves.

21 And the children of Israel, which were come again out of captivity, and all such as had separated themselves unto them from the filthiness of the heathen of the land, to seek the Lᴏʀᴅ God of Israel, did eat,

22 And kept the feast of unleavened bread seven days with joy: for the Lᴏʀᴅ had made them joyful, and turned the heart of the king of Assyria unto them, to strengthen their hands in the work of the house of God, the God of Israel.

CHAPTER 7

NOW after these things, in the reign of Är-ta-xer'xēś king of Persia, Ezra the son of Se-ra-ī'ah, the son of Ăz-a-rī'ah, the son of Hĭl-kī'ah,

2 The son of Shăl'lum, the son of Zā'-dŏk, the son of A-hī'tŭb,

3 The son of Ăm-a-rī'ah, the son of Ăz-a-rī'ah, the son of Me-rā'ioth,

4 The son of Zĕr-a-hī'ah, the son of Ŭz'zi, the son of Bŭk'kī,

5 The son of A-bĭsh'ū-a, the son of Phĭn'e-has, the son of Ĕ-le-ā'zar, the son of Aaron the chief priest:

6 This Ezra went up from Babylon; and he *was* a ready scribe in the law of Moses, which the Lᴏʀᴅ God of Israel had given: and the king granted him all his request, according to the hand of the Lᴏʀᴅ his God upon him.

7 And there went up *some* of the children of Israel, and of the priests, and the Lē'vītes, and the singers, and the porters, and the Nĕth'i-nĭmś, unto Jerusalem, in the seventh year of Är-ta-xer'xēś the king.

8 And he came to Jerusalem in the fifth month, which *was* in the seventh year of the king.

9 For upon the first *day* of the first month began he to go up from Babylon, and on the first *day* of the fifth month came he to Jerusalem, according to the good hand of his God upon him.

10 For Ezra had prepared his heart to seek the law of the Lᴏʀᴅ, and to do *it,* and to teach in Israel statutes and judgments.

19-22. After the dedication of the Temple, the Passover was observed. This was done the next month after the dedication. Great preparations were made. The priests and Levites purified themselves. This purification was important and qualified the priests for holy service. Not all the people were eligible to eat the Passover. Only those who had lived separated lives could partake. This excluded the Samaritans who had intermarried with the heathen nations. **The Lᴏʀᴅ had made them joyful.** The rebuilding the Temple, its dedication, the Passover, and Feast of Unleavened Bread were all possible because of what God had done. They were quick to give Him all the credit for this joyful moment.

III. THE RETURN OF EZRA. 7:1-10:44.

A. His Arrival at Jerusalem. 7:1-10.

7:1. Now after these things. Between the events of chapter 6 and the return of Ezra in chapter 7 is a period of fifty-seven years. Although the people had re-established the Temple worship under Zerubbabel and Jeshua, they were not living in complete obedience to the Law. It was to the task of teaching and preaching the Law that Ezra had resigned himself (vs. 10).

2-5. These verses establish the priestly lineage of Ezra and thus give him the authority to deal with the Law and worship of Jehovah. His lineage is traced all the way back to Aaron, the high priest under Moses.

6. This Ezra went up from Babylon. This statement is connected to the opening statement of verse 1. **He was a ready scribe.** This implies more than just a secretary who copied Scripture. It implies a scholar who was learned in the laws. Besides being a man of zeal, Ezra was a man of great intellect. **The king granted him all his request.** Ezra came to Jerusalem with the sanction of the king. Note the overruling hand of God. Even though the heathen king permitted and sanctioned the return of Ezra, it was ultimately the **hand of the Lᴏʀᴅ** that made the return possible.

7-8. He was accompanied by a group of people that included **the priests, and the Levites, and the singers, and the porters, and the Nethinim.** They left Babylon in the **seventh year of Artaxerxes** and arrived in Jerusalem **in the fifth month.**

9. This gives the directions of the journey. It took exactly five months to go from Babylon to Jerusalem. **The good hand of his God.** Again, the author reminds the reader of the sovereignty of God in this story (see vs. 6).

10. This verse outlines the requirements for serving the Lord. **Ezra had prepared his heart.** God always prepares His servants **to seek the law.** Spiritual maturity and Christian leadership are closely connected to our relationship to the Law. One cannot grow and serve God apart from a commitment to the Word of God (Josh 1:8). **Do it.** Many Chrisitans know the Law but never obey it. Notice that the doing of the Law precedes the teaching of the Law. Practice must always precede preaching. This was true in the life of Jesus (Acts 1:1). **To teach.** Ezra taught from the depth of a pure heart and a consistent life-style. Such teaching is desperately needed today, teaching that emerges from a consistent obedience to the Law.

11 ¶Now this *is* the copy of the letter that the king Är-ta-xer′xēs gave unto Ezra the priest, the scribe, *even* a scribe of the words of the commandments of the Lord, and of his statutes to Israel.

12 Är-ta-xer′xēs, king of kings, unto Ezra the priest, a scribe of the law of the God of heaven, perfect *peace*, and at such a time.

13 I make a decree, that all they of the people of Israel, and *of* his priests and Lē′vītes, in my realm, which are minded of their own freewill to go up to Jerusalem, go with thee.

14 Forasmuch as thou art sent of the king, and of his seven counsellors, to enquire concerning Jū′dah and Jerusalem, according to the law of thy God which *is* in thine hand;

15 And to carry the silver and gold, which the king and his counsellors have freely offered unto the God of Israel, whose habitation *is* in Jerusalem,

16 And all the silver and gold that thou canst find in all the province of Babylon, with the freewill offering of the people, and of the priests, offering willingly for the house of their God which *is* in Jerusalem:

17 That thou mayest buy speedily with this money bullocks, rams, lambs, with their meat offerings and their drink offerings, and offer them upon the altar of the house of your God which *is* in Jerusalem.

18 And whatsoever shall seem good to thee, and to thy brethren, to do with the rest of the silver and the gold, that do after the will of your God.

19 The vessels also that are given thee for the service of the house of thy God, *those* deliver thou before the God of Jerusalem.

20 And whatsoever more shall be needful for the house of thy God, which thou shalt have occasion to bestow, bestow *it* out of the king's treasure house.

21 And I, *even* I Är-ta-xer′xēs the king, do make a decree to all the treasurers which *are* beyond the river, that whatsoever Ezra the priest, the scribe of the law of the God of heaven, shall require of you, it be done speedily,

22 Unto an hundred talents of silver, and to an hundred measures of wheat, and to an hundred baths of wine, and to an hundred baths of oil, and salt without prescribing *how much*.

23 Whatsoever is commanded by the God of heaven, let it be diligently done for the house of the God of heaven: for why should there be wrath against the realm of the king and his sons?

24 Also we certify you, that touching any of the priests and Lē′vītes, singers, porters, Nēth′i-nĭmś, or ministers of this house of God, it shall not be lawful to impose toll, tribute, or custom, upon them.

Verses 11-16 contain the decree of Artaxerxes which Ezra brought with him to Jerusalem.

B. His Commission From Artaxerxes. 7:11-28.

11-12. The priest, the scribe. Ezra is given both titles in this verse. As a scribe he knows the Law of God, and as a priest he practices the Law of God. This is the only place where he is called by both titles. Normally, he is designated by one title or the other, but not by both. **Perfect peace.** This is addressed to Ezra.

13-14. I make a decree. This was more than a letter approving the ministry and return of Ezra. It was a royal decree to which the people must submit and obey. First, he permits those who want to return (of their own free will) to go back with Ezra. **Seven counselors.** These people formed the "supreme court of the realm" (Keil, p. 98). They are referred to in Esther 1:14. **To inquire.** The first job of Ezra was to survey the conditions in **Judah and Jerusalem.** The evaluation was to be performed with respect to the standard of **the law of thy God.** This standard is the only valid measure of spiritual conditions.

15-16. Three specific offerings are mentioned in these verses. First, there was **the silver and gold** given to Ezra by King Artaxerxes and his counselors. Second, there were offerings given to Ezra from the non-Jewish inhabitants of Babylon. Third, Ezra collected offerings from the Jewish population.

17-18. The money was to be utilized to purchase the animals necessary for sacrifice. **And to thy brethren.** This could mean either the elders in Jerusalem or the priests. These people were to be involved in deciding how to utilize the rest of the money. This Jewish settlement was well organized, and there was a specific way of making decisions as outlined in this verse.

19-20. The vessels were to be deposited at the Temple for the worship of God. **And whatsoever more shall be needful.** Artaxerxes recognized that the money Ezra possessed might not be enough to fully establish the worship at Jerusalem; so he permitted them to utilize the money of the royal treasury.

21-22. Ezra could ask up to **a hundred talents of silver.** The treasury contained both silver and food supplies. Whatever was needed for worship was to be made available to Ezra. The priests, Levites, and those involved in the functional service of the Temple were to be exempted from paying taxes.

23-24. Artaxerxes had respect for the God of the Jews. He was giving to Ezra so that the king would be spared from the **wrath** of Jehovah. He was also following the precedent of the Persian kings who hoped to gain the favor of the many deities of the ancient world.

25 And thou, Ezra, after the wisdom of thy God, that *is* in thine hand, set magistrates and judges, which may judge all the people that *are* beyond the river, all such as know the laws of thy God; and teach ye them that know *them* not.

26 And whosoever will not do the law of thy God, and the law of the king, let judgment be executed speedily upon him, whether *it be* unto death, or to banishment, or to confiscation of goods, or to imprisonment.

27 ¶Blessed *be* the LORD God of our fathers, which hath put *such a thing* as this in the king's heart, to beautify the house of the LORD which *is* in Jerusalem:

28 And hath extended mercy unto me before the king, and his counsellors, and before all the king's mighty princes. And I was strengthened as the hand of the LORD my God *was* upon me, and I gathered together out of Israel chief men to go up with me.

CHAPTER 8

THESE *are* now the chief of their fathers, and *this is* the genealogy of them that went up with me from Babylon, in the reign of Är-ta-xẽr′xẽs the king.

2 Of the sons of Phĭn′e-has; Ger′shom: of the sons of Ĭth′a-mär; Daniel: of the sons of David; Hăt′tũsh.

3 Of the sons of Shĕch-a-nī′ah, of the sons of Phã′rŏsh; Zĕch-a-rī′ah: and with him were reckoned by genealogy of the males an hundred and fifty.

4 Of the sons of Pã′hăth-mō′ăb; Ĕ-li-hō-ē′na-ī the son of Zẽr-a-hī′ah, and with him two hundred males.

5 Of the sons of Shĕch-a-nī′ah; the son of Ja-hā′zi-el, and with him three hundred males.

6 Of the sons also of Ā′din; Ē′bĕd the son of Jonathan, and with him fifty males.

7 And of the sons of Ē′lam; Je-shā′iah the son of Ăth-a-lī′ah, and with him seventy males.

8 And of the sons of Shĕph-a-tī′ah; Zĕb-a-dī′ah the son of Michael, and with him fourscore males.

9 Of the sons of Jō′ăb; Ō-ba-dī′ah the son of Je-hī′el, and with him two hundred and eighteen males.

10 And of the sons of Shel′ō-mĭth; the son of Jŏs-i-phī′ah, and with him an hundred and threescore males.

11 And the sons of Bĕb′a-ī; Zĕch-a-rī′ah the son of Bĕb′a-ī, and with him twenty and eight males.

12 And of the sons of Ăz′găd; Jō-hā′-nan the son of Hăk′ka-tăn, and with him an hundred and ten males.

13 And of the last sons of Ăd-on-ī′-kam, whose names *are* these, E-lĭph′e-lĕt, Je-ī′el, and Shem-ā-i′ah, and with them threescore males.

14 Of the sons also of Bĭg′va-ī; Ũ′-tha-ī, and Zăb′bŭd, and with them seventy males.

15 ¶And I gathered them together to the river that runneth to A-hā′va; and there abode we in tents three days: and I viewed the people, and the priests, and found there none of the sons of Levi.

25-26. Ezra was authorized to establish a complete judicial system. The Law was to be enforced, and criminals were to be punished. Four different punishments are outlined for offenders of the Law. They could be executed, excommunicated, stripped of their possessions, or imprisoned. The entire judicial system was to be administered by Jews who understood the Law and its religious implications.

27-28. These verses are not part of the king's decree. Rather, they are Ezra's comments on the king's decree. **Blessed be the LORD God of our fathers.** Ezra was fully aware of who made the return possible. It was God who put this thing **in the king's heart. I was strengthened.** Ezra recognized his own dependence upon God for the work he must do. This great task required complete dependence upon God.

C. His Journey to Jerusalem. 8:1-36.

8:1-14. These verses contain a list of those who returned with Ezra to Jerusalem. The **chief of their fathers,** refers to the heads of each household. There are several important facts to consider from this list. First, the names that appear in this list are similar to those which appear in the list of chapter 2. Those who returned first under Zerubbabel had left parts of their families and relatives behind in Babylon. Now, many of these also returned under the leadership of Ezra. Second, there are twelve families mentioned in this list. This is implied to represent the twelve tribes of Israel (cf. 2:2). Third, there was a total of 1,496 males and fifteen heads who returned with Ezra. This was a much smaller group than the one that had returned with Zerubbabel earlier (cf. ch. 2).

15. And I gathered them. Note the use of the personal pronoun. This chapter begins with the personal pronoun that went up with me (vs. 1). The events described in this chapter are described from Ezra's personal viewpoint. This is different from the previous seven chapters. After reviewing the people,

16 Then sent I for Ĕ-lĭ-ē′zer, for Â′rĭ-el, for Shem-ă-i′ah, and for Ĕl′nā-than, and for Jă′rĭb, and for Ĕl′nā-than, and for Nā′than, and for Zĕch-a-rī′ah, and for Me-shŭl′lam, chief men; also for Joi′a-rĭb, and for Ĕl′nā-than, men of understanding.

17 And I sent them with commandment unto Ĭd′dō the chief at the place Ca-sĭph′ĭ-a, and I told them what they should say unto Ĭd′dō, and to his brethren the Nĕth′i-nĭmś, at the place Ca-sĭph′ĭ-a, that they should bring unto us ministers for the house of our God.

18 And by the good hand of our God upon us they brought us a man of understanding, of the sons of Măh′lĭ, the son of Levi, the son of Israel; and Shĕr-e-bī′ah, with his sons and his brethren, eighteen;

19 And Hăsh-a-bī′ah, and with him Je-shā′iah of the sons of Me-râ′rī, his brethren and their sons, twenty;

20 Also of the Nĕth′i-nĭmś, whom David and the princes had appointed for the service of the Lē′vītes, two hundred and twenty Nĕth′i-nĭmś: all of them were expressed by name.

21 ¶Then I proclaimed a fast there, at the river of A-hă′va, that we might afflict ourselves before our God, to seek of him a right way for us, and for our little ones, and for all our substance.

22 For I was ashamed to require of the king a band of soldiers and horsemen to help us against the enemy in the way: because we had spoken unto the king, saying, The hand of our God is upon all them for good that seek him; but his power and his wrath is against all them that forsake him.

23 So we fasted and besought our God for this: and he was intreated of us.

24 ¶Then I separated twelve of the chief of the priests, Shĕr-e-bī′ah, Hăsh-a-bī′ah, and ten of their brethren with them,

25 And weighed unto them the silver, and the gold, and the vessels, even the offering of the house of our God, which the king, and his counsellors, and his lords, and all Israel there present, had offered:

26 I even weighed unto their hand six hundred and fifty talents of silver, and silver vessels an hundred talents, and of gold an hundred talents;

27 Also twenty basons of gold, of a thousand drams; and two vessels of fine copper, precious as gold.

28 And I said unto them, Ye are holy unto the Lord; the vessels are holy also; and the silver and the gold are a freewill offering unto the Lord God of your fathers.

29 Watch ye, and keep them, until ye weigh them before the chief of the priests and the Lē′vītes, and chief of the fathers of Israel, at Jerusalem, in the chambers of the house of the Lord.

30 So took the priests and the Lē′vītes the weight of the silver, and the gold, and the vessels, to bring them to Jerusalem unto the house of our God.

Ezra was faced with a dilemma. There were no Levites among those who were returning.

16-17. Ezra sent a group of messengers to Iddo. It was apparent that Ezra already had his group organized, for he sends one of the leaders to secure Levites. It is not clear who Iddo is and why Ezra sent to him for help. It is most likely that he was a Levite and **his brethren** were the **Nethinim,** or priest's helpers. Perhaps **Casiphia** was a priestly city inhabited by Levites and Nethinim. Assuming this to be accurate, it would be logical for Ezra to seek Levites from this community to be **ministers for the house.** Ezra was anxious to secure those who could teach the Law, as well as perform worship services.

18-20. The good hand of our God. God was active in every detail of this adventure. They were able to secure forty Levites and two hundred-twenty Nethinim. **All of them were expressed by name,** i.e., they were men of note.

21. I proclaimed a fast. They were ready to leave on their journey, and Ezra realized the importance of depending upon God. This was to implore God for safety and prosperity on their journey. **Afflict ourselves.** This means that they wanted to humble themselves before God.

22-23. Ezra had portrayed God as a mighty and protective God to King Artaxerxes. To then ask for an army to protect their company would be to admit they had a weak God. Ezra wanted to prove to Artaxerxes that the Jews worshiped and served the true God. God was pleased with their desire and was **entreated** of them.

24-30. Ezra chooses twelve priests and twelve Levites and divides the treasures among them. They are charged with bringing them safely to Jerusalem. **And weighed.** This probably refers to some type of inventory of all the vessels. Ezra emphasizes the importance of the vessels. They were **holy** (set apart for the service of God).

31 ¶Then we departed from the river of A-hā′va on the twelfth *day* of the first month, to go unto Jerusalem: and the hand of our God was upon us, and he delivered us from the hand of the enemy, and of such as lay in wait by the way.

32 And we came to Jerusalem, and abode there three days.

33 ¶Now on the fourth day was the silver and the gold and the vessels weighed in the house of our God by the hand of Mĕr′e-mŏth the son of Ū-rī′ah the priest; and with him *was* Ē-le-ā′zar the son of Phĭn′e-has; and with them *was* Jōz′a-băd the son of Jĕsh′u-a, and Nō-a-dī′ah the son of Bĭn′nū-ī, Lē′vītes;

34 By number *and* by weight of every one: and all the weight was written at that time.

35 *Also* the children of those that had been carried away, which were come out of the captivity, offered burnt offerings unto the God of Israel, twelve bullocks for all Israel, ninety and six rams, seventy and seven lambs, twelve he goats *for* a sin offering: all *this was* a burnt offering unto the LORD.

36 And they delivered the king's commissions unto the king's lieutenants, and to the governors on this side the river: and they furthered the people, and the house of God.

CHAPTER 9

NOW when these things were done, the princes came to me, saying, The people of Israel, and the priests, and the Lē′vītes, have not separated themselves from the people of the lands, *doing* according to their abominations, *even* of the Canaanites, the Hittites, the Pĕr′iz-zītes, the Jĕb′u-sītes, the Ammonites, the Moabites, the Egyptians, and the Ăm′ō-rites.

2 For they have taken of their daughters for themselves, and for their sons: so that the holy seed have mingled themselves with the people of *those* lands: yea, the hand of the princes and rulers hath been chief in this trespass.

3 And when I heard this thing, I rent my garment and my mantle, and plucked off the hair of my head and of my beard, and sat down astonied.

4 Then were assembled unto me every one that trembled at the words of the God of Israel, because of the transgression of those that had been carried away; and I sat astonied until the evening sacrifice.

5 ¶And at the evening sacrifice I arose up from my heaviness; and having rent my garment and my mantle, I fell upon my knees, and spread out my hands unto the LORD my God,

6 And said, O my God, I am ashamed and blush to lift up my face to thee, my God: for our iniquities are increased over *our* head, and our trespass is grown up unto the heavens.

7 Since the days of our fathers *have* we *been* in a great trespass unto this

31-32. They leave from the river Ahava on the twelfth day of the first month. They left Babylon on the first day of the first month (7:9). The three days mentioned in verse 15 means that Ezra discovered the lack of Levites after three days. This would permit nine days to receive the Levites they needed. **The hand of our God** (see 7:6, 9, 28; 8:18). The hand of God is observed through all the events of these chapters.

33-34. Now on the fourth day. After a rest of three days (vs. 32) they bring forth the vessels and treasures they have carried from Babylon. By number and by **weight.** Each vessel was numbered and weighed. This was to develop an official document of inventory.

35-36. Those who had returned with Ezra offered both sin offerings and burnt offerings. They also delivered the king's decree to his official representatives throughout the area. As a result, the people of Jerusalem were encouraged, and the worship of God was strengthened.

D. His Prayer and Remorse. 9:1-15.

9:1. The princes came to me. Not all the princes came to Ezra, for many of them were involved in sin. Those who desired purity came to Ezra. Their chief complaint was that the Jews had **not separated themselves from the people of the lands.** The Jewish community was becoming integrated into the heathen nations around Jerusalem.

2. They have taken of their daughters. The lack of separation also involved intermarriage with the Gentile population around them. Intermarriage was forbidden to prevent the children of Israel from going into idolatry. **Holy seed.** This phrase is also used in Isaiah 6:13. **The princes and rulers.** The sin was not limited to the common people. The leaders were just as guilty. It was probably their example and influence that was instrumental in leading the people into sin.

3-4. Ezra's reaction to this report was one of deep remorse and sorrow. He even **plucked** out some of the hair of his head and beard. This symbolized the extreme personal pain he felt because of the people's sin. Ezra gathered those that **trembled at the words of the God of Israel.** These people were in sharp contrast to those who were intermingled with the heathen. They had been true to the Lord. Note that they heard the Lord. A proper concept of God will keep people from a sinful life-style. **God of Israel.** Again the writer emphasizes God's dealing with all of the Jews, and not the tribes of Judah alone.

5-6. The rest of this chapter contains Ezra's prayer. **I arose up from my heaviness.** "His mortification, which had consisted in giving way to sorrow but had certainly likewise been connected with fasting" (Lange, p. 88). He bows in humiliation before God and prays (see I Kgs 8:22). One can sense the great burden of Ezra in the opening statements of his prayer. So great was their sin that it had grown above their **head** and had piled up as high as the **heavens.**

7-8. Ezra recalls that God had punished them because of sin. Until that moment they had been under bondage to foreign

day; and for our iniquities have we, our kings, *and* our priests, been delivered into the hand of the kings of the lands, to the sword, to captivity, and to a spoil, and to confusion of face, as *it is* this day.

8 And now for a little space grace hath been *shewed* from the Lord our God, to leave us a remnant to escape, and to give us a nail in his holy place, that our God may lighten our eyes, and give us a little reviving in our bondage.

9 For we *were* bondmen; yet our God hath not forsaken us in our bondage, but hath extended mercy unto us in the sight of the kings of Persia, to give us a reviving, to set up the house of our God, and to repair the desolations thereof, and to give us a wall in Jū'dah and in Jerusalem.

10 And now, O our God, what shall we say after this? for we have forsaken thy commandments,

11 Which thou hast commanded by thy servants the prophets, saying, The land, unto which ye go to possess it, is an unclean land with the filthiness of the people of the lands, with their abominations, which have filled it from one end to another with their uncleanness.

12 Now therefore give not your daughters unto their sons, neither take their daughters unto your sons, nor seek their peace or their wealth for ever: that ye may be strong, and eat the good of the land, and leave *it* for an inheritance to your children for ever.

13 And after all that is come upon us for our evil deeds, and for our great trespass, seeing that thou our God hast punished us less than our iniquities *deserve*, and hast given us *such* deliverance as this;

14 Should we again break thy commandments, and join in affinity with the people of these abominations? wouldest not thou be angry with us till thou hadst consumed *us*, so that *there should be* no remnant nor escaping?

15 O Lord God of Israel, thou *art* righteous: for we remain yet escaped, as *it is* this day: behold, we *are* before thee in our trespasses: for we cannot stand before thee because of this.

CHAPTER 10

NOW when Ezra had prayed, and when he had confessed, weeping and casting himself down before the house of God, there assembled unto him out of Israel a very great congregation of men and women and children: for the people wept very sore.

2 And Shĕch-a-nī'ah the son of Je-hī'el, *one* of the sons of Ē'lam, answered and said unto Ezra, We have trespassed against our God, and have taken strange wives of the people of the land: yet now there is hope in Israel concerning this thing.

3 Now therefore let us make a covenant with our God to put away all the wives, and such as are born of them, according to the counsel of my lord,

powers. **Now for a little space.** This refers to the time of his prayer. **To give us a nail in his holy place.** This is a figurative expression. This type of nail was put in the wall and used for hanging utensils. The Temple was such a place for the new community. It was a nail on which they could hang their hopes and future. **That our God may lighten our eyes.** This refers to the vitality of a new life. **A little reviving** refers to a bringing of life to this new community.

9-10. We were bondmen. They were still under the rule and authority of the Persian Empire. However, God had allowed them to return, and the heathen emperor had provided the money to rebuild. **And now.** Ezra is building toward this question. God had been merciful to the children of Israel. **What shall we say after this?** They were without excuse. Although God had blessed them and had permitted them to return, they disobeyed His **commandments.**

11-12. Ezra is referring to God's commandments regarding separation (see Deut 7:1-3). **Nor seek their peace or their wealth for ever.** These words come from Deuteronomy 23:7. Christians today are not to seek the wealth or the peace offered by the world, either. Both are temporal and deceiving. Ezra gives the reasons for separation from sin. **That ye may be strong.** Maturity can only come when one's life is separated from sin.

13-14. Ezra pleads to learn from past experience. If God punished sin in the past, then they should learn from that experience and abstain from sin now.

15. Ezra concludes his prayer by appealing to the righteousness of God. This should motivate them to obey God. **For we remain yet escaped.** God had not yet destroyed them because of their sin. Ezra concludes by admitting the sinful condition of the people. It was such that they could not **stand** before God.

E. The Issue of Mixed Marriages. 10:1-17.

10:1. When he had confessed. Prayer and confession always go hand in hand. Sin hinders one's prayer life and must be confessed as the basis of effective prayer. The sorrow and remorse of Ezra had great impact upon the people. **A very great congregation.** A large group of people joined Ezra at the Temple. They also were sorry for the sin of those who had intermarried with the heathen.

2. And Shechaniah . . . said unto Ezra. It is interesting to note that one of the congregation initiated the action. Ezra could have done this, but it was more meaningful coming from the people. Shechaniah begins by confessing their sin. **We have trespassed.** He admits his own sin. **There is hope.** He expresses confidence in the kindness and forgiveness of God.

3. Let us make a covenant. This is the basis for hope. They decide to do something about their sin. They make an agreement (covenant) with God. They **put away all the wives, and such as are born of them.** This seems rather harsh. However,

and of those that tremble at the commandment of our God; and let it be done according to the law.

4 Arise; for *this* matter *belongeth* unto thee: we also *will be* with thee: be of good courage, and do *it*.
5 Then arose Ezra, and made the chief priests, the Lē′vītes, and all Israel, to swear that they should do according to this word. And they sware.
6 Then Ezra rose up from before the house of God, and went into the chamber of Jō-hā′nan the son of E-lī′a-shīb: and *when* he came thither, he did eat no bread, nor drink water: for he mourned because of the transgression of them that had been carried away.
7 And they made proclamation throughout Jū′dah and Jerusalem unto all the children of the captivity, that they should gather themselves together unto Jerusalem;
8 And that whosoever would not come within three days, according to the counsel of the princes and the elders, all his substance should be forfeited, and himself separated from the congregation of those that had been carried away.
9 ¶Then all the men of Jū′dah and Benjamin gathered themselves together unto Jerusalem within three days. It *was* the ninth month, on the twentieth *day* of the month; and all the people sat in the street of the house of God, trembling because of *this* matter, and for the great rain.
10 And Ezra the priest stood up, and said unto them, Ye have transgressed, and have taken strange wives, to increase the trespass of Israel.
11 Now therefore make confession unto the LORD God of your fathers, and do his pleasure: and separate yourselves from the people of the land, and from the strange wives.
12 Then all the congregation answered and said with a loud voice, As thou hast said, so must we do.
13 But the people *are* many, and *it is* a time of much rain, and we are not able to stand without, neither *is this* a work of one day or two: for we are many that have transgressed in this thing.
14 Let now our rulers of all the congregation stand, and let all them which have taken strange wives in our cities come at appointed times, and with them the elders of every city, and the judges thereof, until the fierce wrath of our God for this matter be turned from us.
15 Only Jonathan the son of Ā′sa-hĕl and Jä-ha-zī′ah the son of Tĭk′vah were employed about this *matter*: and Me-shŭl′lam and Shăb′be-thaī the Lē′vīte helped them.
16 And the children of the captivity did so. And Ezra the priest, *with* certain chief of the fathers, after the house of their fathers, and all of them by *their* names, were separated, and sat down

they desired a complete break with the sin that was destroying them. They also put away their children who were born of their heathen wives. Actually, this was logical, since the children remained with their mothers. There may have been exceptions to this standard. It is proper to assume that some children, who were willing to conform to God's law, stayed.

4-6. Arise; for this matter belongeth unto thee. The issue before them involved Ezra. He was the one who would be responsible for fulfilling it. Ezra accepts the responsibility for encouraging the people to follow Shechaniah's advice, and he makes the leaders swear to follow the covenant. Ezra gets up and goes to the **chamber of Johanan,** a room adjacent to the Temple where the priests' garments were stored (note Neh 8:4-9). He goes to this room for the purpose of fasting.

7-9. A proclamation is made by the **princes** and **elders.** Everyone in Jerusalem and Judah is to come to Jerusalem within three days. Failure to respond to this decree would mean that person would lose all his possessions and would be excommunicated from the community. **It was the ninth month, on the twentieth day of the month.** This was the same year in which Ezra returned (7:8). It was the equivalent of the month of December. The weather was cold; and when they came to Jerusalem, it was raining.

10-11. Ezra preaches a short message. This was the message recommended by Shechaniah (vss. 2-3).

12-15. As thou hast said, so must we do. The people recognized that Ezra was correct; it was their duty to obey. **Neither is this a work of one day or two.** There were so many people involved in this sin and there were so many different situations that the people realized it would take a long time to resolve the problem. The princes are appointed to oversee the task. The people are to appear before the **elders of every city, and the judges,** who will ensure that the people put away their heathen wives. Only **Jonathan, Jahaziah,** and two Levites were opposed to this.

16-17. The first day of the tenth month. Ten days after they had gathered together in Jerusalem Ezra met to **examine the matter.** They had put away their wives and had resolved their sin by the **first day of the first month.** The entire process took almost three months.

in the first day of the tenth month to examine the matter.

17 And they made an end with all the men that had taken strange wives by the first day of the first month.

18 ¶And among the sons of the priests there were found that had taken strange wives: namely, of the sons of Jĕsh'u-a the son of Jŏz'a-dăk, and his brethren; Mā-a-sē'iah, and Ĕ-lī-ē'zer, and Jā'rĭb, and Gĕd-a-lī'ah.

19 And they gave their hands that they would put away their wives; and being guilty, they offered a ram of the flock for their trespass.

20 And of the sons of Ĭm'mer; Ha-nā'nĭ, and Zĕb-a-dī'ah.

21 And of the sons of Hā'rĭm; Mā-a-sē'iah, and E-lī'jah, and Shem-ā-i'ah, and Je-hī'el, and Uz-zī'ah.

22 And of the sons of Păsh'ur; Ĕ-lī-ō-ē'na-ī, Mā-a-sē'iah, Ĭsh'ma-el, Ne-thăn'e-el, Jŏz'a-băd, and Ĕl'a-sah.

23 Also of the Lē'vītes; Jŏz'a-băd, and Shĭm'e-ī, and Ke-lā'iah, (the same is Kel'ī-ta,) Pĕth-a-hī'ah, Jū'dah, and Ĕ-lī-ē'zer.

24 Of the singers also; E-lī'a-shĭb: and of the porters; Shăl'lum, and Tē'lĕm, and Ū'rī.

25 Moreover of Israel: of the sons of Pā'rŏsh; Ra-mī'ah, and Je-zī'ah, and Măl-chī'ah, and Mī'a-mĭn, and Ĕ-le-ā'zar, and Măl-chī'jah, and Be-nā'iah.

26 And of the sons of Ē'lam; Măt-ta-nī'ah, Zĕch-a-rī'ah, and Je-hī'el, and Ăb'dī, and Jĕr'e-mŏth, and E-lī'ah.

27 And of the sons of Zăt'tū; Ĕ-lī-ō-ē'na-ī, E-lī'a-shĭb, Măt-ta-nī'ah, and Jĕr'e-mŏth, and Zā'băd, and A-zī'za.

28 Of the sons also of Bĕb'a-ī; Je-hō-hā'nan, Hăn-a-nī'ah, Zăb'baī, and Ăth'laī.

29 And of the sons of Bā'nī; Me-shŭl'-lam, Măl'luch, and Ăd-a-ī'ah, Jāsh'ub, and Shē'al, and Rā'moth.

30 And of the sons of Pā'hăth–mō'ăb; Ăd'na, and Chē'lăl, Be-nā'iah, Mā-a-sē'iah, Măt-ta-nī'ah, Be-zăl'e-el, and Bĭn'-nū-ī, and Ma-năs'seh.

31 And of the sons of Hā'rĭm; Ĕ-lī-ē'zer, Ĭ-shī'jah, Mal-chī'ah, Shem-ā-i'ah, Shĭm'e-on.

32 Benjamin, Măl'luch, and Shĕm-a-rī'ah.

33 Of the sons of Hā'shum; Mat-te-na'ī, Măt-ta-thah, Zā'băd, E-līph'e-lĕt, Jĕr'e-maī, Ma-năs'seh, and Shĭm'e-ī.

34 Of the sons of Bā'nī; Mā-ad'aī, Amram, and Ū'el,

35 Be-nā'iah, Be-dē'iah, Chĕl'luh,

36 Va-nī'ah, Mĕr'e-mŏth, E-lī'a-shĭb,

37 Măt-ta-nī'ah, Măt-te-na'ī, and Jā'a-sau,

38 And Bā'nī, and Bĭn'nū-ī, Shĭm'e-ī,

39 And Shĕl-e-mī'ah, and Nathan, and Ăd-a-ī'ah,

40 Măch-nă-de'baī, Shăsh'a-ī, Shăr'-a-ī,

41 Ă-zar'e-el, and Shĕl-e-mī'ah, Shĕm-a-rī'ah,

42 Shăl'lum, Ăm-a-rī'ah, and Joseph.

43 Of the sons of Nebo; Je-ī'el, Măt-ti-thī'ah, Zā'băd, Ze-bī'na, Jā'dau, and Jō'el, Be-nā'iah.

44 All these had taken strange wives: and some of them had wives by whom they had children.

F. The List of Those With Mixed Marriages. 10:18-44.

18-44. These verses contain a list of those who had strange wives and who put them away. This included priests (vss. 18-22), Levites (vss. 23-24), and those of Israel (vss. 25-43). **They gave their hands.** This expression in verse 19 means they clapped their hands together to signify obedience to their vow.

True revival can only come when God's people are willing to confess their sin (vs. 11) and are willing to obey God (vs. 12). These are two prerequisites for receiving the power of God and are applicable to all generations. It is interesting to note that in this particular chapter they gave public testimony as to their willingness to confess their sin and obey God.

BIBLIOGRAPHY

Ackroyd, P. R. 1 and 2 Chronicles, Ezra and Nehemiah. In *Torch Bible Commentaries*. Richmond: John Knox Press, 1973.

Adeney, W. F. Ezra, Nehemiah and Esther. In *The Expositor's Bible*. London: Hodder & Stoughton, 1893.

Barber, C. J. *Nehemiah & the Dynamics of Effective Leadership*. Neptune, N.J.: Loizeaux Brothers, 1976.

Batten, L. S. *A Critical and Exegetical Commentary on the Books of Ezra and Nehemiah*. New York: Scribner's, 1913.

Campbell, D. K. *Nehemiah: Man in Charge*. Wheaton: Victor Books, 1979.

Coggins, R. J. Ezra and Nehemiah. In *The Cambridge Bible Commentary on the New English Bible*. Cambridge: University Press, 1976.

Crosby, H. Nehemiah. In *A Commentary on the Holy Scriptures*. Ed. by J. P. Lange. Grand Rapids: Zondervan, n.d.

Cumming, J. E. *The Book of Esther*. 2nd ed. London: Religious Tract Society, n.d.

*Keil, C. F. The Books of Ezra, Nehemiah and Esther. In *Biblical Commentary on the Old Testament*. Grand Rapids: Eerdmans, reprinted, 1950.

Kelly, W. *Lectures on Ezra and Nehemiah*. London: Oliphants, 1921.

*Kidner, D. Ezra and Nehemiah. In *Tyndale Old Testament Commentaries*. London: InterVarsity Press, 1979.

Lange, John Peter. *Commentary on the Holy Scriptures*, Vol. II. Grand Rapids: Zondervan, n.d.

Luck, G. C. *Ezra and Nehemiah*. Chicago: Moody, 1961.

McGee, J. Vernon. *An Exposition on the Book of Esther*. Wheaton: Van Kampen Press, 1951.

Myers, J. M. Ezra and Nehemiah. In *The Anchor Bible*. Garden City, New York: Doubleday, 1965.

Raleigh, Alexander. *The Book of Esther*. Edinburgh: Alan and Charles Black, 1880.

Ryle, H. E. Ezra and Nehemiah. In *The Cambridge Bible*. Cambridge: University Press, 1907.

Schultz, F. Ezra. In *A Commentary on the Holy Scriptures*. Ed. by J. P. Lange. Grand Rapids: Zondervan, n.d.

Seume, R. H. *Nehemiah: God's Builder*. Chicago: Moody, 1978.

Thomas, W. Ian. *If I Perish . . . I Perish*. Grand Rapids: Zondervan, 1966.

*Whitcomb, J. C. Ezra, Nehemiah and Esther. In *The Wycliffe Bible Commentary*. Chicago: Moody Press, 1962.

Wilson, R. D. Ezra-Nehemiah. In *International Standard Bible Encyclopedia*. Vol. II. Grand Rapids: Eerdmans, 1946.

*Wright, J. S. Ezra and Nehemiah. In *The New Bible Commentary*. Grand Rapids: Eerdmans, 1953.

———. *The Date of Ezra's Coming to Jerusalem*. London: Tyndale Press, 1958.

*Yamauchi, E. Ezra-Nehemiah. In *The Expositor's Bible Commentary*. Grand Rapids: Zondervan, 1979.

NEHEMIAH

INTRODUCTION

In the Hebrew Masoretic Text the books of Ezra and Nehemiah are considered as one volume. They contain a continuous narrative dealing with the re-establishment of the Jewish community in southern Palestine.

Authorship. Nehemiah is the principal personality in this book which bears his name. It was written by Nehemiah himself (note the use of the personal pronoun) and is in the format of a personal diary. R. K. Harrison, *Introduction to the Old Testament* (pp. 1145-1151), observes that since the books of Nehemiah and Ezra were originally one book, it is likely that Ezra incorporated Nehemiah's memoirs as an appendix to his own book.

The question of the authorship of Nehemiah is bound to the question of the authorship of Ezra (see notes). Critics have objected to the authenticity of this book because of the mention of "Jaddua" (12:11), who Josephus claimed was the high priest in the days of Alexander the Great 330 B.C. On this basis they argue that the book of Nehemiah dates from a later Hellenistic period. However, Josephus also states that Jaddua was a contemporary of Sanballat and Manasseh. While it is possible that Nehemiah may have lived to see the youthful Jaddua, who in turn lived till nearly ninety, it is more likely that Josephus' reference is simply incorrect. Others have argued that the reference to "drams," or Greek drachmas (7:71), is evidence of authorship in the Greek period. However, there is ample evidence of Greek contact with both Babylon and Persia. Drachmas have been discovered in the Persian level at Beth-zur. In view of the biblical testimony and the lack of substantial contrary historical evidence, the authenticity of Nehemiah's authorship in the fifth century B.C. is still reliable.

Date. Despite attempts to prove that Ezra and Nehemiah were written in the third century B.C., it is still more probable that they were written in the fifth century B.C. Contrary views are incompatible with the evidence of Scripture itself. Ezra arrived in Jerusalem in 457 B.C. and Nehemiah in 445 B.C. This is founded on the view that Artaxerxes in 7:1 is Artaxerxes I Longimanus. The date of the writing of Ezra would then be some time after 445 B.C., and the date of Nehemiah would be some time after 433 B.C. (see the discussion of the date of Ezra—cf. also Gleason Archer, *A Survey of Old Testament Introduction*, pp. 395-401).

OUTLINE

COMMENTARY

I. THE ARRIVAL OF NEHEMIAH. 1:1-2:20.

A. Nehemiah Learns of the Conditions of Jerusalem. 1:1-3.

THE words of Nē-he-mī'ah the son of Hăch-a-lī'ah. And it came to pass in the month Chĭs'leu, in the twentieth year, as I was in Shū'shăn the palace,

1:1. The words of Nehemiah. This is the title of the book. Many of the Old Testament prophets begin their writings with a similar statement. **In the month Chisleu.** Chisleu is the ninth month and correlates with December. **In the twentieth year,** that is, the twentieth year of the reign of Artaxerxes. He reigned from 465 to 425 B.C. The events of Nehemiah began in 445 B.C. (J. P. Lange, *Commentary on the Holy Scriptures*, p. 6).

2 That Ha-nā'nī, one of my brethren, came, he and *certain* men of Jū'dah;

2. Hanani was Nehemiah's brother (7:1-2). Nehemiah inquires as to the condition of those who had returned to Jeru-

and I asked them concerning the Jews that had escaped, which were left of the captivity, and concerning Jerusalem.

3 And they said unto me, The remnant that are left of the captivity there in the province *are* in great affliction and reproach: the wall of Jerusalem also *is* broken down, and the gates thereof are burned with fire.

4 ¶And it came to pass, when I heard these words, that I sat down and wept, and mourned *certain* days, and fasted, and prayed before the God of heaven,

5 And said, I beseech thee, O LORD God of heaven, the great and terrible God, that keepeth covenant and mercy for them that love him and observe his commandments:

6 Let thine ear now be attentive, and thine eyes open, that thou mayest hear the prayer of thy servant, which I pray before thee now, day and night, for the children of Israel thy servants, and confess the sins of the children of Israel, which we have sinned against thee: both I and my father's house have sinned.

7 We have dealt very corruptly against thee, and have not kept the commandments, nor the statutes, nor the judgments, which thou commandedst thy servant Moses.

8 Remember, I beseech thee, the word that thou commandedst thy servant Moses, saying, If ye transgress, I will scatter you abroad among the nations:

9 But *if* ye turn unto me, and keep my commandments, and do them; though there were of you cast out unto the uttermost part of heaven, *yet* will I gather them from thence, and will bring them unto the place that I have chosen to set my name there.

10 Now these *are* thy servants and thy people, whom thou hast redeemed by thy great power, and by thy strong hand.

11 O Lord, I beseech thee, let now thine ear be attentive to the prayer of thy servant, and to the prayer of thy servants, who desire to fear thy name: and prosper, I pray thee, thy servant this day, and grant him mercy in the sight of this man. For I was the king's cupbearer.

CHAPTER 2

AND it came to pass in the month Nī'-šăn, in the twentieth year of Är-ta-xerʹ-xĕs the king, *that* wine *was* before him: and I took up the wine, and gave *it* unto the king. Now I had not been *beforetime* sad in his presence.

2 Wherefore the king said unto me, Why *is* thy countenance sad, seeing thou *art* not sick? this *is* nothing *else*

salem. He addresses these people as **the Jews that had escaped.** The idea is that they were delivered or liberated.

3. The response is disheartening. The people were in **great affliction and reproach.** Hanani gives the cause of this reproach. The walls were **broken down.** They had remained like this since the days of Nebuchadnezzar (II Kgs 25:10).

B. Nehemiah's Sorrow and Prayer. 1:4-11.

4. This report brought great sorrow to Nehemiah. He **wept, and mourned . . . , and fasted, and prayed.** His reaction of remorse is similar to that of Ezra when he became aware of the spiritual condition of the remnant (Ezra 9:3, 5; 10:1).

Verses 5-11 contain Nehemiah's prayer.

5. His prayer is addressed to Jehovah, **O LORD.** He is designated as **God of heaven.** This would imply his power over all the events of men. **Terrible.** This is derived from a verb which means "to tremble." He is an "awe-inspiring" God. **That keepeth covenant.** God does not forsake His people; He keeps His agreements and promises. God is faithful to those that **love him** and **observe his commandments.** Several key thoughts in this verse are from Deuteronomy 7:9, 21.

6. Let thine ear now be attentive, and thine eyes open. Compare this with I Kings 8:29, 52 and II Chronicles 6:40. **Day and night.** The concern and sorrow of Nehemiah produced an attitude of continual prayer. **Both I and my father's house have sinned.** Nehemiah does not only recognize that others have sinned, but he first recognizes his own sin.

7-9. Have not kept the commandments, nor the statutes, nor the judgments. This refers to the totality of God's law which the children of Israel had disregarded. After confessing his sin, Nehemiah appeals to the promise of God. **I will scatter you abroad.** God had done that through Nebuchadnezzar. **But if ye turn unto me.** This is the condition upon which Nehemiah is appealing to God. God had promised to regather the Jews if they return to Him.

10-11. Whom thou hast redeemed by thy great power. Nehemiah is appealing on the same basis that Moses appealed. When God wanted to destroy the Jews, Moses interceded and reminded God He had redeemed the Jews. Therefore, how could He now destroy them (Deut 7:8; 9:26, 29)? Nehemiah appeals to the faithfulness of God. Because they **fear** God, God must restore and **prosper** them. **Grant him mercy in the sight of this man.** Nehemiah wants God to move the heart of Artaxerxes so he will be favorable to the request of Nehemiah.

C. Nehemiah Convinced to Return. 2:1-10.

2:1-2. The month Nisan. This is the first month of the Hebrew year, three months after Chisleu (1:1). Nehemiah had spent the three months praying and seeking God's guidance (1:6). **I had not been beforetime sad in his presence.** It was not proper to be sad when in the presence of the king. **Why is thy countenance sad . . . ?** A person cannot effectively hide his emotions. Sadness or joy will always be revealed on the face. The king was able to discern Nehemiah's inner sadness by his distressed face.

but sorrow of heart. Then I was very sore afraid,

3 And said unto the king, Let the king live for ever: why should not my countenance be sad, when the city, the place of my fathers' sepulchres, *lieth* waste, and the gates thereof are consumed with fire?

4 Then the king said unto me, For what dost thou make request? So I prayed to the God of heaven.

5 And I said unto the king, If it please the king, and if thy servant have found favour in thy sight, that thou wouldest send me unto Jū'dah, unto the city of my fathers' sepulchres, that I may build it.

6 And the king said unto me, (the queen also sitting by him,) For how long shall thy journey be? and when wilt thou return? So it pleased the king to send me; and I set him a time.

7 Moreover I said unto the king, If it please the king, let letters be given me to the governors beyond the river, that they may convey me over till I come into Jū'dah;

8 And a letter unto Ā'săph the keeper of the king's forest, that he may give me timber to make beams for the gates of the palace which *appertained* to the house, and for the wall of the city, and for the house that I shall enter into. And the king granted me, according to the good hand of my God upon me.

9 ¶Then I came to the governors beyond the river, and gave them the king's letters. Now the king had sent captains of the army and horsemen with me.

10 When Săn-băl'lat the Hôr'o-nīte, and Tō-bī'ah the servant, the Ammonite, heard *of it*, it grieved them exceedingly that there was come a man to seek the welfare of the children of Israel.

11 ¶So I came to Jerusalem, and was there three days.

12 And I arose in the night, I and some few men with me; neither told I *any* man what my God had put in my heart to do at Jerusalem: neither *was there any* beast with me, save the beast that I rode upon.

13 And I went out by night by the gate of the valley, even before the dragon well, and to the dung port, and viewed the walls of Jerusalem, which were broken down, and the gates thereof were consumed with fire.

14 Then I went on to the gate of the fountain, and to the king's pool: but *there was* no place for the beast *that was* under me to pass.

15 Then went I up in the night by the brook, and viewed the wall, and turned back, and entered by the gate of the valley, and *so* returned.

16 And the rulers knew not whither I went, or what I did; neither had I as yet

3-4. Let the king live for ever. Nehemiah addresses the king with proper respect (Dan 2:4; 3:9). **The city, the place of my fathers' sepulchers.** This unusual description of the city indicates that Nehemiah was originally from Jerusalem. The king inquires as to what Nehemiah wants to do. **So I prayed to the God of heaven.** At this moment of crisis Nehemiah turns to God. Whatever we are and whatever the circumstances, we can pray to God for guidance and strength.

5-6. Nehemiah's answer was direct. **That I may build it.** He wanted to personally supervise the rebuilding of Jerusalem. **So it pleased the king to send me.** The king grants Nehemiah's request. The length of the journey and the time of Nehemiah's return are also discussed.

7-8. Let letters be given me to the governors beyond the river. These were the governors on the west bank of the Euphrates. These letters would provide safe passage through their territory. Nehemiah also requests a letter to **Asaph the keeper of the king's forest . . . the palace which appertained to the house.** There is considerable discussion among commentators as to the identity of this palace. Some think it is Solomon's house, which was located near the Temple. Others think it was a military citadel built as an extension of the Temple and utilized for defensive purposes (Keil and Delitzsch, *Biblical Commentary on the Old Testament*, pp. 166-167). The latter is the more logical of the viewpoints. **For the house that I shall enter into.** This does not refer to Nehemiah's personal home. Rather, it refers to the Temple. The king **granted** Nehemiah all he requested. Note the providential hand of God in all these events. **According to the good hand of my God unto me.**

9-10. The king sent a protective army with Nehemiah. Immediately, Nehemiah is faced with opposition. Sanballat and Tobiah were leaders of the Samaritans and Ammonites. Both hated and despised the Jews.

D. Nehemiah Surveys the Situation. 2:11-20.

Nehemiah arrives in Jerusalem. He evaluates the status of the wall and decides to begin the rebuilding process.

11-12. Was there three days. The first three days he rested. He probably devoted much of this time to prayer. Ezra had begun his mission to Jerusalem in the same way (Ezr 8:32). Nehemiah did not want to call attention to his mission. **Neither told I any man what my God had put in my heart to do at Jerusalem.** Nehemiah had kept his mission to Jerusalem a secret. Probably, he did not want to incite the wrath of Sanballat prior to the building process.

13-15. And I went out by night by the gate of the valley. "The valley gate is the modern gate of the city leading to the valley of Gihon" (Keil and Delitzsch, p. 109). **Dung port.** This was the gate out of which the garbage was taken and then burned. **The gate of the fountain.** This was the gate by the pool of Siloah (3:15). The walls and gates were in such ruin that the **beast** on which Nehemiah sat could not get through. Nehemiah went by the brook Kidron and then returned by **the gate of the valley** (vs. 13).

16-18. Until this point, no one knew what Nehemiah intended to do. **Then said I unto them.** He gathers the people of

told *it* to the Jews, nor to the priests, nor to the nobles, nor to the rulers, nor to the rest that did the work.

17 Then said I unto them, Ye see the distress that we *are* in, how Jerusalem *lieth* waste, and the gates thereof are burned with fire: come, and let us build up the wall of Jerusalem, that we be no more a reproach.

18 Then I told them of the hand of my God which was good upon me; as also the king's words that he had spoken unto me. And they said, Let us rise up and build. So they strengthened their hands for *this* good *work.*

19 But when Săn-băl′lat the Hôr′o-nīte, and Tō-bī′ah the servant, the Ammonite, and Gĕ′shem the Arabian, heard *it*, they laughed us to scorn, and despised us, and said, What *is* this thing that ye do? will ye rebel against the king?

20 Then answered I them, and said unto them, The God of heaven, he will prosper us; therefore we his servants will arise and build: but ye have no portion, nor right, nor memorial, in Jerusalem.

CHAPTER 3

THEN E-lī′a-shĭb the high priest rose up with his brethren the priests, and they builded the sheep gate; they sanctified it, and set up the doors of it; even unto the tower of Mĕ′ah they sanctified it, unto the tower of Hă-nan′ē-el.

2 And next unto him builded the men of Jericho. And next to them builded Zăc′cur the son of Imri.

3 But the fish gate did the sons of Hăs-se-nā′ah build, who *also* laid the beams thereof, and set up the doors thereof, the locks thereof, and the bars thereof.

4 And next unto them repaired Mĕr′e-mŏth the son of Ū-rī′jah, the son of Koz. And next unto them repaired Me-shŭl′lam the son of Bĕr-e-chī′ah, the son of Me-shĕz′a-beel. And next unto them repaired Zā′dŏk the son of Bā′a-na.

5 And next unto them the Te-kō′ītes repaired; but their nobles put not their necks to the work of their Lord.

6 Moreover the old gate repaired Je-hoi′a-da the son of Pa-sē′ah, and Me-shŭl′lam the son of Bĕs-o-dē′iah; they laid the beams thereof, and set up the doors thereof, and the locks thereof, and the bars thereof.

7 And next unto them repaired Mĕl-a-tī′ah the Gĭb′e-o-nīte, and Jā′dŏn the Me-rŏn′o-thīte, the men of Gĭb′e-on, and of Mizpah, unto the throne of the governor on this side the river.

8 Next unto him repaired Ŭz′zī-el the son of Här-hā-i′ah, of the goldsmiths. Next unto him also repaired Hăn-a-nī′ah the son of *one of* the apothecaries,

Jerusalem together in a public meeting. He begins by describing the terrible condition of the city. He then reveals his vision and the purpose that brought him to Jerusalem. **Come, and let us build up the wall of Jerusalem.** Nehemiah calls for a unified effort to accomplish this task. He encourages the people by telling them how God has been working and making the rebuilding possible. **They strengthened their hands for this good work.** This means that they were enthusiastic in their preparations for building the wall.

19-20. But. When one begins a work for God there will always be opposition. Another name is added to the enemy. **Geshem the Arabian.** Sanballat, Tobiah, and Geshem laugh and scorn the efforts of the Jewish community. Nehemiah's answer is rooted in the power of God, who would **prosper** them. As for Sanballat, Tobiah, and Geshem, they had no part whatsoever in Jerusalem. They had set themselves against God.

II. THE BUILDING OF THE WALL. 3:1-7:75.

A. The People Who Rebuilt the Wall. 3:1-32.

3:1. Eliashib the high priest. The rebuilding process is inaugurated by the high priest and the priests. Later in this narrative, Eliashib helps Tobiah and thus promotes the enemies of Jerusalem. **The sheep gate.** This gate was on the eastern part of the wall north of Haram (Keil and Delitzsch, p. 174). Because it was located near the Temple, it was the priests who built it. **They sanctified it** (Heb *qadash*). This means they dedicated the gate after it had been completed. **The tower of Meah . . . unto the tower of Hananeel.** These towers were located between the sheep gate and the fish gate and were adjacent to the Temple area (see 12:39 and Jer 31:38).

2-3. And next unto him builded the men of Jericho. The **next unto him** refers to Eliashib and the priests. Next to Eliashib, the men of Jericho were building. **And next to them.** Beside the men of Jericho, Zaccur was building. **The fish gate.** This gate was located near the fish market. It is also mentioned in II Chronicles 33:14 and Zephaniah 1:10. **The locks thereof, and the bars thereof.** These were the bars and sockets used for locking the gate.

4-7. But their nobles put not their necks to the work of their Lord. Not everyone was sympathetic to the cause of Nehemiah. The wealthy leaders of Tekoa did not participate in the building project. **Moreover the old gate repaired Jehoiada the son of Paseah.** The old gate "must have been in the north wall, east of the present Damascus-gate" (Lange, p. 16). Keil translates this as the "gate of the old wall" (p. 177). **Unto the throne of the governor on this side the river.** The Gibeonites who helped were not under the authority of the governor of Jerusalem. They were responsible to the governor on this side of the Euphrates River. Nevertheless, they assisted in the work.

8-9. The son of one of the apothecaries. These were people who made spices and ointments. They were probably priests (I Chr 9:30). **Fortified** (Heb *'azab*). The literal translation here is "they left Jerusalem unto the broad wall." Keil interprets this

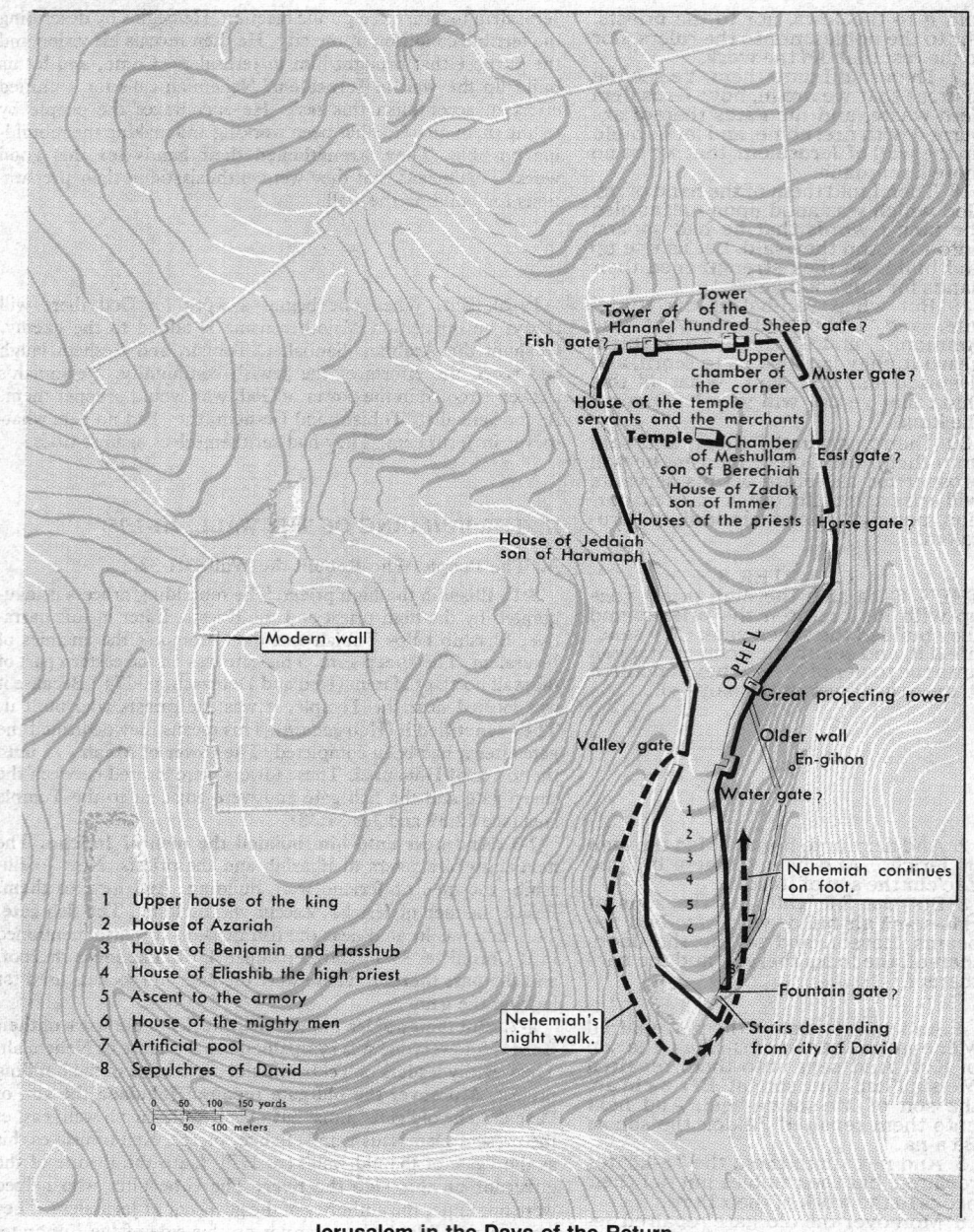

1 Upper house of the king
2 House of Azariah
3 House of Benjamin and Hasshub
4 House of Eliashib the high priest
5 Ascent to the armory
6 House of the mighty men
7 Artificial pool
8 Sepulchres of David

Jerusalem in the Days of the Return

and they fortified Jerusalem unto the broad wall.

9 And next unto them repaired Reph-ā-i'ah the son of Hur, the ruler of the half part of Jerusalem.

10 And next unto them repaired Je-dā'iah the son of Ha-rū'māph, even over against his house. And next unto him repaired Hăt'tŭsh the son of Hăsh-ab-nī'ah.

to mean that they "left Jerusalem untouched as far as the broad wall" (Keil, p. 180). **The ruler of the half part of Jerusalem.** Rephaiah was responsible for half of Jerusalem, and Shallum was responsible for the other half (vs. 12). The government of the early community in Jerusalem was apparently well organized.

10-12. Even over against his house. Jedaiah repaired the part of the wall that was adjacent to his own dwelling place. **The tower of the furnaces.** This lay between the broad wall and the valley gate and served as a defense for the northwestern section of the town. **Shallum . . . ruler of the half part of Jerusalem.**

11 Măl-chī′jah the son of Hā′rĭm, and Hā′shŭb the son of Pā′hăth–mō′ăb, repaired the other piece, and the tower of the furnaces.

12 And next unto him repaired Shăl′lum the son of Hă-lō′hĕsh, the ruler of the half part of Jerusalem, he and his daughters.

13 The valley gate repaired Hā′nun, and the inhabitants of Za-nō′ah; they built it, and set up the doors thereof, the locks thereof, and the bars thereof, and a thousand cubits on the wall unto the dung gate.

14 But the dung gate repaired Măl-chī′ah the son of Rē′chăb, the ruler of part of Bĕth–hăc′ce-rem; he built it, and set up the doors thereof, the locks thereof, and the bars thereof.

15 But the gate of the fountain repaired Shăl′lun the son of Cŏl–hō′zeh, the ruler of part of Mizpah; he built it, and covered it, and set up the doors thereof, the locks thereof, and the bars thereof, and the wall of the pool of Sī-lō′ah by the king's garden, and unto the stairs that go down from the city of David.

16 After him repaired Nē-he-mī′ah the son of Ăz′bŭk, the ruler of the half part of Bĕth′–zûr, unto *the place* over against the sepulchres of David, and to the pool that was made, and unto the house of the mighty.

17 After him repaired the Lē′vītes, Rē′hum the son of Bā′nī. Next unto him repaired Hăsh-a-bī′ah, the ruler of the half part of Keī′lah, in his part.

18 After him repaired their brethren, Băv′a-ī the son of Hĕn′a-dăd, the ruler of the half part of Keī′lah.

19 And next to him repaired Ē′zer the son of Jĕsh′u-a, the ruler of Mizpah, another piece over against the going up to the armoury at the turning *of the wall.*

20 After him Bā′ruch the son of Zăb′baī earnestly repaired the other piece, from the turning *of the wall* unto the door of the house of E-lī′a-shĭb the high priest.

21 After him repaired Mĕr′e-mŏth the son of Ū-rī′jah the son of Koz another piece, from the door of the house of E-lī′a-shĭb even to the end of the house of E-lī′a-shĭb.

22 And after him repaired the priests, the men of the plain.

23 After him repaired Benjamin and Hā′shŭb over against their house. After him repaired Ăz-a-rī′ah the son of Mā-a-sē′iah the son of Ăn-a-nī′ah by his house.

24 After him repaired Bĭn′nū-ī the son of Hĕn′a-dăd another piece, from the house of Ăz-a-rī′ah unto the turning *of the wall,* even unto the corner.

25 Pā′lăl the son of Ū′za-ī, over against the turning *of the wall,* and the tower which lieth out from the king's high house, that *was* by the court of the prison. After him Pe-dā′iah the son of Pā′rŏsh.

26 Moreover the Nĕth′i-nĭmś dwelt in O′phĕl, unto *the place* over against the water gate toward the east, and the tower that lieth out.

27 After them the Te-kō′ītes repaired

See the comments in verse 9. **And his daughters.** Women were involved in this important building project.

13-14. A thousand cubits on the wall unto the dung gate. This describes the distance along the wall between the valley gate and the dung gate. For further discussion on these two gates see chapter 2:13.

15. The gate of the fountain. See 2:15 for a discussion on this gate. **The wall of the pool of Siloah by the king's garden.** This pool was outside the city by the Tyropoeon valley. The king's garden was next to the pool. This garden is also mentioned in II Kings 25:4. **The stairs that go down from the city of David.** These were the steps that lead from the walls down to the king's garden and the pool of Siloah.

16. Unto the place over against the sepulchers of David. These burial places refer to the graves of David and his house and of the various kings of Israel (II Chr 28:27). **And to the pool that was made, and unto the house of the mighty.** The actual location of these two places is still unknown.

17-19. Another piece over against the going up to the armory at the turning of the wall. According to Lange, this armory was probably at the angle in the eastern ophel wall (p. 17).

20-23. Baruch the son of Zabbai earnestly repaired the other piece. It is interesting to note that the zeal and enthusiasm of Baruch is mentioned. He may have been a priest, which would account somewhat for his zealous desire to build (10:6). **And after him repaired the priests, the men of the plain.** The word translated "plain" refers here to the Jordan Valley (Heb *kikar*). These men were from the area of the Jordan Valley. **Over against their house.** Benjamin, Hashub, and Azariah repaired the portion of the wall that was adjacent to their house.

24-25. And the tower which lieth out from the king's high house, that was by the court of the prison. This refers to a tower that was part of Solomon's palace. The court of the prison is also mentioned in Jeremiah 22:2 and was located adjacent to the king's house.

26-31. The Nethinim were the Temple servants. They were originally appointed by David to serve at the Temple (Ezr 8:20). **From above the horse gate repaired the priests.** The horse gate apparently was located between the Temple and the palace. It is mentioned in II Chronicles 23:15 and Jeremiah 31:40. **The**

another piece, over against the great tower that lieth out, even unto the wall of Ō'phĕl.

28 From above the horse gate repaired the priests, every one over against the house.

29 After them repaired Zā'dŏk the son of Ĭm'mer over against his house. After him repaired also Shem-ā-i'ah the son of Shĕch-a-nī'ah, the keeper of the east gate.

30 After him repaired Hăn-a-nī'ah the son of Shĕl-e-mī'ah, and Hā'nun the sixth son of Zā'lăph, another piece. After him repaired Me-shūl'lam the son of Bĕr-e-chī'ah over against his chamber.

31 After him repaired Măl-chī'ah the goldsmith's son unto the place of the Nĕth'i-nĭmś, and of the merchants, over against the gate Mĭph'kăd, and to the going up of the corner.

32 And between the going up of the corner unto the sheep gate repaired the goldsmiths and the merchants.

CHAPTER 4

BUT it came to pass, that when Săn-băl'lat heard that we builded the wall, he was wroth, and took great indignation, and mocked the Jews.

2 And he spake before his brethren and the army of Sa-mā'rī-a, and said, What do these feeble Jews? will they fortify themselves? will they sacrifice? will they make an end in a day? will they revive the stones out of the heaps of the rubbish which are burned?

3 Now Tō-bī'ah the Ammonite was by him, and he said, Even that which they build, if a fox go up, he shall even break down their stone wall.

4 Hear, O our God; for we are despised: and turn their reproach upon their own head, and give them for a prey in the land of captivity:

5 And cover not their iniquity, and let not their sin be blotted out from before thee: for they have provoked thee to anger before the builders.

place of the Nethinim, and of the merchants. This probably refers to the marketplace where they traded animals to be utilized in the sacrificial worship.

32. We can synthesize the chapter by considering the repairing of the main gates and the repairing of the inner gates. The main gates are described as having bars and locks; and the list would include: the sheep gate (vss. 1, 2); the fish gate (vs. 3); the old gate (vs. 6); the valley gate (vs. 13); the dung gate (vs. 14); the fountain gate (vs. 15). The other gates mentioned are the inner gates, such as: the water gate (vs. 26); the horse gate (vs. 28); the east gate (vs. 29); the Miphkad gate (vs. 31). In total there were ten different gates mentioned in the repairing of the wall.

B. Opposition Encountered. 4:1-3.

In chapter 3 the actual repairing is discussed, and the various people who were involved in building and repairing the walls are listed. Chapters 4, 5, and 6 contain a detailed description of this period of time, with special emphasis on those who oppose the rebuilding process.

4:1. But it came to pass. Whenever someone sets out to accomplish a work for God there will always be those who oppose it. Sanballat hears what Nehemiah has done. And mocked the Jews. Sanballat is angry and begins by making fun of the Jews.

2. And the army of Samaria. The rebuilding of Jerusalem had a direct impact on the future of Samaria. "One of the main highways linking the Tigris and Euphrates River Valley to the north with Egypt in the south and Philistia in the west, passes through Jerusalem. With Jerusalem once more a well-protected city, its very location will attract trade and gone will be Samaria's economic supremacy in the land beyond the river" (Cyril J. Barber, *Nehemiah and the Dynamics of Effective Leadership*, pp. 59-60). Sanballat uses the means of criticism and mockery to discourage the Jews. Will they make an end in a day? This refers to the idea that the Jews are completing the task openly during the day.

3. Sanballat is joined by Tobiah in opposing the work. They also criticize the quality of the work.

C. Nehemiah's Prayer. 4:4-12.

4-5. Opposition always brings God's people to their knees in prayer. Hear, O our God. When the forces of evil surround and when we are faced with adversity and discouragement, we must turn to God. It is interesting to note that Nehemiah is driven to prayer eight times during these events. And turn their reproach upon their own head. This prayer for deliverance is based upon the justice and righteousness of God. Nehemiah asks that God would recompense to them according to their sin. For they have provoked thee to anger before the builders. This literally means that they have vexed with alarm the builders (Lange, p. 21).

6 So built we the wall; and all the wall was joined together unto the half thereof: for the people had a mind to work.

7 ¶But it came to pass, *that* when Săn-băl′lat, and Tō-bī′ah, and the Arabians, and the Ammonites, and the Ăsh′dŏd-ītes, heard that the walls of Jerusalem were made up, *and* that the breaches began to be stopped, then they were very wroth,

8 And conspired all of them together to come *and* to fight against Jerusalem, and to hinder it.

9 Nevertheless we made our prayer unto our God, and set a watch against them day and night, because of them.

10 And Jŭ′dah said, The strength of the bearers of burdens is decayed, and *there is* much rubbish; so that we are not able to build the wall.

11 And our adversaries said, They shall not know, neither see, till we come in the midst among them, and slay them, and cause the work to cease.

12 ¶And it came to pass, that when the Jews which dwelt by them came, they said unto us ten times, From all places whence ye shall return unto us *they will be upon you.*

13 Therefore set I in the lower places behind the wall, *and* on the higher places, I even set the people after their families with their swords, their spears, and their bows.

14 And I looked, and rose up, and said unto the nobles, and to the rulers, and to the rest of the people, Be not ye afraid of them: remember the Lord, *which is* great and terrible, and fight for your brethren, your sons, and your daughters, your wives, and your houses.

15 And it came to pass, when our enemies heard that it was known unto us, and God had brought their counsel to nought, that we returned all of us to the wall, every one unto his work.

16 And it came to pass from that time forth, *that* the half of my servants wrought in the work, and the other half of them held both the spears, the shields, and the bows, and the habergeons; and the rulers *were* behind all the house of Jŭ′dah.

17 They which builded on the wall, and they that bare burdens, with those that laded, *every one* with one of his

6. And all the wall was joined together unto the half thereof. This means that they continued to build the wall until its height had reached half of the intended height. **For the people had a mind to work.** In the midst of adversity the people had a unified purpose and a compelling desire to finish the work.

7. In the Hebrew Bible this verse begins as the first verse of chapter 4. The previous six verses in the Hebrew Bible belong to the third chapter. When Sanballat, Tobiah, the Arabians, the Ammonites, and the Ashdodites heard that the work was progressing, **then they were very wroth.**

8-9. These enemies come together and decide to **fight against Jerusalem. Heard that the walls of Jerusalem were made up** (vs. 7). This literally means that the breaches and damages in the walls were bandaged (Keil, p. 202). **Nevertheless we made our prayer unto our God.** Again in the midst of adversity the Jews are driven to God in prayer (see the comments on vs. 4). Besides praying, they **set a watch against them day and night.** The Jews did three things. First, they prayed. Second, they worked. Third, they set guards in order to be ready for battle. Praying, working, and readiness are the three requirements for serving God.

10. The strength of the bearers of burdens is decayed. The overwhelming demands of praying, working, and watching had an adverse effect upon the Jews. It was draining them of their energies, and they were unable to continue. **We are not able to build the wall.**

11-12. Beyond the pressing demands of their work, they also faced the discouragement of their adversaries. They were continuing their work with the fear that at any moment their enemies would strike in battle. The Jews were also faced with a third problem. They were drained from the demands of their work; they were faced with the threat of their enemies; and they were discouraged by Jews from the surrounding communities near Jerusalem. These Jews who lived in the country encouraged those who were building the walls to return home since they were totally surrounded by the enemy. The builders were facing adversity from every possible direction.

D. The Building Continues. 4:13-23.

13. Nehemiah responds to the threat of attack by placing armed detachments of soldiers at the critical places on the wall. These were **the lower places behind the wall.** Where the wall was not totally built up and most susceptible to attack, Nehemiah placed his strongest armed defenses.

14. Be not ye afraid of them: remember the Lord. Nehemiah addresses the congregation and encourages them to place their faith and trust in none other than the Lord. Nehemiah also reminds them that they are fighting for their families and houses. These were important motivations to build and defend the city.

15-18. When Nehemiah is aware that the enemies know the Jews do not fear them, all of the builders return to work. Nehemiah divides up the company; half of them work while the other half are prepared for battle. The work proceeded, and everyone who was involved in the work also carried a weapon. This is symbolic of the Christian who is involved in building for the Lord and, at the same time, in warfare against the devil. We should always be ready to build and to fight. **And he that sounded the trumpet was by me.** Nehemiah had the responsibility of sounding the trumpet to warn of the approaching enemy.

hands wrought in the work, and with the other *hand* held a weapon.

18 For the builders, every one had his sword girded by his side, and *so* builded. And he that sounded the trumpet *was* by me.

19 And I said unto the nobles, and to the rulers, and to the rest of the people, The work *is* great and large, and we are separated upon the wall, one far from another.

20 In what place *therefore* ye hear the sound of the trumpet, resort ye thither unto us: our God shall fight for us.

21 So we laboured in the work: and half of them held the spears from the rising of the morning till the stars appeared.

22 Likewise at the same time said I unto the people, Let every one with his servant lodge within Jerusalem, that in the night they may be a guard to us, and labour on the day.

23 So neither I, nor my brethren, nor my servants, nor the men of the guard which followed me, none of us put off our clothes, *saving that* every one put them off for washing.

CHAPTER 5

AND there was a great cry of the people and of their wives against their brethren the Jews.

2 For there were that said, We, our sons, and our daughters, *are* many: therefore we take up corn *for them*, that we may eat, and live.

3 *Some* also there were that said, We have mortgaged our lands, vineyards, and houses, that we might buy corn, because of the dearth.

4 There were also that said, We have borrowed money for the king's tribute, *and that upon* our lands and vineyards.

5 Yet now our flesh *is* as the flesh of our brethren, our children as their children: and, lo, we bring into bondage our sons and our daughters to be servants, and *some* of our daughters are brought unto bondage *already:* neither *is it* in our power *to redeem them;* for other men have our lands and vineyards.

6 ¶And I was very angry when I heard their cry and these words.

7 Then I consulted with myself, and I rebuked the nobles, and the rulers, and said unto them, Ye exact usury, every one of his brother. And I set a great assembly against them.

8 And I said unto them, We after our ability have redeemed our brethren the Jews, which were sold unto the heathen; and will ye even sell your brethren? or shall they be sold unto us? Then held they their peace, and found nothing *to answer.*

9 Also I said, It *is* not good that ye do: ought ye not to walk in the fear of our God because of the reproach of the heathen our enemies?

19-20. Nehemiah organized the congregation so that when the trumpet was sounded all of the people would congregate to that area. That would signify the point of attack. **Our God shall fight for us.** Again Nehemiah reminds them that God was fighting for them. It was this confidence in the power and ability of God that would give them hope in the midst of the most adverse circumstances.

21-23. The work was very demanding. They worked **from the rising of the morning** until **the stars appeared.** From the crack of dawn until the stars came out they were involved in building the wall. Nehemiah took an extra precaution by asking everyone to reside in Jerusalem during the building process. This was for the security of the city during the night. They were so committed to the building that everyone at all times was prepared to defend the city. **None of us put off our clothes.** They were ready at any moment to defend Jerusalem. As Christians we are never to lay aside our armor but are always to be ready to go to battle.

E. The Problem of Debt. 5:1-19.

5:1-3. The poorer people of the community begin complaining against **their brethren the Jews.** This obviously refers to the richer members of the Jewish community. The first complaint that they made was that they needed corn **that we may eat, and live.** Apparently the situation for the poorer members of the community was rather severe. They had come to the point of desperation and hunger. **We have mortgaged our lands.** Some of the people had mortgaged their properties in order to secure the necessary funds to buy corn.

4-5. Others had borrowed money in order to pay taxes to the king. The problem was compounded by the fact that some of them had sold their children into bondage, and now they could not redeem them. The entire situation was one of destitution. They were without money, food, property, and family.

6-7. Nehemiah was angry when he discovered the injustice of this situation. He gathers the rich members of the community together and brings this injustice to their attention. **Ye exact usury, every one of his brother.** Nehemiah calls all of the Jewish community together for **a great assembly.**

8. Nehemiah reminds them that at various times they had bought back Jews who had been sold into bondage to heathen nations. He reminds them that this is good. However, it is wrong to sell them into bondage. **Then held they their peace.** They had no justification for their injustice.

9. Ought ye not to walk in the fear of our God. Nehemiah reminds them of their obligation to obey and fear the Lord. Proper response to God will prevent them from mistreating their brothers. **Because of the reproach of the heathen our enemies?** If they continued to sell their brethren into bondage, then this will give opportunity for the heathen to criticize and despise them. Nehemiah was conscious of the fact that the heathen would look for every opportunity to mock the Jewish community. Consequently, they were to portray to the outside world a community of love and understanding. This is also true today.

Christians sometimes mistreat one another, and this ultimately gives a bad testimony to the heathen community.

10. I likewise. Nehemiah recognizes that he had been involved in lending money and corn to the poor people. He does not seek to justify his sin, but rather recognizes his own bad conduct for what it is. **Let us leave off this usury.** He encourages the people to make an end of this unjust practice.

11-12. Nehemiah calls for complete restitution. They move to restore the lands and all other properties that had been given. **Also the hundredth part of the money.** This probably refers to the interest placed on the loans. The people agree to restore all properties and to require no interest. Nehemiah signifies the importance of this agreement by taking an oath with the priests that they would fulfill that to which they agreed.

13. Also I shook my lap. Nehemiah gathered his garments and lifted them until he had formed a lap in his garment. By shaking the lap he was symbolizing that anyone who failed to perform their vow would be **shaken out, and emptied.** The congregation responded by saying **Amen, and praised the Lord.** They realized that in obeying the advice of Ezra they were ultimately showing their obedience to the will of God.

14. Nehemiah ruled as governor for twelve years in Jerusalem. During this time he did not eat **the bread of the governor.** He did not take advantage of the money available to him for performing the office of governorship. He was more interested in serving the people than he was in fulfilling a vocation.

15-16. The governors who had ruled before him had heavily taxed the people. However, Nehemiah was gracious and kind. He was motivated to serve the people **because of the fear of God.** Throughout the building of the walls, Nehemiah was always conscious of his relationship to God, and the entire task of rebuilding the walls was done in obedience to God.

17. Nehemiah normally fed one hundred fifty Jews and rulers, and considerable other peoples who came to visit Jerusalem. The implication of this verse is that he did this at his own expense. Although this was part of his governorship, he refused to be reimbursed for doing it.

18. He describes the basic necessities that were prepared for his family and friends every day. **Yet for all this required not I the bread of the governor, because the bondage was heavy upon this people.** The taxes due to the king and the money needed to rebuild the walls were a tremendous burden to the people. Nehemiah refused to add to that burden by demanding additional money to underwrite the expenses of his administration.

19. Think upon me, my God, for good, according to all that I have done for this people. Nehemiah's complete life could be summed up in his desire to serve the Lord and other people. God will always bless a man whose priorities are in these two areas. These were the requirements for leadership. Nehemiah was not interested in position, power, prestige, or possessions. He was simply interested in living in obedience to God and being of service to the people of that Jewish community. Because of his total commitment to the Lord, he was successful in rebuilding the walls of Jerusalem.

F. More Opposition Encountered. 6:1-14.

After experiencing failure when openly opposing the work at

10 I likewise, *and* my brethren, and my servants, might exact of them money and corn: I pray you, let us leave off this usury.

11 Restore, I pray you, to them, even this day, their lands, their vineyards, their oliveyards, and their houses, also the hundredth *part* of the money, and of the corn, the wine, and the oil, that ye exact of them.
12 Then said they, We will restore *them*, and will require nothing of them; so will we do as thou sayest. Then I called the priests, and took an oath of them, that they should do according to this promise.
13 Also I shook my lap, and said, So God shake out every man from his house, and from his labour, that performeth not this promise, even thus be he shaken out, and emptied. And all the congregation said, Amen, and praised the Lord. And the people did according to this promise.
14 ¶Moreover from the time that I was appointed to be their governor in the land of Jū′dah, from the twentieth year even unto the two and thirtieth year of Är-ta-xer′xēs the king, *that is,* twelve years, I and my brethren have not eaten the bread of the governor.
15 But the former governors that *had been* before me were chargeable unto the people, and had taken of them bread and wine, beside forty shekels of silver; yea, even their servants bare rule over the people: but so did not I, because of the fear of God.
16 Yea, also I continued in the work of this wall, neither bought we any land: and all my servants *were* gathered thither unto the work.
17 Moreover *there were* at my table an hundred and fifty of the Jews and rulers, beside those that came unto us from among the heathen that *are* about us.
18 Now *that* which was prepared *for* me daily *was* one ox *and* six choice sheep; also fowls were prepared for me, and once in ten days store of all sorts of wine: yet for all this required not I the bread of the governor, because the bondage was heavy upon this people.
19 Think upon me, my God, for good, *according* to all that I have done for this people.

CHAPTER 6

NOW it came to pass, when Săn-băl'-lat, and Tō-bī'ah, and Gĕ'shem the Arabian, and the rest of our enemies, heard that I had builded the wall, and *that* there was no breach left therein; (though at that time I had not set up the doors upon the gates;)

2 That Săn-băl'lat and Gĕ'shem sent unto me, saying, Come, let us meet together in *some one of* the villages in the plain of Ō'nō. But they thought to do me mischief.

3 And I sent messengers unto them, saying, I *am* doing a great work, so that I cannot come down: why should the work cease, whilst I leave it, and come down to you?

4 Yet they sent unto me four times after this sort; and I answered them after the same manner.

5 ¶Then sent Săn-băl'lat his servant unto me in like manner the fifth time with an open letter in his hand;
6 Wherein *was* written, It is reported among the heathen, and Găsh'mū saith *it, that* thou and the Jews think to rebel: for which cause thou buildest the wall, that thou mayest be their king, according to these words.

7 And thou hast also appointed prophets to preach of thee at Jerusalem, saying, *There is* a king in Jŭ'dah: and now shall it be reported to the king according to these words. Come now therefore, and let us take counsel together.

8 Then I sent unto him, saying, There are no such things done as thou sayest, but thou feignest them out of thine own heart.
9 For they all made us afraid, saying, Their hands shall be weakened from the work, that it be not done. Now therefore, *O God,* strengthen my hands.

Jerusalem, Sanballat and Tobiah changed their tactics in order to defeat Nehemiah.

6:1. The walls have been completed and there was **no breach left therein.**

I had not set up the doors upon the gates. Although the walls were finished, the gates had not been completed. The completion of the gates would include "covering with metal to prevent them from being burned in the event of a siege" (Barber, pp. 96-97).

2. Come, let us meet together in some one of the villages in the plain of Ono. Rather than openly opposing Nehemiah, Sanballat and Geshem now want to join with Nehemiah. Their attitude is that even though they have had differences in the past, they can now formulate a friendship. This has always been one of Satan's weapons. If he cannot openly defeat us, he will seek to integrate us with sin. **But they thought to do me mischief.** Perhaps Sanballat and his accomplices wanted to use this meeting as an opportunity to assassinate Nehemiah. The obvious intent was not to develop a friendship, but rather to get rid of Nehemiah.

3. I am doing a great work, so that I cannot come down. Nehemiah had a proper perspective on his priorities. A continuation of God's work was far more important than the friendship of the world. Nehemiah realized that if he were absent from Jerusalem for a period of time, the work would suffer and might even come to a stop. **Why should the work cease . . . ?** There was no logical reason for the cessation of the work at Jerusalem. The invitation of Sanballat would ultimately frustrate and hurt this work.

4. Yet they sent unto me four times after this sort. Sanballat was persistent in his attempts to divert the work of Nehemiah. This was also true in the life of Christ, for Satan was persistent in seeking to defeat Christ during the temptation (Mt 4:1-11). **And I answered them after the same manner.** Note that Nehemiah did not argue or debate or defend his decision. When a person begins to debate with the enemy, then he takes the first step towards defeat. This was Eve's problem in the Garden of Eden when she attempted to argue and debate with Satan (Gen 3:1-7).

5-6. Sanballat changes his tactics again and delivers a letter to Nehemiah. **It is reported.** The verb that is used here literally means "it is heard" (Keil, p. 217). Sanballat is merely utilizing rumor as a basis upon which to intimidate Nehemiah.

7. And now shall it be reported to the king according to these words. Sanballat implies that he is going to report Nehemiah's intention to rebel to the king. Sanballat hopes that this will upset Nehemiah to the point that he will meet with him in order to clear these suspicions. This attack of Sanballat on the motives of Nehemiah is a well-utilized weapon of Satan. Since people have a tendency to always believe the worst about a person, the character and integrity of many people are ruined by rumor.

8-9. Nehemiah is not fooled by the intimidation of Sanballat; he realizes that the intention of Sanballat is to evil. **But thou feignest them out of thine own heart.** The verb that is used here carries with it the idea of planning something for evil or sinful purposes. **Now therefore, O God, strengthen my hands.** Sanballat had hopes that the Jews would be afraid and that the work would be frustrated upon receiving his letter. However, the people are driven again to the source of their strength. Nehemiah appeals to God to strengthen them in the face of this adversity.

10 ¶Afterward I came unto the house of Shem-ā-i'ah the son of Dĕl-a-ī'ah the son of Me-hĕt'a-beel, who *was* shut up; and he said, Let us meet together in the house of God, within the temple, and let us shut the doors of the temple: for they will come to slay thee; yea, in the night will they come to slay thee.

11 And I said, Should such a man as I flee? and who *is there*, that, *being* as I *am*, would go into the temple to save his life? I will not go in.

12 And, lo, I perceived that God had not sent him; but that he pronounced this prophecy against me: for Tō-bī'ah and Săn-băl'lat had hired him.

13 Therefore *was* he hired, that I should be afraid, and do so, and sin, and *that* they might have *matter* for an evil report, that they might reproach me.

14 My God, think thou upon Tō-bī'ah and Săn-băl'lat according to these their works, and on the prophetess Nō-a-dī'ah, and the rest of the prophets, that would have put me in fear.

15 ¶So the wall was finished in the twenty and fifth *day* of *the month* E'lŭl, in fifty and two days.

16 And it came to pass, that when all our enemies heard *thereof*, and all the heathen that *were* about us saw *these things*, they were much cast down in their own eyes: for they perceived that this work was wrought of our God.

17 ¶Moreover in those days the nobles of Jū'dah sent many letters unto Tō-bī'ah, and *the letters* of Tō-bī'ah came unto them.

18 For *there were* many in Jū'dah sworn unto him, because he *was* the son in law of Shĕch-a-nī'ah the son of Ā'rah; and his son Jō-hā'nan had taken the daughter of Me-shūl'lam the son of Bĕr-e-chī'ah.

19 Also they reported his good deeds before me, and uttered my words to him. *And* Tō-bī'ah sent letters to put me in fear.

CHAPTER 7

NOW it came to pass, when the wall was built, and I had set up the doors, and the porters and the singers and the Lē'vītes were appointed,

2 That I gave my brother Ha-nā'nī, and Hăn-a-nī'ah the ruler of the palace,

10. Having been frustrated again, Sanballat changes his tactics. He hires a prophet by the name of Shemaiah. **Who was shut up.** Apparently, Shemaiah had confined himself to his house in order to imply to Nehemiah that his life was in danger. This would make Nehemiah think that Shemaiah was true to the Lord. Shemaiah wants Nehemiah to go with him to the house of God and to shut themselves in because there was a plan to assassinate Nehemiah.

11-12. Nehemiah refuses to hide in the Temple to save his life. **And, lo, I perceived that God had not sent him.** Nehemiah was always willing to obey and listen to a prophet of God. However, he sensed that Shemaiah had ulterior motives for his message. **Tobiah and Sanballat had hired him.** One of the tragedies of human character is that God's man would change his message for monetary value (I Kgs 22:22).

13. **That I should be afraid, and do so, and sin.** Nehemiah realized that by entering into the Holy Place of the Temple he would be sinning against God. This would be used to assassinate his character and integrity. Since he would have disobeyed the commandments of God, this would have inhibited his ability to lead the people.

14. Notice the response of Nehemiah to all the evil and sinister intents of Tobiah and Sanballat. **My God, think thou upon Tobiah and Sanballat according to these their works.** Nehemiah did not get bitter. He did not seek to retaliate. He did not take justice and vengeance into his own hands. Rather, he committed the entire situation to the Lord. This must always be our response when people mistreat and hurt us. We must trust in God who is the God of justice and the God of vengeance (Deut 32:35).

G. The Wall Completed. 6:15-19.

15. The wall was completed in fifty-two days. It is interesting to note that beyond the adversity and opposition from within and without, the work was completed during the hottest part of the year (Lange, p. 28).

16. The completion of the walls had an unusual effect upon the surrounding heathen nations. **They were much cast down in their own eyes.** They were discouraged and depressed because they recognized that God had intervened and had helped the Jews complete the task.

17-18. Apparently there were a number of Jews and nobles who were in allegiance to Tobiah, **for there were many in Judah sworn unto him.** Since Tobiah was married into a good Jewish family, there were a number of Jews in Jerusalem who felt family loyalty and ties to Tobiah.

19. **And Tobiah sent letters to put me in fear.** These were letters similar in content and character to the letter of Sanballat. Apparently, the letter discussed in this particular chapter was just one of many letters and many attempts to discourage and defeat the work of Nehemiah.

H. The List of Those Who Returned. 7:1-73.

7:1. **And the porters and the singers and the Levites were appointed.** The porters were those who had the responsibility of opening and closing the doors. The singers and Levites normally participated in the Temple worship. However, Nehemiah appoints them to watch over the wall. These three groups of people were charged with the responsibility of the defense of Jerusalem.

2. Nehemiah appoints Hananiah as **the ruler of the palace.** In this position he was responsible to the Persian king for the

charge over Jerusalem: for he *was* a faithful man, and feared God above many.

3 And I said unto them, Let not the gates of Jerusalem be opened until the sun be hot; and while they stand by, let them shut the doors, and bar *them:* and appoint watches of the inhabitants of Jerusalem, every one in his watch, and every one *to be* over against his house.

4 ¶Now the city *was* large and great: but the people *were* few therein, and the houses *were* not builded.

5 And my God put into mine heart to gather together the nobles, and the rulers, and the people, that they might be reckoned by genealogy. And I found a register of the genealogy of them which came up at the first and found written therein,

6 These *are* the children of the province, that went up out of the captivity, of those that had been carried away, whom Něb-u-chad-něz'zar the king of Babylon had carried away, and came again to Jerusalem and to Jū'dah, every one unto his city;

7 Who came with Ze-růb'ba-bel, Jěsh'u-a, Ně-he-mī'ah, Ăz-a-rī'ah, Rā-a-mī'ah, Na-hăm'a-nī, Môr'de-caī, Bĭl'shăn, Mĭs'pe-rěth, Bĭg'va-ī, Ně'hŭm, Bā'a-nah. The number, *I say*, of the men of the people of Israel *was this*;

8 The children of Pâ'rōsh, two thousand an hundred seventy and two.

9 The children of Shěph-a-tī'ah, three hundred seventy and two.

10 The children of Â'rah, six hundred fifty and two.

11 The children of Pā'hăth-mō'ăb, of the children of Jěsh'u-a and Jō'ăb, two thousand and eight hundred *and* eighteen.

12 The children of Ē'lam, a thousand two hundred fifty and four.

13 The children of Zăt'tŭ, eight hundred forty and five.

14 The children of Zăc'ca-ī, seven hundred and threescore.

15 The children of Bĭn'nū-ī, six hundred forty and eight.

16 The children of Běb'a-ī, six hundred twenty and eight.

17 The children of Ăz'găd, two thousand three hundred twenty and two.

18 The children of Ăd-on-ī'kam, six hundred threescore and seven.

19 The children of Bĭg'va-ī, two thousand threescore and seven.

20 The children of Â'din, six hundred fifty and five.

21 The children of Â'ter of Hěz-e-kī'ah, ninety and eight.

22 The children of Hā'shum, three hundred twenty and eight.

23 The children of Bě'zaī, three hundred twenty and four.

24 The children of Hâ'rĭph, an hundred and twelve.

25 The children of Gĭbeon, ninety and five.

26 The men of Běth–lehĕm and Ne-tō'phah, an hundred fourscore and eight.

oversight of Jerusalem. **He was a faithful man, and feared God.** These were the two requirements for leadership. He had been faithful in the rebuilding process, and he had an ultimate fear and respect for God (see 1:2).

3. The command is given concerning the opening and shutting of the gates. The gates were not to be opened until midday, and only when the guards were by them. **And appoint watches of the inhabitants of Jerusalem.** The people were divided into different shifts and were positioned in different places to prepare and warn the city of an attack.

4. Now the city was large and great. Although the walls had been rebuilt, vast portions of the city were still lying in waste. Many of the houses were still in ruins.

5. And my God put into mine heart. Nehemiah was inspired to make a census of the people. **And I found a register of the genealogy of them which came up at the first.** This genealogy is identical with the one listed in Ezra chapter 2. Please note the discussion there.

6-38. These verses list those who returned. Verses 6-25 list families, and verses 26-38 contain the names of cities. There are some apparent discrepancies between the names and numbers of this list and the list of Ezra 2:3-35. They are analyzed and discussed in Ezra 2:64-67.

Many of the names mentioned here are also mentioned in the other lists of Ezra and Nehemiah. Possibly only part of each family returned with Zerubbabel and Jeshua, while the others waited until later to return with Ezra. Lange has suggested that those who were mentioned by family names most likely settled in Jerusalem and those who were listed by city settled in that city.

27 The men of Ăn′a-thŏth, an hundred twenty and eight.
28 The men of Bĕth-ăz′ma-vĕth, forty and two.
29 The men of Kir′jath–jē′a-rĭm, Che-phī′rah, and Bē-ē′rŏth, seven hundred forty and three.
30 The men of Rā′mah and Gā′ba, six hundred twenty and one.
31 The men of Mĭch′măs, an hundred and twenty and two.
32 The men of Bĕth–el and Ā′ī, an hundred twenty and three.
33 The men of the other Nebo, fifty and two.
34 The children of the other Ē′lam, a thousand two hundred fifty and four.
35 The children of Hâ′rĭm, three hundred and twenty.
36 The children of Jericho, three hundred forty and five.
37 The children of Lod, Hā′dĭd, and Ō′nō, seven hundred twenty and one.
38 The children of Se-nā′ah, three thousand nine hundred and thirty.
39 ¶The priests: the children of Je-dā′iah, of the house of Jĕsh′u-a, nine hundred seventy and three.
40 The children of ĭm′mer, a thousand fifty and two.
41 The children of Păsh′ur, a thousand two hundred forty and seven.
42 The children of Hâ′rĭm, a thousand and seventeen.
43 ¶The Lēvītes: the children of Jĕsh′u-a, of Kăd′mĭ-el, *and* of the children of Hō-dē′vah, seventy and four.
44 ¶The singers: the children of Ā′săph, an hundred forty and eight.
45 ¶The porters: the children of Shăl′lum, the children of Ā′ter, the children of Tal′mon, the children of Ăk′kŭb, the children of Hat′ī-ta, the children of Shō′ba-ī, an hundred thirty and eight.
46 ¶The Nĕth′i-nĭmś: the children of Zī′ha, the children of Ha-shŭ′pha, the children of Tăb′ba-ŏth,
47 The children of Ke′rŏs, the children of Sī′a, the children of Pā′don,
48 The children of Lĕb′a-na, the children of Hăg′a-ba, the children of Shăl′ma-ī,
49 The children of Hā′nan, the children of Gĭd′del, the children of Gā′här,
50 The children of Rē-ā-i′ah, the children of Rē′zĭn, the children of Ne-kō′da,
51 The children of Găz′zam, the children of Ŭz′za, the children of Phasē′ah,
52 The children of Bē′saī, the children of Me-ū′nĭm, the children of Ne-phĭsh′e-sĭm,
53 The children of Băk′bŭk, the children of Ha-kū′pha, the children of Här′hûr,
54 The children of Băz′lĭth, the children of Me-hī′da, the children of Här′sha,
55 The children of Bär′kŏs, the children of Sĭs′e-ra, the children of Tā′mah,
56 The children of Ne-zī′ah, the children of Hat′ī-pha.
57 The children of Sŏlomon's servants: the children of Sō′ta-ī, the children of Sŏph′e-rĕth, the children of Pe-rī′da,

39-42. This list of priests is divided into four classes, and it agrees with the classes of priests mentioned in I Chronicles 24:7-18. The names and numbers of this list are identical with those in the list of Ezra 2:36-39.

43-60. The Levites and Solomon's servants are included in this list. Three classes of Levites are listed. First, those who assisted the priests in their duties—Levites in the technical sense—are mentioned. Second, the singers are listed; and, third, so are the doorkeepers. **The Nethinim.** Thirty-five families of the Nethinim are listed, along with the families of Solomon's servants. Both groups were prisoners of war and worked as servants.

58 The children of Jā-a′la, the children of Där′kŏn, the children of Gĭd′del,

59 The children of Shĕph-a-tī′ah, the children of Hăt′til, the children of Pŏch′e-rĕth of Ze-bā′im, the children of Āmon.

60 All the Nĕth′i-nĭmś, and the children of Sòlomon's servants, were three hundred ninety and two.

61 And these were they which went up also from Tĕl-mē′lah, Tĕl-hä-re′sha, Cherub, Äd′dŏn, and Ĭm′mer: but they could not shew their father's house, nor their seed, whether they were of Israel.

62 The children of Dĕl-a-ī′ah, the children of Tō-bī′ah, the children of Ne-kō′da, six hundred forty and two.

63 ¶And of the priests: the children of Ha-bā′iah, the children of Koz, the children of Bar-zĭl′la-ī, which took one of the daughters of Bär-zĭl′la-ī the Gĭleadīte to wife, and was called after their name.

64 These sought their register among those that were reckoned by genealogy, but it was not found: therefore were they, as polluted, put from the priesthood.

65 And the Tir′shā-tha said unto them, that they should not eat of the most holy things, till there stood up a priest with Ú′rĭm and Thŭm′mĭm.

66 ¶The whole congregation together was forty and two thousand three hundred and threescore,

67 Beside their manservants and their maidservants, of whom there were seven thousand three hundred thirty and seven: and they had two hundred forty and five singing men and singing women.

68 Their horses, seven hundred thirty and six: their mules, two hundred forty and five:

69 Their camels, four hundred thirty and five: six thousand seven hundred and twenty asses.

70 ¶And some of the chief of the fathers gave unto the work. The Tir′shā-tha gave to the treasure a thousand drams of gold, fifty basons, five hundred and thirty priests' garments.

71 And some of the chief of the fathers gave to the treasure of the work twenty thousand drams of gold, and two thousand and two hundred pound of silver.

72 And that which the rest of the people gave was twenty thousand drams of gold, and two thousand pound of silver, and threescore and seven priests' garments.

73 So the priests, and the Lĕvites, and the porters, and the singers, and some of the people, and the Nĕth′i-nĭmś, and all Israel, dwelt in their cities; and when the seventh month came, the children of Israel were in their cities.

CHAPTER 8

AND all the people gathered themselves together as one man into the street that was before the water gate; and they spake unto Ezra the scribe to bring the book of the law of Moses,

61-62. They could not show their father's house. They could not prove from which family they descended or **their seed**. Some could not even prove their Jewish ancestry. They never were allowed to have the right of citizenship, although they were allowed to return to Jerusalem. As a result, their names do not appear either in the list of Nehemiah 10:15-28 or in the list of Ezra 10:25-44, both of which indicate who settled the land.

63-65. The priests whose claim to the priesthood could not be proven are listed here. **As polluted.** This pregnant term states that because they could not prove their priesthood they could not serve as priests. **Till there stood up a priest with Urim and with Thummim.** The decision as to whether these priests could serve in the new Temple would be made by the Urim and Thummim. However, there is no evidence that indicates that this ever happened. "On the contrary, the unanimous testimony of the Rabbis, that after the Babylonian exile God no longer manifested His will by the Urim and Thummim, this kind of divine revelation being reckoned by them among the five things which were wanting in the second Temple" (Keil, pp. 44-45).

66-73. The list is concluded with the totals of those who returned, along with their servants, maids, and beasts of burden. The total is 42,360, identical to Ezra 2:40-67. However, in both lists the totals of the individual lists do not add up to 42,360; and they do not agree with one another. Note the following diagram (Keil, p. 45).

	EZRA	NEHEMIAH
Men of Israel	24,144	25,406
Priests	4,289	4,289
Levites	341	360
Nethinim & Servants of Solomon	392	392
Those who could not prove the Israelitish origin	652	642
	29,818	31,089

See the comments on Ezra 2:64-67 for an explanation of these apparent discrepancies.

III. THE REFORMS OF EZRA AND NEHEMIAH. 8:1-13:31.

A. The Law Explained. 8:1-12.

8:1. The last phrase of 7:73 belongs as the introduction to chapter 8. **And when the seventh month came, the children of Israel were in their cities.** At this particular time in the history of the restoration, the people **gathered themselves together as one man into the street that was before the water gate.** The

which the LORD had commanded to Israel.

2 And Ezra the priest brought the law before the congregation both of men and women, and all that could hear with understanding, upon the first day of the seventh month.

3 And he read therein before the street that *was* before the water gate from the morning until midday, before the men and the women, and those that could understand; and the ears of all the people *were attentive* unto the book of the law.

4 And Ezra the scribe stood upon a pulpit of wood, which they had made for the purpose; and beside him stood Măt-ti-thī'ah, and Shē'ma, and An-a-ī'ah, and Ū-rī'jah, and Hīl-kī'ah, and Mā-a-sē'iah, on his right hand; and on his left hand, Pe-dā'iah, and Mīsh'a-el, and Măl-chī'ah, and Hā'shum, and Hăsh-băd'a-na, Zĕch-a-rī'ah, *and* Me-shŭl'lam.

5 And Ezra opened the book in the sight of all the people; (for he was above all the people;) and when he opened it, all the people stood up:

6 And Ezra blessed the LORD, the great God. And all the people answered, Amen, Amen, with lifting up their hands: and they bowed their heads, and worshipped the LORD with *their* faces to the ground.

7 Also Jĕsh'u-a, and Bā'nī, and Shĕr-e-bī'ah, Jā'mīn, Ăk'kŭb, Shăb'be-thaī, Hō-dī'jah, Mā-a-sē'iah, Kel'ī-ta, Ăz-a-rī'ah, Jōz'a-băd, Hā'nan, Pel-ā-i'ah, and the Lēvītes, caused the people to understand the law: and the people *stood* in their place.

8 So they read in the book in the law of God distinctly, and gave the sense, and caused *them* to understand the reading.

9 ¶And Nē-he-mī'ah, which *is* the Tir'shā-tha, and Ezra the priest the scribe, and the Lēvītes that taught the people, said unto all the people, This day *is* holy unto the LORD your God; mourn not, nor weep. For all the people wept, when they heard the words of the law.

10 Then he said unto them, Go your way, eat the fat, and drink the sweet, and send portions unto them for whom nothing is prepared: for *this* day *is* holy

word translated as street in this verse literally means a square or plaza. Adjacent to the Temple was a large square that was suited to public assemblies. The people came to this square to hear the reading of the Law. **Ezra the scribe.** This is the first mention of Ezra in the book of Nehemiah. He had come to Jerusalem thirteen years prior to Nehemiah. His two offices are mentioned in the opening verses of this chapter. He was a scribe and a priest.

2-3. And all that could hear with understanding. This refers to everyone who had the capability of understanding the reading of the Law. **From the morning until midday.** The reading of the Law occupied the time from daylight until noon. This would have been about a six-hour period. According to Lange, one could read approximately one-quarter of the Pentateuch during this time.

4. And Ezra the scribe stood upon a pulpit of wood. This was a large stage that enabled the people to hear the reading more clearly. It is probably the same structure that is referred to in 9:4. Along with Ezra, there were six priests on his right and seven priests on his left. All of these people stood upon the platform.

5. For he was above all the people. This refers to the fact that he was physically located high above the crowd. **And when he opened it, all the people stood up.** There is no indication from Scripture that this was the normal practice when the Law was read. However, out of respect all of the people stood when Ezra read the Law.

6. And Ezra blessed the LORD, the great God. Ezra begins his reading with praising the Lord. The people responded to this thanksgiving by saying **Amen, Amen, with lifting up their hands** (I Tim 2:8). **And they bowed their heads, and worshiped the LORD with their faces to the ground.** This was symbolic of their humility in the presence of God. They felt they were unworthy to lift their faces toward heaven.

7. All the people mentioned in this verse are Levites. **And the Levites, caused the people to understand the law.** Apparently the reading of the Law was interrupted by several events. At certain times the people responded with an amen and by worshiping the Lord. Second, the Levites took time to explain the various portions of the Law to the crowd. Not all of the time was occupied with Ezra's reading.

8. So they read in the book in the law of God distinctly. Apparently, both Ezra and the Levites at various times read directly from the book of the Law. The ultimate purpose of all of the reading was that the people would begin to understand the Law of God. This is still the obligation of preachers today: to take the Word of God, read it distinctly, and cause the people to understand.

9. Apparently, the reading of the Law had a deep and profound effect upon the people. Having been faced with the commandments of God, they realized their sin and were in a state of sorrow. **For all the people wept, when they heard the words of the law.** However, Nehemiah, Ezra, and the Levites reminded the people that **This day is holy unto the LORD your God.** It was important to weep for sin, but this was also a day when they would celebrate one of the Lord's feasts.

10. They were to celebrate the feast by eating, drinking, and sending their food and drink to the poor, who did not have substance wherewith to celebrate the feast. **For the joy of the LORD is your strength.** The joy of God was to be their fortress.

unto our Lord: neither be ye sorry; for the joy of the LORD is your strength.

11 So the Lēvītes stilled all the people, saying, Hold your peace, for the day *is* holy; neither be ye grieved.

12 And all the people went their way to eat, and to drink, and to send portions, and to make great mirth, because they had understood the words that were declared unto them.

13 ¶And on the second day were gathered together the chief of the fathers of all the people, the priests, and the Lēvītes unto Ezra the scribe, even to understand the words of the law.

14 And they found written in the law which the LORD had commanded by Moses, that the children of Israel should dwell in booths in the feast of the seventh month:

15 And that they should publish and proclaim in all their cities, and in Jerusalem, saying, Go forth unto the mount, and fetch olive branches, and pine branches, and myrtle branches, and palm branches, and branches of thick trees, to make booths, as *it is* written.

16 So the people went forth, and brought *them,* and made themselves booths, every one upon the roof of his house, and in their courts, and in the courts of the house of God, and in the street of the water gate, and in the street of the gate of Ē'phra-im.

17 And all the congregation of them that were come again out of the captivity made booths, and sat under the booths: for since the days of Jĕsh'u-a the son of Nun unto that day had not the children of Israel done so. And there was very great gladness.

18 Also day by day, from the first day unto the last day, he read in the book of the law of God. And they kept the feast seven days; and on the eighth day *was* a solemn assembly, according unto the manner.

CHAPTER 9

NOW in the twenty and fourth day of this month the children of Israel were assembled with fasting, and with sackclothes, and earth upon them.

2 And the seed of Israel separated themselves from all strangers, and stood and confessed their sins, and the iniquities of their fathers.

3 And they stood up in their place, and read in the book of the law of the LORD their God *one* fourth part of the day; and *another* fourth part they confessed, and worshipped the LORD their God.

4 Then stood up upon the stairs, of the Lēvītes, Jĕsh'u-a, and Bā'nī, Kăd'-

11-12. The people ceased their grieving and began to celebrate this feast of the new moon.

B. Feast Restored. 8:13-18.

13. The chief of the fathers of all the people, the priests, and the Levites. The various heads of the households and the religious leaders gathered for further exposition of the Law. They desired a deeper and more intimate understanding of what God desired.

14. They discovered that in the seventh month they were to celebrate the Feast of Tabernacles (**booths**). The details of this particular feast are discussed in Leviticus 23:39-43. This feast was to be a reminder of their sojournings in the wilderness.

15. These leaders of the early community make a proclamation that everyone should observe this feast. **Go forth unto the mount.** This refers to the Mount of Olives. They gave specific directions as to what they were to bring and what preparations were to be made. **As it is written.** The directions they gave were in full accordance with the law of God (Lev 23:40).

16. Some of the people who lived in Jerusalem built their booths on top of their house, while others built in the courts of the Temple and in the streets. Those who did not reside in Jerusalem probably built their booths in the streets. All of this celebration occurred within the walls of Jerusalem.

17. For since the days of Jeshua the son of Nun unto that day had not the children of Israel done so. This does not mean that since the times of Joshua they had not celebrated the Feast of Tabernacles. The reference here is that since the days of Joshua, the entire community had not celebrated the feast. Parts of the community kept the feast, but in this particular situation the entire Jewish community was involved in the celebration.

18. He read in the book of the law of God. Each day during the feast Ezra read from the law of God. They observed the feast for seven days; and **on the eighth day was a solemn assembly, according unto the manner.**

C. Confession and Covenant of Priests and Levites. 9:1-38.

9:1. Now in the twenty and fourth day of this month. The events of this chapter occurred two days after the end of the Feast of the Tabernacles. It was a day of fasting and mourning. **And with sackcloth, and earth upon them.** The wearing of sackcloth and the placing of earth upon their heads was a sign of great mourning and sorrow (I Sam 4:12; Job 2:12).

2. And the seed of Israel separated themselves from all strangers. Their sorrow and mourning was evidenced by the fact that they were willing to make a clear separation from the heathen nations around them.

3. The activities consisted of reading the Law for **one fourth part of the day.** This would involve about three hours of listening to the reading of the Law. For another fourth part of the day they **confessed, and worshiped the LORD their God.** Notice the close connection between the reading of the Law, confession, and worship. These should be activities in which we as Christians are involved every day. We should be reading the Word of God, realizing that God's law will lead us to recognize our own unworthiness and sin. After confession is made, then we can worship the Lord.

4-5. Then stood up upon the stairs. This probably refers to the wooden platform that Ezra utilized when he was reading the

mĭ-el, Shĕb-a-nī'ah, Bŭn'nī, Shĕr-e-bī'ah, Bā'nī, and Chen'ā-nī, and cried with a loud voice unto the LORD their God.

5 Then the Lēvītes, Jĕsh'u-a, and Kăd'mĭ-el, Bā'nī, Hăsh-ab-nī'ah, Shĕr-e-bī'ah, Hō-dī'jah, Shĕb-a-nī'ah, and Pĕth-a-hī'ah, said, Stand up and bless the LORD your God for ever and ever: and blessed be thy glorious name, which is exalted above all blessing and praise.

6 Thou, even thou, art LORD alone; thou hast made heaven, the heaven of heavens, with all their host, the earth, and all things that are therein, the seas, and all that is therein, and thou preservest them all; and the host of heaven worshippeth thee.

7 Thou art the LORD the God, who didst choose Abram, and broughtest him forth out of Ur of the Chăl-deĕs, and gavest him the name of Abraham;

8 And foundest his heart faithful before thee, and madest a covenant with him to give the land of the Canaanites, the Hittites, the Ămōrītes, and the Pĕr'-iz-zītes, and the Jĕb'u-sītes, and the Gir'ga-shītes, to give it, I say, to his seed, and hast performed thy words; for thou art righteous:

9 And didst see the affliction of our fathers in Egypt, and heardest their cry by the Red sea;

10 And shewedst signs and wonders upon Pharaoh, and on all his servants, and on all the people of his land: for thou knewest that they dealt proudly against them. So didst thou get thee a name, as it is this day.

11 And thou didst divide the sea before them, so that they went through the midst of the sea on the dry land; and their persecutors thou threwest into the deeps, as a stone into the mighty waters.

12 Moreover thou leddest them in the day by a cloudy pillar; and in the night by a pillar of fire, to give them light in the way wherein they should go.

13 Thou camest down also upon mount Sī'naī, and spakest with them from heaven, and gavest them right judgments, and true laws, good statutes and commandments:

14 And madest known unto them thy holy sabbath, and commandedst them precepts, statutes, and laws, by the hand of Moses thy servant:

15 And gavest them bread from heaven for their hunger, and

Law (8:4). In these two verses there are apparently two distinct activities. First, they **cried with a loud voice unto the LORD their God.** This probably refers to the confession and mourning. In the next verse the Levites said **stand up and bless the LORD your God for ever and ever.** This second activity refers to the worshiping of God.

6. This verse is the beginning of the praise section of the people. They were encouraged by the Levites to praise the Lord and now they begin by enumerating all that God had done for them. Much of what is said in the remainder of the chapter is quoted from other Scripture.

In his commentary, Kyle observes several specific sections of this praise treatise. It begins with the preface acknowledging God's covenant with Abraham. Following that are four specific sections: (1) The deliverance of the children of Israel from Egypt (vss. 9-15); (2) God's provision throughout the wilderness (vss. 16-25); (3) their rebellion in the Promised Land and God's judgment upon them (vss. 26-31); and (4) an entreaty for God to look upon their present affliction and deliver them (vss. 32-37). **Thou, even thou, art LORD alone.** The fact is established that God is Jehovah. He is the self-existent, eternal God of the universe, the one who created and preserves all things.

7. Thou art the LORD the God, who didst choose Abram. This same Jehovah, who was the Creator and Sustainer of the universe, is also the one who chose Abram.

8. God made a covenant, or an agreement, with Abram. This covenant involved two specific promises. First, **to give the land.** God promised Abram a specific geographical area. Second, He promised him posterity. **To his seed.** God's covenant with Abram was to give him a land and that from his seed would come a nation (Gen 15:18; 17:15-16). This covenant is the foundation upon which the rest of God's dealings are reflected. It is because of this covenant that He continues to deal with the rebellious children of Israel. In verses 9-15 the deliverance from Egypt and the passage through the wilderness are discussed. For a detailed discussion on these events, see Exodus chapter 3.

9-14. Didst see the affliction . . . and heardest their cry by the Red Sea. These are the two facts upon which God's deliverance and guidance are based. **As a stone into the mighty waters.** The word mighty here is utilized to mean violent. **And gavest them right judgments, and true laws, good statutes and commandments.** In the Hebrew all of these words are in the singular. Note the adjectives that are used to describe God's law. It is right, true, and good. The language of this verse is similar to the will of God as mentioned in Romans 12:2.

15-16. God miraculously provided for all of their needs in the wilderness. He saw the problem, and He heard their prayer. He

broughtest forth water for them out of the rock for their thirst, and promisedst them that they should go in to possess the land which thou hadst sworn to give them.

16 But they and our fathers dealt proudly, and hardened their necks, and hearkened not to thy commandments,

17 And refused to obey, neither were mindful of thy wonders that thou didst among them; but hardened their necks, and in their rebellion appointed a captain to return to their bondage: but thou *art* a God ready to pardon, gracious and merciful, slow to anger, and of great kindness, and forsookest them not.

18 Yea, when they had made them a molten calf, and said, This *is* thy god that brought thee up out of Egypt, and had wrought great provocations;

19 Yet thou in thy manifold mercies forsookest them not in the wilderness: the pillar of the cloud departed not from them by day, to lead them in the way; neither the pillar of fire by night, to shew them light, and the way wherein they should go.

20 Thou gavest also thy good spirit to instruct them, and withheldest not thy manna from their mouth, and gavest them water for their thirst.

21 Yea, forty years didst thou sustain them in the wilderness, *so that* they lacked nothing; their clothes waxed not old, and their feet swelled not.

22 Moreover thou gavest them kingdoms and nations, and didst divide them into corners: so they possessed the land of Sihon, and the land of the king of Hĕsh'bŏn, and the land of Og king of Bā'shan.

23 Their children also multipliedst thou as the stars of heaven, and broughtest them into the land, concerning which thou hadst promised to their fathers, that they should go in to possess *it*.

24 So the children went in and possessed the land, and thou subduedst before them the inhabitants of the land, the Canaanites, and gavest them into their hands, with their kings, and the people of the land, that they might do with them as they would.

25 And they took strong cities, and a fat land, and possessed houses full of all goods, wells digged, vineyards, and oliveyards, and fruit trees in abundance: so they did eat, and were filled, and became fat, and delighted themselves in thy great goodness.

26 Nevertheless they were disobedient, and rebelled against thee, and cast thy law behind their backs, and slew thy prophets which testified against them to turn them to thee, and they wrought great provocations.

27 Therefore thou deliveredst them

then moved into action to do something about it. Note the many things which God did for the children of Israel. He showed signs and wonders; He divided the Red Sea; He destroyed the Egyptians in the Red Sea; He led them by day and night; He gave them the Law; He gave them bread and water; and He promised **them that they should go in to possess the land which thou hadst sworn to give them. But they and our fathers dealt proudly.** In spite of all the provision that God had made for the children of Israel, they rebelled against God.

17-18. In their rebellion they disobeyed God and **appointed a captain to return to their bondage.** This act of appointing a captain probably refers to Numbers 14:4. **But thou art a God ready to pardon, gracious and merciful.** The character and attributes of God are contrasted with the depravity and disobedience of the children of Israel. In the midst of such rebellion God did not forsake them. The people even made a false image and worshiped that image. This was a deliberate disobedience to the clearly revealed law of God (Ex 32:1-10).

19. Yet thou in thy manifold mercies forsookest them not in the wilderness. It is to our advantage that God is a God of many and multiplied mercies. In spite of their disobedience God continued to lead them.

20. Thou gavest also thy good spirit to instruct them. This refers to the time when God put the spirit of Moses upon the seventy elders. These elders were involved in instructing and making judgment with the children of Israel (Num 11:16-17).

21. So that they lacked nothing. When God leads us through the wilderness, we can be sure that He will supply every need. There is nothing that we need that He cannot and will not provide.

22-25. God divided the kingdom for them and permitted their families to multiply. The children of Israel subdued the land through the leadership of God. **So they did eat, and were filled, and became fat, and delighted themselves in thy great goodness.** When we follow the leadership of God we can be sure that He will fill every longing of our heart. We can become satisfied in Him.

26. Nevertheless they were disobedient, and rebelled against thee. Compare the content of this verse with verse 16. In spite of the fact that God had led them through the wilderness and had allowed them to conquer the land and had provided their every need, they still rebelled. **And cast thy law behind their backs.** Compare this statement with Ezekiel 23:35. **And slew thy prophets.** This could refer to Zechariah (II Chr 24:21) and the many prophets who were killed by Jezebel (I Kgs 18:13).

27-28. The events of these verses are discussed in the book of

into the hand of their enemies, who vexed them: and in the time of their trouble, when they cried unto thee, thou heardest *them* from heaven; and according to thy manifold mercies thou gavest them saviours, who saved them out of the hand of their enemies.

28 But after they had rest, they did evil again before thee: therefore leftest thou them in the hand of their enemies, so that they had the dominion over them: yet when they returned, and cried unto thee, thou heardest *them* from heaven; and many times didst thou deliver them according to thy mercies;

29 And testifiedst against them, that thou mightest bring them again unto thy law: yet they dealt proudly, and hearkened not unto thy commandments, but sinned against thy judgments, (which if a man do, he shall live in them;) and withdrew the shoulder, and hardened their neck, and would not hear.

30 Yet many years didst thou forbear them, and testifiedst against them by thy spirit in thy prophets: yet would they not give ear: therefore gavest thou them into the hand of the people of the lands.

31 Nevertheless for thy great mercies' sake thou didst not utterly consume them, nor forsake them; for thou *art* a gracious and merciful God.

32 Now therefore, our God, the great, the mighty, and the terrible God, who keepest covenant and mercy, let not all the trouble seem little before thee, that hath come upon us, on our kings, on our princes, and on our priests, and on our prophets, and on our fathers, and on all thy people, since the time of the kings of Assyria unto this day.

33 Howbeit thou *art* just in all that is brought upon us; for thou hast done right, but we have done wickedly:

34 Neither have our kings, our princes, our priests, nor our fathers, kept thy law, nor hearkened unto thy commandments and thy testimonies, wherewith thou didst testify against them.

35 For they have not served thee in their kingdom, and in thy great goodness that thou gavest them, and in the large and fat land which thou gavest before them, neither turned they from their wicked works.

36 Behold, we *are* servants this day, and *for* the land that thou gavest unto our fathers to eat the fruit thereof and the good thereof, behold, we *are* servants in it:

37 And it yieldeth much increase unto the kings whom thou hast set over us because of our sins: also they have dominion over our bodies, and over our cattle, at their pleasure, and we *are* in great distress.

38 And because of all this we make a sure *covenant*, and write *it;* and our

Judges. God sent people to oppress the Israelites; and when they repented, He sent a judge to deliver them. Notice that both verses refer to the mercies of God. Verse 27 talks about **thy manifold mercies,** and verse 28 talks about **thy mercies.**

29-30. These two verses occupy the kingdom period of Israel. **Which if a man do, he shall live in them.** This refers to Leviticus 18:5. **And withdrew the shoulder, and hardened their neck.** This refers to throwing back their shoulder in pride and arrogance.

31. Nevertheless for thy great mercies' sake thou didst not utterly consume them, nor forsake them. Again, reference is made to the mercy of God. God's dealings with the children of Israel are founded upon His mercy, for it was His mercy that prevented Him from totally consuming them. Finally, God delivers them into the hand of the peoples of the lands, referring to the Assyrian and the Chaldean invasions.

32. Now therefore, our God. The history of the children of Israel is now brought up to date. They have reviewed God's past dealings, and now they implore God for His continued mercy. **Who keepest covenant and mercy.** The covenant refers back to verse 8 and the Abrahamic covenant. Beyond the fact of the covenant, they implore the mercy of God (see vss. 17, 27, 28, 31).

33. Howbeit thou art just in all that is brought upon us. The people recognized that all of the problems that came from the captivity were well-deserved. **But we have done wickedly.** They recognized their sin.

34-35. The list of people mentioned here is similar to that in verse 32, with the exception of the prophets. Apparently, the prophets suffered from the captivity, but were not one of the causes of the captivity. They lived in obedience to God, but suffered from the disobedience of the rest of Israel.

36-37. The people argue that although others have disobeyed they were the servants of God. **They have dominion over our bodies, and over our cattle, at their pleasure, and we are in great distress.** Although they had returned to the land and the Temple and walls had been restored, they still faced adversity. They were still under bondage to the Persian king, and they were still experiencing a time of trouble.

38. And because of all this we make a sure covenant. On the basis of their repentance and prayer, they made an agree-

princes, Lēvītes, *and* priests, seal *unto it.*

CHAPTER 10

NOW those that sealed *were*, Nē-he-mī′ah, the Tir′shā-tha, the son of Hăch-a-lī′ah, and Zĭd-kī′jah,

2 Se-ra-ī′ah, Ăz-a-rī′ah, Jĕr-e-mī′ah,

3 Păsh′ur, Ăm-a-rī′ah, Măl-chī′jah,

4 Hăt′tŭsh, Shĕb-a-nī′ah, Măl′luch,

5 Hâ′rĭm, Mĕr′e-mŏth, Ō-ba-dī′ah,

6 Daniel, Gĭn′ne-thŏn, Bâ′ruch,

7 Me-shŭl′lam, A-bī′jah, Mĭj′a-mĭn,

8 Mā-a-zī′ah, Bĭl′ga-ī, Shem-a-i′ah: these *were* the priests.

9 And the Lēvītes: both Jĕsh′u-a the son of Ăz-a-nī′ah, Bĭn′nū-ī of the sons of Hĕn′a-dăd, Kăd′mĭ-el;

10 And their brethren, Shĕb-a-nī′ah, Hō-dī′jah, Kel′ī-ta, Pel-ā-i′ah, Hā′nan,

11 Mī′cha, Rĕ′hŏb, Hăsh-a-bī′ah,

12 Zăc′cur, Shĕr-e-bī′ah, Shĕb-a-ni′-ah,

13 Hō-dī′jah, Bā′nī, Ben-ī-nū.

14 The chief of the people; Pâ′rŏsh, Pā′hăth-mō′ăb, Ē′lam, Zăt′thū, Bā′nī,

15 Bŭn′nī, Ăz′găd, Bĕb′a-ī,

16 Ăd-o-nī′jah, Bĭg′va-ī, Ā′din,

17 Ā′ter, Hĭz-kī′jah, Ăz′zur,

18 Hō-dī′jah, Hā′shum, Bē′zaī,

19 Hâ′rĭph, Ăn′a-thŏth, Nēb′a-ī,

20 Măg′pĭ-ăsh, Me-shŭl′lam, Hē′zir,

21 Me-shĕz′a-beel, Zā′dŏk, Jăd-du′a,

22 Pĕl-a-tī′ah, Hā′nan, An-a-ī′ah,

23 Hō-shē′a, Hăn-a-nī′ah, Hā′shŭb,

24 Hăl-lō′hĕsh, Pĭl′e-hä, Shō′bĕk,

25 Rē′hum, Ha-shăb′nah, Mā-a-sē′-iah,

26 And A-hī′jah, Hā′nan, Ā-nan,

27 Măl′luch, Hâ′rĭm, Bā′a-nah.

28 ¶And the rest of the people, the priests, the Lēvītes, the porters, the singers, and the Nĕth′i-nĭmś, and all they that had separated themselves from the people of the lands unto the law of God, their wives, their sons, and their daughters, every one having knowledge, and having understanding;

29 They clave to their brethren, their nobles, and entered into a curse, and into an oath, to walk in God's law, which was given by Moses the servant of God, and to observe and do all the commandments of the Lord our Lord, and his judgments and his statutes;

30 And that we would not give our daughters unto the people of the land, nor take their daughters for our sons:

31 And *if* the people of the land bring ware or any victuals on the sabbath day to sell, *that* we would not buy it of them on the sabbath, or on the holy day: and *that* we would leave the seventh year, and the exaction of every debt.

32 Also we made ordinances for us, to charge ourselves yearly with the third part of a shekel for the service of the house of our God;

ment with God. This agreement was made on a sealed document. They agreed to separate from the heathen and to continue keeping the commandments of God.

D. List of Those Who Sealed Covenant. 10:1-39.

10:1-27. Now those that sealed were. The last verse of chapter 9 is the introduction to the tenth chapter. On the basis of their repentance and prayer, the people made an agreement with God. The agreement was signed and sealed, and the first twenty-seven verses of this chapter enumerate those who sealed and signed the covenant. Note that Nehemiah was the first person to sign the covenant. He is conscious of the fact that he is the leader of the community; and, exercising such leadership, he is the first to sign the covenant.

In verses 1-27 there are three groups of people mentioned. The priests (vss. 1-8), the Levites (vss. 9-13), and the leaders of the people (vss. 14-27).

28. And the rest of the people. There were more people who signed the covenant than just the ones who were mentioned by name. Note the qualifications for those who signed. First, they were separated from evil. And second, they had knowledge and understanding of what they were doing.

29. They clave to their brethren, their nobles. The "rest of the people" mentioned in verse 28 had extreme loyalty to their leaders, who also had signed the covenant. The nature of their covenant was to **walk in God's law.** This is the agreement that is talked about in chapter 9, verse 38. It was an agreement to obey **the commandments of the Lord our Lord.**

30-31. The agreement also included a commitment to remain separate from the heathen nations around them, and they refused to intermarry with the surrounding nations (Ezr 9:2). They also agreed to observe the Sabbath day. They would not buy from anyone or do business on the Sabbath. They also agreed to observe the seventh or sabbatical year (Ex 23:11). **And the exaction of every debt.** For further information on this see Deuteronomy 15:2. The implication of this verse is that they were willing to obey every detail of God's law.

32. For the service of the house of our God. The people recognized the importance of supporting the worship of the Temple. This was part of obedience to God's law. They recognized the need of financially supporting the continuing services of the Temple. **With the third part of a shekel.** This probably is an application of Exodus 30:13, where all men over twenty years old were to give half a shekel to the Lord. Perhaps because of the extreme poverty of the remnant, the tribute was lowered from half a shekel to one third a shekel.

33 For the shewbread, and for the continual meat offering, and for the continual burnt offering, of the sabbaths, of the new moons, for the set feasts, and for the holy *things*, and for the sin offerings to make an atonement for Israel, and *for* all the work of the house of our God.

34 And we cast the lots among the priests, the Lēvītes, and the people, for the wood offering, to bring *it* into the house of our God, after the houses of our fathers, at times appointed year by year, to burn upon the altar of the LORD our God, as *it is* written in the law:

35 And to bring the firstfruits of our ground, and the firstfruits of all fruit of all trees, year by year, unto the house of the LORD:

36 Also the firstborn of our sons, and of our cattle, as *it is* written in the law, and the firstlings of our herds and of our flocks, to bring to the house of our God, unto the priests that minister in the house of our God:

37 And *that* we should bring the firstfruits of our dough, and our offerings, and the fruit of all manner of trees, of wine and of oil, unto the priests, to the chambers of the house of our God; and the tithes of our ground unto the Lēvītes, that the same Lēvītes might have the tithes in all the cities of our tillage.

38 And the priest the son of Aaron shall be with the Lēvītes, when the Lēvītes take tithes: and the Lēvītes shall bring up the tithe of the tithes unto the house of our God, to the chambers, unto the treasure house.

39 For the children of Israel and the children of Levi shall bring the offering of the corn, of the new wine, and the oil, unto the chambers, where *are* the vessels of the sanctuary, and the priests that minister, and the porters, and the singers: and we will not forsake the house of our God.

CHAPTER 11

AND the rulers of the people dwelt at Jerusalem: the rest of the people also cast lots, to bring one of ten to dwell in Jerusalem the holy city, and nine parts *to dwell* in *other* cities.

2 And the people blessed all the men, that willingly offered themselves to dwell at Jerusalem.

3 ¶Now these *are* the chief of the province that dwelt in Jerusalem: but in the cities of Jūdah dwelt every one in his possession in their cities, *to wit,* Israel, the priests, and the Lēvītes, and the Nĕth'ĭ-nĭmś, and the children of Sŏlomon's servants.

4 And at Jerusalem dwelt *certain* of the children of Jūdah, and of the children of Benjamin. Of the children of Jūdah; Ăth-a-ī'ah the son of Uz-zī'ah, the son of Zĕch-a-rī'ah, the son of Ăm-a-

33-34. This offering was to be utilized for the underwriting of the expenses of the Temple. Artaxerxes had provided for the expenses of the Temple (Ezr 7:20); however, the people sense the responsibility to do so on their own.

35-37. And to bring the first fruits of our ground, and the first fruits of all fruit of all trees. This has reference to Leviticus 19:24 and Deuteronomy 26:2. **Also the first-born of our sons.** This refers to the bringing of redemption money as outlined in Numbers 18:15-16. **And that we should bring the first fruits of our dough.** The dough referred to here probably has reference to ground flour.

38. After the people had brought their tithes, then the Levites brought all the tithes up to the Temple (Mal 3:8-12). Tithing was the minimum basis in the Old Testament for giving to God. In the New Testament it is also the minimum basis for our giving to God. However, the emphasis of the New Testament is that we are to give above and beyond our tithe to God. **The Levites shall bring up the tithe of the tithes unto the house of our God.** Apparently, the Levites would tithe of all of the peoples' tithes and give that tithe for the support of the priests.

39. And we will not forsake the house of our God. The people recognized the importance of their loyalty and support of Temple worship. They had determined that they would not let down in that commitment. The New Testament Christian has an equal obligation to be loyal and to support the church.

E. List of Exiles. 11:1-12:26.

11:1-2. The rest of the people also cast lots, to bring one of ten to dwell in Jerusalem the holy city. This was the fulfillment of Nehemiah's desire to expand the population of Jerusalem (7:4-5). **That willingly offered themselves to dwell at Jerusalem.** Beyond those who were chosen by lot to dwell at Jerusalem, some people volunteered to dwell in the city. This was an act of sacrifice and was also a step of faith.

Verses 3-36 contain a list of the inhabitants of Jerusalem and the surrounding areas.

3-4. Two specific families are mentioned here: the children of Judah and the children of Benjamin.

rī'ah, the son of Shĕph-a-tī'ah, the son of
Ma-hă'la-le-el, of the children of Pe'rĕz:

5 And Mā'a-sē'iah the son of Bā'ruch,
the son of Cŏl-hō'zeh, the son of Ha-
zā'iah, the son of Ăd-a-ī'ah, the son of
Joi'a-rīb, the son of Zĕch-a-rī'ah, the
son of Shī-lō'nī.

6 All the sons of Pe'rĕz that dwelt at
Jerusalem *were* four hundred threescore and eight valiant men.

7 And these *are* the sons of Benjamin;
Săl'lū the son of Me-shūl'lam, the son
of Jō'ĕd, the son of Pe-dā'iah, the son of
Kō-la-ī'ah, the son of Mā-a-sē'iah, the
son of Ĭth'ī-el, the son of Je-sā'iah.

8 And after him Găb'ba-ī, Săl'la-ī,
nine hundred twenty and eight.

9 And Jō'el the son of Zĭch'rī *was*
their overseer: and Jūdah the son of Se-
nū'ah *was* second over the city.

10 Of the priests: Je-dā'iah the son of
Joi'a-rīb, Jā'chin.

11 Se-ra-ī'ah the son of Hĭl-kī'ah, the
son of Me-shūl'lam, the son of Zā'dŏk,
the son of Me-rā'ioth, the son of A-hī'-
tūb, *was* the ruler of the house of God.

12 And their brethren that did the
work of the house *were* eight hundred
twenty and two: and Ăd-a-ī'ah the son
of Jer'ō-hăm, the son of Pĕl-a-lī'ah, the
son of Ăm'zī, the son of Zĕch-a-rī'ah,
the son of Păsh'ur, the son of Măl-
chī'ah,

13 And his brethren, chief of the fathers, two hundred forty and two: and
A-măsh'a-ī the son of Ā-zar'e-el, the
son of A-hăs'a-ī, the son of Me-shĭl'le-
mŏth, the son of Ĭm'mer.

14 And their brethren, mighty men of
valour, an hundred twenty and eight:
and their overseer *was* Zăb'dī-el, the
son of *one of* the great men.

15 Also of the Lēvītes: Shem-ā-ī'ah
the son of Hā'shŭb, the son of Ăz'ri-
kam, the son of Hăsh-a-bī'ah, the son of
Bŭn'nī;

16 And Shăb'be-thaī and Jōz'a-băd,
of the chief of the Lēvītes, *had* the oversight of the outward business of the
house of God.

17 And Măt-ta-nī'ah the son of Mī'-
cha, the son of Zăb'dī, the son of Ā'săph
was the principal to begin the thanksgiving in prayer: and Băk-buk-ī'ah the
second among his brethren, and Ăb'da
the son of Shăm-mū'a, the son of Gā'lăl,
the son of Jed'ū-thun.

18 All the Lēvītes in the holy city
were two hundred fourscore and four.

19 Moreover the porters, Ăk'kŭb,
Tăl'mon, and their brethren that kept
the gates, *were* an hundred seventy and
two.

20 ¶And the residue of Israel, of the
priests, *and* the Lēvītes, *were* in all the
cities of Jūdah, every one in his inheritance.

21 But the Nĕth'i-nĭmś dwelt in
Ō'phĕl: and Zī'ha and Gĭs'pa *were* over
the Nĕth'i-nĭmś.

22 The overseer also of the Lēvītes at
Jerusalem *was* Ŭz'zi the son of Bā'nī,
the son of Hăsh-a-bī'ah, the son of Măt-
ta-nī'ah, the son of Mī'cha. Of the sons
of Ā'săph, the singers *were* over the
business of the house of God.

23 For *it was* the king's commandment concerning them, that a certain

5-6. Two heads of the house of Judah are mentioned: Athaiah
of the children of Perez and Maaseiah of the children of Shelah.
There were four hundred and eighty-six **valiant men** of the
family of Perez. Some commentators feel that verse 6 ought to
precede verse 5 (Lange, p. 46).

7-9. The second family mentioned is the Benjamite family.
Two leaders are mentioned: Sallu and Gabbai. Nine hundred
and twenty-eight heads of families are mentioned. **And Judah
the son of Senuah was second over the city.** This probably
refers to the second city, which was part of the city north of the
Temple (Lange, p. 46). Joel and Judah were leaders in the city.

10-14. These verses contain a listing of the various priests and
their families. In this particular record only three of the heads of
the twenty-four classes of priests are mentioned (I Chr 24:17).
The listing that Nehemiah used was probably some copy of the
original listing in I Chronicles 9:13. However, these lists differ
by a total of five hundred and sixty-eight. This is due, most
likely, to scribal error in copying of the records.

Verses 15-19 contain the listing of the Levites.

**15-17. Had the oversight of the outward business of the
house of God.** This refers to the secular aspect of God's worship
(I Chr 26:29). **The principal to begin the thanksgiving in
prayer.** This means that Mattaniah was the one who led in the
praising and singing part of the worship.

18-20. The total number of the Levites within the city was
two hundred and eighty-four. The rest of Israel dwelt in the
cities surrounding Jerusalem.

21-22. But the Nethinim dwelt in Ophel. This particular city
was on the southern slope of Mount Moriah. Uzzi was responsible for the direction of the ministry of the Levites at Jerusalem.
His pedigree is listed as being a part of the sons of Asaph who
were the singers.

**23-24. For it was the king's commandment concerning
them.** This refers to the commandment of Artaxerxes as out-

portion should be for the singers, due for every day.

24 And Pĕth-a-hī′ah the son of Me-shĕz′a-beel, of the children of Ze′rah the son of Jūdah, *was* at the king's hand in all matters concerning the people.

25 And for the villages, with their fields, *some* of the children of Jūdah dwelt at Kir′jath-är′ba, and *in* the villages thereof, and at Dī′bŏn, and *in* the villages thereof, and at Je-kăb′ze-ĕl, and *in* the villages thereof,

26 And at Jĕsh′u-a, and at Mŏl′a-dah, and at Bĕth-phĕ′let,

27 And at Hā′zar-shū′al, and at Be′-er-shĕ′ba, and *in* the villages thereof,

28 And at Ziklag, and at Mek′ō-nah, and in the villages thereof,

29 And at Ĕn-rĭm′mon, and at Zā′re-ah, and at Jär′mŭth,

30 Za-nō′ah, Adŭllam, and *in* their villages, at Lā′chĭsh, and the fields thereof, at A-zē′kah, and *in* the villages thereof. And they dwelt from Be′er-shĕ′ba unto the valley of Hĭn′nom.

31 The children also of Benjamin from Gē′ba *dwelt* at Mĭch′măsh, and A-ī′ja, and Bĕth-el, and *in* their villages,

32 *And* at Ān′a-thŏth, Nob, Ān-a-nī′ah,

33 Hā′zôr, Rā′mah, Gĭt′ta-im,

34 Hā′dĭd, Ze-bō′im, Ne-băl′lat,

35 Lod, and Ō′nō, the valley of craftsmen.

36 And of the Lēvītes *were* divisions in Jūdah, *and* in Benjamin.

CHAPTER 12

NOW these *are* the priests and the Lēvītes that went up with Ze-rŭb′ba-bel the son of Shē-ăl′tī-el, and Jĕsh′u-a: Se-ra-ī′ah, Jĕr-e-mī′ah, Ezra,

2 Ăm-a-rī′ah, Măl′luch, Hăt′tŭsh,

3 Shĕch-a-nī′ah, Rĕ′hum, Mĕr′e-mŏth,

4 Ĭd′dō, Gĭn′ne-thō, A-bī′jah,

5 Mī′a-mĭn, Mā-a-dī′ah, Bĭl′gah,

6 Shem-ā-i′ah, and Joi′a-rĭb, Je-dā′-iah,

7 Săl′lū, Ā′mŏk, Hĭl-kī′ah, Je-dā′iah. These *were* the chief of the priests and of their brethren in the days of Jĕsh′u-a.

8 Moreover the Lēvītes: Jĕsh′u-a, Bĭn′nū-ī, Kăd′mī-el, Shĕr-e-bī′ah, Jū-dah, *and* Măt-ta-nī′ah, which *was* over the thanksgiving, he and his brethren.

9 Also Băk-buk-ī′ah and Ŭn′nī, their brethren, *were* over against them in the watches.

10 ¶ And Jĕsh′u-a begat Joi′a-kĭm, Joi′a-kĭm also begat E-lī′a-shĭb, and E-lī′a-shĭb begat Joi′a-da,

11 And Joi′a-da begat Jonathan, and Jonathan begat Jăd-du′a.

12 And in the days of Joi′a-kĭm were priests, the chief of the fathers: of Se-ra-ī′ah, Mĕr-a-ī′ah; of Jĕr-e-mī′ah, Hăn-a-nī′ah;

13 Of Ezra, Me-shŭl′lam; of Ăm-a-rī′ah, Je-hō-hā′nan;

14 Of Mĕl′i-cu, Jonathan; of Shĕb-a-nī′ah, Joseph;

15 Of Hā′rĭm, Ăd′na; of Me-rā′ioth, Hĕl′ka-ī;

16 Of Ĭd′dō, Zĕch-a-rī′ah; of Gĭn′ne-thŏn, Me-shŭl′lam;

lined in Ezra 7:11ff. Pethahiah was responsible to King Artaxerxes for all matters for the entire community. Uzzi was responsible for the Temple worship, but Pethahiah was responsible for every facet of the new community. He probably acted as an emissary between Nehemiah and the king.

25-30. Various towns and villages are mentioned; they were inhabited by Jews.

31-35. These are the dwelling places of the children of Benjamin.

36. This should literally read "and of the Levites divisions of Judah went to Benjamin." It means that Levites were transferred from areas in Judah and were stationed in certain Benjamite towns (Lange, p. 48).

12:1-7. Now these are the priests and the Levites that went up with Zerubbabel the son of Shealtiel. The first twenty-six verses of this chapter contain a listing of the priests and Levites. Although this list is somewhat different from the listing in chapter 11, it is connected with the desire of Nehemiah to enlarge the population of Jerusalem. Similar lists of priests occur in Ezra 2:36-39, Nehemiah 7:37-42, and in this particular chapter. There are some apparent differences. In Ezra 2 and Nehemiah 7 only four distinct orders of priests are listed. However, in this chapter there are twenty-two distinct families mentioned. According to Lange, twenty-two families are probably part of the four distinct orders mentioned in the other chapters.

8-9. These verses contain the leaders of the Levitical houses. Which was over the thanksgiving. These people were responsible for the thanksgiving and singing part of their worship.

10-11. These verses describe the genealogy of the priests from Jeshua to Jaddua.

12-21. These verses contain a listing of the heads of the priestly houses in Joiakim's time. Joiakim was the high priest during the time of Nehemiah and Ezra.

17 Of A-bī'jah, Zĭch'rī; of Mĭn'i-a-mĭn, of Mō-a-dī'ah, Pĭl'tai;
18 Of Bĭl'gah, Shăm-mū'a; of Shem-ā-i'ah, Je-hŏn'a-than;
19 And of Joi'a-rĭb, Măt-te-na'ī; of Je-dā'iah, Ŭz'zi;
20 Of Săl'la-ī, Kăl'la-ī; of Ā'mŏk, Ē'ber;
21 Of Hĭl-kī'ah, Hăsh-a-bī'ah; of Je-dā'iah, Ne-thăn'e-el.
22 ¶The Lēvītes in the days of E-lī'a-shĭb, Joi'a-da, and Jō-hā'nan, and Jăd-du'a, were recorded chief of the fathers: also the priests, to the reign of Darius the Persian.
23 The sons of Levi, the chief of the fathers, were written in the book of the chronicles, even until the days of Jō-hā'nan the son of E-lī'a-shĭb.
24 And the chief of the Lēvītes: Hăsh-a-bī'ah, Shĕr-e-bī'ah, and Jĕsh'u-a the son of Kăd'mī-el, with their brethren over against them, to praise and to give thanks, according to the commandment of David the man of God, ward over against ward.
25 Măt-ta-nī'ah, and Băk-buk-ī'ah, Ō-ba-dī'ah, Me-shūl'lam, Tăl'mon, Ăk'kŭb, were porters keeping the ward at the thresholds of the gates.
26 These were in the days of Joi'a-kĭm the son of Jĕsh'u-a, the son of Jōz'a-dăk, and in the days of Nē-he-mī'ah the governor, and of Ezra the priest, the scribe.
27 ¶And at the dedication of the wall of Jerusalem they sought the Lēvītes out of all their places, to bring them to Jerusalem, to keep the dedication with gladness, both with thanksgivings, and with singing, with cymbals, psalteries, and with harps.
28 And the sons of the singers gathered themselves together, both out of the plain country round about Jerusalem, and from the villages of Ne-tōph'a-thī;
29 Also from the house of Gilgal, and out of the fields of Gē'ba and Ăz'ma-vĕth: for the singers had builded them villages round about Jerusalem.
30 And the priests and the Lēvītes purified themselves, and purified the people, and the gates, and the wall.

31 Then I brought up the princes of Jūdah upon the wall, and appointed two great companies of them that gave thanks, whereof one went on the right hand upon the wall toward the dung gate:
32 And after them went Hō-sha-i'ah, and half of the princes of Jūdah,
33 And Ăz-a-rī'ah, Ezra, and Me-shūl'lam,
34 Jūdah, and Benjamin, and Shem-ā-i'ah, and Jĕr-e-mī'ah.
35 And certain of the priests' sons with trumpets; namely, Zĕch-a-rī'ah the son of Jonathan, the son of Shem-a-i'ah, the son of Măt-ta-nī'ah, the son of Mī-chā'iah, the son of Zăc'cur, the son Ā'săph:

22-26. These verses contain a listing of the Levites. **These were in the days of Joiakim the son of Jeshua** (vs. 26). Ezra probably came to Jerusalem during the high priesthood of Jeshua. Sometime during the time of Ezra and Nehemiah Eliashib, the son of Jeshua, assumed the priesthood.

F. Dedication of Walls. 12:27-47.

Verses 27-43 contain the historical account of the dedication of the wall of Jerusalem.
27. They sought the Levites out of all their places. The Levites had settled in various places surrounding Jerusalem. They brought them back for the dedication of the wall (11:3). The dedication was to be a time of **gladness, both with thanksgivings, and with singing.**

28-29. And the sons of the singers. There were specific Levitical families whose responsibility involved singing (11:17, 22-23). There were three such families: Asaph, Heman, and Jeduthun.

30. And the priests and the Levites purified themselves. Before they commenced dedication of the walls, the priests realized the necessity for self-purification. This is indeed the basis of our worship of God. Without the purity and holiness of forgiven sin, we cannot effectively communicate with and worship God. Purification involved the offering of certain sacrifices (II Chr 29:20-24).
31. Then I brought up the princes of Judah upon the wall. These were all the leaders from Jerusalem and its surrounding villages and cities. The leadership of the entire Jewish community gathered for the dedication festivities. Ezra divided the people up into companies, or processions.
32-35. These processions advanced in different directions, and as they proceeded they gave thanks and sang psalms.

36 And his brethren, Shem-ā-i′ah, and Ă-zar′ā-ĕl, Mĭl-a-la′ī, Gĭl′ā-laī, Ma-ā′ī, Ne-thăn′e-el, and Jūdah, Ha-nā′nī, with the musical instruments of David the man of God, and Ezra the scribe before them.

37 And at the fountain gate, which was over against them, they went up by the stairs of the city of David, at the going up of the wall, above the house of David, even unto the water gate eastward.

38 And the other *company of them that gave* thanks went over against *them*, and I after them, and the half of the people upon the wall, from beyond the tower of the furnaces even unto the broad wall;

39 And from above the gate of Ē′phra-im, and above the old gate, and above the fish gate, and the tower of Hă-nan′ē-el, and the tower of Mē′ah, even unto the sheep gate: and they stood still in the prison gate.

40 So stood the two *companies of them that gave* thanks in the house of God, and I, and the half of the rulers with me:

41 And the priests; E-lī′a-kĭm, Mă-a-sē′iah, Mĭn′i-a-mĭn, Mĭ-chā′iah, Ē-lĭ-ō-ē′na-ī, Zĕch-a-rī′ah, *and* Hăn-a-nī′ah, with trumpets;

42 And Mă-a-sē′iah, and Shem-ā-i′ah, and Ē-le-ā′zar, and Ūz′zi, and Je-hō-hā′nan, and Măl-chī′jah, and Ē′lam, and Ē′zer. And the singers sang loud, with Jĕz-ra-hī′ah *their* overseer.

43 Also that day they offered great sacrifices, and rejoiced: for God had made them rejoice with great joy: the wives also and the children rejoiced: so that the joy of Jerusalem was heard even afar off.

44 ¶And at that time were some appointed over the chambers for the treasures, for the offerings, for the firstfruits, and for the tithes, to gather into them out of the fields of the cities the portions of the law for the priests and Lēvītes: for Jūdah rejoiced for the priests and for the Lēvītes that waited.

45 And both the singers and the porters kept the ward of their God, and the ward of the purification, according to the commandment of David, *and* of Sŏl′o-mon his son.

46 For in the days of David and Ā′săph of old *there were* chief of the singers, and songs of praise and thanksgiving unto God.

47 And all Israel in the days of Ze-rŭb′ba-bel, and in the days of Nĕ-he-mi′ah, gave the portions of the singers and the porters, every day his portion: and they sanctified *holy things* unto the Lēvītes; and the Lēvītes sanctified *them* unto the children of Aaron.

CHAPTER 13

ON that day they read in the book of

36-38. And Ezra the scribe before them. One of the companies assigned by Nehemiah was headed by Ezra. **And I after them.** The second group was apparently led by Nehemiah himself.

39-42. They proceeded around the city in a different direction. The idea described in these verses is that there were two distinct processions moving in opposite directions. As they walked around the wall, they gave thanks and praised the Lord. After walking around the circumference of the walls, they met at the Temple.

43. Also that day they offered great sacrifices. These sacrifices probably referred to thank offerings. The people would partake and eat of these offerings and rejoice (Lev 3). **The wives also and the children rejoiced.** This moment of great festivity was enjoyed by the entire family. This is important, since the rebuilding and the settling and populating of Jerusalem had involved a commitment by the entire family. Now as a family they could rejoice together in all that God had done for them.

44. And at that time. At the time of dedication certain things were decided upon and outlined. Certain people were appointed to oversee and supervise the **treasures.** These involved three specific things: the offerings, the first fruits, and the tithes. All of these were required by God for the Temple. **For Judah rejoiced.** The people willingly and thankfully gave for the support of the Temple. Although they were paying taxes to the Persian government and were involved in great sacrifice in rebuilding the community, they gladly gave to the Lord.

45. Kept the ward of their God. This means that they performed their required duties. **According to the commandment of David, and of Solomon his son.** This refers to I Chronicles 20:26 and to II Chronicles 8:14.

46. From the time of David onward, singers were an important part of the worship of God. Asaph was the original leader of this element of worship. In the original Hebrew the conjunction between David and Asaph is not there. The idea is that from the days of David, Asaph was the chief of singers. It does not imply that David also was highly involved in the singing.

47. And they sanctified holy things unto the Levites. The concept of the word sanctification is that of consecration. They performed their duties to the Lord in a consecrated and dedicated manner.

G. Reforms of Nehemiah. 13:1-31.

13:1-3. On that day they read in the book of Moses in the

Moses in the audience of the people; and therein was found written, that the Ammonite and the Moabite should not come into the congregation of God for ever;

2 Because they met not the children of Israel with bread and with water, but hired Bā'laam against them, that he should curse them: howbeit our God turned the curse into a blessing.

3 Now it came to pass, when they had heard the law, that they separated from Israel all the mixed multitude.

4 ¶And before this, E-lī'a-shĭb the priest, having the oversight of the chamber of the house of our God, was allied unto Tō-bī'ah:

5 And he had prepared for him a great chamber, where aforetime they laid the meat offerings, the frankincense, and the vessels, and the tithes of the corn, the new wine, and the oil, which was commanded to be given to the Lēvītes, and the singers, and the porters; and the offerings of the priests.

6 But in all this time was not I at Jerusalem: for in the two and thirtieth year of Är-ta-xer'xēš king of Babylon came I unto the king, and after certain days obtained I leave of the king:

7 And I came to Jerusalem, and understood of the evil that E-lī'a-shĭb did for Tō-bī'ah, in preparing him a chamber in the courts of the house of God.

8 And it grieved me sore: therefore I cast forth all the household stuff of Tō-bī'ah out of the chamber.

9 Then I commanded, and they cleansed the chambers: and thither brought I again the vessels of the house of God, with the meat offering and the frankincense.

10 ¶And I perceived that the portions of the Lēvītes had not been given them: for the Lēvītes and the singers, that did the work, were fled every one to his field.

11 Then contended I with the rulers, and said, Why is the house of God forsaken? And I gathered them together, and set them in their place.

12 Then brought all Jūdah the tithe of the corn and the new wine and the oil unto the treasuries.

13 And I made treasurers over the treasuries, Shĕl-e-mī'ah the priest, and Zā'dŏk the scribe, and of the Lēvītes, Pe-dā'iah: and next to them was Hā-nan the son of Zăc'cur, the son of Măt-ta-nī'ah: for they were counted faithful, and their office was to distribute unto their brethren.

14 Remember me, O my God, concerning this, and wipe not out my good deeds that I have done for the house of my God, and for the offices thereof.

audience of the people. That day refers to the day of the dedication of the walls (12:43-44). They read the section of the Law dealing with the Ammonite and Moabite and how the children of Israel were to be separate from them (this refers to Deut 23:3ff.). After hearing the Law, the children of Israel obeyed; and they separated themselves from the heathen people.

4. And before this. The evil of Eliashib occurred during the time when Nehemiah visited Artaxerxes at Susa. Eliashib was **allied unto Tobiah.** The exact alliance is unclear; however, some people feel that Eliashib was in some way related to Tobiah through marriage.

5. And he had prepared for him a great chamber. Apparently, Nehemiah, after building the walls, had to return to Susa for some business. It was during this time that the alliance with Tobiah was inaugurated and established. The chamber which Eliashib utilized originally held a variety of things, such as the meat offerings, the frankincense, the vessels, the tithes.

6. But in all this time was not I at Jerusalem. In the thirty-second year of Artaxerxes Nehemiah returns to the king. He had been at Jerusalem for a period of twelve years and now had to return and make a report of what had happened. **And after certain days obtained I leave of the king.** The extent of Nehemiah's stay at Babylon is uncertain; however, it was probably at least a year's period. Nehemiah is given permission to return again to Jerusalem.

7-9. Upon his return, Nehemiah finds out about the situation with Tobiah. Nehemiah is upset and throws all of Tobiah's belongings out of the chamber. It is interesting to note that in the interest of obtaining the friendship of Tobiah, they had actually taken all of God's vessels out of His house to make provisions for one who opposed the very rebuilding of Jerusalem.

10. And I perceived that the portions of the Levites had not been given them. The people had not been faithful in supporting the work of the Levites. Consequently, they had left the Temple and were working in the fields to make a living.

11. Why is the house of God forsaken? Nehemiah gathers the rulers together and asks why they had disbanded their commitment to serve the Lord. It was the rulers who were responsible for the continuation of God's worship. **And I gathered them together, and set them in their place.** This refers to the Levites. Nehemiah brings them back to Jerusalem and puts them in their proper position of serving God at the Temple.

12-13. The tithing is renewed and brought to the Temple. Nehemiah organizes and appoints people to supervise and oversee the storehouses for the tithes and offerings. These people were also responsible to distribute the needs and necessities to the Levites.

14. This verse contains a prayer. Nehemiah asks God not to forget that he has tried to do right. He asks that God not forget this in light of all of the evil that had come upon the children of Israel.

15 ¶In those days saw I in Jūdah *some* treading wine presses on the sabbath, and bringing in sheaves, and lading asses; as also wine, grapes, and figs, and all *manner of* burdens, which they brought into Jerusalem on the sabbath day: and I testified *against them* in the day wherein they sold victuals.

16 There dwelt men of Tyre also therein, which brought fish, and all manner of ware, and sold on the sabbath unto the children of Jūdah, and in Jerusalem.

17 Then I contended with the nobles of Jūdah, and said unto them, What evil thing *is* this that ye do, and profane the sabbath day?

18 Did not your fathers thus, and did not our God bring all this evil upon us, and upon this city? yet ye bring more wrath upon Israel by profaning the sabbath.

19 And it came to pass, that when the gates of Jerusalem began to be dark before the sabbath, I commanded that the gates should be shut, and charged that they should not be opened till after the sabbath: and *some* of my servants set I at the gates, *that* there should no burden be brought in on the sabbath day.

20 So the merchants and sellers of all kind of ware lodged without Jerusalem once or twice.

21 Then I testified against them, and said unto them, Why lodge ye about the wall? if ye do *so* again, I will lay hands on you. From that time forth came they no *more* on the sabbath.

22 And I commanded the Lē'vītes that they should cleanse themselves, and *that* they should come *and* keep the gates, to sanctify the sabbath day. Remember me, O my God, *concerning* this also, and spare me according to the greatness of thy mercy.

23 ¶In those days also saw I Jews *that* had married wives of Āsh'dŏd, of Ammon, *and* of Moab:

24 And their children spake half in the speech of Āsh'dŏd, and could not speak in the Jews' language, but according to the language of each people.

25 And I contended with them, and cursed them, and smote certain of them, and plucked off their hair, and made them swear by God, *saying*, Ye shall not give your daughters unto their sons, nor take their daughters unto your sons, or for yourselves.

26 Did not Sŏl'o-mon king of Israel sin by these things? yet among many nations was there no king like him, who was beloved of his God, and God made him king over all Israel: nevertheless even him did outlandish women cause to sin.

27 Shall we then hearken unto you to do all this great evil, to transgress against our God in marrying strange wives?

28 And *one* of the sons of Joi'a-da, the

15. Treading wine presses on the sabbath. Beyond the sins that had invaded the Temple worship, the people had also forsaken Sabbath worship. **I testified against them in the day wherein they sold victuals.** They were also selling food on the Sabbath. This desecration of the Sabbath was in complete disobedience to the law of God.

16. There dwelt men of Tyre also therein. Heathen peoples had taken up residence in Jerusalem and were involved in buying, selling, and trading.

17-18. Then I contended with the nobles of Judah. Earlier, he had approached the rulers and asked for accountability. Now he goes a little bit higher and gathers the elite of the community together, inquiring of them concerning their sin. He reminds them that it was because of their desecration of the Sabbath that God had judged Israel.

19-22. Nehemiah begins to enforce Sabbath day worship. He places people at the gates of Jerusalem to shut them when the Sabbath begins and to prevent anyone from bringing materials to buy or sell. **That there should no burden be brought.** These burdens refer to the food and materials that people were selling and buying. The merchants respond by continuing their efforts outside the gates of Jerusalem. Nehemiah corrects this problem by threatening to arrest them. The Sabbath would not be broken without or within the city walls of Jerusalem. Nehemiah commands the Levites to sanctify themselves for Temple worship.

23. In those days also saw I Jews that had married wives of Ashdod. Nehemiah is now made aware of the third problem that had occurred since his absence from Jerusalem. First, there was the alliance with Tobiah. Second, the Levites had forsaken the work of God. Third, the Sabbath had been desecrated; and fourth, the people had intermarried with the heathen nations.

24. The children of these marriages had learned the language of the heathen nations, and they could not speak the language of the Jewish community. This is usually the result of an evil alliance. When we embrace sin, pretty soon we adopt the general life-style of sin; and soon we are absorbed, dominated, and controlled by that sin.

25-27. The action taken by Nehemiah is rather severe. However, it must be interpreted in light of the seriousness of the sin which they had committed. He reminds them that even Solomon in all of his wisdom had been defeated by intermarrying with the heathen nations (I Kgs 11:9-13). **Outlandish women.** The meaning of this word is that they were foreign women (Lange, p. 58). He reminds them that in marrying into the heathen nations they were disobeying a clear command of God.

28. Nehemiah acts in a very severe manner against one of the

son of E-lī′a-shīb the high priest, was son in law to Săn-băl′lat the Hôr′o-nīte: therefore I chased him from me.

29 Remember them, O my God, because they have defiled the priesthood, and the covenant of the priesthood, and of the Lē′vītes.

30 Thus cleansed I them from all strangers, and appointed the wards of the priests and the Lē′vītes, every one in his business;

31 And for the wood offering, at times appointed, and for the firstfruits. Remember me, O my God, for good.

sons of Joiada who had married into the family of Sanballat. Sanballat (2:10) was diametrically opposed to everything that the community stood for; he was the definite enemy of the Jews. One of the priestly line had married into that family. Because of the degradation of the family into which he married and the fact that he was part of the priestly line, Nehemiah excommunicates him from the community. God had given clear direction as to the responsibilities of a priest when it came to marriage (Lev 21:7, 14).

29. Again, Nehemiah inserts a prayer. It begins the same way as the other prayers in this chapter (vss. 14, 22). This prayer is a prayer of confession expressing the fact that they had violated their priesthood and their covenant with God.

30-31. These are the concluding verses that gives a paraphrase of all that Nehemiah did. He caused them to separate from heathen nations and re-establish formal worship of God. The concluding statement of this chapter, and of the book, is a prayer **Remember me, O my God, for good.** This statement occurs four times in this chapter. Again, we are reminded of the importance of prayer in the life of Nehemiah. He was a man who first of all sought to please and obey God; his life was characterized by constant communion and prayer. From the depths of his relationship with God, he was an effective leader of the children of Israel.

(see page 879 for Bibliography to Ezra, Nehemiah, and Esther)

ESTHER

INTRODUCTION

The book of Esther is an exciting story that is a living illustration of the unseen hand of God's providence. Although the name of God is not mentioned in the entire narrative, His overruling sovereignty is seen in every event. This story is also the basis for the celebration of the Jewish feast of Purim. The setting is among the Jewish *diaspora* of the Persian Empire.

Authorship and Date. There can be no doubt that the historicity and canonicity of Esther has been the most debated of all the Old Testament books. Even some Jewish scholars questioned its inclusion in the Old Testament because of the absence of God's name.

There is no indication from the book itself as to its authorship. Some Jewish scholars suggest that Mordecai was the author. Others have proposed either Ezra or Nehemiah, but Gleason Archer, *A Survey of Old Testament Introduction* (p. 403) notes: "for either of these there is no good linguistic evidence, judging from the style or diction of the three books concerned."

The objections to the legitimacy of the book mainly stem from the lack of historical verification of Esther as the wife of Xerxes. While Herodotus refers to Amestris as the Persian Queen, with no mention of Esther or Vashti, it should be remembered that he omits several important names from this period (e.g., Belshazzar). The text does not necessarily imply that Esther became the only "queen," for she may have been one of many in the royal harem. John Whitcomb (*The Wycliffe Bible Commentary*, p. 20ff.) prefers to view her as an unregenerate Hebrew heroine. He dates her marriage at 479-478 B.C. Xerxes died in 465 B.C., and Esther 10:2 implies that his reign had finished. This would date the book sometime in the late fifth century B.C., a period with which it conforms in its historical, cultural, and geographical setting.

OUTLINE

COMMENTARY

I. THE RISE OF ESTHER. 1:1-2:23.

A. The Feast of Ahasuerus. 1:1-9.

NOW it came to pass in the days of A-haś-ū-ě′rus, (this *is* A-haś-ū-ě′rus which reigned, from India even unto Ē-thĭ-ŏ′pĭ-a, *over* an hundred and seven and twenty provinces:)

2 *That* in those days, when the king

1:1. Now it came to pass in the days of Ahasuerus. This opening statement supplies for us the historical setting for the events which follow. All of the events of this book occurred during the time of Ahasuerus, who is mentioned in Ezra chapter 4:6. Ahasuerus is another name for Xerxes. According to F. C. Keil, "the statements also concerning the extent of his kingdom (1:1; 10:1), the manners and customs of the country and court, the capricious and tyrannical character of Ahashverosh, and the historical allusions are suitable only completely to Xerxes" (*Biblical Commentary on the Old Testament*, p. 320). **Ahasuerus which reigned from India even unto Ethiopia.** The fact that Ahasuerus is another name for Xerxes is further substantiated by the defining of the extent of his kingdom. He ruled over one hundred and twenty-seven provinces. Both Ethiopians and Indians paid tribute to Xerxes and served in his army.

2-3. Which was in Shushan the palace. Ahasuerus ruled his

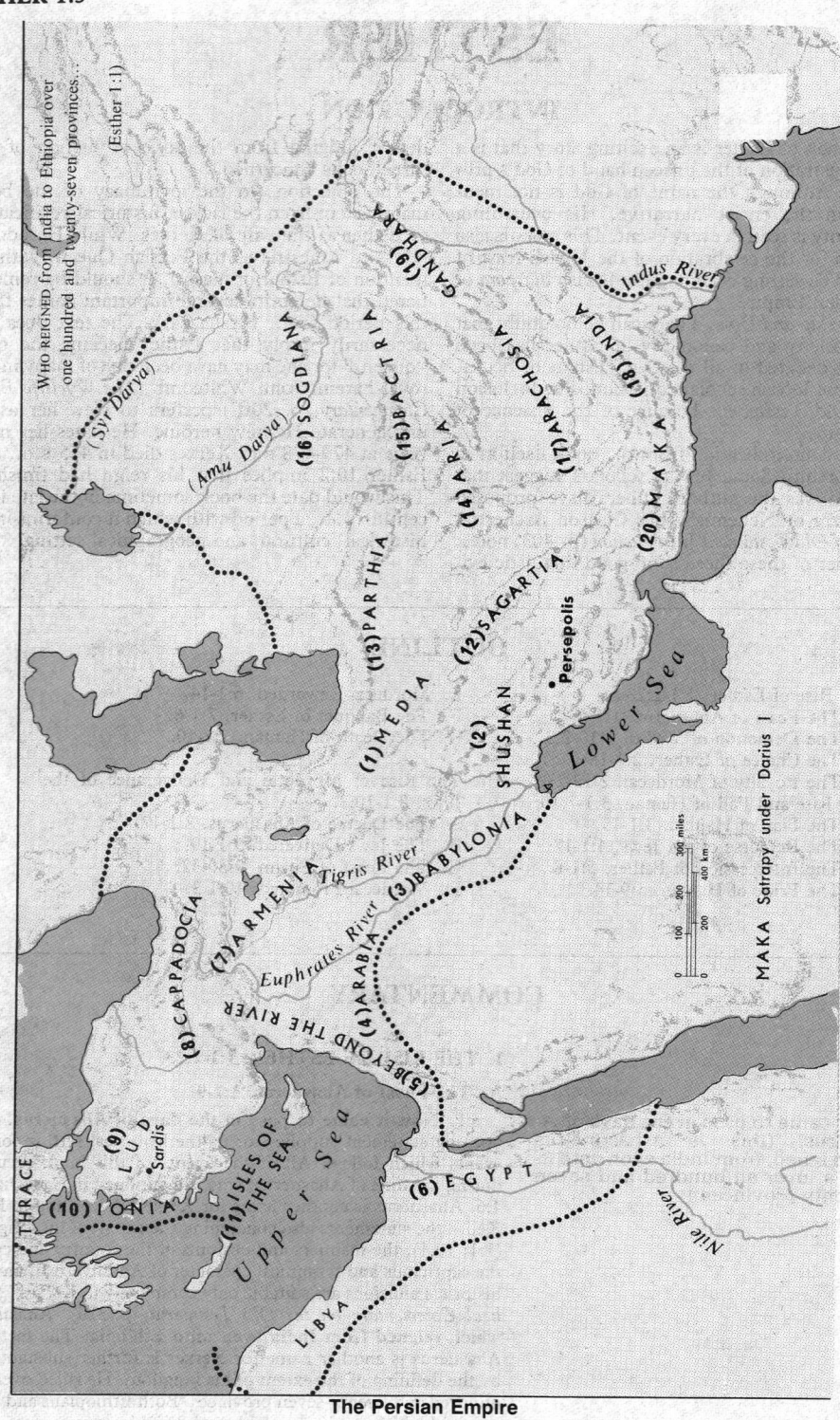

WHO REIGNED FROM India to Ethiopia over
one hundred and twenty-seven provinces...

(Esther 1:1)

(Syr Darya)

(Amu Darya)

(16) SOGDIANA

(15) BACTRIA

(19) GANDHARA

Indus River

(18) INDIA

(14) ARIA

(17) ARACHOSIA

(13) PARTHIA

(20) MAKA

(12) SAGARTIA

Persepolis

(1) MEDIA

(2) SHUSHAN

• Persepolis

Lower Sea

Tigris River

ARMENIA

(3) BABYLONIA

(7) ARMENIA

Euphrates River

(4) ARABIA

(5) BEYOND THE RIVER

CAPPADOCIA

(8) CAPPADOCIA

300 miles

400 km

100 200

200

MAKA Satrapy under Darius I

THRACE

(9) LUD

Sardis

ISLES OF THE SEA

(11) ISLES OF THE SEA

(10) IONIA

Upper Sea

(6) EGYPT

Nile River

LIBYA

The Persian Empire

A-haś-ū-ē'rus sat on the throne of his kingdom, which *was* in Shū'shăn the palace,

3 In the third year of his reign, he made a feast unto all his princes and his servants; the power of Persia and Mē'-dī-a, the nobles and princes of the provinces, *being* before him:

4 When he shewed the riches of his glorious kingdom and the honour of his excellent majesty many days, *even* an hundred and fourscore days.

5 And when these days were expired, the king made a feast unto all the people that were present in Shū'shăn the palace, both unto great and small, seven days, in the court of the garden of the king's palace;

6 *Where were* white, green, and blue, *hangings,* fastened with cords of fine linen and purple to silver rings and pillars of marble: the beds *were of* gold and silver, upon a pavement of red, and blue, and white, and black, marble.

7 And they gave *them* drink in vessels of gold, (the vessels being diverse one from another,) and royal wine in abundance, according to the state of the king.

8 And the drinking *was* according to the law; none did compel: for so the king had appointed to all the officers of his house, that they should do according to every man's pleasure.

9 Also Văsh'tī the queen made a feast for the women *in* the royal house which *belonged* to king A-haś-ū-ē'rus.

10 ¶On the seventh day, when the heart of the king was merry with wine, he commanded Me-hū'man, Bĭz'tha, Här-bō'na, Bĭg'tha, and A-băg'tha, Zē'thär, and Cär'cas, the seven chamberlains that served in the presence of A-haś-ū-ē'rus the king,

11 To bring Văsh'tī the queen before the king with the crown royal, to shew the people and the princes her beauty: for she *was* fair to look on.

12 But the queen Văsh'tī refused to come at the king's commandment by *his* chamberlains: therefore was the king very wroth, and his anger burned in him.

kingdom from its capital in Shushan the palace (Neh 1:1). It was during **the third year of his reign** that his pride caused him to bring together all the leaders of his land to show off his wealth.

4. When he showed the riches of his glorious kingdom. It was during this time of festivity that he displayed all of the glory and majesty of his vast empire. **Even a hundred and fourscore days.** The total period of time mentioned here is one hundred and eighty days. There is a difference of opinion among commentators as to whether or not this actually refers to the fact that the feast itself lasted one hundred and eighty days. Verse 5 refers to the fact that there was a feast of seven days. It would be more likely to assume that the feast and festivities involving the people lasted for one week, whereas, during a hundred-and-eighty-day period he showed the riches of his kingdom. During that one-hundred-and-eighty-day period people could come and go and observe the beauty and power of his kingdom. Perhaps during this period they conferred with each other concerning the administration and expansion of the present empire.

5. The feast mentioned in this verse involved more than just the nobles and princes of verse 3. **All the people that were present in Shushan the palace, both unto great and small.** The people in general were involved in this great feast.

6. Since the banquet took place in an outdoor garden, it is reasonable to assume that all the decorations mentioned in this verse were placed in a large tent that covered the garden. No expense was spared in the preparations for the feast. **The beds were of gold and silver.** These were couches upon which people would sit.

7. The people drank from various kinds of vessels which were made of gold. **And royal wine in abundance.** This would imply that the wine was taken from the king's personal supply and was of an excellent nature.

8. And the drinking was according to the law; none did compel. They drank according to the custom. According to Lange, it was customary for Persians to drink in great abundance. The people were not forced to drink this way; but rather, everyone drank in an abundant manner. **That they should do according to every man's pleasure.** The concept revealed in these verses is that this was a drunken party. People drank to their hearts' content, and there was no limitation put upon their desires for pleasure.

9. Also Vashti the queen made a feast for the women. The name Vashti is a Persian name that literally means, the best. Vashti held a banquet for the women in conjunction with the banquet of her husband.

B. The Demotion of Vashti. 1:10-22.

10. On the seventh day. During the last day of the feast the king desired Vashti to make an appearance. **When the heart of the king was merry with wine.** Since this was the last day of the feast and the banquet guests had been drinking in abundance (vs. 7), the request came from a king who was probably in a highly drunken condition.

11-12. To show the people and the princes her beauty . . . But the queen Vashti refused. Apparently Vashti was apprehensive about appearing at a banquet filled with drunken people. There was no way of determining exactly what would happen in such a situation. She was probably fearful of the moral implications and thus refused the request of the king. Some commentators have speculated that what the king desired was that Vashti ultimately appear naked to the guests, and this is certainly within the realm of possibility. The refusal of the queen infuriated Ahasuerus.

13 ¶Then the king said to the wise men, which knew the times, (for so *was* the king's manner toward all that knew law and judgment:

14 And the next unto him *was* Cär-shē′na, Shē′thär, Ăd′mā-tha, Tär′shĭsh, Me′rēs, Mär′sē-na, *and* Me-mū′can, the seven princes of Persia and Mē′dĭ-a, which saw the king's face, *and* which sat the first in the kingdom;)

15 What shall we do unto the queen Văsh′tī according to law because she hath not performed the commandment of the king A-has-ū-ē′rus by the chamberlains?

16 And Me-mū′can answered before the king and the princes, Văsh′tī the queen hath not done wrong to the king only, but also to all the princes, and to all the people that *are* in all the provinces of the king A-has-ū-ē′rus.

17 For *this* deed of the queen shall come abroad unto all women, so that they shall despise their husbands in their eyes, when it shall be reported, The king A-has-ū-ē′rus commanded Văsh′tī the queen to be brought in before him, but she came not.

18 *Likewise* shall the ladies of Persia and Mē′dĭ-a say this day unto all the king's princes, which have heard of the deed of the queen. Thus *shall there arise* too much contempt and wrath.

19 If it please the king, let there go a royal commandment from him, and let it be written among the laws of the Persians and the Medes, that it be not altered, That Văsh′tī come no more before king A-has-ū-ē′rus; and let the king give her royal estate unto another that is better than she.

20 And when the king's decree which he shall make shall be published throughout all his empire, (for it is great,) all the wives shall give to their husbands honour, both to great and small.

21 And the saying pleased the king and the princes; and the king did according to the word of Me-mū′can:

22 For he sent letters into all the king's provinces, into every province according to the writing thereof, and to every people after their language, that every man should bear rule in his own house, and that *it* should be published according to the language of every people.

CHAPTER 2

AFTER these things, when the wrath of king A-has-ū-ē′rus was appeased, he remembered Văsh′tī, and what she had done, and what was decreed against her.

2 Then said the king's servants that

13. The king sought the counsel of his wise men **which knew the times.** They were people who observed the stars and would advise according to what they observed in the heavens.

14. There were seven princes of Persia who were also consulted for advice. These were probably the ones who knew **law and judgment** (vs. 13). The king sought counsel both from the astrologers and from his lawyers. These are probably the same as those seven princes mentioned in Ezra 7:14.

15-16. The question they discussed was exactly what they should do with the queen since she refused to obey the king's commandment. **Memucan** acts as the spokesman for the princes. He is the last mentioned of the seven princes, and now he speaks in behalf of the entire group. **Vashti the queen hath not done wrong to the king only.** His advice is founded upon the fact that what Vashti did in disobeying the king would have far-reaching implication for all the peoples of the entire kingdom.

17-18. So that they shall despise their husbands in their eyes. What Vashti had done would cause other women to despise or disobey their husbands. The authority of the male members of the kingdom was in jeopardy. Again Memucan amplifies on the ultimate end of Vashti's disobedience. It is interesting to note that he is speaking in this verse even of his own wife. The disobedience of Vashti would affect even the princes who served next to Ahasuerus.

19. Memucan recommends **a royal commandment.** This would involve a royal decree that would be the law of the land. This particular law, according to the Persians and Medes, could not be changed. It involved a decree whereby Vashti would be deposed of her **royal estate,** and her queenship would be given to someone else who was **better than she.** This would mean that even if Vashti showed repentance she could never again be restored to a royal position. Consequently, she could never take revenge upon those who had advised the king to make this edict.

20-22. This severe action would enhance the position of husbands throughout the kingdom. Wives would continue to honor their husbands. Ahasuerus agrees with the advice of the princes and sends **letters into all the king's provinces.** This was considered such a crucial issue that letters concerning the king's action and edict were sent throughout all of the kingdom. It is interesting to note that in recording the decree the primary purpose is emphasized. That purpose was to give credence to the position of each man in his own house. The disobedience of Vashti is actually not mentioned. This was, in reality, secondary to upholding the authority of each husband.

C. The Choice of Esther. 2:1-18.

2:1. After these things. This opening phrase connects the events of chapter 2 with what preceded in chapter 1. Ahasuerus had sent a decree throughout the kingdom that women should honor their husbands. Vashti had been deposed of her royal position, and the great banquet had concluded. According to history, there was probably a three-year period between chapters 1 and 2. **He remembered Vashti.** Now that the event had passed and three years had gone by, Ahasuerus begins to wonder as to whether or not he had done the right thing in being so harsh with Vashti.

2-4. Sensing that perhaps Ahasuerus would restore Vashti and that he would take revenge on those who had counseled him

ministered unto him. Let there be fair young virgins sought for the king:

3 And let the king appoint officers in all the provinces of his kingdom, that they may gather together all the fair young virgins unto Shū'shăn the palace, to the house of the women, unto the custody of Hē'ge the king's chamberlain, keeper of the women; and let their things for purification be given *them*:

4 And let the maiden which pleaseth the king be queen instead of Văsh'tī. And the thing pleased the king; and he did so.

5 ¶*Now* in Shū'shăn the palace there was a certain Jew, whose name *was* Môr'de-caī, the son of Jā'ir, the son of Shĭm'e-ī, the son of Kish, a Benjamite;

6 Who had been carried away from Jerusalem with the captivity which had been carried away with Jĕc-o-nī'ah king of Jū'dah, whom Nĕb-u-chad-nĕz'zar the king of Babylon had carried away.

7 And he brought up Ha-dăs'sah, that *is*, Esther, his uncle's daughter: for she had neither father nor mother, and the maid *was* fair and beautiful; whom Môr'de-caī, when her father and mother were dead, took for his own daughter.

8 ¶So it came to pass, when the king's commandment and his decree was heard, and when many maidens were gathered together unto Shū'shăn the palace, to the custody of Hēg'a-ī, that Esther was brought also unto the king's house, to the custody of Hēg'a-ī, keeper of the women.

9 And the maiden pleased him, and she obtained kindness of him; and he speedily gave her her things for purification, with such things as belonged to her, and seven maidens, *which were* meet to be given her, out of the king's house: and he preferred her and her maids unto the best *place* of the house of the women.

10 Esther had not shewed her people nor her kindred: for Môr'de-caī had charged her that she should not shew *it*.

11 And Môr'de-caī walked every day before the court of the women's house, to know how Esther did, and what should become of her.

12 ¶Now when every maid's turn was come to go in to king A-hăs-ū-ē'rus, after that she had been twelve months, according to the manner of the women, (for so were the days of their purifications accomplished, *to wit*, six months with oil of myrrh, and six months with

to dethrone her, the king's servants advised the king to seek out a new queen. The servants proposed a master plan for the securing of the finest virgins of the kingdom. These women were to be brought to the palace and placed under the custody of Hege. **Hege** was one of the eunuchs responsible for overseeing the king's harem. **And let their things for purification be given them.** This would involve washing and anointing with various oils (see vs. 12).

5. There was a certain Jew, whose name was Mordecai. In this verse we are introduced to one of the principle characters of the narrative. **The son of Kish, a Benjamite.** Some commentators indicate that this means that Esther was a descendant of King Saul (cf. I Sam 9:1; I Chr 8:33).

6. Who had been carried away from Jerusalem with the captivity. Commentators are of a variety of opinions concerning exactly who had been brought from Jerusalem by Nebuchadnezzar. If this refers to Mordecai, it would mean that Mordecai would be between one hundred twenty and one hundred thirty years old when he became prime minister. This is highly unlikely. Probably, it was Mordecai's father or grandfather who came to Babylon during the captivity. Mordecai is also mentioned in Ezra 2:2 and Nehemiah 7:7 as one who returned with Zerubbabel and Joshua. This is probably the same Mordecai. After spending a period of time in Jerusalem he returned to Babylon.

7. And he brought up Hadassah, that is, Esther. Hadassah is her Hebrew name, which means a myrtle; and Esther is her Persian royal name, which means a star. She was the daughter of his father's brother, and after the death of her parents she was adopted by Mordecai. Esther, the second principal person involved in this story, was Mordecai's cousin. She eventually becomes the heroine.

8-9. When the desire of the king was made known throughout his kingdom, Esther was one of the maidens who was placed in the custody of **Hegai**, the eunuch. **And the maiden pleased him, and she obtained kindness of him.** Hegai was impressed with the beauty of Esther, and as a result he gave her additional attention. **And seven maidens, which were meet to be given her.** Seven maids were assigned to wait upon Esther. Hegai also placed Esther in the most beautiful part of the house.

10-11. Her special treatment and rise to prominence was closely related to the secrecy of her Jewish origin. Had Hegai realized that she was a Jew, she probably would not have been treated with such favor. Mordecai was constantly in contact with Esther to determine her progress and her chances of becoming queen.

12-14. The selection process for the new queen now begins. After the women had gone through the process of purification and the anointing and bathing in various oils, they came to the king. Whatever each maiden desired was given in order that they could impress the king. Each maiden went in the evening to the king and returned in the morning **into the second house of the women, to the custody of Shaashgaz.** This particular

sweet odours, and with *other* things for the purifying of the women;)

13 Then thus came *every* maiden unto the king; whatsoever she desired was given her to go with her out of the house of the women unto the king's house.

14 In the evening she went, and on the morrow she returned into the second house of the women, to the custody of Shā-ăsh'găz, the king's chamberlain, which kept the concubines: she came in unto the king no more, except the king delighted in her, and that she were called by name.

15 ¶Now when the turn of Esther, the daughter of Ăb-i-hā'il the uncle of Môr'de-caī, who had taken her for his daughter, was come to go in unto the king, she required nothing but what Hĕg'a-ī the king's chamberlain, the keeper of the women, appointed. And Esther obtained favour in the sight of all them that looked upon her.

16 So Esther was taken unto king A-haṣ-ū-ĕ'rus into his house royal in the tenth month, which *is* the month Tĕ'bĕth, in the seventh year of his reign.

17 And the king loved Esther above all the women, and she obtained grace and favour in his sight more than all the virgins; so that he set the royal crown upon her head, and made her queen instead of Văsh'tī.

18 Then the king made a great feast unto all his princes and his servants, *even* Esther's feast; and he made a release to the provinces, and gave gifts, according to the state of the king.

19 And when the virgins were gathered together the second time, then Môr'de-caī sat in the king's gate.

20 Esther had not *yet* shewed her kindred nor her people; as Môr'de-caī had charged her: for Esther did the commandment of Môr'de-caī, like as when she was brought up with him.

21 ¶In those days, while Môr'de-caī sat in the king's gate, two of the king's chamberlains, Bĭg'than and Te'rĕsh, of those which kept the door, were wroth, and sought to lay hand on the king A-haṣ-ū-ĕ'rus.

22 And the thing was known to Môr'de-caī, who told *it* unto Esther the queen; and Esther certified the king *thereof* in Môr'de-caī's name.

23 And when inquisition was made of the matter, it was found out; therefore they were both hanged on a tree: and it was written in the book of the chronicles before the king.

CHAPTER 3

AFTER these things did king A-haṣ-ū-ĕ'rus promote Hā'man the son of Hăm-

914

eunuch was in charge of the concubines. The maidens only returned to the king at the king's request.

15-16. When Esther's turn came to appear before Ahasuerus, she **required nothing but what Hegai the king's chamberlain, the keeper of the women, appointed.** Hegai understood best the desires of the king, and Esther conformed to those desires as she appeared before the king. Esther went in to the king in the month Tebeth. This particular month probably refers to the Egyptian month Tobi (Lange, p. 44).

17-18. The king loved Esther above everyone else and elevated her to the throne. The implication is that he made her queen at their first meeting. He was so impressed with her beauty and humility and was so overwhelmed at her excellence beyond everyone else that he immediately made her queen. To celebrate her elevation to the throne, the king proclaimed a feast and named it Esther's Feast. **He made a release to the provinces.** This could mean either a relief from taxes or a royal holiday.

D. The Loyalty of Mordecai. 2:19-23.

19. There is some question as to why the virgins were gathered together a second time. The answer to this problem is probably that Ahasuerus was not prevented from loving other virgins and from promoting them to queen. Solomon had seven hundred queens and three hundred concubines (J. P. Lange, *Commentary on the Holy Scriptures*, Vol. II, p. 44).

20-22. Again the writer reminds us that Esther still concealed her heredity. Two persons are introduced in this verse, and their plan to kill the king is revealed to Mordecai. Mordecai reports this to Esther, and an investigation is made. Esther does give Mordecai credit for his loyalty and for reporting the assassination plot.

23. After the investigation **Bigthan and Teresh** are found guilty and **hanged on a tree: and it was written in the Book of the Chronicles before the king.** This seemingly insignificant statement, which concludes the second chapter, is actually the crucial event that later has great bearing on the story. Sometimes events that seem insignificant at the time can turn the entire course of a person's life and even the ultimate course of history.

II. THE RISE AND FALL OF HAMAN. 3:1-7:10.

A. The Plan of Haman. 3:1-15.

3:1. After these things. According to verse 7 of this chapter, the events are taking place in the twelfth year of Ahasuerus,

med'ā-tha the Ā'gag-īte, and advanced him, and set his seat above all the princes that *were* with him.

2 And all the king's servants, that *were* in the king's gate, bowed, and reverenced Hā'man: for the king had so commanded concerning him. But Môr'de-caī bowed not, nor did *him* reverence.

3 Then the king's servants, which *were* in the king's gate, said unto Môr'de-caī, Why transgressest thou the king's commandment?
4 Now it came to pass, when they spake daily unto him, and he hearkened not unto them, that they told Hā'man, to see whether Môr'de-caī's matters would stand: for he had told them that he *was* a Jew.
5 And when Hā'man saw that Môr'de-caī bowed not, nor did him reverence, then was Hā'man full of wrath.
6 And he thought scorn to lay hands on Môr'de-caī alone; for they had shewed him the people of Môr'de-caī: wherefore Hā'man sought to destroy all the Jews that *were* throughout the whole kingdom of A-haš-ū-ē'rus, *even* the people of Môr'de-caī.

7 ¶In the first month, that *is*, the month Nī'sǎn, in the twelfth year of king A-haš-ū-ē'rus, they cast Pur, that *is*, the lot, before Hā'man from day to day, and from month to month, *to* the twelfth *month*, that *is*, the month Ā'där.

8 ¶And Hā'man said unto king A-haš-ū-ē'rus, There is a certain people scattered abroad and dispersed among the people in all the provinces of thy kingdom; and their laws *are* diverse from all people; neither keep they the king's laws: therefore it *is* not for the king's profit to suffer them.

which would mean a period of five years between 2:16 and 3:7. The events of verse 1 occur a short time before the twelfth year. **Did king Ahasuerus promote Haman.** We are now introduced to the villain of the story. Haman becomes the arch enemy of Mordecai, Esther, and the Jewish nation. He is an **Agagite.** Some commentators trace this back to Agag the king of the Amalekites and consequently could consider Haman a descendant of the Amalekite nation. Although this cannot be definitely proved, it is a possibility (I Sam 15:8, 33). If Haman is a descendant of the Amalekite nation, it is interesting to note that Mordecai was a descendant of Saul. It was Saul who killed Agag and defeated the Amalekite nation. The conflict portrayed in this book would then be a conflict that was centuries old. **Set his seat above all the princes that were with him.** Haman was promoted to the highest possible office in the kingdom. The seven princes who gave counsel to Ahasuerus were now secondary to the position of Haman.

2. It was customary for Persians to bow down in reverence to the king. Since Haman had been promoted to a second position in the kingdom, it was also customary to show reverence for his position. **But Mordecai bowed not, nor did him reverence.** Although everyone else was submissive to the authority and position of Haman, Mordecai refused to bow. It was not out of pride that he made the refusal, but rather out of religious conviction (vs. 4). Most commentators believe that the act of bowing down was in essence a religious act and that the people were not only showing reverence for Haman's position but were also worshiping him as a religious god. This would indeed violate the conscience of Mordecai. It was customary for Jews to show reverence by bowing to the ground (cf. I Kgs 1:16). Mordecai refused to bow, not because he did not respect the position, but rather because he refused to worship any god other than Jehovah.

3-4. On questions concerning his refusal to obey the king's commandment, Mordecai replied that **he was a Jew.** It was his loyalty to God that prevented him from showing religious submission and loyalty to a man.

5-6. Then was Haman full of wrath. Haman was furious at the refusal of Mordecai to bow down. His wrath caused him to plan the destruction not only of Mordecai but of all the Jews throughout the kingdom. The vengeance of Haman was not satisfied by destruction of one person; he sought to destroy the entire Jewish nation. Such large massacres were not uncommon to Eastern history. "The caprices of absolute monarchs determine the course of history and in the east human life is not held in much regard" (George Rawlinson, *The Pulpit Commentary*, pp. 62-63).

7. They cast Pur, that is, the lot. In order to accomplish his evil and sinister task, Haman seeks to choose the best day possible to inaugurate his plan. The casting of lots probably refers to the use of astrology. Haman was very much in tune with astrology so that he could find the best day for his plan. Concerning the particular time of his request, see the comments on verse 1.

8. Haman stretches and exaggerates the point in order to fulfill his plan. Although only one person had dared to disobey the king's commandment, Haman gives the impression that all of the Jewish people were living in total disobedience to the king's command.

9 If it please the king, let it be written that they may be destroyed: and I will pay ten thousand talents of silver to the hands of those that have the charge of the business, to bring it into the king's treasuries.

10 And the king took his ring from his hand, and gave it unto Hā'man the son of Hăm-med'ā-tha the Ā'gag-īte, the Jews' enemy.

11 And the king said unto Hā'man, The silver is given to thee, the people also, to do with them as it seemeth good to thee.

12 Then were the king's scribes called on the thirteenth day of the first month, and there was written according to all that Hā'man had commanded unto the king's lieutenants, and to the governors that were over every province, and to the rulers of every people of every province according to the writing thereof, and to every people after their language; in the name of king A-haṣ-ū-ē'rus was it written, and sealed with the king's ring.

13 And the letters were sent by posts into all the king's provinces, to destroy, to kill, and to cause to perish, all Jews, both young and old, little children and women, in one day, even upon the thirteenth day of the twelfth month, which is the month Ā'där, and to take the spoil of them for a prey.

14 The copy of the writing for a commandment to be given in every province was published unto all people, that they should be ready against that day.

15 The posts went out, being hastened by the king's commandment, and the decree was given in Shū'shăn the palace. And the king and Hā'man sat down to drink; but the city Shū'shăn was perplexed.

CHAPTER 4

WHEN Môr'de-caī perceived all that was done, Môr'de-caī rent his clothes, and put on sackcloth with ashes, and went out into the midst of the city, and cried with a loud and a bitter cry;

2 And came even before the king's gate: for none might enter into the king's gate clothed with sackcloth.

3 And in every province, whithersoever the king's commandment and his decree came, there was great mourning among the Jews, and fasting, and weeping, and wailing; and many lay in sackcloth and ashes.

4 ¶So Esther's maids and her chamberlains came and told it her. Then was the queen exceedingly grieved; and she sent raiment to clothe Môr'de-caī, and to take away his sackcloth from him: but he received it not.

5 Then called Esther for Hā'tach, one of the king's chamberlains, whom he had appointed to attend upon her, and gave him a commandment to Môr'de-

9. Haman recommends that they be destroyed and that the ones who carry out the massacre should be rewarded. He presents the Jewish people as a threat to the entire kingdom; and because they were living throughout the entire kingdom, they must be eliminated.

10-11. The king was so impressed with Haman's proposal that he gave him his royal ring. By giving him the ring he was signifying that Haman had the full authority to carry out the destruction of the Jews. **The Jews' enemy.** The word enemy literally means persecutor. The king provides Haman with all of the resources necessary to accomplish his evil task.

12. Haman wasted no time in moving ahead with his plan. The very same month he prepared the decree that was to be sent throughout the entire kingdom. The decree was written in the name of the king and was **sealed with the king's ring.** This decree was as binding and as authoritative as the decree mentioned in 1:19.

13-14. The letters were sent throughout the realm; and the command was given **to destroy, to kill, and to cause to perish, all Jews, both young and old . . . and to take the spoil of them for a prey.** All of the Jews were to be killed on the thirteenth day of the twelfth month. To encourage the people to obey the command, those who destroyed the Jews were also given the advantage of taking their properties and lands. This would provide an incentive for people to destroy the Jewish race. This commandment was made public throughout the entire land.

15. And the king and Haman sat down to drink; but the city Shushan was perplexed. While Haman gloated in the fulfillment of his dream to destroy the Jews, much of the city was perplexed. Perhaps those who were non-Jewish and foreign to Shushan were also concerned that the favor of Haman might go against them; and they, too, might be destroyed at some point.

B. The Remorse of the Jews. 4:1-17.

4:1. Mordecai rent his clothes, and put on sackcloth with ashes. The decree of Ahasuerus for the destruction of the Jews brought about great mourning among the Jewish community, and Mordecai assumed a very prominent role in leading this mourning period. Wearing a hairy garment and putting ashes upon the head were signs of great sorrow and grief (Dan 9:3; Job 2:12). Mordecai went around the city in a state of grief crying with a **loud and a bitter cry.**

2-3. Mordecai even came to the entrance of the palace. However, he could not sit at the king's gate as before since no one could enter the palace mourning. Throughout the entire kingdom there was great mourning among the Jews. Many of them carried their mourning to the extreme; that is they wore sackcloth and ashes (Isa 58:5).

4-6. News of Mordecai's mourning and the fact that he wore sackcloth and ashes reached Esther. Esther sent him clothing to wear, but Mordecai refused to wear it. Perhaps Mordecai's public mourning would be a means by which he could get the attention of Esther. Mordecai's refusal to wear the raiment that Esther sent was probably due to the fact that he desired a personal audience with the queen.

Mordecai's desire was fulfilled and **Hatach** was dispatched to Mordecai to gather the details of his mourning. **To know what it**

caī, to know what it *was*, and why it *was*.

6 So Hă'tach went forth to Môr'de-caī unto the street of the city, which *was* before the king's gate.

7 And Môr'de-caī told him of all that had happened unto him, and of the sum of the money that Hă'man had promised to pay to the king's treasuries for the Jews, to destroy them.

8 Also he gave him the copy of the writing of the decree that was given at Shū'shăn to destroy them, to shew *it* unto Esther, and to declare *it* unto her, and to charge her that she should go in unto the king, to make supplication unto him, and to make request before him for her people.

9 And Hă'tach came and told Esther the words of Môr'de-caī.

10 ¶Again Esther spake unto Hă'-tach, and gave him commandment unto Môr'de-caī;

11 All the king's servants, and the people of the king's provinces, do know, that whosoever, whether man or woman, shall come unto the king into the inner court, who is not called, *there is* one law of his to put *him* to death, except such to whom the king shall hold out the golden sceptre, that he may live: but I have not been called to come in unto the king these thirty days.

12 And they told to Môr'de-caī Esther's words.

13 Then Môr'de-caī commanded to answer Esther, Think not with thyself that thou shalt escape in the king's house, more than all the Jews.

14 For if thou altogether holdest thy peace at this time, *then* shall there enlargement and deliverance arise to the Jews from another place; but thou and thy father's house shall be destroyed: and who knoweth whether thou art come to the kingdom for *such* a time as this?

15 ¶Then Esther bade *them* return Môr'de-caī *this answer*,

16 Go, gather together all the Jews that are present in Shū'shăn, and fast ye for me, and neither eat nor drink three days, night or day: I also and my maidens will fast likewise; and so will I go in unto the king, which *is* not according to the law: and if I perish, I perish.

17 So Môr'de-caī went his way, and did according to all that Esther had commanded him.

CHAPTER 5

NOW it came to pass on the third day, that Esther put on *her* royal *apparel*, and stood in the inner court of the king's house, over against the king's house: and the king sat upon his royal throne in the royal house, over against the gate of the house.

2 And it was so, when the king saw Esther the queen standing in the court, *that* she obtained favour in his sight: and the king held out to Esther the golden sceptre that *was* in his hand. So

was, and why it was. Hatach was to discover the reason and the cause of Mordecai's mourning.

7-8. Mordecai outlined Haman's plan and how that the king had promised to pay money for the destruction of the Jews. Mordecai details the plan to indicate the motive of Haman and to assure Esther that the Jews were not guilty of serious violations of the Law. Mordecai also sent a copy of the document with Hatach so that Esther could read it. **Charge her that she should go in unto the king, to make supplication unto him, and to make request before him for her people.** Mordecai realized that the only hope for the Jewish people was for Esther to intercede on their behalf, and thus gain the favor of the king in protecting the Jews.

9-12. Hatach returned and related all **the words of Mordecai** to Esther. Esther now raises some objections and problems concerning the desire of Mordecai for her to intercede. Since the king resided in the inner court, it was unlawful to approach him unless he had desired for her to come. The penalty for coming before the king and not receiving his favor was the penalty of death. Since the king had not asked for her for thirty days, it was unlikely that he would be desirous to see her now.

13. **Think not with thyself that thou shalt escape in the king's house, more than all the Jews.** Mordecai almost threatened Esther. If all of the Jews are destroyed, she also will be destroyed.

14. Mordecai is confident that if Esther does not intercede, God will utilize some other means for delivering His people. The **another place** mentioned here has clear and definite reference to God Himself. If Esther refuses to intercede, then not only will God deliver His people from another source, but her house and father's house **shall be destroyed.** Mordecai speculates that her advancement to royalty could have been in the providence of God to meet the need in the problem of the present hour.

15-16. Esther sends back an answer to Mordecai. Esther asks that all the Jews be instructed to fast for three days and nights for her. Although God is not specifically mentioned here, again it is implied that the fasting was a means of interceding to God on Esther's behalf. Esther and her maidens also fasted. All of this fasting was designed to invoke the blessing of God on the task. **And if I perish, I perish.** Again, the implication is her implicit trust in God.

17. The chapter concludes with the complete fulfillment of Mordecai's desire. He desired Esther to intercede in behalf of her people, and now this task is accomplished.

C. The Intercession of Esther. 5:1-8.

5:1-2. **Now it came to pass on the third day.** After fasting for three days (4:16), Esther now made her appearance before the king. When the king saw Esther, he extended the golden scepter to her. This indicated that she was free to come before him and that she had found favor in his sight (2:9). **And touched the top of the scepter.** This would probably indicate that she actually kissed the scepter that the king had extended to her.

Esther drew near, and touched the top of the sceptre.

3 Then said the king unto her, What wilt thou, queen Esther? and what *is* thy request? it shall be even given thee to the half of the kingdom.

4 And Esther answered, If *it* seem good unto the king, let the king and Hā′man come this day unto the banquet that I have prepared for him.

5 Then the king said, Cause Hā′man to make haste, that he may do as Esther hath said. So the king and Hā′man came to the banquet that Esther had prepared.

6 ¶And the king said unto Esther at the banquet of wine, What *is* thy petition? and it shall be granted thee: and what *is* thy request? even to the half of the kingdom it shall be performed.

7 Then answered Esther, and said, My petition and my request *is;*

8 If I have found favour in the sight of the king, and if it please the king to grant my petition, and to perform my request, let the king and Hā′man come to the banquet that I shall prepare for them, and I will do to morrow as the king hath said.

9 ¶Then went Hā′man forth that day joyful and with a glad heart: but when Hā′man saw Môr′de-caī in the king's gate, that he stood not up, nor moved for him, he was full of indignation against Môr′de-caī.

10 Nevertheless Hā′man refrained himself: and when he came home, he sent and called for his friends, and Ze′resh his wife.

11 And Hā′man told them of the glory of his riches, and the multitude of his children, and all *the* things wherein the king had promoted him, and how he had advanced him above the princes and servants of the king.

12 Hā′man said moreover, Yea, Esther the queen did let no man come in with the king unto the banquet that she had prepared but myself; and to morrow am I invited unto her also with the king.

13 Yet all this availeth me nothing, so long as I see Môr′de-caī the Jew sitting at the king's gate.

14 Then said Ze′resh his wife and all his friends unto him, Let a gallows be made of fifty cubits high, and to morrow speak thou unto the king that Môr′de-caī may be hanged thereon: then go thou in merrily with the king unto the banquet. And the thing pleased Hā′man; and he caused the gallows to be made.

CHAPTER 6

ON that night could not the king sleep,

918

3-4. What wilt thou, queen Esther? This could be translated as "What ails thee?" (Lange, p. 66). The king expressed that whatever her request is, it will be granted even up to half of the kingdom (Mk 6:23). Esther's request was simple. She desires that the king and Haman come to a banquet that she has prepared for them. Esther has immediately made plans to expose the terrible plot of Haman.

5-6. The king grants her request, and preparations are made for the banquet that evening. It would have been considered a high honor for someone to be invited to dine personally with the king and queen. **The king said unto Esther at the banquet of wine.** Apparently, this particular banquet was a festive occasion; and the king and Haman were in an extremely good mood. Again, the king asks concerning Esther's petition and request.

7-8. My petition and my request is. Apparently, Esther began to reveal the request of her heart, but then she decided against sharing it at this particular time. She continues that if she has found favor before the king, then she would desire another banquet the next day. At that time she would reveal to the king her particular request.

D. The Pride of Haman. 5:9-14.

9. Then went Haman forth that day joyful and with a glad heart. Haman left the banquet elated that he had been invited a second time to dine personally with the king and queen. This was indeed a great honor. It is interesting to note that in the heights of ecstasy, Haman met with his thorn in the flesh, Mordecai. Mordecai refused to give reverence and respect to Haman. **He was full of indignation against Mordecai.**

10-11. Since the decree had been made across the empire to destroy the Jews, Haman refrained himself from taking out his anger on Mordecai. When he arrived home, he called for his friends and his wife to share with them the events of that day, beginning to enumerate all of his riches, promotions, and prestige. These verses outline in detail the vast importance of the position which Haman held. It is as if the author is building Haman to the peaks of prestige and honor so that when he falls his fall will be great.

12-13. All of the events and circumstances of his life to this point were favorable. He has been invited to eat twice and to dine personally with the king and queen. **Yet all this availeth me nothing.** All of his money, power, and prestige do not give satisfaction because Mordecai the Jew is obnoxious in his defiance of Haman's position.

14. His wife and friends give him advice. He should build a gallows and prepare the gallows for the hanging of Mordecai. They suggest that at the banquet the next day Haman get the king's permission to hang Mordecai. **And the thing pleased Haman; and he caused the gallows to be made.** The prospects of hanging Mordecai greatly eased the emotional duress of Haman. Some commentators think that perhaps there was a scribal error in describing the height of the gallows, for fifty cubits would be approximately seventy-five feet in the air. The gallows were made and Haman's wrath and vengeance was appeased.

E. Mordecai Rewarded. 6:1-14.

To this point in the narrative the tide of circumstances has flowed against the Jewish people, but this chapter marks the transition. The tide of circumstances now begins to change in favor of the Jewish nation and against Haman.

6:1-2. On that night could not the king sleep. Throughout

and he commanded to bring the book of records of the chronicles; and they were read before the king.

2 And it was found written, that Môr'de-caī had told of Bĭg'tha-na and Te'rĕsh, two of the king's chamberlains, the keepers of the door, who sought to lay hand on the king A-has-ū-ĕ'rus.

3 And the king said, What honour and dignity hath been done to Môr'de-caī for this? Then said the king's servants that ministered unto him, There is nothing done for him.

4 And the king said, Who *is* in the court? Now Hā'man was come into the outward court of the king's house, to speak unto the king to hang Môr'de-caī on the gallows that he had prepared for him.

5 And the king's servants said unto him, Behold, Hā'man standeth in the court. And the king said, Let him come in.

6 So Hā'man came in. And the king said unto him, What shall be done unto the man whom the king delighteth to honour? Now Hā'man thought in his heart, To whom would the king delight to do honour more than to myself?

7 And Hā'man answered the king, For the man whom the king delighteth to honour,

8 Let the royal apparel be brought which the king *useth* to wear, and the horse that the king rideth upon, and the crown royal which is set upon his head:

9 And let this apparel and horse be delivered to the hand of one of the king's most noble princes, that they may array the man *withal* whom the king delighteth to honour, and bring him on horseback through the street of the city, and proclaim before him, Thus shall it be done to the man whom the king delighteth to honour.

10 Then the king said to Hā'man, Make haste, *and* take the apparel and the horse, as thou hast said, and do even so to Môr'de-caī the Jew, that sitteth at the king's gate: let nothing fail of all that thou hast spoken.

11 Then took Hā'man the apparel and the horse, and arrayed Môr'de-caī, and brought him on horseback through the street of the city, and proclaimed before him, Thus shall it be done unto the man whom the king delighteth to honour.

12 ¶And Môr'de-caī came again to the king's gate. But Hā'man hasted to his house mourning, and having his head covered.

13 And Hā'man told Ze'resh his wife and all his friends every *thing* that had befallen him. Then said his wise men and Ze'resh his wife unto him, If Môr'de-caī *be* of the seed of the Jews, before whom thou hast begun to fall, thou shalt not prevail against him, but shalt surely fall before him.

14 And while they *were* yet talking with him, came the king's chamberlains, and hasted to bring Hā'man unto the banquet that Esther had prepared.

this entire chapter we see in significant fashion the unseen hand of God in the circumstances that occur. After the banquet the king could not sleep, and so he asked for the history books to be brought and read in his presence. These were the Chronicles in which the story of 2:21-23 was written. It is interesting to note that they began reading at the story of Mordecai's integrity when he revealed the plot to assassinate the king. The name **Bigthana** is written as **Bigthan** in 2:21.

3-4. What honor and dignity hath been done to Mordecai for this? The king was anxious to know how Mordecai had been rewarded for his act of loyalty in saving the king's life. The response was that nothing had been given to him for revealing the assassination plot. **Who is in the court?** Normally, an official of high rank was assigned to be in attendance with the king, and Ahasuerus was anxious to know which high official was available so he can converse with him and ask his advice. **Now Haman was come.** Haman had come early in the morning to seek the permission of the king to hang Mordecai on his gallows.

5-6. The king's servants informed the king that Haman was in the court and ushered him into the presence of the king. **What shall be done unto the man whom the king delighteth to honor?** The king was desirous of bringing great honor and respect to Mordecai for the noble deed which he performed. However, Haman assumes that the king is interested in giving honor to him; and so he responds to the king as if he were the one that was going to be honored.

7-9. First, Haman wants the royal apparel to be placed upon the individual. Also, that person should be placed on the king's horse and the royal crown placed upon his head. To give his apparel, horse, and crown to honor a person was indeed an honor of the highest possible degree. Then the king should choose one of his **most noble princes,** and that person would lead the honored individual through the streets of the city proclaiming that this is what the king will do to someone he seeks to honor.

10-11. The king was pleased with Haman's response and informed him that he is to go and do that to Mordecai the Jew. The paradox and humor of this verse is beyond human description. Haman came to the court with the intention of seeking permission to hang Mordecai, and now he must march Mordecai through the streets of the city proclaiming that this is the way the king honors a man in whom he delights. **Let nothing fail of all that thou hast spoken.** The king wishes Haman to fulfill his suggestion to the fullest degree. For Haman to perform this function must have deeply humiliated him.

12-13. After Haman performed this humiliating function he returned home **having his head covered.** This was a sign of remorse and sorrow. However, the advice he received from his wise men added to his sorrow and grief. They predict that this turn of events is but the beginning of the end. **Thou shalt not prevail against him, but shalt surely fall before him.** The counselors of Haman predict that his humiliation is but the beginning of his fall and that he will not prevail or overcome in his struggle against Mordecai.

14. And while they were yet talking with him. As the wise men are revealing to Haman that his end is in sight, the king's chamberlains come to bring Haman to the banquet. Little does he know that this banquet will be his last banquet and that his

CHAPTER 7

SO the king and Hā′man came to banquet with Esther the queen.

2 And the king said again unto Esther on the second day at the banquet of wine, What *is* thy petition, queen Esther? and it shall be granted thee: and what *is* thy request? and it shall be performed, *even* to the half of the kingdom.

3 Then Esther the queen answered and said, If I have found favour in thy sight, O king, and if it please the king, let my life be given me at my petition, and my people at my request:

4 For we are sold, I and my people, to be destroyed, to be slain, and to perish. But if we had been sold for bondmen and bondwomen, I had held my tongue, although the enemy could not countervail the king's damage.

5 ¶Then the king A-haś-ū-ē′rus answered and said unto Esther the queen, Who is he, and where is he, that durst presume in his heart to do so?

6 And Esther said, The adversary and enemy *is* this wicked Hā′man. Then Hā′man was afraid before the king and the queen.

7 ¶And the king arising from the banquet of wine in his wrath *went* into the palace garden: and Hā′man stood up to make request for his life to Esther the queen; for he saw that there was evil determined against him by the king.

8 Then the king returned out of the palace garden into the place of the banquet of wine; and Hā′man was fallen upon the bed whereon Esther *was.* Then said the king, Will he force the queen also before me in the house? As the word went out of the king's mouth, they covered Hā′man's face.

9 And Här-bō′nah, one of the chamberlains, said before the king, Behold also, the gallows fifty cubits high, which Hā′man had made for Môr′de-caī, who had spoken good for the king, standeth in the house of Hā′man. Then the king said, Hang him thereon.

10 So they hanged Hā′man on the gallows that he had prepared for Môr′de-caī. Then was the king's wrath pacified.

CHAPTER 8

ON that day did the king A-haś-ū-ē′rus give the house of Hā′man the Jews' en-

end is nearer than he could possibly imagine. The events of this chapter are startling; and as the chapter concludes, the entire tide of events has turned against Haman. Written in every event of this chapter and through every circumstance is the unseen hand of the sovereign God. God takes the tide of opinion and twists it, and now the accuser of the Jews is about to receive his just reward.

F. The Banquet of Esther. 7:1-6.

7:1-3. So the king and Haman came to banquet. This was the second banquet prepared by Esther for her husband and Haman. **What is thy petition, queen Esther?** This is the second time that the king has asked this question of Esther (cf. 5:6). At this second banquet in the queen's apartment Esther is now ready to give an answer. Esther responds to the king's request by desiring that her life and the life of her people be granted to them.

4. But if we had been sold for bondmen and bondwomen, I had held my tongue, although the enemy could not countervail the king's damage. Her attitude is that if they were simply sold into slavery, she would not question and request her life. However, she felt that the king's interests were also at stake. By losing the Jews, their king would lose a tremendous resource for money and taxes.

5-6. The king was aggravated by the news which Esther expresses. **That durst presume in his heart to do so?** Most of man's evil actions and activities proceed from the heart (Eccl 8:11; Mt 15:19). Finally, the wicked plans of Haman are brought into the open, and Haman trembles in the presence of the king.

G. The Death of Haman. 7:7-10.

7-9. The king leaves the banquet hall in anger and walks through his garden. He does this to appease his anger and also to consider what needed to be done in regards to Haman. Haman remained in the presence of the queen to beg for his life. He realized that his only hope was now to have the queen intercede in his behalf since **there was evil determined against him by the king.** He was fully aware that the intent of the king was now totally against him. When the king returns the scene before him is one of shock. **Haman was fallen upon the bed whereon Esther was.** This would literally be translated that he knelt down where Esther was seated. However, the king assumes the worst. **Will he force the queen also before me in the house?** The word to force here means to trample underfoot, to subdue, to offer violence (Keil, p. 365). The king assumes that Haman has evil immoral intentions with the queen, and immediately he orders Haman's execution. **They covered Haman's face.** This was probably the first step in execution, that of covering the face of the criminal.

10. One of the eunuchs suggests that they hang Haman on the tree or gallows which he had prepared for Mordecai. Indeed, this is the irony of the story. The very object that Haman intended to utilize for the execution of Mordecai was the object upon which he himself died.

III. THE RISE OF MORDECAI AND DELIVERANCE OF JEWS. 8:1-10:3.

A. The Decree of Ahasuerus. 8:1-17.

8:1. Give the house of Haman the Jews' enemy unto Esther the queen. It was common in that culture for the king to

emy unto Esther the queen. And Môr'de-caī came before the king; for Esther had told what he *was* unto her.

2 And the king took off his ring, which he had taken from Hā'man, and gave it unto Môr'de-caī. And Esther set Môr'de-caī over the house of Hā'man.

3 ¶And Esther spake yet again before the king, and fell down at his feet, and besought him with tears to put away the mischief of Hā'man the Ā'gag-īte, and his device that he had devised against the Jews.

4 Then the king held out the golden sceptre toward Esther. So Esther arose, and stood before the king,

5 And said, If it please the king, and if I have found favour in his sight, and the thing *seem* right before the king, and I *be* pleasing in his eyes, let it be written to reverse the letters devised by Hā'man the son of Hǎm-med'ā-tha the Ā'gag-īte, which he wrote to destroy the Jews which *are* in all the king's provinces:

6 For how can I endure to see the evil that shall come unto my people? or how can I endure to see the destruction of my kindred?

7 ¶Then the king A-has-ū-ē'rus said unto Esther the queen and to Môr'de-caī the Jew, Behold, I have given Esther the house of Hā'man, and him they have hanged upon the gallows, because he laid his hand upon the Jews.

8 Write ye also for the Jews, as it liketh you, in the king's name, and seal *it* with the king's ring: for the writing which is written in the king's name, and sealed with the king's ring, may no man reverse.

9 Then were the king's scribes called at that time in the third month, that *is*, the month Sī'văn, on the three and twentieth *day* thereof; and it was written according to all that Môr'de-caī commanded unto the Jews, and to the lieutenants, and the deputies and rulers of the provinces which *are* from India unto Ē-thī-ō'pī-a, an hundred twenty and seven provinces, unto every province according to the writing thereof, and unto every people after their language, and to the Jews according to their writing, and according to their language.

10 And he wrote in the king A-has-ū-ē'rus' name, and sealed *it* with the king's ring, and sent letters by posts on horseback, *and* riders on mules, camels, *and* young dromedaries:

11 Wherein the king granted the Jews which *were* in every city to gather themselves together, and to stand for their life, to destroy, to slay, and to cause to perish, all the power of the people and province that would assault them, *both* little ones and women, and *to take* the spoil of them for a prey,

12 Upon one day in all the provinces of king A-has-ū-ē'rus, *namely*, upon the thirteenth *day* of the twelfth month, which *is* the month Ā'där.

confiscate the lands of criminals. This included all of Haman's property, possessions, and, most likely, all the people in his house. Mordecai is brought before the king, and Esther explains that they are related. **What he was unto her.** This refers to the fact that Mordecai is Esther's foster father.

2. The king gives Mordecai his ring and thereby promotes Mordecai to the highest office in the kingdom, the same position that Haman held (3:10). Mordecai is also appointed as the overseer of all of Haman's properties and possessions.

3. Although Haman is now dead and Mordecai has been promoted in the kingdom, the problem of the decree that had been made to destroy the Jewish people still remains. A specific plan must be devised to avert the previous decree.

4-6. Again the king holds out the golden scepter to Esther (4:11). **And the thing seem right before the king.** The word used here means to be advisable, proper, convenient, advantageous. Esther suggests that letters be written to reverse the plan of Haman. She is asking for a similar edict to the one that was decreed in 3:9 for the destruction of the Jews.

7-9. The king responds by reminding Esther of all that he had already done for Esther and Mordecai. The king authorizes an official decree. It was illegal for him to revoke the previous edict, but their law did permit them to send letters in the king's name which would in effect nullify the previous decree. Mordecai oversees the writing of the letters and they are written in a similar manner to the edict of chapter 3.

10. And sent letters by posts on horseback, and riders on mules, camels, and young dromedaries. Dromedaries here is a saddle horse. To emphasize the urgency of the decree, it was dispersed through the fastest possible means of transportation.

11-12. This verse contains the basic contents of the letters. The Jews were permitted **to stand for their life.** They were given permission to fight for their lives and to defend their property, possessions, and people. This allowed the Jews to organize and to defend with force what they possessed. When they defeated their enemies, they could also take as rewards the possessions of those who opposed them.

13 The copy of the writing for a commandment to be given in every province *was* published unto all people, and that the Jews should be ready against that day to avenge themselves on their enemies.

14 *So* the posts that rode upon mules *and* camels went out, being hastened and pressed on by the king's commandment. And the decree was given at Shū'shăn the palace.

15 ¶And Môr'de-caī went out from the presence of the king in royal apparel of blue and white, and with a great crown of gold, and with a garment of fine linen and purple: and the city of Shū'shăn rejoiced and was glad.

16 The Jews had light, and gladness, and joy, and honour.

17 And in every province, and in every city, whithersoever the king's commandment and his decree came, the Jews had joy and gladness, a feast and a good day. And many of the people of the land became Jews; for the fear of the Jews fell upon them.

CHAPTER 9

NOW in the twelfth month, that *is*, the month Ā'där, on the thirteenth day of the same, when the king's commandment and his decree drew near to be put in execution, in the day that the enemies of the Jews hoped to have power over them, (though it was turned to the contrary, that the Jews had rule over them that hated them;)

2 The Jews gathered themselves together in their cities throughout all the provinces of the king A-haš-ū-ē'rus, to lay hand on such as sought their hurt: and no man could withstand them; for the fear of them fell upon all people.

3 And all the rulers of the provinces, and the lieutenants, and the deputies, and officers of the king, helped the Jews; because the fear of Môr'de-caī fell upon them.

4 For Môr'de-caī *was* great in the king's house, and his fame went out throughout all the provinces: for this man Môr'de-caī waxed greater and greater.

5 Thus the Jews smote all their enemies with the stroke of the sword, and slaughter, and destruction, and did what they would unto those that hated them.

6 And in Shū'shăn the palace the Jews slew and destroyed five hundred men.

7 And Pär-shăn'da-tha, and Dăl'phŏn, and Ăs'pa-tha,

8 And Pōr'ā-tha, and Ad-ā-lī'a, and Ā-rĭd'ā-tha,

9 And Pär-mäsh'ta, and Ā-ris'a-ī, and Ā-rid'a-ī, and Va-jĕz'a-tha,

10 The ten sons of Hā'man the son of Hăm-med'ā-tha, the enemy of the Jews, slew they; but on the spoil laid they not their hand.

11 On that day the number of those that were slain in Shū'shăn the palace was brought before the king.

12 ¶And the king said unto Esther the queen, The Jews have slain and de-

922

13-14. The letter is written and sent throughout the kingdom.

15. Mordecai now appears in a position of prestige and honor. These garments were probably the official uniform of the first minister of the empire. **The city of Shushan rejoiced and was glad.** The most recent decree and edict of Ahasuerus brought great joy to the Jewish community.

16-17. The Jewish community throughout the empire celebrated with a feast, and **many of the people of the land became Jews.** As a result of the strange turn of events, many people became Jewish proselytes; and the Jews gained great respect throughout the kingdom.

B. The Jews Delivered. 9:1-19.

9:1-2. When the king's commandment and his decree drew near to be put in execution. The day was now approaching when the first and second decrees of Ahasuerus were to be carried out. On that particular day the Jews gathered together to **lay hand on such as sought their hurt.** The word used here for to lay means to stretch out the hand and implies that it is for the purpose of killing (2:21, 3:6). **And no man could withstand them.** Again, we have the implication of divine providence. God had intervened and changed the entire course of circumstances to the point where no one was able to withstand the Jewish community.

3. All of the official leaders of the empire assisted the Jews in their fight **because the fear of Mordecai fell upon them.** Mordecai was now the second most powerful man in the empire, and because of his authority and influence, all other officials of the kingdom assisted the Jews.

4-11. For this man Mordecai waxed greater and greater. As time passed the influence and authority of Mordecai increased. The Jews were therefore able to completely defeat their enemies and impart to them the punishment which they had sought to impart to the Jews. In Shushan they **destroyed five hundred men.** They also destroyed the **ten sons of Haman.**

12. The king asks for an accounting of those who were destroyed throughout all of the provinces of the empire. **Now what**

stroyed five hundred men in Shū'shăn the palace, and the ten sons of Hă'man; what have they done in the rest of the king's provinces? now what *is* thy petition? and it shall be granted thee: or what *is* thy request further? and it shall be done.

13 Then said Esther, If it please the king, let it be granted to the Jews which *are* in Shū'shăn to do to morrow also according unto this day's decree, and let Hă'man's ten sons be hanged upon the gallows.

14 And the king commanded it so to be done: and the decree was given at Shū'shăn; and they hanged Hă'man's ten sons.

15 For the Jews that *were* in Shū'shăn gathered themselves together on the fourteenth day also of the month Ā'där, and slew three hundred men at Shū'shăn; but on the prey they laid not their hand.

16 But the other Jews that *were* in the king's provinces gathered themselves together, and stood for their lives, and had rest from their enemies, and slew of their foes seventy and five thousand, but they laid not their hands on the prey,

17 On the thirteenth day of the month Ā'där; and on the fourteenth day of the same rested they, and made it a day of feasting and gladness.

18 But the Jews that *were* at Shū'shăn assembled together on the thirteenth *day* thereof, and on the fourteenth thereof; and on the fifteenth *day* of the same they rested, and made it a day of feasting and gladness.

19 Therefore the Jews of the villages that dwelt in the unwalled towns, made the fourteenth day of the month Ā'där *a day* of gladness and feasting, and a good day, and of sending portions one to another.

20 ¶And Môr'de-caī wrote these things, and sent letters unto all the Jews that *were* in all the provinces of the king A-hăs-ū-ē'rus, *both* nigh and far,

21 To stablish *this* among them, that they should keep the fourteenth day of the month Ā'där, and the fifteenth day of the same, yearly,

22 As the days wherein the Jews rested from their enemies, and the month which was turned unto them from sorrow to joy, and from mourning into a good day: that they should make them days of feasting and joy, and of sending portions one to another, and gifts to the poor.

23 And the Jews undertook to do as they had begun, and as Môr'de-caī had written unto them;

24 Because Hă'man the son of Hăm-med'ä-tha, the Ā'gag-īte, the enemy of all the Jews, had devised against the Jews to destroy them, and had cast Pur, that *is*, the lot, to consume them, and to destroy them;

25 But when *Esther* came before the king, he commanded by letters that his wicked device, which he devised

is thy petition? and it shall be granted thee. Perhaps the king was thinking that if there were five hundred enemies in Shushan that there were many thousands of enemies throughout the kingdom. That being so, then the Jews still had a considerable number of enemies who did not come out into the open to fight them. The king was perhaps concerned about the continued safety of the Jewish community and was desirous of what else he could do to insure their safety.

13-14. Esther asks for a one-day extension to hunt out and destroy any further enemies in Shushan. She also requests that the ten sons of Haman who were already dead be publicly hanged upon a gallows. Esther's requests were granted.

15-19. On the second day an additional three hundred people were killed. Throughout all of the provinces the Jews killed seventy-five thousand enemies. They rested on the next day and proclaimed a day of feasting and gladness throughout the empire. However, at the palace they celebrated a day later than the rest of the empire. This was due to the fact that the king permitted them an additional day to bring to justice other enemies of the Jews. All of the Jews celebrated their deliverance.

C. The Feast of Purim. 9:20-32.

20-22. Mordecai proclaimed throughout the kingdom that the Jews were to establish the fourteenth and fifteenth days of the month of Adar as official feasts. The celebration of the feasts was to involve feasting and giving of gifts to each other and giving to the poor.

23-25. And the Jews undertook to do as they had begun. The Jewish community had already celebrated their deliverance, and Mordecai's letter was simply to make that an official annual custom. The intervention of Esther is mentioned, as well as her important role in turning the favor of the king towards the Jews and against Haman.

against the Jews, should return upon his own head, and that he and his sons should be hanged on the gallows.

26 Wherefore they called these days Pū′rĭm after the name of Pur. Therefore for all the words of this letter, and *of that* which they had seen concerning this matter, and which had come unto them,

27 The Jews ordained, and took upon them, and upon their seed, and upon all such as joined themselves unto them, so as it should not fail, that they would keep these two days according to their writing, and according to their *appointed* time every year;

28 And *that* these days *should be* remembered and kept throughout every generation, every family, every province, and every city; and *that* these days of Pū′rĭm should not fail from among the Jews, nor the memorial of them perish from their seed.

29 Then Esther the queen, the daughter of Ăb-i-hā′il, and Mŏr′de-caī the Jew, wrote with all authority, to confirm this second letter of Pū′rĭm.

30 And he sent the letters unto all the Jews, to the hundred twenty and seven provinces of the kingdom of A-has-ū-ē′rus, *with* words of peace and truth,

31 To confirm these days of Pū′rĭm in their times *appointed*, according as Mŏr′de-caī the Jew and Esther the queen had enjoined them, and as they had decreed for themselves and for their seed, the matters of the fastings and their cry.

32 And the decree of Esther confirmed these matters of Pū′rĭm; and it was written in the book.

CHAPTER 10

AND the king A-has-ū-ē′rus laid a tribute upon the land, and *upon* the isles of the sea.

2 And all the acts of his power and of his might, and the declaration of the greatness of Mŏr′de-caī, whereunto the king advanced him, *are* they not written in the book of the chronicles of the kings of Mē′dĭ-a and Persia?

3 For Mŏr′de-caī the Jew *was* next unto king A-has-ū-ē′rus, and great among the Jews, and accepted of the multitude of his brethren, seeking the wealth of his people, and speaking peace to all his seed.

26-28. The feast is officially named the feast of Purim from the word Pur. This feast is still celebrated by Jews; and as part of the festivities, the entire book of Esther is read in public. When the name of Haman is mentioned, the people respond by booing and jeering; and when the name of Mordecai is mentioned, the people clap and cheer. The feast is a very happy, festive occasion. The Jewish community responds positively to the letters of Mordecai and covenants to keep this feast each year.

29-32. A second letter was sent from Esther and from Mordecai concerning further instructions for the feast of Purim. It was sent throughout all of the provinces to the Jews, confirming the times when the feast should be celebrated and that it should also involve a period of **fastings and their cry.** Time was to be designated during the feast of Purim to fast and mourn. This would be followed by festivities and joy. The fasting and mourning was a very integral part of the events (4:1, 16), and the feast was now established.

D. Mordecai Promoted. 10:1-3.

10:1. The book ends by again reminding the readers of the prominence of Mordecai and the Jews throughout the kingdom of Ahasuerus.

2. The declaration of the greatness of Mordecai. Along with the acts of power and might of Ahasuerus, the authority and influence of Mordecai was also written in the history books of the kings of Media and Persia. It was indeed a great honor for a Jew to be mentioned in the history of the Medo-Persian empire.

3. Seeking the wealth of his people, and speaking peace to all his seed. Mordecai was a kind and generous man who was interested in helping other people. The book concludes with this statement. By doing so it reminds us of the complete contrast between Mordecai and Haman.

(see page 879 for Bibliography to Ezra, Nehemiah, and Esther)

JOB

INTRODUCTION

Job is one of the most highly praised literary works known to man and was so regarded by Tennyson and Carlyle, in addition to Martin Luther and a host of biblical scholars. The beauty of the original in Hebrew may well put the book of Job in a class by itself. However, scholars agree that it is much easier to praise the work than to understand it.

In our English Bible, the book of Job is the first of five poetic books (also Psalms, Proverbs, Ecclesiastes, and Song of Solomon), and of these it is the first classified as Wisdom Literature (also Proverbs and Ecclesiastes).

Name. The book takes its name from the central character in the story, as is the case with a number of books in the Old Testament. The Hebrew name is *'Iyōb.* The English rendering of the name is based on the Latin *Iob,* which was derived from the Greek *'Iwb.* The meaning and derivation are uncertain. However, some possibilities as to root sources for the name suggested by various scholars are: enemy, foe, the persecuted one, enmity, or hostility (based on Hebrew roots); return, repent, or the penitent one (based on Arabic roots); where is my father? (based on Egyptian or Akkadian roots).

The possibility that the name was invented to characterize a fictional hero is no longer defended by the majority of recent authorities, for the antiquity and authenticity of the name are both well documented. It was a common Semitic name as early as the second millennium B.C.

Literary Form. When approached from the standpoint of literary style, the book falls naturally into three unequal divisions: (1) A prose prologue (1-2); (2) a poetic dialogue (3-42:6); and (3) a prose epilogue (42:7-17). For the sake of manageability, it is best to divide the large middle section by content: the dialogues between Job and his visitors (3:1-31:40), the discourse of Elihu (32:1-37:24), and the intervention of Yahweh (38:1-42:6), thus giving us five sections.

The book of Job belongs to the literary genre called Wisdom Literature and shares some superficial similarities with extra-biblical literature from Egypt and other areas of the ancient Near East. However, the inspired author of Job points us to the one true God as the source of answers to our deepest problems, and not to man; his approach is monotheistic, not polytheistic or humanistic; and he glorifies God, not man.

The formal literary classification of this book has been the subject of a great deal of discussion over the centuries, much of it related to the historicity of Job. Most of the suggestions can be put into one of the following categories:

1. History. Job actually lived, and the details related in the story could be classified as historical.

2. Historical poem. Job actually lived; and the basic core of the story is historically true, though the author has been allowed certain freedom to put the story in a beautiful poetic form.

3. Didactic parable. Job would be a fictional representative of "every man" in a parable designed to teach a spiritual truth. A variation of this approach suggests that Job represents the nation Israel.

4. Epic poem. Job is seen by some liberal scholars as being the legendary epic hero in a folk-story, such as Gilgamesh was in the famous variations on a Mesopotamian theme, or Achilles in Homer's epic works.

5. Drama. Some have contended that this work was intended to be acted out before an audience and was thus a forerunner of, or copied from, Greek drama (depending on the date assigned to the book of Job).

6. Pious fiction. A small group of scholars would see no need to try to classify this work as any of the above but would simply say it was the fictional product of a pious Near Eastern sage or "philosopher" grappling with deep philosophical issues.

In a very real sense, the book of Job shares features with various literary forms, and does not wholly fall into any specific literary category. It is one of a kind. However, the soundest, and most God-honoring, approach would be either the first or, with care, the second. For the Holy Spirit to allow truth to be communicated in the form of poetry does not make it less true, for some of the most precious scriptural truths we have are found in the five poetical books of the Bible. This does, however, require that a person interpret Job as poetry, rather than narrative history (like Kings or Acts).

Certainly, Job was an historical person (see Ezk 14:14, 20 and Jas 5:11) and is considered so by other Bible writers, though those who deny divine inspiration of the Scriptures say that other biblical references to the person of Job simply reflect knowledge of the legend about such a character in the Jewish literary tradition. However, the approach that does the least violence to the scriptural record is that Job actually lived, and his experiences were substantially as recorded in this book. At the same time, it is recognized that the superb poetical style of this work has compelled general agreement that the treatment should not be literal, but free. Moreover, the semi-poetic long style of both the prologue and the epilogue also suggests a free, figurative treatment of some details.

Date and Authorship. It is widely accepted that the basic core of the story of Job is ancient, and the setting obviously patriarchal. However, the date of the writing of the book is a problem separate from the question of the date of the historical setting.

Job lived during the patriarchal period and was

probably a contemporary of Isaac, Jacob, or Joseph. One of his visitors was called Bildad the Shuhite (8:1), or son of Shuah; and Shuah was the youngest son of Abraham by his second wife Keturah (Gen 25:2). The religious details mentioned reflect a primitive period of religious development. There are no priests; and the father, or patriarch of the clan, offers the sacrifice for his family. There is no central tabernacle or Temple, and no mention of the Law or any other Israelite institution.

Other historical details gleaned from the story show: the Sabeans and Chaldeans are still marauding nomads; wealth consists mainly of servants and livestock; Job lived a very long time (the same as other patriarchs); and the unit of money used (42:11) is found elsewhere only in Genesis 33:19 and Joshua 24:32, both in reference to Jacob.

Another approach to dating the historical setting has been to establish the locality of Job's homeland, "the land of Uz." Three basic approaches have been suggested: (1) Uz may never have existed since it is merely a fictitious name in a poem. This view is rejected by conservative scholars as being neither historically nor theologically sound. (2) The "northern theory," which would place Uz to the north and east of Damascus. (3) The "southern theory," which would place it to the south and east of Damascus, between Edom and Northern Arabia. Ancient tradition places Job's home in Hauran, to the east of the Sea of Galilee; and some Bible maps shade in the land of Uz large enough to take in both theories, but the weight leans to a location near Edom to the southeast of Damascus (cf. Jer 25:20; Lam 4:21).

Questions concerning the unity of the book in its present form complicate the quest to discover the author. The issues that raise the most controversy are: (1) whether the same author wrote the epilogue/prologue and the poetic body of the work; (2) whether chapters 24-27 are seriously disarranged; and (3) whether the original version contained the poem on wisdom (28), the Elihu discourses (32-37), and God's intervention in chapters 38-41.

There is no compelling reason to assume that one hand did not write/edit/compile all the book at an early date and probably the first time the oral story was put in writing. The possible scrambling around of some of the material in chapters 24-27 by later editors would not alter the divine inspiration of the content. It is more reasonable to assume that all the sections in the book were there from the beginning than to assume that wholesale cut-and-paste alterations by later hands could have produced the literary masterpiece that all recognize the book of Job to be. The structural unity of the whole and the interrelationship between the parts argue for the integrity of the present text.

As one would expect, there have been many views put forward concerning possible authors, or periods when an anonymous author might have written such a work. Among them are the following: (1) Moses (Ancient Hebrew tradition held that Moses wrote it while in the desert of Midian (Ex 2:15), which bordered on the land of Edom. The Israelites, Midianites and descendants of Job were

of common ancestry and could have easily shared a story like that of Job.); (2) the Golden Age of Hebrew literature during time of Solomon; (3) during the Babylonian captivity; (4) post-exilic, during fifth or fourth centuries B.C.; and (5) Maccabean period in second century B.C.

Job is almost certainly not a Hebrew; and he lived, suffered, and died outside of Israel. When would a Jewish author have been likely to present profound spiritual insights to Jewish readers using a non-Jewish hero in a non-Jewish setting? During or after the Babylonian exile, or during the Maccabean revolt? Not likely. These were times of extreme nationalism and anti-foreign sentiment.

The most likely period is almost certainly during the reign of Solomon. This was probably the most cosmopolitan period of Jewish history; for there was much trade with other peoples, foreigners were used in the construction of the Temple and the king's palace, and Wisdom Literature was in vogue. The themes touched on in this book speak to the human condition afresh in every generation, and there may well have been recurring periods of interest in the book of Job at later periods; but the arguments for a late date of authorship are not compelling and create more problems than they solve.

Theme and Purpose. There are as many different views on this as there are on the other critical problems related to the book of Job. Some suggested themes are:

1. Patience. The oldest view as to the intention of the writer is to show the patience of a good man in the midst of trials and testing. This is reflected in some ancient Jewish writers and found in James 5:11.

2. Human suffering. Some maintain that the author is wrestling with the universal problem of evil and human suffering and how a good God could permit this.

3. Suffering of the Righteous. Others stress that it is not universal suffering that concerns the author, but why God would permit His righteous and godly servants to suffer. The ungodly deserve their suffering, for it is the natural result of their sin, so the argument goes; but if a man is as faithful and obedient to God as he knows how to be and still meets calamity, that situation causes a crisis of faith and is the true point of tension in the book.

4. Refute conventional wisdom. A variation on the above-mentioned theme would have the purpose of the author refuting the commonly held view, sometimes called exact retribution or terrestrial eschatology, that all suffering is due to sin and all blessing is due to righteousness. The obvious implication of this prevailing "orthodox" view would be that the poorer one was the more sinful he must be, and the wealthier one was the more righteous he must have been to deserve such blessings. Since Job had been very wealthy (children, cattle, servants, and good health) this proved that God had prospered him for his faithfulness and when he suddenly lost everything, the logical implication was that he had sinned grievously and had fallen from God's favor. Although this might be true in many cases, Job knows it is not true in his case and resents the implication, hence the underlying conflict in the story.

5. *Theodicy.* A justification of God's conduct toward man and a defense of His goodness, as well as His omnipotence, in view of the existence of evil and suffering.

6. *Remoteness and transcendence of God.* According to this view, Job's real problem did not lie in the fact of his suffering; his real problem was in the fact that God was hidden from him. He could not find God, nor get a response from Him. Job felt lonely, overwhelmed, helpless, cut off from God, and abandoned. His problem was solved when God spoke to him out of the whirlwind (Ralph L. Smith, *Job: A Study in Providence and Faith,* pp. 13-14).

7. *Religious motivation is selfishness.* Satan (the adversary) makes the accusation that religion is basically a selfish and self-serving activity done in order to obtain blessings from God. "Doth Job fear God for nought?" (1:9). Satan questions Job's motives and implies that loyalty and obedience to God can be bought. This serious charge cannot go unchallenged, and it is God's permission for Satan to test Job's disinterested faithfulness that underlies the sequence of events that follow. After Job passes the first test, Satan obtains permission to increase the pressure (2:4-5) in an effort to determine what Job's price might be; but in spite of his doubts and anguish, Job never denounces God and proves that his integrity was not for sale.

8. *Doubt.* Some emphasize a religious person's struggle with doubt in the face of unexplained suffering and trial and see the root problem as basically philosophical rather than theological. God must act in a way that is reasonable and logical to the mind of man.

9. *Rebellion and pride.* This view concentrates on the poetic dialogue portion of the book and interprets Job's problem as being essentially rebellion against the will of God. The root of that rebellion is pride. Job is upset because he has lost his position of power, prestige, and honor in the community (ch. 29), more than a genuine grief for the loss of his family and wealth as such (Clyde Francisco, *A Man Called Job,* p. 56).

Each of these nine themes is touched on in one way or another in this marvelous book, and that reflects its depth and complexity. However, those who consider the book of Job to be a definitive treatment of the problem of evil and suffering from a humanistic and philosophical point of view are disappointed. That "problem remains the most dif-

ficult and crucial for theology, and all attempts at a rational solution have fallen short of satisfaction" to the unregenerate mind, as Immanuel Kant demonstrated in his monograph "On the Failure of All Philosophical Attempts in Theodicy" in *The Interpreter's Dictionary of the Bible,* vol. 2, p. 922.

While praising the book, we must not overlook its limitations. The book of Job was written centuries before the advent of Jesus Christ and does not contain all the answers, for revelation was incomplete. Many key doctrines, such as repentance, faith, grace, atonement, the Messiah, eternal life, and resurrection, are foreshadowed in Job and are accurate as far as they go; but their complete meaning awaited the coming of the Lord Jesus Christ and the writing of the New Testament.

There is a very real sense in which we can say, however, that the book of Job shows us that there is a benevolent divine purpose running through the sufferings of the godly, and that life's bitterest enigmas are reconcilable with this purpose did we but know the facts. Of course, Job did not know the facts laid out for us in the prologue and epilogue; indeed, the whole point of the book would have been lost had he known what God was up to. Job's friends did not know the reason behind his trials either, and they too were philosophizing in the dark with very limited information. However, we are meant to see that there was an explanation, even though Job and his friends did not know it, so that when baffling affliction comes to us we may believe that the same holds good in our own case— that there is a purpose for it in the counsel of heaven, and a foreknown outcome of blessing.

Herein lies the message of the book: there was an explanation, but Job did not know it, and was not meant to know it. Because of failure to appreciate this, the book has been said by some to present a problem without a solution (Marvin H. Pope, Job in *The Anchor Bible,* p. LXVIII.); but when we see that the central theme is really only one aspect of the problem—Why do the godly suffer?—the book is far from presenting a problem without a solution. The solution is clearly stated in the prologue: God permitted Job's trials to prove that a person could love God for Himself without thought of reward, and that a loving, sovereign God is always in control though our own knowledge and understanding are limited (J. Sidlow Baxter, *Explore the Book,* vol. 3, pp. 26-28). The book of Job thus makes its contribution to the central message of the entire Bible and calls all people to unconditional consecration to a sovereign God.

OUTLINE

COMMENTARY

I. PROLOGUE. 1:1-2:13.

A. Job's Family and Background. 1:1-5.

THERE was a man in the land of Uz, whose name *was* Job; and that man was perfect and upright, and one that feared God, and eschewed evil.

1:1. There was a man in the land of Uz, whose name was Job. The exact location of the land of Uz is not certain, but it was probably east of Canaan and has come to be associated with Edomite influence. It is not likely that Job or any of the characters in this book were Israelites; they were real people, not nameless symbolic characters in a work of fiction. Like the patriarchs in Genesis, Job is depicted as a prosperous seminomad living on the edge of the desert east of Canaan, near a town.

And that man was perfect and upright, and one that feared God, and eschewed evil. Four characteristics are attributed to Job, and all are favorable. **Perfect.** Not sinless; Job never claimed to be sinless and this was never claimed for him. He practiced what he preached. He was whole, well-balanced, a man of integrity, open, transparent; and he lived up to the light that he had. The root verb carries the idea of being complete, well rounded, wholesome, sound, and blameless. **Upright.** This relates to his relationship with others and means straight, faithful, loyal; he was a man of high moral character. The two root words **perfect** and **upright** are also found together in Psalms 25:21 and 37:37. Taken together they indicate the peak of human moral achievement. **Feared God.** Biblical Hebrew has no word that would translate directly "a religious person." The Old Testament writers expressed it as one who **feared God**, and this to them was the beginning and the end of wisdom. Here the word for God is "Elohim," rather than Yahweh. Job had a high and holy concept of God, and as a result he hated evil. **Eschewed** (avoided) **evil.** As a result of Job's fear, reverence, respect for God, he avoided and turned away from evil. He rejected the evil thing and as a deliberate act of will turned aside from temptation and opportunities to do wrong. His outward walk conformed to his inner convictions. Being for something (**God**) also implies being against something (**evil**).

The writer intentionally uses these four character traits together and repeats them in 1:8 and 2:3 to describe as strongly as possible the sincere goodness and integrity of Job. Any one of the four would be taken as a compliment by the average person, but taken together they multiply the impact of what the writer wants us to understand about Job. The stage is being set for what is to follow in Job's life.

2 And there were born unto him seven sons and three daughters.

2. And there were born unto him seven sons and three daughters. An ideal family. The use of **seven** and **three** (the largest number being sons, also ideal) adding up to ten is characteristic of Semitic thought, but it must not on that account be considered an invention. God is capable of doing that. Note that although Job was a wealthy and powerful man and the father of ten children, he had only one wife. Some Old Testament personalities are known to have had more than one wife, but the Bible never commends them for it. Part of the strength of Job's ideal family was that all of his children were by one woman, and she was his legal wife. After Job's trials and tribulations, seven sons and three daughters are again given to him; and since no mention is made of the death of his wife, or a new marriage, it is assumed that his second family was by the same wife. Having lived in the times of the patriarchs when life spans were long, Job lived to see the grandchildren of his second family (42:16).

3 His substance also was seven thousand sheep, and three thousand camels, and five hundred yoke of oxen, and five hundred she asses, and a very great household; so that this man was the greatest of all the men of the east.

3. His substance also was seven thousand sheep, and three thousand camels, and five hundred yoke of oxen, and five hundred she asses, and a very great household. The highest expression of God's blessing was a large family, but the next most important demonstration of God's favor was taken to be the quantity of livestock one possessed. Sheep were valued for food and wool. Camels, the trucks of that day, were valuable for transportation and were considered status symbols. At times they were also ridden in battle. Oxen and asses were considered working stock; and although no mention is made of specific land holdings in acres, the amount must have been considerable to need such a number of animals for plowing and other chores related to agriculture. Job also had a large number of servants. Most of them probably were involved in work related to agriculture and the tending of livestock. It is probable, however, that he lived part of the year in the country in tents and part of the year in town in a house, and he would also have needed sufficient servants to staff all of these domestic operations.

So that this man was the greatest of all the men of the east. A wealthy, powerful, important man, but also a happy family man, and a godly man. Job was known and respected over a wide area among the many tribes and peoples to the east of Israel.

4 And his sons went and feasted in their houses, every one his day; and sent and called for their three sisters to eat and to drink with them.

4. And his sons went and feasted in their houses, every one his day; and sent and called for their three sisters to eat and to drink with them. Each of the seven sons seems to have had his own house, though it is not specifically stated that they were married. It is not certain what the special **day** was, though some take it to be a birthday. Delitzsch disagrees with that view (*Biblical Commentary on the Book of Job*, vol. I, p. 50) and states "The text understood simply as it stands, speaks of a weekly round (Oehler and others). The seven sons took it in turn to dine with one another the week round, and did not forget their sisters in the loneliness of the parental home, but added them to their number." Pope (p. 8) states just as emphatically that it is "not to be assumed that since there were seven sons and seven days to the week that Job's sons and daughters engaged in incessant rounds of feasting. The feast was doubtless an annual affair, most likely the feast of ingathering at the year's end" (c.f. Ex 23:16; Lev 23:5-8, 34-44; Num 29:35; II Chr 7:9).

We see here a remarkably close family, with love and affection expressed among the brothers and sisters and their father. The sisters are obviously unmarried, or their husbands would have been invited. As Robert Gordis points out (*The Book of Job: Commentary, New Translation, and Special Studies*, p. 11), the sisters must still be young, "another indication that Job, both in the prose and poetry, is conceived of not as an aged patriarch,

929

but as being in the midst of his vigorous years (cf. 15:10)." This would also lend support to the idea that he would still be capable of fathering ten more children at the end of the book, and his wife young enough to bear them.

5 And it was so, when the days of their feasting were gone about, that Job sent and sanctified them, and rose up early in the morning, and offered burnt offerings according to the number of them all: for Job said, It may be that my sons have sinned, and cursed God in their hearts. Thus did Job continually.

5. Offered burnt offerings according to the number of them all: for Job said, It may be that my sons have sinned, and cursed God in their hearts. Thus did Job continually. Job here recognizes the internal nature of sin. His concern was not that his children might have committed one of the more common sins of the flesh, but the internal, motivational, sins of mind, heart, or attitude. In this case he feared that during the feast they may have cursed (in Heb lit., bless) God in their hearts. Perhaps the main emphasis in verses 4 and 5 is not on Job's wealth or how well his children got along together, but on the seriousness with which he approached his duties as head of the family, as priest, as well as father, before God for his sons. He was obviously concerned for the spiritual welfare of his children. For some reason there is no mention of offering sacrifices for his daughters, his wife, or himself. His greatest fear seems to be that his sons would sin (miss the mark). As Smith points out (*Job: A Study in Providence and Faith*, p. 22), "It is interesting that the sin of cursing God was the one which Job feared in his children; the one which Satan said Job would commit; and the one Job almost committed, not through the work of Satan, but through the *comfort* of his friends!"

B. The Controversy of Satan with God. 1:6-22:

1. God grants Satan permission to test Job. 1:6-12.

6 ¶Now there was a day when the sons of God came to present themselves before the LORD, and Satan came also among them.

6. Now there was a day when the sons of God came to present themselves before the LORD, and Satan came also among them. Having introduced the readers to his central character, Job, the author now shifts the scene from earth to heaven; and when the curtain rises again, we find God (Yahweh) on His throne before the heavenly court. **The sons of God.** Literally, sons of Elohim or divine beings. In this context they are the angels who serve God's court in heaven and also act as His messengers. There is no polytheism here; these divine beings are not to be worshiped. They have no authority of their own and can only do what God commands or permits them to do. The deliberations of the heavenly council were secret. Only certain prophets received revelations as to what transpired there. As we are told in Amos 3:7, "Surely the Lord God will do nothing, but he revealeth his secret unto his servants the prophets." But Job was not a prophet and knew nothing of the activities of the heavenly court. The dramatic force of the book depends on his not knowing; for had he known, the experiences to follow would have lost their impact.

7 And the LORD said unto Satan, Whence comest thou? Then Satan answered the LORD, and said, From going to and fro in the earth, and from walking up and down in it.

7. And the LORD said unto Satan, Whence comest thou? Then Satan answered the LORD, and said, From going to and fro in the earth, and from walking up and down in it. Satan means adversary, and carries the definite article, as in Zechariah 3:1-2; it is thus a title "the adversary" and not a proper name in this context. The Satan may or may not be one of the members of the divine court, but he presents himself with the others to report on his activities. The idea of a heavenly court with Yahweh enthroned as king is presented in I Kings 22:19; Isaiah 6; and Zechariah 3-4. As Pope points out (pp. 10-11), "Herodotus tells us that the royal secret police in Persia were called 'the eyes and ears of the King.' Both in the present passage and in Zechariah 4:10 the verb used for the action of the Satan and of the roving eyes is *shūt*, 'roam, rove' which is probably more than mere wordplay." S.D. Luzatto has already suggested that the title Satan is derived from this root and that the Satan was a kind of spy roaming the earth and reporting to God on the evil he found therein. Since he must have appeared to men as their enemy and accuser, they named him the Satan from a verb meaning to accuse. Hence, the blending of the various functions, or roles, of the Satan in Scripture. If he found nothing wrong to report, he might cause trouble, tempt the victim, or provoke damaging reactions, attitudes, words, and actions. This is what he did in the Garden of Eden. In I Peter 5:8 he is depicted as a roaring lion roaming about seeking prey. Thus, Satan is called in various places throughout the Bible the adversary, deceiver, devil, great dragon, old serpent, enemy, accuser, tempter, persecuter and prosecutor of the faithful, and the adversary of God.

The spies of the king during the Persian Empire have been used by some scholars as part of their case for dating the book of Job in the Persian period or post-exilic period. However, even Pope admits (p. 11), "certainly the Persians did not invent spying and secret police and informers, which must have developed very early . . . The Persian court may have contributed something to the idea of the Satan, but the background is much older. . . ." This is a very weak argument for a late date in the case of the book of Job (see the Introduction for discussion concerning the date of the book of Job).

And the LORD said. As Satan's master, the Lord begins the conversation. Servants do not initiate conversation with the Sovereign, and Satan is clearly a created and limited being subject to God's authority. Also, since God did not address anyone but the Satan, it may indicate that he was an intruder and not a regular member of the heavenly court.

8 And the LORD said unto Satan, Hast thou considered my servant Job, that *there is* none like him in the earth, a perfect and an upright man, one that feareth God, and escheweth evil?

8. And the LORD said unto Satan, Hast thou considered my servant Job, that there is none like him in the earth, a perfect and an upright man, one that feareth God, and escheweth evil? After Satan's brief answer to the Lord's direct question (vs. 7), God continues the dialogue with a second question. **Hast thou considered . . . ?** It is assumed that Satan had surely noticed Job because of his exemplary life, the characteristics of which are repeated for the second time at the end of this verse. However, Satan does not jump to attack Job; it is God who calls attention to Job. **My servant Job.** For God to call Job **my servant** was quite a compliment and puts Job in a very select company along with Moses, Caleb, David, Isaiah, Zerubbabel, the prophets, and the Suffering Servant (Isa 52:13). Job is called God's servant four times in the epilogue.

9 Then Satan answered the LORD, and said, Doth Job fear God for nought?

9. Then Satan answered the LORD, and said, Doth Job fear God for nought? Satan does not question or contradict any of the Lord's statements about the moral quality of Job's life (vss. 1, 8). The adversary acknowledges the facts, but questions Job's motives. Here we see the exposed nerve of the drama, the central theme of the story, the crux of the issue that provoked the series of trials and sufferings that brought Job to near despair. The main question being dealt with then is not why people suffer, but rather why people serve God.

10 Hast not thou made an hedge about him, and about his house, and about all that he hath on every side? thou hast blessed the work of his hands, and his substance is increased in the land.

10. Hast not thou made a hedge about him, and about his house, and about all that he hath on every side? thou hast blessed the work of his hands, and his substance is increased in the land. This verse teaches an important truth: God does bless the faithful and prosper them. He did put a protective **hedge** around Job, but we must beware of thinking that by our good works we can require God to do so. God is sovereign; and though He often blesses those who serve Him, we can not compel Him to do so, and none is ever sinless, or good enough, to demand blessings from God as his just reward for faithful service. However, by implication, those who love God and seek to serve Him with all their heart have a **hedge** about them today. Satan cannot touch them unless God allows it, and then only for a purpose; but through sin and unbelief one can abandon the protection of God (not the same as loss of salvation) and leave himself open to the attacks of Satan.

11 But put forth thine hand now, and touch all that he hath, and he will curse thee to thy face.

11. But put forth thine hand now, and touch all that he hath, and he will curse thee to thy face. Here in verses 10-11 Satan is up to his old tricks. He denies what God affirms, as he did in Eden, sees evil where God sees good, and acknowledges no love towards God in the world that is not rooted in self-love. He is sarcastic, cynical, negative, critical, suspicious, reflecting his own egotistical, selfish nature in all that he says and does. Satan accuses Job of serving God because it pays. A true servant of the Lord does not sell himself to God, he gives himself to God, and without conditions. Satan implies that love and loyalty can be bought, and that everything, and everyone, has a price. Satan gets some of us pretty cheap, but not so Job.

Satan reasons this way: Job is faithful to God because of the blessings he receives. He has it made; so he would be a fool not to "be religious." But if God should take away the blessings, i.e., business, livelihood, family, home, money, friends, and status in the community, then Job would no longer have any reason to serve God. As a matter of fact, he is probably so used to thinking of all these things as the work of his own hands, he will turn on God and curse Him to His face for taking away Job's things. Why men serve God, then, is the issue. (1) Some serve Him out of fear. If they don't, something bad will happen to them, they reason. (2) Some serve God to cash in on the promises of peace, joy, material blessings, and earthly rewards of various kinds in this life. (3) Others serve God for pretty much the same rewards as in (2), though they think of them as coming "in the next life," i.e., stars in their crown.

Not that there isn't any truth in these three positions, but the Scripture is clear. We are to love and serve God simply because He is God. We must come to love Him for who He is, not what He gives us now or later. Stewardship testimonies have a tendency to be weak at this point. "Tithe, for a mere ten percent of your present income given to God will prosper you beyond your wildest dreams." Statements like it pays and it works focus on what it will do for us, not what it will do for God or His work.

12 And the LORD said unto Satan, Behold, all that he hath *is* in thy power; only upon himself put not forth thine hand. So Satan went forth from the presence of the LORD.

12. And the LORD said unto Satan, Behold, all that he hath is in thy power; only upon himself put not forth thine hand. So Satan went forth from the presence of the LORD. God was so confident of the purity and integrity of Job's inner motives (not just his outer actions, which are all we can see) that he challenged Satan to find fault with him and, after setting limits on Satan's power, allows the adversary to strip Job of his material prosperity. The divine permission is accompanied by a divine command. **Upon himself put not forth thine hand** is not a suggestion. The turmoil that Satan was to bring into Job's happy, tranquil life goes beyond the normal trials and temptations which we are all subject to as members of a fallen race. Job had handled those very well; now the pressure is increased. The curtain falls on the heavenly scene as Satan withdraws from the Lord's presence.

2. Satan takes away Job's wealth and children. 1:13-19.

13. And there was a day when his sons and his daughters were eating and drinking wine in their eldest brother's house. The next scene shifts the action back to earth. The Adversary chooses to hit Job where it will hurt the most and the next time strikes all of Job's children as they are gathered together in one place. This would also be the day that faithful Job worshiped the Lord and sacrificed to Him on behalf of his children, and thus felt confident of the Lord's protection and favor.

13 ¶And there was a day when his sons and his daughters *were* eating and drinking wine in their eldest brother's house:

14 And there came a messenger unto Job, and said, The oxen were plowing, and the asses feeding beside them:
15 And the Sa-bē′anś fell *upon them,* and took them away; yea, they have slain the servants with the edge of the

14-19. And there came a messenger unto Job, and said, The oxen were plowing, and the asses feeding beside them. The first of four messengers comes running up to Job panting and excited as we see the terrible unfolding of Satan's attacks on **my servant Job** (vs. 8), perfect and upright, who fears God and avoids evil. "The hedge" that Satan complained of has been

sword; and I only am escaped alone to tell thee.

16 While he *was* yet speaking, there came also another, and said, The fire of God is fallen from heaven, and hath burned up the sheep, and the servants, and consumed them; and I only am escaped alone to tell thee.

17 While he *was* yet speaking, there came also another, and said, The Chăl-dē'anś made out three bands, and fell upon the camels, and have carried them away, yea, and slain the servants with the edge of the sword; and I only am escaped alone to tell thee.

18 While he *was* yet speaking, there came also another, and said, Thy sons and thy daughters *were* eating and drinking wine in their eldest brother's house:

19 And, behold, there came a great wind from the wilderness, and smote the four corners of the house, and it fell upon the young men, and they are dead; and I only am escaped alone to tell thee.

20 Then Job arose, and rent his mantle, and shaved his head, and fell down upon the ground, and worshipped,

21 And said, Naked came I out of my mother's womb, and naked shall I return thither: the LORD gave, and the LORD hath taken away; blessed be the name of the LORD.

taken away, and Job reels under the relentless blows of the adversary as one after the other of his possessions are stripped away.

Having been let in on the plot by the author, we understand what is taking place and who is responsible. Job has not had that "behind the scenes" glimpse, so he is dumbfounded by it all.

The impact of the story is intensified by its compression. The catastrophes themselves are not narrated for us. As Gordis points out (p. 16), "We are informed of the disaster exactly as Job hears it, in the impassioned words of each breathless survivor." Each messenger was a survivor of one of the catastrophes and a servant of Job. As far as we can tell, of his hundreds of servants the only ones left to Job were the four Satan spared to be the tragic messengers. The word for "messenger" is the same word used in Hebrew for "angel." Job's losses were complete, sudden, and inexplicable. They fall into two categories. Of course, we know in this case that all four tragedies had a supernatural cause; but humanly speaking, the philosophers like to distinguish between an "evil" deed that has a "natural" cause and one that has a "human" cause. In Job's case there are two of each, in an alternating pattern: (1) **Sabeans**, verse 15, loss of oxen and asses, human agency; (2) **Fire**, verse 16, loss of sheep, natural; (3) **Chaldeans**, verse 17, loss of camels, human agency; and (4) **A great wind**, verses 18-19, death of all ten children, natural disaster. In each of the first three cases servants were killed; combined with the death of Job's children, there was loss of human life in all four catastrophes.

Some critics take the fact that all of these events happened the same day and the messengers arrived one on the heels of the other as evidence that we are dealing with an artificially contrived work of fiction. The better answer is the one already given. All of these events did happen on the same day, and almost simultaneously; for Satan's plan required the ten children being under one roof, and then he struck.

It is interesting to note that Satan had the power to motivate the Sabeans and Chaldeans to kill Job's servants and steal his livestock. Satan also has some control over nature and the weather, for he was responsible for "the fire of God" (probably reflecting its intensity not source) and "the great wind" that killed Job's children. Even though Satan has some power over people and nature, it does not begin to rival God's power. "Greater is he that is in you than he that is in the world." Satan has no creative power, but is permitted limited power to manipulate what God has brought into being.

3. Job remains faithful. 1:20-22.

20. Then Job arose, and rent his mantle, and shaved his head, and fell down upon the ground, and worshiped. After the loss of his beloved children and all his sources of wealth, he fell to the ground in submission and humility and worshiped. In addition to the emotional blow of losing all his children in one day was the loss of his posterity. His line would end. From one minute to the next he was wiped out financially, and with the actual loss went the more subtle loss of his high position in the community. He went from the most wealthy and powerful man in the East to a nobody overnight. The Adversary had done his work well, but to no avail. Instead of cursing God, as Satan said he would, and as most of us would have done, Job worshiped.

21. And said, Naked came I out of my mother's womb, and naked shall I return thither: the LORD gave, and the LORD hath taken away; blessed be the name of the LORD. A remarkable statement for anyone to make, and particularly under the circumstances. What would you have said? Would you have waved your fist in the air instead and cried out, "Why me?" Many a church member has cursed God to His face and left the church for good over much less than Job suffered. There is also

22 In all this Job sinned not, nor charged God foolishly.

CHAPTER 2

AGAIN there was a day when the sons of God came to present themselves before the LORD, and Satan came also among them to present himself before the LORD.

2 And the LORD said unto Satan, From whence comest thou? And Satan answered the LORD, and said, From going to and fro in the earth, and from walking up and down in it.

3 And the LORD said unto Satan, Hast thou considered my servant Job, that *there is* none like him in the earth, a perfect and an upright man, one that feareth God, and escheweth evil? and still he holdeth fast his integrity, although thou movedst me against him, to destroy him without cause.

4 And Satan answered the LORD, and said, Skin for skin, yea, all that a man hath will he give for his life.

5 But put forth thine hand now, and touch his bone and his flesh, and he will curse thee to thy face.

a good lesson in stewardship here. Job knew that he was merely a steward of his possessions, not their owner; even his children really belonged to God. If they belong to God, the true owner, He has every right to take them when He pleases. Job knew he would have to give it all back to God when he died, and only one further step was required to acknowledge God's right to take it all back earlier.

22. In all this Job sinned not, nor charged God foolishly. Satan failed. In spite of his tremendous losses and legitimate grief, Job did not impute anything wrong to God, much less curse him to His face. This does not mean that Job understood why all these things happened to him, but he did recognize God's sovereign rights over His creation. Every believer must come to the point that Job did in vss. 20-22. We must continue to love God and serve Him, no matter what happens, trusting that God will work it all out for His glory and our ultimate good. That is what faith and trust are all about, and only that kind of mature and tested faith will see us through when our world falls in on us.

C. Satan's Second Request of God. 2:1-10.

1. Satan's second request also granted. 2:1-6.

2:1-3. Again there was a day when the sons of God came to present themselves before the LORD, and Satan came also among them to present himself before the LORD. The scene shifts once more from earth to heaven. Verses 1-3 repeat basically the same scene we found in 1:6-8. The four character traits that Job was praised for in 1:1 and 1:8 are repeated for the third time here in verse 3 with the addition: **And still he holdeth fast his integrity, although thou movedst me against him, to destroy him without cause.** Both God and Satan acknowledge that Job has steadfastly maintained his integrity under the most adverse circumstances. Later, in 27:6 Job stubbornly holds fast to the same claim of innocence stated by the Lord Himself here in verse 3. What had happened to Job was **without cause** in Job's life, but God would use it to draw Job closer to Himself and make him wiser and happier in the end. Clearly, much suffering in this world is the result of sin; but not all suffering falls in that category, as in Job's case. Job was not sinless, but there was no direct cause and effect relationship between his life and the suffering he experienced. Satan had insisted that Job served the Lord for gain and that every man has his price. If that were true, they had not yet reached Job's price, but the adversary would not have had to work nearly so hard to reach the price or pressure level where the average believer's faith would begin to crumble.

4-5. And Satan answered the LORD, and said, Skin for skin, yea, all that a man hath will he give for his life. But put forth thine hand now, and touch his bone and his flesh, and he will curse thee to thy face. Satan does not give up easily, and he again denies what God affirms. His second accusation against Job is even more insidious than the first, and the ancient proverb **Skin for skin** seems to imply that, when you come right down to it, man is so selfish and self-centered he will always sacrifice someone else's skin to save his own, even his own family. **All that a man hath will he give for his life.** The adversary says that anyone would give up all his possessions to save his life; that is no big thing for Job to do. He further implies that Job's pious response to the losses (1:20-22) was a faked act to stop the attacks while he still had his life and good health. In other words, Job shrewdly said what God wanted to hear, but was not sincere. Satan again assumes everyone is like he is, and in all too many cases he is right. **Touch his bone and his flesh.** The **hedge** of protection had been removed from Job's family and possessions before; now Satan requests that God's protection be taken from the person of Job, and the second stage of suffering will surely produce what the first did not, the destruction of Job's confidence in God and a rebellious cursing of God for allowing so much pain and suffering in the life of His faithful servant.

6 And the LORD said unto Satan, Behold, he is in thine hand; but save his life.

6. And the LORD said unto Satan, Behold, he is in thine hand; but save his life. God again sets limits on Satan's authority; indeed, Satan could not lay hands on a faithful servant of the Lord at all apart from God's permissive will. The condition imposed is both reasonable and necessary. If Satan was allowed to take Job's life, there would be no way to evaluate the effects of the testing of Job's faithfulness. Satan in his own right does not have the authority to take the life of a faithful believer.

2. Job's health broken. 2:7-8.

7 ¶So went Satan forth from the presence of the LORD, and smote Job with sore boils from the sole of his foot unto his crown.

8 And he took him a potsherd to scrape himself withal; and he sat down among the ashes.

7-8. So went Satan forth from the presence of the LORD, and smote Job with sore boils from the sole of his foot unto his crown. And he took him a potsherd to scrape himself withal; and he sat down among the ashes. Here we have another shift from the heavenly court back to earth, and the next time we see Job he is afflicted with a disease that outwardly manifests itself in boils, or open sores, for all to see. Much has been written about the nature of Job's sickness, and guesses range from leprosy to elephantiasis to simple boils (though an acute case since they cover his entire body); but it is not necessary to identify the disease to get the message. The **hedge** of protection has been lifted from Job, and his body has been wracked with a loathsome affliction that prohibits him from meeting with his friends and functioning in any way in the community. To the loss of family, wealth, and prestige are added the physical pain of his illness and the new role of a virtual outcast sitting alone outside the city, probably in the garbage heap. The LXX says "on the dung hill." We note that whatever the disease was, Satan did it; and this establishes his power to inflict people, even believers, with disease.

3. Job's continued faithfulness. 2:9-10.

9 ¶Then said his wife unto him, Dost thou still retain thine integrity? curse God, and die.

9. Then said his wife unto him, Dost thou still retain thine integrity? curse God, and die. The debate concerning how to interpret the words of Job's wife has raged on for centuries. As far back as the additional wording in the LXX, and later the Muslim tradition as reflected in the Koran, there has been an attempt to soften the impact of the literal meaning of her words. In more recent times liberal scholars have advocated a similar soft position. They would interpret the passage to say that in her deep love for her husband she could not stand to see him suffer any longer and advised him to **curse God, and die** as a theological means of committing suicide since to curse God would presumably bring death.

Another school of thought has been less kind to her. St. John Chrysostom, St. Augustine, Calvin, and others have seen her as an additional trial for Job to pass through. After all, she advised her husband to do the very thing that Satan had been trying to get him to do: curse God. Some have even gone so far as to suggest that Satan left her with Job on purpose, rather than eliminate her with the children, knowing she would make life harder for Job rather than easier. Indeed, one of Job's problems now is that his wife was not taken.

In her defense, it must be recognized that she suffered as much or more than Job at the loss of all her children, having gone through labor ten times, and all the work and anxiety of guiding seven sons and three daughters through childhood, youth, and on to young adulthood, only to see them all snatched away. With her once wealthy husband now sitting in the ashes on the edge of a burning dung heap, her social standing was also reduced to that level, and she could not hide her bitterness.

Sometimes the wife is the spiritual leader of a family, and the husband profits from God's blessings on her and the children. In this case the husband was the spiritual head of the family, as it should be; and his wife was unable to cope with their sudden change of fortune. Her position may well have been more promising as a widow than as the wife of a sick man sitting in the city dump scraping himself with a broken piece of pottery. In that sense she may have wished her husband dead in encouraging him to "curse God and die." **Dost thou still retain thine integrity?** She recognized that Job was responding to his suffering in a mature and proper manner; but her reaction, by implication, would be the opposite of mature and proper.

10 But he said unto her, Thou speakest as one of the foolish women speaketh. What? shall we receive good at the hand of God, and shall we not receive evil? In all this did not Job sin with his lips.

10. But he said unto her, Thou speakest as one of the foolish women speaketh. What? shall we receive good at the hand of God, and shall we not receive evil? In all this did not Job sin with his lips. Job obviously does not see his wife's statement in verse 9 as the devoted concern of a loving wife. He realizes that she was advising him to violate his integrity, the result of which would be to prove Satan's charge valid. He calls her suggestion **foolish.** The root word in Hebrew translated "foolish" and "fool" in the KJV means blindness to spiritual truth, rather than intellectual weakness. It implies moral weakness, rather than mental weakness. This kind of spiritual weakness is often referred to as "foolishness" in the Wisdom Literature of the Old Testament.

Receive good . . . and shall we not receive evil? Believing in a sovereign God, everything stopped there for Job. Even if Satan was the agent, Job saw both good and evil as coming from God ultimately, either through His active or permissive will. God is also capable of turning the evil acts of Satan into benefit for His servants, as in the case of Joseph and his brothers. "Ye thought evil against me; but God meant it unto good" (Gen 50:19-20).

In all this did not Job sin with his lips. The genuineness of his character has been established. Here is a man who would never use his religion for personal gain or position. Satan was rebuffed, defeated, and overcome, and does not appear again in the book. As Kline says (*Wycliffe Bible Commentary*, p. 462), "A man must continue to fear God even when his world flies apart and life strands him, like Job, in stunned bewilderment on the refuse heap."

D. Job's Three Friends Arrive. 2:11-13.

11 ¶Now when Job's three friends heard of all this evil that was come upon him, they came every one from his own place: Ĕl'i-phăz the Tē'man-īte, and Bildad the Shū'hīte, and Zō'phar the Nā'a-math-īte; for they had made an appointment together to come to mourn with him and to comfort him.

11. Now when Job's three friends heard of all this evil that was come upon him, they came every one from his own place; Eliphaz the Temanite, and Bildad the Shuhite, and Zophar the Naamathite: for they had made an appointment together to come to mourn with him and to comfort him. Verses 11-13 introduce us to three of Job's closest friends, and they will be with us through all but the last few verses of the rest of the book. These verses also form a bridge between the prose and poetic sections of the book. We do not know how long Job had been in this lowly condition; but it must have taken at least a matter of months for word to have reached his friends to the East and for them to communicate among themselves about it, set a date to meet and travel together, then actually make the trip and arrive in Job's presence.

Some scholars see an abrupt change in the Job of chapter 3 onward and assume a new author is involved, or possibly the artificial wedding of two ancient legends is the cause. A more logical answer would be that the devastating effects of self-pity and an unduly prolonged morbid introspection have caused Job, over a period of time and not abruptly in 3:1, to feel that he has been treated unjustly and to feel sorry for himself.

"The names of the friends are all drawn from the Pentateuch, primarily from the genealogy of Esau in Genesis 36" (Gordis, pp. 22-23.) **Eliphaz the Temanite.** Eliphaz, whose name probably means "God is as fine gold," is mentioned in Genesis 36:4 and I Chronicles 1:35-36; and Teman is the son of Eliphaz (Gen 36:11). Eliphaz is the oldest, and probably the most prominent, of the visitors. He takes the lead, advances the most important ideas, and is usually supported by the others. His speeches reflect a man steeped in the wisdom of his age and of a philosophical bent. **Bildad the Shuhite.** The name Bildad does not occur outside this book, but the two elements that combine to make the name have analogies in the biblical text. He appears to be scholarly and cites the traditions of his people as his authority. There was a man named Shuah, the youngest son of Abraham by his second wife Keturah (Gen 25:2 and I Chr 1:32), who was a brother of Midian.

Zophar the Naamathite. Zophar is the LXX rendering of Genesis 36:11 (Sepho). According to Gordis, it contains the same consonants as Zippor, the father of Balak, King of Moab (Num 22:2). Naamah is the name of a female descendant of Cain through Lamech, a sister of Tubal-cain (Gen 4:21-22), and an Ammorite princess married to King Solomon (I Kgs 14:21). It is also the name of a village in Palestine (Josh 15:41), and a town in northwestern Arabia called Jebel-el-Naameh. Zophar was the most dogmatic and legalistic of the three. He also rebukes Job most severely in chapter 11 for trying to discover the reasons why God does what He does. The LXX calls all three of the visiting friends kings.

The twofold purpose of the friends was **to mourn with him** and to **comfort him.** It is obvious that the three friends originally came to show sincere sympathy to a friend going through an extremely difficult time. The mourning would be for the loss of his children. They had no idea of the discussion that was to follow, or that would end by calling their dear friend a secret sinner and a hypocrite.

12 And when they lifted up their eyes afar off, and knew him not, they lifted up their voice, and wept; and they rent every one his mantle, and sprinkled dust upon their heads toward heaven.

12. And when they lifted up their eyes afar off, and knew him not, they lifted up their voice, and wept; and they rent every one his mantle, and sprinkled dust upon their heads toward heaven. Though the friends knew what had happened to Job, they were completely unprepared for what they saw. He had changed so much in physical appearance they did not even recognize him at first. They remembered a healthy, robust, cheerful, respected, prosperous Job with a fine house in town, servants, expensive clothing, many **friends,** and a wonderful family. They found a thin, pale, gaunt, dirty, diseased, lonely, friendless, broken, pathetic figure crouched like an animal on the town dung heap, or city dump. They gasped in horror and disbelief, then wept as the realization sunk in that this really was their long-time friend Job. From all indications, at this point they were sincere in their grief and desire to comfort Job. Note too that there is no mention of any of the dozens, even hundreds, of local friends of Job going to all the trouble these three did, nor indeed even his wife. We should not sell the three friends short. Tearing the outer garment and putting dirt on the head were traditional symbolic acts of grief as the friends entered into Job's experience as best they could.

13 So they sat down with him upon the ground seven days and seven nights, and none spake a word unto him: for they saw that *his* grief was very great.

13. So they sat down with him upon the ground seven days and seven nights, and none spake a word unto him: for they saw that his grief was very great. Seven days and nights was the traditional period of mourning for the dead (Gen 50:10; I Sam 31:13). Although a few assume that the mourning was for the death of Job's children, most take it to be related to Job himself and his degraded situation, humanly speaking. Not everyone agrees as to why the friends remained silent for seven days. Some cite the Hebrew tradition that the person in mourning must speak to the visitor first. In that case, it would have been impolite for the three friends to break the silence. Others see in the silence a confusion on the part of the friends concerning what to say. For additional possibilities with regard to this silence see Albert Barnes, *The Book of Job*, pp. 36-37.

Job needed understanding, empathy, and confidence to be shown in him. Instead, he got judgment, condemnation, and sermons. A careful study of the following discourses should be required study for those who plan to counsel people. George Adam Smith writes, "The author shows how all three comforters of Job misunderstood the heart; how little they have fathomed human experience; how easily worn out their love and patience; how they prefer to vindicate their own views of God to saving the soul of their brother; and how above all they commit the sin of not perceiving that God Himself may be working directly in that brother's heart, and purposes to teach them more than they can ever teach him. Love was what he looked for, and trust: but they gave him argument which for a time only drove him further from God" (*Modern Criticism and the Old Testament*, pp. 298-299).

There is one redeeming factor in the actions of the friends. What they had to say about Job they said to his face, and not to others behind his back.

II. THE DISCUSSION CYCLES BETWEEN JOB AND HIS FRIENDS. 3:1-31:40.

A. Job's Lament. 3:1-26.

1. He curses the day of his birth. 3:1-10.

3:1. After this. After the seven days of silence. This verse connects the poetical section now beginning to the prose prologue which ended with the last verses of chapter 2. **Opened Job his mouth** is a common literary structure to call attention to what is about to be said. It is also found in the New Testament, such as the introduction to the Sermon on the Mount (Mt 5:2). **And cursed his day.** Job, not one of his visitors, breaks the silence of seven days and seven nights; and when he does, it is not with a casual greeting to his friends or small talk. He opens with vengeance and curses the day he was born. The last recorded words he is known to have spoken are found in 2:9-10, where he chided his wife for expecting only good and never evil from God. We do not know how many weeks or months may have passed between his conversation with his wife and the arrival of his friends, but when the week of silence has passed in their presence and Job speaks again his former buoyancy has turned to bitterness, his patience to pity (self-pity, the worst kind), and his integrity to ingratitude.

Poetically, this is a beautiful chapter, though the sentiments expressed are negative. As unlikely as it may seem, many people in sorrow have found solace in this chapter; for it helps them to understand that others have walked through dark valleys before them and have gone on to the light and joy on the other side to happy, fruitful lives.

Job seems to be talking to himself (a soliloquy), or at least to no one in particular. At this point he is not addressing his friends or God. This chapter is not really part of the discourse cycles to follow. Job is mostly verbalizing his innermost thoughts and feelings in a spontaneous outburst of anguish, misery, and despair. In a way, it was a cry for help. Possibly the most chilling factor in it all is that Job seems so alone. For the first time since he can remember, God seems hidden to him, out of reach; his wife of many years is no longer there to support and encourage him; his children are all dead; his closest friends misunderstand rather than comprehend. Loneliness overwhelms Job, and it is with good reason that this chapter is called a lament.

2. Job does not curse God, as Satan had predicted and as his wife advised; but rather, he turned the curse in on himself and the day of his birth. Note the similarity between verses 2-10 and

---

CHAPTER 3

AFTER this opened Job his mouth, and cursed his day.

2 And Job spake, and said,

Jeremiah 20:14-18 where Jeremiah also cursed the day of his birth. A key word in the structure of these verses related to the curse is **let,** and it appears at least once in every verse, except 10. In some verses it appears more than once. There is also a repeated play on the words, day/night and light/darkness, in these verses.

3 Let the day perish wherein I was born, and the night *in which* it was said, There is a man child conceived.

3. Let the day perish wherein I was born, and the night in which it was said, There is a man child conceived. This verse introduces, and summarizes, the theme of this passage. Job curses **the day** he was **born** (vss. 4-5) and **the night** he was **conceived** (vss. 6-10). The writer devotes five verses to the night of conception, as the most guilty time if indeed a curse is to be directed at a time, and two of imprecation against the day of his birth. They are in reverse order, but Gordis (p. 32) deals with this well when he states that the sequence "has troubled some commentators, as though the verse were a physiological report rather than a line of poetry. The poet needs two terms which he uses as synonyms to express his entrance into the world, so that it is irrelevant whether Job laments his birth or his conception first." The curse is not directed just at his day of birth as such, but against his life in general, now so full of anguish and pain that he wishes he had never been born. For the writer's purpose, the poetic parallelism found in day of birth and night of conception become as one. It is not uncommon for a person to wish he could die, a person with a terminal illness for instance; but to wish that one had never even been born, thus throwing out the good years with the bad, is one step further down the ladder of depression.

4 Let that day be darkness; let not God regard it from above, neither let the light shine upon it.
5 Let darkness and the shadow of death stain it; let a cloud dwell upon it; let the blackness of the day terrify it.

4-5. Let that day be darkness. A poetic elaboration on Job's curse against **the day . . . I was born** (vs. 3). He wishes away **that day** into oblivion as though it could be undone. Of course it cannot. Another play on the day/light to night/darkness theme.

6 *As for* that night, let darkness seize upon it; let it not be joined unto the days of the year, let it not come into the number of the months.
7 Lo, let that night be solitary, let no joyful voice come therein.
8 Let them curse it that curse the day, who are ready to raise up their mourning.
9 Let the stars of the twilight thereof be dark; let it look for light, but *have* none; neither let it see the dawning of the day:
10 Because it shut not up the doors of my *mother's* womb, nor hid sorrow from mine eyes.

6-10. As for that night. These verses are a poetic elaboration on Job's curse against **that night** of his conception. This passage is much more expressive in Hebrew than in English, due to the lack of different words for **darkness** in English. As Pope points out so well, "The Semitic languages have a wealth of words for darkness, since besides its literal sense it symbolized everything that was evil, as well as fearsome and mysterious; cf. 12:25; Ex 20:21; II Sam 22:29; Isa 5:20; Ps 82:5; Prov 4:19; Mt 6:23" (p. 29). Job wishes that the night of his conception could be blotted out of the calendar of time.

In verse 8 **their mourning** would be better translated **leviathan** (41:1), an ancient mythological beast or sea monster and a symbol for the opposition to God's cosmic order; if he were aroused, chaos would be the result. Job thus seems to be wishing that the world had been returned to a state of chaos, or destroyed, before his birth. In such a case, of course, his birth would never have taken place.

Some scholars think of this entire passage (3:1-10) as an imprecatory poem, similar to some of the imprecatory psalms (cf. Ps 35, 52, 58, 109, 137 and others). Imprecate means to curse or invoke evil upon someone or something. Compared with the pious and patient Job we knew in chapters 1-2, these are strange words indeed to be flowing from his mouth. It seemed to him that God didn't care about him any more. He lost faith that God cared, but never doubted that He was in control. That was the crux of Job's confusion. He had been elevated to the highest peak, then dragged into the deepest pit. It is here, in a situation of seeming hopelessness, that God will begin to help Job put his life back together. The lesson seems to be that if there is hope for someone as stricken as Job, there is certainly hope for people like you and me.

2. He asks why he did not die at birth. 3:11-19.

The key word let of the former imprecatory section is replaced by why in this section of lamentation. Verses 11-12 are a series of repeated Why did I not rhetorical questions, followed by For now should I have (vs. 13) and a series of statements reflecting the current concept of death (vss. 13-19). In the first ten verses Job states in various ways that he wishes he had never been born. In these verses he laments that since he was born, he wishes he had died at birth (vs. 11) or been aborted (vs. 16). The sufferer's mind dwells on other ways in which he might have escaped his misery.

11 Why died I not from the womb? why did I not give up the ghost when I came out of the belly?
12 Why did the knees prevent me? or why the breasts that I should suck?

11-12. Why died I not from the womb? A rhetorical question lamenting that he did not die immediately upon birth. Some see a reference to being stillborn. The result is the same. Why did the knees prevent me? It is not clear whose knees are meant. It could be the mother's knees, the midwife's knees, or the father's knees as a symbol that the child was legitimate and accepted by the father or grandfather. It is said that Joseph's grandchildren were born upon his knees (Gen 30:3; 50:23). Why the breasts that I should suck? Poetic parallel. Receiving a child to the breast, or upon one's knees, both were symbolic ways of recognizing parenthood.

13 For now should I have lain still and been quiet, I should have slept: then had I been at rest,
14 With kings and counsellors of the earth, which built desolate places for themselves;
15 Or with princes that had gold, who filled their houses with silver:
16 Or as an hidden untimely birth I had not been; as infants which never saw light.

13-16. Lain still . . . been quiet . . . have slept . . . been at rest. Different ways of saying Job would have been dead. The words chosen imply a time of peace, quiet, and rest. His suffering would end. Kings . . . counselors . . . princes. In the realm of the dead he would be with the great of the earth. He is now excluded from their company in life. As a hidden untimely birth . . . as infants which never saw light. Another of Job's morbid flights of imagination. He asks, rhetorically, why he was not aborted as a dead fetus, a miscarriage which is discarded, passing directly from the womb to the grave without ever seeing light.

17 There the wicked cease from troubling; and there the weary be at rest.
18 There the prisoners rest together; they hear not the voice of the oppressor.
19 The small and great are there; and the servant is free from his master.

17-19. Wicked . . . weary . . . prisoners . . . small . . . great . . . servant . . . master. All sorts of people are there together. The abused servant and his master both must die. Cease . . . rest . . . free. Job sees death not as the enemy, but as the bearer of rest. He is a sick man, and his views are warped by his condition. His extreme suffering has blinded him, at least for the moment. Satan must have rejoiced to hear God's faithful servant speak so; and since the result of Job's testing was unknown to the adversary (Satan is not all-knowing), he may have even cherished the idea of snatching victory from the jaws of defeat. As Ralph Smith points out, this is not the typical biblical attitude toward Sheol, the place of the dead, not even in the book of Job as a whole. Death is the normal end to a long life of righteousness (5:26), but sudden and premature death was viewed in early Israel as the result of wickedness (24:19, 34:20). Sheol is presented as a place of no return (7:10; 10:21; 16:22), of gloom and deep darkness (10:21), of uncleanness (9:31), rottenness (13:28), pain (14:22), fire (31:12), without wisdom (28:20-22), and a place that is open to the view of God (26:5-6) (p. 35).

3. He cries out in his misery. 3:20-26.

20 Wherefore is light given to him that is in misery, and life unto the bitter in soul;
21 Which long for death, but it cometh not; and dig for it more than for hid treasures;
22 Which rejoice exceedingly, and are glad, when they can find the grave?

20-22. Job's mind shifts from the imagined peace of Sheol back to the misery of this life as he now perceives it. Wherefore (vs. 20) should read why as in verse 23. Job asks two more rhetorical questions, each beginning with Why and elaborating on them. Why is light given? (cf. vss. 20, 23). Job wished he had never been born, or having been born, that he had died as an infant. Since none of that happened, why cannot he die now, he asks? Why does God insist on giving the light of day, or life, to someone experiencing such misery and bitterness that he only wants to die? Why must life continue? Light and life are equated, as darkness and death are equated in other passages in Job. Dig for it more than for hid treasures (vs. 21). To dig for something, to search or seek avidly, shows very strong desire to find something. In this case the object of such strong desire is death. **Rejoice exceedingly, and are glad, when they can find the grave?** They are happy and relieved when the object of their search for death, or **the grave,** is found. Job is so low physically, mentally, and emotionally that if he had been allowed to die he would have rejoiced with enthusiasm.

23 *Why is light given* to a man whose way is hid, and whom God hath hedged in?

23. A man whose way is hid, and whom God hath hedged in? Job now shifts his questioning from the plight of mankind in general to his own particular case. He appears as one trying to find his **way** out of a maze. The way is unmarked and confusing, the exit hidden; the harder he tries to get out, to see or understand, the greater his frustration. He feels boxed in, or **hedged in;** and on top of it all he senses that somehow the God he serves, loves, and trusts is not helping him out, but is rather responsible for the hedge. The **hedge** of protection (1:10) has become an imprisoning hedge; whereas before it locked harm out, it now seems to Job that it has him locked in.

24 For my sighing cometh before I eat, and my roarings are poured out like the waters.
25 For the thing which I greatly feared is come upon me, and that which I was afraid of is come unto me.
26 I was not in safety, neither had I rest, neither was I quiet; yet trouble came.

24-26. My sighing cometh before I eat. His sighing and weeping are as regular a part of his daily life as eating. **The thing which I greatly feared is come upon me.** His greatest fears become almost like self-fulfilling prophecies, or as D. David Garland puts it (*Job: A Study Guide Commentary*, p. 29) "Somewhat like a hypochondriac, he had but to fear an affliction and it would overtake him." **I was not in safety, . . . rest, neither . . . quiet; yet trouble came.** There was no rest, peace, nor quiet for Job. Troubles came one on top of the other and kept on coming. Job is still feeling sorry for himself. There is no thought of his possible sin, pride, rebellious spirit, or need for repentance, only the wish to be dead. He thus ends his soliloquy in the same tone on which he began it, one of hopelessness and the vanity of life.

B. The First Cycle of Discussion. 4:1-14:22.

The chapters which follow are variously called cycles of discussion, speeches, debate, dialogue, or discourses (4:1-31:40). There are three such cycles in which Eliphaz speaks and Job replies, then Bildad speaks and Job replies, then Zophar speaks and Job replies. This pattern of three speeches and replies repeats itself three times (with the exception of the third cycle in which Zophar does not speak). The three cycles of three are followed by the interventions of Elihu (32:1-37:24), and then God Himself (38:1-41:34). Job finally repents (42:1-6) and in a prose epilogue is restored to health and prosperity (42:7-17).

1. The speech of Eliphaz. 4:1-5:27.

Eliphaz is the first to speak in each of the three cycles. He was probably the oldest, wisest, most experienced (he refers often to his personal experiences) and most respected of the three visiting friends. He begins softly, almost apologetically, and does everything he can to be considerate of Job's feelings without being false to his own religious convictions. Eliphaz shares with his two friends the conviction that Job is guilty of some secret unconfessed sin, but each of the three approach the problem with a different concept of authority. Eliphaz bases his argument on personal experience; Bildad bases his on tradition; and Zophar bases his on legalistic dogmatism. Job and his friends share the same basic theology, and much of what the friends say is true; it just doesn't fit Job's case.

In his first discourse Eliphaz touches on four doctrinal truths, as Gordis (p. 41) so well points out that: (1) The righteous are never destroyed, but the wicked are sure to be punished either in their own persons or through their children (4:7-11). (2) **All** men are imperfect in the eyes of God; therefore, even the suffering of the righteous has its justification (4:17-21). In view of these two great truths it is foolish for Job to lose patience and

CHAPTER 4

THEN Ĕl´i-phăz the Tē´man-īte answered and said,

2 If we assay to commune with thee,
wilt thou be grieved? but who can
withhold himself from speaking?

3 Behold, thou hast instructed many,
and thou hast strengthened the weak
hands.

4 Thy words have upholden him that
was falling, and thou hast strengthened
the feeble knees.

5 But now it is come upon thee, and
thou faintest; it toucheth thee, and thou
art troubled.

6 Is not this thy fear, thy confidence,
thy hope, and the uprightness of thy
ways?

7 Remember, I pray thee, who ever
perished, being innocent? or where
were the righteous cut off?

8 Even as I have seen, they that plow
iniquity, and sow wickedness, reap the
same.

9 By the blast of God they perish, and
by the breath of his nostrils are they
consumed.

10 The roaring of the lion, and the
voice of the fierce lion, and the teeth of
the young lions, are broken.

11 The old lion perisheth for lack of
prey, and the stout lion's whelps are
scattered abroad.

surrender his faith in the divine government of the world. (3)
Neither God nor His universe can fairly be charged with the
creation of sin and suffering, because evil is a result of free will.
Since man wills to sin, he must be prepared to suffer (5:6). (4)
Suffering serves at times to discipline and instruct the righteous,
and thus guards them against evil doing (5:17-26). Eliphaz
closes his first discourse by calling upon Job to recognize and
accept the four basic truths he has proclaimed (5:27).

4:1-4. Eliphaz exhorts Job to think back to the good days
when he advised others and remember what he had said to them
when they were passing through trying times. **Eliphaz,** the
oldest, most respected, and most urbane of the friends, opens
the discussion. **Wilt thou be grieved?** He begins with a question. Would Job be grieved, annoyed, offended, weary, upset, if
he ventured to speak? **But who can withhold himself from
speaking?** He follows with a second question. Who can keep
silent any longer after listening to Job's lament? **Thou hast
instructed many . . . strengthened the weak hands . . . upholden him that was falling . . . strengthened the feeble
knees.** Job had been a source of strength and encouragement to
others in their suffering. He was righteous, upright, avoided
evil, feared God, was a faithful husband and father, and was
sought out by others for advice and counsel when they had
serious problems.

5-6. But now it is come upon thee, and thou faintest. Job
had counseled others how to react to adversity, so Eliphaz says
essentially, "Job, practice what you preach." These verses are
better understood as the sincere comments of a friend who wants
to help, rather than sarcasm or false politeness. **Is not this thy
fear, thy confidence, thy hope, and the uprightness of thy
ways?** Isn't your **confidence** still in your **fear** and respect for
God, and isn't your **hope** still shown by the **uprightness** of your
ways? Eliphaz seems to be asking "Down deep, aren't you the
same person you were before?"

**7. Remember, I pray thee, who ever perished, being inno-
cent?** Another question, asking Job to think back and try to
remember from his own experience if he can recall a case of a
truly innocent person who **perished** (lit., was cut off) or met
with total disaster. Eliphaz is experience-oriented and orthodox
in his theology. He accepts the orthodox doctrine that the
righteous are never destroyed, not just because it is the orthodox
view, but also because experience seems to bear it out. By
implication, if this has happened to Job, he could not be all that
innocent; he is hiding something.

**8-9. Even as I have seen, they that plow iniquity, and sow
wickedness, reap the same.**
Another reference to personal experience; **I have seen.** The
plow-sow-reap analogy, like the "reap what you sow" of the
New Testament, is true, but does not apply to Job. **They perish
. . . are they consumed.** Death and evil-doing seem to be linked
in the mind of Eliphaz, as in the "perish" of verse 7. But Job is
alive, so there is hope. Nevertheless, nothing in Job's circumstance points to innocence; and gradually the comforting turns
to accusation and the friendly discussion to a heated courtroom
scene. Who is on trial? At first Job, but eventually each of the
friends and even God Himself seems to be the accused in a court
of human justice.

10-11. The lion. Five different Hebrew words for lion are
used in these two verses. The strong, roaring lion is used as a
symbol for evildoers here; but God is even more powerful and is
able to break their **teeth** and silence them until they become
weak from lack of food and die, and their young are **scattered.**
Men who planned evil reaped it, just as lions with no teeth die.
Both similes are intended to teach that the ungodly, and they
alone, perish.

The argument of Eliphaz is close-knit, consistent, and

grounded solidly in the orthodox religious view of his day. The same God who can break the teeth of the lion (the ungodly) and cause them to perish (vs. 11) can see to it that evil men reap what they sow and perish (vs. 9) and assure that the righteous do not perish (never die suddenly, prematurely, or unnaturally), as we see in verse 7. This is a clear statement of a doctrine based on works.

12-16. Job does not seem to be impressed so far, so experience-oriented Eliphaz shares a personal testimony with the group concerning a mysterious experience in a vision. **Secretly brought to me . . . In thoughts from the visions of the night . . . fear came upon me, and trembling . . . Then a spirit passed before my face . . . an image was before mine eyes . . . and I heard a voice.** Eliphaz takes five verses to introduce us to his mystical and frightening experience before he tells us what his spirit visitor said. Gordis observes: "It is noteworthy that the most graphic and circumstantial description of the process of revelation occurs not in the Prophets, but here in Wisdom Literature! While the Prophets were basically concerned with the content rather than the mode of Divine communication, Eliphaz depicts in detail the vision (vss. 12-16) that served as the medium for the message (vss. 17-21)."

A spirit. The same Hebrew word can mean wind, or spirit. It is clear that spirit is intended in this passage, however, though most of the humanistic commentators prefer wind or breeze due to their disbelief in the supernatural. Some Jewish scholars prefer wind out of their desire to avoid any approximation of an "image" of God. The sacred writer makes clear in verse 16 that a spirit, or supernatural personality, was present, and spoke to him. **It stood still, but I could not discern the form thereof: an image was before mine eyes, there was silence, and I heard a voice, saying.** A breeze does not have form and cannot speak. Some seek a psychological explanation, but someone who sees forms and hears voices would be classified as mentally deranged if the form and voice did not exist. No one has ever seriously questioned the sanity of either Eliphaz or the author of Job.

17-21. Shall mortal man be more just than God? Shall a man be more pure than his Maker? Job never said he was more wise or righteous than God, but he did imply that God had treated him unjustly; and he will say so more clearly as the dialogue cycles progress. Eliphaz thus takes this opportunity to remind Job of a second religious truth: all men are imperfect in the eyes of God, so even the suffering of the righteous has its justification. These five verses are a poetic reinforcement of that thought. Note that God revealed this truth to Eliphaz, not Job, so he must have needed that spiritual insight at the time. Whether the Lord led Eliphaz to share it now with Job, or he did so because it seemed appropriate, is not clear. But the Spirit did lead the writer of Job to include the vision of Eliphaz in the sacred text.

5:1-7. To which of the saints wilt thou turn? Holy ones, angels, or saints (KJV). Eliphaz reminds Job that righteousness will triumph, and warns him against impatient anger in the face of temporary injustice. He then questions who else other than God could Job turn to to resolve his problem? No angel, saint, or pagan god can intercede for him. The unrighteous are called **foolish** and **silly,** or simple. **Wrath,** anger, vexation, worry and **envy,** jealousy are seen as characteristics of the foolish person. The fool, or unrighteous person, often appears to be **taking root** and to be prospering when suddenly his home shows that he has been cursed. From his home the curse progresses to **His children** and his **harvest,** or livelihood. **Affliction cometh not forth of the dust.** Some see in this verse a reinforcement of the idea that God, or nature, is not the source of evil in the world but

12 Now a thing was secretly brought to me, and mine ear received a little thereof.

13 In thoughts from the visions of the night, when deep sleep falleth on men.

14 Fear came upon me, and trembling, which made all my bones to shake.

15 Then a spirit passed before my face; the hair of my flesh stood up:

16 It stood still, but I could not discern the form thereof: an image *was* before mine eyes, *there was* silence, and I heard a voice, *saying,*

17 Shall mortal man be more just than God? shall a man be more pure than his maker?

18 Behold, he put no trust in his servants; and his angels he charged with folly:

19 How much less *in* them that dwell in houses of clay, whose foundation *is* in the dust, *which* are crushed before the moth?

20 They are destroyed from morning to evening: they perish for ever without any regarding *it.*

21 Doth not their excellency *which is* in them go away? they die, even without wisdom.

CHAPTER 5

CALL now, if there be any that will answer thee; and to which of the saints wilt thou turn?

2 For wrath killeth the foolish man, and envy slayeth the silly one.

3 I have seen the foolish taking root: but suddenly I cursed his habitation.

4 His children are far from safety, and they are crushed in the gate, neither *is there* any to deliver *them.*

5 Whose harvest the hungry eateth up, and taketh it even out of the thorns, and the robber swalloweth up their substance.

6 Although affliction cometh not

943

forth of the dust, neither doth trouble spring out of the ground;

7 Yet man is born unto trouble, as the sparks fly upward.

8 I would seek unto God, and unto God would I commit my cause:

9 Which doeth great things and unsearchable; marvellous things without number:

10 Who giveth rain upon the earth, and sendeth waters upon the fields:

11 To set up on high those that be low; that those which mourn may be exalted to safety.

12 He disappointeth the devices of the crafty, so that their hands cannot perform *their* enterprise.

13 He taketh the wise in their own craftiness: and the counsel of the froward is carried headlong.

14 They meet with darkness in the daytime, and grope in the noonday as in the night.

15 But he saveth the poor from the sword, from their mouth, and from the hand of the mighty.

16 So the poor hath hope, and iniquity stoppeth her mouth.

17 Behold, happy *is* the man whom God correcteth: therefore despise not thou the chastening of the Almighty:

18 For he maketh sore, and bindeth up: he woundeth, and his hands make whole.

19 He shall deliver thee in six troubles: yea, in seven there shall no evil touch thee.

20 In famine he shall redeem thee from death: and in war from the power of the sword.

21 Thou shalt be hid from the scourge of the tongue: neither shalt thou be afraid of destruction when it cometh.

22 At destruction and famine thou shalt laugh: neither shalt thou be afraid of the beasts of the earth.

23 For thou shalt be in league with the stones of the field: and the beasts of the field shall be at peace with thee.

24 And thou shalt know that thy tabernacle *shall be* in peace; and thou shalt visit thy habitation, and shalt not sin.

25 Thou shalt know also that thy seed *shall be* great, and thine offspring as the grass of the earth.

26 Thou shalt come to *thy* grave in a full age, like as a shock of corn cometh in in his season.

27 Lo this, we have searched it, so it *is;* hear it, and know thou *it* for thy good.

CHAPTER 6

BUT Job answered and said,

2 Oh that my grief were throughly weighed, and my calamity laid in the balances together!

3 For now it would be heavier than the sand of the sea: therefore my words are swallowed up.

4 For the arrows of the Almighty *are* within me, the poison whereof drinketh

man. Others see here a repetition of the regiving and sowing theme; Job's **affliction** and **trouble** did not just spring out of the ground without being sown there earlier by him. **Yet man is born unto trouble.** Eliphaz says that in a sense trouble and affliction are our lot as a natural result of the fallen human condition. There is no sense in getting yourself all worked up over things that cannot be helped.

8-16. I would seek unto God, and unto God would I commit my cause. Eliphaz now turns his gaze from the human condition and draws our attention to God. He suggests that Job commit his cause to God. Of course, Job feels that he is doing that, but almost in the sense of challenging God, not in humble submission. Job dares to demand justice, not grace. There follows a series of beautiful, poetic stanzas describing the mystery, greatness, and wisdom of God. He is Lord of nature, knowledge, and justice. Such a God deserves our awe, reverence, and trust, argues Eliphaz; and we can surely surrender our cause to the Lord with confidence. Having observed God's past actions (5:9-16), he believes that Job should trust God's mercy and not keep insisting on his innocence. As general spiritual advice, what Eliphaz says has much merit; but having been let in on the secret of God's challenge to Satan, we know that in this case Job is right.

17-27. Behold, happy is the man whom God correcteth: therefore despise not thou the chastening of the Almighty. Eliphaz now introduces the concept of suffering as a means whereby God **correcteth** and provides **chastening.** Elihu deals with this idea at some length later in the book (see also Prov 3:11-12 and Heb 12:5-11). The suggestion here is that God has brought these troubles into Job's life as a form of discipline with a view toward getting him to repent. In this case the suffering should be a cause for happiness, and thus lead to restoration. God **maketh sore,** but he also **bindeth up** or heals (vs. 18). He **shall deliver** from **troubles** (vs. 19), **famine . . . death . . . war** (vs. 20), **the scourge of the tongue** (vs. 21), **destruction,** and the **beasts** (vs. 22). Notice that the tongue, gossip, slander, and backbiting are considered as damaging as war, disease, and hunger. **Thy seed shall be great** (vs. 25). **Thou shalt come to thy grave in a full age** (vs. 26). These are the most highly regarded blessings in Job's day, a numerous and fine family and good health until finally one dies in **full age** with his loved ones gathered around. Job was to be blessed by God with just such a later life and death (42:10-17) because of his faithfulness and eventual humility (42:1-6). Eliphaz closes by asking Job to acknowledge that what he has said is true, **for thy good.** He has said much that is true, but he has not been much help to Job.

2. Job's reply to Eliphaz. 6:1-7:21.

Each of Job's replies is in two parts. The first part is always directed at the human speaker, in this case Eliphaz (ch. 6); and the second part is directed to God (ch. 7).

6:1-7. Job appears not to have paid any attention to the elaborate argument of Eliphaz, but continues his lament as though speaking into space at no one in particular. If his **grief** could be **weighed** it would be **heavier than the sand of the sea.** A poetic way of saying his suffering is unimaginably heavy, and thus unbearable (vss. 2-3). **The arrows of the Almighty are within me, the poison** (vs. 4). Job speaks of his troubles as arrows shot into him by God, and the poison as causing a fever

up my spirit: the terrors of God do set themselves in array against me.

5 Doth the wild ass bray when he hath grass? or loweth the ox over his fodder?

6 Can that which is unsavoury be eaten without salt? or is there *any* taste in the white of an egg?

7 The things *that* my soul refused to touch *are* as my sorrowful meat.

8 Oh that I might have my request; and that God would grant *me* the thing that I long for!

9 Even that it would please God to destroy me; that he would let loose his hand, and cut me off!

10 Then should I yet have comfort; yea, I would harden myself in sorrow: let him not spare; for I have not concealed the words of the Holy One.

11 What *is* my strength, that I should hope? and what *is* mine end, that I should prolong my life?

12 *Is* my strength the strength of stones? or *is* my flesh of brass?

13 *Is* not my help in me? and is wisdom driven quite from me?

14 To him that is afflicted pity *should be shewed* from his friend; but he forsaketh the fear of the Almighty.

15 My brethren have dealt deceitfully as a brook, *and* as the stream of brooks they pass away;

16 Which are blackish by reason of the ice, *and* wherein the snow is hid:

17 What time they wax warm, they vanish: when it is hot, they are consumed out of their place.

18 The paths of their way are turned aside; they go to nothing, and perish.

19 The troops of Tē′ma looked, the companies of Shē′ba waited for them.

20 They were confounded because they had hoped; they came thither, and were ashamed.

21 For now ye are nothing; ye see *my* casting down, and are afraid.

22 Did I say, Bring unto me? or, Give a reward for me of your substance?

23 Or, Deliver me from the enemy's hand? or, Redeem me from the hand of the mighty?

24 Teach me, and I will hold my tongue: and cause me to understand wherein I have erred.

25 How forcible are right words! but what doth your arguing reprove?

26 Do ye imagine to reprove words, and the speeches of one that is desperate, *which are* as wind?

27 Yea, ye overwhelm the fatherless, and ye dig *a pit* for your friend.

28 Now therefore be content, look upon me; for *it is* evident unto you if I lie.

29 Return, I pray you, let it not be iniquity; yea, return again, my righteousness *is* in it.

30 Is there iniquity in my tongue? cannot my taste discern perverse things?

CHAPTER 7

IS there not an appointed time to man

to rage through his body that **drinketh up,** or soaks up, uses up, diminishes his breath or **spirit.** Poison on arrows is not mentioned elsewhere in the Bible, and the metaphor may refer to infection in his system resulting from arrow wounds. Another possible rendering would be "my spirit drinks up their poison."

Verses 5 and 6 are questions that suppose an answer of no, and verse 7 closes with the lament that all of this is like rotten or spoiled food put before him which he refuses to touch. If he was given good food (justice, understanding, love), he would not grieve as he does, but make happy sounds like an animal does with good grass, not braying with hunger.

8-13. Job repeats his wish to die with the comment that after all, he is not made of stone or metal; he can take just so much. He still does not respond to the issues raised by Eliphaz.

14-30. Job finally directs himself to his friends in general, but not to Eliphaz in particular; and though he reproaches his friends for not being more understanding, he does not make reference to the theological issues raised in the discourse of Eliphaz. He seems to be responding more to the tone of what Eliphaz said than the content. Job thought he could at least count on his best friends for **pity,** kindness, and understanding, not condemnation. However, they are like a **stream** that has dried up just when you need water the most. In all this he is still responding to what he perceives to be a judgmental attitude on the part of his friends, not the actual words spoken to him.

Cause me to understand wherein I have erred. It is unclear whether Job is being sarcastic, or is admitting the possibility that he might have done something wrong unintentionally, with far-reaching consequences of which he is unaware. He is probably asking them to stop making indirect and general accusations and make direct, concrete charges against him if they know of any. Job then asks if they think he would really lie to their faces; are they calling him a liar, too (vs. 28)? Do they also think that Job does not even know when he is doing wrong (v. 30)? They have implied such, but have given no proof.

7:1-10. Job likens human life to forced service in the army,

upon earth? *are not* his days also like the days of an hireling?

2 As a servant earnestly desireth the shadow, and as an hireling looketh for *the reward of* his work:

3 So am I made to possess months of vanity, and wearisome nights are appointed to me.

4 When I lie down, I say, When shall I arise, and the night be gone? and I am full of tossings to and fro unto the dawning of the day.

5 My flesh is clothed with worms and clods of dust; my skin is broken, and become loathsome.

6 My days are swifter than a weaver's shuttle, and are spent without hope.

7 O remember that my life *is* wind: mine eye shall no more see good.

8 The eye of him that hath seen me shall see me no *more:* thine eyes *are* upon me, and I *am* not.

9 *As* the cloud is consumed and vanisheth away: so he that goeth down to the grave shall come up no *more.*

10 He shall return no more to his house, neither shall his place know him any more.

11 Therefore I will not refrain my mouth; I will speak in the anguish of my spirit; I will complain in the bitterness of my soul.

12 *Am* I a sea, or a whale, that thou settest a watch over me?

13 When I say, My bed shall comfort me, my couch shall ease my complaint;

14 Then thou scarest me with dreams, and terrifiest me through visions:

15 So that my soul chooseth strangling, *and* death rather than my life.

16 I loathe *it;* I would not live alway: let me alone; for my days *are* vanity.

17 What *is* man, that thou shouldest magnify him? and that thou shouldest set thine heart upon him?

18 And *that* thou shouldest visit him every morning, *and* try him every moment?

19 How long wilt thou not depart from me, nor let me alone till I swallow down my spittle?

20 I have sinned; what shall I do unto thee, O thou preserver of men? why hast thou set me as a mark against thee, so that I am a burden to myself?

21 And why dost thou not pardon my transgression, and take away mine iniquity? for now shall I sleep in the dust; and thou shalt seek me in the morning, but I *shall* not *be.*

CHAPTER 8

THEN answered Bildad the Shū'hīte, and said,

2 How long wilt thou speak these *things?* and *how long shall* the words of thy mouth *be like* a strong wind?

3 Doth God pervert judgment? or doth the Almighty pervert justice?

4 If thy children have sinned against

the mercenary or **hireling,** and the lowly lot of a **servant,** or literally a slave. Job identifies with these hopeless elements of society in his day and says that, like them, life for him is empty and without meaning. He is in such pain he tosses and turns all night, unable to even get peace and rest through sleep as most people do (vss. 3-4). His own flesh is rotting, wormy, and putrid (vs. 5). In one sense life drags agonizingly along (vs. 4), especially the sleepless nights; yet in another sense life seems to be slipping swiftly from his grasp (vs. 6).

In verses 7-10 Job comments on the transitory nature of life, likening it to **wind** (vs. 7) and a **cloud** (vs. 9); and this leads him once again to the idea of death (vs. 10). These verses are a transition passage; and due to the poetical nature of the material, it is not clear exactly when Job turns from his friends and begins addressing God. It is clear, however, that by verse 12 he is continuing his lament and directing it to God.

11-21. Job decides that since all of the foregoing is true (vss. 1-10), he has nothing to lose and might as well not hold anything back, but tell God what he really thinks. After all, what worse could God do to him?

In verse 12 a better translation would be sea monster, which must be watched carefully. Kline comments (p. 468): "To judge from the incessant surveillance kept over him, Job says, one would think he was the chaos-monster (a mythological figure, cf. 3:8) threatening the stability of the universe." When he tries to sleep, even if his diseased body (vs. 4) does not torment him briefly, God does, with **dreams** and **visions** (vss. 13-14), so that again he wishes he could die (vss. 15-16).

In verses 17-21 Job accuses God of spying on him and watching his every move. In Psalm 8 the watch-care of God over His creation is seen in a positive sense. In his physical pain and mental anguish Job turns that watching into a negative trait. **I have sinned** (vs. 20). This is really a conditional structure in Hebrew and would best be rendered as a question: "Even if I have sinned, what harm has that done to you?" This is not an admission of guilt, but an argument against the way God has dealt with him. Job closes his discourse with the urgent request that God forgive him, if indeed he has sinned, before it is too late (vs. 21).

The biblical revelation is progressive, and at this early stage the doctrine of eternal life was not yet understood clearly. Job's idea is that if there is to be any vindication, forgiveness, or wrongs righted, it must take place in this life to have any meaning.

3. The speech of Bildad. 8:1-22.

8:1-3. Without the social amenities and cultural courtesy shown by Eliphaz, Bildad leaps headlong into the fray. He calls Job a windbag full of hot air (vss. 1-2) and goes directly to the heart of Job's lament—the implication that God is unjust (vs. 3). Bildad, the traditionalist, wastes no time in vague philosophy about the human condition, but sticks to the specific case of Job. Ignoring Job's complaint that his friends had let him down by being judgmental rather than sympathetic, and knowing that the deepest of all griefs for a parent is the death of a child, Bildad goes straight for the jugular.

4. If thy children have sinned. It is not really a question the way it is put here, but rather a statement of Bildad's conviction

him, and he have cast them away for their transgression;

5 If thou wouldest seek unto God betimes, and make thy supplication to the Almighty;
6 If thou *wert* pure and upright; surely now he would awake for thee, and make the habitation of thy righteousness prosperous.
7 Though thy beginning was small, yet thy latter end should greatly increase.

8 For enquire, I pray thee, of the former age, and prepare thyself to the search of their fathers:
9 (For we *are but of* yesterday, and know nothing, because our days upon earth *are* a shadow:)
10 Shall not they teach thee, *and* tell thee, and utter words out of their heart?

11 Can the rush grow up without mire? can the flag grow without water?
12 Whilst it *is* yet in his greenness, *and* not cut down, it withereth before any *other* herb.
13 So *are* the paths of all that forget God; and the hypocrite's hope shall perish:
14 Whose hope shall be cut off, and whose trust *shall be* a spider's web.
15 He shall lean upon his house, but it shall not stand: he shall hold it fast, but it shall not endure.
16 He *is* green before the sun, and his branch shooteth forth in his garden.
17 His roots are wrapped about the heap, *and* seeth the place of stones.
18 If he destroy him from his place, then *it* shall deny him, *saying*, I have not seen thee.
19 Behold, this *is* the joy of his way, and out of the earth shall others grow.
20 Behold, God will not cast away a perfect *man*, neither will he help the evil doers:
21 Till he fill thy mouth with laughing and thy lips with rejoicing.
22 They that hate thee shall be clothed with shame; and the dwelling place of the wicked shall come to nought.

CHAPTER 9
THEN Job answered and said,
2 I know *it is* so of a truth: but how should man be just with God?

that Job's children died as a result of their sin. In Bildad's mind the traditional law of sowing and reaping demanded that conclusion. Job's children reaped a violent and untimely death; so they must have sown evil. Though Job is suffering, God has not taken his life; so there is still hope for him.

5-7. If thou wouldest seek unto God. If Job will pray with sincere **supplication to the Almighty,** and if he really is innocent, as he has been insisting, then it follows that a just God would reward him with a prosperous **habitation** once more; and he will yet be greatly increased. Bildad is trying to interject a positive note, but he is obviously the most dogmatic and legalistic of the three friends. It is a fearful thing to fall into the hands of a self-appointed defender of orthodoxy who attempts to defend God's honor by guessing about possible breaches of honor in the life of a friend and guesses wrong. Bildad had no facts; and having been allowed to listen in on the conversation between God and Satan, we know that the charges brought against Job and his children were false.

8-10. For inquire, I pray thee, of the former age. Bildad goes on to bolster his case with the assertion that the traditional wisdom of the sages **of the former age,** will support his position. His conclusion is basically the same as that of Eliphaz; but he appeals to scholarly tradition, rather than a mystical experience, as the source of his authority. **Our days upon earth are a shadow.** The life of one person is too brief and fleeting to acquire much understanding, but the accumulated wisdom of past generations is another matter and can be relied upon to **teach thee** with more authority.

11-20. Can the **rush** or reed grow without water? No. This plant represents **all that forget God; and the hypocrite's hope shall perish** (vs. 13). Bildad uses a traditional proverb to show that the law of sowing and reaping is as certain as the laws of biology; the person who forgets God is cut off in the midst of his prosperity, just as surely as plants die when deprived of water. Trust in anything other than God is as flimsy as a **spider's web** (vs. 14). A **house** so weak it falls down if you lean on it (vs. 15) and another plant (vss. 16-18) are used to illustrate the same basic truth, and Bildad closes with the assertion that **God will not cast away a perfect man** nor help an evil one (vss. 19-20).

21-22. With the singlemindedness of the typical legalist, Bildad has not wavered in his theme or allowed himself to be distracted. Neither is he expounding the idea of retribution (sowing and reaping) in the abstract. He has Job in mind, and Job is guilty; but if he will admit his guilt, God will yet return laughter and joy to his life (vs. 21) and curse Job's enemies (vs. 22). In other words, Job's life would once more manifest the outward signs that were traditionally associated with a person under God's blessing and protection in their culture.

4. Job's reply to Bildad. 9:1-10:22.

In this discourse Job responds to some of the statements of Eliphaz, as well as those of Bildad.
9:1-3. Job acknowledges the truth of what his two friends have said so far concerning the lack of righteousness in the creature as opposed to the Creator. Verse 2 would be better paraphrased, "Yes, I know you are right when you ask, How

947

3 If he will contend with him, he cannot answer him one of a thousand.

4 *He is* wise in heart, and mighty in strength: who hath hardened *himself* against him, and hath prospered?
5 Which removeth the mountains, and they know not: which overturneth them in his anger.
6 Which shaketh the earth out of her place, and the pillars thereof tremble.
7 Which commandeth the sun, and it riseth not; and sealeth up the stars.
8 Which alone spreadeth out the heavens, and treadeth upon the waves of the sea.
9 Which maketh Ärc-tū′rus, Ō-rī′on, and Plē′ia-dēs, and the chambers of the south.
10 Which doeth great things past finding out; yea, and wonders without number.
11 Lo, he goeth by me, and I see *him* not: he passeth on also, but I perceive him not.
12 Behold, he taketh away, who can hinder him? who will say unto him, What doest thou?
13 *If* God will not withdraw his anger, the proud helpers do stoop under him.
14 How much less shall I answer him, *and* choose out my words *to reason* with him?

15 Whom, though I were righteous, *yet* would I not answer, *but* I would make supplication to my judge.
16 If I had called, and he had answered me; *yet* would I not believe that he had hearkened unto my voice.
17 For he breaketh me with a tempest, and multiplieth my wounds without cause.
18 He will not suffer me to take my breath, but filleth me with bitterness.
19 If *I speak* of strength, lo, *he is* strong: and if of judgment, who shall set me a time *to plead?*
20 If I justify myself, mine own mouth shall condemn me: *if I say,* I *am* perfect, it shall also prove me perverse.
21 *Though* I *were* perfect, *yet* would I not know my soul: I would despise my life.
22 This *is* one *thing,* therefore I said *it,* He destroyeth the perfect and the wicked.
23 If the scourge slay suddenly, he will laugh at the trial of the innocent.
24 The earth is given into the hand of the wicked: he covereth the faces of the judges thereof; if not, where, *and* who *is* he?

can a man dare presume to be just before God?" He accepts here the basic message communicated to Eliphaz in his mystical dream (4:17). It should be noted, however, that the main idea of this word for **just** means to be vindicated in the sense of a court declaring in one's favor. **If he will contend with him, he cannot answer him one of a thousand.** Job would like to challenge, or **contend with,** God to gain acquittal, or be found innocent or just. But how? Such a contest could not be equal, for God is too **wise** and **mighty** (vs. 4).

4-12. Verses 4 through 12 constitute a beautiful poetic tribute to the majesty and power of God. Job has never questioned the existence of God, as some moderns do when faced with suffering and unfortunate events they cannot understand; nor has he questioned the power of God. His question has to do with whether God has been just in his particular case. The emphasis in these verses tends to be on the negative aspects of God's power: **removeth . . . overturneth them in his anger** (vs. 5), **shaketh . . . tremble** (vs. 6), **sun . . . riseth not; and sealeth up the stars** (vs. 7), **spreadeth out . . . treadeth upon** (vs. 8), **maketh** (vs. 9), **doeth great things past finding out** (vs. 10), **see him not** (vs. 11), **he taketh away, who can hinder him?** (vs. 12).

13-14. A clearer rendering of verse 13 is given by Gordis (p. 105), "God will not restrain His wrath, beneath which Rahab's helpers crouched." Job turns to a well-known folk story of his day about Rahab, a sea monster like a dragon. She symbolized chaos and had to be conquered so that an orderly creation could take place. She was not alone in her opposition to God, but the dragon and all her helpers put together could not stand against God's anger (cf. 26:12; Isa 51:9; Ps 89:10). That being so, **How much less shall I answer him. . . ?**

15-20. Job now openly toys with the idea of summoning God into court in these verses, but he does not believe that God would actually listen to Job's charges against Him anyway. A more likely result, Job speculates, is that He would come in a **tempest** or whirlwind and **multiplieth** his afflictions, leaving him out of breath, tired, and filled **with bitterness.** If this is a test of **strength,** there is no contest and the very idea is ridiculous, says Job. If it is a court proceeding, or **judgment,** who would even dare set up the appointment on the court calendar and allow Job a time to plead? He is so confused by now that even though he knows he is innocent, he would probably get his words twisted and **mine own mouth shall condemn me.**

21-24. In his diseased and bitter state Job questions that there is any moral order in the world: **He destroyeth the perfect and the wicked.** Based on his own experience, Job concludes that **innocent** people suffer and **wicked** people prosper.

So Eliphaz and Bildad are both wrong, and Job's former concept of a divine providence giving moral stability to the universe must also be wrong. God must be responsible for all this injustice since no one is strong enough to resist Him. If not God, then **who?**

The fate of the wicked and the righteous in this life is the same. Job concludes that you cannot judge the moral quality of a person's life by the outer appearance or prosperity, and in that he is right. His friends should have observed that too. Another consideration is that none of those involved in the debate considered the possibility that God could be showing His love in the merciful death of the righteous in some circumstances. Ellison (p. 45) observes, "We normally see what we want to see, and overlook or minimize that which does not suit our theories. The teaching of the Wise was based on carefully selected facts. When Job had to suffer, his eyes were opened to the suffering around him; when he felt the smart of injustice, he saw for the first time clearly the prevalence of injustice around him. We know that Job's friends were wrong; we must not jump to the conclusion that Job was right. They and he alike are giving us partial views of reality."

25-35. Job now turns from his indictment of how God runs the world back to his own problems. He feels that life is slipping away from him and uses three similes to express that idea. "Job compares his life to a runner, a skiff, and a vulture. Each is not only swifter than the preceding, but suggests an additional nuance—the runner represents speed, the papyrus skiff adds the idea of fragility and the vulture the theme of cruelty. Life is brief, precarious, cruel" (Gordis, p. 109). Job feels it would be of no use to force himself to smile and think positively about his situation when his obvious deep **sorrows** and circumstance seem to indicate that God is holding something against him and does not consider him innocent. No matter how hard he tries to cleanse or purify himself, he cannot really vindicate himself; and God would not find him clean anyway. Job cries out for a **daysman**, umpire, advocate, impartial judge, who could arbitrate between God and him, someone neutral who was not afraid of God. This would suppose Job and God being put on the same level and the **daysman** being superior in authority to them both in order to assure a fair and impartial hearing. Of course such a thing is impossible, and Job knows it; but he imagines that only in such a case would he be treated fairly. Since that situation can never be, the next best thing would be for God to **take his rod away from me**, take the pressure off and not threaten violence so that Job would not be afraid of the truth as he sees it without **fear.**

10:1-22. With the outspokenness that comes from weariness and despair, Job continues his lament and directs it to God. He maintains his innocence. **Thou knowest that I am not wicked** (vs. 7). He acknowledges God's power as Creator, **Thine hands have made me** (vs. 8); but with a twist he refers to his life as **clay** (vs. 9), **milk** (vs. 10), and a spirit which **clothed me with skin and flesh** (vs. 11).

Because God continues to keep the pressure on him, **Thou huntest me as a fierce lion** (vs. 16) Job again wishes he were dead (vss. 18-20), adding the pitiful plea that since he is not dead and his remaining days appear to be so few, couldn't God please leave him alone and let him have **comfort a little** (vs. 20) before he goes on to the dreary place of the dead, **whence I shall not return** (vs. 21) and **where the light is as darkness** (vs. 22). The Hebrew word for the place of the dead (good and bad people alike went there) is Sheol. In describing Sheol here four different words for **darkness** are used. The Hebrews, Edomites, and many other Near Eastern peoples shared this view of death. It is a far cry from the blessed state of the redeemed revealed to us in the New Testament.

---

25 Now my days are swifter than a post: they flee away, they see no good.

26 They are passed away as the swift ships: as the eagle *that* hasteth to the prey.

27 If I say, I will forget my complaint, I will leave off my heaviness, and comfort *myself:*

28 I am afraid of all my sorrows, I know that thou wilt not hold me innocent.

29 *If* I be wicked, why then labour I in vain?

30 If I wash myself with snow water, and make my hands never so clean;

31 Yet shalt thou plunge me in the ditch, and mine own clothes shall abhor me.

32 For *he is* not a man, as I *am, that* I should answer him, *and* we should come together in judgment.

33 Neither is there any days man betwixt us, *that* might lay his hand upon us both.

34 Let him take his rod away from me, and let not his fear terrify me:

35 *Then* would I speak, and not fear him; but *it is* not so with me.

CHAPTER 10

MY soul is weary of my life; I will leave my complaint upon myself; I will speak in the bitterness of my soul.

2 I will say unto God, Do not condemn me; shew me wherefore thou contendest with me.

3 *Is it* good unto thee that thou shouldest oppress, that thou shouldest despise the work of thine hands, and shine upon the counsel of the wicked?

4 Hast thou eyes of flesh? or seest thou as man seeth?

5 *Are* thy days as the days of man? *are* thy years as man's days,

6 That thou enquirest after mine iniquity, and searchest after my sin?

7 Thou knowest that I am not wicked; and *there is* none that can deliver out of thine hand.

8 Thine hands have made me and fashioned me together round about; yet thou dost destroy me.

9 Remember, I beseech thee, that thou hast made me as the clay; and wilt thou bring me into dust again?

10 Hast thou not poured me out as milk, and curdled me like cheese?

11 Thou hast clothed me with skin and flesh, and hast fenced me with bones and sinews.

12 Thou hast granted me life and favour, and thy visitation hath preserved my spirit.

13 And these *things* hast thou hid in

thine heart: I know that this *is* with
thee.

14 If I sin, then thou markest me, and
thou wilt not acquit me from mine iniquity.

15 If I be wicked, woe unto me; and *if*
I be righteous, *yet* will I not lift up my
head. *I am* full of confusion; therefore
see thou mine affliction;

16 For it increaseth. Thou huntest me
as a fierce lion: and again thou shewest
thyself marvellous upon me.

17 Thou renewest thy witnesses
against me, and increasest thine indignation upon me; changes and war *are*
against me.

18 Wherefore then hast thou brought
me forth out of the womb? Oh that I
had given up the ghost, and no eye had
seen me!

19 I should have been as though I had
not been; I should have been carried
from the womb to the grave.

20 *Are* not my days few? cease *then,
and* let me alone, that I may take comfort a little,

21 Before I go *whence* I shall not return, *even* to the land of darkness and
the shadow of death;

22 A land of darkness, as darkness *itself; and of* the shadow of death,
without any order, and *where* the light
is as darkness.

CHAPTER 11

THEN answered Zo′phar the Nā′a-
math-īte, and said,

2 Should not the multitude of words
be answered? and should a man full of
talk be justified?

3 Should thy lies make men hold their
peace? and when thou mockest, shall
no man make thee ashamed?

4 For thou hast said, My doctrine *is*
pure, and I am clean in thine eyes.

5 But oh that God would speak, and
open his lips against thee;

6 And that he would shew thee the
secrets of wisdom, that *they are* double
to that which is! Know therefore that
God exacteth of thee *less* than thine
iniquity *deserveth.*

7 Canst thou by searching find out
God? canst thou find out the Almighty
unto perfection?

8 *It is* as high as heaven; what canst
thou do? deeper than hell; what canst
thou know?

9 The measure thereof *is* longer than
the earth, and broader than the sea.

10 If he cut off, and shut up, or gather
together, then who can hinder him?

11 For he knoweth vain men: he seeth
wickedness also; will he not then consider *it?*

12 For vain man would be wise,
though man be born *like* a wild ass's
colt.

13 If thou prepare thine heart, and
stretch out thine hands toward him;

14 If iniquity *be* in thine hand, put it
far away, and let not wickedness dwell
in thy tabernacles.

15 For then shalt thou lift up thy face
without spot; yea, thou shalt be stedfast, and shalt not fear:

16 Because thou shalt forget *thy* mis-

5. The speech of Zophar. 11:1-20.

It is assumed by most scholars that Zophar was the youngest
of Job's three friends. However, he is direct and cutting in his
accusations and does not bother with introductory pleasantries,
perhaps because he has already heard his two friends speak and
has heard Job's bitter comments directed to them and to God.
Unlike Eliphaz, he cites no mystical vision or personal observation; and unlike Bildad, he does not cite the traditions of the
fathers. Zophar is a dogmatist; things are either black or white
to him. He sees no ambiguity in Job's suffering condition and
assumes his guilt. What's more, he doesn't like Job's attitude
and thinks he is a disrespectful, complaining old man. Elliott
(p. 23) thinks that "Eliphaz was the poet and spiritual man who
sees visions and dreams dreams; Bildad was the man who rested
on authority and appealed to tradition; Zophar is the man of
worldly wisdom and common sense. In some respects he is the
most offensive of the three."

11:1-6. Zophar thinks that Job's protestations of innocence
are a lot of self-serving hot air and Job is nothing but **a man full
of talk.** He calls Job's **multitude of words** rantings and babblings and accuses him of mocking both man and God. Zophar's
general tone is one of reproof, condemnation, and righteous
indignation. He accuses Job of lying and hypocrisy and can
hardly wait for God to defend Himself and finally give the
whining, self-righteous old man what he really deserves. Job has
been insisting that God has been too harsh with him, but Zophar
feels that on the contrary, God has been too easy on him; for
surely Job's hidden sin must be terrible indeed for God to treat
him this way in the first place.

7-12. Zophar accuses Job of arguing with God as though he
knew the deep things of God, then defends God's sovereignty
and greatness, or infinity, in this case. Of course, the height and
depth and the length and breadth of God are beyond human
comprehension. God has absolute power, and in the affairs of
men he acts as judge and jury. There is no appeal, which is what
Job had complained of; but Zophar arrives at a different conclusion than Job. God's exercise of supreme authority is justified
because he knows men through and through and can recognize a
worthless man on sight.

13-20. Zophar continues to express his deep conviction that
Job is a sinner. He begins to get personal and stresses the you as
he advises Job to repent and turn away from wickedness. If he
does that, God will surely forgive him, restore him, and banish
all fear and suffering. Zophar can't let it end on that positive
note, so he closes with a reminder of the terrible plight that
awaits the wicked.

ery, *and* remember *it* as waters *that* pass away:

17 And *thine* age shall be clearer than the noonday; thou shalt shine forth, thou shalt be as the morning.

18 And thou shalt be secure, because there is hope; yea, thou shalt dig *about thee, and* thou shalt take thy rest in safety.

19 Also thou shalt lie down, and none shall make *thee* afraid; yea, many shall make suit unto thee.

20 But the eyes of the wicked shall fail, and they shall not escape, and their hope *shall be as* the giving up of the ghost.

CHAPTER 12

AND Job answered and said,

2 No doubt but ye *are* the people, and wisdom shall die with you.

3 But I have understanding as well as you; I *am* not inferior to you: yea, who knoweth not such things as these?

4 I am *as* one mocked of his neighbour, who calleth upon God, and he answereth him: the just upright *man is* laughed to scorn.

5 He that is ready to slip with *his* feet *is as* a lamp despised in the thought of him that is at ease.

6 The tabernacles of robbers prosper, and they that provoke God are secure; into whose hand God bringeth *abundantly*.

7 But ask now the beasts, and they shall teach thee; and the fowls of the air, and they shall tell thee:

8 Or speak to the earth, and it shall teach thee: and the fishes of the sea shall declare unto thee.

9 Who knoweth not in all these that the hand of the LORD hath wrought this?

10 In whose hand *is* the soul of every living thing, and the breath of all mankind.

11 Doth not the ear try words? and the mouth taste his meat?

12 With the ancient *is* wisdom; and in length of days understanding.

13 With him *is* wisdom and strength, he hath counsel and understanding.

14 Behold, he breaketh down, and it cannot be built again: he shutteth up a man, and there can be no opening.

15 Behold, he withholdeth the waters, and they dry up: also he sendeth them out, and they overturn the earth.

16 With him *is* strength and wisdom: the deceived and the deceiver *are* his.

17 He leadeth counsellors away spoiled, and maketh the judges fools.

18 He looseth the bond of kings, and girdeth their loins with a girdle.

19 He leadeth princes away spoiled, and overthroweth the mighty.

20 He removeth away the speech of the trusty, and taketh away the understanding of the aged.

21 He poureth contempt upon princes, and weakeneth the strength of the mighty.

22 He discovereth deep things out of

6. Job's reply to Zophar. 12:1-13:28.

12:1-6. All three of Job's friends have spoken now; and Job's reply, his closing speech of the first cycle, is his most extensive intervention to this point. Job opens with a sarcastic reference to the comments of all three visitors, not just Zophar, and accuses them of talking as if all wisdom began, and will end, with them. He classifies their arguments as shallow and commonplace; he already knew everything they had said. As a matter of fact, everyone knows those things, he adds sarcastically (vs. 3).

The thought is broken as Job turns away from his friends and in on himself again in self-pity. Here is a man who had many prayers answered, who was known far and wide as a just and blameless man, and is now a laughing stock to all his friends and neighbors. But God has ignored his former righteous life and turned on him, making him a joke to all. Yet criminals and idol worshipers are secure and at peace. Job's point is that he is living proof that God does not always reward goodness and punish evil, as his three visitors have been insisting.

7-12. Job repeats some of the things his friends said about God in nature and ironically turns their arguments back on them. They had praised God as the Creator. Fine, he can do that too; but that is not really the problem.

13-25. Job has never doubted God's power; and he is just as capable as his friends of listing the things God can do, as he does here. But his list has a negative tone and emphasizes God's destructive power. It tells us more about the depth of Job's bitterness and frustration than it does about God.

darkness, and bringeth out to light the shadow of death.

23 He increaseth the nations, and destroyeth them: he enlargeth the nations, and straiteneth them *again.*

24 He taketh away the heart of the chief of the people of the earth, and causeth them to wander in a wilderness *where there is* no way.

25 They grope in the dark without light, and he maketh them to stagger like *a* drunken *man.*

CHAPTER 13

LO, mine eye hath seen all *this,* mine ear hath heard and understood it.

2 What ye know, *the same* do I know also: I *am* not inferior unto you.

3 Surely I would speak to the Almighty, and I desire to reason with God.

4 But ye *are* forgers of lies, ye *are* all physicians of no value.

5 O that ye would altogether hold your peace! and it should be your wisdom.

6 Hear now my reasoning, and hearken to the pleadings of my lips.

7 Will ye speak wickedly for God? and talk deceitfully for him?

8 Will ye accept his person? will ye contend for God?

9 Is it good that he should search you out? or as one man mocketh another, do ye *so* mock him?

10 He will surely reprove you, if ye do secretly accept persons.

11 Shall not his excellency make you afraid? and his dread fall upon you?

12 Your remembrances *are* like unto ashes, your bodies to bodies of clay.

13 Hold your peace, let me alone, that I may speak, and let come on me what *will.*

14 Wherefore do I take my flesh in my teeth, and put my life in mine hand?

15 Though he slay me, yet will I trust in him: but I will maintain mine own ways before him.

16 He also *shall be* my salvation: for an hypocrite shall not come before him.

17 Hear diligently my speech, and my declaration with your ears.

18 Behold now, I have ordered *my* cause; I know that I shall be justified.

19 Who *is* he *that* will plead with me? for now, if I hold my tongue, I shall give up the ghost.

20 Only do not two *things* unto me: then will I not hide myself from thee.

21 Withdraw thine hand far from me: and let not thy dread make me afraid.

22 Then call thou, and I will answer: or let me speak, and answer thou me.

23 How many *are* mine iniquities and sins? make me to know my transgression and my sin.

24 Wherefore hidest thou thy face, and holdest me for thine enemy?

25 Wilt thou break a leaf driven to and fro? and wilt thou pursue the dry stubble?

26 For thou writest bitter things against me, and makest me to possess the iniquities of my youth.

27 Thou puttest my feet also in the stocks, and lookest narrowly unto all

13:1-12. Job once again betrays how deeply he resents the attitude and accusations of his friends. **I am not inferior unto you.** He repeats that he already knew all the traditional wisdom they had shared with him, and they had shed no new light on the problem. Anyway, he would rather discuss it with God and not them. He accuses them of being liars who pretend to be physicians of the soul, but who have failed miserably to diagnose his malady, self-appointed defenders of God, false lawyers who have misrepresented God and will have to answer for it.

13-28. After his strong, even harsh, denunciation of the judgments of his friends, Job turns his attention to God once more, as he has done in each reply to a friend. He defends his integrity again and declares his willingness to risk all in that defense, even though it might mean death. **Though he slay me, yet will I trust in him** (v. 15). This familar rendering is not quite the best translation of the Hebrew text, but it is "thoroughly Job like, and in some measure the final solution of the book of Job" (Delitzsch, p. 215). As to his integrity and innocence, Job does not back down in the slightest. Like a lawyer in court, he has **ordered** his **cause,** or better said, prepared his case. If granted a fair trial, he will not run and hide as Adam did (vss. 20-21), but request that God withdraw His Mighty hand and let him speak freely. He then asks God for the specific sins that could have warranted such treatment (vs. 23) and ends on a bitter note, speaking of man **as a rotten thing** or a garment that is moth-eaten (vs. 28).

my paths; thou settest a print upon the
heels of my feet.

28 And he, as a rotten thing, consumeth, as a garment that is moth eaten.

CHAPTER 14

MAN *that is* born of a woman *is* of few
days, and full of trouble.

2 He cometh forth like a flower, and
is cut down: he fleeth also as a shadow,
and continueth not.

3 And dost thou open thine eyes upon
such an one, and bringest me into judgment with thee?

4 Who can bring a clean *thing* out of
an unclean? not one.

5 Seeing his days *are* determined, the
number of his months *are* with thee,
thou hast appointed his bounds that he
cannot pass;

6 Turn from him, that he may rest, till
he shall accomplish, as an hireling, his
day.

7 For there is hope of a tree, if it be
cut down, that it will sprout again, and
that the tender branch thereof will not
cease.

8 Though the root thereof wax old in
the earth, and the stock thereof die in
the ground;

9 *Yet* through the scent of water it
will bud, and bring forth boughs like a
plant.

10 But man dieth, and wasteth away:
yea, man giveth up the ghost, and
where *is* he?

11 *As* the waters fail from the sea,
and the flood decayeth and drieth up:

12 So man lieth down, and riseth not:
till the heavens *be* no more, they shall
not awake, nor be raised out of their
sleep.

13 O that thou wouldest hide me in
the grave, that thou wouldest keep me
secret, until thy wrath be past, that
thou wouldest appoint me a set time,
and remember me!

14 If a man die, shall he live *again?* all
the days of my appointed time will I
wait, till my change come.

15 Thou shalt call, and I will answer
thee: thou wilt have a desire to the
work of thine hands.

16 For now thou numberest my
steps: dost thou not watch over my sin?

17 My transgression *is* sealed up in a
bag, and thou sewest up mine iniquity.

18 And surely the mountain falling
cometh to nought, and the rock is removed out of his place.

19 The waters wear the stones: thou
washest away the things which grow
out of the dust of the earth; and thou
destroyest the hope of man.

20 Thou prevailest for ever against
him, and he passeth: thou changest his
countenance, and sendest him away.

21 His sons come to honour, and he
knoweth *it* not; and they are brought
low, but he perceiveth *it* not of them.

22 But his flesh upon him shall have
pain, and his soul within him shall
mourn.

CHAPTER 15

THEN answered Ĕl'i-phăz the Tē'man-
īte, and said,

7. *Job speaks to God. 14:1-22.*

14:1-22. This chapter is a beautiful, but sad, poem in which
Job meditates upon the human condition and the brevity of life.
Notice the tone. **Few days, and full of trouble** (vs. 1), **a flower
. . . cut down, . . . a shadow** which disappears (vs. 2). Job feels
that God spies on men so that at the slightest misstep He can
bring the offender **into judgment** (vs. 3). Since God has already
set all kinds of limits and bounds on mankind, why not let up
the pressure a little and let man enjoy life, or **rest** (vs. 6)? No
man is perfect, or sinless, argues Job; so what harm would there
be in dealing with all men, not just Job, less severely? Man is the
highest of God's creations on the earth; yet there is more hope
for a tree than for man, for a sprout may yet spring forth from a
stump.

If a man die, shall he live again? (vs. 14). Job raises an
important question, but the context reflects that he expected the
answer to be no, in this verse. Job "despairs of anything beyond
death except existence in Sheol, which is not real life" (Kline,
p. 473). Job concludes on a note of **pain** and mourning (vs. 22).
With this verse the first cycle of speeches ends. Job surely must
not have thought it possible to be any more miserable than he
already was, or receive any harsher criticism from his friends
than he had already heard; but that is just what happened. It got
worse instead of better.

C. The Second Cycle of Discussion. 15:1-21:34.

1. *Eliphaz's second speech. 15:1-35.*

15:1-3. Eliphaz's second speech is the opening of the second
round of discussion, and its sharpness forewarns us that the

2 Should a wise man utter vain knowledge, and fill his belly with the east wind?
3 Should he reason with unprofitable talk? or with speeches wherewith he can do no good?

4 Yea, thou castest off fear, and restrainest prayer before God.

5 For thy mouth uttereth thine iniquity, and thou choosest the tongue of the crafty.
6 Thine own mouth condemneth thee, and not I: yea, thine own lips testify against thee.
7 Art thou the first man that was born? or wast thou made before the hills?

8 Hast thou heard the secret of God? and dost thou restrain wisdom to thyself?
9 What knowest thou, that we know not? what understandest thou, which is not in us?
10 With us are both the gray headed and very aged men, much elder than thy father.
11 Are the consolations of God small with thee? is there any secret thing with thee?
12 Why doth thine heart carry thee away? and what do thy eyes wink at,
13 That thou turnest thy spirit against God, and lettest such words go out of thy mouth?
14 What is man, that he should be clean? and he which is born of a woman, that he should be righteous?
15 Behold, he putteth no trust in his saints; yea, the heavens are not clean in his sight.
16 How much more abominable and filthy is man, which drinketh iniquity like water?
17 I will shew thee, hear me; and that which I have seen I will declare;
18 Which wise men have told from their fathers, and have not hid it:
19 Unto whom alone the earth was given, and no stranger passed among them.
20 The wicked man travaileth with pain all his days, and the number of years is hidden to the oppressor.
21 A dreadful sound is in his ears: in prosperity the destroyer shall come upon him.

intensity will increase in the second act of the verbal battle between Job and his friends. The urbane and sophisticated Eliphaz is much less courteous than he was before. All three of Job's friends are upset at what they consider his arrogance, and frustrated by his unwillingness to accept their interpretation of events and the accompanying theological implications.

Vain knowledge . . . wind? To Eliphaz, Job has proven he is not a wise man by the **vain knowledge** he has been repeating; to the contrary, Job seems full of hot air and his haughty talk is both **unprofitable** and useless.

4. In verse 4 a more serious accusation is leveled against Job. His position is not just harmful to himself, but to others. Since divine reward in this present life for good deeds and divine punishment for evil deeds are seen as the foundation of religion and public morality, they fear that Job's arguments will undermine **fear** of God and, by extension, eventually undermine social order and morality. Job's position strikes at the very roots of their religious interpretations of the meaning of life and death, good and evil. For this reason Eliphaz doesn't just accuse Job of pride or foolish talk but of sacrilege and heresy.

5-7. In his first intervention Eliphaz seemed to consider Job a sincere man, though sincerely wrong; but now he changes his tone and suspects that Job is really corrupt at heart, and therefore his **mouth uttereth thine iniquity,** meaning your sinful heart teaches your mouth to speak **iniquity** and to choose **crafty** speech. Eliphaz insists he does not have to invent support for such charges, for Job has condemned himself with his **own mouth. Art thou the first man that was born?** Though some scholars see a reference here to a pagan superman myth, Eliphaz is clearly saying that Job pretends to be wisdom personified; and "since Job has presumed to criticize God, Eliphaz sarcastically asks whether he claims to be as wise as Adam before the Fall" (Gordis, p. 161).

8-16. Eliphaz takes many of the arguments used earlier by Job against his friends and turns them back on Job in verses 8-16. He then asks if Job was "as old as the hills," had been present in the council of God, knew all they knew and more, even though they were older than he (and by implication, therefore wiser), and knew all secrets. These are not really attacks on his friends, though directed at them, but attacks on God, Eliphaz reasons (vs. 13). In verse 14 the concept of total human depravity is repeated, with the addition that if even the angels (**saints,** or holy ones) and the **heavens** are not perfect, pure, clean in God's sight, how can corrupt man (Job) pretend to be so.

17-35. In a manner typical of Eliphaz, personal observation is cited as authority: **that which I have seen.** He then launches into a catalog of the terrors that assail the wicked and assures Job that their final end is destruction. Job had complained that evil men seem to prosper and live in peace. Eliphaz is saying in essence not so, and any appearance of prosperity is temporary.

22 He believeth not that he shall return out of darkness, and he is waited for of the sword.

23 He wandereth abroad for bread, *saying*, Where *is it?* he knoweth that the day of darkness is ready at his hand.

24 Trouble and anguish shall make him afraid; they shall prevail against him, as a king ready to the battle.

25 For he stretcheth out his hand against God, and strengtheneth himself against the Almighty.

26 He runneth upon him, *even* on *his* neck, upon the thick bosses of his bucklers:

27 Because he covereth his face with his fatness, and maketh collops of fat on *his* flanks.

28 And he dwelleth in desolate cities, *and* in houses which no man inhabiteth, which are ready to become heaps.

29 He shall not be rich, neither shall his substance continue, neither shall he prolong the perfection thereof upon the earth.

30 He shall not depart out of darkness; the flame shall dry up his branches, and by the breath of his mouth shall he go away.

31 Let not him that is deceived trust in vanity: for vanity shall be his recompence.

32 It shall be accomplished before his time, and his branch shall not be green.

33 He shall shake off his unripe grape as the vine, and shall cast off his flower as the olive.

34 For the congregation of hypocrites *shall be* desolate, and fire shall consume the tabernacles of bribery.

35 They conceive mischief, and bring forth vanity, and their belly prepareth deceit.

CHAPTER 16

THEN Job answered and said,

2 I have heard many such things: miserable comforters *are* ye all.

3 Shall vain words have an end? or what emboldeneth thee that thou answerest?

4 I also could speak as ye *do:* if your soul were in my soul's stead, I could heap up words against you, and shake mine head at you.

5 *But* I would strengthen you with my mouth, and the moving of my lips should assuage *your grief.*

6 Though I speak, my grief is not assuaged: and *though* I forbear, what am I eased?

7 But now he hath made me weary: thou hast made desolate all my company.

8 And thou hast filled me with wrinkles, *which* is a witness *against me:* and my leanness rising up in me beareth witness to my face.

9 He teareth *me* in his wrath, who hateth me: he gnasheth upon me with his teeth; mine enemy sharpeneth his eyes upon me.

10 They have gaped upon me with their mouth; they have smitten me upon the cheek reproachfully; they have gathered themselves together against me.

2. *Job's second reply to Eliphaz. 16:1-17:16.*

16:1-17. The exchange of insults between Job and his friends continues. If they could change places, it would be easy for Job to bombard his friends with shallow platitudes, as they have done to him (vss. 4-5). He doesn't really want their pity, but rather that they share his righteous indignation that an injustice has been done. Of course, the reader knows Job is right, because he has been let in on the exchange between God and the Satan in the first two chapters; but if we knew no more than the three friends know, we might say something similar to what they are saying. We all have a tendency to jump to hasty conclusions based on only partial evidence. Beginning with verse 6 Job lapses into another lament and repeats many of the ideas he has expressed earlier.

11 God hath delivered me to the ungodly, and turned me over into the hands of the wicked.

12 I was at ease, but he hath broken me asunder: he hath also taken *me* by my neck, and shaken me to pieces, and set me up for his mark.

13 His archers compass me round about, he cleaveth my reins asunder, and doth not spare; he poureth out my gall upon the ground.

14 He breaketh me with breach upon breach, he runneth upon me like a giant.

15 I have sewed sackcloth upon my skin, and defiled my horn in the dust.

16 My face is foul with weeping, and on my eyelids *is* the shadow of death;

17 Not for *any* injustice in mine hands: also my prayer *is* pure.

18 O earth, cover not thou my blood, and let my cry have no place.

19 Also now, behold, my witness *is* in heaven, and my record *is* on high.

20 My friends scorn me: *but* mine eye poureth out *tears* unto God.

21 O that one might plead for a man with God, as a man *pleadeth* for his neighbour!

22 When a few years are come, then I shall go the way *whence* I shall not return.

CHAPTER 17

MY breath is corrupt, my days are extinct, the graves *are ready* for me.

2 *Are there* not mockers with me? and doth not mine eye continue in their provocation?

3 Lay down now, put me in a surety with thee; who *is* he *that* will strike hands with me?

4 For thou hast hid their heart from understanding: therefore shalt thou not exalt *them*.

5 He that speaketh flattery to *his* friends, even the eyes of his children shall fail.

6 He hath made me also a byword of the people; and aforetime I was as a tabret.

7 Mine eye also is dim by reason of sorrow, and all my members *are* as a shadow.

8 Upright *men* shall be astonied at this, and the innocent shall stir up himself against the hypocrite.

9 The righteous also shall hold on his way, and he that hath clean hands shall be stronger and stronger.

10 But as for you all, do ye return, and come now: for I cannot find *one* wise *man* among you.

11 My days are past, my purposes are broken off, *even* the thoughts of my heart.

12 They change the night into day: the light *is* short because of darkness.

13 If I wait, the grave *is* mine house: I have made my bed in the darkness.

14 I have said to corruption, Thou *art*

18-22. O earth, cover not thou my blood. We are reminded of the blood of innocent Abel crying out from the ground in Genesis 4:10. Job fears he may soon die; but he wants his blood to continue to bear witness to his innocence after his death, just as he has done while yet alive, until the record is set straight. **Behold, my witness is in heaven.** The witness is not identified. Job has already mentioned the need of a mediator (9:33). We may well be seeing here the development of a new level of faith in Job—mediator (9:33), **witness** (16:19), and **Redeemer** (19:25). From our side of the cross and empty tomb we can look back and see the longing of the human heart for a mediator/witness/redeemer and praise God that this need was met in Jesus Christ our Lord. We must also realize that while Job's friends were wrong in assuming that he was being punished for some great sin against God, they were right in stating that no man is righteous enough to stand alone before a holy God and plead his own merits as sufficient to warrant right standing with God.

17:1-16. Job laments his loss of the respect of neighbors and friends. **Are there not mockers with me?** It hurt as deeply as the material losses he has suffered. The total loss of standing in the community is like rubbing salt in his open wounds.

Verse 1 would be better translated, "My spirit is broken, my days are being cut short, and the grave (lit., graves) waits for me." Broken in body and spirit, he feels the grave is near. In verses 1-5 Job addresses himself to God; and in the customary business and legal language of the day, he asks the Lord to be his guarantor and to pledge the necessary **surety** with Himself since none else can or will. This is an interesting picture of what Jesus Christ did.

Beginning with verse 6, Job again addresses himself to the men before him and laments his pitiful state as a spectacle before men, and his crushed condition a byword among his neighbors. He fears that all hope for righting this wrong will go to the grave with him, but we later learn that God did not let it happen.

my father: to the worm, *Thou art* my mother, and my sister.

15 And where *is* now my hope? as for my hope, who shall see it?

16 They shall go down to the bars of the pit, when *our* rest together *is* in the dust.

CHAPTER 18

THEN answered Bildad the Shū'hīte, and said,

2 How long *will it be ere* ye make an end of words? mark, and afterwards we will speak.

3 Wherefore are we counted as beasts, *and* reputed vile in your sight?

4 He teareth himself in his anger: shall the earth be forsaken for thee? and shall the rock be removed out of his place?

5 Yea, the light of the wicked shall be put out, and the spark of his fire shall not shine.

6 The light shall be dark in his tabernacle, and his candle shall be put out with him.

7 The steps of his strength shall be straitened, and his own counsel shall cast him down.

8 For he is cast into a net by his own feet, and he walketh upon a snare.

9 The gin shall take *him* by the heel, *and* the robber shall prevail against him.

10 The snare *is* laid for him in the ground, and a trap for him in the way.

11 Terrors shall make him afraid on every side, and shall drive him to his feet.

12 His strength shall be hungerbitten, and destruction *shall be* ready at his side.

13 It shall devour the strength of his skin: *even* the firstborn of death shall devour his strength.

14 His confidence shall be rooted out of his tabernacle, and it shall bring him to the king of terrors.

15 It shall dwell in his tabernacle, because *it is* none of his: brimstone shall be scattered upon his habitation.

16 His roots shall be dried up beneath, and above shall his branch be cut off.

17 His remembrance shall perish from the earth, and he shall have no name in the street.

18 He shall be driven from light into darkness, and chased out of the world.

19 He shall neither have son nor nephew among his people, nor any remaining in his dwellings.

20 They that come after *him* shall be astonied at his day, as they that went before were affrighted.

21 Surely such *are* the dwellings of the wicked, and this *is* the place *of him that* knoweth not God.

CHAPTER 19

THEN Job answered and said,

2 How long will ye vex my soul, and break me in pieces with words?

3 These ten times have ye reproached me: ye are not ashamed *that* ye make yourselves strange to me.

4 And be it indeed *that* I have erred, mine error remaineth with myself.

5 If indeed ye will magnify *your-*

3. Bildad's second speech. 18:1-21.

18:1-21. Bildad lashes out at Job and accuses him of insulting the intelligence of his three visitors. **How long will it be ere ye make an end of words?** Bildad has missed Job's hints that he is searching for sympathy, a witness to his innocence, and comfort; and he launches into a harsh and vivid description of the punishment reserved for sinners. The wicked will not escape. His person, his family, even his name, all will be destroyed, insists Bildad. **His remembrance shall perish from the earth, and he shall have no name in the street.** It is also his intention that Job see himself in this word picture of the ruin and misery which awaits the wicked in general, much of which Job has experienced already.

4. Job's second reply to Bildad. 19:1-29.

19:1-5. Job opens this speech much as he has the others, reproving his friends for their uncomprehending attitude and maintaining his innocence.

selves against me, and plead against me my reproach:

6 Know now that God hath overthrown me, and hath compassed me with his net.

7 Behold, I cry out of wrong, but I am not heard: I cry aloud, but *there is* no judgment.

8 He hath fenced up my way that I cannot pass, and he hath set darkness in my paths.

9 He hath stripped me of my glory, and taken the crown *from* my head.

10 He hath destroyed me on every side, and I am gone: and mine hope hath he removed like a tree.

11 He hath also kindled his wrath against me, and he counteth me unto him as *one of* his enemies.

12 His troops come together, and raise up their way against me, and encamp round about my tabernacle.

13 He hath put my brethren far from me, and mine acquaintance are verily estranged from me.

14 My kinsfolk have failed, and my familiar friends have forgotten me.

15 They that dwell in mine house, and my maids, count me for a stranger: I am an alien in their sight.

16 I called my servant, and he gave *me* no answer; I intreated him with my mouth.

17 My breath is strange to my wife, though I intreated for the children's *sake* of mine own body.

18 Yea, young children despised me; I arose, and they spake against me.

19 All my inward friends abhorred me: and they whom I loved are turned against me.

20 My bone cleaveth to my skin and to my flesh, and I am escaped with the skin of my teeth.

21 Have pity upon me, have pity upon me, O ye my friends; for the hand of God hath touched me.

22 Why do ye persecute me as God, and are not satisfied with my flesh?

23 Oh that my words were now written! oh that they were printed in a book!

24 That they were graven with an iron pen and lead in the rock for ever!

25 For I know *that* my redeemer liveth, and *that* he shall stand at the latter *day* upon the earth:

26 And *though* after my skin *worms* destroy this *body*, yet in my flesh shall I see God:

27 Whom I shall see for myself, and mine eyes shall behold, and not another; *though* my reins be consumed within me.

28 But ye should say, Why persecute we him, seeing the root of the matter is found in me?

29 Be ye afraid of the sword: for wrath *bringeth* the punishments of the sword, that ye may know *there is* a judgment.

CHAPTER 20

THEN answered Zŏ′phar the Nā′a-math-īte, and said,

2 Therefore do my thoughts cause me to answer, and for *this* I make haste.

3 I have heard the check of my

6-13. Job again openly lays the responsibility for his condition at God's feet. As has already been noted, Job fails to distinguish between God's permissive will and His direct, active will. Job has also not taken seriously the possibility that the Satan is real and active in human affairs; he does not mention the Adversary once, either directly or indirectly. Other faithful men and women down through the ages have made the same mistake of disregarding the activity of Satan, and this has complicated their efforts to interpret what was taking place in their lives and in the world. The opposite error is also to be guarded against, which is making Satan seem so powerful that one falls into a form of dualism with good and bad gods of almost equal power. The Adversary depicted in the inspired Word of God is a created being of limited power.

14-29. Job laments the very negative effect his situation has had on his personal relationship and the estrangement it has produced between him and his friends, relatives, wife, and even servants and neighbors' children. He finally breaks down in verses 20-24 and makes an open plea for pity. Closing this chapter, in verses 25-29, we find Job climbing out of the pit of despair to scale the heights of faith, especially in verses 25-27, to utter some of the most beautiful words recorded in Scripture. **For I know that my Redeemer liveth, and that he shall stand at the latter day upon the earth: and though after my skin worms destroy this body, yet in my flesh shall I see God.** "In a passionate outburst, Job demands that his words be permanently engraved on a monument so that he may ultimately find vindication (vs. 24). In an ecstatic vision he is carried to the pinnacle of faith. In his unshakable assurance that there must be justice in the world, he sees the God of righteousness rising to his defense. God is not merely an arbiter waiting to judge him fairly, or even a witness ready to testify on his behalf, but a Redeemer who will fight his cause, even at the end of time. His faith reaches a new pinnacle in another respect as well. Earlier he had seen his witness in the heavens; now he sees his vindicator on the earth" (Gordis, (p. 195).

Then Job is suddenly jarred back to the reality of his present earthly situation, and he turns on his friends with the warning that their persistent persecution of an innocent man will bring the sword of judgment down on their own heads.

5. *Zophar's second speech. 20:1-29.*

20:1-29. Ignoring Job's plea for pity, and the lofty insights concerning a Redeemer in the preceding chapter, Zophar merely reacts against what he considers to be personal insults by Job, then launches into another discourse on the short-lived nature of the supposed prosperity of the wicked. **Knowest thou not . . .**

reproach, and the spirit of my under-standing causeth me to answer.

4 Knowest thou *not* this of old, since man was placed upon earth,

5 That the triumphing of the wicked *is* short, and the joy of the hypocrite *but* for a moment?

6 Though his excellency mount up to the heavens, and his head reach unto the clouds;

7 *Yet* he shall perish for ever like his own dung: they which have seen him shall say, Where *is* he?

8 He shall fly away as a dream, and shall not be found: yea, he shall be chased away as a vision of the night.

9 The eye also *which* saw him shall *see him* no more; neither shall his place any more behold him.

10 His children shall seek to please the poor, and his hands shall restore their goods.

11 His bones are full *of the sin* of his youth, which shall lie down with him in the dust.

12 Though wickedness be sweet in his mouth, *though* he hide it under his tongue;

13 *Though* he spare it, and forsake it not; but keep it still within his mouth:

14 *Yet* his meat in his bowels is turned, *it is* the gall of asps within him.

15 He hath swallowed down riches, and he shall vomit them up again: God shall cast them out of his belly.

16 He shall suck the poison of asps: the viper's tongue shall slay him.

17 He shall not see the rivers, the floods, the brooks of honey and butter.

18 That which he laboured for shall he restore, and shall not swallow *it* down: according to *his* substance *shall* the restitution *be*, and he shall not rejoice *therein*.

19 Because he hath oppressed *and* hath forsaken the poor; *because* he hath violently taken away an house which he builded not;

20 Surely he shall not feel quietness in his belly, he shall not save of that which he desired.

21 There shall none of his meat be left; therefore shall no man look for his goods.

22 In the fulness of his sufficiency he shall be in straits: every hand of the wicked shall come upon him.

23 *When* he is about to fill his belly, *God* shall cast the fury of his wrath upon him, and shall rain *it* upon him while he is eating.

24 He shall flee from the iron weapon, *and* the bow of steel shall strike him through.

25 It is drawn, and cometh out of the body; yea, the glittering sword cometh out of his gall: terrors *are* upon him.

26 All darkness *shall be* hid in his secret places: a fire not blown shall consume him; it shall go ill with him that is left in his tabernacle.

27 The heaven shall reveal his iniquity; and the earth shall rise up against him.

28 The increase of his house shall depart, *and his goods* shall flow away in the day of his wrath.

29 This *is* the portion of a wicked man

that the triumphing of the wicked is short . . . ? The orthodox position on the matter has been stated already, repeatedly, by Eliphaz and Bildad, as well as by Zophar himself in his first speech. He has nothing new to add to the argument here. Unable to really understand Job and unwilling to compromise with what he considers serious doctrinal error, he can do nothing more than repeat himself in a slightly more dogmatic fashion. **He shall flee from the iron weapon, and the bow of steel shall strike him through.** He makes the misery and ruin that await the wicked sound truly terrible; and we would agree with much that he says, except that we know he includes Job among the **wicked.** Before we are overly harsh with the friends, let us take into account again that if they knew what we know they would have reacted differently too.

from God, and the heritage appointed unto him by God.

CHAPTER 21

BUT Job answered and said,

2 Hear diligently my speech, and let this be your consolations.

3 Suffer me that I may speak; and after that I have spoken, mock on.

4 As for me, *is* my complaint to man? and if *it were so,* why should not my spirit be troubled?

5 Mark me, and be astonished, and lay *your* hand upon *your* mouth.

6 Even when I remember I am afraid, and trembling taketh hold on my flesh.

7 Wherefore do the wicked live, become old, yea, are mighty in power?

8 Their seed is established in their sight with them, and their offspring before their eyes.

9 Their houses *are* safe from fear, neither *is* the rod of God upon them.

10 Their bull gendereth, and faileth not; their cow calveth, and casteth not her calf.

11 They send forth their little ones like a flock, and their children dance.

12 They take the timbrel and harp, and rejoice at the sound of the organ.

13 They spend their days in wealth, and in a moment go down to the grave.

14 Therefore they say unto God, Depart from us; for we desire not the knowledge of thy ways.

15 What *is* the Almighty, that we should serve him? and what profit should we have, if we pray unto him?

16 Lo, their good *is* not in their hand: the counsel of the wicked is far from me.

17 How oft is the candle of the wicked put out! and *how oft* cometh their destruction upon them! *God* distributeth sorrows in his anger.

18 They are as stubble before the wind, and as chaff that the storm carrieth away.

19 God layeth up his iniquity for his children: he rewardeth him, and he shall know *it.*

20 His eyes shall see his destruction, and he shall drink of the wrath of the Almighty.

21 For what pleasure *hath* he in his house after him, when the number of his months is cut off in the midst?

22 Shall *any* teach God knowledge? seeing he judgeth those that are high.

23 One dieth in his full strength, being wholly at ease and quiet.

24 His breasts are full of milk, and his bones are moistened with marrow.

25 And another dieth in the bitterness of his soul, and never eateth with pleasure.

26 They shall lie down alike in the dust, and the worms shall cover them.

6. *Job's second reply to Zophar. 21:1-34.*

This is Job's last reply in the second cycle of discussion. This time he does not turn aside to address some of his remarks to God; all of his barbs and sarcasm are reserved for the friends. In replying to Zophar, he deals with some examples that had been cited by Eliphaz, and Bildad as well. All three had agreed concerning the punishment of the wicked and the prosperity of the righteous in this life, so in a sense Job lumps them all together in this reply.

21:1-6. Job opens his remarks by requesting their attention while he speaks, knowing that when he finishes they will renew their mocking criticism. Job is getting more impatient and troubled; and he asks them to look at him, **Mark me,** and be appalled, **and be astonished** and see if he is not justified. When he thinks about his own condition, he is **afraid,** dismayed, appalled. He is stunned to **remember** what has happened and to know **trembling taketh hold.** Talk comes cheaply for the friends; they have not been through what Job has experienced.

7-22. Job turns his attention from himself to the issue of the prosperity of the wicked. To make their point, the three friends had idealized, and somewhat overstated, their case. They said the wicked always died young, suffered, had sickly children, failed in business, had no friends, and died in misery. On the other hand, Job may exaggerate the prosperity of the sinner. He describes the contentment, happiness, healthy children, prosperous business, fertile livestock, and peaceful death of the wicked. He reminds his friends that they had said such prosperity would be only temporary and the wicked would lose all before they died. But how often does that really happen, asks Job? Well, you say **God layeth up his iniquity for his children** (vs. 19), but why the children? Would it not be better to punish the wicked man himself so that **he shall know it** (vs. 19), reasons Job. It would be better to let his own eyes **see his destruction** and experience **the wrath of the Almighty** (vs. 20) directly.

23-26. Job continues his bitter attack by denouncing the view of the friends that at death there would be a moment of truth and God would surely set things right. The KJV is not very clear, but the sense of verses 23-26 is that the rich man (implied wicked man) dies content, secure, well nourished, and at ease. On the other hand, others (vs. 25) die in bitterness, poverty (implied righteous man) without ever having experienced the good things of life. Yet, God seems indifferent to all this, says Job, and **They shall lie down alike in the dust, and the worms shall cover them.**

27 Behold, I know your thoughts, and the devices *which* ye wrongfully imagine against me.

28 For ye say, Where *is* the house of the prince? and where *are* the dwelling places of the wicked?

29 Have ye not asked them that go by the way? and do ye not know their tokens,

30 That the wicked is reserved to the day of destruction? they shall be brought forth to the day of wrath.

31 Who shall declare his way to his face? and who shall repay him *what* he hath done?

32 Yet shall he be brought to the grave, and shall remain in the tomb.

33 The clods of the valley shall be sweet unto him, and every man shall draw after him, as *there are* innumerable before him.

34 How then comfort ye me in vain, seeing in your answers there remaineth falsehood?

CHAPTER 22

THEN Ĕl'i-phăz the Tē'man-īte answered and said,

2 Can a man be profitable unto God, as he that is wise may be profitable unto himself?

3 *Is it* any pleasure to the Almighty, that thou art righteous? or *is it* gain *to him*, that thou makest thy ways perfect?

4 Will he reprove thee for fear of thee? will he enter with thee into judgment?

5 *Is* not thy wickedness great? and thine iniquities infinite?

Job was, of course, limited in his understanding due to this early period of history and the corresponding lack of the progressive revelation that would make so many things clear later. Job could not really come to grips with a judgment after death when all wrongs would be made right. He wanted them made right now, in this life, even though he had caught a brief glimpse of the possibility of a bodily resurrection in 19:25-27.

27-34. Job continues his sarcastic attack on the position of Zophar, which he considers to be wide of the truth. The friends had made reference to the destruction of the dwelling of the wicked. Job says you can ask even the travelers passing by where the big house of the prince is located, knowing that most princes were greedy men who exploited the weak, accepted bribes and kick-backs, and lived by plunder of one sort or another. Yet, their big, beautiful houses stood strong and secure for all to see. They were not cast down and destroyed as Zophar had said. When the rich, wicked man dies, he is **brought to the grave** (vs. 32) with great pomp and a splendid funeral. He rests in a beautiful, undefiled tomb; and **the clods of the valley shall be sweet unto him** (vs. 33). Job wraps up his discourse with the rejoinder that since all the above is true, your attempt to comfort me with the statements you have made is futile and **in vain** (vs. 34) and your supposed **answers** are **falsehood** (vs. 34).

Of course, Job has his position, just as his friends cited extreme cases to the contrary in support of their position. The true message to be seen is that neither is correct, in that there is no direct connection between one's outer prosperity and inner spirituality. God's people are numbered among all levels of society: rich, middle-class, and poor. There are also unrighteous people who are rich, middle-class, and poor. The personal faith and trust in God is what matters.

D. The Third Cycle of Discussion. 22:1-31:40.

1. *Eliphaz's third speech. 22:1-30.*

22:1-5. Eliphaz goes straight to the attack without the usual courtesies. As a matter of fact, he is no longer content to speak of Job's wrongdoings in general terms, but accuses him of a long list of specific, but imagined, sins. However, he must first deal with Job's insistence that God has dealt unjustly with him. Eliphaz does that through a series of rhetorical questions (vss. 2-4); the implied answer to each is negative. The argument is that since God is so great and complete in Himself, there is nothing we can do for Him, no need we can meet, nothing Job could do to benefit him. Therefore, God could have no ulterior motive in dealing with Job. God rewards or punishes in a disinterested way according to our works, insists Eliphaz; and there is nothing personal about it.

Job is a complex book. We know from the first two chapters that, as a matter of fact, God was pleased with Job's upright life (1:8; 2:3); and it was because of this that he was being tested. That does not fit into the preconceived theological structure of Eliphaz, so such a thought had never occurred to him. Even though Job had consistently maintained his innocence and implied that something like that must be the case (that he was being tested because of his faith, not because of his sin), Eliphaz's rigid, legalistic doctrinal position caused him to reject that as a possibility. It was simply beyond his capacity to comprehend such an interpretation. That is probably one of the main messages the author is trying to communicate through this work.

Since Eliphaz's thinking excluded such severe testing (as Job had experienced) of a truly righteous man, that left two alternatives: either God was unjust, or Job was unrighteous. Obviously, Eliphaz would reject the former as impossible; so the latter must be true. Since the theory he held did not fit the facts,

6 For thou hast taken a pledge from thy brother for nought, and stripped the naked of their clothing.

7 Thou hast not given water to the weary to drink, and thou hast withholden bread from the hungry.

8 But *as for* the mighty man, he had the earth; and the honourable man dwelt in it.

9 Thou hast sent widows away empty, and the arms of the fatherless have been broken.

10 Therefore snares *are* round about thee, and sudden fear troubleth thee;

11 Or darkness, *that* thou canst not see; and abundance of waters cover thee.

12 *Is* not God in the height of heaven? and behold the height of the stars, how high they are!

13 And thou sayest, How doth God know? can he judge through the dark cloud?

14 Thick clouds *are* a covering to him, that he seeth not; and he walketh in the circuit of heaven.

15 Hast thou marked the old way which wicked men have trodden?

16 Which were cut down out of time, whose foundation was overflown with a flood:

17 Which said unto God, Depart from us: and what can the Almighty do for them?

18 Yet he filled their houses with good *things:* but the counsel of the wicked is far from me.

19 The righteous see *it*, and are glad: and the innocent laugh them to scorn.

20 Whereas our substance is not cut down, but the remnant of them the fire consumeth.

21 Acquaint now thyself with him, and be at peace: thereby good shall come unto thee.

22 Receive, I pray thee, the law from his mouth, and lay up his words in thine heart.

23 If thou return to the Almighty, thou shalt be built up, thou shalt put away iniquity far from thy tabernacles.

24 Then shalt thou lay up gold as dust, and the *gold* of Ō'phir as the stones of the brooks.

25 Yea, the Almighty shall be thy defence, and thou shalt have plenty of silver.

26 For then shalt thou have thy delight in the Almighty, and shalt lift up thy face unto God.

27 Thou shalt make thy prayer unto him, and he shall hear thee, and thou shalt pay thy vows.

28 Thou shalt also decree a thing, and it shall be established unto thee: and the light shall shine upon thy ways.

29 When *men* are cast down, then thou shalt say, *There is* lifting up; and he shall save the humble person.

30 He shall deliver the island of the innocent: and it is delivered by the pureness of thine hands.

Eliphaz resorts to the time-honored strategy of adjusting the facts to fit the theory. This he does by cataloging the imagined sins of Job in the following verses. We know these things are not true. The accusations are not based on fact, but theory, and are the product of Eliphaz's preconceived ideas about God and man.

6-14. The sins mentioned here give us an interesting insight into the ethical standards of that day and culture. The offenses are not the laboring man's stealing and cheating, but those most likely to be associated with the abuses of power and wealth, reflecting Job's former elevated status. Job is accused of taking advantage of a **brother** in need by making a loan then taking his pledge clothing when he could not pay on time (a form of loan sharking). The borrower was a kinsman; so Job would have done doubly wrong if it were true. He should have helped a needy relative without collateral (an object of **pledge**) and seems to have given little in return, **for nought** (vs. 6).

In a dry land, where settlements were often many miles apart, the refusal to share water and food with a needy traveler was considered a grave offense (vs. 7). There are sins of omission as well as commission in the list. Job is also supposed to have exploited the poor in shady land deals (vs. 8) and callously withheld help from widows and orphans (vs. 9). This had to be the explanation for Job's tragic situation (vss. 10-11). Maybe Job thinks God does not know these things (vss. 12-14). Job, in turn, specifically denies these charges in chapter 31.

15-20. In verses 15-20 Eliphaz accuses Job of being like the most godless men he could think of, probably the sinful generation washed away in the Flood. In chapter 21 Job had spoken of such people, but gave them a happy ending. Eliphaz responds to that by saying they were judged by God and met a tragic end. Eliphaz is right concerning the Flood, but Job was right in observing that he knew godless men that died a natural death surrounded by their ill-gotten gain.

21-30. Eliphaz urges Job to repent and be reconciled to God. It is assumed that by being restored to favor with God, his material prosperity will also be restored. Actually, this is a beautiful passage and contains much truth. Unfortunately, it is directed at the wrong person and closes with a works approach to finding favor with God.

CHAPTER 23

THEN Job answered and said,

2 Even to day *is* my complaint bitter: my stroke is heavier than my groaning.

3 Oh that I knew where I might find him! *that* I might come *even* to his seat!

4 I would order *my* cause before him, and fill my mouth with arguments.

5 I would know the words *which* he would answer me, and understand what he would say unto me.

6 Will he plead against me with *his* great power? No; but he would put *strength* in me.

7 There the righteous might dispute with him; so should I be delivered for ever from my judge.

8 Behold, I go forward, but he *is* not *there;* and backward, but I cannot perceive him:

9 On the left hand, where he doth work, but I cannot behold *him;* he hideth himself on the right hand, that I cannot see *him;*

10 But he knoweth the way that I take: *when* he hath tried me, I shall come forth as gold.

11 My foot hath held his steps, his way have I kept, and not declined.

12 Neither have I gone back from the commandment of his lips; I have esteemed the words of his mouth more than my necessary *food.*

13 But he *is* in one *mind,* and who can turn him? and *what* his soul desireth, even *that* he doeth.

14 For he performeth *the thing that is* appointed for me: and many such *things are* with him.

15 Therefore am I troubled at his presence: when I consider, I am afraid of him.

16 For God maketh my heart soft, and the Almighty troubleth me:

17 Because I was not cut off before the darkness, *neither* hath he covered the darkness from my face.

CHAPTER 24

WHY, seeing times are not hidden from the Almighty, do they that know him not see his days?

2 *Some* remove the landmarks; they violently take away flocks, and feed *thereof.*

3 They drive away the ass of the fatherless, they take the widow's ox for a pledge.

4 They turn the needy out of the way: the poor of the earth hide themselves together.

5 Behold, *as* wild asses in the desert, go they forth to their work; rising betimes for a prey: the wilderness *yieldeth* food for them *and* for *their* children.

6 They reap *every one* his corn in the field: and they gather the vintage of the wicked.

7 They cause the naked to lodge without clothing, that *they* have no covering in the cold.

8 They are wet with the showers of the mountains, and embrace the rock for want of a shelter.

9 They pluck the fatherless from the breast, and take a pledge of the poor.

2. Job's third reply to Eliphaz. 23:1-24:25.

23:1-9. Job's search for the hidden, or silent, God continues; and he repeats his desire to present his case before God as a lawyer would (vss. 2-4), not only to defend his innocence but to hear what God would say in reply to clear up the problem of why that haunts Job (vs. 5). Of course, God does not always respond in the way we desire, especially if we seek Him with an improper attitude or for the wrong reason. For those of us who stand on this side of the cross and empty tomb, the remoteness of God has ended. In Jesus Christ God has revealed Himself clearly.

10-17. Job felt he had been faithful to God; and when tried, he would come through it all **as gold.** Since this was true, and the darkness he was experiencing must also be from God, he was left confused and afraid. **Because I was not cut off before the darkness, neither hath he covered the darkness from my face.**

24:1-11. New insights are gained into the ethical standards of the day in this chapter, which is basically a list of crimes and is thus a description of criminals as perceived in Job's day. The moral standards are seen to be amazingly high, and the arguments show a remarkable degree of sensitivity to the plight of the poor and defenseless. Job asks why God doesn't set a time of judgment when all is revealed since many of God's people never see the promised hour of vindication and retribution fall upon the unrighteous. Of course, there will be such a day; but Job wants to see it happen immediately.

10 They cause *him* to go naked without clothing, and they take away the sheaf *from* the hungry;

11 *Which* make oil within their walls, *and* tread *their* winepresses, and suffer thirst.

12 Men groan from out of the city, and the soul of the wounded crieth out: yet God layeth not folly *to them.*

13 They are of those that rebel against the light; they know not the ways thereof, nor abide in the paths thereof.

14 The murderer rising with the light killeth the poor and needy, and in the night is as a thief.

15 The eye also of the adulterer waiteth for the twilight, saying, No eye shall see me: and disguiseth *his* face.

16 In the dark they dig through houses, *which* they had marked for themselves in the daytime: they know not the light.

17 For the morning *is* to them even as the shadow of death: if *one* know *them,* they *are in* the terrors of the shadow of death.

18 He *is* swift as the waters; their portion is cursed in the earth: he beholdeth not the way of the vineyards.

19 Drought and heat consume the snow waters: *so doth* the grave *those which* have sinned.

20 The womb shall forget him; the worm shall feed sweetly on him; he shall be no more remembered; and wickedness shall be broken as a tree.

21 He evil entreateth the barren *that* beareth not: and doeth not good to the widow.

22 He draweth also the mighty with his power: he riseth up, and no *man* is sure of life.

23 *Though* it be given him *to be* in safety, whereon he resteth; yet his eyes *are* upon their ways.

24 They are exalted for a little while, but are gone and brought low; they are taken out of the way as all *other,* and cut off as the tops of the ears of corn.

25 And if *it be* not *so* now, who will make me a liar, and make my speech nothing worth?

CHAPTER 25

THEN answered Bildad the Shū'hīte, and said,

2 Dominion and fear *are* with him, he maketh peace in his high places.

3 Is there any number of his armies? and upon whom doth not his light arise?

4 How then can man be justified with God? or how can he be clean *that is* born of a woman?

5 Behold even to the moon, and it shineth not; yea, the stars are not pure in his sight.

6 How much less man, *that is* a worm? and the son of man, *which is* a worm?

CHAPTER 26

BUT Job answered and said,

2 How hast thou helped *him that is* without power? *how* savest thou the arm *that hath* no strength?

12-17. The children of darkness are evil men who sin under cover of night, and darkness symbolizes their wickedness. Light is seen as representing goodness and decency.

18-25. A change takes place. Job is quoting back Eliphaz's argument to him, so verse 18 should begin, "You say that" (implied), so that the transition is clear. Job repeats the standard argument they had used against him, that the success of evil men was more apparent than real and in any case, was of short duration. Job disagrees with this position, as he has stated repeatedly throughout the book, then closes with the challenge that his position conforms more to reality than theirs. And if that is not so, prove it! **Who will make me a liar . . . ?**

3. Bildad's third speech. 25:1-6.

Some scholars question the arrangement of much of the material found in chapters 25-31. However, they disagree among themselves as to how best to rectify the problem; and there are as many different rearrangements as commentators.

25:1-6. Bildad's brief reply adds nothing new to the discussion. He merely repeats an argument found many times already: Since God is so mighty, and man is but **a worm** in comparison (vs. 6), how does Job dare to stand before God and claim to be clean? Even the stars could not make such a claim (vs. 5).

With Bildad's last resort to the holiness and sovereignty of God as a clinching argument, the speeches of the three friends come to an end.

4. Job's third reply to Bildad. 26:1-14.

The arguments which insist that 26:1-14 are dislocated are not compelling. They are entirely appropriate to the development of the discussion.

26:1-4. Job replies to Bildad in a very sarcastic tone, implying that Bildad seems to think God would be **without power** if he didn't help Him, lacking in **strength** and **wisdom,** and in need of human defenders. Job then raises the question of the source

3 How hast thou counselled *him that hath* no wisdom? and *how* hast thou plentifully declared the thing as it is?

4 To whom hast thou uttered words? and whose spirit came from thee?

5 Dead *things* are formed from under the waters, and the inhabitants thereof.

6 Hell *is* naked before him, and destruction hath no covering.

7 He stretcheth out the north over the empty place, *and* hangeth the earth upon nothing.

8 He bindeth up the waters in his thick clouds; and the cloud is not rent under them.

9 He holdeth back the face of his throne, *and* spreadeth his cloud upon it.

10 He hath compassed the waters with bounds, until the day and night come to an end.

11 The pillars of heaven tremble and are astonished at his reproof.

12 He divideth the sea with his power, and by his understanding he smiteth through the proud.

13 By his spirit he hath garnished the heavens; his hand hath formed the crooked serpent.

14 Lo, these *are* parts of his ways: but how little a portion is heard of him? but the thunder of his power who can understand?

CHAPTER 27

MOREOVER Job continued his parable, and said,

2 *As* God liveth, *who* hath taken away my judgment; and the Almighty, *who* hath vexed my soul;

3 All the while my breath *is* in me, and the spirit of God *is* in my nostrils;

4 My lips shall not speak wickedness, nor my tongue utter deceit.

5 God forbid that I should justify you: till I die I will not remove mine integrity from me.

6 My righteousness I hold fast, and will not let it go: my heart shall not reproach *me* so long as I live.

7 Let mine enemy be as the wicked, and he that riseth up against me as the unrighteous.

8 For what *is* the hope of the hypocrite, though he hath gained, when God taketh away his soul?

9 Will God hear his cry when trouble cometh upon him?

10 Will he delight himself in the Almighty? will he always call upon God?

11 I will teach you by the hand of God: *that* which *is* with the Almighty will I not conceal.

12 Behold, all ye yourselves have seen *it*; why then are ye thus altogether vain?

13 This *is* the portion of a wicked man with God, and the heritage of oppressors, *which* they shall receive of the Almighty.

14 If his children be multiplied, *it is* for the sword: and his offspring shall not be satisfied with bread.

15 Those that remain of him shall be buried in death: and his widows shall not weep.

16 Though he heap up silver as the dust, and prepare raiment as the clay;

17 He may prepare *it*, but the just

of Bildad's counsel. Whose **spirit,** or literally breath, is behind such words?

5-14. These verses constitute an impressive display of Job's understanding of the greatness, power, and majesty of God, and reinforce Job's insistence that he does not need his friends' wisdom on this matter. God's power extends over the living and dead, north and south, sun and moon, the clouds and waters, and all this is but **how little a portion** of His power. **Who can understand?**

5. Job's last reply to Bildad and his friends collectively. 27:1-31:40.

27:1-6. Zophar declines to reply a third time, so Job speaks up once again in what becomes his final speech of the dialogue section of the book. Job makes it clear that he is still innocent of the charges of wrongdoing brought against him by his three friends, and he has no intention of changing his position now.

7-23. The seeming prosperity of the wicked is not what it appears. Some scholars attribute this passage to Zophar and find in these verses at least part of his missing third speech. However, it is more likely to be Job speaking; and the plural structure reflects that more than one person is being addressed, which would not be the case if Zophar were speaking to Job. Job may well have in mind the unbending **wicked** (vs. 7) men who called him wicked. The hopeless plight of evil men is described here in vivid detail, and their seeming prosperity is seen to be fleeting. The traditional symbols of prosperity are heaped upon the wicked in this poetic section, e.g., children, money, houses, and then taken away one by one as in the end **Terrors take hold on him as waters** (vs. 20). In these verses Job takes many of the accusations his friends had brought against him and hurls them back at his visitors, saying in effect, Yes, I agree as to the fate of wicked men, but if anyone here needs to be reminded of the fate of wrongdoers it is you, not me.

shall put *it* on, and the innocent shall divide the silver.

18 He buildeth his house as a moth, and as a booth *that* the keeper maketh.

19 The rich man shall lie down, but he shall not be gathered: he openeth his eyes, and he *is* not.

20 Terrors take hold on him as waters, a tempest stealeth him away in the night.

21 The east wind carrieth him away, and he departeth: and as a storm hurleth him out of his place.

22 For *God* shall cast upon him, and not spare: he would fain flee out of his hand.

23 *Men* shall clap their hands at him, and shall hiss him out of his place.

CHAPTER 28

SURELY there is a vein for the silver, and a place for gold *where* they fine *it*.

2 Iron is taken out of the earth, and brass *is* molten *out of* the stone.

3 He setteth an end to darkness, and searcheth out all perfection: the stones of darkness, and the shadow of death.

4 The flood breaketh out from the inhabitant: *even the waters* forgotten of the foot: they are dried up, they are gone away from men.

5 *As for* the earth, out of it cometh bread: and under it is turned up as it were fire.

6 The stones of it *are* the place of sapphires: and it hath dust of gold.

7 *There is* a path which no fowl knoweth, and which the vulture's eye hath not seen:

8 The lion's whelps have not trodden it, nor the fierce lion passed by it.

9 He putteth forth his hand upon the rock; he overturneth the mountains by the roots.

10 He cutteth out rivers among the rocks; and his eye seeth every precious thing.

11 He bindeth the floods from overflowing; and *the thing that is* hid bringeth he forth to light.

12 But where shall wisdom be found? and where *is* the place of understanding?

13 Man knoweth not the price thereof; neither is it found in the land of the living.

14 The depth saith, It *is* not in me: and the sea saith, *It is* not with me.

15 It cannot be gotten for gold, neither shall silver be weighed *for* the price thereof.

16 It cannot be valued with the gold of Ōphir, with the precious onyx, or the sapphire.

17 The gold and the crystal cannot equal it: and the exchange of it *shall not be for* jewels of fine gold.

18 No mention shall be made of coral, or of pearls: for the price of wisdom *is* above rubies.

19 The topaz of Ē-thĭ-ō'pĭ-a shall not equal it, neither shall it be valued with pure gold.

20 Whence then cometh wisdom? and where *is* the place of understanding?

21 Seeing it is hid from the eyes of all

28:1-28. The first eleven verses are a poetic cataloging of various metals and precious stones and how they are acquired, leading up to the key verse of the chapter, **But where shall wisdom be found? And where is the place of understanding?** (vs. 12). The reader is then assured that true wisdom is beyond price and cannot be purchased, but has its source in God (vss. 23-28). The questions raised in verse 12 are finally answered in verse 28: **Behold, the fear of the LORD, that is wisdom; and to depart from evil is understanding.**

living, and kept close from the fowls of the air.

22 Destruction and death say, We have heard the fame thereof with our ears.

23 God understandeth the way thereof, and he knoweth the place thereof.

24 For he looketh to the ends of the earth, *and* seeth under the whole heaven;

25 To make the weight for the winds; and he weigheth the waters by measure.

26 When he made a decree for the rain, and a way for the lightning of the thunder:

27 Then did he see it, and declare it; he prepared it, yea, and searched it out.

28 And unto man he said, Behold, the fear of the Lord, that *is* wisdom; and to depart from evil *is* understanding.

CHAPTER 29

MOREOVER Job continued his parable, and said,

2 Oh that I were as *in* months past, as *in* the days *when* God preserved me;

3 When his candle shined upon my head, *and when* by his light I walked *through* darkness;

4 As I was in the days of my youth, when the secret of God *was* upon my tabernacle;

5 When the Almighty *was* yet with me, *when* my children *were* about me;

6 When I washed my steps with butter, and the rock poured me out rivers of oil;

7 When I went out to the gate through the city, *when* I prepared my seat in the street!

8 The young men saw me, and hid themselves: and the aged arose, *and* stood up.

9 The princes refrained talking, and laid *their* hand on their mouth.

10 The nobles held their peace, and their tongue cleaved to the roof of their mouth.

11 When the ear heard *me,* then it blessed me; and when the eye saw *me,* it gave witness to me:

12 Because I delivered the poor that cried, and the fatherless, and *him that had* none to help him.

13 The blessing of him that was ready to perish came upon me: and I caused the widow's heart to sing for joy.

14 I put on righteousness, and it clothed me: my judgment *was* as a robe and a diadem.

15 I was eyes to the blind, and feet *was* I to the lame.

16 I *was* a father to the poor: and the cause *which* I knew not I searched out.

17 And I brake the jaws of the wicked, and plucked the spoil out of his teeth.

18 Then I said, I shall die in my nest,

29:1. In chapter 29 Job recalls his former happiness. The first verse of this chapter introduces chapters 29 and 30, which are contrasted; chapter 29 speaks of Job's past prosperity, while chapter 30 bewails his present suffering. Job feels cut off from both God and man; but it was not always so, as he tells us so eloquently in this chapter. It is not clear if he is addressing God or his three friends; maybe both, maybe neither. A number of writers have aptly called this passage Job's soliloquy.

2-6. Job speaks of former material blessings. He feels very much alone. His children are all dead; his wealth is gone; he stands abandoned by God and misunderstood by wife and friends. A black wave of self-pity sweeps over him, and he tries to fight off depression by recalling happier times. In these six verses he speaks of former material blessings.

7-10. Job speaks of former greatness. Young and old, rich and poor, respected Job and showed deference to him. **When I went out to the gate . . . The nobles held their peace.** He was truly one of the greatest men of the East (see also vss. 21-25).

11-20. Job speaks of former social concern. Job was not an amoral Oriental despot. He did not gain his former wealth dishonestly, nor by exploiting the poor and weak. His comments reflect a sense of morality and social conscience that escapes most wealthy men of our day. He was the defender, deliverer, liberator, advocate of the poor (vss. 12, 16), fatherless (vs. 12), widow (vs. 13), lame and blind (vs. 15). Job was a friend to the most needy and defenseless elements of society. At the same time, he opposed evil men and prospered. The world says the way to get ahead is just the opposite; yet his enemies did not contradict any of these claims.

and I shall multiply *my* days as the sand.

19 My root *was* spread out by the waters, and the dew lay all night upon my branch.

20 My glory *was* fresh in me, and my bow was renewed in my hand.

21 Unto me *men* gave ear, and waited, and kept silence at my counsel.

22 After my words they spake not again; and my speech dropped upon them.

23 And they waited for me as for the rain; and they opened their mouth wide *as* for the latter rain.

24 *If* I laughed on them, they believed *it* not; and the light of my countenance they cast not down.

25 I chose out their way, and sat chief, and dwelt as a king in the army, as one *that* comforteth the mourners.

21-25. Job's former greatness is reemphasized as he speaks of the kind of power and prestige that other people only dream of. **He sat chief, and dwelt as a king,** even among the nobles of his people.

CHAPTER 30

BUT now *they that are* younger than I have me in derision, whose fathers I would have disdained to have set with the dogs of my flock.

2 Yea, whereto *might* the strength of their hands *profit* me, in whom old age was perished?

3 For want and famine *they were* solitary; fleeing into the wilderness in former time desolate and waste.

4 Who cut up mallows by the bushes, and juniper roots *for* their meat.

5 They were driven forth from among *men*, (they cried after them as *after* a thief;)

6 To dwell in the cliffs of the valleys, *in* caves of the earth, and *in* the rocks.

7 Among the bushes they brayed; under the nettles they were gathered together.

8 *They were* children of fools, yea, children of base men: they were viler than the earth.

9 And now am I their song, yea, I am their byword.

10 They abhor me, they flee far from me, and spare not to spit in my face.

11 Because he hath loosed my cord, and afflicted me, they have also let loose the bridle before me.

12 Upon *my* right *hand* rise the youth; they push away my feet, and they raise up against me the ways of their destruction.

13 They mar my path, they set forward my calamity, they have no helper.

14 They came *upon me* as a wide breaking in *of waters:* in the desolation they rolled themselves *upon me.*

15 Terrors are turned upon me: they pursue my soul as the wind: and my welfare passeth away as a cloud.

16 And now my soul is poured out upon me; the days of affliction have taken hold upon me.

17 My bones are pierced in me in the night season: and my sinews take no rest.

18 By the great force *of my disease* is my garment changed: it bindeth me about as the collar of my coat.

19 He hath cast me into the mire, and I am become like dust and ashes.

20 I cry unto thee, and thou dost not

30:1-31. Job speaks of his present suffering. **But now** sets the stage for the contrast between his past prosperity and his present pathetic state. **They that are younger . . . whose fathers I would have disdained.** From the chief of princes, Job is now the object of contempt and cruel pranks by the most useless elements of society. The remainder of the chapter is another lament as Job recites in vivid language the agony of his physical suffering. In addition to that, we see again his mental and emotional alienation, as well as anguish, in realizing that although he reached out before to the needy and downtrodden, they do not now reach out in sympathy to him (vss. 24-26). Job stands fast. Rejected by his former wealthy colleagues, scorned by the poor as not really one of them, abandoned by his wife, and seemingly unable to communicate with God, Job is finally about to cave in and say whatever is necessary to save himself. But Job refuses! He again lifts his head, reaffirms his integrity, and stands fast.

hear me: I stand up, and thou regardest me *not*.

21 Thou art become cruel to me: with thy strong hand thou opposest thyself against me.

22 Thou liftest me up to the wind; thou causest me to ride *upon it*, and dissolvest my substance.

23 For I know *that* thou wilt bring me to death, and *to* the house appointed for all living.

24 Howbeit he will not stretch out *his* hand to the grave, though they cry in his destruction.

25 Did not I weep for him that was in trouble? was *not* my soul grieved for the poor?

26 When I looked for good, then evil came *unto me:* and when I waited for light, there came darkness.

27 My bowels boiled, and rested not: the days of affliction prevented me.

28 I went mourning without the sun: I stood up, *and* I cried in the congregation.

29 I am a brother to dragons, and a companion to owls.

30 My skin is black upon me, and my bones are burned with heat.

31 My harp also is *turned* to mourning, and my organ into the voice of them that weep.

CHAPTER 31

I MADE a covenant with mine eyes: why then should I think upon a maid?

2 For what portion of God *is there* from above? and *what* inheritance of the Almighty from on high?

3 *Is* not destruction to the wicked? and a strange *punishment* to the workers of iniquity?

4 Doth not he see my ways, and count all my steps?

5 If I have walked with vanity, or if my foot hath hasted to deceit;

6 Let me be weighed in an even balance that God may know mine integrity.

7 If my step hath turned out of the way, and mine heart walked after mine eyes, and if any blot hath cleaved to mine hands;

8 *Then* let me sow, and let another eat; yea, let my offspring be rooted out.

9 If mine heart have been deceived by a woman, or *if* I have laid wait at my neighbour's door;

10 *Then* let my wife grind unto another, and let others bow down upon her.

11 For this *is* an heinous crime; yea, it *is* an iniquity *to be punished by* the judges.

12 For it *is* a fire *that* consumeth to destruction, and would root out all mine increase.

13 If I did despise the cause of my manservant or of my maidservant, when they contended with me;

14 What then shall I do when God riseth up? and when he visiteth, what shall I answer him?

15 Did not he that made me in the womb make him? and did not one fashion us in the womb?

16 If I have withheld the poor from

Chapter 31 is a series of oaths, called oaths of innocence (see Ex 22:10-11; Num 5:11-31; I Kgs 8:31-32; Ps 7:3-5). There was in ancient Israel the custom, or law, that required anyone who claimed to be innocent when he was accused of a crime to go to the sanctuary and take the oath of innocence. Job swears his innocence and calls down God's wrath upon himself if he does not tell the truth. We have here one of the highest standards of ethical behavior found in Scripture, plus the realization that sinful acts begin in the heart. Job not only declares his innocence of the offenses leveled at him by his three accusers, he adds inner thoughts and attitudes more difficult to detect and reflecting his high standards toward unseen sins, too.

"He has been sensitive to the deeper and less obvious forms of unethical behavior to which even good men are liable. He has been free from the arrogance that comes with wealth. He has never rejoiced in the discomfiture of his foes. He has not feared the tyranny of the mob, nor has he been ashamed to confess his errors in public. The outer integrity of his actions has been a reflection of the inner probity of his spirit" (Gordis, p. 339).

31:1-4. Sexual morality. Covenant with mine eyes conveys the truth that lustful acts are preceded by lustful looks and thoughts. Job determined in his heart to exercise the will power necessary not to think lustful thoughts about young maidens. He disciplined himself not to take the second look that leads to lust. The verb used here does not mean to "glance briefly," but rather to "gaze, stare or look intently."

5-8. Business ethics. The word **vanity** here would be better translated deceitfulness, lying, falsehood or trickery and probably has reference to deceptive or dishonest business practices. Verse 7 seems to imply taking bribes or some other unethical way of getting ahead, taking the possessions of others, such as small objects that **cleaved to mine hands.**

9-12. Adultery. Job seems to imply sexual sin with a married woman here, rather than the young maid of verse 1. If he had done such a thing, his wife might be made the servant and concubine of another. **This is a heinous crime.**

13-15. Treatment of employees. This is a remarkably enlightened passage for the time, showing that Job knew he must answer to God for his treatment of servants. **What then shall I do when God riseth up? And when he visiteth, what shall I answer him?** They were not by nature inferior to him; the same God made them all. Thus, Job denies having taken advantage of his servants in any way.

16-23. Social concern. Job denies having exploited the poor, widows, fatherless, or any other sort of disadvantaged person.

their desire, or have caused tne eyes of the widow to fail;

17 Or have eaten my morsel myself alone, and the fatherless hath not eaten thereof;

18 (For from my youth he was brought up with me, as *with* a father, and I have guided her from my mother's womb;)

19 If I have seen any perish for want of clothing, or any poor without covering;

20 If his loins have not blessed me, and *if* he were *not* warmed with the fleece of my sheep;

21 If I have lifted up my hand against the fatherless, when I saw my help in the gate:

22 *Then* let mine arm fall from my shoulder blade, and mine arm be broken from the bone.

23 For destruction *from* God *was* a terror to me, and by reason of his highness I could not endure.

24 If I have made gold my hope, or have said to the fine gold, *Thou art* my confidence;

25 If I rejoiced because my wealth *was* great, and because mine hand had gotten much;

26 If I beheld the sun when it shined, or the moon walking *in* brightness;

27 And my heart hath been secretly enticed, or my mouth hath kissed my hand:

28 This also *were* an iniquity *to be punished by* the judge: for I should have denied the God *that is* above.

29 If I rejoiced at the destruction of him that hated me, or lifted up myself when evil found him:

30 Neither have I suffered my mouth to sin by wishing a curse to his soul.

31 If the men of my tabernacle said not, Oh that we had of his flesh! we cannot be satisfied.

32 The stranger did not lodge in the street: *but* I opened my doors to the traveller.

33 If I covered my transgressions as Adam, by hiding mine iniquity in my bosom:

34 Did I fear a great multitude, or did the contempt of families terrify me, that I kept silence, *and* went not out of the door?

35 Oh that one would hear me! behold, my desire *is,* that the Almighty would answer me, and *that* mine adversary had written a book.

36 Surely I would take it upon my shoulder, *and* bind it *as* a crown to me.

37 I would declare unto him the number of my steps; as a prince would I go near unto him.

38 If my land cry against me, or that the furrows likewise thereof complain;

39 If I have eaten the fruits thereof without money, or have caused the owners thereof to lose their life:

40 Let thistles grow instead of wheat, and cockle instead of barley. The words of Job are ended.

To the contrary, he asserts he has shared his goods and food with them. He also acknowledges that all men will be judged by God concerning this very matter, as well as other sins (vss. 23, 28).

24-25. Greed. Continuing with his rhetorical questions as an oath of innocence, Job denies a spirit of greed concerning his wealth in general, and gold in particular. He refutes the idea that he hoarded wealth like a miser and used it to oppress others.

26-28. Idolatry. The worship of sun and moon is the only matter in this chapter not directly related to interpersonal relations and ethical standards. Some writers think that the gold and wealth of verses 24-25 should be joined to these verses as a form of idolatry, however. The object of our worship is not totally unrelated to morality, however; and Job denies that he made gold his god, or that he worshiped nature and heavenly bodies as his pagan neighbors. If he had he would **have denied the God that is above.**

29-32. Generosity. Job states that he has not gloated over the misfortunes of his enemies (vs. 29), nor wished them dead through curse or incantation (vs. 30). It is likely that verses 31-32 refer to Job's hospitality to strangers and travelers. Some see a denial of any homosexual activities ever happening in Job's tent. The implication is that if travelers were forced to sleep in the streets at night they might be attacked by degenerate men. However, Job always gave them food, shelter and protection. **I opened my doors to the traveler.**

33-34. Courage. Job maintains he has the inner strength and courage to admit when he is wrong (vs. 33) and not to cover his **transgressions as Adam.** He further states that neither fear of the crowd nor peer pressure have ever kept him from speaking out against evil (vs. 34).

35-37. Job again appeals to God to judge if all he has said is true or not. **That mine adversary had written a book.** He does not fear the verdict; rather, he would like to have it in writing so that he could display it proudly. Job would answer any questions and declare to God anything He might wish to ask about his life.

38-40. Let thistles grow instead of wheat. Job repeats his willingness to suffer the consequences if all he has said in his defense is not true. **The words of Job are ended.**

III. THE INTERVENTION OF ELIHU. 32:1-37:24.

A. Elihu's Anger. 32:1-22.

The next six chapters record the intervention of a young man not mentioned before. Great pains are taken to establish his

CHAPTER 32

SO these three men ceased to answer Job, because he *was* righteous in his own eyes.

2 Then was kindled the wrath of E-lī′hū the son of Băr′a-chĕl the Bū′zīte, of the kindred of Ram: against Job was his wrath kindled, because he justified himself rather than God.

3 Also against his three friends was his wrath kindled, because they had found no answer, and *yet* had condemned Job.

4 Now E-lī′hū had waited till Job had spoken, because they *were* elder than he.

5 When E-lī′hū saw that *there was* no answer in the mouth of *these* three men, then his wrath was kindled.

6 And E-lī′hū the son of Băr′a-chĕl the Bū′zīte answered and said, I *am* young, and ye *are* very old; wherefore I was afraid, and durst not shew you mine opinion.

7 I said, Days should speak, and multitude of years should teach wisdom.

8 But *there is* a spirit in man: and the inspiration of the Almighty giveth them understanding.

9 Great men are not *always* wise: neither do the aged understand judgment.

10 Therefore I said, Hearken to me; I also will shew mine opinion.

11 Behold, I waited for your words; I gave ear to your reasons, whilst ye searched out what to say.

12 Yea, I attended unto you, and, behold, *there was* none of you that convinced Job, *or* that answered his words:

13 Lest ye should say, We have found out wisdom: God thrusteth him down, not man.

14 Now he hath not directed *his* words against me: neither will I answer him with your speeches.

15 They were amazed, they answered no more: they left off speaking.

16 When I had waited, (for they spake not, but stood still, *and* answered no more;)

17 *I said,* I will answer also my part, I also will shew mine opinion.

18 For I am full of matter, the spirit within me constraineth me.

19 Behold, my belly *is* as wine *which* hath no vent; it is ready to burst like new bottles.

20 I will speak, that I may be refreshed: I will open my lips and answer.

21 Let me not, I pray you, accept any man's person, neither let me give flattering titles unto man.

22 For I know not to give flattering titles; *in so doing* my maker would soon take me away.

CHAPTER 33

WHEREFORE, Job, I pray thee, hear

identity as a real person, and not a mere symbol in a religious parable.

32:1-5. Elihu, the son of Barachel the Buzite, of the kindred of Ram. Elihu seems to be one of many onlookers who have been listening intently to the running debate between Job and his three friends. A brief silence has settled over the group as Job has finished his defense; and the other three men decline to argue further, seeing that Job continues to maintain his innocence no matter what they say. The impetuous, idealistic, young Elihu can stand it no longer and breaks the silence. The fact that he is angry with the lack of progress in the proceedings is mentioned four times in the first five verses. He is not only angry with Job for questioning God's justice, but also with Job's three friends for defending God's honor so poorly. The three friends have maintained that God is just and suffering is the result of sin. Job is suffering; therefore, Job has sinned. Based on his own experience, Job has come to deny all of that: he has not sinned, but is suffering; therefore, God is unjust. Elihu tries to stake out the middle ground between the two extremes. His main thesis is that God is always just, and suffering is sometimes the result of sin; but sometimes God uses suffering to discipline or instruct basically sincere and good persons.

6-22. Elihu knows his culture well enough to understand that his youth is against him in this situation. The elders are assumed to be wiser than the young, so he begins with an apology for daring to intervene in a discussion among elders. But he couldn't help himself. He felt that both sides had missed some opportunities to make good points, and that both sides were defending too narrow a position. He was about to burst in his frustration and eagerness to get into the fray (vss. 19-20). Elihu concludes his opening speech with the promise not to take sides in the debate (vss. 21-22).

B. Elihu Addresses Job: God Uses Pain to Chasten Men. 33:1-33.

33:1-33. Elihu turns his attention to Job now and his address

my speeches, and hearken to all my words.

2 Behold, now I have opened my mouth, my tongue hath spoken in my mouth.

3 My words *shall be of* the uprightness of my heart: and my lips shall utter knowledge clearly.

4 The spirit of God hath made me, and the breath of the Almighty hath given me life.

5 If thou canst answer me, set *thy words* in order before me, stand up.

6 Behold, I *am* according to thy wish in God's stead: I also am formed out of the clay.

7 Behold, my terror shall not make thee afraid, neither shall my hand be heavy upon thee.

8 Surely thou hast spoken in mine hearing, and I have heard the voice of *thy* words, *saying*,

9 I am clean without transgression, I *am* innocent; neither *is there* iniquity in me.

10 Behold, he findeth occasions against me, he counteth me for his enemy,

11 He putteth my feet in the stocks, he marketh all my paths.

12 Behold, *in* this thou art not just: I will answer thee, that God is greater than man.

13 Why dost thou strive against him? for he giveth not account of any of his matters.

14 For God speaketh once, yea twice, *yet man* perceiveth it not.

15 In a dream, in a vision of the night, when deep sleep falleth upon men, in slumberings upon the bed;

16 Then he openeth the ears of men, and sealeth their instruction,

17 That he may withdraw man *from his* purpose, and hide pride from man.

18 He keepeth back his soul from the pit, and his life from perishing by the sword.

19 He is chastened also with pain upon his bed, and the multitude of his bones with strong *pain*:

20 So that his life abhorreth bread, and his soul dainty meat.

21 His flesh is consumed away, that it cannot be seen; and his bones *that* were not seen stick out.

22 Yea, his soul draweth near unto the grave, and his life to the destroyers.

23 If there be a messenger with him, an interpreter, one among a thousand, to shew unto man his uprightness:

24 Then he is gracious unto him, and saith, Deliver him from going down to the pit: I have found a ransom.

25 His flesh shall be fresher than a child's: he shall return to the days of his youth:

26 He shall pray unto God, and he will be favourable unto him: and he shall see his face with joy: for he will render unto man his righteousness.

27 He looketh upon men, and *if any* say, I have sinned, and perverted *that which was* right, and it profited me not;

28 He will deliver his soul from going into the pit, and his life shall see the light.

takes the form of a challenge. In vss. 4-7 Elihu assures Job that they are both human and that the same **Spirit of God** has formed them both of the same clay. He seems to be referring to Job's earlier charge that God intimidates him with threats of violence and terror rather than answer him (9:34; 13:21). Elihu assures Job that no such situation exists between them as two mortals; so let's see if Job can answer him. Elihu then enumerates some of the charges Job has made against God and says Job was wrong in each case. **God is greater than man** (vs. 12). It should not surprise anyone that God does not respond directly to all our questions, but it is not accurate to say that He is hidden and does not communicate with men, argues Elihu. He then mentions three ways in which God reveals Himself to man: (1) In dreams and visions (vss. 15-18); (2) by chastening man through pain and suffering (vss. 19-22); and (3) by heavenly messengers or angels (vss. 23-25). The purpose of God in all this is always good and just. God seeks to **Deliver him from going down to the pit** (vs. 24).

29 Lo, all these *things* worketh God oftentimes with man,

30 To bring back his soul from the pit, to be enlightened with the light of the living.

31 Mark well, O Job, hearken unto me: hold thy peace, and I will speak.

32 If thou hast anything to say, answer me: speak, for I desire to justify thee.

33 If not, hearken unto me: hold thy peace, and I shall teach thee wisdom.

CHAPTER 34

FURTHERMORE E-li′hū answered and said,

2 Hear my words, O ye wise *men;* and give ear unto me, ye that have knowledge.

3 For the ear trieth words, as the mouth tasteth meat.

4 Let us choose to us judgment: let us know among ourselves what *is* good.

5 For Job hath said, I am righteous: and God hath taken away my judgment.

6 Should I lie against my right? my wound *is* incurable without transgression.

7 What man *is* like Job, *who* drinketh up scorning like water?

8 Which goeth in company with the workers of iniquity, and walketh with wicked men.

9 For he hath said, It profiteth a man nothing that he should delight himself with God.

10 Therefore hearken unto me ye men of understanding: far be it from God, *that he should do* wickedness; and *from* the Almighty, *that he should commit* iniquity.

11 For the work of a man shall he render unto him, and cause every man to find according to *his* ways.

12 Yea, surely God will not do wickedly, neither will the Almighty pervert judgment.

13 Who hath given him a charge over the earth? or who hath disposed the whole world?

14 If he set his heart upon man *if* he gather unto himself his spirit and his breath;

15 All flesh shall perish together, and man shall turn again unto dust.

16 If now *thou hast* understanding, hear this: hearken to the voice of my words.

17 Shall even he that hateth right govern? and wilt thou condemn him that is most just?

18 *Is it fit* to say to a king, *Thou art* wicked? *and* to princes, *Ye are* ungodly?

19 *How much less to him* that accepteth not the persons of princes, nor regardeth the rich more than the poor? for they all *are* the work of his hands.

20 In a moment shall they die, and the people shall be troubled at midnight, and pass away: and the mighty shall be taken away without hand.

21 For his eyes *are* upon the ways of man, and he seeth all his goings.

22 *There is* no darkness, nor shadow

C. God Is Not Unjust. 34:1–35:16.

34:1-37. Elihu defends God's justice, and suspects that Job has questioned it to bolster his own pretended innocence. God could destroy all men if He chose (vss. 14-15) and is sovereign. As a general rule, men reap what they sow in this life. If God delays someone's punishment, it is for a reason. It may be because the misrule of evil princes constitutes in itself a penalty upon sinners, since these tyrants are instruments of God's justice at work in the destiny of individuals or nations. Or has Job considered that God may be seeking their genuine repentance through pain? How dare Job question all this? He thus **addeth rebellion unto his sin** (vs. 37). By arguing against God's justice, Job just makes things worse for himself. **He clappeth his hands among us** (vs. 37). He claps his hands against God is the sense, and that would be a sign of impatience or indignation in Job's culture. On top of all that, he **multiplieth his words against God** (vs. 37). Job has allowed his pain to turn him into a person with a rebellious spirit and a bad attitude, says Elihu.

of death, where the workers of iniquity may hide themselves.

23 For he will not lay upon man more *than right;* that he should enter into judgment with God.

24 He shall break in pieces mighty men without number, and set others in their stead.

25 Therefore he knoweth their works, and he overturneth *them* in the night, so that they are destroyed.

26 He striketh them as wicked men in the open sight of others;

27 Because they turned back from him, and would not consider any of his ways:

28 So that they cause the cry of the poor to come unto him, and he heareth the cry of the afflicted.

29 When he giveth quietness, who then can make trouble? and when he hideth *his* face, who then can behold him? whether *it be done* against a nation, or against a man only:

30 That the hypocrite reign not, lest the people be ensnared.

31 Surely it is meet to be said unto God, I have borne *chastisement,* I will not offend *any more:*

32 *That* which I see not teach thou me: if I have done iniquity, I will do no more.

33 *Should it be* according to thy mind? he will recompense it, whether thou refuse, or whether thou choose; and not I: therefore speak what thou knowest.

34 Let men of understanding tell me, and let a wise man hearken unto me.

35 Job hath spoken without knowledge, and his words *were* without wisdom.

36 My desire *is that* Job may be tried unto the end because of *his* answers for wicked men.

37 For he addeth rebellion unto his sin, he clappeth *his hands* among us, and multiplieth his words against God.

CHAPTER 35

E-LI'HU spake moreover, and said,

2 Thinkest thou this to be right, *that* thou saidst, My righteousness *is* more than God's?

3 For thou saidst, What advantage will it be unto thee? *and,* What profit shall I have, *if I be cleansed* from my sin?

4 I will answer thee, and thy companions with thee.

5 Look unto the heavens, and see; and behold the clouds *which* are higher than thou.

6 If thou sinnest, what doest thou against him? or *if* thy transgressions be multiplied, what doest thou unto him?

7 If thou be righteous, what givest thou him? or what receiveth he of thine hand?

8 Thy wickedness *may hurt* a man as thou *art;* and thy righteousness *may profit* the son of man.

9 By reason of the multitude of oppressions they make *the oppressed* to cry: they cry out by reason of the arm of the mighty.

10 But none saith, Where *is* God my maker, who giveth songs in the night;

35:1-16. Job has charged that it doesn't matter whether one is sinful or righteous and has cited his own case as an example; Elihu reminds him of those words and proceeds to deal with that problem (vss. 1-3). He feels that Job's three friends failed to deal with that issue adequately when it came up earlier; so he wants them to listen, too (vs. 4). Elihu then calls their attention to the heavens and reminds them that God is so mighty that He has nothing to gain or lose, thus no ulterior motive, in regard to man's behavior (vss. 5-7). However, other people are affected by our deeds, for good or ill (vs. 8). As to the delay, or even lack of help from God when the oppressed cry out, Elihu suggests they are simply unhappy because of pain but do not really want to turn to God or have closer fellowship with Him (vs. 10). Their motives are unworthy; and when freed, they merely return to their evil living as before. They forget God's former blessings. They may be oppressed now and in pain, but they are basically evil men full of pride and vanity (vss. 12-13). If God does not respond to those who try to use Him but show no genuine repentance, then He will surely not listen to someone who calls Him unjust, either (vss. 14-16). Elihu implies that, like the proud and vain men mentioned above, Job is crying out from pain, but not piety. Job, of all people, should know better; but he, too, speaks **in vain** and **without knowledge** (vs. 16), concludes Elihu.

11 Who teacheth us more than the beasts of the earth, and maketh us wiser than the fowls of heaven?

12 There they cry, but none giveth answer, because of the pride of evil men.

13 Surely God will not hear vanity, neither will the Almighty regard it.

14 Although thou sayest thou shalt not see him, *yet* judgment *is* before him; therefore trust thou in him.

15 But now, because *it is* not *so,* he hath visited in his anger; yet he knoweth *it* not in great extremity:

16 Therefore doth Job open his mouth in vain; he multiplieth words without knowledge.

CHAPTER 36

E-Lǐ'HŬ also proceeded, and said,

2 Suffer me a little, and I will shew thee that *I have* yet to speak on God's behalf.

3 I will fetch my knowledge from afar, and will ascribe righteousness to my Maker.

4 For truly my words *shall* not *be* false: he that is perfect in knowledge *is* with thee.

5 Behold, God *is* mighty, and despiseth not *any: he is* mighty in strength *and* wisdom.

6 He preserveth not the life of the wicked: but giveth right to the poor.

7 He withdraweth not his eyes from the righteous: but with kings *are they* on the throne; yea, he doth establish them for ever, and they are exalted.

8 And if *they be* bound in fetters, *and* be holden in cords of affliction;

9 Then he sheweth them their work, and their transgressions that they have exceeded.

10 He openeth also their ear to discipline, and commandeth that they return from iniquity.

11 If they obey and serve *him,* they shall spend their days in prosperity, and their years in pleasures.

12 But if they obey not, they shall perish by the sword, and they shall die without knowledge.

13 But the hypocrites in heart heap up wrath: they cry not when he bindeth them.

14 They die in youth, and their life *is* among the unclean.

15 He delivereth the poor in his affliction, and openeth their ears in oppression.

16 Even so would he have removed thee out of the strait *into* a broad place, where *there is* no straitness: and that which should be set on thy table *should be* full of fatness.

17 But thou hast fulfilled the judgment of the wicked: judgment and justice take hold *on thee.*

18 Because *there is* wrath, *beware* lest he take thee away with *his* stroke: then a great ransom cannot deliver thee.

19 Will he esteem thy riches? *no,* not gold, nor all the forces of strength.

20 Desire not the night, when people are cut off in their place.

21 Take heed, regard not iniquity: for

D. God Is Just and Mighty. 36:1-37:24.

36:1-23. Elihu pauses to get his breath then requests their attention again, asking them to bear with him a little longer; for he is truly a wise man and still has important things to say (vss. 1-4). **God is mighty.** He knows each person's case, and understands (vs. 5). The **wicked** and the **poor** get what they have coming (vs. 6), and many **righteous** men have been **exalted** by God to positions of great authority (vs. 7). If they then suffer, it will be because they have sinned, probably through pride and arrogance; and God will reveal this to them (vss. 8-10). If they respond to God's instructions as they should, all will go well for them (vs. 11); but if they are disobedient, they will suffer the consequences (vss. 12-14). Elihu then applies the above principles to Job. He tries to convince Job that this is what God is attempting to teach him through his suffering (vss. 17-23).

this hast thou chosen rather than affliction.

22 Behold, God exalteth by his power: who teacheth like him?

23 Who hath enjoined him his way?
or who can say, Thou hast wrought iniquity?

24 Remember that thou magnify his
work, which men behold.

25 Every man may see it; man may
behold *it* afar off.

26 Behold, God *is* great, and we know
him not, neither can the number of his
years be searched out.

27 For he maketh small the drops of
water: they pour down rain according
to the vapour thereof:

28 Which the clouds do drop *and* distil upon man abundantly.

29 Also can *any* understand the
spreadings of the clouds, *or* the noise of
his tabernacle?

30 Behold, he spreadeth his light
upon it, and covereth the bottom of the
sea.

31 For by them judgeth he the people; he giveth meat in abundance.

32 With clouds he covereth the light;
and commandeth it *not to shine* by *the
cloud* that cometh betwixt.

33 The noise thereof sheweth concerning it, the cattle also concerning
the vapour.

CHAPTER 37

AT this also my heart trembleth, and is
moved out of his place.

2 Hear attentively the noise of his
voice, and the sound *that* goeth out of
his mouth.

3 He directeth it under the whole
heaven, and his lightning unto the ends
of the earth.

4 After it a voice roareth: he thundereth with the voice of his excellency;
and he will not stay them when his
voice is heard.

5 God thundereth marvellously with
his voice; great things doeth he, which
we cannot comprehend.

6 For he saith to the snow, Be thou *on*
the earth; likewise to the small rain,
and to the great rain of his strength.

7 He sealeth up the hand of every
man; that all men may know his work.

8 Then the beasts go into dens, and
remain in their places.

9 Out of the south cometh the whirlwind: and cold out of the north.

10 By the breath of God frost is given:
and the breadth of the waters is
straitened.

11 Also by watering he wearieth the
thick cloud: he scattereth his bright
cloud:

12 And it is turned round about by his
counsels: that they may do whatsoever
he commandeth them upon the face of
the world in the earth.

13 He causeth it to come, whether for
correction, or for his land, or for mercy.

14 Hearken unto this, O Job: stand
still, and consider the wondrous works
of God.

15 Dost thou know when God disposed them, and caused the light of his
cloud to shine?

24-37:24. The gathering clouds Elihu mentioned before have
produced a thunder shower and he now uses the rain, wind,
thunder, and lightning to illustrate God's power and glory.

16 Dost thou know the balancings of the clouds, the wondrous works of him which is perfect in knowledge?

17 How thy garments *are* warm, when he quieteth the earth by the south *wind?*

18 Hast thou with him spread out the sky, *which is* strong, *and* as a molten looking glass?

19 Teach us what we shall say unto him; *for* we cannot order *our speech* by reason of darkness.

20 Shall it be told him that I speak? if a man speak, surely he shall be swallowed up.

21 And now *men* see not the bright light which *is* in the clouds: but the wind passeth, and cleanseth them.

22 Fair weather cometh out of the north: with God *is* terrible majesty.

23 *Touching* the Almighty, we cannot find him out: *he is* excellent in power, and in judgment, and in plenty of justice: he will not afflict.

24 Men do therefore fear him: he respecteth not any *that are* wise of heart.

CHAPTER 38

THEN the LORD answered Job out of the whirlwind, and said,

2 Who *is* this that darkeneth counsel by words without knowledge?

3 Gird up now thy loins like a man: for I will demand of thee, and answer thou me.

4 Where wast thou when I laid the foundations of the earth? declare, if thou hast understanding.

5 Who hath laid the measures thereof, if thou knowest? or who hath stretched the line upon it?

6 Whereupon are the foundations thereof fastened? or who laid the corner stone thereof;

7 When the morning stars sang together, and all the sons of God shouted for joy?

8 Or *who* shut up the sea with doors, when it brake forth, *as if* it had issued out of the womb?

9 When I made the cloud the garment thereof, and thick darkness a swaddlingband for it,

10 And brake up for it my decreed *place*, and set bars and doors,

11 And said, Hitherto shalt thou come, but no further: and here shall thy proud waves be stayed?

12 Hast thou commanded the morning since thy days; *and* caused the dayspring to know his place;

13 That it might take hold of the ends of the earth, that the wicked might be shaken out of it?

14 It is turned as clay *to* the seal; and they stand as a garment.

15 And from the wicked their light is

IV. THE THEOPHANY: GOD SPEAKS. 38:1-42:6.

Job had, many times, expressed the desire to have God appear and answer his questions; but the heavens were silent. Now they are rent by a whirlwind, and Job's wish is granted; but the experience is not what Job had expected. True, the silence is broken; but God did not really answer Job's philosophical questions. He responded to the mystery of suffering with the mystery of Himself. God reveals Himself as Yahweh (JHWH) in this passage, which is one of many in which the Lord is associated with a whirlwind and/or thunder-lightning-storm-quake (Ex 19:16; Jud 5:4-5; II Sam 22:8-16; Ps 18:7-15; 50:3; 68:8; Nah 1:3-5; Hab 3:3-6; Zech 9:14).

A. God Challenges Job. 38:1-39:30.

38:1. Then the LORD answered Job out of the whirlwind, and said. God (Yahweh) spoke to Job directly; He did not speak to Elihu or the three friends though they probably heard the voice also and saw whatever Job saw. (God did speak to them a short time later, 42:7-9; they heard His voice and obeyed). Since God is a Spirit (Jn 4:24), the appearance would be similar to that found in Deuteronomy 4:12: "And the LORD spake unto you out of the midst of the fire: ye heard the voice of the words, but saw no similitude; only ye heard a voice."

2-3. God's first words were, in effect, "Who do you think you are, questioning Me?" No wasted small-talk or indirect approach. He continues, **Gird up now thy loins like a man; for I will demand of thee, and answer thou me.** Interpreted being "Here I come, ready or not!"

4-39:30. The rest of chapter 38 and all of chapter 39 are a relation of the mystery and grandeur of creation, and by implication the might and wisdom required of a God who could create such a universe. In contrast to all of this, man appears weak, finite, and very limited in understanding indeed. The comparison of the Creator's greatness and man's creatureliness is not lost on Job.

withholden, and the high arm shall be broken.

16 Hast thou entered into the springs of the sea? or hast thou walked in the search of the depth?

17 Have the gates of death been opened unto thee? or hast thou seen the doors of the shadow of death?

18 Hast thou perceived the breadth of the earth? declare if thou knowest it all.

19 Where *is* the way *where* light dwelleth? and *as for* darkness, where *is* the place thereof,

20 That thou shouldest take it to the bound thereof, and that thou shouldest know the paths *to* the house thereof ?

21 Knowest thou *it*, because thou wast then born? or *because* the number of thy days *is* great?

22 Hast thou entered into the treasures of the snow? or hast thou seen the treasures of the hail,

23 Which I have reserved against the time of trouble, against the day of battle and war?

24 By what way is the light parted, *which* scattereth the east wind upon the earth?

25 Who hath divided a watercourse for the overflowing of waters, or a way for the lightning of thunder;

26 To cause it to rain on the earth, *where* no man *is*; *on* the wilderness, wherein *there is* no man;

27 To satisfy the desolate and waste *ground*; and to cause the bud of the tender herb to spring forth?

28 Hath the rain a father? or who hath begotten the drops of dew?

29 Out of whose womb came the ice? and the hoary frost of heaven, who hath gendered it?

30 The waters are hid as *with* a stone, and the face of the deep is frozen.

31 Canst thou bind the sweet influences of Plē'ia-dēs, or loose the bands of Ō-rī'on?

32 Canst thou bring forth Măz'za-rŏth in his season? or canst thou guide Ärc-tū'rus with his sons?

33 Knowest thou the ordinances of heaven? canst thou set the dominion thereof in the earth?

34 Canst thou lift up thy voice to the clouds, that abundance of waters may cover thee?

35 Canst thou send lightnings, that they may go, and say unto thee, Here we *are*?

36 Who hath put wisdom in the inward parts? or who hath given understanding to the heart?

37 Who can number the clouds in wisdom? or who can stay the bottles of heaven,

38 When the dust groweth into hardness, and the clods cleave fast together?

39 Wilt thou hunt the prey for the lion? or fill the appetite of the young lions,

40 When they couch in *their* dens, *and* abide in the covert to lie in wait?

41 Who provideth for the raven his food? when his young ones cry unto God, they wander for lack of meat.

CHAPTER 39

KNOWEST thou the time when the wild goats of the rock bring forth? *or* canst thou mark when the hinds do calve?

2 Canst thou number the months *that* they fulfil? or knowest thou the time when they bring forth?

3 They bow themselves, they bring forth their young ones, they cast out their sorrows.

4 Their young ones are in good liking, they grow up with corn; they go forth, and return not unto them.

5 Who hath sent out the wild ass free? or who hath loosed the bands of the wild ass?

6 Whose house I have made the wilderness, and the barren land his dwellings.

7 He scorneth the multitude of the city, neither regardeth he the crying of the driver.

8 The range of the mountains *is* his pasture, and he searcheth after every green thing.

9 Will the unicorn be willing to serve thee, or abide by thy crib?

10 Canst thou bind the unicorn with his band in the furrow? or will he harrow the valleys after thee?

11 Wilt thou trust him, because his strength *is* great? or wilt thou leave thy labour to him?

12 Wilt thou believe him, that he will bring home thy seed, and gather *it into* thy barn?

13 *Gavest thou* the goodly wings unto the peacocks? or wings and feathers unto the ostrich?

14 Which leaveth her eggs in the earth, and warmeth them in dust,

15 And forgetteth that the foot may crush them, or that the wild beast may break them.

16 She is hardened against her young ones, as though *they were* not hers: her labour is in vain without fear;

17 Because God hath deprived her of wisdom, neither hath he imparted to her understanding.

18 What time she lifteth up herself on high, she scorneth the horse and his rider.

19 Hast thou given the horse strength? hast thou clothed his neck with thunder?

20 Canst thou make him afraid as a grasshopper? the glory of his nostrils *is* terrible.

21 He paweth in the valley, and rejoiceth in *his* strength: he goeth on to meet the armed men.

22 He mocketh at fear, and is not affrighted; neither turneth he back from the sword.

23 The quiver rattleth against him, the glittering spear and the shield.

24 He swalloweth the ground with fierceness and rage: neither believeth he that *it is* the sound of the trumpet.

25 He saith among the trumpets, Ha, ha; and he smelleth the battle afar off, the thunder of the captains, and the shouting.

26 Doth the hawk fly by thy wisdom,

and stretch her wings toward the south?

27 Doth the eagle mount up at thy command, and make her nest on high?

28 She dwelleth and abideth on the rock, upon the crag of the rock, and the strong place.

29 From thence she seeketh the prey, *and* her eyes behold afar off.

30 Her young ones also suck up blood: and where the slain *are*, there *is* she.

CHAPTER 40

MOREOVER the Lord answered Job, and said,

2 Shall he that contendeth with the Almighty instruct *him?* he that reproveth God, let him answer it.

3 ¶Then Job answered the Lord, and said,

4 Behold, I am vile; what shall I answer thee? I will lay mine hand upon my mouth.

5 Once have I spoken; but I will not answer: yea, twice; but I will proceed no further.

6 ¶Then answered the Lord unto Job out of the whirlwind, and said,

7 Gird up thy loins now like a man: I will demand of thee, and declare thou unto me.

8 Wilt thou also disannul my judgment? wilt thou condemn me, that thou mayest be righteous?

9 Hast thou an arm like God? or canst thou thunder with a voice like him?

10 Deck thyself now *with* majesty and excellency; and array thyself with glory and beauty.

11 Cast abroad the rage of thy wrath: and behold every one *that is* proud, and abase him.

12 Look on every one *that is* proud, *and* bring him low; and tread down the wicked in their place.

13 Hide them in the dust together; *and* bind their faces in secret.

14 Then will I also confess unto thee that thine own right hand can save thee.

15 ¶Behold now behemoth, which I made with thee; he eateth grass as an ox.

16 Lo now, his strength *is* in his loins, and his force *is* in the navel of his belly.

17 He moveth his tail like a cedar: the sinews of his stones are wrapped together.

18 His bones *are as* strong pieces of brass; his bones *are* like bars of iron.

19 He *is* the chief of the ways of God: he that made him can make his sword to approach *unto* him.

20 Surely the mountains bring him forth food, where all the beasts of the field play.

21 He lieth under the shady trees, in the covert of the reed, and fens.

22 The shady trees cover him *with* their shadow; the willows of the brook compass him about.

23 Behold, he drinketh up a river, *and* hasteth not: he trusteth that he can draw up Jordan into his mouth.

24 He taketh it with his eyes: *his* nose pierceth through snares.

B. Job's Humble Submission. 40:1-5.

40:1-5. The Lord pauses and asks Job to respond (vss. 1-2). **Shall he that contendeth with the Almighty instruct him?** Job is awed by God's majesty and puts his hand over his mouth, vowing to contend with God no more. **I will proceed no further.**

C. God's Second Speech. 40:6-41:34.

6-41:34. The Lord again speaks out of the whirlwind and accuses Job of playing God, even to the extent of condemning God in order to justify himself. God challenges Job to demonstrate his power if he thinks he is equal to the Omnipotent. **Hast thou an arm like God? Or canst thou thunder with a voice like him?** (40:9). The rest of chapter 40 and all of chapter 41 relate the power of God over nature and imply that the God who could create the powerful beasts **behemoth** (40:15) and **leviathan** (41:1) is far superior to any puny man.

CHAPTER 41

CANST thou draw out leviathan with an hook? or his tongue with a cord *which* thou lettest down?

2 Canst thou put an hook into his nose? or bore his jaw through with a thorn?

3 Will he make many supplications unto thee? will he speak soft *words* unto thee?

4 Will he make a covenant with thee? wilt thou take him for a servant for ever?

5 Wilt thou play with him as *with* a bird? or wilt thou bind him for thy maidens?

6 Shall the companions make a banquet of him? shall they part him among the merchants?

7 Canst thou fill his skin with barbed irons? or his head with fish spears?

8 Lay thine hand upon him, remember the battle, do no more.

9 Behold, the hope of him is in vain: shall not *one* be cast down even at the sight of him?

10 None *is so* fierce that dare stir him up: who then is able to stand before me?

11 Who hath prevented me, that I should repay *him? whatsoever is* under the whole heaven is mine.

12 I will not conceal his parts, nor his power, nor his comely proportion.

13 Who can discover the face of his garment? *or* who can come *to him* with his double bridle?

14 Who can open the doors of his face? his teeth *are* terrible round about.

15 *His* scales *are his* pride, shut up together *as with* a close seal.

16 One is so near to another, that no air can come between them.

17 They are joined one to another, they stick together, that they cannot be sundered.

18 By his neesings a light doth shine, and his eyes *are* like the eyelids of the morning.

19 Out of his mouth go burning lamps, *and* sparks of fire leap out.

20 Out of his nostrils goeth smoke, as *out* of a seething pot or caldron.

21 His breath kindleth coals, and a flame goeth out of his mouth.

22 In his neck remaineth strength, and sorrow is turned into joy before him.

23 The flakes of his flesh are joined together: they are firm in themselves; they cannot be moved.

24 His heart is as firm as a stone; yea, as hard as a piece of the nether *millstone.*

25 When he raiseth up himself, the mighty are afraid: by reason of breakings they purify themselves.

26 The sword of him that layeth at him cannot hold: the spear, the dart, nor the habergeon.

27 He esteemeth iron as straw, *and* brass as rotten wood.

28 The arrow cannot make him flee: slingstones are turned with him into stubble.

29 Darts are counted as stubble: he laugheth at the shaking of a spear.

30 Sharp stones *are* under him: he spreadeth sharp pointed things upon the mire.
31 He maketh the deep to boil like a pot: he maketh the sea like a pot of ointment.
32 He maketh a path to shine after him; *one* would think the deep *to be* hoary.
33 Upon earth there is not his like, who is made without fear.
34 He beholdeth all high *things:* he *is* a king over all the children of pride.

CHAPTER 42

THEN Job answered the LORD, and said,
2 I know that thou canst do every *thing,* and *that* no thought can be withholden from thee.
3 Who *is* he that hideth counsel without knowledge? therefore have I uttered that I understood not; things too wonderful for me, which I knew not.
4 Hear, I beseech thee, and I will speak: I will demand of thee, and declare thou unto me.
5 I have heard of thee by the hearing of the ear: but now mine eye seeth thee.
6 Wherefore I abhor *myself,* and repent in dust and ashes.

7 ¶And it was *so,* that after the LORD had spoken these words unto Job, the LORD said to Ĕl'i-phăz the Tē'man-īte, My wrath is kindled against thee, and against thy two friends: for ye have not spoken of me *the thing that is* right, as my servant Job *hath.*
8 Therefore take unto you now seven bullocks and seven rams, and go to my servant Job, and offer up for yourselves a burnt offering; and my servant Job shall pray for you: for him will I accept: lest I deal with you *after your* folly, in that ye have not spoken of me *the thing which is* right, like my servant Job.
9 ¶So Ĕl'i-phăz the Tē'man-īte and Bildad the Shū'hīte *and* Zō'phar the Nā'a-math-īte went, and did according as the LORD commanded them: the LORD also accepted Job.

10 And the LORD turned the captivity of Job, when he prayed for his friends: also the LORD gave Job twice as much as he had before.
11 Then came there unto him all his

D. Job Repentant. 42:1-6.

42:1-6. Job had responded the first time (40:1-5) with silence and his hand over his mouth. Now he humbly repents, having seen God's power, wisdom, and love demonstrated. He now confesses that he spoke foolishly and without understanding. Before, his knowledge of God was second-hand, but now it is first-hand, his own personal experience. **I have heard of thee by the hearing of the ear; but now mine eye seeth thee.** All of his questions have not been answered, but they no longer are burning issues. Job has been transformed by his personal encounter with God. **Wherefore I abhor myself, and repent in dust and ashes.**

V. EPILOGUE. 42:7-17.

Job's repentance and submission end the poetic section of the book. The prose-style narrative found in the first two chapters resumes here.

Some modern scholars think the restoration of Job ruins the story. This attitude is usually taken by liberals who assume the book of Job to be some sort of protest written by an ancient civil rights activist to call attention to the existence of injustice in the world. If, however, the point of the story is precisely what the text itself claims it to be, to show that unselfish and disinterested piety is indeed possible in this world, then justice demands Job's restoration; and the story ends logically.

A. Job's Prayer for His Friends. 42:7-9.

7-9. The Lord speaks to **Eliphaz** directly but includes **thy two friends** and condemns them, for they **have not spoken of me the thing that is right.** God thus shows His rejection of their simplistic, almost mechanical, view that all suffering is the result of sin and the degree of suffering is always in direct proportion to the awfulness of the sin. That Elihu is not included in the Lord's censure does not necessarily show a lack of unity in the work, but could well reflect that Elihu did not share the three friends' theological errors at this point.

It is also noteworthy that the Lord refers to **my servant Job** four times in this passage and publicly approves Job once more. Not that everything spoken by Job was correct, nor that everything spoken by his friends was false; but the overall direction of their thinking is meant. To make the point clear, the friends are required to sacrifice **seven bullocks and seven rams;** and Job must pray for them. Thus, the story ends with all the relationships healed. Job forgives the three friends and intercedes for them, their relationship with God is restored, Job's relationship with God is also restored, and Job's relationship with relatives and community is restored in the following verses.

B. God Restores the Fortunes of Job. 42:10-17.

10-16. In praying unselfishly for others, Job's material blessings are restored. Job was faithful; Satan was wrong (and does not appear in the epilogue); and God is vindicated. Job's livestock is restored twofold; he receives more sons and daughters; and he lives to see his descendants for **four generations.** God

brethren, and all his sisters, and all they that had been of his acquaintance before, and did eat bread with him in his house: and they bemoaned him, and comforted him over all the evil that the Lord had brought upon him: every man also gave him a piece of money, and every one an earring of gold.

12 So the Lord blessed the latter end of Job more than his beginning: for he had fourteen thousand sheep, and six thousand camels, and a thousand yoke of oxen, and a thousand she asses.

13 He had also seven sons and three daughters.

14 And he called the name of the first, Je-mī′ma; and the name of the second, Ke-zī′a; and the name of the third, Kĕr′en-hăp′puch.

15 And in all the land were no women found so fair as the daughters of Job: and their father gave them inheritance among their brethren.

16 After this lived Job an hundred and forty years, and saw his sons, and his sons' sons, even four generations.

17 So Job died, being old and full of days.

had protected Job with a **hedge** (1:10) in the beginning, as Satan had noted sarcastically; Job was faithful without the hedge, and it would appear that God restored the hedge of blessings for Job's integrity in the end. Nowhere in the book did it say that God does not reward faithfulness, only that the kind of faithfulness He rewards is true worship of Himself, regardless of rewards.

17. So Job died, being old and full of days, a fitting ending to a story of true worship and integrity in the face of extreme adversity. How much greater should be our faith on this side of the cross and empty tomb!

BIBLIOGRAPHY

Allen, Clifton J. ed. *The Broadman Bible Commentary*. Vol. 4. Nashville: Broadman Press, 1971.

Anderson, Francis I. *Job: An Introduction and Commentary*. Downers Grove, Ill.: InterVarsity Press, 1977.

Barnes, Albert. *Notes, Critical, Illustrative, and Practical on the Book of Job*. 2 vols. New York: Leavitt, Trow and Co., 1844.

*Blackwood, A. W. *Out of the Whirlwind: A Study of Job*. Grand Rapids: Baker, 1979.

Blair, J. Allen. *Living Patiently: A Devotional Study of the Book of Job*. Neptune, N.J.: Loizeaux Brothers, Inc., 1966.

Caryl, Joseph. *An Exposition with Practical Observations Upon the Book of Job*. 12 vols. London, 1647-1666.

Delitzsch, F. *Biblical Commentary on the Book of Job*. 2 vols. Grand Rapids: Eerdmans, 1970.

Ellicott, Charles John. *Ellicott's Commentary on the Whole Bible*. Vol. IV. Grand Rapids: Zondervan, 1959.

*Ellison, H. L. *A Study of Job: From Tragedy to Triumph*. Grand Rapids: Zondervan, 1970.

Garland, D. David. *Job: A Study Guide Commentary*. Grand Rapids: Zondervan, 1971.

Gordis, Robert. *The Book of Job: Commentary, New Translation and Special Studies*. New York: The Jewish Theological Seminary of America, 1978.

Hanson, Anthony and Miriam. *The Book of Job: A Commentary*. New York: Collier Books, 1962.

*Inch, M. A. *My Servant Job*. Grand Rapids: Baker, 1979.

*Kline, Meredith. Job. In *Wycliffe Bible Commentary*. Chicago: Moody Press, 1962.

McGee, J. Vernon. *Job*. Pasadena, Calif.: Thru the Bible Books, 1977.

*Ridout, S. *The Book of Job*. New York: Loizeaux Brothers, Inc., 1919.

Smith, Ralph L. *Job: A Study in Providence and Faith*. Nashville: Convention Press, 1971.

Strahan, James. *The Book of Job*. 2nd ed. Edinburgh: T. and T. Clark, 1914.

THE PSALMS

INTRODUCTION

Value of the Psalms. The Psalms have always occupied a place of special affection in the hearts of God's people. Israel rejoiced together and lamented together by voicing the Psalms, and these poetic masterpieces constituted a vital element in the public and private worship of ancient Israel. Likewise, the early church quickly adopted the Psalms as part of their praise to God (e.g., I Cor 14:15, 26; Eph 5:19). Tertullian, in the second century, noted that in his day the Psalms were sung at the agape feasts of the church.

The historic impact of the Psalms cannot be overstated. Jerome claimed the Psalms were "continually to be heard in the fields and vineyards of Palestine." Jeremy Taylor mentions that the primitive church "would admit no man to the superior orders of the clergy unless among other prerequired dispositions he could say all David's Psalter by heart" (see his *Works,* Vol. viii, p. 507). Origen, Eusebius, Basil, Chrysostom, Athanasius, Ambrose, Augustine, and Jerome all wrote commentaries on the Psalms.

These sacred songs of the Hebrews not only provide a sketch of Israel's praise to God, but also provide a mirror into which one can peer and see himself and his emotions reflected. As Calvin said in the Preface to his *Commentary on the Psalms,* these writings "impel every one of us to self-examination, that of all the infirmities to which we are liable, and all the sins of which we are so full, none may remain hidden." To this Luther adds, "If you want to see the holy Christian church painted in glowing colors and in a form which is really alive, and if you want to do this in a miniature, you must get hold of the Psalter, and there you will have in your possession a fine, clear, pure mirror which will show you what Christianity really is" (see the second Preface to the *German Psalter,* 1528).

The Name of the Psalms. Although the Hebrew name for this entire collection was the Book of Praises (Heb *sēper tehilīm*), the New Testament designation "the Psalms" (Lk 20:42; 24:44; Acts 1:20; 13:33) finds its origin in the Septuagint, where the Codex Vaticanus of the LXX title the Psalms *psalmoi,* ultimately meaning poems that are sung to the accompaniment of stringed instruments. The Greek *psalmoi* relates to the Hebrew *mizmōr,* which occurs in the inscriptions of fifty-seven psalms. The Latin Vulgate follows the LXX, *Liber Psalmorum;* and from this our English word "Psalms" is derived. Luther and most German Bibles ascribe to these poems the designation "The Psalter."

Authorship. As one thumbs through the Psalms, it becomes immediately obvious that many psalms bear a superscription above them. Lyrical compositions of the Hebrews from the earliest times frequently had such superscriptions (cf. Ex 15:1; Jud 5:1; I Sam 2:1; II Sam 23:1; Jon 2:1; Hab 3:1). Those superscriptions, which name the authors

of the Psalms, list David as the author of seventy-three psalms (3-9; 11-32; 34-41; 51-65; 68-70; 86; 101; 103; 108-110; 122; 124; 131; 133; 138-145); Asaph (cf. I Chr 16:4-5) as the author of twelve psalms (50, 73-83); and the sons of Korah (cf. Num 16) as the authors or more probably those to whom were dedicated twelve psalms (42; 43; 44-49; 84; 85; 87; 88). Psalm 43 is unnamed, but it usually is considered in the group of the sons of Korah because it occurs second in a series of Korahite psalms. Also, Psalm 88 receives the double designation of "A song or psalm for the sons of Korah" and "A Maschil of Heman the Ezrahite." Heman (cf. I Chr 15:17) is probably the author and the "sons of Korah" a category designation or a guild of singers.

In addition, two psalms are ascribed to Solomon (72; 127), one to Ethan (89), and one to Moses (90). This leaves forty-nine "orphan psalms" (1; 2; 10; 33; 66-67; 71; 91-100; 102; 104-107; 111-121; 123; 125-126; 128-130; 132; 134-137; 146-150), all of which are anonymous, but many of which are authored by the above-mentioned psalmists.

Date of composition. Higher critics continually reject the psalm superscriptions as being inaccurate and of little value. One might expect such an attack, however, in light of the fact that the contents of these superscriptions affirm the early authorship of the Psalms. Yet, all Hebrew Bibles regularly include these superscriptions in the numbered verses, thus raising the number of verses in a given psalm by one or two digits.

The Psalms were composed over the course of many years (see J. Patton, *Canaanite Parallels in the Book of Psalms* for early parallels to the biblical psalms in the Ras Shamra tablets of Ugarit). However, the psalms were begun to be collected into a body of literature only in the time of David. "Since David had such a genuine interest in establishing worship and began the liturgical use of some of them, it is reasonable to associate the early collections with him as king of Israel (I Chr 15-16)" (Samuel Schultz, *The Old Testament Speaks,* p. 286). "Hezekiah may have been responsible for arranging the first three books (Ps 1-89) of the Psalter. At least in his time there were collections of David's and Asaph's psalms (II Chr 29:30)" (Edward J. Young, *An Introduction to the Old Testament,* p. 306).

The chief objection in dating the Psalms is to those composed by David. Many modern liberal scholars hold to a post-exilic origin of the psalms said to be authored by David. Eissfeldt traces the poetry of the Hebrews to the cult songs of the Canaanites and thus finds justification in a late dating of the Psalms in order to give Israel adequate time to incorporate Canaanite motifs into their own compositions. Duhm, Cornhill, and others place the Davidic psalms in the Maccabean period. Thus, Hitzig identifies the author of Psalms 1 and 2 with the Maccabean prince Alexander Jannaeus (103-76 B.C.). Even worse, Olshausen marks the reign of Jannaeus' father, John Hyrcanus (135-107 B.C.), as the time when the latest psalms were composed and when the collection as we now possess it was made.

There is, however, no legitimate reason for rejecting Davidic authorship of the seventy-three psalms ascribed to him. Princeton scholar Robert Dick Wilson and others have shown the compatibility of David's authorship with the content of each Davidic psalm. David's name is closely associated in the Old Testament as a skillful musician (I Sam 16:16-18; Amos 6:5) and poet (II Sam 1:17-27). He is called ". . . the sweet psalmist of Israel . . ." (II Sam 23:1). As a man of rich and varied experience, David had the background to be a poet-psalmist, and most of the psalms ascribed to him reflect some period in his life (cf. 23; 51; 57; et al.). Again, the New Testament bears witness of David's psalm-writing activity (cf. 2 with Acts 4:25-26; 16 with Acts 2:25-28; 32 with Rom 4:6-8; 69 with Acts 1:16-20; etc.). Such witness must be considered conclusive.

Classification of the Psalms. Since even a casual reading of the Psalms impresses the conviction that the psalms themselves are greatly varied in subject and substance, many attempts at classification have been made. Pioneer work in this field was done by the German form critic Herman Günkel. Günkel attempted to liken the Psalms of Israel to existing Near Eastern practices, such as cultic worship or the annual enthronement Festival of the Kings. Consequently, Günkel lists the following categories of classification: hymns, personal laments, personal songs of praise, national laments, national songs of praise, songs of pilgrimage, wisdom poems, Torah liturgies, royal psalms, and mixed types of psalms.

Artur Weiser reduces Günkel's categories to three, i.e., hymns, laments, and thanksgivings; but essentially his is a collective and simplified version of Günkel's list. All form critics classify the Psalms upon the assumption of a tenuous presupposition. Heidelberg University professor Claus Westermann characteristically states: "The Psalms have developed out of Israel's public worship. Each one individually contains within itself a worship event. It is a part of the worship life. Even though the events lying behind the Psalms can often no longer be perceived, nevertheless they are always to be assumed. When one listens to a psalm, one should not ask: 'What ideas does it contain?' but rather: 'What is being fulfilled in the words of this psalm?'" (*Handbook to the Old Testament*, p. 216).

The search for a supposed event lying behind the Psalms and an overemphasis on form and structure in their content have blinded the critics' eyes to the real message of the Psalms. Robert Pfeiffer, himself a liberal, concludes: "Numerous problems cannot be solved finally for lack of evidence, so that a satisfactory classification of the Psalms . . . cannot be achieved. . . . No scheme of classification can do full justice to the wealth of literary forms and religious contents of the Psalter" (*The Books of the Old Testament*, p. 201).

Schultz (p. 287) presents a suggestive, but not comprehensive, classification, based mainly on content instead of cultic worship practices. His categories and some examples of each are:

I. Prayers of the Righteous-17; 20; 25; 50; 44; etc.
II. Penitential Psalms-6; 32; 38; 51; 102; etc.
III. Psalms of Praise-65; 95-100; 111-118; 146-150; etc.
IV. Pilgrim Psalms-120-134.
V. Historical Psalms-78; 105; 106; etc.
VI. Messianic Psalms-2; 22; 40; 45; 72; 110; etc.
VII. Alphabetic Psalms-25; 34; 111; 112; 119; etc.

These categories represent psalms in which the righteous appeal to God for assistance or vindication, and where sincere repentance from sin is evident. A dominant note in the Psalms is that of praise, as seen above. The Pilgrim Psalms are sometimes listed as "Songs of Ascents" or "Songs of Degrees" which may have been sung by the Jews as they ascended the heights of Jerusalem for annual festivals. The category of historical psalms presents those that rehearse the great victories Jehovah has won for Israel. Perhaps the most important category is that of the messianic psalms, which forecast the presence and person of the Messiah in the New Testament. And, finally, alphabetic psalms make use of acrostic arrangements or alphabetic arrangements to add to the beauty of the psalm in the Hebrew.

Form of Poetry. Early Hebrew poetry had neither rhyme nor meter, and neither was adopted into Jewish poetry until the seventh century A.D. "In Hebrew poetry rhyme does not exist, and it is more accurate to speak of rhythm rather than meter. There is a rhythmic accentuation in each clause, and a rhythmic balance of clauses, but no metrical system dependent upon the quality or number of syllables or accents in each line" (J.G.S.S. Thompson in *The New Bible Dictionary*, ed. by J. D. Douglas, p. 1055).

Since the Hebrews did not employ a "roses are red" approach to poetry, what approach did they use? In a 1753 treatise, Oxford professor Bishop Robert Lowth noted that the distinctive feature of Hebrew poetry was parallelism. "Every verse must consist of at least two members, the second of which must, more or less completely, satisfy the expectation raised by the first" (J. A. Robinson, *Poetry and Poets of the Old Testament*, p. 11ff.). The two or more members of a verse show a parallel relationship to each other.

Four basic types of parallelisms have been distinguished: (1) synonymous, the thought of the first line is repeated exactly, but with different words, in the second line (e.g., 49:1); (2) antithetical, the first line is affirmed by a contrast, or exact opposite, in the second line (e.g., 37:21), (3) synthetic, the statement in the first line serves as the basis for the statement in the second line, which fulfills it (e.g., 19:7-10); and (4) climactic, the first line is incomplete, but the second line draws from it and completes it (e.g., 29:1).

Acrosticism is another interesting feature of Hebrew poetry exhibited in the Psalms. A notable example of acrosticism is Psalm 119. This psalm is set in twenty-two stanzas, each containing eight verses. Above each stanza is a letter of the Hebrew alphabet, because each of the eight verses within a stanza begins with the same Hebrew letter. For example, verses 1-8 each begin with an *'aleph*, verses 9-16 each begin with a *beth*, etc. Other examples of acrosticism may be found in Psalms 9, 34, and 37.

Musical Technical Notations. A number of curious musical or technical terms appear in the superscriptions over the Psalms. Briefly explained, these are: (1) *Mizmor*, meaning psalm, comes from a root word meaning to pluck and refers to the psalms sung to stringed accompaniment. Fifty-seven psalms are thus designated (3-6; 8; 9; 12; 13; 15; 17; 19-24; 29-31; 38; 40-41; 47-51; 62-68; 73; 75-77; 79-80; 82-85; 78; 88; 92; 98; 100-101; 108-110; 139-141; 143); (2) *shir*, meaning song or a joyful melody, is included in the superscription of thirty psalms, twelve of them in conjunction with *mizmor* (30; 46; 48; 65-68; 75-76; 83; 87-88; 92; 108; 120-134; 145); (3) *maschil*, meaning instructive, probably denotes a psalm with didactic or meditative quality and occurs thirteen times (32; 42; 44-45; 52-55; 74; 78; 88-89; 142); (4) *michtam*, perhaps meaning a golden psalm or a mystery poem (16; 56-60); (5) *tephillah*, meaning prayer (17; 86; 90; 102; 142); (6) *tehillah*, meaning praise (145); and (7) *shiggaion*, perhaps meaning "dirge," although again the meaning is not clear, is used only once (7).

Three musical notations that frequently occur are: (1) *Lamnatseach*, which is usually translated "To the chief musician," indicates a psalm of the choirmaster, perhaps assigned to him to rehearse the choirs of Israel for public worship and this expression is found in the superscription of a full fifty-two psalms (4-6; 8-9; 11-14; 18-22; 31; 36; 39-42; 44-47; 49; 51-62; 64-70; 80-81; 84-85; 88; 109; 139-140); (2) *ma'aloth*, variously translated as "Songs of Ascent" or "Songs of Degrees," were psalms sung by pilgrims ascending the hills of Jerusalem in order to celebrate the three annual feasts (120-134 cf. 122:1-3); and (3) *selah* does not occur in the superscription but at the end of a strophe and appears seventy-one times in thirty-nine different psalms. *Selah* may either mean to play forte or lift up the voice in an increase of volume, or it may indicate a dramatic pause for musical effect. (3-4; 7; 9; 20-21; 24; 32; 39; 44; 46; 47-50; 52; 54-55; 57; 59-62; 66-68; 75-77; 81-85; 87-89; 140; 143).

Purpose. In his *Introduction* (p. 399), Carl Cornhill portrays the purpose of the Psalms as the "hymn, prayer, and religious instruction book of the community of the Second Temple." Others, such as Günkel (*Einleitung in die Psalmen*) and Sigmund Mowinckel (*Psalmenstudien*), view the Psalms as set in the *milieu* of ancient Near Eastern cultic worship and claim the Psalms are but the Hebrew accommodation of pagan rituals. But such conclusions are without foundation in fact and are grossly unwarranted.

Whereas once modern scholarship saw the Psalms as primarily a vehicle for public and corporate worship in cultic Israel, more and more the emphasis has been placed on the individual. Thus, today, the purpose of the Psalms is rightly seen as being the outcries of praise and pleading from the hearts of some of God's choicest servants.

On occasion, it was the purpose of the poet to cry out against evil and call for God's righteous wrath to fall upon the wicked. When such is the case, the psalm is usually called an "imprecatory psalm." Some of these imprecations are but brief reflections from the heart of the pious author. Others, such as those found in Psalms 35, 69, and 109, are lengthy tirades against wickedness and arise out of true piety and fear of the Lord. The psalmist is not being vindictive, he is but seeking the Lord's righteous aid in dealing with the avowed enemies of God.

It is apparent that the purpose of some psalms is to illuminate the life and death of the coming Messiah. These psalms are the messianic psalms. In the past theologians have perhaps read too much into the messianic psalms, claiming messianic character even for psalms in which it was not present. St. Augustine, for example, in his *Expositions on the Psalms*, regarded practically all the psalms as messianic. This, too, was a tendency of the Reformers. In reaction to this, form critics have allowed the pendulum to swing the other way. Thus, Günkel concludes, "The eschatology of the psalms offers no Messianic features of a sort such as bygone generations have erroneously sought to find" (p. 330).

But the fact that the New Testament sees something messianic in a number of psalms (e.g., 8; 16; 22; 31; 69; 110; etc.) cannot be denied. While conservative scholars may disagree on the number of messianic psalms, the existence of such psalms is certain, and those messianic elements of the Psalms will be featured in this commentary.

It is a mistake, as liberal scholars have done, to regard the Psalms as Temple hymns used exclusively in cultic worship. "The Psalter, rather, is primarily a manual and guide and model for the devotional needs of the individual believer. It is a book of prayer and praise, to be meditated upon by the believer, that he may thereby learn to praise God and pray to Him" (Young, p. 309).

Special Features. In the pages that follow, brief comments will be made on each one of the one hundred fifty psalms. In addition, two other features should be noted. First, each psalm has been appropriately titled. The title usually arises from the dominant theme of the psalm. Secondly, each psalm is accompanied by a sentence summary which is designed to give a bird's-eye view of the psalm's contents, or theme. Perhaps these features will help the reader to more successfully accomplish the purpose of the Psalms, i.e., "that he may thereby learn to praise God and pray to Him."

OUTLINE

COMMENTARY

I. PSALMS 1:1-41:13.

A. The Two Ways. 1:1-6.

THEME: The secret of true happiness is found only in God and His Word.

The Psalms, like our Lord's Sermon on the Mount, begin with a beatitude. Although not specifically written as an introduction to the Psalter, the first psalm provides a basis for all the psalms that follow. It compares the happiness found in the Lord with the sadness of those who do not know Him.

BLESSED is the man that walketh not in the counsel of the ungodly, nor standeth in the way of sinners, nor sitteth in the seat of the scornful.

1:1. The unnamed psalmist describes the godly man, both negatively (vs. 1) and positively (vss. 2-3). Negatively, he lists three types of sinners, three expressions of sin, and three places of sin that are available to, but not frequented by, the godly man. In ascending order they are: **Walketh not in the counsel of the ungodly,** i.e., his conduct is not shaped by worldly standards; **nor standeth in the way of sinners,** i.e., he does not make his association with evil men; and **nor sitteth in the seat of the scornful,** i.e., he has no fellowship with those who scorn God.

2 But his delight is in the law of the LORD; and in his law doth he meditate day and night.

2. Positively, the godly man is one who delights in the **law of the LORD.** The law (Heb *tôrah*) **of the LORD** is clearly to be understood as more than Moses' law. It is synonymous with the Word of God (cf. 78:5; Josh 1:7; II Kgs 17:13; 21:8, etc.). Hence, it is in the Word of God he doth **meditate day and night.** To **meditate** means to discuss or ponder. As Thomas a Kempis quaintly put it, "I have no rest, but in a nook, with *the* Book." That's meditation.

3 And he shall be like a tree planted by the rivers of water, that bringeth forth his fruit in his season; his leaf also shall not wither; and whatsoever he doeth shall prosper.
4 The ungodly are not so: but are like the chaff which the wind driveth away.

3-4. Lastly, the godly man is described as **a tree planted by the rivers of water.** The verb **planted** (Heb *shatal*) indicates that the godly man did not accidently, nor under his own initiative, take root. He is rooted fast in order that he may bring **forth his fruit.** The purpose of God's planting a man in the fertile soil of His grace is always the production of fruit (cf. Eph 2:8-10; Col 1:9-10). **The ungodly are not so.** The contrast here is striking. The character of the ungodly man is **like the chaff.** Those who are not planted by the **rivers of water** (i.e., the Word of God) are not saved and therefore are intrinsically worthless, without substance and easily carried away.

5 Therefore the ungodly shall not stand in the judgment, nor sinners in the congregation of the righteous.

5. Positively, the ungodly are described as those who cannot **stand in the judgment.** When they are brought before the judgment bar of God, they have no retort to God's just condemnation of their ungodliness (see the comments on 130:3).

988

6 For the LORD knoweth the way of the righteous: but the way of the ungodly shall perish.

6. The secret of the godly man's success is not found in his godliness, but in that **the LORD knoweth the way of the righteous.** Our loving Lord attends to and provides for those who live godly lives before Him (101:6; Prov 12:10; Hos 13:5). In contrast, all the plans and hopes of the ungodly will end in disappointment and ruin (37:13; 146:9; Prov 4:19).

Two men, two ways, two destinies. One leads to life and blessedness; the other, without God and His Word, is a dead-end street, leading but to death. No one can seriously read this psalm and not examine his own destiny. If we're going to go to God's heaven, we have to go in God's way. Jesus Christ said, "I am the way, the truth, and the life: no man cometh unto the Father, but by me" (Jn 14:6).

B. Christ the Messiah and King. 2:1-12.

THEME: Man's rebellion against God is futile because God has anointed Christ as the King of the earth.

Although unnamed, that this psalm is Davidic is established in Acts 4:25; and that it is the second psalm, is noted in Acts 13:33. Though many of the warlike events of David's life may have suggested the imagery, this psalm is nonetheless a messianic portrayal of the millennial reign of Jesus Christ.

PSALM 2
WHY do the heathen rage, and the people imagine a vain thing?
2 The kings of the earth set themselves, and the rulers take counsel together, against the LORD, and against his anointed, *saying,*

2:1-2. Why do the heathen rage, and the people imagine a vain thing? What is it that ails the **heathen** (Heb *gōy*), the Gentiles, and what causes the masses to plan that which is destined to come to nought? What causes the **kings of the earth** and the **rulers** to band together in mutual purpose against **the LORD** and **his Anointed? His Anointed** is an obvious reference to Christ Jesus; for anointing was conferred on prophets (Isa 6:1), priests (Ex 30:30), and kings (I Sam 10:1), and only Jesus Christ can claim all three offices. The answer to these questions is found in the next verse.

3 Let us break their bands asunder, and cast away their cords from us.

3. Let us break their bands asunder, and cast away their cords. The heathen rage and constantly devise ways to thwart the purpose of God because they do not like the constraints of God's law, Bible morality, or Christian conduct. They prefer to be a law unto themselves, to establish their own conduct by what feels right to them.

4 He tnat sitteth in the heavens shall laugh: the LORD shall have them in derision.
5 Then shall he speak unto them in his wrath, and vex them in his sore displeasure.
6 Yet have I set my king upon my holy hill of Zion.

4-6. He that sitteth in the heavens shall laugh . . . and vex them . . . Yet have I set my King. God's laughter does not arise from humor. **Laugh** and **derision** are anthropomorphisms, meaning that God views puny man's rebellion as utterly preposterous and scornful. God plans to establish His Anointed as King on **my holy hill of Zion.** Without denying a possible reference to David here, this must be primarily understood that the Anointed of God on Mount Zion depicts Christ Jesus in His millennial reign.

7 I will declare the decree: the LORD hath said unto me, Thou *art* my Son; this day have I begotten thee.

7. This day have I begotten thee. Luke makes reference to this verse in the context of resurrection (Acts 13:29-37), indicating that God raised up Jesus from the dead so that His eternal purpose might continue unabated.

8 Ask of me, and I shall give *thee* the heathen *for* thine inheritance, and the uttermost parts of the earth *for* thy possession.
9 Thou shalt break them with a rod of iron; thou shalt dash them in pieces like a potter's vessel.

8-9. I shall give thee the heathen for thine inheritance. In the millennial kingdom the Lord's enemies will be subject to His terrible power (Job 4:9; II Thess 2:8), just as His people are to His profound grace (110:2-3). Christ deals with the nations as the righteous Judge.

10 Be wise now therefore, O ye kings: be instructed, ye judges of the earth.
11 Serve the LORD with fear, and rejoice with trembling.
12 Kiss the Son, lest he be angry, and ye perish *from* the way, when his wrath is kindled but a little. Blessed *are* all they that put their trust in him.

10-12. In light of this, five important instructions are given to the totality of God's creation: **Be wise . . . be instructed . . . Serve the LORD . . . rejoice . . . Kiss the Son.** To **Kiss the Son** means more than to pay unwilling homage to Him. It means to embrace Him, depend entirely upon Him, to kiss Him and not be ashamed of that fact (cf. Song 8:1). "Kiss the Son is the Old Testament way of saying, '. . . Believe on the Lord Jesus Christ, and thou shalt be saved . . .' (Acts 16:31)"—George Gill.

PSALM 3

LORD, how are they increased that trouble me! many *are* they that rise up against me.

2 Many *there be* which say of my soul, *There is* no help for him in God. Sē'lah.

3 But thou, O LORD, *art* a shield for me; my glory, and the lifter up of mine head.

4 I cried unto the LORD with my voice, and he heard me out of his holy hill. Sē'-lah.

5 I laid me down and slept; I awaked; for the LORD sustained me.

6 I will not be afraid of ten thousands of people, that have set *themselves* against me round about.

7 Arise, O LORD; save me, O my God: for thou hast smitten all mine enemies *upon* the cheek bone; thou hast broken the teeth of the ungodly.

8 Salvation *belongeth* unto the LORD: thy blessing *is* upon thy people. Sē'lah.

PSALM 4

HEAR me when I call, O God of my righteousness: thou hast enlarged me *when I was* in distress; have mercy upon me, and hear my prayer.

2 O ye sons of men, how long *will ye turn* my glory into shame? *how long* will ye love vanity, *and* seek after leasing? Sē'lah.

3 But know that the LORD hath set apart him that is godly for himself: the LORD will hear when I call unto him.

4 Stand in awe, and sin not: commune with your own heart upon your bed, and be still. Sē'lah.

5 Offer the sacrifices of righteousness, and put your trust in the LORD.

6 *There be* many that say, Who will shew us *any* good? LORD, lift thou up the light of thy countenance upon us.

7 Thou hast put gladness in my heart, more than in the time *that* their corn and their wine increased.

8 I will both lay me down in peace, and sleep: for thou, LORD, only makest me dwell in safety.

C. A Psalm of Security. 3:1-8.

THEME: An oppressed righteous man looks confidently to salvation from the Lord.

The historical background for this psalm is found in II Samuel 15-17 where David had to take flight from his own palace to hide himself from his rebellious son Absalom. Many refer to this as a morning prayer to God.

3:1-6. There is no help for him in God. With the troubles of the king mounting, many of his distrustful friends deduced that David was doomed to death. Thus, they exclaimed that God had forsaken him. David's confidence is not shaken. To him the Lord is a **shield**, his **glory**, and the **lifter up** of his head. He is certain the Lord will hear and answer his prayer in this time of need.

7-8. David's psalm of security comes to a conclusion with the statement that the Lord has **smitten all mine enemies upon the cheek bone**, the point of contact which inflicts the greatest pain and the highest degree of insult (cf. I Kgs 22:24; Job 16:10; Mic 5:1). He joyfully exclaims, **Salvation belongeth unto the LORD.** God is the Author and Originator of our salvation, and David glories in the fact that salvation, as God's gift to him, is certain.

D. An Evening Psalm of Trust. 4:1-8.

THEME: The godly man in distress may quietly repose in the arms of God.

The historical occasion for this psalm was probably the same as the former one. David prays for additional help from God and admonishes his enemies that it is useless to attack the servant of God.

4:1-2. Have mercy upon me, and hear my prayer is David's usual cry, repeated in hundreds of varied forms throughout these poetic writings (cf. 5:2; 6:2; 9:13; 27:7; 30:10, etc.). **O ye sons of men.** This is a title of honor or dignity and means men of prominence. The psalmist's appeal is perhaps to Joab, Abishai, or others of his own party whose activities were a disgrace to David. Joab's treachery and falsehood were especially well-known (cf. II Sam 3:27; 20:8-10).

3-6. David's quiet confidence that he has been set apart to God enables him to feel certain that **the LORD will hear when I call unto him.** A godly man, saved and set apart by God, has the same certainty in any generation. **Stand in awe, and sin not** is probably more meaningfully translated, "Be ye angry, and sin not . . ." and has the sanction of Paul in Ephesians 4:26 for such a rendering. The sinner should reconsider his actions each night upon his pillow and repent of his sin.

7-8. As for David, there was **gladness** in his heart, the type of gladness that is enjoyed by the farmer at harvest time. **I will both lay me down in peace, and sleep;** for there is nothing to fear when the righteous are in a right relationship to God.

E. A Morning Prayer. 5:1-12.

THEME: A righteous man prays that God will destroy his wicked enemies.

The most probable date for this psalm is shortly after the revolt of Absalom, when David was keenly aware of the machinations and conspiracies against him. The psalm is best

PSALM 5

GIVE ear to my words, O Lord, consider my meditation.

2 Hearken unto the voice of my cry, my King, and my God: for unto thee will I pray.

3 My voice shalt thou hear in the morning, O Lord; in the morning will I direct *my prayer* unto thee, and will look up.

4 For thou *art* not a God that hath pleasure in wickedness: neither shall evil dwell with thee.

5 The foolish shall not stand in thy sight: thou hatest all workers of iniquity.

6 Thou shalt destroy them that speak leasing: the Lord will abhor the bloody and deceitful man.

7 But as for me, I will come *into* thy house in the multitude of thy mercy: *and* in thy fear will I worship toward thy holy temple.

8 Lead me, O Lord, in thy righteousness because of mine enemies; make thy way straight before my face.

9 For *there is* no faithfulness in their mouth; their inward part *is* very wickedness; their throat *is* an open sepulchre; they flatter with their tongue.

10 Destroy thou them, O God; let them fall by their own counsels; cast them out in the multitude of their transgressions; for they have rebelled against thee.

11 But let all those that put their trust in thee rejoice: let them ever shout for joy, because thou defendest them: let them also that love thy name be joyful in thee.

12 For thou, Lord, wilt bless the righteous; with favour wilt thou compass him as *with* a shield.

PSALM 6

O LORD, rebuke me not in thine anger, neither chasten me in thy hot displeasure.

2 Have mercy upon me, O Lord; for I *am* weak: O Lord, heal me; for my bones are vexed.

3 My soul is also sore vexed: but thou, O Lord, how long?

4 Return, O Lord, deliver my soul: oh save me for thy mercies' sake.

5 For in death *there is* no remembrance of thee: in the grave who shall give thee thanks?

6 I am weary with my groaning; all the night make I my bed to swim; I water my couch with my tears.

---

divided into two parts: preliminaries to prayer (vss. 1-7), and petition and praise (vss. 8-12).

5:1-3. Give ear to my words. Such cries are common to the psalmist and represent almost a groaning, as in Romans 8:26-27. **In the morning will I direct my prayer unto thee, and will look up.** Here David makes use of two military terms. His prayer is marshalled (Heb 'arak) and put into battle array. Secondly, after praying, he acts as a spy, scanning (Heb tsapah) the heavens to see the results of his prayer. When the righteous pray to God, they should expect results (Jas 5:16).

4-7. These verses represent David's rehearsing the holiness of God (vss. 4-6) and the determination of the psalmist that **in thy fear will I worship toward thy holy temple.** David's worship is never without a reverent sense of God's sovereignty and perfect holiness.

8. Lead me, O Lord, in thy righteousness . . . make thy way straight before my face. David now utters his actual prayer, petitioning God to lead him in a righteous path, in contrast to that of his enemies, and to make that path plainly known to him (cf. 25:5; 27:11).

9-10. A description of the lying, wicked transgressors who have rebelled against God and attacked His man David is presented here. This same description is graphically used by Paul in depicting the wickedness of unsaved men (cf. Rom 3:13ff.).

11-12. A final note of rejoicing is recorded for those who have **put their trust** in God. The reason is threefold: (1) **thou defendest them;** (2) **thou, Lord, wilt bless the righteous;** and (3) **wilt thou compass him as with a shield.** The righteous need not fear what their enemies can do to them; we are but a prayer away from divine assistance and protection.

F. The First Penitential Psalm. 6:1-10.

THEME: *The moan of a saint, and the mercy of his God.*

This is commonly called the first of the Penitential Psalms. The others are Psalms 32; 38; 51; 130; 143. David is seen in deeper distress of soul than hitherto noted. II Samuel presents many occasions which would bring such distress to David's soul.

6:1-4. O Lord, rebuke me not in thine anger. David is very conscious that he deserves to be rebuked, but he does not want the sovereign God to destroy him with a rebuke. Thus, he prays, **Have mercy upon me, O Lord.** Mercy is sought from God for the psalmist's physical well-being (vs. 2), as well as his spiritual well-being (vss. 3-4).

5. In the grave who shall give thee thanks? This statement does not represent any incredulity on the part of the author about his future state, but is merely a contrast between the scenes of life and the grave (Heb she'ōl). Churchyards are silent reminders of once vocal witnesses for the Lord. David bargains with the Lord that if his life is spared he will praise the Lord continually.

6-7. So penitent is the psalmist that he exclaims, **I water my couch with my tears.** Night after night he drenches his bed because of a realization of his sin. As the English Puritan divine

7 Mine eye is consumed because of grief; it waxeth old because of all mine enemies.

8 Depart from me, all ye workers of iniquity; for the Lord hath heard the voice of my weeping.

9 The Lord hath heard my supplication; the Lord will receive my prayer.

10 Let all mine enemies be ashamed and sore vexed: let them return *and* be ashamed suddenly.

PSALM 7

O LORD my God, in thee do I put my trust: save me from all them that persecute me, and deliver me:

2 Lest he tear my soul like a lion, rending *it* in pieces, while *there is* none to deliver.

3 O Lord my God, if I have done this; if there be iniquity in my hands;

4 If I have rewarded evil unto him that was at peace with me; (yea, I have delivered him that without cause is mine enemy:)

5 Let the enemy persecute my soul, and take *it*; yea, let him tread down my life upon the earth, and lay mine honour in the dust. Sĕ'lah.

6 Arise, O Lord, in thine anger, lift up thyself because of the rage of mine enemies: and awake for me *to* the judgment *that* thou hast commanded.

7 So shall the congregation of the people compass thee about: for their sakes therefore return thou on high.

8 The Lord shall judge the people: judge me, O Lord, according to my righteousness, and according to mine integrity *that is* in me.

9 Oh let the wickedness of the wicked come to an end; but establish the just: for the righteous God trieth the hearts and reins.

10 My defence *is* of God, which saveth the upright in heart.

11 God judgeth the righteous, and God is angry *with the wicked* every day.

12 If he turn not, he will whet his sword; he hath bent his bow, and made it ready.

13 He hath also prepared for him the

John Trapp said, "That eye of his that had looked and lusted after his neighbour's wife is now dimmed and darkened with grief and indignation. He had wept himself almost blind."

8-10. David's sudden shift in tone and his shout, **Depart from me, all ye workers of iniquity,** indicate that he is certain his plea for mercy has been heard. Therefore, all those who plague or criticize him are suddenly rebuked. His prayer ends; and his proclamation begins, based on God's answer to his prayer.

G. Song of the Slandered Saint. 7:1-17.

THEME: *When the innocent saint's integrity is questioned, his only defense is God.*

The occasion for the composition of this psalm is given in the superscription. David had been slandered by one named **Cush the Benjamite.** This man is most likely identified with: (1) Saul (Hengstenberg), Cush being a play on words for Saul's father's name Kish; (2) Shimei (cf. II Sam 16:5-13), represented under a feigned name; or (3) a cohort of Saul named Cush who was also a Benjamite (Spurgeon) and an accuser in the court of Saul. An identification with Shimei seems unlikely. A previously unnamed conspirator named Cush may be the preferable interpretation.

7:1-2. David opens with a positive statement, **O Lord my God, in thee do I put my trust** (cf. 11; 31; 71). He prays for deliverance from an enemy who is stronger than the others. **Lest he tear my soul like a lion.** This singular **he** is probably King Saul, to whom Cush has made false statements concerning David. The simile of the lion is a frequent one in the Psalms (see 10:9; 17:12; 22:13, 21; etc.).

3-5. David feels that he has the right to cry out to God against Saul; for twice, in the cave of Adullam and in the slumbering camp, he had spared the king's life. **If I have done this,** i.e., that for which he has been charged by Cush the Benjamite; **if there be iniquity in my hands,** i.e., if he has committed a criminal act toward Saul; **if I have rewarded evil unto him . . . that without cause is mine enemy,** i.e., if David has in mercy allowed to escape him who was his enemy. If any of these be true, David's prayer is fourfold: (1) **Let the enemy persecute my soul;** (2) let the enemy **take it;** (3) **let him tread down my life upon the earth;** and (4) let him **lay mine honor in the dust.** Falsely accused, David takes no revenge, knowing that evil for good is devil-like, evil for evil is beast-like, good for good is man-like, good for evil is Godlike.

6. Arise, O Lord . . . and awake for me to the judgment that thou hast commanded. David now appeals to the God of mercy to ascend to the judgment seat. He does so in true piety, knowing that the judgment of God is ordained, or **commanded.**

7-16. Judge me, O Lord . . . according to mine integrity that is in me (lit., which is on me, cf. Job 29:24). The righteous need not fear the judgment of God, for their **defense is of God.** God's righteous judgment makes everything right. The divine law of retribution is seen here. When we do not retaliate for slanderous remarks made against us and instead ". . . give place unto (God's) wrath . . ." (Rom 12:19), God makes sure that when someone digs a ditch for us to fall into, that false accuser is the one who is **fallen into the ditch which he made** (cf. 9:15-16; 35:8; 57:6; Prov 26:27; 28:10, etc.). Haman is a striking example of this principle (cf. Est 7:7-10).

instruments of death; he ordaineth his arrows against the persecutors.

14 Behold, he travaileth with iniquity, and hath conceived mischief, and brought forth falsehood.

15 He made a pit, and digged it, and is fallen into the ditch which he made.

16 His mischief shall return upon his own head, and his violent dealing shall come down upon his own pate.

17 I will praise the LORD according to his righteousness: and will sing praise to the name of the LORD most high.

PSALM 8

O LORD our Lord, how excellent is thy name in all the earth! who hast set thy glory above the heavens.

2 Out of the mouth of babes and sucklings hast thou ordained strength because of thine enemies, that thou mightest still the enemy and the avenger.

3 When I consider thy heavens, the work of thy fingers, the moon and the stars, which thou hast ordained;

4 What is man, that thou art mindful of him? and the son of man, that thou visitest him?

5 For thou hast made him a little lower than the angels, and hast crowned him with glory and honour.

6 Thou madest him to have dominion over the works of thy hands: thou hast put all things under his feet:

7 All sheep and oxen, yea, and the beasts of the field;

8 The fowl of the air, and the fish of the sea, and whatsoever passeth through the paths of the seas.

9 O LORD our Lord, how excellent is thy name in all the earth!

PSALM 9

I WILL praise thee, O LORD, with my whole heart; I will shew forth all thy marvellous works.

2 I will be glad and rejoice in thee: I will sing praise to thy name, O thou most High.

3 When mine enemies are turned

17. I will praise the LORD. In another characteristically abrupt transition, David bursts into a song of praise to Jehovah for deliverance from slanderous men.

H. Our Excellent Lord. 8:1-9.

THEME: *A Messianic Psalm emphasizing the humanity of Christ and His ultimate victory as the Son of Man.*

The meaning of the word **Gittith** (Heb *'al-hagittî*) in the superscription has been a matter of much debate. Some think it refers to Gath and view this as a **psalm of David,** sung after the killing of Goliath. Others translate the Hebrew as referring to a tune sung by the treaders of the winepress. Since the term is found in the superscriptions of two other psalms (81 and 84), both of which are joyous, it may be assumed that this is a hymn of delight. David rejoices in God's creation, this being the first of the so-called nature psalms (cf. 19; 29; 65; 104).

8:1-2. How excellent is thy name. The name **O Lord our Lord** could be translated "Jehovah, who art our sovereign Lord and Master." His name alone is glorious and worthy of praise; it is praised even **Out of the mouth of babes and sucklings.** Perhaps David has reference to himself as a young man when he received strength to **still the enemy and the avenger.**

3-8. The psalmist now considers the heavens. The life of a shepherd would afford David frequent opportunity to do just that. With the vastness of the universe to ponder, including the **moon and the stars,** David cannot help but ask, **what is man, that thou art mindful of him?** In comparison with the lofty grandeur of the stars of heaven, man indeed appears to be of little significance and wholly unworthy of God's attention. Yet, God has made man, **a little lower than the angels** (Heb *'elōhîm*), to be the crown of His creation and have dominion over all living things.

Yet, whereas the position of man (Gen 1:26-28) was once supreme, it has been ruined by the fall. That which the first Adam lost in the fall, the Last Adam has more than regained. **The son of man** will rule all of creation, and we will reign with Him as heirs of God and joint-heirs with Christ (Rom 8:17).

9. O LORD our LORD, how excellent is thy name in all the earth! The psalmist ends, as he began, with an expression of the wisdom and worthiness of God.

I. Praise for God's Justice. 9:1-20.

THEME: *The judgment of God upon all is always just to all.*

Psalm 9 may be the first of the so-called Alphabetic Psalms. Both this psalm and the one which follows employ a loose and irregular acrostic, so loose and irregular that many consider Psalm 25 to be the first "Alphabetic Psalm." That Psalms 9 and 10 are very closely connected cannot be denied. In fact, both the Septuagint and the Vulgate consider these to be one psalm; but distinct differences do manifest themselves.

9:1-2. I will praise thee, O Lord. Heartfelt gratitude always finds utterance. **I will show forth all thy marvelous works.** Gratitude for one mercy frequently refreshes the memory of a thousand others.

3-6. For thou hast maintained my right and my cause. In these verses David praises the Lord for making him victor over

back, they shall fall and perish at thy presence.

4 For thou hast maintained my right and my cause; thou satest in the throne judging right.

5 Thou hast rebuked the heathen, thou hast destroyed the wicked, thou hast put out their name for ever and ever.

6 O thou enemy, destructions are come to a perpetual end: and thou hast destroyed cities; their memorial is perished with them.

7 But the LORD shall endure for ever: he hath prepared his throne for judgment.

8 And he shall judge the world in righteousness, he shall minister judgment to the people in uprightness.

9 The LORD also will be a refuge for the oppressed, a refuge in times of trouble.

10 And they that know thy name will put their trust in thee: for thou, LORD, hast not forsaken them that seek thee.

11 Sing praises to the LORD, which dwelleth in Zion: declare among the people his doings.

12 When he maketh inquisition for blood, he remembereth them: he forgetteth not the cry of the humble.

13 Have mercy upon me, O LORD; consider my trouble *which I suffer* of them that hate me, thou that liftest me up from the gates of death:

14 That I may shew forth all thy praise in the gates of the daughter of Zion: I will rejoice in thy salvation.

15 The heathen are sunk down in the pit *that* they made: in the net which they hid is their own foot taken.

16 The LORD is known *by* the judgment *which* he executeth: the wicked is snared in the work of his own hands. Hĭg-gā'iŏn. Sĕ'lah.

17 The wicked shall be turned into hell, *and* all the nations that forget God.

18 For the needy shall not alway be forgotten: the expectation of the poor shall *not* perish for ever.

19 Arise, O LORD; let not man prevail: let the heathen be judged in thy sight.

20 Put them in fear, O LORD: *that* the nations may know themselves *to be but* men. Sĕ'lah.

PSALM 10

WHY standest thou afar off, O LORD? *why* hidest thou *thyself* in times of trouble?

all his enemies. But this mighty man of God uniformly ascribes his military successes, not to his own ability or the valor of his soldiers, but expressly to the might of his mighty God.

7-12. But the LORD shall endure for ever (lit., the Lord is seated, upon His throne, for ever). Judgment upon David's enemies comes from the Lord. This is true of us as well, for **he shall judge the world in righteousness.** The **he** is emphatic, He Himself, Jehovah, and not another (see Jn 5:22 for the application of the name Jehovah or LORD to Jesus Christ). **And they that know thy name will put their trust in thee.** As always, to know the name of the Lord is tantamount to putting one's trust in the Lord as Saviour. The Lord's name is a reflection of His Person (cf. Mt 12:21).

13-18. Have mercy upon me, O LORD. The consideration of God's judgment prompts the psalmist to plead for mercy. What a wonderfully quaint expression David uses in describing the Lord as **thou that liftest me up from the gates of death.** These gates are obviously to be contrasted with **the gates of the daughter of Zion.** This is, of course, the city of Jerusalem. David views his life as being snatched from the gates of death in order that he may praise the name of the Lord in the gates of the city. Our attitude should be the same. **Higgaion. Selah** (vs. 16). **Higgaion** means "meditation"; and, combined with **Selah**, it seems to denote a pause of unusual duration and solemnity.

19-20. An appeal to God. **Arise, O LORD . . . Put them in fear, O LORD: that the nations may know themselves to be but men. Selah.** As Calvin observes, "The original word for men is *'enōsh* and therefore it is a prayer that they may know themselves to be but miserable, frail, and dying men. The word is in the singular number, but it is used collectively." David prays that all men everywhere will reflect on their frail nature (cf. 8:4) and refrain from rebellion against God.

J. The Cry of the Oppressed. 10:1-18.

THEME: A prayer and praise for God's intervention in the oppression by the wicked one.

Although unnamed and untitled, Psalm 10 is obviously that composition of David. This conclusion is justified in that the character of this psalm is quite similar to that of Psalm 9; the content, however, is quite dissimilar. Here, the psalmist mourns God's apparent indifference to his troubles; it is the heart-cry of every true believer who is oppressed and depicts the genuine test of faith.

10:1. Why standest thou afar off, O LORD? Why hidest thou thyself in times of trouble? These two questions capsulize the concern of the psalmist. David humanly feels that after God has delivered Israel from Egyptian bondage and from the clutch of foreign foes, He has now removed Himself as the Protector of

2 The wicked in *his* pride doth persecute the poor: let them be taken in the devices that they have imagined.

3 For the wicked boasteth of his heart's desire, and blesseth the covetous, *whom* the LORD abhorreth.

4 The wicked, through the pride of his countenance, will not seek *after* God: God *is* not in all his thoughts.

5 His ways are always grievous; thy judgments *are* far above out of his sight: *as for* all his enemies, he puffeth at them.

6 He hath said in his heart, I shall not be moved: for *I shall* never *be* in adversity.

7 His mouth is full of cursing and deceit and fraud: under his tongue *is* mischief and vanity.

8 He sitteth in the lurking places of the villages: in the secret places doth he murder the innocent: his eyes are privily set against the poor.

9 He lieth in wait secretly as a lion in his den: he lieth in wait to catch the poor: he doth catch the poor, when he draweth him into his net.

10 He croucheth, *and* humbleth himself, that the poor may fall by his strong ones.

11 He hath said in his heart, God hath forgotten: he hideth his face; he will never *see it.*

12 Arise, O LORD; O God, lift up thine hand: forget not the humble.

13 Wherefore doth the wicked contemn God? he hath said in his heart, Thou wilt not require *it.*

14 Thou hast seen *it;* for thou beholdest mischief and spite, to requite *it* with thy hand: the poor committeth himself unto thee; thou art the helper of the fatherless.

15 Break thou the arm of the wicked and the evil *man:* seek out his wickedness *till* thou find none.

16 The LORD *is* King for ever and ever: the heathen are perished out of his land.

17 LORD, thou hast heard the desire of the humble: thou wilt prepare their heart, thou wilt cause thine ear to hear:

18 To judge the fatherless and the oppressed, that the man of the earth may no more oppress.

Israel. The Lord who is "a very present help in trouble" appears now to be hiding Himself. This human complaint is also shared by Isaiah (Isa 45:15) and by Job (Job 23:9).

2-11. These verses paint a graphic description of the wicked one who is the oppressor. The basis of his wickedness is encompassed in verses 2 and 3 by the words **pride** and **boasteth.** All other offenses described herein find their root in pride and boasting.

In his pride, the wicked one will **persecute the poor** (vs. 2). These are the poor in spirit whom Jesus mentions in the Sermon on the Mount (Mt 5:3). The wicked one **boasteth of his heart's desire,** giving vocal expression to the greed of his soul (vs. 3). **God is not in all his thoughts** (vs. 4). This self-opinionated sinner schemes as if God did not exist. **Thy judgments are far above out of his sight** (vs. 5). The wicked one does not believe God will intervene in behalf of the righteous oppressed and does not foresee the calamity of his ways (vs. 6).

Like a three-headed serpent, **His mouth is full of cursing and deceit and fraud** (vs. 7). Not only does this wicked one curse God, but through guile and extortion he leads others astray as well. **In the secret places doth he murder the innocent** (vs. 8). As a highway brigand, he lies in wait to ensnare the saint, **he lieth in wait to catch the poor** (vs. 9). Crouched for the kill and looking harmless (vs. 10), the wicked one assures himself, **God hath forgotten: he hideth his face; he will never see it** (vs. 11). Convinced that God will not intervene, the wicked one goes about his task of deceit, terror, and oppression.

Although historically there were many domestic oppressors in David's reign to whom these verses can be applied, nevertheless it is hard to escape the conclusion that these verses prophetically describe the deceitful career of the Antichrist. Through pride and boasting, the Antichrist will attempt to deceive the entire world, oppressing the righteous, lurking in hiding places for the saints (Rev 13-19).

12-15. The description of the activities of the wicked one finished, the psalmist now addresses God in the bold language of faith. A call to action is issued: **Arise, O LORD; O God, lift up thine hand** (vs. 12). God is not standing aloof from the oppression, for **Thou hast seen it** (vs. 14). G. Rawlinson observes, "The most emphatic contradiction that was possible to the wicked man's 'he will never see it' (vs. 11). God sees, notes, bears in mind, and never forgets, every act of wrong-doing that men commit, and especially acts of oppression" (p. 35). **Break thou the arm of the wicked and the evil man** (vs. 15) is a prayer that the wicked one may lose his strength and cease his tyranny through the power of almighty God.

16-18. This psalm ends with a song of thanksgiving to the Lord, the great King. It began on a note of concern and defeat; it concludes on a note of confidence and triumph. **The LORD is King for ever and ever** (cf. 29:10; 146:10). The Antichrist cannot prohibit the establishment of God's kingdom. God will hear **the desire of the humble** and answer their prayer to ferret out the wicked one and destroy him. **To judge the fatherless and the oppressed** is to vindicate the oppressed, judging between them and their oppressors. The **man of the earth** will be defeated by the man from heaven (Rev 19:11-21).

K. Confidence in God. 11:1-7.

THEME: *God's providence watches most carefully over those who put their trust in Him.*

Ascribed **To the chief musician,** this **psalm of David** does not admit the circumstances under which it was composed. It is obvious that David was in deep distress; and the most likely period of the psalmist's life that gave rise to such distress was either his residence in the court of Saul, when the king was

PSALM 11

IN the Lord put I my trust: how say ye to my soul, Flee *as* a bird to your mountain?

2 For, lo, the wicked bend *their* bow, they make ready their arrow upon the string, that they may privily shoot at the upright in heart.
3 If the foundations be destroyed, what can the righteous do?

4 The Lord *is* in his holy temple, the Lord's throne *is* in heaven: his eyes behold, his eyelids try, the children of men.
5 The Lord trieth the righteous: but the wicked and him that loveth violence his soul hateth.
6 Upon the wicked he shall rain snares, fire and brimstone, and an horrible tempest: *this shall be* the portion of their cup.
7 For the righteous Lord loveth righteousness; his countenance doth behold the upright.

PSALM 12

HELP, Lord; for the godly man ceaseth; for the faithful fail from among the children of men.

2 They speak vanity every one with his neighbour: *with* flattering lips *and* with a double heart do they speak.
3 The Lord shall cut off all flattering lips, *and* the tongue that speaketh proud things:
4 Who have said, With our tongue will we prevail; our lips *are* our own: who *is* lord over us?
5 For the oppression of the poor, for the sighing of the needy, now will I arise, saith the Lord; I will set *him* in safety *from him that* puffeth at him.

provoked to jealousy, or when David, as king himself, lived under the duress of his son Absalom's rebellion.

11:1. In the Lord I put my trust: how say ye to my soul, Flee as a bird to your mountain? In a time of distress and persecution, David had put his trust in the right place. His friends had given him advice that no one who has put his trust in the Lord could follow. **Flee as a bird to your mountain** is probably a proverbial expression for seeking shelter and safety. David cannot run away from his problems; he can but trust in the Lord.

2-3. When a society spawns those who would **bend their bow** and **shoot at the upright in heart,** it is evidence that the foundations of righteousness are being shaken. The psalmist's rhetorical question, **If the foundations be destroyed, what can the righteous do?** is answered by the psalmist in his first declaration. **In the Lord I put my trust** (vs. 1).

4-7. In the face of his timid advisors, David expresses absolute faith and trust in the God of heaven. **The Lord is in his holy temple, the Lord's throne is in heaven.** The expression that Jehovah reigns supremely in His heavenly temple is equivalent to our twentieth-century expression, "God is still on the throne." The true believer must be aware that when troubles come and God tests the righteous, He is yet in total control of our every situation. **Upon the wicked he shall rain snares, fire and brimstone, and a horrible tempest.** Divine displeasure is always followed by divine punishment. The snares (Heb *pach*) which treacherous men have laid for the godly, God will turn against those who would destroy the righteous and bring upon them fire, brimstone, and a "wrathwind." David is confident that this will happen because **the righteous Lord loveth righteousness.** The psalmist need not flee to the mountains to escape difficulty; he need only live righteously, for the Lord is righteous and the very nature of Jehovah is to defend those who are just.

L. Words: Perverse and Pure. 12:1-8.

THEME: *Living a godly life in a godless environment.*

This Davidic Psalm is headed, **To the chief musician upon Sheminith. Upon Sheminith** (Heb *'al-hashemīnīt*), signifying the eighth, is of uncertain meaning, but may mean to play by octaves or perhaps an instrument for the eighth key, the bass as opposed to the treble (cf. 46; I Chr 15:20).

12:1. Help, Lord; for the godly man ceaseth. The cry, **Help, Lord** is described by Spurgeon as, "a short, but sweet, but suggestive, seasonable, and serviceable prayer; a kind of angel's sword, and to be turned every way and to be used on all occasions." This is a universal cry and a timeless plea for mercy against treachery on every side.

2-5. In describing the unbridled speech of the ungodly, the psalmist notes that they speak **with flattering lips and with a double heart.** Flattery is but treachery in disguise. The Chinese consider a man of two hearts to be a very base individual because he believes one thing with his heart but says another with his mouth. Such action will not be tolerated, for **The Lord shall cut off all flattering lips.**

Three proud claims are made by those with a double heart. They say: (1) **With our tongue will we prevail,** i.e., whatever we desire we can accomplish through our tongues by persuasion and deception; (2) **our lips are our own,** i.e., no one can control the flatterer's lips but himself; and (3) **who is lord over us?,** i.e., who can interfere with what we say or impede our saying it? The ungodly man is convinced that he may make any claim, tell any lie, voice any deception and not stand under judgment for his actions.

But this is not the case, for **now will I arise, saith the Lord.** Jehovah highly resolves that those who are oppressed by the

6 The words of the Lord *are* pure words: *as* silver tried in a furnace of earth, purified seven times.

7 Thou shalt keep them, O Lord, thou shalt preserve them from this generation for ever.

8 The wicked walk on every side, when the vilest men are exalted.

PSALM 13

HOW long wilt thou forget me, O Lord? for ever? how long wilt thou hide thy face from me?

2 How long shall I take counsel in my soul, *having* sorrow in my heart daily? how long shall mine enemy be exalted over me?

3 Consider *and* hear me, O Lord my God: lighten mine eyes, lest I sleep the sleep *of* death;

4 Lest mine enemy say, I have prevailed against him; *and* those that trouble me rejoice when I am moved.

5 But I have trusted in thy mercy; my heart shall rejoice in thy salvation.

6 I will sing unto the Lord, because he hath dealt bountifully with me.

---

tongues of vanity will be put in a place of safety, and those who oppress the poor and needy will be punished for puffing at them with lying lips.

6-8. The words of the Lord are pure words: as silver tried in a furnace of earth, purified seven times. What a contrast between the vain words of men and the pure words of God. While the words of men are vanity, the words of God are purity; while men speak with flattering lips, God speaks with tested lips.

The words of God and the Word of God have passed through the furnace of persecution, philosophical disputation, scientific reasoning, and literary criticism; but they have not lost one precious ounce of their purity. God preserves and keeps those who are oppressed and needy because He keeps His word. Even when **The wicked walk on every side,** as a result of vile men being in positions of authority, we may still trust the Word of God, knowing that ". . . all things work together for good to them that love God, to them who are the called according to his purpose" (Rom 8:28).

M. Protest, Prayer, Praise. 13:1-6.

THEME: *Yearning for help from God and believing that help is on its way.*

Perhaps written while still under the persecution of Saul, in this psalm David exhibits the progression toward God a true believer must take when he finds himself confronted with intolerable circumstances. David's first reaction is that God has abandoned him, and he protests this supposed abandonment. Then David comes to realize that God never abandons His children; he thus prays for God to give him victory. Having bathed his protest in prayer, David is led quite naturally to the confidence that God will deliver him; and thus this psalm erupts in a final note of praise.

13:1-2. In the face of adverse circumstances, David questions God on four fronts. **How long wilt thou forget me, O Lord? for ever?** Although God cannot forget His own, frequently we feel as though we have been forgotten by Him, or that He has hidden His face from us. David wrestled all night with plans to escape his enemy, and day after day he experienced the futility of those plans. Although he could not understand, and thus questioned God, note that an answer was never given. David's restless protest erupted into prayer before God answered.

3-4. Consider and hear me, O Lord my God. Now comes the joy of morning after a night of weeping. Now comes the prayer of faith, a petition pure and simple. Through it all David still refers to Jehovah as **My God.** David will prevail against his enemy from his knees. The prayer of David asks for nothing but that the honor of God be identified with the deliverance of His servant.

5-6. There is an inseparable link between the elements of verses 5 and 6, the note of David's praise. **My heart shall rejoice in thy salvation.** Trust in God is always rewarded by salvation; salvation always provides the opportunity for the redeemed of the Lord to sing unto the Lord; and joyous praise to God always brings increased bounty from God.

What a reversal is seen in this psalm. Faith has climbed out of the cellar of despair and has ascended the heights of God's bounty. The feeling of isolation from God and the rejoicing of salvation in God are only separated by prayer to God.

N. The Depravity of Man. 14:1-7.

THEME: *God's reaction to the universal corruption of mankind.*

Anyone who is aware that in Romans 3:1-12 Paul appeals to this psalm in support of his contention that man is universally depraved, must then also be aware of the special difficulty in interpreting this psalm. The verbs appear in the perfect tense and therefore would ordinarily be considered past action. The question becomes, at what point did the events of this psalm actually take place?

Some have appealed to the mention of the **captivity** of God's people in verse 7 to indicate that this psalm was written during the Babylonian captivity and therefore can not have been written by David. But **captivity** is often used metaphorically in Scripture (cf. Job 42:10; Ezk 16:53; Rom 7:23; II Cor 10:5; Eph 4:8; etc.). Perhaps the perfect tense in these verbs indicates that the psalmist has a number of events that indicate the depravity of man in mind, e.g., the Flood, the Tower of Babel, Sodom and Gomorrah, etc.

PSALM 14

THE fool hath said in his heart, *There is* no God. They are corrupt, they have done abominable works, *there is* none that doeth good.

2 The Lord looked down from heaven upon the children of men, to see if there were any that did understand, *and* seek God.

3 They are all gone aside, they are *all* together become filthy: *there is* none that doeth good, no, not one.

14:1-3. The fool hath said in his heart, There is no God. This interpretation may be borne out by the fact that even though the word **fool** in verse 1 is singular, nevertheless the pronouns which refer to it are plural. **The fool** (Heb *nabal*) is without an article and therefore is to be taken in the generic sense. Perhaps the verb **hath said** (Heb *'amar*) can be translated has always said. Whether in Noah's, Moses', or David's time, or our own, fools have always said that there is no God. **They are corrupt.** Literally, this means that they have corrupted themselves (cf. Gen 6:12; Jud 2:19). Atheism relaxes moral restraints and is thus usually accompanied by corruption. **They have done abominable works,** the natural consequence of a corrupt heart. **There is none that doeth good,** i.e., spiritual good to be looked upon favorably by God.

The Lord looked down from heaven. God is not a tyrant who punishes blindly; He is just and holy. In response to God's divine surveillance of mankind **to see if there were any that did understand, and seek God,** the universal conclusion is that **They are all gone aside, they are all together become filthy.** Not one human being understands the goodness of God, nor does one by himself seek God in salvation (see I Cor 2:14).

The conclusion to the matter is this: **There is none that doeth good, no, not one.** In surveying all history, the psalmist comes to the conclusion that, subsequent to the fall of man, no one has ever existed whom God could describe as morally good.

4 Have all the workers of iniquity no knowledge? who eat up my people *as* they eat bread, and call not upon the Lord.

5 There were they in great fear: for God *is* in the generation of the righteous.

6 Ye have shamed the counsel of the poor, because the Lord *is* his refuge.

4-6. Have all the workers of iniquity no knowledge? This exclamation appears to be put into the mouth of God. It seems incomprehensible that those outside of Christ are unaware of the results of their corruption. They ridicule, rob, and reduce to desperation those who live righteously before God as easily as they eat bread. And yet, they **call not upon the Lord.** Corruption breeds callousness toward God, for "How then shall they call on him in whom they have not believed?" (Rom 10:14).

There were they in great fear. In the midst of their corruption, an indescribable panic seized the unbeliever, because God's people cannot be attacked without provoking God to action. The unrighteous have **shamed the counsel of the poor, because the Lord is his refuge.** The ungodly taunt the godly about the existence of God, slandering His presence and power to work among those who believe in Him. Yet, the very Jehovah who the fool claims does not exist is the refuge for those who put their trust in Him.

7 Oh that the salvation of Israel *were come* out of Zion! when the Lord bringeth back the captivity of his people, Jacob shall rejoice, *and* Israel shall be glad.

7. Oh that the salvation of Israel were come out of Zion! Natural enough is it to see this closing prayer, for nothing would set the folly of the fool to flight more than the salvation of Israel. When the ultimate salvation of God's people shall be effected (Rom 11), when the salvation of the "generation of the righteous" shall come to pass, then not only **Jacob shall rejoice, and Israel shall be glad;** but the fool will no longer be able to deceive his own heart that there is no God.

O. Walk, Work, Word. 15:1-5.

THEME: Those who are fit for communion with God may be known by conformity to His Law.

This psalm of David gives no indication of the occasion upon which it was written. Like Psalm 24, to which it bears a striking resemblance, its composition was in some respect connected with the establishment of the tabernacle on the holy hill of Zion.

PSALM 15

LORD, who shall abide in thy tabernacle? who shall dwell in thy holy hill?

2 He that walketh uprightly, and worketh righteousness, and speaketh the truth in his heart.

3 *He that* backbiteth not with his tongue, nor doeth evil to his neighbour, nor taketh up a reproach against his neighbour.

4 In whose eyes a vile person is contemned; but he honoureth them that fear the LORD. *He that* sweareth to *his own* hurt, and changeth not.

5 *He that* putteth not out his money to usury, nor taketh reward against the innocent. He that doeth these *things* shall never be moved.

15:1. This verse asks Jehovah the question, **who shall abide in thy tabernacle? Who shall dwell in thy holy hill?** Who is to approach the throne of God in holiness? What qualifications are there for service in the tabernacle?

2. The answer to these questions is found in verse 2, an elaboration of which is recorded in verses 3, 4, and 5. David responds, **He that walketh uprightly, and worketh righteousness, and speaketh the truth in his heart.** No man can stand before the Lord unless he possesses an upright walk, a righteous work, and a true word.

3-5. Seen negatively, one whose word is true is one who gives observance to the ninth commandment, **He that backbiteth not with his tongue.** One whose work is righteous does not do evil to his neighbor or spread an ill report concerning his neighbor. He prefers to keep silent and let the ill report die.

One who is interested in serving the Lord in His holy hill will never be interested in profiting financially at the expense of others; and thus, he **putteth not out his money to usury,** nor can he ever stoop to bribery in taking reward against the innocent. When a man lives righteously, there is no storm that can uproot him from the soil of God's service.

P. The Psalm of the Resurrection. 16:1-11.

THEME: A Messianic Psalm revealing the mystery of the resurrection of Christ.

This psalm is noted as a **Michtam of David.** We have not met with this term heretofore; but 56, 58, 59, and 60 are also called michtams. The word **Michtam** may be understood to mean the Golden Psalm, or may simply be derivative of the word signifying to hide, indicating the depth of a doctrinal and spiritual truth that is a mystery. Such an interpretation fits well with this psalm.

We are not left to human interpreters to unlock the secrets of this golden mystery. According to the Apostle Peter (Acts 2:25) and the Apostle Paul (Acts 13:35), this psalm relates to Christ. It expresses His feeling of human emotion when, during His sufferings and death, he called on God to preserve Him.

PSALM 16

PRESERVE me, O God: for in thee do I put my trust.

2 *O my soul,* thou hast said unto the LORD, Thou *art* my Lord: my goodness *extendeth* not to thee;

3 *But* to the saints that *are* in the earth, and *to* the excellent, in whom *is* all my delight.

4 Their sorrows shall be multiplied *that* hasten *after* another *god:* their drink offerings of blood will I not offer, nor take up their names into my lips.

16:1. Preserve me, O God. As body-guards surround a king and shepherds protect their flocks, so the psalmist appeals to God, whose name is EL (the Omnipotent One), preserve him. One of the great names of God is the Preserver of Men (Job 7:20). As our Mediator, the Lord Jesus Christ has expressly promised such preservation (Isa 49:7-8).

2-3. Thou hast said unto the LORD. Some translators prefer this Hebrew verb *'amarte* to be translated as *'amarti,* I have said. If the traditional rendering is maintained, the insertion of **O my soul** is necessary to express the meaning of the psalmist's cry.

My goodness extendeth not to thee; but to the saints that are in the earth. Two possible interpretations may be admitted here. First, the Lord's goodness (Heb *tōbah,* i.e., happiness) extendeth not to God (taking the Heb *'al* to mean "besides" or "beyond"), indicating that the omnipotent God is the sole source of Christ's goodness or happiness. The second interpretation is that the Lord's goodness or merit is not on account of Thee, i.e., is not for God's benefit. This interpretation is more constant with the messianic character of the psalm. It is also reflected in Christ's great high priestly prayer recorded in John 17.

4. Their sorrows shall be multiplied that hasten after another God. This is the only sad note in the entire psalm. The psalmist notes that God will multiply the sorrows of those who woo or wed other gods. **Nor take up their names into my lips.**

5 The LORD *is* the portion of mine inheritance and of my cup: thou maintainest my lot.
6 The lines are fallen unto me in pleasant *places;* yea, I have a goodly heritage.
7 I will bless the LORD, who hath given me counsel: my reins also instruct me in the night seasons.

8 I have set the LORD always before me: because *he is* at my right hand, I shall not be moved.
9 Therefore my heart is glad, and my glory rejoiceth: my flesh also shall rest in hope.

10 For thou wilt not leave my soul in hell; neither wilt thou suffer thine Holy One to see corruption.
11 Thou wilt shew me the path of life: in thy presence *is* fulness of joy; at thy right hand *there are* pleasures for evermore.

PSALM 17

HEAR the right, O LORD, attend unto my cry, give ear unto my prayer, *that* goeth not out of feigned lips.
2 Let my sentence come forth from thy presence; let thine eyes behold the things that are equal.
3 Thou hast proved mine heart; thou hast visited *me* in the night; thou hast tried me, *and* shalt find nothing; I am purposed *that* my mouth shall not transgress.
4 Concerning the works of men, by

The Mosaic law forbade the mention of the names of foreign gods by the Israelites (Ex 23:13; Deut 12:3).

5-7. There was no need for either the psalmist or the Messiah Himself to seek after another god, for Jehovah is **the portion of mine inheritance.** The Omnipotent God is all the portion one needs. **The lines are fallen unto me in pleasant places.** Notwithstanding all the sorrows that marred His coming to Jerusalem, the Lord Jesus could exclaim that Jerusalem was an abode of pleasure for Him. **I will bless the LORD, who hath given me counsel.** Jesus not only prays to the Father, but praises Him as well. All that the Lord said and did on this earth was at the direct counsel of God the Father (Jn 7:16; 8:28; 12:49-50). Whether alone on the hillsides of Galilee or in the Garden of Gethsemane, Jesus spent many nights of profitable communion with the Father in preparation for His crucifixion.

8-9. I have set the LORD always before me, i.e., the psalmist continually realized the presence of God, as did the Saviour. The apostle translated this passage, "I foresaw the Lord always before my face . . ." (Acts 2:25). **I shall not be moved,** i.e., with the Father's continual divine support, nothing could dissuade the Lord Jesus from keeping His destined appointment with death. **Therefore my heart is glad, and my glory rejoiceth.** Faith in God brings gladness to the inner man and the expression of joy to the lips.

10-11. For thou wilt not leave my soul in hell. The Lord Jesus was not disappointed in His hope in the Father. He declared his confidence that God would not allow His soul to remain in hell (Heb *She'ōl*, the grave). The verb in this clause (Heb *'azab*) means to forsake, abandon, or surrender. The Lord Jesus did not expect God the Father to deliver Him from the ordeal of death and the grave, but from the dominion of death and the grave. He actually died and was placed in the grave, but the grave could not hold Him. What a great encouragement to all true believers; die we must, but rise we shall.

Neither wilt thou suffer thine Holy One to see corruption. The translation of the Hebrew *shachat* by the English word **corruption** (Gr *diaphthora* in the LXX) squares well with our understanding that on the third day, when the women came to embalm the body, the Lord Jesus had risen from the dead, totally free from physical decay (Acts 13:35).

Thou wilt show me the path of life. As the first begotten from the dead, the first-born of every creature, Jesus was the first to trod the path from death to life. He will certainly not be the last, for He promised every believer, ". . . because I live, ye shall live also" (Jn 14:19).

Q. A Petition to Heaven. 17:1-15.

THEME: *David's prayer to God for divine intervention and protection from the persecutions of earth.*

This psalm is termed a prayer because the language of petition is predominant. David would not have been a man after God's own heart, had he not been a man of prayer. The time in David's life to which this psalm belongs is uncertain, but it is quite likely that Saul is the leader of those who oppose him. I Samuel 23:24ff. fits the situation of the psalm very well.

17:1-4. Hear the right, O LORD, attend unto my cry. The psalmist here, and in frequent other places, assumes that he is on the right side and has been unjustly persecuted. The earnestness of his prayer is indicated by the word **cry** (Heb *rinnah*), a word that means a shout or outcry. Having been wrongly judged by his enemies, David weeps and laments, petitioning the Lord to allow his sentence to **come forth from thy presence** and knowing that the Lord God is always right in His judgment.

Thou hast proved mine heart. The motives of the psalmist have been tested by the Lord, examined closely, and proven to be true. **By the word of thy lips I have kept me from the paths**

the word of thy lips I have kept *me from* the paths of the destroyer.

5 Hold up my goings in thy paths, *that* my footsteps slip not.
6 I have called upon thee, for thou wilt hear me, O God: incline thine ear unto me, *and hear* my speech.
7 Shew thy marvellous lovingkindness, O thou that savest by thy right hand them which put their trust *in thee* from those that rise up *against them.*
8 Keep me as the apple of the eye, hide me under the shadow of thy wings,
9 From the wicked that oppress me, *from* my deadly enemies, *who* compass me about.

10 They are inclosed in their own fat: with their mouth they speak proudly.
11 They have now compassed us in our steps: they have set their eyes bowing down to the earth;
12 Like as a lion *that* is greedy of his prey, and as it were a young lion lurking in secret places.

13 Arise, O LORD, disappoint him, cast him down: deliver my soul from the wicked, *which is* thy sword:
14 From men *which are* thy hand, O LORD, from men of the world, *which have* their portion in *this* life, and whose belly thou fillest with thy hid *treasure:* they are full of children, and leave the rest of their *substance* to their babes.
15 As for me, I will behold thy face in righteousness: I shall be satisfied, when I awake, with thy likeness.

PSALM 18
I WILL love thee, O LORD, my strength.
2 The LORD *is* my rock, and my for-

of the destroyer. By attending carefully unto the Word of God and taking heed to it (119:11), David knew that he had avoided the courses of the wicked one (cf. I Sam 24:4-10).

5-9. It is not easy to always live righteously, even when things are going well. But when we are being persecuted, and that falsely, it is most difficult to live in a right manner. **Hold up my goings in thy paths, that my footsteps slip not.** Only the Lord God of heaven, as He directs us through His Word, can keep our paths right and our spirits bright when we are falsely accused.

O God: incline thine ear unto me. David is asking the Sovereign of the universe to bend His ear out of heaven and touch it to his lips. His faith strengthened, he petitions, **Show thy marvelous loving-kindness.** The loving-kindness that led the Israelites across the Red Sea, as well as sent Jesus Christ to the cross, is sought by the psalmist, especially in a tangible form, i.e., his deliverance from the oppressors.

Keep me as the apple of the eye. This same simile is used in Deuteronomy 32:10. The eye is the most precious organ of the body; and the pupil is the most precious point of the most precious organ. As the eye is hedged about with the eyebrows, fenced in by the eyelashes, and given the curtain of the eyelids, so too does the psalmist petition for God's protective covering, a covering which shall hide him **under the shadow of thy wings, from the wicked that oppress** him.

10-12. David's descriptive analysis of his enemy begins with **They are inclosed in their own fat: with their mouth they speak proudly.** These wicked foes have been guilty of the double sin of gluttony and pride. As a bull lowers his head, looks downward, and charges toward his victim with mighty force, so too the enemies of David **have set their eyes bowing down to the earth.** They are **like as a lion that is greedy of his prey.** The only animal more treacherous than a lion is **a young lion lurking in secret places, a hungry lion in the strength of his youth.**

13-15. **Arise, O LORD . . . deliver my soul from the wicked, which is thy sword.** David knows he has lived righteously before the Lord God and his enemy has not. Therefore, he confidently cries for deliverance from those who have received all that the good earth could produce and have passed their substance on to their children totally without thankfulness to God.

David wants no part of that bounty and fatness. **As for me, I will behold thy face in righteousness.** The wicked may joy in his prosperity and wrongly defame the psalmist, but David prefers to live righteously in the face of God. **I shall be satisfied, when I awake, with thy likeness.** Like John, he has the confidence that, "it doth not appear what we shall be: but we know that when He shall appear, we shall be like Him; for we shall see Him as He is" (I Jn 3:2).

R. Thankful Reflection. 18:1-50.

THEME: In retrospect the goodness of the Lord gives rise to David's song of praise.

The superscription over this psalm gives the occasion for his deliverance. It was penned by David after he became king of Israel. But David refers to himself as **the servant of the LORD,** without a single reference to his royalty. Apparently, he counted it a higher honor to be the Lord's servant than to be Israel's king.

The second verse of this song is quoted in the New Testament in Hebrews 2:13; verse 49 is quoted in Romans 15:9. Both of these quotes are presented as the words of the Lord Jesus; and thus, although this psalm is in the historical context of King David, a king greater than David can readily be found in these verses.

18:1-3. David's high resolve to love the Lord constitutes the first segment of this psalm. The Hebrew word used for love

tress, and my deliverer; my God, my strength, in whom I will trust; my buckler, and the horn of my salvation, *and* my high tower.

3 I will call upon the LORD, *who is worthy* to be praised: so shall I be saved from mine enemies.

4 The sorrows of death compassed me, and the floods of ungodly men made me afraid.

5 The sorrows of hell compassed me about: the snares of death prevented me.

6 In my distress I called upon the LORD, and cried unto my God: he heard my voice out of his temple, and my cry came before him, *even* into his ears.

7 Then the earth shook and trembled; the foundations also of the hills moved and were shaken, because he was wroth.

8 There went up a smoke out of his nostrils, and fire out of his mouth devoured: coals were kindled by it.

9 He bowed the heavens also, and came down: and darkness *was* under his feet.

10 And he rode upon a cherub, and did fly: yea, he did fly upon the wings of the wind.

11 He made darkness his secret place; his pavilion round about him *were* dark waters *and* thick clouds of the skies.

12 At the brightness *that was* before him his thick clouds passed, hail *stones* and coals of fire.

13 The LORD also thundered in the heavens, and the Highest gave his voice; hail *stones* and coals of fire.

14 Yea, he sent out his arrows, and scattered them; and he shot out lightnings, and discomfited them.

15 Then the channels of waters were seen, and the foundations of the world were discovered at thy rebuke, O LORD, at the blast of the breath of thy nostrils.

16 He sent from above, he took me, he drew me out of many waters.

17 He delivered me from my strong enemy, and from them which hated me: for they were too strong for me.

(Heb *racham*) denotes the tenderest affection and is elsewhere used only of God's love toward man.

As if he cannot find sufficient expression to indicate his love for God, the psalmist engages in a lively series of epithets for the Lord. **The LORD is my rock.** The Lord is a dwelling place among the crags, (Heb *sela'*). **And my fortress** (cf. 144:2). This is a fortified, though natural, stronghold. **And my deliverer.** Not just an inanimate defense, but a living protector. **My God,** the personal divine being who holds my future. **My strength** (lit., "my rock," as translated in Ex 17:6; 33:21-22; Deut 32:4, 15, 18, 31; etc., cf. Isa 26:4). Here it is a firm rock, an unchangeable rock, a symbol of strength. **My buckler,** both an offensive and defensive weapon to shield from the arrow or the sword. **And the horn of my salvation,** an emblem of strength. As the means of attack or defense in some of the strongest animals, the horn is a frequent emblem of power (cf. Deut 33:17; Lk 1:69). **And my high tower** is a rocky citadel well beyond the reach of the enemy; and from its heights, one who abides therein may confidently survey a crumbling world around him. It is a worthy observation that these epithets for God start with the rock beneath our feet and end with the high tower above our heads, i.e., those who trust in the Lord are equipped with God's provision from head to toe.

4-5. The situation of the psalmist was grave indeed. Engulfed by **The sorrows of death** (lit., the cord of death), surrounded by **ungodly men** (lit., sons of Belial), and chased by **The sorrows of hell** (lit., the cords of Sheol), there was nowhere to turn but to God. Spurgeon observes, "From all sides the hell-hounds barked furiously. A cordon of devils hemmed in the hunted man of God; every way of escape was closed up. Satan knows how to blockade our coasts with the iron war-ships of sorrow, but, blessed be God, the port of all prayer is still open. . . ."

6-15. David did the only thing he could do, that which he was in the habit of doing. **In my distress I called upon the LORD.** In reaction to Jehovah's hearing the prayer of the psalmist, **the earth shook and trembled,** an event not without precedent in this land. **There went up a smoke out of his nostrils.** This is an Oriental way of expressing fierce wrath. The entire description is designed to depict the majesty of God who **bowed the heavens also, and came down** to help his child.

And he rode upon a cherub, and did fly. Frequently in the Old Testament, the cherubim are said to be the chariots of God. The storm clouds thickened with the presence of the Lord God; and **The LORD also thundered in the heavens, and the Highest gave his voice.** Darkness, hailstones, thunder, and lightning are all fit accompaniment for the flames of vengeance when God relieves the distress of His own.

When reading this account, one cannot help but be mindful of the events that took place at the crucifixion of our Lord. It was dark and ominous that day too as ". . . the veil of the temple was rent in twain from the top to the bottom; and the earth did quake, and the rocks rent; And the graves were opened . . ." (Mt 27:51-52).

16-24. In rehearsing his deliverance, the psalmist gives the credit to God. God has delivered him from his **strong enemy.** In the case of David, this is undoubtedly a reference to Saul; in the case of the Lord Jesus, the son of David, it is a reference to Satan. God frustrated the designs of Saul at Gilboa (I Sam

18 They prevented me in the day of my calamity: but the Lord was my stay.

19 He brought me forth also into a large place; he delivered me, because he delighted in me.

20 The Lord rewarded me according to my righteousness; according to the cleanness of my hands hath he recompensed me.

21 For I have kept the ways of the Lord, and have not wickedly departed from my God.

22 For all his judgments were before me, and I did not put away his statutes from me.

23 I was also upright before him, and I kept myself from mine iniquity.

24 Therefore hath the Lord recompensed me according to my righteousness, according to the cleanness of my hands in his eyesight.

25 With the merciful thou wilt shew thyself merciful; with an upright man thou wilt shew thyself upright;

26 With the pure thou wilt shew thyself pure; and with the froward thou wilt shew thyself froward.

27 For thou wilt save the afflicted people; but wilt bring down high looks.

28 For thou wilt light my candle: the Lord my God will enlighten my darkness.

29 For by thee I have run through a troop; and by my God have I leaped over a wall.

30 As for God, his way is perfect: the word of the Lord is tried: he is a buckler to all those that trust in him.

31 For who is God save the Lord? or who is a rock save our God?

32 It is God that girdeth me with strength, and maketh my way perfect.

33 He maketh my feet like hinds' feet, and setteth me upon my high places.

34 He teacheth my hands to war, so that a bow of steel is broken by mine arms.

35 Thou hast also given me the shield of thy salvation: and thy right hand hath holden me up, and thy gentleness hath made me great.

36 Thou hast enlarged my steps under me, that my feet did not slip.

37 I have pursued mine enemies, and overtaken them: neither did I turn again till they were consumed.

38 I have wounded them that they were not able to rise: they are fallen under my feet.

39 For thou hast girded me with strength unto the battle: thou hast subdued under me those that rose up against me.

40 Thou hast also given me the necks of mine enemies; that I might destroy them that hate me.

41 They cried, but there was none to save them: even unto the Lord, but he answered them not.

42 Then did I beat them small as the dust before the wind: I did cast them out as the dirt in the streets.

43 Thou hast delivered me from the strivings of the people; and thou hast made me the head of the heathen: a

31:1-4), as He frustrated the designs of Satan at Calvary (Lk 24:1-7).

Deliverance for the psalmist meant being brought **into a large place,** a place of safety, as contrasted with the snares of distress found in the places of ambush (4:1). **Because he delighted in me.** David understands his deliverance to be entirely the fruit of God's grace, free and sovereign. **The Lord rewarded me according to my righteousness.** David does not mean he is absolutely blameless, any more than Job means blamelessness by his "integrity" (cf. Job 27:5; 31:6). His sincere and honest claims are that **I have kept the ways of the Lord, and have not wickedly departed from my God.**

What was the secret of David's upright living? **I did not put away his statutes from me.** David was constantly mindful to study the Scriptures. Righteous living begins with a knowledge of what is righteous. Backsliding begins with a dusty Bible.

25-28. In these verses David gives a principle (vs. 25), examples of that principle (vss. 26-27), and a delightful promise (vs. 28). The principle is this: **With the merciful thou wilt show thyself merciful.** The dealings of the Lord are always just. He metes out to men every man according to his measure. God measures the area of a man's land by the same rod with which that man measures the area of others' land. **For thou wilt light my candle** means that David has full assurance that, since he has lived uprightly, God will be his light in his darkest hour. All who live righteously in Christ Jesus have that same promise.

29-45. Using the language of war, David ascribes his victories to the power of God. **As for God, his way is perfect: the word of the Lord is tried.** The psalmist expresses perfect faith in the righteousness of God's path. **For who is God save the Lord?** As in Exodus 20:3 and Deuteronomy 32:39, absolute confidence is placed in Jehovah, the one and only God, the deliverer of His people.

David is convinced that his battle record is due to the Lord's hand upon him. **He maketh my feet like hinds' feet.** The Israelites reckoned agility, endurance, and swiftness as the highest of warlike qualities. The rapidity of David's conquests must be attributed to the enabling of the Lord God. **He teacheth my hands to war, so that a bow of steel is broken by mine arms. A bow of steel** (Heb nechûshah) indicates a bow of brass or bonze; steel was unknown at this period. **Thou hast also given me the shield of thy salvation.** As God has provided the offensive weapons for the believer, likewise He provides adequate defensive weapons. **Thy right hand hath holden me up.** The right hand is always spoken of as the arm of greatest strength (cf. 44:3; 45:4; 48:10; etc.).

I have wounded them that they were not able to rise is an expression of the remarkable fact that the nations David subdued were unable to revolt during his lifetime. **For thou hast girded me with strength unto the battle.** David consistently acknowledges that his victorious efforts are solely due to the God who enabled him.

His enemies cried, **but there was none to save them: even unto the Lord, but he answered them not.** Seeing the victory of David, the enemy, as a last resort, even cried out unto Jehovah for victory; but victory was denied to the ungodly. **I did cast them out as the dirt in the streets.**

Verse 43, with the antithesis between **people** (Heb 'am) and **heathen** (Heb gōy), is obviously messianic in nature. The people are the Jews; the heathen are the Gentiles. The Lord Jesus was not only delivered from the strivings of the Jews, but as the Saviour of the world, He has been made the Head of all people. This can never literally be said of David, and thus it must be

people *whom* I have not known shall serve me.

44 As soon as they hear of me, they shall obey me: the strangers shall submit themselves unto me.

45 The strangers shall fade away, and be afraid out of their close places.

46 The LORD liveth; and blessed *be* my rock; and let the God of my salvation be exalted.

47 *It is* God that avengeth me, and subdueth the people under me.

48 He delivereth me from mine enemies: yea, thou liftest me up above those that rise up against me: thou hast delivered me from the violent man.

49 Therefore will I give thanks unto thee, O LORD, among the heathen, and sing praises unto thy name.

50 Great deliverance giveth he to his king; and sheweth mercy to his anointed, to David, and to his seed for evermore.

PSALM 19

THE heavens declare the glory of God; and the firmament sheweth his handywork.

2 Day unto day uttereth speech, and night unto night sheweth knowledge.

3 *There is* no speech nor language, *where* their voice is not heard.

4 Their line is gone out through all the earth, and their words to the end of the world. In them hath he set a tabernacle for the sun,

5 Which *is* as a bridegroom coming out of his chamber, *and* rejoiceth as a strong man to run a race.

6 His going forth *is* from the end of the heaven, and his circuit unto the ends of it: and there is nothing hid from the heat thereof.

7 The law of the LORD *is* perfect, converting the soul: the testimony of the LORD *is* sure, making wise the simple.

explained as a messianic prophecy. **A people whom I have not known shall serve me. As soon as they hear of me, they shall obey me.** These words can only aptly apply to the conversion of the Gentiles (cf. Acts 10:34-48; 13:48; 17:11; 18:8; etc.). The remarkable expansion of the church into Gentile territory in the first century is the fulfillment of this messianic prophecy.

46-50. The epilogue of this psalm brings into focus both David and Christ. **The LORD liveth** is a cry of victory. David did not have to avenge himself when he was wrongfully accused and maligned; for **It is God that avengeth me,** a concept reiterated by Paul in Romans 12:19. The name of Jehovah is to be exalted among the heathen, for **Great deliverance giveth he to his king. Deliverance** is plural, indicating how complete and manifold the salvation of the Lord is. **And showeth mercy to his anointed, to David, and to his seed for evermore.**

The psalm ends on a strong messianic note. Not only does Paul cite verse 49 in Romans 15:9 with reference to David's Lord, but the references to **seed** and **for evermore** clearly indicate that this passage is carried well beyond the psalmist and depicts the deliverance of the Messiah-Saviour from the enemy Satan. As great as the deliverance of David was, the resurrection of Christ was much greater.

S. Witnesses to God's Glory. 19:1-14.

THEME: *The harmonious revelation of God's glory as seen by His world and His Word.*

This psalm seems to naturally divide itself into three parts: the witness of God's glory by His creation (vss. 1-6); the witness of God's glory by His law (vss. 7-11); and the witness of God's glory in comparison to man (vss. 12-14).

Some incorrectly argue that this psalm could not have been written by David because the Law had not achieved a position of prominence in David's day. However, the historical record of I Kings 2:1-4 indicates that David held the Law in very high regard, and therefore he should not be questioned as the author of this psalm.

19:1. The heavens declare the glory of God. The heavens are plural because there are various spheres represented, i.e., the heavens of clouds, the solar heavens, deep space, the throne of God, etc. **The glory of God** is the sum of all of God's perfections (24:7-9; Rom 1:20). The vastness of space declares the magnitude of our God. The energy of a thousand suns is but a token of His divine energy. The perfect timing of planetary movements declares His precision. And yet, the multifaceted declaration of the heavens only begins to show the great glory of God. **The firmament showeth his handiwork** may be designed as an expression of the most readily visible evidence of God's presence in the universe.

2-6. Day unto day and **night unto night** the creation of God emits speech testifying to the person of God. **There is no speech nor language, where their voice is not heard.** The creation of God speaks without sound or language, but with great pictorial wonder that is understood throughout the world (cf. Rom 1:20).

The psalmist now zeroes in on one particular body of the heavens: the sun. In fact, the heavens are described as **a tabernacle for the sun.** It is there that the sun encamps and marches as a mighty monarch across the skies, arising every morning as a **bridegroom coming out of his chamber,** indicating that the sun bursts forth every day from the night chamber in the strength of youth. **His circuit unto the ends of it** indicates that as the sun blazes across the sky, it finds no boundary from which its heat can be hidden.

7. The witness to the glory of God now turns to the testimony of the Law of the Lord. **The law of the LORD is perfect.** By this is not meant simply the law of Moses, but the entire doctrine of

God, the whole body of scriptural truth. **Converting the soul,** or better, restoring the soul. The word used here (Heb *shūb*) is the normal word for restoration from decay (80:19), from sorrow (Ruth 4:15), or from death (I Kgs 17:21-22).

8 The statutes of the LORD *are* right, rejoicing the heart: the commandment of the LORD *is* pure, enlightening the eyes.

8. The statutes of the LORD are right. The precepts and decrees of the Lord are founded in His righteousness and, therefore, are righteous themselves. **The commandment of the LORD is pure.** It is no alloy, polluted, adulterated, or diluted; it is the sincere milk of the Word.

9 The fear of the LORD *is* clean, enduring for ever: the judgments of the LORD *are* true *and* righteous altogether.

9. The fear of the LORD is clean, enduring for ever. To respect and reverence the Lord God brings cleanliness of soul and, thus, everlasting life. Filthiness brings decay, but cleanliness brings incorruptibility. **The judgments of the LORD are true and righteous altogether.** Taken separately or corporately, God's judgments are manifestly pure and righteous.

10 More to be desired *are they* than gold, yea, than much fine gold: sweeter also than honey and the honeycomb.
11 Moreover by them is thy servant warned: *and* in keeping of them *there is* great reward.

10-11. More to be desired are they than gold, yea, than much fine gold. The words of God's Word are more precious than the finest commodity man possesses. **Sweeter also than honey and the honeycomb** may be designed to show the elderly the desirability of God's Word, just as gold is designed to show the young that the Word is to be desired. The appeal is universal, whether gold or honey. **In keeping of them there is great reward.** Although the wicked may seem to prosper on every hand, we must be assured that keeping the commandments of God's Word will prove to our ultimate benefit.

12 Who can understand *his* errors? cleanse thou me from secret *faults.*
13 Keep back thy servant also from presumptuous *sins;* let them not have dominion over me: then shall I be upright, and I shall be innocent from the great transgression.
14 Let the words of my mouth, and the meditation of my heart, be acceptable in thy sight, O LORD, my strength, and my redeemer.

12-14. Who can understand his errors? There is no one who can discern all of his sins. But he who knows the Word best knows himself best. **Cleanse thou me from secret faults.** Not only does the psalmist pray for cleansing from sins unknown to him, but he also prays **Keep back thy servant also from presumptuous sins,** those willful, intentional, deliberate sins that are personified as tyrants and strive to make the servant of God a servant of sin. We must utter the preventative prayer, "And lead us not into temptation, but deliver us from evil . . ." (Mt 6:13). **Then shall I be upright,** or blameless (Gr *amōmos* in the LXX). The believer knows he can never be sinless in this life, but he must strive to be blameless.

Let the words of my mouth, and the meditation of my heart. The psalmist closes this inspiring psalm with a sweet prayer. He asks that his words and thoughts be equal. Words of the mouth are a sham if they are not backed up by meditation of the heart. **Be acceptable in thy sight.** David's greatest concern as a servant of the Lord is his own acceptability to his Master. This concern is also reflected by Paul in the New Testament (II Cor 5:8-10).

The prayer concludes with the psalmist's reiteration that Jehovah is **my strength, and my redeemer.** David has surveyed the wonderful heavens that declare the glory of God; he has looked into the wonderful Word of God that declares His glory; and he has seen himself in light of these two creations of God. He has recognized the completeness of God's creation, the perfection of His Word, and his own sinful condition. Therefore, he can do nothing less than conclude with a prayer for God to sanctify him constantly.

T. A National Anthem. 20:1-9.

THEME: *A prayer for the deliverance of the king as he prepares to enter battle.*

Psalms 20 and 21 have been called "an antiphonal war anthem." Psalm 20 offers the prayers of God's people for their king as he prepares for battle; Psalm 21 expresses thanksgiving after the victory. David is the author of these psalms, but the occasion for their writing is difficult to determine.

The ultimate intent of this psalm is probably not for David as much as for David's Lord, the great Captain of salvation. The reference in verse 1 to **the day of trouble** for Jacob is probably a reference to the Great Tribulation in which the Messiah, Jesus

PSALM 20

THE LORD hear thee in the day of trouble; the name of the God of Jacob defend thee;

2 Send thee help from the sanctuary, and strengthen thee out of Zion;

3 Remember all thy offerings, and accept thy burnt sacrifice; Sĕ'lah.

4 Grant thee according to thine own heart, and fulfil all thy counsel.

5 We will rejoice in thy salvation, and in the name of our God we will set up *our* banners: the LORD fulfil all thy petitions.

6 Now know I that the LORD saveth his anointed; he will hear him from his holy heaven with the saving strength of his right hand.

7 Some *trust* in chariots, and some in horses: but we will remember the name of the LORD our God.

8 They are brought down and fallen: but we are risen, and stand upright.

9 Save, LORD: let the king hear us when we call.

PSALM 21

THE king shall joy in thy strength, O LORD; and in thy salvation how greatly shall he rejoice!

2 Thou hast given him his heart's desire, and hast not withholden the request of his lips. Sĕ'lah.

3 For thou preventest him with the blessings of goodness: thou settest a crown of pure gold on his head.

4 He asked life of thee, *and* thou gavest *it* him, *even* length of days for ever and ever.

5 His glory *is* great in thy salvation: honour and majesty hast thou laid upon him.

6 For thou hast made him most blessed for ever: thou hast made him exceeding glad with thy countenance.

Christ, will ride forth in victory against Satan and his forces (Rev 19:11-21).

20:1-5. In days of distress the people's prayer for their king is, **the name of the God of Jacob defend thee.** When God puts His name on the line, He also puts His reputation as a Deliverer on the line. Thus, the prayer is not simply that God deliver the king, but that the God of Jacob prove Himself again as a Deliverer.

A most important petition in this prayer is, **remember all thy offerings, and accept thy burnt sacrifice.** Before kings went to war, they always offered sacrifices unto their God, and the acceptance of their sacrifices would assure success in battle. **Grant thee according to thine own heart,** i.e., whatever the heart's desire of the Lord is with regard to this battle. This is the "thy will be done" of ancient Israel. **And in the name of our God we will set up our banners.** Confident that God will hear their plea, the people promised to plant their banners on enemies' forts and strongholds in the name of the Lord.

6-9. Now know I that the LORD saveth his anointed. The use of the first person singular marks a change of speaker. Whereas the congregation has been praising the Lord and petitioning Him for the safety of the king, now either the king himself or the high priest takes the lead in the prayer. Whether the anointed King David or the Messiah Jesus enters the battle, God will assure victory **with the saving strength of his right hand.**

Some trust in chariots. Chariots and horses were the most dreaded war machines of David's day. The Syrians were especially noted for their fierceness in driving chariots armed with scythes that mowed down the enemy like grass. The chariots and horses of David's enemies made quite an imposing comparison to David's trust in the Lord. Their trust in war machines did not bring them victory, but David's confidence in the saving power of Jehovah assured him of victory. The psalmist is already certain of the answer when he prays, **Save, LORD: let the king hear us when we call.**

U. A National Thanksgiving. 21:1-13.

THEME: *A psalm of praise for the devastating victory given by God to His anointed.*

This psalm is a companion to the preceding one. Psalm 20 is essentially a psalm of intercession; Psalm 21 is essentially a psalm of thanksgiving. Again, the messianic character of this psalm is evident in that although the victory was completely David's, nevertheless ultimate victory comes only to the "seed of David." The Davidic authorship of this psalm has been questioned, but on insufficient grounds.

21:1-6. The first six verses, which represent a direct thanksgiving to God offered by the people on behalf of their king, are replete with allusions that may be taken to refer to David's King, the King of Kings.

The king shall joy in thy strength, O LORD. Salvation, which was confidently anticipated in 20:5, 6, and 9, has now been experienced; and to pray for something and receive it necessitates an additional prayer of thanksgiving. **For thou preventest him with the blessings of goodness.** The word **preventest** signifies to go before or precede. Thus, even now, before the victory of the King at Armageddon has been won, the blessings of goodness are ours; and we are assured of victory because God always causes us to triumph. **Thou settest a crown of pure gold on his head.** The Lord Jesus exchanged His crown of thorns for a crown of pure gold, because He is the victor.

He asked life of thee, and thou gavest it him, even length of days for ever and ever. Although it can be said that David asked for life from the Lord God, it can never be said that he received length of days for ever and ever. This can only refer to the King of David the king, King Jesus Christ. **Honor and majesty hast thou laid upon him.** Once at the depth of shame (Phil 2:6-8; Heb 12:2), Jesus Christ, the victor, has now been placed at the height of glory. **Thou hast made him exceeding glad with thy countenance.** The presence and countenance of God the Father gives the Son incomparable joy.

7-12. The outcome of the statement **the king trusteth in the Lord** is found in verses 7 through 12. Jehovah shall make the enemies of the king **as a fiery oven in the time of thine anger.** Those whose anger raged within themselves and who burned in wrath against the great king, shall themselves be the victim of the fire of God's wrath. **Their fruit shalt thou destroy from the earth.** By order of King David, Joab remained in Edom, ". . . until he had cut off every male . . ." (I Kgs 11:16). **For they intended evil against thee.** He who intends evil against any of God's saints intends evil against God Himself. **They imagined a mischievous device, which they are not able to perform.** The victory is secure in Christ Jesus, and therefore all the Evil One can do is imagine or devise evil against us. He cannot exercise it.

7 For the king trusteth in the Lord, and through the mercy of the most High he shall not be moved.
8 Thine hand shall find out all thine enemies: thy right hand shall find out those that hate thee.
9 Thou shalt make them as a fiery oven in the time of thine anger: the Lord shall swallow them up in his wrath, and the fire shall devour them.
10 Their fruit shalt thou destroy from the earth, and their seed from among the children of men.
11 For they intended evil against thee: they imagined a mischievous device, *which* they are not able *to perform.*
12 Therefore shalt thou make them turn their back, *when* thou shalt make ready *thine arrows* upon thy strings against the face of them.
13 Be thou exalted, Lord, in thine own strength: *so* will we sing and praise thy power.

13. Be thou exalted, Lord. This concluding doxology may relate to both Psalm 20 and 21. It describes the strength, the praise, and the power due the Lord God of heaven. Throughout all the ages, God has been pleased to display His grace and power in defeating the oppressor.

V. The Crucifixion Psalm. 22:1-31.

THEME: A psalm which depicts the victorious suffering of Christ on the cross of Calvary.

This psalm of David is addressed **To the chief musician upon Aijeleth Shahar.** The meaning of these words is obscure. Most interpreters agree in translating them hind of the morning, but a great difference exists in the understanding of these words. At best, we can say it is an enigmatic phrase for which we do not have a precise interpretation.

The greatest difficulty in interpreting this psalm is the question of its intention. Some scholars interpret it personally, indicating that David, the author, lived through these experiences and describes them in the psalm. Others, like Hengstenberg, believe the ideal interpretation is best. This interpretation allows for these experiences not to have been known by only one man, but to be the combined experiences of an ideal righteous person, the sort of experiences a person would have if he were entirely righteous. Still others, following Buttenwieser, assume this psalm to refer to a national experience only, i.e., the details relating to the nation Israel, especially in the Exile. But the proper approach is the prophetic interpretation of this passage.

The citation of verse 1 by our Saviour on the cross and the quotation of verse 18 by John (Jn 19:24) and of verse 22 by the author of Hebrews (Heb 2:12) as fulfilled in Christ, clearly indicate that the New Testament writers understood this psalm to be messianic in nature. In addition, there are a number of circumstances described that cannot apply to David. The conclusion to be drawn, then, is that David prophetically wrote a description of Jesus Christ hanging between heaven and earth on the cross of Calvary.

PSALM 22
MY God, my God, why hast thou forsaken me? *why art thou so* far from helping me, *and from* the words of my roaring?

22:1. My God, my God, why hast thou forsaken me? This is the unmistakably similar and startling cry of Calvary: *Eli, Eli, lama sabacthani?* (Mt 27:46). This complaint did not arise out of Christ's need to know the deep-seated reasons for God's absence. Rather, it arose out of the incomprehensibility of it all. Certainly, God had forsaken the Lord Jesus in those moments on the cross, but the reason was that He had made Him who knew no sin to be sin for us (II Cor 5:21). God turned His back on the sin He hated, not the Son He loved.

Why art thou so far from helping me, and from the words of my roaring? The Man of Sorrows had prayed in the Garden and along the pathway to Calvary to such an extent that He was nearly speechless on the cross. His utterings, because of severe pain and heartache, have been reduced to **words of roaring.** From a diaphram sagging in pain and a heart filled with sorrow, Christ inquired of the incomprehensibility of His solitude on the cross.

2 O my God, I cry in the daytime, but thou hearest not; and in the night season, and am not silent.

3 But thou *art* holy, *O thou* that inhabitest the praises of Israel.

4 Our fathers trusted in thee: they trusted, and thou didst deliver them.

5 They cried unto thee, and were delivered: they trusted in thee, and were not confounded.

2-5. O my God, I cry in the daytime, but thou hearest not, rather, thou answerest not. The speaker is in no way concerned with God's faithfulness in hearing Him. God does not refrain from delivering the Messiah because He lacks the power to deliver Him. Whether the Mighty One chooses to deliver Christ or not, the Lord Jesus concludes, **But thou art holy.** Unanswered prayer cannot be traced to the unfaithfulness of God. **Our fathers trusted in thee . . . and thou didst deliver them . . . they trusted in thee, and were not confounded.** The outcry on the cross did not go unheard; simply, in the loving plan of God, it went unheeded.

6 But I *am* a worm, and no man; a reproach of men, and despised of the people.

7 All they that see me laugh me to scorn: they shoot out the lip, they shake the head, *saying,*

8 He trusted on the LORD *that* he would deliver him: let him deliver him, seeing he delighted in him.

6-8. But I am a worm, and no man (cf. Job 25:6; Isa 41:14). The worm is a symbol of extreme weakness and helplessness, something to be trodden down, unnoticed, and despised. **A reproach of men, and despised of the people.** Jesus had become a byword and a proverb to the scorners; so despised was He that the very people who once would have crowned Him now expressed their desire to have a murderer released instead of the Lord of Glory (Acts 3:14; cf. Isa 49:7; 53:3; Mt 27:39). **All they that see me laugh me to scorn,** cruel mocking that was fulfilled in Luke 23:35.

They shoot out the lip, they shake the head. These further gestures of contempt are fulfilled in Matthew 27:39 and Mark 15:29. **He trusted on the LORD . . . let him deliver him.** Matthew records that this text was cited by the scribes and elders who witnessed the crucifixion and applied it to the Lord in scorn (Mt 27:43).

9 But thou *art* he that took me out of the womb: thou didst make me hope *when I was* upon my mother's breasts.

10 I was cast upon thee from the womb: thou *art* my God from my mother's belly.

11 Be not far from me; for trouble *is* near; for *there is* none to help.

9-11. I was cast upon thee from the womb. Although in certain respects this may be said of every individual, it is most appropriate for the God-man to say (cf. Lk 2:40, 49, 52). God the Son and God the Father had never been separated until that eventful moment at Calvary. Thus, the Son cried, **Be not far from me . . . for there is none to help.** This obviously cannot apply to David, for he had never been in such straits. But the Lord Jesus found no man to stand beside him at the cross. All had fled; there was none to help.

12 Many bulls have compassed me: strong *bulls* of Bā′shan have beset me round.

13 They gaped upon me *with* their mouths, *as* a ravening and a roaring lion.

12-13. Many bulls have compassed me: strong bulls of Bashan have beset me round. When the Lord Jesus looked down from the cross He saw the priests, rulers, scribes, Pharisees, and others gathered around Him like an infuriated herd of wild bulls. They were like the strong bulls of Bashan, the richest pasture land in Palestine that produced the largest and strongest animals (Ezk 39:18; cf. Amos 4:1).

They gaped upon me with their mouths. The metaphor now turns from the threatening bulls to the ravenous lions who are eager to devour their prey with their monstrous jaws. Like roaring lions, the crowd howled and longed to tear the Saviour to pieces.

14 I am poured out like water, and all my bones are out of joint; my heart is like wax; it is melted in the midst of my bowels.

14. I am poured out like water. So utterly spent was the body of the Lord on the cross that He felt as if He were water that had been poured out upon the earth. **All my bones are out of joint.** As if distended upon a rack, the process of crucifixion had undoubtedly stretched the body of the Lord out of recognizable human shape. **My heart is like wax.** The intense pain and suffering of the cross is matched only by the intense pain of

15 My strength is dried up like a potsherd; and my tongue cleaveth to my jaws; and thou hast brought me into the dust of death.

16 For dogs have compassed me: the assembly of the wicked have inclosed me: they pierced my hands and my feet.

17 I may tell all my bones: they look *and* stare upon me.

18 They part my garments among them, and cast lots upon my vesture.

19 But be not thou far from me, O LORD: O my strength, haste thee to help me.

20 Deliver my soul from the sword; my darling from the power of the dog.

21 Save me from the lion's mouth: for thou hast heard me from the horns of the unicorns.

22 I will declare thy name unto my brethren: in the midst of the congregation will I praise thee.

23 Ye that fear the LORD, praise him; all ye the seed of Jacob, glorify him; and fear him, all ye the seed of Israel.

24 For he hath not despised nor abhorred the affliction of the afflicted; neither hath he hid his face from him; but when he cried unto him, he heard.

25 My praise *shall be* of thee in the great congregation: I will pay my vows before them that fear him.

26 The meek shall eat and be satisfied: they shall praise the LORD that seek him: your heart shall live for ever.

27 All the ends of the world shall remember and turn unto the LORD: and all the kindreds of the nations shall worship before thee.

28 For the kingdom *is* the LORD's: and he *is* the governor among the nations.

29 All *they that be* fat upon earth shall eat and worship: all they that go down to the dust shall bow before him: and none can keep alive his own soul.

bearing the sins of mankind, and thus the Lord Jesus musters the usual internal feelings.

15. My strength is dried up like a potsherd. Here Christ likens Himself to a piece of broken earthenware that has been fired in a kiln to such an extent that the last drop of moisture is driven out of the clay. **My tongue cleaveth to my jaws.** The complete debility witnessed here gives rise to a tormenting thirst that fastens the tongue to the jaws and causes the Lord to cry out, ". . . I thirst . . ." (Jn 19:28).

16-17. For dogs have compassed me. Unlike the ruling class, whom the Lord likens to lions with gaping mouths, here He undoubtedly has in mind the Roman soldiers who laid rough hands upon Him (Mt 27:27-35). **They pierced my hands and my feet.** If there thus far had been any doubt that this psalm refers directly to the Messiah Jesus Christ, all doubt is swept away in the flood of this statement. No one who truly loves the Lord can pass this verse without a tearful eye. **I may tell all my bones: they look and stare upon me,** (cf. Mt 27:39). So emaciated was Jesus from His fastings and so distended was His body from the posture on the cross that it was possible to count the bones of His body. What an awesome sight it must have been.

18. They part my garments among them, and cast lots upon my vesture. To the victor belongs the spoils, and in the Roman society that usually meant the executioners received the garments of the executed. So noteworthy was this fulfillment of prophecy in the conduct of the soldiers at the crucifixion that all four of the evangelists record it (Mt 27:35; Mk 15:24; Lk 23:34; Jn 19:24).

19-21. But be not thou far from me, O LORD. The Suffering Servant was convinced that He had not been forsaken by God. God's back had been turned upon sin; but, nevertheless, He was there ready to help. **Deliver my soul from the sword** may well be a reference to the authority of the Roman governor. **My darling from the power of the dog.** By **my darling** there is no doubt that the soul is intended, both here and in Psalm 35:17. It is the most precious thing that a man possesses (Mt 16:26).

22-25. The task of crucifixion and atonement complete, the Lord Jesus now bursts into a song of praise. He vows that He will **declare thy name unto my brethren.** The benefit of salvation is always a benefit to those who believe, the brethren. With Him we declare the praise of the Lord, both the **seed of Jacob** and **all ye the seed of Israel,** and more importantly, **The great congregation.** The reason for this outburst of praise is that God the Father **hath not despised nor abhorred the affliction of the afflicted; neither hath he hid his face from him.** The seeming passivity of God during the ordeal of the cross was only that, seeming passivity. He allowed Christ Jesus to bear the sins of mankind alone, but He never allowed Him to be alone.

26-28. The meek shall eat and be satisfied. The Messiah now addresses Himself to the results of His suffering and death. Those who were famished and who had no spiritual sustenance may now eat of the finished work of Christ until they are full. **Your heart shall live for ever.** Not only does the Lord promise satisfaction through His death, He promises immortality as well.

All the ends of the world shall remember and turn unto the LORD. Looking to the whole world as a mission field, the Lord Jesus envisions countless Gentiles turning unto Him for salvation. **For the kingdom is the LORD's: and he is the governor among the nations.** The promise of Isaiah 9:6, given of the Messiah, ". . . the government shall be upon His shoulder . . ." will be realized when the King of Kings comes to establish His millennial reign upon this earth.

29-31. In the closing verses of this psalm the universality of the Lord's kingdom is seen. **All they that be fat upon earth shall eat and worship.** Not only do the meek eat, but the rich and prosperous may find the Lord as well. In fact, whether great

30 A seed shall serve him; it shall be accounted to the Lord for a generation.
31 They shall come, and shall declare his righteousness unto a people that shall be born, that he hath done *this*.

PSALM 23

THE LORD *is* my shepherd; I shall not want.

2 He maketh me to lie down in green pastures: he leadeth me beside the still waters.

---

or small, wealthy or a pauper, **All they that go down to the dust shall bow before him** (Phil 2:10-11).

But until the time of this Kingdom Age, how shall the message of salvation be kept alive? **A seed shall serve him; it shall be accounted to the LORD for a generation.** God always has a remnant; His people are always present. **They shall come, and shall declare his righteousness unto a people that shall be born.** Generation after generation will see those who come to Christ through the grace of God. The message of the crucifixion will never grow old, nor can it.

W. The Shepherd Psalm. 23:1-6.

THEME: The Chief Shepherd leads His own even as a shepherd tends his flocks.

This is the pearl of the Psalms. No other pastoral poem is loved so well and is so highly prized as Psalm 23. As observed by Maclaren, "The world could spare many a large book better than this sunny little psalm."

To attack Davidic authorship of Psalm 23 is foolish; the subject matter and poetic style are clearly that of David. But at what period in David's life did he compose this psalm? Only two possibilities exist: in his early shepherd's life or in his later years. We cannot judge which it is for certain, but the question has no bearing on the spiritual impact of the psalm.

23:1. The LORD is my shepherd. The metaphor of the shepherd is frequently found in Scripture (Isa 40:11; 49:9-10; Jer 31:10; Ezk 34:6-19). That the Lord Jesus chose to show His relation to His people by the figure of a shepherd (Jn 10:11-19; 26-28; Heb 13:20; I Pet 2:25; 5:4; Rev 7:17) makes it evident that **the LORD** spoken of here is the Lord Jesus Christ.

What condescension that the infinite Lord would characterize Himself as a finite shepherd. But the most important element in this phrase is the little word **my**. What right does the psalmist, or any man, have to call the Lord Jehovah **my shepherd**? The answer is found in the preceding psalm, which depicted the death of the Lord Jesus on the cross. The Lord Jesus said, "I am the good shepherd: the good shepherd giveth his life for the sheep" (Jn 10:11). No one has the right to consider himself a sheep of the Lord unless his nature has been renewed by the Spirit of God. Unconverted men are never pictured as sheep, but as goats.

I shall not want. Each of us is aware of the four freedoms, enumerated by U.S. President Franklin D. Roosevelt: the freedom from want, the freedom from fear, the freedom of speech, and the freedom of religion. However, the psalmist goes one better. The sheep of the Lord's pasture possess five freedoms. The first is freedom from want. Those who abide in the presence of the shepherd never lack for temporal things (cf. 50:10; 84:11; Phil 4:19).

2. In continuing the thought that the Good Shepherd brings us freedom from want, the psalmist notes, **He maketh me to lie down in green pastures.** Interpretations of this phrase have generally followed along two lines. Some, like Spurgeon, have understood **green pastures** to be the place of most substantial feeding for the sheep. Others see a reference to the Lord's rest in the phrase **he maketh me to lie down in green pastures.** Since the green pastures of Palestine are so few and far between, the sheep must be led from pasture to pasture. When once a pasture is found, it is there they rest before moving on to the next pasture. Coupled with the expression, **he leadeth me beside the still waters,** we see the perfect balance between rest and activity.

He leadeth me beside the still waters. The reaffirming metaphor of the still waters assumes the same role as that of the green pastures. Just as the grass of the green pastures is deep enough to lie in, so also we must understand that still waters run deep. Any deep experience with the Shepherd can only be accomplished by time spent with the Shepherd, as the words **lie down** indicate.

3. He restoreth my soul. Not only is physical sustenance provided by the Good Shepherd, but spiritual restoration is provided as well. When the soul becomes sorrowful, He revives it. When our spirit becomes weak, He reinvigorates it. We have freedom from depletion, for every time we would stray, as a sheep would, He brings us back.

He leadeth me in the paths of righteousness. The word translated **paths** (Heb *ma'gal*) means the ways clearly marked by wheeled traffic. These are not rabbit trails to oblivion but are the paths of pleasantness and peace (Prov 3:17). For what purpose does the Good Shepherd lead us in the paths of righteousness? **For his name's sake.** The leading of the Lord is accomplished out of pure grace. It is to the honor of the Great Shepherd that we keep the commandments of the Word and walk in the narrow way of righteousness.

4. Yea, though I walk through the valley of the shadow of death. In the course of the late afternoon, the shepherd may find himself walking through deep ravines overhung with high cliffs which cause intermittent shadows. The sheep would naturally have an aversion to this darkness as a cover for beasts of prey; yet with the shepherd to lead them, there is nothing to fear.

I will fear no evil. The shadow of death is nothing to fear. As the shadow of the sword cannot kill, the shadow of death cannot destroy. Because the Lord Jesus has taken the sting out of death, we can say with the psalmist, **I will fear no evil.**

But how is it that we do not fear evil? Previously, the psalmist referred to God as **he**; now he refers to Him with a more intimate **thou. For thou art with me.** The intimacy of the statement **The Lord is my shepherd** is now seen in his direct address to the God of heaven. When we come to know God personally through His Son Jesus Christ, the death barrier is shattered. All who have trusted in Christ as Saviour are not only free from want, but have freedom from the fear of death as well.

Thy rod and thy staff they comfort me. The rod (Heb *shēbet*) and staff (Heb *mish'enet*) are symbols of the shepherd's office. By them, he guides the sheep. Perhaps a crook and a club, these are the ensigns of the sovereignty of the shepherd over his sheep. When passing through the shadowy ravine, the sheep know that the gentle tap of the shepherd's crook or of his rod is designed for their safe passage. Thus, they heed that gentle leading.

5. Thou preparest a table before me in the presence of mine enemies. Unlike the account of Gideon and his three hundred soldiers (Jud 7:6), the Lord does not command us to hastily snatch a meal in the presence of our enemies, but actually prepares a table before us in the presence of our enemies. Nothing is hurried; there is no confusion. We are with the Great Shepherd, and even in the midst of our enemies there is perfect peace.

Thou anointest my head with oil. The shepherd would carry a small flask of oil to anoint the scratched face of sheep that had to find their food among the thorns and thistles. But in the imagery of the psalmist, with relation to the Christian today, the anointing of our heads with oil must be taken to mean the filling of the Holy Spirit of God. It is by Him that we have an unction (I Jn 2:20) without which we cannot be a believer-priest.

My cup runneth over. This expressive metaphor means that not only has our cup been filled to the brim, but it runs over the brim, indicating a state of bliss rarely experienced in this life. If this statement relates to the preceding one, in the life of the believer it means that we may be continually filled to overflowing with the Spirit of God.

6. Surely goodness and mercy shall follow me all the days of my life. So certain is the psalmist that these twin graces will follow him that he begins his summary statement with a heav-

3 He restoreth my soul: he leadeth me in the paths of righteousness for his name's sake.

4 Yea, though I walk through the valley of the shadow of death, I will fear no evil: for thou *art* with me; thy rod and thy staff they comfort me.

5 Thou preparest a table before me in the presence of mine enemies: thou anointest my head with oil; my cup runneth over.

6 Surely goodness and mercy shall follow me all the days of my life: and I

will dwell in the house of the LORD for ever.

enly "verily" or **surely. Goodness** and **mercy** will not simply follow, but will pursue him. The verb used here (Heb *radap*) is used elsewhere in a predominantly hostile sense. That it is given a benevolent sense here makes its usage even more striking. These graces actively seek us out when we walk with the Good Shepherd. They are present with us in times of feasting, as well as times of fasting **all the days of my life.**

And I will dwell in the house of the LORD for ever. The prayer of 27:4 is a certain reality to the psalmist. The **house of the LORD** does not indicate a temple or church, but rather communion with God. The fact that we shall dwell in the house of the Lord forever indicates sonship, for a servant never abides in the house. As a child of God who walks in the path of the Good Shepherd, I am always at home with God. This is the fifth of the five freedoms: freedom from desertion. The Shepherd has promised me, ". . . I will never leave thee, nor forsake thee" (Heb 13:5); and whether through the green pastures, the still waters, through the valley of death, or in the presence of mine enemies, I know He is always there.

X. The Ascension Psalm. 24:1-10.

THEME: The song of joy which accompanies the return of the King of Glory to His kingdom.

The inscription indicates that David is the author of this psalm. Its contents make it quite possible that it was written on the return of the ark of the covenant from the house of Obed-Edom to the tent prepared for it in Jerusalem after it had been captured by the Philistines in the days of Eli (II Sam 6:12ff.). In fact, the words are not unsuitable for the sacred dance with which David led the processional.

24:1-3. The earth is the LORD's, and the fullness thereof. God's glory has already been manifested in Psalm 19 from a consideration of the heavens (vss. 1-6). Here that glory is manifested from the other half of the creation, i.e., the earth. There can be no question but that the King of Glory is the Lord of the earth. **For he hath founded it upon the seas, and established it upon the floods.** The Lord God lifted the earth above the flood and the seas, making it a fit habitation for man (cf. Gen 1:9). He founded it, established it, created it, and sustains it (cf. Col 1:17).

If it is possible that this psalm was sung on the ascent to the tabernacle, it may be assumed that it was sung antiphonally. Two choirs were used, one to sing the questions, the other to respond with the answers. The first choir now sings, **Who shall ascend into the hill of the LORD? Or who shall stand in his holy place?** What type of man is worthy to be brought into contact with a God of such might and glory? Who can ascend to God's hill, i.e., God's highest heaven? Or who shall stand in the tabernacle of God to serve him? The other choir now responds with the appropriate answers.

4-6. He that hath clean hands. Whoever would draw nigh to the presence of a holy God must be totally freed from any visible, vestigial habits of sin. But more is necessary. **A pure heart.** The outside of the bowl may be clean; but before we eat from it, we are interested in the state of the inside.

He shall receive the blessing from the LORD, and righteousness from the God of his salvation. Those who are pure in thought, word, and deed are sure to receive the blessing of God (cf. Mt 5:8). But such blessing is God's gift that accompanies righteousness, itself the gift from God.

O Jacob. It is difficult to understand the expression **O Jacob** in this context. It is possible to regard **Jacob** as being in apposition with **generation** and to translate this verse, **This is the generation of them that seek him, that seek thy face, O Jacob.** After all, a race of men is not indicated here, but a quality of mankind, those who have clean hands and a pure heart.

PSALM 24

THE earth *is* the LORD's, and the fulness thereof; the world, and they that dwell therein.

2 For he hath founded it upon the seas, and established it upon the floods.

3 Who shall ascend into the hill of the LORD? or who shall stand in his holy place?

4 He that hath clean hands, and a pure heart; who hath not lifted up his soul unto vanity, nor sworn deceitfully.

5 He shall receive the blessing from the LORD, and righteousness from the God of his salvation.

6 This *is* the generation of them that seek him, that seek thy face, O Jacob. Se'lah.

7 Lift up your heads, O ye gates; and be ye lift up, ye everlasting doors; and the King of glory shall come in.
8 Who *is* this King of glory? The LORD strong and mighty, the LORD mighty in battle.
9 Lift up your heads, O ye gates; even lift *them* up, ye everlasting doors; and the King of glory shall come in.
10 Who is this King of glory? The LORD of hosts, he *is* the King of glory. Sĕ′lah.

PSALM 25

UNTO thee, O LORD, do I lift up my soul.
2 O my God, I trust in thee: let me not be ashamed, let not mine enemies triumph over me.
3 Yea, let none that wait on thee be ashamed: let them be ashamed which transgress without cause.

4 Shew me thy ways, O LORD; teach me thy paths.
5 Lead me in thy truth, and teach me: for thou *art* the God of my salvation; on thee do I wait all the day.
6 Remember, O LORD, thy tender mercies and thy lovingkindnesses; for they *have been* ever of old.
7 Remember not the sins of my youth, nor my transgressions: according to thy mercy remember thou me for thy goodness' sake, O LORD.

8 Good and upright *is* the LORD: therefore will he teach sinners in the way.
9 The meek will he guide in judgment: and the meek will he teach his way.
10 All the paths of the LORD *are* mercy and truth unto such as keep his covenant and his testimonies.
11 For thy name's sake, O LORD, pardon mine iniquity; for it *is* great.

12 What man *is* he that feareth the

7-10. As the ancient Israelites began to ascend the hills to Jerusalem with the ark of the covenant, they joyously sang, **Lift up your heads, O ye gates; and be ye lifted up, ye everlasting doors; and the King of glory shall come in.** The choirs call for the personified gates of Jerusalem to lift up their heads and for the doors to be lifted up. It is no ordinary God who is going to enter the tabernacle; it is the Shekinah glory. The reference to the King of Glory begs the question from the other choir, **Who is this King of glory?** The refrain is the epithet for God **The LORD strong and mighty, the LORD mighty in battle.** The Lord of Hosts was well known to the Israelites by this time (cf. I Sam 1:11; II Sam 5:10; 6:2; 7:26-27; etc.). He is the mighty God, **The LORD of hosts, he is the King of glory.**

Y. The Second Penitential Psalm. 25:1-22.

THEME: *David's cry to God for forgiveness of sin and help in the face of affliction.*

This second of the seven Penitential Psalms is also the second psalm with an acrostic arrangement (see introduction). As a result of being bound by the acrostical device in which the first word of each strophe begins with a consecutive letter of the alphabet, the thought of this psalm does not flow as freely as is the case in other psalms. Yet, there is some continuity to the psalm.

25:1-3. **Unto thee, O LORD, do I lift up my soul.** David does not simply uplift his eyes or hands in prayer, but the true spirit of prayer is one in which the soul is uplifted. **O my God, I trust in thee.** David has already shown he has drawn closer to Jehovah by using the more personal expression **my God.** Let not **mine enemies triumph over me. Yea, let none that wait on thee be ashamed.** What David desires for himself he also desires for all those who love God.

4-7. **Show me thy ways, O LORD; teach me thy paths.** This echo of the prayer of Moses when his people were rebellious at Sinai (Ex 33:13) is reiterated by David here and elsewhere (cf. 27:11; 86:11). There appears to be a difference between **Show** and **teach. Teach** carries the thought of a father helping a little child learn, of giving specific ethical instruction. But greater is **Lead me in thy truth, and teach me.** To show the ways of the Lord and make them visible, is very basic. The next higher step is to teach them. But the higher step yet is to lead in the ways of truth, to provide example as well as instruction. This is David's prayer: that the Lord would lead him in His truth.

The double remembrance that follows is significant. First, David pleads that the Lord would remember **thy tender mercies and thy loving-kindnesses.** God's mercy and kindness are everlasting. The psalmist knows that if God continues that characteristic, He will then **Remember not the sins of my youth, nor my transgressions.** It is on the basis of God's everlasting mercy that David prays that the wanton follies of his youth would not impair his present desire to be led by the Lord God. **According to thy mercy remember thou me for thy goodness' sake, O LORD.**

8-11. These verses are a meditation upon the attributes and acts of the Lord. **Good and upright is the LORD.** Because the Lord is good, He will not abandon sinners, but will reclaim, purge, and show them the way of the cross so that they may live righteously. **All the paths of the LORD are mercy and truth unto such as keep his covenant and his testimonies.** God's rule is without exception. Anyone who will come to the Lord may claim the promise of God for salvation and be assured, as was David, that the Lord will remember the sins of his youth and his transgressions no more. **For thy name's sake, O LORD, pardon mine iniquity; for it is great.** His appeal for pardon is for the sake of the name of the Lord, i.e., for the honor of that name.

12-15. These verses contain another series of reflections by

1013

LORD? him shall he teach in the way *that* he shall choose.

13 His soul shall dwell at ease; and his seed shall inherit the earth.

14 The secret of the LORD *is* with them that fear him; and he will shew them his covenant.

15 Mine eyes *are* ever toward the LORD; for he shall pluck my feet out of the net.

16 Turn thee unto me, and have mercy upon me; for I *am* desolate and afflicted.

17 The troubles of my heart are enlarged: *O* bring thou me out of my distresses.

18 Look upon mine affliction and my pain; and forgive all my sins.

19 Consider mine enemies; for they are many; and they hate me with cruel hatred.

20 O keep my soul, and deliver me: let me not be ashamed; for I put my trust in thee.

21 Let integrity and uprightness preserve me; for I wait on thee.

22 Redeem Israel, O God, out of all his troubles.

PSALM 26

JUDGE me, O LORD; for I have walked in mine integrity: I have trusted also in the LORD; *therefore* I shall not slide.

2 Examine me, O LORD, and prove me; try my reins and my heart.

3 For thy lovingkindness *is* before mine eyes: and I have walked in thy truth.

4 I have not sat with vain persons, neither will I go in with dissemblers.

5 I have hated the congregation of evil doers; and will not sit with the wicked.

the psalmist. **What man is he that feareth the LORD?** Every man who fears the Lord shall be shown the way of obedience by the Lord. **His soul shall dwell at ease,** or rather in bliss, because he will keep the commandments of the Lord and know that he has lived righteously. **His seed shall inherit the earth;** that is, his posterity after him shall continue to prosper because of his righteousness. **The secret of the LORD is with them that fear him.** The friendship of the Lord is with those who fear Him. God favors with His presence those who trust and love Him.

16-21. The psalmist now returns to prayer. **Turn thee unto me, and have mercy upon me.** David assumes that his personal sin has been the cause of God turning His back on him. Thus, he pleads for mercy. His prayer is no less than **forgive all my sins.** He has repented of them all; he now seeks the Lord's forgiveness of them all. **O keep my soul, and deliver me: let me not be ashamed; for I put my trust in thee.** David is as concerned about the reflection his salvation will have on the Lord God as he is about what it will mean to him. This thought is seen again in the next verse: **Let integrity and uprightness preserve me; for I wait on thee.** This can scarcely be his own inherent integrity and uprightness, for he has already confessed the lack of those in verse 11. Rather, he waits upon the Lord God who is Himself upright and who the psalmist feels is alone capable of forgiving his sin.

22. Redeem Israel, O God, out of all his troubles. Some have supposed that this concluding prayer was added during the period of the captivity. It certainly stands outside the alphabetical arrangement of the psalm. Nevertheless, as we have seen in verse 11, David is not opposed to bringing prayers to the Lord when a particular problem strikes his mind.

Z. A Plea for Vindication. 26:1-12.

THEME: *David's plea for examination and vindication by the Lord on the basis of his avowed integrity.*

In this psalm David appears as a man enduring great reproach. As such, he is a type of the Great Son of David, Jesus Christ the Lord, and is an encouraging example for all of us who bear the burden of slander to take that burden to the throne of grace.

It is quite obvious that the psalmist has been falsely accused, but David's references to personal righteousness are not to convince God that he should not be defamed. David is not sinlessly perfect. We must understand those references in relation to verse 11, which clearly cancels out the spirit of self-righteousness. As a man greatly defamed, he simply rises in protest, asking the Lord God, who knows the psalmist's inner motives, to vindicate him and protect him from his enemies.

26:1-2. Judge me, O LORD; for I have walked in mine integrity. David begs to be judged in his own integrity because he has done all God has asked. He has trusted in God; he has walked in God's commandments; and he is free of the offense for which he has been slandered. **Examine me, O LORD, and prove me; try my reins and my heart.** The psalmist wants to be reassured by God that there is no improper motive in his obtaining the crown or in the way he has exercised his duties as king.

3-5. David now embarks on a sixfold enumeration of his integrity. First, **For thy loving-kindness is before mine eyes.** The unsaved sits with God's law before his eyes, but the believer can meditate and reflect on the loving-kindness of God continually. Second, **and I have walked in thy truth.** God's truth is God's Law (119:42-44), and only the person who has experienced God's grace can make such a claim. Third, **I have not sat with vain persons.** Similar to 1:1, David indicates that he has not consorted with light or frivolous persons, those who have nothing but vanity in their hearts. Fourth, **neither will I go in**

with dissemblers. Dissemblers are hypocrites and are not those with whom the Christians should cultivate communion. The psalmist will not associate with those "Having a form of godliness, but denying the power thereof . . ." (II Tim 3:5).

Fifth, **I have hated the congregation of evildoers.** Those who have experienced the grace of God in salvation must hate such gatherings and assemblies and have no part in them. Sixth, the psalmist **will not sit with the wicked.** Those who would sit at the table of the Great King must be careful at whose tables they presently sit.

6-7. I will wash mine hands in innocency: so will I compass thine altar, O LORD. Here is the high point of the psalm. David would publicly avow himself to be altogether free from the accusations made against him and totally blameless. Such freedom from blame is necessary to approach the altar of God. **That I may publish with the voice of thanksgiving.** The purpose of having a clean heart is not simply to be clean before the Lord, but to be a cleansed vessel ready for use by the Master.

8. LORD, I have loved the habitation of thy house. All true believers will love to assemble themselves in God's house, not only to fellowship with other believers but simply to be in **the place where thine honor dwelleth.** We must take care that services conducted in the house of God indeed honor God, because His honor dwells there.

9-10. Gather not my soul with sinners, nor my life with bloody men. David continues his prayer by asking that God not unite him with sinners, particularly the bloodthirsty brand of sinner, i.e., wicked men, assassins, murderers, etc. For they are full of mischief and bribes.

11-12. But as for me, I will walk in mine integrity; rather, I will continue to walk in mine integrity. **My foot standeth in an even place.** He will stand upon the level ground of the Law of God, knowing that conformity to God's Law and His Word, will never cause him to stumble. **In the congregations will I bless the LORD.** In all the assemblies of the people for public worship, David acknowledges his duty to speak a word of praise for the Lord (22:22, 25; 27:6; 35:18; 40:9-10; 68:26; etc.).

AA. A Psalm of Confidence. 27:1-14.

THEME: *The psalmist confidently praises the Lord who is his light and his salvation.*

This delightful psalm has been attacked as a composition of two writers. Critics have noted the great transition in thought which occurs between verses 6 and 7, but it is idle speculation to assume that these were two psalms written by two men and joined together later. The two parts of the psalm are so totally unalike and so totally distinct that no arranger or editor would ever unite them. Besides, it is characteristic of David's writing to engage in such sharp transitions.

The whole tone of this psalm fits the period of David's flight from Absalom. In fact, verse 10 may refer to the situation described in I Samuel 22:3-4. At this time, David had to especially wait confidently upon the Lord.

27:1-3. The LORD is my light and my salvation; whom shall I fear? This strong affirmation is reminiscent of the words of John 1:7-9; 12:35-36, 46; and I John 1:5. It is an acknowledgement of total confidence in God. **Whom shall I fear** has its New Testament counterpart in, "If God be for us, who can be against us?" (Rom 8:31).

4-5. One thing have I desired of the LORD . . . that I may dwell in the house of the LORD all the days of my life. Amid his joy, David's heart still desires one thing. When he took flight from Absalom, he also took flight from Jerusalem and had to

---

6 I will wash mine hands in innocency: so will I compass thine altar, O LORD:
7 That I may publish with the voice of thanksgiving, and tell of all thy wondrous works.

8 LORD, I have loved the habitation of thy house, and the place where thine honour dwelleth.

9 Gather not my soul with sinners, nor my life with bloody men;
10 In whose hands *is* mischief, and their right hand is full of bribes.

11 But as for me, I will walk in mine integrity: redeem me, and be merciful unto me.
12 My foot standeth in an even place: in the congregations will I bless the LORD.

PSALM 27

THE LORD *is* my light and my salvation; whom shall I fear? the LORD *is* the strength of my life; of whom shall I be afraid?
2 When the wicked, *even* mine enemies and my foes, came upon me to eat up my flesh, they stumbled and fell.
3 Though an host should encamp against me, my heart shall not fear: though war should rise against me, in this *will* I *be* confident.
4 One *thing* have I desired of the LORD, that will I seek after; that I may dwell in the house of the LORD all the days of my life, to behold the beauty of

the LORD, and to enquire in his temple.

5 For in the time of trouble he shall hide me in his pavilion: in the secret of his tabernacle shall he hide me; he shall set me up upon a rock.

6 And now shall mine head be lifted up above mine enemies round about me: therefore will I offer in his tabernacle sacrifices of joy; I will sing, yea, I will sing praises unto the LORD.

7 Hear, O LORD, *when* I cry with my voice: have mercy also upon me, and answer me.
8 *When thou saidst,* Seek ye my face; my heart said unto thee, Thy face, LORD, will I seek.
9 Hide not thy face *far* from me; put not thy servant away in anger: thou hast been my help; leave me not, neither forsake me, O God of my salvation.
10 When my father and my mother forsake me, then the LORD will take me up.

11 Teach me thy way, O LORD, and lead me in a plain path, because of mine enemies.
12 Deliver me not over unto the will of mine enemies: for false witnesses are risen up against me, and such as breathe out cruelty.
13 *I had fainted,* unless I had believed to see the goodness of the LORD in the land of the living.
14 Wait on the LORD: be of good courage, and he shall strengthen thine heart: wait, I say, on the LORD.

PSALM 28
UNTO thee will I cry, O LORD my rock; be not silent to me: lest, *if* thou be silent to me, I become like them that go down into the pit.
2 Hear the voice of my supplications, when I cry unto thee, when I lift up my hands toward thy holy oracle.

3 Draw me not away with the wicked, and with the workers of iniquity, which speak peace to their neighbours, but mischief *is* in their hearts.
4 Give them according to their deeds, and according to the wickedness of

leave the Temple behind, an expression applied to the tabernacle in David's time. The king longs to return to the house of the Lord God with an intensity exhibited by few Christians today. **He shall hide me in his pavilion.** He wants to be hid in the refuge of God Himself. He desires for God to wrap His arms around him and set him **upon a rock** (cf. 18:2; 61:2).

6. And now shall mine head be lifted up above mine enemies round about me. The situation is grave indeed, but David exhibits total confidence in God's ability to protect him. Since he will not worry, he resolves **I will sing, yea, I will sing praises unto the LORD.**

7-9. Hear, O LORD. The tone now drastically changes. The rhythm of jubilation is now the dole of mourning. David pleads for the Lord to hear him when he cries, an expression not uncommon in the Psalms. The double expression **Seek ye my face . . . Hide not thy face far from me** shows David's dependence upon the Lord for an answer to his prayer.

10. When my father and my mother forsake me, then the LORD will take me up. Again, David expresses confidence that God will not forsake him. This expression is proverbial and is not designed to indicate that David's mother and father had forsaken him. They had probably been dead for years.

11-13. Lead me in a plain path. David now continues his prayer by asking that the Lord make his way to be a level one, a path traversing a flat or smooth country. The reason is that **False witnesses are risen up against me.** Such had breathed out cruelty or violence against the king, who was himself upright in heart.

14. Wait on the LORD. This exhortation is given by the psalmist, not to others, but to himself. If he tarries for the Lord, the Lord will show His goodness to him. In the meantime, **be of good courage.** The psalmist has now convinced himself that the Lord God would strengthen his heart in the day of trouble if he would only **wait, I say, on the LORD,** advice which we cannot fail to heed.

BB. A Prayer for Deliverance. 28:1-9.
THEME: *David prays to God in a time of trouble and in anticipation praises Him for relief.*

The superscription over this psalm ascribes it to David, and there is no reason to question this. It was probably composed when Absalom rose in rebellion against his father. Absalom's men could well be described in verses 3 and 5 and their rebellious fate described in verse 4. Thus, the prayer is made for the people and their king (vs. 8).

28:1-2. Unto thee will I cry, O LORD my rock. The Lord as a **rock** is a familiar figure in David's psalms (cf. 18:2; 27:5; 31:2-3; 40:2; 61:2; 62:2; etc.). David is concerned that if the Lord does not hear him, he will become **like them that go down into the pit,** into Sheol, or the grave. Hence, he begs the Lord God to hear his cry **when I lift up my hands,** a common practice while Israel was in prayer (cf. I Kgs 8:22, 54; Lam 2:19). The king's hands were lifted **toward thy holy oracle** (Heb *debîr*), toward the inner sanctuary of the Holy Place.

3-5. David begins his denunciation of the wicked with the prayer, **Draw me not away with the wicked.** The metaphor he uses is that of the hunter drawing his prey into a net. The psalmist prays that he will not share the fate of the wicked **which speak peace to their neighbors, but mischief is in their hearts.** Hypocrisy is the special form of wickedness mentioned here.

their endeavours: give them after the work of their hands; render to them their desert.

5 Because they regard not the works of the LORD, nor the operation of his hands, he shall destroy them, and not build them up.

6 Blessed be the LORD, because he hath heard the voice of my supplications.

7 The LORD is my strength and my shield; my heart trusted in him, and I am helped: therefore my heart greatly rejoiceth; and with my song will I praise him.

8 The LORD is their strength, and he is the saving strength of his anointed.

9 Save thy people, and bless thine inheritance: feed them also, and lift them up for ever.

PSALM 29

GIVE unto the LORD, O ye mighty, give unto the LORD glory and strength.

2 Give unto the LORD the glory due unto his name; worship the LORD in the beauty of holiness.

3 The voice of the LORD is upon the waters: the God of glory thundereth: the LORD is upon many waters.

4 The voice of the LORD is powerful; the voice of the LORD is full of majesty.

5 The voice of the LORD breaketh the cedars; yea, the LORD breaketh the cedars of Lebanon.

6 He maketh them also to skip like a calf; Lebanon and Sīr'i-on like a young unicorn.

7 The voice of the LORD divideth the flames of fire.

Give them according to their deeds . . . give them after the work of their hands. So corrupted are the moral natures of his enemies that David asks the Lord to give them exact retribution for the evils they have given him. **Because they regard not the works of the LORD, nor the operation of his hands.** These wicked men do not retain the knowledge of God in their minds. They do not ascribe the works of His hands to Him. This denunciation is similar to that of Paul in Romans 1 (especially Rom 1:21, 28). David is simply calling upon God to deal righteously with those who are wicked.

6-7. Blessed be the LORD. Suddenly, and characteristically, David changes tone drastically. From the plaintive tone of the preceding verses, he now turns to rejoicing and thanksgiving, **The LORD is my strength and my shield** (cf. 18:1-2; 119:114). **My heart trusted in him, and I am helped.** David's heart, which was in despair, is now in great rejoicing because it trusted in the Lord.

8-9. The LORD is their strength. The welfare of the king and his kingdom are inextricably bound together. As God strengthens him, he strengthens them; **and he is the saving strength of his anointed.**

Save thy people, and bless thine inheritance. In the finale of his prayer the psalmist pleads for God to continue doing what He is already doing, i.e., saving and blessing His inheritance. **Feed them also,** as a shepherd feeds his flock (cf. 23:1-2; Isa 40:11). **And lift them up for ever.** David finishes his prayer with a petition that Israel shall be exalted through the triumph of her king. Although this occurred in history with David, it will occur most notably in prophecy with the Son of David, Jesus Christ.

CC. The Thunder Psalm. 29:1-11.

THEME: *The glory of the Lord as it is revealed in a thunder storm.*

This psalm expresses God's working through His natural creation. It is a psalm of David and reflects the certain awe that a shepherd would naturally have had for thunder. Yet, our English word **thundereth** does not do justice to the expression frequently translated **the voice of the LORD** (Heb *qōl Yahweh*). The eleven verses of this psalm manifest a deep sensitivity toward the voice of the Lord in the storm.

29:1-2. Give unto the LORD, O ye mighty. It is considerably disputed among scholars to whom the expression **O ye mighty** refers. Most understand this to refer to the holy angels, while others assume it to be a reference to the heathen or the mighty ones of the earth in general. Whoever the mighty ones are, they ascribe to the Lord God that **glory** which alone is His. **Worship the LORD in the beauty of holiness.** Although this may mean to worship Him in the vestments of the priests, it more likely means that we are to worship Him in a holy ornament of meekness and a quiet spirit (I Pet 3:4).

3-4. The description of the Lord's power in the thunderstorm now begins with a typically Davidic transition. **The voice of the LORD,** which has already been identified with the thunder in 18:13, is **upon the waters.** This should be interpreted as the waters stored up in the clouds high in the air. **The God of glory thundereth.** The psalmist views God Himself as active in the thunderstorm. **The voice of the LORD is powerful.**

5-6. The voice of the LORD breaketh the cedars. As the thunderstorm rages on, the flashes of lightning strike the great cedars of Lebanon splitting them and breaking them down. **He maketh them also to skip like a calf,** a statement that represents the way thunder reverberates among the mountains. **Lebanon and Sirion like a young unicorn.** Lebanon and Sirion, or Hermon (Deut 3:9), are the two principal mountains of Palestine.

7-9. The voice of the LORD divideth the flames of fire. This may mean to hew a place out in the skies through which the

8 The voice of the LORD shaketh the wilderness; the LORD shaketh the wilderness of Kā′desh.

9 The voice of the LORD maketh the hinds to calve, and discovereth the forests: and in his temple doth every one speak of *his* glory.

10 The LORD sitteth upon the flood; yea, the LORD sitteth King for ever.

11 The LORD will give strength unto his people; the LORD will bless his people with peace.

PSALM 30

I WILL extol thee, O LORD; for thou hast lifted me up, and hast not made my foes to rejoice over me.

2 O LORD my God, I cried unto thee, and thou hast healed me.

3 O LORD, thou hast brought up my soul from the grave: thou hast kept me alive, that I should not go down to the pit.

4 Sing unto the LORD, O ye saints of his, and give thanks at the remembrance of his holiness.

5 For his anger *endureth but* a moment; in his favour *is* life: weeping may endure for a night, but joy *cometh* in the morning.

6 And in my prosperity I said, I shall never be moved.

7 LORD, by thy favour thou hast made my mountain to stand strong: thou didst hide thy face, *and* I was troubled.

8 I cried to thee, O LORD; and unto the LORD I made supplication.

9 What profit *is there* in my blood, when I go down to the pit? Shall the dust praise thee? shall it declare thy truth?

10 Hear, O LORD, and have mercy upon me: LORD, be thou my helper.

11 Thou hast turned for me my

lightning passes. **The LORD shaketh the wilderness of Kadesh.** Kadesh represents the opposite direction of Palestine from the cedars of Lebanon and, thus, indicates that the thunderstorm of the Lord extends throughout the entirety of the Holy Land. **The voice of the LORD maketh the hinds to calve.** So fierce is the thunderstorm that it inaugurates birth.

10-11. The LORD sitteth upon the flood, probably not a reference to the Great Deluge, but rather to the floods accompanying the storm. **The LORD will bless his people with peace.** The God who is able to cause havoc in the thunderstorm is also able to bring peace in the midst of the storm.

DD. The Dedication Psalm. 30:1-12.

THEME: *Praise to God on the occasion of the consecration of the site of the Temple.*

To a greater degree than usual, the interpretation of this psalm depends on its occasion for writing. There is no question but that David is the author, but why did he write this psalm? The superscription over the psalm reads, **A psalm and song at the dedication of the house of David.** Obviously, this cannot refer to the building of the Temple; for David did not see such a building. But the historical outline of II Samuel 24 and I Chronicles 21 provides a perfect framework into which we may place Psalm 30, describing the purchase, the erection of an altar, and the dedication by David of the threshing floor of Araunah. It seems likely that the dedication of this site, upon which later David's son would build the glorious Solomonic Temple, is meant by the superscription of the psalm.

30:1-3. I will extol thee, O LORD, a promise of praise. **For thou hast lifted me up.** The image used here is that of a bucket drawing water out of a well. The psalmist views himself as having been pulled from the mire of tribulation. **Thou hast healed me.** The plague that came upon the people of Israel as a result of their king's sin (see II Sam 24 or I Chron 21) brought both mental and physical suffering to the land. David's healing was the removal of that plague. **O LORD, thou hast brought up my soul from the grave.** It was as if David was on the very edge of death itself when the Lord brought him back into a position of favor.

4-5. Sing unto the LORD. In the midst of desolation the psalmist manages a song of praise unto the Lord. **For his anger endureth but a moment; in his favor is life.** The meaning is reinforced by the expression **Weeping may endure for a night, but joy cometh in the morning.** Weeping all night is common for the restless heart. But when we lay those burdens at the feet of Jesus, the Sun of Righteousness, joy comes in the morning to relieve us of that burden (I Pet 5:7; cf. Job 33:26; Isa 26:20; 54:7).

6-7. And in my prosperity I said, I shall never be moved. Prosperity had worked an ill effect on the psalmist and had made him self-confident and proud. But something happened; **thou didst hide thy face, and I was troubled.** When God was displeased, He turned his face from him; and suddenly David realized the folly of his ways (I Chr 21:7-12). A dreadful plague which killed 70,000 men in one day was sent. Feeling the coolness of God's face turned from him, David was indeed troubled.

8-9. I cried to thee, O LORD (cf. II Sam 24:17; I Chr 21:17). David's question to God was a legitimate one: **What profit is there in my blood, when I go down to the pit?** Would there be advantage to God if He killed His servant with the plague? **Shall the dust praise thee?** In death, the mouth of God's servant would be silent, as silent as the dust.

10-12. Hear, O LORD . . . be thou my helper. A prayer for God's mercy is quickly uttered (cf. 54:4; Heb 13:6). But the prayer uttered in distress also exhibits a confidence in the result.

mourning into dancing: thou hast put off my sackcloth, and girded me with gladness;

12 To the end that *my* glory may sing praise to thee, and not be silent. O Lord my God, I will give thanks unto thee for ever.

PSALM 31

IN thee, O Lord, do I put my trust; let me never be ashamed: deliver me in thy righteousness.

2 Bow down thine ear to me; deliver me speedily: be thou my strong rock, for an house of defence to save me.

3 For thou *art* my rock and my fortress; therefore for thy name's sake lead me, and guide me.

4 Pull me out of the net that they have laid privily for me: for thou *art* my strength.

5 Into thine hand I commit my spirit: thou hast redeemed me, O Lord God of truth.

6 I have hated them that regard lying vanities: but I trust in the Lord.

7 I will be glad and rejoice in thy mercy: for thou hast considered my trouble; thou hast known my soul in adversities;

8 And hast not shut me up into the hand of the enemy: thou hast set my feet in a large room.

9 Have mercy upon me, O Lord, for I am in trouble: mine eye is consumed with grief, *yea* my soul and my belly.

10 For my life is spent with grief, and my years with sighing: my strength faileth because of mine iniquity, and my bones are consumed.

11 I was a reproach among all mine enemies, but especially among my neighbours, and a fear to mine acquaintance: they that did see me without fled from me.

12 I am forgotten as a dead man out of mind: I am like a broken vessel.

13 For I have heard the slander of many: fear *was* on every side: while they took counsel together against me, they devised to take away my life.

14 But I trusted in thee, O Lord: I said, Thou *art* my God.

15 My times *are* in thy hand: deliver me from the hand of mine enemies, and from them that persecute me.

16 Make thy face to shine upon thy servant: save me for thy mercies' sake.

17 Let me not be ashamed, O Lord; for I have called upon thee: let the wicked be ashamed, *and* let them be silent in the grave.

Thou hast turned for me my mourning into dancing. Suddenly, all was changed. God had done a wonderful thing in the life of David His servant; and David could only say **O Lord my God, I will give thanks unto thee for ever.**

EE. A Psalm of Fear and Faith. 31:1-24.

THEME: *The prayer of a believer in time of deep distress and the resulting confidence in God.*

In the main part, this psalm is a cry for deliverance from pressing danger or trouble; yet it is interspersed with passages of faith and culminates in a great hymn of praise and confidence toward God. It is unquestionably a psalm of David, and the occasion for writing is either David's escape from the treachery of the men of Keilah (I Sam 23) or more probably the later period of treachery under the rebellion of Absalom.

31:1-4. The introductory verses of the psalm are filled with many familiar and favorite Davidic expressions. There is the expression of trust, **In thee, O Lord, do I put my trust.** There is the familiar expression calling upon God to hear him, **Bow down thine ear to me.** His common expression of calm assurance is seen in the phrase **be thou my strong rock.** Again, we are familiar with **For thou art my rock and my fortress,** all of which make David's authorship of this psalm a certainty. His cry for help now is seen. **Pull me out of the net that they have laid privily for me.**

5. Into thine hand I commit my spirit. When David uttered these words, he was not thinking of a final committal of his soul to the Lord, but rather of a constant committal of himself and his situation to the delivering hand of God. But our Lord's adoption of these words and application of them on the cross have given them a special meaning far beyond their original intent.

6-8. After a characteristic expression of hatred toward those who engage in idolatrous practices, the psalmist continues, **I will be glad and rejoice in thy mercy.** Anticipating God's mercy for which he had prayed (vss. 2-4), the psalmist now delights in that anticipated mercy. **Thou hast set my feet in a large room.** When the Lord brings deliverance, we are not cramped or confined or hindered in any way; but we are given room to roam, freedom to serve Him.

9-10. Mine eye is consumed with grief. The metaphors used in this verse are all identical and are intended to indicate how great the sorrow of soul David has endured. **For my life is spent with grief, and my years with sighing.** David's present troubles, he is certain, began years ago, perhaps at the time he committed his great sin (cf. II Sam 11:4-17).

11-14. I was a reproach among all mine enemies. The psalmist knows that he has become a reproach to those around him. **I am forgotten as a dead man out of mind.** Once removed from the capital, David assumes himself to be no more than a deposed king. His assumption of self-worthlessness is seen in the phrase, **I am like a broken vessel,** something only to be thrown away. **But I trusted in thee, O Lord: I said, Thou art my God.** Seeing himself for the miserable wretch he was, David turned his eyes toward the Father.

15-16. My times are in thy hand. David knew that all the varied events of his life were in the hand of the Lord God of heaven and he need not fear. What a great statement of faith coming from the depths of depression. His prayer was, **Make thy face to shine upon thy servant.**

17-18. Let me not be ashamed . . . let the wicked be ashamed. Coming from a pious heart, this double request arises as much out of concern for the sanctity of the Lord's name as it does for the reputation of the Lord's man. **Let the lying lips be**

18 Let the lying lips be put to silence; which speak grievous things proudly and contemptuously against the righteous.

19 *Oh* how great *is* thy goodness, which thou hast laid up for them that fear thee; *which* thou hast wrought for them that trust in thee before the sons of men!

20 Thou shalt hide them in the secret of thy presence from the pride of man: thou shalt keep them secretly in a pavilion from the strife of tongues.

21 Blessed *be* the LORD: for he hath shewed me his marvellous kindness in a strong city.

22 For I said in my haste, I am cut off from before thine eyes: nevertheless thou heardest the voice of my supplications when I cried unto thee.

23 O love the LORD, all ye his saints: for the LORD preserveth the faithful, and plentifully rewardeth the proud doer.

24 Be of good courage, and he shall strengthen your heart, all ye that hope in the LORD.

PSALM 32

BLESSED *is* he whose transgression *is* forgiven, *whose* sin *is* covered.

2 Blessed *is* the man unto whom the LORD imputeth not iniquity, and in whose spirit *there is* no guile.

3 When I kept silence, my bones waxed old through my roaring all the day long.

4 For day and night thy hand was heavy upon me: my moisture is turned into the drought of summer. Sě'lah.

5 I acknowledged my sin unto thee, and mine iniquity have I not hid. I said, I will confess my transgressions unto the LORD; and thou forgavest the iniquity of my sin. Sě'lah.

6 For this shall every one that is godly pray unto thee in a time when thou mayest be found: surely in the floods of great waters they shall not come nigh unto him.

7 Thou *art* my hiding place; thou shalt preserve me from trouble; thou shalt compass me about with songs of deliverance. Sě'lah.

8 I will instruct thee and teach thee in

put to silence. II Samuel 16:7, 8; 17:1-3 provide ample evidence that David had been slandered by lying lips.

19-21. Oh how great is thy goodness. David quickly turns from prayer to praise in the four verses that follow. **Thou shalt keep them secretly in a pavilion from the strife of tongues.** Speaking poetically, the psalmist paints a beautiful picture of the protection of God for His own. God keeps His own in a **pavilion,** a place in which they may receive relief from the heat of the day and protection from their enemies **in a strong city,** or a fortified city.

22. For I said in my haste, I am cut off. David admits that his faith had wavered. Now in coming back to the Lord, he is admitting that he spoke too hastily, something each of us has frequent occasion to admit to the Lord.

23-24. O love the LORD, all ye his saints. It is almost as if David is portraying his life on a stage. He has now come to the conclusion, the last act. He seems to turn away from the other actors and look directly into the faces of the audience, saying the last two verses of this psalm to them. The psalmist has one final word of advice to the audience: **Be of good courage, and he shall strengthen your heart.**

FF. The Blessedness of Forgiveness. 32:1-11.

THEME: A psalm of instruction relating the blessings that come to a man who has experienced God's forgiveness.

The superscription of this psalm is, **A psalm of David. A Maschil.** This is to indicate that it is a psalm of instruction (see Introduction). That David wrote this glorious psalm is proved not only by this heading, but by the words of the Apostle Paul in Romans 4:6-8.

32:1-2. Blessed is he whose transgression is forgiven, whose sin is covered. The truly happy man is one whose transgressions have been forgiven. The active agent in the forgiveness of sin is always God; He forgives and covers our sin. The idea of covering sin is at the very root of our atonement, i.e., the blood of Jesus Christ covers all our sins and hides them from the presence of God. **Blessed is the man unto whom the LORD imputeth not iniquity.** This is the third in the trilogy of blessing: a man is blessed whose transgression is forgiven, whose sin is covered, unto whom the Lord does not impute iniquity.

3-4. When I kept silence, my bones waxed old. As long as the psalmist did not acknowledge his sin, he suffered the grievous pain, both bodily and mentally, of that sin. Unconfessed sin arrests the heart of man and causes him great distress. **My moisture is turned into the drought of summer.** The sap of his soul, the vital principle of his life, had been drained from him by the heat of God's wrath.

5. I acknowledged my sin unto thee, and mine iniquity have I not hid. The psalmist did not attempt to gloss over his sin, nor to conceal it from the God of heaven. **I said, I will confess my transgressions unto the LORD.** This, the I John 1:9 principle, is the only real answer to the forgiveness of sin. Sin cannot be hidden; it must be faced, confessed, and openly dealt with.

6-8. For this shall every one that is godly pray unto thee in a time when thou mayest be found. The day will come when judgment will fall upon unconfessed sin, and in that day the Saviour will not be found to make our confession to. We must indeed seek the Lord while He may be found. **Thou art my hiding place.** This expression, found elsewhere in the Psalms (17:8; 27:5; 31:20; 143:9), is a favorite one, graphically displaying the Lord God as a shelter from trouble when the enemy compasses us about.

the way which thou shalt go: I will guide thee with mine eye.

9 Be ye not as the horse, *or* as the mule, *which* have no understanding: whose mouth must be held in with bit and bridle, lest they come near unto thee.

10 Many sorrows *shall be* to the wicked: but he that trusteth in the LORD, mercy shall compass him about.

11 Be glad in the LORD, and rejoice, ye righteous: and shout for joy, all *ye that are* upright in heart.

PSALM 33

REJOICE in the LORD, O ye righteous: *for* praise is comely for the upright.

2 Praise the LORD with harp: sing unto him with the psaltery *and* an instrument of ten strings.

3 Sing unto him a new song; play skilfully with a loud noise.

4 For the word of the LORD *is* right; and all his works *are done* in truth.

5 He loveth righteousness and judgment: the earth is full of the goodness of the LORD.

6 By the word of the LORD were the heavens made; and all the host of them by the breath of his mouth.

7 He gathereth the waters of the sea together as an heap: he layeth up the depth in storehouses.

8 Let all the earth fear the LORD: let all the inhabitants of the world stand in awe of him.

9 For he spake, and it was *done;* he commanded, and it stood fast.

10 The LORD bringeth the counsel of the heathen to nought: he maketh the devices of the people of none effect.

11 The counsel of the LORD standeth for ever, the thoughts of his heart to all generations.

12 Blessed *is* the nation whose God *is* the LORD: *and* the people *whom* he hath chosen for his own inheritance.

13 The LORD looketh from heaven; he beholdeth all the sons of men.

14 From the place of his habitation he looketh upon all the inhabitants of the earth.

15 He fashioneth their hearts alike; he considereth all their works.

9-10. Be ye not as the horse, or as the mule. The horse and the mule were excusable for their actions because they had no understanding or discernment, but Israel was inexcusable. If she would not learn to live in light of the Lord's Law, she would experience what all wicked individuals experience, i.e., **Many sorrows shall be to the wicked.** In direct opposition to this, **he that trusteth in the LORD, mercy shall compass him about.**

11. Be glad in the LORD, and rejoice, ye righteous. Happiness is not only our privilege; it is our duty as well. **And shout for joy, all ye that are upright in heart.** David's psalms almost always end with a note of joy, or at least in a tone of encouragement.

GG. A Psalm of Rejoicing. 33:1-22.

THEME: A call to lively and joyous praise to God for His glorious attributes and works.

Psalm 33 is one of the orphan psalms. It has no title in Hebrew, and an author is not named. Some manuscripts have Psalm 33 joined to Psalm 32, forming one psalm; but the difference in subject matter and tone render it highly improbable that the two psalms should be joined. The LXX makes David the author, but it has no support from the Hebrew to do this. The psalm does exhibit, however, much Davidic character.

33:1-4. The psalm begins with a call to extol the Lord God of heaven. Specifically, we are to **Praise the LORD with harp,** a small, simple instrument of triangular framework, made of wood crossed by seven strings. **Sing unto him with the psaltery and an instrument of ten strings.** The psaltery (Heb *nēbel*) is further described as an instrument of ten strings (cf. 92:3; 144:9). **Play skillfully with a loud noise.** It is a sin to praise God in a slovenly manner. **For the word of the LORD is right.**

5-7. By the word of the LORD were the heavens made. God is to be praised, not only for His personal goodness, but for the greatness of His creation as well. **He gathereth the waters of the sea together as a heap.** Although this is an allusion to Genesis 1:8, we cannot help but remember the accounts of Exodus 15:8 and Joshua 3:13-16. In each instance, the same Hebrew word (Heb *nēd*) is used and translated **a heap.**

8-9. Let all the earth fear the LORD. All the inhabitants of the earth must forsake their idols and regard only the living God Jehovah as the Supreme Being. **For he spake, and it was done; he commanded, and it stood fast.** He spoke the heavens into existence. And not only so, but He commanded His creation to stand fast; and thus the planetary bodies of every universe maintain their position by the power of the Almighty's Word.

10-11. The counsel of the LORD standeth for ever. As opposed to the decrees of His enemies, God never changes His purpose; His decrees are not frustrated, and His designs are always accomplished. **The thoughts of his heart to all generations.** The plan of the Lord God is carried throughout generations, age after age, because it is settled and sure in heaven.

12. Blessed is the nation whose God is the LORD. The next phrase must be linked to this one, **the people whom he hath chosen for his own inheritance.** He speaks here of the blessing on the nation Israel which accompanies their election as God's chosen people. Yet, any nation that aligns itself with the Lord God can expect His blessing.

13-15. The LORD looketh from heaven . . . From the place of his habitation he looketh upon all the inhabitants of the earth. It is a great comfort for those who live righteously to know that all their acts are beheld by the Lord; it should be a great concern to those who live unrighteously. **He fashioneth their hearts alike.** By this is meant that the hearts of all men are equally fashioned by the Lord, the king's heart as well as the

1021

16 There is no king saved by the multitude of an host: a mighty man is not delivered by much strength.

17 An horse *is* a vain thing for safety: neither shall he deliver *any* by his great strength.

18 Behold, the eye of the LORD *is* upon them that fear him, upon them that hope in his mercy;

19 To deliver their soul from death, and to keep them alive in famine.

20 Our soul waiteth for the LORD: he *is* our help and our shield.

21 For our heart shall rejoice in him, because we have trusted in his holy name.

22 Let thy mercy, O LORD, be upon us, according as we hope in thee.

PSALM 34

I WILL bless the LORD at all times: his praise *shall* continually *be* in my mouth.

2 My soul shall make her boast in the LORD: the humble shall hear *thereof,* and be glad.

3 O magnify the LORD with me, and let us exalt his name together.

4 I sought the LORD, and he heard me, and delivered me from all my fears.

5 They looked unto him, and were lightened: and their faces were not ashamed.

6 This poor man cried, and the LORD heard *him,* and saved him out of all his troubles.

7 The angel of the LORD encampeth round about them that fear him, and delivereth them.

8 O taste and see that the LORD *is* good: blessed *is* the man *that* trusteth in him.

9 O fear the LORD, ye his saints: for *there is* no want to them that fear him.

10 The young lions do lack, and suffer hunger: but they that seek the LORD shall not want any *thing.*

11 Come, ye children, hearken unto me: I will teach you the fear of the LORD.

beggar's heart. **He considereth all their works.** God does not simply view the acts of men from heaven; He ponders and judges them as well.

16-17. There is no king saved by the multitude of a host. Safety is not in numbers when one runs counter to the purpose of God. **A horse is a vain thing for safety.** The psalmist calls the horse a deceitful confidence. With all his cavalry, Sennacherib was no match for one angel of the Lord.

18-21. Behold. Look. Something better is coming. **The eye of the LORD is upon them that fear him.** Those who fear God need fear nothing else. **To deliver their soul from death, and to keep them alive in famine.** Whatever the Lord's eye can observe, His sovereign hand can preserve. **For our heart shall rejoice in him, because we have trusted in his holy name.** The duty that was commanded of us in the first verse is carried out here. We who are to rejoice in the Lord must never be caught short in praising Him.

22. Let thy mercy, O LORD, be upon us. The final verse of this delightful psalm is an appeal for mercy, but not just a blanket appeal. The psalmist appeals to the Lord to show mercy on us **according as we hope in thee.** In the words of the Master, ". . . According to your faith be it unto you" (Mt 9:29).

HH. A Psalm of Praise and Instruction. 34:1-22.

THEME: After praising God for gracious treatment, the psalmist instructs others on the providential care of the righteous.

This third alphabetical psalm bears a striking resemblance to Psalm 25. The superscription over the psalm, claiming to give occasion for its writing, says, **A psalm of David, when he changed his behavior before Abimelech; who drove him away, and he departed.** A brief account of these happenings is recorded in I Samuel 21:10-15. In the psalm David does not parade his sinfulness, but rather spends his time praising the Lord for His grace.

34:1-3. I will bless the LORD at all times. The psalmist's resolve is fixed. In every situation and under every circumstance, he is determined to bless the Lord. But more than that, his blessing of the Lord will not just be in his heart, but **his praise shall continually be in my mouth . . . O magnify the LORD with me, and let us exalt his name together.** David extends a call for Israel to come and praise Jehovah with him. The reasons that such praise is justified are listed in verses 4-10.

4-7. They looked unto him, and were lightened. This simply means that when men in need look to the Lord Jesus, their countenances are immediately brightened or cheered because of the One to whom they look. **This poor man cried, and the LORD heard him.** The poor man is a reference to David himself, else the demonstrative this would not have been used. Returning to his own case, he makes note that a single prayer **saved him out of all his troubles.** The reason the deliverance could be enacted so quickly was **The angel of the LORD encampeth round about them that fear him, and delivereth them.** This is not just an angel of the Lord, but "the captain of the LORD's host" who appeared to Joshua (Josh 5:15), the Lord Jesus Christ manifesting Himself in the Old Testament.

8-10. O taste and see that the LORD is good. Put the matter to the test of experience (cf. I Pet 2:3). We must test Him and fear Him, for **there is no want to them that fear him.** Jehovah will not allow His faithful servants to starve, nor to lack in any of the necessities of life. **They that seek the LORD shall not want any good thing.**

11-12. Suddenly, David's praise for the Lord gives way to teaching others. He calls to them **Come, ye children, hearken unto me: I will teach you the fear of the LORD.** What can a man

12 What man *is he that* desireth life, *and* loveth *many* days, that he may see good?

13 Keep thy tongue from evil, and thy lips from speaking guile.

14 Depart from evil, and do good; seek peace, and pursue it.

15 The eyes of the LORD *are* upon the righteous, and his ears *are open* unto their cry.

16 The face of the LORD *is* against them that do evil, to cut off the remembrance of them from the earth.

17 *The righteous* cry, and the LORD heareth, and delivereth them out of all their troubles.

18 The LORD *is* nigh unto them that are of a broken heart; and saveth such as be of a contrite spirit.

19 Many *are* the afflictions of the righteous: but the LORD delivereth him out of them all.

20 He keepeth all his bones: not one of them is broken.

21 Evil shall slay the wicked: and they that hate the righteous shall be desolate.

22 The LORD redeemeth the soul of his servants: and none of them that trust in him shall be desolate.

PSALM 35

PLEAD *my cause,* O LORD, with them that strive with me: fight against them that fight against me.

do if he desires a long life and good days all his life? It is to this that David now addresses himself.

13-14. Keep thy tongue from evil. Sins of the tongue have been abundantly noted in the Psalms (5:9; 10:7; 12:3; 15:3; 50:19; 57:4; 73:8-9; etc.). **Depart from evil, and do good.** Now some positive and negative advice. **Depart from evil** means to go away from evil, to avoid it as one would avoid a plague. Positively, once one has departed from evil, he may **do good.** It is not simply enough to lack evil; one must possess good. In addition, **seek peace, and pursue it.** Peace is not a magnet that seeks out the hunter; it is a commodity woven in the fabric of distress which must be tirelessly extricated by its seeker.

15-16. The eyes of the LORD are upon the righteous. The eyes and the ears of the Lord are always open to those who live righteously, and no righteous act ever escapes God's eye. Conversely, **The face of the LORD is against them that do evil.** God is never indifferent to the deeds of sinful men.

17-18. The righteous cry, and the LORD heareth . . . The LORD is nigh unto them that are of a broken heart. The Lord does not hear the cry of the proud; but when we live righteously and humbly, He is always near in friendship to receive and console us. Broken hearts are only broken in this life. **And saveth such as be of a contrite spirit.** Literally, the **contrite spirit** is the beaten-out spirit (Heb *daka'*). It implies a spirit that has been hammered and is in a state of submission to whatever God has for it.

19. Many are the afflictions of the righteous. For the Christian, afflictions come from every point of the compass (cf. Job 36:8-10; Acts 14:22; I Cor 15:19; II Tim 3:12; Heb 11:33-38; 12:5-10; etc.). **But the LORD delivereth him out of them all.** Whenever God has allowed tribulation to do its perfect work in purging, molding, and shaping us, He will then remove that tribulation from us.

20-21. He keepeth all his bones: not one of them is broken. The **bones** are the entire frame of the body, that which provides structure to the entire body. As not a bone of the Lord's body was broken at His crucifixion, not a bone of the body of Christ, the church, will be broken, harmed, segmented or lost. **And they that hate the righteous shall be desolate.** Although they are a formidable group now, those who have caused hurt and who have hated all who live righteously will one day find themselves forsaken, wretched and alone.

22. The LORD redeemeth the soul of his servants. With great price and great power the Lord Jesus has severed the soul of the redeemed from the bands of Satan. Our souls have been emancipated, by the paying of a price. The ransom—Jesus Christ. **And none of them that trust in him shall be desolate.** What a tremendous promise with which to conclude this psalm!

II. A Prayer for Rescue. 35:1-28.

THEME: *The psalmist invokes God's deliverance from the oppression and malice of those who strive against him.*

The psalm exhibits many of the characteristics of David's style, particularly his early style, i.e., abruptness, graphic images, sudden transitions. Those close to the psalmist have developed an intense enmity against him. Although it is difficult to fix the time of writing with great accuracy, many points of correspondence between this psalm and the experiences of David's early life as a fugitive from Saul are seen (cf. I Sam 20-26, especially I Sam 24:12-15).

35:1. Plead my cause, O LORD, with them that strive with me. It is good to know that we have One who pleads our cause for us. The accuser of the brethren shall be met face to face with the Advocate of the brethren. The second hemistich, **fight against them that fight against me,** is added to provide the setting out of which the psalmist cries.

2 Take hold of shield and buckler, and stand up for mine help.

3 Draw out also the spear, and stop *the way* against them that persecute me: say unto my soul, I *am* thy salvation.

4 Let them be confounded and put to shame that seek after my soul: let them be turned back and brought to confusion that devise my hurt.

5 Let them be as chaff before the wind: and let the angel of the LORD chase *them.*

6 Let their way be dark and slippery: and let the angel of the LORD persecute them.

7 For without cause have they hid for me their net *in* a pit, *which* without cause they have digged for my soul.

8 Let destruction come upon him at unawares; and let his net that he hath hid catch himself: into that very destruction let him fall.

9 And my soul shall be joyful in the LORD: it shall rejoice in his salvation.

10 All my bones shall say, LORD, who *is* like unto thee, which deliverest the poor from him that is too strong for him, yea, the poor and the needy from him that spoileth him?

11 False witnesses did rise up; they laid to my charge *things* that I knew not.

12 They rewarded me evil for good *to* the spoiling of my soul.

13 But as for me, when they were sick, my clothing *was* sackcloth: I humbled my soul with fasting; and my prayer returned into mine own bosom.

14 I behaved myself as though *he had been* my friend *or* brother: I bowed down heavily, as one that mourneth *for his* mother.

15 But in mine adversity they rejoiced, and gathered themselves together: *yea,* the abjects gathered themselves together against me, and I knew *it* not; they did tear *me,* and ceased not:

16 With hypocritical mockers in feasts, they gnashed upon me with their teeth.

17 Lord, how long wilt thou look on? rescue my soul from their destructions, my darling from the lions.

18 I will give thee thanks in the great congregation: I will praise thee among much people.

19 Let not them that are mine enemies wrongfully rejoice over me: *neither* let them wink with the eye that hate me without a cause.

20 For they speak not peace: but they devise deceitful matters against *them that are* quiet in the land.

21 Yea, they opened their mouth wide against me, *and* said, Aha, aha, our eye hath seen *it.*

2-3. Take hold of shield and buckler. In these verses the Lord is pictured as coming forth arrayed for battle and placing Himself between His servant and his enemies. The **shield** (Heb *magēn*) was the smaller hand weapon of war; the **buckler** (Heb *tsinah*) was that protection which covers the whole body. **Draw out also the spear.**

4-6. Let them be confounded and put to shame that seek after my soul. Disappointment is always the portion of those who seek vengeance against the righteous. **Let them be as chaff before the wind.** Chaff is a type of whatever is futile, worthless, or vain. **And let the angel of the LORD persecute them.** In the name of unflinching justice, no foothold will be found for these persecutors with the angel of the Lord, God's avenger, at their heels.

7-8. For without cause have they hid for me their net in a pit. Their action toward the psalmist was totally without provocation on his part. To those who stalk the righteous, God is swift and deadly in His retribution. **Let his net that he hath hid catch himself.** This is the Haman principle, a *lex talionis,* poetic justice (cf. 9:15-16; 57:6; 141:10).

9-10. And my soul shall be joyful in the LORD . . . All my bones shall say, LORD, who is like unto thee. Here is a sudden transition from imprecatory prayer to thanksgiving. David envisions himself now rescued, and he wants to ascribe honor to the Lord. As if his tongue were not enough to praise the Lord, his whole anatomy quakes with gratitude.

11-12. False witnesses did rise up. An age-old device in persecuting the righteous is to enlist the help of false witnesses. David was accused by Saul (". . . seeketh thy hurt . . . ," I Sam 24:9) in much the same way our Lord was falsely accused at His trial and crucifixion. **They rewarded me evil for good.** His accusers robbed David of all the comforts of home, his innocent name, and a quiet soul.

13-14. I bowed down heavily, as one that mourneth for his mother. The psalmist bowed his head as mourners do. He engaged in the extreme and exaggerated manifestations of both joy and grief that were characteristic of his Oriental society (see Herodotus, viii. p. 99). David behaved himself very well indeed.

15-16. But in mine adversity they rejoiced. His enemies did not reciprocate his good conduct. As in the case of Job (Job 30:1-14), they **gathered themselves together. With hypocritical mockers in feasts, they gnashed upon me with their teeth.** Like professional buffoons who attend a great man's table and spoil the occasion by their ribald behavior, these classless clods speak fiercely and angrily against the psalmist like angry dogs which gnarl and show their teeth.

17-18. LORD, how long wilt thou look on? How long? is the common cry of sufferers (6:3; 13:1; 79:5; 89:46; Job 19:2; Hab 1:2; Rev 6:10). David questions whether the Lord will continue to be a mere spectator or will rescue His darling from the lions. **I will give thee thanks in the great congregation.** David's flutter of faith does not daunt his strong belief that he will be delivered by the Lord. Friend and foe alike will hear of the glory of the Lord from the psalmist.

19-21. Neither let them wink with the eye that hate me without a cause. The winking of the eye was a sign of congratulations at the ruin of a victim over which they had completely triumphed. David prays that he will be spared this scornful gesture. **They devise deceitful matters against them that are quiet in the land.** Riotous men charge others with sedition. Such was the case when the Lord Jesus was charged with seeking to overthrow Caesar. David too has now felt the cold edge of the sharp tongue of the unscrupulous. **Aha, aha, our eye**

hath seen it. Triumphantly and in derision they scorn, Ha Ha. We have seen our enemies' downfall.

22-23. O LORD: keep not silence. His petition now becomes more intense. As he draws to a close, he becomes more pointed in his prayer. **O LORD, be not far from me.** This is the cry to be the fourth Man in the fire with him, to be the unseen angel in the lion's den. **Awake to my judgment.** The psalmist calls on God to wake, not that He was asleep, but as an appeal for God to manifest Himself.

24-28. Finally, the psalmist utters a number of appeals to the Lord God. Each is in the hortatory mood: **Let them not say in their hearts. Let them not say. Let them be ashamed. Let them be clothed with shame. Let them shout for joy. Let the LORD be magnified.** David prays for shame and confusion to be brought upon those who would bring shame and confusion upon him. When David's enemies are put to flight and are silenced, David's friends will come forth to shout with joy and be glad. Through it all, his great request is **Let the LORD be magnified.** And for the good and bad that he has been through with the Lord, the psalmist vows **And my tongue shall speak of thy righteousness and of thy praise all the day long.**

JJ. The Contrast Psalm. 36:1-12.

THEME: *The wickedness of man contrasted with the steadfastness of God.*

Instead of the usual contrast between the wicked man and the godly man, which can be seen in 1:1-6; 4:2-3; 5:10-11; etc., here the psalmist makes a brilliant contrast between the wicked man and God. The wicked man is characterized in the first four verses; the character of God is portrayed in the next five.

There is little internal evidence to assist us in determining the date and authorship of this psalm. However, since nothing conflicts with Davidic authorship, such tradition must be maintained.

36:1. The first verse of this psalm presents us with a rather thorny textual problem. It is indeed difficult to translate; in fact, in the Hebrew, the first word (Heb *ne'um*) meaning an utterance or an oracle doesn't even occur in the English translation (lit., the original text reads, An oracle of transgression). If we understand the initial phrase to read, An oracle about transgression, this would mean the psalmist is saying that down deep in his heart he was given insight about what was really wrong with the wicked. This insight came not by reasoning nor by intuition, but by divine revelation. God revealed the character of the wicked to the psalmist, just as He revealed His own divine character. **There is no fear of God before his eyes.** However we translate the first half of this verse, there is no question that the person being described belongs to that class of fools who say in their hearts there is no God (14:1).

2-3. The continued description of the wicked person deepens our impression of him. **For he flattereth himself in his own eyes.** He alone counts his achievements as worthwhile. **He hath left off to be wise, and to do good.** Apparently, there was a time when the wicked man could act with some degree of wisdom. But that time is now gone; he now acts wicked consistently.

4. He deviseth mischief upon his bed. In the night when God-fearing men are in innocent slumber and meditating on the goodness of God, the wicked man, with the devil for his bedfellow, lies awake devising wicked schemes against others (cf. Prov 4:16; Mic 2:1). **He abhorreth not evil.** So calloused has he become that he has no contempt or abhorrence at all for evil; he even rejoices in it.

5. Thy mercy, O LORD, is in the heavens. God's mercy, or rather His loving-kindness, His steadfast love (Heb *chesed*), is like a canopy over all creatures of the earth. **And thy faithful-**

---

22 *This* thou hast seen, O LORD: keep not silence: O Lord, be not far from me.
23 Stir up thyself, and awake to my judgment, *even* unto my cause, my God and my Lord.

24 Judge me, O LORD my God, according to thy righteousness; and let them not rejoice over me.
25 Let them not say in their hearts, Ah, so would we have it: let them not say, We have swallowed him up.
26 Let them be ashamed and brought to confusion together that rejoice at mine hurt: let them be clothed with shame and dishonour that magnify *themselves* against me.
27 Let them shout for joy, and be glad, that favour my righteous cause: yea, let them say continually, Let the LORD be magnified, which hath pleasure in the prosperity of his servant.
28 And my tongue shall speak of thy righteousness *and* of thy praise all the day long.

PSALM 36

THE transgression of the wicked saith within my heart, *that there is* no fear of God before his eyes.

2 For he flattereth himself in his own eyes, until his iniquity be found to be hateful.
3 The words of his mouth *are* iniquity and deceit: he hath left off to be wise, *and* to do good.

4 He deviseth mischief upon his bed; he setteth himself in a way *that is* not good; he abhorreth not evil.

5 Thy mercy, O LORD, *is* in the heavens; *and* thy faithfulness *reacheth* unto the clouds.

ness reaches unto the clouds. God exhibits an unswerving fidelity toward His creation; He never falters, never fails, never forgets.

6 Thy righteousness *is* like the great mountains; thy judgments *are* a great deep: O LORD, thou preservest man and beast.

6. Thy righteousness is like the great mountains, in the Hebrew idiom, "the mountains of God." Like the majestic Alps or snowcapped Mount Hermon, the righteousness of God is unshakable, lofty, sublime, unmovable. It will always be there; it can be relied upon. **O LORD, thou preservest man and beast.** Another tremendous characteristic of God is His attention to the innumerable birds, the abundance of fish, and the infinite armies of insects, as well as the increasing population of men. All would have no sustenance were it not for the providential care of God.

7 How excellent *is* thy lovingkindness, O God! therefore the children of men put their trust under the shadow of thy wings.

7. How excellent is thy loving-kindness, O God! The steadfast love of God warrants additional mention. The psalmist calls it excellent or precious, more precious than any other attribute. Without it, the other attributes would be meaningless. Because of it, men can put their trust **under the shadow of thy wings.**

8 They shall be abundantly satisfied with the fatness of thy house; and thou shalt make them drink of the river of thy pleasures.

8. They shall be abundantly satisfied with the fatness of thy house. Although God's **house** is typified by heaven, nevertheless, every place we reside, when we are under the wings of the Lord, we may find abundant blessing (cf. 91:1, 4). **Thou shalt make them drink of the river of thy pleasures** (lit., the river of thy Edens). Our loving God gives us access to the exhaustless fountains of paradise, a stream like that which watered Eden (cf. Isa 51:3; 55:1; Jn 4:14; 7:37-38).

9 For with thee *is* the fountain of life: in thy light shall we see light.

9. For with thee is the fountain of life. One can hardly fail to note how much of John's theology finds its root in this verse. The ultimate source of all life is God. As He is the sole source of natural life, likewise He is also the sole source of spiritual life (30:5; 66:9; Jn 1:4; 6:57; 7:37-39; etc.). **In thy light shall we see light.** Here we must be aware of John's statements in John 1:4-5, 9; I John 1:5-7. Light is the glory of life. Life in the darkness is more death than life. God is life and light.

10 O continue thy lovingkindness unto them that know thee; and thy righteousness to the upright in heart.
11 Let not the foot of pride come against me, and let not the hand of the wicked remove me.
12 There are the workers of iniquity fallen: they are cast down, and shall not be able to rise.

10-12. The final verses of this psalm are an intercessory prayer to God that He will protect the righteous from the assaults of the ungodly. **O continue thy loving-kindness unto them that know thee.** David's prayer is not grandiose; he asks no more than a continuance of the past expression of God's love, His steadfast love and mercy.

There are the workers of iniquity fallen. At some point, **there,** on a spot before his eyes, the psalmist envisions his foes as vanquished. **They are cast down, and shall not be able to rise.** The defeat of the ungodly and all the powers of hell will be final. Whereas the righteous may fall into misfortune repeatedly and be recovered (Prov 24:16), the evil workers will fall and perish.

KK. The Inheritance Psalm. 37:1-40.

THEME: The psalmist struggles with the enigma of the prosperity of the wicked and the affliction of the righteous.

Psalm 37 is another of the Alphabetic, or acrostic, Psalms. This is a psalm of David in his old age (cf. vs. 25), a psalm in which he reflects upon his years of experience. Although his thoughts do not flow freely because of the fetter of the acrostic form, nevertheless this psalm, with its sententious sayings, resembles the book of Proverbs. The subject matter is the age-old question, "Why do the wicked prosper, when the righteous are afflicted?" Other classic treatments of this question are found in Psalm 49, Psalm 73, and the whole book of Job.

37:1. Fret not thyself because of evildoers. This psalm begins with the first great lesson on how to live in light of the wicked who prosper around us. That lesson is, **Fret not.** Don't be concerned, for the verses that follow explain that the righteous are in a much better position than the wicked.

PSALM 37
FRET not thyself because of evildoers, neither be thou envious against the workers of iniquity.

2 For they shall soon be cut down like the grass, and wither as the green herb.

2. For they shall soon be cut down like the grass. As Job's friend Zophar noted, "the triumphing of the wicked is short, and the joy of the hypocrite but for a moment" (Job 20:5). Why should the righteous be envious of that?

3 Trust in the LORD, and do good; *so* shalt thou dwell in the land, and verily thou shalt be fed.

3. Trust in the LORD. If those around you live wickedly and prosper, here is the second lesson that the psalmist would teach us. The cure for fretting is faith. Regardless of the circumstances around us, we must still trust in the Lord. But there is more, **and do good.** True faith always produces good works. A faith that trusts in the Lord will find active outlet. **And verily thou shalt be fed.** The Good Shepherd is always present to care for His sheep. Feed on this thought, and you will fret not.

4 Delight thyself also in the LORD; and he shall give thee the desires of thine heart.

4. Delight thyself also in the LORD. Here is the third lesson we must learn. If we make the Lord God the object of our affection, our meditation, and our activity, then we will find ourselves rejoicing in the Spirit. Evildoers delight in their position; but as a child of God, if you delight in yours, you will never envy theirs. **And he shall give thee the desires of thine heart.** When we find pleasure in the Lord God, we will then be rewarded with our innermost desires; we will have all that God intends for us to have.

5 Commit thy way unto the LORD; trust also in him; and he shall bring *it* to pass.
6 And he shall bring forth thy righteousness as the light, and thy judgment as the noonday.

5-6. Commit thy way unto the LORD. The psalmist now teaches us a fourth lesson in understanding why the wicked apparently prosper while we are afflicted. To have that peace and understanding, we must cast ourselves and our lives unreservedly upon God, yield ourselves wholly to Him, and cultivate the habit of placing our lives in His hands. There can be no better medicine to dispel envy and fretting. **And he shall bring forth thy righteousness as the light.** If the prosperity of the wicked causes us to fret, we can always be assured that God will ultimately make things right. Our righteous living will be brought to light.

7 Rest in the LORD, and wait patiently for him: fret not thyself because of him who prospereth in his way, because of the man who bringeth wicked devices to pass.

7. And now the fifth lesson that the psalmist would teach: **Rest in the LORD, and wait patiently for him.** Literally, this means to be silent, not to murmur. That is, do not make any complaint when the wicked prosper around us. To fulfill this lesson requires a special unction of grace. We must recognize that God is fully in control of the situation and simply wait for Him to work it out to our good and His glory. Synchronize your life with His timetable, and you will have learned this fifth lesson well.

8 Cease from anger, and forsake wrath: fret not thyself in any wise to do evil.
9 For evildoers shall be cut off: but those that wait upon the LORD, they shall inherit the earth.
10 For yet a little while, and the wicked *shall* not *be*; yea, thou shalt diligently consider his place, and it *shall* not *be*.

8-10. The basic premise of the psalm given, what follows is proverbial advice concerning the inheritance of the wicked, as opposed to the inheritance of the righteous. As we cease fretting about those who prosper around us and forsake our wrath, we can see more clearly that **evildoers shall be cut off.** Those who are evildoers will certainly, sooner or later, be cut down, as the scythe cuts down the grass of the field. Although we may only partially see this prophecy fulfilled in our lifetime, it will find its complete fulfillment in ". . . new heavens and a new earth, wherein dwelleth righteousness" (II Pet 3:13).

11 But the meek shall inherit the earth; and shall delight themselves in the abundance of peace.

11. But the meek shall inherit the earth. This prophecy was reiterated by the Lord Jesus (Mt 5:5). **And shall delight themselves in the abundance of peace.** The meek may never enjoy an abundance, but why should they care? An abundance of peace is theirs, and that is far better.

12 The wicked plotteth against the just, and gnasheth upon him with his teeth.
13 The Lord shall laugh at him: for he seeth that his day is coming.
14 The wicked have drawn out the sword, and have bent their bow, to cast down the poor and needy, *and* to slay such as be of upright conversation.
15 Their sword shall enter into their own heart, and their bows shall be broken.
16 A little that a righteous man hath

12-17. The wicked plotteth against the just. But we should not fear their plans, for **The LORD shall laugh at him.** God, who sees the end from the beginning, knows the day is coming when the wicked shall no longer prosper.

A fine proverb is **A little that a righteous man hath is better than the riches of many wicked** (cf. Prov 15:16; 16:8). It is better to cast your lot, though a poor one it may be, with the righteous than to live in luxury with the wicked. **For the arms of the wicked shall be broken.** God will destroy the strength of the strong. He has a way of making incapable men out of implacable men.

is better than the riches of many wicked.

17 For the arms of the wicked shall be broken: but the LORD upholdeth the righteous.

18 The LORD knoweth the days of the upright: and their inheritance shall be for ever.

19 They shall not be ashamed in the evil time: and in the days of famine they shall be satisfied.

18-19. The LORD knoweth the days of the upright. No calamity of which God is unaware can befall us; no financial disaster, no life-robbing illness, can affect us without His knowledge. **And their inheritance shall be for ever.** In contrast to the wicked, who are quickly cut off, those who live righteously have an eternal inheritance, an inheritance ". . . incorruptible, and undefiled, and that fadeth not away, reserved in heaven for you" (I Pet 1:4). **They shall not be ashamed in the evil time.** Even if we fall into trying situations, we know that God is simply purifying us (Job 36:8-11), making us better servants and more understanding comforters (II Cor 1:1-4).

20 But the wicked shall perish, and the enemies of the LORD *shall be* as the fat of lambs: they shall consume; into smoke shall they consume away.

21 The wicked borroweth, and payeth not again: but the righteous sheweth mercy, and giveth.

22 For *such as be* blessed of him shall inherit the earth; and *they that be* cursed of him shall be cut off.

20-22. The wicked are entirely different. The wicked borroweth, and payeth not again. One of the characteristics of a wicked man is that he borrows with a light heart, having no intention of repaying. But the righteous **showeth mercy, and giveth.** Characteristic of the righteous person is that he freely gives of himself and all that he has.

23 The steps of a *good* man are ordered by the LORD: and he delighteth in his way.

24 Though he fall, he shall not be utterly cast down: for the LORD upholdeth *him with* his hand.

23-24. The steps of a good man are ordered by the LORD. Why should a righteous person be concerned about his future? If a man lives righteously, that is, if he is a good man and has committed his way unto the Lord, the steps which lead to his inheritance are designed by the Lord. **Though he fall, he shall not be utterly cast down.** A good man is never dealt a fatal blow by the wicked of this world. The reason is clear; **For the LORD upholdeth him with his hand.**

25 I have been young, and *now* am old; yet have I not seen the righteous forsaken, nor his seed begging bread.

25. Yet have I not seen the righteous forsaken. David's observation has been that the righteous are never forsaken by God, even if circumstances appear to be to the contrary. **Nor his seed begging bread.** Although the righteous and his seed may have occasions of scarcity, they are never left to be continual vagabonds to beg from house to house.

26 *He is* ever merciful, and lendeth; and his seed *is* blessed.

27 Depart from evil, and do good; and dwell for evermore.

28 For the LORD loveth judgment, and forsaketh not his saints; they are preserved for ever: but the seed of the wicked shall be cut off.

29 The righteous shall inherit the land, and dwell therein for ever.

30 The mouth of the righteous speaketh wisdom, and his tongue talketh of judgment.

31 The law of his God *is* in his heart; none of his steps shall slide.

26-31. The psalmist now turns his attention to the righteous in his relationship to the Lord. **He is ever merciful, and lendeth.** The righteous man has a generous impulse that causes him constantly to be a giver. The righteous are preserved, **but the seed of the wicked shall be cut off.** The thought that the wicked and his posterity shall both be cut off from the land of the living (Isa 53:8) is repeated frequently in this psalm. **The mouth of the righteous speaketh wisdom.** A man's character is frequently betrayed by his tongue. **The law of his God is in his heart** (cf. 40:8; 119:11; Deut 6:6; Isa 51:7). Because the godly has the law of God in his heart, **none of his steps shall slide.**

32 The wicked watcheth the righteous, and seeketh to slay him.

33 The LORD will not leave him in his hand, nor condemn him when he is judged.

34 Wait on the LORD, and keep his way, and he shall exalt thee to inherit the land: when the wicked are cut off, thou shalt see *it*.

32-34. The wicked watcheth the righteous, and seeketh to slay him. The life of a righteous individual is a reproach to one living wickedly. If it were not for the grace of God and the law of the land, the righteous would be massacred by the wicked. Although a righteous man may at times fall prey to the devices of the wicked, **The LORD will not leave him in his hand.**

Wait on the LORD, and keep his way, and he shall exalt thee to inherit the land. We must wait in obedience as a servant, in hope as an heir, in expectation as a believer. But waiting is not simply being passive; for while we wait, we **keep his way.** We walk in the way of righteousness and thus have the promise of an incorruptible inheritance.

35 I have seen the wicked in great power, and spreading himself like a green bay tree.

35-36. I have seen the wicked . . . spreading himself like a green bay tree. Like a tree in its own native soil, growing luxuriantly, branching heavily, leafy and green, the wicked

36 Yet he passed away, and, lo, he *was* not: yea, I sought him, but he could not be found.

37 Mark the perfect *man*, and behold the upright: for the end of *that* man *is* peace.
38 But the transgressors shall be destroyed together: the end of the wicked shall be cut off.

39 But the salvation of the righteous *is* of the LORD: *he is* their strength in the time of trouble.
40 And the LORD shall help them, and deliver them: he shall deliver them from the wicked, and save them, because they trust in him.

PSALM 38

O LORD, rebuke me not in thy wrath: neither chasten me in thy hot displeasure.
2 For thine arrows stick fast in me, and thy hand presseth me sore.

3 *There is* no soundness in my flesh because of thine anger; neither *is there any* rest in my bones because of my sin.
4 For mine iniquities are gone over mine head: as an heavy burden they are too heavy for me.
5 My wounds stink *and* are corrupt because of my foolishness.
6 I am troubled; I am bowed down greatly; I go mourning all the day long.
7 For my loins are filled with a loathsome *disease:* and *there is* no soundness in my flesh.
8 I am feeble and sore broken: I have roared by reason of the disquietness of my heart.
9 Lord, all my desire *is* before thee; and my groaning is not hid from thee.
10 My heart panteth, my strength faileth me: as for the light of mine eyes, it also is gone from me.
11 My lovers and my friends stand aloof from my sore; and my kinsmen stand afar off.
12 They also that seek after my life lay snares *for me:* and they that seek my hurt speak mischievous things, and imagine deceits all the day long.

prosper. This is a graphic picture of how the influence of the wicked is felt. But what is the end result? **Yet he passed away, and, lo, he was not.** Death makes a clean sweep of all, both trees and men. One day he whose prosperity is now legend will be searched for and not found.

37-38. Mark the perfect man, and behold the upright. The closing advice from the psalmist is that, having seen the downfall of the wicked portrayed, we would be wise to give our attention to the man who lives uprightly, perfectly, and righteously. **For the end of that man is peace. But the transgressors shall be destroyed together.** The theme of this psalm is now repeated: common ruin awaits those who have joined in common rebellion against God. The sword of Damocles is above their heads; they are not to be envied.

39-40. But the salvation of the righteous is of the LORD. Here is David's doctrine of grace. The very marrow of the gospel is the acknowledgement that **Salvation belongeth unto the LORD** (3:8). The righteous man comes to appreciate that the Lord God is the designer, the initiator, and the end of his salvation.

LL. The Prayer of a Suffering Penitent. 38:1-22.

THEME: *The psalmist confesses his sin and cries to God for forgiveness during a time of physical suffering.*

The superscription over the psalm reads **A psalm of David, to bring to remembrance.** David felt that he had been forgotten by God because he had sinned and was desperately ill. This is one of the Penitential Psalms, and it is recited by many churches on Ash Wednesday. Of all the Penitential Psalms, this one exhibits, perhaps the most severe state of body and mind.

38:1-2. O LORD, rebuke me not in thy wrath. The psalmist knew he had sinned and a rebuke was necessary. His initial prayer, therefore, was not for the cessation of the rebuke, but for the removal of God's wrath from it. The believer can withstand God's rebuke and His chastening, but he cannot withstand divine wrath. **For thine arrows stick fast in me.** The metaphor of God's **arrows** used as chastisement is not unfamiliar in Scripture (cf. 7:13; 18:14; 45:5; 64:7; 77:17; Job 6:4). By God's arrows the psalmist means physical, mental, and spiritual infirmities.

3-8. In the verses that follow, a brief description of the psalmist's anguish is given. **There is no soundness in my flesh,** i.e., no vitality, no strength, no health. **Neither is there any rest in my bones.** His whole body was given to continual aching and unrest (cf. 6:2; 22:14; 31:10) because of his sin against God. **I am troubled; I am bowed down greatly.** Each of these expressions may refer to his physical condition. He is also bent over and bowed down, as in old age or suffering from rheumatism or a similar malady. **I have roared by reason of the disquietness of my heart.** His aches and pains have given rise to frequent groanings. The sounds of death have accompanied his illness.

9-10. LORD, all my desire is before thee; and my groaning is not hid from thee. In the midst of great distress and pain, the psalmist indicates a flicker of hope for his recovery. That hope stems from the fact that the Good Physician hears his groanings and understands his dilemma.

11-12. My lovers and my friends stand aloof from my sore. His near acquaintances and relatives have kept their distance from his suffering. The psalmist feels himself to be ". . . stricken, smitten of God . . ." (Isa 53:4). As the Lord's acquaintances gazed at the cross from a distance, the plight of the psalmist typifies that loneliness. **They also that seek after my life lay snares for me.** All day long, those who hated Him spoke malignity against Him.

13 But I, as a deaf *man*, heard not; and *I was* as a dumb man *that* openeth not his mouth.

14 Thus I was as a man that heareth not, and in whose mouth *are* no reproofs.

15 For in thee, O LORD, do I hope: thou wilt hear, O Lord my God.

16 For I said, *Hear me*, lest *otherwise* they should rejoice over me: when my foot slippeth, they magnify *themselves* against me.

17 For I *am* ready to halt, and my sorrow *is* continually before me.

18 For I will declare mine iniquity; I will be sorry for my sin.

19 But mine enemies *are* lively, *and* they are strong: and they that hate me wrongfully are multiplied.

20 They also that render evil for good are mine adversaries; because I follow *the thing that* good *is*.

21 Forsake me not, O LORD: O my God, be not far from me.

22 Make haste to help me, O Lord my salvation.

PSALM 39

I SAID, I will take heed to my ways, that I sin not with my tongue: I will keep my mouth with a bridle, while the wicked is before me.

2 I was dumb with silence, I held my peace, *even* from good; and my sorrow was stirred.

3 My heart was hot within me, while I was musing the fire burned: *then* spake I with my tongue,

4 LORD, make me to know mine end, and the measure of my days, what it *is*: that I may know how frail I *am*.

5 Behold, thou hast made my days *as* an handbreadth; and mine age *is* as nothing before thee: verily every man

13-16. But I, as a deaf man, heard not . . . as a dumb man that openeth not his mouth. The brave silence of David is eminently typical of our Lord Jesus. Throughout the ordeal of His trial and crucifixion, He was as a sheep before the slaughter, totally free from self-defense (cf. Isa 53:7; Mt 26:63; 27:14; I Pet 2:23). **For in thee, O LORD, do I hope**. The psalmist acted as he did because he knew the Lord had **maintained my right and my cause** (9:4). His sole prayer was **Hear me, lest otherwise they should rejoice over me**.

17-20. For I am ready to halt. The psalmist knows that with his tottering footsteps he is constantly in danger of falling. The distress of stumbling is continually before him. But his resolve is great, **For I will declare mine iniquity; I will be sorry for my sin**. He knows he has sinned, and something must be done about that sin. He must pursue the twin children of grace, i.e., confession and contrition. David declared his iniquity and was sorry for his sin.

While the psalmist lies half-lifeless on his sickbed, his enemies **are lively, and they are strong**. He is near death; they are full of life. **They that hate me wrongfully are multiplied**. This expression fits well with the days of Absalom's conspiracy, when increasingly more people forsook David and joined the party of Absalom (II Sam 15:12-13). His enemies render evil for good, **because I follow the thing that good is**.

21-22. Forsake me not, O LORD. This is the first of three final petitions. As the others, it is frequently found in the Psalms (cf. 27:9; 71:9, 18; 119:8). David need not worry; God never forsakes His own. **O my God, be not far from me** (cf. 22:19; 35:22; 71:12). The final petition is **Make haste to help me, O LORD my salvation** (cf. 22:19; 31:2; 40:13; 70:1; 71:12). This cry always shows imminent peril. The psalmist knew he was in danger from both his enemies and his severe physical condition. But in the midst of that danger he cried out to God in a faith that always conquers.

MM. The Broken Resolution Psalm. 39:1-13.

THEME: The psalmist promises restraint, fails in his promise, and prays to God for divine compassion.

This is a very unusual psalm. The title assigns it to David and indicates that he committed the composition for musical arrangement to the choirmaster of the time, a man named **Jeduthun**, one of the chief musicians in David's service. We have thus far not encountered such a dedication in the Psalms. Delitzsch summarizes that Jeduthun was, "the name of one of David's three musicians, the third after Asaph and Heman (I Chr 16:41ff.; 25:1ff.; II Chr 5:12; 35:15) undoubtedly the same person as Etham (I Chr 15:19), a name which after the appointments at Gibeon (I Chr 16) was changed to Jeduthan."

39:1-2. I said, I will take heed to my ways, that I sin not with my tongue. The psalmist undertakes a steady resolve to be circumspect in what issues from his mouth. He does not wish to give vent to his innermost feelings **while the wicked is before me**. In order to avoid the embarrassment of complaint, he says, **I was dumb with silence, I held my peace, even from good**. Literally, the psalmist was as speechless as if he had been tongueless. Neither good nor bad came from his mouth.

3-6. My heart was hot within me. Bitterness rubbed against anguish and caused the spark of complaint. **While I was musing the fire burned**. As he thought about the situation around him, his own affliction, and the wicked who pursued him, the commitment to his resolve weakened. **Then spake I with my tongue, LORD, make me to know mine end**. His request to know his end is not that of Job who desired to be cut off at once (Job 6:9; 7:15; 14:13). Instead, weary of life, the psalmist requests to know **the measure of my days, what it is**. David

at his best state *is* altogether vanity. Sĕ'lah.

6 Surely every man walketh in a vain shew: surely they are disquieted in vain: he heapeth up *riches*, and knoweth not who shall gather them.

7 And now, Lord, what wait I for? my hope *is* in thee.
8 Deliver me from all my transgressions: make me not the reproach of the foolish.

9 I was dumb, I opened not my mouth; because thou didst *it.*
10 Remove thy stroke away from me: I am consumed by the blow of thine hand.
11 When thou with rebukes dost correct man for iniquity, thou makest his beauty to consume away like a moth: surely every man *is* vanity. Sĕ'lah.

12 Hear my prayer, O Lord, and give ear unto my cry; hold not thy peace at my tears: for I *am* a stranger with thee, *and* a sojourner, as all my fathers *were*.
13 O spare me, that I may recover strength, before I go hence, and be no more.

PSALM 40
I WAITED patiently for the Lord; and he inclined unto me, and heard my cry.

wanted to know the number of his days to be assured his trial would soon be over.

Surely every man walketh in a vain show. To the despondent psalmist, life is but a passing pageant. As he surveys those around him, the anguished psalmist notes that man **heapeth up riches, and knoweth not who shall gather them.** With little preparation for eternity, man is solely interested in the existential now. And yet, all that he amasses for himself, he must leave behind (cf. Job 27:16-17; Eccl 2:18, 21).

7-8. In the midst of despondency, the conscience of the psalmist is awakened to the fact, **And now, Lord, what wait I for? My hope is in thee.** He has fallen prey to the despair of vanity. Where shall he turn? Out of the depths comes the voice of faith. **My hope is in thee. Deliver me from all my transgressions.** As he begins his prayer, David's first task is to confess his sin of discouragement. His approach to God quickens within him a sense of the need for pardon of his sin.

9-11. I was dumb, I opened not my mouth; because thou didst it. David recognizes that his afflictions came from God. This enabled him to keep silence while the ungodly were in his sight. Now he continues his prayer, asking the Lord God to remove the heavy hand of chastisement from him, knowing that the rebuke of the Lord makes the beauty of a man to be consumed like the moth. This simply means that his health and strength were taken from him while the Lord chastised him. In light of that, his only conclusion can be **surely every man is vanity.** Without God, life is vain; and the living of life is a vain display of futility.

12-13. Hear my prayer, O Lord. The call for divine attendance unto the psalmist's prayer is accompanied with the request, **hold not thy peace at my tears.** Frequently, tears speak more eloquently than a thousand tongues. The sincerity of a tear does not go unnoticed by God. Tearfully then, the psalmist prays, **O spare me, that I may recover strength, before I go hence, and be no more.** The psalmist is no longer anxious for death, although he is well aware that death is his lot. Instead, he requests a breathing space, a time of refreshment before he is **no more.**

NN. Christ Our Sacrifice. 40:1-17.

THEME: *A psalm of David's anguish depicting the greater anguish in the sufferings of Christ.*

Psalm 40 is dedicated **To the chief musician,** which probably indicates that the psalm was intended for public worship. The author of the psalm was David, and it may be conjectured that he penned this writing on his restoration to the throne after the usurpation of Absalom.

It is evident that this is a Messianic Psalm. Verses 6-8 are quoted in Hebrews 10:5-9, as the words of Christ. But it is quite likely that David, in expressing the Lord's restoration of him from the door of death to the throne of Israel, is also prophetically describing the anguish and crucifixion of Christ, the Son of David. Thus, even if the New Testament had not quoted Psalm 40 in reference to Christ, the very context of this psalm would have indicated its Messianic character.

40:1. I waited patiently for the Lord; and he inclined unto me, and heard my cry. The common Hebrew idiom of waiting patiently on the Lord, coupled with the expressive anthropomorphism of the Lord God bending forward toward the psalmist, constitute a beautiful picture of God's concern and care for those who cry out to Him. Patient waiting upon God was frequently evidenced in the life of the Lord Jesus. Throughout the ordeal of the Passion Week, the agony in the Garden, the trial and mockings, and the crucifixion, Christ Jesus patiently waited upon God the Father to perform the work of atonement.

2 He brought me up also out of an horrible pit, out of the miry clay, and set my feet upon a rock, *and* established my goings.

3 And he hath put a new song in my mouth, *even* praise unto our God: many shall see *it*, and fear, and shall trust in the LORD.

4 Blessed *is* that man that maketh the LORD his trust, and respecteth not the proud, nor such as turn aside to lies.

5 Many, O LORD my God, *are* thy wonderful works *which* thou hast done, and thy thoughts *which are* to usward: they cannot be reckoned up in order unto thee: *if* I would declare and speak *of them*, they are more than can be numbered.

6 Sacrifice and offering thou didst not desire; mine ears hast thou opened: burnt offering and sin offering hast thou not required.

7 Then said I, Lo, I come: in the volume of the book *it is* written of me,

8 I delight to do thy will, O my God: yea, thy law *is* within my heart.

9 I have preached righteousness in the great congregation: lo, I have not refrained my lips, O LORD, thou knowest.

10 I have not hid thy righteousness within my heart; I have declared thy faithfulness and thy salvation: I have not concealed thy lovingkindness and thy truth from the great congregation.

11 Withhold not thou thy tender mercies from me, O LORD: let thy loving kindness and thy truth continually preserve me.

12 For innumerable evils have compassed me about: mine iniquities have taken hold upon me, so that I am not able to look up; they are more than the hairs of mine head: therefore my heart faileth me.

The proverbial patience of Job on the dung hill does not equal the patience of Christ on the cross.

2. He brought me up also out of a horrible pit (lit., a pit of tumult, uproar, or noise). The **pit** is synonymous with the grave; and the Lord Jesus, who patiently waited upon the Lord God, received the fruit of that patience when after His crucifixion He was raised from the dead **out of the miry clay**.

3-4. And he hath put a new song in my mouth. With death destroyed, Satan defeated, and hell subdued, a new song is now sung by the Master. It is a song resplendent with righteousness, a song of victory. **Many shall see it, and fear, and shall trust in the LORD.** An innumerable multitude shall see the sufferings of the Lord, the atonement which He provided for them, their shameful condition, and through grace shall trust in the Lord for salvation. To this thought the psalmist can add only **Blessed is that man that maketh the LORD his trust.**

5. Many, O LORD my God, are thy wondrous works . . . they are more than can be numbered. All of life teems with evidence of God's handiwork: creation, redemption, the skies and seas, the love of the home, etc. Human mathematics cannot possibly total the wonderful works of God. Their sum is so great as to forbid analysis or numeration.

6. Sacrifice and offering thou didst not desire; mine ears hast thou opened. This verse, attributed to the lips of Jesus, is quoted in Hebrews 10:5 as, ". . . Sacrifice and offering thou wouldest not, but a body hast thou prepared me." The difference in the verse is accounted for by circumstance. **Burnt offering and sin offering hast thou not required.** In this verse the psalmist specifies four specific kinds of offerings: **Sacrifice** (Heb *zebach;* Gr *thysia*) the ordinary sacrifice of a victim at the altar; **offering** (Heb *minchah;* Gr *prosphora*) the meal offering of flour with oil and frankincense; **burnt offering** (Heb *'ōlah;* Gr *holokautōma*) the whole burnt offering; and **sin offering** (Heb *chata'ah;* Gr *peri hamartias*) the sin or trespass offering. None of these, by the blood of bulls and goats, could make adequate atonement for our sins. Only the blood of Jesus Christ could do that (Heb 9).

7-10. In the volume of the book it is written of me. The pages of both testaments are replete with testimony of Jesus Christ. This claim could not be made of David alone, but only of David's Messiah. **I have preached righteousness in the great congregation.** Not only did great hoards of people hear the Lord as He spoke to them on the Galilean hills, but His whole life was a sermon. He taught of God's salvation openly in the Temple, as well as the synagogue. He lived as an example of God's righteousness wherever He went.

11. At this point, the supplication segment of the psalm begins. As a man, the psalmist could think of the lovingkindness of God just mentioned and pray **Withhold not thou thy tender mercies from me, O LORD.** But how much more appropriate for the Lord Jesus dying upon the cross to say these words.

12. For innumerable evils have compassed me about. From every quarter the devil drew his best weapons and aimed them squarely at the Lord of Glory. **Mine iniquities have taken hold upon me, so that I am not able to look up.** Although this is a Messianic Psalm and certain references cannot be but to the Lord Jesus, nevertheless it was penned by David and a violent wresting of language is not necessary to see both David and His Lord in this psalm. It is not unreasonable to assume that the psalmist's reference here was never intended to be messianic, and therefore a problem does not really exist. David just cries out that his sins are more than the hairs of his head, and he is thoroughly repentant of them.

13 Be pleased, O Lord, to deliver me: O Lord, make haste to help me.

14 Let them be ashamed and confounded together that seek after my soul to destroy it; let them be driven backward and put to shame that wish me evil.

15 Let them be desolate for a reward of their shame that say unto me, Aha, aha.

16 Let all those that seek thee rejoice and be glad in thee: let such as love thy salvation say continually, The Lord be magnified.

17 But I *am* poor and needy; *yet* the Lord thinketh upon me: thou *art* my help and my deliverer; make no tarrying, O my God.

PSALM 41

BLESSED *is* he that considereth the poor: the Lord will deliver him in time of trouble.

2 The Lord will preserve him, and keep him alive; *and* he shall be blessed upon the earth: and thou wilt not deliver him unto the will of his enemies.

3 The Lord will strengthen him upon the bed of languishing: thou wilt make all his bed in his sickness.

4 I said, Lord, be merciful unto me: heal my soul; for I have sinned against thee.

5 Mine enemies speak evil of me, When shall he die, and his name perish?

6 And if he come to see *me*, he speaketh vanity: his heart gathereth iniquity to itself; *when* he goeth abroad, he telleth *it*.

7 All that hate me whisper together

13-17. Be pleased, O Lord, to deliver me. This plaintive cry for deliverance, both Davidic in light of the rebellion of Absalom and messianic in light of Gethsemane, shows the gravity of the situation. With due piety the psalmist calls, **Let them be ashamed and confounded together that seek after my soul to destroy it . . . Let them be desolate for a reward of their shame that say unto me, Aha, aha.** Whether a prayer of David or a prophecy, the result is the same. Satan constantly seeks the destruction of the Saviour and His people. Many in Israel laughed at the King when he was deposed from his throne and fled in terror. The Jewish rulers, the Roman soldiers, and the street people of Jerusalem screamed, "Ah" at the Son of God as He endured the shame of the cross (see Mk 15:29). This prayer is that the ungodly will not long relish in the plight of the godly.

The Lord be magnified. But I am poor and needy; yet the Lord thinketh upon me. The Man of Sorrows closes this psalm with yet another appeal based on His need as He hung between heaven and earth dying for us. His disciples had forsaken Him, His friends had departed, His call was to the Lord God Jehovah, His deliverer, **make no tarrying, O my God.** In perfect faith, just as the psalmist had called upon the Lord God and had expected deliverance, so too the Son of God, in perfect faith, called upon His Father to hasten His deliverance through death because that would also hasten His resurrection to life.

OO. Abuse and Assurance. 41:1-13.

THEME: *The prayer of a sick man beset by cruel enemies.*

The title, **To the chief musician. A psalm of David,** indicates the importance of the psalm; for it was dedicated to the chief of the musicians. David celebrates the blessedness of those who have compassion upon the poor, while he contrasts and condemns those who neglect their friends during times of distress. Finally, he prays for God's mercy in light of his circumstances and asks that God will vindicate his cause.

A point of messianic contact is made at verse 9, which Jesus quoted of Judas in John 13:18. This does not necessarily make the entire psalm messianic in nature; for the words uttered by the psalmist were spoken of his **friend** (vs. 9), yet were no less designed of God to be applied to Judas Iscariot.

41:1-3. Blessed is he that considereth the poor. David makes a statement of fact and then gives proof for that statement. The psalmist concluded the preceding psalm by calling himself **poor and needy** (40:17). This one he begins by commending those who **considereth the poor,** who regard the afflicted affectionately. **The Lord will preserve him, and keep him alive.** God will give length of days to anyone who considers the plight of the poor. **Thou wilt make all his bed in his sickness.** Here is a tender phrase. The Hebrew verb meaning to change (Heb *hapak*) is used which literally means to rearrange the covers, fluff up the pillow, and in general make the bed more comfortable to lie in. All this is to the man who has tender regard for the poor.

4-6. I said, Lord, be merciful unto me. David now turns to his own case. He, too, has suffered great afflictions, both of body and mind. However, he does not fail to recognize his own sin. **Mine enemies speak evil of me.** David has been the object of calumny, misrepresentation, and abuse. Israel's hearts have been stolen away by Absalom in his misrepresentation of his father David (II Sam 15:3-4). Shimei also greatly abused and cursed the king (II Sam 16:5-8). Speaking of his enemies, the psalmist notes, **his heart gathereth iniquity to itself; when he goeth abroad, he telleth it.** An apparent reference to Ahithophel, this friend/enemy made a show of his friendship with David, complimenting him freely to his face, but misrepresenting him behind his back.

7-8. All that hate me whisper together against me. A whis-

against me: against me do they devise my hurt.

8 An evil disease, *say they*, cleaveth fast unto him: and *now* that he lieth he shall rise up no more.

9 Yea, mine own familiar friend, in whom I trusted, which did eat of my bread, hath lifted up *his* heel against me.

10 But thou, O LORD, be merciful unto me, and raise me up, that I may requite them.

11 By this I know that thou favourest me, because mine enemy doth not triumph over me.

12 And as for me, thou upholdest me in mine integrity, and settest me before thy face for ever.

13 Blessed *be* the LORD God of Israel from everlasting, and to everlasting. Amen, and Amen.

PSALM 42

AS the hart panteth after the water brooks, so panteth my soul after thee, O God.

2 My soul thirsteth for God, for the living God: when shall I come and appear before God?

3 My tears have been my meat day

per campaign had been launched against the king. Part of that campaign was **An evil disease, say they, cleaveth fast unto him** (lit., a thing of Belial). This may mean either a physical or moral evil. Whatever the disease, David's enemies used it to great advantage in misrepresenting and abusing him.

9. Yea, mine own familiar friend, in whom I trusted, (lit., the man of my peace). This obviously refers to Ahithophel, for he is called "the man of my peace" since he was one of David's official counselors (II Sam 15:12). **Hath lifted up his heel against me.** As David's friend, Ahithophel defected from the king and joined in Absalom's conspiracy (see II Sam 15:12, 31; 16:15-23; 17:1-23).

It is evident that there is a messianic connotation given to this verse because the Lord Jesus quoted it in speaking of Judas Iscariot in John 13:18. Although David, the type of Christ, said, **Yea, mine own familiar friend, in whom I trusted,** nevertheless Jesus Christ, the antitype, deleted the reference to trusting, when he used it of Judas. As Ahithophel had eaten bread with David, so too Judas dipped in the same dish with his Lord. Ahithophel is a type of Judas, as David is a type of Christ.

10-11. But thou, O LORD, be merciful unto me. David prays for the Lord's mercy so that he may rise up against his traitor, not in private revenge, but in justification of his office as the chosen king of Israel (cf. Rom 13:4). Why does he feel he can do this? **By this I know that thou favorest me.** God delighted in David in choosing him to be king, and his victory over Absalom and Ahithophel will prove God's delight.

12. And as for me, thou upholdest me in mine integrity, and settest me before thy face for ever. David's innocence and righteousness before the sight of God caused him to be held in divine surveillance all the days of his life. Long after his enemies had been defeated, David was still a man after God's own heart.

13. Blessed be the LORD God of Israel from everlasting, and to everlasting. Amen, and Amen. Although this doxology fits perfectly well with this psalm, it is likely that it was an addition to the entire first book of Psalms. Each of the five books of the Psalter closes with such a doxology (cf. 72:18ff.; 89:52; 106:48).

II. PSALMS 42:1-72:20.

A. Longing for God. 42:1-11.

THEME: A psalm of rare beauty and passion exhibiting the writer's intense longing for God.

The superscription over this psalm reads **To the chief musician. A Maschil, for the sons of Korah.** If we are to understand this heading like those which have preceded it, the authorship of this psalm must be ascribed to the sons of Korah, a Levitical family of singers who perhaps accompanied David in exile. However, many expositors are of the opinion that the psalm was written by David on the occasion of his flight from his son Absalom (II Sam 17:24), having crossed the fords of the Jordan near Jericho and ascended the eastern heights, taking refuge in Mahanaim (II Sam 19:32). Though the date and authorship of this psalm cannot be said with great certainty, there is no doubt as to the locality from which it was written. The writer was in the land beyond the Jordan near the mountain ridges of Mount Hermon (vs. 6). From there he pines for the presence of God and His sanctuary in Jerusalem.

42:1-2. As the hart panteth after the water brooks, so panteth my soul after thee, O God. After a tiring, yet lifesaving, run the hart instinctively seeks after the river. Barred from public worship, David, too, was homesick for the Lord God, **the living God.** His very self, his deepest person, had an insatiable desire for the presence of God.

3-4. My tears have been my meat day and night. David's

and night, while they continually say unto me, Where *is* thy God?

4 When I remember these *things*, I pour out my soul in me: for I had gone with the multitude, I went with them to the house of God, with the voice of joy and praise, with a multitude that kept holyday.

5 Why art thou cast down, O my soul? and *why* art thou disquieted in me? hope thou in God: for I shall yet praise him *for* the help of his countenance.

6 O my God, my soul is cast down within me: therefore will I remember thee from the land of Jordan, and of the Her′mon-ītes, from the hill Mī′zär.

7 Deep calleth unto deep at the noise of thy waterspouts: all thy waves and thy billows are gone over me.

8 *Yet* the LORD will command his lovingkindness in the daytime, and in the night his song *shall be* with me, *and* my prayer unto the God of my life.

9 I will say unto God my rock, Why hast thou forgotten me? why go I mourning because of the oppression of the enemy?

10 *As* with a sword in my bones, mine enemies reproach me; while they say daily unto me, Where *is* thy God?

11 Why art thou cast down, O my soul? and why art thou disquieted within me? hope thou in God: for I shall yet praise him, *who is* the health of my countenance, and my God.

PSALM 43

JUDGE me, O God, and plead my cause against an ungodly nation: O deliver me from the deceitful and unjust man.

2 For thou *art* the God of my strength: why dost thou cast me off? why go I mourning because of the oppression of the enemy?

3 O send out thy light and thy truth: let them lead me; let them bring me unto thy holy hill, and to thy tabernacles.

4 Then will I go unto the altar of God, unto God my exceeding joy: yea, upon the harp will I praise thee, O God my God.

banishment from the house of God did not bring him to indifference. On the contrary, being shut out from the Old Testament presence of God in the sanctuary intensified David's desire to commune with God. **I had gone with the multitude, I went with them to the house of God.** With what great fondness the psalmist remembers his former free access to the house of God and the frequency of his attendance there. These painful reflections of the days when he mingled with the pious throng initiate his cry of despair.

5-6. Why art thou cast down, O my soul? This is a descriptive term of extreme dejection, i.e., why has my soul been brought very low? **And why art thou disquieted in me?**, i.e., why do you make a roaring noise like the sea moaning over me (cf. 46:3; Jer 4:19; 5:22). But the psalmist's dejection is not so great that he has forgotten the solution to that dejection. **Hope thou in God** (cf. 33:22; 39:7, etc.). **From the land of Jordan, and of the Hermonites.** Here, David localizes the place of his lament. He is in Transjordan on that mountain that begins with Hermon in the north and extends south through the entirety of Transjordan.

7. Deep calleth unto deep at the noise of thy waterspouts. The psalmist's misfortunes did not come singly, but in tandem. Wave after wave of the troubled seas had swallowed him up, yet he knew where to find hope.

8-9. Yet the LORD will command his loving-kindness in the daytime, and in the night. No day will ever dawn in which the child of God is found forsaken by God. **I will say unto God my rock, Why hast thou forgotten me?** God never forgets His own, even though in our circumstances it may humanly appear that He does (cf. 9:12; 37:28). The historical record indicates clearly that David had not been forsaken (II Sam 19:9-40).

10-11. The slanders of David's enemies were like daggers in his bones. As they taunted him saying, **Where is thy God?**, he could but reply to himself, **Why art thou cast down, O my soul?** Repeating the earlier phrase of dismay, the answer still remains the same: **Hope thou in God.** God is always faithful.

B. The Light and Truth Psalm. 43:1-5.

THEME: *A prayer for deliverance from the deceitful and for guidance by the light and truth of God.*

There is no title to this psalm, but presumably it is written by the same writer as Psalm 42. In fact, there is a close relationship between the two psalms. The refrain of verses 6 and 11 of Psalm 42 appears as the conclusion of Psalm 43. Psalm 43 brings the unresolved issues of Psalm 42 to a conclusion. The remarkable coincidence of thought and language in these two psalms has led many scholars to believe that they were originally one psalm. The lack of a superscription over Psalm 43 may be additional evidence for this hypothesis. Yet, each psalm is complete in itself, although they bear a relationship to each other.

43:1-2. Judge me, O God, and plead my cause against an ungodly nation. The psalmist is aware that men frequently misjudge the motives of the righteous. Therefore, God's intervention is asked in the struggle between David and his enemy. **For thou art the God of my strength,** i.e., the God in whom lies all my strength (28:7). Again the cry **why dost thou cast me off?** is equivalent to saying, "Why have you forgotten me?" Again, God has not forgotten the psalmist; he only assumes so.

3-4. O send out thy light and thy truth: let them lead me. God's piercing light and searching truth will vindicate the character of the psalmist. As the pillar of fire and the cloud led the Israelites into the Promised Land, so David now pleads that God's **light** and **truth** will lead him back to Jerusalem and to the worship of God in His sanctuary. **Let them bring me unto thy holy hill, and to thy tabernacles.** It is the great desire of David's

5 Why art thou cast down, O my
soul? and why art thou disquieted
within me? hope in God: for I shall yet
praise him, *who is* the health of my
countenance, and my God.

PSALM 44

WE have heard with our ears, O God,
our fathers have told us, *what* work
thou didst in their days, in the times of
old.

2 *How* thou didst drive out the
heathen with thy hand, and plantedst
them; *how* thou didst afflict the people,
and cast them out.

3 For they got not the land in possession by their own sword, neither did
their own arm save them: but thy right
hand, and thine arm, and the light of
thy countenance, because thou hadst a
favour unto them.

4 Thou art my King, O God: command deliverances for Jacob.

5 Through thee will we push down
our enemies: through thy name will we
tread them under that rise up against
us.

6 For I will not trust in my bow,
neither shall my sword save me.

7 But thou hast saved us from our enemies, and hast put them to shame that
hated us.

8 In God we boast all the day long,
and praise thy name for ever. Sē'lah.

9 But thou hast cast off, and put us to
shame; and goest not forth with our armies.

10 Thou makest us to turn back from
the enemy: and they which hate us
spoil for themselves.

11 Thou hast given us like sheep *appointed* for meat; and hast scattered us
among the heathen.

12 Thou sellest thy people for nought,
and dost not increase *thy wealth* by
their price.

13 Thou makest us a reproach to our
neighbours, a scorn and a derision to
them that are round about us.

14 Thou makest us a byword among
the heathen, a shaking of the head
among the people.

15 My confusion *is* continually before me, and the shame of my face hath
covered me,

16 For the voice of him that reproach-

heart to be able to return to Jerusalem and worship freely in the
tabernacle.

5. For the third and final time he repeats the refrain **Why art
thou cast down, O my soul?** Three times the question has been
asked; three times the answer has been **Hope in God,** or a
similar expression. Notwithstanding the present woes of the
psalmist, he yet has occasion to praise God; for he anticipates a
soon return to the city of the Great King.

C. God's Hidden Face. 44:1-26.

*THEME: A psalm of praise for past deliverance and for deliver-
ance from present troubles.*

The superscription over the psalm reads **To the chief musician for the sons of Korah. A Maschil.** Similar to the title over
Psalm 42, the authorship of this psalm is even more in question.
It appears safe to assume that this psalm was written during the
time of David, but not necessarily by him. Psalm 44 does not
have the Davidic ring to it that Psalms 42 and 43 had. Calvin
claims that if we know nothing else about this psalm we ought to
know that it was written by anyone other than David. It may be
that some Israelite patriot sings out his psalm of faith and sorrow
here while his countrymen experience a disturbing military
setback.

**44:1-3. Our fathers have told us, what work thou didst in
their days, in the times of old.** The Mosaic law required all
Israelites to teach their children of God's dealings with their
nation (see Ex 10:2; 12:26-27; 13:8-10, etc.). It was handed
down by oral tradition **How thou didst drive out the heathen
with thy hand.** The conquest of Canaan was accomplished by
the power of God's hand. **For they got not the land in possession by their own sword.** Canaan was not conquered without
Israel's armies, but neither were they the conquerors of Canaan.
The Lord alone can be considered the conqueror of the Promised Land.

**4-8. Thou art my king, O God: command deliverances for
Jacob.** At the command of the king, the psalmist fully expected
continued deliverance from the enemies of Israel as his forefathers had seen it. **Through thee will we push down our
enemies,** i.e., we will overthrow and prostrate our enemies.
Those who oppress Israel will be trodden underfoot. Thus, **In
God we boast all the day long, and praise thy name for ever.
Selah.** Praise should be perpetual; and for the many blessings
which God has performed in the past, the psalmist must continue to praise Him in the present. But suddenly this was not the
case.

9-12. At this stage of the psalm, a loud and bitter complaint is
uttered to God by the psalmist. The psalmist's complaint is that
Israel has had to retreat from her enemies, and he charges that
Jehovah **hast scattered us among the heathen.** The armies of
Israel had been dispersed throughout foreign countries, and
many had been taken captive. **Thou sellest thy people for
nought, and dost not increase thy wealth by their price.** Here
the complaint was that God had allowed Israel's enemies to have
power over her without great difficulty, without causing the
victory to be dearly bought as one who pays a great price. Israel
had been defeated so easily that the psalmist concluded that God
had abandoned her.

13-16. Thou makest us a reproach to our neighbors (cf.
43:10; 79:4; 80:6). The Israelite armies had become so
weakened that her enemy neighbors laughed her to scorn. **Thou
makest us a byword among the heathen, a shaking of the head
among the people.** The misery of Israel was so great that
eventually the very name, Jew, became a byword for misery.

eth and blasphemeth; by reason of the enemy and avenger.

17 All this is come upon us; yet have we not forgotten thee, neither have we dealt falsely in thy covenant.

18 Our heart is not turned back, neither have our steps declined from thy way;

19 Though thou hast sore broken us in the place of dragons, and covered us with the shadow of death.

20 If we have forgotten the name of our God, or stretched out our hands to a strange god;

21 Shall not God search this out? for he knoweth the secrets of the heart.

22 Yea, for thy sake are we killed all the day long; we are counted as sheep for the slaughter.

23 Awake, why sleepest thou, O Lord? arise, cast us not off for ever.

24 Wherefore hidest thou thy face, and forgettest our affliction and our oppression?

25 For our soul is bowed down to the dust: our belly cleaveth unto the earth.

26 Arise for our help, and redeem us for thy mercies' sake.

PSALM 45

MY heart is inditing a good matter: I speak of the things which I have made touching the king: my tongue is the pen of a ready writer.

17-22. All this is come upon us; yet have we not forgotten thee . . . neither have our steps declined from thy way. The confusion in the mind of the psalmist is evident. Israel had maintained her sincerity and consistency in worshiping Jehovah. With respect to God's Law, they had not strayed from the right path. Though Israel had been brought into a **place of dragons,** i.e., in a desolate region where jackals abound (cf. Isa 13:22; 34:13), God's people had not forgotten the name of Jehovah. In addition, Israel had not **stretched out our hands to a strange god,** or the idols of Canaan. Thus, the psalmist can confidently say, **shall not God search this out? For he knoweth the secrets of the heart.** Had Israel been guilty of idolatry, how could that have been concealed from God? But no idolatry was present; how then can the psalmist justify God's treatment of Israel? **Yea, for thy sake are we killed all the day long.** The suffering of Israel was not on account of her desertion from God but, on the contrary, was the cause of her fidelity to God. She suffered as sheep before the slaughter **for thy sake.**

23-26. Awake, why sleepest thou, O Lord? The psalmist does not really believe that Jehovah sleeps. The heathen might imagine so of their gods (I Kgs 18:27), but not an Israelite. An Israelite would be sure that **he that keepeth Israel shall neither slumber nor sleep** (121:4). The writer consciously uses an anthropomorphism, simply intending to call God to action.

Wherefore hidest thou thy face? The patriot of Israel understands that God must have turned His face away from Israel, else she would be enjoying the success of her forefathers (cf. 15:1; 27:9; 69:17, etc.). **For our soul is bowed down to the dust.** This is a very poetic way of saying that Israel has been brought very low, humbled, as it were, even to the earth. She lies prostrate in the dust, defeated by a godless foe. **Arise for our help, and redeem us for thy mercies' sake.** Here is the psalmist's final plea; he prays for redemption and mercy. He cannot understand his circumstances. He cannot see his way clear; he can only see his way up.

D. The Marriage of the King. 45:1-17.

THEME: *A heavenly wedding song rejoicing in the union of Christ the Bridegroom and His bride the church.*

This psalm possesses an unusually long and complicated title, perhaps to mark its royalty or deep import. The title is **To the chief musician upon Shoshannim, for the sons of Korah. A Maschil, A song of loves.** As elsewhere the psalm is addressed **to the chief musician,** the head of the tabernacle choir. The word **Shoshannim** literally means lilies; but exactly what upon lilies means is difficult to say. Similar expressions occur in three other psalms (60; 69; 80). Perhaps it is descriptive of a trumpet-like instrument shaped like lilies or denotes some tune or melody according to which the psalm is to be rendered. In any case, this poetic title is followed by the designation **for the sons of Korah,** which either indicates authorship by these Levitical singers or dedication to them. It is a didactic psalm, as indicated by the word **Maschil;** but the title concludes with **A song of loves** (Heb *yedīdōt*), which probably refers to the subject matter of the psalm.

The psalm itself is an epithalamium, or wedding hymn, which would ordinarily be sung at a royal wedding. The well-focused spiritual eye will see Jesus Christ the Lord in this psalm and His marriage as the Bridegroom to the bride, His church. The quotation of verses 6 and 7 in Hebrews 1:8-9, as applicable to Christ, is conclusive evidence that this is a messianic hymn of praise to the marriage of the Lamb.

45:1-2. My heart is inditing a good matter (lit., my heart bubbles up or boils over with a good matter). The psalmist is so overjoyed with the opportunity to speak good things of his king that he cannot contain himself. **My tongue is the pen of a ready**

2 Thou art fairer than the children of men: grace is poured into thy lips: therefore God hath blessed thee for ever.

3 Gird thy sword upon *thy* thigh, O *most* mighty, with thy glory and thy majesty.
4 And in thy majesty ride prosperously because of truth and meekness *and* righteousness; and thy right hand shall teach thee terrible things.
5 Thine arrows *are* sharp in the heart of the king's enemies; *whereby* the people fall under thee.

6 Thy throne, O God, *is* for ever and ever: the sceptre of thy kingdom *is* a right sceptre.

7 Thou lovest righteousness, and hatest wickedness: therefore God, thy God, hath anointed thee with the oil of gladness above thy fellows.
8 All thy garments *smell* of myrrh, and aloes, *and* cassia, out of the ivory palaces, whereby they have made thee glad.

9 Kings' daughters *were* among thy honourable women: upon thy right hand did stand the queen in gold of Ōʹphir.

10 Hearken, O daughter, and consider, and incline thine ear; forget also thine own people, and thy father's house;
11 So shall the king greatly desire thy beauty: for he *is* thy Lord; and worship thou him.

12 And the daughter of Tyre *shall be there* with a gift; *even* the rich among the people shall intreat thy favour.
13 The king's daughter *is* all glorious within: her clothing *is* of wrought gold.
14 She shall be brought unto the king in raiment of needlework: the virgins her companions that follow her shall be brought unto thee.
15 With gladness and rejoicing shall

writer, a mere instrument of the mind of God. **Grace is poured into thy lips.** That which proceeds from the mouth of the fairest Lord Jesus corresponds to the grace that is found within His heart. One word from the Lord Jesus dissolved the heart of Saul of Tarsus, turning him from the persecutor of righteousness to the preacher of righteousness.

3-5. Gird thy sword upon thy thigh. The king is instructed to array himself in the majesty of a warrior prepared for battle. However, He is not coming to do battle, but to secure His bride. The sword is simply part of His formal attire. **And in thy majesty ride prosperously, because of truth and meekness and righteousness.** Here a majestic and pompous scene unfolds. The picture is that of Christ coming at the Rapture of the church in full adornment for His bride. He rides with the virtues of truth, meekness, and righteousness. **Thine arrows are sharp in the heart of the King's enemies.** His Majesty has aimed not at the heads of men, but rather at their hearts, and has won them to Him because He loved them.

6. Thy throne, O God, is for ever and ever: the scepter of thy kingdom is a right scepter. This can be addressed to none but the Lord Jesus. No earthly king could possibly claim this promise. The psalmist joyfully exclaims the perpetuity of his King. When perpetuity is promised to the throne of David (89:4, 36-37; II Sam 7:13-16), it is only as that throne is continued in the reign of David's son, Christ Jesus.

7-8. Thou lovest righteousness, and hatest wickedness. The Lord Jesus is not neutral on the question of right or wrong. God will not commit rule and authority to one who will not rule righteously. **Therefore God, thy God, hath anointed thee with the oil of gladness above thy fellows.** At Oriental feasts it was customary to pour oil on the heads of distinguished guests. But the Messiah was anointed by God Himself, and the anointing intended is that of Christ's exaltation over all others. This exaltation followed His voluntary humiliation and condescension (cf. Phil 2:9; Heb 2:9).

All thy garments smell of myrrh, and aloes, and cassia. The Messiah is delightful in every respect. Not only has His head been anointed with oil, but His garments carry the fragrance of the most precious and rarest spices.

9. Kings' daughters were among thy honorable women. As the marriage scene begins to unfold, we note that the bride's entourage is glorious as well. The daughters of kings are in the attendance of nobility. Spiritually, every believer is a king's daughter and a member of the royal family of heaven. **Upon thy right hand did stand the queen in gold of Ophir.** The bride, Christ's church, is poetically depicted as the queen in gold of Ophir, the most precious gold available to the Israelite kingdom.

10-11. Forget also thine own people, and thy father's house. The bride, having been introduced, is now spoken to directly. The bride must break all her relationships, separating herself forever from all that she has known since birth, and cling only to her husband, the king. At the Rapture of the church we, as the bride of Christ, will leave behind all that we have known since birth and shall go to be with the Groom, the Lord Jesus, and live in his kingdom for ever and ever. And what should our response be to his love for us? **Worship thou him.** Our response to His love for us can only be a reciprocating love for Him.

12-15. And the daughter of Tyre shall be there with a gift. Tyre is a type of heathenism in the Scriptures (cf. Isa 49:18-23; 56:6-8; 60:3-14). When the King comes for His bride, there will be no lack of others, the unsaved, who will then entreat the Lord for mercy towards them. But the wedding plans have been made in eternity past; the Bridegroom has arrived, and now it is too late. Depicted as the king's daughter, the church is said to be **all glorious within.** The beauty of the redeemed is not an external beauty only, but an internal beauty as well. Through the sanc-

they be brought: they shall enter into the king's palace.

16 Instead of thy fathers shall be thy children, whom thou mayest make princes in all the earth.
17 I will make thy name to be remembered in all generations: therefore shall the people praise thee for ever and ever.

PSALM 46
GOD *is* our refuge and strength, a very present help in trouble.

2 Therefore will not we fear, though the earth be removed, and though the mountains be carried into the midst of the sea;
3 *Though* the waters thereof roar *and* be troubled, *though* the mountains shake with the swelling thereof. Sĕ'lah.

4 *There is* a river, the streams whereof shall make glad the city of God, the holy *place* of the tabernacles of the most High.
5 God *is* in the midst of her; she shall not be moved: God shall help her, *and that* right early.

6 The heathen raged, the kingdoms were moved: he uttered his voice, the earth melted.
7 The LORD of hosts *is* with us; the God of Jacob *is* our refuge. Sĕ'lah.

8 Come, behold the works of the LORD, what desolations he hath made in the earth.
9 He maketh wars to cease unto the end of the earth; he breaketh the bow, and cutteth the spear in sunder; he burneth the chariot in the fire.

tifying power of the Holy Spirit, Christ's bride, the church, will become altogether beautiful. **They shall enter into the King's palace.** The grand and glorious palace of the King, the place that Jesus is today preparing for us (Jn 14:1-3), will one day be the scene of the marriage of the Lamb.

16-17. In conclusion, the psalmist once again addresses the Bridegroom. The emphasis shifts from His ancestry to His progeny. This is yet another way of showing the continuity and perpetuity of the line of Christ. **I will make thy name to be remembered in all generations.** Names renowned in one generation are frequently unknown to the next. But the name of the Lord Jesus Christ, our Bridegroom, a name which is above every name, shall never be forgotten generation on end.

E. The Reformer's Psalm. 46:1-11.
THEME: A psalm of consolation in God and holy confidence in His desire to save Israel.

Another psalm ascribed to the sons of Korah and dedicated **To the chief musician,** this was a favorite of Martin Luther. The expression **A song upon Alamoth** most probably denotes either the treble, a part sung by female voices (the word meaning virgins), or some appropriately high-keyed instrument (cf. 6, title; I Chr 15:19-21).

It is difficult to discern exactly what situation may have called forth this hymn of praise. Perhaps the historical situation that best fits the tone of this psalm was the deliverance that took place in the days of Hezekiah the king (701 B.C.) when Sennacherib's forces were miraculously smitten by the angel of the Lord and the 185,000 Assyrians lay dead on the ground (II Kgs 19:20-37).

46:1. God is our refuge and strength, a very present help in trouble. While other nations boasted in their impregnable castles perched high on inaccessible cliffs secured with iron gates and protected by fierce warriors, Israel was in a safer position than them all. God was her refuge and her strength.

2-3. Therefore will not we fear. Though writing beautiful poetry, the psalmist couches his language in reason. Israel will proceed in a reasonable manner, regardless of the situation around her, because she knows God is in her midst. **Though the earth be removed . . . the mountains be carried into the midst of the sea,** nevertheless, Israel will remain calm. The metaphors of these verses are designed to encompass whatever violent disturbances Israel may encounter. **Selah.** What a powerful thought; let's dwell on it a moment.

4-5. There is a river, the streams whereof shall make glad the city of God. The city of God was threatened by neighboring nations, but the inhabitants of Jerusalem were calmly trusting in God for protection. How could that be? The answer is that ever since the Garden of Eden, God has always had a river to bring peace to His own. It is the river of God's grace. The psalmist is so certain of God's grace in bringing about victory that he exclaims, **God shall help her, and that right early.**

6-7. The heathen raged, the kingdoms were moved. The nations rose up in fury against God's people, but all to no avail; for **The LORD of hosts is with us; the God of Jacob is our refuge.** God has innumerable angels at His command (68:17; II Kgs 6:16-17; Mt 26:53), and Jehovah has covenanted with Israel to be a refuge to them and those who live righteously before Him.

8-9. Come, behold the works of the LORD, what desolations he hath made in the earth. When the morning light broke, the joyful citizens of Jerusalem were invited to go view the remains of their enemies that they may see with what power Jehovah has undertaken in their behalf. God had completely devastated His enemy. **He breaketh the bow, and cutteth the spear in sunder; he burneth the chariot in the fire.** All the

10 Be still, and know that I *am* God: I will be exalted among the heathen, I will be exalted in the earth.
11 The LORD of hosts *is* with us; the God of Jacob *is* our refuge. Sē'lah.

offensive weapons of the enemy were no match for God. The war chariots, which were largely employed by the Assyrians and formed the main strength of the army of Sennacherib (II Kgs 19:23), were utterly destroyed by the power of His might.

10-11. Be still, and know that I am God. These words appear to be addressed not to the enemy, but to Israel herself. What joy is brought to our souls when we are confronted with a problem which has no solution, and yet God works it out for our good and His glory. It is good for us, on occasion, just to stand still and watch the mighty hand of God intently. Then we too will know **The LORD of hosts is with us, the God of Jacob is our refuge. Selah.**

F. King of the Earth. 47:1-9.

THEME: A call to the nations of the earth to praise Jehovah as their King.

Again, the superscription reads **To the chief musician. A psalm for the sons of Korah.** Here, as elsewhere, the author is anonymous and may be identified either as the sons of Korah, David, or one of David's associates. However, the tone is definitely Davidic.

That the psalm is messianic is evident. The majority of the rabbinical interpreters regard it as messianic. Most older Christian expositors suppose it to have been written on the occasion of the removal of the ark to Mount Zion (II Sam 6) and to be a prophecy of the ascension of Christ, His kingly rule, and His taking a place of majesty on the right hand of the Father.

PSALM 47

O CLAP your hands, all ye people; shout unto God with the voice of triumph.
2 For the LORD most high *is* terrible; *he is* a great King over all the earth.
3 He shall subdue the people under us, and the nations under our feet.
4 He shall choose our inheritance for us, the excellency of Jacob whom he loved. Sē'lah.

47:1-4. O clap your hands, all ye people; shout unto God with the voice of triumph. It is not just Israel who is to rejoice at divine triumph, but the world at large. Their voices are to keep tune with their hands and join them in praise to God. **For the LORD most high is terrible.** The victorious God is awesome to contemplate (cf. 65:5; 68:35; 76:7-9; Deut 7:21). **He is a great King over all the earth.** Not over Israel only, but unto the uttermost parts of the earth, over every nation, the aisles of the sea and the continents of the world (cf. 95:3-4; 96:10; 97:1; etc.). **He shall choose our inheritance for us.** God originally chose Canaan as the habitation of His people (Gen 12:1-7). Later, under David and Solomon He enlarged the boundaries (Gen 15:18). Ultimately, He will rule the world with a rod of iron, through the Son of David, i.e., the Lord Jesus Christ.

5 God is gone up with a shout, the LORD with the sound of a trumpet.
6 Sing praises to God, sing praises: sing praises unto our King, sing praises.
7 For God *is* the King of all the earth: sing ye praises with understanding.
8 God reigneth over the heathen: God sitteth upon the throne of his holiness.
9 The princes of the people are gathered together, *even* the people of the God of Abraham: for the shields of the earth *belong* unto God: he is greatly exalted.

5-9. God is gone up with a shout, the LORD with the sound of a trumpet. The ascending or descending of God is frequently associated with a shout and a trumpet (cf. I Thess 4:16). When He has ascended to His throne on high, His subjects are advised to, **Sing praises to God . . . For God is the King of all the earth.** The extent of the jubilation is seen in that five times the whole earth is called upon to sing praises to God. A great King He is indeed.

God reigneth over the heathen . . . The princes of the people are gathered together. The psalmist confidently looks forward to the day when God will unite all people during the millennial reign of Christ. There comes One after David who is mighty and **a great King over all the earth** (vs. 2). That One is Jesus Christ the Lord. The insignia of pomp, the weapons of war, **the shields of the earth belong unto God.** In that day no one will raise his voice against the reign of the Great King, and Jesus Christ will rule supremely with a rod of iron (Rev 19:15).

G. Jerusalem the Golden. 48:1-14.

THEME: A psalm praising the greatness of God and Mount Zion, His dwelling place.

Many have pointed out the similarities between this psalm and Psalm 46. Luther takes it for granted that David wrote this psalm, saying, "David is here celebrating the truth of God." However, Calvin disagrees, indicating, "It is easy to gather from

PSALM 48

GREAT *is* the LORD, and greatly to be praised in the city of our God, *in* the mountain of his holiness.

2 Beautiful for situation, the joy of the whole earth, *is* mount Zion, *on* the sides of the north, the city of the great King.

3 God is known in her palaces for a refuge.

4 For, lo, the kings were assembled, they passed by together.

5 They saw *it, and* so they marvelled; they were troubled, *and* hasted away.

6 Fear took hold upon them there, *and* pain, as of a woman in travail.

7 Thou breakest the ships of Tärshĭsh with an east wind.

8 As we have heard, so have we seen in the city of the LORD of hosts, in the city of our God: God will establish it for ever. Sĕ'lah.

9 We have thought of thy lovingkindness, O God, in the midst of thy temple.

10 According to thy name, O God, so *is* thy praise unto the ends of the earth: thy right hand is full of righteousness.

11 Let mount Zion rejoice, let the daughters of Jūdah be glad, because of thy judgments.

12 Walk about Zion, and go round about her: tell the towers thereof.

13 Mark ye well her bulwarks, consider her palaces; that ye may tell *it* to the generation following.

14 For this God *is* our God for ever and ever: he will be our guide *even* unto death.

the subject matter of the psalm that it was composed after the death of David." Clarke, Hengstenberg, Ainsworth, and others agree. Perowne sees this psalm as a celebration of the deliverance of Jerusalem from the army of Sennacherib (II Kgs 18:19; Isa 36). Leupold agrees, but admits that the events of the days of Jehoshaphat (II Chr 20) might also qualify to establish the occasion for this psalm.

48:1-3. Great is the LORD, and greatly to be praised in the city of our God. Long before the misguided cry of the Ephesians, ". . . Great is Diana . . ." (Acts 19:28), the people of God had good reason to sing the praises of Jehovah. He had identified Himself with the people of God, Israel, and with the **mountain of his holiness,** Mount Zion, the city of Jerusalem. There, more than anywhere in the world, is God to be praised.

Beautiful for situation . . . is mount Zion (lit., beautiful for elevation). Rising aloft in beauty, the city of Jerusalem was remarkable topographically; for it was set on the summit of one of the numerous hills of Judaea. Early called the "Queen of the East," Jerusalem is indeed **the joy of the whole earth** (cf. Lam 2:15). It was the unique claim of Jerusalem to be **the city of the great King.** There **God is known,** and in that city the worship of Jehovah is centered.

4-6. The kings were assembled . . . They saw it . . . and hasted away. If this psalm refers to the miraculous deliverance of Jerusalem during the days of Jehoshaphat the king, these verses can be easily understood as a reference to the events of II Chronicles 20. **Fear took hold upon them there, and pain, as of a woman in travail.** The destruction of Sennacherib's host was totally unperceived until it was accomplished (II Kgs 19:35).

7-8. Thou breakest the ships of Tarshish with an east wind. I Kings 22:48 describes the fleet, Jehoshaphat's **ships of Tarshish** which "were broken at Ezion-geber." **God will establish it for ever.** The psalmist concludes that if God could spare Mount Zion from this great catastrophe, He would spare **the city of the great King** (vs. 2) forever. All that belongs to God belongs to Him eternally.

9-14. We have thought of thy loving-kindness, O God. The attempt to destroy the city of God now past, the psalmist can join the people of God in the midst of His Temple praising that deliverance. **Let Mount Zion rejoice, let the daughters of Judah be glad.** The psalmist encourages God's praise to rise to a crescendo in the Holy City. The praise of Israel will peak when she takes note of how glorious God has made her capital. **Walk about Zion, and go round about her: tell the towers thereof. Mark ye well her bulwarks, consider her palaces.** A leisurely stroll around the city of Jerusalem will allow the hearts of the Jews to swell with admiration. They should count the towers of the city and take note that none of them have crumbled. They should consider the strength of her ramparts, and they should examine with great care the beauty of her palaces. Once they had assessed the goodness of God in giving them this jewel, they should **tell it to the generation following. For this God is our God for ever and ever.**

It is a fruitful exercise when each of us takes stock of the blessings of God in our lives and recognizes how good He has been to us. **He will be our guide even unto death,** as He has been the guide of His chosen people. We can but reiterate the sentiment of the psalmist, **Great is the Lord and greatly to be praised** (vs. 1).

H. The Vanity of Wealth. 49:1-20.

THEME: It is God, not riches, that redeems the soul.

This psalm is designed as a vindication of the ways of God in the face of the fortunes enjoyed by the wicked of this world. It is not a simple homily that encourages us to bear up in the face of

PSALM 49

HEAR this, all ye people; give ear, all ye inhabitants of the world:

2 Both low and high, rich and poor, together.

3 My mouth shall speak of wisdom; and the meditation of my heart *shall be* of understanding.

4 I will incline mine ear to a parable: I will open my dark saying upon the harp.

5 Wherefore should I fear in the days of evil, *when* the iniquity of my heels shall compass me about?

6 They that trust in their wealth, and boast themselves in the multitude of their riches;

7 None *of them* can by any means redeem his brother, nor give to God a ransom for him:

8 (For the redemption of their soul *is* precious, and it ceaseth for ever:)

9 That he should still live for ever, *and* not see corruption.

10 For he seeth *that* wise men die, likewise the fool and the brutish person perish, and leave their wealth to others.

11 Their inward thought *is, that* their houses *shall continue* for ever, *and* their dwelling places to all generations; they call *their* lands after their own names.

12 Nevertheless man *being* in honour abideth not: he is like the beasts *that* perish.

13 This their way *is* their folly: yet their posterity approve their sayings. Sĕ'lah.

14 Like sheep they are laid in the grave; death shall feed on them; and the upright shall have dominion over them in the morning; and their beauty shall consume in the grave from their dwelling.

15 But God will redeem my soul from the power of the grave: for he shall receive me. Sĕ'lah.

apparent iniquity. Instead, it goes to the heart of the matter. That God will not only not forsake His own, but will one day redeem them to Himself, is a greater ground for consolation than rationalizing the wealth of the wicked.

Leupold says, "It is practically impossible to make any safe pronouncements on the identity of the author and the time of composition. For beyond the sons of Korah we have nothing to guide our thinking on this score . . . ."

49:1-4. Hear this, all ye people; give ear, all ye inhabitants of the world. Like Psalm 47, this psalm is addressed to all men everywhere. The **rich and poor, together** are instructed to listen to the psalmist, for his **mouth shall speak of wisdom.** The psalmist is determined to share with the world what God has taught him. He will do so in a **parable,** by opening a **dark saying.** In the Old Testament a parable refers to an enigmatical saying, which usually includes a metaphor, also.

5-6. Wherefore should I fear in the days of evil, when the iniquity of my heels shall compass me about? The psalmist's faith in God and God's promise to sustain him is strong. Therefore, when iniquitous men lie in wait to ensnare him, the psalmist has no fears. He knows the ground of his faith is greater than the ground of **They that trust in their wealth.**

7-8. None of them can by any means redeem his brother, nor give to God a ransom for him. This is a poetic way of saying that with all their riches, the wealthy cannot amass sufficient riches to rescue themselves or their family from death. **For the redemption of their soul is precious,** and only the blood of Jesus Christ can satisfactorily atone for our sins (Heb 9:10).

9-10. That he should still live for ever, and not see corruption. When the blood of Jesus Christ is applied to our sins, the natural consequence is life everlasting (Jn 5:24; I Jn 5:12). But such is not the case for those who attempt to buy their ransom with their own wealth. **For he seeth that wise men die, likewise the fool and the brutish person perish.** The law of mortality, ". . . it is appointed unto man once to die, but after this the judgment" (Heb 9:27), applies to all. **And leave their wealth to others.** It is a sad commentary on our society when those who have amassed a great deal of wealth look to that wealth for salvation. It is even sadder when they find out that they must leave all of that behind them; for man brings nothing into this world, and he will take nothing out. How foolish is the folly of trusting in riches.

11-13. Their inward thought is, that their houses shall continue for ever. Many look to their families to carry on the tradition of their wealth. These vain trusters in their wealth **call their lands after their own names.** We all must remember that, although the honor of a man may live on in his family estate bearing his name, nevertheless the man himself **abideth not: he is like the beasts that perish.** Sinful man has no more promise of continuance on the earth than do the animals. **This their way is their folly.** The course of conduct that they have chosen, described in verses 7-12, is a falacious and foolish one.

14-15. Like sheep they are laid in the grave. All men, whether rich or poor, will one day be laid in the grave, should the Lord not return before their death. But there is a sparkle of hope for those that have claimed Christ as Saviour. **The upright shall have dominion over them in the morning.** There is a resurrection morning coming, however; and it will initiate a day that never ends, the day of the righteous.

The solution to the psalmist's dark saying is this: **God will redeem my soul from the power of the grave: for he shall receive me. Selah.** The hope of resurrection pervades this passage. As God took "Enoch . . . and he was not . . ." (Gen 4:24), so the psalmist would be resurrected from his dwelling place in the grave.

16 Be not thou afraid when one is made rich, when the glory of his house is increased;

17 For when he dieth he shall carry nothing away: his glory shall not descend after him.

18 Though while he lived he blessed his soul: and *men* will praise thee, when thou doest well to thyself.

19 He shall go to the generation of his fathers; they shall never see light.

20 Man *that is* in honour, and understandeth not, is like the beasts *that* perish.

PSALM 50

THE mighty God, *even* the Lord, hath spoken, and called the earth from the rising of the sun unto the going down thereof.

2 Out of Zion, the perfection of beauty, God hath shined.

3 Our God shall come, and shall not keep silence: a fire shall devour before him, and it shall be very tempestuous round about him.

4 He shall call to the heavens from above, and to the earth, that he may judge his people.

5 Gather my saints together unto me; those that have made a covenant with me by sacrifice.

6 And the heavens shall declare his righteousness: for God *is* judge himself. Sĕ'lah.

7 Hear, O my people, and I will speak; O Israel, and I will testify against thee: I *am* God, *even* thy God.

8 I will not reprove thee for thy sacrifices or thy burnt offerings, *to have been* continually before me.

9 I will take no bullock out of thy house, *nor* he goats out of thy folds.

10 For every beast of the forest *is* mine, *and* the cattle upon a thousand hills.

11 I know all the fowls of the mountains: and the wild beasts of the field *are* mine.

16-18. Be not thou afraid when one is made rich . . . for when he dieth he shall carry nothing away. The psalmist concludes by repeating and confirming the general lesson of this psalm. There is no reason for perplexity, no grounds for fear, when the righteous man sees the wicked growing rich and prospering around him. **Though while he lived he blessed his soul.** While the foolish man who trusted in his wealth is alive, he thinks himself to be happy and congratulates himself on his good fortune. But self-praise in this life is worthless with regard to eternity.

19-20. He shall go to the generation of his fathers; they shall never see light. What a tragedy it is for a man, whether wealthy or poor, to leave this life without the Lord Jesus as Saviour! Even if he is a man of honor and well-respected, he must understand that without the Lord Jesus he is **like the beasts that perish.**

I. True Worship. 50:1-23.

THEME: A blistering indictment against hypocrisy and formalism in worship.

This is the first of the psalms of Asaph. The son of Berachiah, of the family of Gershom (I Chr 6:39; 15:17), **Asaph** was an eminent musician appointed by David to preside over the sacred choral services of Israel (I Chr 16:5). The descendants of Asaph are recorded as Choristers of the Temple (I Chr 25:1-2; II Chr 20:14, etc.). Asaph himself was a celebrated poet (II Chr 29:30; Neh 12:46); and twelve psalms (50; 73-83) bear his name, though some of these (74; 75; 79) were probably written by his descendants, ". . . the sons of Asaph . . ." (I Chr 25:1).

50:1-3. The mighty God, even the Lord, hath spoken. The grandeur of this psalm is seen as it begins with a combination of three names for God, i.e., El, Elohim, and Jehovah (found only here and in Josh 22:22). The Mighty One, The Self-Existent One, the "Lord God of gods" is depicted as summoning all the nations of the earth together to hear His pronouncement. **Out of Zion, the perfection of beauty, God hath shined** (cf. 48:2; Lam 2:15; I Maccabees 2:12). The radiance of the Lord God has shone out of His holy hill in Zion. The presence of God is a magnificent sight; **a fire shall devour before him, and it shall be very tempestuous round about him.** Flames and the hurricane are frequently described as the attendants of divine presence. This may be seen in all His theophanies (see 18:13; 97:2-5; Ex 19:16; I Kgs 19:11; Job 38:1; Acts 2:2; Rev 4:5, etc.).

4-6. He shall call to the heavens from above. In this solemn scene the Lord God is seen as bringing together angels and men, the upper and lower worlds, to witness His judgment. **Gather my saints together unto me.** The winged messengers of God are commanded to gather the throng of Israel together, those who **have made a covenant with me by sacrifice.** God doesn't want a single Israelite to miss this scene. **And the heavens shall declare his righteousness: for God is judge himself.** God will send no deputy, no lieutenant, no angel to do His work of judgment. This is a task He must do Himself.

7-11. Hear, O my people, and I will speak. Gathering the faithful of Israel together, the God of gods will now indicate what type of worship is acceptable to Him. **I will not reprove thee for thy sacrifices or thy burnt offerings.** While His chosen people abounded in outward sacrifice and burnt offerings, they seriously neglected the sacrifice of heart devotion toward Him. **I will take no bullock out of thy house . . . for every beast of the forest is mine, and the cattle upon a thousand hills.** Jehovah sought the love of Israel and her complete obedience. But simple giving to God a bullock or goat could never appease Him, for every beast of the forest and all the cattle upon a thousand hills already belong to Him. He had no need of beasts; He sought only heart dedication.

12 If I were hungry, I would not tell thee: for the world *is* mine, and the fulness thereof.
13 Will I eat the flesh of bulls, or drink the blood of goats?

14 Offer unto God thanksgiving; and pay thy vows unto the most High:
15 And call upon me in the day of trouble: I will deliver thee, and thou shalt glorify me.

16 But unto the wicked God saith, What hast thou to do to declare my statutes, or *that* thou shouldest take my covenant in thy mouth?
17 Seeing thou hatest instruction, and casteth my words behind thee.

18 When thou sawest a thief, then thou consentedst with him, and hast been partaker with adulterers.
19 Thou givest thy mouth to evil, and thy tongue frameth deceit.
20 Thou sittest *and* speakest against thy brother; thou slanderest thine own mother's son.
21 These *things* hast thou done, and I kept silence; thou thoughtest that I was altogether *such an one* as thyself: *but* I will reprove thee, and set *them* in order before thine eyes.
22 Now consider this, ye that forget God, lest I tear *you* in pieces, and *there be* none to deliver.
23 Whoso offereth praise glorifieth me: and to him that ordereth *his* conversation *aright* will I shew the salvation of God.

PSALM 51

HAVE mercy upon me, O God, according to thy lovingkindness: according unto the multitude of thy tender mercies blot out my transgressions.
2 Wash me throughly from mine iniquity, and cleanse me from my sin.

12-13. If I were hungry, I would not tell thee: for the world is mine, and the fullness thereof. What a strange concept, a hungry God. If it were possible for God to be hungry, He would have no reason to tell man; for the entire world and everything in it already belong to Him. **Will I eat the flesh of bulls, or drink the blood of goats?** Ancient Near East texts are filled with stories of the pagan gods cowering around the sacrifices offered to them, savagely devouring the flesh of bulls, and drinking the blood of goats. Jehovah indignantly separates Himself from that kind of deity.

14-15. Offer unto God thanksgiving; and pay thy vows unto the Most High. It is not the sacrifice that brings pleasure to God, but rather the willing and cheerful attitude of the sacrificer. The one acceptable sacrifice to God is praise and thanksgiving out of a pure heart.

16-17. But unto the wicked God saith. The psalmist now addresses the wicked Israelites because they knew God's law. They took it upon themselves to enforce that law against others (Rom 2:18-20), but they did not actually obey that law themselves, as verses 18-20 indicate. **Seeing thou hatest instruction, and castest my words behind thee.** These wicked Israelites knew God's law; but they did not heed it, metaphorically casting it behind them as refuse.

18-23. When thou sawest a thief, then thou consentedst with him. They did not actually participate in robberies, but gave their consent for them to occur. In God's eyes this made them accessories to robbery. **Thy tongue frameth deceit.** Wicked Israelites had become famous for their conniving and deceitful practices. **Thou slanderest thine own mother's son.** Even their nearest relatives were not immune to the wickedly active mouths of the Israelites. **These things hast thou done, and I kept silence.** Since Jehovah had allowed wicked Israel to continue in her folly for a season, she felt that God had become indifferent to her sin.

J. A Psalm of Contrition, Confession, and Conversion. 51:1-19.

THEME: David pleads for God's mercy and forgiveness in light of his great sin.

The superscription of this deeply moving Penitential Psalm identifies David as the author. It was written sometime after his great sin with Bath-sheba (II Sam 11:3-4).

Unbelievable though it may seem, some modern critical scholars have questioned David's authorship of this psalm. It is objected that the statement in verse 4, **Against thee, thee only, have I sinned,** takes no account of the great wrong done to both Bath-sheba and Uriah. But David had learned what great saints of God have always known; and that is that regardless of who is affected by our sin, God is always the ultimate target of sin (cf. Joseph, Gen 39:9; Paul, Acts 9:4). It has been most strenuously objected that David could not possibly be the author of the last two verses of the psalm. Thus, it is assumed by many Bible scholars, that these verses are later additions (cf. Scroggie, Perowne, Rawlinson, et al.). Such an assumption, held even by some conservative scholars, is not necessary. Luther was right when he said, "Two parts constitute true repentance; first that a man recognize sin, then that he recognize what grace is." Regardless, Davidic authorship of all the verses of Psalm 51 must be maintained.

51:1-2. Have mercy upon me, O God. David begins his penitence with a plea for mercy. He addresses God (Heb *'Elōhîm*) in a way that shows himself feeling unworthy to utter the covenant name of Jehovah. **According unto the multitude of thy tender mercies blot out my transgressions** (lit., rebellion, cf. 19:13; 32:1). David's initial plea for mercy is quickly followed by the plea that his sins be blotted out, as from a register,

3 For I acknowledge my transgressions: and my sin *is* ever before me.
4 Against thee, thee only, have I sinned, and done *this* evil in thy sight: that thou mightest be justified when thou speakest, *and* be clear when thou judgest.

5 Behold, I was shapen in iniquity; and in sin did my mother conceive me.
6 Behold, thou desirest truth in the inward parts: and in the hidden *part* thou shalt make me to know wisdom.

7 Purge me with hyssop, and I shall be clean: wash me, and I shall be whiter than snow.
8 Make me to hear joy and gladness; *that* the bones *which* thou hast broken may rejoice.
9 Hide thy face from my sins, and blot out all mine iniquities.
10 Create in me a clean heart, O God; and renew a right spirit within me.
11 Cast me not away from thy presence; and take not thy holy spirit from me.
12 Restore unto me the joy of thy salvation; and uphold me *with thy* free spirit.

13 *Then* will I teach transgressors thy ways; and sinners shall be converted unto thee.
14 Deliver me from bloodguiltiness, O God, thou God of my salvation: *and* my tongue shall sing aloud of thy righteousness.
15 O Lord, open thou my lips; and my mouth shall shew forth thy praise.

16 For thou desirest not sacrifice; else would I give *it*: thou delightest not in burnt offering.
17 The sacrifices of God *are* a broken spirit: a broken and a contrite heart, O God, thou wilt not despise.

a record book of sin accurately kept by God (cf. Ex 32:32; Isa 43:25; 44:22). **Wash me thoroughly . . . and cleanse me.** As Spurgeon observes, "The hypocrite is content if his garments be washed; but the true suppliant cries, 'wash me.'"

3-4. My sin is ever before me. The first step in repentance is contrition for sin. David has shown such contrition. The second step is confession of sin. True confession is acknowledging your sin to God and admitting that you cannot deal with it alone (I Jn 1:9). **Against thee, thee only, have I sinned.** There can scarcely be sins that more directly harm mankind than adultery and murder. Yet, David is aware that all sin culminates in wrong against the Being and will of God. There is no such thing as private sin. Regardless of whom we hurt when we sin, God is always hurt the worst. **And done this evil in thy sight.** David has a keen consciousness that he has committed his moral iniquity in the full view of Jehovah God.

5-6. Behold, I was shapen in iniquity. It cannot intelligently be denied that David here speaks of original sin. He claims that the source of his life is just as polluted as its streams. He has a natural bent from birth towards sin, as do we all. Given the option, we would choose wrong every time. **In sin did my mother conceive me.** This verse does not indicate that David was conceived out of wedlock; his mother was chaste, the Lord's handmaid. Rather, his intent is to trace a congenital depravity which is asserted not only here, but also in 58:3; Job 14:14, and implied in Isaiah 43:27; Hosea 6:7; etc. God desires purity **in the inward part,** but it is the wisdom of God to know that we are impure from the very moment of conception. Hence, David does not try to excuse his sin, but simply to acknowledge it.

7-12. There is a noticeable progression in the prayer of David which begins each of these verses. **Purge me** is the cry to remove defilement. According to the Levitical law, hyssop alone could cleanse one from contact with a corpse (Num 19:18) or from the defilement of leprosy (Lev 14:4). **Wash me** implies a thorough, deep cleansing as a man washes his garments, and not simply as he washes his skin. **Make me** is a prayer to experience the joy and gladness that comes from receiving God's forgiveness. **Hide thy face from my sins** is the psalmist's plea for God not to view him as he really is, i.e., a sinner. **Create in me a clean heart** shows that David is interested in more than just forgiveness of sins. He is interested in the creative power of God making him a new creature with a new, clean heart. **Cast me not away from thy presence** extends David's plea to include the possibility of constant fellowship with God because of the renewed right spirit within the psalmist. **Restore unto me the joy of thy salvation** is David's prayer to return to the conscious favor of God and to know that he walks again hand in hand with his creator. And finally, **uphold me** means to preserve me from falling, by the power of God's spirit.

13-15. Then will I teach transgressors thy ways. With his sin confessed and forgiven, David is ready to live a **converted** life for his Lord. His first responsibility is to teach transgressors the ways of God so as to prevent their making the same mistakes he did. His intent, like that of all faithful servants of the Lord, is that **sinners shall be converted unto thee.** Since God has delivered David from the guilt of shedding blood (5:6; II Sam 12:9-10), the psalmist's tongue would ever **sing aloud of thy righteousness** and his lips and **mouth shall show forth thy praise.**

16-17. For thou desirest not sacrifice . . . thou delightest not in burnt offering. The Mosaic law allows no reconciliation or sacrifice for the sins of adultery and murder. David correctly recognizes that the only acceptable sacrifices **are a broken spirit: a broken and a contrite heart.** God does not want a show of ceremony when we sin. Rather, God delights in a quiet softening of the heart and a personal contrition and confession of sin.

18 Do good in thy good pleasure unto Zion: build thou the walls of Jerusalem.
19 Then shalt thou be pleased with the sacrifices of righteousness, with burnt offering and whole burnt offering: then shall they offer bullocks upon thine altar.

PSALM 52

WHY boastest thou thyself in mischief, O mighty man? the goodness of God *endureth* continually.
2 Thy tongue deviseth mischiefs; like a sharp razor, working deceitfully.
3 Thou lovest evil more than good; *and* lying rather than to speak righteousness. Sĕ'lah.
4 Thou lovest all devouring words, O *thou* deceitful tongue.

5 God shall likewise destroy thee for ever, he shall take thee away, and pluck thee out of *thy* dwelling place, and root thee out of the land of the living. Sĕ'lah.
6 The righteous also shall see, and fear, and shall laugh at him:
7 Lo, *this is* the man *that* made not God his strength; but trusted in the abundance of his riches, *and* strengthened himself in his wickedness.

8 But I *am* like a green olive tree in the house of God: I trust in the mercy of God for ever and ever.
9 I will praise thee for ever, because thou hast done *it:* and I will wait on thy name; for *it is* good before thy saints.

18-19. Do good in thy good pleasure unto Zion. It is quite characteristic of David to pass from personal prayer to prayer for his kingdom. He prays that God will not reject **the sacrifices of righteousness, with burnt offering and whole burnt offering.** David knew full well that people rise only as high as their leadership and that he must right himself with God if Israel were to be blessed. As a true leader, he concludes his personal prayer of penitence with a prayer for God's blessing on his nation.

K. The Doom of the Evildoer. 52:1-9.

THEME: The boast of the wicked over the righteous is vain, for God cares for His people.

The superscription is authentic; and hence, it is our best guide to the origin and authorship of this psalm. It was written by David when Doeg the Edomite apprised Saul the King that David had visited Ahimelech the priest (I Sam 21:1-9). The biting denunciation of the mighty man by David is a result of the fact that Doeg's betrayal led to a fearful massacre (I Sam 22:11-19). The psalm consists of three strophes of four, three, and two verses respectively.

52:1-4. Why boasteth thou thyself in mischief, O mighty man? Doeg is called a mighty man or tyrant because he was ". . . the chiefest of the herdmen that belonged to Saul" (I Sam 21:7). **Thy tongue deviseth mischiefs,** destructive malignities of the worst kind. Doeg told the king a half truth; he told Saul that David had visited the priest Ahimelech. But he did not tell Saul the circumstances; and thus he gave the impression that Ahimelech was being disloyal to the king. As a base individual, Doeg did this because he loved **lying rather than to speak righteousness.** Doeg's actions appear to justify the conclusion that he did evil simply for the sake of doing evil. His **deceitful tongue** was craftily used to bring death and ruin to others.

5-7. After a brief allusion to Doeg's sin, David describes the fate of the sinner. **God shall likewise destroy thee . . . and pluck thee out of thy dwelling place, and root thee out of the land of the living.** As Doeg had destroyed the entire house of Ahimelech save one (I Sam 22:17-20), so God would root him and his family out of the land of the living. **Lo, this is the man that made not God his strength; but trusted in the abundance of his riches.** In order to secure the good pleasure of the king, Doeg had unscrupulously become an instrument of cruelty. He did so in order to obtain an award from Saul. But he received his reward from a greater king than Saul and was destroyed for his wickedness.

8-9. Here the psalmist contrasts those who live righteously with the wickedness of Doeg. **But I am like a green olive tree in the house of God.** Doeg was about to be plucked up and rooted out of the land of the living. In contrast, those who **trust in the mercy of God for ever and ever** will remain fruitful as a green olive tree in God's house.

L. The Depravity of Man. 53:1-6.

THEME: God's reaction to the universal corruption of mankind.

Even a fledgling Bible student will immediately recognize the similarities between this psalm and Psalm 14. It is incorrect, however, to call this psalm a rescindment of the 14th. It is not a repetition, but more of a revision sung by the same author under a different set of circumstances. Although the situation referred to here is quite similar to that which confronted Israel at the hands of the Assyrians in the days of Hezekiah and Isaiah (II Kgs 18:9ff.), nevertheless, this situation is not altogether unlike many in David's time.

The superscription, **To the chief musician upon Mahalath. A Maschil. A psalm of David,** accurately depicts the time and intent of the psalm. It is almost impossible to say what the word **Mahalath** means, but in some forms the word refers to disease

PSALM 53

THE fool hath said in his heart, *There is* no God. Corrupt are they, and have done abominable iniquity: *there is* none that doeth good.

2 God looked down from heaven upon the children of men, to see if there were *any* that did understand, that did seek God.

3 Every one of them is gone back: they are altogether become filthy; *there is* none that doeth good, no, not one.

4 Have the workers of iniquity no knowledge? who eat up my people *as* they eat bread: they have not called upon God.

5 There were they in great fear, *where* no fear was: for God hath scattered the bones of him that encampeth *against* thee: thou hast put *them* to shame, because God hath despised them.

6 Oh that the salvation of Israel *were* come out of Zion! When God bringeth back the captivity of his people, Jacob shall rejoice, *and* Israel shall be glad.

PSALM 54

SAVE me, O God, by thy name, and judge me by thy strength.

2 Hear my prayer, O God; give ear to the words of my mouth.

3 For strangers are risen up against me, and oppressors seek after my soul: they have not set God before them. Sē'-lah.

4 Behold, God *is* mine helper: the Lord *is* with them that uphold my soul.

5 He shall reward evil unto mine enemies: cut them off in thy truth.

6 I will freely sacrifice unto thee: I will praise thy name, O Lord; for *it is* good.

7 For he hath delivered me out of all

or sickness. Undoubtedly, the sickness to which he refers is the depravity of man, the human condition that is recalled by the psalmist a second time in this psalm.

53:1-2. Verses 1 and 2 are practically identical with the same verses of Psalm 14, with the exception that the name Jehovah is replaced by the term Elohim as the first word in verse 2 (see 14:1-2).

3-4. Every one of them is gone back is equivalent to **They are all gone aside** in 14:3. The effect is the same. The psalmist sees the universality of a practical atheism that denies the presence, power, and provisions of God.

5. There were they in great fear, where no fear was. David sees the coming end of the ungodly as the ultimate triumph of those who fear God. Whereas they once boasted fearlessly of their disbelief in God, now circumstances have made it such that they must cower in fear at His presence. **For God hath scattered the bones of him that encampeth against thee.** Many and mighty were the hosts that besieged Jerusalem, but they were all defeated and dispelled in fear at the prowess of God. **Thou hast put them to shame, because God hath despised them.** Here 14:6 reads, **Ye have shamed the counsel of the poor, because the Lord is his refuge.** The tenor is entirely different. In this psalm those who scoff at God are laughed to scorn because of their vanity. How unsettling it is to be such a fool and be despised of God.

6. Oh that the salvation of Israel were come out of Zion! This verse is identical with 14:7, except for the substitution of Elohim for Jehovah. God will ultimately be victorious and will reign from His city Jerusalem. When the ultimate salvation of God's people shall be accomplished (Rom 11), when the salvation of the generation of the righteous shall come to pass, then not only **Jacob shall rejoice, and Israel shall be glad,** but the fool will no longer be able to deceive his own heart by thinking that there is no God.

M. God Is My Helper. 54:1-7.

THEME: *A psalm of assured deliverance because of divine aid.*

The superscription of this psalm is most instructive. It is a psalm dedicated **To the chief musician,** or choir director. The psalm is designed to be played **on Neginoth,** or stringed instruments, and is a **Maschil,** a didactic poem. The author is David, and the occasion is when David was being persecuted by Saul. David had taken refuge with six hundred men at Keliah; but, warned by Abiathar the son of Ahimelech that the men at Keliah were not to be trusted, he escaped into the wilderness of Ziph.

54:1-3. Save me, O God . . . Hear my prayer, O God. In desperation the psalmist cries out for God to save him and judge or vindicate him by divine might. His prayer is earnest because **oppressors seek after my soul.** This phrase is identical to that used in I Samuel 23:15, when David was in the wilderness of Ziph and ". . . saw that Saul was come out to seek his life." Unlike the psalmist, his oppressors **have not set God before them.** Frequently, good men are hated for the sake of God; or evil men totally disregard God.

4-7. Behold, God is mine helper. The clause between verses 3 and 4 is intentional and is marked by a **Selah.** In pondering his enemies, David suddenly looks from them and up to God. **He shall reward evil unto mine enemies.** The work of the Ziphites was intended for evil, and now they shall have their wages. David's confidence has now risen to certainty. Spontaneously, he vows to God, **I will freely sacrifice unto thee.** So

trouble: and mine eye hath seen *his desire* upon mine enemies.

certain is his deliverance that the psalmist offers a vow by anticipation. **I will praise thy name, O Lord.** How good is the name of God, **For he hath delivered me out of all trouble.** The psalmist treats the future as if it were the past. While he was yet troubled by the Ziphites, he speaks to God as if He had already delivered him.

N. Betrayed by a Friend. 55:1-23.

THEME: *A prayer of confidence in the face of distress and treachery.*

Modern critics have almost unanimously denied the Davidic authorship of this psalm. Hitzig assumes it was written by Jeremiah, Pashur being the familiar friend of the psalm. Ewald thinks the psalm was written during the last century before the Captivity, inferring that verse 10 depicts the city in a state of siege. But such conjectures are groundless, and there is no reason to doubt the Davidic authorship of the psalm.

The usual occasion ascribed to this psalm is that of Absalom's rebellion (II Sam 15:18). If this be the case, the treacherous person of verses 12-14, 20, and 21 is to be identified with Ahithophel. But the intent of the psalm may go beyond the era of sorrow marked by Absalom's rebellion and point to the suffering of our Lord at the hand of His familiar friend, the betrayer Judas. One cannot escape noticing the similarities between this aspect of the psalmist's life and that of his Great Descendant.

55:1-3. Give ear to my prayer . . . hide not thyself from my supplication. Attend unto me, and hear me. David does what any believer who loves God would do when in distress; he comes boldly to the throne of grace. His plea that God would not hide Himself from the psalmist's supplication prophetically rings of that dark day at Calvary when Jesus Christ said, "My God, my God, why hast thou forsaken me?" (Mt 27:46).

4-5. My heart is sore pained within me. The attacks of his enemies have so deeply grieved the psalmist that his spirit writhes in agony. David's pain and anguish parallel that of our Lord in the garden when his soul was ". . . exceeding sorrowful even unto death . . ." (Mt 26:38). **Fearfulness and trembling are come upon me.** So great was the psalmist's fear that he began trembling. There was good reason to be swallowed up in horror.

6-8. Oh that I had wings like a dove! David's natural tendency was to flee his oppressor. He would escape his troubles and problems as a dove would escape the snares of the fowler.

PSALM 55

GIVE ear to my prayer, O God; and hide not thyself from my supplication.

2 Attend unto me, and hear me: I mourn in my complaint, and make a noise;

3 Because of the voice of the enemy, because of the oppression of the wicked: for they cast iniquity upon me, and in wrath they hate me.

4 My heart is sore pained within me: and the terrors of death are fallen upon me.

5 Fearfulness and trembling are come upon me, and horror hath overwhelmed me.

6 And I said, Oh that I had wings like a dove! *for then* would I fly away, and be at rest.

7 Lo, *then* would I wander far off, *and* remain in the wilderness. Sĕ'lah.

8 I would hasten my escape from the windy storm *and* tempest.

9 Destroy, O Lord, *and* divide their tongues: for I have seen violence and strife in the city.

10 Day and night they go about it upon the walls thereof: mischief also and sorrow *are* in the midst of it.

11 Wickedness *is* in the midst thereof: deceit and guile depart not from her streets.

9-11. At this point the righteous indignation of David spills forth. He cries prophetically unto Jehovah, **Destroy, O Lord, and divide their tongues.** Oh that God would put his enemies to rout by making another Babel, setting them at cross-purposes and causing confusion in their counsels of war.

David now describes the situation in his capital city, Jerusalem. **I have seen violence and strife in the city . . . upon the walls thereof . . . in the midst of it . . . deceit and guile depart not from her streets.** If, historically, this account speaks of Absalom's rebellion, then the conspirators to overthrow King David have met in the dark alleys of Jerusalem both day and night spreading vicious lies against the king. How similar the situation for the Son of David to cry, "O Jerusalem, Jerusalem, . . . how often would I have gathered thy children together, even as a hen gathereth her chickens under her wings, and ye would not!" (Mt 23:37).

12 For *it was* not an enemy *that* reproached me; then I could have

12-14. For it was not an enemy that reproached me; then I could have borne it. If Ahithophel is intended, it is known that

borne *it:* neither *was it* he that hated me *that* did magnify *himself* against me; then I would have hid myself from him:

13 But *it was* thou, a man mine equal, my guide, and mine acquaintance.

14 We took sweet counsel together, *and* walked unto the house of God in company.

15 Let death seize upon them, *and* let them go down quick into hell: for wickedness *is* in their dwellings, *and* among them.

16 As for me, I will call upon God; and the LORD shall save me.

17 Evening, and morning, and at noon, will I pray, and cry aloud: and he shall hear my voice.

18 He hath delivered my soul in peace from the battle *that was* against me: for there were many with me.

19 God shall hear, and afflict them, even he that abideth of old. Sĕ'lah. Because they have no changes, therefore they fear not God.

20 He hath put forth his hands against such as be at peace with him: he hath broken his covenant.

21 *The words* of his mouth were smoother than butter, but war *was* in his heart: his words were softer than oil, yet *were* they drawn swords.

22 Cast thy burden upon the LORD, and he shall sustain thee: he shall never suffer the righteous to be moved.

23 But thou, O God, shalt bring them down into the pit of destruction: bloody and deceitful men shall not live out half their days; but I will trust in thee.

Ahithophel was ". . . David's counselor . . ." (II Sam 15:12). Whoever is intended, he betrayed his friend and went over to the side of the enemy. How much easier it is to be attacked by an open enemy than by a friend. **But it was thou.** This is David's *Et tu, Brute?* It is the sentiment of the Master in the garden, ". . . Judas, betrayest thou the Son of Man . . . ?" (Lk 22:48). The one who betrayed was **mine acquaintance** (cf. Mt 26:50-51). The traitor was one who had been treated lovingly and trusted explicitly. With his friends he had **walked unto the house of God in company** (cf. Jn 2:13-25).

15. Let them go down quick into hell. It is likely that this imprecation of David was not intended to be fulfilled literally. Yet, the deaths of Ahithophel (II Sam 17:23), Absalom (II Sam 18:14-15), and many of Absalom's followers (II Sam 18:7-8) were literal fulfillments of this prophetic imprecation.

16-17. As for me, I will call upon God. David does not intend to return evil for evil. His prayer arises from the heart of a pious lover of God, and not from a vengeful despot. Rather, **Evening, and morning, and at noon, will I pray, and cry aloud.**

18-20. He hath delivered my soul in peace from the battle. Pious faith foresees that which has not yet occurred. David sees his deliverance, yet future, as a present fact; and he is convinced that **God shall hear, and afflict them.**

21. The words of his mouth were smoother than butter . . . his words were softer than oil. In describing the adversary of David, Spurgeon says, "He lauded and larded the man he hoped to devour. He buttered him with flattery and then battered him with malice . . . soft, smooth, oily words are most plentiful where truth and sincerity are most scarce." It will be remembered that even as Judah planted the kiss of betrayal on the cheek of Jesus, he said, ". . . Master, Master . . ." (Mk 14:45).

22-23. Cast thy burden upon the LORD, and he shall sustain thee. In confident resolution, the psalmist suggests that when treacherously treated by those whom we have trusted, the wise course of action is to unburden ourselves to the Lord. The burden, literally portion (Heb *yehab*), has been assigned to us by the Lord; and He will sustain us in what He assigns. **He shall never suffer the righteous to be moved.** Like the rooted tree that sways in the wind, those who live righteously may be disturbed, distressed, or discouraged; but they shall never be shaken or uprooted. **Bloody and deceitful men shall not live out half their days.** His statement about the half-life of the wicked is not intended to be a universal law, but David has more than once outlived his oppressors. Sin shortens life; therefore, David resolves, **but I will trust in thee.** The pious psalmist will not reciprocate violence for violence, but will commit his oppressors unto God and live above their oppression.

O. A Psalm of Fear and Faith. 56:1-13.

THEME: *The complaint of one who, though oppressed by enemies, nevertheless trusts in God.*

The superscription over this psalm is a bit complicated. It is addressed **To the chief musician upon Jonath-elem-rechokim.** Jonath-elem-rechokim has been variously translated as "silent dove among the strangers," "the dove of silence in distant places," and "the dove of the distant Terebinths." This designation is either a melody by that name, to which the psalm was to be performed; or it is an enigmatical form of denoting the subject of the psalm. This is the second Golden Psalm, the first being Psalm 16, to which it bears great likeness. It is a golden mystery of David on the occasion when he was detained in Gath

PSALM 56

BE merciful unto me, O God: for man would swallow me up; he fighting daily oppresseth me.

2 Mine enemies would daily swallow me up: for *they be* many that fight against me, O thou most High.

3 What time I am afraid, I will trust in thee.

4 In God I will praise his word, in God I have put my trust; I will not fear what flesh can do unto me.

5 Every day they wrest my words: all their thoughts *are* against me for evil.

6 They gather themselves together, they hide themselves, they mark my steps, when they wait for my soul.

7 Shall they escape by iniquity? in *thine* anger cast down the people, O God.

8 Thou tellest my wanderings: put thou my tears into thy bottle: *are they* not in thy book?

9 When I cry *unto thee,* then shall mine enemies turn back: this I know; for God *is* for me.

10 In God will I praise *his* word: in the LORD will I praise *his* word.

11 In God have I put my trust: I will not be afraid what man can do unto me.

12 Thy vows *are* upon me, O God: I will render praises unto thee.

13 For thou hast delivered my soul from death: *wilt* not *thou deliver* my feet from falling, that I may walk before God in the light of the living?

by the Philistines (I Sam 21:11-16; 27-29). David was like a dove in a strange land whose captivity gives rise to a mixture of fear and faith.

56:1-2. Be merciful unto me, O God . . . Mine enemies would daily swallow me up. The company of the Philistines oppressing David on this occasion seemed numberless (I Sam 29:2-9). They gave him no interval of relief, oppressing him daily. How encouraging it is to see the sweet spirit of the psalmist plead to the mercy of God for help.

3-4. What time I am afraid, I will trust in thee. David was no coward; but he was not given to false fearlessness, either. His natural inclination to fear was swallowed up in his quiet resolve, **I will trust in thee.** What is it that gives David the confidence to trust in God? **In God I will praise his word . . . I will not fear what flesh can do unto me.** In times of distress David is driven to his familiarity with the Scriptures. With great fidelity God always performs what He has promised. Hence, David will not fear what flesh can do to him.

5-7. Every day they wrest my words. All who live righteously should expect those who do not live righteously to continually extort meanings from what the righteous say. **They hide themselves, they mark my steps.** The psalmist's oppressors lay an ambush for him because they are entirely bent on doing him evil. In fear and frustration the psalmist cries out, **Shall they escape by iniquity?** Will God not judge these oppressors for their sin?

8-9. Thou tellest my wanderings. Suddenly, David answers his own question. Just as the Philistines mark the psalmist's steps, so too the Father observes in every detail the wanderings of His own. Confident that his goings are constantly viewed by God, David prays, **put thou my tears into thy bottle: are they not in thy book?** The purpose of the metaphor, no doubt, was to indicate that God was aware of his wanderings. So too, God was aware of his sorrows. How exact and precise is His interest in and knowledge of us.

10-11. In God will I praise his word . . . In God have I put my trust. Fear having been swallowed up in faith, the time has come to praise the Lord. The psalmist again can repeat, **I will not be afraid what man can do unto me.** Should the whole race become his enemy, David is convinced that with God on his side he is a majority.

12-13. Thy vows are upon me, O God . . . For thou hast delivered my soul from death. Under the duress of affliction, the psalmist has made vows of thankfulness to God. These vows are now due. Making vows is commendable only if fulfillment follows. Many foxhole vows are made and too quickly forgotten. David resolves that he will not forget to fulfill his vow.

Wilt not thou deliver my feet from falling, that I may walk before God in the light of the living? God had snatched him from the jaws of death; would He not preserve him on the path of life? Constant continuation is the mark of true spirituality. David had been through a traumatic experience with the Philistines and had relied heavily on God to preserve him. But his maturity is now seen in his expression of continued reliance on God to walk in the light of the living.

P. Prayer and Praise Amid Perils. 57:1-11.

THEME: A confident cry amid cruel enemies and a resolve to praise God for deliverance.

The superscription over this psalm shows that it bears a unique relationship to those which precede and follow it. **Altaschith** (lit., destroy not). Psalm 47 is the first of three consecutive psalms to bear this title. This may well be a reference to David's leniency on the life of King Saul.

David, the author of Psalm 57, is said to have written this psalm when he fled from Saul in the cave. The LXX renders

PSALM 57

BE merciful unto me, O God, be merciful unto me: for my soul trusteth in thee: yea, in the shadow of thy wings will I make my refuge, until *these* calamities be overpast.

2 I will cry unto God most high; unto God that performeth *all things* for me.
3 He shall send from heaven, and save me *from* the reproach of him that would swallow me up. Se̅'lah. God shall send forth his mercy and his truth.
4 My soul *is* among lions: *and* I lie *even among* them that are set on fire, *even* the sons of men, whose teeth *are* spears and arrows, and their tongue a sharp sword.
5 Be thou exalted, O God, above the heavens; *let* thy glory *be* above all the earth.

6 They have prepared a net for my steps; my soul is bowed down: they have digged a pit before me, into the midst whereof they are fallen *themselves.* Se̅'lah.
7 My heart is fixed, O God, my heart is fixed: I will sing and give praise.

8 Awake up, my glory; awake, psaltery and harp: I *myself* will awake early.
9 I will praise thee, O Lord, among the people: I will sing unto thee among the nations.
10 For thy mercy *is* great unto the heavens, and thy truth unto the clouds.

11 Be thou exalted, O God, above the heavens: *let* thy glory *be* above all the earth.

PSALM 58

DO ye indeed speak righteousness, O congregation? do ye judge uprightly, O ye sons of men?
2 Yea, in heart ye work wickedness; ye weigh the violence of your hands in the earth.

this, "into the cave." Thus, there are two occasions upon which this psalm could have been penned. The first was at the cave of Adullam in the valley of the Philistines (I Sam 22); the other was at the cave of En-gedi along the limestone banks of the western Dead Sea (I Sam 24).

57:1. Be merciful unto me . . . in the shadow of thy wings will I make my refuge. To the cry for mercy paralleling the preceding psalm, David now adds the metaphor of the wings. This metaphor was first used in Deuteronomy 32:11 and is a favorite one in the Psalms (cf. 17:8; 36:7; 61:4; 63:7; 91:4). The psalmist will not simply hide in the cave, but under the shadow of the wings of the Mighty One who made the cave.

2-3. I will cry unto God most high . . . that performeth all things for me. His prayer ascends to One much higher than his enemies, to his heavenly Friend. Those who would swallow David up must first defeat his God, an impossible task; for **God shall send forth his mercy and his truth.**

4-5. I lie even among them that are set on fire. Those who seek David's life are like burning firebrands, and he is in the midst of them. So fierce are they that he describes their teeth as **spears and arrows, and their tongue a sharp sword.** These carnivorous foes would tear him limb from limb had they the chance. In the midst of this distress, David's thoughts turn immediately to God. His prayer is, **Be thou exalted, O God, above the heavens.**

6-7. In very poetic language the psalmist depicts the treachery of those who oppress him. **They have digged a pit before me** (cf. 7:15; 119:85). The first note of triumph occurs here, following on the heels of his refrain of praise to God. The concept of the wicked falling into the pit that they have dug for the oppressed is a familiar one in the Psalms (cf. 7:15; 9:15; 39:8; 141:10). **O God, my heart is fixed.** In the midst of his storm he has resolved to trust in God; he is confident of deliverance.

8-10. Awake up, my glory; awake, psaltery and harp. Poetically, the psalmist calls for his greatest intellect to give thought to praising the Lord. Likewise, his fingers will fly in joy over the strings of the psaltery and harp. Foreigners to the covenant of God will also hear the psalmist sing praises to the Lord; for His **Mercy is great unto the heavens, and thy truth unto the clouds.** The mercy of God is more sublime than the vaulted skies, and the truth of God is above the clouds. God's creation is great, but creation's God is greater.

11. Be thou exalted, O God, above the heavens. Once again, the psalmist closes with a refrain of exaltation. God's glory is greater than any on earth or above the earth. David need not fear his desperate situation; neither should we.

Q. Judgment on Unjust Judges. 58:1-11.

THEME: A bold and indignant outcry against judicial corruption and unrighteous judges.

This psalm is the second "destroy not" of David, **Altaschith,** another **Michtam of David,** a psalm of golden secret or mystery. The occasion for this psalm is not stated, although Delitzsch believes it arises from an event in David's life during the rebellion of Absalom. It must be pointed out, however, that at no time did David deliver such a sharp denunciation of his son as this psalm is. Rather, he was much more lenient to Absalom (II Sam 18:33).

58:1-2. Do ye indeed speak righteousness, O congregation? The psalmist's indictment here is not of the people, but of the mighty ones who judge the people. He clarifies with the question **Do ye judge uprightly, O ye sons of men?** Both questions are asked in bitter irony. **In heart ye work wickedness; ye weigh the violence of your hands in the earth.** These men, who sat as judges and pretended with indignation to abhor the crimes

3 The wicked are estranged from the womb: they go astray as soon as they be born, speaking lies.

4 Their poison *is* like the poison of a serpent: *they are* like the deaf adder *that* stoppeth her ear;
5 Which will not hearken to the voice of charmers, charming never so wisely.

6 Break their teeth, O God, in their mouth: break out the great teeth of the young lions, O LORD.
7 Let them melt away as waters *which* run continually: *when* he bendeth *his bow to shoot* his arrows, let them be as cut in pieces.
8 As a snail *which* melteth, let *every one of them* pass away: *like* the untimely birth of a woman, *that* they may not see the sun.
9 Before your pots can feel the thorns, he shall take them away as with a whirlwind, both living, and in *his* wrath.

10 The righteous shall rejoice when he seeth the vengeance: he shall wash his feet in the blood of the wicked.
11 So that a man shall say, Verily *there is* a reward for the righteous: verily he is a God that judgeth in the earth.

PSALM 59
DELIVER me from mine enemies, O my God: defend me from them that rise up against me.
2 Deliver me from the workers of iniquity, and save me from bloody men.

of those they judged, were in their very hearts committing even greater crimes. With cold and calculating manner, even as they heard the Law, they devised means to break it.

3. The wicked are estranged from the womb. Using the language of hyperbole, David enunciates the doctrine of original sin. Is it possible that the moment we draw our first breath we are culpable for sin and accountable to God? Is it possible that a child strays with his first step? Hear the Word of the Lord: **They go astray as soon as they be born, speaking lies.** One does not have to teach a child to lie, but rather must break him of the habit.

4-5. Their poison is like the poison of a serpent. Unjust judges who speak lies, unregenerated men who slander the righteous, are unreasonable like the serpent **that stoppeth her ear**, i.e., will not harken to the mesmerizing tunes of the charmer.

6-9. The psalmist now advances a number of figures depicting the utter ruin to which God will bring the unjust judge. **Break their teeth, O God, in their mouth.** In order to render the serpent harmless, the snake charmers sometimes would beat out the poison fangs of the serpent with a stone. David desires that God would render the unjust judges as harmless. **As a snail which melteth, let every one of them pass away.** In the Ancient Near East it was thought that the slimy track left by a snail as it crawled along was subtracted from his substance and, given enough time, the snail would become smaller and smaller until it had wasted away. **Like the untimely birth of a woman, that they may not see the sun.** Here the wicked are likened to human abortions. Heaven was created by the God of love as the end and eternal destiny of man; but when man falls short of the glory of God and does not obtain the purpose of his being, he is an eternal abortion.

Before your pots can feel the thorns. This is a picture of the enemy encircling the camp, lighting thorns and briars underneath their pots to heat their celebration victory. But before they can partake of one morsel of food, God sends the whirlwind of His wrath to sweep away the fire, the pot, the meat, and those who would eat.

10-11. The righteous shall rejoice when he seeth the vengeance. The psalmist knows that when the wicked are defeated there will be no pious and heartless tears shed for them. Rather, the congregation of the righteous shall say a hearty Amen to the condemnation of the wicked. The end result of God's judgment upon the unjust judges will be that every man of the earth will know **there is a reward for the righteous: verily he is a God that judgeth in the earth.** Wickedness will not prevail long; God always rewards righteousness righteously. God and time will heal the wounds of unjust judges.

R. A Prayer for Deliverance from Malicious Foes. 59:1-17.

THEME: The psalmist cries for deliverance from oppression from violent and wicked enemies.

The final in the trilogy of the "destroy not" golden mysteries of David, the superscription of this psalm places the occasion as **when Saul sent, and they watched the house to kill him.** Critical scholars have questioned the Davidic authorship of this psalm on the basis that the references to **all the heathen** (vss. 5, 8) and to **my people** (vs. 11) would best refer to enemies who were foreigners, rather than to Saul and his men. But both the Hebrew and the LXX contain the superscription concerning Saul.

59:1-2. Deliver me from mine enemies, O my God . . . and save me from bloody men. Deliverance from enemies and oppressors is the almost constant cry of David (see 22:20; 25:20; 31:1-2, 15; 35:17; 40:13; 43:1; etc.); but here David seems to remember how often Saul sought to assassinate him,

3 For, lo, they lie in wait for my soul: the mighty are gathered against me; not *for* my transgression, nor *for* my sin, O LORD.

4 They run and prepare themselves without *my* fault: awake to help me, and behold.

5 Thou therefore, O LORD God of hosts, the God of Israel, awake to visit all the heathen: be not merciful to any wicked transgressors. Sĕ'lah.

6 They return at evening: they make a noise like a dog, and go round about the city.

7 Behold, they belch out with their mouth: swords *are* in their lips: for who, *say they*, doth hear?

8 But thou, O LORD, shalt laugh at them; thou shalt have all the heathen in derision.

9 *Because of* his strength will I wait upon thee: for God *is* my defence.

10 The God of my mercy shall prevent me: God shall let me see *my desire* upon mine enemies.

11 Slay them not, lest my people forget: scatter them by thy power; and bring them down, O Lord our shield.

12 *For* the sin of their mouth *and* the words of their lips let them even be taken in their pride: and for cursing and lying *which* they speak.

13 Consume *them* in wrath, consume *them*, that they *may* not *be:* and let them know that God ruleth in Jacob unto the ends of the earth. Sĕ'lah.

14 And at evening let them return; *and* let them make a noise like a dog, and go round about the city.

15 Let them wander up and down for meat, and grudge if they be not satisfied.

16 But I will sing of thy power; yea, I will sing aloud of thy mercy in the morning: for thou hast been my defence and refuge in the day of my trouble.

17 Unto thee, O my strength, will I sing: for God *is* my defence, *and* the God of my mercy.

and thus he cries out to God to stay the hand of this bloodthirsty and jealous king.

3-4. They lie in wait for my soul . . . They run and prepare themselves without my fault. Saul sent his emissaries to David's house ". . . to watch him, and to slay him in the morning" (I Sam 19:11). This is an apparent reference to **lie in wait for my soul,** which the psalmist depicts here. His only fault was to be the popular rival of the envious king.

5. Thou therefore, O LORD God of hosts, the God of Israel, awake to visit all the heathen (cf. 69:6, also a Davidic Psalm). David pleads with his Lord, the God of hosts, the God of Israel, as if to win the Lord's favor through the variety of names by which he addresses God. **All the heathen** is emphatic and means those heathen both within and without the covenant. It simply means all who live ungodly lives. The psalmist appreciates God's love and mercy on the behalf of men but prays, **be not merciful to any wicked transgressors.**

6-7. They make a noise like a dog. Comparing Saul's men to despised and loathesome Eastern dogs, David says they **go round about the city** snarling and growling, quarreling amongst themselves. In addition, **they belch out with their mouth.** As John Gill observes, Saul's men bubble out as a fountain bubbles out water; but from their mouths come only wickedness and venom. **For who, say they, doth hear?** They are free from all restraint because they do not fear the God of heaven or the king of Israel.

8-10. But thou, O LORD, shalt laugh at them. Saul's men had been made fools of by Michal, David's wife (cf. I Sam 19:12). In His providence God had arranged the malicious enemies of His anointed to be made the object of ridicule. **The God of my mercy shall prevent me.** A twinkle of confidence now shines through. David is convinced that God would meet him with preventing mercy in the time of need.

11-13. David prays a strange request: **Slay them not, lest my people forget.** So great was the sin of Israel's king and his men that David begged the Lord God not to sweep them away too quickly. He wants Israel to keep the Lord's justice in mind so that she does not stray as Saul had strayed. All eyes were on Israel; and so that the ends of the earth would know **that God ruleth in Jacob,** it was necessary that Saul's men be consumed in the wrath of God.

14-15. Here the psalmist repeats his description of verse 6 but adds, **Let them wander up and down for meat, and grudge if they be not satisfied.** Like ravenous dogs, they would encircle the house of David; and if he would not come out, they would remain there all night. This they appear to have done (I Sam 19:11-15).

16-17. Now comes the psalmist's great resolve. Being confident of his deliverance, he promises **I will sing of thy power . . . of thy mercy in the morning.** Notice that the wicked howl and the righteous sing. In the morning David would sing of his deliverance. After David had escaped from Saul (I Sam 19:12), he joined Samuel at Ramah; and then he could freely sing of God's strength, **for God is my defense, and the God of my mercy.**

S. A Confident Prayer in a Time of War. 60:1-12.

THEME: *David prayed to God for the thrill of victory after he had experienced the agony of defeat.*

The very lengthy superscription of this psalm (only that of Psalm 18 is longer) is the most helpful guide to interpreting this prayer. The **chief musician** is instructed to conduct the public performance of this psalm **upon Shushan-eduth.** This is best interpreted as "the Lily of Testimony" and is probably a refer-

PSALM 60

O GOD, thou hast cast us off, thou hast scattered us, thou hast been displeased; O turn thyself to us again.

2 Thou hast made the earth to tremble; thou hast broken it: heal the breaches thereof; for it shaketh.

3 Thou hast shewed thy people hard things: thou hast made us to drink the wine of astonishment.

4 Thou hast given a banner to them that fear thee, that it may be displayed because of the truth. Sĕ'lah.

5 That thy beloved may be delivered; save with thy right hand, and hear me.

6 God hath spoken in his holiness; I will rejoice, I will divide Shĕ'chem, and mete out the valley of Sŭc'coth.

7 Gilead is mine, and Ma-năs'seh is mine; Ē'phra-im also is the strength of mine head; Jū'dah is my lawgiver;

8 Moab is my washpot; over Edom will I cast out my shoe: Philistia, triumph thou because of me.

ence to a tune for the rendition of the psalm. **Michtam of David** announces that it is a teaching psalm and seems to imply that it was intended to be taught to Israel and preserved in her memory (cf. Deut 31:9-13). The setting of the psalm is described in the words, **when he strove with Aram-naharaim and with Aram-zobah. Aram-naharaim** (lit., Aram of the Two Rivers, i.e., Tigris and Euphrates, which identifies the land of Mesopotamia. **Aram-zobah** is placed eastward of Hamath. Both sites are mentioned in I Chronicles 19:6.

From reading the accounts of II Samuel 8:13-14; I Kings 11:15-16; and I Chronicles 18:12-13, we may historically construct the details that lead to the writing of this psalm. David's armies were in the far northeast of his kingdom, engaged in his first Syrian campaign. The Edomites, in the extreme southeast, took advantage of this situation to invade Palestine. When news of the Edomite invasion reached David, he immediately dispatched Joab and some of the forces to deal with them. A severe battle ensued in the Valley of Salt, near the southern extremity of the Dead Sea, and the Edomites suffered a crushing defeat from which they never recovered.

60:1-3. Israel had clamored for a king because her citizens were uneasy about the political stability of the nation. Saul was made that king, but the great disaster at Gilboa ended the reign of Saul. David inherited insurmountable problems; and now, while fighting the Syrians to the north, his kingdom had been invaded by the Edomites to the south. It is in this context that he cries, **O God, thou hast cast us off . . . thou hast been displeased.** David felt that Israel had been cast aside by God, shunned with contempt. No greater calamity can occur in the life of God's people than to be a castaway from him (cf. I Cor 9:27).

Thou hast made the earth to tremble . . . thou hast made us to drink the wine of astonishment. The government and military were in upheaval; nothing was stable. The priests had been murdered by Saul, and the military power of Israel had been broken by the Philistines. It was as if an earthquake had shaken the land. David had learned that the wine of the vineyard of sin is squeezed from the grapes of God's wrath.

4-5. Thou hast given a banner to them that fear thee. The psalmist compares the salvation that the Lord brings to His people with a high banner, the banner of salvation. It is only beneath this banner **That thy beloved may be delivered,** an apparent reference to David, who was the Lord's beloved, and to Israel at large.

6-8. Confident of victory, the king surveys the land that will soon be his, to the glory of God. **I will divide Shechem, and mete out the valley of Succoth.** Shechem was an important territory that had not yet yielded to David's government. It was also the chief town of central Canaan (I Kgs 12:25). **The valley of Succoth** (Gen 33:17) east of Shechem, where father Jacob had once pitched his tent, was also where his rightful heirs would now plow the soil. **Gilead is mine, and Manasseh is mine.** Gilead and Manasseh represent the large portion of territory east of the Jordan River; Gilead was the territory to the north (Gen 37:25), and Manasseh was the territory to the south (Num 32:39-42; Josh 17:1).

Ephraim also is the strength of mine head; Judah is my lawgiver. Ephraim is so named because not only did it hold the central position in the western region, but also all the military power of that tribe was under the command of David. Judah is called the **lawgiver** because it was within her territory that civil power was concentrated. The king was a member of that tribe, and all judicial proclamations came from her midst (cf. 78:68; I Sam 16:1; II Sam 2:4; 5:1-3).

Moab is my washpot; over Edom will I cast out my shoe: Philistia, triumph thou because of me. Implying that Moab will be reduced to slavery, the psalmist refers to that nation as his washpot. The reference to Edom is in keeping with the washing of feet, where a person would throw his shoe to someone who would then clean it while his foot was being washed. This person would be a lowly servant or slave.

9 Who will bring me *into* the strong city? who will lead me into Edom?
10 *Wilt* not thou, O God, *which* hadst cast us off? and *thou*, O God, *which* didst not go out with our armies?

9-10. Who will bring me into the strong city? . . . Wilt not thou, O God, which hadst cast us off? The strong city of Moab is an evident reference to Sela, known in modern Jordan as Petra. It was a hidden city of enormous strength, hewn for the main part out of the side of cliffs and accessible only through a frightful siq, a narrow passageway overhung on both sides by gigantic precipices.

11 Give us help from trouble: for vain *is* the help of man.
12 Through God we shall do valiantly: for he *it is that* shall tread down our enemies.

11-12. Vain is the help of man. If David was to lead Israel to the great nation she would become, he would have to look clearly to the help of the Lord God and not to the strength of his armies or alliances with other nations. The king resolves **Through God we shall do valiantly.** Here is the unbeatable tandem. As Adam Clarke once observed, "In war these two must be joined, and indeed in all actions: he, we; God and man." We are called upon to fight; but, as soldiers of the cross, we must remember that it is only **through God** that we shall be victorious (cf. Gal 2:20).

T. A Prayer of an Exiled Ruler. 61:1-8.

THEME: *The prayer of a banished ruler turns to confident praise that God will spare his life and line.*

This psalm, both composed and performed by the psalmist David, is addressed **To the chief musician upon Neginah.** We have encountered this expression elsewhere (Heb *bingīnōt;* cf. 4; 6; 54-55; 67; 76) translated **with stringed instruments.** Here, however, it is used in the singular (Heb *'al negīnat*) and should be translated "upon a stringed instrument." It is evident that David wrote this psalm while he was undergoing some form of banishment. The most likely historical situation is that reported in II Samuel 17:27, where David had to take refuge in Mahanaim while fleeing before his son Absalom.

PSALM 61
HEAR my cry, O God; attend unto my prayer.

61:1. Hear my cry, O God; attend unto my prayer. Once again, in grave earnest the psalmist lifts his voice to his only hope, the Lord God. The softest whisper of prayer never goes unheard; the breath of prayer is never exhaled in vain.

2 From the end of the earth will I cry unto thee, when my heart is overwhelmed: lead me to the rock *that* is higher than I.
3 For thou hast been a shelter for me, *and* a strong tower from the enemy.

2-3. From the end of the earth will I cry unto thee . . . Lead me to the rock that is higher than I. Banishment from his capital city was not nearly so difficult for David as banishment from the religious center of his life. He had but one prayer: **Lead me to the rock that is higher than I,** the rock that is too high for me. Some have regarded this rock as Mount Zion, but unquestionably the Rock is God Himself (cf. 62:2, 6-7). Here we have the deity of Jesus Christ. It is the Person of this Rock that David says **hast been a shelter for me, and a strong tower from the enemy.** The **strong tower** (Heb *migdal*) is not a mere refuge, but a great fortress (cf. Ex 14:2).

4 I will abide in thy tabernacle for ever: I will trust in the covert of thy wings. Sĕ'lah.
5 For thou, O God, hast heard my vows: thou hast given *me* the heritage of those that fear thy name.

4-5. I will abide in thy tabernacle for ever . . . For thou, O God, hast heard my vows. Here David seeks to return to the dwelling place of God, to enjoy the fellowship of God once again. **Thou hast given me the heritage of those that fear thy name.** With all those who have trusted in God, the psalmist joins himself as an heir, heirs of God and joint-heirs with Jesus Christ (Rom 8:17).

6 Thou wilt prolong the king's life: *and* his years as many generations.
7 He shall abide before God for ever: O prepare mercy and truth, *which* may preserve him.

6-7. Now the psalmist breaks forth in confident praise that God **wilt prolong the king's life: and his years as many generations.** Of which King does he speak? Certainly he is interested in his own life as the king of Israel. But the best interpretation here is the Messianic one. The psalmist is lifted above himself and sees the dynasty of the Son of David, Jesus Christ the Lord, who reigns forevermore. And what is it that shall preserve this king forever and ever? **Mercy and truth, which may preserve**

8 So will I sing praise unto thy name for ever, that I may daily perform my vows.

PSALM 62

TRULY my soul waiteth upon God: from him *cometh* my salvation.
2 He only *is* my rock and my salvation; *he is* my defence; I shall not be greatly moved.

3 How long will ye imagine mischief against a man? ye shall be slain all of you: as a bowing wall *shall ye be, and as* a tottering fence.
4 They only consult to cast *him* down from his excellency: they delight in lies: they bless with their mouth, but they curse inwardly. Sĕ'lah.

5 My soul, wait thou only upon God; for my expectation *is* from him.
6 He only *is* my rock and my salvation: *he is* my defence; I shall not be moved.
7 In God *is* my salvation and my glory: the rock of my strength, *and* my refuge, *is* in God.
8 Trust in him at all times; ye people, pour out your heart before him: God *is* a refuge for us. Sĕ'lah.

9 Surely men of low degree *are* vanity, *and* men of high degree *are* a lie: to be laid in the balance, they *are* altogether *lighter than* vanity.
10 Trust not in oppression, and become not vain in robbery: if riches increase, set not your heart *upon them.*

---

him. It is the high attributes of mercy and truth that make the dynasty of David continue successfully through Jesus Christ. It is His mercy and His truth that guarantee that continuation.

8. Having been drawn from the depths of despair to the height of glory, the psalmist resolves **So will I sing praise unto thy name for ever.** His prayer has been answered; his song shall be perpetual.

U. God Only Is My Salvation. 62:1-12.

THEME: A noble assertion of calm assurance in God in the midst of distress.

This Davidic Psalm, probably belonging to the time of Absalom's rebellion and addressed **To the chief musician,** is dedicated **to Jeduthun.** We have encountered this man before (on his identification see Ps 39), and shall do so again (see Ps 77; 89). A distinctive feature of this psalm is the repeated use (6 times) of the word **only** (Heb *'ak*). The psalm, 12 verses in length, is equally divided into three segments by the word **Selah** (vss. 4, 8).

62:1-2. Truly my soul waiteth upon God. The particle (Heb *'ak*) may be rendered **only** in a restrictive manner, or **truly** in an affirmative manner. Regardless, we must understand that God only is our salvation and God surely is our salvation. To wait upon God is the habitual practice of faith. No language of praise is nearly as meaningful to God as the patient silence of those who wait upon Him. For David, God is his **rock . . . salvation . . . defense,** lofty fortress, anchor, hiding place, etc. **I shall not be greatly moved.** The adverb **greatly** indicates that the psalmist is like a tree swaying in the wind, bent but not broken, as a ship moored in the harbor is buffeted but not destroyed.

3-4. Ye shall be slain all of you: as a bowing wall shall ye be, and as a tottering fence. How persistent are those who imagine mischief against the righteous. Some commentators have interpreted the **bowing wall** and **tottering fence** as references to David, but it makes better sense to understand them as a contrast to David who shall not be greatly moved. It is his enemies who shall be slain who are bowing and tottering. It is they who **consult to cast him down from his excellency.** They will be unsuccessful, even though they use the double weapons of blessing and cursing. **They bless with their mouth, but they curse inwardly.** Public flattery and private character assassination are favorite tricks of those who imagine mischief against the righteous.

5-8. The second segment begins almost identically as the first: **My soul, wait thou only upon God.** It is only from Him that the psalmist can expect salvation. The psalmist addresses God as **my expectation . . . my rock . . . my salvation . . . my defense . . . my salvation . . . my glory . . . my strength, and my refuge.** All these are personal references to the character of God. Notice how his confidence grows. The more he contrasts God with those who would do him mischief, the more the psalmist sees the absolute strength of his position in God. In light of this, David's advice to all is **Trust in him at all times . . . pour out your heart before him.**

9-10. Having surveyed the heights of the glorious God, now the psalmist surveys the depths of man's vanity. Beginning this third segment of his psalm with the affirmative use of the word **only,** the psalmist is convinced that, unlike God, man is nothing but vanity. The crowds of ancient Jerusalem cried "Hosanna!" one day and "Crucify Him!" the next. **They are altogether lighter than vanity.** When wealth is gained by oppression or through embezzlement or common robbery, it makes little sense to trust in it. And even **if riches increase** through honest industry, the psalmist advises, **set not your heart upon them.** All that man is, and all that man has in this life, is vanity; "For what shall it profit a man, if he shall gain the whole world, and lose his own soul?" (Mk 8:36).

11-12. God hath spoken once; twice have I heard this. What God spoke once, the psalmist heard twice, in the sense that he first heard with his ears and then with his heart believing. What was it that he heard and understood? **That power belongeth unto God. Also unto thee, O LORD, belongeth mercy.** The tandem of power and mercy are delicately balanced in God. Although omnipotent, the sovereign God will not do what His mercy prevents Him from doing. His most potent attribute is balanced with His most tender attribute. God will never use His divine strength to crush us; but He will break us, shape us, and mold us in His will.

V. A Song of Satisfaction. 63:1-11.

THEME: *A hungry and thirsting soul finds relief in God.*

Chrysostom testifies that, "It was decreed and ordained by the primitive fathers, that no day should pass without the public singing of this psalm." Again, this ancient preacher observes that "the spirit and soul of the whole book of Psalms is contracted into this psalm" (*Sermon LXVI.*; *Works*, Vol. III. pp. 156-157). This gem of a morning psalm is a reflection of David's experience when he fled before his son Absalom.

63:1-2. O God, thou art my God. In Hebrew this psalm begins *'elōhīm 'ēlī.* The plural title, followed by the single title, may suggest the Trinity of God. It will be remembered that *'ēlī* is the same word with which our Lord cried out upon the cross to the Father, "My God, my God, why hast thou forsaken me?" (Mt 27:46). **Early will I seek thee.** Note how eager the psalmist is to speak with his God. This is because he judges those extra hours of sleep less profitable than his hours spent with God. **My soul thirsteth for thee, my flesh longeth for thee.** The psalmist refers to both the **soul** and **flesh** is order to denote his whole being. He has an insatiable longing to fellowship with God. The psalmist seeks the Lord as one seeks water **in a dry and thirsty land,** perhaps an allusion to a literal fact (II Sam 16:2; 17:29).

David's desire is **to see thy power and thy glory.** As he is now on the run and cannot attend the sanctuary, David cries for his God. It is important to note, however, that he cries less to see the sanctuary of his God than he does to see the God of his sanctuary. Our delight should be in the Lord.

3-4. Thy loving-kindness is better than life. Life is dear, but God is much dearer. The psalmist is saying that divine favor is better than life. **Thus will I bless thee while I live** is the Old Testament equivalent of "For to me to live is Christ . . ." (Phil 1:21).

5-7. My soul shall be satisfied as with marrow and fatness. The king remembered with delight the sacrificial feasts of the sanctuary. Now, unable to sacrifice at the great altar, his soul would be equally blessed **when I remember thee upon my bed, and meditate on thee in the night watches.** Lying awake at night, the psalmist would have a hymn-sing of the mind. He would **remember** and **meditate.** Meditation always brings more sweetness than does mere remembrance. All of this, **Because thou hast been my help.**

8. My soul followeth hard after thee. The soul of the psalmist was glued to God. So closely did he follow Him that the psalmist was at one with God. This was only possible, however, because **thy right hand upholdeth me.** David's consistency in following the Lord is a tribute to the Lord's strength, not David's ability.

9-10. Those that seek my soul . . . shall go into the lower parts of the earth. Those who seek after his soul shall be slain, and the grave shall cover them. **They shall fall by the sword: they shall be a portion for foxes.** David's enemies would not

PSALM 63

O GOD, thou *art* my God; early will I seek thee: my soul thirsteth for thee, my flesh longeth for thee in a dry and thirsty land, where no water is;

2 To see thy power and thy glory, so *as* I have seen thee in the sanctuary.

3 Because thy lovingkindness *is* better than life, my lips shall praise thee.

4 Thus will I bless thee while I live: I will lift up my hands in thy name.

5 My soul shall be satisfied as *with* marrow and fatness; and my mouth shall praise *thee* with joyful lips:

6 When I remember thee upon my bed, *and* meditate on thee in the *night* watches.

7 Because thou hast been my help, therefore in the shadow of thy wings will I rejoice.

8 My soul followeth hard after thee: thy right hand upholdeth me.

9 But those *that* seek my soul, to destroy *it*, shall go into the lower parts of the earth.

11 God hath spoken once; twice have I heard this; that power *belongeth* unto God.

12 Also unto thee, O Lord, *belongeth* mercy: for thou renderest to every man according to his work.

10 They shall fall by the sword: they shall be a portion for foxes.

11 But the king shall rejoice in God; every one that sweareth by him shall glory: but the mouth of them that speak lies shall be stopped.

PSALM 64

HEAR my voice, O God, in my prayer: preserve my life from fear of the enemy.

2 Hide me from the secret counsel of the wicked; from the insurrection of the workers of iniquity:

3 Who whet their tongue like a sword, and bend their bows to shoot their arrows, even bitter words:

4 That they may shoot in secret at the perfect: suddenly do they shoot at him, and fear not.

5 They encourage themselves in an evil matter: they commune of laying snares privily; they say, Who shall see them?

6 They search out iniquities; they accomplish a diligent search: both the inward thought of every one of them, and the heart, is deep.

7 But God shall shoot at them with an arrow; suddenly shall they be wounded.

8 So they shall make their own tongue to fall upon themselves: all that see them shall flee away.

9 And all men shall fear, and shall declare the work of God; for they shall wisely consider of his doing.

10 The righteous shall be glad in the LORD, and shall trust in him; and all the upright in heart shall glory.

see their design fulfilled. Rather, they would become the food for jackals (cf. II Sam 18:6-8).

11. Every one that sweareth by him shall glory. Those who swear by the name of God show themselves to be loyal to God and will be upheld by Him in the time of danger (cf. Deut 6:13; Isa 65:16). When we swear our oath of allegiance to the Lord God, we never have reason to fear.

W. Complaint and Consolation. 64:1-10.

THEME: *The psalmist's complaint against the hurtful tongue of his enemy and his consolation that God will defend him.*

That this is a psalm of David cannot be seriously contested. It may fit equally well into two periods of David's life, when Doeg criticized David before he came to the throne (cf. 52; I Sam 22) or the period of Absalom's rebellion when Ahithophel's tongue gave evil counsel (55; II Sam 15-17).

As is the psalmist's common practice, the psalm opens with a cry to God against the machinations of his enemies, describes at length the methods they used to accomplish their ends, and concludes with a confident prediction of their sudden and utter demise.

64:1-2. Hear my voice . . . preserve my life . . . Hide me. In times of deep distress it is often helpful to pray aloud to God. David spent much time praying aloud and asking the Lord God to preserve his life from his enemy. His great concern was **the secret counsel of the wicked.** In concert his enemies held closed-door sessions to devise mischief against the psalmist. But once those sessions were complete and a plan was devised, David's prayer continues for protection **from the insurrection of the workers of iniquity.**

3-4. David describes his oppressors as those who **whet their tongue like a sword, and bend their bows.** To **whet** (Heb *shanan*) means to sharpen by repeated motion or friction. The enemies of the king repeatedly used slander as their master weapon against him. Shunning combat in the open battlefield, they **shoot in secret at the perfect.**

5-6. They encourage themselves . . . they commune of laying snares privily . . . They search out iniquities; they accomplish a diligent search. These artisans of hell do not rely on superficial planning. In concert they pool the sagacity of Satan's slaves and conduct a diligent search seeking the most cunningly devised means of discrediting the Lord's righteous.

7-8. But God. Two of the greatest words in the English Bible provide us with the greatest contrast between the complaint of the psalmist and his consolation. By himself he is sure to fail; but the king is not by himself. **God shall shoot at them with an arrow.** God will interpose.

9-10. The end result of the interposition of God is that men will flee from cursing the righteous and fear God. So great will that fear be that they **shall declare the work of God; for they shall wisely consider of his doing.** Not only will the fate of David's enemies cause widespread fear and alarm; but seeing their demise, those who have been indifferent toward God shall seriously consider their relationship with the Almighty. And what will be the end of the righteous? **The righteous shall be glad in the LORD, and shall trust in him.**

X. A Harvest Hymn of Praise. 65:1-13.

THEME: *A psalm and song of David which sings to God, "How great Thou art."*

The superscription, which consigns this psalm to the care of **the chief musician,** indicates that it is both a **psalm** (Heb *mizmōr*) and **song** (Heb *shīr*). This would make it akin to a lyrical poem.

Davidic authorship has sometimes been questioned, but on

PSALM 65

PRAISE waiteth for thee, O God, in Sion: and unto thee shall the vow be performed.

2 O thou that hearest prayer, unto thee shall all flesh come.

3 Iniquities prevail against me: *as for* our transgressions, thou shalt purge them away.

4 Blessed *is the man whom* thou choosest, and causest to approach *unto thee, that* he may dwell in thy courts: we shall be satisfied with the goodness of thy house, *even* of thy holy temple.

5 *By* terrible things in righteousness wilt thou answer us, O God of our salvation; *who art* the confidence of all the ends of the earth, and of them that are afar off *upon* the sea:

6 Which by his strength setteth fast the mountains; *being* girded with power:

7 Which stilleth the noise of the seas, the noise of their waves, and the tumult of the people.

8 They also that dwell in the uttermost parts are afraid at thy tokens: thou makest the outgoings of the morning and evening to rejoice.

9 Thou visitest the earth, and waterest it: thou greatly enrichest it with the river of God, *which* is full of water: thou preparest them corn, when thou hast so provided for it.

10 Thou waterest the ridges thereof abundantly: thou settlest the furrows thereof: thou makest it soft with showers: thou blessest the springing thereof.

11 Thou crownest the year with thy goodness; and thy paths drop fatness.

12 They drop *upon* the pastures of the wilderness: and the little hills rejoice on every side.

13 The pastures are clothed with flocks; the valleys also are covered over with corn; they shout for joy, they also sing.

insufficient grounds. From the allusions in verses 7-8, it appears that it was composed during a time of great political convulsion. It is obviously a harvest hymn of praise, designed to be sung on any occasion of thanksgiving, and not a ritual associated with the festival of the annual enthronement of Yahweh.

65:1-3. Praise waiteth for thee, O God in Zion. The most fitting praise to God is that which waits in silence, anticipating God's goodness rather than creating a disturbing tumult of praise. **O thou that hearest prayer.** What a delightful name for the God that David served. Hearing prayer is a necessary attribute of a loving God. He is the One who supersedes all false gods and to whom ultimately **shall all flesh come.** Such devotion belongs to the Lord God of Heaven only, and one day He will have it.

4. Blessed is the man whom thou choosest, and causest to approach unto thee. The blessings of God flow to His chosen nation Israel (Deut 7:6) and to all who are drawn to Him by faith. Among the peculiar privileges of the chosen is the privilege of dwelling in the courts of God, **even of thy holy temple.** David foresaw this as Israel's privilege. The believer foresees it as his privilege in the courts of heaven.

5-8. By terrible things in righteousness wilt thou answer us, O God of our salvation. God exhibits His grace when He hears our prayers; He exhibits His glory when He answers them. The prayers of the righteous are heard and answered, regardless of their location. Those who are at **the ends of the earth** and those **that are afar off upon the sea** can look to God in confidence that He will hear their prayers.

There is good reason for this **confidence.** The God to whom we pray is the One who **setteth fast the mountains . . .** and **stilleth the noise of the seas.** The mountains sit in silent majesty as an emblem of God's strength and firmness. The seas, far beyond the control of men, are tamed by this great God. Likewise tamed by Him is **the tumult of the people.** No man is too far away, nor too far removed, from God not to be **afraid at thy tokens.** Indications of the mighty power of God are everywhere, and the hearts of men everywhere are filled with awe.

9-10. Thou visitest the earth, and waterest it . . . thou preparest them corn . . . thou settlest the furrows thereof: thou makest it soft with showers. The fool thanks Mother Nature; the wise man knows that it is God that has visited the earth and watered it (cf. 147:18; Job 36:27-28; 37:6; 38:26-28; Jer 5:24; Mt 5:45). God's store of water in the clouds, here referred to as **the river of God,** is given by a loving God to prepare the corn, the fruit of harvest time. **Thou blessest the springing thereof.** God sends the latter rains in the early spring to insure that the vegetables will be lucious and the fruit juicy.

11-13. Thou crownest the year with thy goodness. God always brings what He begins to fruition. Perhaps the greatest display of the goodness of God, apart from our own salvation, is the golden grain of summer. **Thy paths drop fatness.** Fertility and abundance abound, and the footsteps of God are noticed everywhere. **They drop upon the pastures of the wilderness.** God's showers of blessing not only fall gently to the ground at the habitations of man, but even in the wilderness as well. **The pastures are clothed with flocks,** a scene well-known to the psalmist, for any shepherd of the Judaean hill country. **The valleys also are covered over with corn.** Those areas of his homeland not covered with flocks were producing grain bountifully. God is so good; what can nature do but join the voice of man to articulate His goodness? **They shout for joy, they also sing.**

Y. A Call to Worship. 66:1-20.

THEME: *A hymn of praise which summons men to worship the Lord God of Israel.*

PSALM 66

MAKE a joyful noise unto God, all ye
lands:
2 Sing forth the honour of his name:
make his praise glorious.
3 Say unto God, How terrible *art thou
in* thy works! through the greatness of
thy power shall thine enemies submit
themselves unto thee.
4 All the earth shall worship thee,
and shall sing unto thee; they shall sing
to thy name. Sĕ′lah.
5 Come and see the works of God: *he
is* terrible *in his* doing toward the children of men.

6 He turned the sea into dry *land:*
they went through the flood on foot:
there did we rejoice in him.
7 He ruleth by his power for ever; his
eyes behold the nations: let not the rebellious exalt themselves. Sĕ′lah.

8 O bless our God, ye people, and
make the voice of his praise to be
heard:
9 Which holdeth our soul in life, and
suffereth not our feet to be moved.

10 For thou, O God, hast proved us:
thou hast tried us, as silver is tried.
11 Thou broughtest us into the net;
thou laidst affliction upon our loins.
12 Thou hast caused men to ride over
our heads; we went through fire and
through water: but thou broughtest us
out into a wealthy *place.*

13 I will go into thy house with burnt
offerings: I will pay thee my vows,
14 Which my lips have uttered, and
my mouth hath spoken, when I was in
trouble.
15 I will offer unto thee burnt sacrifices of fatlings, with the incense of
rams; I will offer bullocks with goats.
Sĕ′lah.

This **song or psalm,** designed to be sung as well as spoken, celebrates the great deeds of God on behalf of His people and calls upon all nations to rejoice with them. It was apparently composed as a result of a special deliverance that had come to the children of Israel, a deliverance of such magnitude that the Jews alone could not give sufficient praise to their God. Thus, the psalm expresses a universal call to praise the Lord God of Israel.

66:1-4. Make a joyful noise unto God, all ye lands. So good is God that all the earth is invited to join in Israel's praise of Him. That praise is evidenced in the words **sing . . . say . . . worship.** A thankful heart should reflect to Him **How terrible art thou in thy works!** The power of God is so awesome that even His enemies shall be brought to forced submission under His feet.

5. Come and see the works of God. The psalmist now begins to recount how awesome God is when He defends His people. The children of men can but stand and tremble in the presence of the God of Abraham, Isaac, and Jacob.

6-7. He turned the sea into dry land . . . He ruleth by his power for ever. It is obvious that the writer is recounting the glorious event of the crossing of the Red Sea (Ex 14). Jehovah had proved His love for Israel; He had proved His presence with them; He had proved His power to them; He had proved His purpose to Pharaoh. This is an historical lesson to anyone who would say, "Who is the LORD, that I should obey His voice . . . ?"

8-9. O bless our God, ye people . . . which holdeth our soul in life, and suffereth not our feet to be moved. Although all the world will praise Him, the people of God must lead the way. Their voices must be heard long and loud in praising the God who gives us life and enables us to keep it.

10-12. For thou, O God, hast proved us. Many a calamity had been sent as a trial to prove and purify (cf. 7:9; 11:5). Spurgeon says, "God had one son without sin, but he never had a son without trial. Why ought we to complain if we are subjected to the rule which is common to all the family, and from which so much benefit has flowed to them?" **Thou hast tried us, as silver is tried,** referring to the prolonged process of refining this precious metal (cf. 12:6; Prov 17:3; 25:4; Isa 1:22, 25; 48:10; Zech 13:9; Mal 3:3; I Cor 3:12-15).

Thou broughtest us into the net . . . Thou hast caused men to ride over our heads. Frequent were the occasions when Israel in Egypt was like a bird in the nest of the fowler or a fish in the net of the fisherman. **We went through fire and through water.** Fire and water are antithetical, but both are deadly. In both the Egyptian brick kilns and the waters of the Nile, Israel had been oppressed; **but thou broughtest us out into a wealthy place.** God did not forsake His people in Egypt. He brought them into a place of refreshment, the land that flows with milk and honey. This has always been the testimony of the people of God.

13-15. When the psalmist surveys the great hand of God upon His people, it drives him to a sense of personal indebtedness to Jehovah. Thus, from corporate praise he turns to personal worship. **I will go into thy house.** This phrase is usually advanced as justification for late authorship of this psalm. It must be remembered, however, that the tabernacle as well as the "House of God." **I will pay thee my vows.** The Psalms bear witness to the importance of this practice (cf. 22:25; 50:14; 56:12; 61:8; 65:1; 116:14-18; 132:2). As is frequently the case, the psalmist made his vows to the Lord **When I was in trouble.** Vows should be hesitantly made, but once made, heartily kept. Thus, in keeping his vows, the psalmist will offer burnt offerings; **of fatlings** (cf. I Sam 15:9; II Sam 6:13; Ezk 39:18) **with**

the incense of rams (the savory odor of rams) and of **bullocks with goats** (cf. I Kgs 18:23, 26).

16-17. Come and hear . . . and I will declare what he hath done for my soul. Earlier we were invited to **Come and see** (vs. 5). Now, in faith we are asked to draw unto the psalmist while he declares with his mouth and extols with his tongue the great goodness of God.

18-20. If I regard iniquity in my heart, the LORD will not hear me. All believers on occasion harbor sin without aversion to it. Sin must be properly confessed (I Jn 1:9) before God can effectually be addressed. For examples in Scripture see Job 27:9; 31:27; Proverbs 15:29; 28:9; Isaiah 1:15; Zechariah 7:13; John 9:31; etc.

In confirmation that the psalmist did not harbor secret sin is his confidence, **but verily God hath heard me.** A great God who brings us through fire and water and hears our prayers certainly deserves our worship and praise. Thus, it is fitting that this psalm concludes with a special blessing, **Blessed be God, which hath not turned away my prayer, nor his mercy from me.**

Z. A Missionary Hymn of Praise. 67:1-7.

THEME: *A psalm reflecting Israel, as God's priest to the nations.*

Committed **To the chief musician** and to be played on **Neginoth** (stringed instruments), this is **A psalm or song.** Like the one preceding it, Psalm 67 is anonymous; and estimates of its dates and authorship range from, it "may have been composed either in the time of Hezekiah . . . or at a time subsequent to the return from the Exile," (Perowne) to "almost certainly it was written by Hezekiah" (Scroggie), to "no author's name is given, but it would be a bold man who should attempt to prove that David did not write it" (Spurgeon).

67:1-2. God be merciful unto us, and bless us; and cause his face to shine upon us. This echo of Aaron (Num 6:24-26) need not necessarily be the utterance of the priest. The prayer of this verse is threefold: first for mercy, the prerequisite for salvation; then for blessing, the accompaniment of salvation; and finally for divine favor, the end of salvation. **Thy saving health** (Heb *yeshū'ah*) occurs more than seventy times in the Hebrew Bible, and in more than fifty instances it is translated salvation (sometimes translated as help, welfare, deliverance, and twice translated health, see 42:5, 11); but only here is it translated **saving health.** The verse has nothing whatsoever to do with divine healing or salvational healing, but is to be understood in the singular sense as salvation among all nations.

3-5. Let the people praise thee, O God; let all the people praise thee. In both clauses the prayer is that all the peoples of the world will one day praise the God of Israel. When the wishes of this chorus become fact, the prayer of verse 2, **that thy way may be known upon earth,** will also become fact. Now the crux of the psalm: when shall men know the way of God? When shall His salvation be seen of all nations? When shall the people praise Him? Verse 4 provides the answer. **For thou shalt judge the people righteously, and govern the nations upon earth.** When the kingdoms of this world become the kingdoms of our God, when Jesus Christ sits upon the throne of David to rule His millennial kingdom, then, and only then, shall the nations praise the Lord.

6-7. Then shall the earth yield her increase. This quotation from Leviticus 26:4 is designed to show that the curse placed upon this planet by sin (Gen 3:17-18) can only be removed by salvation. When the Lord Jesus Christ reigns in righteousness this earth shall yield a harvest more abundant than humanly conceivable. **And God, even our own God, shall bless us . . . and all the ends of the earth shall fear him.** One day the earth

PSALM 67

GOD be merciful unto us, and bless us; *and* cause his face to shine upon us; Sē'-lah.

2 That thy way may be known upon earth, thy saving health among all nations.

3 Let the people praise thee, O God; let all the people praise thee.

4 O let the nations be glad and sing for joy: for thou shalt judge the people righteously, and govern the nations upon earth. Sē'lah.

5 Let the people praise thee, O God; let all the people praise thee.

6 *Then* shall the earth yield her increase; *and* God, *even* our own God, shall bless us.

7 God shall bless us; and all the ends of the earth shall fear him.

16 Come *and* hear, all ye that fear God, and I will declare what he hath done for my soul.

17 I cried unto him with my mouth, and he was extolled with my tongue.

18 If I regard iniquity in my heart, the Lord will not hear *me:*

19 *But* verily God hath heard *me;* he hath attended to the voice of my prayer.

20 Blessed *be* God, which hath not turned away my prayer, nor his mercy from me.

shall be full of the knowledge and the fear of the Lord, ". . . as the waters cover the sea" (Isa 11:9).

AA. The Triumphant Ascension. 68:1-35.

THEME: *A song of praise to the ascended God who brings salvation to all nations.*

Psalm 68 is obviously a hymn of praise for victories complete and the ascension of the King to Mount Zion. The majority of interpreters suppose it to be written when the ark was removed from the house of God at Obed-edom to Mount Zion (II Sam 6). This is the view of Plumer, Spurgeon, and others. The superscription reads, **To the chief musician. A psalm or song of David.** Not only is the style typically Davidic, but there is tremendous external evidence; David's authorship is ascribed by the Hebrew, Chaldee, Syriac, Arabic, Septuagint, Ethiopic, and Vulgate editions of the Old Testament.

Most older theologians hold the psalm to be messianic. They see the dominant theme of the psalm to be Christ in history, especially His resurrection and ascension to the right hand of the Father and the victory of the church over the world because of the ascended Christ, the Head of the church. To some, this prophecy was so clear that they saw no historical interpretation. Yet a more moderate and reasonable interpretation is that the psalm is messianic, yet has a double fulfillment seen in the history of Israel as the ascension of the King to Mount Zion, and the history of God's church as dominated by the ascension of Christ to heaven. One of the chief arguments for a messianic interpretation is that this was the apparent understanding of the Apostle Paul, for he quotes vs. 18 and applies these verses to Christ in Ephesians 4:8-11 (see the comments on vs. 18).

68:1-6. Let God arise, let his enemies be scattered . . . as smoke is driven away . . . as wax melteth before the fire. The prophetic prayer is that the enemies of God would be scattered before Him, using the double simile of smoke that is dispersed by the wind and wax that disappears before a hot fire (cf. 22:14; 97:5). As the wicked are destroyed, the righteous praise God for His goodness to them (cf. 52:6; 58:10; 64:7-10; etc.). This rejoicing takes the form of **Sing . . . sing praises . . . extol him . . . and rejoice.**

A father of the fatherless . . . is God in his holy habitation. God, in His majestic seat in the highest heaven, is not withdrawn from His creation. He is a defender of the oppressed and downtrodden (cf. Isa 1:17). **God setteth the solitary in families,** i.e., He gives homes and families to those who are solitary outcasts and wanderers, and sets the prisoner free.

PSALM 68

LET God arise, let his enemies be scattered: let them also that hate him flee before him.

2 As smoke is driven away, *so* drive *them* away: as wax melteth before the fire, *so* let the wicked perish at the presence of God.

3 But let the righteous be glad; let them rejoice before God: yea, let them exceedingly rejoice.

4 Sing unto God, sing praises to his name: extol him that rideth upon the heavens by his name JAH, and rejoice before him.

5 A father of the fatherless, and a judge of the widows, *is* God in his holy habitation.

6 God setteth the solitary in families: he bringeth out those which are bound with chains: but the rebellious dwell in a dry *land.*

7 O God, when thou wentest forth before thy people, when thou didst march through the wilderness; Sĕ'lah:

8 The earth shook, the heavens also dropped at the presence of God: *even* Sĭ'naĭ itself *was moved* at the presence of God, the God of Israel.

9 Thou, O God, didst send a plentiful rain, whereby thou didst confirm thine inheritance, when it was weary.

10 Thy congregation hath dwelt therein: thou, O God, hast prepared of thy goodness for the poor.

11 The Lord gave the word: great *was* the company of those that published *it.*

12 Kings of armies did flee apace: and she that tarried at home divided the spoil.

13 Though ye have lien among the pots, *yet shall ye be as* the wings of a

7-10. Verses 7-8 are an echo of the Song of Deborah (Jud 5:4-5) and recall the events of Exodus 13:20-22. During the march from Egypt to Sinai **Thou, O God, didst send a plentiful rain.** This is not meant to be a literal rain, but rather a shower of blessings, i.e., manna, quail, water out of the rock, innumerable victories, protection from enemies, etc. **Thy congregation hath dwelt therein.** The congregation (Heb *chayah;* lit., the troop; cf. II Sam 23:11-13) indicates the military prominence of the people of Israel.

11-14. The Lord gave the word: great was the company of those that published it. When God sounded the battle cry from the ark of the covenant, a great company roused the troops of Israel to fight. The result was fleeing enemy armies on too numerous occasions to mention. **Though ye have lain among the pots.** The word translated **pots** (Heb *shepatayim*) is more properly understood to mean "sheepfolds."

dove covered with silver, and her feathers with yellow gold.

14 When the Almighty scattered kings in it, it was *white* as snow in Săl'-mon.

15 The hill of God *is as* the hill of Bā'-shan; an high hill *as* the hill of Bā'shan.

16 Why leap ye, ye high hills? *this is* the hill *which* God desireth to dwell in; yea, the LORD will dwell *in it* for ever.

17 The chariots of God *are* twenty thousand, *even* thousands of angels: the Lord *is* among them, *as in* Sī'naī, in the holy *place*.

18 Thou hast ascended on high, thou hast led captivity captive: thou hast received gifts for men; yea, *for* the rebellious also, that the LORD God might dwell *among them*.

19 Blessed *be* the Lord, *who* daily loadeth us *with benefits, even* the God of our salvation. Sē'lah.

20 *He that is* our God *is* the God of salvation; and unto GOD the Lord *belong* the issues from death.

21 But God shall wound the head of his enemies, *and* the hairy scalp of such an one as goeth on still in his trespasses.

22 The Lord said, I will bring again from Bā'shan, I will bring *my people* again from the depths of the sea:

23 That thy foot may be dipped in the blood of *thine* enemies, *and* the tongue of thy dogs in the same.

24 They have seen thy goings, O God; *even* the goings of my God, my King, in the sanctuary.

25 The singers went before, the players on instruments *followed* after; among *them were* the damsels playing with timbrels.

26 Bless ye God in the congregations, *even* the Lord, from the fountain of Israel.

27 There *is* little Benjamin *with* their ruler, the princes of Jŭ'dah *and* their council, the princes of Zĕb'u-lun, *and* the princes of Năph'ta-lī.

28 Thy God hath commanded thy strength: strengthen, O God, that which thou hast wrought for us.

29 Because of thy temple at Jeru-

Here a challenge is thrown to Israel. When God calls the troops to battle, will they continue their pastoral life, lying among the sheepfolds; or will they, like the Reubenites in the war against Sisera, abide in their prosperity and riches rather than answer the call? Will Israel be as **a dove covered with silver, and her feathers with yellow gold?** Salmon (Zalmon) is a hill adjacent to Shechem mentioned in Judges 9:48. It was covered with a thick black forest. The use of this figure is designed to show that the power of the Almighty God is so great that He can change the complexion of a battle as quickly as He changes the dark forest of Salmon with the white snow.

15-18. The hill of God is as the hill of Bashan . . . Why leap ye, ye high hills? This is the hill which God desireth. The hill, or mountain, of Basham could well refer to Mount Hermon, the highest snowcapped peak in the Middle East. The psalmist's intent was to show that Israel would be victorious by divine design, rather than human ingenuity. The **chariots of God** are thousands upon thousands of angels; and they surround the Almighty God in His **holy place,** both with reference to the ark of the covenant in the tabernacle on Mount Zion and God's throne in Heaven.

There are three major clauses that constitute verse 18. They are: (1) **Thou hast ascended on high;** (2) **thou hast led captivity captive;** and (3) **thou hast received gifts for men.** What do these clauses describe historically? **Thou hast ascended on high** means ascended into the sanctuary on Mount Zion. It refers to one of the occasions when the ark was transferred there (cf. II Sam 6:12-19; I Chr 15:11-28). **Thou hast led captivity captive** indicates that many have been captured and taken prisoner in Israel's struggle to secure Canaan. **Thou hast received gifts for men** indicates that tribute has been paid by Israel's enemies to the chosen nation of God. But, in light of Ephesians 4, the messianic interpretation must carry us far beyond this.

19-23. When thought is given to the throne of God being established in heaven, and historically on Mount Zion, the psalmist can do little but praise the Lord. **Blessed be the LORD, who daily loadeth us with benefits, even the God of our salvation. Selah.** Jehovah is not a God far removed from Israel, but one who bears Israel's burdens day by day and is alone her salvation. Unto this God **belong the issues from death.** God mysteriously brings those who are dead both physically and spiritually to life. Jehovah is the God who brings down the proud, i.e., **the hairy scalp.**

Jehovah is the God who **will bring my people . . . that thy foot may be dipped in the blood of thine enemies.** This poetic metaphor, used in Isaiah 63:1-3, shows the utter domination of God and His people over their enemies. Prophetically, it shows the utter domination of the ascended Lord over the kingdoms of this world.

24-27. When the ark of the covenant was taken up to Mount Zion, all the people watched the procession. It is specifically noted **the singers went before, the players on instruments followed after,** because the reverse was true with Assyrian musical processions. All the tribes of Israel were present, but only four are mentioned here as representatives. **There is little Benjamin with their ruler,** the royal tribe that gave Israel her first king. **The princes of Judah,** the second royal tribe that gave Israel her second king and her coming King. The tribes of **Zebulun and Naphtali** were the learned tribes of Israel.

28-31. Thy God hath commanded thy strength. It is fixed in the eternal design of God that Israel shall be strong and shall remain forever. Messianically, it is fixed in the eternal design of God that Christ Jesus shall rule the world with a rod of iron forever. As men would bring presents to Solomon in the great

salem shall kings bring presents unto thee.

30 Rebuke the company of spearmen, the multitude of the bulls, with the calves of the people, *till every one* submit himself with pieces of silver: scatter thou the people *that* delight in war.

31 Princes shall come out of Egypt; Ē-thĭ-ō'pĭ-a soon stretch out her hands unto God.

32 Sing unto God, ye kingdoms of the earth; O sing praises unto the Lord; Sē'-lah:

33 To him that rideth upon the heavens of heavens, *which were* of old; lo, he doth send out his voice, *and that a* mighty voice.

34 Ascribe ye strength unto God: his excellency *is* over Israel, and his strength *is* in the clouds.

35 O God, *thou art* terrible out of thy holy places: the God of Israel *is* he that giveth strength and power unto *his* people. Blessed *be* God.

PSALM 69

SAVE me, O God; for the waters are come in unto *my* soul.

2 I sink in deep mire, where *there is* no standing: I am come into deep waters, where the floods overflow me.

3 I am weary of my crying: my throat is dried: mine eyes fail while I wait for my God.

4 They that hate me without a cause are more than the hairs of mine head: they that would destroy me, *being* mine enemies wrongfully, are mighty: then I restored *that* which I took not away.

5 O God, thou knowest my foolishness; and my sins are not hid from thee.

6 Let not them that wait on thee, O

1064

Temple of Jerusalem, so too during the Millennium the Son of Solomon who sits on that throne, the Lord Jesus Christ Himself, shall be the recipient of the praise and presents of all men.

Rebuke the company of spearmen . . . of the bulls . . . till every one submit himself with pieces of silver. The spearmen literally refers to the wild beast of the reeds, presumably the crocodile. This is evidentially a symbolic description of Egypt. The **bulls** represent Assyria. Together, Egypt and Assyria represent Israel's enemy forces which, when rebuked by God, shall bring tribute to Israel's divine Son, Jesus Christ. One day the whole world will fall at His feet: **Princes shall come out of Egypt; Ethiopia shall soon stretch out her hands unto God.**

32-35. The end is in sight. The historical victories of Israel past and present only point to the coming mighty victory at Armageddon and the establishment of the kingdom of God on this earth with its center of government at Jerusalem (Isa 2:2-4). Thus, all the kingdoms of the earth shall **sing praises unto the LORD . . . that rideth upon the heavens.** The day will come when every nation will recognize that there is a God in heaven, the highest heaven (cf. Deut 10:140; I Kgs 8:27).

BB. A Cry of Distress. 69:1-36.

THEME: A plea for God not to hide His face from His troubled servant.

For the second time (Ps 45 being the first), we have a psalm addressed **To the chief musician upon Shoshannim,** (upon the lilies). Both the Hebrew and the LXX attribute this psalm to David; St. Paul also quotes it as Davidic in Romans 11:9. No unanswerable objections to David's authorship can be mustered.

An important feature of this psalm is its messianic character. With the exception of Psalm 22, no portion of the Old Testament is more frequently quoted by the New Testament writers. Just as obvious, however, is the fact that some of these verses must refer only to David and not to the Son of David. It would have been impossible, for example, for Christ to have acknowledged sin, as is done in verse 5. Likewise, at the point of our Lord's greatest persecution, when He uttered, ". . . Father, forgive them; for they know not what they do . . ." (Lk 23:34) the psalmist is seen to say, **Add iniquity unto their iniquity: and let them not come into thy righteousness** (vs. 27). It is thus evident that portions of the psalm were designed strictly for the author.

69:1-4. Save me, O God; for the waters are come in unto my soul. I sink in deep mire. So deeply had sorrows penetrated his soul that the psalmist begins his cry of despair with a common, proverbial expression of great distress (cf. 18:4; 42:7; 88:7, 17; Job 22:11; 27:20). The waters of sorrow that remained outside the psalmist's life would be disturbing, but those which made their way into the hold of his life would be disastrous.

I am weary of my crying: my throat is dried. The psalmist and his Great Son both honestly prayed to God. In the Garden of Gethsemane, the Lord Jesus prayed until He sweat great drops as if it were blood. Long and fervent pleading had scorched His throat until it was too parched to verbalize His prayers. **They that hate me without a cause are more than the hairs of mine head.** For the most part, David had lived righteously before God. Yet, the Lord Jesus lived even more righteously (without sin) and nonetheless was hated without reason. **They that would destroy me . . . are mighty.** It was bad enough that our Lord's enemies were many; they were mighty as well. **Then I restored that which I took not away** refers to the fact that Jesus was presumed guilty and paid the penalty for sin that was not His own.

5-8. O God, thou knowest my foolishness; and my sins are not hid from thee. David may have uttered these words, but certainly not Christ the Lord. The Father was well aware of

Lord GOD of hosts, be ashamed for my sake: let not those that seek thee be confounded for my sake, O God of Israel.

7 Because for thy sake I have borne reproach; shame hath covered my face.

8 I am become a stranger unto my brethren, and an alien unto my mother's children.

9 For the zeal of thine house hath eaten me up; and the reproaches of them that reproached thee are fallen upon me.

10 When I wept, *and chastened* my soul with fasting, that was to my reproach.

11 I made sackcloth also my garment; and I became a proverb to them.

12 They that sit in the gate speak against me; and I *was* the song of the drunkards.

13 But as for me, my prayer *is* unto thee, O LORD, *in* an acceptable time: O God, in the multitude of thy mercy hear me, in the truth of thy salvation.

14 Deliver me out of the mire, and let me not sink: let me be delivered from them that hate me, and out of the deep waters.

15 Let not the waterflood overflow me, neither let the deep swallow me up, and let not the pit shut her mouth upon me.

16 Hear me, O LORD; for thy loving-kindness *is* good: turn unto me according to the multitude of thy tender mercies.

17 And hide not thy face from thy servant; for I am in trouble: hear me speedily.

18 Draw nigh unto my soul, *and* redeem it: deliver me because of mine enemies.

19 Thou hast known my reproach, and my shame, and my dishonour: mine adversaries *are* all before thee.

20 Reproach hath broken my heart; and I am full of heaviness: and I looked *for some* to take pity, but *there was* none; and for comforters, but I found none.

David's foolishness. But the **sins** of the Lord Jesus, should this verse be applied prophetically to Him, must be viewed as those sins imputed to Him, i.e., the sins of the world, not His own.

Let not them . . . be ashamed for my sake. The psalmist is concerned that his supposed desertion by God would be the cause for shame by those who trusted in God. **Because for thy sake I have borne reproach; shame hath covered my face.** The reproach that King David bore is completely overshadowed by that of his descendant. The Lord Jesus undertook to do the Father's will, and it took Him to Calvary. He endured the shame of the cross and the railing accusations of an ungrateful mob. **I am become a stranger unto my brethren,** as the Apostle John recorded, "He came unto his own, and his own received him not" (Jn 1:11). **An alien unto my mother's children.** As the preference of David over his elder brethren aroused their jealousy (I Sam 16:6-13), so too the Son of David was alien to the younger children of Mary during His earthly ministry (Jn 7:5); but they joined His followers after His resurrection (Acts 1:14).

9-12. For the zeal of thine house hath eaten me up. David's zeal for the house of God was seen when he established a dwelling place on Mount Zion (II Sam 6:12-19) when he desired to build a permanent dwelling place for God (132:2-5; II Sam 7:2), when he collected materials for the building of a magnificent Temple (I Chr 28:11-18; 29:2-5), and when he left directions to his son Solomon concerning the erection of the Temple (I Chr 28:9-10, 20). **When I wept, and chastened my soul with fasting, that was to my reproach.** Nothing David nor his Great Descendant did would please their oppressors. Having resolved to hate them, their enemies even reproached the weeping and fasting of King David and King Jesus.

I made sackcloth also my garment. We know David did this, and it is not improbable that Jesus did it as well. Sackcloth was the common garb of a mourner, and the Lord Jesus had many occasions to lament the sinful condition of His creatures. **I was the song of the drunkards.** So intense was the hatred of the mob that the name Jesus became a byword, a proverb, the ballad of buffoons.

13-15. It was the Lord Jesus' resolve that He would not retaliate for the cruelty perpetrated on Him. Rather, He would pray to God **Deliver me out of the mire, and let me not sink . . . Let not the waterflood overflow me . . . and let not the pit shut her mouth upon me.** One cannot help but remember the occasion of Jonah being swallowed up in the deep. As Jonah came forth from the abyss of woe after three days, so too our Lord would come forth. The grave enclosed, but could not hold, Him.

16-18. Hear me, O Lord; for thy loving-kindness is good . . . And hide not thy face from thy servant. In an appeal to the Father's love, kindness, and mercy, David cries out to God to make His presence known (cf. 10:1; 13:1; 22:24; 27:9; etc.). In the Garden of Gethsemane the Son of David did the same. **Deliver me because of mine enemies.** The Lord Jesus Christ's cry was not for deliverance from the cross, but through the cross to renewed communion, joy and glory with the Father and Spirit.

19-21. Thou hast known my reproach . . . shame . . . dishonor. This triad is designed to show the great suffering, shame, and contempt poured out upon the Lord as He hung upon the cross. God the Father was not unaware of what God the Son endured. **Reproach hath broken my heart.** Surrounded by His enemies and deserted by His friends, the Lord Jesus was heartbroken; but He did not die of a broken heart. He freely gave His life as a ransom for our sin. **I am full of heaviness.** The

21 They gave me also gall for my meat; and in my thirst they gave me vinegar to drink.

insults hurled at Him caused His head to bow low and be full of sickness. **I looked for some to take pity . . . and for comforters, but I found none.** No one stood by to offer a kind word or a sympathetic tear. Although He could have called ten thousand angels, Jesus Christ died alone for you and me.

In my thirst they gave me vinegar to drink. When upon Calvary's cross Christ uttered the words "I thirst," those who stood by "filled a sponge with vinegar, and put it upon hyssop, and put it to His mouth. When Jesus therefore had received the vinegar, he said, It is finished: and he bowed his head, and gave up the ghost" (cf. 22:16-18; Jn 19:28-30).

22 Let their table become a snare before them: and *that which should have been* for *their* welfare, *let it become* a trap.
23 Let their eyes be darkened, that they see not; and make their loins continually to shake.
24 Pour out thine indignation upon them, and let thy wrathful anger take hold of them.
25 Let their habitation be desolate; *and* let none dwell in their tents.
26 For they persecute *him* whom thou hast smitten; and they talk to the grief of those whom thou hast wounded.
27 Add iniquity unto their iniquity: and let them not come into thy righteousness.
28 Let them be blotted out of the book of the living, and not be written with the righteous.

22-28. Here David and our Lord part company. Thus far the verses of this psalm have followed closely the lives of both David and Jesus Christ. At this point severe imprecations are uttered, imprecations unknown to the dying Saviour.

Let their table become a snare before them. As the wicked oppressors of the king had laid snares for him, they would themselves become snared by the **welfare,** or good things, of their own tables. **Pour out thine indignation upon them.** Be angry with them and show divine anger in a way that they will not escape. **Let their habitation be desolate; and let none dwell in their tents.** Let their posterity be destroyed so that there is no mention of their name after them.

For they persecute him whom thou hast smitten. David had undergone affliction at the hand of God, and it is the characteristic of ungodly men to add persecution to those who already suffer affliction at God's hand. **Let them not come into thy righteousness.** Let them not receive of the gift of thy grace, i.e., salvation. **Let them be blotted out of the book of the living.** Let not their names appear in the Lamb's Book of Life.

29 But I *am* poor and sorrowful: let thy salvation, O God, set me up on high.
30 I will praise the name of God with a song, and will magnify him with thanksgiving.
31 *This* also shall please the LORD better than an ox *or* bullock that hath horns and hoofs.
32 The humble shall see *this, and* be glad: and your heart shall live that seek God.
33 For the LORD heareth the poor, and despiseth not his prisoners.

29-33. With these severe imprecations now behind him, the psalmist assumes a milder tone, intermingled with thankfulness and praise. **Let thy salvation, O God, set me up on high.** By way of contrast to the imprecation, David asks for blessing on his behalf. He resolves **I will praise the name of God with a song . . . This also shall please the LORD better than an ox or bullock.** There is no sacrifice as acceptable to God as the sacrifice of a heart filled with thanksgiving to God and overflowing with His praise. **The humble shall see this, and be glad.** Great joy will come to those humble of heart when David is once again restored to the majesty of his throne. Likewise, the humble rejoiced on Easter Sunday morning when Jesus of Nazareth was found to be raised from the dead. **For the LORD heareth the poor.** God despises no man; and no prayer that is honest and sincere and delivered from one of God's children, regardless of his earthly stature, is ever unheard and unheeded.

34 Let the heaven and earth praise him, the seas, and every thing that moveth therein.
35 For God will save Zion, and will build the cities of Jū'dah: that they may dwell there, and have it in possession.
36 The seed also of his servants shall inherit it: and they that love his name shall dwell therein.

34-36. The psalmist now issues a doxology of praise. He calls upon **the heaven and earth** to praise the Lord. This includes the **seas, and every thing that moveth therein.** And why is David so confident of God's worthiness to be praised? **For God will save Zion, and will build the cities of Judah . . . The seed also of his servants shall inherit it.** God will consistently deliver and watch over His great city, and the inheritance of the people of Israel will be the cities of Judah. God will maintain them and keep them from decay. **And they that love his name shall dwell therein.** What confidence and great praise concludes a psalm that began in deep waters! How gracious is the change, and how wonderful is the God who executes such change. Jesus Christ will one day sit on the throne of David in David's city, God's city, Jerusalem. He who has suffered much at the hands of oppressors will one day rule the world from the city of His oppression (Isa 62; Zech 2).

CC. A Plea for Divine Haste. 70:1-5.

THEME: *The psalmist's prayer for a speedy deliverance by God.* This psalm is a repetition, with some variations, of the last

PSALM 70

MAKE *haste*, O God, to deliver me; make haste to help me, O Lord.

2 Let them be ashamed and confounded that seek after my soul: let them be turned backward, and put to confusion, that desire my hurt.

3 Let them be turned back for a reward of their shame that say, Aha, aha.

4 Let all those that seek thee rejoice and be glad in thee: and let such as love thy salvation say continually, Let God be magnified.

5 But I *am* poor and needy: make haste unto me, O God: thou *art* my help and my deliverer; O Lord, make no tarrying.

PSALM 71

IN thee, O Lord, do I put my trust: let me never be put to confusion.

2 Deliver me in thy righteousness, and cause me to escape: incline thine ear unto me, and save me.

3 Be thou my strong habitation, whereunto I may continually resort: thou hast given commandment to save me; for thou *art* my rock and my fortress.

4 Deliver me, O my God, out of the hand of the wicked, out of the hand of the unrighteous and cruel man.

5 For thou *art* my hope, O Lord God: *thou art* my trust from my youth.

6 By thee have I been holden up from the womb: thou art he that took me out of my mother's bowels: my praise *shall be* continually of thee.

7 I am as a wonder unto many; but thou *art* my strong refuge.

five verses of Psalm 40. This is the second psalm in which such a repetition has been seen (see 53 which is a rehearsal of 14). The Apostle Paul said, "To write the same things to you, to me indeed is not grievous, but for you it is safe" (Phil 3:1). This seems to be the practice of the psalmist as well.

The title ascribes authorship to David, and there is no reason to doubt this. David appears to have written the full-length psalm and to have excerpted from 40:13-17 and altered for a special occasion these verses. Since the next psalm (71) is untitled, some have suggested that 70 and 71 constitute a single psalm.

70:1-5. A full treatment of these verses is given in 40:13-17. **Make haste, O God, to deliver me; make haste to help me, O Lord.** In 40:13 we find the phrase "Be pleased, O Lord, to deliver me." Here "be pleased" is omitted, presumably to increase the urgency of the request. **Let them be ashamed and confounded** (40:14 adds "together"). It is the desire of the psalmist that those who seek his life would be **put to confusion.** Thus, he prays, **Let them be turned back for a reward of their shame that say, Aha, aha** (40:15 has, "Let them be desolate," but though here milder the meaning is the same). **Let such as love thy salvation say continually, Let God be magnified.** This doxology is recorded in 40:16 as, "The Lord be magnified." Either way, the direction of praise is always toward God. **But I am poor and needy; make haste unto me, O God.** This appears to be a deliberate variation from 40:17, which reads, "yet the Lord thinketh upon me." The praise and prayer of the final clauses is virtually identical with 40:17. **Thou art my help and my deliverer; O Lord, make no tarrying** ("Make no tarrying, O my God" in 40:17).

DD. A Psalm of Old Age. 71:1-24.

THEME: A plea by an aged saint not to be cast off.

This is the psalm of an aged saint who is in some sort of trouble and keeps crying out for deliverance. Although there is no inscription in Hebrew, in the LXX it is titled "a Psalm of David, of the sons of Jonadab, and of those who were first led captive." This is obviously a composite title and a contradictory one. However, it has led many scholars to believe that it was a favorite psalm with the Rechabites and the earlier exiles. Therefore, they have ascribed this psalm to Jeremiah or one of his scribes (Perowne, Scroggie, et al.). Nonetheless, its proximity to Psalm 70 and close relationship with Psalms 22; 31; 35; and 40 (all Davidic Psalms) make David's authorship a real possibility (Plumer, Clarke, Kay, Scott, et al.).

71:1-3. In thee, O Lord, do I put my trust: let me never be put to confusion. The Lord God Jehovah deserves our trust and confidence. As long as we trust Him and His Word, confusion will never be the result of that trust. **Incline thine ear unto me, and save me.** Here the call is for the God of heaven to stoop and listen to the whispers of an old man. But when this aged saint whispers, it is not blasphemy to the Lord, but a heartfelt request: **Be thou my strong habitation, whereunto I may continually resort.**

4-6. Deliver me, O my God, out of the hand of the wicked. David characteristically singles out from his adversaries an individual from whom he asks to be delivered (cf. 13:2; 17:13; 18:17, 48; 35:8; 41:6, 9, 11; etc.). **For thou art my hope, O Lord God . . . thou art he that took me out of my mother's bowels.** God has been the psalmist's hope since before he drew his first breath. All these years he has trusted in God, and there is no reason to believe that God will not be his hope now that he has passed the meridian of his life.

7-12. I am as a wonder unto many. The word **wonder** (Heb *môpēt*) means a prodigy, a token. The psalmist was a marvelous example of God's punishments. This interpretation is supported

8 Let my mouth be filled *with* thy praise *and with* thy honour all the day.

9 Cast me not off in the time of old age; forsake me not when my strength faileth.

10 For mine enemies speak against me; and they that lay wait for my soul take counsel together,

11 Saying, God hath forsaken him: persecute and take him; for *there is* none to deliver *him*.

12 O God, be not far from me: O my God, make haste for my help.

13 Let them be confounded *and* consumed that are adversaries to my soul; let them be covered *with* reproach and dishonour that seek my hurt.

14 But I will hope continually, and will yet praise thee more and more.

15 My mouth shall shew forth thy righteousness *and* thy salvation all the day; for I know not the numbers *thereof*.

16 I will go in the strength of the Lord GOD: I will make mention of thy righteousness, *even* of thine only.

17 O God, thou hast taught me from my youth: and hitherto have I declared thy wondrous works.

18 Now also when I am old and greyheaded, O God, forsake me not; until I have shewed thy strength unto *this* generation, *and* thy power to every one *that* is to come.

19 Thy righteousness also, O God, *is* very high, who hast done great things: O God, who *is* like unto thee!

20 *Thou,* which hast shewed me great and sore troubles, shalt quicken me again, and shalt bring me up again from the depths of the earth.

21 Thou shalt increase my greatness, and comfort me on every side.

22 I will also praise thee with the psaltery, *even* thy truth, O my God: unto thee will I sing with the harp, O thou Holy One of Israel.

23 My lips shall greatly rejoice when I sing unto thee; and my soul, which thou hast redeemed.

24 My tongue also shall talk of thy righteousness all the day long: for they are confounded, for they are brought unto shame, that seek my hurt.

by Deuteronomy 28:46 and would explain why David, a man after God's own heart, was so frequently oppressed and troubled. Nonetheless, his resolve was **Let my mouth be filled with thy praise and with thy honor all the day.** He couples with this the prayer, **Cast me not off in the time of old age.** The enemies of the righteous take counsel together of the old saints **saying, God hath forsaken him.** But there is someone to deliver us even in old age. With the psalmist we may pray, **O God, be not far from me: O my God, make haste for my help.** Nearness to God and the certainty of His constant presence are our conscious security.

13-15. After the imprecation of verse 13, in which the aged saint asks that his enemies be **confounded and consumed** as well as **covered with reproach and dishonor,** he contrasts himself with those who seek his hurt by promising, **My mouth shall show forth thy righteousness and thy salvation all the day.** The resolve of this aged saint to continually praise the Lord God **all the day** is deepened by his recognition **for I know not the numbers thereof.** He knew the sweetness of his salvation; he knew the glory of the days in which he walked with the Lord; but he did not know how many days remained for him to do so.

16-18. **I will go in the strength of the Lord GOD.** Now, robbed of his physical strength, the psalmist does not reduce his praise to God, but simply recognizes that his comings and goings are in the Lord's strength. **O God, thou hast taught me from my youth.** Like Samuel and Timothy, the psalmist has been raised in a God-fearing environment. He has learned well of the goodness of God and has **declared thy wondrous works.** His one concern was that he would be robbed of life before he was able to relate the power and glory of God to the present generation. Therefore, he prays, **Now also when I am old and grayheaded, O God, forsake me not; until I have showed thy strength unto this generation.**

19-21. **Thy righteousness also, O God, is very high, who hast done great things.** Exalted and unsearchable are the riches of God. He had showed the psalmist great and sore trouble, but this aged saint was confident that God **shalt quicken me again, and shalt bring me up again from the depths of the earth.** Heavy and severe trials would not claim the life of the psalmist until God was ready to take him home. Even in old age, as he remained true and faithful praising Jehovah's **greatness, and comfort,** his stature and consolation would only increase.

22-24. Therefore, the aging psalmist resolves, **I will also praise thee with the psaltery. My lips shall greatly rejoice.** The sudden burst of renewed vitality and determination can scarcely be unnoticed. The psalmist is not a bitter old man, pining away and cursing his longevity. Rather, he is seeking new ways, both vocal and instrumental, to praise the **Holy One of Israel . . . My tongue also shall talk of thy righteousness all the day long.** His theme will not be the good old days, the glory that once was his, or the ills of the present generation. Let others resort to that; he shall praise the righteousness of Jehovah from morning till night.

EE. The Reign of the Righteous King. 72:1-20.

THEME: *A prayer for Solomon's reign and a prediction of Christ in millennial reign.*

The superscription of this psalm reads, **A psalm for Solomon.** However, many scholars feel that **A psalm for Solomon** ought to be more properly rendered, "A Psalm of Solomon" (including Leupold, Perowne, Scroggie, et al.). Delitzsch contends that the psalm bears the marks both of Solomon's style and time. The expressions of the psalm are arranged in distichs, like the proverb; and the character of the poetry is reflected. These are elements of Solomonic style. Beyond this, the allusions to Sheba and to Tarshish, and the extent of the kingdom all harmonize with the reign of Solomon better than with the reign of David. The closing verse of the psalm is therefore foreseen to conclude the second book of the Psalms, and not to ascribe Davidic authorship to this particular psalm.

This psalm speaks of the messianic reign of Christ in the Millennium. The Targum of this psalm paraphrases the first verse to read, "O God, give thy judgments to the King's Messiah, and thy justice to the Son of King David." To this Midrash Tehillim adds the explanation, "This is the King Messiah, for it is said, And a stem shall go forth from the root of Jesse." To argue, therefore, that this psalm is not messianic ignores Jewish tradition and the plain meaning of the text.

72:1-4. Give the king thy judgments, O God. Israel was a theocracy. The right to reign was not only transmitted by descent, but also by divine right. Israel's kings were but viceroys of the greater King. God would give His judgment unto the ruler who would then exercise divinely-invested leadership. **And thy righteousness unto the king's son.** Solomon was both the king and the son of the king. The right to reign arose from both inherited and intrinsic authority. Such is the case with our Lord Jesus, who has power in Himself and also royal dignity given to Him of His Father.

He shall judge thy people with righteousness. When the judgment of the king is the judgment of God, the natural consequence is a righteous judgment. **And thy poor with judgment.** Too frequently partiality has been shown to the rich; the Messiah King is no respecter of persons. One day His righteousness will even pervade **The mountains . . . and the little hills.** He shall be the protectorate of the poor. **And shall break in pieces the oppressor.** On God's hatred of oppression and oppressors see Exodus 3:9; Leviticus 25:14; Job 27:13; Isaiah 16:14; etc.

5-7. The righteous government of the king will be characterized by the fear of God. That fear will exist as long as his messianic government exists, **as long as the sun and moon endure.** The reign of the Messiah, as well as that of His ancestor Solomon, will be one of refreshment and will **come down like rain upon the mown grass,** i.e., softly and gently. **In his days shall the righteous flourish.** When Jesus Christ rules and reigns on this earth, it will be a day of an **abundance of peace** such as this earth has never before experienced.

8-11. The universality of Messiah's reign upon the earth is seen in these verses. Not entirely applicable to Solomon, this universality attests to the messianic interpretation of this psalm. **He shall have dominion also from sea to sea.** Israel's promised dominion extended only as far as the Great River (Gen 15:18), which was also the boundary of Solomon's kingdom on the east (I Kgs 4:21, 24). The Son of Solomon, Jesus Christ, will govern a kingdom that reaches to the world's end.

They that dwell in the wilderness shall bow before him. Those wild and lawless people who have never been made to fall beneath the yoke will gladly submit themselves to the Messiah. **The kings of Tarshish and of the isles shall bring presents.** Tarshish is probably Tartessus in Spain, well known to the Israelites in the days of Solomon (I Kgs 10:22; II Chr 9:21). **The isles** probably indicate those multiple islands that dot the Mediterranean Sea. The merchant princes of far and near shall fall under Christ's reign. **The kings of Sheba and Seba shall offer gifts.** We must distinguish between Sheba and Seba, as did the writer of Genesis (Gen 10:7). **Sheba** was in southeastern Arabia, and **Seba** was located on the Middle Nile. From far and near gifts will flow to the exalted ruler. **Yea, all kings shall fall down before him: all nations shall serve him** (Phil 2:10-11).

12-15. The theme of Messiah's redemption of the poor and needy is prevalent in these verses. The worldly proverb says that God helps those who help themselves. The Word of God says,

PSALM 72

GIVE the king thy judgments, O God, and thy righteousness unto the king's son.

2 He shall judge thy people with righteousness, and thy poor with judgment.

3 The mountains shall bring peace to the people, and the little hills, by righteousness.

4 He shall judge the poor of the people, he shall save the children of the needy, and shall break in pieces the oppressor.

5 They shall fear thee as long as the sun and moon endure, throughout all generations.

6 He shall come down like rain upon the mown grass: as showers *that* water the earth.

7 In his days shall the righteous flourish; and abundance of peace so long as the moon endureth.

8 He shall have dominion also from sea to sea, and from the river unto the ends of the earth.

9 They that dwell in the wilderness shall bow before him; and his enemies shall lick the dust.

10 The kings of Tärshish and of the isles shall bring presents: the kings of Shĕ'ba and Sĕ'ba shall offer gifts.

11 Yea, all kings shall fall down before him: all nations shall serve him.

12 For he shall deliver the needy when he crieth; the poor also, and *him* that hath no helper.

13 He shall spare the poor and needy, and shall save the souls of the needy.

14 He shall redeem their soul from deceit and violence: and precious shall their blood be in his sight.

15 And he shall live, and to him shall be given of the gold of Shē′ba: prayer also shall be made for him continually; *and* daily shall he be praised.

16 There shall be an handful of corn in the earth upon the top of the mountains; the fruit thereof shall shake like Lebanon: and *they* of the city shall flourish like grass of the earth.

17 His name shall endure for ever: his name shall be continued as long as the sun: and *men* shall be blessed in him: all nations shall call him blessed.

18 Blessed *be* the LORD God, the God of Israel, who only doeth wondrous things.

19 And blessed *be* his glorious name for ever: and let the whole earth be filled *with* his glory; Amen, and Amen.

20 The prayers of David the son of Jesse are ended.

He shall spare the poor and needy, and shall save the souls of the needy. The clear teaching of Scripture is that God helps those who cannot help themselves. The special tenderness toward the poor and lowly is one of the main features of Christ's kingdom (Isa 11:4; 29:19; 41:17; etc.). This was illustrated by our Lord's ministry upon this earth (cf. Mt 11:5; Lk 4:18). **Precious shall their blood be in his sight.** The reign of Christ will be one of righteousness, not tyranny; and no war shall take the blood of any man during the millennial reign. **Prayer also shall be made for him continually.** Messiah's reign will not only be one of righteousness, but one of prayer as well. **And daily shall he be praised.** He who is perpetually available for prayer is also perpetually worthy of honor.

16-17. There shall be a handful of corn in the earth upon the top of the mountains. A handful (Heb *pisah*) is better understood as a heap of corn or an abundance of corn. This is to imply that His reign is not a time of famine, but rather a time of peace. **The fruit thereof shall shake like Lebanon.** The meaning is that the harvest of grain will be so plentiful that it will rustle in the wind like the mighty cedars of Lebanon in the mountain breezes. **His name shall endure for ever.** The name which is above every name, the name of Jesus, **shall be continued as long as the sun.** There shall be no end to His kingdom, nor to His praise. With the words, **all nations shall call him blessed,** the psalm comes to a conclusion. What follows is a doxology and explanation concerning the prayers of David.

18-20. The prayer **blessed be his glorious name for ever** is a summary note of praise that relates to the main feature of this psalm, i.e, that the name of the Lord Jesus Christ is an exalted name and His messianic kingdom an exalted kingdom. The final prayer of the psalm is, **let the whole earth be filled with his glory. Amen, and Amen.**

III. PSALMS 73:1–89:52.

A. The Prosperity of the Wicked. 73:1-28.

THEME: Why do the wicked seemingly prosper and the righteous seemingly go unrewarded?

This is the second psalm ascribed to Asaph, and the first of eleven consecutive psalms in this book which bear his name. In II Chronicles 29:30 King Hezekiah invites the Levites to sing, ". . . the words of David and of Asaph the seer. . . ." Also, in Nehemiah 12:46 David and Asaph are mentioned together, but distinct from ". . . chief of the singers. . . ." This is apparently to point them out as authors of psalmody, and not merely performers.

This psalm deals with the same perplexing subject as that of Psalm 37, curiously the transposition of Psalm 73. It is also the subject of Psalm 49 and the entire book of Job. How can an infinitely powerful God be good and still allow the wicked to appear to prosper and the righteous to be in want? In Psalm 37 the advice given is to wait on the Lord, for all will be made right in this world. In Psalm 73, however, the psalmist is not simply content to wait; but he expects a full and definite recompense in the future.

PSALM 73

TRULY God *is* good to Israel, *even* to such as are of a clean heart.

2 But as for me, my feet were almost gone; my steps had well nigh slipped.

73:1-2. Truly God is good to Israel, even to such as are of a clean heart. In spite of first appearances, God is good to Israel, at least to true Israel. True Israel are those pious Israelites who are not merely ceremoniously clean, but are clean in heart and mind as well. **But as for me, my feet were almost gone.** Asaph knew that he was part of true Israel, but he doubted God's goodness and righteousness on his behalf. This doubting heart had caused his slipping feet to ebb even further from God. **My steps had well-nigh slipped.** So overwhelming were the circumstances in his life that Asaph was in great danger of a disgraceful fall. He had nearly slipped from the rock of faith into the abyss of skepticism.

3 For I was envious at the foolish, *when* I saw the prosperity of the wicked.

4 For *there are* no bands in their death: but their strength *is* firm.

5 They *are* not in trouble *as other* men; neither are they plagued like *other* men.

6 Therefore pride compasseth them about as a chain; violence covereth them *as a* garment.

3-6. For I was envious at the foolish, when I saw the prosperity of the wicked. The foolish (Heb *halal*) is the generic title of all who are wicked. They are arrogant, vain, boasters, and proud. By their ostentation they invite envy, and Asaph had fallen prey.

Why was Asaph envious of the foolish? He lists his reasons. **For there are no bands in their death.** A similar complaint can be seen by Job who says of the wicked, "They spend their days in wealth and in a moment go down to the grave" (Job 21:13). The notion was very prevalent in the Ancient Near East that a quiet death meant a happy life thereafter. It puzzled Asaph, as it did Job, that the wicked died painlessly. **They are not in trouble as other men.** This may be Oriental hyperbole, for all men have some trouble. But comparatively, Asaph noticed that the wicked had less difficulty in life than those who live righteously. **Neither are they plagued like other men.** Other men (Heb *'adam*) means the whole human race. God did not seem to chasten the wicked as He did others. **Therefore pride compasseth them about as a chain.** So pompous were the wicked that they appeared to flaunt their pride to Asaph by wearing it around their neck as a chain.

7 Their eyes stand out with fatness: they have more than heart could wish.

8 They are corrupt, and speak wickedly *concerning* oppression: they speak loftily.

9 They set their mouth against the heavens, and their tongue walketh through the earth.

10 Therefore his people return hither: and waters of a full *cup* are wrung out to them.

7-10. Their eyes stand out with fatness. The eyes of the wicked ever gloat upon the luxuries around them; and thus, they are bugged out from their fat and bloated faces, ever pompously surveying their possessions (cf. 17:10; Job 15:27). **They have more than heart could wish.** Like King Midas of old, all that they touch turns to gold. The plenty of the pompous leads them to great sin against God. **They are corrupt, and speak wickedly . . . they speak loftily.** Their corruption urges them to scoff at the righteous and speak oppressively as an oracle would to a menial servant. But their verbal sin against God's righteous ones leads them to even greater sin against God Himself. **They set their mouth against the heavens.** Since there is no fear of God in their hearts, **their tongue walketh through the earth** busily employed in backbiting, lying, boasting, and blasphemy. Consequently, God's people are driven to fly to Him for shelter. **Waters of a full cup are wrung out to them.** Tears flow freely from the righteous when the uninhibited blasphemies of the wicked are allowed to continue unassuaged.

11 And they say, How doth God know? and is there knowledge in the most High?

12 Behold, these *are* the ungodly, who prosper in the world; they increase *in* riches.

13 Verily I have cleansed my heart *in* vain, and washed my hands in innocency.

14 For all the day long have I been plagued, and chastened every morning.

11-14. And they say, How doth God know? And is there knowledge in the Most High? Soon these impious oppressors are convinced that their deeds are unobserved in heaven. How much wiser they would have been to recognize with David, **my sins are not hid from thee** (69:5). When Asaph views the ungodly who prosper in the world, he comes to the faulty conclusion that his holiness and obedience are in vain. **Verily I have cleansed my heart in vain, and washed my hands in innocency.** He was innocent; the ungodly were guilty. He was poor; they were rich. He was afflicted; they were at peace. **For all the day long have I been plagued, and chastened every morning.** From dawn's early light to evening's dark night, he was continually chastened (cf. Job 7:18). How could God be just and allow this to happen?

15 If I say, I will speak thus; behold, I should offend *against* the generation of thy children.

16 When I thought to know this, it *was* too painful for me;

17 Until I went into the sanctuary of God; *then* understood I their end.

18 Surely thou didst set them in slippery places: thou castedst them down into destruction.

15-18. Now Asaph faces a moral dilemma. **If I say, I will speak thus; behold, I should offend against the generation of thy children.** For the psalmist to utter his deep discouragement, he is faced with the possibility of spreading discontent among the brethren who are faithful to God. As Asaph meditated upon this thought, he came to the conclusion that to open his mouth against the God who loved him **was too painful for me.**

Until I went into the sanctuary of God. By his own admission, he removed himself from the apparent disarray of his world to the order and harmony of God's sanctuary; **then understood I their end.** Now he views the world through the enlight-

19 How are they *brought* into desolation, as in a moment! they are utterly consumed with terrors.
20 As a dream when *one* awaketh; *so*, O Lord, when thou awakest, thou shalt despise their image.
21 Thus my heart was grieved, and I was pricked in my reins.
22 So foolish *was* I, and ignorant: I was *as* a beast before thee.

23 Nevertheless I *am* continually with thee: thou hast holden *me* by my right hand.
24 Thou shalt guide me with thy counsel, and afterward receive me *to* glory.
25 Whom have I in heaven *but thee?* and *there is* none upon earth *that* I desire beside thee.
26 My flesh and my heart faileth: *but* God *is* the strength of my heart, and my portion for ever.

27 For, lo, they that are far from thee shall perish: thou hast destroyed all them that go a whoring from thee.
28 But *it is* good for me to draw near to God: I have put my trust in the Lord GOD, that I may declare all thy works.

ened eyes of grace, and envy no longer gnaws at his heart. That he sees the divine hand of God purposely placing prosperity in the path of these sinners is evidenced from his exclamation, **Surely thou didst set them in slippery places.** Their position is dangerous at best. God allowed them to prosper only to cause their wickedness to stand out in bold relief when they would be cast **down into destruction.**

19-22. How are they brought into desolation, as in a moment! Headlong they fall into destruction, despite their golden chains and beautiful apparel. **They are utterly consumed with terrors.** No one who blasphemes God or charges heaven escapes judgment. Asaph likened the period of their prosperity to a **dream when one awaketh.** Prosperity lasts for the moment; eternal punishment or reward lasts forever.

Thus my heart was grieved, and I was pricked in my reins. Literally, he is saying that his heart was soured; and he suffers in his most inward organs, the kidneys or **reins** (Heb *kilyah*). This is the usual Old Testament designation for extreme internal affliction. Asaph's only conclusion can be, **So foolish was I, and ignorant: I was as a beast before thee.**

23-26. Thou hast holden me by my right hand. It was God who upheld him and kept him from slipping when his feet were almost gone (vs. 2). God was his **guide** and **counsel.** Asaph is clearly aware that it will be God who shall **afterward receive me to glory.** As Enoch walked with God and received a reception into glory, so the psalmist anticipates the same response. **Whom have I in heaven but thee? There is none upon earth . . . besides thee.** "Who is there in all the host of heaven on whom I can rely except my God?" **God is the strength of my heart, and my portion for ever.** Convinced now that God would never fail him, Asaph has little trouble accepting the apparent prosperity of the wicked in the face of his own distress.

27-28. They that are far from thee shall perish. God is the source of all life, and those who stray from Him stray from the source of eternal life. We must abide in Him to live. **Thou hast destroyed all them that go a whoring from thee.** The jealous God will not permit the righteous to be alienated from Him. **But it is good for me to draw near to God.** The greater our nearness to God, the less we are affected by the attractions of sin. No longer would Asaph hesitate or vacillate. He has resolved, **I have put my trust in the Lord GOD.**

B. Fiery Trials for God's People. 74:1-23.

THEME: *The deep misery of the Jews erupts into a complaint born of faith.*

Psalm 74 depicts the pathetic condition of God's chosen nation. Jerusalem is fallen into **perpetual desolations** (vs. 3), and the enemy violates the Temple (vs. 3). The sanctuary's intricate and beautifully carved work is battered with axes and hammers (vs. 6). The destruction of the Temple is complete (vs. 7), and the nation is seen to be without a prophet (vs. 9). A foreign devil blasphemes the name of the Lord God (vs. 10). Israel is depicted in a state of utter chaos and spiritual disarray.

Scholars have advanced three possible historical events to which this psalm may refer. They are: (1) the invasion of the Egyptian Pharaoh Shishak; (2) the invasion of the Babylonian Nebuchadnezzar; or (3) the invasion of the Seleucid King Antiochus Epiphanes. Each of these possibilities raises as many questions as it answers.

What then is to be made of the inscription **A Maschil of Asaph?** Some who hold one of the latter two views above completely disregard this superscription. Others believe that indeed the psalm was composed by an Asaph, but a different person from the contemporary of David.

It must be remembered, however, that Asaph, the contemporary of David, was not only a musician and psalmist, but also

PSALM 74

O GOD, why hast thou cast *us* off for ever? *why* doth thine anger smoke against the sheep of thy pasture?
2 Remember thy congregation, *which* thou hast purchased of old; the rod of thine inheritance, *which* thou hast redeemed; this mount Zion, wherein thou hast dwelt.
3 Lift up thy feet unto the perpetual desolations; *even* all *that* the enemy hath done wickedly in the sanctuary.

4 Thine enemies roar in the midst of thy congregations; they set up their ensigns *for* signs.
5 *A man* was famous according as he had lifted up axes upon the thick trees.
6 But now they break down the carved work thereof at once with axes and hammers.
7 They have cast fire into thy sanctuary, they have defiled *by casting down* the dwelling place of thy name to the ground.
8 They said in their hearts, Let us destroy them together: they have burned up all the synagogues of God in the land.
9 We see not our signs: *there is* no more any prophet: neither *is there* among us any that knoweth how long.

10 O God, how long shall the adversary reproach? shall the enemy blaspheme thy name for ever?
11 Why withdrawest thou thy hand, even thy right hand? pluck *it* out of thy bosom.

12 For God *is* my King of old, working salvation in the midst of the earth.
13 Thou didst divide the sea by thy strength: thou brakest the heads of the dragons in the waters.
14 Thou brakest the heads of leviathan in pieces, *and* gavest him *to be*

a seer (Heb *chōzeh* cf. II Chr 29:30). Therefore, it is highly possible, and indeed likely, that this psalm is not historical at all, but rather prophetic. This view certainly relieves the interpretation of much difficulty. Perhaps Asaph is giving a full examination of the subject of future Jewish tribulation and prophetically groups together the most appalling incidents that result in the desolation of the Temple and Holy City from the time of Nebuchadnezzar to the days of Titus (A.D. 70).

74:1-3. O God, why hast thou cast us off for ever? Here the psalmist's appeal betrays the extremity of distress that Israel must endure. **Why doth thine anger smoke against the sheep of thy pasture?** Since Israel is the object of His care and the sheep of His pasture, defenseless and totally dependent upon God, Israel must have sinned a great sin in order to have made God's anger **smoke** hot and furious (cf. 18:18; 104:32; 144:5). Thus, in behalf of Israel, Asaph pleads, **Remember thy congregation, which thou hast purchased of old.** The writer bids God to look upon the blood mark that graces His own sheep and not to forget the price of His redemption for them. **The rod of thine inheritance, which thou hast redeemed** (lit., the tribe of thine inheritance). Asaph begs God to not forget His chosen people. **Lift up thy feet unto the perpetual desolations.** Would Jehovah sit by and watch His own land made a wilderness, His own city in **mount Zion** made a desolation? **The enemy hath done wickedly in the sanctuary.**

4-9. The first act of foreign oppressors, after they had captured the house of God in Jerusalem, was always to **set up their ensigns for signs.** These tokens of victory were idolatrous emblems of war set alongside God's altar as an insult to and contempt for their vanquished foe, and Jehovah their God. The day was when **A man was famous according as he had lifted up axes upon the thick trees.** Those once renowned for felling the great cedars and preparing them to build temples now contemptuously **break down the carved work thereof at once with axes and hammers.** The **carved work** (Heb *pitūchīm*) was the Temple wall (cf. I Kgs 6:29). The invaders undertook this task of desecration to show the gods' contempt for Israel's Temple and to plunder the gold with which it was overlaid (I Kgs 6:22, 32, 35).

They said in their hearts, Let us destroy them together. Consequently, this destruction began at the Temple by setting fire to the sanctuary. The Temple of Solomon was burned by Nebuchadnezzar (II Kgs 25:9; II Chr 36:19). The Temple of Herod the Great was burned in the siege of Jerusalem by Titus (A.D. 70). From Jerusalem the oppressors moved throughout Israel and **burned up all the synagogues of God in the land.** These were simply meeting places for prayer.

We see not our signs. No Urim and Thummim were visible on the High Priest's garment, and no shekinah descended from heaven, flowing through the cherubim and filling the Temple. Each time a foreign army marched into Jerusalem the question was the same: How long would God allow this to happen to His people? The answer is, **neither is there among us any that knoweth how long.**

10-11. Suddenly Asaph breaks into prayer. He asks the dual question, how long and why? **Shall the enemy blaspheme thy name for ever?** Is it possible that God has cast off His people? **Why withdrawest thou thy hand, even thy right hand?** Why does Jehovah withhold His right hand of power from expelling the oppressors?

12-17. His prayer completed, the psalmist is renewed in comfort and confidence when he remembers **God is my King of old, working salvation in the midst of the earth.** Israel's God has a history of restoring her to Himself and removing her from the clutches of her adversaries. For example, **Thou didst divide the sea by thy strength.** This is an obvious reference to Exodus 14:21 (cf. 77:16; 78:13; 106:9). **Thou brakest the heads of the**

meat to the people inhabiting the wilderness.

15 Thou didst cleave the fountain and the flood: thou driedst up mighty rivers.

16 The day *is* thine, the night also *is* thine: thou hast prepared the light and the sun.

17 Thou hast set all the borders of the earth: thou hast made summer and winter.

18 Remember this, *that* the enemy hath reproached, O LORD, and *that* the foolish people have blasphemed thy name.

19 O deliver not the soul of thy turtledove unto the multitude *of the wicked:* forget not the congregation of thy poor for ever.

20 Have respect unto the covenant: for the dark places of the earth are full of the habitations of cruelty.

21 O let not the oppressed return ashamed: let the poor and needy praise thy name.

22 Arise, O God, plead thine own cause: remember how the foolish man reproacheth thee daily.

23 Forget not the voice of thine enemies: the tumult of those that rise up against thee increaseth continually.

PSALM 75

UNTO thee, O God, do we give thanks, *unto thee* do we give thanks: for *that* thy name is near thy wondrous works declare.

2 When I shall receive the congregation I will judge uprightly.

3 The earth and all the inhabitants thereof are dissolved: I bear up the pillars of it. Se'lah.

4 I said unto the fools, Deal not foolishly: and to the wicked, Lift not up the horn:

5 Lift not up your horn on high: speak *not with* a stiff neck.

dragons in the waters. Thou brakest the heads of leviathan in pieces. The dragon (Heb *tanin*) was frequently used as a symbol of Egypt (cf. Isa 51:9; Ezk 29:3; 32:2).

Another example was **Thou didst cleave the fountain and the flood.** The word **flood** (Heb *nachal*, lit., torrent, cf. Ex 17:6; Num 20:11). This probably refers to the fountain that was released when Moses smote the rock and a perpetual stream flowed forth in the wilderness. Still another example is **thou driedst up mighty rivers.** This is a reference to the miraculous crossing of the Jordan (cf. Josh 3:13). The day and night alike are His, for **thou hast prepared the light and the sun.** Certainly, He who has arranged the seasons and the hours of daylight and darkness can arrange for the deliverance of His own people.

18-23. The psalmist calls upon God to remember that Israel has been reproached and **that the foolish people have blasphemed thy name.** The word translated **foolish** (Heb *nabal*) designates a folly that is akin to wickedness. The psalmist bids God to keep Israel as His pet **turtledove** and not to forget **the congregation of thy poor for ever.** In order to do this, Jehovah must **Have respect unto the covenant,** probably the covenant made with Abraham, Isaac, and Jacob, assuring their descendants perpetual possession of Canaan.

Thus, the psalmist concludes his prayer by begging, **Arise, O God, plead thine own cause.** He calls upon God to assert Himself, to show His power and avenge His defiant foes. **Remember how the foolish man reproacheth thee daily.** Jehovah is begged to remember that it is He that is reproached by the oppressor of Israel, and not His people. Asaph therefore calls on God to **Forget not the voice of thine enemies.** The righteous God never forgets insults of this kind; He always remembers and punishes.

C. The Sovereignty of God. 75:1-10.

THEME: *An expression of confidence in the righteousness of God the Sovereign Judge.*

Addressed to the chief musician, **Altaschith** in the title is probably a musical term. It occurs also in the titles of Psalms 57, 58, and 59. The title also ascribes this psalm to **Asaph.**

The fact that this psalm follows Psalm 74 is not unimportant. The preceding psalm concludes with the prayer, **Arise, O God, plead thine own cause . . . Forget not the voice of thine enemies . . .** (74:22-23). This psalm appears to be an answer to those challenges. It is a confident expression of the sovereign God's ability to judge uprightly and to superintend the affairs of men.

75:1. Unto thee, O God, do we give thanks. The psalmist is joyful because **thy name is near thy wondrous works declare.** Reviewing the previous deliverances of Israel by Jehovah, God causes Asaph to anticipate further deliverance and divine aid.

2-5. It is clear that the speaker of verses 3 and 4 is God, while the speaker of verse 1 and verses 6-9 is the psalmist. God may also be the speaker of verses 4-5 and 10; however, this is uncertain.

When I shall receive the congregation I will judge uprightly (lit., when I shall have reached the appointed or set time). God will judge the nations, but He will do so at His own time. At the judgment of God **The earth and all the inhabitants thereof are dissolved.** This is apparently a poetic way of saying that no one on the earth will be able to withstand the righteous judgment of God. Thus, God warns the wicked, **Deal not foolishly . . . lift not up your horn on high: speak not with a stiff neck.** The meaning here is apparently that the fool is not to flex his muscle in the face of God. To be humbled, or cast down, was often represented by the figure of breaking or cutting off the horn (see vs. 10). The phrase **a stiff neck** is one common in the Pen-

6 For promotion *cometh* neither from the east, nor from the west, nor from the south.
7 But God *is* the judge: he putteth down one, and setteth up another.
8 For in the hand of the LORD *there is* a cup, and the wine is red; it is full of mixture; and he poureth out of the same: but the dregs thereof, all the wicked of the earth shall wring *them* out, *and* drink *them*.

9 But I will declare for ever; I will sing praises to the God of Jacob.
10 All the horns of the wicked also will I cut off; *but* the horns of the righteous shall be exalted.

PSALM 76

IN Jū'dah *is* God known: his name *is* great in Israel.
2 In Sā'lem also is his tabernacle, and his dwelling place in Zion.
3 There brake he the arrows of the bow, the shield, and the sword, and the battle. Sē'lah.

tateuch (Ex 32:9; 33:3, 5; 34:9; Deut 9:6, 13; 10:16; 31:27) and expresses arrogancy, obstinance, or pride.

6-8. For promotion cometh neither from the east, nor from the west, nor from the south. The Hebrew word rendered **promotion** is from the same root used in verses 4-5, 7, and 10, in which it is translated **shall be exalted, lift** or **setteth up.** It is a very expressive and emphatic word, signifying deliverance from trouble or a lifting up when all those who encompass you have helped to put you down. In the face of those who have been lifted up by pride and strength, the psalmist is convinced that his elevation, or exaltation, comes neither from the east, nor the west, nor the south; **But God is the judge.** It is God who is sovereign and **putteth down one, and setteth up another** (cf. I Sam 2:7; Dan 2:21; 4:17).

For in the hand of the LORD there is a cup, and the wine is red. The cup of God's fury filled with blood red wine will ultimately find expression at the great battle of Armageddon (cf. Isa 51:22; Jer 25:15). It is here that Jesus Christ, the conquering God, ". . . shall rule them with a rod of iron: and he treadeth the winepress of the fierceness and wrath of Almighty God" (Rev 19:15). So complete will God's judgment be on those who walk wickedly that even **the dregs** that settle to the bottom of the cup will be ingested by them. When God's wrath is poured out on the foolish, self-willed sinner, it will be a complete and devastating punishment.

9-10. But I will declare for ever; I will sing praises to the God of Jacob. Those who live righteously will not see God's wrath, but will sing His praises. God's eternal promise to the righteous, is **All the horns of the wicked also will I cut off; but the horns of the righteous shall be exalted.** The pomp and power of mighty men are no match for the wrath of God. Jehovah, who will one day make all things right, will exalt those who have lived righteously but have been dealt with treacherously by the fools of this world. The sovereign God is still in control. "If God be for us, who can be against us?" (Rom 8:31).

D. The God of the Meek. 76:1-12.

THEME: Even the wrath of men shall praise the protection of God for Israel.

As Delitzsch notes, no psalm has a greater right to follow Psalm 75 than this one. They form a pair: Psalm 75 prepares the way for the imminent divine judgment, which Psalm 76 celebrates as having taken place.

The inscription reads, **To the chief musician on Neginoth.** The reference to Neginoth (i.e., stringed instrument), may also be noted in 4:1; 6:1; 54:1; 61:1; 67:1. The precentor is instructed to perform the song to the music of stringed instruments. It is a **psalm or song of Asaph,** or perhaps one of his descendants.

Attempts to establish the historical situation out of which this psalm arose frequently point to the Assyrian invasion under Sennacherib (701 B.C.) as is recorded in Isaiah 36-37. Most Old Testament scholars agree with this understanding (cf. Hengstenberg, Alexander, Perowne, etc.). The psalm celebrates the continued protection of God for His chosen people.

76:1-3. In Judah is God known: his name is great in Israel. In commenting on this verse, Tholuck notes, "The tribe of Judah designates the entire nation." However, if the event that occasioned this psalm is the defeat of the armies of Sennacherib, it is much more likely that Judah designates the tribes of the south, i.e., Judah and Benjamin. The ten secessionists are referred to in the second clause.

In Salem also is his tabernacle, and his dwelling place in Zion. Salem is the shortened form of Jerusalem. **There brake he the arrows of the bow, the shield, and the sword, and the**

4 Thou *art* more glorious *and* excellent than the mountains of prey.
5 The stouthearted are spoiled, they have slept their sleep: and none of the men of might have found their hands.
6 At thy rebuke, O God of Jacob, both the chariot and horse are cast into a dead sleep.

7 Thou, *even* thou, *art* to be feared: and who may stand in thy sight when once thou art angry?
8 Thou didst cause judgment to be heard from heaven; the earth feared, and was still,
9 When God arose to judgment, to save all the meek of the earth. Sē′lah.

10 Surely the wrath of man shall praise thee: the remainder of wrath shalt thou restrain.
11 Vow, and pay unto the LORD your God: let all that be round about him bring presents unto him that ought to be feared.
12 He shall cut off the spirit of princes: *he is* terrible to the kings of the earth.

PSALM 77

I CRIED unto God with my voice, *even* unto God with my voice; and he gave ear unto me.
2 In the day of my trouble I sought the Lord: my sore ran in the night, and ceased not: my soul refused to be comforted.
3 I remembered God, and was troubled: I complained, and my spirit was overwhelmed. Sē′lah.

battle. With sublime ease, the God of Israel repelled the attackers of Jerusalem and defended His habitation.

4-6. Thou art more glorious and excellent than the mountains of prey. Here the psalmist appears to address God directly. Although the invading armies are comparable to mountains in greatness, yet Jehovah, the God Of Israel, is far more glorious and excellent. **The stout-hearted are spoiled.** This begins a vivid description of the catastrophe that befell Sennacherib, or any other invader with whom this psalm may be identified. Those who came to spoil were spoiled by Jehovah. **They have slept their sleep,** i.e., when it was time for battle they were found to be asleep, even the sleep of death. **Both the chariot and horse are cast into a dead sleep.** At the mere word of God the cavalries of the oppressors were stopped.

7-9. Thou, even thou, art to be feared. Jehovah God alone should be the object of their reverence and awe. **Who may stand in thy sight when once thou art angry?** A recurring theme throughout the Bible (see 130:3), the psalmist asks who will be able to stand in the judgment of God. **Thou didst cause judgment to be heard from heaven; the earth feared, and was still, when God arose to judgment.** When God rises for judgment, all men are silenced and are subservient to His glory. **To save all the meek of the earth.** The sovereign God has a special eye toward those who cannot help themselves and are at the mercy of others. This is seen in the statement of God the Son, "Blessed are the meek: for they shall inherit the earth" (Mt 5:5).

10-12. Surely the wrath of man shall praise thee. When vengeful men breathe out threatenings against God, Jehovah simply places His trumpet to their lips and allows them to sound the clarion call to His praise. **Vow, and pay unto the LORD your God: let all that be round about him bring presents unto him that ought to be feared.** Now the people of Israel are addressed directly. During the time of their distress they would undoubtedly have made vows to God. Now that deliverance has come, they are called upon to pay those vows; and not Israel only but all those round about her who have been oppressed, should now bring their presents unto the One who is to be feared (lit., unto the Terrible One). For **he is terrible to the kings of the earth.**

E. Consolation by Recollection. 77:1-20.

THEME: A personal lament that eventuates in private confidence toward God.

It is impossible to assign a date to this psalm, even though Delitzsch has carefully traced the coincidences in expression between Habbakuk 3:10-15 and verses 16-20 of this psalm. The inscription addresses **the chief musician, to Jeduthun.** With regard to this man, we know very little. The name occurs several times in the historic books of Scripture (cf. I Chr 16:38, 41-42; 25:1, 3, 6; II Chr 5:12; 29:14; Neh 11:17). Leupold suggests that **to Jeduthun** means that the psalm is to be rendered as Jeduthun was accustomed to rendering psalms.

77:1-3. I cried unto God with my voice . . . In the day of my trouble I sought the Lord. Although this psalm, at least the first half of it, is marked by extreme sadness, nevertheless the psalmist begins rightly with a prayer. That which begins with prayer usually ends with victory. This was not simply silent prayer; but with his voice he gave utterance to God, and God **gave ear unto me.** All day long his great distress drove him to God (cf. Gen 35:3; Hab 3:16). **My sore ran in the night.** It appears this clause is better translated, "My hand was stretched out in the night," referring to his continued prayer throughout the night.

I remembered God, and was troubled. The source of great delight to a man of faith had become the object of dread to the man of sorrow. As John Owens notes, "All had once been well

4 Thou holdest mine eyes waking: I am so troubled that I cannot speak.
5 I have considered the days of old, the years of ancient times.
6 I call to remembrance my song in the night: I commune with mine own heart: and my spirit made diligent search.

7 Will the Lord cast off for ever? and will he be favourable no more?
8 Is his mercy clean gone for ever? doth *his* promise fail for evermore?
9 Hath God forgotten to be gracious? hath he in anger shut up his tender mercies? Sĕ'lah.

10 And I said, This *is* my infirmity: *but I will remember* the years of the right hand of the most High.
11 I will remember the works of the LORD: surely I will remember thy wonders of old.
12 I will meditate also of all thy work, and talk of thy doings.

13 Thy way, O God, *is* in the sanctuary: who *is* so great a God as *our* God?
14 Thou *art* the God that doest wonders: thou hast declared thy strength among the people.
15 Thou hast with *thine* arm redeemed thy people, the sons of Jacob and Joseph. Sĕ'lah.

16 The waters saw thee, O God, the waters saw thee; they were afraid: the depths also were troubled.
17 The clouds poured out water: the skies sent out a sound: thine arrows also went abroad.
18 The voice of thy thunder *was* in the heaven: the lightnings lightened the world: the earth trembled and shook.
19 Thy way *is* in the sea, and thy path in the great waters, and thy footsteps are not known.
20 Thou leddest thy people like a flock by the hand of Moses and Aaron.

between God and the psalmist, and whereas formerly his remembrance of God brought him joy, now his own sin caused that remembrance to bring discomfort." **I complained, and my spirit was overwhelmed.** The more the psalmist considered his present condition, the more he complained about it to God.

4-6. The psalmist went to bed hoping to drown his sorrows with sleep. But God would not have it be so. **Thou holdest mine eyes waking.** Sleep is the great comforter, but it forsakes the sorrowful and increases his discomfort so that **I am so troubled that I cannot speak.** Sleepless and speechless, the psalmist can but consider **the days of old, the years of ancient times.** If no comfort could be found in his present situation, the psalmist was willing to ransack his memory in order to call to mind God's doings in the past (cf. vss. 14-19). **My spirit made diligent search.** As Adam Clarke notes, the verb for **search** (Heb *chapas*) signifies such an investigation as in our phrase, to leave no stone unturned.

7-9. The psalmist now advances a series of six questions in a *reductio ad absurdum* argument. **Will the LORD cast off for ever?** God would perhaps leave His people for a time, but would He do so indefinitely? **Will he be favorable no more?** Would God's good will toward Israel never be seen again? **Is his mercy clean gone for ever?** If His chosen people do not see His love or favor, will they not at least see His mercy? **Doth his promise fail for evermore?** Would God fail to meet the conditions of His covenant with Israel? **Hath God forgotten to be gracious?** The metaphor here is taken from a spring, the mouth of which is closed so that waters can no longer run through the existing channel. **Hath he in anger shut up his tender mercies?** Does God no longer yearn for His beloved nation?

10-12. I said, This is my infirmity. The fault is not with God, but with the psalmist himself. He confesses that his unbelief is a weakness, a folly, a sin. He resolves, **Surely I will remember thy wonders of old.** Whatever else may fall into oblivion in his mind, the psalmist cannot forget the marvelous works of the Lord in days gone by. **I will meditate also of all thy work.** But more than that, he is determined to **talk of thy doings.** As Spurgeon says, "A meditative man should be a talker, otherwise he is a mental miser, a mill which grinds corn only for the miller."

13-15. Who is so great a God as our God? In Him the qualities of goodness and greatness are blended. God is great, and God is good. **Thou hast declared thy strength among the people** Not only Israel, but also Egypt, Edom, Philistia, and all other nations have seen the power of Jehovah. God is awesome in the sight of many heathen nations (cf. Ex 15:14-16). **Thou hast with thine arm redeemed thy people, the sons of Jacob and Joseph.**

16-20. The waters saw thee, O God, the waters saw thee. This expression is highly poetical because in the mind of the psalmist it is ironic that the waters can see God, but man cannot discern Him. **The clouds poured out water.** As if to join in praise for the deliverance of God's people, the elements of the lower atmosphere assisted in the overthrow of Egypt. **The skies sent out a sound.** The higher regions uttered a voice which, in light of the next verse, is obviously a reference to thunder (cf. 68:33). **Thine arrows also went abroad.** Lightning sizzles across the sky in an awesome display of the might of Jehovah (cf. 18:14; II Sam 22:15). **The earth trembled and shook.** Joining the atmosphere, the earth quaked and reverberated at the presence of the miracle-working God.

Thy way is in the sea, and thy path in the great waters. God had made a way for the Israelites to escape the treacheries of Pharaoh and his armies. In the deep secret channels of the Red Sea, God had prepared the pathway. **Thy footsteps are not known.** It is not for man to attempt to understand the way God

GIVE ear, O my people, *to* my law: incline your ears to the words of my mouth.

2 I will open my mouth in a parable: I will utter dark sayings of old:

3 Which we have heard and known, and our fathers have told us.

PSALM 78

4 We will not hide *them* from their children, shewing to the generation to come the praises of the LORD, and his strength, and his wonderful works that he hath done.

5 For he established a testimony in Jacob, and appointed a law in Israel, which he commanded our fathers, that they should make them known to their children:

6 That the generation to come might know *them, even* the children *which* should be born; *who* should arise and declare *them* to their children:

7 That they might set their hope in God, and not forget the works of God, but keep his commandments:

8 And might not be as their fathers, a stubborn and rebellious generation; a generation *that* set not their heart aright, and whose spirit was not stedfast with God.

9 The children of E'phra-im, *being* armed, *and* carrying bows, turned back in the day of battle.

10 They kept not the covenant of God, and refused to walk in his law;

11 And forgat his works, and his wonders that he had shewed them.

12 Marvellous things did he in the

leads, but simply to trust the way He leads. **Thou leddest thy people like a flock by the hand of Moses and Aaron.** From the tempests of the storm the psalmist concludes with the tenderness of the shepherd. Notice that it is God who leads His people by the hand of His servants Moses and Aaron. When we have successfully traversed the depths of despair, we will be able to look back and recognize that we have been led through by the Shepherd and Bishop of our souls (I Pet 2:25).

F. God's Hand in Israel's History. 78:1-72.

THEME: *Lessons from history that faithful Israelite parents are to teach their children.*

This is the first and the longest of the Historical Psalms. The inscription indicates that it is **A Maschil of Asaph,** and there is little reason to doubt that the man by this name who was the contemporary of David is the author (cf. I Chr 25:1; II Chr 29:30).

78:1-3. Give ear. As the psalmist calls his people to listen to the history of Israel, he begs them, **incline your ears to the words of my mouth,** i.e., bow your stiff necks and stretch forward to catch every word. **I will open my mouth in a parable.** Their history was a living allegory to the Israelites and a source of spiritual truth to all who followed, for "all these things happened unto them for examples: and they are written for our admonition . . ." (I Cor 10:11). **I will utter dark sayings of old.** These enigmas of antiquity (Heb *chîdôt*) are, literally, riddles (cf. Jud 14:12). Here, the enigmas seem to be the historical facts mentioned in the subsequent part of the psalm, which will help unravel in the minds of the Israelites the method of God's dealings with them.

4-8. As they had received from their fathers, so now the present generation would pass the history of God's working in Israel on to their children with greater understanding. **We will not hide them from their children.**

God had **established a testimony in Jacob, and appointed a law in Israel** that from generation to generation there would be oral transmission of the divine dealings with Israel. There was to be absolute continuity throughout the years in this instruction process. Adam Clarke notes that five generations appear to be mentioned: (1) **fathers;** (2) **their children;** (3) **the generation to come;** (4) and **their children;** (5) and **their children.**

Verses 6-8 present six reasons why parents are to instruct their children in the things of the Lord. They are: (1) **That the generation to come might know them,** i.e., have a personal knowledge of their ancestors' rebellion against God; (2) **and declare them to their children** for a perpetual knowledge of the same; (3) **that they might set their hope in God,** for faith cometh by hearing; (4) **and not forget the works of God,** which could not happen if they were perpetually reminded of them; (5) **but keep his commandments,** being doers of the Word and not hearers only; and (6) **and might not be as their fathers,** whose stubbornness was legendary (cf. Deut 9:27; Jud 2:19; Jer 3:17; 7:24; 9:14; 11:8; etc.).

9-11. The psalmist abruptly changes his subject from Israel at large to **The children of Ephraim** in particular. Ephraim was the leading tribe of Israel from the appointment of Joshua as Moses' successor until the establishment of Saul as king. The importance of Ephraim appears in Judges 3:27; 7:24; 8:1-2; 10:9; 12:1-6; *et al.* The children of Ephraim were **armed, and carrying bows,** but they failed in faith and courage and were defeated **in the day of battle.** The Ephraimites broke their covenant with God (cf. Deut 29:25; 31:20; I Kgs 19:10, 14; etc.) and **refused to walk in his law** (cf. Jud 2:11-13; 8:33; 10:10). Because of this, Ephraim's descendants quickly forgot God's marvelous works and wonders.

12-16. The psalmist now begins to recount some of those

sight of their fathers, in the land of Egypt, *in* the field of Zō'an.

13 He divided the sea, and caused them to pass through; and he made the waters to stand as an heap.

14 In the daytime also he led them with a cloud, and all the night with a light of fire.

15 He clave the rocks in the wilderness, and gave *them* drink as *out of* the great depths.

16 He brought streams also out of the rock, and caused waters to run down like rivers.

17 And they sinned yet more against him by provoking the most High in the wilderness.

18 And they tempted God in their heart by asking meat for their lust.

19 Yea, they spake against God; they said, Can God furnish a table in the wilderness?

20 Behold, he smote the rock, that the waters gushed out, and the streams overflowed; can he give bread also? can he provide flesh for his people?

21 Therefore the LORD heard *this*, and was wroth: so a fire was kindled against Jacob, and anger also came up against Israel;

22 Because they believed not in God, and trusted not in his salvation:

23 Though he had commanded the clouds from above, and opened the doors of heaven,

24 And had rained down manna upon them to eat, and had given them of the corn of heaven.

25 Man did eat angels' food: he sent them meat to the full.

26 He caused an east wind to blow in the heaven: and by his power he brought in the south wind.

27 He rained flesh also upon them as dust, and feathered fowls like as the sand of the sea:

28 And he let *it* fall in the midst of their camp, round about their habitations.

29 So they did eat, and were well filled: for he gave them their own desire;

30 They were not estranged from their lust. But while their meat *was* yet in their mouths,

31 The wrath of God came upon them, and slew the fattest of them, and smote down the chosen *men* of Israel.

32 For all this they sinned still, and believed not for his wondrous works.

33 Therefore their days did he consume in vanity, and their years in trouble.

34 When he slew them, then they sought him: and they returned and enquired early after God.

35 And they remembered that God

works and wonders, **Marvelous things** which God did **in the land of Egypt, in the field of Zoan.** Zoan was one of the principal capitals and royal abodes of the Pharaoh (Isa 19:11, 13; 30:4). The **field of Zoan** was a beautiful alluvial plain surrounding the city.

Among the great and marvelous works of God and wonders performed by His hand was that **He divided the sea** (Ex 14:21-22), **and caused them to pass through.** God was always leading His people, **in the daytime . . . with a cloud** and at **night with a light of fire** (Ex 13:21-22, etc.). In addition, God **clave the rocks in the wilderness, and . . . brought streams also out of the rock.** Although the primary reference is obviously to Exodus 17:6 and Numbers 20:8-11, nevertheless the rocks were typical of Christ (I Cor 10:4). He is the Great Rock upon whom the church is built and in whom our relationship with the God of Israel is based.

17-20. And they sinned yet more against him. Ironically, the more God did in behalf of Israel, the more Israel sinned in response. **They tempted God in their heart by asking meat for their lust. Tempted God** means to try His patience over and over again. **Can God furnish a table in the wilderness?** God had allowed water to gush out of the rock and bread to miraculously appear before them, but could **he provide flesh for his people?** In evil unbelief and ingratitude, like lustful animals, the people clamored for more.

21-22. Therefore the LORD heard this, and was wroth. Israel had committed the master sin. **They believed not in God, and trusted not in his salvation.** God is willing to save to the uttermost all who come to Him in faith, but the requirement of salvation is always faith. Israel had proved herself faithless before God.

23-31. Though he had commanded the clouds from above is a dependent clause that stands in relationship to **they were not estranged from their lust** (vs. 30). Each of the intervening clauses and phrases is designed to show the goodness of God in behalf of Israel and to point out, in bold relief, the result that Israel still was not **estranged from their lust.**

God **had rained down manna upon them to eat** (cf. Ex 16:13-14), which because it was like the coriander seed and was found in grain, is called **the corn of heaven** (cf. 105:40; Ex 16:4; Jn 6:6-7). **Man did eat angels' food.** These ungrateful paupers did not feast on the food of kings, but the food of angels. Such is God's grace.

God provided favorable conditions, **the south wind** blowing softly (cf. Acts 27:13); and **flesh . . . and feathered fowls** fell in the midst of Israel's camp. Not only did Israel have an abundance of food and water; but, due to the goodness of God, they had quails and an enormous number of birds divinely provided right to their doorstep. **So they did eat, and were well filled.** The loving God who owed them nothing **gave them their own desire.** Yet, satiated, they were not satisfied. As Calvin noted, "A great abundance will not extinguish the fire of a depraved appetite." **They were not estranged from their lust.** Thus, while they were still munching on the goodness of God's provision, He **slew the fattest of them, and smote down the chosen men of Israel.**

32-35. For all this they sinned still, and believed not for his wondrous works. Neither gratitude for the favors they had received (vss. 13-17), nor alarm at the punishments inflicted (vs. 31), had any effect on this stubborn and stiffnecked people. They continued to spew out the venom of their ingratitude and consequently knew the bitterness of days consumed **in vanity** and years wasted **in trouble.**

When he slew them, then they sought him (cf. Ex 32:28, 35; 33:4, 10; Num 11:33; 16:48-49; etc.). The heart that only death

was their rock, and the high God their redeemer,

36 Nevertheless they did flatter him with their mouth, and they lied unto him with their tongues.
37 For their heart was not right with him, neither were they stedfast in his covenant.

38 But he, *being* full of compassion, forgave *their* iniquity, and destroyed *them* not: yea, many a time turned he his anger away, and did not stir up all his wrath.
39 For he remembered that they *were* but flesh; a wind that passeth away, and cometh not again.

40 How oft did they provoke him in the wilderness, *and* grieve him in the desert!
41 Yea, they turned back and tempted God, and limited the Holy One of Israel.

42 They remembered not his hand, *nor* the day when he delivered them from the enemy.
43 How he had wrought his signs in Egypt, and his wonders in the field of Zŏ'an:
44 And had turned their rivers into blood; and their floods that they could not drink.
45 He sent divers sorts of flies among them, which devoured them; and frogs, which destroyed them.
46 He gave also their increase unto the caterpiller, and their labour unto the locust.
47 He destroyed their vines with hail, and their sycomore trees with frost.
48 He gave up their cattle also to the hail, and their flocks to hot thunderbolts.
49 He cast upon them the fierceness of his anger, wrath, and indignation, and trouble, by sending evil angels *among them.*

50 He made a way to his anger; he spared not their soul from death, but gave their life over to the pestilence;
51 And smote all the firstborn in Egypt; the chief of *their* strength in the tabernacles of Ham:
52 But made his own people to go forth like sheep, and guided them in the wilderness like a flock.
53 And he led them on safely, so that they feared not: but the sea overwhelmed their enemies.
54 And he brought them to the border of his sanctuary, *even to* this mountain, *which* his right hand had purchased.

can make tender is hard, indeed. Even the deepest reprobate calls for the minister on his deathbed. Suddenly, at the most dire extremity of their lives **They remembered that God was their rock, and the high God their redeemer.**

36-37. Nevertheless they did flatter him with their mouth, and they lied unto him with their tongues. All they did or said when they were alarmed by the prospective judgment of God was a mere pretense, an attempt to flatter and win the favor of the righteous God. The kings of the earth may enjoy flattery, but the King of Kings abhors it; for **their heart was not right with him.**

38-39. One might expect that God would immediately destroy ungrateful hypocrites from off the face of the earth. **But he, being full of compassion, forgave their iniquity, and destroyed them not.** Though they were full of flattery, He was full of mercy. Many times God turned His anger away from Israel; for though they were forgetful of Him, He was ever mindful of them. **They were but flesh,** weak, frail, and erring. Man is **a wind that passeth away, and cometh not again.** Man's life is but a breath, ". . . a vapor, that appeareth for a little time, and then vanisheth away" (Jas 4:14).

40-41. Both God and Israel were consistent; He was consistently merciful, and they were consistently rebellious. **How oft did they provoke him . . . and grieve him . . . they turned back and tempted God, and limited the Holy One of Israel.** It is difficult to interpret how the Israelites could limit (Heb *tawah*) or "pain" God. Perhaps they set a limit to His power in their minds only. Possibly their iniquity limited the good He could do for them. But in the only other place where the Hebrew word occurs (Ezk 9:4), it means to set a mark upon someone or to insult someone. They thought of the Holy One of Israel very much to be one such as themselves (50:21).

42-49. Beyond forgetting God's miraculous delivery of Israel from Egypt, **They remembered not his hand . . . how he had wrought his signs in Egypt.** What follows is a catalog of the works and wonders of God in the lives of the Israelites during their bondage. God **had turned their rivers into blood** (Ex 7:19-20); **He sent divers sorts of flies among them** (Ex 8:24). In addition, God sent **frogs . . . the caterpillar** (Heb *chasil*), and **. . . the locust. Their vines . . . and their sycamore trees** were also destroyed by the **fierceness of his anger.** In divine judgment God usually protects the animals from such destruction, but in the case of the Egyptians He withdrew those safeguards and **gave up their cattle also to the hail, and their flocks to hot thunderbolts.** With the trees and vines destroyed and the cattle and sheep dead, famine was inevitable for Egypt.

Yet, the final blow of God was the heaviest, His final arrow the sharpest. His **anger, wrath, and indignation, and trouble** are all seen to their greatest degree when the divinely-dispatched **evil angels** swooped down among the Egyptians that Passover night and slew the **first-born.** This plague, and this one alone, resulted in the release of the Jews.

50-55. Continuing to describe God's activity in behalf of Israel, the psalmist says, **He made a way to his anger . . . and smote all the first-born in Egypt.** No exceptions were made; Pharaoh lost his first-born too. **The chief of their strength in the tabernacles of Ham.** This is a restatement of the previous clause, undoubtedly for emphasis. In great contrast to the slaughter and pestilence of the Egyptians, God **made his own people to go forth like sheep.** The nation Egypt was individually slain; the nation of Israel was collectively saved. As a flock of sheep, they were led from bondage safely through the wilderness while **the sea overwhelmed their enemies.**

Once the wilderness journey was completed, God **brought them to the border of his sanctuary,** an apparent reference to

55 He cast out the heathen also before them, and divided them an inheritance by line, and made the tribes of Israel to dwell in their tents.

56 Yet they tempted and provoked the most high God, and kept not his testimonies:
57 But turned back, and dealt unfaithfully like their fathers: they were turned aside like a deceitful bow.
58 For they provoked him to anger with their high places, and moved him to jealousy with their graven images.
59 When God heard *this*, he was wroth, and greatly abhorred Israel:
60 So that he forsook the tabernacle of Shī′lōh, the tent *which* he placed among men;
61 And delivered his strength into captivity, and his glory into the enemy's hand.
62 He gave his people over also unto the sword; and was wroth with his inheritance.
63 The fire consumed their young men; and their maidens were not given to marriage.
64 Their priests fell by the sword; and their widows made no lamentation.
65 Then the LORD awaked as one out of sleep, *and* like a mighty man that shouteth by reason of wine.
66 And he smote his enemies in the hinder parts: he put them to a perpetual reproach.
67 Moreover he refused the tabernacle of Joseph, and chose not the tribe of E′phra-im:
68 But chose the tribe of Jū′dah, the mount Zion which he loved.
69 And he built his sanctuary like high *palaces*, like the earth which he hath established for ever.
70 He chose David also his servant, and took him from the sheepfolds:
71 From following the ewes great with young he brought him to feed Jacob his people, and Israel his inheritance.
72 So he fed them according to the integrity of his heart; and guided them by the skilfulness of his hands.

the Holy Land (Ex 15:17) and the River Jordan, its eastern boundary. But more than this, God brought the second generation of Israelites **even to this mountain**, Mount Zion, which would become the capital of the Promised Land. In addition, **He cast out the heathen also before them** (cf. 44:2; Ex 34:24; Deut 7:1; I Kgs 21:26).

In a final example of God's grace to Israel, the psalmist notes that God **divided them an inheritance by line,** that is divided the land to the tribes by lot and measure as He had determined. As an added display of His grace, God **made the tribes of Israel to dwell in their tents,** i.e., in the houses of the heathen.

56-58. Yet they tempted and provoked the most high God. They **turned back . . '. they were turned aside like a deceitful bow.** The Israelites are here described as being unfaithful to God; and they soon recoiled into their natural state as a bow recoils and returns to the "C" curvature when tension is removed from it. The people had provoked God to jealousy **with their high places,** and . . . **their graven images.**

59-64. When God heard this, he was wroth, and greatly abhorred Israel. From this point to the end of the psalm, God's reaction to Israel's rebellion is recorded. Israel becomes greatly abhorred by the God who chose them, blessed them, and made everlasting promises to them. **He forsook the tabernacle of Shiloh.** The tabernacle of the congregation was first erected under Joshua (Josh 18) at Shiloh, a city of Ephraim. Here the sanctuary stayed throughout the period of the judges (Jud 18:31; I Sam 1:3, 24). God **forsook** this tabernacle when the ark of the covenant fell into the hands of the Philistines, Israel's hated enemy. **The fire consumed their young men,** perhaps a literal reference to Nadab and Abihu (Lev 10:1-2). **Their priests fell by the sword,** undoubtedly a reference to Hophni and Phinehas (I Sam 4:11).

65-66. Then the LORD awaked as one out of sleep. God had been justly inactive while Israel was being punished, but He **awaked** to exert His almighty power once again, defeating Israel's foes (cf. 7:6; 35:23; 73:20). **He smote his enemies in the hinder parts.** This may specifically be a reference to I Samuel 5:6-12.

67-69. Again, the narrative of God's dealings with Israel is brought into sharp focus with His dealings with Ephraim. God had honored Ephraim; but because of the sins of Israel, God **chose the tribe of Judah, the mount Zion which he loved.** Instead of the hills of Ephraim, Mount Zion became the beloved place of God (87:2). It was here that God **built his sanctuary like high palaces** (lit., like the heights), an apparent reference to the heights of heaven, (cf. Job 11:8; 22:12).

70-72. He chose David also his servant (cf. I Sam 16:1, 12). It was by the foreknowledge and determinate counsel of God that He **took him from the sheepfolds** (cf. I Sam 16:11, 19; II Sam 7:8). This rags-to-riches story is God's, not David's. God took the young David from feeding the **ewes great with young . . . to feed Jacob his people, and Israel his inheritance. So he fed them according to the integrity of his heart.** In general, David performed his task of governing Israel faithfully. He was upright before God; and, although on occasion he faltered and fell into sin, nevertheless he was unfeigned in his sincerity and allegiance to God. As for the people of God's choosing, David **guided them by the skillfulness of his hands.**

Psalm 78 is like a long voyage over a stormy sea. At best, the history of Israel is a checkered one. But the psalmist has intended the last stanza of this lengthy psalm to show that through all the chastenings and rebellions of Israel, God's plan has not been deterred nor altered. God will establish a kingdom over which Jesus Christ, the Prince of the house of David, will rule. God has not cast away His people Israel (cf. Rom 11).

G. A Psalm of Lament. 79:1-13.

THEME: *A lament for the destruction of Jerusalem and a call for righteous retribution.*

This psalm treats times of invasion and oppression. Asaph was a patriot who frequently found himself rehearsing the history of his nation and calling for God to restore the integrity of His divine name by rendering a reproach on His enemies.

Most commentators are agreed that this psalm bears a close relation to Psalm 74. If the author of these two psalms is the great Asaph, he is then speaking prophetically of Jerusalem's destruction. If he is one of Asaph's descendants, he may be speaking of its destruction historically.

Yet, we may possibly take the liberty to suggest that the similarities between Psalm 74 and Psalm 79 are by design, and are not coincidental. If the great contemporary of David wrote Psalm 74 and was speaking prophetically of Jerusalem's future destruction, Psalm 79 may intentionally parallel Psalm 74, even if it were written by one of Asaph's descendants whose design it was to record the destruction of Jerusalem and show with what great accuracy his ancestor wrote.

79:1-4. O God, the heathen are come into thine inheritance. It is a cry of utter amazement and horror that strangers have been allowed to violate the territorial integrity of the land of Israel. **Thy holy temple have they defiled.** Not only have the heathen entered the land, but they have profaned the sanctuary of God and have arrogantly defiled the Temple by breaking into it, seizing its treasures and ornaments (Jer 52:17-23), and, finally, setting fire to it (Jer 52:13). **They have laid Jerusalem on heaps.** This was certainly not done either by Shishak or by Antiochus Epiphanes, but was done, as prophesied (Jer 9:11; 26:18; Mic 3:12), by the Babylonians.

The dead bodies of thy servants have they given to be meat unto the fowls. So ruthless were the invaders that they cared not at all to bury those whom they had destroyed. Their bodies became food for the fowls, and **the flesh of thy saints** became prey for hyenas and jackals. Those who remained alive were carried into captivity and became **a reproach to our neighbors, a scorn and derision.**

5-8. The eternal cry of those who have been righteous, yet are afflicted, is, **How long, LORD? Wilt thou be angry for ever?** (cf. 6:3; 90:13; Rev 6:10). The cry of those who pray to God in sincerity is that He will pour out His wrath upon those **kingdoms that have not called upon thy name.** Their prayer is for holy vengeance on those only who had refused to know the Lord God, not those who had no occasion to know Him. The heart of their prayer is seen in the petition, **Let thy tender mercies speedily prevent us; for we are brought very low.** The prayer is that the mercy of God will come to them speedily because their numbers are greatly depleted (lit., we are greatly thinned).

9-12. The psalmist now masterfully pleads for God to do three things in behalf of his people: (1) **Help us;** (2) **deliver us;** and (3) **purge away our sins.** He recognizes the sin of his people and confesses it as such. His concern is that the name of God would be blasphemed among the heathen if Jehovah did not rescue His own (cf. 23:3; 25:11; 34:3; Ezk 36:22). **Where is their God?** is a legitimate question for the heathen to ask if God does not avenge **the blood of thy servants which is shed.** When the captive Israelites could not sing and did not dare shout, they prayed, **Let the sighing of the prisoner come before thee.** The prayer of the sighing prisoners was that God would punish those who had punished His people seven times as much as they had done to Israel.

PSALM 79

O GOD, the heathen are come into thine inheritance; thy holy temple have they defiled; they have laid Jerusalem on heaps.

2 The dead bodies of thy servants have they given *to be* meat unto the fowls of the heaven, the flesh of thy saints unto the beasts of the earth.

3 Their blood have they shed like water round about Jerusalem; and *there was* none to bury *them*.

4 We are become a reproach to our neighbours, a scorn and derision to them that are round about us.

5 How long, LORD? wilt thou be angry for ever? shall thy jealousy burn like fire?

6 Pour out thy wrath upon the heathen that have not known thee, and upon the kingdoms that have not called upon thy name.

7 For they have devoured Jacob, and laid waste his dwelling place.

8 O remember not against us former iniquities: let thy tender mercies speedily prevent us: for we are brought very low.

9 Help us, O God of our salvation, for the glory of thy name: and deliver us, and purge away our sins, for thy name's sake.

10 Wherefore should the heathen say, Where *is* their God? let him be known among the heathen in our sight *by* the revenging of the blood of thy servants *which is* shed.

11 Let the sighing of the prisoner come before thee; according to the greatness of thy power preserve thou those that are appointed to die;

12 And render unto our neighbours sevenfold into their bosom their reproach, wherewith they have reproached thee, O Lord.

13 So we thy people and sheep of thy pasture will give thee thanks for ever: we will shew forth thy praise to all generations.

13. So we thy people and sheep of thy pasture will give thee thanks for ever. The punishment of the heathen who had defiled, devoured, and destroyed the inheritance of God would be the subject of continued thankfulness. The captives would resolve **We will show forth thy praise to all generations.**

H. A Psalm of the Vine. 80:1-19.

THEME: A prayer for the national restoration of Israel, God's vine.

This is the fourth time we have encountered a song **upon Shoshannim,** or the lilies. Previously, we have seen this designation in Psalms 45, 60, and 69. Here, the word occurs in conjunction with **eduth,** which signifies testimony, as was the case in Psalm 60.

The author of the psalm is Asaph and again may either be the contemporary of David, in which case he is speaking prophetically, or more probably one of Asaph's school or descendants. If this be the case, it appears that this psalm was written after the deportation of the northern tribes to Assyria by an Asaphite of the southern kingdom.

PSALM 80

GIVE ear, O Shepherd of Israel, thou that leadest Joseph like a flock; thou that dwellest *between* the cherubims, shine forth.

2 Before Ē′phra-im and Benjamin and Ma-năs′seh stir up thy strength, and come *and* save us.

80:1-2. Give ear, O Shepherd of Israel. The title **Shepherd of Israel** is a new one; but, given the present metaphor, it is by far the best one available. **Thou that leadest Joseph like a flock.** This term may refer to the ten tribes of which Joseph's sons, Manasseh and Ephraim, were the recognized leaders. **Thou that dwellest between the cherubim.** A particular reference to the God of Israel; Jehovah was the only God who dwelt upon the mercy seat between the cherubim. And now for his first petition: **Shine forth.** "Stretch forth thine hand for our assistance, that the mouth of them that speak iniquities may be shut"—Savanarola. **Ephraim and Benjamin and Manasseh** were the descendants of Jacob's beloved Rachel; and as tribes, they marched together in the wilderness following immediately behind the ark of the covenant (Num 2:17-24; 10:21-24). **Come and save us** is a recognition that salvation comes only with the presence of the Lord.

3 Turn us again, O God, and cause thy face to shine; and we shall be saved.

3. Turn us again, O God. The first of three such refrains, the psalmist does not pray, Turn our captivity, but **Turn us.** The Israelites do not need a new turn of circumstances, but a new turn of character. **Cause thy face to shine** is a way of praying for God to be favorable to us, to smile on us.

4 O LORD God of hosts, how long wilt thou be angry against the prayer of thy people?

5 Thou feedest them with the bread of tears; and givest them tears to drink in great measure.

6 Thou makest us a strife unto our neighbours: and our enemies laugh among themselves.

4-6. As is frequently seen in the Psalms, here is another **how long** appeal. **How long wilt thou be angry against the prayer of thy people?** (lit., How long wilt thou smoke?, cf. 74:1). In spite of the smoking incense of their prayers, how long would the smoke of God's wrath descend upon them? In their misery the Jews have had **bread of tears** to eat and **tears to drink in great measure** (Heb *shalish*), from the Hebrew word that means a third part of an ephah (cf. Isa 40:12), approximately four times as large as the usual drinking cup. **Our enemies laugh among themselves.** The always jealous Edom and Moab rejoiced at Israel's troubles and found malicious mirth in her miseries.

7 Turn us again, O God of hosts, and cause thy face to shine; and we shall be saved.

7. Turn us again, O God of hosts. Here, the refrain occurs for the second time, but with the variation **O God of hosts,** instead of **O God.** The more we approach the Lord in prayer, the more we will be impressed with the greatness of His person. **Cause thy face to shine.**

8 Thou hast brought a vine out of Egypt: thou hast cast out the heathen, and planted it.

9 Thou preparedst *room* before it, and didst cause it to take deep root, and it filled the land.

10 The hills were covered with the shadow of it, and the boughs thereof *were like* the goodly cedars.

8-11. From this verse to the end, the psalmist uses the metaphor of a vine for Israel. Everything said to happen to the vine has happened to Israel in her history. **Thou hast brought a vine out of Egypt: thou hast cast out the heathen.** Though small in appearance and frail in beginning, yet the vine of Israel was the chosen of the Lord; and once He **planted it,** He **didst cause it to take deep root, and it filled the land.** Not only the fertile valleys, but **The hills were covered** with its boughs described in their strength as like **the goodly cedars.** The

11 She sent out her boughs unto the sea, and her branches unto the river.

ever-increasing tentacles of the vine stretched **unto the sea,** a reference to the Mediterranean, and **unto the river,** the Euphrates.

In the golden age of Israel under David and Solomon, the vine had reached gigantic proportions; and the fruit of the vine was enjoyed throughout the Middle East. But history has shown that the vine's strength would soon be cut off.

12 Why hast thou *then* broken down her hedges, so that all they which pass by the way do pluck her?
13 The boar out of the wood doth waste it, and the wild beast of the field doth devour it.

12-13. Why hast thou then broken down her hedges, so that all they which pass by the way do pluck her? In the Ancient Near East vineyards were always enclosed with stone fences (cf. Isa 5:5). The psalmist wonders why God has broken down those fences so that any passerby has the opportunity to pluck her grapes, i.e., ravage and plunder her (cf. 89:40-41). **The boar out of the wood doth waste it.** About the size of and resembling a donkey, a wild boar is swift and possesses razor-like tusks sufficient to rip a dog asunder. For the northern kingdom the wild boar may refer to Tiglath-Pileser (II Kgs 15:19), or Assyrian power in general.

14 Return, we beseech thee, O God of hosts: look down from heaven, and behold, and visit this vine;

14. Return, we beseech thee, O God of hosts. In this modified refrain the psalmist calls upon God not to close His eyes to Israel's plight, but to **look down from heaven, and behold, and visit this vine.**

15 And the vineyard which thy right hand hath planted, and the branch *that* thou madest strong for thyself.
16 *It is* burned with fire, *it is* cut down: they perish at the rebuke of thy countenance.

15-16. This Asaphite prayer was necessary because the vineyard that God had planted in the Promised Land was **burned with fire** and **cut down.** Like a dry and lifeless tinderbox forest, Israel had been burned and hacked away by the cruel ax of plunderous invaders. **They perish at the rebuke of thy countenance.** Here the metaphor is disbanded.

17 Let thy hand be upon the man of thy right hand, upon the son of man *whom* thou madest strong for thyself.
18 So will not we go back from thee: quicken us, and we will call upon thy name.

17-18. With God's favor withdrawn from them because of Israel's sin, destruction would be inevitable. Therefore, the psalmist prays **Let thy hand be upon the man of thy right hand, upon the son of man.** Although the express intent of the psalmist may be for God to restore Ephraim to a position of leadership among the tribes, nevertheless one cannot escape the conclusion that ultimately the **man of thy right hand** for whom the psalmist prays is none other than the Messiah, the **son of man,** the Lord Jesus Christ. Jesus Christ will one day sit upon David's throne and rule his kingdom and the world from the capital city of Israel—Jerusalem (Zech 2:12; 14:1-4, 16, 17).

Quicken us, and we will call upon thy name. As the Lord Jesus is life to the believer today, so, too, as Messiah of Israel, He will bring life to the now spiritually dead people of God. He will make them alive, and in turn they will call upon Him for salvation (Rom 9:11; 11:26). The order is always God's quickening (Eph 2:1) and man's response (Rom 10:13).

19 Turn us again, O LORD God of hosts, cause thy face to shine; and we shall be saved.

19. Turn us again, O LORD God of hosts. The psalm is closed by a third refrain, one in which there is yet another advance in the psalmist's relationship with His God. First, there was **Turn us again, O God** (vs. 3); then **Turn us again, O God of hosts** (vs. 7); now, in the most perfect form, **Turn us again, O LORD God of hosts** where the incommunicable name of Jehovah, the great "I AM" (cf. Ex 3:14) is introduced. As the psalmist's prayer progressed, so did his faith and increasing sensitivity to his personal relationship with God. Thus, he can confidently conclude his prayer, **cause thy face to shine, and we shall be saved.**

I. A Psalm of Missed Blessings. 81:1-16.

THEME: *A plea for loyalty and fidelity in view of all that God has done for His people.*

The inscription **To the chief musician upon Gittith. A psalm of Asaph** is difficult to interpret. **Gittith** could mean either after the Gathian manner, or to be sung according to the tune that was used when the winepress (Heb *gat*) was trodden. We may agree with Alexander who says, "In the absence of any proof to the contrary, the Asaph of this title must be assumed to be the

PSALM 81

SING aloud unto God our strength: make a joyful noise unto the God of Jacob.

2 Take a psalm, and bring hither the timbrel, the pleasant harp with the psaltery.

3 Blow up the trumpet in the new moon, in the time appointed, on our solemn feast day.

4 For this *was* a statute for Israel, *and* a law of the God of Jacob.

5 This he ordained in Joseph *for* a testimony, when he went out through the land of Egypt: *where* I heard a language *that* I understood not.

6 I removed his shoulder from the burden: his hands were delivered from the pots.

7 Thou calledst in trouble, and I delivered thee; I answered thee in the secret place of thunder: I proved thee at the waters of Měr'i-bah. Sē'lah.

8 Hear, O my people, and I will testify unto thee: O Israel, if thou wilt hearken unto me;

9 There shall no strange god be in thee; neither shalt thou worship any strange god.

10 I *am* the LORD thy God, which brought thee out of the land of Egypt: open thy mouth wide, and I will fill it.

11 But my people would not hearken to my voice; and Israel would none of me.

12 So I gave them up unto their own hearts' lust: *and* they walked in their own counsels.

13 Oh that my people had hearkened unto me, *and* Israel had walked in my ways!

14 I should soon have subdued their enemies, and turned my hand against their adversaries.

15 The haters of the LORD should have submitted themselves unto him:

contemporary of David." Hengstenberg, Tholuck, and others agree. Since the northern kingdom may be addressed in verse 5, it appears to be pre-exilic in construction. In fact, the whole tenure of the psalm points to those problems which vexed Israel long before the captivity.

81:1-3. Sing aloud unto God. The psalmist calls the people to sing aloud; for the heartiest praise is due the Lord, and loud singing is usually indicative of earnestness and sincerity (cf. 33:3; 98:4; II Chr 20:19; Neh 12:42; etc.). **Make a joyful noise unto the God of Jacob.**

The **timbrel** (Heb *tōp*) is what we would today call a tambourine; it was played mainly at the hands of women. It is mentioned three times in the Psalms (81:2; 149:3; and 150:4). **The psaltery** (Heb *nebel*) is translated in the Genevan Version as viol, the ancient six-stringed guitar. The loudness of the timbrel and the body of the psaltery would be joined by the sweetness of **the pleasant harp** and the **trumpet** on the **solemn feast day,** meaning either the Passover, Feast of Tabernacles, or Feast of Trumpets.

4-5. This he ordained in Joseph for a testimony. The nation is called Joseph's here probably because in Egypt it would have been known as Joseph's family. The mention of Joseph and the passing out **through the land of Egypt** strongly hints that this psalm may refer to the Passover.

Suddenly, there is an abrupt change. **Where I heard a language that I understood not.** It can scarcely be held that these words belong to the context of verse 5. Surely, we are required to understand them as the voice of the Lord. We may translate them, "The discourse of one whom I had not known (i.e., of God) did I hear."

6-7. Jehovah begins by reminding Israel of His favors toward them while they were in captivity. **I removed his shoulder from the burden** is an obvious reference to their freedom from slavery. **His hands were delivered from the pots,** which may be the bricklayer's baskets, hanging one at each end of a yoke laid across Jewish shoulders. When the Israelites called upon God, He delivered them and answered them **in the secret place of thunder,** which appears to refer to the pillar of the cloud (cf. Ex 14:24). Once again, He proved Himself **at the waters of Meribah** (cf. Ex 17:7).

8-10. If Israel will now only **hearken unto me,** God will teach her things she yet needs to know. **There shall no strange god be in thee.** But more than that, **neither shalt thou worship any strange god.** Having the idol in the home could only lead to the eventual worship of the idol. Therefore, God rebukes both possession and prostration before any strange god (cf. Ex 20:3; Deut 5:7). **Open thy mouth wide, and I will fill it.** Over and over again God has proven Himself capable of meeting our greatest needs.

11-12. Because the people of Israel, God's chosen people, would not hearken unto His voice, Jehovah regretfully indicates **So I gave them up unto their own hearts' lust: and they walked in their own counsels.** God's spirit will not always strive with men (Gen 6:3). If we persist in our evil courses, after a time God will withdraw from us His restraining grace (cf. Rom 1:24, 26, 28). He who would persist in sin is a fool, for no one knows that he has crossed the boundary of God's grace until it is too late.

13-16. I should soon have subdued their enemies, and turned my hand against their adversaries. Israel was still surrounded by enemies anxious for their destruction; but God, if He pleased, could easily subdue and brush them away in a moment. If only Israel would repent and return to Him, it would please Him to do so. **The haters of the LORD should have submitted themselves unto him.** It is the awesome power of the Almighty God that keeps the fiercest opponents of God's

but their time should have endured for ever.

16 He should have fed them also with the finest of the wheat: and with honey out of the rock should I have satisfied thee.

people in check. The closer we live to Him, the more subdued those who hate Him become.

He should have fed them also with the finest of the wheat (lit., with the fat of the wheat, 147:14; Deut 32:14). Had they remained true to their God, famine would have been unknown to Israel. **And with honey out of the rock should I have satisfied thee.** The expression **honey out of the rock,** is taken from Deuteronomy 32:13. **Wheat** and **honey** are metaphors to show the temporal and spiritual blessings that God gives to those who love Him. As John Gill notes, "The rock spiritually and mystically designs Christ, the rock of salvation, I Corinthians 10:4." How important it is that we be faithful to God and sing and hearken unto Him. It is then, and only then, that we shall be satisfied by Him.

J. The Judgment of Unjust Judges. 82:1-8.

THEME: *A denunciation of the corrupt judges in Israel who oppress the people.*

In this psalm Asaph deviates from the usual pattern of psalms and hymns that are direct expressions of praise to God. He saw much bribery and corruption in the government of his day; and, while David punished it with the sword, he lashed out against it with his pen.

Thus, unlike Psalm 50, in which Asaph depicts God judging His people, in this psalm he shows God judging His judges. It is a solemn rebuke, in prophetic language, to those who are pledged to uphold the Mosaic law by their office, but yet have trampled upon it for their own selfish ends. Instead of living righteously, these unjust judges had shown favor to wicked persons who were powerful and wealthy. Asaph appeals to them to discharge their duties faithfully and uprightly and to cease their prejudicial treatment of the poor, the fatherless, and the defenseless.

PSALM 82

GOD standeth in the congregation of the mighty; he judgeth among the gods.

82:1. God standeth in the congregation of the mighty; he judgeth among the gods. The divine Onlooker in every court-room is Almighty God. He views the judgments of the world's judges and knows the thoughts and intents of their hearts. Since he stands in the congregation of the mighty (lit., in the congregation of God), i.e., the Divine assembly (cf. Job 1:6; 2:1; Isa 6:1-2; etc.), it behooves each judge to conduct himself uprightly and righteously before that congregation.

He judgeth among the gods. This expression has led some to understand that this psalm is actually addressed to the minor gods of a pagan pantheon (see Leupold). Yet, in the highly poetic language of the Psalms, it is natural for civil governors, especially those entrusted with the administration of justice, to be likened to **gods** over men.

2 How long will ye judge unjustly, and accept the persons of the wicked? Sē'lah.

2. How long will ye judge unjustly, and accept the persons of the wicked? The unjust judges had judged unjustly. They had respected the wicked and had no respect for the righteous. Thus, the familiar **How long. . . ?** cry of the psalmist.

3 Defend the poor and fatherless: do justice to the afflicted and needy.
4 Deliver the poor and needy: rid *them* out of the hand of the wicked.

3-4. Defend the poor and fatherless . . . the afflicted and needy. Here the psalmist's plea appears to be that the judges be less interested in the bribes of wealthy men and more interested in justice for the common man. The psalmist prays that God will rescue the poor and needy **out of the hand of the wicked** judges.

5 They know not, neither will they understand; they walk on in darkness: all the foundations of the earth are out of course.

5. They know not, neither will they understand. What a deplorable situation a nation finds itself in when its justices are devoid of moral judgment. Asaph could see just such a lack of understanding among the judges of his day; and he could only describe the situation thus: **All the foundations of the earth are out of course.** When the fundamental basis of society, the very principles of morality, are not followed by the judges, the very fabric of the nation is shaken.

6 I have said, Ye *are* gods; and all of you *are* children of the most High.

6-7. Ye are gods . . . But ye shall die like men (cf. Ex 21:6; 22:8-9; Deut 1:17; II Chr 19:6). But even though these men

7 But ye shall die like men, and fall like one of the princes.

have held lofty positions, they must not forget that great men die, just as common men do. Even God's representatives in judgment must one day die and face judgment themselves (Heb 9:27). **And fall like one of the princes.** The princes are the tyrants of the land, and tyrants seldom go to their graves in peace. Asaph warned that if a judge chooses to live as a tyrant, he must expect to die as a tyrant.

8 Arise, O God, judge the earth: for thou shalt inherit all nations.

8. Arise, O God, judge the earth. The words of God (vss. 2-7) now being ended, the psalmist calls upon Him at once to proceed to the judgment of unjust judges. The call to arise is a metaphor taken from the common gesture of judges who sit as they hear the case and arise to pronounce a sentence.

For thou shalt inherit all nations. All who are poor and needy, all who are afflicted and fatherless, all who are downtrodden and have received unjust justice should take heart: your day of justice is coming. The Messiah, the true God, the Son of the Most High (Jn 10:34) to whom God has committed all judgment, will one day take a hand personally in this misgoverned world and be its true Judge.

K. Encircled by Enemies. 83:1-18.

THEME: A plea to God for protection from those all around.

The inscription indicates that this is **A song or psalm of Asaph.** When these two words (Heb *shĭr, mizmōr*) occur together, the meaning appears to be a lyric poem that is designed to be sung.

We cannot be absolutely certain about the historical situation for which this psalm was composed. The most likely time period into which it fits is that of Jehoshaphat. This is the view of Tholuck, Hengstenberg, Alexander, Clarke, Delitzsch, Kay, and a host of others; for there are striking coincidences between the record of II Chronicles 20:1-25 and this psalm. It is highly likely that Psalm 83 was written by one of the Asaphites, the sons of Asaph, a Levite named Jahaziel of the days of Jehoshaphat (cf. II Chr 20:14).

PSALM 83

KEEP not thou silence, O God: hold not thy peace, and be not still, O God.

83:1. Keep not thou silence, O God. The most deafening silence is divine silence in the midst of human clamor. Here the psalmist appeals to El, the Mighty One, who is entreated to act and speak because the nation Israel is in great jeopardy.

2 For, lo, thine enemies make a tumult: and they that hate thee have lifted up the head.
3 They have taken crafty counsel against thy people, and consulted against thy hidden ones.
4 They have said, Come, and let us cut them off from *being* a nation; that the name of Israel may be no more in remembrance.

2-4. Thine enemies make a tumult. The enemies of Israel are always the enemies of God. They are now making a roaring like the roaring of the sea (cf. 46:3; Isa 17:12). **They have taken crafty counsel against thy people.** They formed a treacherous confederation against God's chosen people. **Come, and let us cut them off from being a nation** was the common objective of Israel's enemies (cf. 138:7; II Kgs 24:2; II Chr 20:11; I Macc 3:35; 5:2). Their ultimate objective was **that the name of Israel may be no more in remembrance** (cf. 34:16; 109:13; Ex 17:14; Deut 32:26).

5 For they have consulted together with one consent: they are confederate against thee:
6 The tabernacles of Edom, and the Ĭsh′ma-el-ītes; of Moab, and the Hă′-gar-ēnes;
7 Gē′bal, and Ammon, and Ăm′a-lĕk; the Philistines with the inhabitants of Tyre;
8 Assur also is joined with them: they have holpen the children of Lot. Sē′lah.

5-8. The confederacy consisted of **Edom,** among the bitterest of Israel's enemies. **The Ishmaelites,** seizing this opportunity to continue the old grudge between the child of the bondwoman and the son of a freewoman, **Moab,** born of incest and a persistent adversary of Israel (Num 22:6; Jud 3:12-30; I Sam 14:47; II Kgs 1:1; 3:4-27), **and the Hagarenes,** mentioned only here and in I Chronicles 5:10, 19-20, probably a branch of the Ishmaelites named after Hagar, Ishmael's mother (Gen 25:12).

Other enemies in the confederacy included: **Gebal,** south of the Dead Sea toward Petra, or the Phoenician city in the region of Tyre and Sidon mentioned in Ezekiel 27:9 and alluded to in Joshua 13:5 and I Kings 5:18; **Ammon,** the perpetual enemy of the Jewish people; **Amalek,** the grandson of Esau and the son of Eliphaz by a concubine, Timna (Gen 36:12); **the Philistines,** remembered in infamy in Israel; **with the inhabitants of Tyre** friendly in early times (II Sam 5:11; I Kgs 5:1-18) but hostile in the later history of Israel rejoicing at the destruction of Jerusalem (Ezk 26:2); and **Assur**, at this time a petty nation but destined to become the great Assyrian Empire.

They have helped the children of Lot. Each of these nations has joined the confederacy of which the principal powers were the children of Lot, i.e., the Moabites and Ammonites (cf. Gen 19:37-38; Deut 2:9, 19). The enemies of Israel surrounded the Promised Land. Although there may be no particular historical occasion in which this was the case, nonetheless it indicates that the Lord's people were troubled on every side (cf. II Cor 4:8).

9 Do unto them as *unto* the Mĭd'ĭ-an-ītes; as *to* Sĭs'e-ra, as *to* Jā'bin, at the brook of Kī'son:

10 *Which* perished at Ĕn-dôr: they became *as* dung for the earth.

11 Make their nobles like Ō'reb, and like Zē'eb: yea, all their princes as Zē'-bah, and as Zăl-mŭn'na:

12 Who said, Let us take to ourselves the houses of God in possession.

9-12. Appealing to the precedent of past deliverances, the psalmist prays, **Do unto them as unto the Midianites,** probably an allusion to the days of Gideon (cf. Jud 7:19-25; 8:1-7), **as to Sisera, as to Jaban, at the brook of Kison,** where God raised a tiny brook into a raging sea and swept away Israel's enemies in a sudden torrent. **Make their nobles like Oreb . . . Zeeb . . . Zebah . . . Zalmunna.** Oreb and Zeeb were the ringleaders of the Midianites and were slain at a rock and a winepress by the Ephraimites (Jud 7:25). **Zebah** and **Zalmunna** were the kings of Midian who were captured and slain by Gideon himself (Jud 8:21). They fell by the hands of God when they attempted to rob God.

13 O my God, make them like a wheel; as the stubble before the wind.

14 As the fire burneth a wood, and as the flame setteth the mountains on fire;

15 So persecute them with thy tempest, and make them afraid with thy storm.

16 Fill their faces with shame; that they may seek thy name, O LORD.

17 Let them be confounded and troubled for ever; yea, let them be put to shame, and perish;

18 That *men* may know that thou, whose name alone *is* JE-HŌ'VAH, *art* the most high over all the earth.

13-15. Make them like a wheel (cf. Isa 17:13). The psalmist prays that the confederation will be driven away and scattered **as the stubble before the wind;** as mountains are burned with fire and forests destroyed, **So persecute them with thy tempest.**

16-18. Fill their faces with shame . . . Let them be confounded and troubled for ever. It is the psalmist's desire that this confederation never again seek the destruction of Jehovah's people or Israel's God. Like Hezekiah (Isa 37:20), the great desire of the psalmist in the defeat of Israel's enemies is **that men may know that thou, whose name alone is JEHOVAH, art the Most High over all the earth.** No greater delight can come to the heart of God's oppressed people than to see their oppressors come to grips with the God whose name is Jehovah **that they may seek thy name, O LORD** (vs. 16).

L. The Pearl of Psalms. 84:1-12.

THEME: An eloquent expression of the love of God's servant for God's sanctuary.

The character of this psalm is very much akin to that of Psalms 42 and 43. Although the expression, **A psalm for the sons of Korah,** may indicate the authorship of the psalm; nevertheless, many believe that David is actually the author. Spurgeon says that it exhales of "a Davidic perfume." Calvin notes, "in all probability David was its author." Luther also speaks of David as the author of this psalm, and the Syriac version of the Psalms ascribes it to him.

PSALM 84

HOW amiable *are* thy tabernacles, O LORD of hosts!

2 My soul longeth, yea, even fainteth for the courts of the LORD: my heart and my flesh crieth out for the living God.

3 Yea, the sparrow hath found an house, and the swallow a nest for herself, where she may lay her young, *even* thine altars, O LORD of hosts, my King, and my God.

4 Blessed *are* they that dwell in thy house: they will be still praising thee. Sē'lah.

5 Blessed *is* the man whose strength

84:1-4. How amiable are thy tabernacles. How inexpressibly lovely, or dear, are the tabernacles of the Lord; the psalmist does not even attempt to describe them. He uses the plural of tabernacles, as Alexander points out, because it has reference to the subdivisions and appurtenances of the sanctuary. **My soul longeth, yea, even fainteth for the courts of the LORD.** The word **fainteth** (Heb *kalah*) signifies to be consumed with longing. Today one would say: I'm dying to visit your house, Lord.

The **sparrow** and the **swallow** have found nests for themselves in the trees that grew within the sacred enclosure. For one wistful moment the psalmist appears to wish himself the good fortune of these birds. **Blessed are they that dwell in thy house,** those who are constantly engaged in the service of the tabernacle. **They will be still praising thee.** Surely, the psalmist reasons, their tongues would never be still and their mouths would never cease magnifying the Lord.

5-8. Blessed is the man . . . Who passing through the valley

is in thee; in whose heart *are* the ways *of them.*

6 *Who* passing through the valley of Bā′ca make it a well; the rain also filleth the pools.

7 They go from strength to strength, *every one of them* in Zion appeareth before God.

8 O LORD God of hosts, hear my prayer: give ear, O God of Jacob. Sē′-lah.

9 Behold, O God our shield, and look upon the face of thine anointed.

10 For a day in thy courts *is* better than a thousand. I had rather be a doorkeeper in the house of my God, than to dwell in the tents of wickedness.

11 For the LORD God *is* a sun and shield: the LORD will give grace and glory: no good *thing* will he withhold from them that walk uprightly.

12 O LORD of hosts, blessed *is* the man that trusteth in thee.

PSALM 85

LORD, thou hast been favourable unto thy land: thou hast brought back the captivity of Jacob.

2 Thou hast forgiven the iniquity of thy people, thou hast covered all their sin. Sē′lah.

3 Thou hast taken away all thy wrath: thou hast turned *thyself* from the fierceness of thine anger.

---

of Baca make it a well. Perhaps the same as the Valley of Bochim, mentioned in Judges 2:1, 5, or the Valley of the Mulberry Tree (II Sam 5:23-24; I Chr 14:14-15), the meaning of the expression is that the man who finds his **strength** in God will never be without a **well** of comfort in a dry and barren land. He who makes his way to the house of God, a journey which under ordinary circumstances saps the traveler's strength in proportion to the distance traveled, finds that the promise of worshiping in God's sanctuary will enable him to **go from strength to strength,** i.e., gain strength as he nears God's house.

9-10. O God . . . look upon the face of thine anointed. Here the psalmist prays that God would regard the king with favor and that the light of divine countenance would shine on him. **For a day in thy courts is better than a thousand** days spent elsewhere. **I had rather be a doorkeeper in the house of my God, than to dwell in the tents of wickedness.** The text literally reads: I had rather be a doorkeeper at the threshold of God's house and never be able to enter therein than to dwell on the inside of the tent of the wicked.

11-12. The LORD God is a sun and shield. In Him we find both warmth and protection. His steady rays direct our paths. Yet, when we encounter trouble, He is our shield, the one who preserves our going out and coming in. In due time **the LORD will give grace and glory.** When we receive the free gift of God's grace, it secures the promise of heaven's glory.

The psalmist concludes this pearl of psalms by indicating that **the man that trusteth** in the **LORD** of hosts has the wonderful promise from the Lord that **no good thing will he withhold from them that walk uprightly** (cf. 34:10; I Cor 2:9; I Tim 4:8).

M. The Restoration of Israel. 85:1-13.

THEME: *A promise of future blessing for Israel in a golden age of universal peace.*

The inscription to Psalm 85 reads **To the chief musician. A psalm for the sons of Korah.** It is likely, however, that David is the author of the psalm. To assert this means automatically a denial of the most common interpretations of Psalm 85.

Because of the reference to **the captivity** in verse 1, and the total lack of any distinct or definite historical allusions in the rest of the psalm, the most common belief among scholars today is that this psalm was written either at the time of Zerubbabel (Ezr 3:4), or more likely during the days of Ezra and Nehemiah (Ezr 9:10; Neh 2-4).

Yet, beyond the historical allusion found in verse 1, our commentators are hard pressed to interpret the rest of the psalm historically. In fact, there are many allusions in this psalm that have no historical reference. For example, verse 10 declares, **Mercy and truth are met together; righteousness and peace have kissed each other.** There is surely no day nor epic in history in which this can have been said to be historically a fact. Thus, regardless of what historical setting can be supposed for this psalm, it appears that the most appropriate interpretation is not historical at all, but prophetic. The psalm must speak not of the return of Israel to Palestine from the Babylonian captivity, but the future restoration of Israel and the inauguration of the millennial reign of Jesus Christ on this earth. It is from that perspective that we interpret this psalm.

85:1-4. In recalling that the Lord had in past times been favorable to the land of Israel, the psalmist is reminded **thou hast brought back the captivity of Jacob.** It is this expression that brings most scholars to the conclusion that Psalm 85 refers to a time after the Babylonian captivity. Yet, many commentators freely admit that this clause does not necessitate reference to a historical event. Plumer says, "To turn captivity, or bring back captivity is to relieve from sore evils. The man of Uz was never a prisoner to his enemies, and yet God turned his captiv-

4 Turn us, O God of our salvation, and cause thine anger toward us to cease.

ity, Job 42:10. The design of the psalmist is to recall former deliverances for the encouragement of hope and prayer."

The word for **captivity** (Heb *shebît*) is used metaphorically for calamities short of an actual historical captivity. It is not the psalmist's intent to point to a specific event, but to remind those to whom he writes that God has often been favorable unto Israel. Jehovah has often brought Israel back from severe tribulation to glory and has frequently **forgiven the iniquity** of the people and **covered all their sin. Thou hast taken away all thy wrath: thou hast turned thyself from the fierceness of thine anger.** The forgiveness of sin implies a cessation of wrath. Having removed the sin, the anger is removed, also. Yet, the psalmist must pray, **Turn us, O God of our salvation, and cause thine anger toward us to cease.**

Together, these verses seem to point to a time when judgments are over for Israel forever. Yet, the Scriptures clearly indicate that the greatest tribulation the nation Israel will ever undergo is yet future (see Jer 30:7; Ezr 22:17-22; Dan 12:1). God's chosen people have gone through awful sufferings and persecutions in the past. The Jews have had tribulation in Egypt, Babylon, Assyria, Russia, Rome, Germany, and elsewhere. But all those tribulations pale into insignificance when we think of the Great Tribulation, the time of Jacob's trouble. This will be Israel's darkest hour (see the detailed prophecy of these events in Revelation 12).

5 Wilt thou be angry with us for ever? wilt thou draw out thine anger to all generations?
6 Wilt thou not revive us again: that thy people may rejoice in thee?
7 Shew us thy mercy, O LORD, and grant us thy salvation.

5-7. In seeking to discern whether God's punishment on Israel would continue forever, the psalmist asks, **Wilt thou be angry with us for ever? Wilt thou not revive us again . . . ?** (lit., wilt thou not return and revive us?). The punishment that Israel has received **to all generations** at the hands of cruel men and at the hands of a just God will cease forever in that great millennial day of Christ's reign on earth. It is to this reign that the psalmist appeals. Will not the Lord return and revive His chosen nation? Will He not put an end to the time of Jacob's trouble? In faith the psalmist can but pray, **Show us thy mercy, O LORD, and grant us thy salvation.**

8 I will hear what God the LORD will speak: for he will speak peace unto his people, and to his saints: but let them not turn again to folly.
9 Surely his salvation *is* nigh them that fear him; that glory may dwell in our land.

8-9. Having offered an earnest prayer on behalf of an afflicted nation, the psalmist now awaits a response from God. **He will speak peace unto his people, and to his saints.** God will not always chide Israel. The seven-year period of tribulation, which is yet future for Israel, will come to a conclusion with the return of the **God of our salvation** (vs. 4; cf. Rev 19:11-16).

When the psalmist thinks of these great promises of God toward Israel, he can but conclude, **Surely his salvation is nigh them that fear him.** Once again the **glory** of God will dwell in the land of Israel, but not the shekinah glory this time. The glory that dwells in Israel during the future millennial reign of Christ will be the glory of God Himself, Jesus Christ (cf. Jn 1:1, 14; Acts 7:55).

10 Mercy and truth are met together; righteousness and peace have kissed each other.
11 Truth shall spring out of the earth; and righteousness shall look down from heaven.

10-11. **Mercy and truth are met together; righteousness and peace have kissed each other.** The full revelation of mercy and truth meeting and righteousness and peace kissing is only seen in the future. Today, mercy and truth do not meet; righteousness and peace do not kiss; they are not even on speaking terms. We do not have peace today because we do not have righteousness in this world. Peace will only come with the arrival of the Prince of Peace, and righteousness with the King of Righteousness (see Isa 11-12).

During the future one-thousand-year reign of the Lord Jesus Christ on this earth, **Truth shall spring out of the earth; and righteousness shall look down from heaven.** With the reign of Jesus, the Messiah, on this earth there shall be a phenomenal growth of righteousness among men. Earth shall yield the flowers of truth, and heaven shall shine with the stars of holiness. There has never been a day in the history of the world to date when this can be said to be the case.

12 Yea, the Lord shall give *that which is* good; and our land shall yield her increase.

13 Righteousness shall go before him; and shall set *us* in the way of his steps.

12-13. Our land shall yield her increase. During the one thousand years of Christ's reign the curse of barrenness placed upon the ground because of sin will be removed. Even the animals and reptiles will lose their ferocity. The just society promised by human leaders for centuries, but never produced, will at last be realized.

Righteousness shall go before him. During the Millennium all roads will not lead to Rome, but to Jerusalem and to the feet of Jesus Christ the Righteous. Calvin explains this as, "the prevalence and unobstructed course of righteousness." In that day Christ will establish the right pattern for life and His servants shall walk in His footsteps in righteousness. **He shall set us in the way of his steps.**

Although the world has not yet seen such an hour, nevertheless, the promises of God are sure. Jesus will return to this earth to establish a reign of righteousness and restore Israel to righteous prominence as His chosen people. In this the psalmist rejoices.

N. A Prayer of Praise. 86:1-17.

THEME: A mosaic prayer consisting of fragments from other psalms and Scriptures.

This is one of the five psalms entitled Tephillahs or prayers. The others are Psalms 17, 90, 102 and 142. Since a prayer is irregular in construction, the psalm does not lend itself easily to strophical arrangement.

Although at first it may not be evident to the reader, this psalm is actually a mosaic pieced together by adapting sections of other psalms. The psalms from which this psalm draws materials are 25-28 and 54-57, all of which are Davidic Psalms. In addition, there are thoughts that parallel those found in Exodus, Deuteronomy, Isaiah, and Jeremiah. Because of the character of this psalm, the question of authorship is naturally raised. Inserted among a series of Korahite Psalms, this is the only one in the third book ascribed to David. Many scholars today are quite willing to brush this psalm aside and deny Davidic authorship, claiming that it was edited by someone in a later period. Yet, Davidic authorship can be reasonably maintained.

PSALM 86

BOW down thine ear, O Lord, hear me: for I *am* poor and needy.

2 Preserve my soul; for I *am* holy: O thou my God, save thy servant that trusteth in thee.

3 Be merciful unto me, O Lord: for I cry unto thee daily.

4 Rejoice the soul of thy servant: for unto thee, O Lord, do I lift up my soul.

86:1-4. Bow down thine ear, O Lord, hear me. This form of address is common in devotional literature (cf. 17:6; 31:2; 45:10; Prov 22:17). **Preserve my soul.** God is not only the Creator of men, but the Preserver as well (Job 7:20; 10:12). It is the delight of God to **preserve the souls of his saints** (97:10). **For I am holy.** The psalmist only indicates sincerity and innocence in the wake of unjust charges made against him. Lest any should suppose that David trusted in his own holiness, he immediately declared his trust in God, **O thou my God, save thy servant that trusteth in thee. Be merciful unto me, O Lord: for I cry unto thee daily** (lit., all day long). The man who is in the habit of speaking frequently with God will never wonder whether God hears him in the day of his trouble. **Unto thee, O Lord, do I lift up my soul.**

5 For thou, Lord, *art* good, and ready to forgive; and plenteous in mercy unto all them that call upon thee.

5. For thou, Lord, art good, and ready to forgive. Although the word translated **ready to forgive** (Heb *salach*) occurs only here, nevertheless the context clearly implies that it means God is gracious, a pardoner, forgiving, and one who will show **mercy unto all them that call** unto Him (cf. Ex 34:6; Joel 2:13).

6 Give ear, O Lord, unto my prayer; and attend to the voice of my supplications.

7 In the day of my trouble I will call upon thee: for thou wilt answer me.

6-7. After a sincere expression of praise, the psalmist now calls upon the Lord to hear his **supplications** in a manner consistent with other psalms (cf. 17:1; 55:2; 61:1; etc.). The psalmist does not simply petition God in his heart, but gives **voice** unto his prayers, fully confident that **thou wilt answer me** (cf. vs. 5).

8 Among the gods *there is* none like

8. Another note of praise and adoration is seen in David's declaration **among the gods there is none like unto thee, O**

unto thee, O Lord; neither *are there any works* like unto thy works.

9 All nations whom thou hast made shall come and worship before thee, O Lord; and shall glorify thy name.
10 For thou *art* great, and doest wondrous things: thou *art* God alone.

11 Teach me thy way, O Lord; I will walk in thy truth: unite my heart to fear thy name.
12 I will praise thee, O Lord my God, with all my heart: and I will glorify thy name for evermore.
13 For great *is* thy mercy toward me: and thou hast delivered my soul from the lowest hell.

14 O God, the proud are risen against me, and the assemblies of violent *men* have sought after my soul; and have not set thee before them.
15 But thou, O Lord, *art* a God full of compassion, and gracious, longsuffering, and plenteous in mercy and truth.

16 O turn unto me, and have mercy upon me; give thy strength unto thy servant, and save the son of thine handmaid.
17 Shew me a token for good; that they which hate me may see *it*, and be ashamed: because thou, Lord, hast holpen me, and comforted me.

PSALM 87

HIS foundation *is* in the holy mountains.
2 The Lord loveth the gates of Zion more than all the dwellings of Jacob.
3 Glorious things are spoken of thee, O city of God. Sĕ'lah.

Lord. The imaginary gods of the heathen could not compare to the reality of Jehovah. David could confidently say that any alleged works of the heathen gods were not **like unto thy works** (Deut 3:24).

9-10. All nations whom thou hast made shall come and worship before thee, O Lord; and shall glorify thy name. As in the preceding psalm, David appears to be praising the Lord that the God of all nations will one day inaugurate the glorious reign of universal peace in which the Lord Jesus Christ will rule the nations with a rod of iron (Rev 19:15). Then all the peoples of the earth will recognize the universal authority of the Messiah, Jesus Christ, and worship Him accordingly (cf. Isa 42:1; 49:6; 60:3-5; Ob 21; Zech 8:22-23).

11-13. Teach me thy way, O Lord; I will walk in thy truth. This same thought is expressed elsewhere in the Psalms (cf. 25:4; 27:11; 119:33). The psalmist prays that his heart will be brought into unity in the fear of God. Then he will praise the Lord God with all his heart and **glorify thy name for evermore.** His reason is clear. He is thankful for God's great mercy, recognizing that God has delivered his soul **from the lowest hell.** Every sinner deserves God's wrath. But for violating the sixth and seventh commandments David perceived himself to deserve the most dreadful of punishments, i.e., the lowest concentric circle of hell.

14-15. Again, the psalmist returns to a mournful tone. **The proud are risen against me, and the assemblies of violent men have sought after my soul.** Whereas the proud are violent, the Lord is a God who is **full of compassion, and gracious, longsuffering, and plenteous in mercy and truth.** The expression **full of compassion** (Heb *rachūm*) is very emphatic; it signifies the tenderness parents have toward their children.

16-17. David concludes his psalm with a series of requests: **turn . . . have mercy . . . give thy strength . . . save the son of thine handmaid . . . Show me a token for good.** The psalmist recognized that he did not deserve these favors. Nevertheless, he asks for them, begging the grace of God to give him strength to overcome the proud and violent men. **That they which hate me may see it, and be ashamed.** The psalmist's deliverance would be his enemies' shame; it would show that his God, Jehovah, alone was God. The days of his life would do in microcosm what the glorious reign of His Great Son, Jesus Christ, would do in macrocosm.

O. Zion: City of God. 87:1-7.

THEME: A prophetic portrait of the glories of Zion.

This **psalm or song for the sons of Korah** gives little indication of authorship or the occasion for its writing. Most scholars believe that it was written by one of the attendants of Korah during the days of Hezekiah. The reference to Egypt as **Rahab** (vs. 4) is in favor of this interpretation; for Isaiah himself, the chief prophet of Hezekiah's days, called Egypt Rahab (Isa 30:7).

This beautiful little psalm sings the praises of the universality of the Messiah's kingdom. It also sings of the glories of Jerusalem, the capital of the Messiah's kingdom. God chose it, founded it, loved it, and will forever care for it. Jerusalem will one day be the center city of the world, the capital of Jesus Christ, the Son of David. Psalm 87 fits well into the framework of history depicted by such prophecies as Isaiah 2:2-4; 4:2-6; 19:21-24; 25:6-9; 66:7-22; Zephaniah 3:14-20, and many others.

87:1-3. His foundation is in the holy mountains. God's foundation, i.e., the city which He has founded as the capital of His theocratic kingdom, has been divinely established in the hill country of Judaea, the mountain of holiness (cf. 3:4; Zech 2:12). **The Lord loveth the gates of Zion.** God loved the walls of the city of Jerusalem because He chose it to be the center of His theocracy. He also chose it to be the site of Solomon's Temple,

4 I will make mention of Rahab and Babylon to them that know me: behold Philistia, and Tyre, with E-thǐ-ō'pǐ-a; this *man* was born there.

5 And of Zion it shall be said, This and that man was born in her: and the highest himself shall establish her.

6 The LORD shall count, when he writeth up the people, *that* this *man* was born there. Sē'lah.

7 As well the singers as the players on instruments *shall be there:* all my springs *are* in thee.

as well as the future site and center of the kingdom of Christ upon this earth.

Glorious things are spoken of thee, O city of God. God Himself had inspired holy men to write of the glories of Jerusalem. The fame of this wondrous city extended to the ends of the earth (cf. Mt 12:42; Lk 11:31). **Selah.** Pause and meditate a moment on the glories of Jerusalem.

4-6. In the verses that follow it is the determination of the God of Israel that Zion shall be the center of His activities in the earth. Speaking of the prophetic future, Jehovah God promises, **I will make mention of Rahab and Babylon to them that know me.** In Job 26:12, **Rahab** is the name of a fierce monster of the deep, commonly believed to be the crocodile. In Psalm 89:10 there can be little doubt, however, that Rahab is a reference to Egypt, **thou hast broken Rahab in pieces;** for the crocodile of the Nile was taken to be the symbol of the Egyptian kingdom (see also Isaiah 51:9). **Babylon** is the counterpart of Egypt, a nation equally antagonistic to Israel and as much her enemy to the east as Egypt was to the south.

Philistia, and Tyre, with Ethiopia. Other hostile nations as well shall be counted among the number of those who are at peace with God's people (cf. 83:7; II Chr 12:3; 14:9-13). **This man was born there** contrasts the lowliness and insignificance of those who are born in Egypt, Babylon, Philistia, Tyre, or Ethiopia, with the truly great prophets, judges, and kings of Jerusalem (cf. Gen 19:9; I Sam 21:15; I Kgs 22:27; Mt 12:24; 26:61; etc.).

And of Zion it shall be said, This and that man was born in her. The Hebrew word used for man (Heb *'ish*) is not the common name for man (Heb *'adam*), but one which is used to designate someone of distinction and honor. **The LORD shall count . . . that this man was born there.** God is the keeper of accurate and perfect records. Every man in the kingdom of Christ will be known by God the Father, and every citizen of that kingdom shall be registered by God for exceptional privileges.

7. The singers as the players on instruments shall be there. The sorrows that the city of Jerusalem has endured for centuries will find themselves excluded from the new Jerusalem. **All my springs are in thee.** Every source of joy and happiness in life will be found in God's New Jerusalem.

P. A Psalm of Sadness. 88:1-18.

THEME: *The darkest, most mournful psalm in the Psalter.*

This psalm is unique in the fact that it is the only psalm in which the outpouring of the burdened heart of the psalmist to God fails to bring relief or consolation.

Yet, as terrible as the despair of the psalmist is, we are not here faced with utter despair. No one who really despairs will pray, for prayer is the proof of lingering hope. Even in the midst of despair the psalmist recognizes that should there be any hope, it will only be found in God (vss. 1-2, 9, 13). Regardless of his circumstances, in the back of his mind the psalmist entertained the thought that God would provide salvation.

The superscription indicates that it is **A song or psalm for the sons of Korah to the chief musician.** Thus, it is catalogued among the Korahite Psalms. However, the author appears to be one **Heman the Ezrahite.** Who this man was is not fully known. There was a Heman, a wise man, alluded to in I Kings 4:31 who is the brother of Ethan, and one of the five sons of Zerah (I Chr 2:6), the son of Judah, and hence called the **Ezrahite.** Another man named Heman, a man of David's day, was one of the trio of the chief musicians, "Heman, Asaph, Ethan" (I Chr 15:19) and is mentioned as a singer in I Chronicles 6:33; 15:17; 25:4-6.

Whichever man is the author of the psalm, it is a **Maschil** or didactic poem to be played upon **Mahalath Leannoth. Maha-**

PSALM 88

O LORD God of my salvation, I have cried day *and* night before thee:
2 Let my prayer come before thee: incline thine ear unto my cry;

3 For my soul is full of troubles: and my life draweth nigh unto the grave.
4 I am counted with them that go down into the pit: I am as a man *that hath* no strength:
5 Free among the dead, like the slain that lie in the grave, whom thou rememberest no more: and they are cut off from thy hand.

6 Thou hast laid me in the lowest pit, in darkness, in the deeps.
7 Thy wrath lieth hard upon me, and thou hast afflicted *me* with all thy waves. Sē'lah.

8 Thou hast put away mine acquaintance far from me; thou hast made me an abomination unto them: *I am* shut up, and I cannot come forth.
9 Mine eye mourneth by reason of affliction: LORD, I have called daily upon thee, I have stretched out my hands unto thee.

10 Wilt thou shew wonders to the dead? shall the dead arise *and* praise thee? Sē'lah.
11 Shall thy lovingkindness be declared in the grave? *or* thy faithfulness in destruction?
12 Shall thy wonders be known in the dark? and thy righteousness in the land of forgetfulness?

13 But unto thee have I cried, O LORD; and in the morning shall my prayer prevent thee.

14 LORD, why castest thou off my soul? *why* hidest thou thy face from me?
15 I *am* afflicted and ready to die from *my* youth up: *while* I suffer thy terrors I am distracted.

lath Leannoth may refer to the tune to which this psalm is sung or to a particular musical instrument that is plaintive in tone. Rabbi Kimchi and other Jewish writers assert that this was a wind instrument similar to the flute and was played on occasions of great sorrow or lamentation.

88:1-2. O LORD God of my salvation. The one ray of hope in the entire psalm is removed by some by an emendation. But the LXX supports the Hebrew text and is thoroughly in harmony with the rest of Scripture, which teaches us that the saint of God is never in utter despair. **I have cried day and night before thee . . . incline thine ear unto my cry.** These verses represent a single sliver of light in the gloomiest of psalms.

3-5. With a trouble-filled soul, the psalmist was convinced that his **life draweth nigh unto the grave.** The word **grave** (Heb *she'ōl;* Gr *hades*) refers to the unseen world, the place of departed spirits (cf. Job 10:21-22). **I am counted with them that go down into the pit.** The psalmist sees himself reckoned as one who is about to die. Weak and feeble, he is **free among the dead,** i.e., cast out among the dead. **And they are cut off from thy hand.** Heman felt as if God had smitten him mortally and laid him among the corpses upon whom God would execute divine justice.

6-7. Thou hast laid me in the lowest pit, metaphorically meaning the deepest calamity that ultimately issues in death. **In darkness, in the deeps.** So great are his afflictions that he has been laid to rest in the depths of calamity where no sunlight ray of hope can ever reach. The psalmist clearly recognizes the source of his difficulty; his sin has caused God to be angry with him. He says, **Thy wrath lieth hard upon me.**

8-9. Thou hast put away mine acquaintance far from me (cf. 31:11; see also the similar complaint of Job 19:13-14). **Thou hast made me an abomination unto them.** Likewise, see the sentiment of Job (cf. Job 9:31; 19:19; 30:10). Whatever the psalmist's affliction, it had turned his friends into enemies. Cursed by men, the psalmist lamented, **I am shut up, and I cannot come forth.** This probably indicates that being considered unclean, or suspected of being unclean, the psalmist was banished from his people (cf. Lev 13:4-33).

Mine eye mourneth by reason of affliction. The psalmist had cried his eyes out. In an attitude of earnest prayer, Heman assumed the appropriate position of one who calls earnestly unto God. **I have stretched out my hands unto thee.**

10-12. Wilt thou show wonders to the dead? Shall the dead arise and praise thee? The psalmist doubts that God will show the glories of His grace to those who are in the grave. Conversely, he is sure that those who are dead (Heb *repa'îm* lit., the shades, designating shadowy ghosts) shall not arise out of their graves to praise God.

Shall thy loving-kindness be declared in the grave? The psalmist is useless to the Lord in his present condition, and even more so in his eventual demise. **Shall thy wonders be known in the dark? and thy righteousness in the land of forgetfulness? The land of forgetfulness** is obviously a euphemism for sheol. The psalmist's argument is that if he dies in his present condition, how will that bring glory to God?

13. Regardless of his present condition, the psalmist has not abandoned prayer. **But unto thee have I cried, O LORD; and in the morning shall my prayer prevent thee.** He would arise before the dawn and begin to pray before the sun was up.

14-15. Now for the hard question. **LORD, why castest thou off my soul?** Speaking as one who is greatly grieved, as Job had done, the psalmist cries unto the Lord God for answers to his dilemma. **Why hidest thou thy face from me?** Is God insensitive to his affliction? Why does God allow this affliction to continue?

I am afflicted and ready to die from my youth up. The

psalmist's affliction has lasted so long that he cannot remember when he lived without it. It has been a daily part of his life since his youth. He has suffered the terrors of affliction to the extent that he is now **distracted,** i.e., exhausted.

16 Thy fierce wrath goeth over me; thy terrors have cut me off.
17 They came round about me daily like water; they compassed me about together.

16-17. Again, Heman recognizes God's anger on his life. **Thy fierce wrath goeth over me,** i.e., overwhelms me like a mighty flood. The terrors of his affliction **came round about me daily like water.** The psalmist viewed himself as being overwhelmed by his affliction and in the process of continual drowning.

18 Lover and friend hast thou put far from me, *and* **mine acquaintance into darkness.**

18. Lover and friend hast thou put far from me, and mine acquaintance into darkness. So deeply distressed is the psalmist that he finds no friends eager to help him. He is all alone; he bears the anger of God alone. The psalm ends with no resolution to his problem, and the psalmist's affliction continues.

Q. The Davidic Covenant Psalm. 89:1-52.

THEME: A psalm expressing confidence and concern over the Lord's covenant with David.

According to the inscription, this psalm is a **Maschil of Ethan the Ezrahite.** The date of this psalm will depend entirely upon our identification of Ethan. If the author is considered to be the brother of Heman, the poet of Psalm 88 and one of the five sons of Zerah (I Chr 2:6), the son of Judah, then he must be considered as the same man named Jeduthun (cf. I Chr 25:6; 16:41-42) and a contemporary of Solomon. If he was one of Solomon's wives' counselors, much of what he wrote will have to be interpreted prophetically. That this psalm is Messianic is generally admitted, and this assertion is proven by its contents and quotations in the New Testament.

PSALM 89

I WILL sing of the mercies of the LORD for ever: with my mouth will I make known thy faithfulness to all generations.
2 For I have said, Mercy shall be built up for ever: thy faithfulness shalt thou establish in the very heavens.

89:1-2. I will sing of the mercies of the LORD for ever. This one short verse contains a summary of the whole psalm. It is the delight of this psalmist to magnify the mercies of God. **Mercies,** either in the singular or plural, occurs in verses 2, 14, 24, 28, 33, 49. In verses 33 and 49 it is rendered **loving-kindness,** but it is the same word in Hebrew. The psalmist has a devout resolve to **make known thy faithfulness to all generations.** The twin subjects of this psalm are the **mercies** (Heb *chesed*) of the Lord and the **faithfulness** (Heb *'emūnah*) of the Lord. **Faithfulness** is seen in verses 2, 5, 8, 24, 33, and 49. In verse 49 it is rendered **truth.** Like a glorious edifice, **Mercy shall be built up for ever.** Like the stars of the sky, **thy faithfulness shalt thou establish in the very heavens.**

3 I have made a covenant with my chosen, I have sworn unto David my servant,
4 Thy seed will I establish for ever, and build up thy throne to all generations. Se'lah.

3-4. God's promise to David is the foundation and very ground upon which the psalmist's hope and confidence is built. Quoting the exact words of the Lord God revealed to him by the Holy Spirit, the psalmist utters a condensed version of the original covenant given to David. **I have sworn unto David my servant** (cf. 132:11; II Sam 7:11-16). **Thy seed will I establish for ever** (cf. 130:12; II Sam 7:12-13). **And build up thy throne to all generations.** The immediate fulfillment of this promise was found in Solomon and his descendants. But the first chapter of the New Testament begins by indicating that it is Jesus, the seed of David, who is the Christ and in whom the everlasting kingdom would be preserved.

5 And the heavens shall praise thy wonders, O LORD: thy faithfulness also in the congregation of the saints.
6 For who in the heaven can be compared unto the LORD? *who* among the sons of the mighty can be likened unto the LORD?
7 God is greatly to be feared in the assembly of the saints, and to be had in reverence of all *them that are* about him.

5-7. And the heavens shall praise thy wonders. This is not a reference to the stars of heaven, as in Psalm 19:1, but to the inhabitants of heaven, i.e., the angelic host (cf. 96:6; Job 15:15; Heb 1:6). **The congregation of the saints,** those redeemed and living on this earth, also shall praise the mighty wonders of God.

For who in the heaven can be compared unto the LORD? There is no one among the angels of heaven suited to rival Jehovah in glory. **Who among the sons of the mighty can be likened unto the LORD?** There are no princes of the earth who can equal the Lord God in majesty and might. Thus, the psalmist concludes, **God is greatly to be feared in the assembly of**

8 O LORD God of hosts, who *is* a strong LORD like unto thee? or to thy faithfulness round about thee?

9 Thou rulest the raging of the sea: when the waves thereof arise, thou stillest them.

10 Thou hast broken Rahab in pieces, as one that is slain; thou hast scattered thine enemies with thy strong arm.

11 The heavens *are* thine, the earth also *is* thine: *as for* the world and the fulness thereof, thou hast founded them.

12 The north and the south thou hast created them: Tā'bor and Her'mon shall rejoice in thy name.

13 Thou hast a mighty arm: strong is thy hand, *and* high is thy right hand.

14 Justice and judgment *are* the habitation of thy throne: mercy and truth shall go before thy face.

15 Blessed *is* the people that know the joyful sound: they shall walk, O LORD, in the light of thy countenance.

16 In thy name shall they rejoice all the day: and in thy righteousness shall they be exalted.

17 For thou *art* the glory of their strength: and in thy favour our horn shall be exalted.

18 For the LORD *is* our defence; and the Holy One of Israel *is* our king.

19 Then thou spakest in vision to thy holy one, and saidst, I have laid help upon *one that is* mighty; I have exalted *one* chosen out of the people.

20 I have found David my servant; with my holy oil have I anointed him:

21 With whom my hand shall be established: mine arm also shall strengthen him.

22 The enemy shall not exact upon him; nor the son of wickedness afflict him.

the saints. He is so marvelous that He is to be held **in reverence of all them that are about him.**

8-10. O LORD God of hosts, who is a strong LORD like unto thee? A more poetic reading may be: Who is strong like unto thee, O JAH? **Thou rulest the raging of the sea.** God's power over the sea is a frequent scene in the Old Testament verifying His greatness (cf. 107:29; Job 38:8-11; Prov 8:29; Jer 5:22; etc.). **When the waves thereof arise, thou stillest them** (cf. 65:7; 107:23-30; Mt 8:26-27).

The psalmist's intent appears to be to show that Jehovah is the absolute Sovereign over the physical realm. From the natural kingdom he turns to the human kingdom and notes **thou hast broken Rahab in pieces, as one that is slain.** Egypt, here called Rahab (cf. 87:4), was crushed like a corpse beneath the chariot wheels of God's people. The impious Pharaoh and his mighty hosts are no match for the mighty JAH (68:4).

11-12. A quick survey of the world around him brings the psalmist to testify that all his eyes may behold was created by Jehovah. **The heavens are thine** (cf. 8:3; 33:6; 115:16); **the earth also is thine** (cf. 24:1); **the world and the fullness thereof,** i.e., all the habitable and cultivated earth and the fruit thereof belonged to the Creator (cf. 50:12).

The north and the south thou hast created them. These geographical designations are a poetic expression of the universality of God's creation. **Tabor and Hermon** complete that poetic description. Mount Tabor is situated on the west bank of the Jordan River, and from its summit the Mediterranean Sea can be seen (cf. Jer 46:18). Mount Hermon stands to the north of Tabor on the east side of the Jordan (cf. 42:6). The prominence of these two mountains is used poetically to designate the third and fourth points of the compass.

13-14. Beginning with the anthropomorphisms of God's **mighty arm: strong . . . hand, and . . . right hand,** the psalmist leaves the physical realm to show Jehovah's supremacy in the ethical realm as well. **Justice and judgment are the habitation of thy throne.** The king who shall sit upon the throne of David can do no wrong and can make no improper judgments, nor dispense any inappropriate justice.

15-18. Blessed is the people that know the joyful sound. An apparent reference to the happiness that accompanies Jewish festivals (cf. 27:6; 81:1; Lev 25:9; Num 10:2, 9), there is a real sense in which only those who have experienced the grace of God have heard **the joyful sound. In thy name shall they rejoice all the day . . . For thou art the glory of their strength . . . For the LORD is our defense.** It is little wonder that the redeemed of the ages are joyful. The God who rules the physical and ethical realms is their strength and shield. **The Holy One of Israel is our King.** He who protects should also govern; he who defends is acknowledged as king.

19-21. Then thou spakest in vision to thy holy one. The reference is undoubtedly to the revelation to Nathan, since it was in the form of a vision (cf. I Chr 17:15) to his Holy One(s) God said, **I have laid help upon one that is mighty; I have exalted one chosen out of the people.** Even before he slew the great giant Goliath, David was mighty from his youth as is evidenced by the slaughter of the lion and the bear (I Sam 17:34-36). As if to remove all doubt with regard to who has been chosen out of the people, Jehovah continues, **I have found David my servant** (cf. I Sam 16:1; Acts 13:22) **with my holy oil have I anointed him** (cf. I Sam 16:13). Not only has God established David as the king and anointed him with oil, he is also determined to aid him permanently. **Mine arm also shall strengthen him.**

22-23. And I will beat down his foes before his face, and plague them that hate him. The passages that most nearly identify this promise as a historical event are II Samuel 7:9 and

23 And I will beat down his foes before his face, and plague them that hate him.

24 But my faithfulness and my mercy *shall be* with him: and in my name shall his horn be exalted.

25 I will set his hand also in the sea, and his right hand in the rivers.

26 He shall cry unto me, Thou *art* my father, my God, and the rock of my salvation.

27 Also I will make him *my* firstborn, higher than the kings of the earth.

28 My mercy will I keep for him for evermore, and my covenant shall stand fast with him.

29 His seed also will I make *to endure* for ever, and his throne as the days of heaven.

30 If his children forsake my law, and walk not in my judgments;

31 If they break my statutes, and keep not my commandments;

32 Then will I visit their transgression with the rod, and their iniquity with stripes.

33 Nevertheless my lovingkindness will I not utterly take from him, nor suffer my faithfulness to fail.

34 My covenant will I not break, nor alter the thing that is gone out of my lips.

35 Once have I sworn by my holiness that I will not lie unto David.

36 His seed shall endure for ever, and his throne as the sun before me.

37 It shall be established for ever as the moon, and *as* a faithful witness in heaven. Sĕ′lah.

38 But thou hast cast off and abhorred, thou hast been wroth with thine anointed.

39 Thou hast made void the covenant of thy servant: thou hast profaned his crown *by casting it* to the ground.

II Samuel 22:40-44. Both David and his Greater Son, Jesus Christ, were afflicted by enemies; but neither of them was ever overthrown.

24-26. But my faithfulness and my mercy shall be with him . . . I will set his hand also in the sea, and his right hand in the rivers. How God exalted both David and Christ is fully declared in I Chronicles 17:7, Romans 1:4, and Philippians 2:9-11. **He shall cry unto me, Thou art my father, my God, and the rock of my salvation.** For the fulfillment of these promises in the life of David see II Samuel 7:14 and 22:2-3, 47. The Son of God was also in the habit of crying unto Jehovah and calling Him Father (cf. Jn 17: 1, 5, 11, 21, 24-25). In Matthew 27:46 He fulfilled the promise of 22:1 by crying unto the Father and calling Him, **my God.**

27-29. I will make him my first-born, higher than the kings of the earth. In the society of the Ancient Near East the first-born had special privileges. Although God gave David power, excellence, and majesty, even over the surrounding nations (II Sam 5:11-12; I Chr 14:17), yet this prophecy has never had its complete fulfillment in David, but only in Christ. Six times the Lord Jesus is declared to be the first-born of God (cf. Rom 8:29; Col 1:15, 18; Heb 1:6; 12:23; Rev 1:5). As King of Kings and Lord of Lords (Rev 19:16), Jesus Christ is **higher than the kings of the earth.** As the sole heir to the Davidic Covenant and, consequently, to the throne of David, Jesus will have perfect dominion over all the kings of the earth and all the angels of creation (cf. Prov 8:15-16; Dan 2:21; Mk 1:27; Eph 1:20-21; Phil 2:9-11; Col 2:10, 15).

My covenant shall stand fast with him. In no case has God ever broken a covenant. With David, as a type of Christ, the covenant was given in much assurance (cf. vss. 3, 34; II Sam 23:5; Jer 33:20-21). To the Lord Jesus Christ that covenant is even more secure, for it was ratified by both the oath of God and the blood of Christ; and it cannot be canceled or annulled. **His seed also will I make to endure for ever, and his throne as the days of heaven.** The seed of David lives on in the person of Jesus Christ, and the seed of Christ lives on in the person of the believer. **As the days of heaven** never cease, so the kingdom of Christ shall never come to an end.

30-32. With the promise of this great covenant came a warning that David's **children** should not forsake God's **law** or His **judgments,** and they must not break His **statutes** or His **commandments.** The divine promise was that if they did, **then will I visit their transgression with the rod, and their iniquity with stripes.** Unfortunately, David's children did forsake God's law and neglected to walk in His judgments; and the history recorded in Kings and Chronicles amply testifies to the fact that God visited their transgression with the rod.

33-35. Regardless of how faithless the descendants of David had been, God had purposed in His heart that **loving-kindness will I not utterly take from him, nor suffer my faithfulness to fail.** Although the immediate seed of David had failed God, the seed of David would not fail. Because He could swear by no greater than Himself, Jehovah had sworn by His **holiness** the very essence of His nature.

36-37. The final promise seen in this psalm is that David's **seed shall endure for ever.** Perpetuity is characteristic of those things established by God. The kingdom divinely established was that of David and his seed, the Lord Jesus Christ. It will be before the face of God as long as **the sun** and **the moon.**

38-41. Suddenly, there is an abrupt change. **But thou hast cast off and abhorred.** The Lord had promised not to cast off the seed of David, and yet it looked as if He had done so. Everywhere men of Israel were convinced that God had **been wroth with thine anointed,** i.e., that person and family in which the kingdom had been invested. **Thou hast made void the**

40 Thou hast broken down all his hedges; thou hast brought his strong holds to ruin.
41 All that pass by the way spoil him: he is a reproach to his neighbours.

42 Thou hast set up the right hand of his adversaries; thou hast made all his enemies to rejoice.
43 Thou hast also turned the edge of his sword, and hast not made him to stand in the battle.
44 Thou hast made his glory to cease, and cast his throne down to the ground.
45 The days of his youth hast thou shortened: thou hast covered him with shame. Sĕ'lah.

46 How long, LORD? wilt thou hide thyself for ever? shall thy wrath burn like fire?
47 Remember how short my time is: wherefore hast thou made all men in vain?
48 What man *is he that* liveth, and shall not see death? shall he deliver his soul from the hand of the grave? Sĕ'lah.

49 Lord, where *are* thy former loving-kindnesses, *which* thou swarest unto David in thy truth?
50 Remember, Lord, the reproach of thy servants; *how* I do bear in my bosom *the reproach of* all the mighty people;
51 Wherewith thine enemies have reproached, O LORD; wherewith they have reproached the footsteps of thine anointed.
52 Blessed *be* the LORD for evermore. Amen, and Amen.

covenant of thy servant. Made void is found only here and in Lamentations 2:7, where it is rendered "abhorred." In both instances it expresses strong aversion. Thou hast profaned his crown by casting it to the ground. The royal family had been brought very low in the years subsequent to David. It was said of the king that his lands, defenses, and walled cities were destroyed; and All that pass by the way spoil him. He is a reproach to his neighbors. The armies of the world passing by the devastated Holy City would say in jest: Is this the anointed of the Lord? Is this the capital of the everlasting kingdom? The seed of David was likewise ridiculed and became a reproach to his neighbors (cf. Mt 27:39-40).

42-45. Each of these verses is designed to show the depths to which the kingdom of David had fallen. Thou hast set up the right hand of his adversaries, i.e., you have exalted them over Israel. Thou hast also turned the edge of his sword. Apparently this expression indicates that the weapons of warfare for Israel were rendered powerless for either attack or defense.

With swords incapable of striking a blow, it would be impossible for the Israelites to stand in the battle. Of David and his descendants it was believed that God had covered him with shame. Most particularly, this phrase seems well suited to Jehoiachin who was put in prison by Nebuchadnezzar and made to wear ". . . prison garments . . ." (cf. II Kgs 25:29) for many years. To the Israelites it appeared that the throne had been cast to the ground forever.

46-48. The psalmist could but ask, How long, LORD? Wilt thou hide thyself for ever? This is not an uncommon plea for the psalmist (cf. 13:1; 74:10; 79:5). Remember how short my time is was the plea of the psalmist for God to remember the brevity of human life. What man is he that liveth, and shall not see death? There is none. Not by strength, nor wisdom, nor wealth, nor virtue shall a man deliver his soul from the hand of the grave? Selah. Give serious consideration to that.

49-51. In light of these truths, the psalmist must ask, LORD, where are thy former loving-kindnesses, which thou swarest unto David in thy truth? This is his basic question. Where is the fulfillment of the promise of a perpetual kingdom? He has felt the scorn and ridicule of his countrymen, as well as God's enemies who have reproached him. Every step of David and his descendants made them a reproach to their neighbors (cf. 44:13; 79:4; Neh 1:3; 2:17; etc.).

52. Blessed be the LORD for evermore. From the psalmist's viewpoint, the covenant of David had been destroyed and would probably never be renewed. From our vantage point, the covenant was not destroyed and need not be renewed because God's Son, Jesus Christ our Lord "was made of the seed of David according to the flesh; And declared to be the Son of God with power . . ." (Rom 1:3-4). The day will come when the seventh angel shall sound his trumpet and great voices in heaven will say, "The kingdoms of this world are become the kingdoms of our Lord, and of His Christ; and He shall reign for ever and ever" (Rev 11:15).

IV. PSALMS 90:1-106:48.

A. A Prayer of Moses. 90:1-17.

THEME: *A prayer for eternal wisdom in light of the transitory nature of man.*

The superscription over this psalm reads, A prayer of Moses the man of God. This is most remarkable in that no other psalm is ascribed to Moses, nor indeed is any of a time period earlier than that of David. Some have objected to Mosaic authorship mainly because verse 10 ascribes the average lifespan to seventy years, and that is said to be in conflict with the known age of Moses himself (Deut 34:7). However, the Pentateuch clearly depicts Moses' longevity as an exception. Even Caleb speaks of his strength at eighty-five as being quite beyond the ordinary (Josh 14:10). In spite of the critics, Mosaic authorship of this psalm is attested by all the ancient versions of the Old Testament, as well as by such commentators as Luther, Calvin, Gill, Tholuck, Hengstenberg, etc.

PSALM 90

LORD, thou hast been our dwelling place in all generations.
2 Before the mountains were brought forth, or ever thou hadst formed the earth and the world, even from everlasting to everlasting, thou *art* God.

90:1-2. LORD, thou has been our dwelling place in all generations. In reflecting on the past, Moses recognizes that the dwelling place of God's people has never been in a geographical locality, but rather has always been in Jehovah Himself.

Before the mountains were brought forth. Mountains are always mentioned as the grandest and most ancient of God's works. **Or ever thou hadst formed the earth and the world.** Before the earth had left the blueprint of God's mind to become the product of His creative fingers, God was gloriously present. **Even from everlasting to everlasting, thou art God.** Before anything else was, God was. From everlasting to everlasting (cf. 93:2; Prov 8:23; Mic 5:2; Hab 1:12) indicates that God's lifetime has no beginning and can have no end. He is the eternal God, the Great "I AM" (Ex 3:14).

3 Thou turnest man to destruction; and sayest, Return, ye children of men.
4 For a thousand years in thy sight *are but* as yesterday when it is past, and *as* a watch in the night.

3-4. Thou turnest man to destruction. So frail is man in the presence of the Almighty God that He who brought man into creation with a word possesses the power to bring him to destruction with a word. **For a thousand years in thy sight are but as yesterday when it is past.** God is above time: it does not exist for Him. ". . . one day is with the Lord as a thousand years, and a thousand years as one day" (II Pet 3:8). With God a thousand years is but **as a watch in the night.** To the eternal God, no sooner has a thousand years begun than it is done, as one who sleeps through the watch of a night.

5 Thou carriest them away as with a flood; they are *as* a sleep: in the morning *they are* like grass *which* groweth up.
6 In the morning it flourisheth, and groweth up; in the evening it is cut down, and withereth.

5-6. Thou carriest them away as with a flood. As the torrent rushes through the riverbed and washes away everything in its path, so the timeless God removes the children of men with equal rapidity. **In the morning they are like grass which groweth up** (cf. 37:2; 72:16; 92:7; 103:15; Isa 40:7). In the morning the grass of the field covers the meadows with the beauty of youth. As an example of the vibrancy and vitality of young life, morning grass **flourisheth, and groweth up.** The whole day lies before it. But **in the evening it is cut down, and withereth** (cf. 102:4, 11; 103:15-16; Isa 40:7; Jas 1:10-11). Inevitably the scythe of old age reaps the blossom of youth.

7 For we are consumed by thine anger, and by thy wrath are we troubled.
8 Thou hast set our iniquities before thee, our secret *sins* in the light of thy countenance.

7-8. The psalmist now turns his reflections from life in general to the present situation of the Israelite wanderers. All of the original generation but two would be cut down by the scythe of death before they would enter the Promised Land. Moses knew why. **For we are consumed by thine anger . . . Thou hast set our iniquities before thee.** Moses was fully aware that God had not hidden His face from their iniquities, but rather displayed **our secret sins in the light of thy countenance.**

9 For all our days are passed away in thy wrath: we spend our years as a tale *that is told.*
10 The days of our years *are* threescore years and ten; and if by reason of strength *they be* fourscore years, yet *is* their strength labour and sorrow; for it is soon cut off, and we fly away.
11 Who knoweth the power of thine anger? even according to thy fear, *so is* thy wrath.

9-11. For all our days are passed away in thy wrath. From the hard taskmasters of Egypt to the wrath of an angry God displeased at their sin, Moses' people had known little in life but trouble. **We spend our years as a tale that is told.** The Hebrew reads, "We consume our years like a groan (Heb *kemō hegeh*)." Life is swift; and for those who live in iniquity, not at all sweet.

The days of our years are threescore years and ten. Moses died at the age of one hundred twenty (Deut 34:7) and Aaron at the age of one hundred twenty-three (Num 33:39). But these are clearly exceptional cases. Should one live beyond those allotted years, there was little reason to boast in longevity; for those lengthened years wrought only **labor and sorrow.** Even if we live to be eighty or more, our life is a short span, indeed; and all too quickly **we fly away.**

12 So teach *us* to number our days,

12. What should be our prayer in light of the transitoriness of

that we may apply *our* hearts unto wisdom.

13 Return, O Lord, how long? and let it repent thee concerning thy servants.
14 O satisfy us early with thy mercy; that we may rejoice and be glad all our days.
15 Make us glad according to the days *wherein* thou hast afflicted us, *and* the years *wherein* we have seen evil.

16 Let thy work appear unto thy servants, and thy glory unto their children.
17 And let the beauty of the Lord our God be upon us: and establish thou the work of our hands upon us; yea, the work of our hands establish thou it.

PSALM 91

HE that dwelleth in the secret place of the most High shall abide under the shadow of the Almighty.
2 I will say of the Lord, *He is* my refuge and my fortress: my God; in him will I trust.

3 Surely he shall deliver thee from the snare of the fowler, *and* from the noisome pestilence.
4 He shall cover thee with his feathers, and under his wings shalt thou trust: his truth *shall be thy* shield and buckler.

our lives? Moses' answer is, **So teach us to number our days, that we may apply our hearts unto wisdom.**

13-15. Return, O Lord, how long? i.e., how long will it be before you turn from your anger? **And let it repent thee concerning thy servants.** The psalmist appeals to the mighty God to relent in His anger and **satisfy us early with thy mercy.** Since man's life is as the grass which flourisheth and then is cut down, it is imperative that God early turn His anger to mercy if Moses and his people are to **rejoice and be glad all our days.** The request to **Make us glad according to the days wherein thou hast afflicted us** is a prayer that God will proportion their time of joy to the years they have spent in sorrow.

16-17. Finally, the psalmist prays that the **work** of God would appear unto the Israelites, **thy servants.** The work that Moses desires is one that will show God's **glory unto their children.** Undoubtedly, the psalmist is speaking of the establishment of Israel in the Promised Land.

And let the beauty of the Lord our God be upon us. Although Moses' generation will not see the Promised Land, nonetheless they pray for God's blessing to rest upon them. To emphasize this final prayer, there is repetition of the phrase **establish thou the work of our hands upon us.**

B. The Secret Place Psalm. 91:1-16.

THEME: "This is the most distinguished jewel among all the psalms of consolation"—Luther.

Like the majority in this present book, this psalm is anonymous and without title. It was the practice of Jewish interpreters to assign the authorship of an unnamed psalm to the writer of the last named psalm. If this be so, this is another psalm of Moses, the man of God. It is in striking contrast with Psalm 90. Psalm 90 is somber; this psalm is cheerful. That psalm is one of concern; Psalm 91 is one of comfort. Some of the motifs in Psalm 91 correspond well to the life of Moses (**the noisome pestilence,** vs. 3; **the terror by night,** vs. 5; **the pestilence that walketh in darkness,** vs. 6; **A thousand shall fall at thy side . . . but it shall not come nigh thee,** vs. 7; **neither shall any plague come nigh thy dwelling,** vs. 10; **he shall give his angels charge over thee,** vs. 11; etc.). These and other references are reminiscent of the plagues on Egypt, the Passover night, and Israel's escape from bondage; and they speak strongly for Mosaic authorship.

91:1-2. He that dwelleth in the secret place of the Most High shall abide under the shadow of the Almighty. This is a great promise of blessing to believers. Yet, the promise is not made to all who believe, but only to those who are willing to make their abode in the secret place, to sit down or take up residence there. The words **shall abide** (Heb *lūn*) signify to pass the night. They imply a constant and continuous dwelling, and not just a temporary visitation during trouble or calamity. Psalm 91 is a promise to those who take up residence in the secret place.

He is my refuge and my fortress: my God. That God is a refuge (cf. 18:2; 144:2) and a God who can be trusted (cf. 31:6; 55:23; 56:3; 61:4; etc.) is a frequent theme of the Psalms. Yet, it is of little comfort that God is a refuge or a fortress unless we are able to say He is **my refuge and my fortress.**

3-4. Constant fellowship with the Lord Jesus Christ, who is **the secret place of the Most High,** bring us most assuredly to deliverance **from the snare of the fowler** (cf. 124:7; Prov 6:5), i.e., the devil who, like one who traps birds, skillfully prepares a snare for God's servants, **and from the noisome pestilence.** **Pestilence** comes from the Hebrew (Heb *dabar*), which signifies to speak or speak out. The pestilence appears to be something spoken, something proclaimed by God among the people. The LXX renders it (Gr *thanatos*) death.

5 Thou shalt not be afraid for the terror by night; *nor* for the arrow *that* flieth by day;
6 *Nor* for the pestilence *that* walketh in darkness; *nor* for the destruction *that* wasteth at noonday.

7 A thousand shall fall at thy side, and ten thousand at thy right hand; *but* it shall not come nigh thee.
8 Only with thine eyes shalt thou behold and see the reward of the wicked.
9 Because thou hast made the LORD, *which is* my refuge, *even* the most High, thy habitation;
10 There shall no evil befall thee, neither shall any plague come nigh thy dwelling.

11 For he shall give his angels charge over thee, to keep thee in all thy ways.
12 They shall bear thee up in *their* hands, lest thou dash thy foot against a stone.
13 Thou shalt tread upon the lion and adder: the young lion and the dragon shalt thou trample under feet.

14 Because he hath set his love upon me, therefore will I deliver him: I will

Whatever this great danger may be, we need not fear it; for **He shall cover thee with his feathers, and under his wings shalt thou trust.** In loving condescension, God likens Himself to a mother hen sheltering her young from the hawks of the sky and the snares of the field. **His truth shall be thy shield and buckler.** God's faithfulness and veracity will constitute our double armor, i.e., the shield borne on the arm and the buckler, which was the coat of mail giving protection to every part of the warrior's body.

5-6. In typically poetic style, the psalmist beautifully portrays that God's protection of those who dwell in the secret place is constant, never failing day or night. **Thou shalt not be afraid for the terror by night,** a probable reference to robbers (cf. Job 24:14-16; Jer 49:9; Ob 5), **nor for the arrow that flieth by day,** perhaps a reference to open warfare (cf. Job 6:4). **Nor for the pestilence that walketh in darkness,** a poetic picture of the grim reaper stalking the night looking for victims; **nor for the destruction that wasteth at noonday.** The word rendered **destruction** (Heb *qeteb*) here and in Deuteronomy 32:24 is rendered by the LXX (Gr *daimonion*) meaning the demon of the day, i.e., sunstroke (cf. 121:6).

The Hebrews were accustomed to dividing the twenty-four hours of a day and night into four equal parts, i.e., evening (6 P.M.-12 A.M.), midnight (12 A.M.-6 A.M.), morning (6 A.M.-12 P.M.), and midday (12 P.M.-6 P.M.). When we are willing to take up our residence in the secret place of the Most High and abide under the shadow of the Almighty, we are assured of round-the-clock, twenty-four-hour protection from the devil and his angels.

7-10. In these verses the poet notices that while we are untouched in the shelter of the secret place **A thousand shall fall at thy side, and ten thousand at thy right hand.** The scythe of death shall reap a mortal toll all around **but it shall not come nigh thee.** This promise was graphically etched in Israelite memories that bloody Passover night in Egypt, when the death angel passed through the land and the first-born was executed by the judgment of the Lord. **Neither shall any plague come nigh thy dwelling.** No evil befell the Israelites; for as God had promised, **thou hast made the LORD, which is my refuge, even the Most High, thy habitation.**

11-13. The psalmist now identifies the agent of this continual coverage we enjoy when we are in constant fellowship as the Lord Jesus, God's **secret place. He shall give his angels charge over thee.** Dwellers in the secret place are under the constant care of angels (Heb 1:13-14), and it is comforting to note that the word is not singular but plural, angels. Caring properly for us is more than a one angel job. The angels are said to bear us up lest we **dash thy foot against a stone.** How tender it is to know that they bear us **in their hands,** as a nurse would give tender loving care to a small child.

Thou shalt tread upon the lion and adder: the young lion and the dragon shalt thou trample under feet. It was a common mark of complete victory when the vanquished foe lay prostrate on the ground and the conqueror placed his foot on the lifeless body of his enemy. From this practice came the metaphor of treading underfoot, indicating complete victory (cf. 7:5; 44:5; 60:12; etc.). The **lion** poetically represents an open and ardent foe. The **adder** is symbolic of a more secret and malignant foe. Regardless of the snare placed in our path by Satan, when we abide under the shadow of the Almighty, both open and secret enemies will be vanquished. The repetition for emphasis and embellishment indicates the **young lion and the dragon,** the lion in the strength of its youth and the most dreadful type of serpent, are no match for God's ministering spirits.

14-16. A dramatic change is seen in these verses. It is evident that the speaker here is none other than Jehovah Himself. He

set him on high, because he hath known my name.

15 He shall call upon me, and I will answer him: I *will be* with him in trouble; I will deliver him, and honour him.

16 With long life will I satisfy him, and shew him my salvation.

addresses the one who **hath set his love upon me,** i.e., the one who is willing to dwell in the secret place. To run to the Lord Jesus when we are in trouble is not to show Him the consistent love necessary to receive the promises of this psalm. But when we take up residence in the house of His fellowship, when we set our love on Him, then God makes astounding promises.

Therefore will I deliver him, a ratification of verses 3, 7, 10-15, and a frequent promise in the Old Testament. **I will set him on high,** i.e., either meaning far above the dangers which plague this world or to exalt Him above His fellows and bring honor to Him. The reason is **because he hath known my name.** Knowing the name of God is equivalent to knowing Him personally.

He shall call upon me, and I will answer him. "Call unto me, and I will answer thee, and show thee great and mighty things, which thou knowest not" (Jer 33:3), **I will be with him in trouble** (cf. 46:1, whenever trouble comes God is already there), **I will deliver him, and honor him.** The man who honors God with his love and willingness to forsake the world will ultimately be honored by God.

With long life will I satisfy him (1:3; 34:12; 37:3). This promise is in marked contrast to the apparent despair of the preceding psalm, which describes long life as **labor and sorrow** (90:10). What can the difference be? The difference is the reality of verse 1. **And show him my salvation.** To see the salvation of God is to see beyond today and to know that, ". . . the sufferings of this present time are not worthy to be compared with the glory which shall be revealed in us" (Rom 8:18).

C. The Sabbath Psalm. 92:1-15.

THEME: A psalm to contemplate the precious works of the hands of God.

The superscription indicates that this is **A psalm or song for the sabbath day.** Beyond this, nothing is known of the author or occasion for the composition of this psalm. In the Mishnah (*Tamid* 6:4) it is recorded that this psalm was appointed to be used in the Temple service on the Sabbath. The inscription with regard to the Sabbath Day is preserved in the best Hebrew manuscripts, as well as the Chaldee, Arabic, Septuagint, Ethiopic, and Vulgate. The title in the Targum, "Of the First Adam," indicates the opinion of the older rabbis that this psalm may have been written by Adam himself. Although Adamic authorship is as well attested in the Chaldee version, nevertheless few Christian scholars give credence to this assertion.

92:1-3. It is a good thing to give thanks unto the LORD. To praise God does our hearts good; it is right morally and ethically to do so. As the birds sing His praises, let us **sing praises unto thy name, O Most High.** It is appropriate that with the freshness of a new day we sing forth the **loving-kindness** of God **in the morning.** This prayer ought to continue throughout the day and come to a close with praise of **thy faithfulness every night.** Not only shall our voices be raised to God, but we praise Him as well **upon an instrument of ten strings, and upon the psaltery; upon the harp.** Both vocal and instrumental praises to God are fitting in the Jewish Sabbath service.

4-6. For thou, LORD, hast made me glad through thy work. The mere contemplation of divine work, either creation or providence, floods the heart of the psalmist with joy. **I will triumph in the works of thy hands.** The word **triumph** (Heb *ranan*) is sometimes rendered cry or shout for joy. In the first sentence of this verse the psalmist expresses the unity of God's work; in the second he praises the variety of God's works. When he surveys all that God has done, he can but exclaim, **O LORD, how great are thy works!** The works of Jehovah are great in number, great in design, great in glory, and great in conse-

PSALM 92

IT is a good *thing* to give thanks unto the LORD, and to sing praises unto thy name, O most High:

2 To shew forth thy lovingkindness in the morning, and thy faithfulness every night,

3 Upon an instrument of ten strings, and upon the psaltery; upon the harp with a solemn sound.

4 For thou, LORD, hast made me glad through thy work: I will triumph in the works of thy hands.

5 O LORD, how great are thy works! *and* thy thoughts are very deep.

6 A brutish man knoweth not; neither doth a fool understand this.

quence. **Thy thoughts are very deep** is an expression reminiscent of St. Paul's expression of praise to God, "O the depth of the riches both of the wisdom and knowledge of God! how unsearchable are his judgments, and his ways past finding out!" (Rom 11:33).

What a sharp contrast is drawn between the one who praises God's loving-kindness every morning and His faithfulness every night, and the **brutish man,** i.e., a rude, uncultivated, stupid man who never contemplates the wonderful depths of God's love. Whether he is an intellectual philosopher or a menial laborer, he has no conception of Jehovah God and is blind and insensitive to the things of God. By divine appraisal he is thought to be **a fool.**

7 When the wicked spring as the grass, and when all the workers of iniquity do flourish; it is that they shall be destroyed for ever:

8 But thou, LORD, *art most* high for evermore.

9 For, lo, thine enemies, O LORD, for, lo, thine enemies shall perish; all the workers of iniquity shall be scattered.

7-9. The wicked spring as the grass . . . all the workers of iniquity do flourish. Although this is a theme that disturbed both Job (Job 21:7-21) and Asaph (73:2-15), the prosperity of the wicked does not seem to trouble our psalmist here. He is convinced that when the wicked gather together in abundance and apparent strength, as the flourishing grass, **they shall be destroyed for ever** (cf. 73:18-20). On the other hand, **thou, LORD, art most high for evermore.** God is consistently and gloriously exalted, seated upon His throne in the heavens and unaffected either by the efforts or by the fall of the wicked. Glory be to His name!

For, lo, thine enemies shall perish; all the workers of iniquity shall be scattered. The psalmist takes great comfort in the fact that although the workers of iniquity have gathered themselves together against God, nonetheless their forces shall be dispersed, their evil designs destroyed, and themselves defeated.

10 But my horn shalt thou exalt like *the horn of* an unicorn: I shall be anointed with fresh oil.

11 Mine eye also shall see *my desire* on mine enemies, *and* mine ears shall hear *my desire* of the wicked that rise up against me.

10-11. But my horn shalt thou exalt like the horn of a unicorn. The horn of an animal was used for protection and raised high in glorious victory (cf. Lk 1:69). The psalmist is confident that he will be victorious over the enemies of God and that he will have his horn, a figure of speech borrowed from the animals, exalted like **the horn of a unicorn.** Like the Assyrian, the Hebrew word for unicorn (Heb *re'em*) indicates a wild ox. With the vigor of one who had been **anointed with fresh oil,** and entering battle with certain divine aid, the psalmist could confidently say, **Mine eye also shall see my desire on mine enemies.**

12 The righteous shall flourish like the palm tree: he shall grow like a cedar in Lebanon.

13 Those that be planted in the house of the LORD shall flourish in the courts of our God.

12-13. The psalmist now contrasts the life of the righteous with that of the wicked. Whereas the workers of iniquity are likened unto grass which flourisheth for a short time and then is destroyed forever, **The righteous shall flourish like the palm tree,** the queen of all trees in antiquity. The palm was luxurious and lovely and would grow in those unlikely areas where others would not. To add to the figure, the righteous **shall grow like a cedar in Lebanon** (cf. II Kgs 14:9; Song 5:15; Ezk 31:3-9; Amos 2:9; Zech 11:1).

Those that be planted in the house of the LORD shall flourish in the courts of our God. Referring to the righteous, the psalmist correctly concludes that the greater wisdom is shown in living righteously, rather than living wickedly.

14 They shall still bring forth fruit in old age; they shall be fat and flourishing;

15 To shew that the LORD *is* upright: *he is* my rock, and *there is* no unrighteousness in him.

14-15. Those who are righteous and flourish in the courts of God, making their habitation in the secret place of the Most High, **shall still bring forth fruit in old age** and be **fat and flourishing.** Aged believers are sweet testimonies to the constant presence and provision of God. They can truly say, "The longer I serve Him, the sweeter it grows."

Of Jehovah the promise concludes, **he is my rock, and there is no unrighteousness in him.** Even in the years of failing health, on the Sabbath day a Jew could come to the Temple and give praise to God for being the rock of his salvation. **It is a good thing to give thanks . . . and to sing praises unto thy name, O Most High** (vs. 1).

PSALM 93

THE LORD reigneth, he is clothed with majesty; the LORD is clothed with strength, *wherewith* he hath girded himself: the world also is stablished, that it cannot be moved.
2 Thy throne *is* established of old: thou *art* from everlasting.

3 The floods have lifted up, O LORD, the floods have lifted up their voice; the floods lift up their waves.
4 The LORD on high *is* mightier than the noise of many waters, *yea, than* the mighty waves of the sea.

5 Thy testimonies are very sure: holiness becometh thine house, O LORD, for ever.

D. The Lord Is King. 93:1-5.

THEME: A celebration of Jehovah as Sovereign of the universe.
Although this psalm has no inscription, the Syriac, Arabic, Septuagint, Ethiopic, and Vulgate versions of the Old Testament ascribe it to David as author. It is a psalm that praises the majesty of God as Creator.

"The subject of the psalm is the kingdom of God; not of nature and providence, but of grace; the kingdom of Messiah"—John Gill. Here we see the majesty of the divine Sovereign as His program moves unimpeded through history, from creation to consummation.

93:1-2. The LORD reigneth, he is clothed with majesty; the LORD is clothed with strength. Literally, the initial expression is that the Lord is become King (cf. 10:16; 47:6; 96:10; 97:1; etc.). Although men have not always recognized His sovereignty, nonetheless Jehovah is clothed with majesty and strength, which is proven by the fact that **the world also is stablished, that it cannot be moved.** God has set both the boundaries of the stars and the seas. He is the majestic God who has firmly established His sovereignty in the world. **Thy throne is established of old: thou art from everlasting.** The design of Satan has always been to thwart the purpose of God and to usurp His throne; but God has always been King, both in heaven and in earth. God is not a temporal King, but an eternal one (cf. 90:2; Prov 8:23; Isa 63:15; Mic 5:2; Hab 1:12; etc.).

3-4. The floods have lifted up their voice. Angry men who have joined Satan's rebellion have spewed out their venomous hatred for God, as the waves of the sea lash against the shore. Yet, as the wicked lift their voices in opposition to the sovereignty of God, it is to no avail; for **The LORD on high is mightier than the noise of many waters, yea, than the mighty waves of the sea.** Jehovah is self-existent and omnipotent. His purpose will be fulfilled; it cannot be thwarted.

5. Thy testimonies are very sure. Although the teachings of other religions are subject to change and their holy books are discredited in error, nevertheless the throne of God is fixed in heaven and all His revelation is infallible. **Holiness becometh thine house, O LORD for ever.** The sovereign Lord who is King will not permit a corruption of His perfect plan. No one can thwart the purpose of God. He is the Lord God, who reigneth and is clothed with majesty.

E. The Lord God of Vengeances. 94:1-23.

THEME: A painful cry for vengeance on the oppressors of the righteous.
The LXX calls this psalm, "A Lyric Psalm of David, for the Fourth Day of the Week." Although the author of this psalm is unnamed, the Syriac, Arabic, Ethiopic, and Vulgate agree with the LXX on Davidic authorship.

Scholars are divided over the identification of David's enemies upon whom God's vengeance is called. Delitzsch and Kirkpatrick are of the opinion that they are foreign enemies, while Maclaren and Rawlinson understand them to be domestic.

Whichever the case, the psalmist calls upon the God of vengeance to cut them off. Many have wondered at the appropriateness of such a psalm. Some have suggested that the psalmist exhibits a strong sense of unforgiving retribution. But as Maclaren observes, "There are times when no thought of God is so full of strength as that he is the 'God of recompenses' as Jeremiah calls Him (Jer 51:56) and when the longing of good men is that he would flash forth and slay evil by the brightness of His coming." The psalm concludes with an expression of quiet confidence that God's righteousness will be manifested ultimately. Although the faithful would rather take God's wrath into their own hands, nevertheless they have learned to

PSALM 94

O LORD God, to whom vengeance belongeth; O God, to whom vengeance belongeth, shew thyself.
2 Lift up thyself, thou judge of the earth: render a reward to the proud.

3 LORD, how long shall the wicked, how long shall the wicked triumph?
4 *How long* shall they utter *and* speak hard things? *and* all the workers of iniquity boast themselves?

5 They break in pieces thy people, O LORD, and afflict thine heritage.
6 They slay the widow and the stranger, and murder the fatherless.
7 Yet they say, The LORD shall not see, neither shall the God of Jacob regard *it*.

8 Understand, ye brutish among the people: and *ye* fools, when will ye be wise?
9 He that planted the ear, shall he not hear? he that formed the eye, shall he not see?
10 He that chastiseth the heathen, shall not he correct? he that teacheth man knowledge, *shall not he know?*
11 The LORD knoweth the thoughts of man, that they *are* vanity.

12 Blessed *is* the man whom thou chastenest, O LORD, and teachest him out of thy law;
13 That thou mayest give him rest from the days of adversity, until the pit be digged for the wicked.

14 For the LORD will not cast off his people, neither will he forsake his inheritance.
15 But judgment shall return unto righteousness: and all the upright in heart shall follow it.

". . . give place unto wrath . . ." (Rom 12:19) and allow the wicked to reap what they have sown.

94:1-2. O LORD God, to whom vengeance belongeth. God is frequently mentioned as the one to whom ". . . belongeth vengeance, and recompense . . ." (Deut 32:35), or is sometimes directly called, ". . . the LORD God of recompenses . . ." (Jer 51:56). Here again, it is God the avenger who is asked to **show thyself,** i.e., shine forth in justice and **Lift up thyself,** i.e., rouse thyself to **render a reward to the proud.** Since God alone is the **judge of the earth** (cf. 58:11; Gen 18:25), He alone is able to righteously avenge those who are afflicted.

3-4. The natural question from those who are oppressed is, **How long shall the wicked triumph? How long shall they utter and speak hard things?** The casual reader of the Psalms will soon notice that the question **How long?** is a frequent lamentation in the Psalms. It is asked by David (6:3; 13:1-2; 35:17; 94:3-4); the psalms of Asaph record the question twice (74:10; 80:4); and Moses asks it but once (90:13). Such a cry is both one of impatience and one of faith in the fact that in His own time God will show Himself and render a reward to the proud. Thus, perhaps the most difficult answer to the prayer **How long?** is the answer: not yet.

5-7. They break in pieces thy people, O LORD; literally, they crush or oppress (cf. Prov 22:22; Isa 3:15) **and afflict thine heritage.** Here is a strong plea for divine intervention; for those afflicted by the wicked are none other than the elect of God, His people, His inheritance. **They slay the widow and the stranger, and murder the fatherless.** This is not an uncommon practice in the Old Testament (cf. Isa 1:17-23; 10:2; Ezk 22:6-9; Mal 3:5; etc.). The wicked stoop to the most inhumane practices because they believe **The LORD shall not see, neither shall the God of Jacob regard it.**

8-11. Understand, ye brutish among the people. Even among God's people there were some who supposed God would not see or regard their sin (cf. 10:11, 13; 92:6). How stupid and foolish people are who feel that **He that planted the ear** and **He that formed the eye** shall not hear of their sin nor see their iniquity. It is totally unreasonable.

He that teacheth man knowledge, shall not he know? The last clause of this question, **shall not he know?** is in italics in *The Open Bible,* indicating that it is not part of the original text. There, the sentence comes to an abrupt end, as if to imply that examples of how foolish the brutish man is, need not continue. It is abruptly cut off so that the psalmist may come to a conclusion: **The LORD knoweth the thoughts of man, that they are vanity.** Our minds are quickly drawn to Ecclesiastes 2:14-15, where the same thought is expressed.

12-13. Blessed is the man whom thou chastenest, O LORD. The blessedness of chastening is the theme of 89:32-33; II Samuel 7:14-15; Job 5:17; and numerous New Testament passages. Coupled with the blessedness of chastening is that of teaching **out of thy law.** The book and the rod, the law and chastening, go together. The reason for chastening and teaching is **that thou mayest give him rest from the days of adversity, until the pit be digged for the wicked.** Trials and afflictions are but a means to an end, and the end is rest from our labors (Heb 4:9). There is also an end for the wicked, i.e., **the pit** (cf. 9:1; 35:7-8).

14-15. For the LORD will not cast off his people . . . But judgment shall return unto righteousness. The faithful God will never cast off His people utterly (cf. Deut 4:31; I Sam 12:22; I Kgs 6:13; Isa 41:17). God is faithful to His people until the end and has not cast them away (Rom 11), even though there were wicked workers among them. They can be assured that God's justice shall prevail, and **all the upright in heart shall follow it.** Ultimately, this must be a reference to the righteous rule of the Messiah on this earth, the Son of David. The coming

16 Who will rise up for me against the evildoers? *or* who will stand up for me against the workers of iniquity?

17 Unless the LORD *had been* my help, my soul had almost dwelt in silence.

18 When I said, My foot slippeth; thy mercy, O LORD, held me up.

19 In the multitude of my thoughts within me thy comforts delight my soul.

20 Shall the throne of iniquity have fellowship with thee, which frameth mischief by a law?

21 They gather themselves together against the soul of the righteous, and condemn the innocent blood.

22 But the LORD is my defence; and my God *is* the rock of my refuge.

23 And he shall bring upon them their own iniquity, and shall cut them off in their own wickedness; *yea*, the LORD our God shall cut them off.

one-thousand-year reign of Jesus Christ on this planet is proof positive that God has not cast off His people.

16. In the meantime, the psalmist makes a plea: **Who will rise up for me against the evildoers?** Where are the champions of God who will come out to fight Goliath? Where are today's men like Martin Luther who will say, "Here I take my stand; I cannot do otherwise: May God be my help! Amen"?

17-19. The psalmist quickly realizes that without Jehovah's help, he has no cause for optimism. **Unless the LORD had been my help, my soul had almost dwelt in silence.** Had God not divinely aided him, he would be dead. He recognized the necessity of God being the champion for Israel when he said, **My foot slippeth; thy mercy, O LORD, held me up.** When the psalmist was at his greatest weakness, he felt his greatest strength, the strength of the Lord. **In the multitude of my thoughts within me thy comforts delight my soul.** The questionings, forebodings, anxieties, and perplexing thoughts which pervaded the mind of the psalmist while he was being persecuted were no less than a multitude. Yet, through it all he had learned to trust in God.

20-21. Shall the throne of iniquity have fellowship with thee, which frameth mischief by a law? Will the wicked in high places, who by law decree wrong against the psalmist ever make an alliance with God? Can those who use the law for evil purposes call upon God to justify their actions? **They gather themselves together against the soul of the righteous, and condemn the innocent blood.** There are so many who use their high offices wrongly that they can gather in a company and in their treachery murder those who are innocent of all crimes (cf. 10:8; II Kgs 21:16; 24:4; Prov 6:17; Isa 1:21; 59:3, 7; Jer 7:6; 22:3, 17; etc.).

22-23. Yet for all this, the psalmist does not despair. Let the wicked gather in crowds to persecute and shed innocent blood. Let unjust judges hand down judgments that are contrary to righteousness. The psalmist is committed that **the LORD is my defense; and my God is the rock of my refuge.** He finds sweet trust and faith in the promises of God.

And he shall bring upon them their own iniquity, and shall cut them off in their own wickedness. Like Haman, who was hanged upon the gallows he had prepared for Mordecai (Est 7:9), God has a way that brings those who do wickedly to fall into their own snare (cf. 7:15; 35:8; 57:6; 141:9-10). **The LORD our God shall cut them off,** i.e., destroy or exterminate them. God will not tolerate wickedness. Wickedness that remains unchecked and unrepented will not go unnoticed.

F. Praise Out of Provocation. 95:1-11.

THEME: *A psalm of worship to the Lord, a Great God and a Great King.*

Psalms 95 to 100 have a common theme that is undoubtable. They all begin with a summons to praise the Lord God, though each is distinctive in that praise, with Psalm 95 as the keynote. There is nothing in these psalms that warrants a specific date for their composition. Many scholars see in them the type of praise that would have been characteristic of Israel after their return from the Babylonian captivity, and some say that they were composed for the dedication of the second Temple. Yet, there is nothing historical in these psalms to warrant such precise dating.

In addition, the Syriac, Arabic, Septuagint, Ethiopic, and Vulgate editions all ascribe Psalm 95 to David. The writer of the Hebrews appears to concur, ascribing an allusion from Psalm 95 to David (Heb 4:7). There is nothing in Psalm 95 that is uncharacteristic of David's writing, and since the psalm is not dated by historical evidence, there is little reason not to assume Davidic authorship.

Many feel that this psalm is Messianic in character. Rabbi Kimchi saw in it a reference to the days of the Messiah. Luther says, "The whole of this Psalm is to be referred to Christ." Gill agrees, "It belongs to the times of Messiah." If the subject of the psalm is the Messiah's exaltation and kingdom, this is confirmed in the Epistle to the Hebrews, especially chapters 3 and 4. Yet, though it is Messianic, it still has reference to the people of God throughout all ages to come.

PSALM 95

O COME, let us sing unto the LORD: let us make a joyful noise to the rock of our salvation.

2 Let us come before his presence with thanksgiving, and make a joyful noise unto him with psalms.

95:1-2. O come, let us sing unto the LORD: let us make a joyful noise to the rock of our salvation. If other nations can enthusiastically worship their false gods, should not the people of God be more enthusiastic in their worship of Jehovah? To **make a joyful noise** (Heb *rûa'*) signifies to make a loud noise, either with the voice or with instruments. **Let us come before his presence with thanksgiving.** The reference here is probably to the presence of God above the mercy seat in the Holy of Holies of the tabernacle. Although God is everywhere, He is peculiarly present in those places sanctified and set apart unto Him.

3 For the LORD *is* a great God, and a great King above all gods.

4 In his hand *are* the deep places of the earth: the strength of the hills *is* his also.

5 The sea *is* his, and he made it: and his hands formed the dry *land*.

3-5. The psalmist now gives his reasons for calling Israel to praise God: **For the LORD is a great God, and a great King above all gods.** As Adam Clarke notes, "The Supreme Being has three names here: El, Jehovah, and Elohim, and we should apply none of these to false gods. The first implies His strength; the second, His being and essence; the third, His covenant relation to mankind. In public worship these are the views we should entertain of the Divine Being."

6 O come, let us worship and bow down: let us kneel before the LORD our maker.

7 For he *is* our God; and we *are* the people of his pasture, and the sheep of his hand. To day if ye will hear his voice,

6-7a. O come, let us worship and bow down: let us kneel before the LORD our maker. We are to remember that the God we worship is not only our friend, but our Creator as well. We should worship in a style that is accompanied by a recognition of our position before Him. He is the **LORD our maker,** i.e., the one who has created, redeemed, and made us **the people of his pasture, and the sheep of his hand.**

8 Harden not your heart, as in the provocation, *and* as *in* the day of temptation in the wilderness:

9 When your fathers tempted me, proved me, and saw my work.

7b-9. Today if ye will hear his voice, harden not your heart, as in the provocation. In a role that is unnecessary for the King above all gods, Jehovah cries out to His people to **hear** and not **harden.** He calls them to repentant hearts, in contrast to their actions in the provocation, i.e., at Meribah (Ex 17:2-7). He calls them to an attitude unlike that displayed **in the day of temptation in the wilderness,** i.e., in the day of Massah (Ex 17:2-7) that **your fathers tempted me, proved me, and saw my work.** Over and over again the Israelites put God to needless tests, demanding new miracles and tokens of His presence.

10 Forty years long was I grieved with *this* generation, and said, It *is* a people that do err in their heart, and they have not known my ways:

11 Unto whom I sware in my wrath that they should not enter into my rest.

10-11. Forty years long was I grieved with this generation. As the eternal mind of God viewed the generation of Israelites in the wilderness, He recalled that they were **a people that do err in their heart, and they have not known my ways.** This expression literally indicates that the Israelites were a people who were wanderers in heart more than they were wanderers in foot.

Unto whom I sware in my wrath that they should not enter into my rest. If the manna and miracles would not satisfy the stiffnecked Israelites, God knew that the land which flowed with milk and honey would not satisfy them either. Therefore, He swore (cf. Num 14:21-23; Deut 1:34-35) that none of this original generation of gripers, save Joshua and Caleb, would ever enter the Promised Land.

G. A Grand Missionary Hymn. 96:1-13.

THEME: "An Exhortation to Praise God, Addressed not to Jews only, but to all nations"—John Calvin.

Although the authorship of this psalm is ascribed to David by the Syriac, Arabic, Ethiopic, Septuagint, and Vulgate, the contents of this psalm occur as well, with very little change, in I Chronicles 16:23-33; and there (I Chr 16:7) authorship is ascribed to David. Yet, many commentators ascribe the psalm

PSALM 96

O SING unto the LORD a new song: sing unto the LORD, all the earth.
2 Sing unto the LORD, bless his name; shew forth his salvation from day to day.
3 Declare his glory among the heathen, his wonders among all people.

4 For the LORD *is* great, and greatly to be praised: he *is* to be feared above all gods.
5 For all the gods of the nations *are* idols: but the LORD made the heavens.
6 Honour and majesty *are* before him: strength and beauty *are* in his sanctuary.

7 Give unto the LORD, O ye kindreds of the people, give unto the LORD glory and strength.
8 Give unto the LORD the glory *due unto* his name: bring an offering, and come into his courts.
9 O worship the LORD in the beauty of holiness: fear before him, all the earth.

10 Say among the heathen *that* the LORD reigneth: the world also shall be established that it shall not be moved: he shall judge the people righteously.
11 Let the heavens rejoice, and let the earth be glad; let the sea roar, and the fulness thereof.
12 Let the field be joyful, and all that *is* therein: then shall all the trees of the wood rejoice
13 Before the LORD: for he cometh, for he cometh to judge the earth: he shall judge the world with righteousness, and the people with his truth.

to some post-exilic writer, or to Isaiah during the time of Hezekiah's reformation. There is no ground for reasonable doubt that David wrote this psalm.

This psalm, as all the psalms in the joyful collection 95-100, is cast in a broad eschatological outlook. The heart of the psalm beats with the hope of the Lord's coming. The Syriac version calls it, "A prophecy concerning the advent of Christ and the calling of the Gentiles who should believe in Him."

96:1-3. If the call to **sing unto the LORD a new song** is not made to Israel alone, but to **all the earth,** Jew and Gentile alike, from all the ends of the earth shall come the song of praise to Jehovah. **Sing unto the LORD, bless his name** (cf. 100:4; 145:1, 10, 21; etc.). This is the third in a trilogy of calls to sing unto the Lord. **Show forth his salvation from day to day,** i.e., publish His salvation or make it known. Spread the good tidings. **Declare his glory among the heathen, his wonders among all people.** The wonder of the gospel of God's redeeming grace is not to be published in Israel only, but unto the ends of the earth. It is God's design that all mankind hear the good news of the gospel (cf. 2:8; 47:1, 8; 138:4; Mt 28:19-20; Mk 16:15; Lk 24:46-47; Jn 20:21; Acts 1:8; etc.).

4-6. Unlike the petty deities of the heathen gods who were unworthy of the slightest adoration, **the LORD is great, and greatly to be praised.** Praise should be proportionate to its object. The same is true of respect and fear. **God is to be feared above all gods.** And for what reason? **For all the gods of the nations are idols,** i.e., mere images of wood and stone, nothings, vanities. The Creator God is worthy of **Honor and majesty . . . strength and beauty.**

7-9. The first six verses each commenced with an exhortation to sing unto the Lord. Here, using a similar trilogy, the psalmist calls upon the universe to **Give unto the LORD.** All the families of the peoples of the earth, Jewish and pagan alike, are to give unto the Lord **glory and strength . . . the glory due unto his name. Bring an offering, and come into his courts.** The parallel expression in I Chronicles 16:29 is ". . . come before him. . . ." Our offering today, Christ having made our atonement, is the offering of ourselves, presenting our bodies as a living sacrifice, holy and acceptable unto God (Rom 12:1-2). **O worship the LORD in the beauty of holiness.** Originally, this must have meant holy attire, or the vestments suited for holy service.

10-13. Say among the heathen that the LORD reigneth. All the world must know that the Christ of the cross is the coming King who will rule from the throne of David in the Millennium. This is just as certain as the world is **established that it shall not be moved.** Tyrants rise and fall today; but in that great millennial day, Jesus Christ **shall judge the people righteously.**

The sure knowledge of this fact is in itself a cause for rejoicing. Both above and below that joy is manifested. **Let the heavens rejoice, and let the earth be glad.** A great symphony of nature will joyfully shout the praises of the Creator God **Let the sea roar . . . Let the field be joyful . . . then shall all the trees of the wood rejoice before the LORD.** In that day all the earth shall rejoice, **for he cometh to judge the earth.** Though the courts of men may exhibit miscarriages of justice, at the court of God **he shall judge the world with righteousness, and the people with his truth.**

How absolutely essential it is that each one who has experienced the grace of God in salvation **show forth his salvation from day to day** (vs. 2) and **Declare his glory among the heathen** (vs. 3). For in the great day of God's judgment, the dead, small and great, shall stand before God and shall be ". . . judged out of those things which were written in the books, according to their works" (Rev 20:11-15).

PSALM 97

THE LORD reigneth; let the earth re-joice; let the multitude of isles be glad *thereof.*

H. Jehovah Is King. 97:1-12.

THEME: A psalm prophesying the righteous reign of Messiah as King of the earth.

Perhaps Clarke most succinctly summarizes the question of authorship for this psalm when he says, "Who the author was is uncertain: it is much in the spirit of David's finest compositions: and yet many learned men suppose it was written to celebrate the Lord's power and goodness in the restoration of the Jews from Babylonish captivity."

Regardless of the authorship, the psalm is certainly messianic. The Syriac version says it is "A Psalm of David, in which he foretells the advent of Christ. He also insinuates in it His last coming." To this Calvin adds, "The description which we have of the kingdom of God in this Psalm does not apply to the state of it under the law. We may infer, accordingly, that it contains a prediction of that kingdom of Christ . . ."

97:1. The LORD reigneth. That Jehovah reigns is the watch-word of this psalm. Everything in it relates to this one truth, i.e., Jehovah reigns in the world. Nearly all conservative commentators appear to miss the point of this statement. Even Spurgeon refers the psalm to the first advent of Christ and says that it is the essence of the gospel proclamation that Jehovah reigneth, and the foundation of the gospel is the kingdom of God. Yet, the description of the events in this psalm did not occur at the first coming of Christ as a babe in Bethlehem. They are so drastically different from those early days of Christianity that they cannot be attributed even to poetry. But they perfectly relate to His Second Coming to this earth to establish His kingdom of one thousand years upon the earth. Only then will the prayer be true, **let the earth rejoice; let the multitude of isles be glad thereof.** While other reigns have brought blood-shed and tears and while others have been reigns of terror, the reign of Jehovah God, the Lord Jesus Christ, upon this earth will be one of absolute righteousness; for the Sun of Righteousness shall heal all nations from the heartaches of the Tribulation (Mal 4:2).

2 Clouds and darkness *are* round about him: righteousness and judg-ment *are* the habitation of his throne.

2. The characteristics of the Lord's earthly millennial reign are now enumerated by the psalmist. **Clouds and darkness are round about him** (cf. Ex 19:16, 18; Deut 4:11; 5:22; I Kgs 8:12). As the Lord revealed Himself at Sinai, so His essential deity must be shrouded forever from the view of man. **Righteousness and judgment are the habitation of his throne.** Righteousness is an immutable attribute of God. Christ will be the King reigning in righteousness (Isa 32:1), and righteousness shall be the girdle of His loins (Isa 11:5).

3 A fire goeth before him, and burn-eth up his enemies round about.

3. A fire goeth before him, and burneth up his enemies round about. The righteous reign of Jesus Christ on this earth will be preceded by the fire of God's wrath, which will go before Him to sweep the evil from His pathway (cf. Isa 42:25). The awful days of the Tribulation will bring the enemies of the Lord God to their knees as His coming is accompanied by a divinely directed inferno (see the trumpet judgments of Rev 8:7-10).

4 His lightnings enlightened the world: the earth saw, and trembled.

4. His lightnings enlightened the world: the earth saw, and trembled. The lightnings of God, which precede His second coming to earth, are mentioned four times in the book of Revelation (cf. Rev 4:5; 8:5; 11:19; 16:18). Two things must be noted from these verses. First, they relate to those events that pave the way for the coming of Christ to establish His kingdom upon the earth. They will occur at the end of the great battle of Armageddon when Jesus will rule and reign from the throne of David for one thousand years, for these events did not occur when Jesus Christ came to be born in the stable of Beth-lehem. Second, it should be noted that with each verse there is a progressive worsening of judgment upon the world. The only hope for this world is the righteous reign of Jesus Christ upon

5 The hills melted like wax at the presence of the LORD, at the presence of the Lord of the whole earth.
6 The heavens declare his righteousness, and all the people see his glory.

7 Confounded be all they that serve graven images, that boast themselves of idols: worship him, all ye gods.

8 Zion heard, and was glad; and the daughters of Jŭ'dah rejoiced because of thy judgments, O LORD.
9 For thou, LORD, art high above all the earth: thou art exalted far above all gods.

10 Ye that love the LORD, hate evil: he preserveth the souls of his saints; he delivereth them out of the hand of the wicked.

11 Light is sown for the righteous, and gladness for the upright in heart.
12 Rejoice in the LORD, ye righteous; and give thanks at the remembrance of his holiness.

PSALM 98
O SING unto the LORD a new song; for he hath done marvellous things: his

1110

the earth. For the Christian living today there is another hope, a blessed hope (Tit 2:13, cf. I Thess 4:13-18).

5-6. **The hills melted like wax at the presence of the LORD.** Not only is there ample reference to this event in the prophecy of Revelation, but the Apostle Peter himself prophesied it (II Pet 3:10-12). **The heavens declare his righteousness, and all the people see his glory.** Just as the heavens declare the glory of God in His creation, so too they will declare His righteous judgments on a wicked earth (see Jesus' prophecy in Mt 24:29-30).

7. **Confounded be all they that serve graven images, that boast themselves of idols.** The Apocalypse records the dramatic return of the Lord to establish His kingdom upon the earth (Rev 19:11, 14, 16). In those days all who have received the mark of the beast and who have fallen down to worship his image (Rev 19:20) shall be cast alive into a lake of fire burning with brimstone. For seven long years the Tribulation Period has raged upon the earth, but those who have boasted in their idols will boast no more. As Spurgeon says, "He who boasts of an idol makes idle boast."

It would be ludicrous to apply these preceding verses to the first advent of the Lord Jesus in Beth-lehem. They are clearly eschatological in nature; they are perfectly suited to the second coming of the Lord of glory.

8-9. **Zion heard, and was glad; and the daughters of Judah rejoiced because of thy judgments, O LORD.** It is little wonder that Jerusalem, and all the daughters of Judah, will rejoice and be glad during the millennial reign of Jesus Christ. In that day the Jews will see their Messiah and King **exalted far above all gods;** for the presence of God will be fully recognized, and fellowship with Him will be experienced as never before (cf. Ezk 37:27-28; Zech 2:2, 10-13).

10. In light of these wonderful promises, how should His people respond? **Ye that love the LORD, hate evil.** Here is an exhortation to the faithful. We have a moral obligation to do so because the God who hates evil, and has taught us to do the same, is the one who **preserveth the souls of his saints.** God has delivered us **out of the hand of the wicked** by His nail-scarred hands and has placed us in the hand of the Father where we are preserved, for ". . . no man is able to pluck them out of my Father's hand" (Jn 10:29). Our salvation and preservation are only as sure as the hand of God is sure.

11-12. **Light is sown for the righteous, and gladness for the upright in heart.** God, who is light, has shown His grace to those who would live righteously and has caused rejoicing in their hearts. What then must our response be? **Rejoice in the LORD, ye righteous; and give thanks at the remembrance of his holiness.**

I. A New Song. 98:1-9.

THEME: An exuberant psalm of praise unto the Lord.

The questions related to the preceding three psalms bear on this one as well. While it is possible that the occasion for its writing is the joyous return of the Israelites from Babylonian captivity, nonetheless there is nothing which would prohibit David from being the author of the psalm. While it is true that portions of this psalm bear the image of Isaiah 40-65, it is more likely that the prophet adapted the language of David than that an unknown writer here adopted the language of Isaiah. The usual array of ancient versions ascribe Davidic authorship to the psalm. The inscription of the psalm in Hebrew is the single word *mizmôr,* **A psalm.** It is again a messianic psalm that speaks eschatologically of the great Millennium of David's Greater Son, Jesus Christ.

98:1-3. **O sing unto the LORD a new song.** Psalm 96, a twin psalm to this one, opens in an identical fashion. Throughout the

right hand, and his holy arm, hath gotten him the victory.

2 The LORD hath made known his salvation: his righteousness hath he openly shewed in the sight of the heathen.

3 He hath remembered his mercy and his truth toward the house of Israel: all the ends of the earth have seen the salvation of our God.

4 Make a joyful noise unto the LORD, all the earth: make a loud noise, and rejoice, and sing praise.

5 Sing unto the LORD with the harp; with the harp, and the voice of a psalm.

6 With trumpets and sound of cornets make a joyful noise before the LORD, the King.

7 Let the sea roar, and the fulness thereof; the world, and they that dwell therein.

8 Let the floods clap their hands: let the hills be joyful together

9 Before the LORD; fcr he cometh to judge the earth: with righteousness shall he judge the world, and the people with equity.

history of Israel God **hath done marvelous things,** but in the prophecy of the psalm the words **his right hand, and his holy arm, hath gotten him the victory** must refer to the decisive victory of the forces of Christ at the great battle of Armageddon (Rev 16:14-16; 19:11-16). It is then that the salvation of the Lord will be universally known, and **his righteousness hath he openly showed in the sight of the heathen.** Jew and Gentile alike will participate in the Millennial Kingdom of our Lord, for **He hath remembered his mercy and his truth toward the house of Israel** (Rom 11:25-32; Rev 12:1-6; cf. Jer 30:7). But God in His grace will bring salvation and peace to more than Israel in that day, for **all the ends of the earth have seen the salvation of our God.**

4-6. The only appropriate response to the prophetic promise of the millennial reign of Jesus Christ upon this earth is to **Make a joyful noise unto the LORD, all the earth.** The song of praise that we utter to God is to be **a loud noise** of rejoicing and praise. Loudness of the voice was regarded as indicating earnestness of the heart (cf. II Chr 20:19; Ezr 3:13; Neh 12:42; etc.). We are to **Sing unto the LORD with the harp** as an accompanying instrument.

With **the voice of a psalm,** i.e., with a voice of melody or in a melodious manner, **With trumpets and sound of cornet make a joyful noise before the LORD, the King.** The word for **trumpets** (Heb *chatsōtserōt*) is used only here in the Psalms. These were the straight trumpets, as can be seen on the Arch of Titus, which were used by the priests for giving signals (cf. Num 10:2-10; I Chr 15:24, 28; etc.). The **cornet** (Heb *shōpar*) was the ordinary curved trumpet or horn. The words **the LORD, the King** (lit., the king, Jehovah) mark out distinctly the person to whom our praise is to be directed. It is Jehovah, as King of all kings and Lord of all lords, who is worthy of praise. It is Jesus Christ, the millennial King, who shall receive this praise.

7-9. Not only will the voices of man sing the praises of God, but His natural creation shall praise Him as well. Thus, the psalmist prays, **Let the sea roar . . . the world, and they that dwell therein.** The entire world of God's creation shall join in the praise of their Messiah and Redeemer. **For he cometh to judge the earth: with righteousness shall he judge the world, and the people with equity.** Echoing the words of 96:10, as well as verse 13, this verse joins in a parade of verses throughout the Old Testament predicting the righteous reign of Jesus Christ upon this earth, His millennial reign (cf. 72:7; 85:10; Isa 46:13; 51:5; etc.). Surely the righteous Judge is worthy of our praise.

J. Holy, Holy, Holy. 99:1-9.

THEME: A psalm praising the holiness of Christ's reign upon the earth.

This is the last of the series of royal psalms, psalms which celebrate and prophetically announce the millennial reign of Christ. The first in this series was Psalm 93. It began **The LORD reigneth.** Psalm 97 also began **The LORD reigneth.** Now Psalm 99 completes the trilogy by echoing **The LORD reigneth.**

Each of these psalms relates to the establishment of the Davidic kingdom upon this earth by David's Great Descendant, Jesus Christ. Together they anticipate this event with joy. They form a universal anthem in which the tongues of men and the forces of nature join together to praise the coming of the Lord.

Like the psalms before it in this series, the Syriac, Arabic, Septuagint, Ethiopic, and Vulgate editions of the Psalms all ascribe this psalm to David. But whereas many commentators tenaciously held to a post-exilic event that aroused a psalmist to pen those psalms, they are curiously silent on this one. It is evident that the psalm could not have been written after the beginning of the Babylonian captivity; for in verse 1 God is

PSALM 99

THE LORD reigneth; let the people tremble: he sitteth *between* the cherubims; let the earth be moved.

2 The LORD *is* great in Zion; and he *is* high above all the people.

3 Let them praise thy great and terrible name; *for* it *is* holy.

4 The king's strength also loveth judgment; thou dost establish equity, thou executest judgment and righteousness in Jacob.

5 Exalt ye the LORD our God, and worship at his footstool; *for* he *is* holy.

6 Moses and Aaron among his priests, and Samuel among them that call upon his name; they called upon the LORD, and he answered them.

7 He spake unto them in the cloudy pillar: they kept his testimonies, and the ordinance *that* he gave them.

8 Thou answeredst them, O LORD our God: thou wast a God that forgavest them, though thou tookest vengeance of their inventions.

9 Exalt the LORD our God, and worship at his holy hill; for the LORD our God *is* holy.

represented as sitting **between the cherubim,** which were never heard of again after the Babylonian captivity.

99:1-3. The LORD reigneth; let the people tremble. Rabbi Jarchi understands this last clause to refer to the war of Gog and Magog. Although it could refer to that battle, nevertheless, in keeping with the preceding psalms, this is probably a reference to the day when Jesus Christ shall ". . . smite the nations: and he shall rule them with a rod of iron: and he treadeth the winepress of the fierceness and wrath of Almighty God" (Rev 19:15).

The LORD is great in Zion; and he is high above all the people. During Christ's millennial reign on earth, Jerusalem will become the center of the world (cf. Isa 2:2-4; Jer 31:6; Mic 4:1; Zech 2:10-11). The city of Zion will be the center of Christ's kingdom and government (cf. Jer 3:17; 30:16-17; 31:6, 23; Ezk 43:5-6; Joel 3:17; Mic 4:7; Zech 8:2-3). Hence, all the people are to praise the **great and terrible name** of the Lord. His name is great; for He, the Creator of all things, is great (cf. 76:1; Josh 7:9). It is terrible because He is an awesome God (89:7; 111:9; Gen 28:17; Ex 15:11). But most of all, His name is to be praised, **for it is holy.** The name of God was viewed by the Hebrew commentators as so holy that the tetragrammaton, the four Hebrew letters (*YHWH*) which make up the name Jehovah or *YAHWEH*, would not even be pronounced out of reverence to His name.

4-5. Here the psalmist returns to a prevalent theme in the preceding psalms i.e., the righteousness and justice of Christ's millennial reign. **Thou dost establish equity, thou executest judgment and righteousness in Jacob.** The pronoun is emphatic: Thou, even thou, an expression equivalent to, Thou only. It is the Lord Jesus, the Lord of Lords, who is the righteous Judge of the earth. Therefore, **Exalt ye the LORD our God, and worship at his footstool.** The **footstool** of God is the ark of the covenant; for when the Hebrews viewed God as sitting enthroned between the cherubim, His feet, as it were, rested upon the mercy seat, the lid of the ark of the covenant (cf. 132:7; I Chr 28:2; Isa 60:13; Lam 2:1). In light of the apocalyptic character of this psalm, however, this may be a veiled reference to the promise of 110:1, to Jesus the coming King of the earth.

Again, this segment of the psalm concludes, **for he is holy.** This is the second time the psalmist has struck this chord. It is to this aspect of the character of God that Psalm 99 is dedicated.

6-8. As witness to the holiness of God, the psalmist now alludes to several historical figures who came to appreciate God's holiness; **Moses and Aaron among his priests. Samuel,** who witnessed the judgment of the Lord on Eli's house, like Moses, performed sacerdotal functions (cf. Ex 17:15; 24:7-8; Lev 8:15-30; I Sam 9:13; 16:3, 5). All three of these men were intercessors, i.e., **they called upon the LORD, and he answered them.**

He spake unto them in the cloudy pillar. This is true of Moses and Aaron (cf. Ex 16:10-11; 17:6; 19:9, 18-19, 24; 20:21-22). How God spoke to Samuel is seen from I Samuel 3:10; 7:9-10. In answering them Jehovah proved that He was **a God that forgavest them, though thou tookest vengeance of their inventions.** Both Moses and Aaron angered God at the waters of strife (cf. 106:32; Num 20:12-13). Samuel received the vengeance of God for installing his sons as his successors; his judgeship came to an end through undue leniency toward his sons, Joel and Abiah (I Sam 8:1-5).

9. Exalt the LORD our God, and worship at his holy hill. This is the second time that this title for Jehovah our God is used. In the next clause it is repeated yet a third time. Jehovah is to be worshiped in Zion, **his holy hill,** the capital city of Christ's millennial kingdom. The reason is clear, and it has been given twice before at the end of each major stanza (cf. vss. 3, 5). **For the LORD our God is holy.** What a fitting climax to a psalm dedicated to praising the holiness of God and the millennial king.

K. A Psalm of Praise. 100:1-5.

THEME: A jubilant summons to give thanksgiving unto Jehovah.

If we are correct in understanding Psalms 93-99 as a corpus of psalms relating to the millennial reign of Christ, one great prophetic oratorio, then, as is suggested by Perowne, Psalm 100 may be regarded as the doxology which closes this strain. Among the psalms of praise and thanksgiving this one is pre-eminent, rising to a crescendo of joy and grandeur.

Although it most specifically relates to the praise given to Messiah where He reigns on the throne of His father David, nevertheless there is no historical data in the Psalms to date it accurately. It is a universal call for all men to give thanksgiving to the Lord Jehovah. The Arabic indicates David as the author, and there is certainly nothing in the Psalms that forbids our regarding the sweet singer of Israel as the composer. The inscription simply says, **A psalm of praise.** This is the only psalm to bear this precise inscription. The joy and thanksgiving flows so freely in this beloved poem that the whole of the psalm runs to a conclusion without any natural breaks or divisions.

100:1-2. Make a joyful noise unto the LORD, all ye lands. This is a repetition of the fourth verse of Psalm 98. It signifies to give a glad shout and worshipful praise unto Jehovah. **All ye lands** is the same as "all the earth" in 98:4. It is a universal call to praise and thanksgiving to the King of Kings. **Serve the LORD with gladness,** an emphatic word (Heb 'abad). Almost every clause of this psalm contains a similar call. Service to God is not only done out of obedience and a sense of debt; it is also done out of a sense of gratitude (cf. Eph 2:8-10; Col 3:17, 23-24). **Come before his presence with singing.** Singing requires lips of thanksgiving and triumph, as the word is rendered in 63:5; Job 3:7; 20:5. Let the whole earth join in singing His praises.

3. Know ye that the LORD he is God. Jehovah alone is God and worthy of our praise (Heb 11:6). **It is he that hath made us, and not we ourselves.** Just as there is no such thing as a self-made man, so too there is no such thing as a spontaneously generated man. The theory of evolution miserably fails to deal adequately with the facts of nature or history. **We are his people, and the sheep of his pasture** (cf. 74:1; 79:13; 95:7). What a blessed picture of the tenderness with which we are related to God. How beautifully John 10 depicts our relationship to the Good Shepherd.

4. Enter into his gates with thanksgiving, and into his courts with praise. Although the mention of **gates** and **courts** is usually indicative of temple worship, nonetheless this is also a metaphorical reference to the very presence of the Lord God. It is a call to worship, a call to praise, and a call to thanksgiving. **Be thankful unto him, and bless his name.** Giving thanks unto God is the joyous privilege of all who love Him.

5. For the LORD is good; his mercy is everlasting. The psalmist now gives his threefold rationale for making a joyful noise unto the Lord. First, the Lord is good (106:1; 118:1; 125:3; 136:1; 145:9; I Chr 16:34; II Chr 5:13; 7:3; Ezr 3:11; etc.). Second, God is everlastingly merciful. It is frequent refrain in the Psalms that, **his mercy endureth for ever** (cf. 118:1-4, 29; 136:1-26). Third, a joyful noise is to be made unto the Lord God, for **his truth endureth to all generations.** Jehovah is no fickle God, promising and then not performing. He is faithful generation after generation. He is God; He does not change. **Make a joyful noise unto the LORD, all ye lands** (vs. 1).

PSALM 100

MAKE a joyful noise unto the LORD, all ye lands.

2 Serve the LORD with gladness: come before his presence with singing.

3 Know ye that the LORD he *is* God: *it is* he *that* hath made us, and not we ourselves; *we are* his people, and the sheep of his pasture.

4 Enter into his gates with thanksgiving, *and* into his courts with praise: be thankful unto him, *and* bless his name.

5 For the LORD *is* good; his mercy *is* everlasting; and his truth *endureth* to all generations.

PSALM 101

I WILL sing of mercy and judgment: unto thee, O Lord, will I sing.

2 I will behave myself wisely in a perfect way. O when wilt thou come unto me? I will walk within my house with a perfect heart.

3 I will set no wicked thing before mine eyes: I hate the work of them that turn aside; *it* shall not cleave to me.

4 A froward heart shall depart from me: I will not know a wicked *person*.

5 Whoso privily slandereth his neighbour, him will I cut off: him that hath an high look and a proud heart will not I suffer.

6 Mine eyes *shall be* upon the faithful of the land, that they may dwell with me: he that walketh in a perfect way, he shall serve me.

7 He that worketh deceit shall not dwell within my house: he that telleth lies shall not tarry in my sight.

8 I will early destroy all the wicked of the land; that I may cut off all wicked doers from the city of the Lord.

L. Royal Resolutions. 101:1-8.

THEME: *A psalm of the king who resolves to rule righteously.*

The inscription of this psalm attributes it to David, and there is no good reason for not assuming its accuracy. As Maclaren notes, "The contents of this psalm go far toward confirming the correctness of the superscription in ascribing it to David."

The subject of the psalm is the rightful conduct and proper principles for the rule of the godly king. As Luther maintained, we have here *ein Regentenspiegel*, "a mirror for magistrates." It expresses the pious resolutionists, who purpose that in all aspects of His reign, God will be magnified.

101:1-2. I will sing of mercy and judgment. With the very first words of this psalm we see the absolute resolve of the king. He would extol both the sweet and the bitter, the pleasant experiences of life as king and the hardships. **I will behave myself wisely in a perfect way.** The psalmist aspires to behave himself in wisdom. Although David's resolve was commendable, at times his life did not square with his resolution (cf. II Sam 12). **I will walk within my house with a perfect heart.** It is easier for most men to walk with a perfect heart before the world than before their own families, but David resolves to walk blamelessly before those who know him best.

3-4. His resolution continues, not now concerning personal piety, but concerning those who would frequent his presence. **I will set no wicked thing before mine eyes.** The king is determined not to gaze with pleasure on that in which God has no pleasure. **I hate the work of them that turn aside,** i.e., that depart from the right way. **It shall not cleave to me.** He is determined neither to look with indifference on the sins of those around him nor to permit their sins to rub off on him.

A froward heart shall depart from me. Thomas Chalmers understands frowardness as "from-wardness" and says that it is "giving way to sudden impulses of anger, or quick conception, and casting it forth in words or deeds of impetuous violence." **I will not know a wicked person.** David is determined that those who are corrupt in character and crooked in heart will be denied entrance into his court.

5-6. Continuing his theme concerning those who will be disbarred from his fellowship, David says, **Whoso privily slandereth his neighbor, him will I cut off.** Slandering one's neighbor has always been considered a heinous crime (cf. 15:3; 31:13; 50:20; etc.). It betrays a reprobate heart and an untrustworthy manner. **Him that hath a high look and a proud heart will not I suffer** (cf. 131:1). No servant of pride or a domineering spirit would ever be a servant of Israel's camp. In contrast, David shall choose **the faithful of the land . . . he that walketh in a perfect way** to become responsible members of his court. David reasoned that men who are faithful to God will likely be faithful to men as well.

7-8. Lapsing into a reaffirmation that the one who **worketh deceit** and **he that telleth lies** shall not even be tolerated in David's presence, he finally resolves, **I will early destroy all the wicked of the land,** i.e., day after day he would make it his practice to free the palace from evildoers. **That I may cut off all wicked doers from the city of the Lord.** Jerusalem was to be the Holy City, and the king resolved to make it so. Every nation ought to long for men of government who have the same resolve as King David.

M. The Afflicted Messiah. 102:1-28.

THEME: *The plaintive cry of an abandoned and afflicted soul.*

The inscription of this psalm is entirely unique. It reads **A prayer of the afflicted, when he is overwhelmed, and poureth out his complaint before the Lord.** This title stands quite alone among the titles prefixed to the Psalms. It describes the character of the psalm and marks the circumstances under which it was given. In all other inscriptions there is either a musical or an historical notation.

Three major opinions prevail respecting the time of composition for this psalm. Some hold that it was written after the return of Ezra with the command to rebuild the Temple and thus relates to the state of affairs mentioned in Nehemiah 1:3-11. In this case the author is probably Nehemiah, Ezra, or some contemporary. Others view the psalm as having been written during the later time of the captivity. Accordingly, both Jeremiah and Daniel have been suggested as the author of the psalm. Others view the psalm as entirely prophetic, relating to no historical situation and therefore probably written by David. Hengstenberg and Alexander hold to this view.

Although it is curious that such scholars as Calvin and Tholuck, or even Hengstenberg and Spurgeon, do not address this as a messianic psalm it is nonetheless clearly to be included among those psalms that refer to the Messiah, Jesus Christ. That this ode is messianic is determined by inscription itself. In Hebrews 1:10-12 the author directly applies to Jesus Christ verses 25-27 of this psalm, substantially as they are found in the LXX. The author's intent is clearly to show that the Son of God is above the angels. A long line of expositors from the time of St. Augustine down to this day may be cited as holding a messianic view of Psalm 102.

102:1-2. Hear my prayer, O LORD, and let my cry come unto thee (cf. 27:7; 39:12; 54:2; 55:1; etc.). The words **prayer** and **cry** explain each other and express the great earnestness and urgency of the psalmist's petition. **Hide not thy face from me in the day when I am in trouble** (cf. 13:1; 27:9; 44:24; 69:17; 88:14). The plea continues, **incline thine ear unto me**, a frequently occurring petition (cf. 17:6; 31:2; 45:10; 71:2; 86:1; 88:2). **In the day when I call answer me speedily.** As Alexander notes, "We find here accumulated nearly all the phrases used by David to express the same ideas elsewhere." There is a definite progression to these petitions: **Hear . . . Hide not . . . incline . . . answer.**

3-5. For my days are consumed like smoke (perhaps, in smoke), i.e., they disappear and pass away into nothingness. **My bones are burned as a hearth** (perhaps, as a firebrand, cf. 31:10; 32:3; 42:10; Isa 33:14). **My heart is smitten, and withered like grass.** Clarke observes, "The metaphor here is taken from grass cut down in the meadow. It is first *smitten* with the scythe, and then *withered* by the sun." So great is this sufferer's pain that he forgets even to eat his bread. So weary is he from groaning that the psalmist says, **my bones cleave to my skin,** as if his bones were covered with skin only, no muscle (cf. Job 19:20; Lam 4:8).

6-7. I am like a pelican of the wilderness. The word here rendered **pelican** (Heb *qa'at*) may have come from a verb that signifies to vomit. The female pelican has under her bill a large pouch in which she carries quantities of food for her young. When she wishes to give them nourishment, she regurgitates their food and thus feeds them. Hence, the Hebrew name. Hence also the ability of the pelican to remain in solitude in the wilderness. **I am like an owl of the desert.** The owl haunts the ruins, wastes, or desolations of desert places (cf. Ezr 9:9; Isa 51:3; Ezk 33:24; 38:12). It, too, remains alone. **I . . . am as a sparrow alone upon the housetop.**

Each of these metaphors is designed to show the solitude of the psalmist in his agony. Since this psalm is messianic in nature, these metaphors describe the awful loneliness of Jesus during those last hours which led to His crucifixion.

8-10. The enemies of the Messiah reproached Him, a word implying great insolence, defiance, and railing. Those that were

PSALM 102

HEAR my prayer, O LORD, and let my cry come unto thee.
2 Hide not thy face from me in the day when I am in trouble; incline thine ear unto me: in the day when I call answer me speedily.

3 For my days are consumed like smoke, and my bones are burned as an hearth.
4 My heart is smitten, and withered like grass; so that I forget to eat my bread.
5 By reason of the voice of my groaning my bones cleave to my skin.

6 I am like a pelican of the wilderness: I am like an owl of the desert.
7 I watch, and am as a sparrow alone upon the house top.

8 Mine enemies reproach me all the

day; *and* they that are mad against me are sworn against me.

9 For I have eaten ashes like bread, and mingled my drink with weeping,

10 Because of thine indignation and thy wrath: for thou hast lifted me up, and cast me down.

11 My days *are* like a shadow that declineth; and I am withered like grass.

12 But thou, O LORD, shalt endure for ever; and thy remembrance unto all generations.

13 Thou shalt arise, *and* have mercy upon Zion: for the time to favour her, yea, the set time, is come.

14 For thy servants take pleasure in her stones, and favour the dust thereof.

15 So the heathen shall fear the name of the LORD, and all the kings of the earth thy glory.

16 When the LORD shall build up Zion, he shall appear in his glory.

17 He will regard the prayer of the destitute, and not despise their prayer.

18 This shall be written for the generation to come: and the people which shall be created shall praise the LORD.

19 For he hath looked down from the height of his sanctuary; from heaven did the LORD behold the earth;

20 To hear the groaning of the prisoner; to loose those that are appointed to death;

21 To declare the name of the LORD in Zion, and his praise in Jerusalem;

22 When the people are gathered together, and the kingdoms, to serve the LORD.

mad against Jesus Christ had **sworn against** Him, i.e., they had used Him as their curse. To eat **ashes like bread** is to say that the ashes of humiliation have been His bread. Likewise, to mingle the drink with tears is a figure of great distress and humiliation (cf. 42:3; 80:5). The relationship of God the Son to God the Father on that crucifixion day is seen in the expression **because of thine indignation and thy wrath: for thou hast lifted me up, and cast me down.** The psalmist is the recipient of divine wrath without a notation of cause. Nothing is said of his personal sin. Messianically, Jesus was the recipient of divine wrath upon the cross without accompanying personal sin. But the purpose of Christ's receiving God's indignation is clear: "For he (God the Father) hath made him (God the Son) to be sin for us, who knew no sin; that we might be made the righteousness of God in him" (II Cor 5:21).

11. My days are like a shadow that declineth (lit., that stretches out or lengthens as shadows do when the day comes to a conclusion). **I am withered like grass.** The I (Heb '*ani*) is emphatic. Not only have the psalmist's days come to an end, but they have come to an end as he himself is altogether scorched and dried up as the mown grass. How closely these echo the sentiments of the Lord Jesus on the cross (cf. Jn 19:28-30).

12-14. Suddenly, there is an abrupt change. Here the second part of the psalm begins, and the psalmist sees God's readiness to help both the city of Zion and himself. In contrast to his own declining days, the psalmist notes, **But thou, O LORD, shall endure for ever; and thy remembrance unto all generations.** It seems natural for the brevity of human life to be contrasted with the eternality of God. **Thou shalt arise, and have mercy upon Zion.** The Almighty will not allow the city of Zion, which represents God's people, to be desolate. **The set time, is come.** This expression is explained by what follows. **For thy servants take pleasure in her stones, and favor the dust thereof.** This verse, more than any other in the psalm, would seem to point to the rebuilding of Jerusalem (Neh 4:2, 10) as the occasion for the writing of this psalm. But the idea of desolation is frequently applied to the people of God just before a great, personal manifestation of God to them. Although the restoration of a destroyed city is the natural implication in the poetic language of the psalmist, it may not be the only interpretation.

15-17. When the LORD shall build up Zion, he shall appear in his glory. The verbs in this verse, and that of the next verse, are in the preterite, meaning the prophetic psalmist sees as certain those things not yet accomplished. He prophetically foresees a day when the Lord shall once again restore the greatness of His kingdom in Zion and **the heathen shall fear the name of the LORD, and all the kings of the earth thy glory.** Given a Messianic interpretation of the psalm, this restoration of Zion equally fits the millennial reign of Christ upon this earth as it does the historic rebuilding of Zion during the days of Ezra and Nehemiah.

18-22. Let the mercies of God through the coming Messiah **be written for the generation to come.** It is the great God of Israel who **hath looked down from the height of his sanctuary.** The psalmist pictures God in the sanctuary of the heavens, earnestly and thoroughly inquiring about the state of affairs of His people below. He hears the groaning of a **prisoner**, one who is bound by affliction and unable to help himself, one like Jesus Christ hanging upon the cross. The Lord God looks down to **loose those that are appointed to death,** i.e., the children of death, those doomed to death. God will praise His name in Zion, in Jerusalem, **when the people are gathered together, and the kingdoms, to serve the LORD.** This cannot be interpreted accurately in any other way but messianically. The fullness of God's capital city will only be seen during the messianic reign of Jesus Christ upon this earth, His kingdom, millennial reign.

23 He weakened my strength in the way; he shortened my days.
24 I said, O my God, take me not away in the midst of my days: thy years *are* throughout all generations.

25 Of old hast thou laid the foundation of the earth: and the heavens *are* the work of thy hands.
26 They shall perish, but thou shalt endure: yea, all of them shall wax old like a garment; as a vesture shalt thou change them, and they shall be changed:
27 But thou *art* the same, and thy years shall have no end.

28 The children of thy servants shall continue, and their seed shall be established before thee.

PSALM 103

BLESS the LORD, O my soul: and all that is within me, *bless* his holy name.
2 Bless the LORD, O my soul, and forget not all his benefits:

23-24. Again, the beginning of a third strophe can be seen. The psalmist begins with an acknowledgement of his weakness, couched in the confidence that God, who is everlasting, will perpetually protect His own. **He weakened my strength in the way; he shortened my days.** A weakened sufferer is pictured as coming to an end prematurely. **I said, O my God, take me not away in the midst of my days,** i.e., "O my Father, if it be possible, let this cup pass from me . . ." (Mt 26:39).

25-27. **Of old hast thou laid the foundation of the earth** (cf. Isa 48:13). **The heavens are the work of thy hands** (cf. 89:11; Gen 1:1, 7; 2:4). **They shall perish** (cf. Isa 51:6; 65:17; Mt 24:35; Mk 13:31; Lk 21:33; II Pet 3:7, 10, 12), **but thou shalt endure** (cf. 9:7). **All of them shall wax old like a garment** (cf. Isa 51:6), **as a vesture shalt thou change them, and they shall be changed** (cf. Isa 65:17; 66:22; II Pet 3:13; Rev 21:1). **But thou art the same,** i.e., "thou art the eternal one, infinite and unchangeable" (cf. Isa 41:4; 43:10), **and thy years shall have no end.** "We cannot be mistaken in applying this language to Jesus. We have the authority of heaven itself for so doing, Heb 1:10-12" (Plumer, p. 909).

28. **The children of thy servants shall continue, and their seed shall be established before thee.** All who come to the Messiah, the Lord Jesus, in faith and love (89:36; Gal 3:7) shall continue, be established, and have an everlasting inheritance. The eternal God does not forsake His own. With what burst of confidence this psalm concludes after a rather gloomy beginning in solitude. Though we may be alone, as God's children, we are never abandoned or annihilated. The solitude of Jesus on the cross and His reception into the hands of God the Father prove that for all of us.

N. The Pinnacle of Praise. 103:1-22.

THEME: *A pure note of praise for God's mercy in forgiving sin.*
So beautiful is this psalm that Spurgeon says, "There is too much in this Psalm for a thousand pens to write, it is one of those all-comprehending Scriptures which is a Bible in itself, and it might alone almost suffice for the hymn-book of the Church." Henry's first remark on the psalm is, "This Psalm calls more for devotion than exposition."
This delightful note of praise for the mercies of the Lord carries the superscription, **A psalm of David.** Although it has been quite fashionable to deny Davidic authorship of this psalm, there is insufficient reason to do so. The Hebrew and all the ancient versions list David as its author. The argument for a later date of the psalm is built upon supposed Aramaic terminal forms that this psalm has in common with 116; 124; 129; and 139; but those so-called Aramaisms are not a true index of date. The same forms occur in II Kings 4:1-7. Also, similarities with words found in Job and the latter chapters of Isaiah do not necessitate a late date for this psalm. This psalm may be the original from which these authors borrowed. Thus, holding to the old Jewish tradition of Davidic authorship appears to be sound.
This delightful psalm consists of 22 verses, the exact number of letters in the Hebrew alphabet. It concludes with the words with which it began, **Bless the LORD, O my soul.** It is, therefore, a composition of praise by the psalmist to the covenant of God of Israel whom he loved so dearly.
103:1-2. **Bless the LORD, O my soul: and all that is within me.** David calls upon his soul, his immortal nature, which he defines as all that is within him, all his senses and faculties (cf. 5:9; 49:11) to bless the holy name of God. By stirring the innermost self to magnify the Lord, the psalmist has remembered the law of gratitude. **Forget not all his benefits.** The word rendered **benefits** (Heb *gemŭl*) means an act or work, and

1117

3 Who forgiveth all thine iniquities;
who healeth all thy diseases;
4 Who redeemeth thy life from destruction; who crowneth thee with
lovingkindness and tender mercies;
5 Who satisfieth thy mouth with
good *things; so that* thy youth is
renewed like the eagle's.

6 The LORD executeth righteousness
and judgment for all that are oppressed.
7 He made known his ways unto
Moses, his acts unto the children of
Israel.

8 The LORD *is* merciful and gracious,
slow to anger, and plenteous in mercy.
9 He will not always chide: neither
will he keep *his anger* for ever.
10 He hath not dealt with us after our
sins; nor rewarded us according to our
iniquities.

11 For as the heaven is high above the
earth, *so* great is his mercy toward
them that fear him.
12 As far as the east is from the west,
so far hath he removed our transgressions from us.
13 Like as a father pitieth *his* children, *so* the LORD pitieth them that fear
him.

14 For he knoweth our frame; he
remembereth that we *are* dust.
15 *As for* man, his days *are* as grass:
as a flower of the field, so he
flourisheth.
16 For the wind passeth over it, and it

consequently the recompense of what a man deserves for his act.
The psalmist is literally prepared to count his many blessings
and name them one by one.

3-5. David begins his list of blessings with the note that he
praises the God **who forgiveth all thine iniquities,** the greatest
benefit we can receive from God. It is significant that the
psalmist's praise to God is for the Almighty who **forgiveth,** a
continual forgiving, of iniquities and **who healeth all thy diseases.**

Third in the list of the benefits the psalmist will not forget is
that God is the one **who redeemeth thy life from destruction,**
both by purchase through the blood of Jesus Christ and by the
power of His mighty hand. Redemption always constitutes one
of the sweetest notes of the redeemeds' chorus. **Who crowneth
thee with loving-kindness and tender mercies** (cf. 8:5; 18:50;
23:6; etc.); **who satisfieth thy mouth with good things.** Regardless of our age, when we find joy and happiness in blessing the
name of the Lord and recounting all His benefits to us, the
strength of our youth **is renewed like the eagle's.** We have the
strength to soar over the problems that face us daily because we
have a heart satisfied with God.

6-7. **The LORD executeth righteousness and judgment for
all that are oppressed.** The care of the oppressed is a recurring
feature in the Holy Scriptures (cf. 9:9; 10:18; 79:21; 146:7; Ex
2:23-24; Jud 2:18; Job 35:9-14; Isa 1:17; etc.). **He made known
his ways unto Moses.** Although God's ways are ". . . past
finding out" by man (Rom 11:33), yet it is an act of sovereign
grace and condescending love when the Lord God reveals Himself to any individual. Throughout the wilderness journey God
revealed Himself continually, although mysteriously, to both
Moses and **the children of Israel.**

8-10. The psalmist now turns his attention completely to
praising God for His divine character. **The LORD is merciful
and gracious, slow to anger, and plenteous in mercy.** As is
seen in Exodus 34:6, this was part of the revelation God made to
Moses. Both here and in 86:15 the psalmist is found to echo the
words of Moses. **He will not always chide: neither will he keep
his anger for ever.** Jehovah will not always contend with those
who sin (Isa 57:16; cf. Jer 3:5, 12). His anger bears no grudges
and harbors no resentments. He is not implacable; He is a God
who will accept repentance (Ezk 18:27) and atonement (I Jn
2:2).

One of the most praiseworthy characteristics of God is that **He
hath not dealt with us after our sins; nor rewarded us according to our iniquities.** God does not punish us as we deserve, else
each of us would be consigned to the lowest hell. We ought to
praise the Lord for what He has not done to us, as well as for
what He has done for us.

11-13. **For as the heaven is high above the earth, so great is
his mercy** (36:5). **As far as the east is from the west, so far
hath he removed our transgressions from us.** Sin is removed
by the miracle of God's love and Christ's atonement. His mercy
is the cause, and the extent of forgiveness is described by the
largest measure which the earth can render. The reason for this
wondrous mercy is clear, **Like as a father pitieth his children,
so the LORD pitieth them that fear him** (cf. Deut 32:6; Job
10:8; Isa 29:16; 63:16; 64:8; etc.). Like the reverence and
respect of a child to his father, so too when we exhibit that godly
fear (Heb 12:28) toward God, His great mercy is extended
toward us.

14-16. The mercy of God is the natural extension of His
omniscience. **For he knoweth our frame; he remembereth that
we are dust** (cf. Gen 2:7; 3:19; Job 34:15; etc.). Man is fragile,
feeble, and when left to himself, helpless. **His days are as grass**
(cf. 37:2; 90:5-6; 102:11; Isa 40:6-8; etc.). They are **as a flower
of the field** (cf. Job 14:2; Isa 28:1; 40:6; Jas 1:10; I Pet 1:24;

is gone; and the place thereof shall know it no more.

17 But the mercy of the LORD *is* from everlasting to everlasting upon them that fear him, and his righteousness unto children's children;
18 To such as keep his covenant, and to those that remember his commandments to do them.

19 The LORD hath prepared his throne in the heavens; and his kingdom ruleth over all.

20 Bless the LORD, ye his angels, that excel in strength, that do his commandments, hearkening unto the voice of his word.
21 Bless ye the LORD, all *ye* his hosts; *ye* ministers of his, that do his pleasure.
22 Bless the LORD, all his works in all places of his dominion: bless the LORD, O my soul.

PSALM 104

BLESS the LORD, O my soul. O LORD my God, thou art very great; thou art clothed with honour and majesty.

etc.), which may brilliantly fragrance his world but is short-lived. **For the wind passeth over it, and it is gone** (lit., it is not).

17-18. But the mercy of the LORD is from everlasting to everlasting upon them that fear him. The psalmist here contrasts the fleeting character of man's life with the everlasting character of God's mercy. Divine mercy is **from everlasting,** indicating that from eternity past the Lord viewed His own through the eyes of mercy. And divine mercy is **to everlasting,** an equally precious thought. Jehovah does not change, as His mercy is without beginning, so it is without end. Yet, that mercy is **upon them that fear him** only, and **his righteousness unto children's children.** But this too has the conditional element, **to such as keep his covenant.** God's mercy cannot be claimed until it is claimed by His grace. We do not know God's mercy until we know it in His son, Jesus Christ.

19. The LORD hath prepared his throne in the heavens; and his kingdom ruleth over all. In preparation for the grand finale of praise to God, the psalmist depicts the incomparable majesty of God as He sits on His throne **prepared** (lit., established in the heavens). He rules over all the kingdoms of the world, a promise that will find its ultimate fulfillment when "The kingdoms of this world are become the kingdoms of our Lord, and of His Christ; and he shall reign for ever and ever" (Rev 11:15).

20-22. This final triad of verses forms a trilogy of praise to God. Three times the expression **Bless the LORD** is used to call God's creation, all of His creation, to praise Him. The **angels, that excel in strength** are perhaps those called "archangels" in the New Testament (I Thess 4:16; Jude 9), the highest and most glorious beings that surround the throne of God (Rev 8:2, 6; 10:1) and **do his commandments. All ye his hosts; ye ministers of his, that do his pleasure** may refer to angels of lesser stature, the multitude of the hosts of heaven that appeared to the shepherds of Beth-lehem (Lk 2:13) and are elsewhere referred to in Scripture (cf. 24:10; 148:2; Isa 40:26; Mt 25:31; Mk 8:38; Lk 9:26; Heb 12:22; Jude 14). Finally, **all his works in all places of his dominion** (19:1-4; 145:10; 148:7-13) may refer to the material universe, which is now invited to join the archangels, the angelic hosts, and the soul of the psalmist in blessing the Lord. **Bless the LORD, O my soul** is not only the keynote of this psalm; it is the conclusion of it as well.

O. The Creation Psalm. 104:1-35.

THEME: *A poet's version of the creation chapters of Genesis.*

Although neither the Hebrew nor the Chaldee versions ascribe a title to this psalm, nevertheless the Syriac, Arabic, Septuagint, Ethiopic, and Vulgate list David as its author. The close relationship with the last psalm may bear out that contention.

This psalm is very unique because it is the only example of ancient poetry in which there is a distinct recognition that the universe was created by and is totally dependent on a creator. In fact, this is the main theme of the poem.

Although this psalm shows familiarity with the Genesis creation story, it does not follow it slavishly. It is not merely a copy of the original, but has an originality of its own. It is a poet's eye view of the creative work of God, but in some respects it is even a more striking record of creation than that of Genesis.

104:1a. Bless the LORD, O my soul. O LORD my God, thou art very great. Immediately, the keynote for the psalm is set. It begins and ends like the one which precedes it. A psalm that praises the Creator and His creation can only begin with the statement that the Lord is **very great.** Yet, this is a remarkable blending of faith and fear; the psalmist speaks the unspeakable name of Jehovah with holy reverence, and yet personalizes Jehovah by calling Him **my God.**

2 Who coverest *thyself* with light as *with* a garment: who stretchest out the heavens like a curtain:

3 Who layeth the beams of his chambers in the waters: who maketh the clouds his chariot: who walketh upon the wings of the wind:

4 Who maketh his angels spirits; his ministers a flaming fire:

5 *Who* laid the foundations of the earth, *that* it should not be removed for ever.

6 Thou coveredst it with the deep as *with* a garment: the waters stood above the mountains.

7 At thy rebuke they fled; at the voice of thy thunder they hasted away.

8 They go up by the mountains; they go down by the valleys unto the place which thou hast founded for them.

9 Thou hast set a bound that they may not pass over; that they turn not again to cover the earth.

10 He sendeth the springs into the valleys, *which* run among the hills.

11 They give drink to every beast of the field: the wild asses quench their thirst.

12 By them shall the fowls of the heaven have their habitation, *which* sing among the branches.

13 He watereth the hills from his chambers: the earth is satisfied with the fruit of thy works.

14 He causeth the grass to grow for the cattle, and herb for the service of man: that he may bring forth food out of the earth;

15 And wine *that* maketh glad the heart of man, *and* oil to make *his* face to shine, and bread *which* strengtheneth man's heart.

16 The trees of the LORD are full *of sap;* the cedars of Lebanon, which he hath planted;

17 Where the birds make their nests: *as for* the stork, the fir trees *are* her house.

18 The high hills *are* a refuge for the wild goats; *and* the rocks for the conies.

1b-6. Thou art clothed with honor and majesty, i.e., you have robed yourself with glory and grandeur. **Who coverest thyself with light as with a garment.** Light was the first thing created (Gen 1:3) and, Jehovah shrouds Himself in it, veiling His hidden glory from the rest of His creation.

It is God **who stretchest out the heavens like a curtain,** i.e., like a canopy (cf. Isa 40:22; 42:5; 44:24), and **who layeth the beams of his chambers in the waters,** i.e., makes the clouds the flooring of His heavens and **his chariot** (cf. Isa 19:1). The anthropomorphism continues as the psalmist notes that God **walketh upon the wings of the wind** (18:10).

Jehovah also makes **his angels spirits,** messengers of the wind (Heb *rûach* meaning both spirit and wind), **his ministers a flaming fire** (cf. Hebrews 1:7 where this passage refers to angels). God wrapped **the foundations of the earth** in aquatic clothing and concealed the highest mountains in a watery womb.

7-9. Yet it was not the design of Jehovah that the earth should remain in this condition, and thus **At thy rebuke they fled,** i.e., the waters shifted into the places established by God (Gen 1:9). At the command of God waters by the **mountains** and **valleys** flowed to **the place which thou hast founded for them.** Except for the Great Deluge, which for the purpose of his poetry is excluded by the poet, God had **set a bound** for the waters **that they may not pass over** (cf. Job 38:10-11; Jer 5:22).

10-12. He sendeth the springs into the valleys . . . They give drink to every beast of the field. God has designed the mountain streams that flow where the animals graze, and in His mercy He cares for all of His creation (cf. 104:27; 145:15-16; Ex 20:10; 23:19; Deut 25:4; Jn 4:11; etc.). **By them** (i.e., by the springs), **shall the fowls of the heaven have their habitation** when the streams water the trees in which the birds filled their nests. John Wesley reminds us that the music of birds was the first song of thanksgiving which was offered from the earth. All of God's creation praises His name.

13-15. These verses perfectly illustrate how God coordinates nature. **He watereth the hills from his chambers.** Even those high hills that cannot be moistened by the streams receive their moisture from God's own heaven. The rain falls upon the peaks of the mountains, and **the earth is satisfied.** Because of God's coordinated plan for nature, **He causeth the grass to grow for the cattle, and herb for the service of man.** God has seen to it that **food** for every one of His creatures arises **out of the earth.** And not only food, but **wine that maketh glad the heart of man** (Num 15:5, 7; Jud 9:12-13; Prov 31:6-7) is given to God's creation. The word **wine** (Heb *yayin*, Gr *oinos*) can indicate any form of the juice of the grape that might be made into a beverage.

With **wine** God also gave to man **oil to make his face to shine, and bread which strengtheneth man's heart.** Such oil was used for various purposes, i.e., to avoid intoxication, to improve the health, to perfume the body, or to shine the face as an emblem of joy. God sees to it that man has all he needs; and thus, it is not without consequence that the Promised Land is said to have produced in abundance these three: wine, oil, and bread (cf. Deut 8:8; 9:14; II Kgs 18:32).

16-18. The trees of the LORD . . . the cedars of Lebanon, which he hath planted; where the birds make their nests. Even the trees have their fill of God's moisture and have grown tall and stately like the cedars of Lebanon (cf. 29:5-6; 92:12). Again, the coordination of God's nature is seen. The moisture waters the trees, which makes provision for the birds to house themselves. God's mercy is seen throughout all His creation. **The high hills are a refuge for the wild goats** (i.e., the ibex, an animal of agility). **The rocks for the conies** (i.e., rabbits or marmots), ". . . a feeble folk, yet makes their houses in the rocks" (Prov 30:26).

19 He appointed the moon for seasons: the sun knoweth his going down.
20 Thou makest darkness and it is night: wherein all the beasts of the forest do creep *forth*.
21 The young lions roar after their prey, and seek their meat from God.
22 The sun ariseth, they gather themselves together, and lay them down in their dens.
23 Man goeth forth unto his work and to his labour until the evening.

24 O LORD, how manifold are thy works! in wisdom hast thou made them all: the earth is full of thy riches.

25 *So is* this great and wide sea, wherein *are* things creeping innumerable, both small and great beasts.
26 There go the ships: *there is* that leviathan, *whom* thou hast made to play therein.

27 These wait all upon thee; that thou mayest give *them* their meat in due season.
28 *That* thou givest them they gather: thou openest thine hand, they are filled with good.
29 Thou hidest thy face, they are troubled: thou takest away their breath, they die, and return to their dust.
30 Thou sendest forth thy spirit, they are created: and thou renewest the face of the earth.

31 The glory of the LORD shall endure for ever: the LORD shall rejoice in his works.
32 He looketh on the earth, and it trembleth: he toucheth the hills, and they smoke.

33 I will sing unto the LORD as long as I live: I will sing praise to my God while I have my being.
34 My meditation of him shall be sweet: I will be glad in the LORD.

35 Let the sinners be consumed out of the earth, and let the wicked be no more. Bless thou the LORD, O my soul. Praise ye the LORD.

19-23. Now the psalmist turns his attention to God's coordination of the heavens. **He appointed the moon for seasons** (cf. Gen 1:14). The Jewish calendar was a lunar calendar; dates followed the movements of the moon. Thus, the Jewish psalmist viewed the moon as all-important in setting the seasons. **The sun knoweth his going down** (i.e., a poetic picture of the sun knowing when it is time to set). **Thou makest darkness, and it is night.** It is at night that **all the beasts of the forests do creep forth** and the primeval jungle comes alive with action. **The young lions roar after their prey,** stalking the night forests seeking God's provision for their own sustenance. And then **The sun ariseth,** which causes the jungle to rest when the lions and beasts of the forest **lay them down in their dens.**

How beautifully God has arranged His creation. **Man goeth forth unto his work and to his labor until the evening.** Then man must rest from his labors; and when he does, the predatory animals arise from their daylight rest to prowl the jungles at night. God coordinates nature by the coordinated alternation of the sun and moon.

24. With such a marvelous illustration before his eyes, the psalmist can but cry, **O LORD, how manifold are thy works! In wisdom hast thou made them all: the earth is full of thy riches.**

25-26. Finally, the psalmist turns his attention beneath the sea to the **things creeping innumerable, both small and great beasts.** The abundant life of the sea is again living proof of God's control over His creatures. In the sea **go the ships;** and in the same waters **there is that leviathan,** probably in this case a whale **whom thou hast made to play therein.** The huge whale has made the waters of the world his playground while at the same time the shipping lanes are used for man's commerce. How wonderful is God's coordination of His creatures.

27-30. These verses represent a summarization of all the realms of God's creation considered by the psalmist. His conclusion is that, regardless of the realm, **These wait all upon thee,** Jehovah God. All God must do is simply open His hand, and **they are filled with good.** The whole of creation must recognize that, as it did not come into existence by itself, it cannot maintain existence by itself.

Thou hidest thy face, they are troubled. If God withdraws the light of His countenance from His living creatures, they are confounded (cf. 30:7). He who gave them breath should He take away that breath; **they die, and return to their dust,** the dust from which they were formed. The psalmist knows nothing of spontaneous generation; God sends forth His **spirit,** and **they are created.** The fallacies of evolution did not cloud his understanding of the marvelous creative hand of God.

31-32. Theories of generation may come and go; but because of the remarkable creation of God, **The glory of the LORD shall endure for ever.** It is His creation, **He looketh on the earth, and it trembleth,** perhaps a poetic reference to earthquakes and earth tremors. **He toucheth the hills, and they smoke.** Mount Sinai quaked and smoked at the presence of God and we too must stand in awe at the incredible power of God as evidenced through His creation.

33-34. In light of all that the mind of the psalmist has recalled, his resolve must be that **I will sing unto the LORD as long as I live: I will sing praise to my God while I have my being.** The psalmist knows he will sing the praises of God until the end of his days; the Christian knows he will sing the praises of his God well beyond his days. **My meditation of him shall be sweet** both to God and to me. **I will be glad in the LORD** (cf. 32:11; 33:1; etc.). Being glad in God is a form of praising Him.

35. **Let the sinners be consumed out of the earth, and let the wicked be no more.** Those who are a blot on God's creation, the spoilers, are to be removed. Then the whole world will join the psalmist with praising, **Bless thou the LORD, O my soul.**

This oft-repeated phrase now gives way to a new phrase, **Praise ye the LORD** (Heb *halelū-yah*). This is the first time the word *Hallelujah* occurs in the Psalms. The great God Jehovah creates and sustains; He cleanses and saves. *Hallelujah!*

P. The Abrahamic Covenant Psalm. 105:1-45.

THEME: *A psalm of praise for God's mercy toward Israel in her early history.*

Like the two which precede it, this psalm and the next are a pair; and they conclude Book IV of the Psalter. Together they are closely related to Psalm 78. Psalm 105 tells how God treated Israel; Psalm 106 tells how Israel treated God. The keynote of the first psalm is the Lord's grace; the keynote of the second is the people's disgrace. In Psalm 105 our eyes are continually fixed on the magnificence of the works of the Lord. In Psalm 106 they are fixed on Israel's ingratitude and impenitence. In Psalm 78 both these approaches are blended by emphasizing that God's mighty works and the proper responses to them are to be taught to every generation.

Hengstenberg and others have held that since the psalm deals at length with the early history of Israel, the design of the psalmist was to encourage the exiles in the Babylonian captivity. No ancient version names any author; and neither the Hebrew or Chaldee prefixes any title. The Syriac says the psalm is anonymous. Yet, Davidic authorship cannot be ruled out. The first fifteen verses are found in I Chronicles 16:8-22, with some slight variations. Of these words I Chronicles 16:7 records, "Then on that day David delivered first this psalm to thank the Lord into the hand of Asaph and his brethren." What follows this statement is substantially the same as the first fifteen verses of this psalm. Although a later writer may have been familiar with the work of David, who would be more familiar with it than the author himself? Thus, Davidic authorship is a very viable possibility.

105:1-3. As is his practice, the psalmist begins with a call to **Give thanks unto the LORD** (cf. 106:1; 107:1; 111:1; 136:1; 138:1). Accompanying the invitation to **Give thanks** is the invitation to **call upon his name,** i.e., come to Him with praise and petition, and to **make known his deeds among the people,** i.e., the heathen nations (cf. 18:49; 57:9; Isa 12:4). A fourth and fifth invitation accompany these three: **Sing unto him,** i.e., praise His name with song and music, and **talk ye of all his wondrous works** (cf. 119:27, 46). But the joyful invitation is not yet complete; and the psalmist invites us to **Glory ye in his holy name** as much or more than the world does in riches and fame, and **let the heart of them rejoice that seek the LORD** (cf. 33:21).

4-6. To the above sevenfold invitation the psalmist now invites us to join him in two additional praiseworthy activities. **Seek the LORD . . . his strength . . . his face,** i.e., His person, His support, and His favor, and **Remember his marvelous works** (rendered "miracles" in the LXX, Gr *ta terata autou*). Though an invitation to all the redeemed, these nine activities are the special delight of the **seed of Abraham** and the **children of Jacob his chosen.**

7-11. Here the psalmist gives the basis for God's dealings with His people, i.e., the Abrahamic Covenant. The covenant is issued from Jehovah; **He is the LORD our God.** After identifying the One who initiates the covenant, the poet next identifies the universal dominion of Jehovah God; **his judgments are in all the earth.** He then praises God's historic faithfulness; **He hath remembered his covenant for ever.** The covenant was **made with Abraham** (Gen 15:18), yet God consigned **his oath unto Isaac** (Gen 26:2-5) **and confirmed the same unto Jacob for a law** (Gen 28:10-15) **to Israel for an everlasting covenant,** i.e., to Jacob after his name was changed to Israel (cf. Gen 35:10-12).

PSALM 105

O GIVE thanks unto the LORD; call upon his name: make known his deeds among the people.

2 Sing unto him, sing psalms unto him: talk ye of all his wondrous works.

3 Glory ye in his holy name: let the heart of them rejoice that seek the LORD.

4 Seek the LORD, and his strength: seek his face evermore.

5 Remember his marvellous works that he hath done; his wonders, and the judgments of his mouth;

6 O ye seed of Abraham his servant, ye children of Jacob his chosen.

7 He *is* the LORD our God: his judgments *are* in all the earth.

8 He hath remembered his covenant for ever, the word *which* he commanded to a thousand generations.

9 Which *covenant* he made with Abraham, and his oath unto Isaac;

10 And confirmed the same unto Jacob for a law, *and* to Israel *for* an everlasting covenant:

11 Saying, Unto thee will I give the land of Canaan, the lot of your inheritance:

The substance of the Abrahamic Covenant was God's promise that **Unto thee will I give the land of Canaan, the lot of your inheritance** (cf. Gen 13:15; 17:8; 26:3; 28:13).

12-15. This covenant was made when the descendants of Abraham could easily be counted, for **they were but a few men in number.** The time when God cut a covenant with Abraham was when he and his family **went from one nation to another,** a reference to the migration of the Patriarchs from one region to another, one tribe to another. Yet, through it all God **suffered no man to do them wrong,** a probable reference to the punishment inflicted on Pharaoh (Gen 12:17) and on Abimelech of Gerar (Gen 20:3, 7, 18).

God had warned those whom His chosen servants would encounter, **Touch not mine anointed, and do my prophets no harm.** Although Abraham, Isaac, and Jacob had no external anointing, nevertheless the implication of this command is clear. They had been specifically set apart by God to His service; and when those whom they encountered attempted to do them evil, such as Pharaoh and Abimelech, God hedged them about with His mighty hand. The same thing is true today of those set apart by God for His service. God's man is indestructible until he has finished the task God has called him to do.

16-19. The poet now begins to recount how God's family was led into Egypt. **Moreover he called for a famine upon the land.** For God to call for a famine is the same as to create a famine. What He **called for** immediately comes into existence (Gen 1:3). **He brake the whole staff of bread** (cf. Lev 26:26; Isa 3:1). So severe was the famine that God created in Canaan (cf. Gen 41:1; 42:5; 43:1), that the very staff of life was destroyed. **He sent a man before them, even Joseph, who was sold for a servant** (cf. Gen 37:28, 36; 39:1). Man views Joseph's life as being **sold;** God views him as being **sent.** Joseph **was laid in iron** and his feet bound **with fetters . . . until the time that his word came,** i.e., came to pass (cf. Gen 40:20-22). **The word of the LORD tried him.** The word tried (Heb *tsarap*) means assayed (cf. 12:6; 17:3; 18:30). Though shamefully treated and with fetter-bruised feet, Joseph had come through his ordeal as gold from the refiner's fire, more pure and lustrous.

20-22. **The king sent and loosed him** (Gen 41:14), **He made him lord of his house, and ruler of all his substance** (Gen 41:40). As ruler of the house of Pharaoh, he who once was bound in prison could now **bind his princes at his pleasure.** Joseph had become Pharaoh's prime minister with next to absolute power. His wisdom and prowess in political economy made it possible for him to **teach his senators wisdom,** being wiser than any of them (Gen 41:38-39).

23-25. **Israel also came into Egypt; and Jacob sojourned in the land of Ham.** Yet, while lodging in Egypt, God **increased his people greatly; and made them stronger than their enemies.** The family of Jacob multiplied rapidly (cf. Ex 1:7, 12, 20) and grew in might until the sons of Ham recognized that "the people of the children of Israel are more and mightier than we" (Ex 1:9). By prospering Israel more than the native Egyptians, God **turned their heart to hate his people, to deal subtilely with his servants** (Ex 1:10).

26-27. Just as God **sent** the man Joseph into Egyptian bondage, so too God **sent Moses his servant** to deliver His people. On the mission of Moses, see Exodus 3:10-18; 4:1-9. Aaron's mission is recorded in Exodus 4:14-17. Both **Moses . . . and Aaron . . . showed his signs among them, and wonders in the land of Ham.** Aaron initiated the signs (Ex 7:10, 19-20; 8:6, 17), and Moses continued them (Ex 9:10, 23; 10:13, 22).

28-36. Now the psalmist begins to enumerate the signs and wonders that God did in the land of Egypt. **He sent darkness** (Ex 10:21-23) . . . **He turned their waters into blood** (Ex 7:20-21) . . . **Their land brought forth frogs in abundance** (Ex

---

12 When they were *but* a few men in number; yea, very few, and strangers in it.

13 When they went from one nation to another, from *one* kingdom to another people;

14 He suffered no man to do them wrong: yea, he reproved kings for their sakes;

15 *Saying,* Touch not mine anointed, and do my prophets no harm.

16 Moreover he called for a famine upon the land: he brake the whole staff of bread.

17 He sent a man before them, *even* Joseph, *who* was sold for a servant:

18 Whose feet they hurt with fetters: he was laid in iron:

19 Until the time that his word came: the word of the LORD tried him.

20 The king sent and loosed him; *even* the ruler of the people, and let him go free.

21 He made him lord of his house, and ruler of all his substance:

22 To bind his princes at his pleasure; and teach his senators wisdom.

23 Israel also came into Egypt; and Jacob sojourned in the land of Ham.

24 And he increased his people greatly; and made them stronger than their enemies.

25 He turned their heart to hate his people, to deal subtilly with his servants.

26 He sent Moses his servant; *and* Aaron whom he had chosen.

27 They shewed his signs among them, and wonders in the land of Ham.

28 He sent darkness, and made it dark; and they rebelled not against his word.

29 He turned their waters into blood,
and slew their fish.

30 Their land brought forth frogs in
abundance, in the chambers of their
kings.

31 He spake, and there came divers
sorts of flies, *and* lice in all their coasts.

32 He gave them hail for rain, *and*
flaming fire in their land.

33 He smote their vines also and their
fig trees; and brake the trees of their
coasts.

34 He spake, and the locusts came,
and caterpillers, and that without number,

35 And did eat up all the herbs in their
land, and devoured the fruit of their
ground.

36 He smote also all the firstborn in
their land, the chief of all their strength.

37 He brought them forth also with
silver and gold: and *there was* not one
feeble *person* among their tribes.

38 Egypt was glad when they departed: for the fear of them fell upon
them.

39 He spread a cloud for a covering;
and fire to give light in the night.

40 *The people* asked, and he brought
quails, and satisfied them with the
bread of heaven.

41 He opened the rock, and the waters
gushed out; they ran in the dry
places *like* a river.

42 For he remembered his holy promise, *and* Abraham his servant.

43 And he brought forth his people
with joy, *and* his chosen with gladness:

44 And gave them the lands of the
heathen: and they inherited the labour
of the people;

45 That they might observe his statutes, and keep his laws. Praise ye the
LORD.

8:6) . . . **and there came divers sorts of flies** (Ex 8:21), probably gnats or biting insects which alight on the moist part of the eyelids and nostrils, **and lice** (Ex 8:17), a common annoyance in Egypt. **He gave them hail for rain, and flaming fire** (Ex 9:23) which broke down **their vines also and their fig trees** (cf. 78:47; Ex 9:25). **He spake and the locusts came, and caterpillars** (Ex 10:13-14). But the crushing blow to the Egyptians, the master blow, came when God **smote also all the first-born in their land** (Ex 12:29). Through the mighty hand of God the powerful Pharaoh of Egypt was brought to his knees.

37-38. Exodus 12:35-36 records that the Israelites received from their neighbors **silver and gold,** which they brought with them out of the land, perhaps as reparations. None were left behind, **not one feeble person among their tribes.** The oppressed Israelites were anxious to leave, but no more so than their oppressors; for **Egypt was glad when they departed** (Ex 11:1, 8; 12:31, 33).

39-41. Not only had God displayed His mercy in delivering His chosen people from the bands of Egyptian bondage, He also displayed great mercy when **He spread a cloud for a covering; and fire to give light in the night.** When the Israelites murmured because of their diet, **he brought quails, and satisfied them with the bread of heaven.** Although the quails provided the Israelites with only periodic food, the manna was fresh every morning. But what would they drink in their wilderness journey? **He opened the rock, and the waters gushed out** (Ex 17:5-6; Num 20:8-11). God was truly merciful to His murmuring people; and the last verse of the psalm gives the reason.

42-45. Three acts of God proved His love and faithfulness to Israel: (1) **he remembered his holy promise, and Abraham his servant,** i.e., the Abrahamic Covenant, to bring the descendants of Abraham into the Promised Land; (2) **he brought forth his people with joy,** initially forced from the land of bondage, but ultimately into the land of blessing; and (3) **He gave them the lands of the heathen** (cf. Josh 8-12) in which **they inherited the labor of the people** (cf. Deut 6:10-11). These three singular acts of God, more than any others, proved His love and faithfulness to Israel.

But why did He do it? Why did He endure with longsuffering such ungrateful people? The answer, **that they might observe his statutes, and keep his laws.** Just the very thought of this process brings the psalmist to conclude with a "Hallelujah," **Praise ye the LORD** (cf. 104:35; 106:1, 48; 111:1; 112:1; 113:1; etc.).

Q. A National Confession of Sin. 106:1-48.

THEME: Amid praise, the psalmist confesses the sins of a nation.

This is the first of the truly Hallelujah psalms, i.e., the psalms beginning with the phrase **Praise ye the LORD** (*Hallelu-Jah*). The others are 111-113; 135; 146-150. Eight of these ten psalms (all but 111 and 112) also end with the same phrase. Psalms 104 and 105 end with the phrase, but do not begin with it.

On the authorship of the psalm little is known. The psalm has no title, but it may safely be said that whoever wrote the preceding psalm also wrote this one. Many ascribe the psalm to David; for the first verse and the last two verses, except the Hallelujahs, are taken from I Chronicles 16:34-36, almost certainly penned by David. But the expression, **gather us from among the heathen** (vs. 47), has led many interpreters to believe that this psalm was written during the conditions that prevailed only after the Exile or during it.

The most notable feature of the psalm is the rehearsal of the sins of Israel with intent to make confession for them. The psalm begins and ends with *Hallelujah;* the verses between are filled with the mournful details of Israel's sin.

PSALM 106

PRAISE ye the LORD. O give thanks unto the LORD; for *he is* good: for his mercy *endureth* for ever.

2 Who can utter the mighty acts of the LORD? *who* can shew forth all his praise?

3 Blessed *are* they that keep judgment, *and* he that doeth righteousness at all times.

4 Remember me, O LORD, with the favour *that thou bearest unto* thy people: O visit me with thy salvation;

5 That I may see the good of thy chosen, that I may rejoice in the gladness of thy nation, that I may glory with thine inheritance.

6 We have sinned with our fathers, we have committed iniquity, we have done wickedly.

7 Our fathers understood not thy wonders in Egypt; they remembered not the multitude of thy mercies; but provoked *him* at the sea, *even* at the Red sea.

8 Nevertheless he saved them for his name's sake, that he might make his mighty power to be known.

9 He rebuked the Red sea also, and it was dried up: so he led them through the depths, as through the wilderness.

10 And he saved them from the hand of him that hated *them,* and redeemed them from the hand of the enemy.

11 And the waters covered their enemies: there was not one of them left.

12 Then believed they his words; they sang his praise.

13 They soon forgat his works; they waited not for his counsel:

14 But lusted exceedingly in the wilderness, and tempted God in the desert.

15 And he gave them their request; but sent leanness into their soul.

16 They envied Moses also in the camp, *and* Aaron the saint of the LORD.

17 The earth opened and swallowed up Dā'than, and covered the company of A-bī'ram.

18 And a fire was kindled in their company; the flame burned up the wicked.

106:1-3. Praise ye the LORD. Hallelujah, Praise ye Jah. **For his mercy endureth for ever.** Although this is the first time this phrase occurs in the Psalms, the Chronicles indicate that it was used at the dedication of David's tabernacle (I Chr 16:34, 41) and again at the dedication of the Temple (II Chr 5:13).

Who can utter the mighty acts of the LORD? (92:5; Job 11:7-9; Isa 40:12-17; Rom 11:33-36). "For what canst thou say of Him, what, I repeat, canst thou adequately say of Him, who is sublimer than all loftiness . . . greater than all majesty, and mightier than all might, richer than all riches, wiser than all wisdom . . . more merciful than all mercy?"—Tertullian.

4-5. Remember me, O LORD . . . . O visit me with thy salvation (cf. 18:35; 85:7). The psalmist bids Jehovah to bring salvation to his house. Jesus said of Zaccheus, "This day is salvation come to this house . . ." (Lk 19:9), for He himself had come to the household of Zacchaeus. The psalmist begs God to make Himself known to him, **that I may see the good of thy chosen, that I may rejoice in the gladness of thy nation, that I may glory with thine inheritance.**

6-7. Here begins the long national confession for the sins of Israel. Verse 6 is the summary statement, indicating the certainty of Israel's sin by the threefold expressions, **We have sinned . . . we have committed iniquity, we have done wickedly.** The Israelites saw the miraculous plagues by which they were delivered from Egyptian bondage, and yet **Our fathers understood not thy wonders in Egypt.** Accompanying the sin of a lack of understanding is the double sin of a lack of memory: **They remembered not the multitude of thy mercies** (cf. 69:16; Isa 63:7; Lam 3:32). This led to the provocation of Jehovah **at the Red Sea** (cf. Ex 14:11-12).

8-12. When God could find no justification for showing mercy on Israel, He seized that opportunity to display His power. **He saved them for his name's sake, that he might make his mighty power to be known.** The Hebrew poet notes that at the very rebuke of God **the Red Sea . . . was dried up** (cf. Ex 14:21-22). **He saved them from the hand of him that hated them,** i.e., the Pharaoh of the Exodus (cf. Ex 2:23; 3:9; 5:6-19), **And redeemed them from the hand of the enemy.** God's deliverance of the Israelites is constantly referred to as a "redemption" (cf. 74:2; 107:2; Ex 6:6-7; 15:16; etc.). **And the waters covered their enemies** (cf. Ex 14:28-30; 15:10) until **There was not one of them left.** God never does anything half-way. The enemies of Israel were completely destroyed; and as a result **Then believed they his words; they sang his praise,** probably an allusion to the "Song of Moses" (Ex 15:1-18).

13-15. With such a great deliverance to be called to their memory, it is almost incredible that **They soon forgat his works** and waited no longer to see the unfolding plan of God, i.e., **his counsel.** Instead, they **lusted exceedingly in the wilderness, and tempted God in the desert.** Israel's lustful desire **sent leanness into their soul,** i.e., dissatisfaction or bitterness. After eating of the quails for a full month, the food became "loathsome" to them (Num 11:20).

16-18. Now the psalmist becomes more pointed in his confession of Israel's sin. He passes to the sin of Korah, Dathan, and Abiram who **envied Moses also in the camp** and became jealous of his high position, assigned by God Himself (Ex 3:10; 4:1-17). They also expressed jealousy over **Aaron the saint of the LORD.** The result of their jealousy was devastating: **The earth opened and swallowed up Dathan, and covered the**

19 They made a calf in Hōʹrĕb, and worshipped the molten image.
20 Thus they changed their glory into the similitude of an ox that eateth grass.

21 They forgat God their saviour, which had done great things in Egypt;
22 Wondrous works in the land of Ham, *and* terrible things by the Red sea.
23 Therefore he said that he would destroy them, had not Moses his chosen stood before him in the breach, to turn away his wrath, lest he should destroy *them.*

24 Yea, they despised the pleasant land, they believed not his word:
25 But murmured in their tents, *and* hearkened not unto the voice of the LORD.
26 Therefore he lifted up his hand against them, to overthrow them in the wilderness:
27 To overthrow their seed also among the nations, and to scatter them in the lands.

28 They joined themselves also unto Bāʹal-pēʹōr, and ate the sacrifices of the dead.
29 Thus they provoked *him* to anger with their inventions: and the plague brake in upon them.

30 Then stood up Phĭnʹe-has, and executed judgment: and *so* the plague was stayed.
31 And that was counted unto him for righteousness unto all generations for evermore.

32 They angered *him* also at the waters of strife, so that it went ill with Moses for their sakes:
33 Because they provoked his spirit, so that he spake unadvisedly with his lips.
34 They did not destroy the nations, concerning whom the LORD commanded them:
35 But were mingled among the heathen, and learned their works.

36 And they served their idols: which were a snare unto them.

company of Abiram (cf. Num 26:9-11). Meanwhile, **the flame burned up the wicked,** a reference to Korah and company (cf. Deut 11:6).

19-20. The crimes of Israel continue to be described. **They made a calf in Horeb,** the very place where they had solemnly pledged themselves to obey the Law of the Lord, **and worshiped the molten image** (cf. Ex 32:4, 24; Deut 9:8-16). **Thus they changed their glory into the similitude of an ox that eateth grass.** This phrase expresses the contempt which the psalmist has for the gods of Egypt. He undoubtedly has in mind not only the golden calf, but Apis, or Serapis, the god of Egypt fashioned as a black bull with a white streak along the back and a half-moon white mark on his right shoulder.

21-23. Unfortunately for Israel, remembering the golden calf involved forgetting God. In Egypt, God had overcome all the idols, all the gods; and yet **They forgat God their saviour** who had done **wondrous works in the land of Ham** (cf. 78:51; 105:23, 27), **and terrible things by the Red Sea** (cf. Ex 14:24, 27-30). As a result, God promised that He would destroy the Israelites; and he would have done so **had not Moses his chosen stood before him in the breach, to turn away his wrath** (cf. Ex 32:11-13, 31-34).

24-27. It was bad enough that **they despised the pleasant land,** the land which floweth with milk and honey; but even worse, **they believed not his word,** i.e., His promise to give them the land (Gen 15:18-21; Ex 23:31). Here is the root of sin. Because the Israelites murmured instead of praising God for His promise to them, **Therefore he lifted up his hand against them . . . to overthrow their seed also among the nations, and to scatter them in the lands.** Perhaps either a historical or prophetical reference to the captivity, it is certain that the judgment of God fell upon Israel when she was "overthrown" in the wilderness (Num 14:29, 32, 37) and scattered throughout the land (cf. Lev 26:33; Deut 28:64).

28-29. The worship of the golden calf was but the initial step in a descending pattern of debauchery. **They joined themselves also unto Baal-peor.** In the worship of Baal-peor the Israelites gave up their bodies to shameful lusts, and in the orgy which occurred under the guise of religion, they forsook the living God and chose to sacrifice to the dead idols of Baal. **Thus they provoked him** (Jehovah) **to anger with their inventions** (i.e., with their lustful practices): **and the plague brake in upon them** (i.e., the judicial slaughter inflicted by the command of Moses, Num 25:4-8).

30-31. Then stood up Phinehas and executed judgment. God always has His champions who rise to the occasion, even in the worst of times. Slain were the men who joined themselves to the women of Baal-peor; and because of the action of Phinehas (Num 25:7-8), not only was the plague stayed but **that was counted unto him for righteousness unto all generations for evermore** (cf. Num 25:11-13), i.e., the praise awarded to Phinehas here became an everlasting testimony to him even though his ". . . everlasting priesthood . . ." has passed away.

32-35. They angered him also at the waters of strife (the waters of Meribah) **so that it went ill with Moses for their sakes.** The gentleness and patience of Moses finally gave way to anger, so **that he spake unadvisedly with his lips,** not blasphemously but hastily, making his rash utterance (Num 20:10). Continuing the catalogue of Israel's sins for which the psalmist must make a national confession, he does not forget that **They did not destroy the nations . . . but were mingled among the heathen, and learned their works.** Once comfortably settled into the land, the Israelites failed to drive the heathen out of the land, which they had been commanded to do.

36-39. Suddenly, the sins of Israel take on a more heinous character. Not only did they serve idols that ensnared them, but

37 Yea, they sacrificed their sons and their daughters unto devils,

38 And shed innocent blood, *even* the blood of their sons and of their daughters, whom they sacrificed unto the idols of Canaan: and the land was polluted with blood.

39 Thus were they defiled with their own works, and went a whoring with their own inventions.

40 Therefore was the wrath of the LORD kindled against his people, insomuch that he abhorred his own inheritance.

41 And he gave them into the hand of the heathen; and they that hated them ruled over them.

42 Their enemies also oppressed them, and they were brought into subjection under their hand.

43 Many times did he deliver them; but they provoked *him* with their counsel, and were brought low for their iniquity.

44 Nevertheless he regarded their affliction, when he heard their cry:

45 And he remembered for them his covenant, and repented according to the multitude of his mercies.

46 He made them also to be pitied of all those that carried them captives.

47 Save us, O LORD our God, and gather us from among the heathen, to give thanks unto thy holy name, *and* to triumph in thy praise.

48 Blessed *be* the LORD God of Israel from everlasting to everlasting: and let all the people say, Amen. Praise ye the LORD.

they sacrificed their sons and their daughters unto devils, i.e., they shed innocent blood by slaying their sons and daughters and offering them to Molech (cf. Lev 18:21; Deut 18:10; II Kgs 3:27; Jer 7:31; Ezk 23:37), a horrible god of whom the designation devils is thoroughly accurate (cf. Lev 17:7; Deut 32:17; II Chr 11:15; I Cor 10:20-21). So gross was their sin that the land was polluted with blood, contrary to the commandments given in Numbers 35:33. But that the Israelites went a whoring with their own inventions, after having been the recipients of the goodness of God, is sheer ingratitude and totally inexcusable.

40-42. The divine response was swift and severe. Therefore was the wrath of the LORD kindled against his people . . . And he gave them into the hand of the heathen. Being delivered on frequent occasions into the bondage of those that hated them is done partly for punishment and partly in order to lead to repentance. Because of Israel's sin, Their enemies also oppressed them (cf. Jud 4:3; 10:8; I Sam 9:16; etc.). Hated men ruled over them.

43-46. Yet, God's wrath is always tempered with His mercy. Many times did he deliver them, i.e., by Othniel (Jud 3:9), by Ehud (Jud 3:15-29), by Shamgar (Jud 3:31), by Samson (Jud 15:8-20), and by David (II Sam 5:22-25). Still, they provoked him with their counsel, and were brought low for their iniquity. If God were not gracious, this would be the end of the story. But God is full of mercy and grace; therefore, he regarded their affliction, when he heard their cry. Notwithstanding all their provocations, rebellions, and murmurings, God still heard their prayers and pitied them. And he remembered for them his covenant, the sure foundation of His mercy, and repented according to the multitude of his mercies (cf. Ex 32:14; II Sam 24:16; I Chr 21:15; Jer 26:19; etc.). God's apparent change of course in this microscopic segment of time cannot be understood to clash with the declaration, ". . . he is not a man, that he should repent" (I Sam 15:29). The telescopic plan of God remains the same; our microscopic view of our present situation is changed.

47. In a concluding prayer the psalmist now utters either a historical allusion to his present situation, or a prophetic petition for what is certain to be the case, given the sins of Israel. Save us, O LORD our God, and gather us from among the heathen. Having been subdued by the heathen throughout their history, the single concern of the psalmist is that they might be gathered together again in freedom so that Israel may give thanks unto thy holy name, and to triumph in thy praise.

48. Blessed be the LORD God of Israel from everlasting to everlasting. Not only is this verse a fitting conclusion to the God who forgives Israel's sins, but it also fittingly concludes this book of the Psalms, Book IV (cf. 41:13; 72:19; 89:52). And let all the people say, Amen. The other terminal psalms end with Amen, and Amen, but here the single Amen is used in order to give way to a Hallelujah. Praise ye the LORD.

V. PSALMS 107:1-150:6.

A. God's Wonderful Works. 107:1-43.

THEME: A song of the redeemed celebrating providential deliverances.

The fifth and last book of the Psalter begins with this psalm. Nevertheless, the close relationship between this psalm and the two that precede it has been noted by many authors. Delitzsch says that they "form a trilogy in the strictest sense, and are in all probability a tripartite whole from the hand of one author." Most modern authors regard this as a thanksgiving psalm first composed for the deliverance from Babylonian captivity. The

PSALM 107

O GIVE thanks unto the LORD, for *he is* good: for his mercy *endureth* for ever.

2 Let the redeemed of the LORD say *so*, whom he hath redeemed from the hand of the enemy;

3 And gathered them out of the lands, from the east, and from the west, from the north, and from the south.

4 They wandered in the wilderness in a solitary way; they found no city to dwell in.

5 Hungry and thirsty, their soul fainted in them.

6 Then they cried unto the LORD in their trouble, *and* he delivered them out of their distresses.

7 And he led them forth by the right way, that they might go to a city of habitation.

8 Oh that *men* would praise the LORD *for* his goodness, and *for* his wonderful works to the children of men!

9 For he satisfieth the longing soul, and filleth the hungry soul with goodness.

10 Such as sit in darkness and in the shadow of death, *being* bound in affliction and iron;

11 Because they rebelled against the words of God, and contemned the counsel of the most High:

12 Therefore he brought down their heart with labour; they fell down and *there was* none to help.

13 Then they cried unto the LORD in their trouble, *and* he saved them out of their distresses.

14 He brought them out of darkness and the shadow of death, and brake their bands in sunder.

psalm should be viewed simply as a celebration of God's providential deliverance of His own and may be sung by any man of any era in any life situation who has experienced the goodness of the Lord and His wonderful works to the children of men.

107:1-3. O give thanks unto the LORD (cf. 106:1; 108:1; 136:1) . . . **Let the redeemed of the LORD say so.** Whatever others may say of the Lord God and His mercy, those who have been redeemed out of the hand of the enemy have a peculiar song to sing; for they have a peculiar redemption. **And gathered them out of the lands, from the east . . . west . . . north . . . south.** The Lord is in the business of redeeming people from the four corners of the earth to call out a people for His own. Gathering together always follows redemption, just as fellowship always follows salvation.

4-7. The psalmist now begins to describe a life situation from which the redeemed have been delivered by the power of God. Some who have been gathered from out of the land have been delivered from wanderings. **They wandered in the wilderness in a solitary way** through the trackless and trailless sands of the burning desert. **They found no city to dwell in.** As is usually the case, the wanderers described in these verses were **Hungry and thirsty,** getting weaker by the moment. In their extremity **Then they cried unto the LORD in their trouble;** and as is the case with God when one seriously calls unto Him, **he delivered them out of their distresses.** In addition, **he led them forth by the right way.** God does not lead in paths of crookedness but only in a straight line to a worthy end, i.e., **a city of habitation.** When men have failed to gain access to that eternal city by their own ways, God shows the straight way, the narrow way that leads to eternal life.

8-9. Here the refrain occurs for the first time in the psalm. Note its repetition in verses 15, 21, and 31. But to each refrain is attached a concluding verse that explains why the refrain is not simply a vain repetition, but an appropriate note of praise for that life situation. **Oh that men would praise the LORD** (the one thing God desires from us) **for his goodness, and for his wonderful works to the children of men!** The children of men know something of God's goodness, as do the children of God. ". . . he maketh the sun to rise on the evil and on the good, and sendeth rain on the just and on the unjust" (Mt 5:45). But it is only the **redeemed of the LORD** (vs. 2) who may sing the praises of God's redemption.

For he satisfieth the longing soul (Heb *nepesh shōqēqah*), i.e., the soul that thirsts for salvation, **and filleth the hungry soul with goodness.** In this summary of the lost traveler's experience, the spiritual implication is evident. The Lord plants within us a longing which He and He alone can satisfy.

10-12. Now the psalmist turns his attention to deliverance from prison. He graphically portrays the enslaved as ones who **sit in darkness and in the shadow of death, being bound in affliction and iron.** The cell is dark, but the threat of execution hangs over the prisoners causes a gloom to pervade the prison. **Because they rebelled against the words of God, and contemned the counsel of the Most High.** Men are condemned to the shadow of death because they have rebelled against the words of God and have not received the words of life. It is for this reason that they are brought down with labor, presumably a reference to the hard labor of the prisoner, and are left alone where **there was none to help.**

13-14. This is the second time we have seen the people in deep distress cry unto the Lord for help (cf. vss. 6, 19, 28). **Then they cried unto the LORD in their trouble;** there is no hint of a prayer until then. **And he saved them out of their distresses.** This was done by bringing **them out of darkness and the shadow of death** and removing their bonds from them. Spiritually, this is a perfect picture of salvation. Paul tells us that

15 Oh that *men* would praise the LORD *for* his goodness, and *for* his wonderful works to the children of men!

16 For he hath broken the gates of brass, and cut the bars of iron in sunder.

17 Fools because of their transgression, and because of their iniquities, are afflicted.

18 Their soul abhorreth all manner of meat; and they draw near unto the gates of death.

19 Then they cry unto the LORD in their trouble, *and* he saveth them out of their distresses.

20 He sent his word, and healed them, and delivered *them* from their destructions.

21 Oh that *men* would praise the LORD *for* his goodness, and *for* his wonderful works to the children of men!

22 And let them sacrifice the sacrifices of thanksgiving, and declare his works with rejoicing.

23 They that go down to the sea in ships, that do business in great waters;

24 These see the works of the LORD, and his wonders in the deep.

25 For he commandeth, and raiseth the stormy wind, which lifteth up the waves thereof.

26 They mount up to the heaven, they go down again to the depths: their soul is melted because of trouble.

27 They reel to and fro, and stagger like a drunken man, and are at their wit's end.

28 Then they cry unto the LORD in their trouble, and he bringeth them out of their distresses.

29 He maketh the storm a calm, so that the waves thereof are still.

30 Then are they glad because they be quiet; so he bringeth them unto their desired haven.

31 Oh that *men* would praise the LORD *for* his goodness, and *for* his wonderful works to the children of men!

32 Let them exalt him also in the congregation of the people, and praise him in the assembly of the elders.

it is God, "Who delivered us from so great a death, and doth deliver . . ." (II Cor 1:10).

15-16. Again the refrain, **Oh that men would praise the LORD for his goodness,** which is not merely a repetition of verse 8, but a song of thanksgiving sung by those who have been delivered from the chains of darkness. **And for his wonderful works to the children of men!** When the dungeon doors fly open and the chains of iron are snapped, the natural response is thanksgiving to God. **For he hath broken the gates of brass, and cut the bars of iron in sunder.**

17-18. **Fools, because of their transgression, and because of their iniquities, are afflicted.** With this notation the psalmist begins the third segment of his psalm, describing God's deliverance from sickness. While it is not always possible to ascribe sickness to foolish sin, nonetheless, some sicknesses are the direct result of foolish acts. Because of the transgressors' sickness, **Their soul abhorreth all manner of meat.** The appetite of the fool departs from him when he is sick; even the best of food is nauseous. Because of a lack of nourishment, **they draw near unto the gates of death.**

19-20. Again notice the cry of the distressed. **Then they cry unto the LORD in their trouble,** and as usual He saved them. This time salvation came as **He sent his word, and healed them, and delivered them from their destructions.** Man is not always healed by the skill of the surgeon; he is sometimes healed by the simple word of the Lord.

21-22. As twice before, the refrain is repeated, **Oh that men would praise the LORD for his goodness, and for his wonderful works to the children of men!** A man rescued from disease, whether physical or spiritual, must praise Jehovah Rophi, the healing God (Ex 15:26). **And let them sacrifice the sacrifices of thanksgiving.** If we sacrifice to pay doctors and hospitals exorbitant fees for healing, how much more willing ought we be to sacrifice unto the Great Physician who healed us of a soul sick with sin.

23-24. With these verses begin a fourth and final segment of deliverance, i.e., deliverance from the sea. This life situation is addressed to them **that go down to the sea in ships.** One of the great advantages of being a sailor is that **these see the works of the LORD, and his wonders in the deep.** The works of the Lord referred to here are those tempests and storms that suddenly arise on the seas and cause awe in even the most seasoned sailor (Acts 27:14-44; II Cor 11:25).

25-27. The psalmist pictures the sailor at the complete mercy of God when being tossed to and fro by a raging sea. It is the Lord Jehovah who **commandeth, and raiseth the stormy wind, which lifteth up the waves thereof.** As the mariner attempts to ride out the storm, his ship seems to **mount up to the heaven** as it rises high on the crest of the waves and then **go down again to the depths** as it plummets to the surface of the sea between the waves. Regardless of how salty these sailors may be, **their soul is melted because of trouble;** and their intrepid toughness is broken by the command of God.

28-30. As before, when man is at his **wit's end,** then he will call unto the Lord in his trouble; and the Lord will bring him out of his distress. The Lord **maketh the storm a calm, so that the waves thereof are still** (cf. Mk 4:35-41). Regardless of how fierce the storm, when men cry unto God for help, **he bringeth them unto their desired haven.**

31-32. The refrain is repeated for the final time. **Oh that men would praise the LORD for his goodness, and for his wonderful works to the children of men!** As the sea sounds forth the praises of God, so too let the sailors who have returned to a safe haven praise the Lord for His goodness. **Let them exalt him also in the congregation of the people, and praise him in the**

33 He turneth rivers into a wilderness, and the watersprings into dry ground;
34 A fruitful land into barrenness, for the wickedness of them that dwell therein.
35 He turneth the wilderness into a standing water, and dry ground into watersprings.

36 And there he maketh the hungry to dwell, that they may prepare a city for habitation;
37 And sow the fields, and plant vineyards, which may yield fruits of increase.
38 He blesseth them also, so that they are multiplied greatly; and suffereth not their cattle to decrease.
39 Again, they are minished and brought low through oppression, affliction, and sorrow.
40 He poureth contempt upon princes, and causeth them to wander in the wilderness, *where there is* no way.

41 Yet setteth he the poor on high from affliction, and maketh *him* families like a flock.
42 The righteous shall see *it*, and rejoice: and all iniquity shall stop her mouth.

43 Whoso *is* wise, and will observe these *things*, even they shall understand the lovingkindness of the Lord.

assembly of the elders. It is not enough to praise the Lord secretly or privately for great deliverances. **Let the redeemed of the Lord say so** (vs. 2), publicly, before the assembly of the elders and anyone else who would listen.

33-35. Now the psalmist embarks upon an epilogue given in praise of God's sovereignty. Jehovah can, if it is His purpose, turn **rivers into a wilderness, and the watersprings into dry ground.** God has full control over nature and can take back His blessings, should He desire, or render them of no avail. **A fruitful land into barrenness, for the wickedness of them that dwell therein.** Should a nation not humble herself and pray and seek the face of the Lord and turn from her wicked ways (II Chr 7:14), then her mountains, prairies, and oceans will become a land of barrenness. God will not withhold judgment from those who live wickedly before Him.

But should repentance come, He can just as easily turn **the wilderness into a standing water, and dry ground into watersprings.** The whole earth is at the mercy of the Lord God who brings judgment on wickedness.

36-38. When God restores a nation to favor, **there he maketh the hungry to dwell . . . and sow the fields, and plant vineyards, which may yield fruits of increase.** It is a divine fact of nature: wickedness brings dearth; repentance brings blessing. **He blesseth them also, so that they are multiplied greatly.** God's blessing is in everything, i.e., in the abundance of rain, of crops, of vineyards, and of cattle.

39-40. Again, they are minished and brought low through oppression, affliction, and sorrow. As men change, so do their circumstances. Israel had her ups and downs; believers have theirs. When we fall into the valleys of sin and are brought low, we know that **He poureth contempt upon princes, and causeth them to wander in the wilderness, where there is no way.**

41-42. In contrast, **Yet setteth he the poor on high from affliction, and maketh him families like a flock.** Here, the working of God's providence is seen. Whether one is a prince or pauper is not the issue; the issue is whether we are repentant before God. Though we are poor; if we live righteously and faithfully for God, we shall prosper. And not only this, but **The righteous shall see it, and rejoice.** When the prince is in despair and the pauper is above affliction, the righteous shall understand through the eyes of faith why this unnatural situation exists. But **all iniquity shall stop her mouth.** It is a tremendous thing when divine providence so rules in the affairs of men as to silence the boastings and the blasphemies of ungodly men.

43. The psalmist concludes with a warning and a promise. **Whoso is wise, and will observe these things, even they shall understand the loving-kindness of the Lord.** Let us recognize that the deliverances we experience come from the good hand of God, and let us know that when we are delivered from afflictions and distresses, our deliverance has not come by chance or our own cunning, but that, "The steps of a good man are ordered by the Lord" (37:23). Let us ever be mindful that the redeemed of the Lord are to "praise the Lord for his goodness, and for his wonderful works to the children of men!" (vs. 8).

B. Valiant God, Valiant Warrior. 108:1-13.

THEME: *A jubilant national hymn of confidence in God.*

It will be immediately noticed that this psalm consists of two other portions of Scripture almost identical with these verses. The first half is similar to 57:7-11, and the latter half is almost identical to 60:5-12. The chief difference between them is that this psalm substitutes Yahweh for Adonai in verse 3. The superscription says that this is **A song or psalm of David.** It is idle speculation to question whether or not David actually placed two portions of his previous works together in this psalm or

PSALM 108

O GOD, my heart is fixed: I will sing and give praise, even with my glory.

2 Awake, psaltery and harp: I *myself* will awake early.

3 I will praise thee, O LORD, among the people: and I will sing praises unto thee among the nations.

4 For thy mercy *is* great above the heavens: and thy truth *reacheth* unto the clouds.

5 Be thou exalted, O God, above the heavens: and thy glory above all the earth;

6 That thy beloved may be delivered: save *with* thy right hand, and answer me.

7 God hath spoken in his holiness; I will rejoice, I will divide Shĕ′chem, and mete out the valley of Sŭc′coth.

8 Gilead *is* mine; Ma-năs′seh *is* mine; Ē′phra-im also *is* the strength of mine head; Jū′dah *is* my lawgiver;

9 Moab *is* my washpot; over Edom will I cast out my shoe; over Philistia will I triumph.

10 Who will bring me into the strong city? who will lead me into Edom?

some later poet adapted them to circumstances of his own. As Spurgeon has aptly noted, "The Holy Spirit is not so short of expressions that He needs to repeat Himself . . . there must be some intention in the arrangement of two former divine utterances in a new connection." The meaningful repetition of a song of praise to God is never out of place.

108:1-2. O God, my heart is fixed. The fixed heart is an unperturbed heart. It is a heart that vows to **sing and give praise, even with my glory,** i.e., with all my intellect, my skill, my resources, my self. **Awake, psaltery and harp.** As if to sing the praises of God by voice alone were not enough, the psalmist calls upon his fingers to pluck the well-tuned strings of the psaltery and harp in accompanying his song of praise. But more than that, **I myself will awake early.** The psalmist is determined to sing the praises of God anew each morning before he encounters others who may delay or deter him from doing so.

3-4. In these verses David's double resolution is undergirded by a double reason. **I will praise thee, O LORD . . . and I will sing praises unto thee . . . For thy mercy is great above the heavens: and thy truth reacheth unto the clouds.** David was not in the habit of praising the Lord only when he was before a company of the Lord's people. He had committed himself to praising the Lord always, even before unbelievers.

5. After such a worthy commitment to God comes a meaningful refrain. **Be thou exalted, O God, above the heavens.** As His mercy and truth are above the heavens, so is God's essence and glory.

6. Now that the psalmist has praised the Lord God, his prayer will follow that praise. This is always the proper order. From his representative position as king of Israel he prays that **thy beloved may be delivered: save with thy right hand, and answer me.** When the king felt the swift and sure hand of divine deliverance, all the nation would experience that same deliverance.

7-10. Encouraged by the promise of deliverance, David began to act vigorously against his enemies, even as in this psalm he vows to do. **I will divide Shechem, and mete out the valley of Succoth.** Shechem was west and Succoth east of the Jordan Valley. By naming them together he implies that he will possess the whole land on both sides of the river. **Gilead is mine; Manasseh is mine.** Gilead is the fine fertile mountainous region lying east of the Jordan and was held in considerable part by the tribe of Gad. Manasseh, the eldest son of Joseph, received the fine grazing land of Bashan. **Ephraim also is the strength of mine head.** It was this tribe that furnished David with more than twenty thousand "mighty men of valour, famous throughout of the house of their fathers." **Judah is my lawgiver** is a clear allusion to Genesis 49:10. "No government could stand, which was not resident in Judah," says Calvin.

Moab is my washpot. This nation, which had shown no friendly spirit at all toward the Israelites and which constituted one of its most detested rivals, is now understood to be one of David's most menial subjects. The meaning of the psalmist is that he would reduce Moab to a very low condition of servitude, and this he certainly did (cf. II Sam 8:2; I Chr 18:1-2). **Over Edom will I cast out my shoe.** Likewise, the once proud Edomite Empire would be reduced to servitude under the leadership of Almighty God through His servant David. Finally, **over Philistia will I triumph.** David had done so in his youth, and he would surely do so again. II Samuel 8:1 notes, ". . . David smote the Philistines, and subdued them. . . ."

Now David rhetorically seeks an affirmation with regard to who will cause him to be victorious. He asks, **Who will bring me into the strong city?** (presumably Petra, the rose-rock capital of the Edomite Empire). **Who will lead me into Edom?** There could be but one answer.

11 *Wilt* not *thou,* O God, *who* hast cast us off ? and wilt not thou, O God, go forth with our hosts?
12 Give us help from trouble: for vain *is* the help of man.
13 Through God we shall do valiantly: for he *it is that* shall tread down our enemies.

11-13. **Wilt not thou, O God . . . Give us help from trouble: for vain is the help of man.** Divine help was but a sincere prayer away. Petra was impregnable, and David was well aware that he could not take the city by human aid alone. Thus, the psalmist confidently concludes, **Through God we shall do valiantly.** Our hidden strength, our secret weapon, is the power of God. It is from that source that we draw courage, wisdom, and strength. **For he it is that shall tread down our enemies.** "What shall we then say to these things? If God be for us, who can be against us?" (Rom 8:31). "I can do all things through Christ which strengtheneth me" (Phil 4:13).

C. A Plea for Vengeance. 109:1-31.

THEME: *The psalmist cries unto God for the punishment of the wicked.*

The superscription of this psalm reads, **To the chief musician. A psalm of David.** If this inscription is to be accepted, and there is no valid reason not to ascribe this ode to David since Peter does so in Acts 1:16, then we have here not "the ravings of a malicious misanthrope," but a psalm that begins with a tender appeal to God because of the retribution of the psalmist's enemy (vss. 1-5) and concludes with a distressed cry to God for help (vss. 21-31). If there is a historic occasion to which this psalm refers, some find it in the persecutions of Saul urged on by Doeg. Others feel that it has reference to the rebellion of Absalom and the treachery of Ahithophel. Whatever the case, the primary reference of this psalm is to be seen in the historic events of the life of David.

This is the last of the psalms of imprecation and brings them to a concerted crescendo. It is the severest of its kind in the Psalter and has caused much serious discussion among scholars. As Maclaren notes: "The combination of devout meekness and trust with the fiery imprecations in the core of the Psalm is startling to Christian consciousness."

An obvious distinction must be made between the Old Testament covenant of the Law and the New Testament covenant of grace. Men of the Old Testament stage of revelation did not have the example of the Saviour, nor His teachings concerning love and justice; and it would be unreasonable to expect them to understand that things, once overlooked in the Old Testament, are now understood by us as inexcusable in the New (Mt 5:43-48; 19:8-9; Lk 9:51-56).

PSALM 109

HOLD not thy peace, O God of my praise;
2 For the mouth of the wicked and the mouth of the deceitful are opened against me: they have spoken against me with a lying tongue.
3 They compassed me about also with words of hatred; and fought against me without *a* cause.

109:1-3. Hold not thy peace, O God of my praise (cf. 28:1; 35:22; 39:12). The psalmist prays for God to break His solemn silence and silence those who slander Him. In the arsenal of weapons available to Satan none is more deadly than **the mouth of the wicked and the mouth of the deceitful.** Calumny and misrepresentation are double fiends that stalk the righteous constantly. **They have spoken against me with a lying tongue . . . with words of hatred.** David was calumniated by Saul (I Sam 22:7-13), Absalom (II Sam 15:3-4), Shimei (II Sam 16:8), and others. Yet, like David, we should not be overly concerned when our enemies fight against us **without a cause;** for the Lord Jesus Himself said, ". . . They hated me without a cause" (Jn 15:25). He too was severely accused (Mt 11:19; 12:24; 26:60-61; Lk 23:2; etc.).

4 For my love they are my adversaries: but I *give myself unto* prayer.
5 And they have rewarded me evil for good, and hatred for my love.

4-5. For my love they are my adversaries. Just as his Great Descendant, David found that his enemies reciprocated hatred for love. Yet, in such a deplorable situation the psalmist gave himself to the proper response: **But I give myself unto prayer.** The psalmist had resolved not to retaliate, but to pray for his enemies even though they had **rewarded me evil for good, and hatred for my love.**

At this point the psalmist, a man made from a gentle mold and remarkably free of the spirit of revenge, lashes out imprecations against those who slander him. Throughout the ages saints have been perplexed at this psalm, for what is now said is so out of character for David. Yet, his righteous indignation is given vent in these verses as we have never seen it before.

6 Set thou a wicked man over him: and let Satan stand at his right hand.

7 When he shall be judged, let him be condemned: and let his prayer become sin.

6-7. Set thou a wicked man over him. "The first thing that the psalmist asks is, that his foe might be subjected to the evil of having a man placed over him like himself;—a man regardless of justice, truth, and right; a man who would respect character and propriety no more than he had himself done"—Albert Barnes. **Let Satan stand at his right hand.** Should not the father of lies stand near his children? Satan (Heb *satan*) means an adversary, or an accuser. He stands at the right hand of the wicked man so that **When he shall be judged, let him be condemned.**

8 Let his days be few; *and* let another take his office.

9 Let his children be fatherless, and his wife a widow.

10 Let his children be continually vagabonds, and beg: let them seek *their bread* also out of their desolate places.

8-10. Let his days be few. There was a divine promise that **bloody and deceitful men shall not live out half their days.** (55:23; cf. Prov 10:27; Eccl 7:17). **Let another take his office.** The LXX and other versions which follow it render the word **office** (Heb *pequdah*) as bishopric or superintendence. Is it any wonder that St. Peter applied this verse to Judas (Acts 1:20)? He saw at once in the speedy death of Judas a fulfillment of this sentence and a reason for the appointment of a successor who should fill his bishopric. For that reason many have regarded this as a messianic psalm, but it is difficult to see how the words of this psalm could be placed in the mouth of our Lord Jesus.

Let his children be fatherless, and his wife a widow. As would be the case should his days be few, the wicked man would leave fatherless children and a husbandless wife behind. **Let his children be continually vagabonds, and beg,** having neither home nor food. **Let them seek their bread also out of their desolate places.** Beyond the days of the tyrant's life, his family must endure the universal detestation and total lack of social welfare that accompanies the misuse of wealth or the abuse of power.

11 Let the extortioner catch all that he hath; and let the strangers spoil his labour.

12 Let there be none to extend mercy unto him: neither let there be any to favour his fatherless children.

11-12. Let the extortioner catch all that he hath; and let the strangers spoil his labor. The **extortioner** (Heb *nashah*) is actually a creditor or usurer, a man who loans money at inflated interest rates. Wealth that is amassed by oppression seldom lasts to the third generation, and thus David prays that **the strangers** would remove the ill-gotten gains of the wicked man from his fatherless children and husbandless wife. **Let there be none to extend mercy unto him . . . any to favor his fatherless children.** He who had never extended mercy to others, now shall be mercilessly treated.

13 Let his posterity be cut off; *and* in the generation following let their name be blotted out.

14 Let the iniquity of his fathers be remembered with the LORD; and let not the sin of his mother be blotted out.

15 Let them be before the LORD continually, that he may cut off the memory of them from the earth.

13-15. Continuing his imprecation against the family of the wicked man, David asks, **Let his posterity be cut off . . . their name be blotted out.** With no grandchildren, the family would soon come to an end; and their very name would be forgotten (cf. 37:28; Job 18:18; Prov 10:7). In our system of justice today this next imprecation is perhaps the most difficult of all for us to accept. **Let the iniquity of his fathers be remembered with the LORD; and let not the sin of his mother be blotted out.** Simply, this calls for the threatening of Exodus 20:5 to take effect and for God not to forget the sins of the wicked man in dealing with the wicked man's children. The sins of their mother ought not be erased from God's memory; and thus, they are visited on them, just as Jezebel's sins were visited on her children. The end result of this divine remembrance is **that he may cut off the memory of them from the earth.**

16 Because that he remembered not to shew mercy, but persecuted the poor and needy man, that he might even slay the broken in heart.

16. How could David pray for such dastardly consequences? The psalmist answers, **Because that he remembered not to show mercy, but persecuted the poor and needy man, that he might even slay the broken in heart.** He who would not remember mercy will not receive mercy. The wicked had **persecuted the poor and needy man.** Should not he be punished under the law? Should not he who slew the **broken in heart** also be slain?

17 As he loved cursing, so let it come

17-19. In one final, but totally distinct, burst of imprecation the psalmist turns to another characteristic of the wicked man.

unto him: as he delighted not in blessing, so let it be far from him.

18 As he clothed himself with cursing like as with his garment, so let it come into his bowels like water, and like oil into his bones.

19 Let it be unto him as the garment which covereth him, and for a girdle wherewith he is girded continually.

20 Let this be the reward of mine adversaries from the LORD, and of them that speak evil against my soul.

21 But do thou for me, O GOD the Lord, for thy name's sake: because thy mercy is good, deliver thou me.

22 For I am poor and needy, and my heart is wounded within me.

23 I am gone like the shadow when it declineth: I am tossed up and down as the locust.

24 My knees are weak through fasting; and my flesh faileth of fatness.

25 I became also a reproach unto them: when they looked upon me they shaked their heads.

26 Help me, O LORD my God: O save me according to thy mercy:

27 That they may know that this is thy hand; that thou, LORD, hast done it.

28 Let them curse, but bless thou: when they arise, let them be ashamed; but let thy servant rejoice.

29 Let mine adversaries be clothed with shame, and let them cover themselves with their own confusion, as with a mantle.

30 I will greatly praise the LORD with my mouth; yea, I will praise him among the multitude.

31 For he shall stand at the right hand of the poor, to save him from those that condemn his soul.

As he loved cursing, so let it come unto him. David's enemy who the most **loved cursing** was Shimei (II Sam 16:5-13). Whoever this singular enemy of the psalmist may be, **he delighted not in blessing;** and thus the psalmist prays, **so let it be far from him.** As he never enjoyed dispensing blessing, never let him enjoy receiving it. **As he clothed himself with cursing like as with his garment** (cf. 10:7; 59:12; 62:4), as extreme malevolence fit him as a cloak, **so let it come into his bowels like water, and like oil into his bones.** The sense seems to be that as he freely cursed others, the wicked man would now be **girded continually,** both outwardly and inwardly, with the fruit of that cursing.

20. Here is found a summation of the entire imprecation. What does the evil conduct of the wicked man remit to him? **Let this be the reward of mine adversaries from the LORD.** The wage of wickedness is condemnation, answerless prayers, fatherless children, a husbandless widow, a merciless creditor, an unremembered family, and a life with no blessing.

21-25. Almost as suddenly as David entered the verses of imprecation (vss. 6-20), now he leaves them behind and turns to God in a prolonged prayer, entreating Him for deliverance, blessing, and triumph over his enemies. **But do thou for me, O God the Lord, for thy name's sake.** It is for the sake of God's good name that the psalmist prays for his own deliverance. **Because thy mercy is good, deliver thou me,** not because the psalmist is good but because God's mercy is good. **For I am poor and needy** (cf. vs. 16), even an appropriate description for an oppressed king, **and my heart is wounded within me** through the undeserving cruelty and remorseless slander of his enemies. **I am gone like the shadow when it declineth** (cf. 102:11), i.e., a mere shadow of a man about to disappear from the face of the earth. **I am tossed up and down as the locust,** i.e., about to be swept away from the face of the earth (cf. Ex 10:19; Joel 2:20; Nah 3:17). **I became also a reproach unto them: when they looked upon me they shook their heads.** Words alone were not sufficient to express the scorn his enemies had for David. They resorted to lampooning him with gestures of detestation, much as they did the Lord Jesus Himself (cf. Mt 27:30).

26-27. The psalmist was indeed brought very low; but as was his established practice, when brought low he raised himself high in prayer. **Help me, O LORD my God: O save me according to thy mercy.** David's concern is not so much for himself as it is **that they may know that this is thy hand; that thou, LORD, hast done it.** David wants his deliverance to come in such a conspicuous way that ungodly men will be forced to see the good hand of God upon him (Neh 2:8; Ezr 7:9; 8:18). The good will be David's; the glory will be God's.

28-29. Let them curse, but bless thou. David has resolved that it doesn't matter if men curse him as long as God blesses him. "Men's curses are impotent, God's blessings are omnipotent"—Matthew Henry. **When they arise, let them be ashamed; but let thy servant rejoice.** When this is true, the psalmist's **adversaries** will be clothed with shame and must **cover themselves with their own confusion, as with a mantle.** Instead of the cursing that once clothed the wicked, their covering will now be shame and confusion because of the psalmist's vindication and salvation by God. Praise be to God.

30-31. I will greatly praise the LORD with my mouth. Enthusiastically and loudly, the psalmist resolves to extol the name of the righteous Lord, not simply to himself, but **among the multitude. For he shall stand at the right hand of the poor, to save him from those that condemn his soul.** We may rest assured that when we face our hour of greatest trial, when we are slandered mercilessly and are repaid hatred for love, God will be by our side ready to deliver us.

D. The Lord Messiah. 110:1-7.

THEME: A Davidic Psalm praising Jesus Christ as Lord, King, Priest, and exalted Messiah.

Psalm 110 is quoted more frequently in the New Testament than any other psalm. Augustine said that this psalm is brief in the number of words, but great in the weight of its thought.

While there are those who attempt to deny the Davidic authorship of this psalm, this is done out of a purely critical bias. The inscription of the psalm reads, **A psalm of David.** According to our Lord's comment on the psalm, found in three of the Gospels (cf. Mt 22:43-45; Mk 12:35-37; Lk 20:41-44), David was understood to be the author of this psalm even by the Lord Jesus Himself.

That the psalm is messianic is almost universally acknowledged. In fact, Alexander says, "This is the counterpart of the Second Psalm, completing the prophetic picture of the conquering Messiah . . . any other application is ridiculous." In disputing with the Pharisees, the Lord Jesus appealed to the first verse of this psalm (see Mt 22:41-45; Mk 12:35-37). Both Davidic authorship and the messianic character of this psalm are well attested by the Lord Jesus in the New Testament. David was moved by the Holy Ghost to clearly write, not of himself or another earthly ruler, but of the Lord Jesus Christ, David's Messiah and King. There is no double reference here; the psalm does not refer primarily to David and secondarily to his Great Son, the Lord Jesus. Rather, this psalm clearly refers only to the Messiah, the Great Descendant of the Son of Jesse.

110:1. The LORD said unto my Lord. Jehovah said unto *Adonai. Adonai* is a title of respect given to any potentate, even God Himself. It is applied here to one who is the master of the psalmist, for David calls him **my LORD.** Given David's position in the Israelite kingdom, this verse can only refer to the Messiah. Historically, the Jews have generally understood this psalm with a Messianic reference (cf. Midrashim Tehillim, Bereshith Rabba, etc.). Jehovah speaks directly to David's master and bids him to **Sit thou at my right hand.** This represents the third step in the exaltation of the Lord Jesus. The first step in His exaltation was His resurrection; the second step was His ascension into heaven. Now He is bid to take up residence at the right hand of royal power, the place of permanent honor (cf. I Kgs 2:19; Eph 1:20; Heb 1:13).

Until I make thine enemies thy footstool. To place the foot upon the neck of a defeated foe was a common practice of Oriental conquerors. The meaning of this language is explained historically in Joshua 10:24. Having completed His atoning work, Jesus Christ ". . . must reign, till he hath put all enemies under his feet" (I Cor 15:25). This clause, indeed this whole verse, is fully expounded in I Corinthians 15:24-28 (cf. Mt 19:28; II Tim 2:12; Rev 3:21).

2. The LORD shall send the rod of thy strength out of Zion. The **rod of thy strength,** or strong scepter, is a poetic expression for His ruling power (cf. Jer 48:17; Ezk 19:11). The ruling power of the Messiah was to go forth from Jerusalem, Zion's city of our God (cf. Acts 1:4-8; 2:1-4). **Rule thou in the midst of thine enemies.** The rule and reign of Jesus Christ during this age is not one of power and bloodshed, but rather of conquering love and grace. One day, however, when the curtain of God's grace comes crashing down and the curtain of His wrath is raised, ". . . he shall rule them with a rod of iron: and he treadeth the winepress of the fierceness and wrath of Almighty God" (Rev 19:15).

3. Thy people shall be willing in the day of thy power. Because of the power of the gospel and of the mighty hand of the Lord God, the servants of the Saviour will be willingly ruled by the Messiah. Men under the influence of the gospel do not

---

PSALM 110

THE LORD said unto my Lord, Sit thou at my right hand, until I make thine enemies thy footstool.

2 The LORD shall send the rod of thy strength out of Zion: rule thou in the midst of thine enemies.

3 Thy people *shall be* willing in the day of thy power, in the beauties of holiness from the womb of the morning: thou hast the dew of thy youth.

render themselves to the service of the King out of fear, but **in the beauties of holiness**, i.e., in holy obedience to the one who is at once Priest and King. **From the womb of the morning: thou hast the dew of thy youth.** As the dew falls fresh every morning and is perpetually resupplied, so too are those who fall to the message of God's redeeming grace and join the ranks of the saved.

4 The LORD hath sworn, and will not repent, Thou *art* **a priest for ever after the order of Mĕl-chĭz′e-dĕk.**

4. We have now reached the heart of this psalm. There is a change, an abrupt change, in the figure used of the Messiah. Whereas, the Messiah had been bidden to rule over His enemies from the right hand of God by God's decree, now, in similar decree, He is bidden to continue forever in His function as a priest. Thus, Jesus Christ is both King and Priest.

Not only had the Lord sworn by decree that the Messiah would be a priest forever; he also decreed that he should be a priest forever **after the order of Melchizedek.** Melchizedek's office was exceptional; none preceded or succeeded him. He comes upon the pages of history mysteriously, blessing Abraham and receiving tithes; and he vanished from the scene among honors that show that he was greater than the founder of the chosen nation.

5 The Lord at thy right hand shall strike through kings in the day of his wrath.

5. **The LORD at thy right hand shall strike through kings in the day of his wrath.** Previously (vs. 1), David's *Adonai* was described as sitting at the right hand of Jehovah. Now, addressing the Messiah, the psalmist refers to Jehovah as the *Adonai* at the right hand of the Messiah. He stands at Messiah's right hand (cf. 16:8; 121:5) to protect, defend, and insure His victory. As King of the Jews during His days upon the earth, Jesus Christ subdued men by His divine grace. But now, positioned at the right hand of Jehovah and with Jehovah as His right hand of strength, He **shall strike through kings in the day of his wrath.** There is a time for grace and patience; there is a time for vengeance and wrath.

6 He shall judge among the heathen, he shall fill *the places* **with the dead bodies; he shall wound the heads over many countries.**

6. **He shall judge among the heathen, he shall fill the places with the dead bodies.** It is difficult not to see in this verse a direct reference to the coming day of God's wrath when the priest-king shall come to this earth as ". . . KING OF KINGS, AND LORD OF LORDS" (see Rev 19:16-18). In that day, Jesus Christ the Messiah **shall wound the heads over many countries.** That will be the culmination of a pattern of victory created before the foundation of the world. The eternal Messiah is the eternal Priest; the eternal Priest is the eternal King; the eternal King is the eternal Judge; the eternal Judge is the eternal Lord.

7 He shall drink of the brook in the way: therefore shall he lift up the head.

7. **He shall drink of the brook in the way: therefore shall he lift up the head.** This concluding and summary verse is apparently designed to show the Messiah's singleness of purpose. Nothing will thwart the plan of God. **Therefore shall he lift up the head.** The attacks of Satan shall not cause the march of Christ to faint, let alone fail. He will gloriously proceed in the conquest of the nations. His victory is certain; He incessantly pursues it.

E. In Praise of God's Works. 111:1-10.

THEME: An alphabetic psalm praising the Lord for His works of creation and redemption.

This psalm is a pure Alphabetic Psalm. Each sentence begins with a letter of the Hebrew alphabet, and in order. This acrostic form is also found in 9-10; 25; 34; 37; 112; 118; and 145. But in this psalm, and the one which follows, not only do the letters of the alphabet mark the beginning of the verses; but they also mark the beginning of several clauses within the verses. The psalm consists of ten verses, the first eight of which are couplets and the last two of which are triplets. These couplets and triplets make twenty-two lines, the exact number of letters in the Hebrew alphabet.

It also must be noted that another series of Hallelujah psalms

PSALM 111

PRAISE ye the LORD. I will praise the LORD with *my* whole heart, in the assembly of the upright, and *in* the congregation.

2 The works of the LORD *are* great, sought out of all them that have pleasure therein.
3 His work *is* honourable and glorious: and his righteousness endureth for ever.
4 He hath made his wonderful works to be remembered: the LORD *is* gracious and full of compassion.

5 He hath given meat unto them that fear him: he will ever be mindful of his covenant.
6 He hath shewed his people the power of his works, that he may give them the heritage of the heathen.

7 The works of his hands *are* verity and judgment; all his commandments *are* sure.
8 They stand fast for ever and ever, *and are* done in truth and uprightness.

9 He sent redemption unto his people: he hath commanded his covenant for ever: holy and reverend *is* his name.

10 The fear of the LORD *is* the beginning of wisdom: a good understanding have all they that do *his* commandments: his praise endureth for ever.

begin with this psalm (cf. Ps 111-117), as they all either begin or end with **Praise ye the LORD** (Heb *halelū yah*). There is no title to this psalm of praise. The author is unknown, and conjectures have ranged from David to someone in the post-exilic period.

111:1. In addition to the hallelujah that begins this psalm, the resolve of the psalmist is seen: **I will praise the LORD . . . in the assembly of the upright, and in the congregation.** The psalmist is committed to praise the Lord with his whole heart (cf. 9:1; 119:34, 58, 69), both before the few who are upright in heart (before whom praise is easy) and the many **in the congregation** (before whom praise is more difficult).

2-4a. The reason for such praise is clearly delineated. **The works of the LORD are great.** In design, number, excellence, and deliverance God has performed mightily for His people. God's works are **sought out of all them that have pleasure therein.** This word (Heb *derūshīm*) means objects of study and is etymologically connected with the word *madrasha*, which is a place of study and research, i.e., a college. Great works ought not go by unnoticed but ought to be studied, delved into, researched, and enjoyed.

His work is honorable and glorious. In the previous verse the psalmist spoke of the **works of the LORD.** Here, He speaks of a single, honorable, glorious **work** of the Lord. It is a work so preeminently divine that it eclipses all other works. It is undoubtedly the work of salvation, redemption. **His righteousness endureth for ever.** No other work can be compared with that of salvation. No other work so honors both the Saviour and the saved, or brings more glory to God and good to us. **He hath made his wonderful works to be remembered.** It is God's design that what He has done for His people should be memorable and easily recalled.

4b-6. The LORD is gracious and full of compassion (cf. 103:13). **He hath given meat unto them that fear him.** The **meat** spoken of here has been variously understood as the manna provided for the wandering Israelites, the lamb provided for the Passover, and the spoil by which the Israelites were enriched from their enemies. The intent of the verse is to show that God favors those who fear Him. **He hath showed his people the power of his works, that he may give them the heritage of the heathen.** All Israel saw what God performed in their behalf. They saw the power of His physical works and of His matchless spiritual wonders. This same power is available to all who come to the righteous Lord in faith.

7-8. That which God does is never artificial or false, for the works of His hands are **verity and judgment,** truth and justice. God never acts capriciously. **All his commandments are sure. They stand fast for ever and ever.** As the mood of a nation changes, so do the laws of that nation; but the laws of God are established and settled forever. All that He does has been done in **truth and uprightness.**

9. He sent redemption unto his people. Perhaps the redemption from Egypt (Ex 6:6) is especially in the psalmist's mind. **Holy and reverend is his name.** Reverend is often translated terrible (Hab 1:7), as seen in 45:4, or dreadful. It is a participle literally meaning to be feared. It is important to note that it is the name of the Lord that is reverend, not His servants.

10. The fear of the LORD is the beginning of wisdom (cf. Prov 1:7; 9:10; Eccl 1:16). "In this passage 'fear' is not to be understood as referring to the first or elementary principles of piety, as in I John 4:18, but is comprehensive of all true godliness, or the worship of God"—John Calvin. **Fear** is the first principle and chief element in godliness. **A good understanding have all they that do his commandments.** It is our obedience to God that proves we have mastered the first elements of wisdom, i.e., the fear of the Lord. No one who disavows the claims of God upon him can lay any claim to godly intelligence. Regardless of how it is viewed by the world at large, **The fear of the Lord** is both the chief aim and the chief proof of wisdom. We evidence that wisdom when we say **his praise endureth for ever.**

F. The Blessings of Godly Living. 112:1-10.

THEME: *A psalm in praise of God's blessing toward those who live uprightly.*

With the preceding psalm, this one has been called a twin psalm. Both are Alphabetical Psalms and in both the letters of the alphabet mark the beginning of the verses and clauses within the verses. Psalm 111-112 have almost identical structures: both have ten verses, the first eight of which are couplets and the last two are triplets; and both have twenty-two lines, the number of letters in the Hebrew alphabet.

Although the structure of these psalms is quite similar, their emphases are very different. Whereas Psalm 111 deals with the Lord who is to be feared, Psalm 112 deals with the man who fears the Lord. In 111 the mighty deeds of God, His glory and righteousness, are celebrated. In 112 the righteousness and uprightness of the man of God are highlighted. The first sets forth God, His character and work. The second sets forth man, his character and work for God. Hence, they are twin psalms, both acrostic and parallel, but with very different intent.

112:1. Blessed is the man that feareth the Lord, that delighteth greatly in his commandments. The closing thought of Psalm 111 is continued and expanded here. The fear of the Lord is the beginning of wisdom, and such fear brings great gain to the godly man. That fear is manifested in the fact that the righteous man **delighteth greatly** in God's commandments. At all times the believer is to "Let the word of Christ dwell in you richly in all wisdom . . ." (Col 3:16).

2-3. His seed shall be mighty upon the earth. This phrase was used of Nimrod in Genesis 10:8. However, the word **mighty** (Heb *gibōr*) may well be understood as "wealthy" or "prosperous" (Ruth 2:1; I Sam 9:1). When a man lives a godly life, generations after him are blessed as well. **And his righteousness endureth for ever.** When the godly man prospers, he does not forsake righteousness. Prosperity does not destroy his holiness.

4. Unto the upright there ariseth light in the darkness. The man who **delighteth greatly** (vs. 1) in the commandments of God and in His Word is never in the dark about dispersing the wealth that he has accumulated. The Word, which is a lamp unto our feet and a light unto our path, is also a guide to being **gracious, and full of compassion, and righteous.** These words are spoken of God in the fourth verse of Psalm 111; now they are used of God's servant who faithfully metes out to those in need a portion of the wealth and riches given unto him by God.

5-6. A good man sheweth favor, and lendeth. A man who is **full of compassion** will not sit idly by while his neighbor is in need. His kindness and graciousness will lead him to lend to those in necessity (cf. 37:26; Deut 15:8, 11). The word translated **lendeth** (Heb *lawah*) means to join one's self to another, to cleave to him, to form a union between borrower and lender. **He will guide his affairs with discretion.** He will do all things decently and in order. His prosperity will be established both before God and man, and **the righteous shall be in everlasting remembrance.** Generous and compassionate righteousness is never forgotten.

7-8. He shall not be afraid of evil tidings. That is not to say that evil tidings will not come; but the righteous man will face them in the confidence of God, for **his heart is established, he shall not be afraid** until the conflict is over and he knows his enemies have been vanquished.

9. He hath dispersed, he hath given to the poor. Out of the reservoir given to him by God, the righteous man has systematically shared with those in need. As a consequence, **his righ-**

PSALM 112

PRAISE ye the Lord. Blessed *is* the man *that* feareth the Lord, *that* delighteth greatly in his commandments.

2 His seed shall be mighty upon earth: the generation of the upright shall be blessed.
3 Wealth and riches *shall be* in his house: and his righteousness endureth for ever.

4 Unto the upright there ariseth light in the darkness: he *is* gracious, and full of compassion, and righteous.

5 A good man sheweth favour, and lendeth: he will guide his affairs with discretion.
6 Surely he shall not be moved for ever: the righteous shall be in everlasting remembrance.

7 He shall not be afraid of evil tidings: his heart is fixed, trusting in the Lord.
8 His heart *is* established, he shall not be afraid, until he see *his desire* upon his enemies.

9 He hath dispersed, he hath given to the poor; his righteousness endureth

for ever; his horn shall be exalted with honour.

10 The wicked shall see *it*, and be grieved; he shall gnash with his teeth, and melt away: the desire of the wicked shall perish.

PSALM 113

PRAISE ye the LORD. Praise, O ye servants of the LORD, praise the name of the LORD.
2 Blessed be the name of the LORD from this time forth and for evermore.
3 From the rising of the sun unto the going down of the same the LORD's name *is* to be praised.

4 The LORD *is* high above all nations, *and* his glory above the heavens.
5 Who *is* like unto the LORD our God, who dwelleth on high,
6 Who humbleth *himself* to behold the things that are in heaven, and in the earth!

7 He raiseth up the poor out of the dust, *and* lifteth the needy out of the dunghill;
8 That he may set *him* with princes, *even* with the princes of his people.
9 He maketh the barren woman to keep house, *and to be* a joyful mother of children. Praise ye the LORD.

teousness endureth for ever. His horn shall be exalted with honor. In general, the man who lives righteously and shares with those who live in poverty will be honored by all men.

10. The wicked shall see it, and be grieved. It is difficult enough for the wicked to see the righteous prosper; it is even more difficult to hear the righteous receive the praise of other men. So difficult is it that the wicked **shall gnash with his teeth, and melt away** (cf. 35:16; 37:12; Job 16:9; Lam 2:16; Acts 7:54). When the wicked view the prosperity of the righteous, their hatred is so great that they shall simply pine away in their grief. **The desire of the wicked shall perish** (cf. 1:6). The words **the wicked** (Heb *rasha*ʿ) are used emphatically by the Jews to denote one who never gives to the poor himself and cannot endure the sight of righteous men who share with the poor. When the wicked man is unable to see his desire, i.e., the financial downfall of the righteous man, that wicked man shall perish in pity and poverty.

G. The Greatness of the Lord God. 113:1-9.

THEME: A psalm of praise to the unique God of Israel.
Like the two preceding it, this psalm is without title. Some commentators have ascribed it to Samuel, others to David, still others to a post-exilic writer. The authorship is unknown, but with this psalm begins The Hallel (from the Hebrew *halal*, which is used seventy-six times in the Psalter and means praise). The Hallel consists of Psalms 113-118 and was reserved for use on the three great feasts of the Jews, i.e., Passover, Weeks, and Tabernacles, and for both the New Moon celebration and Dedication.

113:1-3. Praise ye the LORD. An essential feature of the ancient festivals held by the Israelites was praise to Jehovah. **Blessed be the name of the LORD from this time forth and for evermore.** If as servants of the Lord we have never praised His name, let us start now and continue to praise His name forever. **From the rising of the sun unto the going down of the same the LORD's name is to be praised.** From dawn's early light till the day's dark night, praise the name of Jehovah.

4-6. The LORD is high above all nations, the Lord of all lords, **and his glory above the heavens.** He outshines all of His creatures and His creation. He is above them all. The psalmist issues a challenge that is never answered: **Who is like unto the LORD our God?** No ancient god can be compared to Him; no modern technology can be compared to Him; no futuristic wisdom can be compared to Him. He is eternal, unchangeable, omniscient, omnipotent, and omnipresent. He is totally unique. He is God.

One of the most unbelievable characteristics of the God who is above all heavens and **who dwelleth on high** is that He is also the God **who humbleth himself to behold the things that are in heaven, and in the earth!** The heathen philosophers were totally unprepared to conceive of such a God who could at once be high above the heavens and at the same time stoop to be interested in the daily affairs of men. It is a condescension for God even to regard **the things that are in heaven,** since the very ". . . heavens are not clean in his sight" (Job 15:15).

7-9. As an example of the condescension of this great God, the psalmist notes that Jehovah is the God who **raiseth up the poor out of the dust, and lifteth the needy out of the dunghill.** While heaven is full of His glory, earth is full of His mercy. God is in the habit of lifting man from the depths of his experience as a destitute and downtrodden individual and raising him in order **that he may set him with princes.** God takes the castaways from the ash heap of life and makes them champions.

He maketh the barren woman to keep house, and to be a joyful mother of children. The power of God is unlimited. Not only can He make a prince out of a pauper, but He can make a mother out of a barren woman. With such a unique and wonderful God, it is little wonder that the psalmist concludes where he began, **Praise ye the LORD** (Hallelujah).

H. A Psalm of the Exodus. 114:1-8.

THEME: A beautiful psalm recalling God's power in leading the children of Israel from Egypt.

Although this psalm has been ascribed variously to as diverse possible authors as Shadrach, Meshach, and Abed-nego, to Esther or Mordecai, nevertheless the author is unknown. The beauty of the psalm, however, completely overshadows the question of authorship. Of it Clarke says, "It is elegantly and energetically composed." Maclaren says, "This Psalm is a little gem." And Spurgeon notes, "True poetry has here reached its climax: no human has ever been able to equal, much less to excel, the grandeur of this Psalm."

The structure of the psalm is poetically perfect. It consists of four strophes, each of two verses; each of these verses consists of two lines that are parallelistic. Thus, in Hebrew the beauty of the psalm can easily be detected.

114:1-2. When Israel went out of Egypt, the house of Jacob from a people of strange language. The psalm begins with the same abruptness with which Israel came out of Egypt. Joseph had gone down into Egypt, followed by the family of his father. There they multiplied greatly and indeed became **the house of Jacob.** Jehovah called them out of Egyptian bondage, for **Judah was his sanctuary, and Israel his dominion.** The land of Judah and the kingdom of Israel have always been special real estate to God.

3-4. Speaking of Israel's removal from Egypt to the land of Judah, the psalmist says, **The sea saw it, and fled** (Ex 14:19-24): **Jordan was driven back** (Josh 3:13-17). The miracles performed at the Red Sea and the Jordan River marked the beginning and end of Israel's long journey to the Promised Land. They made natural parallels to which the psalmist could allude (cf. Hab 3:8). **The mountains skipped like rams, and the little hills like lambs.** That the mountains **skipped like rams** may be a poetic reference to an earthquake; for when Israel entered Canaan, Judges 5:4 says, ". . . the earth trembled. . . ." Earthquakes are not uncommon in that area, and it is not impossible that God may have used a divinely directed earthquake to perform the miracle of stopping the waters of Jordan.

5-6. Now the psalmist taunts the creation in light of God's absolute dominance over it. **What ailed thee, O thou sea, that thou fleddest?** The Red Sea had bordered on the might of Pharaoh and had never quivered at his presence. Yet, when God led His people through, the sea fled. **What ailed thee . . . ye mountains, that ye skipped like rams . . . ?** What would cause the mountains to quake at precisely the moment the Israelites were about to enter the flooded waters of the Jordan? There can be but one answer: the omnipotent majesty of God.

7-8. Tremble, thou earth, at the presence of the Lord. The word **tremble** (Heb *chūl*) literally means to be in pain or have the pangs of a woman in childbirth. The convulsions of nature that accompanied the Exodus are poetically likened to the birth of a child. What could that nation do save worship their God Jehovah **which turned the rock into a standing water, the flint into a fountain of waters** (cf. Ex 17:6; Num 20:11). How wonderful and merciful is our God of deliverance.

I. In Praise of Monotheism. 115:1-18.

THEME: A favorable comparison of our one God to the idols of the heathen.

Although the authorship of this psalm has been variously ascribed to David at the beginning of his reign, to Mordecai and Esther, to Shadrach, Meshach, and Abed-nego, and to Heze-

PSALM 114

WHEN Israel went out of Egypt, the house of Jacob from a people of strange language;
2 Jŭ′dah was his sanctuary, *and* Israel his dominion.

3 The sea saw *it*, and fled: Jordan was driven back.
4 The mountains skipped like rams, *and* the little hills like lambs.

5 What *ailed* thee, O thou sea, that thou fleddest? thou Jordan, *that* thou wast driven back?
6 Ye mountains, *that* ye skipped like rams; *and* ye little hills, like lambs?

7 Tremble, thou earth, at the presence of the Lord, at the presence of the God of Jacob;
8 Which turned the rock *into* a standing water, the flint into a fountain of waters.

victim had seized the mind of the psalmist. Death and hell (Heb *she'ōl*) are frequently associated in Scripture, as they are connected in the prayer of Hezekiah (Isa 38:10, 18). (3) **I found trouble and sorrow.** On top of all this, the psalmist encountered anguish and woe (cf. Isa 38:12-17).

Prayer is never out of season, but it is significant that the psalmist records **Then called I upon the name of the LORD.** There are many who never think of calling upon the name of Jehovah until the conditions of verse 3 grasp for their souls. This was the case of Hezekiah as he, ". . . turned his face toward the wall, and prayed unto the Lord" (Isa 38:2). **I beseech thee, deliver my soul.**

5-6. The God who answers prayer shows Himself to be both **Gracious . . . and righteous.** In His mercy **The LORD preserveth the simple.** The expression **the simple** means those who are without guile, who are pure and without hypocrisy (cf. 19:7). **I was brought low, and he helped me.** The word translated **brought low** (Heb *dalal*) signifies to be drawn dry. The metaphor is taken from brooks, rivers, or ponds that are dried up.

7-8. The psalmist calls for his own soul to rest from the disquietude of those horrors that have come crashing in upon him. He is convinced that Jehovah has dealt **bountifully** with him in giving a threefold deliverance: **My soul from death, mine eyes from tears, and my feet from falling.** He was delivered as in 7:4; 18:19; 91:15. When God delivers us, it is a complete deliverance.

9-11. **I will walk before the LORD in the land of the living,** i.e., to walk a heavenly walk before a watching world. **I believed, therefore have I spoken.** He would never pray unto God unless he had faith that God would hear and answer his prayer. In his great affliction, the psalmist admitted that in his haste he had said, **All men are liars.** He means that during his period of distress, he found no man who was a friend to him.

12-14. The psalmist is now prepared to ask the question, **What shall I render unto the LORD for all his benefits toward me?** He wisely sets aside his fretting and consternation about the falsehood of man and turns his attention to ways in which he may repay the veracity and sincerity of God. Thus, the psalmist resolved, **I will take the cup of salvation.** The **cup of salvation** (Heb *yeshū'ah*) symbolized the cup used at the Passover supper (18:50; 28:8; 53:6). Like Zion, having drunk of the ". . . cup of trembling . . ." (cf. Isa 51:17, 22), the psalmist must now drink of the **cup of salvation.** This is an act of worship, just as much as calling upon **the name of the LORD** and paying **my vows unto the LORD** in the presence of all His people.

15-16. **Precious in the sight of the LORD is the death of his saints.** It is a matter of no little consequence or indifference to God when one of His saints dies. In Him are the issues of life and death (68:20), and the death of a saintly mother or father, an innocent child, or a godly pastor, does not pass unnoticed by a **gracious . . . and righteous** (vs. 5) God. To such a God the psalmist can but say, **O LORD, truly I am thy servant.** The God who cares for us in His mercy deserves to have our grateful service. Not only should we be His servants, but **the son of thine handmaid.** We are a servant born in His house of a servant, and thus we are doubly His servant.

17-19. **I will offer . . . and will call upon the name of the LORD. I will pay my vows.** As the psalmist continues his grateful resolutions, he prepares to give to the Lord the **sacrifice of thanksgiving.** This is not an actual sacrifice, but rather a heart filled with grateful praise to which is given voice. **In the courts of the LORD's house, in the midst of thee, O Jerusalem.** Thanksgiving was always most appropriately offered in the place where God had ordained that He should be worshiped. In the Holy City, in the holy place of that city, the psalmist would be

5 Gracious *is* the LORD, and righteous; yea, our God *is* merciful.
6 The LORD preserveth the simple: I was brought low, and he helped me.

7 Return unto thy rest, O my soul; for the LORD hath dealt bountifully with thee.
8 For thou hast delivered my soul from death, mine eyes from tears, *and* my feet from falling.

9 I will walk before the LORD in the land of the living.
10 I believed, therefore have I spoken: I was greatly afflicted:
11 I said in my haste, All men *are* liars.

12 What shall I render unto the LORD *for* all his benefits toward me?
13 I will take the cup of salvation, and call upon the name of the LORD.
14 I will pay my vows unto the LORD now in the presence of all his people.

15 Precious in the sight of the LORD *is* the death of his saints.
16 O LORD, truly I *am* thy servant; I *am* thy servant, *and* the son of thine handmaid: thou hast loosed my bonds.

17 I will offer to thee the sacrifice of thanksgiving, and will call upon the name of the LORD.
18 I will pay my vows unto the LORD now in the presence of all his people.
19 In the courts of the LORD's house, in the midst of thee, O Jerusalem. Praise ye the LORD.

careful to bring his praise, his vows, and his thanksgiving to Jehovah. **Praise ye the LORD.**

K. All Nations Praise. 117:1-2.

THEME: A call for universal praise unto Jehovah, whose truth endureth forever.

This is the shortest psalm in the Psalter; it has only seventeen words in the Hebrew, sixteen if the final Hallelujah is regarded as one. The brevity of this psalm does not in any way warrant the conclusion that it is a fragment, an addendum to Psalm 116 or a prefix to Psalm 118.

Though brief, the contents of this psalm have been praised by man. "This Psalm, which is very little in its letter, is exceedingly large in its spirit; for, bursting beyond all bounds of race or nationality, it calls upon all mankind to praise the name of the Lord"—Spurgeon. "This psalm manifests a breadth of outlook and a depth of insight that is amazing"—Leupold. "This is a prophecy concerning Christ; that all peoples, out of all kingdoms and islands, shall know Christ in His kingdom"—Luther. "It was in Israel the equivalent of the doxology in the Christian church"—Scroggie.

117:1. O praise the LORD, all ye nations. As in Romans 15:11, here is an exhortation to the Gentile nations to glorify the God of Israel, Jehovah. The Gentiles (Heb *gōyim*) will share in the goodness of God to Israel and thus are invited here to share in His praise (cf. 2:1, 8; 9:5, 15, 19-20; etc.). **Praise him, all ye people.** The word used here for **praise** is different from the one used in the first clause. John Gill notes that this latter word is more frequently used in the Chaldee, Syriac, Arabic, and Ethiopic languages and signifies the celebration of the praises of God with high voice. The use of two separate verbs to call upon the nations to praise the Lord is undoubtedly designed to emphasize the necessity of such praise.

2. For his merciful kindness is great toward us. In Christ Jesus God has shown mercy mixed with kindness in the very highest degree. Nothing has ever blessed the hearts and minds of the nations of the earth as the message of the gospel of Christ has. **The truth of the LORD endureth for ever.** The gospel brings everlasting life (Jn 3:16) and consolation (II Thess 2:16) to all who believe, Jew and Gentile alike. God has kept His covenant with Abraham that through him should all nations of the earth be blessed. When the psalmist considers the great mercy, kindness, and truth of Jehovah, there is no better expression of his amazement at the love of God than **Praise ye the LORD,** hallelujah.

L. A Resounding Hymn of Praise. 118:1-29.

THEME: The psalm which Martin Luther considered his favorite, his very own.

Throughout the centuries the authorship of this psalm has been hotly contested. While many conservative commentators like Calvin, Henry, Spurgeon, and others hold to the Davidic authorship of the psalm, most recent commentators look to the time after the Exile for its composition.

To what extent is the psalm messianic? Calvin notes, "Let us remember that it was the design of the Spirit, under the figure of this temporal kingdom, to describe the eternal and spiritual kingdom of God's Son, even as David represented Christ." With regard to this interpretation, one might examine Matthew 21:42-46; Mark 12:10-12; Luke 20:17-18; Acts 4:10-12. Spurgeon cautions, "But at the same time it could not have been intended that every particular line and sentence should be read in reference to the Messiah, for this requires very great ingenuity, and ingenius interpretations are seldom true."

Martin Luther dedicated his translation of this psalm to the Abbot Frederick of Nuremburg. In that dedication he noted:

PSALM 117

O PRAISE the LORD, all ye nations: praise him, all ye people.

2 For his merciful kindness is great toward us: and the truth of the LORD *endureth* for ever. Praise ye the LORD.

PSALM 118

O GIVE thanks unto the LORD; for *he is* good: because his mercy *endureth* for ever.

2 Let Israel now say, that his mercy *endureth* for ever.
3 Let the house of Aaron now say, that his mercy *endureth* for ever.
4 Let them now that fear the LORD say, that his mercy *endureth* for ever.

5 I called upon the LORD in distress: the LORD answered me, *and set me* in a large place.

6 The LORD *is* on my side; I will not fear: what can man do unto me?
7 The LORD taketh my part with them that help me: therefore shall I see *my desire* upon them that hate me.

8 *It is* better to trust in the LORD than to put confidence in man.
9 *It is* better to trust in the LORD than to put confidence in princes.
10 All nations compassed me about: but in the name of the LORD will I destroy them.
11 They compassed me about; yea, they compassed me about: but in the name of the LORD I will destroy them.
12 They compassed me about like bees; they are quenched as the fire of thorns: for in the name of the LORD I will destroy them.
13 Thou hast thrust sore at me that I might fall: but the LORD helped me.
14 The LORD *is* my strength and song, and is become my salvation.

15 The voice of rejoicing and salvation *is* in the tabernacles of the righteous: the right hand of the LORD doeth valiantly.
16 The right hand of the LORD is ex-

"This is my Psalm, my chosen Psalm . . . . It has saved me from many a pressing danger, from which neither emperor, nor kings, nor sages, nor saints could have saved me. It is my friend; dearer to me than all the honours and power of the earth . . . . But it may be objected that this psalm is common to all; no one has a right to call it his own. Yes; but Christ is also common to all, and yet Christ is mine." Luther is not the sole reader of this psalm for whom a blessing awaits; it brings praise to the hearts of all who read it.

118:1. O give thanks unto the LORD. A grateful heart needs to give expression to that gratitude. The Lord is deserving of our thanksgiving; **for he is good,** one of His essential attributes, and **because his mercy endureth for ever,** an integral part of His goodness.

2-4. Let Israel now say. . . . Let the house of Aaron now say. . . . Let them now that fear the LORD say. Israel should be particularly thankful for the mercy of Jehovah because she had sinned in Egypt and provoked the Lord again and again in the wilderness. Yet **his mercy endureth for ever.** The sons of Aaron were the closest to God, for they were set apart for private service to Jehovah. More than Israel in general, they should appreciate that **his mercy endureth for ever.** As if the psalmist had neglected someone who did not belong to Israel, he calls upon all who reverence the God of Israel to remember **that his mercy endureth for ever.**

5. I called upon the LORD in distress (lit., from the straight place) out of the narrow gorge. From the straits in which the psalmist found himself and his nation, a prayer is made to Jehovah and **The LORD answered me, and set me in a large place** (lit., in the open plain) removing him from the defile of disaster to the basin of blessing.

6-7. The LORD is on my side; I will not fear: what can man do unto me? ". . . If God be for us, who can be against us?" (Rom 8:31). Having been rescued by Jehovah, the psalmist had no reason to fear the destructive designs of man. He was convinced that **The LORD taketh my part with them that help me.** Jehovah had condescended to stand shoulder to shoulder with the psalmist and his comrades.

8-9. These two verses record the wisest of God's wisdom. **It is better to trust in the LORD than to put confidence in man.** Given all the time there is, God will never fail.

10-12. All nations compassed me about in order to destroy me **but in the name of the LORD I will destroy them.** Confident of victory because he has put his trust in the Lord, the psalmist remembers his enemies swarming about him **like bees.** But the battle was his to be won; and he envisions them **quenched as the fire of thorns,** a fire that quickly kindles into a blaze, but soon dies away. We may rest assured that when God is ours, so is the victory.

13-14. As if addressing his enemy directly, the psalmist says, **Thou hast thrust sore at me that I might fall: but the LORD helped me.** The psalmist would spar with his enemies because he knew that their purpose would be frustrated by God. **The LORD is my strength and song, and is become my salvation.** What a trio! Jehovah provides strength for the conflict, song for the victory, and salvation for the soul. Augustine explains the expression **and is become my salvation,** to mean "not that he hath become anything which he was not before, but because His people, when they believed on Him, became what they were not before."

15-16. The voice of rejoicing and salvation is in the tabernacles of the righteous. Within the tents of those who live righteously before Jehovah, there is the sound of music, i.e., **rejoicing and salvation.** The verse and chorus of their song are identical, i.e., **The right hand of the LORD doeth valiantly.** The

alted: the right hand of the LORD doeth valiantly.

17 I shall not die, but live, and declare the works of the LORD.

18 The LORD hath chastened me sore: but he hath not given me over unto death.

19 Open to me the gates of righteousness: I will go into them, and I will praise the LORD:

20 This gate of the LORD, into which the righteous shall enter.

21 I will praise thee: for thou hast heard me, and art become my salvation.

22 The stone which the builders refused is become the head stone of the corner.

23 This is the LORD's doing; it is marvellous in our eyes.

24 This is the day which the LORD hath made; we will rejoice and be glad in it.

25 Save now, I beseech thee, O LORD: O LORD, I beseech thee, send now prosperity.

26 Blessed be he that cometh in the name of the LORD: we have blessed you out of the house of the LORD.

27 God is the LORD, which hath shewed us light: bind the sacrifice with cords, even unto the horns of the altar.

refrain of the psalm is very similar, i.e., **The right hand of the LORD is exalted.**

17-18. I shall not die, but live, and declare the works of the LORD. The psalmist is convinced that his life will not be taken from him, even if the nations compass about him (vs. 10). God's man is indestructible until he has finished the work God has given him to do.

19-20. These verses may have been sung by the people upon reaching the entrance to the Temple. **Open to me the gates of righteousness . . . this gate of the LORD, into which the righteous shall enter.** Within the palace of the Great King, the psalmist would go in for one purpose and one purpose alone, i.e., **I will praise the LORD.**

21. Again he repeats, **I will praise thee.** God is to be praised because He hears our prayers (vs. 5) and has become our salvation (vs. 14).

22-23. The stone which the builders refused is become the head stone of the corner. Although this verse may refer to Israel or the Temple, it undoubtedly has as its primary referent the Lord Jesus Christ Himself. He is the living stone, the precious stone. The Messiah that the Jews rejected will one day be anointed King on the throne of David. The Saviour which the world rejected will one day be "KING OF KINGS, AND LORD OF LORDS" (Rev 19:16). Jesus Christ is the cornerstone of His church, that which holds it together, and that upon which it is built. **This is the LORD's doing; it is marvelous in our eyes.** The resurrection and exalted position of the Lord Jesus were not the work of men, for they had rejected Him. It was the work of Almighty God.

24. This is the day which the LORD hath made; we will rejoice and be glad in it. Various interpretations of this verse have been given. But if verse 24 is to be understood in the context of Jesus Christ, the Messiah, this **day** may well refer to the most remarkable day in history, the day in which Jesus Christ rose from the grave. That day began a whole new era of rejoicing by those who believed; for the Lord Jesus Himself said, ". . . because I live, ye shall live also" (Jn 14:19). As Adam introduced a day of sadness, so the Chief Cornerstone introduced a day of resurrection hope. It is little wonder that through the eyes of faith the psalmist concludes, **we will rejoice and be glad in it.**

25. Save now . . . O LORD, I beseech thee, send now prosperity. Those who understand David as the author of the psalm see here the king's petition for the Lord's blessing upon his reign. Those who understand the psalm to have been written during the days of Ezra and Nehemiah regard it as a prayer for the return of prosperity to the capital city of Jerusalem.

26. Blessed be he that cometh in the name of the LORD. He that cometh was one of the usual titles for the Messiah among the Jews. **We have blessed you out of the house of the LORD** appears to be a benediction used by the priests of the Temple. It was their privilege to participate in a sacrificial system that pointed toward the day when the Messiah would come **in the name of the LORD.**

27. God is the LORD, which hath showed us light. "God is Jehovah," but this is more than simply an allusion to the priestly blessing, "Jehovah make His face shine upon thee." In the messianic context, it must mean that Jehovah has showed unto us the Messiah, the Light of the World. He has delivered us from the powers of darkness and has translated us into the kingdom of His own dear Son. **Bind the sacrifice with cords, even unto the horns of the altar.** This is a particularly difficult phrase. Perhaps it is simply a prophetic identification that more than the blood of bulls and goats, the blood of Christ, the Light of the World, shall ". . . purge your conscience from dead works to serve the living God" (Heb 9:13-14).

28 Thou *art* my God, and I will praise thee: thou *art* my God, I will exalt thee.

29 O give thanks unto the LORD; for *he is* good: for his mercy *endureth* for ever.

28. Thou art my God, and I will praise thee . . . I will exalt thee. This resolve comes as a direct result of the psalmist's recollection that Jehovah has heard his prayer and has become his salvation (cf. vss. 5, 14, 21).

29. O give thanks unto the LORD for the same two reasons which he enumerated in verse 1. The psalm concludes as it began, making a complete circle of joyous praise to God. It is a resounding hymn of praise, an antiphonal song sung on joyous occasions. Yet, the latter portion of the psalm, which is messianic in character, helps us to understand that God's mercy did not cease with the captivity of His nation Israel; but in the Lord Jesus Christ, the heir to the throne of David, **his mercy endureth for ever.**

M. The Great Psalm. 119:1-176.

THEME: *A psalm dedicated to the praise of God's Word.*

This is the longest and most elaborate of the alphabetic psalms. While there are eight other acrostic psalms (9; 10; 25; 34; 37; 111; 112; 145), this one far exceeds the others in splendor.

The psalm is arranged in twenty-two stanzas, corresponding to the twenty-two letters of the Hebrew alphabet. Each stanza is composed of eight verses, each verse having but two members. The first line of each couplet begins with a letter of the alphabet and each of the eight verses in that stanza begins with the same letter. In our English Bibles the word supplied on top of each stanza is the name of that Hebrew letter, by which the Hebrews both wrote and counted.

With this acrostic arrangement and a predetermined length for the psalm, including each stanza, the author is remarkably unshackled from a mechanistic poetry. However, apart from the continuous praise of the Word of God, little or no theme can be discerned running through the verses of the psalm. Henry comments, "This Psalm is a chest of gold rings, not a chain of gold links." What we have here is a group of meaningful and purposeful declarations about the Word of God.

The author of the psalm is unknown. Still, the song is Davidic in tone and expression and squares with David's experiences at many interesting points. Clarke notes, "Though the most judicious interpreters assign it to the time of the Babylonian captivity; yet there are so many things in it descriptive of David's state, experience, and affairs, that I am led to think it might have come from his pen." Although there is little in the psalm to give us a positive identification of the author, David is as likely as any.

The Masoretes observed that in every verse but one (vs. 122) there is a direct reference to the Law under one of ten legal names found in the psalm. Yet, others do not find a reference to God's Word or His law in verse 132; and still others, strictly speaking, disregard the word *mishpat*, usually meaning **judgment**, as a reference to the Law in verses 84, 90, 121, 149, and 156. However, the great preponderance of verses contain at least one word which identifies the law of God, and that in itself is remarkable.

Although Psalm 119 is lengthy, it is not tiresome. Its subject, the Word of God, is more than worthy of its one hundred seventy-six verses.

119:1-3. Blessed are the undefiled in the way, who walk in the law of the LORD (lit., O the blessedness, cf. 1:1). The **undefiled** are those who live uprightly (cf. 18:23), those who are perfect or complete (18:30, 32), those who walk sincerely (cf. 15:2). The **way** is undoubtedly the way of righteousness (cf. 1:6; 23:3; etc.). The verbs of these sentences indicate the lifestyles of those who are blessed by God, who **walk . . . keep . . . seek.**

4-8. Then shall I not be ashamed, when I have respect unto all thy commandments. Shame always follows transgression. In

PSALM 119
ALEPH

BLESSED *are* the undefiled in the way, who walk in the law of the LORD.

2 Blessed *are* they that keep his testimonies, *and that* seek him with the whole heart.

3 They also do no iniquity: they walk in his ways.

4 Thou hast commanded *us* to keep thy precepts diligently.

5 O that my ways were directed to keep thy statutes!

6 Then shall I not be ashamed, when I have respect unto all thy commandments.

7 I will praise thee with uprightness of heart, when I shall have learned thy righteous judgments.

8 I will keep thy statutes: O forsake me not utterly.

BETH

9 Wherewithal shall a young man cleanse his way? by taking heed *thereto* according to thy word.

10 With my whole heart have I sought thee: O let me not wander from thy commandments.

11 Thy word have I hid in mine heart, that I might not sin against thee.

12 Blessed *art* thou, O LORD: teach me thy statutes.

13 With my lips have I declared all the judgments of thy mouth.

14 I have rejoiced in the way of thy testimonies, as *much as* in all riches.

15 I will meditate in thy precepts, and have respect unto thy ways.

16 I will delight myself in thy statutes: I will not forget thy word.

GIMEL

17 Deal bountifully with thy servant, *that* I may live, and keep thy word.

18 Open thou mine eyes, that I may behold wondrous things out of thy law.

19 I am a stranger in the earth: hide not thy commandments from me.

20 My soul breaketh for the longing *that it hath* unto thy judgments at all times.

21 Thou hast rebuked the proud *that are* cursed, which do err from thy commandments.

22 Remove from me reproach and contempt; for I have kept thy testimonies.

23 Princes also did sit *and* speak against me: *but* thy servant did meditate in thy statutes.

24 Thy testimonies also *are* my delight *and* my counsellors.

DALETH

25 My soul cleaveth unto the dust: quicken thou me according to thy word.

26 I have declared my ways, and thou heardest me: teach me thy statutes.

27 Make me to understand the way of thy precepts: so shall I talk of thy wondrous works.

28 My soul melteth for heaviness:

order to escape shame, we must be vigilant and constant in obeying the Word of God. "Among the snares of Satan, amid such thick darkness and so great insensibility as ours, the utmost vigilance and caution are necessary, if we would aim at being entirely exempted from blame"—Calvin.

9. **Wherewithal shall a young man cleanse his way?** (lit., with what shall a youth cleanse his path?). The word rendered **his way** (Heb *'ōrach*) signifies a track, a rut, such as would have been made by the wheel of a cart. A young sinner has not beaten a broad path, but rather has transgressed again and again in the same manner, creating a sinful rut. How shall he escape? **By taking heed thereto according to thy word.** Heeding the Word of God leads to a godly life-style. Ignoring the Word of God leads to a godless rut.

10-11. **With my whole heart have I sought thee** (cf. vs. 2). Because the psalmist has sincerely and genuinely sought the blessing of God through obedience to His Word, he prays that God would not permit him to deviate accidentally or deliberately from His commandments. **Thy word** (Heb *'imrah*) is literally "thy promise." To have the promises of God secretly laid up in our hearts is a good defense against being surprised by sin.

12-16. **I have rejoiced in the way of thy testimonies, as much as in all riches.** The psalmist has taken more delight in the doctrines of God's Word than he has in the dollars of this world. **I will meditate in thy precepts** (cf. vss. 23, 48, 78, 148). **I will not forget thy word;** that which we have laid up in our hearts (vs. 11) and upon which we have meditated ceaselessly (vs. 15), will never be forgotten.

17-20. **Open thou mine eyes, that I may behold wondrous things out of thy law.** As Thomas Manton observes, "The Hebrew phrase signifieth 'unveil mine eyes'. . . . Paul's cure of his natural blindness is a fit emblem of our cure of spiritual blindness: 'Immediately there fell from his eyes as it had been scales: and he received sight forthwith . . .' (Acts 9:18)." **I am a stranger in the earth** (cf. 39:12; Heb 11:13-16). Since the psalmist is not native born, but a sojourner here, he needs the roadmap of God's commandments in order to find his way back to his home with God.

21-24. As he winds his way through life, the psalmist had been slandered by even the rulers and captains of this world; **but thy servant did meditate in thy statutes.** He paid no attention to the calumnies and barbs hurled at him, but rather found comfort and solace in meditating upon the Word of God. **Thy testimonies also are my delight and my counselors.** When the world went one way, the psalmist went the other as counseled by God's Word.

25-29. **My soul cleaveth unto the dust: quicken thou me according to thy word.** When in a state of depression, the psalmist recognized that his soul had adhered to the dust as if he were already dead and buried. Yet ". . . the word of God is quick, (alive) and powerful, and sharper than any two-edged sword . . . ." (Heb 4:12). Reading, meditating, and obeying it would raise him to life and health again. **My soul melteth for heaviness: strengthen thou me according unto thy word,** an expression of similar sentiment to that of verse 25.

strengthen thou me according unto thy word.

29 Remove from me the way of lying: and grant me thy law graciously.

30 I have chosen the way of truth: thy judgments have I laid *before me.*

31 I have stuck unto thy testimonies: O LORD, put me not to shame.

32 I will run the way of thy commandments, when thou shalt enlarge my heart.

HE

33 Teach me, O LORD, the way of thy statutes; and I shall keep it *unto* the end.

34 Give me understanding, and I shall keep thy law; yea, I shall observe it with *my* whole heart.

35 Make me to go in the path of thy commandments; for therein do I delight.

36 Incline my heart unto thy testimonies, and not to covetousness.

37 Turn away mine eyes from beholding vanity; *and* quicken thou me in thy way.

38 Stablish thy word unto thy servant, who *is* devoted to thy fear.

39 Turn away my reproach which I fear: for thy judgments *are* good.

40 Behold, I have longed after thy precepts: quicken me in thy righteousness.

VAU

41 Let thy mercies come also unto me, O LORD, *even* thy salvation, according to thy word.

42 So shall I have wherewith to answer him that reproacheth me: for I trust in thy word.

43 And take not the word of truth utterly out of my mouth; for I have hoped in thy judgments.

44 So shall I keep thy law continually for ever and ever.

45 And I will walk at liberty: for I seek thy precepts.

46 I will speak of thy testimonies also before kings, and will not be ashamed.

47 And I will delight myself in thy commandments, which I have loved.

48 My hands also will I lift up unto thy commandments, which I have loved; and I will meditate in thy statutes.

ZAIN

49 Remember the word unto thy servant, upon which thou hast caused me to hope.

50 This *is* my comfort in my affliction: for thy word hath quickened me.

51 The proud have had me greatly in derision: *yet* have I not declined from thy law.

52 I remembered thy judgments of old, O LORD; and have comforted myself.

53 Horror hath taken hold upon me

30-32. I have chosen the way of truth . . . I have stuck unto thy testimonies. The psalmist contrasts himself with those who have chosen the **way of lying** (vs. 29). By choosing the truthful path, the psalmist has had to cleave or cling steadfastly to the testimonies of God. Therefore, he prays, **O LORD, put me not to shame.**

33-40. Teach me, O LORD, the way of thy statutes. If there is an underlying theme to this psalm, surely this is it. The psalmist is convinced that if the Lord will but teach him His law, **I shall observe it with my whole heart.**

41-44. Each verse of this stanza begins with a *waw* conjunctive. God had pledged that He would grant mercy and salvation to all His faithful servants (Deut 28:1-13). Armed with that promise, the psalmist was confident that he would be able to **answer him that reproacheth me.** Still, he recognized that it was God Himself that would put **the word of truth** in his mouth and thus prayed that God would not remove it when he was reproached. The goodness and mercy of God exhibited in answered prayer was enough to cause the psalmist to determine, **So shall I keep thy law continually for ever and ever.**

45-48. "Five things David promiseth himself here in the strength of God's grace. 1. That he should be free and easy in his duties: **I will walk at liberty:** freed from that which is evil, not hampered with the fetters of my own corruptions, and free to do that which is good. 2. That he should be bold and courageous in his duty: **I will speak of thy testimonies also before kings.** 3. That he should be cheerful and pleasant in his duty: **I will delight myself in thy commandments,** in conversing with them, in conforming to them. 4. That he should be diligent and vigorous in his duty: **My hands also will I lift up unto thy commandments;** which notes not only a vehement desire towards them but close application of mind to the observance of them. 5. That he should be thoughtful and considerate in his duty: **I will meditate in thy statutes**"—Matthew Henry.

49-52. Remember the word unto thy servant . . . I remembered thy judgments of old, O LORD. As the psalmist requests Jehovah to remember His promises to the faithful, he reminds Jehovah that he himself has remembered the very principles of God's government. It is the Word of God that brings him **comfort in my affliction.** Though **the proud** laughed at him in derision, nevertheless, **have I not declined from thy law.** Having found comfort in the law of God, the psalmist knew that there was no reason to turn aside from that Law when he was ridiculed.

53-56. Horror hath taken hold upon me because of the wicked that forsake thy law. The word **horror** (Heb *zal'apah*)

because of the wicked that forsake thy law.

54 Thy statutes have been my songs in the house of my pilgrimage.

55 I have remembered thy name, O LORD, in the night, and have kept thy law.

56 This I had, because I kept thy precepts.

CHETH

57 *Thou art* my portion, O LORD: I have said that I would keep thy words.

58 I intreated thy favour with *my* whole heart: be merciful unto me according to thy word.

59 I thought on my ways, and turned my feet unto thy testimonies.

60 I made haste, and delayed not to keep thy commandments.

61 The bands of the wicked have robbed me: *but* I have not forgotten thy law.

62 At midnight I will rise to give thanks unto thee because of thy righteous judgments.

63 I *am* a companion of all *them* that fear thee, and of them that keep thy precepts.

64 The earth, O LORD, is full of thy mercy: teach me thy statutes.

TETH

65 Thou hast dealt well with thy servant, O LORD, according unto thy word.

66 Teach me good judgment and knowledge: for I have believed thy commandments.

67 Before I was afflicted I went astray: but now have I kept thy word.

68 Thou *art* good, and doest good; teach me thy statutes.

69 The proud have forged a lie against me: *but* I will keep thy precepts with *my* whole heart.

70 Their heart is as fat as grease; *but* I delight in thy law.

71 *It is* good for me that I have been afflicted; that I might learn thy statutes.

72 The law of thy mouth *is* better unto me than thousands of gold and silver.

JOD

73 Thy hands have made me and fashioned me: give me understanding, that I may learn thy commandments.

74 They that fear thee will be glad when they see me; because I have hoped in thy word.

75 I know, O LORD, that thy judgments *are* right, and *that* thou in faithfulness hast afflicted me.

76 Let, I pray thee, thy merciful kindness be for my comfort, according to thy word unto thy servant.

77 Let thy tender mercies come unto

signifies a burning tempest or desert storm (cf. 11:6). Here, it signifies the mental anguish that came over the psalmist when he contemplated the fate of the wicked who had forsaken God's Law. **I have remembered thy name, O LORD, in the night, and have kept thy law.** To the one who delights to keep God's law, God will give more grace to keep it. There is never a time in which it is improper to turn to God and meditate upon His name. His name, and it alone, will calm the mental anguish caused by the vision of horror from all that awaits those who forsake God's law.

57-60. Thou art my portion, O LORD (cf. 73:26; 142:5; see also Num 18:20; Josh 13:33). If the Lord God is all we have, fear not: He is all we need. Martin Luther used to counsel every Christian to answer all temptations with the words, "I am a Christian." That is equal to saying to temptation, **Thou art my portion, O LORD.** Temptation flees from us when we find in God everything we need. **I entreated thy favor with my whole heart.** The Hebrew expresses great earnestness, humility, and supplication. **I thought on my ways . . . I made haste, and delayed not to keep thy commandments.**

61-64. Although the snares of the wicked have entrapped him, the psalmist is determined not to forget the law of God. He resolves, **At midnight I will rise to give thanks unto thee because of thy righteous judgments.** "He had praised God in the courts of the Lord's house, and yet he will do it in his bed-chamber. Public worship will not excuse us from secret worship"—Matthew Henry. **I am a companion of all them that fear thee.** The psalmist will love all those who love God.

65-72. Before I was afflicted I went astray: but now have I kept thy word . . . It is good for me that I have been afflicted: that I might learn thy statutes. David had well recognized that the humility of affliction, the stones of adversity, were God's gift to him to draw him closer to God. Although the wicked had propagated a lie against the psalmist (cf. vss. 22-23, 42, 78, etc.), and **Their heart is as fat as grease,** i.e., insensitive to spiritual things (cf. 17:10; Isa 6:10), nonetheless the psalmist is convinced that **The law of thy mouth is better unto me than thousands of gold and silver.** The Word of God is to be more highly valued than gold and silver.

73-74. Thy hands have made me and fashioned me: (cf. 100:3; 138:8; 139:14; Deut 32:6; Job 10:8) **give me understanding, that I may learn thy commandments.** Here is an acknowledgement from the psalmist that he has his existence from God. He reasons that since God has fashioned him, He will also teach him. As this is the case, **They that fear thee will be glad when they see me; because I have hoped in thy word.** The intention of the psalmist is that all who see him will rejoice in the fact that God does not forsake His own.

75-80. Fully aware that the judgments of Jehovah are righteous, the psalmist recognizes that it is by those judgments **that thou in faithfulness hast afflicted me.** Should a father intend to disown and banish his child, he would correct him no more. But when he intends to keep him and enjoy his presence forever, he makes sure that he faithfully "afflicts" the child. **Let, I pray thee, thy merciful kindness be for my comfort.** After affliction,

me, that I may live: for thy law *is* my delight.

78 Let the proud be ashamed: for they dealt perversely with me without a cause: *but* I will meditate in thy precepts.

79 Let those that fear thee turn unto me, and those that have known thy testimonies.

80 Let my heart be sound in thy statutes; that I be not ashamed.

CAPH

81 My soul fainteth for thy salvation: *but* I hope in thy word.

82 Mine eyes fail for thy word, saying, When wilt thou comfort me?

83 For I am become like a bottle in the smoke; *yet* do I not forget thy statutes.

84 How many *are* the days of thy servant? when wilt thou execute judgment on them that persecute me?

85 The proud have digged pits for me, which *are* not after thy law.

86 All thy commandments *are* faithful: they persecute me wrongfully; help thou me.

87 They had almost consumed me upon earth; but I forsook not thy precepts.

88 Quicken me after thy lovingkindness; so shall I keep the testimony of thy mouth.

LAMED

89 For ever, O LORD, thy word is settled in heaven.

90 Thy faithfulness *is* unto all generations: thou hast established the earth, and it abideth.

91 They continue this day according to thine ordinances: for all *are* thy servants.

92 Unless thy law *had been* my delights, I should then have perished in mine affliction.

93 I will never forget thy precepts: for with them thou hast quickened me.

94 I *am* thine, save me; for I have sought thy precepts.

95 The wicked have waited for me to destroy me: *but* I will consider thy testimonies.

there was need for divine comfort. **Let thy tender mercies come unto me, that I may live.** After affliction, the psalmist was nigh unto death. It was only by God's mercy that he would live. **Let the proud be ashamed** (cf. 35:4, 26; 40:14; 70:2; 83:17; etc.). His fourth petition was, **Let those that fear thee turn unto me.** After affliction, it was necessary that the psalmist recover the confidence of his friends and that they return to him. **Let my heart be sound in thy statutes.** What a fitting conclusion to his prayer.

81-83. My soul fainteth for thy salvation: but I hope in thy word. The psalmist is committed that regardless of the circumstances which cause him to faint in soul (not in body), he would continue to place his trust in the Word of God. In the early seventeenth century Samuel Rutherford said, "Believe under a cloud, and wait for him when there is no moonlight nor starlight."

Mine eyes fail for thy word. . . . For I am become like a bottle in the smoke. The simile here is very vivid. In the Ancient Near East bottles were commonly made of animal skins and covered with dust and smoke. They were unsightly. This is a striking picture of the psalmist's own spiritual state. He had waited for the Lord to come and in spirit had become dried up by the pressure placed upon him. Relentless enemies taunted his faith in God. Still the psalmist has resolved, **yet do I not forget thy statutes.**

84-88. How many are the days of thy servant? i.e., how little time do I have left? The psalmist had good reason to ask such a question. **The proud have digged pits for me . . . They had almost consumed me upon earth.** Regular attempts had been made by the psalmist's enemies to end his days. Yet, through it all the psalmist's conviction remained that **All thy commandments are faithful** (lit., are faithfulness). He does not lash out against his enemies, but simply whispers the prayer, **help thou me.** Says Matthew Henry, "'God help me' is an excellent, comprehensive prayer; it is a pity it should ever be used lightly and as a bye-word." **Quicken me after thy lovingkindness** (cf. vss. 25, 37, 50, 107, 149, 156, 159). It is the "quickening" of God through His life-giving grace that enables the servant of God to **keep the testimony of thy mouth.**

89. For ever, O LORD, thy word is settled in heaven. The psalmist praises God that His Word is not only settled and unchangeable, but it is also settled and unchangeable far from the reach of men, **in heaven.** Because of its perfect author, precise inscription, and permanent habitation, the Word of God is unsurpassable, undeniable, and unchangeable.

90-92. Thomas Chalmers observes that "in these verses there is affirmed to be an analogy between the Word of God and the works of God . . . It is said of both in the 91st verse, **They continue this day according to thine ordinances: for all are thy servant's;** thereby identifying the sureness of that Word which proceeded from his lips, with the unfailing unconstancy of that Nature which was formed and is upholden by His hands." Both the Word and the world are secure in God's faithfulness unto all generations. The psalmist recognizes that **Unless thy law had been my delights, I should then have perished in mine affliction** (cf. vss. 16, 24, 35, 47, 70, 77). God's faithfulness, coupled with our love for His Word, will see us through any adversity.

93-96. Once again, the psalmist resolves that **I will never forget thy precepts: for with them thou hast quickened me.** The quickening Spirit delights to work by the Word of God. Once quickened, we are quickened forever and thus can unremittently pray to God, **I am thine, save me.** Even when **The wicked have waited for me to destroy me,** we must not again

96 I have seen an end of all perfection: *but* thy commandment *is* exceeding broad.

MEM

97 O how I love thy law! it *is* my meditation all the day.
98 Thou through thy commandments hast made me wiser than mine enemies: for they *are* ever with me.
99 I have more understanding than all my teachers: for thy testimonies *are* my meditation.
100 I understand more than the ancients, because I keep thy precepts.

101 I have refrained my feet from every evil way, that I might keep thy word.
102 I have not departed from thy judgments: for thou hast taught me.
103 How sweet are thy words unto my taste! *yea, sweeter* than honey to my mouth!
104 Through thy precepts I get understanding: therefore I hate every false way.

NUN

105 Thy word *is* a lamp unto my feet, and a light unto my path.

106 I have sworn, and I will perform *it,* that I will keep thy righteous judgments.
107 I am afflicted very much: quicken me, O LORD, according unto thy word.

108 Accept, I beseech thee, the freewill offerings of my mouth, O LORD, and teach me thy judgments.
109 My soul *is* continually in my hand: yet do I not forget thy law.
110 The wicked have laid a snare for me: yet I erred not from thy precepts.
111 Thy testimonies have I taken as an heritage for ever: for they *are* the rejoicing of my heart.
112 I have inclined mine heart to perform thy statutes alway, *even unto* the end.

SAMECH

113 I hate *vain* thoughts: but thy law do I love.
114 Thou *art* my hiding place and my shield: I hope in thy word.
115 Depart from me, ye evildoers: for I will keep the commandments of my God.
116 Uphold me according unto thy word, that I may live: and let me not be ashamed of my hope.
117 Hold thou me up, and I shall be safe: and I will have respect unto thy statutes continually.
118 Thou hast trodden down all them

seek salvation but simply **consider thy testimonies.** When we look confidently to the Word of Promise and daily trust the provision of God's grace, we are testifying not only to our salvation by God's grace, but also to the fact that "For ever, O LORD, thy word is settled in heaven" (vs. 89).

97-100. O how I love thy law! It is my meditation all the day. The word **love** is in the preterite form, meaning that it has been and still is the habit of the psalmist to love the law of God. The psalmist delights in the fact that he has fallen deeply in love with the law of God. Armed with divine wisdom, the psalmist is assured that he is **wiser** than his enemies, he has **more understanding** than all his teachers, and he understands **more than the ancients.** The cunning and craft of worldly men is no match for the wisdom of God. As long as the psalmist did not attempt to match wit with his enemies but wholly relied on God's Word for direction, he was assured of victory.

101-104. I have refrained my feet from every evil way, that I might keep thy word. This was the intention of the psalmist; it is a good intention, although he had to admit that he had not always successfully refrained from evil (cf. vss. 67, 176). We cannot willingly live in sin when we have a sincere desire to keep God's law. **How sweet are thy words unto my taste! yea, sweeter than honey to my mouth!** This metaphor is not new to the psalmist (cf. vss. 14, 16, 40, 47), but it is one that pervades this poetic masterpiece.

105. Thy word is a lamp unto my feet, and a light unto my path. The words used in description of God's Word are carefully chosen. It is both a **lamp** and a **light.** These metaphors are probably allusions to the lamps and torches carried at night by Eastern caravans. The heavenly design of God's Word is not to confuse, camouflage, or cover over the kernel of truth, but to reveal the Word as truth.

106-107. I have sworn, and I will perform it. The psalmist solemnly swears to **keep thy righteous judgments** and, as Calvin notes, "By the Word swear, he intimates that he had solemnly pledged himself to God not to alter his determination." For his resolve, the psalmist had only received affliction. This necessitates his call, **quicken me, O LORD, according unto thy word.**

108-112. My soul is continually in my hand: yet do I not forget thy law. Here the psalmist wishes to depict how fragile his life is. His soul is constantly in danger, for **The wicked have laid a snare** for him. Nonetheless, he had not forgotten God's law and had **inclined mine heart to perform thy statutes always, even unto the end.** Neither the frailty of life nor the snare of the wicked would deter the psalmist from living faithfully for the Lord until his final breath.

113-117. I hate vain thoughts: but thy law do I love. Simple dislike of evil is not sufficient for the man of God; perfect hatred against all manner and degree of evil is. Such hatred prompts the psalmist to say, **Depart from me, ye evildoers.** There is no fellowship between light and darkness, between righteousness and unrighteousness (II Cor 10:16). In order to ensure his separation from sin, the psalmist pleads with Jehovah to **Uphold me according unto thy word . . . Hold thou me up, and I shall be safe.** He is totally dependent upon God's sustaining grace as promised in His inspired Word.

118-120. Thou hast trodden down all them that err from thy statutes: for their deceit is falsehood. Chrysostom ex-

that err from thy statutes: for their deceit *is* falsehood.

119 Thou puttest away all the wicked of the earth *like* dross: therefore I love thy testimonies.

120 My flesh trembleth for fear of thee; and I am afraid of thy judgments.

AIN

121 I have done judgment and justice: leave me not to mine oppressors.

122 Be surety for thy servant for good: let not the proud oppress me.

123 Mine eyes fail for thy salvation, and for the word of thy righteousness.

124 Deal with thy servant according unto thy mercy, and teach me thy statutes.

125 I *am* thy servant; give me understanding, that I may know thy testimonies.

126 *it is* time for *thee*, Lord, to work: *for* they have made void thy law.

127 Therefore I love thy commandments above gold; yea, above fine gold.

128 Therefore I esteem all *thy* precepts *concerning* all *things to be* right; *and* I hate every false way.

PE

129 Thy testimonies *are* wonderful: therefore doth my soul keep them.

130 The entrance of thy words giveth light; it giveth understanding unto the simple.

131 I opened my mouth, and panted: for I longed for thy commandments.

132 Look thou upon me, and be merciful unto me, as thou usest to do unto those that love thy name.

133 Order my steps in thy word: and let not any iniquity have dominion over me.

134 Deliver me from the oppression of man: so will I keep thy precepts.

135 Make thy face to shine upon thy servant; and teach me thy statutes.

136 Rivers of waters run down mine eyes, because they keep not thy law.

TZADDI

137 Righteous *art* thou, O Lord, and upright *are* thy judgments.

138 Thy testimonies *that* thou hast commanded *are* righteous and very faithful.

139 My zeal hath consumed me, because mine enemies have forgotten thy words.

pounds the text, "God will make them ignominious and comtemptible." **Thou puttest away all the wicked of the earth like dross.** Although it may not be entirely possible now for the righteous to live separated from the wicked, the day will come when God will purge the world with a refiner's fire. Those who live His testimonies will be removed from the dross of this earth, and those who do not will be ushered to the great white throne judgment (Rev 20:11-15) from which there is no departure except to the lake of fire.

121-125. Be surety for thy servant for good (cf. Job 17:3; Isa 38:14). The word **surety** (Heb *'arab*) is the same as is rendered in Genesis 43:9; 44:32; Proverbs 6:1; 11:15; 20:16; 27:13, and elsewhere. It means a pledge with which something is obtained, the full result of purchase to follow. The Puritan John Gill observes, "What David prays to God to be for him, that Christ is for all His people: Hebrews 7:22."

126-128. It is time for thee, Lord, to work. The psalmist discerned that the time had come for God to move into history, for the Messiah to come, for a work of salvation to be done among sinful men. In anticipation of that blessed day which God had promised, the psalmist says, **Therefore I love thy commandments above gold; yea, above fine gold.** The image employed here brings to our minds a picture of the miser; his heart and his treasure are in his gold. How miserly the man of God ought to be, having his heart and his treasure in the gold of God's Word.

129-130. Thy testimonies are wonderful . . . The entrance of thy words giveth light. The Scriptures are wonderful in their subject matter, the manner in which they were written, and the eternal effects which they produce. It is the **entrance** (lit., opening), i.e., the unfolding or unveiling, of the words of God that give light to the darkened soul. That which the human mind cannot comprehend by itself (I Cor 2:14) is comprehended through the divine aid of the Spirit of God.

131-134. Look thou upon me, and be merciful unto me, as thou usest to do unto those that love thy name; literally, according to the judgment belonging to them that love Thy Name, which may mean "as is just to them." But the word for judgment (Heb *mishpat*) is frequently used in the sense of "custom" (see Perowne). The psalmist begs that God will **Order my steps in thy word** in the same way that He had ordered the steps of those righteous men who preceded him. The word **order** (Heb *kūn*) means to make firm, to walk without halting. If no iniquity is to have dominion over us, our steps must be established by the Word of God (cf. 40:2).

135-136. Make thy face to shine upon thy servant. Oh how we need the blessing of God in order to walk uprightly and perform adequately for Him. "Thy ministers can pronounce the Word, but cannot impart the Spirit; they may entertain the fancy with the charms of eloquence, but if thou art silent they do not inflame the heart . . . . therefore do Thou, O Lord my God, Eternal Truth! speak to my soul! lest, being outwardly warm, but not inwardly quickened I die, and be found unfruitful"— Thomas a Kempis (1380-1471).

137-138. Righteous art thou, O Lord (cf. 7:9; 11:7; 25:8; 116:5; 145:17) . . . **Thy testimonies that thou hast commanded art righteous and very faithful** (lit., righteousness and very faithfulness). God never alters with time; we may fruitfully meditate upon His righteous nature because that nature never changes.

139-142. My zeal hath consumed me. The heat of intention is zeal. The psalmist's zeal was a holy warmth, emanating from his conviction that **Thy word is very pure.** God's Word had

140 Thy word *is* very pure: therefore thy servant loveth it.

141 I *am* small and despised: *yet* do not I forget thy precepts.

142 Thy righteousness *is* an everlasting righteousness, and thy law *is* the truth.

143 Trouble and anguish have taken hold on me: *yet* thy commandments *are* my delights.

144 The righteousness of thy testimonies *is* everlasting: give me understanding, and I shall live.

KOPH

145 I cried with *my* whole heart; hear me, O Lord: I will keep thy statutes.

146 I cried unto thee; save me, and I shall keep thy testimonies.

147 I prevented the dawning of the morning, and cried: I hoped in thy word.

148 Mine eyes prevent the *night* watches, that I might meditate in thy word.

149 Hear my voice according unto thy lovingkindness: O Lord, quicken me according to thy judgment.

150 They draw nigh that follow after mischief: they are far from thy law.

151 Thou *art* near, O Lord; and all thy commandments *are* truth.

152 Concerning thy testimonies, I have known of old that thou hast founded them for ever.

RESH

153 Consider mine affliction, and deliver me: for I do not forget thy law.

154 Plead my cause, and deliver me: quicken me according to thy word.

155 Salvation *is* far from the wicked: for they seek not thy statutes.

156 Great *are* thy tender mercies, O Lord: quicken me according to thy judgments.

157 Many *are* my persecutors and mine enemies; *yet* do I not decline from thy testimonies.

158 I beheld the transgressors, and was grieved; because they kept not thy word.

159 Consider how I love thy precepts: quicken me, O Lord, according to thy lovingkindness.

160 Thy word *is* true *from* the beginning: and every one of thy righteous judgments *endureth* for ever.

proved itself to be tried, refined, and purified like gold in the furnace, and also, absolutely perfect, inerrant, and infallible. No wonder **Thy righteousness is an everlasting righteousness, and thy law is the truth.** With God there is ". . . no variableness, neither shadow of turning" (Jas 1:17). Hence, with His holy and righteous Word there is also no variableness nor shadow of turning.

143-144. Even though trouble and anguish had taken hold upon the psalmist, nevertheless he delighted in the commandments of God; for **the righteousness of thy testimonies is everlasting.** His simple prayer to God is that Jehovah may give him full understanding of His commandments, their depth, their breadth, and their exceeding excellence.

145-146. I cried with my whole heart . . . I cried unto thee; save me. With earnest and patient prayer the psalmist voiced his desire that God would supply his greatest need, i.e., grace for salvation. With enemies all around and a deep sense of personal guilt, David could only turn toward the Lord God for salvation.

147-149. So intense was his prayer that he confessed, **I prevented the dawning of the morning.** Before the light broke through the shadows of night, the psalmist was already prevailing upon God in prayer. "It is a grievous thing if the rays of the rising sun find thee lazy and ashamed in thy bed, and the bright light strike on eyes still weighed down with slumbering sloth"—Ambrose. **Mine eyes prevent the night watches, that I might meditate in thy word.** The Jews, like the Greeks and Romans, divided the night into military watches instead of hours. Accompanying the prevailing prayer of the psalmist was a meditation in the Word of God. Prayer and reading the Word preceded the dawning of the day and continued unto the watches of the night. That is the secret of getting ahold of God.

150-152. They draw nigh that follow after mischief. . . . Thou art near, O Lord. Though those who would threaten the psalmist have pursued him and have come near unto him, he is confident that there is One nearer him than his adversaries, i.e., Jehovah God. Through testing and adversity he had learned that the Word of God is true.

153-156. Consider mine affliction, and deliver me. . . . Plead my cause, and deliver me (cf. 35:1; 43:1; Mic 7:9). God will **plead** the **cause** of His servants when He avenges the injustices done to them by their enemies. Thus, the psalmist can say, **Salvation is far from the wicked.** The Lord is ready to pardon, but He will not pardon an impenitent sinner. By their own actions, men of impenitent hearts have put salvation far from them. Nevertheless, **Great are thy tender mercies, O Lord.**

157-160. David's attitude toward his oppressors was not a calloused one. He had many persecutors; yet he says, **I beheld the transgressors, and was grieved; because they kept not thy word.** In his book, *The Saints' Everlasting Rest,* Puritan Richard Baxter (1615-1691) writes of our appropriate concern for those who live around us and yet have not kept the Word of God. He says, "Oh, if you have the hearts of Christians or of men in you, let them yearn towards your poor ignorant, ungodly neighbors . . . Dost thou live close by them, or meet them in the streets, or labour with them, or travel with them . . . and say nothing to them of their souls, or the life to come? If their houses were on fire, thou wouldst run and help them; and wilt thou not help them when their souls are almost at the fire of Hell?"

After a thorough examination of the testimonies, commandments, precepts, statutes, etc., of God's Word, the psalmist can come but to one sure conclusion: **Thy word is true.** Oh that each reader of this psalm would come to the same certain conclusion.

SCHIN

161 Princes have persecuted me without a cause: but my heart standeth in awe of thy word.
162 I rejoice at thy word, as one that findeth great spoil.
163 I hate and abhor lying: *but* thy law do I love.

161-163. Though princes and great men had persecuted him unjustly and unmercilessly, nevertheless the heart of the psalmist **standeth in awe of thy word.** The overpowering presence of the Word of God in the mind of God's servant sustained him under the most severe circumstances. Thus the psalmist could rejoice in the Word of God **as one that findeth great spoil.** The riches of God's Word only come to those who have disciplined themselves to battle the enemies of time, apathy, and irregularity with regard to the reading of God's Word. Anyone who gives himself to such a rewarding practice will be able to say with the psalmist, **I hate and abhor lying.** Not only **hate** lying, nor simply **abhor** it, but **hate and abhor lying** is the responsibility of one who loves the law of God.

164 Seven times a day do I praise thee because of thy righteous judgments.
165 Great peace have they which love thy law: and nothing shall offend them.
166 LORD, I have hoped for thy salvation, and done thy commandments.
167 My soul hath kept thy testimonies; and I love them exceedingly.
168 I have kept thy precepts and thy testimonies: for all my ways *are* before thee.

164-168. Seven times a day do I praise thee, because of thy righteous judgments. Such judgments brought him **Great peace** amidst the tempests of his life. The **peace** (Heb *shalōm*) that David received was not just a feeling of tranquility or safety, but an overwhelming sense of wholeness, completion, and well-being. Things were well with David; for he could say, **I have kept thy precepts and thy testimonies.** The word rendered **kept** (Heb *shamar*) signifies to keep diligently, studiously, or exactly.

TAU

169 Let my cry come near before thee, O LORD: give me understanding according to thy word.
170 Let my supplication come before thee: deliver me according to thy word.
171 My lips shall utter praise, when thou hast taught me thy statutes.
172 My tongue shall speak of thy word: for all thy commandments *are* righteousness.

169-172. The last stanza of this great psalm is the psalmist's prayer to God, praise for salvation, and confession for personal sin. **Let my cry come near before thee, O LORD.** The psalmist views as his greatest need an **understanding according to thy word.** To give understanding of the Word of God is the special work of the Spirit of God. This was the first petition in the psalmist's prayer. His second petition was like unto it: **Let my supplication come before thee.** It did him no good to pray for understanding if God would not hear his prayer. Then he prays, **deliver me according to thy word.** It is good to note that his prayer for deliverance did not precede his prayer for understanding. From his prayer the psalmist passes on to a note of praise. **My lips shall utter praise. . . . My tongue shall speak of thy word.** We can no more praise the Lord God appropriately than we can pray to Him, unless the Spirit of God is our teacher.

173 Let thine hand help me; for I have chosen thy precepts.
174 I have longed for thy salvation, O LORD; and thy law *is* my delight.
175 Let my soul live, and it shall praise thee; and let thy judgments help me.
176 I have gone astray like a lost sheep; seek thy servant; for I do not forget thy commandments.

173-176. I have longed for thy salvation, O LORD. . . . Let my soul live, and it shall praise thee. It was the delight of the psalmist to meditate in the law of God because he had received God's salvation. His soul had been made alive by God's spirit, and it was now his responsibility to praise the living Lord. **Thy law is my delight.** "Religion will decay or flourish as it is our duty or our delight." The psalmist delighted in the Word of God; and spontaneously, joyously, and purposefully engrossed himself in God's Holy Word.

I have gone astray like a lost sheep. This is a frequent figure in the Scriptures (cf. Isa 53:6; Jer 50:6; Mt 10:6; 15:24). Lost sheep never find their own way back to the shepherd; and thus, having admitted his depravity and personal sin, the psalmist's final prayer is, **seek thy servant; for I do not forget thy commandments.** The result of this inquiry was that no man was found to seek God in and of himself. The psalmist knew that his sins separated him from the Lord God of heaven and that **Salvation is far from the wicked** (vs. 155). Yet, he also knew that **Great are thy tender mercies** (vs. 156). The law of God had ever been in his mind; He had meditated on it and longed for it (vss. 15, 20, 40). But the Law could not bring salvation to him; only the Lord God could do that. Thus, he ends his psalm with a note of dependency upon the grace of God: **Seek thy servant.**

THE SONGS OF ASCENTS.

The next fifteen psalms form a collection by themselves, sometimes aptly called the Little Psalter. Ten of these fifteen psalms are anonymous; four are attributed to David; one to Solomon. They appear to be in five groups of three psalms in each group. With one exception, the Psalm 132, they are all short and similar in tone, diction, rhythm, and form.

Each of the psalms carries the superscription, **A song of degrees,** sometimes translated as, "A Song of Ascents," or "A Song of Steps."

From the Hebrew designation of these psalms (Heb *shir hama'alōt*) four major interpretations have evolved. Since the word could be translated "steps," some interpreters have understood these psalms to build from the first verse to the last in a step-like progression. Others interpret the term as a starting point from which the psalms will be sung. The actual steps of the sanctuary, leading up to the Court of the Men, are understood by many as those steps upon which the psalms will be sung. Another interpretation understands these songs as designed to be sung by the children of Israel as they ascended the hills of Judaea *en route* to the Holy City after they have been released from Babylonian captivity. The final interpretation is that they were sung on any occasion that drew the Israelites to go up to Jerusalem or to the Holy Place (cf. I Sam 1:3); for they were joyous occasions that would necessitate the singing of songs such as those found in the Little Psalter.

N. A Prayer Against Slander. 120:1-7.

THEME: *A petition to God for deliverance from those with deceitful tongues.*

This is one of the anonymous psalms of the Songs of Degrees. Calvin, Patrick, and Henry ascribe it to David as the probable author, but this cannot be said for sure. Others ascribe it to Solomon, Ezra, Haggai, Zechariah, or Malachi. Those who hold to Davidic authorship suppose it to have been written when Doeg and his accomplices drove David from his capital by their slander.

As to classification, this psalm is a lament. The author voices a petition to God for preservation in the face of lying lips; and there are noticeable points of contact with Psalms 64; 140; and 142.

PSALM 120

IN my distress I cried unto the LORD, and he heard me.
2 Deliver my soul, O LORD, from lying lips, *and* from a deceitful tongue.

120:1-2. In my distress I cried unto the LORD. The specific distress intended can only be conjectured, but there is no distress so grievous as that occasioned by slander. The psalmist could retaliate; or he could retain that distress within himself. But the wisest course he could follow is the one he chose when he **cried unto the LORD.** His prayer was, **Deliver my soul, O LORD, from lying lips, and from a deceitful tongue.** Since that fateful day in the Garden of Eden, lips created to praise the name of the Lord have been prone to curse that name and speak evil of his anointed.

3 What shall be given unto thee? or what shall be done unto thee, thou false tongue?
4 Sharp arrows of the mighty, with coals of juniper.

3-4. What shall be given unto thee? The psalmist addresses those who slander him and says, "What punishment will God inflict upon you for speaking falsely of me?" He then conjectures what that punishment may be. **Sharp arrows of the mighty, with coals of juniper.** God has reserved the sharpest arrows of the mighty for them and the most torturous coals of punishment. It is not without significance that all liars ". . . shall have their part in the lake which burneth with fire and brimstone . . ." (Rev 21:8).

5 Woe is me, that I sojourn in Mē'sĕch, *that* I dwell in the tents of Kē'dar!
6 My soul hath long dwelt with him that hateth peace.
7 I *am for* peace: but when I speak, they *are* for war.

5-7. Woe is me. Two things concern the psalmist at the present moment: **That I sojourn in Mesech, that I dwell in the tents of Kedar!** Plumer notes, "Mesech or Meshech was the son of Japheth, Genesis 10:2; Kedar was a son of Ishmael (Gen 25:13). Though of different origin, their descendants seem to have had much the same manner, habits, and dispositions, all of them being idolaters, fierce and cruel."

The psalmist is speaking metaphorically here, for Israel never sojourned **in Mesech** or dwelt **in the tents of Kedar.** He is simply indicating that this would be a cruel fate indeed, for **My soul hath long dwelt with him that hateth peace.** The psalmist did nothing to elicit the slanderous remarks of his neighbors. **I am for peace: but when I speak, they are for war.** The centuries have not changed the situation, for the Middle East is today as volatile as it was in the day of the psalmist.

O. Jehovah: Keeper of Israel. 121:1-8.

THEME: *A beautiful expression of trust in the Maker of heaven and earth and the Keeper of Israel.*

We know nothing of this psalm's authorship, although its design is one of comfort and consolation. "This is a Psalm of consolation wherein the psalmist from his own experience, exhorts the godly to a constancy of faith, and to an expectation of help and defense from God"—Luther. It is in marked contrast to the preceding psalm, which was a complaint unto God. The key to our understanding of this psalm is the word **keep** (Heb *shamar*). The Creator of the universe is also the Keeper of both the nation Israel and individual Israelites. This is the theme of Psalm 121.

121:1-2. I will lift up mine eyes unto the hills, from whence cometh my help. The meaning of this verse is not clear. Perhaps the meaning could be, "If I lift up mine eyes to the hills," so as to participate in the idolatrous worship which was prevalent in the hillsides of Judaea, **from whence cometh my help?** Or the psalmist may be asking, "Shall I lift up mine eyes unto the hills?" Many significant events in the life of Israel and her forefathers took place on the mountains (cf. Gen 22:2ff.; Ex 3:1-2; 19:3ff.; I Kgs 19:8; etc.). But these events did not always issue in **help** from the Lord. Regardless of whether we interpret this first verse as a determination on the part of the psalmist to look to the holy hills of Jerusalem (87:1; 125:2), or as to whether or not he should look to these holy hills, or as a contrast with those who looked to the hills in idolatrous worship, nonetheless, the psalmist has resolved that his help does not come from the hills themselves; but **My help cometh from the LORD, which made heaven and earth.**

3-4. He will not suffer thy foot to be moved. "The sliding of the foot is a frequent description of misfortune, for example, Psalm 38:16; 66:9; and a very natural one in mountainous Canaan, where a single slip of the foot was often attended with great danger. The language here naturally refers to complete, lasting misfortune"—Hengstenberg. **Behold, he that keepeth Israel shall neither slumber nor sleep.** The Lord God puts a garrison around us with His holy angels, so that even while we sleep we are confident of protection because He never sleeps. The attacks of Satan never catch our God off guard.

5-6. To the expression that is the theme of this psalm, **The LORD is thy keeper,** the psalmist adds, **the LORD is thy shade upon thy right hand.** The word **shade** (Heb *tsel*) literally means a shadow; and it is a graphic description of the protection which the Lord God gives when we "abide under the shadow of the Almighty" (cf. 91:1). **The sun shall not smite thee by day, nor the moon by night.** The scorching heat of the Palestinian sun is no match for the protection provided by the ever-vigilant Jehovah.

7-8. "The threefold expression, **shall preserve thee . . . thy soul . . . thy going out and thy coming in,** marks the completeness of the protection vouchsafed, extending to all that the man is and that he does"—Perowne. Jehovah promises to preserve our movements, from morning to evening, from infancy to old age, **from this time forth, and even for evermore.**

PSALM 121

I WILL lift up mine eyes unto the hills, from whence cometh my help.
2 My help *cometh* from the LORD, which made heaven and earth.

3 He will not suffer thy foot to be moved: he that keepeth thee will not slumber.
4 Behold, he that keepeth Israel shall neither slumber nor sleep.

5 The LORD *is* thy keeper: the LORD *is* thy shade upon thy right hand.
6 The sun shall not smite thee by day, nor the moon by night.

7 The LORD shall preserve thee from all evil: he shall preserve thy soul.
8 The LORD shall preserve thy going out and thy coming in from this time forth, and even for evermore.

PSALM 122

I WAS glad when they said unto me,
Let us go into the house of the LORD.
2 Our feet shall stand within thy
gates, O Jerusalem.

3 Jerusalem is builded as a city that is
compact together:
4 Whither the tribes go up, the tribes
of the LORD, unto the testimony of
Israel, to give thanks unto the name of
the LORD.
5 For there are set thrones of judgment, the thrones of the house of David.

6 Pray for the peace of Jerusalem:
they shall prosper that love thee.
7 Peace be within thy walls, and prosperity within thy palaces.
8 For my brethren and companions'
sakes, I will now say, Peace be within
thee.
9 Because of the house of the LORD
our God I will seek thy good.

P. Jerusalem: City of Pilgrims. 122:1-9.

THEME: *A pilgrim's prayer for the peace of Jerusalem.*

This is the first Song of Degrees to which an author's name is
attached. The superscription ascribes this psalm to David; and
though the Septuagint and Vulgate omit this ascription,
nonetheless, the internal evidence of the psalm is strongly in
favor of Davidic authorship.

**122:1-2. I was glad when they said unto me, Let us go into
the house of the LORD** (cf. 5:7; 28:2; 138:2). The heart that
delights in worship of God will always delight in the place
appointed for worship. Although the Lord God may be worshiped anywhere, the tabernacle, and later the Temple, became
the focal point for the worship of God in Israel. Today the house
of the Lord is a common expression for the church, the place set
apart and sanctified for God's use alone. How glad we ought to
be today upon every occasion to attend the house of God.

3-5. Jerusalem is builded as a city that is compact together.
This is probably a reference to the compact shape of the ancient
city of Jerusalem. Built over the southeast ridge of the Ophel
Mount, the city of David was bordered by the Kidron Valley on
the east and the Valley of Hinnom on the south. Because of this
compactness, Solomon, David's son, extended the city to the
north and west from the threshing-floor of Araunah the Jebusite
that David had purchased for the building of the Temple
(II Sam 24:16).

**Whither the tribes go up . . . to give thanks unto the name
of the LORD.** This points to a time before the dispersion of **the
tribes,** which rendered such a regular going up an impossibility.
Their purpose in ascending the hill of Jerusalem was both civil
and religious. **For there are set thrones of judgment, the
thrones of the house of David.** Not only did they attend the
House of the Lord, but they attended the palace of David as
well.

6-9. Pray for the peace of Jerusalem. Peace in Exodus 18:7
and elsewhere refers to welfare; in 35:27 it refers to prosperity.
Every true Israelite was to pray for the tranquility and prosperity of Jerusalem. Ultimately, to pray for the peace of Jerusalem
is to pray that the Prince of Peace will soon establish His
kingdom upon this earth with Jerusalem as His capital (Isa 62;
Zech 2).

They shall prosper that love thee. A covert threat, at the
same time it is a promise. It parallels the promise of Genesis
12:3. Those who love Jerusalem and pray for her peace shall
prosper; those who seek her demise shall lack her prosperity.
Peace be within thy walls, and prosperity within thy palaces.
David knows that God will bless the city because it is there that
the house of the LORD our God is located. The tabernacle set
up by David in Jerusalem was called **the house of the LORD** in
5:7; 27:4; 52:8; and 55:14. Hence, if for no other reason, we
ought to pray for the peace of Jerusalem because God's people
are there, and God's house was there.

Q. Psalm of the Eyes. 123:1-4.

THEME: *The prayer of a distressed psalmist as he turns his eyes
toward God.*

Many ancient writers called this psalm *Oculus Sperans* (the eye
of hope). Says Luther, "This is a deep sigh of a pained heart,
which looks round on all sides, and seeks friends, protectors,
and comforters, but can find none . . . what shouldest thou do,
then when the world despises and insults thee? Turn thy eyes
thither, and see that God with His beloved angels and His elect
looks down upon thee, rejoices in thee, and loves thee."

The psalm itself is not sublime, but is quiet, subdued, and of
a submissive tone. It expresses a single thought and does so with
singular effect. The psalmist is in trouble, and he looks to God

PSALM 123

UNTO thee lift I up mine eyes, O thou that dwellest in the heavens.

2 Behold, as the eyes of servants *look* unto the hand of their masters, *and* as the eyes of a maiden unto the hand of her mistress; so our eyes *wait* upon the LORD our God, until that he have mercy upon us.

3 Have mercy upon us, O LORD, have mercy upon us: for we are exceedingly filled with contempt.
4 Our soul is exceedingly filled with the scorning of those that are at ease, *and* with the contempt of the proud.

PSALM 124

IF *it had not been* the LORD who was on our side, now may Israel say;
2 If *it had not been* the LORD who was on our side, when men rose up against us:
3 Then they had swallowed us up quick, when their wrath was kindled against us:

4 Then the waters had overwhelmed us, the stream had gone over our soul:
5 Then the proud waters had gone over our soul.

for deliverance. To attempt an identification of the author would be sheer conjecture, although the Syriac version ascribes it to David.

123:1. Unto thee lift I up mine eyes. "He who previously lifted his eyes unto the hills, now hath raised his heart's eyes to the Lord Himself"—The Venerable Bede. The statement here is much bolder than that of 121:1. There is no question here concerning whom the psalmist looks to for help; he looks to Jehovah, **thou that dwellest in the heavens** (cf. 2:4; 11:4; Isa 57:15; 66:1). The psalmist knows where his God is; Jehovah is not on a journey like Baal, but dwells in the heavens. Hence, there is no time day or night in which our God may not be approached in prayer.

2. Behold, as the eyes of servants look unto the hand of their masters . . . so our eyes wait upon the LORD our God. A beautiful smile is used to indicate the psalmist's watchfulness in prayer. Oriental servants were accustomed to sit in the corner of a room with their hands folded in their laps, watching the eyes of their masters and waiting for the slightest indication that the master desired their services. The psalmist has cast his eyes upon God; and he is looking steadfastly into the heavens, seeking to do the bidding of his heavenly Master.

3-4. Have mercy upon us . . . for we are exceedingly filled with contempt. To be **exceedingly filled** means to have the appetite fully satisfied. The idea here is that there is so much contempt for the psalmist that he could experience no more. More than that, his **soul is exceedingly filled with the scorning of those that are at ease.** Those who have never experienced distress scorn the distress of others. But the psalmist has done the only thing a godly individual in his situation could do. When the eyes of the scornful are turned on him, the psalmist knew not to look back. He knew where his help originated, and thus he looked solely to the Lord God for mercy.

R. Divine Deliverance. 124:1-8.

THEME: *Praise to the LORD who was on our side.*

The superscription over this psalm reads, **A song of degrees of David.** Although the psalm is ascribed to David, many modern critics adhere to the belief that the psalm was written at the proclamation of Cyrus when the Israelite captives were permitted to return to their land. Indeed, the Septuagint, Syriac, Arabic, Ethiopic, and Vulgate editions of this psalm omit the ascription of authorship to David. Nonetheless, there is nothing in the psalm which could not have been the experience of David, or at least his understanding of Israel's past deliverances by God. Calvin, Henry, Hengstenberg, and other scholars assume Davidic authorship. The importance of the so-called Aramaisms, which some feel indicates a later date than the time of David, has been effectively disputed.

124:1-3. If it had not been the LORD who was on our side. The opening sentence of this psalm is abrupt and, at best, a fragment. The abundance of italicized words in the AV indicates how fragmentary these expressions are. **When men rose up against us.** It appeared to the psalmist as if all the nations of mankind were operating in concert against the chosen nation, Israel. Had the Lord not been on their side, **then they had swallowed us up quick.** The word **quick** (Heb *chay*) is not an adverb, quickly, but an adjective, meaning alive. When the **wrath** of Israel's enemy **was kindled against** them, God's people would surely have been swallowed alive had it not been that the Lord was on their side.

4-5. There is an obvious progression in these verses in the use of the water metaphor. **Then the waters had overwhelmed us, the stream had gone over our soul: then the proud waters had gone over our soul.** The flood of opposition would have swelled over the heads of the Israelites like the waters of the Red Sea had

1159

6 Blessed be the LORD, who hath not given us as a prey to their teeth.

7 Our soul is escaped as a bird out of the snare of the fowlers: the snare is broken, and we are escaped.

8 Our help is in the name of the LORD, who made heaven and earth.

PSALM 125

THEY that trust in the LORD shall be as mount Zion which cannot be removed, but abideth for ever.

2 As the mountains are round about Jerusalem, so the LORD is round about his people from henceforth even for ever.

3 For the rod of the wicked shall not rest upon the lot of the righteous; lest the righteous put forth their hands unto iniquity.

4 Do good, O LORD, unto those that be good, and to them that are upright in their hearts.

5 As for such as turn aside unto their crooked ways, the LORD shall lead them forth with the workers of iniquity: but peace shall be upon Israel.

it not been that the Lord was on their side. So also, the rushing torrent would surely have drowned their souls; the proud waters able to capsize the largest vessel and drown the greatest men would have gone over their souls; and Israel's antagonists would have been victorious over them.

6-8. Blessed be the LORD who was their Life Preserver. Not only did He keep them from drowning in the waters of despair; but, abruptly changing the metaphor, Jehovah also prevented Israel's enemy from devouring them **as a prey to their teeth.** Again, the metaphor changes to indicate that they were well within the grasp of the enemy; but as a bird escapes **out of the snare of the fowlers** (cf. 91:3; 140:5; 141:10), so too by divine aid **the snare is broken, and we are escaped.** Setting the metaphors aside, the psalmist clearly recognizes that **Our help is in the name of the LORD, who made heaven and earth.** As long as the heavens and earth remain, we are assured of divine deliverance.

S. A Hymn of Trust. 125:1-5.

THEME: Praise to the God who surrounds His people.

On the authorship or occasion of this psalm little can be said with certainty, though most scholars agree that the psalm best fits the times of Nehemiah. Clarke thinks this ode may have been occasioned by the opposition of Sanballat and his associates. Scott compares the situation created by the invasion of Sennacherib to Jerusalem. Others associate it with various events in the life of David.

125:1. They that trust in the LORD shall be as mount Zion. The psalmist chooses the most graphic analogy of which he is aware to illustrate how safe one is who has placed his trust in Jehovah. Every Israelite knew that Mount Zion **cannot be removed, but abideth for ever.** We shall be like the great mountain if we but place our trust in God. Like the mountain of God (Isa 28:16), the child of God cannot be removed and abides for eternity.

2. As the mountains are round about Jerusalem, so the LORD is round about his people. As the mountains that encircle the Holy City stand as silent sentinels guarding her gates, so too God silently stands in the shadows of our lives, protecting us from the assaults of the wicked one (cf. Zech 2:4-5; II Kgs 6:17).

3. For the rod of the wicked shall not rest upon the lot of the righteous. The people of God should not expect immunity from the scepter of wickedness any more than the city of God was immune from attack. God has promised to keep us through trials, not from them. Still, God would not permit Jerusalem to be trodden down by the Gentiles forever, **lest the righteous put forth their hands unto iniquity.** God will not try men beyond their strength (I Cor 10:13). He will not allow the siege to last forever.

4. Do good, O LORD, unto those that be good. Repay goodness with goodness. Man can only be considered good because the good in us is God in us. Therefore, he asks God to continue His watchful care over **them that are upright in their hearts** and garrison them as the mountains do Jerusalem.

5. In contrast, those who turn aside unto **crooked ways, the LORD shall lead them forth with the workers of iniquity.** The word translated **crooked ways** (Heb 'aqalqal) occurs here only and as "highways" in Judges 5:6. It means side roads that deviate from the straight path of right. Men who are upright in their hearts, such as David, are the object of God's watch over us; men who are workers of iniquity, such as Saul or Ahithophel, are objects of God's wrath. **But peace shall be upon Israel** is actually a prayer, Peace be upon Israel, and is a fitting benediction to this hymn of trust.

T. Captivity Turned. 126:1-6.

THEME: Praise for the reversal of captivity and a prayer for an increased reversal.

Although we have no clue as to the author of this psalm, most commentators assume the occasion to be the restoration of Israel from Babylonian captivity. The Syriac version ascribes it to Haggai and Zechariah; other versions ascribe it to Ezra. If the psalm refers specifically to the restoration of the Jews, it falls quite nicely into the historic account given in Ezra 6:22; Nehemiah 12:43. However, if the psalm refers to one of the many other restorations of Israel from desperate situations, the author must remain anonymous.

Of much greater consequence is the question of interpretation. Should we, with the majority of interpreters, understand this psalm to be a message of praise to God for the first wave of immigration back to Palestine after the Babylonian captivity? Or should we see the Captivity as that of the Holy City, Jerusalem, and therefore this psalm to have reference to any one of a number of occasions on which Jerusalem was besieged? Or is the psalm Messianic as well as historical, with the call for a restoration from captivity in verse 4 to be understood as the national restoration of Israel when the Messiah returns in power and great glory?

Each interpretation presents us with problems. The messianic interpretation appears forced. Those who hold that the psalm is a praise and prayer from those returning from Babylonian captivity must wrestle with the question of whether **Zion** is used of the captives themselves or of the city of Jerusalem. Those who understand the captivity to be that of the Holy City are faced with a somewhat obvious reference in verse 4 to subsequent waves of emigration from captivity. All things being considered, perhaps the most likely interpretation is that this psalm records the joy of those Israelites who have returned from the Exile.

126:1-3. When the Lord turned again the captivity of Zion, we were like them that dream. The Chaldee, Syriac, and Arabic version of this psalm place the verbs of verse 1 in the future tense. But the Septuagint, Ethiopic, Vulgate versions, as well as the commentators Calvin, Edwards, Hengstenberg. Alexander, and others, agree with the AV that the verbs are in the preterite. Although the phrase **turned again the captivity** does not necessarily express any more than relief from a great distress (14:7; 63:6; 85:1), it appears to refer to the Babylonian captivity here. So overjoyed were the captives that the announcement of their release made them **like them that dream.** Their mouths were filled **with laughter and . . . with singing** because **The Lord hath done great things for us.** The captivity had been great; the deliverance was even greater. Great deliverance demanded great praise.

4. Turn again our captivity, O Lord, as the streams in the south. This prayer is that Jehovah will show His kindness to the multitudes of those yet remaining in Babylon as He had on the remnant already returned. The simile used to express this, **as the streams in the south,** is a reference to the torrents in the Negev region of southern Palestine. These wadis, stream beds, are dry eleven months out of the year; but when the rainy season comes, they are quickly filled and become torrential rivers (68:9; Josh 15:9; cf. Job 6:15). The point of the comparison is that the joy expressed at the reappearing of these raging torrents, so sorely missed for eleven months of the year, is akin to that of the anticipated return of all of Israel to her homeland.

5. They that sow in tears shall reap in joy. No metaphor is more frequently used in both Testaments than that of the farmer sowing and reaping. Thus, this verse is as much a proverb as a prayer; it suits all times and all situations. Our faithfulness in bearing the seed of the Word of God to the unsaved carries with it the promise of future harvests. "Winners of souls are first

PSALM 126

WHEN the Lord turned again the captivity of Zion, we were like them that dream.

2 Then was our mouth filled with laughter, and our tongue with singing: then said they among the heathen, The Lord hath done great things for them.

3 The Lord hath done great things for us; *whereof* we are glad.

4 Turn again our captivity, O Lord, as the streams in the south.

5 They that sow in tears shall reap in joy.

6 He that goeth forth and weepeth, bearing precious seed, shall doubtless come again with rejoicing, bringing his sheaves *with him.*

weepers for souls. As there is no burden without travail, so is there no spiritual harvest without painful tillage. When our own hearts are broken with grief at man's transgression we shall break other men's hearts"—Spurgeon.

6. He that goeth forth and weepeth . . . shall doubtless come again with rejoicing. The gerund construction in verse 6a (as in II Sam 3:16; 15:30; Jer 50:4) depicts the continual passing along. Israel was continually faithful in captivity, and thus God restored her to Zion. If the people of God today are equally faithful in scattering the precious seed of God's Word, we are promised the faithfulness of God in bringing in the sheaves. The proverb is true in any application. God's guarantee is: precious tears, precious seed, precious reward.

U. Reliance on God. 127:1-5.

THEME: The folly of human effort that does not rely on the Lord.

This is the center psalm of the Little Psalter, containing the fifteen Songs of Degrees. It is the only one ascribed to Solomon; in fact, only one other psalm (72) is ascribed to him. We may read the superscription either as **A song of degrees for Solomon** (AV) or "A son of degrees of Solomon." The form of the Hebrew is the same in either case. Henry, Gill, Spurgeon, and others feel that David was the author and that the psalm was written **for Solomon** his son. But Calvin, Edwards, Scott, Hengstenberg, Alexander, and others follow the Chaldee and Vulgate editions in understanding the psalm to be a hymn "of Solomon." Solomon wrote one thousand and five songs (cf. I Kgs 4:32). Perhaps this is one of them.

It is apparent that the point of this psalm is that all human effort that does not rely on the power and goodness of God is useless. The psalmist deals with four aspects of human life: social (vs. 1a), civic (vs. 1b), business (vs. 2), and domestic (vss. 3-5). In each of these there is a clear and unmistakable emphasis on the necessity of reliance upon God.

PSALM 127

EXCEPT the LORD build the house, they labour in vain that build it: except the LORD keep the city, the watchman waketh *but* in vain.

127:1. Except the LORD build the house, they labor in vain that build it. In order to prove that all our efforts are fruitless if God is not in them, the psalmist begins with the metaphor of a house. A house built without the blessing of the Lord is a house built upon the sand. In everything we undertake we must begin by seeking the blessing of the Lord God.

Except the LORD keep the city, the watchman waketh but in vain. Turning from social to civic life, the psalmist advances that the unseen watchman of every city is Jehovah Himself. The constant vigilance of a sentinel is without reward if he watches alone.

2 *It is* vain for you to rise up early, to sit up late, to eat the bread of sorrows: *for* so he giveth his beloved sleep.

2. It is vain for you to rise up early, to sit up late, to eat the bread of sorrows. It must be noted that the psalmist is not counseling against early rising (cf. 63:1). His intent is to show us that nothing is accomplished by rising early or staying up late simply to fret about real or potential problems. Being eaten up with envy when others receive a promotion and we do not is to eat the bread of sorrows. It is just as vain as building a house without the Lord's blessing.

3 Lo, children *are* an heritage of the LORD: *and* the fruit of the womb *is his* reward.

3. Lo, children are a heritage of the LORD. Here is another mode of building up a house, i.e., raising a household or family. The reason a man builds a house is to build a home. Children are a heritage that Jehovah must give. Given this biblical perspective on children, it is little wonder that the people of God always abhor abortion. **The fruit of the womb is his reward.** God gives children, not as a penalty, but as a privilege.

4 As arrows *are* in the hand of a mighty man; so *are* children of the youth.
5 Happy *is* the man that hath his quiver full of them: they shall not be

4-5. As arrows are in the hand of a mighty man; so are children of the youth. If parents have acted as good stewards of God's gift to them, children born to young parents are a great source of comfort and protection in old age. Fighting men are happy when their strength and swiftness are gone, and yet their

ashamed, but they shall speak with the enemies in the gate.

PSALM 128

BLESSED *is* every one that feareth the LORD; that walketh in his ways.

2 For thou shalt eat the labour of thine hands: happy *shalt* thou *be*, and *it shall be* well with thee.

3 Thy wife *shall be* as a fruitful vine by the sides of thine house: thy children like olive plants round about thy table.

4 Behold, that thus shall the man be blessed that feareth the LORD.

5 The LORD shall bless thee out of Zion: and thou shalt see the good of Jerusalem all the days of thy life.

6 Yea, thou shalt see thy children's children, *and* peace upon Israel.

---

arrows fly straight to the target. Likewise, children can be the extension of our lives, doing what we could never do, in our sunset years. **Happy is the man that hath his quiver full of them.** As the old German proverb says, "Many children make many prayers, and many prayers bring much blessing." **They shall not be ashamed, but they shall speak with the enemies in the gate.** A man is particularly fortunate if his sons support him in the city gate in his old age. This is where persons generally congregated and business was transacted. A stalwart and well-bred son could represent his father well in such transactions and prevent unscrupulous men from taking advantage of a man of age. Recognized as a gift from God and raised in a Christian home, children are a blessing indeed.

V. Home, Sweet Home. 128:1-6.

THEME: A psalm extolling the blessings of family life.

The design of this psalm is obvious. It is to show that the basis of domestic tranquility and happiness is true fear of the Lord God. Little wonder that Luther says it is "a wedding Psalm for Christians." Henry styles it "a Psalm for families." The happy man is one who fears God and finds joy in the company of his family.

128:1. Blessed is every one that feareth the LORD. In a psalm dedicated to marriage and family, it is significant that the initial thought is that the domestic state of affairs is only as happy as the Lord is feared. The obvious emphasis here is on **every one**, without regard to sex, family position, or any other kind of distinction. Fearing the Lord is not enough; following Him is necessary as well.

2. For thou shalt eat the labor of thine hands. God is a God of laborers. We are not to have our hands outstretched for blessings, but rather are to be busy in working to achieve them. This is especially true in the family relationship. Martin Luther noted, "This must they learn also which are married, that they must labour. For the law of nature requireth that the husband should sustain and nourish his wife and his children. . . ." Labor without God is vain; labor with God is value.

3. Thy wife shall be as a fruitful vine by the sides of thine house. A man who fears God and labors with his hands finds his greatest fruitfulness in his wife and children. The wife is not likened to thorns or briers, but to the fertility and tenderness of a vine. **By the sides of thine house** does not indicate that she is outside the house, but rather vines were always within the courtyard located in the center of Oriental homes. The simile is designed to indicate that a man is happy when his wife is within his house, keeping the home and being the center of God's love there. **Thy children like olive plants round about thy table.** Olive trees are craggy and indestructible. They never die; sprouts keep growing from the roots running along the ground. The psalmist says that a man is happy when even in his old age children spring up around his table, just as the lifeless root of an olive tree can give rise to new plants.

4-5. Behold. . . . The LORD shall bless thee out of Zion. To the Jew, all blessings were regarded as arising out of Zion, the earthly dwelling place of God. Specifically, happy was the man who saw **the good of Jerusalem,** the good fortune or prosperity of the Holy City, all the days of his life.

6. Yea, thou shalt see thy children's children. Solomon said that "Children's children are the crown of old men . . ." (Prov 17:6). To see his children's children was the crowning blessing granted to Job in his second period of blessing (Job 42:16). It is the promise God makes to all men who fear the Lord. **Peace . . . upon Israel,** just as the concluding phrase of Psalm 125 was a favorite formula of the Hebrew people. It is a concluding prayer and benediction, "Let God's own heritage be at peace."

PSALM 129

MANY a time have they afflicted me from my youth, may Israel now say:

2 Many a time have they afflicted me from my youth: yet they have not prevailed against me.

3 The plowers plowed upon my back: they made long their furrows.
4 The LORD *is* righteous: he hath cut asunder the cords of the wicked.

5 Let them all be confounded and turned back that hate Zion.
6 Let them be as the grass *upon* the housetops, which withereth afore it groweth up:
7 Wherewith the mower filleth not his hand; nor he that bindeth sheaves his bosom.

8 Neither do they which go by say, The blessing of the LORD *be* upon you: we bless you in the name of the LORD.

W. Affliction and Retribution. 129:1-8.

THEME: *A psalm rehearsing Israel's past afflictions and the future judgment on her enemies.*

With regard to critical material, little can be said of this psalm. To conjecture on the authorship or occasion would be foolish. Some feel the psalm fits best with the times and circumstances of Hezekiah; others suppose the psalm to have been written after the captivity. All is conjecture.

The psalm has much in common with Psalm 124. It treats the same general theme in the same manner and even has a similar form of repetition in the first verse. The psalm consists of two parts, the first four verses being a retrospect of Israel's afflictions and the last four verses being an anticipation of righteous judgment upon her oppressors.

129:1-2. Many a time have they afflicted me from my youth. Israel has recollection of many fierce and treacherous afflictions by her enemies. The afflictions of God's chosen people began from her youth, her infancy as a nation (cf. Isa 47:12, 15; Jer 2:2; 22:21; 48:11; Ezk 16:4; 23:3; Hos 2:15; 11:1). The afflictions began early and have never ceased. **Yet they have not prevailed against me.** Although God will allow His own to be afflicted, He will never allow them to be annihilated.

3-4. The plowers plowed upon my back: they made long their furrows. Those who scourged Israel tore the flesh of her national back as a plowman would plow furrows in a field. They were treated as criminals and subjected to the cruel lashes of a whip. "God fails not to sow blessings in the furrows, which the plowers plow upon the back of the church"—Jeremy Taylor (1613-1667). Although the devil never makes short furrows, God always plants the seed of forgiveness in those furrows.

Through it all the Israelites can say, **The LORD is righteous.** Whatever those who afflict Israel may be, she remains certain that Jehovah remains just. **He hath cut asunder the cords of the wicked.** Luther, Calvin, Gill, Alexander, and others understand this to mean the cord used in plowing to attach the oxen to the plow. The righteous Lord will not allow His chosen people to receive more affliction than they can bear (cf. I Cor 10:13).

5-7. The retrospect of past afflictions now completed, the psalmist anticipates godly retribution on the afflicters. Thus, the imprecation begins, **Let them all be confounded and turned back that hate Zion.** John Gill observes, Let them be turned back "from pursuing their designs and accomplishing them; as the Assyrian monarch was, who had a hook put into his nose, and a bridle in his lips, and was turned back by the way he came, Isaiah 37:29."

Let them be as the grass upon the housetops, which withereth afore it groweth up. Frequently, in the crevices of the Palestinian roof wild grasses would begin to take root. They would sprout in the hot Eastern sun, and then because there is not sufficient earth or moisture to sustain that growth, the grass would die away before it reached to maturity. With it the ancient **mower filleth not his hand; nor he that bindeth sheaves his bosom.** There was no harvest to be clutched close to the chest and joyfully carried home from housetop grass.

8. Neither do they which go by say, The blessing of the LORD be upon you: we bless you in the name of the LORD. In harvest times it was customary for men to bless each other in the name of the Lord. As they would pass by a field of harvesters, they would say, **The blessing of the LORD be upon you** (cf. Ruth 2:4). The psalmist warned against pronouncing the blessings of the Lord indiscriminately. Those who live ungodly lives should never be told, "God bless you"; for to do so is to wish God's assistance on their ungodliness. No one dare say to the oppressors of God's chosen people, **The blessing of the LORD be upon you.**

X. Out of the Depths. 130:1-8.

THEME: A cry to God for the forgiveness of sin.

This is the sixth of the seven penitential psalms (6; 32; 38; 51; 106; 130; 143). This psalm is unique, however, in that the focus of the psalm is on sin itself, and not the consequences of sin. The psalm highlights the horrendousness of sin. Yet, the themes of forgiveness and redemption are also to be seen. In fact, this combination of themes inspired Luther to note the similarities between Psalm 130 and the Pauline Epistles (he also noted that similarity in 32; 51; and 143).

The authorship of this psalm is uncertain. Luther, Calvin, Henry, Patrick, and Edwards all regard David as the author. On the other hand, Scroggie is convinced that the psalm relates to Hezekiah's experience as recorded in Isaiah 38. Hengstenberg and Perowne feel that the vocabulary of the psalm, especially the words **attentive** and **forgiveness**, betray a later date. **Attentive** is found elsewhere only in II Chronicles 6:40; 7:15; and **forgiveness** is found elsewhere only in Nehemiah 9:17; Daniel 9:9. Thus, the question of authorship must remain open.

PSALM 130

OUT of the depths have I cried unto thee, O LORD.
2 Lord, hear my voice: let thine ears be attentive to the voice of my supplications.

130:1-2. Out of the depths have I cried unto thee, O LORD (cf. 69:2, 14; Isa 51:10; Ezk 27:34). **The depths** are the lowest abysses to which the soul can sink. From the lowest point in his life the psalmist cries unto God. **LORD . . . let thine ears be attentive.** All the psalmist asks is that Jehovah hear his supplications.

3 If thou, LORD, shouldst mark iniquities, O LORD, who shall stand?

3. Yet, there is a fly in the ointment. The psalmist questions, **If thou, LORD, shouldest mark iniquities, O Lord, who shall stand?** If the Lord Jehovah should diligently observe our sins, who among men would be able to withstand the scrutiny of His omniscient purity? This is a question that dots the pages of the Bible (cf. 76:7; I Sam 6:20; Nah 1:6; Mal 3:2; Rev 6:17). If God observes our sin closely, who shall be able to stand in His sight? "Therefore being justified by faith, we have peace with God through out Lord Jesus Christ: By whom also we have access by faith into this grace wherein we stand . . ." (Rom 5:1-2). As sinners, the only opportunity we have to stand firmly on the solid rock of His grace is the grace with which we were saved.

4 But *there is* forgiveness with thee, that thou mayest be feared.

4. **But there is forgiveness with thee, that thou mayest be feared. Forgiveness** (Heb *selîchah*), although used only here and in Daniel 9:9 and Nehemiah 9:17, is promised throughout the Scriptures (cf. 25:13; 32:1; Ex 34:7; I Kgs 8:30, 34, 36, 39; I Jn 1:9; etc.). The piety of the psalmist allows him to see one purpose only for divine forgiveness of sins, i.e., **that thou mayest be feared.**

5 I wait for the LORD, my soul doth wait, and in his word do I hope.
6 My soul *waiteth* for the Lord more than they that watch for the morning: *I say, more than* they that watch for the morning.

5-6. **I wait for the LORD . . . and in his word do I hope.** Hoping and waiting are inseparably united. All who would hope must wait. The psalmist firmly believed that God was gracious and forgiving, and out of that confident faith sprang the well-spring of hope. **More than they that watch for the morning,** the psalmist would hopefully wait for the Lord's deliverance. As much as the watchman anticipated the dawn that would end his nightly duties, so the psalmist anticipated the Lord's gracious deliverance.

7 Let Israel hope in the LORD: for with the LORD *there is* mercy, and with him *is* plenteous redemption.
8 And he shall redeem Israel from all his iniquities.

7-8. Why should Israel hope in Jehovah? Two reasons: (1) **With the LORD there is mercy;** and (2) **with him is plenteous redemption.** The psalmist is confident that he will be rescued from his dire condition because he places his hope and trust in a merciful God who has more than enough redemption to spare. **And he shall redeem Israel from all his iniquities.** In his *Paradise Lost*, Milton has Satan say, "Then farewell hope, and with hope, farewell fear!" But contrary to Satan, the psalmist, and all who put their hope in God, has no reason to fear; for he has the promise that paradise once lost is found again in the mercy of God.

PSALM 131

LORD, my heart is not haughty, nor mine eyes lofty: neither do I exercise myself in great matters, or in things too high for me.

2 Surely I have behaved and quieted myself, as a child that is weaned of his mother: my soul *is* even as a weaned child.

3 Let Israel hope in the LORD from henceforth and for ever.

PSALM 132

LORD, remember David, *and* all his afflictions:

2 How he sware unto the LORD, *and* vowed unto the mighty *God* of Jacob;

3 Surely I will not come into the tabernacle of my house, nor go up into my bed;

Y. A Song of Humility. 131:1-3.

THEME: A psalm celebrating the blessedness of the man who is meek and lowly in spirit.

This unpretentious psalm is one of the great gems of the Psalter. Its teaching on humility parallels such New Testament passages as Matthew 19:3; James 4:6; I Peter 5:5. The superscription indicates this is **A song of degrees of David.** Both the Syriac and Vulgate editions agree with this inscription, as do Calvin, Henry, Gill, Tholuck, Hengstenberg, Alexander, and others. It is a song both by David and of David; he is its author, as well as its subject.

131:1. LORD, my heart is not haughty. Literally, the psalmist says that his heart is not lifted up (cf. II Chr 26:16; 32:25).His heart is not exalted, lifted high by pride. **Nor mine eyes lofty.** Since the psalmist's heart had not been lifted up with pride, his eye did not seek that upon which pride feeds. **Neither do I exercise myself in great matters, or in things too high for me.** David did not attempt to delve into the secret of God's purposes, or into the sovereign design of God.

2. Surely I have behaved . . . myself, as a child that is weaned of his mother. The original Hebrew records this statement in the form of an oath, a phrase of asseveration. From what had the psalmist been weaned? William Jay (1769-1853) answers, "Self-sufficiency, self-will, self-seeking. From creatures and the things of the world—not, indeed, as to their use, but as to any dependence upon them for his happiness and portion."

3. Let Israel hope in the LORD from henceforth and for ever. One who is weaned from self automatically thinks of others. Based on his own experience with the Lord, David exhorts all Israel to humbly recognize Jehovah as their source of hope. Each one who names the name of Christ Jesus as Saviour has that same source of hope.

Z. An Habitation for the Mighty God. 132:1-18.

THEME: A prayer for God's blessing on His holy habitation.

Of all the Songs of Degrees, this is by far the longest. It also differs from the others in rhythm and content. It is a prayer that the promises made by God to David will find no cause to be unfulfilled.

Authorship of this psalm is difficult to determine. Lightfoot and Gill both regard it as Davidic; Rabbi Kimchi agrees. The majority of ancient interpreters regard this psalm as a prayer of David. But the references to David in verses 1, 10-11, and 17 lead many to believe he was not its author. Edwards, Henry, and Scott confidently ascribe it to Solomon; Clarke, Hengstenberg, and Alexander give it a later date. Hengstenberg places it in the days of Ezra and Nehemiah, but the ark did not survive the captivity, having disappeared after the destruction of Solomon's Temple. Thus, it is unlikely that the psalm is post-exilic. Scroggie, as he does with each of the psalms in this group, ascribes the authorship to Hezekiah, but with little credence. Perhaps it is best understood as Davidic or Solomonic.

132:1-2. LORD, remember David. At the outset of the psalm the writer calls upon Jehovah to remember the afflictions of David and the theocratic kingdom that he represents. The request to **remember** is not simply to bring to mind, but to bless. **How he sware unto the LORD, and vowed unto the mighty God of Jacob.** Even while being afflicted, David was moved by his devotion toward Jehovah and made a mighty vow that was sealed by an oath.

3-5. Surely I will not come into the tabernacle of my house . . . . until I find out a place for the LORD. David's vow was that he would not settle comfortably into his own substantial house (cf. II Sam 5:11) until he had established a permanent

4 I will not give sleep to mine eyes, *or* slumber to mine eyelids,
5 Until I find out a place for the LORD, an habitation for the mighty *God* of Jacob.

6 Lo, we heard of it at Ĕph′ra-täh: we found it in the fields of the wood.
7 We will go into his tabernacles: we will worship at his footstool.

8 Arise, O LORD, into thy rest; thou, and the ark of thy strength.
9 Let thy priests be clothed with righteousness; and let thy saints shout for joy.
10 For thy servant David's sake turn not away the face of thine anointed.

11 The LORD hath sworn *in* truth unto David; he will not turn from it; Of the fruit of thy body will I set upon thy throne.
12 If thy children will keep my covenant and my testimony that I shall teach them, their children shall also sit upon thy throne for evermore.

13 For the LORD hath chosen Zion; he hath desired *it* for his habitation.
14 This *is* my rest for ever: here will I dwell; for I have desired it.

15 I will abundantly bless her provision: I will satisfy her poor with bread.
16 I will also clothe her priests with salvation: and her saints shall shout aloud for joy.

17 There will I make the horn of David to bud: I have ordained a lamp for mine anointed.

resting place for the ark of God. In his work *"Les Pseaumes, avec des Reflexions,"* published in 1700, Pasquier Quesnel correctly observes, "This admirable zeal of this pious king condemns the indifference of those who leave the sacred places which are dependent upon their care in a condition of shameful neglect, while they lavish all their care to make for themselves sumptuous houses."

6-7. Lo, we heard of it at Ephratah, we found it in the fields of the wood. Although some believe that Ephratah is in the northern region of Ephraim where Samuel's father lived, it is far more likely that this is a reference to the ancient name of Beth-lehem (Gen 48:7) mentioned here as the place where David heard about the ark of the covenant as a boy. The ark had been carried into battle against the Philistines and was lost to the enemy. When the ark was rediscovered, it was found **in the fields of the wood,** Kirjath-jearim, a town the name of which means city of the woods.

With the prospect of a permanent dwelling place for the ark, the psalmist resolves, **We will go into his tabernacles: we will worship at his footstool.** The Lord's **footstool** mentioned here was either the ark of the covenant itself, or the place where it would stand in the Holy of Holies.

8-10. In piety, the psalmist calls upon Jehovah, **Arise, O LORD. . . . Let thy priests be clothed with righteousness.** Here is a call for a permanent dwelling-place for the ark of the covenant and a corresponding righteous priesthood to attend unto the ark. **For thy servant David's sake turn not away the face of thine anointed.** The frequency with which God is called upon to answer prayer for David's sake (cf. I Kgs 11:12-13; 15:4; II Kgs 8:19; etc.) shows that the psalmist is convinced that the covenant God has made with him will not be broken.

11-12. Because the Lord God has sworn unto David, **he will not turn from it.** One such covenant promise is God's pledge to David, **Of the fruit of thy body will I set upon thy throne.** Jehovah had promised perpetuity to the line of David. The Lord Jesus was born ". . . of the house and lineage of David" (Lk 2:4). He bears a unique right to sit upon the throne of David, and during His one thousand year reign upon this earth He will do just that. Still, God made this covenant conditional: **If thy children will keep my covenant and my testimony.** Many of the kings in David's line did not fulfill this condition, and after the enslavement of Jehoiachin (II Kgs 24:10-16) it appeared that the line of David would be obliterated. Yet, the line was preserved, through the grace of God, because the True Seed of David fulfilled this covenant-keeping condition.

13-14. For the LORD hath chosen Zion; he hath desired it for his habitation. Zion, the city of David, was also **the city of the great King** (48:2). It is the only city that God has called His own, the one of which He has said, **here will I dwell; for I have desired it.**

15-16. I will satisfy her poor with bread. The inhabitants of Jerusalem, though poor, will never be destitute. They have God's word on it. **I will also clothe her priests with salvation.** The psalmist's prayer in verse 9 is Jehovah's pleasure in verse 16. To be clothed in righteousness is tantamount to being clothed with salvation.

17. There will I make the horn of David to bud. The budding of the horn is a metaphor taken from such beautiful creatures as stags, red deer, etc., whose chief beauty and strength were found in their horns. As Rawlinson says, "The 'horn of David' budded most gloriously when 'a rod came forth out of the stem of Jesse, and a branch grew out of his roots, and the Spirit of the Lord rested upon' (Isa 11:1-2)—in other words, when Messiah appeared, and re-established the Davidian kingdom, which thenceforth has endured, and will endure for ever." **I have ordained a lamp for mine anointed.** Here, the

18 His enemies will I clothe with shame: but upon himself shall his crown flourish.

metaphor is changed again, but the intent is the same. The lamp was used to enlighten or shed light upon the glory of David's house; and David was often promised a lamp (cf. I Kgs 11:36; 15:4; II Kgs 8:19; II Chr 21:7). In Christ, the Light of the World, that lamp was given.

18. His enemies will I clothe with shame. What a contrast with the clothing provided for the priests (cf. vss. 9, 16). The enemies of David's line, and most specifically of the Lord Jesus Himself, will be utterly defeated and must wear the garments of sin and shame forever. How much more blessed to wear the garment of salvation as David did, even with **all his afflictions** (vs. 1). In Christ shall his dynasty be victorious, and **upon himself shall his crown flourish.**

AA. Blessed Unity. 133:1-3.

THEME: A psalm in praise of unity and brotherly harmony.

Superscription of this psalm reads, **A song of degrees of David.** Although the Syriac and Vulgate editions of the Psalms join the Hebrew in ascribing this psalm to David, the Targum and some manuscripts of the Septuagint lack this heading. Calvin, Edwards, Scott, Tholuck, Alexander, Spurgeon, and others all see no reason to deny Davidic authorship. Assuming the validity of the superscription then, upon what occasion did David compose this beautiful psalm? Some think it refers to the termination of the civil war between Saul and David. Others see in it the conclusion of Absalom's rebellion. Still others point to I Chronicles 12:38, which records the narrative of the tribes of Israel laying down their arms against one another and rallying behind David as their king at Hebron.

PSALM 133

BEHOLD, how good and how pleasant *it is* for brethren to dwell together in unity!

133:1. Behold, how good and how pleasant it is for brethren to dwell together in unity! Although the word for **brethren** (Heb *'ach*) is used in the sense of those who are descended from a common ancestor (Gen 13:8; Ex 2:11; Acts 7:26; etc.), nonetheless the implication of this psalm is that it is good for brethren in Christ to dwell together in unity. "If there be but one God, as God is one, so let them that serve Him be one. This is what Christ prayed so heartily for. 'That they may be one': John 17:21. Christians should be one"—Thomas Watson.

2 *It is* like the precious ointment upon the head, that ran down upon the beard, *even* Aaron's beard: that went down to the skirts of his garments;

2. David recognized that in the very profuse anointing of Aaron with oil at his installation as High Priest there was a conducive analogy of brotherly love. **It is like the precious ointment upon the head, that ran down upon the beard . . . to the skirts of his garments.** The anointing oil was not simply sprinkled on the head of Aaron, but the vessel was emptied upon him so that it flowed down from the head, over his beard, and all the way to the skirts of his sacerdotal robes. As abundantly and extravagantly as the oil was used at the installation of a high priest, so abundantly and extravagantly is unity to characterize those who dwell together in the Lord.

3 As the dew of Her′mon, *and as the dew* that descended upon the mountains of Zion: for there the LORD commanded the blessing, *even* life for evermore.

3. In characteristic Davidic style, the psalmist quickly enhances his writing with another analogy. **As the dew of Hermon, and as the dew that descended upon the mountains of Zion.** Like the dew which covers Palestine from the mountains of the north to the mountains of the south, so unity is to blanket the brotherhood of believers from north to south, east to west. **For there the LORD commanded the blessing, even life for evermore.** "God commands His blessing where peace is cultivated; by which is meant, that He testifies how much He is pleased with concord amongst men, by showering blessings upon them."—John Calvin.

BB. The Night Watch. 134:1-3.

THEME: An exhortation to praise the Lord in the house of the Lord.

With this Song of Degrees the Little Psalter is terminated.

PSALM 134

BEHOLD, bless ye the LORD, all ye servants of the LORD, which by night stand in the house of the LORD.

2 Lift up your hands in the sanctuary, and bless the LORD.

3 The LORD that made heaven and earth bless thee out of Zion.

PSALM 135

PRAISE ye the LORD. Praise ye the name of the LORD; praise him, O ye servants of the LORD.

2 Ye that stand in the house of the LORD, in the courts of the house of our God,

3 Praise the LORD; for the LORD is good: sing praises unto his name; for it is pleasant.

4 For the LORD hath chosen Jacob unto himself, and Israel for his peculiar treasure.

5 For I know that the LORD is great, and that our Lord is above all gods.

6 Whatsoever the LORD pleased, that did he in heaven, and in earth, in the seas, and all deep places.

7 He causeth the vapours to ascend from the ends of the earth; he maketh lightnings for the rain; he bringeth the wind out of his treasuries.

Most scholars are curiously silent with regard to the authorship of this psalm. The Syriac version ascribes it to David, but few others do. The origin and setting of the psalm have been the subject of much speculation. Luther thought it was an exhortation to all priests in every age to attend faithfully to their priestly duties, but all attempts to place the occasion for this psalm are mere speculation.

134:1-2. Behold. The psalm begins with a demonstrative adverb. It is a forceful, Hello. **Bless ye the LORD.** This is the express task of those who are **servants of the LORD.** A servant should always speak well of his master. Servants of Jehovah certainly have cause to do so. The servants addressed in this psalm are those **which by night stand in the house of the LORD.** Who is being addressed here? Those consecrated to guarding the Temple through the hours of night and are charged with the responsibility of praising the Lord even during the hours while others sleep. **Lift up your hands in the sanctuary, and bless the LORD.** Lifting up the hands was the posture of prayer and praise (63:4; 119:48; 141:2) and was indicative of expectancy.

3. Now comes the response. As those who had kept the night watch scatter and make their way one by one, they report to those who have replaced them. **The LORD that made heaven and earth** (cf. 115:15; 121:2; 124:8; 146:6; Gen 1:1) **bless thee out of Zion** (cf. 20:2; 53:6; 128:5). The priests who throughout the night had been called upon to bless God on behalf of the people, now blessed the people on behalf of God.

CC. An Anthology of Praise. 135:1-21.

THEME: A composite psalm calling for praise unto Jehovah.

At once the reader is struck with the fact that this psalm is a mosaic, the psalmist quoting from existing psalms and other biblical sources. That the psalmist selects portions of previous compositions that were inspired of God does not in any way lessen the inspiration of this psalm. As Maclaren notes, "The flowers are arranged in a new bouquet, because the poet had long delighted in their fragrance."

This is a Hallelujah psalm that remains untitled in the original text. Its composition has been ascribed to various periods of history, from Hezekiah to the days after the Exile. The psalm has an apparent antiphonal arrangement and is therefore generally assumed to have been composed for Temple worship. Still, few clues that would help us identify its author are offered.

135:1-3. Praise ye the LORD (Heb *halelū yah*). **Ye that stand in the house of the Lord . . . praise the LORD.** The servants called upon to praise Jehovah in the house of God are the priests, the Levites, and the people, i.e., all those who enter the courts of the Temple. The reason for this necessary praise is clear: **For the LORD is good** (cf. 86:5; 119:68). His glorious name is worthy of our praise, **for it is pleasant** (cf. 52:9; 54:6).

4. For the LORD hath chosen Jacob unto himself, and Israel for his peculiar treasure. In the minds of the Israelites the foremost reason for praising Jehovah was the election of the Jewish people as the chosen nation of God. Being a **peculiar treasure** imposed both rights and awesome responsibilities (cf. 33:12; 105:6; Deut 7:6-7; Amos 3:2).

5-7. For I know that the LORD is great. Those who would sincerely sing Jehovah's praise must be convinced that **our LORD is above all gods.** Jupiter does not rule in the heavens; Neptune does not rule the sea; Pluto does not rule the lower regions of the earth. Jehovah rules them all. **Whatsoever the LORD pleased, that did he.** In a very poetic way the psalmist shows that Jehovah is the King of the earth.

Not only does Jehovah create as He wills, He controls as He wills as well. **He causeth the vapors to ascend** (cf. Jer 10:13; 51:16) . . . **he maketh lightnings for the rain** (i.e., to accom-

8 Who smote the firstborn of Egypt, both of man and beast.

9 *Who* sent tokens and wonders into the midst of thee, O Egypt, upon Pharaoh, and upon all his servants.

10 Who smote great nations, and slew mighty kings;

11 Sihon king of the Ăm′o-rītes, and Og king of Bă′shan, and all the kingdoms of Canaan:

12 And gave their land *for* an heritage, an heritage unto Israel his people.

13 Thy name, O Lord, *endureth* for ever; *and* thy memorial, O Lord, throughout all generations.

14 For the Lord will judge his people, and he will repent himself concerning his servants.

15 The idols of the heathen *are* silver and gold, the work of men's hands.

16 They have mouths, but they speak not; eyes have they, but they see not;

17 They have ears, but they hear not; neither is there *any* breath in their mouths.

18 They that make them are like unto them: *so is* every one that trusteth in them.

19 Bless the Lord, O house of Israel: bless the Lord, O house of Aaron:

20 Bless the Lord, O house of Levi: ye that fear the Lord, bless the Lord.

21 Blessed be the Lord out of Zion, which dwelleth at Jerusalem. Praise ye the Lord.

pany the rain); **he bringeth the wind out of his treasuries** (i.e., storehouses, cf. 33:7), where God keeps all the elements of the earth (cf. Job 38:22; Virgil's *Aeneid* 2:25).

8-12. To continue his theme of God's sovereignty, the psalmist now looks beyond God's created nature to His creatures. Not only does the sovereign God do what He wills with His creation, He interjects Himself at will in the lives of His creatures. Jehovah **smote the first-born of Egypt . . . smote great nations, and slew mighty kings.** The most spectacular of the plagues upon the Egyptians was the final plague of the death of the first-born. The plagues fell **upon Pharaoh, and upon all his servants** (Ex 7:21; 8:4, 11, 17, 24; 9:6, 11, 25; 10:4-6, 14-15; 12:30). **Sihon king of the Amorites,** (Num 21:24; Deut 2:33) **and Og king of Bashan** (cf. Num 21:35; Deut 3:3) were notable among the mighty kings who were slain before Israel. Their land became **a heritage unto Israel** (cf. 78:55; 136:21; Ex 6:8).

13-14. Immutability is a glory that belongs to all the attributes of God. Thus, the psalmist says, **Thy name, O Lord, endureth for ever . . . throughout all generations.** The promises of God are as good as His name. When as God's people we are wronged, we need never fear; **For the Lord will judge his people** (cf. 54:1-3; Ex 2:23-24; 3:7-9; 6:6). **He will repent himself concerning his servants.** When God has chastised us for our sins, He will not continue to punish us, but will repent or relent of that chastisement. The book of Judges is a perfect illustration of the validity of this truth.

15-18. Contrary to the people of God, men of the world choose not to worship and praise Jehovah, but rather **the work of men's hands** (cf. Rom 1:22-25). Though the idols of the heathen are **silver and gold** and have **mouths . . . eyes . . . ears,** they cannot speak, see, or hear. What is worse, **They that make them are like unto them** and **every one that trusteth in them** shall perish without God.

19-21. It is altogether fitting that such a psalm which begins with the triple call to praise Jehovah (vs. 1) should conclude with a quadruple call to bless Jehovah (vss. 19-20). **Bless the Lord, O house of Israel . . . O house of Aaron . . . O house of Levi,** and all **ye that fear the Lord.** With the call for the Israelites to bless Jehovah's name, the psalmist includes a call to the priests of Aaron (cf. 115:10,12; 118:3) and Levi (cf. 115:11, 13), the two orders of the priesthood. The priests and laity alike are to **bless the Lord.** As God gives His people blessings "out of Zion" (134:3), so too is He to be praised **out of Zion;** for it is here that Jehovah **dwelleth at Jerusalem** (cf. 48:1-3; 76:2).

DD. Mercy Without Duration. 136:1-26.

THEME: A thanksgiving psalm for God's enduring mercy.

The similarities between this psalm and the preceding one are obvious even to the casual reader. That was a psalm of praise; this is a psalm of thanksgiving. Yet the topics covered in the two psalms are nearly identical.

In the Babylonian Talmud (*Pesachim* 118) this psalm, with its twenty-six responses, is denoted The Great Hallel, to distinguish it from The Hallel, which comprises Psalms 113-118. The structure of this psalm is unique in the Psalter. The first line of each verse addresses a topic in which the psalmist recognizes evidence of God's mercy. The second line of each verse is a kind of refrain or response. This refrain is identical in each verse.

We do not possess a clue as to who the author of the psalm may have been. Many scholars refer it to the times of David; others give it a later date. Apparently, the psalm was sung in Solomon's temple (II Chr 7:3, 6) and by the armies of Jehoshaphat when they sang themselves to victory in the wilderness of Tekoa.

PSALM 136

O GIVE thanks unto the LORD; for *he is* good: for his mercy *endureth* for ever.

2 O give thanks unto the God of gods: for his mercy *endureth* for ever.

3 O give thanks to the Lord of lords: for his mercy *endureth* for ever.

4 To him who alone doeth great wonders: for his mercy *endureth* for ever.

5 To him that by wisdom made the heavens: for his mercy *endureth* for ever.

6 To him that stretched out the earth above the waters: for his mercy *endureth* for ever.

7 To him that made great lights: for his mercy *endureth* for ever:

8 The sun to rule by day: for his mercy *endureth* for ever:

9 The moon and stars to rule by night: for his mercy *endureth* for ever.

10 To him that smote Egypt in their firstborn: for his mercy *endureth* for ever:

11 And brought out Israel from among them: for his mercy *endureth* for ever:

12 With a strong hand, and with a stretched out arm: for his mercy *endureth* for ever.

13 To him which divided the Red sea into parts: for his mercy *endureth* for ever:

14 And made Israel to pass through the midst of it: for his mercy *endureth* for ever:

15 But overthrew Pharaoh and his host in the Red sea: for his mercy *endureth* for ever.

16 To him which led his people through the wilderness: for his mercy *endureth* for ever.

17 To him which smote great kings: for his mercy *endureth* for ever:

18 And slew famous kings: for his mercy *endureth* for ever:

19 Sihon king of the Ăm′o-rītes: for his mercy *endureth* for ever:

20 And Og the king of Bā′shan: for his mercy *endureth* for ever:

21 And gave their land for an heritage: for his mercy *endureth* for ever:

22 *Even* an heritage unto Israel his servant: for his mercy *endureth* for ever.

23 Who remembered us in our low estate: for his mercy *endureth* for ever:

24 And hath redeemed us from our enemies: for his mercy *endureth* for ever.

25 Who giveth food to all flesh: for his mercy *endureth* for ever.

136:1-3. O give thanks unto the LORD. This verse is identical with 106:1; 107:1; and 118:1. It is a formula found elsewhere in the Old Testament as well (cf. II Chr 5:13; Ezr 3:11). Thanksgiving is to be given to Jehovah **for he is good,** which invokes the refrain, **for his mercy endureth for ever.** In the second verse the psalmist intensifies his thoughts by indicating that thanks is to be given unto **the God of gods.** This phrase first occurs in Deuteronomy 10:17 and is a Hebrew superlative meaning that God is far above all other gods. The appellation **Lord of lords** also occurs for the first time in Deuteronomy 10:17. It was a favorite expression for Jesus Christ in the New Testament having been used both by the Apostle Paul (I Tim 6:15) and the Apostle John (Rev 17:14; 19:16).

4-6. Having begun the first triad of verses with the expression **O give thanks** (vs. 1), the psalmist begins the next triad with **To him.** We are to give thanks to Him **who alone doeth great wonders** (cf. 72:18) who **by wisdom made the heavens** (cf. Prov 3:19; Eph 1:11), and who **stretched out the earth above the waters** (cf. 24:2; Isa 42:5; 44:24). "There are three things here declared of God; that He doeth *wonders,* and that the wonders He doeth are *great;* that He *only* doeth them"—Augustine.

7-9. The next triad of verses continues the identification of the works of Him who is worthy of our great thanks. **To him that made great lights** (cf. Gen 1:14-16) **the sun to rule the day** (cf. Gen 1:16), "the lantern of the world" as Copernicus named the sun, **the moon and stars to rule by night** (cf. Gen 1:16, 18). It is this same God whose **mercy endureth for ever.**

10-12. Now the psalmist turns his attention from the creative activity of the merciful God to His salvational activity. Thanks is to be given **To him that smote Egypt in their first-born.** At this point the parallelism with Psalm 135 begins and continues to the end of verse 22. The one worthy of our thanks is Him who **brought out Israel from among them** (cf. Ex 12:51; 14:19-31) **with a strong hand, and with a stretched out arm** (cf. Ex 6:6; Deut 7:8, 19; Neh 1:10).

13-15. Continuing to refer to Israel's great deliverance by the mercy of Jehovah, the psalmist gives thanks **To him which divideth the Red Sea into parts** (cf. Ex 14:21) **and made Israel to pass through the midst of it** (cf. Ex 14:22, 29; 15:19) but **overthrew Pharaoh and his host in the Red Sea** (cf. Ex 14:27-28; 15:1-10). The word for **overthrew** (Heb *na'ar*) literally means shaked off as a tree would shake off its foliage (Isa 33:9). So mighty is Jehovah God that He was responsible for bringing down the most powerful monarch in the world as a giant oak would shake off its leaves in the breeze.

16-18. The Exodus from Egyptian bondage by no means concluded the mercy of God in behalf of Israel. Thanksgiving is to be given **To him which led his people through the wilderness** (cf. Ex 13:20-22; 40:36-38; Deut 8:15) **To him which smote great kings** (see comment on Ps 135:10) **and slew famous kings,** two of which are about to be singled out as noteworthy.

19-22. Sihon king of the Amorites. . . . and Og the king of Bashan were the two most mighty kings who stood in the way of Israel's successful entrance into the Promised Land. Still, they were no match for the God whose **mercy endureth for ever.** Thus, He **gave their land for a heritage** unto Israel (cf. Josh 12:1-6). It was **a heritage unto Israel his servant,** the nation chosen both son and servant of Jehovah.

23-26. Enough reason has already been given why Israel should **give thanks unto the LORD** (vs. 1), **unto the God of Gods** (vs. 2), and unto **the Lord of lords** (vs. 3). Yet, the psalmist poetically finds one more avenue to describe the mercy of the Lord which endures forever. Thanks is to be given unto Jehovah, **Who remembered us in our low estate.** Although this

26 O give thanks unto the God of heaven: for his mercy *endureth* for ever.

may refer to the Babylonian captivity, it more likely refers to the Egyptian captivity or any other time in which Israel was humiliated by her enemies. It was the God whose mercy was without duration who **hath redeemed us from our enemies,** snatched us from our adversaries. This is the same God **Who giveth food to all flesh,** both to man and the animals (cf. 104:27; 145:15; 147:9; Job 38:41). Such a merciful God deals kindly and tenderly with all His creatures.

When the psalmist recalls the great grace of God and the infinite, enduring mercy of Jehovah, he can but conclude his thoughts by saying, **O give thanks unto the God of heaven.** This particular name for Jehovah is found no where else in the Psalms. It is an expressive designation for the glorious God who is far above the pestilences and annoyances of the earth, and yet not so far above these that He cannot redeem His people from them. Is it little wonder, then, that the psalmist found it appropriate to repeat some twenty-six times the refrain, **for his mercy endureth for ever.**

EE. Babylon and Jerusalem. 137:1-9.

THEME: A psalm of exile commencing with lament and concluding with imprecation.

Although the Syriac version ascribes this psalm to David, understanding it to be prophetic, most scholars agree with Alexander that this psalm is "the most direct and striking reminiscence of the Babylonish exile in the whole Psalter." The real question seems to be whether or not this psalm was written during the Exile or after the Exile. Calvin, Henry, Edwards, Patrick, and others point to verses 4-6, which appear to be written during captivity, and verses 8-9, which anticipate the overthrow of Babylon, as evidence that the psalm was composed while the exiles were still captive. Tholuck, Hengstenberg, Perowne, and others see the past tenses of the verbs in verses 1-3 as evidence that the psalmist wrote shortly after his release from captivity.

The psalm begins with a personal lament for the treatment received by the exiles. But soon the psalmist turns his attention from the pathetic tale of his captivity to a strong indictment and natural resentment toward his enemy. This resentment grows out of the terrible wrongs that have been done to Jerusalem and her people. It arises out of patriotism and national pride. Yet, it is bitter and indicative of a heart that has not been touched by the love of God.

PSALM 137

BY the rivers of Babylon, there we sat down, yea, we wept, when we remembered Zion.

2 We hanged our harps upon the willows in the midst thereof.

3 For there they that carried us away captive required of us a song; and they that wasted us *required of us* mirth, *saying,* Sing us *one* of the songs of Zion.

137:1-3. **By the rivers of Babylon, there we sat down, yea, we wept, when we remembered Zion.** The Euphrates, Tigris, and the canals that crisscross Babylonia between these rivers became the places of lament for the captives. It was here they **sat down,** which "implies that the burst of grief was a long one, and also that it was looked on by the captives as some relaxation and repose"—Chrysostom. The purpose of sitting by the watercourses and canals of Babylon was to weep. The weeping (Heb *bakah*) was a mourning, a bewailing, which this the most expressive Hebrew verb of deep grief indicates. Such weeping was when the exiles **remembered Zion.**

Symbolic of their grief, **We hanged our harps upon the willows.** The drooping branches of the weeping willow provided a most somber setting for the Jews to sit along the banks of the Babylonian watercourses and weep for their city. But, as if to add injury to insult, when the Babylonians carried the Jews into captivity, **they that wasted us required of us mirth.** Just as the Philistines had earlier made sport of blind Samson, now the Babylonians ridicule their captives, saying, **Sing us one of the songs of Zion.**

4 How shall we sing the LORD's song in a strange land?

4-6. They asked themselves, **How shall we sing the LORD's song in a strange land?** How would it be possible to sing the songs of Jehovah among the uncircumcised? **If I forget thee, O**

5 If I forget thee, O Jerusalem, let my right hand forget *her cunning.*

6 If I do not remember thee, let my tongue cleave to the roof of my mouth; if I prefer not Jerusalem above my chief joy.

7 Remember, O LORD, the children of E′dom in the day of Jerusalem; who said, Rase *it,* rase *it, even* to the foundation thereof.

8 O daughter of Babylon, who art to be destroyed; happy *shall he be,* that rewardeth thee as thou hast served us.

9 Happy *shall he be,* that taketh and dasheth thy little ones against the stones.

Jerusalem, let my right hand forget. The AV supplies the words, **her cunning,** to complete the thought of this resolve. The Jews understand it to be better that their right hand lose its ability to play the harp than to play for these ruthless dogs. **If I prefer not Jerusalem above my chief joy.** The captives reasoned that if they could not sing and play to the praise of Jehovah before those who were in full agreement with those praises, they would not sing and play at all.

7-9. Suddenly, the tone of the psalm shifts from recollection of Jerusalem to a strong indictment and fierce imprecation of those who aided in their captivity. The psalmist begs Jehovah to remember **the children of Edom.** The Jews were their brothers (Amos 1:11; Ob 10), their neighbors (Mk 3:8), their confederates (Jer 27:3) and one time their allies (Ob 7). But **in the day of Jerusalem,** that is, in the day in which Jerusalem fell to the Babylonians, the Edomites took part with her enemies and rejoiced at the destruction of Jerusalem (Ezk 25:12; 35:5; Lam 4:21-22; Ob 10-14). Edom urged the Babylonians, **Rase it, rase it, even to the foundation thereof.** At this grand opportunity, the inherent hatred between Edom and Judah boiled over into an ungodly delight.

Now the psalmist turns his attention to the devastaters of Israel themselves. **O daughter of Babylon . . . happy shall he be, that rewardeth thee as thou hast served us.** In full prediction of the future devastation by Cyrus, the Jews rejoiced in the principle of *lex talionis,* an eye for an eye retaliation. **Happy shall he be, that taketh and dasheth thy little ones against the stones.** Here, the psalmist wishes upon the Babylonians the worst calamities of war (cf. II Kgs 8:12; Isa 13:16-18; Hos 10:14; 13:16; Nah 3:10). The murder of innocent children was a fact of ancient warfare. The Babylonians had committed more than their share of such atrocities in the massacres of whole families as they moved across the Ancient Near East. But such senseless killing can never be condoned by the Christian. The psalmist who penned these words wrote from national pride and patriotism, not from a heart filled with the truth of the second great commandment, ". . . Thou shalt love thy neighbor as thyself" (Mt 22:39).

We should not allow the final imprecation of this psalm to mar our admiration for the Israelites who, while captives in Babylon, did not make music for their enemies, but rather stalwartly sat in silence and solitude, preferring to remain faithful to their holy city and their holy God and allow Him to deal in righteous justice with their enemies.

FF. A Psalm of Boldness. 138:1-8.

THEME: The resolve of the psalmist to boldly praise the Lord.

The Davidic authorship of this psalm is advanced by the Hebrew, Syriac, Chaldee, Arabic, Septuagint, Ethiopic, and Vulgate editions of the Psalms. Likewise, most scholars from the early centuries on recognize David's authorship of this psalm. The internal evidence for such authorship is strong as well.

138:1-3. Before the gods will I sing praise unto thee. A variety of interpretations has been advanced for the **gods** (Heb *'elōhîm*) mentioned here. The LXX, Vulgate, Ethiopic, and Arabic translates the word "angels." Luther, Calvin, and a host of other commentators agree. The Chaldee interprets the word as "judges," and the Syriac understands it to be "kings." But perhaps the real intent is that the psalmist has resolved to praise God in the presence of the gods of the heathen, i.e., in the sight and scorn of those who worship idols (for a similar expression see 23:5 in the Heb).

PSALM 138

I WILL praise thee with my whole heart: before the gods will I sing praise unto thee.

2 I will worship toward thy holy temple, and praise thy name for thy lovingkindness and for thy truth: for thou hast magnified thy word above all thy name.

3 In the day when I cried thou answeredst me, *and* strengthenedst me *with* strength in my soul.

I will worship toward thy holy temple. Some have contended that the mention of a Temple here precludes Davidic authorship. But David uses the same language in psalms that are unquestionably his (cf. 5:7; 11:4; 18:6; etc.). It is obvious that he is referring to the tabernacle where he would go to praise the **loving-kindness** and **truth** of the Lord God. There are two reasons for doing so. First, **for thou hast magnified thy word above all thy name.** God has a greater reward for the words of His mouth than for the works of His hand. Heaven and earth shall pass away, but not one jot or one tittle of what He has spoken shall ever pass away. David's other reason for praising the name of the Lord God was that **In the day when I cried thou answeredst me, and strengthenedst me with strength in my soul.** To the believer committed to praise God with his whole heart in the face of the world's ridicule, soul strength is more important than body strength.

4-6. All the kings of the earth shall praise thee, O LORD. In a very small sense this promise was fulfilled with regard to David; but in the strictest sense, this statement is prophetic in nature. It will only fully be complete when the Messiah, Jesus Christ, assumes the throne of David. Then these heathen kings shall no longer sing of their idols and false gods; but **they shall sing in the ways of the LORD.** And why is this so? **For great is the glory of the LORD.** As example of this greatness, David indicates that **Though the LORD be high, yet hath he respect unto the lowly.** God is no respecter of persons. Princes and paupers alike are the recipients of His mercy. **But the proud he knoweth afar off.** This shows God's utter disdain for a proud person. He does not draw the proud near unto Him, but keeps them at a distance until, like the potter's vessel, they are dashed in pieces by their pride.

7-8. These final verses display the confidence of David as he walks uprightly before the Lord. He is convinced that though his walk frequently takes him **in the midst of trouble,** nevertheless God would sustain his life. **Thy right hand shall save me.** With one hand God will hold the enemy at bay; with the other He will securely protect His anointed (cf. 18:35; 63:8; 108:6; etc.).

Thus, the Lord will complete the work which He has begun in the psalmist (cf. Phil 1:6). But the psalmist's confidence does not prohibit him from whispering a prayer unto the Lord God. **Forsake not the works of thine own hands.**

GG. God and Man. 139:1-24.

THEME: *The relationship between the omniscient, omnipresent, omnipotent God and man His creation.*

The superscription to this psalm reads, **To the chief musician. A psalm of David.** However, some scholars have pointed to the presence of Aramaisms as evidence of a later date. Also, some copies of the LXX ascribe the psalm both to David and to Zechariah. Origen notes that some MSS even add the words "in the dispersion." Yet, this tacking on of expressions in the superscription of a psalm cannot be seen as having any validity. Also, the Aramaic coloring of the psalm, as well as others psalms, has become less and less important to recent scholars in attempting to date the Psalms. Therefore, we must accept the Davidic authorship of Psalm 139, as indicated in the Hebrew MS.

This is a strikingly beautiful psalm, said by some to be the most beautiful. It deals with the three great attributes of God; i.e., His omniscience, His omnipresence, and His omnipotence. Jehovah God is clearly the object of this hymn of praise.

139:1-3. O LORD, thou hast searched me, and known me. Addressing the all-knowing God, the psalmist notes that he has been **searched** (Heb *chaqar*), which originally meant to dig, a word applied to the search for precious metals (Job 28:3) but here metaphorically used of a moral inquisition. Yet it must be remembered that although we search God's word and world to know about Him, He intuitively knows us. The psalmist admits, **Thou knowest my downsitting and mine uprising.** Every move

---

4 All the kings of the earth shall praise thee, O LORD, when they hear the words of thy mouth.
5 Yea, they shall sing in the ways of the LORD: for great *is* the glory of the LORD.
6 Though the LORD *be* high, yet hath he respect unto the lowly: but the proud he knoweth afar off.

7 Though I walk in the midst of trouble, thou wilt revive me: thou shalt stretch forth thine hand against the wrath of mine enemies, and thy right hand shall save me.
8 The LORD will perfect *that which* concerneth me: thy mercy, O LORD, *endureth* for ever: forsake not the works of thine own hands.

PSALM 139

O LORD, thou hast searched me, and known *me.*
2 Thou knowest my downsitting and mine uprising, thou understandest my thought afar off.
3 Thou compassest my path and my lying down, and art acquainted *with* all my ways.

he makes is observed by the Lord God. **Thou understandest my thought afar off,** i.e., before it is fully formed. **Thou compassest my path and my lying down. Compassest** (Heb *zarah*) literally means to sift or winnow. God is so intimately aware of all our ways that He has literally sifted our seconds to insure our well-being.

4-5. More than that, **there is not a word in my tongue, but, lo, O LORD, thou knowest it altogether.** If the omniscience of God allows Him to know our thoughts even before they are developed in our mind, why should we think that He does not know our words even before they are formed by our tongues? No, **Thou hast beset me behind and before.** "Behind us there is God recording our sins, or in grace blotting out the remembrance of them; and before us there is God foreknowing all our deeds, and providing for all our wants. We cannot turn back and so escape Him, for He is behind; we cannot go forward and outmarch Him, for He is before"—Spurgeon.

6. Having been made aware of the wonderful omniscience of Jehovah, the psalmist must humbly admit, **Such knowledge is too wonderful for me; it is high, I cannot attain unto it.** To be aware that Jehovah knows everything about the psalmist is knowledge that surpasses his comprehension, and even his imagination.

7. This knowledge is a source of both comfort and concern to the psalmist. He asks, **Whither shall I go from thy Spirit?** Here, the transition is made from God's omniscience to God's omnipresence. **Whither shall I flee from thy presence?** "A heathen philosopher once asked, 'Where is God?' The Christian answered, 'Let me first ask you, where is He not?' "—John Arrowsmith (1602-1659).

8-10. The psalmist is theorizing in his own mind what Jonah had learned in fact. When Jonah sought to flee from the presence of God, he found himself to be more perceptibly and redemptively in His presence (cf. Jer 23:24). The psalmist says, **If I ascend up into heaven, thou art there.** Man can certainly not escape the divine presence by ascending into the heaven of Heavens. **If I make my bed in hell, behold thou art there.** Descending into the lowest imaginable depths of the dead, then spreading his mat for a bed (a very unlikely possibility), will not alleviate either the comfort or concern that the psalmist has for the presence of God.

If I take the wings of the morning, perhaps a metaphorical reference to sunbeams, morning clouds, or even the incalculable velocity of light, **and dwell in the uttermost parts of the sea,** the area between the heavens and hell, nonetheless **even there shall thy hand lead me.** God is magnificently present wherever we are.

11-12. Unable to escape the presence of God in space, the psalmist theorizes that it may be possible to escape His omnipresence in time. **If I say, Surely the darkness shall cover me.** Would it be possible for the inky blackness of night to shield us from the presence of God? The psalmist quickly answers his own question. **The darkness hideth not from thee.** The light of God's divine essence penetrates every dark place and makes the deepest darkness to radiate as the brightest light.

13. Having addressed God's omniscience (vss. 1-6) and omnipresence (vss. 7-12), the psalmist now turns his attention to God's omnipotence (vss. 13-18). **For thou hast possessed my reins.** The ancient Hebrews regarded the **reins** as the seat of sensation and feeling, as well as that of desire and longing (73:21; Job 16:13; 19:27). The word (Heb *kilyah*) literally signifies the kidneys, but it is poetically used of the inner nature generally (16:7; Jer 20:12). God knows and has power over our innermost personality. **Thou hast covered me in my mother's womb.** As Albert Barnes notes, "The word here rendered cover (vs. 11) (Heb *sakak*) means properly to interweave; to weave; to

4 For *there is* not a word in my tongue, *but,* lo, O LORD, thou knowest it altogether.
5 Thou hast beset me behind and before, and laid thine hand upon me.

6 *Such* knowledge *is* too wonderful for me; it is high, I cannot *attain* unto it.

7 Whither shall I go from thy spirit? or whither shall I flee from thy presence?

8 If I ascend up into heaven, thou *art* there: if I make my bed in hell, behold, thou *art there.*
9 *If* I take the wings of the morning, *and* dwell in the uttermost parts of the sea;
10 Even there shall thy hand lead me, and thy right hand shall hold me.

11 If I say, Surely the darkness shall cover me; even the night shall be light about me.
12 Yea, the darkness hideth not from thee; but the night shineth as the day: the darkness and the light *are* both alike *to thee.*

13 For thou hast possessed my reins: thou hast covered me in my mother's womb.

knit together, and the (literal translation would be, 'thou hast woven me in my mother's womb,' meaning that God had put his parts together as one who weaves cloth, or who makes a basket." The weaving of the bones, tissue, and organs of the fetal unborn are under the control and guardianship of God.

14 I will praise thee; for I am fearfully and wonderfully made: marvellous *are* thy works; and *that* my soul knoweth right well.

14. There is cause to praise Jehovah, **for I am fearfully and wonderfully made.** The wonderfulness of the human body is so great that those who study the cells of the brain, the articulation of the limbs, or the smooth functioning of the body organs stand in awe at how wonderful this creation of God really is. In honesty, every student of the human anatomy must say to God, **marvelous are thy works.**

15 My substance was not hid from thee, when I was made in secret, *and* curiously wrought in the lowest parts of the earth.

15. My substance was not hid from thee when I was made in secret. The substantial part of a man's being, i.e., the bones which make up his frame, may not be visible to the naked eye; but it is certainly not hidden from the eyes of God. He has power over the formation of the skeletal body while it is yet in the womb. It is being formed **in secret** and is **curiously wrought in the lowest parts of the earth,** a poetic reference to the womb. "A great artist will often labour alone in his studio, and not suffer his work to be seen until it is finished; even so did the Lord fashion us when no eye beheld us, and the veil was not lifted till every member was complete"—Spurgeon. All of our veins, muscles, nerves, etc., were woven together by God, embroidered with great skill, before the world got its first look at us.

16 Thine eyes did see my substance, yet being unperfect; and in thy book all *my members* were written, *which* in continuance were fashioned, when *as yet there was* none of them.

16. Thine eyes did see my substance, yet being unperfect. The word **substance** (Heb *gōlem*) is not the same as the word **substance** in verse 15. This is the only usage of the word in the Bible (although *galam* occurs in II Kgs 2:8 and is translated wrapped together). The word means anything that is rolled together as a ball, a wrapped and unformed mass, "the still unformed embryonic mass" (Hengstenberg). Most scholars understand it to mean the fetus or the embryo in the womb. The psalmist is saying that the omnipotence of God guided the very formation of life in the womb, that life being yet an **unperfect** or unformed embryonic mass, yet **in continuance** for in the course of time was being **fashioned** daily in fetal form. **When as yet there was none of them,** God had written in His book **all my members.** In the mind of God, poetically referred to as the book of God, the blueprint for life is clearly charted, so that from the very moment of conception, God begins to fashion the members of the body, even before they are recognizable.

Given this truth, it is little wonder that those who have faithfully followed the Judaeo-Christian faith have understood life to begin at the moment of conception, and not at birth. They, too, have solidly stood in opposition to the taking of that human life by abortion.

17 How precious also are thy thoughts unto me, O God! how great is the sum of them!
18 *If* I should count them, they are more in number than the sand: when I awake, I am still with thee.

17-18. If the work of God in forming the fetus is precious, how much more precious **are thy thoughts,** the thoughts of God, toward His creation. **How great is the sum of them!** Were we to total them they would be immeasurable. **If I should count them, they are more in number than the sand.** "If all is glorious deeds my song would tell, the shore's unnumbered stones I might recount as well"—Pindar (B.C. 518-442). More than the sands of the sea are the delightful thoughts of God toward us.

19 Surely thou wilt slay the wicked, O God: depart from me therefore, ye bloody men.
20 For they speak against thee wickedly, *and* thine enemies take *thy name* in vain.

19-20. Surely thou wilt slay the wicked, O God (cf. 5:6, 10; 7:9-13; 9:19; 10:15; 21:8-12; etc.). God, who has seen the transgressions of the wicked, even those covertly done within the womb, will surely not allow such crimes to go unpunished. Thus, the psalmist bids depart the **bloody men** who **speak against thee wickedly, and . . . take thy name in vain;** literally, "thine enemies lift up (their soul) to vanity" (cf. 24:4). The psalmist has resolved to have nothing to do with such sinners.

21 Do not I hate them, O LORD, that

21-22. Do not I hate them, O LORD . . . I hate them with

hate thee? and am not I grieved with those that rise up against thee?

22 I hate them with perfect hatred: I count them mine enemies.

23 Search me, O God, and know my heart: try me, and know my thoughts:

24 And see if *there be any* wicked way in me, and lead me in the way everlasting.

PSALM 140

DELIVER me, O LORD, from the evil man: preserve me from the violent man;

2 Which imagine mischiefs in *their* heart; continually are they gathered together *for* war.

3 They have sharpened their tongues like a serpent; adders' poison *is* under their lips. Sē'lah.

4 Keep me, O LORD, from the hands of the wicked; preserve me from the violent man; who have purposed to overthrow my goings.

5 The proud have hid a snare for me,

---

perfect hatred. Of the psalmist Spurgeon says that "he was a good hater, for he hated only those who hated good." The psalmist could not remain neutral on the matter of those who hate God. **And am not I grieved with those that rise up against thee?** He was disgusted with, nauseated by, and loathed those men who unjustly raised their hatred against God. **I count them mine enemies.**

23-24. David would be no accomplice to the sinner. He disowns them and clings to God. Having begun this psalm with the statement, **O LORD, thou hast searched me, and known me** (vs. 1), he now concludes with a similar prayer, **Search me, O God, and know my heart.** The psalmist is asking the Lord to examine him to see if he has accurately represented his feelings toward the omniscience, omnipresence, and omnipotence of God. **See if there be any wicked way in me.** Test for secret sins. The end result of such testing for the psalmist will be, **lead me in the way everlasting** (lit., the way that leadeth to everlasting life). How blessed it is for a man to lead such a godly life that he can submit himself to divine scrutiny and be confident that he is a man of God walking in the way of God.

HH. A Cry for Deliverance. 140:1-13.

THEME: *A hunted man calls upon God for deliverance from the evil and violent man.*

All the ancient versions ascribe this psalm of supplication to David. The internal evidence for the psalm substantiates this identification; yet, the greater question relates to the occasion in David's life for which the psalm was composed. It obviously describes his troubles during the time of Saul, Doeg, Ahithophel, and Absalom (I Sam 22-23). Spurgeon says, "The life of David wherein he comes in contact with Saul and Doeg is the best explanation of this Psalm." The Syriac version relates it solely to the time when Saul attempted to kill David with a spear. Theodoret, on the other hand, relates the occasion for composition to the time when Doeg and the Ziphites were pursuing David. In fact, however, the exact identification is sheer conjecture.

It has been noted that, together with the following three psalms, this one constitutes a distinct group. Each of these four psalms bears the same characteristics, including David's name as author. Three of them are called **A psalm;** one is called **A Maschil** (a psalm of instruction). In these psalms the circumstances of David are all similar. An implacable foe seeks his destruction, and the psalmist in turn seeks deliverance from God.

140:1-3. **Deliver me, O LORD, from the evil man.** David's prayer is not directed toward any individual, but rather toward the species of wicked men in general. Evil in the hearts of men soon drives them to become bitter and malicious. That malice produces **the violent man,** from whom David pleads the Lord will preserve him. Violent men are those who **imagine mischiefs in their heart** (cf. 28:3; 36:4; 62:3) and who continually are **gathered together for war** (cf. 68:30; 120:7). In order to graphically portray the maliciousness of evil and violent men, David notes that **They have sharpened their tongues like a serpent** (cf. 52:2; 57:4; 59:7; 64:3). This is apparently a description of the way in which a serpent darts out his tongue before he inflicts a wound. **Adders' poison is under their lips** (cf. 58:4; Rom 3:15). Those who maliciously speak evil of the unjustly afflicted do so with tongues as laden with poison as the fangs of a serpent. **Selah** marks the completion of the first stanza.

4-5. **Keep me . . . preserve me** is a modified repetition of the first verse. Yet, here the psalmist becomes even more specific. He desires not simply to be kept from the evil man, but **from the hands of the wicked** in their attempt **To overthrow my goings.** So cunning is the proud man that he has laid a variety of

and cords; they have spread a net by the wayside; they have set gins for me. Sĕ'lah.

6 I said unto the LORD, Thou *art* my God: hear the voice of my supplications, O LORD.
7 O GOD the Lord, the strength of my salvation, thou hast covered my head in the day of battle.
8 Grant not, O LORD, the desires of the wicked: further not his wicked device; *lest* they exalt themselves. Sĕ'lah.

9 *As for* the head of those that compass me about, let the mischief of their own lips cover them.
10 Let burning coals fall upon them: let them be cast into the fire; into deep pits, that they rise not up again.
11 Let not an evil speaker be established in the earth: evil shall hunt the violent man to overthrow *him*.

12 I know that the LORD will maintain the cause of the afflicted, *and* the right of the poor.
13 Surely the righteous shall give thanks unto thy name: the upright shall dwell in thy presence.

traps for the psalmist. These traps include **a snare** and **gins,** a type of snare (cf. 11:6; 69:22; 91:3; 119:110; 124:7; Job 18:9). Some snares were operated by ropes or **cords.** Others used **a net,** which was set simply **by the wayside** where one would think it safe to travel. How crafty indeed are those wicked and violent men who seek the downfall of the righteous. Selah, the conclusion of the second stanza.

6-8. In the midst of his turmoil, David has a clear and confident assurance of divine deliverance. The expressions of this prayer are characteristically Davidic. He said unto Jehovah, **Thou art my GOD** and petitioned, **hear the voice of my supplications, O LORD** (cf. 31:14; 143:1). **O God the LORD,** *Yahweh Adonai,* is both the strength of his salvation and shield **in the day of battle.** Goliath had his armor-bearer, as did Saul. But David looked confidently toward Jehovah to protect his head from the arrows and spears of the wicked and violent man. Thus he prays to Jehovah that **the desires of the wicked** would be thwarted, **lest they exalt themselves. Selah** terminates the third stanza and gives rise to a thoughtful consideration of his prayer.

9-11. At this point, a concluding imprecation is voiced. David contrasts **the head of those that compass me about** with his own head, which God has covered in the day of battle. As the wicked and violent man has attempted to inflict injury to the psalmist's head, so he prays, **let the mischief of their own lips cover them.** Here again is a striking example of *lex talionis,* the law of retaliation. David simply prays that God will do to the violent man what he has desired to do to the psalmist. **Let burning coals fall upon them,** in order that they be convinced their destruction is divinely directed. Those who had **spread a net by the wayside** (vs. 5) in order to entrap the righteous, would themselves fall into deep pits **that they rise not up again.** May God direct that **evil shall hunt the violent man to overthrow him.** He hunted the good, and now he shall be hunted by his own evil. He was violent; he shall be violently hunted down. Sin is its own punishment.

12-13. In a concluding note of confidence, the psalmist indicates, **I know that the LORD will maintain the cause of the afflicted, and the right of the poor.** Those who had been slandered knew that Jehovah always cares that the truth be made manifest. Those who were poverty-stricken always knew that the wealthy and prosperous were not nearly as blessed as those who lived righteously before God. **The upright shall dwell in thy presence.** The result of God's punishment on the wicked and His deliverance of the righteous is eternal banishment from the presence of God for those who are evil and eternal blessing in the presence of God for those who live righteously.

II. A Psalm of Censorship. 141:1-10.

THEME: *David's prayer that God will not permit him to speak ill of those who have done ill to him.*

In this psalm of supplication David is once again in danger. The superscription, **A psalm of David,** is not to be refuted. There is no serious objection to authorship by David; no historical fact in the psalm is in opposition to the known facts of his life. Some have assigned it to the time of his persecution by Saul, others to the period of Absalom's rebellion.

Plumer notes, "The scope of this ode is clearly a prayer for grace to restrain his temper and his tongue in a time of wanton injuries received from those, whom he had never wronged." From the days of the early church this psalm has been regarded as an evening prayer to be used in the vespers (cf. vs. 2); Psalm 63 was the corresponding morning prayer.

141:1-2. David was in the habit of crying unto the Lord God, as many of the psalms testify. But when he was in deep distress, he would always pray, **make haste unto me . . . when I cry**

PSALM 141
LORD, I cry unto thee: make haste unto me; give ear unto my voice, when I cry unto thee.

2 Let my prayer be set forth before thee *as* incense; *and* the lifting up of my hands *as* the evening sacrifice.

3 Set a watch, O LORD, before my mouth; keep the door of my lips.
4 Incline not my heart to *any* evil thing, to practise wicked works with men that work iniquity: and let me not eat of their dainties.

5 Let the righteous smite me; *it shall be* a kindness: and let him reprove me; *it shall be* an excellent oil, *which* shall not break my head: for yet my prayer also *shall be* in their calamities.

6 When their judges are overthrown in stony places, they shall hear my words; for they are sweet.

7 Our bones are scattered at the grave's mouth, as when one cutteth and cleaveth *wood* upon the earth.

8 But mine eyes *are* unto thee, O GOD the Lord: in thee is my trust; leave not my soul destitute.
9 Keep me from the snares *which*

unto thee (cf. 22:19; 31:2; 38:22; 40:17; etc.). To the urgent prayer for help the psalmist adds, **Let my prayer be set forth before thee as incense.** For a prayer to **be set forth** (Heb *kūn*) means to fit, to establish, to make firm. The psalmist asks that his prayer would not soon dissipate or be feeble, but that it would be solid, strong, and secure. **And the lifting up of my hands as the evening sacrifice** was a familiar form of worship and sacrifice to Jehovah (cf. Hos 14:3).

3-4. **Set a watch, O LORD, before my mouth,** watching and praying are often joined together in Scripture. Yet, in this case the **watch** is a divinely appointed keeper of the door to David's lips. Having a hasty, impetuous temper, David knew he must submit himself to divine censorship or defile his mouth with malicious retaliation on those who had assailed him. He prays that Jehovah will not permit him **to practice wicked works with men that work iniquity,** to run with those who run wide of God. More than this, David asks, **let me not eat of their dainties.** If we work with the wicked, we shall soon eat with them. David does not want to share in their wickedness or wantonness to any degree, especially to enjoy their sinful life of luxury. The road to disaster is lined with the banquet of wicked pleasures.

5. **Let the righteous smite me; it shall be a kindness.** At best, this verse is difficult to interpret. If it bears a relationship to the preceding verses, it is probably correct to regard the **righteous** as a righteous man and not, as Hengstenberg and Alexander understand the term, referring to God. It appears that the psalmist prays that some righteous friend of his might reprove him sharply if he yielded to the temptation to practice wicked works with men that work iniquity. Such a reproof would even be a kindness to him. In fact, he describes it as **an excellent oil, which shall not break my head.** For a righteous friend to smite the psalmist with a reproof should he waver in his determination not to keep company with the wicked, would not be a head-breaking blow, but rather an act of godly kindness, This act of kindness would be returned, says the psalmist, in that **my prayer also shall be in their calamities.** One kind reproof deserves a reciprocating kind reproof.

6. **When their judges are overthrown in stony places, they shall hear my words; for they are sweet.** A wide variety of interpretations have been given to these words. To whom does the word **judges** (Heb *shōpēt*), i.e., leaders, refer? Some, like Spurgeon, understand these to be the righteous leaders among the Israelites. But many others see here a reference to David's enemies and the grievous calamities which shall befall them, metaphorically expressed as being cast down into the crevices of the rock. Either interpretation is plausible.

7. Instead of a verse of despair, as many interpreters regard it, this verse appears to be a note of comfort and hope. **Our bones are scattered at the grave's mouth, as when one cutteth and cleaveth wood upon the earth.** In the AV the word **wood** is in italics, since it is not included in the Hebrew text. If we regard the **cutteth and cleaveth** to be of the earth itself, the psalmist is referring to plowing a parcel of land. On the plowed earth lay the scattered bones of God's saints, unburied and at the very door of Sheol. Here these bones await the resurrection of the just; for they are not sown unto death and destruction, but unto new life. It is as if the psalmist were paralleling the ancient Job when he said, "Though he slay me, yet will I trust in him: but I will maintain mine own ways before him. He also shall be my salvation: for an hypocrite shall not come before him" (Job 13:15-16).

8-10. The last verse gives rise to a confident conclusion. Rather than gazing downward to **the grave's mouth,** the psalmist gazes upward toward the Lord God. It is there that his eyes are fixed, for he trusts that Jehovah will **leave not my soul destitute** (lit., pour not out my soul, but keep it in thy cup of

they have laid for me, and the gins of the workers of iniquity.

10 Let the wicked fall into their own nets, whilst that I withal escape.

PSALM 142

I CRIED unto the LORD with my voice; with my voice unto the LORD did I make my supplication.

2 I poured out my complaint before him; I shewed before him my trouble.

3 When my spirit was overwhelmed within me, then thou knewest my path. In the way wherein I walked have they privily laid a snare for me.

4 I looked on *my* right hand, and beheld, but *there was* no man that would know me: refuge failed me; no man cared for my soul.

salvation, cf. Isa 53:12). As he prayed in the preceding psalm (cf. 140:5), David prays, **Keep me from the snares which they have laid for me, and the gins of the workers of iniquity.** Previously in this psalm (vs. 3), the writer asks God to keep his mouth; now he asks God to keep him. He may pray to God, **Let the wicked fall into their own nets,** a form of divinely appointed retaliation, but his great concern is that he conduct himself uprightly in the presence of God and his enemies.

JJ. A Psalm of Solitude. 142:1-7.

THEME: *A cry for divine aid from the cavern of despair.*

The superscription of this psalm is significant. It reads, **A Maschil of David. A prayer when he was in the cave.** The word **Maschil** occurs in the title of thirteen psalms (those of David: 32; 52-55; 142; those of Korah: 42; 44-45; those of Asaph: 74; 78; those of Heman: 88; and those of Ethan: 89). A maschil is a teaching psalm designed to give moral as well as practical instruction.

The psalm is said to have been written by David **when he was in the cave.** There are two notable occasions when David hid in a cave while fleeing from pursuit. The first was in the cave of Adullam (I Sam 22), and the second was in the cave of En-gedi (I Sam 24). Expositors are divided as to the occasion to which this psalm refers. Hengstenberg and Alexander understand this psalm to be speaking of cave life in general, and not to a specific occasion of hiding in a cave. Yet, it is most likely that the psalmist composed this ode in either Adullam or En-gedi.

This is one of four psalms that have the word, prayer, in the title (cf. 86; 90; 102). It is also found in the caption to Habakkuk 3:1. The psalm is probably called a prayer because the petition of the psalmist is the characteristic feature of the psalm.

142:1-2. I cried unto the LORD with my voice. The fact that the expression **with my voice** is repeated indicates that he prayed aloud and therefore earnestly (cf. 3:4; 27:7; 64:1; 77:1; 130:1-2; etc.). The psalmist had been the victim of oppression. David knew he had to tell someone of his trouble; and thus, **I poured out my complaint before him,** i.e., **the Lord.** Had he poured out his complaint before men, he would only have received token sympathy, or no sympathy at all. Thus, he did not publish his sorrows before the world, but took them to the one who could assuage them.

3. When my spirit was overwhelmed within me, then thou knewest my path. David is indeed in deep despair. His soul does not despair, but rather his spirit. The dejection of the spirit (Heb *rūach*) is a much more sorrowful condition than the fainting of the soul (Heb *nepesh*). Compare 143:3-4 with John 12:27 and John 13:21. The psalmist was aware that God knew **they privily laid a snare for me.** This is by no means the first time the psalmist has lamented the snare that his oppressors have laid for him (cf. 140:5; 141:9-10).

4. I looked on my right hand, and beheld, but there was no man that would know me. It is preferable to understand the first two verbs of this statement as imperatives (look on the right hand, and see). Not only had the psalmist been unable to discover faithful friends in his moment of despair, but he invites the all-knowing God to look and see that the friends have deserted him.

Given the fact that David was surrounded by a band of loyal subjects when he made this statement, in what sense are we to understand that he has no true friends? Perhaps the language of the Apostle Paul in Philippians 2:20 is an analogy: ". . . I have no man likeminded. . . ." He is saying that he has no man "of equal soul" to him, no man who shared his burdens and dreams and visions to the degree which he would be willing to share them. **No man cared for my soul.** No man looked after his soul (cf. Jer 30:17).

5 I cried unto thee, O Lord: I said, Thou *art* my refuge *and* my portion in the land of the living.

6 Attend unto my cry; for I am brought very low: deliver me from my persecutors; for they are stronger than I.

7 Bring my soul out of prison, that I may praise thy name: the righteous shall compass me about; for thou shalt deal bountifully with me.

PSALM 143

HEAR my prayer, O Lord, give ear to my supplications: in thy faithfulness answer me, *and* in thy righteousness.

2 And enter not into judgment with thy servant: for in thy sight shall no man living be justified.

3 For the enemy hath persecuted my soul; he hath smitten my life down to the ground; he hath made me to dwell in darkness, as those that have been long dead.

4 Therefore is my spirit overwhelmed

5-6. In the midst of the solitude of despair, David made an appropriate response when he cried unto the Lord and said, **Thou art my refuge and my portion in the land of the living.** What a grand confession this was. Frequently, David had looked upon God as his refuge (cf. 9:9; 18:1-2; 57:1; 59:9, 16-17). To that he adds that God is his **portion,** or "inheritance" (cf. 16:5; 73:26). Yet, the psalmist is not content with having an audience with God. He wants God to **Attend unto my cry.** David prays that God will not only hear but act and **deliver me from my persecutors; for they are stronger than I.** In the cave of Adullam David's persecutors were Saul and the thousands in the armies of Israel (I Sam 22:1-2). When he hid at En-gedi, David was being pursued by Saul and three thousand chosen men out of all Israel (I Sam 24:2). At other times Saul, Doeg, the Ziphites, and the armies of Saul hunted David in the mountains (I Sam 26:20). It is little wonder that the psalmist admitted his persecutors were stronger than he.

7. In the concluding clause of his supplication David requests, **Bring my soul out of prison, that I may praise thy name.** The word **prison** is used as a metaphor for trouble and distress (cf. 88:8; 107:10-14). Again, David's intent is that by his rescue the name of Jehovah may be praised. With his rescue David was convinced that **the righteous shall compass me about,** circle about him like a crown, as the word (Heb *katar*) signifies. The Targum says, "For my sake the righteous will make to thee a crown of praise." Viewing David's cause as their own, those who live rightly before God will glory in the psalmist's deliverance (cf. 35:27; 40:16).

KK. Prayer of the Overwhelmed Spirit. 143:1-12.

THEME: A psalm of complaint and prayer to God.

The inscription for this psalm reads, **A psalm of David;** and the psalm gives us little reason to question this inscription. In fact, the Arabic, Septuagint, Ethiopic, and Vulgate versions refer it to the rebellion of Absalom. This addition may be questioned. However, most scholars feel that the psalm itself is a composite largely taken from previous Davidic Psalms; and therefore, they ascribe Psalm 143 to a post-exilic poet. But before we conclude that David did not pen this psalm, we must ask why he could not have similar thoughts while under distress to those that he had previously penned in similar situations. Many commentators are too quick to view those psalms toward the end of the Psalter as non-Davidic, and we find no good basis for claiming that this psalm is a late compilation of Davidic thoughts, rather than a psalm of David himself.

143:1-2. Hear my prayer . . . give ear . . . answer me . . . . And enter not into judgment. Again and again the psalmist has petitioned Jehovah to hear his supplication. This time he calls for an answer to arise out of God's **faithfulness** and **righteousness.** His prayer turns to pleading when he asks that God not enter into judgment with David His servant. The reason is clear: **For in thy sight shall no man living be justified** (cf. 130:3). David knew he could not justify his unrighteous life; and therefore he begs God not to judge him. But today we know that God has already entered into judgment with His Son, Jesus Christ the Righteous, and has laid upon Him the iniquity of us all. We cannot stand in God's judgment unless we stand in the righteousness provided by Christ Jesus (Rom 5:2). "So far from being able to answer for my sins, I cannot answer even for my righteousness"—Bernard of Clairvaux (1091-1153).

3-4. In by now a common complaint, he pours out his heart to God that his enemy has persecuted his soul and **hath smitten my life down to the ground.** His assailant has hurled him to the ground, if not physically then in depressing his spirit. **He hath made me to dwell in darkness, as those that have been long dead;** he has dwelt in gloom and unhappiness as if he had

within me; my heart within me is desolate.

5 I remember the days of old; I meditate on all thy works; I muse on the work of thy hands.
6 I stretch forth my hands unto thee: my soul *thirsteth* after thee, as a thirsty land. Sĕ'lah.

7 Hear me speedily, O LORD: my spirit faileth: hide not thy face from me, lest I be like unto them that go down into the pit.
8 Cause me to hear thy lovingkindness in the morning; for in thee do I trust: cause me to know the way wherein I should walk; for I lift up my soul unto thee.

9 Deliver me, O LORD, from mine enemies: I flee unto thee to hide me.
10 Teach me to do thy will; for thou *art* my God: thy spirit *is* good; lead me into the land of uprightness.

11 Quicken me, O LORD, for thy name's sake: for thy righteousness' sake bring my soul out of trouble.
12 And of thy mercy cut off mine enemies, and destroy all them that afflict my soul: for I *am* thy servant.

already entered Sheol (cf. Lam 3:6). The enemy who threw him to the ground in spirit would lay him lower still in the underworld of departed spirits. Hence, the psalmist can but say, **Therefore is my spirit overwhelmed within me.** His spirit was faint (cf. 77:3), and his **heart** was **desolate** within him (cf. 40:15). The psalmist was completely overwhelmed by the implacable hatred of the enemy toward him.

5-6. With little future to look toward, and the present an unpleasant experience, the psalmist began to **remember the days of old . . . meditate on all thy works . . . muse on the work of thy hands.** He remembered those good things God had done for him in the past (cf. 77:5, 10-11), and he meditated on the work of God throughout the history of Israel. He mused at the creative activity of God in nature (cf. 77:12). When he remembered, meditated, and mused on God's goodness, it turned his complaint to the point that he began to **stretch forth my hands unto thee;** and he allowed his soul to thirst after God, **as a thirsty land. Selah,** not only a pause that marks the first division of the psalm, but also a call to think about that which has just been said.

7-8. Here, the direct prayer that was announced in verse 1 actually begins. Because of the psalmist's desperate situation, with his spirit overwhelmed and failing, he prays, **Hear me speedily, O LORD . . . lest I be like unto them that go down into the pit.** Frequently, we hear people lightly say: "If I don't get to do this or that I'll just die." In essence, the psalmist says if God doesn't hear his prayer, he'll die. God is not only his first resort in the time of trouble, He is the psalmist's last resort as well.

In order to insure that he does not **go down into the pit,** the psalmist prays to God, **Cause me to hear thy loving-kindness in the morning;** i.e., early, speedily, at the breaking of the dawn (cf. 46:5; 90:14). An early answer from God would be the only remedy for the psalmist's distress. He continues his pleading: **cause me to know the way wherein I should walk.** Here, the prayer is that God would illumine the psalmist in such a way that he would perceive the right course to follow (cf. 5:8).

9-10. Deliver me, O LORD, from mine enemies . . . Teach me to do thy will . . . lead me into the land of uprightness. By fleeing unto the Lord to hide, the psalmist is assured of deliverance from his enemies. But the immediate deliverance of the psalmist was not enough for him; he begged God to **Teach** him the divine will and to **lead** him into uprightness. And when we do the will of God, He leads us **into the land of uprightness** (lit., along a land of smoothness). "The land of plainness, a land where no wickedness of men, and malice of Satan, vex the soul from day to day; a land where no rough paths and crooked turns lengthen out the traveller's weary journey; but where all is like the smooth pasture-land of Reuben (Deut 3:16-20; Josh 13:15-23), a fit place for flocks to lie down"—Andrew Bonar.

11-12. The prayer of David recorded in these last verses exhibits a remarkable usage of verbs. His prayer was: **Hear me** (vs. 7); **Cause me** (vs. 8); **Deliver me** (vs. 9); **Teach me** (vs. 10); **lead me** (vs. 10) and now **Quicken me.** The final segment of his prayer is a petition for fresh spiritual life from God (cf. 119:25, 37, 50, 88, 93, etc.). The psalmist felt himself overwhelmed in spirit and near the pit of death. It was only a matter of time until the man of God prayed, **Quicken me, O LORD, for thy name's sake.** David was convinced that God would quicken him because He is a living and loving God, one who would not forsake His own but would rather **bring my soul out of trouble. . . . and destroy all them that afflict my soul.**

This prayer is raised by holy hands unto God based on two reasons: (1) **For thy righteousness' sake** (vs. 11); and (2) **for I am thy servant** (vs. 12). The servant of God was entitled to the protection of his master (cf. 27:9; 69:17; 86:2, 4, 16; 116:16;

etc.). Being the servant of God is an elevated, not a demeaning, position. The Roman emperor Theodosius (346-395) considered it to be a title of greater dignity to be God's servant than to be emperor of Rome. The Lord Jesus Himself, who was equal in every respect to the Father, was not ashamed of the title servant (cf. Isa 53:11). To be the faithful servant of God gives us the privilege to call upon our Master in times of distress, when our spirits are overwhelmed, and ask Him to hear us speedily and deliver us from our enemies.

LL. The Happy People Psalm. 144:1-15.

THEME: A psalm of praise to the Lord from a man fulfilled by God's salvation.

Nearly all the ancient versions ascribe this psalm to David. Most of the older commentators agree with these versions, e.g., Luther, Calvin, Patrick, Edwards, Henry, Clarke, Scott, and Hengstenberg. Alexander is typical when he says, "The Davidic origin of this psalm is as marked as that of any in the Psalter." Rabbi Kimchi understands this psalm as a reference to the events mentioned in II Samuel 5. The LXX states that the psalm was composed in honor of David's victory over Goliath; the Syriac version even attributes it to the occasion of David's slaying of Asaph, the brother of Goliath. These additions to the simple inscription **A psalm of David,** however, are highly unreliable.

As other psalms in this group (Psalms 138-145) ascribed to David, this one gives the appearance of a compilation. The majority of modern commentators are agreed that the psalm is not Davidic in origin, but rather a collection of Davidic thoughts from previous psalms. Although Psalm 18 appears to be the most closely aligned with this one, many quotations from 8; 33; 102-104 are also clearly discernible. One may compare verses 1 and 2 with 18:2, 34, 36-37; verses 5-8 with 18:9, 14-16, 44-45; and verse 10 with 18:50.

A satellite critical problem relates to verses 12-15. These verses differ completely from the first eleven verses of Psalm 144. Again, most commentators today view the first eleven verses as a collection of Davidic sayings, to which a later psalmist added the last four verses. Perowne says, "It is hardly probable, however, that this concluding portion is the work of the Poet who compiled the rest of the Psalm: it is more probable that he has here transcribed a fragment of some ancient Poem, in which were portrayed the happiness and prosperity of the nation in its brightest days,—under David, it may have been, or at the beginning of the reign of Solomon." Although Perowne holds that the latter portion of the psalm is "plainly a fragment," nonetheless in a footnote he must admit, "Yet in all MSS. and editions and versions, ancient and modern, it is joined to the first part as one Psalm." It must be remembered, however, that David characteristically is given to sudden transitions in his writing. This may account for the difference in subject matter in verses 12-15. Also, we must remember that the use of Davidic material in verses 1-11 is equally as strong an argument for Davidic authorship as it is for a later compiler. Therefore, the accuracy of the superscription is assumed, and we agree with Schmidt who holds that we have here *ein originales Kunstwerk,* "an original work of art."

144:1-2. Blessed be the LORD my strength (lit., my rock, Heb *tsūr*). Here the word **blessed,** as in 5:12; 18:46; 28:6; etc., is a term of benediction. He does not simply ascribe blessing to the gods, but to Jehovah, the Lord God of Israel who **teacheth my hands to war, and my fingers to fight.** Probably, the immediate reference here is to the use of a bow, the hands holding the weapon and the fingers drawing the string. But Jehovah is far more to the psalmist than his military mentor. By using multiplied metaphors he describes the Lord God as his

PSALM 144

BLESSED *be* the LORD my strength, which teacheth my hands to war, *and* my fingers to fight:

2 My goodness, and my fortress; my high tower, and my deliverer; my shield, and *he* in whom I trust; who subdueth my people under me.

3 LORD, what *is* man, that thou takest knowledge of him! *or* the son of man, that thou makest account of him!
4 Man is like to vanity: his days *are* as a shadow that passeth away.

5 Bow thy heavens, O LORD, and come down: touch the mountains, and they shall smoke.
6 Cast forth lightning, and scatter them: shoot out thine arrows, and destroy them.

7 Send thine hand from above; rid me, and deliver me out of great waters, from the hand of strange children;
8 Whose mouth speaketh vanity, and their right hand *is* a right hand of falsehood.

9 I will sing a new song unto thee, O God: upon a psaltery *and* an instrument of ten strings will I sing praises unto thee.
10 *It is he* that giveth salvation unto kings: who delivereth David his servant from the hurtful sword.

11 Rid me, and deliver me from the hand of strange children, whose mouth speaketh vanity, and their right hand *is* a right hand of falsehood:

goodness . . . fortress . . . high tower . . . deliverer . . . shield. Although each of these metaphors is interesting, none is more interesting than that of the fortress. David uses a unique word (Heb *metsūdah*), which is translated hold in I Samuel 24:22 and I Chronicles 12:8. Many scholars believe that when David took flight from King Saul his men and he sought safety at the fortress of Masada, the hold. Masada is located about two and one-half miles from the western shore of the Dead Sea and is a plateau imposingly rising about thirteen hundred feet from the valley below it. In the mind of the psalmist, no better physical fortress could be conjured up to depict the strength of Jehovah in his behalf.

3-4. LORD, what is man, that thou takest knowledge of him! (cf. 8:4; Job 7:14-18). Why would the glorious God take note of minute man? Or the son of man, that thou makest account of him! The son of man here is not a designation for the Lord Jesus, as it occurs elsewhere in the Scriptures. Son of man (Heb *ben-'enōsh*) indicates one weaker than man himself, i.e., not made of God as man is but made of woman as the son of man is. Man is like to vanity (lit., to a breath, cf. 39:5; 62:9). Man is like nothing at all, just a puff of air. His days are as a shadow that passeth away (cf. 102:11; 109:23). His life is but a shadow, a vague resemblance of existence.

5-6. Bow thy heavens, O LORD, and come down. Here, the psalmist's prayer changes from praise to invocation. Having ascribed blessedness unto Jehovah, he now invokes the aid of Jehovah. Taking his metaphor from 18:9, the psalmist asks Jehovah to extend Himself from the heavens and come down to the aid of man. "This was never so remarkably fulfilled as in the incarnation of Jesus Christ, when heaven and earth were, as it were, brought together. . . . But this will be more remarkably filled still by Christ's second coming, when He will indeed bring all heaven down with Him—viz. all the inhabitants of heaven"—Jonathan Edwards.

Touch the mountains, and they shall smoke. Here is an invocation for God to do what He had done at Sinai (cf. 18:7-14; Ex 19:16, 18; Deut 4:11). Cast forth lightning . . . shoot out thine arrows. The psalmist understands even the very wonders of nature to be the divine artillery of heaven. Simply, at the word of God the enemy shall be put to flight.

7-8. Send thine hand from above . . . deliver me out of great waters, a common metaphor in the Psalms for danger or peril. Rid me . . . from the hand of strange children (lit., sons of strangers). "He calls them strangers, not in respect of generic origin, but character and disposition"—John Calvin. David wants rid of those foes whose mouth speaketh vanity (cf. 18:45) and their right hand is a right hand of falsehood. The right hand was always lifted in taking a solemn oath (cf. Ezk 20:15); these strange children have no intent in keeping their oaths.

9-10. I will sing a new song unto thee, O God. Here, the psalmist returns to his theme of praising God (cf. vss. 1-4). With renewed vigor he will sing praises to the Lord, not just the old songs again but entirely new songs of praise. Upon a psaltery and an instrument of ten strings. As the strange children spoke with a mouth of vanity and raised their right hand in a vain oath, the psalmist will distinguish himself by speaking with a mouth of praise and employing his hands in praise toward the Lord. His reason is clear: It is he that giveth salvation unto kings, a sacrosanctness and a divine preservation, who delivereth David his servant from the hurtful sword.

11. Rid me, and deliver me appears almost as a refrain as it is found similarly in verses 7-8. There is sufficient reason for David's prayer for riddance from the wicked and for gracious presence of Jehovah. If the wicked are removed from the life of Israel and Jehovah's presence fills that life, the consequences are all blessed.

12 That our sons *may be* as plants grown up in their youth; *that* our daughters *may be* as corner stones, polished *after* the similitude of a palace:

13 *That* our garners *may be* full, affording all manner of store: *that* our sheep may bring forth thousands and ten thousands in our streets.

14 *That* our oxen *may be* strong to labour; *that there be* no breaking in, nor going out; *that there be* no complaining in our streets.

12-14. David now enumerates some of those consequences: (1) **That our sons may be as plants grown up in their youth** (lit., grown large). Without wickedness, the young men will be like green plants, grown up, healthy, strong, and beautiful (cf. 115:14-15; 127:4-5; 128:3). (2) **That our daughters may be as corner stones, polished after the similitude of a palace.** Henry observes, "Thy daughter's families are united and connected to their mutual strength, as the parts of a building are by a corner stone; and when they are graceful and beautiful both in body and mind, they are then polished after the similitude of a nice and curious structure." The daughters are the "sculptured angles, and ornament, of a palace". (3) **That our garners may be full,** the storage bins of Israel filled to capacity with **all manner of store.** (4) **That our sheep may bring forth thousands and ten thousands in our streets** (lit., in our fields). The word rendered **streets** (Heb *chûts*) refers to open places, rather than within houses. It is translated "fields" in Job 5:10 and Proverbs 8:26. (5) **That our oxen may be strong to labor,** healthy and fit to bear the heavy burden of an abundant harvest (cf. I Chr 12:40). (6) **That there be no breaking in, nor going out,** no breach in the walls which would invite marauders and no removal of the population into captivity by forced emigration. (7) **That there be no complaining in our streets.** The word **complaining** does not occur elsewhere in the Psalter. But this is clearly a prayer that there be no cry of sorrow (cf. Isa 24:11; Jer 14:2; 46:12) in our open places, i.e., the places where the people gathered for assembly near the gate of the city (cf. II Chr 32:6; Neh 8:1).

This sevenfold blessing which results from being rid of and delivered from the **strange children** (vs. 11) is fully described in the conclusion of the next verse.

15 Happy *is that* people, that is in such a case: *yea*, happy *is that* people, whose God *is* the Lord.

15. **Happy is that people, whose God is the Lord.** There is a repetition of **happy** in this verse. The first part of the text relates to temporal blessings that come from being rid of **the strange children.** The second half of the text relates to the spiritual blessings that come to those who, having been rid of the **strange children,** recognize that **God is the Lord** and Jehovah is truly God. Israel's prosperity, as well as that of all the faithful, depends entirely on the faithfulness of Jehovah.

MM. The Crown Jewel of Praise. 145:1-21.

THEME: David's alphabetical hymn of praise to the glory and greatness of God.

Psalm 145 is perhaps the richest selection in the Psalter. It has been appropriately called "The *Te Deum* of the Old Testament," "This exquisite Psalm," "A magnificent ode of praise," and other equally fitting plaudits to its beauty and brilliance. It is the last of the psalms ascribed to David and is the first of the final group of psalms (Psalm 145-150) in the Psalter. This psalm alone bears the title *tehilah*, meaning "a Praise," a word that in the plural is given to the whole Psalter (Heb *tehilīm*). Psalm 145 is the capstone of all the acrostic, or alphabetic, psalms (see also 9-10; 25; 34; 37; 111-112; 119). Like four other acrostic psalms (9-10; 25; 34), this one is incomplete: the Hebrew alphabet having twenty-two letters, only twenty-one verses appearing in this psalm. The letter *nūn* is omitted, but the LXX attempts to restore this "missing" verse with dubious effort. Both the Septuagint and the Vulgate add the following at the *nūn:* "The Lord is faithful in all his words; and holy in all His works." Since, however, the latter part of this addition is taken from verse 17, and since no other ancient versions except the Syriac and those which follow the LXX recognize this addition, it is not included in modern translations of the Psalms.

Although there seems to be little reason to question Davidic authorship, many scholars do question it. Even Perowne says, "There can in this case be no doubt that the inscription is not to

PSALM 145

I WILL extol thee, my God, O king; and
I will bless thy name for ever and ever.
2 Every day will I bless thee; and I
will praise thy name for ever and ever.

3 Great *is* the LORD, and greatly to be
praised; and his greatness *is* unsearchable.

4 One generation shall praise thy
works to another, and shall declare thy
mighty acts.

5 I will speak of the glorious honour
of thy majesty, and of thy wondrous
works.

6 And *men* shall speak of the might of
thy terrible acts: and I will declare thy
greatness.

7 They shall abundantly utter the
memory of thy great goodness, and shall
sing of thy righteousness.

8 The LORD *is* gracious, and full of
compassion; slow to anger, and of
great mercy.

9 The LORD *is* good to all: and his tender mercies *are* over all his works.

10 All thy works shall praise thee, O
LORD; and thy saints shall bless thee.

11 They shall speak of the glory of thy
kingdom, and talk of thy power;

12 To make known to the sons of men
his mighty acts, and the glorious majesty of his kingdom.

13 Thy kingdom *is* an everlasting
kingdom, and thy dominion *endureth*
throughout all generations.

be trusted." While it is true that there is no known historic
occasion to which this psalm can be attributed, nonetheless it
bears the marks of Davidic authorship. The Aramaic words that
are said to prove a late date for this psalm are noted; nonetheless, these so-called Aramaisms fall far short of being convincing.

145:1-2. I will extol thee, my God, O King. David, who was
God's choice for king, extolled God as his king. How wonderful
it is when the king on earth recognizes that he is but a subregent
of the king of earth. **Every day will I bless thee,** an emphatic
repetition of his previous promise to **bless thy name for ever
and ever.** To bless the name of God is to praise Him, and that he
promises as well **for ever and ever.**

3-4. Great is the LORD, and greatly to be praised (cf. 48:1;
96:4). **His greatness is unsearchable** (lit., of His greatness
there is no search, cf. Rom 11:33). So great is Jehovah that men
cannot begin to search His greatness, (cf. Job 5:9; 9:10; Prov
25:3) where the same words are used for **unsearchable** (Heb *'ēn
cheqer*). God's plan for the propagation of our knowledge of the
unsearchable greatness of Jehovah is that **One generation shall
praise thy works to another, and shall declare thy mighty acts.**

**5-7. I will speak of the glorious honor of thy majesty, and of
thy wondrous works.** It is very fitting that the king should
speak of the adorable glory of the majesty of the King of Kings.
David dare not hand the worship of God to others or relegate it
to any lesser subject than the king himself. The **majesty** and
wondrous works of Jehovah are worthy of the highest praise.
Some of these works are the **terrible acts,** awesome acts, which
show both God's wrath and His grace. David commits, **I will
declare thy greatness,** an attribute of God that is found everywhere in all His works.

Personally, the psalmist has now made a fivefold promise to
Jehovah: (1) **I will extol thee** (vs. 1); (2) **Every day will I bless
thee** (vs. 2); (3) **I will praise thy name for ever and ever** (vs. 2);
(4) **I will speak of the glorious honor of thy majesty** (vs. 5); and
(5) **I will declare thy greatness** (vs. 6). To this personal resolve
he adds, that all men **shall abundantly utter the memory of thy
great goodness, and shall sing of thy righteousness.** The imputed righteousness of Jesus Christ that we enjoy as believers is
perhaps the most worthy subject of all about which we may sing.
Therefore, let us praise His **great goodness** and **righteousness.**

**8-10. The LORD is gracious, and full of compassion; slow
to anger, and of great mercy.** What a quartet of attributes.
Similar notes of praise to Jehovah are recorded in 86:5, 15;
103:8; Exodus 34:6-7; Numbers 14:18. It is the graciousness of
Jehovah that leads Him to be **full of compassion.** "In God there
is no passion, only compassion"—Richard Rothe (1799-1867).
This compassion leads Him to be **slow to anger, and of great
mercy.** With such attributes it is little wonder that **The LORD is
good to all: and his tender mercies are over all his works.** The
Lord makes the sun to rise on the evil as well as the good, and
He sends rain upon the just as well as the unjust (cf. Mt 5:45).
**All thy works shall praise thee, O LORD; and thy saints shall
bless thee.** Both God's created realm (cf. 148:2-13) and the
realm of those ones devoted to His service recognized the complete mercy that underlies all the works of God. Truly, He is a
great God.

11-13. Speaking generally about the mercies of God that
underlie all His works, the psalmist's mind is naturally drawn to
some of those things that best indicate the greatness of God's
mercy. The first to which he addresses himself is the kingdom of
God. All the world **shall speak of the glory of thy kingdom, and
talk of thy power.** And why not? God's kingdom **is an everlasting kingdom** (cf. 146:10; Dan 2:44; 4:3, 34; I Tim 1:17) **and thy
dominion endureth throughout all generations.** This customary phrase (cf. 33:11; 45:17; 49:11; 61:6; etc.) is used to contrast

14 The LORD upholdeth all that fall, and raiseth up all *those that be* bowed down.

15 The eyes of all wait upon thee; and thou givest them their meat in due season.

16 Thou openest thine hand, and satisfiest the desire of every living thing.

17 The LORD *is* righteous in all his ways, and holy in all his works.

18 The LORD *is* nigh unto all them that call upon him, to all that call upon him in truth.

19 He will fulfil the desire of them that fear him: he also will hear their cry, and will save them.

20 The LORD preserveth all them that love him: but all the wicked will he destroy.

21 My mouth shall speak the praise of the LORD: and let all flesh bless his holy name for ever and ever.

the kingdom of men, which one day shall cease, with the kingdom of God, which is everlasting. It is not men's kingdoms about which **the sons of men** will make known **mighty acts,** but of **the glorious majesty of his kingdom.**

14-17. A second subject about which the saints of the Lord shall bless Jehovah is that **The LORD upholdeth all that fall, and raiseth up all those that be bowed down.** Those **that fall** (Heb *nōpelīm*) are those that are too weak to keep themselves stable. They must rely on someone greater than themselves. The gracious God is always there for us to rely upon. He not only lifts us up when we fall, but he holds us up when we are **bowed down** (cf. 146:8). How wonderful it is to know that the Lord who reigns in glorious majesty is not so far above us that He cannot condescend to lift us up and hold us up when we fall. Those who are despondent and discouraged can find encouragement in the God of all comfort (II Cor 1:3-4). **The LORD is righteous in all his ways, and holy in all his works.** Both the ways and works of God are worthy of our praise. It is God's way to give us all that we need, and it is for this reason that He gives us **meat in due season** (cf. 104:21, 27; 136:25; 147:9). It is through His righteousness that He opens His hand and satisfies **the desire of every living thing.** Only God can be the ultimate satisfaction for His creation.

18-20. Finally, a third reason for praising the Lord is enumerated by the psalmist. **The LORD is nigh unto all them that call upon him** (cf. 34:18; 46:1; 119:151; Deut 4:7; etc.) **to all that call upon him in truth.** Those who offer their prayers in genuine faith know that the Lord is never too busy to hear them, nor in His will to answer them. "Oppressions and afflictions make man cry, and cries and supplications make God hear"— John Calvin. **He also will hear their cry, and will save them,** fulfilling their desires and preserving **all them that love him** (cf. 31:23; 97:10). When we are in need, our responsibility is to call upon the Lord, to fear Him, and to love Him. In turn, God promises to be near us, to fulfill our desires, to hear our cries, to save us, and to preserve us. However, such is not the case with the wicked; for **all the wicked will he destroy.** The severity of God is always contrasted with His goodness. In order to maintain His righteousness, God must deal with the wicked in their wickedness. The verb **destroy** (Heb *shamad*) means to ruin or exterminate. God will never tolerate wickedness; He will always exterminate it (cf. Deut 2:22; Amos 2:4).

21. **My mouth shall speak the praise of the LORD.** This psalm of praise ends as it began (cf. vss. 1-2). The psalmist will not be silent, but will praise the name of Jehovah forever. **Let all flesh bless his holy name for ever and ever.** No one has a monopoly on the praise of the Lord God. **All flesh** indicates that all of the created beings of God are designed to reflect praise to Him. When we do not reflect praise to the name of His holiness, we fail to accomplish the purpose for our existence.

NN. A Psalm of Trust. 146:1-10.

THEME: *A call for men to put their trust in God, rather than in princes.*

The last five psalms end the Psalter with a cluster of Hallelujah psalms. In addition to Psalms 113-118, Psalms 146-150 constitute a Hallel in the Jewish Talmudic tradition. None of these psalms has a superscription, but the majority of commentators today understand them to be of late origin. The Syriac, Arabic, Septuagint, and Vulgate all ascribe the Psalms to Haggai and Zechariah, inscriptions that are felt to embody a true tradition by Tholuck, Hengstenberg, Alexander, Perowne, Leupold, and others. Some of the earlier commentators, Calvin, Patrick, Henry, Scott, and Plumer, etc., nevertheless hold to Davidic authorship of at least some of these psalms.

Since many of the psalms in the Psalter have depicted life in

PSALM 146

PRAISE ye the LORD. Praise the LORD, O my soul.

2 While I live will I praise the LORD: I will sing praises unto my God while I have any being.

3 Put not your trust in princes, *nor* in the son of man, in whom *there is* no help.

4 His breath goeth forth, he returneth to his earth; in that very day his thoughts perish.

5 Happy *is he* that *hath* the God of Jacob for his help, whose hope *is* in the LORD his God:

6 Which made heaven, and earth, the sea, and all that therein *is:* which keepeth truth for ever:

7 Which executeth judgment for the oppressed: which giveth food to the hungry. The LORD looseth the prisoners:

8 The LORD openeth *the eyes of* the blind: the LORD raiseth them that are bowed down: the LORD loveth the righteous:

9 The LORD preserveth the strangers; he relieveth the fatherless and widow: but the way of the wicked he turneth upside down.

the depths of despair, the psalmist being falsely accused and greatly abused by the enemy, it is a joy to find a Psalter being completed with psalms wholly dedicated to the praise of the Lord God Jehovah. In fact, addressing this group of Hallelujah psalms with which the Psalter closes, Spurgeon says, "The rest of our journey lies through the Delectable Mountains. All is praise to the close of the book. The key is high-pitched; the music is upon the high-sounding cymbals. Oh for a heart full of joyful gratitude, that we may run, and leap, and glorify God, even as these Psalms do."

146:1-2. Praise ye the LORD (cf. 111:1). **Praise the LORD, O my soul** (cf. 103:1-2; 104:1). What the psalmist preached, he practiced. He would not dare call upon us to praise the Lord without himself having first done so. He resolves **While I live will I praise the LORD.** Life as we know it now does not go on forever. It is our moral duty to praise God while we have life, for no man shall praise Him from the grave.

3-4. Put not your trust in princes (cf. 118:9). Should this psalm have been written by David, this warning comes from a prince himself. But regardless, Israel was frequently guilty of trusting those nations around her (i.e., Egypt, Isa 30:2; 36:6; or Assyria, II Kgs 16:7) instead of trusting God. To look to mankind for help is foolish indeed, for **His breath goeth forth, he returneth to his earth.** Men are untrustworthy; for when they die, as we all must, their souls return to the God who breathed life into them initially, and their bodies to the dust of the ground out of which they were created (cf. Gen 2:7). It is appointed unto man once to die, and **in that very day his thoughts perish.** As the Puritan, Thomas Watson, observed, "At death a man sees all those thoughts which were not spent on God to be fruitless. All worldly, vain thoughts, in the day of death perish and come to nothing. What good will the whole globe of the world do at such a time?"

5-7. In delightful contrast to the one who puts his trust in princes or the son of man, these verses depict the joy that comes from trusting in God. **Happy is he that hath the God of Jacob for his help, whose hope is in the LORD his God.** The **God of Jacob** is a favorite expression of the latter psalms, where it appears to supersede the phrase, the God of Israel (cf. 76:6; 81:1, 4; 84:8; 94:7; 114:7; 132:2, 5; etc.). He is the God who **made heaven, and earth, the sea, and all that therein is,** i.e., He is the creator God (cf. Jn 1; Col 1; Heb 1). But more than that, He is a God who keeps His promises and **executeth judgment for the oppressed . . . giveth food to the hungry . . . looseth the prisoners.** God is swift to execute perfect judgment (cf. 103:6). He is just as swift to see to the welfare of those who are hungry (cf. 145:15-16). And He is equally swift to loose prisoners from dungeons (cf. Jeremiah from his dungeon, Jer 37:16-17; Daniel from his lions' den, Dan 6:23; or Peter from the prison, Acts 12:7-10). He is a God worthy of all praise.

8-9. LORD openeth the eyes of the blind . . . raiseth them that are bowed down . . . loveth the righteous. When the psalmist says that God opens the eyes of the blind, he means that literally and figuratively. God opens physically blinded eyes (cf. Deut 28:28-29; Job 12:25; Isa 59:9-10), and He opens spiritually blinded eyes (cf. Isa 29:18; 42:7, 18; 43:8). On numerous occasions in the New Testament, the Lord Jesus both gave sight to the physically blind and discernment to the spiritually blind. Also, Jehovah and Jesus console the bereaved, and give solace to despondent, bringing comfort to those who despair.

The LORD preserveth the strangers; he relieveth the fatherless and widow. God's goodness leads Him to protect those who cannot protect themselves. Strangers, the fatherless, and widows are the constant object of God's providential care (cf. 82:3; Ex 22:21-22; Lev 19:33-34; Deut 10:18; Job 29:12; Jer 7:6; etc.). **But the way of the wicked he turneth upside down**

10 The LORD shall reign for ever, *even* thy God, O Zion, unto all generations. Praise ye the LORD.

PSALM 147

PRAISE ye the LORD: for *it is* good to sing praises unto our God; for *it is* pleasant; *and* praise is comely.

2 The LORD doth build up Jerusalem: he gathereth together the outcasts of Israel.
3 He healeth the broken in heart, and bindeth up their wounds.
4 He telleth the number of the stars; he calleth them all by *their* names.

5 Great *is* our Lord, and of great power: his understanding *is* infinite.
6 The LORD lifteth up the meek: he casteth the wicked down to the ground.

(cf. 145:20; Isa 1:28). God's divine protection for His saints stems from the same character that leads Him to overturn the plans and schemes of the wicked. The words **turneth upside down** (Heb *'awat*) mean to bend or curve, to make crooked or distort. This same word is applied to the conduct of the wicked in 119:78. As they have made their paths perverse, God will distort and overturn their evil plans. No one seeks to destroy the fatherless or widow without coming under the condemnation of God's wrath.

10. The LORD shall reign for ever, even thy God, O Zion, unto all generations. This concluding verse is both a statement and a prayer. Jehovah is king, and of His kingdom there shall be no end. He is never overthrown; He does not abdicate; He does not die in office. He cannot give up His crown, neither can He lose it. This thought in itself is enough to make the psalmist shout, **Praise ye the LORD.**

OO. Great Is the Lord. 147:1-20.

THEME: *A psalm of praise to Jehovah, the God of Zion.*

Although there are a few very respectful writers who ascribe this psalm to David, making it a prophecy, generally it is assigned to the time of the dedication of the city wall (Neh 12:27-43) when the gates and bars were erected for the security and prosperity of the city (cf. vs. 13; Neh 7:1-3). The events of verse 2 may well be an allusion to this event. The object of praise in this psalm is the God of Israel and the God of nature whose name occurred herein as *Yahweh, Yah, 'Elōhīm,* and *'Adōnay.* The closeness of the God of Israel to nature is seen in verses 4, 8-9, 14, 16-18.

The psalm appears to divide itself into three stanzas or strophes, each beginning with a note of praise (vss. 1-6; vss. 7-11; vss. 12-20). The LXX, however, offers verses 12-20 as a separate psalm, thus evening the count of psalms which had departed from the Hebrew when the LXX combined Psalms 9 and 10. But this "very blessed Psalm of thanksgiving," as Luther calls it, appears to be a unified whole, occurring in three stanzas.

147:1. Praise ye the LORD: for it is good to sing praises unto our God (cf. 92:1); **for it is pleasant** (135:3) **and praise is comely,** or suitable for such a God. It is good to sing praises unto God for it is right; it is right because Jehovah is a God worth praising, as the psalmist will now substantiate.

2-4. These verses seem to connect the greatness of God to the rebuilding of the walls of Jerusalem and to His overall superintendence of nature. God is worth our praise because **The LORD doth build up Jerusalem,** and because **he gathereth together the outcasts of Israel.** During the course of these rebuilding events, God **healeth the broken in heart, and bindeth up their wounds.** God is not only the rebuilder of walls, but the healer of hearts as well.

But in addition to that, Jehovah is so great that **He telleth the number of the stars; he calleth them all by their names** (cf. Job 9:9; Isa 40:26). As in the last decade of the twentieth century man has begun to reach out to the stars, finite man must remember that God is so intimately aware of His creation that he knows those stars by name. Assigning names to the stars is not done frivolously, but as a sign of dominion. Each of the heavenly bodies are under the sovereignty of God. ". . . the stars in their courses fought against Sisera" (Jud 5:20); at the permission of God ". . . the sun stood still . . ." to give Josuha a complete victory (Josh 10:12). God not only intimately knows His stellar creation, He rules in that creation as well.

5-6. No wonder the psalmist must say, **Great is our LORD, and of great power: his understanding is infinite.** Jehovah is at once omnipotent and omniscient. Of His understanding there is no number; God is incomprehensible. Yet, His works are not

7 Sing unto the LORD with thanksgiving; sing praise upon the harp unto our God:
8 Who covereth the heaven with clouds, who prepareth rain for the earth, who maketh grass to grow upon the mountains.
9 He giveth to the beast his food, *and* to the young ravens which cry.

10 He delighteth not in the strength of the horse: he taketh not pleasure in the legs of a man.
11 The LORD taketh pleasure in them that fear him, in those that hope in his mercy.

12 Praise the LORD, O Jerusalem; praise thy God, O Zion.

13 For he hath strengthened the bars of thy gates; he hath blessed thy children within thee.
14 He maketh peace *in* thy borders, *and* filleth thee with the finest of the wheat.

15 He sendeth forth his commandment *upon* earth: his word runneth very swiftly.
16 He giveth snow like wool: he scattereth the hoarfrost like ashes.
17 He casteth forth his ice like morsels: who can stand before his cold?
18 He sendeth out his word, and melteth them: he causeth his wind to blow, *and* the waters flow.

incomprehensible; for **The LORD lifteth up the meek** (cf. 145:14; 146:8), and **he casteth the wicked down to the ground** (cf. 146:9). God reverses the order of nature. **The meek,** who are cast down in this life, are raised up by God. **The wicked,** who raise themselves in this life, are cast down to the ground by God. He is not only omniscient and omnipotent, He is omnirighteous as well.

7-9. Again, referring to nature, the psalmist begs that we sing to the God **who covereth the heaven with clouds, who prepareth rain for the earth** (cf. 104:13; Job 38:25-41), **who maketh grass to grow upon the mountains.** Here again, God's providence in nature is seen. Clouds are not caused by an act of mother nature or by accident, but they are produced by God Himself. From the clouds He prepares rain so that the grass may grow upon the mountains. But the cycle does not end there; for God **giveth to the beast his food,** a reference to the grass that grows upon the mountains, **and to the young ravens which cry.** Even those of God's creation which do not contribute directly to man's benefit receive the watchful care of Jehovah.

10-11. These verses do not mean to indicate that God takes no glory in horses or men. Obviously, He does; the God who is big enough to know every star by name is also small enough to know each of us by name. **He delighteth not in the strength of the horse: he taketh not pleasure in the legs of a man.** These two clauses obviously are intended to describe the cavalry and infantry, those forces that constitute the military strength of nations. Warriors trust in the cavalries; monarchs in their infantries.

God is not interested in the physical and material might of nations. Rather, **The Lord taketh pleasure in them that fear him, in those that hope in his mercy.** God takes little account of those nations who build up mighty arsenals of weapons and yet, do not fear God or find their hope in His mercy. What an indictment this is on the military super powers of the world who have forgotten God in their quest for superiority.

12. **Praise the LORD, O Jerusalem; praise thy God, O Zion.** These exhortations to praise, like those of verse 1 and verse 7, are directed specifically toward the inhabitants of Jerusalem. They appear to be a reminder, as Jerusalem is rebuilt, that God is not interested in Israel's military might nearly as much as He is interested in her fear and reverence.

13-14. Speaking of Jerusalem, the psalmist notes that God **hath strengthened the bars of thy gates,** the strong wooden beams that were positioned on either side of the city gates (cf. Neh 3:3, 6, 13-15; 7:3). **He hath blessed thy children within thee.** External security is worthless without internal happiness. **He maketh peace in thy borders.** With the completion of the walls of Jerusalem, the troubles caused by Sanballat, Tobiah, and Geshem came to an end. Israel began to enjoy a period of relative peace and tranquility. How ironic that this same city today is the perennial eye of the Middle East hurricane. Jehovah also **filleth thee with the finest of the wheat** (lit., with the fat of the wheat). For the prosperity of Nehemiah's times see Nehemiah 10:28-39; 12:44-47; 13:12-15. Peace is always attended with plenty.

15-18. So authoritative are the commandments of God **upon earth** that when He gives a command to nature, **his word runneth very swiftly** and is always obeyed. Some of those commands follow. **He giveth snow like wool.** Little in the realm of nature can compare to the loveliness of new fallen snow. Though rare in most parts of Palestine, snow does occasionally fall, even in Jerusalem. When God scatters His snow, it falls in flakes like fleecy wool. **He scattereth the hoar frost like ashes.** As a mighty volcano belches out its ashes that cover the ground, or as the towering inferno of a forest fire litters the hills with ash, so too it is God who scatters the frost upon the ground each morning. **He casteth forth his ice like morsels,** literally, like crumbs, as a man would scatter bread crumbs to feed the birds. A penetrating question: **Who can stand before his cold?** One cannot continue his normal life style in the dead of winter without taking appropriate measures to keep warm. But God will help us in our effort, for **He sendeth out his word, and melteth them** (vs. 15). All God must do is speak His Word, and the ice is melted. **He causeth his wind to blow, and the waters flow.** Even the seasons are controlled by God. He brings ice and snow, and then the warm spring winds which cause the ice to melt and the water to flow again. How great is this God of nature!

19 He sheweth his word unto Jacob, his statutes and his judgments unto Israel.

20 He hath not dealt so with any nation: and as for his judgments, they have not known them. Praise ye the LORD.

19-20. As if to show that the purpose of this psalm is to praise the God of Israel and the God of Nature, the psalmist now concludes his ode by praising the God of Israel. **He showeth his word unto Jacob, his statutes and his judgments unto Israel.** The God who is the creator God is also the revealer God. He has most specifically revealed Himself to His chosen nation, Israel. **He hath not dealt so with any nation** as He has with His most favorite nation. The heathen nations had not know God's **judgments.** Since ". . . unto whomsoever much is given, of him shall much be required . . ." (Lk 12:48), and since Israel was the object of special favor and had an intimate knowledge of God, Jehovah requires of them, **Praise ye the LORD.** "God deals in a singular way of mercy with His people, and therefore expects singular praises from His people"—Joseph Alleine (1634-1668). Those who know God best ought to praise Him most.

PP. The Creation Chorus. 148:1-14.

THEME: A joyful song in which all of God's creation is invited to praise Him.

Spurgeon describes this psalm as "one indivisible," and so it is. He says, "it is a Psalm of nature and of grace. As a flash of lightning flames through space, and enwraps both heaven and earth in one vestment of glory, so doth the adoration of the Lord in the psalm light up all the universe and cause to glow the radiance of praise."

It is unknown who the author of the psalm is. While Patrick ascribes it to David, few others do. There seems to be little reason for ascribing it to Haggai and Zechariah, as the Septuagint does. The question of authorship matters little. More important is the beauty of the psalm. As Henry notes, this psalm is "a most solemn and earnest call to all creatures, according to their capacity, to praise their Creator, and to show forth His eternal power and Godhead." The psalm reflects the unified view of nature, as it is a call to all of God's creation to praise Him. This includes both animate and inanimate creation. One might ask when all of God's creation has praised Him, including the sun and moon, the stars, the hail, snow, mountains, and hills. To this most would answer that the psalm is poetic in nature and is not to be taken literally. Such may not be the case, however. Since all of creation was cursed with man's fall (Gen 3:15-24), all of creation ". . . was made subject to vanity . . ." and ". . . groaneth and travaileth in pain together until now" (Rom 8:20, 22). But the day will come when ". . . the creature itself also shall be delivered from this bondage of corruption into the glorious liberty of the children of God" (Rom 8:21). Thus, if this psalm is interpreted prophetically, the day will come when, ". . . every creature which is in heaven, and on the earth, and under the earth, and such as are in the sea, and all that are in them," will sing, "Blessing, and honor, and glory, and power, be unto him that sitteth upon the throne, and unto the Lamb for ever and ever" (Rev 5:13). This will only occur when ". . . The kingdoms of this world are become the kingdoms of our Lord, and of his Christ; and he shall reign for ever and ever" (Rev

PSALM 148

PRAISE ye the LORD. Praise ye the LORD from the heavens: praise him in the heights.

2 Praise ye him, all his angels: praise ye him, all his hosts.

3 Praise ye him, sun and moon: praise him, all ye stars of light.

4 Praise him, ye heavens of heavens, and ye waters that be above the heavens.

5 Let them praise the name of the LORD: for he commanded, and they were created.

6 He hath also stablished them for ever and ever: he hath made a decree which shall not pass.

7 Praise the LORD from the earth, ye dragons, and all deeps:

8 Fire, and hail; snow, and vapours; stormy wind fulfilling his word:

9 Mountains, and all hills; fruitful trees, and all cedars:

10 Beasts, and all cattle; creeping things, and flying fowl:

11 Kings of the earth, and all people; princes, and all judges of the earth:

12 Both young men, and maidens; old men, and children:

11:15). During the millennial reign of Jesus Christ on this earth, the prophecy of this psalm will be entirely fulfilled.

So blessed is Psalm 148 that it early was imitated by an interpolation in the LXX. The additions to Daniel 3, known as "the Song of the Three Holy Children," are in effect an expansion of this psalm. In addition, John Milton in his *Paradise Lost* (Book V, line 153 ff.) has imitated this psalm, elegantly placing it in the mouth of our first parents, Adam and Eve, as their morning hymn in the state of innocency. Many, too, have noted the similarities between Psalm 148 and The Hymn of Saint Francis of Assisi, who referred to the sun as our "honourable brother" and addresses the cricket as his "sister," inviting all of God's creation to praise him.

148:1-4. Praise ye the LORD from the heavens: praise him in the heights. The Puritan John Trapp notes that in framing the world, God began in the heavens and wrought downward; so in this exhortation to all creatures, the psalmist proceeds to praise the Lord from the heavens downward. Praise to God ought to begin in the most exalted regions of creation. That praise is not only to be **from** the heavens, but also in the heights. Jehovah is to be praised by **all his angels** (cf. 103:20-21) and **all his hosts**, those **ministers of his, that do his pleasure** (103:21). The angels praised God when they sang their *Gloria in Excelsis* at the Incarnation of Christ, and they ministered unto Him after His temptation and before His crucifixion. Again, the psalmist calls upon them to **Praise ye him.**

What the animate hosts of heaven must do, so must the inanimate. **Sun and moon . . . stars of light. . . . heavens of heavens, and ye waters that be above the heavens** are to praise the Lord. The joint rulers of day and night are to be paired in praise for Jehovah. They are joined by the **stars of light**, which twinkle their praises every night. Although Luther understood the **heavens of heavens** to mean all heavenly regions, it more properly corresponds to the phrase "the third heaven" in the New Testament. The highest heaven of heavens is to join the atmospheric heaven, represented by the **waters**, and the spatial heaven, represented by the **sun and moon**, in praising Jehovah. This is the psalmist's way of indicating that all three heavens must give praise to their Creator, and all bodies contained therein, both animate and inanimate.

5-6. Now the psalmist advances his reason for calling upon the heavens to praise the Lord: **For he commanded, and they were created** (Gen 1:3, 6, 9, 11, 14-15, etc.). All creation came into being at the express word of God (33:8). But not only did Jehovah command the creation, **He hath also stablished them for ever and ever** (cf. 89:37). The continued existence of all the celestial wonder is totally dependent upon the Creator who brought them into existence. **He hath made a decree which shall not pass** (cf. Gen 8:22; Jer 31:35-36; 33:25).

7-12. Verse 7 is a counterpart to verse 1. As the first six verses issue a call to the heights of heaven to praise Jehovah, the next six issue that same call to the inhabitants of earth. **Praise the LORD from the earth.** Included in the representative lists of those on earth who are called upon to praise Jehovah are the **dragons** (Heb *tanîn*), a word that may denote whales, sharks, or sea monsters of any kind (Job 30:29; Ezk 29:3), **fire, and hail**, the hot phenomenon of nature, and **snow, and vapor**, the cool phenomenon of nature. Next, the psalmist calls upon the mountains and all hills, those towering such as Hermon and those tapering such as Tabor, the **fruitful trees, and all cedars**, fruit trees and forest trees alike, to praise the Lord. In addition, all **beasts, and all cattle**, both fierce and tame animals, **creeping things** (cf. 104:25; Gen 1:24-25, 30), **and flying fowl** (lit., bird of wing), are to join in the song of praise. Man himself is not exempt, for the psalmist calls upon the **kings of the earth . . . princes, and all judges. . . . both young men, and maidens;**

13 Let them praise the name of the LORD: for his name alone is excellent; his glory *is* above the earth and heaven.
14 He also exalteth the horn of his people, the praise of all his saints; *even* of the children of Israel, a people near unto him. Praise ye the LORD.

old men, and children to join the creation chorus. Age, sex, or station in life should not be a deterrent to praising the Lord.

13-14. The psalmist's concluding remarks exhibit his burden throughout the psalm. **Let them praise the name of the LORD.** And for what reason? **For his name alone is excellent; his glory is above the earth and heaven** (cf. 8:1; 19:1; 57:5, 11; 63:2; 89:17; etc.). In all heaven and earth only Jehovah's name, which is representative of His person, is worthy of our praise. His glory is not simply above the earth, but above heaven as well. He is the ultimate end of all praise.

He also exalteth the horn of his people. He increases the glory and strength of those who praise Him. Most particularly, Jehovah has exalted **the children of Israel, a people near unto him,** a nearness that results from being the object of His choosing. God draws nigh to His peculiar people (69:18) and then draws them nigh unto Him (Jer 30:21). Although all of creation will be represented in the creation chorus, Israel, the apple of God's eye, will be prominently featured in that chorus. For this and all the other blessings of God the psalmist must conclude as he began with a call to **Praise ye the LORD.**

QQ. The Victory Psalm. 149:1-9.

THEME: A jubilant and exaltant psalm in celebration of victory.
Like the other psalms of this Hallel, Psalm 149 appears to fit best at a later date in Israel's history. Still, many good authors believe it not beyond the realm of possibility for David to have written this psalm. The question remains open.

Over the centuries this psalm has been misunderstood and misused. As Delitzsch correctly points out, it was by means of this psalm that Casper Sciopius in his *Clarion of the Sacred War* (*Classicum Belli Sacri*) inflamed the Roman Catholic princes to initiate the Thirty Years' War. So inflammatory was that work that it was said to have been written not with ink but with blood. It was also with this psalm that the Protestant Thomas Münzer initiated the War of the Peasant. Delitzsch cautions, "We see from these and other instances, that when in her interpretation of such a Psalm the church forgets the words of the Apostle, 'the weapons of our warfare are not carnal' (II Cor 10:4), she falls back upon the ground of the Old Testament . . . round which even the Jews themselves did not venture to maintain. . . . Therefore the Christian must transpose the letter of this Psalm into the spirit of the New Testament."

How are we to explain the militant attitude of this psalm? Leupold hypothesizes a situation in which the children of Israel have been granted great victory, but anticipate still future victories. At the same time, their existence is threatened by the enemies around them who would drive them into the sea. They pray to God that as they take up arms against their foes they would achieve additional victories. Then Leupold asks, "To be in such a situation and to hope to use arms successfully—is that blood thirstiness? Can nothing be said in defense of such an attitude? Was it an holy business when Joshua fought the Amalekites (Ex 17:11-13)? Or when Gideon took up the sword against the Midianites (Jud 7:20)? Or when Asa had to fight the Ethiopians (II Chr 14:10ff.)? Or when Nehemiah had the builders of the wall gird on their weapons as they built (Neh 4:16)? With these situations in mind, we shall feel reluctant to tribute to the persons here involved anything blood thirsty or unwholesome."

Yet, the New Testament church must still find application of this psalm for them as well. It is for this reason that many biblical scholars interpret this psalm prophetically. The ultimate victory to which the psalm looks must be understood messianically. Seen through the eyes of the New Testament, and with considerable theological hindsight, this psalm can never be in-

PSALM 149

PRAISE ye the LORD. Sing unto the LORD a new song, *and* his praise in the congregation of saints.
2 Let Israel rejoice in him that made him: let the children of Zion be joyful in their King.
3 Let them praise his name in the dance: let them sing praises unto him with the timbrel and harp.

terpreted as a twentieth-century call to arms against those who do not share our love for the Lord God.

149:1-3. Immediately after the call to **Praise ye the LORD,** the normal introduction of a hallelujah psalm, the author continues with a call to **Sing unto the LORD a new song.** For the Israelite the **new song** may well have been an account of his deliverance from captivity (cf. 33:3). The deliverance may even have been one of those under the leadership of Nehemiah (Neh 4:7-23; 6:2-16). But for the saint of today, the **new song** is of the release from eternal captivity, the captivity and penalty of sin. The new song is a song of salvation. As Augustine once said, "The old man hath an old song, the new man a new song. The Old Testament is an old song, the New Testament is a new song . . . Whoso loveth earthly things singeth an old song: let him that desireth to sing a new song love the things of eternity."

For the Lord God to receive our new song is pleasure to His ears. But for Him to receive **his praise in the congregation of saints** is like receiving a diamond-studded crown as opposed to a solitaire crown. Personal praise is sweet to God, but the praise of a congregation of saints is sweeter still. Therefore, **let Israel rejoice in him that made him** (cf. 95:6). The ground of Israel's praise is that they are **the children of Zion** and therefore ought to be **joyful in their King** (cf. Jud 8:23; I Sam 8:6-7; 10:19; 12:12; etc.). Israel was not to be joyful because of what their King had done for them, but to be joyful in their King. Our joy in God stems from the fact that He is God, not from what He can do for us.

Let them praise his name in the dance . . . with the timbrel and harp. In the life of early Israel dancing was one of the most expressive modes of religious joy (cf. Ex 15:20; II Sam 6:14-16). In the New Testament we are counseled to be ". . . admonishing one another in psalms and hymns and spititual songs, singing with grace in your hearts to the Lord" (Col 3:16). Nowhere are we told that dancing is to accompany that singing. The **timbrel** (Heb *tōp*) was employed by David in all the festivities of religion (cf. II Sam 6:5). Three kinds of such instrument existed in the Old Testament: one was round, another square or oblong, a third consisted of two squares separated by a bar. Each of them was beaten with the hand and was used as accompaniment to the **harp** (Heb *kinōr*), the stringed instrument upon which David was skilled (cf. I Sam 16:23; 18:10; 19:9).

4 For the LORD taketh pleasure in his people: he will beautify the meek with salvation.
5 Let the saints be joyful in glory: let them sing aloud upon their beds.
6 *Let* the high *praises* of God *be* in their mouth, and a two-edged sword in their hand;

4-6. For the LORD taketh pleasure in his people. What wonderful condescension is seen that the mighty Jehovah, the One who has given us a new song, would take pleasure in our praise of Him. Truly, He is the prime example of one who condescends to men of low estate. **He will beautify the meek with salvation.** The expression **the meek** (Heb *'anaw*) means those who are poor and afflicted. The term came to be applied to those who were merciful persons, those who would patiently submit to the chastisements of God and suffer for His sake.

The very mention of God's salvation is enough to cause **the saints** to be joyful and **sing aloud upon their beds.** Even confined by sickness, shut in, or during the loneliness of the midnight hours, saints of God know that they are not alone and are encouraged to **Let the high praises of God be in their mouth** (lit., in their throat, cf. Isa 58:1).

But the saints of God are not always depicted as languishing upon their beds during the midnight hours. Praise and power go hand in hand. They also are depicted with **a two-edged sword in their hand.** For the Israelites, this was a literal weapon. In Nehemiah's time they were used against a violent enemy (Neh 4:13, 16, 17-18). Sanballat, Tobiah, and Geshem were threatening the virtual destruction of the program for rebuilding Jerusalem's wall. For Israel the two-edged sword in their hand was literal and deadly.

It is no coincidence, however, that the book of Hebrews

describes the Word of God as ". . . quick, and powerful, and sharper than any two-edged sword . . ." (Heb 4:12). Today, converts are not made with a steel sword, but with the quickening power of the Word of God. We fight against principalities and powers; we fight in the power of God's Spirit. Metaphorically, for those who have a new song to sing, the song of redemption by the blood of Jesus Christ, the two-edged sword is to be used against the prince of the power of the air (see also Rev 19:12-15).

7 To execute vengeance upon the heathen, *and* punishments upon the people;
8 To bind their kings with chains, and their nobles with fetters of iron;
9 To execute upon them the judgment written: this honour have all his saints. Praise ye the LORD.

7-9. When the Israelites returned to Canaan, it was their responsibility to execute vengeance upon the heathen, and punishments upon the peoples. This was the righteous judgment of God upon a godless people. Israel was to bind their kings with chains, and their nobles with fetters of iron, even as Nebuchadnezzar had bound Zedekiah with fetters of brass (cf. II Kgs 25:7). All these victories for the Israelites will bring glory to God.

Although the New Testament saint cannot literally claim these promises for his own, nevertheless, one can see a prophecy herein. The prophets of the Old Testament foretold of the glorious conquests of the heathen world by the gospel. These conquests are by the sword of the Word, not by the sword of steel. They ultimately come when the living Word of God establishes His one thousand year reign upon this earth. At that time He will come to execute vengeance. . . . to bind their kings and to bring honor to all his saints (cf. Rev 19:11-21); and both Old and New Testament saints will be able to join together to say, Praise ye the LORD.

RR. The Grand Finale of Praise. 150:1-6.

THEME: *A most noble psalm; a fit conclusion to a most noble collection of psalms.*

It is of interest that the first and last psalms of the Psalter have but six verses. The first is a psalm of blessing, the last a psalm of praise. One can easily recognize the propriety of having this psalm serve as a termination of the entire collection; for no psalm rises more grandly from verse to verse, or comes to a conclusion in a nobler manner. Thirteen times in this short psalm the verb praise (Heb *halal*) is used. It is indeed a grand hymn of praise. Some have ascribed it to Ezra; others, not unreasonably believe David to be the author. Regardless, we have here a full-blown symphony of praise to *YAH*.

In his characteristic style, Maclaren notes, "The Psalm is more than an artistic close of the Psalter; it is a prophecy of the last result of the devout life, and in its unclouded sunniness, as well as in its universality, it proclaims the certain end of the weary years for the individual and for the world." As such, this is a psalm of great triumph.

PSALM 150
PRAISE ye the LORD. Praise God in his sanctuary: praise him in the firmament of his power.

150:1. Praise ye the LORD. To all who read this psalm, to all in heaven and all in earth, to all who are aware of the excellency of God's greatness, to all who have experienced His grace, to all who have been warmed by His love, this is an exhortation. Praise God in his sanctuary. This expression has been variously understood by scholars. The Vulgate renders it, "in His holy places." Luther, in his German version, translates it, "in His holiness." The Septuagint renders it, "in His holy ones." It is a phrase designed to indicate that God, the strong God, is to be praised in the holiness of His Temple, His tabernacle, His church, and in the bodies of those who are the temple of the Holy Spirit (I Cor 3:16). A holy God is to be worshiped in a holy place. But in addition, we are to praise him in the firmament of his power, that great expanse above us which shows His power and glory. This verse tells us who is to be praised; i.e., *YAH*, the strong God. It also tells us where He is to be praised.

2 Praise him for his mighty acts:

2. Praise him for his mighty acts, those acts of omnipotence in creation, redemption, and sovereignty. Praise him according

praise him according to his excellent greatness.

3 Praise him with the sound of the trumpet: praise him with the psaltery and harp.
4 Praise him with the timbrel and dance: praise him with stringed instruments and organs.
5 Praise him upon the loud cymbals: praise him upon the high sounding cymbals.

6 Let every thing that hath breath praise the LORD. Praise ye the LORD.

to his excellent greatness. Not only is God to be praised for His mighty acts, but He is to be praised as well for being Himself, excellent and great. It was through that excellent greatness that He brought the Israelites safely through the Red Sea (Ex 15). It was by that excellent greatness that Deborah and the Israelites were delivered from the host of Sisera (Jud 5). And it by that excellent greatness that we today are delivered from the prince of the power of the air (Eph 2:1-10). This verse tells us why God is to be praised.

3-5. These verses tell us how God is to be praised. They represent a full orchestra of instruments upon which we are to praise Him. They represent the wind, the strings, and the percussion instruments. Praise him with the sound of the trumpet (Heb shōpar), a wind instrument. Originally a cow's or ram's horn, the shōpar was employed in making announcements or calling the people together in a time of worship or war. The word itself in Hebrew means bright or clear, and thus was used as an instrument to give a clarion call for a special occasion. Praise him with the psaltery (Heb nēbel), a large portable harp. This instrument of ten strings was chiefly used in religious services and was struck with a plectrum or pick. The harp (Heb kinōr), which comes from the word meaning to twang, was the first musical instrument mentioned in the Bible (Gen 4:21).

Praise him with the timbrel (Heb tōp) a percussion instrument like a tambourine that was struck with the hand. Praise him with stringed instruments (Heb minīm), derived from a root word meaning "division" or "distribution." This instrument is also mentioned in 45:8; 68:23 and is simply an instrument of multiple strings. The organs (Heb 'ūgab) are simply, as the Targum renders it, pipes. They also were one of the first instruments mentioned in the Bible (Gen 4:21) and were probably instruments which consisted of a collection of reeds.

Praise him upon the loud cymbals (Heb tseltselīm), the clanging cymbals that give a clear but sharp sound. Praise him upon the high-sounding cymbals, apparently to be distinguished as finger-cymbals or castanets. This concludes the repertoire of instruments upon which the Lord is to be praised.

6. As we have been told who is to be praised, where God is to be praised, why God is to be praised, and how God is to be praised, now the last verse of this psalm, and indeed the last verse of the entire Psalter, is a joyous admonition simply to praise the Lord. Let everything that hath breath praise the LORD (lit., all breath or the whole of breath praise the Lord). Vocal joins instrumental in lifting up God's praises. Ultimately, the day will come when, ". . . every creature which is in heaven, and on the earth, and under the earth, and such as are in the sea, and all that are in them, heard I saying, Blessing, and honor, and glory, and power, be unto him that sitteth upon the throne, and unto the Lamb for ever and ever" (Rev 5:13). That will be the ultimate day of praise for the Lord Jesus Christ. But until that grand and glorious day, Praise ye the LORD.

BIBLIOGRAPHY

*Alexander, J. A. *The Psalms*. 3 vols. New York: Baker and Scribner, 1851.

Bonar, Andrew A. *Christ and His Church in the Book of Psalms*. Grand Rapids: Kregel Publications, 1978.

Calvin, John. *Commentary of the Book of Psalms*. Trans. by James Anderson. 5 vols. Grand Rapids: Eerdmans, 1949.

Cheyne, Thomas Kelly. *The Book of Psalms*. London: Kegan, Paul, 1888.

*Clarke, Arthur G. *Analytical Studies in the Psalms*. Kilmarnock: Ritchey, n.d.

*Delitzsch, Franz. *Biblical Commentary on the Psalms*. Trans. by Francis Bolton. 3 vols. Edinburgh: T. & T. Clark, 1880.

Gaebelein, Arno Clemens. *The Book of Psalms*. New York: Our Hope Publications, 1939.

*Hengstenberg, Ernst Wilhelm. *A Commentary on the Psalms*. Trans. by P. Fairbairn. 3 vols. Edinburgh: T. & T. Clark, 1876.

Horne, George. *A Commentary on the Book of Psalms*. Edinburgh: Thomas Nelson, 1840.

Kirkpatrick, Alexander Francis. *The Book of Psalms*. Cambridge: University Press, 1951.

Leslie, Elmer A. *The Psalms*. New York: Abingdon-Cokesbury Press, 1949.

*Leupold, Herbert Carl. *Exposition of the Psalms*. Grand Rapids: Baker Book House, 1970.

Luther, Martin. *A Commentary on the Psalms Called Psalms of Degrees*. London: W. Simpkin and R. Marshall, 1819.

Maclaren, Alexander. *The Psalms*. 3 vols. London: Hodder and Stoughton, 1893.

Meyer, Frederick Brotherton. *F. B. Meyer on the Psalms*. Grand Rapids: Zondervan Publishing House, n.d.

Murphy, James G. *A Critical and Exegetical Commentary on the Book of Psalms*. Edinburgh: T. & T. Clark, 1875.

Oesterley, W. O. E. *The Psalms*. 2 vols. London: SPCK, 1939.

*Perowne, John James Stewart. *The Book of Psalms*. 2 vols. London: Bell and Daldy, 1864.

*Plumer, William S. *Studies in the Book of Psalms*. Philadelphia: J. B. Lippincott & Co., 1866.

Scroggie, W. Graham. *The Psalms*. 3 vols. London: Pickering & Ingles, Ltd., 1948.

*Spurgeon, Charles Haddon. *The Treasury of David*. 6 vols. Grand Rapids: Zondervan Publishing House, 1950.

Tholuck, Augustus. *A Translation and Commentary of the Book of Psalms*. Trans. by J. Isidor Mombert. Philadelphia: William S. & Alfred Martien, 1858.

PROVERBS

INTRODUCTION

Proverbial teaching represents one of the most ancient forms of instruction; and the book of Proverbs belongs to that segment of the Old Testament that is commonly called the Wisdom Literature. For Israel, the Wisdom Literature consisted of Job, Proverbs, Ecclesiastes, and certain Psalms in the Masoretic canon. Ecclesiasticus and the Wisdom of Solomon are Apocryphal additions to the corpus of the Wisdom Literature. (James Wood, *Wisdom Literature* (London: Gerald Duckworth, 1967, pp. 1-7; and Roland Murphy, "Assumptions and Problems in Old Testament Wisdom Research," *CBQ*, 29, 1967, p. 410).

This literature was composed by the Israelite wise men (*Chakamin*). In the time of Jeremiah these wise men were ranked with the priests and prophets as spiritual leaders in Israel (Jer 18:18). They fulfilled the role of counselors in Israel; and the close association between wisdom and counsel is frequently observed in the Old Testament (cf. Daniel 1:4, 17, 20; 4:18, 27; Jer 49:7).

These wisdom counselors were often responsible for the major operation of government and held positions of great prominence, and as such they were related to both wisdom and kingship. Frequently they were members of the royal court. A land was blessed when the king was a wise man, and the wisdom traditions are closely attached to Solomon and Hezekiah (see R.B.Y. Scott, "Solomon and the Beginnings of Wisdom in Israel" pp. 262-79). The wisdom of Solomon is said to have surpassed the wisdom of all the peoples of the East, and all the wisdom of Egypt (I Kings 4:30). We should not restrict the teaching of wisdom to a special hierarchy of men within the State. Parents and village wise men, as well as teachers (William McKane, *Proverbs*, pp. 36-40), were included in the ranks of wisdom's men.

Israel was surrounded by nations whose history was rich in Wisdom Literature (R.B.Y. Scott, *The Study of the Wisdom Literature*, pp. 36-39). Beyond the borders of Israel large collections of Wisdom Literature have been found in Egypt and Mesopotamia (William McKane, *Proverbs*, p. 55). At least two Canaanite proverbs are found in the Tel-el-Armana letters. There is hardly any basis for doubting that the Israelites drew from the great cultured traditions of the world in which they lived. However, the Israelite sages were not mere copyists who borrowed materials indiscriminately from other people. They made the heritage of wisdom from the ancient cultures their own. When we read the Wisdom Literature of the Old Testament, we are reading literature that is Israelite, formed and preserved in the context of Yahwistic religion. (Marvin Tate, *The Broadman Bible Commentary-Proverbs*, p. 3).

In the international arena of wisdom, the Wisdom Literature of Israel was unique in that it constituted the chief storehouse of moral instruction and practical wisdom for the chosen people of Yahweh. The literature recognized three classes of people who desperately needed wisdom's counsel: the fool, the simple, and the scorner (see 1:22). The wisdom teacher pleads with all in Israel to forsake the way of the fool, the simple, and the scorner. There is a ". . . wisdom of this world . . ." (I Cor 2:1-8; Jas 3:13-18), and there is the divine wisdom that comes from above. In Proverbs, these two types of wisdom are pictured as lovely women. Wisdom beckons men to follow her into the path of blessing and success. Folly calls men to follow her to the path of rebellion and self-fulfillment that ultimately leads to hell.

The description of wisdom in Proverbs 8:22-31 leads to the conviction that Jesus Christ is the ultimate embodiment of the wisdom of God (I Cor 1:24, 30). Wisdom is eternal (8:22-26), the Creator of all things (8:27-29) and the Beloved of God (8:30-31), (see Jn 1:1-2; Col 1:15-19). To yield our lives to Jesus Christ is the ultimate act of wisdom; to be in Him is to be in the wisdom of God. Proverbs is of immense value to the man who has entered into covenant with the Lord through Jesus Christ, for in this book the child of God is instructed in the way of wisdom.

Authorship and Date. The ancients regarded this collection of proverbs as wholly the composition of Solomon. The fact that Solomon spoke some 3000 proverbs (I Kgs 4:32) led early to the conviction that 800 verses of Proverbs were the product of his hand. The application of historical criticism led to the conclusion that direct Solomonic authorship of any major part of Proverbs was highly improbable (Marvin Tate, *The Broadman Bible Commentary*, Proverbs, p. 4). This conclusion is unwarranted. The bitter disappointments, the skeptical darkness, and the weary heart Solomon incurred through trusting his own wisdom make him a probable instructor for Israel's youth. In his wish to save them from the folly of his misspent energies, he penned these proverbs. No major evidence exists for disavowing his authorship.

The date of writing can be fixed only in general terms. Solomon's reign is to be placed in the tenth century B.C., and the proverbs originate with him in that era. R.B.Y. Scott and G. Von Rad have pointed to supporting evidence for the development of Wisdom Literature in Israel in Solomon's reign; and although they hold that Solomonic authorship is uncertain, they do not disavow it (R.B.Y. Scott, *The Anchor Bible-Proverbs*, pp. 12-13).

OUTLINE

COMMENTARY

I. THE TITLE, PURPOSE, AND MOTTO OF THE BOOK. 1:1-7.

The introduction expresses the author's intention to provide a book that will serve for the moral and intellectual training of Israel's youth. The mission does not end there, however; for even the educated man can study these proverbs to his profit.

THE proverbs of Sŏl'o-mon the son of David, king of Israel;

1:1. The Proverbs of Solomon the son of David, king of Israel. The Hebrew word *mashal* has a broader connotation than the English word proverb. The *mashal* is not just a short, pithy saying. It is a profound or mysterious utterance that possesses effective power (Num 23:7; Jer 24:9). The prosperity of Solomon's reign (I Kgs 4:20) provided a fitting time for the compos-

1199

2 To know wisdom and instruction; to perceive the words of understanding;

3 To receive the instruction of wisdom, justice, and judgment, and equity;

4 To give subtilty to the simple, to the young man knowledge and discretion.

5 A wise *man* will hear, and will increase learning; and a man of understanding shall attain unto wise counsels:

6 To understand a proverb, and the interpretation; the words of the wise, and their dark sayings.

7 ¶The fear of the LORD *is* the beginning of knowledge: *but* fools despise wisdom and instruction.

8 My son, hear the instruction of thy father, and forsake not the law of thy mother:

ing of these reflective proverbs. The charm of prosperity called forth this impassioned plea to refuse the path of the fool.

2-3. To know wisdom and instruction. The proverbs are written that one might find the path of wisdom. Wisdom is the subject and goal of education in the Wisdom School, moral discipline is its method and process (R.B.Y. Scott, *The Anchor Bible-Proverbs*, p. 36). Instruction (Heb *mūsar*) is the companion of wisdom. This word represents that discipline which enables a man to keep himself under control (cf. Eph 4:14; II Pet 1:6).

To perceive the words of understanding. A disciplined encounter with wisdom will produce a perceptive spirit (cf. Heb 5:14). The senses will be exercised to discern both good and evil. That discernment, when yoked with instruction, produces understanding (Heb *bīnah*), or practical wisdom that manifests itself in justice, judgment, and equity. The first of the three terms describes that which is fitting according to the will of the supreme Judge, the second that which is customarily considered good among men, and the third that which is straightforward, honorable, and upright.

4. To give subtilty to the simple. The simple are, literally, those who are open to good impressions but can be easily led astray (cf. 8:5; 14:15). To these wisdom's instruction will bring subtilty (Heb *'armah*), the ability to seize the opportunities for good. (cf. Mt 10:16; Lk 16:8; Eph 5:16). The term **young man** is used of any age from birth to about the twentieth year (C. J. Ellicott, *Proverbs*, p. 305). To the young living in the prosperous times of Solomon's reign, wisdom would bring discretion or, rather, thoughtfulness.

5-6. A wise man will hear. It is not only the young who will profit from these proverbs. The wise, through careful attention, increase learning. The **man of understanding shall attain unto wise counsels** (lit., find steering or master the art of seamanship). He will be able to guide himself and others across the troubled waters of this life. Wisdom will also aid in the dissolution of dark sayings, literally knots, like Samson's riddle (Jud 14:12).

7. The fear of the LORD is the beginning of knowledge. This verse is somewhat independent and has often been linked with verse 9 rather than verses 1-6. It seems to fit better with the introduction, or perhaps it should be considered an independent matter standing between the preface and the first admonitory discourse (chs. 1-9) It is the motto for the entire collection.

The fear of the LORD. To hold in awe or fear is used in varying ways in the Old Testament. It may imply numinous awe (Job 37:23-24) or respect (Ex 9:30). Here, Solomon is clearly teaching that belief in God is the necessary prelude to the understanding of truth and the acquisition of any knowledge. **Beginning** is literally first in order of importance: the first principle. Whybray suggests that a real understanding of the term *fear* in the Wisdom Literature is dependent on observing the close connection between the fear of Yahweh and education. In many passages the fear of Yahweh is to be taught and learned as in Ps 34:11-14; Deut 17:18-20; II Kgs 17:25-38 (R. B. Whybray, *Wisdom in Proverbs*, p. 97). The beginning of all knowledge is grounded in the fear of Yahweh. **Fools despise wisdom and instruction.** The *evilim* are the self-willed, headstrong sons in Israel who will hear no advice.

II. A FATHER'S PRAISE OF WISDOM. 1:8-9:18.

A. Wisdom's Warning Against the Enticement of Sinners. 1:8-19.

8-9. My son. This is the customary form of address in Wisdom Books. The term is probably used because the primary responsibility for the instruction of sons lay with the father (cf.

9 For they *shall be* an ornament of grace unto thy head, and chains about thy neck.

10 ¶My son, if sinners entice thee, consent thou not.
11 If they say, Come with us, let us lay wait for blood, let us lurk privily for the innocent without cause:
12 Let us swallow them up alive as the grave; and whole, as those that go down into the pit:
13 We shall find all precious substance, we shall fill our houses with spoil:
14 Cast in thy lot among us; let us all have one purse:
15 My son, walk not thou in the way with them; refrain thy foot from their path:
16 For their feet run to evil, and make haste to shed blood.
17 Surely in vain the net is spread in the sight of any bird.
18 And they lay wait for their *own* blood; they lurk privily for their *own* lives.
19 So *are* the ways of every one that is greedy of gain; *which* taketh away the life of the owners thereof.

20 ¶Wisdom crieth without; she uttereth her voice in the streets:
21 She crieth in the chief place of concourse, in the openings of the gates: in the city she uttereth her words, *saying,*
22 How long, ye simple ones, will ye love simplicity? and the scorners delight in their scorning, and fools hate knowledge?

23 Turn you at my reproof: behold, I will pour out my spirit unto you, I will make known my words unto you.

24 ¶Because I have called, and ye re-

Deut 6:7; I Kgs 2:9). **Forsake not the law of thy mother.** The mother's teaching is also of great value (cf. 6:20; 10:1; 15:20; 20:20; 30:17). Parental teachings are not meant to constitute a heavy burden, but **shall be an ornament of grace unto thy head, and chains about thy neck.** The word for ornament is a rare word from the root to wind or twist; hence a turban. Authority and honor were marked by this special headdress. The necklace was also a masculine adornment given to a young man when he was embarking upon new responsibilities, here, perhaps, to serve as a reminder of his moral heritage.

10-19. If sinners entice thee. In this verse an admonition against robbery and violence begins. The insecurity of life in the wild Palestinian countryside provided a tempting opportunity for livelihood through plunder. Such became sinners by profession: let us lay wait for blood; let us lurk privily. The two verbs both signify to lie in wait for and to lay snares artfully. These seasoned robbers plunder the innocent. In verses 17-19 the folly of their acts is cited. They reason that they will come to great wealth. In reality, they scheme their own destruction. Yahweh will bring punishment upon them; the net which they have hidden will be used by the Lord to snare their own feet (cf. Ps 9:15). **In vain the net is spread in the sight of any bird.** Birds are wiser than these. Birds know enough to stay away from nets. These, however, are fashioning the nets for their own capture. They shall ultimately lose their lives, and it is their blood that will be spilled. **So are the ways of every one that is greedy of gain.**

Like a boomerang their acts of violence will come back upon them. There is an order in the universe. What men sow they do reap. When greed becomes the owner of a man's life, that man is destined for destruction.

B. Wisdom's Plea. 1:20-33.

20-22. The plea of wisdom continues, and we meet the person of wisdom. Wisdom appears in this section as a female. **Wisdom crieth . . . in the streets.** In the places of public concourse wisdom raises her voice. It is interesting to note how in her many activities wisdom parallels the works of the Lord Jesus Christ as He is depicted in the New Testament. She cries where traffic converges at the gateways of the fortified cities. **How long,** she cries! Her cry is addressed to three classes of persons. The simple ones are those who are open to good influences, but are also too open to those who influence for evil. Life is simple, for them for they are in pursuit of simple pleasure; and little else interests them. The scorner (Heb *lēts*) despises that which is godly and takes pride in his evil works. The name (Heb *lēts*) seems to have arisen in Solomon's time when prosperity allowed for the growth of such indifference and pride. Thirdly, wisdom addresses herself to the fools (Heb *kesīlīm*). These are those stupid persons who are totally confident in their own wisdom. They believe they have things all figured out without God's aid (cf. Isa 28:14). Wisdom cannot bear the sight of these sinners moving off toward hell and destruction without crying out (cf. Lk 19:41; Rom 9:2).

23. Turn you at my reproof: behold, I will pour out my spirit unto you. Wisdom pleads with men to turn, and the reward for that turning is her spirit. She promises to pour out her spirit; literally, her spirit will flow or gush upon those who turn. There may be an echo here of the prophetic promises of the pouring out of the Holy Spirit (Isa 44:3; Joel 2:28-29). **I will make known my words.** Wisdom will also increase the knowledge of those who turn. A similar promise is found in Psalm 25:14. The secret of the Lord is with them that fear Him. Blessing and revelation is for those who will turn, and judgment awaits those who will not.

24-31. Because I have called. In these verses wisdom ha-

fused; I have stretched out my hand, and no man regarded;

25 But ye have set at nought all my counsel, and would none of my reproof:

26 I also will laugh at your calamity; I will mock when your fear cometh;

27 When your fear cometh as desolation, and your destruction cometh as a whirlwind; when distress and anguish cometh upon you.

28 Then shall they call upon me, but I will not answer; they shall seek me early, but they shall not find me:

29 For that they hated knowledge, and did not choose the fear of the LORD:

30 They would none of my counsel: they despised all my reproof.

31 Therefore shall they eat of the fruit of their own way, and be filled with their own devices.

32 For the turning away of the simple shall slay them, and the prosperity of fools shall destroy them.

33 But whoso hearkeneth unto me shall dwell safely, and shall be quiet from fear of evil.

CHAPTER 2

MY son, if thou wilt receive my words, and hide my commandments with thee;

2 So that thou incline thine ear unto wisdom, and apply thine heart to understanding;

3 Yea, if thou criest after knowledge, and liftest up thy voice for understanding;

4 If thou seekest her as silver, and searchest for her as for hid treasures;

5 Then shalt thou understand the fear of the LORD, and find the knowledge of God.

6 For the LORD giveth wisdom: out of his mouth cometh knowledge and understanding.

7 He layeth up sound wisdom for the righteous: he is a buckler to them that walk uprightly.

8 He keepeth the paths of judgment, and preserveth the way of his saints.

9 Then shalt thou understand righteousness, and judgment, and equity; yea, every good path.

10 ¶When wisdom entereth into thine heart, and knowledge is pleasant unto thy soul;

rangues her audience with the vocabulary of a wisdom teacher and the stance of a prophet (William McKane, *Proverbs*, p. 274). Luther translates verse 24; "Because I call and ye refuse, . . . to stretch forth the hand in order to beckon to one as a signal of need for help" (cf. Isa 65:2). They feel no need of Yahweh's assistance. **I also will laugh at your calamity; I will mock when your fear cometh.** The softness of Yahweh's mercy vanishes in the presence of such self-reliance, and in its place comes a resolute look of anger. Laughter fills the lungs of wisdom, and mockery rides her countenance as she beholds the destruction of the fool's dreams and possessions. When they (the simple, the scorner, and the fool) call, she will not answer. They shall seek wisdom early, but she shall not be found. They who would not choose the fear of the Lord as a worthy complement to their efforts shall eat of the fruit of their own way. Theirs was the joy of independence; but that joy is destined to turn to bitterness of soul, for it has cut them off from Yahweh for eternity.

32-33. Their turning away and their prosperity has produced a false sense of well-being that leads them to destruction. **But whoso hearkeneth unto me shall dwell safely, and shall be quiet.** He who hears wisdom and embraces her shall dwell in the place of safety and shall not be afraid of evil tidings. (cf. Ps 112:7; Ps 37).

C. Wisdom's Value. 2:1-22.

2:1-4. Wisdom continues her pleading and points to the path that men should travel. The words **path(s)** or **way(s)** are used many times in this section (see 2:8-9, 13, 15, 18-20; 3:17; 4:11, 14, 18-19).

Men are challenged to hide or, literally, store up the teachings of wisdom. The verbs in verses 1-4 are expressive and strong: **receive, hide, liftest up, criest after, incline thine ear, apply thine heart, seekest,** and **searchest.** As miners labor fervently to obtain silver, so men are admonished to seek wisdom with equal fervor. Hunting for hidden treasure was always of keenest interest (cf. Mt 13:44); men must seek wisdom with a similar zeal. They must cry after her.

5-8. **Then shalt thou understand the fear of the LORD, and find the knowledge of God.** Such zealousness is counseled because of its fruitful consequences. The young man who cries out for understanding will find the knowledge of God. It is the highest of all gifts to know God who is the giver of all things that are good (cf. Jn 17:3). The knowledge of God will include the fear of the Lord, which is clearly represented in Scripture as the most valuable possession of man (cf. Eccl 12:13).

To those who enter cheerfully and zealously upon this quest the Lord gives wisdom. Even as James will later record; ". . . God, that giveth to all men liberally, and upbraideth not . . ." (Jas 1:5). The Lord alone can give this gift, for He alone is the source of knowledge and understanding. **Sound wisdom** (Heb *tûshiyah*) in verse 7 carries the idea of power for furtherance or advancement. The Lord will respond with favor to those who seek to walk uprightly before Him. He will be a shield to all who walk blamelessly. He protects those who walk in the paths of justice. He preserveth the way of His saints (Heb *chasîdîm*), literally, those who are His ardent worshipers. In the Maccabean period the *chasîdîm* were those who were voluntarily devoted to the Law (I Mac 2:42), as opposed to those who favored amalgamating Judaism with Greek Culture.

9-15. The moral understanding that results from the pursuit of wisdom was given in verses 1-4. Now we are informed of the results obtained when wisdom enters a man: you will understand righteousness and justice and equity, every good path. This pleasant result is due to the fact that wisdom has made its way into the mind and has found a welcome reception in the soul

11 Discretion shall preserve thee, understanding shall keep thee:
12 To deliver thee from the way of the evil *man,* from the man that speaketh froward things;
13 Who leave the paths of uprightness, to walk in the ways of darkness;
14 Who rejoice to do evil, *and* delight in the frowardness of the wicked;
15 Whose ways *are* crooked, and *they* froward in their paths:
16 To deliver thee from the strange woman, *even* from the stranger *which* flattereth with her words;
17 Which forsaketh the guide of her youth, and forgetteth the covenant of her God.
18 For her house inclineth unto death, and her paths unto the dead.
19 None that go unto her return again, neither take they hold of the paths of life.

20 That thou mayest walk in the way of good *men,* and keep the paths of the righteous.
21 For the upright shall dwell in the land, and the perfect shall remain in it.
22 But the wicked shall be cut off from the earth, and the transgressors shall be rooted out of it.

CHAPTER 3

MY son, forget not my law; but let thine heart keep my commandments:
2 For length of days, and long life, and peace, shall they add to thee.
3 Let not mercy and truth forsake thee: bind them about thy neck; write them upon the table of thine heart:
4 So shalt thou find favour and good understanding in the sight of God and man.
5 ¶Trust in the LORD with all thine heart; and lean not unto thine own understanding.
6 In all thy ways acknowledge him, and he shall direct thy paths.
7 Be not wise in thine own eyes: fear the LORD, and depart from evil.
8 It shall be health to thy navel, and marrow to thy bones.
9 Honour the LORD with thy substance, and with the firstfruits of all thine increase:
10 So shall thy barns be filled with plenty, and thy presses shall burst out with new wine.
11 ¶My son, despise not the chastening of the LORD; neither be weary of his correction:
12 For whom the LORD loveth he correcteth; even as a father the son *in whom* he delighteth.

of man. This receptive man is now guarded by discretion and understanding. Discretion is an alert guardedness against the froward (Heb *tahpukah*), i.e., those who represent or distort of the truth. When wisdom is pleasant to your soul, you are preserved from men who practice the distortion of the truth.

16-19. Guardedness will also keep the young man from sexual sin. Two epithets are used here for the evil woman. She is strange (Heb *zarah*) or the stranger (Heb *nakriyah*). The first term implied a woman who was a part of another family while the second term implied one who belonged to another nation. Solomon's practice of marrying foreign women seems to have become a commonplace cause of corruption in Israel (cf. I Kgs 11:1) She forsakes the guide of her youth and forgetteth the covenant of her God. These women leave their husbands with whom they have lived intimately during the days of their youth. They also forget the marriage covenant that they made in the presence of God (Mal 2:14) and prefer to play the role of the harlot (see Toy, *International Critical Commentary.—Proverbs,* p. 47).

The house of this woman is a dangerous place to visit, for she and her house incline (lit., sink down) unto death and the dead. The dead are the inhabitants of sheol (lit., the place of shadows), for here the dead are but shadows of their former selves in their impoverished state (cf. Isa 14:10). None who go in unto her return, neither do they take hold of the path of life again.

20-22. The upright shall dwell in the land. The promise to Abraham and his seed envisioned a dwelling in the land; this phrase became emblematic for the highest earthly prosperity. This highest of all blessings was reserved for those who obey faithfully Yahweh's commandments (Gen 17:8; Deut 4:1; Jer 23:5-6; Mt 5:5). The wicked will be uprooted (Heb *nasach*), literally torn up by the roots and cast out of the land.

D. Wisdom's True Discipline. 3:1-4:27.

3:1-12. Solomon challenges the young man to an appreciation of wisdom's ability to direct. This first section of chapter 8 consists of six quatrains, each of which begins with an exhortation and closes with a promise of blessing for compliance. Men are exhorted to listen, to trust, to obey, to fear, to honor, and to submit to the Lord. To bind God's word to one's neck and to write His commandments upon the heart is a testimony of mercy (loyalty) and truth (fidelity). The motivation for loyalty and faithfulness is found in verses 2 and 4. Verse 2 promises a life that is fit to be called life, the extension of days and a peace of mind of which the ungodly know nothing (cf. Isa 48:22; 57:21). Verses 3-4 promise favor with God and man. The directions resemble the figurative orders with regard to the Law given in Exodus 13:9 and Deuteronomy 6:8. This inner and outer appreciation for the commandments of God will produce good success before God and men.

In verse 5 wisdom enjoins trust in the Lord. This is a plea for the entire commitment of all that one is or ever hopes to be to the providential directing and provisioning of Yahweh. All reliance on our own understanding (insights) must be forever relinquished and replaced by a total trust in his ability to make a straight and profitable path for our feet (Eccl 10:10). **Be not wise in thine own eyes.** In opposition to the efforts of man, wisdom suggests that we take notice of God; that we humbly recognize him as that one who can best control the affairs of our lives; that we **fear the LORD, and depart from evil.** He who fears the Lord and walks not in the vanity of self-conceit will be delivered from evil (cf. Gen 3:5). This approach to life will have the effect of producing health in the navel, the lifeline of the body for one who is in a state of dependency. Trusting will also provide relief for dryness of bones. Marrow is literally watering, i.e., refreshing. Bones will be continuously refreshed as a man trusts in Yahweh (Job 21:24).

Honor the LORD with thy substance, and with the first fruits of all thine increase. Trusting is always evidenced in the area of man's stewardship. Wisdom admonishes man to bring gifts to his Lord (Isa 43:23). The first fruits belong to the Lord (Deut 18:4; 26:2). To refuse to bring them to the storehouse is to rob Yahweh and is indicative of the greatest dishonor (Mal 3:10). The barns and presses of Israel will be filled if these covenanting sons will honor the Lord with tithes and offerings.

Despise not the chastening of the LORD. All men sin and bring dishonor upon the Lord. Those who enjoy His great blessing will at times experience His chastening, for Yahweh corrects every son whom He receives (Heb 12:5-13). These times of chastening are a sign of both His displeasure and love. When He sends difficulties into the lives of His children, He is not to be regarded as a vindictive despot, but rather as a loving father who diligently corrects His children. **Neither be weary of his correction.** Man is born in sin and practices the art of sinning arduously before he meets the God of grace. Thus, the Lord's hand of correction is often found upon us shepherding us away from sin. We must not weary of this hand upon us or despise its gentle and persistent presence, a presence that is always grounded in His faithfulness (I Cor 10:13). A humble submission is an essential adjunct to our growth in spiritual truth (I Pet 5:6).

13-18. Two short poems in praise of wisdom are inserted in this didactic section. The first poem is in praise of the benefits of wisdom. Three pictures of wisdom are presented to portray her incomparable worth. **Happy is the man that findeth wisdom.** This means, literally, how blessed is the blessedness of the man who finds wisdom (cf. 8:34; Ps 1:1; Mt 5:3-11). His condition is far superior to that of the man who finds silver, gold, or rubies. **She is more precious than rubies . . . Length of days is in her right hand.** The merchandise of this world is good, but it cannot give a man meaning in life or eternal life. Wisdom can give the gift of life, as well as riches and honor. Her ways are the paths of peace. Peace is the highest reward in the New Testament for the life of dependence upon God (Phil 4:6, 7). **She is a tree of life** for those who grasp her. The tree of life is probably an allusion to Genesis 2 and 3. No mention is made of it except in 11:30; 13:12; 15:4 and Revelation 2:7; 22:2. The tree or vine is often symbolic in Scripture of life (cf. Jn 15:1-11). Wisdom is of immense profit, for she alone leads to the path of peace and life.

19-20. This bride poem is a single quatrain that may at one time have belonged to a longer poem. Here wisdom is once again personified, and some degree of independent existence is postulated for wisdom, an existence that predates the beginning of the universe.

The LORD by wisdom hath founded the earth. This passage anticipates passages like John 1:3 and Colossians 1:17. Wisdom's existence antedates all of creation. Wisdom is seen as an independent creative power who **founded the earth . . . established the heavens. By his knowledge, the depths are broken up, and the clouds drop down the dew.** (cf. Gen 7:11; Job 38:8). Surely this is a reference to that One who upholds all things by the word of His power: the Lord Jesus Christ. Wisdom is the divine mediatrix between God and men (Keil and Delitzsch, *Proverbs*, p. 41).

21-26. The primary purpose of this section is to call attention to the security that wisdom gives and the importance of unbroken vigilance in the maintenance of fellowship with wisdom. The keeping of sound wisdom and discretion at the center of

13 ¶Happy *is* the man *that* findeth wisdom, and the man *that* getteth understanding.

14 For the merchandise of it *is* better than the merchandise of silver, and the gain thereof than fine gold.

15 She *is* more precious than rubies: and all the things thou canst desire are not to be compared unto her.

16 Length of days *is* in her right hand; *and* in her left hand riches and honour.

17 Her ways *are* ways of pleasantness, and all her paths *are* peace.

18 She *is* a tree of life to them that lay hold upon her: and happy *is* every one that retaineth her.

19 The LORD by wisdom hath founded the earth; by understanding hath he established the heavens.

20 By his knowledge the depths are broken up, and the clouds drop down the dew.

21 ¶My son, let not them depart from thine eyes: keep sound wisdom and discretion:

22 So shall they be life unto thy soul, and grace to thy neck.

23 Then shalt thou walk in thy way safely, and thy foot shall not stumble.

24 When thou liest down, thou shalt not be afraid: yea, thou shalt lie down, and thy sleep shall be sweet.

25 Be not afraid of sudden fear, neither of the desolation of the wicked, when it cometh.

26 For the LORD shall be thy confidence, and shall keep thy foot from being taken.

27 ¶Withhold not good from them to whom it is due, when it is in the power of thine hand to do it.

28 Say not unto thy neighbour, Go, and come again, and to morrow I will give; when thou hast it by thee.

29 Devise not evil against thy neighbour, seeing he dwelleth securely by thee.

30 Strive not with a man without cause, if he have done thee no harm.

31 ¶Envy thou not the oppressor, and choose none of his ways.

32 For the froward is abomination to the LORD: but his secret is with the righteous.

33 The curse of the LORD is in the house of the wicked: but he blesseth the habitation of the just.

34 Surely he scorneth the scorners: but he giveth grace unto the lowly.

35 The wise shall inherit glory: but shame shall be the promotion of fools.

CHAPTER 4

HEAR, ye children, the instruction of a father, and attend to know understanding.

2 For I give you good doctrine, forsake ye not my law.

3 For I was my father's son, tender and only beloved in the sight of my mother.

4 He taught me also, and said unto me, Let thine heart retain my words: keep my commandments, and live.

5 Get wisdom, get understanding: forget it not; neither decline from the words of my mouth.

6 Forsake her not, and she shall preserve thee: love her, and she shall keep thee.

7 Wisdom is the principal thing; therefore get wisdom: and with all thy getting get understanding.

8 Exalt her, and she shall promote thee: she shall bring thee to honour, when thou dost embrace her.

9 She shall give to thine head an ornament of grace: a crown of glory shall she deliver to thee.

10 Hear, O my son, and receive my sayings; and the years of thy life shall be many.

11 I have taught thee in the way of wisdom; I have led thee in right paths.

12 When thou goest, thy steps shall not be straitened; and when thou runnest, thou shalt not stumble.

13 Take fast hold of instruction; let her not go: keep her; for she is thy life.

14 ¶Enter not into the path of the

one's eyes (vision) will demand a consistent effort. **Depart from thine eyes** is literally to escape or slip away. Careful attention to the practice of common sense and resourcefulness will result in life and security. Sound wisdom will insure a walk free from care and full of trust. Anxiety will not affix itself to such a man, for he trusts God so totally that fear will be unable to ensnare him. His confidence is not in himself, but in Yahweh. Yahweh will keep his foot from the snare. This man goes under the double guard of the ". . . peace of God . . ." (Phil 4:7) and the ". . . power of God . . ." (I Pet 1:5). He will not then need to fear the destruction that will overcome the wicked.

27-35. Attention is once again directed to the practice of wisdom. The man who would live well must be a good neighbor. Jesus exhorted his disciples to make to themselves ". . . friends of the mammon of unrighteousness . . ." (Lk 16:9), remembering that they were stewards of all that God had given. The poor and the neighbor are to be specific objects of that stewardship. The good neighbor meets his obligations, does not take advantage of an unsuspecting neighbor, avoids the arousing of trouble with a man who has done him no harm, and does not envy the man who has gotten his gain through the practice of violence. The froward (underhanded or devious) man is an abomination to Yahweh. The expression is used several times in Proverbs and is related to ethical and social flaws in the conduct of men (William McKane, *Proverbs,* p. 301). It can be translated repulsive. The perverse are an abomination to the Lord, but the righteous are those to whom He conveys his secrets. Literally, they are those in whom He has confidence (Heb *sōd*), i.e., those with whom He has fellowship and enjoys unity. It is a great honor for a man to belong to the *sōd* of Yahweh. Yahweh's curse dwells in the house of the wicked. Shame lifts the scorner up; and as he rises in his shame, God sweeps him with scorn off the stage of human history and into hell. This is the promotion of fools.

4:1-9. Solomon presents the example of one beloved son, probably himself, as an admonition to proper pursuits for the many sons. It is not his advice alone that he offers, but rather the good doctrine received in the home of his father David. David taught Solomon (I Chr 28:9, 10) to seek wisdom. **Get wisdom** was David's instruction to Solomon. The doubling of the verb makes the demand more vehement. The highest achievement in the universe is the attainment of wisdom. Get her! At any cost! **Wisdom is the principal thing.** Love her and embrace her as you would one whom you deeply love. Embraced wisdom will lift you up and **bring thee to honor** (I Sam 2:30). She will place upon your head a graceful wreath. The ornament of grace and crown of glory were ornaments that the bride placed on the bridegroom.

10-19. In these verses the way of wisdom is contrasted with the ruinous **path of the wicked.** The choice that lies before Israel as Yahweh's people is developed here. To heed the sayings or words of Yahweh is to inherit the blessing of many years of life. The word is in the plural here as though Solomon intends to add eternity to time. Life itself is threatened when we refuse to heed these admonitions. Those who will not hear are destined to stumble, while the path of the "hearers" is illumined by the light of the Lord (Ps 27:1). The path of the righteous shines brighter and brighter, ultimately leading wisdom's sons into the

wicked, and go not in the way of evil *men*.

15 Avoid it, pass not by it, turn from it, and pass away.

16 For they sleep not, except they have done mischief; and their sleep is taken away, unless they cause *some* to fall.

17 For they eat the bread of wickedness, and drink the wine of violence.

18 But the path of the just *is* as the shining light, that shineth more and more unto the perfect day.

19 The way of the wicked *is* as darkness: they know not at what they stumble.

20 ¶My son, attend to my words; incline thine ear unto my sayings.

21 Let them not depart from thine eyes; keep them in the midst of thine heart.

22 For they *are* life unto those that find them, and health to all their flesh.

23 ¶Keep thy heart with all diligence; for out of it *are* the issues of life.

24 Put away from thee a froward mouth, and perverse lips put far from thee.

25 Let thine eyes look right on, and let thine eyelids look straight before thee.

26 Ponder the path of thy feet, and let all thy ways be established.

27 Turn not to the right hand nor to the left: remove thy foot from evil.

CHAPTER 5

MY son, attend unto my wisdom, *and* bow thine ear to my understanding:

2 That thou mayest regard discretion, and *that* thy lips may keep knowledge.

3 ¶For the lips of a strange woman drop *as* an honeycomb, and her mouth *is* smoother than oil:

4 But her end is bitter as wormwood, sharp as a two-edged sword.

5 Her feet go down to death; her steps take hold on hell.

6 Lest thou shouldest ponder the path of life, her ways are moveable, *that* thou canst not know *them*.

7 Hear me now therefore, O ye children, and depart not from the words of my mouth.

8 Remove thy way far from her, and come not nigh the door of her house:

9 Lest thou give thine honour unto others, and thy years unto the cruel:

10 Lest strangers be filled with thy wealth; and thy labours *be* in the house of a stranger;

11 And thou mourn at the last, when thy flesh and thy body are consumed,

12 And say, How have I hated instruction, and my heart despised reproof;

13 And have not obeyed the voice of my teachers, nor inclined mine ear to them that instructed me!

14 I was almost in all evil in the midst of the congregation and assembly.

very presence of that One who is the Light of the World. Solomon pleads with men to avoid at all cost the path of the wicked. On that path you will meet men who are so ungodly that they cannot sleep until they have harmed some soul. Men who **drink the wine of violence** and **eat the bread of wickedness.**

20-27. Verse 23 reads Guard your heart above everything else you have because it determines what kind of life you will live. The great burden of wisdom is for purity of heart. A pure heart leads into the light of verse 18 and is health to the entire body. The heart is the control center for all of life, and the tongue is controlled by the heart (Lk 6:45). A froward mouth reveals a heart filled with pride. Lips that are filled with scorn and arrogance have their roots in a scorner's heart. The issues of life reveal the contents of the heart. Solomon exhorts all to keep the commandments of Yahweh in the midst of the heart and to carefully keep the eyes and feet centered in the ways of the Lord without deviation. The concern of the wise man for the holiness of the whole person is evidenced in these verses.

E. Wisdom's Counsel on Sexuality. 5:1-23.

5:1-14. Solomon now points with unmistakable clarity to those persons and mistakes which, if not diligently avoided, will usher men into the path of darkness. In this chapter the young man is warned of the bitter consequence of involvement with the strange woman. Solomon encourages marital fidelity by graphically portraying the joys of sexual union with the wife of your youth.

The adulteress, with her lips and charming words, is an object of extreme excitement for the young man. Alas, the end of involvement with her is the bitterness of wormwood. Wormwood is the bitter gall of the LXX, a poison when ingested. The man who embraces her will find no mercy. Her smooth mouth, when kissed, becomes a sharp two-edged sword that severs him from the blessing of wisdom. The adulteress offers young men the luxury of sexual ecstasy without the commitment of marriage, but she is a totally irresponsible character. Her course turns first one way then another; her ways are movable and unpredictable. She is fickle, seeking only to satisfy her own depraved desires. Only one thing is certain; she and all who travel with her are bound for the kingdom of the dead (sheol). Sheol is the place of those dying without the blessing of God, a place reserved for all who refuse to ponder the path of life.

The method recommended for avoiding the adulteress is found in verses 7-8. Solomon advises that the young man keep away from her. **Come not nigh the door of her house.**

Sober reflection may also help to keep you from her door. Consider what can happen if you involve yourself with such a woman. It will cost you your honor if you get within her grasp, not to mention your money and hard-earned gains which will wind up in her hands or the hands of her associates. Consider also that the best years of your life will be given unto this cruel temptress and her associates whose sole object is plunder. Through her avaricious demands all of a man's substance will gradually pass over into other hands. The end of such a fool is a

15 ¶Drink waters out of thine own cistern, and running waters out of thine own well.

16 Let thy fountains be dispersed abroad, *and* rivers of waters in the streets.

17 Let them be only thine own, and not strangers' with thee.

18 Let thy fountain be blessed: and rejoice with the wife of thy youth.

19 *Let her be as* the loving hind and pleasant roe; let her breasts satisfy thee at all times; and be thou ravished always with her love.

20 And why wilt thou, my son, be ravished with a strange woman, and embrace the bosom of a stranger?

21 For the ways of man *are* before the eyes of the LORD, and he pondereth all his goings.

22 His own iniquities shall take the wicked himself, and he shall be holden with the cords of his sins.

23 He shall die without instruction; and in the greatness of his folly he shall go astray.

CHAPTER 6

MY son, if thou be surety for thy friend, *if* thou hast stricken thy hand with a stranger,

2 Thou art snared with the words of thy mouth, thou art taken with the words of thy mouth.

3 Do this now, my son, and deliver thyself, when thou art come into the hand of thy friend; go, humble thyself, and make sure thy friend.

4 Give not sleep to thine eyes, nor slumber to thine eyelids.

5 Deliver thyself as a roe from the

body consumed. This destruction of body and flesh signifies the total destruction that awaits the libertine.

The libertine can then be heard to say in his state of abject poverty of body and soul, How could I have been so foolish as to have hated instruction? Solomon himself had shared in the spirit of the libertine, and he makes his confession in verse 14. **I was almost in all evil.** At one point in his life he had tried all the pleasures of this world. He might have committed any sin openly before all the congregation. His eyes were opened, however; and he was led by wisdom to walk as a true son of the covenant. Now he shares illuminating wisdom with all and warns of the public disgrace that must be theirs if they walk with the adulteress and fall under the open censure of the congregation and assembly.

15-23. Solomon now urges his readers to follow sexual purity through faithfulness to the institution of marriage. He pictures in vivid terms the delights that marriage can afford, as opposed to the misery of sexual impurity. The adulteress contends that stolen waters are sweet (9:17), but drinking is an allusion to the satisfactions of conjugal love. The same figure is used in Song of Solomon 4:15, where a wife is compared to a well of living water. The word of God consistently commends and commands total fidelity to the marriage partner as the path to sexual satisfaction.

Many different interpretations have been suggested for verse 16. The content would seem to support viewing the sentence as an interrogative. In light of what has been said, shall your fountain (semen) flow abroad as waters in the street? The response is found in verses 15 and 17. No! **Let them be only thine own.** Let the fruit of your reproductive powers be shared only with your wife and not with strangers. The consequences of such fidelity will be a joyous union between a man and the wife with whom he has covenanted in his youth.

The ecstasy that fidelity can bring is celebrated in verses 18 and 19. The ecstatic joy of the lover is summed up in the word ravished, which is used elsewhere of the staggering gait of the intoxicated (Isa 28:7). The hind and roe have always been chosen by the Oriental poets as figures of human beauty because of their grace, speed, and lustrous eyes. Wisdom does not regret the sexual pleasures that a man can find with the wife of his youth and marvels that in the face of such pleasure any would be so foolish as to embrace the fickle adulteress. The Lord ponders all the goings of man and has assigned bitter and severe consequences to the sin of sexual promiscuity. Sexual sin ruthlessly incarcerates the participants. The cords of this sin wrap themselves around the very soul of the participant until he cannot free himself, even though he may desire freedom. His persistent lack of self-control has led him beyond the place where he might be instructed. His great folly has led him beyond the reach of God's grace (Jn 12:24, Rom 1:28-32;). **He shall die without instruction.** McKane thinks in terms of a corpse that has been wrapped in a shroud. The shroud in this case is his sexual folly (William McKane, *Proverbs*, p. 313).

F. Wisdom's Counsel on Pitfalls. 6:1-35.

6:1-5. The matter of personal conduct is still in view in this chapter. Chapter 5 has dealt with that area of life which Solomon deemed in most imminent danger to the young in Israel. In chapter 6 Solomon moves to a consideration of other areas in which a young man might be guilty of any misconduct that could lead to dishonor. The man who orders his conduct in accordance with the instruction given here will be saved from many failures.

The warning against becoming surety is repeated several times in Proverbs (11:15; 20:16; 22:26; 27:13). The frequent warnings that are given against giving security for others are to

hand *of the hunter,* and as a bird from the hand of the fowler.

6 ¶Go to the ant, thou sluggard; consider her ways, and be wise:

7 Which having no guide, overseer, or ruler,

8 Provideth her meat in the summer, *and* gathereth her food in the harvest.

9 How long wilt thou sleep, O sluggard? when wilt thou arise out of thy sleep?

10 *Yet* a little sleep, a little slumber, a little folding of the hands to sleep:

11 So shall thy poverty come as one that travelleth, and thy want as an armed man.

12 ¶A naughty person, a wicked man, walketh with a froward mouth.

13 He winketh with his eyes, he speaketh with his feet, he teacheth with his fingers;

14 Frowardness *is* in his heart, he deviseth mischief continually; he soweth discord.

15 Therefore shall his calamity come suddenly; suddenly shall he be broken without remedy.

16 ¶These six *things* doth the LORD hate: yea, seven *are* an abomination unto him:

17 A proud look, a lying tongue, and hands that shed innocent blood,

18 An heart that deviseth wicked imaginations, feet that be swift in running to mischief,

19 A false witness *that* speaketh lies, and he that soweth discord among brethren.

be explained by the severe consequences that could result from such practices. According to Hebrew jurisprudence, a man's goods could be confiscated and he himself might be sold into slavery if the person with whom he stood as surety failed to meet his obligations (Neh 5:1-5).

It seems unlikely that these strong admonitions are directed toward the ordinary lending of money to members of one's community, though that, too, may lead to difficulties. Solomon wishes to produce in young men a proper sense of the complications that can often attend financial and business arrangements. The warning, then, is against risking irreparable harm. If through careless words or vanity one has done so, no time is to be lost in obtaining release from the arrangement, which apparently has been agreed to but not yet carried into effect (R.B.V. Scott, *The Anchor Bible-Proverbs,* p. 58).

A man must understand the severity of his situation. He is as vulnerable as a roe (gazelle) is to the hunter and the bird is to the fowler. It would seem that pride often furnished the incentive to suretyship. The desire to be thought well of often led a man to strike hands even with the knowledge that he was totally unable to assume such a serious responsibility. If thus deluded, a man must humble himself, admit his vulnerability, and take no rest until he has freed himself from this unwise commitment.

6-11. Go to the ant, thou sluggard; consider her ways, and be wise. This small creature models proper virtues for the foolish man. Forethought and prudence are virtues that are constantly applauded by wisdom. The loafer (Heb *asel*) is the object of much scorn in Proverbs. Here he is commanded to consider or judge the ant and observe its wisdom. The ant, ever working on its own impulse, is proverbial as an emblem of industry (J. P. Lange, *A Commentary on the Holy Scriptures—Proverbs,* p. 84). The ant plans at harvest time for the cold months of winter; the wise man should be equally alert to the future and plan to meet its contingencies. The ant also demonstrates the wonder of self-directedness. He works, having no guide or command barked from the mouth of a superior. Working is cemented to his character and represents his free and personal response to all that surrounds him.

The slothful sleeper stands in stark contrast to our industrious model. He folds his arms, a well-known posture for one who is preparing to go to sleep (Eccl 4:5). His hands are folded in sloth, rather than extended in expectancy. Poverty and want shall be his reward. The form of the Hebrew here is intensive. While the sluggard sleeps, poverty is coming on swiftly; and it shall assail him with the sudden force of a highwayman. The sleeper will be utterly defenseless.

12-19. Seven types of deceitful action are depicted in these verses. These deceptive traits will characterize the sluggard, for in every part of his being he is devoted to folly. His mouth is filled with *'iqshūt* (lit., distortions or twisting of the truth). His eyes are winking, an allusion to the malicious tattler and scandalmonger who fills his lying tale with winks. The winks suggest that only part is really being told and that the person being maligned is even worse than one could possibly imagine. His feet and hands are used to call attention to things that would be better left unnoticed. His heart is absorbed with the devising of evil and the stirring up of strife, and he is committed to the scattering of his evil tares wherever wheat fields are found. This man has an appointment with the Lord. **Suddenly shall he be broken.** He shall be shattered as a potter's vessel (Isa 30:14) without hope of remedy.

These six things doth the LORD hate. These verses represent a climax to the instruction of verses 12-15. Yahweh hates six things, but there is a seventh thing that he hates the worst of all. This numerical form of proverb, to which the name of *Middah* is given by later writers, is found also in chapter 30:15-16, 18-19,

21-23, 29-31; and in all these instances the number first named is increased by one (C. J. Ellicott, *Proverbs*, p. 314).

A proud look He has ever detested, for such a look renders a man unfit for the reception of grace. A lying tongue betrays a deceitful heart. This heart of deceit soon joins hands with those who plot the shedding of innocent blood. The shedding of blood emboldens a man's heart to every evil imagination and the pursuit of every evil mischief. The pursuits of such a man have grave implications for the covenant community, for this man's lies produce continuous **discord among brethren.**

20-26. In view of the Lord's disdain for such actions, Solomon returns now to the enjoining of a proper response to Yahweh's statutes. **Keep thy father's commandment.** The opening verses on parental instruction have been adapted from Deuteronomy 6:7 11:19. The commandments and teachings of parents should be highly treasured and worn over the heart like an expensive locket or ring which hangs from a necklace. The function of these commandments and teachings are like those of the Torah in Deuteronomy 6:6-9. These commandments will be a lamp pointing the proper direction for the journey. The commandments, when closely followed, are unique in their ability to protect the young man from the evil woman and bring him into the way of life. The consequences of yielding to such a woman are severe. She so ensnares her worshipers that they reduce themselves to their last morsel of bread for her services.

20 ¶My son, keep thy father's commandment, and forsake not the law of thy mother:
21 Bind them continually upon thine heart, *and* tie them about thy neck.
22 When thou goest, it shall lead thee; when thou sleepest, it shall keep thee; and *when* thou awakest, it shall talk with thee.
23 For the commandment *is* a lamp; and the law *is* light; and reproofs of instruction *are* the way of life:
24 To keep thee from the evil woman, from the flattery of the tongue of a strange woman.
25 Lust not after her beauty in thine heart; neither let her take thee with her eyelids.
26 For by means of a whorish woman *a man is brought* to a piece of bread: and the adulteress will hunt for the precious life.
27 Can a man take fire in his bosom, and his clothes not be burned?
28 Can one go upon hot coals, and his feet not be burned?
29 So he that goeth in to his neighbour's wife; whosoever toucheth her shall not be innocent.
30 *Men* do not despise a thief, if he steal to satisfy his soul when he is hungry;
31 But *if* he be found, he shall restore sevenfold; he shall give all the substance of his house.
32 *But* whoso committeth adultery with a woman lacketh understanding: he *that* doeth it destroyeth his own soul.
33 A wound and dishonour shall he get; and his reproach shall not be wiped away.
34 For jealousy *is* the rage of a man: therefore he will not spare in the day of vengeance.
35 He will not regard any ransom; neither will he rest content, though thou givest many gifts.

27-35. A man may protest that it needn't go that far. However, the man who pursues the adulteress is like a man who is carrying fire in his clothes. Can this be done without a man's clothes burning from his body? Can a man walk on hot coals without burning his feet? The answer is an obvious no. Adultery is simply playing with fire. The man who plays with the fire of adultery will not continue in innocence. No exceptions exist! Such a man will not go unpunished. The man who becomes a thief because of hunger will receive the pity of some. He may even be allowed to make restoration. The Law required a two-, four-, five-, or sevenfold compensation (Ex 22). However, the man who commits adultery is in a completely different category. He is a man who has no sense. He destroys himself and has no hope of getting out of the penalty for his sin. He will get only wounds and dishonor, and his disgrace is never to be erased. The wounds (Heb *nega'*) may designate the blows that the adulterer will receive from the jealous husband whose jealousy is like a fire burning fiercely. No amount of ransom or payment will appease jealousy. Eventually, that jealous rage will culminate in a day of vengeance for the wounded husband. Little wonder Joseph said, ". . . How then can I do this great wickedness, and sin against God?" (Gen 39:9).

CHAPTER 7
MY son, keep my words, and lay up my commandments with thee.
2 Keep my commandments, and live; and my law as the apple of thine eye.
3 Bind them upon thy fingers, write them upon the table of thine heart.
4 Say unto wisdom, Thou *art* my sister; and call understanding *thy* kinswoman:
5 That they may keep thee from the strange woman, from the stranger *which* flattereth with her words.

G. Wisdom's Despisers Portrayed. 7:1-27.

7:1-5. The usual introduction with its commendation of wisdom as a guide for life is followed by a vivid description of the seduction of a young man by a married woman. The verbs in verses 1-3 are strong and active, asking for concentration and retention on the part of the student (William McKane, *Proverbs*, p. 332). The terms **words, commandments,** and **teachings** (Heb *torah*) are shared by the Wisdom Literature with the Pentateuch, Prophets, and Psalms. These terms are used to designate the authoritative nature of wisdom teaching. The young man is asked to keep these laws **as the apple of thine eye.** Literally, he is to keep them "as the little pupil in thine eye," or as the little man in thine eye (J. P. Lange, *A Commentary on the Holy Scriptures—Proverbs*, p. 90). The pupil is the light of the

1209

eye and very precious. To damage it is to spend one's life in darkness. In like manner, the teaching of the wise man is precious. To fail to appreciate and appropriate it personally is to risk a life spent in darkness.

Bind them upon thy fingers is a way of indicating that these teachings should be ever before men's eyes. A literal interpretation of these commands in Exodus 13:9 and Deuteronomy 6:8 led to the use of prayer fillets and phylacteries among the Jewish people. Texts of Scripture were copied, enclosed in a leather case, and tied to forehead and arm at the time of prayer. The phylactery for the left arm was wound around it seven times and then seven times around the middle finger.

Solomon admonishes the importance of writing these commandments upon the heart as well. For the man of wisdom, the commandments of God are not merely external ornaments, but rather truths to be assimilated and joined to the very being of a man in order that they may have an effectual voice in all he purposes to do. This deep relationship with wisdom is as one's kinsman, the only safeguard to the sensuous offerings of the strange woman. The kinsman was that member of the family group who protected the other members from the open disgrace of poverty. Wisdom alone can protect from the disgrace of impious relationship with the strange woman.

6-9. With the perspicuity of an eyewitness, Solomon brings before us a scene that has been duplicated thousands of times. The young man is once again beseeched to ponder with care the dangers that accompany fraternizing with the strange woman. From his window Solomon beholds the simple one, literally the inexperienced one, a man not yet vicious, but eager to expand his exposure to the things of this world. He is near a corner. The punctuation represents the corner as hers, possibly the corner of her house. It is the place where she habitually stalks her prey, and the young man knowing this eagerly seeks to encounter her. In the black and dark night he seeks to establish contact.

10-23. A careful description of the adulteress is now given. She is a woman who lives "at fever temperature" (William McKane, *Proverbs*, p. 336). Her heart is guarded and inaccessible, subtle, a walled fortress that none can ascend. She wears the attire of a harlot unashamedly. She is loud and stubborn, literally ungovernable, like a wild heifer that will not submit its neck to the yoke (Hos 4:16). **Now is she without . . . in the streets.** She is not a keeper at home, as St. Paul advises (Tit 2:5). Her joy is to be in the streets where she can ply her wares on the simple. She delights to catch and kiss the simple, wooing them to her bed. Feigning devotion to this young lover, she says, **Therefore came I forth . . . diligently to seek thy face, and I have found thee.** Her advances are brisk and subtle. **I have peace offerings with me; this day have I payed my vows.** She has only recently fulfilled religious vows. She had offered the peace offering. A purely voluntary offering, the remainder of which must be eaten before the passing of two days in accordance with Leviticus 7:16. To this religious meal she invites the young man. He is told that it is for him, and only him, that she has prepared this meal. For him she has decked her bed with the myrrh of Arabia and the cinnamon of Africa and Ceylon. Come, is her plea; for the goodman, her husband, is gone, and all is ready for them to enjoy a night of conjugal bliss. All that is lacking is his consent, and that he is only too eager to give. He goes as an ox to the slaughter and is fettered in the stocks, like a bird caught in a trap. But the great tragedy is that he does not realize that it will cost him his life. The liver was prominent in ancient writings as the seat of sexual desire. A dart will strike through his liver. This can mean that the husband will return and kill the offenders (man and woman), or have others, who are legally appointed to do so, kill them. It may be, however, that our young man proves to be his own assassin. The illicit passions

6 ¶For at the window of my house I looked through my casement,
7 And beheld among the simple ones, I discerned among the youths, a young man void of understanding,
8 Passing through the street near her corner; and he went the way to her house,
9 In the twilight, in the evening, in the black and dark night:

10 And, behold, there met him a woman *with* the attire of an harlot, and subtil of heart.
11 (She *is* loud and stubborn; her feet abide not in her house:
12 Now *is she* without, now in the streets, and lieth in wait at every corner.)
13 So she caught him, and kissed him, *and* with an impudent face said unto him,
14 *I have* peace offerings with me; this day have I payed my vows.
15 Therefore came I forth to meet thee, diligently to seek thy face, and I have found thee.
16 I have decked my bed with coverings of tapestry, with carved *works*, with fine linen of Egypt.
17 I have perfumed my bed with myrrh, aloes, and cinnamon.
18 Come, let us take our fill of love until the morning: let us solace ourselves with loves.
19 For the goodman *is* not at home, he is gone a long journey:
20 He hath taken a bag of money with him, *and* will come home at the day appointed.
21 With her much fair speech she caused him to yield, with the flattering of her lips she forced him.
22 He goeth after her straightway, as an ox goeth to the slaughter, or as a fool to the correction of the stocks;
23 Till a dart strike through his liver;

as a bird hasteth to the snare, and knoweth not that it *is* for his life.

24 ¶Hearken unto me now therefore, O ye children, and attend to the words of my mouth.

25 Let not thine heart decline to her ways, go not astray in her paths.

26 For she hath cast down many wounded: yea, many strong *men* have been slain by her.

27 Her house *is* the way to hell, going down to the chambers of death.

CHAPTER 8

DOTH not wisdom cry? and understanding put forth her voice?

2 She standeth in the top of high places, by the way in the places of the paths.

3 She crieth at the gates, at the entry of the city, at the coming in at the doors.

4 Unto you, O men, I call; and my voice *is* to the sons of man.

5 O ye simple, understand wisdom: and, ye fools, be ye of an understanding heart.

6 Hear; for I will speak of excellent things; and the opening of my lips *shall be* right things.

7 For my mouth shall speak truth; and wickedness *is* an abomination to my lips.

8 All the words of my mouth *are* in righteousness; *there is* nothing froward or perverse in them.

9 They *are* all plain to him that understandeth, and right to them that find knowledge.

10 Receive my instruction, and not silver; and knowledge rather than choice gold.

11 For wisdom *is* better than rubies; and all the things that may be desired are not to be compared to it.

12 I wisdom dwell with prudence, and find out knowledge of witty inventions.

13 The fear of the Lord *is* to hate evil: pride, and arrogancy, and the evil way, and the froward mouth, do I hate.

14 Counsel *is* mine, and sound wisdom: I *am* understanding; I have strength.

15 By me kings reign, and princes decree justice.

16 By me princes rule, and nobles, *even* all the judges of the earth.

17 I love them that love me; and those that seek me early shall find me.

18 Riches and honour *are* with me; *yea,* durable riches and righteousness.

19 My fruit *is* better than gold, yea, than fine gold; and my revenue than choice silver.

20 I lead in the way of righteousness, in the midst of the paths of judgment:

21 That I may cause those that love me to inherit substance; and I will fill their treasures.

22 The Lord possessed me in the beginning of his way, before his works of old.

23 I was set up from everlasting,

which she has lighted in him will surely bring him to hell itself if he does not repent and forsake the way of the adulteress.

24-27. Let not thine heart decline to her ways. Wisdom instruction is addressed to the heart (mind or will) of man because the basic decisions which control the flow of a man's life are made in this willing center. The optimism of the text resides in the emphasis on man's ability to make the right decision. Sobering, however, is the conclusion. Many strong men have been slain by her, and the chambers of her house are in reality the chambers of death. These **simple ones** (vs. 7) will be ruined if they do not direct their hearts into the pursuit of wisdom (see 1:4, 22).

H. Wisdom's Defense. 8:1-36.

8:1-5. Once again wisdom speaks openly in the high places and gates. Wisdom does not speak with a seductive voice under the cover of darkness; she stands in the higher parts of the city and goes to every place where people in numbers are apt to be found. She works at the intersections and before the large gates of the city. She is not willing that any should perish. (cf. II Pet 3:9).

Her message is for all; the men (great ones) and the sons of men (those of interim ranks) alike are objects of her concern. She pleads with the simple and the fool to exert their understanding and to direct their hearts.

6-11. The words of wisdom are excellent, i.e., noble or princely. From the mouth of wisdom proceeds only those things that are right and true. The speech of wisdom is contrasted with the speech of the adulterous woman in verse 8. The man of wisdom will be able to discern the speech of righteousness and the utterance that is an abomination. **They are all plain to him.** The words of wisdom are to those who practice hearing them of greater value than silver, gold, or jewels.

12-36. I wisdom dwell with prudence. Dwell is *shakan,* which means, literally, to inhabit. Wisdom has settled down and taken up her abode with prudence. Prudence is right knowledge for special times which, if understood, can do much to better a man's position in the arena of human affairs. Wisdom's possession of knowledge and ability to construct witty inventions, i.e., well-thought-out plans, makes her a grand ally. She is a prepared counselor who can ably guide men in the craft of living well. She is eager to guide, but a word of caution is in order. In keeping with 6:16-19, certain traits of character are hated by wisdom and will abort her influence on a man's life.

from the beginning, or ever the earth was.

24 When *there were* no depths, I was brought forth; when *there were* no fountains abounding with water.

25 Before the mountains were settled, before the hills was I brought forth:

26 While as yet he had not made the earth, nor the fields, nor the highest part of the dust of the world.

27 When he prepared the heavens, I *was* there: when he set a compass upon the face of the depth:

28 When he established the clouds above: when he strengthened the fountains of the deep:

29 When he gave to the sea his decree, that the waters should not pass his commandment: when he appointed the foundations of the earth:

30 Then I was by him, *as* one brought up *with him:* and I was daily *his* delight, rejoicing always before him;

31 Rejoicing in the habitable part of his earth; and my delights *were* with the sons of men.

32 Now therefore hearken unto me, O ye children: for blessed *are they that* keep my ways.

33 Hear instruction, and be wise, and refuse it not.

34 Blessed *is* the man that heareth me, watching daily at my gates, waiting at the posts of my doors.

35 For whoso findeth me findeth life, and shall obtain favour of the LORD.

36 But he that sinneth against me wrongeth his own soul: all they that hate me love death.

CHAPTER 9

WISDOM hath builded her house, she hath hewn out her seven pillars:

2 She hath killed her beasts; she hath mingled her wine; she hath also furnished her table.

3 She hath sent forth her maidens: she crieth upon the highest places of the city,

4 Whoso *is* simple, let him turn in hither: *as for* him that wanteth understanding, she saith to him,

5 Come, eat of my bread, and drink of the wine *which* I have mingled.

6 Forsake the foolish, and live; and go in the way of understanding.

7 He that reproveth a scorner getteth to himself shame: and he that rebuketh a wicked *man getteth* himself a blot.

8 Reprove not a scorner, lest he hate thee: rebuke a wise man, and he will love thee.

9 Give *instruction* to a wise *man,* and

I. Wisdom's Banquet. 9:1-18.

9:1-6. Chapter 7 described the house of the harlot and her invitation to the simple one. In this chapter we are informed that wisdom has built her house and invites men to come to the banquet she has prepared. The seven pillars suggest the splendor of the house wisdom has built. The number seven often represents that which is sacred and holy in Scripture. The house of wisdom is thus constituted a holy dwelling by means of the emblematic number. Wisdom provides an elaborate banquet for all who will come. Animals have been slain, and the wine has been flavored with spices to give it the best possible flavor. The maidens who attend wisdom are then sent forth to summon the guests (cf. Mt 22). They cry from the highest places so that all may hear the gracious invitation (Mt 10:27). Her compassion is expressed in her sincere interest in those simple ones who, through want of experience and lack of sound judgment, are so apt to go astray (II Pet 3:9). To those who might all too eagerly eat the poisoned bread of idleness and sin, wisdom freely offers her bread, which gives life and understanding to the eater (Isa 55:1; Jn 6:35). The eating of wisdom's bread and the drinking of her cup will strengthen the resolve to forsake the foolish. Banqueting with wisdom does not send men out addled and disillusioned, but rather filled with an understanding of that which is true and productive.

7-12. He that reproveth a scorner getteth to himself shame. Wisdom recognizes the hardened, those who will only mock at her preachments. She does not approve of giving that which is holy to the dogs or of the casting of her pearls before swine (Mt 7:6). The wisdom teacher ought not to waste his time with the incorrigible, but rather seek those who demonstrate some fear of the Lord. The demonstration of such fear will provide the

he will be yet wiser: teach a just *man*, and he will increase in learning.

10 The fear of the LORD *is* the beginning of wisdom: and the knowledge of the holy *is* understanding.

11 For by me thy days shall be multiplied, and the years of thy life shall be increased.

12 If thou be wise, thou shalt be wise for thyself: but *if* thou scornest, thou alone shalt bear *it*.

13 ¶A foolish woman *is* clamorous: *she is* simple, and knoweth nothing.

14 For she sitteth at the door of her house, on a seat in the high places of the city,

15 To call passengers who go right on their ways:

16 Whoso *is* simple, let him turn in hither: and *as for* him that wanteth understanding, she saith to him,

17 Stolen waters are sweet, and bread *eaten* in secret is pleasant.

18 But he knoweth not that the dead *are* there; *and that* her guests *are* in the depths of hell.

CHAPTER 10

THE proverbs of Sŏl'o-mon. A wise son maketh a glad father: but a foolish son *is* the heaviness of his mother.

2 Treasures of wickedness profit nothing: but righteousness delivereth from death.

3 The LORD will not suffer the soul of the righteous to famish: but he casteth away the substance of the wicked.

4 He becometh poor that dealeth *with* a slack hand: but the hand of the diligent maketh rich.

5 He that gathereth in summer *is* a wise son: *but* he that sleepeth in harvest *is* a son that causeth shame.

6 Blessings *are* upon the head of the just: but violence covereth the mouth of the wicked.

7 The memory of the just *is* blessed: but the name of the wicked shall rot.

8 The wise in heart will receive commandments: but a prating fool shall fall.

9 He that walketh uprightly walketh surely: but he that perverteth his ways shall be known.

10 He that winketh with the eye caus-

foundation for a purposeful dialogue on the benefits of wisdom. The instruction of such men will result in their gaining a deeper appreciation for wisdom and holiness. The scorner, according to verse 12, must accept sole responsibility for his cynicism. He has so hardened himself that he is beyond the reach of reason and love. Wisdom counsels that such a man should not be approached with the instruction of wisdom. To those who have, wisdom counsels the giving of more. From those who have not, wisdom counsels complete withdrawal (Mt 13:13; 25:29).

13-18. A foolish woman is clamorous. Wisdom counsels complete separation from the scorner. Wisdom also counsels complete separation from the foolish woman. The man who would embrace wisdom must eschew them both. She, like wisdom, has a house. She, like wisdom, is particularly interested in the simple youth. She sits at her door and clamors forth a message to all who pass by. The primary emphasis here is on the nature of the invitation that she extends. Wisdom invites men as a teacher, while the foolish woman invites men as a lover, wishing to use them for her own personal pleasure. Those who heed wisdom's plea are led into life (vs. 6), while those who accept the invitation of the foolish woman to partake of her water and bread are led to death. Her house is the very vestibule of sheol, the very throat of hell which, when entered, leads one irresistibly down into hell.

III. THE PROVERBS OF SOLOMON. 10:1-22:16.

A. Wisdom's Instruction on Rewards. 10:1-32.

10:1. We now enter upon the second division of the book. The collections in this section are made up largely of wisdom sentences that have no larger immediate context. This contrasts quite sharply with the well-compacted discourse of the first nine chapters. Although each verse is complete in itself, it is obvious that the collector has attempted to put together verses that relate to similar subject matter. The section is authored by Solomon and extends to 22:16. **A wise son maketh a glad father** (vs. 1). This general thought is designed to serve as an introduction to the entire collection. A son who walks with wisdom is a great delight to his parents, while one who rejects instruction and plays the fool is a source of great sorrow.

2-7. These verses compare the earthly lot of the wicked and the righteous. Six verses arranged in three pairs accomplish the task. The doer of wrong is rewarded with the treasures of wickedness, and these treasures will not enable him to avert the sudden death that awaits the wicked. Yahweh will strip away the substance of the wicked. The righteous man, one who deals not with a slack hand, will be delivered from death; and the Lord will not suffer his soul to famish. Yahweh is the moral governor of the universe, and He renders to all their due.

The idle hand of the sluggard ultimately will bring him poverty, but diligence will make a man rich. Disciplined application of one's energies was considered a primary virtue by the wise men. Poverty and shame are the byproducts of sleeping in harvest; blessing and a good reputation are the lot of the diligent. Violence and a reputation that rots are the lot of the sluggard. The memory of such a man smolders and disappears from history as a thing abhorrent; but the memory of the just will be revered, for he leaves the world a richer place.

8-10. Three more proverbs are given contrasting the way of the wise with the way of the fool. The wise are ever ready to receive commandments from Yahweh and His servants. The self-willed prater will listen to no one and is destined to fall. The steps of the fool are filled with uncertainty; the abundance of his words serves only to point him out as a man who is anchored to uncertainties. The winking eye suggests that his speech can

eth sorrow: but a prating fool shall fall.

11 The mouth of a righteous *man is* a well of life: but violence covereth the mouth of the wicked.

12 Hatred stirreth up strifes: but love covereth all sins.

13 In the lips of him that hath understanding wisdom is found: but a rod *is* for the back of him that is void of understanding.

14 Wise *men* lay up knowledge: but the mouth of the foolish *is* near destruction.

15 The rich man's wealth *is* his strong city: the destruction of the poor *is* their poverty.

16 The labour of the righteous *tendeth* to life: the fruit of the wicked to sin.

17 He *is in* the way of life that keepeth instruction: but he that refuseth reproof erreth.

18 He that hideth hatred *with* lying lips, and he that uttereth a slander, *is* a fool.

19 In the multitude of words there wanteth not sin: but he that refraineth his lips *is* wise.

20 The tongue of the just *is as* choice silver: the heart of the wicked *is* little worth.

21 The lips of the righteous feed many: but fools die for want of wisdom.

22 The blessing of the LORD, it maketh rich, and he addeth no sorrow with it.

23 *It is* as sport to a fool to do mischief: but a man of understanding hath wisdom.

24 The fear of the wicked, it shall come upon him: but the desire of the righteous shall be granted.

25 As the whirlwind passeth, so *is* the wicked no *more:* but the righteous *is* an everlasting foundation.

26 As vinegar to the teeth, and as smoke to the eyes, so *is* the sluggard to them that send him.

27 The fear of the LORD prolongeth days: but the years of the wicked shall be shortened.

28 The hope of the righteous *shall be* gladness: but the expectation of the wicked shall perish.

29 The way of the LORD *is* strength to the upright: but destruction *shall be* to the workers of iniquity.

30 The righteous shall never be removed: but the wicked shall not inhabit the earth.

never be taken at face value. Violence accompanies him everywhere.

11-14. A contrast between the mouth of the righteous and the mouth of the wicked is undertaken in these verses. The mouth of the righteous is a well of life because of the edifying character of its utterances. The mouth of the wicked is filled with words of deceit that are designed to conceal violent intentions. The wicked are constantly rehashing old feuds with the hope that strife will be rekindled. In contrast, the words of the wise are conciliatory (cf. Jas 5:20; I Pet 4:8).

Sooner or later the fool's merited punishment overtakes him. None exhibited more clearly the contrast of these verses than Solomon and his son Rehoboam. Solomon waited on the Lord for a wise and understanding heart; Rehoboam trusted his own wisdom and received a rod for his back (I Kgs 12:8-19). In summary, Solomon summarizes the significance of speech. The wise lay up knowledge and are careful stewards of their speech. They avoid squandering words and fashion them with understanding to fit them properly to time and place (Eccl 12:10). The fool practices no such carefulness. He is constantly causing havoc and destruction through his ill-chosen words. He doesn't even know what awkward or dangerous thing he will say next.

15-22. Seven proverbs now are used to provide instruction on the proper use of wealth. First, Solomon instructs on the benefits of wealth. Wealth is worthy of pursuit, since it affords an actual protection for a man against his enemies. The poor, on the other hand, are in grave danger; for they have little resource with which to establish a defense against the vicissitudes of this life. The achievement of wealth serves two ends. The wise man should employ the gains of his toil to enhance his walk in this life. All that the wicked man acquires serves only to deepen his journey into sin; for he lacks the discipline to properly administer his wealth, and he refuses instruction. He ignores reproof and causes many to err (cf. Jer 42:20). He conceals inner hatred beneath lying or flattering lips. In addition to being a malignant flatterer, the man is a slanderer who intends the assassination of others through well-chosen words. Verse 21 prophesies death for this fool. An overabundance of words carelessly chosen must ultimately incur the judgment of the Lord and the neighbors (cf. Mt 12:36). **The lips of the righteous,** however, feed many through words of encouragement and comfort. **The blessing of the LORD** will bring riches to such a man; and these riches, properly attained and administered, will bring no sorrow to that man.

23-30. The wicked and the righteous are contrasted in the proverbs. The fool gets his sport, i.e., his enjoyment, through the execution of his evil plottings. The man of understanding gets his enjoyment through the faithful practice of wisdom. The wicked, who are pledged to the continuous plotting of mischief, secretly fear that one day their evil will return to haunt them. Solomon articulates a theory of retribution. What they have done to others will be done to them. The righteous, however, have submitted themselves to the will of God and desire only the accomplishment of His will in their lives and in the lives of others. Those who delight in Yahweh are daily His delight, and He will grant them the desires of their hearts.

When a storm sweeps over the wicked, they shall be carried away; for they lack any depth of soul. The man of understanding has anchored himself on the foundation of righteousness; and the advent of the storm finds such a man firmly anchored there. The sluggard has passed his time in idleness with no thought for the impending storm. He has failed to realize that his life is a mission and a message constantly read by Yahweh and others. He is an obnoxious character. He is like **vinegar to the teeth, and as smoke to the eyes** of his employer. He comprehends at no level his responsibility for faithfulness to his appointed missions. He is an irritation in the eyes of all that is holy and his **years . . . shall be shortened.** His expectations will perish, for he lacks the discipline necessary to make them become realities; destruction shall attend his every venture. This man can expect a shortened life and, ultimately, total and eternal death. Verse 30 reflects the promises of the Lord to Israel concerning the land. The promise of the land, however, contained a conditional element. To dwell in the land the covenanters must respond positively to the laws of Yahweh. To fail in this matter of persistent obedience is to incur the wrath of Yahweh and be cut out of the land. Like Cain, they became vagabonds and were ultimately dispersed among the nations.

The man of understanding fears Yahweh and disciplines himself to carefully fulfill his appointed tasks. Yahweh rewards such a man with length of days, gladness of heart, and strength to continue in the path of life. The righteous shall dwell in the land, and they shall never be removed.

31-32. Again, compare the mouths of the righteous and the wicked. The mouths of the righteous put forth wisdom; acceptable or fitting words flow from the mouth of the righteous (cf. Eccl 12:10; Lk 4:22). The mouth of the wicked is filled with interpretations and distortions of the truth, and such sinning with the tongue will be severely judged (cf Mt 12:36).

B. Wisdom's Instruction on the Aspects of Wickedness. 11:1-31.

11:1-9. A false balance is abomination to the LORD. A similar proverb occurs in 20:23, and the praise of just weights is given in 16:11 and 20:10. The recurrence of this message suggests that this form of cheating may have become common in Solomon's reign when commerce was flourishing in Israel. In such affluence common honesty is often eroded. Several proverbs are now given to govern a man's proper deportment in his relationship with his neighbors. Yahweh delights in a just weight, for a true weight bespeaks a proper regard for the dignity of one's neighbor. Pride, or a concern for self-advancement that is devoid of a concern for others, is the dynamic that is behind this breach of ethics. Such callousness is an abomination to the Lord.

The fruit of such indifference will be personal disgrace, or destruction. The lowly are those who conceal or renounce themselves in the interest of meeting the needs of others. With these men of integrity the wisdom of God resides.

Fraudulent persons who pervert the truth lose the favor of Yahweh and are destroyed under the sponsorship of their own wickedness (vs. 5). Their total destruction will be accomplished in that great day of Yahweh's eschatological wrath. Riches will profit nothing in that day. Righteousness alone will deliver in that day, but righteousness is also profitable for directing a man in all the days that the Lord gives him until he faces the day of judgment. The practice of righteousness smooths the difficulties that beset the path of wisdom's man. The practice of evil darkens the path until a man grovels in darkness, uncertain of where his steps are leading him. The naughtiness (strong passions) of the wicked inexorably draws them to destruction.

When the wicked die, their expectation of worldly prosperity ceases to be an achievable objective. Misfortune passes by the righteous and instead falls upon the wicked (cf. 21:18). The righteous man can, and ultimately will, be delivered from anything. The impure hypocrite will attempt the destruction of his righteous neighbor, but the man of wisdom will be delivered in or from the situation by his knowledge of the protective power of Yahweh, a power that serves righteousness and acts in the interest of the oppressed.

10-14. The effect of the righteous and the wicked on their community is discussed. The city should rejoice at the prosper-

---

31 The mouth of the just bringeth forth wisdom: but the froward tongue shall be cut out.

32 The lips of the righteous know what is acceptable: but the mouth of the wicked *speaketh* frowardness.

CHAPTER 11

A FALSE balance *is* abomination to the LORD: but a just weight *is* his delight.

2 *When* pride cometh, then cometh shame: but with the lowly *is* wisdom.

3 The integrity of the upright shall guide them: but the perverseness of transgressors shall destroy them.

4 Riches profit not in the day of wrath: but righteousness delivereth from death.

5 The righteousness of the perfect shall direct his way: but the wicked shall fall by his own wickedness.

6 The righteousness of the upright shall deliver them: but transgressors shall be taken in *their own* naughtiness.

7 When a wicked man dieth, *his* expectation shall perish: and the hope of unjust *men* perisheth.

8 The righteous is delivered out of trouble, and the wicked cometh in his stead.

9 An hypocrite with *his* mouth destroyeth his neighbour: but through knowledge shall the just be delivered.

10 When it goeth well with the

righteous, the city rejoiceth: and when the wicked perish, *there is* shouting.

11 By the blessing of the upright the city is exalted: but it is overthrown by the mouth of the wicked.

12 He that is void of wisdom despiseth his neighbour: but a man of understanding holdeth his peace.

13 A talebearer revealeth secrets: but he that is of a faithful spirit concealeth the matter.

14 Where no counsel *is*, the people fall: but in the multitude of counsellors *there is* safety.

15 He that is surety for a stranger shall smart *for it:* and he that hateth suretiship is sure.

16 A gracious woman retaineth honour: and strong *men* retain riches.

17 The merciful man doeth good to his own soul: but *he that is* cruel troubleth his own flesh.

18 The wicked worketh a deceitful work: but to him that soweth righteousness *shall be* a sure reward.

19 As righteousness *tendeth* to life: so he that pursueth evil *pursueth it* to his own death.

20 They that are of a froward heart *are* abomination to the LORD: but *such as are* upright in *their* way *are* his delight.

21 *Though* hand *join* in hand, the wicked shall not be unpunished: but the seed of the righteous shall be delivered.

22 *As* a jewel of gold in a swine's snout, *so is* a fair woman which is without discretion.

23 The desire of the righteous *is* only good: *but* the expectation of the wicked *is* wrath.

24 There is that scattereth, and yet increaseth; and *there is* that withholdeth more than is meet, but *it tendeth* to poverty.

25 The liberal soul shall be made fat: and he that watereth shall be watered also himself.

26 He that withholdeth corn, the

ity of the righteous and at the downfall of the wicked. The salutary words and acts of the righteous cause a city to be exalted. The blessing of the righteous within the city is often cited in the Wisdom Literature (cf. Eccl 9:14). Intercessory prayer is only one of their unique contributions (Gen 18:23; Ezr 6:10; Jer 29:7). The mouth of the wicked is filled with contempt. He does not sympathize with the problems of his neighbor. He spreads abroad any secret flaw that he has uncovered and brings great distress upon all by his destructive and often fraudulent talebearing. The man of understanding holds his peace. He is not hasty to condemn or speak, knowing that he may be mistaken in his analysis of the matter. He is pledged to the wisdom of silence or concealment as the best course of action. This tact does much to ensure the tranquility of life within the city. The preservation of a city depends upon the presence of a goodly number of such men. In the multitude of such counselors there is safety, and their absence will almost certainly cause the people to fall.

15-23. A man will escape the anxieties of 6:3-5 if he avoids fellowship with those who desire financial assistance often. He that hateth suretyship (cosigning) will be better off than those who get themselves entangled in spurious financial entanglements.

Verse 16 begins an unusual contrast between men and women. The gracious woman is able to retain honor, whereas the strong (energetic) man is able to retain riches. Grace and energy are needed to retain the characteristics of life most prized by Yahweh. Mercy (Heb *chesed*), i.e., loyalty, is also necessary for success in life, for loyalty and dependability are necessary for the continuance of relationships. The self-centered, ruthless man ultimately troubleth his own flesh. In keeping with the theology of retribution, his cruel conduct ultimately causes the destruction of his own soul. The gains of such a man are evanescent; the fruit of his deceitful work slips between his fingers. In contrast, the sower of righteousness builds a sure reward for himself.

Righteousness leads one into the beauty of life, whereas the pursuit of evil leads only to death. The pursuers of evil are an abomination to the Lord, an object of his eternal hatred (Rom 9:13). Those who practice the pursuit of righteousness are Yahweh's delight. **Though hand join in hand** is a Hebrew idiom that is similar to the English idiom, Here is my hand on it; it should be translated here, Be assured! These evil men will not go unpunished; you can be assured of that. The wicked can expect only frustration and punishment.

The righteous, on the other hand, will be delivered; and their vigorous pursuit of righteousness will be wholly vindicated.

In verse 22 we have two incongruities, the gold ring in the swine's snout and the beautiful woman who has no discretion. The earthy humor, in marked contrast to the moralizing context, suggests that this is a colloquial saying (R.B.Y. Scott, *The Anchor Bible,* Proverbs, p. 88). The gold ring and discretion represent ornaments of wisdom. It is sad to see a gold ring so out of place, and it is equally sad to see beauty wasted on a person who continuously practices indiscretion. Such waste can only expect to meet with divine disfavor. The righteous would desire good, i.e., the proper conjunction of ornaments with personalities. The unrighteous may only expect to be visited with Yahweh's wrath.

24-31. Three proverbs against avarice are now given. The man who scatters his substance with benevolence will increase the more in wealth and blessings. There is an old epitaph which says: What we spent, we had; what we saved, we lost; what we gave, we have. Many withhold from others only to discover all too suddenly that they are in great want. Liberality fattens the soul. Yahweh recompenses with faithful correspondence the

people shall curse him: but blessing *shall be* upon the head of him that selleth *it*.

27 He that diligently seeketh good procureth favour: but he that seeketh mischief, it shall come unto him.

28 He that trusteth in his riches shall fall; but the righteous shall flourish as a branch.

29 He that troubleth his own house shall inherit the wind: and the fool *shall be* servant to the wise of heart.

30 The fruit of the righteous *is* a tree of life; and he that winneth souls *is* wise.

31 Behold, the righteous shall be recompensed in the earth: much more the wicked and the sinner.

CHAPTER 12

WHOSO loveth instruction loveth knowledge: but he that hateth reproof *is* brutish.

2 A good *man* obtaineth favour of the LORD: but a man of wicked devices will he condemn.

3 A man shall not be established by wickedness: but the root of the righteous shall not be moved.

4 A virtuous woman *is* a crown to her husband: but she that maketh ashamed *is* as rottenness in his bones.

5 The thoughts of the righteous *are* right: *but* the counsels of the wicked *are* deceit.

6 The words of the wicked *are* to lie in wait for blood: but the mouth of the upright shall deliver them.

7 The wicked are overthrown, and *are* not: but the house of the righteous shall stand.

8 A man shall be commended according to his wisdom: but he that is of a perverse heart shall be despised.

9 *He that is* despised, and hath a servant, *is* better than he that honoureth himself, and lacketh bread.

10 A righteous *man* regardeth the life of his beast: but the tender mercies of the wicked *are* cruel.

11 He that tilleth his land shall be satisfied with bread: but he that followeth vain *persons is* void of understanding.

giving of man. The man who withholds corn to force the price to exorbitant heights will be cursed by the people, but the blessing of the Lord and man will be upon that man who sells at a fair price. He who practices good in this manner will procure favor with Yahweh and man. He who practices avarice will reap a turbulent life for himself. The principle of retribution is once again presented. That man may think that he can trust in his accumulated riches for security, but he shall fall even while the righteous flourish as a branch (green leaf). The righteous alone are connected with an unfailing source of sustenance.

Avarice will ultimately bring great trouble to a man's household as well, for his destruction will leave his family nothing to inherit. Ultimately, the fools of the world will become the slaves of the wise man who has managed his affairs in accord with the commandments of Yahweh.

The righteous man is a source of life to many. By the power of his spirit and example, the wise man gains many souls for wisdom's battle against fools. The company of the wise shall be recompensed by God for their misdeeds; how much more shall the wicked and the sinner (cf. I Pet 4:18) receive a deserved retribution for their sins.

C. Wisdom's Instruction on Contrasting Conducts. 12:1-28.

12:1-3. He who hates the reproof, which is so necessary for the development of self-discipline, is brutish. Only the man who loves instruction will increase his storehouse of knowledge.

The good man is benevolent toward others and merits divine favor, but the man who plots evil against others is condemned by the Lord. The good man knows a measure of security in this world, for he knows the God who makes all things beautiful in their time (Eccl 3:11). The righteous are firmly rooted and shall not be moved, while the ungodly are like the chaff which the wind blows away.

4-11. These proverbs examine the blessings and evils encountered in domestic life and explain the causes of both. A central figure in wisdom's home is the virtuous woman. She is possessed of a moral power that manifests itself in her godly character and domestic activity. The crown, or garland, is an emblem of renown. She bestows honor upon her husband.

Solomon contrasts her with the wife who brings shame upon her husband. She is like a cancer that saps his strength and ultimately causes his total collapse.

The thought life of those who love instruction is pure, and it is from such a thought life that righteous actions spring. The wicked are controlled by a murderous disposition. Their words and deeds seek the destruction of the righteous, while the mouth of the upright delivers those who would be trapped in the ambush of the wicked. The wicked are overthrown, for they lack security. The house of the righteous will stand because it is built upon the fear of the Lord (cf. Mt 7:24-27).

Men will be rewarded justly. The wise will be commended according to the degree that they faithfully practice wisdom's precepts, and the perverse will be despised by all (cf. I Sam 2:30). The man who does most of his work himself and keeps only one servant is commended above the man who honors himself with many servants whom he cannot afford and brings himself to such poverty that he cannot afford to buy bread.

The righteous man who would take proper care of his domestic affairs has a heart for his animals as well. He cares for the feelings and comfort of his beasts. God's own care for the animals is illustrated in the provisions for their care in the Law (Deut 25:4). The wicked man takes no thought for the comfort of dumb animals, and what he calls tender mercies are in reality acts of cruelty.

The man who **tilleth his land** and works hard day after day is certainly better off than the man who dreamingly follows vain

12 The wicked desireth the net of evil *men:* but the root of the righteous yieldeth *fruit.*

13 The wicked is snared by the transgression of *his* lips: but the just shall come out of trouble.

14 A man shall be satisfied with good by the fruit of *his* mouth: and the recompence of a man's hands shall be rendered unto him.

15 The way of a fool *is* right in his own eyes: but he that hearkeneth unto counsel *is* wise.

16 A fool's wrath is presently known: but a prudent *man* covereth shame.

17 *He that* speaketh truth sheweth forth righteousness: but a false witness deceit.

18 There is that speaketh like the piercings of a sword: but the tongue of the wise *is* health.

19 The lip of truth shall be established for ever: but a lying tongue *is* but for a moment.

20 Deceit *is* in the heart of them that imagine evil: but to the counsellors of peace *is* joy.

21 There shall no evil happen to the just: but the wicked shall be filled with mischief.

22 Lying lips *are* abomination to the LORD: but they that deal truly *are* his delight.

23 A prudent man concealeth knowledge: but the heart of fools proclaimeth foolishness.

24 The hand of the diligent shall bear rule: but the slothful shall be under tribute.

25 Heaviness in the heart of man maketh it stoop: but a good word maketh it glad.

26 The righteous *is* more excellent than his neighbour: but the way of the wicked seduceth them.

27 The slothful *man* roasteth not that which he took in hunting: but the substance of a diligent man *is* precious.

28 In the way of righteousness *is* life: and *in* the pathway *thereof there is* no death.

persons. Vain persons may be translated vain things and would then suggest searching for hidden treasures (C. J. Ellicott, *Proverbs*, p. 324). The following of such a course stamps a man devoid of understanding.

12-23. Proverbs that point to virtues and faults in civil relations are collected here. The wicked feed on one another; one wicked man seeks to relieve another evil man of his gains. These men continuously seek the ruin of their fellows. The root of the righteous sponsors the production of much fruit without the infliction of injury on others.

The wicked man is cursed for his words, which are the product of his evil heart. His speech, which is designed to injure others, demonstrates a curious boomerang effect and settles upon the sender with devastating consequences. The just man avoids much of this devastation by discrimination in his speech. Wise, benevolent discourse brings good to such a man, for the works that men sow are always rendered unto them as recompense. The fool cares not for this type of counsel. He artfully rationalizes the propriety of his behavior. The wise man, on the other hand, is a willing listener and an ardent reformer.

Whenever the fool is angry, everybody knows about it immediately. The wise man, in contrast, exercises a prudent self-control and covers that which could produce shame. He waits for the proper moment to attempt to instruct the offender. The wise man always speaks the truth, even when it means confronting the fool. He is particularly careful to speak the truth in judicial matters when he is functioning as a witness. The deceitful witness stands in stark contrast to wisdom's witness. This babbling fool talks incessantly and takes no notice of those whose feelings are wounded because of his inconsiderate chatter. The wise man moves through life with a commitment to speech that heals, and he diligently binds the wounds of those who have fallen prey to the lacerating fool. These verbal assassins will be cut off. In the providence of God they will be dealt with (cf. Ps 64:7-8) and silenced forever. Those who strive for healing and peace shall be established forever (cf. Mt 5:7-9).

The evil man suffers from a malignancy in the heart; the heart of the man who counsels peace is possessed by joy. The givers of wholesome counsel both sow and reap joy. In fact, they are the world's joy, just as the wicked man is this world's malignancy. These men of joy cannot be touched by evil, except God allow it for the accomplishment of His sovereign purposes (cf. I Cor 10:13). God will, however, fill the life of the wicked with all manner of trials that are designed to lead them to repentance (Rom 1:18, 28). In summary, Solomon gives Yahweh's final descriptive word for these liars: they are an abomination. The Lord has no delight in them, but rather turns His love and blessing to those who deal truly, i.e., the prudent men of this world. These special men love enough to practice silence in the presence of others' faults. The fool, in contrast, blurts forth all he knows and suspects indiscriminately.

24-28. The man of sloth will ultimately be forced into servitude. He is too lazy to labor at the appropriate time and will be obliged at a later season to labor as a slave to earn the bare necessities of life. The diligent, who use every provided moment industriously, will ultimately rule over the sluggards.

A heavy heart will work its way through a man's entire being until the whole body is made to stoop. The marked consequences of anxiety are noticed in Scripture, and the sin is sternly opposed (Ps 37:5; Mt 6:25; I Pet 5:7). The man of wisdom will attempt a ministry of healing through the careful use of words. A good word may restore joy to the heart of a man bowed to the earth.

Truly, the righteous are the royalty of this world. It is they who should be followed. However, in this world of appearances the wicked seduce large numbers of simple ones.

The slothful man is so lazy that he will not even prepare game that is already in his hand to eat. Such a man does not appreciate the resource that is in his hand. Only to the man of diligence is substance precious, for he alone knows the price of its attainment. He has paid the price, and in the paying he has learned the preciousness of that which is to be possessed. R.B.Y. Scott translates verse 28, on the road of righteousness there is life and the treading of its path (reading *Netibato* for Mount *Netigah*) is deathlessness (R.B.Y. Scott, *The Anchor Bible*, Proverbs, p. 91). The righteous practice diligence, for such care in living leads to a life which knows no death.

CHAPTER 13

A WISE son *heareth* his father's instruction: but a scorner heareth not rebuke.

2 A man shall eat good by the fruit of *his* mouth: but the soul of the transgressors *shall eat* violence.

3 He that keepeth his mouth keepeth his life: *but* he that openeth wide his lips shall have destruction.

4 The soul of the sluggard desireth, and *hath* nothing: but the soul of the diligent shall be made fat.

5 A righteous *man* hateth lying: but a wicked *man* is loathsome, and cometh to shame.

6 Righteousness keepeth *him that is* upright in the way: but wickedness overthroweth the sinner.

7 There is that maketh himself rich, yet *hath* nothing: *there is* that maketh himself poor, yet *hath* great riches.

8 The ransom of a man's life *are* his riches: but the poor heareth not rebuke.

9 The light of the righteous rejoiceth: but the lamp of the wicked shall be put out.

10 Only by pride cometh contention: but with the well advised *is* wisdom.

11 Wealth *gotten* by vanity shall be diminished: but he that gathereth by labour shall increase.

12 Hope deferred maketh the heart sick: but *when* the desire cometh, *it is* a tree of life.

13 Whoso despiseth the word shall be destroyed: but he that feareth the commandment shall be rewarded.

14 The law of the wise *is* a fountain of life, to depart from the snares of death.

15 Good understanding giveth favour: but the way of transgressors *is* hard.

D. Wisdom's Instruction on Right Living. 13:1-25.

13:1-7. This section consists of the kind of teaching that a father might give to his son or a teacher to his pupil. The scorner's unwillingness to accept rebuke is once again cited. The speech of the good man is life-giving, and he and others are benefited by it. The treacherous have no desire to further righteousness, but rather are filled with a desire for violence and trouble. They often say the first thing that comes into their mind and, consequently, author much destruction. The soul (Heb *nepesh*, i.e., life or appetite) of the sluggard is always filled with the desire for food and the good things of life, but he never receives them. The diligent see the satisfaction of their desires because they faithfully work to accomplish their desired goals.

Truth in the heart is the secret of practical righteousness. Falsehood is an abomination to those who are in the way. The wicked become more odious with the advance of time and are ultimately overthrown by their own sin. It is in the nature of the wicked man to play the hypocrite when it suits his diabolical purposes. At times he feigns riches and then again feigns poverty. The direction his pretense takes is dictated by that which will bring him greatest personal gain (C. Toy, *The International Critical Commentary*, Proverbs, p. 264).

8-12. Several interpretations have been offered for verse 8. The thought seems to be that those who possess riches invariably put their trust in them. The possession of riches allows a man to scorn the one who offers reproof. The poor need worry little about threatenings. Poverty and insignificance are their protection.

The light of the righteous burns brightly, and so the path he traverses is always clearly seen. The lamp of the wicked flares for a moment but, alas, gives out and leaves its carrier in utter darkness to stumble and fall.

Nothing but contention comes from pride. The man who is too proud to receive input from others is certain to experience grave difficulties in his relationships. They are wise who suffer themselves to be advised.

Wealth that is secured in a fraudulent manner vanishes sooner than a breath. A man treasures that for which he has toiled honestly and is careful in the use of it. His substance gradually and progressively increases because of his careful stewardship and hard labor.

The continuous frustration of one's hopes will produce sickness of heart. The translating of desires into realities is a vivifying experience. Realized ambitions provide foundations for growth from which much fruit can spring forth. The fulfillment of desires is a tree of life.

13-15. The man who despises the word of instruction will bring certain ruin upon himself. The awesome power of Yahweh to bring reward or destruction is in view in this passage. To despise Yahweh's commandments is to expose oneself to shame and destruction. He that feareth the commandments will not experience the sorrows of the transgressor and will inherit the promised reward. The righteous, by the performance of his duty, brings life and healing to his neighbors. He is a tree of life

and healing to his neighbors. He is a tree of life who attracts men to himself and induces them to follow him away from the snares of death. Such good understanding brings favor with God and men. The way of the transgressor, in contrast, is rough and barren. He leads others only to the sadness and barrenness of life that is his daily lot.

16-25. The careful actions of the prudent man are here contrasted with those of the fool who openly flaunts his folly. The fool exposes his lack of knowledge to all by his evident lack of discernment. The prudent move cautiously ahead, pondering the counsel of wisdom and realizing that their character is fully demonstrated by words spoken and deeds performed.

16 Every prudent *man* dealeth with knowledge: but a fool layeth open *his* folly.

17 A wicked messenger falleth into mischief: but a faithful ambassador *is* health.

18 Poverty and shame *shall be to* him that refuseth instruction: but he that regardeth reproof shall be honoured.

19 The desire accomplished is sweet to the soul: but *it is* abomination to fools to depart from evil.

20 He that walketh with wise *men* shall be wise: but a companion of fools shall be destroyed.

21 Evil pursueth sinners: but to the righteous good shall be repayed.

22 A good *man* leaveth an inheritance to his children's children: and the wealth of the sinner *is* laid up for the just.

23 Much food *is in* the tillage of the poor: but there is *that is* destroyed for want of judgment.

24 He that spareth his rod hateth his son: but he that loveth him chasteneth him betimes.

25 The righteous eateth to the satisfying of his soul: but the belly of the wicked shall want.

The messenger who runs unsent or betrays his master will fall into trouble as a punishment for his faithfulness. The man who practices loyalty as the ambassador of another is health and blessing to his employers and himself.

Men may feel it beneath their dignity to bow to instruction, but lasting honor will only come to those who humble themselves and receive instructions from those who are in possession of true knowledge. Poverty and shame will be the portion of all who think themselves too advanced for such instruction.

The accomplishment of desired objectives can bring real joy to the soul, but the desires of the fool are directed toward the accomplishment of evil. Evil desires are especially hard to appease since they are grounded in unbridled passion. The evil man considers it an abomination not to pursue the satiation of these insatiable desires. This explains the horrible depths to which depraved men often plunge. Once started on their downward spiral, they feel it an abomination to desist from pressing on into the darkness. Such men stumble on to total destruction, and all who are their companions share their end. Only those who walk with wisdom are safe from these men.

Once again Solomon emphasizes the principle of retribution. The sinner vigorously pursues evil, only to find that evil is pursuing him. The righteous man is vigorous in his pursuit of righteousness, and he too is repaid in kind.

When at last the good man is called away from this world, he leaves the inheritance to his descendants. An honored name and the material gains God has given are his legacy, for he has not squandered his substance nor his reputation. The treasures of the wicked are soon dissipated and pass into the hands of those who, through the faithful practice of discipline, use this world's goods aright.

Because he is diligent, the poor farmer will use every corner of his little farm and will enjoy a greater harvest than his wealthy neighbor who has many more acres that he allows to stand untilled. The man who has little often makes the most of what he has, while the man who enjoys larger privileges often reaps little because of his lack of discipline.

The production of such wasteful attitudes may be prevented if parents faithfully discipline their children in time, i.e., before such faults have firmly rooted themselves. Corporal punishment of children should be patterned after the divine discipline of Hebrews 12. It is not love, but actually a lack of it, that refuses to check those propensities that are sure to lead to future tragedy. The Scriptures declare without hesitation that he who loves his children will correct them.

The righteous may not have a large portion, but to them alone is given the power of enjoyment. They alone know the joy of satisfaction of soul. The wicked, though they be surrounded by abundance, can never attain true satisfaction. They shall always be in want.

CHAPTER 14

EVERY wise woman buildeth her

E. Wisdom's Instruction on the Fear of the LORD. 14:1-35.

14:1. The wise and the foolish woman are now contrasted. The wise woman, by her counsel and personal example, leads

house: but the foolish plucketh it down with her hands.

2 He that walketh in his uprightness feareth the LORD: but *he that is* perverse in his ways despiseth him.

3 In the mouth of the foolish *is* a rod of pride: but the lips of the wise shall preserve them.

4 Where no oxen *are*, the crib *is* clean: but much increase *is* by the strength of the ox.

5 A faithful witness will not lie: but a false witness will utter lies.
6 A scorner seeketh wisdom, and *find-eth it* not: but knowledge *is* easy unto him that understandeth.
7 Go from the presence of a foolish man, when thou perceivest not *in him* the lips of knowledge.

8 The wisdom of the prudent *is* to understand his way: but the folly of fools *is* deceit.

9 Fools make a mock at sin: but among the righteous *there is* favour.

10 The heart knoweth his own bitterness; and a stranger doth not inter-meddle with his joy.
11 The house of the wicked shall be overthrown: but the tabernacle of the upright shall flourish.
12 There is a way which seemeth right unto a man, but the end thereof *are* the ways of death.
13 Even in laughter the heart is sorrowful; and the end of that mirth *is* heaviness.
14 The backslider in heart shall be filled with his own ways: and a good man *shall be satisfied* from himself.

her household in the way that is right and consequently builds up her house. The foolish woman pulls down her household with her own hands. The contrast is ultimately between the constructive nature of wisdom and the destructive nature of folly.

2. Feareth the LORD. The man who fears the Lord will walk in the straight way. The man who walks on the twisted road of perversity, i.e., the road of double dealings, is the man who despises the Lord.

3. The wise man is delivered from many difficulties into which the foolish come by their rash talk. The wise man gives the soft answer that turns away wrath. He is slow to speak and swift to hear. **The lips of the wise shall preserve them.**

4. An empty stable is a clean stable, but it would indeed be a foolish man who would kill his oxen to insure a clean crib. Labor does have its disagreeable aspects. One must work long hours, care for animals, and deny self many things; but labor also has its rewards. The oxen allow a man to increase his efforts and, ultimately, to enjoy a larger reward for efforts expended. The little time spent in cleaning the stalls is more than adequately reimbursed.

5-7. A false witness is committed to the declaration of that which is untrue. The faithful witness will not lie, for he is committed to that which is true. God resists the proud (Jas 4:6). The scorner is thereby disqualified from the possession of wisdom; his heart is filled with pride. None but those to whom God gives it can possess wisdom, for he alone has it to give (I Cor 2:11). To those who fear him, he teaches the precepts of wisdom (Ps 24:11); and they comprehend his teaching with ease. When you perceive that a man's heart has been captured by foolishness, go from such a man with haste. To argue or reason with him is useless. The proper course of action is withdrawal from the company of one whose mouth is filled with foolishness.

8. The prudent are guided by wisdom into the way that is right. The lying fool has no desire for wisdom. The prudent are able to evaluate their walk and see it as God himself views it. The folly of fools is that their perception of their walk in no way corresponds with the Lord's evaluation.

9. Fools are mocked by their sin offerings. God does not accept their offerings, and so they have gone through the motions for nothing since they come with no deep sense of their own sinfulness. The upright, who come to God with a deep sense of inner sin, receive the favor of the Lord, for he is pleased with their offerings.

10. Every heart has its own joys and bitterness that no one else can share. No other person perfectly understands those inner emotions, except the Lord Jesus Christ (cf. Heb 4:15).

11-14. The great **house of the wicked shall be overthrown,** while the little **tabernacle** (tent) **of the upright** shall stand and flourish. The house undoubtedly seems more stable to the uninformed, but it shall be destroyed; for it rests on a foundation of sand. To man the house seems destined to far outlast the tent. **There is a way which seemeth right unto a man,** but the end of that way is always disaster and death. The pursuit of gain, when coupled with man's natural perspective, invariably results in punishment. Even in laughter these men find no lasting satisfaction. Though they laugh, their hearts are not at rest; and their mirth leads them only to the madness of despondency (cf. Ps 36:8). This backslider in heart, i.e., the man who has slid away from God, has his reward. He gets to the full that which he seeks, and to his chagrin he stands ruined and empty in the midst of his gain. The good man will be satisfied from within himself; for his satisfaction does not consist in the pursuit of externalities, but rather in the quiet confidence that he walks with God and labors under the security and provisioning of Yahweh's mighty hand.

15 The simple believeth every word: but the prudent *man* looketh well to his going.
16 A wise *man* feareth, and departeth from evil: but the fool rageth, and is confident.
17 *He that is* soon angry dealeth foolishly: and a man of wicked devices is hated.
18 The simple inherit folly: but the prudent are crowned with knowledge.
19 The evil bow before the good; and the wicked at the gates of the righteous.

20 The poor is hated even of his own neighbour: but the rich *hath* many friends.
21 He that despiseth his neighbour sinneth: but he that hath mercy on the poor, happy *is* he.
22 Do they not err that devise evil? but mercy and truth *shall be* to them that devise good.
23 In all labour there is profit: but the talk of the lips *tendeth* only to penury.
24 The crown of the wise *is* their riches: *but* the foolishness of fools *is* folly.
25 A true witness delivereth souls: but a deceitful *witness* speaketh lies.
26 In the fear of the LORD *is* strong confidence: and his children shall have a place of refuge.
27 The fear of the LORD *is* a fountain of life, to depart from the snares of death.
28 In the multitude of people *is* the king's honour: but in the want of people *is* the destruction of the prince.

29 *He that is* slow to wrath *is* of great understanding: but *he that is* hasty of spirit exalteth folly.
30 A sound heart *is* the life of the flesh: but envy the rottenness of the bones.
31 He that oppresseth the poor reproacheth his Maker: but he that honoureth him hath mercy on the poor.

15-19. The simple man believes every word he hears for he lacks any fixed principle by which to gauge the verity of another's words or ways. In consequence, he often takes the wrong steps and stumbles. The prudent man considers carefully the planting of his feet and ponders the direction in which he is advancing. He fears the dreadful consequences of evil. He refuses to play around with evil, but rather chooses to remove himself from its presence with haste. The fool consistently gives way to passion and is confident that he can master any situation.

The rash fool makes a practice of doing stupid things and is a continuous object of ridicule, but people do not hate him. The man of wicked devices, however, is hated for his cold-blooded acts.

In searching for lawless pleasures the simple inherit much folly, while the knowledge that the prudent have acquired through diligence adorns them like a crown.

Though the realization of verse 19 may not be swift in coming, the truth of the verse is forever settled in heaven. The final retribution of Yahweh finds the wicked bowing at the feet of the holy (Phil 2:10).

20-22. The simple applaud the rich, while the poor are the object of their disgust. Such attitudes are not in keeping with righteousness, and those who hold them sin grievously. God will reward those who are gracious in their dealings with the poor.

23-28. Labor is profitable; for it occupies the mind and hands of a man, thus lessening the danger of his giving way to his corrupt nature. Mere talk i.e., idle talk, results in material and spiritual poverty. One should thus beware of idle talk more than of the hardest physical labor.

The riches of the wise are an adornment that allows the wisdom they have to shine even more brightly. The fool, whatever his possessions, is filled only with folly; and nothing he can bring him to any ultimate profit.

A man who witnesses to the truth will deliver souls from certain death at the hands of some false witness brought against them in a court of law. This verse, when joined to verse five, presents the picture of the faithful and true witness in whose deeds the Lord delights. A deceitful witness is in every way the opposite of the true. His heart and mouth are filled with lies, and many are led to eternal loss because of his deceitful words and acts. The deceitful witness does not fear the Lord. Solomon everywhere teaches the necessity of the fear of Yahweh; to understand this principle is to embrace the supreme duty of man (Eccl 12:13). The man who has learned to fear the Lord has laid hold of a strong confidence and a mighty refuge. This fear is not the paranoia of a frightened bondsman, but the fear of a son that any careless act should bring dishonor upon the father who has loved and given all he possesses for his son. This fear is a fountain of life that serves to nourish the son through every dark forest of circumstance and, ultimately, to deliver him from the snares of death. Yahweh wills that many come to know him in this way, for he is honored as he brings many sons to salvation. He will enjoy the worship of multitudes in that final day (Rev 7:9).

29-35. The man who rules his own spirit wisely is a man of understanding. The Scriptures teach everywhere that the Lord has given to man the ability to govern that which issues from his life (cf. I Cor 14:32). He who refuses to control his spirit and is given to volatile self-expression is of little use to himself or others.

A sound heart is one in which the passions and emotions are under control. Such a heart brings composure and soundness to

32 The wicked is driven away in his wickedness: but the righteous hath hope in his death.

33 Wisdom resteth in the heart of him that hath understanding: but *that which is* in the midst of fools is made known.

34 Righteousness exalteth a nation: but sin *is* a reproach to any people.

35 The king's favour *is* toward a wise servant: but his wrath is *against* him that causeth shame.

CHAPTER 15

A SOFT answer turneth away wrath: but grievous words stir up anger.

2 The tongue of the wise useth knowledge aright: but the mouth of fools poureth out foolishness.

3 The eyes of the LORD *are* in every place, beholding the evil and the good.

4 A wholesome tongue *is* a tree of life: but perverseness therein *is* a breach in the spirit.

5 A fool despiseth his father's instruction: but he that regardeth reproof is prudent.

all of life. A heart filled with violent excitement or envy is the cause of trouble for the entire organism.

All men are the work of God (cf. 22:2; Gen 1:27; Job 31:15). To oppress the poor is to ultimately reproach the God who made all and cares equally for them. The duty to aid the poor is found everywhere in Scripture (Mt 25:40), and he who loves God will value the privilege of ministering to the poor. God, who views the actions of all men, will interpret such acts of kindness as honor bestowed upon himself.

The wicked care not for God and are carried along on the wings of unbridled passion. Ultimately, they are carried into a hopeless eternity to receive their reward, a reward that carries them out from the presence of God into the eternal abyss of hell. The righteous have a better hope in their death. They go to sleep in this world with trustful hope in the coming joy (Job 13:15; Ps 23:4).

Wisdom rests in the heart of the man of understanding. From this center wisdom controls all that the man does and says. The fool does not have wisdom dwelling in his midst. It is mischievous folly that controls him, and this is readily apparent to all who hear his words or behold his deeds.

A nation is exalted when righteousness is in her midst. Just as wisdom in the heart of a man energizes the production of works that merit divine approval, so righteousness in the heart of a nation will enable the production of works that will bring the smile of God upon the nation. Sin in the heart of a nation will be readily assessable, for it will issue in a pollution that will bring reproach upon the people; and God's judgment will soon be seen falling like a hammer. The king's favor rests upon the righteous, but his wrath is destined to burn from the land all pollutants.

F. Wisdom's Instruction on the Cheerful Heart and the Proper Path. 15:1-33.

15:1-2. The power for good and evil that lies in the human tongue is awesome. A soft word will often disarm a man whose heart is bent upon great harm, whereas harsh words serve only to stir up great anger.

The wise man masters the art of producing the right answer at the proper time and place. He often allows angry words to pass unchallenged, for he has his personal feelings in subjection. He knows when to speak; and when he does, he uses his knowledge in such a way that his words are statements that have great profit for his hearers. The fool is always ready with an answer, but men are seldom profited by his foolish contribution.

3. The wise man does not just believe in God; he believes in the God who is always there. In every moment Yahweh is beholding all he says and does. Not one word or deed escapes His knowing eye. He beholds the evil man and weighs each action until his iniquity is full (Gen 15:16). He compassionately watches the good man and is ever ready to come to his aid (Ps 25:15-17).

4. The wholesome tongue in verse 4 should be understood as the healing tongue, the tongue that issues forth healing speech. This therapeutic speech is a tree of life to those who are the grateful recipients of its ministry. The perverse tongue belongs to the man who sows discord. Those around him suffer much, but he is the ultimate loser; for perverse speech will ultimately cause a breach in his spirit, literally a fragmentation of his own personality.

5. The world is filled with young men who think that their insights are superior to those of their fathers. The young often register disdain for the reproof of their elders. The fool seldom cares for the advice of one who has been over the path before him. He is so full of self-confidence that he feels no need for the slightest assistance. The man who regards reproof and thank-

6 In the house of the righteous *is* much treasure: but in the revenues of the wicked is trouble.

7 The lips of the wise disperse knowledge: but the heart of the foolish *doeth* not so.

8 The sacrifice of the wicked *is* an abomination to the LORD: but the prayer of the upright *is* his delight.
9 The way of the wicked *is* an abomination unto the LORD: but he loveth him that followeth after righteousness.

10 Correction *is* grievous unto him that forsaketh the way: *and* he that hateth reproof shall die.
11 Hell and destruction *are* before the LORD: how much more then the hearts of the children of men?
12 A scorner loveth not one that reproveth him: neither will he go unto the wise.
13 A merry heart maketh a cheerful countenance: but by sorrow of the heart the spirit is broken.
14 The heart of him that hath understanding seeketh knowledge: but the mouth of fools feedeth on foolishness.

15 All the days of the afflicted *are* evil: but he that is of a merry heart *hath* a continual feast.

16 Better *is* little with the fear of the LORD than great treasure and trouble therewith.
17 Better *is* a dinner of herbs where love is, than a stalled ox and hatred therewith.

18 A wrathful man stirreth up strife: but *he that is* slow to anger appeaseth strife.
19 The way of the slothful *man is* as an hedge of thorns: but the way of the righteous *is* made plain.
20 A wise son maketh a glad father: but a foolish man despiseth his mother.

fully acknowledges correction is sure to finish life's journey in better fashion than the fool.

6. God's blessing rests upon the house of the righteous. The treasure that is in such a house is undoubtedly the righteousness that becomes at once a sign and a pledge of abiding prosperity. Whatever riches the wicked may pile up, he shall never be truly rich; for he has no part in the true riches, the righteousness and favor of God (cf. Luke 16:11).

7. The lips of the wise are committed to evangelism and discipleship. They are constantly spreading abroad the knowledge God has given them for the profit, blessing, and edification of all humanity. The fool can only utter what is in his heart, and such nonsense is of no permanent value to anyone. In fact, his words, when believed, often produce great harm.

8-9. These verses are among the few in Proverbs that deal directly with the subject of worship. The Lord delights in the prayers of the righteous, for such utterances form the nucleus of all worship. The sacrifices of the wicked, however, are an abomination to Him. The term abomination is found only in Proverbs and Deuteronomy (Deut 7:25, 26; 18:12). Abomination (Heb *tōʿēbah*) denotes something that is abhorrent or repulsive (William McKane, *Proverbs*, p. 486). The Lord removes himself from those whom He abhors.

10-14. A grievous punishment awaits those who forsake the way of wisdom. The Lord will first bring correction that is designed to bring them back into the way (Lev 26:14 ff.). If a man hates this reproof from the Lord and does not move to the place of repentance, the Lord will kill him. No man will be able to fool Yahweh. His evaluation takes into account all the facts, for He is the perfect discerner of the thoughts and intents of the heart. All is open to Him, even the unseen world of hell and destruction (Heb *ʾabadōn*). Destruction is a synonym for sheol, or the grave (R.B.Y. Scott, *The Anchor Bible*, Proverbs, p. 102).

The scorner is incorrigible, and he will not tolerate the company of the wise man who could teach him the way of life. He loves no one if words of reproof must pass between them.

Joy in the heart brightens the countenance. The inner condition of a man always shows in his outward appearance. When there is pain in the heart, the spirit of a man is broken; and the power for effective living vanishes. The heart of man determines the course to be taken. A heart possessed by understanding moves briskly toward greater knowledge, while the heart of the fool ushers him toward greater participation in foolishness.

15. This verse is connected with the thirteenth verse. The man who is depressed sees in each day only those dismal events that serve to increase his already extensive fear. The man whose life is possessed by a merry heart sees such evidences of God's faithfulness that his days are bright and his soul has a **continual feast.** The source of such festivity is the settled conviction that every affliction and blessing has its source in God's love.

16-17. It is better to have little on earth and joy in the heart than to have extensive luxuries accompanied by great trouble. The one who is rejoicing in the Lord can well understand the dear old saint who gave thanks for a bit of bread, an onion, a glass of water, and then joyfully thanked God for "all this and Jesus!" Better is a dish of herbs when love is there. Vegetables represented the diet of the simple poor, while meat was the festive food, especially the flesh of fatted oxen. Better the simple diet with love than festive food shared with those who hate you.

18-22. The commendation of the even-tempered man is the subject of verse 18. He is the man who carefully controls his emotions and is not prone to quarreling. A wrathful man stirs up strife wherever he goes. The man who is slow to anger is able to spread the oil of peace on strife-laden situations.

The slothful man sleeps on a bed of thorns. Every hour of the day he is hedged about by thorns. Most of the thorns, however,

21 Folly *is* joy to *him that is* destitute of wisdom: but a man of understanding walketh uprightly.
22 Without counsel purposes are disappointed: but in the multitude of counsellors they are established.

23 A man hath joy by the answer of his mouth: and a word *spoken* in due season, how good *is it!*
24 The way of life *is* above to the wise, that he may depart from hell beneath.

25 The LORD will destroy the house of the proud: but he will establish the border of the widow.

26 The thoughts of the wicked *are* an abomination to the LORD: but *the words* of the pure *are* pleasant words.

27 He that is greedy of gain troubleth his own house; but he that hateth gifts shall live.

28 The heart of the righteous studieth to answer: but the mouth of the wicked poureth out evil things.
29 The LORD *is* far from the wicked: but he heareth the prayer of the righteous.
30 The light of the eyes rejoiceth the heart: *and* a good report maketh the bones fat.

31 The ear that heareth the reproof of life abideth among the wise.
32 He that refuseth instruction despiseth his own soul: but he that heareth reproof getteth understanding.
33 The fear of the LORD *is* the instruction of wisdom; and before honour *is* humility.

are imagined and serve to provide him with all manner of excuses for not dealing responsibly with the realities of life. The righteous, having been informed of his duty, presses toward the fulfillment of his goals. Such obedience illumines his way and makes plain the path for his feet.

A father's heart will be gladdened when his son chooses to walk in the ways of wisdom. It is a foolish man who considers himself superior to his mother and ignores her loving advice. Such a man will soon lose the path and succumb to fascination with folly.

The man who desires to stay on the plain path would do well to consult with men of spiritual experience, for with a multitude of counselors the right way will be clearly discerned. Collective wisdom is always to be preferred to individual wisdom. Consultation enlarges the possibility of success for individuals and communities.

23-24. The wisest of men are apt to say things that they later regret. Much mischief is done by the tongue. Little wonder that a good and therapeutic answer would be a cause of great joy. Speech of this nature will only be found on the lips of those whose way of life is anchored in God's wisdom. Men who speak therapeutically have stepped on the upward path that leads to heaven. The man of understanding has embraced a way of life that leads ever upward to higher levels of moral purity and responsibility. A reference to heaven is implied by the reference to sheol. This man makes every effort to avoid the hopeless abode of the eternally dying.

25. The house of the proud will not endure, for the Lord will destroy it. His face is forever set against those who exalt themselves. God has perennially been the support of widows and orphans, who need protection from the evil forces and men of this world. Yahweh will establish the borders of the widow. The offense of removing a neighbor's landmark was a common form of oppression, and the threatened punishment is often mentioned in Scripture (cf. Deut 19:14; 27:17). God's curse rested upon any who would remove the ancient landmarks.

26. This evil practice was a fruit of the thought of depraved men. Such men and their wicked plottings are an abomination to the Lord; they are utterly repulsive to him. In contrast, the words of the pure are pleasant words.

27. Man's greed for unjust gain is a perpetual source of woe for the people of this world. Greed leads men to habitually want more than their share. Greed and covetousness have proven the undoing of multitudes. The gifts (bribes) they often accept bring ruin upon themselves and shame upon all who bear their name. The haters of such greed, that is those who refuse to be involved in these ungodly practices, shall live.

28-30. The righteous man understands the potential for good and evil that resides in words. In keeping with this understanding, the man who fears God will weigh his words carefully, lest through a hasty utterance he bring dishonor upon his Lord and cause pain in the life of his neighbor. The wicked show no such consideration.

The Lord will hear the righteous, for He has pledged himself to hear the prayers of the righteous (cf. Jn 15:7). The righteous will have eyes that are sparkling with joy, for they are dynamically linked to the God who cares for them and answers their prayers. **A good report maketh the bones fat.** Good news is always a tonic for both body and soul.

31-33. The ear that hears the reproof that points the way to life will place its owner within the circle of the wise. He who undervalues the benefits of correction despises his own soul; he is in love with death. The man who hears reproof recognizes a responsibility to protect the eternal dimension of his soul life.

The best way to protect the soul from destruction is to embrace the fear of the Lord in every moment. Abiding in that

CHAPTER 16

THE preparations of the heart in man, and the answer of the tongue, *is* from the LORD.

2 All the ways of a man *are* clean in his own eyes; but the LORD weigheth the spirits.

3 Commit thy works unto the LORD, and thy thoughts shall be established.

4 The LORD hath made all *things* for himself: yea, even the wicked for the day of evil.

5 Every one *that is* proud in heart *is* an abomination to the LORD: *though* hand *join* in hand, he shall not be unpunished.

6 By mercy and truth iniquity is purged: and by the fear of the LORD *men* depart from evil.

7 When a man's ways please the LORD, he maketh even his enemies to be at peace with him.

8 Better *is* a little with righteousness than great revenues without right.

9 A man's heart deviseth his way: but the LORD directeth his steps.

10 A divine sentence *is* in the lips of the king: his mouth transgresseth not in judgment.

11 A just weight and balance *are* the LORD's: all the weights of the bag *are* his work.

12 *It is* an abomination to kings to commit wickedness: for the throne is established by righteousness.

13 Righteous lips *are* the delight of kings; and they love him that speaketh right.

14 The wrath of a king *is as* messen-

fear, the man of wisdom affirms that it is in accord with wisdom to humbly acknowledge one's mistakes and faults. A man must receive admonition as coming from the Lord himself, for humility is before honor.

G. Wisdom's Instruction on the LORD's Providential Care. 16:1-33.

16:1-3. Man's limited ability to plan his life is the subject of verse 1. Literally the verse should read: The plans are man's, but from the Lord is the tongue's answer. The close parallel in verse 9 makes the point clear: Whatever man may intend, that which actually eventuates is decided by God. "Man proposes but God disposes." (R.B.Y. Scott, *The Anchor Bible*, Proverbs, p. 106).

According to his own standards, a man may be able to justify all of his actions. The Lord, however, weighs the moral character of every action, and ultimately every action must be submitted to His judgment.

Man is encouraged to commit all of his works unto the Lord. Literally, the challenge is to roll something on someone, or entrust it wholly to him (J. P. Lange, *A Commentary on the Holy Scriptures*, Proverbs, p. 154). The Lord is ever ready to receive our weighty concerns or take charge of them and carry them through to successful completion. The beauty of such an arrangement is that the man who has placed such intensive confidence in Yahweh will never have to worry, and his thoughts will be securely established.

4-9. Yahweh's control of human life is the theme of verses 4-7. **The LORD hath made all things for himself,** that is, to serve His own purposes. Even the wicked are subservient to His eternal purposes. They are destined to experience the day of wrath and receive their well-merited punishment.

The proud in heart are repulsive to the Lord: and though they attempt to resist the Lord's judgment through the power of confederation, they will be broken asunder.

The avoidance of such an awesome encounter with God's wrath can only be accomplished through a faithful alliance with mercy and truth. Mercy and truth will always lead a man to the fear of the Lord, which will allow him to escape the compelling attraction of evil.

The ways of such a man will be a cause of delight to the Lord. This statement has far-reaching implications. If a man's ways are pleasing to the Lord, his enemies will be unable to assail his character. They might even hate him, but they will ultimately be compelled to admit that God is with him. Men should hasten to commit themselves to the Lord with the assurance that such a commitment will bring stability and peace to all of life (cf. vs. 3).

Even if this means being content with little, that is best. Integrity of heart and favor with Yahweh is worth far more than millions coupled with practices that are not right. Verse 9 should be compared with verse 1. The Lord is directing both the righteous and the unrighteous. He is leading the righteous toward eternal blessing, and the wicked He is leading inexorably toward their appointment with divine judgment.

10-15. Preparation for service and leadership is the major theme of this section. The ideal king is contemplated. Only occasionally have earthly rulers arisen who have incarnated the virtues of this ideal ruler. The verses may represent the days of Solomon's youth, when he aspired to judge the people without transgressing justice. **A just weight and balance** are a concern to the king, for they are indispensable as instruments for the proper advance of commerce. Wisdom's ideal king realizes that no evil thought or deed can be tolerated in his life, for the establishment of the throne depends upon his total commitment to righteousness. The righteous king will appreciate those in his

gers of death: but a wise man will pacify it.

15 In the light of the king's countenance *is* life; and his favour *is* as a cloud of the latter rain.

16 How much better *is it* to get wisdom than gold! and to get understanding rather to be chosen than silver!
17 The highway of the upright *is* to depart from evil: he that keepeth his way preserveth his soul.
18 Pride *goeth* before destruction, and an haughty spirit before a fall.
19 Better *it is to be* of an humble spirit with the lowly, than to divide the spoil with the proud.

20 He that handleth a matter wisely shall find good: and whoso trusteth in the LORD, happy *is* he.
21 The wise in heart shall be called prudent: and the sweetness of the lips increaseth learning.
22 Understanding *is* a wellspring of life unto him that hath it: but the instruction of fools *is* folly.
23 The heart of the wise teacheth his mouth, and addeth learning to his lips.
24 Pleasant words *are as* an honeycomb, sweet to the soul, and health to the bones.

25 There is a way that seemeth right unto a man, but the end thereof *are* the ways of death.
26 He that laboureth laboureth for himself; for his mouth craveth it of him.
27 An ungodly man diggeth up evil: and in his lips *there is* as a burning fire.
28 A froward man soweth strife: and a whisperer separateth chief friends.
29 A violent man enticeth his neighbour, and leadeth him into the way *that is* not good.
30 He shutteth his eyes to devise froward things: moving his lips he bringeth evil to pass.

kingdom who share his commitment to **righteous lips.** Such men register their partnership with the king by committing themselves to that which is his delight. The wrath of the king is directed against those who do not seek righteousness. This wrath can be diverted by a quick repentance accompanied by a resolve to pacify his anger.

The friendly countenance of the king is here contrasted with the countenance of wrath. This look of friendliness is compared with the cloud of the latter rain. This rain fell at the end of March, maturing all the crops before the harvest in April. The latter rain was eagerly anticipated and was the source of great blessing for the people. The ideal king is of equal importance to a nation. Without him the nation will wither and die, or at best lead a stunted existence.

16-19. Verse 16, along with verses 8, 19, and 32, belong to a series of proverbs of comparison. These proverbs flow from the pen of one who had a larger portion of this world's blessings than most men ever enjoy (I Kgs 3:12-13). The comparison is between greater and lesser goods. Wisdom and understanding are more valuable because they are more abiding. The security of wisdom also heightens its value. Wisdom preserves a man's soul and is, thus, to be chosen above the precarious delights of evil.

The highway of the upright is the plainly marked way of duty and humility. Men of haughty spirits detest this path and their love for the evil way assures them an imminent destruction. Pride blinds and humility opens the eyes of men to the joys of the lowly. Little wonder the Scriptures admonish all: ". . . Be not high-minded, but fear" (Rom 11:20).

20-24. These verses form a series of epigrams on the value of applied wisdom in the various affairs of life. The man who would have success for his companion needs two things. Wisdom is needed to teach man what to expect from himself, and trust enables a man to discern what he may expect from Yahweh. The matter of verse 20 may refer to the word (Heb *dabar*) of Yahweh. The man who acts wisely with respect to the words of the Lord will find good. The man of wisdom sees more reality in the smallest promises of God's word than in the greatest demonstrations of this world's might. With the psalmist he cries; ". . . Blessed are all they that put their trust in him" (Ps 2:12). Such trust creates men who are wise in heart. Sweetness of lips, i.e., gentle, and persuasive language, will secure for wisdom an ever-widening circle of listeners, thus serving to increase the learning of all.

The blessing of wisdom is primarily found in the enrichment it brings to its possessors. It is a source of unending refreshment in the depths of a man's heart where no secular force can quench its vivifying power. Wisdom is a well-spring of life.

Wisdom also brings to a man skill in utterance and continuously places in his mouth such pleasant words that others often find healing and learning in the instruction that is given. Like honey, the words of the wise have a therapeutic and strengthening value.

25-30. There is a way that seemeth right unto a man. This verse repeats the thought of 14:12. Solomon wishes to reemphasize the danger of refusing the path of wisdom for self-chosen ways that can only end in death. The danger of self-delusion is so real that warning upon warning must be issued against it.

The laboring man is driven on by his desires or hunger. His feeling that he is supplying a pressing need drives him onward. The fall of Adam has shut man out of the garden of delight, and he is condemned to labor for his bread with the sweat of his brow.

An ungodly man diggeth up evil. The perverse man of this world is described in verses 27-30. He is known for his deceitful and crafty dealings. He digs an evil pit for others through his

31 The hoary head *is* a crown of glory, *if* it be found in the way of righteousness.

32 *He that is* slow to anger *is* better than the mighty; and he that ruleth his spirit than he that taketh a city.

33 The lot is cast into the lap; but the whole disposing thereof *is* of the LORD.

CHAPTER 17

BETTER *is* a dry morsel, and quietness therewith, than an house full of sacrifices *with* strife.

2 A wise servant shall have rule over a son that causeth shame, and shall have part of the inheritance among the brethren.

3 The fining pot *is* for silver, and the furnace for gold: but the LORD trieth the hearts.

4 A wicked doer giveth heed to false lips; *and* a liar giveth ear to a naughty tongue.

5 Whoso mocketh the poor reproacheth his Maker: *and* he that is glad at calamities shall not be unpunished.

6 Children's children *are* the crown of old men; and the glory of children *are* their fathers.

malicious plottings and slander. The burning fire or volatile words that pass from his lips have in them the scorching malice of hell. He **soweth strife: and . . . separateth . . . friends.** He is a sterile person devoid of all true affection. His mischievous whispers often produce great harm and separate those who had become dear friends. His malignant deeds are often far more difficult to discern than the violent man, who is readily recognized by all. He is loud and overbearing, but many follow him because of the sheer force of his personality. At the appointed time he moves his eyes and lips to signal the commencement of the mischief he and his confederates have planned. The simple are carried forward into the **way that is not good,** almost as if they are captured by a magnetic spell.

31-32. The agitators who have been described will all be cut off before their time. The hoary head (grey hair) is a crown of glory when it adorns the head of one who is found in the way of the righteous. Hoary heads will be seen among the wicked; but there will be no glory there, only the agony of a body broken in the pursuit of sin. Only the man who has grown old in the pursuit of wisdom is crowned with the glory of God's presence.

A man may reach such a state only through the faithful practice of self-mastery. **He that is slow to anger is better than the mighty.** The ruling of the spirit is seen as the apex of wisdom's application (I Cor 14:32).

33. The lot is cast . . . but the . . . disposing thereof is of the LORD. Throughout the Bible the casting of lots was often used as a method for discovering the divine will (Lev 16:8; Num 26:55; Acts 1:26). Men may cast lots to ascertain what the future will bring, but Yahweh alone decides who will be exalted and who will be brought low.

H. Wisdom's Instruction on Men of Folly. 17:1-28.

17:1-2. The thought of verse 1 is similar to that of 15:17. It is better to have a simple meal in peace than to have feasting with contention. The mention of sacrifices here is an allusion to the practice of provisioning the house with the remains of the sacrifices. A man might have a house filled with such provisions; yet, if their presence was not accompanied by peace at the dinner table, then he might better have a dry morsel of bread and quietness.

A faithful servant is better than a rebellious son. He may take the place of an unworthy son and receive his part of the inheritance. Faithfulness will allow a man to rise from servitude to the status of sonship.

3. The refiner's fining pot and furnace try his metals. Yahweh alone claims the right to try the hearts (I Kgs 8:39). Gold must be placed in the furnace to free it from impurities. The refinement creates a separation between the good and the worthless.

4-5. A wicked heart filled to the brim with corruption gladly attends to the words of false lips. The liar is not content with the sin he is capable of concocting and delights in joining himself to those who speak the same evil language. In verse 5 our attention is once again called to the poor. Any who rejoice over the sudden misfortune of others are actually mocking the God who has providentially visited upon them their affliction. To pour contempt upon the currency of a land is to be contemptuous of the sovereign whose image the coinery bears. To be contemptuous of any of God's creatures is to despise the God who in His sovereignty has stamped his image upon every man, be He poor or rich (Gen 9:6).

6. The cohesion of the family unit is a basic theme of the Old Testament. Keeping the family chains intact was counted a great blessing. In verse 6 there are no gaps in the family. The aged view their children's children and find their youth renewed in

7 Excellent speech becometh not a fool: much less do lying lips a prince.
8 A gift *is as* a precious stone in the eyes of him that hath it: whithersoever it turneth, it prospereth.

9 He that covereth a transgression seeketh love; but he that repeateth a matter separateth *very* friends.

10 A reproof entereth more into a wise man than an hundred stripes into a fool.
11 An evil *man* seeketh only rebellion: therefore a cruel messenger shall be sent against him.
12 Let a bear robbed of her whelps meet a man, rather than a fool in his folly.
13 Whoso rewardeth evil for good, evil shall not depart from his house.

14 The beginning of strife *is as* when one letteth out water: therefore leave off contention, before it be meddled with.
15 He that justifieth the wicked, and he that condemneth the just, even they both *are* abomination to the LORD.
16 Wherefore *is there* a price in the hand of a fool to get wisdom, seeing *he hath* no heart *to it?*

17 A friend loveth at all times, and a brother is born for adversity.
18 A man void of understanding striketh hands, *and* becometh surety in the presence of his friend.

19 He loveth transgression that loveth strife: *and* he that exalteth his gate seeketh destruction.
20 He that hath a froward heart find-

them, while the young revere their fathers and heed well their instruction.

7-8. The speech of a man is always revealing, for the lip is an organ of the heart. Excellent speech reveals an upright heart. Lying lips reveal the heart of a fool. It cannot be otherwise, for out of the abundance of the heart a man speaks. In verse 8 Solomon again considers the influence of a gift, or literally a bribe. A bribe is like a jewel to the eyes of the man who receives it; all his energies are called up by the prospect of such lucrative gain. The promise that such material advancement brings provides great incentive for pushing on so that a man carries his tasks on to successful completion.

9. To cover a transgression does not imply the espousal of a light view of sin. Rather, it counsels a sensitive confrontation of the erring one with the hope of moving him to repentance. Such a mission for the man of wisdom has upon it the seal of secrecy. The man who goes about peddling information gained in the confidentiality of such encounters is an evil person. His evil work has ended many friendships.

10-13. Reprove the fool, and he will rebel with greater passion. Stripes only scourge the back of the fool; they cannot reach his heart, for it lies in a vacuum of rebellion. He ever remains a fool. Reprove a wise man, and he will take it to heart; for he realizes his limitations and is thankful for correction. **An evil man seeketh only rebellion.** He wants only to do his thing. Nothing galls him more than the attempted restraint of authorities. His unrestrainable rebelliousness mandates that he be severely dealt with. Encountering him is like encountering a bear robbed of her whelps. He is like an enraged animal when confronted in his rebellion, and a mighty messenger will be sent against him by Yahweh. Verse 13 expresses once again the principle of retribution. This evil man reaps what he has sown. He has dispensed evil, and **evil shall not depart from his house.**

14-16. The beginning of strife is as when one letteth out water. The drops that ever so gently seep through a tiny hole in the dikes of a reservoir can all too soon swell into a gushing torrent. From such small beginnings arise feuds that cannot be appeased. Lifetime feuds have often started with such meager beginnings and have swelled to unbelievable proportions. If apologies had been immediately forthcoming and sincerely meant, the wound could have been healed immediately. Saint Paul reiterates this in the New Testament when he says, "Be ye angry, and sin not: let not the sun go down upon your wrath" (Eph 4:26).

Men stir up strife when they justify the lawless and condemn the just. Such misuse of judicial authority is repulsive to Yahweh, who wants justice for the innocent and guilty alike. Fools who operate in this manner will remain fools. **Is there a price in the hand of the fool to get wisdom,** for they lack any capacity for change.

17-18. A friend loveth at all times, and a brother is born for adversity. The friend and the brother are related in that the one is the climax of the other. The friend is the companion with whom one shares a general spirit of comradery. Friends are chosen on the basis of congeniality and companionship. The true friend proves himself in adversity by helping whenever and wherever he is needed. Only adversity will allow such an amiable conjunction of spirits, for it alone provides the opportunity for the offerings of love which in truth only brother makes for brother. Though we would desire to befriend many in this way, we must proceed with caution. A man must use great care in his relationships, lest overwhelming liabilities be incurred.

19-21. He that exalteth his gate seeketh destruction. Men often adopt a life-style that is beyond their means. Many seek to transform a simple home into a splendid edifice. Private homes in Solomon's day were often entered through a lofty gateway

eth no good: and he that hath a perverse tongue falleth into mischief.

21 He that begetteth a fool *doeth it* to his sorrow: and the father of a fool hath no joy.

22 A merry heart doeth good *like* a medicine: but a broken spirit drieth the bones.

23 A wicked *man* taketh a gift out of the bosom to pervert the ways of judgment.

24 Wisdom *is* before him that hath understanding; but the eyes of a fool *are* in the ends of the earth.

25 A foolish son *is* a grief to his father, and bitterness to her that bare him.

26 Also to punish the just *is* not good, *nor* to strike princes for equity.

27 He that hath knowledge spareth his words: *and* a man of understanding is of an excellent spirit.

28 Even a fool, when he holdeth his peace, is counted wise: *and* he that shutteth his lips *is esteemed* a man of understanding.

CHAPTER 18

THROUGH desire a man, having separated himself, seeketh *and* intermeddleth with all wisdom.

2 A fool hath no delight in understanding, but that his heart may discover itself.

3 When the wicked cometh, *then* cometh also contempt, and with ignominy reproach.

4 The words of a man's mouth *are as* deep waters, *and* the wellspring of wisdom *as* a flowing brook.

5 *It is* not good to accept the person of the wicked, to overthrow the righteous in judgment.

6 A fool's lips enter into contention, and his mouth calleth for strokes.

7 A fool's mouth *is* his destruction, and his lips *are* the snare of his soul.

8 The words of a talebearer *are* as wounds, and they go down into the innermost parts of the belly.

9 He also that is slothful in his work is brother to him that is a great waster.

10 The name of the LORD *is* a strong tower: the righteous runneth into it, and is safe.

11 The rich man's wealth *is* his strong

that spoke of wealth and social prestige. Folk who did not have the means were often tempted to construct such edifices and brought financial ruin upon themselves. Their pride carried them into financial waters that were beyond their resources. Those who love contention also bring upon themselves ruin. These perverse men stir up mischief and then wind up falling prey to their own devices (Eccl 10:8).

22. A merry heart doeth good like a medicine. When a man feels gloomy, his whole body hurts; his whole life seems as lifeless as a pile of old dried bones. When joy invades the heart of man, it refreshes the whole man.

23. A wicked man taketh a gift out of the bosom to pervert the ways of judgment. Out of the bosom signifies the folds of the dress in which the bribe was concealed, waiting to be delivered into the hand of the judge whose favor it was destined to purchase. Such a judge perverts the way of justice, and God's judgment upon him will be severe.

24. The eyes of a fool are in the ends of the earth. The man of understanding keeps wisdom at the center of his vision. He has one grand object, and that is the gaining of the knowledge of Yahweh. The pursuit of that knowledge is at the top of his list of priorities. The fool has his eyes on the world; he has no settled purpose and skips from one thing to another.

25. The young man who wanders thus, aimlessly out of control, is a cause of great grief to his father and bitterness to her that bore him. To have brought one into the world who despises all restraint and has no settled objectives is a bitter reality to live with day after day.

26-28. Also to punish the just is not good. Rulers are to be a terror to those who do evil. If they become a terror to those who do good, the whole world will be turned upside down. The punishment of the just is an abomination to the Lord. Rebellion against the prince is never encouraged. The man who spares his words evidences knowledge, and the man who keeps a cool head in difficult times is a man of understanding. The shutting of the lips is commended everywhere in wisdom's instruction. Even a fool may be thought wise if he keeps his mouth shut.

I. Wisdom's Instruction on Perils and Blessings. 18:1-24.

18:1-5. Through desire a man, having separated himself. Observations are now made on the behavior of the man who alienates himself from all others. He is an unsociable man who cares only about his selfish concerns. He rails against every sound enterprise (R.B.Y. Scott, *The Anchor Bible*, Proverbs, p. 114). The fool loves to share his opinions, but he has no desire to grasp real understanding. This person will soon become a reproach and will never achieve a position of respect in the community.

The wise man is certain to become a source of enrichment to the members of his community. His words are deep and clear; they are a wellspring continuously sending forth fresh material.

To accept the wicked is not a wise course of action. Yahweh abhors false and biased decisions in the courts of this world and counsels the separation of his people from all who would commit such actions.

6-12. We are often confronted in Scripture with the evil that the tongue inflicts on others. Here we see the honor the tongue can produce for the man himself. The mouth of the fool continuously causes contention and calls forth the strokes of justice. In fact, the fool's mouth eventually will lead him to destruction if its vile production is not curtailed. The fool readily gives his ear to the talebearer and greedily swallows his words as if they were delicious food. (cf. 26:22).

The fool is also a waster of goods and time; he is slothful. He will not give careful attention to work, for his heart is set on the pursuit of other things.

city, and as an high wall in his own conceit.

12 Before destruction the heart of man is haughty, and before honour *is* humility.

13 He that answereth a matter before he heareth *it*, it *is* folly and shame unto him.

14 The spirit of a man will sustain his infirmity; but a wounded spirit who can bear?

15 The heart of the prudent getteth knowledge; and the ear of the wise seeketh knowledge.

16 A man's gift maketh room for him, and bringeth him before great men.

17 *He that is* first in his own cause *seemeth* just; but his neighbour cometh and searcheth him.

18 The lot causeth contentions to cease, and parteth between the mighty.

19 A brother offended *is harder to be won* than a strong city: and *their* contentions *are* like the bars of a castle.

20 A man's belly shall be satisfied with the fruit of his mouth; *and* with the increase of his lips shall he be filled.

21 Death and life *are* in the power of the tongue: and they that love it shall eat the fruit thereof.

22 *Whoso* findeth a wife findeth a good *thing*, and obtaineth favour of the LORD.

23 The poor useth intreaties; but the rich answereth roughly.

24 A man *that hath* friends must shew himself friendly: and there is a friend *that* sticketh closer than a brother.

Men ought to hasten from such a frivolous life-style and run with the righteous to the name of the Lord. The phrase, **name of the LORD,** is used only here in Proverbs. The name represents the Lord himself, His presence and His power. He alone is a strong tower in whom men may find true security.

Men may seek to fortify themselves through other means. The rich man may hope to fortify himself behind walls constructed by his riches and may protest in conceit that he does not need the Lord. However, this haughty man is destined for destruction. The shattering realities of life will reveal the artificiality of the security that those walls afford. Honor, or favor with Yahweh, alone can provide lasting security, humility alone bestows upon a man the honor that leads to the enjoyment of Yahweh's security.

13-15. Rash words spoken without benefit of full information often expose a man to open shame. When all the evidence is gathered, the conclusions of such a man are often proven false. Perhaps the young man is particularly in view here because of his boundless confidence in his ability to correctly analyze all situations. Folly and shame often accompany such boundless optimism.

A spirit of praise often enables a man to rise above the infirmities of the flesh. If that spirit is lost and replaced by a broken spirit, then the defeat of the whole man will quickly ensue. Verse 15 presents the mind that is in direct antithesis to the mind of verse 2. The man of wisdom is constantly seeking knowledge. His ear and his heart are ever open to the instruction of the wise.

16-21. The gifted man need never force himself upon others. The faithful use of his gifts will gain for him recognition that will ultimately make room for him and bring him before great men.

The value of cross-examination is discussed in verse 17. It is always unwise to hear only one side of a case and make a pronouncement. Even the best of men will render a prejudicial accounting of the events that concern them. Wisdom mandates a thorough searching of both parties, preferably with them face to face. This will allow for a careful sifting of statements and guarantee a better grasp of the truth.

When arrangements seemed beyond resolution, the lot was often resorted to for a final settlement of the issue. Men who might otherwise settle their dispute by blows would accept the lot as the judgment of God.

A brother offended is harder to win than a strong city, and his antagonism is like the bars of a castle. The deep animosity that is the fruit of quarreling between brethren is likened in its intensity to the rigid resistance of the city gates against all intrusion. The bursting of these bars was almost impossible, so great was their strength. A brother entrenched behind the bars of wounded pride, unwilling to view the matter from a Godly perspective, is equally impregnable.

The tongue possesses the power for life or for death. He who builds strong bars with his tongue must suffer the guilt and loneliness that ensue, while he who sows well with his lips will provide pleasant fruit for his soul.

22-24. A good wife is a gift from Yahweh. It is not blind chance that brings such a blessed union. She is one of the highest expressions of the Lord's favor.

The rich are apt to harden their hearts against the Lord. Filled with conceit, they are often devoid of kindness and speak roughly. The poor, who have little to lean on but the Lord, have to master the art of entreating. They take great care in their speech to please both God and man.

The acquisition of friends is dependent upon the ability to demonstrate friendliness toward others. He who is a friend himself will always meet others eager to reciprocate his kindness and interest. Friends, however, will often desert or fail you in the time of need. This reality should not lead to pessimism, for there are true friends (cf. 17:17) whose commitments will never waiver. The true friend is rare, and his devotion even surpasses that of a brother by birth.

J. Wisdom's Instruction on Character. 19:1-29.

19:1-3. In these verses the paths of truth and ignorance are contrasted. It is far better to be an unknown pauper and walk before Yahweh in integrity than to possess much and be given to folly and perversity. A lack of knowledge is not an admirable trait. The acquisition of knowledge will take time, and he who attempts to unduly hasten the process may be sinning against knowledge and himself. The man who allows his feet to carry him beyond the maturity of his mind will pervert his way, for he will take many unwise steps. Such a man will be prone to blame the Lord for his failures, and perhaps even become embittered. However, it is his own foolishness that has caused his way to be twisted and hard.

4-5. The wealthy will always have friends, while the poor will seldom be sought out; for they offer little by way of advantage to their compatriots. The poor man may even find himself frequently separated from his neighbors since he lacks the substance to keep up with their life-style.

The true witness delivers souls and the false witness destroys them. The false witness despises his responsibilities as a neighbor. His callous indifference to the needs of others will bring him under severe punishment. He shall not escape, and he will ultimately join all liars in the lake that burns with eternal fire (Rev 21:8).

6-10. The incentive to personal profit is the motive that sponsors many friendships. Every man is friend to him that giveth gifts. The poor, on the other hand, are hated by their brethren. They can't even get people to talk to them, and they are often left poor and helpless without promise of aid.

The man who gets wisdom, or literally develops a sound mind, is the man who gives thought to the proper care of his soul life. God will destroy the oppressors of the poor, and he who cares for his soul will care for the souls of the poor. He who cares for the poor is courting the favor of Yahweh, and to cleave to such understanding will produce much good.

The man who sins against his neighbor through the bearing of false witness will perish. These men will go down broken beneath the righteous judgment of God to endure the unspeakable agony of the liars' eternity.

There is an order in the universe. Although injustice exists, the passing of time will level all who practice oppression. A servant does not rule over princes, nor does the fool enjoy delight. The sovereignty of Yahweh will not allow it to be so.

11-14. There is a worldly viewpoint that believes it better to fight for one's rights than allow a personal affront to go unanswered. Yahweh's wisdom counsels the deferral of anger and the passing over of a transgression. Wisdom's man is ready to overlook the faults of others and pass lightly over insults that would goad a man of lesser sense into intense conflict.

In verse 12 the monarch of the forest is compared to the monarch of the land. When a lion roars, a wise man will take heed. The king's wrath is to be equally dreaded, and his favor is a strengthening force to all who receive it. The foolish son is a multitude of calamities to his father. He is stroke upon stroke to his father's back. Such a son will often be found in the home where a contentious wife abides. When the wife despises the husband's authority, the effect upon the children is always disastrous. Her contentious words are like rain leaking through the roof of a house, spoiling the interior. An Arabic proverb lists three things that make a house unbearable: *tak*, a leak of rainwater; *mak*, a wife's nagging; and *bak*, bugs (Edgar Jones,

CHAPTER 19

BETTER *is* the poor that walketh in his integrity, than *he that is* perverse in his lips, and is a fool.

2 Also, *that* the soul *be* without knowledge, *it is* not good; and he that hasteth with *his* feet sinneth.

3 The foolishness of man perverteth his way: and his heart fretteth against the LORD.

4 Wealth maketh many friends; but the poor is separated from his neighbour.

5 A false witness shall not be unpunished, and *he that* speaketh lies shall not escape.

6 Many will intreat the favour of the prince: and every man *is* a friend to him that giveth gifts.

7 All the brethren of the poor do hate him: how much more do his friends go far from him? he pursueth *them with* words, *yet* they *are* wanting *to him*.

8 He that getteth wisdom loveth his own soul: he that keepeth understanding shall find good.

9 A false witness shall not be unpunished, and *he that* speaketh lies shall perish.

10 Delight is not seemly for a fool; much less for a servant to have rule over princes.

11 The discretion of a man deferreth his anger; and *it is* his glory to pass over a transgression.

12 The king's wrath *is* as the roaring of a lion; but his favour *is* as dew upon the grass.

13 A foolish son *is* the calamity of his father: and the contentions of a wife *are* a continual dropping.

14 House and riches *are* the inheritance of fathers: and a prudent wife *is* from the LORD.

Proverbs and Ecclesiastes, p. 166)! A prudent wife is from the Lord. A good wife is absolutely necessary for the erection of a Godly home. She is not acquired, however, as are other possessions which may be worked for or inherited. She is always to be treasured as a gift from Yahweh.

15 Slothfulness casteth into a deep sleep; and an idle soul shall suffer hunger.

16 He that keepeth the commandment keepeth his own soul; *but* he that despiseth his ways shall die.

17 He that hath pity upon the poor lendeth unto the Lord; and that which he hath given will he pay him again.

18 Chasten thy son while there is hope, and let not thy soul spare for his crying.

19 A man of great wrath shall suffer punishment: for if thou deliver *him,* yet thou must do it again.

15-19. Slothfulness is a sin. Time wasted can never be retrieved, and idleness produces a deep stupor in the soul of a man. Such a man is destined to feel great hunger in body and soul. The man who keeps the commandments of Yahweh preserves his soul from famine. The man who despises Yahweh's way is destined for certain death.

Yahweh is the patron of the poor who often tests the reality of our spiritual profession. Money and goods bestowed upon the poor are in reality bestowed upon the Lord. He takes note of every penny and accepts total responsibility for paying the giver again.

The value of disciplinary action is again attested in verse 18. The father is enjoined to discipline his son while there is hope. We have here a caution against that cruel kindness that kills by withholding reasonable correction (J. P. Lange, *A Commentary on the Holy Scriptures,* Proverbs, p. 173).

If thou deliver him yet thou must do it again. It is foolish to shield a man who cannot control his temper. You may deliver him again and again from the consequences of his great wrath, but there comes a time when he must pay the price for his behavior. Such a man should be left to suffer the consequences of his sin until he learns by punishment what he is incapable of learning in any other way.

20 Hear counsel, and receive instruction, that thou mayest be wise in thy latter end.

21 *There are* many devices in a man's heart; nevertheless the counsel of the Lord, that shall stand.

22 The desire of a man *is* his kindness: and a poor man *is* better than a liar.

23 The fear of the Lord *tendeth* to life: and *he that hath it* shall abide satisfied; he shall not be visited with evil.

24 A slothful *man* hideth his hand in *his* bosom, and will not so much as bring it to his mouth again.

20-24. To despise counsel is to display the heart of the fool. The wise place a high value on instruction, especially when it bears upon it the stamp of Yahweh's wisdom. They know that the theories of men are transitory. Only the counsel of the Lord will stand, and only the man who abides in that counsel will end his life well.

What makes a man desirable is his kindness. A benevolent spirit appeals to all but the most corrupt. The poor man who practices kindness is better than the wealthy man who makes grand promises that never materialize.

The fear of the Lord tendeth to life. Verse 23 is a variation on 14:27. The undisciplined fool enjoys a few moments of joy, but all too soon the darkness of despair surrounds him. Only those who fear misrepresenting a holy God through sinful word or deed can enjoy a satisfied life. They can rest securely, knowing that they shall not be visited by evil. All that comes to them, though it may be meant for evil, is turned by a sovereign God to good purpose in their lives (Gen 50:20; Eccl 3:11; Rom 8:28).

A slothful man hideth his hand in his bosom. Laziness is a terrible sin. It so grips the heart of a man that he ceases to do even those things that are necessary and should be enjoyed. The picture here is extreme, but it represents how lethargy can take command of a person. This sinner is so lazy he prefers to abandon himself to sleep, rather than eat the food provided for him.

25 Smite a scorner, and the simple will beware: and reprove one that hath understanding, *and* he will understand knowledge.

26 He that wasteth *his* father, *and* chaseth away *his* mother, *is* a son that causeth shame, and bringeth reproach.

27 Cease, my son, to hear the instruction *that causeth* to err from the words of knowledge.

28 An ungodly witness scorneth judgment: and the mouth of the wicked devoureth iniquity.

29 Judgments are prepared for scorners, and stripes for the back of fools.

25-29. Smite a scorner, and the simple will beware. Reproof will not turn the scorner from his evil way. Punishment will not dissuade him, but the simple man whose character is not yet formed for good or evil may be led to reflection and repentance as he views the scorner being punished. Verse 26 describes the calloused behavior of a son who treats his parents with cruelty. Bitter indeed are the sorrows upon these parents. **Wasteth** is literally to assail violently, and **chaseth away** is literally to have no patience with or to drive away. This son brings great **reproach** upon his family. A wise son will not listen to all kinds of theories. He will prudently screen all that comes before him and practice great discernment in what he allows his ears to hear. He recognizes that the ears are a doorway to the heart.

When he detects the slightest detriment in what he is hearing, he will cease any further trafficking with such error.

An ungodly witness scorneth judgment. The worthless witness scoffs at justice, and his mouth pours out iniquity, rather than devours iniquity (William McKane, *Proverbs*, p. 529). These scorners will not escape judgment. Judgments are prepared for them, and a solemn accounting awaits these sons of Satan.

CHAPTER 20

WINE *is* a mocker, strong drink *is* raging: and whosoever is deceived thereby is not wise.

2 The fear of a king *is* as the roaring of a lion: *whoso* provoketh him to anger sinneth *against* his own soul.

3 *It is* an honour for a man to cease from strife: but every fool will be meddling.

4 The sluggard will not plow by reason of the cold; *therefore* shall he beg in harvest, and *have* nothing.

5 Counsel in the heart of man *is like* deep water; but a man of understanding will draw it out.

6 Most men will proclaim every one his own goodness: but a faithful man who can find?

7 The just *man* walketh in his integrity: his children *are* blessed after him.

8 A king that sitteth in the throne of judgment scattereth away all evil with his eyes.

9 Who can say, I have made my heart clean, I am pure from my sin?

10 Divers weights, *and* divers measures, both of them *are* alike abomination to the LORD.

11 Even a child is known by his doings, whether his work *be* pure, and whether *it be* right.

12 The hearing ear, and the seeing eye, the LORD hath made even both of them.

13 Love not sleep, lest thou come to poverty; open thine eyes, *and* thou shalt be satisfied with bread.

14 *It is* naught, *it is* naught, saith the buyer: but when he is gone his way, then he boasteth.

15 There is gold, and a multitude of rubies: but the lips of knowledge *are* a precious jewel.

K. Wisdom's Instruction on Means and Ends. 20:1-30.

20:1-3. Various precepts are discussed in this section; if followed they will lead to a life of integrity. Wine appears here personified as an evil demon. The man who allows himself to be deceived by demon rum is a fool, for its power to destroy is seen everywhere in society.

The word of the king is also of great power, and **whoso provoketh him to anger sinneth against his own soul.** Men ought to practice restraint in the presence of such a formidable figure. To provoke him to anger is to put one's life in danger.

It is an honor for a man to cease from strife. To cease from strife is, literally, to remain seated in the presence of a dispute. Here, the practice of a quiet and peaceable demeanor stands in stark contrast to the contentious meddlings of the fool.

4-5. The sluggard is ready to abandon labor under the slightest stimulation. The coming of winter and the industrious activities of others provide no incentive for him. During harvest he must beg from others, for he has nothing to nourish his life.

Counsel in the heart . . . is like deep water. The wise thoughts of a man are hidden deep within his heart, like the water in a deep well. **A man of understanding** knows how to draw them out. He understands how to bring them forth so that their vivifying force can be felt in the lives of men.

6-12. A moral connection exists between the proverbs in this section. **Most men will proclaim every one his own goodness.** Men in general are filled with good intentions; but the faithful man who carries out these intentions is hard to find. **The just man walketh in his integrity.** His integrity is established in the faithful performance of his promises. Such a man will bring Yahweh's blessing upon himself and his children.

The wise king establishes his throne in integrity by pronouncing judgments that cause the scattering away of the evil in his kingdom.

Who can say . . . I am pure. . . ? All men must practice care in living, for the possibility of appearing before the King as Judge is an imminent one. Such a reality ought to force the open admission that none are without sin and enforce the resolve to keep a clean heart. Illegally tampering with weights and measures to increase profits testifies to the lack of integrity in the heart of many.

Even a child is known by his doings. The hearts of men and children are openly revealed for all to see by simply observing their words and deeds (Jer 17:9). The verdict is tragic. All are sinners, and the stench of death hovers above all mankind. Only a remnant are guarded by the fear of Yahweh and the pursuit of integrity. Only a small group hear and see, and the credit for it belongs not to men but to the Lord. **The hearing ear, and the seeing eye, the LORD hath made even both of them.**

13-18. **Love not sleep, lest thou come to poverty.** The man who has received hearing and sight from Yahweh will not sleep his life away, for that would result in a state of poverty, which would render his life a useless tool in Yahweh's hand. He will open his eyes, rise early, work his fields, and, consequently, have plenty of bread for his needs and the needs of others. He will also pay a fair price to others for their produce, rather than attempt to diminish their worth. The bargaining rituals of the

16 Take his garment that is surety *for* a stranger: and take a pledge of him for a strange woman.

17 Bread of deceit *is* sweet to a man; but afterwards his mouth shall be filled with gravel.

18 *Every* purpose is established by counsel: and with good advice make war.

19 He that goeth about *as* a talebearer revealeth secrets: therefore meddle not with him that flattereth with his lips.

20 Whoso curseth his father or his mother, his lamp shall be put out in obscure darkness.

21 An inheritance *may be* gotten hastily at the beginning; but the end thereof shall not be blessed.

22 Say not thou, I will recompense evil; *but* wait on the LORD, and he shall save thee.

23 Divers weights are an abomination unto the LORD; and a false balance *is* not good.

24 Man's goings *are* of the LORD; how can a man then understand his own way?

25 *It is* a snare to the man *who* devoureth *that which is* holy, and after vows to make enquiry.

26 A wise king scattereth the wicked, and bringeth the wheel over them.

27 The spirit of man *is* the candle of the LORD, searching all the inward parts of the belly.

28 Mercy and truth preserve the king: and his throne is upholden by mercy.

29 The glory of young men *is* their strength: and the beauty of old men *is* the grey head.

30 The blueness of a wound cleanseth away evil: so *do* stripes the inward parts of the belly.

Near East are in view here. Gold and rubies are of little value when compared to lips of knowledge. A man must take care that hurtful speech is kept far from his lips.

Ruin and disaster will attend the way of the man who through the unwise use of his lips blunders into dealings with the stranger and the strange woman. Solomon has continually warned against becoming surety for strangers. Now he advises that if man is foolish enough to enter into such arrangements, he is not fit to be trusted. Lend nothing to him without strong security. If needful, take his garments as a pledge that he will repay.

Bread of deceit is sweet to a man. It may seem for a brief moment that prosperity is in the way of the deceiver, but time will prove otherwise. The sweetness of the moment will turn to gravel in the mouth of the deceiver. Deceit never pays.

Verse 18 should be compared with 12:15 and 15:22. The subject here is warfare. Before a man begins what he may not easily end, it is well for him to seek the counsel of the wise (cf. Lk 14:31, 32).

19-21. Meddle not with him that flattereth with his lips. The man who is open with his lips, i.e., cannot keep them shut, is a man to be avoided. He gains access to the secrets of the unwary by the use of flattering speech. His every encounter furnishes material for idle talk with those whom he meets next. Wisdom counsels the avoidance of such a man. Avoid also the man who curses his father or mother. Such a man transgresses the fifth commandment of the Law with boldness (Ex 20:12), and he is destined for certain destruction.

The sense of verse 21 is similiar to that of verse 17. Ill-gotten gains will never produce lasting blessings. Get-rich-quick schemes that subordinate the means to the desired end will always end in personal disaster. **The end thereof shall not be blessed.**

22-25. Say not . . . I will recompense evil. Never seek to repay evil done to you (Deut 32:35; Rom 12:17). God's man can make no greater mistake than to vigorously pursue vengeance. Such a pursuit violates the orders of our divine Commander who said, "Vengeance is mine; I will repay." Yahweh will save all who practice trust. We are to be in submission to His workings in our lives, trusting the power of His hand to deliver us.

The prophet Jeremiah echoes the counsel of Solomon in verse 24. ". . . I know that the way of man is not in himself . . ." It is not in man to direct his steps (Jer 10:23). One alone knows the beginning from the end, and that one is Yahweh. He alone can be trusted to lead on in righteousness. He has said, "I will instruct thee and teach thee in the way which thou shalt go: I will guide thee with mine eye" (Ps 32:8). We will not always understand, but we must always trust (3:5, 6).

It is a snare to the man. Men ought to practice great care in their dealings with Yahweh. Men cause themselves great harm when they thoughtlessly dedicate things to God without tallying their resources to see if they can honor such a commitment (Eccl 5:4-7).

26-30. Verses 26 and 28 deal with the subject of kingship. Verse 26 is closely related to verse 8. **A wise king scattereth the wicked.** The wise king attempts to winnow out, or expunge from society, the lawless. No society is safe when the lawless are allowed to run free; such should be run over with the wheel. A cart was driven over the stalks of corn spread upon the threshing floor, and the good grain was separated from the husk. The wise king runs the wheel of justice across his kingdom. He separates the worthless from the profitable and casts the worthless away, thus ending their corrupting influence.

The spirit of man is the candle of the LORD. Man's spirit was breathed into him by the Lord of creation. The spirit is the candle of the Lord that gives to man an inward light. Man is enabled to think, plan, and weigh matters through the guidance of his spirit. At death, the body of man goes to the dust; and the spirit returns unto the Lord who gave it (Eccl 12:7).

Mercy and truth preserve the king. The love and faithfulness that a king shows to his subjects is not lost on them. They delight in returning love and loyalty to such a monarch. In this reciprocity of love, the security of the throne is safeguarded. In verse 26 the responsibility of the kings to judge the lawless was observed. Here, his responsibility to love the faithful is enjoined.

The beauty of old men is the gray head. A society that worships youth needs the reminder of verse 29. Age in Scripture is an adornment, not a detriment. Gray is beautiful when it adorns the head of a godly man, a man who has dedicated the strength of his youth to the aggressive pursuit of righteousness. Strength, which passes all too soon, must be invested wisely.

The stripes of discipline will leave their black-and-blue wounds upon a child. Such suffering is often required, however, to purge the young man of evil intent. The stripes are prayerfully intended to cleanse the inner heart of a man and should always be attended by the prayer that this desired objective will be realized (Ps 119:75; I Cor 11:32).

L. Wisdom's Instruction on the Law of God. 21:1-31.

21:1-8. The king's heart is in the hand of the LORD. No monarch, regardless of the vastness of his power, can act independently of God. The books of Esther and Daniel fully amplify this principle. Jehovah controls the actions of all sovereigns in the same way He controls the flow of the water in the brooks (cf. Isa 45:1-7).

Every way of a man is right in his own eyes. Men have always been expert in the justification of their personal actions, and men infected with self-righteousness have always constituted one of the Lord's greatest challenges. Yahweh ever sees the hearts of men and casts aside all rationalizing with the crisp rendering of His judgments, which are according to truth.

To do justice and judgment is more acceptable to the LORD. This theme is frequently discussed in the prophets (cf. Hos 6:6; Amos 5:22-24; Mic 6:6-8). In all of these passages, sacrifice is subordinated to those characteristics that are deemed greater in importance. Yahweh always esteems personal righteousness and love for one's neighbor above ceremonial involvements in worship (cf. Isa 58:5-14). A high look and a proud heart render sacrifices unacceptable. Such acts of worship, impregnated with self-exaltation, are always an abomination to the Lord.

The thoughts of the diligent tend only to plenteousness. The diligent man thinks incisively. He is the man who slices through complex issues and devises a successful course of action. He is contrasted with the man whose actions are not well planned and who impetuously ventures forth with great force. His plans usually end in failure.

Treasures accumulated through the practice of deceit and robbery will always be accompanied by vanity and death, a contrast to the man who practices purity. He will shun every form of evil and practice the performance of that which is right (cf. Dan 6:4).

CHAPTER 21

THE king's heart *is* in the hand of the LORD, *as* the rivers of water: he turneth it whithersoever he will.

2 Every way of a man *is* right in his own eyes: but the LORD pondereth the hearts.

3 To do justice and judgment *is* more acceptable to the LORD than sacrifice.

4 An high look, and a proud heart, *and* the plowing of the wicked, *is* sin.

5 The thoughts of the diligent *tend* only to plenteousness; but of every one *that is* hasty only to want.

6 The getting of treasures by a lying tongue *is* a vanity tossed to and fro of them that seek death.

7 The robbery of the wicked shall destroy them; because they refuse to do judgment.

8 The way of man *is* froward and strange: but *as for* the pure, his work *is* right.

9 *It is* better to dwell in a corner of the housetop, than with a brawling woman in a wide house.

10 The soul of the wicked desireth evil: his neighbour findeth no favour in his eyes.

11 When the scorner is punished, the simple is made wise: and when the wise is instructed, he receiveth knowledge.

12 The righteous *man* wisely considereth the house of the wicked: *but God*

9-12. It is better to dwell in a corner of the housetop. The corner of the housetop refers to a small room sometimes used for guests. It was built on the roof near the corner and was accessible only by ladder. The room was small and less comfortable than the quarters below. It is better to dwell in these small quarters than to live in more comfortable quarters with a brawling woman who seeks to rule the house and will not be content unless everything goes her way.

The soul of the wicked desireth evil. The man who seeks to discover goodness in those around him usually finds it. Ob-

overthroweth the wicked for *their* wickedness.

13 Whoso stoppeth his ears at the cry of the poor, he also shall cry himself, but shall not be heard.
14 A gift in secret pacifieth anger: and a reward in the bosom strong wrath.
15 *It is* joy to the just to do judgment: but destruction *shall be* to the workers of iniquity.
16 The man that wandereth out of the way of understanding shall remain in the congregation of the dead.
17 He that loveth pleasure *shall be* a poor man: he that loveth wine and oil shall not be rich.
18 The wicked *shall be* a ransom for the righteous, and the transgressor for the upright.

19 *It is* better to dwell in the wilderness, than with a contentious and an angry woman.
20 *There is* treasure to be desired and oil in the dwelling of the wise; but a foolish man spendeth it up.
21 He that followeth after righteousness and mercy findeth life, righteousness, and honour.
22 A wise *man* scaleth the city of the mighty, and casteth down the strength of the confidence thereof.
23 Whoso keepeth his mouth and his tongue keepeth his soul from troubles.
24 Proud *and* haughty scorner *is* his name, who dealeth in proud wrath.
25 The desire of the slothful killeth him; for his hands refuse to labour.
26 He coveteth greedily all the day long: but the righteous giveth and spareth not.

versely, the man who looks for evil readily finds it. None can please the reciter of evil. He finds fault with everyone and adopts a philosophy of life that stresses his superiority, usually a mask for his fear.

When the scorner is punished. Verse 11 should be compared with 19:25. When the man who resists the truth is allowed to go without open rebuke, his ability to lead the ignorant astray is strengthened. Paul thus counsels the open rebuke of sinners that all may fear (I Tim 5:20). The simple ought also to be spurred to right action by the prosperity of the wise, which they adjudge to be due to their receptive spirit. The judgment is reinforced in the mind of the simple as they view God overthrowing the wicked for their wickedness.

13-18. Whoso stoppeth his ears at the cry of the poor. In 19:17 the proper response to poverty and the Lord's reward for that response was cited. Here, the negative response is addressed. Those who will not heed the cry of the poor shall in their time of need find none who will be responsive to their cries. (cf. Mt 5:7; Jas 2:13). **A gift . . . pacifieth anger.** Nothing staves off hatred so swiftly as the doing of good. If the act is performed in the presence of witnesses, it may be construed as an attempt to gain applause. What occurs between two parties secretly can never be so construed. The angered person can see in that secret only the deep desire for the establishment of peace.

The man who is righteous finds joy in the doing of that which is right, whereas the lawless despise the practice of righteousness. These workers of iniquity think it the highest form of ignorance to trust such promises as Matthew 6:33. They believe that they would be destined for ruin if they did not cheat their neighbor at every opportunity. Such men shall not participate in the resurrection of Isaiah 26:19, but shall pass from the darkness of this life into the retribution of death in the next. They are permanently affixed to the congregation of the dead.

The self-indulgent who love pleasure supremely will always be poor. The wise man knows how to possess and preserve wealth, but the fool squanders it in the pursuit of pleasures. The righteous are delivered out of trouble (cf. Isa 52:1), and the transgressors stand in their place as the recipients of Yahweh's descending judgment. The wicked literally receive the trouble they have planned for the just.

19-26. In verse 19 the contentious woman of 21:9 is once again the subject of discussion. A tent pitched in the desert wastes is a better dwelling place than a palace if it must be shared with her.

Oil in the dwelling of the wise. The fool wastes whatever he has that is of value. The wise man carefully considers the future and uses such resources as he possesses prudently. He can always be counted on to have a precious store of those substances on which the sustaining of his life depends. The man who follows after righteousness will find life. He is a careful steward of his time and talents and thus insures for himself the finding of life, righteousness, and honor. This man can scale the heavy fortifications of the worldly, for even a well defended fortress will soon fall before the sagacious counsel of the wise (cf. Eccl 9:15).

Whoso keepeth his mouth and his tongue, keepeth his soul from troubles. The speech of the wise man keeps him from much of this world's troubles. The careful control of his tongue prevents the utterance of unwise words, however true, that are often the cause of disaster when sent abroad.

The scorner is defined in verse 24. He is the proud, self-willed man who evidences his corruption by unbridled words and wrath. He is proud of his wrath when it ought to be the cause of great shame for him.

The slothful have tremendous desires. They would like to own the world one day, but they lack the disciplined industry

27 The sacrifice of the wicked *is* abomination: how much more, *when* he bringeth it with a wicked mind?

28 A false witness shall perish: but the man that heareth speaketh constantly.
29 A wicked man hardeneth his face: but *as for* the upright, he directeth his way.

30 *There is* no wisdom nor understanding nor counsel against the LORD.
31 The horse *is* prepared against the day of battle: but safety *is* of the LORD.

CHAPTER 22

A *GOOD* name *is* rather to be chosen than great riches, *and* loving favour rather than silver and gold.
2 The rich and poor meet together: the LORD *is* the maker of them all.
3 A prudent *man* forseeth the evil, and hideth himself: but the simple pass on, and are punished.
4 By humility *and* the fear of the LORD *are* riches, and honour, and life.
5 Thorns *and* snares *are* in the way of the froward: he that doth keep his soul shall be far from them.

6 Train up a child in the way he should go: and when he is old, he will not depart from it.
7 The rich ruleth over the poor, and the borrower *is* servant to the lender.
8 He that soweth iniquity shall reap

necessary for the achievement of the smallest goal. Their days are spent in covetous daydreaming, but their **hands refuse to labor.** In contrast, the righteous labor day and night and give to all in need, remembering that they are but stewards of all they possess (Lk 16:9).

27. The sacrifice of the wicked is abomination (see remarks on 15:8, 9, 26; 21:4). Yahweh has given his unalterable pronouncement on the worship of the wicked. It is repulsive to him, a stench to his nostrils. The wicked attend to worship clothed in the garment of hypocrisy. How much greater is the Lord's hatred of those who bring sacrifices and in the same hour are plotting some future wickedness.

28-29. In verse 28 the consequences of bearing false witness are once again presented. Solomon enjoins all to listen carefully, for a good listener is a good witness. He who listens carefully will be able to speak the truth, maintain consistently his position, and thus establish his integrity before all.

The wicked man who has no regard for human life or truth **hardeneth his face** and persists in his false testimony, thus insuring his ultimate damnation. The **upright directeth his way** into life, righteousness, and honor (vs. 21).

30-31. Chapter 21 ends as it began with a statement on the omnipotence of Yahweh. The Lord of Israel holds supremacy over all human wisdom. There is no **counsel against the LORD.** Men are foolish to set their wisdom or understanding against the will of the Lord.

The horse is prepared against the day of battle: but safety is of the LORD. The horse is a symbol of military power. The horse may be employed legitimately in the cause of defense, but Israel's confidence ought never rest in horseflesh. The people of Yahweh must remember that their safety is in the Lord, and in His might alone. Some will trust in chariots, and some will trust in horses; but the people of the covenant will trust in the name of their God (Ps 20:7).

M. Wisdom's Instruction on Cause and Effect. 22:1-16.

22:1-5. A good name is rather to be chosen than great riches. The adjective **good** does not appear in the Masoretic text. **Name** conveys the idea of reputation, or character. A continuous display of that grace that wins love is commended here.

The LORD is the maker of them all. There is a sense in which God is the Father of all, and all men are brothers. "And hath made of one blood all nations of men for to dwell on all the face of the earth . . ." (Acts 17:26). Thrown together in this world and made by the same God, all men ought to render aid one to another.

A prudent man foreseeth the evil. The prudent man is the man who looks ahead and anticipates impending difficulties. He then diligently hides himself in whatever refuge God has provided. The simple comprehend not the dangers that await them, and their destruction is assured in consequence.

By humility and the fear of the LORD are riches, and honor, and life. The rewards for true piety are set forth in verse 4. Humility is the absence of pride, coupled with the presence of a teachable and disciplined spirit. True riches, honor, and eternal life are found in the way of true humility. **Thorns and snares are in the way of the froward.** The diligent shall be kept from such through careful compliance with the commandments of Yahweh.

6-11. Train up a child. The verb, to train, indicates the first instruction that is given to a child, i.e., his early education. This training is designed to open before the child the manner of life for which he is intended. To commence the child's education in this way is of great importance, for the tree follows the bent of its early years.

vanity: and the rod of his anger shall fail.

9 He that hath a bountiful eye shall be blessed; for he giveth of his bread to the poor.

10 Cast out the scorner, and contention shall go out; yea, strife and reproach shall cease.

11 He that loveth pureness of heart, *for* the grace of his lips the king *shall be* his friend.

12 The eyes of the LORD preserve knowledge, and he overthroweth the words of the transgressor.

13 The slothful *man* saith, *There is* a lion without, I shall be slain in the streets.

14 The mouth of strange women *is* a deep pit: he that is abhorred of the LORD shall fall therein.

15 Foolishness *is* bound in the heart of a child; *but* the rod of correction shall drive it far from him.

16 He that oppresseth the poor to increase his *riches, and* he that giveth to the rich, *shall* surely *come* to want.

17 ¶Bow down thine ear, and hear the words of the wise, and apply thine heart unto my knowledge.

18 For *it is* a pleasant thing if thou keep them within thee; they shall withal be fitted in thy lips.

19 That thy trust may be in the LORD, I have made known to thee this day, even to thee.

20 Have not I written to thee excellent things in counsels and knowledge,

21 That I might make thee know the certainty of the words of truth; that thou mightest answer the words of truth to them that send unto thee?

22 Rob not the poor, because he *is* poor: neither oppress the afflicted in the gate:

23 For the LORD will plead their cause, and spoil the soul of those that spoiled them.

The borrower is servant to the lender. Paul advised the Roman Christians to "Owe no man any thing . . ." (Rom 13:8). The bondage of indebtedness is exceedingly cruel. The borrower and the sower of iniquity both face a bleak future. The man who **hath a bountiful eye shall be blessed,** i.e., the generous man. When the wicked man's time comes, he will suffer the full force of the evil he has practiced on others (cf. Isa 14:6).

Cast out the scorner. The moral success of the community depends upon the diligent expulsion of the scoffers who persistently stir up trouble. Chase the scorner away, and strife and reproach shall cease.

For the grace of his lips. The man who loves the truth and can speak it pleasantly will win the approbation of the king (cf. vs. 29; 14:35). The partnership of purity and graciousness produce a man of rare quality who will be prized by a wise leader.

12. The eyes of the LORD preserve knowledge. The eye of the Lord is upon His truth, and He garrisons it about with His power. The watchman metaphor is in view here. The omniscient Yahweh views the speech of all men, evil and good alike. He preserves truth and brings the lies of the deceiver to light.

13. The slothful man saith. The lazy man can think of a million excuses for not going to work. The one before us is absurd. He cannot go out of his house, for he fears confronting a lion. No one has seen a lion for years, but little matter. One excuse is as good as another when your heart is committed to inaction.

14. The mouth of strange women is a deep pit. The lazy are often the particular prey of the promiscuous woman. They have little time to labor but love to boast of their sexual exploits. To fall in with her is to become an object of abhorrence to the Lord (see 2:16-22; chs. 5, 7).

15. Foolishness is bound in the heart of a child. To leave a child to himself is to insure his ruin, for folly is bound to every child's heart. Folly here is *'iwelet,* which is literally, stubbornness. The careful administration of discipline will correct this propensity to arrogance. The rod is the symbol of parental restraint. Applied in love, it will insure the child's proper moral development.

16. He that oppresseth the poor is none the better for his oppressive acts, for the Lord will eventually reduce such a man to poverty. He who relies upon his ability to purchase the favor of the rich will also come upon bad times. The general sense of the proverb is that greed is self-defeating.

IV. THE WORDS OF THE WISE MEN. 22:17-24:34.

A. Wisdom's Instruction on What to Avoid. 22:17-23:11.

17-21. Hear the words of the wise. Wise is in the plural here and may suggest that this section contains proverbs written by others and collected by Solomon. Verse 17 commences a call for alert concentration and disciplined listening. Verse 19 attempts to provide the motivation for listening by pointing to the pleasant consequences obtained when wisdom's truths are internalized. The man who views himself as the envoy of wisdom (**send unto thee** vs. 21) will have excellent counsel, counsel devoid of uncertainty. Yahweh has given to him the **certainty of the words of truth.**

22-23. The LORD will plead their cause. The **gate** refers to the place where court was held. He who is deprived of help in judicial contests and other cases of want should be cared for by the more fortunate. If the ways of justice are perverted, let that man by whom oppression comes beware. The supreme Judge is looking on, and He will render to every man according to his deeds. The Lord will spoil the souls of the oppressors.

24 Make no friendship with an angry man; and with a furious man thou shalt not go:

25 Lest thou learn his ways, and get a snare to thy soul.

26 Be not thou *one* of them that strike hands, *or* of them that are sureties for debts.

27 If thou hast nothing to pay, why should he take away thy bed from under thee?

28 Remove not the ancient landmark, which thy fathers have set.

29 Seest thou a man diligent in his business? he shall stand before kings; he shall not stand before mean *men.*

CHAPTER 23

WHEN thou sittest to eat with a ruler, consider diligently what *is* before thee:

2 And put a knife to thy throat, if thou *be* a man given to appetite.

3 Be not desirous of his dainties: for they *are* deceitful meat.

4 Labour not to be rich: cease from thine own wisdom.

5 Wilt thou set thine eyes upon that which is not? for *riches* certainly make themselves wings; they fly away as an eagle toward heaven.

6 Eat thou not the bread of *him that hath* an evil eye, neither desire thou his dainty meats:

7 For as he thinketh in his heart, so *is* he: Eat and drink, saith he to thee; but his heart *is* not with thee.

8 The morsel *which* thou hast eaten shalt thou vomit up, and lose thy sweet words.

9 Speak not in the ears of a fool: for he will despise the wisdom of thy words.

10 Remove not the old landmark; and enter not into the fields of the fatherless:

11 For their redeemer *is* mighty; he shall plead their cause with thee.

12 Apply thine heart unto instruction, and thine ears to the words of knowledge.

13 Withhold not correction from the child: for *if* thou beatest him with the rod, he shall not die.

14 Thou shalt beat him with the rod, and shalt deliver his soul from hell.

15 My son, if thine heart be wise, my heart shall rejoice, even mine.

16 Yea, my reins shall rejoice, when thy lips speak right things.

17 Let not thine heart envy sinners: but *be thou* in the fear of the LORD all the day long.

18 For surely there is an end; and thine expectation shall not be cut off.

24-27. Make no friendship with an angry man. A man is greatly influenced by his companions, and wisdom counsels the avoidance of bad companions. The danger that one who keeps company with the angry may learn his ways and reap the fruit of anger's evil practices is ever present.

For verses 26 and 27, see 6:1-5 and 11:15. Here, another warning against suretyship is issued. A man must be the worst kind of fool if he enters into business arrangements that will bring him to penury and leave him without even a bed to sleep in.

28-29. Remove not the ancient landmark. The landmark was protected by the ancient laws of Israel. The landmark stood as a memorial of each man's rights as bequeathed to him by his ancestors. Its removal was prohibited in the Torah and censured as a greedy and unjust invasion of a person's rights (Deut 19:14; 27:17).

He shall stand before kings. The man of diligence is marked out for special notice. He is quick to improve his circumstances and pursue opportunities. He shall prosper as Joseph, Nehemiah, and Daniel. He shall stand above the average men of this world and shall minister before kings.

23:1-8. Consider diligently what is before thee. The man who eats at the royal table should remember where he is. Wantonness of appetite should be bridled with the greatest sternness. **A knife to thy throat** is better than an appetite out of control. The dainties are deceitful meat when given by an insincere host. To enjoy them is to place oneself in serious danger.

Riches . . . make themselves wings. The selfish accumulation of wealth is never a worthy goal for the servant of the Lord. Wealth is extremely elusive. Like the eagle, it may suddenly soar to the heavens, placing itself far beyond a man's reach.

As he thinketh in his heart, so is he. The stingy host is pictured in this verse. He carefully calculates the cost of his entertaining, and he entertains solely for the purpose of gaining the goodwill of others. He is a grudging host and does mental arithmetic with each bite. He then seeks to use those whom he reckons his favors have placed in his debt. Ultimately, you will be sorry you ever partook of his gifts and will even wish you could **vomit up.**

9. Speak not in the ears of a fool. Avoid also the fool. To seek to advise him whose heart is filled with folly is to waste one's breath. Pearls of divine wisdom are not to be cast before the swine of this world.

10-11. Their Redeemer is mighty. He who invades the fields of the fatherless in order to enlarge his possessions will learn to his sorrow of the power of their kinsman-redeemer. They may have no near kinsman (Lev 25:25) to redeem their land; yet Yahweh is mighty to deliver (Ex 6:6). He will deliver all who trust His mighty power.

B. Wisdom's Instruction on What to Look For. 23:12-25.

12-16. Apply thine heart. Godly wisdom cannot be lightly picked up or lightly imparted. In view of this fact, a general admonition to *mûsar* (i.e., disciplined training) is given. Such training is of great value for the child; his momentary suffering will preserve him from the ruin that is bound to accompany the undisciplined life.

My reins shall rejoice. In Hebrew poetry the reins represented the seat of the deepest affections. The joy of the father who beholds the love of wisdom in his child's life is inexpressible.

17-18. Let not thine heart envy sinners. The temptation to envy the sinner for his apparent prosperity is a perennial one. To do so is not wise, for their day of reckoning is coming. However much the righteous may suffer, it will be proven at last that they who practice the fear of the Lord will receive the greater reward.

19 Hear thou, my son, and be wise, and guide thine heart in the way.
20 Be not among winebibbers; among riotous eaters of flesh:
21 For the drunkard and the glutton shall come to poverty: and drowsiness shall clothe *a man* with rags.

22 Hearken unto thy father that begat thee, and despise not thy mother when she is old.
23 Buy the truth, and sell *it* not; *also* wisdom, and instruction, and understanding.
24 The father of the righteous shall greatly rejoice: and he that begetteth a wise *child* shall have joy of him.
25 Thy father and thy mother shall be glad, and she that bare thee shall rejoice.

26 My son, give me thine heart, and let thine eyes observe my ways.

27 For a whore *is* a deep ditch; and a strange woman *is* a narrow pit.
28 She also lieth in wait as *for* a prey, and increaseth the transgressors among men.

29 Who hath woe? who hath sorrow? who hath contentions? who hath babbling? who hath wounds without cause? who hath redness of eyes?
30 They that tarry long at the wine; they that go to seek mixed wine.
31 Look not thou upon the wine when it is red, when it giveth his colour in the cup, *when* it moveth itself aright.
32 At the last it biteth like a serpent, and stingeth like an adder.
33 Thine eyes shall behold strange women, and thine heart shall utter perverse things.
34 Yea, thou shalt be as he that lieth down in the midst of the sea, or as he that lieth upon the top of a mast.
35 They have stricken me, *shalt thou say, and* I was not sick; they have beaten me, *and* I felt *it* not: when shall I awake? I will seek it yet again.

CHAPTER 24

BE not thou envious against evil men, neither desire to be with them.
2 For their heart studieth destruction, and their lips talk of mischief.

In the presence of any temporal injustice the remedy is to look to the LORD (17b) and to look ahead with **expectation** (vs. 18).

19-21. Be not among winebibbers. Intemperance in drinking and eating reveals a heart that is not controlled by wisdom. The wise will guide their hearts carefully away from the control of any carnal appetites. Excessive sleep, wine, or foolishness will bring a man to abject poverty. These verses describe men whose minds are twisted, and McKane suggests that these verses are a paradigm on the recalcitrant and incorrigible youth of Deuteronomy 21:20 (William McKane, *Proverbs*, p. 388).

22-25. Hearken unto thy father. The exuberant youth is apt to forget the reverence due to parents whose agility of mind and body have waned. Wisdom protests the generation gap and insists that children who honor their fathers and mothers will enjoy a fruitful communication with the older generation.

Buy the truth, and sell it not. There are some things that ought not to be sold at any price. Wisdom, self-discipline, and understanding are all children of the truth. These can only be obtained from Yahweh and are His gracious gift to the lowly. They are to be obtained without money (Isa 55:1) and are pearls of great price (Mt 13:44-46). Once obtained, they ought never be sold for any price.

The father of the righteous shall greatly rejoice. Parents whose children are convinced of the wisdom of pursuing such treasure are parents whose hearts are filled with joy.

C. Wisdom's Instruction on Snares. 23:26-24:2.

26. In verse 26 one greater than Solomon speaks. Wisdom pleads with her sons to give her their hearts. Nothing less is worthy of the child of God who would walk with the Christ, who is the ultimate wisdom of God.

27-28. A whore is a deep ditch. The man who has given his heart to God will not be able to give it to lesser gods. To the god of sex he may say: My heart belongs to Yahweh. The harlot's plans to decoy such a man from the path of truth will bear no fruit, for he has given his heart to Yahweh. He has nothing left to give her, save Yahweh's pure concern for the salvation of her corrupted soul.

29-35. Who hath woe? In verse 29 a question is posed and a picture is drawn. The picture is of the drunkard whose wounds might have been avoided, for they are self-inflicted wounds. He continuously seeks for wine. Wine here is (Heb *mimsak*) the blended wine that was a mixture of water, wine, honey, and spices. To drink this sparkling brew is tantamount to submitting oneself to the bite of a poisonous snake. The adder is probably the Daboia Xanthia, the largest venomous snake in Palestine. Such venomous brew will cause a man to loosen control of his morals. His speech will be befuddled, and he will walk as a sailor on the decks of a vessel in the midst of a raging storm. This man's senses have been so blunted that he can be beaten and doesn't even remember his pain. No sooner does he end his drunken binge than plans are laid for the next debasing bout with the fruit of the vine.

24:1-2. Be not thou envious against evil. The glamorous lives of the worldly often arouse great envy in young and old alike. In later passages, the antidote to envy is instruction concerning the future destinies of the evil and the righteous, the darkness (24:20) and the glory (23:18) which are to come. The envied sinner is obsessed with all that is negative, and he is destined for eternal separation from the Lord.

3 Through wisdom is an house builded; and by understanding it is established:

4 And by knowledge shall the chambers be filled with all precious and pleasant riches.

5 A wise man *is* strong; yea, a man of knowledge increaseth strength.

6 For by wise counsel thou shalt make thy war: and in multitude of counsellors *there is* safety.

7 Wisdom *is* too high for a fool: he openeth not his mouth in the gate.

8 He that deviseth to do evil shall be called a mischievous person.

9 The thought of foolishness *is* sin: and the scorner *is* an abomination to men.

10 *If* thou faint in the day of adversity, thy strength *is* small.

11 *If* thou forbear to deliver *them that are* drawn unto death, and *those that are* ready to be slain;

12 *If* thou sayest, Behold, we knew it not; doth not he that pondereth the heart consider *it?* and he that keepeth thy soul, doth *not* he know *it?* and shall *not* he render to *every* man according to his works?

13 My son, eat thou honey, because *it is* good; and the honeycomb, *which is* sweet to thy taste:

14 So *shall* the knowledge of wisdom *be* unto thy soul: when thou hast found *it,* then there shall be a reward, and thy expectation shall not be cut off.

15 Lay not wait, O wicked *man,* against the dwelling of the righteous; spoil not his resting place:

16 For a just *man* falleth seven times, and riseth up again: but the wicked shall fall into mischief.

17 Rejoice not when thine enemy falleth, and let not thine heart be glad when he stumbleth:

18 Lest the LORD see *it,* and it displease him, and he turn away his wrath from him.

19 Fret not thyself because of evil *men,* neither be thou envious at the wicked:

20 For there shall be no reward to the evil *man;* the candle of the wicked shall be put out.

21 My son, fear thou the LORD and the king: *and* meddle not with them that are given to change:

22 For their calamity shall rise suddenly; and who knoweth the ruin of them both?

D. Wisdom's Instruction on Values. 24:3-22.

3-6. Through wisdom is a house builded. The building and furnishing of a house should be entrusted to those who possess the requisite skills. The man of understanding will fill his mind with wisdom and will, consequently, establish a solid foundation for living. His house will be well-furnished, a pleasant place in which to dwell. The force of the teaching is that all men ought to do the same. This wise action produces not only a strong house, but a strong man as well. The man who listens carefully to wisdom's counselors will increase his strength and be enabled to wage war successfully.

7. Wisdom is too high for a fool. The fool is too filled with self-will to learn. He protests that the way of wisdom is naive and nonsensical. He knows well that he is unwilling to practice the precepts of righteousness; but when asked what he believes to be a positive course of action, he defers. He is not prepared to contribute anything of a positive nature to the proceedings at the gate.

8-9. A mischievous person. The deviser of evil is called the mischief-maker, or literally the master of schemes (Heb *mezimah* lit., lewdness). He plans the mechanics whereby his evil objectives may be achieved well. He is repulsive to men and Yahweh; for his every thought is sin, and destruction accompanies him everywhere.

10-12. If thou faint in the day of adversity. In verse 10 there is a play on the words **adversity** (Heb *tsarah*) and **small** (Heb *tsar*). Solomon reminds his readers that the time of crisis is in reality a test of strength, an opportunity for a man to demonstrate his mettle. Verses 11 and 12 set forth situations where the character of a man is tested. The obligation to receive a man who is being overwhelmed by oppressors is set forth. Any attempt to avoid the responsibilities for deliverance in such situations is unacceptable. One may not hypocritically plead ignorance. The God who knows you knew will **render to every man according to his works.**

13-14. My son, eat thou honey. Honey is sweet, but Solomon admonishes all to appreciate afresh the sweetness of wisdom to the soul of all who will partake. The strange woman attempts to simulate the sweetness of honey, but in the end her offering turns to bitterness in the soul of man. Wisdom, in contrast, offers an assured reward, an expectation that shall not be disappointed.

15-18. A just man falleth seven times, and riseth up again. A righteous man is hard to keep down. He possesses an inner fortitude that the wicked lack. Faith, engrafted to his soul, has made him strong. The sevenfold fall may refer to misfortunes or moral failures. He will recover from them all, for God's grace is upon him. The malice of the wicked will not avail against the dwelling of the righteous. Love does not inflict sorrow upon others, nor does it gloat over the difficulties others are experiencing. Such gloating displeases the Lord, who returns in boomerang fashion the evil intents upon the head of the perpetrator.

19-20. Fret not thyself because of evil men. The prosperity of evil men should not disturb the righteous (cf. Ps 37:1). These men have no lasting reward, i.e., future. No reward for their earthly toil awaits them in eternity. **The candle of the wicked shall be put out,** and they shall find themselves under the awful darkness of God's judgment.

21-22. Meddle not with them that are given to change. Young men are encouraged to beware of men who are prone to plot intrigue because of their greed for power. These men are given to change (Heb *shōnīm*), i.e., they are men of revolutionary tendencies. They inflict calamity on themselves and those whom they seek to overthrow. Stay far from such a man, lest you share his calamity.

23 These *things* also *belong* to the wise. *It is* not good to have respect of persons in judgment.

24 He that saith unto the wicked, Thou *art* righteous; him shall the people curse, nations shall abhor him:

25 But to them that rebuke *him* shall be delight, and a good blessing shall come upon them.

26 *Every man* shall kiss *his* lips that giveth a right answer.

27 Prepare thy work without, and make it fit for thyself in the field; and afterwards build thine house.

28 Be not a witness against thy neighbour without cause; and deceive *not* with thy lips.

29 Say not, I will do so to him as he hath done to me: I will render to the man according to his work.

30 I went by the field of the slothful, and by the vineyard of the man void of understanding;

31 And, lo, it was all grown over with thorns, *and* nettles had covered the face thereof, and the stone wall thereof was broken down.

32 Then I saw, *and* considered *it* well: I looked upon *it, and* received instruction.

33 *Yet* a little sleep, a little slumber, a little folding of the hands to sleep:

34 So shall thy poverty come *as* one that travelleth; and thy want as an armed man.

CHAPTER 25

THESE *are* also proverbs of Sŏl′o-mon, which the men of Hĕz-e-kī′ah king of Jū′dah copied out

2 *It is* the glory of God to conceal a thing: but the honour of kings *is* to search out a matter.

3 The heaven for height, and the earth for depth, and the heart of kings *is* unsearchable.

4 Take away the dross from the silver, and there shall come forth a vessel for the finer.

5 Take away the wicked *from* before the king, and his throne shall be established in righteousness.

6 Put not forth thyself in the presence of the king, and stand not in the place of great *men:*

7 For better *it is* that it be said unto thee, Come up hither; than that thou shouldest be put lower in the presence

E. Wisdom's Instruction on Preparation. 24:23-34.

23-26. Verse 23 to the end of the chapter seems to represent an appendix to the book's original form.

It is not good to have respect of persons in judgment. To distinguish between persons on the basis of an assigned preference is to turn justice into injustice and thus impair the well-being of the entire nation. Truth spoken, though at times costly, wins gratitude (vs. 26) and has its special charm.

27-29. Afterward build thine house. The matter of priorities is in view in verse 27. The diligent completion of labor in the fields must precede the building of one's house. Perhaps the starting of family life is in view here, as well. One ought to be certain that a well-ordered life has been established before embarking upon marriage.

Be not a witness against thy neighbor without cause. This proverb is aimed at the man who would deliberately seek the destruction of his neighbor through false accusation. Such a man is an abomination to God (6:19). Men who seek revenge are also repulsive to Yahweh. The servant of the Lord must entrust all retribution to the Master's hand, for the Lord has said, ". . . Vengeance is mine; I will repay . . ." (Rom 12:19).

30-34. Nettles had covered the face thereof. The field of the sluggard presents a desolate view. Thorns and nettles flourish everywhere. No fruit is observable, and the walls of stone are broken down (cf. Isa 5:5, 6). The field serves as an apt illustration of the fruit of slothfulness. The sluggard has made too many excuses. The weeds of evil habits have overgrown his soul, and now he is destined for ruin.

V. A FURTHER COLLECTION OF SOLOMON'S PROVERBS (Hezekiah's Collection). 25:1-29:27.

A. The Title. 25:1-29:27.

25:1. This section is composed of the **proverbs of Solomon, which the men of Hezekiah . . . copied.** Copied (from the Heb root *'ateq*) seems to indicate that the scribes were dealing not only with written proverbs, but also with proverbs that were a part of Israel's oral tradition. Hezekiah, in his anxiety to preserve these sacred words from the past, had them brought together in one sacred collection.

B. Wisdom's Instruction Through Comparison. 25:2-28.

2-3. The honor of kings is to search out a matter. The Lord has so ordered the events of a man's life that he is constantly forced to confess the limits of his understanding (Deut 29:29; Eccl 3:11). Though understanding is not easily achieved, the Lord would have those in authority diligently search the sacred Scriptures for His mind and will. This search represents one of man's nobler exercises. Kings are like Yahweh in this regard; their minds are often incomprehensible to the ordinary man.

4-5. His throne shall be established in righteousness. The king needs trustworthy servants and advisors, for violence and wrongdoing will pull down his throne. The removal of dross from the silver produces silver suitable for use by the finer, just as the removal of the lawless is mandated if the throne is to be firmly established.

6-7. Put not forth thyself in the presence of the king. The matter of proper conduct before dignitaries is the subject of these verses. The love of approbation, which leads one to seek selfishly for advancement, is certain to meet with the king's rebuke. A man who attempts to gain recognition in this way is

1243

of the prince whom thine eyes have seen.

8 Go not forth hastily to strive, lest *thou know not* what to do in the end thereof, when thy neighbour hath put thee to shame.

9 Debate thy cause with thy neighbour *himself;* and discover not a secret to another:

10 Lest he that heareth *it* put thee to shame, and thine infamy turn not away.

11 A word fitly spoken *is like* apples of gold in pictures of silver.

12 *As* an earring of gold, and an ornament of fine gold, *so is* a wise reprover upon an obedient ear.

13 As the cold of snow in the time of harvest, *so is* a faithful messenger to them that send him: for he refresheth the soul of his masters.

14 Whoso boasteth himself of a false gift *is like* clouds and wind without rain.

15 By long forbearing is a prince persuaded, and a soft tongue breaketh the bone.

16 Hast thou found honey? eat so much as is sufficient for thee, lest thou be filled therewith, and vomit it.

17 Withdraw thy foot from thy neighbour's house; lest he be weary of thee, and *so* hate thee.

18 A man that beareth false witness against his neighbour *is* a maul, and a sword, and a sharp arrow.

19 Confidence in an unfaithful man in time of trouble *is like* a broken tooth, and a foot out of joint.

20 *As* he that taketh away a garment in cold weather, *and as* vinegar upon nitre, so *is* he that singeth songs to an heavy heart.

21 If thine enemy be hungry, give him bread to eat; and if he be thirsty, give him water to drink:

22 For thou shalt heap coals of fire upon his head, and the LORD shall reward thee.

23 The north wind driveth away rain: so *doth* an angry countenance a backbiting tongue.

24 *It is* better to dwell in the corner of the housetop, than with a brawling woman and in a wide house.

25 *As* cold waters to a thirsty soul, so *is* good news from a far country.

certain to be put to open shame when men of greater reputation arrive on the scene (cf. Lk 14:8-11).

8-10. Go not forth hastily to strive. A man must practice care in relationships in order to avoid conflict with others. He always risks the shame of being proven wrong when all the facts are in. A great deal of trouble could be avoided if people were careful to debate their differences among themselves before spreading abroad the news of their quarrels (cf. Mt 18:15).

11-13. A word fitly spoken. Apples of gold in a framework of silver represent sculptured work for the decoration of expensive buildings. They were objects of great beauty. Equally lovely are the words of wisdom spoken at the proper time. The kindly rebuke of the wise man should be esteemed of greater value than costly presents.

As the cold of snow. The peasants of Lebanon even now store up snow in the clefts of the mountains to cool drinks in the summer heat. This cold snow refreshes the reapers on the warm harvest days, just as a dependable messenger refreshes the soul of his master.

14. Whoso boasteth himself of a false gift. Clouds in the sky awaken in men the hope of showers, and disappointment is experienced when the promise is not realized. So, when a man talks of giving gifts to others but fails to fulfill his promises, he is likewise a cause of great disappointment (cf. Jude 11-13).

15-17. A soft tongue breaketh the bone. The practice of self-control and gentleness subdues even the most obstinate resistance. A refusal to be pushed aside may produce amazing victories.

Hast thou found honey? Self-control is still in view. Many things like honey are good in moderation; but when taken to excess, their effect can be destructive. Too much of a good thing is bad. Too much time spent in the home of a friendly neighbor may turn that friend into an enemy. Familiarity may breed contempt.

18-19. A man that beareth false witness. The false witness seldom considers the devastation that his mischief produces. In reality, his vicious tongue is a warlike weapon, inflicting pain and anguish upon unsuspecting souls. The faithless man cannot be trusted. He is like a bad tooth or a weak tooth, both of which fail you when they are needed.

20. He that taketh away a garment in cold weather. It seems unthinkable that any would be so cruel as to take a man's coat from him in the winter's cold or pour vinegar into a man's cuts (Heb *neter,* i.e., scab). Only the greatest insensitivity would allow a man to follow such a course. At times mirth in the presence of a man whose heart is heavy betrays a similar insensitivity.

21-22. Thou shalt heap coals of fire upon his head. A high ethical standard is set here for dealing with one's enemies. The emphasis here is pragmatic. If you return evil for evil, the battle will escalate and harm will come to all parties. Kindness to an enemy will bring a fire to his soul that may soften angry feelings and melt a destructive resolve (cf. Mt 5:44). Regardless of its effect, the Lord will reward this discipline.

23-25. The north wind. Slander, with all its wicked accoutrements, produces troubled faces just as surely as the north wind darkens the heavens with rain clouds. **A brawling woman** is on the same level with the slanderer. Any lodging is to be preferred to quarters with her (cf. 21:9).

As cold waters to a thirsty soul. Little communication passed between countries in the days of Solomon. Those far removed from kindred and home seldom heard from one another. Words received were precious indeed, like cold water to a thirsty soul.

26 A righteous man falling down before the wicked *is* as a troubled fountain, and a corrupt spring.

27 *It is* not good to eat   much honey: so *for men* to search their own glory *is not* glory.

28 He that *hath* no rule over his own spirit *is like* a city *that is* broken down, *and* without walls.

CHAPTER 26

AS snow in summer, and as rain in harvest, so honour is not seemly for a fool.

2 As the bird by wandering, as the swallow by flying, so the curse causeless shall not come.

3 A whip for the horse, a bridle for the ass, and a rod for the fool's back.

4 Answer not a fool according to his folly, lest thou also be like unto him.

5 Answer a fool according to his folly, lest he be wise in his own conceit.

6 He that sendeth a message by the hand of a fool cutteth off the feet, *and* drinketh damage.

7 The legs of the lame are not equal: so *is* a parable in the mouth of fools.

8 As he that bindeth a stone in a sling, so *is* he that giveth honour to a fool.

9 *As* a thorn goeth up into the hand of a drunkard, so *is* a parable in the mouth of fools.

10 The great *God* that formed all *things* both rewardeth the fool, and rewardeth transgressors.

11 As a dog returneth to his vomit, *so* a fool returneth to his folly.

12 Seest thou a man wise in his own conceit? *there is* more hope of a fool than of him.

26-28. A corrupt spring. The spring in verse 26 has been trampled by men or animals, so that the water has been rendered unfit for human consumption. That which could have been a source of refreshment has now become the source of immense disappointment. This tragedy is paralleled by the righteous man who allows his pure life to be polluted by compromise and involvement with the lawless. He who could have been a source of great blessing has thus become a cause of great sorrow.

It is not good to eat much honey. The necessity of self-control has been highlighted in verse 26. One must practice moderation in all things. Even something as good as honey will have an evil effect if used immoderately. The immoderate practice of self-glorification will also have an evil effect upon a man's life. It is essential that a man **rule over his own spirit**. Ultimately, this is his most important line of defense in this broken world. If a man cannot control his inner life, he will be defenseless. He will be like a city without walls. His enemies will easily plot his destruction.

C. Wisdom's Instruction on Fools and Scoundrels. 26:1-28.

26:1-5. The fool is once again evaluated in verses 1-12. **Honor is not seemly for a fool.** All the elements in verse 1 are out of place and cause great inconvenience. Snow in summer can be deadly. Rain in harvest is destructive; and where a fool is held in honor, much evil will be found.

The **curse causeless shall not come.** The unprovoked curse will miss its intended target because an innocent person is being attacked. It will fly about as a sparrow and may come to rest on the one who maliciously sent it forth.

A rod for the fool's back. The bridle and whip are necessary to curb the reckless ambitions of the horse and the ass. Since the fool will not be ruled by persuasion nor reason, a rod is required to check his rebellious ambitions.

Answer not a fool. The twin sayings of verses 4-5 brings out the dilemma of those who would reason with the fool. The man of wisdom will not dispute with the fool, but will rather answer the fool with a sharp and decisive retort which will challenge his statements and expose his shallowness (cf. II Cor 12:11; 11:16).

6-9. He that sendeth a message by the hand of a fool. The fool is unfit for service. When employed for the accomplishment of a simple task, he makes so many mistakes that it seems as if his feet had been severed from his body, thus rendering him immobile. The sender must view such a messenger as a bitter pill to swallow.

As he that bindeth a stone in a sling. It is a great folly to promote a fool to a position of honor. It is as nonsensical a procedure as tying a stone in a sling, for the stone is there to be slung out. The fool should be thrown out as well.

A parable in the mouth of fools. The lame walk with an uncertain gait. When he who is not a child of wisdom attempts to use the proverbs of wisdom, he speaks with an unevenness that betrays his doublemindedness. What he says hangs limp.

10-12. The great God . . . rewardeth. When fools and transgressors set their minds upon the husks of this world instead of God's provision, He does not deny this shallow fare to them. He grants them their desired reward. Yahweh gives all their just desserts. He renders to all according to their deeds.

As a dog returneth to his vomit. The disgusting picture of the dog who eats the vile eruptions of his stomach is an apt picture of the fool. This man, though he learn of his folly, returns to ingest it with a reckless enthusiasm (cf. II Pet 2:22).

Seest thou a man wise in his own conceit? The fool is an opinionated man, but his stupidity may at least open him to a bit of instruction. The abler man feeds however on the conceit of his abilities and accomplishments. So the publicans and harlots who had foolishly strayed from God were open to the preaching of the Saviour. The Pharisees and lawyers, however, filled with the conceit of their wisdom, rejected the counsel of Jesus against them (Lk 7:30).

13 The slothful *man* saith, *There is* a lion in the way; a lion *is* in the streets.
14 *As* the door turneth upon his hinges, so *doth* the slothful upon his bed.
15 The slothful hideth his hand in *his* bosom; it grieveth him to bring it again to his mouth.
16 The sluggard *is* wiser in his own conceit than seven men that can render a reason.

13-16. Four proverbs against sloth are now given. **There is a lion in the way.** The lazy man is ingenious in the inventing of excuses for his continued indolence. His ability to rationalize is well-cultivated, and he will be the last to see the error of his ways. He never thinks of himself as lazy, but rather as a realist (vs. 13). One could get mugged if he ventures into the street, and so he reasons it is best to stay at home. He never thinks of himself as self-indulgent, but simply as a slow starter in the morning (vs. 14). The slightest exertion is a sorrow to him, and he is grieved by every attempt to speed him up (vs. 15). This man sticks to his opinions and defends his view of things with industry, and the disgust of others leaves him unaffected.

17 He that passeth by, *and* meddleth with strife *belonging* not to him, *is like* one that taketh a dog by the ears.
18 As a mad *man* who casteth firebrands, arrows, and death,
19 So *is* the man *that* deceiveth his neighbour, and saith, Am not I in sport?
20 Where no wood is, *there* the fire goeth out: so where *there is* no talebearer, the strife ceaseth.
21 *As* coals *are* to burning coals, and wood to fire; so *is* a contentious man to kindle strife.
22 The words of a talebearer *are* as wounds, and they go down into the innermost parts of the belly.
23 Burning lips and a wicked heart *are like* a potsherd covered with silver dross.

17-23. Meddleth with strife. Mixing in the disputes of others is foolish and dangerous. To take a wild dog by the ears is risky business. It is better to give mad dogs and mad people a wide berth.

Am not I in sport? The man who finds the injuring of others sport ought to be carefully avoided. He who enjoys deceiving or tripping his neighbor and then passing it off as a joke is in the same class as a madman who hurls about arrows to which some blazing material has been affixed, with no concern for the deadly consequences.

Where there is no talebearer, the strife ceaseth. He who lays no wood upon the fire will cause it to die. He who adds no fuel to a quarrel may bring about the same affect. When there is no whisperer about to inflame persons, strife often ceases. The quarrelsome love to generate ill feelings and contribute the same effect in a situation that the adding of hot coals exercises on a fire. These evil men keep souls inflamed with dissension and hatred.

Burning lips. Fiery protestations of friendship, when issuing from one whose heart is wicked, are to be compared with a potsherd covered with impure silver. The pleasing surface covers the real nature of the interior. Look carefully, and you will see the impurities in the silver, which should then lead to thoughtfulness about the true worth of the vessel.

24 He that hateth dissembleth with his lips, and layeth up deceit within him;
25 When he speaketh fair, believe him not: for *there are* seven abominations in his heart.
26 *Whose* hatred is covered by deceit, his wickedness shall be shewed before the *whole* congregation.
27 Whoso diggeth a pit shall fall therein: and he that rolleth a stone, it will return upon him.
28 A lying tongue hateth *those that are* afflicted by it; and a flattering mouth worketh ruin.

24-28. He that hateth dissembleth. The flatterer covers his malicious heart with charming speech. He should not be trusted. **Seven abominations** represents the intensity of his moral deformity. Verse 26 expresses the confidence that ultimately this hypocrite's wickedness will be revealed in the assembly. In time this one who digs pits for others to fall into will fall into the pit himself. This man is rolling a large stone up a steep incline. He believes the stone to be under his control, but in a careless moment it will break loose and crush him to death. This doctrine of retribution is also taught in Psalm 7:11.

Sins never exist as individual entities. One sin soon joins itself to another. In this case, lying joins itself to hatred. Men afflict because they hate, and their hatred burns ever more brightly against those whom they have afflicted.

D. Wisdom's Instruction on Human Relations. 27:1-27.

27:1-2. Boast not thyself of tomorrow. This is forbidden as well in James 4:13, but there it is on the higher ground that it betrays a lack of submission to the will of God. To defer until tomorrow what could be accomplished today is a sad mistake that has destroyed millions. The uncertainties of health, or reason, or your very life render absolutely necessary the total investment of all one's energies in the present day.

CHAPTER 27
BOAST not thyself of to morrow; for thou knowest not what a day may bring forth.
2 Let another man praise thee, and not thine own mouth; a stranger, and not thine own lips.

Let another man praise thee. Self-praise is also out of place for the man of wisdom and reveals an insensitivity to the fitness of things. Praise is a comely garment; and though we may desire to wear it, it is always better if others place the garment upon us.

3 A stone *is* heavy, and the sand weighty; but a fool's wrath *is* heavier than them both.

4 Wrath *is* cruel, and anger *is* outrageous; but who *is* able to stand before envy?

5 Open rebuke *is* better than secret love.

6 Faithful *are* the wounds of a friend; but the kisses of an enemy *are* deceitful.

7 The full soul loatheth an honeycomb; but to the hungry soul every bitter thing is sweet.

8 As a bird that wandereth from her nest, so *is* a man that wandereth from his place.

9 Ointment and perfume rejoice the heart: so *doth* the sweetness of a man's friend by hearty counsel.

10 Thine own friend, and thy father's friend, forsake not; neither go into thy brother's house in the day of thy calamity: *for* better *is* a neighbour *that is* near than a brother far off.

11 My son, be wise, and make my heart glad, that I may answer him that reproacheth me.

12 A prudent *man* foreseeth the evil, *and* hideth himself; *but* the simple pass on, *and* are punished.

13 Take his garment that is surety for a stranger, and take a pledge of him for a strange woman.

14 He that blesseth his friend with a loud voice, rising early in the morning, it shall be counted a curse to him.

15 A continual dropping in a very

3-4. Wrath is cruel, and anger is outrageous. Nothing is harder to bear than the misguided and uncontrolled anger of the fool. His ill-tempered behavior is a burden far heavier than stone and sand for all who must suffer under it. Wrath and anger are passing tempests however. Jealousy (envy) is far worse, for it abides unchecked and is more cruel than sheol itself.

5-6. Open rebuke is better than secret love. It is better to hear rebuke when it is warranted than to hear of a secret profession of love that never issues in acts of kindness. The reproof of a friend is a valuable adjunct of friendship. The usefulness of friendship is dissipated when loving and faithful reproof is divorced from the relationship. The love that will not speak the truth under the pretense of fearing to inflict pain is, by God's standard, hatred (Lev 19:17). Rebuke, patiently administered, cements and validates friendship rather than loosening it. A man may lavish tokens of affection in time of crisis, but in the end the deceitful intentions of his deepest heart will be unveiled.

7. To the hungry soul every bitter thing is sweet. Moderation is once again the theme. The moderate use of things increases our enjoyment of them. The hungry soul recounts with joy the little treats life affords and is possessed by a spirit of thankfulness. The full of soul are quarrelsome and trample upon that which should be a cause of great delight for them.

8-10. So is a man that wandereth from his place. Yahweh has appointed to every man a place and a task (cf. I Cor 12:18). Man's greatest virtue is his resolve to fill that place and accomplish that task. A man who has wandered from that resolve is like the little bird who has ventured away from the safety of the nest and has hence exposed himself to grave danger.

Hearty counsel. Perfume and ointment are most refreshing to the senses, and the counsel of a friend is equally vivifying to the soul. The tenderness of such counsel heals grave wounds and provides an added source of strength for the bearing of what might otherwise constitute overwhelming sorrows.

Thine own friend, and thy father's friend, forsake not. The values of friendship have been established in previous texts. Your father's friend has proportionately greater value because he is, in a sense, a family heirloom of longstanding fidelity and goodness. When calamity suddenly strikes, a tried friend will often be of far more benefit to you than a member of your own family, whose affections have been weakened by time and distance.

11-14. My son, be wise. The actions of a child always reflect upon his parents. Willfulness and disrespect on the part of the son will generate an indictment of the father. The father who can point to acts of wisdom in the life of his son will have a valued resource to stop the mouth of those who would reproach him (cf. I Thess 2:19, 20; 3:8).

The simple pass on. The man of understanding hastens to remove himself from the presence of evil. He cultivates a perception that allows him to sense its advent before it fully materializes. The simple man cannot discern what is happening and stumbles into much evil, which in turn exposes him to grievous afflictions (see 22:3).

Take his garment. Here is an illustration of the foresight described in verse 12. The verse is a near repetition of 20:16, with a caution to avoid those who practice folly.

He that blesseth his friend with a loud voice. A man who is so eager to express his thankfulness that he begins early in the morning while others are still groggy with sleep is a man who will soon fall into disfavor. His unbridled enthusiasm may indicate deception or naiveté. In either case, he will sooner or later be looked upon as a curse. It matters not only what we say, but how, when, and why we say it (Derek Kidner, *The Proverbs*, p. 166).

15-16. A contentious woman. Rain in Palestine thoroughly

1247

rainy day and a contentious woman are alike.

16 Whosoever hideth her hideth the wind, and the ointment of his right hand, *which* bewrayeth *itself*.

17 Iron sharpeneth iron; so a man sharpeneth the countenance of his friend.
18 Whoso keepeth the fig tree shall eat the fruit thereof: so he that waiteth on his master shall be honoured.
19 As in water face *answereth* to face, so the heart of man to man.
20 Hell and destruction are never full; so the eyes of man are never satisfied.

21 *As* the fining pot for silver, and the furnace for gold; so *is* a man to his praise.
22 Though thou shouldest bray a fool in a mortar among wheat with a pestle, *yet* will not his foolishness depart from him.

23 Be thou diligent to know the state of thy flocks, *and* look well to thy herds.
24 For riches *are* not for ever: and doth the crown *endure* to every generation?
25 The hay appeareth, and the tender grass sheweth itself, and herbs of the mountains are gathered.
26 The lambs *are* for thy clothing, and the goats *are* the price of the field.
27 And *thou shalt have* goats' milk enough for thy food, for the food of thy household, and *for* the maintenance for thy maidens.

CHAPTER 28

THE wicked flee when no man pursueth: but the righteous are bold as a lion.
2 For the transgression of a land many *are* the princes thereof: but by a man of understanding *and* knowledge the state *thereof* shall be prolonged.
3 A poor man that oppresseth the poor *is like* a sweeping rain which leaveth no food.

soaks through the flat earthen roofs, and water leaks in droplets everywhere. It is an annoying situation, perhaps only equalled by the relentless quarrelings of a contentious woman. She is as unsteady as the wind and as slippery as oil; you can never tie her down.

17-20. Iron sharpeneth iron. The wisdom teachers considered the interaction of human personalities to be productive of great good or ill. Friends can sharpen one another even as one piece of metal can sharpen and brighten another through friction. Countenance, like soul, can stand for the man himself.

Shall eat the fruit thereof. The man who carefully tends his fruit trees will enjoy an abundance of fruit. The servant who attends his master's needs and faithfully complies with his wishes will be honored (cf. Mt 25:21). Moffatt points out the correspondence between the two verbs "He who tends . . . ; He who attends to" (cf. II Tim 2:6, 15).

Face answereth to face. As the water faithfully mirrors the likeness of a man's face, so the condition of a man's heart dictates what he will behold in the lives of others. The good see good, and the evil see or manufacture evil. Whatever characteristics our lives manifest, we tend to observe and elicit the same in the lives of others.

The eyes of man are never satisfied. The natural man is never satisfied. Let him get all he can, and he still desires more. The avarice of hell is aflame in his soul. Hell is here the name for the unseen world (Hades). Destruction (Heb *badōn*) is the lowest region of hell (cf. Lk 8:31). Hell is possessed of an avaricious appetite for the souls of men, ever asking for more and more.

21-22. As the fining pot for silver. The fining pot and the furnace test the metals put into them. No hotter crucible exists for the testing of men than the crucible of praise. A man must be of good mettle to survive the testing of the fires of popularity.

Though thou shouldest bray a fool. The pounding of the pestle separates the husk from the wheat. Though you pound a headstrong, self-willed person, he has so entrenched himself in his obstinacy that it cannot be separated from him even with the most violent pounding.

23-27. Look well to thy herds. The last five verses of the chapter stress the peacefulness of the pastoral life. Faithful shepherding will yield provisions for oneself and one's family. Sound animal husbandry is to be preferred to the uncertainty of wealth attained through business transactions. Even regal power is transient. He who works hard day after day and husbands his resources well will have all he needs.

E. Wisdom's Instruction on Pure Religion. 28:1-28.

28:1-3. The wicked flee when no man pursueth. The dread of the perpetual sinner functions without interruption. Fear plagues his every step. The righteous are emboldened by the consciousness that behind them is Yahweh as rear guard (Num 32:23) and before them is God's mercy (Ps 23:6).

For the transgression of a land. Transgression here carries the sense of rebellion. Many pretenders to the throne produce a state of political anarchy. In contrast to that unsettled state, the land that has as its sovereign a wise and understanding ruler who enjoys a long tenure is truly blessed.

A poor man that oppresseth the poor. This proverb seems to be pointing to a magistrate who, originally poor, now seeks to enrich himself by the oppression of the poor over whom he rules. Such a man floods the field of a fruitful people and thus

4 They that forsake the law praise the wicked: but such as keep the law contend with them.

5 Evil men understand not judgment: but they that seek the LORD understand all *things*.

6 Better *is* the poor that walketh in his uprightness, than *he that is* perverse *in his* ways, though he *be* rich.

7 Whoso keepeth the law *is* a wise son: but he that is a companion of riotous *men* shameth his father.

8 He that by usury and unjust gain increaseth his substance, he shall gather it for him that will pity the poor.

9 He that turneth away his ear from hearing the law, even his prayer *shall be* abomination.

10 Whoso causeth the righteous to go astray in an evil way, he shall fall himself into his own pit: but the upright shall have good *things* in possession.

11 The rich man *is* wise in his own conceit; but the poor that hath understanding searcheth him out.

12 When righteous *men* do rejoice, *there is* great glory: but when the wicked rise, a man is hidden.

13 He that covereth his sins shall not prosper: but whoso confesseth and forsaketh *them* shall have mercy.

14 Happy *is* the man that feareth alway: but he that hardeneth his heart shall fall into mischief.

15 *As* a roaring lion, and a ranging bear; *so is* a wicked ruler over the poor people.

16 The prince that wanteth understanding *is* also a great oppressor: but he that hateth covetousness shall prolong *his* days.

17 A man that doeth violence to the blood of *any* person shall flee to the pit; let no man stay him.

18 Whoso walketh uprightly shall be saved: but *he that is* perverse *in his* ways shall fall at once.

19 He that tilleth his land shall have

destroys their potential for prosperity. This man, bereft of compassion, is the impoverishment of a people.

4-5. They that seek the LORD understand all things. Law (Heb *tōrah*) is the law of Jehovah. Those who forsake the Law are, in reality, praising those who pursue lawless practices and are blind to true justice. They preach moral relativity and espouse the development of a society where nothing quite merits punishment. The sight and sounds of moral relativity are abhorred by the righteous, who meet all such pronouncements with aggressive resistance.

6-9. Better is the poor that walketh in his uprightness. The poor man, with all of the disadvantages that attend his poverty, is better, i.e., more honorable, than the rich man, with all of his supposed advantages. The character of the righteous poor mandate a preferential care from Yahweh. **Ways** here is in the dual number and intensifies the idea of double dealing that is always present in the practices of the perverse.

Whoso keepeth the law. Keeping the Law (Heb *tōrah*) is an open manifestation of a righteous intelligence. The companion of a waster will inevitably bring shame upon his parents.

He that by usury . . . increaseth his substance. Wealth gained by unjust usury will not be kept permanently, for God has forbidden such practices (Lev 25:35-37). The true son of the covenant was to be liberal with the poor and lend for nothing. Those who violate this injunction will see their possessions taken from them and given to those who are concerned about the poor (cf. I Sam 15:28; Lk 19:24).

His prayer shall be abomination. The habitual rejection of Torah has unfathomable consequences. Such a person must look in vain for answers to prayer, for in his willful rebellion he has utterly cut himself off from God (cf. Ps 66:18).

10-12. Whoso causeth the righteous to go astray. The evil way is the way of sin into which the upright are betrayed with ruinous consequences. Those who deliberately turn the righteous into these paths incur the judgment of Yahweh. Yahweh pledges himself to cast these men into the pits that they have dug for another (cf. Num 31:15, 16, with 8; see also 26:27).

The rich man is wise in his own conceit. The rich are often filled with pride; but the poor man sees through him and, knowing his weaknesses, easily outstrips him in the struggle for true prosperity (cf. I Cor 1:26-28). When the righteous triumph, all the people rejoice. In contrast, when the evil rule, men must hide themselves to insure their safety (Amos 5:13).

13-14. He that coverth his sins shall not prosper. God and men cover sins. God covers with the blood of His Christ, and men with the shame of hypocrisy. Confession is the divinely appointed method for obtaining the mercy and blessing of God. Confession, when accompanied by forsaking, brings prosperity in the life of the child of God.

Happy is the man that feareth always. Happiness belongs to the man who lives in holy dread of violating God's will by the practice of sin in any of its heinous forms. The sensitivity of this man is set in contrast to the hardness of heart that characterizes the perpetual sinner.

15-16. As a roaring lion. The oppressive reign of a wicked ruler is compared to the viciousness of attacking animals. Lacking true understanding, these vicious persons fail to recognize that the security of the throne is related to the welfare of their subjects. The ruler who hates such senseless oppression will bring stability and length of days to his reign.

17-22. A man that doeth violence. The man who is guilty of murder is under the sentence of death, and no one should try to inhibit his hasty execution. The offender himself, once his conscience is awakened, hastens to relieve himself of the burden of his crime. He hastens to his punishment, rather than face the public executioners.

plenty of bread: but he that followeth after vain *persons* shall have poverty enough.

20 A faithful man shall abound with blessings: but he that maketh haste to be rich shall not be innocent.

21 To have respect of persons *is* not good: for for a piece of bread *that* man will transgress.

22 He that hasteth to be rich *hath* an evil eye, and considereth not that poverty shall come upon him.

23 He that rebuketh a man afterwards shall find more favour than he that flattereth with the tongue.

24 Whoso robbeth his father or his mother, and saith, It is no transgression; the same *is* the companion of a destroyer.

25 He that is of a proud heart stirreth up strife: but he that putteth his trust in the Lord shall be made fat.

26 He that trusteth in his own heart is a fool: but whoso walketh wisely, he shall be delivered.

27 He that giveth unto the poor shall not lack: but he that hideth his eyes shall have many a curse.

28 When the wicked rise, men hide themselves: but when they perish, the righteous increase.

CHAPTER 29

HE, that being often reproved hardeneth *his* neck, shall suddenly be destroyed, and that without remedy.

2 When the righteous are in authority, the people rejoice: but when the wicked beareth rule, the people mourn.

3 Whoso loveth wisdom rejoiceth his father: but he that keepeth company with harlots spendeth *his* substance.

4 The king by judgment establisheth the land: but he that receiveth gifts overthroweth it.

5 A man that flattereth his neighbour spreadeth a net for his feet.

6 In the transgression of an evil man *there is* a snare: but the righteous doth sing and rejoice.

7 The righteous considereth the cause of the poor: *but* the wicked regardeth not to know *it*.

8 Scornful men bring a city into a snare: but wise *men* turn away wrath.

9 *If* a wise man contendeth with a

Whoso walketh uprightly shall be saved. Day-by-day practical salvation from failure and sin is in view here. The man who purposes in his heart to cleave to the laws of Yahweh will be saved from much that vexes the soul of the perverse man.

He that tilleth . . . shall have plenty of bread. Habits of diligence are reinforced by the blessings of God. The prodigal (Lk 15) is a type of the man who followeth after vain persons. He was quickly reduced to poverty and through repentance found his way back to the richness of fellowship with his father. The faithful man will receive the Lord's blessing. The man who abandons principles in the quick pursuit of riches will find himself under the judgment of God. The man who keeps faith with biblical principles will prosper, and those who abandon these principles will wind up selling their souls for a piece of bread. **Poverty shall come upon him.**

23-24. He that rebuketh a man. He who rebukes a man in accordance with the precepts of God will be of great value to all. The flatterer may please the object of his flattery, but he will ultimately be of little value to anyone.

Whoso robbeth his father or his mother. Shall he who robs father or mother make light of it? He is next door to a murderer. This robbery often reached real refinement (cf. Mk 7:11).

25-26. He that is of a proud heart stirreth up strife. The man who is directed by pride will always be stirring up strife as he contends with others for the preeminence. The man whose trust is not in this kind of maneuvering but in the Lord will be richly rewarded (Mt 6:19-34). The man who trusts in his own heart is a fool and will wander in deception and darkness. He who trusts in the Lord will walk in His light and enjoy His continuing deliverance.

27-28. He that giveth unto the poor shall not lack. Giving to the poor is persistently commended by Solomon. Those who cover their eyes to ignore the sight of the teeming millions in poverty cannot enjoy the blessing of God. The poor seem to be left in this world as a constant test of the reality of man's commitment to Yahweh (see 11:24).

When the wicked rise. Righteous men must hide themselves when the lawless rise to power, for they are ever the object of hatred to these evil people. When the unrighteous are overthrown, the righteous visibly increase because of the climate that is created by the absence of plunder and lawless practices.

F. Wisdom's Instruction on God and Society. 29:1-27.

29:1-4. He that being often reproved. The man who defends himself when censored and defiantly carries his evil thoughts to completion is insuring his destruction. He shall be shattered as a potter's vessel, with no possibility of repair. This theme is presented in 1:24-33 and Jeremiah 19:10-11.

When the righteous are in authority. When the righteous attain to power, the people are garmented in gladness. When the wicked are in ascendance, the people are clothed in the garb of mourning. A father is clothed with gladness when his son loves wisdom and eschews the company of harlots. The land is clothed in mourning when a king who receives bribes is on the throne, and the king who practices justice establishes the land.

5-7. A man that flattereth. Flattery is the saying of what the heart does not mean with the intention of misleading or obtaining favor. Such action is designed to ensnare the unwary. The transgressions of these evil men forge a chain that binds them steadfastly to a treadmill of evil. The innocent go singing and rejoicing on their way, free from sin's entangling power.

8-9. Scornful men bring a city into a snare. Men of derision provoke the party spirit that resides in the community to an excited state. They add fuel to the fires of division and set the city aflame. The wise ever seek reconciliation. Peaceable wis-

foolish man, whether he rage or laugh, *there is* no rest.

10 The bloodthirsty hate the upright: but the just seek his soul.
11 A fool uttereth all his mind: but a wise *man* keepeth it in till afterwards.
12 If a ruler hearken to lies, all his servants *are* wicked.

13 The poor and the deceitful man meet together: the LORD lighteneth both their eyes.
14 The king that faithfully judgeth the poor, his throne shall be established for ever.

15 The rod and reproof give wisdom: but a child left *to himself* bringeth his mother to shame.
16 When the wicked are multiplied, transgression increaseth: but the righteous shall see their fall.
17 Correct thy son, and he shall give thee rest; yea, he shall give delight unto thy soul.
18 Where *there is* no vision, the people perish: but he that keepeth the law, happy *is* he.

19 A servant will not be corrected by words: for though he understand he will not answer.
20 Seest thou a man *that is* hasty in his words? *there is* more hope of a fool than of him.

21 He that delicately bringeth up his servant from a child shall have him become *his* son at the length.

22 An angry man stirreth up strife, and a furious man aboundeth in transgression.
23 A man's pride shall bring him low: but honour shall uphold the humble in spirit.

24 Whoso is partner with a thief hateth his own soul: he heareth cursing, and bewrayeth *it* not.

dom works and waits for godly solutions (Jas 3:13-18). There is no reasoning with the fool. Certain of the accuracy of his opinions, he is beyond the reach of reason. Whether he smiles or raves, the result is always the same; he returns to embrace his own opinions. There can be no happy ending to any involvement with him.

10-12. The bloodthirsty hate the upright. There is a strong antipathy between the evil and the righteous man. Line 2 might best be translated: And as for the upright they seek his life.

A fool uttereth all his mind. His mind is literally his spirit or, from the context, his anger. The fool pours out all his wrath, but the wise man holds it back. If the adverb indicates repression, the verb (used in Heb 10 and Ps: 89:9 of the stilling of a storm) speaks of anger overcome, not merely checked (Derek Kidner, *The Proverbs*, p. 175).

If a ruler harken to lies. The servants of a ruler are apt to become like the ruler and accommodate themselves to his practices. If the ruler prefers falsehood to the truth, his servants will become able liars.

13-14. The LORD lighteneth both their eyes. The Lord gives life to all men, rich and poor alike. The moneylender might use his superior economic power to oppress the poor, but he had better remember that they both meet together under the watchful eye of the Lord. Faithfulness to the poor does much to establish the throne.

15-18. The rod and reproof give wisdom. The child who is exempted from discipline and allowed to govern his life according to the dictates of his own will is destined to bring shame upon his home. The society that does not practice the disciplining of its children is destined to be overrun by the wicked who feel they can practice all manner of evil with impunity. Though this sad state may continue for a time, the righteous will ultimately witness the total overthrow of the wicked (cf. Ps 54:7). Loving discipline will produce children who will be a cause of delight for aging parents. **Where there is no vision** the people perish. The context here would suggest a vision of the potential for good that the proper discipline of children possesses for the development of a godly society. Perish means, literally, to run wild. Where there is no vision for the proper discipline of children, a society produces a generation of young people who have no regard for the law and literally run wild.

19-20. A servant will not be corrected by words. The LXX reads "a stubborn servant." Verbal correction accomplishes little with men who deliberately refuse to obey commands. Sterner measures are needed, for it is only the fear of punishment that alters the resolve of these unprincipled and self-willed persons.

Seest thou a man that is hasty in his words? The fool may be taught better habits of speech through careful instruction. The man who speaks with haste outclasses the fool. His tongue is set on fire of hell, and he is destined for certain judgment unless he repents of his evil speech (see 26:12).

21. Become his son at the length. Trusted slaves sometimes rose to positions of prominence and became heirs of their master's property. To handle a slave tenderly could open the way to his gaining possession of all his master's goods. He could take the place of a man's son.

22-23. An angry man stirreth up strife. The passionate man abounds (Heb *rab*) literally, is rich in, transgressions.

Pride shall bring him low. Anger and pride always go together. Pride seals a man off from learning and is a precursor of impending destruction. The lowly (lit., the sufferers) who trust in the Lord are destined for honor.

24. Whoso is partner with a thief. A suicidal complicity is in view here. The man who forms a partnership with a thief in reality despises his own life. Eventually the thief will be

25 The fear of man bringeth a snare: but whoso putteth his trust in the LORD shall be safe.
26 Many seek the ruler's favour; but *every* man's judgment *cometh* from the LORD.

27 An unjust man *is* an abomination to the just: and *he that is* upright in the way *is* abomination to the wicked.

CHAPTER 30

THE words of Ā'gur the son of Jā'keh, *even* the prophecy: the man spake unto Ĭth'Ĭ-el, even unto Ĭth'Ĭ-el and Ū'cal,
2 Surely I *am* more brutish than *any* man, and have not the understanding of a man.
3 I neither learned wisdom, nor have the knowledge of the holy.
4 Who hath ascended up into heaven, or descended? who hath gathered the wind in his fists? who hath bound the waters in a garment? who hath established all the ends of the earth? what *is* his name, and what *is* his son's name, if thou canst tell?

5 Every word of God *is* pure: he *is* a

apprehended. Anyone who has any information with regard to the criminal's actions should present that information to the court. He has heard much. If he remains silent, he must share the thief's punishment.

25-26. The fear of man bringeth a snare. Trembling before men is a malicious sin. Tremblers will all too soon become the tools of wicked men. Perhaps fear motivated the accomplice to silence in verse 24. Man must fear only Yahweh, and he who fears him will fear no man (cf. Gal 1:10). They who trust the Lord will be set on high, i.e., beyond man's reach.

Every man's judgment cometh from the LORD. Many seek the approval of earthly leaders, but in reality this approval means little. All men are servants of appetites and pressures. Leaders are subject to irrationality and instability, which robs their intervention of all certainty. The cultivating of the ruler's favor is, then, a vain pursuit; for God alone determines the destinies of men.

27. An unjust man is an abomination. Two families are locked in mortal combat on planet earth: the unjust who cherish the devious and the upright who cherish righteousness. The enmity may be masked, but nothing can mend it; there can be no treaty of peace.

VI. THE WORDS OF AGUR. 30:1-33.

A. Wisdom's Instruction on the Knowledge of God. 30:1-4.

30:1-4. There were many sages besides Solomon (I Kgs 4:30-31). The identity of Agur is uncertain, and there is no need to find here a nom de plume for Solomon. The term prophecy (Heb *masa'*) emphasizes the authority of what is being given and expresses the nature of the message that the prophet bore to his hearers (Isa 13:1-2).

To Ithiel and Ucal. Various interpretations of the text have been suggested. The ancient versions do not translate the text with proper names. Kidner suggests that the Hebrew consonants of this phrase can be revocalized to read: I have wearied myself, O God, and come to an end (Derek Kidner, *The Proverbs*, p. 178). The two names, then, are meant to typify the plight of man as he grows faint in his attempts to pursue God in his own strength.

I am more brutish than any man. Our author is mindful of his own finitude as a member of a fallen humanity. His ignorance and narrow experience as a mere human are the cause of profound humility.

Have the knowledge of the holy. A deep sense of his limitations and lack of intelligence in the great matters that exercise his soul are here confessed. What he is about to communicate is not the byproduct of his reasoning, but the result of the Lord opening his understanding.

Who hath ascended up into heaven. Wisdom must be a gift (cf. Eccl 2:26; Jas 1:5). Man's inability to obtain it is amplified in this verse, which is in its entirety a commentary on the transcendence of God. The questions are designed to contrast man's finiteness with Yahweh's sovereignty. Who curtains the waters of the heavens and keeps them from falling on the earth? What is His son's name? No words can adequately describe the sovereign God of the universe. The only revelation we have of this infinite God is in His Son. The name of this Son at this point in the history of redemption was unknown. The concluding clauses of this energetic passage are easily interpreted if we admit that the ancient Jews had some obscure idea of a plurality in the divine nature (J. Pye Smith, *Scripture Testimony*, p. 496). The messianic psalms had already spoken of "the son" who is the ultimate fulfillment of all that is wisdom.

B. Wisdom's Instruction on the Word of God. 30:5-6.

5-6. Every word of God is pure. Every word that God speaks

shield unto them that put their trust in him.

6 Add thou not unto his words, lest he reprove thee, and thou be found a liar.

7 Two *things* have I required of thee; deny me *them* not before I die:

8 Remove far from me vanity and lies: give me neither poverty nor riches; feed me with food convenient for me:

9 Lest I be full, and deny *thee*, and say, Who *is* the LORD? or lest I be poor, and steal, and take the name of my God *in vain.*

10 Accuse not a servant unto his master, lest he curse thee, and thou be found guilty.

11 *There is* a generation *that* curseth their father, and doth not bless their mother.

12 *There is* a generation *that are* pure in their own eyes, and *yet* is not washed from their filthiness.

13 *There is* a generation, O how lofty are their eyes! and their eyelids are lifted up.

14 *There is* a generation, whose teeth *are as* swords, and their jaw teeth *as* knives, to devour the poor from off the earth, and the needy from *among* men.

15 The horseleach hath two daughters, *crying,* Give, give. There are three *things that* are never satisfied, *yea,* four *things* say not, *It is* enough:

16 The grave; and the barren womb; the earth *that* is not filled with water; and the fire *that* saith not, *It is* enough.

17 The eye *that* mocketh at *his* father, and despiseth to obey *his* mother, the ravens of the valley shall pick it out, and the young eagles shall eat it.

18 There be three *things which are* too wonderful for me, yea, four which I know not:

19 The way of an eagle in the air; the way of a serpent upon a rock; the way of a ship in the midst of the sea; and the way of a man with a maid.

20 Such *is* the way of an adulterous woman; she eateth, and wipeth her mouth, and saith, I have done no wickedness.

is truth. The name for God is *'Elōah*, which is used commonly in Job. Pure is literally smelted or refined. Every word of God has been tested and proven in the furnace of man's experience and His promises are a **shield unto them that put their trust in him.** His words cannot be improved upon and it is folly to seek to do so.

C. Wisdom's Instruction on Prayer. 30:7-9.

7-9. Two things have I required of thee. Agur utters a double petition to the Lord. Keep deceit and lies from me. Cause me to eat the food allotted to me. The two requests concern character and the circumstances that endanger the wise development of character. Help me Lord, before I die, to handle wisely the portion that falls to me under the providential guidance of your almighty hand, is his request. Such aid is needed, lest pride or poverty cause him to handle the name of God with disrespect and he find fault with the Lord.

D. Wisdom's Instruction on Another Man's Servant. 30:10.

10. Agur ends his upward look and now begins to look about him. **Accuse not a servant.** The incitement to slander and betrayal is inveighed against. The slanderer ever runs the risk of insulting the wrong person and reaping the wrath of that encounter.

E. Wisdom's Instruction on the Classification of Persons. 30:11-14.

11-14. There is a generation. Four times in verses 11-14 the word **generation** occurs. The existence of a circle of men who display the arrogance prayed against in verses 7-9 is now presented. The picture is one of a downward spiral as we move from the rebellious child to the brutal practices of reprobate adults. Pride is at the heart of this and is seen corrupting a man's attitude toward his superiors (vs. 11), himself (vs. 12), the world at large (vs. 13), and his inferiors (vs. 14).

F. Wisdom's Instruction on Insatiable Things. 30:15-16.

15-16. The horseleech hath two daughters. The leech is a reference to the bloodsucking horseleech that was common in Palestine. The ugly creature serves as an emblem of insatiable greed. If it could speak, it would say, Give! Give! Give!

Three things that are never satisfied, yea, four things say not, It is enough. The leech, with his insatiable thirst for blood, has served to introduce an insatiable quartet. The grave never says, I have enough (cf. 15:11); neither do the barren womb or the earth upon which rain falls. Yet there is a fourth. Fire devours all that stands before it and cries, it is not enough.

G. Wisdom's Instruction on the Turbulent Son. 30:17.

17. All these are but a type of man who restlessly mocks at his father and despises all authority. Such a man is an abomination to the Lord. In his evil ambition he cries, Give! Give! The birds of the heaven will feast upon his evil flesh.

H. Wisdom's Instruction on Wonderful Things. 30:18-20.

18-20. There be three things which are too wonderful for me. Four marvels are enumerated here, with a fifth affixed. Some commentators, following the Wisdom of Solomon 5:10-11, have sought a common denominator in the idea of movement that leaves no trace behind; but it would be better sought in the easy mastery, by the appropriate agent, of elements as difficult to negotiate as air, rock, sea, and the young woman. The fifth, and unnatural, marvel is that of a person utterly at ease and in her element in sin; an act of adultery is as unremarkable to her as a meal (Derek Kidner, *The Proverbs*, p. 180).

21 For three *things* the earth is disquieted, and for four *which* it cannot bear:

22 For a servant when he reigneth; and a fool when he is filled with meat;

23 For an odious *woman* when she is married; and an handmaid that is heir to her mistress.

24 There be four *things which are* little upon the earth, but they *are* exceeding wise:

25 The ants *are* a people not strong, yet they prepare their meat in the summer;

26 The conies *are but* a feeble folk, yet make they their houses in the rocks;

27 The locusts have no king, yet go they forth all of them by bands;

28 The spider taketh hold with her hands, and is in kings' palaces.

29 There be three *things* which go well, yea, four are comely in going:

30 A lion *which is* strongest among beasts, and turneth not away for any;

31 A greyhound; an he goat also; and a king, against whom *there is* no rising up.

32 If thou hast done foolishly in lifting up thyself, or if thou hast thought evil, *lay* thine hand upon thy mouth.

33 Surely the churning of milk bringeth forth butter, and the wringing of the nose bringeth forth blood: so the forcing of wrath bringeth forth strife.

CHAPTER 31

THE words of king Lěm'ū-el, the prophecy that his mother taught him.

2 What, my son? and what, the son of my womb? and what, the son of my vows?

3 Give not thy strength unto women, nor thy ways to that which destroyeth kings.

4 *It is* not for kings, O Lěm'ū-el, *it is* not for kings to drink wine; nor for princes strong drink:

I. Wisdom's Instruction on Intolerable Things. 30:21-23.

21-23. For three things the earth is disquieted. Under three things the earth trembles; under four it cannot bear up. Four intolerable things that cause society to tremble and issue in intolerable consequences are now enumerated.

A servant when he reigneth. Sudden elevation to prominence of men of low degree can have ruinous consequences. **Fool** here is *nabal*. He is a man filled (Ps 14:1) with self and is, in consequence, a cause of great mischief. **An odious woman.** The woman in view here is the one who seemed destined for eternal singleness but at last captured a man. Her conquest goes to her head, and she lords it over those who were once her peers. **A handmaid** who takes the place of her former mistress is also odious in her profuse revelry.

J. Wisdom's Instruction on Little Things. 30:24-28.

24-28. Four things which are little upon the earth. Four animals who in spite of their small size are possessed of attributes that serve as a source of instruction for man are now described.

The ant models the advisability of carefully planning ahead to meet future contingencies. The conies, or badgers, are only about as big as a rabbit. Their Hebrew name (*shapan*) signifies a hider. The animal is named for its habit of living in the cleft of rocks, a resourcefulness that gains for him a high degree of security. The locusts model organization and discipline. The spider (lizard) models the use of resources beyond one's own to enhance one's security and enjoyment of life.

K. Wisdom's Instruction on Comely Things. 30:29-31.

29-31. Four are comely in going. Four creatures who are stately in their demeanor are now listed. The unflinching lion is first. His boldness serves as a model for all. The second in the series has been variously understood. A beast girt in the loins or like the greyhound is intended. The animal models the persistent and disciplined pursuit of objectives. The he goat is a climber, mounting ever higher. Last is the king who marches on with vigorous resolve, trampling his conquered foes.

L. Wisdom's Closing Words. 30:32-33.

32-33. Lay thine hand upon thy mouth. The teachings of Agur close with instruction for the person who is about to, or has allowed himself to, get pridefully out of hand. Such pride is apt to lead to tragic consequences, which are summarized under the term pressing or wringing. The same word is used in Hebrew for churning, wringing, and forcing. The verse would then read, For as pressure on milk produces butter, and pressure on the nose produces blood, so pressure on wrath produces anger. The practice of humility forestalls the accumulation of such pressure.

VII. THE WORDS OF LEMUEL. 31:1-9.

A. Wisdom's Instruction on Duty. 31:1-4.

31:1-4. Despite the fact that nothing is known elsewhere of Lemuel, there is no good reason for refusing to recognize the term as a proper name. The exact meaning of the name is uncertain, but it probably contains the idea of belonging to God or dedicated to God.

What, my son? . . . Give not thy strength. The exclamations are affectionately reproachful. The mother reminds him of truths she has taught and the shame that will be his if he allows that instruction to slip from him. He is of great importance to her (vs. 2a), and she has vowed him to God (vs. 2b). Therefore, he must take heed to not give himself to that which destroyeth.

5 Lest they drink, and forget the law, and pervert the judgment of any of the afflicted.

6 Give strong drink unto him that is ready to perish, and wine unto those that be of heavy hearts.

7 Let him drink, and forget his poverty, and remember his misery no more.

8 Open thy mouth for the dumb in the cause of all such as are appointed to destruction.

9 Open thy mouth, judge righteously, and plead the cause of the poor and needy.

10 ¶Who can find a virtuous woman? for her price is far above rubies.

11 The heart of her husband doth safely trust in her, so that he shall have no need of spoil.

12 She will do him good and not evil all the days of her life.

13 She seeketh wool, and flax, and worketh willingly with her hands.

14 She is like the merchants' ships; she bringeth her food from afar.

15 She riseth also while it is yet night, and giveth meat to her household, and a portion to her maidens.

16 She considereth a field, and buyeth it: with the fruit of her hands she planteth a vineyard.

17 She girdeth her loins with strength, and strengtheneth her arms.

18 She perceiveth that her merchandise is good: her candle goeth not out by night.

19 She layeth her hands to the spindle, and her hands hold the distaff.

20 She stretcheth out her hand to the poor; yea, she reacheth forth her hands to the needy.

21 She is not afraid of the snow for her household: for all her household are clothed with scarlet.

22 She maketh herself coverings of tapestry; her clothing is silk and purple.

23 Her husband is known in the gates, when he sitteth among the elders of the land.

24 She maketh fine linen, and selleth it; and delivereth girdles unto the merchant.

25 Strength and honour are her clothing; and she shall rejoice in time to come.

26 She openeth her mouth with wisdom; and in her tongue is the law of kindness.

27 She looketh well to the ways of her household, and eateth not the bread of idleness.

28 Her children arise up, and call her blessed; her husband also, and he praiseth her.

29 Many daughters have done virtuously, but thou excellest them all.

30 Favour is deceitful, and beauty is vain: but a woman that feareth the LORD, she shall be praised.

B. Wisdom's Instruction on Intemperance. 31:5-7.

5-7. The drinking of wine will lead to the perversion of justice (Isa 5:22, 23). Wine should only be given to him that is ready to perish, for this represents an advantageous use of God's gift (cf. I Tim 5:23). The pious women of Jerusalem used to offer wine to those condemned to crucifixion in order to deaden their misery. This was offered to the Lord Jesus (Mt 27:34), but he refused it; for He wished to keep His mind clear to the last as He took upon himself the sins of all mankind.

C. Wisdom's Instruction on Justice. 31:8-9.

8-9. Open thy mouth for the dumb. The dumb are those who cannot get a fair hearing for themselves (lit., the insecure and timid). Since they may be crushed by their antagonists, speak on their behalf. **Plead the cause of the poor and needy.**

VIII. WISDOM'S ALPHABET ON WIFELY EXCELLENCE. 31:10-31.

10-27. This section is written in the form of an acrostic; the composition is constructed with 22 verses. The initial letter of each couplet follows the normal order of the Hebrew alphabet. The thought of 28:22 is probably a distinct section, and not a continuation of the teachings of Lemuel's mother.

Who can find a virtuous woman? The Hebrew *chayil* is translated in other places as strong, wealthy, and able. Literally, the question asks, Who can find a fine wife?

So that he shall have no need of spoil (lit., shall have no lack of gain). His substance is constantly increasing because of the prudent care she exercises over his resources.

And worketh willingly with her hands. She enjoys providing for her family and therefore works uncomplainingly. Her activities apparently extend beyond those normally associated with the housewife. **Like the merchants' ships** is probably idiomatic for her work beyond the domestic context (William McKane, *Proverbs*, p. 667). **She seeketh wool . . . considereth a field, and buyeth it.** The virtuous wife is efficient in matters of business. She is famous for the way she looks after her household, and her priorities dictate the investment of her energies there (vss. 13, 19, 21, 22, 27, 28). She provides her family with adequate clothing (vss. 21-22). The term scarlet probably suggests quality. She is energetic in meeting the needs of her family and confident in her ability to meet the challenges of the future (vs. 25). She is keenly alive to the sorrows of the needy and aids them with all her power.

She so enhances the performance of her husband that he is well known in the gates (vs. 23). Free from domestic squabbling, he is able to contribute to public life.

28-31. Verses 28 and 29 describe the praise which this excellent woman receives from her husband and sons. Verse 29 is a statement from the husband.

Favor is deceitful, and beauty is vain. Charm and beauty are not abiding attributes and are therefore not worthy of praise. Contrasted with them is the disposition to fear the Lord. This disposition has eternal consequences and is therefore worthy of

31 Give her of the fruit of her hands; and let her own works praise her in the gates.

praise. The real worth of a woman is her devotion to God. She should be given the praise she deserves. She is no slave of a master husband, but a person in her own right who takes a full and honored place in the life of home and community (Marvin Tate, *The Broadman Commentary*, Proverbs, p. 99).

BIBLIOGRAPHY

*Bridges, Charles. *An Exposition of Proverbs*. Grand Rapids: Zondervan Publishing House, reprinted, 1959.

*Delitzsch, Franz. *Biblical Commentary on the Proverbs of Solomon*. Grand Rapids: Eerdmans Publishing Company, reprinted, 1970.

Fritsch, Charles T. The Book of Proverbs. In *The Interpreter's Bible*, Vol. IV. Ed. by George Arthur Buttrick. Nashville: Abingdon Press, 1955.

Horton, R. F. The Book of Proverbs. In *The Expositor's Bible*. New York: A. C. Armstrong and Son, 1902.

Jones, Edgar. Proverbs and Ecclesiastes. In *Torch Bible Commentaries*. New York: MacMillan Company, 1961.

*Kidner, Derek. The Proverbs. In *The Tyndale Old Testament Commentaries*. Chicago: InterVarsity Press, 1964.

Lange, John. Proverbs. In *Commentary on the Holy Scriptures*. New York: Charles Scribners Sons, 1886.

Luther, Martin. Proverbs. In *Luther's Works*. St. Louis: Concordia Publishing House, 1972.

McKane, William. Proverbs. In *The Old Testament Library*. Philadelphia: The Westminster Press, 1970.

Miller, John. *A Commentary on the Proverbs*. New York: Anson D. F. Randolph and Company, 1872.

Oesterley, W. O. E. The Book of Proverbs. In *Westminster Commentaries*. London: Methuen and Company, Ltd., 1929.

Parker, Joseph. The Proverbs. In *The People's Bible*. New York: Funk and Wagnalls Co., n.d.

Rylaarsdam, J. Coert. Proverbs, Ecclesiastes, Song of Solomon. In *The Layman's Bible Commentary*, Vol. 10. Richmond, Va.: John Knox Press, 1964.

Scott, R. B. Y. Proverbs, Ecclesiastes. In *The Anchor Bible*, Vol. 18. Garden City, New York: Doubleday and Company, 1965.

Spence, H. D. M. and J. S. Exell. Proverbs. In *The Pulpit Commentary*. Chicago: Wilcox and Follett Co., n.d.

*Tate, Marvin, E. Proverbs. In *The Broadman Commentary*. Nashville: Broadman Press, 1971.

Toy, Crawford H. A Critical and Exegetical Commentary on the Book of Proverbs. In *The International Commentary*. Edinburgh: T. & T. Clark, 1959.

Whybray, R. N. Wisdom in Proverbs. In *Studies in Biblical Theology*, No. 45. Naperville, Ill.: Alec R. Allenson, Inc., 1965.

ECCLESIASTES

INTRODUCTION

Purpose. In the book of Ecclesiastes we witness the efforts of the wisdom teacher as he endeavors to lead young men into the path of true wisdom. Perhaps the young man was inclined to equate wisdom with wide knowledge and to suppose that one gains wisdom by assiduous book work (12:12). This sophomoric attitude is perennially affixed to human nature. Perhaps the young man cared not for wisdom, but rather spent his time in the pursuit of pleasure and personal satisfaction. Our teacher of wisdom has carefully constructed his discourse in the firm hope that young men shall be persuaded to avoid these dead-end streets and enter upon that path which alone leads to true profit. Many have experienced the power of this book to accomplish that task in their lives. B. H. Carroll testified that, in the days of his infidelity, Ecclesiastes exerted an unearthly power over him, exposing the emptiness of his life and pointing him to God (B. H. Carroll, *Jesus the Christ*, p. 19).

The English title Ecclesiastes was adopted from the Vulgate (Latin). In Hebrew the title reads, *The Words of Qoheleth, the Son of David, King in Jerusalem.* The term *Qoheleth* is rare, occurring only seven times in Ecclesiastes and nowhere else in the canonical Hebrew writings. *Qoheleth* (written Koheleth by some) is the feminine singular participle of the otherwise nonexistent form of *qahal.* Jerome translated the word as *concionator.* Luther translated it *Der Prediger*, which means, the Preacher. The word designates the function of the leader who speaks in the assembly. Hence, the translation "preacher" is approximately correct (E. J. Young, *An Introduction to Old Testament*, p. 347). From 12:9 we know that our instructor is a presenter of wisdom, teaching knowledge to the people, scrutinizing, evaluating, and arranging many proverbs in his search for words that will suitably move his hearers to the path of profit and truth. Hence, he is a preacher in the finest sense of the tradition, and not a philosophizer as some have suggested. His contribution to men's education is based squarely upon his interaction with the words "goads, and . . . nails" which have been given by one shepherd (12:11) and are not the product of his own cognitive powers (12:9).

Our preacher poses a question that all mankind must face: what profit does man achieve through his life under the sun? What does man gain (Heb *yithron*)? This word is unique to Ecclesiastes and is drawn from the world of business. The term here is not used, however, in a mercenary sense, but rather to raise the important issue of meaning and profit for all of life. Our author here shares the concern of our Lord Jesus Christ when he asks the question, "For what shall it profit a man, if he shall gain the whole world, and lose his own soul?" (Mk 8:36). If a man gain all the knowledge and experience, all the pleasures of this world, what would be the remaining or abiding benefit or happiness which he would achieve? Our author confirms that all such pursuits are vain, i.e., as empty as steam. He points man to the only path that leads to true profit: a wholehearted commitment to the better way, the way of duty, which man can only walk upon if he fears God and keeps His commandments.

Authorship. The Preacher identifies himself as "the son of David, king in Jerusalem" (1:1), but the name of the author never appears in the book. In the twelfth verse of the first chapter the author states; "I the Preacher (*Qoheleth*) was king over Israel in Jerusalem." Since Solomon was the only son of David who was king over Israel, there can be no doubt that he is meant by the appellation *Qoheleth.* This is fully corroborated by the allusion to events and circumstances throughout the book that are unmistakably connected with the life of the great monarch. Compare, for instance, Ecclesiastes 1:16 with I Kings 3:12; Ecclesiastes 2:4-10 with I Kings 4:27-32, 7:1-8, 9:7-19, 10:24-29; Ecclesiastes 7:20 with I Kings 8:46; Ecclesiastes 7:28 with I Kings 11:1-8; Ecclesiastes 12:9 with I Kings 4:32 (C. D. Ginsburg, *The Song of Songs and Qoheleth*, p. 244).

According to the tradition of the synagogue, the book of Ecclesiastes is attributed to Solomon, son of David. One Rabbinic source declares that he wrote the Song of Songs, with its accent on love, in his youth; Proverbs, with its emphasis on practical problems, in his maturity; and Ecclesiastes with its emphasis on the vanity of life, in old age (Midrash, *Shir Hashirim Rabba*, 1:1, Sec. 10). In a very old Tannaitic source the order of the Kethubim is given as Ruth, Psalms, Job, Proverbs, Ecclesiastes, Canticles, Lamentations, Daniel, Esther, Ezra, and Chronicles. That Solomon is regarded as the author of Ecclesiastes is clear from its position between Proverbs and Canticles, both of which are specifically attributed to Solomon in the superscriptions of the biblical text itself (Gordis, *Koheleth, the Man and His World*, p. 39). Today Solomonic authorship is not widely held and is rejected by most orthodox Protestant scholars (E. J. Young, *Introduction to Old Testament*, p. 347). Their contention is that the author is following the tradition of much of the ancient Jewish literature when he selects a famous personage as his mouthpiece, and no one was better suited for his purposes than Solomon. The era of Solomon was the era of splendor, and Solomon was the founder of the wisdom movement. Therefore, seeking to speak as profoundly as possible about life, the author of this book says, in effect, "What would Solomon have said?" But this does not tell us who he was (Rylaarsdam, Ecclesiastes, in *The Layman's Bible Commentary*, p. 94).

One question must be raised regarding this approach to the question of the book's authorship. If it was the author's intention to palm his work off as the work of Solomon, why did he use the enigmatic name of *Qoheleth*? Wouldn't he have used the name "Solomon" directly, as happened time without number in the Pseudepigrapha, roughly contemporaneous with our book (Gordis, p. 40). In actuality, the fact that the author makes no effort to imply Solomon's authorship, but rather takes on the guise of "the Son of David," could indicate that the device was employed by Solomon to avoid an express statement of his authorship of the treatise. It would prove extremely effective for Solomon to pass judgment on the true value of wisdom and luxury, for who in Israel could better do so. Any who came after him could only repeat what Solomon had already done (2:12). This tradition of Solomonic authorship guaranteed the book a place in the canon of Scripture. Often the denial of Solomonic authorship is related to attempts to give the book a very late date and prove extensive Greek influence on the author. Dahood has urged that we consider a strong Phoenician influence, but the evidence for this is hardly visible. Rather, our author is in the mainstream of the Ancient Near Eastern wisdom movement, especially the Mesopotamian literature (Murphy, *Ecclesiastes*, p. 54). The time of writing is fixed at a much earlier date by the discovery of Hebrew fragments found at Qumran which indicate that there was a copy of the book in circulation about 150 B.C. (T. Muilenburg, *Bulletin of the American Schools of Oriental Research* 135 1954 pp. 20-28).

Many scholars have detected the hands of glossators throughout the work and refuse to view it as a united discourse, but no outline of the work based on this viewpoint has achieved any widespread support.

In the following commentary Solomon is viewed as the mature collector and assembler of wisdom giving the young disciple the fruits of his own experience and reflection (Packer, *Knowing God*, p. 94). He lays bare the superficiality of the standard assertions of his age and exposes the corruption that has been shrouded in the midst of affluence and habit. With unflinching commitment he stands as a Preacher pointing the way to the path of true profit. In so doing he points across the centuries to that One who reveals in himself the fulness of God's wisdom. We desperately need Solomon's message to aid us in our endeavor to lay bare the hollow beliefs of our own time and point men to the life of profit that is to be found in Jesus Christ who is the wisdom of God and who alone is profit in this life (Phil 3:7-8).

OUTLINE

I. The Wisdom Preacher Poses the Question of True Profit. 1:1-3.
II. The Wisdom Preacher Points to Life Under the Sun. 1:4-15.
III. The Wisdom Preacher Points to Dead End Streets Experienced in the Pursuit of Profit. 1:16-2:23.
IV. The Wisdom Preacher Points the Way to True Profit. 2:24-6:10.
  A. Faith in the Hand of God. 2:24-26.
  B. Faith in God's Control. 3:1-22.
  C. A Proper Response to God's Call to Community. 4:1-16.
  D. A Proper Response to God's Call to Worship. 5:1-9.
  E. A Proper Response to God's Call to Joyful Labor. 5:10-6:9.
  F. A Summary Statement. 6:10.
V. The Wisdom Preacher Introduces and Expands the Practical Application of His Message on Profit. 6:11-8:17.
VI. The Wisdom Preacher Continues to Enjoin the Practical Application of His Message on Profit in Spite of Life's Many Perplexities. 9:1-12:8.
VII. The Wisdom Preacher Summarizes His Mission, Method, and Message. 12:9-14.

COMMENTARY

I. THE WISDOM PREACHER POSES THE QUESTION OF TRUE PROFIT. 1:1-3.

THE words of the Preacher, the son of David, king in Jerusalem.

2 Vanity of vanities, saith the Preacher, vanity of vanities; all *is* vanity.

3 What profit hath a man of all his labour which he taketh under the sun?

1:1. The words of the Preacher, the son of David, king in Jerusalem. The superscription serves to introduce us to the preacher, whose vocational involvements in teaching, researching, editing, and creative writing have given rise to an inescapable burden to address the nation of Israel. His mission and method are more fully developed in 12:9ff.

2-3. Vanity of vanities, saith the Preacher. The Preacher expresses the theme of his discourse in verses 2 and 3. An exclamation and a question provide the foundation from which he moves, sensitively and courageously, to unfold the words of the wise (12:11). The words are not his own; for they are given to him by the one shepherd, i.e., Israel's Shepherd (12:11). The

Preacher first points to the all-inclusive vanity of man's existence as he lives his life under the sun. *Hebel*, or vanity, is one of the Preacher's favorite words. It is used thirty-five times in the book (lit., the word means breath or vapor). Here the Hebrew idiom for the superlative is used, as in King of Kings. Vanity is used elsewhere to express that which is transient or worthless (Ps 39:6-7; 94:11). The writer's thesis is that everything man experiences in his life under the sun is empty of meaning or worth, both in itself and because of its transience. Hence, all man's restless activities, his efforts to achieve something, are ultimately futile. He attempts to demonstrate this thesis from experience (R. B. Y. Scott, *Proverbs-Ecclesiastes*, p. 209).

However, this is not the Preacher's major thesis. It merely provides the background against which he asks the question, **What profit hath a man of all his labor which he taketh under the sun?** Here is the hard reality to which our Preacher addresses himself. In a world of superlative vanity, what profit can a man attain? Profit (Heb *yitrōn*) signifies that which remains over, either as here, clear gain, profit, or that which has the preeminence, i.e., superiority, precedence, or is the foremost (Delitzsch, *Ecclesiastes*, p. 219). This word occurs only in this book and serves our Preacher uniquely in his desire to raise the issue of profit as it relates to the whole law of man's life under the sun. The key to understanding the message of the Preacher is encountered here in these opening verses. The natural man is under the sun in a fallen world, a world where he reaps day after day the full implications of Adam's disobedience and death (Gen 2:17 and Rom 5:12).

The Preacher's words serve to provide the only proper assessment of man's crooked and groaning world (1:15; Rom 8:22-23). The positive pronouncements are garnered from that repository of given truths that the God of wisdom has granted to man (12:11). The **goads,** or negative words of the Preacher, summarize the experiences of man which are meant to exercise and drive him back to God (12:11; 1:13). The **nails** (12:11) are those positive words of wisdom that are given to man from "The Shepherd" to secure him and anchor his soul till by faith he is delivered to a land where the question of profit is fully answered in the blessing of the presence of our God and His Christ. Any temptation to view this question as a purely negative assessment of life under the sun must be abandoned as we hear the Preacher's exposition of the wisdom nails which fasten his faith to God.

II. THE WISDOM PREACHER POINTS TO LIFE UNDER THE SUN. 1:4-15.

4-8. One generation passeth away. Our Preacher has first called attention to the vanity of life. He now proceeds to give a more complete exposition of that vanity. The first evidence for vanity is that neither the ceaseless round of motion in the world of nature, nor the toil and efforts of man, change anything. The generations of man are continuously changing. Ceaselessly do fresh ones appear on the scene, but, Oh misery! The earth against which the curse recorded in Genesis 3:17-19 was pronounced, on which it is impossible to realize permanent results or to arrive at abiding happiness, and where men find themselves hemmed in on all hands, that remains (E. W. Hengstenberg, *Ecclesiastes*, p. 51).

The sun also ariseth. The same futile round of things is seen as we view the sun. Between its rising and setting it seems to pant (Heb *sha'ap*) along its trail. It seems never to make any progress, for it must hasten in order to get back to the place where it regularly rises in order that it may rise again.

The wind . . . whirleth about continually. The wind and the rivers are also a part of nature's endless round. They may at first seem less rigidly governed than the sun; but alas, they too come

4 *One* generation passeth away, and *another* generation cometh: but the earth abideth for ever.

5 The sun also ariseth, and the sun goeth down, and hasteth to his place where he arose.

6 The wind goeth toward the south, and turneth about unto the north; it whirleth about continually, and the wind returneth again according to his circuits.

7 All the rivers run into the sea; yet the sea *is* not full; unto the place from whence the rivers come, thither they return again.

8 All things *are* full of labour; man cannot utter *it:* the eye is not satisfied with seeing, nor the ear filled with hearing.

9 The thing that hath been, it *is that* which shall be; and that which is done *is* that which shall be done: and *there is* no new *thing* under the sun.

10 Is there *any* thing whereof it may be said, See, this *is* new? it hath been already of old time, which was before us.

11 *There is* no remembrance of former *things;* neither shall there be *any* remembrance of *things* that are to come with *those* that shall come after.

12 ¶I the Preacher was king over Israel in Jerusalem.

13 And I gave my heart to seek and search out by wisdom concerning all *things* that are done under heaven: this sore travail hath God given to the sons of man to be exercised therewith.

14 I have seen all the works that are done under the sun; and, behold, all *is* vanity and vexation of spirit.

15 *That which is* crooked cannot be made straight: and that which is wanting cannot be numbered.

16 I communed with mine own heart, saying, Lo, I am come to great estate, and have gotten more wisdom than all *they* that have been before me in Jerusalem: yea, my heart had great experience of wisdom and knowledge.

17 And I gave my heart to know wisdom, and to know madness and folly: I

back to the points from which they have commenced (Job 36:27). This relentless monotony, with no observable achievement, in reality symbolizes man's failure to accomplish anything. Man, like the elements, seems to be constantly repeating himself. Verse 8 sums up this incessant cycling by pronouncing it an unutterable weariness.

9-11. No new thing. Verse 9 represents a sweeping commentary on the history of humanity and is not meant as a pronouncement about inventions. Everything that man can observe bears the stamp of monotonous sameness. **Is there any thing . . . new?** The Preacher, having affirmed that nothing new happens under the sun, explains that what seems to man to be new is only so because of man's limited knowledge. A better grasp of history would reveal that the particular phenomenon had also occurred in years gone by.

There is no remembrance of former things. Man may hope to establish such a reputation for greatness that he will never be forgotten. Alas! "Men of former generations forgot all too quickly that which preceded them; and coming generations will repeat their error. However, all that has been said in these verses is not the unhappy lament of a chronic pessimist. All that needs to be borne in mind is the basic declaration of verse 3. If you consider purely earthly values, what are you profited? What do you achieve? What is left to you as your portion? You shall be merely a helpless victim of the dreary human condition, part of the ceaseless round of futile action. All this is, of course, an indirect way of saying: Do not rule out or eliminate the higher values" (Leupold, *Ecclesiastes,* p. 50).

12-15. I gave my heart to seek and search out. What can the Preacher say to men who must live under this oppressive burden? His response is twofold. No matter how thoroughly a man investigates all of these phenomena, he cannot comprehend them (cf. 3:11). A total quest for wisdom all too soon produces the realization that you are achieving nothing, are straightening out none of the many things that are crooked, and are unable to even add up all of the things that are lacking in this world.

A momentous utterance now falls from the Preacher's lips. This task of wrestling with the crooked and reasoning in the face of an oppressive cyclical world is God's gift to His creatures who live in the fallen world. The task exercises (1:13) man to the point where he confesses vanity and vexation of spirit (1:14) as his daily lot. Thus exercised, man lifts his eyes to look beyond the crooked creation and view the Creator who has implanted eternity in his heart (3:11). Only a man whose heart is thus exercised may escape vain existence and discover the path to profit.

III. THE WISDOM PREACHER POINTS TO DEAD-END STREETS EXPERIENCED IN THE PURSUIT OF PROFIT. 1:16-2:23.

There was a time in the life of our Preacher when he had not grasped an important principle. He did not appreciate that the world is a vast gymnasium where God exercises His creation, compassionately and consistently pointing out to all the futility of life without Him and faithfully pledging himself to the creation of a people for His name's sake, a people brought to himself through the trials of Egypt and the glories of the Exodus exercisings.

16-18. I communed with mine own heart. The fledgling student is apt to think that the gaining of earthly wisdom and knowledge will lead to a true sense of inner satisfaction. The Preacher says no. The heart here represents the seat of the intellectual faculties. Knowledge in the mind of a man cannot make the crooked world straight. In fact, great knowledge, when placed against the background of this world's crookedness, becomes a source of great sorrow and pain. The more we

perceived that this also is vexation of spirit.

18 For in much wisdom *is* much grief: and he that increaseth knowledge increaseth sorrow.

CHAPTER 2

I SAID in mine heart, Go to now, I will prove thee with mirth, therefore enjoy pleasure: and, behold, this also *is* vanity.

2 I said of laughter, *It is* mad: and of mirth, What doeth it?

3 I sought in mine heart to give myself unto wine, yet acquainting mine heart with wisdom; and to lay hold on folly, till I might see what *was* that good for the sons of men, which they should do under the heaven all the days of their life.

4 I made me great works; I builded me houses; I planted me vineyards:

5 I made me gardens and orchards, and I planted trees in them of all *kind of* fruits:

6 I made me pools of water, to water therewith the wood that bringeth forth trees:

7 I got *me* servants and maidens, and had servants born in my house; also I had great possessions of great and small cattle above all that were in Jerusalem before me:

8 I gathered me also silver and gold, and the peculiar treasure of kings and of the provinces: I gat me men singers and women singers, and the delights of the sons of men, *as* musical instruments, and that of all sorts.

9 So I was great, and increased more than all that were before me in Jerusalem: also my wisdom remained with me.

10 And whatsoever mine eyes desired I kept not from them, I withheld not my heart from any joy; for my heart rejoiced in all my labour: and this was my portion of all my labour.

11 Then I looked on all the works that my hands had wrought, and on the labour that I had laboured to do: and, behold, all *was* vanity and vexation of spirit, and *there was* no profit under the sun.

12 ¶And I turned myself to behold wisdom, and madness, and folly: for what *can* the man *do* that cometh after the king? *even* that which hath been already done.

13 Then I saw that wisdom excelleth folly, as far as light excelleth darkness.

know the more we realize we need to know. No! Earthly wisdom will not satisfy.

2:1-3. I said in mine heart, Go to now . . . enjoy pleasure. The splendors of Solomon's court were known to all (cf. I Kgs 5-10). The Preacher now recounts his attempts to find something of value or profit in the pursuit of those pleasures that the wealth of such a court afforded. He temporarily hung all of his inhibitions in the closet and entered into the pursuit of pleasure with zest. For a time he occupied the seat of the Epicurean. He sought, literally searched out, the satisfactions that could be achieved by giving himself to wine.

Thus he plunged into frivolity, but part of him hung back from a wholehearted commitment to pleasure. **I . . . yet acquainting mine heart with wisdom.** The Preacher resolved to give his body to the enjoyment of pleasure, but yet hoped that wisdom would hold the reins of his mind and thus preserve him from total ruin of mind and body. **To lay hold on.** The pursuit we are to remember had only one objective: the discovery of what was good. This he did not to revel in sensuality, but rather to see if he, with all the vast resources at his command, could not discover how to sweeten the years of man's existence, few and bitter, contrasted with the ever-ending objects of nature (Ginsburg, p. 278).

The abandonment to pleasure represents then a misguided attempt, but nonetheless an attempt to answer the questions posed in 1:3. **What profit hath a man . . . ?**

4-11. I made me great works. In the RSV the term "things" serves as a synonym for all the created phenomena that are cited in verses 4-6. From the pursuit of wisdom the Preacher turned his energies to the creation of a world within the crooked world; a world all his own filled with his own creations. **Houses** (I Chr 28:4, 11), **vineyards** (I Chr 27:27), and **orchards**, literally parks, fill his secular Eden. **Servants** and **singers** populated his edenic garden, and for him there was no forbidden fruit (cf. 2:10; Gen 2:16-17). In all of this he kept his league with wisdom (vs. 9) and with every new creature act he questioned his heart as to that "thing's" ability to add meaning and profit to his life under the sun.

This was my portion (vs. 10) was the thought of his heart. Alas, before the words had passed from his lips the yield of all that he had labored to do turned to steam, and emptiness of heart ensued. The "things" didn't produce fulfillment and meaning. The dream of constructing his own Eden was proving as elusive as the wind.

12-17. I turned myself to behold. The poignant verdict of verse 11 is further explored in this section. **I turned** implies a deeper investigation into the relative values of wisdom and folly. Perhaps there are those who have not yet been convinced that the pursuit of pleasure for pleasure's sake holds no permanent profit for man. If **the king** has failed in his experiment, what

14 The wise man's eyes *are* in his head; but the fool walketh in darkness: and I myself perceived also that one event happeneth to them all.

15 Then said I in my heart, As it happeneth to the fool, so it happeneth even to me; and why was I then more wise? Then I said in my heart, that this also *is* vanity.

16 For *there is* no remembrance of the wise more than of the fool for ever; seeing that which now *is* in the days to come shall all be forgotten. And how dieth the wise *man?* as the fool.

17 Therefore I hated life; because the work that is wrought under the sun *is* grievous unto me: for all *is* vanity and vexation of spirit.

18 ¶Yea, I hated all my labour which I had taken under the sun: because I should leave it unto the man that shall be after me.

19 And who knoweth whether he shall be a wise man or a fool? yet shall he have rule over all my labour wherein I have laboured, and wherein I have shewed myself wise under the sun. This *is* also vanity.

20 Therefore I went about to cause my heart to despair of all the labour which I took under the sun.

21 For there is a man whose labour *is* in wisdom, and in knowledge, and in equity; yet to a man that hath not laboured therein shall he leave it *for* his portion. This also *is* vanity and a great evil.

22 For what hath man of all his labour, and of the vexation of his heart, wherein he hath laboured under the sun?

23 For all his days *are* sorrows, and his travail grief; yea, his heart taketh not rest in the night. This is also vanity.

24 ¶*There is* nothing better for a man, *than* that he should eat and drink, and *that* he should make his soul enjoy good in his labour. This also I saw, that it *was* from the hand of God.

25 For who can eat, or who else can hasten *hereunto*, more than I?

26 For *God* giveth to a man that *is* good in his sight wisdom, and knowledge, and joy: but to the sinner he giveth travail, to gather and to heap up, that he may give to *him that is* good before God. This also *is* vanity and vexation of spirit.

likelihood is there that a private person should be more successful? (Ellicott, *Ecclesiastes,* p. 369). All of humanity hovers between the pursuit of wisdom and the pursuit of folly as the two possible ways to profit for man. Here our Preacher provides a radical assessment of the two ways. The method employed is that of interpreting a thing by reference to its opposite.

Wisdom, when compared with folly, manifests some striking advantages. These advantages are stated in verses 13ff. Wisdom compares with folly as light compares to darkness. An antithetical proverb is employed in verse 14 to again illustrate the superiority of wisdom. **The wise man's eyes are in his head.** Wisdom sees; it is not blind. The man who pursues wisdom is comforted by a great light in his inner heart, while the devotee of folly stumbles on in darkness. **Wisdom excelleth folly.** Excel is the word for good or profit (cf. 5:11). Our Preacher avows that wisdom leads to the path of profit.

One event happeneth to them all. The value of mental attainments has been fully explored, but in the end the confession of their inability to satisfy is framed on the Preacher's lips. Although wisdom is certainly preferable to folly, the pursuers of both are subject to a common lot. One event unites all. The Preacher suffers from no illusion about life under the sun, and he does not seek to soften perplexing issues. Death brings about the extinction of every project and robs every man of the enjoyment of dignity. The fool and the wise man die alike. **Therefore I hated life.**

18-23. Yea, I hated all my labor. The hard reality of death has forced a pained admission from the Preacher. In the presence of such a common leveler as death, he can only question the ultimate value of toil. Death cancels the lasting value of the wise man's labors. The elusive quality of one's work and possessions causes the Preacher to despair. Life under the sun, devoid of knowledge of God's hand, is susceptible to no other interpretation. To leave the fruit of all one's labor to one who may indeed be a fool surely constitutes one of life's most bitter disappointments. The days of a man are therefore filled with travail, and at night upon his bed he can find no rest for his grief-stricken heart. Labor then cannot provide man with the key to profit in this life. Where then may a man look?

IV. THE WISDOM PREACHER POINTS THE WAY TO TRUE PROFIT. 2:24—6:10.

A. Faith in the Hand of God. 2:24-26.

24-26. There is nothing better for a man. The Preacher has demonstrated the profitlessness of those things that man customarily considers profitable. When put to a practical and exhaustive test, these "things" are proven to be as empty of profit as vapor or steam. They are of no profit for man in his life under the sun.

Now the Preacher reaches beyond the sun and points to higher spiritual truths which if embraced will lead to the path of true profit. Leupold translates verse 24, "It is not a good thing in man that he can eat and drink and enjoy life." Man left to himself under the sun cannot find the path to joy and profit. He has a hunger for eternity and a desire to fit all the pieces of a broken world together, but he cannot do it (3:11). This inability to put it all together is God's gift to all men who dwell in the crooked world.

This universal blessing causes all men everywhere to be exercised concerning the potential for a life of meaning and profit. **For who can eat.** Leupold translates verse 25, "For who can eat and who can have enjoyment apart from him?" He who abounded in all good things (2:1-10) found that it was not within his power to enjoy them (2:2-11). The ability to enjoy anything in this world is always a gift from God. No enjoyment of any kind is obtainable "apart from Him."

For God giveth to a man that is good. The hand of God sovereignly exercises man with the objective of bringing him to repentance. God's gifts are often related to man's receptivity. To the man who pleases God He grants the matchless gifts of wisdom, plus knowledge and joy. The good are those who are not habitual sinners, as contrasted with those who habitually practice sin. To the man who lives in sin He gives the travail of gathering and heaping up "things," only to see them evaporate. God further vexes the sinner by giving all he has amassed to him whom God deems worthy. Surely such an experience is, for the sinner, vanity and vexation of spirit. His is a poor existence indeed. Especially impoverished is he when compared to the man who recognizes and revels in the hand of God (Neh 2:8; I Pet 5:6).

CHAPTER 3

TO every *thing there is* a season, and a time to every purpose under the heaven:

2 A time to be born, and a time to die; a time to plant, and a time to pluck up *that which is* planted;

3 A time to kill, and a time to heal; a time to break down, and a time to build up;

4 A time to weep, and a time to laugh; a time to mourn, and a time to dance;

5 A time to cast away stones, and a time to gather stones together; a time to embrace, and a time to refrain from embracing;

6 A time to get, and a time to lose; a time to keep, and a time to cast away;

7 A time to rend, and a time to sew; a time to keep silence, and a time to speak;

8 A time to love, and a time to hate; a time of war, and a time of peace.

9 What profit hath he that worketh in that wherein he laboureth?

10 I have seen the travail, which God hath given to the sons of men to be exercised in it.

11 He hath made every *thing* beautiful in his time: also he hath set the world in their heart, so that no man can find out the work that God maketh from the beginning to the end.

12 I know that *there is* no good in them, but for *a man* to rejoice, and to do good in his life.

B. Faith in God's Control. 3:1-22.

3:1-10. To every thing there is a season. The Preacher is far from holding that events in this world are simply a haphazard jumble. He is aware of something that mysteriously rules and orders every event; he usually refers to this phenomenon by the neutral word **time** and thereby touches on the fact that every activity and every event is subject to a certain determinism (G. Von Rad, *Wisdom in Israel*, p. 228). Man does not control the world or time; God does. God steers us into the future with His hand, and He is absolutely in control of all events. The different types of activities enumerated in verses 1-8 are divine activities, each of which is brought to pass in accord with a divine schemata. The word **time** occurs twenty-eight times. Fourteen pairs of opposites are used in an effort to cover every conceivable experience of man under the sun.

These events enter our lives at will, and we seem helpless to control their arrival and departure. This sense of helplessness produces a measure of travail (vs. 10) and causes all men to once again raise the question of profit (vs. 9). Can man achieve a profitable outcome in a world which seems so capricious?

God hath given to the sons of men. In the presence of such mystery, our Preacher was not left without a rudder. Man's inability to control the events of life, man's travail over insoluble difficulties, is once again viewed as God's gift to man. Men who are continuously troubled by events under the sun are exercised to lift their eyes above the sun and search for the Creator. Men who recognize their tragic limitations are more open to the message of God's supreme control.

11-12. He hath made every thing beautiful in his time. This verse is one of the most important in the Old Testament. It not only affirms God's sovereignty, but also His compassion. Everything that God makes, or that happens, is the gift of God, purposeful, to be desired, and beautiful (fitting). Among the things mentioned in verses 2-8, there are, it is true, many that are unpleasant; but at the time, when God sends them, they are not only good, but even beautiful. These things, which in and of themselves are painful, must consequently occur in such a connection that they shall further the good purposes of God. Only at the fit season are they beautiful, and then they form an indispensable link in the chain of the worlds events (Hengstenberg, p. 106).

He hath set the world in their heart. God has not created man without the ability to appreciate the importance of what he is doing. He has implanted eternity in the heart of man. To give into the heart is a Hebraism for giving or speaking in a flattering way (Luther, *Ecclesiastes*, p. 53). Man alone has within him the

13 And also that every man should eat and drink, and enjoy the good of all his labour, it *is* the gift of God.

14 I know that, whatsoever God doeth, it shall be for ever: nothing can be put to it, nor any thing taken from it: and God doeth *it*, that *men* should fear before him.

15 That which hath been is now; and that which is to be hath already been; and God requireth that which is past.

16 And moreover I saw under the sun the place of judgment, *that* wickedness *was* there; and the place of righteousness, *that* iniquity *was* there.

17 I said in mine heart, God shall judge the righteous and the wicked: for *there is* a time there for every purpose and for every work.

18 I said in mine heart concerning the estate of the sons of men, that God might manifest them, and that they might see that they themselves are beasts.

19 For that which befalleth the sons of men befalleth beasts; even one thing befalleth them: as the one dieth, so dieth the other; yea, they have all one breath; so that a man hath no preeminence above a beast: for all *is* vanity.

20 All go unto one place; all are of the dust, and all turn to dust again.

21 Who knoweth the spirit of man that goeth upward, and the spirit of the beast that goeth downward to the earth?

22 Wherefore I perceive that *there is* nothing better, than that a man should rejoice in his own works; for that *is* his

ability to appreciate what God is doing. It is beyond man to reason out the significance of each time event. He cannot know, even if he torments himself, the hours when events will come to pass. Indeed, to attempt the unraveling of the future is an exercise forbidden to man (Isa 47:12). He can, however, in the spirit of Romans 8:28 know that God is working all things together for His good and with the knowledge of that reality he can enter into the path of profit and joy.

There is no good in them. In a world controlled by God and not by man there is nothing better for a man to do than to enjoy the things that are present and leave the future to God.

13. It is the gift of God. The decision to break with anxiety and travail is not a decision that man is free to make. It is not in his ability to do it. He may will it, but he cannot perform it (Rom 7:18). The ability to enjoy the things that are presented and to have a joyful heart is the gift of God.

14. Whatsoever God doeth, it shall be for ever. The conclusion that is offered in verses 14-15 has been carefully formulated. All of the preceding observations concerning God's supreme control over all things lead the Preacher to advance a final conclusion. When man realizes that everything God does is unchangeable and compares the vanity and uncertainty of his efforts with those of God, he is forced to accept the conclusion of the Preacher: God must be feared! All of the exercising of man is directed toward the accomplishment of that fear in the heart of man. The fear of God alone makes possible that fruitful and filial relationship between God and man that leads man to the good and profitable life. Properly understood, fear is that attribute of humanity that opens the mind of man to the reality that everything depends upon God's achievements. The man who confesses His absolute control needs only fear the rejection of that confession. For in the rejection of that confession man leaves the path of profit and stumbles out into darkness.

15-20. God requireth that which is past. Nothing is now that has not already been, and everything that is, owes its existence to the requiring God. God sets all in order and seeks to address all men as they experience the events of His allotment. He seeks the persecuted and shall deliver them at the appointed time. **I said in mine heart, God shall judge the righteous and the wicked.**

God's rule is always rendered somewhat enigmatic when we consider the plight of the suffering and the oppressive character of the unjust. Here the Preacher provides some insight concerning the crookedness of society. God will judge. God has appointed a time for all things. Some will petition the Preacher and question why God has delayed the time of judgment. Such questions only serve to point out man's wretched unwillingness to abide under the conviction of 3:11. God is refraining from judgment in order that men might properly be exposed as the depraved beings they are. Man may object to this cruel designation, but it does not change the truth.

Two facts are given in support of this evaluation of man's nature. Man continuously practices greed and cunning in all of his dealings and even corrupts his courts of justice (vs. 16). Secondly, man shares the same earthly destiny as the beast. Since the Fall (Gen 3:19) man, like the beast, is on his journey from dust to dust. Man, who fancies himself to be like God, is in reality more like the beast. This is our Preacher's anthropology. Man who divorces himself from the requiring God, is doomed to a life of vanity.

21-22. Who knoweth the spirit of man that goeth upward. Many commentators portray our Preacher here as a confused figure who is uncertain of man's destiny after death. Those interpreters who maintain that the author is expressing doubt here have the author contradicting himself, for in 12:7 he claims that **the spirit shall return unto God who gave it.** Leupold

portion: for who shall bring him to see what shall be after him?

CHAPTER 4

SO I returned, and considered all the oppressions that are done under the sun: and behold the tears of *such as were* oppressed, and they had no comforter; and on the side of their oppressors *there was* power; but they had no comforter.

2 Wherefore I praised the dead which are already dead more than the living which are yet alive.

3 Yea, better *is he* than both they, which hath not yet been, who hath not seen the evil work that is done under the sun.

4 ¶Again, I considered all travail, and every right work, that for this a man is envied of his neighbour. This *is* also vanity and vexation of spirit.

5 ¶The fool foldeth his hands together, and eateth his own flesh.

6 Better *is* an handful *with* quietness, than both the hands full *with* travail and vexation of spirit.

7 ¶Then I returned, and I saw vanity under the sun.

8 There is one *alone*, and *there is* not a second; yea, he hath neither child nor brother: yet *is there* no end of all his labour; neither is his eye satisfied with riches; neither *saith he*, For whom do I labour, and bereave my soul of good? This *is* also vanity, yea, it *is* a sore travail.

renders verse 21, "There are not many who take to heart as they ought to the fact that the spirit of man goeth upward, and that the spirit of the beast goeth downward to the earth." True, man often resembles the beast, but if he would only keep God in the picture, he would recognize that he, unlike the beast, must stand before the God of judgment.

The Preacher concludes in verse 22 the argument he advanced in verses 16-20. As we live under the sun mindful of the "time event" labeled judgment, we should never forget that we are destined to participate in it. This caution is not meant to produce a morbid sense of confinement or dull resignation. Rather, man is to **Rejoice in his own works** and not fret about the works of others or the uncertainty of the future. Man's portion is to do the business of the day and take pleasure in it, realizing that both the deed and the ability to enjoy the doing of it are gifts from the hand of God. Such knowledge separates man from the beasts.

C. A Proper Response to God's Call to Community. 4:1-16.

Only the man who affirms in faith the sovereignty of God can experience profit in this life. His life will be profitable, but not without enigma. Injustice, death, and oppression will continue to vex his righteous soul. Even the follower of wisdom cannot thoroughly discern the work of God. These enigmas will not turn the pursuer of wisdom into a beast, but will rather cause him to heed God's call with a deepened sense of devotion. First he will heed God's call to community.

4:1-3. They had no comforter. The tragedy of men who are victims of beastly oppression is cited here. The man who faces these powerful oppressors alone is better off dead. We may think this a defeatist attitude; yet as we survey the whole of life and view the awesome power of the oppressors, we must also confess alarm. The unborn are surely more fortunate than the dead or the oppressed, for they have not yet had to suffer the sight of the great wickedness that is done under the sun.

4-5. A man is envied. The man who achieves great skill in his profession is envied by his neighbor. The hostile, pernicious acts that flow from envy are documented everywhere in Scripture. This spirit of rivalry renders the achievement of greatness a lonely and empty accomplishment. One may suggest that the way to avoid the frustrations which rivalry produces is to do nothing. The Preacher labels such thinking the prating of fools. **The fool foldeth his hands together, and eateth his own flesh.** The fool resigns all ambition to perform a successful work. He sits in seething anger, overcome by a sense of life's futility, and literally feeds on his own flesh. He becomes a veritable bundle of psychosomatic disturbances.

6. Better is a handful with quietness. In contrast to the excessive toil of the envious and the bitter resignation of the fool, we view in this verse the model of the man of wisdom. He adopts a course of action recommended as a golden mean between the self-ruinous sloth of the fool and the vexatious toil of the workaholic.

7-8. There is one alone. The Preacher points now to the dilemma of the one alone whose heart is set on the gathering of riches. Since his heart is committed to the acquisition of riches for himself, he never takes the time to relate significantly to others in his community. He is the typical miser. If he has children, he has no time for them. The pursuit of riches so thoroughly absorbs his energies that he shuts himself away from all others.

This typical miser is heard in conversation with himself after he has gathered his fortune. From his restless and lonely heart

9 ¶Two *are* better than one; because they have a good reward for their labour.

10 For if they fall, the one will lift up his fellow: but woe to him *that is* alone when he falleth; for *he hath* not another to help him up.

11 Again, if two lie together, then they have heat: but how can one be warm *alone?*

12 And if one prevail against him, two shall withstand him; and a threefold cord is not quickly broken.

13 ¶Better *is* a poor and a wise child than an old and foolish king, who will no more be admonished.

14 For out of prison he cometh to reign; whereas also *he that is* born in his kingdom becometh poor.

15 I considered all the living which walk under the sun, with the second child that shall stand up in his stead.

16 *There is* no end of all the people, *even* of all that have been before them: they also that come after shall not rejoice in him. Surely this also *is* vanity and vexation of spirit.

CHAPTER 5

KEEP thy foot when thou goest to the house of God, and be more ready to hear, than to give the sacrifice of fools: for they consider not that they do evil.

---

comes the question, **For whom do I labor . . . ?** No profit can be discovered in the midst of such loneliness. God created man for fellowship, and loneliness is a paralysis in the heart of man (Gen 2:18). Since no one profits from his labor and he himself cannot (for his eye cannot be satisfied), the whole enterprise must be pronounced profitless and vain.

9-12. Two are better than one. There is great profit in men holding faithfully to one another. The profit in such commitment is illustrated in three examples. If two journey together and one trips and falls, his faithful companion will help him to his feet. Lodging was not always available for travelers, and a man alone often felt keenly the cold of the night. However, two men traveling together could warm one another by snuggling together. A man alone who is about to be overcome by any onslaught may be kept from ruin through the helpful hand of his friend. Such companionship is of inestimable value and is certainly a profit to all who possess it.

A threefold cord is not quickly broken. The alliance of three is meant to represent a complete unity. Hence, the complete adoration of God, both by His angels in heaven and man on earth, consisted in the invocation of a threefold "holy" on the part of the celestial beings (Isa 6:3), three annual visits to Jerusalem, and three terrestrial worshipers (Ex 23:14; Ps 55:18; Dan 6:11) (Ginsburg, p. 330). In making a strong cord, three threads were used. The three threads may symbolize the man, the friend, and the God who has brought them both together and given birth in their spirits to the burden for companionship.

13-16. Better is a poor and a wise child than an old and foolish king. Even those who hold high offices are not exempt from wisdom's teaching on the need for community. They may choose to think that they need no one, that they can stand alone. The situation here described is an illustration that amplifies that propensity. The usual honor accorded to gray hairs may be lost to men who forsake all sociability and seek only the enlargement of their own riches. The poor young man who practices wisdom's teaching on community will find profit in this life. The old foolish king who will no longer hear the words of wisdom, preferring to trust in his own power and go it alone, will come to ruin.

For out of prison he cometh to reign. Though the king bind such a youth in his prison, he will ultimately come forth to reign. History is replete with accounts of those who, born in poverty, have by wisdom and magnanimity raised themselves to positions of honor. History is likewise filled with the sad testimony of others who, born with the right to reign, have lost it all through their indifference to the needs of others in their kingdom. The second, i.e., the youth of verse 13 who hears the admonition of the wisdom Preacher comes to the head of all the people. All will do homage to him as their king.

They also that come after shall not rejoice in him. The fate of earthly monarchs is a tenuous fate; they rise and fall with alarming suddenness. The Preacher ends his illustration with the demise of the child king. He too falls under the grinding wheel of history. All this kingly business is empty chasing of the wind; it is better to have a few good friends and embrace the teaching of wisdom on the threefold cord. This will bring a man to lasting profit. All else is evanescent.

D. A Proper Response to God's Call to Worship. 5:1-9.

5:1. Keep thy foot when thou goest to the house of God. In order to hold to the path of true wisdom and profit, a man must also recognize the need for reverence and honesty in worship. Our Preacher admonishes the practice of discretion in the performance of acts of worship. The words **keep thy foot** convey the seriousness of a man's attendance at God's house.

In speaking of worship the Preacher points to three elements:

(1) the going to the Temple in verse 1; (2) prayer in verses 1-2; and (3) vows in verses 3-6. **Be more ready to hear, than to give the sacrifice of fools.** The man who worships properly is a careful listener. To hear implies not only hearing, but understanding and obedience as well. The fool offers sacrifices in a mechanical manner, but the man of wisdom is responsive to the teachings and prayers of the Temple service (cf. I Sam 15:22, Jer 7:21-34, Prov 21:3). The fool's casual approach to worship is a great evil. The New Testament is equally sharp in its condemnation of the casual worshiper (Mt 7:21ff.; 23:16ff.; I Cor 11:27ff.). No amount of emphasis on grace can justify taking liberties with God, for the very concept of grace demands gratitude; and gratitude cannot be casual (Derek Kidner, *A Time to Mourn and a Time to Dance*, p. 53).

2 Be not rash with thy mouth, and let not thine heart be hasty to utter *any* thing before God: for God *is* in heaven, and thou upon earth: therefore let thy words be few.

2. Be not rash with thy mouth. The proper worship of man stands in stark contrast to the worship of the fool. The wise worshiper is a careful listener whose heart is bent upon obedience. The fool's worship is punctuated by braggadocio, his foolish heart manifesting itself in rash and rapid chatter. This incessant speech-making betrays a shallow perception of God's character. One who truly understands the divine and supreme station of God will be captured by awe, and his words will be few.

3 For a dream cometh through the multitude of business; and a fool's voice *is known* by multitude of words.

3. A dream cometh through the multitude of business. The main thrust here is the demonstration of a cause-and-effect relationship. The person who frets over a multitude of things shall surely fall to dreaming of those things in the night. The heavy burdens of the day act as an effectual cause of dreams in the night. In the same manner the heart of the fool becomes the effectual cause of a multitude of words.

4 When thou vowest a vow unto God, defer not to pay it; for *he hath* no pleasure in fools: pay that which thou hast vowed.
5 Better *is it* that thou shouldest not vow, than that thou shouldest vow and not pay.
6 Suffer not thy mouth to cause thy flesh to sin; neither say thou before the angel, that it *was* an error: wherefore should God be angry at thy voice, and destroy the work of thine hands?

4-6. When thou vowest a vow unto God. A wise man must watch his words. The fool makes rash promises to God. The fool's mouth traverses terrain that his heart has no intention of traversing. This is an exercise fraught with danger. The Preacher warns all to exercise extreme care in the making of promises to God. A man must never defer the payment of vows made to God. It is better not to vow, than to vow and not pay.

Suffer not thy mouth to cause thy flesh to sin. The messenger (angel) spoken of is the priest to whom the guilty fool makes his appeal for atonement (Mal 2:7-8). The maker of rash vows desires the priest to offer for him a trespass offering. Under the premise that his vow was an error, he expects to thus dispose of his sin. Those who trifle with vows in this way are reminded that such shallowness is an affront to God. Far from being a marginal error, this failure to fulfill a sacred promise is a sin that merits God's full judgment (cf. Deut 23:21). God's just anger will surely result in the destruction of the works of such a person's hands.

7 For in the multitude of dreams and many words *there are* also *divers* vanities: but fear thou God.
8 ¶If thou seest the oppression of the poor, and violent perverting of judgment and justice in a province, marvel not at the matter: for *he that is* higher than the highest regardeth; and *there be* higher than they.
9 ¶Moreover the profit of the earth is for all: the king *himself* is served by the field.

7-9. In the multitude of dreams and many words. Men who are engaged in the pursuit of vanities cannot avoid rash chattering. They love to incessantly talk of their exploits and future schemes. They long for some great break in the future that will provide them with ample opportunity to demonstrate the greatness of their abilities. The man of wisdom is never to emulate these purposeless ones who in their schemings allow the present to pass by unattended and wasted.

The path to profit and meaning in life can only be found by the man who breaks with such profitless practices and pursues a right relationship to God. Here we are confronted with that deep spiritual principle that is the cornerstone of all profit for time and eternity: **fear thou God.**

The fool will be quick to defend his approach to life. He will say that there is a need for fast talking and the employment of limited deception in order to get ahead in this old world. The problems of exploitation and oppression on the part of earthly rulers render such practices a practical necessity.

Marvel not at the matter. The Preacher disagrees. In the case of such irregularities we are not to marvel (cf. I Pet 4:12). Those who suffer from oppression should consider the way to true profit to be this: the problem of injustice must be resolved by designated leadership. Rulers are to rule for good (Rom 13), and it is an advantage to the country that they are there. Their presence may not always further justice, but their absence is sure to guarantee anarchy. One higher than they, Jehovah, will ultimately judge perfectly the quality of their rule. In summary then, we can only keep to the path of profit when we worship with proper fear the God who demands holiness in speech and avoid in every situation making the sacrifice of the fool.

E. A Proper Response to God's Call to Joyful Labor. 5:10-6:9.

The Preacher now gives wisdom's instruction on the subject of labor. Profit is not to be found in idle talk and dreaming, but the incessant laborer may also miss it if he is not informed by wisdom's caution. The teaching begins with a series of reasons why the accumulation of wealth as the singular goal of labor is a vain objective (5:10-17; 6:1-9) and proceeds to a proper view of the place of labor in a man's life (5:12a, 18-20).

10-11. He that loveth silver shall not be satisfied. Here the Preacher provides the first of several reasons why labor ought not to be employed solely as a means for the accumulation of wealth. The love of wealth never produces satisfaction, but rather a craving that can never be satisfied. The man whose God is mammon will experience only emptiness (cf. I Tim 6:9ff.). Man who has been created with eternity in his heart can never be satisfied with the nourishment of mammon.

The accumulation of wealth also attracts a wide variety of parasites. The fruit of a man's labor is vigorously consumed by an ever-growing group of spongers. The wealthy man enjoys a form of profit. He may enjoy viewing the fruit of his labor. Such profit is rather sterile, however; for while he views his riches, they are dissipating, and he is thus goaded to seek larger accumulations. He knows no rest.

12-17. The sleep of a laboring man is sweet. The poor rich man gets no rest. When he is not absorbed in the multiplication of his wealth, his energies must be given to the protection of his gain. This perpetual concern he takes into the night, and he seldom gets a good night's sleep. The desire for wealth is so consuming that it can only end in the destruction of his entire life. The simple laborer, whose life is unencumbered by massive accumulation, is free from such vexatious care and enjoys the sweetness of sleep. Even if the poor man's meal may not be quite sufficient, physical weariness has made his body ready to sleep. As for the rich man, his very abundance of means imposes a disadvantage upon him (Leupold, p. 127).

There is a sore evil. A climax is reached in verse 13. First, the Preacher has shown the inability of riches to satisfy. Then he has shown how they rob a man of sleep; finally he points out that the keeping of riches is an evil in itself. The man who has struggled for riches considered them **good,** but in reality they are **evil.** This applies of course to a man who is totally absorbed with life under the sun. Such a man keeps riches to his own hurt. There is a tragic prophecy in Isaiah 22:23 ff. that illustrates the Preacher's point. The man who accumulates wealth is like a nail fastened to the wall upon which an unbearable burden has been placed. After a time the burden crashes to the floor. Men and nails can bear only so much. Greed results in a man placing upon himself unbearable burdens, and the end of that foolishness is destruction. Worse than that, the fortune that he has killed himself to accumulate can be lost in a moment; and he can be reduced to such penury that there will be nothing in his hand. Even if he doesn't lose his possessions, he will certainly be

10 He that loveth silver shall not be satisfied with silver; nor he that loveth abundance with increase: this *is* also vanity.
11 When goods increase, they are increased that eat them: and what good *is there* to the owners thereof, saving the beholding *of them* with their eyes?

12 The sleep of a labouring man *is* sweet, whether he eat little or much: but the abundance of the rich will not suffer him to sleep.
13 There is a sore evil *which* I have seen under the sun, *namely* riches kept for the owners thereof to their hurt.
14 But those riches perish by evil travail: and he begetteth a son, and *there is* nothing in his hand.
15 As he came forth of his mother's womb, naked shall he return to go as he came, and shall take nothing of his labour, which he may carry away in his hand.
16 And this also *is* a sore evil, *that* in all points as he came, so shall he go: and what profit hath he that hath laboured for the wind?
17 All his days also he eateth in darkness, and *he hath* much sorrow and wrath with his sickness.

18 ¶Behold *that* which I have seen: *it is* good and comely *for one* to eat and to drink, and to enjoy the good of all his labour that he taketh under the sun all the days of his life, which God giveth him: for it *is* his portion.

19 Every man also to whom God hath given riches and wealth, and hath given him power to eat thereof, and to take his portion, and to rejoice in his labour; this *is* the gift of God.

20 For he shall not much remember the days of his life; because God answereth *him* in the joy of his heart.

CHAPTER 6

THERE is an evil which I have seen under the sun, and it *is* common among men:

2 A man to whom God hath given riches, wealth, and honour, so that he wanteth nothing for his soul of all that he desireth, yet God giveth him not power to eat thereof, but a stranger eateth it: this *is* vanity, and it *is* an evil disease.

3 ¶If a man beget an hundred *children*, and live many years, so that the days of his years be many, and his soul be not filled with good, and also *that* he have no burial; I say, *that* an untimely birth *is* better than he.

4 For he cometh in with vanity, and departeth in darkness, and his name shall be covered with darkness.

5 Moreover he hath not seen the sun, nor known *any thing*: this hath more rest than the other.

6 Yea, though he live a thousand years twice *told*, yet hath he seen no good: do not all go to one place?

separated from them in death. He came into this world **naked**, and he will go into eternity in similar fashion. He will carry nothing **away in his hand** (I Tim 6:7). Truly, such a man has labored for the wind and has reaped the whirlwind. All his days have been spent in darkness, sickness, and anger. He has found no profit in his journey. He whose God is mammon is a man to be pitied.

18-20. The improper use of labor and its rewards has been thoroughly explored. Mingled with the Preacher's words on the prostitution of life's forces is a clear statement on the proper function of labor. The embracing of wisdom's teaching will be rewarded with the sweetness of sleep (vs. 12).

It is good and comely for one to eat and to drink, and to enjoy. Here our Preacher is led back to the conclusion he stated in 2:24 and 3:12, 22. In contrast to the greedy person and the disappointing life which is his portion, the Preacher recommends the adoption of a perspective that will allow one to enjoy the simple things of this life. The key words in this section of the message are God and gift. Man must view all of the good that passes to him as the gift of God. Wealth and possessions are of no ultimate significance; they neither disclose nor help man to attain a divinely appointed destiny. God does not give them for that (vs. 19), but for the sweetening of life day by day (Rylaarsdam, p. 114). These are man's portion in life and should be celebrated as gifts, rather than allowed to promote a spirit of avarice. Wisdom counsels a state of determined rejoicing, whether the menu be steak or hamburger, and the ability to achieve such a perspective is in itself a gift of God. This joyous achievement of emancipation from avarice and greed is described more fully in verse 20. The man who achieves this recommended perspective enjoys a heart-joy that makes the circumstances of a given day inconsequential, for God causes him to be continuously occupied with joy.

6:1-6. There is an evil which I have seen under the sun. The perspective counseled by our Preacher of wisdom in 5:18-20 is not embraced by many. The common lot of man is markedly different. They labor in the pursuit of wealth with such abandonment that they risk total failure in this life. The masses never rise above avarice; theirs is a grievous misery. For even though God allows them the acquisition of wealth and honor, he withholds from them the ability to enjoy their acquisitions. Surrounded by abundance, they are unable to enjoy even the smallest elements of the beauty that surrounds them. Their unrest is heightened as they view the evident satisfaction that others are able to derive from the fruits of their labor.

Long life has always been viewed as a token of good fortune. However, for these men whose souls are destitute of enjoyment, long life is a curse. Long life (Prov. 3:16; 4:10) and many children (Ps 127:3-5; 128:3-4; Prov 17:6) were considered great blessings. Proper burial was considered very important, and to be denied it was considered a great curse (Jer 16:4). These men have wealth, children, and long life; but they have no enjoyment in life and no honor in death. It would have been better for them if they had not been born. As undesirable as an untimely birth is with its attendant obscurity, i.e., never acquiring a name, never seeing the sun, and never knowing anything, yet all the vexations of the poor in their vulnerable and wretched pursuit of wealth are spared such a person. Such a person has rest, and rest eternally eludes our miser. Though he live a thousand years twice over, it is of no profit to him; for God has withheld the power of enjoyment from him, and in the end his experience is the same as that of the man born dead.

Do not all go to one place? This must be interpreted so as to fit the context. The sameness of the lot of all people cannot be the outstanding thought. The nature of that place is under consideration only in that all have the same experiences there;

1269

whatever they may have failed to achieve during the span of their earthly existence cannot be retrieved in that one place. That one feature of that place is commonly conceded: it is not a place for making up lost opportunities (Leupold, p. 139).

7 All the labour of man is for his mouth, and yet the appetite is not filled.

8 For what hath the wise more than the fool? what hath the poor, that knoweth to walk before the living?

9 Better is the sight of the eyes than the wandering of the desire: this is also vanity and vexation of spirit.

7-9. All the labor of man is for his mouth, and yet the appetite is not filled. The matter of man's inability to find satisfaction is further explored. The tragic state of the natural man cut off from God is developed poignantly in these verses. The natural man toils ultimately for himself. His desire to satisfy himself is insatiable; but satisfaction continuously evades him, and his appetites are never appeased.

Even some of the covenant people manifest traces of this malignancy. The wise man is uniformly a child of God, whereas the fool is a stranger to the covenant, usually a Gentile. The poor man is also a member of the covenant community and is limited in the amount of this world's goods that he possesses. The people of Israel alone knew how to walk in the way of wisdom and profit, for they alone possessed the statutes of God (Deut 4:5-6).

The covenant people are rebuked in verse 9 for allowing their desires to stray. They are guilty of a lustful search for satisfaction and profit. This is particularly reprehensible since they have received so much as gifts from the hand of the Lord. They have beheld with their eyes all of the good gifts that God has given to them as a nation. They should have regarded these gifts and their giver as the truly profitable objects of worship and refrained from giving unbridled rein to their desires. Such carnal pursuits are in reality only an empty chasing after the wind. Our Preacher of wisdom points to the path of true profit as he counsels the curbing of the appetite and the embracing of that life of wisdom which was first advocated in 2:24-26.

F. A Summary Statement 6:10.

10 ¶That which hath been is named already, and it is known that it is man: neither may he contend with him that is mightier than he.

10. Neither may he contend with him that is mightier than he. In verse 10 the Preacher summarizes the rationale for the life he advocates by once again calling man's attention to the sovereignty of God. The type of being man is, proclaims the Preacher, is fully revealed by the name that God has given him long ago. His name is 'adam, and earthen men tend to be earthy. The Preacher has pointed out the folly in pursuing the earthy and has taught the way to lasting profit. Men may wish to rebel against this instruction; but the opulent are, after all, only frail creatures, unable to contend with the Almighty (Ginsburg, p. 366). No frail being may contend with the Lord, who is infinitely stronger than himself, and hope to prevail. God has supreme control over all things; all matters are in His hand (Isa 45:9 ff.). Man is on the earth, and God is in heaven (5:2). The only proper response of man to such a Being is to hold Him in awe and dutifully submit to His every requirement. This response will be totally elucidated in 12:13, but we are even now pointed toward it.

V. THE WISDOM PREACHER INTRODUCES AND EXPANDS THE PRACTICAL APPLICATION OF HIS MESSAGE ON PROFIT. 6:11-8:17.

11 Seeing there be many things that increase vanity, what is man the better?

12 For who knoweth what is good for man in this life, all the days of his vain life which he spendeth as a shadow? for who can tell a man what shall be after him under the sun?

11-12. The list of all things that increase vanity has been carefully compiled. The accumulation of things has been pronounced a vain and unprofitable goal, for things can be lost so easily and must be relinquished at death. Our Preacher now once again raises the question that he hopes every man will ask of himself: What is the way to profit?

Who knoweth what is good for man . . . ? In verse 12 the dilemma is reiterated. No man is able to discern what is to follow the situation in which he presently finds himself. The present, then, is filled with things that increase vanity, and the future is shrouded in deep shadows. In the presence of such uncertainty, who knows what is good for man?

CHAPTER 7

A GOOD name *is* better than precious ointment; and the day of death than the day of one's birth.

2 ¶*It is* better to go to the house of mourning, than to go to the house of feasting: for that *is* the end of all men; and the living will lay *it* to his heart.

3 Sorrow *is* better than laughter: for by the sadness of the countenance the heart is made better.

4 The heart of the wise *is* in the house of mourning; but the heart of fools *is* in the house of mirth.

5 *It is* better to hear the rebuke of the wise, than for a man to hear the song of fools.

6 For as the crackling of thorns under a pot, so *is* the laughter of the fool: this also *is* vanity.

7 ¶Surely oppression maketh a wise man mad; and a gift destroyeth the heart.

8 Better *is* the end of a thing than the beginning thereof: *and* the patient in spirit *is* better than the proud in spirit.

9 Be not hasty in thy spirit to be angry: for anger resteth in the bosom of fools.

10 Say not thou, What is *the cause* that the former days were better than these? for thou dost not enquire wisely concerning this.

11 ¶Wisdom *is* good with an inheritance: and *by it there is* profit to them that see the sun.

12 For wisdom *is* a defence, *and* money *is* a defence: but the excellency of knowledge *is, that* wisdom giveth life to them that have it.

13 Consider the work of God: for who can make *that* straight, which he hath made crooked?

14 In the day of prosperity be joyful, but in the day of adversity consider: God also hath set the one over against the other, to the end that man should find nothing after him.

7:1-4. A good name is better than precious ointment. The question with which the preceding chapter has closed, **Who knoweth what is good for man in this life . . . ?** is now answered. The Preacher commences an expansive list of those things that are good for man and, if pursued, will ultimately lead into the way of true profit. A good reputation is of greater value than precious ointment. Ointment refers to an expensive, liquid, perfumed oil that was used on joyful occasions (Amos 6:6; Ps 45:7). The possession of a good name is to be preferred to the possession of such ointment. A man will have a good name if he heeds the following admonitions of the Preacher. The contemplation of the day of death is more fruitful than contemplating the day of one's birth. Whereas the latter is of limited profit, the former brings sober and salutary thoughts to the heart of a man. Hence, the heart is made better.

Thus **sorrow is better than laughter,** for it fosters the growth of a sober frame of mind, which tends to keep one in the way of profit. The heart of the fool rejoices only in mirth and eschews the valuable lessons that can only be learned in the place of mourning. Much of God's gentle chastening of His children can be understood when it is informed by the instruction of this text (cf. Heb 12:3-15; II Cor 12:9-10).

5-7. It is better to hear the rebuke of the wise, than . . . the song of fools. The way to profit is to be kept by patiently hearing the rebuke of the wise. The pleasing words of the fool are like thorns placed under a kettle. Anticipation may run high as the immediate crackling sound occurs, but little lasting good can come of it. This flash of fire fails to produce any substantial heat. In like manner, the shallow speech and laughter of the fool is never productive of lasting good.

In verse 7 the means by which the cackling fool has fallen to such non-substantive living is identified. Some have become fools because they have refused to hear faithful rebuke and have chosen rather to pursue a course of oppression and corruption. The Preacher warns that those who practice oppression and relish the gain brought by bribes are destined for madness.

8-10. Better is the end of a thing than the beginning. Since a true appraisal of any enterprise can only be made from the vantage point of its completion, the end is, the Preacher of wisdom reminds us, better than the beginning. However, the end is frequently arrived at very slowly, and the man who would find profit in this life must be a patient man. He must faithfully resist any and all desire to pride and anger. In his waiting for the end of the matter, he must never fall to idealizing the good old days; for such an attitude will greatly curtail his effectiveness in the present. Profit can only be found by those who are truly alive to the present.

11-14. Wisdom is good with an inheritance. In likening wisdom to an inheritance, the Preacher establishes the fact that an inheritance is to be a permanent possession of a man, which, especially in Israel, was received from parents and passed on to children. The permanence of such a possession is emphasized. This treasure abides with a man through all manner of vicissitudes (Leupold, p. 158). The secular inheritance may be lost or stolen and must certainly be surrendered at death, but wisdom is profitable in this life and in the life to come and cannot be taken from us if we do not wish to surrender it. Wisdom and wealth are both desirable, and each affords a measure of protection for their possessors. However, the preeminence of wisdom is that it alone gives life. Wisdom grants a higher reward, a higher life that cannot be smothered, submerged or lost in the waves of uncertainty that surge over man. This higher life is possible because we recognize the supreme governor of all things and bow to His sovereignty. He is all-powerful, and man cannot change the times which He has arranged in accordance with His

15 All *things* have I seen in the days of my vanity: there is a just *man* that perisheth in his righteousness, and there is a wicked *man* that prolongeth *his life* in his wickedness.

16 Be not righteous over much; neither make thyself over wise: why shouldest thou destroy thyself?

17 Be not over much wicked, neither be thou foolish: why shouldest thou die before thy time?

18 *It is* good that thou shouldest take hold of this; yea, also from this withdraw not thine hand: for he that feareth God shall come forth of them all.

19 Wisdom strengtheneth the wise more than ten mighty *men* which are in the city.

20 For *there is* not a just man upon earth, that doeth good, and sinneth not.

21 Also take no heed unto all words that are spoken; lest thou hear thy servant curse thee:

22 For oftentimes also thine own heart knoweth that thou thyself likewise hast cursed others.

23 All this have I proved by wisdom: I said, I will be wise; but it *was* far from me.

24 That which is far off, and exceeding deep, who can find it out?

25 I applied mine heart to know and to search, and to seek out wisdom, and the reason *of things*, and to know the wickedness of folly, even of foolishness *and* madness:

26 And I find more bitter than death the woman, whose heart *is* snares and nets, *and* her hands *as* bands: whoso pleaseth God shall escape from her; but the sinner shall be taken by her.

27 Behold, this have I found, saith the preacher, *counting* one by one, to find out the account:

28 Which yet my soul seeketh, but I find not: one man among a thousand have I found; but a woman among all those have I not found.

29 Lo, this only have I found, that God hath made man upright; but they have sought out many inventions.

divine pleasure. Man is called to joyful consideration of the fact that God is doing all things with the end in view of bringing man to Himself as the ultimate profit in this life.

15-18. There is a just man that perisheth in his righteousness. Wisdom is not only able to point us to that One who alone marks the way to profit, but wisdom proves itself a valuable possession in days of suffering. In illustrating verses 13 and 14 cases are now cited, illustrating that God works in a way that often seems crooked or puzzling to man. The suffering of the righteous and the seeming prosperity of the wicked has always constituted a great perplexity for the people of God.

Another perplexing problem for the man who would earnestly serve God is that of the overly righteous. These are the persons Malachi complains about in 2:17 and 3:12-13 of his book, a people beyond repentance because they were so impressed with their works-righteousness. The wisdom Preacher counsels the avoidance of such a superficial view of righteousness, for it will most certainly lead its adherents to destruction.

Some simpleton may gather from the Preacher's admonition against over-righteousness that the best course to pursue is one of open wickedness. He who makes such an assumption deserves the title *Kasak* (stupid fool). Like the over-righteous man, he too is the cause of his own destruction. In his case he is apt to end his life prematurely because of his wicked practices. The path to profit may only be kept by those men of wisdom who eschew overly righteous and overly wicked behavior and practice consistently the fear of God.

19-22. Wisdom strengtheneth the wise more than ten mighty men. Wisdom, when pursued to the conclusion formulated in verse 18, is a strong ally that places itself at a man's side and proves a valuable companion in combat. Such a close alliance is needed because we are all guilty of sin. Only wisdom can lead a man to profit in the presence of this universal malady. Wisdom will aid in the establishment of self-control, which will keep man from being overly offended when he observes sin in the lives of others or when he is victimized by the sins of others. When he is maligned by others, wisdom teaches him that he has maligned as well; and therefore he does not allow the words of others to detract him from his major objective, the practice of that wisdom which leads to profit.

23-29. All this have I proved by wisdom. It is good to persistently pursue wisdom, but one must confess that the perfect achievement of the goal is far from every man. In his finite state man cannot plumb the depths of what the sovereign God is doing (3:11). The events of life are complex, and we will never be able to plumb their depths. There was certainly nothing superficial about Solomon's attempt to solve the riddles of life under the sun. The intensity of his search is indicated by the three infinitives: know, explore, and seek. The task was not unproductive, however. The earnest seeking did prove the wickedness of folly and the blindness that issues from it.

This blindness in humanity is discernable in both men and women. It is observed in the woman whose heart is a snare and who binds men with the subtlety of her sensual wares. He who pleases God, i.e., "he who seeks happiness wisely" (Gordis), will escape her wiles. The sinner is easily ensnared by her, since sexual lust represents one of man's gravest temptations.

The woman displays her foolishness by the indiscriminate use of her body, while the man displays his foolishness through being enamored with inventiveness. **God hath made man upright.** The term designates the normal state for man, the state that is in adequate correspondence with the divine standard. Were man still in the condition in which he was created, wisdom would be the easy approach; for the possession of wisdom is part of the normal condition and character of man (Hengstenberg, p. 188).

The more man employs his creativity, the prouder he becomes of his intellect and the less need he feels for the Creator. In consequence, he draws further and further away from God. God made man to fellowship with wisdom; but, failing to abide in that normative state, man has pursued the clever manipulation of things in place of the persistent fear of the God who created all things.

Solomon suggests that one man in a thousand has discovered the way of wisdom and profit, the inference being that the path that leads to wisdom is narrow and found by only a few (cf. Mt 7:13). Among the Jewish "wisdom persons" that Solomon has known, none have been women. This disparaging estimate of the female is common in countries where polygamy is practiced (see, e.g. Ecclesiasticus 25:24, 42:13). However, the failure to discover a woman of wisdom is to be laid at Solomon's feet. The wisdom woman of Proverbs 31 and Song of Solomon can only be known through the monogamous right-man—right-woman relationship. The wisdom woman, in Song of Solomon, gives her heart alone to that man who has given his heart to her with an inviolable pledge of commitment (Song 8:6). Solomon had given his heart to his harem, and thus he exempted himself from the ecstasy of an intimate relationship with a woman of wisdom.

8:1-5. Who is as the wise man? and who knoweth the interpretation of a thing? In a world where wisdom is seldom seen, the Preacher commends the wise man. The interrogative frequently is used for an emphatic negative, i.e., 'no one can be compared with the wise man, and with him who knows the import of this view of life.' (Ginsburg, p. 390). The insight that wisdom brings to a man allows him to know the true interpretation to be placed upon events and brings a joy that is indicated in the shining of the face (Ps 19:8). The hardness of the face, when viewed in the light of Deuteronomy 28:50 and Daniel 8:23, suggests a sinful and rebellious heart. The face then mirrors the personality. The shining countenance is a reflection of a new joy that has been born in a soul that has entered into the narrow way of wisdom. The man who wishes to stay in the narrow way of wisdom is admonished by the Preacher to practice certain truths in the day-to-day practical affairs of life.

One of the primary truths to be practiced is that of obedience to authority, though exactly what level of authority Solomon has in mind is difficult to prove from the text. Leupold feels that the **king** (vs. 2) is a reference to Jehovah (Leupold, p. 185). Perhaps the king should be taken as a political ruler and the passage viewed as an Old Testament parallel to Romans 13. The oath of God is an oath of allegiance to a government made in the name of God. The man who appears before the king must be very careful in his conduct. He must never appear overly anxious to depart, lest the king should suspect some intrigue. Unless one desired certain death, departure from the presence of a monarch could be made only after the proper signal was given.

The submissive man will never participate in evil and consequently will not have to experience the ruler's power of judgment. To incur the wrath of one who possesses such power would indeed constitute a foolish course of action. A man ought to be very careful about questioning the actions of such a powerful figure. Faithful compliance with his laws will preserve a man from evil (Rom 13:3-4).

The first half of verse 5 is a quotation of Proverbs 19:16, and the last half is added by the Preacher. The Preacher believes that the wise man alone knows of **time and judgment.** That is, he knows that God keeps His own counsels (3:1-12) and that He does not share the knowledge of His purpose with mortals. For the sages, the power and the wisdom of the king stand as a challenge to moral obedience; for *Qoheleth,* they become the symbol of God in His mysteriousness (Rylaarsdam, p. 121).

6-13. Because to every purpose there is time and judgment.

CHAPTER 8

WHO *is* as the wise *man?* and who knoweth the interpretation of a thing? a man's wisdom maketh his face to shine, and the boldness of his face shall be changed.

2 I *counsel thee* to keep the king's commandment, and *that* in regard to the oath of God.

3 Be not hasty to go out of his sight: stand not in an evil thing; for he doeth whatsoever pleaseth him.

4 Where the word of a king is, *there is* power: and who may say unto him, What doest thou?

5 Whoso keepeth the commandment shall feel no evil thing: and a wise man's heart discerneth both time and judgment.

6 Because to every purpose there is

time and judgment, therefore the misery of man *is* great upon him.

7 For he knoweth not that which shall be: for who can tell him when it shall be?

8 *There is* no man that hath power over the spirit to retain the spirit; neither *hath he* power in the day of death: and *there is* no discharge in *that* war; neither shall wickedness deliver those that are given to it.

9 All this have I seen, and applied my heart unto every work that is done under the sun: *there is* a time wherein one man ruleth over another to his own hurt.

10 And so I saw the wicked buried, who had come and gone from the place of the holy, and they were forgotten in the city where they had so done: this *is* also vanity.

11 Because sentence against an evil work is not executed speedily, therefore the heart of the sons of men is fully set in them to do evil.

12 Though a sinner do evil an hundred times, and his *days* be prolonged, yet surely I know that it shall be well with them that fear God, which fear before him:

13 But it shall not be well with the wicked, neither shall he prolong *his* days, *which are* as a shadow; because he feareth not before God.

14 There is a vanity which is done upon the earth; that there be just *men*, unto whom it happeneth according to the work of the wicked; again, there be wicked *men*, to whom it happeneth according to the work of the righteous: I said that this also *is* vanity.

15 Then I commended mirth, because a man hath no better thing under the sun, than to eat, and to drink, and to be merry: for that shall abide with him of his labour the days of his life, which God giveth him under the sun.

16 ¶When I applied mine heart to know wisdom, and to see the business that is done upon the earth: (for also *there is that* neither day nor night seeth sleep with his eyes:)

17 Then I beheld all the work of God, that a man cannot find out the work that is done under the sun: because though a man labour to seek *it* out, yet he shall not find *it;* yea farther; though a wise *man* think to know *it,* yet shall he not be able to find *it.*

CHAPTER 9
FOR all this I considered in my heart even to declare all this, that the righteous, and the wise, and their

The Preacher admonishes that much of man's misery is related to the fact that God rightly judges the works of the inventive man and the snaring woman. We do not know the time of God's judgment, but we may know that it is rooted in man's rebellion and that "man's evil is great upon him" (Scott, p. 241), i.e., man is crushed beneath the weight of his own evil.

Death, too, is oppressive and must be faced by all men; for there is no discharge from the demands of death's war on humanity. Inventive man has never yet found a way to get around death's demands. The authors of oppression think that they shall get away with their evil since God does not judge them immediately (vs. 11). The man of wisdom waits, knowingly affirming that the way to ultimate profit in this life and the next is the fear of God. Ultimately, those who practice evil will receive a full recompense for their deeds. They may enjoy long life, but their end will be tragic and without profit since they have not practiced the fear of God.

14-17. There is a vanity which is done upon the earth; that there be just men, unto whom it happeneth according to the work of the wicked. Although the man of wisdom can affirm by faith the ultimate profitableness of fearing God, the earth still remains a place of vanity. Life under the sun is in many ways an enigma. The wicked often prosper, and the righteous often suffer. This is certainly problematical and may cause a man to initially posit the profitableness of pursuing pleasure. However, as the wisdom Preacher has already shown, this is a hasty and superficial decision and cannot lead to the path of true profit.

The pursuit of wisdom and knowledge knows its limitations as well. The more one studies, the more enigmas that are observed. If a man attempts to answer all these enigmas, he is troubled day and night and becomes a stranger to sleep.

The Preacher once again affirms the inappropriateness of these shallow responses to the perplexities of life. The man of wisdom acknowledges that he does not know, nor will he ever know, the ways in which God effects His sovereign purposes (3:11; Deut 29:29; Isa 55:8). In the presence of such a lack of knowledge, wisdom's man refuses to occupy the seat of the pessimist, but rather commits everything to God. It is the sovereign Lord of the universe who is at work. It is His work that is beyond our comprehension; but because it is His work we know that it is holy and beautiful, for He is holy and beautiful and can do nothing that would in any way violate his character. The man of wisdom trusts in the Lord with all of his heart. He leans not upon his own understanding. He acknowledges the hand of God as sovereign over all his ways and completely trusts in the direction of that hand (Prov 3:5-6).

VI. THE WISDOM PREACHER CONTINUES TO ENJOIN THE PRACTICAL APPLICATION OF HIS MESSAGE ON PROFIT IN SPITE OF LIFE'S MANY PERPLEXITIES. 9:1-12:8.

9:1-6. No man knoweth either love or hatred by all that is before them. Before the Preacher moves aggressively to the positive affirmations of the final chapters, he takes care to insure

works, *are* in the hand of God: no man knoweth either love or hatred *by* all *that is* before them.

2 All *things come* alike to all: *there is* one event to the righteous, and to the wicked; to the good and to the clean, and to the unclean; to him that sacrificeth, and to him that sacrificeth not: as *is* the good, so *is* the sinner; *and* he that sweareth, as *he* that feareth an oath.

3 This *is* an evil among all *things* that are done under the sun, that *there is* one event unto all: yea, also the heart of the sons of men is full of evil, and madness *is* in their heart while they live, and after that *they go* to the dead.

4 For to him that is joined to all the living there is hope: for a living dog is better than a dead lion.

5 For the living know that they shall die: but the dead know not any thing, neither have they any more a reward; for the memory of them is forgotten.

6 Also their love, and their hatred, and their envy, is now perished; neither have they any more a portion for ever in any *thing* that is done under the sun.

7 ¶Go thy way, eat thy bread with joy, and drink thy wine with a merry heart; for God now accepteth thy works.

8 Let thy garments be always white; and let thy head lack no ointment.

9 Live joyfully with the wife whom thou lovest all the days of the life of thy

that wisdom's man will be building on nothing short of hard reality. In 8:16-17 he has stated that man may never comprehend the purposes of God. Man may affirm the beauty of these "time events" (3:11), but the rationale for their interrelationships evades him.

Having expressed himself fully on the important point of God's inscrutability, the Preacher now invites meditation upon the implications of this important teaching. The righteous and the wise, and all of their works, are in the hand of God. Anything may happen to anyone. Just as the same fate overtakes man and beast (3:19-20), so fate makes no distinction among men on moral grounds (Scott, p. 246). The people of God have throughout their history been tempted to cynicism because of the difficulties they encounter (Mal 1:2ff.). This tendency leads our Preacher to urge the application of wisdom's message on profit in spite of the perplexities.

The Preacher affirms that all men, the righteous and the unrighteous, are in the hand of God. Men do not direct the course of their lives; all persons and the works that they do are in the hands of God, and He does as He pleases. In fact, an objective surveillance of the events which occur in our lives furnishes a mixture of evidence which, in the final analysis, does little to establish absolutely God's love or hatred of an individual man. The fates and fortunes of all men seem remarkably similar. The wisdom of men would certainly provide a more amenable deity. Righteous man would surely create a God who would immediately reward the righteous and judge the wicked, and such a God was clearly envisioned by the religious friends of Job. What actually happens is very different.

The sinner and the saint seem to share a common lot. The sinner's freedom from divine punishment causes him to fill his heart with madness and rebellion while he lives. The vision of death as the universal obliteration breeds madness in the hearts of those who do not companion with wisdom. The Hebrew word translated madness implies a blindness to the true issues. These poor men are blinded all the days of their miserable existence. They lack the ability to see things rightly, for they have refused the profit of wisdom's illumination. Hence, from their darkness and evil they go to death. They pass from death to death.

The wisdom Preacher treasures the hope that these deluded men might repent before they must go to the place of the dead. As long as they are **joined to all the living there is hope,** or as another proverb in verse 4 states, **A living dog is better than a dead lion.** The contemptibles who scavenge the Jerusalem streets are better off than a dead lion.

The living know that they shall die. Although at first this seems a pointless advantage, in reality the possession of this knowledge represents a great advantage. As long as a man is alive and is experiencing the grace of God as it encounters him in the various "time events" of his days, there is the possibility that he may be moved to consider his ways. Such consideration may lead a man to the discovery of true profit (Jn 14:6) and prepare him to meet the requiring God (Heb 9:27). Once the spirit travels upward, the possibility for a man to consider his ways is over. He then meets the sovereign Judge of the universe and receives an infallible estimate of the profitableness of the life he has lived (Rev 20:12; I Cor 3:9-15). For the unrepentant sinner this evaluation will launch him into an empty and hopeless eternity.

7-10. Not much more can be said about the perplexing similarity between the fate of the godly and the ungodly. All that results is a word of caution lest the man of wisdom allow this perplexing situation to reduce him to pessimism and inaction. Once again, the Preacher points the way to ultimate profit, a way that is to be persistently pursued in spite of the presence of perplexity and enigma. Under the very cloud of death, this

vanity, which he hath given thee under the sun, all the days of thy vanity: for that *is* thy portion in *this* life, and in thy labour which thou takest under the sun.

10 Whatsoever thy hand findeth to do, do *it* with thy might; for *there is* no work, nor device, nor knowledge, nor wisdom, in the grave, whither thou goest.

life-affirming spirit illumines the rest of the passage. We are to savor the joys of life and not allow ourselves to get mired down in its vexatious problems. As responsible beings, we are to make ourselves enjoy the little gifts of God (2:24, 3:12, 13, 22; 5:18; 6:12; 8:15). The Preacher continuously confronts man with this teaching in the fear that its seeming simplicity will render it an object of scorn by men who seek greater profits in this world. A thankful spirit for the graces of life is a must, for he who would discover profit on his sojourn through life.

One more thing is needful. Men need the inner conviction of God's approval and acceptance of those who seek to walk before Him in righteousness. Though God may give few outward tokens of His approval of our course, we must be convinced in our heart that He is delighted with our decision to rest in Him and follow His laws. Men must affirm the 'positive will of God' (G. Von Rad, p. 457). Believe this and say thank you for all of life, and you will know profit in this world and the next.

Keep your garments white and anoint your head with fragrant spiced oil, counsels the Preacher. These are symbols of festivity and joy (cf. Est 8:15, Ps 45:7). A man ought to get himself a wife and bask in the sunshine of her love (cf. Song of Solomon). A man must love that wife all the days of his life and prize her as one of God's choicest gifts. Here the emphasis is on monogamy and the intensity of relationship which the man and woman are to share a relationship that would not be possible in a polygamous structure. The companionship shared between a right-man and a right-woman joined in the bond of love will provide one of life's greatest rewards for men and women who labor under the sun (4:9).

Men filled with the knowledge of these wise principles should enter upon the tasks of the hour with great verve. Whatever the task, man must see it as a gift from the Lord and enter into its challenge with an awareness that He will hold us accountable for what we do with His provisions (3:17, 5:8, 11:9, 12:14). When the spirit goeth upward, there is no opportunity for making up tasks left undone. Jesus expresses the same thought when He says, "I must work the works of him that sent me, while it is day: the night cometh, when no man can work" (Jn 9:4).

11 ¶I returned, and saw under the sun, that the race *is* not to the swift, nor the battle to the strong, neither yet bread to the wise, nor yet riches to men of understanding, nor yet favour to men of skill; but time and chance happeneth to them all.

12 For man also knoweth not his time: as the fishes that are taken in an evil net, and as the birds that are caught in the snare; so *are* the sons of men snared in an evil time, when it falleth suddenly upon them.

13 ¶This wisdom have I seen also under the sun, and it *seemed* great unto me:

14 *There was* a little city, and few men within it; and there came a great king against it, and besieged it, and built great bulwarks against it:

15 Now there was found in it a poor wise man, and he by his wisdom delivered the city; yet no man remembered that same poor man.

16 Then said I, Wisdom *is* better than strength: nevertheless the poor man's wisdom *is* despised, and his words are not heard.

17 The words of wise *men are* heard in quiet more than the cry of him that ruleth among fools.

18 Wisdom *is* better than weapons of

11-18. I returned, and saw under the sun, that the race is not to the swift, nor the battle to the strong. Do these things, affirms the Preacher; for only the diligent practice of them will lead to true profit, profit that transcends the enigmatic ordering of events in time. Do these things because the uncertainty of life hangs like a scepter above you as you live under the sun. The race is not always to the swift, nor the battle to the strong, nor bread to men of wisdom, nor yet riches to men of understanding, nor favors for men of skill. Evil times and unfavorable circumstances fall on each of these, and they come with alarming suddenness and seeming capriciousness. Yes, even as I give wisdom's teaching, says the Preacher, "I am mindful of these perplexing enigmas. Do not think that I am blind to them. But I believe that even though the man of wisdom may be despised and forgotten, still wisdom delivers. One sinner destroys much good, but the way of wisdom is still the better way."

God's hero in this world is the poor wise man who is ready to do his part, even though men will despise him, refuse to hear his words, and ultimately forget him. Such a man is, however, a man compelled by a sense of duty. He continues to speak the words of wisdom, regardless of the response of others. He has found the way to profit, and duty compels him to share it with all. He is the Preacher of wisdom. Perhaps our Preacher himself is the "poor wise man" of the parable.

The words of the Preacher will only be heard by those who have an inner quietness. These hear the words of the wise man more readily than the fool hears the harsh overbearing cry of the

war: but one sinner destroyeth much good.

CHAPTER 10

DEAD flies cause the ointment of the apothecary to send forth a stinking savour: *so doth* a little folly him that is in reputation for wisdom *and* honour.

2 A wise man's heart *is* at his right hand; but a fool's heart at his left.

3 Yea also, when he that is a fool walketh by the way, his wisdom faileth *him*, and he saith to every one *that* he *is* a fool.

4 If the spirit of the ruler rise up against thee, leave not thy place; for yielding pacifieth great offences.

5 There is an evil *which* I have seen under the sun, as an error *which* proceedeth from the ruler:

6 Folly is set in great dignity, and the rich sit in low place.

7 I have seen servants upon horses, and princes walking as servants upon the earth.

8 He that diggeth a pit shall fall into it; and whoso breaketh an hedge, a serpent shall bite him.

9 Whoso removeth stones shall be hurt therewith; *and* he that cleaveth wood shall be endangered thereby.

10 If the iron be blunt, and he do not whet the edge, then must he put to more strength: but wisdom *is* profitable to direct.

11 Surely the serpent will bite without enchantment; and a babbler is no better.

ruler. Wisdom is better than the mightiest weapons of war, but one sinner can destroy many of wisdom's accomplishments.

10:1-11. Dead flies cause the ointment of the apothecary to send forth a stinking savor. The man who would remain in the way of profit must take scrupulous care to keep even the smallest grain of folly from taking root in his life. The little fly who has rested amidst the sweet scent of a costly ointment will ultimately be the cause of the ointment's total corruption. The Preacher alludes to an everyday occurrence that has passed into a proverb. Just as the insignificant fetid fly has the power of corrupting a quantity of precious perfume by imparting unto it it's offensive smell, so a little folly has often shown itself more weighty and powerful than glorious wisdom. From the disagreeable effect which the presence of dead flies in precious moistures produces in the sultry climate of the East arose the Arabic proverb, "A fly is nothing, yet it produces loathsomeness" (Ginsburg, p. 423). The toleration of the slightest folly in the life of a man of reputation will soon cause his reputation to have a stinking savor.

The wise man's mind is consistently directed toward his right hand. In the language of the Scripture the right hand suggests that which is honorable (Lk 1:11), and the left hand that which is sinister and evil (Mt 25:41). The mind of the wise man is dominated by thoughts of duty, while the mind of the fool runs persistently to evil. The little wisdom that the fool possesses fails him when he walks and talks in the market place. His commitment to left handed action confirms the fact that he is a fool.

His foolhardiness is evidenced most blatantly in his total disregard for authority. When the leftist finds himself at cross-purposes with the king, he enters into spirited protestation that is devoid of respect: he defies the ruler. The Preacher counsels a more submissive attitude toward those who are in positions of authority. The wisdom man practices a controlled submission, and his yielding often puts an end to potentially explosive situations. Such carefulness allows time for a ruler to reconsider his decisions and perhaps reverse an original decision that was not in a man's favor. This counsel is necessary, for men are often ruled by monarchs who lack wisdom. Many rulers will elevate folly and denigrate wisdom, and they will give power and prestige to the unworthy. In such situations, the man of wisdom should practice the control of self and speech. A man will be helped in his endeavor to achieve self control if he remembers the destiny of these foolish leaders.

In reality, these men of folly are digging their own graves. Their lack of attention to duty has opened a great crevice in their kingdom, and eventually they will fall into it. Others ought to learn from this as well. He who digs a pit is bound to fall into it sooner or later. Inattention to duty is also compared to the breaking down of walls. Passive indifference to the norms of God's laws is always destructive. Men who pursue such a course of action risk great harm to themselves, for no one ever knows when a venomous strike will find its way to his flesh. Quarrying and the cutting down of trees are both operations which are not free from danger. Those who will avoid the embracing of duty are like the man who works with a dull axe. He expends vast amounts of energy and makes a great deal of noise, but when all is finished he has accomplished little. His safety is precarious, and he can count on no lasting profit for all his labor.

In contrast to the fruitless labor of the fool, the man of wisdom enjoys the advantage of wisdom's direction. Wisdom is an advantage (Heb *yitrōn*), for it gives success. In verse 11 there is no advantage in the charmer. A contrasting summation is intended by the Preacher in verses 10-11. In a world where folly is often set in high places, a man needs the profitable direction of

12 The words of a wise man's mouth *are* gracious; but the lips of a fool will swallow up himself.

13 The beginning of the words of his mouth *is* foolishness: and the end of his talk *is* mischievous madness.

14 A fool also is full of words: a man cannot tell what shall be; and what shall be after him, who can tell him?

15 The labour of the foolish wearieth every one of them, because he knoweth not how to go to the city.

16 ¶Woe to thee, O land, when thy king *is* a child, and thy princes eat in the morning!

17 Blessed *art* thou, O land, when thy king *is* the son of nobles, and thy princes eat in due season, for strength, and not for drunkenness!

18 ¶By much slothfulness the building decayeth; and through idleness of the hands the house droppeth through.

19 ¶A feast is made for laughter, and wine maketh merry: but money answereth all *things*.

20 ¶Curse not the king, no not in thy thought; and curse not the rich in thy bedchamber: for a bird of the air shall carry the voice, and that which hath wings shall tell the matter.

CHAPTER 11

CAST thy bread upon the waters: for thou shalt find it after many days.

2 Give a portion to seven, and also to eight; for thou knowest not what evil shall be upon the earth.

3 If the clouds be full of rain, they empty *themselves* upon the earth: and if the tree fall toward the south, or toward the north, in the place where the tree falleth, there it shall be.

4 He that observeth the wind shall not sow; and he that regardeth the clouds shall not reap.

5 As thou knowest not what *is* the way of the spirit, *nor* how the bones *do grow* in the womb of her that is with

wisdom to avoid the venomous bite of serpentine rulers. Just as the serpent may be kept from biting through the careful work of the charmer, so may the serpentine ruler be kept from ruling against the man who carefully employs the charm of wisdom. In Isaiah 26:16 the word for charming (Heb *lachash*) is used for prayer. The wisdom Preacher points to the way of profit in the presence of such evil rulers. To deal wisely with these serpentine rulers, one ought to practice well the charm of prayer (Dan 6).

12-15. The words of a wise man's mouth are gracious. The fool will offend the ruler and go to death because of his inability to discern the right words for the moment as he appears before the ruler. Wisdom's man has been delivered again and again because he has received wisdom from on high as to the mode of charming serpentine rulers (cf. David, Joseph, Paul, and Jesus). The fool reveals only his mischievous madness when he opens his mouth. It cannot be otherwise, for he walks in darkness. He's so confused that he can't even follow the signs pointing to the city. He can't even read a roadmap. This man of the left hand is walking in total and complete darkness. He is a man thrashing in the water and going nowhere; and it wearies a man of wisdom to even watch his unprofitable motion.

16-20. Woe to thee, O land, when thy king is a child, and thy princes eat in the morning. Woe is the lot of that land that has such an addled figure for its monarch. Woe to that land that is led by a man of such immaturity, one who is so little aware of duty and responsibility that he must be called a child. He is a ruler who knows so little of honor and duty that when he arises in the morning he never considers the affairs of state, but hastens rather to feasting and revelry. The lot of the citizens in such a land will indeed be a hard one. The Preacher then compares the blessedness of the land where the rulers eat for strength and not for revelry. The land where the rulers are truly noble is certain to be a far better place for the man of wisdom to dwell.

The childish ruler is certain to lead his woeful land into corruption and collapse. Meals are prepared for drunken revelry, and all of life is calculated to heighten hilarity. Money is the charmer in this kind of kingdom. Money buys "things," and things are thought to be profit in this land.

The state of such a land is tragic. God has created people to love others and use things, but in this land that is devoid of wisdom people love things and use people. Be careful, however, what you say against the childish ruler; and be careful when you say it. Do not speak lightly of this unworthy ruler. Do not even allow yourself to practice seditious thoughts; for if they are allowed to ferment in your mind, they may eventually give birth to an ill-advised utterance. Such an utterance will probably prove unfortunate and could ultimately produce tragic consequences. Do not beat your head against this formidable wall. Do not sacrifice your life to such a fool. Practice the art of prayer (charming), and thereby insure the providential guidance of the Lord in all of your dealings with such a despot.

11:1-8. Cast thy bread upon the waters: for thou shalt find it after many days. In view of the perplexing problems that man must face, it is not at all amazing that many become extremely pessimistic. However, the Preacher admonishes all to avoid selfishness, self-centeredness, and pessimism. Put away from yourself that narrow-heartedness that in times of perplexity and injustice so easily captures the heart, is the firm admonition of the Preacher. To illustrate further, our Preacher employs an illustration from the commerce of the sea. Let your bread of charity go out upon the waters, as ships do in their travels, carrying precious cargo hither and yon. Solomon's vessels returned from Tarshish once in three years, bringing rich treasures to his kingdom (I Kgs 10:22). Their return was only possible because they had been sent. If the venture had not been

child: even so thou knowest not the works of God who maketh all.

6 In the morning sow thy seed, and in the evening withhold not thine hand: for thou knowest not whether shall prosper, either this or that, or whether they both *shall be* alike good.

7 ¶Truly the light *is* sweet, and a pleasant *thing it is* for the eyes to behold the sun:

8 But if a man live many years, *and* rejoice in them all; yet let him remember the days of darkness; for they shall be many. All that cometh *is* vanity.

9 ¶Rejoice, O young man, in thy youth; and let thy heart cheer thee in the days of thy youth, and walk in the ways of thine heart, and in the sight of thine eyes: but know thou, that for all these *things* God will bring thee into judgment.

10 Therefore remove sorrow from

undertaken in faith, the day of reward could not have come. In like manner, men who would find profit in life under the sun must send their bread out upon the waters. The more ships a man sends forth, the better will be his return.

The teaching has both a commercial and a moral application. The Preacher counsels a diversification of investments lest evil strike and destroy your entire fortune. Give to many, so that in your day of need you may encounter at least one who in gratitude will assist you. The addition of the words, also to eight, serves the purpose of indicating that the number seven did not mark the limit of the extent of our benevolence: not, "at the utmost seven," but, seven and more (Hengstenberg, p. 236).

Man does not know when evil will come, but he can know this: the evil day will come. Just as certainly as clouds filled with rain will drop that rain to the earth, so is the certainty of evil's arrival. When it falls, it is as heavy as a large, old tree. Men will be unable to move it once it has landed. Where it lands it must stay until age has dissipated it or wiser measures are taken to remove it, but the man upon whom it falls is totally unable to free himself from its oppressive weight. However, don't stand around observing rain clouds. Don't stand gazing idly at the clouds, wondering when and where the rain is going to fall. Don't allow your actions to be governed by the capricious conditions of life under the sun. **Sow.** Sow because it is the honorable thing to do. True, the value of what you are doing is shrouded in mystery, as is the formation of the child in the womb. Man does not know what God is doing, but that lack of knowledge is never to serve as a cause for inactivity. Man must do his work and enjoy the present life, though it is beyond his powers to determine the future (Scott, p. 252).

The way to profit is to be found in the fields in the early sowing of the seed. It is to be found in the expenditure of all one's might in every minute of every day. In the evening the man of wisdom is still sending out the ships and sowing the seeds of benevolence and industry. He is involved in a multiplicity of givings. He blesses many and invests widely, for he knows not what seeds will find fertile soil and spring forth in life. Perhaps on a good day all will prosper. That, however, is not the concern of wisdom's man. He is constrained to benevolence in every opportune moment, for he knows that ultimate profit is in the way of a man who is possessed by such worthy motives. Such faithful action in a world of perplexity will ultimately prove the better course of action. While persisting in faithful action, the Preacher admonishes man to remember that life is sweet.

Man ought to thank God for the opportunity to behold the sun. It is profitable for man to adopt this attitude in the presence of perplexity; for as Jesus said, "The night is coming when man works no more." Remember that, and you will do all you can with a grateful heart; for death awaits all men, and there is no commissioning of ships or sowing of seed in the grave. The grave is void of opportunities to practice benevolence, and the possibility of laboring for God ceases when one passes out from under the light of the sun. Had the Preacher possessed the light of the New Testament revelation, he might have said more. The information he possesses here, however, allowed him to speak well. Faithfulness in life is the way to profit. Man who practices faithfulness will go from this life to the judgment of God and fare well (5:20, 7:18, 12:13, 14).

9-10. Rejoice, O young man, in thy youth. Perhaps the young man who reads this treatise of the wisdom Preacher will want to cast it aside as too weighty and serious for his youthful heart. To our wisdom Preacher, life affords few greater tragedies than the wasted energies of youth. The careful description of old age is calculated to produce a desire in the heart of the young to enjoy life. The caution concerning God's judgment is designed

thy heart, and put away evil from thy flesh: for childhood and youth *are* vanity.

CHAPTER 12

REMEMBER now thy Creator in the days of thy youth, while the evil days come not, nor the years draw nigh, when thou shalt say, I have no pleasure in them;

2 While the sun, or the light, or the moon, or the stars, be not darkened, nor the clouds return after the rain:

3 In the day when the keepers of the house shall tremble, and the strong men shall bow themselves, and the grinders cease because they are few, and those that look out of the windows be darkened,

4 And the doors shall be shut in the streets, when the sound of the grinding is low, and he shall rise up at the voice of the bird, and all the daughters of musick shall be brought low;

5 Also *when* they shall be afraid of *that which is* high, and fears *shall be* in the way, and the almond tree shall flourish, and the grasshopper shall be a burden, and desire shall fail: because man goeth to his long home, and the mourners go about the streets:

6 Or ever the silver cord be loosed, or the golden bowl be broken, or the pitcher be broken at the fountain, or the wheel broken at the cistern.

7 Then shall the dust return to the earth as it was: and the spirit shall return unto God who gave it.

8 ¶Vanity of vanities, saith the preacher; all *is* vanity.

to keep the young in the way of true profit as they pursue that enjoyment. To the young, our Preacher of wisdom addresses a final appeal. What will our wisdom Preacher say to the youth of Israel? Will he exhort them to prayer and fasting? No, the Preacher exhorts the young man to rejoice.

Rejoice in your youth; let thy heart cheer thee (Prov 14:30, 15:13). Cheerfully enjoy all of God's gifts. Hearing, sight, strength, mind; enjoy it all. Celebrate each of these faculties as the gifts of God, but remember He has not given you these gifts to squander foolishly. There will be a day of accounting, so do all with a consciousness that at a future point you are to stand before the sovereign Judge of the universe. A man must put away from himself all that would be displeasing to God, for these things will ultimately blunt his ability to achieve true joy. Fretfulness over existing circumstances (vexation) will rob a man of that joy. A man must therefore purge a fretful spirit from himself.

The time is coming when bodily decay will set in and the enjoyment of life will be circumscribed by the failings of the flesh. Youth cannot be held onto, admonishes the Preacher; so be certain that you use its resources well. Remember your Creator! The Berleburger Bible remarks, "In the noble time of youth turn betimes to God, and do not sacrifice its bloom to the devil; do not devote merely the dregs of thy years to God and put off till late the work of conversion." The young man is exhorted to remember his Creator before the evil days come, when his susceptibility to pleasure has ceased and he is forced to reflect upon a wasted existence.

12:1-8. In the day when the keepers of the house shall tremble. Chapter 12 contains the moving "Allegory of Old Age." A poignant picture of senility that is partly metaphorical and partly literal affords a dynamic reinforcement of the Preacher's instruction to remember the Creator in the days of youth. The opportunity for remembrance will soon be over, and what will replace it will drastically limit a man's ability to enjoy life under the sun. In old age life takes on the characteristics of the dark, cold Palestinian winter, when storm after storm hides the heavenly luminaries.

Each phrase of the allegory is designed to describe the waning of strength in a specific organ of the body (Talmud, B. Shad. 152 A; Midrash; Ibn Ezra). The keepers of the house are the hands and arms. It is their specific duty to guard the house from intrusion. In old age they tremble so severely that they can no longer move swiftly to the defense of the body. The strong men refer to the legs. They are thus designated because they are supported by the largest muscles of the body (Ps 147:10; Song 5:15). In old age, the legs fail and the knees grow weak. The grinding women are the teeth. The mouth is the mill. It is difficult for the mill to function effectively when the teeth become few in number. They that look out of the windows are no doubt the eyes whose ability to perceive images lessens with the passing of the years.

The door is a symbol of interchange with the outside world. The doors that are shut represent the deafness that cuts the elderly person off from the sounds of the city. The sound of the grinding of grain, which was heard daily about the Oriental home, is scarcely discernible to the old man. Rising at the sound of the bird suggests the light sleeping habits developed in old age which cause awakening to coincide with the rising of the birds. All times become indistinct to the aged person, due to an inability to hear that which is transpiring about him. Singing, as well as any real appreciation of music, has become a thing of the past.

Increasing age also brings with it a fear of high places. There is the constant fear of a fall that may result in broken bones. Even the road (sidewalks) brings terror; for there is the continual danger of stumbling, and this danger is complicated by the presence of increased traffic.

The almond tree blossoms are a reference to the white hair that appears upon the head as an external sign of internal physical decay. The white signifies the time of the end. The walk of the old man is compared to that of the grasshopper. His whole body is nothing but skin and bones. His bones stick out, and his body is exhausted. He is nothing but an image of death (Luther, p. 181).

The older person has lost all lightness of body and mind. All desires, physical and mental, fail as life begins to ebb out like the retreating tide. The professional wailers have drawn near to this man's home, waiting with expectation to be hired for his funeral. What the professional mourners are waiting for is described in verses 6 and 7. The beauty and fragility of the human frame are captured here. It is a masterpiece, as delicate in its construction as the greatest work of art, yet as fragile as a piece of pottery. In the end it is as useless as a broken lamp, a shattered pitcher, and a broken wheel. The silver cord held the golden bowl or lamp; and when it snapped, the lamp fell to the ground, dissolving itself into a myriad of pieces. The burning lamp is a common symbol for life (cf. I Kgs 11:36, Prov 13:9). When the wheel and the pitcher are broken at the well, no more water can be drawn. The well with all its treasures is then beyond the reach of man. Light and water are common symbols for life.

Man, with his aged and broken frame, is like the broken wheel and the shattered pottery. He looks out at all that life has to offer, but he has no tools that will allow him to interact with all he sees. His body will soon dissolve into dust; and his spirit, or the breath of his life, will return unto the God who originally gave it (Job 34:14-15, Gen 2:7). This section closes with the same admonition with which the Preacher began. Man under the sun is compelled to confess the vanity of all secular striving as he views the final destiny of the groaning human frame (Rom 8:23).

Certainly, this portrait of aging is calculated to cause the young to stop and ponder the direction in which they are going. The assurance of a common destiny is evidenced everywhere by the sighings of the aged. Beyond that vanity, however, lies a common confrontation between the spirits of men and the Lord who breathed them into being (Heb 9:27).

VII. THE WISDOM PREACHER SUMMARIZES HIS MISSION, METHOD, AND MESSAGE. 12:9-14.

9 And moreover, because the preacher was wise, he still taught the people knowledge; yea, he gave good heed, and sought out, and set in order many proverbs.
10 The preacher sought to find out acceptable words: and that which was written was upright, even words of truth.
11 The words of the wise are as goads, and as nails fastened by the masters of assemblies, which are given from one shepherd.

9-11. And moreover, because the preacher was wise, he still taught the people knowledge. In spite of the vanity that is cemented to the existence of man, our Preacher has held to wisdom and admonishes all men to do the same. Even the greatest vanity, death, is transcended by the reality that man must appear before God after the shattering of the earthen vessel. The reality of this confrontation presses upon the heart of the Preacher and forces from him the pursuit of a particular path, a path which he believes will alone bring man into the enjoyment of true profit. In verses 8-9 the Preacher summarizes his mission. In this world of vanity the Preacher is committed to the impartation of knowledge. Men must hear the word of the Lord; it is his conviction that people perish for lack of knowledge. He is thus committed to being a herald of God's truth. He has carefully pondered all that makes up life under the sun and has attempted to find the deeper meaning of things. Once he arrived at the true meaning of things, he skillfully set down many proverbs. The Hebrews loved good proverbs that were skillfully arranged and artistically grouped. Solomon was a master in the art of proverbial construction (I Kgs 5:12). The wisdom Preacher's mission in life is to inform the people through the careful choice of suitable proverbs that will fit the need and minister grace to the hearer (Lk 4:22).

The wisdom Preacher's arsenal of proverbs is designed to perform two tasks. The Preacher here pays tribute to the stimulation (goads) afforded by the writings of the wise and the firm support (fixed nails) that they give to human life (Gordis, p. 350). The Preacher desires not only to minister pleasantly, but also to minister truthfully. Perfect candor and truthfulness have characterized all his efforts. He is the man of grace and truth (cf. Jn 1:14). God, in His revelation of wisdom to the world, gave great attention to form and content. Our wisdom Preacher has taken equal care in the construction of his message. His message of grace and truth has a double effect upon the world that hears it, serving as goads and as stakes. The purpose of the goad is to stir the slumbering to action. The goad was a sharp stick that was used to convince sluggish animals to move with greater haste into a desired path. The wisdom Preacher uses many proverbs designed to goad men and women out of their spiritual indifference and into a firm resolve to embrace the wisdom of God. Ecclesiastes has been filled with goads.

The purpose of the stake, or fixed nail, is to provide a secure place to which a man may anchor himself during the stormy days of his life under the sun. These stakes furnish man with mental and spiritual anchorage. All of these collected sayings, be they goad or stake, are given by the one Shepherd of Israel (Ps 80:1) who through His words is both anchor and goad to the people whom He loves. With these words the Preacher, master as he is, pays unwitting tribute to the greatest wisdom teacher of all: our Lord. His sayings have both these marks supremely, just as they also excel by the criterion of verse 10 as **acceptable words** and **words of truth.** They marry felicity with fearlessness, partners which should not be put asunder (Kidner, p. 106).

12 And further, by these, my son, be admonished: of making many books *there is* no end; and much study *is* a weariness of the flesh.

13 ¶Let us hear the conclusion of the whole matter: Fear God, and keep his commandments: for this is the whole *duty* of man.

14 For God shall bring every work into judgment, with every secret thing, whether *it be* good, or whether *it be* evil.

12-14. With these verses the Preacher concludes his message. First, as a good author, he considers the work of his mind and hands to be qualitatively superior to that of the regular secular fare. The superiority of his offering is due to the source from which it has been derived. The proverbs are God's gift to man. Other productions, when studied, will bring only weariness of flesh (II Tim 3:7). These collected proverbs from the Lord minister life to the hearer, and they alone point the way to true profit for man under the sun. The collected proverbs are able to point a man to profit because they alone admonish in such a way that the faithful hearer is led into the fear of God.

Life is totally profitless without God-connectedness. Profit exists only for those who fear God and keep His commandments. This is the grand conclusion of the wisdom Preacher. The order in the original text is, "God thou shalt fear." Fear of God is that reverential awe that emerges when we, with our lack of holiness, are met with the righteous demands of His holiness (Isa 6). Its total effect is to produce in man an unquestioning obedience to all of God's revealed will. Viewing God in this manner and complying with all of His revealed commandments is the inescapable duty of all men. Rebels will not comply, but the man of wisdom dares to commend and practice no other life.

In verse 14 a further reason is given for practicing the fear of God and obeying His commandments. The Preacher announces a heavenly tribunal at which **every work,** and every **secret thing** shall be brought into judgment. After the thoughtful conjunction of goads and stakes, after the careful admission of perplexity, after the clear challenge to the performance of duty, the author ends his Preaching. He ends by enunciating with lucid clarity the reality of a day of judgment. Only in the New Testament is the doctrine of a day of judgment more clearly proclaimed. It is a day when God shall judge the secrets of men (Rom. 2:16), bring to light the hidden things of darkness, and make manifest the counsels of every heart (I Cor 4:5), a day when the absolute profit of every deed and thought will be assigned by that One who judges in righteousness and truth.

When every detail has been examined, the way to profit will be universally acclaimed to rest in that One through whom all things are yours (I Cor 3:21), that One who is the wisdom of God, Jesus the Christ. In that day our Preacher will be heard pronouncing a resonant Amen.

BIBLIOGRAPHY

Barton, G. A. The Book of Ecclesiastes. In *International Critical Commentary*. Edinburgh: T.&T. Clark, 1908.

Bridges, Charles. *An Exposition of the Book of Ecclesiastes*. London: Banner of Truth, reprinted, 1960.

Delitzsch, F. Commentary on Song of Songs and Ecclesiastes. In *Commentaries on the Old Testament*. Grand Rapids: Eerdmans, reprinted, 1950.

*Ginsburg, C. D. *The Song of Songs and Qoheleth*. New York: Ktav Publishing House, 1970.

Gordis, Robert. *Koheleth The Man and His World-A Study of Ecclesiastes*. New York: Schocken Books, 1968.

*Hengstenberg, E. W. *A Commentary on Ecclesiastes*. Minneapolis: James and Klock Christian Publishing Co., 1977.

Jones, E. Proverbs and Ecclesiastes. In *The Torch Bible Commentaries*. London: SCM Press, 1961.

Kidner, Derek. *A Time to Mourn, and A Time to Dance: Ecclesiastes & the Way of the World*. Downers Grove: InterVarsity Press, 1976.

*Leupold, N. C. *Exposition of Ecclesiastes*. Grand Rapids: Baker Book House, n.d.

Luther, M. *Notes on Ecclesiastes*. Saint Louis: Concordia, reprinted, 1972.

Rylaarsdam, J. D. Proverbs, Ecclesiastes, The Song of Solomon. In *The Layman's Bible Commentary*. Richmond: John Knox Press, 1964.

Scott, R. B. Y. Proverbs and Ecclesiastes. In *The Anchor Bible*. New York: Doubleday and Company, Inc., 1965.

Von Rad, Gerhard. *Wisdom in Israel*. New York: Abingdon Press, 1972.

Zockler, O. "Ecclesiastes." In *Commentary on the Holy Scriptures*. Ed. by J. P. Lange. Grand Rapids: Zondervan, reprinted, n.d.

SONG OF SOLOMON

INTRODUCTION

Here is undoubtedly one of the most beautiful books in the Bible. How sad that it is so often neglected. Many pass by the Song of Solomon confused or embarrassed by the simple beauty of its words. This ought not to be, for all Scripture is authored by the blessed Holy Spirit; and this song is no exception.

Characteristics. The Song of Solomon exhibits all the characteristics of the best Hebrew poetry. The Song abounds in imagery drawn from both country and urban life, and its language is full of vitality.

The scenes are not always chronological. Some paragraphs are obviously retrospective, and others clearly look ahead in anticipation. Whether Solomon himself understood the import of his writing we do not know. It is clear to all who read the book that the Holy Spirit intends it as a testimony to the true nature of love.

Synopsis. The Song is told primarily from the standpoint of a Shulamite maiden. She is a member of a family in Shunem; her father is apparently deceased; and her brothers have become responsible for the maintenance of the family. Their livelihood is obtained from shepherding flocks and caring for vineyards.

In the course of her shepherding duties the maiden meets and falls in love with a young shepherd. The brothers do not approve and attempt to hinder any further development of their relationship.

One day the maiden sets out to visit the countryside. On her way she meets King Solomon with his entourage returning from an excursion to his northern territories. Solomon is struck by her great beauty and remands her to the care of the ladies of his court. She cannot escape and is eventually taken to Solomon's splendid palace at Jerusalem.

Solomon attempts every conceivable ploy to win her affection. She refuses him consistently because her thoughts are filled with the memory of her absent shepherd-lover. She cannot forget her vow of love to him. Solomon eventually realizes that she is not to be his and, impressed by her devotion to her shepherd, he grants her permission to return home.

The Shulamite maiden is overjoyed. She immediately sends word to the beloved to come and take her back to her family and the land of their betrothal. The Song ends with a beautiful description of their homeward journey.

Purpose. The Song furnishes the saints of all ages with the language of holy love and challenges the saints of every dispensation to an ardent devotion and fidelity in the presence of God's love. Such loyalty and devotion to God and mate are aptly illustrated by the conduct of the Shulamite maiden in the "Song of songs" (1:1).

Authorship. The Solomonic authorship has at times been denied. However, there are many interesting internal arguments for the authorship of Solomon. There is the reference to the horses in Pharaoh's chariots at 1:9, which compares to a similar reference in I Kings 10:28, 29. Also, the towns mentioned in the Song of Songs point to a time when there was a single kingdom in Israel, which would have been the case prior to the death of Solomon. Solomonic authorship was universally accepted in ancient times, and no convincing reasons have been advanced to warrant its rejection.

Interpretation. Approaches to the interpretation of the book have varied. Historically, four approaches have held prominence:

1. Allegorical. This method of interpretation treats biblical narratives in a nonliteral manner. One looks beyond the literal meaning of the words and constructs new and more spiritual meanings. Jewish scholars who followed this approach saw in the Song a message relating the special union between Jehovah and Israel. Many of the early church fathers employed this approach and found in the Song a message of God's love for the church.

2. Typical. This view sees in the Song a portrayal of the love between Christ, the Bridegroom, and the church, His bride.

3. Literal. This view sees the book as a collection of love songs or poems that is designed to extol human love.

4. Dramatic. This approach suggests that the Song is a drama. Solomon has fallen in love with the Shulamite who has already given her heart to her shepherd. This view is advocated by Franz Delitzsch and is essentially the view espoused in this commentary.

OUTLINE

Steadfastly Loyal to the Absent Shepherd. 5:9-7:10.
A. Love Challenged. 5:9.
B. The Shepherd Described. 5:10-16.
C. Love Challenged. 6:1.
D. Devotion Expressed. 6:2-3.
E. Seduction Attempted. 6:4-7:9.
F. Devotion Expressed. 7:10.

IV. Salvation Accomplished and the Shulamite Rejoices in the Presence of the Shepherd-Lover. 7:11-8:14.
A. Devotion Expressed. 7:11-8:4.
B. The Journey Homeward. 8:5.
C. Commitment Desired. 8:6-7.
D. History Recounted. 8:8-12.
E. Conclusion. 8:13-14.

COMMENTARY

I. INTRODUCTION. 1:1.

1:1. The title is suggestive of the Song's superlative character. Solomon wrote one thousand and five songs (I Kgs 4:32), and this is the grandest of all his songs. Compare such Hebrew idioms as "King of Kings," "Holy of Holies," "Lord of Lords," and "Vanity of Vanities." In the Midrash we read that the Song of Songs is "the most praiseworthy, most excellent, most highly treasured among the Songs." This is the Song of Songs because it speaks of Love's great victory over all temptations to infidelity.

II. SEPARATION ACCOMPLISHED AND THE SHULAMITE REFLECTS SADLY UPON THE ABSENCE OF HER SHEPHERD-LOVER. 1:2-5:8.

A. The Shulamite Abducted. 1:2-2:7.

THE song of songs, which *is* Sŏl'o-mon's.

2 Let him kiss me with the kisses of his mouth: for thy love *is* better than wine.

2. **Let him kiss me with the kisses of his mouth.** The Shulamite does not name the person whose kiss she desires. For her, there is only one such person. The memories of her shepherd's love are fresh upon her heart; yet, she longs for a sweet token of it. The heart of the bride-to-be is filled with longing for the absent bridegroom. The kiss is a token of honest love and affection between blood relations and friends (Gen 29:11; I Sam 10:1; Ps 2:12).

In comparing such love with wine, the heart of the comparison is not the intoxicating power of wine, but primarily its sweetness. In Scripture, beverage wine (Heb *yayin*) is distinguished from strong drink (Heb *shēkar*). Wine exhilarates but its effects are evanescent. Love effects a much more endearing and permanent response.

3 Because of the savour of thy good ointments thy name *is as* ointment poured forth, therefore do the virgins love thee.

3. **Because of the savor of thy good ointments thy name is as ointment poured forth.** Many are the ointments that are highly prized by the peoples of the East. These oils, which are compounds of precious and fragrant ingredients, were used in the anointing of kings and priests, as well as honored guests. (Ex 30:22-33; I Sam 16:13; Jn 12:3). To the Shulamite maiden the sweet perfumes symbolize the many graces that were evidently prominent in her beloved's character.

The beloved's very name is filled with a holy aroma. His name is to her as the name of that one who is wonderful. (Isa 9:6). So wonderful is the name that it cannot be kept in a box or container, as was the usual custom, but rather must be poured forth that all may know its sweetness.

All who are pure and whose affections have not been pledged to another are attracted to this fragrant shepherd. The Shulamite recognizes this and feels that many other virgins besides her are attracted to the shepherd with admiring devotion and love.

4 Draw me, we will run after thee: the king hath brought me into his chambers: we will be glad and rejoice in

4. **Draw me, we will run after thee: the King hath brought me into his chambers.** Her heart's desire is to be united with the shepherd once again. She desires to escape from the chambers of the king with her attendants. She cries out for the

thee, we will remember thy love more than wine: the upright love thee.

5 ¶I *am* black, but comely, O ye daughters of Jerusalem, as the tents of Kē'dar, as the curtains of Sŏl'o-mon.

6 Look not upon me, because I *am* black, because the sun hath looked upon me: my mother's children were angry with me; they made me the keeper of the vineyards; *but* mine own vineyard have I not kept.

7 Tell me, O thou whom my soul loveth, where thou feedest, where thou makest *thy flock* to rest at noon: for why should I be as one that turneth aside by the flocks of thy companions?

8 ¶If thou know not, O thou fairest among women, go thy way forth by the footsteps of the flock, and feed thy kids beside the shepherds' tents.

9 I have compared thee, O my love, to a company of horses in Pharaoh's chariots.

10 Thy cheeks are comely with rows of *jewels*, thy neck with chains *of gold*.

shepherd-lover to draw them after him, that they may run to the place of freedom with him.

The king has taken her forcibly to his private apartments. Eastern potentates allowed none but their favored friends to their inner chamber. Here in this hidden place she is kept as the private property of the king.

She finds no delight in the pleasures of the kings' court. Her delight is in the companionship of that one to whom she has betrothed her affections and undying loyalty. He alone is her cause of rejoicing. The wine represents the gifts of the king. In the presence of such gifts she steadfastly prefers the love and the person of the shepherd. **The upright love thee.** The Hebrew is "in uprightness" and suggests that it is not at all surprising that the shepherd is the object of such love.

5. I am black, but comely, O ye daughters of Jerusalem. This verse represents what is called an alternative in Hebrew poetry. The verse should read: I am dark as the tents of Kedar, but comely as the curtains of Solomon. The Shulamite's complexion is deeply sunburnt (cf. vs. 6) from the open life of the country. **Kedar** refers to a nomadic tribe that roamed the deserts of Northwest Arabia. Their tents were made of skins that were very dark in color and were rather unsightly. In contrast, the curtains of Solomon were lavishly beautiful. Our country maiden expresses with frankness the difference in appearance which the sun has wrought upon her.

6. Look not upon me, because I am black, because the sun hath looked upon me: my mother's children were angry with me; they made me the keeper of the vineyards; but mine own vineyard have I not kept. The Shulamite maiden had received many curious looks from the daughters of Jerusalem and quite probably a few jeering comments. **Look not** could be translated Do not stare at me with disdain. She proceeds to explain the reasons for her blackness. Her brothers had consigned to her the task of keeping the vineyards. These brothers appear toward the end of the Song as the rigorous guardians of their younger sister. One is led to suppose that the Shulamite's own father was deceased and that sons of the first or second marriage ruled in the house of the Shulamite's mother. With the object of keeping the young maiden from her shepherd-lover, they banished her to a place beyond his ready reach. Under the pressure of her tasks in the vineyards, she had little time to care for her own physical needs. In the interest of separating the two lovers the brothers had assigned her difficult tasks that did not allow her time for any of the beauty care in which the average young lady might indulge. Her task was indeed a hard one. Vinedressers were among the poorer classes in the land of Israel (II Kgs 25:12). In the millennial kingdom freedom from this toil is among the promised blessings to Israel (Isa 61:5).

7. Tell me, O thou whom my soul loveth, where thou feedest, where thou makest thy flock to rest at noon. Her desire is to know the location of the shepherd whom she loves. Ginsburg suggests that **turneth aside** be translated to roam or to wander (p. 136). Knowing the whereabouts of her shepherd will thus prevent the necessity of her roaming amongst the flocks of his fellow shepherds in search of him.

8. If thou know not. The court ladies, hearing the maiden's plea, bid her to depart and search for the shepherd. **Fairest among women** is undoubtedly meant in an ironical sense. They would be glad to see this rival depart. Keeping near the **kids beside the shepherds' tents** she would undoubtedly find her lover.

9-11. I have compared thee, O my love. Ginsburg and Clarke are agreed that Solomon begins to speak here. He first praises her beauty and gracefulness by comparing her to his stately chariot steed. Such steeds were ornamented with costly harnesses and the most elegant of headgear. In return for her

11 We will make thee borders of gold with studs of silver.

12 ¶While the king *sitteth* at his table, my spikenard sendeth forth the smell thereof.
13 A bundle of myrrh *is* my well-beloved unto me; he shall lie all night betwixt my breasts.
14 My beloved *is* unto me *as* a cluster of camphire in the vineyard of Ĕn-gē´dī.

15 Behold, thou *art* fair, my love; behold, thou *art* fair; thou *hast* doves' eyes.
16 Behold, thou *art* fair, my beloved, yea, pleasant: also our bed *is* green.
17 The beams of our house *are* cedar, *and* our rafters of fir.

CHAPTER 2

I *AM* the rose of Shä´ron, *and* the lily of the valleys.

2 As the lily among thorns, so *is* my love among the daughters.
3 As the apple tree among the trees of the wood, so *is* my beloved among the sons. I sat down under his shadow with great delight, and his fruit *was* sweet to my taste.

4 He brought me to the banqueting house, and his banner over me *was* love.

5 Stay me with flagons, comfort me with apples: for I *am* sick of love.
6 His left hand *is* under my head, and his right hand doth embrace me.

7 I charge you, O ye daughters of Jerusalem, by the roes, and by the hinds of the field, that ye stir not up, nor awake *my* love, till he please.

affirmative response to his advances, the king promises costly gifts. She is indeed beautiful, but with the expensive adornments which he will give her she will have an unsurpassable beauty. She is to have necklaces of silver discs and gold beads. Such jewelry is to replace the poor ornaments worn by the maiden, perhaps the gifts of her shepherd-lover.

12-14. While the King sitteth at his table. Literally, while the king reclines in his circle of friends. Spikenard is strictly a product of India and a costly perfume (*Int. Bible.*, p. 109). My beloved. The Hebrew *dōd* (beloved) is used twenty-five times by the Shulamite and seven times by others. It always refers to the shepherd-lover. This fact provides an important clue to the interpretation of the Song. The bundle of myrrh is a scent bag or sachet worn in the bosom and suspended from the neck on a silk thread. The Shulamite confesses that her beloved is to her what this delightful perfume is to others. In her heart's eye he was as close to her as the sachet of myrrh nestled between her breasts. He is also to be likened to the camphire in the vineyards of En-gedi. En-gedi is a lush oasis below a plateau overlooking the Dead Sea. Her loved one is like a beautiful flower. Henna flowers are from a privet-like shrub bearing small, inconspicuous but fragrant white to yellow blossoms (Clarke, p. 42).

15-17. The Shulamite now relates an intimate dialogue between the shepherd and herself. She begins with the words of the shepherd. Thou art fair (*yapeh*, lit., beautiful or comely). Its double use here indicates the ardor of the young man's love for the beautiful maiden. The dove is symbolic of gentleness (cf. Mt 10:16). They are also known for fidelity, having only one mate for life. Verses 16-17 contain the reply of the Shulamite. She replies that he, too, is comely. More than that, he is pleasant, i.e., luxuriant; and their place of meeting was also luxuriant. Their couch did not have the artificial beauty of Solomon's. Their couch was the green carpet of the fields, and their palace consisted of the beautiful cedar, and our rafters of fir.

2:1. I am the rose of Sharon. The Plain of Sharon was famous for its flowers and pasture lands. The maiden is saying, I am merely a flower of the plain. I am only one among a host of others. Why, she is asking, would you choose me?

2-3. As the lily among thorns. Thorns or brambles are a sign of the curse God placed upon the ground (Gen 3:17, 18). No, he replies, you are not ordinary. You are as the beautiful lily among a bouquet of thorns. You are as the apple tree (*tapûach*), she replies (lit., a cultivated tree), a tree of great value, like the citrus tree, which stands out conspicuously from the ordinary trees of the forest. Delightedly, she sits under his shadow. Sat down speaks of rest, and fruit tells of the refreshment she receives from being in his presence.

4. Banqueting house. Perhaps she now suggests an arbor of vines, a special place where they partook of simple meals. A contrast may be in her mind as she has now witnessed the ornate canopy spread above the host and principal guest at Solomon's meals. Her shepherd had no such expensive banner. His banner over me was love.

5-6. Stay me with flagons. Love and longing for her absent lover have literally weakened her to the point of exhaustion. She appeals to the women of the harem to bring her flagons (i.e., lit., cakes of raisins and citron). Citrons were famous for their reviving powers. Verse 6 is probably best understood as an expression of longing, O that his left hand is under my head.

7. I charge you . . . stir not up, nor awake my love. Having stated her warm and undiminished attachment to her beloved shepherd, the Shulamite addresses the court ladies who, as we have seen, tried to gain her affections for the king (Ginsburg, p. 143).

8 ¶The voice of my beloved! behold, he cometh leaping upon the mountains, skipping upon the hills.

9 My beloved is like a roe or a young hart: behold, he standeth behind our wall, he looketh forth at the windows, shewing himself through the lattice.

10 My beloved spake, and said unto me, Rise up, my love, my fair one, and come away.

11 For, lo, the winter is past, the rain is over *and* gone;

12 The flowers appear on the earth; the time of the singing *of birds* is come, and the voice of the turtle is heard in our land;

13 The fig tree putteth forth her green figs, and the vines *with* the tender grape give a *good* smell. Arise, my love, my fair one, and come away.

14 O my dove, *that art* in the clefts of the rock, in the secret *places* of the stairs, let me see thy countenance, let me hear thy voice; for sweet *is* thy voice, and thy countenance *is* comely.

15 Take us the foxes, the little foxes, that spoil the vines: for our vines *have* tender grapes.

16 ¶My beloved *is* mine, and I *am* his: he feedeth among the lilies.

17 Until the day break, and the shadows flee away, turn, my beloved, and be thou like a roe or a young hart upon the mountains of Be'ther.

CHAPTER 3

BY night on my bed I sought him whom my soul loveth: I sought him, but I found him not.

2 I will rise now, and go about the city in the streets, and in the broad ways I will seek him whom my soul loveth: I sought him, but I found him not.

3 The watchmen that go about the city found me: *to whom I said*, Saw ye him whom my soul loveth?

4 *It was* but a little that I passed from

B. The Beginnings of Love Described. 2:8-3:5.

8-9. The voice of my beloved! The speakers in these verses are the Shulamite and the court ladies. In 1:6 the maiden had spoken of the ill treatment she received from her brothers. She now informs the court ladies of the reason for that treatment. She describes the coming of the sheperd as the surefooted stag or gazelle, covering difficult mountain terrain. No obstacle could keep him from his love. Soon he is behind the wall; he looketh forth at the windows. He approaches the wall of the village, and from there he moves to the windows where she beholds him peering through the lattice. In Eastern lands windows are unglazed and of latticework so closely set together that a person outside cannot see what is taking place within, yet anyone inside can see all that goes on outside.

10-11. Rise up, my love. The Shulamite here records the words of the shepherd. He urges her to come with him to enjoy the charm of the fields, for winter and the rains have ceased.

12. The voice of the turtle is heard in our land. The time of singing (*zamir*) has arrived. The voices of the bulbul (nightingale) abounded in the wooded valleys, filling the air in early spring with the rich cadence of their notes (*Tristrans Nat. His. of the Bible*, p. 160). The turtle (Heb *tōr*) is the turtledove. It is a migrating bird, and its advent marks the return of spring (Jer 8:7).

13. The fig tree putteth forth her green figs. In Palestine the first crop of ripe figs appears in the early spring and ripens in early June. Literally, the line might read, the fig tree sweetens her green figs and the vines are in blossom (Ginsburg p. 146).

14. O my dove, that art in the clefts of the rock. The maiden cloistered in her house is as unapproachable as the dove who selects the lofty cliffs and the deep ravine for its roosting place. In poetic language, the shepherd seeks to overcome her timidity. He appeals to her to put aside her shyness and let him see her countenance and hear her voice.

15. The little foxes, that spoil the vines. The Shulamite here recounts the response of her brothers to the shepherd's invitation. To prevent any further involvement from materializing, the brothers command her to go to the vineyard, to catch the foxes (cf. 1:6a). The young foxes were especially injurious to the vineyard. Both young foxes and jackals are known to work havoc in Palestinian vineyards. They play among the vines, dig holes, and spoil fences. Although carnivorous, they are also fond of young shoots and grapes; so they need to be trapped or driven away before the fruit begins to ripen (Clarke, p. 52).

16-17. The maiden is heard in reply to her brothers. She will not be separated from her beloved, and she knows where he is. They may keep them apart for a time, but she has settled the matter in her mind; **My beloved is mine, and I am his.** She then turns to the shepherd and expresses her desire that he would return when the day breaks and the shadows flee away and her work in the vineyard is completed. She adjures him to come with the same dexterity and speed that brought him to her side initially. **Bether** means separation or division. She pleads with him to span the mountains of their separation.

3:1-5. By night on my bed. It appears that the shepherd was not able to return in the evening as they had hoped. This passage and 5:2-7 are usually interpreted as dream sequences. These nightly dreams, which are born in the midst of her longing for his return, soon turn to nightmares. His delay awakened in her the apprehension that some disaster may have befallen him. She decided to **seek him who my soul loveth.** While on the search, she met the watchmen and immediately inquired of them if they had seen him. Shortly after her encounter with the watchmen, she found her shepherd and held him tightly, fearing that she

them, but I found him whom my soul loveth: I held him, and would not let him go, until I had brought him into my mother's house, and into the chamber of her that conceived me.

5 I charge you, O ye daughters of Jerusalem, by the roes, and by the hinds of the field, that ye stir not up, nor awake my love, till he please.

6 ¶Who is this that cometh out of the wilderness like pillars of smoke, perfumed with myrrh and frankincense, with all powders of the merchant?

7 Behold his bed, which is Sŏl'o-mon's; threescore valiant men are about it, of the valiant of Israel.
8 They all hold swords, being expert in war: every man hath his sword upon his thigh because of fear in the night.
9 King Sŏl'o-mon made himself a chariot of the wood of Lebanon.
10 He made the pillars thereof of silver, the bottom thereof of gold, the covering of it of purple, the midst thereof being paved with love, for the daughters of Jerusalem.

11 Go forth, O ye daughters of Zion, and behold king Sŏl'o-mon with the crown wherewith his mother crowned him in the day of his espousals, and in the day of the gladness of his heart.

CHAPTER 4

BEHOLD, thou art fair, my love; behold, thou art fair; thou hast doves' eyes within thy locks: thy hair is as a flock of goats, that appear from mount Gilead.

2 Thy teeth are like a flock of sheep that are even shorn, which came up from the washing; whereof every one

might lose him again (Mt 28:9; Jn 20:17). Her love, though ardent, was chaste and proper love. She desired that he accompany her to meet her mother, whose decision she hoped would countermand the harsh decisions of her brothers. One who had improper thoughts would hardly take her lover to her mother's bedchamber. Having expressed her deep love for the shepherd, she once again pleads with the ladies of the court to desist from their attempts to persuade her to love Solomon. She had met her right man and she wishes not to give her love to any other (cf. Rev 2:4).

C. The Journey to Jerusalem. 3:6-11.

6. Who is this . . . ? A change in the situation is reflected in these verses. We are now provided with insight which helps us to understand how the maiden's abduction occurred. Solomon's encampment has been broken up, and the caravan has moved from the neighborhood of the Shulamite's home. It is now described by spectators who view the train moving toward Jerusalem. "What is this commotion?" asks the spectator as he views the caravan moving out of the open country toward the cultivated areas which surround the city. In the countryside the caravan comes upon the unsuspecting maiden (cf. 6:4-13). The **pillars of smoke** were the incense that was customarily burned at the head of important processions. Such incense served to purify the air of offensive odors.

7-10. Behold his bed, literally, the litter or the palanquin. Another spectator, recognizing at a distance the litter with the king's bodyguard surrounding it, exclaims that Solomon's cortege is approaching. Sixty men chosen especially for their skill with weapons have been chosen to protect the cortege from night attack. A brief description of the palanquin is given in verses 9-10. It was constructed of the woods of Lebanon: cedar, cypress, fir, and pine. The oak rest (bottom), against which the occupant leaned, was covered with gold and the royal crimson colors. The pillars that supported the weight of the litter were generally painted with flowers, and short sentences were written on the walls which expressed the power of the king.

The middle of the litter was paved with expressions of love by the daughters of Jerusalem.

11. Go forth, O ye daughters of Zion. As the cortege draws near to the city, one of the spectators calls the daughters of Zion to come out to view the monarch and his crown. The crown here is not the crown of royalty, but the nuptial chaplet worn by a bridegroom. He is wearing the crown his mother gave him when he was married.

D. The Shepherd Appears. 4:1-5:1.

4:1. Behold, thou art fair. The shepherd now appears upon the scene. Concerned for her welfare amid the splendor and temptation of Solomon's court, he has sped to Jerusalem to seek her out. When he finds her, he encourages her at this critical point in her life by once again expressing his undiminished affection for her. Using striking poetic language, he enumerates her charms. The perfect proportion of her body is mentioned. It is well to remind ourselves that such a description of a female's physical attractions is not to be judged by our Western standards (Clarke, p. 60). Easterners were far less inhibited in this area.

Thy hair is as a flock of goats. Her locks (tsamah) are as beautiful as Mount Gilead covered with the shaggy goat herd. The hair of Oriental goats is exceedingly delicate, soft (Gen 27:16), long, and black (I Sam 19:13); and when the sun shines upon it, it reflects such a glare that the eye can hardly bear the luster (Ginsburg, p. 154).

2-5. Thy teeth. Her teeth are as white as newly washed sheep. **Bear twins.** The Hebrew word literally means to make double or to occur in pairs. The perfect and regular rows of her

bear twins, and none *is* barren among them.

3 Thy lips *are* like a thread of scarlet, and thy speech *is* comely: thy temples *are* like a piece of a pomegranate within thy locks.

4 Thy neck *is* like the tower of David builded for an armoury, whereon there hang a thousand bucklers, all shields of mighty men.

5 Thy two breasts *are* like two young roes that are twins, which feed among the lilies.

6 Until the day break, and the shadows flee away, I will get me to the mountain of myrrh, and to the hill of frankincense.

7 Thou *art* all fair, my love; *there is* no spot in thee.

8 ¶Come with me from Lebanon, *my* spouse, with me from Lebanon: look from the top of A-mā′na, from the top of She′nir and Her′mon, from the lions' dens, from the mountains of the leopards.

9 Thou hast ravished my heart, my sister, *my* spouse; thou hast ravished my heart with one of thine eyes, with one chain of thy neck.

10 How fair is thy love, my sister, *my* spouse! how much better is thy love than wine! and the smell of thine ointments than all spices!

11 Thy lips, O *my* spouse, drop *as* the honeycomb: honey and milk *are* under thy tongue; and the smell of thy garments *is* like the smell of Lebanon.

12 A garden inclosed *is* my sister, *my* spouse; a spring shut up, a fountain sealed.

13 Thy plants *are* an orchard of pomegranates, with pleasant fruits; camphire, with spikenard,

14 Spikenard and saffron; calamus and cinnamon, with all trees of frankincense; myrrh and aloes, with all the chief spices:

15 A fountain of gardens, a well of living waters, and streams from Lebanon.

16 ¶Awake, O north wind; and come, thou south; blow upon my garden, *that* the spices thereof may flow out. Let my beloved come into his garden, and eat his pleasant fruits.

teeth are exactly paired, and not one tooth is missing. **Thy lips are like a thread of scarlet.** Her lips are not unduly thick, and they have a natural red tone which signifies good health. **Thy temples** or the upper part of her cheeks resemble the interior of a pomegranate; they have a rosy hue. This also symbolizes health and attractiveness to the shepherd. **Thy neck is like the tower of David.** The tower of David (Neh 3:25-27) was at the summit of Zion and was made of white marble. The interior of the tower was embellished with an innumerable store of weapons and trophies from David's many victories (cf. Ezk 27:10, 11). She is a mighty one, and she can withstand the temptation that Solomon shall place before her. **Thy two breasts.** Among Orientals there is a greater freedom to discuss the female bosom, and it was often bared in public for the feeding of infants. The beauty of her breasts suggests to him that she has reached womanhood and is eligible for marriage.

6. I will get me to the mountain of myrrh. The shepherd informs the maiden that a temporary separation is to be endured. The mountains of myrrh and the hill of frankincense were probably certain localities about the royal palace (Lange, p. 86). Perhaps he must go there to plot their escape from the court.

7-9. Thou art all fair. The shepherd speaks afresh, and once again his mouth is filled with praise for her impeccable beauty. **Come with me.** He desires to aid her in her planned escape and thus insure an immediate exit to the beauty of the mountains of Lebanon. From the safety of those heights they shall be able to avoid the king (lions) and the leopards (his courtiers). **Thou hast ravished my heart,** literally, put heart into me. The great courage that he feels is due to the renewed knowledge of her continued love for him. One look into her eyes and the renewed sight of her beautiful neck has incarcerated him as with a mighty chain.

10-16. My sister, my spouse! Love in this verse is in the plural (Heb *dōdīm*). **Sister** speaks of blood relationship. It does not imply that she was related to him, but only that he felt an endearment for her that was broader than sexual desire. **My spouse,** speaks of the covenant of love into which they each have freely entered. She has indicated to him, you are my right man and I will forsake all others for you. He has said to her, you are my bride and for you I forsake all others and covenant to cleave unto you all the days of my life.

His ravished heart continues on in praise of her beauty. **Thy lips** are like the **honeycomb** (Heb *nōpet*, i.e., virgin honey). Her speech was as sweet as honey and as wholesome as milk. **The smell of thy garments.** Everything about her smells good to him. Garments in Scripture often symbolize the conduct of the person (cf. Ps 45:8).

A garden inclosed. Her heart belongs only to him. She has told him so, and his heart can safely trust in her word (Prov 31:11). Note the frequent occurrence of **my** in verses 12, 16, and 5:1. **Shut up . . . sealed** (vs. 12). In the East, gardens are frequently barred to the public, not only to secure the desired privacy but to conserve the water supply and preserve it from pollution. Water is scarce and therefore precious (Clarke, p. 69). Equally precious to the shepherd is this virtuous woman who has voluntarily sealed herself off for him alone.

Thy plants. She is a garden to the shepherd, but not just an ordinary garden. She is an orchard filled with the most costly trees and producing the most pleasant of fruits. Orchard is from the Persian word *paradis* and means, literally, paradise. The pomegranate was the chosen symbol of fruitfulness (for **camphire** or henna see 1:13; for spikenard see 1:13-14). **Saffron** appears only here in the Old Testament. It was esteemed for its flavoring and medicinal properties. **Calamus** was an aromatic cane coming from Arabia and India. **Cinnamon**

was also used as a perfume. **With all trees** which served in the making of incense she is to be likened. **Frankincense** was a whitish resin and was used with cinnamon and calamus in the production of the holy incense (Ex 30:24). It was also added to the meal offering and seems to symbolize personal righteousness (Lev 2:1, 2). **Myrrh** is the gum resin which came from an incision in a tree of the terebinth order. The substance hardens into a brown, translucent substance. It had a bitter taste, but a pleasant odor. **Aloe** was a resinous oil extracted from the trunk of certain trees.

Having described the maiden's physical charms in verses 1-7, the shepherd turned to consider the graces of her character in verses 8-16. The most pleasant things he can think of do not serve to fully express the beauty of his faithful Shulamite. **All the chief spices** only serve to begin to recount her fairness.

To finish the picture of this charming garden, he introduces streams, wells, and a cooling wind to waft abroad the delightful scent of his lovely sister bride. The shepherd desires that others should be benefited by her graces as well as himself.

5:1. The last two lines of verse 16 are from the lips of the Shulamite. If my person really resembles such a paradise, this garden with all of its productions is yours, all yours. To him she gives the treasures that she had locked away from King Solomon. The day of their formal union is fully anticipated in these verses.

The chapter division here seems inappropriate. The shepherd gives an immediate and excited response to her expression of total commitment. The verbs are in the perfect tense and are best understood in the modified sense known to grammarians as the perfect of confidence or certainty, anticipating in time the fulfillment of some purpose or cherished hope (Clarke, p. 71). "I will come into my garden; I will gather my myrrh with my spice; I will eat; I will drink," would thus be the preferable translation. The end of verse 1 would probably best be understood as an expression of sympathy and encouragement from some of the ladies of the court who may have been looking on at a distance.

CHAPTER 5

I AM come into my garden, my sister, *my* spouse: I have gathered my myrrh with my spice; I have eaten my honeycomb with my honey; I have drunk my wine with my milk: eat, O friends; drink, yea, drink abundantly, O beloved.

E. The Advancement of Love Recounted. 5:2-8.

2. The shepherd is absent as this section opens (cf. 4:6). Most are agreed that the second main division of the Song commences at this point. The Shulamite relates to the court ladies a second dream in which she experienced the fear of losing her beloved. In all likelihood the dream may be placed chronologically right after the one recorded in 3:1-4. **I sleep.** The story that began in chapter 3 is greatly amplified. The sympathies extended by the ladies of the court have encouraged her to share more deeply her love for the shepherd. To accomplish this she recounts an additional dream. In her dream the shepherd knocks at her door, and she hears him asking for admittance: **Open to me.** His language is suggestive of the moral purity he assigns to her; she is **my love** (cf. 1:15), **my dove** (cf. 2:14), **my undefiled. My head is filled with dew.** He appears at her door drenched with dew. The dew falls heavily in the East and saturates the clothes.

2 ¶ I sleep, but my heart waketh: *it is* the voice of my beloved that knocketh, *saying,* Open to me, my sister, my love, my dove, my undefiled: for my head is filled with dew, *and* my locks with the drops of the night.

3. I have put off my coat. The tunic was an undergarment that covered the entire body and was removed before retiring. She desires to answer his knock, but maidenly modesty holds her back. She has already washed her feet and retired to her bed.

3 I have put off my coat; how shall I put it on? I have washed my feet; how shall I defile them?

4. My beloved put in his hand. The hole is an aperture made in the door above the lock for the insertion of the hand with the key. A caller might also be seen through this opening. It was a safety precaution that allowed a certain measure of security for the person opening the door (cf. Acts 12:13-16). **Put in** might be better translated withdrew. Unsuccessful in his attempt to gain entrance, he withdrew his hand from the opening and left. Recognizing that his departure has been initiated, her bowels or

4 My beloved put in his hand by the hole *of the door*, and my bowels were moved for him.

5 I rose up to open to my beloved; and my hands dropped *with* myrrh, and my fingers *with* sweet smelling myrrh, upon the handles of the lock.

6 I opened to my beloved; but my beloved had withdrawn himself, *and was* gone: my soul failed when he spake: I sought him, but I could not find him; I called him, but he gave me no answer.

7 The watchmen that went about the city found me, they smote me, they wounded me; the keepers of the walls took away my vail from me.

8 I charge you, O daughters of Jerusalem, if ye find my beloved, that ye tell him, that I *am* sick of love.

9 ¶What *is* thy beloved more than *another* beloved, O thou fairest among women? what *is* thy beloved more than *another* beloved, that thou dost so charge us?

10 ¶My beloved *is* white and ruddy, the chiefest among ten thousand.

11 His head *is as* the most fine gold, his locks *are* bushy, *and* black as a raven.
12 His eyes *are* as *the eyes* of doves by the rivers of waters, washed with milk, *and* fitly set.
13 His cheeks *are* as a bed of spices, *as* sweet flowers: his lips *like* lilies, dropping sweet smelling myrrh.
14 His hands *are as* gold rings set with the beryl: his belly *is as* bright ivory overlaid *with* sapphires.
15 His legs *are* as pillars of marble, set upon sockets of fine gold: his countenance *is* as Lebanon, excellent as the cedars.
16 His mouth *is* most sweet: yea, he *is* altogether lovely. This *is* my beloved, and this *is* my friend, O daughters of Jerusalem.

CHAPTER 6
WHITHER is thy beloved gone, O thou

heart, i.e., the seat of her emotions, was set in a condition of turmoil.

5. I rose up. The cessation of his knock caused her great alarm. At once she hastened to the door. In grasping the bolt of the door, her hands came into contact with the **myrrh** which the shepherd had poured upon the bolts.

6-7. My beloved had withdrawn himself (lit., had turned away). The Hebrew indicates a turning with deep distress. **My soul failed.** We are not informed of the shepherd's response; his words are not recorded. We only know that in retreating **he spake** and her heart sunk. **I sought him.** Into the dark of the night she pursues him, calling after him; but he is not to be found. In the city she meets with ill treatment at the hands of the watchmen. The veil (Heb *redid*) is a type of shawl that Eastern women placed over their shoulders and head when going out doors. The face was also covered, hence the translation veil. These guardians of the city wrench it from her and treat her as a wanton woman.

8. I am sick of love. Having informed the ladies of the court of the seeming callousness with which she had treated her shepherd, she is anxious to impress upon them the genuine quality of her feelings. You tell him that I am sick with love if you see him, is her admonition. In 2:5 this lovesickness resulted from excess of joy at the presence of her beloved; now it arose from excess of pain at his absence.

III. SEDUCTION ATTEMPTED AND THE SHULAMITE REMAINS STEADFASTLY LOYAL TO THE ABSENT SHEPHERD. 5:9-7:10.

A. Love Challenged. 5:9.

9. What is thy beloved more than another beloved. The court ladies began to ask satirical questions meant to deride the maiden and the shepherd. The Shulamite responds with a lengthy description of her beloved designed to delineate the superiority of his charms.

B. The Shepherd Described. 5:10-16.

10. My beloved is white and ruddy. His countenance is a perfect mixture of white and red. He is clear of skin and rosy red. He is also **chiefest** (a standard-bearer) among ten thousand. He stands out from the multitudes, even as the standard-bearer stands out from the multitude of regular soldiers.

11-16. His head is as the most fine gold (lit., gold of gold). Gold that has been doubly refined. His **eyes** with irises surrounded by clear white were perfectly spaced and are set as gems in a ring. His beard upon his **cheeks** is compared to beds of aromatic plants. His lips are pictured as the dispensers of spices and myrrh. His **hands** resemble golden cylinders, and his body reminds her of polished ivory. His legs are symbols of strength and stability. They are pillars of marble or alabaster set upon foundations of purest gold. **His mouth.** The members of the shepherd have been described in striking terms. He is, however, no inanimate statue. Most pleasing of all is the voice that emanates from this noble and commanding shepherd. His voice is altogether lovely, i.e., melodious.

This is my beloved, and this is my friend. Emphatically and with joy, she concludes, "This is my beloved! This is my friend!" Friend is used for the first time here by the Shulamite. These symbols of companionship, i.e., sister and friend, are important contributions to the biblical doctrine of love. The man or woman is not merely a sexual object, but in every sense a companion as well.

C. Love Challenged. 6:1.

6:1. Whither is thy beloved gone . . . ? Satire may be inhe-

fairest among women? whither is thy beloved turned aside? that we may seek him with thee.

2 ¶My beloved is gone down into his garden, to the beds of spices, to feed in the gardens, and to gather lilies.
3 I *am* my beloved's, and my beloved *is* mine: he feedeth among the lilies.

4 ¶Thou *art* beautiful, O my love, as Tir'zah, comely as Jerusalem, terrible as *an army* with banners.
5 Turn away thine eyes from me, for they have overcome me: thy hair *is* as a flock of goats that appear from Gilead.
6 Thy teeth *are* as a flock of sheep which go up from the washing, whereof every one beareth twins, and *there is* not one barren among them.
7 As a piece of a pomegranate *are* thy temples within thy locks.

8 There are threescore queens, and fourscore concubines, and virgins without number.
9 My dove, my undefiled is *but* one; she *is* the *only* one of her mother, she *is* the choice *one* of her that bare her. The daughters saw her, and blessed her; *yea*, the queens and the concubines, and they praised her.
10 ¶Who *is* she *that* looketh forth as the morning, fair as the moon, clear as the sun, *and* terrible as *an army* with banners?

11 I went down into the garden of nuts to see the fruits of the valley, *and* to see whether the vine flourished, *and* the pomegranates budded.
12 Or ever I was aware, my soul made me *like* the chariots of Am-mi'-na-dib.

13 Return, return, O Shū'lam-īte; return, return, that we may look upon thee. What will ye see in the Shū'lam-īte? As it were the company of two armies.

rent in this question. With mock sincerity the ladies of the court offer to seek out such a marvelously endowed person. They would like to share his company themselves.

D. Devotion Expressed. 6:2-3.

2-3. She informs them that his affections are solely hers. **I am my beloved's, and my beloved is mine.** Her reply to the question of his whereabouts is vague. She simply replies that he is gone to the garden to gather lilies.

E. Seduction Attempted. 6:4-7:9.

4-7. No sooner had the grand attestation of her beloved's character passed from the maiden's lips than Solomon appears and attempts once again to dissuade her from her unbending commitment.

Thou art beautiful, O my love, as Tirzah. Tirzah was the royal residence of Israel's kings after the revolt of Rehoboam. It was a city of tremendous beauty and was therefore named Tirzah, or delightful. **Terrible** is, literally, imposing or awe-inspiring. She was as wonderful to look at as many companies of warriors gathered around their respective banners, a sight that was a cause of special delight to a king. These awesome hosts are seen in the eyes of the Shulamite, and Solomon begs her to remove them from his gaze. They overcome him or, literally, cause him to be filled with awe. For verses 6 and 7 see 4:1-3.

8-10. There are threescore queens, literally, I have three-score queens, etc., but **My dove, my undefiled is but one.** The flattery extended here surpasses all that Solomon has yet given. Though he is surrounded by an innumerable group of beautiful women, the Shulamite is the loveliest of all. Her beauty has also been praised by the women of the court. Verse 10 is a summary of the words spoken by the court ladies on the occasion of their first encounter with the maiden. They were compelled to acknowledge her beauty. The rising morning, with its red light looking down from heaven and over the mountains (Joel 2:2), the beautiful and placid complexion of the **moon**, and the grandiose and resplendent appearance of the **sun**, have often afforded, both to the Oriental and to the Greek and Latin writers, exquisite similes for beauty and grandeur (Ginsburg, p. 174).

11-12. I went down into the garden of nuts. The Shulamite speaks here and explains to Solomon how the first meeting came about. It was not by design that her life became intertwined with the royal cortege. She had gone to the valley to gather fruit and herbs for her family. On her way to the valley, her progress was interrupted by an encounter with the royal cortege. Before she was aware of what was happening, she had been abducted and placed on the chariots of the great prince who is among my people, i.e., Solomon. Thus, she explains to Solomon how she came to be the subject of praise before the ladies of the court.

13. Return, return, O Shulamite. In the Hebrew Bible the seventh chapter begins here. The Shulamite has explained how she came to the notice of the king. Noting their interest, she began to retreat hastily while they cried for her return. In response to their entreaty she turns and asks, **What will ye see in the Shulamite?** i.e., What can you possibly see in a rustic country girl?

The men are heard in their reply; **As it were the company of two armies.** Literally, we look upon the Shulamite as one looks upon the dance of the Mahanaim. They see in her something that resembles the dance of the Mahanaim, something as magnificent and transporting as the dance of the angel host east of the Jordan on Jacob's return home to the Promised Land. See Genesis 32:1-3, to which passage there is an unmistakable allusion here, as Dopke, Delitzsch, Hengstenberg, and Meir correctly assume (Lange, p. 115). She represents for them the

CHAPTER 7

HOW beautiful are thy feet with shoes, O prince's daughter! the joints of thy thighs *are* like jewels, the work of the hands of a cunning workman.

2 Thy navel *is like* a round goblet, *which* wanteth not liquor: thy belly *is like* an heap of wheat set about with lilies.

3 Thy two breasts *are* like two young roes *that are* twins.

4 Thy neck *is* as a tower of ivory; thine eyes *like* the fishpools in Hĕsh'-bŏn, by the gate of Băth–răb'bĭm: thy nose *is* as the tower of Lebanon which looketh toward Damascus.

5 Thine head upon thee *is* like Car-mel, and the hair of thine head like purple; the king *is* held in the galleries.

6 How fair and how pleasant art thou, O love, for delights!

7 This thy stature is like to a palm tree, and thy breasts to clusters *of* grapes.

8 I said, I will go up to the palm tree, I will take hold of the boughs thereof: now also thy breasts shall be as clusters of the vine, and the smell of thy nose like apples;

9 And the roof of thy mouth like the best wine for my beloved, that goeth *down* sweetly, causing the lips of those that are asleep to speak.

charming view of a festive choir expressing their joy in jubilant dance.

7:1. Solomon continues his praise of her beauty and advances his attempt to dissuade the maiden's faithful affection for her shepherd-lover by describing ten of her features that he finds particularly beautiful. **How beautiful are thy feet.** Solomon first expresses appreciation for her feet and thighs. She walks with feet which are gracefully arched. Her thighs are rounded (Heb *chamūq*), or curving. When she walked, she seemed as one of magnificent bearing whose thighs had been molded by a master craftsman.

2. Thy navel is like a round goblet. Navel may denote the lower abdomen, and in Arabic the word was frequently translated secret part. Liquor (lit., mixed wine) was wine mixed with spice to improve on its ability to excite. Solomon's interest in her is sexual, and he describes that interest in the most seductive terms. **Thy belly is like a heap of wheat.** The appearance of heaps of wheat, which one might see in long parallel lines on the threshing floors in any village, was a sight that was well pleasing to every child in Israel. The color of wheat was regarded as a most pleasing color for the human body. The mixing of flowers with the harvested crop was a testimony to joy.

3. Thy two breasts (cf. notes at 4:5).

4. Thy neck (cf. with 4:4). **Thine eyes like the fishpools.** Heshbon was a town west of Amman. Literally, the name is translated intelligence. At one time it was a royal city of the Amorites, but now only its ruins remain. Near the main gate of this city were two reservoirs called Bath-rabbim (i.e., daughters of many). These were reportedly pools of unusual beauty. **Thy nose.** The tower of Lebanon must have contained a projection that was famous for its beauty. Her nose is to him similarly wonderfully proportioned.

5. Thine head upon thee is like Carmel. The marginal reading crimson, from Heb *karmil*, preserves the parallelism with the next clause better. Her flowing tresses and beautiful colored head are a source of great delight to Solomon. The king is literally captivated by them.

6. O love. Solomon now makes a final and almost desperate attempt to win the affection of the Shulamite. He presses his attentions with language that is unrestrained. The obvious intention is the satisfaction of his own carnal desires.

7. This thy stature is like to a palm tree. The palm tree (Heb *tamar*) often represents feminine beauty in the literature of the East. To the weary traveler the tree indicated the presence of water and the promise of fruit.

8. I said, I will . . . I will. The king now expresses the direction which his passions have urged him to pursue. **The boughs** are small stumps or protuberances left from the cutoff, or fallen, fronds. He wishes to climb these and partake of the fruit. These verses are satiated with his desire for immediate and total sexual satisfaction.

9. The king described the Shulamite's charms as possessing the stimulating power of mixed wine. He thus seeks to excuse the ardent expressions of his personal interest in her. The Shulamite interrupts his words with these words. **Wine for my beloved that goeth down sweetly.** Her love in its entirety is for the shepherd, and all of it must be saved for him. The closing words are difficult to interpret. Perhaps Solomon is heard here closing out his attempts with these words causing slumbering, literally unresponsive, lips to speak. She has spoken of little with him, but her love for the shepherd causes her lips to speak of her faithfulness.

10 ¶I *am* my beloved's, and his desire *is* toward me.

F. Devotion Expressed. 7:10.

10. I am my beloved's. The Shulamite here verbalizes her final rejection of Solomon's advances. **His desire is toward me.** The king is only an intruder on a heart that has already been pledged to another. She loves the shepherd because she realizes his deep love for her (cf. I Jn 4:19).

IV. SALVATION ACCOMPLISHED AND THE SHULAMITE REJOICES IN THE PRESENCE OF THE SHEPHERD-LOVER. 7:11-8:14.

A. Devotion Expressed. 7:11-8:4.

11 Come, my beloved, let us go forth into the field; let us lodge in the villages.

11. Come, my beloved. At this juncture in the Song the shepherd has once again moved on the scene. The maiden, overjoyed at his presence, urges a hasty withdrawal from the presence of Solomon and his retinue. **Let us.** The open air of the fields would be deeply appreciated after the stifling moral atmosphere of the king's court. The villages are much to be preferred to the noise and business of Jerusalem.

12 Let us get up early to the vineyards; let us see if the vine flourish, *whether* the tender grape appear, *and* the pomegranates bud forth: there will I give thee my loves.

12. Let us. Togetherness is the theme of this verse. Let us together visit those places upon which my thoughts have centered much in these days of captivity. She longs for the vineyards and the blossoms. Once returned to the security and beauty of this natural sanctuary, she promises him suitable tokens of her love.

13 The mandrakes give a smell, and at our gates *are* all manner of pleasant *fruits*, new and old, *which* I have laid up for thee, O my beloved.

13. The mandrakes. Another reason for hastening to that beautiful place is the *dūdā'îm*, or love apples. Many luscious fruits that have delighted their tastebuds await them once again in that final place of memory. This may refer in poetic language to her longing for the day when they shall be united in marriage.

CHAPTER 8

O THAT thou *wert* as my brother, that sucked the breasts of my mother! *when* I should find thee without, I would kiss thee; yea, I should not be despised.

2 I would lead thee, *and* bring thee into my mother's house, *who* would instruct me: I would cause thee to drink of spiced wine of the juice of my pomegranate.

3 His left hand *should be* under my head, and his right hand should embrace me.

8:1-3. O that thou wert as my brother. If he had but been her brother, she might have kissed him openly without reproach. She had not dared to openly display her affection for him and wishes that their familiar relationship had been such that it would have allowed them a far greater amount of companioning and sharing. The pomegranate juice was particularly esteemed as a fruit drink. She would have brought him into her **mother's house**, ruling out any clandestine motivation for this togetherness. **His left hand.** Exhausted by her moral combat with Solomon, she now wishes the gentle hand of her shepherd-lover to support her exhausted frame that she may rest and gain strength for their coming journey.

4 I charge you, O daughters of Jerusalem, that ye stir not up, nor awake *my* love, until he please.

4. I charge you. In this last scene before the Shulamite and the shepherd depart from the king's court, the Shulamite once again charges the court ladies that they never again try to draw her affection away from her shepherd. He is her beloved, and she will remain faithful to him forever.

B. The Journey Homeward. 8:5.

5 ¶Who *is* this that cometh up from the wilderness, leaning upon her beloved? I raised thee up under the apple tree: there thy mother brought thee forth: there she brought thee forth *that* bare thee.

5. Who is this . . . ? Convinced that the Shulamite's heart, indeed, belongs to another, Solomon dismisses her. In this verse we hear the response of the local villagers as the couple approaches their beloved home. **I raised thee up under the apple tree** (lit., I awakened your love here under this apple tree). Once again on familiar ground, their hearts are lifted to reminiscence. Here is the tree under which the shepherd had won her heart. There, beneath that tree, her mother had consented to their betrothal.

C. Commitment Desired. 8:6-7.

6 Set me as a seal upon thine heart, as a seal upon thine arm: for love *is* strong as death; jealousy *is* cruel as the grave: the coals thereof *are* coals of fire, *which hath* a most vehement flame.

7 Many waters cannot quench love,

6-7. The maiden, mindful of what passion can do to a man, urges a commitment to utter faithfulness from the shepherd. She admonishes him to set her as a seal, i.e., to indelibly imprint her upon his heart and his arm like the imprinting of a seal that forever ratifies a contract. She covets a settled assurance of his unwavering love. Her love for him is like a raging flame and is as

neither can the floods drown it: if a man would give all the substance of his house for love, it would utterly be contemned.

8 ¶We have a little sister, and she hath no breasts: what shall we do for our sister in the day when she shall be spoken for?

9 If she *be* a wall, we will build upon her a palace of silver: and if she *be* a door, we will inclose her with boards of cedar.

10 I *am* a wall, and my breasts like towers: then was I in his eyes as one that found favour.

11 Sŏl'o-mon had a vineyard at Bā'al-hā'mon; he let out the vineyard unto keepers; every one for the fruit thereof was to bring a thousand *pieces* of silver.

12 My vineyard, which *is* mine, *is* before me: thou, O Sŏl'o-mon, *must have* a thousand, and those that keep the fruit thereof two hundred.

13 Thou that dwellest in the gardens, the companions hearken to thy voice: cause me to hear *it*.

14 ¶Make haste, my beloved, and be thou like to a roe or to a young hart upon the mountains of spices.

strong as death. It is utterly irreversible. No earthly influence can destroy or drown her love for him. It cannot be bought, for it is a spontaneous gift; and all she asks is the love of his heart and the strength of his arm for abiding protection.

D. History Recounted. 8:8-12.

8-9. We have a little sister. Here she remembers a day when she was not yet of marriageable age. Her brothers are heard to express their desire to protect her. **If she be a wall** (i.e., a careful and godly woman they will give her a worthy dowry). **If she be a door** (i.e., giving ready access to lovers they will restrict her liberty). Her brothers were filled with a cautious spirit as they fulfilled the role of her deceased father. Now she would no longer need their protection, for the strong arm of her beloved bore upon it the seal of her love; and he would protect her all the days of her life.

10. I am a wall. She has kept herself chaste. She had resisted all the advances of Solomon and could now utter, without fear of dissenting opinion, that she was a wall. Her breasts had grown to beautiful proportions, but she had grown in moral understanding as well; so she never took lightly Jehovah's gift of femininity. Now there is one in whose eyes she has found favor. The time of her marriage is at hand; and, based upon her continuous chastity and compliance with the wishes of her brothers, she now desires them to fulfill their promise of a dowry.

11-12. Solomon had a vineyard. The proof of unbending morality is offered in this verse. Solomon had offered her a large vineyard in Baal-hamon if she would but compromise herself with him. The vineyard was so large that he let it out to a number of tenants, and each of them paid a thousand shekels annually and had two hundred shekels left for himself. She was truly a virtuous woman, and now she asks her brothers for the vineyard that she reasons ought to belong to her. Solomon is welcome to all the revenue and tenants he wants, but she is content with a small vineyard as a dowry and the companionship of her shepherd-lover.

E. Conclusion. 8:13-14.

13-14. In the gardens. In closing, the Shulamite has finished dealing with her brothers and wants once again to be joined to her shepherd. He has gone to the garden where he visits with his companions whom he has not seen for a while. His voice is heard in their midst. She cries for his hasty return that she may hear his voice. **Make haste.** Too long they have been separated. Now united, she longs for his voice and presence. Unrelentlessly she beseeches him to always hasten to her side with the speed of the swift-footed gazelle.

Thus the Song ends with an unparalleled testimony to the heights of joy that can be achieved by both male and female through the practice of absolute fidelity to the commands of Yahweh and the seal of marital love. Nowhere else in all the Scriptures is the character of faithful love so carefully described, a love that has its base in God's love for all of His children in every era of redemptive history, a love which is only possible for those who realize that both the ability to love and the objects to be loved are gifts from the Lord.

BIBLIOGRAPHY

*Burrowes, George. *A Commentary On The Song of Solomon*. London: The Banner of Truth Trust, 1958.

Clarke, Arthur G. *The Song of Songs*. Kansas City: Walterick Publishers, n.d.

Delitzsch, Franz. *Commentary on the Song of Songs*. Grand Rapids: Eerdmans Publishing Co., reprinted 1950.

*Gill, John. *An Exposition of the Song of Solomon*. Marshallton, Del.: The National Foundation for Christian Education, n.d.

*Ginsburg, Christian D. *The Song of Songs and Qoheleth*. New York: Ktav Publishing House, Inc., 1970.

Gordis, Robert. *Song of Songs: A Study, Modern Translation and Commentary*. New York: Jewish Theological Seminary of America, 1954.

Guthrie, D. and J.A. Motyer. *The New Bible Commentary, Revised*. Grand Rapids: Eerdmans Publishing Co., 1970.

Harper. A Song of Songs. In *Cambridge Bible*. New York: Macmillan Company, 1902.

Knight, E. Song of Songs. In *Torch Bible Commentaries*. New York: Macmillan Company, 1955.

LaBotz, Paul. *The Romance of the Ages*. Grand Rapids: Kregel Publications, 1965.

Meek, T. J. The Song of Songs. In *The Interpreter's Bible*, Vol. V. Ed. by George Arthur Buttrick. Nashville: Abingdon Press, 1956.

Rowley, H.H. The Interpretation of the Song of Songs. In *The Servant of the Lord and other Essays on the Old Testament*. London: Lutterworth Press, 1965.

Rylaarsdam, J.C. *Proverbs, Ecclesiastes, Song of Solomon*. In *Layman's Bible Commentary*. Richmond: John Knox Press, 1964.

Schonfield, Hugh J. *The Song of Songs*. New York: The New American Library, 1959.

The Book of

ISAIAH

INTRODUCTION

Isaiah stands at the peak of the Old Testament as the literary genius of the prophets of Israel. His book is the longest of the prophets and looks further into the future than any of its contemporaries. This amazing book of prophecy includes Isaiah's unique prophecies regarding Immanuel and the Suffering Servant.

Isaiah, the son of Amoz, was one of the most prominent citizens of Jerusalem, having access to both the royal and priestly leadership of the nation of Judah. *Yeshaʻ-Yahu* (translated as Joshua) means "the Lord is salvation." The significance of his name is revealed in his prophetic ministry, for he came on the scene of Judah's history at a time when it was of the utmost importance that the people realize that salvation was of the Lord, and not merely by man's own efforts. Isaiah found himself standing against the threat of rising imperialism by Assyria and the emergence of a spirit of universalism which began to turn his people from the concept of a theocracy to that of dependence upon an alliance with the surrounding nations of the Near East.

Historical Setting. Isaiah's long life spanned the rule of several kings. Born during the reign of Uzziah, Isaiah was called to his prophetic ministry the year the king died (740 B.C.). The prophet's birth, then, was likely to have been ca. 770-760 B.C. Jotham came to the throne and reigned from 750 to 732 B.C. He was followed by Ahaz (732-715 B.C.), and finally by Hezekiah (ca. 716-686 B.C.). In his early years Isaiah saw Judah in a time of prosperity and military strength. Soon, however, the rise of Tiglath-pileser III (or Pul) in Assyria became a constant threat to Judah's safety. Rapid change came upon Israel; Menahem died, Pekahiah was murdered, and by 740 B.C. Pekah seized the throne in Samaria. The same year, Uzziah died in Judah. Pekah immediately began an aggressive anti-Assyrian policy. At the same time, however, a pro-Assyrian party was gaining influence in Judah. At this juncture, Ahaz came to the throne of Judah. Having rejected the prophet's advice, Ahaz continued the pro-Assyrian policy. Little else is heard of Isaiah during the reign of Ahaz.

With the accession of Hezekiah to the throne, a new day came upon Judah. Pursuing a policy of reforms, the new king repaired and cleansed the Temple and returned to emphasizing the Mosaic law in determining national ethics. During these years as Hezekiah's chief advisor, Isaiah became a prime figure. How long the prophet lived beyond his associations with Hezekiah (ca. 700 B.C.) we do not know. Possibly, he lived until 680 B.C., when Sennacherib died. Tradition says that he was sawn in half by Manasseh, the evil king who followed Hezekiah (cf. Heb 11:37; Josephus, *Antiquities*, 10:3:1; and the pseudepigraphical book, *The Ascension of Isaiah*).

Authorship. Modern scholarship has severely criticized the unity and authenticity of the book of Isaiah since the late eighteenth century. The critics' arguments center on the stylistic differences between the first (chs. 1-39) and second (chs. 40-66) portions of the book and on the nature of predictive prophecy. The critical position runs parallel to the rise of anti-supernatural rationalism among European philosophers. Doderlein, Eichhorn, and Rosenmueller became the major advocates of the Deutero-Isaiah theory. Duhm added a third "Isaiah" and pushed the date of some of the material back to the first century B.C. With the discovery of the Dead Sea Scroll, 1 Q ISA (St. Mark's Manuscript), dating from at least 100 B.C., this view must now be rejected. There is no evidence of disunity in this document, which is the oldest known extant copy of Isaiah. (For a thorough discussion of this manuscript, see M. Mansoor, *The Dead Sea Scrolls*, pp. 69-81; for a recent defense of multiple [more than three] authorship of the book of Isaiah, see W. L. Holladay, *Isaiah: Scroll of a Prophetic Heritage;* in defense of the unity of Isaiah by a single author, see O. T. Allis, *The Unity Of Isaiah;* E. J. Young, *Who Wrote Isaiah?;* G. Archer, *A Survey of Old Testament Introduction*, pp. 314-339; R. K. Harrison, *Introduction to the Old Testament*, pp. 764-800; also the commentaries of Hengstenberg, Alexander, Delitzsch, and Young.)

The arguments in favor of the source division of Isaiah are based on theme, subject matter, language, style, and theological ideas. Critics especially object to the predictive naming of Cyrus in 44:26-28. Archer (p. 321) argues: "If there can be no such thing as fulfilled prophecy, it becomes logically necessary to explain all apparent fulfillments as mere *vaticinia ex eventu*, that is, prophecies after the event." In the meantime, there is more than adequate proof for the unity and reliability of the book. While the foreign policy shifts from Assyria in the first half of the book to Babylon in the second half, that in no way limits the genuineness of that portion of Isaiah's prophecy. Throughout the second portion of this book, the author shows great familiarity with Palestine, but not with Babylon. In 40:9 he views the cities of Judah as still standing.

The arguments based upon language and style prove the view of those who believe in the unity of Isaiah as well as that of the critics. There are as many stylistic similarities between one part and the other as there are alleged differences. The title, "Holy One of Israel," occurs twelve times in the first portion and fourteen times in the second. There are also many literary similarities to the writings of the prophet Micah, an eighth-century contemporary of Isaiah.

It should also be observed that all the New

Testament writers clearly regarded the author of "first" and "second" Isaiah as the same person (see Mt 3:3; 12:17-18; Lk 3:4; Jn 12:38-41; Acts 8:28-34; Rom 10:16, 20). The strongest argument of all is that Jesus Himself quoted from both "parts" of Isaiah equally, ascribing all the statements to the prophet Isaiah. One must reduce his Christology to the accommodation view, or worse, in order to hold to the multiple authorship view of Isaiah's prophecies. In light of all these matters, it must be concluded that there is ample evidence for the unity and authenticity of the book. It must also be observed that there is absolutely no available external evidence to refute the historicity of Isaiah the man, nor the book he has written dating from the eighth century B.C. That this book should stand at the head of the seventeen prophetic works is most appropriate in light of its impressive grandeur, dignity of expression, and dramatic style.

The Prophet and the Prophetic Ministry. The prophetical histories are followed in the Hebrew canon by the prophetical books of prediction. The two form a unit in the middle portion of the threefold canon, under the common term *nebi'im* (prophets). They are distinguished as the *hari'shonim* (former prophets) and *ha'acherōnim* (latter prophets).

The usage of *nabiy'* designates the prophet as a spokesman for God. Though often radical in his approach, the nineteenth-century Dutch theologian Kuenen, of the University of Leyden, rightly asked for a re-examination of the office and work of the prophet because of the orthodox overemphasis upon the merely predictive aspect of prophecy. However, this does not allow for the opposite extreme, throwing out all predictive aspects of prophecy. It is true that prophecy has its roots in history. In some cases, however, it also has a definite reference to the future. That reference is taken from the writer's historical standpoint; the prophet does speak primarily to men of his own time, and his message springs out of the circumstances in which he lives. Yet, for all this, the source of that message is supernatural, not natural. Ellison (*Men Spake from God*, p. 14) writes: "It is derived neither from observation nor intellectual thought, but from admission to the council chamber of God, from knowing God and speaking with Him."

Thompson (*Old Testament View of Revelation*, p. 40) traces this concept, noting that the prophet is admitted to God's council chamber, where God "revealeth his secret" (Amos 3:7). "Reveal" (*galah*) means uncover (I Sam 9:15—"uncovering of the ear"). He concludes that when God uncovers the prophet's ear, He reveals what is hidden (II Sam 7:27), so that the prophet in turn "perceives" and "gives heed to" what the Lord said (Jer 23:18).

It is obvious, therefore, that the "spirit of God" is necessary for prophetic inspiration (Isa 30:1ff.). Thus, it was by the Spirit that the Word of the Lord was communicated to the prophet and by the Spirit that the Word was mediated to the people. This communion with God was indispensable to the prophetic consciousness as a medium of revelation, so that under the guidance of the Holy Spirit prophecy can sometimes be quite startling in the individuality and definiteness of its prediction of even remote events. So we see the full picture of prophecy as both a forthtelling of God's messages and a foretelling of God's actions. Through this means God continued to energize the prophet to speak for Him. Isaiah was such a man, addressing himself to his own times as he brought God's direction to the kings of Judah and also a man seeing far into the future of God's plans for His people.

Isaiah has been described as the most notable figure, after David, in the entire history of Israel. In the face of national crises he practically guided the helm of the state in Hezekiah's day, encouraging Jerusalem to hold out against the Assyrian invasion when all others were ready to submit. He has been called the most powerful statesman in Jerusalem. His main distinction, however, was moral and intellectual, rather than political. His influence upon Hebrew polity and religion was great and lasting. His literary efforts may be termed the classical period in Hebrew literature. That his book should stand at the head of the seventeen prophetic works is no mistake. All who have an appreciation for literature must be impressed by Isaiah's combined excellence of style. The grandeur and dignity are paralleled by a liveliness of energy and profusion of imagery. His rich style can be seen in his forceful plays on words, vivid descriptions, and dramatic rhetorical touches. He was, without doubt, the "Prince of Prophets."

OUTLINE

COMMENTARY

I. PROPHETIC CONDEMNATION. 1:1-35:10.

A. Prophecies Against Judah and Jerusalem. 1:1-12:6.

1. Coming judgment and blessing. 1:1-5:30.

a. Condemnation of Judah. 1:1-31.

THE vision of Isaiah the son of Amoz, which he saw concerning Jū'dah and Jerusalem in the days of Uz-zī'ah, Jō'tham, Ahaz, *and* Hĕz-e-kī'ah, kings of Jū'dah.

1:1. Vision is the technical term for divine revelation (Heb *shazōn*) to the mind of the prophet. This refers to the entire prophetic epic which follows. Calvin (p. 6) notes that the term here signifies the prophecy as a whole, rather than a specific vision (Heb *mar'eh*). Some (Smith, p. 4) have suggested that this chapter was actually written late in Isaiah's life and serves as both an introduction to his prophecies and a summary of them. **Isaiah** means "Jehovah is salvation" (Heb *yesha'-yahu*). He is called the son of **Amoz** (courageous). **Uzziah** is also known as Azariah, who reigned from 767-740 B.C. He was a contemporary of Tiglath-pileser III of Assyria, who later invaded Israel. **Jotham** ruled as co-regent with Uzziah (ca. 750-740), and alone from 740-736 B.C. He was succeeded by **Ahaz** who ruled from 736-716 B.C. He was a wicked and idolatrous king who rejected Isaiah's offer of help. However, his son **Hezekiah** was one of Judah's greatest spiritual kings. He ruled as co-regent from 726-716 and as sole king from 716-698 B.C. During his reign there was a major spiritual revival and nationwide religious reform. He was especially close to the prophet Isaiah who exercised his greatest influence during his reign. He was a contemporary of Sennacherib of Assyria, who invaded Judah in 701 B.C., during his reign.

2 ¶Hear, O heavens, and give ear, O earth: for the LORD hath spoken, I have nourished and brought up children, and they have rebelled against me.

2-4. Isaiah pictures the sin of the people of Judah (southern kingdom) as **children** rebelling against their parents. The opening verses of this chapter serve as a "Great Arraignment" of the chosen people. God is pictured as both the prosecutor and the

3 The ox knoweth his owner, and the ass his master's crib: *but* Israel doth not know, my people doth not consider.

4 Ah sinful nation, a people laden with iniquity, a seed of evildoers, children that are corrupters: they have forsaken the LORD, they have provoked the Holy One of Israel unto anger, they are gone away backward.

5 Why should ye be stricken any more? ye will revolt more and more: the whole head is sick, and the whole heart faint.

6 From the sole of the foot even unto the head *there is* no soundness in it; *but* wounds, and bruises, and putrifying sores: they have not been closed, neither bound up, neither mollified with ointment.

7 Your country *is* desolate, your cities *are* burned with fire: your land, strangers devour it in your presence, and *it is* desolate, as overthrown by strangers.

8 And the daughter of Zion is left as a cottage in a vineyard, as a lodge in a garden of cucumbers, as a besieged city.

9 Except the LORD of hosts had left unto us a very small remnant, we should have been as Sodom, *and* we should have been like unto Go-mŏr'rah.

10 ¶Hear the word of the LORD, ye rulers of Sodom; give ear unto the law of our God, ye people of Go-mŏr'rah.

11 To what purpose *is* the multitude of your sacrifices unto me? saith the LORD: I am full of the burnt offerings of rams, and the fat of fed beasts; and I delight not in the blood of bullocks, or of lambs, or of he goats.

12 When ye come to appear before me, who hath required this at your hand, to tread my courts?

13 Bring no more vain oblations; incense is an abomination unto me; the new moons and sabbaths, the calling of assemblies, I cannot away with; *it is* iniquity, even the solemn meeting.

14 Your new moons and your appointed feasts my soul hateth: they are a trouble unto me; I am weary to bear *them.*

judge. Both the **heavens and . . . earth** are called as witnesses. **The LORD** is the covenant name of God (Jehovah, Heb *Yahweh*) and is used to depict the covenant relationship between God and His people. Fitch (p. 563) notes the use of the emphatic pronouns: "Even my children, those whom I have reared, even they have rebelled." The reference to the **ox** and the **ass** indicates that even dumb animals have enough sense to know whom they should follow. The **crib** refers to a feeding trough, not a bed. The fact that Israel **doth not know** implies a deliberate and self-willed disobedience. Hence, Judah is called a **sinful nation.** **Sinful** is a participial form of the verb *chata'*, meaning to miss the mark or to offend by sinful actions. Archer (p. 609) observes that it implies missing the proper goal of life, and therefore missing the way that God has ordained. The nation's **iniquity** (Heb *'awa*, meaning to bend or twist) is pictured as being so great that it is like a wagon **laden** with a heavy load. They are referred to as a **seed of evildoers,** implying that their parents were unspiritual and that they too will likely continue the same trend. Thus, they are called **children that are corrupters.** They have corrupted the way of God and followed after their own way. Therefore, they have **forsaken** the Lord altogether and have provoked **the Holy One of Israel.** This title is undoubtedly Isaiah's favorite reference for God. **The Holy One** (Heb *qadosh*) is the transcendent God Himself. It should be noted that the title **Holy One of Israel** appears twelve times in the first half of the book and fourteen times in the last half of the book, providing excellent internal evidence for the unity of authorship of the entire book (see Slotki, p. 23).

5-9. The southern kingdom is pictured as having suffered a brutal assault and being virtually left for dead. The prophet pictures the nation as being bruised from the **sole of the foot even unto the head.** He sees the nation as hopelessly wounded with open sores that have not been **closed, neither bound up.** These open wounds are but an evidence of the real spiritual sickness of the nation. **The whole heart faint** (better, sick). Thus, he pictures a sickness of soul as the real cause of Judah's impending political collapse. The statement that **Your country is desolate . . . burned with fire,** does not necessarily mean that this condition is due to the invasion of Sennacherib, as some have suggested (Fitch, p. 563), but may simply refer to the general condition of the land at an even earlier time. The reference to a **cottage in a vineyard** or a **lodge in a garden** is to a temporary shelter against marauding bands. The **very small remnant** (Heb *saird*), refers to the remnant of true believers for whose sakes God would yet spare the land.

10-15. The prophet addressed the people of Judah as if they were the inhabitants of **Sodom** and **Gomorrah.** Archer (p. 610) calls Isaiah's criticism of the superficial worship of Jewish legalism the "sinful subterfuge of hypocritical worship." The rejection of sacrifices (Heb *zebach*) and offerings (Heb *'aloth*) is not a rejection of the sacrificial system as such, but a condemnation of their unrepented use of it. The "sacrifices" were animals offered to God for the payment of sin. The **burnt offerings** are actually ascension offerings that ascend up into the presence of God. They represent the concept that one's offerings to the Lord are totally consumed and surrendered unto Him. This is exactly where the Israelites of Isaiah's day were failing. In many ways they were still acknowledging the outward trappings and legal ceremonies of the sacrificial system without any real heart for the things of God. Therefore, their various religious trappings are condemned severely as the prophet speaks for God Himself. **Vain oblations** are, literally, worthless offerings. Even the **solemn** meeting (Heb *'asarah*) was looked upon as a sinful gather-

15 And when ye spread forth your hands, I will hide mine eyes from you: yea, when ye make many prayers, I will not hear: your hands are full of blood.

16 Wash you, make you clean; put away the evil of your doings from before mine eyes; cease to do evil;

17 Learn to do well; seek judgment, relieve the oppressed, judge the fatherless, plead for the widow.

18 ¶Come now, and let us reason together, saith the LORD: though your sins be as scarlet, they shall be as white as snow; though they be red like crimson, they shall be as wool.

19 If ye be willing and obedient, ye shall eat the good of the land:

20 But if ye refuse and rebel, ye shall be devoured with the sword: for the mouth of the LORD hath spoken it.

21 ¶How is the faithful city become an harlot! it was full of judgment; righteousness lodged in it; but now murderers.

22 Thy silver is become dross, thy wine mixed with water:

23 Thy princes are rebellious, and companions of thieves: every one loveth gifts, and followeth after rewards: they judge not the fatherless, neither doth the cause of the widow come unto them.

24 Therefore saith the Lord, the LORD of hosts, the mighty One of Israel, Ah, I will ease me of mine adversaries, and avenge me of mine enemies:

25 And I will turn my hand upon thee, and purely purge away thy dross, and take away all thy tin:

26 And I will restore thy judges as at the first, and thy counsellors as at the beginning: afterward thou shalt be called, The city of righteousness, the faithful city.

27 Zion shall be redeemed with judgment, and her converts with righteousness.

28 And the destruction of the transgressors and of the sinners shall be

ing because of the wrong motives in their hearts. **Your appointed feasts** (Heb *mo'adim*) probably refers to the three major religious events of the Hebrew calendar: Passover, Pentecost, and Tabernacles. Even the **prayers** of the unrepentant will be rejected.

16-20. In the midst of this severe warning by the prophet of God comes an invitation to choose between pardon and destruction. **Wash you** does not indicate that the sinner may cleanse himself, but rather that he must accept the cleansing which is offered to him from the Lord. That such cleansing will be complete in its effects is illustrated by the contrast: **cease to do evil; learn to do well.** Isaiah indicates that this will come about when they genuinely repent and **put away** their evil and shall totally turn to the Lord. Notice the interchangeable use of justice (Heb *mishpat*) and judge (Heb *shapat*). In the Hebrew mind there was no true justice without judgment, and there was no judgment without justice. The verb judge (*shiphetū*) in reference to the poor, not only means to be concerned for the poor, but to deliver the poor (as in the case of the use of the word in the book of Judges). The prophet's appeal to come and **reason together** shows God's gracious invitation to all men. This is another legal term meaning to implead one another. Notice that sin is described here as being **scarlet** and **red like crimson**, not black. While the colors indicate the crimson dye of the scarlet worm, which is absolutely colorfast and indelible, it also refers to their blood-guiltiness before God. Thus, Delitzsch (p. 98) is correct when he observes that the changing of colors from indelible red to snowy white is symbolic of the life-changing grace of God. Calvin (p. 21) notes that God stands ever ready to cleanse us and to forgive us when we turn to Him. He also observes that the destiny of the people of Israel was in their own hands. If they were **willing** to turn from their wickedness (repentance) and to continue to be **obedient** (confession), they would **eat the good of the land.** Many are willing, at least in their initial intention, but alas are not persistent in their obedience and therefore they never experience the full blessing that God has for them. To rebel is to bring certain and immediate judgment upon themselves. The statement **for the mouth of the LORD hath spoken it** indicates the solemn finality with which God has spoken. It also reveals the divine origin of Isaiah's message; it was the message of God Himself.

21-31. The concluding passage is supplementary to the rest of the chapter. It serves as a reminder to the people of Judah that they are in danger of judgment; and yet, at the very point of their peril, God is willing to offer them salvation. The **faithful** who were filled with **righteousness** are now replaced by harlots and murderers! The **silver** has become **dross**, the **wine** diluted; and the rulers are now the **companions of thieves.** Here the Lord is spoken of as the **mighty One of Israel** who will judge His enemies. In that day He will make Jerusalem to become the **city of righteousness, the faithful city.** Archer (p. 612) correctly notes that while this may have begun to be fulfilled with the formation of the New Testament church, it will only receive its ultimate fulfillment in the millennial kingdom.

together, and they that forsake the LORD shall be consumed.

29 For they shall be ashamed of the oaks which ye have desired, and ye shall be confounded for the gardens that ye have chosen.

30 For ye shall be as an oak whose leaf fadeth, and as a garden that hath no water.

31 And the strong shall be as tow, and the maker of it as a spark, and they shall both burn together, and none shall quench them.

CHAPTER 2

THE word that Isaiah the son of Amoz saw concerning Jū'dah and Jerusalem.

2 And it shall come to pass in the last days, that the mountain of the LORD's house shall be established in the top of the mountains, and shall be exalted above the hills; and all nations shall flow unto it.

3 And many people shall go and say, Come ye, and let us go up to the mountain of the LORD, to the house of the God of Jacob; and he will teach us of his ways, and we will walk in his paths: for out of Zion shall go forth the law, and the word of the LORD from Jerusalem.

4 And he shall judge among the nations, and shall rebuke many people: and they shall beat their swords into plowshares, and their spears into pruninghooks: nation shall not lift up sword against nation, neither shall they learn war any more.

5 ¶O house of Jacob, come ye, and let us walk in the light of the LORD.

6 Therefore thou hast forsaken thy people the house of Jacob, because they be replenished from the east, and are soothsayers like the Philistines, and they please themselves in the children of strangers.

7 Their land also is full of silver and gold, neither is there any end of their treasures; their land is also full of horses, neither is there any end of their chariots:

8 Their land also is full of idols; they worship the work of their own hands, that which their own fingers have made:

9 And the mean man boweth down, and the great man humbleth himself: therefore forgive them not.

10 ¶Enter into the rock, and hide thee in the dust, for fear of the LORD, and for the glory of his majesty.

b. Cleansing of Zion. 2:1-4:6.

2:1-5. The phrase **The word that Isaiah . . . saw** indicates that this is a separate prophecy from that of chapter 1. These verses are repeated in a somewhat different form in Micah 4:1-4. We are now transported into the messianic age when the Holy City shall be the center of the earth and all nations shall come to it to learn the ways of God. It should be noted that this universal emphasis will not be fulfilled in the days of Israel's earthly kingdom, nor in the days of the church, but in the **last days**. This points our attention to the millennial future when Israel's kingdom shall become a reality only during the time when the Messiah shall rule after the church age. The **mountain of the LORD's house** refers to Mount Zion, formerly known as Mount Moriah, on which the various temples of Israel were built. In Isaiah's day, the Temple of Solomon was still standing. The implication of this passage is that in the millennial kingdom there will once again be a Temple in Jerusalem which shall serve as the focal point of the worship of Jesus Christ during His kingdom rule on earth. God's kingdom is pictured as being **exalted above the hills,** i.e., the kingdoms of this world. **All nations** refers to the gentile nations (Heb goyim). Both the **law** (torah) and the **word** (debar) are pictured as continually (present tense) going forth from the presence of the Lord. Christ Himself **shall judge among the nations.** This will be that time when He shall rule with a "rod of iron" (Rev 2:27) upon the earth and compel all nations to practice justice toward one another. This will be a time of complete international peace and safety unlike any other time in the history of the world. To try to apply this passage to the church age is ridiculous. Notice that Christ Himself is pictured as the **judge** (shaphat) who shall discern and direct the affairs of all nations during His millennial kingdom. Thus, the weapons of war shall be turned into tools of peace and economic productivity.

6-9. The phrase **replenished from the east** meant that they had become filled with the pagan influences from Assyria and Babylon to the east. From their Philistine neighbors they followed the false idea of **soothsayers** (Heb 'anan, meaning to cloud or cover). The idea of the Hebrew word itself implies that the soothsayer clouded over the truth, rather than shedding any genuine light on the truth. (On Philistine religious practices, see E. Hindson, The Philistines and the Old Testament, pp. 25-35.) The accusation that they **please themselves** refers to the making of treaties with those who did not know the Lord. The prosperity of Judah under the rule of Uzziah is described in verses 7-8, but only with the reminder that such prosperity had led to an innate materialism. With prosperity had come religious compromise, so that the land was **full of idols. The mean man** refers to the lower class of society and the **great man** to the upper class. Both were bowing to the idols of the pagan nations. Therefore, the announcement of God's judgment and its severity is simply stated, **forgive them not.**

10-22. Isaiah warns his listeners to "run for cover" because the judgment of God will come with certainty on those who have rejected His Word. The prophet announces the great extent of

11 The lofty looks of man shall be humbled, and the haughtiness of men shall be bowed down, and the LORD alone shall be exalted in that day.

12 For the day of the LORD of hosts shall be upon every one that is proud and lofty, and upon every one that is lifted up; and he shall be brought low:

13 And upon all the cedars of Lebanon, that are high and lifted up, and upon all the oaks of Bā'shan,

14 And upon all the high mountains, and upon all the hills that are lifted up,

15 And upon every high tower, and upon every fenced wall,

16 And upon all the ships of Tär'shĭsh, and upon all pleasant pictures.

17 And the loftiness of man shall be bowed down, and the haughtiness of men shall be made low: and the LORD alone shall be exalted in that day.

18 And the idols he shall utterly abolish.

19 And they shall go into the holes of the rocks, and into the caves of the earth, for fear of the LORD, and for the glory of his majesty, when he ariseth to shake terribly the earth.

20 In that day a man shall cast his idols of silver, and his idols of gold, which they made each one for himself to worship, to the moles and to the bats;

21 To go into the clefts of the rocks, and into the tops of the ragged rocks, for fear of the LORD, and for the glory of his majesty, when he ariseth to shake terribly the earth.

22 Cease ye from man, whose breath is in his nostrils: for wherein is he to be accounted of?

CHAPTER 3

FOR, behold, the Lord, the LORD of hosts, doth take away from Jerusalem and from Jū'dah the stay and the staff, the whole stay of bread, and the whole stay of water.

2 The mighty man, and the man of war, the judge, and the prophet, and the prudent, and the ancient,

3 The captain of fifty, and the honourable man, and the counsellor, and the cunning artificer, and the eloquent orator.

4 And I will give children to be their princes, and babes shall rule over them.

5 And the people shall be oppressed, every one by another, and every one by his neighbour: the child shall behave himself proudly against the ancient, and the base against the honourable.

6 When a man shall take hold of his brother of the house of his father, saying, Thou hast clothing, be thou our ruler, and let this ruin be under thy hand:

7 In that day shall he swear, saying, I will not be an healer; for in my house is neither bread nor clothing: make me not a ruler of the people.

8 For Jerusalem is ruined, and Jū'dah is fallen: because their tongue and their doings are against the LORD, to provoke the eyes of his glory.

God's judgment as the day of the LORD. Prophetically, this refers to the final overthrow of all human government, which shall precede the coming of Christ as King (cf. II Thess 1:7-2:12; II Pet 3:12). The references to cedars and oaks and mountains and hills are symbols of human sufficiency and strength. Ships of Tarshish is a reference to the merchant fleet of western Europe at the other extremity of the Mediterranean Sea (possibly even as far away as Spain). The reference in verse 19 to holes of the rocks as hiding places in the time when God shall shake terribly the earth is reminiscent of Revelation 6:15. The destruction in view here seems cataclysmic in nature and may well refer to some great final nuclear destruction, during which man can only find safety in the caves of the earth. Cease ye from man means to cease putting your trust in man whose very breath is in the hand of God Himself.

3:1-8. In this chapter the prophet denounces the private sins of the affluent upper class of Judah by warning them that God will take away their leadership. The stay and the staff are two genders of the same noun, emphasizing in the Hebrew idiom "all kinds of things." The meaning of the statement is that everything on which they are depending for their survival as a nation will be taken from them. The mighty man (Heb gibbōr, the heroic leader) . . . the judge (shaphat) . . . the prophet (nabiy') . . . the prudent (quoses, the diviner) . . . the counselor (yō'its) . . . and the eloquent orator (lachash, enchanter or prayer). In place of these national leaders God tells them that He will give them children . . . and babes to rule over them. In other words, He will allow their competent leaders to be replaced by incompetent rulers. The instability of the nation will eventually become so bad that the people will be oppressed by one another and the child shall behave himself proudly against the ancient (zaqen, aged man or elder). Archer (p. 614) notes that this was actually fulfilled when Manasseh came to the throne at the age of twelve to begin his long and wicked reign. It was certainly also true politically in the instability and childish behavior of Judah's last three kings (Jehoiakim, Jehoiachin, and Zedekiah). Within twenty years after the death of King Josiah they allowed the country to fall into total ruin. Thou hast clothing (Heb simla, outer garment or mantle). In the coming days of desolation this ordinary garment would mark a man as a man of wealth. Those who could not afford an outer garment would come in their underwear and plead with him to be ruler over them! However, Isaiah warned that even he would refuse to rule over them and be to them a healer (Heb chobesh, a comforter). The statement that Jerusalem is ruined, and Judah is

9 The shew of their countenance doth witness against them; and they declare their sin as Sodom, they hide *it* not. Woe unto their soul! for they have rewarded evil unto themselves.

10 Say ye to the righteous, that *it shall be* well *with him:* for they shall eat the fruit of their doings.

11 Woe unto the wicked! *it shall be* ill *with him:* for the reward of his hands shall be given him.

12 *As for* my people, children *are* their oppressors, and women rule over them. O my people, they which lead thee cause *thee* to err, and destroy the way of thy paths.

13 ¶The LORD standeth up to plead, and standeth to judge the people.

14 The LORD will enter into judgment with the ancients of his people, and the princes thereof: for ye have eaten up the vineyard; the spoil of the poor *is* in your houses.

15 What mean ye *that* ye beat my people to pieces, and grind the faces of the poor? saith the Lord GOD of hosts.

16 ¶Moreover the LORD saith, Because the daughters of Zion are haughty, and walk with stretched forth necks and wanton eyes, walking and mincing *as* they go, and making a tinkling with their feet:

17 Therefore the Lord will smite with a scab the crown of the head of the daughters of Zion, and the LORD will discover their secret parts.

18 In that day the Lord will take away the bravery of *their* tinkling ornaments *about their* feet, and *their* cauls, and *their* round tires like the moon,

19 The chains, and the bracelets, and the mufflers,

20 The bonnets, and the ornaments of the legs, and the headbands, and the tablets, and the earrings,

21 The rings, and nose jewels,

22 The changeable suits of apparel, and the mantles, and the wimples, and the crisping pins,

23 The glasses, and the fine linen, and the hoods, and the vails.

24 And it shall come to pass, *that* instead of sweet smell there shall be stink; and instead of a girdle a rent; and instead of well set hair baldness; and instead of a stomacher a girding of sackcloth; *and* burning instead of beauty.

25 Thy men shall fall by the sword, and thy mighty in the war.

26 And her gates shall lament and mourn; and she *being* desolate shall sit upon the ground.

CHAPTER 4

AND in that day seven women shall take hold of one man, saying, We will eat our own bread, and wear our own apparel: only let us be called by thy name, to take away our reproach.

fallen is stated in the prophetic perfect, as if this future event were already a fact. Though it would be nearly one hundred and fifty years until it would actually come to pass, God considered it already done. The process that would eventually lead to Judah's fall was already in motion. There would be times of reprieve under Hezekiah and Josiah, but the eventual destruction was an inevitable reality.

9-15. The show of their countenance (Heb *hakarath penēyhes*) should be read "the look of their faces" rather than "their respecting of persons." The idea was that their faces reveal their sin, as in the parallel phrase **they declare their sin as Sodom.** The Bible clearly emphasizes that one's true heart condition is often revealed on one's face. Again, the emphasis **children are their oppressors, and women rule over them** indicates the utter failure of the male leadership in the society of Judah. The implication of the entire chapter is that when male leadership fails, it will naturally be replaced by female leadership and incompetent childish leadership. The chapter is not meant to be an indictment against women, but against the oppressive attitude of female dominance in light of masculine weakness. Every ancient country in the world knew the necessity of strong male leadership in the face of potential war. Failure always meant eventual and certain doom.

16-26. The prophet Isaiah now begins a diatribe against the haughty and fashionable women of Jerusalem who were more concerned about the latest fads in jewelry, hair style, and dress than they were in the spiritual well-being of the nation. The **daughters of Zion** are variously described as being **haughty** (proud) and **wanton** (suggestive). The NASB reads: "Because the daughters of Zion are proud, And walk with heads held high and seductive eyes, And go along with mincing steps, And tinkle the bangles on their feet. . ." (vs. 16). Thus, the prophet warns that the Lord will take away all of their adornments. Again the NASB reads: ". . . their anklets, headbands, crescent ornaments, dangling earrings, bracelets, veils, headdresses, ankle chains, sashes, perfume boxes, amulets, finger rings, nose rings, festal robes, outer tunics, cloaks, money purses, hand mirrors, undergarments, turbans, and veils" (vss. 18-23). Instead of delighting in these female dainties, they will perish with the men of the nation. Therefore, in the coming day of captivity, instead of **sweet smell** (perfume), theirs shall be a **stink** (putrefaction); and **instead of a girdle a rent** (better, instead of a belt, a rope) . . . **instead of a stomacher** (better, a robe), they will wear sackcloth and ashes. The passage closes by warning that the **men** shall fall by the sword in battle and the women will be sold off as slaves. In the ancient Near East the humiliation of slavery usually included being stripped naked, chained together, and marched off into captivity to be sold as a servant or worse.

4:1-6. The first verse serves as a summary of the preceding chapter. As a result of the devastation of the land, conditions will become so bad that **seven women shall take hold of one man,** meaning that the male population will be so devastated

2 ¶In that day shall the branch of the LORD be beautiful and glorious, and the fruit of the earth *shall be* excellent and comely for them that are escaped of Israel.

3 And it shall come to pass, *that he that is* left in Zion, and *he that* remaineth in Jerusalem, shall be called holy, *even* every one that is written among the living in Jerusalem:

4 When the Lord shall have washed away the filth of the daughters of Zion, and shall have purged the blood of Jerusalem from the midst thereof by the spirit of judgment, and by the spirit of burning.

5 And the LORD will create upon every dwelling place of mount Zion, and upon her assemblies, a cloud and smoke by day, and the shining of a flaming fire by night: for upon all the glory *shall be* a defence.

6 And there shall be a tabernacle for a shadow in the daytime from the heat, and for a place of refuge, and for a covert from storm and from rain.

CHAPTER 5

NOW will I sing to my wellbeloved a song of my beloved touching his vineyard. My wellbeloved hath a vineyard in a very fruitful hill:

2 And he fenced it, and gathered out the stones thereof, and planted it with the choicest vine, and built a tower in the midst of it, and also made a winepress therein: and he looked that it should bring forth grapes, and it brought forth wild grapes.

3 And now, O inhabitants of Jerusalem, and men of Jū'dah, judge, I pray you, betwixt me and my vineyard.

4 What could have been done more to my vineyard, that I have not done in it? wherefore, when I looked that it should bring forth grapes, brought it forth wild grapes?

5 And now go to; I will tell you what I will do to my vineyard: I will take away

that there will be seven women for every surviving man in the nation. This section ends with a promise of future blessing and protection and gives us an indication of the literary style Isaiah uses throughout the entire book. Those who argue for the multiple authorship of Isaiah try to place this section in the latter period. Instead of viewing this as an indication of Isaiah's consistent style throughout, they misinterpret the nature of the book by reading their presupposition back into this section. There was no question at one time that this chapter was authentically attributed to Isaiah himself. The problem is that he goes drastically from a warning of judgment to a message of comfort. It is obvious to the unbiased reader that this is his style throughout the entire book, from chapter 1 through chapter 66. **The branch of the LORD** (vs. 2) is a reference to the Messiah Himself. In the midst of the severity of the prophet's warning of judgment there bursts this glorious promise of hope for the future. **Branch** is also used as a title for the Messiah in Jeremiah 23:5; 33:15; cf. "BRANCH" in Zechariah 3:8; 6:12. In contrast with the worldly beauty of the society women of Jerusalem, there will be found in Him the **beautiful** and **glorious** features of the true Israel. The idea again is that the Branch (lit., sprout) will burst forth in fruitful blessing as the answer to the desolation of judgment which shall precede it. The reference to **he that is left in Zion** comes from the Hebrew word *pelēta*, meaning the remnant who have escaped. Thus, the promise here is not to the entire nation, but to a believing remnant who would yet escape the coming judgments of God (cf. Rom 11:5). These will be those who are blessed of God and enter the Millennium, when once again the **cloud** of glory shall rule them by day and the pillar of **fire** shall guide them by night. The phrase **for upon all the glory shall be a defence** should be read: the glory shall be spread over like a canopy (of protection). Thus, the presence of God Himself is symbolized by His glory once again being with the nation of Israel. A study of the glory of God in the Scripture will reveal that it is virtually synonymous with the presence of God Himself. Where God is, there His glory is revealed. The chapter ends with a promise that in those days a **tabernacle** shall stand as the **place of refuge** on Mount Zion. The term tabernacle (Heb *sukkah*) literally means a sheltering pavilion. That it refers to the millennial Temple is most likely indeed. In this scene Delitzsch (p. 158) also sees paradise restored. The prophet pictures the mountain of Zion roofed over with a cloud of smoke by day and a shining, flaming fire by night. This is none other than the mountain of the house of the Lord. Here shall His Temple once again stand during the millennial kingdom, and all the nations shall come to it for protection.

c. Charge against Israel. 5:1-30.

5:1-7. These verses comprise a parable of the **vineyard**, which symbolizes the nation of Israel (this figure also appears in Jer 12:10). It is called the **song of my beloved** (*dōdi*, favored one or loved one). It resembles the same concept as the Song of Solomon, only in this passage it becomes a song of lament. The beloved one is the Lord Himself. Israel is the vineyard which has been properly cared for and yet has brought **wild grapes**. Fitch (p. 566) notes that the setting is one of a fertile vineyard set on the sunny slopes of a rocky hill, with the winepress hollowed out of the rock and the walls and towers of defense built about it. Yet, in spite of this preparation, it still becomes unproductive. The imagery is illustrative of the idea that spiritually God has prepared Israel to bring forth fruit unto Himself and yet she has only brought forth the **wild grapes** of sin. Therefore, God denounces it with judgment to come, indicating the coming Babylonian captivity. The phrases **he looked for judgment** (*mishpat*), **but behold oppression** (*mispach*); **for righteousness** (*tsedaqah*), **but behold a cry** (*tse'aqah*) represent a

the hedge thereof, and it shall be eaten up; *and* break down the wall thereof, and it shall be trodden down:

6 And I will lay it waste: it shall not be pruned, nor digged; but there shall come up briers and thorns: I will also command the clouds that they rain no rain upon it.

7 For the vineyard of the LORD of hosts *is* the house of Israel, and the men of Jū′dah his pleasant plant: and he looked for judgment, but behold oppression; for righteousness, but behold a cry.

8 ¶Woe unto them that join house to house, *that* lay field to field, till *there be* no place, that they may be placed alone in the midst of the earth!

9 In mine ears *said* the LORD of hosts, Of a truth many houses shall be desolate, *even* great and fair, without inhabitant.

10 Yea, ten acres of vineyard shall yield one bath, and the seed of an homer shall yield an ephah.

11 ¶Woe unto them that rise up early in the morning, *that* they may follow strong drink; that continue until night, *till* wine inflame them!

12 And the harp, and the viol, the tabret, and pipe, and wine, are in their feasts: but they regard not the work of the LORD, neither consider the operation of his hands.

13 Therefore my people are gone into captivity, because *they have* no knowledge: and their honourable men *are* famished, and their multitude dried up with thirst.

14 Therefore hell hath enlarged herself, and opened her mouth without measure: and their glory, and their multitude, and their pomp, and he that rejoiceth, shall descend into it.

15 And the mean man shall be brought down, and the mighty man shall be humbled, and the eyes of the lofty shall be humbled:

16 But the LORD of hosts shall be exalted in judgment, and God that is holy shall be sanctified in righteousness.

17 Then shall the lambs feed after their manner, and the waste places of the fat ones shall strangers eat.

18 ¶Woe unto them that draw iniquity with cords of vanity, and sin as it were with a cart rope:

19 That say, Let him make speed, *and* hasten his work, that we may see *it:* and let the counsel of the Holy One of Israel draw nigh and come, that we may know *it!*

20 Woe unto them that call evil good, and good evil; that put darkness for light, and light for darkness; that put bitter for sweet, and sweet for bitter!

21 Woe unto *them that are* wise in their own eyes, and prudent in their own sight!

22 Woe unto *them that are* mighty to drink wine, and men of strength to mingle strong drink:

23 Which justify the wicked for reward, and take away the righteousness of the righteous from him!

24 Therefore as the fire devoureth the stubble, and the flame consumeth the chaff, *so* their root shall be as rotten-

play-on-words to emphasize the prophet's point that the judgment of God would bring the opposite of what they expected.

8-25. In this section the prophet pronounces a sixfold **Woe** (Heb *hōy*) upon the sins of the nation of Judah. **Join house to house,** meaning that they are greedy landgrabbers. By foreclosing mortgages, the wealthy landowners acquired all the adjoining land to form huge estates. **Acres** (lit., yokes, i.e., as much as could be plowed by a yoke of oxen in a single day). A **bath** was a liquid measure equivalent to a **ephah** of dry measure (each about eight gallons). A **homer** was about eighty-three gallons. The idea is that the yield would be barely one-tenth of the amount sown. The second woe is against drunkenness and them that **follow strong drink** (Heb *shēkar*, fermented drink). Their immediate punishment would be **captivity** and their ultimate punishment would be **hell** itself (Hades or Sheol). The imagery of verse 14 indicates that the people are so ungodly that they go dancing and parading into hell, which **opened her mouth** to receive them. The third woe states that their sin is so open that they literally **draw iniquity with cords** as one would pull a cart rope. The idea is that they are sinning with such deliberate willfulness it is as if they are parading their sin in front of God as one would pull a cart rope in order to parade some great idol in a procession. The people of Judah are pictured as literally parading their sin before God. The fourth woe states that they now **call evil good, and good evil.** That is, they have now reversed moral standards completely; and that which should be disdained is being honored before them. The fifth woe is against those that are **wise in their own eyes,** meaning their pride of self-wisdom and self-determination will ultimately lead them to destruction. The sixth woe is also against drinking, this time with the emphasis upon those who **mingle strong drink** (Heb *shēkar*), as opposed to the regular word for wine (Heb *yayēn*), which is also prohibited. In this drunken state their justification of the wicked is the cause of God's wrathful judgment which shall fall upon them because they despised the **word of the Holy One of Israel.** The phrase **his anger is not turned away, but his hand is stretched out still** refers to the fact that God's hand of judgment is still going to be upon the people and His wrath will not yet be abated.

ness, and their blossom shall go up as dust: because they have cast away the law of the LORD of hosts, and despised the word of the Holy One of Israel.

25 Therefore is the anger of the LORD kindled against his people, and he hath stretched forth his hand against them, and hath smitten them: and the hills did tremble, and their carcases *were* torn in the midst of the streets. For all this his anger is not turned away, but his hand *is* stretched out still.

26 ¶And he will lift up an ensign to the nations from far, and will hiss unto them from the end of the earth: and, behold, they shall come with speed swiftly:

27 None shall be weary nor stumble among them; none shall slumber nor sleep; neither shall the girdle of their loins be loosed, nor the latchet of their shoes be broken:

28 Whose arrows *are* sharp, and all their bows bent, their horses' hoofs shall be counted like flint, and their wheels like a whirlwind:

29 Their roaring *shall be* like a lion, they shall roar like young lions: yea, they shall roar, and lay hold of the prey, and shall carry *it* away safe, and none shall deliver *it*.

30 And in that day they shall roar against them like the roaring of the sea: and if *one* look unto the land, behold darkness *and* sorrow, and the light is darkened in the heavens thereof.

CHAPTER 6

IN the year that king Uz-zi′ah died I saw also the Lord sitting upon a throne, high and lifted up, and his train filled the temple.

2 Above it stood the seraphims: each one had six wings; with twain he covered his face, and with twain he covered his feet, and with twain he did fly.

3 And one cried unto another, and said, Holy, holy, holy, *is* the LORD of hosts: the whole earth *is* full of his glory.

4 And the posts of the door moved at the voice of him that cried, and the house was filled with smoke.

26-30. Again Isaiah injects a word of hope in the midst of his prophecy of doom. He shall raise an **ensign** (lit., banner) and shall **hiss** (whistle) at the nations to come to do His bidding. Thus, the banner is that of the declaration of war, and the invading nations are those nations that shall eventually destroy Israel (especially Assyria and Babylon). The point of this statement is that the judgment of the nation of Israel is ultimately in the hands of God Himself, not the nations.

2. Call of Isaiah. 6:1-13.

a. His confrontation. 6:1-4.

6:1-4. In this chapter the prophet Isaiah recounts his call to the prophetic ministry, which undoubtedly occurred many years prior to this writing. He dates it from the **year that king Uzziah died**, which was in 740 B.C. In many ways this marked the passing of a golden age in the southern kingdom of Judah. Uzziah had been a godly king, in spite of his sinful intrusion into the priest's office ten years prior to his death. For this act of rebellion he had been struck with leprosy and lived in isolation until the time of his death. Nevertheless, Isaiah recognized that with the passing of Uzziah the nation of Israel was in trouble from a human standpoint. No leader appeared on the scene who seemed capable of reversing a process of decadence that had already begun during Uzziah's years of isolation. Thus, burdened and overwrought with the pressures of the hour, Isaiah came to the Temple to pray. It was here in Solomon's Temple that he had a vision of God which gave him a renewed concept of who the Lord was. Thus, he states that he saw **the Lord sitting upon a throne**. This undoubtedly represents the throne of heaven (see Rev 4:2). **His train** refers to His royal robes. Thus, Isaiah sees God sitting upon the throne of the universe, dressed in His royal robes. What Isaiah needed to realize afresh was that God Himself was still upon the throne! While human rulers may come and go, the believer needs to be reminded again and again that God is still in control of the affairs of this world. He is in fact ruling from heaven, and He often overrules the sinful actions of men to bring glory to Himself. The **seraphim** (a transliteration of "burning ones") are six-winged creatures who constantly fly in the presence of God declaring His threefold holiness. The fact that they are burning indicates that they are literally continually burning up in the presence of the glory of God. **Holy, holy, holy** (Heb *qadōsh*). This threefold declaration of God's holiness is often taken as an indication of the triune God in the Old Testament. Note in verse 8 that when God speaks, He uses the plural pronoun **us**. The Hebrew text makes it clear that Isaiah saw the **Lord** (*Adonai*) sitting upon the throne and that it was the LORD (Jehovah) whom the seraphs worshiped, substantiating that Jehovah and *Adonai* were One and the same. This declaration was to draw attention to the fact of God's **glory** (Heb *kabōd*, splendor). This is the same term used of the glory of God which appeared unto Moses in the book of Exodus. It is synonymous with the manifestation of God's presence. The cloud of **smoke** which filled the Temple was the radiant cloud of His glory.

b. His confession. 6:5.

5 Then said I, Woe *is* me! for I am undone; because I *am* a man of unclean lips, and I dwell in the midst of a people of unclean lips: for mine eyes have seen the King, the LORD of hosts.

5. Having seen God in the full light of His holiness, Isaiah pronounces the prophetic **Woe** upon himself. This was a legal charge (lit., I am ruined or I am dead). His self-evaluation: **I am undone** (Heb from *damah*, meaning to be dumb or silent, to perish or to be destroyed). His response is exactly that which shall be true of every unbeliever who stands before the throne of God in the day of judgment. It is a statement of total self-condemnation, literally meaning: "I am speechless . . . I am dead!" It is a picture of the unregenerate man, who will be able to offer no legitimate excuse for himself in the face-to-face confrontation with the thrice Holy God. He will be left speechless and will pronounce his own condemnation! He further recognized that he was **unclean** (Heb *tamē'*, defiled or polluted). This self-evaluation is made in light of the fact that he has seen **the King, the LORD of hosts** (*hamelek Yahweh tseba'oth*). Thus, the heavenly King is identified as Jehovah Himself who is called the **LORD of hosts** 62 times in the book of Isaiah. This title appears 285 times altogether throughout the Old Testament. Psalm 24:10 states: "The LORD of hosts, he is the King of glory!" The term conveys the concept of a glorious King in all His splendor who leads the armies of heaven in triumph. It is no wonder that Isaiah fell in self-condemnation before this infinite and eternal God, before whom he saw himself in all of his sinful finitude.

c. His consecration. 6:6-7.

6 Then flew one of the seraphims unto me, having a live coal in his hand, *which* he had taken with the tongs from off the altar:
7 And he laid *it* upon my mouth, and said, Lo, this hath touched thy lips; and thine iniquity is taken away, and thy sin purged.

6-7. It was Isaiah's confession of his personal sin that brought the response of God's cleansing to equip him for service to the Lord. The **seraphim** (fiery one) flew to the **altar** (Heb *mizbeach*, place of blood sacrifice). Girdlestone, *Synonyms* (p. 194) notes that the rabbinic writers also called it the *paraclete*, meaning the place of expiation or intercession. The **coal** has no redemptive ability of its own, but is represented as having been taken from the altar of a burnt offering (Heb *'olah*). Used in the causative voice, it signifies to ascend or cause to go up. The idea is that the burnt offering was literally burned up in complete devotion to God. It was only in this sense that the coal, which had been taken from the blood altar could be used as the means of cleansing so that it could be said **Lo . . . is . . . thy sin purged.** The imagery, of course, is figurative since the burning coal would have literally burned his mouth. It symbolizes the application of the cleansing of God on the basis of the shedding of blood on the altar of sacrifice. God offers a means of consecration to Isaiah; he gladly accepts it in light of seeing himself for what he really is: a condemned sinner.

d. His call. 6:8.

8 Also I heard the voice of the Lord, saying, Whom shall I send, and who will go for us? Then said I, Here *am* I; send me.

8. Isaiah states that he heard the **voice of the Lord** (*Adonai*) asking whom He should send and **who will go for us?** While some have attempted to view this plural pronoun as referring to God and the angelic host, it is more obvious (in the context of the passage) that the plural refers to himself (as in Gen 1:26). Having experienced such a radical transformation from unworthiness to that of divine consecration of his total being, the changed and cleansed Isaiah simply responds immediately and

9 And he said, Go, and tell this people, Hear ye indeed, but understand not; and see ye indeed, but perceive not.

10 Make the heart of this people fat, and make their ears heavy, and shut their eyes; lest they see with their eyes, and hear with their ears, and understand with their heart, and convert, and be healed.

11 Then said I, Lord, how long? And he answered, Until the cities be wasted without inhabitant, and the houses without man, and the land be utterly desolate,

12 And the LORD have removed men far away, and there be a great forsaking in the midst of the land.

13 But yet in it shall be a tenth, and it shall return, and shall be eaten: as a teil tree, and as an oak, whose substance is in them, when they cast their leaves: so the holy seed shall be the substance thereof.

CHAPTER 7

AND it came to pass in the days of Ahaz the son of Jō'tham, the son of Uz-zī'ah, king of Jū'dah, that Rĕ'zĭn the king of Syria, and Pĕ'kah the son of Rĕm-a-lī'ah, king of Israel, went up toward Jerusalem to war against it, but could not prevail against it.

2 And it was told the house of David, saying, Syria is confederate with Ē'phra-im. And his heart was moved, and the heart of his people, as the trees of the wood are moved with the wind.

spontaneously: **Here am I; send me.** Leupold (p. 136) comments: "After the vision, Isaiah is no longer the man he was. He has undergone a radical change of insight and attitude. Being absolved and having the burden of guilt taken from off his conscience, he possesses a new freedom and new compelling insights that make him an instrument far more fit for service than he could have been otherwise."

e. *His commission. 6:9-13.*

9-13. In commissioning Isaiah to become His prophet, God warns him that his ministry, for the most part, will fall upon deaf ears. **Hear ye indeed, but understand not** should be read "keep on hearing" as the syntax of the sentence indicates. In other words, Israel will continue to listen to the prophet's message but will not really respond with believing faith. Their rejection will be such that it will be the same as if they had never heard and never seen. **Make the heart . . . fat . . . ears heavy . . . shut their eyes** indicates a ministry of reprobation. The more he preaches and they reject his message, the more hardened they will become toward the Lord. Thus, they will not believe and be converted that they might be **healed.** Probably stunned by this statement, Isaiah asks the question, **Lord, how long?** God's answer, that He would continue to preach this message until the cities were desolate and only a remnant survived, indicated that his message would be pertinent to Israel up until the time of the Babylonian captivity. Yet, he is reminded that his ministry will not be totally in vain; for a **tenth . . . shall return.** This is also indicated in the next chapter in the symbolic name of the prophet's son Shear-jashub (a remnant shall return). Verse 13 indicates that even this remnant shall be **eaten** as a tree and that only a **holy seed** shall be left of that. The **teil** tree and the **oak** are both mentioned here; both are especially capable of reproducing from tiny shoots left from their stumps. The idea in this passage is that Judah will continue to rebel against the message of God until they are taken in the Babylonian captivity and only a tenth of them shall ever return; and even that remnant shall later be devastated again, and only a tiny remnant (**holy seed**) shall actually remain.

3. Coming of the Child Immanuel. 7:1-12:6.

a. *His miraculous birth. 7:1-25.*

7:1-2. The Immanuel prophecy is one of the most controversial for interpreters in all of the book of Isaiah. In these chapters we see the prophet confronting the pagan King Ahaz of Judah; the sign of the virgin's Son, Immanuel; the predicted Assyrian invasion; the birth of the prophet's own son; and the coming Child who will rule on David's throne. It is interesting that children play an important role in these chapters. Each is mentioned as a **sign.** In the interpretation of this passage, three basic positions have historically been taken by commentators: (1) That Immanuel is the Messiah; (2) that He is a Person living in the prophet's own day; and (3) that He is somehow both. From the time of the reformers the single messianic viewpoint was clearly held by most (Calvin, Luther, Lowth, Gill). However, with a rise of the liberal view that rejected any messianic fulfillment in this passage (Michaelis, Ewald, Driver, Duhm), some Evangelicals developed a dual-fulfillment view of the passage (Barnes, Keith, MacClaren, Naegelsbach). This approach views the prophecy as both a reference to an immediate event in Isaiah's own day, as well as a distant reference to the coming of the Messiah. It should be noted that no one ever held such a view until after the non-messianic view became popular in liberal circles. In the meantime, many great commentators held to the single messianic viewpoint (Hengstenberg, Alexander, Delitzsch, Cheyne, Orelli).

The Syrian-Samarian alliance against Judah is in view in verse 1. According to II Kings 15:37; they had already begun a seige of Judah in the days of Jotham. It is obvious that their intention was to replace Ahaz with their own puppet-king who would cooperate with their ambitions. **Rezin the king of Syria** was the last king to reign in Damascus. He was later killed by Tiglath-pileser who invaded Syria and slew her king and carried many of the Syrians into captivity (see II Kgs 16:9). **Pekah the son of Remaliah** was the king of northern Israel from 740-732 B.C. He had usurped the throne by murdering his predecessor, Peka-hiah, and was himself murdered by his successor, Hoshea (the last king of Israel). The reference to the **house of David** is to the Davidic line of kings in Judah (hence, in this passage Ahaz himself). **Syria is confederate with Ephraim** (northern Israel). The verb "resting" (*nachah*) may refer to a confederation. But since these two nations were already in an alliance with one another, it is more likely that this refers to a friendly halt of the Syrian troops within Israel's territory. This is what panicked Ahaz into realizing that Syria had not returned home, but was preparing a second invasion. It was at this time that he decided to call on the aid of Tiglath-pileser of Assyria for help. The incident in this chapter is generally dated at 734 B.C.

3 Then said the LORD unto Isaiah, Go forth now to meet Ahaz, thou, and Shě′-ar-jā′shub thy son, at the end of the conduit of the upper pool in the high-way of the fuller's field;

4 And say unto him, Take heed, and be quiet; fear not, neither be faint-hearted for the two tails of these smok-ing firebrands, for the fierce anger of Rē′zĭn with Syria, and of the son of Rĕm-a-lī′ah.

5 Because Syria, Ē′phra-im, and the son of Rĕm-a-lī′ah, have taken evil counsel against thee, saying,

6 Let us go up against Jū′dah, and vex it, and let us make a breach therein for us, and set a king in the midst of it, *even* the son of Tā′be-al:

7 Thus saith the Lord GOD, It shall not stand, neither shall it come to pass.

3-7. At this point the Lord (*Yahweh*) intervened and sent Isaiah to warn Ahaz against this unnecessary alliance with the very nation that would eventually invade Judah as well. To understand the geography of this political situation one must remember that Assyria was north of Syria, which was north of Israel, which was north of Judah. Therefore, Syria was desper-ately in need of an ally (Israel) to withstand the Assyrian inva-sion. However, Israel did not prove to be enough of an ally; and they were attempting to bring Judah into the alliance as well. Accompanying the prophet was **Shear-jashub** (i.e., a remnant shall return), his son, whose name is symbolically indicative of hope. These specific details emphasize God's dealing with His people in actual history. Young (I, p. 271) takes Jennings to task for "spiritualizing away" these descriptions. The meaning of the prophet's son's name is that a remnant shall survive, therefore the king does not need to be in a panic. The location at **the end of the conduit of the upper pool in the highway of the fuller's field** is the same place that the Assyrian Rab-shakeh later stood to challenge another Judaean king (Isa 36:2). Isaiah, who dares to confront the king, has words of calm and reassurance: **Take heed, and be quiet.** He refers to the invading kings as **smoking firebrands** (lit., smoldering sticks). Though they have devised evil against the throne of David by attempting to set up the **son of Tabeal,** the prophet's message is that they will not succeed because God has other purposes for that throne. It must be reserved for the coming of the Messiah (Anointed One). Isaiah's message is that their plan shall **not stand, neither . . . come to pass.**

8 For the head of Syria *is* Damascus, and the head of Damascus *is* Rē′zĭn; and within threescore and five years shall Ē′phra-im be broken, that it be not a people.

9 And the head of Ē′phra-im *is* Sa-mâ′rĭ-a, and the head of Sa-mâ′rĭ-a *is* Rĕm-a-lī′ah's son. If ye will not believe, surely ye shall not be established.

8-9. This section contains two affirmations and two predic-tions. The affirmations relate to Syria and Ephraim, and the predictions relate to Ephraim and Judah. **The head of Syria is Damascus** means that Damascus is the capital of the Syrian kingdom. **The head of Damascus is Rezin** refers to his being the king who ruled in that city. **The head of Ephraim is Samaria** means that Samaria was the capital of Ephraim, and **Remaliah's son** is a reference to Pekah. **Threescore and five years** refers to the fact that within sixty-five years the northern kingdom of Israel would fall and be taken into captivity (by Assyria). **If ye will not believe, surely ye shall not be estab-lished** is the promise to the Judaean king. In other words, if Judah will believe, she can stand; if not, she too will fall. The phrase is actually poetic, similar to "if ye have not faith, ye cannot have staith."

10 ¶Moreover the LORD spake again unto Ahaz, saying,

11 Ask thee a sign of the LORD thy God; ask it either in the depth, or in the height above.

12 But Ahaz said, I will not ask, neither will I tempt the LORD.

13 And he said, Hear ye now, O house of David; Is it a small thing for you to weary men, but will ye weary my God also?

14 Therefore the Lord himself shall give you a sign; Behold, a virgin shall conceive, and bear a son, and shall call his name Im-măn′ū-el.

10-13. The LORD spake again unto Ahaz. This very pertinent section of the Immanuel prophecy begins by calling attention to the **LORD** (*Yahweh*) as the One actually addressing King Ahaz. Isaiah's message is now viewed as one of both potential hope and impending doom. Thus, "as the spokesman of the Lord, he urges Ahaz to **Ask thee a sign** (Heb *'oth*) generally referring to a miraculous intervention of God. While liberal commentators have attempted to deny that the use of the word demands a miracle in the attempted event" (Gray, p. 124), nevertheless, it is obvious that nothing short of a miracle would deliver Ahaz from his predicament. However, the king surprisingly responded that he would **not ask, neither . . . tempt the LORD.** His response has been viewed by virtually all commentators of every type as being a pious ploy to avoid having to deal directly with God or the prophet. Ahaz could have chosen any sign to attest God's message of hope as delivered by the prophet; but he refused, and therefore God chose His own sign to give to Ahaz. The prophet's prediction is addressed now to the **house of David**; since the royal Davidic line was at stake, the people would need some means of confidence in trusting that God's chosen kingly line would be maintained for all generations. In time this royal line would be eliminated in Israel. Yet, out of this apparently cut-down stump there would spring forth a Branch of hope for the future. Thus, the prophecies of this entire section must be viewed as a unity. There is a Child who is going to come to rule in Israel who will be the fulfillment of all these prophecies.

14. Therefore (Heb *laken*) is a connective word often used by the prophets to introduce a divine declaration. In this context it is a transitory word used to unify verse 14 with the preceding statements. **The Lord** here is *Adonai*. It was common to interchange this term Lord for the tetragrammaton (four-consonant spelling of Yahweh). (See the references in E. Würthwein, *The Text of the Old Testament*, p. 146.) Since Jehovah (Yahweh) was the personal name of God as revealed to His covenant people, it is likely here that the reference to Him as *Adonai* was to emphasize that He was, in fact, not the personal God of the unbelieving Ahaz. **Behold** (*hineh*) is always used to arrest the attention. When used with a participle, it is an interjection, introducing either a present or future action. Delitzsch (p. 216) argues that it always introduces a future occurrence, whereas Young (*Studies*, p. 161) argues that it should be taken as a verbal adjective expressing present conditions. The real significance of the term is in its calling attention to an important birth (see similar forms of announcements in Gen 16:11; Jud 13:5). Thus, we are to look with anticipation to the virgin and her son who are announced as the central figures of this prophecy. The real questions in this passage are, "Who is the virgin, and who is Immanuel?" **A virgin** should better be read "the virgin." The use of the Hebrew definite article *ha* in connection with the woman in the passage indicates that a definite woman is in view to the mind of the prophet (see Lindbolm, *A Survey of the Immanuel Section of Isaiah*, p. 19). Hengstenberg (*Christology*, II, p. 44) emphasizes that the relationship of *hineh* to the article in *ha'almah* is best explained by the present tense of the context, so that the girl is present to the inward perception of the prophet. That she is definitely a specific girl is obvious. When he refers to her specifically as "the" virgin, it is highly unlikely that he meant to refer to any woman who might bear a child in the next few months. The word **virgin** is the unique and uncommon Hebrew word *'almah*. The more commonly used word for virgin is *bethûlah*; but in spite of its frequent usage to denote a virgin, it is in at least two passages (Deut 22:19; Joel 1:8) used to refer to a married woman. Therefore, Isaiah's choice of the rare word *'almah* better signifies virginity than the more common term *bethûlah*. While it is true that *'almah* can be translated "young woman," it is never intended in the Hebrew language to deny the legitimacy of that young woman's virginity! Even the prominent Jewish scholar, Cyrus Gordon, notes that the LXX translates 'almah by the Greek word parthenos, which always means "virgin." It should be remembered that the LXX is a Jewish translation made in pre-Christian Alexandria, Egypt. It represents a Jewish interpretation of Isaiah 7:14 that is much earlier than Matthew's use of the same word parthenos when referring back to the Isaiah 7:14 passage (Mt 1:23). Had Isaiah chosen to use the word bethûlah instead of 'almah, the liberals, who seem determined to deny the messianic predictive element of this verse, could just have easily argued that Isaiah did not intend to predict the virgin birth of the coming Messiah, or else he would have used the more scarce, yet technically correct, term 'alah! No one has done a better job of evaluating the meaning of this word than Young, Studies, pp. 143-198; he should be consulted for further information. **Shall conceive** (Heb harah) should actually be translated "is pregnant." It is neither a verb nor a participle, but a feminine adjective connected with an active participle (bearing); and it denotes that the scene is present to the prophet's view. Alexander (p. 121) discusses this point at length with conclusive evidence to show that the **virgin** is already pregnant and bearing a son. Thus, we can not escape the conclusion that this is a picture of the virgin birth of Christ Himself. The context makes it clear that the virgin is pregnant and is still a virgin! **Immanuel** is the symbolic name of the child, meaning "God with us." Smith (I, p. 131) argues that it is impossible to disassociate the Immanuel of this passage from that who is mentioned in connection with the land in chapter 8 and the Prince of four names in chapter 9. It is obvious that Matthew regarded this Immanuel to be none other than Jesus Christ Himself. He thus quotes this prophecy as being fulfilled in the virgin birth of Christ (Mt 1:23). He considers it to be of divine origin, stating that it was "spoken of the Lord by the prophet" (Mt 1:22). He therefore recognized that the sign given in Isaiah 7:14 was authored by God and delivered to Ahaz through the prophet. Even if one attempts to argue that Matthew merely followed the LXX in using parthenos, he followed the source that represented the oldest available interpretation of Isaiah 7:14. His contextual usage of hina plārōtha is certainly indicative of his understanding the passage to contain a definitely predictive element. There can be no doubt that until the rise of so-called "modern" scholarship, those closest historically to the actual statement by the prophet Isaiah have always taken it to be a prediction of the miraculous virgin birth of the coming Messiah. (For a thorough study of this entire prophecy see E. Hindson, Isaiah's Immanuel.)

15 Butter and honey shall he eat, that he may know to refuse the evil, and choose the good.
16 For before the child shall know to refuse the evil, and choose the good, the land that thou abhorrest shall be forsaken of both her kings.

15-16. **Butter and honey** is a reference to the best of food, not the worst of food. The context, including verse 22 (**abundance of milk . . . and honey**), indicates that this diet is due to the scarcity of people in the land. Though the land is virtually desolate, the few people left have the best of food available to them. Virtually everyone agrees that the statement **before the child shall know to refuse the evil** indicates about two years of age. **The land that thou abhorrest** is a reference to Syria and Ephraim. It is obvious that the statement is taken to mean that before the child could grow to the age of two, the enemy nations would lose **both her kings**. The question is often raised as to how this relates to the prediction of the virgin birth of Christ if, in actuality, He is not to be born yet for many years. Cowles (p. 55) argues that Isaiah saw the vision of the future event as if it were already happening and continues to speak as though the child were growing before his very eyes. Thus, he carries this "present condition" into the contemporary situation. The infancy of this child will symbolize the fact that the desolation of Judah at Ahaz's time will be short-lived, for the enemy kings

17 ¶The Lord shall bring upon thee, and upon thy people, and upon thy father's house, days that have not come from the day that Ē'phra-im departed from Jū'dah; *even* the king of Assyria.

18 And it shall come to pass in that day, *that* the Lord shall hiss for the fly that *is* in the uttermost part of the rivers of Egypt, and for the bee that *is* in the land of Assyria.

19 And they shall come, and shall rest all of them in the desolate valleys, and in the holes of the rocks, and upon all thorns, and upon all bushes.

20 In the same day shall the Lord shave with a razor that is hired, *namely*, by them beyond the river, by the king of Assyria, the head, and the hair of the feet: and it shall also consume the beard.

21 And it shall come to pass in that day, *that* a man shall nourish a young cow, and two sheep;

22 And it shall come to pass, for the abundance of milk *that* they shall give he shall eat butter: for butter and honey shall every one eat that is left in the land.

23 And it shall come to pass in that day, *that* every place shall be, where there were a thousand vines at a thousand silverlings, it shall *even* be for briers and thorns.

24 With arrows and with bows shall *men* come thither; because all the land shall become briers and thorns.

25 And *on* all hills that shall be digged with the mattock, there shall not come thither the fear of briers and thorns: but it shall be for the sending forth of oxen, and for the treading of lesser cattle.

CHAPTER 8

MOREOVER the Lord said unto me, Take thee a great roll, and write in it

will soon be rendered powerless. Delitzsch (p. 221) takes the reference to indicate a time parallel to the child's reaching the age of discernment. Thus, the prophecy does have significance and relevance to Ahaz, even though it predicts the yet future virgin birth of the Messiah. In the meantime, Ahaz is not to attempt an alliance with Assyria, because such an alliance will later create even more problems for Judah. The king is called upon to trust God Himself to protect the Davidic line at the present time; in less than two years Judah's enemies would be defeated. The situation certainly has a parallel in the Old Testament in Exodus 3:12, where the promise that Israel would worship at Mount Sinai is given to Moses, obviously guaranteeing that they would first be delivered out of Egypt. In Isaiah's time the throne of David had to be spared in order for the Messiah eventually to reign upon it. Thus, Isaiah's prediction of the coming of the virgin-born Son can literally look down through history to the time of Christ, while the time-indicator of His growing to discernment within a couple of years of His birth is used to illustrate the fact that within a couple of years Judah would be rid of her nemesis. The Baptist Hebrew scholar, J.W. Watts, in *A Distinctive Translation of Isaiah with an Interpretive Outline* (p. 16), notes that the construction here is an imperfect, which must be interpreted as a subjunctive of possibility. This indicates that the period of time involved in the child's experience is a mere possibility. This possibility is then used by the prophet to measure the period of time in which Syria and Ephraim will be laid waste by Assyria.

17-25. The day that Ephraim departed from Judah refers back to the time of the division of the kingdom between the northern and southern tribes after the death of Solomon in 931 B.C. **The king of Assyria** is then named as the source of the coming destruction upon Israel, which eventually fell to that nation in 722 B.C. (For a brief but excellent survey, see H. W. Saggs, "The Assyrians," in *POTT*, pp. 156-178.) **The fly** is appropriately used as a symbol for the land of **Egypt** (coming from the wet Delta region); and the **bee** is used as a symbol of Assyria, where these insects are also in abundance. The symbolism is used of a numberless host (**hiss**, lit., whistle). The population will be so devastated by this invasion that there will be an **abundance of milk . . . butter . . . and honey.** For the most part, however, this is a picture of devastation; for where there were many vines, there shall now be only **briers and thorns.** Again, the prophet ends with a ray of hope; for those who are left and are willing to farm the land, it will yet send forth some nourishment.

b. His magnificent land. 8:1-10:34.

8:1-4. Isaiah is commanded to take a **great roll** (scroll) and write upon it the symbolic name **Maher-shalal-hash-baz** (lit.,

with a man's pen concerning Mā′-her–shăl′al–hăsh′–băz,

2 And I took unto me faithful witnesses to record, Ū-rī′ah the priest, and Zěch-a-rī′ah the son of Je-běr-e-chī′ah.

3 And I went unto the prophetess; and she conceived, and bare a son. Then said the Lord to me, Call his name Mā′her–shăl′al–hăsh′–băz,

4 For before the child shall have knowledge to cry, My father, and my mother, the riches of Damascus and the spoil of Sa-mâ′rī-a shall be taken away before the king of Assyria.

5 ¶The Lord spake also unto me again, saying,

6 Forasmuch as this people refuseth the waters of Shī-lō′ah that go softly, and rejoice in Rē′zĭn and Rěm-a-lī′ah's son;

7 Now therefore, behold, the Lord bringeth up upon them the waters of the river, strong and many, even the king of Assyria, and all his glory: and he shall come up over all his channels, and go over all his banks;

8 And he shall pass through Jū′dah; he shall overflow and go over, he shall reach even to the neck; and the stretching out of his wings shall fill the breadth of thy land, O Ĭm-măn′ū-el.

9 ¶Associate yourselves, O ye people, and ye shall be broken in pieces; and give ear, all ye of far countries: gird yourselves, and ye shall be broken in pieces; gird yourselves, and ye shall be broken in pieces.

10 Take counsel together, and it shall come to nought; speak the word, and it shall not stand: for God is with us.

11 For the Lord spake thus to me with a strong hand, and instructed me that I should not walk in the way of this people, saying,

12 Say ye not, A confederacy, to all them to whom this people shall say, A confederacy; neither fear ye their fear, nor be afraid.

13 Sanctify the Lord of hosts himself; and let him be your fear, and let him be your dread.

14 And he shall be for a sanctuary; but for a stone of stumbling and for a rock of offence to both the houses of Israel, for a gin and for a snare to the inhabitants of Jerusalem.

15 And many among them shall stumble, and fall, and be broken, and be snared, and be taken.

16 Bind up the testimony, seal the law among my disciples.

17 And I will wait upon the Lord, that hideth his face from the house of Jacob, and I will look for him.

18 Behold, I and the children whom the Lord hath given me are for signs and for wonders in Israel from the Lord of hosts, which dwelleth in mount Zion.

speed the spoil, hurry the prey). His name was to symbolize the successful Assyrian conquest of Damascus and Samaria. Thus, both kingdoms would be crushed before this child would be old enough to say **father** and **mother** (i.e., two to three years). **Uriah** is referred to as one of the **faithful witnesses** to the significance of this event. Some have seen a parallel between him and a man of a similar name in II Kings 16; however, this is not clearly indicated. **Zechariah** (one of twenty-eight men so named in the OT) is distinguished here as the **son of Jeberechiah.**

5-10. The waters of Shiloah refer to the waters of the pool of Siloam. The gradual gradient which brought these waters into the pool was such that they flowed quietly and peacefully. Even in the New Testament this pool is referred to as a place of healing (Jn 9:7). Therefore, because of their refusal to trust the peaceful blessings of the Lord and their dependence instead upon wicked leaders, God will bring upon them **the waters of the river** (contrasted to those of the gentle pool). This phrase is used figuratively of the overflowing of the army of the **king of Assyria.** Thus, Isaiah names in advance the nation which shall be responsible for the conquest and destruction of Israel. This invasion shall even **pass through Judah** and shall overflow **even to the neck.** The indication of Isaiah's prophecy is that the Assyrian invasion will eventually wipe out the northern kingdom and nearly drown the southern kingdom, which shall narrowly escape (this is actually detailed in the historical account in Isa 36-37). Thus, the invasion is referred to as filling **the breadth of thy land, O Immanuel.** This clearly states that the land belongs to Immanuel, indicating that He is no ordinary person born in the days of the prophet Isaiah. He is more than that, for He is the One who owns the land Himself. Since the Old Testament makes it clear that God is in fact the landowner of Israel (Gen 12:7), this must indicate that Immanuel is God Himself! Thus, the invading nations are told that their alliances will ultimately **not stand** against Judah because **God is with us.** There can be no real doubt that the usage of these terms in this chapter are intended to connect it with the preceding prophecy of the virgin birth of Immanuel and to serve as a link to the further prediction of His birth as King in chapter 9.

11-18. The Lord (*Yahweh*) speaks personally to the prophet with a **strong hand,** referring to the common method of Jewish parental discipline. Thus, Isaiah is **instructed** (Heb *yasar*, to chasten) not to follow the attitude (**walk in the way**) of the people, nor is he to be intimidated by their threat that he is forming a **confederacy** (better, a conspiracy, see ASV). The true believers in Jehovah are not to **fear,** but to Sanctify (Heb *quediyshū*), **the Lord of hosts.** He shall be a **sanctuary** (Heb *miqdash*) to those who trust Him; but to those who reject Him, He shall be a **stone of stumbling and . . rock of offence** to **both the houses of Israel** (i.e., north and south). This verse is quoted in both Romans 9:33 and I Peter 2:8 as predictively referring to Jesus Christ. If we are to take the inspiration of the New Testament writers seriously, we must again see the predictive connection of the entire Immanuel passage as it is literally fulfilled in the life and ministry of Christ. A **gin** is a trap. **Many among them shall stumble** on this **rock of offence.** The meaning of the entire passage is that instead of finding asylum in the Lord, these unbelievers would stumble over Him in disbelief. **My disciples** refers to those who have accepted the message of the prophet Isaiah. Delitzsch (p. 237) holds that it is the prophet's prayer to Jehovah to seal these truths to His disciples (rather than viewing them as God's own disciples). The prophet closes this section by stating that he and his **children** are intended to be **signs and . . . wonders** to the nation of Israel.

19 And when they shall say unto you, Seek unto them that have familiar spirits, and unto wizards that peep, and that mutter: should not a people seek unto their God? for the living to the dead?

20 To the law and to the testimony: if they speak not according to this word, *it is* because *there is* no light in them.

21 And they shall pass through it, hardly bestead and hungry: and it shall come to pass, that when they shall be hungry, they shall fret themselves, and curse their king and their God, and look upward.

22 And they shall look unto the earth; and behold trouble and darkness, dimness of anguish; and *they shall be* driven to darkness.

CHAPTER 9

NEVERTHELESS the dimness *shall* not *be* such as *was* in her vexation, when at the first he lightly afflicted the land of Zĕb'u-lun and the land of Năph'ta-lī, and afterward did more grievously afflict *her by* the way of the sea, beyond Jordan, in Galilee of the nations.

2 The people that walked in darkness have seen a great light: they that dwell in the land of the shadow of death, upon them hath the light shined.

3 Thou hast multiplied the nation, *and* not increased the joy: they joy before thee according to the joy in harvest, *and* as *men* rejoice when they divide the spoil.

4 For thou hast broken the yoke of his burden, and the staff of his shoulder, the rod of his oppressor, as in the day of Mĭd'ĭ-an.

5 For every battle of the warrior *is* with confused noise, and garments rolled in blood; but *this* shall be with burning *and* fuel of fire.

6 For unto us a child is born, unto us a son is given: and the government shall be upon his shoulder: and his name shall be called Wonderful, Counsellor,

Because of their sign-ificant names, they were to serve as a sign of warning to the people of Israel, especially those of Zion (Jerusalem).

19-22. Familiar spirits refers to female witches and **wizards** (**soothsayers**) that **peep, and . . . mutter** (better, chirp and whisper). In these times of great distress the people were actually consorting to witchcraft instead of turning to God. The messenger warns that they are not to seek these mediums **for the living to the dead.** Verse 19 in the RSV reads: ". . . Should they consult the dead on behalf of the living?" The passage clearly speaks against the cult of spiritism which is one of the oldest pagan religions known to mankind. True Old Testament religion, like Christianity, forbade such practices because there was **no light** in them. The guideline of verse 20 clearly states that **the law** (*tōrah*) **and . . . the testimony** (*te'ūdah*, precept) are clearly declared to be the basis of interpreting any claim to divine revelation. Thus, those who neglect this standard of truth shall find no answer at all in their day of **anguish** and shall be driven even further into the impenetrable **darkness.**

9:1-5. This chapter opens with another striking messianic prophecy of the coming of the child Immanuel who, though He is not named as such in this chapter, is obviously the Child that is to be born and shall rule upon the throne of David. Verse 1 continues the thought of the previous chapter. The **dimness** of Israel's rejection was especially prevalent in the northern tribal areas of **Zebulun** and **Naphtali,** which suffered grievously under the Assyrian invasion that was shortly forthcoming. In a striking Old Testament passage **Galilee** is actually named and identified with **the nations** (Heb *goyim,* lit., Gentiles). To them who had walked in darkness the promise is made of the coming of a **great light,** which is quoted in Matthew 4:15-16 as being "fulfilled" in the coming of Christ and His ministry in Galilee. This is also alluded to in Luke 1:79. Watts (p. 20) notes that the word **not** in verse 3 is a mistranslation that distorts the entire meaning of the verse. He notes that the Masoretic recommendation was to read "its" instead of "not." In the original they are identical in sound and similar in form (Heb *lo',* not, and *loh,* its). Evidently some scribe mistakenly miscopied the manuscript, accidently confusing the two words. The coming of this Great Light shall break the **yoke of his burden** and the **rod of his oppressor,** indicating the total victory of Jesus Christ over the enemies of His people. The promise in verse 5 actually extends to the time when the garments of battle shall be consumed and used no more. Obviously, it represents a millennial promise of peace in the future. It should also be noted that the verbs in this section are virtually all prophetic perfects, which is highly unusual in one brief passage. As a rule, the prophet normally used only one or two at a time. These verbs are actually stated in the present tense as if they were already happening (e.g., people "walking" in darkness; light "shining" upon them). Yet, they refer to future events that shall yet come to pass. In essence, the prophet makes his prediction of the future event with such certitude and finality that he states it in the present tense as if it was already a fact. That the prophet expected his prediction to come true in actual history is obvious by his very usage of terminology. (On the significance of this syntactical construction, see *Gesenius' Hebrew Grammar* [Cautzsch-Cowley edition, p. 312ff.]; on the message and ministry of the prophets, see Schultz, *The Prophets Speak,* and Young, *My Servants the Prophets.*)

6-7. The Gift-Child in this passage is certainly to be understood as the same person as the Immanuel who appeared earlier. This Child is certainly none other than the virgin's son. Contrasted with the Syrian-Ephraimitic coalition, this Child brings

The mighty God, The everlasting Father, The Prince of Peace.

7 Of the increase of *his* government and peace *there shall be* no end, upon the throne of David, and upon his kingdom, to order it, and to establish it with judgment and with justice from henceforth even for ever. The zeal of the LORD of hosts will perform this.

8 ¶The Lord sent a word into Jacob, and it hath lighted upon Israel.

9 And all the people shall know, *even* E'phra-im and the inhabitant of Sa-mâ'rī-a, that say in the pride and stoutness of heart,

10 The bricks are fallen down, but we will build with hewn stones: the sycomores are cut down, but we will change *them into* cedars.

11 Therefore the LORD shall set up the adversaries of Rē'zĭn against him, and join his enemies together;

12 The Syrians before, and the Philistines behind; and they shall devour Israel with open mouth. For all this his anger is not turned away, but his hand *is* stretched out still.

13 ¶For the people turneth not unto him that smiteth them, neither do they seek the LORD of hosts.

14 Therefore the LORD will cut off from Israel head and tail, branch and rush, in one day.

15 The ancient and honourable, he *is*

deliverance to the people of God. Again, using the prophetic perfect, the prophet speaks of Him as though He were already born! Even the text of the Targum supports a messianic interpretation of this passage. The concept of a Messiah who is both the Son of David and the Son of God is also stated in Psalm 2:7. Notice also the play-on-words between **child is born** (Heb *yalad*, to be delivered, as in birth) and a **son is given** (Heb *natan*). Some have suggested that there is a distinction between the human birth of the Child and the divine gift of the Son. While the usage of the verbs is not conclusive, it is interesting to note that the same idea appears in Isaiah 42:1 where God gives His Spirit to His Servant. The real significance of this unique Child comes in His fourfold name. **Wonderful, Counselor** (*pele' yō'ets*) is actually one title in the Hebrew (based upon the Masoretic accentuation). "Wonder," from *pele'*, is indicative of that which is miraculously accomplished by God Himself (see Harris, *Theological Word Book of the Old Testament*, II, p. 723). The two words of this title are actually an appositional genitive and may be rendered "a wonder of a counselor" or "a wonderful counselor." The term "counselor" is often used in parallel with "king" (e.g., Mic 4:9), so that the emphasis here implies that of God-like counsel of a God-like King. **The mighty God** (Heb *'el gibbōr*). This is the strongest of the titles with reference to deity. In the book of Isaiah *'el* is always used of God and never refers to man (e.g., 10:21). *Gibbōr* means "hero." Whether it is used as an appositional genitive or adjectivally, in either case it is an epithet that indicates deity. There is, therefore, every indication that the Child is **The mighty God** Himself! Obviously, such a revelation explains how the Child in 7:14 could be born miraculously of a virgin and how He could symbolically be called Immanuel (God with Us). **The everlasting Father** (Heb *'abiy-'ad*) is a peculiar expression literally meaning Father of Eternity. He is the Lord of eternity, as well as the Author of eternal life. He is "of old, from everlasting" (Mic 5:2). Here we clearly see how the throne of David, which is to be forever, is to be preserved. It will seat a ruler who Himself is Eternal! **The Prince of Peace** (Heb *shar-shalōm*). Rather than a warring monarch, He who is the Mighty God will be a benevolent Father, bringing a peace that will be eternally established in His kingdom. His reign shall be characterized by a rule of peace on earth because He is the very embodiment of peace itself. Thus, the obscure figure of Immanuel in 7:14 is now brought to clear light. We know of His kingdom, throne, world rule, peaceful reign, and eternal kingdom, as well as His virgin birth. More than this, we know who He is—God Himself incarnate!

8-12. Isaiah now warns that **Ephraim** (northern Israel) will not heed the warning of the Lord; in her pride she will assume that she can rebuild with the **bricks** that **are fallen down.** This refers to the invasion of Israel by Tiglath-pileser in 732 B.C. The Ephraimites are still boasting that they can rebuild their devastated country and make it stronger and more glorious than ever before. However, the prophet warns that their former allies, the **Syrians** (to the north) and the **Philistines** (to the south), will turn against Ephraim and shall **devour Israel.** This prediction is followed by a recurring statement that now appears in this section: **For all this his anger is not turned away, but his hand is stretched out still,** meaning that His anger is not abated but His hand of judgment is still stretched out in anger against Israel.

13-21. In spite of this discipline from the Lord, **the people turneth not unto him.** "To turn" means to repent (from the Heb *shūb*). Thus, the meaning of this statement is that they had refused to repent and turn again to the Lord. It is clear in the Old Testament that the concept of repentance included a change

the head; and the prophet that teacheth lies, he *is* the tail.

16 For the leaders of this people cause *them* to err; and *they that are* led of them *are* destroyed.

17 Therefore the Lord shall have no joy in their young men, neither shall have mercy on their fatherless and widows: for every one *is* an hypocrite and an evildoer, and every mouth speaketh folly. For all this his anger is not turned away, but his hand *is* stretched out still.

18 ¶For wickedness burneth as the fire: it shall devour the briers and thorns, and shall kindle in the thickets of the forest, and they shall mount up *like* the lifting up of smoke.

19 Through the wrath of the LORD of hosts is the land darkened, and the people shall be as the fuel of the fire: no man shall spare his brother.

20 And he shall snatch on the right hand, and be hungry; and he shall eat on the left hand, and they shall not be satisfied: they shall eat every man the flesh of his own arm:

21 Ma-năs′seh, Ē′phra-ĭm; and Ē′phra-ĭm, Ma-năs′seh: *and* they together shall *be* against Jū′dah. For all this his anger is not turned away, but his hand *is* stretched out still.

CHAPTER 10

WOE unto them that decree unrighteous decrees, and that write grievousness *which* they have prescribed.

2 To turn aside the needy from judgment, and to take away the right from the poor of my people, that widows may be their prey, and *that* they may rob the fatherless!

3 And what will ye do in the day of visitation, and in the desolation *which* shall come from far? to whom will ye flee for help? and where will ye leave your glory?

4 Without me they shall bow down under the prisoners, and they shall fall under the slain. For all this his anger is not turned away, but his hand *is* stretched out still.

5 ¶O Assyrian, the rod of mine anger, and the staff in their hand is mine indignation.

6 I will send him against an hypocritical nation, and against the people of my wrath will I give him a charge, to take the spoil, and to take the prey, and to tread them down like the mire of the streets.

7 Howbeit he meaneth not so, neither doth his heart think so; but *it is* in his heart to destroy and cut off nations not a few.

8 For he saith, *Are* not my princes altogether kings?

9 *Is* not Căl′nō as Căr′che-mĭsh? *is* not Hă′măth as Ăr′păd? *is* not Sa-mā′rĭ-a as Damascus?

10 As my hand hath found the kingdoms of the idols, and whose graven images did excel them of Jerusalem and of Sa-mā′rĭ-a:

11 Shall I not, as I have done unto Sa-mā′rĭ-a and her idols, so do to Jerusalem and her idols?

12 Wherefore it shall come to pass, *that* when the Lord hath performed his

of direction, as well as a change of mind. Therefore, the prophet pictures Israel as a tree felled before the presence of Jehovah. **Branch and rush** means "branch and root." The **ancient** (lit., elder) and the **prophet that teacheth lies** together will be cut off by the Lord. The statement that the **leaders of this people cause them to err** is reminiscent of the prophet's message in chapter 3. Notice that **joy** and **mercy** are used interchangeably in verse 17, where the Lord says that He will extend neither to these people because **every one is a hypocrite.** Because of Israel's spiritual condition, this predicted judgment is irrevocable. Therefore, the warning refrain is again repeated: **For all this his anger is not turned away. . . .** The imagery of the closing verses of this section is that of a devouring **fire** which is burning out of control in the forest and shall certainly burn up these dried and fallen trees previously described. The tragedy is that the prophet is really talking about **people** who actually **shall be as the fuel of the fire.** The two major political tribes in the north, **Manasseh** and **Ephraim,** are both singled out for the brunt of God's judgment.

10:1-4. A prophetic **Woe** is pronounced against those administrators who have perverted justice with **unrighteous decrees.** Those governmental officials who have abused their positions of authority by oppressing the people, especially the poor, are to be brought before God's bar of justice. In the coming invasion they will lose all their **glory.** Notice that this loss of glory is associated with their being **Without me.** To lose the presence of God is to lose His glory, and to lose His glory is to lose His presence (cf. Ezk 8-11). Again, the poetic strophe is repeated: **For all this his anger is not turned away. . . .**

5-19. By the sovereign will of God the **Assyrian** was to serve as His **rod of . . . anger.** Like an offended father dealing with a disobedient son, God indicates that He is using the nation of Assyria to give His people Israel a well-deserved spanking. Verse 7 makes it clear that Assyria does not intend to be the instrument of Jehovah. **Howbeit he meaneth not so** indicates that the Assyrians did not intend to cooperate with God, but they had no choice in the matter! Their intention was simply to **destroy and cut off nations.** The cities listed in verse 9 are on a direct line from Nineveh (capital of Assyria) to Jerusalem (capital of Judah). All of them had fallen to the invading Assyrian army. Notice that **Samaria** is listed as having already fallen, and **Jerusalem** is under threat because of **her idols.** As is always the case, people who know the Lord are usually a bit restrained in their sin; thus, their **idols** did not excel those of the foreign nations. In other words, it was rather ridiculous for them to permit idol worship of pagan gods in the first place when their devotion to these gods was less than the other nations which had already fallen. Then, the prophet, speaking for God, explains that when he has finished dealing with Jerusalem, he will **punish . . . the king of Assyria.** The Lord will make it clear to the Assyrians that they have not conquered in the strength of their own might, but only as He has permitted them to do. This

whole work upon mount Zion and on Jerusalem, I will punish the fruit of the stout heart of the king of Assyria, and the glory of his high looks.

13 For he saith, By the strength of my hand I have done it, and by my wisdom; for I am prudent: and I have removed the bounds of the people, and have robbed their treasures, and I have put down the inhabitants like a valiant man:

14 And my hand hath found as a nest the riches of the people: and as one gathereth eggs that are left, have I gathered all the earth; and there was none that moved the wing, or opened the mouth, or peeped.

15 Shall the axe boast itself against him that heweth therewith? or shall the saw magnify itself against him that shaketh it? as if the rod should shake itself against them that lift it up, or as if the staff should lift up itself, as if it were no wood.

16 Therefore shall the Lord, the Lord of hosts, send among his fat ones leanness; and under his glory he shall kindle a burning like the burning of a fire.

17 And the light of Israel shall be for a fire, and his Holy One for a flame: and it shall burn and devour his thorns and his briers in one day;

18 And shall consume the glory of his forest, and of his fruitful field, both soul and body: and they shall be as when a standardbearer fainteth.

19 And the rest of the trees of his forest shall be few, that a child may write them.

20 ¶And it shall come to pass in that day, that the remnant of Israel, and such as are escaped of the house of Jacob, shall no more again stay upon him that smote them; but shall stay upon the LORD, the Holy One of Israel, in truth.

21 The remnant shall return, even the remnant of Jacob, unto the mighty God.

22 For though thy people Israel be as the sand of the sea, yet a remnant of them shall return: the consumption decreed shall overflow with righteousness.

23 For the Lord GOD of hosts shall make a consumption, even determined, in the midst of all the land.

24 ¶Therefore thus saith the Lord GOD of hosts, O my people that dwellest in Zion, be not afraid of the Assyrian: he shall smite thee with a rod, and shall lift up his staff against thee, after the manner of Egypt.

25 For yet a very little while, and the indignation shall cease, and mine anger in their destruction.

26 And the LORD of hosts shall stir up a scourge for him according to the slaughter of Mĭd'ĭ-an at the rock of Ō'reb: and as his rod was upon the sea, so shall he lift it up after the manner of Egypt.

27 And it shall come to pass in that day, that his burden shall be taken away from off thy shoulder, and his yoke from off thy neck, and the yoke

passage clearly teaches that the power of nations is no greater than the permission of God. They can go no further than God will allow them to go! This point is pictured by the illustration of the **axe** boasting against the hewer who is using it. It is not the axe that cuts down the tree, but the man who swings the axe. In the mind of God, Assyria is nothing more than a tool in His hand. Of the cut-down trees, the Lord Himself shall serve as a **flame** and **fire** and shall **burn** them up and **consume** them. When He is finished, the remaining **trees** shall be few, so **few** that a child may **write them** (count them). It is interesting to note that since wood was so scarce in Assyria, the Assyrians were also famous for cutting down their enemies' trees after they had conquered their nation.

20-34. In this section the prophet Isaiah makes a prediction that was to come true within his own lifetime (see ch. 37-38). **The remnant of Israel** are those who will come to believe in the LORD, **the Holy One of Israel.** In light of his previous statements, verse 21 ties together the earlier and latter aspects of this prophecy. **The remnant shall return** is reminiscent of the name of the prophet's son, Shear-jashab. That they will return unto **the mighty God** calls the reader's attention back to the divine title of 9:6. **Thy people Israel** are referred to as a **remnant,** indicating that the northern tribes were not totally lost in their dispersion by Assyria; a small remnant would one day return. The prophet's message is clear: the northern kingdom shall fall to Assyria, whereas the southern kingdom shall also be invaded but shall not be utterly destroyed. Later, Isaiah will direct his attention to the fact that the destruction of Judah will arise from another source altogether—Babylon. God's intervention is related to the **slaughter of Midian at the rock of Oreb** which took place centuries earlier in the days of Gideon (Jud 7:25). **The anointing** is taken by virtually all commentators to better read "fatness," referring to the weight of the yoke. The cities listed in verses 28-32 are those lesser towns which shall be taken by the coming Assyrian invasion which will cause the invader to **shake his hand against the mount . . . of Jerusalem.** In spite of his early success, the invading Assyrians will miraculously be stopped when **the LORD of hosts, shall lop the bough with terror.** The prediction is that God will stop the invasion by divine intervention. This is the historical claim of the book, as well in 37:36 where the **angel of the LORD** slays the invading Assyrian army. (The Assyrian account of this invasion is given in the Sennacherib Chronicle in Bauer, *Akkadische Lesestücke* (I, pp. 90-96); for an English translation, see D. J. Wiseman in *POTT*, pp. 64-70.)

shall be destroyed because of the anointing.

28 He is come to Ā-i′ăth, he is passed to Mĭg′rŏn; at Mĭch′măsh he hath laid up his carriages:

29 They are gone over the passage: they have taken up their lodging at Gē′ba; Rā′mah is afraid; Gĭb′e-ah of Saul is fled.

30 Lift up thy voice, O daughter of Găl′lĭm: cause it to be heard unto Lā′ĭsh, O poor Ăn′a-thŏth.

31 Măd-mē′nah is removed; the inhabitants of Gē′bĭm gather themselves to flee.

32 As yet shall he remain at Nob that day: he shall shake his hand *against* the mount of the daughter of Zion, the hill of Jerusalem.

33 Behold, the Lord, the Lord of hosts, shall lop the bough with terror: and the high ones of stature *shall* be hewn down, and the haughty shall be humbled.

34 And he shall cut down the thickets of the forest with iron, and Lebanon shall fall by a mighty one.

CHAPTER 11

AND there shall come forth a rod out of the stem of Jesse, and a Branch shall grow out of his roots:

2 And the spirit of the Lord shall rest upon him, the spirit of wisdom and understanding, the spirit of counsel and might, the spirit of knowledge and of the fear of the Lord;

3 And shall make him of quick understanding in the fear of the Lord: and he shall not judge after the sight of his eyes, neither reprove after the hearing of his ears:

4 But with righteousness shall he judge the poor, and reprove with equity for the meek of the earth: and he shall smite the earth: with the rod of his mouth, and with the breath of his lips shall he slay the wicked.

5 And righteousness shall be the girdle of his loins, and faithfulness the girdle of his reins.

c. His millennial reign. 11:1-12:6.

11:1-5. The time of the Messiah's coming was undoubtedly a great puzzle in Old Testament times. Isaiah's prophecies in chapters 7-9 indicate that Immanuel, the virgin-born, divine Child is soon to appear. However, in this chapter we are given a clear indication that His coming will be in the yet distant future. Isaiah predicts that the "tree" of the line of David will be cut down and that a shoot must grow out of the root stock of Jesse before the tree can flourish again. Isaiah's point is to show that the kingdom has sunk so low that the Davidic line will apparently be cut down, and yet somehow will spring forth again in the person of the Messiah. The prophet predicts that a **rod** (Heb *shoter*, shoot or sprout) shall come forth out of the **stem** (Heb *geza‘*, root stock or stump) of **Jesse** (David's father and the forefather of the Davidic line). The imagery of the prophet is that of a felled tree out of whose stump a twig would sprout and from whose roots a **Branch** (Heb *netser*, shoot) would flourish again. In verse 2 this **shoot** is personalized as an individual ruler—the Messiah Himself! **The spirit of the Lord** apparently refers to the sevenfold Holy Spirit of God (cf. Rev 4:5). The **spirit** (Heb *rūach*) is described in a sevenfold personification of **wisdom . . . understanding . . . counsel . . . might . . . knowledge . . . fear of the Lord.** Young (I, p. 381) notes that this verse is a genitive of causality in which these qualities appear in three pairs. Thus, the reference is not to seven separate spirits. Delitzsch (p. 282) notes that the words for **counsel** and **might** are the same as were used in 9:6 to describe the divine Child. Certainly the parallel of this statement to that of chapter 9 is amazingly similar. The phrase **And shall make him of quick understanding** in verse 3 should literally be translated "delights to smell," indicating His extreme sensitivity to the fear of God. The picture is that the Messiah rejoices in the fear of the Lord just as if an offering has been brought to Him. The form is not a finite verb but an infinite construct (lit., His smelling with delight). Because the Spirit of God is upon Him, the Messiah will not **judge after the sight of his eyes;** for He shall have true spiritual vision. He shall **neither reprove** (settle) matters after the **hearing of his ears.** Rather, the basis of His judgment and His vindication of the poor shall be **with righteousness** (Heb *tsedeq*). It is this righteousness that is the basis of His millennial reign. Thus, He shall rule the earth with the **the rod** (*shebet*, scepter) **of his mouth,** indicating that the rule of the Messiah

6 The wolf also shall dwell with the lamb, and the leopard shall lie down with the kid; and the calf and the young lion and the fatling together; and a little child shall lead them.
7 And the cow and the bear shall feed; their young ones shall lie down together; and the lion shall eat straw like the ox.
8 And the sucking child shall play on the hole of the asp, and the weaned child shall put his hand on the cockatrice' den.
9 They shall not hurt nor destroy in all my holy mountain: for the earth shall be full of the knowledge of the LORD, as the waters cover the sea.

10 And in that day there shall be a root of Jesse, which shall stand for an ensign of the people; to it shall the Gentiles seek: and his rest shall be glorious.
11 And it shall come to pass in that day, *that* the Lord shall set his hand again the second time to recover the remnant of his people, which shall be left, from Assyria, and from Egypt, and from Păth'rŏs, and from Cush, and from Ē'lam, and from Shī'när, and from Hă'măth, and from the islands of the sea.
12 And he shall set up an ensign for the nations, and shall assemble the outcasts of Israel, and gather together the dispersed of Jū'dah from the four corners of the earth.
13 The envy also of Ē'phra-im shall depart, and the adversaries of Jū'dah shall be cut off: Ē'phra-im shall not envy Jū'dah, and Jū'dah shall not vex Ē'phra-im.
14 But they shall fly upon the shoulders of the Philistines toward the west; they shall spoil them of the east together: they shall lay their hand upon Ē'dom and Moab; and the children of Ammon shall obey them.
15 And the LORD shall utterly destroy the tongue of the Egyptian sea; and with his mighty wind shall he shake his hand over the river, and shall smite it in the seven streams, and make *men* go over dryshod.
16 And there shall be an highway for the remnant of his people, which shall be left, from Assyria; like as it was to Israel in the day that he came up out of the land of Egypt.

shall be by the power of His spoken Word, even to the extent that He shall slay the wicked with His **breath** (cf. Rev 19:15). It is His righteousness that shall be the **girdle** (belt) that holds together the spiritual greatness of His kingdom on earth.

6-9. The quality of the Messiah's kingdom will be one of complete peace and harmony. The dangerous predatory animals, **wolf . . . leopard . . . lion . . . bear,** are to be taken as literal, and not symbolic of various types of hostile people. It is obvious in these verses that these ravenous animals are set in deliberate contrast against the more defenseless **lamb . . . kid . . . calf . . . cow . . . ox.** The reference to a **little child** and the **sucking child** shows that there will not only be harmony between men in the Messiah's kingdom, but there will also be harmony between the animals and between man and the animal kingdom. Verse 7 goes even further to indicate that the **lion shall eat straw,** indicating a change of diet from carnivorous to vegetarian. To "spiritualize" this passage away in defense of an amillennial position is totally unfair to the text. If we are to assume that a real Messiah shall come forth and rule in real righteousness, then we must also view this era of real peace as extending to the real animal world as well. Even the **cockatrice** (snake) shall be rendered harmless, even to the small child. This unparalleled time of spiritual and natural peace will result from the fact that the **earth shall be full of the knowledge of the LORD.** Isaiah now introduces his Jewish readers to a new, universal emphasis on the salvation of the Lord. Not only will there be a remnant spared in Judah, but the day is coming when this divine Messiah shall rule the entire world.

10-16. The Messiah is again referred to as a **root** (Heb *shoresh*) **of Jesse** as in 11:1. The prophet reemphasizes the fact that this glorious coming kingdom will be the result of the shoot which shall bud forth from the apparently cut-down tree of David's line. The Messiah shall **stand for an ensign** (banner) **of the people** (Heb *'amiy*, the term normally applied to the Jewish people). Yet, Isaiah goes on to say that it is this banner that the **Gentiles** (*gōyim*) **seek.** Thus, there can be no doubt that Isaiah is predicting a coming time of salvation for the Gentiles as well as the Jews. **His rest** is, literally, "place of rest" or "resting place." In either case it represents the place where God has settled down to rule. The Hebrew word is also used in 7:2 and forms an interesting contrast: in the former case Ahaz was worried because Syria was resting with Ephraim and here those who trust in God are sharing in His **glorious** rest. Again, note that the glory of God (*kabōd*) is synonymous with the presence of God. Therefore, one must conclude that the Messiah who is ruling in this glorious Kingdom is none other than God Himself. Thus, the Old Testament here provides ample witness to the deity of Christ. The prophet Isaiah then makes it clear that this shall **come to pass** by a **second** restoration of the Jews. This clearly excludes a reference to the return under Zerubbabel in 537 B.C. It indicates a national restoration of the **remnant** of the Jews from every possible direction. **Assyria** was to the northeast; **Egypt** was to the southwest; **Pathros** is Upper Egypt; **Cush** is Ethiopia in Africa; **Elam** was on the Persian Gulf, near **Shinar,** or Babylon; **Hamath** was located on the Orontes River in northern Syria. Amillennial commentators (e.g., Young, I, p. 398) attempt to view this statement in light of all national distinction being abolished in Christ. They then view the **Philistines** as the "enemies of the Church!" This view is highly unlikely in light of the literalness with which the prophet speaks of **Judah** and **Ephraim** in the same context. Archer (p. 621) views this passage from a premillennial position, noting that the Christian Israelites who have been converted by the gospel are then used of God to reach their yet unconverted neighboring nations, Philistia, Edom, and Moab. This will take place at the beginning of the millennial kingdom. Even the natural barriers of the Euphrates

CHAPTER 12

AND in that day thou shalt say, O LORD, I will praise thee: though thou wast angry with me, thine anger is turned away, and thou comfortedst me.

2 Behold, God *is* my salvation; I will trust, and not be afraid: for the LORD JEHOVAH *is* my strength and *my* song; he also is become my salvation.

3 Therefore with joy shall ye draw water out of the wells of salvation.

4 And in that day shall ye say, Praise the LORD, call upon his name, declare his doings among the people, make mention that his name is exalted.

5 Sing unto the LORD; for he hath done excellent things: this *is* known in all the earth.

6 Cry out and shout, thou inhabitant of Zion: for great *is* the Holy One of Israel in the midst of thee.

CHAPTER 13

THE burden of Babylon, which Isaiah the son of Amoz did see.

2 Lift ye up a banner upon the high mountain, exalt the voice unto them,

and the Red Sea will miraculously be removed at this time, and communication between these formerly hostile nations will be natural and unimpeded during the reign of the Prince of Peace.

12:1-6. In the twelfth chapter the prophet Isaiah, speaking for the blessed millennial believers, bursts into a song of triumphant praise. Thus, the chapter serves as a dramatic climax to the Immanuel prophecy. God's **anger** (Heb *'aph*, wrath) is no longer directed toward the people of Judah, but has been **turned away** (*yashob* from *shūb*). Therefore, he declares **I will praise thee.** This verb is in the imperfect and expresses continual action. Thus, he boldly proclaims: **Behold, God is my salvation. Behold** is a construct and serves as a dramatic climax in this doxology of praise. It is used to announce the momentous truth which in the Hebrew literally reads "My salvation is God Himself!" Here, undoubtedly, is the culmination of the prophet's introduction of his mysterious character—Immanuel (God with us). The name of God (*'el*) is used in parallel with **the Lord JEHOVAH** (Heb *yah yahweh*). It is He who is our **strength . . . song . . . salvation.** This verse is quite similar to the song of deliverance sung by the people of Israel after the crossing of the Red Sea (Ex 15:2). The reference in verse 3 to **water out of the wells of salvation** is certainly reminiscent of John 4:14 and follows biblical precedent in using the symbol of water as a type of salvation (cf. Ex 15:27; Num 20:2; Isa 41:17; Rev 7:17). In commenting on this verse, Calvin (p. 185) states: "By figure of speech, in which a part is taken for the whole, he declares that everything necessary for a supporting life flows to us from the undeserved goodness of God." Thus, the prophet states that in that day shall men **call upon his name,** which the New Testament reminds us is the only basis of our salvation. Young (I, p. 406) correctly notes that in Oriental culture one's name is associated with his nature and character. Thus, His name is His very being; His name is Himself. Not only is His name to be declared, but also **his doings** (i.e., the mighty deeds of Yahweh). Thus, all preaching must include the declaration of who the Saviour is and what it is that He has done for us. Verse 5 declares that He has done **excellent things** (lit., majestic things). These great things are to be preached to the whole world and sung and shouted aloud, **for great is the Holy One of Israel.** In the beautiful language of this triumphant doxology, Isaiah brings this section of his prophecy to a close.

Viewing the entire context of the Immanuel passage, we are taken from a time when the nation of Israel is trembling in fear for the future of the throne of David to a time of unparalleled exaltation of the One who shall sit upon that throne during His great millennial reign upon the earth. In between, we are introduced to Immanuel, the virgin's son, who is indeed "God with us." Next, we are told that He is to identify with the land; for it is His land. Further, He is described as the Gift-Child who will assume the government of His kingdom. We are further told that He is Himself the **mighty God** (10:21), whose rule will bring peace through His wonderful counsel. Finally, we are told that before He comes, the tree of David will be reduced to a stump. Yet, Judah need not fear; for the time will yet come when God's King will sit on that throne as a Branch that sprouts from the root-stock of Jesse into an everlasting kingdom. To the Christian there can be no doubt that this entire passage speaks of only One Person: Jesus Christ the King!

B. Prophecies Against the Nations. 13:1-23:18.

1. Concerning Babylon. 13:1-14:32.

13:1-5. This section of Isaiah's prophecy concerns the message of God's judgment against Israel's neighbors. Not only will God judge His people for their sins, but He will also judge the pagan nations surrounding Israel. (For a study of Israel's rela-

shake the hand, that they may go into the gates of the nobles.

3 I have commanded my sanctified ones, I have also called my mighty ones for mine anger, *even* them that rejoice in my highness.

4 The noise of a multitude in the mountains, like as of a great people; a tumultuous noise of the kingdoms of nations gathered together: the LORD of hosts mustereth the host of the battle.

5 They come from a far country, from the end of heaven, *even* the LORD, and the weapons of his indignation, to destroy the whole land.

6 ¶Howl ye; for the day of the LORD *is* at hand; it shall come as a destruction from the Almighty.

7 Therefore shall all hands be faint, and every man's heart shall melt:

8 And they shall be afraid: pangs and sorrows shall take hold of them; they shall be in pain as a woman that travaileth: they shall be amazed one at another; their faces *shall be as* flames.

9 Behold, the day of the LORD cometh, cruel both with wrath and fierce anger, to lay the land desolate: and he shall destroy the sinners thereof out of it.

10 For the stars of heaven and the constellations thereof shall not give their light: the sun shall be darkened in his going forth, and the moon shall not cause her light to shine.

11 And I will punish the world for *their* evil, and the wicked for their iniquity; and I will cause the arrogancy of the proud to cease, and will lay low the haughtiness of the terrible.

12 I will make a man more precious than fine gold; even a man than the golden wedge of Oʹphir.

13 Therefore I will shake the heavens, and the earth shall remove out of her place, in the wrath of the LORD of hosts, and in the day of his fierce anger.

14 And it shall be as the chased roe, and as a sheep that no man taketh up: they shall every man turn to his own people, and flee every one into his own land.

15 Every one that is found shall be thrust through; and every one that is joined *unto them* shall fall by the sword.

16 Their children also shall be dashed to pieces before their eyes; their houses shall be spoiled, and their wives ravished.

17 Behold, I will stir up the Medes against them, which shall not regard

tionship to her neighbors throughout her history, see F. F. Bruce, *Israel and the Nations*.) The message of this chapter deals with the nation of Babylon, which would eventually carry Judah into captivity. Nevertheless, the prophet Isaiah sees into the future to a time beyond that captivity when Babylon itself shall be taken captive. (For excellent surveys of the history and archaeology of ancient Babylon, see W. G. Lambert, "The Babylonians and Chaldeans," *POTT*, pp. 179-198; A. Parrot, *Babylon and the Old Testament*; H. W. F. Saggs, *The Greatness That Was Babylon*.) The prophet's message of judgment begins with an emphasis on the word **burden** (Heb *massāʾ*), which may also be rendered "oracle." Thus, the word itself has a twofold meaning, emphasizing both the burden of divine judgment which must be "lifted up" and the voice of the prophet which must be "lifted up" against the sins of the nation. The fact that Isaiah **did see** these events implies that he saw them in a vision as if they were actually happening. His message calls for a **banner** (lit., ensign) against the **nobles**, i.e., the chief leaders of the Babylonians. The **sanctified ones** is probably a reference to the invasion of the Media-Persian armies that would one day come against Babylon. They are viewed as being God's agents of judgment against Babylon. The idea in this statement is that God has literally ordained them to overthrow Babylon. Thus, **the LORD of hosts** is viewed as the One who is calling the armies of the world to battle. This clearly indicates that God uses the wrath of men against each other to bring about His purposes in the world.

6-18. Isaiah's reference to the **day of the LORD** is both eschatological and immediate. The **destruction** which He has in view is clearly the fall of Babylon that will come in 539 B.C. Archer (p. 621) notes that "this fall of Babylon is prophetically typical of the overthrow of latter-day Babylon (Rev 14:8)." Just as Babylon will suffer a terrible judgment at the hands of the Medes and Persians, so shall the "Babylon" of the last days suffer **destruction from the Almighty**. Thus, the **day of the LORD**, which is coming in such utter desolation that the **stars** and **sun** shall be darkened, is a time when God will punish the entire **world** (Heb *tēbēl*). This obviously points to a time of judgment beyond that of the Chaldean Empire. That God will make a **man more precious than fine gold** indicates the scarcity of men that will exist after this awful destruction when God will **shake** the heavens and the earth. The most amazing statement in this prophecy is the naming of the **Medes** in verse 17 (cf. chs. 44-45, where Cyrus is also named in advance as the leader of the invasion). Historically, the Medes rose to power in Iran before the Persians and were more known to Western Asia in the time of Isaiah than were the Persians. (For the historical development of this period and the relationship between the Medes and Persians see R. Ghirshman, *Iran*; K. N. Schoville, "Mesopotamia," in *Biblical Archaeology in Focus*, pp. 173-217; G. Widengren, "The Persians," in *POTT*) The fact that this verse appears in the early part of the book of Isaiah and yet names the Medes in advance as the conquerors of Babylon is in itself a significant argument against the dual authorship of the prophecy, especially since that view assumes that the second half of the book was written at a later period of time when it would have been more likely to name the Medes as the second part names Cyrus. The ultimate issue between liberals and conservatives on the interpretation of Isaiah really has to do with the supernatural nature of predictive prophecy. If one decides *a priori* that advance predictions are an impossibility, he will then have to explain away such predictions when he finds them clearly stated in the text.

silver; and *as for* gold, they shall not delight in it.

18 *Their* bows also shall dash the young men to pieces; and they shall have no pity on the fruit of the womb; their eye shall not spare children.

19 And Babylon, the glory of kingdoms, the beauty of the Chăl′dees′ excellency, shall be as when God overthrew Sodom and Go-mŏr′rah.

20 It shall never be inhabited, neither shall it be dwelt in from generation to generation: neither shall the Arabian pitch tent there; neither shall the shepherds make their fold there.

21 But wild beasts of the desert shall lie there; and their houses shall be full of doleful creatures; and owls shall dwell there, and satyrs shall dance there.

22 And the wild beasts of the islands shall cry in their desolate houses, and dragons in *their* pleasant palaces: and her time *is* near to come, and her days shall not be prolonged.

CHAPTER 14

FOR the Lord will have mercy on Jacob, and will yet choose Israel, and set them in their own land: and the strangers shall be joined with them, and they shall cleave to the house of Jacob.

2 And the people shall take them, and bring them to their place: and the house of Israel shall possess them in the land of the Lord for servants and handmaids: and they shall take them captives, whose captives they were; and they shall rule over their oppressors.

3 And it shall come to pass in the day that the Lord shall give thee rest from thy sorrow, and from thy fear, and from the hard bondage wherein thou wast made to serve.

4 That thou shalt take up this proverb against the king of Babylon, and say, How hath the oppressor ceased! the golden city ceased!

5 The Lord hath broken the staff of the wicked, *and* the sceptre of the rulers.

6 He who smote the people in wrath with a continual stroke, he that ruled the nations in anger, is persecuted, *and* none hindereth.

7 The whole earth is at rest, *and* is quiet: they break forth into singing.

8 Yea, the fir trees rejoice at thee, *and* the cedars of Lebanon, *saying,* Since thou art laid down, no feller is come up against us.

9 Hell from beneath is moved for thee to meet *thee* at thy coming: it stirreth up the dead for thee, *even* all the chief ones of the earth; it hath raised up from their thrones all the kings of the nations.

10 All they shall speak and say unto

19-22. Isaiah closes this chapter with the statement that **the glory** of Babylon and the **beauty** of the Chaldeans shall one day be no more. He likens the destruction of this great city to the time when God overthrew **Sodom and Gomorrah.** The splendor of ancient Babylon was indeed spectacular, covering over 1000 acres surrounded by a double-walled system of defense that encircled the city. These walls were over 85 feet thick and 11 miles long, with the outer walls being approximately 25 feet wide and reinforced with towers every 65 feet. There were eight major city gates named after various Babylonian deities (e.g., Ishtar). The city was dominated by a seven-story ziggurat, 288 feet high, known as the Tower of Babylon. It was constructed from nearly 60 million fired bricks. On the top of it stood the temple of Marduk. The Greek historian Herodotus claimed that it contained a solid gold statue of Marduk weighing 52,000 pounds! The predictive judgment that **It shall never be inhabited** was eventually fulfilled literally. By the seventh century A.D., the site of ancient Babylon was completely desolate; and it has never been rebuilt. That the **Arabian** would not pitch his tent there is interesting in light of the fact that to this day the Arabic-speaking population regards this site with a superstitious dread. The reference to **wild beasts** needs not be taken to mean demons but, literally, wild animals. Since the city shall become **desolate,** it would naturally become uninhabited. The reference to **owls . . . satyrs . . . dragons** is better read ostriches, goats, and jackals.

14:1-11. This section forms a song of triumph over the vanquished Babylon. The hated nation that would send Judah into captivity will herself be judged severely by God. In spite of all of God's displeasure with Israel, there is yet coming a time when He will have **mercy on Jacob** and will **choose Israel.** This has reference to a time of coming restoration when God will once again return His people to **their own land.** Isaiah was able to see through the corridor of time to the captivity of Israel in Babylon, the subsequent fall of Babylon, and the return of Israel to her own land. Notice that God is viewed as the Landowner since the land of Israel is called the **land of the Lord.** The **proverb against the king of Babylon** is also one of rejoicing for God's deliverance of His people. Archer (p. 622) takes verse 8 as a literal reference to the **fir trees** and **cedars,** since they were spared from the normal deforestation of the Babylonians. **Hell** (Heb *Sheol*) is the Old Testament name for the abode of the dead. It includes Hades, which is the fiery-like place of judgment for the unsaved. Thus, the ungodly rulers of former ages are pictured here as welcoming the king of Babylon into hell. In the imagery of this passage the Babylonian king is viewed as actually parading into hell where he is met by the **kings of the nations** (Gentiles) who are astounded that he has become **weak as we.** Their only malicious satisfaction was that the king of Babylon has had his brief earthly glory extinguished, even as was theirs.

thee, Art thou also become weak as we? art thou become like unto us?

11 Thy pomp is brought down to the grave, *and* the noise of thy viols: the worm is spread under thee, and the worms cover thee.

12 How art thou fallen from heaven, O Lū'cĭf-er, son of the morning! how art thou cut down to the ground, which didst weaken the nations!

13 For thou hast said in thine heart, I will ascend into heaven, I will exalt my throne above the stars of God: I will sit also upon the mount of the congregation, in the sides of the north:

14 I will ascend above the heights of the clouds; I will be like the most High.

15 Yet thou shalt be brought down to hell, to the sides of the pit.

16 They that see thee shall narrowly look upon thee, *and* consider thee, *saying, Is* this the man that made the earth to tremble, that did shake kingdoms;

17 *That* made the world as a wilderness, and destroyed the cities thereof; *that* opened not the house of his prisoners?

18 All the kings of the nations, *even* all of them, lie in glory, every one in his own house.

19 But thou art cast out of thy grave like an abominable branch, *and as* the raiment of those that are slain, thrust through with a sword, that go down to the stones of the pit; as a carcase trodden under feet.

20 Thou shalt not be joined with them in burial, because thou hast destroyed thy land, *and* slain thy people: the seed of evildoers shall never be renowned.

21 Prepare slaughter for his children for the iniquity of their fathers; that they do not rise, nor possess the land, nor fill the face of the world with cities.

22 For I will rise up against them, saith the LORD of hosts, and cut off from Babylon the name, and remnant, and son, and nephew, saith the LORD.

23 I will also make it a possession for the bittern, and pools of water: and I will sweep it with the besom of destruction, saith the LORD of hosts.

24 ¶The LORD of hosts hath sworn, saying, Surely as I have thought, so shall it come to pass; and as I have purposed, *so* shall it stand:

25 That I will break the Assyrian in my land, and upon my mountains tread him under foot: then shall his yoke depart from off them, and his burden depart from off their shoulders.

26 This *is* the purpose that is purposed upon the whole earth: and this *is* the hand that is stretched out upon all the nations.

27 For the LORD of hosts hath purposed, and who shall disannul *it?* and his hand *is* stretched out, and who shall turn it back?

12-23. The reference to **Lucifer** is most certainly to Satan himself. The real issue of interpretation in this passage is whether Satan is to be viewed literally as the referent of the prophecy in these verses, or whether he is to be viewed as the power behind the throne of the Babylonian king (see Young, I, p. 441). In either case, we are given a clear picture of the certain destruction that always follows pride. It seems most likely that Isaiah is using the fall of Satan, which is an assumed fact, to illustrate the fall of the Babylonian king (who is simply a prototype and not necessarily a specific king such as Belshazzar). Tertullian seems to have been the first to interpret this passage as referring to the fall of Satan (cf. Lk 10:18). Since the fall of Satan is actually yet future (see Rev 9:1), it would seem that the prophet is again speaking in the present tense with the sure assurance of the future fulfillment of his prediction. He sees the rise of Babylon to a point of prominence that it had not yet achieved in his own day; yet beyond that he sees the demise of this same nation. He views her kings as attempting to ascend into heaven by the divine claims that they would make for themselves and their kingdom; then he pictures them as falling from heaven just as certainly as Lucifer himself shall one day fall under the judgment of God. Therefore, it is not inappropriate to understand the words of verses 13-14 as the attitude of Satan himself. Five times the personal pronoun **I** is used to emphasize the selfish determination of both Satan and Satan-empowered men to replace God Himself as the rightful ruler of this world. The name **Lucifer** is actually the Roman designation for the Morning Star. The Hebrew (*helēl*) means "the bright one." This reference illustrates the fact that the morning star speedily disappears before the far greater splendor of the rising sun. Hence, though Satan may appear as an "angel of light," he shall be banished to outer darkness by the coming of the Son of God. (On the preposterous divine claim of the Babylonian kings, see Saggs, pp. 342-369.) Certainly, such claims were parallel to and inspired by the ultimate claim of Satan himself! He, too, will be **brought down to hell** in the final judgment of God (see Rev 20:10). In the meantime, the king of Babylon will no longer be a threat to the nations of the earth. Instead of fearing him, they shall cast him out like an **abominable branch**. The tragedy of national judgment is that it falls upon every generation, including the **children**. For those who rise up in defiance against God, there is nothing ahead for them but disaster, because **I will rise up against them** is the promise of the Lord. He will **cut off** . . . **Babylon.** Thus, it is that this once mighty nation which caused the kings of the earth to tremble is now but a dusty reminder of a bygone kingdom of another era.

24-32. As a part of the same **burden**, the prophet now turns his attention to Assyria. This reference clearly shows a distinction between Babylon and Assyria on the part of the prophet Isaiah. Liberal critics (cf. R. Pfeiffer, *Introduction to the Old Testament*, pp. 443-447) have tried to argue that the entire passage originally referred to Assyria and that the reference to Babylon is a later insertion. However, it should be noted that Jeremiah, Zephaniah, and Ezekiel all refer to this same passage as having to do with Babylon. For a defense of the conservative position, see Young (p. 410ff.). Therefore, the passage is speaking to both enemy nations which shall come from Mesopotamia: Babylon and Assyria. God promises to **break** (*shebor*) the Assyrian nation **upon my mountains** (the Judaean hills). This would be fulfilled in Isaiah's own lifetime when the destruction

28 ¶In the year that king Ahaz died was this burden.

29 ¶Rejoice not thou, whole Palestina, because the rod of him that smote thee is broken: for out of the serpent's root shall come forth a cockatrice, and his fruit *shall be* a fiery flying serpent.

30 And the firstborn of the poor shall feed, and the needy shall lie down in safety: and I will kill thy root with famine, and he shall slay thy remnant.

31 Howl, O gate; cry, O city; thou, whole Palestina, *art* dissolved: for there shall come from the north a smoke, and none *shall be* alone in his appointed times.

32 What shall *one* then answer the messengers of the nation? That the Lord hath founded Zion, and the poor of his people shall trust in it.

CHAPTER 15

THE burden of Moab. Because in the night Ar of Moab is laid waste, *and* brought to silence; because in the night Kir of Moab is laid waste, *and* brought to silence;

2 He is gone up to Bā'jĭth, and to Dĭ'bŏn, the high places, to weep: Moab shall howl over Nebo, and over Mĕd'e-ba: on all their heads *shall be* baldness, *and* every beard cut off.

3 In their streets they shall gird themselves with sackcloth: on the tops of their houses, and in their streets, every one shall howl, weeping abundantly.

4 And Hĕsh'bŏn shall cry, and Ĕ-le-ā'leh: their voices shall be heard *even* unto Jā'hăz: therefore the armed soldiers of Moab shall cry out; his life shall be grievous unto him.

5 My heart shall cry out for Moab; his fugitives *shall flee* unto Zō'ar, an heifer of three years old: for by the mounting up of Lū'hĭth with weeping shall they go it up; for in the way of Hôr-o-nā'im they shall raise up a cry of destruction.

6 For the waters of Nĭm'rĭm shall be desolate: for the hay is withered away, the grass faileth, there is no green thing.

7 Therefore the abundance they have gotten, and that which they have laid up, shall they carry away to the brook of the willows.

8 For the cry is gone round about the borders of Moab; the howling thereof unto Ĕg'la-im, and the howling thereof unto Be'er-ē'lĭm.

9 For the waters of Dĭ'mon shall be full of blood: for I will bring more upon Dĭ'mon, lions upon him that escapeth of Moab, and upon the remnant of the land.

---

wrought by the angel of the Lord on the Assyrian army of Sennacherib would weaken Assyria and lead to her ultimate downfall (37:36). The further statement that God's **hand** is still **stretched out** means that His hand of judgment is still coming against the nations for their rebellion against Him. The fact that the Lord has **purposed** (*ya'ats*) means that man cannot annul what God has determined to bring to pass. Isaiah then dates this vision (**burden**) **In the year that king Ahaz died** (727 B.C.). The chapter ends with a brief statement against **Palestina** (or Philistia). The prophet's warning is that just because the **rod** of Assyria shall be broken, don't you rejoice against Israel, because out of the **serpent's root** there shall come forth a further serpent and his fruit shall be a **fiery flying serpent.** In other words, the rise of Babylon to world power out of the demise of Assyria will make it such that the latter shall be worse than the former. Thus, the Philistines who had been brought under subjection to the Israelites since the days of David (see E. Hindson, *The Philistines and the Old Testament,* pp. 170-173) are warned not to attempt a rebellion against Israel themselves because they too face a greater enemy **from the north** (i.e., Babylon). Thus, the first burden of the prophet deals extensively with the nation of Babylon. Isaiah then appends a brief warning to both Assyria and Philistia as well.

2. Concerning Moab. 15:1-16:14.

15:1-9. The burden of Moab encompasses the entire eastern Transjordan. Prophecy opens with a historic reminder of the fall of **Ar,** the capital of Moab, and **Kir,** their chief fortress. After the death of Ahab, the Israelite king, Moab had broken away and refused to pay the annual tribute (II Kgs 3:5ff.). Eventually, Jehoram, Ahab's son, aided by Jehoshaphat of Judah, invaded Moab, capturing the capital and destroying its chief fortress. Thus, Isaiah reminds Moab of that terrible time of earlier destruction that again threatened this rebellious nation. (On the history and archaeology of Moab, see A. H. van Zyl, *The Moabites;* J. R. Bartlett, "The Moabites and Edomites," in *POTT,* pp. 229-258; N. Glueck, *The Other Side of the Jordan.*) As this chapter unfolds, it actually becomes a "prophetic lament" as the prophet weeps over the coming Assyrian invasion of Moab. **Bajith . . . Dibon . . . Nebo . . . Medeba . . . Heshbon . . . Elealeh . . . Jahaz . . .** form a list of Moabite cities that will be overrun by the coming Assyrian invasion. The prediction states that they will fall **in the night,** which Delitzsch (p. 323) takes as absolute and Young (I, p. 456) views as a construct, "in the night of." Of these cities which dotted the Moabite territory, Dibon was north of the Arnon River, one of the four major tributaries that divides the plateau of Transjordan. It formed the northern boundary between Moab and Ammon. Dibon had at one time belonged to the Israelites and was now a center of pagan idolatry. Nebo and Medeba are actually mountains which at that time were within the borders of Moab. Nebo was the mountain from which Moses had viewed the Promised Land (Deut 32:49). Heshbon had previously been the capital of Sihon (Num 21:26). Elealeh was one mile from Heshbon. Jahaz was some distance away and was the place where Sihon had fought against the Israelites (Num 21:23). **Zoar** was one of the cities of the plain to which Lot attempted to flee (Gen 19:23). It should be remembered that Lot was the forefather of the Moabites. This city was often resorted to by fleeing Moabites. The imagery of a **heifer of three years old** conveys the idea that Moab is simply a young and untamed calf. She lacks the discernment to submit to the yoke of God's direction; thus, her end shall be her own destruction. **Nimrim** was an oasis of Moab near the Dead Sea. The desolation of the terrible invasion will leave the land so parched that there will be **no green thing.** The location of **Eglaim** and **Beer-elim** is unknown. The reference to the **waters**

CHAPTER 16

SEND ye the lamb to the ruler of the land from Sē′la to the wilderness, unto the mount of the daughter of Zion.

2 For it shall be, *that*, as a wandering bird cast out of the nest, *so* the daughters of Moab shall be at the fords of Arnon.

3 Take counsel, execute judgment; make thy shadow as the night in the midst of the noonday; hide the outcasts; bewray not him that wandereth.

4 Let mine outcasts dwell with thee, Moab; be thou a covert to them from the face of the spoiler: for the extortioner is at an end, the spoiler ceaseth, the oppressors are consumed out of the land.

5 And in mercy shall the throne be established: and he shall sit upon it in truth in the tabernacle of David, judging, and seeking judgment, and hasting righteousness.

6 ¶We have heard of the pride of Moab; *he is* very proud: *even* of his haughtiness, and his pride, and his wrath: *but* his lies *shall* not *be* so.

7 Therefore shall Moab howl for Moab, every one shall howl: for the foundations of Kĭr–hăr′e–sĕth shall ye mourn; surely *they are* stricken.

8 For the fields of Hĕsh′bŏn languish, *and* the vine of Sĭb′mah: the lords of the heathen have broken down the principal plants thereof, they are come *even* unto Jā′zer, they wandered *through* the wilderness: her branches are stretched out, they are gone over the sea.

9 Therefore I will bewail with the weeping of Jā′zer the vine of Sĭb′mah: I will water thee with my tears, O Hĕsh′bŏn, and Ĕ-le-ā′leh: for the shouting for thy summer fruits and for thy harvest is fallen.

10 And gladness is taken away, and joy out of the plentiful field; and in the vineyards there shall be no singing, neither shall there be shouting: the treaders shall tread out no wine in *their* presses; I have made *their* vintage shouting to cease.

11 Wherefore my bowels shall sound like an harp for Moab, and mine inward parts for Kĭr–hă′rĕsh.

12 And it shall come to pass, when it is seen that Moab is weary on the high place, that he shall come to his sanctuary to pray; but he shall not prevail.

13 This *is* the word that the LORD hath spoken concerning Moab since that time.

14 But now the LORD hath spoken, saying, Within three years, as the years of an hireling, and the glory of Moab shall be contemned, with all that great multitude; and the remnant *shall be* very small *and* feeble.

CHAPTER 17

THE burden of Damascus. Behold, Da-

of Dimon being **full of blood** represents a play-on-words between the Hebrew for blood (*dām*) and Dimon, which may be a deliberate variation of the more familiar name of Dibon. H. Orlinsky has argued that Dimon is the correct spelling (*JBL*, Mar 1959, p. 28). The **lions** probably refer to the winged symbols of Assyrian power. Yet, in spite of all of this, a **remnant** shall still be left in the land.

16:1-14. The only hope for Moab will be found in making peace with Judah. **Send ye the lamb** meant to pay tribute to the Davidic dynasty. **Sela** refers to Petra, the capital of Edom. This city, well-known in Bible prophecy (see Ezk 35; Ob), was cut into the face of the rock at the end of the narrow gorge known as Es-Siq which protected the magnificent Ed-Djerra, the facade of the temple which was cut out of solid rock. This was a natural hiding place for the Moabites as well as the Edomites with whom they were in confederation. Isaiah urges them to send a peace offering from this hiding place to **Zion.** Just as Moab had to run to Petra for protection, so God asks them to **Let mine outcasts dwell with thee.** Most premillennial commentators take this to mean that Israel will flee during the last days into ancient Petra for refuge from the invading army from the north. Others see this merely as a reference to their flight there in the time of the Assyrian/Babylonian invasions. The reference to One sitting on the **throne** in the **tabernacle of David** (vs. 5) would seem to place this passage in a millennial context, when Christ shall sit upon the throne of David and extend His mercy toward the remnant of Moab. The reason for Moab's problems is given as the **pride of Moab.** This is clearly demonstrated in the prideful bragging of King Mesha in his inscriptions on the "Moab Stone." Therefore, proud Moab shall **howl** for itself during the coming invasion of the Assyrian army. Her fields are pictured as desolate, and her joy has turned to tears. The rejoicing and gladness in the terrorist vineyard of Moab shall cease and be replaced by the tragic wail of anguish. The prophecy closes with an elegy about Moab's fall. Moab is to become **weary on the high place,** referring to the temples of her pagan gods. Her prayers shall **not prevail** and her god, which in reality is no god, shall be unable to help her. Chemosh was the god of the Moabites and was known for his severe retribution. Mesha offered his son, the heir to the throne, as a burnt offering to Chemosh because of the disastrous defeat he had suffered against Israel (see II Kgs 3:4-27). The coming disaster is dated **Within three years.** Just as **a hireling** (hired servant) keeps precise and exact records of his servitude, so shall God keep His records of Moab's rebellion and its resulting consequences.

3. Concerning Damascus (Syria). 17:1-14.

17:1-14. The **burden of Damascus** refers to the capital city

mascus is taken away from *being* a city, and it shall be a ruinous heap.

2 The cities of Ar'ŏ-er *are* forsaken: they shall be for flocks, which shall lie down, and none shall make *them* afraid.

3 The fortress also shall cease from E'phra-im, and the kingdom from Damascus, and the remnant of Syria: they shall be as the glory of the children of Israel, saith the LORD of hosts.

4 And in that day it shall come to pass, *that* the glory of Jacob shall be made thin, and the fatness of his flesh shall wax lean.

5 And it shall be as when the harvestman gathereth the corn, and reapeth the ears with his arm; and it shall be as he that gathereth ears in the valley of Rĕph'a-im.

6 Yet gleaning grapes shall be left in it, as the shaking of an olive tree, two *or* three berries in the top of the uppermost bough, four *or* five in the outmost fruitful branches thereof, saith the LORD God of Israel.

7 At that day shall a man look to his Maker, and his eyes shall have respect to the Holy One of Israel.

8 And he shall not look to the altars, the work of his hands, neither shall respect *that* which his fingers have made, either the groves, or the images.

9 In that day shall his strong cities be as a forsaken bough, and an uppermost branch, which they left because of the children of Israel: and there shall be desolation.

10 Because thou hast forgotten the God of thy salvation, and hast not been mindful of the rock of thy strength, therefore shalt thou plant pleasant plants, and shalt set it with strange slips:

11 In the day shalt thou make thy plant to grow, and in the morning shalt thou make thy seed to flourish: *but* the harvest *shall be* a heap in the day of grief and of desperate sorrow.

12 ¶Woe to the multitude of many people, *which* make a noise like the noise of the seas; and to the rushing of nations, *that* make a rushing like the rushing of mighty waters!

13 The nations shall rush like the rushing of many waters: but *God* shall rebuke them, and they shall flee far off, and shall be chased as the chaff of the mountains before the wind, and like a rolling thing before the whirlwind.

14 And behold at eveningtide trouble; *and* before the morning he *is* not. This *is* the portion of them that spoil us, and the lot of them that rob us.

CHAPTER 18

WOE to the land shadowing with wings, which *is* beyond the rivers of E-thĭ-ō'pĭ-a:

2 That sendeth ambassadors by the sea, even in vessels of bulrushes upon the waters, *saying,* Go, ye swift messengers, to a nation scattered and peeled, to a people terrible from their beginning hitherto; a nation meted out and trodden down, whose land the rivers have spoiled!

of Syria, Israel's neighbor to the north. Archer (p. 623) notes that this chapter is contemporaneous with chapter 7 and predicts the downfall of the northern coalition between Syria and Ephraim. Tiglath-pileser of Assyria would leave Damascus in a heap of ruins in 732 B.C., as well as its basal cities including **Aroer.** (On the Syrians or Aramaeans see A. Malamat, *The Aramaeans;* R. T. O'Callaghan, *Aram Naharaim;* and M. F. Unger, *Israel and the Aramaeans of Damascus.*) In his prophecy of the coming judgment of Syria, Isaiah indicates that her failure will also spell the downfall of **Ephraim** (northern Israel). Thus, **Jacob** (Israel) **shall be made thin** refers to the time of famine which shall follow the devastation of the Assyrian army in the north. Like the final stalks of wheat or olives left from an earlier harvest, after this invasion only a pitiful remnant of the ten northern tribes would remain in the land. This prediction looks beyond the immediate invasion to the final deportation of Israel by Sargon of Assyria in 722 B.C. As in all tragic events, this invasion shall cause man to look to his **Maker** (an interesting reference to God the Creator). Thus, the people shall get their eyes off the **altars,** which are the work of their own hands, and shall look to the **Holy One of Israel.** For **groves** read *Asherim* (female deities). Throughout his prophecies Isaiah sounds the note of impending doom and then raises a glimmer of hope for restitution. Though these allied nations shall rush **like the rushing of mighty waters** in their sweeping entrance into Syria, nevertheless **God shall rebuke them.** Again we see that in the midst of judgment God extends His mercy even to Israel's pagan neighbors whom He will not allow to be completely wiped out.

4. Concerning Ethiopia. 18:1-7.

18:1-7. The prophet now turns his attention to the land of **Ethiopia** (lit., Cush), which he views as swarming with insects whose **wings** are **shadowing** the land by their multitude. Isaiah would seem to be referring to the frequent plagues of insects which have caused such devastating famine in Africa throughout her history, rather than to the tsetse fly which is referred to by Young (I, p. 474). The reference to **vessels of bulrushes** is certainly to the papyrus boats which Roman historians claimed were made by the Egyptians. It is likely that the Ethiopians had

3 All ye inhabitants of the world, and dwellers on the earth, see ye, when he lifteth up an ensign on the mountains; and when he bloweth a trumpet, hear ye.

4 For so the LORD said unto me, I will take my rest, and I will consider in my dwelling place like a clear heat upon herbs, *and* like a cloud of dew in the heat of harvest.

5 For afore the harvest, when the bud is perfect, and the sour grape is ripening in the flower, he shall both cut off the sprigs with pruning hooks, and take away *and* cut down the branches.

6 They shall be left together unto the fowls of the mountains, and to the beasts of the earth: and the fowls shall summer upon them, and all the beasts of the earth shall winter upon them.

7 ¶In that time shall the present be brought unto the LORD of hosts of a people scattered and peeled, and from a people terrible from their beginning hitherto; a nation meted out and trodden under foot, whose land the rivers have spoiled, to the place of the name of the LORD of hosts, the mount Zion.

CHAPTER 19

THE burden of Egypt. Behold, the LORD rideth upon a swift cloud, and shall come into Egypt: and the idols of Egypt shall be moved at his presence, and the heart of Egypt shall melt in the midst of it.

2 And I will set the Egyptians against the Egyptians: and they shall fight every one against his brother, and every one against his neighbour; city against city, *and* kingdom against kingdom.

3 And the spirit of Egypt shall fail in the midst thereof; and I will destroy the counsel thereof: and they shall seek to the idols, and to the charmers, and to them that have familiar spirits, and to the wizards.

4 And the Egyptians will I give over into the hand of a cruel lord; and a fierce king shall rule over them, saith the Lord, the LORD of hosts.

5 And the waters shall fail from the sea, and the river shall be wasted and dried up.

6 And they shall turn the rivers far away; *and* the brooks of defence shall be emptied and dried up: the reeds and flags shall wither.

7 The paper reeds by the brooks, by the mouth of the brooks, and every thing sown by the brooks, shall wither, be driven away, and be no *more*.

8 The fishers also shall mourn, and all they that cast angle into the brooks shall lament, and they that spread nets upon the waters shall languish.

9 Moreover they that work in fine flax, and they that weave networks, shall be confounded.

10 And they shall be broken in the purposes thereof, all that make sluices *and* ponds for fish.

11 Surely the princes of Zō'an *are* fools, the counsel of the wise counsellors of Pharaoh is become brutish: how

constant contact with Egypt and at times even ruled Egypt (in 714 B.C. a new Ethiopian dynasty was established over Egypt). That these papyrus boats would be adequate to sail up the Red Sea to the Israelite port city is certainly now a well-established fact. The Ethiopian dynasty (Egypt's twenty-fifth) had been established by Piankhi, whose son Shabaka (called "So" in II Kgs 17:4) encouraged Israel's last king, Hoshea, in a final and unsuccessful revolt against Assyria. He later attempted to form an alliance with Merodach-baladan of Babylon and Hezekiah of Judah against the Assyrians as well. Sennacherib finally crushed the Ethiopian-Egyptian forces at Eltekeh in 701 B.C. This failure is illustrated by that of a destroyed crop which is cut down even before the time of her **ripening.** Thus, at the height of her power the Ethiopian dynasty shall fail. Yet again Isaiah ends with a message of hope. The reference to **a people scattered and peeled** should read "tall and dark-skinned." The phrase, **whose land the rivers have spoiled** (vs. 2), should be read "Whose land the rivers divide" (ASV), referring to the Ethiopians as coming from the land where the blue Nile joins the white Nile. Because of their pride, they too would be **trodden under foot** by the Assyrians. And yet the prophet looks beyond this time to a day when the Ethiopians would pay tribute to the **LORD of hosts** and would come to **mount Zion** as believers in the true God (Acts 8:26-40).

5. *Concerning Egypt. 19:1-20:6.*

19:1-10. The burden of Egypt begins one of Isaiah's most unusual prophecies in that it is both a message of judgment and of blessing to come upon Egypt. It reflects a time in Judah's history when her tendency was to depend upon an Egyptian alliance against the threat of Assyria. Thus, the prophet warns against such an alliance; it would cause the people of Judah to depend upon a foreign army rather than upon the divine and sovereign protection of her God. (On Egyptian history and archaeology, see J. H. Breasted, *A History of Egypt;* A. H. Gardiner, *Egypt of the Pharaohs;* G. Steindorff and K. C. Seele, *When Egypt Ruled the East;* J. A. Wilson, *The Culture of Ancient Egypt.* On the Biblical and prophetic significance of Egypt, see W. M. Smith, *Egypt in Biblical Prophecy.*) Isaiah pictures the coming Egyptian civil war between the competing Ethiopian and Libyan dynasties as resulting from the intervention of **the LORD** (*Yahweh*). Therefore, God states that He **set the Egyptians against the Egyptians** (an interesting allusion which also came true during the Six-Day-War in 1967). The seventh-century B.C. civil catastrophe weakened Egypt so that the entire political coalition of Egyptians, Ethiopians, and Libyans fell to Esar-haddon of Assyria in 671 B.C. God's judgment of Egypt embraces four major aspects of Egyptian life—government, religion, wealth, and wisdom. All of this is pictured as failing in the immediate future. **Idols . . . charmers . . . familiar spirits . . . wizards** refer to the various aspects of Egyptian religion, which was dominated by the occult. (See the development of this in J. J. Davis, *Moses and the Gods of Egypt; Mummies, Men and Madness.*) The **cruel lord** and **fierce king** is a reference to the Assyrian overlords who were to dominate Egypt for nearly twenty years. Verses 5-10 refer to a severe drought which shall follow. At that time the Nile River shall cease to overflow its banks. The floods were needed annually in order to properly irrigate the farmers' fields. This failure would result in the economic ruin of Egypt. Everything in the Nile shall be destroyed including **paper reeds** (papyrus).

11-17. Next, Isaiah predicts the failure of Egyptian wisdom, which was the height of the pride of Egypt's culture. **Princes of Zoan** is a reference to the kings' northeastern capital of Tanis

say ye unto Pharaoh, I *am* the son of the wise, the son of ancient kings?

12 Where *are* they? where *are* thy wise *men?* and let them tell thee now, and let them know what the LORD of hosts hath purposed upon Egypt.

13 The princes of Zõ'an are become fools, the princes of Noph are deceived; they have also seduced Egypt, *even they that are* the stay of the tribes thereof.

14 The LORD hath mingled a perverse spirit in the midst thereof: and they have caused Egypt to err in every work thereof, as a drunken *man* staggereth in his vomit.

15 Neither shall there be *any* work for Egypt, which the head or tail, branch or rush, may do.

16 In that day shall Egypt be like unto women: and it shall be afraid and fear because of the shaking of the hand of the LORD of hosts, which he shaketh over it.

17 And the land of Jū'dah shall be a terror unto Egypt, every one that maketh mention thereof shall be afraid in himself, because of the counsel of the LORD of hosts, which he hath determined against it.

18 In that day shall five cities in the land of Egypt speak the language of Canaan, and swear to the LORD of hosts; one shall be called, The city of destruction.

19 In that day shall there be an altar to the LORD in the midst of the land of Egypt, and a pillar at the border thereof to the LORD.

20 And it shall be for a sign and for a witness unto the LORD of hosts in the land of Egypt: for they shall cry unto the LORD because of the oppressors, and he shall send them a saviour, and a great one, and he shall deliver them.

21 And the LORD shall be known to Egypt, and the Egyptians shall know the LORD in that day, and shall do sacrifice and oblation; yea, they shall vow a vow unto the LORD, and perform *it*.

22 And the LORD shall smite Egypt: he shall smite and heal *it:* and they shall return *even* to the LORD, and he shall be intreated of them, and shall heal them.

23 In that day shall there be a highway out of Egypt to Assyria, and the Assyrian shall come into Egypt, and the Egyptian into Assyria, and the Egyptians shall serve with the Assyrians.

24 In that day shall Israel be the third with Egypt and with Assyria, *even* a blessing in the midst of the land:

25 Whom the LORD of hosts shall bless, saying, Blessed *be* Egypt my people, and Assyria the work of my hands, and Israel mine inheritance.

CHAPTER 20

IN the year that Tartan came unto Āsh'dōd, (when Sär'gŏn the king of Assyria sent him,) and fought against Āsh'dōd, and took it.

2 At the same time spake the LORD by Isaiah the son of Amoz, saying, Go and loose the sackcloth from off thy loins, and put off thy shoe from thy foot. And he did so, walking naked and barefoot.

near the Sinai border. **Noph** is ancient Memphis, located at the apex of the Delta. All of this confusion, the prophet indicates, will come as a result of the fact that Jehovah has **mingled a perverse spirit** among the Egyptians to cause them to err in their discernment. Again, we must note the prophet's view of the sovereign intervention of God in the affairs of men. Egypt's fear is likened unto that of **women** who naturally stand trembling in a time of war because of all the tragedy and uncertainty that it brings. **Judah shall be a terror unto Egypt** refers to the weakened condition of Egypt being such that even little Judah now frightens them. This is not likely a reference to the Christian conversion of Egypt during the time of the early church (see Eusebius, Cyrill, Jerome, and Calvin).

18-25. The city of destruction comes from a deliberate alteration of the name Heliopolis, "City of the Sun." The prophet sees a day when Egypt shall be converted to the knowledge of Jehovah. The prediction of an **altar to the LORD** in Egypt was technically fulfilled during the reign of Ptolemy VI by a priest named Onias. There is some debate by commentators as to whether the **savior, and a great one** is a reference to the coming of Alexander the Great who would expel Near Eastern rule from Egypt or a reference to the coming of Christ Himself. That the context of the latter part of the prophecy goes beyond the immediate crisis to the time of messianic deliverance is obvious by the universal blessing described in these verses. While Egyptians have certainly been converted to Christianity throughout its history, the implication of verse 21 is that there is coming a time when all Egypt shall be saved. God promises that He will also heal the nation which He has smitten. The closing verses definitely seem to look beyond any immediate prospect for an Egyptian-Assyrian-Israelite alliance to the time of blessing in the millennial kingdom. Boutflower (p. 312) views this passage as a "peep down through the long-drawn vista of the future." He likens the prophet to one standing on a mountain peak peering through an awesome thunderstorm of God's judgment and envisioning a cruel lord who shall come from Assyria to rule over the Egyptians. Beyond that, he sees a great Saviour or deliverer who shall also come to bring God's blessing upon the Egyptians. The fact that a **highway** can run from Egypt to Assyria through the land of Israel indicates a time of such peace as the world has never known. Egypt and Assyria will be **Blessed** by the Lord, not just because they are at peace with Israel, but because they have become **my people** saith the Lord.

20:1-6. This oracle is related to the previous chapter but extends the prediction even further. It was probably delivered at a different time since it is dated **In the year** of the Assyrian invasion (711 B.C.) of the Philistine coast. **Tartan** is the Akkadian term for "general." He was sent by Sargon to subdue the Philistine city of Ashdod. (For details, see H. Tadmor, "Philistia under Assyrian Rule," *Biblical Archaeologist* (1966), pp.

3 And the LORD said, Like as my servant Isaiah hath walked naked and barefoot three years *for* a sign and wonder upon Egypt and upon Ē-thǐ-ō′pǐ-a;

4 So shall the king of Assyria lead away the Egyptians prisoners, and the Ē-thǐ-ō′pǐ-ans captives, young and old, naked and barefoot, even with *their* buttocks uncovered, to the shame of Egypt.

5 And they shall be afraid and ashamed of Ē-thǐ-ō′pǐ-a their expectation, and of Egypt their glory.

6 And the inhabitant of this isle shall say in that day, Behold, such *is* our expectation, whither we flee for help to be delivered from the king of Assyria: and how shall we escape?

CHAPTER 21

THE burden of the desert of the sea. As whirlwinds in the south pass through; *so* it cometh from the desert, from a terrible land.

2 A grievous vision is declared unto me; the treacherous dealer dealeth treacherously, and the spoiler spoileth. Go up, O Ē′lam: besiege, O Mē′dǐ-a; all the sighing thereof have I made to cease.

3 Therefore are my loins filled with pain: pangs have taken hold upon me, as the pangs of a woman that travaileth: I was bowed down at the hearing *of it;* I was dismayed at the seeing *of it.*

4 My heart panted, fearfulness affrighted me: the night of my pleasure hath he turned into fear unto me.

5 Prepare the table, watch in the watchtower, eat, drink: arise, ye princes, *and* anoint the shield.

6 For thus hath the LORD said unto me, Go, set a watchman, let him declare what he seeth.

7 And he saw a chariot *with* a couple of horsemen, a chariot of asses, *and* a chariot of camels; and he hearkened diligently with much heed:

8 And he cried, A lion: My lord, I stand continually upon the watchtower in the daytime, and I am set in my ward whole nights:

9 And, behold, here cometh a chariot of men, *with* a couple of horsemen. And he answered and said, Babylon is fallen, is fallen; and all the graven images of her gods he hath broken unto the ground.

10 O my threshing, and the corn of

86-102; on the extensive excavations recently done at Ashdod, see M. Dothan, *Ashdod, A City of the Philistine Pentapolis.*) Azuri, the king of Ashdod, was deposed by Sargon's general; and a revolt by Iatna was suppressed. God then spoke to Isaiah and told him to become a living illustration of His coming judgment on the Egyptians by **walking naked and barefoot.** This passage has provoked a great deal of controversy, and at least one commentator (Archer) has refused to even comment on it! Leupold (I, p. 326) prefers the view that the **sackcloth** (Heb *saq,* hairy mantle) refers to a coarse outer garment that would have gone over an undergarment, or tunic. He argues that the prophet went about barefoot and in his undergarment as a shocking means of gaining the attention of the people to the severity of his prediction. He prefers not to view the prophet as literally naked. Young (II, p. 54), however, views the prophet as literally being naked. Verse 3 indicates that his walking naked and barefoot was a **sign** (*'ōth*) and **wonder** (*mōpeth*). This drastic move symbolized the fact that the **Egyptians . . . and Ethiopians,** both young and old, would be taken away **naked and barefoot** into captivity. That their **buttocks** (*shēth*) would be **uncovered** would seem to indicate that his nakedness was real. In either case, one must remember that the matter of nakedness is viewed much differently in more primitive cultures than it is in the modern western world. That prisoners were transferred in such a condition is clearly illustrated in *ANET,* pp. 296, 326, 332. The Assyrians, in particular, usually stripped their captives naked and deported them. Those who were killed were also stripped and had their skin peeled (fileted) while they were still alive! Thus, Isaiah's drastic action is predictive of a horrible and horrifying event which shall soon come upon Egypt. (For further details of Assyrian practices, see G. Roux, *Ancient Iraq.*)

6. *Concerning the desert (Babylon). 21:1-10.*

21:1-10. This prophecy is introduced as the **burden of the desert of the sea.** The ASV reads "wilderness of the sea." Archer (p. 624) takes this as a reference to the alluvial plain of Babylonia, whereas Young (II, p. 61) takes it as a reference to Media and Persia, which were beyond the Persian Gulf from Babylon. Since the fall of Babylon is in view in verse 9, it would appear that the **burden** is against that nation. Thus, **Elam** and **Media** are viewed as going up against Babylon. Elam was located to the east of Babylon on the other side of the Persian Gulf, whereas Media was far to the north across the Zagros Mountains. In between the two lay the great Persian Empire. Both were better known in Isaiah's day than Persia, which would eventually come to have power over the entire Near East. Isaiah sees the events as a **vision** in which he is transported into the future to observe the Media-Persian invasion of Babylon. Thus, he predicts the fall of the very nation that will eventually conquer and deport his own nation. His reference to the **night of my pleasure** may well be a reference to Belshazzar's banquet in Daniel 5. In one night self-sufficient Babylon fell to her invaders in 539 B.C. Thus, the apostle John repeats Isaiah's solemn statement in the book of Revelation with double emphasis: **Babylon is fallen, is fallen!**

my floor: that which I have heard of the LORD of hosts, the God of Israel, have I declared unto you.

11 ¶The burden of Dū'mah. He calleth to me out of Sē'ir, Watchman, what of the night? Watchman, what of the night?

12 The watchman said, The morning cometh, and also the night: if ye will enquire, enquire ye: return, come.

13 ¶The burden upon Arabia. In the forest in Arabia shall ye lodge, O ye travelling companies of Dĕd'a-nīm.

14 The inhabitants of the land of Tĕ'ma brought water to him that was thirsty, they prevented with their bread him that fled.

15 For they fled from the swords, from the drawn sword, and from the bent bow, and from the grievousness of war.

16 For thus hath the LORD said unto me, Within a year, according to the years of an hireling, and all the glory of Kē'dar shall fail:

17 And the residue of the number of archers, the mighty men of the children of Kē'dar, shall be diminished: for the LORD God of Israel hath spoken it.

CHAPTER 22

THE burden of the valley of vision. What aileth thee now, that thou art wholly gone up to the housetops?

2 Thou that art full of stirs, a tumultuous city, a joyous city: thy slain men are not slain with the sword, nor dead in battle.

3 All thy rulers are fled together, they are bound by the archers: all that are found in thee are bound together, which have fled from far.

4 Therefore said I, Look away from me; I will weep bitterly, labour not to comfort me, because of the spoiling of the daughter of my people.

5 For it is a day of trouble, and of treading down, and of perplexity by the Lord GOD of hosts in the valley of vision, breaking down the walls, and of crying to the mountains.

6 And Ē'lam bare the quiver with chariots of men and horsemen, and Kir uncovered the shield.

7 And it shall come to pass, that thy choicest valleys shall be full of chariots, and the horsemen shall set themselves in array at the gate.

8 ¶And he discovered the covering of Jū'dah, and thou didst look in that day to the armour of the house of the forest.

9 Ye have seen also the breaches of the city of David, that they are many: and ye gathered together the waters of the lower pool.

10 And ye have numbered the houses of Jerusalem, and the houses have ye broken down to fortify the wall.

7. Concerning Edom. 21:11-12.

11-12. The burden of Dumah refers to Edom, which was south of Moab. **Seir** is another name for the same area. They were the descendants of Esau and were (generally) the enemies of Israel. Isaiah announces to the Edomites of Seir that the "silence" of their land shall be due to the defeat and bondage which shall befall them. Isaiah is called a **watchman** (*shomer*). He warns that both **morning** and **also the night** are coming. Again, his message is one of impending judgment which can be averted by their willingness to **return** (from Heb *shūb*). Thus, Edom is pictured as hiding in Seir, wondering if it is safe to come out; and the prophet calls back to them that they should return unto the Lord in whom alone they can find safety.

8. Concerning Arabia. 21:13-17.

13-17. The burden upon Arabia refers to the various Arabian tribes of the desert beyond Edom. Earlier, these Arab tribes had allied with the Philistines in an invasion of Jerusalem in the days of Jehoram, but they were later defeated by Uzziah. Now they are warned of the coming judgment that will fall upon them as a result of the Assyrian invasion. **Dedanim** is a reference to Dedan, a region in Arabia. The Assyrians first invaded this area in 732 B.C. and again in 725 B.C. These desert cameleers would have been no match for the well-armed Assyrian infantry and cavalry. **Tema** was an oasis that became famous during the Babylonian period, for it was here that Nabonidus spent much of his time while Belshazzar ruled over Babylon. Again, the time is dated in accordance with the **years of a hireling** (hired servant). **Kedar** designates a tribe of Ishmaelite descent. The prophet's message ends with a note of severity; the glory of Kedar, the Arabian tribes, shall fail because the **LORD God of Israel hath spoken it!**

9. Concerning the valley of vision (Jerusalem). 22:1-25.

22:1-14. The burden (*massa'*) **of the valley of vision** stands in apposition to the *chazūth* concerning Babylon and the Arab nations. Delitzsch (p. 389) notes that "these four prophecies were not composed in the tetralogical form in which they are grouped together here, but were joined together at a later period in a group of this kind on account of their close affinity." Together they form the picture of a gathering storm that dumps its greatest torrents upon Jerusalem herself. Jerusalem was located upon two hills in the midst of the valleys surrounded by dominating mountain ranges. As such, it is appropriate to call it the **valley of vision.** It was here also that many of God's servants received their revelations of His message. The coming of the invading (Babylonian) army has caused the people to go up into the **housetops** to observe the siege of the city. Isaiah then reminds them that they are not yet **slain,** but they will soon face death. The **rulers** are pictured as being **fled together,** leaving the people of the city defenseless and helpless before their enemies. Isaiah's personal heartache over this condition is clearly expressed in verse 4: **I will weep bitterly.** One of the obvious characteristics of the Old Testament prophets was their brokenness over the sin of their people and their personal heartache over the impending judgment that was coming upon them. It should be noted that these prophets never delighted in the judgment that was coming upon their country. They always viewed the divine retribution with the greatest of personal agony and concern. Under the inspiration of the Holy Spirit, the prophet gives a precisely detailed account of the coming Babylonian siege (589-587 B.C.). He even notes that the warriors of **Kir** and **Elam** are coming as mercenaries of the Babylonians, prepared for war with quivers opened and shields uncovered. Thus, it will be that the **choicest valleys,** which had known the blessing of prosperity, shall now be **full of chariots** of the

11 Ye made also a ditch between the two walls for the water of the old pool: but ye have not looked unto the maker thereof, neither had respect unto him that fashioned it long ago.

12 And in that day did the Lord GOD of hosts call to weeping, and to mourning, and to baldness, and to girding with sackcloth:

13 And behold joy and gladness, slaying oxen, and killing sheep, eating flesh, and drinking wine: let us eat and drink; for tomorrow we shall die.

14 And it was revealed in mine ears by the LORD of hosts, Surely this iniquity shall not be purged from you till ye die, saith the Lord GOD of hosts.

15 ¶Thus saith the Lord GOD of hosts, Go, get thee unto this treasurer, *even* unto Shĕb′na, which *is* over the house, *and say,*

16 What hast thou here? and whom hast thou here, that thou hast hewed thee out a sepulchre here, *as* he that heweth him out a sepulchre on high, *and* that graveth an habitation for himself in a rock?

17 Behold, the LORD will carry thee away with a mighty captivity, and will surely cover thee.

18 He will surely violently turn and toss thee *like* a ball into a large country: there shalt thou die, and there the chariots of thy glory *shall be* the shame of thy lord's house.

19 And I will drive thee from thy station, and from thy state shall he pull thee down.

20 ¶And it shall come to pass in that day, that I will call my servant E-lī′a-kĭm the son of Hĭl-kī′ah:

21 And I will clothe him with thy robe, and strengthen him with thy girdle, and I will commit thy government into his hand: and he shall be a father to the inhabitants of Jerusalem, and to the house of Jū′dah.

22 And the key of the house of David will I lay upon his shoulder; so he shall open, and none shall shut; and he shall shut, and none shall open.

23 And I will fasten him *as* a nail in a sure place; and he shall be for a glorious throne to his father's house.

24 And they shall hang upon him all the glory of his father's house, the offspring and the issue, all vessels of small quantity, from the vessels of cups, even to all the vessels of flagons.

25 In that day, saith the LORD of hosts, shall the nail that is fastened in the sure place be removed, and be cut down, and fall; and the burden that *was* upon it shall be cut off: for the LORD hath spoken *it*.

CHAPTER 23

THE burden of Tyre. Howl, ye ships of Tär′shĭsh; for it is laid waste, so that there is no house, no entering in: from the land of Chĭt′tĭm it is revealed to them.

2 Be still, ye inhabitants of the isle; thou whom the merchants of Zī′don, that pass over the sea, have replenished.

3 And by great waters the seed of

invading army. But instead of turning to the Lord for their help, the people will turn to the **armor of the house of the forest** (the arsenals or forest houses) that had been built as early as the days of Solomon. They will attempt to fortify the **breaches of the city** and the **waters of the lower pool.** The prophet goes on to state that even the houses will be **broken down to fortify the wall.** All of these preparations, the prophet warns, will be worthless because they have **not looked unto the maker thereof.** He has called for **weeping . . . mourning . . . sackcloth** (repentance); but instead, the people have developed the attitude of **eat and drink; for tomorrow we shall die.**

15-25. In the last part of the chapter Isaiah turns his attention to an internal matter in the affairs of Jerusalem during his own time. **Shebna** is referred to as the **treasurer;** apparently, he was the royal chamberlain who was the leader of the pro-Egyptian faction in Jerusalem. Thinking that his position was secure, he had already ordered a large **sepulcher** (tomb) to be raised in memory of himself. Instead, Isaiah predicted that he would soon be demoted from his office and would eventually die a pauper in a far country. Delitzsch (p. 401) notes the boldness and freedom with which Isaiah rebuked a public official of such wealth and position. Those interested in sports will be intrigued by the reference to his being thrown **like a ball** into a far country. Second Kings 18:18 indicates that he, Shebna, was replaced by **Eliakim** as early as 701 B.C. The overall impression of the passage is that Shebna would die in captivity in Babylon in his old age. Eliakim came to authority and power under the reign of Hezekiah as his prime minister. Thus, his **robe** was a sign of his royal authority as the king's chief advisor. **The key of the house of David** refers to his responsibility in advising and protecting the Davidic line. The process of opening and shutting refers to his absolute authority in civil affairs. God then promises that he will **fasten him as a nail in a sure place,** referring to a large peg built into the wall of houses in that day which was virtually irremovable. The idea was that Eliakim would enjoy the permanence of his position while Shebna would not. Archer (p. 625) is probably correct in interpreting the final verse as referring not to Eliakim himself, but to his descendants who would assume that they are as secure as he and would find that one day their **nail** would be removed (e.g., at the time of the Babylonian invasion).

10. Concerning Tyre (Phoenicia). 23:1-18.

23:1-12. The burden of Tyre extends the prophet's message to Israel's neighboring nations to the northeastern Mediterranean coastal kingdom of the Phoenicians. (On their history and significance, see D. R. Ap-Thomas, in "The Phoenicians," *POTT*, pp. 259-286; D. Baramaki, *Phoenicia and the Phoenicians;* D. Harden, *The Phoenicians;* S. Moscati, *The World of the Phoenicians.*) These ancient merchanteers of the Mediterranean were ethnically related to the Caananites (cf. Gen 10) and derived their name *Phoinikoi* from the Greeks who simply called

Sī'hôr, the harvest of the river, *is* her revenue; and she is a mart of nations.

4 Be thou ashamed, O Zī'don: for the sea hath spoken, *even* the strength of the sea, saying, I travail not, nor bring forth children, neither do I nourish up young men, *nor* bring up virgins.

5 As at the report concerning Egypt, *so* shall they be sorely pained at the report of Tyre.

6 Pass ye over to Tär'shĭsh; howl, ye inhabitants of the isle.

7 *Is* this your joyous *city,* whose antiquity *is* of ancient days? her own feet shall carry her afar off to sojourn.

8 Who hath taken this counsel against Tyre, the crowning *city,* whose merchants *are* princes, whose traffickers *are* the honourable of the earth?

9 The Lord of hosts hath purposed it, to stain the pride of all glory, *and* to bring into contempt all the honourable of the earth.

10 Pass through thy land as a river, O daughter of Tär'shĭsh: *there is* no more strength.

11 He stretched out his hand over the sea, he shook the kingdoms: the Lord hath given a commandment against the merchant *city,* to destroy the strong holds thereof.

12 And he said, Thou shalt no more rejoice, O thou oppressed virgin, daughter of Zī'don: arise, pass over to Chĭt'tĭm; there also shalt thou have no rest.

13 Behold the land of the Chăl-dē'-ans; this people was not, *till* the Assyrian founded it for them that dwell in the wilderness: they set up the towers thereof, they raised up the palaces thereof; *and* he brought it to ruin.

14 Howl, ye ships of Tär'shĭsh: for your strength is laid waste.

15 And it shall come to pass in that day, that Tyre shall be forgotten seventy years, according to the days of one king: after the end of seventy years shall Tyre sing as an harlot.

16 Take an harp, go about the city, thou harlot that hast been forgotten; make sweet melody, sing many songs, that thou mayest be remembered.

17 ¶And it shall come to pass after the end of seventy years, that the Lord will visit Tyre, and she shall turn to her hire, and shall commit fornication with

them the "purple-folk," deriving this title from their famous purple dye which they extracted from the sea snails off the coast. They were the great merchants of the ancient Near East, and their well-established commercial shipping enterprise is well verified prior to 260 B.C. In ancient times their timber-carrying ships from Byblos engaged in extensive trade with the Egyptian pharaohs, even providing the cedar ship for Khufu, the Cheops of pyramid fame. Tyre and neighboring **Zidon** (Sidon) are more well-known in biblical passages. Jezebel, the ruthless queen of Israel, was the daughter of the king of Tyre and Zidon. Her ungodly tactics are representative of the pagan Phoenician commercialism that dominated their entire society. The matter in view here by the prophet is the coming total destruction of this ancient city, which was the crown of the Phoenician commercial enterprise. **Tarshish** is the common designation for the westernmost part of the Mediterranean basin, possibly referring to Spain. **Chittim** refers to the island of Cyprus that lay off the coast of the Mediterranean from Tyre. The implication of this passage is that the fall of Tyre would mean the ruin of the commercial trading ventures of Cyprus and Western Europe, especially for the Phoenician colonies scattered throughout the Mediterranean region. **Sihor** refers to a branch of the Nile River in Egypt and therefore can be taken as a general designation for Egypt itself. Thus, the prophet predicts that the prosperous trade between Egypt and Phoenicia will cease. Even neighboring **Zidon** will be shocked at the utter destruction and calamity that shall come upon Tyre. The name of this chief port city, which lay to the south of Zidon, comes from the Greek word for "rock," referring to the rocky promontories on which the city sits, overlooking its protected harbor. Tyre also occupies an unusual place in Old Testament history, for it was from here that David's friend Hiram supplied the wood that was necessary for the building of Solomon's temple. Later, Tyre was dominated by the Assyrians, but managed to break free; and it was during this period of renewed prosperity that the prophetic condemnations of Isaiah and, later, Ezekiel (27, 28) were uttered. Ezekiel predicted that the entire city would be thrown into the sea, which was fulfilled during the long siege and razing of the city by the Babylonian king Nebuchadnezzar. Only the island city escaped, and it was completely demolished in 332 B.C. by the Greek emperor Alexander the Great. Thus, this **joyous** and **ancient** city would no longer be the crowning jewel of the Phoenician Empire because the **Lord of hosts hath purposed it.** Such statements were given by the Old Testament prophets with absolute finality. Therefore, the prophet pictures the Lord as the One who **shook the kingdoms** and has commanded the fall of the **merchant city.**

13-18. The reference to the **land of the Chaldeans** has caused some interpretive difficulty. Since Nebuchadnezzar the Chaldean was the one who besieged and destroyed Tyre, it would appear that these Babylonians/Chaldeans are definitely the invaders that are in view in the passage. Archer (p. 626) incorrectly follows the Berkeley Version in translating this as a vocative, implying that **Assyrian** forces would destroy Tyre. Young (II, p. 134) correctly translates and interprets this passage to mean that Assyria, which rose to power earlier than the Neo-Babylonian Empire, viewed the dwellers in the Chaldean desert as insignificant in comparison to themselves. Thus, Isaiah refers to the fact that **this people was not,** meaning that the Chaldeans had not previously risen to any significance in Assyro-Babylonia. Since the Chaldean establishment of Babylon was just beginning to take place in Isaiah's own day, his statement about raising her **towers** and **palaces** is amazing, indeed. The closing four verses of this passage are written in prose and form a contrast to the preceding poetic style. That these events **shall come to pass** is the prophet's expression for emphasizing the

all the kingdoms of the world upon the face of the earth.

18 And her merchandise and her hire shall be holiness to the LORD; it shall not be treasured nor laid up; for her merchandise shall be for them that dwell before the LORD, to eat sufficiently, and for durable clothing.

predictive nature of his declaration. Like the coming Babylonian captivity of the Jews, **Tyre shall be forgotten seventy years.** This would indicate that the initial destruction of the city would be so severe that for the lifespan of **one king** the city would be virtually forgotten by the nations of the world. After that, Tyre would have to **sing as a harlot,** meaning that she would no longer enjoy her independence and would have to pander to the lusts and desires of her conquerors like a woman of the streets. The reference to her **songs** seems to indicate an old, worn, and used harlot who is no longer desired, who sings songs of enticement because she has lost her natural beauty. Buksbazen (p. 234) notes that Isaiah compares Tyre to a pathetic old harlot who is forced by poverty and old age to go out into the streets to ply her trade and seek her former customers. Like all of Isaiah's prophecies, this one begins with a statement of severe judgment; yet, it ends with a word of hope. There will come a time in which **the LORD will visit Tyre** and allow her to continue her commercial enterprise, and even beyond that there will come a time when her **merchandise** shall eventually be **holiness to the LORD.** As the prophet closes this series of prophetic judgments on Israel's neighbors, he once again reminds us that there will come a time (in the millennial kingdom) when they shall share in Israel's blessing.

C. Predictions of the Great Tribulation and the Millennial Kingdom (I). 24:1-27:13.

This section of Isaiah's prophecies has been called the "little apocalypse"; it looks beyond the immediate judgment of the gentile nations to the time of final judgments over them during the Tribulation Period and the ushering in of the messianic kingdom. These chapters function as an appropriate finale, a closing triumph of God over the nations of the world. In them we have some of Isaiah's most amazing predictions to be found anywhere in his book.

1. Tragedies of the Tribulation Period. 24:1-23.

This chapter begins Isaiah's prophecy of a coming universal judgment upon all the nations of the earth, which is to be followed by the universal blessing of the coming messianic kingdom. A proper interpretation of chapter 24 must certainly be based upon its comparison and relationship to chapters 25-27. This chapter has been variously interpreted by commentators. Eusebius and Jerome seem to be the first Christian commentators to interpret this passage as a prediction of the end of the world. Even the older Jewish commentators, who saw the first part of the chapter as referring to the Assyro-Babylonian invasions, nevertheless viewed the last part of the chapter in relation to the wars of Gog and Magog in the days of the Messiah. Calvin viewed it as a prophecy against both Israel and her contemporary neighbors. Luther applied it to the desolation of Judaea by the Romans. The interpretive issue rests upon the use of the Hebrew word 'erets, which may be translated either "land" or "earth." If it is to be translated "land," the extent of the desolations would be limited to the land of Judah itself. This view is favored by Alexander, Barnes, Calvin, Gesenius, Hitzig, Lowth, and MacRae (with the latter applying the passage to both an immediate judgment upon Israel and an ultimate eschatological judgment as well). The universal, apocalyptic view is taken by Archer, Buksbazen, Delitzsch, Fitch, Leupold, and Young. The context of the chapter certainly favors the universal view of the judgment statements, since they are followed by universal statements of blessing. Worldwide judgment is viewed as preceding a time of world-embracing salvation. The result of this judgment will be that a remnant shall be saved from the earth and will praise the glory and majesty of God. Young (II, p. 146) states that this judgment is "not local but universal, one

CHAPTER 24

BEHOLD, the LORD maketh the earth empty, and maketh it waste, and turneth it upside down, and scattereth abroad the inhabitants thereof.

2 And it shall be, as with the people, so with the priest; as with the servant, so with his master; as with the maid, so with her mistress; as with the buyer, so with the seller; as with the lender, so with the borrower; as with the taker of usury, so with the giver of usury to him.

3 The land shall be utterly emptied, and utterly spoiled: for the LORD hath spoken this word.

4 The earth mourneth *and* fadeth away, the world languisheth *and* fadeth away, the haughty people of the earth do languish.

5 The earth also is defiled under the inhabitants thereof; because they have transgressed the laws, changed the ordinance, broken the everlasting covenant.

6 Therefore hath the curse devoured the earth, and they that dwell therein are desolate: therefore the inhabitants of the earth are burned, and few men left.

7 The new wine mourneth, the vine languisheth, all the merryhearted do sigh.

8 The mirth of tabrets ceaseth, the noise of them that rejoice endeth, the joy of the harp ceaseth.

9 They shall not drink wine with a song; strong drink shall be bitter to them that drink it.

10 The city of confusion is broken down: every house is shut up, that no man may come in.

11 *There is* a crying for wine in the streets; all joy is darkened, the mirth of the land is gone.

12 In the city is left desolation, and the gate is smitten with destruction.

which will cover the entire covenant-breaking earth; and in this judgment the theocratic nation, Judah, will also be included." He also correctly notes that the real theme of this section is not judgment and blessing so much as it is the divine intervention of God. He is the God who will move to judge the nations of the world, and He is also the God who will intervene to establish His kingdom upon the earth. The Hebrew of this section is replete with assonances and alliterations. Leupold (I, p. 375) notes that this section is also filled with past-tense verbs that may be classed as "prophetic perfects." Thus, the prophet sees these events, which are yet future, as though they had already happened. Such was the absolute certitude with which the prophet predicted the judgment of God. This would imply an irrevocable judgment, rather than a conditional and provisional threat of judgment.

24:1-12. The LORD (*Yahweh*) moves in cataclysmic judgment upon the **earth** (*'erets*). The devastating nature of the context would imply that it should be translated **earth. The LORD maketh the earth empty** (*bōqeq*), **and . . . waste** (*bōleqah*). The verb **turneth it upside down** may better be translated "distorts" or "changes its face." The idea is that Jehovah empties the earth and lays it waste through the means of war and leaves it so devastated and distorted that it is unrecognizable. The few remaining survivors **scattereth abroad.** Every class of society will be affected: **People . . . priest . . . servant . . . master,** etc. MacRae ("Some Principles in the Interpretation of Isaiah as Illustrated by Chapter 24," in *NPOT*, p. 151ff.) correctly notes that one of the problems in interpreting this passage is the interchangeable use of the word *'erets*, which occurs nine times in the first thirteen verses. The AV translates it "earth" six times and "land" three times, whereas the RSV translates it "earth" each time. Naturally, the translation of the word greatly influences the interpretation of the passage. Thus, **land** should be read "earth." The proof that this is the proper interpretation of the passage comes in verse 4, where **earth** (*'erets*) is used in parallel with the word *world* (*tēbēl*). Only Leupold and Young emphasize this point. Young (II, p. 154) quotes Kittel in asserting that *tēbēl* is never restricted to the land of Judah, but always refers to the inhabited world in its entirety. Thus, from common Hebrew poetic usage we are given a clear interpretation within the passage itself as to the meaning of *'erets*. It is undoubtedly the "whole world" that the prophet has in view in this passage. Therefore, the **inhabitants** are to be viewed as the peoples of the earth who have **transgressed** the moral laws (*torōth*) of God. The **covenant** is not to be limited to God's covenant with Israel alone; it should be viewed as the "covenant of ancient times." Hence, the violation is one of Divine Law itself. Since all the earth has broken God's moral laws, the **curse devoured the earth.** Looking down through the corridor of time, Isaiah sees an era when the entire world shall come under the judgment and retribution of a righteous God. The inhabitants of the earth are spoken of as being **desolate** and **burned** (*harū*, meaning charred). As a result of universal transgression, mankind is almost totally obliterated from the face of the earth. Whether this has direct implication to the potential of nuclear warfare is certainly not made clear in the passage; but in light of the modern situation, it must be taken as a definite possibility. The **city of confusion** (*qiryah tohū*) should be translated "city of chaos" or "emptiness." Note that *tohū* is the same word that is used in Genesis 1:2 to describe the empty and chaotic initial state of the earth. This city does not necessarily refer to Jerusalem or Babylon. It is merely used to describe the desolation of cities in general. Notice the more common word *'iyr* for **city** in verse 12. The idea conveyed in the passage is that the cities of the earth will be wasted and empty as a result of this universal destruction.

13 ¶When thus it shall be in the midst of the land among the people, *there shall be* as the shaking of an olive tree, *and* as the gleaning grapes when the vintage is done.

14 They shall lift up their voice, they shall sing for the majesty of the LORD, they shall cry aloud from the sea.

15 Wherefore glorify ye the LORD in the fires, *even* the name of the LORD God of Israel in the isles of the sea.

16 ¶From the uttermost part of the earth have we heard songs, *even* glory to the righteous. But I said, My leanness, my leanness, woe unto me! the treacherous dealers have dealt treacherously; yea, the treacherous dealers have dealt very treacherously.

17 Fear, and the pit, and the snare, *are* upon thee, O inhabitant of the earth.

18 And it shall come to pass, *that* he who fleeth from the noise of the fear shall fall into the pit; and he that cometh up out of the midst of the pit shall be taken in the snare: for the windows from on high are open, and the foundations of the earth do shake.

19 The earth is utterly broken down, the earth is clean dissolved, the earth is moved exceedingly.

20 The earth shall reel to and fro like a drunkard, and shall be removed like a cottage; and the transgression thereof shall be heavy upon it; and it shall fall, and not rise again.

21 And it shall come to pass in that day, *that* the LORD shall punish the host of the high ones *that are* on high, and the kings of the earth upon the earth.

22 And they shall be gathered together, *as* prisoners are gathered in the pit, and shall be shut up in the prison, and after many days shall they be visited.

23 Then the moon shall be confounded, and the sun ashamed, when the LORD of hosts shall reign in mount Zion, and in Jerusalem, and before his ancients gloriously.

13-23. The universal nature of the eschatological judgment that is announced in this passage is made even more clear and certain in the latter half of the chapter. The worldwide devastation is so total that it will leave the people of the earth **as the shaking of an olive tree.** The meaning is that when a great wind storm shakes a ripened olive tree, it would naturally blow most of the fruit away, leaving only negligible remains. The use of the word **shaking** (*kenoqep*) in this passage should not be interpreted as referring to an earthquake. The remnant that remains shall **lift up their voice** and **shall sing** in recognition of God's divine deliverance of them from the Great Tribulation (cf. Mt 24:22, "And except those days should be shortened, there should no flesh be saved: but for the elect's sake those days shall be shortened"). **Glorify ye the LORD in the fires** (*urim*) should be translated "sunlit places" (i.e., the east), in contrast to those who shall cry out loud **from the sea** (i.e., the west). The reference is not to "fires of persecution," as stated by McRae (p. 154). The reference to the **uttermost part of the earth** would again emphasize the universal nature of the prophecy in this passage. The phrase **glory to the righteous** should be taken as a reference to the righteous ones (people of God) and not to God Himself since He is nowhere called by the term *tsadik*. **Fear . . . the pit . . . the snare** are all assonances in the Hebrew. The idea is that one who runs from the **noise of the fear** shall eventually fall into the **pit,** and both he that cometh out and he who climbs out of the pit shall be **taken in the snare.** The meaning of all of this is certainly poetic and difficult to determine. However, it is to be understood in relation to the fact that the **foundations of the earth do shake.** The language of this passage is certainly reminiscent of Ezekiel 38:19-20 and Haggai 2:6-7, and possibly even I Peter 3:10-11. Verse 19, which is translated **utterly broken down . . . clean dissolved . . . moved exceedingly** in the AV, is actually stated in the Hebrew to be "broken, cracked, and shaken." In each case a *hithpolel* perfect verb follows an infinitive absolute. The emphasis of the statement is certainly upon the earthquake-like disaster that shall shake the entire earth. This would clearly place the eschatological focus of the passage in the Tribulation Period, rather than referring to a localized earthquake in the land of Israel. The nature of this statement is not to emphasize that the land has been devastated due to war, but that it has been destroyed by the natural catastrophe of an earthquake. The further designation that the **earth shall reel to and fro like a drunkard** would indicate a further severe eschatological judgment of God upon the earth that throws it off its axis. The reference to the **windows from on high** is certainly reminiscent of the Noahic flood but it is not to be taken as referring to such. In other words, this ultimate cataclysmic and apocalyptic judgment of the earth will be of the same severe proportions as the Flood was in Noah's day. It will literally rock the very stability of the planet itself as a reminder that the people of the earth have rebelled against God. In spite of impending doom, the passage concludes with another ray of hope. The Hebrew word *paqad* is translated **punish** in verse 21 and **visited** in verse 22. It actually conveys the idea of divine intervention. The idea is that the Lord shall intervene in regard to the **host of the high ones** (Satanic powers) and the **kings of the earth** (earthly powers). They all are referred to as **gathered in the pit . . . shut up . . . many days.** After that period of time, **shall they be visited** (lit., punished). Notice the obvious parallel to Revelation 20:1-3, where Satan is bound in the bottomless pit for a thousand years and then is loosed for a "little season," only to be finally cast into the Lake of Fire! This shall be followed by the fact that the **LORD of hosts shall reign in mount Zion, and in Jerusalem.** His glorious reign shall be such that it shall outshine the moon and the sun. Thus Isaiah began his prophecy with a message of worldwide judgment that shall come during

CHAPTER 25

O LORD, thou *art* my God; I will exalt thee, I will praise thy name; for thou hast done wonderful *things; thy* counsels of old *are* faithfulness *and* truth.

2 For thou hast made of a city an heap; *of* a defenced city a ruin: a palace of strangers to be no city; it shall never be built.

3 Therefore shall the strong people glorify thee, the city of the terrible nations shall fear thee.

4 For thou hast been a strength to the poor, a strength to the needy in his distress, a refuge from the storm, a shadow from the heat, when the blast of the terrible ones *is* as a storm *against* the wall.

5 Thou shalt bring down the noise of strangers, as the heat in a dry place; *even* the heat with the shadow of a cloud: the branch of the terrible ones shall be brought low.

6 ¶And in this mountain shall the LORD of hosts make unto all people a feast of fat things, a feast of wines on the lees, of fat things full of marrow, of wines on the lees well refined.

7 And he will destroy in this mountain the face of the covering cast over all people, and the vail that is spread over all nations.

8 He will swallow up death in victory; and the Lord GOD will wipe away tears from off all faces; and the rebuke of his people shall he take away from off all the earth: for the LORD hath spoken *it*.

9 ¶And it shall be said in that day, Lo, this *is* our God; we have waited for him, and he will save us: this *is* the LORD; we have waited for him, we will be glad and rejoice in his salvation.

10 For in this mountain shall the hand of the LORD rest, and Moab shall be trodden down under him, even as straw is trodden down for the dunghill.

11 And he shall spread forth his hands in the midst of them, as he that swimmeth spreadeth forth *his hands* to swim: and he shall bring down their pride together with the spoils of their hands.

12 And the fortress of the high fort of thy walls shall he bring down, lay low, *and* bring to the ground, *even* to the dust.

CHAPTER 26

IN THAT day shall this song be sung in the land of Jū′dah; We have a strong city; salvation will *God* appoint *for* walls and bulwarks.

2 Open ye the gates, that the righteous nation which keepeth the truth may enter in.

3 Thou wilt keep *him* in perfect peace, *whose* mind *is* stayed *on thee:* because he trusteth in thee.

4 Trust ye in the LORD for ever: for in the LORD JE-HŌ′VAH *is* everlasting strength:

5 ¶For he bringeth down them that dwell on high; the lofty city, he layeth it

the Tribulation Period and closed this chapter with a glorious ray of hope that, in spite of all this, the King, the Lord Himself, shall reign in Jerusalem!

2. Triumphs of the kingdom age. 25:1-27:13.

25:1-12. This chapter begins with a song of exultation and praise: **O LORD, thou art my God.** The survivors of the Great Tribulation Period cannot proclaim the marvelous intervention of God on their behalf in too exulted and exuberant language. The cities of mankind have fallen into **ruin,** and the people therefore finally **fear** God. He is the One alone who has been a **refuge from the storm** of His own judgment. Thus, the proud nations of the world are **brought low** before the majesty of the mighty God. A great celebration shall take place in **this mountain** (Zion). **All people** refers to those nations that have survived the Tribulation Period and go into the blessings of the millennial kingdom. They should be distinguished from the gentile church, which is the bride of Christ. The banquet described here is not the Marriage Supper of the Lamb (see Archer, p. 626), but the time of spiritual and material blessing that shall prevail in the kingdom. **Wines on the lees** refers to dregs of filtered wine, which was not always necessarily fermented. It was certainly not always served in its fermented state either. (See the article on "Wine," in the *Zondervan Pictorial Bible Dictionary*, pp. 894-895.) The **veil** is not a reference to the veil of the Temple that would be rent later, but the **covering** of death that hangs over **all nations** as a result of the recently completed devastations of the Tribulation Period. **He will destroy** (in verse 7) should read "He will swallow up," coming, as it does, from the same verb (*bila'*) as the phrase in verse 8, **He will swallow up death in victory** (cf. I Cor 15:54). Moreover **the Lord GOD will wipe away tears** (cf. Rev 7:17). Again, there can be no doubt that in this passage Isaiah intends to look to the distant future as he speaks of the time of unparalleled peace that shall occur during the millennial kingdom as a result of the intervention of God Himself. Thus, the people can rejoice in the fact that though they have waited through all these years of human devastation, it has been worth it because **Lo, this is our God!**

26:1-11. This chapter opens the Great Song of Praise that is sung in the land of **Judah** (lit., praise). The picture is one of the redeemed who enter the millennial kingdom. Notice that the **walls and bulwarks** are not physical, but spiritual. **Salvation** is God's total provision for His people's needs. Verse 2 indicates that the city (New Jerusalem) has never yet been opened; hence, the command, **Open ye the gates** so that the **righteous nation** may enter into the place of God's blessing. Certainly, historic Judah had entered into Jerusalem many times. But this passage has in view that time at the end of the age when saved Israel shall come up in her redemption to the New Jerusalem to a place of honor unparalleled in her history. The promise that **Thou wilt keep him in perfect peace** literally reads "peace, peace" (*shalōm*

low; he layeth it low, *even* to the ground; he bringeth it *even* to the dust.

6 The foot shall tread it down, *even* the feet of the poor, *and* the steps of the needy.

7 The way of the just *is* uprightness: thou, most upright, dost weigh the path of the just.

8 Yea, in the way of thy judgments, O Lord, have we waited for thee; the desire of *our* soul *is* to thy name, and to the remembrance of thee.

9 With my soul have I desired thee in the night; yea, with my spirit within me will I seek thee early: for when thy judgments *are* in the earth, the inhabitants of the world will learn righteousness.

10 Let favour be shewed to the wicked, *yet* will he not learn righteousness; in the land of uprightness will he deal unjustly, and will not behold the majesty of the Lord.

11 Lord, *when* thy hand is lifted up, they will not see: *but* they shall see, and be ashamed for *their* envy at the people; yea, the fire of thine enemies shall devour them.

12 ¶ Lord, thou wilt ordain peace for us: for thou also hast wrought all our works in us.

13 O Lord our God, *other* lords beside thee have had dominion over us: *but* by thee only will we make mention of thy name.

14 *They are* dead, they shall not live; *they are* deceased, they shall not rise: therefore hast thou visited and destroyed them, and made all their memory to perish.

15 Thou hast increased the nation, O Lord, thou hast increased the nation: thou art glorified: thou hadst removed *it* far *unto* all the ends of the earth.

16 Lord, in trouble have they visited thee, they poured out a prayer *when* thy chastening *was* upon them.

17 Like as a woman with child, *that* draweth near the time of her delivery, is in pain, *and* crieth out in her pangs; so have we been in thy sight, O Lord.

18 We have been with child, we have been in pain, we have as it were brought forth wind; we have not wrought any deliverance in the earth; neither have the inhabitants of the world fallen.

19 Thy dead *men* shall live, *together with* my dead body shall they arise. Awake and sing, ye that dwell in dust: for thy dew *is as* the dew of herbs, and the earth shall cast out the dead.

20 ¶ Come, my people, enter thou into thy chambers, and shut thy doors about thee: hide thyself as it were for a little moment, until the indignation be overpast.

21 For, behold, the Lord cometh out of his place to punish the inhabitants of the earth for their iniquity: the earth also shall disclose her blood, and shall no more cover her slain.

CHAPTER 27
IN that day the Lord with his sore and

shalōm). This double emphasis indicates a peace that goes beyond human comprehension. It is a peace that really is a peace. To have one's **mind . . . stayed** (*samak*, "to lean upon," or to be "sustained") is used in parallel with **trusteth,** indicating that when one does in fact trust the Lord totally, he will lean upon Him entirely and be sustained by Him alone. God's great promise is that those who will put their trust in Him shall be completely secure. That spiritual stability mitigates against mental instability is the constant promise of God throughout the Scripture. **Trust** (*batach*) indicates not only a confidence in something but a "careless security" that comes from that confidence (*Theological Wordbook of the Old Testament*, I, p. 101). Notice also that the object of one's faith or trust is as important as the act of trusting. Here the object of faith is **the Lord Jehovah**! Isaiah then contrasts the **way of the just** with the unjust. **The just** have upheld His **judgments . . . have . . . waited for thee . . . desired thee.** The prophet then makes one of the outstanding observations found anywhere in the Bible. In verse 10 he raises the hypothetical issue of showing **favor . . . to the wicked;** and yet, if he will not **learn righteousness,** then Isaiah's conclusion is that even in the **land of uprightness** (heavenly kingdom) he will deal **unjustly.** His point is that God does not allow unredeemed sinners into His kingdom because they would ultimately wreck it. Those who have not been content to walk in the ways of the Lord in this life would certainly not be content to do so in the next life, either.

12-21. Next, Isaiah predicts that God will **ordain peace** for His elect ones whose salvation is the result of His work in them. The reference to **other lords** is apparently to other gods that they had previously worshiped. Now they must recognize that **They are dead.** The meaning of the passage is quite clear in light of Israel's prolonged idolatry. Those gods that never really did exist could not deliver them, and their only hope is in Jehovah Himself. He is such that He can even make the **memory** of a pagan nation or god to disappear. The prophet recognizes that God would not regather the very nation He had **removed . . . unto all the ends of the earth** through the process of the dispersion in the land of Israel. Verse 19 is certainly one of the strongest indications of physical resurrection found anywhere in the Old Testament. **Thy dead men shall live . . . my dead body shall they arise.** Those who have previously died are called upon to **Awake and sing, ye that dwell in the dust.** The prophet further predicts that the **earth shall cast out the dead.** The language here is certainly reminiscent of Daniel 12:2. That the Old Testament clearly teaches the resurrection of the physical body is obvious from this passage, as well as others. The chapter ends with God urging His people to **hide** themselves for **a little moment.** The passing over of **the indignation** (*za'am*, indignant denunciation) may refer to the survival of the Jewish remnant during the Tribulation Period. Finally, **the Lord** Himself has to intervene in order to punish the wicked and to vindicate the righteous.

27:1-13. The reference to **leviathan** has provoked a great deal

great and strong sword shall punish leviathan the piercing serpent, even leviathan that crooked serpent; and he shall slay the dragon that *is* in the sea.

2 ¶In that day sing ye unto her, A vineyard of red wine.

3 I the LORD do keep it; I will water it every moment: lest *any* hurt it, I will keep it night and day.

4 Fury *is* not in me: who would set the briers *and* thorns against me in battle? I would go through them, I would burn them together.

5 Or let him take hold of my strength, *that* he may make peace with me; *and* he shall make peace with me.

6 He shall cause them that come of Jacob to take root: Israel shall blossom and bud, and fill the face of the world with fruit.

7 Hath he smitten him, as he smote those that smote him? *or* is he slain according to the slaughter of them that are slain by him?

8 In measure, when it shooteth forth, thou wilt debate with it: he stayeth his rough wind in the day of the east wind.

9 By this therefore shall the iniquity of Jacob be purged; and this *is* all the fruit to take away his sin; when he maketh all the stones of the altar as chalkstones that are beaten in sunder, the groves and images shall not stand up.

10 Yet the defenced city *shall be* desolate, *and* the habitation forsaken, and left like a wilderness: there shall the calf feed, and there shall he lie down, and consume the branches thereof.

11 When the boughs thereof are withered, they shall be broken off: the women come, *and* set them on fire: for it *is* a people of no understanding: therefore he that made them will not have mercy on them, and he that formed them will shew them no favour.

12 And it shall come to pass in that day, *that* the LORD shall beat off from the channel of the river unto the stream of Egypt, and ye shall be gathered one by one, O ye children of Israel.

13 And it shall come to pass in that day, *that* the great trumpet shall be blown, and they shall come which were ready to perish in the land of Assyria, and the outcasts in the land of Egypt, and shall worship the LORD in the holy mount at Jerusalem.

of controversy among commentators. Some see parallels in Babylonian, Hittite, and Ugaritic literature. It is generally suggested that the symbolic-mythical creature of the Ancient Near East is used as a "figure of speech" to describe the enemy nations; they are a monster whom Jehovah shall defeat. However, in view of the millennial context of this passage and the fact that Leviathan is also referred to as **that crooked serpent . . . the dragon,** the text indicates that Isaiah has the victory of the Lord over Satan in view (cf. Rev 20:2). Rather than using the imagery of Leviathan as a symbol of the monstrous enemies of Israel, it seems much more appropriate that the prophet would use this mythical symbol to represent the monster of monsters—Satan himself! The prophet then bursts into a joyful song of the **vineyard** of the Lord. This vineyard shall succeed because **I the LORD do keep it.** God promises to water and protect this vineyard from the **briers and thorns** (enemies of Israel). Because of the time of blessing that shall accompany the millennial kingdom, God can say that **Fury is not in me.** This will be a time when the nations shall **make peace** with the Lord. The Israelites who have wandered from place to place shall **take root** and shall **blossom and bud.** Israel is pictured as having been **smitten** by the Lord throughout her history. But this shall ultimately cause **the iniquity of Jacob** to **be purged.** The **stones** of the heathen altars shall be as **chalkstones** (limestones) that have been ground to dusty powder. **The defenced city** (vs. 10) is not a reference to the impregnable capitals of Israel's conquerors; it refers to the fact that during the millennial kingdom **defenced** cities shall be empty because they shall need no walls. In this age of peace and prosperity, when all the world shall worship the Lord Jehovah, such cities shall be emptied; the people shall have no need of them. Verse 12 reiterates Israel's ultimate boundary from **the channel of the river** (i.e., Euphrates) in the north unto the **stream of Egypt** (probably the border stream, *Wady el-Arish,* rather than the Nile) to the south. The promise of the passage is that the **children of Israel** shall be **gathered one by one** into the land that had been originally promised to their forefathers. Those who had been scattered from **Assyria** to **Egypt** shall not perish, but shall return and shall **worship** the Lord in the **holy mount** (Zion) at **Jerusalem.** There can be no doubt that the apocalypse of Isaiah ends with the triumph of the Jewish people during the kingdom age, in which not only they shall worship at Jerusalem, but all the nations shall come to Jerusalem to worship God as well. Thus, this part of Isaiah's prophecy ends with both a universal and a particular emphasis. The nations shall come to Israel and shall recognize that their God is the true God; and the Jews themselves shall return in national conversion and revival, having come to know the Lord Himself.

D. Perilous Woes Upon Israel and Judah. 28:1-33:24.

In the prophecies of this section we see an entirely different setting. Young (II, p. 263) dates these prophecies from the time of Hezekiah. Each **woe** announces the final and certain impending doom that God has pronounced against the various peoples of these prophecies. It is not inappropriate to translate the word **woe** (*hōy*) as "doomed" in reference to a legal sentence of death. The context of the passage indicates that though Israel had suffered greatly from Assyria's infringement, Samaria, the capital city, had not yet fallen. This was a cause of great pride on the part of the Samaritans and is the background of the strong denunciation of the first **Woe.**

1. Woe to Ephraim (Israel). 28:1-29.

28:1-13. The first **Woe** is pronounced on the **crown of pride . . . the drunkards of Ephraim.** The reference is obviously to Samaria, the capital city of Ephraim, which was situated on a

CHAPTER 28

WOE to the crown of pride, to the drunkards of E'phra-im, whose glorious beauty *is* a fading flower, which *are* on the head of the fat valleys of them that are overcome with wine!

2 Behold, the Lord hath a mighty and strong one, which as a tempest of hail *and* a destroying storm, as a flood of mighty waters overflowing, shall cast down to the earth with the hand.

3 The crown of pride, the drunkards of É'phra-im, shall be trodden under feet:

4 And the glorious beauty, which *is* on the head of the fat valley, shall be a fading flower, *and* as the hasty fruit before the summer; which *when* he that looketh upon it seeth, while *it* is yet in his hand he eateth it up.

5 ¶In that day shall the LORD of hosts be for a crown of glory, and for a diadem of beauty, unto the residue of his people,

6 And for a spirit of judgment to him that sitteth in judgment, and for strength to them that turn the battle to the gate.

7 But they also have erred through wine, and through strong drink are out of the way; the priest and the prophet have erred through strong drink, they are swallowed up of wine, they are out of the way through strong drink; they err in vision, they stumble *in* judgment.

8 For all tables are full of vomit *and* filthiness, *so that there is* no place clean.

9 Whom shall he teach knowledge? and whom shall he make to understand doctrine? *them that are* weaned from the milk, *and* drawn from the breasts.

10 For precept *must be* upon precept, precept upon precept; line upon line, line upon line; here a little, *and* there a little:

11 For with stammering lips and another tongue will he speak to this people.

12 To whom he said, This *is* the rest wherewith ye may cause the weary to rest; and this *is* the refreshing: yet they would not hear.

13 But the word of the LORD was unto them precept upon precept, precept upon precept; line upon line, line upon line; here a little, *and* there a little; that they might go, and fall backward, and be broken, and snared, and taken.

14 ¶Wherefore hear the word of the LORD, ye scornful men, that rule this people which *is* in Jerusalem.

15 Because ye have said, We have made a covenant with death, and with hell are we at agreement; when the overflowing scourge shall pass through, it shall not come unto us: for we have made lies our refuge, and under falsehood have we hid ourselves:

16 Therefore thus saith the Lord GOD, Behold, I lay in Zion for a foundation a stone, a tried stone, a precious corner *stone*, a sure foundation: he that believeth shall not make haste.

17 Judgment also will I lay to the line, and righteousness to the plummet: and the hail shall sweep away the refuge of lies, and the waters shall overflow the hiding place.

18 And your covenant with death

hill that resembled a crown. Thus, **crown** has a topological significance, as well as referring to the capital of the northern kingdom. Ephraim is described as the **crown of pride** (vs. 1), whereas the Lord is called the **crown of glory** (vs. 5). The **mighty and strong one** refers to Assyria, who shall come in like a **destroying storm** and **waters overflowing** and shall sweep Samaria away into captivity. This was fulfilled in 722 B.C. by Shalmaneser. Again, in the midst of his pronouncement of judgment Isaiah offers a token of hope to the **residue** (remnant) **of his people,** who shall survive this devastating invasion. To them the Lord shall be a **crown of glory** and a **diadem of beauty.** To those who will acknowledge the rulership of Jehovah, there will yet be the opportunity for God's blessing. Immediately, Isaiah again turns his attention to the problem at hand because the people have **erred through wine . . . strong drink.** Both **priest** and **prophet** have joined the debauchery of the nation. Notice the interrelationship between pride and drunkenness throughout this passage. Also note that drinking leads the people **out of the way,** that is, out of the path of righteousness. The drunkenness of the people, leaders, and clergy of Ephraim is so severe that the prophet states that their tables are **full of vomit.** Isaiah then raises the question of how God can teach these people when they are in such a condition. They are incapable of receiving **knowledge** or **doctrine** (*shemū'ah,* the message). The familiar reference to **precept upon precept; line upon line** is to be taken negatively, not positively. The word **for** introduces the statement quoted by the prophet from the people who are weary of listening to his prophecies. In essence, they are complaining that his repetitious message is petty and annoying: "rule upon rule" (taking *tsaw* as a shortened form of *mitswah,* "rule" or "commandment") and "line upon line" (lit., plumbline). The idea is that the people are complaining that all they ever hear from this prophet is one rule and one standard after another, and they are weary of it because they have never learned to obey the One who is the Source of all law. Young (II, p. 276) observes that **here a little, and there a little** refers to the fact that the people did not understand the prophet's message in its fullness, but merely regarded it as "incoherent, disparate bits of instruction cast here and there." Instead, God must speak to them with **stammering lips** (unintelligible mutterings) and **another tongue** (that of the Assyrians, which was virtually incomprehensible to the Hebrews). The idea is that since they will not listen to God's message and they consider it a mere repetition of annoying bits of rules and regulations, God will speak to them through the Assyrian captivity. Thus, the **word of the LORD** will ultimately be **precept upon precept** to them because they are so slow to learn His truth.

14-19. The prophet turns his attention for a moment to the people of **Jerusalem** who have made a **covenant with death, and with hell** (*sheōl* is used here as a synonym for death). In the context the idea seems to be that since Ephraim is going to be destroyed by the Assyrian invasion, the Judaeans of Jerusalem are foolish to think that a pro-Assyrian covenant is going to protect them. Thus, the prophet warns against such an alliance with the **overflowing scourge** of the Assyrians who shall pass through the land. He pictures the people as hiding under the **lies** and **falsehood** of their ill-fated hope that the invader will somehow be benevolent to them. In contrast to their covenant, God promises to **lay in Zion . . . a precious corner stone, a sure foundation.** By referring to the New Testament quotations of this verse, it is clear that in Scripture the **corner stone** is ultimately the person of Jesus Christ Himself (cf. I Pet 2:6; and the quotation in Rom 9:33 of Isa 8:14). To those who believe on Christ, He becomes a cornerstone of **sure foundation,** but to those who reject Him, He becomes the "stumbling stone." Note

shall be disannulled, and your agreement with hell shall not stand; when the overflowing scourge shall pass through, then ye shall be trodden down by it.

19 From the time that it goeth forth it shall take you: for morning by morning shall it pass over, by day and by night: and it shall be a vexation only *to* understand the report.

20 For the bed is shorter than that *a man* can stretch himself *on it:* and the covering narrower than that he can wrap himself in it.

21 For the LORD shall rise up as *in* mount Per'a-zĭm, he shall be wroth as *in* the valley of Gĭb'e-on, that he may do his work, his strange work; and bring to pass his act, his strange act.

22 Now therefore be ye not mockers, lest your bands be made strong: for I have heard from the Lord GOD of hosts a consumption, even determined upon the whole earth.

23 ¶Give ye ear, and hear my voice; hearken, and hear my speech.

24 Doth the plowman plow all day to sow? doth he open and break the clods of his ground?

25 When he hath made plain the face thereof, doth he not cast abroad the fitches, and scatter the cummin, and cast in the principal wheat and the appointed barley and the rie in their place?

26 For his God doth instruct him to discretion, *and* doth teach him.

27 For the fitches are not threshed with a threshing instrument, neither is a cart wheel turned about upon the cummin; but the fitches are beaten out with a staff, and the cummin with a rod.

28 Bread *corn* is bruised; because he will not ever be threshing it, nor break *it with* the wheel of his cart, nor bruise it *with* his horsemen.

29 This also cometh forth from the LORD of hosts, *which* is wonderful in counsel, *and* excellent in working.

CHAPTER 29

WOE to Ā'rĭ-el, to Ā'rĭ-el, the city *where David dwelt!* add ye year to year; let them kill sacrifices.

2 Yet I will distress Ā'rĭ-el, and there shall be heaviness and sorrow: and it shall be unto me as Ā'rĭ-el.

3 And I will camp against thee round about, and will lay siege against thee

that the prophecy is introduced by the words **Therefore** and **Behold** (as in the case of 7:14). Isaiah uses this device to gain his listeners' attention to a great messianic truth. The people of Judah have been overconfident in their alliances with their neighboring nations. These alliances can only bring about certain destruction; therefore, the Lord must act to save His people. The word used here for Lord is *adonay*, referring to the "Sovereign One." The Stone that is to be laid is erected by God's own initiative. It is the work of God, and not the work of man; therefore, it is irremovable. The imagery may refer back to Genesis 49:24, where the "mighty God of Jacob" is called the "stone of Israel." The verb **lay** is actually in the past tense, indicating that God's action has already been accomplished. Young (I, p. 286) states: "The decree of God goes back to eternity; the plan of salvation has been determined, and it is to be accomplished in time." Delitzsch (II, p. 10) "what is historically realized has had an eternal existence, and indeed an ideal pre-existence even in the heart of history itself." The stone is also referred to as a **tried stone**, or better, a "stone of testing," i.e., a "touch stone." Because God has established His foundation in Zion, the intended **covenant with death shall be disannulled.** Thus, Judah's desire to trust in alliances, whether with Assyria or Egypt, shall be disannulled by God Himself.

20-29. Such agreements are illustrated humorously by the **bed is shorter than that a man can stretch himself on it** or the **covering** that is **narrower than that he can wrap himself in it.** This clever illustration emphasizes the frustration of attempting to rest or sleep in such a manner and illustrates the futility the Israelites will experience in trying to rest upon their alliances, which shall have their shortcomings. The idea clearly emphasizes that even with Egyptian aid, Judah's resources would be wretchedly insufficient to meet the threat of Assyria. The reference is to **mount Perazim,** the place where David defeated the Philistines (II Sam 5:20). Now God will perform a **strange act,** in that He will turn against His disobedient children instead of fighting for them. The chapter closes with a parable of the farmer. Isaiah emphasizes that the **plowman** does not plow just for the sake of plowing; rather, he plows that he might sow and reap a crop. For **fitches** (*qetsach*) read "black cummin," a plant having small black seeds used for seasoning. **Cummin** is a plant common to Western Asia cultivated from the earliest times. It resembles the caraway in flavor and appearance and was generally grown as a condiment (*New Bible Dictionary,* p. 282). Both are still commonly **beaten out with a staff** in the harvesting process by nomads. The prophet's point in this parable is that even the farmer understands the laws of nature which must necessarily be followed in order to reap a crop. Like the farmer, the LORD of hosts is not just going through the motions of divine activity; but rather, He intends to harvest a crop. Just as the farmer acts with prudence and wisdom, so does the Lord who is **wonderful in counsel** and **excellent in working.** Both His wisdom and works are beyond the imagination and comprehension of finite man. No wonder the Apostle Paul proclaimed: "O the depth of the riches both of the wisdom and knowledge of God! How unsearchable are his judgments, and his ways past finding out!" (Rom 11:33).

2. Woe to Ariel (Jerusalem). 29:1-24.

29:1-12. The next prophetic **Woe** is ascribed to **Ariel, the city where David dwelt!** This parallel name for Jerusalem emphasizes the fact that it was the "altar-hearth" of God, i.e., the sacrificial center of Israel's worship. Robinson (p. 110) notes that David first inaugurated the true worship of Jehovah on Mount Zion. But now Jerusalem's worship had become a meaningless and heartless formality. Isaiah speaks with irony

with a mount, and I will raise forts against thee.

4 And thou shalt be brought down, *and* shalt speak out of the ground, and thy speech shall be low out of the dust, and thy voice shall be, as of one that hath a familiar spirit, out of the ground, and thy speech shall whisper out of the dust.

5 Moreover the multitude of thy strangers shall be like small dust, and the multitude of the terrible ones *shall be* as chaff that passeth away: yea, it shall be at an instant suddenly.

6 Thou shalt be visited of the LORD of hosts with thunder, and with earthquake, and great noise, with storm and tempest, and the flame of devouring fire.

7 And the multitude of all the nations that fight against Â′rĭ-el, even all that fight against her and her munition, and that distress her, shall be as a dream of a night vision.

8 It shall even be as when an hungry *man* dreameth, and, behold, he eateth; but he awaketh, and his soul is empty: or as when a thirsty man dreameth, and, behold, he drinketh; but he awaketh, and, behold, *he is* faint, and his soul hath appetite: so shall the multitude of all the nations be, that fight against mount Zion.

9 ¶Stay yourselves, and wonder; cry ye out, and cry: they are drunken, but not with wine; they stagger, but not with strong drink.

10 For the LORD hath poured out upon you the spirit of deep sleep, and hath closed your eyes: the prophets and your rulers, the seers hath he covered.

11 And the vision of all is become unto you as the words of a book that is sealed, which *men* deliver to one that is learned, saying, Read this, I pray thee: and he saith, I cannot; for it *is* sealed:

12 And the book is delivered to him that is not learned, saying, Read this, I pray thee: and he saith, I am not learned.

13 ¶Wherefore the Lord said, Forasmuch as this people draw near *me* with their mouth, and with their lips do honour me, but have removed their heart far from me, and their fear toward me is taught by the precept of men:

14 Therefore, behold, I will proceed to do a marvellous work among this people, *even* a marvellous work and a wonder: for the wisdom of their wise *men* shall perish, and the understanding of their prudent *men* shall be hid.

15 Woe unto them that seek deep to hide their counsel from the LORD, and their works are in the dark, and they say, Who seeth us? and who knoweth us?

16 Surely your turning of things upside down shall be esteemed as the potter's clay: for shall the work say of him that made it, He made me not? or shall the thing framed say of him that framed it, He had no understanding?

17 ¶*Is* it not yet a very little while, and Lebanon shall be turned into a fruitful

when he commands **add ye year to year; let them kill sacrifices.** His attitude is that empty religion, endlessly continuing its animal sacrifices year after year, will not be able to stop the judgment of God. The parallel statements, **I will distress Ariel . . . and it shall be unto me as Ariel,** means that God will bring judgment upon Jerusalem through the simultaneous invasions of Assyria and Babylon; thereby, it will become **Ariel** ("fire-hearth") to Him. In other words, God will take this city that has been the pride and joy of His people and turn it into what it in fact is, a place of burnt sacrifice. The meaning of the passage is rather clear. Because of her sin, the city, which was known for its burnt offerings unto the Lord, shall in turn become a burnt offering unto the Lord. The city does not stand a chance because Jehovah announces that **I will camp against thee . . . thou shalt be brought down . . . Thou shalt be visited of the LORD of hosts.** God's "visitation" is one of judgment that shall be accompanied by **thunder . . . earthquake . . . great noise . . . storm . . . tempest** and **devouring fire.** There can be no question that the prophet intends to refer to the severity of the coming Babylonian invasion, although he does not yet name the invader. The prophet then announces that all of this will be like a bad **dream** that shall come upon the people of Israel. He cleverly likens it to a man who is dreaming of eating or drinking, only to awaken hungry and thirsty. Then he changes the imagery to remind them that they are **drunken, but not with wine.** They are drunken with their own self-indulgence which has caused them not to hear the message of God. It is as if God has **poured out upon you the spirit of deep sleep** (*tardēmah*, lit., used in Scripture as a "divine anesthetic"). There is definitely a note of reprobation in these words, which are similar to those quoted in Romans 9 by the Apostle Paul. Through the prophet's writings they have the **words of a book;** but because of their unbelief, it appears to them to be **sealed.** (On the inability of man to open the divine message to himself, see Rev 5:1-8.) Thus, the message goes forth, but without divine intervention, to bring faith and repentance to the heart of man; he cannot, in and of himself, receive it.

13-24. Kidner (p. 607) notes that Jesus saw this verse as the very epitome of pharisaism (Mk 7:6ff.). The idea the statement conveys is that the Jewish people **honor** the Lord with their **mouth, and with their lips,** rather than their **heart** (*leb,* the general OT designation for mind, emotions, and will). The prophet further notes that their **fear** (*yir'ah,* reverence) was merely an outward and intellectual accommodation **taught by the precept of men.** Isaiah uses the verse as a protasis, with the apodosis in the following verse. His point is to emphasize that their accommodation of God is purely external, and therefore their worship is hypocritical. It does not represent a genuine, heartfelt fear of God in an act of true reverence and worship. The apodosis is expressed in the idea that since the people will not do what is right toward God, then God must do what is right toward them. The terms a **marvelous work and a wonder** should actually read "doing wondrously and a wonder." This paronomasia of double emphasis, strengthens the thought and, thus, better gains the attention of the listener. The nation which prides itself in its own **wisdom** and **understanding** shall ultimately **perish.** The Scripture makes it clear throughout that God is not impressed with mere intellectual worship, but demands a surrender of one's total being to Himself. A further woe is pronounced on those who seek to **hide their counsel from the**

field, and the fruitful field shall be esteemed as a forest?

18 And in that day shall the deaf hear the words of the book, and the eyes of the blind shall see out of obscurity, and out of darkness.

19 The meek also shall increase *their* joy in the LORD, and the poor among men shall rejoice in the Holy One of Israel.

20 For the terrible one is brought to nought, and the scorner is consumed, and all that watch for iniquity are cut off:

21 That make a man an offender for a word, and lay a snare for him that reproveth in the gate, and turn aside the just for a thing of nought.

22 Therefore thus saith the LORD, who redeemed Abraham, concerning the house of Jacob, Jacob shall not now be ashamed, neither shall his face now wax pale.

23 But when he seeth his children, the work of mine hands, in the midst of him, they shall sanctify my name, and sanctify the Holy One of Jacob, and shall fear the God of Israel.

24 They also that erred in spirit shall come to understanding, and they that murmured shall learn doctrine.

CHAPTER 30

WOE to the rebellious children, saith the LORD, that take counsel, but not of me; and that cover with a covering, but not of my spirit, that they may add sin to sin:

2 That walk to go down into Egypt, and have not asked at my mouth; to strengthen themselves in the strength of Pharaoh, and to trust in the shadow of Egypt!

3 Therefore shall the strength of Pharaoh be your shame, and the trust in the shadow of Egypt *your* confusion.

4 For his princes were at Zō'an, and his ambassadors came to Hā'nēs.

5 They were all ashamed of a people *that* could not profit them, nor be an help nor profit, but a shame, and also a reproach.

6 The burden of the beasts of the south: into the land of trouble and anguish, from whence *come* the young and old lion, the viper and fiery flying serpent, they will carry their riches upon the shoulders of young asses, and their treasures upon the bunches of camels, to a people *that* shall not profit them.

7 For the Egyptians shall help in vain, and to no purpose: therefore have I cried concerning this, Their strength *is* to sit still.

8 ¶Now go, write it before them in a table, and note it in a book, that it may

LORD. The prophet denounces them for attempting to hide their plans and devices from the omniscient God. He likens them to **potter's clay** that rebels against the potter as if he had **no understanding**. The implication is that when we depend upon our own devices instead of surrendering to the Lord, we act as if God did not have the wisdom or ability to help us. All such self-sufficient manipulation by men is a direct reflection on their inability to trust the nature and character of God. Instead of the intellectual leaders of Israel following the Lord, the **deaf . . . blind . . . meek . . . poor** shall **rejoice** in Him. The word **men** ('*adam*) is the common Hebrew designation for "all mankind," which would imply that these truths were fulfilled, not only in Jesus' preaching to the lost people of Israel (Mt 11:5), but to all men everywhere, including the Gentiles. The ideology here is reminiscent of that of Jesus' conversation with the woman at the well. He emphasized to her that the place of one's worship was not as important as that we "worship him in spirit and in truth" (Jn 4:24). Isaiah further criticizes the severe external religious code of his day, noting that it makes a **man an offender for a word** or a **thing of nought**. The idea here is that formal, external, petty religion begins to nitpick at things that are inconsequential as far as God is concerned. Again, as in his previous prophecies, the prophet ends with a word of hope for the **children** of another generation who shall **sanctify** (from Heb *qedōsh*, holy) the **Holy One of Jacob** and shall **fear** ('*arats*, to be in awe or dread) the **God of Israel**. The chapter ends with Isaiah's admonition that those who have **erred in spirit** shall come to **understanding** by learning **doctrine** (*leqach*, teaching). Notice that the Scripture makes it clear that a proper knowledge of God must rest upon a proper doctrine of God.

3. Woe to rebellious children (Judah). 30:1-33.

30:1-7. The **rebellious children** in view in this passage are clearly indicated by the context to be the people of Judah, who are determined to **go down into Egypt**, that is, to seek an alliance with the Egyptians to protect themselves against the possibility of an Assyrian invasion. Speaking through the prophet, God reminds His people that they are willing to **take counsel** of everyone but Him. Therefore, they **cover with a covering** of self-effort; they deal with man's problems by human opinions. But God reminds them that this approach is **not of my spirit** (*rūchiy*). Kidner (p. 607) notes that "ten years earlier, Isaiah had dissuaded Judah from playing Egypt's game against Assyria (ch. 20); now the mood has hardened, and Judah's envoys are on their way." **His princes** seem to refer to Pharaoh's officials. **Hanes** is mentioned in the Bible only here; apparently it was near **Zoan** (Tanis), the largest Egyptian city near the Israelites' border. It was the capital of the twenty-first and twenty-second dynasties of Egypt. Young (II, p. 338) understands this passage to refer to Israel's ambassadors who have gone down to Egypt, a land that cannot profit them. However, the context seems to be the opposite; Israel's ambassadors have gone down to Egypt, and the Egyptians have become ashamed of them because they cannot **profit** from them. Thus, the reference to the **beasts of the south** is that of the great trading caravans that desired to carry off **their treasures upon the . . . camels**. However, Israel's impoverished condition while under attack from the Assyrians, will prevent the Egyptians from profiting; and Egypt will ultimately fail to support Israel in its time of need. The prophet's emphasis is that because it will not profit them to risk their lives for the sake of little Judah, the **Egyptians shall help in vain.** He then turns his imagery around by emphasizing that even if they want to help, they cannot because: **Their strength is to sit still!**

8-17. The prophet is commanded by God to write His message in a **table** (tablet) and **book** (*sepher*). The parallel expres-

be for the time to come for ever and ever:

9 That this *is* a rebellious people, lying children, children *that* will not hear the law of the LORD:

10 Which say to the seers. See not; and to the prophets, Prophesy not unto us right things, speak unto us smooth things, prophesy deceits:

11 Get you out of the way, turn aside out of the path, cause the Holy One of Israel to cease from before us.

12 Wherefore thus saith the Holy One of Israel, Because ye despise this word, and trust in oppression and perverseness, and stay thereon:

13 Therefore this iniquity shall be to you as a breach ready to fall, swelling out in a high wall, whose breaking cometh suddenly at an instant.

14 And he shall break it as the breaking of the potters' vessel that is broken in pieces; he shall not spare: so that there shall not be found in the bursting of it a sherd to take fire from the hearth, or to take water *withal* out of the pit.

15 For thus saith the Lord GOD, the Holy One of Israel; In returning and rest shall ye be saved; in quietness and in confidence shall be your strength: and ye would not.

16 But ye said, No; for we will flee upon horses; therefore shall ye flee: and, We will ride upon the swift; therefore shall they that pursue you be swift.

17 One thousand *shall flee* at the rebuke of one; at the rebuke of five shall ye flee: till ye be left as a beacon upon the top of a mountain, and as an ensign on an hill.

18 And therefore will the LORD wait, that he may be gracious unto you, and therefore will he be exalted, that he may have mercy upon you: for the LORD *is* a God of judgment: blessed *are* all they that wait for him.

19 ¶For the people shall dwell in Zion at Jerusalem: thou shalt weep no more: he will be very gracious unto thee at the voice of thy cry; when he shall hear it, he will answer thee.

20 And *though* the Lord give you the bread of adversity, and the water of affliction, yet shall not thy teachers be removed into a corner any more, but thine eyes shall see thy teachers:

21 And thine ears shall hear a word behind thee, saying, This *is* the way, walk ye in it, when ye turn to the right hand, and when ye turn to the left.

22 Ye shall defile also the covering of thy graven images of silver, and the ornament of thy molten images of gold: thou shalt cast them away as a menstruous cloth; thou shalt say unto it, Get thee hence.

23 Then shall he give the rain of thy seed, that thou shalt sow the ground withal; and bread of the increase of the earth, and it shall be fat and plenteous: in that day shall thy cattle feed in large pastures.

24 The oxen likewise and the young asses that ear the ground shall eat clean provender, which hath been win-

sions are really a single command to do the same thing. He is to write down His message **for the time to come** (or for succeeding generations to read). What he is to note is that the people of Judah are a **rebellious people;** they will not listen to the Word of the Lord. The prophet pictures the sinner as willing to listen to lies, but not to the truth! Prophets were also called **seers** (*ro'iym*). To them, in reality the rebellious people of Judah are saying, **See not . . . Prophesy not.** Instead of God's truth, they would rather hear **smooth things** and **deceits.** Their attitude was much like that of many today who do not want to be confronted with the severity of God's demands. They would rather listen only to **smooth** messages that tickle the ear, but do not confront the heart. Like those of a reprobate mind in Romans 1:28, they want their preachers to **cause the Holy One of Israel to cease from before us.** Such is the depth of their conviction that they do not even want to face the reality of God. Therefore, God's judgment shall be swift and unsparing on those that **despise this word.** He shall break the people as a **potters' vessel,** and He shall **not spare.** All of this shall come upon them, the prophet reminds, because they had refused the salvation offered by the **Holy One of Israel.** While the nation was busy sending out messengers and caravans laden with goods to procure the favor of Egypt, God, by contrast, was calling upon them to simply trust in Him. **Returning and rest** suggests a genuine turning unto God in true conversion and a resting upon the grace of God as the basis of salvation. Some have likened **returning** (*shūbah*) unto repentance and **rest** (*nachath*) unto faith. The idea of the text is that activity will not bring about salvation. Therefore, fleeing **upon horses** is worthless. If the people think that they can escape by their own means, then God reminds them that those who pursue them will be swifter than they. Rather, God's plan is that they should find salvation **in quietness and in confidence** (in submission and in faith). The tragedy of this gracious offer by God is summarized in the words **and ye would not.**

18-33. As so often before, Isaiah sees a gleam of hope for the future. Because God is **gracious** and has been willing to **wait** for His people to turn to Him, He will certainly bless them that **wait for him.** Waiting is viewed here as a confident and dependent trust in God. He will do this because He is a **God of judgment** (*mishpat*, justice). To those who are crying because of His judgments, He promises to hear the **voice of thy cry.** It is one thing to cry in agony because of calamity; it is another thing to cry unto God in genuine repentance. Because they were not willing to listen to the message of God's prophets, they will have to learn through the **bread of adversity, and the water of affliction.** These appositional genitives clearly indicate that God does teach us through the circumstances of life. Because they had been unwilling to listen to the prophets of God (**teachers**), they will be forced to listen to God's message through the awful circumstances that lie ahead. In the meantime, they will hear **a word** (*dabar*) **behind thee.** This has been variously interpreted as a divine admonition, the voice of the teachers who follow their students to admonish them from going astray, or the voice of a shepherd who follows his flocks in order to give them safe direction (see Barnes, I, p. 457, for various examples). Alexander (p. 481) notes that the LXX makes it the voice of "seducers." The immediate context seems to best fit the idea that it is the voice of their teachers whom they have left behind and who continue to call them to walk in **the way** (i.e., the way of God). Kelley (p. 279) notes that the Masoretic Text has a plural subject (**teachers**) followed by a singular verb, whereas the Dead Sea Scroll of Isaiah has both a plural subject and a plural verb. The context of the passage seems to indicate that the prophets have gone into hiding because of persecution; and when they reappear to correct the people, they should follow their guid-

nowed with the shovel and with the fan.

25 And there shall be upon every high mountain, and upon every high hill, rivers *and* streams of waters in the day of the great slaughter, when the towers fall.

26 Moreover the light of the moon shall be as the light of the sun, and the light of the sun shall be sevenfold, as the light of seven days, in the day that the LORD bindeth up the breach of his people, and healeth the stroke of their wound.

27 ¶Behold, the name of the LORD cometh from far, burning *with* his anger, and the burden *thereof is* heavy: his lips are full of indignation, and his tongue as a devouring fire:

28 And his breath, as an overflowing stream, shall reach to the midst of the neck, to sift the nations with the sieve of vanity: and *there shall be* a bridle in the jaws of the people, causing *them* to err.

29 Ye shall have a song, as in the night *when* a holy solemnity is kept; and gladness of heart, as when one goeth with a pipe to come into the mountain of the LORD, to the mighty One of Israel.

30 And the LORD shall cause his glorious voice to be heard, and shall shew the lighting down of his arm, with the indignation of *his* anger, and *with* the flame of a devouring fire, *with* scattering, and tempest, and hailstones.

31 For through the voice of the LORD shall the Assyrian be beaten down, *which* smote him with a rod.

32 And *in* every place where the grounded staff shall pass, which the LORD shall lay upon him, *it* shall be with tabrets and harps: and in battles of shaking will he fight with it.

33 For Tŏ′phet *is* ordained of old; yea, for the king it is prepared; he hath made *it* deep *and* large: the pile thereof *is* fire and much wood; the breath of the LORD, like a stream of brimstone, doth kindle it.

CHAPTER 31

WOE to them that go down to Egypt for help; and stay on horses, and trust in chariots, because *they are* many; and in horsemen, because they are very strong; but they look not unto the Holy One of Israel, neither seek the LORD!

2 Yet he also *is* wise, and will bring evil, and will not call back his words: but will arise against the house of the evildoers, and against the help of them that work iniquity.

3 Now the Egyptians *are* men, and not God; and their horses flesh, and not spirit. When the LORD shall stretch out his hand, both he that helpeth shall fall, and he that is holpen shall fall down, and they all shall fail together.

4 For thus hath the LORD spoken unto me, Like as the lion and the young lion roaring on his prey, when a multitude of shepherds is called forth against him, *he* will not be afraid of their voice, nor abase himself for the noise of them:

ance. Isaiah urges them to cast out their **graven images** in order that God might bless them with the **bread of the increase of the earth.** Then a day of national healing will come for the people of Israel. God is pictured as coming in judgment upon the gentile nations, **full of indignation** (wrath) and **as a devouring fire. The name of the LORD** (*shem-Yahweh*) must refer to the Lord Himself (see Calvin, p. 406), not merely to a revelation of His words. In contrast to those who worshiped man-made, visible gods, the Lord Jehovah, who is known only by His name, the Invisible One, shall reveal Himself **as a devouring fire** and an **overflowing stream** (the language is reminiscent of II Thess 2:8; Rev 14:20). So severe will the judgment of God be that it will be revealed with **lighting . . . indignation . . . flame . . . tempest,** etc. In spite of all this, the Jewish people shall have a **song, as in the night.** Those who are surrendered to the Lord in obedience shall have **gladness of heart,** in spite of the severe judgments which shall come upon the world. This verse is a reminder that God always gives His children a **song . . . in the night,** no matter how dark the circumstances may become. The immediate context of the passage applies this judgment to **the Assyrian.** Though God will use him as the rod of His judgment against Israel, He will then turn and judge Assyria as well. It is for Him that **Tophet is ordained of old.** *Tophet* may be translated "hearth" or "firepit." It represents the place in the Valley of Hinnom, below the hill of Zion on the southwest corner of Jerusalem, where human sacrifices were burned in offering to the god Moloch. This terrible practice had gone on since the days of Ahaz (II Kgs 23:10) and special furnaces were utilized for this purpose. *Tophet* is used as a symbol of the fires of hell where the **breath of the LORD, like a stream of brimstone,** kindles the flame!

4. *Woe to the compromisers. 31:1-32:20.*

31:1-9. Isaiah turns his attention again to those who would advocate a pro-Egyptian alliance for the protection and defense of Judah. He observes that they **stay** (*yisha'ĕnū*, lean) **on horses** and **trust in chariots.** He reminds them that the **Egyptians are men . . . and their horses flesh,** in contrast to **God** who is a **spirit.** In other words, disaster awaits those who put their confidence in human and material strength, rather than in the Lord. The great failure of the people of Judah is that they are not willing to **look . . . unto . . . neither seek the LORD!** Unlike Egypt, who will flee in the day of confrontation, the Lord will defend His people **Like as the lion** resisting the shepherds. In contrast to the tenacity of the lion, the Lord will defend Jerusalem **As birds flying.** The imagery here is that of a mother bird hovering over her young in order to protect them. The parallel imagery, however, of the flying birds and lions belies the imagery of the national symbol of Judah's great enemies, Assyria and Babylon: the winged lion! The verb **passing over** is from the same root as *pesah*, or "passover." The promise is that the same God who delivered His children from Egypt in the Passover will again miraculously intervene on their behalf against **the**

so shall the LORD of hosts come down to fight for mount Zion, and for the hill thereof.

5 As birds flying, so will the LORD of hosts defend Jerusalem; defending also he will deliver *it; and* passing over he will preserve *it.*

6 ¶Turn ye unto *him from* whom the children of Israel have deeply revolted.

7 For in that day every man shall cast away his idols of silver, and his idols of gold, which your own hands have made unto you *for* a sin.

8 Then shall the Assyrian fall with the sword, not of a mighty man; and the sword, not of a mean man, shall devour him: but he shall flee from the sword, and his young men shall be discomfited.

9 And he shall pass over to his strong hold for fear, and his princes shall be afraid of the ensign, saith the LORD, whose fire *is* in Zion, and his furnace in Jerusalem.

CHAPTER 32

BEHOLD, a king shall reign in righteousness, and princes shall rule in judgment.

2 And a man shall be as an hiding place from the wind, and a covert from the tempest; as rivers of water in a dry place, as the shadow of a great rock in a weary land.

3 And the eyes of them that see shall not be dim, and the ears of them that hear shall hearken.

4 The heart also of the rash shall understand knowledge, and the tongue of the stammerers shall be ready to speak plainly.

5 The vile person shall be no more called liberal, nor the churl said *to be* bountiful.

6 For the vile person will speak villany, and his heart will work iniquity, to practise hypocrisy, and to utter error against the LORD, to make empty the soul of the hungry, and he will cause the drink of the thirsty to fail.

7 The instruments also of the churl *are* evil: he deviseth wicked devices to destroy the poor with lying words, even when the needy speaketh right.

8 But the liberal deviseth liberal things; and by liberal things shall he stand.

9 ¶Rise up, ye women that are at ease; hear my voice, ye careless daughters; give ear unto my speech.

10 Many days and years shall ye be troubled, ye careless women: for the vintage shall fail, the gathering shall not come.

11 Tremble, ye women that are at ease; be troubled, ye careless ones: strip you, and make you bare, and gird *sackcloth* upon *your* loins.

12 They shall lament for the teats, for the pleasant fields, for the fruitful vine.

13 Upon the land of my people shall come up thorns *and* briers; yea, upon all the houses of joy *in* the joyous city:

14 Because the palaces shall be forsaken; the multitude of the city shall be left; the forts and towers shall be for

Assyrian. Verse 8 contains the amazing prediction that this invading army would not **fall** by the sword, but would **flee** from the sword (37:36). Therefore, the prophet calls on the people to **Turn** (*shūvu,* turn back or repent). This is the very heart of Isaiah's message. Israel's only hope is to repent and return to the Lord. Years of international manipulation and alliances will only lead to her ultimate downfall. If there is any hope for her future, it is in turning again to Jehovah. This is virtually the same message that John the Baptist was still declaring at the end of the Old Testament era. His was still a ministry of preparation: "Repent ye; for the Kingdom of Heaven is at hand" (Mt 3:2). By contrast, Jesus' message was "Believe ye that I am He that should come?"

32:1-20. The great interpretive issue in this passage is found in the first verse; who is the **king** that shall **reign in righteousness?** Those rejecting the messianic interpretation in favor of Hezekiah include Luther, Calvin, Alexander, Barnes, Cheyne, and Kelley. Delitzsch and Leupold struggle between both views, and Kidner avoids the issue altogether! Archer, Buksbazen, Fitch, and Young hold strongly to the viewpoint that the king in this passage is the Messiah, Jesus Christ Himself. Archer (p. 631) argues that only Christ can be the "perfect King of Israel" in view in this passage. Buksbazen (p. 267) observes: "No historical king ever fitted this description, which must be understood as a further elaboration of Isaiah's vision of the King Messiah." Young (II, p. 385) notes that a messianic government where **righteousness** and **judgment** (justice) are in the foreground is in view here. Young states: "Isaiah is not talking about a government that is only partially righteous; he is speaking of one that is completely righteous." Thus, the prophecy goes beyond merely the king himself, but is a reference to his entire governing body. No such description adequately or properly fits even the best of Judah's kings, even Hezekiah. The prophet is speaking of a time when godly conditions that shall be **as the shadow of a great rock in a weary land** shall prevail. He sees a time when the blind shall see, the deaf shall hear, and the ignorant shall **understand knowledge** (*da'at,* moral cognition or personal discernment, not doctrine). Thus, the prophet sees a day when people will not only know the teaching about God (for that was true in the prophet's own time), but when morality shall be based upon spiritual knowledge. It will also be a time when all immoral societal evaluations shall be reversed. For example, the **vile person** shall no longer be called **liberal** (gracious). Notice that the term liberal should be taken as a personal quality, not a theological position! Again the prophet turns his attention to the **careless women** who are **at ease** in Judah. Thus, he issues a stern warning to the worldly minded society women of Jerusalem—the devastation of war could plunge them into utter poverty. Virtually every Judaean city was ransacked in 701 B.C. by the invading Assyrian army. The destruction will be so severe that the women will beat upon their **teats** (breasts) as a sign of sorrow. The land that they have loved and from which they have enjoyed so much bounty shall be **forsaken.** As always, the prophet immediately turns from this picture of devastation to beam a ray of hope upon the scene. He sees a time of complete national conversion for Israel in the future, when the **spirit** shall be **poured upon us** (cf. Joel 2:28). When this occurs, there shall

dens for ever, a joy of wild asses, a pasture of flocks;

15 Until the spirit be poured upon us from on high, and the wilderness be a fruitful field, and the fruitful field be counted for a forest.

16 Then judgment shall dwell in the wilderness, and righteousness remain in the fruitful field.

17 And the work of righteousness shall be peace; and the effect of righteousness quietness and assurance for ever.

18 And my people shall dwell in a peaceable habitation, and in sure dwellings, and in quiet resting places;

19 When it shall hail, coming down on the forest; and the city shall be low in a low place.

20 Blessed *are* ye that sow beside all waters, that send forth *thither* the feet of the ox and the ass.

CHAPTER 33

WOE to thee that spoilest, and thou *wast* not spoiled; and dealest treacherously, and they dealt not treacherously with thee! when thou shalt cease to spoil, thou shalt be spoiled; *and* when thou shalt make an end to deal treacherously, they shall deal treacherously with thee.

2 O Lord, be gracious unto us; we have waited for thee: be thou their arm every morning, our salvation also in the time of trouble.

3 At the noise of the tumult the people fled; at the lifting up of thyself the nations were scattered.

4 And your spoil shall be gathered *like* the gathering of the caterpiller: as the running to and fro of locusts shall he run upon them.

5 The Lord is exalted; for he dwelleth on high: he hath filled Zion with judgment and righteousness.

6 And wisdom and knowledge shall be the stability of thy times, *and* strength of salvation: the fear of the Lord *is* his treasure.

7 Behold, their valiant ones shall cry without: the ambassadors of peace shall weep bitterly.

8 The highways lie waste, the wayfaring man ceaseth: he hath broken the covenant, he hath despised the cities, he regardeth no man.

9 The earth mourneth *and* languisheth: Lebanon is ashamed *and* hewn down: Shăr'on is like a wilderness; and Bā'shan and Carmel shake off *their* fruits.

10 ¶Now will I rise, saith the Lord; now will I be exalted; now will I lift up myself.

11 Ye shall conceive chaff, ye shall bring forth stubble: your breath, *as* fire, shall devour you.

12 And the people shall be *as* the burnings of lime: *as* thorns cut up shall they be burned in the fire.

be **judgment** (justice) . . . **righteousness** . . . **peace** . . . **for ever!** It is then that Isaiah foresees a **peaceable habitation** for the Jewish people (**my people**) during the millennial kingdom, in contrast to the years of downtrodden devastation that they have experienced throughout the centuries.

5. *Woe to the spoilers (invaders). 33:1-24.*

33:1-12. Isaiah ends his pronouncement of **Woe** upon the kingdoms of Israel and Judah with a pronouncement of a final devastation that shall come upon the land in the last days. The judgments on Israel in this chapter stand in contrast to the judgments that shall come upon the nations in the next chapter. The setting of both is during the Tribulation Period. This chapter is an admitted puzzle to most commentators. Eusebius seems to have been the first to apply it to the day of judgment and the end of the world. Michaelis and Gill alone limit the prediction to the coming of the Antichrist. Kidner (p. 608) admits it refers to "other kinds" besides that of Isaiah's own day. Alexander (II, p. 19) follows Calvin in suggesting that the prophecy "extends both to the past and the future . . . (including) . . . the destruction of the antichrist." Barnes, Delitzsch, Leupold, and Young all interpret this prophecy as having to do with the fall of Assyria after its aborted siege of Jerusalem. Sennacherib is then viewed as the one who breaks the covenant in verse 8. While the passage certainly has some parallels to the Assyrian invasion, it extends so far beyond it that even Young (II, p. 421) admits the messianic nature of the king in verse 17 and in the closing verses of the chapter. To fail to see the invasion of the Antichrist as the subject of the opening verses of the chapter is to miss its entire point! While he is not named as such in the passage, we should remember that he is only called by that designation in a few passages (I Jn 2:18,22; 4:3; II Jn 7). Compare the "man of sin" (II Thess 2:1-12) with the "woeful king" (Dan 11:36-45). Thus, **thee that spoilest** and was **not spoiled** is a reference to the Antichrist and his kingdom. Israel is pictured as crying out to the Lord for His grace so that He might be their **salvation** (*yeshū'athenū*, deliverance, the word coming from the derivative of the name Joshua or in Greek, Jesus). **The time of trouble** refers to the Tribulation Period. It will be during this time that the Jewish people will finally recognize that Jesus is their Messiah and turn to Him for salvation (cf. Zech 12:10; 13:6; Rom 11:26; Ezk 36:24-29; 37:11-14; Rev 11:1-19; 12:10-17). The invading army is likened unto an insect horde of **locusts** that shall cover the land of Israel. The only thing that shall sustain the Jewish people during this awful invasion is the **wisdom and knowledge . . . of salvation.** Having turned to Christ as their Saviour, the converted Jewish nation shall be sustained through this terrible time of the Tribulation by a renewed personal relationship with the God of salvation. The **valiant ones** (*'erelam*) should be translated "heroes," rather than "inhabitants of Ariel." **The ambassadors of peace** would refer to those who have attempted to keep the very delicate balance of peace in the world. They are weeping bitterly because they now realize that their attempts have been futile. The fact that the **highways lie waste** is an indication of the complete devastation that results from the invading horde. **He hath broken the covenant . . . he regardeth no man** is certainly reminiscent of Daniel 9:27, which refers to the Antichrist. Note that Daniel, living many years after the Assyrian and Babylonian invasions, still sees a time in the distant future when the Antichrist will break his covenant with Israel. It is to this same covenant that Isaiah refers in this passage. The one who had promised to uphold and defend Israel now turns against her during the Tribulation Period. A converted Israel was never part of his plan; and, therefore, he breaks his covenant (*beriyth*) and turns against her. **Lebanon . . . Sharon . . . Bashan . . . Carmel** refer to the most fertile regions of Israel, which now lie in devastation. When all looks hopeless and Israel is convinced that she cannot save herself or depend on her alliance with the "spoiler," then God decides to move. **Now will I rise . . . be exalted . . . lift up myself.** Each of these action verbs begins with the Hebrew letter *aleph*. They clearly indicate the idea that after a period of inactivity, God will stand up to act in history. "Exalt" is the same verb that Isaiah later uses of the exaltation of the **servant** of the Lord (52:13). Instead of further destroying the people of God, the prophet reminds the invader that his **breath, as fire** shall turn and destroy him.

13-24. Though the "spoiler's" breath has devoured him like fire, the prophet makes it clear that it is really the person of God Himself who is **the devouring fire.** So awesome is the judgment of God that only the righteous shall be spared (cf. Mt 24:22). The eschatological nature of the entire passage is made completely clear by the reference to the **king in his beauty** who shall appear unto Israel. Young (II, p. 421) is correct in noting that this passage is not at all applicable to Hezekiah's reign. Here is a King who shall reign in all the splendor of His royalty. He is a King who is victorious in a sense that was not true of the historic kings of Judah. He is the King of the redeemed Israel of the millennial kingdom who reigns in the **land that is very far off** (land of great distances). The prophet sees both the King and His kingdom. The description is reminiscent of the magnitude of the New Jerusalem in Revelation 21:16-17, where it is described as a habitation of 1,500 cubic miles. During the Millennium of peace on earth, there shall be no need of the normal provisions of war because **Thou shalt not see a fierce people,** meaning that none shall attempt war anymore. Therefore, Jerusalem will be a **quiet habitation** during this time of worldwide peace. The reference to a **tabernacle** (lit., tent) **that shall not be taken down** simply refers to the nomadic custom of setting up and taking down one's tent. There is not necessarily a reference to the millennial Temple in this passage. The reference to **rivers and streams** is reminiscent of Revelation 22. All that Israel shall need will be fulfilled in the Lord her God; for in the millennial kingdom He shall be the **judge** (*shaphat*) . . . **lawgiver** (*chaqaq*, from engraver) . . . **king** (*melek*). Thus, it is in this threefold capacity that **he will save us.**

13 ¶Hear, ye *that are* far off, what I have done; and, ye *that are* near, acknowledge my might.

14 The sinners in Zion are afraid; fearfulness hath surprised the hypocrites. Who among us shall dwell with the devouring fire? who among us shall dwell with everlasting burnings?

15 He that walketh righteously, and speaketh uprightly; he that despiseth the gain of oppressions, that shaketh his hands from holding of bribes, that stoppeth his ears from hearing of blood, and shutteth his eyes from seeing evil;

16 He shall dwell on high: his place of defence *shall be* the munitions of rocks: bread shall be given him; his waters *shall be* sure.

17 Thine eyes shall see the king in his beauty: they shall behold the land that is very far off.

18 Thine heart shall meditate terror. Where *is* the scribe? where *is* the receiver? where *is* he that counted the towers?

19 Thou shalt not see a fierce people, a people of a deeper speech than thou canst perceive; of a stammering tongue, *that thou canst* not understand.

20 Look upon Zion, the city of our solemnities: thine eyes shall see Jerusalem a quiet habitation, a tabernacle *that* shall not be taken down; not one of the stakes thereof shall ever be removed, neither shall any of the cords thereof be broken.

21 But there the glorious Lord *will be* unto us a place of broad rivers *and* streams; wherein shall go no galley with oars, neither shall gallant ship pass thereby.

22 For the Lord *is* our judge, the Lord *is* our lawgiver, the Lord *is* our king; he will save us.

23 Thy tacklings are loosed; they could not well strengthen their mast, they could not spread the sail: then is

the prey of a great spoil divided; the lame take the prey.

24 And the inhabitant shall not say, I am sick: the people that dwell therein *shall be* forgiven *their* iniquity.

CHAPTER 34

COME near, ye nations, to hear; and hearken, ye people: let the earth hear, and all that is therein; the world, and all things that come forth of it.

2 For the indignation of the LORD *is* upon all nations, and *his* fury upon all their armies: he hath utterly destroyed them, he hath delivered them to the slaughter.

3 Their slain also shall be cast out, and their stink shall come up out of their carcases, and the mountains shall be melted with their blood.

4 And all the host of heaven shall be dissolved, and the heavens shall be rolled together as a scroll: and all their host shall fall down, as the leaf falleth off from the vine, and as a falling *fig* from the fig tree.

5 For my sword shall be bathed in heaven: behold, it shall come down upon Ĭ-dū-mē´a, and upon the people of my curse, to judgment.

6 The sword of the LORD is filled with blood, it is made fat with fatness, *and* with the blood of lambs and goats, with the fat of the kidneys of rams: for the LORD hath a sacrifice in Bŏz´rah, and a great slaughter in the land of Ĭ-dū-mē´a.

7 And the unicorns shall come down with them, and the bullocks with the bulls; and their land shall be soaked with blood, and their dust made fat with fatness.

8 For *it is* the day of the LORD's vengeance, *and* the year of recompences for the controversy of Zion.

9 And the streams thereof shall be turned into pitch, and the dust thereof into brimstone, and the land thereof shall become burning pitch.

10 It shall not be quenched night nor day; the smoke thereof shall go up for ever: from generation to generation it shall lie waste; none shall pass through it for ever and ever.

11 But the cormorant and the bittern shall possess it; the owl also and the raven shall dwell in it: and he shall stretch out upon it the line of confusion, and the stones of emptiness.

12 They shall call the nobles thereof to the kingdom, but none *shall be* there, and all her princes shall be nothing.

13 And thorns shall come up in her palaces, nettles and brambles in the fortresses thereof: and it shall be an

E. Predictions of the Great Tribulation and Millennial Kingdom (II). 34:1-35:10.

1. Bitterness of the Tribulation Period. 34:1-17.

34:1-10. The closing two chapters of the first section of Isaiah's prophecies are purely apocalyptic in nature. The object of God's judicial wrath will be the **nations . . . the earth . . . the world.** Archer (p. 633) correctly observes: "Here we have depicted the scene of the carnage that will ensue upon the Battle of Armageddon." **The indignation** (*qetsep*, wrath or retributive justice) and **fury** (*chemah*, hot displeasure) is poured out upon **all nations** (*gōyim*, Gentiles). **Mountains shall be melted** refers to the great physical changes in the earth as a result of the devastation of the Tribulation Period. **The host of heaven** may refer to the Satanic angels (demons) and their powers, which shall also be destroyed. The language of verse 4 is certainly parallel to II Peter 3:10. The verb **shall be dissolved** (*namaqū*, melt, or vanish) is similar to the New Testament Greek word *luō*, meaning to loosen or melt. In both passages the idea seems to be that the Battle of Armageddon will be so severe that the earth and the atmospheric heavens (lower heavens) shall be **rolled together as a scroll.** While there has been much speculation about what this means, one thing is obviously clear. This apocalyptic judgment will be so cataclysmic that it will affect both the earth and the atmosphere, and it will usher in **new heavens and a new earth** (65:17). The destruction of mankind is personified in the judgment of God falling upon **Idumea** (Edom). The Edomites had been Israel's enemies throughout her history; and they were a particular illustration of Gentile self-sufficiency during the days of Isaiah, when their Nabataean Petra was thriving. (See J. I. Lawlor, *The Nabataeans in Historical Perspective.*) This devastation will be so great that it is called **a sacrifice in Bozrah** (see also 63:1-4). Bozrah was a city in Edom known for shepherding. **Unicorns** (*re'emim*) is an unfortunate translation in the AV that should be rendered "wild oxen." Young (II, p. 434) notes: "So all-embracing and widespread is the slaughter that together with the lambs and goats, the ordinary animals of sacrifice, the wild oxen also will fall." **The day of the LORD's vengeance** refers to the Battle of Armageddon. Though this particular name is only found in Revelation 16:16, throughout the Bible it is certainly descriptive of the final devastation that culminates at the end of the Tribulation Period (cf. "day of the LORD": Joel 2:2; Zeph 1:15; Zech 14:1; Mal 4:5; "time of trouble": Dan 12:1; "time of Jacob's trouble": Jer 30:7; "hour of his judgment": Rev 14:7; "the wrath to come": I Thess 1:10; "the wrath of the Lamb": Rev 6:16-17). The fiery nature of this judgment is such that it cannot refer to any historic battle in ancient Israel. **Pitch . . . brimstone . . . smoke** are mentioned as lasting **for ever.** Attempts to view this as a local destruction in past history are futile in light of the severe, universal description given in this passage. Jeremiah 49:18 clearly states that Edom will be destroyed like Sodom and Gomorrah. Since the land still exists today as a part of Transjordan, the fulfillment of the passage must be viewed as still in the future.

11-17. The desolation and depopulation of Edom becomes a symbol of God's judgment on the Christ-denying nations of the world; and Edom figuratively appears as "Babylon" in the book of Revelation (ch. 18). Instead of a great civilization, it shall become the habitation of wild animals. For **cormorant** read "pelican," and for **bittern** read "porcupine." The depopulation of the area is emphasized in the words **confusion** (*tohū*) and **emptiness** (*bohū*), which are the same words used in Genesis 1:2 where they are translated "without form, and void." Instead of a great civilization, it shall become a **habitation of dragons** (*tha-*

habitation of dragons, *and* a court for owls.

14 The wild beasts of the desert shall also meet with the wild beasts of the island, and the satyr shall cry to his fellow: the screech owl also shall rest there, and find for herself a place of rest.

15 There shall the great owl make her nest, and lay, and hatch, and gather under her shadow: there shall the vultures also be gathered, every one with her mate.

16 ¶Seek ye out of the book of the LORD, and read: no one of these shall fail, none shall want her mate: for my mouth it hath commanded, and his spirit it hath gathered them.

17 And he hath cast the lot for them, and his hand hath divided it unto them by line: they shall possess it for ever, from generation to generation shall they dwell therein.

CHAPTER 35

THE wilderness and the solitary place shall be glad for them; and the desert shall rejoice, and blossom as the rose.

2 It shall blossom abundantly, and rejoice even with joy and singing: the glory of Lebanon shall be given unto it, the excellency of Carmel and Shâr'on, they shall see the glory of the LORD, *and* the excellency of our God.

3 Strengthen ye the weak hands, and confirm the feeble knees.

4 Say to them *that are* of a fearful heart, Be strong, fear not: behold, your God will come *with* vengeance, *even* God *with* a recompence; he will come and save you.

5 Then the eyes of the blind shall be opened, and the ears of the deaf shall be unstopped.

6 Then shall the lame *man* leap as an hart, and the tongue of the dumb sing: for in the wilderness shall waters break out, and streams in the desert.

7 And the parched ground shall become a pool, and the thirsty land springs of water: in the habitation of dragons, where each lay, *shall be* grass with reeds and rushes.

8 And an highway shall be there, and a way, and it shall be called The way of holiness; the unclean shall not pass over it; but it *shall be* for those: the wayfaring men, though fools, shall not err *therein*.

9 No lion shall be there, nor *any* ravenous beast shall go up thereon, it shall not be found there; but the redeemed shall walk *there*:

10 And the ransomed of the LORD shall return, and come to Zion with songs and everlasting joy upon their heads: they shall obtain joy and gladness, and sorrow and sighing shall flee away.

niym, jackals), meaning that the depopulated areas of the world shall become the habitation of wild scavenger-like animals. Though Young sees a possible reference to demons in these statements (II, p. 440), it is not likely; and Alexander's view that this is merely a list of wild animals is to be preferred. For **satyr** read "shaggy goat." The chapter ends with a reference to the **book of the LORD,** which is apparently the book of inspired prophecies and probably refers to Isaiah's own writing. So severe will this coming eschatological judgment be, the reader needs to be reminded that it is part of the divinely inspired prophetic Scripture; and therefore, it will certainly come to pass as God has predicted it.

2. Blessings of the kingdom age. 35:1-10.

35:1-10. After the great and awesome destruction predicted in the preceding chapter, the prophet turns again to a message of hope for the future. There shall come a time when the **desert shall rejoice, and blossom as the rose.** In the millennial kingdom of the coming Messiah, all spiritual evil, as well as physical catastrophe, shall be reversed; and the land, as well as the people, shall be blessed. The reference to the **glory of Lebanon** and the **excellency of Carmel and Sharon** is to the beautiful and fertile areas of the Promised Land. The prediction here is that even the desert areas of Israel shall one day blossom more beautifully than the grandeur of the cedar forests of Lebanon, etc. The prophet urges the people to **Strengthen** (encourage) one another. **Weak hands** and **feeble knees** refer to the failing endurance of the Jewish people. The prophet recognizes that his people, persecuted over these many centuries, will need to encourage themselves in the knowledge of the coming fulfillment of God's promised blessings to them. To his downtrodden, elect nation the prophet urges valiance and vigilance, because **your God will come with vengeance** (*naqam*, revenge). Again, it should be noted that ultimately God's acts of judgment are acts of mercy. For the great judgment of the Tribulation Period shall cut off the unrighteous and usher in a time of unparalleled blessing and prosperity on the earth for all mankind. The **blind . . . deaf . . . lame . . . dumb** shall all be restored. The wilderness shall blossom, and there shall be **streams in the desert** (from which is taken the title of Mrs. Cowman's famous devotional book). Again, for **dragons** read "jackals." The formerly **parched ground** shall now spring forth with water and shall blossom abundantly. The **highway** is emphasized, in contrast to the imagery of a desolate desert, which is an endless maze of shifting sands where there are no roads to guide the traveler. Isaiah, however, sees a time when there shall be a distinct highway that shall lead to the New Jerusalem. It shall be called the **way of holiness** (*derek haqodesh*), and it shall be reserved for the saved and **ransomed** of the Tribulation Period who shall enter into the millennial kingdom. The reference to **fools** is figurative, meaning that even a foolish traveler, who normally could not find his way through the desert, could not miss his destination if he were on the Highway of Holiness. Even nature itself shall be changed, and wild animals shall no longer prey upon men. The **unclean** shall not walk there, for it is reserved only for the **redeemed.** This great prophecy ends with the promise that the **ransomed of the LORD shall return, and come to Zion,** referring to the heavenly Jerusalem. It is there that everlasting joy shall be their possession, and **sorrow and sighing** shall disappear forever. Here is the beautiful picture now of the saved people of God living in peace, joy, and harmony in the blessed millennial kingdom of the Messiah.

II. Historic Consideration. 36:1-39:8.

Standing like a beacon in the middle of Isaiah's prophecies is this historical interlude that records the fulfillment of the prophet's predictions concerning the overthrow of Assyria and the threat of a new invasion from Babylon. The text shifts from poetry to prose. It is parallel to the account given in II Kings 18 and II Chronicles 32. This historic narrative serves as a transition from the first half of the book, in which Assyria is in the foreground as Israel's major enemy, to the last half of the book, in which Babylon is the prominent threat to Israel's future security.

A. Looking Back to the Assyrian Invasion. 36:1-37:38.

1. Hezekiah's trouble: Sennacherib. 36:1-22.

36:1-3. In the irony of history, Hezekiah would come to the throne at a time when Judah was once again threatened by an invasion from the north. Thus, Isaiah jumps historically from the threat of King Ahaz, an unbeliever, to the renewed threat in the days of Hezekiah, a believer. **The fourteenth year of king Hezekiah** represents a chronological problem in the text. Apparently, there was a copyist's error; and an *M* was substituted for an *h*, changing "twenty-fourth" to **fourteenth**. Virtually all commentators are agreed that **fourteenth** is incorrect, though several different explanations are given. Archer (p. 634) follows Nägelsbach (p. 372) in suggesting that this is the fourteenth year after Hezekiah's sickness. However, both Isaiah and the parallel passage in Kings explicitly state that the date is from the fourteenth year of the king and make no reference at all to his intervening sickness. Young (II, p. 540ff.) rejects the more liberal interpretation of Albright and Bright that would date the ascension of Hezekiah at 715 B.C., and also the views of Kissane and Nägelsbach in favor of the textual emendation from "twenty-fourth" to "fourteen." He notes that this would make Hezekiah's revolt at about 703 B.C., two years before Sennacherib's invasion, which occurred in 701 B.C. (For a detailed discussion of this question, see Young, "The Reign of Hezekiah," in *Commentary II*, pp. 540-555; H. Tadmor, "The Campaigns of Sargon II of Assur," *Journal of Cuneiform Studies*, 12 (1958), pp. 22-40; *contra*, S. Shultz, *The Old Testament Speaks*, pp. 209-215, follows E. R. Thiele, *A Chronology of the Hebrew Kings*, p. 99ff. in suggesting the 716-715 B.C. date for Hezekiah's ascension to the throne. Assyrian records date this invasion as 701 B.C.) **Sennacherib** ruled Assyria from 705-681 B.C. When he first came to the throne, he ousted Merodach-baladan (see ch. 39), the usurper King of Babylon. It was probably just prior to this that he had sent envoys to Hezekiah of Judah, which would indicate that the chapters related here are actually out of chronological order. Late in 702 B.C. Sennacherib defeated the Chaldean and Elamite allies, and Merodach-baladan escaped to Elam. The invasion mentioned in this chapter was brought on by Hezekiah's revolt. He had seized Padi, the pro-Assyrian ruler of Ekron (see Jud 1:18), strengthened the fortifications of the city, and improved the water supply by building the Siloam tunnel (II Kgs 20:20). The initial campaign against the **cities of Judah** was relatively successful as the Assyrians swept through the area, with Ashkelon suffering the worst. The *Chronicle of Sennacherib* claims that he captured forty-six towns and over 200,000 people. He himself took part in the siege and capture of Lachish, and from there he sent officers to demand the surrender of Jerusalem. His own account of besieging of Jerusalem on

CHAPTER 36

NOW it came to pass in the fourteenth year of king Hĕz-e-kī'ah, *that* Sen-nāch'e-rĭb king of Assyria came up against all the defenced cities of Jū'dah, and took them.

2 And the king of Assyria sent Răb'-sha-keh from Lā'chĭsh to Jerusalem unto king Hĕz-e-kī'ah with a great army. And he stood by the conduit of the upper pool in the highway of the fuller's field.

3 Then came forth unto him E-lī'a-kĭm, Hĭl-kī'ah's son, which was over the house, and Shĕb'na the scribe, and Jō'ah, Ā'săph's son, the recorder.

the Taylor Prism states: "I shut him (Hezekiah) up like a caged bird within his royal capital." (The Akkadian text may be found in T. Bauer, *Akkadische Lesestücke*, pp. 88-96; for English translation see D. W. Thomas, in *POTT*, pp. 64-69.)

4 And Răb'sha-keh said unto them, Say ye now to Hĕz-e-kī'ah, Thus saith the great king, the king of Assyria, What confidence *is* this wherein thou trustest?

5 I say, *sayest thou,* (but *they are but* vain words) *I have* counsel and strength for war: now on whom dost thou trust, that thou rebellest against me?

6 Lo, thou trustest in the staff of this broken reed, on Egypt; whereon if a man lean, it will go into his hand, and pierce it: so *is* Pharaoh king of Egypt to all that trust in him.

7 But if thou say to me, We trust in the LORD our God: *is it* not he, whose high places and whose altars Hĕz-e-kī'ah hath taken away, and said to Jū'dah and to Jerusalem, Ye shall worship before this altar?

8 Now therefore give pledges, I pray thee, to my master the king of Assyria, and I will give thee two thousand horses, if thou be able on thy part to set riders upon them.

9 How then wilt thou turn away the face of one captain of the least of my master's servants, and put thy trust on Egypt for chariots and for horsemen?

10 And am I now come up without the LORD against this land to destroy it? the LORD said unto me, Go up against this land, and destroy it.

11 Then said E-lī'a-kĭm and Shĕb'na and Jō'ah unto Răb'sha-keh, Speak, I pray thee, unto thy servants in the Syrian language; for we understand *it:* and speak not to us in the Jews' language, in the ears of the people that *are* on the wall.

12 But Răb'sha-keh said, Hath my master sent me to thy master and to thee to speak these words? *hath he* not *sent me* to the men that sit upon the wall, that they may eat their own dung, and drink their own piss with you?

13 Then Răb'sha-keh stood, and cried with a loud voice in the Jews' language, and said, Hear ye the words of the great king, the king of Assyria.

14 Thus saith the king, Let not Hĕz-e-kī'ah deceive you: for he shall not be able to deliver you.

15 Neither let Hĕz-e-kī'ah make you trust in the LORD, saying, The LORD will surely deliver us: this city shall not be delivered into the hand of the king of Assyria.

16 Hearken not to Hĕz-e-kī'ah: for thus saith the king of Assyria, Make *an* agreement with me *by* a present, and come out to me: and eat ye every one of his vine, and every one of his fig tree, and drink ye every one the waters of his own cistern;

17 Until I come and take you away to a land like your own land, a land of corn

4-10. Rab-shakeh is a title not a proper name. It means "chief cupbearer" and is probably the title of a high court official. Thus, it is appropriate to refer to him as "the Rab-shakeh." Notice that he comes to the very spot where years earlier Isaiah the prophet had confronted Ahaz (see 7:3). **Of the conduit of the upper pool in . . . the fuller's field.** It was here that Ahaz had refused to trust the Lord and instead chose to turn to Assyria for help. Now some thirty years later, the nation he had thought to trust stands ready to attack Jerusalem. The reference to **Eliakim** shows him superior to **Shebna** (see 22:20). The Rab-shakeh stands and belittles Hezekiah, while at the same time demanding the complete surrender of the city to the **great king, the king of Assyria** (i.e., Sennacherib). The issue of his tirade becomes the matter of **whom dost thou trust.** The Assyrian official belittles Egypt, referring to it as a **broken reed** and indicating that anyone who would lean on it would pierce through his own hand. He then attacked their confidence in **the LORD,** and at this point shows his ignorance by assuming that it was His **high places** and **altars** which Hezekiah had earlier destroyed. Hebrew history shows that these were the altars of Baal and the gods of the pagans. In reality, Hezekiah had brought about a great spiritual return to the worship of Jehovah. The demand to **give pledges** means to pay tribute. Again, the officer makes fun of the Israelites by suggesting that if he were to give them two thousand horses, they could not even set enough riders on them to be able to use them. Finally, in an attempt to scare the people, the Rab-shakeh tells them that **the LORD said unto me, Go up against this land, and destroy it.** The context of the passage reveals ultimately that his claim was false. While God did at times use Assyria as a rod of His judgment against His people (especially northern Israel), He had not ordered the destruction of Jerusalem at this time. This would become evident in the succeeding events.

11-22. Fearful that the words of the Rab-shakeh would upset and startle the common people, the Jewish representatives request that he speak to them in the **Syrian language** (Aramaic), instead of in the **Jews' language** (*yehūdith*, Judaean or Jewish). This was the common designation for the Hebrew dialect of the southern kingdom; and it was an appropriate term to use at this period of time when the northern tribes had already been taken into captivity by Assyria. Aramaic was the language of the Aramaean states of Syria and northwestern Mesopotamia. However, during the period of the Assyrian empire, Aramaic replaced Akkadian as the common language of international diplomacy. In time it became the common language of the entire Near East. (On the nature and significance of the Aramaic language, see H. H. Rowley, *The Aramaic of the Old Testament;* A. F. Johns, *A Short Grammar of Biblical Aramaic;* and the article on "Language of the Old Testament," in the *New Bible Dictionary* pp. 712-713.) In reaction to their request, the Rab-shakeh responded that, in the first place, he was not really there to speak to them, but was sent to address the **men that sit upon the wall.** Therefore, he **cried with a loud voice in the Jews' language** so that all could hear him. Thus, the attempt by the Jewish leaders to quiet his verbal assault only provoked him to a worse response. The Assyrian official contrasts **the great king, the king of Assyria** with **Hezekiah.** He charges the people not to listen to Hezekiah or let him **make you trust in the LORD.** Instead, he calls for them to **Make an agreement with me by a present,** meaning to make an alliance to pay tribute to Assyria. An ancient city under siege was in great threat of famine, and he also played on this in his reminder that they could each eat of

and wine, a land of bread and vineyards.

18 *Beware* lest Hĕz-e-kī'ah persuade you, saying, The LORD will deliver us. Hath any of the gods of the nations delivered his land out of the hand of the king of Assyria?

19 Where *are* the gods of Hā'mᾰth and Ar'phᾰd? where *are* the gods of Sĕph-ar-vā'im? and have they delivered Sa-mā'rī-a out of my hand?

20 Who *are they* among all the gods of these lands, that have delivered their land out of my hand, that the LORD should deliver Jerusalem out of my hand?

21 But they held their peace, and answered him not a word: for the king's commandment was, saying, Answer him not.

22 Then came E-lī'a-kĭm, the son of Hĭl-kī'ah, that *was* over the household, and Shĕb'na the scribe, and Jō'ah, the son of Ā'sᾰph, the recorder, to Hĕz-e-kī'ah with their clothes rent, and told him the words of Rᾰb'sha-keh.

CHAPTER 37

AND it came to pass, when king Hĕz-e-kī'ah heard *it*, that he rent his clothes, and covered himself with sackcloth, and went into the house of the LORD.

2 And he sent E-lī'a-kĭm, who *was* over the household, and Shĕb'na the scribe, and the elders of the priests covered with sackcloth, unto Isaiah the prophet the son of Amoz.

3 And they said unto him, Thus saith Hĕz-e-kī'ah, This day *is* a day of trouble, and of rebuke, and of blasphemy: for the children are come to the birth, and *there is* not strength to bring forth.

4 It may be the LORD thy God will hear the words of Rᾰb'sha-keh, whom the king of Assyria his master hath sent to reproach the living God, and will reprove the words which the LORD thy God hath heard: wherefore lift up *thy* prayer for the remnant that is left.

5 So the servants of king Hĕz-e-kī'ah came to Isaiah.

6 And Isaiah said unto them, Thus shall ye say unto your master, Thus saith the LORD, Be not afraid of the words that thou hast heard, wherewith the servants of the king of Assyria have blasphemed me.

7 Behold, I will send a blast upon him, and he shall hear a rumour, and return to his own land; and I will cause him to fall by the sword in his own land.

8 ¶ So Rᾰb'sha-keh returned, and found the king of Assyria warring against Lĭb'nah: for he had heard that he was departed from Lā'chĭsh.

9 And he heard say concerning Tir'hā-kah king of Ē-thī-ō'pĭ-a, He is come forth to make war with thee. And when he heard *it*, he sent messengers to Hĕz-e-kī'ah, saying,

10 Thus shall ye speak to Hĕz-e-kī'ah king of Jū'dah, saying, Let not thy God, in whom thou trustest, deceive thee, saying, Jerusalem shall not be given into the hand of the king of Assyria.

11 Behold, thou hast heard what the kings of Assyria have done to all lands

their own food if they would but surrender to the Assyrians. Unfortunately, the Assyrians only considered Jehovah to be like the **gods of Hamath . . . Arphad . . . Sepharvaim** (cities of Syria which had already fallen to the Assyrians). He also refers to **Samaria** (northern Israel) as also having fallen to them. His question is, if these gods could not deliver their lands out of the hand of Sennacherib, then how did Hezekiah expect Jehovah (*Yahweh*) to deliver **Jerusalem out of my hand?** But in obedience to the king's previous commandment, they **held their peace** and did not respond to the threats of the Rab-shakeh. Instead, they came in before the king **with their clothes rent** and told him of the Rab-shakeh's demands.

2. Hezekiah's triumph: Angel of the Lord. 37:1-38.

37:1-13. Horrified by the demands of the Assyrians, King Hezekiah **rent his clothes** (a sign of mourning) and went into **the house of the LORD** (the Temple). He then sent **Eliakim** and **Shebna** to get **Isaiah the prophet.** The king recognized that **This day is a day of trouble;** and as such, it becomes a picture of all such days of trouble predicted in the Scripture. His only hope is that the Lord will have heard the words of the Rab-shakeh and will **reprove** them as a reproach against the **living God.** Thus, the king goes to **prayer** for the **remnant** of survivors left within the besieged city. It should be observed that Hezekiah's kingdom was in danger of extermination, and he fully realized that only God could intervene to spare him. In the meantime, in contrast to the fear of everyone else, the prophet **Isaiah** spoke with great confidence, urging the people to **Be not afraid of the words that thou hast heard** because God has interpreted those words to mean that they have **blasphemed** Him. Therefore, the prophet promises a miraculous deliverance by the Lord who will send a **blast** (*rûach*, spirit) upon the invaders. The use of the word *rûach* has caused much confusion in translation. Modern versions prefer the more literal rendering "spirit" (see RSV, NEB, NASB, NIV). The idea of a **blast** is too harsh and is perhaps an adaptation of Calvin's translation, which conveys the idea that God would "carry him away as with a wind." Leupold (I, p. 562) suggests that the translation "spirit" is inadequate; it should really convey the idea of resolve or impulse. The idea of the text seems to be that God will intervene and impose a "spirit of confusion" or a cowardly "impulse" upon the Assyrian king as a result of his hearing a **rumor** (*shemûah*, report). While most commentators have taken this to mean that he would hear the rumor of a renewed Ethiopian invasion from the South, Alexander (II, p. 55) follows Henderson in suggesting that the "report" that chased him off was that of the destruction of his army before Jerusalem while he himself was absent. In either case, **Tirhakah, king of Ethiopia** is reported in verse 9 to have advanced toward the Assyrian army. The reference to **Tirhakah** also has caused some difficulty to various commentators due to our insufficient knowledge of the history of that time. Tirhakah was certainly the most famous ruler of the twenty-fifth dynasty (the Ethiopian dynasty) of Egypt. He succeeded Shabataka in 690 B.C. and reigned until 664 B.C. It has been commonly thought that he was born about 710 B.C. and would have been too young to command an army in 701 B.C. This argument, however, is not conclusive. While

by destroying them utterly; and shalt thou be delivered?

12 Have the gods of the nations delivered them which my fathers have destroyed, as Gō´zăn, and Hâ´ran, and Rē´zĕph, and the children of Eden which were in Te-lăs´sar?

13 Where is the king of Hā´măth, and the king of Är´phăd, and the king of the city of Sĕph-ar-vā´im, Hē´na, and Ī´vah?

14 ¶And Hĕz-e-kī´ah received the letter from the hand of the messengers, and read it: and Hĕz-e-kī´ah went up unto the house of the LORD, and spread it before the LORD.

15 And Hĕz-e-kī´ah prayed unto the LORD, saying,

16 O LORD of hosts, God of Israel, that dwellest between the cherubims, that art the God, even thou alone, of all the kingdoms of the earth: thou hast made heaven and earth.

17 Incline thine ear, O LORD, and hear; open thine eyes, O LORD, and see: and hear all the words of Sen-nách´e-rīb, which hath sent to reproach the living God.

18 Of a truth, LORD, the kings of Assyria have laid waste all the nations, and their countries,

19 And have cast their gods into the fire: for they were no gods, but the work of men's hands, wood and stone: therefore they have destroyed them.

20 Now therefore, O LORD our God, save us from his hand, that all the kingdoms of the earth may know that thou art the LORD, even thou only.

21 ¶Then Isaiah the son of Amoz sent unto Hĕz-e-kī´ah, saying, Thus saith the LORD God of Israel, Whereas thou hast prayed to me against Sen-nách´e-rīb king of Assyria:

22 This is the word which the LORD hath spoken concerning him; The virgin, the daughter of Zion, hath despised thee, and laughed thee to scorn; the daughter of Jerusalem hath shaken her head at thee.

23 Whom hast thou reproached and blasphemed? and against whom hast thou exalted thy voice, and lifted up thine eyes on high? even against the Holy One of Israel.

24 By thy servants hast thou reproached the Lord, and hast said, By the multitude of my chariots am I come up to the height of the mountains, to the sides of Lebanon; and I will cut down the tall cedars thereof, and the choice fir trees thereof: and I will enter into the height of his border, and the forest of his Carmel.

25 I have digged, and drunk water; and with the sole of my feet have I dried up all the rivers of the besieged places.

26 Hast thou not heard long ago, how I have done it; and of ancient times, that I have formed it? now have I brought it to pass, that thou shouldest be to lay waste defenced cities into ruinous heaps.

27 Therefore their inhabitants were

Young (II, p. 478) suggests that he may be called king in this text proleptically (in anticipation of his later reign), it is also possible that the date of his birth is an insufficient basis for making a judgment. It was not uncommon for boy-kings to actually symbolically lead an army whose military command was under that of his chief generals. Since his father, Pianki, had died in 710 B.C., this was certainly possible. In either case, the result of this rumor was that Sennacherib hurriedly sent messengers again to Hezekiah king of Judah urging his immediate surrender. Again the messenger reminded the Judaean king of the failure of gods of the nations which they had already conquered.

14-32. This time Hezekiah received the letter (lit., letters) from the messengers of the Assyrian king. Having read it, he returned to the house of the LORD (the Temple) and spread them out before the LORD. This was a symbolic action of his utter dependence upon God. He was literally bringing the threat before the Lord, and therewith he prayed unto the LORD. He begins with a recognition of who God is, describing Him as the LORD of hosts, God of Israel. He thereby acknowledged that the God of Heaven was indeed the God of Israel. He also designates Him as the One who dwelled between the cherubim (which stood symbolically on the ark of the covenant and between which the glory of God was manifested). His ultimate recognition was that thou art the God, even thou alone. Here was a king with all of his authority and dignity broken in total humiliation before the One true God who alone was over all the kingdoms of the earth. Hezekiah then reminded the Lord, as only we finite beings are want to do, that the words of Sennacherib were in reality sent to reproach the living God. Hezekiah acknowledged that it was true that the kings of Assyria had laid waste the other nations and cities that they had invaded and had cast their gods into the fire. However, the Judaean king correctly recognized the failure of these gods because they were in reality no gods (lo' 'elohiym). The Hebrew designation is such that it negates the word gods. Hezekiah recognized that an article that was nothing more than the work of men's hands could in no way save or deliver people. The most humble and genuine aspect of his prayer is expressed in verse 20 where he asks God to save us so that the kingdoms of the earth may know that thou art the LORD. It was this sincere request that brought the miraculous answer of Jehovah on behalf of the penitent Jewish king. Isaiah then responded by sending his own message to Hezekiah, acknowledging that Whereas thou hast prayed, God would miraculously intervene on his behalf. The invader is pictured as a military rapist who would attack The virgin, the daughter of Zion (Jerusalem). God's response is that while He has allowed Assyria to conquer the northern kingdom, because of their rebellion against Him, He will not allow them to conquer Judah (the southern kingdom), lest they conclude that they have done it by their own might. Therefore, God reminds them: I have done it . . . I brought it to pass. The Bible clearly indicates that military invasions of the ancient Near Eastern nations against Israel were all part of God's omniscient plan. Thus, the reference to my hook in thy nose indicates God's divine control over the affairs of nations and their armies. To the remnant that is escaped God promises that they shall take root downward, and bear fruit upward, meaning that Judah would be given a divine reprieve to continue its prosperity as a nation.

of small power, they were dismayed and confounded: they were *as* the grass of the field, and *as* the green herb, *as* the grass on the housetops, and *as corn* blasted before it be grown up.

28 But I know thy abode, and thy going out, and thy coming in, and thy rage against me.

29 Because thy rage against me, and thy tumult, is come up into mine ears, therefore will I put my hook in thy nose, and my bridle in thy lips, and I will turn thee back by the way by which thou camest.

30 And this *shall be* a sign unto thee, Ye shall eat *this* year such as groweth of itself; and the second year that which springeth of the same: and in the third year sow ye, and reap, and plant vineyards, and eat the fruit thereof.

31 And the remnant that is escaped of the house of Jū′dah shall again take root downward, and bear fruit upward:

32 For out of Jerusalem shall go forth a remnant, and they that escape out of mount Zion: the zeal of the LORD of hosts shall do this.

33 Therefore thus saith the LORD concerning the king of Assyria, He shall not come into this city, nor shoot an arrow there, nor come before it with shields, nor cast a bank against it.

34 By the way that he came, by the same shall he return, and shall not come into this city, saith the LORD.

35 For I will defend this city to save it for mine own sake, and for my servant David's sake.

36 ¶Then the angel of the LORD went forth, and smote in the camp of the Assyrians a hundred and fourscore and five thousand: and when they arose early in the morning, behold, they *were* all dead corpses.

37 So Sen-nǎch′e-rĭb king of Assyria departed, and went and returned, and dwelt at Nĭn′e-veh.

38 And it came to pass, as he was worshipping in the house of Nĭs′rŏch his god, that A-drăm′me-lĕch and Sha-rē′zer his sons smote him with the sword; and they escaped into the land of Är-mē′nĭ-a: and Ē′sar-hăd′don his son reigned in his stead.

33-38. Having listened to the threats of the king of Assyria, God now responds with a message of His own! The subject of that message is the **king of Assyria** (Sennacherib). God announces: **He shall not come into this city. . . . By the way that he came, by the same shall he return.** The Lord then announces that He will defend the city for **my servant David's sake.** Thus, God's intervention is on behalf of the Davidic (and hence, messianic) line. Verse 36 must stand as one of the most amazing statements in all the Bible. **The angel of the LORD** is often a reference to Christ Himself and should be so taken in this passage. The idea then is that the mighty Assyrian army is no match for Him (see Gen 18:1-33; Josh 5:13-6:5; Jud 6:11-23). The indication of the passage is that the angel of the Lord **went forth** (*yetse'*, the verb commonly used for setting out to battle) and **smote** (*yakeh*, struck) 185,000 in the **camp of the Assyrians.** No explanation is given as to how this actually occurred. The parallel account in II Kings 19:35 adds the words "And it came to pass that night," indicating that it happened the very night after Isaiah had delivered the Lord's message. Just as the angel of the Lord had gone forth at the time of the Passover and smote the Egyptians, so now He smites the military encampment of the Assyrians as well. Some have suggested that the soldiers may have actually died from bubonic plague because of the Greek historian Herodotus' account indicating that Sennacherib had been compelled to retreat from Palestine because of "field mice." While it is certainly possible that God may have used this method, the indication of the Scripture is that this was no mere natural phenomenon, but was a direct and divine intervention of the Lord God Himself. The closing phrase of the statement, **behold, they were all dead corpses,** is actually more forceful in the Hebrew: "Behold! all of them, corpses, dead ones!" At any rate, the combined fact of the Ethiopian-Egyptian invasion from the south and the report of the devastation of his troops at Jerusalem caused Sennacherib to return to the Assyrian capital at **Nineveh.** (For a description of the rise and fall of this powerful city, see A. Parrot, *Nineveh and the Old Testament.*) It was there that he would eventually face assassination at the hand of his own sons nearly twenty years later in 681 B.C. **Nisroch his god** was an intentional misspelling of Marduk, the patron god of the Assyrians and Babylonians. The names of his assassins, **Adrammelech and Sharezer,** are known in Akkadian as Adad-milki and Shar-usur. They are referred to as having escaped into the **land of Armenia** (ASV, "Ararat"). Armenian tradition actually records the names of these two men; they are stated to have founded influential dynasties in the land that now forms the southernmost part of Russia. **Esar-haddon,** the son of Sennacherib, is then stated to have taken over the reign of the Assyrian Empire. He ruled from 681-669 B.C., having served earlier as the viceroy of Babylon under the authority of his father. He lived to be a powerful king, and eventually he defeated Tirhakah and brought Egypt under his control. He died in 669 B.C. at Haran. Thus, the chapter ends with the absolute victory of Jehovah over the threatening Assyrians and thereby completes the Assyrian portion of Isaiah's prophecies. He now uses the next two chapters to turn the reader's attention to a new threat on the distant horizon: Babylon.

B. Looking Ahead to the Babylonian Captivity. 38:1-39:8.

It is generally accepted that the two chapters that follow are out of order chronologically, and they serve as a literary introduction to the coming Babylonian captivity. The prophet's attention shifts from Assyria to Babylon as the major threat to the nation of Judah. Hezekiah, the godly king, is still the major subject of this historic interlude.

1. Hezekiah's sickness and prayer. 38:1-22.

38:1-8. This chapter simply opens with the direct statement that Hezekiah was **sick unto death.** We are not given any indication as to the nature of that sickness. **Isaiah** came to the king to announce that the sickness was **unto death.** This indicates that God had a definite purpose in allowing this sickness to come into Hezekiah's life and that He was in control of these events. The simple announcement **thou shalt die, and not live** was enough to send anyone into depression and soul-searching seriousness. Deeply moved by this austere announcement, Hezekiah **prayed** and **wept sore.** The king reminded the Lord that he had **walked** before Him **in truth** and with a **perfect heart.** He was making no claim to sinless perfection, for the Hebrew *shalem* literally means "whole." Thus, what Hezekiah was really emphasizing was not that he was perfect, but that he had served the Lord with his whole heart. His brief, but serious, prayer was answered: **I have heard thy prayer, I have seen thy tears.** The tender touch of this statement reminds us of the goodness and grace of our loving God who delights to answer the prayers of His servants. In response to Hezekiah's request, the Lord promised that He would add unto his days **fifteen years.** In addition, He also promised that He would deliver the city of Jerusalem out of the hand of the **king of Assyria.** Again, this would indicate that the events in this chapter occurred prior to the events in the two previous chapters. In light of the miraculous intervention of God to spare Hezekiah's life, it is no wonder that he was able to pray for God to spare the city of Jerusalem as well. This would also shed further light on the reason why he had such trust and confidence in God and why the Rab-shakeh felt compelled to undermine that confidence. In an attitude of marked contrast to that of his predecessor Ahaz, Hezekiah asked the Lord for a **sign** (*'oth*). This is especially emphasized in the parallel passage in II Kings 20:8. Like most of Isaiah's announcements of great prophetic consequence, this one is also introduced with the interjection **behold!** The prophet's account is shorter than that given in II Kings, where Hezekiah is asked to choose whether he desires the shadow to go forward ten degrees or to go backward ten degrees. Realizing that it is more likely that it would eventually go down, the king asked that it would return backwards ten degrees. It is generally assumed that the amount of time lost was about twenty minutes; however, since we know very little of the nature of the sundial used in those days, this is difficult to determine with precision. The phrase **shadow of the degrees** (*'eth-tsel hama'alōth*) may also be

CHAPTER 38

IN those days was Hĕz-e-kī'ah sick unto death. And Isaiah the prophet the son of Amoz came unto him, and said unto him, Thus saith the LORD, Set thine house in order: for thou shalt die, and not live.

2 Then Hĕz-e-kī'ah turned his face toward the wall, and prayed unto the LORD,

3 And said, Remember now, O LORD, I beseech thee, how I have walked before thee in truth and with a perfect heart, and have done *that which is* good in thy sight. And Hĕz-e-kī'ah wept sore.

4 Then came the word of the LORD to Isaiah, saying,

5 Go, and say to Hĕz-e-kī'ah, Thus saith the LORD, the God of David thy father, I have heard thy prayer, I have seen thy tears: behold, I will add unto thy days fifteen years.

6 And I will deliver thee and this city out of the hand of the king of Assyria: and I will defend this city.

7 And this *shall be* a sign unto thee from the LORD, that the LORD will do this thing that he hath spoken;

8 Behold, I will bring again the shadow of the degrees, which is gone down in the sun dial of Ahaz, ten degrees backward. So the sun returned ten degrees, by which degrees it was gone down.

translated "the shadow of the steps." Jerome understands the "steps" to refer to degree markers on the sundial, whereas Josephus takes the word to refer to literal steps. This interpretation understands the sun to have cast a shadow on the steps by means of a pillar and thereby to have served as an indication of the passing of time. **In the sun dial of Ahaz** actually reads, "in the steps of Ahaz with the sun." Young (II, p. 514) notes that this refers to the place where the shadow falls (whether on a dial or on the steps). In contrast to the passage in Kings, Isaiah emphasizes that the **sun returned ten degrees.** There is no contradiction between the two passages; here there is a further explanation on the part of the prophet that God used the sun as the means of producing this result. There can be no doubt that a supernatural miracle was involved and that this was no ordinary providential working of God. Conjecture as to whether this involved an actual reverse rotation of the earth, or some other geophysical means, is certainly left unexplained by the text. The real key to understanding the passage is the emphasis that Isaiah placed earlier on the miraculous **sign** (vs. 7) which was to give hope to the ailing monarch that his life would be spared.

9-14. In response to his renewed hope for deliverance from his illness, Hezekiah sings a poetic song of praise unto the Lord. **The writing** (*miktab*) **of Hezekiah king of Judah** clearly indicates that he was the author of this "song of deliverance," which he wrote during the time of his recovery. The psalm reflects on the king's attitudes during the early stages of his sickness. The phrase **in the cutting off** (*demiy*, pause) **of my days** seems to refer to the period of time when the king sensed that his life was about to come to an end. **The gates of the grave** (*sheol*) expresses the destination to which all Old Testament peoples went. In Christian theology, it is generally held that *sheol* had two compartments: Paradise and Hades. The unusual statement, **I shall not see the Lord . . . in the land of the living** (*'erets hachayiym*), does not refer to Judah, but to the abode of the living: earth. The implication of this statement is not necessarily that Hezekiah expected to see the unseen God, but that he would no longer be able to observe God's workings among men. In view of the chronology of this passage, there was certainly one great work ahead in the deliverance of Jerusalem from the Assyrians, and he would see it with his own eyes. He also distinguishes **the inhabitants of the world** (*chadel*) from those in *sheol*. He further regrets that his **age is departed,** i.e., his "years are spent," and are **removed . . . as a shepherd's tent.** This undoubtedly refers to the transient nature of Bedouin tents which can be so easily taken down and moved with little advance notice. The further reference to a **weaver** pictures the finished work of a weaver when he rolls up the cloth on a roller and then cuts it off from the larger bolt. Expecting that his life has come to an end and nothing more remains than for him to be cut off and rolled up, Hezekiah pictures God as a **lion** waiting to devour him. He then views himself as a **crane or a swallow** helplessly awaiting his own destruction.

9 ¶The writing of Hĕz-e-kī'ah king of Jū'dah, when he had been sick, and was recovered of his sickness:

10 I said in the cutting off of my days, I shall go to the gates of the grave: I am deprived of the residue of my years.

11 I said, I shall not see the LORD, *even* the LORD, in the land of the living: I shall behold man no more with the inhabitants of the world.

12 Mine age is departed, and is removed from me as a shepherd's tent: I have cut off like a weaver my life: he will cut me off with pining sickness: from day *even* to night wilt thou make an end of me.

13 I reckoned till morning, *that,* as a lion, so will he break all my bones: from day *even* to night wilt thou make an end of me.

14 Like a crane *or* a swallow, so did I chatter: I did mourn as a dove: mine eyes fail *with looking* upward: O LORD, I am oppressed; undertake for me.

15 What shall I say? he hath both spoken unto me, and himself hath done *it:* I shall go softly all my years in the bitterness of my soul.

16 O LORD, by these *things* men live, and in all these *things is* the life of my spirit: so wilt thou recover me, and make me to live.

17 Behold, for peace I had great bitterness: but thou hast in love to my soul *delivered it* from the pit of corruption: for thou hast cast all my sins behind thy back.

18 For the grave cannot praise thee, death can *not* celebrate thee: they that

15-22. The "song of deliverance" changes its expression with the words **What shall I say?** The idea is that Hezekiah has been so stunned by God's promise of an extension of his life that he is speechless before the mercy of Jehovah. **I shall go softly** means that he was humbled before the Lord and can no longer live in a proud or haughty manner; he will spend the remainder of his years in humility before the Lord. **In the bitterness of my soul** should read "on account of the bitterness of my soul." Hezekiah is not saying that he shall remain bitter, but that he would live the rest of his life in humble submission to God, realizing that He was the only One that could deliver him from the bitterness of death. The phrase **for peace I had great bitterness** should actually be reversed: "My bitterness turned to peace." The song ends in a great exaltation of the opportunity of the **living** to

shall wither, and the whirlwind shall take them away as stubble.

25 To whom then will ye liken me, or shall I be equal? saith the Holy One.

26 Lift up your eyes on high, and behold who hath created these *things,* that bringeth out their host by number: he calleth them all by names by the greatness of his might, for that *he is* strong in power; not one faileth.

27 Why sayest thou, O Jacob, and speakest, O Israel, My way is hid from the LORD, and my judgment is passed over from my God?

28 Hast thou not known? hast thou not heard, *that* the everlasting God, the LORD, the Creator of the ends of the earth, fainteth not, neither is weary? *there is* no searching of his understanding.

29 He giveth power to the faint; and to *them that have* no might he increaseth strength.

30 Even the youths shall faint and be weary, and the young men shall utterly fall:

31 But they that wait upon the LORD shall renew their strength; they shall mount up with wings as eagles; they shall run, and not be weary; *and* they shall walk, and not faint.

CHAPTER 41

KEEP silence before me, O islands; and let the people renew *their* strength: let them come near; then let them speak: let us come near together to judgment.

2 Who raised up the righteous *man* from the east, called him to his foot, gave the nations before him, and made *him* rule over kings? he gave *them* as the dust to his sword, *and* as driven stubble to his bow.

3 He pursued them, *and* passed safely; *even* by the way *that* he had not gone with his feet.

4 Who hath wrought and done *it,* calling the generations from the beginning? I the LORD, the first, and with the last; I *am* he.

5 The isles saw *it,* and feared; the ends of the earth were afraid, drew near, and came.

6 They helped every one his neighbour; and *every one* said to his brother, Be of good courage.

7 So the carpenter encouraged the goldsmith, *and* he that smootheth *with* the hammer him that smote the anvil, saying, It *is* ready for the sodering: and he fastened it with nails, *that* it should not be moved.

8 But thou, Israel, *art* my servant, Ja-

the earth refers to the Lord God and clearly indicates that the earth is round and not flat! In addition, this God **stretcheth out the heavens as a curtain, and . . . as a tent.** The word translated **curtain** (*doq*) is a *hapax legomenon* and indicates something very thin. Isaiah, therefore, is emphasizing that for God it was no greater task to set out the heavens in order than it would be for someone to stretch forth a thin veil in the wind. He is called **the Holy One** and is pictured as controlling the heavens **on high,** even as He providentially controls the events on earth. His prominence over the stars is indicated in verse 26, where He **created** them and **calleth them all by names.** In light of God's omniscience, as well as His omnipresence, the prophet asks Israel why it is that she thinks her **way is hid from the LORD.** As the **Creator of the ends of the earth,** He is so great that He never wearies; and there is no comprehending of the magnitude of His being. Rather than being able to give to Him, He is the One who must give to us in order for our needs to be met. While He is incomprehensible, He is, nevertheless, knowable. While He meets our every need, we may in turn serve Him as well. The chapter closes with the contrast between **youths,** and those that **wait** (*qōey,* waiters) **upon the LORD,** who shall run, walk, and fly. Alexander (II, p. 116) argues that **wait** has the connotation of patience rather than serving. Thus, it is not just those who serve the Lord who shall renew their strength, but those who are patiently awaiting the fulfillment of His promises. MacRae (pp. 31-49) views this entire section from chapters 40-48 as a great "symphony," with chapter 40 serving as the "overture."

41:1-7. In this chapter the nations are pictured as coming before the presence of God, and in recognition of His sovereignty they must **keep silence before me.** Notice the same idea in Revelation 8:1, where there was ". . . silence in heaven . . ." before the announcement of God was made. God appeals to the nations to **come near** that they might speak together of **judgment** (*mishpat,* justice). The nations (**islands**) are summoned before the presence of the mighty God to answer His questions. This time the rhetorical questions are addressed to the unbelieving gentile kingdoms. The answers to those questions are designed to bring recognition to the true God who has brought the circumstances into existence. **The righteous man from the east** is certainly a reference to Cyrus the Great of Persia (558-529 B.C.). Though he is not named until 44:28, he is introduced in this passage as one who is raised up from the east to fulfill the will of God. Both the Hebrew and the LXX translate righteousness (*tsedek*) as a noun, rather than as an adjective, as in the AV. It is God Himself who has raised up righteousness toward His people in the deliverance that shall be provided by Cyrus the Great. MacRae (p. 55) is correct when he states: "Thus there is not necessarily any statement here regarding the character of Cyrus but rather regarding God's purpose in enabling Cyrus to carry on his great career of conquest." God is pictured by the prophet Isaiah as the one who **gave the nations** unto Cyrus and his Persian Empire. Thus, it would come to pass that Israel's two greatest enemies, Assyria and Babylon, would both fall in the future. While in the book of Daniel Persia is certainly viewed as a gentile kingdom, it is also true that the deliverance which they wrought for the Jews is looked upon as God's divine intervention on the behalf of His people. The Lord is the One who is sovereign over history because He is **the first, and with the last** (cf. Rev 1:11). The prophet's message is one of encouragement for the nation of Israel which one day would be **fastened . . . with nails,** meaning that there would come a time when the nation would no longer be subject to dispersion and would be established immovable by the Lord God.

8-9. Thou, Israel, art my servant. This is the first reference to the Servant of the Lord who becomes so prominent in these

cob whom I have chosen, the seed of Abraham my friend.

9 Thou whom I have taken from the ends of the earth, and called thee from the chief men thereof, and said unto thee, Thou art my servant; I have chosen thee, and not cast thee away.

10 ¶Fear thou not; for I am with thee: be not dismayed; for I am thy God: I will strengthen thee; yea, I will help thee; yea, I will uphold thee with the right hand of my righteousness.

11 Behold, all they that were incensed against thee shall be ashamed and confounded: they shall be as nothing; and they that strive with thee shall perish.

12 Thou shalt seek them, and shalt not find them, even them that contended with thee: they that war against thee shall be as nothing, and as a thing of nought.

13 For I the LORD thy God will hold thy right hand, saying unto thee, Fear not; I will help thee.

14 Fear not, thou worm Jacob, and ye men of Israel; I will help thee, saith the LORD, and thy redeemer, the Holy One of Israel.

15 Behold, I will make thee a new sharp threshing instrument having teeth: thou shalt thresh the mountains, and beat them small, and shalt make the hills as chaff.

16 Thou shalt fan them, and the wind shall carry them away, and the whirlwind shall scatter them: and thou shalt

chapters. Here the servant is pictured as the believing element of Israel, as opposed to the unbelieving gentile nations. Her national heritage is traced through **Abraham**, who is referred to as the **friend** of God, and also to **Jacob** (Israel). Thus, the national heritage of the Israelites is traced to both Abraham and his grandson Jacob. Even though they are weak in and of themselves, God has chosen each of them to be His **servant**. There has naturally been great debate among Jewish and Christian commentators as to the identity of the Servant of Lord throughout these passages. There can be no doubt in this reference that God is speaking of Israel as His Servant-Nation; however, this does not limit all of the servant references to the nation. Many of them are personified as an individual (see 42:1). The designation **servant** ('ebed) means a slave or bondman. It is derived from the Hebrew root word meaning "to work" or "to serve." The term is used frequently throughout this section by the prophet (cf. 42:19; 44:1-2, 21; 45:4; 48:20; 52:13). Leupold (II, p. 46) notes that the basic meaning of the term is that of a "slave"; yet, in this passage it has connotations that are entirely honorable and bespeak of the close intimacy between the master and his servant. He views this statement as a reassurance to Israel that even though Cyrus may fulfill some servant-like functions for God, this in no way cancels out Israel's election by God to be His servant. Whereas the election is often spoken of in the prophets as dating from the time of the Exodus, Isaiah traces it all the way back to Abraham himself. The word **servant** is used far more in this section of Isaiah than in any other part of the book. Thus, the servant is briefly introduced in this chapter and is described throughout the succeeding chapters, reaching its great climax in 52:13-53:12. Here the use of the term, then, is one of reassurance to the nation of Israel. Even though God will raise up a deliverer from outside the nation, He has not yet forsaken the nation. Abraham is designated as **my friend** ('ohabiy, lit., my lover). It is interesting to note that this same concept is picked up in the Koran (1:25), where Abraham is referred to as: "the Upright" and the one whom God took as His "friend" (Arab chalil, he who loves me). Even the Arabic name Abdallah is similar to the name Abraham in that it designates a friend or worshiper of Allah.

10-20. In order to learn this lesson of faith, Israel must pass through the humiliation of an exile and the bondage of captivity in order to see that the deliverance of God through Cyrus reaffirms His covenant commitment to His people. Thus, He reassures Israel: **I am with thee . . . I am thy God.** To encourage His people, God promises that those nations that have oppressed Israel **shall perish.** In this regard it should be noted that Assyria and Babylon, Israel's two greatest antagonists, have long since vanished. The designation, **thou worm Jacob,** is but a reminder to the Israelites of their ultimate frailty and need for God. It is the Lord who promises to be their **Redeemer** (go'el). (On the historical basis of the concept of redemption, see D. A. Legett, The Levirate and Goel Institutions in the Old Testament; on the theological aspects of redemption, see J. Murray, Redemption Accomplished and Applied.) The title the **Holy One of Israel** (qedōsh yisra'el) is one of the prophet Isaiah's favorite designations for the Lord Jehovah. As a title for God, it appears as frequently in the second half of his prophecy as it does in the first half. Verses 17-19 provide a beautiful picture of God's provision of water to abundantly supply the need of His people. These statements are of particular significance to people living in desert and arid regions. God promises to provide **rivers . . . fountains . . . springs of water.** Because of this supply, He will also plant various trees in the wilderness: the **cedar . . . shittah** (acacia) **. . . myrtle . . . oil tree** ('ets shemen, possibly a wild olive) **. . . fir . . . pine . . . box** (or boxwood). Archer (p. 638) and Young (III, p. 93) both follow Delitzsch (II, p. 167) in

rejoice in the LORD, and shalt glory in the Holy One of Israel.

17 When the poor and needy seek water, and there is none, and their tongue faileth for thirst, I the LORD will hear them, I the God of Israel will not forsake them.

18 I will open rivers in high places, and fountains in the midst of the valleys: I will make the wilderness a pool of water, and the dry land springs of water.

19 I will plant in the wilderness the cedar, the shittah tree, and the myrtle, and the oil tree; I will set in the desert the fir tree, and the pine, and the box tree together:

20 That they may see, and know, and consider, and understand together, that the hand of the LORD hath done this, and the Holy One of Israel hath created it.

21 ¶Produce your cause, saith the LORD; bring forth your strong reasons, saith the King of Jacob.

22 Let them bring them forth, and shew us what shall happen: let them shew the former things, what they be, that we may consider them, and know the latter end of them; or declare us things for to come.

23 Shew the things that are to come hereafter, that we may know that ye are gods: yea, do good, or do evil, that we may be dismayed, and behold it together.

24 Behold, ye are of nothing, and your work of nought: an abomination is he that chooseth you.

25 I have raised up one from the north, and he shall come: from the rising of the sun shall he call upon my name: and he shall come upon princes as upon morter, and as the potter treadeth clay.

26 Who hath declared from the beginning, that we may know? and beforetime, that we may say, He is righteous? yea, there is none that sheweth, yea, there is none that declareth, yea, there is none that heareth your words.

27 The first shall say to Zion, Behold, behold them: and I will give to Jerusalem one that bringeth good tidings.

28 For I beheld, and there was no man; even among them, and there was no counsellor, that, when I asked of them, could answer a word.

29 Behold, they are all vanity; their works are nothing: their molten images are wind and confusion.

emphasizing that the seven species of trees symbolize the perfection of God's work on behalf of His people. Young further notes that these trees are all common to Syria and Palestine and would not likely have been well-known to a Second Isaiah who supposedly lived in Babylon all of his life. (For an extensive development of this idea see R. L. Alden, "Isaiah and Wood," in *The Law and the Prophets*, pp. 377-387.)

21-29. Having promised to bless His people Israel, the Lord now challenges the gods of the heathen nations in verses 21-29. He challenges them to **produce your cause** (set forth your case) and to bring forth your **strong reasons** (arguments). Here the Lord is referred to as the **King of Jacob**, recognizing His ultimate authority over His people. The gods of the nations are challenged to both predict the future and explain the meaning of the past. But they can do neither, because they are in fact not gods at all. MacRae (p. 57) notes "The emphasis on the inability of heathen gods to predict the future points to one of the great themes of this section, the argument from fulfilled prophecy, which, like the emphasis on God's creative power, is stressed more often in this section of Isaiah than almost anywhere else in the Bible." (On the nature and significance of predictive prophecy, see W. J. Beecher, *The Prophets and the Promise*; R. D. Culver, "Were the Old Testament Prophecies Really Prophetic?" in *Can I Trust My Bible?* A. G. Kirkpatrick, *The Doctrine of the Prophets*; S. J. Schultz, *The Prophets Speak*; L. J. Wood, *The Prophets of Israel*; E. J. Young, *My Servants the Prophets*; for a liberal perspective cf. G. C. Oxtoby, *Prediction and Fulfillment in the Bible*.) The law of Moses laid down the stipulation of exact fulfillment of predictive utterances as an evidence of the divine authority and genuineness of the prophet's message (Deut 18:21-22). According to Jeremiah 28, the verification of the prophet's word by the events of history as the fulfillment of that prediction was the evidence of the truth of his message. Nonfulfillment was an indication of false prophecy. Therefore, fulfillment constitutes the evidence of the genuineness of the prophecy. In commenting on this passage, H. E. Freeman, *An Introduction to the Old Testament Prophets* (p. 112) states: "In Isaiah 41:21-23 the significance of the relationship between prophecy and fulfillment is seen when God disdainfully challenged the idol-gods, in which Israel vainly trusted, to predict events lying in the distant future; their fulfillment would be proof of the existence and authority of these gods. However, the idol-gods could announce no predictions, whereas God, knowing the end from the beginning of all events, again and again demonstrated the truth of the word of His prophets through the fulfillment of their forecasts and signs." In the New Testament era, the very first Christian sermon preached by Peter quoted the fulfillment of prophecy as an example of the authenticity of Christ. (Acts 2:16, 22-23, 25, 30-31, 37-40). Even Jesus Himself authenticated His authority as a messenger of God by predicting His own resurrection (Mt 12:38-40; Jn 2:13-22). To reassure John the Baptist that He was indeed the Messiah, Jesus quoted the fulfillment of Old Testament prophecies (Mt 11:2-6). The challenge to the false gods is that they should declare **what shall**

happen . . . the former things . . . the latter end . . . things for to come. Thus, the challenge of the Lord to these idols is that they should predict something—anything! Something close at hand, soon to be fulfilled, or something far to the distant future would suffice. The wording implies that if they could make any kind of prediction, this would be indicative of the reality of their existence. The challenge here laid down is that the idols predict the future. Young (III, p. 98) notes that this illustrates the true method of Christian apologetics in which falsehood is placed upon the defensive. The fact that Isaiah would record this challenge is indicative of the fact that he deliberately intended his statements to be taken as prophetic predictions of future events. In light of his own challenge, Isaiah immediately refers again to the **one from the north** (Cyrus) whom he will specifically name later. This deliverer is a temporal one and is not to be confused with the ultimate deliverer, the Messiah. That He comes from both the **north** and the **rising of the sun** (east) fits perfectly with a Palestinian writer's designation of the Media-Persia Empire. The geographical designation does not fit well with a supposed "Second Isaiah" in Babylon. That he will **call upon my name** has been questioned, but it may simply refer to acknowledgment rather than salvation. Certainly in Ezra 1 we have an example of Cyrus' recognition of Jehovah. The chapter ends with the confident declaration that the prophet, as God's spokesman, shall predict this deliverer in advance. **Behold them** calls attention to the fulfillment of these predictions, which are intended to arrest the attention of the nation of Judah. In the meantime, there was **no man . . . no counselor** among the idols of the heathen to make or explain such predictions.

2. Promise of the Servant. 42:1-45:25.

With the identification of the **servant** as a person in this chapter, rather than a mere personification of the nation of Israel, a new and glorious element of Isaiah's predictions begins to unfold. Nägelsbach (p. 448) notes that Cyrus is looked upon as the servant of the Lord without being called so and that Israel is clearly identified as such in the previous chapter. Both, he argues, have their roots in Him who is the servant of Jehovah in the highest sense: the Messiah! David Baron, *The Servant of Jehovah*, pp. 10-32, provides an extensive study of both ancient and modern Jewish interpretations of this passage, showing that prior to the time of Christ, it was generally interpreted by the rabbis as being messianic in nature. Such support may be found readily in the Babylonian Talmud and Rabbinic Midrashim, with Jonathan ben Uzziel (first century A.D.) being the chief exponent of the messianic view. Both Abrabanel and Alsheck clearly admit that the older (earlier) Jewish interpretation is messianic. Baron concludes that until Rashi (A.D. 1040-1105) applied it to the Jewish nation, the messianic interpretation of this chapter was "almost universally adopted by the Jews." The earliest known reference of an attempt to interpret the Servant of the Lord always to be only the Jewish nation is actually stated by the Christian writer Origen (A.D. 185-253) who refers to his attempt to explain the prophecy to a particular rabbi who offered the "counter-explanation" that the fulfillment of this passage was national and not personal. Alexander (II, p. 130) states: "This ancient doctrine of the Jewish church, and of the great majority of Christian writers, is that the Servant of the Lord is the Messiah." H. L. Ellison, *The Message of the Old Testament* (p. 64) says: "History shows us that there were only a few in Israel who had begun to take this revelation seriously by the time of our Lord, and there is no evidence that any of these had penetrated into its real meaning. There are elements in it that baffled men before Jesus of Nazareth made it luminous by fulfilling it. Even so today it baffles those who refuse to see Him as its fulfiller. In these Servant passages we find traits of the

King, of the Prophet, and of the High Priest so united that they point to only one who was truly all three."

42:1-4. The **servant . . . mine elect** is none other than Christ Jesus Himself. **Elect** does not mean choice or excellent, except by implication. Strictly translated, *chiyriy* actually means one chosen or set apart for a definite purpose. The phrase, **I have put my spirit** (rūach) **upon him,** indicates that the Servant is a person. In light of this obvious statement in Hebrew, many liberal commentators have attempted to identify the Servant here as Cyrus. However, Alexander (II, p. 129) observes, "The office thus ascribed to the servant of Jehovah, both here and in the following context, as a teacher of the truth, makes the description wholly inappropriate to Cyrus." It is much more obvious that these passages in the book of Isaiah present a corporate identity between the Messiah and His people Israel. (On this subject see, H. W. Robinson, *Corporate Personality in Ancient Israel.*) As the Messiah, Christ is the One who emerges as the individual who is representative of the entire nation. Thus, it is not inappropriate to speak of both the nation and the Messiah as the Servant of the Lord. The New Testament clearly quotes this passage as being fulfilled in the person of Jesus Christ (Mt 12:18-21). Certainly other allusions to this may be found in Zechariah 3:8 and Philippians 2:7, with a possible further allusion in the words spoken by the Father on the occasion of the descent of the Holy Spirit upon Jesus: "This is my beloved Son, in whom I am well pleased" (Mt 3:17). It is interesting to note that the Greek word *pais* translates both "son" and "servant." The ministry of the Servant of the Lord will be to bring forth **judgment** (*mishpat*, "justice") **to the Gentiles.** While it is true that Jesus' early ministry was directed to the "house of Israel," it is, nevertheless, obvious that His ultimate ministry was to extend to the Gentiles as well. Of all of the Old Testament prophets, Isaiah saw this fact most clearly. (For a thorough discussion of this see T. C. Vriezen, *An Outline of Old Testament Theology,* pp. 349-373.) Throughout these closing chapters of Isaiah's prophecy, it becomes more and more evident that he foresees a time of gentile salvation. Therefore, the election of Israel as the chosen people of God is not viewed as an end in itself, but rather as a means toward the goal of the salvation of the nations. This is to be accomplished not merely by national means, but by the coming of a personal Messiah and Saviour. The basic humility of the Messiah is emphasized by the seven negative verbs that are used to describe Him in verses 2-4. In contrast to the loud and ostentatious worldly conqueror who loudly proclaims his deeds, the Servant of the Lord will not cry aloud, nor lift up His voice in praise of Himself. The emphasis here is not that He will not speak, but that His teaching will be accomplished through quiet instruction, rather than through loud proclamation. He is also viewed as One who takes mercy on the **bruised** and the broken. **Smoking flax** refers to the burning wick and is used symbolically of those who are endangered. The idea of the passage is that the Servant will take mercy on the weak. Several ridiculous allegorical interpretations have been proposed for this passage and are quite unnecessary. The simple point of the passage is that the Messiah will come, not as a worldly king or conqueror, as the Jews so expected Him to come, but as the humble Servant of the Lord. He will **not fail** in His purpose until He accomplishes **judgment** (justice) **in the earth.** His work will not be limited to Israel, but will extend to the whole world, again pointing out the universality of His ministry. Young (III, p. 116) states: "Cyrus' kingdom was to be limited in extent, and Moses' law was directed to the Israelites; the Servant's law and his kingdom know no barriers of nationality and race."

5-16. God the LORD is pictured as the Creator who **created** (*bara'*) the heavens and **stretched them out** (*natah*) and **spread**

CHAPTER 42

BEHOLD my servant, whom I uphold; mine elect, *in whom* my soul delighteth; I have put my spirit upon him: he shall bring forth judgment to the Gentiles.

2 He shall not cry, nor lift up, nor cause his voice to be heard in the street.

3 A bruised reed shall he not break, and the smoking flax shall he not quench: he shall bring forth judgment unto truth.

4 He shall not fail nor be discouraged, till he have set judgment in the earth: and the isles shall wait for his law.

5 ¶Thus saith God the LORD, he that created the heavens, and stretched

them out; he that spread forth the earth, and that which cometh out of it; he that giveth breath unto the people upon it, and spirit to them that walk therein:

6 I the Lord have called thee in righteousness, and will hold thine hand, and will keep thee, and give thee for a covenant of the people, for a light of the Gentiles;

7 To open the blind eyes, to bring out the prisoners from the prison, and them that sit in darkness out of the prison house.

8 I am the Lord: that is my name: and my glory will I not give to another, neither my praise to graven images.

9 Behold, the former things are come to pass, and new things do I declare: before they spring forth I tell you of them.

10 ¶Sing unto the Lord a new song, and his praise from the end of the earth, ye that go down to the sea, and all that is therein; the isles, and the inhabitants thereof.

11 Let the wilderness and the cities thereof lift up their voice, the villages that Kē′dar doth inhabit: let the inhabitants of the rock sing, let them shout from the top of the mountains.

12 Let them give glory unto the Lord, and declare his praise in the islands.

13 The Lord shall go forth as a mighty man, he shall stir up jealousy like a man of war: he shall cry, yea, roar; he shall prevail against his enemies.

14 I have long time holden my peace; I have been still, and refrained myself: now will I cry like a travailing woman; I will destroy and devour at once.

15 I will make waste mountains and hills, and dry up all their herbs; and I will make the rivers islands, and I will dry up the pools.

16 And I will bring the blind by a way that they knew not; I will lead them in paths that they have not known: I will make darkness light before them, and crooked things straight. These things will I do unto them, and not forsake them.

17 They shall be turned back, they shall be greatly ashamed, that trust in graven images, that say to the molten images, Ye are our gods.

18 ¶Hear, ye deaf; and look, ye blind, that ye may see.

19 Who is blind, but my servant? or deaf, as my messenger that I sent? who is blind as he that is perfect, and blind as the Lord's servant?

20 Seeing many things, but thou observest not; opening the ears, but he heareth not.

21 The Lord is well pleased for his righteousness' sake; he will magnify the law, and make it honourable.

22 But this is a people robbed and spoiled; they are all of them snared in holes, and they are hid in prison houses: they are for a prey, and none delivereth; for a spoil, and none saith, Restore.

23 Who among you will give ear to

forth (raqa‘) the earth. As the Creator of the world, He is the One who gives both breath (neshamah) and spirit (rûach) to the people ('am, the common designation for the "people" of God.) Notice the contrast between the terms "people" ('am) and Gentiles (gōyim, nations). The ministry of the Messiah is described in verse 6 as a covenant (beriyth) to the Jews and a light ('ōr) to the gentile nations. His purpose will be to open the blind eyes and to bring out the prisoners from the prison. The statement here is very similar to that of Isaiah 61:1-2, which the New Testament definitely states was fulfilled in Jesus Christ (cf. Lk 14:18; II Tim 2:26; Heb 2:14-15). I am the Lord (Yahweh): that is my name. This affirmation draws our attention to the fact that it is the Lord Jehovah who will call forth His Servant, put His spirit upon Him, and send Him forth both to His covenant people Israel and to the gentile nations of the world. Thus, we see a clear affirmation of and prediction of the twofold ministry of the Messiah. The Lord Himself proclaims His greatness in predicting the former things as well as the new things which shall come to pass even as He has predicted. Therefore, the prophet responds with a new song or praise to the Lord from the ends of the earth. This universal praise will be the result of the worldwide message of salvation which the Servant of the Lord shall proclaim. Thus, verses 10-13 must be viewed as the Gentiles singing praise for their deliverance and conversion. In contrast to the quiet and submissive ministry of the Servant, the Lord shall go forth as a mighty man . . . like a man of war in verse 13. Herein we have clearly delineated the twofold aspects of the advent of Christ. In His first coming, He will be the meek and lowly Servant and in His second coming in judgment upon the world He shall go forth as a man of war. The devastation described in verses 14-16 is reminiscent of that of the Tribulation Period in which the mountains and hills are destroyed and the rivers are dried up (cf. Rev 8:7-9:21). As always in Isaiah's prophecies there is a message of hope in the midst of his announcement of destruction. The blind are those that are spiritually blind and who will come to the light of God's glorious truth.

17-25. In this section the prophet contrasts the faith of those who believe in God, to the idolatry of those who trust in graven images. These are they who shall be greatly ashamed. In the imagery of these verses, it becomes clear that the deaf and the blind are the unbelieving element of the nation of Israel. The question Who is blind, but my servant? is directed at Israel as the servant-nation of the Lord. This identification of Israel's spiritual weakness points all the more clearly to the need for a personal Servant-Messiah who shall deliver Israel from her spiritual bondage. The people of Israel are robbed and spoiled because they have sinned against the Lord God. Thus, the prophet asks the question: Who gave Jacob for a spoil, and Israel to the robbers? The answer is, the Lord! He is the ultimate source of Israel's judgment and devastation; yet, the prophet bemoans: he laid it not to heart, that is, he did not repent as a result of these judgments. One of the great tragedies of man's dealings with God is his inability to internalize the working of God in the midst of his own circumstances. In other words, we may fully experience the hand of God upon us through an act of His judgment and, nevertheless, refuse to acknowledge it as such.

7 And who, as I, shall call, and shall declare it, and set it in order for me, since I appointed the ancient people? and the things that are coming, and shall come, let them shew unto them.

8 Fear ye not, neither be afraid: have not I told thee from that time, and have declared *it?* ye *are* even my witnesses. Is there a God beside me? yea, *there is* no God; I know not *any.*

book of Isaiah, the prophet stresses the significance of the election of Israel as the people of God. The phrase **formed thee from the womb** identifies God's activity on behalf of His people from the very beginning. Jacob is paralleled to **Jesurun** (upright one, cf. Deut 32:15). The pouring out of **water** is paralleled to the pouring out of God's **spirit upon thy seed.** Archer (p. 640) correctly relates this to the coming of the Holy Spirit at Pentecost in Acts 2. The futuristic nature of this promise would indicate that in the future there was yet coming a time when this would happen. Verse 6 is one of the most unusual passages in all of the Old Testament prophetic scripture. It emphasizes the oneness of God by stating that **beside me there is no God.** Yet, at the same time, it distinguishes between **the LORD the King of Israel** and **his Redeemer the LORD of hosts.** The personal name *Yahweh* is used of both the King and His Redeemer, the one referring to God the Father and the other referring to God the Son. God's sovereignty is then emphasized by the fact that He alone is able to predict the future. The question is raised as to who else can predict the **things that are coming** with the kind of accuracy that He can. God calls the people to be His **witnesses** to the fact that He can indeed predict events in advance of their fulfillment. This issue becomes one of the great theological problems of the Old Testament. Those who are determined to deny the possibility of supernatural prediction of specific events in advance seem determined to interpret such predictions right out of the Bible, even contradicting the interpretion of the same events by the New Testament writers. Thus, the modern critic sets himself up, not only as a judge of the Old Testament scripture, but as critic of the inspired New Testament as well! (On the use of the Old Testament by New Testament writers, cf. F. F. Bruce, *New Testament Development of Old Testament Themes;* R. T. France, *Jesus and the Old Testament;* L. J. Kuyper, *The Scripture Unbroken;* R. V. G. Tasker, *The Old Testament in the New Testament.*) With the words of the prophet, God asks the question: **Is there a God beside me?** Then, He proceeds to answer His own question; **there is no God; I know not any.** What God is stating here is that He is the ultimate authority on divinity! In order to prove His statement, he accuses the other "gods" of being nothing more than idols made by men.

9 They that make a graven image *are* all of them vanity; and their delectable things shall not profit; and they *are* their own witnesses; they see not, nor know; that they may be ashamed.

10 Who hath formed a god, or molten a graven image *that* is profitable for nothing?

11 Behold, all his fellows shall be ashamed: and the workmen, they *are* of men: let them all be gathered together, let them stand up; *yet* they shall fear, *and* they shall be ashamed together.

12 The smith with the tongs both worketh in the coals, and fashioneth it with hammers, and worketh it with the strength of his arms: yea, he is hungry, and his strength faileth: he drinketh no water, and is faint.

13 The carpenter stretcheth out *his* rule; he marketh it out with a line; he fitteth it with planes, and he marketh it out with the compass, and maketh it after the figure of a man, according to the beauty of a man; that it may remain in the house.

14 He heweth him down cedars, and taketh the cypress and the oak, which he strengtheneth for himself among

9-20. This exposé of idolatry is the most powerful in all of the Bible! Here the prophet Isaiah, serving as the spokesman of Jehovah, shows the utter foolishness of polytheistic idolatry. (On the uniqueness of Israelite worship as opposed to pagan idolatry, see W. Dyrness, *Themes in Old Testament Theology,* pp. 143-160 and C. J. Labuschagne, *The Incomparability of Yahweh in the Old Testament,* pp. 142-153). The **graven image** (carved idol) is called **vanity** (nothingness). **Delectable things** refer to the extreme adornment of idols with gold, silver, and precious stones. The prophet announces his verdict that the idols themselves are **their own witnesses** (*'edeyhim*). They testify against themselves that they **see not, nor know.** Because of their own helpless condition, they are ultimately **ashamed** (*yeboshū,* meaning to dry up). Thus, these helpless idols leave their devotees without help or hope. The prophet continues his sarcastic and satirical attack by announcing that a god who is nothing more than a carved image is **profitable for nothing.** Thus, he berates the **fellows** (*habarim,* companions) or other idols. He also suggests that the **workmen** (artisans), as well as the devotees, shall be **ashamed** (dried up). Both the **smith** (iron worker) and the **carpenter** (woodworker) design and construct the idol of natural materials and form it in the **figure of a man, according to the beauty of a man.** Thus, the prophet exposes the basic fallacy of idolatry, a god made in the image of man. By contrast, the Bible teaches that man is made in the personal image of God. Isaiah carries his argument even further by

the trees of the forest: he planteth an ash, and the rain doth nourish *it.*

15 Then shall it be for a man to burn: for he will take thereof, and warm himself; yea, he kindleth *it,* and baketh bread; yea, he maketh a god, and worshippeth *it;* he maketh it a graven image, and falleth down thereto.

16 He burneth part thereof in the fire; with part thereof he eateth flesh; he roasteth roast, and is satisfied: yea, he warmeth *himself,* and saith, Aha, I am warm, I have seen the fire:

17 And the residue thereof he maketh a god, *even* his graven image: he falleth down unto it, and worshippeth *it,* and prayeth unto it, and saith, Deliver me; for thou *art* my god.

18 They have not known nor understood: for he hath shut their eyes, that they cannot see; *and* their hearts, that they cannot understand.

19 And none considereth in his heart, neither *is there* knowledge nor understanding to say, I have burned part of it in the fire; yea, also I have baked bread upon the coals thereof; I have roasted flesh, and eaten *it:* and shall I make the residue thereof an abomination? shall I fall down to the stock of a tree?

20 He feedeth on ashes: a deceived heart hath turned him aside, that he cannot deliver his soul, nor say, *Is there* not a lie in my right hand?

21 ¶Remember these, O Jacob and Israel; for thou *art* my servant: I have formed thee; thou *art* my servant: O Israel, thou shalt not be forgotten of me.

22 I have blotted out, as a thick cloud, thy transgressions, and, as a cloud, thy sins: return unto me; for I have redeemed thee.

23 Sing, O ye heavens; for the LORD hath done *it:* shout, ye lower parts of the earth: break forth into singing, ye mountains, O forest, and every tree therein: for the LORD hath redeemed Jacob, and glorified himself in Israel.

24 Thus saith the LORD, thy redeemer, and he that formed thee from the womb, I *am* the LORD that maketh all *things;* that stretcheth forth the heavens alone; that spreadeth abroad the earth by myself;

25 That frustrateth the tokens of the liars, and maketh diviners mad; that turneth wise *men* backward, and maketh their knowledge foolish;

26 That confirmeth the word of his servant, and performeth the counsel of his messengers; that saith to Jerusalem, Thou shalt be inhabited; and to the cities of Jū'dah, Ye shall be built, and I will raise up the decayed places thereof:

27 That saith to the deep, Be dry, and I will dry up thy rivers:

pointing out that when a man cuts down **the trees of the forest,** he may take part of them to build a fire and **warm himself;** and he may take another part to build a fire so that he **baketh bread,** and of another part **he maketh a god, and worshipeth it.** The utter stupidity of idolatry and pagan religion is exposed here to the most scathing attack in the entire Bible. What is worse is not only that the pagan would worship this so-called god, but that he **prayeth unto it** and expects it to deliver him. Isaiah is overwhelmed at the illogical stupidity of such reasoning. He condemns the idol worshipers for shutting their **eyes** and their **hearts.** Thus it is that they **cannot see** and **cannot understand** truth in the spiritual realm. To the mind of God, such idolatry is an **abomination** (*thō'ebah,* abhorrence). The prophet's criticism of one who would worship an idol carved from the same tree that he would use for firewood is that **He feedeth on ashes.** The ultimate problem of the unbeliever, whether he be an idolator or a modern agnostic, is that he has a **deceived** (*hūthal,* cheated) **heart.** His ultimate condemnation shall be that he **cannot deliver his soul** from judgment because what he holds in his **right hand** (i.e., an idol) is really a **lie.**

21-27. The prophet turns now to **Israel** who is once again reminded that he is the **servant** of the Lord. Having pointed out the foolishness of idolatry, He reminds His people of their proper relationship to Him. Kelley (p. 316) notes that the LXX and the Dead Sea Scroll (1QIsa) exhibit a slightly different reading: "Do not forget me." In relation to the doctrine of salvation (soteriology), it should be noted of the Lord that He has **blotted out** their transgressions and has **redeemed** them; and yet, He urges them to **return** (*shūbah,* repent) **unto me.** (On the theological significance of redemption in the Old Testament, see R. Youngblood, "Redemption," in *The Heart of the Old Testament,* pp. 97-106.) All of creation is to burst forth in singing and praise because of the Lord's redemption. He is identified as **thy Redeemer** (*go'el*), and His redemption is correlated to His creative action. He is the One that **formed thee from the womb . . . maketh all things . . . stretcheth forth the heavens . . . spreadeth abroad the earth.** He is the omnipotent Creator who has called Israel to be His people from eternity past, and He is the omniscient and sovereign Lord of history Who **frustrateth the tokens of the liars** (*'ophōth badiym,* the signs of the babblers). What is more, He **maketh diviners** (soothsayers or predictors) **mad** by overturning their false predictions. In charting the numerico-climactic structure of this poem of the transcendence of God (vv. 24-28), Allis (p. 65ff.) notes that the declaration **I am the LORD** (*Yahweh*) stands at the beginning of the poem as the subject of all that follows. His argument is that the name of Cyrus cannot be a later insertion because it falls into the essential meter of the strophes of the poem. Schultz, *The Old Testament Speaks* (p. 316), notes that the name Jehovah, or Lord, occurs 421 times in Isaiah—228 times in chapters 1-39 and 193 times in 40-66, underscoring the unity of the book's authorship by the equal distribution of its usage. Nine times the English word **that** is used to identify the activity of the Lord. Thus, the passage follows in perfect meter, leading up to the identification of Cyrus by name. Thus, it is announced that **Jerusalem . . . shalt be inhabited** and that the **cities of Judah**

. . . **shall be built.** To accomplish this, God will raise up a deliverer of His own to accomplish this astounding deed.

28 That saith of Cyrus, *He is* my shepherd, and shall perform all my pleasure: even saying to Jerusalem, Thou shalt be built; and to the temple, Thy foundation shall be laid.

28. The naming of Cyrus more than one hundred years in advance by the prophet Isaiah has become a great stumbling block to liberal theologians who refuse to acknowledge the reality and possibility of predictive prophecy. At this point the *a priori* supposition of the unbelieving scholar will cause him to deny that this prediction of Cyrus by name actually occurred prior to the fact. At the same time, the presupposition of the believing scholar will cause him to accept this statement as a prediction of a future event (not the restatement of an already established fact as if it were yet going to happen). Until there is such evidence to cause us to view this passage otherwise, there is no basis within the text itself to deny the predictive nature of this statement. In this verse the reader is brought to the apex of a great truth. The God who created the world and who is sovereign over history itself can predict the future. Naegelsbach (p. 487) states: "What is nearest as well as what is most remote is equally present to him." One is left with a choice of believing that God either spoke through His prophets, or He did not. Young, *My Servants the Prophets* (p. 189), states: "There remains but one alternative. It is to accept the claims of the prophets at face value. If we do this, we discover that all fits into its proper place. The wonderous message which came forth from the lips of the prophets was not of human origination. It came from God." The entire purpose of this prediction is to let Israel know that when it does come to pass, their deliverance is from the Lord and not from Cyrus. By contrast to Jehovah, Cyrus is as nothing; for he is merely an instrument in the hand of God. **Cyrus** (Heb *kōresh*; Persian *kūrush*) is similar to the Greek word *kurios* (lord). Thus, his name may have been an early dynastic title. (See D. J. Wiseman, "Cyrus," in *NBD*, p. 286; J. C. Whitcomb, "Cyrus in the Prophecies of Isaiah," in *The Law and the Prophets*, pp. 388-401.) He was a Persian king of the Achaemenid dynasty who ruled from 559-530 B.C. In Persian history he is known as Cyrus II, or Cyrus the Great. He was the grandson of Cyrus I who was a contemporary of Ashurbanipal of Assyria and may have possibly been known to Isaiah in the prophet's latter years. In 549 B.C. he conquered his mother's father, Astyages, the Median overlord, and founded the Persian Empire. He soon marched through Assyria, and in 546 he overthrew Croesus and the kingdom of Lydia. On October 16, 539 B.C. his army conquered Babylon and deposed Belshazzar (see comments on Dan 5). The prediction of his name nearly 150 years in advance should not seem incomprehensible in light of the prediction of Josiah by name nearly 300 years in advance (I Kgs 13:2). He is called **my shepherd** in that he is destined to rule the people of Israel during a time when they have no national ruler of their own. Though this term is normally applied to Christ (Ezk 34:23), God Himself (Isa 40:11), and the kings of Israel (II Sam 5:2), it is used here of Cyrus because he will be permitted to perform this shepherding function over God's people by gathering the "lost sheep" of the house of Israel back into their land. Young (III, p. 193) notes that in this sense Cyrus is a type of the Lord's Servant, the true Messiah and Shepherd of His people. He will not only allow the people of Judah to return to their homeland, but will personally decree the rebuilding of **Jerusalem** and the **foundation** of the **temple.** Thus, the words of Ezra 1:2 quote his official decree; "The Lord God of Heaven hath given me all the kingdoms of the earth and has charged me to build Him an house . . ." Josephus (*Antiq.* XI. 1:1) claims that Cyrus made this decree in full knowledge of the prediction of him which had been made in the book of Isaiah. The discovery of the *Cyrus Cylinder* (dating from 536 B.C.) throws further light on his attitude of restoration. In the first year after his conquest of Babylon he issued a decree by which he "gathered together all the inhabitants (who were exiled) and returned them to their homes." In the same decree, he restored their deities and renovated their temples. Since the Jews had no images and their restoration would have meant little at that time to the balance of world power, the prophet views this benevolent move as an act of God. If this is in fact a prediction made a century and a half ahead of time, then it is one of the greatest prophecies in all of the Bible. If, as the liberals suppose, it is merely a statement after the fact, it is hardly worthy of any significance at all. That the prophet Isaiah considered himself to be an actual spokesman for God is indicated by the 122 references to this fact which he makes throughout this book (see this listing by Young, *My Servants the Prophets*, pp. 171-175). There can be no doubt that the prophet himself considered his words which he proclaimed actually to be the words of God. Young (p. 176) concludes: "The prophets believe themselves to be the recipients of Divine revelation because as a matter of fact they actually were the recipients of Divine revelation."

CHAPTER 45

THUS saith the LORD to his anointed, to Cyrus, whose right hand I have holden, to subdue nations before him; and I will loose the loins of kings, to open before him the two leaved gates; and the gates shall not be shut;

2 I will go before thee, and make the crooked places straight: I will break in pieces the gates of brass, and cut in sunder the bars of iron:

3 And I will give thee the treasures of darkness, and hidden riches of secret places, that thou mayest know that I, the LORD, which call *thee* by thy name, *am* the God of Israel.

4 For Jacob my servant's sake, and Israel mine elect, I have even called thee by thy name: I have surnamed thee, though thou hast not known me.

45:1-4. The prophet Isaiah continues with an emphasis on the divine origination of his message: **Thus saith the LORD.** It is Jehovah God who will set an open gate of world conquest before Cyrus. The Persian king is called by the designation His **anointed** (*meshiyaḥ*, messiah or christ). This is the only place in Scripture where this title is used of a Gentile. It was normally used to designate priests (Lev 4:3-5), reigning kings (I Sam 24:6-10), and, in a metaphorical sense, the patriarchs (Ps 105:15). Kelley (p. 318) notes: "Oddly enough, it is never used in the Old Testament as a title for the future messianic king." The origin of the term certainly comes from the Israelite custom of anointing those who would assume positions of leadership in the nation with oil. The term is generally associated with the messianic expectation of the Jewish people. He shares this title in a symbolic and metaphoric sense as a deliverer of God's people from their Babylonian bondage. Though not generally mentioned in any commentary, it should also be observed that God's purpose in so designating Cyrus as being under His authority may well have been intended to keep the focus of the attention of His people upon the Lord Himself. Certainly, an event as startlingly wonderful as the return of the Judaean captives to their homeland by this Persian potentate could have easily caused the people to worship him, instead of their God. Thus, the prophet's predictive description of the coming warrior-king may well have served to help the Jews keep him in proper perspective as an underlord to the Lord God of Hosts. God further promises to **subdue nations before him** and certainly many fell under His control (e.g., Media, Assyria, Babylon, Lydia, etc.). (For a detailed history and account of the Persian Empire see R. Ghirshman, *Iran: The Story of Persia from Earliest Times;* A. T. Olmstead, *History of the Persian Empire;* G. Widengren, "The Persians," in *POTT*, pp. 312-357.) The statement **the gates shall not be shut** may have possible reference to Cyrus' relatively easy conquest of Babylon in 539 B.C. By an ingenious strategem, a Persian contingent diverted the course of the Euphrates River and thus entered the city via the dry river-bed and opened the gates to the main army from the inside. Thinking their city to be invincible and impregnable, the Babylonians were shocked and easily overrun. Seventeen days later, Cyrus himself entered the city in peace as a victorious conqueror, thus bringing an end to the Neo-Babylonian Empire. Verse 3 emphasizes that **I, the LORD** will perform this great conquest on Cyrus' behalf **For Jacob my servant's sake.** Both verse 3 and verse 4 emphasize that it is for this reason that **I have even called thee by thy name.** This would certainly reinforce the conservative view that Cyrus was named in advance by Isaiah the prophet himself. What purpose would there be to acknowledging a world conqueror by name after the fact? The LORD who has called Cyrus by his name identifies Himself as the **God of Israel.** The passage also makes it clear that Cyrus may have known His name, but that he **hast not known me.** This statement makes it clear that Cyrus was merely a tool used by God to accomplish His great purpose. The inscription on the *Cyrus Cylinder* attributes his successes to Marduk, the god of Babylon, whom he addresses as "my lord." (For an English translation, see *ANET*, p. 316; *POTT*, pp. 92-94.) That he acknowledged Yahweh as the legitimate God of the Israelites is also obvious as well. Thus, it is clear that he was not personally converted to true faith in the Lord. Nevertheless, he served as God's means of turning the direction of history at that time. Even the Greek historian, Herodotus, saw in his rise the turning point of all Greek history! F. F. Bruce, *Israel and the Nations* (p. 97) notes that he affected Near Eastern history for more than 1,500 years as a consequence of his actions. MacRae (p. 30) notes that the various statements about Cyrus bring out these basic facts: (1) God raised up Cyrus for His own purposes; (2) the great successes of this Persian king went beyond those of any previously known conqueror; (3) the coming of Cyrus was predicted by name far in advance; (4) Cyrus was to serve as both a temporary shepherd and messiah to God's people; and (5) God's purpose in blessing him was to make him an instrument for delivering Israel from the captivity and returning her to Jerusalem. Therefore, God is the author of both the destruction of Jerusalem and her subsequent deliverance. Whereas, Jeremiah speaks of the time of this deliverance (II Chr 36:21), Isaiah speaks of the agent of this deliverance who will be Cyrus, the king of Persia.

5-12. Again, the Lord proclaims His uniqueness in that there is **no God beside me.** The Old Testament message is not that Jehovah was one of the many gods of the nations of the ancient world, but that He was the One and the only God over the entire world. He is unique in that He alone can predict names in advance. The phrase **I . . . create evil** refers to physical evil or calamitous consequences, rather than moral evil. Young (III, p. 200) disagrees with Delitzsch in viewing this as sinful evil that is allowed to exist in the world by the *decretum absolutum* of God who has foreordained whatever comes to pass. However, he cautions that this must be viewed in light of the biblical teaching of the responsibility of the individual as well and warns against the extremes of both hyper-Calvinism and Arminianism. In either case, God is not to be viewed as the author of sin by any means. (On the doctrine of sin, see J. O. Buswell, "The Origin and Nature of Sin," in *Basic Christian Doctrines*, pp. 103-109; G. C. Berkouwer, *Sin: Studies in Dogmatics*). Verses 8-10 constitute a unit, with each verse beginning with the Hebrew letter, *H.* **Drop down, ye heavens, from above . . . pour down righteousness** is a prayer for God to intervene in human history. The imagery is that of a refreshing rain upon a fertile field, which causes it to spring forth abundantly. Hence, the prayer: **Let the earth open, and let them bring forth salvation, and let righteousness spring up together.** This wonderful picture is that of the blessing of God coming down from above and beneath simultaneously. It is concluded by the simple statement, **I the LORD have created it,** indicating that God is the source of spiritual refreshing. R. Sprauge, *Lectures on Revival*, took this as the key passage for his book. Two **Woes** are pronounced on those that reject the Lord. Those who would resist the will and work of God are pictured as **clay** resisting the potter (for a similar imagery, cf. Jer 18:6; Rom 9:20). Such rejection is as ridiculous as one questioning his father or mother as to why he (or she) had begotten him. Thus, God is pictured as **his Maker.** He challenges the unbeliever to **Ask me of things to come concerning my sons.** Thereby, He challenges the unbeliever to

5 I *am* the LORD, and *there is* none else, *there is* no God beside me: I girded thee, though thou hast not known me:

6 That they may know from the rising of the sun, and from the west, that *there is* none beside me. I *am* the LORD, and *there is* none else.

7 I form the light, and create darkness: I make peace, and create evil: I the LORD do all these *things.*

8 Drop down, ye heavens, from above, and let the skies pour down righteousness: let the earth open, and let them bring forth salvation, and let righteousness spring up together; I the LORD have created it.

9 Woe unto him that striveth with his Maker! *Let* the potsherd *strive* with the potsherds of the earth. Shall the clay say to him that fashioneth it, What makest thou? or thy work, He hath no hands?

10 Woe unto him that saith unto *his* father, What begettest thou? or to the woman, What hast thou brought forth?

11 Thus saith the LORD, the Holy One of Israel, and his Maker, Ask me of things to come concerning my sons, and concerning the work of my hands command ye me.

12 I have made the earth, and created man upon it: I, *even* my hands, have stretched out the heavens, and all their host have I commanded.

13 I have raised him up in righteousness, and I will direct all his ways: he shall build my city, and he shall let go my captives, not for price nor reward, saith the LORD of hosts.

14 Thus saith the LORD, The labour of Egypt, and merchandise of Ē-thī-ō′pĭ-a and of the Sa-bē′ans, men of stature, shall come over unto thee, and they shall be thine: they shall come after thee; in chains they shall come over, and they shall fall down unto thee, they shall make supplication unto thee, saying, Surely God is in thee; and there is none else, there is no God.

15 Verily thou art a God that hidest thyself, O God of Israel, the Saviour.

16 They shall be ashamed, and also confounded, all of them: they shall go to confusion together that are makers of idols.

17 But Israel shall be saved in the LORD with an everlasting salvation: ye shall not be ashamed nor confounded world without end.

18 For thus saith the LORD that created the heavens; God himself that formed the earth and made it; he hath established it, he created it not in vain, he formed it to be inhabited: I am the LORD; and there is none else.

19 I have not spoken in secret, in a dark place of the earth: I said not unto the seed of Jacob, Seek ye me in vain: I the LORD speak righteousness, I declare things that are right.

20 ¶Assemble yourselves and come; draw near together, ye that are escaped of the nations: they have no knowledge that set up the wood of their graven image, and pray unto a god that cannot save.

21 Tell ye, and bring them near; yea, let them take counsel together: who hath declared this from ancient time? who hath told it from that time? have not I the LORD? and there is no God else beside me; a just God and a Saviour; there is none beside me.

22 Look unto me, and be ye saved, all the ends of the earth: for I am God, and there is none else.

23 I have sworn by myself, the word is gone out of my mouth in righteousness, and shall not return, That unto me every knee shall bow, every tongue shall swear.

24 Surely, shall one say, in the LORD have I righteousness and strength: even to him shall men come; and all that are incensed against him shall be ashamed.

25 In the LORD shall all the seed of Israel be justified, and shall glory.

in turn challenge His ability to predict the future as it relates to His people. **Command ye me** is better translated "commit to me," following the normal idiomatic usage.

13-19. Cyrus is again addressed in verse 13 as the one who has been **raised . . . up in righteousness** and who **shall build my city,** and shall **let go my captives.** This does not imply that Cyrus is himself a believer, but that the fact that God has raised him up on the world scene is an act of His own righteousness. That Cyrus the Great was willing to subsidize the reconstruction of Jerusalem and its Temple without any monetary gain to himself is a fact of history. In essence, God has answered His own challenge to make a specific prediction about the future events that would affect His people. The passage then looks forward to a time when **Egypt . . . Ethiopia . . . the Sabeans** (Arabs) shall **fall down** and acknowledge that Jehovah is the only God. While this probably has its fullest and final application in the millennial kingdom, it should also be noted that there were extensive Christian churches established in these areas during the early centuries of church history. The profound truth of verse 15 is that God cannot be known apart from His revelation of Himself to man. Thus, He is a **God that hidest;** and yet, at the same time, He is **the Saviour.** The idol-worshipers are pictured as perishing, **But Israel shall be saved.** In spite of the coming Babylonian captivity, and the subsequent return of the Jews under the beneficent hand of Cyrus, there would still come an **everlasting salvation** to the Jews from the Messiah who would arise from among them. The purpose of God's creation is clearly stated to be the habitation of the earth and the salvation of mankind. God is clearly stated to be the Creator who **formed the earth and made it.** Throughout this passage, the main Hebrew verbs for creation are constantly used interchangeably (yoster, forming; 'asah, making; bara', creating).

20-25. God calls His people to **Assemble** themselves from among the **nations** (Gentiles) and return unto Him. The Lord is not only superior to the idols of **wood,** but He is the One who has **declared this from ancient time,** meaning that He is the One who can predict the future with the precision and accuracy that only the True God can do. Thus, He is both **a just God** and **a Saviour** to those who will come unto Him. His invitation is to all the peoples of the earth: **Look unto me, and be ye saved, all the ends of the earth: for I am God, and there is none else.** It was upon hearing a sermon preached upon this text that Charles Spurgeon, the famous English Baptist pastor, was converted. This glorious invitation is similar to that of Jesus, who said, "Come unto me, all ye that labor . . . and I will give you rest" (Mt 11:28). His gracious invitation is followed by the absolute statement that **unto me every knee shall bow, every tongue shall swear** (cf. Phil 2:10). God's promise is made **in righteousness** and shall not **return** (be reported of). Since the Lord God is the One who alone is the source of our salvation, we also may say, **in the LORD have I righteousness and strength.** See the enlightening study by N. H. Snaith, "The Righteousness of God" and "The Salvation of God," in The Distinctive Ideas of the Old Testament, pp. 51-93, where he notes that in Isaiah righteousness becomes synonymous with salvation. The chapter ends with the sweeping affirmation, **In the LORD shall all the seed of Israel be justified,** which is virtually quoted by the Apostle Paul in Romans 11:26. J. Murray, The Epistle to the Romans (II, p. 96ff.) concludes that this refers to the restoration of Israel to the gospel and is correlative to Israel turning from unbelief to faith. The spiritual heritage of Israel is the salvation of the Lord, and it is to that salvation that Israel herself shall return after her present era of unbelief. In fact, this has always been the pattern of her pilgrimage throughout her history. She comes to know the Lord and then as a nation tragically rejects Him, only to ultimately be captured afresh by Him.

3. Prophecy of Deliverance. 46:1-48:22.

46:1-4. Isaiah's prediction of deliverance for the people of Israel begins with a recognition of the supremacy of the Lord over the false gods of the nations. **Bel** and **Nebo** were the two most prominent deities in the Babylonian religious system. The name **Bel** is a derivative of Baal and signifies Marduk, the patron deity of Babylon. **Nebo** was the son of Bel/Marduk and was especially worshiped at Borsippa. His name is found in the name of Nebuchadnezzar, the great Babylonian king. The idea in this passage is that Babylonian religion shall fall in recognition before the Lord God. The description of their **idols** being carried away upon **beasts** and **carriages** may have reference to the attempt of the Babylonian people to flee from the coming Persian conquest. Whereas the heathen had to carry their gods, Jehovah was the One who carried His people. These reminders are especially significant in light of the fact that Isaiah wrote this passage prior to the Babylonian captivity. If that in fact is true, then it becomes clear that his purpose is to cause the people of Israel not to be swept away with the gods of Babylon, but to recognize that they too shall be taken into captivity, even as the children of Israel were. Reading this book long after the fact makes it difficult for us to imagine the tremendous pressure that must have been upon the Jews to forsake the worship of Jehovah and to accept the gods of their conquerors. Thus, it is that Isaiah declares that these gods themselves shall also fail to deliver their people.

5-13. Speaking through the prophet, God again continues His tirade against the gods of the nations. The rhetorical question, **To whom will ye liken me, and make me equal, and compare me?** implies the obvious answer—no one! This unseen God, who is not represented by any image, is superior to all the idol-gods of the gentile nations. These gods are nothing more than the product of the craftsman and the **goldsmith.** Their gods are nothing more than handmade images which must be borne **upon the shoulder.** They must be carried from place to place, whereas the God of Israel is the One who carries nations from place to place. God then answers His own question declaring, **I am God, and there is none else; I am God, and there is none like me.** He is the unique and incomprehensible, personal God. His uniqueness is found in His **Declaring the end from the beginning . . . the things that are not yet done.** Again, the strongest argument put forth for the reality of the Lord God and the proof of His singular distinctiveness is His ability to predict the future. Again and again, the book of Isaiah emphasizes the reality of predictive prophecy. In this book, prophecy is not viewed as human guesswork, nor history written after the fact; it is the unique revelation of the supernatural God of Israel. His predictions are associated with His **counsel** and His **pleasure.** Young (III, p. 227) notes: "He can thus predict the future for the future is the unfolding of what He has Himself already determined." Thus, He knows what He is going to do, because He alone controls what He is going to do. The Lord's **pleasure** is that which He pleases to do. In other words, history is the unfolding of His will. While the Bible recognizes the individual responsibility of man for his own actions, it also clearly teaches God's ability to overrule those actions to bring about His ultimate purposes. The **ravenous bird from the east** is undoubtedly Cyrus of Persia. In his own initiative to conquer the nations of the Near East, he is the one who comes from a **far country** to perform the will of God. By contrast, the **stouthearted** ("hardhearted") are those that are **far from righteousness.** Here, righteousness is again synonymous with salvation. There seems to be an obvious contrast between the conqueror that God shall

CHAPTER 46

BEL boweth down, Nebo stoopeth, their idols were upon the beasts, and upon the cattle: your carriages *were* heavy loaden; *they are* a burden to the weary beast.

2 They stoop, they bow down together; they could not deliver the burden, but themselves are gone into captivity.

3 ¶Hearken unto me, O house of Jacob, and all the remnant of the house of Israel, which are borne *by me* from the belly, which are carried from the womb:

4 And *even* to *your* old age I *am* he; and *even* to hoar hairs will I carry *you:* I have made, and I will bear; even I will carry, and will deliver *you.*

5 ¶To whom will ye liken me, and make *me* equal, and compare me, that we may be like?

6 They lavish gold out of the bag, and weigh silver in the balance, *and* hire a goldsmith; and he maketh it a god: they fall down, yea, they worship.

7 They bear him upon the shoulder, they carry him, and set him in his place, and he standeth; from his place shall he not remove: yea, *one* shall cry unto him, yet can he not answer, nor save him out of his trouble.

8 Remember this, and shew yourselves men: bring *it* again to mind, O ye transgressors.

9 Remember the former things of old: for I *am* God, and *there is* none else; I *am* God, and *there is* none like me,

10 Declaring the end from the beginning, and from ancient times *the things* that are not *yet* done, saying, My counsel shall stand, and I will do all my pleasure:

11 Calling a ravenous bird from the east, the man that executeth my counsel from a far country: yea, I have spoken *it,* I will also bring it to pass; I have purposed *it,* I will also do it.

12 ¶Hearken unto me, ye stouthearted, that *are* far from righteousness:

13 I bring near my righteousness; it shall not be far off, and my salvation shall not tarry: and I will place salvation in Zion for Israel my glory.

CHAPTER 47

COME down, and sit in the dust, O virgin daughter of Babylon, sit on the ground: *there is* no throne, O daughter of the Chăl-dē´anś: for thou shalt no more be called tender and delicate.

2 Take the millstones, and grind meal; uncover thy locks, make bare the leg, uncover the thigh, pass over the rivers.

3 Thy nakedness shall be uncovered, yea, thy shame shall be seen: I will take vengeance, and I will not meet *thee as a* man.

4 ¶*As for* our redeemer, the LORD of hosts *is* his name, the Holy One of Israel.

5 Sit thou silent, and get thee into darkness, O daughter of the Chăl-dē´anś: for thou shalt no more be called, The lady of kingdoms.

6 I was wroth with my people, I have polluted mine inheritance, and given them into thine hand: thou didst shew them no mercy; upon the ancient hast thou very heavily laid thy yoke.

7 And thou saidst, I shall be a lady for ever: *so* that thou didst not lay these *things* to thy heart, neither didst remember the latter end of it.

8 Therefore hear now this, *thou that art* given to pleasures, that dwellest carelessly, that sayest in thine heart, I *am,* and none else beside me; I shall not sit *as* a widow, neither shall I know the loss of children:

9 But these two *things* shall come to thee in a moment in one day, the loss of children, and widowhood: they shall come upon thee in their perfection for the multitude of thy sorceries, *and* for the great abundance of thine enchantments.

10 For thou hast trusted in thy wickedness: thou hast said, None seeth me. Thy wisdom and thy knowledge, it hath perverted thee; and thou hast said

bring from the **far country** and His salvation, which **shall not be far off** but is ever present to those who will receive it. Thus it is that the **salvation** of the Lord **shall not tarry,** but is always available to those that will seek Him. Compare this statement with that of Hebrews 10:37, "For yet a little while, and he that shall come will come, and will not tarry," as well as the similar statement in Habakkuk 2:3. The idea conveyed here is that while from man's perspective it may appear that the deliverance of God is tarrying (or waiting), in the timetable of God everything is being done with divine precision. To the eternal God, with whom all time is ever present, His deliverance **shall not tarry.**

47:1-6. The prophet Isaiah now sees a time when the imposing conqueror, Babylon, shall itself be deposed; and, thus, he pictures her as the **virgin daughter of Babylon** who can do no more than **sit in the dust.** This interesting use of terms reminds us that ancient Babylon, in spite of all its splendor, was in reality a kingdom built upon the dust of the desert of Shinar. **Chaldeans** were the elite ruling class of the Neo-Babylonian Empire. This passage represents a song of triumph over vanquished Babylon. Cast down from her imperial tower, she is reduced to the disgraceful status of a half-naked slave girl grinding meal with **millstones.** What is worse, she must **sit on the ground.** To not sit upon a chair was regarded in Babylon as a sign of degradation. Thus, the nation itself is illustrated by the imagery of a girl who is deposed from her throne and now functions as a slave girl. The commands to **uncover thy locks** (*tsammah,* tresses of hair) . . . **make bare the leg, uncover the thigh** are not to be taken as steps of intentional action, but rather the result of her captivity. Delitzsch (II, p. 238) states: "She has to leave her place as a prisoner of war, and, laying aside all feminine modesty, to wade through the rivers upon which she borders." **Thy nakedness shall be uncovered** clearly indicates that in the ancient world both the uncovered head and the uncovered leg were considered to be **nakedness.** That captive prisoners of war were often taken into captivity naked is well attested by ancient carvings and inscriptions (see *ANEP,* p. 285ff.). Such shame is coming upon Babylon that she shall no more be called **The lady** (mistress) **of kingdoms.** It is most certain that this imagery is the basis of viewing Babylon as the "great whore" in Revelation 18:3. Whereas, in the New Testament passage, Babylon is used as a symbol of gentile world powers, here it is to be taken with specific reference to the ancient kingdom itself. The prophet, speaking for God, further explains that he has only allowed Babylon to come to power and to conquer Judah because He was **wroth with my people.** Again, the reminder of Scripture was that Babylon has not come to power by herself, but by the divine permission of God Himself.

7-15. The unrepentant attitude of Babylon is that she will last forever as the "queen" of the ancient world. **I shall be a lady** (*gebareth,* mistress) **for ever.** While Alexander (II, p. 200) regards the rendering "queen" as being weak and favors the translation "mistress," it seems obvious from the context of the passage that she was in reality both! Therefore, because Babylon has been unwilling to take these matters **to . . . heart** and, instead, has been given to **pleasures,** she shall suffer the loss of **two things:** her children and her husband. In the ancient world it was considered the greatest of tragedies to be both widowed and childless. God is predicting that in the days ahead both conditions will come upon Babylon politically. In spite of her great prosperity as the queen of the ancient world, she shall be brought down into the dust as a young slave girl or as a widow who sits on the ground in shock and dismay. This great failure shall come in spite of the **abundance of thine enchantments.** Babylonian religion was replete with **sorceries . . . astrologers . . . stargazers . . . prognosticators** who claimed to be able to

in thine heart, I *am*, and none else beside me.

11 Therefore shall evil come upon thee; thou shalt not know from whence it riseth: and mischief shall fall upon thee; thou shalt not be able to put it off: and desolation shall come upon thee suddenly, *which* thou shalt not know.

12 Stand now with thine enchantments, and with the multitude of thy sorceries, wherein thou hast laboured from thy youth; if so be thou shalt be able to profit, if so be thou mayest prevail.

13 Thou art wearied in the multitude of thy counsels. Let now the astrologers, the stargazers, the monthly prognosticators, stand up, and save thee from *these things* that shall come upon thee.

14 Behold, they shall be as stubble; the fire shall burn them; they shall not deliver themselves from the power of the flame: *there shall* not *be* a coal to warm at, *nor* fire to sit before it.

15 Thus shall they be unto thee with whom thou hast laboured, *even* thy merchants, from thy youth: they shall wander every one to his quarter; none shall save thee.

CHAPTER 48

HEAR ye this, O house of Jacob, which are called by the name of Israel, and are come forth out of the waters of Jūʹdah, which swear by the name of the LORD, and make mention of the God of Israel, *but* not in truth, nor in righteousness.

2 For they call themselves of the holy city, and stay themselves upon the God of Israel; The LORD of hosts *is* his name.

3 I have declared the former things from the beginning; and they went forth out of my mouth, and I shewed them; I did *them* suddenly, and they came to pass.

4 Because I knew that thou *art* obstinate, and thy neck *is* an iron sinew, and thy brow brass;

5 I have even from the beginning declared *it* to thee; before it came to pass I shewed *it* thee: lest thou shouldest say, Mine idol hath done them, and my graven image, and my molten image, hath commanded them.

6 Thou hast heard, see all this; and will not ye declare *it?* I have shewed thee new things from this time, even hidden things, and thou didst not know them.

7 They are created now, and not from the beginning; even before the day when thou heardest them not; lest thou shouldest say, Behold, I knew them.

8 Yea, thou heardest not; yea, thou knewest not; yea, from that time *that* thine ear was not opened: for I knew that thou wouldest deal very treacherously, and wast called a transgressor from the womb.

9 ¶For my name's sake will I defer mine anger, and for my praise will I refrain for thee, that I cut thee not off.

10 Behold, I have refined thee, but not with silver; I have chosen thee in the furnace of affliction.

11 For mine own sake, *even* for mine own sake, will I do *it:* for how should

tell the future from the astrological times of the stars. The culture of ancient Babylon included both the science of astronomy and the religion of astrology. (On the nature of Babylonian religion, see H. W. F. Saggs, *The Greatness That Was Babylon*, pp. 288-341.) Because of the pagan origin of astrology, it should be obvious to Christians that its concepts and practice have no place in true Christianity. Those who are worried about their astrological signs would do better to come to personal faith in the God of the heavens!

48:1-11. This message is addressed to the **house of Jacob** in its totality, which includes both **Israel** and **Judah**. Here God admonishes the hypocrites among His people who **make mention of the God of Israel** (i.e., give lip service to Him) but do not follow **in truth, nor in righteousness** (i.e., are not really saved). He proceeds to say that they both call themselves by His name and by that of the **holy city**, but in reality their heart is far from Him. In spite of their seeming piety, many of these Israelites practiced idolatry on the side, and thus it is that the Lord reminds them again of His ability to predict the future lest they attribute their success to their own **idol** or their **graven image**. Because the Lord is the one true God, He alone can reveal the **former things . . . new things . . . hidden things.** In spite of His prediction of coming judgment, God reminds them that only the true and living God could predict such a deportation to Babylon more than a hundred years in advance. Archer (p. 643) notes: "No human being, not even a demon-inspired devotee of idols, can accurately and specifically foretell events that far ahead." The meaning of verses 7 and 8 is (in essence) that God is telling the Jewish people that He knew even before He called them **from the womb** that they would sin against Him in spite of His great prophetic prediction. Fitch (p. 596) translates: "You have heard: you now see it before your eyes: why will you not admit and confess that this is indeed the act of Jehovah?" In spite of all the tragic judgments that will come upon Judah and Israel, God reminds them **I have chosen** (tried) **thee in the furnace of affliction.** We are here reminded that even God's acts of judgment are ultimately acts of mercy. The reason for His severe treatment of His people is that they might emerge from their afflictions minus the dross of their sin and that they might reflect His glory and greatness among them. Thus, this chapter is a celebration of divine mercy which always determines the activity of God on the behalf of His people. Though they deserve to be obliterated from the face of the earth, nevertheless, He will preserve them.

my name be polluted? and I will not give my glory unto another.

12 ¶Hearken unto me, O Jacob and Israel, my called; I *am* he; I *am* the first, I also *am* the last.

13 Mine hand also hath laid the foundation of the earth, and my right hand hath spanned the heavens: *when* I call unto them, they stand up together.

14 All ye, assemble yourselves, and hear; which among them hath declared these *things?* The LORD hath loved him: he will do his pleasure on Babylon, and his arm *shall be on* the Chăl-dē′anś.

15 I, *even* I, have spoken; yea, I have called him: I have brought him, and he shall make his way prosperous.

16 ¶Come ye near unto me, hear ye this; I have not spoken in secret from the beginning; from the time that it was, there *am* I: and now the Lord GOD, and his Spirit, hath sent me.

17 Thus saith the LORD, thy Redeemer, the Holy One of Israel; I *am* the LORD thy God which teacheth thee to profit, which leadeth thee by the way *that* thou shouldest go.

18 O that thou hadst hearkened to my commandments! then had thy peace been as a river and thy righteousness as the waves of the sea:

19 Thy seed also had been as the sand, and the offspring of thy bowels like the gravel thereof; his name should not have been cut off nor destroyed from before me.

20 ¶Go ye forth of Babylon, flee ye from the Chăl-dē′anś, with a voice of singing declare ye, tell this, utter it *even* to the end of the earth; say ye, The LORD hath redeemed his servant Jacob.

21 And they thirsted not *when* he led them through the deserts: he caused the waters to flow out of the rock for them: he clave the rock also, and the waters gushed out.

22 *There is* no peace, saith the LORD, unto the wicked.

12-22. Both **Jacob and Israel** are referred to as **my called** (chosen). In spite of all their failures, God reminds them that He has called them and chosen them to be His people. Further, God states that with His own **hand** He laid the **foundation of the earth** and has **spanned the heavens.** His omniscient power over the creation is such that when He calls nature to obedience, both heaven and earth **stand up together** (that is, they literally obey Him instantly). This assemblage of nature shall be shocked by God's persistent love for the Jewish people. And it is because of this simple fact that **The LORD hath loved him** (Israel) that He shall bring judgment (His pleasure) on **Babylon** and the **Chaldeans.** Just as God's message of the faithful pledge of His love to His people was one of encouragement to Israel in the Old Testament, so it is a promise of blessing to the New Testament church as well. Because all of us are sinners, we deserve the wrath of God against our sins; and yet, all of nature stands in awe of the fact that He loves us! He will not allow us to be destroyed, even though destruction is what we deserve. Notice the distinction in verse 16 between **the Lord GOD and his Spirit,** implying that while they are One, they are not one and the same. Several titles are used for God in verse 17. He is recognized as **the LORD** (*Yahweh*), **thy Redeemer** (*go'al*), **the Holy One of Israel** (*quedōsh yisra'el*). It is He who teaches them to **profit** (both spiritually and financially). In harmony with the teaching of the book of Proverbs, Isaiah emphasizes the total blessing of prosperity from God upon those who have surrendered to His Lordship and authority. However, this blessing does not come by accident, but only by obedience to his **commandments.** This obedience will bring **peace . . . as a river** and **righteousness as the waves of the sea,** meaning that the blessing of God would continually flow in their direction. Because of God's love for His people, they shall not be **cut off** from the face of the earth. He has promised them an eternal inheritance, and they shall receive it. **Go ye forth of Babylon** is a promise to the Israelites of their future deliverance. Again, we note the distinctive characteristic of Isaiah's style in which he announces impending judgment and immediately follows that announcement with a ray of hope for future blessing. He has clearly predicted the coming Babylonian invasion of Judah and their subsequent captivity. Now he looks beyond that captivity to their release and their return which shall result in the redemption of **Jacob.** Though His people may come under temporary judgment, they still have access to the God of peace. By contrast, however, **There is no peace . . . unto the wicked.** To those who turn their back on God, there is only worry and vexation. True peace comes only from one source: God Himself, the Lord of peace!

B. Prince of Peace. 49:1-57:21.

In this section of Isaiah's prophecy two words become predominant: servant and salvation. Kaiser (p. 215) notes that the corporate figure of the "servant" is already observable in the use of the form twenty times in Isaiah 40-53 and in the plural form ten times in Isaiah 54-66. He observes: "To demonstrate that the servant is a collective term as well as an individual term representing the whole group can be done from two sets of data: (1) the servant is all Israel in twelve out of twenty singular references (41:8-10; 43:8-13; 43:14-44:5; 44:6-8, 21-23; 44:24-45:13; 48:1, 7, 10-12, 17); (2) The four great servant songs of Isaiah (42:1-7; 49:1-6; 50:4-9; 52:13-53:12) all present the Servant as an individual who ministers to Israel. Therein lies one of the greatest puzzles of those scholars who reject corporate solidarity of the Servant." He further notes that in the four Servant Songs many of the individual's titles or descriptions are matched by identical ascriptions made of Israel in the Isaianic poems, for example:

as with sweet wine: and all flesh shall know that I the LORD *am* thy Saviour and thy Redeemer, the mighty One of Jacob.

CHAPTER 50

THUS saith the LORD, Where *is* the bill of your mother's divorcement, whom I have put away? or which of my creditors *is it* to whom I have sold you? Behold, for your iniquities have ye sold yourselves, and for your transgressions is your mother put away.

2 Wherefore, when I came, *was there* no man? when I called, *was there* none to answer? Is my hand shortened at all, that it cannot redeem? or have I no power to deliver? behold, at my rebuke I dry up the sea, I make the rivers a wilderness: their fish stinketh, because *there is* no water, and dieth for thirst.

3 I clothe the heavens with blackness, and I make sackcloth their covering.

4 ¶The Lord GOD hath given me the tongue of the learned, that I should know how to speak a word in season to *him that is* weary: he wakeneth morning by morning, he wakeneth mine ear to hear as the learned.

5 The Lord GOD hath opened mine ear, and I was not rebellious, neither turned away back.

6 I gave my back to the smiters, and my cheeks to them that plucked off the hair: I hid not my face from shame and spitting.

7 For the Lord GOD will help me; therefore shall I not be confounded: therefore have I set my face like a flint, and I know that I shall not be ashamed.

8 *He is* near that justifieth me; who will contend with me? let us stand together: who *is* mine adversary? let him come near to me.

9 Behold, the Lord GOD will help me; who *is* he *that* shall condemn me? lo, they all shall wax old as a garment; the moth shall eat them up.

10 ¶Who *is* among you that feareth the LORD, that obeyeth the voice of his servant, that walketh *in* darkness, and hath no light? let him trust in the name of the LORD, and stay upon his God.

11 Behold, all ye that kindle a fire, that compass *yourselves* about with sparks: walk in the light of your fire, and in the sparks *that* ye have kindled. This shall ye have of mine hand; ye shall lie down in sorrow.

50:1-11. This chapter begins with an emphasis on the Lord's unbreakable commitment of spiritual "marriage" to His people, Israel. The question **Where is the bill of your mother's divorcement?** is rhetorical, and the answer implied is that there is none. This should be seen in contrast with Jeremiah 3:8, where the Lord clearly states that He divorced Israel and threatens to do the same to Judah. However, in light of Isaiah's statement (though made at an earlier time), it would appear that God never actually divorced the Davidic kingdom. Though they have **sold** themselves and attempted to **put away** (divorce) themselves, God's love for them is still faithful. He who can miraculously deal with nature can also **deliver** (save) those who will trust in Him. Four times in these verses the Servant uses the designation **the Lord GOD** ('*adonay Yahweh*), at the beginning of verses 4, 5, 7, and 9. The majestic emphasis of this designation is to call the reader's attention to the fact that it is this God who has "clothed the heavens" that shall empower his servant. **The tongue of the learned** implies "educated" as well as wise, in that he will be able to **speak a word in season** to those who are **weary**. The meaning of this passage is that God Himself shall so equip His Servant, the Messiah, that He shall speak as an educated scholar and at the same time shall speak with the practical ability to meet the needs of people. It should not surprise us, therefore, that in the New Testament the scribes and Pharisees were "astonished" at Jesus' speaking abilities. The chapter is heightened by the definite prophecy of Christ's suffering which would occur at the time of His crucifixion. **I gave my back to the smiters** is quoted in Matthew 27:26 in relation to the scourging which Christ received outside Pilate's hall. **My cheeks to them that plucked off the hair** refers to their plucking out the hair of His beard. The reference to **spitting** in His face is certainly verified in Matthew 26:67 in relation to Jesus. Here, the Servant is again personified as an individual; and it cannot refer to the nation as a whole. Even to the amillennial commentator, the passage cannot refer to the church. It must refer to the only One who endured such suffering, and that One is Jesus Christ! This is one of the clearest prophecies of the Old Testament (along with that of ch. 53) of the death of Christ to be found anywhere in the Bible. In spite of the great suffering that lies ahead of Him, the Servant will not turn back because He has set His **face like a flint** (a description used of Christ in Lk 9:51) toward this goal. This passage throws light on the New Testament statement that He set his face "toward Jerusalem," helping us understand that it was not His determination to go to the geographical location that so beset Him, but His willingness to go to the place of crucifixion and thus fulfill the plan of God. None shall be able to stand with Him at that time, for it is the Lord God who **justifieth** (*matsediyq iy*, my justifier) Him. Young (III, p. 302) notes that "justify" is used in strictly a forensic sense, just as in the New Testament, where it means to "declare to be just." In light of God's severe accusations against Israel because of her sin, it would seem that she is not a candidate for this task. Only the Messiah who comes forth from Israel in His sinlessness can be pronounced "just" in and of Himself and, thereby, become the Justifier of those who would **trust in the . . . LORD.** By contrast, those who would find confidence and warmth in the fires of this world shall **lie down in sorrow** or go to the grave in hopelessness. On the other hand, those who trust in the justification of the Servant of the Lord shall have hope of everlasting life.

CHAPTER 51

HEARKEN to me, ye that follow after righteousness, ye that seek the Lord: look unto the rock *whence* ye are hewn, and to the hole of the pit *whence* ye are digged.

2 Look unto Abraham your father, and unto Sarah *that* bare you: for I called him alone, and blessed him, and increased him.

3 For the Lord shall comfort Zion: he will comfort all her waste places; and he will make her wilderness like Eden, and her desert like the garden of the Lord; joy and gladness shall be found therein, thanksgiving, and the voice of melody.

4 ¶Hearken unto me, my people; and give ear unto me, O my nation: for a law shall proceed from me, and I will make my judgment to rest for a light of the people.

5 My righteousness *is* near; my salvation is gone forth, and mine arms shall judge the people; the isles shall wait upon me, and on mine arm shall they trust.

6 Lift up your eyes to the heavens, and look upon the earth beneath: for the heavens shall vanish away like smoke, and the earth shall wax old like a garment, and they that dwell therein shall die in like manner: but my salvation shall be for ever, and my righteousness shall not be abolished.

7 ¶Hearken unto me, ye that know righteousness, the people in whose heart *is* my law; fear ye not the reproach of men, neither be ye afraid of their revilings.

8 For the moth shall eat them up like a garment, and the worm shall eat them like wool: but my righteousness shall be for ever, and my salvation from generation to generation.

9 ¶Awake, awake, put on strength, O arm of the Lord; awake, as in the ancient days, in the generations of old. *Art* thou not it that hath cut Rahab, *and* wounded the dragon?

10 *Art* thou not it which hath dried the sea, the waters of the great deep; that hath made the depths of the sea a way for the ransomed to pass over?

11 Therefore the redeemed of the Lord shall return, and come with singing unto Zion; and everlasting joy *shall be* upon their head: they shall obtain gladness and joy; *and* sorrow and mourning shall flee away.

12 I, *even* I, *am* he that comforteth you: who *art* thou, that thou shouldest be afraid of a man *that* shall die, and of the son of man *which* shall be made *as* grass;

13 And forgettest the Lord thy maker, that hath stretched forth the heavens, and laid the foundations of the earth; and hast feared continually every day because of the fury of the oppressor, as if he were ready to destroy? and where *is* the fury of the oppressor?

14 The captive exile hasteneth that he may be loosed, and that he should

2. His compassion. 51:1-53:12.

51:1-8. In emphasizing His love to His people, God reminds them to **look unto the rock whence ye are hewn.** That rock is associated with **Abraham your father** in verse 2. By contrast, **the hole of the pit whence ye are digged** must refer to the inauspicious circumstances from which they were called to nationhood. God makes it clear that Israel has been blessed because He **called him . . . blessed him . . . increased him.** (from *rabah*, to enlarge to greatness). Because of God's covenant with Abraham, He will ultimately bless Israel and **comfort Zion.** Notice the parallel between **waste places . . . wilderness . . . desert** which shall be **like Eden.** By contrast to desolation, He shall bring such abundant blessing that it shall result in **joy . . . gladness . . . thanksgiving . . . melody.** God specifies the Jewish people as **my nation,** emphasizing their special and unique relationship to Him. But it shall extend beyond them, as well; for now the peoples of the nations and the **isles** are also called *'amiy.* Verse 6 makes it clear that there is coming a day when the **heavens shall vanish away . . . and the earth.** Isaiah sees through the corridor of human history to a time when the heavens (atmospheric) and the earth shall be no more. He likens the earth to an **old . . . garment,** meaning that the earth would literally wear out (a fact which is borne out by the second law of thermodynamics). The inhabitants of the earth **shall die in like manner,** indicating the frailty of human life apart from God who is the source of all life. By contrast, His **salvation shall be for ever.** Again, notice that salvation is used in parallel with **righteousness.** The righteous are those **people in whose heart is my law.** The **law** here refers to God's moral law, which is the standard by which He shall judge the nations of the earth. All those who submit to Him through faith and trust in His grace shall experience His salvation, which shall be longer lasting than the temporal heavens and earth. Thus it is that His **righteousness** and his **salvation** shall endure **from generation to generation** (i.e., **for ever**).

9-16. Like the psalmist, the prophet urges that God **awake, as in the ancient days.** This is not to imply that God is asleep, but that his endurance has reached an end; and in desperation he is calling upon the Lord to intervene in the affairs of men. **Rahab** (broad expanse) and **dragon** (*tannin,* monster, often refers to the crocodile) are used in symbols for Egypt and are also associated with the power of God over chaos in the creation. The translation in the AV is unfortunate and implies an almost mythological connotation. In reality, the text is merely indicating that God is the One who has "cut" and "wounded" Egypt and **dried . . . the waters of the great deep** in the process of delivering His people from bondage. They are the **ransomed** and **redeemed** ones who shall return **with singing unto Zion.** The imagery here bears the idea that just as God delivered His people from Egypt with a mighty miraculous hand that dried up the Red Sea, so will He redeem them from Babylon (by implication) or any other nation to which they have been dispersed; and they shall be gathered again to His holy land. **Everlasting joy** (*simechath,* to rejoice with all one's heart and soul) **shall be upon their head** (an idiomatic phrase for characteristic of). The idea in this statement is that God's people shall be so blessed by His action on their behalf that joy shall characterize their very being, and as a result **mourning shall flee away.** Therefore, there is no reason for His people to be afraid of **man** or the **son of man,** referring to human beings. The contrast is drawn between fearing mortal man and fearing one's Creator. The implication of verse 13 is that when one does not remember who

not die in the pit, nor that his bread should fail.

15 But I *am* the LORD thy God, that divided the sea, whose waves roared: The LORD of hosts *is* his name.

16 And I have put my words in thy mouth, and I have covered thee in the shadow of mine hand, that I may plant the heavens, and lay the foundations of the earth, and say unto Zion, Thou *art* my people.

17 ¶Awake, awake, stand up, O Jerusalem, which hast drunk at the hand of the LORD the cup of his fury; thou hast drunken the dregs of the cup of trembling, *and* wrung *them* out.

18 *There is* none to guide her among all the sons *whom* she hath brought forth; neither *is there any* that taketh her by the hand of all the sons *that* she hath brought up.

19 These two *things* are come unto thee; who shall be sorry for thee? desolation, and destruction, and the famine, and the sword: by whom shall I comfort thee?

20 Thy sons have fainted, they lie at the head of all the streets, as a wild bull in a net: they are full of the fury of the LORD, the rebuke of thy God.

21 ¶Therefore hear now this, thou afflicted, and drunken, but not with wine:

22 Thus saith thy Lord the LORD, and thy God *that* pleadeth the cause of his people, Behold, I have taken out of thine hand the cup of trembling, *even* the dregs of the cup of my fury; thou shalt no more drink it again:

23 But I will put it into the hand of them that afflict thee; which have said to thy soul, Bow down, that we may go over: and thou hast laid thy body as the ground, and as the street, to them that went over.

CHAPTER 52

AWAKE, awake; put on thy strength, O Zion; put on thy beautiful garments, O Jerusalem, the holy city: for henceforth there shall no more come into thee the uncircumcised and the unclean.

2 Shake thyself from the dust; arise, *and* sit down, O Jerusalem: loose thyself from the bands of thy neck, O captive daughter of Zion.

3 For thus saith the LORD, Ye have sold yourselves for nought; and ye shall be redeemed without money.

4 For thus saith the Lord GOD, My people went down aforetime into Egypt to sojourn there; and the Assyrian oppressed them without cause.

5 Now therefore, what have I here, saith the LORD, that my people is taken away for nought? they that rule over them make them to howl, saith the LORD; and my name continually every day *is* blasphemed.

6 Therefore my people shall know my name: therefore *they shall know* in that day that I *am* he that doth speak: behold, *it is* I.

God really is and what He has done, he will always fear men, rather than Him. The **oppressor** who is ready **to destroy** is ultimately Satan. The rhetorical question, **where is the fury of the oppressor?** implies that it is nowhere. It has disappeared! For **captive exile** read "He that is bowed down" (as a slave) shall be **loosed** (set free). Who is He that can set the captives free? It is no other than **the LORD thy God,** the One who has conquered nature itself and, thereby, delivered His people. He is the One who is the source of the prophet's inspiration. **I have put my words in thy mouth** certainly implies a plenary and verbal inspiration of the prophet, whose message came from God Himself.

17-23. God calls **Jerusalem** to **awake** from her spiritual drunkenness. While she has fallen away from the Lord, she has become drunk on the **cup of his fury.** The idea of the passage is not that God has made her drunk, but that her sin has brought about her spiritual drunkenness, which has resulted in the judgment of God upon her. So staggered is she in her condition that she cannot walk, and there is **none to guide her.** Because of her sin **desolation, and destruction, and the famine, and the sword** have all come upon her. In light of this great devastation, God asked the question: **by whom shall I comfort thee?** They are unable to help themselves as a result of their devastation, and they are **as a wild bull** (*oryx*) who has been caught in the net of their own frustration. However, this contrast sets the stage for God to announce that He considers the Captivity sufficient penalty for Israel and that a new era of forgiveness and blessing is about to dawn upon them. **Therefore hear now this** is stated to get their attention. The Israelites are said to be **drunken, but not with wine,** meaning that they are **drunken** or intoxicated by their own sins. God announces that, though He is the One who has poured out His **cup of . . . fury** upon them, they shall not have to drink of it again because He is the One that **pleadeth the cause** (from the root *rūb*, to contend or debate) **of his people.** The term is a legal one and identifies the Lord as the advocate, or defense attorney, for His people. Notice that the verse interchangeably uses the three common designations for God: *Adonay, Yahweh, Elohim,* each appearing the one after the other consecutively in the Hebrew text. God makes it clear that He will no longer allow His people to be trodden underfoot, but shall raise them up in an hour of glorious victory.

52:1-6. The theme of God's deliverance for His people is now developed and reaches its greatest extent in the introduction of the Servant of the Lord who shall suffer for the sins of His people that they might be forgiven by God. The pinnacle of **Zion** is told to **put on thy strength,** and the city of **Jerusalem** is told to put on her **beautiful garments** (robes). She shall no longer be a servant girl, trodden underfoot by the gentile nations; but she shall once again be **the holy city.** The prophet foresees the time in the Millennium when the **uncircumcised and the unclean** (unsaved) shall no longer enter into the city of God. Thus, He tells her to shake the **dust** of her captivity off her and recognize that she sold herself **for nought,** that is, she had sold herself into sin and had profited nothing thereby. By contrast, God promises that she shall be **redeemed without money.** The Old Testament concept of redemption is based on the person of the redeemer (*go'el*) who had to be a free man himself, who was related by the flesh (a kinsman), and who was willing to pay the price of redemption in order to redeem one from slavery, orphanhood, or widowhood. In the book of Ruth we find this concept as it was practiced in the ancient agrarian culture of Israel illustrated. In the New Testament we see it fulfilled in the redemption which shall be accomplished by Jesus Christ who has become our Kinsman-Redeemer by means of His incarnation and His atonement. The imagery of the statement here by the prophet is that God sold His people into captivity for nothing and shall redeem them without money as well. God points out in verse 4 that their captivity in both **Egypt** and under the **Assyrian** was unprovoked. That is, the Jews did not deliberately incite the provocation of the Egyptians or the Assyrians; they had provoked the Lord because of their sin, and in turn God had used those nations as His instrument of judgment against His own people. Because of this God observes that His **name continually every day is blasphemed.** The nations have berated Him because of the failure of His people, and even the Jews themselves have questioned His care of them. Because of this, the Lord states that He will deliver His people, not because they deserve it, but for His own name's sake.

7-12. As the passage moves on to greater heights, the time of desolation begins to fade into oblivion in light of the glory which shall come. The reference to the **beautiful . . . feet of him that bringeth good tidings** is certainly familiar from the New Testament (Rom 10:15; Eph 6:15). **Tidings** (*mebaser*) means to "preach or carry good news." It certainly anticipates the gospel (good news) of the New Testament. The good news of God's message is that of **peace** (*shalōm*) and **salvation** (*yeshūʻah,* the basis of the name Joshua or Jesus). In contrast to the degradation that Israel had known under its foreign captors, they would come to the final realization that **Thy God reigneth!** Instead of announcing a message of impending judgment or doom, the **watchmen** shall lift up their voices and **sing** praises unto the King of Zion who has delivered His people. **The Lord shall bring again Zion** means that He shall bring the people of Israel back into their own land. Thus, all the people shall **break forth into joy,** singing praises unto the God who has **redeemed Jerusalem.** The salvation of God is illustrated by the Lord making **bare his holy arm** (rolling up His sleeves) in order to deliver His people before the nations of all the earth. No longer shall His people be downtrodden by their sins, but they shall be sanctified and march in victory. **The Lord,** who is the source of their strength, will both go **before** them and shall also be their **rearward.** The idea here is that God shall both march before His people and behind them as the total provision for their protection.

7

7 ¶How beautiful upon the mountains are the feet of him that bringeth good tidings, that publisheth peace; that bringeth good tidings of good, that publisheth salvation; that saith unto Zion, Thy God reigneth!

8 Thy watchmen shall lift up the voice; with the voice together shall they sing: for they shall see eye to eye, when the Lord shall bring again Zion.

9 Break forth into joy, sing together, ye waste places of Jerusalem: for the Lord hath comforted his people, he hath redeemed Jerusalem.

10 The Lord hath made bare his holy arm in the eyes of all the nations; and all the ends of the earth shall see the salvation of our God.

11 ¶Depart ye, depart ye, go ye out from thence, touch no unclean *thing;* go ye out of the midst of her; be ye clean, that bear the vessels of the Lord.

12 For ye shall not go out with haste, nor go by flight: for the Lord will go before you; and the God of Israel *will be* your rereward.

13 ¶Behold, my servant shall deal prudently, he shall be exalted and extolled, and be very high.

14 As many were astonied at thee; his visage was so marred more than any man, and his form more than the sons of men:

15 So shall he sprinkle many nations; the kings shall shut their mouths at him: for *that* which had not been told them shall they see; and *that* which they had not heard shall they consider.

13-15. Because of the chapter divisions which the Authorized Version followed, this passage stands at the end of chapter 52. Actually, it goes with chapter 53. The subject of both passages is the **servant** of the Lord, individualized here as the Messiah who shall come to suffer for our sins. He is the new David who comes to reestablish the Davidic line as the King of Israel. He is the same One who is the miraculously born Son of the Virgin, Immanuel, God with us. He is the Branch who springs up out of the stump of the Davidic line. He is the Holy One of Israel Himself. He would bring in a New Exodus and a New Redemption for the people of Israel. This Servant would personally rule the world and yet be the One to suffer on behalf of all humanity. Though coming in the form of a humble Servant, He will be **exalted and extolled, and be very high.** The combination of *rūm* (to exalt) and *nasa'* (to lift up) is intransitive and refers to the same subject. This unusual designation is found only in Isaiah 33:10 and here, but nowhere else in the Prophets. This exaltation is not merely limited to His prosperity, but it also refers to an exaltation of spiritual glory. The verbs represent a stative force, with a modifying adverb, thus pointing to a final stage of exaltation. Thus, He will not remain in the period of humiliation which is described here, but shall rise above it (cf. Phil 2:9-11; Acts 3:13, 26). The threefold emphasis of His exaltation is to underscore its magnitude and certitude. While it may contain a veiled reference to His resurrection, ascension, and sitting at the right hand of the Father, it certainly embodies all of that. Young (III, pp. 336-338) notes that the construction of verse 14 involves that of a statement (protasis) followed by a parenthetical observation, followed by another parenthesis, and a final apodosis. He suggests the following arrangement:

Protasis: "even as many were astonished at thee"
Parenthesis: (so was His appearance disfigured from men, and his form from the sons of men)
Second Parenthesis: (so shall He sprinkle many nations)
Apodosis: kings shall shut their mouths at Him, etc.

There seems to be a deliberate contrast between the **many** who are **astonished** (astonied) and the **kings** who shall **shut their mouths at him.** The idea here is that both the common man, as well as the great potentate, shall stand speechless and in awe of Him. Thus, Christ emerges as the great King of His people. His **visage** refers to His appearance (or face), which would become so **marred** (disfigured) in His beatings and scourgings that He would be virtually unrecognizable. The verb **shall he sprinkle** (*yezeh* comes from the root *nazah*, meaning to squirt or sprinkle in the sense of expiation) is a technical term found in the Mosaic law for the sprinkling of blood as a cleansing or purifying rite (see Vriezen, p. 204). For examples of sprinkling both water and blood ceremonially, see Leviticus 4:6; 8:11; 14:7. This was the activity of the priest in order to obtain ceremonial purification. It has no reference to the idea of sprinkling infants (or adults) with water as the New Testament rite of baptism. The waters of baptism do not cleanse or purify; they merely identify the believer with his Saviour. (On the nature and significance of New Testament baptism, see G. R. Beasley—Murray, *Baptism in the New Testament;* A. Gilmore, *Christian Baptism;* R. E. O White, *Biblical Doctrine of Initiation.*) Young (III, p. 338-339) states: "The purpose of the sprinkling was not decontamination, but to obtain ritual purity; hence the one who does the sprinkling must himself be pure and innocent. It is the work of a priest that is here set forth, and the purpose of this work is to bring purification and cleansing to others." Therefore, the Servant of the Lord is viewed as our High Priest who offers the ultimate sacrifice of Himself which shall astonish the world, but expiate the wrath of God. It is interesting to observe that those who are so quick to deny the messianic and Christological interpretation of this passage as something unthinkable—that God would demand the sacrifice of His Son—are, nevertheless, at the same time, those who are quick to view Israel as the Suffering Servant in His stead. In other words, they are more willing to see a nation suffering these atrocities in order to somehow "atone" for the sins of the world, rather than recognizing that there is only One who can mediate between God and man—Christ Jesus! It is in His substitutionary and expiatory atonement that purification is possible to mankind. (On the necessity of the death of Christ as the means of atonement, see J. Denney, *The Death of Christ;* R. Lightner, *The Death Christ Died;* J. Owen, *The Death of Death.* On the nature and extent of the atonement, see G. Smeaton, *The Atonement According to Christ and His Apostles;* L. Morris, "The Atonement," in *Basic Christian Doctrine,* pp. 152-157.)

Before this Suffering Servant, the nations of the world are rendered speechless as they observe this almost unbelievable demonstration of God's love. They stand in reverent awe before the divine Son of God Who "loved them and gave himself for them." These are they who were not the people of God, but the Gentiles (*gōyim*). It is no wonder that a gentile believer has written that great hymn, "There is a Fountain Filled with Blood, drawn from Immanuel's veins, and sinners plunged beneath that flood, lose all their guilty stains! "

CHAPTER 53

WHO hath believed our report? and to whom is the arm of the LORD revealed?

53:1. In the prophecies of Isaiah the Servant of the Lord represents both all Israel, as well as an individual Messiah who ministers to Israel and who atones for the sins of the Gentiles. In this passage we see the personal Messiah who alone can atone for sin. His message is rejected (vs. 1); His person is refused (vs. 2); and His mission is misunderstood (vs. 3). Nevertheless, His vicarious suffering would bring atonement between God and man (vss. 4-6); and though He would suffer (vs. 7) death (vs. 8) and burial (vs. 9), He would ultimately be exalted (vss. 10-12). Kaiser (p. 217) notes: "The result of the Servant's suffering was that the 'seed' would 'possess the nations'; for their tent would be enlarged, the ropes lengthened, and the pegs driven in deeper (54:2-3). Yahweh would then be 'the God of the whole earth' (54:5; 49:6)." (The expositions of this passage are many; and in addition to the standard commentaries, the reader should consult D. Baron, *The Servant of Jehovah;* J. Brown, *The Sufferings and Glories of the Messiah;* R. D. Culver, *The Sufferings and the Glory of the Lord's Righteous Servant;* T. W. Manson, *The Servant Messiah.* For a liberal perspective, see H. H. Rowley, *The Servant of the Lord and Other Essays in the Old Testament;* and the comments of C. Westermann, *Isaiah 40-66,* pp. 255-269.) The latter vacillates between whether the servant is Christ or Israel to such an extent that he finally concludes that the "church's confession as it is given in the Apostle's Creed . . . is far more important than quotations from Isa. 52ff. here and there in the New Testament." We could perhaps excuse the unbelief of Jewish scholarship which is "blinded" in this present church age, but such unbelief on the part of liberal Protestant theologians is without excuse! To miss the fact that the person of Jesus Christ (the Messiah) is the central figure in this passage is to stumble in unbelief over the Cornerstone and Foundation of all the gospel. The rhetorical question **Who hath believed our report?** is more of an explanation than an interrogation. It does not demand a negative response; it is merely designed to call attention to the lack of faith in the world in general. Culver (p. 43) notes: "Historically speaking, Israel rejected the spoken message God gave them about their Messiah." Yet, the Scripture clearly maintains that a remnant of Israel would come to faith in Him. MacRae (p. 133) translates: "Who would have believed what we have heard?" The Hebrew word for "report" (*shemu'athenū*) is a passive participle, literally meaning "that which we have heard." Young (III, p. 341) follows Hengstenberg in noting that while the kings of the earth were speechless in view of what they had not "heard" (*shame'ū*), it is the prophet's message which he has "heard" (*shemu'athenū*) that is to be ignored by many. Brown (pp. 200-201) asks the question as to who is speaking here and suggests that it is the apostles and that the **report** is none other than the gospel which they preached. While this is certainly possible if one were to push the implicit meaning of Isaiah's prophecy as far as possible, it is not likely. Rather, it would appear that Isaiah is the chief speaker and the plurality of **our** would extend to the prophets in general. If we hold that the Old Testament prophecies are in fact an inspired message from God Himself, then it is fully appropriate for the prophet to identify himself with all those spokesmen of God's divine message. Baron (p. 68) notes that the **arm of the LORD** is the emblem of divine power which has already been referred to in 51:9; 52:10. Thus, it is used as a metonymy for the Lord's "strength" (cf. Jer 17:5). To have believed the report of the prophets and have been the recipient of the revelation of the arm of God is to have surrendered one's self by faith to the person and authority of the Lord God. As the passage develops, it would seem clear that Isaiah is suggesting here that while this revelation and declaration of truth is all too clear to him as a prophet of God, it will not be believed and received by the majority of the people.

2 For he shall grow up before him as a tender plant, and as a root out of a dry

2. The phrase **he shall grow up before him as a tender plant** has often been associated with the inauspicious early life of

ground: he hath no form nor comeliness; and when we shall see him, *there is* no beauty that we should desire him.

3 He is despised and rejected of men; a man of sorrows, and acquainted with grief: and we hid as it were *our* faces from him; he was despised, and we esteemed him not.

4 ¶Surely he hath borne our griefs, and carried our sorrows: yet we did esteem him stricken, smitten of God, and afflicted.

Christ. The term **tender plant** (*yōneq*, suckling) refers to the "shoot" which shall spring up out of the decayed stump of Jesse (the Davidic line), whereas while men might expect a magnificent "plant of reknown," the Messiah shall appear with inauspicious and humble beginnings. Thus, the appearance of the messianic Servant of the Lord upon the earth is expressed as the almost unobservable tender "sprout" that shall spring up out of the kingly line of Israel at a time when it is least expected. **Before him** should be taken as referring to God Himself. The **root out of a dry ground** would reinforce this same concept. To all human observation, the Davidic line shall be cut down forever. Its potential for producing a messianic king is thought to be dried up indeed. There is no way that the imagery here is to be taken as referring to the unmarried state of the Virgin Mary. While acknowledging that such an interpretation is without warrant, Young (III, p. 342) suggests that it refers to the "lowly conditions and background in which the servant was to appear." This would also seem unlikely and unnecessary; for the real issue in view here is the condition of the Davidic line, or as Baron (p. 70) expresses it, "The proud cedar of the Davidic monarchy (which) has been felled." **No form nor comeliness** denote the Servant's humiliation, rather than His personal appearance. For **beauty** read "elegance." The meaning of this passage is not that the Messiah will be homely or ugly, but that He will be common. He will not appear on the scene in the regalia of a king. Nothing could better describe the humble appearance of Jesus as a simple rabbi.

3. The prophet uses a series of predicates, with an assumed subject (the Servant), to provide a more detailed description than in the previous verse. The Messiah is described as being both **despised** (from *bazah*, to disdain or scorn) and **rejected** (*chadal*, abandon) **of men** (*'ishim*, referring to individual men, rather than mankind). By contrast, He is described as a **man** (*'iysh*) **of sorrows** (*make'obōth*, severe pains) and **acquainted with grief** (*choliy*, sicknesses or injuries). This is a most appropriate description for one who would be physically crucified for our sins and thereby suffer both pains and injuries. It is in regard to His awful personal suffering that **we hid as it were our faces from him.** The vivid and detailed descriptions of Christ's crucifixion given in the Gospels clearly indicate the severity of His physical suffering: the agony in the garden; His battered face; the severe scourging; and the torture of the Crucifixion itself. In spite of the great agony of His suffering, **He was despised** (rejected), **and we esteemed** (*chashabenuhū*, valued) **him not.** The meaning of this passage is that the prophet is speaking for the nation of Israel generically. It states that in light of the common origin and physical suffering of the Messiah, in our spiritual blindness we would not value Him to be the King and Lord that He really was. Thus it is that God's greatest gift is not even valued by those who in their unbelief fail to see His real significance.

4. In the opening verses of this section the prophet describes the suffering of Christ in His crucifixion in great detail. Verse 4 begins with the affirmative particle, **Surely,** which directs our attention to that which follows. He is none other than the person of the coming Messiah who serves as the substitute for **our** (mankind's) sins. Young (III, p. 345) notes: "In contrast to the order of the previous verse (*griefs; sicknesses*), we now have *sicknesses,* then *griefs.* To be noted is the juxtaposition of *us* and *He.* We may render: *The sicknesses of us He bore.* This contrast brings to the fore the idea of substitution, which characterizes this section of the chapter." The verb "to bear" (*nasa'*) means more than to take away. It connotes the idea of lifting up or carrying. Thus, the passage emphasizes the fact that Christ, who is Himself sinless, is the sin-bearer who carries our weight of sin and, therefore, bears the punishment which that sin deserves.

5 But he *was* wounded for our transgressions, *he was* bruised for our iniquities: the chastisement of our peace *was* upon him; and with his stripes we are healed.

For **griefs** read sicknesses. These are spiritual infirmities that parallel **sorrows** (anguish). In emphasizing this same idea, the New Testament states: "Who his own self bare our sins in his own body on the tree" (I Pet 2:24). The terminology in this verse is not intended to indicate that Christ merely became a fellow sufferer with mankind, or that He merely died for the physical effects of our sin. Instead of properly understanding the purpose of His substitutionary atonement, the prophet predicts that **we** (mankind in general, and perhaps the Jews in particular) falsely assumed that He was **stricken, smitten of God**. Three severe verbs describe this process: *nagu'a* (plagued); *mukeh* (struck); *me'uneh* (afflicted).

5. While this is the assumption of men in general, the prophet makes it clear that in reality the Messiah will not be judged by God because of any failure of His own, but rather He is the one who will be **wounded** (*mecholal*, pierced through) **for our transgressions** (sins). The precise choice of words by the prophet could not express the nature of Christ's death by crucifixion more appropriately. The verb **bruised** translates the Hebrew word *daka'*, meaning to be crushed. Holladay, *A Concise Hebrew and Aramaic Lexicon* (p. 70), notes that its parallel forms include "oppressed," or "beat to pieces." The imagery of the word is derived from that of a man crushing grapes in a winepress. Christ is pictured in 63:1-4 as treading the winepress of God's wrath upon the unbelieving nations of the world. He had the right to bring judgment against wickedness because He was Himself crushed **for our iniquities** (from *'avon*, moral evil or fault, including the idea of punishment as well). While the doctrine of the atonement does not rest upon this passage alone, it is obvious that this passage gives clear support to that doctrine. Young (III, p. 348) states: "Isaiah is in reality declaring that he bore the guilt of our sins . . . we are saying that he bore the punishment that was due to us because of those sins, and that is to say that he was our substitute." The vicarious atonement of Christ is clearly taught in this passage. A secondary reference to the actual suffering involved in the crucifixion may be found, but the major emphasis of this statement is toward the substitutionary nature of His death for our sins. In light of the severe language (**wounded** and **bruised**) used in this passage, it is obvious that the wrath of God for all sin for all time was poured out upon Christ who "became sin for us" (II Cor 5:21). **Chastisement** (*mosar*, correction, or discipline) **of our peace** (*shalom*) refers to that which procured our peace. The peace which only God can give is the fruit of our salvation and is concomitant with it. Thus, it is only by His substitutionary atonement that we may be saved and experience peace with God and, by our continued obedience, also the peace of God. The final phrase, referring to His **stripes** (*chaburah*, bruises or wounds), must be viewed in its poetic parallel with the two previous statements, which relate to spiritual iniquity. While many have attempted to read physical healing into this text, it simply is not there. MacRae (p. 139) correctly observes that the healing described in this verse is spiritual in nature. While God may choose to grant us physical healing, He is under no obligation to do so. By contrast, the statements in this verse are all definitely guaranteed to the recipient. It is sometimes argued that Christ's crucifixion is the basis of our salvation and that His scourging is the basis of our healing. This is an unfortunate misreading of the obvious intention of the text. The entire context deals with the problem of our **transgressions** and **iniquities** and the means of our **peace** that we may be spiritually healed. Notice the double parallel emphasis of the verse:

His action	*Our Need*
Wounded	**Transgressions**
Bruised	**Iniquities**

Chastisement   Peace
Stripes   Healed

The verb **healed** (from *rapah*, to mend or cure) may refer to physical healing; but, more extensively, it indicates a condition of being made whole. Within the book of Isaiah it is used of the healing and forgiveness of the gentile nations (19:22; 57:18). In view of the spiritual provision that is met by the atonement of Christ, it would not be inappropriate to translate it as "by his stripes we are forgiven."

6-7. All we (*kullanu*, all of us) is both the beginning and ending word of this verse. The comparative **like sheep** is used to illustrate the desperate condition of mankind. Because of our spiritual blindness (similar to the near blindness of sheep) and our lack of a shepherd for our souls, we sinners have the constant tendency to go **astray** (*ta 'iynū*, pluperfect, we had turned astray). Notice that **all** and **every** are used in parallel, emphasizing the totality of sinful humanity. Our **own way** is used in parallel with **gone astray**. Thus, in light of the imagery the force of the passage is clear. Since sheep are especially prone to wander off with little or no sense of direction and cannot find their own way home, they serve as a perfect illustration of lost and sinful humanity which, in and of itself, cannot come to the Saviour without divine assistance. Therefore, in the New Testament Christ is pictured as the seeking Shepherd who deliberately goes searching for the lost sheep (cf. Jn 10:1-18, where Jesus is pictured as the "good shepherd"; Mt 9:36, where He is moved with compassion for the people whom He views as ". . . sheep having no shepherd"; Mt 18:11-14, where the Shepherd leaves the "ninety and nine" and goes seeking for the one that is "gone astray"). Again, this verse emphasizes the substitutionary nature of the atonement with the phrase, **the LORD hath laid on him the iniquity of us all.** The causative verb *paga'* means to punish by violence, or to strike violently. Interestingly, it also carries the idea of intercession, which is how it is translated in verse 12 of this same chapter (see *TWOT*, p. 715). The idea conveyed in this verse is that the wrath of God, which should violently strike us, is expiated by the fact that it has struck upon our Lord Christ instead. This is the dynamic of the concept of the atonement of Christ. We who fully deserve the entire penalty and punishment for our sins have been set free not only by God's grace, but by the fact that in His grace He has poured out His wrath against sin upon His own Son! This also gives us greater insight into the nature of Christ's suffering on the cross—the spiritual agony of bearing our sins being far greater than the physical torture which He endured. Because of His willingness to die for our sins, Christ was **oppressed** (*nigas*, meaning to exert demanding pressure). The word is a derivative of taskmaster, or slave driver. The idea expressed in this verse is that though the Messiah would come to do away with all such oppression (Isa 9:4), He would quietly endure it Himself in order to accomplish our salvation. The second verb **he was afflicted** (*na'aneh*, from the basic meaning of browbeating and often used in relation to self-chastisement) emphasizes the fact that His suffering was vicarious and voluntary. This verb is the center of the sentence; and the two following clauses are circumstantial, expressing the conditions under which the Servant was afflicted. Young (III, p. 350) suggests that the clause may be rendered, "and he suffered himself to be afflicted." What is clear in this passage is that He offers no self-defense or protest. The fact that He opened not His mouth is illustrated by the imagery of a **lamb** being brought to **the slaughter.** Again, the prophet Isaiah could not have chosen more appropriate terminology to depict the coming Messiah who would lay down His life for sinners and thereby be designated the "Lamb of God" (see Jn 1:29, where John the

6 All we like sheep have gone astray; we have turned every one to his own way; and the LORD hath laid on him the iniquity of us all.
7 He was oppressed, and he was afflicted, yet he opened not his mouth: he is brought as a lamb to the slaughter, and as a sheep before her shearers is dumb, so he openeth not his mouth.

8 He was taken from prison and from judgment: and who shall declare his generation? for he was cut off out of the land of the living: for the transgression of my people was he stricken.

9 And he made his grave with the wicked, and with the rich in his death; because he had done no violence, neither *was any* deceit in his mouth.

Baptist refers to Him as being the one who "taketh away the sin of the world"; Rev 5:6,12, where the resurrected Christ appears in heaven as the slain Lamb of God who alone, is able to open the scroll of God's judgment).

8-9. Under the inspiration of the Holy Spirit, the prophet Isaiah further details with unbelievable accuracy and precision the exact events related to the crucifixion death and subsequent burial of Jesus Christ. **He was taken from prison** (*otser*, oppression or restraint) **and from judgment** (*mishpat*, justice). In view of the details of Christ's illegitimate trials held in the middle of the night by the Sanhedrin and in the early morning by Pilate, the Roman official, this designation could not be more appropriate. **Who shall declare** is better translated "who has considered." **His generation** refers to His potential life. In view of His crucifixion, the force of the passage is thus rendered, "who seriously considered his life and all of its potential." The verb **he was cut off** (*nigezar*, always means a violent death. Notice the verbs of action (**he was taken** and **he was cut off**), which indicate the passivity of the Servant. He has not brought this action upon Himself by any misconduct of His own; He is the victim of the actions and decisions of others. This proper balance recognizes the biblical truth that Christ both willingly laid down His life for our sins and those who crucified Him were personally responsible for their actions. The ultimate purpose of His death is emphasized again by the last phrase of the verse: **for the transgression of my people was he stricken** (violently killed). There is no way that this verse can honestly be applied to the nation of Israel as the Servant of God, to the exclusion of an individual messianic Servant; for national Israel has never been completely **cut off** out of the land of the living. While it is true that she has suffered probably greater than any nation on earth, the Bible makes it clear that she has suffered because of her own hardness and sin. Like the Gentiles, she, too, must come to personal faith in Jesus Christ as her Lord and Messiah if she is to experience again the full blessing of God. MacRae (p. 143) notes that the details of verse 8 form an "inorganic" prophecy; that is, the prediction of incidental features that do not relate directly to the major prediction further the divine objective by proving that what occurs is actually the event predicted. Thus, the reference to the Servant's making His **grave with the wicked** (*resha'iym*, criminals) was certainly fulfilled in Christ's crucifixion and death between two thieves (Mt 27:38). Since Jewish criminals always received an ignominious burial, the additional phrase, **and with the rich in his death,** cannot imply that He was buried with rich criminals. Rather, it teaches that though He died in association with criminals, He was, nevertheless, "with the rich." The Hebrew conjunction may be translated **and,** but may also be translated "but" or "yet," and frequently is. Technically, the singular noun reads "a rich man." There can be no serious doubt that this refers to Jesus being buried in the borrowed tomb of Joseph of Arimathea (Mt 27:57).

10 Yet it pleased the LORD to bruise him; he hath put *him* to grief: when thou shalt make his soul an offering for sin, he shall see *his* seed, he shall prolong *his* days, and the pleasure of the LORD shall prosper in his hand.

10. While the wicked men were personally responsible for the death of Christ, this passage makes it clear that the ultimate cause of His death was the plan and purpose of God. **It pleased the LORD to bruise** (from *daka'*, to crush) **him.** This refers back to the same condition in verse 5, where He was **bruised for our iniquities.** The combination of the two statements clearly indicates that the substitutionary atonement of Christ was always the master plan of God the Father. The verb **put him to grief** may be rendered "made Him sick." The Qumran Scroll (1Q Isa) reads *wychllhw,* "that He might pierce Him." Some have questioned why God would be **pleased** to allow the crucifixion of His own Son. However, this statement must be seen in light of the ultimate purpose of the Crucifixion, which is the salvation of **his seed** (see Mt 5:9; i.e., those who would come to believe in Him would thus become the "children of God"). Since Christ had no physical lineage of His own, His **seed** must be viewed (in the spiritual sense) as those who have been born of God as a result of His atonement. Therefore, if there is to be a redeemed people, there must be an expiatory sacrifice that provides a vicarious atonement for the salvation of mankind. Without such an atonement there can ultimately be no redeemed people of God, whether Jewish or Gentile. (On the necessity of the atonement of Christ on the cross, see S. Charnock, *Christ Crucified*; H. Guillabaud, *Why the Cross?* L. Morris, *Apostolic Preaching of the Cross* and *The Cross in the New Testament*; R. Nicole, "The Nature of Redemption," in *Christian Faith and Modern Theology*, pp. 191-222). The strength of the passage rests on the statement that the Lord would make **his soul** (*naphesh*) **an offering for sin** (*asham*, guilt offering). This involves the "trespass offering" that is commanded and described in Numbers 5:5ff. (For a thorough discussion of its meaning, see Girdlestone, *Synonyms of the Old Testament* (pp. 201-222) and Hengstenberg, *Dissertations on the Genuineness of the Pentateuch* (II, pp. 174-179). The verb **shalt make** (*sym*) means to place or designate. Thus, the Lord God designates the significance of this offering, but is not Himself the Offerer. Young (III, p. 354) notes that in verse 12 the Servant receives the reward for His work which proves that it is He Himself who offers the sacrifice. The offering of His **soul** represents the giving of His very life as an oblation to God. Since the Lord Jesus Christ was sinless, He is not making a "trespass offering" for His own sin; it is for our sin. The rest of the verse describes the results that will follow His sacrifice of Himself. The phrase **he shall prolong his days** indicates that the Servant's ministry will not end with His death. MacRae (p. 145) notes that since the previous verses clearly indicate the violent nature of His death, it carries a strong suggestion of physical resurrection. Thus it is that God's promise of an eternal perpetuity to David and his seed (II Sam 7:13-16; Ps 21:5) is to be fulfilled in the extension (or prolonging) of the years of the Servant of the Lord who shall live forever. **The pleasure of the LORD** refers to God's ultimate purposes, which shall be accomplished by the death and resurrection of the Servant. Calvin (p. 731) states: "Isaiah could not have better expressed the infinite love of Christ toward us than by declaring that He takes the highest delight in our salvation, and that He rests in it as the fruit of His labors."

11. **The travail of his soul** refers again to His substitutionary suffering, which causes God to be **satisfied** (*yiseba'*, filled or satisfied). The phrase **by his knowledge** (*beda'tô*, through His knowledge) has been viewed as being both subjective (the Servant accomplishes justification by His own knowledge) and objective (our knowledge of His sacrifice leads to our justification). Archer (p. 647) argues that it must be construed as an objective genitive meaning "by the knowledge of Him" (as Saviour) shall we be justified. Alexander (II, p. 305) argues: "The only satisfactory construction is the passive one which makes the phrase mean 'by the knowledge of Him' upon the part of others; and this is determined by the whole connection to mean practical experimental knowledge, involving faith and self-appropriation of the Messiah's righteousness." Young (III, p. 357) observes that: "In this context the Servant appears, not as a teacher, but as a Saviour. He does not justify men, by His righteous knowledge, but by bearing their iniquities." **Righteous servant** is better read "my Servant as a righteous One." The ultimate purpose of the coming of the Servant is not merely to teach the way to God, but to provide the way to God through His atonement. This is fully borne out in the words **justify many**. On the basis of His personal righteousness (*tsâdîq*) He will justify (*yasedîyq*) those for whom **he shall bear their iniquities.** Thus, there is no justification without the provision of the

11 He shall see of the travail of his soul, *and* shall be satisfied: by his knowledge shall my righteous servant justify many; for he shall bear their iniquities.

12 Therefore will I divide him a *portion* with the great, and he shall divide the spoil with the strong; because he hath poured out his soul unto death: and he was numbered with the transgressors; and he bare the sin of many, and made intercession for the transgressors.

CHAPTER 54

SING, O barren, thou *that* didst not bear; break forth into singing, and cry aloud, thou *that* didst not travail with child: for more *are* the children of the desolate than the children of the married wife, saith the LORD.

2 Enlarge the place of thy tent, and let them stretch forth the curtains of thine habitations: spare not, lengthen thy cords, and strengthen thy stakes;

3 For thou shalt break forth on the right hand and on the left; and thy seed shall inherit the Gentiles, and make the desolate cities to be inhabited.

4 Fear not; for thou shalt not be ashamed: neither be thou confounded; for thou shalt not be put to shame: for thou shalt forget the shame of thy youth, and shalt not remember the reproach of thy widowhood any more.

Righteous One who must bear our sins if we are to be forgiven our sins.

12. The chapter ends with the glorification and exaltation of the Servant of the Lord. **Therefore** calls our attention to the great work of atonement which has proceeded, and which is the basis of the exaltation which follows. The parallel to Philippians 2:9 ("Wherefore God also hath highly exalted him . . .") is clear. The verb and its object, **will I divide him,** actually reads, "I will divide to Him." The idea is that His **portion** shall be comparable to that of the **great** (*barabbym*) and the **strong** (*'asûmîm,* mighty). Delitzsch (II, p. 339) attempts to draw a parallel to them and the **many** at the end of the verse. However, this seems quite unlikely. Rather, the meaning of the text would seem to be that He shares the **spoil** of His victory on the same level and in the same manner as any other great conqueror. This is not to imply that Christ is merely on the level of a human king; rather it emphasizes the victorious nature of His atonement as a conquest of sinners for whom He died. His great exaltation has been given by God the Father because **He hath poured out** (*he'erah,* to expose or make naked) **his soul unto death.** The meaning of this phrase clearly indicates that the divine Son of God fully exposed Himself to the naked reality of death on our behalf! In the process of His crucifixion He was **numbered with the transgressors** (criminals, i.e., the two thieves) **and he bare the sin of many** (*rabbym,* a large or great number). His **intercession** refers to the high priestly work of the Servant of the Lord who makes that intercession on the basis of His own substitutionary expiation. By virtue of that atoning work alone the sinner has a ground of acceptance before God. This chapter stands as the greatest epitome of Old Testament prophecy, for with unparalleled intricate accuracy, it clearly predicts the theological significance of the atoning death of Christ. It is certainly appropriate to call this chapter the "Gospel of Isaiah."

3. His consolation. 54:1—55:13.

54:1-4. This chapter portrays the results of the atoning work of the Servant of the Lord and adds a further description to the previous chapter. Here we see the universal extent of the Servant's work as it extends to all nations. In chapters 40:1-52:12 there is constant reference to the words **Jacob, Jerusalem,** and **Zion.** But in 52:13-57:21 the national designations for Israel almost never appear. The view of the prophet is toward the application of the atonement of the Servant to the entire world. Kidner (p. 619) likens these chapters in the following manner: "In Christian terms, the Calvary of ch. 53 is followed by the growing church of ch. 54 and the gospel call of ch. 55." The gentile nations are depicted as a **barren** and **desolate** woman who breaks forth into songs of praise because of her recent (assumed) **marriage** and **children.** The imagery here is used simply to illustrate the concept that whereas the Gentiles were estranged from God, in contrast to the Israelites who are depicted here as the **married wife,** they shall now be united to the Lord and bear spiritual descendants. In a direct allusion to this passage in Galatians 4:27, the Apostle Paul likens the growth of the true church to the story of Sarah and Hagar. However, he reverses the imagery; and the Jews become Hagar, and the Christians are Sarah. The idea, however, is quite clear. In the Old Testament Israel is represented as the wife of Jehovah, and in the New Testament the church is illustrated as the wife of Christ. Thus, the New Testament gentile church must spread out like a Bedouin enlarging His **tent.** The imagery of the verse captures the idea of one pulling up his tent **stakes,** lengthening his **cords** (ropes), extending the area of his dwelling, and repositioning and anchoring the tent **stakes.** Kelley (p. 346), a Baptist commentator, is quick to note that this verse served as the text for William Carey's famous sermon on world missions delivered on May 31, 1792, before a group of Baptist ministers at Kettering, England. His efforts eventually led to the formation of the Baptist Missionary Society, which became the forerunner of the modern missionary movement. The passage certainly teaches a great spiritual lesson, in that any expansion program for the cause of Christ must include the extension of one's faith and a recommitment to the ground-stake of truth. **Thy seed shall inherit the Gentiles** is not so much a reference to Israel conquering the Gentiles as it is to the true gentile church which shall come from the previously unsaved gentile nations.

5-10. God is pictured in these verses as both the **Maker** and the **husband** of the Gentiles. Verse 5 makes it clear that He is the same One who is also the **Redeemer** of all men and yet still is the **Holy One of Israel.** Therefore, the imagery of this passage views both Israel and the gentile nations as being "married" to Him in the church that He shall establish. Thus, He is called the **God of the whole earth** (*'arets*, world). In the mind of God, the initial refusal of the Gentiles is looked upon as being **For a small moment.** However, it shall be replenished with **great mercies** by which the Lord shall gather the nations unto Himself and His new bride, the church! Though she was forsaken for a **moment** when God turned away from the Gentiles in preferring the election of Abraham (Gen 12), now He will take **great mercies** (*rachamyim*, compassion) and with **everlasting kindness** (*chesed*, loyal love). (For an excellent discussion of this term, see N. H. Smith, "The Covenant-Love of God," in *Distinctive Ideas of the Old Testament*, pp. 94-130.) This section ends with the prophet using the illustration of the **waters of Noah** (the Noahic flood) as an illustration of the fact that as God stopped the Flood and promised never again to destroy the earth in such a matter, so He now promises to stop His judgment of the gentile nations and establish **the covenant of my peace** with them. This prophetically looks forward to the New Covenant and the church of the New Testament era.

11-17. The new gentile bride of the Lord is described as having foundations that are laid of **stones with fair colors** (beautiful colors). The gem-built city is the New Jerusalem. This language is certainly reflected in the description of Revelation 21:10-27. The passage even looks beyond the church age to the millennial kingdom when Jewish and gentile saints shall dwell together in **peace.** The Lord promises that those who **gather together** against this great city shall utterly fail. The chapter ends with the great promise that **No weapon** that is brought against her **shall prosper** (succeed). **Every tongue** (by implication, accusation) that shall come against her in **judgment** (a formal accusation, rather than irresponsible gossip) shall be stopped. The implication of the passage is that while people may complain against or gossip about the human inadequacies of the church, there shall ultimately be no formal accusation that shall stand against her because the **heritage** (*nachalath*, inheritance) of these **servants** of the Lord is **righteousness** (from *tsedeq*). Thus, their testimony in the world is not dependent upon their own self-righteousness, but upon the free gift of His righteousness, which He has given them. The passage ends with the final affirmation, **saith the LORD,** which serves as an "Amen" to the truth that has just been stated.

55:1-7. The free gift of God's righteousness that is made available through the salvation He alone provides is emphasized in the opening verse, where everyone that **thirsteth** (referring

5 For thy Maker *is* thine husband; the LORD of hosts *is* his name; and thy Redeemer the Holy One of Israel: The God of the whole earth shall he be called.

6 For the LORD hath called thee as a woman forsaken and grieved in spirit, and a wife of youth, when thou wast refused, saith thy God.

7 For a small moment have I forsaken thee; but with great mercies will I gather thee.

8 In a little wrath I hid my face from thee for a moment; but with everlasting kindness will I have mercy on thee, saith the LORD thy Redeemer.

9 For this *is as* the waters of Noah unto me: for *as* I have sworn that the waters of Noah should no more go over the earth; so have I sworn that I would not be wroth with thee, nor rebuke thee.

10 For the mountains shall depart, and the hills be removed; but my kindness shall not depart from thee, neither shall the covenant of my peace be removed, saith the LORD that hath mercy on thee.

11 ¶O thou afflicted, tossed with tempest, *and* not comforted, behold, I will lay thy stones with fair colours, and lay thy foundations with sapphires.

12 And I will make thy windows of agates, and thy gates of carbuncles, and all thy borders of pleasant stones.

13 And all thy children *shall be* taught of the LORD; and great *shall be* the peace of thy children.

14 In righteousness shalt thou be established: thou shalt be far from oppression: for thou shalt not fear: and from terror; for it shall not come near thee.

15 Behold, they shall surely gather together, *but* not by me: whosoever shall gather together against thee shall fall for thy sake.

16 Behold, I have created the smith that bloweth the coals in the fire, and that bringeth forth an instrument for his work; and I have created the waster to destroy.

17 No weapon that is formed against thee shall prosper; and every tongue *that* shall rise against thee in judgment thou shalt condemn. This *is* the heritage of the servants of the LORD, and their righteousness *is* of me, saith the LORD.

CHAPTER 55

HO, every one that thirsteth, come ye to the waters, and he that hath no money: come ye, buy, and eat; yea, come, buy wine and milk without money and without price.

2 Wherefore do ye spend money for *that which is* not bread? and your labour for *that which* satisfieth not? hearken diligently unto me, and eat ye *that which is* good, and let your soul delight itself in fatness.

3 Incline your ear, and come unto me: hear, and your soul shall live; and I will make an everlasting covenant with you, *even* the sure mercies of David.

4 Behold, I have given him for a witness to the people, a leader and commander to the people.

5 Behold, thou shalt call a nation *that* thou knowest not, and nations *that* knew not thee shall run unto thee because of the LORD thy God, and for the Holy One of Israel; for he hath glorified thee.

6 ¶Seek ye the LORD while he may be found, call ye upon him while he is near:

7 Let the wicked forsake his way, and the unrighteous man his thoughts: and let him return unto the LORD, and he will have mercy upon him; and to our God, for he will abundantly pardon.

8 ¶For my thoughts *are* not your thoughts, neither *are* your ways my ways, saith the LORD.

9 For as the heavens are higher than the earth, so are my ways higher than your ways, and my thoughts than your thoughts.

10 For as the rain cometh down, and the snow from heaven, and returneth not thither, but watereth the earth, and maketh it bring forth and bud, that it may give seed to the sower, and bread to the eater:

11 So shall my word be that goeth forth out of my mouth: it shall not return unto me void, but it shall accom-

to spiritual need) is invited to **come ye to the waters**. The invitation is open to all who are willing to come, and they may **come** and **buy** with **no money**. The imagery is that of a person who is given the opportunity to go to the marketplace to purchase whatever he would desire without money. Therefore, the prophet urges them to not spend **money** (representative of self effort) for that which is **not bread** (spiritually satisfying). The text certainly indicates that it is a waste of one's time and effort to seek that which is ultimately not satisfying to his soul. It is possible to get caught up in the material blessings of life and miss its whole purpose. At the same time, the imagery of this verse appropriately describes those who continue attempting to work their way to heaven while never discovering the free gift of God, that is, the "Bread of Life." To those who will receive Him, God promises to make an **everlasting covenant** based upon the **sure mercies (*chesed*) of David**. This clearly indicates that the covenant that God will establish with the church is essentially the same type of covenant He had already established with Israel. Both are based upon His "steadfast love." While Delitzsch (II, p. 355) holds that David was the **witness** (*ed*) to Christ through his composition of the Psalms, this is highly unlikely. The **witness** in the passage is the Messiah. Young (III, p. 378) observes that in this context the suffix of the verb "I will give," refers to the seed of David, the Messiah. He is the One who is to be the witness of God by bringing the message of God to the people of Israel. He is also described as a **leader** (*nagid*, prince) and a **commander** (*metsaveh*). These descriptions fit well with His prophetic and princely functions as the Messiah. Because God will have **glorified** the Messiah, the **nations** (*goyi*, gentiles) who have not previously known Him, shall come to the Lord (Jehovah). The invitation **Seek ye the LORD . . . call ye upon him** is conditioned by the phrases, **while he may be found** and **while he is near**. The indication of the *niphal* tense implies that God's invitation to the sinner is open at all times, but the sinner may come only when he is called. This must be viewed in light of the New Testament statement, "There is none that understandeth, there is none that seeketh after God" (Rom 3:11). In both the Old and New Testament scriptures we find a balance between divine sovereignty and human responsibility in the matter of eternal salvation. God "calls" and "elects," while man "chooses" and "believes." Lest anyone presume upon the grace of God, the warning of this text is to seek the Lord while one is under conviction to do so. That as an aspect of true believing faith, repentance is involved in our salvation is clearly indicated by verse 7. The **wicked** is to **forsake** (*ya`azob*, to turn or refuse) **his way** and let him **return** (*vashob*, to turn or repent) **unto the LORD**. To those who genuinely repent and turn to Him, God promises **mercy** and **pardon**. (On the relationship of repentance to salvation, see the evangelical classic, H. A. Ironside, *Except Ye Repent*.)

The **Holy One of Israel** (Isaiah's favorite designation for the Lord Jehovah).

8-13. To those who are overwhelmed by the doctrine of salvation as it relates to the purposes of God, the Lord reminds that His **thoughts** (*machashebeth*, purposes, or intentions) and His **ways** (*derachay*, directions) are **higher** than ours. That the Bible teaches that God's eternal purposes are beyond our full comprehension is obvious. While aspects of the person and work of God are knowable, and even communicable to man, God Himself is ultimately incomprehensible in the totality of His person and His purposes. (This is discussed at length by H. Bavinck, *The Doctrine of God*, pp. 13-25); A. Hoekema, "The Attributes of God: The Communicable Attributes," in *Basic Christian Doctrines*, pp. 28-34; F. Klooster, "The Attributes of God: The Incommunicable Attributes," in *Basic Christian Doctrines*, pp. 21-27; R. Lightner, *The God of the Bible*; and J. I. Packer, *Knowing God*.) Ultimately, the purpose of God in bring-

plish that which I please, and it shall prosper in the thing whereto I sent it.

12 For ye shall go out with joy, and be led forth with peace: the mountains and the hills shall break forth before you into singing, and all the trees of the field shall clap their hands.

13 Instead of the thorn shall come up the fir tree, and instead of the brier shall come up the myrtle tree: and it shall be to the LORD for a name, for an everlasting sign that shall not be cut off.

CHAPTER 56

THUS saith the LORD, Keep ye judgment, and do justice: for my salvation is near to come, and my righteousness to be revealed.

2 Blessed is the man that doeth this, and the son of man that layeth hold on it; that keepeth the sabbath from polluting it, and keepeth his hand from doing any evil.

3 ¶Neither let the son of the stranger, that hath joined himself to the LORD, speak, saying, The LORD hath utterly separated me from his people: neither let the eunuch say, Behold, I am a dry tree.

4 For thus saith the LORD unto the eunuchs that keep my sabbaths, and choose the things that please me, and take hold of my covenant;

5 Even unto them will I give in mine house and within my walls a place and a name better than of sons and of daughters: I will give them an everlasting name, that shall not be cut off.

6 Also the sons of the stranger, that join themselves to the LORD, to serve him, and to love the name of the LORD, to be his servants, every one that keepeth the sabbath from polluting it, and taketh hold of my covenant;

ing men to salvation is accomplished by the preaching of His **word**. The Word of God is that which proceeds from His **mouth**. Thus, the description provided here is quite in line with the New Testament teaching of inspired, or God-breathed (Gr *theopneustos*) Scriptures. Thus, God reveals Himself to man through the Word which He reveals by means of inspiration to His spokesmen. Young (III, p. 384) notes: "The reference is to His propositional revelation, and the origin of this propositional revelation (as also in II Tim 3:16) is in God Himself." (For a discussion of divine revelation in relation to the message of the prophets, see Young, *My Servants the Prophets*, pp. 161-190; and his *Thy Word Is Truth*, pp. 65-82. On inspiration and revelation, see N. Geisler, ed., *Inerrancy*; C. F. H. Henry, ed., *Revelation and the Bible*, and his *God, Revelation and Authority*; J. W. Montgomery, ed., *God's Inerrant Word*.) The end result of the Word of God accomplishing the purpose to which He sends it is that it shall **not return** unto Him **void** (in vain). The Word of God is not sent forth in vanity; but rather, it accomplishes the purposes to which God sent it in announcing His salvation to all mankind. Those who believe and receive His message shall experience **joy** and **peace**. The evidence of salvation is clearly indicated to be a fruitful **tree**, as opposed to that which can only produce a **thorn** or **brier**. This is in line with the New Testament teaching found in Matthew 7:16-20, where the Scripture uses fruitfulness as an evidence of genuine salvation. While the production of fruit does not earn one's salvation, it certainly does evidence it. Such a spiritually productive and fruitful life shall stand as a **name** and an **everlasting sign**, and it shall not be **cut off** (destroyed because it is indestructible). The name is that designation which God shall give to His people; it shall never be blotted out, and they themselves who are the receptacles of His everlasting life shall remain as a miraculous **sign** of His grace for all eternity.

4. His condemnation. 56:1-57:21.

56:1-6. In contrast to His message of salvation and blessing to those who repent and turn from sin, this chapter introduces God's message of condemnation to those who refuse to repent. Both **salvation** and **righteousness** are going to be revealed shortly. Therefore, the prophet urges the people to **Keep ye judgment** (*mishpat*, justice) and **do justice** (*tsedaqah*, righteousness). The interchangeable usage of these terms is common to Isaiah's style. Despite this, critical scholars, following the lead of Duhm, have attempted to designate this very chapter as the beginning of the work of Trito-Isaiah, a Palestinian Jew who supposedly lived after the time of the Exile and the subsequent return to Judah. There is absolutely no evidence anywhere for this assumption, and all attempts to find any within the text, grammar, and vocabulary of these chapters have found absolutely nothing to support it. The greatest argument against the critical view is the fact that Jesus Himself quoted Isaiah 61:1 and applied it to Himself, referring to Isaiah as the author. To deny the Isaianic authorship of these chapters is to deny the intelligence or the integrity of Jesus Christ. The relationship to the previous chapter is clearly established in the activity of the **blessed** man who turns away from **doing any evil**. The passage serves as an admonition to believers to maintain their testimony by their consistent and godly life. The keeping of the **sabbath** is especially enjoined on God-fearing Jews as a covenant sign and testimony. However, even the **stranger** (Gentile) and the **eunuch** (unmarried or childless) can find a place of blessing among the people of God. To them an **everlasting name** (cf. 55:13) that shall **not be cut off** (blotted out) is better than sons and daughters. The gracious invitation of God to the Gentiles has already been mentioned several times, and it is further strengthened by the invitation of verse 6, which is extended to

7 Even them will I bring to my holy mountain, and make them joyful in my house of prayer: their burnt offerings and their sacrifices *shall be* accepted upon mine altar; for mine house shall be called an house of prayer for all people.

8 The Lord God which gathereth the outcasts of Israel saith, Yet will I gather *others* to him, beside those that are gathered unto him.

9 ¶All ye beasts of the field, come to devour, yea, all ye beasts in the forest.

10 His watchmen *are* blind: they are all ignorant, they *are* all dumb dogs, they cannot bark; sleeping, lying down, loving to slumber.

11 Yea, *they are* greedy dogs *which* can never have enough, and they *are* shepherds *that* cannot understand: they all look to their own way, every one for his gain, from his quarter.

12 Come ye, *say they*, I will fetch wine, and we will fill ourselves with strong drink; and to morrow shall be as this day, *and* much more abundant.

CHAPTER 57

THE righteous perisheth, and no man layeth *it* to heart: and merciful men *are* taken away, none considering that the righteous is taken away from the evil *to come*.

2 He shall enter into peace: they shall rest in their beds, *each one* walking *in* his uprightness.

3 ¶But draw near hither, ye sons of the sorceress, the seed of the adulterer and the whore.

4 Against whom do ye sport yourselves? against whom make ye a wide mouth, *and* draw out the tongue? *are ye* not children of transgression, a seed of falsehood,

5 Enflaming yourselves with idols under every green tree, slaying the children in the valleys under the clifts of the rocks?

6 Among the smooth *stones* of the stream *is* thy portion; they, they *are* thy lot: even to them hast thou poured a drink offering, thou hast offered a meat offering. Should I receive comfort in these?

7 Upon a lofty and high mountain hast thou set thy bed: even thither wentest thou up to offer sacrifice.

8 Behind the doors also and the posts hast thou set up thy remembrance: for thou hast discovered *thyself to another* than me, and art gone up; thou hast enlarged thy bed, and made thee a cov-

the sons of the stranger. Those who are willing to love and serve the Lord may partake of His covenant.

7-12. To those who trust Him, God extends acceptance in His Temple, which shall be called **a house of prayer for all people.** This phrase was quoted by Jesus (Mt. 21:13) in His dispute with the moneychangers, and it is also referred to in Malachi 1:11 and Hebrews 13:15. Therefore, verse 8 makes it clear that through the ministry of the Messiah God is not only gathering the **outcasts** (sinners) **of Israel** to himself, but also **others** (Gentiles) as well. The chapter ends with an indictment of the **watchmen** who **are blind . . . ignorant . . . dumb dogs.** Archer (p. 649) suggests that they are the self-seeking, professional prophets of Isaiah's own day whose degenerate morality prevailed in the reign of Manasseh. Delitzsch (II, p. 366) who notes similar designations of the prophet as a "watchman" (Ez 33:1-9; Jer 29:1-32). This is also the view of Young (III, p. 620) sees them as the leaders of Israel in general, and Kidner (p. 396) sees them as both. In either case, it was especially the prophet's responsibility to serve as a spiritual watchman (in this case, watchdog) for the nation. Isaiah's complaint is that the prophets in general are failing as are the people who falsely assume that **tomorrow shall be as this day.** This has always been the worldly philosophy of those who neither take time to foresee the coming judgment of God, nor His offer of salvation to those who will repent. Instead, they continue on as before, falsely assuming that the next day will bring opportunity for more of the same. To such the warning of the Apostle James is appropriate where he reminds us that ". . . ye know not what shall be on the morrow. For what is your life? It is even a vapor, that appeareth for a little time, and then vanisheth away" (see Jas 4:13-17). He goes on to state that those who rejoice in their "boastings" of what they shall do on the next day are an offense to God, since "all such rejoicing is evil." The thrust of both the prophet's statement and the apostle's warning is that no man can boast of tomorrow, and every man must be ready to meet God today.

57:1-12. The message begun at the end of the last chapter is continued throughout this chapter. Isaiah is probably dealing with the immoral conditions that prevailed at the end of his own lifetime during the reign of King Manasseh, who ". . . shed innocent blood very much, till he had filled Jerusalem from one end to another . . ." (II Kgs 21:16). Thus, his lament was that **the righteous perisheth.** He struggles with the suffering of the godly and the apparent success of the ungodly and is consoled only by the thought that **the righteous is taken away from the evil to come** (the coming Babylonian captivity). These righteous martyrs would actually be saved from the coming atrocity of Judah's exile by entering into the **peace** of their **rest** in Paradise. The idol-worshipers are described as **sons of the sorceress** and the **seed of the adulterer.** Religious infidelity is often described by the prophets as spiritual adultery. While these apostate worshipers make **sport** (fun) against the Lord, they continue **Enflaming** (*hanēḥamim*, arousing sexual desire) themselves with idols. The use of the *niphal* participle is analogous to the cultic orgies which were often practiced as a part of pagan religions. The prophet points out the grossest aspect of primitive religion: ritual sex orgies and infant sacrifices. **Slaying the children** refers to the practice of child sacrifice that was especially prevalent among the Canaanites and Amorites. (For a discussion, see J. L. Kelso, "The Great Apostasy," in *Archaeology and the Ancient Testament*, pp. 156-161; W. F. Albright, *Yahweh and the Gods of Canaan*.) This practice was not common among the Babylonians, and that fact would serve as another argument in favor of the unity of Isaiah. The author is dealing with it as a present reality among his people. The reference to **clifts of the rocks** is uniquely Isaianic, occurring only here and in 2:21. Such a description is also certainly fitting for Palestine, but not for Babylon. For **stream** read "valley" (ASV). It was there that the people poured out a **drink offering** (or libation). These offerings were associated with freewill offerings in Israel, but according to Deut 32:38 they were also a common feature of heathen cultic rituals. They also offered a **meat** offering (*minchah*, food or meal offering). In a further extension of this description of their spiritual adultery, the prophet describes the idolater as setting his **bed** upon a **high mountain** (high place, the common designation for a pagan altar site); and he further observes that the idolater has **enlarged thy bed**, a reference to worshiping several pagan gods at once. In spite of everything that was wrong with idolatry and the primitive and pagan religions that went with it, the people of Judah remained enamored with it. The entire context of this chapter would mitigate against it having been written by a post-exilic Palestinian Jew, for the Babylonian activity cured the Israelites of the problem of idolatry once for all. Isaiah is writing at a time (in the eighth century B.C.) when the people of Judah were still indulging in idol worship. He condemns these practices as going to the **king** (the Father-gods of the Canaanite pantheon) and sending **messengers** (i.e., priests) to make their spiritual negotiations, which shall ultimately lead them all **unto hell** (*she'ōl*, the place of the dead which included both paradise and hades). Therefore, the prophet has drawn a sharp contrast between the righteous who shall suffer, but nevertheless enter into the place of peace (paradise), and the transgressors who shall ultimately end up in hell (hades) because their **righteousness** and their **works shall not profit** them at all. The only means by which man may gain access into heaven is on the basis of the righteousness of God. Self-righteousness, within the religion of Israel or outside it in pagan ritual cults, shall never enable man to come into the presence of God.

13-21. While the religious compromises of the idol-worshiping Jews shall profit them nothing, the Scripture now declares that whoever shall put **his trust** in the Lord Jehovah shall **possess** and **inherit** the land. The phrase **cast ye up, prepare the way** is a technical term for constructing a highway by heaping up a mound of earth and stones in order to build up the surface of the road. God is described as the **high and lofty One** whose name, which is **Holy** (*qādôsh*), describes His true character. Yet, this transcendent God is also a personal Saviour. He inhabits both **eternity** and the **heart of the contrite ones** (*daka'*, broken or repentant). Thus, this Old Testament passage envisions the New Testament truth that God both dwells in the eternal heavens and in the hearts of those who will receive Him. He promises to **revive** (from *chayah*, to quicken or restore) those that are of a **contrite and humble spirit**. Herein we learn one of the great lessons of the spiritual life: revival comes only to those who are humble and broken before God. It is impossible to concoct a revival by mere self-effort and organizational enthusiasm. One may conduct a meeting by such a means, but there will be no genuine revival. Revival comes when the people of God set aside their idols and find a renewed and total dependence upon the Lord God Himself. (On the nature and significance of spiritual revival, see E. Hindson, *Glory in the Church: The Coming Revival*; W. Sprague, *Lectures on Revival*; O. Winslow, *Personal Declension and Revival of Religion in the Soul*.) Speaking to the prophet, God proceeds to announce that He would not **contend for ever** (from *ryb*, referring to the outward manifestation of God's wrath) against those whose **spirit** (*ruach*) would **fail** (faint) before His presence. The **souls** (*neshamoth*, lit., breaths, a term used as an equivalent for soul) are those human souls who are created by God and are so inadequate in themselves. Thus, this passage contains a great promise of hope to those who in their own spiritual inadequacy and brokenness

enant with them; thou lovedst their bed where thou sawest *it*.

9 And thou wentest to the king with ointment, and didst increase thy perfumes, and didst send thy messengers far off, and didst debase *thyself even* unto hell.

10 Thou art wearied in the greatness of thy way; *yet* saidst thou not, There is no hope: thou hast found the life of thine hand; therefore thou wast not grieved.

11 And of whom hast thou been afraid or feared, that thou hast lied, and hast not remembered me, nor laid *it* to thy heart? have not I held my peace even of old, and thou fearest me not?

12 I will declare thy righteousness, and thy works; for they shall not profit thee.

13 When thou criest, let thy companies deliver thee; but the wind shall carry them all away; vanity shall take *them*: but he that putteth his trust in me shall possess the land, and shall inherit my holy mountain.

14 And shall say, Cast ye up, cast ye up, prepare the way, take up the stumblingblock out of the way of my people.

15 For thus saith the high and lofty One that inhabiteth eternity, whose name *is* Holy; I dwell in the high and holy *place*, with him also *that is* of a contrite and humble spirit, to revive the spirit of the humble, and to revive the heart of the contrite ones.

16 For I will not contend for ever, neither will I be always wroth: for the spirit should fail before me, and the souls *which* I have made.

17 For the iniquity of his covetousness was I wroth, and smote him: I hid me, and was wroth, and he went on frowardly in the way of his heart.

18 I have seen his ways, and will heal him: I will lead him also, and will restore comforts unto him and to his mourners.

19 I create the fruit of the lips; Peace, peace to *him that is* far off, and to *him that is* near, saith the LORD; and I will heal him.

20 But the wicked *are* like the troubled sea, when it cannot rest, whose waters cast up mire and dirt.

21 *There is* no peace, saith my God, to the wicked.

throw themselves before the mercy of God, who shall revive them and restore them to a right relationship with Him. To these revived believers the Lord promises peace; but, by contrast, **There is no peace . . . to the wicked** who are described as a **troubled** (restless) **sea**. In a strong declaration of His holiness and sovereignty, God states that He will bring peace to the contrite and trouble to the rebellious. Whether man acknowledges God or not, He is the One who rules over the affairs of our lives.

C. Program of Peace. 58:1–66:24.

The closing chapters of the book of Isaiah introduce us to the Messiah's program of peace for the world. Here we are lifted beyond the first coming of Christ to the time of His second coming. In these chapters we see Christ as Lord, Judge, and King of the universe.

1. Conditions for peace. 58:1-59:21.

58:1-2. This chapter introduces a new series of prophecies. Vine (p. 188) and Delitzsch (p. 384) observe that these prophecies contain all three elements of the prophetic address: rebuke, warning, and promise. Isaiah is commissioned to serve as God's preacher for the condemnation of Israel's sin. Verse 1 begins with an admonition to **Cry aloud**. The emphasis on the spoken word is clearly demonstrated with the addition of the word **aloud**. This comes from the Hebrew *begarōn*, which means with the throat. Isaiah is commanded to preach at the top of his voice (Ps 115:7; 149:6). It parallels the sound of a trumpet (*shophar*). This is not the normal word for a trumpet; but rather, it refers to a ram's horn, which was utilized to sound a signal (Holladay, *CHAL*, pp. 304-305). God wants the prophet to sound a loud, clear, complete warning to His people. The second part of the verse gives the content of Isaiah's message. He is to **show . . . their transgression. Transgression** is from the root word *pasha'*, which means to revolt or rebel (Holladay, p. 300). The sin of Israel was that of conscious rebellion against God's law. God's minister has the responsibility of addressing the sins and rebellion of God's people. **My people** is equivalent to the **house of Jacob.** The reason for such strong confrontational preaching is given in verse 2. In spite of their rebellion and sin, Israel continued to act as if they were a righteous nation that genuinely sought after God. Their rebellion and sin was wrapped in a cloak of hypocrisy. The verse begins in the Hebrew with "and me," According to Young (III, p. 416), this "me" is emphatic. It implies that God Himself was highly insulted that they should act in such a hypocritical fashion. They performed their religious activities **daily** (lit., day by day). They **seek** (Heb *darash*, to inquire about, worship) and they **delight** (Heb *chapē*, to take pleasure, to desire). These two words imply a strong religious commitment. On the basis of their so-called religion and righteous activity, they **ask of me the ordinances of justice.** The **ordinances of justice** could be literally translated as the judgments of righteousness. This is a direct reference to the intervention of God on their behalf to deliver them and destroy their enemies. They also desire in **approaching to God. Approaching** comes from the root word *qarab*, which means to draw near and is utilized in some passages in reference to sexual intercourse (Holladay, *CHAL*, p. 324). This refers to an intimate drawing near of two people.

3-4. These verses express the self-righteous hypocritical attitude of Israel and God's response to that attitude. The people were proud of their fasting and were objecting that God was disregarding their fast. The only fast required by law was a fast for the Day of Atonement (Lev 16:29ff.; Num 29:7). **We afflicted our soul,** which means to oppress, humble, and bruise (Harris,

CHAPTER 58

CRY aloud, spare not, lift up thy voice like a trumpet, and shew my people their transgression, and the house of Jacob their sins.

2 Yet they seek me daily, and delight to know my ways, as a nation that did righteousness, and forsook not the ordinance of their God: they ask of me the ordinances of justice; they take delight in approaching to God.

3 Wherefore have we fasted, say *they,* and thou seest not? wherefore have we afflicted our soul, and thou takest no knowledge? Behold, in the day of your fast ye find pleasure, and exact all your labours.

4 Behold, ye fast for strife and debate, and to smite with the fist of

wickedness: ye shall not fast as ye do this day, to make your voice to be heard on high.

5 Is it such a fast that I have chosen? a day for a man to afflict his soul? is it to bow down his head as a bulrush, and to spread sackcloth and ashes under him? wilt thou call this a fast, and an acceptable day to the LORD?

6 Is not this the fast that I have chosen? to loose the bands of wickedness, to undo the heavy burdens, and to let the oppressed go free, and that ye break every yoke?

7 Is it not to deal thy bread to the hungry, and that thou bring the poor that are cast out to thy house? when thou seest the naked, that thou cover him; and that thou hide not thyself from thine own flesh?

TWOT, p. 1651). This is probably a direct reference to fasting (see Ezra 9:5). God objected to their fast on the grounds that they integrated their fasting with their **pleasure**. Along with their own pleasure, they **exact all your labors** (lit., your toilers you drive hard). These were people that were pleasure-oriented and were consumed with their work in order to make money. God is not objecting to fasting. In fact, fasting is a very legitimate expressor of our worship of God. However, the purpose of fasting is to draw us nearer to God. These people utilized fasting for their own interests and totally ignored the opportunity to draw near to God. God outlines the results of their fasting in verse 4. Their external righteousness resulted in **strife and debate**, rather than drawing them nearer to God and nearer to each other. These hypocrites became divided to the point where they expressed their contention and violence. The **fist of wickedness** is a reference to a clenched fist and implies a striking of each other in sin. God clearly states that they did not fast for their **voice to be heard on high.** The true purpose of fasting is so that our heart would be acceptable to God. **On high** is a direct reference to heaven. These people did not fast that their voice would be heard in heaven. They fasted for self-motivated reasons.

5-7. In these verses God describes the characteristics of a true fast, one that He accepts. He utilizes a series of rhetorical questions through which to communicate the characteristics of true fasting. These characteristics are indeed a contrast to the hypocrisy of Israel. In verse 5 God explains that Israel has conformed to the outward characteristics of fasting but that fasting is much more than conformity to certain external criteria. The meaning of verse 5 is that even though a person may **bow down his head** and **spread sackcloth and ashes**, these external manifestations alone do not constitute fasting. God opens with a question asking the children of Israel: "Have I chosen a fast like this?" **A day for a man to afflict his soul.** The word **afflict** is a synonym for fasting (see comments on vs. 3). The bending, or bowing down, of the head and the utilization of sackcloth and ashes are demonstrations of mock repentance. Though these can be signs of true repentance (I Kgs 21:27-29), God is vitally interested in the heart attitude out of which fasting is motivated. In verses 6-7 God outlines the true characteristics of fasting. True fasting is demonstrated in a sacrificial love on behalf of other people. In other words, when someone fasts in order to draw near to God, the legitimate consequence of his experience will be a greater desire to love and help other people. The principle communicated here is that the closer I get to God, the more conscious I will become of the needs of others. In verse 6 God gives the negative characteristics of true fasting. **To loose the bands of wickedness. To loose** comes from the Hebrew root *patach* (which means to open). This is a reference to a removal of a bondage placed upon another person. Young (III, p. 419) implies that this could be a reference to the release of slaves that were held unjustly. **The heavy burdens** referred to in the second phrase could be literally translated "to undo the bands of the yoke." **Yoke** (*motah*) refers to the collar or harness placed on the animal's head. When this was taken out of the way, the animal attached to the plow was set free. In verse 7 God outlines the positive characteristics of true fasting. True fasting will be characterized by a willingness to share food and clothing with those who are in need. **And that thou hide not thyself from thine own flesh?** Though this refers specifically to their own family (Gen 29:14) it also refers to mankind in general. One who desires intimate fellowship with God will have a compassion for all men everywhere. Here we have a mandate to be involved in meeting not only spiritual needs of others, but also physical needs. The believer must not ignore a world that is hungry and

8 ¶Then shall thy light break forth as the morning, and thine health shall spring forth speedily: and thy righteousness shall go before thee; the glory of the LORD shall be thy rereward.

9 Then shalt thou call, and the LORD shall answer; thou shalt cry, and he shall say, Here I am. If thou take away from the midst of thee the yoke, the putting forth of the finger, and speaking vanity;

10 And if thou draw out thy soul to the hungry, and satisfy the afflicted soul: then shall thy light rise in obscurity, and thy darkness be as the noon day:

11 And the LORD shall guide thee continually, and satisfy thy soul in drought, and make fat thy bones: and thou shalt be like a watered garden, and like a spring of water, whose waters fail not.

12 And they that shall be of thee shall build the old waste places: thou shalt raise up the foundations of many generations; and thou shalt be called, The repairer of the breach, The restorer of paths to dwell in.

in need of clothing, but must sacrifice to ultimately minister to their spiritual need as well.

8. These verses contain the promises of God to those who meet His spiritual conditions. Then. Only when God's conditions have been fulfilled will God's promises be realized. The emphasis here is that then, and only then, will God's promises be realized. First, God promises light in the midst of darkness. The verb break forth comes from the root word *baqa'* (to split, to break through), to invade; Harkavy, *Hebrew and Chaldee Dictionary*, p. 66). This word is used in 59:5 to speak of the hatching of eggs and in 35:6 to describe water gushing forth. God promises an invasion and bursting forth of light to replace the darkness in our lives. Second, God promises healing. Thine health, (lit. healing; shall spring forth (from the Hebrew root *tsamach*, this refers to the "healing of a wound," *CHAL*, p. 307). When these first two promises are considered together, God extends both light and life to those who worship Him appropriately (see Jn 1:4-5). Third, God promises protection. Thy righteousness shall go before thee refers not to their own religious works, but rather the Lord Himself (Isa 54:17). The glory of the Lord shall be thy rereward, or their rearguard. When the people learn to love others, they will progress as a mighty caravan with the Lord Himself and His righteousness leading the way and His glory as their rear protection. Young (III, p. 421) suggests that God's glory is "His declarative glory manifested in His works, or perhaps the Lord Himself in glorious manifestation."

9-11. The fourth promise is that of answered prayer; and the LORD shall answer. In these verses the prophet reemphasizes God's conditions and His promises. His conditions fall into two categories. God demands personal integrity, as well as a love which is demonstrated in helping others. They were to put away the yoke (see comment, vs. 6), and they were to stop putting forth of the finger. Putting forth comes from the root verb *shelach*, which means to stretch forth (*CHAL*, p. 423). This refers to a pointing of the finger. This was a gesture of contempt, and among Arabs it was used to bring misfortune on others. The idea is to stop pointing an accusative finger of spiritual superiority at other people. And speaking vanity. This is a reference to false information and probably refers to the strife and debate mentioned in verse 4. After establishing the personal characteristics necessary for acceptance with God, the prophet goes on to remind the people again of their obligation to others. If thou draw out thy soul to the hungry. God demands that we share ourselves with those in need. The afflicted soul is probably a synonym for the hungry one. The prophet follows with a series of promises for those who are in a proper relationship with God and are actively involved in ministering to others. First, God promises light in darkness and the noonday sun in gloom. This is a reference to the joyful state that follows a time of sorrow. Second, God promises to guide thee continually (lit., always). Third, He will satisfy their soul in drought (Heb *tsachtsachôth*), scorched land or desert place, *CHAL*, p. 305). Fourth, God promises to make fat thy bones. This refers to the strengthening of the bones to make them "loose or ready for action" (Delitzsch, II, p. 392). Fifth, God promises them prosperity like a watered garden. Isaiah often used this illustration to describe God's blessings (30:25; 33:21; 41:17). Sixth, Israel would be like a spring of water, whose waters fail not. This implies the outpouring of God's grace upon them (see Eph 2:7).

12. These individual promises, enumerated in verses 10-11 are climaxed by an ultimate promise of revival and restoration. The words of thee refer to the fact that the descendants of the people to whom Isaiah was preaching would one day rebuild the destroyed walls and foundations of Jerusalem. Clearly, the

preacher is addressing those living prior to the Exile and comforting them with the thought that their descendants would one day rebuild Jerusalem. These people would be called **The repairer of the breach.** The word **repairer** comes from the root word *gadar*, which means to erect a wall. Clear reference is made to the rebuilding of the walls of Jerusalem. The last phrase, **The restorer of paths to dwell in,** refers to a rebuilding of places to live in order that the land would be reinhabited.

13-14. In light of these glorious promises, Isaiah again reminds the people of God's conditions. These conditions apparently fall into three categories: man's responsibility to God, man's responsibility to others, and man's responsibility to God's self. In verses 13-14 Isaiah reminds the people of God's conditions in relation to the sabbath. **If thou turn,** Young (III, p. 426) suggests that the "sabbath is a place upon which one walks. Possibly the thought is that the sabbath is holy ground and therefore the unsanctified foot is not to walk upon it." This idea is further emphasized in the next statement. People are not to utilize God's day as a time for doing pleasure. Sabbath is to be **a delight** (from the root word *'oneg* which means enjoyment or great delight). This sabbath is to be honored in three ways: by not doing one's own things, nor seeking pleasure, nor speaking idle talk. Then the people would delight themselves, not only in the sabbath, but also in the Lord Himself. **And I will cause thee to ride upon the high places of the earth. The high places of the earth** refers in particular to the Promised Land, and according to Vine (p. 190) it indicates "the thought of their sovereign rights and dominant positions, and that not only over the land but over the nations as well." It is clearly indicated in Scripture that Israel has a unique position in the plan and program of God for all nations. This statement further substantiates that unique position of blessing. They would also partake of the heritage of Jacob or become recipients of the blessings of inhabiting Palestine. These warnings and promises are concluded with a powerful statement: **for the mouth of the Lord hath spoken it.** What Isaiah has proclaimed has not been the proclamation of his own mouth, but it is the very word of Jehovah Himself.

13 ¶If thou turn away thy foot from the sabbath, *from* doing thy pleasure on my holy day; and call the sabbath a delight, the holy of the Lord, honourable; and shalt honour him, not doing thine own ways, nor finding thine own pleasure, nor speaking *thine own words*:

14 Then shalt thou delight thyself in the Lord; and I will cause thee to ride upon the high places of the earth, and feed thee with the heritage of Jacob thy father: for the mouth of the Lord hath spoken *it*.

CHAPTER 59

BEHOLD, the Lord's hand is not shortened, that it cannot save; neither his ear heavy, that it cannot hear:

2 But your iniquities have separated between you and your God, and your sins have hid *his* face from you, that he will not hear.

3 For your hands are defiled with blood, and your fingers with iniquity; your lips have spoken lies, your tongue hath muttered perverseness.

59:1-3. This chapter is a continuation of the judgments enumerated in the previous chapter regarding Israel's hypocrisy. This entire chapter is devoted to defining and exposing the sins of the people. Isaiah reminds the people that God has not lost His power to save them. God's hand is not **shortened** (Heb root *qatsar*). The idea is that God's hand was long enough to extend its influence to save them. God both hears and understands their need for deliverance and has the capability within Himself to provide that deliverance. However, that deliverance has not come. There was a separation based on their sin. **Have separated** is from the root word *badal*, which means to be separated, excluded, set apart. In this passage it refers to a central wall or partition that divided the people of God from the person of God. **And your sins have hid his face from you.** The verb translated **have hid** comes from the root *satat*. It means to hide, or to keep secret (*CHAL*, p. 260). The face of God refers to the presence of God, and the prophet is communicating the fact that our sins hide or veil the face of God. We must recognize that our sin often becomes a major hindrance to receiving answered prayers from God. In verse 3 Isaiah substantiates his accusations of the previous verse. He utilizes various members of the body (hands, fingers, lips, and tongue) to publicly expose the sin of the people. Their sin is both in action, thus the description of **hands and fingers,** and in word, thus the description of **lips and tongue.** The very hands that the people lifted in prayer to God were defiled with blood (see also 1:15). Their sin also involved what they said and thought. **Your tongue hath muttered perverseness.** The verb translated **muttered** comes from the Hebrew *hagah* which is a common word in the Old Testament for

4 None calleth for justice, nor *any* pleadeth for truth: they trust in vanity, and speak lies; they conceive mischief, and bring forth iniquity.

5 They hatch cockatrice' eggs, and weave the spider's web: he that eateth of their eggs dieth, and that which is crushed breaketh out into a viper.

6 Their webs shall not become garments, neither shall they cover themselves with their works: their works *are* works of iniquity, and the act of violence *is* in their hands.

7 Their feet run to evil, and they make haste to shed innocent blood: their thoughts *are* thoughts of iniquity; wasting and destruction *are* in their paths.

8 The way of peace they know not; and *there is* no judgment in their goings: they have made them crooked paths: whosoever goeth therein shall not know peace.

9 ¶ Therefore is judgment far from us, neither doth justice overtake us: we wait for light, but behold obscurity; for brightness, *but* we walk in darkness.

10 We grope for the wall like the blind, and we grope as if *we had* no eyes: we stumble at noon day as in the night; we *are* in desolate places as dead men.

11 We roar all like bears, and mourn sore like doves: we look for judgment, but *there is* none; for salvation, *but* it is far off from us.

meditation. Isaiah condemns their thoughts, their language, and their activity.

4-8. The prophet continues his exposition of sin. **None call-eth for justice.** The word translated justice is the Hebrew word *tsedeq*, which refers to that which is right and clearly implies legal rightness or righteousness (Holladay p. 303). This prob-ably refers to the fact that no one is calling for public justice in regards to transgression and law breaking. **Nor any pleadeth for truth** could be literally translated "it is not judged in truth." The execution of legal justice is always predicated on a clear understanding and application of truth. **They trust in vanity.** The verb in this clause is an infinitive absolute and implies a continuous action. The people were constantly trusting in things. The word vanity is the Hebrew word *tohu*, which means a wasteland or nothingness. This is the same word that is utilized in Genesis 1:2 when the earth is described "without form." These people were constantly putting their trust in emptiness. **They conceive mischief, and bring forth iniquity.** They hatch **cockatrice eggs.** They hatch *bastlisk's* eggs. This refers to the hatching of poisonous snakes. The prophet con-tinues his illustration by the utilization of a **spider's web.** These webs are used to ensnare other people. The emphasis of this verse is upon the effects of the vipers. If the eggs are eaten, one dies; and when the egg is crushed, it gives birth to more vipers. This verse emphasizes the cancerous growth and devastating results of sin. Just as a spider's web cannot serve as a covering for the spider, so these wicked works of rebellion can never serve as a covering in the sight of God. **Their feet run to evil** is a phrase often used in Scripture to describe one's walk or life-style. The eagerness of their sinful intentions is described by the verb **run.** Paul uses these statements as the basis for his argu-ment of universal corruption in Romans 3:15-17. **The way of peace they know not.** Three words for a path are utilized in this verse. **The way** refers to "a high road on an embankment; their goings refers to a carriage road; and crooked paths refers to a footpath formed by a constant passing to and fro of travelers" (Delitzsch II, p. 398). If one follows in their path they will never know peace (*shalom*) which is repeated on numerous occasions in the book of Isaiah.

9-11. In this verse Isaiah begins to speak in the first person. He now includes himself with the people of Israel. **Therefore.** Because of their sinful life-style and their perverted directions, Isaiah reminds them that they are suffering the consequences of their sin. **Judgment far from us.** Judgment is the Hebrew word *mišpat*, which refers to a "legal decision" or "justice" (Holla-day, p. 221). The idea implied is that the just decision of God related to their deliverance had escaped them. Therefore, God would not intervene and deliver them. **Neither doth justice overtake us.** The word translated **justice** here is the Hebrew word *tsedaqah*, which means righteousness or to be right, have a just cause. This is a reference to salvation. The people continue in the darkness of their sin with no immediate hope of light and brightness. They are described as blind men feeling their way along a wall for a way of escape, but that escape eludes them; and even though it is bright, they stumble as if they were in darkness. This is a clear reference to spiritual blindness whereby men seek to escape, but no way of escape confronts them (Jn 12:40; Isa 6:10). **We are in desolate places as dead men.** This is a difficult phrase to translate and interpret. The New Amer-ican Standard translates it "among those who are vigorous we are like dead men." The idea is that although they are physically healthy, they are spiritually dead (see Paul's argument in Eph 2). In this verse Isaiah continues his indictment of the people's spiritual blindness by comparing them to bears and doves. They are like bears who hunt the flock and walk around growling with evil intent and at the same time mourn and moan like doves. He concludes this section by going back to the promise he established in verse 9. **For salvation, but it is far off from us.** The words peace, judgment, light, righteousness, brightness, all are descriptive of God's divine salvation. All of their hopes in regard to this salvation turn to emptiness. "All their looking for righteousness and salvation turns out again and again to be nothing but self deception, when the time for their coming seems close at hand" (Delitzsch, II, p. 401).

12-15. In these verses the prophet confesses his sins and the sins of the people. Since they were under God's judgment for their sin, it was imperative that they confess their sin; for it was that sin that was separating them from God (see vs. 1). **For our transgressions are multiplied.** Their apostasy and rebellion against God had greatly increased. Although they sinned as if God did not exist, God knew and was aware of all of their sins; and those sins were a witness against them. The people knew their sin. In verse 13 Isaiah clearly articulates the transgressions and rebellions mentioned in verse 12. He gets directly to the heart of the matter. **In transgressing and lying against the Lord.** The word transgression is the Hebrew word *pesha'*, which should be translated as rebellion or revolt (Holladay, p. 300). They were guilty of conscious rebellion against God's law. The word translated **lying** is the Hebrew word *kachash*, which means to deny or disown (Holladay, pp. 154-155). They had rebelled against God, and in so doing they had disowned or denied the Lord. They were **departing away from our God.** This is also a clear reference to apostasy or turning back from following God. They were **conceiving** (i.e., pregnant with falsehood) and, from the depths of their evil hearts, uttering **falsehood.** In verses 14-15, the prophet describes the terrible condition of society, as opposed in verse 13 to the awful condition of the people within that society. In that evil society, justice (*mishpat*) is **turned away backward** (*hissig*, which is utilized to describe the removal of boundaries, Delitzsch, p. 402). The proper boundaries of justice in society have been destroyed. Thus, **justice** (righteousness) also stands afar off. There is no place for righteousness in a land filled with sin. Truth can no longer occupy the open public places. Because she has **fallen in the street,** truth is conspicuously absent in the marketplace, where judgment is pronounced. **Truth faileth** (is lacking or lit., left behind). The one who decides to turn aside from evil becomes easy prey. The great controversy of the ages between good and evil is described here. Those who desire to live right and submit to truth are the antithesis of an evil and wicked society. However, all of these evils in society were known to God who abhorred them.

16-18. After observing the personal sin of His people (vs. 13) and the corporate sin of society (vss. 14-15), God observes that there was no one to stand for truth and intercede in behalf of a sinful society. There was no one to stand against the tide of sin and corruption. **And wondered that there was no intercessor.** The word "wonder" implies that God was astonished that there was no one capable of standing between a sinful people and His impending judgment. Because there was no one to stand as a mediator, God had prepared to do so Himself. His salvation would be wrought through His power (**his arm . . . and his righteousness**). In verse 17 Isaiah describes the clothing that God had already prepared for the salvation of Israel. The righteousness of which He speaks is His acting according to that which is right in judging sin and delivering His people. The breastplate and helmet are also described as the armor of the Christian in Ephesians 6:14-15. He was also clothed with the garments of vengeance (judgment, and zeal) indicating deep genuine concern for the welfare of His people. It is interesting to note that no specific weapons are mentioned. God will visit His people and judge sin with the power of His own arm. The

12 For our transgressions are multiplied before thee, and our sins testify against us: for our transgressions are with us; and *as for* our iniquities, we know them;

13 In transgressing and lying against the Lord, and departing away from our God, speaking oppression and revolt, conceiving and uttering from the heart words of falsehood.

14 And judgment is turned away backward, and justice standeth afar off: for truth is fallen in the street, and equity cannot enter.

15 Yea, truth faileth; and he *that* departeth from evil maketh himself a prey: and the LORD saw *it,* and it displeased him that *there was* no judgment.

16 ¶And he saw that *there was* no man, and wondered that *there was* no intercessor: therefore his arm brought salvation unto him; and his righteousness, it sustained him.

17 For he put on righteousness as a breastplate, and an helmet of salvation upon his head; and he put on the garments of vengeance *for* clothing, and was clad with zeal as a cloak.

18 According to *their* deeds, accordingly he will repay, fury to his adversaries, recompence to his enemies; to the islands he will repay recompence.

19 So shall they fear the name of the Lord from the west, and his glory from the rising of the sun. When the enemy shall come in like a flood, the Spirit of the Lord shall lift up a standard against him.

20 ¶And the Redeemer shall come to Zion, and unto them that turn from transgression in Jacob, saith the Lord.

21 As for me, this *is* my covenant with them, saith the Lord; My spirit that *is* upon thee, and my words which I have put in thy mouth, shall not depart out of thy mouth, nor out of the mouth of thy seed, nor out of the mouth of thy seed's seed, saith the Lord, from henceforth and for ever.

CHAPTER 60

ARISE, shine; for thy light is come, and the glory of the Lord is risen upon thee.

judgment spoken of in verse 18 is a judgment of nations. The islands mentioned probably refer to God's judgment upon the gentile nations. The adversaries and enemies probably refer to the rebellious people of Israel. Their rebellion had placed them in a position of being an enemy of God. When God comes in judgment, no one escapes His judgment.

19-21. These verses are a logical consequence of the judgment of God. They describe the time when God will be worshiped by all people on the earth. This is a direct reference to the millenial kingdom. **So shall they fear the name of the Lord.** The word **fear** is from the root word *yare'*. This word means to fear or to reverence God. When used in reference to God, it involves more than an emotional feeling. It applies to worship and carries the connotation of respecting and honoring God. Isaiah clearly states that people from the west and from the east will reverence and worship God (*TWOT*, pp. 399-400). The second phrase in this verse is introduced by the word *ki* (lit., for). The latter part of the verse gives the reason why the entire world will worship the Lord. **When the enemy shall come in like a flood, the spirit of the Lord shall lift up a standard against him.** This is an unusual construction, and its meaning is difficult to ascertain. Young (III, p. 440) gives a good translation and interpretation of this phrase: "The thought of the verse then is that whenever the enemy comes upon God's people, like a flood of all engulfing water racing down a narrow wadi, the Lord in the very midst of the flood raises a standard, thus showing that he is in control of the situation." This is a great promise for God's people. Whenever the flood of circumstances is on the verge of sweeping us into oblivion, God raises a dam to stem the tide and thus delivers His people. Even now there are people all over the world who worship His people. God who in His sovereignty intervenes in the affairs of mankind to deliver His people. **The Redeemer shall come to Zion.** The Redeemer mentioned is the One who pays the price in order to establish freedom. The preposition that precedes Zion should be translated as "for." The Redeemer who is coming is coming for the benefit of Zion (see Rom 11:26). Paul translates it in Romans "from Zion," which is also within the meaning of this preposition. God is coming for those who have turned from their rebellion to Him. In light of the extensive rebellion of Israel and the depravity that gripped their society, one wonders why God would continue His dealings with them and extend His grace to them. In verse 21 Isaiah gives us the answer. **This is my covenant with them.** In some ways this covenant is actually a repetition of the covenant of Genesis. The God who comes in judgment is also the God who will keep His covenant with His people. **And my words which I have put in thy mouth, shall not depart out of thy mouth.** Apparently, this is a direct reference to the word spoken to Joshua in Joshua 1:8. God reminds His people of their glorious heritage that extends back to the Abrahamic covenant and to His promises given when they entered the Promised Land (see Gen 17:4). The authority of this covenant is established by the repetition of the statement **saith the Lord.** This covenant is also an eternal covenant, **from henceforth and for ever.** The church is not Israel in the New Testament era, nor has God finished His dealings with the children of Israel. His covenant is permanent and eternal.

2. Character of peace. 60:1-62:12.

60:1. This opening verse is a continuation of the thoughts of chapter 59 which concluded with the covenant-keeping God who would come in behalf of Zion as its Redeemer. This message now reaches a climactic announcement of hope: **Arise, shine.** This command is given to Zion and Jerusalem. She who was under the judgment of God, smitten upon the ground, and groping in darkness, is now commanded to **arise** (Heb *qûmy*, which means to stand up or rise up). This word implies that God will also give Israel the capability of standing up. The second command is **shine**. This is indeed a contrast to the terrible spiritual condition described in 59:10. The reason that Israel is able to rise and shine is that their **light is come, and the glory of the LORD is risen upon thee.** In stating this promise, Isaiah utilizes the prophetic perfect. He is so certain of the fulfillment of this promise that he describes it as if it had already occurred. The verb translated as **risen** is the Hebrew *zarach* and is often used to describe the rising of the sun (Mal 3:20). As the sun rises to dispel the darkness, so the glory of the Lord will rise to dispel spiritual darkness for Israel.

2 For, behold, the darkness shall cover the earth, and gross darkness the people: but the LORD shall arise upon thee, and his glory shall be seen upon thee.

2. The glory of the Lord described in verse 1 is contrasted with the darkness of the hour that will precede His coming. **The darkness shall cover the earth.** This darkness refers to sin, rebellion, and sorrow upon the earth. Note that it is to cover all of the earth—not just Israel. **And gross darkness** (*'arapel* which means gloom and sometimes refers to heavy clouds, Holladay, p. 284). Again, in the last part of the verse Isaiah reminds the people of Israel that the Lord will rise to dispel the darkness. In the previous verse, both the Lord and His glory are the subjects of the same verb; however, in this verse the Lord and His glory are separated into two phrases. There are some who would indicate that these verses have a direct reference to the first coming of Jesus Christ (Jn 1:14–16; I Jn 1:2). Although it is true that God revealed His glory through the coming of Christ to the earth, the entire context of this chapter indicates that this glory is the glory of the millennial kingdom.

3 And the Gentiles shall come to thy light, and kings to the brightness of thy rising.

4 Lift up thine eyes round about, and see: all they gather themselves together: thy sons come to thee: thy sons and thy daughters shall be nursed at thy side.

5 Then thou shalt see, and flow together, and thine heart shall fear, and be enlarged; because the abundance of the sea shall be converted unto thee, the forces of the Gentiles shall come unto thee.

3–5. And the Gentiles shall come. This refers to the fact that all of the nations (*gōyim*) of the earth will be attracted to the Light. The verb used here literally means that the nations would walk. The preposition **to** could also be translated as in or with reference to the Light. Even official heads of state would perform their homage to the Light. Again, one must remember that the Light is not the light of Zion, but rather the beauty and radiance of the Lord as shining upon Zion. The people are ultimately attracted not to Israel, but to the Lord. Verse 4 refers to the regathering of the children of Israel from all parts of the earth. This is clearly emphasized by the utilization of the terminology **thy sons and thy daughters.** Jerusalem is likened to a mother who gathers her children back in the security of the home. **Thy daughters shall be nursed at thy side** (lit., and your daughters on the side shall be supported). This is a reference to the Oriental custom of carrying children on the hips. **And flow together** (from the verb *nahar*, which means to shine or be radiant). The idea conveyed is that when Israel would see this happen, their face would light up or become radiant. **And thine heart shall fear** ("tremble in fear") **and be enlarged** (lit., swell). This describes the deep and heartfelt emotion of the people of Israel. **The abundance of the sea** is a reference to the riches of the gentile nations that will all be delivered to Israel. **The forces** (the wealth) **of the Gentiles shall come unto thee.**

6 The multitude of camels shall cover thee, the dromedaries of Mid'i-an and E'phah; all they from She'ba shall come: they shall bring gold and incense; and they shall shew forth the praises of the LORD.

7 All the flocks of Ke'dar shall be gathered together unto thee, the rams of Ne-ba'i̇oth shall minister unto thee: they shall come up with acceptance on mine altar, and I will glorify the house of my glory.

8 Who are these that fly as a cloud, and as the doves to their windows?

9 Surely the isles shall wait for me, and the ships of Tar'shish first, to bring

6–9. These verses contain a listing of all of the gifts and wealth that will be brought to Israel. Ancient traders traveling in caravans of camels will come from **Sheba**, a district in Arabia, most likely, modern-day Yemen. They would bring gold and incense and would **show forth the praises of the LORD.** People from **Kedar** (the second son of Ishmael, Gen 25:13) whose posterity lived between Syria and Mesopotamia and the **rams of Nebaioth** will come to Zion. The people of Nebaioth are always mentioned in reference to Kedar or the descendants of Ishmael. They will use their flocks as a sacrificial offering to God. This verse clearly teaches that animal sacrifice will be a part of the millenial kingdom. Having described the immigration from the east, the prophet now looks toward the west and asks the question, **Who are these that fly as a cloud, and as the doves**

thy sons from far, their silver and their gold with them, unto the name of the Lord, thy God, and to the Holy One of Israel, because he hath glorified thee.

10 And the sons of strangers shall build up thy walls, and their kings shall minister unto thee: for in my wrath I smote thee, but in my favour have I had mercy on thee.
11 Therefore thy gates shall be open continually; they shall not be shut day nor night; that *men* may bring unto thee the forces of the Gentiles, and *that* their kings *may be* brought.
12 For the nation and kingdom that will not serve thee shall perish; yea, *those* nations shall be utterly wasted.

13 The glory of Lebanon shall come unto thee, the fir tree, the pine tree, and the box together, to beautify the place of my sanctuary; and I will make the place of my feet glorious.
14 The sons also of them that afflicted thee shall come bending unto thee; and all they that despised thee shall bow themselves down at the soles of thy feet; and they shall call thee, The city of the Lord, The Zion of the Holy One of Israel.
15 Whereas thou hast been forsaken and hated, so that no man went through thee, I will make thee an eternal excellency, a joy of many generations.
16 Thou shalt also suck the milk of the Gentiles, and shalt suck the breast of kings: and thou shalt know that I the Lord *am* thy Saviour and thy Redeemer, the mighty One of Jacob.

to their windows? This is a description of a fleet of ships who are swiftly approaching Israel. They are described as doves returning to their shelter. Verse 9 contains the answer to the question of the previous verse. **The isles shall wait for me.** This is a direct reference to the coastlands of the Mediterranean Sea. The ships will not only bring the people of Israel from other lands, but they will also contain silver and gold. Again, the prophet reminds us that all of these people are attracted to the Lord. **God had glorified thee** (from the Hebrew word *pa'ar*, meaning to shine, to glitter, to glow, Harkavy, p. 588). The idea is that God had beautified or caused Israel to shine forth with His glory.

10-12. These verses describe the rebuilding of Jerusalem. **The sons of strangers** indicates that foreigners will be involved in the building of Jerusalem's walls. This is a dramatic divergence from past dealings between Israel and the Gentiles. It was foreigners who destroyed the walls and who were hostile towards Israel. Now, they come and assist in helping Jerusalem. The reason for the dramatic change is found in the last two phrases of verse 10: God had dealt with Israel in judgment, and then in grace. It was not really foreigners who had destroyed the walls of Jerusalem; rather, it was the wickedness of the people and the judgment of God that had destroyed them. Faithful to His covenant and promises, God now shows mercy; and the city is rebuilt. **Therefore thy gates shall be open continually.** The gates served as a means by which to defend the city. Now that all the world was turning in favor to Jerusalem, there was no longer need for the gates to be closed. All previous hostilities had been reconciled, and there was no fear of an attack upon Jerusalem. John utilizes this phrase in the book of the Revelation when describing the heavenly Jerusalem (Rev 21:25). The continual opening of the gates would allow people to bring **the forces of the Gentiles** (lit., the wealth of the Gentiles). Those who refuse allegiance to Jerusalem will perish and will be destroyed. This is a clear reference to the millennial kingdom when Christ will rule with a rod of iron. Some commentators imply that this passage refers to the rebuilding of Jerusalem after the Exile, and others imply that it refers to the coming of Christ when all nations will be affected by His death and resurrection. However, this verse clearly contradicts either of these positions. The only legitimate interpretation is to apply this to the millennial kingdom. (On the millennial age, see C. L. Feinberg, *Millennialism*; A. McClain, *The Greatness of the Kingdom*; G. N. Peters, *The Theocratic Kingdom*; N. West, *The Thousand Years*.)

13-16. These verses describe in detail the worship which is performed at Jerusalem. Special attention is centered around the sanctuary where this worship takes place. In verse 13 the sanctuary will be a beautiful place, and the **glory of Lebanon** (her fir, pine, and box trees) will be a vital part of the structure. **I will make the place of my feet glorious.** This is another reference to the Temple (1 Chr 28:2). Even those who had previously hated and oppressed Zion will come **bending unto thee.** They will also **bow themselves down at the soles of thy feet.** This implies a falling at one's feet and clinging to the feet for mercy. They will call the city **The city of the Lord** (Jehovah or *Yahveh*). The prophet describes an important contrast. Instead of being ignored, forsaken, and hated, Israel will now have **an eternal excellency.** Notice that this excellency is eternal and a **joy of many generations** (lit., a joy of generation and generation). This can only be interpreted to mean the millennial kingdom and, ultimately, the heavenly Jerusalem. The opening phrases of verse 16 emphasize that as a mother gives milk for the sustenance of her child, so the nations will give of their life for the substance of Israel. **The breast of kings** refers to the quality of the resources received by Israel. In the latter part of this verse Isaiah reminds the people again that it is not the inherent worth

17 For brass I will bring gold, and for iron I will bring silver, and for wood brass, and for stones iron: I will also make thy officers peace, and thine exactors righteousness.
18 Violence shall no more be heard in thy land, wasting nor destruction within thy borders; but thou shalt call thy walls Salvation, and thy gates Praise.

19 The sun shall be no more thy light by day; neither for brightness shall the moon give light unto thee: but the LORD shall be unto thee an everlasting light, and thy God thy glory.
20 Thy sun shall no more go down; neither shall thy moon withdraw itself: for the LORD shall be thine everlasting light, and the days of thy mourning shall be ended.
21 Thy people also *shall be* all righteous: they shall inherit the land for ever, the branch of my planting, the work of my hands, that I may be glorified.
22 A little one shall become a thousand, and a small one a strong nation: I the LORD will hasten it in his time.

CHAPTER 61

THE Spirit of the Lord GOD *is* upon me; because the LORD hath anointed me to preach good tidings unto the meek; he hath sent me to bind up the brokenhearted, to proclaim liberty to the captives, and the opening of the prison to *them that are bound;*

of Israel that brings this to pass; but rather, it is the Lord thy **Savior and . . . Redeemer** (see 49:26).

17-18. There will be both outward beauty and inward stability in this city. Good materials, such as **brass, iron, wood,** and **stones,** will be replaced with **gold** and **silver.** This will be accomplished by God Himself. This is emphasized by the two verbs, **I will bring,** and **I will also make.** Beyond the outward beauty there will be inner stability. **Thy officers peace.** The word **officers** could be translated as governors and has a direct reference to the government. God will bring peace to the government. **And thine exactors** (Heb *nagas,* overseer, taskmaster, tax collector, with direct reference to the officials of government, Holladay, p. 227). These officials will be righteous (see the contrast in 59:14). Violence, and the resulting waste and destruction, will be eliminated. The very walls of the city will be called **Salvation, and thy gates Praise.** People will recognize the very borders of Jerusalem as salvation and will enter into that salvation with praise to the One who made it possible.

19-22. In these verses the prophet concludes the thoughts he began in verse 1. He returns to the description of the city as being filled with the **brightness** and glory of the Lord. The opening statement of verse 19 could be translated: "there shall not be to thee anymore the sun for light." This construction is similar to the opening statement of the first commandment. There shall not be to thee any other gods. The glory of the Lord will so fill Jerusalem that no other gods will be worshiped. The Apostle John utilizes this same description for the new Jerusalem (Rev 21:23; 22:5). Again, in verse 20 the emphasis is upon light. Leupold (II, p. 316) suggests that in the Old Testament light symbolizes two things: the presence of God and salvation. The fact that the sun will not set nor the moon disappear implies an eternal consistency. **The days of thy mourning shall be ended.** The days of thy mourning refers to the dark days when sin overwhelmed the world (see vs. 2). These days are now **ended** (from the Hebrew word *shalam,* which means to be full or completed, Harkavy, p. 726). To complete God's program on God's time sequence, the days of apostasy and darkness have been fully completed. Having described the city and the Temple, the prophet now describes the inhabitants. The **people** shall be **righteous** (referring to theological righteousness as imputed by faith to the recipients, see 35:8; 52:1; 53:11). Their possession of the land is to be permanent, which is a fulfillment of the promise to Abraham (Gen 12:1, 7; 15:18). These people would be a **branch of my planting** and the **work of my hands,** implying that they would receive their care and nourishment from God Himself. **That I may be glorified.** All of the fulfillment of these promises will ultimately glorify the source—God Himself. **A little one** probably refers to a person with few children, and a **small one** probably indicates someone in a humble position. God promises them numerical increase and also an expansion of joyous fellowship. **I the LORD** (*Yahweh* or Jehovah) **will hasten it in his time** (lit., fulfill it rapidly). The glorious prospects of this chapter will be accomplished; and in His sovereignty, Jehovah will bring it to pass.

61:1. In chapter 60 Isaiah introduces and describes the glorious kingdom that has been promised by Jehovah. Conspicuously absent in that chapter is the King that rules over the kingdom. In this chapter Isaiah introduces the One who will rule. The identity of the speaker can only be determined by examining the words of Jesus in Luke 4:17-21. After Jesus read from this passage in the synagogue, He concluded by making this statement ". . . this day is this scripture fulfilled in your ears" (Lk 4:21). It is amazing to note that liberal commentators go to extensive lengths in identifying the speaker of this chapter, and they totally ignore the words of Jesus. Westermann (p. 366) identifies the speaker as Trito-Isaiah who has received a call

2 To proclaim the acceptable year of the Lord, and the day of vengeance of our God; to comfort all that mourn;

3 To appoint unto them that mourn in Zion, to give unto them beauty for ashes, the oil of joy for mourning, the garment of praise for the spirit of heaviness; that they might be called trees of righteousness, the planting of the Lord, that he might be glorified.

4 ¶And they shall build the old wastes, they shall raise up the former

similar to that of Deutero-Isaiah. **The spirit of the Lord God is upon me.** This opening statement is a powerful witness to the Trinity. It speaks of the **Lord God** (*Adonai Yahweh*). This same title is also used for God in 50:4-9. The **me** upon whom the **spirit** rests is obviously the Lord Jesus Christ (Lk 4:17-21). And it is the Spirit (Holy Spirit) which rests upon Christ. In these designations we have the clear teaching of the Trinity in the Old Testament. The reason the Spirit of God is on Christ is that the Lord **hath anointed me.** The Hebrew word is *mashach* which indicates a pouring on of oil to set apart a person for a specific office. In the Old Testament people were appointed to be kings, prophets, or priests. Although the anointing here emphasizes the prophetic nature of Christ's ministry, Jesus is the anointed Prophet, Priest, and King! Isaiah then identifies the specific ministry of this God-anointed prophet. In describing His ministry, he extends beyond the normal boundaries of a prophet's ministry. He is, first of all, **to preach good tidings.** This is from the verb *basar*, which means to announce or bring glad tidings. This is a clear reference to the proclamation of the gospel and to the priority of evangelism. It is interesting to note that this is mentioned first because this was the foremost objective of Christ in coming to the earth. Second, Christ will **bind up the brokenhearted.** He will come to place bandages of healing on broken hearts. This refers to hearts that have been broken by sin and guilt. Third, He will **proclaim** (*qara*) **liberty.** In the Hebrew this phrase is the same phrase utilized when describing the proclamation of freedom at the Year of Jubilee, when all those who were in slavery were set free. **The opening of the prison.** This could be literally translated "and to the bound one's complete opening."

2-3. Fourth, Messiah will **proclaim** (*qara*) **the acceptable year of the Lord.** It is interesting to note that when Jesus quoted from this passage, He stopped after this phrase and then proclaimed that what has been stated has already been fulfilled in their eyes. Jesus did not come for the **day of vengeance of our God.** He came in the fullness of time to save sinners. The next time He comes He will come with vengeance to judge the world. The fact that Jesus stopped prior to the **day of vengeance** clearly indicates that during His first advent, He had no intention of setting up an earthly kingdom such as is described in chapter 60. Fifth, Christ was **to comfort all that mourn** after His great and awesome judgments. Sixth, He would exchange the evidences of mourning with the evidences of rejoicing. The recipients of these blessings would be those who are broken because of their personal sin and the terrible condition of their society. Their **ashes** would be exchanged for **beauty.** This is the same root word that is used to describe the glory and the radiance of Jehovah who is the Light of Jerusalem. This would imply that God will give of His own radiance in exchange for the ashes of repentance. He will give them **the oil of joy** to replace their mourning (Ps 45:8). He will give them **the garment of praise for the spirit of heaviness.** They will receive an outer mantle of praise to replace the spirit of heaviness (lit., the spirit of infirmity). The prophet then identifies the ultimate results of this messianic ministry. The people would be called **trees of righteousness.** The word translated **trees** is from the Hebrew word *'ayl* and could be translated as a strong tree, oak, or sometimes as a mighty one. The oak tree represents greatness, strength, and a tree capable of enduring all of the adverse elements of nature. God's righteousness is that which makes His people as oak trees. Again, the final conclusion is that which makes His people as **that he might be glorified.** This is a repetition of 60:21.

4-6. They refer to the subject of **shall build the old wastes** and also those mentioned in verse 3 who mourn in Zion. Their repentance has been turned to joy, and their joy will ultimately lead them to rebuild the city. The **old wastes** refers to the building of ancient ruins. Delitzsch (II, p. 428) suggests that these ancient ruins extend beyond the geographic boundaries of Palestine and implies a rebuilding of all ancient ruins. Cities and lands that have been desolate for many generations will be reinhabited. The verse suggests a program of worldwide rebuilding and renewal. **And strangers** (*zariym*) **shall stand** is often translated as enemies. During this time of Israel's glory, even her enemies **shall stand**. The word translated **stand** is the word '*amad*, which means to stand or to serve, and implies one who stands before the king ready to serve him (Harkavy, p. 529). Those with former hostilities to Israel would stand as servants ready to perform whatever tasks she deemed necessary. This. They would be shepherds, **plowmen**, and **vinedressers**. This era will be a time of great cooperation between Jew and Gentile, former friend and foe. Israel will occupy a place of special significance in this new kingdom. They would be **Priests of the LORD**. This is in keeping with God's promise to Moses that His people would become a kingdom of priests (Ex 19:6). They would also be **Ministers of our God**. The word translated **ministers** (*mesharethiy*) could also be translated as servant and would indicate some noble service performed by Israel. It is interesting to note that the prophet distinguishes the fact that Israel does not lose its national identity. Although God's program has changed in the New Testament era, there will come a time when God again will restore Israel to a place of prominence. In light of this and many other passages of Scripture, it is impossible to legitimately interpret the church as simply an extension of Israel from the Old Testament. Israel maintains its identity in the future. Israel will be the recipients of the riches and wealth of the gentile nations.

7-9. God would replace their darkness and shame with the grace of His blessings. **Ye shall have double.** This means that they would receive double blessing and glory due to God's desolation. As they possess the land, **they will be recipients of the manifold blessings of God**; thus, **they shall possess the double**. The Hebrew word **double** is *misheneh*, which refers to a doubling or a repetition. This signifies the extent of God's blessings that would be manifold; they would be duplicated. This blessing would be accompanied by **everlasting joy**. Again, the only legitimate interpretation is that all of these promises will be finally fulfilled during the millennial reign of Christ. God loves **judgment** (that which is right), and God hates **robbery for burnt offering**. This is probably not a reference to stealing in regards to sacrifices, but rather the unjust robbery imposed on the children of Israel during their captivity. In essence, the heathen had robbed Israel of that which was most meaningful: their sacrificial system. God will also **direct their work in truth**, which implies that He will place the result of their work in security. In other words, what they are doing will not be in vain. All of these qualities of God in regards to His people are predicated upon His **everlasting covenant with them**. All the people of the world will recognize that God has blessed His people. All **that see them shall acknowledge them**. This could be literally translated as they will certainly recognize them for what they are, that is, a people blessed by God Himself.

10-11. After enumerating the many blessings of God upon His people, the chapter concludes with an exuberant and joyous song of praise to Jehovah. **I will greatly rejoice.** The tremendous emphasis of this opening statement is somewhat lost in the English translation. The opening statement should be literally translated "rejoicing I will rejoice." When the writers sought to emphasize a point in Hebrew, they did so by repeating the word (see Isa 6:3). The joy spoken of in this verse is not

desolations, and they shall repair the waste cities, the desolations of many generations.

5 And strangers shall stand and feed your flocks, and the sons of the alien *shall be* your plowmen and your vinedressers.

6 But ye shall be named the Priests of the LORD: *men* shall call you the Ministers of our God: ye shall eat the riches of the Gentiles, and in their glory shall ye boast yourselves.

7 For your shame *ye shall have* double; and *for* confusion they shall rejoice in their portion: therefore in their land they shall possess the double: everlasting joy shall be unto them.

8 For I the LORD love judgment, I hate robbery for burnt offering; and I will direct their work in truth, and I will make an everlasting covenant with them.

9 And their seed shall be known among the Gentiles, and their offspring among the people: all that see them shall acknowledge them, that they are the seed *which* the LORD hath blessed.

10 I will greatly rejoice in the LORD, my soul shall be joyful in my God; for he hath clothed me with the garments of salvation, he hath covered me with the robe of righteousness, as a bridegroom decketh *himself* with ornaments, and as a bride adorneth *herself* with her jewels.

11 For as the earth bringeth forth her

bud, and as the garden causeth the things that are sown in it to spring forth; so the Lord God will cause righteousness and praise to spring forth before all the nations.

CHAPTER 62

FOR Zion's sake will I not hold my peace, and for Jerusalem's sake I will not rest, until the righteousness thereof go forth as brightness, and the salvation thereof as a lamp that burneth.

2 And the Gentiles shall see thy righteousness, and all kings thy glory: and thou shalt be called by a new name, which the mouth of the Lord shall name.

3 Thou shalt also be a crown of glory in the hand of the Lord, and a royal diadem in the hand of thy God.

4 Thou shalt no more be termed Forsaken; neither shall thy land any more be termed Desolate: but thou shalt be called Hĕph'zi-bah, and thy land Bĕü'-lah: for the Lord delighteth in thee, and thy land shall be married.

5 For as a young man marrieth a virgin, so shall thy sons marry thee: and as

simply an external, emotional state predicated upon circumstances, it is an inner joy, for it comes from the **soul**. This joy was a result of the fact that God had clothed them with **the garments of salvation** and **the robe of righteousness**. These two phrases are synonymous and speak of salvation. Salvation is receiving the imputed righteousness of God Himself. The glorious nature of these garments and their resplendent beauty can be observed in the latter part of the verse where they are paralleled to the garments of a bridegroom and bride. The bridegroom is described as wearing a large turban similar to that worn by the priest, and the direct implication is that it is only through sacrifice that these garments are available. The beauty and pride of the bride in her marriage jewels describe the feeling and excitement of being clothed in the righteousness of God. The words of Edward Mote, in his hymn, "The Solid Rock," are so appropriate, "When He shall come with trumpet sound, O may I then in Him be found, Dressed in His righteousness alone, Faultless to stand before the throne. On Christ, the solid Rock, I stand—All other ground is sinking sand." Verse 11 contains a comparison. Isaiah confirms that as surely as in His creative power God brings forth natural life, so God will also cause **righteousness and praise to spring forth before all the nations.**

62:1-2. If this part of Isaiah was strictly organized according to chronology, this chapter would actually precede chapter 60. The content outlines the situations which are preparatory to the deliverance of Zion and the establishment of Christ's kingdom. Commentators differ as to who is speaking in this chapter. Some perceive that it is the prophet himself, while others indicate that it is the Lord. Apparently, verse 6 indicates that the speaker is the Lord Himself. God's desire to fulfill His promise to **Zion** and **Jerusalem** is emphasized in its opening statement. God would not be still, and He will not rest until His promise is fulfilled. There is an interesting parallel in the two verbs mentioned here. God promised He would not be at **peace**; even further, He emphasized that He would not even **rest** until He had fulfilled His covenant with Zion. **Righteousness** will be as *nōgah*, which is the light that bursts through the night (Prov 4:18). **Salvation** will be as a torch that burns. As the sun rises in the glory of the morning, so would the deliverance and salvation of Israel arise against the darkness of sin. **And the Gentiles shall see.** The verb translated **shall see** is the Hebrew word *rā'āh*, which means to gaze, to perceive, to become aware of (Holladay, p. 328). The Gentiles will do more than observe this glory. They will look at it attentively. Note that **all kings** will see their glory. The glory of Jerusalem will exceed the cosmopolitan glory of all the kings of the earth combined. **Thou shalt be called by a new name**, which implies a specific name is not mentioned, this phrase implies a new change. Just as a Christian is a new creation in Christ, so also Israel will experience a radical change from that which has been normal previously. Jehovah will determine this new name. The verb *naqab* means to pierce, to mark, and to "designate in a signal and distinguishing manner" (Delitzsch, II, p. 435). The name will be a clear designation of their new estate.

3-5. Israel will be a **crown of glory**. The word translated **diadem** is the same root word used to describe the headdress of the high priest. Note that the crown and headdress are not on the head of Jehovah; but rather, both are in His hand. Two different Hebrew words are translated as **hand**. The first indicates the open hand, which implies power; and the second denotes the palm, which indicates the function of displaying an object. The idea is that God is displaying Zion in all of her glory, which is ultimately a manifestation of His redeeming power. One could also deduce from this that Israel will be a nation of kings and priests. In verse 4 the names by which the city and the land had been known would be changed because of God's blessings. Zion would no longer be called **Forsaken.** It had been known as *'azûbah* which means that Zion had been forsaken by Jehovah, but now she would be called *chephtsibah* (lit., my delight is in her). The land that was formerly called *shemamah* (a desolate place referring to the desert) would now be called *be'ulah* (lit., married). **And thy land shall be married.** The land will be strongly attached to the Lord; and the Lord, as the Husband, will serve as the protector of His bride. This relationship is further described with the joy experienced in the marriage ceremony. The word that is translated married (from ba'al) could also be translated to rule over, to take possession, or to marry (Holladay, p. 43). **So shall thy God rejoice over thee.** Note that rejoicing occurs both from God and towards God. In 61:10 the people rejoice in what God has done, and in 62:5 God rejoices with the people as He fulfills His covenant relationship on their behalf.

6-7. I have set watchmen upon thy walls. God appoints **watchmen** (overseers) for the further protection of His people. The identity of these watchmen is somewhat difficult to assess. Some believe that they are spiritual watchmen whose primary occupation is to continue in prayer. Others utilize Daniel 4:18 and I Kings 22:19 to suggest that they could be angels. Since there is no indication of military purpose in this passage, they most likely are intercessors who pray for the final peace of Jerusalem. **They are not to hold their peace day or night.** This could be literally translated as "all the day and all the night always they shall not be silent." The thought of continual, persistent intercessory prayer continues in verse 7. They are to persistently pray **till he establish.** This word indicates the idea of making ready or preparing oneself. Thus, the prophets are both to sound a warning to and intercede in prayer for the people.

8-9. The unique balance between human intercession and divine sovereignty is demonstrated here. God appoints watchmen to continually intercede until He fulfills His promise to Jerusalem. In these particular verses God's sovereignty and His power to fulfill His promises are indicated. **The LORD hath sworn.** The promise of God is confirmed by an oath established through His right hand and His strong arm. The particular formation of this oath is similar to that in 22:14. God promises that strangers will no longer ravish and plunder the land. It indicates that even this plundering of Israel was within the providence and plan of God. Since God indicates He will permit it no longer, it is logical to assume that when it occurred, it was by His permission. The plundering of one's crops was considered as a clear evidence of God's judgment upon that person (Deut 28:30-33). In verse 9 God guarantees that the people who planted the corn would eat it and those who gathered the grapes would drink it.

10-12. These last verses contain the command for the people to prepare themselves for the coming exalted state of Zion. The prophet utilizes repetition in order to emphasize the importance of the message. Verse 10 begins **Go through, go through.** The message communicated is that God's people all over the world were to pass through the gates of their cities and prepare themselves to return to Jerusalem. It could also refer to the passing through the gates of Jerusalem. For additional comments on repeated imperatives, see also 40:11; 51:9, 17; 52:1; 57:14; 65:1. The second repeated, emphatic imperative is **cast up, cast up the highway.** The people were not only to leave the gates of their heathen cities to prepare for their journey, but they were also to throw up the road; and in so doing they lifted up a banner above the nations. The raising of this banner would indicate that their actions would be visible to nations far and wide. The proclama-

---

the bridegroom rejoiceth over the bride, *so* shall thy God rejoice over thee.

6 ¶I have set watchmen upon thy walls, O Jerusalem, *which* shall never hold their peace day nor night: ye that make mention of the LORD, keep not silence.

7 And give him no rest, till he establish, and till he make Jerusalem a praise in the earth.

8 The LORD hath sworn by his right hand, and by the arm of his strength, Surely I will no more give thy corn *to be* meat for thine enemies; and the sons of the stranger shall not drink thy wine, for the which thou hast laboured:

9 But they that have gathered it shall eat it, and praise the LORD; and they that have brought it together shall drink it in the courts of my holiness.

10 ¶Go through, go through the gates; prepare ye the way of the people; cast up, cast up the highway; gather out the stones; lift up a standard for the people.

11 Behold, the LORD hath proclaimed unto the end of the world, Say ye to the daughter of Zion, Behold, thy salvation cometh; behold, his reward *is* with him, and his work before him.

12 And they shall call them, The holy people, The redeemed of the LORD: and thou shalt be called, Sought out, A city not forsaken.

CHAPTER 63

WHO *is* this that cometh from E'dom, with dyed garments from Bŏz'rah? this *that is* glorious in his apparel, traveling in the greatness of his strength? I that speak in righteousness, mighty to save.

2 Wherefore *art thou* red in thine apparel, and thy garments like him that treadeth in the winefat?

3 I have trodden the winepress alone; and of the people *there was* none with me: for I will tread them in mine anger, and trample them in my fury; and their blood shall be sprinkled upon my garments, and I will stain all my raiment.

63:1-3. The prophet asks a question, and then that question is answered. **Edom** is representative of all those who hate Israel. The Edomites were descendants of Esau (Gen 36:1, 8-9), and throughout their history they practiced hostile intent toward Israel (Amos 1:11-12). The destruction of all those who oppose God and His people is implied in the destruction of Edom. It is interesting to note that when Jerusalem was destroyed, the Edomites sided with the captors and applauded the destruction of Israel. **Bozrah** was the capital city of Edom. **With dyed garments** (*shamats* which means to be heavy or to be dyed in red; Harkavy, p. 180). The reason for these bright red garments is given in verses 2-3. The phrase **traveling in the greatness of his strength** could be translated as inclining in his great power. The Person answers by stating that He is great in word and in deed. He comes in righteousness to judge sin and those who hate His people. He is also **mighty to save** (or to deliver). Who is this person with bright red garments that promises great words and deeds? The clue to his identity can be deciphered by comparing a similar passage in Revelation 19:13: "And he was clothed with a vesture dipped in blood: and his name is called The Word of God." This person who comes in judgment is none other than Jesus Christ the Messiah. An interesting parallel is that the one who speaks in 63:1 is the same One who is called "The Word of God" in Revelation 19:13. Having addressed His identity with the first question, the prophet now asks a second question concerning His red garments. Obviously, red was not the normal color of these garments. They were like the garments of one who had been treading upon the grapes in the winepress. Those garments were as if they had been stained by red wine (see 5:2). The Lord answers the prophet's question: **I have trodden the winepress alone.** The word used here for winepress is different and occurs only in this passage and in Haggai 2:16. It designates the place where the grapes were crushed or broken (Isa 53:5). Although the description of Christ in this passage refers to His coming in judgment, this opening statement implies the Crucifixion. Because Christ did go through the winepress alone, He has the legitimate right to return in righteous judgment upon the earth. This mighty deliverer now comes in vengeance. The word trans-

tion that **salvation cometh** is made to the **end of the world.** Since this salvation is personified in the next phrase, **his reward, his work** probably refers to the salvation refers to more than a coming kingdom; it refers to a coming King. The reward spoken of here probably refers to a large multitude of people making their way back to Jerusalem in anticipation of the coming glory. These people would be called **The holy people** (from the Hebrew word *qadash* which means to be holy, withheld from ordinary use, belonging to the sanctuary; Holladay, p. 313). God had intended for His people to be a holy people (Ex 19:6); and now, in their final hour of glorification this promise is fully realized. This holiness is predicated upon God's redemption. They are **The redeemed of the LORD.** They would be called **Sought out.** This is from the word *derishah* and is the opposite of the Hebrew word '*azuvah*, which means forsaken. They will be a **city not forsaken.** This implies that Israel will now have permanent inhabitants and that God's grace, mercy, and love will never depart from the city.

3. Consummation of peace. 63:1-66:24.

Having listed God's conditions for peace in chapters 58-59 and having described the character of that peace and the resultant glory that comes to Zion in chapters 60-62, the prophet now looks to the consummation of that peace in these last chapters. Yet, it appears that Israel is surrounded by hostile enemies. How could she rise to such glory and prominence when there were so many people who desired her extinction? The answer to this question is explained in this section.

4 For the day of vengeance *is* in mine heart, and the year of my redeemed is come.

5 And I looked, and *there was* none to help; and I wondered that *there was* none to uphold: therefore mine own arm brought salvation unto me; and my fury, it upheld me.

6 And I will tread down the people in mine anger, and make them drunk in my fury, and I will bring down their strength to the earth.

7 ¶ I will mention the lovingkindnesses of the LORD, *and* the praises of the LORD, according to all that the LORD hath bestowed on us, and the great goodness toward the house of Israel, which he hath bestowed on them according to his mercies, and according to the multitude of his lovingkindnesses.

8 For he said, Surely they *are* my people, children *that* will not lie: so he was their Saviour.

9 In all their affliction he was afflicted, and the angel of his presence saved them: in his love and in his pity he redeemed them; and he bare them, and carried them all the days of old.

lated **blood** is *netsach*, which refers to juice and, in reference to people, blood, and gore (*CHAL*, p. 244). **And I will stain all my raiment.** The judgment will be so severe and universal that ultimately all of His garments will be stained with the blood of nations.

4-6. **The day** and **the year** both refer to the specific time of God's judgment. It was **in mine heart.** This implies that the coming vengeance was in the purposes and plans of God. It was to be a time of **vengeance** (see 61:2), and yet it would be the time of **my redeemed** (62:12). In the completion of His wrath and judgment, **there was none to help.** There was no one capable of executing such judgment upon the earth. **And I wondered** (lit., I was astonished). **There was none to uphold** (there was none upholding or none maintaining justice and righteousness). Only God's arm brought deliverance, and His **fury** (wrath) . . . **upheld me.** The verb **upheld** is the same word translated earlier in the verse as to **uphold.** Verse 6 describes in the judgment of God by utilizing three verbs, each of them listed in a specific order of progression. **I will tread . . . and make them drunk . . . I will bring down.** Again, the figurative language of a winepress is utilized in this verse. God will trample them as in a winepress; they will become intoxicated with God's fury, and ultimately they will be destroyed. **And I will bring down** means that God will pour out **their strength** (*netsach* or their juice, which implies their life's blood). The judgment will be so severe that the lifeblood of the nations will be poured out on the earth. This passage is strikingly similar to Revelation 19, where Jesus Christ is described in His final revelation upon the earth. Christ will come to ". . . judge and make war . . ." (Rev 19:11), He will be clothed ". . . with a vesture dipped in blood" (Rev 19:13), and "he treadeth the winepress of the fierceness and wrath of Almighty God" (Rev 19:15). The flowing of the blood mentioned in verse 6 parallels the great judgment of Revelation 14:20. "And the winepress was trodden without the city, and blood came out of the winepress, even unto the horse bridles, by the space of a thousand and six hundred furlongs." The clear implication of this passage is the coming of Christ for His final conflict with Satan and his forces. At that time He comes in righteousness and judgment to destroy those who oppose His purpose. The rest of this chapter and the following chapter contain a prayer of thanksgiving, confession, and intercession. Chapters 65-66 articulate the answer to the prophet's prayer. God will reject His apostate people and will be faithful to the remnant.

7-9. There is a sharp distinction in the person speaking between verse 6 and verse 7. In verse 6 the Lord is speaking, and in verse 7ff. the prophet speaks. **I will mention.** This could be translated as I will celebrate. This celebration is centered around the **loving kindnesses** of God's grace (*chasedey*). It is a celebration of God's grace as extended in His kindness toward His people. This word is also in the plural and indicates the abundance of God's mercies to Israel. The prayer begins with thanksgiving and praise and conforms to the guidelines of Psalm 23. He celebrates **the great goodness toward the house of Israel.** The word **goodness** (*tub*) refers to God's beneficent goodness. **According to his mercies** is the word *rachamim*, which refers to His deepest, sympathizing tenderness (Delitzsch, II, p. 451). God's dealings with His sinful people is rooted in His grace, His deepest sympathy and His inherent goodness. Israel was God's people. They were the recipients of a covenant relationship with Jehovah. **Children that will not lie.** God demanded obedience to His law on the part of those who were His children. The last statement could be translated "and He became to them a Saviour" (*moshiyac*), a word utilized frequently by Isaiah in 40-66. **In all their affliction he was afflicted.** There is strong disagreement between translators as to the specific translation of

10 But they rebelled, and vexed his holy Spirit: therefore he was turned to be their enemy, and he fought against them.

11 Then he remembered the days of old, Moses *and* his people, *saying,* Where *is* he that brought them up out of the sea with the shepherd of his flock? where *is* he that put his holy Spirit within him?

12 That led *them* by the right hand of Moses with his glorious arm, dividing the water before them, to make himself an everlasting name?

13 That led them through the deep, as an horse in the wilderness, *that* they should not stumble?

14 As a beast goeth down into the valley, the Spirit of the LORD caused him to rest: so didst thou lead thy people, to make thyself a glorious name.

this statement. Some translate it "in all their distress, there was no distress"; some translate it "in their affliction, he was not an enemy"; but the AV renders the best translation. The thought communicated is that in all our affliction God Himself bears those same sorrows. Calvin (p. 839) notes: "In order to move us more powerfully and draw us to Himself, the Lord accommodates Himself to the manner of man, by attributing to Himself all the affection, love and compassion which a father can have." **And the angel of his presence saved them.** The word **angel** means messenger, and God provided this protection in answer to His promise (Ex 23:20-23; 14:19; 33:14-15). This refers to the presence of the Lord Himself, ". . . My presence shall go with thee, and I will give thee rest" (Ex 33:14). **He redeemed them; and he bare them, and carried them.** As a mother carefully carried and cares for her children, so the Lord carried and cares for His people. This redemption is rooted in His love and His *shemlah* (his forgiving gentleness) toward His people.

10-11. But they. This introductory phrase is emphatic. In spite of all of God's good intentions toward His people, they were ungrateful and rebellious. **And vexed his holy Spirit.** This was the nature, or the description, of their rebellion. **Vexed** is from *'atsab*, which means to afflict, or to grieve, or to pain. This idea is similar to the one conveyed in Ephesians 4:30. Note again in these verses a specific reference to the Trinity. Jehovah extended His mercy to His people; He sent His angel (Christ) to deliver them, but they rebelled and grieved His Holy Spirit (see also comments on 61:1), and Jehovah became their enemy. This was accomplished in Israel's history by allowing heathen nations to conquer and plunder Israel. There are a number of textual difficulties in verse 11. **Then he remembered.** The first critical issue is the subject of this verb. Is God referred to as remembering, or could it be that the people should be the subject of the verb? In the overall context of the verse, it is more legitimate to assume that the people are the subject of the verb. Assuming that to be true, the next problem has to do with the relationship of **Moses** to the phrase. The only reasonable interpretation is that Moses is inserted parenthetically to indicate the specific period of history to which the writer is referring. Leupold (II, p. 349) treats the second part of the verse as follows: "Strike the final *m* of the second word (a clear case of dittography). Then the object of this participle is the word 'shepherd' which is not plural construct (shepherds of) but a singular construct to be written with the final *h*. This makes Moses the one whom the Lord brought up from the sea, and the one in whose midst He put His Holy Spirit." **Put his holy Spirit within him?** This could be translated as "He put His Holy Spirit in the midst of them." In the Old Testament economy, the Holy Spirit came upon people and dwelt in their midst; whereas, in the New Testament the Holy Spirit lives within people (Eph 5:18).

12-14. These verses describe God's dealings with the children of Israel in delivering them from Egyptian bondage and leading them through the wilderness. The opening statement of vs. 12 could be translated "who at the right hand of Moses causes the arm of His glory to go." The idea is that the right hand of Moses (place of his strength) was guided by the glorious arm of the Lord. The prophet emphasizes the cooperation between the human and the divine. The children of Israel were led by Moses' hand, and in turn Moses was guided by the hand of God. **Dividing the water.** This word means to split or cleave the water (*boq'*). The miracle of the dividing of the waters would be an event long remembered by Israel. **That led them through the deep.** This is a reference to the crossing of the Red Sea (Ps 106:9). Paul utilizes this event in dealing with the subject of temptation in I Corinthians 10:2. The passing through the depths is likened to baptism. This symbolism would further substantiate the mode of baptism to be that of immersion. God also led them in such a way that they would not stumble. The **horse** is used to illustrate the fact that they were able to walk with all obstacles cleared from their path. **As a beast goeth down into the valley.** The word **beast** could be translated as cattle, and in this beautiful illustration God communicates a tremendous truth. Like cattle who leave the barren, cold mountains to go down into the valley where they find abundant pastureland, so **the Spirit of the LORD caused him to rest** (see Deut 12:9; Ps 105:11). This is a direct reference to their entrance into the land of Canaan where God gave them rest. By doing this, God would make **thyself a glorious name** (or a beautiful name). This leading of God in behalf of His people could be paralleled to the leadership of a shepherd leading his flock (for a Psalm of Thanksgiving in behalf of God's deliverance, see Ps 78).

15 ¶Look down from heaven, and behold from the habitation of thy holiness and of thy glory: where *is* thy zeal and thy strength, the sounding of thy bowels and of thy mercies toward me? are they restrained?

16 Doubtless thou *art* our father, though Abraham be ignorant of us, and Israel acknowledge us not: thou, O LORD, *art* our father, our redeemer; thy name *is* from everlasting.

17 ¶O LORD, why hast thou made us to err from thy ways, *and* hardened our heart from thy fear? Return for thy servants' sake, the tribes of thine inheritance.

18 The people of thy holiness have possessed *it* but a little while: our adversaries have trodden down thy sanctuary.

19 We are *thine:* thou never barest rule over them; they were not called by thy name.

15-19. The prophet makes an appeal for God to hear him. Heaven is indicated as **the habitation of thy holiness and of thy glory.** The word **habitation** (*mᵉwbul*) could be translated as the dwelling place, but that does not indicate that God's presence is localized there (see I Kgs 8:49). **Where is thy zeal and thy strength?** The prophet is referring to the zeal and the deliverance that God had effected for His people in leading them from Egypt into Canaan. The idea is not that God had lost His zeal or strength, but rather that He is withholding it from His people. **The sounding of thy bowels.** Though this is a rather crude statement, it was a colloquialism utilized to express love, concern, and sympathy. **Doubtless.** This phrase could be translated "for you are our Father," and indicates the reason why the prophet is praying. Although the figure of God as a Father is a rare expression in the Old Testament, it is nevertheless an expression of deep love and concern. Isaiah furthers this analogy by describing Israel as God's son. The sole fatherhood of God is emphasized by the fact that their natural fathers could not help them. The words **ignorant** and **acknowledge** are utilized to communicate the fact that even though Abraham and Israel were distinguished patriarchs, they were incapable of helping Israel in their predicament. The prophet is emphasizing a spiritual relationship between God as the Father and Israel as the children, whereas Abraham and Jacob represent a natural relationship. The last phrase of this verse could be translated as "our Redeemer; from everlasting is your name." Jehovah, Israel's Father, had always been their one-and-only Redeemer. **Why hast thou made us to err from thy ways . . . ?** This could be translated as "Why do you make us wander, Jehovah?" God does not cause anyone to sin. The idea implied here is that God allowed them to wander because of their sin and because of their disobedience He had **hardened our heart.** The word translated **hardened** is a more emphatic word than the normal *qashah.* **Return for thy servants' sake.** This verb **return** (*shûb* means to turn around and is sometimes translated with the idea of conversion or repentance; Harakvy, p. 700) is in the imperative. The presumption of the prophet in commanding God to return is based on the fact that the people are His servants. The prophet is appealing to God's covenant relationship with His people. Verse 18 begins with the word *mits'ar* (lit., for a little). This indicates a short duration of time, a phrase that modifies both statements in the verse. The people of Israel had possessed the land for a little while, and their adversaries had **trodden down thy sanctuary** for a little while. The first fulfillment of this prophecy was during the Babylonian exile when God's temple was totally destroyed, but their temples would be destroyed again in 63 B.C. and in A.D. 70 by the Roman armies. **We are thine.** This is a peculiar phrase and should be translated as "We are from forever." This emphasizes the fact that Israel had been chosen from eternity as God's people. **Thou never barest rule**

CHAPTER 64

OH that thou wouldest rend the heavens, that thou wouldest come down, that the mountains might flow down at thy presence,

2 As *when* the melting fire burneth, the fire causeth the waters to boil, to make thy name known to thine adversaries, *that* the nations may tremble at thy presence!

3 When thou didst terrible things *which* we looked not for, thou camest down, the mountains flowed down at thy presence.

4 For since the beginning of the world *men* have not heard, nor perceived by the ear, neither hath the eye seen, O God, beside thee, *what* he hath prepared for him that waiteth for him.

5 Thou meetest him that rejoiceth and worketh righteousness, *those that* remember thee in thy ways: behold, thou art wroth; for we have sinned: in those is continuance, and we shall be saved.

6 But we are all as an unclean *thing,* and all our righteousnesses *are* as filthy rags: and we all do fade as a leaf; and

over them, God had not ruled over Israel's enemies in a personal way as He had ruled over Israel.

64:1. Verse 1 of this chapter is actually a part of 63:19 in the original divisions of the Hebrew Bible. Isaiah appeals for God's direct intervention into the affairs of Israel. The figure here is one of significance. Delitzsch (II, p. 463) comments: "Israel felt itself to be separated from the world beyond by a thick party-wall, resembling an impenetrable black cloud." Isaiah appeals to God to split or tear apart that separating cloud. He desires for the mountains to **flow down** (*nazal*). This would indicate the melting of mountains and, as a result, the judgment fire of God. The reference to clouds and the Lord splitting the clouds definitely points to the second coming of Christ. "Behold, he cometh with clouds; and every eye shall see him . . .," (Rev 1:7). The melting of the mountains is also indicated when the Lord returns: ". . . and the earth shall melt with fervent heat, the earth also and the works that are therein shall be burned up" (II Pet 3:10).

2-5. The melting fire burneth (lit., as burns the fire brushwood). It refers to the burning of brush. This phrase, along with the phrase describing fire burning boiling water, are both descriptive of the plea for the Lord to come down. Fire is often utilized as a description of God's judgment (1:31; 10:17; 65:5). The result of His coming in judgment will be **to make thy name known** (or lit., to cause to make known thy name). Just as the mountains melted at His presence, so also the nations would tremble before Him. Verse 3 is a rephrasing of the previous two verses and continues the thought of God's judgment. **Terrible things.** This is from the Hebrew word *yare'* which means to fear, or to hold in honor. These words refer to mighty acts of God which cause people to fear and respect Him. Verse 4 contains the reasons why the prophet implores God to come down and pronounce judgment on the earth. The eternal character of God is introduced in the opening emphatic statement of the verse. **For since the beginning** could be translated "And from forever." Two verbs are utilized to describe hearing **not heard, nor perceived.** They are the same two verbs that appear at the very beginning of the book (1:2). The idea of hearing, perceiving, and seeing God refers to "recognizing His existence through the perception of His works" (Delitzsch, II, p. 466). Isaiah refers to this recognition of a God who works on behalf of those that **waiteth for him.** Paul utilizes this verse as the basis for I Corinthians 2:9, but he does not give an exact quotation from Isaiah. Verse 4 is one that is extremely difficult to interpret. Alexander (II, p. 431) has said of this passage: "There is perhaps no sentence in Isaiah, or indeed in the Old Testament, which has more divided and perplexed interpreters, or on which the ingenuity and learning of modern writers have thrown less light." **Thou meetest.** This verb implies the idea of a meeting that involves helping. God will meet with and help those who **rejoiceth and worketh righteousness.** When God comes in final judgment on behalf of Israel, not all of Israel will be looking forward to that coming or will live in belief. God only comes on behalf of those who are faithful to Him. **Those that remember thee in thy ways.** This could be literally translated as "in your ways they remember you." It emphasizes the fact that when God intervenes on behalf of His people, they will remember Him for what He has done. God was angry **for we have sinned.** This is the word *chata',* which means to miss, or to fail. The Old Testament concept of sin was a falling short of God's standard or mark. **In those is continuance.** This is literally translated as "in them is eternity." It refers to the fact that in God's ways or dealings with His people, there is perpetuity of eternity.

6-9. *Kullanu* or **all** (of us) are unclean. This refers to all those who are making confession (see ch. 53). The word **unclean** is the word *tame'* and is a technical term utilized to describe legal impurity (Lev 5:2; 7:19). The people were recognizing that because they had fallen short of God's standard, they were as those who were required by law to cry unclean. All of their right living amounted to **filthy rags**. **Filthy rags** refers to the menstrual periods of a woman. The last two figures in verse 6 go together. In the fading of a leaf, reference is made to the gradual losing of one's vitality and strength. Ultimately, they would be swept away with the wind as a leaf is blown across the earth after falling from the tree. "The people were robbed by their sins of all vital strength and energy, like dry leaves, which the guilt and punishment springing from sin carried off as a very easy prey" (Delitzsch, II, p. 471). **And there is none that calleth upon thy name.** Because of the depravity of their nature and the complexities of their sin, the people had forgotten God. **And hast consumed us, because of our iniquities.** The word **consumed** is *wattemūgenū* (lit., thou hast melted us). The people had melted like wax. They had lost all their strength because of their sin. Verse 8 begins with a change in thought. **But now.** In spite of their sinful condition and in spite of the fact that they had been melted like wax, the prophet reminds Jehovah that He is **our father.** There is hope in spite of their deplorable condition. God was still their Father; and as such, He still loved them and could intervene on their behalf (see 63:16). This relationship is further described in the form of a potter and the clay. The word **potter** could be translated as "the one who formed us" (see 29:16; 45:9). The **clay** represents that which is pliable and submissive, and the potter represents the One who has absolute authority over the clay. **Be not wroth very sore.** The prophet implores God not to be angry (lit., into strength). In other words, don't be angry to the full extent of your strength or power. Had God vexed His full anger against sin, He would have utterly destroyed the people. **Neither remember iniquity for ever,** or not in a sense of retribution for eternity. The prophet is pleading for mercy on the basis of their sin. They recognize that judgment is just, but they are throwing themselves on the mercy of God. **We beseech thee,** or we pray to you, to remember that **we are all thy people.**

10-12. The prophet again reminds God of His covenant relationship and that their substantive basis for mercy is that they are God's people. The prophet again asks God to intervene, not only on behalf of His people, but also on behalf of His land. He sees a time ahead when the land is in desolation; the land is a desert and the cities, especially the Holy City, Jerusalem, is a desolation. Note the step-by-step progression in the prayer. He begins in general with the **holy cities,** then progresses to **Jerusalem,** the chiefest of holy cities, and finally, to the Temple itself. The Temple had been burned with fire and destroyed. This implies the literal burning of the Temple (Jer 52:13). Finally, the prophet concludes his prayer. He asks three questions, with the obvious answer to each question being negative. In the Hebrew the verse begins with "over these things." Because of the desolation of the land, Jerusalem, and the Temple, will you restrain yourself from hearing and answering our prayer? **Hold thy peace** refers to being silent. **Afflict us very sore** (*me'ōd* which means exceedingly). The prophet is asking God not to judge them with all of His strength and to the full extreme. The answer to this prayer is given in the last two chapters of the book.

65:1-10. In response to the prayer of the previous chapter, God speaks to the Gentiles who have come to trust in His salvation. **I am found of them that sought me** not refers to the election of the Gentiles as the New Testament church of God. The fact that God has declared Himself unto a **nation** (*gōy*, gentile nation) is indicative of His sovereign election. This verse is quoted by the Apostle Paul (Rom 10:20) in relation to the unconditional election of the Gentiles as the people of God. The

1419

---

our iniquities, like the wind, have taken us away.

7 And *there is* none that calleth upon thy name, that stirreth up himself to take hold of thee: for thou hast hid thy face from us, and hast consumed us, because of our iniquities.

8 But now, O LORD, thou *art* our father; we *are* the clay, and thou our potter; and we all *are* the work of thy hand.

9 Be not wroth very sore, O LORD, neither remember iniquity for ever: behold, see, we beseech thee, we *are* all thy people.

10 Thy holy cities are a wilderness, Zion is a wilderness, Jerusalem a desolation.

11 Our holy and our beautiful house, where our fathers praised thee, is burned up with fire: and all our pleasant things are laid waste.

12 Wilt thou refrain thyself for these *things*, O LORD? wilt thou hold thy peace, and afflict us very sore?

CHAPTER 65

I AM sought of *them that* asked not *for me; I* am found of *them that* sought me not: I said, Behold me, behold me, unto a nation *that* was not called by my name.

2 I have spread out my hands all the day unto a rebellious people, which walketh in a way *that was* not good, after their own thoughts;

3 A people that provoketh me to anger continually to my face; that sacrificeth in gardens, and burneth incense upon altars of brick;

4 Which remain among the graves, and lodge in the monuments, which eat swine's flesh, and broth of abominable *things is in* their vessels;

5 Which say, Stand by thyself, come not near to me; for I am holier than thou. These are a smoke in my nose, a fire that burneth all the day.

6 Behold, *it is* written before me: I will not keep silence, but will recompense, even recompense into their bosom,

7 Your iniquities, and the iniquities of your fathers together, saith the LORD, which have burned incense upon the mountains, and blasphemed me upon the hills: therefore will I measure their former work into their bosom.

8 ¶ Thus saith the LORD, As the new wine is found in the cluster, and one saith, Destroy it not; for a blessing *is in* it: so will I do for my servants' sakes, that I may not destroy them all.

9 And I will bring forth a seed out of Jacob, and out of Ju´dah an inheritor of my mountains: and mine elect shall inherit it, and my servants shall dwell there.

10 And Shar´on shall be a fold of flocks, and the valley of A´chor a place for the herds to lie down in, for my people that have sought me.

11 ¶ But ye *are* they that forsake the LORD, that forget my holy mountain, that prepare a table for that troop, and that furnish the drink offering unto that number.

12 Therefore will I number you to the sword, and ye shall all bow down to the slaughter: because when I called, ye did not answer; when I spake, ye did not hear; but did evil before mine eyes, and did choose *that* wherein I delighted not.

13 Therefore thus saith the Lord GOD, Behold, my servants shall eat, but ye shall be hungry: behold, my servants shall drink, but ye shall be thirsty: behold, my servants shall rejoice, but ye shall be ashamed:

14 Behold, my servants shall sing for joy of heart, but ye shall cry for sorrow of heart, and shall howl for vexation of spirit.

15 And ye shall leave your name for a curse unto my chosen: for the Lord GOD shall slay thee, and call his servants by another name:

16 That he who blesseth himself in the earth shall bless himself in the God of truth; and he that sweareth in the

rebellious people are the Jews who have refused God's gracious offer of salvation and provoketh (from 'abar, to alienate) the Lord's anger by their attitude that: I am holier than thou. Because of Israel's election as the covenant people of God, their false assumption was that this was an election to privilege and not to responsibility. In time they falsely assumed that their election as the chosen (vs. 15) nation was based on some merit of their own. (On the significance of the election of Israel, see J. B. Payne, *The Theology of the Older Testament*, pp. 177-194; G. Vos, *Biblical Theology*, pp. 127-141; R. Youngblood, *The Heart of the Old Testament*, pp. 17-35. On the relationship of election to the covenant, see W. Dyrness, *Themes in Old Testament Theology*, pp. 112-126; H. H. Rowley, *The Biblical Doctrine of Election*, pp. 69-89.) God further announces His coming judgment on Israel because she has blasphemed me upon the hills, a reference to the pagan worshiping at the pagan altars of the high places. Though they deserve to be destroyed, God promises that he will not destroy them all. This clearly indicates that the successive judgments of God against the Jewish people shall never be such as to cause their extermination. He will always keep a remnant of His people for Himself. Within that physical remnant is yet a further spiritual remnant of believing Israelites. They are called a seed out of Jacob . . . mine elect. The language here is reminiscent of Romans 11:1-5, where the Apostle Paul raises the question of whether God has cast away His people. In answering his own question, the apostle states that "God hath not cast away his people which he foreknew"; and then he observes that "at this present time also there is a remnant according to the election of grace." The prediction has a twofold significance, in that there will be a saved remnant of Jews who will come to faith in Christ during the church age; and there will be an even greater believing remnant who shall be blessed during the millennial kingdom of Christ when the plain of Sharon (to the west) and the valley of Achor (to the east) shall both blossom abundantly in an atmosphere of peace and prosperity. Young (III, p. 508) takes the amillennial view in suggesting that this does not represent a physical return of the Jews to Palestine. Archer (p. 653), holding the premillennial view, sees this as a time of prosperity during the time of the millennial age, when the latter-day Israel shall again enjoy the special blessings of God.

11-16. This message of the coming consolation of the Messiah is interrupted with a statement of condemnation to those that **forsake the LORD.** Instead of enjoying the blessing and prosperity of God, they shall remain **hungry . . . thirsty . . . ashamed.** By contrast, the **servants shall sing for joy of heart.** Notice that the term **servants** is now being used in the plural for all those believers who have come to faith in God by the means of the atonement of the Servant. **Joy of heart** actually means goodness (tôb) of heart and is contrasted to the **sorrow of heart** (grief or anguish) which shall characterize the unbelievers. **Vexation of spirit** actually means brokenness of spirit. The apostate, unbelieving Jews are described as a **curse unto my chosen,** so that God shall call **his servants by another name.** Many see in this a possible reference to saved Israelites being known as Christians. Their **former troubles** (tribulations) shall be **forgotten** as the peoples of the earth come to bless and swear by the **God of truth** ('amen). Hence, He is the "God of Amen!" Whatever He decrees or declares shall stand as truth!

17-20. At this point the prophet Isaiah sees further into the future than any other Old Testament prophet. He looks down beyond the church age, the Tribulation Period, and the millennial kingdom, to the new heavens and a new earth (cf. Rev 21:1ff.). This brand new world is the result of the creation of God. The verb bōrē' (from bara') is only used in the simple (Qual) stem with God as its subject. It is the same word used in Genesis 1 to describe the creative activity of God. While the new heavens and a new earth specifically refer to the eternal state, the reference here may be taken as an overview to all that follows: for the child dying in verse 20 is certainly not an experience of the eternal state, but of the earthly millennial kingdom. God shall also create Jerusalem a rejoicing. Instead of a city that has been trodden underfoot of the Gentiles, Jerusalem emerges as the great city of joy, meaning that she shall become an object of joy. The former (things) refers to the former heavens and earth. Thus, we are suddenly thrust into the celestial future where there shall be new heavens, a new earth, and a New Jerusalem. The grandeur and magnitude of this new Creation shall be such as to cause people to forget about the former Creation. As beautiful as our present world is, even under the curse of sin, the beauty of the world to come will obliterate even the finest of its memories. In this great city of celestial joy weeping and crying shall be no more. Surely the Apostle John captured this same picture when he saw into the future when "... God shall wipe away all tears from their eyes; and there shall be no more death, neither sorrow, nor crying, neither shall there be any more pain: for the former things are passed away" (Rev 21:4). In this kingdom to come, time itself shall begin to fade away; and both the infant and the old man shall die a hundred years old, means that if someone were to die at a hundred, he would be considered a mere child. However, by contrast, death shall cut off the sinner without hesitation. While amillennial commentators attempt to relate this promise to eternity, it is an utter impossibility to do so. Here we have the blessedness of the millennial kingdom of Christ in view. It is a time when men shall have the potential of living for a thousand years; hence, anyone who shall die at a hundred shall be looked upon as a mere child. This era is not the restoration of Paradise, but the restoration of the pre-Flood patriarchal era. It is a time when Christ shall rule the earth with a rod of iron and the gentile nations shall accept His authority or be cut off. It is a time when children shall yet be born, when there are still sinners, and when life on this earth shall proceed as before.

21-25. The inhabitants of this era shall build houses ... plant vineyards, etc. It is a time when there is neither slave labor nor socialism, for every man shall enjoy the work of their hands. Thus, no one shall labor in vain; but he shall have the opportunity to plant and harvest his own crop. Mine elect refers to the saved Israelites of the Tribulation Period who shall go into the millennial kingdom under the banner of God's blessed provision. This period of time shall be long (1000 years). The greatest blessing of the millennial kingdom shall be instantaneously answered prayer. Before they call, I will answer is God's promise to His people. In this present age, we too have the confidence that God hears and answers our prayers; however, we must often await His proper timing in that answer. By contrast, the millennial age shall be characterized by instantly answered prayers that God shall fulfill even before we ask! All of nature shall be changed, as well as the conditions of mankind. The wolf and the lion are contrasted with the lamb and the bullock; but they will

1421

earth shall swear by the God of truth: because the former troubles are forgotten, and because they are hid from mine eyes.

17 ¶For, behold, I create new heavens and a new earth: and the former shall not be remembered, nor come into mind.

18 But be ye glad and rejoice for ever in that which I create: for, behold, I create Jerusalem a rejoicing, and her people a joy.

19 And I will rejoice in Jerusalem, and joy in my people: and the voice of weeping shall be no more heard in her, nor the voice of crying.

20 There shall be no more thence an infant of days, nor an old man that hath not filled his days: for the child shall die an hundred years old: but the sinner being an hundred years old shall be accursed.

21 And they shall build houses, and inhabit them; and they shall plant vineyards, and eat the fruit of them.

22 They shall not build, and another inhabit; they shall not plant, and another eat: for as the days of a tree are the days of my people, and mine elect shall long enjoy the work of their hands.

23 They shall not labour in vain, nor bring forth for trouble; for they are the seed of the blessed of the LORD, and their offspring with them.

24 And it shall come to pass, that before they call, I will answer; and while they are yet speaking, I will hear.

25 The wolf and the lamb shall feed together, and the lion shall eat straw like the bullock: and dust shall be the

serpent's meat. They shall not hurt nor destroy in all my holy mountain, saith the LORD.

CHAPTER 66

THUS saith the LORD, The heaven is my throne, and the earth is my footstool: where is the house that ye build unto me? and where is the place of my rest?

2 For all those things hath mine hand made, and all those things have been, saith the LORD: but to this man will I look, even to him that is poor and of a contrite spirit, and trembleth at my word.

3 He that killeth an ox is as if he slew a man; he that sacrificeth a lamb, as if he cut off a dog's neck; he that offereth an oblation, as if he offered swine's blood; he that burneth incense, as if he blessed an idol. Yea, they have chosen their own ways, and their soul delighteth in their abominations.

4 I also will choose their delusions, and will bring their fears upon them; because when I called, none did answer; when I spake, they did not hear: but they did evil before mine eyes, and chose that in which I delighted not.

5 ¶Hear the word of the LORD, ye that tremble at his word: Your brethren that hated you, that cast you out for my name's sake, said, Let the LORD be glorified: but he shall appear to your joy, and they shall be ashamed.

6 ¶A voice of noise from the city, a voice from the temple, a voice of the LORD that rendereth recompence to his enemies.

7 Before she travailed, she brought forth; before her pain came, she was delivered of a man child.

8 Who hath heard such a thing? who hath seen such things? Shall the earth be made to bring forth in one day? or shall a nation be born at once? for as soon as Zion travailed, she brought forth her children.

9 Shall I bring to the birth, and not cause to bring forth? saith the LORD: shall I cause to bring forth, and shut the womb? saith thy God.

feed together. This would indicate that during the Millennium the carnivorous diet of certain animals shall be changed, and there shall be peace in the animal kingdom as well as among men. However, to remind us that this is not yet heaven, but Christ's rule upon the earth, we are cautioned, **And dust shall be the serpent's meat** (an idiom for bite the dust), while the other predatory animals have become tame and harmless. Though Satan shall be bound for a thousand years during Christ's millennial reign upon the earth (Rev 20:2), he shall yet be released one more time for one final act of rebellion. Thus, the serpent remains in the dust as a symbolic reminder that Christ's final and ultimate triumph over him is yet to come.

66:1–4. Isaiah's final prophecy begins with the assertive, **Thus saith the LORD** (*Yahweh*). The passage points to the magnitude and immensity of God, who is greater than the heavens themselves. He is the God who does not really need a temple. The **heaven** (celestial) is His **throne**, and the **earth** is His **footstool**. This passage makes it clear that there is no **house** or **place** that man can build that shall contain or confine God. Even Solomon's temple, in which the glory of the Lord dwelt as a representation of His presence with Israel, can only be referred to as the dwelling place of God in a symbolic sense. While there will be a Temple during the millennial kingdom, there is no need for a Temple in eternity. The Apostle John catches the same vision in the Apocalypse when he says, "And I saw no temple therein: for the Lord God Almighty and the Lamb are the temple of it" (Rev 21:22). While men may build a structure to honor God, he can in no way build anything that will accommodate Him in all of His majesty. Rather than dwelling in a Temple made with human hands, God's desire is to dwell in men who are of a **poor and . . . contrite spirit.** These are they in whom He delights according to 57:15. Thus, Isaiah foresees the New Testament doctrine of the indwelling of the Spirit of God in the temple of man's body (1 Cor 6:19). In contrast to this reality of true spiritual life, God makes it clear that He no longer delights in the **abominations** of Israel's empty ritual and animal sacrifice. Merely going through the outward form of ritual religion is nothing more than a series of **delusions** (*ta'alûl*, vexations). Instead of answering the call of God to personal repentance and faith, they **chose . . . evil.**

5–9. In contrast to the judgment of the unbelievers, God promises a marvelous deliverance to the repentant remnant that **tremble at his word.** These are the ones who were **hated** by the unsaved and were **cast . . . out** for the Lord's **name's sake.** The prophet emphasizes that the Lord shall be **glorified** (from *kabod*, divine splendor) in His saints when **he shall appear** (from *ra'ah*, to come near). The Hebrew root word is similar to that of a bird of prey dropping down from the heavens. It refers to the second coming of the Lord. The prophet further describes a woman bringing forth a **man child** before she travailed in pain. The prophet then asks the question, **who hath heard such a thing?** While God is judging His enemies, Israel is pictured as being born in a day (**shall a nation be born at once?**) Zion is pictured as the mother who is speedily bringing forth **children.** While it has been customary for commentators to view this as the church (spiritual Israel) quickly springing up and spreading across the world, it should rather be viewed as converted Israel who will come to faith during the Tribulation Period and quickly spread the message of the gospel around the world. (For a unique Jewish-Christian perspective see A. W. Kac, *The Messianic Hope;* and *The Rebirth of the State of Israel;* cf. also T. LaHaye, *The Beginning of the End;* H. Lindsell, *The Gathering Storm; World Events and the Return of Christ;* J. Phillips, *Only God Can Prophesy!*) Even Kidner (p. 624) admits that these events, "clearly concern the end-time." The question asked in verse 9, **Shall I bring to the birth, and not cause to bring**

forth?, is rhetorical and implies the answer, no! In essence, the Lord is saying, "Should I bring Israel this far through all of these difficulties and not bring forth converted Israel to the full blessing of the Millennium?" The answer, by implication, is that He will in fact do so.

10-16. All those that both **love and mourn** for the Holy City are commanded to **Rejoice ye with Jerusalem.** The imagery of a mother nursing her baby with fresh milk is illustrative of the nations of the world that shall look once again to Jerusalem for spiritual nourishment. This shall occur during the millennial kingdom when Jerusalem shall again be God's "capital" on earth. It is during that time that she shall experience **peace . . . like a river and glory . . . like a flowing stream.** Then shall the Gentiles be as a baby who **shall be borne upon her sides, and be dandled upon her knees.** This touching picture is that of a loving mother who carefully carries her child upon her hip and bounces him gently upon her knees. The image of **peace . . . like a river** is taken from the figure of a mighty river, which represents a never-dwindling supply of water that continues as a source of nourishment and refreshment without interruption. The ultimate source of all spiritual life, of course, is God Himself. As God extends a spiritual rebirth to the nation of Israel during the time of her darkest hours, she will become the channel of God's blessing to the Gentiles, which is a purpose that she never really fulfilled in the Old Testament era. In her national conversion and rebirth, Israel's **bones shall flourish** (cf. Ezk 37). For those who do not receive the Lord but remain in unbelief, **the LORD will come with fire . . . like a whirlwind . . . with fury . . . with flames of fire.** The imagery here is certainly reflected in II Thessalonians 1:7-8, where Christ is pictured in His second coming as returning to earth in fiery judgment on the unrighteous. So severe will that judgment be that Isaiah notes the **slain of the LORD shall be many!**

17-19. Those who seek salvation in the religious abominations of man shall **be consumed together.** Thus, the religion of the last days is described as an **abomination** (*hashequets*, the hateful thing). Because God knows both their **works** and their **thoughts,** He shall come in furious judgment upon them. But while God shall judge the wicked and unrighteous nations of this world, He shall, at the same time, **gather all nations and tongues.** The context of these verses indicates that this gathering is one of blessing which results in their seeing His **glory.** In order to accomplish this, the Lord states that He will set a **sign** (*'ôth,* miracle) among them. That sign is the miraculous re-gathering and rebirth of the nation of Israel. **I will send those that escape** refers to those converted Israelites who shall escape the Tribulation to come and shall be sent by God as Christian believers **unto the nations.** The names given in the text are those nations that were on the farthest extremities of the Mediterranean world. **Tarshish** refers to western Europe, or possibly Spain. **Pul** (Put) and **Lud** were regions of North Africa. **Tubal** was on the Turkish-Russian border, and **Javan** refers to Greece. The names serve as an example of the universality of the mission which converted Israel will have in succeeding the church in taking the message of God to the nations. Thus, they shall **declare** (from *nagad,* meaning to boldly announce by word of mouth) the Lord's **glory** (*kebôdy*). While the actual meaning of the word conveys the idea of splendor or glory, its forty-five usages in the Old Testament are always associated with a visible manifestation of God. This is directly related to God's self-disclosure and His desire to dwell among men (see *TWOT,* pp. 426-428). That this reference should be taken in relation to the preaching of the gospel is obvious. It is as the gospel of Jesus Christ is preached and men come to know Him that they come to experience His glory dwelling in them personally.

20-24. Not only will the nations come **to my holy mountain**

---

10 Rejoice ye with Jerusalem, and be glad with her, all ye that love her: rejoice for joy with her, all ye that mourn for her:

11 That ye may suck, and be satisfied with the breasts of her consolations; that ye may milk out, and be delighted with the abundance of her glory.

12 For thus saith the LORD, Behold, I will extend peace to her like a river, and the glory of the Gentiles like a flowing stream: then shall ye suck, ye shall be borne upon *her* sides, and be dandled upon *her* knees.

13 As one whom his mother comforteth, so will I comfort you; and ye shall be comforted in Jerusalem.

14 And when ye see *this,* your heart shall rejoice, and your bones shall flourish like an herb: and the hand of the LORD shall be known toward his servants, and *his* indignation toward his enemies.

15 For, behold, the LORD will come with fire, and with his chariots like a whirlwind, to render his anger with fury, and his rebuke with flames of fire.

16 For by fire and by his sword will the LORD plead with all flesh: and the slain of the LORD shall be many.

17 They that sanctify themselves, and purify themselves in the gardens behind one *tree* in the midst, eating swine's flesh, and the abomination, and the mouse, shall be consumed together, saith the LORD.

18 For I *know* their works and their thoughts: it shall come, that I will gather all nations and tongues; and they shall come, and see my glory.

19 And I will set a sign among them, and I will send those that escape of them unto the nations, *to* Tar'shish, Pul, and Lud, that draw the bow, *to* Tū'bal, and Jā'van, *to* the isles afar off, that have not heard my fame, neither have seen my glory; and they shall declare my glory among the Gentiles.

20 And they shall bring all your

1423

brethren *for* an offering unto the LORD out of all nations upon horses, and in chariots, and in litters, and upon mules, and upon swift beasts, to my holy mountain Jerusalem, saith the LORD, as the children of Israel bring an offering in a clean vessel into the house of the LORD.

21 And I will also take of them for priests *and* for Lē′vites, saith the LORD.

22 For as the new heavens and the new earth, which I will make, shall remain before me, saith the LORD, so shall your seed and your name remain.

23 And it shall come to pass, *that* from one new moon to another, and from one sabbath to another, shall all flesh come to worship before me, saith the LORD.

24 And they shall go forth, and look upon the carcases of the men that have transgressed against me: for their worm shall not die, neither shall their fire be quenched; and they shall be an abhorring unto all flesh.

Jerusalem during the millennial kingdom, but God promises to take **priests** and **Levites** from among them to serve Him. The chapter ends with a wonderful and awful promise of God's perpetuity. The promise is that the **new heavens and the new earth shall remain** forever. This will usher in the final state of glorification, which shall be an unchanging state for both the redeemed and the damned. Not only shall the nations worship regularly at Jerusalem during the Millennium, but the people of God throughout all eternity shall come to worship in the New Jerusalem. **All flesh** refers to all of the redeemed of the Lord. These alone shall **come to worship . . . the LORD.** Isaiah's universalism is not a message of universal salvation regardless of one's faith, but a universal kingdom with the awesome purged out of it! Thus, the book ends with the awesome statement that the redeemed shall **go forth, and look upon the carcases of the men that have transgressed against me.** While the imagery may be drawn from the fact that one could stand in the Temple at Jerusalem and look down into the valley of Hinnom (from which the imagery for hell is drawn), nevertheless, the scene here seems rather to be that of the redeemed of heaven, in their final, glorified, and fixed state. Those who are described as suffering are undoubtedly in the lake of fire where **their worm shall not die, neither shall their fire be quenched** (Mk 9:44; Rev 20:14-15). The question is often asked of this statement as to whether or not the saved will be able to see those who are in hell. The obvious answer is, Yes! In our final and fixed state, we would be able to see our dearest loved one in the lake of fire and be able to say, "The judge of all the earth has done right!" In our finite human state we could never bear such a sight. The awesome closing of this marvelous book of prophecy is a reminder to every believer of our responsibility to personal witnessing and soul-winning. There is a real hell to be avoided, and all those who do not receive Jesus Christ as their personal Saviour shall go there. Of these awesome words, S. C. Thexton, *Isaiah 40-66,* pp. 154-155, said "They remind us that from the gate of Heaven there is a road to Hell; and that before every man there lies the choice between the way of life and the way of death."

Thus, the book of Isaiah ends much as it began, with a message of both impending doom and potential deliverance. In this greatest of the Old Testament prophets we see one recurring theme: Jesus Christ, the Virgin's son, Immanuel, the Branch of the Lord, the Mighty God, the Prince of Peace, the coming Messiah, the Suffering Servant, the glorious King! "To him give all the prophets witness . . ." (Acts 10:43).

BIBLIOGRAPHY

*Alexander, J. A. *The Prophecies of Isaiah.* 2 vols. New York: Wiley & Putnam, 1846, reprinted Grand Rapids: Zondervan, 1970.

*Archer, G. L. Isaiah. In *The Wycliffe Bible Commentary.* Ed. by C. Pfeiffer and E. Harrison. Chicago: Moody Press, 1962.

Barnes, A. *Notes on the Old Testament: Isaiah.* 2 vols. Grand Rapids: Baker, reprinted, 1964.

Buksbazen, V. *The Prophet Isaiah.* Collingswood, N.J.: Spearhead Press, 1971.

Calvin, J. *Commentary on the Book of the Prophet Isaiah.* Grand Rapids: Associated Publishers, reprinted, 1970.

Cheyne, T. K. *The Prophecies of Isaiah.* 2 vols. New York: Whitaker, 1888.

*Delitzsch, F. *Biblical Commentary on Isaiah.* 2 vols. Grand Rapids: Eerdmans, reprinted, 1949.

Fitch, W. Isaiah. In *The New Bible Commentary.* Ed. by F. Davidson. Grand Rapids: Eerdmans, 1954.

Gray, G. The Book of Isaiah. 2 vols. In *International Critical Commentary.* New York: Scribner's Sons, 1912.

*Hindson, E. E. *Isaiah's Immanuel.* Philadelphia: Presbyterian & Reformed, 1978.

Jennings, F. C. *Studies in Isaiah.* New York: Loizeaux Brothers, 1950.

Kidner, D. Isaiah. In *New Bible Commentary: Revised.* Grand Rapids: Eerdmans, 1970.

*Leupold, H. C. *Exposition of Isaiah.* 2 vols. Grand Rapids: Baker, 1968.

Lowth, R. *Isaiah.* 2 vols. Boston: Buckingham, 1815.

MacRae, A. A. *The Gospel of Isaiah.* Chicago: Moody Press, 1977.

Martin, A. Isaiah: "The Salvation of Jehovah." Chicago: Moody Press, 1962.

*Nägelsbach, C. The Prophet Isaiah. In *A Commentary on the Holy Scriptures.* Ed. by J. P. Lange. New York: Scribner's Sons, 1906.

Orelli, C. von. *The Prophecies of Isaiah.* London: T. & T. Clark, 1895.

Robinson, G. L. *The Book of Isaiah.* Grand Rapids: Baker, reprinted, 1964.

Rowlinson, G. Isaiah. 2 vols. In *The Pulpit Commentary.* London and New York: Funk and Wagnalls, 1913.

Smith, G. A. *The Book of Isaiah.* 2 vols. New York: Harper & Brothers, 1927.

Vine, W. E. Isaiah: *Prophecies, Promises, Warnings.* London: Oliphants, 1953.

Watts, J. W. *A Distinctive Translation of Isaiah with an Interpretative Outline.* New Orleans: New Orleans Baptist Seminary, 1979.

Wordsworth, W. A. *En-Roeh: The Prophecies of Isaiah the Seer.* Edinburgh: T. & T. Clark, 1939.

*Young, E. J. *The Book of Isaiah.* 3 vols. Grand Rapids: Eerdmans, 1972.

JEREMIAH

INTRODUCTION

The Life and Times of Jeremiah. Nearly one hundred years after Isaiah, Jeremiah appears on the scene. In order to understand the book, one must comprehend the political and social conditions of Judah and its neighboring nations. Assyria had reached its zenith when Sargon III took Samaria in 721 B.C. For the next century Assyria was troubled on all sides. Sennacherib nearly captured Jerusalem in the fourteenth year of Hezekiah (701-700 B.C.; see II Kgs 18:13-19:37; Isa 36-37), but he was miraculously defeated by "the angel of the LORD." His son, Esar-haddon, did not make any important expeditions into Palestine, except for the brief rebellion of Manasseh, Hezekiah's son, for which he was taken to Babylon and shortly thereafter released (II Chr 33).

Ashurbanipal, Esarhaddon's successor, made expeditions into Egypt, dividing that country into twelve small principalities and thus relieving Judah of the Egyptian threat. However, Psamtik (Psammetichus) reunited Egypt, momentarily reviving its glory and posing a new threat to Judah. In time Manasseh died. His son, Amon, reigned for two years and was then succeeded by his son, Josiah. The Assyrian Empire continued to decline during the last quarter of the seventh century B.C.

Early Life. During the reign of the wicked tyrant, Manasseh, Jeremiah was born to Hilkiah, priest of Anathoth, in the land of Benjamin (1:1). This is not Hilkiah the High Priest mentioned in II Kings 22:8 (see A. W. Streane, *Jeremiah and Lamentations* for a defense of Hilkiah as the High Priest), since: (1) the name is too common; (2) the manner in which Hilkiah is mentioned is inconsistent with his being the High Priest; and (3) the priests at Anathoth were of the house of Ithamar line of Eleazar from Zadok on.

Jeremiah was about twenty years old when called to be a prophet in the thirteenth year (626 B.C.) of the reign of Josiah (1:2). He felt immature and unable to speak to men, but God touched his mouth (1:9). Until he was obliged to leave, Jeremiah stayed in Anathoth, his native city. He stayed there in order to escape persecution from his fellow townsmen (11:21) and even his own family who had declared him a dangerous fanatic (12:6). He keenly felt this opposition, crying out to God for judgment (11:18-21; 12:3). He then took up residence in Jerusalem.

Jeremiah prophesied during the reigns of five successive kings of Judah (Josiah, eighteen years; Jehoahaz, three months; Jehoiakim, eleven years; Jehoiachin, three months; and Zedekiah, eleven years and five months). He also prophesied during the occupation by Nebuchadnezzar and the exile in Egypt. His ministry covered about fifty years. Throughout Jeremiah's life he was in almost constant danger from the townsmen (11:21), the priests and prophets (26:8-9), Jehoiakim (36:19, 26), and the military (38:4). However, he remained faithful to the Lord and his calling in spite of persecution.

Under Josiah (640-608 B.C.). Five years after Jeremiah's call, the last great revival occurred under Josiah. Although Jeremiah probably did not participate in the revival, he was greatly influenced by the newly found book of Deuteronomy.

In 607 B.C. Pharaoh Necho, son of Psamtik, landed in the Bay of Acco and marched across northern Palestine, intending to fight the Assyrians at the Euphrates River. Josiah, fearing that if Syria fell to Necho it would mean the end of Judah, intercepted him at Megiddo. The armies of Judah were defeated; and Josiah, mortally wounded, died on his way to Jerusalem (II Kgs 23:29ff.; II Chr 35:20ff.). Jeremiah lamented his death (II Chr 35:25).

Under Jehoahaz (608 B.C.). The people passed by Eliakim, Josiah's eldest son, and appointed Jehoahaz (Shallum), his youngest brother, king (I Chr 3:15; II Chr 36:1). After a three-month reign, Necho bound Jehoahaz at Riblah in northern Syria and exiled him to Egypt where he died. Jeremiah prophesied that he would not return (22:10-12). There is no other mention of Jeremiah during his brief reign.

Under Jehoiakim (608-597 B.C.). Necho took Eliakim and made him a vassal king under the name of Jehoiakim (II Kgs 23:30-35; II Chr 36:1-4). Pro-Egyptian and pro-Babylonian parties vied for the favor of the policymakers in the court, with the Egyptian party being dominant at this time. Jeremiah seemed to be the chief proponent of the Babylonians (Chaldeans) being the way of safety and was, therefore, accused of treason and urged to be executed by the priests and prophets (ch. 26). Jeremiah escaped for a time due to the intervention of the princes (26:16-24).

In 605 B.C., the fourth year of Jehoiakim's reign (the third according to Daniel 1:1, which uses a different dating system), the crown-prince of Babylon, Nebuchadnezzar, defeated Necho at Carchemish (as Jeremiah predicted 46:1-12), an ancient Hittite city on the west bank of the Euphrates River (II Chr 35:20). This was one of two great events (the other being the fall of Jerusalem, 586 B.C.) in the life of Jeremiah. Judah now exchanged an Egyptian yoke for a Babylonian one. Nebuchadnezzar's pursuit of Necho, stopped only by the death of his father, Nabopolassar, resulted in the first invasion of Jerusalem and the deportation of some of the Hebrews to Babylon (Daniel among them). This first invasion of Jerusalem marks the beginning of the seventy year Babylonian captivity

In 607 B.C., Nineveh, capital of the tottering Assyrian Empire, fell to the Babylonians under Nabopolassar, threatening all the countries washed by the Mediterranean, the realm Pharaoh Necho had just added to his empire. Conflict between the two nations could not long be avoided.

foretold by Jeremiah (25:11) just prior to the invasion.

Jehoiakim kept his oath of allegiance to Nebuchadnezzar for three years, at which time he refused to pay his yearly tribute (an act tantamount to a declaration of independence). The Babylonian armies invaded Judah, devastating the land (II Kgs 24:1-2), and eventually encircled Jerusalem. However, by this time Jehoiachin (age eighteen, II Kgs 24:8) had ascended the throne upon his father's death (predicted by Jeremiah, 22:13-19).

Under Jehoiachin (597 B.C.). After a brief reign of only one hundred days, the "young lion" (Ezk 19:5) Jehoiachin (Jeconiah or Coniah) unconditionally surrendered and was deported to Babylon (as predicted by Jeremiah, 22:24-30), along with many nobles and artisans. He was imprisoned for thirty-seven years until he was released by Evil-merodach, Nebuchadnezzar's son (II Kgs 25:27 ff.). Jeremiah sent a letter of condolence to those who shared the captivity with the royal family (chs. 29-31).

Under Zedekiah (597-586 B.C.). Nebuchadnezzar appointed Jehoiachin's uncle, Mattaniah, to the throne and changed his name to Zedekiah (II Kgs 24:8-17; II Chr 36:10). Although weak in character, Zedekiah protected Jeremiah and consulted him secretly (for fear of the princes), though he never carried out his advice (38:14-28). Jeremiah's persecution reached its climax under Zedekiah, especially during the long Babylonian siege. With the approach of the Egyptian army the Babylonians withdrew temporarily, but Jeremiah prophesied they would return (37:7-8). The irritated princes used Jeremiah's departure from the city as a pretext of accusing him of desertion. He was thrown into a prison, then transferred by Zedekiah to the more pleasant court of the guards (37:11-21). With judgment at hand, Jeremiah now prophesied the return of the nation (chs. 32-33). As the siege wore on, the princes had the prophet thrown into a dungeon to die (38:1-6). Ebedmelech, a royal eunuch, took compassion on Jeremiah and had him transferred from the slime pit back to the court of the guard, where he remained until Jerusalem was taken (38:7-28).

This was the last and most bitter cup Jeremiah had to drink. He had preached repentance, but the people of Judah failed to repent. He had advised the kings to submit to Babylon, but they refused. He had counseled the remnant to remain in the land, but they fled to Egypt.

Even in Egypt, Jeremiah continued trying to turn the rebellious people to the Lord (ch. 44). Now between seventy and eighty years old, the prophet delivered his last predictions from Tahpanhes (Daphne) in Lower Egypt (43:8-44:30). Nothing further is recorded of his life. Three traditions have existed concerning his death: (1) a Christian tradition that he was stoned by the Jews at Tahpanhes (Jerome; Tertullion); (2) an Alexandrian tradition that his bones were brought to the city of Alexandria by Alexander the Great; and (3) a Jewish tradition that he, along with Baruch, escaped to Babylon. Jeremiah probably died in Egypt.

Like many great men, Jeremiah was despised in his life, but applauded in death. From being of no account as a prophet, he came to be considered one of the greatest and was called "the Prophet" (cf. Deut 18:15; Mt 16:14; Jn 1:21; 6:14; 7:40).

The Man and His Message. Jeremiah was called to the prophetic office at a most unhappy time in the history of Judah. Both politically and morally, the nation was at a low ebb. God had earlier sent His prophets, but the people would not hear (7:25; 44:4). When the effects of Josiah's revival wore off, the nation plunged on in unbelief, and Jeremiah was called to warn the people of impending judgment. The great theme that runs through the book is that of judgment against Judah. Because of idolatry the people deserved the punishment of God. Even in his call it was intimated to Jeremiah that his message would be one of condemnation, rather than salvation (1:10, 18-19).

The fate of the apostate nation predicted in Deuteronomy 28-30 was now inevitable, and Jeremiah saw Babylon as the instrument of judgment in the hands of God. Judah would be conquered by Babylon. Therefore, it is only wise to surrender, for the sake of the city and the lives of the people.

All the desperate people had to cling to was their nationalism; and, thus, they not only completely rejected the message, but the man as well. Considered a traitor, Jeremiah was persecuted by the mighty and the lowly alike.

However, against this dark background of warning and judgment there is also a message of hope. Some of the most glorious messianic prophecies of the Old Testament appear in Jeremiah. Like Isaiah a century before, he saw Christ's day. He saw Rachel weeping for her children while being carried into captivity (31:15). Matthew saw a further fulfillment of this prophecy in the slaying of the innocents (Mt 2:17, 18). His prophecy of the righteous Branch (chs. 23, 31, 33) is referred to by Zechariah concerning the birth of Christ (Lk 1:78). His prophecy of the new covenant is discussed in Hebrews 8:8-13 and 10:15-17 and is referred to by Christ at the last Passover (Lk 22:20). Christ referred to Jeremiah when He cleansed the Temple (7:9-11; Mk 11:17); and the book of Revelation refers to him many times, particularly with regard to the overthrow of "Babylon" (cf. 17:10—Rev

JEREMIAH

2:23; cf. 25:10—Rev 18:22-23; cf. 51:7-9, 45, 64— Rev 14:8; 17:2-4; 18:2-5, 21).

Because of the autobiographical nature of the book, Jeremiah's character is better known than any other Hebrew prophet. Jeremiah's confessions (10:23, 24; 11:18-12:6; 15:10-21; 17:9-11, 14-18; 18:18-23; 20:7-18; etc.) show the spirit of a man who was retiring, sensitive, and fearful, yet clung tenaciously to his task in spite of persecution.

Jeremiah was especially a preacher of personal religion, the religion of the heart (the word "heart" occurs seventy-one times). The old covenant would be replaced with a new one—one written on men's hearts (31:31-34).

With sorrow he saw his message rejected by the many and received by the few. Because of his immense sorrow at the impenitence of the people, he has been given the title of "the weeping prophet."

Authorship. It has never been seriously doubted that Jeremiah was the author of this book, although some modern critical scholars have credited substantial parts to later authors and editors. In chapter 36:1-2 the Lord commanded Jeremiah to write in a "roll of a book" all his prophecies from Josiah unto the present (the fourth year of Jehoiakim). Therefore, the text itself declares that Jeremiah was the author. But Liberal critics suggest three sources for the book: (1) Jeremiah himself wrote or dictated to Baruch, his amanuensis; (2) a biography of Jeremiah written shortly after his death (perhaps by Baruch); and (3) various editions of later authorship (see J. Hastings, *A Dictionary of the Bible*, p. 575ff for a discussion of the critical view). Numerous conservative scholars have exposed the untenable nature of the above arguments, pointing out that Baruch was too pious a man to have tampered with Jeremiah's prophecies, and that there is simply no evidence to support the view of later additions and interpolations (see C. F. Keil, *The Prophecies of Jeremiah*, p. 25ff., and E. J. Young, *An Introduction to the Old Testament*, p. 243ff). "Though Jeremiah was one of the most read of the prophets," states Lange (J. P. Lange, *A Commentary on the Holy Scriptures, Jeremiah-Lamentations*, p. 14), "his text has been handed down to us, on the whole, pure and unadulterated."

Date and Place of Writing. The bulk of the prophecies were given and written in Jerusalem during the forty-one years of Jeremiah's ministry under Judah's last five kings (626-586 B.C.). The final segments of the book were dictated to Baruch, Jeremiah's secretary, during the five years of his life in Tahpanhes, Egypt. It is possible that chapter 52 (the historical appendix) was the work of Baruch, who may have survived the restoration of Jehoiachin after Nebuchadnezzar's death (563 B.C.).

While accepting the Jeremianic origin of the book, it is impossible to say exactly when it was placed in its final form. The first roll was destroyed by Jehoiakim, and a second one was written with several additions (36:32). Perhaps the final form took place during the exile in Egypt.

Style. Jeremiah is a book of prophetic oracles, or sermons, with autobiographical and historical material giving the background to the oracles. The character of the prophet is reflected in his writings. While lacking the glowing and flowing language of Isaiah, Jeremiah's beauty is in his clear and simple style. He is both a humble servant and a prophet of sorrow. A lack of ornament would be expected. His style is also rich with frequent repetitions (2:28 repeated in 11:13; 5:9, 29 repeated in 9:9; 6:13-15 repeated in 8:10-12; 7:14 repeated in 26:6; 10:12-16 repeated in 51:15-19; 11:20 repeated in 20:12; 15:2 repeated in 43:11; etc.). This is not a sign of degeneration of the prophetic gift, but rather is to be expected with the theme of judgment. The prophet also frequently uses the language of the other prophets, especially the book of Deuteronomy. Jeremiah had not been given the prophetic credentials granted to his predecessors. His predictions were not fulfilled immediately. He performed no miracles. Rather, the word of the Lord was a reproach to him, and a derision daily (20:7). Therefore, he was anxious to vindicate himself and his message by showing the continuity between himself and the older prophets—that idolatry and national crimes would bring the judgment of God and the overthrow of the nation (cf. 23:5, 6 and 33:15 with Isa 4:2 and 51 with Isa 13 and 47; 10:3-5 with Isa 40:19, 20; 48 with Isa 15; 31:9 with Isa 42:16; 14:10 with Hos 8:13; 10:25 with Ps 79:6; 10:13 with Ps 135:7). Jeremiah also employs numerous illustrations throughout his writings.

Chronological Order. To the western mind, the book does not follow a logical order. The order is not chronological, but rather by cognate subject matter. The lack of chronological order is evidently intentional. In spite of this fact, it is possible to date many of the sections, for they contain specific chronological notations. The messages that are dated are as follows: In Josiah's reign: 1:2; 3:6. In Jehoiakim's reign: 22:18; 25:1; 26:1; 35:1; 36:1; 45:1. In Zedekiah's reign: 21:1; 24:1, 8; 27:3, 12; 28:1; 29:3; 32:1; 37:1; 38:5; 39:1; 49:34; 51:59. And in Egypt: 43:7-9; 44:1 (For a thorough discussion of the chronology, see Young, p. 250ff.).

Authenticity. The Old Testament contains several explicit references to the book of Jeremiah. Daniel refers to Jeremiah's prediction of the seventy-year captivity (Dan 9:2). II Chronicles 36:21 and Ezra 1:1 both confirm the book. The Apocrypha, Josephus, and the New Testament also confirm the prophecy of Jeremiah. Matthew 2:17-18 quotes Jeremiah 31:15, while Jeremiah 7:11 is quoted in Matthew 21:13, Mark 11:17, and Luke 19:46. Jeremiah 31:31-34 is quoted in Hebrews 8:8-12. As has already been noted, the book of Revelation contains several allusions to Jeremiah. Two archaeological discoveries of this century have also confirmed the book of Jeremiah. Professor Petrie discovered the ruins of "Pharaoh's house" at Tahpanhes. The house had only one entry with a wide paved area, exactly as described by Jeremiah (ch. 43).

In 1935, and again in 1938, several ostraca (broken pieces of pottery with writing on them) were discovered at Lachish in the Judaean foothills. The Lachish Letters, as they were named, shed much interesting light on the last days of Judah (588-586 B.C.). They were written in ancient Hebrew script during the time of Jeremiah when Lachish was besieged by the Babylonians.

In one letter a description is given of the princes closely corresponding to Jeremiah's description (38:4). There is also mention of "the prophet" whose message is "Beware," perhaps a reference to Jeremiah. The description found in these letters confirms the descriptions Jeremiah gives of the same period (see H. Torcyzner, Lachish I, The Lachish Letters and J. B. Pritchard, Ancient Near Eastern Texts).

OUTLINE

THE words of Jĕr-e-mī'ah the son of Hĭlkī'ah, of the priests that were in Ān-a-thŏth in the land of Benjamin:

2 To whom the word of the LORD came in the days of Jō-sī'ah the son of Amon king of Jū'dah, in the thirteenth year of his reign.

3 It came also in the days of Je-hoi'a-kim the son of Jō-sī'ah king of Jū'dah, unto the end of the eleventh year of Zĕd-e-kī'ah the son of Jō-sī'ah king of Jū'dah, unto the carrying away of Jerusalem captive in the fifth month.

4 ¶Then the word of the LORD came unto me, saying,

5 Before I formed thee in the belly I knew thee; and before thou camest forth out of the womb I sanctified thee, and I ordained thee a prophet unto the nations.

6 Then said I, Ah, Lord GOD! behold, I cannot speak: for I am a child.

7 But the LORD said unto me, Say not, I am a child: for thou shalt go to all that I shall send thee, and whatsoever I command thee thou shalt speak.

8 Be not afraid of their faces: for I am with thee to deliver thee, saith the LORD.

9 Then the LORD put forth his hand, and touched my mouth. And the LORD said unto me, Behold, I have put my words in thy mouth.

10 See, I have this day set thee over the nations and over the kingdoms, to

COMMENTARY

I. INTRODUCTION. 1:1-19.

A. The Superscription. 1:1-3.

1:1. **The words of Jeremiah.** Departing from the more common introductions to the prophetical books ("burden," "utterance," "vision," "the word of the Lord which came," etc.), Jeremiah introduces his prophecy with **the words of Jeremiah.** As with similar superscriptions (Eccl 1:1; Song 1:1; Amos 1:1), the reason for its use is due to the fact that not only prophecies are contained herewith, but also much of the personal history of the author. However, verse 2 does employ the standard formula.

The name **Jeremiah** (the Lord exalts) was very common and was used for no less than eight other biblical personages (35:3; II Kgs 23:30-31; I Chr 5:24; 12:4, 10, 13; Neh 10:2; 12:1).

The son of Hilkiah. Because of the small number of proper names among the Hebrews, it was necessary for purposes of distinction to employ the father's name as well.

2-3. The double superscription **the days of Josiah . . . and also in the days of Jehoiakim . . .** does not exclude the prophecies given at Mizpah and Egypt, but rather emphasizes that the bulk of the prophecies were given before the fall of Jerusalem. The exclusion of Jehoahaz and Jehoiachin in the list of kings is due to their brief reigns of only three months each. Therefore, Jeremiah's ministry covered a forty-one-year period under the theocracy. Since the years of his stay in Egypt are not given, it is impossible to state the entire length of his ministry (perhaps fifty years).

B. Jeremiah's Call to Be God's Prophet. 1:4-10.

4. Jeremiah's call was not some whim or fanciful dream, but rather a supernatural, divine revelation vouchsafed to him. Here, he employs the familiar formula **the word of the LORD came unto me,** a powerful credential for the prophets.

5. Even before he was conceived, God **knew** him. The knowing is more than acquaintance; it means approval (Ps 1:6; Gen 18:19; Nah 1:7) or selection (Gen 39:6; Amos 3:2). The preordination of individuals is a common theme in the Old Testament as well as the New (Isa 45:4; 49:1; Ps 139:16). This theme is also found in pagan literature. The Assyrian king, Ashurbanipal states in his 'Annals' that the gods "in the body of his mother have made (him) to rule Assyria." Like Samson (Jud 13:3ff.), John the Baptist (Lk 1:15) Paul (Gal 1:15-16), and others, the prophet was chosen and set apart for special service while still in his mother's womb. "The three clauses of verse 5 give the three moments whereof the choosing consists: God has chosen him, has consecrated him, and has installed him as prophet" (C. F. Keil, *The Prophecies of Jeremiah*, pp. 39-40).

6-8. The task would be difficult; but since the prophet was called by God, he would have divine enablement. Yet, Jeremiah laments **Ah . . . !** (cf. Josh 7:7; II Kgs 3:10). He does not plead inability like Moses (Ex 4:10), but rather the inexperience of his youth (cf. Solomon, I Kgs 3:7). The word for **child** means a young man (even to forty-five years of age, Ex 33:11). The length of his prophetic ministry shows that Jeremiah was probably in his early twenties at this time. Unlike Moses, who angered the Lord by his repeated excuses (Ex 3:11, 13; 4:1, 10, 13), Jeremiah needed only a little encouragement. This the Lord does, as well as promising deliverance.

9-10. With the opposition of the prophet broken, the Lord proceeded to the solemn act of inauguration. The symbolic, though historical, act of touching the lips of the prophet was a sign that God would frame in his mouth what he would speak. In the same manner, Isaiah's lips were touched with a hot coal (Isa 6:7; cf. Ezk 2:8-10; Dan 10:16). The expression **I have put** my words in thy mouth, was a divine pledge of inspiration, whereby ". . . holy men of God spake as they were moved by the Holy Ghost" (II Pet 1:21).

The second part of the inauguration was the conferring of authority and the commissioning of the prophet. He was not only authorized for the task but he was empowered. God never calls without also providing the enablement. God made him an overseer of the nations. The prophetic coin of Jeremiah was to have two sides—a positive and a negative. By his words he would destroy, and . . . build. The former was done by the prophesying of divine judgment (the bulk of his ministry), and the latter by the prophesying of divine mercy.

C. Signs Confirming Jeremiah's Call. 1:11-19.

11-12. Two signs were given the prophet as sort of an outline of his prophetic ministry. The first was that of a rod of an almond tree. The Hebrew name for almond is wakeful; it is the first tree in Palestine to wake from its winter sleep, beginning to blossom in January. God interprets this symbol in verse 12 as the certain fulfillment of His Word. Jeremiah uses a play on similar sounding words here between almond tree (Heb *shaqād*) and I will hasten (Heb *shōqēd*, meaning watchover). To make this rod (Heb *maqēl*, stick or branch) a rod of correction, as do some commentators (cf. Lange pp. 22-23 and Keil pp. 42-43), seems to force the meaning. The symbol of the almond rod or branch was intended only to assure the prophet of the certain fulfillment of his prophecies. The contents of his preaching-judgment would be illustrated by the second symbol.

13-16. The second sign was that of a seething pot. The word for pot (Heb *sîr*) is a large caldron in which vegetables or meat for many persons can be cooked (II Kgs 4:38ff.; Ezk 24:3ff.). The foe to the north. The interpretation is given in verse 15 that Judah and Jerusalem will be destroyed by peoples from the north. As the pot boils over and spills out on the hearth, so disaster from the north will run over the land of Judah.

I will utter my judgments against them, says the Lord. This expression, peculiar to Jeremiah (cf. 4:12; 12:1; 39:5; 52:9), has the sense of a lawsuit, including both the examination of the accused and the judicial sentence (39:5; 52:9). The people deserve this judgment because they have worshiped other gods, as well as the works of their own hands, i.e., idols.

17-19. Chapter 1 concludes with a charge to Jeremiah to fulfill his calling and another promise of divine enablement. Gird up thy loins is an Oriental expression meaning to equip oneself or get ready for service. Since these people wore long robes, it was imperative for them to tuck the long robe under a belt around the waist in order to run, work, or fight. As Jeremiah was given an offensive stand in verses 9-10, here in verses 18-19 he is given a defensive stand. As a defenced (fortified) city, and an iron pillar, and brazen walls would defy the assaults of an enemy, so God would protect His servant Jeremiah.

II. PROPHETIC ORACLES AGAINST THE THEOCRACY. 2:1-45:5.

A. During the Reigns of Josiah and Jehoiakim. 2:1-20:18.

1. First message: national apostasy. 2:1-3:5.

a. God's faithfulness, the people's unfaithfulness. 2:1-19.

2:1-3. This first oracle begins with a review of God's faithfulness to His people. Moreover connects the first oracle to Jere-

root out, and to pull down, and to destroy, and to throw down, to build, and to plant.

11 ¶Moreover the word of the Lord came unto me, saying, Jĕr'e-mī'ah, what seest thou? And I said, I see a rod of an almond tree.

12 Then said the Lord unto me, Thou hast well seen: for I will hasten my word to perform it.

13 And the word of the Lord came unto me the second time, saying, What seest thou? And I said, I see a seething pot; and the face thereof *is* toward the north.

14 Then the Lord said unto me, Out of the north an evil shall break forth upon all the inhabitants of the land.

15 For, lo, I will call all the families of the kingdoms of the north, saith the Lord; and they shall come, and they shall set every one his throne at the entering of the gates of Jerusalem, and against all the walls thereof round about, and against all the cities of Jū'-dah.

16 And I will utter my judgments against them touching all their wickedness, who have forsaken me, and have burned incense unto other gods, and worshipped the works of their own hands.

17 ¶Thou therefore gird up thy loins, and arise, and speak unto them all that I command thee: be not dismayed at their faces, lest I confound thee before them.

18 For, behold, I have made thee this day a defenced city, and an iron pillar, and brasen walls against the whole land, against the kings of Jū'dah, against the princes thereof, against the priests thereof, and against the people of the land.

19 And they shall fight against thee; but they shall not prevail against thee; for I *am* with thee, saith the Lord, to deliver thee.

CHAPTER 2

MOREOVER the word of the Lord came to me, saying,

2 Go and cry in the ears of Jerusalem, saying, Thus saith the LORD; I remember thee, the kindness of thy youth, the love of thine espousals, when thou wentest after me in the wilderness, in a land that was not sown.

3 Israel was holiness unto the LORD, and the firstfruits of his increase: all that devour him shall offend; evil shall come upon them, saith the LORD.

4 ¶Hear ye the word of the LORD, O house of Jacob, and all the families of the house of Israel:

5 Thus saith the LORD, What iniquity have your fathers found in me, that they are gone far from me, and have walked after vanity, and are become vain?

6 Neither said they, Where is the LORD that brought us up out of the land of Egypt, that led us through the wilderness, through a land of deserts and of pits, through a land of drought, and of the shadow of death, through a land that no man passed through, and where no man dwelt?

7 And I brought you into a plentiful country, to eat the fruit thereof and the goodness thereof; but when ye entered, ye defiled my land, and made mine heritage an abomination.

8 The priests said not, Where is the LORD? and they that handle the law knew me not: the pastors also transgressed against me, and the prophets prophesied by Ba'al, and walked after things that do not profit.

9 ¶Wherefore I will yet plead with you, saith the LORD, and with your children's children will I plead.

10 For pass over the isles of Chĭt'tĭm, and see; and send unto Kē'dar, and consider diligently, and see if there be such a thing.

11 Hath a nation changed their gods, which are yet no gods? but my people have changed their glory for that which doth not profit.

12 Be astonished, O ye heavens, at this, and be horribly afraid, be ye very desolate, saith the LORD.

13 For my people have committed two evils; they have forsaken me the fountain of living waters, and hewed them out cisterns, broken cisterns, that can hold no water.

miah's call. **The kindness of thy youth, the love of thine espousals** can refer to God's love and kindness to Israel, or Israel's kindness and love for God. The latter is the most natural understanding of the passage; yet the abundance of favors were God's to Israel. Israel showed perversity, rather than kindness (Ex 14:11-12; 15:24; 32:1-7). Therefore, these were the kindnesses Israel experienced from God in her youth (Deut 32:16-17; Ezk 16:5-6). The **espousals** were the periods between God's betrothal to Israel at the Exodus and the formal marriage ceremony at Mt. Sinai. Verse 6 shows that it was God who led them through the wilderness and not the people who went after Him.

4-7. The review of God's faithfulness to His people is followed by an indictment of the nation's apostasy. The Lord brought them into a **plentiful** land, but they **defiled** it (with idolatry and the sacrifices of their own children, Ps 106:37). With this they made themselves (**mine heritage**, Deut 32:9; I Sam 10:1; I Kgs 8:51; Ps 28:9, etc.) an abomination.

Holiness unto the LORD is an expression of consecration, while **first fruits of his increase** is an expression of God's produce. As the first fruits of the land belonged to Him (Ex 23:19; Num 18:12-13), so Israel belonged to God as His first fruits among the nations. Here, also, is another of God's promises to protect His people and bring judgment on those who harm the apple of His eye.

8. Even the three primary classes of leaders established by God had turned against Him, as did the common people. The **priests** were to expound the law (Mal 2:6-7), yet were silent. The **pastors** (lit., shepherds or leaders) were not religious, but civil, leaders (3:15). Under the theocracy their duty was to lead the people in the way of the Lord, yet they themselves transgressed His way. The **prophets** were to reclaim the people from apostasy, yet they encouraged it by pretending to have oracles from **Baal**, the false Phoenician god.

9-12. Yet, in His mercy God continued to plead with His people. However, Israel is more of an abomination than the heathen. Go to the west to **Chittim** (Cyprus), later the maritime coast of the Mediterranean, especially Greece, Num 24:24; Isa 23:1; Dan 11:30) or to the east to **Kedar**, the Arab lands, states the prophet. In all the heathen lands not one who forsakes his own gods for others will be found. Israel alone does this.

13. The people had committed **two evils**. First, they had forsaken the Lord, **the fountain of living waters**. Isaiah had already used this imagery of God's blessing (Isa 44:3), and Jesus later alluded to it (Jn 4:10-15; 7:37-39). The second sin was that of idolatry, i.e., **broken cisterns**. To people living in an arid land where the search for fountains of fresh water and good cisterns to hold it was a daily priority, this imagery was a powerful object lesson.

14-19. As a result of these two great sins, Israel had lost her freedom and had become a slave, first to Assyria and then to Egypt. The **young lions** refers to Assyria (see Isaiah's description of the Assyrian invasion, 5:29). **Noph** is a colloquial Semitic or Egyptian pronunciation of Memphis, the capital of Lower (i.e., Northern) Egypt, located near Cairo. **Tahapanes** was an ancient border fortress city located on the caravan road from Egypt to Palestine and the East. Later, the remnant of Jews fled here after the fall of Jerusalem (43:1-7). **Backslidings** is used in the plural because of the numerous defections of the people. This is a recurring theme in Jeremiah, found thirteen times (2:19; 3:6, 8, 11, 12, 14, 22; 5:6; 8:5; 14:7; 31:22; 49:4), and only four other times in the rest of Scripture (Prov 14:14; Hos 4:16; 11:7; 14:4).

b. Divine judgment. 2:20-37.

20-22. The indictment against Israel is given with several vivid images. As a stubborn ox, they have sinned; and through the **yoke** and the **bands** of God's law they have been broken. The **high hill** and **green tree** are examples of the places of idolatry (Deut 12:2; Isa 57:5, 7).

The vine is a familiar figure in Scripture (cf. Isa 5:2; Jn 15:1-7), but here Israel has become a degenerate vine. Their sin has been so great that there is nothing they can do to cleanse it, **thine iniquity is marked before me. Nitre** is an Egyptian alkali mineral and **soap** or potash was used for washing.

23-25. Israel is also likened to a lustful prostitute (cf. vs. 20). To show the debauchery of the nation's idolatry, she is called a **dromedary**, a female ass that has not yet had a foal.

26-28. As a **thief** is ashamed, so is the nation Israel. Not only the people, but the leaders also are thieves. And how foolish their idolatry. Gods made with their own hands will not help in the day of trouble. **Grove** (see 17:1 note).

29-37. Generation after generation has been a thoughtless, thankless people. The **attire** of the bride was an ornament that the bride assumed on her wedding day and was the mark of her being married. She would, therefore, cherish this token. But not so Israel, which had forgotten her husband. Their sin of idolatry was compounded by teaching it to their children and to others.

14. ¶ Is Israel a servant? is he a homeborn slave? why is he spoiled?

15. The young lions roared upon him, and yelled, and they made his land waste: his cities are burned without inhabitant.

16. Also the children of Noph and Tăhăp′a-nês have broken the crown of thy head.

17. Hast thou not procured this unto thyself, in that thou hast forsaken the Lord thy God, when he led thee by the way?

18. And now what hast thou to do in the way of Egypt, to drink the waters of Sī′hôr? or what hast thou to do in the way of Assyria, to drink the waters of the river?

19. Thine own wickedness shall correct thee, and thy backslidings shall reprove thee: know therefore and see that it is an evil thing and bitter, that thou hast forsaken the Lord thy God, and that my fear is not in thee, saith the Lord God of hosts.

20. For of old time I have broken thy yoke, and burst thy bands; and thou saidst, I will not transgress; when upon every high hill and under every green tree thou wanderest, playing the harlot.

21. Yet I had planted thee a noble vine, wholly a right seed: how then art thou turned into the degenerate plant of a strange vine unto me?

22. For though thou wash thee with nitre, and take thee much soap, yet thine iniquity is marked before me, saith the Lord God.

23. How canst thou say, I am not polluted, I have not gone after Bā′al-ĭm? see thy way in the valley, know what thou hast done: thou art a swift dromedary traversing her ways;

24. A wild ass used to the wilderness, that snuffeth up the wind at her pleasure; in her occasion who can turn her away? all they that seek her will not weary themselves; in her month they shall find her.

25. Withhold thy foot from being unshod, and thy throat from thirst: but thou saidst, There is no hope: no; for I have loved strangers, and after them will I go.

26. As the thief is ashamed when he is found, so is the house of Israel ashamed; they, their kings, their princes, and their priests, and their prophets,

27. Saying to a stock, Thou art my father; and to a stone, Thou hast brought me forth: for they have turned their back unto me, and not their face: but in the time of their trouble they will say, Arise, and save us.

28. But where are thy gods that thou hast made thee? let them arise, if they can save thee in the time of thy trouble: for according to the number of thy cities are thy gods, O Jū′dah.

29. Wherefore will ye plead with me? ye all have transgressed against me, saith the Lord.

30. In vain have I smitten your children; they received no correction: your own sword hath devoured your prophets, like a destroying lion.

31 ¶O generation, see ye the word of the LORD. Have I been a wilderness unto Israel? a land of darkness? wherefore say my people, We are lords; we will come no more unto thee?

32 Can a maid forget her ornaments, or a bride her attire? yet my people have forgotten me days without number.

33 Why trimmest thou thy way to seek love? therefore hast thou also taught the wicked ones thy ways.

34 Also in thy skirts is found the blood of the souls of the poor innocents: I have not found it by secret search, but upon all these.

35 Yet thou sayest, Because I am innocent, surely his anger shall turn from me. Behold, I will plead with thee, because thou sayest, I have not sinned.

36 Why gaddest thou about so much to change thy way? thou also shalt be ashamed of Egypt, as thou wast ashamed of Assyria.

37 Yea, thou shalt go forth from him, and thine hands upon thine head: for the LORD hath rejected thy confidences, and thou shalt not prosper in them.

CHAPTER 3

THEY say, If a man put away his wife, and she go from him, and become another man's, shall he return unto her again? shall not that land be greatly polluted? but thou hast played the harlot with many lovers; yet return again to me, saith the LORD.

2 Lift up thine eyes unto the high places, and see where thou hast not been lien with. In the ways hast thou sat for them, as the Arabian in the wilderness: and thou hast polluted the land with thy whoredoms and with thy wickedness.

3 Therefore the showers have been witholden, and there hath been no latter rain; and thou hadst a whore's forehead, thou refusedst to be ashamed.

4 Wilt thou not from this time cry unto me, My father, thou art the guide of my youth?

5 Will he reserve his anger for ever? will he keep it to the end? Behold, thou hast spoken and done evil things as thou couldest.

---

c. The results of infidelity. 3:1-5.

Although some scholars believe that the first 5 verses of chapter 3 are part of Jeremiah's second oracle (see Lange, p. 45 ff.), the substance of verse 5 and the new heading in verse 6, along with the context, show that it forms the conclusion to oracle one in chapter 2.

3:1. If a man put away his wife . . . unto her again? Apostate Israel is compared to the divorced wife as represented in the Law (Deut 24:1-4). The Mosaic law forbade a man to take back his wife if she had married another, even if her second husband had died or divorced her. Adultery pollutes the land (cf. Lev 18:25, 27); and Israel had committed spiritual adultery, **played the harlot,** with many false gods. She glibly thought she could simply return to the Lord. But not so. **Yet return again to me.** Rather, "Thinkest thou to return?" This is not an invitation for Israel to return, as seems to be suggested by the AV; but a strong rebuke of the idolatrous nation. Could the nation simply return to the Lord after their idolatrous harlotry, when the Deuteronomic law forbids it in the physical relationship? Earlier, her idolatry was portrayed with the imagery of an animal; now she is called a harlot.

2-5. High places (lit., bare-topped hills) were favorite places for idolatrous worship. **In the ways hast thou sat.** Like the prostitutes who enticed passers-by along the roads, so had Israel enticed other gods (cf. Gen 38:14; Prov 7:12). Idolatrous altars had actually been erected at road intersections and the gates of the cities (II Kgs 23:8; Ezk 16:25). Also, like the **Arabian,** the Bedouin who lies in wait for travelers in order to plunder them, so Israel sought after idolatry and thus desecrated the land. **Showers . . . latter rain.** God judged the nation by withholding rain (14:1ff.; Amos 4:7ff.), not necessarily the early rains (which break the summer drought), but simply any showers. **Latter rain** comes during March and April in order to bring the crops to fruition and harvest. **Wilt thou not . . . cry . . . ?** Israel had called upon the Lord, but only with lip service. Even the revival under Josiah was not a heart revival among the people. **Thou hast spoken and done evil.** Over and over they promised to repent and return to the Lord; yet they continued in their sin.

So debased were they that they had even offered their children to Molech, one of the Canaanite gods collectively called Baalim, in the valley of Hinnom. Therefore, they were guilty of the **blood of the souls of the poor innocents.**

---

2. Second message: warnings and repentance. 3:6-6:30.

Jeremiah's second oracle is a continuation of the condemnation found in the first, with the addition of a promise of pardon for genuine repentance. The captive northern kingdom, Israel, is cited as a warning to the southern kingdom, Judah.

a. Judah's apostasy greater than Israel's, 3:6-25.

6-10. Three hundred years previously, the ten tribes of the north revolted against both the Temple in Jerusalem and the throne of David (church and state). In chapter 2 "Israel" means the entire nation, but in Jeremiah's second oracle it means the northern kingdom. **Backsliding Israel** had worshiped other gods **upon every high mountain and under every green tree,** i.e., the high places of pagan idolatry. God in His grace and love had sent His prophets unto them with the message, **Turn thou unto me.** Yet, Israel refused to repent. So debased were the idolatrous practices of Israel that they even involved the act of adultery with **stones and with stocks** (trees). Because of her spiritual adultery, God gave her a divorce; and the northern kingdom fell to Assyria in 721 B.C.

Yet, her **treacherous sister Judah** (they both came from the common stock of Abraham and Jacob) did not learn her lessons from the punishment of Israel. Judah **feignedly** pretended to repent, but not with her whole heart. Josiah genuinely turned to the Lord (II Kgs 23:25), but the people only complied outwardly (II Chr 34:32; 35:17). God promised that as He removed Israel, so he would remove Judah from the land (II Kgs 23:27). The Almighty knows no religion of insincerity.

11. Judah's sin was worse than Israel's. Israel had openly revolted from Jehovah from the day that Jeroboam set up the golden calves (I Kgs 12:19-33). Only one northern king, Jehoahaz, "sought the Lord," and then only under Syrian oppression (II Kgs 13:4-5). Yet, backsliding Israel made no attempt to conceal her condition. On the other hand, **treacherous Judah** was lukewarm, wanting both God and Baal (lukewarmness is one of the greatest sins against Christ, cf. Rev 3:15-16). Judah had greater privileges than Israel (divinely ordained kings, priests, the Temple of captive Israel, etc.), and therefore was more guilty.

12-13. God called Israel to repentance and promised her pardon and restitution. **North.** Israel was now captive in Assyria. Her confession must be clear and specific: (1) **thou hast transgressed against the LORD;** (2) **and hast scattered thy ways to the strangers;** and (3) **have not obeyed my voice.**

14-15. The promise of regathering is not only to the Lord but to the land as well. Those regathered will be small, only a remnant, **one of a city, and two of a family.** They will have leaders who fear and love the Lord. **Pastors** (lit., shepherds), civil leaders who will be obedient to God (cf. 2:8, 26; 23:4).

16-18. The Old Testament prophets refused to accept the divided kingdom as final. Here, Jeremiah saw the reunification of both Israel (vs. 14) and Judah (vs. 18). This is a literal return to a literal Zion. The words of this passage are too plain and explicit to spiritualize (cf. chs. 30-31). The **ark of the covenant,** in which the law of God was kept, was no longer needed because God's law was written on men's hearts (cf. 31:31-34). In the millennial kingdom the ark will no longer be God's throne (Ex 25:22), but Jerusalem from which He rules the nations of the world (Rev 21:22). This is the last mention of the ark. After it was brought into the Temple, I Kings 8:6, it is not mentioned again in the historical books. It is possible that what was only the

---

6 ¶ The LORD said also unto me in the days of Jo-si'ah the king, Hast thou seen that which backsliding Israel hath done? she is gone up upon every high mountain and under every green tree, and there hath played the harlot.

7 And I said after she had done all these things, Turn thou unto me. But she returned not. And her treacherous sister Ju'dah saw it.

8 And I saw, when for all the causes whereby backsliding Israel committed adultery I had put her away, and given her a bill of divorce; yet her treacherous sister Ju'dah feared not, but went and played the harlot also.

9 And it came to pass through the lightness of her whoredom, that she defiled the land, and committed adultery with stones and with stocks.

10 And yet for all this her treacherous sister Ju'dah hath not turned unto me with her whole heart, but feignedly, saith the LORD.

11 ¶ And the LORD said unto me, The backsliding Israel hath justified herself more than treacherous Ju'dah.

12 Go and proclaim these words toward the north, and say, Return, thou backsliding Israel, saith the LORD; and I will not cause mine anger to fall upon you: for I am merciful, saith the LORD, and I will not keep anger for ever.

13 Only acknowledge thine iniquity, that thou hast transgressed against the LORD thy God, and hast scattered thy ways to the strangers under every green tree, and ye have not obeyed my voice, saith the LORD.

14 Turn, O backsliding children, saith the LORD; for I am married unto you: and I will take you one of a city, and two of a family, and I will bring you to Zion:

15 And I will give you pastors according to mine heart, which shall feed you with knowledge and understanding.

16 And it shall come to pass, when ye be multiplied and increased in the land, in those days, saith the LORD, they shall say no more, The ark of the covenant of the LORD: neither shall it come to mind: neither shall they remember it; neither shall they visit it; neither shall that be done any more.

17 At that time they shall call Jerusalem the throne of the LORD; and all the nations shall be gathered unto it, to the name of the LORD, to Jerusalem: neither shall they walk any more after the imagination of their evil heart.

18 In those days the house of Jū'dah shall walk with the house of Israel, and they shall come together out of the land of the north to the land that I have given for an inheritance unto your fathers.

19 But I said, How shall I put thee among the children, and give thee a pleasant land, a goodly heritage of the hosts of nations? and I said, Thou shalt call me, My father; and shalt not turn away from me.

20 Surely as a wife treacherously departeth from her husband, so have ye dealt treacherously with me, O house of Israel, saith the Lord.

21 ¶A voice was heard upon the high places, weeping and supplications of the children of Israel: for they have perverted their way, and they have forgotten the Lord their God.

22 Return, ye backsliding children, and I will heal your backslidings. Behold, we come unto thee; for thou art the Lord our God.

23 Truly in vain is salvation hoped for from the hills, and from the multitude of mountains: truly in the Lord our God is the salvation of Israel.

24 For shame hath devoured the labour of our fathers from our youth; their flocks and their herds, their sons and their daughters.

25 We lie down in our shame, and our confusion covereth us: for we have sinned against the Lord our God, we and our fathers, from our youth even unto this day, and have not obeyed the voice of the Lord our God.

CHAPTER 4

IF thou wilt return, O Israel, saith the Lord, return unto me: and if thou wilt put away thine abominations out of my sight, then shalt thou not remove.

2 And thou shalt swear, The Lord liveth, in truth, in judgment, and in righteousness; and the nations shall bless themselves in him, and in him shall they glory.

3 ¶For thus saith the Lord to the men of Jū'dah and Jerusalem, Break up your fallow ground, and sow not among thorns.

4 Circumcise yourselves to the Lord, and take away the foreskins of your heart, ye men of Jū'dah and inhabitants of Jerusalem: lest my fury come forth like fire, and burn that none can quench it, because of the evil of your doings.

5 Declare ye in Jū'dah, and publish in Jerusalem; and say, Blow ye the trumpet in the land; cry, gather together, and say, Assemble yourselves, and let us go into the defenced cities.

6 Set up the standard toward Zion: retire, stay not: for I will bring evil from the north, and a great destruction.

7 The lion is come up from his thick-

testimony of God's presence became an obstacle to knowing Him, see II Kgs 18:4. The **imagination of their evil heart** (stubbornness) will finally be taken away. Apart from Deuteronomy 29:19 and Psalms 81:12, "imagination" is found exclusively in Jeremiah (3:17; 7:24; 9:14; 11:8; 13:10; 16:12; 18:12; 23:17).

19-25. God had expected His people to say **My father,** but they had lived in contempt of their spiritual heritage. Yet, Jehovah graciously invited them to return. Judah is referred to here as a woman. In Hebrew law, daughters did not have the same inheritance as their brothers. But here, God promises a good inheritance if they will only repent. The **high places** (vs. 21), **hills and mountains** (vs. 23), the places of Canaanite worship, are vain. Man-made religion is useless, for **salvation is from God alone. For shame hath devoured.** The shameful thing is a euphemism for "Baal" (the evil substitute for true worship of God, cf. Hos 2:17).

b. The foe from the north. 4:1-31.

4:1-2. Again God calls on His people to return to Him in repentance. The **return** (Heb *shûb*) may mean "return from exile," but also has a deeper meaning. Jeremiah attached great importance to true repentance and returning to Jehovah (15:19; cf. 3:1, 12-14, 22; 8:4-7; 15:5-9; 23:14).

3-5. Circumcise yourselves. All Jewish boys were circumcised at eight days old as a sign of having entered into covenant relationship with God (Gen 17:1-14). But no external sign can make a man God's child without an accompanying circumcision of the heart, mind, and will (cf. Rom 2:28-29). The people's hearts must be circumcised by the removal of all false pride. The only alternative is God's fiery wrath.

6. Jeremiah gives a preview of Judah's collapse, and it fills him with horror (vss. 19-31). **I will bring evil from the north.** The **north** was a perpetual symbol of threat to Israel. The foe from the **north** here is not identified, and Jeremiah's words are too general to apply it to any one invader. Some have held that it refers to the Scythians, barbarous Indo-European tribes, or perhaps Babylon. Jeremiah explicitly refers to Babylon in later prophecies; and probably Babylon is referred to here as well. However, the foe is the instrument of God for His judgment of His people.

7-10. Three symbols of the invaders are given. **The lion**

...et, and the destroyer of the Gentiles is on his way; he is gone forth from his place to make thy land desolate; *and* thy cities shall be laid waste, without an inhabitant.

8 For this gird you with sackcloth, lament and howl: for the fierce anger of the LORD is not turned back from us.

9 And it shall come to pass at that day, saith the LORD, *that* the heart of the king shall perish, and the heart of the princes; and the priests shall be astonished, and the prophets shall wonder.

10 Then said I, Ah, Lord GOD! surely thou hast greatly deceived this people and Jerusalem, saying, Ye shall have peace; whereas the sword reacheth unto the soul.

11 At that time shall it be said to this people and to Jerusalem, A dry wind of the high places in the wilderness toward the daughter of my people, not to fan, nor to cleanse,

12 *Even* a full wind from those *places* shall come unto me: now also will I give sentence against them.

13 Behold, he shall come up as clouds, and his chariots *shall be* as a whirlwind: his horses are swifter than eagles. Woe unto us! for we are spoiled.

14 O Jerusalem, wash thine heart from wickedness, that thou mayest be saved. How long shall thy vain thoughts lodge within thee?

15 For a voice declareth from Dan, and publisheth affliction from mount E′phra-im.

16 Make ye mention to the nations; behold, publish against Jerusalem, *that* watchers come from a far country, and give out their voice against the cities of Ju′dah.

17 As keepers of a field, are they against her round about; because she hath been rebellious against me, saith the LORD.

18 Thy way and thy doings have procured these *things* unto thee; this *is* thy wickedness, because it is bitter, because it reacheth unto thine heart.

19 ¶My bowels, my bowels! I am pained at my very heart; my heart maketh a noise in me; I cannot hold my peace, because thou hast heard, O my soul, the sound of the trumpet, the alarm of war.

20 Destruction upon destruction is cried: for the whole land is spoiled: suddenly are my tents spoiled, *and* my curtains in a moment.

21 How long shall I see the standard, *and* hear the sound of the trumpet?

22 For my people *is* foolish, they have not known me; they *are* sottish children, and they have none understanding: they *are* wise to do evil, but to do good they have no knowledge.

23 I beheld the earth, and, lo, *it was* without form, and void; and the heavens, and they *had* no light.

24 I beheld the mountains, and, lo, they trembled, and all the hills moved lightly.

25 I beheld, and, lo, *there was* no man, and all the birds of the heavens were fled.

comes from the thicket to destroy not only the cities of Judah but also the **Gentiles**, the nations. The lion is a prototype of Gog (Ezk 38-39), and the Antichrist (Rev 13:17). **Thou hast greatly deceived.** God never deceives His people. The leaders were blaming God because He had allowed the false prophets to cry, "Peace! peace!" (cf. ch. 28). But God had warned the people of Israel many times through His true prophets.

11-15. The second symbol of destruction was the **dry wind**, the sirocco, a fearful hot east wind that fell upon Palestine in the spring and fall and could last three to seven days. Sirocco would not only cause great discomfort to the people, but also destroy their crops. So too, the foe from the north would destroy both life and livelihood. The only door of escape was to **wash thine heart from wickedness. Dan.** The northernmost town in Israel would be the first to be invaded. **Ephraim.** The largest territory of Israel to cross before reaching Jerusalem.

16-18. The **watchers** (besiegers); thirdly, symbolize the eyes of divine judgment. Judah would be surrounded as hunters surround an animal, making escape impossible.

19-22. The first picture of Jeremiah's internal emotion with the coming invasion is expressed in Hebrew fashion in terms of the body. **My bowels** (anguish, distress) were regarded as the seat of the emotions. The prophets often speak in the past or present tense of events that are yet future. This shows that what God proposes to do is as good as done. **Have not known** refers to experiential knowledge that governs action (cf. Hos 4:1; Isa 1:3). **Wise to do evil,** just the opposite of Paul's desire for the saints at Rome (Rom 16:19).

23-26. A graphic, poetic description is given by the prophet of the destruction of the land. Described in terms of the primeval chaos (Gen 1:2), the invading armies have left the land **without form, and void.** Archaeological excavations have shown that every one of the cities that existed in Jeremiah's day were completely destroyed. Desolation was everywhere. Man, birds, even the mountains and heavens, which are so permanent, were affected. This is more than simply a picture of the impending

1437

26 I beheld, and, lo, the fruitful place was a wilderness, and all the cities thereof were broken down, at the presence of the LORD, and by his fierce anger.

27 For thus hath the LORD said, The whole land shall be desolate; yet will I not make a full end.

28 For this shall the earth mourn, and the heavens above be black: because I have spoken it, I have purposed it, and will not repent, neither will I turn back from it.

29 The whole city shall flee for the noise of the horsemen and bowmen; they shall go into thickets, and climb up upon the rocks: every city shall be forsaken, and not a man dwell therein.

30 And when thou art spoiled, what wilt thou do? Though thou clothest thyself with crimson, though thou deckest thee with ornaments of gold, though thou rentest thy face with painting, in vain shalt thou make thyself fair; thy lovers will despise thee, they will seek thy life.

31 For I have heard a voice as of a woman in travail, and the anguish as of her that bringeth forth her first child, the voice of the daughter of Zion, that bewaileth herself, that spreadeth her hands, saying, Woe is me now! for my soul is wearied because of murderers.

CHAPTER 5

RUN ye to and fro through the streets of Jerusalem, and see now, and know, and seek in the broad places thereof, if ye can find a man, if there be any that executeth judgment, that seeketh the truth; and I will pardon it.

2 And though they say, The LORD liveth; surely they swear falsely.

3 O LORD, are not thine eyes upon the truth? thou hast stricken them, but they have not grieved; thou hast consumed them, but they have refused to receive correction: they have made their faces harder than a rock; they have refused to return.

4 Therefore I said, Surely these are poor; they are foolish: for they know not the way of the LORD, nor the judgment of their God.

5 I will get me unto the great men, and will speak unto them; for they have known the way of the LORD, and the judgment of their God: but these have altogether broken the yoke, and burst the bonds.

6 Wherefore a lion out of the forest shall slay them, and a wolf of the evenings shall spoil them: a leopard shall watch over their cities: every one that goeth out thence shall be torn in pieces: because their transgressions are many, and their backslidings are increased.

7 How shall I pardon thee for this? thy children have forsaken me, and sworn by them that are no gods: when I had fed them to the full, they then committed adultery, and assembled themselves by troops in the harlots' houses.

8 They were as fed horses in the morning: every one neighed after his neighbour's wife.

9 Shall I not visit for these things? saith the LORD: and shall not my soul be avenged on such a nation as this?

invasion. It is also a picture of the devastation man brings upon himself when he rebels against God's purpose for his life. The believer, however, has the promise of a new heaven and a new earth (Isa 65:17-25; Rev 21:1-22:5).

27-29. Yet will I not make a full end. In the midst of destruction, God's purpose also included mercy. The people would return to the land after the exile.

30-31. The agony of Jerusalem will be like a prostitute being murdered by her clientele. **The daughter of Zion** is a personification of Judah or Jerusalem (4:11; 6:2, 23, 26; 8:19, 21; 9:1; 14:17), and also Egypt (46:11) and Babylon (50:42). Instead of turning to Jehovah, the people still are unrepentant and seek foreign aid.

c. The national corruption. 5:1-31.

5:1-5. As Diogenes, the Greek philosopher, went through the streets of Athens looking for an honest man, so Jeremiah is commanded to search Jerusalem and Judah for a righteous man, one that executeth **judgment,** i.e., justice. He searched among the common people, in the **broad places** and city squares, but he found none. The prophet reasoned this was because they did not know the **judgment** of God. Here (as well as in vs. 5 and II Kgs 17:26) the word means the "law of God." Jeremiah then searched among the **great men,** the leaders; but they were no better. If even one righteous man were found, perhaps the Lord would spare the city for the sake of this one (cf. Gen 18:22-33). This is an example of prophetic overemphasis in order to press home the truth of the universal depravity of Judah. There were, of course, a few who were still faithful to Jehovah (for example, Baruch, Jeremiah's secretary; those who hid Jeremiah and Baruch from Jehoiakim, 36:26; Zephaniah, the High Priest during the reign of Zedekiah; Ebed-melech the Ethiopian, 38:7-13; and Jeremiah himself). But the vast majority of the people were given wholly to idolatry and promiscuous indulgence.

6-9. The prophet again (cf. 4:7) resorts to an animal metaphor (lion, wolf, and leopard) to reveal God's judgment on the nation. Dante used the same metaphor in the *Inferno.* The idolatry of the nation is spoken again in terms of sexual license, **committed adultery.** They were like well-fed unrestrained stallions. **Visit.** In relation to sin, this means to punish.

10. ¶Go ye up upon her walls, and destroy; but make not a full end: take away her battlements; for they are not the LORD's.

11 For the house of Israel and the house of Ju'dah have dealt very treacherously against me, saith the LORD.

12 They have belied the LORD, and said, It is not he; neither shall evil come upon us; neither shall we see sword nor famine:

13 And the prophets shall become wind, and the word is not in them: thus shall it be done unto them.

14 Wherefore thus saith the LORD God of hosts, Because ye speak this word, behold, I will make my words in thy mouth fire, and this people wood, and it shall devour them.

15 Lo, I will bring a nation upon you from far, O house of Israel, saith the LORD; it is a mighty nation, it is an ancient nation, a nation whose language thou knowest not, neither understandest what they say.

16 Their quiver is as an open sepulchre, they are all mighty men.

17 And they shall eat up thine harvest, and thy bread, which thy sons and thy daughters should eat: they shall eat up thy flocks and thine herds: they shall eat up thy vines and thy fig trees: they shall impoverish thy fenced cities, wherein thou trustedst, with the sword.

18 Nevertheless in those days, saith the LORD, I will not make a full end with you.

19 And it shall come to pass, when ye shall say, Wherefore doeth the LORD our God all these things unto us? then shalt thou answer them, Like as ye have forsaken me, and served strange gods in your land, so shall ye serve strangers in a land that is not yours.

20 ¶Declare this in the house of Jacob, and publish it in Ju'dah, saying,

21 Hear now this, O foolish people, and without understanding; which have eyes, and see not; which have ears, and hear not:

22 Fear ye not me? saith the LORD: will ye not tremble at my presence, which have placed the sand for the bound of the sea by a perpetual decree, that it cannot pass it: and though the waves thereof toss themselves, yet can they not prevail: though they roar, yet can they not pass over it?

23 But this people hath a revolting and a rebellious heart; they are revolted and gone.

24 Neither say they in their heart, Let us now fear the LORD our God, that giveth rain, both the former and the latter, in his season: he reserveth unto us the appointed weeks of the harvest.

25 ¶Your iniquities have turned away

10. Jerusalem is compared to a vineyard soon to be destroyed. The foreign nation is seen as an instrument of judgment in the hand of the Lord. God called the enemy to scale the vineyard walls (not vine-rows as some have supposed, since they would have to scale the walls in order to destroy the vines). The enemy was to destroy the vineyard and carry off her battlements (branches) that God had disowned because they were unfruitful and worthless. Yet, the vine was to remain alive. The judgment was not to be the final rejection.

11-23. Both Israel and Judah had rejected the Lord. They had scoffed at the prophets' warnings and, therefore, had disregarded God as well. The people wanted to hear the false prophets rather than the true prophets. ". . . Judah's serving a foreign power in exile is fitting retribution for its serving foreign gods at home (cf. 9:12-16; 16:10-13; 22:8ff.; Deut 29:24-26; I Kgs 9:8ff.). It is a tribute to the work which Jeremiah did for his people, that when the exile came they were not shattered by it, but, accepting it as God's punishment, turned to God to seek in a new way their life from him" (H. Conliffe-Jones, Jeremiah, p. 72).

24. The wickedness of Judah is seen also in her ingratitude. One example is given here, ingratitude for daily food. God manifested His faithfulness by sending the former and the latter rains. The former, or early, rains (October to December) were essential to soften the land for planting after the hot summer season. The latter rains came in March and April just before the harvest season. God kept His covenant, but not so the people.

25-29. The people were wholly given to deceit, oppression,

these *things*, and your sins have withholden good *things* from you.

26 For among my people are found wicked *men*: they lay wait, as he that setteth snares; they set a trap, they catch men.

27 As a cage is full of birds, so *are* their houses full of deceit: therefore they are become great, and waxen rich.

28 They are waxen fat, they shine: yea, they overpass the deeds of the wicked: they judge not the cause, the cause of the fatherless, yet they prosper; and the right of the needy do they not judge.

29 Shall I not visit for these *things?* saith the Lord: shall not my soul be avenged on such a nation as this?

30 ¶A wonderful and horrible thing is committed in the land;

31 The prophets prophesy falsely, and the priests bear rule by their means; and my people love *to have it* so: and what will ye do in the end thereof?

CHAPTER 6

O YE children of Benjamin, gather yourselves to flee out of the midst of Jerusalem, and blow the trumpet in Te-ko′a, and set up a sign of fire in Bĕth-hăc′ce-rem: for evil appeareth out of the north, and great destruction.

2 I have likened the daughter of Zion to a comely and delicate *woman.*

3 The shepherds with their flocks shall come unto her; they shall pitch their tents against her round about; they shall feed every one in his place.

4 Prepare ye war against her; arise, and let us go up at noon. Woe unto us! for the day goeth away, for the shadows of the evening are stretched out.

5 Arise, and let us go by night, and let us destroy her palaces.

6 ¶For thus hath the Lord of hosts said, Hew ye down trees, and cast a mount against Jerusalem: this *is* the city to be visited; she *is* wholly oppression in the midst of her.

7 As a fountain casteth out her waters, so she casteth out her wickedness: violence and spoil is heard in her; before me continually *is* grief and wounds.

8 Be thou instructed, O Jerusalem, lest my soul depart from thee; lest I make thee desolate, a land not inhabited.

9 ¶Thus saith the Lord of hosts, They shall throughly glean the remnant of Israel as a vine: turn back thine hand as a grapegatherer into the baskets.

10 To whom shall I speak, and give warning, that they may hear? behold, their ear *is* uncircumcised, and they cannot hearken: behold, the word of the Lord is unto them a reproach; they have no delight in it.

11 Therefore I am full of the fury of the Lord; I am weary with holding in: I will pour it out upon the children abroad, and upon the assembly of young men together: for even the hus-

and wickedness. Jeremiah cried out against the prosperity of the wicked and was assured that retribution would come in God's appointed time (cf. Deut 24:17-22).

30-31. The people were satisfied with a totally corrupt government. The prophets were telling the people what they wanted to hear. But not so with Jeremiah. He took his orders from the One who knew what the people needed. If their healing required bitter medicine, that is what they would get. "It is seldom possible to provide painless cures for the ills of the spirit." (W. Harrelson, *Jeremiah, Prophet to the Nations,* pp. 39-40.)

d. The inevitable disaster. 6:1-30.

6:1-3. Jerusalem would be besieged by the foe from the north and would fall amid great suffering. Since the enemy would come from the north, the people were to flee to the south. **Tekoa** twelve miles south of Jerusalem, was the home of the prophet Amos. **Beth-haccerem.** Its identity is not certain. Some believe it to be modern Ain Karim, four and a half miles west of Jerusalem. The people were warned to flee from religious corruption (II Tim 2; II Cor 6; Rev 18).

4-6. The invaders were like the shepherds whose flocks strip away the covering of the land. **Noon.** It was not usual to attack during the heat of the day. However, this army will not stop for rest, but will continue to attack right through the night.

7. **Fountain . . . wickedness.** The people of Jerusalem had an ever-renewing fresh supply of wickedness, just the opposite of Jesus' picture of the ". . . well of water springing up into everlasting life" (Jn 4:14).

8-14. Jeremiah was bidden by the Lord to go back to the city and search again (as he did in ch. 5) in order to glean any remnant grapes on God's vine. However, the people had **uncircumcised** ears (cf. Acts 7:51). God's word was a reproach to them. They listened to the false prophet who cried **Peace, peace,** even in the midst of calamity.

15-19. Over and over, year after year, Jeremiah had warned the people; but they flatly refused. **Watchmen.** In a wicked, unprotected land a watchman was vital in order to warn others of impending danger. However, all of the watchmen God sent met with the same stubborn reply. **We will not hearken.** Therefore, the **nations** were called upon to acknowledge the justice of Jehovah's dealings with so rebellious a people.

20-26. Sheba is modern Yemen, an Arabian city famous for its incense (cf. Isa 43:24). **Sweet cane.** Calamus, an Indian aromatic reed (cf. Isa 43:24; Ex 30:23). Since the invitation to repentance was rejected, the prophet mourned for the inevitable judgment upon the city. The foe from the north would be cruel and merciless.

27-30. The message closes with God's attempts to purge His people, illustrated in three pictures related to metals: (1) Jeremiah is the Lord's assayer to **try** His people. As precious metals

1441

---

band with the wife shall be taken, the aged with *him that is* full of days.

12 And their houses shall be turned unto others, *with their* fields and wives together; for I will stretch out my hand upon the inhabitants of the land, saith the LORD.

13 For from the least of them even unto the greatest of them every one *is* given to covetousness; and from the prophet even unto the priest every one dealeth falsely.

14 They have healed also the hurt of *the daughter* of my people slightly, saying, Peace, peace; when *there is* no peace.

15 Were they ashamed when they had committed abomination? nay, they were not at all ashamed, neither could they blush: therefore they shall fall among them that fall: at the time *that* I visit them they shall be cast down, saith the LORD.

16 Thus saith the LORD, Stand ye in the ways, and see, and ask for the old paths, where *is* the good way, and walk therein, and ye shall find rest for your souls. But they said, We will not walk *therein*.

17 Also I set watchmen over you, *saying*, Hearken to the sound of the trumpet. But they said, We will not hearken.

18 ¶ Therefore hear, ye nations, and know, O congregation, what *is* among them.

19 Hear, O earth: behold, I will bring evil upon this people, *even* the fruit of their thoughts, because they have not hearkened unto my words, nor to my law, but rejected it.

20 To what purpose cometh there to me incense from She'ba, and the sweet cane from a far country? your burnt offerings *are* not acceptable, nor your sacrifices sweet unto me.

21 Therefore thus saith the LORD, Behold, I will lay stumblingblocks before this people, and the fathers and the sons together shall fall upon them; the neighbour and his friend shall perish.

22 Thus saith the LORD, Behold, a people cometh from the north country, and a great nation shall be raised from the sides of the earth.

23 They shall lay hold on bow and spear; they are cruel, and have no mercy; their voice roareth like the sea; and they ride upon horses, set in array as men for war against thee, O daughter of Zion.

24 We have heard the fame thereof: our hands wax feeble: anguish hath taken hold of us, *and* pain, as of a woman in travail.

25 Go not forth into the field, nor walk by the way; for the sword of the enemy *and* fear *is* on every side.

26 ¶ O daughter of my people, gird *thee* with sackcloth, and wallow thyself in ashes: make thee mourning, *as* for an only son, most bitter lamentation: for the spoiler shall suddenly come upon us.

27 I have set thee *for* a tower *and* a fortress among my people, that thou mayest know and try their way.

28 They are all grievous revolters, walking with slanders: *they are* brass and iron; they are all corrupters.

29 The bellows are burned, the lead is consumed of the fire; the founder melteth in vain: for the wicked are not plucked away.

30 Reprobate silver shall *men* call them, because the LORD hath rejected them.

CHAPTER 7

THE word that came to Jĕr'ĕ-mī'ah from the LORD, saying,

2 Stand in the gate of the LORD's house, and proclaim there this word, and say, Hear the word of the LORD, all *ye of* Jū'dah, that enter in at these gates to worship the LORD.

3 Thus saith the LORD of hosts, the God of Israel, Amend your ways and your doings, and I will cause you to dwell in this place.

4 Trust ye not in lying words, saying, The temple of the LORD, The temple of the LORD, The temple of the LORD, *are* these.

5 For if ye throughly amend your ways and your doings; if ye throughly execute judgment between a man and his neighbour;

6 *If* ye oppress not the stranger, the fatherless, and the widow, and shed not innocent blood in this place, neither walk after other gods to your hurt:

7 Then will I cause you to dwell in this place, in the land that I gave to your fathers, for ever and ever.

8 ¶Behold, ye trust in lying words, that cannot profit.

9 Will ye steal, murder, and commit adultery, and swear falsely, and burn incense unto Bā'al, and walk after other gods whom ye know not;

10 And come and stand before me in this house, which is called by my name, and say, We are delivered to do all these abominations?

11 Is this house, which is called by my name, become a den of robbers in your eyes? Behold, even I have seen *it*, saith the LORD.

12 But go ye now unto my place which was in Shī'lŏh, where I set my

a. Rebuke of a superstitious faith. 7:1-8:17.

The people's faith and trust were in a building, the Temple, rather than in Jehovah. They reasoned that no foreign power could destroy the house belonging to God. Isaiah's teaching about the presence of God in Jerusalem (Isa 8:18; 28:16) was confirmed by the Assyrian deliverance in 701 B.C. (II Kgs 19:35). Along with Josiah's reform (621 B.C.), this gave the people confidence that the Temple could not be destroyed. Jeremiah shows that true worship includes repentance from sin and repudiation of idolatry.

7:1-3. All ye of Judah. This sermon was probably delivered at one of the three annual pilgrim feasts when Jerusalem would have been crowded with many visitors.

4-7. The temple of the LORD. The Temple had become a fetish. Originated by the lies of the false prophets, the people chimed this religious chant. **Stranger.** The Mosaic law had strict conditions on the treatment of strangers (sojourners), the fatherless, and widows (Ex 22:20; 23:9; Deut 24:17).

8-9. Jeremiah complained that God's people were treating His covenant as license for immoral living. How can they repudiate the commandments (five are mentioned) and rejoice in the power of God at the same time?

10-11. We are delivered. The second religious chant (cf. vs. 4). The people lived in gross sin in everyday life. Then, at the religious hour they came before God in His house and gave lip service to Him. They had turned God's house into a den of thieves, the same situation that Jesus faced centuries later (cf. Mt 21:13; Mk 11:17; Lk 19:46).

12. The tabernacle was located at **Shiloh,** eighteen miles north of Jerusalem, during the early days of Israel. In the days of Eli, probably after the battle of Eben-ezer in 1050 B.C. (I Sam 4;

are tested, so must the people of God be tested; (2) the people are likened to **brass** (bronze) and **iron,** representing imprudence and obstinacy; and (3) the people are also likened to **reprobate** (contaminated) **silver** because the Lord has rejected them.

3. Third message: Threat of exile. 7:1-10:25.

The third message is called the Temple Sermon, because it was delivered at the gate of the Temple. This was Jeremiah's first public act requiring great courage, because it set him in opposition to the people, prophets, priests, and kings alike. This was the basis of his later persecutions; yet, through it all he was determined to be faithful to Jehovah and his calling.

Most of the messages from chapters 7-20 were delivered during the reign of Jehoiakim. However, without the actual dates given in the text, some could have been during the reign of Josiah. Probably chapter 26 is a brief resume of this sermon and its effects. If this is the case, then it gives the historical background of this sermon during the reign of Jehoiakim (26:1).

Ps 78:60), the city was destroyed by the Philistines and the ark taken. The destruction of **Shiloh** should have been a lesson to Judah. Because of the people's sin, God would also destroy the Temple in Jerusalem.

13-15. Rising up early, a favorite expression of Jeremiah (7:25; 11:7; 25:3ff.; 26:5; 29:19; 32:33; 35:14ff.; 44:4), showing God's persistent activity with Judah from morning to night. **Ephraim.** The leading tribe of the northern kingdom, exiled in 721 B.C. (cf. II Kgs 17:23; Isa 7:2-17).

16-17. Jeremiah was forbidden to intercede for his people (cf. Moses, Ex 32:32; Num 14:13-19). The sin of Judah had been so terrible that the prophet felt a revulsion within himself at interceding for her. Amos had a similar experience (Amos 7:1-9). Judah was so settled in her sin that she was the cause of great sorrow, not only to our prophet, but also to Jehovah.

18-20. Queen of heaven was the fertility goddess, Ashtoreth, (Astarte or Ishtar), worshiped in Assyria and Babylon. Her worship involved sexual immorality. **Provoke me to anger,** another favorite expression of Jeremiah (8:19; 11:17; 25:6ff.; 32:29ff.; 44:3, 8).

21-28. Jeremiah urged the people to get their priorities right. He did not deny the sacrifices because God instructed them (Lev 1-7). Rather he opposed the empty ritualism the people had given to the sacrifices and contrasted it with the obedience God demands (cf. I Sam 15:22). **Put your burnt offerings.** Since the offerings had lost all their sacred significance, Jeremiah said they might as well eat the burnt offerings, which were wholly offered to God, as well as the other offerings that they were accustomed to eating.

name at the first, and see what I did to it for the wickedness of my people Israel.

13 And now, because ye have done all these works, saith the LORD, and I spake unto you, rising up early and speaking, but ye heard not; and I called you, but ye answered not;

14 Therefore will I do unto *this* house, which is called by my name, wherein ye trust, and unto the place which I gave to you and to your fathers, as I have done to Shī'lōh.

15 And I will cast you out of my sight, as I have cast out all your brethren, *even* the whole seed of Ē'phra-im.

16 Therefore pray not thou for this people, neither lift up cry nor prayer for them, neither make intercession to me: for I will not hear thee.

17 ¶ Seest thou not what they do in the cities of Jū'dah and in the streets of Jerusalem?

18 The children gather wood, and the fathers kindle the fire, and the women knead *their* dough, to make cakes to the queen of heaven, and to pour out drink offerings unto other gods, that they may provoke me to anger.

19 Do they provoke me to anger? saith the LORD: *do they* not *provoke* themselves to the confusion of their own faces?

20 Therefore thus saith the Lord GOD; Behold, mine anger and my fury shall be poured out upon this place, upon man, and upon beast, and upon the trees of the field, and upon the fruit of the ground; and it shall burn, and shall not be quenched.

21 ¶ Thus saith the LORD of hosts, the God of Israel; Put your burnt offerings unto your sacrifices, and eat flesh.

22 For I spake not unto your fathers, nor commanded them in the day that I brought them out of the land of Egypt, concerning burnt offerings or sacrifices:

23 But this thing commanded I them, saying, Obey my voice, and I will be your God, and ye shall be my people: and walk ye in all the ways that I have commanded you, that it may be well unto you.

24 But they hearkened not, nor inclined their ear, but walked in the counsels *and* in the imagination of their evil heart, and went backward, and not forward.

25 Since the day that your fathers came forth out of the land of Egypt unto this day I have even sent unto you all my servants the prophets, daily rising up early and sending *them*:

26 Yet they hearkened not unto me, nor inclined their ear, but hardened their neck: they did worse than their fathers.

27 Therefore thou shalt speak all these words unto them; but they will not hearken to thee: thou shalt also call unto them; but they will not answer thee.

28 But thou shalt say unto them, This *is* a nation that obeyeth not the voice of the LORD their God, nor receiveth cor-

rection: truth is perished, and is cut off from their mouth.

29 ¶Cut off thine hair, O Jerusalem, and cast it away, and take up a lamentation on high places; for the Lord hath rejected and forsaken the generation of his wrath.

30 For the children of Jŭ́dah have done evil in my sight, saith the Lord: they have set their abominations in the house which is called by my name, to pollute it.

31 And they have built the high places of Tṓ́phet, which is in the valley of the son of Hĭn̄́nom, to burn their sons and their daughters in the fire; which I commanded them not, neither came it into my heart.

32 ¶Therefore, behold, the days come, saith the Lord, that it shall no more be called Tṓ́phet, nor the valley of the son of Hĭn̄́nom, but the valley of slaughter: for they shall bury in Tṓ́phet, till there be no place.

33 And the carcases of this people shall be meat for the fowls of the heaven, and for the beasts of the earth; and none shall fray them away.

34 Then will I cause to cease from the cities of Jŭ́dah, and from the streets of Jerusalem, the voice of mirth, and the voice of gladness, the voice of the bridegroom, and the voice of the bride: for the land shall be desolate.

CHAPTER 8

AT that time, saith the Lord, they shall bring out the bones of the kings of Jŭ́dah, and the bones of his princes, and the bones of the priests, and the bones of the prophets, and the bones of the inhabitants of Jerusalem, out of their graves:

2 And they shall spread them before the sun, and the moon, and all the host of heaven, whom they have loved, and whom they have served, and after whom they have walked, and whom they have sought, and whom they have worshipped: they shall not be gathered, nor be buried; they shall be for dung upon the face of the earth.

3 And death shall be chosen rather than life by all the residue of them that remain of this evil family, which remain in all the places whither I have driven them, saith the Lord of hosts.

4 ¶Moreover thou shalt say unto them, Thus saith the Lord; Shall they fall, and not arise? shall he turn away, and not return?

5 Why then is this people of Jerusalem slidden back by a perpetual backsliding? they hold fast deceit, they refuse to return.

6 I hearkened and heard, but they spake not aright: no man repented him of his wickedness, saying, What have I done? every one turned to his course, as the horse rusheth into the battle.

7 Yea, the stork in the heaven knoweth her appointed times; and the turtle and the crane and the swallow observe the time of their coming; but my people know not the judgment of the Lord.

8 How do ye say, We are wise, and the law of the Lord is with us? Lo, cer-

29-34. God complains about two things as this chapter closes: the idolatrous worship in the Temple and the building of the high place in the valley of Hinnom. **Abominations** were the idols in the Temple introduced by Manasseh (II Kgs 21:1-9), destroyed by Josiah (II Kgs 23:4-14), and now reintroduced. **Tophet** was the high place in the valley, or **son of Hinnom**, southwest of Jerusalem, where the people sacrificed their children to Molech, an Ammonite deity (II Kgs 16:3; 21:6). Human sacrifice meant the repudiation of the covenant and a regression into barbarism. Because of the enormity of the destruction of Judah the **valley of . . . Hinnom**, where they sacrificed their own children, will become the **valley of slaughter**, where they themselves will be killed. The holy place will be defiled by becoming a burying ground; the corpses will be defiled by being left unburied (cf. 16:4; 19:7; 34:20).

8:1-3. **They shall bring out the bones.** The enemy will desecrate the graves, a common practice in the warfare of that day (Amos 2:1). **Host of heaven.** The worship of the planets or the gods of the planets was introduced by Ahaz and Manasseh (II Kgs 21:5; 23:12).

4-7. Jeremiah illustrates the unnaturalness of Judah's backsliding by referring to the migratory birds. They know, live by, or obey their **appointed times**, their migratory instincts. Thus, they are obeying God's will for them. It should be natural for man, who lives at a higher level, to do the same; but Judah is a **perpetual** backslider.

8-12. God's ministers (scribes, prophets, and priests) do not teach the Word of God. The scribes were guilty because they

tainly in vain made he *it*; the pen of the scribes *is* in vain.

9 The wise *men* are ashamed, they are dismayed and taken: lo, they have rejected the word of the LORD; and what wisdom *is* in them?

10 Therefore will I give their wives unto others, *and* their fields to them that shall inherit *them*: for every one from the least even unto the greatest is given to covetousness, from the prophet even unto the priest every one dealeth falsely.

11 For they have healed the hurt of the daughter of my people slightly, saying, Peace, peace; when *there is* no peace.

12 Were they ashamed when they had committed abomination? nay, they were not at all ashamed, neither could they blush: therefore shall they fall among them that fall: in the time of their visitation they shall be cast down, saith the LORD.

13 I will surely consume them, saith the LORD: *there shall be* no grapes on the vine, nor figs on the fig tree, and the leaf shall fade; and *the things that* I have given them shall pass away from them.

14 ¶ Why do we sit still? assemble yourselves, and let us enter into the defenced cities, and let us be silent there: for the LORD our God hath put us to silence, and given us water of gall to drink, because we have sinned against the LORD.

15 We looked for peace, but no good *came; and* for a time of health, and behold trouble!

16 The snorting of his horses was heard from Dan: the whole land trembled at the sound of the neighing of his strong ones; for they are come, and have devoured the land, and all that is in it; the city, and those that dwell therein.

17 For, behold, I will send serpents, cockatrices, among you, which *will* not *be* charmed, and they shall bite you, saith the LORD.

18 ¶ *When* I would comfort myself against sorrow, my heart *is* faint in me.

19 Behold the voice of the cry of the daughter of my people because of them that dwell in a far country: *Is* not the LORD in Zion? *is* not her king in her? Why have they provoked me to anger with their graven images, *and* with strange vanities?

20 The harvest is past, the summer is ended, and we are not saved.

21 For the hurt of the daughter of my people am I hurt; I am black; astonishment hath taken hold on me.

22 *Is there* no balm in Gilead; *is there* no physician there? why then is not the

wrote falsely; the prophets and priests were guilty because they spoke falsely.

13-17. God became disappointed with His vineyard. This is a recurring theme in Scripture (cf. 5:10-11; 6:9; Isa 5:1-7; Lk 13:6-9). Therefore, doom was inevitable. God's pronouncements of judgment were brief. **I will surely** (utterly) **consume** (vs. 13) and **I will send serpents** (vs. 17). **Cockatrices** (adders).

b. Lamentations for sinners. 8:18-9:26.

18. Since the grace of God was at their disposal, yet was rejected, Jeremiah was overcome with grief for the people. His heart cried out with several lamentations. These lamentations and God's answers (usually judgment) alternate as follows: lamentation (8:18-9:6), reason for judgment (9:7-9); lamentation (9:10-11), reason for judgment (9:12-16); lamentation (17-22), final words of Jehovah (saving glory 23-24, and ultimate judgment, 25-26).

19. A far country. From the length and breadth of the land. **Strange vanities.** Foreign idols.

20-21. Harvest and **summer** represent the two successive phases of the harvest season. The grain harvest was from April to June. The fruit harvest was later. If the former failed, the people could still look forward to the latter. But if both failed, famine was inevitable. For Judah, the harvest season was over; and no fruit had been stored for the winter ahead. Therefore, **we are not saved.**

22. Balm in Gilead. A resin from the styrax tree in Gilead, across the Jordan from Anathoth. This healing ointment was

1445

health of the daughter of my people re-covered?

CHAPTER 9

OH that my head were waters, and mine eyes a fountain of tears, that I might weep day and night for the slain of the daughter of my people!

2 Oh that I had in the wilderness a lodging place of wayfaring men; that I might leave my people, and go from them! for they *be* all adulterers, an assembly of treacherous men.

3 And they bend their tongues *like* their bow *for* lies: but they are not valiant for the truth upon the earth; for they proceed from evil to evil, and they know not me, saith the Lord.

4 Take ye heed every one of his neighbour, and trust ye not in any brother: for every brother will utterly supplant, and every neighbour will walk with slanders.

5 And they will deceive every one his neighbour, and will not speak the truth: they have taught their tongue to speak lies, *and* weary themselves to commit iniquity.

6 Thine habitation *is* in the midst of deceit; through deceit they refuse to know me, saith the Lord.

7 Therefore thus saith the Lord of hosts, Behold, I will melt them, and try them; for how shall I do for the daughter of my people?

8 Their tongue *is* as an arrow shot out; it speaketh deceit: *one* speaketh peaceably to his neighbour with his mouth, but in heart he layeth his wait.

9 ¶Shall I not visit them for these *things?* saith the Lord: shall not my soul be avenged on such a nation as this?

10 For the mountains will I take up a weeping and wailing, and for the habitations of the wilderness a lamentation, because they are burned up, so that none can pass through *them;* neither can *men* hear the voice of the cattle; both the fowl of the heavens and the beast are fled; they are gone.

11 And I will make Jerusalem heaps, *and* a den of dragons; and I will make the cities of Ju′dah desolate, without an inhabitant.

12 ¶Who *is* the wise man, that may understand this? and *who is* he to whom the mouth of the Lord hath spoken, that he may declare it, for what the land perisheth *and* is burned up like a wilderness, that none passeth through?

13 And the Lord saith, Because they have forsaken my law which I set before them, and have not obeyed my voice, neither walked therein;

14 But have walked after the imagination of their own heart, and after Ba′al-im, which their fathers taught them:

15 Therefore thus saith the Lord of hosts, the God of Israel; Behold, I will feed them, *even* this people, with wormwood, and give them water of gall to drink.

16 I will scatter them also among the heathen, whom neither they nor their fathers have known: and I will send a sword after them, till I have consumed them.

---

known from patriarchal days (Gen 37:25) and was exported (46:11; 51:8; Ezk 27:17).

9:1-2. The utter degradation of the people was so abominable that Jeremiah wanted to separate himself from them. **Lodging place.** Better to be in a traveller's hut in the desert with all its discomforts than dwell with the **adulterers** (breakers of the covenant) in comfort.

3-9. Jeremiah now decried the sins of the tongue: lies, slander, double-dealing, deceit, etc. This life-style destroys a knowledge of God and a proper relationship with Him. God answered Jeremiah's complaint by showing him that there is no alternative but divine judgment (chs. 7-9).

10-16. Jeremiah's second lament was for the **habitations of the wilderness.** The land will be desolate; the birds will be taken away; and only scavengers will be left. **Dragons** (jackals). God answered that there will be judgment for their forsaking His Law, disobedience, stubbornness, and idolatry.

Two terms are used to describe the bitter afflictions that will come upon the people: **wormwood,** a bitter tasting plant and therefore a symbol of sorrow; and **gall,** a poisonous bitter herb.

17 ¶Thus saith the LORD of hosts, Consider ye, and call for the mourning women, that they may come; and send for cunning women, that they may come:

18 And let them make haste, and take up a wailing for us, that our eyes may run down with tears, and our eyelids gush out with waters.

19 For a voice of wailing is heard out of Zion, How are we spoiled! we are greatly confounded, because we have forsaken the land, because our dwellings have cast us out.

20 Yet hear the word of the LORD, O ye women, and let your ear receive the word of his mouth, and teach your daughters wailing, and every one her neighbour lamentation.

21 For death is come up into our windows, and is entered into our palaces, to cut off the children from without, and the young men from the streets.

22 Speak, Thus saith the LORD, Even the carcases of men shall fall as dung upon the open field, and as the handful after the harvestman, and none shall gather them.

23 ¶Thus saith the LORD, Let not the wise man glory in his wisdom, neither let the mighty man glory in his might, let not the rich man glory in his riches:

24 But let him that glorieth glory in this, that he understandeth and knoweth me, that I am the LORD which exercise lovingkindness, judgment, and righteousness, in the earth: for in these things I delight, saith the LORD.

25 ¶Behold, the days come, saith the LORD, that I will punish all them which are circumcised with the uncircumcised;

26 Egypt, and Ju'dah, and Edom, and the children of Ammon, and Moab, and all that are in the utmost corners, that dwell in the wilderness: for all these nations are uncircumcised, and all the house of Israel are uncircumcised in the heart.

CHAPTER 10

HEAR ye the word which the LORD speaketh unto you, O house of Israel:

2 Thus saith the LORD, Learn not the way of the heathen, and be not dismayed at the signs of heaven; for the heathen are dismayed at them.

3 For the customs of the people are vain: for one cutteth a tree out of the forest, the work of the hands of the workman, with the axe.

4 They deck it with silver and with gold: they fasten it with nails and with hammers, that it move not.

5 They are upright as the palm tree, but speak not: they must needs be borne, because they cannot go. Be not afraid of them; for they cannot do evil, neither also is it in them to do good.

6 Forasmuch as there is none like unto thee, O LORD; thou art great, and thy name is great in might.

7 Who would not fear thee, O King of nations? for to thee doth it appertain: forasmuch as among all the wise men of the nations, and in all their kingdoms, there is none like unto thee.

17-22. Jeremiah's third lamentation was in the form of a death dirge. **Mourning women.** Professional mourners, who excited mourning in others (cf. Mt 9:23; Mk 5:38) and recited death dirges (II Chr 35:25). Now they will really have something to mourn for, i.e., the destruction of life, houses, and land.

23-26. God answered with two universal truths: (1) salvation is for all who know God (vss. 23-24); and (2) judgment is for all who are unbelievers in heart (vss. 25-26). Judah cannot rely on circumcision to protect her (cf. 7:1-15), for circumcision was also practiced by other nations. Therefore, it is no substitute for the pure heart demanded by God (cf. Mt 5:8; I Cor 7:19; Rom 2:25). All the nations mentioned here practiced physical circumcision (Gen 17:22-26; Ezk 31:18; 32:19, 32). Only the Philistines are singled out in the Old Testament as being uncircumcised. Spiritually, all these nations were **uncircumcised in the heart,** but so too was Judah. **Utmost corners.** Cut the corners of their hair. Some of the Arabian tribes shaved off the hair of their temples in honor of their gods, a practice forbidden to the people of God (Lev 19:27).

c. *The living God versus lifeless idols.* 10:1-25.

The prophet concludes his temple message by painting a picture of the broad scope of God's relationship to the nations (vss. 1-11), to nature (vss. 12-13), and to mankind (vss. 14-25). 10:1-5. Jeremiah begins with a charge on the fallacy of worshiping idols. The **heathen** (nations) fear the potentially destructive elements of nature. **Signs of heaven** are eclipses, comets, lightning, etc. They manufacture gods out of the trees of the forest and then cover them with **silver and with gold.** But these practices are **vain,** worthless. These man-made gods are speechless and impotent, like a scarecrow in the field, **upright as the palm tree.**

6-18. By contrast, the living God is **great.** Jeremiah declares, **there is none like unto thee.** The wise men of the nations are **brutish** (stupid) and **foolish.** God's majesty is exalted. He is the **King of nations.** He is the **true God . . . the living God, and an everlasting king.** He is the **LORD of hosts.** Tarshish was located either in southern Spain or the island of Sicily and was a source of metals (cf. Ezk 27:12; Jon 1:3). **Uphaz** is unknown.

1447

8 But they are altogether brutish and foolish: the stock *is* a doctrine of vanities.

9 Silver spread into plates is brought from Tär'shĭsh, and gold from Ū'phăz, the work of the workman, and of the hands of the founder: blue and purple *is* their clothing: they *are* all the work of cunning *men*.

10 But the LORD *is* the true God, he *is* the living God, and an everlasting king: at his wrath the earth shall tremble, and the nations shall not be able to abide his indignation.

11 Thus shall ye say unto them, The gods that have not made the heavens and the earth, *even* they shall perish from the earth, and from under these heavens.

12 He hath made the earth by his power, he hath established the world by his wisdom, and hath stretched out the heavens by his discretion.

13 When he uttereth his voice, *there is* a multitude of waters in the heavens, and he causeth the vapours to ascend from the ends of the earth; he maketh lightnings with rain, and bringeth forth the wind out of his treasures.

14 Every man is brutish in *his* knowledge: every founder is confounded by the graven image: for his molten image *is* falsehood, and *there is* no breath in them.

15 They *are* vanity, *and* the work of errors: in the time of their visitation they shall perish.

16 The portion of Jacob *is* not like them: for he *is* the former of all *things*; and Israel *is* the rod of his inheritance: The LORD of hosts *is* his name.

17 ¶ Gather up thy wares out of the land, O inhabitant of the fortress.

18 For thus saith the LORD, Behold, I will sling out the inhabitants of the land at this once, and will distress them, that they may find *it* so.

19 ¶ Woe is me for my hurt! my wound is grievous: but I said, Truly this *is* a grief, and I must bear it.

20 My tabernacle is spoiled, and all my cords are broken: my children are gone forth of me, and they *are* not: *there is* none to stretch forth my tent any more, and to set up my curtains.

21 For the pastors are become brutish, and have not sought the LORD: therefore they shall not prosper, and all their flocks shall be scattered.

22 Behold, the noise of the bruit is come, and a great commotion out of the north country, to make the cities of Jū'dah desolate, *and* a den of dragons.

23 ¶ O LORD, I know that the way of man *is* not in himself: *it is* not in man that walketh to direct his steps.

24 O LORD, correct me, but with judgment; not in thine anger, lest thou bring me to nothing.

25 Pour out thy fury upon the heathen that know thee not, and upon the families that call not on thy name: for they have eaten up Jacob, and de-

---

Some believe it might be Ophir (1 Kgs 9:28; 10:11; Isa 13:12), a gold-producing territory on the southwest coast of Arabia. **Tremble.** Both earthquakes and political disasters are seen as judgments from God. Verse 11 is the only verse in Jeremiah that is given in Aramaic, the language of international diplomacy in that day. **Gather up thy wares.** The prophet warns them to get ready to flee, for God is going to bring judgment.

19-22. Judah replies in terms of her pain, expressed as a mother bereft of her children (cf. Isa 49:14-23; 54: 1-3). **Pastors.** Shepherds (cf. 2:8, note). **Dragons.** Jackals.

23-25. The chapter concludes with a prayer of the prophet. Scholars are not agreed as to whether these are Jeremiah's words to himself or to the people. Both interpretations are possible and meaningful. The former interpretation understands the prayer to be Jeremiah's final submission to God's direction in his life, while the latter interpretation views it as his prayer for a yet future penitent Judah.

4. *Fourth message: The broken covenant. 11:1-13:27.*

The messages found in chapters 2 through 10 were delivered by Jeremiah on the streets and in the Temple without any particular reference to his own life. However, in chapters 11

voured him, and consumed him, and have made his habitation desolate.

CHAPTER 11

THE word that came to Jĕr'e-mī'ah from the LORD, saying,

2 Hear ye the words of this covenant, and speak unto the men of Jū'dah, and to the inhabitants of Jerusalem;

3 And say thou unto them, Thus saith the LORD God of Israel; Cursed be the man that obeyeth not the words of this covenant,

4 Which I commanded your fathers in the day that I brought them forth out of the land of Egypt, from the iron furnace, saying, Obey my voice, and do them, according to all which I command you: so shall ye be my people, and I will be your God:

5 That I may perform the oath which I have sworn unto your fathers, to give them a land flowing with milk and honey, as it is this day. Then answered I, and said, So be it, O LORD.

6 Then the LORD said unto me, Proclaim all these words in the cities of Jū'dah, and in the streets of Jerusalem, saying, Hear ye the words of this covenant, and do them.

7 For I earnestly protested unto your fathers in the day that I brought them up out of the land of Egypt, even unto this day, rising early and protesting, saying, Obey my voice.

8 Yet they obeyed not, nor inclined their ear, but walked every one in the imagination of their evil heart: therefore I will bring upon them all the words of this covenant, which I commanded them to do; but they did them not.

9 And the LORD said unto me, A conspiracy is found among the men of Jū'dah, and among the inhabitants of Jerusalem.

10 They are turned back to the iniquities of their forefathers, which refused to hear my words; and they went after other gods to serve them: the house of Israel and the house of Jū'dah have broken my covenant which I made with their fathers.

11 Therefore thus saith the LORD, Behold, I will bring evil upon them, which they shall not be able to escape; and though they shall cry unto me, I will not hearken unto them.

12 Then shall the cities of Jū'dah and inhabitants of Jerusalem go, and cry

through 20 his personal struggles are interwoven into his messages.

Critical scholars have completely denied Jeremiah's authorship of 11:1-14 and have attributed it to so-called Deuteronomic authors. These were supposedly a group of authors who composed Deuteronomy, Joshua, Judges, Samuel, Kings and parts of Jeremiah during the Exile (see E. W. Nicholson, *The Book of the Prophet Jeremiah*, p. 10ff.; p. 107ff.; and p. 154). However, the text declares that this is **The word that came to Jeremiah from the LORD;** and there is no reason to doubt its authenticity. The covenant referred to in 11:2-6 is not some Deuteronomic Covenant compiled as a result of Josiah's reform, but the covenant given by God to Israel at Sinai (see T. Laetsch, *Bible Commentary, Jeremiah*, p. 126). Jeremiah championed this covenant, as is seen in this message.

a. The broken covenant. 11:1-17.

11:1-2. God gives two commands regarding His covenant. The first, **Hear,** used six times in this message, always denotes a sense of obey. Obedience is a primary demand of the Covenant God (Ex 19:5; I Sam 15:22; Ps 50:7-23; Mal 4:4). The second command is **speak.** Everyone who hears is also to tell the words of the covenant.

3-8. Cursed (cf. Deut 27:11-26). In the application of the covenant there were blessings for obedience and cursings for disobedience. This was also the pattern of the Suzerain King Treaties of the ancient Near East (see M. Kline, *Treaty of the Great King*). **Iron furnace.** A furnace in which iron was smelted and thus a figure of a place of severe suffering (Deut 4:20; I Kgs 8:51). Verse 5 is a summary of the teachings of the book of Deuteronomy. **I will bring . . . covenant.** A repetition of the threats of the covenant (cf. Deut 8:19; 28:15ff.).

9-14. Although warned many times, both Israel and Judah had broken the covenant and had joined themselves to idols. Even after the revival under Josiah the present generation had returned to the sins of their forefathers. Therefore, Jeremiah reaffirmed the consequences of breaking the covenant, which was judgment. **Conspiracy.** The breaking of the covenant was the first of three conspiracies in this message. It was a national conspiracy against God. So widespread was their idolatry that their idols were more numerous than the streets of Jerusalem and the cities in Judah. **Shameful thing** (see 3:24 note). The covenant had been broken; therefore, there was no reason to intercede for the people. **I will not hear them.**

unto the gods unto whom they offer incense: but they shall not save them at all in the time of their trouble.

13 For *according to* the number of thy cities were thy gods, O Jū'dah; and *according to* the number of the streets of Jerusalem have ye set up altars to *that* shameful thing, *even* altars to burn incense unto Bā'al.

14 Therefore pray not thou for this people, neither lift up a cry or prayer for them: for I will not hear *them* in the time that they cry unto me for their trouble.

15 What hath my beloved to do in mine house, *seeing* she hath wrought lewdness with many, and the holy flesh is passed from thee? when thou doest evil, then thou rejoicest.

16 The LORD called thy name, A green olive tree, fair, *and* of goodly fruit: with the noise of a great tumult he hath kindled fire upon it, and the branches of it are broken.

17 For the LORD of hosts, that planted thee, hath pronounced evil against thee, for the evil of the house of Israel and of the house of Jū'dah, which they have done against themselves to provoke me to anger in offering incense unto Bā'al.

18 ¶And the LORD hath given me knowledge *of it*, and I know *it*: then thou shewedst me their doings.

19 But I was like a lamb *or* an ox *that* is brought to the slaughter; and I knew not that they had devised devices against me, *saying*, Let us destroy the tree with the fruit thereof, and let us cut him off from the land of the living, that his name may be no more remembered.

20 But, O LORD of hosts, that judgest righteously, that triest the reins and the heart, let me see thy vengeance on them: for unto thee have I revealed my cause.

21 Therefore thus saith the LORD of the men of Ăn'a-thŏth, that seek thy life, saying, Prophesy not in the name of the LORD, that thou die not by our hand:

22 Therefore thus saith the LORD of hosts, Behold, I will punish them: the young men shall die by the sword; their sons and their daughters shall die by famine:

23 And there shall be no remnant of them: for I will bring evil upon the men of Ăn'a-thŏth, *even* the year of their visitation.

CHAPTER 12

RIGHTEOUS *art* thou, O LORD, when I plead with thee: yet let me talk with thee of *thy* judgments: Wherefore doth the way of the wicked prosper? *wherefore* are all they happy that deal very treacherously?

2 Thou hast planted them, yea, they have taken root: they grow; yea, they bring forth fruit: thou *art* near in their mouth, and far from their reins.

3 But thou, O LORD, knowest me: thou hast seen me, and tried mine heart toward thee: pull them out like sheep for the slaughter, and prepare them for the day of slaughter.

15-17. Like Solomon, who was called Jehovah's beloved one (II Sam 12:24), so too Judah and Jerusalem had been the Lord's beloved (cf. Ps 78:68ff.; 87:2). But because of her sins, Judah no longer had any right to God's **house**, the Temple. In the days of her youth God regarded Judah as a **green olive tree**. Extremely valuable in Palestine, the olive tree was a source of oil for light, cooking, body ointment, medicine, etc. It was also the symbol of prosperity, beauty, and the Holy Spirit and His gifts (cf. Ps 45:7; Acts 10:38). Judah was like a great olive tree (cf. Ps 52:8; Hos 14:6); but having been struck by **fire** (lightning), in a **great tumult** (great storm), her beauty is now marred. Paul used this verse for the text of his discussion in Romans 11:17-24.

b. The plot against Jeremiah's life. 11:18-12:17.

18. The men of Anathoth plotted against Jeremiah. When men reject God's Word, they also will reject God's messenger. With the rejection of the covenant comes the rejection of the preacher of the covenant. This is the second conspiracy.

19-23. Jeremiah's reaction to their threats was that of a **lamb**, a tame lamb, therefore trustful and unsuspecting. Jeremiah appeals to God who alone can judge **righteously**. The **reins**, kidneys, were thought by the Hebrews to be the seat of emotions (cf. Prov 23:16; Ps 16:7; 73:21; Job 19:27). The **heart** (Heb *lēb*) was thought to be the seat of the understanding (cf. 5:21). Thus, when it is said that Jehovah "tries" (i.e., tests or examines) the reins and heart, it means He is cognizant of man's emotions and affections as well as his purposes and thoughts (cf. 17:10; 20:12; Ps 7:9; 26:2).

12:1-6. Jeremiah pleads with God in regard to the impending vengeance. Along with many of the Old Testament saints, Jeremiah faces the problem of the prosperity of the wicked, and he asks for the destruction of the wicked. The people had mocked Jeremiah by saying that **He shall not see our last end** meaning they would survive him so that he would not see his predictions fulfilled. But God had promised him that in due time the wicked would receive their just deserts. Judgment would fall upon them as in the **swelling of Jordan**, i.e., the thick undergrowth along the sides of the Jordan that was infested with wild animals and consequently very dangerous (49:19; Zech 11:3). Even his relatives had dealt **treacherously** with him. This was the third conspiracy.

4 How long shall the land mourn, and the herbs of every field wither, for the wickedness of them that dwell therein? the beasts are consumed, and the birds; because they said, He shall not see our last end.

5 ¶If thou hast run with the footmen, and they have wearied thee, then how canst thou contend with horses? and *if* in the land of peace, *wherein* thou trustedst, *they wearied thee,* then how wilt thou do in the swelling of Jordan?

6 For even thy brethren, and the house of thy father, even they have dealt treacherously with thee; yea, they have called a multitude after thee: believe them not, though they speak fair words unto thee.

7 ¶I have forsaken mine house, I have left mine heritage; I have given the dearly beloved of my soul into the hand of her enemies.

8 Mine heritage is unto me as a lion in the forest; it crieth out against me: therefore have I hated it.

9 Mine heritage *is* unto me *as* a speckled bird, the birds round about *are* against her; come ye, assemble all the beasts of the field, come to devour.

10 Many pastors have destroyed my vineyard, they have trodden my portion under foot, they have made my pleasant portion a desolate wilderness.

11 They have made it desolate, *and being* desolate it mourneth unto me; the whole land is made desolate, because no man layeth *it* to heart.

12 The spoilers are come upon all high places through the wilderness: for the sword of the LORD shall devour from the *one* end of the land even to the *other* end of the land: no flesh shall have peace.

13 They have sown wheat, but shall reap thorns: they have put themselves to pain, *but* shall not profit: and they shall be ashamed of your revenues because of the fierce anger of the LORD.

14 ¶Thus saith the LORD against all mine evil neighbours, that touch the inheritance which I have caused my people Israel to inherit; Behold, I will pluck them out of their land, and pluck out the house of Jū′dah from among them.

15 And it shall come to pass, after that I have plucked them out I will return, and have compassion on them, and will bring them again, every man to his heritage, and every man to his land.

16 And it shall come to pass, if they will diligently learn the ways of my people, to swear by my name, The LORD liveth; as they taught my people to swear by Bā′al; then shall they be built in the midst of my people.

17 But if they will not obey, I will utterly pluck up and destroy that nation, saith the LORD.

CHAPTER 13

THUS saith the LORD unto me, Go and get thee a linen girdle, and put it upon thy loins, and put it not in water.

2 So I got a girdle according to the word of the LORD, and put *it* on my loins.

3 And the word of the LORD came unto me the second time, saying,

7-13. Here, the Lord, rather than the prophet, laments over Judah. It was too late to plead for the people. Jehovah had **forsaken** them. Since the covenant had been broken, judgment was the only option. **Speckled bird** means a bird of unusual plumage often attacked by other birds. In addition to birds, several other figures of speech are used to describe Israel: **house, heritage, beloved, lion, beasts, vineyard and portion.** Jeremiah fearlessly and courageously declared God's judgment upon the nation.

"The world today needs more Jeremiahs who, in the midst of opposition, are true to the standard of the Bible, patient in the proclamation of the gospel, gentle in the hands of persecutors, committed to the protective care of the Chief Shepherd, and burdened for the souls of lost men and women. Satan and the world may conspire against a servant of God, but the conspiracy is really against God, and God is invincible!" (I.L. Jensen, *Jeremiah and Lamentations,* p. 48).

14-17. The chapter concludes with God's declaration against the **evil neighbors,** the nations. They, too, will be punished if they don't repent. Although Judah will be **plucked . . . out,** yet God will have compassion on her and return her to the land.

c. Dramatic signs of impending judgment. 13:1-27.

13:1-2. Jeremiah is told to purchase and wear a **girdle,** a loincloth or belt. This was a piece of cloth fastened tightly around the loins in order to hold up the long upper garment while walking or working.

3-7. The Lord then commanded Jeremiah to hide the loincloth in the cleft of a rock by the River Euphrates. He returned

4 Take the girdle that thou hast got, which is upon thy loins, and arise, go to Eū-phrā'tēs, and hide it there in a hole of the rock.

5 So I went, and hid it by Eū-phrā'tēs, as the LORD commanded me.

6 And it came to pass after many days, that the LORD said unto me, Arise, go to Eū-phrā'tēs, and take the girdle from thence, which I commanded thee to hide there.

7 Then I went to Eū-phrā'tēs, and digged, and took the girdle from the place where I had hid it: and, behold, the girdle was marred, it was profitable for nothing.

8 Then the word of the LORD came unto me, saying,

9 Thus saith the LORD, After this manner will I mar the pride of Jū'dah, and the great pride of Jerusalem.

10 This evil people, which refuse to hear my words, which walk in the imagination of their heart, and walk after other gods, to serve them, and to worship them, shall even be as this girdle, which is good for nothing.

11 For as the girdle cleaveth to the loins of a man, so have I caused to cleave unto me the whole house of Israel and the whole house of Jū'dah, saith the LORD; that they might be unto me for a people, and for a name, and for a praise, and for a glory: but they would not hear.

12 ¶ Therefore thou shalt speak unto them this word; Thus saith the LORD God of Israel, Every bottle shall be filled with wine: and they shall say unto thee, Do we not certainly know that every bottle shall be filled with wine?

13 Then shalt thou say unto them, Thus saith the LORD, Behold, I will fill all the inhabitants of this land, even the kings that sit upon David's throne, and the priests, and the prophets, and all the inhabitants of Jerusalem, with drunkenness.

14 And I will dash them one against another, even the fathers and the sons together, saith the LORD: I will not pity, nor spare, nor have mercy, but destroy them.

15 ¶ Hear ye, and give ear; be not proud: for the LORD hath spoken.

16 Give glory to the LORD your God, before he cause darkness, and before your feet stumble upon the dark mountains, and, while ye look for light, he turn it into the shadow of death, and make it gross darkness.

17 But if ye will not hear it, my soul shall weep in secret places for your pride; and mine eye shall weep sore, and run down with tears, because the LORD's flock is carried away captive.

18 Say unto the king and to the queen, Humble yourselves, sit down: for your principalities shall come down, even the crown of your glory.

19 The cities of the south shall be

home and was commanded to return to the Euphrates and remove the loincloth. He finds it marred by the moisture and no longer usable. Since the Euphrates is about two hundred fifty miles from Jerusalem, many have denied that Jeremiah actually made those two journeys; and many attempts have been made at alternate interpretations. Some have changed the Hebrew word slightly, rendering it Ephrath, the ancient name for Beth-lehem (Gen 35:19) or the modern Wadi Forah three miles northeast of Anathoth (Josh 21:18).

Others, holding to a literal meaning of **Euphrates**, have understood this account to be a parable or vision. However, as several conservative scholars have pointed out (cf. Keil, p. 230 ff.; Streane, pp. 102-103, Laetsch, p. 137), the entire account is presented as a command. Euphrates is understood elsewhere as actually the river Euphrates (51:63); and Jeremiah was absent from Jerusalem during part of Jehoiakim's reign, making possible a trip to Babylon. This might also account for Nebuchadnezzar's kind treatment of Jeremiah after the fall of Jerusalem (39:11).

8-11. God interprets the sign of the loincloth. The white loincloth symbolizes the original purity of the nation in fellowship with the Lord. However, because of their sin, God marred the **pride of Judah** by the judgment of the captivity. The captivity would not change the heart; only self-judgment would do that. As the loincloth clings to the loins of a man, so God would cause Israel and Judah to cling to Him.

12-14. The sign of the wine bottles. **Bottle.** The Hebrew term can mean either an animal skin or an earthen jar (cf. 48:12; Isa 30:14; Jn 2:6ff.). The wine jars filled to the brim symbolized the drunkenness of the people and their ruin under divine judgment. Judah shall be filled, not with the joy of the Lord, but with a delusion which shall bring judgment. **Drunkenness** was a common symbol of irrationality and helplessness. This would be the plight of the people in captivity (25:15-28; Ezk 23:31-34; Isa 51:17-18).

15-17. Jeremiah warned the people about the sin of pride. By rejecting the light they would receive the darkness of judgment, as a traveler in the mountains is suddenly overtaken by darkness.

18-19. The prophet now chants a dirge for the **king** and **queen** (probably the queen-mother who held a powerful position in the ancient Orient, see I Kgs 15:13). This was no doubt "Jehoiachin" and the queen mother, both of whom were captives in Babylon (II Kgs 24:12-15). **The cities of the south shall be**

army from the north would march along the fertile coastal plain, capturing the outlying cities before it attacked Jerusalem.

20-27. Already Jeremiah saw the enemy from the north approaching and pronounced a woe upon Jerusalem. Judah shall be **made bare**, violently stripped of all in which she gloried. Judah was so entrenched in her sin that she could not change. It would be easier for an **Ethiopian** to change his skin or a **leopard** his spots than for Judah to do good. Judah preferred the filth of her harlotry to the purity offered by God.

5. Fifth message: The drought. 14:1-17:27.

This fifth message was given during a time of war and famine. Although there were periods of war at the close of the reigns of Jehoiachin and Zedekiah, this message was probably given during the reign of Jehoiakim. In a land where rainfall is marginal, a drought can have far-reaching effects. As a consequence of the people's sin, a severe drought had come upon the land.

Though hated, ridiculed, and mocked, Jeremiah's heart ached when he saw the people suffering. In his prayer for the people, Jeremiah's intense intercessory character is seen. His intercession is the greatest example of the heart of our Lord Jesus in the Old Testament.

a. The drought. 14:1-22.

14:1-6. The severe drought brought anguish on everyone in Judah, from the poor to the rich. The **nobles** sent their children to the **pits** (cisterns) in search of water, but to no avail. The **plowmen**, representing the masses, could not till the **chapt** (cracked) earth. The **hind** had forsaken her young because there was no **grass**. **Covered their heads** is an expression of grief (cf. II Sam 15:30; 19:4).

7-9. The people appeal to God for relief. Their intercession is based on a confession of sin, an interested God (not a disinterested **stranger . . . wayfaring man** — traveler), an able God, and a present God (**in the midst of us**) whom Judah still calls by His **name**.

10-12. However, because they continue in their sin the LORD

---

shut up, and none shall open them: Jū'-dah shall be carried away captive all of it, it shall be wholly carried away captive.

20 Lift up your eyes, and behold them that come from the north: where is the flock that was given thee, thy beautiful flock?

21 What wilt thou say when he shall punish thee? for thou hast taught them to be captains, and as chief over thee: shall not sorrows take thee, as a woman in travail?

22 ¶And if thou say in thine heart, Wherefore come these things upon me? For the greatness of thine iniquity are thy skirts discovered, and thy heels made bare.

23 Can the Ē-thī-ō'pĭ-an change his skin, or the leopard his spots? then may ye also do good, that are accustomed to do evil.

24 Therefore will I scatter them as the stubble that passeth away by the wind of the wilderness.

25 This is thy lot, the portion of thy measures from me, saith the LORD; because thou hast forgotten me, and trusted in falsehood.

26 Therefore will I discover thy skirts upon thy face, that thy shame may appear.

27 I have seen thine adulteries and thy neighings, the lewdness of thy whoredom, and thine abominations on the hills in the fields. Woe unto thee, O Jerusalem! wilt thou not be made clean? when shall it once be?

CHAPTER 14

THE word of the LORD that came to Jĕr'e-mī'ah concerning the dearth.

2 Jū'dah mourneth, and the gates thereof languish; they are black unto the ground; and the cry of Jerusalem is gone up.

3 And their nobles have sent their little ones to the waters: they came to the pits, and found no water; they returned with their vessels empty; they were ashamed and confounded, and covered their heads.

4 Because the ground is chapt, for there was no rain in the earth, the plowmen were ashamed, they covered their heads.

5 Yea, the hind also calved in the field, and forsook it, because there was no grass.

6 And the wild asses did stand in the high places, they snuffed up the wind like dragons; their eyes did fail, because there was no grass.

7 ¶O LORD, though our iniquities testify against us, do thou it for thy name's sake: for our backslidings are many; we have sinned against thee.

8 O the hope of Israel, the saviour thereof in time of trouble, why shouldest thou be as a stranger in the land, and as a wayfaring man that turneth aside to tarry for a night?

9 Why shouldest thou be as a man astonied, as a mighty man that cannot save? yet thou, O LORD, art in the midst of us, and we are called by thy name; leave us not.

10 ¶Thus saith the LORD unto this

people. Thus have they loved to wander, they have not refrained their feet, therefore the LORD doth not accept them; he will now remember their iniquity, and visit their sins.

11 Then said the LORD unto me, Pray not for this people for *their* good.

12 When they fast, I will not hear their cry; and when they offer offering and an oblation, I will not accept them; but I will consume them by the sword, and by the famine, and by the pestilence.

13 ¶Then said I, Ah, Lord GOD! behold, the prophets say unto them, Ye shall not see the sword, neither shall ye have famine; but I will give you assured peace in this place.

14 Then the LORD said unto me, The prophets prophesy lies in my name: I sent them not, neither have I commanded them, neither spake unto them; they prophesy unto you a false vision and divination, and a thing of nought, and the deceit of their heart.

15 Therefore thus saith the LORD concerning the prophets that prophesy in my name, and I sent them not, yet they say, Sword and famine shall not be in this land: By sword and famine shall those prophets be consumed.

16 And the people to whom they prophesy shall be cast out in the streets of Jerusalem because of the famine and the sword; and they shall have none to bury them, them, their wives, nor their sons, nor their daughters: for I will pour their wickedness upon them.

17 ¶Therefore thou shalt say this word unto them; Let mine eyes run down with tears night and day, and let them not cease: for the virgin daughter of my people is broken with a great breach, with a very grievous blow.

18 If I go forth into the field, then behold the slain with the sword! and if I enter into the city, then behold them that are sick with famine! yea, both the prophet and the priest go about into a land that they know not.

19 Hast thou utterly rejected Ju'dah? hath thy soul lothed Zion? why hast thou smitten us, and *there is* no healing for us? we looked for peace, and *there is* no good; and for the time of healing, and behold trouble!

20 We acknowledge, O LORD, our wickedness, *and* the iniquity of our fathers: for we have sinned against thee.

21 Do not abhor *us*, for thy name's sake, do not disgrace the throne of thy glory: remember, break not thy covenant with us.

22 Are there any among the vanities of the Gentiles that can cause rain? or can the heavens give showers? *art* not thou, O LORD our God? therefore we will wait upon thee: for thou hast made all these *things*.

CHAPTER 15

THEN said the LORD unto me, Though Moses and Samuel stood before me, *yet* my mind *could* not *be* toward this people: cast *them* out of my sight, and let them go forth.

doth not accept them, i.e., God will not listen. **To visit** meant to punish. Judgment is coming, but Jeremiah is forbidden to pray for the people because their fastings and sacrifices have not been from the heart. **Sword, famine, and pestilence** were all regarded as punishments sent from God. The three together imply a full scale judgment (cf. 16:4; 24:10; Ezk 14:21; Rev 6:8; 18:8).

13-18. Jeremiah pleads for the people and excuses their actions on the basis of the false prophets who cried **peace.** God answers that the prophets will be judged, but that still does not absolve the people. **Virgin** (see 18:13 note).

19-22. Again Jeremiah intercedes for the people. He appeals for healing, **no healing for us;** for forgiveness, **we have sinned;** for God's honor, **do not disgrace the throne;** and finally for God's providence, **we will wait.**

b. Inevitable judgment. 15:1-21.

15:1. Jeremiah was despondent and felt rejected as an intercessor because of God's answer. But no amount of intercession could avail, not even the great intercessors **Moses** and **Samuel** (Ex 32:1-14, 30-32; Num 14:13-24; Deut 9:18-20, 25-29; 1 Sam 7:8ff.; 12:19-23; Ps 99:6-8). **Cast them out of my sight.** Not that God didn't want His people, but their rejection of Him and His purposes for them was the cause of their captivity.

2-4. Jeremiah's unpopular task was to preach **death, sword, famine** and **captivity** (see 14:12 note). Political subjugation was inevitable. Nothing could avert the impending disaster.

2 And it shall come to pass, if they say unto thee, Whither shall we go forth? then thou shalt tell them, Thus saith the LORD; Such as *are* for death, to death; and such as *are* for the sword, to the sword; and such as *are* for the famine, to the famine; and such as *are* for the captivity, to the captivity.

3 And I will appoint over them four kinds, saith the LORD: the sword to slay, and the dogs to tear, and the fowls of the heaven, and the beasts of the earth, to devour and destroy.

4 And I will cause them to be removed into all kingdoms of the earth, because of Ma-năs´seh the son of Hĕz-e-kī´ah king of Jū´dah, for *that* which he did in Jerusalem.

5 For who shall have pity upon thee, O Jerusalem? or who shall bemoan thee? or who shall go aside to ask how thou doest?

6 Thou hast forsaken me, saith the LORD, thou art gone backward: therefore will I stretch out my hand against thee, and destroy thee; I am weary with repenting.

7 And I will fan them with a fan in the gates of the land; I will bereave *them* of children, I will destroy my people, *since* they return not from their ways.

8 Their widows are increased to me above the sand of the seas: I have brought upon them against the mother of the young men a spoiler at noonday: I have caused *him* to fall upon it suddenly, and terrors upon the city.

9 She that hath borne seven languisheth: she hath given up the ghost; her sun is gone down while *it was* yet day: she hath been ashamed and confounded: and the residue of them will I deliver to the sword before their enemies, saith the LORD.

10 ¶Woe is me, my mother, that thou hast borne me a man of strife and a man of contention to the whole earth! I have neither lent on usury, nor men have lent to me on usury; *yet* every one of them doth curse me.

11 The LORD said, Verily it shall be well with thy remnant; verily I will cause the enemy to entreat thee *well* in the time of evil and in the time of affliction.

12 Shall iron break the northern iron and the steel?

13 Thy substance and thy treasures will I give to the spoil without price, and *that* for all thy sins, even in all thy borders.

14 And I will make *thee* to pass with thine enemies into a land *which* thou knowest not: for a fire is kindled in mine anger, *which* shall burn upon you.

15 ¶O LORD, thou knowest: remember me, and visit me, and revenge me of my persecutors; take me not away in thy longsuffering: know that for thy sake I have suffered rebuke.

16 Thy words were found, and I did eat them; and thy word was unto me the joy and rejoicing of mine heart: for I

5-9. Fan them with a fan, like the farmer who scatters the chaff so God will winnow His people (compare John the Baptist's use of winnowing in Mat 3:12). **I have brought,** a prophetic perfect in which action that is yet future is spoken in terms of already being completed. **Borne seven.** The mother of seven children is a Hebrew type of complete happiness (cf. I Sam 2:5; Ruth 4:15). However, her happiness is now the source of great sorrow, for none will escape the judgment of God.

10-14. Jeremiah now comes to the lowest point in his career. Friendless, forsaken, discouraged, frustrated, he even despairs of life itself. But God had not forsaken him. Eventually good would come of this hopeless situation.

15-21. Jeremiah was reminded of his special call and this strengthened him. **Thy words . . . I did eat them.** As soon as God's words came to the prophet, he eagerly received them. **Because of thy hand.** An expression of divine inspiration (cf. Ezk 1:3; I Kgs 18:46; Isa 8:11). **Liar.** A dried-up watercourse or brook. **If thou return.** If Jeremiah will return to his work, his words will continue to have divine authority. **Fenced brazen wall** (see 1:19 note).

1455

am called by thy name, O Lord God of hosts.

17 I sat not in the assembly of the mockers, nor rejoiced; I sat alone because of thy hand: for thou hast filled me with indignation.

18 Why is my pain perpetual, and my wound incurable, *which* refuseth to be healed? wilt thou be altogether unto me as a liar, *and as* waters *that fail?*

19 ¶Therefore thus saith the LORD, If thou return, then will I bring thee again, *and* thou shalt stand before me: and if thou take forth the precious from the vile, thou shalt be as my mouth: let them return unto thee; but return not thou unto them.

20 And I will make thee unto this people a fenced brasen wall: and they shall fight against thee, but they shall not prevail against thee: for I *am* with thee to save thee and to deliver thee, saith the LORD.

21 And I will deliver thee out of the hand of the wicked, and I will redeem thee out of the hand of the terrible.

CHAPTER 16

THE word of the LORD came also unto me, saying,

2 Thou shalt not take thee a wife, neither shalt thou have sons or daughters in this place.

3 For thus saith the LORD concerning the sons and concerning the daughters that are born in this place, and concerning their mothers that bare them, and concerning their fathers that begat them in this land;

4 They shall die of grievous deaths; they shall not be lamented; neither shall they be buried; *but* they shall be as dung upon the face of the earth: and they shall be consumed by the sword, and by famine; and their carcases shall be meat for the fowls of heaven, and for the beasts of the earth.

5 For thus saith the LORD, Enter not into the house of mourning, neither go to lament nor bemoan them: for I have taken away my peace from this people, saith the LORD, *even* lovingkindness and mercies.

6 Both the great and the small shall die in this land: they shall not be buried, neither shall *men* lament for them, nor cut themselves, nor make themselves bald for them:

7 Neither shall *men* tear *themselves* for them in mourning, to comfort them for the dead; neither shall *men* give them the cup of consolation to drink for their father or for their mother.

8 Thou shalt not also go into the house of feasting, to sit with them to eat and to drink.

9 For thus saith the LORD of hosts, the God of Israel; Behold, I will cause to cease out of this place in your eyes, and in your days, the voice of mirth, and the voice of gladness, the voice of the bridegroom, and the voice of the bride.

10 ¶And it shall come to pass, when thou shalt shew this people all these words, and they shall say unto thee, Wherefore hath the LORD pronounced all this great evil against us? or what *is* our iniquity? or what *is* our sin that we

c. *Sign of the unmarried prophet.* 16:1-21.

16:1-5. The domestic life of the prophets was frequently used to reinforce their messages (cf. Hos 1:2-9; Isa 15-27). Isaiah and Hosea named their children for their principle ideas. However, God commanded Jeremiah to remain unmarried. Remaining single in that society was unheard of. Therefore, Jeremiah became a living symbol of the coming judgment. Considering the impending crisis, this was no time or place to have a family. Compare Paul's advice against marriage in view of an impending crisis, I Corinthians 7:26-27. **Grievous deaths.** Because of the severity of the judgment, entire families would be left with no burials.

6-9. Cut themselves . . . bald. Self-mutilation and shaving the head for the dead were forbidden (Deut 14:1; Lev 19:27-28). Yet, these practices are referred to here (cf. 41:4-5; 47:5; Amos 8:10; Mic 1:16; Isa 22:12). **Tear themselves. Break bread.** It was a custom for mourners to fast until the evening before the funeral. Their friends would then prepare a meal and serve it to them along with the **cup of consolation** (cf. II Sam 1:12; 12:16-23).

10-13. The people will respond, What have we done to deserve the Exile? Jeremiah will be the lone spokesman of God's judgment; pointing out their wickedness.

have committed against the LORD our God?

11 Then shalt thou say unto them, Because your fathers have forsaken me, saith the LORD, and have walked after other gods, and have served them, and have worshipped them, and have forsaken me, and have not kept my law;

12 And ye have done worse than your fathers; for, behold, ye walk every one after the imagination of his evil heart, that they may not hearken unto me:

13 Therefore will I cast you out of this land into a land that ye know not, *neither* ye nor your fathers; and there shall ye serve other gods day and night; where I will not shew you favour.

14 ¶ Therefore, behold, the days come, saith the LORD, that it shall no more be said, The LORD liveth, that brought up the children of Israel out of the land of Egypt;

15 But, The LORD liveth, that brought up the children of Israel from the land of the north, and from all the lands whither he had driven them: and I will bring them again into their land that I gave unto their fathers.

16 ¶ Behold, I will send for many fishers, saith the LORD, and they shall fish them; and after will I send for many hunters, and they shall hunt them from every mountain, and from every hill, and out of the holes of the rocks.

17 For mine eyes *are* upon all their ways: they are not hid from my face, neither is their iniquity hid from mine eyes.

18 And first I will recompense their iniquity and their sin double; because they have defiled my land, they have filled mine inheritance with the carcases of their detestable and abominable things.

19 O LORD, my strength, and my fortress, and my refuge in the day of affliction, the Gentiles shall come unto thee from the ends of the earth, and shall say, Surely our fathers have inherited lies, vanity, and *things wherein there is* no profit.

20 Shall a man make gods unto himself, and they *are* no gods?

21 Therefore, behold, I will this once cause them to know, I will cause them to know mine hand and my might; and they shall know that my name *is* The LORD.

CHAPTER 17

THE sin of Jú'dah *is* written with a pen of iron, *and* with the point of a diamond: *it is* graven upon the table of their heart, and upon the horns of your altars;

2 Whilst their children remember their altars and their groves by the green trees upon the high hills.

3 O my mountain in the field, I will give thy substance *and* all thy treasures to the spoil, *and* thy high places for sin, throughout all thy borders.

4 And thou, even thyself, shalt discontinue from thine heritage that I gave thee; and I will cause thee to serve thine enemies in the land which thou knowest not; for ye have kindled a fire

14-15. However, they would experience a new Exodus; and the captivity would change the Jews' testimony of God's deliverance. Prior to the Babylonian exile, Canaan had been known as the land to which God brought His people from Egyptian bondage; but after the captivity it would be known as the place to which God brought His people from the **north**.

16-18. There was no escape from God's judgment. As Jeremiah had been bidden to glean among the people (6:9), and as God had used the winnowing process (15:5-9), so now God was sending **fishers** for a large catch and **hunters** to entrap all who had previously escaped.

19-21. The power and might of the true God will be seen, for Gentiles will be converted. **They shall know that my name is The LORD.**

d. *The human heart and the Sabbath. 17:1-27.*

Judah's sin was indelible; her downfall, inevitable. Yet, she is again promised that if only her people would repent and turn to the Lord, Jerusalem would remain forever.

17:1-4. Pen of iron. As an iron stylus cuts indelible inscriptions on stone, so was Judah's sin permanently engraved on her hard heart. **Horns of your altars,** a symbol of Old Testament worship. Sacrificial blood was smeared on the horns of the altar (Ex 29:12; Lev 4:7; 8:15; 16:18), and fugitives were safe from pursuit when they laid hold of the horns (I Kgs 1:50ff.; 2:28). **Groves.** Asherim, wooden poles that stood by the Canaanite altars. Ashera was the Canaanite goddess of fertility. **Green trees . . . high hills** (see 2:20 note).

in mine anger, which shall burn for ever.

5 ¶Thus saith the LORD; Cursed be the man that trusteth in man, and maketh flesh his arm, and whose heart departeth from the LORD.

6 For he shall be like the heath in the desert, and shall not see when good cometh; but shall inhabit the parched places in the wilderness, in a salt land and not inhabited.

7 ¶Blessed is the man that trusteth in the LORD, and whose hope the LORD is.

8 For he shall be as a tree planted by the waters, and that spreadeth out her roots by the river, and shall not see when heat cometh, but her leaf shall be green; and shall not be careful in the year of drought, neither shall cease from yielding fruit.

9 ¶The heart is deceitful above all things, and desperately wicked: who can know it?

10 I the LORD search the heart, I try the reins, even to give every man according to his ways, and according to the fruit of his doings.

11 As the partridge sitteth on eggs, and hatcheth them not; so he that getteth riches, and not by right, shall leave them in the midst of his days, and at his end shall be a fool.

12 ¶A glorious high throne from the beginning is the place of our sanctuary.

13 O LORD, the hope of Israel, all that forsake thee shall be ashamed, and they that depart from me shall be written in the earth, because they have forsaken the LORD, the fountain of living waters.

14 Heal me, O LORD, and I shall be healed; save me, and I shall be saved: for thou art my praise.

15 Behold, they say unto me, where is the word of the LORD? let it come now.

16 As for me, I have not hastened from being a pastor to follow thee: neither have I desired the woeful day; thou knowest: that which came out of my lips was right before thee.

17 Be not a terror unto me: thou art my hope in the day of evil.

18 Let them be confounded that persecute me, but let not me be confounded: let them be dismayed, but let not me be dismayed: bring upon them the day of evil, and destroy them with double destruction.

19 ¶Thus said the LORD unto me; Go and stand in the gate of the children of the people, whereby the kings of Judah come in, and by the which they go out, and in all the gates of Jerusalem;

20 And say unto them, Hear ye the word of the LORD, ye kings of Judah, and all Judah, and all the inhabitants of Jerusalem, that enter in by these gates;

21 Thus saith the LORD; Take heed to yourselves, and bear no burden on the sabbath day, nor bring it in by the gates of Jerusalem;

22 Neither carry forth a burden out of your houses on the sabbath day, neither do ye any work, but hallow ye the sabbath day, as I commanded your fathers.

23 But they obeyed not, neither in-

5-8. Judah's last kings were constantly seeking help from each other against the Babylonian threat, whereas they should have turned to God. **Heath.** A bare or dry tree. When a man trusts in God, he is like a "tree planted by the . . . water" (cf. Ps 1:3).

9.13. Sin is like a disease of the **heart**, the inner being. **Wicked.** Corrupt. **Reins** (see 11:20 note).

14-18. Jeremiah's prayer. He had not forsaken his calling; he will remain faithful.

19-27. Disregard for the Sabbath, instituted by God (Ex 20:8-11), was symptomatic of the nation's general disobedience. Jeremiah was not concerned for a ritual, but rather for the Sabbath as a sign of God's sanctifying Judah (Ex 31:13). **Plain.** The Shephelah or lowlands west of Jerusalem. **Mountains.** The hill country of Judah. **South.** The Negev or arid region south of Hebron.

clined their ear, but made their neck stiff, that they might not hear, nor receive instruction.

24 And it shall come to pass, if ye diligently hearken unto me, saith the LORD, to bring in no burden through the gates of this city on the sabbath day, but hallow the sabbath day, to do no work therein;

25 Then shall there enter into the gates of this city kings and princes sitting upon the throne of David, riding in chariots and on horses, they, and their princes, the men of Jū′dah, and the inhabitants of Jerusalem: and this city shall remain for ever.

26 And they shall come from the cities of Jū′dah, and from the places about Jerusalem, and from the land of Benjamin, and from the plain, and from the mountains, and from the south, bringing burnt offerings, and sacrifices, and meat offerings, and incense, and bringing sacrifices of praise, unto the house of the LORD.

27 But if ye will not hearken unto me to hallow the sabbath day, and not to bear a burden, even entering in at the gates of Jerusalem on the sabbath day; then will I kindle a fire in the gates thereof, and it shall devour the palaces of Jerusalem, and it shall not be quenched.

CHAPTER 18

THE word which came to Jĕr′e-mī′ah from the LORD, saying,

2 Arise, and go down to the potter's house, and there I will cause thee to hear my words.

3 Then I went down to the potter's house, and, behold, he wrought a work on the wheels.

4 And the vessel that he made of clay was marred in the hand of the potter: so he made it again another vessel, as seemed good to the potter to make it.

5 Then the word of the LORD came to me, saying,

6 O house of Israel, cannot I do with you as this potter? saith the LORD. Behold, as the clay is in the potter's hand, so are ye in mine hand, O house of Israel.

7 At what instant I shall speak concerning a nation, and concerning a kingdom, to pluck up, and to pull down, and to destroy it;

8 If that nation, against whom I have pronounced, turn from their evil, I will repent of the evil that I thought to do unto them.

9 And at what instant I shall speak concerning a nation, and concerning a kingdom, to build and to plant it;

10 If it do evil in my sight, that it obey not my voice, then I will repent of the good, wherewith I said I would benefit them.

11 Now therefore go to, speak to the men of Jū′dah, and to the inhabitants of Jerusalem, saying, Thus saith the LORD; Behold, I frame evil against you, and devise a device against you: return ye now every one from his evil way, and make your ways and your doings good.

12 And they said, There is no hope: but we will walk after our own devices,

6. Sixth message: The sign of the potter. 18:1-20:18.

Pottery-making was a familiar sight throughout the ancient Near East. Therefore, it was quite natural for Jeremiah to employ this symbol. Jeremiah used many symbols (marred loincloth, ch. 3; celibacy, ch. 16; the potter's clay, ch. 18; the yoke, ch. 27; and the purchased field, ch. 32) to gain a hearing for his preaching and reinforce his message. This message summarizes the thrust of Jeremiah's oracles (the long-suffering of God and the sure judgment of God) under Josiah and Jehoiakim.

a. Visit to the potter's house. 18:1-23.

18:1-6. Jeremiah was commanded to go to the **potter's house** in order to learn a lesson. The potter's house was probably located in the southern section of the city, or perhaps in the potter's field south of Jerusalem, just beyond the Valley of Hinnom. **Wheels**, two circular stones connected by a vertical shaft. The potter could sit at the wheel, spinning the lower stone with his feet and causing the upper disc to rotate. This enabled both hands to be free in order to work the clay. Should the vessel become marred or any impurity detected, the potter would not discard the clay, but simply remold it into **another vessel.**

7-12. So too, God had the right to remold His people. In His sovereignty He could **pluck up,** judge (vs. 7) or **build,** bless (vs. 9). The analogy breaks down henceforth because Judah still had the responsibility of choosing righteousness, **turn from their evil** (vs. 8) or sin **do evil** (vs. 10). Judgment already pronounced could be averted by repentance (vs. 11). The Hebrew word for **frame** in verse 11 is from the same root as potter, a deliberate choice on the part of the prophet in order to show them that the nation would be molded by the Exile.

and we will every one do the imagination of his evil heart.

13 Therefore thus saith the LORD; Ask ye now among the heathen, who hath heard such things: the virgin of Israel hath done a very horrible thing.

14 Will *a man* leave the snow of Lebanon *which cometh* from the rock of the field? *or* shall the cold flowing waters that come from another place be forsaken?

15 Because my people hath forgotten me, they have burned incense to vanity, and they have caused them to stumble in their ways *from* the ancient paths, to walk in paths, *in* a way not cast up;

16 To make their land desolate, *and a* perpetual hissing; every one that passeth thereby shall be astonished, and wag his head.

17 I will scatter them as with an east wind before the enemy; I will shew them the back, and not the face, in the day of their calamity.

18 ¶Then said they, Come, and let us devise devices against Jere-mi'ah: for the law shall not perish from the priest, nor counsel from the wise, nor the word from the prophet. Come, and let us smite him with the tongue, and let us not give heed to any of his words.

19 Give heed to me, O LORD, and hearken to the voice of them that contend with me.

20 Shall evil be recompensed for good? for they have digged a pit for my soul. Remember that I stood before thee to speak good for them, *and* to turn away thy wrath from them.

21 Therefore deliver up their children to the famine, and pour out their *blood* by the force of the sword; and let their wives be bereaved of their children, and *be* widows; and let their men *be* put to death; *let* their young men *be* slain by the sword in battle.

22 Let a cry be heard from their houses, when thou shalt bring a troop suddenly upon them: for they have digged a pit to take me, and hid snares for my feet.

23 Yet, LORD, thou knowest all their counsel against me to slay *me:* forgive not their iniquity, neither blot out their sin from thy sight, but let them be overthrown before thee; deal *thus* with them in the time of thine anger.

CHAPTER 19

THUS saith the LORD, Go and get a potter's earthen bottle, and *take of* the ancients of the people, and of the ancients of the priests;

2 And go forth unto the valley of the son of Hin'nom, which *is* by the entry of the east gate, and proclaim there the words that I shall tell thee,

3 And say, Hear ye the word of the LORD, O kings of Ju'dah, and inhabitants of Jerusalem; Thus saith the LORD of hosts, the God of Israel; Behold, I will bring evil upon this place, the which whosoever heareth, his ears shall tingle.

4 Because they have forsaken me, and have estranged this place, and have burned incense in it unto other

13-17. Virgin of Israel, a saying for the people collectively (cf. 14:17). Judah's sin was unheard of among the nations and unnatural. Mount Hermon in **Lebanon,** like a **rock** rising out of the **field,** is covered with snow year round. Even the **cold flowing waters** from this foreign place do not cease to flow. Yet, Judah, God's own, has forsaken Him. The result? **I will scatter them,** cried the Lord.

18. The reaction of the people against Jeremiah's sermon was so great that they not only slandered him, but also plotted to take his life. This shows the unrepentant attitude of their hearts. One false charge **(smite him with the tongue)** brought against the prophet was the non-fulfillment of his prophecies, a crime punishable by death (Deut 18:20-22).

19-23. This caused the prophet to experience another extremely low period. He prayed passionately that his enemies might be punished. This seemed rather shocking, but Jeremiah's refusal to forgive his enemies simply reiterated the Lord's refusal to forgive them and pronouncement of judgment upon them (7:16; 14:10, 12; 15:1, 6; 16:5; cf. Mt 23:12-36; I Cor 16:22; Gal 1:8-9; I Jn 5:16).

b. The shattered vessel. 19:1-13.

This second symbol was an extension of the first. It was another sign that God will smash the idolatry-ridden people. The marred vessel taught God's sovereignty, long-suffering, and the consequences of rejecting His invitation. The broken vessel taught the extent and inevitability of the impending judgment. As long as the vessel was pliable, it could be remolded by the potter; but once it was baked, it could no longer be molded.

19:1-9. Ancients. The elders. **Valley of . . . Hinnom** (see 7:31 note). **East gate.** The Potsherd Gate (later called the Dung Gate, Neh 2:13) led to the Valley of Hinnom and was probably a place where broken pottery was deposited. **Blood of innocents,** the offering of their sons to Molech (cf. II Kgs 23:10). **Tophet** (see 7:31 note). **Eat the flesh.** The siege of the city will be so bad that the people will resort to cannibalism (cf. Deut 28:53). This prediction was fulfilled in Lamentations 4:10.

gods, whom neither they nor their fathers have known, nor the kings of Jū′dah, and have filled this place with the blood of innocents;

5 They have built also the high places of Bā′al, to burn their sons with fire for burnt offerings unto Bā′al, which I commanded not, nor spake it, neither came it into my mind:

6 Therefore, behold, the days come, saith the LORD, that this place shall no more be called Tō′phet, nor The valley of the son of Hin′nom, but The valley of slaughter.

7 And I will make void the counsel of Jū′dah and Jerusalem in this place; and I will cause them to fall by the sword before their enemies, and by the hands of them that seek their lives: and their carcases will I give to be meat for the fowls of the heaven, and for the beasts of the earth.

8 And I will make this city desolate, and an hissing; every one that passeth thereby shall be astonished and hiss because of all the plagues thereof.

9 And I will cause them to eat the flesh of their sons and the flesh of their daughters, and they shall eat every one the flesh of his friend in the siege and straitness, wherewith their enemies, and they that seek their lives, shall straiten them.

10 Then shalt thou break the bottle in the sight of the men that go with thee, 11 And shalt say unto them, Thus saith the LORD of hosts; Even so will I break this people and this city, as one breaketh a potter's vessel, that cannot be made whole again: and they shall bury them in Tō′phet, till there be no place to bury.

12 Thus will I do unto this place, saith the LORD, and to the inhabitants thereof, and even make this city as Tō′phet:

13 And the houses of Jerusalem, and the houses of the kings of Jū′dah, shall be defiled as the place of Tō′phet, because of all the houses upon whose roofs they have burned incense unto all the host of heaven, and have poured out drink offerings unto other gods.

14 Then came Jĕr′e-mī′ah from Tō′phet, whither the LORD had sent him to prophesy; and he stood in the court of the LORD's house; and said to all the people,

15 Thus saith the LORD of hosts, the God of Israel; Behold, I will bring upon this city and upon all her towns all the evil that I have pronounced against it, because they have hardened their necks, that they might not hear my words.

CHAPTER 20

NOW Păsh′ur the son of Ĭm′mer the priest, who was also chief governor in the house of the LORD, heard that Jĕr′e-mī′ah prophesied these things.

2 Then Păsh′ur smote Jĕr′e-mī′ah the prophet, and put him in the stocks that were in the high gate of Benjamin, which was by the house of the LORD.

3 And it came to pass on the morrow,

10-11. Jeremiah delivered his message of doom to the elders and priests in the Valley of Hinnom. The object lesson of breaking the bottle was devastating. As the jar was irrevocably destroyed, so too God will destroy Judah.

12-13. He continued to describe the destruction of Jerusalem. **Roofs.** The flat rooftops of Oriental houses had many legitimate uses (cf. Jud 16:27; I Sam 9:26; II Sam 11:2; Neh 8:16; Mt 10:27; Acts 10:9), but the people of Jerusalem had used their rooftops for the worship of astral deities such as Astarte or Ashtaroth (cf. 32:29; Zeph 1:5). Cuneiform texts discovered at Ras Shamra included a religious ritual for such occasions. Since these rooftops had been the places of idolatrous worship, God would also destroy them.

c. *Pashur's persecution of Jeremiah. 19:14-20:18.*

14-15. Jeremiah repeated his sermon in the court of the Temple where Pashur, chief of the temple police, arrested him.

20:1-2. **The chief governor** was the chief officer of the Temple in charge of security. **Smote.** Jeremiah was beaten with forty stripes (reduced slightly in Paul's day, cf. II Cor 11:24, for fear of exceeding the legal limit, Deut 25:3). Then he was placed in the **stocks,** a scaffold affair where the prisoner's hands and legs were detained in a contorted position, producing cramped muscles (cf. 29:26; II Chr 16:10).

3-6. Upon his release the next morning, Jeremiah pro-

that Păsh'ur brought forth Jĕr'e-mī'ah out of the stocks. Then said Jĕr'e-mī'ah unto him, The LORD hath not called thy name Păsh'ur, but Mā-gŏr-mĭs'sa-bĭb.

4 For thus saith the LORD, Behold, I will make thee a terror to thyself, and to all thy friends; and they shall fall by the sword of their enemies, and thine eyes shall behold it: and I will give all Jū'dah into the hand of the king of Băb'y-lon, and he shall carry them captive into Băb'y-lon, and shall slay them with the sword.

5 Moreover I will deliver all the strength of this city, and all the labours thereof, and all the precious things thereof, and all the treasures of the kings of Jū'dah will I give into the hand of their enemies, which shall spoil them, and take them, and carry them to Băb'y-lon.

6 And thou, Păsh'ur, and all that dwell in thine house shall go into captivity: and thou shalt come to Băb'y-lon, and there thou shalt die, and shalt be buried there, thou, and all thy friends, to whom thou hast prophesied lies.

7 ¶O LORD, thou hast deceived me, and I was deceived: thou art stronger than I, and hast prevailed: I am in derision daily, every one mocketh me.

8 For since I spake, I cried out, I cried violence and spoil; because the word of the LORD was made a reproach unto me, and a derision, daily.

9 Then I said, I will not make mention of him, nor speak any more in his name. But his word was in mine heart as a burning fire shut up in my bones, and I was weary with forbearing, and I could not stay.

10 For I heard the defaming of many, fear on every side. Report, say they, and we will report it. All my familiars watched for my halting, saying, Peradventure he will be enticed, and we shall prevail against him, and we shall take our revenge on him.

11 But the LORD is with me as a mighty terrible one: therefore my persecutors shall stumble, and they shall not prevail: they shall be greatly ashamed; for they shall not prosper: their everlasting confusion shall never be forgotten.

12 But, O LORD of hosts, that triest the righteous, and seest the reins and the heart, let me see thy vengeance on them: for unto thee have I opened my cause.

13 Sing unto the LORD, praise ye the LORD: for he hath delivered the soul of the poor from the hand of evildoers.

14 ¶Cursed be the day wherein I was born: let not the day wherein my mother bare me be blessed.

15 Cursed be the man who brought tidings to my father, saying, A man child is born unto thee; making him very glad.

16 And let that man be as the cities which the LORD overthrew, and repented not: and let him hear the cry in the morning, and the shouting at noontide;

17 Because he slew me not from the womb; or that my mother might have

---

nounced two judgments. The first was upon **Pashur**. His name would be changed to **Magor-missabib**, a **terror** (cf. 6:25; 20:10; 25:8-11; 46:5; 49:29; Ps 31:13) because he would be a terror to himself, as well as his friends. The second judgment was against Judah. For the first time, Babylon was identified as the foe from the North. This confirmed Isaiah's prophecy of the previous century (Isa 39:6,7).

7-13. Since many of Jeremiah's prophecies were not fulfilled immediately, the people ridiculed him; and this was a cause of great sorrow to the prophet. He was not a hard, thick-skinned man, and it hurt to be ridiculed. Yet, he did not give up because he was driven by the compulsion of his calling, **Fear on every side**, the same Hebrew words as *Magor-missabib*, used in verse 3. The fact that God was with him, however, was more than compensation for Jeremiah's loss of his friends.

14-18. Jeremiah gave in to despair and even cursed the day of his birth. The prophet's mood fluctuated between confident faith (vss. 11-13) and utter misery (vss. 14-18). **Cities.** Sodom and Gomorrah. **Shouting.** War cry.

B. From Jehoiakim Until Jerusalem's Destruction. 21:1-39:18.

As the first messages of Jeremiah occurred during the reigns of Josiah and Jehoiakim, most of these later messages came during the reign of Zedekiah, the last king of Judah. Zedekiah's revolt against Nebuchadnezzar was the political cause of the Babylonian invasion. However, the real cause was spiritual, the revolt of the people against almighty God.

1. Zedekiah and the people's punishment. 21:1-29:32.

Chapters 21-29 tell of the sure captivity of Judah. The fall was inevitable because judgment had been decreed by God (21:1-25:38), as well as announced by His prophet (26:1-29:32). The judgment of God is spelled out more clearly in this section than ever before.

a. Zedekiah's enquiry and Jeremiah's response. 21:1-14.

The king and his counselors came to Jeremiah to seek a word of comfort from the Lord in the face of the Babylonian siege of Jerusalem (vss. 1-3). But there was no answer of comfort. The only hope lay in surrender.

21:1-2. Pashur. A different one from 20:1-6. **Zephaniah.** A temple official (cf. 29:25; 37:3; 52:24). **Nebuchadrezzar.** This is Nebuchadnezzar, king of Babylon, but the Hebrew prefers the *n*, while the Aramaic, the Babylonian tongue, prefers the *r*. Jeremiah's spelling is therefore closer to the original.

3-7. Chaldeans, originally a name given to a semi-nomadic tribe of northern Arabia. Several Chaldeans became king of Babylon and established a dynasty. Eventually the term was applied generally to the Babylonians (Ezk 23:23; Dan 3:8). **I myself will fight.** The Babylonians were God's agents for the punishment of rebellious Judah.

8-14. Jeremiah now brings a message to the royal house. **Judgment in the morning.** Oriental kings would dispense justice in the morning before the heat of the day (II Sam 15:2-6). Thus, even in the midst of destruction God was concerned with social justice within His people. **Valley, and rock of the plain.** Verses 13 and 14 are difficult but probably are a description of Jerusalem with its valleys and rocky hills. Thus, the inhabitants thought the city impregnable.

---

been my grave, and her womb *to be* always great *with me.*

18 Wherefore came I forth out of the womb to see labour and sorrow, that my days should be consumed with shame?

CHAPTER 21

THE word which came unto Jĕr'e-mī'ah from the Lord, when king Zĕd-e-kī'ah sent unto him Păsh'ur the son of Mĕl-chī'ah, and Zĕph-a-nī'ah the son of Mā-a-sē'iah the priest, saying,

2 Enquire, I pray thee, of the Lord for us; for Nĕb-u-chad-rĕz'zar king of Babylon maketh war against us; if so be that the Lord will deal with us according to all his wondrous works, that he may go up from us.

3 ¶ Then said Jĕr'e-mī'ah unto them, Thus shall ye say to Zĕd-e-kī'ah:

4 Thus saith the Lord God of Israel; Behold, I will turn back the weapons of war that *are* in your hands, wherewith ye fight against the king of Babylon, and *against* the Chal-dē'ans, which besiege you without the walls, and I will assemble them into the midst of this city.

5 And I myself will fight against you with an outstretched hand and with a strong arm, even in anger, and in fury, and in great wrath.

6 And I will smite the inhabitants of this city, both man and beast: they shall die of a great pestilence.

7 And afterward, saith the Lord, I will deliver Zĕd-e-kī'ah king of Ju'dah, and his servants, and the people, and such as are left in this city from the pestilence, from the sword, and from the famine, into the hand of Nĕb-u-chad-rĕz'zar king of Babylon, and into the hand of their enemies, and into the hand of those that seek their life: and he shall smite them with the edge of the sword; he shall not spare them, neither have pity, nor have mercy.

8 ¶ And unto this people thou shalt say, Thus saith the Lord; Behold, I set before you the way of life, and the way of death.

9 He that abideth in this city shall die by the sword, and by the famine, and by the pestilence: but he that goeth out, and falleth to the Chal-dē'ans that besiege you, he shall live, and his life shall be unto him for a prey.

10 For I have set my face against this city for evil, and not for good, saith the Lord: it shall be given into the hand of

the king of Babylon, and he shall burn it with fire.

11 ¶And touching the house of the king of Jū'dah, say, Hear ye the word of the LORD;

12 O house of David, thus saith the LORD: Execute judgment in the morning, and deliver *him that is* spoiled out of the hand of the oppressor, lest my fury go out like fire, and burn that none can quench *it*, because of the evil of your doings.

13 Behold, I *am* against thee, O inhabitant of the valley, *and* rock of the plain, saith the LORD; which say, Who shall come down against us? or who shall enter into our habitations?

14 But I will punish you according to the fruit of your doings, saith the LORD: and I will kindle a fire in the forest thereof, and it shall devour all things round about it.

CHAPTER 22

THUS saith the LORD; Go down to the house of the king of Jū'dah, and speak there this word,

2 And say, Hear the word of the LORD, O king of Jū'dah, that sittest upon the throne of David, thou, and thy servants, and thy people that enter in by these gates:

3 Thus saith the LORD; Execute ye judgment and righteousness, and deliver the spoiled out of the hand of the oppressor: and do no wrong, do no violence to the stranger, the fatherless, nor the widow, neither shed innocent blood in this place.

4 For if ye do this thing indeed, then shall there enter in by the gates of this house kings sitting upon the throne of David, riding in chariots and on horses, he, and his servants, and his people.

5 But if ye will not hear these words, I swear by myself, saith the LORD, that this house shall become a desolation.

6 For thus saith the LORD unto the king's house of Jū'dah; Thou *art* Gilead unto me, *and* the head of Lebanon: *yet* surely I will make thee a wilderness, *and* cities *which* are not inhabited.

7 And I will prepare destroyers against thee, every one with his weapons: and they shall cut down thy choice cedars, and cast *them* into the fire.

8 And many nations shall pass by this city, and they shall say every man to his neighbour, Wherefore hath the LORD done thus unto this great city?

9 Then they shall answer, Because they have forsaken the covenant of the LORD their God, and worshipped other gods, and served them.

10 ¶Weep ye not for the dead, neither bemoan him: *but* weep sore for him that goeth away: for he shall return no more, nor see his native country.

11 For thus saith the LORD touching Shăl'lum the son of Jō-sī'ah king of Jū'dah, which reigned instead of Jō-sī'ah his father, which went forth out of this place; He shall not return thither any more:

12 But he shall die in the place whither they have led him captive, and shall see this land no more.

13 ¶Woe unto him that buildeth his

b. Warnings for the kings of Judah. 22:1-30.

22:1-9. Chapter 22 contains messages to several kings of Judah. Verses 1 through 9 are an introduction to these oracles with a warning to the kings of Judah (cf. II Sam 12:1ff.). Unlike David, however, the present kings were unrepentant (see Ps 51). **Execute ye judgment.** Since Judah was a theocracy, it was the king's responsibility to establish justice and enforce moral law and social justice. **I swear by myself,** swearing by Himself (cf. Gen 22:16; Isa 45:23; Heb 6:13-18)," states R. K. Harrison, "He is maintaining His rights as the initiator of the covenant relationship" (*Jeremiah and Lamentations,* p. 117).

10-12. Jeremiah's second oracle was addressed to **Shallum,** Jehoahaz (I Chr 3:15), who succeeded his father Josiah when he was killed at Megiddo. After only a three-month reign, Shallum was carried to Egypt. He was not to mourn for his father, but for his own fate; for Jeremiah predicted he would never return to Judah. And so it was that Jehoahaz became the first leader of Judah to die in exile.

13-23. Jeremiah now brings a message of warning to the

house by unrighteousness, and his chambers by wrong; *that* useth his neighbour's service without wages, and giveth him not for his work;

14 That saith, I will build me a wide house and large chambers, and cutteth him out windows; and it is cieled with cedar, and painted with vermilion.

15 Shalt thou reign, because thou closest *thyself* in cedar? did not thy father eat and drink, and do judgment and justice, *and then it was* well with him?

16 He judged the cause of the poor and needy; then *it was* well *with him: was* not this to know me? saith the LORD.

17 But thine eyes and thine heart are not but for thy covetousness, and for to shed innocent blood, and for oppression, and for violence, to do *it.*

18 Therefore thus saith the LORD concerning Je-hoi'a-kim the son of Jo-si'ah king of Ju'dah; They shall not lament for him, *saying,* Ah my brother! or, Ah sister! they shall not lament for him, *saying,* Ah lord! or, Ah his glory!

19 He shall be buried with the burial of an ass, drawn and cast forth beyond the gates of Jerusalem.

20 ¶ Go up to Lebanon, and cry; and lift up thy voice in Ba'shan, and cry from the passages: for all thy lovers are destroyed.

21 I spake unto thee in thy prosperity; *but* thou saidst, I will not hear. This *hath been* thy manner from thy youth, that thou obeyedst not my voice.

22 The wind shall eat up all thy pastors, and thy lovers shall go into captivity: surely then shalt thou be ashamed and confounded for all thy wickedness.

23 O inhabitant of Lebanon, that makest thy nest in the cedars, how gracious shalt thou be when pangs come upon thee, the pain as of a woman in travail!

24 *As* I live, saith the LORD, though Co-ni'ah the son of Je-hoi'a-kim king of Ju'dah were the signet upon my right hand, yet would I pluck thee thence;

25 And I will give thee into the hand of them that seek thy life, and into the hand *of them* whose face thou fearest, even into the hand of Neb-u-chad-rez'zar king of Babylon, and into the hand of the Chal-de'ans.

26 And I will cast thee out, and thy mother that bare thee, into another country, where ye were not born; and there shall ye die.

27 But to the land whereunto they desire to return, thither shall they not return.

28 *Is* this man Co-ni'ah a despised broken idol? *is he* a vessel wherein *is* no pleasure? wherefore are they cast out, he and his seed, and are cast into a land which they know not?

29 O earth, earth, earth, hear the word of the LORD.

30 Thus saith the LORD, Write ye this man childless, a man *that* shall not prosper in his days: for no man of his seed shall prosper, sitting upon the throne of David, and ruling any more in Ju'dah.

oppressive, covetous, idolater Jehoiakim. Jehoiakim had built his palace with forced labor and heavy taxes (II Kgs 23:35). This callous exploitation of the people was contrary to the Law (Lev 19:13; Deut 24:14). He had allowed pagan gods to flourish like those in Egypt (Ezk 8:5-17) and was much like the wicked Manasseh (cf. II Kgs 24:3). Jeremiah contrasted his palace, elaborately decorated with cedars from Lebanon, to the humble reign of his father Josiah.

Because of his wicked deeds, Jehoiakim would not be given a royal funeral (cf. II Kgs 24:6). Instead, he would be dumped on the garbage heap with the **burial of an ass**, as a dead donkey is dragged outside the city and left to rot.

24-30. The last judgment of this chapter is pronounced upon Jehoiachin, who reigned for only three months and was deported to Babylon. **Coniah** is Jehoiachin here and in 37:1. He is also called Jeconiah in 24:1; 27:20 (cf. II Kgs 24:8-16; 25:27-30). **Signet,** the royal insignia. Such rings had great value (Song 8:6; Hag 2:23). In taking off the signet, Jehovah had rejected his leadership. God cannot remain in fellowship with a rebellious sinner, since implicit obedience to Him is absolutely necessary for fellowship (cf. Heb 10:36).

Jehoiachin, as well as his mother Nehoshta (II Kgs 24:6, 8, 15), would be exiled to Babylon, never to return. **Childless.** The prophecy does not mean that he would not have any children, for he had seven sons (I Chr 3:17-18) and is also mentioned in the messianic line (Mt 1:12). Rather, he would be childless by divine judgment, i.e., have no physical descendant to sit upon David's throne. Christ's dynastic right to the throne of David came through his foster father Joseph, who was of the line of Jeconiah (Mt 1:12, 16); but His physical descent came through Mary, whose genealogy is traced through Nathan, rather than Solomon, to David (cf. Mt 1:17; Lk 3:31). If Joseph had been the father of Jesus, the Lord would not be able to occupy David's throne; and Luke 1:32-33 would contradict this prophecy.

c. False prophets and the righteous Branch. 23:1-40.

The wicked kings of the previous oracle, along with the other wicked rulers and leaders of Judah (vss. 1 and 2), are compared

CHAPTER 23

WOE be unto the pastors that destroy and scatter the sheep of my pasture! saith the LORD.

2 Therefore thus saith the LORD God of Israel against the pastors that feed my people; Ye have scattered my flock, and driven them away, and have not visited them: behold, I will visit upon you the evil of your doings, saith the LORD.

3 And I will gather the remnant of my flock out of all countries whither I have driven them, and will bring them again to their folds; and they shall be fruitful and increase.

4 And I will set up shepherds over them which shall feed them: and they shall fear no more, nor be dismayed, neither shall they be lacking, saith the LORD.

5 Behold, the days come, saith the LORD, that I will raise unto David a righteous Branch, and a King shall reign and prosper, and shall execute judgment and justice in the earth.

6 In his days Judah shall be saved, and Israel shall dwell safely: and this is his name whereby he shall be called, THE LORD OUR RIGHTEOUSNESS.

7 Therefore, behold, the days come, saith the LORD, that they shall no more say, The LORD liveth, which brought up the children of Israel out of the land of Egypt;

8 But, The LORD liveth, which brought up and which led the seed of the house of Israel out of the north country, and from all countries whither I had driven them: and they shall dwell in their own land.

with the coming righteous king, the Messiah. Jesus Christ is the perfect Prophet, Priest, and King. These three Old Testament offices were types of the messianic offices. Yet, the prophets, priests, and kings of Judah did not live up to their names. King David's greater Son, the King of Kings and Lord of Lords, is seen here as the only hope of Judah.

23:1-2. Pastors. Unrighteous rulers (see 2:8 note). By right of their office, the kings of Judah had exerted a tremendous influence on the people, scattering them away from God. Driven them away, the very opposite of the shepherd's duty, i.e., to go before the flock and lead them to pasture or the fold (Isa 40:11; Jn 10:3-4).

3-4. I will gather the remnant. As the kings of Judah had scattered the people of God, so God would regather the nation. There is a double fulfillment of this prophecy. The first fulfillment occurred after the Babylonian exile when the remnant returned to Israel. However, this peaceful and righteous rule was short-lived. By the time of Malachi, the last Old Testament prophet (400 B.C.), Israel had degenerated again into idolatry and immorality. Permanent peace and a truly righteous reign would not come until the Messiah, the righteous Branch, would reign for a thousand years. Although verses 3-8 presuppose the Exile, this does not mean Jeremiah could not have written them. The prediction of restoration after the Exile was common among the pre-exilic prophets (cf. Amos 9:11-15; Isa 11:1-16; 44:24-45:13; etc.). See the note on verses 7-8 for the second fulfillment of this prophecy.

5-8. Behold, the days come. Jeremiah uses this introductory formula fourteen times in the book to prepare a message of hope for the future (7:32; 9:25; 16:14; 19:6; 23:5, 7; 31:27, 31, 38; 33:14; 48:12; 49:2; 51:47, 52). In verses 5-8 we have one of the great messianic prophecies of Jeremiah and the Old Testament. Branch (Heb tsemach), is a messianic metaphor (cf. 33:15; Zech 3:8; 6:12; Isa 4:2-4). The Branch was not an individual twig or branch of a tree, but a sprout from a root, forming a second tree (cf. Gen 19:25; Ps 65:10; Isa 61:11; Ezk 16:7; 17:9, 10). Therefore, out of the fallen dynasty of Israel life would spring through an individual Messiah, upon whom the nation's, as well as the world's hopes, would rest.

The second fulfillment of the prophecy of Israel's regathering and the righteous Branch will occur during the millennial reign following the Great Tribulation. That this prophecy has not yet been realized is clearly seen in such statements as judgment and justice (vs. 5), Israel shall dwell safely (vs. 6), they shall no more say . . . land of Egypt (vs. 7) and But, The LORD liveth . . . out of the north country (vs. 8).

Judgment and justice have not yet occurred on a local, let alone a worldwide, scale. This can only come during the Millennium. Israel has not, is she presently, dwelling safely in the land, but in the Millennium she will. The greatest feast celebrated today among the Jews is the Feast of the Passover (the deliverance from Egyptian bondage). Yet, verses 7 and 8 prophesy that the day will come when the house of Israel will no longer celebrate the Passover, but will rejoice that the Lord has led the seed of the house of Israel out of the north country. That day has not yet occurred and awaits the second advent of our Lord Jesus Christ.

His name shall then be called THE LORD OUR RIGHTEOUSNESS, the One who secures our vindication. This title may possibly be a play on the name Zedekiah (the Lord is my righteousness), in contrast to his wicked character. The King of Babylon changed his name from Mattaniah to Zedekiah, no doubt for political reasons. Zedekiah never lived up to his name, but the coming Messiah will.

9-13. Jeremiah had been persecuted by the false priests and false prophets (27:16-22; 28; 29:8-9). They were false prophets because they neither loved nor walked close to the Lord (cf. 29:23) and because they prophesied peace when God had proclaimed destruction. Jeremiah fiercely denounced them.

14-32. So great was their adultery and falsehood that Jeremiah likened them to **Sodom and Gomorrah**. This was an even greater sin than the Baal worship of the Samaritan prophets. **Wormwood . . . gall** (see 9:15 note). **Counsel.** The same word (Heb *sôd*) means both counsel and council. The Old Testament depicts a heavenly council to which the true prophets were evidently admitted (cf. Amos 3:7; Ps 82:1; 89:7; I Kgs 22:19-22; Job 1:1-2:7; Isa 6:1-13). **Visions . . . dreams** (vss. 16, 25, 28). Dreams were a legitimate means of divine revelation (cf. Num 12:6; I Sam 28:6; Joel 2:28; Zech 1:7-6:8), but the false prophets' dreams were not from God, being self-induced (cf. vss. 16-20; 25-27; 30-32). Our Lord also warned of the false prophets in the last days (Mt 24:5, 11). God told the false prophets to go ahead and tell their dreams; but **He that hath my word, let him speak my word faithfully.** Jeremiah had apparently not received his message through dreams, but in a better way (note comparison of **chaff** to **wheat**, vs. 28). We are not told exactly how Jeremiah received the word of the Lord.

9 ¶Mine heart within me is broken because of the prophets; all my bones shake; I am like a drunken man, and like a man whom wine hath overcome, because of the LORD, and because of the words of his holiness.

10 For the land is full of adulterers; for because of swearing the land mourneth: the pleasant places of the wilderness are dried up, and their course is evil, and their force *is* not right.

11 For both prophet and priest are profane; yea, in my house have I found their wickedness, saith the LORD.

12 Wherefore their way shall be unto them as slippery *ways* in the darkness: they shall be driven on, and fall therein: for I will bring evil upon them, *even* the year of their visitation, saith the LORD.

13 And I have seen folly in the prophets of Sa-mā'rī-a; they prophesied in Bā'al, and caused my people Israel to err.

14 I have seen also in the prophets of Jerusalem an horrible thing: they commit adultery, and walk in lies: they strengthen also the hands of evildoers, that none doth return from his wickedness: they are all of them unto me as Sodom, and the inhabitants thereof as Go-mŏr'rah.

15 Therefore thus saith the LORD of hosts concerning the prophets; Behold, I will feed them with wormwood, and make them drink the water of gall: for from the prophets of Jerusalem is profaneness gone forth into all the land.

16 Thus saith the LORD of hosts, Hearken not unto the words of the prophets that prophesy unto you: they make you vain: they speak a vision of their own heart, *and* not out of the mouth of the LORD.

17 They say still unto them that despise me, The LORD hath said, Ye shall have peace; and they say unto every one that walketh after the imagination of his own heart, No evil shall come upon you.

18 For who hath stood in the counsel of the LORD, and hath perceived and heard his word? who hath marked his word, and heard *it*?

19 Behold, a whirlwind of the LORD is gone forth in fury, even a grievous whirlwind: it shall fall grievously upon the head of the wicked.

20 The anger of the LORD shall not return, until he have executed, and till he have performed the thoughts of his heart: in the latter days ye shall consider it perfectly.

21 I have not sent these prophets, yet they ran: I have not spoken to them, yet they prophesied.

22 But if they had stood in my counsel, and had caused my people to hear my words, then they should have turned them from their evil way, and from the evil of their doings.

23 *Am* I a God at hand, saith the LORD, and not a God afar off?

24 Can any hide himself in secret places that I shall not see him? saith the

LORD. Do not I fill heaven and earth? saith the LORD.

25 I have heard what the prophets said, that prophesy lies in my name, saying, I have dreamed, I have dreamed.

26 How long shall *this* be in the heart of the prophets that prophesy lies? yea, *they* are prophets of the deceit of their own heart;

27 Which think to cause my people to forget my name by their dreams which they tell every man to his neighbour, as their fathers have forgotten my name for Ba'al.

28 The prophet that hath a dream, let him tell a dream; and he that hath my word, let him speak my word faithfully. What *is* the chaff to the wheat? saith the LORD.

29 *Is* not my word like as a fire? saith the LORD; and like a hammer *that* breaketh the rock in pieces?

30 Therefore, behold, I *am* against the prophets, saith the LORD, that steal my words every one from his neighbour.

31 Behold, I *am* against the prophets, saith the LORD, that use their tongues, and say, He saith.

32 Behold, I *am* against them that prophesy false dreams, saith the LORD, and do tell them, and cause my people to err by their lies, and by their lightness; yet I sent them not, nor commanded them: therefore they shall not profit this people at all, saith the LORD.

33 ¶ And when this people, or the prophet, or a priest, shall ask thee, saying, What *is* the burden of the LORD? thou shalt then say unto them, What burden? I will even forsake you, saith the LORD.

34 And *as for* the prophet, and the priest, and the people, that shall say, The burden of the LORD, I will even punish that man and his house.

35 Thus shall ye say every one to his neighbour, and every one to his brother, What hath the LORD answered? and, What hath the LORD spoken?

36 And the burden of the LORD shall ye mention no more: for every man's word shall be his burden; for ye have perverted the words of the living God, of the LORD of hosts our God.

37 Thus shalt thou say to the prophet, What hath the LORD answered thee? and, What hath the LORD spoken?

38 But since ye say, The burden of the LORD; therefore thus saith the LORD; Because ye say this word, The burden of the LORD, and I have sent unto you, saying, Ye shall not say, The burden of the LORD;

39 Therefore, behold, I, even I, will utterly forget you, and I will forsake you, and the city that I gave you and your fathers, *and cast you* out of my presence:

40 And I will bring an everlasting reproach upon you, and a perpetual shame, which shall not be forgotten.

33-40. Burden (Heb *maśā'*) has a double meaning: utterance and burden. Jeremiah's word from God was a burden to the people. Since they had refused the burden of covenant responsibilities, God would refuse them as too much of a burden to carry. Because of the shameful abuse of this prophetic term, it would no longer be used (vss. 34-35). Since the false prophets would persist in their disdain for God and His Word, God would bring **an everlasting reproach** and **a perpetual shame** upon them. Let us, too, beware of the false prophet of our day whose preaching is a compromise, whose personal character is fraudulent, whose dreams are lies, whose message is a perversion of the Word of God, and whose end is the lake of fire (Rev 19:20).

d. *Sign of the two baskets of figs. 24:1-10.*

The people of Jerusalem were constantly contrasting themselves with the people of the captivity. Now God does the contrasting, and the inhabitants of Jerusalem do not fare too well. Jeremiah is given a vision of a fresh basket of figs and a rotten basket of figs. The good figs symbolize the best of the people who were, in 597 B.C., carried to Babylon with Jehoiachin, here called Jeconiah (cf. 22:20-30). God promises to bless the exiles and return them to the land.

The bad figs symbolize the apostates who remained in the land to support the wicked Zedekiah, who was determined, with the help of Egypt, to resist Babylon (II Kgs 24:10-20). As the bad figs are thrown away, so God will discard this apostate people. The people of Judah could not miss this graphic contrast with the exiled Jews.

CHAPTER 24

THE LORD shewed me, and, behold, two baskets of figs were set before the temple of the LORD, after that Neb-u-chad-rez'zar king of Babylon had carried away captive Jec-o-ni'ah the son of Je-hoi'a-kim king of Ju'dah, and the princes of Ju'dah, with the carpenters and smiths, from Jerusalem, and had brought them to Babylon.

2 One basket *had* very good figs, *even* like the figs *that are* first ripe: and the other basket *had* very naughty figs, which could not be eaten, they were so bad.

3 Then said the LORD unto me, What seest thou, Jer'e-mi'ah? And I said, Figs; the good figs, very good; and the evil, very evil, that cannot be eaten, they are so evil.

4 ¶Again the word of the LORD came unto me, saying,

5 Thus saith the LORD, the God of Israel; Like these good figs, so will I acknowledge them that are carried away captive of Ju'dah, whom I have sent out of this place into the land of the Chal-de'ans for *their* good.

6 For I will set mine eyes upon them for good, and I will bring them again to this land: and I will build them, and not pull *them* down; and I will plant them, and not pluck *them* up.

7 And I will give them an heart to know me, that I *am* the LORD: and they shall be my people, and I will be their God: for they shall return unto me with their whole heart.

8 ¶And as the evil figs, which cannot be eaten, they are so evil; surely thus saith the LORD, So will I give Zed-e-ki'ah the king of Ju'dah, and his princes, and the residue of Jerusalem, that remain in this land, and them that dwell in the land of Egypt:

9 And I will deliver them to be removed into all the kingdoms of the earth for *their* hurt, *to be* a reproach and a proverb, a taunt and a curse, in all places whither I shall drive them.

10 And I will send the sword, the famine, and the pestilence, among them, till they be consumed from off the land that I gave unto them and to their fathers.

CHAPTER 25

THE word that came to Jer'e-mi'ah concerning all the people of Ju'dah in the fourth year of Je-hoi'a-kim the son of Jo-si'ah king of Ju'dah, that *was* the first year of Neb-u-chad-rez'zar king of Babylon;

2 The which Jer'e-mi'ah the prophet spake unto all the people of Ju'dah, and to all the inhabitants of Jerusalem, saying,

3 From the thirteenth year of Jo-si'ah the son of Amon king of Ju'dah, even unto this day, that *is* the three and twentieth year, the word of the LORD

24:1. The LORD showed me. An expression of divine inspiration (cf. Ex 25:9; Zech 1:20; 3:1; Amos 7:1, 4, 7). **Carpenters and smiths,** the skilled artisans and construction workers. Nebuchadnezzar needed the educated, the skilled, and the military people for his building program in Babylon, as well as his military campaigns abroad. Only the poor were left in the land.

2-5. First ripe. The early figs which came in June, as compared with summer figs of August and the winter figs of November. The Hebrews considered the early figs as a delicacy (cf. Isa 28:4; Hos 9:10; Mic 7:1). **Naughty,** i.e., bad. The same Hebrew word is translated bad later in this verse and evil in verses 3 and 8. The idea of the reference is that one basket had very good figs, like the early figs, and the other basket had very bad, or rotten, figs.

6-7. God's blessing upon the exiles would be both physical and spiritual. Physically, the captives would be brought back into the land. Spiritually, the captives would be given a new heart to return to the Lord and serve Him.

8-10. Them that dwell in the land of Egypt, were those captured by Pharaoh Necho, or perhaps Palestinian fugitives from the Chaldeans. **To be removed,** to be a horror, an object of terror, a perturbation (see Laetsch, p. 147). **Consumed from off the land.** The fulfillment of the prophecy occurred in A.D. 70 when the Romans under Titus devastated Jerusalem (as our Lord also predicted, cf. Matt 23:38).

e. Prediction of the Babylonian invasion and exile. 25:1-38.

25:1-8. The first year of Nebuchadrezzar (Nebuchadnezzar preferred spelling). Earlier scholars considered this an anachronism in which the fourth year of Jehoiakim was equated with the third year of that same king in Daniel 1:1. However, it is now universally accepted as an accurate account since the Palestinian method of chronology was different from the Babylonian. In Palestine the accession year was counted as the first year of the king's reign, whereas in Babylon the accession year was reckoned separately, being followed by the first year of the actual reign.

This message is specifically dated during the fourth year of King Jehoiakim (605 B.C.). Jeremiah, now at the mid point of his career, had been warning the people of coming judgment for twenty-three years. Even before him, God had sent His prophets to warn the people; but their message of repentance, with the promise of remaining in the land, had fallen on deaf ears. The result of disobedience would be seventy years of captivity, not only for Judah but also for the surrounding nations. The cup of fury from the Lord would be no respecter of persons. Babylon, too, would not escape. After the seventy-year captivity, divine punishment would fall upon Babylon for its sins. The message concludes with another warning concerning the false leaders of the people, a recurring theme in the book.

hath come unto me, and I have spoken unto you, rising early and speaking; but ye have not hearkened.

4 And the LORD hath sent unto you all his servants the prophets, rising early and sending them; but ye have not hearkened, nor inclined your ear to hear.

5 They said, Turn ye again now every one from his evil way, and from the evil of your doings, and dwell in the land that the LORD hath given unto you and to your fathers for ever and ever:

6 And go not after other gods to serve them, and to worship them, and provoke me not to anger with the works of your hands; and I will do you no hurt.

7 Yet ye have not hearkened unto me, saith the LORD, that ye might provoke me to anger with the works of your hands, to your own hurt.

8 ¶ Therefore thus saith the LORD of hosts; Because ye have not heard my words,

9 Behold, I will send and take all the families of the north, saith the LORD, and Nĕb-u-chad-rĕz´zar the king of Babylon, my servant, and will bring them against this land, and against the inhabitants thereof, and against all these nations round about, and will utterly destroy them, and make them an astonishment, and an hissing, and perpetual desolations.

10 Moreover I will take from them the voice of mirth, and the voice of gladness, the voice of the bridegroom, and the voice of the bride, the sound of the millstones, and the light of the candle.

11 And this whole land shall be a desolation, and an astonishment; and these nations shall serve the king of Babylon seventy years.

12 ¶ And it shall come to pass, when seventy years are accomplished, that I will punish the king of Babylon, and that nation, saith the LORD, for their iniquity, and the land of the Chal-dē´ans, and will make it perpetual desolations.

13 And I will bring upon that land all my words which I have pronounced against it, even all that is written in this book, which Jĕr´e-mī´ah hath prophesied against all the nations.

14 For many nations and great kings shall serve themselves of them also: and I will recompense them according to their deeds, and according to the works of their own hands.

15 ¶ For thus saith the LORD God of Israel unto me; Take the wine cup of this fury at my hand, and cause all the nations, to whom I send thee, to drink it.

16 And they shall drink, and be moved, and be mad, because of the sword that I will send among them.

17 Then took I the cup at the LORD's hand, and made all the nations to drink, unto whom the LORD had sent me:

18 To wit, Jerusalem, and the cities of Jū´dah, and the kings thereof, and the princes thereof, to make them a desola-

9-10. My servant. Judah had not listened to God's servants, the prophets. Now they would be forced to heed a different kind of servant, Nebuchadnezzar, who was unconsciously doing the will of God (cf. 27:6; 43:10; see Isaiah 45:1 where Cyrus is called God's anointed).

11-14. Seventy years, an approximate figure, since from the first year of Nebuchadnezzar and the deportation of Jehoiakin (605 B.C.) to the first year of Cyrus (538 B.C.) and his decree permitting the exiles to return (cf. Zech 1:12; II Chr 36:20-23) is not quite seventy years. Some scholars reckon the captivity from the destruction of the Temple (586 B.C.) to the completion of the Temple's reconstruction (516 B.C.). However, the former reckoning is preferred. **Many nations** specifically the Medes and Persians who overthrew Babylon under Cyrus.

Verses 15-38 are a summary of the prophecies against the foreign nations. All the nations mentioned in chapters 46-51 are included here, except Damascus. Therefore, these verses serve as an introduction to that section. For this reason, the Septuagint placed chapters 46-51 in this message. However, chronologically these chapters are best left in their original Hebrew order, since the main burden of Jeremiah is the testing of Judah. This summary, on the eve of the destruction of Jerusalem is included as an assurance to God's people that judgment would also fall upon the nations. The nations not mentioned in chapters 46-51 are commented on here.

15-28. The wine cup of this fury. This is an intoxicating cup, a symbol of divine wrath (cf. 13:12ff.; 49:12; Isa 51:17, 22; Zech 12:2). **Pharaoh king of Egypt** was Pharaoh Necho. **Mingled people** were foreigners residing in Egypt (Ionians, Carians, and Phoenicians, mercenaries in the Egyptian army). **Uz** was the home of Job (Job 1:1; cf. Lam 4:21) located in Transjordan, Edomite territory (Gen 10:23; 22:21; 36:28; Lam 4:21). **Azzah** (vs. 20), is Gaza. **Isles** was the Coastland, the Mediterranean coasts and islands. **Tema** was an Arab tribe living in the deserts of Syria (cf. Gen 25:15-16; Isa 21:14; Job 6:19). **Buz** was a tribe descended from Nahor, Abraham's brother (Gen 22:21). **Utmost corners** (see 9:26 note). **Zimri** is unknown. **Sheshach,**

tion, an astonishment, an hissing, and a curse; as *it is* this day;

19 Pharaoh king of Egypt, and his servants, and his princes, and all his people;

20 And all the mingled people, and all the kings of the land of Uz, and all the kings of the land of the Philistines, and Ash'ke-lon, and Az'zah, and Ekron, and the remnant of Ash'dod,

21 Edom, and Moab, and the children of Ammon,

22 And all the kings of Ty'rus, and all the kings of Zi'don, and the kings of the isles which *are* beyond the sea,

23 De'dan, and Te'ma, and Buz, and all *that are* in the utmost corners,

24 And all the kings of Arabia, and all the kings of the mingled people that dwell in the desert,

25 And all the kings of Zimri, and all the kings of E'lam, and all the kings of the Medes,

26 And all the kings of the north, far and near, one with another, and all the kingdoms of the world, which *are* upon the face of the earth: and the king of She'shach shall drink after them.

27 Therefore thou shalt say unto them, Thus saith the LORD of hosts, the God of Israel; Drink ye, and be drunken, and spue, and fall, and rise no more, because of the sword which I will send among you.

28 And it shall be, if they refuse to take the cup at thine hand to drink, then shalt thou say unto them, Thus saith the LORD of hosts: Ye shall certainly drink.

29 For, lo, I begin to bring evil on the city which is called by my name, and should ye be utterly unpunished? Ye shall not be unpunished: for I will call for a sword upon all the inhabitants of the earth, saith the LORD of hosts.

30 Therefore prophesy thou against them all these words, and say unto them, The LORD shall roar from on high, and utter his voice from his holy habitation; he shall mightily roar upon his habitation; he shall give a shout, as they that tread *the grapes*, against all the inhabitants of the earth.

31 A noise shall come *even* to the ends of the earth; for the LORD hath a controversy with the nations, he will plead with all flesh; he will give them *that are* wicked to the sword, saith the LORD.

32 Thus saith the LORD of hosts, Behold, evil shall go forth from nation to nation, and a great whirlwind shall be raised up from the coasts of the earth.

33 And the slain of the LORD shall be at that day from *one* end of the earth even unto the *other* end of the earth: they shall not be lamented, neither gathered, nor buried; they shall be dung upon the ground.

34 ¶Howl, ye shepherds, and cry; and wallow yourselves *in the ashes*, ye principal of the flock: for the days of your slaughter and of your dispersions are accomplished; and ye shall fall like a pleasant vessel.

35 And the shepherds shall have no way to flee, nor the principal of the flock to escape.

a cipher for Babylon, is a cryptogram in which the last letter of the Hebrew alphabet is substituted for the first, the next to last for the second, the third from the last for the third, etc.

The wrath of God inescapably will fall upon these nations, beginning with God's own people Judah; not one can refuse to drink the cup of wrath. But this cup can in no way compare to the cup of divine wrath our Lord Jesus drank to atone for the sins of the world (Lk 22:42).

29. Should ye be utterly unpunished. No sin is mentioned against the nations. However, God was about to destroy His people because of their idolatry, so He tacitly indicted the nations with the same offense.

30-38. A poetic section concludes this chapter in which God pours out His vengeance against His rebellious people. So great is God's indictment upon mankind that the victims of the coming disaster will be like **dung,** manure upon the ground. Both **shepherds** (the rulers) and **habitations** (their people) will be destroyed. This prophecy is not only descriptive of God's judgment upon Judah and the nations following the seventy-year captivity, but also **His** judgment upon apostate Israel and the nations which will culminate in the second coming of Christ (Mt 24:30; Rev 1:4-19). The warnings of Jeremiah some two and one-half millennia ago need to be heeded by the ungodly nations of our day, who are **drunken** and, unless they repent, will **rise no more** (vs. 27).

36 A voice of the cry of the shepherds, and an howling of the principal of the flock, *shall be heard:* for the Lord hath spoiled their pasture.

37 And the peaceable habitations are cut down because of the fierce anger of the Lord.

38 He hath forsaken his covert, as the lion: for their land is desolate because of the fierceness of the oppressor, and because of his fierce anger.

CHAPTER 26

IN the beginning of the reign of Jehoi′a-kim the son of Jo-si′ah king of Ju′dah came this word from the Lord, saying,

2 Thus saith the Lord; Stand in the court of the Lord's house, and speak unto all the cities of Ju′dah, which come to worship in the Lord's house, all the words that I command thee to speak unto them; diminish not a word:

3 If so be they will hearken, and turn every man from his evil way, that I may repent me of the evil, which I purpose to do unto them because of the evil of their doings.

4 And thou shalt say unto them, Thus saith the Lord; If ye will not hearken to me, to walk in my law, which I have set before you,

5 To hearken to the words of my servants the prophets, whom I sent unto you, both rising up early, and sending *them,* but ye have not hearkened;

6 Then will I make this house like Shi′loh, and will make this city a curse to all the nations of the earth.

7 So the priests and the prophets and all the people heard Jer′e-mi′ah speaking these words in the house of the Lord.

8 ¶ Now it came to pass, when Jer′e-mi′ah had made an end of speaking all that the Lord had commanded *him* to speak unto all the people, that the priests and the prophets and all the people took him, saying, Thou shalt surely die.

9 Why hast thou prophesied in the name of the Lord, saying, This house shall be like Shi′loh, and this city shall be desolate without an inhabitant? And all the people were gathered against Jer′e-mi′ah in the house of the Lord.

10 ¶ When the princes of Ju′dah heard these things, then they came up from the king's house unto the house of the Lord, and sat down in the entry of the new gate of the Lord's *house.*

11 Then spake the priests and the prophets unto the princes and to all the people, saying, This man *is* worthy to die; for he hath prophesied against this city, as ye have heard with your ears.

12 ¶ Then spake Jer′e-mi′ah unto all the princes and to all the people, saying, The Lord sent me to prophesy against this house and against this city all the words that ye have heard.

13 Therefore now amend your ways and your doings, and obey the voice of the Lord your God; and the Lord will repent him of the evil that he hath pronounced against you.

14 As for me, behold, I am in your

f. Jeremiah's life in danger, 26:1-24.

26:1-5. The historical background of the Temple Sermon (7:1-8:17) is given in this chapter. Early in the reign of Jehoiakim, Jeremiah was commanded to bring his message of repentance, or disaster, to the people of Judah in front of the Temple. The message is summarized here in one sentence (vss. 4-6) and declared that the destruction of the Temple would be the price for national disobedience.

Arrested and falsely accused by the priests and false prophets, Jeremiah was acquitted by the testimony of Ahikam and some of the wise court officials (citing the revival under Hezekiah that came as a result of the people's repentance after the preaching of the prophet Micah). Determined to stop the divine message of judgment, Jehoiakim vented his anger against a lesser adversary, the prophet Urijah. Having fled to Egypt for protection, Urijah was apprehended by Elnathan, returned to Jehoiakim, and executed.

6-16. Shiloh (see 7:12 note). **Curse.** The nations would make fun of Jerusalem in cursing others by saying, "I hope you become a desolation, just like Jerusalem." **Prophets.** The LXX adds the word "false," and this is certainly in agreement with the context since these were false prophets. These false prophets were so enraged with Jeremiah's message that they demanded his death. **Princes** were the good rulers appointed by Josiah. **Innocent blood.** Jeremiah's personal defense and appeal to his innocence won the hearts of the rulers, who could find no fault in him (compare Pilate with Jesus, Jn 19:4).

hand: do with me as seemeth good and meet unto you.

15 But know ye for certain, that if ye put me to death, ye shall surely bring innocent blood upon yourselves, and upon this city, and upon the inhabitants thereof: for of a truth the LORD hath sent me unto you to speak all these words in your ears.

16 ¶ Then said the princes and all the people unto the priests and to the prophets; This man is not worthy to die: for he hath spoken to us in the name of the LORD our God.

17 Then rose up certain of the elders of the land, and spake to all the assembly of the people, saying,

18 Mī'cah the Mō'ras-thite prophesied in the days of Hĕz-e-kī'ah king of Jū'dah, and spake to all the people of Jū'dah, saying, Thus saith the LORD of hosts; Zion shall be plowed like a field, and Jerusalem shall become heaps, and the mountain of the house as the high places of a forest.

19 Did Hĕz-e-kī'ah king of Jū'dah and all Jū'dah put him at all to death? did he not fear the LORD, and besought the LORD, and the LORD repented him of the evil which he had pronounced against them? Thus might we procure great evil against our souls.

20 And there was also a man that prophesied in the name of the LORD, U-rī'jah the son of Shĕm-a-ī'ah of Kir'jăth-jē'a-rim, who prophesied against this city and against this land according to all the words of Jĕr'e-mī'ah:

21 And when Je-hoi'a-kĭm the king, with all his mighty men, and all the princes, heard his words, the king sought to put him to death: but when U-rī'jah heard it, he was afraid, and fled, and went into Egypt;

22 And Je-hoi'a-kĭm the king sent men into Egypt, namely, Ĕl'nā-than the son of Ăch'bôr, and certain men with him into Egypt.

23 And they fetched forth U-rī'jah out of Egypt, and brought him unto Je-hoi'a-kĭm the king; who slew him with the sword, and cast his dead body into the graves of the common people.

24 Nevertheless the hand of A-hī'kam the son of Shā'phan was with Jĕr'e-mī'ah, that they should not give him into the hand of the people to put him to death.

CHAPTER 27

IN the beginning of the reign of Je-hoi'a-kĭm the son of Jō-sī'ah king of Jū'dah came this word unto Jĕr'e-mī'ah from the LORD, saying,

2 Thus saith the LORD to me; Make

---

wise men of the city. **Micah the Morasthite.** The writing prophet Micah from the town of Moresheth near Gath (Mic 1:14). In the elders' appeal to Micah (cf. Mic 1:1ff.) they give an unprecedented direct quotation of Micah 3:12.

17-19. Elders were usually rulers, but here probably the aged

20-23. Urijah the son of Shemaiah. Apart from this passage, nothing is known of this prophet. He is among the many unsung heroes of the faith who have witnessed, suffered and have died for the Lord they loved (cf. Heb 11:36-40). We can learn the lesson of total surrender to the will of God in the lives of Jeremiah and Urijah. Jeremiah was allowed to live, but God took Urijah home to his eternal reward. **Kirjath-jearim** originally was a Gibeonite city (Josh 9:17) where the ark was kept for 20 years (I Sam 7:2) and was located about nine miles west of Jerusalem on the road to Jaffa. **Elnathan** (cf. 36:12, 25) was, perhaps, Jehoiakim's father-in-law (II Kgs 24:8) and therefore the most likely court official to institute extradition proceedings with Egypt for Urijah.

24. Ahikam was a court official, a member of the deputation sent by Josiah to the prophetess Huldah (II Kgs 22:12ff.; II Chr 34:20-21) and the father of Gedaliah, the governor of Judah appointed by Nebuchadnezzar (39:14; II Kgs 25:22).

g. The sign of the yokes. 27:1-28:17.

27:1. Jehoiakim. Zedekiah. As is stated in verses 3, 12, and 20, Zedekiah was reigning at the time. Some Hebrew manuscripts, as well as the Syriac version, mention Zedekiah, which is correct (cf. 28:1). The Septuagint omits the verse. Probably this discrepancy arose from a miscopy of 26:1. The context shows that Zedekiah is certainly correct.

Although Zedekiah had been placed upon the Judaean throne by Nebuchadnezzar, he, along with the neighboring kings, was planning a rebellion. Jeremiah's message from the Lord was that this rebellion would be futile. By saddling the bonds and yokes about Jeremiah's neck, God graphically demonstrated the unalterable Babylonian captivity of Judah and her allies (see I Kgs 22:11 for a similar sign).

2-4. Bonds. The thongs that bound the wooden yokes together symbolized the hopelessness of trying to throw off the

1473

JEREMIAH 27:3

thee bonds and yokes, and put them upon thy neck.

3 And send them to the king of Edom, and to the king of Moab, and to the king of the Ammonites, and to the king of Tyrus, and to the king of Zī'don, by the hand of the messengers which come to Jerusalem unto Zĕd-e-kī'ah king of Jū'dah:

4 And command them to say unto their masters, Thus saith the Lord of hosts, the God of Israel; Thus shall ye say unto your masters;

5 I have made the earth, the man and the beast that are upon the ground, by my great power and by my outstretched arm, and have given it unto whom it seemed meet unto me.

6 And now have I given all these lands into the hand of Nĕb-u-chad-nĕz'zar the king of Babylon, my servant; and the beasts of the field have I given him also to serve him.

7 And all nations shall serve him, and his son, and his son's son, until the very time of his land come: and then many nations and great kings shall serve themselves of him.

8 And it shall come to pass, that the nation and kingdom which will not serve the same Nĕb-u-chad-nĕz'zar the king of Babylon, and that will not put their neck under the yoke of the king of Babylon, that nation will I punish, saith the Lord, with the sword, and with the famine, and with the pestilence, until I have consumed them by his hand.

9 Therefore hearken not ye to your prophets, nor to your diviners, nor to your dreamers, nor to your enchanters, nor to your sorcerers, which speak unto you, saying, Ye shall not serve the king of Babylon:

10 For they prophesy a lie unto you, to remove you far from your land; and that I should drive you out, and ye should perish.

11 But the nations that bring their neck under the yoke of the king of Babylon, and serve him, those will I let remain still in their own land, saith the Lord; and they shall till it, and dwell therein.

12 ¶ I spake also to Zĕd-e-kī'ah king of Jū'dah according to all these words, saying, Bring your necks under the yoke of the king of Babylon, and serve him and his people, and live.

13 Why will ye die, thou and thy people, by the sword, by the famine, and by the pestilence, as the Lord hath spoken against the nation that will not serve the king of Babylon?

14 Therefore hearken not unto the words of the prophets that speak unto you, saying, Ye shall not serve the king of Babylon: for they prophesy a lie unto you.

15 For I have not sent them, saith the Lord, yet they prophesy a lie in my name; that I might drive you out, and that ye might perish, ye, and the prophets that prophesy unto you.

16 Also I spake to the priests and to all this people, saying, Thus saith the Lord; Hearken not to the words of your prophets that prophesy unto you,

Babylonian bondage. **Send them.** Probably only one yoke was worn by Jeremiah and word was simply sent to the other nations. The LXX omits the word **them. Moab . . . Zion** (see chs. 47-49 note).

5-8. Revolt against Nebuchadnezzar would be futile since he had been ordained by God for this work (see 25:9 note). **His son, and his son's son.** A Hebrew idiom meaning a very long time.

9-11. Diviners . . . enchanters. In addition to the false priests and false prophets, the national crisis had given birth to various soothsayers and religious quacks. The false message of peace was heartily accepted by the people. The prophets mention a wide variety of these diviners (Isa 44:25; 47:13; Ezk 21:21; Hos 4:12).

12-15. Here, Jeremiah declares his message to the weak, vacillating Zedekiah. If Zedekiah would submit to Babylon, Jerusalem could be spared.

16-22. Jeremiah's message to Zedekiah was repeated to the priests and people. **Vessels,** the expensive religious treasures stored in the Temple (1 Kgs 7:15-39). Nebuchadnezzar had carried them off to Babylon during his second invasion (597

saying, Behold, the vessels of the LORD's house shall now shortly be brought again from Babylon: for they prophesy a lie unto you.

17 Hearken not unto them: serve the king of Babylon, and live: wherefore should this city be laid waste?

18 But if they be prophets, and if the word of the LORD be with them, let them now make intercession to the LORD of hosts, that the vessels which are left in the house of the LORD, and in the house of the king of Jū′dah, and at Jerusalem, go not to Babylon.

19 ¶For thus saith the LORD of hosts concerning the pillars, and concerning the sea, and concerning the bases, and concerning the residue of the vessels that remain in this city,

20 Which Nĕb-u-chad-nĕz′zar king of Babylon took not, when he carried away captive Jĕc-o-nī′ah the son of Je-hoī′a-kĭm king of Jū′dah from Jerusalem to Babylon, and all the nobles of Jū′dah and Jerusalem;

21 Yea, thus saith the LORD of hosts, the God of Israel, concerning the vessels that remain in the house of the LORD, and in the house of the king of Jū′dah and of Jerusalem;

22 They shall be carried to Babylon, and there shall they be until the day that I visit them, saith the LORD; then will I bring them up, and restore them to this place.

CHAPTER 28

AND it came to pass the same year, in the beginning of the reign of Zĕd-e-kī′-ah king of Jū′dah, in the fourth year, and in the fifth month, that Hăn-a-nī′ah the son of Ā′zur the prophet, which was of Gibeon, spake unto me in the house of the LORD, in the presence of the priests and of all the people, saying,

2 Thus speaketh the LORD of hosts, the God of Israel, saying, I have broken the yoke of the king of Babylon.

3 Within two full years will I bring again into this place all the vessels of the LORD's house, that Nĕb-u-chad-nĕz′zar king of Babylon took away from this place, and carried them to Babylon:

4 And I will bring again to this place Jĕc-o-nī′ah the son of Je-hoī′a-kĭm king of Jū′dah, with all the captives of Jū′dah, that went into Babylon, saith the LORD: for I will break the yoke of the king of Babylon.

5 ¶Then the prophet Jĕr′e-mī′ah said unto the prophet Hăn-a-nī′ah in the presence of the priests, and in the presence of all the people that stood in the house of the LORD,

6 Even the prophet Jĕr′e-mī′ah said, Amen: the LORD do so: the LORD perform thy words which thou hast prophesied, to bring again the vessels of the LORD's house, and all that is carried away captive, from Babylon into this place.

7 Nevertheless hear thou now this word that I speak in thine ears, and in the ears of all the people;

8 The prophets that have been before me and before thee of old prophesied both against many countries, and

B.C., cf. II Kgs 24:8-16). The promise of their return by the false prophets encouraged the people to rebel against Babylon. However, Jeremiah predicted that the **pillars**, and **sea** and the **bases** (cf. I Kgs 7:15-26), the largest and heaviest vessels that had not been taken the first time, would be taken next. This prophecy was fulfilled in 52:17.

28:1-5. Shortly after the events of chapter 27, during that same year, one of the false prophets, **Hananiah the son of Azur** (apart from this reference nothing else is known of him), prophesied that in two years God would break the yoke of Nebuchadnezzar and would return the stolen vessels, King Jehoiachin (Jeconiah, see 22:24 note), and the other captives. This deceptive prophecy was exactly the opposite of what Jeremiah had prophesied (22:26, 27; 27:16).

6-9. Jeremiah replied, perhaps ironically, **Amen**. So be it. Would that it be true. However, time will tell. Apparently, Jeremiah didn't have a word from the Lord at this time; but the true test of a prophet was absolute fulfillment (Deut 18:22).

1476

against great kingdoms, of war, and of evil and of pestilence.

9 The prophet which prophesieth of peace, when the word of the prophet shall come to pass, *then* shall the prophet be known, that the LORD hath truly sent him.

10 ¶Then Hăn-a-nī´ah the prophet took the yoke from off the prophet Jĕr-e-mī´ah's neck, and brake it.

11 And Hăn-a-nī´ah spake in the presence of all the people, saying, Thus saith the LORD; Even so will I break the yoke of Nĕb-u-chad-nĕz´zar king of Băb-ylon from the neck of all nations within the space of two full years. And the prophet Jĕr-e-mī´ah went his way.

12 ¶Then the word of the LORD came unto Jĕr-e-mī´ah *the prophet*, after that Hăn-a-nī´ah the prophet had broken the yoke from off the neck of the prophet Jĕr-e-mī´ah, saying,

13 Go and tell Hăn-a-nī´ah, saying, Thus saith the LORD: Thou hast broken the yokes of wood; but thou shalt make for them the yokes of iron.

14 For thus saith the LORD of hosts, the God of Israel; I have put a yoke of iron upon the neck of all these nations, that they may serve Nĕb-u-chad-nĕz´zar king of Babylon; and they shall serve him: and I have given him the beasts of the field also.

15 ¶Then said the prophet Jĕr-e-mī´ah unto Hăn-a-nī´ah the prophet, Hear now, Hăn-a-nī´ah; The LORD hath not sent thee; but thou makest this people to trust in a lie.

16 Therefore thus saith the LORD; Behold, I will cast thee from off the face of the earth: this year thou shalt die, because thou hast taught rebellion against the LORD.

17 So Hăn-a-nī´ah the prophet died the same year in the seventh month.

CHAPTER 29

NOW these are the words of the letter that Jĕr-e-mī´ah the prophet sent from Jerusalem unto the residue of the elders which were carried away captives, and to the priests, and to the prophets, and to all the people whom Nĕb-u-chad-nĕz´zar had carried away captive from Jerusalem to Babylon;

2 (After that Jĕc-o-nī´ah the king, and the queen, and the eunuchs, the princes of Jū´dah and Jerusalem, and the carpenters, and the smiths, were departed from Jerusalem;)

3 By the hand of Ĕl´a-sah the son of Shā´phan, and Gĕm-a-rī´ah the son of Hĭl-kī´ah, (whom Zĕd-e-kī´ah king of Jū´dah sent unto Babylon to Nĕb-u-chad-nĕz´zar king of Babylon) saying,

4 Thus saith the LORD of hosts, the God of Israel, unto all that are carried away captives, whom I have caused to be carried away from Jerusalem unto Babylon;

5 Build ye houses, and dwell *in them*; and plant gardens, and eat the fruit of them;

6 Take ye wives, and beget sons and daughters; and take wives for your sons, and give your daughters to husbands, that they may bear sons and

h. *Jeremiah's letter to the exiles*. 29:1-32.

Word had reached Jeremiah that, like Hananiah, some of the exiled prophets were predicting a speedy fall of Babylon and the immediate return of the exiles.

In 597 B.C. Nebuchadnezzar deported King Jehoiachin and the best of the people to Babylon. During the reign of Zedekiah, probably within two years of the deportation, Jeremiah opened this letter to the captives advising them to settle in the land, multiply, and become peaceful, law-abiding exiles because the exile would be long (vss. 1-9). Yet, there was hope of return. After the seventy-year captivity God would bring His people back into the land (vss. 10-19). However, they must not follow the wicked counsel and example of the false prophets, such as Ahab and Zedekiah (vss. 20-23).

29:1-3. **The elders . . . priests . . . prophets**. The whole community of exiles, of which these were representatives. **Jeconiah**. Jehoiachin, (see 22-24 note). **The queen**. The queen-mother (II Kgs 24:15). **Elasah** and **Gemariah** were the two ambassadors sent by Zedekiah to Babylon, who also delivered Jeremiah's letter. Elasah may have been the brother of Ahikam, who protected Jeremiah from Jehoiakim (26:24). Gemariah, not to be confused with Gemariah, the son of the secretary Shaphan (36:10), is unknown beyond this passage. Apparently, his was a popular name at this time since the Lachish Letters also mention a "Gemaryahu son of Hitsilyahu" (see D. W. Thomas ed., *Documents from Old Testament Times*, p. 213).

4-9. Although the Psalmist pictures the exiles weeping in Babylon (Ps 137:4), they were not slaves but deportees. The Babylonians permitted the Jews to congregate in their own settlements. Tel-abib, near Nippur on the River Chebar (also known as the Grand Canal), was perhaps the largest settlement. From here Ezekiel conducted his prophetic ministry. Since the exile would be seventy years, Jeremiah encouraged them to build homes, marry, and settle down, which the exiles were free to do. Jeremiah's counsel to pray for the peace of Babylon (vs. 7) and be loyal to her has been a principle that has preserved the Jews through the centuries. Some of the Jews became so

10-11. Hananiah impudently broke the yoke about Jeremiah's neck as a sign of his prophecy. Perhaps he was so bold because he had heard of the revolt in Babylon at this time. According to the *Babylonian Chronicle*, at this same time Nebuchadnezzar was engaged in quelling civil rebellion at home.

12-17. When Jeremiah received a word from the Lord, it was much stricter than before. The yoke of wood would become a yoke of iron, God's absolute resolve to punish Judah. Since Hananiah had taught **rebellion against the LORD**, he would die. And so it happened. Hananiah's prophecy did not come true, and his rapid death was a demonstration of God's judgement upon apostasy and rebellion (cf. Deut 13:5; Ezk 11:13; Acts 5:1-11).

prosperous in Babylon that they chose to remain there when Cyrus decreed their return.

10-23. Seventy years. (see 25:11 note). **An expected end. A** future and a hope. These promises extend far beyond the return from Babylon, but first Judah would undergo persecution (vss. 12-14). **Vile figs** (see ch. 24). **To be removed** means tossed about from one nation to another. **Ahab** and **Zedekiah** were two false prophets of which nothing more is known beyond this passage. **Roasted in the fire** was a common Babylonian punishment (cf. Dan 3:6). This atrocity definitely dates this passage during the Neo-Babylonian period of Nebuchadnezzar, since under the Persians, who regarded fire as sacred, a different form of capital punishment (ingestion by lions) was employed (cf. Dan 6:16).

daughters; that ye may be increased there, and not diminished.

7 And seek the peace of the city whither I have caused you to be carried away captives, and pray unto the LORD for it: for in the peace thereof shall ye have peace.

8 ¶For thus saith the LORD of hosts, the God of Israel; Let not your prophets and your diviners, that *be* in the midst of you, deceive you, neither hearken to your dreams which ye cause to be dreamed.

9 For they prophesy falsely unto you in my name: I have not sent them, saith the LORD.

10 ¶For thus saith the LORD, That after seventy years be accomplished at Babylon I will visit you, and perform my good word toward you, in causing you to return to this place.

11 For I know the thoughts that I think toward you, saith the LORD, thoughts of peace, and not of evil, to give you an expected end.

12 Then shall ye call upon me, and ye shall go and pray unto me, and I will hearken unto you.

13 And ye shall seek me, and find *me*, when ye shall search for me with all your heart.

14 And I will be found of you, saith the LORD: and I will turn away your captivity, and I will gather you from all the nations, and from all the places whither I have driven you, saith the LORD; and I will bring you again into the place whence I caused you to be carried away captive.

15 ¶Because ye have said, The LORD hath raised us up prophets in Babylon;

16 *Know* that thus saith the LORD of the king that sitteth upon the throne of David, and of all the people that dwelleth in this city, *and* of your brethren that are not gone forth with you into captivity;

17 Thus saith the LORD of hosts; Behold, I will send upon them the sword, the famine, and the pestilence, and will make them like vile figs, that cannot be eaten, they are so evil.

18 And I will persecute them with the sword, with the famine, and with the pestilence, and will deliver them to be removed to all the kingdoms of the earth, to be a curse, and an astonishment, and an hissing, and a reproach, among all the nations whither I have driven them:

19 Because they have not hearkened to my words, saith the LORD, which I have sent unto them by my servants the prophets, rising up early and sending *them*; but ye would not hear, saith the LORD.

20 ¶Hear ye therefore the word of the LORD, all ye of the captivity, whom I have sent from Jerusalem to Babylon:

21 Thus saith the LORD of hosts, the God of Israel, of Ahab the son of Kō-la-ī'ah, and of Zĕd-e-kī'ah the son of Mā-a-sē'iah, which prophesy a lie unto you in my name; Behold, I will deliver them into the hand of Nĕb-u-chad-rĕz'zar king of Babylon; and he shall slay them before your eyes;

22 And of them shall be taken up a

curse by all the captivity of Jū́dah which are in Babylon, saying, The LORD make thee like Zĕd-e-kī́ah and like A'hab, whom the king of Babylon roasted in the fire;

23 Because they have committed villany in Israel, and have committed adultery with their neighbours' wives, and have spoken lying words in my name, which I have not commanded them; even I know, and am a witness, saith the LORD.

24 ¶ Thus shalt thou also speak to Shĕm-a-ī́ah the Nē-hĕl'a-mīte, saying,

25 Thus speaketh the LORD of hosts, the God of Israel, saying, Because thou hast sent letters in thy name unto all the people that are at Jerusalem, and to Zĕph-a-nī́ah the son of Mā-a-sḗiah the priest, and to all the priests, saying,

26 The LORD hath made thee priest in the stead of Je-hoī́a-da the priest, that ye should be officers in the house of the LORD, for every man that is mad, and maketh himself a prophet, that thou shouldest put him in prison, and in the stocks.

27 Now therefore why hast thou not reproved Jĕr-e-mī́ah of Ăn'a-thŏth, which maketh himself a prophet to you?

28 For therefore he sent unto us in Babylon, saying, This captivity is long: build ye houses, and dwell in them; and plant gardens, and eat the fruit of them.

29 And Zĕph-a-nī́ah the priest read this letter in the ears of Jĕr'e-mī'ah the prophet.

30 Then came the word of the LORD unto Jĕr'e-mī'ah saying,

31 Send to all them of the captivity, saying, Thus saith the LORD concerning Shĕm-a-ī́ah the Nē-hĕl'a-mīte; Because that Shĕm-a-ī́ah hath prophesied unto you, and I sent him not, and he caused you to trust in a lie;

32 Therefore thus saith the LORD; Behold, I will punish Shĕm-a-ī́ah the Nē-hĕl'a-mīte, and his seed: he shall not have a man to dwell among this people; neither shall he behold the good that I will do for my people, saith the LORD, because he hath taught rebellion against the LORD.

CHAPTER 30

THE word that came to Jĕr'e-mī'ah from the LORD, saying,

2 Thus speaketh the LORD God of Israel, saying, Write thee all the words that I have spoken unto thee in a book.

3 For, lo, the days come, saith the LORD, that I will bring again the captivity of my people Israel and Jū́dah, saith the LORD: and I will cause them to return to the land that I gave to their fathers, and they shall possess it.

---

prophet, protested to the Jerusalem authorities about Jeremiah's letter and asked that he be reprimanded. The patronymic sense of **Nehelamite** (or perhaps also after an otherwise unknown village) is to be preferred to the sense of a play on the word *chalam*, to dream, since the form does not occur elsewhere. **Zephaniah the son of Maaseiah** a temple official (cf. 21:1; 37:3; 52:24) read the letter to Jeremiah. The text of the letter is given in verses 26-28. Jeremiah then sent another letter to the exiles, condemning Shemaiah and predicting that neither he nor his descendants would see the day of the return from Babylonian exile (vs. 32).

2. The future messianic kingdom. 30:1-33:26.

The biographical sequence is interrupted by chapters 30-33. The message of impending disaster for national apostasy is counterbalanced here with a message of comfort and future hope. Frequently called the "Book of Consolation," due to its message of comfort, this section points far beyond the return from Babylon to the end of the age, the Day of the Lord and the fulfillment of God's promise to Israel in the Millennium.

Here, on the eve of the darkest hour of Israel's history, the prophet is given the vision of the nation's ultimate deliverance from both physical and spiritual bondage. Although chapters 30 and 31 are not dated, they were probably written either during the siege of Jerusalem or immediately thereafter. Chapters 32 and 33 are dated during the siege (the tenth year of Zedekiah's reign) while Jeremiah was imprisoned in the court of the guard. Liberal critics often give many of these aphorisms a late exilic date. However, the internal evidence attests to their Jeremianic authorship.

a. The promise of the new covenant. 30:1-31:40.

30:1-3. Verses 1 through 3 form a superscription for this entire section. Over half of Jeremiah's message thus far has been "pluck up and . . . break down" (cf. 1:10). Now the prophet is able to deliver the other side of his prophetic call, a message of "build and . . . plant" (cf. 1:10). **Bring again the captivity of my people Israel and Judah.** This is a promise of a literal return of both Israel and Judah, not just the latter to the land (cf. Mt. 24; Mk. 24; Rom. 11; Dan. Rev.). Some commentators spiritualize these promises to Israel and Judah. "The promise of a physical return to Canaan (30:4-20)" states Laetsch, "ended with the abrogation of the Old Covenant and is no longer part of God's covenant with His people in the latter days" (Laetsch, p. 244). However, to spiritualize the specific promises to Israel and Judah in this section, transferring them to the church, does a grave injustice to the text. Numerous references to a literal future restoration are given in this section. **Possess it.** In the days of Zerubbabel after the captivity, the land was not possessed. Although a few Jews from the northern tribes returned with the remnant of

---

24-32. Shemaiah the Nehelamite, another exiled false

---

a. ...

Judah, there was no regathering of Israel. Revelation 7 speaks of 12,000 from each tribe, which even if this number is topological implies a large group. The promised return is not simply the return from Babylon, but the future millennial kingdom.

4-7. Before the promises of blessings there must be the judgment of God upon Israel and the nations (cf. Amos 5:18-20; Isa 2:12-22; 34:1-15; Zeph 1:2-3:8; Zech 14:1-8, 12-15). The return gathering and end-time restoration of **Israel and . . . Judah will** be preceded by the Great Tribulation (cf. Mt 24:21; Rev 7:14). **Every man . . . travail.** The intense anguish of the Great Tribulation with parturient imagery. Men will hold their thighs in pain as a woman in labor. **Jacob's trouble** is the Great Tribulation. As the church, the saints of this age, will be kept from the Great Tribulation (Rev 3:10; I Thess 1:10), so the tribulation saints will be **saved out of it.**

8-11. That day. The Day of the Lord (cf. 46:10; Isa 13:6; Lam 2:22; Ezk 30:3; Joel 1:15; 2:1). **Yoke.** The last Gentile power (cf. Rev 13). **David their king** was not David, the son of Jesse or some other King David (since the return from Babylon, the Jews have never had a king named David), but the messianic Son of David, the Lord Jesus Christ (cf. Hos 3:5; Ezk 34:23). The declaration of Gabriel (cf. Lk 1:32-33) was never fulfilled during the first advent of Christ, but it will be at His second. **And Jacob shall . . . be in rest.** From the return under Ezra, Nehemiah, and Zerubbabel until the destruction of Jerusalem under Titus (A.D. 70) even unto this day, Israel has seen nothing but unrest and warfare. The fulfillment of this prophecy is yet future. **Scattered.** Although God has scattered His people, He has promised that He will **not make a full end** of them, but will one day cause them to return to Him and the land.

12-17. The incurable wounds of Israel will be healed (cf. 8:22; Joel 2:25), and those who have oppressed Israel will be punished. **Lovers,** the surrounding nations upon which Judah relied for help against Babylon.

18-24. Jerusalem will be rebuilt, and its splendor will rival that of the days of David and Solomon. **Heap** (Heb *tel*), the same word used by the Arabs today to identify the mounds of ancient cities. In the ancient Near East, when a city was destroyed, a new city would be built upon the rubble of the old. With repeated destruction and rebuilding, many layers of civilization would be built up in a *tel*. **Nobles . . . governor.** The

4 ¶And these *are* the words that the Lord spake concerning Israel and concerning Ju'dah.

5 For thus saith the Lord; We have heard a voice of trembling, of fear, and not of peace.

6 Ask ye now, and see whether a man doth travail with child? wherefore do I see every man with his hands on his loins, as a woman in travail, and all faces are turned into paleness?

7 Alas! for that day *is* great, so that none *is* like it: it *is* even the time of Jacob's trouble; but he shall be saved out of it.

8 For it shall come to pass in that day, saith the Lord of hosts, *that* I will break his yoke from off thy neck, and will burst thy bonds, and strangers shall no more serve themselves of him:

9 But they shall serve the Lord their God, and David their king, whom I will raise up unto them.

10 ¶ Therefore fear thou not, O my servant Jacob, saith the Lord; neither be dismayed, O Israel: for, lo, I will save thee from afar, and thy seed from the land of their captivity; and Jacob shall return, and shall be in rest, and be quiet, and none shall make *him* afraid.

11 For I *am* with thee, saith the Lord, to save thee: though I make a full end of all nations whither I have scattered thee, yet will I not make a full end of thee: but I will correct thee in measure, and will not leave thee altogether unpunished.

12 For thus saith the Lord, Thy bruise *is* incurable, *and* thy wound *is* grievous.

13 *There is* none to plead thy cause, that thou mayest be bound up: thou hast no healing medicines.

14 All thy lovers have forgotten thee; they seek thee not; for I have wounded thee with the wound of an enemy, with the chastisement of a cruel one, for the multitude of thine iniquity; *because* thy sins were increased.

15 Why criest thou for thine affliction? thy sorrow *is* incurable for the multitude of thine iniquity: *because* thy sins were increased, I have done these things unto thee.

16 Therefore all they that devour thee shall be devoured; and all thine adversaries, every one of them, shall go into captivity; and they that spoil thee shall be a spoil, and all that prey upon thee will I give for a prey.

17 For I will restore health unto thee, and I will heal thee of thy wounds, saith the Lord; because they called thee an Outcast, *saying,* This *is* Zion, whom no man seeketh after.

18 ¶Thus saith the Lord; Behold, I will bring again the captivity of Jacob's tents, and have mercy on his dwellingplaces; and the city shall be builded upon her own heap, and the palace shall remain after the manner thereof.

19 And out of them shall proceed thanksgiving and the voice of them

that make merry; and I will multiply them, and they shall not be few; I will also glorify them, and they shall not be small.

20 Their children also shall be as aforetime, and their congregation shall be established before me, and I will punish all that oppress them.

21 And their nobles shall be of themselves, and their governor shall proceed from the midst of them; and I will cause him to draw near, and he shall approach unto me: for who is this that engaged his heart to approach unto me? saith the LORD.

22 And ye shall be my people, and I will be your God.

23 ¶ Behold, the whirlwind of the LORD goeth forth with fury, a continuing whirlwind: it shall fall with pain upon the head of the wicked.

24 The fierce anger of the LORD shall not return, until he have done it, and until he have performed the intents of his heart: in the latter days ye shall consider it.

CHAPTER 31

AT the same time, saith the LORD, will I be the God of all the families of Israel, and they shall be my people.

2 Thus saith the LORD, The people which were left of the sword found grace in the wilderness; even Israel, when I went to cause him to rest.

3 The LORD hath appeared of old unto me, saying, Yea, I have loved thee with an everlasting love: therefore with lovingkindness have I drawn thee.

4 Again I will build thee, and thou shalt be built, O virgin of Israel: thou shalt again be adorned with thy tabrets, and shalt go forth in the dances of them that make merry.

5 Thou shalt yet plant vines upon the mountains of Sa-mā'rĭ-a: the planters shall plant, and shall eat them as common things.

6 For there shall be a day, that the watchman upon the mount Ē'phrā-ĭm shall cry, Arise ye, and let us go up to Zion unto the LORD our God.

7 For thus saith the LORD; Sing with gladness for Jacob, and shout among the chief of the nations: publish ye, praise ye, and say, O LORD, save thy people, the remnant of Israel.

8 Behold, I will bring them from the north country, and gather them from the coasts of the earth, and with them the blind and the lame, the woman with child and her that travaileth with child together: a great company shall return thither.

9 They shall come with weeping, and with supplications will I lead them: I will cause them to walk by the rivers of waters in a straight way, wherein they shall not stumble: for I am a father to Israel, and Ē'phrā-ĭm is my firstborn.

10 ¶ Hear the word of the LORD, O ye nations, and declare it in the isles afar off, and say, He that scattered Israel will gather him, and keep him, as a shepherd doth his flock.

11 For the LORD hath redeemed Jacob, and ransomed him from the hand of him that was stronger than he.

1480

King who shall reign over them. Since he shall be of themselves, this can only refer to the kingdom reign of the Messiah. My people . . . your God. This beautiful description of the glory of restored Israel could only refer to the yet future reign of Christ. Fierce anger. The judgment of God which must precede His blessings.

31:1-6. Chapter 31 continues the general theme of the glorious hope of a restored Israel and the establishment of a new covenant with them. Will I be the God. The covenant to Abraham (cf. Gen 17:7) will finally be realized when God is God of all the families of Israel. Wilderness. The Exodus (Ex 14; Deut 34) or perhaps the land of exile. Of old. From afar (cf. 30:10). I have loved thee. It is God's love for Israel, not their love for Him (cf. I Jn 4:10), that is the basis of their salvation. Virgin of Israel. Israel is personified as a virgin, emphasizing God's protection for her as a virgin. Tabrets, timbrels, hand drums used to accompany dancing (cf. Ex 15:20). Eat them as common things. As the fruit was not eaten during the first three years and the fourth year given unto the Lord, yet could be redeemed and eaten (Lev 19:23-25; Deut 20:6), so Israel would one day live off the land. Watchmen. One stationed upon the mountains to proclaim the festivals (cf. Isa 52). Here, the watchman on mount Ephraim (the center of the northern kingdom) indicates the reunion of the nation (cf. Isa 11:13).

7-14. North country. The foe from the North (see Introduction). Coasts. The ends of the earth. Father to Israel. God was not revealed as a father in any individual sense in the Old Testament. He was the Most High, the Almighty, the All-Sufficient. Only through the Lord Jesus Christ is He revealed as Father to us. Isles, coasts. Gather him, and keep him. Not a temporary restoration but a permanent regathering, never to be scattered again. Redeemed Jacob. God's purpose in redemption cannot be thwarted. As He had redeemed Israel from the hand of Pharaoh, so too He would redeem them from the hand of Nebuchadnezzar and all other oppressors, as well as from the time of Jacob's trouble. Shall not sorrow any more at all. A beautiful picture of the bliss of God's people, which can only be fulfilled in the millennial kingdom.

12 Therefore they shall come and sing in the height of Zion, and shall flow together to the goodness of the LORD, for wheat, and for wine, and for oil, and for the young of the flock and of the herd: and their soul shall be as a watered garden; and they shall not sorrow any more at all.

13 Then shall the virgin rejoice in the dance, both young men and old together: for I will turn their mourning into joy, and will comfort them, and make them rejoice from their sorrow.

14 And I will satiate the soul of the priests with fatness, and my people shall be satisfied with my goodness, saith the LORD.

15 ¶ Thus saith the LORD; A voice was heard in Rā′mah, lamentation, *and* bitter weeping; Rachel weeping for her children refused to be comforted for her children, because they *were* not.

16 Thus saith the LORD; Refrain thy voice from weeping, and thine eyes from tears: for thy work shall be rewarded, saith the LORD; and they shall come again from the land of the enemy.

17 And there is hope in thine end, saith the LORD, that thy children shall come again to their own border.

18 ¶ I have surely heard E′phra-im bemoaning himself *thus*; Thou hast chastised me, and I was chastised, as a bullock unaccustomed *to the yoke:* turn thou me, and I shall be turned; for thou *art* the LORD my God.

19 Surely after that I was turned, I repented; and after that I was instructed, I smote upon *my* thigh: I was ashamed, yea, even confounded, because I did bear the reproach of my youth.

20 *Is* E′phra-im my dear son? *is he a* pleasant child? for since I spake against him, I do earnestly remember him still: therefore my bowels are troubled for him; I will surely have mercy upon him, saith the LORD.

21 Set thee up waymarks, make thee high heaps: set thine heart toward the highway, *even* the way *which* thou wentest: turn again, O virgin of Israel, turn again to these thy cities.

22 ¶ How long wilt thou go about, O thou backsliding daughter? for the LORD hath created a new thing in the earth, A woman shall compass a man.

23 Thus saith the LORD of hosts, the God of Israel; As yet they shall use this speech in the land of Jū′dah and in the cities thereof, when I shall bring again their captivity; The LORD bless thee, O habitation of justice, *and* mountain of holiness.

24 And there shall dwell in Jū′dah itself, and in all the cities thereof together, husbandmen, and they *that* go forth with flocks.

25 For I have satiated the weary soul, and I have replenished every sorrowful soul.

26 Upon this I awaked, and beheld; and my sleep was sweet unto me.

27 ¶ Behold, the days come, saith the LORD, that I will sow the house of Israel and the house of Jū′dah with the seed of man, and with the seed of beast.

15-17. Ramah. A settlement in the area of Gibeon and Beeroth (cf. Josh 18:25), about five miles north of Jerusalem and where Jeremiah was released from his bonds (cf. 40:1). Jeremiah employs a beautiful figure here of **Rachel weeping** from her grave over her descendants, the people of Ephraim and Benjamin. Matthew saw a partial fulfillment of this prophecy in the slaughter of the innocent children in Bethlehem (the exact location of Rachel's tomb is a matter of dispute). However, verses 16-17 make it clear that there is a further fulfillment, since Rachel will be comforted when her children **come again from the land of the enemy** and **come again to their own border.** Peter's reference to Joel is a similar use of a twofold application of prophecy (Acts 2:16-21; cf. Joel 2:28-32).

18-22. Jeremiah now predicts the repentance of the Northern tribes. **Ephraim** is Israel. Ephraim was the favored grandson of Rachel, whom Jacob treated as his first-born. Here, as well as in other portions of Scripture, Ephraim is considered as the representative head of the ten northern tribes. **Smote upon my thigh.** Among the Hebrews, as well as the Persians, Greeks, and others, smiting on the thigh was a sign of great sorrow (Ezk 21:12). **Bowels** (see 4:19 note). **A woman shall compass a man.** Whereas the man (Jehovah) embraced (encompassed) the woman (Israel) in love, in the latter days Israel (the woman) would return to her husband (God).

23-30. Jeremiah now turns to Judah, who will also be restored. **Habitation of justice, and mountain of holiness.** This prophecy is yet future. The Jews must be brought back into the land and established in the fear of God in order for this to be accomplished. **Husbandmen.** Farmers. **My sleep was sweet.** Although Jeremiah repudiated dreams (23:25-28), here he was like a man asleep while God gave him this vision. He awakens with a sweet confidence in God's purpose for His people. **The fathers have eaten . . . on edge,** a common proverb (cf. Ezk 18:2-4). It was not God's anger, but the sins of the people, that had brought judgment upon them.

1482

28 And it shall come to pass, *that like* as I have watched over them, to pluck up, and to break down, and to throw down, and to destroy, and to afflict; so will I watch over them to build, and to plant, saith the LORD.

29 In those days they shall say no more, The fathers have eaten a sour grape, and the children's teeth are set on edge.

30 But every one shall die for his own iniquity: every man that eateth the sour grape, his teeth shall be set on edge.

31 ¶Behold, the days come, saith the LORD, that I will make a new covenant with the house of Israel and with the house of Jū′dah:

32 Not according to the covenant that I made with their fathers in the day that I took them by the hand to bring them out of the land of Egypt; which my covenant they brake, although I was an husband unto them, saith the LORD:

33 But this *shall be* the covenant that I will make with the house of Israel; Af-ter those days, saith the LORD, I will put my law in their inward parts, and write it in their hearts; and will be their God, and they shall be my people.

34 And they shall teach no more every man his neighbour, and every man his brother, saying, Know the LORD: for they shall all know me, from the least of them unto the greatest of them, saith the LORD: for I will forgive their iniquity, and I will remember their sin no more.

35 ¶Thus saith the LORD, which giv-eth the sun for a light by day, *and* the ordinances of the moon and of the stars for a light by night, which divideth the sea when the waves thereof roar; The LORD of hosts *is* his name:

36 If those ordinances depart from before me, saith the LORD, *then* the seed of Israel also shall cease from being a nation before me for ever.

37 Thus saith the LORD; If heaven above can be measured, and the foun-dations of the earth searched out be-neath, I will also cast off all the seed of Israel for all that they have done, saith the LORD.

38 ¶Behold, the days come, saith the LORD, that the city shall be built to the LORD from the tower of Hă-nan′ĕ-el unto the gate of the corner.

39 And the measuring line shall yet go forth over against it upon the hill Gā′reb, and shall compass about to Gō′-ăth.

40 And the whole valley of the dead bodies, and of the ashes, and all the fields unto the brook of Kidron, unto the corner of the horse gate toward the east, *shall be* holy unto the LORD; it shall not be plucked up, nor thrown down any more for ever.

b. Jeremiah's faith in the restoration. 32:1-44.

Chapter 32 provides a tangible demonstration of Jeremiah's faith in God's promise to restore His people. The final siege of Jerusalem was well under way. Anathoth, the birthplace of

31-34. Frequent mention is made in the Old Testament to the covenant of God with Israel (Ex 19:3-8; 24:3-8; Deut 29:1-29). Jeremiah, however, declares that Israel has broken that cove-nant (7:21-26; 11:1-13) and that God will one day make a new covenant with His people. This remarkable prophecy states that the new covenant will be made in the last day (vss. 31, 33), the parties of the covenant will be both Israel and Judah (v. 31); the terms of the covenant are a knowledge of God and forgiveness of sin (vs. 34); the perpetuity of the people of the covenant (vss. 35-37) and the guarantee of the covenant is the rebuilt city of Jerusalem (vss. 38-40). The book of Hebrews teaches that the Lord Jesus Christ instituted the new covenant by His vicarious atonement (Heb 7:22; 8:7-13; 10:15-22). Although certain fea-tures of this covenant have been fulfilled in the church, verse 31 states explicitly that the covenant will one day be ratified with a repentant Israel and Judah.

35-37. The preservation of the Hebrew people over the cen-turies can only be attributed to the miraculous fulfillment of this divine promise to them. Over the centuries dictators, religious leaders, and entire nations have tried to eliminate the Jew; but God's promise still remains. In A.D. 70 Titus killed 1,300,000 Jews when he captured Jerusalem. In eighth-century France and Spain, Jews were persecuted and burned at the stake. With the establishment of Islam in 622, most Arabian Jews were killed. England banished all Jews in 1020. The eleventh-century Cru-saders were as cruel to the Jews as they were to the Muslims. Blamed for the European Black Plague (1350), over one-half of the Jews in Europe were murdered. Thousands of Jews died in the Roman Catholic Inquisition (1411). Under the Russian czars, thousands of Jews were murdered. During World War I many European towns instituted local massacres of Jews. In the Ukraine alone over twelve hundred such pogroms took place. With Hitler's slaughter of six million Jews, the most devastating genocide in world history occurred. The Jew today is one of the greatest proofs of the promises of God.

38-40. The dimensions of the rebuilt Jerusalem are given from the **tower of Hananeel** (the northeast corner, II Kgs 14:13; II Chr 26:9) to **Gareb . . . Goath** (probably the south-west and southeast corners) to the **valley of the dead bodies** (the Valley of Hinnom, see 7:31 note). **The brook of Kidron**, which flows into the Valley of Hinnom, forms the eastern boundary of the city. The **horse gate** was located at the south-east corner of the Temple (cf. Neh 3:28). **Shall not be plucked up, nor thrown down any more for ever.** Another promise that awaits fulfillment during the millennial reign of Christ.

Jeremiah, had already fallen to the Babylonians. While imprisoned in the house of the king, Jeremiah purchased a piece of property in Anathoth from his opportunist cousin, Hanameel. Because of the desperate plight of the nation, the purchase of a piece of property, now in enemy hands, would have been absolutely foolish. However, Jeremiah's action in purchasing the property was a clear demonstration to all of his faith in the promised restoration.

32:1-2. Tenth year. The siege began in the ninth year of Zedekiah's reign (39:1). Except for a short reprieve from the Egyptian forces (37:5), the siege lasted for eighteen months into the tenth year of Zedekiah when Jerusalem finally fell.

CHAPTER 32

THE word that came to Jĕr´e-mī´ah from the LORD in the tenth year of Zĕd-e-kī´ah king of Jū´dah, which *was* the eighteenth year of Nĕb-u-chad-rĕz-zar.

2 For then the king of Babylon's army besieged Jerusalem: and Jĕr´e-mī´ah the prophet was shut up in the court of the prison, which *was* in the king of Jū´-ah's house.

3 For Zĕd-e-kī´ah king of Jū´dah had shut him up, saying, Wherefore dost thou prophesy, and say, Thus saith the LORD, Behold, I will give this city into the hand of the king of Babylon, and he shall take it:

4 And Zĕd-e-kī´ah king of Jū´dah shall not escape out of the hand of the Chăl-dē´ans, but shall surely be delivered into the hand of the king of Babylon, and shall speak with him mouth to mouth, and his eyes shall behold his eyes;

5 And he shall lead Zĕd-e-kī´ah to Babylon, and there shall he be until I visit him, saith the LORD: though ye fight with the Chăl-dē´ans, ye shall not prosper.

6 ¶ And Jĕr´e-mī´ah said, The word of the LORD came unto me, saying,

7 Behold, Hă-nam´é-el the son of Shăl´lum thine uncle shall come unto thee, saying, Buy thee my field that *is* in Ăn´a-thôth: for the right of redemption *is* thine to buy *it*.

8 So Hă-nam´é-el mine uncle's son came to me in the court of the prison according to the word of the LORD, and said unto me, Buy my field, I pray thee, that *is* in Ăn´a-thôth, which *is* in the country of Benjamin: for the right of inheritance *is* thine, and the redemption *is* thine; buy *it* for thyself. Then I knew that this *was* the word of the LORD.

9 And I bought the field of Hă-nam´é-el my uncle's son, that *was* in Ăn´a-thôth, and weighed him the money, *even* seventeen shekels of silver.

10 And I subscribed the evidence, and sealed *it*, and took witnesses, and weighed *him* the money in the balances.

11 So I took the evidence of the purchase, *both* that which was sealed *according* to the law and custom, and that which was open:

12 And I gave the evidence of the purchase unto Bā´ruch the son of Ne-rī´ah, the son of Mă-a-sē´iah, in the sight of Hă-nam´é-el mine uncle's *son*, and in the presence of the witnesses that subscribed the book of the purchase, before all the Jews that sat in the court of the prison.

13 ¶ And I charged Bā´ruch before them, saying,

14 Thus saith the LORD of hosts, the God of Israel; Take these evidences, this evidence of the purchase, both which is sealed, and this evidence

3-15. Parenthetically, verses 3-5 are an explanation as to why Jeremiah was imprisoned. **Right of redemption.** The law of redemption (Lev 25:23-28) granted that a near relative could redeem property under certain conditions and thus keep it in the family. **Weighed him the money.** Before coinage was introduced (sixth century B.C.), money was weighed in silver and gold (cf. Gen 23:16). **Seventeen shekels.** The actual value is unknown. Proper legal procedures were followed, consisting of a signed deed (**subscribed the evidence**) and witnesses. From the Jewish military colony in Elephantine (495 B.C.), an island in the Nile, we have learned that duplicate deeds were written on papyrus. One copy was rolled up and sealed to prevent tampering, while the other was left open for easy reference (see D. W. Thomas, p. 256ff.).

Baruch. This is the first mention of Jeremiah's faithful amanuensis who was responsible for preparing the documents under the prophet's direction. **Earthen vessel.** Valuable documents were commonly placed in pottery jars. Many of the Dead Sea scrolls, as well as papyri from Elephantine, were preserved in earthenware. Pitch was generally used to seal the jars. Once the land was repopulated, these sealed deeds would allow the rightful owner to reclaim the family patrimony. This is a key to the understanding of the vision of the seven-sealed book in Revelation. This title-deed to the world remains sealed until the rightful owner, the Lord Jesus Christ, claims His inheritance.

which is open; and put them in an earthen vessel, that they may continue many days.

15 For thus saith the Lord of hosts, the God of Israel; Houses and fields and vineyards shall be possessed again in this land.

16 ¶Now when I had delivered the evidence of the purchase unto Bä′ruch the son of Ne-rī′ah, I prayed unto the Lord, saying,

17 Ah Lord God! behold, thou hast made the heaven and the earth by thy great power and stretched out arm, *and* there is nothing too hard for thee:

18 Thou shewest lovingkindness unto thousands, and recompensest the iniquity of the fathers into the bosom of their children after them: the Great, the Mighty God, the Lord of hosts, *is* his name,

19 Great in counsel, and mighty in work: for thine eyes are open upon all the ways of the sons of men: to give every one according to his ways, and according to the fruit of his doings:

20 Which hast set signs and wonders in the land of Egypt, *even* unto this day, and in Israel, and among *other* men; and hast made thee a name, as at this day;

21 And hast brought forth thy people Israel out of the land of Egypt with signs, and with wonders, and with a strong hand, and with a stretched out arm, and with great terror;

22 And hast given them this land, which thou didst swear to their fathers to give them, a land flowing with milk and honey;

23 And they came in, and possessed it; but they obeyed not thy voice, neither walked in thy law; they have done nothing of all that thou commandedst them to do: therefore thou hast caused all this evil to come upon them:

24 Behold the mounts, they are come unto the city to take it: and the city is given into the hand of the Chăl-dē′ans, that fight against it, because of the sword, and of the famine, and of the pestilence: and what thou hast spoken is come to pass; and, behold, thou seest *it.*

25 And thou hast said unto me, O Lord God, Buy thee the field for money, and take witnesses; for the city is given into the hand of the Chăl-dē′ans.

26 ¶Then came the word of the Lord unto Jĕr-e-mī′ah, saying,

27 Behold, I *am* the Lord, the God of all flesh: is there any thing too hard for me?

28 Therefore thus saith the Lord; Behold, I will give this city into the hand of the Chăl-dē′ans, and into the hand of Nĕb-u-chad-rĕz′zar king of Babylon, and he shall take it:

29 And the Chăl-dē′ans, that fight against this city, shall come and set fire on this city, and burn it with the houses, upon whose roofs they have offered incense unto Bä′al, and poured out drink offerings unto other gods, to provoke me to anger.

30 For the children of Israel and the children of Jū′dah have only done evil before me from their youth: for the

16-25. Jeremiah had second thoughts after the purchase and responded with a prayer of doubt and anguish of spirit. The prophet cannot understand why God would ask him to purchase the property with the immediate destruction of the city in sight. Yet, nothing is too hard for God (cf. vs. 17); and Jeremiah's obedience and faith is an example for us to follow in similar circumstances.

26-44. God replied, using Jeremiah's own words (vs. 27 cf. vs. 17). God comforted His prophet by reassuring him that although the city will be destroyed there will one day be a restoration. **Abominations:** Idols. Pagan gods were inhabiting the Temple (see 7:30 note). **High places . . . Molech** (see 7:31 note).

children of Israel have only provoked me to anger with the work of their hands, saith the LORD.

31 For this city hath been to me *as a* provocation of mine anger and of my fury from the day that they built it even unto this day; that I should remove it from before my face,

32 Because of all the evil of the children of Israel and of the children of Jū́-dah, which they have done to provoke me to anger, they, their kings, their princes, their priests, and their prophets, and the men of Jū́dah, and the inhabitants of Jerusalem.

33 And they have turned unto me the back, and not the face: though I taught them, rising up early and teaching *them,* yet they have not hearkened to receive instruction.

34 But they set their abominations in the house, which is called by my name, to defile it.

35 And they built the high places of Bā́al, which are in the valley of the son of Hĭńnom, to cause their sons and their daughters to pass through *the fire* unto Mṓlĕch; which I commanded them not, neither came it into my mind, that they should do this abomination, to cause Jū́dah to sin.

36 ¶ And now therefore thus saith the LORD, the God of Israel, concerning this city, whereof ye say, It shall be delivered into the hand of the king of Babylon by the sword, and by the famine, and by the pestilence;

37 Behold, I will gather them out of all countries, whither I have driven them in mine anger, and in my fury, and in great wrath: and I will bring them again unto this place, and I will cause them to dwell safely:

38 And they shall be my people, and I will be their God:

39 And I will give them one heart, and one way, that they may fear me for ever, for the good of them, and of their children after them:

40 And I will make an everlasting covenant with them, that I will not turn away from them, to do them good; but I will put my fear in their hearts, that they shall not depart from me.

41 Yea, I will rejoice over them to do them good, and I will plant them in this land assuredly with my whole heart and with my whole soul.

42 For thus saith the LORD; Like as I have brought all this great evil upon this people, so will I bring upon them all the good that I have promised them.

43 And fields shall be bought in this land, whereof ye say, *It is* desolate without man or beast; it is given into the hand of the Chăl-dḗ́ans.

44 Men shall buy fields for money, and subscribe evidences, and seal *them,* and take witnesses in the land of Benjamin, and in the places about Jerusalem, and in the cities of Jū́dah, and in the cities of the mountains, and in the cities of the valley, and in the cities of the south: for I will cause their captivity to return, saith the LORD.

CHAPTER 33

MOREOVER the word of the LORD

c. Prophecy of the Davidic kingdom. 33:1-26.

33:1. Verse 1 indicates that this is a continuation of the

came unto Jĕr'e-mī'ah the second time, while he was yet shut up in the court of the prison, saying,

2 Thus saith the LORD the maker there-of, the LORD that formed it, to estab-lish it; the LORD is his name;

3 Call unto me, and I will answer thee, and shew thee great and mighty things, which thou knowest not.

4 For thus saith the LORD, the God of Israel, concerning the houses of this city, and concerning the houses of the kings of Jū'dah, which are thrown down by the mounts, and by the sword;

5 They come to fight with the Chal-dē'ans, but it is to fill them with the dead bodies of men, whom I have slain in mine anger and in my fury, and for all whose wickedness I have hid my face from this city.

6 Behold, I will bring it health and cure, and I will cure them, and will re-veal unto them the abundance of peace and truth.

7 And I will cause the captivity of Jū'-dah and the captivity of Israel to re-turn, and will build them, as at the first.

8 And I will cleanse them from all their iniquity, whereby they have sinned against me; and I will pardon all their iniquities, whereby they have sinned, and whereby they have trans-gressed against me.

9 And it shall be to me a name of joy, a praise and an honour before all the nations of the earth, which shall hear all the good that I do unto them: and they shall fear and tremble for all the goodness and for all the prosperity that I procure unto it.

10 ¶Thus saith the LORD; Again there shall be heard in this place, which ye say shall be desolate without man and without beast, even in the cities of Jū'-dah, and in the streets of Jerusalem, that are desolate, without man, and without inhabitant, and without beast,

11 The voice of joy, and the voice of gladness, the voice of the bridegroom, and the voice of the bride, the voice of them that shall say, Praise the LORD of hosts: for the LORD is good; for his mercy endureth for ever: and of them that shall bring the sacrifice of praise into the house of the LORD. For I will cause to return the captivity of the land, as at the first, saith the LORD.

12 ¶Thus saith the LORD of hosts; Again in this place, which is desolate without man and without beast, and in all the cities thereof, shall be an habita-tion of shepherds causing their flocks to lie down.

13 In the cities of the mountains, in the cities of the vale, and in the cities of the south, and in the land of Benjamin, and in the places about Jerusalem, and in the cities of Jū'dah, shall the flocks pass again under the hands of him that telleth them, saith the LORD.

14 Behold, the days come, saith the LORD, that I will perform that good thing which I have promised unto the house of Israel and to the house of Jū'-dah.

15 ¶In those days, and at that time, will I cause the Branch of righteous-

prophecy given to Jeremiah while he was shut up in the court of the prison. Jerusalem will be rebuilt and will be ruled by a righteous king.

2-13. **The maker thereof** means the Maker of the Earth. God here pledges the unchanging faithfulness of His being for the fulfillment of His promises to His people. **Mighty.** Inaccessible, hidden. The mysteries of eternity are available to the believer only through a call unto the Lord. **Thrown down by the mounts.** During the siege, the buildings near the city walls were torn down in order to provide more space for defense by the soldiers. **It.** Jerusalem. **Praise the LORD.** The liturgical formula of praise used in the Temple (Ps 135:1) will once again be upon the lips of Israel. **Return the captivity of the land.** Return to the land. **Shepherds . . . flocks.** Imagery of peace, rather than war and devastation. **Vale.** The Shephelah, the low hills and valleys between the coastal plains and the Judean hill country. **South.** The Negev (see 17:26 note).

14-18. The question of how God will accomplish His promise is answered in these verses. He will raise up a **Branch of righteousness** of the line of David, a King who will reign in righteousness. Some years earlier, a similar message had been given identifying the King as *Yahweh Tsidqenu*, Jehovah our Righteousness. **The LORD our righteousness.** The righteous

ness to grow up unto David; and he shall execute judgment and righteousness in the land.

16 In those days shall Jū'dah be saved, and Jerusalem shall dwell safely: and this *is the name* wherewith she shall be called, The LORD our righteousness.

17 ¶For thus saith the LORD; David shall never want a man to sit upon the throne of the house of Israel;

18 Neither shall the priests the Levites want a man before me to offer burnt offerings, and to kindle meat offerings, and to do sacrifice continually.

19 ¶And the word of the LORD came unto Jeremiah, saying,

20 Thus saith the LORD, If ye can break my covenant of the day, and my covenant of the night, and that there should not be day and night in their season;

21 *Then* may also my covenant be broken with David my servant, that he should not have a son to reign upon his throne; and with the Levites the priests, my ministers.

22 As the host of heaven cannot be numbered, neither the sand of the sea measured: so will I multiply the seed of David my servant, and the Levites that minister unto me.

23 ¶Moreover the word of the LORD came to Jēr-e-mī'ah, saying,

24 Considerest thou not what this people have spoken, saying, The two families which the LORD hath chosen, he hath even cast them off? thus they have despised my people, that they should be no more a nation before them.

25 ¶Thus saith the LORD; If my covenant *be* not with day and night, *and if* I have not appointed the ordinances of heaven and earth;

26 Then will I cast away the seed of Jacob, and David my servant, *so* that I will not take *any* of his seed *to be* rulers over the seed of Abraham, Isaac, and Jacob: for I will cause their captivity to return, and have mercy on them.

CHAPTER 34

THE word which came unto Jēr-e-mī'ah from the LORD, when Nēb-u-chad-nēz'zar king of Babylon, and all his army, and all the kingdoms of the earth of his dominion, and all the people, fought against Jerusalem, and against all the cities thereof, saying,

2 Thus saith the LORD, the God of Israel; Go and speak to Zĕd-e-kī'ah king of Jū'dah, and tell him, Thus saith the LORD; Behold, I will give this city into the hand of the king of Babylon, and he shall burn it with fire:

3 And thou shalt not escape out of his hand, but shalt surely be taken, and delivered into his hand: and thine eyes shall behold the eyes of the king of Babylon, and he shall speak with thee mouth to mouth, and thou shalt go to Babylon.

4 Yet hear the word of the LORD, O Zĕd-e-kī'ah king of Jū'dah; Thus saith the LORD of thee, Thou shalt not die by the sword:

5 *But* thou shalt die in peace: and

rule of a righteous king will bring about a righteous city. Of the twenty Davidic kings who reigned over Judah from David to the captivity, most of them were evil and unworthy of the name of David. In chapters 22 and 23 Jeremiah had bitterly indicted the family line. However, now he prophesies that one great King would come and reign in righteousness. With Jeremiah, we still look forward to that righteous reign of the Righteous Branch of David, the Lord Jesus Christ.

19-26. The surety of God's promise of the Righteous Branch is His covenant of day and night. Since the covenant of day and night cannot be broken, neither can His covenant with David (cf. II Sam 7:8-16). Reminiscent of God's promise of seed to Abraham (Gen 22:17), He also promises David's seed to be as the **host of heaven** and the **sand of the sea.**

3. *Warning to Zedekiah. 34:1-22.*

34:1-6. **All the kingdoms,** The Chaldean army was composed of several units from previously subjugated nations. **Jerusalem.** Here, as well as in other portions of Scripture, Jerusalem stands for the entire nation. **Thou shalt die in peace** was a conditional promise based on Zedekiah's surrender to Nebuchadnezzar. Since he refused to surrender, Zedekiah's eyes were put out; and he died in a Babylonian prison (39:7; 52:8-11; II Kgs 25:5-7; Ezk 12:13). Josephus tells us that Nebuchadnezzar honored the king's remains with a magnificent funeral (*Antiq.* 10. 8, 7). **Burn odors** were the ceremonial incense-burning at a funeral (cf. II Chr 16:14; 21:19).

with the burnings of thy fathers, the former kings which were before thee, so shall they burn odours for thee; and they will lament thee, saying, Ah lord! for I have pronounced the word, saith the LORD.

6 Then Jĕr′e-mī′ah the prophet spake all these words unto Zĕd-e-kī′ah king of Jū′dah in Jerusalem,

7 When the king of Babylon's army fought against Jerusalem, and against all the cities of Jū′dah that were left, against Lā′chish, and against A-zē′kah: for these defenced cities remained of the cities of Jū′dah.

8 ¶ This is the word that came unto Jĕr-e-mī′ah from the LORD, after that the king Zĕd-e-kī′ah had made a covenant with all the people which were at Jerusalem, to proclaim liberty unto them;

9 That every man should let his manservant, and every man his maidservant, being an Hebrew or an Hebrewess, go free; that none should serve himself of them to wit, of a Jew his brother.

10 Now when all the princes, and all the people, which had entered into the covenant, heard that every one should let his manservant, and every one his maidservant, go free, that none should serve themselves of them any more, then they obeyed, and let them go.

11 But afterward they turned, and caused the servants and the handmaids, whom they had let go free, to return, and brought them into subjection for servants and for handmaids.

12 ¶ Therefore the word of the LORD came to Jĕr-e-mī′ah from the LORD, saying,

13 Thus saith the LORD, the God of Israel; I made a covenant with your fathers in the day that I brought them forth out of the land of Egypt, out of the house of bondmen, saying,

14 At the end of seven years let ye go every man his brother an Hebrew, which hath been sold unto thee; and when he hath served thee six years, thou shalt let him go free from thee: but your fathers hearkened not unto me, neither inclined their ear.

15 And ye were now turned, and had done right in my sight, in proclaiming liberty every man to his neighbour; and ye had made a covenant before me in the house which is called by my name:

16 But ye turned and polluted my name, and caused every man his servant, and every man his handmaid, whom he had set at liberty at their pleasure, to return, and brought them into subjection, to be unto you for servants and for handmaids.

17 Therefore thus saith the LORD; Ye have not hearkened unto me, in proclaiming liberty, every one to his

7. Lachish was a large twenty-two-acre military town (Tell ed-Duweir) about thirty miles southwest of Jerusalem and fifteen miles west of Hebron. It was of immense strategic importance, since it guarded the road from Jerusalem to the Nile valley. **Azekah** (Tell ez-Zakariyeh) was another military fortress eighteen miles west-southwest of the capital, some eleven miles north of Lachish. In 1935, the Wellcome Archaeological Research Expedition discovered eighteen ostraca (three others were discovered in 1938) with inscriptions in ancient Hebrew. These Lachish Letters are dated between the two Babylonian sieges of Lachish (598-587 B.C.) and illustrate the Hebrew current in the time of Jeremiah. Both Lachish and Azekah would have to fall before Jerusalem could be captured.

8-22. Zedekiah, hoping to procure God's favor by fulfilling the commands of the Law (Ex 21:1ff.; Lev 25:39-41), released the Hebrew slaves. Shortly thereafter, the Egyptian army attacked the Babylonians, forcing the latter to lift the siege of Jerusalem temporarily in order to regroup and attack the advancing Egyptians (cf. 37:1-10). Zedekiah and the slave owners reneged on the liberation of the slaves and incurred the guilt of profaning God's name since He had been witness to the covenant (vss. 11-16; cf. Deut 15:12ff). **Seven years.** Hebrew slaves, according to the Law (Ex 21:2; Deut 15:1-15), could only be held for six years and then had to be released the seventh year. Here, the year of liberation has been included with the six years of servitude. **Cut the calf in twain.** This was the ancient Babylonian method of ratifying a covenant (cf. Gen 15:9-17), whereby the sacrificial victim was cut in half, and the covenant parties would pass between the parts. The implication was that those who violated the covenant could expect to meet the same end as the calf.

brother, and every man to his neighbour: behold, I proclaim a liberty for you, saith the LORD, to the sword, to the pestilence, and to the famine; and I will make you to be removed into all the kingdoms of the earth.

18 And I will give the men that have transgressed my covenant, which have not performed the words of the covenant which they had made before me, when they cut the calf in twain, and passed between the parts thereof,

19 The princes of Jū́dah, and the princes of Jerusalem, the eunuchs, and the priests, and all the people of the land, which passed between the parts of the calf;

20 I will even give them into the hand of their enemies, and into the hand of them that seek their life: and their dead bodies shall be for meat unto the fowls of the heaven, and to the beasts of the earth.

21 And Zĕd-e-kī́ah king of Jū́dah and his princes will I give into the hand of their enemies, and into the hand of them that seek their life, and into the hand of the king of Babylon's army, which are gone up from you.

22 Behold, I will command, saith the LORD, and cause them to return to this city; and they shall fight against it, and take it, and burn it with fire: and I will make the cities of Jū́dah a desolation without an inhabitant.

CHAPTER 35

THE word which came unto Jĕr̄́e-mī́ah from the LORD in the days of Je-hoi̇́a-kim the son of Jō-sī́ah king of Jū́dah, saying,

2 Go unto the house of the Rḗ́chab-ites, and speak unto them, and bring them into the house of the LORD, into one of the chambers, and give them wine to drink.

3 Then I took Jā-az-a-nī́ah the son of Jĕr̄́e-mī́ah, the son of Hā̆b-a-zī-nī́ah, and his brethren, and all his sons, and the whole house of the Rḗ́chab-ites;

4 And I brought them into the house of the LORD, into the chamber of the sons of Hā́nan, the son of Ig-da-lī́ah, a man of God, which was by the chamber of the princes, which was above the chamber of Mā-a-sḗ́iah the son of Shăl̄́lum, the keeper of the door.

5 And I set before the sons of the house of the Rḗ́chab-ites pots full of wine, and cups, and I said unto them, Drink ye wine.

6 But they said, We will drink no wine: for Jŏn̄́a-dăb the son of Rḗ́chab our father commanded us, saying, Ye shall drink no wine, neither ye, nor your sons for ever:

7 Neither shall ye build house, nor sow seed, nor plant vineyard, nor have any: but all your days ye shall dwell in tents; that ye may live many days in the land where ye be strangers.

8 Thus have we obeyed the voice of Jŏn̄́a-dăb the son of Rḗ́chab our father in all that he hath charged us, to drink no wine all our days, we, our wives, our sons, nor our daughters;

9 Nor to build houses for us to dwell

4. The loyalty of the Rechabites. 35:1-19.

35:1-19. Written during the reign of Jehoiakim (probably during an early siege of Jerusalem), chapter 35 reveals the glaring sin of disobedience described in the previous chapter. Jeremiah was sent by God to test the loyalty of the Rechabites, a branch of the Kenites founded by Jonadab, the son of Rechab (Num 10:29-32; Jud 1:16; II Kgs 10:15-23; I Chr 2:55). During the reign of Jehu (841-814 B.C.) the Rechabites assisted in the eradication of the Baalim from Israel (II Kgs 10:15-23). They avoided the corrupting influences of the city life, living as semi-nomads in tents and drinking no wine. Wine drinking was excessive in the ancient Near East and formed a vital part of Canaanite worship. The Nazirites also took a vow for a similar life-style (Num 6:1-21) as the Rechabites.

Since the armies of Nebuchadnezzar were ravaging the countryside, the Rechabites took refuge in Jerusalem. God, knowing the outcome of the test, had Jeremiah offer them wine to drink. When they refused on the basis of obedience to their father, God used this as an object lesson to Judah of their disobedience to Him. Judah would reap judgment for their disobedience (vs. 14), while the Rechabites would have an eternal relationship with God for their obedience. **House of the Rechabites.** Clan or group. The house was the Rechabites' religious community. **Jaazaniah** was probably the leader of the Rechabite community. This name also appears in the Lachish Letters, Ostracon I (see Thomas, p. 213). **Keeper of the door.** An ancient priestly office responsible for the allocation of funds for Temple repairs (cf. 52:24; II Kgs 12:10; 25:18).

in: neither have we vineyard, nor field, nor seed:

10 But we have dwelt in tents, and have obeyed, and done according to all that Jŏn´a-dăb our father commanded us.

11 But it came to pass, when Nĕb-u-chad-rĕz´zar king of Babylon came up into the land, that we said, Come, and let us go to Jerusalem for fear of the army of the Chăl-dē´anś, and for fear of the army of the Syrians: so we dwell at Jerusalem.

12 ¶ Then came the word of the LORD unto Jĕr´e-mī´ah, saying,

13 Thus saith the LORD of hosts, the God of Israel; Go and tell the men of Jū´dah and the inhabitants of Jeru-salem, Will ye not receive instruction to hearken to my words? saith the LORD.

14 The words of Jŏn´a-dăb the son of Rē´chăb, that he commanded his sons not to drink wine, are performed; for unto this day they drink none, but obey their father's commandment: not-withstanding I have spoken unto you, rising early and speaking; but ye hearkened not unto me.

15 I have sent also unto you all my servants the prophets, rising up early and sending them, saying, Return ye now every man from his evil way, and amend your doings, and go not after other gods to serve them, and ye shall dwell in the land which I have given to you and to your fathers: but ye have not inclined your ear, nor hearkened unto me.

16 Because the sons of Jŏn´a-dăb the son of Rē´chăb have performed the commandment of their father, which he commanded them: but this people hath not hearkened unto me:

17 Therefore thus saith the LORD God of hosts, the God of Israel; Behold, I will bring upon Jū´dah and upon all the inhabitants of Jerusalem all the evil that I have pronounced against them: because I have spoken unto them, but they have not heard; and I have called unto them, but they have not answered.

18 ¶ And Jĕr´e-mī´ah said unto the house of the Rē´chab-ites, Thus saith the LORD of hosts, the God of Israel; Be-cause ye have obeyed the command-ment of Jŏn´a-dăb your father, and kept all his precepts, and done according unto all that he hath commanded you:

19 Therefore thus saith the LORD of hosts, the God of Israel; Jŏn´a-dăb the son of Rē´chăb shall not want a man to stand before me for ever.

CHAPTER 36

AND it came to pass in the fourth year of Je-hoī´a-kĭm the son of Jō-sī´ah king of Jū´dah, that this word came unto Jĕr´e-mī´ah from the LORD, saying,

5. Jehoiakim's opposition. 36:1-32.

36:1. With chapter 36 we have the first actual recording of Jeremiah's prophecy. In the fourth year of the reign of Jehoiakim (see 25:1ff.) God commanded His prophet to write down his oracles. Jeremiah dictated these words to Baruch, his faithful friend and secretary, who wrote them upon a scroll. It was as common in those days for a professional man to dictate to a secretary as it is today. Once completed, Baruch read the scroll to the people at the Temple, then to the princes, who advised Baruch and Jeremiah to hide while they read the scroll to the king. Jehoiakim violently reacted to the prophecy and destroyed the scroll. Jeremiah was then instructed to compile a new scroll with several additional words.

2-7. A roll of a book. A blank (perhaps papyrus) scroll on which a text was written in parallel columns necessitating the unrolling of it as one read. The actual contents of the scroll are unknown, although it was probably an anthology of all the prophet's prophecies to date (626-605 B.C.). **Baruch** was Jeremiah's secretary (see 32:12 note). **Shut up.** Although this same Hebrew word is used for imprisonment (33:1; 39:15), here it simply means detainment. Jeremiah was free to escape at will (vs. 19), and God hid His prophet and Baruch from the evil monarch (vs. 26). **Fasting day.** Fasts at this time were being proclaimed for the national crisis. Although this actual fast is unknown, it ensured a crowd for the reading of the scroll. **Will return every one from his evil way.** The prophecy was conditional; failure to repent would seal the nation's doom.

8-10. With the completion of the writing, Baruch reads the scroll in the Temple on the fast day. **Fifth year . . . ninth month.** December. Some commentators believe that the monarch's regnal year was reckoned from October, the seventh month, making this December of 605 B.C., rather than a year later. **Gemariah** (see 29:3 note) **The higher court.** The inner court of I Kings 6:36; 7:12.

11-19. Michaiah, Gemariah's son reported the reading of the scroll to the conclave of princes meeting in the King's house. **Elishama** was the secretary; perhaps he can be identified with the Elishama of 41:1 and II Kings 25:25. **Elnathan.** (see 26:22). This name is confirmed by Ostracon III at Lachish (Thomas, p. 214). **Jehudi** was otherwise unknown; but he must have been a man of some importance, since his genealogy is traced to the third generation. The princes, though fearful of Jeremiah, were sympathetic to him and instructed Baruch to hide the prophet while they read the scroll to the king.

2 Take thee a roll of a book, and write therein all the words that I have spoken unto thee against Israel, and against Jū́dah, and against all the nations, from the day I spake unto thee, from the days of Jō-sī́ah, even unto this day.

3 It may be that the house of Jū́dah will hear all the evil which I purpose to do unto them; that they may return every man from his evil way; that I may forgive their iniquity and their sin.

4 Then Jeremiah called Bā́ruch the son of Ne-rī́ah: and Bā́ruch wrote from the mouth of Jĕr'e-mī́ah all the words of the LORD, which he had spoken unto him, upon a roll of a book.

5 And Jĕr'e-mī́ah commanded Bā́ruch, saying, I am shut up; I cannot go into the house of the LORD:

6 Therefore go thou, and read in the roll, which thou hast written from my mouth, the words of the LORD in the ears of the people in the LORD's house upon the fasting day: and also thou shalt read them in the ears of all Jū́dah that come out of their cities.

7 It may be they will present their supplication before the LORD, and will return every one from his evil way: for great is the anger and the fury that the LORD hath pronounced against this people.

8 And Bā́ruch the son of Ne-rī́ah did according to all that Jĕr'e-mī́ah the prophet commanded him, reading in the book the words of the LORD in the LORD's house.

9 And it came to pass in the fifth year of Je-hoī́a-kĭm the son of Jō-sī́ah king of Jū́dah, in the ninth month, that they proclaimed a fast before the LORD to all the people in Jerusalem, and to all the people that came from the cities of Jū́dah unto Jerusalem.

10 Then read Bā́ruch in the book the words of Jĕr'e-mī́ah in the house of the LORD, in the chamber of Gĕm-a-rī́ah the son of Shā́phan the scribe, in the higher court, at the entry of the new gate of the LORD's house, in the ears of all the people.

11 ¶When Mī-chā́iah the son of Gĕm-a-rī́ah, the son of Shā́phan, had heard out of the book all the words of the LORD,

12 Then he went down into the king's house, into the scribe's chamber: and, lo, all the princes sat there, even E-lĭsh́-a-ma the scribe, and Dĕl-a-ī́ah the son of Shĕm-a-ī́ah, and Ĕl'nā-than the son of Ăch́bŏr, and Gĕm-a-rī́ah the son of Shā́phan, and Zĕd-e-kī́ah the son of Hăn-a-nī́ah, and all the princes.

13 Then Mī-chā́iah declared unto them all the words that he had heard, when Bā́ruch read the book in the ears of the people.

14 Therefore all the princes sent Je-hū́dī the son of Nĕth-a-nī́ah, the son of Shĕl-e-mī́ah, the son of Cū́shī, unto Bā́ruch, saying, Take in thine hand the roll wherein thou hast read in the ears of the people, and come. So Bā́ruch the son of Ne-rī́ah took the roll in his hand, and came unto them.

15 And they said unto him, Sit down

now, and read it in our ears. So Bả′ruch read it in their ears.

16 Now it came to pass, when they had heard all the words, they were afraid both one and other, and said unto Bả′ruch, We will surely tell the king of all these words.

17 And they asked Bả′ruch, saying, Tell us now, How didst thou write all these words at his mouth?

18 Then Bả′ruch answered them, He pronounced all these words unto me with his mouth, and I wrote them with ink in the book.

19 Then said the princes unto Bả′ruch, Go, hide thee, thou and Jẽr′e-mī′-ah; and let no man know where ye be.

20 ¶And they went in to the king into the court, but they laid up the roll in the chamber of E-lī′sh′a-ma the scribe, and told all the words in the ears of the king.

21 So the king sent Je-hū′dī to fetch the roll: and he took it out of E-lī′sh′a-ma the scribe's chamber. And Je-hū′dī read it in the ears of the king, and in the ears of all the princes which stood beside the king.

22 Now the king sat in the winterhouse in the ninth month: and there was a fire on the hearth burning before him.

23 And it came to pass, that when Je-hū′dī had read three or four leaves, he cut it with the penknife, and cast it into the fire that was on the hearth, until all the roll was consumed in the fire that was on the hearth.

24 Yet they were not afraid, nor rent their garments, neither the king, nor any of his servants that heard all these words.

25 Nevertheless Ĕl′nā-than and Dĕl-a-ī′ah and Gĕm-a-rī′ah had made intercession to the king that he would not burn the roll: but he would not hear them.

26 But the king commanded Je-răh′me-el the son of Hăm′me-lĕch, and Se-ra-ī′ah the son of Ăz′rī-el, and Shĕl-e-mī′ah the son of Ăb′de-el, to take Bả′ruch the scribe and Jẽr-e-mī′ah the prophet: but the LORD hid them.

27 ¶Then the word of the LORD came to Jẽr-e-mī′ah, after that the king had burned the roll, and the words which Bả′ruch wrote at the mouth of Jẽr-e-mī′-ah, saying,

28 Take thee again another roll, and write in it all the former words that were in the first roll, which Je-hoi′a-kīm the king of Jū′dah hath burned.

29 And thou shalt say to Je-hoi′a-kīm king of Jū′dah, Thus saith the LORD; Thou hast burned this roll, saying, Why hast thou written therein, saying, The king of Babylon shall certainly come and destroy this land, and shall cause to cease from thence man and beast?

30 Therefore thus saith the LORD of Je-hoi′a-kīm king of Jū′dah: He shall have none to sit upon the throne of Da′-vid: and his dead body shall be cast out in the day to the heat, and in the night to the frost.

31 And I will punish him and his seed and his servants for their iniquity; and I

20-26. Jehudi now reads the scroll before Jehoiakim, who with impassioned rage cuts each column and burns it in a fire. **Winter house**. The winterized portion of the palace. In two-story Palestinian homes, the ground floor was generally used during the winter, while the upper floor with its superior ventilation was used in the summer. **Hearth**. Since the Jewish calendar began in the Spring, this was the month of December when Jerusalem can be quite chilly and occasionally even experience snow. **Penknife**. A scribe's knife used for sharpening reed pens and for trimming or cutting papyrus rolls. **Leaves**. Columns. **Yet they were not afraid**. Baruch is astonished at the lack of respect and fear of the word of the Lord. He expected the king and the princes to express a repentant spirit, as Josiah did when he heard the Law read (II Kgs 22:11). **Jerahmeel the son of Hammelech**. Jerahmeel, the king's son, otherwise unknown, may be an honorific title for a member of the royal household (cf. 39:6; I Kgs 22:26). **The LORD hid them**. The Hebrew text makes it clear that Jeremiah and Baruch would have suffered the same fate as **Urijah** (26:20-23), except for divine intervention. The LXX is less forceful with its translation "and they were hidden."

27-32. After Jehoiakim destroyed the first scroll, Jeremiah, while in hiding, was commanded to rewrite his prophecy (vs. 32) with additional predictions (vs. 28) concerning **David** (vs. 30). Since Jehoiakim burned the original scroll, he would be punished by being deprived of a permanent successor. This prediction was literally fulfilled, as Jehoiachin his son reigned for only three months before he was exiled. **Dead body**. Although the exact manner of Jehoiakim's death is not recorded, some have conjectured, on the basis of this verse, that he died in a palace coup (see 22:19 note). **Many like words**. Jehoiakim could burn the scroll of Jeremiah, but he could not destroy the Word of God; so today men may burn the paper, but they will never destroy "The Book."

will bring upon them, and upon the inhabitants of Jerusalem, and upon the men of Jū́dah, all the evil that I have pronounced against them; but they hearkened not.

32 ¶Then took Jĕr′e-mī′ah another roll, and gave it to Bâr′uch the scribe, the son of Ne-rī′ah: who wrote therein from the mouth of Jĕr′e-mī′ah all the words of the book which Jĕ-hoī′a-kĭm king of Jū́dah had burned in the fire: and there were added besides unto them many like words.

CHAPTER 37

AND king Zĕd-e-kī′ah the son of Jō-sī′ah reigned instead of Co-nī′ah the son of Jĕ-hoī′a-kĭm, whom Nĕb-u-chad-rĕz′zar king of Babylon made king in the land of Jū́dah.

2 But neither he, nor his servants, nor the people of the land, did hearken unto the words of the LORD, which he spake by the prophet Jĕr′e-mī′ah.

3 And Zĕd-e-kī′ah the king sent Je-hū′cal the son of Shĕl-e-mī′ah and Zĕph-a-nī′ah the son of Mā-a-sē′iah the priest to the prophet Jĕr′e-mī′ah, saying, Pray now unto the LORD our God for us.

4 Now Jĕr′e-mī′ah came in and went out among the people: for they had not put him into prison.

5 Then Pharaoh's army was come forth out of Egypt: and when the Chăl-dē′ans that besieged Jerusalem heard tidings of them, they departed from Jerusalem.

6 ¶Then came the word of the LORD unto the prophet Jĕr′e-mī′ah, saying,

7 Thus saith the LORD, the God of Israel; Thus shall ye say to the king of Jū́dah, that sent you unto me to enquire of me; Behold, Pharaoh's army, which is come forth to help you, shall return to Egypt into their own land.

8 And the Chăl-dē′ans shall come again, and fight against this city, and take it, and burn it with fire.

9 ¶Thus saith the LORD; Deceive not yourselves, saying, The Chăl-dē′ans shall surely depart from us: for they shall not depart.

10 For though ye had smitten the whole army of the Chăl-dē′ans that fight against you, and there remained but wounded men among them, yet should they rise up every man in his tent, and burn this city with fire.

11 ¶And it came to pass, that when the army of the Chăl-dē′ans was broken up from Jerusalem for fear of Pharaoh's army,

12 Then Jĕr′e-mī′ah went forth out of Jerusalem to go into the land of Benjamin, to separate himself thence in the midst of the people.

13 And when he was in the gate of Benjamin, a captain of the ward was there, whose name was Ĭ-rī′jah, the son of Shĕl-e-mī′ah, the son of Hăn-a-nī′ah; and he took Jĕr′e-mī′ah the prophet, saying, Thou fallest away to the Chăl-dē′ans.

14 Then said Jĕr′e-mī′ah, It is false; I fall not away to the Chăl-dē′ans. But he hearkened not to him: so Ĭ-rī′jah took

6. The siege of Jerusalem. 37:1—39:18.

The following three chapters tell of the dismal days of the siege and fall of Jerusalem.

a. Jeremiah's interview with Zedekiah. 37:1-10.

During the reign of the weak and vacillating Zedekiah, Nebuchadnezzar besieged Jerusalem. When Pharaoh Hophra's army came to Zedekiah's aid, the Chaldeans withdrew from Jerusalem. God sent Jeremiah to Zedekiah with the warning not to place hope in Egypt, for they would be defeated and the siege of Jerusalem resumed.

37:1-4. Whom Nebuchadnezzar . . . made king. Nebuchadnezzar made Zedekiah, not Coniah (Jehoiachin), king over Judah. The AV follows the Hebrew word order, which is somewhat confusing. **Jehucal** is called **Jucal** in 38:1-6, where he urges the execution of Jeremiah for treason. Here Jehucal is sent by Zedekiah to ask Jeremiah to intercede for the people. Zedekiah was not strong-willed like Jehoiakim. Being weak and vacillating, he was led by the whims of the evil princes who came to power during the reign of Jehoiakim. A similar deputation was sent by Zedekiah to Jeremiah in chapter 21. Although there are many similarities, the two events are separate. The former occurred during the siege, while the latter took place when the siege was temporarily lifted.

5-10. Pharaoh's army. Pharaoh Hophra (cf. 44:30), who reigned from 589 to 570 B.C. and supported Zedekiah's revolt against Nebuchadnezzar (Ezk 17:11-21). **Wounded men.** This forceful expression demonstrates that God is never at a loss for means to accomplish His purposes (cf. Mt 3:9). Even if the Babylonian army were reduced to only wounded men, God would raise them up out of their tents and burn this city with fire.

b. Jeremiah's imprisonment. 37:11—38:13.

11. Jeremiah took advantage of the lifting of the siege to visit Anathoth, but he was falsely accused of treason and placed in prison.

12-15. Separate himself thence. A difficult Hebrew construction often translated to receive his portion there. **Gate of Benjamin.** A gate in the north wall of the city and leading to the Benjamite territory (38:7; Zech 14:10). **Captain of the ward.** Sentinel. **Irijah.** Otherwise unknown. **Princes.** Rulers who were much more hostile toward Jeremiah than those under Jehoiakim. **Jonathan.** Otherwise unknown. His house was converted into an emergency prison in order to house the many suspected deserters (cf. 38:19; 39:9; 52:15).

1494

Jĕr'e-mī'ah, and brought him to the princes.

15 Wherefore the princes were wroth with Jĕr'e-mī'ah, and smote him, and put him in prison in the house of Jona-than the scribe: for they had made that the prison.

16 ¶ When Jĕr'e-mī'ah was entered into the dungeon, and into the cabins, and Jĕr'e-mī'ah had remained there many days;

17 Then Zĕd-e-kī'ah the king sent, and took him out: and the king asked him secretly in his house, and said, Is there any word from the Lord? And Jĕr'e-mī'ah said, There is: for, said he, thou shalt be delivered into the hand of the king of Babylon.

18 Moreover Jĕr'e-mī'ah said unto king Zĕd-e-kī'ah, What have I offended against thee, or against thy servants, or against this people, that ye have put me in prison?

19 Where are now your prophets which prophesied unto you, saying, The king of Babylon shall not come against you, nor against this land?

20 Therefore hear now, I pray thee, O my lord the king: let my supplication, I pray thee, be accepted before thee; that thou cause me not to return to the house of Jonathan the scribe, lest I die there.

21 Then Zĕd-e-kī'ah the king com-manded that they should commit Jĕr'e-mī'ah into the court of the prison, and that they should give him daily a piece of bread out of the bakers' street, until all the bread in the city were spent. Thus Jĕr'e-mī'ah remained in the court of the prison.

CHAPTER 38

THEN Shĕph-a-tī'ah the son of Mǎt-tan, and Gĕd-a-lī'ah the son of Pǎsh'ur, and Jū'cal the son of Shĕl-e-mī'ah, and Pǎsh'ur the son of Mǎl-chī'ah, heard the words that Jĕr'e-mī'ah had spoken unto all the people, saying,

2 Thus saith the Lord, He that re-maineth in this city shall die by the sword, by the famine, and by the pesti-lence: but he that goeth forth to the Chǎl-dē'ans shall live; for he shall have his life for a prey, and shall live.

3 Thus saith the Lord, This city shall surely be given into the hand of the king of Babylon's army, which shall take it.

4 Therefore the princes said unto the king, We beseech thee, let this man be put to death: for thus he weakeneth the hands of the men of war that remain in this city, and the hands of all the peo-ple, in speaking such words unto them: for this man seeketh not the wel-fare of this people, but the hurt.

5 Then Zĕd-e-kī'ah the king said, Be-hold, he is in your hand: for the king is not he that can do any thing against you.

6 Then took they Jĕr'e-mī'ah and cast him into the dungeon of Mǎl-chī'ah the son of Hǎm'me-lech, that was in the court of the prison: and they let down Jĕr'e-mī'ah with cords. And in the dun-

16-21 While in prison, Zedekiah secretly (for fear of the princes) inquired of Jeremiah if there was any word from the Lord. Again the reply was one of inevitable doom. Jeremiah took the opportunity to request more humane conditions. Zede-kiah asserted himself at least long enough to transfer the prophet from the unsanitary subterranean dungeon to a more suitable prison. **Cabins.** Cells or vaults. **Court of the prison.** The palace prison was not a maximum-security facility, such as the dungeon of 37:15 and 38:6 was. **Piece of bread.** Loaf of bread. **Bakers' street.** A name typical of the ancient Near East (and even today) where each trade or craft had its own street.

The prophet's stay in the court of the prison was short-lived. The princes besought Zedekiah to put Jeremiah to death for weakening the morale of the fighting forces. The king ac-quiesced, and the princes cast Jeremiah into a waterless cistern letting him down by cords to the bottom of the pit, where he sank into the mire and was left to die. This was Jeremiah's ultimate test. God, however, intervened and used an insignifi-cant person Ebed-melech, an Ethiopian eunuch, to rescue His prophet.

38:1-13. Shephatiah. A princely ruler who is otherwise un-known. **Gedaliah.** Not the governor who was assassinated (39:14; 40:5; 41:18). He is otherwise unknown. **Jucal** (see 37:3 note). **Pashur** (see 21:2 note). **He weakeneth the hands.** He is a traitor. The same accusation was made against certain people in Jerusalem by an anonymous patriotic official in one of the Lachish Letters (Ostracon VI). **He is in your hand.** Zedekiah was secretly in sympathy with Jeremiah; but, consumed by fear, he released Jeremiah to the princes (compare Pilate's treatment of Jesus, Jn 18:28-19:16). **Dungeon.** Cistern. Cisterns were very common in the ancient Near East. Water was collected in them in the winter rainy season and was stored for use during the dry summer (cf. II Kgs 18:31; Prov 5:15). Since the water had been consumed from this cistern, Jeremiah sank into the mud and would have suffocated except for the intervention of Ebed-melech who persuaded Zedekiah to change his mind again. **Ethiopian.** Ethiopia (Kush) means the upper area of the Nile and not the present land of that name. The Ethiopians were dark-skinned (13:23); and due to their skill in commerce, many were wealthy (Isa 43:3; 45:14). **Eunuchs.** Generally, designation for a court or palace official (cf. 29:2; Gen 39:1), here, however, it may actually refer to a foreign castrate who was the only one who cared enough to save the prophet. **Thirty men.** One He-brew manuscript and the LXX read three men, which seems to be more appropriate.

geon *there was* no water, but mire: so Jĕr´e-mī´ah sunk in the mire.

7 ¶Now when Ē´bed-mĕ´lech the Ē-thī-ō´pǐ-an, one of the eunuchs which was in the king's house, heard that they had put Jĕr´e-mī´ah in the dungeon; the king then sitting in the gate of Ben-jamin;

8 Ē´bed-mĕ´lech went forth out of the king's house, and spake to the king, saying,

9 My lord the king, these men have done evil in all that they have done to Jĕr´e-mī´ah the prophet, whom they have cast into the dungeon; and he is like to die for hunger in the place where he is: for *there is* no more bread in the city.

10 Then the king commanded Ē´bed-mĕ´lech the Ē-thī-ō´pǐ-an, saying, Take from hence thirty men with thee, and take up Jĕr´e-mī´ah the prophet out of the dungeon, before he die.

11 So Ē´bed-mĕ´lech took the men with him, and went into the house of the king under the treasury, and took thence old cast clouts and old rotten rags, and let them down by cords into the dungeon to Jĕr´e-mī´ah.

12 And Ē´bed-mĕ´lech the Ē-thī-ō´pǐ-an said unto Jĕr´e-mī´ah, Put now these old cast clouts and rotten rags under thine armholes under the cords. And Jĕr´e-mī´ah did so.

13 So they drew up Jĕr´e-mī´ah with cords and took him up out of the dungeon: and Jĕr´e-mī´ah remained in the court of the prison.

14 ¶Then Zĕd-e-kī´ah the king sent, and took Jĕr´e-mī´ah the prophet unto him into the third entry that *is* in the house of the LORD: and the king said unto Jĕr´e-mī´ah, I will ask thee a thing; hide nothing from me.

15 Then Jĕr´e-mī´ah said unto Zĕd-e-kī´ah, If I declare *it* unto thee, wilt thou not surely put me to death? and if I give thee counsel, wilt thou not hearken unto me?

16 So Zĕd-e-kī´ah the king sware secretly unto Jĕr´e-mī´ah saying, *As the* LORD liveth, that made us this soul, I will not put thee to death, neither will I give thee into the hand of these men that seek thy life.

17 Then said Jĕr´e-mī´ah unto Zĕd-e-kī´ah, Thus saith the LORD, the God of hosts, the God of Israel; If thou wilt assuredly go forth unto the king of Babylon's princes, then thy soul shall live, and this city shall not be burned with fire; and thou shalt live, and thine house:

18 But if thou wilt not go forth to the king of Babylon's princes, then shall this city be given into the hand of the Chăl-dē´ans, and they shall burn it with fire, and thou shalt not escape out of their hand.

19 And Zĕd-e-kī´ah the king said unto Jĕr´e-mī´ah, I am afraid of the Jews that are fallen to the Chăl-dē´ans, lest they deliver me into their hand, and they mock me.

20 But Jĕr´e-mī´ah said, They shall not deliver *thee*. Obey, I beseech thee, the voice of the LORD, which I speak

c. A final appeal. 38:14-28.

Zedekiah, one last time, calls for Jeremiah to give him a word from the Lord. The message is still the same. Unless Zedekiah surrenders, the city will be burned and the inhabitants either killed or exiled.

14-28. Third entry. Perhaps the royal entry (cf. II Kgs 16:18). **Thy soul shall live.** Your life will be spared. In ancient warfare rebel kings were usually mutilated and put to death. Unless he obeyed the word of the Lord, the prospects for Zedekiah were not pleasant. **Jews that are fallen.** Zedekiah's vacillating nature is seen again as he tacitly agrees that Nebuchadnezzar will spare his life, yet he is afraid of the Jews who had already deserted the Babylonians. **All the women . . . back.** Jeremiah sees the palace women chanting an elegiac poem. This lament is in a qinah measure (see the introduction to Lamentations).

JEREMIAH 38:21

unto thee: so it shall be well with thee, and thy soul shall live.

21 But if thou refuse to go forth, this *is* the word that the Lord hath shewed me:

22 And, behold, all the women that are left in the king of Ju'dah's house *shall be* brought forth to the king of Baby-lon's princes, and those women shall say, Thy friends have set thee on, and have prevailed against thee: thy feet are sunk in the mire, *and* they are turned away back.

23 So they shall bring out all thy wives and thy children to the Chal-de'-ans: and thou shalt not escape out of their hand, but shalt be taken by the hand of the king of Babylon: and thou shalt cause this city to be burned with fire.

24 ¶ Then said Zed-e-ki'ah unto Jer-e-mi'ah, Let no man know of these words, and thou shalt not die.

25 But if the princes hear that I have talked with thee, and they come unto thee, and say unto thee, Declare unto us now what thou hast said unto the king, hide it not from us, and we will not put thee to death; also what the king said unto thee:

26 Then thou shalt say unto them, I presented my supplication before the king, that he would not cause me to re-turn to Jonathan's house, to die there.

27 Then came all the princes unto Jer-e-mi'ah, and asked him: and he told them according to all these words that the king had commanded. So they left off speaking with him; for the matter was not perceived.

28 So Jer-e-mi'ah abode in the court of the prison until the day that Jeru-salem was taken: and he was *there* when Jerusalem was taken.

CHAPTER 39

IN the ninth year of Zed-e-ki'ah king of Ju'dah, in the tenth month, came Neb-u-chad-rez'zar king of Babylon and all his army against Jerusalem, and they besieged it.

2 *And* in the eleventh year of Zed-e-ki'ah, in the fourth month, the ninth day of the month, the city was broken up.

3 And all the princes of the king of Babylon came in, and sat in the middle gate, *even* Ner'gal-sha-re'zer, Sam'gar-ne'bo, Sar'se-kim, Rab-sa-ris, Ner'-gal-sha-re'zer, Rab'-mag, with all the residue of the princes of the king of Babylon.

4 ¶ And it came to pass, *that* when Zed-e-ki'ah the king of Ju'dah saw them, and all the men of war, then they fled, and went forth out of the city by night, by the way of the king's garden, by the gate betwixt the two walls: and he went out the way of the plain.

5 But the Chal-de'ans' army pursued after them, and overtook Zed-e-ki'ah in the plains of Jericho: and when they had taken him, they brought him up to Rib'lah in the land of Ha'math, where he gave judgment upon him.

6 Then the king of Babylon slew the

d. The fall of Jerusalem, 39:1-18.

After a year-and-a-half siege, Jerusalem finally fell to the Babylonians. The siege began in January of 587 B.C. and, except for a brief interval of false hope in the summer (37:11), continued until 586 B.C. when all hope collapsed. Zedekiah escaped by night, but was captured by the Chaldean army in the plains of Jericho and taken to Nebuchadnezzar at Riblah. Nebuchadnez-zar slew Zedekiah's sons before his own eyes, blinded him, and sent him in shackles to Babylon. Except for 39:3 and 14, a greater description of the capture and destruction of Jerusalem is given in the historical appendix in chapter 52 (cf. II Kgs 25:1-12; II Chr 36:17-21). Nebuzaradan, the military governor, carried the inhabitants of Jerusalem off into Babylon; and only the poor were left to attend the fields and vineyards.

39:1-3. With the finding of a clay prism listing high officials of the Babylonian court, much light has been shed upon this verse. Three officials and their titles are listed here, rather than six different persons. **Nergal-sharezer,** the **Samgar-nebo** (the meaning of his title is unknown) and **Nergal-sharezer, Sarsechim,** the **Rab-saris** (chief of the eunuchs) and **Nergal-sharezer,** the **Rab-mag** (the meaning of this title is also unknown).

4-10. The king's garden was located near the Pool of Siloam (cf. Neh 3:15). **The gate** between the two walls was probably the Fountain Gate (Neh 2:14; 12:37). **The plain.** The plain (Heb *Arabah*) was the deep Jordan Valley north of the Dead Sea. **Nebuzar-adan the captain of the guard.** He was the military governor of Nebuchadnezzar who arrived a month after the city had fallen (52:12). This name appears on several Babylonian lists as the chief baker. Since the noun translated guard comes from the root meaning to kill, it can then mean butcher, cook, or executioner.

sons of Zĕd-e-kī'ah in Rĭb'lah before his eyes: also the king of Babylon slew all the nobles of Jū'dah.

7 Moreover he put out Zĕd-e-kī'ah's eyes, and bound him with chains, to carry him to Babylon.

8 And the Chăl-dē'ans burned the king's house, and the houses of the people, with fire, and brake down the walls of Jerusalem.

9 ¶Then Nĕb'u-zar-ā'dan the captain of the guard carried away captive into Babylon the remnant of the people that remained in the city, and those that fell away, that fell to him, with the rest of the people that remained.

10 But Nĕb'u-zar-ā'dan the captain of the guard left of the poor of the people, which had nothing, in the land of Jū'dah, and gave them vineyards and fields at the same time.

11 ¶Now Nĕb'u-chad-rĕz'zar king of Babylon gave charge concerning Jĕr-e-mī'ah to Nĕb'u-zar-ā'dan the captain of the guard, saying,

12 Take him, and look well to him, and do him no harm; but do unto him even as he shall say unto thee.

13 So Nĕb'u-zar-ā'dan the captain of the guard sent, and Nĕb-u-shăs'băn, Răb'-sa-rĭs, and Ner'găl-sha-rē'zer, Răb'-măg, and all the king of Babylon's princes;

14 Even they sent, and took Jĕr'e-mī'ah out of the court of the prison, and committed him unto Gĕd-a-lī'ah the son of A-hī'kam the son of Shā'phan, that he should carry him home: so he dwelt among the people.

15 ¶Now the word of the LORD came unto Jĕr'e-mī'ah, while he was shut up in the court of the prison, saying,

16 Go and speak to E'bed-mĕ'lech the E-thī-ō'pi-an, saying, Thus saith the LORD of hosts, the God of Israel; Behold, I will bring my words upon this city for evil, and not for good; and they shall be *accomplished* in that day before thee.

17 But I will deliver thee in that day, saith the LORD: and thou shalt not be given into the hand of the men of whom thou art afraid.

18 For I will surely deliver thee, and thou shalt not fall by the sword, but thy life shall be for a prey unto thee: because thou hast put thy trust in me, saith the LORD.

CHAPTER 40

THE word that came to Jĕr'e-mī'ah from the LORD, after that Nĕb'u-zar-ā'dan the captain of the guard had let him go from Rā'mah, when he had taken him being bound in chains among all that were carried away captive of Jerusalem and Jū'dah, which were carried away captive unto Babylon.

11-14. God did not forget His promise to deliver His prophet (1:8). Nebuchadnezzar instructed Nebuzar-adan to treat Jeremiah with the deference and respect of their own Babylonian seers. Although some have questioned Nebuchadnezzar's kind treatment of Jeremiah, his name was no doubt on the intelligence list Nebuchadnezzar received concerning pro-Babylonians in Jerusalem. **Gedaliah** was the Hebrew puppet governor appointed by Nebuchadnezzar to rule over the poor people left in the land. He was later assassinated by Ishmael (41:2). **Ahikam** was the man who saved Jeremiah's life earlier (26:24).

15-18. The chapter closes with a divine promise of deliverance for Ebed-melech, the Ethiopian who persuaded Zedekiah to release Jeremiah from the slimy pit dungeon. **While he was shut up** means while he was still in the court of the prison. Chronologically, this oracle should come at the end of chapter 38, when Jeremiah had spoken privately with Zedekiah. **Men of whom thou art afraid.** Ebed-melech was afraid of being punished by the princes who wanted revenge for his accusations of their cruel and inhuman behavior toward Jeremiah. However, his faith in God and the courageous demonstration of that faith was rewarded with the divine promise of security. God never forgets His own. Even as He delivered His prophet (vss. 11-14), He also delivered His lowly servant (vss. 15-18).

C. After the Fall of Jerusalem. 40:1—45:5.

The last years of Jeremiah's life were spent in mournful retrospect of a people who refused to heed his message. Choosing to remain with the remnant of Judah after the fall of Jerusalem, rather than the ease of perhaps a political pension in Babylon, he was then forced to go with that remnant to idolatrous Egypt where he died.

1. Jeremiah's ministry to the remnant in the land. 40:1—42:22.

a. Jeremiah chooses to remain with Gedaliah. 40:1-6.

40:1. Ramah. A Benjamite town (modern Er-Ram) about five miles north of Jerusalem. This town had been selected as a general staging-area from which the deportees would leave for Babylon. The apparent discrepancy of Jeremiah's release from Jerusalem (39:11-14) and Ramah (40:1) has two possible explanations. Because of Ramah's close proximity to Jerusalem, it may have been omitted from the first account. More probably, though, Jeremiah was released in Jerusalem and, caught up

2 And the captain of the guard took Jĕr-e-mī'ah, and said unto him, The Lord thy God hath pronounced this evil upon this place.

3 Now the Lord hath brought it, and done according as he hath said: because ye have sinned against the Lord, and have not obeyed his voice, therefore this thing is come upon you.

4 And now, behold, I loose thee this day from the chains which were upon thine hand. If it seem good unto thee to come with me into Babylon, come; and I will look well unto thee: but if it seem ill unto thee to come with me into Babylon, forbear: behold, all the land is before thee: whither it seemeth good and convenient for thee to go, thither go.

5 Now while he was not yet gone back, he said, Go back also to Gĕd-a-lī'ah the son of A-hī'kam the son of Shā'phan, whom the king of Babylon hath made governor over the cities of Jū'dah, and dwell with him among the people: or go wheresoever it seemeth convenient unto thee to go. So the captain of the guard gave him victuals and a reward, and let him go.

6 Then went Jĕr'e-mī'ah unto Gĕd-a-lī'ah the son of A-hī'kam to Mizpah; and dwelt with him among the people that were left in the land.

7 Now when all the captains of the forces which were in the fields, even they and their men, heard that the king of Babylon had made Gĕd-a-lī'ah the son of A-hī'kam governor in the land, and had committed unto him men, and women, and children, and of the poor of the land, of them that were not carried away captive to Babylon;

8 Then they came to Gĕd-a-lī'ah to Mizpah, even Ish'ma-el the son of Nĕth-a-nī'ah, and Jō-hā'nan and Jona'than the sons of Ka-rē'ah, and Se-ra-ī'ah the son of Tan'hu-meth, and the sons of E'phai the Ne-tŏph'a-thīte, and Jĕz-a-nī'ah the son of a Mā-ăch'a-thīte, they and their men.

9 And Gĕd-a-lī'ah the son of A-hī'kam the son of Shā'phan sware unto them and to their men, saying, Fear not to serve the Chăl-dē'ans: dwell in the land, and serve the king of Babylon, and it shall be well with you.

10 As for me, behold, I will dwell at Mizpah, to serve the Chăl-dē'ans, which will come unto us: but ye, gather ye wine, and summer fruits, and oil, and put them in your vessels, and dwell in your cities that ye have taken.

11 Likewise when all the Jews that were in Moab, and among the Ammonites, and in Edom, and that were in all the countries, heard that the king of Babylon had left a remnant of Jū'dah, and that he had set over them Gĕd-a-lī'ah the son of A-hī'kam the son of Shā'phan;

12 Even all the Jews returned out of all places whither they were driven, and came to the land of Jū'dah, to Gĕd-a-lī'ah, unto Mizpah, and gathered wine and summer fruits very much.

13 ¶ Moreover Jō-hā'nan the son of

c. *The plot against Gedaliah.* 40:13-16.

13-16. Not all the Jews were reconciled to their subjection to

among the deportees, he was shackled and brought to Ramah. After this embarrassing error, Jeremiah was again released at Ramah.

2-4. Critics have had a heyday with this speech of Nebuzaradan in which the Babylonian general sounds more like a Hebrew prophet. No doubt the Babylonians had received several intelligence reports concerning Jeremiah's stand and activities. The Assyrians also studied the religious beliefs and practices of their enemies for use in psychological warfare (II Kgs 18:22, 33-35). It is in keeping with the message of Jeremiah that a pagan would comprehend the metaphysical causes for Judah's denial sooner than the Israelites themselves. **Ye have sinned.** The people have sinned.

5-6. **Gedaliah the son of Ahikam** (see 39:14 note). In 1935 a seal inscribed "belonging to Gedaliah, the one who is over the house" was found in the ashes left by Nebuchadnezzar when he burned Lachish. **Mizpah**, Gedaliah's headquarters were about seven miles north of Jerusalem. It is identified with Tell en-Nasbeh.

b. *Gedaliah's governorship.* 40:7-12.

7-12. In addition to the poor people, there were bands of guerrilla warriors roaming the Judean countryside. Gedaliah's responsibility was to help the remnant settle down, till the land, and pay tribute to Babylon from the harvest. Economic and political stability could only be obtained by pacifying the bands of guerrillas. It is a tribute to Gedaliah that he was able to do this without military action. One by one, at least six different guerrilla leaders became convinced of his ability to lead them without reprisal from the Babylonians.

The length of his governorship is not recorded. Some (i.e., Leslie) have held that he ruled for only two months. However, the circumstances seem to indicate a longer period. The three deportations (see 52:28-30 note) to Babylon suggest a five-year governorship. His successful rule came to a tragic end when he was assassinated by Ishmael, one of the guerrilla leaders.

Ishmael was a guerrilla leader of a royal family (II Kgs 25:25) who became a turncoat and assassinated Gedaliah (41:2). **Joha-nan** was the loyal lieutenant of Gedaliah; he rescued the captives from Ishmael and then led the remnant to Egypt. **Seraiah.** He, along with the sons of **Ephai**, came from the village of Netophah near Beth-lehem (II Kgs 25:23). **Jezaniah.** An abbreviated form of Jazaniah (35:3; Ezk 8:11; 11:1). He also was loyal to Gedaliah. In 1932 an agate seal with the inscription, "Belonging to Jaazaniah, servant of the King," was found at Mizpah.

Ka-rē'ah, and all the captains of the forces that were in the fields, came to Gĕd-a-lī'ah to Mizpah,

14 And said unto him, Dost thou certainly know that Bă'a-lis the king of the Ammonites hath sent Ish'ma-el the son of Nĕth-a-nī'ah to slay thee? But Gĕd-a-lī'ah the son of A-hī'kam believed them not.

15 Then Jŏ-hā'nan the son of Ka-rē'ah spake to Gĕd-a-lī'ah in Mizpah secretly, saying, Let me go, I pray thee, and I will slay Ish'ma-el the son of Nĕth-a-nī'ah, and no man shall know it: wherefore should he slay thee, that all the Jews which are gathered unto thee should be scattered, and the remnant in Jū'dah perish?

16 But Gĕd-a-lī'ah the son of A-hī'kam said unto Jŏ-hā'nan the son of Ka-rē'ah, Thou shalt not do this thing: for thou speakest falsely of Ish'ma-el.

CHAPTER 41

NOW it came to pass in the seventh month, that Ish'ma-el the son of Nĕth-a-nī'ah the son of E-lish'a-ma, of the seed royal, and the princes of the king, even ten men with him, came unto Gĕd-a-lī'ah the son of A-hī'kam to Mizpah; and there they did eat bread together in Mizpah.

2 Then arose Ish'ma-el the son of Nĕth-a-nī'ah, and the ten men that were with him, and smote Gĕd-a-lī'ah the son of A-hī'kam the son of Shā'phan with the sword, and slew him, whom the king of Babylon had made governor over the land.

3 Ish'ma-el also slew all the Jews that were with him, even with Gĕd-a-lī'ah, at Mizpah, the Chăl-dē'ans that were found there, and the men of war.

4 And it came to pass the second day after he had slain Gĕd-a-lī'ah, and no man knew it,

5 That there came certain from Shē'chem, from Shī'lōh, and from Sa-mā'rĭ-a, even fourscore men, having their beards shaven, and their clothes rent, and having cut themselves, with offerings and incense in their hand, to bring them to the house of the LORD.

6 And Ish'ma-el the son of Nĕth-a-nī'ah went forth from Mizpah to meet them, weeping all along as he went: and it came to pass, as he met them, he said unto them, Come to Gĕd-a-lī'ah the son of A-hī'kam.

7 And it was so, when they came into the midst of the city, that Ish'ma-el the son of Nĕth-a-nī'ah slew them, and cast them into the midst of the pit, he, and the men that were with him.

8 But ten men were found among them that said unto Ish'ma-el, Slay us not: for we have treasures in the field, of wheat, and of barley, and of oil, and of honey. So he forbare, and slew them not among their brethren.

9 Now the pit wherein Ish'ma-el had cast all the dead bodies of the men, whom he had slain because of Gĕd-a-lī'ah, was it which Ā'sa the king had made for fear of Bă'a-sha king of Israel: and Ish'ma-el the son of Nĕth-a-nī'ah filled it with them that were slain.

10 Then Ish'ma-el carried away cap-

Babylon. So, Baalis, King of the Ammonites, wanting to harass Nebuchadnezzar without danger to himself, found a willing assassin in Ishmael. Johanan warned Gedaliah of the plot against his life, but he refused to believe it. Gedaliah also refused Johanan's pragmatic offer to slay the assassin (vss. 15-16).

d. The assassination of Gedaliah. 41:1-18.

41:1-4. Seventh month. October. This tragic event was marked in later Judaism by a fast in October. Seed royal. It has been suggested that one reason why Ishmael wanted to kill Gedaliah was because, being of royal blood, he wanted to avenge the injustices done to his relative, Zedekiah. Hospitality was held as sacred in the ancient Near East. Therefore, Ishmael's treacherous act broke all the laws of Oriental hospitality.

The assassination of Gedaliah might be explained on the grounds of a warped patriotism, but the senseless massacre of seventy pilgrims defies explanation.

5-9. Beards shaven . . . clothes rent . . . cut themselves. All these are tokens of mourning, although the Law forbids self-inflicted cuts (Lev 19:28; 21:5; Deut 14:1). These pilgrims were on their way to the ruins of the Jerusalem Temple in order to sacrifice. Ten pilgrims were spared by Ishmael because of the promise of their staples that were hid in the fields. Cisterns were often used as storage places.

10-18. Ishmael abducted the remnant at Mizpah and headed

tive all the residue of the people that were in Mizpah, even the king's daughters, and all the people that remained in Mizpah, whom Nĕb′u-zar-ā′dan the captain of the guard had committed to Gĕd-a-lī′ah the son of A-hī′kam: and Ish′ma-el the son of Nĕth-a-nī′ah carried them away captive, and departed to go over to the Ammonites.

11 ¶But when Jŏ-hā′nan the son of Ka-rē′ah, and all the captains of the forces that were with him, heard of all the evil that Ish′ma-el the son of Nĕth-a-nī′ah had done,

12 Then they took all the men, and went to fight with Ish′ma-el the son of Nĕth-a-nī′ah, and found him by the great waters that are in Gibeon.

13 Now it came to pass, *that* when all the people which were with Ish′ma-el saw Jŏ-hā′nan the son of Ka-rē′ah, and all the captains of the forces that were with him, then they were glad.

14 So all the people that Ish′ma-el had carried away captive from Mizpah cast about and returned, and went unto Jŏ-hā′nan the son of Ka-rē′ah.

15 But Ish′ma-el the son of Nĕth-a-nī′-ah escaped from Jŏ-hā′nan with eight men, and went to the Ammonites.

16 Then took Jŏ-hā′nan the son of Ka-rē′ah, and all the captains of the forces that were with him, all the remnant of the people whom he had recovered from Ish′ma-el the son of Nĕth-a-nī′ah, from Mizpah, after *that* he had slain Gĕd-a-lī′ah the son of A-hī′kam, *even* mighty men of war, and the women, and the children, and the eunuchs, whom he had brought again from Gibeon:

17 And they departed, and dwelt in the habitation of Chĭm′hăm, which is by Bĕth′-le-hĕm, to go to enter into Egypt,

18 Because of the Chăl-dē′ans: for they were afraid of them, because Ish′ma-el the son of Nĕth-a-nī′ah had slain Gĕd-a-lī′ah the son of A-hī′kam, whom the king of Babylon made governor in the land.

CHAPTER 42

THEN all the captains of the forces, and Jŏ-hā′nan the son of Ka-rē′ah, and Jĕz-a-nī′ah the son of Hō-sha-ī′ah, and all the people from the least even unto the greatest, came near,

2 And said unto Jĕr-e-mī′ah the prophet, Let, we beseech thee, our supplication be accepted before thee, and pray for us unto the Lord thy God, even for all this remnant; (for we are left *but* a few of many, as thine eyes do behold us:)

3 That the Lord thy God may shew us the way wherein we may walk, and the thing that we may do.

4 Then Jĕr-e-mī′ah the prophet said unto them, I have heard *you*; behold, I will pray unto the Lord your God according to your words; and it shall come to pass, *that* whatsoever thing the Lord shall answer you, I will declare *it* unto you: I will keep nothing back from you.

5 Then they said to Jĕr-e-mī′ah, The Lord be a true and faithful witness be-

e. Jeremiah the intercessor, 42:1-22.

Jeremiah's counsel had previously been spurned by kings, prophets, and the people. However, the remnant now wanted Jeremiah to seek God's guidance for them and promised to obey it. When the message of God came, there was a promise of blessing for remaining in the land and a warning of sure punishment (famine and death) should they flee into Egypt.

42:1-22. Jezaniah the son of Hoshaiah. Not the Jezaniah of 40:8, but Azariah the son of Hoshaiah. **After ten days.** God's answers do not always come immediately but in His own good time. **Will I build you** (see 1:10 note). **Cause you to return to your own land.** Cause you to dwell or remain in the land. **The sword . . . Egypt.** These denunciations were fulfilled when the Babylonians invaded Egypt. **Ye dissembled in your hearts.** You have done evil against your own souls, i.e., to your ruin.

for the Ammonites. Johanan intercepted him, freeing the refugees; but in the struggle Ishmael and eight of his men escaped. **Great waters.** A pool at Gibeon, probably the rock-hewn cistern found at El-jib, Gibeon, some three miles southwest of Tell en-Nasbeh. **Habitation of Chimham.** The lodging-place of Chimham, probably a caravanserai near Beth-lehem. From here the remnant left for Egypt because of fear of reprisal from the Babylonians for the assassination of Gedaliah.

tween us, if we do not even according to all things for the which the LORD thy God shall send thee to us.

6 Whether *it be* good, or whether *it be* evil, we will obey the voice of the LORD our God, to whom we send thee; that it may be well with us, when we obey the voice of the LORD our God.

7 ¶And it came to pass after ten days, that the word of the LORD came unto Jĕr′e-mī′ah.

8 Then called he Jŏ-hā′nan the son of Ka-rē′ah, and all the captains of the forces which *were* with him, and all the people from the least even to the greatest,

9 And said unto them, Thus saith the LORD, the God of Israel, unto whom ye sent me to present your supplication before him;

10 If ye will still abide in this land, then will I build you, and not pull *you* down, and I will plant you, and not pluck *you* up: for I repent me of the evil that I have done unto you.

11 Be not afraid of the king of Babylon, of whom ye are afraid; be not afraid of him, saith the LORD: for I *am* with you to save you, and to deliver you from his hand.

12 And I will shew mercies unto you, that he may have mercy upon you, and cause you to return to your own land.

13 But if ye say, We will not dwell in this land, neither obey the voice of the LORD your God,

14 Saying, No; but we will go into the land of Egypt, where we shall see no war, nor hear the sound of the trumpet, nor have hunger of bread; and there will we dwell:

15 And now therefore hear the word of the LORD, ye remnant of Jū′dah; Thus saith the LORD of hosts, the God of Israel; If ye wholly set your faces to enter into Egypt, and go to sojourn there;

16 Then it shall come to pass, *that* the sword, which ye feared, shall overtake you there in the land of Egypt, and the famine, whereof ye were afraid, shall follow close after you there in Egypt; and there ye shall die.

17 So shall it be with all the men that set their faces to go into Egypt to sojourn there; they shall die by the sword, by the famine, and by the pestilence: and none of them shall remain or escape from the evil that I will bring upon them.

18 For thus saith the LORD of hosts, the God of Israel; As mine anger and my fury hath been poured forth upon the inhabitants of Jerusalem; so shall my fury be poured forth upon you, when ye shall enter into Egypt: and ye shall be an execration, and an astonishment, and a curse, and a reproach; and ye shall see this place no more.

19 ¶The LORD hath said concerning you, O ye remnant of Jū′dah; Go ye not into Egypt: know certainly that I have admonished you this day.

20 For ye dissembled in your hearts, when ye sent me unto the LORD your God, saying, Pray for us unto the LORD our God; and according unto all that the LORD our God shall say, so declare unto us, and we will do *it*.

21 And now I have this day declared *it* to you; but ye have not obeyed the voice of the Lord your God, nor any thing for the which he hath sent me unto you.

22 Now therefore know certainly that ye shall die by the sword, by the famine, and by the pestilence, in the place whither ye desire to go *and* to sojourn.

CHAPTER 43

AND it came to pass, *that* when Jĕr-e-mī'ah had made an end of speaking unto all the people all the words of the Lord their God, for which the Lord their God had sent him to them, *even* all these words,

2 Then spake Ăz-a-rī'ah the son of Hŏ-sha-ī'ah, and Jŏ-hā'nan the son of Ka-rē'ah, and all the proud men, saying unto Jĕr-e-mī'ah, Thou speakest falsely: the Lord our God hath not sent thee to say, Go not into Egypt to sojourn there:

3 But Bā'ruch the son of Ne-rī'ah setteth thee on against us, for to deliver us into the hand of the Chăl-dē'ans, that they might put us to death, and carry us away captives into Babylon.

4 So Jŏ-hā'nan the son of Ka-rē'ah, and all the captains of the forces, and all the people, obeyed not the voice of the Lord, to dwell in the land of Jū'dah.

5 But Jŏ-hā'nan the son of Ka-rē'ah, and all the captains of the forces, took all the remnant of Jū'dah, that were returned from all nations, whither they had been driven, to dwell in the land of Jū'dah;

6 *Even* men, and women, and children, and the king's daughters, and every person that Nĕb'u-zar-ă'dan the captain of the guard had left with Gĕd-a-lī'ah the son of A-hī'kam the son of Shā'phan, and Jĕr-e-mī'ah the prophet, and Bā'ruch the son of Ne-rī'ah.

7 So they came into the land of Egypt: for they obeyed not the voice of the Lord: thus came they even to Tăh'pan-hēs.

8 ¶ Then came the word of the Lord unto Jĕr-e-mī'ah in Tăh'pan-hēs, saying,

9 Take great stones in thine hand,

2. *Jeremiah's ministry in Egypt. 43:1-45:5.*

Refusing to heed the counsel of Jeremiah, the remnant forced the prophet and Baruch to accompany them to Egypt. Jeremiah's sojourn in Egypt was extremely unpleasant, due to his rejection by his countrymen and the open idolatry in the land. Jeremiah probably died in Egypt (see Introduction).

a. The flight into Egypt. 43:1-7.

43:1. Despite the vindication of Jeremiah's message and his personal integrity by the fall of Jerusalem, the people accused him of lying about the will of God. Although the evidence was to the contrary, the people accused him of being a tool in the hands of his secretary, Baruch. Realizing that it was hopeless to reprove a scorner (Prov 9:8; cf. 10:8; 17:10), Jeremiah did not even give a reply to their accusation (the same attitude as Jesus before the council, Mt 26:60-63).

2-7. **Azariah the son of Hoshaiah** (see 42:1 note). **Baruch the son of Neriah** (see 32:12 note). **Returned from all nations.** The Chaldean war had forced many Jews to flee to neighboring countries. Having now returned, many accompanied Johanan to Egypt. We cannot be sure if Jeremiah was physically forced into Egypt, or if his sense of duty compelled him to accompany the remnant. **Tahpanhes.** A frontier city in the east Delta region, located at modern Tell Defneh, about twenty-seven miles southwest of Port Said. It has also been identified with the Pelusian Daphnai mentioned by Herodotus.

b. Prediction of Nebuchadnezzar's conquest of Egypt. 43:8-13.

8. God instructed Jeremiah to demonstrate his message by a dramatic sign. Earlier in Jeremiah's ministry, he had used other dramatic signs (the girdle 13:1-11; the wine bottle 13:12-17; the potter 18:1-19:15; the yokes 27:1-29:17). Jeremiah buried large stones in the pavement in front of the Pharaoh's governmental headquarters at Tahpanhes, stating that Nebuchadnezzar would build his throne upon these stones. Although the Judaean remnant had buried itself in Egypt, they too would feel the weight of Nebuchadnezzar, as did their counterparts who were exiled in Babylon. Although we still await historical confirmation of a total Babylonian reduction of Egypt, we do know that Nebuchadnezzar did invade the land. Josephus tells us that in his twenty-third year, Nebuchadnezzar invaded Egypt, slew the Pharaoh, set up another, and carried the Jewish remnant to Babylon (*Antiq.* x. ix. 7). A fragmentary inscription, now in the British Museum, records that Nebuchadnezzar actually invaded Egypt in 568 B.C. when Amasis (570-526 B.C.) was Pharaoh. Amasis seems to have heeded the warning and thereafter remained on good terms with the Babylonians.

9-13. **The clay in the brickkiln.** The mortar of the pavement.

and hide them in the clay in the brickkiln, which *is* at the entry of Pharaoh's house in Tăh'pan-hēs, in the sight of the men of Jū'dah.

10 And say unto them, Thus saith the LORD of hosts, the God of Israel; Behold, I will send and take Nĕb-u-chad-rĕz'zar the king of Babylon, my servant, and will set his throne upon these stones that I have hid; and he shall spread his royal pavilion over them.

11 And when he cometh, he shall smite the land of Egypt, *and deliver* such as *are* for death to death; and such *as are* for captivity to captivity; and such *as are* for the sword to the sword.

12 And I will kindle a fire in the houses of the gods of Egypt; and he shall burn them, and carry them away captives: and he shall array himself with the land of Egypt, as a shepherd putteth on his garment; and he shall go forth from thence in peace.

13 He shall break also the images of Bĕth-shē'mĕsh, that *is* in the land of Egypt; and the houses of the gods of the Egyptians shall he burn with fire.

CHAPTER 44

THE word that came to Jĕr'e-mī'ah concerning all the Jews which dwell in the land of Egypt, which dwell at Mig'dŏl, and at Tăh'pan-hēs, and at Noph, and in the country of Păth'rŏs, saying,

2 Thus saith the LORD of hosts, the God of Israel; Ye have seen all the evil that I have brought upon Jerusalem, and upon all the cities of Jū'dah; and, behold, this day they *are* a desolation, and no man dwelleth therein,

3 Because of their wickedness which they have committed to provoke me to anger, in that they went to burn incense, *and* to serve other gods, whom they knew not, *neither* they, ye, nor your fathers.

4 Howbeit I sent unto you all my servants the prophets, rising early and sending *them*, saying, Oh, do not this abominable thing that I hate.

5 But they hearkened not, nor inclined their ear to turn from their wickedness, to burn no incense unto other gods.

6 Wherefore my fury and mine anger was poured forth, and was kindled in the cities of Jū'dah and in the streets of Jerusalem; and they are wasted *and* desolate, as at this day.

7 Therefore now thus saith the LORD, the God of hosts, the God of Israel; Wherefore commit ye *this* great evil against your souls, to cut off from you man and woman, child and suckling, out of Jū'dah, to leave you none to remain;

8 In that ye provoke me unto wrath with the works of your hands, burning incense unto other gods in the land of Egypt, whither ye be gone to dwell, that ye might cut yourselves off, and that ye might be a curse and a reproach among all the nations of the earth?

9 Have ye forgotten the wickedness of your fathers, and the wickedness of the kings of Jū'dah, and the wickedness of their wives, and your own wickedness, and the wickedness of your

Sir Flinders Petrie, who extensively excavated Tahpanhes, found a paved area in front of the royal palace which he identified with this reference. The Elephantine papyri also speak of the "king's house" at Tahpanhes. **Carry them away captives.** Frequently, conquering kings would carry off the foreign idols. **Array himself . . . garment.** This vivid simile demonstrates that as the shepherd picks pieces of grass, insects, etc. from his coat, so Nebuchadnezzar will pick the land of Egypt clean. **Beth-shemesh.** Not the Palestinian Beth-shemesh (I Sam 6:9-20), but probably the Egyptian city of Heliopolis (called On in Gen 41:45), modern Tell el-Husn, near Cairo. Beth-shemesh literally means "the house (temple) of the sun." In ancient days Heliopolis was the center of worship of the sun-god, Re (Isa 19:18). **Images.** The obelisks of Heliopolis.

c. Jeremiah's plea. 44:1-30.

We have here the last effort of Jeremiah to convince the Israelites to abandon their idolatry. A great assembly of Jews, both the present refugees from Palestine and Jews who had emigrated to Egypt before the fall of Jerusalem, were addressed by Jeremiah. The sins of the past had continued into the present, and again Jeremiah had brought the message of divine judgment.

44:1-8. Migdol. Tell el-Heir, eleven miles south of Pelusium on the northeast border of Egypt. **Tahpanhes** (see 43:7 note). **Noph.** The Hebrew name for Memphis, capital of Lower Egypt (northern Egypt), some fourteen miles south of Cairo. **Pathros.** The general name for Upper Egypt (southern Egypt). Since the Nile is one of the few rivers in the world that flows north, the designations upper and lower are just the opposite of their normal meanings. That these four cities are mentioned shows that the Jews had migrated throughout Egypt.

9-16. Your wives. Jeremiah castigates the women for enticing their husbands into idolatry, a practice which began in the Solomonic period. **Such as shall escape.** Apart from a few fugitives (cf. 44:28), none of the remnant that sought refuge in

wives, which they have committed in the land of Jū′dah, and in the streets of Jerusalem?

10 They are not humbled even unto this day, neither have they feared, nor walked in my law, nor in my statutes, that I set before you and before your fathers.

11 ¶ Therefore thus saith the LORD of hosts, the God of Israel; Behold, I will set my face against you for evil, and to cut off all Jū′dah.

12 And I will take the remnant of Jū′dah, that have set their faces to go into the land of Egypt to sojourn there, and they shall all be consumed, and fall in the land of Egypt; they shall even be consumed by the sword and by the famine: they shall die, from the least even unto the greatest, by the sword and by the famine: and they shall be an execration, and an astonishment, and a curse, and a reproach.

13 For I will punish them that dwell in the land of Egypt, as I have punished Jerusalem, by the sword, by the famine, and by the pestilence:

14 So that none of the remnant of Jū′-dah, which are gone into the land of Egypt to sojourn there, shall escape or remain, that they should return into the land of Jū′dah, to the which they have a desire to return to dwell there: for none shall return but such as shall escape.

15 ¶ Then all the men which knew that their wives had burned incense unto other gods, and all the women that stood by, a great multitude, even all the people that dwelt in the land of Egypt, in Păth′rŏs, answered Jĕr′e-mī′ah, saying,

16 As for the word that thou hast spoken unto us in the name of the LORD, we will not hearken unto thee.

17 But we will certainly do whatsoever thing goeth forth out of our own mouth, to burn incense unto the queen of heaven, and to pour out drink offerings unto her, as we have done, we, and our fathers, our kings, and our princes, in the cities of Jū′dah, and in the streets of Jerusalem: for then had we plenty of victuals, and were well, and saw no evil.

18 But since we left off to burn incense to the queen of heaven, and to pour out drink offerings unto her, we have wanted all things, and have been consumed by the sword and by the famine.

19 And when we burned incense to the queen of heaven, and poured out drink offerings unto her, did we make her cakes to worship her, and pour out drink offerings unto her, without our men?

20 ¶ Then Jĕr′e-mī′ah said unto all the people, to the men, and to the women, and to all the people which had given him that answer, saying,

21 The incense that ye burned in the cities of Jū′dah, and in the streets of Je-rusalem, ye, and your fathers, your kings, and your princes, and the people of the land, did not the LORD remember them, and came it not into his mind?

22 So that the LORD could no longer bear, because of the evil of your doings,

Egypt would escape. The ungrateful Hebrews scornfully reply, ascribing all their success to the worship of the Queen of heaven.

17-19. Queen of heaven (see 7:18 note). **For then had we plenty.** The people attributed their earlier prosperity to their worship of the pagan cultic forms, but the revival under Josiah had forbidden all pagan worship. The people blamed the Chal-dean war, and its related hardship, to that revival. What an example of man's depravity! **Cakes.** Models of the Queen of heaven. **Without our men.** According to the law, a vow made by a woman rested upon the consent of her husband, who had the power to annul it if he didn't approve (Num 30:7-15). Thus, the pagan worship condemned by the prophet had the full approval of the Hebrew husbands.

20-25. With the insolent reply of the remnant, Jeremiah deli-vered his last message. The idolatry and apostasy of the people will be the nemesis of the remnant in Egypt. Jeremiah ends his prophecy as he began. Because of continued disobedience, di-vine retribution was inevitable.

and because of the abominations which ye have committed; therefore is your land a desolation, and an astonishment, and a curse, without an inhabitant, as at this day.

23 Because ye have burned incense, and because ye have sinned against the LORD, and have not obeyed the voice of the LORD, nor walked in his law, nor in his statutes, nor in his testimonies; therefore this evil is happened unto you, as at this day.

24 Moreover Jẽr-e-mĩ´ah said unto all the people, and to all the women, Hear the word of the LORD, all Jũ´dah that are in the land of Egypt:

25 Thus saith the LORD of hosts, the God of Israel, saying; Ye and your wives have both spoken with your mouths, and fulfilled with your hand, saying, We will surely perform our vows that we have vowed, to burn incense to the queen of heaven, and to pour out drink offerings unto her: ye will surely accomplish your vows, and surely perform your vows.

26 Therefore hear ye the word of the LORD, all Jũ´dah that dwell in the land of Egypt; Behold, I have sworn by my great name, saith the LORD, that my name shall no more be named in the mouth of any man of Jũ´dah in all the land of Egypt, saying, The Lord GOD liveth.

27 Behold, I will watch over them for evil, and not for good: and all the men of Jũ´dah that are in the land of Egypt shall be consumed by the sword and by the famine, until there be an end of them.

28 Yet a small number that escape the sword shall return out of the land of Egypt into the land of Jũ´dah, and all the remnant of Jũ´dah, that are gone into the land of Egypt to sojourn there, shall know whose words shall stand, mine, or their's.

29 ¶ And this shall be a sign unto you, saith the LORD, that I will punish you in this place, that ye may know that my words shall surely stand against you for evil:

30 Thus saith the LORD; Behold, I will give Phã´raõh-hõph´ra king of Egypt into the hand of his enemies, and into the hand of them that seek his life; as I gave Zĕd-e-kĩ´ah king of Jũ´dah into the hand of Nĕb-u-chad-rĕz´zar king of Bab´y-lon, his enemy, and that sought his life.

CHAPTER 45

THE word that Jẽr-e-mĩ´ah the prophet spake unto Bã´ruch the son of Nē-rĩ´ah, when he had written these words in a book at the mouth of Jẽr-e-mĩ´ah, in the fourth year of Jē-hoi´a-kĩm the son of Jõ-sĩ´ah king of Jũ´dah, saying,

2 Thus saith the LORD, the God of Israel, unto thee, O Bã´ruch;

3 Thou didst say, Woe is me now! for the LORD hath added grief to my sorrow; I fainted in my sighing, and I find no rest.

4 Thus shalt thou say unto him, The LORD saith thus; Behold, that which I have built will I break down, and that

26-30. My name shall no more be named. The present generation of Jews in Egypt perished and did not name the name of the Lord. However, later, during the inter-testamental period, a large Jewish population in Egypt repented and worshiped the Lord. The prophecy is therefore conditional. **Sign.** The downfall of Pharaoh Hophra would be a sign to the Egyptian Jews of their own destruction. The fourth king of the Twenty-Sixth Dynasty, Pharaoh Hophra reigned from 588-569 B.C. He had tried to help the beleaguered city of Jerusalem, but he withdrew in face of Babylonian opposition (37:5). In 564 B.C. Hophra was assassinated by Ahmosis II (Amasis 569-526 B.C.), a court official and founder of the Twenty- Seventh (Libyan) Dynasty.

d. Message to Baruch. 45:1-5.

Three supplemental messages occur at the end of the book of Jeremiah: the message to Baruch (45:1-5); the message to foreign nations (46:1-51:64); and the historical appendix (52:1-34). Chronologically, this oracle should follow 36:8, as it is a recapitulation of an event occurring in the fourth year of Jehoiakim (604 B.C.). Since the theme of chapter 36 was the scroll, and not the scribe, this message was placed here.

45:1-5. Baruch had been told at the beginning of his ministry of the difficulties ahead (cf. 1:10; 36:1-4). Like Jeremiah, Baruch became discouraged in the work. God rebuked him and encouraged him with the promise of sparing his life. Jeremiah reminded Baruch of God's sorrow in destroying the people and the land for which He had so long labored. Yet, because of their disobedience and apostasy, such a catastrophe was inevitable.

which I have planted I will pluck up, even this whole land.

5 And seekest thou great things for thyself? seek *them* not: for, behold, I will bring evil upon all flesh, saith the LORD: but thy life will I give unto thee for a prey in all places whither thou goest.

CHAPTER 46

THE word of the LORD which came to Jĕr'e-mī'ah the prophet against the Gentiles;

2 Against Egypt, against the army of Phâ'raōh-ne'chō king of Egypt, which was by the river Eû-phrā'tēs in Câr'che-mish, which Něb-u-chad-rĕz'zar king of Babylon smote in the fourth year of Je-hoi'a-kim the son of Jŏ-sī'ah king of Jū'dah.

3 Order ye the buckler and shield, and draw near to battle.

4 Harness the horses; and get up, ye horsemen, and stand forth with *your* helmets; furbish the spears, *and* put on the brigandines.

5 Wherefore have I seen them dismayed *and* turned away back? and their mighty ones are beaten down, and are fled apace, and look not back: for fear *was* round about, saith the LORD.

6 Let not the swift flee away, nor the mighty man escape; they shall stumble, and fall toward the north by the river Eû-phrā'tēs.

7 Who *is* this *that* cometh up as a flood, whose waters are moved as the rivers?

8 Egypt riseth up like a flood, and *his* waters are moved like the rivers: and he saith, I will go up, *and* will cover the earth; I will destroy the city and the inhabitants thereof.

9 Come up, ye horses; and rage, ye chariots; and let the mighty men come forth; the Ē-thī-ō'pī-ans and the Lĭb'y-ans that handle the shield; and the

III. PROPHETIC ORACLES AGAINST FOREIGN NATIONS. 46:1-51:64.

Jeremiah had been commissioned by God as "a prophet unto the nations" (1:5; cf. 1:10), as well as to Israel. This ministry to the Gentile nations was found in other Hebrew prophets as well (Amos 1:3-2:5; Isa 13-23; Ezk 25-32). Since these nations had sinned greatly, God's judgment would also come upon them.

Chronologically, these oracles could have been placed after chapter 25 (the LXX places them after 25:13a). However, these oracles are relegated to a supplement because the prophet's main purpose in the book is to describe God's judgment. The order follows a general geographical pattern from west to east. The LXX follows a different order, but the content is basically the same. Since Jeremiah's purpose was to describe God's judgment, rather than the particular sins which caused that judgment, there is little reference to actual national sins in these oracles.

A. Against Egypt. 46:1-28.

46:1. Verse 1 is a superscription for the entire section. Jeremiah frequently used superscriptions (cf. 1:1-3; 14:1; 30:1-3; 47:1; 49:34). **Gentiles. Nations.**

2-3. Verse 2 begins a poetic song about Nebuchadnezzar's victory over Pharaoh Necho at Carchemish. Interpretative songs are found in other portions of Scripture as well (cf. Jud 5; Ezk 21:9-17). **Pharaoh-necho** was the second ruler of the Twenty-Sixth Dynasty, reigning from 609 to 593 B.C. One of the most powerful kings of Egypt, Necho killed Josiah at Megiddo in 609 B.C. when the latter attempted to stop the Egyptian army from going to help the Assyrians in beleaguered Harran (II Kgs 23:29-35). **Carchemish** was an important military city of the Hittites. It was located near a ford of the Euphrates River in Northern Syria, some four hundred miles north-northeast of Jerusalem. This city commanded the approaches to the former Hittite Empire to the northwest, to the southwest the approaches to the Mediterranean coast, and to the east the Euphrates Valley. Here in 605 B.C. a decisive battle that altered the course of Oriental history was fought: Necho and his Egyptian forces had attempted to stop Nebuchadnezzar at Carchemish and bolster the faltering Assyrian Empire. Egypt was defeated, and Nebuchadnezzar's pursuit of Necho was halted only by the death of his father Nabopolassar. Babylon now dominated not only Mesopotamia, but also the Levant, the eastern coastline of the Mediterranean.

4-12. Brigandines. Coats of mail. **Who is this that cometh up as a flood . . . ?** The flood is a word borrowed from Egypt; it means the Nile River. **Rivers.** The plural is used to designate the irrigation canals of the Nile. The onrushing Egyptians were like the Nile when it inundates the surrounding countryside. Isaiah used this same figure of speech to describe the Assyrians (Isa 8:7). **He saith.** The pharaoh. **Ethiopians** (Heb *kûsh*), **Libyans** (Heb *pûṭ*), **Lydians** (Heb *lûdîm*). These North-African nations supplied mercenary soldiers for Egypt. **The day of the Lord God of hosts.** The reference is to the judgment of God upon the nations, and not the judgment associated with the second coming of Christ. **Gilead.** The proverbial home of balm (see 8:22 note).

13-26. In verses 13-26 Jeremiah prophesies the complete devastation of Egypt by Nebuchadnezzar. **Migdol . . . Noph** (see 44:1 note). **Tahpanhes** (see 43:7 note). **Swept away.** The Hebrew word *nischap* (swept away) has sometimes been divided as NAS CHAP and translated Apis (*chap*) fled (cf. LXX, RSV). Apis was the Egyptian bull-deity. In ancient near-eastern thought, to conquer a nation meant to conquer their gods as well. This image of Apis probably influenced the Hebrews into idolatry (cf. Ex 32:4-5; I Kgs 12:28-29). **Is but a noise.** Loud-mouth, a disrespectful nickname given to the pharaoh. Originally, it was probably a pun whose meaning has been lost. **Tabor.** Rising some 1,843 feet above sea level, this mountain is located about five and a half miles southeast of Nazareth. **Carmel.** A mountain range that extends into the Mediterranean forming the southern boundary of the Bay of Akko (Acre). Its highest peak is only 1,742 feet. Neither Tabor nor Carmel are large, but they are conspicuous in relation to the neighboring terrain. Likewise, Nebuchadnezzar will tower over other monarchs, including Necho. **Hired men.** Mercenary soldiers (Ionians and Carians) hired by Psammetichus and retained by his successor Necho. **It cannot be searched.** Impenetrable. **The multitude of No.** Amun (Amon) of Thebes. Amun was the chief deity of Thebes (No), the capital of Upper (southern) Egypt. During the Middle Kingdom, Amun achieved national importance. By this time his qualities coalesced with those of Re, the sun-god; and he became the national deity, Amun-Re. **It shall be inhabited.** Egypt will be destroyed, but it will be rebuilt (cf. Ezk 29:13-15).

Lȳdī-ans, that handle *and* bend the bow.

10 For this *is* the day of the Lord God of hosts, a day of vengeance, that he may avenge him of his adversaries: and the sword shall devour, and it shall be satiate and made drunk with their blood: for the Lord God of hosts hath a sacrifice in the north country by the river Eu-phrā'tēs.

11 Go up into Gilead, and take balm, O virgin, the daughter of Egypt: in vain shalt thou use many medicines; *for* thou shalt not be cured.

12 The nations have heard of thy shame, and thy cry hath filled the land: for the mighty man hath stumbled against the mighty, *and* they are fallen both together.

13 ¶ The word that the LORD spake to Jĕre-mī'ah the prophet, how Nĕb-u-chad-rĕz'zar king of Babylon should come *and* smite the land of Egypt.

14 Declare ye in Egypt, and publish in Mĭg'dŏl, and publish in Noph and in Tăh'pan-hēs: say ye, Stand fast, and prepare thee; for the sword shall devour round about thee.

15 Why are thy valiant *men* swept away? they stood not, because the LORD did drive them.

16 He made many to fall, yea, one fell upon another: and they said, Arise, and let us go again to our own people, and to the land of our nativity, from the oppressing sword.

17 They did cry there, Pharaoh king of Egypt *is but* a noise; he hath passed the time appointed.

18 *As* I live, saith the King, whose name *is* the LORD of hosts, Surely as Tā'bor *is* among the mountains, and as Carmel by the sea, *so* shall he come.

19 O thou daughter dwelling in Egypt, furnish thyself to go into captivity: for Noph shall be waste and desolate without an inhabitant.

20 Egypt *is like* a very fair heifer, *but* destruction cometh; it cometh out of the north.

21 Also her hired men *are* in the midst of her like fatted bullocks; for they also are turned back, *and* are fled away together: they did not stand, because the day of their calamity was come upon them, *and* the time of their visitation.

22 The voice thereof shall go like a serpent; for they shall march with an army, and come against her with axes, as hewers of wood.

23 They shall cut down her forest, saith the LORD, though it cannot be searched; because they are more than the grasshoppers, and *are* innumerable.

24 The daughter of Egypt shall be confounded; she shall be delivered into the hand of the people of the north.

25 The LORD of hosts, the God of Israel, saith; Behold, I will punish the multitude of No, and Pharaoh, and Egypt, with their gods, and their kings; even Pharaoh, and *all* them that trust in him:

26 And I will deliver them into the hand of those that seek their lives, and into the hand of Nĕb-u-chad-rĕz'zar king of Babylon, and into the hand of

his servants; and afterward it shall be inhabited, as in the days of old, saith the Lord.

27 ¶But fear not thou, O my servant Jacob, and be not dismayed, O Israel: for, behold, I will save thee from afar off, and thy seed from the land of their captivity; and Jacob shall return, and be in rest and at ease, and none shall make *him* afraid.

28 Fear thou not, O Jacob my servant, saith the Lord: for I *am* with thee; for I will make a full end of all the nations whither I have driven thee: but I will not make a full end of thee, but correct thee in measure; yet will I not leave thee wholly unpunished.

CHAPTER 47

THE word of the Lord that came to Jere-mi'ah the prophet, against the Philistines, before that Pharaoh smote Ga'za.

2 Thus saith the Lord; Behold, waters rise up out of the north, and shall be an overflowing flood, and shall overflow the land, and all that is therein; the city, and them that dwell therein: then the men shall cry, and all the inhabitants of the land shall howl.

3 At the noise of the stamping of the hoofs of his strong *horses*, at the rushing of his chariots, *and* at the rumbling of his wheels, the fathers shall not look back to *their* children for feebleness of hands;

4 Because of the day that cometh to spoil all the Philistines, *and* to cut off from Tyrus and Zi'don every helper that remaineth: for the Lord will spoil the Philistines, the remnant of the country of Caph'tor.

5 Baldness is come upon Ga'za; Ash'ke-lon is cut off *with* the remnant of their valley: how long wilt thou cut thyself?

6 O thou sword of the Lord, how long *will it be* ere thou be quiet? put up thyself into thy scabbard, rest, and be still.

7 How can it be quiet, seeing the Lord hath given it a charge against Ash'ke-lon, and against the sea shore? there hath he appointed it.

C. Against Moab. 48:1-47.

Descendants of Moab, the son of Lot's eldest daughter (Gen 19:37), the Moabites inhabited the tableland southeast of the Dead Sea. In the patriarchal period they were generally friendly with the Israelites. However, they refused to grant Israel permission to cross their land into the Promised Land; and the Moabite king summoned Balaam to curse them (Num 22:24). This engendered a bitterness that endured for centuries (cf. Neh 13:1). The Moabite women also beguiled the Israelites into idolatry (Num 25:1-3). From this time onward there was intermittent war between the Hebrews and the Moabites until David subdued them (II Sam 8:2, 12). Assyria controlled Moab during the eighth century until the former's demise. Nebuchadnezzar again subdued the Moabites, who then dissolved as a nation. Ruth, the great-grandmother of David, was a Moabitess and thus the blood of Moab flowed through the veins of Jesus.

The other major prophets (Isa 15-16; Ezk 25:8-11; Dan 11:41) and two minor prophets (Amos 2:1-3; Zeph 2:8-9) also pronounced oracles against Moab. Although there are many similar-

27-28. After the denunciation of Egypt, Jeremiah gave a bright ray of hope for captive Israel. This same hope was given in 30:10-11 (see comments on that passage).

B. Against Philistia. 47:1-7.

Ancient contenders against the Hebrews for possession of Palestine, the Philistines inhabited the coastal plain of southern Palestine. The five principal cities of the Philistines were Ashdod, Gaza, Ashkelon, Gath, and Ekron (Josh 13:3; I Sam 6:17). Except for Gath, which is in the Shephelah, they were situated in the coastal plain. Although they were subjugated by David, the Philistines maintained their independence throughout the Divided Kingdom. With the numerous battles fought on the Philistine plain came their gradual demise; they were finally absorbed by the Maccabees during the latter half of the second century B.C.

Here Jeremiah prophesies their doom. Other great prophets likewise delivered oracles against the Philistines (Amos 1:6-8; Isa 14:28-31; Ezk 25:15-17; Zeph 2:4-7).

47:1-7. Before that Pharaoh smote Gaza. The chronological reference here is somewhat confusing. Perhaps the attack may have occurred during Necho's campaign against Megiddo (609 B.C.). **Out of the north,** Babylon. So great will the panic from Nebuchadnezzar's invasion be that fathers will even abandon their children. **Tyrus** (Tyre) **and Zidon** (Sidon) were the two great Phoenician maritime cities. Any help that may come from these cities would be prevented from reaching Philistia. **Caphtor** was the Old Testament designation for Crete, the home of the Philistines prior to their migration to Palestine (Amos 9:7; Deut 2:23). **Baldness** was a symbol of mourning (cf. 16:6), or perhaps a description of the complete destruction of Gaza. **Gaza** was the most southerly of the five Philistine cities located on the great caravan route between Syria and Egypt. **Ashkelon** was located twelve miles north-northeast of Gaza on the Via Maris, the road to the sea. Zechariah foretold that Ashkelon would see the destruction of Tyre and then be destroyed herself (Zech 9:5). **Their valley.** The LXX reads the Anakim, the aboriginal inhabitants of Palestine. However, this is pure conjecture. **Put up thyself into thy scabbard.** Man's response to God's judgment is always appeasement and evasion. Jeremiah's question is: **How can it be quiet, seeing the Lord hath given it a charge . . . ?** Without repentance, judgment is inevitable (Rom 6:23; Gal 6:7-8).

ities between Jeremiah's oracle and that of Isaiah, it is not a direct quotation or copy. Numerous Moabite cities and places are mentioned in the oracle. We will comment on only the more significant ones. The content of the message, rather than the geographical details, is what is important. Moab will be destroyed because she had trusted in her own strength (vs. 7), rather than in the Lord. This "Maginot Line psychology," as Andrew W. Blackwood, Jr. calls it, still plagues us today. We trust in our weapons and our treaties, rather than the Lord. The materialistic religion of modern man is like the sin of ancient Moab—and Moab fell.

CHAPTER 48

AGAINST Moab thus saith the LORD of hosts, the God of Israel: Woe unto Nebo! for it is spoiled: Kir-i-a-thā'im is confounded and taken: Mĭs'găb is confounded and dismayed.

2 There shall be no more praise of Moab: in Hĕsh'bŏn they have devised evil against it; come, and let us cut it off from being a nation. Also thou shalt be cut down, O Măd'mĕn; the sword shall pursue thee.

3 A voice of crying shall be from Hŏr-o-nā'im, spoiling and great destruction.

4 Moab is destroyed; her little ones have caused a cry to be heard.

5 For in the going up of Lū'hĭth continual weeping shall go up; for in the going down of Hŏr-o-nā'im the enemies have heard a cry of destruction.

6 ¶Flee, save your lives, and be like the heath in the wilderness.

7 For because thou hast trusted in thy works and in thy treasures, thou shalt also be taken: and Chē'mŏsh shall go forth into captivity with his priests and his princes together.

8 And the spoiler shall come upon every city, and no city shall escape: the valley also shall perish, and the plain shall be destroyed, as the LORD hath spoken.

9 Give wings unto Moab, that it may flee and get away: for the cities thereof shall be desolate, without any to dwell therein.

10 Cursed be he that doeth the work of the LORD deceitfully, and cursed be he that keepeth back his sword from blood.

11 ¶Moab hath been at ease from his youth, and he hath settled on his lees, and hath not been emptied from vessel to vessel, neither hath he gone into captivity: therefore his taste remained in him, and his scent is not changed.

12 Therefore, behold, the days come, saith the LORD, that I will send unto him wanderers, that shall cause him to wander, and shall empty his vessels, and break their bottles.

13 And Moab shall be ashamed of Chē'mŏsh, as the house of Israel was ashamed of Bĕth-el their confidence.

14 ¶How say ye, We are mighty and strong men for the war?

15 Moab is spoiled, and gone up out of her cities, and his chosen young men are gone down to the slaughter, saith the King, whose name is the LORD of hosts.

16 The calamity of Moab is near to come, and his affliction hasteth fast.

17 All ye that are about him, bemoan him; and all ye that know his name,

48:1-10. **Nebo.** Not Mount Nebo, from which Moses saw the Promised Land (Deut 34), but rather (due to the Hebrew verb form) the city built by the Reubenites south of Heshbon (Num 32:3, 38). The city of Nebo was named on the Moabite Stone, erected by King Mesha of Moab (ca. 840 B.C.) to commemorate his victory over Israel (see II Kgs 3:4-27 note). **Kiriathaim,** also mentioned on the Moabite Stone, was a city once occupied by the Hebrews (Num 32:37) and is identified with modern El Quraiyat (fifteen miles south of Mount Nebo). **Heshbon.** Jeremiah here uses a play on words. In Hebrew the word *evil* sounds like the word for the city of Heshbon. **Madmen.** Another untranslatable play on words. This is a Moabite city, otherwise unknown. **The going up of Luhith.** The ascent to Luhith. **The going down of Horonaim.** The descent to Horanaim, another town mentioned on the Moabite Stone. **Heath in the wilderness.** The meaning is uncertain. It is derived from a Hebrew verb meaning to be naked. It probably has reference to loneliness, isolation, and destruction. **Chemosh.** The national god of the Moabites (II Kgs 3:27), to whom child sacrifices were offered (vss. 13, 46; Num 21:29; I Kgs 11:7, 33; II Kgs 23:13). Solomon erected a high place for Chemosh (I Kgs 11:7) that was later destroyed by Josiah (II Kgs 23:13). **Go forth into captivity.** In ancient Near Eastern warfare the custom was to carry off the idols of captive peoples. **Valley.** The Jordan Valley. **Plain.** The tableland of Moab.

11-17. **Lees.** Sediment. Moab was famous for its vineyards (vs. 32; cf. Isa 16:8-11). When wine settles on the sediment produced by fermentation, it becomes contaminated; but it could be purified by pouring from jar to jar through a strainer. Moab, however, was like bile contaminated wine, or lees. Isolated as it was, Moab had become soft through ease and prosperity. **Wanderers . . . bottles.** The process of decanting would destroy Moab, rather than purify her. **Beth-el** was the rival worship center to Jerusalem established by Jeroboam and a thorn in the side of Israel (I Kgs 12:26-33).

say, How is the strong staff broken, *and* the beautiful rod!

18 Thou daughter that dost inhabit Dĭ′bŏn, come down from *thy* glory, and sit in thirst; for the spoiler of Moab shall come upon thee, *and* he shall destroy thy strong holds.

19 O inhabitant of Ar′ŏ-er, stand by the way, and espy; ask him that fleeth, and her that escapeth, *and* say, What is done?

20 Moab is confounded; for it is broken down: howl and cry; tell ye it in Ar′non, that Moab is spoiled.

21 And judgment is come upon the plain country; upon Hŏ′lŏn, and upon Ja-hā′zah, and upon Mĕph′a-ăth,

22 And upon Dĭ′bŏn, and upon Nebo, and upon Bĕth-dĭb-la-thā′im,

23 And upon Kir′ĭ-a-thā′im, and upon Bĕth-gā′mul, and upon Bĕth-mē′ŏn,

24 And upon Kĕr′ĭ-ŏth, and upon Bŏz′rah, and upon all the cities of the land of Moab, far or near.

25 The horn of Moab is cut off, and his arm is broken, saith the LORD.

26 ¶Make ye him drunken: for he magnified *himself* against the LORD: Moab also shall wallow in his vomit, and he also shall be in derision.

27 For was not Israel a derision unto thee? was he found among thieves? for since thou spakest of him, thou skippedst for joy.

28 O ye that dwell in Moab, leave the cities, and dwell in the rock, and be like the dove *that* maketh her nest in the sides of the hole's mouth.

29 We have heard the pride of Moab, (he is exceeding proud) his loftiness, and his arrogancy, and his pride, and the haughtiness of his heart.

30 I know his wrath, saith the LORD, but *it shall* not *be so*; his lies shall not so effect *it*.

31 Therefore will I howl for Moab, and I will cry out for all Moab; *mine heart* shall mourn for the men of Kir-he′res.

32 O vine of Sĭb′mah, I will weep for thee with the weeping of Jā′zer: thy plants are gone over the sea, they reach even to the sea of Jā′zer: the spoiler is fallen upon thy summer fruits and upon thy vintage.

33 And joy and gladness is taken from the plentiful field, and from the land of Moab; and I have caused wine to fail from the winepresses: none shall tread with shouting; *their* shouting *shall be* no shouting.

34 From the cry of Hĕsh′bŏn *even* unto E′le-ā′leh, *and even* unto Jā′hăz, have they uttered their voice, from Zō′ar *even* unto Hŏr-ō-nā′im, *as* an heifer of three years old: for the waters also of Nimrim shall be desolate.

35 Moreover I will cause to cease in Moab, saith the LORD, him that offereth in the high places, and him that burneth incense to his gods.

36 Therefore mine heart shall sound for Moab like pipes, and mine heart shall sound like pipes for the men of Kir-he′res: because the riches *that* he hath gotten are perished.

37 For every head *shall be* bald, and

18-25. Dibon. Modern Diban, a town about eighteen miles south of Mt. Nebo and thirteen miles east of the Dead Sea, near the Arnon River. The Moabite Stone was discovered here in 1868. Arnon. The wadi on the east side of the Dead Sea, opposite En-gedi. It trenchantly divides the tableland forming the boundary between Ammon to the north and Moab to the south (Jud 11:18). Holon, Jahazah, Mephaath, Bethdiblathaim, Beth-gamul, Beth-meon, Kerioth, Bozrah. All were cities of Moab.

26-34. Drunken. Because of Moab's pride she will be made drunk with terror from divine wrath (see 25:15-29). The sides of the hole's mouth. The sides of the deep gorge. Jeremiah here refers to the deep gorge of the Arnon, which is about 1700 feet deep and narrows from about two miles at the top to only forty yards at the floor. Sibmah, Jazer. Villages near Heshbon. The entire area was noted for its vineyards. Zoar. Probably the smallest city of the Plain. Lot fled here for refuge (Gen 19:20-30). As an heifer of three years old. The LXX treats this as a place name, Eglath Shelishiyah.

35-47. With the simile of an unwanted pot, Jeremiah describes the destruction and discarding of Moab (see 22:28 where Jeremiah applies this simile to Jehoiachin). Numbers 21:28-29 provide the background for Jeremiah's remarks in verses 45-46. Balaam's oracles against Moab were now about to be fulfilled. Moab, however, will one day be restored, just as God had promised to restore Israel and Judah.

every beard clipped: upon all the hands *shall be* cuttings, and upon the loins sackcloth.

38 *There shall be* lamentation generally upon all the housetops of Moab, and in the streets thereof: for I have broken Moab like a vessel wherein *is* no pleasure, saith the LORD.

39 They shall howl, *saying*, How is it broken down! how hath Moab turned the back with shame! so shall Moab be a derision and a dismaying to all them about him.

40 For thus saith the LORD; Behold, he shall fly as an eagle, and shall spread his wings over Moab.

41 Kē'rĭ-ŏth is taken, and the strong holds are surprised, and the mighty men's hearts in Moab at that day shall be as the heart of a woman in her pangs.

42 And Moab shall be destroyed from *being* a people, because he hath magnified *himself* against the LORD.

43 Fear, and the pit, and the snare, *shall be* upon thee, O inhabitant of Moab, saith the LORD.

44 He that fleeth from the fear shall fall into the pit; and he that getteth up out of the pit shall be taken in the snare: for I will bring upon it, *even* upon Moab, the year of their visitation, saith the LORD.

45 They that stood under the shadow of Hēsh'bŏn because of the force: but a fire shall come forth out of Hēsh'bŏn, and a flame from the midst of Sihon, and shall devour the corner of Moab, and the crown of the head of the tumultuous ones.

46 Woe be unto thee, O Moab! the people of Chē'mŏsh perisheth: for thy sons are taken captives, and thy daughters captives.

47 Yet will I bring again the captivity of Moab in the latter days, saith the LORD. Thus far *is* the judgment of Moab.

CHAPTER 49

CONCERNING the Ammonites, thus saith the LORD; Hath Israel no sons? hath he no heir? why *then* doth their king inherit Gad, and his people dwell in his cities?

2 Therefore, behold, the days come, saith the LORD, that I will cause an alarm of war to be heard in Răb'bah of the Ammonites; and it shall be a desolate heap, and her daughters shall be burned with fire: then shall Israel be heir unto them that were his heirs, saith the LORD.

3 Howl, O Hēsh'bŏn, for Āī is spoiled: cry, ye daughters of Răb'bah, gird you with sackcloth; lament, and run to and fro by the hedges; for their king shall go into captivity, *and* his priests and his princes together.

4 Wherefore gloriest thou in the valleys, thy flowing valley, O backsliding daughter? that trusted in her treasures, *saying*, Who shall come unto me?

5 Behold, I will bring a fear upon thee, saith the Lord God of hosts from all those that be about thee; and ye shall be driven out every man right forth; and none shall gather up him that wandereth.

D. Against Ammon. 49:1-6.

Descended from Benjamin, son of Lot (like the Moabites they were a product of incest, Gen 19:38), the Ammonites inhabited the territory east of the Jordan (Transjordan) between the Arnon and Jabbok rivers. Because they joined the Moabites in retaining Balaam to curse Israel, they were excluded from Israel and Ammon (e.g., Jud 3:13; 10:6-18). David captured their capital (II Sam 11:1); but during Jehoshaphat's reign, the Ammonites invaded Judah (II Chr 20:1-30). They harassed Jehoiakim (II Kgs 24:2) and helped destroy the emasculated administration of Gedaliah (40:11-14; II Kgs 25:25). Other Hebrew prophets also proclaimed oracles against the Ammonites (Ezk 21:20; 25:1-7; Amos 1:13-14; Zeph 2:8-11).

49:1-6. **Hath Israel no sons?** Jeremiah probably makes reference here to the Assyrian invasion of Israel (732 B.C.) After the deportation of the Israelites, the Ammonites inhabited the territory of Gad in Transjordan. **Their king.** The Greek, Syriac and Latin texts understood this as *Milcom* (with a slight change of the vowels). Milcom was the national Ammonite god, also known as Molech. Children were offered as sacrifices to him, despite the stern prohibition of the Old Testament law (Lev 18:21; 20:1-5). **Rabbah** the capital of Ammon, located fourteen miles northeast of Heshbon on the Jabbok River. **Ai** probably was a town in Ammon, rather than the Ai captured by Joshua (Josh 8:1-29), since this reference omits the article. **Treasures.** Ammon trusted in her isolation and materialism, but the seeds of sin always bring a harvest of judgment (Gal 6:7-8).

E. Against Edom. 49:7-22.

Descendants of Esau (Gen 36:1-19), the Edomites inhabited the Transjordan territory south of the Dead Sea from the Zered River to the Gulf of Aqaba. This mountainous country was formerly known as the land of Seir (Gen 32:3; Num 24:18). The great caravan route, the King's Highway (Num 20:14-18), passed along the eastern plateau of Edom. Hostilities and bitterness were abundant between the Hebrews and the Edomites (I Kgs 11:15-16; II Kgs 14:7; II Chr 25:11-12; 28:17); but despite this

6 And afterward I will bring again the captivity of the children of Ammon, saith the LORD.

7 ¶Concerning Edom, thus saith the LORD of hosts; Is wisdom no more in Tē′man? is counsel perished from the prudent? is their wisdom vanished?

8 Flee ye, turn back, dwell deep, O inhabitants of Dē′dan; for I will bring the calamity of Esau upon him, the time that I will visit him.

9 If grapegatherers come to thee, would they not leave some gleaning grapes? if thieves by night, they will destroy till they have enough.

10 But I have made Esau bare, I have uncovered his secret places, and he shall not be able to hide himself: his seed is spoiled, and his brethren, and his neighbours, and he is not.

11 Leave thy fatherless children, I will preserve them alive; and let thy widows trust in me.

12 For thus saith the LORD; Behold, they whose judgment was not to drink of the cup have assuredly drunken; and art thou he that shall altogether go unpunished? thou shalt not go unpunished, but thou shalt surely drink of it.

13 For I have sworn by myself, saith the LORD, that Bōz′rah shall become a desolation, a reproach, a waste, and a curse; and all the cities thereof shall be perpetual wastes.

14 I have heard a rumour from the LORD, and an ambassador is sent unto the heathen, saying, Gather ye together, and come against her, and rise up to the battle.

15 For, lo, I will make thee small among the heathen, and despised among men.

16 Thy terribleness hath deceived thee, and the pride of thine heart, O thou that dwellest in the clefts of the rock, that holdest the height of the hill: though thou shouldest make thy nest as high as the eagle, I will bring thee down from thence, saith the LORD.

17 Also Edom shall be a desolation: every one that goeth by it shall be astonished, and shall hiss at all the plagues thereof.

18 As in the overthrow of Sodom and Go-mŏr′rah and the neighbour cities thereof, saith the LORD, no man shall abide there, neither shall a son of man dwell in it.

19 Behold, he shall come up like a lion from the swelling of Jordan against the habitation of the strong: but I will suddenly make him run away from her: and who is a chosen man, that I may appoint over her? for who is like me? and who will appoint me the time? and who is that shepherd that will stand before me?

20 Therefore hear the counsel of the LORD, that he hath taken against Edom; and his purposes, that he hath pur-

God forbade the Israelites to abuse them (Deut 23:7ff.). The Edomites supported the Babylonian siege of Jerusalem and rejoiced when the beleaguered city fell (Ps 137:7). The LXX and the New Testament call Edom by its Greek name, Idumaea. Edom is also included in the imprecatory oracles of other Old Testament prophets (Ezk 25:12-14; 35:1-15; Joel 3:19; Amos 9:12; Ob 1:16). The theme and content of this oracle is similar to Obadiah: no mercy will be shown Edom for God's judgment will be complete and final.

7-13. Teman. A tribe living in northern Edom who derived their name from the grandson of Esau (Gen 36:11). The Temanites were renowned in the ancient Near East for their wisdom. Job's comforter Eliphaz was from Teman (Job 2:11). **Dedan.** Descendants of Ham, this tribe living in the south of Edom was known for its commercial interest (25:23; Gen 10:7; 25:3; Ezk 25:13; 27:15, 20; Isa 21:13). **Visit him.** Punish him. **Secret places.** God will completely destroy Edom, and no one will be able to hide from divine judgment.

14-22. This prophecy concerning the fall of Edom saw its initial fulfillment in the third century B.C. when the Edomites were dispossessed by the Nabateans. Those who escaped were later subdued by the Maccabees and incorporated into the Jewish people. **Rock.** Sela, the rose-red city of Petra, capital of Edom. Verses 19-21 are repeated again in 50:44-46, where they are applied to Babylon. **The swelling of Jordan** (see 12:5 note).

posed against the inhabitants of Tē´-man: Surely the least of the flock shall draw them out: surely he shall make their habitations desolate with them.

21 The earth is moved at the noise of their fall, at the cry the noise thereof was heard in the Red sea.

22 Behold, he shall come up and fly as the eagle, and spread his wings over Bŏz´rah: and at that day shall the heart of the mighty men of Edom be as the heart of a woman in her pangs.

23 ¶Concerning Damascus. Hā´măth is confounded, and Ar´pad: for they have heard evil tidings: they are faint-hearted; there is sorrow on the sea; it cannot be quiet.

24 Damascus is waxed feeble, and turneth herself to flee, and fear hath seized on her: anguish and sorrows have taken her, as a woman in travail.

25 How is the city of praise not left, the city of my joy!

26 Therefore her young men shall fall in her streets, and all the men of war shall be cut off in that day, saith the LORD of hosts.

27 And I will kindle a fire in the wall of Damascus, and it shall consume the palaces of Bĕn-hā´dăd.

28 ¶Concerning Kē´dar, and concerning the kingdoms of Hā´zŏr, which Nĕb-u-chad-rĕz´zar king of Babylon shall smite, thus saith the LORD; Arise ye, go up to Kē´dar, and spoil the men of the east.

29 Their tents and their flocks shall they take away: they shall take to themselves their curtains, and all their vessels, and their camels; and they shall cry unto them, Fear is on every side.

30 ¶Flee, get you far off, dwell deep, O ye inhabitants of Hā´zŏr, saith the LORD; for Nĕb-u-chad-rĕz´zar king of Babylon hath taken counsel against you, and hath conceived a purpose against you.

31 Arise, get you up unto the wealthy nation, that dwelleth without care, saith the LORD, which have neither gates nor bars, which dwell alone.

32 And their camels shall be a booty, and the multitude of their cattle a spoil: and I will scatter into all winds them that are in the utmost corners; and I will bring their calamity from all sides thereof, saith the LORD.

33 And Hā´zŏr shall be a dwelling for dragons, and a desolation for ever: there shall no man abide there, nor any son of man dwell in it.

34 ¶The word of the LORD that came to Jĕr´e-mī´ah the prophet against Ē´-lam in the beginning of the reign of Zĕd´e-kī´ah king of Jū´dah, saying,

35 Thus saith the LORD of hosts; Behold, I will break the bow of Ē´lam, the chief of their might.

36 And upon Ē´lam will I bring the four winds from the four quarters of heaven, and will scatter them toward all those winds; and there shall be no nation whither the outcasts of Ē´lam shall not come.

37 For I will cause Ē´lam to be dismayed before their enemies, and before them that seek their life: and I will

F. Against Damascus. 49:23-27.

Damascus was the chief city of Syria and was located at the intersection of three major caravan routes. Damascus is an old city (Gen 14:15), but little is known about it during Jeremiah's time. In 732 B.C. Tiglath-pileser of Assyria captured the city. Later, it was subdued by the Egyptians and then the Babylonians. Amos 1:3-5 also records an oracle against Damascus.

23-27. Hamath. A city about one hundred ten miles north of Damascus and on the Orontes River. One of the chief trade routes from Asia Minor to the south passed through this city. Arpad was an important fortress north of Hamath. It is identified with Tel Erfad about twenty miles northwest of Aleppo (about 200 miles north of Damascus). Ben-hadad. The name was borne by several Syrian kings (I Kgs 15:18; 20:1; II Kgs 6:24; 8:7; 13:3). It is impossible to determine which king is meant here.

G. Against Arabia (Kedar and Hazor). 49:28-33.

This oracle is directed to the little-known Arabian tribes located in the Syrian desert east of Palestine. They are warned to flee the worst effects of the coming calamity.

28-33. Kedar. A Bedouin tribe descended from Ishmael (Gen 25:13), living in the Syro-Arabian desert. The name also applies to Bedouins in general. They were renowned for their skilled archers, trading, and flocks (Song 1:5; Isa 21:13-17; 42:11; 60:7; Ezk 27:21). Hazor. This was not the city of northern Palestine (Josh 11:1-13; 12:19), but the desert region east of Palestine. The name may also be used collectively of the permanent villages in the area. Thus, the phrase "Kedar and Hazor" may mean both the nomadic (migratory) and semi-nomadic (settlement dwellers) of the desert. These peoples are not mentioned in Jeremiah's list of nations that will drink the cup of divine wrath, but Arab peoples and towns are mentioned (25:23-24). Josephus tells of the Babylonian invasion of the Arab territory (Contra Apion I, 19). This invasion is also recorded in the Babylonian Chronicle. Fear is on every side. Jeremiah here employs one of his favorite phrases (cf. 6:25; 20:10; 46:5) to describe the panic that will result from this unexpected attack. That are in the utmost corners. Who cut the corners of their hair (see 9:26 note).

H. Against Elam. 49:34-39.

34-39. An extremely ancient civilization, Elam lies east of Babylon and is bordered by Assyria and Media on the north, the Persian Gulf on the south and Persia on the east. A powerful nation during the second millennium B.C. (Gen 14:1-11), Elam was conquered by Ashurbanipal of Assyria about 640 B.C. When Nineveh fell, Elam regained its independence and later helped to overthrow Babylon.

Some question why Jeremiah was concerned about such a distant nation (Susa, its capital was over seven hundred miles from Jerusalem). However, with Elam's proximity to Babylon and the Jews deported there with Zedekiah (II Kgs 24:14), this oracle would have brought hope, not only for the Jews in Jerusalem, but the exiles in Babylon as well. Jeremiah's theme is

bring evil upon them, even my fierce anger, saith the LORD; and I will send the sword after them, till I have consumed them:

38 And I will set my throne in Ē'lam, and will destroy from thence the king and the princes, saith the LORD.

39 ¶But it shall come to pass in the latter days, *that* I will bring again the captivity of Ē'lam, saith the LORD.

CHAPTER 50

THE word that the LORD spake against Babylon *and* against the land of the Chăl-dē'ănš by Jĕr'ĕ-mī'ăh the prophet.

2 Declare ye among the nations, and publish, and set up a standard; publish, *and* conceal not: say, Babylon is taken, Bel is confounded, Mē-rō'dăch is broken in pieces; her idols are confounded, her images are broken in pieces.

3 For out of the north there cometh up a nation against her, which shall make her land desolate, and none shall dwell therein: they shall remove, they shall depart, both man and beast.

4 ¶In those days, and in that time, saith the LORD, the children of Israel shall come, they and the children of Jū'dah together, going and weeping: they shall go, and seek the LORD their God.

5 They shall ask the way to Zion with

that God is in control. He controls all nations, both near and far. Not even the vaunted Elamite archers will be able to resist the divine judgment (cf. 25:25; Isa 22:6; Ezk 32:24). My throne to be set up is God's righteous judgment upon sinful people. Despite the awful judgment, there is the promise of a future restoration (vs. 39) of Elam. On the day of Pentecost there were Elamites present in Jerusalem (Acts 2:9).

I. Against Babylon. 50:1-51:64.

50:1. The Babylonians, or Chaldeans as they were frequently called, were descended from a semi-nomadic tribe that settled near Ur in Mesopotamia in the third millennium B.C. Situated some fifty miles south of modern Baghdad on the Euphrates River, Babylon became the chief city of the Babylonians. From the time of Abraham until the fall of the first Dynasty (1596 B.C.), Babylon was a dominant influence in Mesopotamia. Under Hammurabi (ca. 1704-1662 B.C.), the First Dynasty reached its greatest height. Renowned for its jurisprudence, The Law Code of Hammurabi was carried off by the Elamites and not unearthed until 1901 by J. de Morgan at Susa, biblical Shushan. For the next several centuries Babylon was at the mercy of several Near Eastern kings until it became a vassal of the growing Assyrian Empire. In 626 B.C. Nabopolassar founded an independent dynasty known as the neo-Babylonian or Chaldean regime. Under Nabopolassar and his son Nebuchadnezzar II, ancient Babylon attained its greatest splendor, becoming the most powerful empire of that day (see Introduction for further details).

Some have doubted that Jeremiah could have written this oracle since the divine judgment upon Babylon seems to contradict the prophet's thesis that Nebuchadnezzar was God's servant of judgment upon Judah. Jeremiah did urge the people of Jerusalem to submit to Nebuchadnezzar (27:6) and even urged the Jews to pray for the welfare of Babylon (29:7). However, Jeremiah also teaches that God is sovereign, not Nebuchadnezzar. He is over nations (1:10). He may have permitted Nebuchadnezzar to be his servant of judgment, but the heathen Babylonians will be punished for their sins of pride and rapacity. Jeremiah was not a politician, but a prophet. He was not a member of the pro-Babylonian party, but a declarer of God's truth. His themes of judgment and restoration occur again in this oracle. Babylon will fall, never to be restored (50:39); but the Jews will return from Babylonian exile.

In 539 B.C. Cyrus the Persian conquered Babylon without a battle. He was almost welcomed as a liberator from the misrule of Nebuchadnezzar's successors. Reversing the Assyro-Babylonian policy of deportation, he decreed that the exiles could return to their own countries. Many Jews were repatriated and rebuilt Jerusalem.

2-20. Bel . . . Merodach. Only one deity. Bel is a cognate of the Hebrew word meaning lord. Merodach is the Hebrew spelling of *Marduk*, the chief god of Babylon, the sun-god and creator. **Her idols.** A term used disparagingly of pagan idols (Lev 26:30; Deut 29:17; I Kgs 15:12). Ezekiel uses this term some thirty-eight times. **Out of the north.** The Jews used the term north colloquially to refer to the location of anything sinister. Here, no doubt, the reference is to Persia. **Shepherds** (see 23:1 note). **Wholly desolate . . . plagues.** Cyrus did not destroy Babylon when he captured it in 539 B.C.; but the walls were later destroyed by Darius Hystaspis (514 B.C.), and the city continued to decline until it ceased to exist in the Christian era. **Carmel, Bashan, Ephraim, Gilead.** These are the fertile lands to which Israel will return, in contrast to Babylon, which was once fertile and will become a desert (cf. 16).

their faces thitherward, *saying*, Come, and let us join ourselves to the LORD in a perpetual covenant *that* shall not be forgotten.

6 My people hath been lost sheep: their shepherds have caused them to go astray, they have turned them away *on* the mountains: they have gone from mountain to hill, they have forgotten their restingplace.

7 All that found them have devoured them: and their adversaries said, We offend not, because they have sinned against the LORD, the habitation of justice, even the LORD, the hope of their fathers.

8 Remove out of the midst of Babylon, and go forth out of the land of the Chăl-dē′ans, and be as the he goats before the flocks.

9 ¶For, lo, I will raise and cause to come up against Babylon an assembly of great nations from the north country: and they shall set themselves in array against her; from thence she shall be taken: their arrows *shall be* as of a mighty expert man; none shall return in vain.

10 And Chăl-dē′a shall be a spoil: all that spoil her shall be satisfied, saith the LORD.

11 Because ye were glad, because ye rejoiced, O ye destroyers of mine heritage, because ye are grown fat as the heifer at grass, and bellow as bulls;

12 Your mother shall be sore confounded; she that bare you shall be ashamed: behold, the hindermost of the nations *shall be* a wilderness, a dry land, and a desert.

13 Because of the wrath of the LORD it shall not be inhabited, but it shall be wholly desolate: every one that goeth by Babylon shall be astonished, and hiss at all her plagues.

14 Put yourselves in array against Babylon round about: all ye that bend the bow, shoot at her, spare no arrows: for she hath sinned against the LORD.

15 Shout against her round about: she hath given her hand: her foundations are fallen, her walls are thrown down: for it *is* the vengeance of the LORD: take vengeance upon her; as she hath done, do unto her.

16 Cut off the sower from Babylon, and him that handleth the sickle in the time of harvest: for fear of the oppressing sword they shall turn every one to his people, and they shall flee every one to his own land.

17 ¶Israel *is* a scattered sheep; the lions have driven *him* away: first the king of Assyria hath devoured him; and last this Nĕb-u-chad-rĕz′zar king of Babylon hath broken his bones.

18 Therefore thus saith the LORD of hosts, the God of Israel; Behold, I will punish the king of Babylon and his land, as I have punished the king of Assyria.

19 And I will bring Israel again to his habitation, and he shall feed on Carmel and Bā′shan, and his soul shall be satisfied upon mount Ē′phra-im and Gilead.

20 In those days, and in that time, saith the LORD, the iniquity of Israel shall be sought for, and *there shall be*

none; and the sins of Jū'dah, and they shall not be found: for I will pardon them whom I reserve.

21 ¶Go up against the land of Mer-a-thā'im, even against it, and against the inhabitants of Pē'kŏd: waste and utterly destroy after them, saith the LORD, and do according to all that I have commanded thee.

22 A sound of battle is in the land, and of great destruction.

23 How is the hammer of the whole earth cut asunder and broken! how is Babylon become a desolation among the nations!

24 I have laid a snare for thee, and thou art also taken, O Babylon, and thou wast not aware: thou art found, and also caught, because thou hast striven against the LORD.

25 The LORD hath opened his armoury, and hath brought forth the weapons of his indignation: for this is the work of the Lord GOD of hosts in the land of the Chăl-dē'ans.

26 Come against her from the utmost border, open her storehouses: cast her up as heaps, and destroy her utterly: let nothing of her be left.

27 Slay all her bullocks; let them go down to the slaughter: woe unto them! for their day is come, the time of their visitation.

28 The voice of them that flee and escape out of the land of Babylon, to declare in Zion the vengeance of the LORD our God, the vengeance of his temple.

29 Call together the archers against Babylon: all ye that bend the bow, camp against it round about; let none thereof escape: recompense her according to her work; according to all that she hath done, do unto her: for she hath been proud against the LORD, against the Holy One of Israel.

30 Therefore shall her young men fall in the streets, and all her men of war shall be cut off in that day, saith the LORD.

31 Behold, I am against thee, O thou most proud, saith the Lord GOD of hosts: for thy day is come, the time that I will visit thee.

32 And the most proud shall stumble and fall, and none shall raise him up: and I will kindle a fire in his cities, and it shall devour all round about him.

33 ¶Thus saith the LORD of hosts; The children of Israel and the children of Jū'dah were oppressed together: and all that took them captives held them fast; they refused to let them go.

34 Their Redeemer is strong; the LORD of hosts is his name: he shall throughly plead their cause, that he may give rest to the land, and disquiet the inhabitants of Babylon.

35 ¶A sword is upon the Chăl-dē'ans, saith the LORD, and upon the inhabitants of Babylon, and upon her princes, and upon her wise men.

36 A sword is upon the liars; and they shall dote: a sword is upon her mighty men; and they shall be dismayed.

37 A sword is upon their horses, and upon their chariots, and upon all the mingled people that are in the midst of her: and they shall become as women: a

21-46. Merathaim. A sarcastic wordplay on Marmarati, the name for southern Babylon, meaning double bitterness. **Pekod.** Another sarcastic wordplay meaning punishment for Pugudu (cf. Ezk 23:23), an eastern Babylonian tribe. **Sword.** Five times the Lord calls for a sword to smite the Babylonians. **Dote.** Become fools. **Wild beasts.** Even today Bedouins avoid Babylon as the habitat of wild animals and evil spirits. **No more inhabited . . . generation.** A quote from Isaiah 13:19-20.

sword *is* upon her treasures; and they shall be robbed.

38 A drought *is* upon her waters; and they shall be dried up: for it *is* the land of graven images, and they are mad upon *their* idols.

39 Therefore the wild beasts of the desert with the wild beasts of the islands shall dwell *there*, and the owls shall dwell therein: and it shall be no more inhabited for ever; neither shall it be dwelt in from generation to generation.

40 As God overthrew Sodom and Gomor'rah and the neighbour *cities* thereof, saith the LORD; *so* shall no man abide there, neither shall any son of man dwell therein.

41 Behold, a people shall come from the north, and a great nation, and many kings shall be raised up from the coasts of the earth.

42 They shall hold the bow and the lance: they are cruel, and will not shew mercy: their voice shall roar like the sea, and they shall ride upon horses, *every one* put in array, like a man to the battle, against thee, O daughter of Babylon.

43 The king of Babylon hath heard the report of them, and his hands waxed feeble: anguish took hold of him, *and* pangs as of a woman in travail.

44 Behold, he shall come up like a lion from the swelling of Jordan unto the habitation of the strong: but I will make them suddenly run away from her: and who *is* a chosen *man, that* I may appoint over her? for who *is* like me? and who will appoint me the time? and who *is* that shepherd that will stand before me?

45 Therefore hear ye the counsel of the LORD, that he hath taken against Babylon; and his purposes, that he hath purposed against the land of the Chal-de'ans: Surely the least of the flock shall draw them out: surely he shall make *their* habitation desolate with them.

46 At the noise of the taking of Babylon the earth is moved, and the cry is heard among the nations.

CHAPTER 51

THUS saith the LORD; Behold, I will raise up against Babylon, and against them that dwell in the midst of them that rise up against me, a destroying wind;

2 And will send unto Babylon fanners, that shall fan her, and shall empty her land: for in the day of trouble they shall be against her round about.

3 Against *him that* bendeth let the archer bend his bow, and against *him that* lifteth himself up in his brigandine: and spare ye not her young men; destroy ye utterly all her host.

4 Thus the slain shall fall in the land of the Chal-de'ans, and *they that are* thrust through in her streets.

5 For Israel *hath* not *been* forsaken, nor Ju'dah of his God, of the LORD of hosts; though their land was filled with sin against the Holy One of Israel.

51:1-24. Chapter 51 continues the description of God's judgment upon Babylon with the imagery of Oriental winnowing of grain. **In the midst of them that rise up against me.** Them that dwell in Chaldea. The Hebrew *lēb-qamay* is a cipher for Chaldea (cf. 25:26). **Brigandine** (see 46:4 note). **Medes.** An ancient people who lived east of the Zagros Mountains, south of the Caspian Sea. The Medes became a formidable power in the Ancient Near East about a century before Jeremiah's time. With Nebuchadnezzar's marriage to Amytic, granddaughter of Cyaxares, king of the Medes, the Babylonians and Medes became allies and jointly destroyed Nineveh. However, upon the death of Nebuchadnezzar the Medo-Babylonian alliance fell apart. With Cyrus, the Persian King, the Medes overthrew Babylon in 539 B.C., forming the Medo-Persian Empire (cf. Isa 13:17-19; 21:2, 9; Dan 5:28, 31; 8:20). **Many waters.** The many irrigation canals of Babylon. Babylon was a fertile land, due to its outstanding irrigation system. However, when God's judgment

6 Flee out of the midst of Babylon, and deliver every man his soul: be not cut off in her iniquity; for this *is* the time of the Lord's vengeance; he will render unto her a recompence.

7 Babylon *hath been* a golden cup in the Lord's hand, that made all the earth drunken: the nations have drunken of her wine; therefore the nations are mad.

8 Babylon is suddenly fallen and destroyed: howl for her; take balm for her pain, if so be she may be healed.

9 We would have healed Babylon, but she is not healed: forsake her, and let us go every one into his own country: for her judgement reacheth unto heaven, and is lifted up *even* to the skies.

10 The Lord hath brought forth our righteousness: come, and let us declare in Zion the work of the Lord our God.

11 Make bright the arrows; gather the shields: the Lord hath raised up the spirit of the kings of the Medes: for his device *is* against Babylon, to destroy it; because it *is* the vengeance of the Lord, the vengeance of his temple.

12 Set up the standard upon the walls of Babylon, make the watch strong, set up the watchmen, prepare the ambushes: for the Lord hath both devised and done that which he spake against the inhabitants of Babylon.

13 O thou that dwellest upon many waters, abundant in treasures, thine end is come, *and* the measure of thy covetousness.

14 The Lord of hosts hath sworn by himself, *saying,* Surely I will fill thee with men, as with caterpillers; and they shall lift up a shout against thee.

15 He hath made the earth by his power, he hath established the world by his wisdom, and hath stretched out the heaven by his understanding.

16 When he uttereth *his* voice, *there is* a multitude of waters in the heavens; and he causeth the vapours to ascend from the ends of the earth: he maketh lightnings with rain, and bringeth forth the wind out of his treasures.

17 Every man is brutish by *his* knowledge; every founder is confounded by the graven image: for his molten image *is* falsehood, and *there is* no breath in them.

18 They *are* vanity, the work of errors: in the time of their visitation they shall perish.

19 The portion of Jacob *is* not like them; for he *is* the former of all *things:* and *Israel is* the rod of his inheritance: the Lord of hosts *is* his name.

20 Thou *art* my battle axe *and* weapons of war: for with thee will I break in pieces the nations, and with thee will I destroy kingdoms;

21 And with thee will I break in pieces the horse and his rider; and with thee will I break in pieces the chariot and his rider;

22 With thee also will I break in pieces man and woman; and with thee will I break in pieces old and young; and with thee will I break in pieces the young man and the maid;

1518

---

would come, the land would become a desert (50:16). **Caterpillars.** Probably locusts (cf. Joel 1:1-12).

23 I will also break in pieces with thee the shepherd and his flock; and with thee will I break in pieces the husbandman and his yoke of oxen; and with thee will I break in pieces captains and rulers.

24 And I will render unto Babylon and to all the inhabitants of Chăl-dē'a all their evil that they have done in Zion in your sight, saith the LORD.

25 Behold, I am against thee, O destroying mountain, saith the LORD, which destroyest all the earth: and I will stretch out mine hand upon thee, and roll thee down from the rocks, and will make thee a burnt mountain.

26 And they shall not take of thee a stone for a corner, nor a stone for foundations; but thou shalt be desolate for ever, saith the LORD.

27 Set ye up a standard in the land, blow the trumpet among the nations, prepare the nations against her, call together against her the kingdoms of Ăr'a-răt, Mĭn'nĭ, and Ăsh'che-năz; appoint a captain against her; cause the horses to come up as the rough caterpillers.

28 Prepare against her the nations with the kings of the Medes, the captains thereof, and all the rulers thereof, and all the land of his dominion.

29 And the land shall tremble and sorrow: for every purpose of the LORD shall be performed against Babylon, to make the land of Babylon a desolation without an inhabitant.

30 The mighty men of Babylon have forborn to fight, they have remained in their holds: their might hath failed; they became as women: they have burned her dwellingplaces; her bars are broken.

31 One post shall run to meet another, and one messenger to meet another, to shew the king of Babylon that his city is taken at one end,

32 And that the passages are stopped, and the reeds they have burned with fire, and the men of war are affrighted.

33 For thus saith the LORD of hosts, the God of Israel; The daughter of Babylon is like a threshingfloor, it is time to thresh her; yet a little while, and the time of her harvest shall come.

34 Nĕb-u-chad-rĕz'zar the king of Babylon hath devoured me, he hath crushed me, he hath made me an empty vessel, he hath swallowed me up like a dragon, he hath filled his belly with my delicates, he hath cast me out.

35 The violence done to me and to my flesh be upon Babylon, shall the inhabitant of Zion say; and my blood upon the inhabitants of Chăl-dē'a, shall Jerusalem say.

36 Therefore thus saith the LORD; Behold, I will plead thy cause, and take vengeance for thee; and I will dry up her sea, and make her springs dry.

37 And Babylon shall become heaps, a dwellingplace for dragons, and astonishment, and an hissing, without an inhabitant.

38 They shall roar together like lions: they shall yell as lions' whelps.

25-58. **O destroying mountain.** A symbol for a powerful nation since Babylon is located on a plain. **Ararat, Minni, Ashchenaz.** In addition to Media, God also calls other nations to be His arm of judgment upon Babylon. Ararat was located northwest of Lake Van in Armenia. Minni was also in Armenia, and Ashkenaz was her ally. This tribe was descended from the eldest son of Gomer (Gen 10:3; I Chr 1:6). **Dragon.** Monster. Like a monster Nebuchadnezzar had ingested Judah, and for this his land would be punished. **Sheshach.** A cipher for Babylon (see 25:26 note). **Sea** is a poetic reference to the invading armies. **That which he hath swallowed up.** The Jewish exiles.

39 In their heat I will make their feasts, and I will make them drunken, that they may rejoice, and sleep a perpetual sleep, and not wake, saith the LORD.

40 I will bring them down like lambs to the slaughter, like rams with he goats.

41 How is Shē′shăch taken! and how is the praise of the whole earth surprised! how is Babylon become an astonishment among the nations!

42 The sea is come up upon Babylon: she is covered with the multitude of the waves thereof.

43 Her cities are a desolation, a dry land, and a wilderness, a land wherein no man dwelleth, neither doth any son of man pass thereby.

44 And I will punish Bel in Babylon, and I will bring forth out of his mouth that which he hath swallowed up: and the nations shall not flow together any more unto him: yea, the wall of Babylon shall fall.

45 My people, go ye out of the midst of her, and deliver ye every man his soul from the fierce anger of the LORD.

46 And lest your heart faint, and ye fear for the rumour that shall be heard in the land; a rumour shall both come in *one year, and after that in another year* shall come a rumour, and violence in the land, ruler against ruler.

47 Therefore, behold, the days come, that I will do judgment upon the graven images of Babylon: and her whole land shall be confounded, and all her slain shall fall in the midst of her.

48 Then the heaven and the earth, and all that *is* therein, shall sing for Babylon: for the spoilers shall come unto her from the north, saith the LORD.

49 As Babylon *hath* caused the slain of Israel to fall, so at Babylon shall fall the slain of all the earth.

50 Ye that have escaped the sword, go away, stand not still: remember the LORD afar off, and let Jerusalem come into your mind.

51 We are confounded, because we have heard reproach: shame hath covered our faces: for strangers are come into the sanctuaries of the LORD's house.

52 Wherefore, behold, the days come, saith the LORD, that I will do judgment upon her graven images: and through all her land the wounded shall groan.

53 Though Babylon should mount up to heaven, and though she should fortify the height of her strength, yet from me shall spoilers come unto her, saith the LORD.

54 A sound of a cry *cometh* from Babylon, and great destruction from the land of the Chăl-dē′ăns:

55 Because the LORD hath spoiled Babylon, and destroyed out of her the great voice; when her waves do roar like great waters, a noise of their voice is uttered:

56 Because the spoiler is come upon her, even upon Babylon, and her mighty men are taken, every one of

their bows is broken: for the Lord God of recompences shall surely requite.

57 And I will make drunk her princes, and her wise *men*, her captains, and her rulers, and her mighty men: and they shall sleep a perpetual sleep, and not wake, saith the King, whose name *is* the Lord of hosts.

58 Thus saith the Lord of hosts; The broad walls of Babylon shall be utterly broken, and her high gates shall be burned with fire; and the people shall labour in vain, and the folk in the fire, and they shall be weary.

59 ¶The word which Jĕr'e-mī'ah the prophet commanded Sĕ-ra-ī'ah the son of Nē-rī'ah, the son of Mā-a-sē'iah, when he went with Zĕd-e-kī'ah the king of Jū'dah into Babylon in the fourth year of his reign. And *this* Se-ra-ī'ah *was* a quiet prince.

60 So Jĕr'e-mī'ah wrote in a book all the evil that should come upon Babylon, *even* all these words that are written against Babylon.

61 And Jĕr'e-mī'ah said to Se-ra-ī'ah, When thou comest to Babylon, and shalt see, and shalt read all these words;

62 Then shalt thou say, O Lord, thou hast spoken against this place, to cut it off, that none shall remain in it, neither man nor beast, but that it shall be desolate for ever.

63 And it shall be, when thou hast made an end of reading this book, *that* thou shalt bind a stone to it, and cast it into the midst of Eū-phrā'tēs:

64 And thou shalt say, Thus shall Babylon sink, and shall not rise from the evil that I will bring upon her: and they shall be weary. Thus far *are* the words of Jĕr'e-mī'ah.

CHAPTER 52

ZĔD-E-KĪ'AH *was* one and twenty years old when he began to reign, and he reigned eleven years in Jerusalem. And his mother's name *was* Ha-mū'tal the daughter of Jĕr'e-mī'ah of Lĭb'nah.

2 And he did *that* which *was* evil in the eyes of the Lord, according to all that Je-hoī'a-kĭm had done.

3 For through the anger of the Lord it came to pass in Jerusalem and Jū'dah, till he had cast them out from his presence, that Zĕd-e-kī'ah rebelled against the king of Babylon.

4 ¶And it came to pass in the ninth year of his reign, in the tenth month, in the tenth day of the month, *that* Nĕb-u-chad-rĕz'zar king of Babylon came, he and all his army, against Jerusalem, and pitched against it, and built forts against it round about.

5 So the city was besieged unto the eleventh year of king Zĕd-e-kī'ah.

6 And in the fourth month, in the ninth day of the month, the famine was sore in the city, so that there was no bread for the people of the land.

7 Then the city was broken up, and all the men of war fled, and went forth out of the city by night by the way of the gate between the two walls, which *was* by the king's garden: (now the Chăl-dē'-

59-64. Jeremiah adds an appendix to the oracle against Babylon, instructing Seraiah to read the oracle to the exiles and then bind it with a stone and cast it into the Euphrates as a visual symbol of the sinking of Babylon. **Seraiah the son of Neriah.** He was not the one who helped arrest Jeremiah (36:26), but the brother of Baruch (32:12). **In the fourth year.** Some type of diplomatic mission was engaged in by Zedekiah during his fourth year of reign. It was not uncommon for vassal kings to visit the capital of the empire occasionally to assure the emperor of their loyalty. **A quiet prince.** The title of a quartermaster who arranged for food and lodging for diplomatic delegations.

IV. HISTORICAL APPENDIX: THE FALL OF JERUSALEM AND RELATED EVENTS. 52:1-34.

Chapter 52 is nearly identical with II Kings 24:18-25:30, although it does give some historical particulars more fully. The material in II Kings that is omitted in this chapter is found in chapters 40 through 43. It is possible that this historical appendix was added to Jeremiah's writings to show how his prophecies were fulfilled. In no way would this detract from the Jeremianic authorship of the book, since 51:64 affirms: "Thus far are the words of Jeremiah."

A. The Fall and Captivity of Judah. 52:1-30.

52:1-23. Zedekiah (see Introduction). **Hamutal** was the wife of Josiah and the mother of Jehoahaz and Zedekiah (cf. II Kgs 23:31; 24:18). **Jeremiah of Libnah.** Obviously, not the prophet. **Jehoiakim** (see Introduction). Zedekiah fled the city through the Arabah (Plain), the fault in which the Jordan and the Dead Sea are located. **King's garden.** A garden located on the south of Jerusalem near the Kedron Valley. **Tenth day.** II Kings 25:8 records the seventh day. The difference may be the interval between the arrival of **Nebuzar-adan** and the beginning of the destruction of the city.

ans̱ were by the city round about:) and they went by the way of the plain.

8 But the army of the Chăl-dē′ans̱ pursued after the king, and overtook Zĕd-e-kī′ah in the plains of Jericho; and all his army was scattered from him.

9 Then they took the king, and carried him up unto the king of Baby-lon to Rĭb′lah in the land of Hā′măth; where he gave judgment upon him.

10 And the king of Babylon slew the sons of Zĕd-e-kī′ah before his eyes: he slew also all the princes of Jū′dah in Rĭb′lah.

11 Then he put out the eyes of Zĕd-e-kī′ah; and the king of Babylon bound him in chains, and carried him to Baby-lon, and put him in prison till the day of his death.

12 ¶Now in the fifth month, in the tenth day of the month, which was the nineteenth year of Nĕb-u-chad-rĕz′zar king of Babylon, came Nĕb-u-zar-ā′dan, captain of the guard, which served the king of Babylon, into Jeru-salem,

13 And burned the house of the LORD, and the king's house; and all the houses of Jerusalem, and all the houses of the great men, burned he with fire:

14 And all the army of the Chăl-dē′ans, that were with the captain of the guard, brake down all the walls of Jeru-salem round about.

15 Then Nĕb′u-zar-ā′dan the captain of the guard carried away captive cer-tain of the poor of the people, and the residue of the people that remained in the city, and those that fell away, that fell to the king of Babylon, and the rest of the multitude.

16 But Nĕb′u-zar-ā′dan the captain of the guard left certain of the poor of the land for vinedressers and for hus-bandmen.

17 Also the pillars of brass that were in the house of the LORD, and the bases, and the brasen sea that was in the house of the LORD, the Chăl-dē′ans̱ brake, and carried all the brass of them to Babylon.

18 The caldrons also, and the shovels, and the snuffers, and the bowls, and the spoons, and all the vessels of brass wherewith they ministered, took they away.

19 And the basons, and the firepans, and the bowls, and the caldrons, and the candlesticks, and the spoons, and the cups; that which was of gold in gold, and that which was of silver in sil-ver, took the captain of the guard away.

20 The two pillars, one sea, and twelve brasen bulls that were under the bases, which king Sŏlŏmon had made in the house of the LORD: the brass of all these vessels was without weight.

21 And concerning the pillars, the height of one pillar was eighteen cubits; and a fillet of twelve cubits did compass it; and the thickness thereof was four fingers: it was hollow.

22 And a chapiter of brass was upon it: and the height of one chapiter was five cubits, with network and pomegran-ates upon the chapiters round about, all of brass. The second pillar also and

the pomegranates were like unto these.

23 And there were ninety and six pomegranates on a side; and all the pomegranates upon the network were an hundred round about.

24 ¶And the captain of the guard took Se-ra-i′ah the chief priest, and Zĕph-a-nī′ah the second priest, and the three keepers of the door:

25 He took also out of the city an eunuch, which had the charge of the men of war; and seven men of them that were near the king's person, which were found in the city; and the principal scribe of the host, who mustered the people of the land; and threescore men of the people of the land, that were found in the midst of the city.

26 So Nĕb′u-zar-a′dan the captain of the guard took them, and brought them to the king of Babylon to Rĭb′lah.

27 And the king of Babylon smote them, and put them to death in Rĭb′lah in the land of Hā′măth. Thus Jū′dah was carried away captive out of his own land.

28 This is the people whom Nĕb-u-chad-rĕz′zar carried away captive: in the seventh year three thousand Jews and three and twenty.

29 In the eighteenth year of Nĕb-u-chad-rĕz′zar he carried away captive from Jerusalem eight hundred thirty and two persons:

30 In the three and twentieth year of Nĕb-u-chad-rĕz′zar Nĕb′u-zar-a′dan the captain of the guard carried away captive of the Jews seven hundred forty and five persons: all the persons were four thousand and six hundred.

31 ¶And it came to pass in the seven and thirtieth year of the captivity of Je-hoi′a-chin king of Jū′dah, in the twelfth month, in the five and twentieth day of the month, that E′vil-mĕ-ro′dach king of Babylon in the first year of his reign lifted up the head of Je-hoi′a-chin king of Jū′dah, and brought him forth out of prison,

32 And spake kindly unto him, and set his throne above the throne of the kings that were with him in Babylon,

33 And changed his prison garments: and he did continually eat bread before him all the days of his life.

34 And for his diet, there was a continual diet given him of the king of Babylon, every day a portion until the day of his death, all the days of his life.

24. **Seraiah** (see 51:59 note). **Zephaniah** (see 29:25 note). **The principal scribe of the host.** The secretary of the army's commander.

25-30. Three deportations are given in this passage. The first was during the seventh year of Nebuchadnezzar. The disparity of dates between verses 12 and 29 is due to the difference between the use of the Hebrew dating system in one and the Babylonian system in the other. The larger number of exiles in II Kings 24:12-16 probably includes the women and children, while Jeremiah only includes the men (see Mt 14:21).

The second deportation occurred in the **Eighteenth** year of Nebuchadnezzar (the time of the destruction of Jerusalem). The disparity of dates between verse 12 and 29 (also the seventh year of 52:28 and the eighth year of II Kgs 24:12-16) is due to the different systems of dating the reigns of Oriental kings. One would count his reign from the beginning of the first year, the other from the end of the first year.

The third deportation is only mentioned here. Probably this deportation was to punish the Jews for the assassination of Gedaliah (see notes on chs. 40 and 41).

B. The Liberation of Jehoiachin. 52:31-34.

31-34. **Jehoiachin** (see Introduction). **Evil-merodach.** The son of Nebuchadnezzar, he reigned for only one year. **Lifted up the head,** i.e., looked upon with favor. During the excavations of R. Koldewey (1899-1917), several cuneiform tablets were discovered in a building near the famous Ishtar Gate in Babylon. These tablets confirm the liberation of Jehoiachin by Evil-merodach (see D. W. Thomas, p. 84ff.). **A continual diet given him.** An Oriental expression for a government pension. Thus ends the book of Jeremiah, with Judah in captivity as he had prophesied.

BIBLIOGRAPHY

Albrekton, Bertil. *Studies in the Text and Theology of the Book of Lamentations.* Lund: G.W.K. Gleerup, 1963.

Ball, C. J., and W. H. Bennett. The Book of Jeremiah. In *The Expositors' Bible.* New York: George H. Doran Co., n.d.

Cawley, F. and A. R. Millard. Jeremiah. In *New Bible Commentary: Revised.* Grand Rapids: Eerdmans, 1970.

Cheyne, T. K. The Lamentations of Jeremiah. In *The Pulpit Commentary.* Grand Rapids: Eerdmans, 1950.

Clark, Adam. *Clark's Commentary.* New York: The Methodist Book Concern, n.d.

Gottwald, Norman K. *Studies in the Book of Lamentations.* Naperville, Ill.: Alec R. Allenson, 1962.

Harrelson, W. *Jeremiah, Prophet to the Nations.* Philadelphia: Judson Press, 1959.

*Harrison, R. K. *Jeremiah and Lamentations.* Downers Grove, Ill.: InterVarsity, 1973.

Jensen, Irving L. *Jeremiah and Lamentations.* Chicago: Moody Press, 1966.

Keil, C. F. and F. Delitzsch. Jeremiah. In the *Commentaries on the Old Testament.* Vol. II. Grand Rapids: Eerdmans, 1967.

Kinsler, F. Ross. *Inductive Study of the Book of Jeremiah.* South Pasadena, Ca.: William Carey Library, 1971.

Knight, G. A. F. *Esther, Song of Songs, Lamentations.* London: S.C.M. Press, 1955.

*Laetsch, T. *Bible Commentary: Jeremiah.* Saint Louis: Concordia, 1965.

Lange, J. Lamentations. In the *Commentary on the Holy Scriptures.* Grand Rapids: Zondervan.

Leslie, E. A. *Jeremiah.* Nashville: Abingdon Press, 1954.

Meek, Theophile J., and Wm. P. Merrill. Lamentations. In *The Interpreter's Bible.* New York: Abingdon Press, 1956.

Morgan, G. Campbell. *Studies in the Prophecy of Jeremiah.* Westwood, N.J.: Fleming H. Revell Co., 1955.

Nicholson, E. W. *The Book of the Prophet Jeremiah.* Cambridge, England: Cambridge University Press, 1973.

Peake, A. S., ed. Jeremiah and Lamentations. In *The New Century Bible.* Edinburgh: T.C. and E.C. Jack, 1910.

Smith, George Adam. *Jeremiah.* 4th ed. Garden City: Doubleday, Doran and Co., 1929.

Stephens-Hodge, L. E. H. Lamentations. In *The New Bible Commentary.* Ed. by Frances Davidson. Grand Rapids: Eerdmans, 1960.

Streane, A. W. Jeremiah and Lamentations. In *The Cambridge Bible For Schools and Colleges.* Ed. by J. J. S. Perowne. Cambridge, England: Cambridge University Press, 1895.

Thompson, J. A. The Book of Jeremiah. In *The New International Commentary.* Grand Rapids: Eerdmans, 1979.

Von Orelli, C. *The Prophecies of Jeremiah.* Edinburgh: T. & T. Clark, 1889.

LAMENTATIONS

INTRODUCTION

Lamentations consists of five beautiful elegiac poems, one for each chapter. These elegies, or songs of mourning, express the grief of the poet at the utter ruin of Jerusalem. Dirge poetry was not unique to Israel, but rather common in the ancient Near East. The Sumerians were the first to write dirge poetry over the destruction of some great city. The lament over Ur is one of the most celebrated elegies of the ancient Near East.

Title. The title in the original (Heb *'ēkah*) comes from the opening word and means, "Alas!" The Talmud named the book "Qinoth Lamentations or Elegies." The Septuagint, the Greek version of the Old Testament, translated this title Threnoi (Gr *thrēnos*) "Lamentations." The Latin version was Lamentationes, from which we have our English title, Lamentations.

Place in canon. In the Hebrew Bible, Lamentations is in the third division, the Hagiographa (Sacred Writings) and forms one of the Megilloth or five rolls (Song, Ruth, Lamentations, Ecclesiastes, and Esther). Jesus also recognized this threefold division of the Old Testament (Lk 24:44). The Septuagint, Latin Vulgate, and our English versions place it between Jeremiah and Ezekiel.

Literary Form. The composition of the book is not only poetical, but alphabetical, with the exception of Chapter 5. Written as if for a national funeral, the first four chapters have the rhythm of a dirge and are written as acrostics. In chapters 1, 2, and 4, each of the 22 verses begins with a new letter of the Hebrew alphabet: the first, *'alep*, the second, *bēt*, the third *gimel*, etc. The third chapter has three verses to each Hebrew letter, making sixty-six verses in all. Psalm 119 is a good example of this arrangement. Chapter 1 follows the usual order of the Hebrew alphabet, but in chapters 2, 3, and 4 the letters *'ayin* and *pē'* are transposed (cf. Ps 34). Chapter 5 has twenty-two verses but they are not in alphabetical order. Jensen summarizes the possible reasons for the use of the acrostic device as follows: "(1) as an aid to memorization; (2) as a symbol of the fullness of the people's grief (i.e. from A to Z); (3) to confine the expression of boundless grief by the limiting device of an acrostic" (*Jeremiah and Lamentations*, p. 123).

The Hebrew meter is called *qînôt* (Lamentations) and corresponds to our English elegiac poetry. Instead of the usual balance in Hebrew poetry, this meter has the second part as an imperfect echo of the first. A lively three or four beats to the first phrase is followed by a sad two or three beats to the second, giving the effect of a dying plaintive tune. This was the strain used by the mourning women in their laments for the dead (cf. Jer 9:17; Amos 5:2). This "limping verse" was adopted by the prophets in order to put the listener into a mood corresponding to their melancholy utterance. Everyone understood the melody.

Authorship. Although the book itself does not name its author, both Jewish and Christian traditions have attributed authorship to Jeremiah. Both Josephus and Jerome believed that II Chronicles 35:25 refers to Lamentations. This verse shows that Jeremiah wrote elegies; this lament for Josiah, however, is not our present book since it is a lamentation for Jerusalem rather than Josiah. If Jeremiah committed his Josiahan elegies to writing, they have been lost.

Several scholars (Chaney, Ewald, Eissfeldt, Pfeiffer, etc.) have denied the Jeremianic authorship of Lamentations, citing the unreliability of the Jeremianic tradition, the unworthiness of Jeremiah to produce the alphabetical scheme, supposed differences in sentiment, etc. However, these arguments are extremely precarious. The long Jeremianic tradition includes not only the LXX but the Targum of Jonathan, the Vulgate, many church fathers, and numerous later commentators. There is also strong internal evidence for Jeremianic authorship, including: (1) the local color and detail of an eyewitness; (2) numerous similarities between the prophecy and poetry; (3) the reflection of the sensitive temperament of Jeremiah in Lamentations; and (4) the absence of the name Jeremiah showing that no other eyewitness could have composed the elegies and at the same time ignored the great prophet. (For a complete discussion of authorship see: Lange, *Commentary on the Holy Scriptures-Lamentations*, p. 6ff.; Keil, *Keil and Delitzsch Commentaries on The Old Testament–Lamentations*, p. 339ff.; and Young, *An Introduction to the Old Testament*, p. 362ff.). In the book of Jeremiah we have predictions of the destruction of Judah and Jerusalem and the author's eyewitness account of their fulfillment. In Lamentations we have the author's expressions of his sorrow at the calamities and desolation of the city and her people (cf. Lk 13:34-35; 19:41-44 for Christ's lament over Jerusalem).

Purpose. To the people of Judah, the fall of Jerusalem meant more than just the destruction of their nation's capital. It contained the Temple of Jehovah, where God had chosen to live with His people (Deut 16:16; Ps 87). When Jerusalem was destroyed and the Temple desecrated, the people knew that God had given them over to the enemy. God had rejected them because of their sin and corruption.

Composed probably during the three-month interval between the burning of Jerusalem and the departure of the remnant to Egypt (Jer 39:2; 41:1, 18; 43:7), Lamentations is a description of the woes of the people interspersed with messages of exhortation to repentance and promises of God's mercy (3:22-26, 31-33, 40-41, 57-58; 4:22; 5:19, 21). Jerusalem is pictured as a widowed and disgraced princess. Following the destruction of Jerusalem in A.D. 70 at the hands of the Romans, the conquering general Titus erected an arch in Rome picturing Israel as a woman mourning. The daughters of Jerusalem also sought to wail such a dirge over Jesus at His death (Lk 23:27-31).

In the Jewish tradition, the book of Lamentations was and still is read in the synagogue during the fast on the ninth of *Ab* (mid-July) to commemorate the destruction of Jerusalem by the Babylonians in 586 B.C., as well as the Roman destruction of the city in A.D. 70. The book is also recited by pious Jews at the Western Wall (Wailing Wall) in Jerusalem every Friday. Roman Catholics have designated the last three days of Holy Week as a special time to read Lamentations, one regrets to say, have too often neglected the reading of

these solemn poems. Yet in these days of personal, national, and international crises (and disaster) the message of this book is a challenge to repent of sins, personal, national, and international, and to commit ourselves afresh to God's steadfast love. Though this love is ever present and outgoing, a holy and just God must surely judge unrepentant sinners" (*The Wycliffe Bible Commentary*, p. 696).

Since Lamentations looks back in mourning to the destruction of Jerusalem, as the book of Jeremiah looked forward to that event with a solemn warning, Jeremiah's poetry forms a perfect sequel to his prophecy.

OUTLINE

COMMENTARY

I. THE FIRST LAMENT—THE RUINED CITY OF JERUSALEM. 1:1-22.

A. The Utter Destruction of the City. 1:1-11.

Each of the five chapters of Lamentations expresses grief over the destruction of Jerusalem, but the first poem gives the most poignant weeping. The first half of this poem describes the utter destruction of the capital city caused by her grievous sin.

1:1. Become as a widow. Cities are often referred to as the mothers of their inhabitants, the kings as husbands, and the princes as children. Therefore, when these are taken from them, they are represented as childless widows. **Princess among the provinces.** Israel is no longer a super-power among the nations, but rather she is now a widow.

2-3. Her lovers . . . her friends. Nations who once vied for her friendship are now her enemies. The allies to whom she looked for help have deserted her.

HOW doth the city sit solitary, *that was* full of people! *how* is she become as a widow! *she that was* great among the nations, *and* princess among the provinces, *how* is she become tributary!

2 She weepeth sore in the night, and her tears are on her cheeks: among all her lovers she hath none to comfort *her:* all her friends have dealt treacherously with her, they are become her enemies.

3 Ju'dah is gone into captivity because of affliction, and because of great servitude: she dwelleth among the heathen, she findeth no rest: all her persecutors overtook her between the straits.

4 The ways of Zion do mourn, because none come to the solemn feasts:

4-6. Solemn feasts (cf. Ex 23:14-17) included special occasions (II Chr 30:22) and weekly sabbaths (Lev 23:2-3). The roads leading to the city were no longer busy thoroughfares filled with pilgrims attending the festivals (cf. Ps 42:1-4). No one attended her religious feasts. **Her virgins.** Probably a reference to the female choirs who took part in the services (cf. Jer 31:13; Ps 68:25). Because of her continuing sin, her inhabitants were deported and her leaders were like malnourished deer (**harts**) unable to escape the hunters. All the splendor, beauty, pride, and glory of Jerusalem was gone. Everywhere the poet looked, he found destruction and oppression.

7-11. Jerusalem remembered. "They had loved to roam," observes Laetsch, "now they are condemned to roam. In her wanderings scattered throughout the earth (Jer 9:16; 18:17; 30:11), afflicted and homeless Judah too late remembers 'all her pleasant things,' all her precious possessions she had in the days of old, gracious gifts of her Lord, to be cherished highly. She had despised both the gifts and the giver. Now nothing remains but affliction and wanderings and grievous sins (vs. 8), filthy sins, defiling her skirts (vs. 9; cf. Jer 2:34), manifest in spite of her self-righteousness, her formal worship, her hypocritical boasting (Jer 7:4ff.), sins unforgiven" (*Bible Commentary-Jeremiah*, p. 379).

These verses picture Judah as turning her back in naked shame. Those who had honored her now despise her. Heathen nations, which were forbidden religious communion with Israel, now plunder and desecrate her holiest places. The people are starving, having already exchanged their precious things for available sustenance. Jerusalem's grievous sin has brought grievous suffering (note the cry to God in vs. 9 is repeated in vs. 11).

B. Jerusalem Bewails Her Desolate Condition. 1:12-19.

12-13. Is it nothing to you . . . ? Is it not of concern to you? Do you not care? In the second half of this poem, the city personified bewails her affliction. Her pathetic appeal summons passers-by to look on and consider her sorrowful dilemma. **The day of his fierce anger.** Many people today want to ignore the severity of God's wrath. This inability to realize that true goodness does not indulge evil often keeps people from seeking God's grace.

14. Transgressions . . . wreathed, and come up upon my neck. The Lord has taken the sins of the people and has woven them into a strong rope to keep the yoke of subjection secure.

15-16. An assembly. Jehovah calls an assembly, not for Judah, but for her enemies. Judah is as one in a **winepress.** Her young men are as clusters of grapes, whose lifeblood has been trodden out in the winepress of affliction. A winepress is sometimes used in Scripture as a picture of divine judgment (Isa 63:1-6; Rev 14:19-20; 19:15). The city weeps uncontrollably for her children, and there is no one to comfort her.

17-19. I called for my lovers. With outstretched hands Zion's call for help from those around her goes unheeded. The Lord has commanded Jacob's neighbors to be her adversaries. Jerusalem is treated as an unclean thing. He who was to be an example of holiness to the nations (Deut 4:4-9; Lev 11:44) has become unclean, as a **menstruous woman.**

---

all her gates are desolate: her priests sigh, her virgins are afflicted, and she *is* in bitterness.

5 Her adversaries are the chief, her enemies prosper; for the LORD hath afflicted her for the multitude of her transgressions: her children are gone into captivity before the enemy.

6 And from the daughter of Zion all her beauty is departed: her princes are become like harts *that* find no pasture, and they are gone without strength before the pursuer.

7 Jerusalem remembered in the days of her affliction and of her miseries all her pleasant things that she had in the days of old, when her people fell into the hand of the enemy, and none did help her: the adversaries saw her, *and* did mock at her sabbaths.

8 Jerusalem hath grievously sinned; therefore she is removed: all that honoured her despise her, because they have seen her nakedness: yea, she sigheth, and turneth backward.

9 Her filthiness *is* in her skirts; she remembereth not her last end; therefore she came down wonderfully: she had no comforter. O LORD, behold my affliction: for the enemy hath magnified *himself*.

10 The adversary hath spread out his hand upon all her pleasant things: for she hath seen *that* the heathen entered into her sanctuary, whom thou didst command *that* they should not enter into thy congregation.

11 All her people sigh, they seek bread; they have given their pleasant things for meat to relieve the soul: see, O LORD, and consider; for I am become vile.

12 ¶*Is it* nothing to you, all ye that pass by? behold, and see if there be any sorrow like unto my sorrow, which is done unto me, wherewith the LORD hath afflicted *me* in the day of his fierce anger.

13 From above hath he sent fire into my bones, and it prevaileth against them: he hath spread a net for my feet, he hath turned me back: he hath made me desolate *and* faint all the day.

14 The yoke of my transgressions is bound by his hand: they are wreathed, *and* come up upon my neck: he hath made my strength to fall, the LORD hath delivered me into *their* hands, *from whom* I am not able to rise up.

15 The LORD hath trodden under foot all my mighty *men* in the midst of me: he hath called an assembly against me to crush my young men: the LORD hath trodden the virgin, the daughter of Judah, *as* in a winepress.

16 For these *things* I weep; mine eye, mine eye runneth down with water, because the comforter that should relieve my soul is far from me: my children are desolate, because the enemy prevailed.

17 Zion spreadeth forth her hands, *and there is* none to comfort her: the LORD hath commanded concerning Jacob, *that* his adversaries *should be* round about him: Jerusalem is as a menstruous woman among them.

18 ¶The LORD is righteous; for I have rebelled against his commandment:

hear, I pray you, all people, and behold my sorrow: my virgins and my young men are gone into captivity.

19 I called for my lovers, *but* they deceived me: my priests and mine elders gave up the ghost in the city, while they sought their meat to relieve their souls.

20 Behold, O LORD; for I *am* in distress: my bowels are troubled; mine heart is turned within me; for I have grievously rebelled: abroad the sword bereaveth, at home *there is* as death.

21 They have heard that I sigh: *there is* none to comfort me: all mine enemies have heard of my trouble; they are glad that thou hast done *it:* thou wilt *bring* the day *that* thou hast called, and they shall be like unto me.

22 Let all their wickedness come before thee; and do unto them, as thou hast done unto me for all my transgressions: for my sighs *are* many, and my heart *is* faint.

CHAPTER 2

HOW hath the LORD covered the daughter of Zion with a cloud in his anger, *and* cast down from heaven unto the earth the beauty of Israel, and remembered not his footstool in the day of his anger!

2 The LORD hath swallowed up all the habitations of Jacob, and hath not pitied: he hath thrown down in his wrath the strong holds of the daughter of Judah; he hath brought *them* down to the ground: he hath polluted the kingdom and the princes thereof.

3 He hath cut off in *his* fierce anger all the horn of Israel: he hath drawn back his right hand from before the enemy, and he burned against Jacob like a flaming fire, *which* devoureth round about.

4 He hath bent his bow like an enemy: he stood with his right hand as an adversary, and slew all *that were* pleasant to the eye in the tabernacle of the daughter of Zion: he poured out his fury like fire.

5 The Lord was as an enemy: he hath swallowed up Israel, he hath swallowed up all her palaces: he hath destroyed his strong holds, and hath increased in the daughter of Judah mourning and lamentation.

6 And he hath violently taken away his tabernacle, as *if it were of* a garden: he hath destroyed his places of the assembly: the LORD hath caused the solemn feasts and sabbaths to be forgotten in Zion, and hath despised in the indignation of his anger the king and the priest.

7 The LORD hath cast off his altar, he hath abhorred his sanctuary, he hath given up into the hand of the enemy the walls of her palaces; they have made a noise in the house of the LORD, as in the day of a solemn feast.

8 The LORD hath purposed to destroy the wall of the daughter of Zion: he hath stretched out a line, he hath not withdrawn his hand from destroying: therefore he made the rampart and the wall to lament; they languished together.

C. A Prayer for Vindication. 1:20-22.

20-22. Finding no compassion among men, Judah turns to Jehovah with a prayer that her joyful enemies will someday suffer her mournful misfortune. This is entirely in keeping with God's prophecy on the nations (Isa 10:12-21; Hab 2:5-17; Jer 25:12-14).

II. THE SECOND LAMENT—JERUSALEM UNDER JUDGMENT. 2:1-22.

Israel had imagined that she occupied a privileged position among the nations because of her covenant relationship to God, but she had forgotten the moral and spiritual obligations of the covenant. She who had sown to the wind was now reaping the whirlwind. Approximately forty descriptions of divine judgment affecting every aspect of Jewish life are given in this chapter.

A. Judgment Follows Sin. 2:1-10.

2:1-5. Footstool. In all of the judgments unleashed upon Judah and Jerusalem, none was so astonishing as the Lord's rejecting His footstool, i.e., the ark of the covenant (1 Chr 28:2), which was destroyed along with the Temple. **Habitations** (vs. 2). The place where the shepherds lived with their flocks in the open village areas of Judaea. Both the habitations and the **strongholds,** the fortified towns, had been destroyed. **Hath brought them down.** The humiliation of Judah, which had been reduced to a position below all the other nations. **Horn of Israel** (vs. 3), is a favorite Old Testament symbol of power and strength (cf. I Sam 2:1). As a consuming fire (Heb 12:29, Deut 4:24) the Lord had taken away every means of both offense and defense available to the kingdom. God not only delivered His people to the enemy, but also fought against them Himself. **The tabernacle of the daughter of Zion** (vs. 4). Her tent is not the Temple, which is never referred to as anything but that of Jehovah, but rather her house, i.e., the city of her dwelling. The Lord has become as an enemy and multiplied the **mourning and lamentation** (vs. 5) of the people.

6-10. Violently taken away his tabernacle. With the destruction of Jerusalem, Jehovah's temple and its sacred institutions are destroyed. (Note verses 5-7.) **hath destroyed his strongholds . . . his tabernacle . . . his places of the assembly . . . his altar . . . his sanctuary. Wall of the daughter of Zion** (vs. 8). A metonymy for the city of Jerusalem, i.e., the Lord hath purposed to destroy the city of Jerusalem. God's plumbline of destruction is so complete as to extend to the **wall** (vs. 8). Her **law** is no longer taught and there is no **vision,** i.e., revelation from the Lord. The rulers of Jerusalem sit silently in deep sorrow, while her **virgins** hang their heads in shame. **Elders** (vs. 10). In the patriarchal culture, elders were the heads of families. Now they are the civil leaders (cf. Jud 8:14; I Sam 8:4; I Kgs 8:1-3; 20:7; II Kgs 10:1; etc.).

B. The Reflections of the Eyewitness. 2:11-19.

11-12. Mine eyes do fail with tears. The author vividly portrays his physical and emotional distress at the suffering of his people. **My liver is poured upon the earth.** Since the liver was regarded as the seat of the emotions, this is a metaphorical description of the poet's anguish of soul. The heart of the prophet is broken at the sight of small children crying for food and drink, of infants breathing their last on their mother's breasts.

13-14. What thing shall I liken to thee . . . ? Jeremiah is at a loss to find any situation with which to compare Zion's irreparable ruin. The false prophets must bear a large share in the doom of the nation, since they did not expose and castigate the sin of the people. Rather they delivered empty messages of peace and future prosperity (cf. Jer 2:5; 10:15; 14:13; 16:19; etc.), resulting in banishment from their land.

15-16. Clap their hands. Jerusalem's enemies mock her devastation. Clapping hands was a gesture of delight over another's injury. The hissing and wagging of the head showed scorn and ridicule. Jerusalem was the envy of her neighboring nations; they longed for her destruction and blessed the day of her ruin.

17-18. The LORD hath done . . . devised. The prophet emphasizes the fact that God has now executed the judgment of which He had long before warned (Lev 26:14ff.; Deut 28:15ff.). The people were driven to pray for mercy. **Apple of thine eye** (vs. 18). Compare this word meaning "pupil of the eye" with Deuteronomy 32:10, Psalm 17:8; and Zechariah 2:8.

19. In the beginning of the watches. The twelve hours of the night were divided into three units of four hours each (cf. Jud 7:19). Each unit was called a watch. Therefore, the lament was uttered at specific intervals during the night to remind the remnant that their sorrows were God's punishment for earlier sin.

C. A Prayer for Mercy. 2:20-22.

20-22. Consider to whom thou hast done this. Do you realize, Lord, what people you are afflicting? The Jewish nation always pointed with pride to their special relationship with Jehovah. However, now children were being eaten by those who bore them (cannibalism, a most reprehensible crime against humanity, was resorted to by the Hebrews only as a last desper-

9 Her gates are sunk into the ground; he hath destroyed and broken her bars: her king and her princes are among the Gentiles: the law is no more; her prophets also find no vision from the LORD.

10 The elders of the daughter of Zion sit upon the ground, and keep silence: they have cast up dust upon their heads; they have girded themselves with sackcloth: the virgins of Jerusalem hang down their heads to the ground.

11 Mine eyes do fail with tears, my bowels are troubled, my liver is poured upon the earth, for the destruction of the daughter of my people; because the children and the sucklings swoon in the streets of the city.

12 They say to their mothers, Where is corn and wine? when they swooned as the wounded in the streets of the city, when their soul was poured out into their mothers' bosom.

13 What thing shall I take to witness for thee? what thing shall I liken to thee, O daughter of Jerusalem? what shall I equal to thee, that I may comfort thee, O virgin daughter of Zion? for thy breach is great like the sea: who can heal thee?

14 Thy prophets have seen vain and foolish things for thee: and they have not discovered thine iniquity, to turn away thy captivity; but have seen for thee false burdens and causes of banishment.

15 All that pass by clap their hands at thee, they hiss and wag their head at the daughter of Jerusalem, saying, Is this the city that men call The perfection of beauty, The joy of the whole earth?

16 All thine enemies have opened their mouth against thee: they hiss and gnash the teeth: they say, We have swallowed her up: certainly this is the day that we looked for; we have found, we have seen it.

17 The LORD hath done that which he had devised; he hath fulfilled his word that he had commanded in the days of old: he hath thrown down, and hath not pitied: and he hath caused thine enemy to rejoice over thee, he hath set up the horn of thine adversaries.

18 Their heart cried unto the LORD, O wall of the daughter of Zion, let tears run down like a river day and night: give thyself no rest; let not the apple of thine eye cease.

19 Arise, cry out in the night: in the beginning of the watches pour out thine heart like water before the face of the LORD: lift up thy hands toward him for the life of thy young children, that faint for hunger in the top of every street.

20 Behold, O LORD, and consider to whom thou hast done this. Shall the women eat their fruit, and children of a span long? shall the priest and the prophet be slain in the sanctuary of the Lord?

21 The young and the old lie on the

ground in the streets: my virgins and my young men are fallen by the sword; thou hast slain *them* in the day of thine anger; thou hast killed, *and* not pitied.

22 Thou hast called as in a solemn day my terrors round about, so that in the day of the LORD's anger none escaped nor remained: those that I have swaddled and brought up hath mine enemy consumed.

CHAPTER 3

I AM the man *that* hath seen affliction by the rod of his wrath.

2 He hath led me, and brought *me into* darkness, but not *into* light.

3 Surely against me is he turned; he turneth his hand *against me* all the day.

4 My flesh and my skin hath he made old; he hath broken my bones.

5 He hath builded against me, and compassed *me* with gall and travail.

6 He hath set me in dark places, as *they that* be dead of old.

7 He hath hedged me about, that I cannot get out: he hath made my chain heavy.

8 Also when I cry and shout, he shutteth out my prayer.

9 He hath inclosed my ways with hewn stone, he hath made my paths crooked.

10 He was unto me *as* a bear lying in wait, *and as* a lion in secret places.

11 He hath turned aside my ways, and pulled me in pieces: he hath made me desolate.

12 He hath bent his bow, and set me as a mark for the arrow.

13 He hath caused the arrows of his quiver to enter into my reins.

14 I was a derision to all my people; *and* their song all the day.

15 He hath filled me with bitterness, he hath made me drunken with wormwood.

16 He hath also broken my teeth with gravel stones, he hath covered me with ashes.

17 And thou hast removed my soul far off from peace: I forgat prosperity.

18 And I said, My strength and my hope is perished from the LORD:

19 Remembering mine affliction and

ate act, cf. II Kgs 6:26-29); **priest and prophet** alike were massacred in the Temple; **young and old** lie unburied in the street; **virgins, young women and young men** are fallen by the sword. The slaughter of the young meant the destruction of an entire generation. With the complaint that no one could escape God's judgment, this poem, like the first (cf. 1:20), concludes with deep sorrow.

III. THE THIRD LAMENT—JEREMIAH'S SUFFERING REPRESENTATIVE, 3:1-66.

The high point of the book of Lamentations comes in this third poem. The brightest and most hopeful picture in the book is painted here. As man's hope arises out of a sea of hard experience, so in this poem the stanza about hope (vss. 19-42) is surrounded by two stanzas about affliction. This elegy summarizes the basic message of Lamentations and is also a foreshadowing of the sufferings of Christ (cf. Isa 53; Ps 22).

A. God's Servant Sorrows. 3:1-18.

3:1-2. I am the man. The personal pronoun changes from "I" (vss. 1-24) to "we" (vss. 22, 40-47) and back to "I" (vss. 48-66) again. This is not simply Jeremiah or some other Israelite weeping over the injustices he had to bear from his peers. Here Jeremiah speaks as an individual member or the nation expressing grief over the ruin of the city and its people. Jeremiah is a representative of all the godly who were afflicted in the fall of Judah and Jerusalem (Jer 15:15-18; 38:6). **Rod of his wrath.** God could and would use pagan nations as His instruments of punishment upon Israel (cf. Isa 10:5).

3-13. Turneth his hand. In contrast to the benevolent hand of God in guiding Israel in the Exodus and her subsequent history, now the hand of God is turned upon her in judgment. **Gall** (vs. 5). It was a bitter and poisonous herb (Deut 29:18; Jer 8:14; 9:15; Hos 10:4). The term was also applied to the bile (Job 16:13) and the poison of serpents (Job 20:14, 16). The Romans gave criminals this bitter potion to strengthen them for crucifixion. Jesus refused it and chose to bear the punishment alone (Mt 27:34; cf. Ps 69:21).

These verses contain a more detailed account of God's chastening. The representative poet suffers a physical wasting away; his light (Ps 143:3) and freedom are gone. **Hedged me about** (vs. 7). This was a form of torture made popular by the Assyrians, whereby a prisoner was walled-up in a confined space. There is no way out, no possible escape (cf. Job 3:23; 19:8). Even his prayers go unheard (cf. Job 30:20). How aptly this describes the nation. **Arrow** (vs. 12). A common metaphor for persecution (Ps 38:1-2; Job 6:4; 16:12-14).

14-18. Derision. Laughingstock. As Jeremiah was a laughingstock to the nation, so Judah had become the laughingstock of the entire Near East. **Wormwood** (vs. 15). A bitter-plant growing in the deserts of Palestine and Syria, which became a symbol of calamity and injustice. **Gravel stones.** A punishment whereby foreign substances, especially sand, were mixed with food (cf. Ex 32:20). Many Egyptian mummies exhibit worn-down teeth from such practices. Here Judah's teeth are broken because God has given her stones to eat as punishment for her idolatry. The prophet had become an object of ridicule and scoffing. In this pitiful condition there was no room for thoughts of peace and prosperity, even strength and hope seem forever gone (vss. 17-18).

B. Jeremiah Recalls God's Faithfulness. 3:19-38.

19-21. Remembrance. Here the prophet makes the transition from the desperate complaint to hope. Realizing that thoughts of his affliction only serve to keep his soul low, he brings to mind truth that will give him hope.

22-27. Mercies. (Heb *chesed*) means loyalty or devotion, especially in relationship to the covenant and God as its author. Out of the faithfulness of His covenant God grants mercy. His mercy is limitless and can never fail. **Great is thy faithfulness.** The very fact that there still exists a remnant of His people proves the steadfastness of God's mercy and inheritance (Num 18:20). If the Lord is kind to those who hope in Him, then it follows that we ought to be patient while waiting for His help in suffering. **Yoke in his youth.** A person needs more discipline while he is young than in his mature years. Therefore, it is good for man to suffer in his youth, that he may learn to exercise himself in patient waiting upon the Lord.

28-30. Keepeth silence. A form of resignation to God's will (cf. Ps 39:2; 94:17). The result of early discipline is a humble spirit. **Mouth in the dust** (vs. 29). This Oriental expression of complete submission by throwing oneself on the ground is a silent confession of unworthiness. **His cheek to him that smiteth him** (vs. 30). Another gesture of complete submission. The prophet Micah had predicted that the king of Israel would be smitten upon the cheek during the siege (Mic 5:1). Now Jerusalem is submissive to God's judgment. The highest expression of this submission is found in our Lord Jesus Christ just before the crucifixion (cf. Mt 26:67; Lk 22:64; Jn 18:22; 19:3) when the innocent Lamb of God suffered for our sin in obedience to the will of the Father (cf. Mt 26:39) and without any retaliation (I Pet 2:21ff.).

31-33. He doth not afflict willingly. Three certainties are given to comfort the afflicted. The first is in verse 31: there will be an end to the sorrow. The second is in verse 32: He shows compassion according to the fulness of grace. The third is given in verse 35: God does not delight to send sorrow and pain to his children, but chastisement is a necessary part of spiritual growth.

34-38. The Lord approveth not. Our Lord does not approve of cruelty, injustice, or subversion. God is sovereign and the supreme Arbiter of human affairs. Like Isaiah (45:7), Jeremiah attributes the whole range of moral values to the **Most High.**

C. A Call for Repentance. 3:39-54.

39-42. Wherefore doth a living man complain . . . ? Since nothing can happen to us without God's knowledge, we should endure suffering patiently and without protest, trusting God will work out all things for the good (cf. Rom 8:28). The transgressor has no right at all to complain about the punishment for his sins (cf. I Pet 2:19ff.). Rather, we should **search and try our ways** (vs. 40), which will always cause us to return to the Lord. Let us lift up our hearts, not merely our hands, in earnest prayer. We have sinned, and God has **not pardoned** because His justice must punish sin.

43-47. Thou hast . . . persecuted us. Jeremiah again returns to the theme of affliction. The Lord's wrath forms an impenetrable cover over the prayers of the people. Having slain without pity, God makes them as rubbish in the land. Tearful, desolate, and destroyed, Judah must listen to the taunting cries of her enemies.

---

my misery, the wormwood and the gall.

20 My soul hath them still in remembrance, and is humbled in me.

21 This I recall to my mind, therefore have I hope.

22 ¶It is of the LORD's mercies that we are not consumed, because his compassions fail not.

23 They are new every morning: great is thy faithfulness.

24 The LORD is my portion, saith my soul; therefore will I hope in him.

25 The LORD is good unto them that wait for him, to the soul that seeketh him.

26 It is good that a man should both hope and quietly wait for the salvation of the LORD.

27 It is good for a man that he bear the yoke in his youth.

28 He sitteth alone and keepeth silence, because he hath borne it upon him.

29 He putteth his mouth in the dust; if so be there may be hope.

30 He giveth his cheek to him that smiteth him: he is filled full with reproach.

31 For the Lord will not cast off for ever:

32 But though he cause grief, yet will he have compassion according to the multitude of his mercies.

33 For he doth not afflict willingly nor grieve the children of men.

34 To crush under his feet all the prisoners of the earth,

35 To turn aside the right of a man before the face of the most High,

36 To subvert a man in his cause, the Lord approveth not.

37 ¶Who is he that saith, and it cometh to pass, when the Lord commandeth it not?

38 Out of the mouth of the most High proceedeth not evil and good?

39 Wherefore doth a living man complain, a man for the punishment of his sins?

40 Let us search and try our ways, and turn again to the LORD.

41 Let us lift up our hearts with our hands unto God in the heavens.

42 We have transgressed and have rebelled: thou hast not pardoned.

43 Thou hast covered with anger, and persecuted us: thou hast slain, thou hast not pitied.

44 Thou hast covered thyself with a cloud, that our prayer should not pass through.

45 Thou hast made us as the offscouring and refuse in the midst of the people.

46 All our enemies have opened their mouths against us.

47 Fear and a snare is come upon us, desolation and destruction.

48 Mine eye runneth down with rivers of water for the destruction of the daughter of my people.

49 Mine eye trickleth down, and ceaseth not, without any intermission,

50 Till the LORD look down, and behold from heaven.

51 Mine eye affecteth mine heart because of all the daughters of my city.

52 Mine enemies chased me sore, like a bird, without cause.

53 They have cut off my life in the dungeon, and cast a stone upon me.

54 Waters flowed over mine head; then I said, I am cut off.

55 ¶ I called upon thy name, O LORD, out of the low dungeon.

56 Thou hast heard my voice: hide not thine ear at my breathing, at my cry.

57 Thou drewest near in the day that I called upon thee: thou saidst, Fear not.

58 O LORD, thou hast pleaded the causes of my soul; thou hast redeemed my life.

59 O LORD, thou hast seen my wrong: judge thou my cause.

60 Thou hast seen all their vengeance and all their imaginations against me.

61 Thou hast heard their reproach, O LORD, and all their imaginations against me;

62 The lips of those that rose up against me, and their device against me all the day.

63 Behold their sitting down, and their rising up; I am their musick.

64 Render unto them a recompence, O LORD, according to the work of their hands.

65 Give them sorrow of heart, thy curse unto them.

66 Persecute and destroy them in anger from under the heavens of the LORD.

CHAPTER 4

HOW is the gold become dim! how is the most fine gold changed! the stones of the sanctuary are poured out in the top of every street.

2 The precious sons of Zion, comparable to fine gold, how are they esteemed as earthen pitchers, the work of the hands of the potter!

3 Even the sea monsters draw out the breast, they give suck to their young ones: the daughter of my people is become cruel, like the ostriches in the wilderness.

4 The tongue of the sucking child cleaveth to the roof of his mouth for thirst: the young children ask bread, and no man breaketh it unto them.

5 They that did feed delicately are desolate in the streets: they that were brought up in scarlet embrace dunghills.

6 For the punishment of the iniquity

48-51. **Mine eye trickleth down.** Jeremiah's tears over the destruction of his people will flow until Jehovah looks down from heaven (cf. Jer 9:1).

52-54. **Mine enemies chased me sore.** Without excuse for their hatred, the prophet's enemies hunted him down, cast him into a well, and sought to destroy his life by casting in stones upon him. Thus, Jeremiah used a picture of his own experience to illustrate the sufferings that had come upon the godly Israelites (Jer 38:6ff).

D. A Prayer for Retribution. 3:55-66.

55-58. **I called upon thy name.** Jeremiah recalls his prayer for deliverance from the circumstances that could have ended his life. Jehovah's answer to this desperate prayer was **Fear not.** With this answer, the prophet is confident of God's redemption.

59-66. **Thou hast seen.** Confident that God has seen all the wrong done to both Judah and her suffering representative, Jeremiah concludes that the Lord will deal justly with the enemy.

IV. THE FOURTH LAMENT—THE SUFFERING PEOPLE OF JERUSALEM. 4:1-22.

This fourth lament consists of Jeremiah's contrast of the happy conditions of former days with the present devastation of Jerusalem. The vivid descriptions of this chapter prove, beyond doubt, authorship by an eyewitness. First, the fate of the city is described; then the prophet gives the reasons for the unbelievable devastation.

A. The Siege and the Pitiful State of Zion's Nobility. 4:1-12.

4:1-2. **The precious sons of Zion.** The people of Jerusalem had considered themselves as gold in comparison to the other nations because of their covenant relationship with God. Now they had been discarded as broken pieces of pottery, and their bodies were scattered throughout all the streets.

3-5. **The daughter of my people is become cruel.** Even animals of prey care for their offspring better than the people of Jerusalem have been forced to treat their young. **Ostriches,** especially, are noted as cruel and indifferent to the needs of their young (cf. Job 39:13-17). The nursing child dies of thirst, and young children lack food; while their mothers, like the ostriches of the desert, ignore their cries. Once well-fed and cared for, the nobles now perish while seeking garbage in the street. **Scarlet.** A mark of wealth.

6. **Greater than the punishment of the sin of Sodom.** Jeru-

salem's greater sin has brought the greater punishment. While Sodom's destruction was sudden and by the hand of God, Jerusalem's ruin came by the hand of man and brought prolonged torment.

7-9. Her Nazarites. Distinguished ones, i.e., nobility. Once handsome and healthy, her princes now appear dull, shriveled, and dying. The nobility cannot be distinguished from the peasants because the famine has reduced everyone to a state of malnutrition and starvation. Better to die by the sword than by the slow process of starvation.

10-12. Pitiful women have sodden their own children. Tenderhearted women have been driven to this most horrible crime of boiling and then eating their own children. This fearful state of things shows that the Lord has fully poured out His wrath upon Jerusalem and His people. No one would have imagined that the enemies of Jerusalem could have entered her gates and caused such devastation.

B. The Consequences and Sin of the Corrupt Spiritual Leaders. 4:13-20.

This judgment of wrath is a consequence of the sins of the prophets and priests (vss. 13-16), as well as their vain trust in the help of man (vss. 17-20).

13-16. Shed the blood of the just. These spiritual leaders had shed the blood of the innocent and just. They had even attempted to add Jeremiah to their list (cf. Jer 26:8). Having defiled themselves with the blood of the righteous, they are now shunned and abhorred by the people and treated as lepers and unceremoniously cast out of the city. Without honor or respect, they wander the countryside as vagabonds.

17-20. Watched for a nation. All hope for aid from a foreign country has been admitted as vain, and escape is not an alternative. **Laid wait . . . in the wilderness** (vs. 19). In order to prevent the remnant from making any further leagues with Egypt, the Babylonians set up ambush points south of Judah in the desert. Even the king has been captured. **The anointed.** Zedekiah (Jer 52:7-11). Zedekiah was a weak king who took Jeremiah's advice only in times of severe crisis (Jer 21:1-7; 37:17-21; 38:14-28). Since, however, he was the Lord's anointed, his office is recognized here, rather than his character or his leadership.

C. The Promise of Punishment for Edom. 4:21-22.

21-22. Haughty and gloating, Edom watches with joy at Judah's ruin. Now the prophet turns and, pointing a finger at her sin, foretells the judgment of Edom (cf. Ob 8-14). (The Edomites were descendants of Esau, brother of Jacob, Gen 25:30; 36:1.)

---

of the daughter of my people is greater than the punishment of the sin of Sodom, that was overthrown as in a moment, and no hands stayed on her.

7 Her Nazarites were purer than snow, they were whiter than milk, they were more ruddy in body than rubies, their polishing *was* of sapphire:

8 Their visage is blacker than a coal; they are not known in the streets: their skin cleaveth to their bones; it is withered, it is become like a stick.

9 *They that be* slain with the sword are better than *they that be* slain with hunger: for these pine away, stricken through for *want* of the fruits of the field.

10 The hands of the pitiful women have sodden their own children: they were their meat in the destruction of the daughter of my people.

11 The LORD hath accomplished his fury; he hath poured out his fierce anger, and hath kindled a fire in Zion, and it hath devoured the foundations thereof.

12 The kings of the earth, and all the inhabitants of the world, would not have believed that the adversary and the enemy should have entered into the gates of Jerusalem.

13 For the sins of her prophets, *and* the iniquities of her priests, that have shed the blood of the just in the midst of her,

14 They have wandered *as* blind *men* in the streets, they have polluted themselves with blood, so that men could not touch their garments.

15 They cried unto them, Depart ye; *it is* unclean; depart, depart, touch not: when they fled away and wandered, they said among the heathen, They shall no more sojourn *there*.

16 The anger of the LORD hath divided them; he will no more regard them: they respected not the persons of the priests, they favoured not the elders.

17 As for us, our eyes as yet failed for our vain help: in our watching we have watched for a nation *that* could not save *us*.

18 They hunt our steps, that we cannot go in our streets: our end is near, our days are fulfilled; for our end is come.

19 Our persecutors are swifter than the eagles of the heaven: they pursued us upon the mountains, they laid wait for us in the wilderness.

20 The breath of our nostrils, the anointed of the LORD, was taken in their pits, of whom we said, Under his shadow we shall live among the heathen.

21 Rejoice and be glad, O daughter of Edom, that dwellest in the land of Uz; the cup also shall pass through unto thee: thou shalt be drunken, and shalt make thyself naked.

22 The punishment of thine iniquity is accomplished, O daughter of Zion; he will no more carry thee away into captivity: he will visit thine iniquity, O daughter of Edom; he will discover thy sins.

CHAPTER 5

REMEMBER, O LORD, what is come upon us: consider, and behold our reproach.

2 Our inheritance is turned to strangers, our houses to aliens.

3 We are orphans and fatherless, our mothers *are* as widows.

4 We have drunken our water for money; our wood is sold unto us.

5 Our necks *are* under persecution: we labour, *and* have no rest.

6 We have given the hand *to* the Egyptians, *and to* the Assyrians, to be satisfied with bread.

7 Our fathers have sinned, *and are* not; and we have borne their iniquities.

8 Servants have ruled over us: *there is* none that doth deliver *us* out of their hand.

9 We gat our bread with *the peril of* our lives because of the sword of the wilderness.

10 Our skin was black like an oven because of the terrible famine.

11 They ravished the women in Zion, *and* the maids in the cities of Judah.

12 Princes are hanged up by their hand: the faces of elders were not honoured.

13 They took the young men to grind, and the children fell under the wood.

14 The elders have ceased from the gate, the young men from their musick.

15 The joy of our heart is ceased; our dance is turned into mourning.

16 The crown is fallen *from* our head: woe unto us, that we have sinned!

17 For this our heart is faint; for these *things* our eyes are dim.

18 Because of the mountain of Zion, which is desolate, the foxes walk upon it.

19 Thou, O LORD, remainest for ever; thy throne from generation to generation.

20 Wherefore dost thou forget us for ever, *and* forsake us so long time?

21 Turn thou us unto thee, O LORD, and we shall be turned; renew our days as of old.

22 But thou hast utterly rejected us; thou art very wroth against us.

(see page 1524 for Bibliography to Jeremiah and Lamentations)

V. THE FIFTH LAMENT—A PLEA FOR MERCY. 5:1-22.

A. Jerusalem Pleads for God to Look upon Her Humiliation. 5:1-18.

5:1. Remember, O LORD, what is come upon us. Jerusalem cries out to Jehovah to regard her disgrace.

2-5. She has lost land and houses to strangers; loved ones are gone. The people now have to pay their enemies for those necessities which are rightly their own, and they are forced to perform hard labor without rest.

6. We have given the hand. To give the hand is a sign of submission or subjection. In order to go on living, Judah finds herself begging bread from her enemies.

7-10. Our fathers have sinned. While the speakers do not consider themselves innocent (vs. 16), they do recognize the previous generations' sins and their effect. The people are now ruled by those who were formerly servants, and they must risk their lives to obtain their daily food. **Sword of the wilderness.** The Bedouins raided and often killed those supplying their bread. The comparison of their skin to an oven does not refer to the blackness of an oven, but to the fire burning in it. The fever of famine is one of the usual aftermaths of war.

11-13. Specific cases of suffering are listed here, such as rape, the shameful treatment of the nobility, and the oppressive tasks given youths and children.

14-18. Joy . . . turned into mourning. The gate was not only for conducting public affairs, but was also a place of assembly for social entertainment. All public meetings and enjoyment have been suspended. Judah has fallen from her position of honor and power among the nations. She recognizes the cause as sin. This sorrow culminates in the realization that Mount Zion lies in desolation. The holy mount on which the house of God stood is now desolate and overrun by wild animals.

B. A Prayer for Divine Restoration. 5:19-22.

19. Remainest for ever. The earthly dwelling place of Jehovah may lie in ruin, but His throne endures forever.

20-22. Wherefore. Since His throne endures forever in heaven, He cannot allow His kingdom (people) to perish on earth. **Turn** (vs. 21). "To restore and to build Jerusalem," is the prayer on the heart of the prophet (Dan 9:25). Without repentance and conversion there can be no restoration to the former relationship. **Utterly rejected** (vs. 22). The construction of the verse implies, "Surely you won't reject us forever?" (cf. Hab 3:2). As L.E.H. Stephens-Hodge notes, "Suffering has done its work, the prodigal has come to himself and is ready to arise and go to his father" (*The New Bible Commentary*, p. 644).

EZEKIEL

INTRODUCTION

The Man. Very little is known about the man Ezekiel, although he was a contemporary of Jeremiah. Jeremiah was a prophet, mainly to the Jews, in Jerusalem before the city fell in 586 B.C. Daniel, also, was a prophet at this same time, mainly in the court of King Nebuchadnezzar in Babylonia.

Name. In Hebrew the name Ezekiel means God strengthens. God made the prophet strong to resist the opposition of a hardened and rebellious people (cf. 3:8-9).

Birth. If the phrase "thirtieth year" of 1:1 refers to Ezekiel's age at that time (593 B.C.), then he was born in 623 B.C. This would have been during the reign of the good King Josiah. He then would have lived his boyhood years during the great reformation of that period when the Law was discovered in the Temple in 621 B.C. (cf. II Kgs 22:8ff. and 23).

Family. Ezekiel was like Jeremiah in that he was of a priestly heritage. He was the son of Buzi (1:3). His father may have been of the Zadok line (1:3; 40:46; 44:15). He was married (24:18) and loved his wife dearly (24:16). The darkest day of his life was when the Lord announced to him the siege of Jerusalem (24:2) and then the death of his beloved wife (24:15-18).

In Exile. When Ezekiel was about 18 years old, the Babylonians made their first invasion into Palestine and carried away Daniel (ca. 605 B.C.). Then in 597 B.C. they came again and took Ezekiel among the captives (1:2; 33:21; II Kgs 24:10-17). Some of the exiles were made slaves; others were imprisoned; and many were allowed to settle down in their own homes. In the providence of God, Ezekiel was one of those granted such liberty (cf. Ezr 2:59; Neh 7:61; Jer 29:1-7).

His home was Tel-abib (3:15), a principal colony of the exiles near the famous city of Babylon. Ezekiel's home became a meeting place where the Jewish elders often came to receive counsel (8:1; 14:1; 20:1).

Ezekiel dates his ministry precisely. He was taken captive in the year 597 B.C., which is evident from 33:21. In this passage he speaks of his captivity as occurring in the twelfth year before the time when the city of Jerusalem was destroyed, which came in 586 B.C. Then, in 40:1 he speaks of an event that occurred in the twenty-fifth year of his captivity; he says this was "in the fourteenth year after that the city was smitten."

Call and Commission. Ezekiel indicates that his call to the prophetic ministry came in "the fifth year of King Jehoiachin's captivity" (1:2). This would have been 593-592 B.C. He continued in service at least until the twenty-seventh year of his captivity, according to 29:17. This would have been 571 B.C. He may have continued longer in the ministry, but this is the last reported date in the book.

Message. There are at least five recurrent themes that run through the book. The first relates to the character of God and is the otherness of God. Eze-

kiel was a priest, and it would be inevitable that he was most concerned with the holiness of God. "This was not a moral quality, though it could and did show itself in moral actions (cf. Isa 5:16b)" (Taylor, *Ezekiel: An Introduction and Commentary*, p. 40). Holiness is a word expressing a relationship with the root meaning of *qōdesh*, to be separate. Thus, it involved being cut off from ordinary relationships for the purpose of serving a peculiar function, one belonging to God, the Holy One. "The God of Israel did not simply possess this quality; He was it. Everything connected with Him derived holiness from Him. So there could be a holy place where He was worshiped, holy people who acted as His ministers, holy garments that they wore and holy equipment that they used. His name was holy, His people Israel were holy (even when they were living unrighteously), and the place which He made His dwelling was His holy mountain" (Taylor, p. 41). Chapters 1-3 direct one's attention to the sense of otherness and majesty as it presents the vision of the Lord riding upon His chariot-throne.

The second emphasis in the book relates to the sinfulness of Israel. Three passages (16:1-63; 20:1-31; 23:1-49) employ the use of allegory to depict the story of Israel's persistent unfaithfulness to the gracious covenant of God. More specifically, in chapter eight the wrongdoings that were happening in the Temple are cited. These were religious deviations, including idolatry, animal worship, nature worship, and sun worship. They all illustrated the degree of syncretism that was affecting the worship of God in Jerusalem.

These practices provided abundant justification for God's decision to slaughter the people of Jerusalem, reminiscent of the Passover plague (9:5ff.), and to bring a destruction upon the city as in the days of Sodom and Gomorrah (10:2).

A third theme is the inevitable fact of judgment in the face of these bold and brazen sinful practices. Messages of judgment had been given to the people for many years prior to Ezekiel, but now judgment was imminent. "God's message to him was that the God who spoke would also act: 'I the LORD have spoken and I will do it' (17:24; 22:14; 24:14; 36:36; 37:14)" (Taylor, p. 44).

The people could no longer shrug off the warning of judgment with the excuse that nothing had happened so far (12:22), or that all of the prophecies applied to the distant future (12:27). As 12:28 records, "Therefore say unto them, Thus saith the LORD GOD; There shall none of my words be prolonged any more, but the word which I have spoken shall be done. . . ."

In light of the previous concepts, a fourth theme is evident, that of individual responsibility. In the face of inevitable judgment, the possibility of the salvation of a remnant is projected. This appears even in the prediction of destruction (5:3, 10; 6:8; 9:4). Ezekiel's purpose in acting as a watchman is that the wicked man may turn and save his life (3:18). This is explicitly stated in 18:1-29, where he takes pains "to say that every man is treated as an individual by God. What happens to him is not dependent purely on heredity (his father's sins), nor yet on environment (the nation's sins), but is conditioned by personal choice" (Taylor, p. 45). Thus, each Israelite had the personal responsibility of committing his life to God.

Finally, in light of all this there is the promise of a future restoration. Repentance is for the individual and has implications for the community as a whole. The new Israel will be brought to life miraculously by the working of God's Spirit. The new bones will live (37:5). There will be no old divisions of Israel and Judah to tear apart (37:17). The people will enjoy the blessings of the everlasting covenant expressed as "and they shall be my people, and I will be their God" (cf. 11:20; 14:11; 36:28; 37:23, 27). At the head of the nation will be David my servant as the Messiah King (37:24ff.). He will rule justly, and out from the sanctuary in the new Jerusalem "will flow the symbolical river of life to water the waste places of the earth" (Taylor, p. 46) from 47:1-12.

The Book. Much of the book consists of direct addresses of the Lord to Ezekiel, indicated by "and the word of the LORD came unto me, saying." Prose and poetry are intermingled. The book abounds with visions, parables, allegories, apocalyptic imagery, and various symbolic acts. Jerome said that Ezekiel was "an ocean and labyrinth of the mysteries of God."

Ezekiel was methodical in his recording events and dates. His messages are dated, twelve of them, with the year cited: 1:1-2; 8:1; 20:1; 24:1; 26:1; 29:1; 30:20; 31:1; 32:1; 32:17; and 40:1.

Visions. Ezekiel is known as the prophet of visions. The very first verse says, "... the heavens were opened, and I saw visions of God." Note the visions recorded by Ezekiel: (1) cherubim, 1:4-28 (vision of God); (2) roll or scroll, 2:9-3:3; (3) plain, 3:22-23; and (4) Jerusalem (including four abominations in the Temple, 8:1-18; inhabitants slain, 9:1-11; city destroyed by fire, 10:1-22; and the Lord departs from the city, 11:1-25); (5) dry bones, 37:1-10; and (6) new temple, etc., 40:1-48:35.

Symbolic Actions. God told Ezekiel, "... I have set thee for a sign unto the house of Israel" (12:6). Ezekiel, probably more than any other prophet, taught by symbolic actions. His actions were revelatory in nature and produced the desired effect, "at least upon the hearts of the serious-minded, causing them to ask what these things meant (12:9; 24:19; 37:18)" (Jensen, *Survey of the Old Testament,* p. 365). Some of the actions included: (1) sign of the brick, 4:1-3; (2) prophet's posture, 4:4-8; (3) famine, 4:9-17; (4) knife and razor, 5:1-17; (5) house moving, 12:1-7, 17-20; (6) sharpened sword, 21:1-17; (7) Nebuchadnezzar's sword, 21:18-23; (8) smelting furnace, 22:17-31; (9) Ezekiel's wife's death, 24:15-18; and (10) two sticks, 37:15-17. Each of these signs depicted events beginning with the siege and fall of Jerusalem and culminating in the future restoration of Israel and Judah. They depict the captivity and the captor, Nebuchadnezzar of Babylon.

Allegories. Allegories are stories intended to teach spiritual lessons. John Bunyan's work, *Pilgrim's Progress,* is a good example of an allegory. In Ezekiel, allegories teach by words, whereas the symbolic actions teach by actual events. The following constitute allegories in Ezekiel: (1) the vine, 15:1-8; (2) the faithless wife, 16:1-63; (3) the two eagles, 17:1-21; (4) the cedar, 17:22-24; (5) the two women, 23:1-49; and (6) the boiling caldron, 24:1-14.

Apocalyptic Imagery. Daniel and Revelation are the two books of the Bible usually classified by this terminology. But Ezekiel contains much such future prophecies which contain much symbol and imagery (note: 6:1-14; 7:5-12; 20:33-44; 28:25, 26; 34:25-31; 36:8-15, 33-36; 38:1-23; 39:1-29; and 47:1-12). See Jensen (p. 367) for the many resemblances between Ezekiel and the book of Revelation.

Prominent Subjects. First, Ezekiel's call and commission (2:1-3:27). Like other prophets, he received a vision of God that caused him to prostrate himself before His sovereign Maker (1:26-28; cf. Isaiah's vision in Isa 6 and John's vision in Rev 1:10-18). Isaiah emphasized God's holiness; Ezekiel, His power, majesty, and government; and John, His love. Second, the glory and majesty of God (1:1b, 28b; 3:12, 23).

Third, messianic prophecies: (1) the Lord, the sanctuary, 11:16-20; (2) the wonderful cedar sprig, 17:22-24; (3) the rightful King, 21:26, 27; (4) the faithful Shepherd, 34:11-31; (5) the great purification, 36:25-35; (6) the great Resurrection, 37:1-14; (7) the great reunion, 37:21-28; and (8) the overthrow of Gog, 38:1-39:29; and (9) the life-giving stream, 47:1-12, (Pearson, p. 705).

Fourth, the future resurrection of Israel, 37:1-48:35. Note 39:25, 28-29: "... Now will I bring again the captivity of Jacob, and have mercy upon the whole house of Israel . . . Then shall they know that I am the LORD their God, which caused them to be led into captivity among the heathen: but I have gathered them unto their own land, and have left none of them any more there . . . for I have poured out my spirit upon the house of Israel. . ."

Key Words and Verses. The phrase "son of man" appears over ninety times in Ezekiel, and the prophet is the one so designated. "The title was symbolic of Ezekiel's identity with the people to whom he was sent, even as Jesus, the Son of man, was so identified (It appears almost ninety times in the Gospels). This title was Jesus' favorite title of Himself" (Jensen, p. 371). The phrase "glory of the God of Israel" or "glory of the LORD" appears eleven times in the first eleven chapters. "LORD GOD" appears over two hundred times. "The word of the LORD came unto me" appears forty-nine times; "I shall (will) be sanctified" appears six times; 20:41; 28:22, 25; 36:23; 38:16; 39:27. And the phrase, "The hand of the LORD was upon me," or similar phrases, appears seven times in 1:3; 3:14, 22; 8:1; 33:22; 37:1; 40:1. The book of Ezekiel is to *System of Interpretation.*

be viewed in a perspective wherein the events stated as historical are accurate and the events that have not yet taken place at the time of their prophetic utterance will take place in the future. This has occurred as it relates to the fall of Jerusalem in 586 B.C. and as it pertained to the seven nations surrounding her. The events relating to Israel's future regathering, her salvation, the building of the Temple, and details concerning the land are all to be understood as awaiting their literal fulfillment.

Though there is much use made of symbolism, it is not to be interpreted allegorically. The symbol depicts that which is real in a manner to which ordinary language could not do justice, as for ex-

ample the vision of the glory of the Lord. The vision of the Temple is not to be seen as symbolical, but as that which literally will be.

Also, the past and future events of Ezekiel are viewed in a dispensational framework. Israel past and future is distinct from the body of Christ, the New Testament church. Israel's chastisement will be concluded in the Tribulation period following the catching away of the church in the Rapture. At the Second Advent, when Christ comes back to earth, Israel will be regathered and saved, her enemies destroyed, the Temple rebuilt, and memorial sacrificial worship instituted; and a reign of justice, equity, and peace will be established with Christ as the King.

OUTLINE

I. Ezekiel's Call and Commissioning. 1:1-3:27.
  A. Ezekiel's Situation. 1:1-3.
  B. Ezekiel's Vision of God. 1:4-28.
  C. Ezekiel's Call. 2:1-10.
  D. Ezekiel's Commissioning. 3:1-27.
II. Prophecies Against Judah and Jerusalem. 4:1-24:27.
  A. Prediction of the Siege and Doom of Jerusalem. 4:1-8:18.
  B. Departure of the Glory of the Lord. 9:1-11:25.
  C. Burden of the Prince and False Prophets. 12:1-15:8.
  D. Adultery of Israel. 16:1-17:24.
  E. Lamentation for the Princes of Israel. 18:1-19:14.
  F. History of Israel: Past and Future. 20:1-49.
  G. Sword of the Lord. 21:1-32.
  H. Jerusalem Condemned and Destroyed. 22:1-24:27.
III. Prophecies Against Seven Foreign Nations. 25:1-32:32.
  A. Judgment on Ammon. 25:1-7.
  B. Judgment on Moab. 25:8-11.
  C. Judgment on Edom. 25:12-14.
  D. Judgment on Philistia. 25:15-17.
  E. Judgment on Tyre. 26:1-28:19.
  F. Judgment on Sidon. 28:20-26.
  G. Judgment on Egypt. 29:1-32:32.
IV. Prophecies Concerning Israel's Future Restoration. 33:1-39:29.
  A. Ezekiel's Appointment as a Watchman. 33:1-33.
  B. Israel's Shepherds. 34:1-31.
  C. The Rebirth of the Nation. 35:1-36:38.
  D. The Resuscitation of the Nation. 37:1-14.
  E. The Reuniting of the Nation. 37:15-28.
  F. The Victory of the Nation over Gog and Magog. 38:1-39:29.
V. Prophecies Concerning Israel in the Millennial Kingdom. 40:1-48:35.
  A. A New Temple. 40:1-43:27.
  B. A New Service of Worship. 44:1-46:24.
  C. A New Holy Land. 47:1-48:35.

COMMENTARY

I. EZEKIEL'S CALL AND COMMISSIONING. 1:1-3:27.

A. Ezekiel's Situation. 1:1-3.

NOW it came to pass in the thirtieth year, in the fourth *month*, in the fifth *day* of the month, as I *was* among the captives by the river of Chebar, *that* the heavens were opened, and I saw visions of God.

1:1. In the thirtieth year. Since the time of Origen (ca. A.D. 185-254), this has been held to be a reference to the prophet's age. According to Numbers 4:3-4, this is the age when priests began their ministry. There are many other proposed interpretations: (1) thirtieth year of Jehoiachin's age, 593-592 B.C.; (2) thirtieth year after Josiah's reform, 585 B.C.; (3) thirtieth year of the current jubilee period; (4) thirtieth year of the neo-Babylonian Empire, 606-605 B.C.; (5) thirtieth year of Manasseh, 667 B.C.; and (6) thirtieth year of Artaxerxes III, 328 B.C.

In the fourth. This would have been mid-June to mid-July, if one reckons from the first month being mid-March to mid-April.

Among the captives (lit., the captivity). Lofthouse concludes from this term and the use of **among** that the exiles had by then formed themselves into a community (Fisch, p. 2).

2 In the fifth day of the month, which was the fifth year of king Je·hoi´a·chin's captivity,

3 The word of the LORD came expressly unto E·ze´ki·el the priest, the son of Bu´zi, in the land of the Chal·de´ans by the river Che´bar; and the hand of the LORD was there upon him.

4 ¶ And I looked, and, behold, a whirlwind came out of the north, a great cloud, and a fire infolding itself, and a brightness was about it, and out of the

By the river of Chebar. This has been tentatively identified with the *naru kabari*, or "great river," referred to in two cuneiform texts from Nippur. "It was the name given to an irrigation canal which brought the waters of the Euphrates in a loop southeastwards from Babylon via Nippur and back to the main river near Uruk (biblical Erech)" (Taylor, pp. 21-22). Along this river Ezekiel made his home at the community of Tel-abib (3:15).

The heavens were opened. This is comparable with the drawing of the stage curtain. It is a passive of the verb, indicating Ezekiel was not responsible for this action, but as verse 3 reveals, the LORD is the initiator of the action.

And I saw visions of God. The Hebrew may indicate "Divine visions," i.e., concerning God or devised by Him. Certainly, both concepts are involved.

2-3. King Jehoiachin. He was the eighteenth and the next to last king of Judah. He was the son of a diminutive tyrant, Jehoiakim; and he was the grandson of the godly king Josiah. His name means, The Lord establishes. Having been enthroned by Pharaoh Necho of Egypt, he only reigned three months. He was deported to Babylon by Nebuchadnezzar in the year 597 B.C., along with the upper classes (II Kgs 24:8-16). He was released by Amel Marduk (Evil Merodach), son of Nebuchadnezzar in 560 B.C. Jeremiah (Jer 22:20-30) and Ezekiel (19:5-9) appear sympathetic toward him. It was his grandson, Zerubbabel, who appears in the messianic line (cf. I Chr 3:17-19; Ezr 3:8; Mt 1:11-12). Jehoiachin's captivity. This was the fifth year (June-July, 592 B.C.) of his captivity. It is the first of fourteen date references in the book of Ezekiel (cf. 1:2; 3:16; 8:1; 20:1; 24:1; 26:1; 29:1; 29:17; 30:20; 31:1; 32:1; 33:21; 40:1). He was the first prophet to date his messages chronologically. "The vision occurred at a most appropriate time, because in that year a plot against the Babylonian invader was being planned by patriots in Jerusalem and some exiles in Babylon. Ezekiel, like Jeremiah, saw in this movement a rebellion against God's judgment and therefore a threat to the national existence. During the critical years which preceded the fall of Jerusalem, his addresses were in the nature of exhortation against this dangerous policy and a prediction of the final fall of Jerusalem" (Fisch, p. 2). The word of the LORD. The reference is to the message in chapter 2, which follows the vision of chapter 1. The expression associated with the Old Testament prophet (I Sam 15:10; I Kgs 12:22; Isa 38:4; Jer 1:2; Hos 1:1; Joel 1:1). Came expressly (lit., being was, the verb being duplicated for the sake of emphasis). Thus, the phrase denotes the solemnity of the experience. The hand of the LORD was there upon him, an expression describing a condition that indicates a supernatural influence upon the prophet as the source of his revelation (see also 3:14,22; 8:1; 33:22; 37:1; 40:1). Thirteen Hebrew manuscripts and the Septuagint, Syriac, and Arabic versions read "upon me." LORD expresses the covenant name for God in the Old Testament. The theme of the book of Ezekiel centers around the covenant that resulted from Judah's breaking the covenant with the LORD (Ex 3:13-14; 6:3).

B. Ezekiel's Vision of God: 1:4-28.

Ezekiel's call came in the form of a theophany, a manifestation of God in the midst of a storm. He describes his vision in much greater detail than the theophanies of Moses (Ex 24:9ff., 33), Isaiah (ch. 6), Jeremiah (1:4-10), Daniel (7:9ff.), or Amos (7:15).

4. A whirlwind came out of the north. God appears in a whirlwind and a cloud in Exodus 9:24; 19:16; Judges 5:4; 1 Kings 19:11; Psalms 29; Zechariah 9:14. North quite frequently indicates the direction from which the majority of Israel's enemies approached them. The Babylonian Empire extended from

midst thereof as the colour of amber, out of the midst of the fire.

5 Also out of the midst thereof *came* the likeness of four living creatures. And this *was* their appearance; they had the likeness of a man.

6 And every one had four faces, and every one had four wings.

7 And their feet *were* straight feet; and the sole of their feet *was* like the sole of a calf's foot: and they sparkled like the colour of burnished brass.

8 And *they had* the hands of a man under their wings on their four sides; and they four had their faces and their wings.

9 Their wings *were* joined one to another; they turned not when they went; they went every one straight forward.

10 As for the likeness of their faces, they four had the face of a man, and the face of a lion, on the right side: and they four had the face of an ox on the left side; they four also had the face of an eagle.

11 Thus *were* their faces: and their wings *were* stretched upward; two *wings* of every one *were* joined one to another, and two covered their bodies.

12 And they went every one straight forward: whither the spirit was to go, they went; *and* they turned not when they went.

13 As for the likeness of the living creatures, their appearance *was* like burning coals of fire, *and* like the appearance of lamps: it went up and down among the living creatures; and the fire was bright, and out of the fire went forth lightning.

14 And the living creatures ran and returned as the appearance of a flash of lightning.

15 ¶Now as I beheld the living creatures, behold one wheel upon the earth by the living creatures, with his four faces.

16 The appearance of the wheels and their work *was* like unto the colour of a beryl: and they four had one likeness: and their appearance and their work *was* as it were a wheel in the middle of a wheel.

17 When they went, they went upon their four sides: *and* they turned not when they went.

18 As for their rings, they were so high that they were dreadful; and their rings *were* full of eyes round about them four.

19 And when the living creatures went, the wheels went by them: and when the living creatures were lifted up from the earth, the wheels were lifted up.

20 Whithersoever the spirit was to go, they went, thither *was their* spirit to go: and the wheels were lifted up over against them: for the spirit of the living creature *was* in the wheels.

21 When those went, *these* went; and when those stood, *these* stood: and when those were lifted up from the earth, the wheels were lifted up over against them: for the spirit of the living creature *was* in the wheels.

the land of the Chaldeans to the north of the Holy Land (cf. Jer 1:14 which says, "Out of the north an evil shall break forth . . .").

5-9. Four living creatures. These are identified in 10:15 as cherubim. Cherubim are special angelic beings consistently associated with God's holiness (28:14; Isa 6:3).

10-11. Their faces . . . man . . . lion . . . ox . . . eagle. All power, glory, and authority belong to God. However, He uses rational intelligences to govern, including the angelic host. The face of **man** may well represent the realm of intelligence among God's creatures; the face of the **lion**, the majesty of His creation; the face of the **ox**, the patient service that creation returns to Him; and the face of the **eagle**, swiftness to see and bring judgment where needed.

12. Straight forward. Since cherubim are ministering spirits of the Lord, they do not deviate from their assigned task (Heb 1:14). Their task, shortly, would be to carry out God's judgment upon a sinning nation.

13-14. Coals of fire is used here as a symbol of judgment and holiness. By such means, Isaiah's lips were purged (Isa 6:7). Note the coals of fire upon the altar to burn the sacrifices as substitutes for the sinners. The fire of judgment seen here in the vision was soon to be exercised upon the unrepentant remnant still in the land.

15-23. Wheel . . . wheels. Obviously, the wheels are used symbolically. A wheel symbolizes movement. In His government God never is static, but is always moving. The idolatrous remnant was saying judgment would not come. However, God's reward or judgment will never fail to come. **Wheel in the middle of a wheel.** The symbolic wheels were so constructed as to enable movement in any direction, thus speaking of His power to work anywhere. **Full of eyes** speaks of the One who is all-seeing and all-knowing. God is omniscient and omnipresent.

EZEKIEL 1:22

22 And the likeness of the firmament upon the heads of the living creature was as the colour of the terrible crystal, stretched forth over their heads above.

23 And under the firmament were their wings straight, the one toward the other: every one had two, which covered on this side, and every one had two, which covered on that side, their bodies.

24 And when they went, I heard the noise of their wings, like the noise of great waters, as the voice of the Almighty, the voice of speech, as the noise of an host: when they stood, they let down their wings.

25 And there was a voice from the firmament that was over their heads, when they stood, and had let down their wings.

26 ¶ And above the firmament that was over their heads was the likeness of a throne, as the appearance of a sapphire stone: and upon the likeness of the throne was the likeness as the appearance of a man above upon it.

27 And I saw as the colour of amber, as the appearance of fire round about within it, from the appearance of his loins even upward, and from the appearance of his loins even downward, I saw as it were the appearance of fire, and it had brightness round about.

28 As the appearance of the bow that is in the cloud in the day of rain, so was the appearance of the brightness round about. This was the appearance of the likeness of the glory of the Lord. And when I saw it, I fell upon my face, and I heard a voice of one that spake.

CHAPTER 2

AND he said unto me, Son of man, stand upon thy feet, and I will speak unto thee.

24. Noise of their wings. The noise coming from the cherubim's wings is likened unto the noise of a great body of water, or the voice of the Almighty, or the noise of an army in movement. This is the same Hebrew word expressing the noise or sound that Adam and Eve heard in the garden in Genesis 3, rendered "voice" in the KJV. The symbolism is that of unlimited strength and power. Nothing can deter God from accomplishing His plans of judgment, and even angels have frequently been used in executing His judgment (II Kgs 7:6; Dan 10:6).

25-27. Let down their wings. The complete obedience and attention of the cherubim is noted here. They never minister according to their own design, but according to His bidding. **Man.** The symbol God could use when referring to Himself was that of a man. Man has been created in His image, rationally, emotionally, and volitionally, though on a finite level.

28. Likeness of the glory of the Lord. The Lord was not seen by Ezekiel in actuality, but only in symbolical likeness. But even this was of such splendor and glory that Ezekiel fell on his face. Such is consistently the case when man has seen the glory of the Lord, as for example Moses (Ex 19:16); Isaiah (Isa 6:5); Paul (Acts 9:4); and John (Rev 1:17).

C. Ezekiel's Call. 2:1-10.

Ezekiel is addressed as Son of man. The context here would indicate that his human weakness was in view, in contrast to the strength of deity. For the superhuman task about to be given to him, he needed supernatural enablement that he did not have; thus, God the Spirit indwelt him for his work.

Being now indwelt by the Spirit of God, he is commissioned to go to the house of Israel, which has been, and continues to be, rebellious. Terms such as rebellious, stubborn, and obstinate are used to describe the nation. They are even likened to this-tles, thorns, and scorpions standing in opposition to him.

But Ezekiel is given special preparation for the task. First, he is given the message from God to eat and assimilate. He is forewarned that Israel will not receive the message. And finally, he who was naturally fearful will now be made harder in spirit than even the rebellious house of Israel. This will enable him to tell them God's message whether they believe it or not. With this preparation he is directed to go to the exiles already in captivity.

2:1. Son of man is an emphatic form of **man,** occurring over ninety times in the book to remind Ezekiel that, in contrast to the majestic God, he was merely a mortal man. Our Lord in His earthly ministry also took this title to Himself. It indicated His perfect identification with man, so as to enable Him to be our perfect substitute. The blood of animal sacrifice was only a temporary covering for sin, whereas He shed blood for the expiation (full removal) of our sins (Heb 2:14; 10:4). **Stand upon thy feet.** Awestruck by the majestic sight of the divine glory, the prophet had fallen upon his face (1:28). He is now bidden to stand on his feet and be prepared to receive God's message.

2-3. The spirit entered into me. In contrast to the Holy Spirit indwelling all believers of our present age, in Old Testament times He came upon some individuals by sovereign choice for the divine enablement needed for superhuman tasks. It was not universal among those who trusted in God, nor was it a permanent indwelling. Ezekiel was now enabled for his divine commission by the very Spirit of God indwelling him. "God's words revived him and 'spirit' entered him—not necessarily 'the Spirit,' as in RSV, but spiritual energy which he felt within him, strengthening him and infusing his whole body" (Taylor, p. 61). This last view does not seem to be sufficient, as the Holy Spirit is referred elsewhere in the book in the same manner (cf. 3:12, 14, 24; 8:3; 11:1, 5, 24; 37:1; 43:5).

4-8. Impudent children and stiffhearted (lit. the sons, stiffaced and hardhearted). Israel's problem was not one of ignorance, but rather a deliberate and obstinate rebellion to the known will of God. **Briers . . . thorns . . . scorpions.** As these in the natural realm stand in resistance to the traveler and laborer, so Israel will resist the message Ezekiel will bring from the Lord. **Speak my words.** As a prophet from the Lord, it was God's message, even the very words, that he was to proclaim. The people will respond negatively and perhaps even threaten him with harm, but he shall speak faithfully and not be discouraged.

9-10. Roll . . . lamentations . . . mourning . . . woe. In his vision Ezekiel saw a leather scroll opened so both sides could be seen. The message no doubt dealt with Israel's past history of disobedience, idolatry, bloodshed, chastisement, and woe over her impending judgment. In 3:1-3 we see him assimilating this message; and the following chapters deal with the prophet bringing such a message.

D. Ezekiel's Commissioning. 3:1-27.

3:1-7. Eat that thou findest; eat this roll, and go speak. The eating is associated with the command to **go** and **speak** the words of God to the house of Israel. The Lord touched Jeremiah's mouth (Jer 1:9), but gave Ezekiel a scroll to eat. "Implicit in the reception of God's word, symbolized by the eating of the scroll, was the acceptance of the responsibility to utter it at God's direction" (Taylor, p. 64).

Compare Jeremiah 20:9: ". . . in mine heart as a burning fire shut up in my bones, and I was weary with forbearing, and I could not stay," which expresses the inner compulsion of the true prophet sent by God. In much the same way, Peter and John testified before the Sanhedrin: "We cannot but speak the things which we have seen and heard" (Acts 4:20).

2 And the spirit entered into me when he spake unto me, and set me upon my feet, that I heard him that spake unto me.

3 And he said unto me, Son of man, I send thee to the children of Israel, to a rebellious nation that hath rebelled against me: they and their fathers have transgressed against me, *even* unto this very day.

4 For *they are* impudent children and stiffhearted. I do send thee unto them; and thou shalt say unto them, Thus saith the Lord God.

5 And they, whether they will hear, or whether they will forbear, (for they *are* a rebellious house,) yet shall know that there hath been a prophet among them.

6 ¶And thou, son of man, be not afraid of them, neither be afraid of their words, though briers and thorns *be* with thee, and thou dost dwell among scorpions: be not afraid of their words, nor be dismayed at their looks, though they *be* a rebellious house.

7 And thou shalt speak my words unto them, whether they will hear, or whether they will forbear: for they *are* most rebellious.

8 But thou, son of man, hear what I say unto thee; Be not thou rebellious like that rebellious house: open thy mouth, and eat that I give thee.

9 ¶And when I looked, behold, an hand *was* sent unto me; and, lo, a roll of a book *was* therein;

10 And he spread it before me; and it *was* written within and without: and *there was* written therein lamentations, and mourning, and woe.

CHAPTER 3

MOREOVER he said unto me, Son of man, eat that thou findest; eat this roll, and go speak unto the house of Israel.

2 So I opened my mouth, and he caused me to eat that roll.

3 And he said unto me, Son of man, cause thy belly to eat, and fill thy bowels with this roll that I give thee. Then did I eat *it*; and it was in my mouth as honey for sweetness.

4 ¶And he said unto me, Son of man, go, get thee unto the house of Israel, and speak with my words unto them.

5 For thou *art* not sent to a people of a strange speech and of an hard language, *but* to the house of Israel;

6 Not to many people of a strange speech and of an hard language, whose words thou canst not understand. Surely, had I sent thee to them, they would have hearkened unto thee.

7 But the house of Israel will not hearken unto thee; for they will not hearken unto me: for all the house of Israel *are* impudent and hardhearted.

8 Behold, I have made thy face strong against their faces, and thy forehead strong against their foreheads.

9 As an adamant harder than flint have I made thy forehead: fear them not, neither be dismayed at their looks, though they be a rebellious house.

10 Moreover he said unto me, Son of man, all my words that I shall speak unto thee receive in thine heart, and hear with thine ears.

11 And go, get thee to them of the captivity, unto the children of thy people, and speak unto them, and tell them, Thus saith the Lord God; whether they will hear, or whether they will forbear.

12 Then the spirit took me up, and I heard behind me a voice of a great rushing, saying, Blessed be the glory of the Lord from his place.

13 I heard also the noise of the wings of the living creatures that touched one another, and the noise of the wheels over against them, and a noise of a great rushing.

14 So the spirit lifted me up, and took me away, and I went in bitterness, in the heat of my spirit; but the hand of the Lord was strong upon me.

15 ¶ Then I came to them of the captivity at Tĕl-a'bĭb, that dwelt by the river of Chē'băr, and I sat where they sat, and remained there astonished among them seven days.

16 And it came to pass at the end of seven days, that the word of the Lord came unto me, saying,

17 Son of man, I have made thee a watchman unto the house of Israel: therefore hear the word at my mouth, and give them warning from me.

18 When I say unto the wicked, Thou shalt surely die; and thou givest him not warning, nor speakest to warn the wicked from his wicked way, to save his life; the same wicked man shall die in his iniquity; but his blood will I require at thine hand.

8-10. I have made thy face strong (hard) . . . As an adamant. As special preparation against the stubbornness of Israel, Ezekiel will be steeled in nerve and courage for whatever opposition he may face. Symbolically, he will be made as hard as adamant. This word is used frequently by Isaiah meaning "thorn-bushes." In Jeremiah 17:1 it is translated "diamond" and denotes the point of an engraving implement. It also appears figuratively to describe hardness of heart (Zech 7:12). Unless we are dealing with two different words, the only connecting link with the present use is that of sharpness, which comes out clearly in Jeremiah 17:1, "with the point of a diamond: it is graven."

11. Get thee to them of the captivity. Two groups of exiles had already been brought to Babylon, one in 606 B.C., and another in 597 B.C. Ezekiel was sent to them to show God's justice in their being chastened. The very fact of Ezekiel being sent to them indicates God's love and compassion by pleading with them to repent and turn to Him.

12-14. The Spirit bodily transported Ezekiel to the exiles at Tel-abib on the large irrigation canal at Chebar. His ministry to them was in the form of seven days of complete silence among them. He thereby communicated a message most terrible and awesome to them, and it caused great consternation.

Thereupon, he was commanded to go to the plain, where the Lord would have further instructions for him. There he saw a repeat of the vision of the glory of the Lord seen earlier. He was told to go to his house, where he would be bound; and he was told that he would be dumb. However, between intermittent periods of dumbness he was to speak to the rebellious house the message that the Lord would give to him.

After seven days of ministry in silence, he was told to be a watchman over Israel in moral matters. As such, he was to warn the wicked to turn from his way and to warn the righteous, but erring, one to turn from his way. These individuals, whether warned or not, would be held individually accountable for their actions. The prophet would be cleared of guilt if he warned them of their wicked ways, even if they did not repent. But if he did not warn them, he would be guilty of their blood.

Spirit took me up (vs. 12). Ezekiel appears to have been bodily carried by the Spirit. Furthermore, while being transported, he seems to be aware that he was in the fiery chariot that he had seen previously in connection with the vision of the glory of the Lord (ch. 1). This would be an encouragement to follow through in ministering to his people by means of acting out symbolically the sign messages. The evangelist Philip was similarly carried away by the Spirit (Acts 8:39). But later, Ezekiel seems to have been transported to Jerusalem in vision only, not actually in body (8:3; 11:24).

15. I sat where they sat. As Job's three friends sat in silence with him for seven days (Job 2:13), thus comforting him, so Ezekiel entered into anguish for his people in view of the calamities that he knew would come upon them. They did become greatly aroused, but apparently were not yet told of the coming judgment.

16-19. Watchman. The responsibility of a watchman to warn of a coming enemy was well understood (II Kgs 9:17-20), as well as the guilt of manslaughter if he failed to warn his people. In this passage the same principle is applied to warning of moral issues.

19 Yet if thou warn the wicked, and he turn not from his wickedness, nor from his wicked way, he shall die in his iniquity; but thou hast delivered thy soul.

20 Again, When a righteous *man* doth turn from his righteousness, and commit iniquity, and I lay a stumbling-block before him, he shall die: because thou hast not given him warning, he shall die in his sin, and his righteousness which he hath done shall not be remembered; but his blood will I require at thine hand.

21 Nevertheless if thou warn the righteous *man*, that the righteous sin not, and he doth not sin, he shall surely live, because he is warned; also thou hast delivered thy soul.

22 ¶And the hand of the LORD was there upon me; and he said unto me, Arise, go forth into the plain, and I will there talk with thee.

23 Then I arose, and went forth into the plain: and, behold, the glory of the LORD stood there, as the glory which I saw by the river of Chē'bär: and I fell on my face.

24 Then the spirit entered into me, and set me upon my feet, and spake with me, and said unto me, Go, shut thyself within thine house.

25 But thou, O son of man, behold, they shall put bands upon thee, and shall bind thee with them, and thou shalt not go out among them:

26 And I will make thy tongue cleave to the roof of thy mouth, that thou shalt be dumb, and shalt not be to them a reprover: for they are a rebellious house.

27 But when I speak with thee, I will open thy mouth, and thou shalt say unto them, Thus saith the Lord GOD; He that heareth, let him hear; and he that forbeareth, let him forbear: for they are a rebellious house.

CHAPTER 4

THOU also, son of man, take thee a tile, and lay it before thee, and pourtray upon it the city, *even* Jerusalem:

2 And lay siege against it, and build a fort against it, and cast a mount against it; set the camp also against it, and set *battering* rams against it round about.

3 Moreover take thou unto thee an iron pan, and set it *for* a wall of iron between thee and the city: and set thy face against it, and it shall be besieged, and thou shalt lay siege against it. This *shall be* a sign to the house of Israel.

4 Lie thou also upon thy left side, and lay the iniquity of the house of Israel upon it: *according* to the number of the days that thou shalt lie upon it thou shalt bear their iniquity.

5 For I have laid upon thee the years of their iniquity, according to the number of the days, three hundred and ninety days: so shalt thou bear the iniquity of the house of Israel.

6 And when thou hast accomplished them, lie again on thy right side, and thou shalt bear the iniquity of the house of Jū'dah forty days: I have appointed thee each day for a year.

7 Therefore thou shalt set thy face to-

20-27. **I lay a stumbling block before him.** James 1:13 very clearly indicates that God never leads an individual into ways of sin or error. However, God does permit the evil effects of sin to run their courses when persisted in.

It should be noted that in this passage the death of the righteous man is entirely a physical matter, not one of eternal, spiritual death. **Go, shut thyself within thine house.** This was a withdrawal from public life, though individuals could still come see him. It may also indicate that the masses were given up to their way and the emphasis would now be on ministering to concerned individuals. **Put bands upon thee.** Nowhere in the book do we find evidence of actual physical violence upon the prophet, though admittedly this is an argument from silence. Some have suggested that it may have reference to bands of moral restraint, such as the people's rejection of the prophet's warning against their sin and impending judgment. **Thou shalt be dumb.** The dumbness of the prophet may have a double significance. First, his message would have divine authentication if he could speak only when relaying the message from the Lord. Secondly, it certainly would remove the temptation any prophet might have to speak flattering words to the people, rather than God's words.

II. PROPHECIES AGAINST JUDAH AND JERUSALEM. 4:1-24:27.

A. Prediction of the Siege and Doom of Jerusalem. 4:1-8:18.

4:1-17. Chapter 4 predicts the coming siege and famine of Jerusalem. This is graphically done by the prophet, just as the Lord instructed him to do it. Ezekiel took a clay tablet and sketched the city of Jerusalem on it. To picture the siege of an invading force, he built forts around it from which to shoot arrows. Mounds of dirt were moved against the wall, and battering rams were placed in position from which to hurl rocks. An iron pan was set in position as protection against arrows and spears coming from behind the wall, and the army was pitched round about in tents.

Ezekiel lay on his left side behind the iron pan for three hundred ninety days, depicting bearing punishment for Israel's iniquity, and forty days on his right side depicting bearing punishment for Judah's iniquity. Doing this, he shall bare his arm as in combat and prophesy against it. Terrible famine develops within the city, as symbolized by Ezekiel eating bread made of mixed grain measured out in the small amount of twenty shekels (ounces) a day and drinking but one hin (quart) of water a day. To his horror, he shall prepare the food in a defiling manner, contrary to the Levitical law. The Lord said this shall be the way you will eat your food (in a defiled manner) in the nations where you will be banished.

In verse 1 he is told to **take thee a tile.** The bricks, or tile, were larger in those days than in ours. They were at least 13" by 13" by 4". It was large enough to accommodate a plan of the city.

ward the siege of Jerusalem, and thine arm *shall* be uncovered, and thou shalt prophesy against it.

8 And, behold, I will lay bands upon thee, and thou shalt not turn thee from one side to another, till thou hast ended the days of thy siege.

9 ¶Take thou also unto thee wheat, and barley, and beans, and lentiles, and millet, and fitches, and put them in one vessel, and make thee bread thereof, *according* to the number of the days that thou shalt lie upon thy side, three hundred and ninety days shalt thou eat thereof.

10 And thy meat which thou shalt eat *shall* be by weight, twenty shekels a day: from time to time shalt thou eat it.

11 Thou shalt drink also water by measure, the sixth part of an hin: from time to time shalt thou drink.

12 And thou shalt eat it *as* barley cakes, and thou shalt bake it with dung that cometh out of man, in their sight.

13 And the Lord said, Even thus shall the children of Israel eat their defiled bread among the Gentiles, whither I will drive them.

14 Then said I, Ah Lord God! behold, my soul hath not been polluted: for from my youth up even till now have I not eaten of that which dieth of itself, or is torn in pieces; neither came there abominable flesh into my mouth.

15 Then he said unto me, Lo, I have given thee cow's dung for man's dung, and thou shalt prepare thy bread therewith.

16 Moreover he said unto me, Son of man, behold, I will break the staff of bread in Jerusalem: and they shall eat bread by weight, and with care; and they shall drink water by measure, and with astonishment.

17 That they may want bread and water, and be astonied one with another, and consume away for their iniquity.

CHAPTER 5

AND thou, son of man, take thee a sharp knife, take thee a barber's razor, and cause *it* to pass upon thine head and upon thy beard: then take thee the balances to weigh, and divide *the hair.*

2 Thou shalt burn with fire a third part in the midst of the city, when the days of the siege are fulfilled: and thou shalt take a third part, *and* smite about it with a knife: and a third part thou shalt scatter in the wind; and I will draw out a sword after them.

He drew a picture of Jerusalem, built a **fort**, which was a siege wall or tower, then connected the two with **battering rams**, or ramps, and arranged an army **camp** (soldiers) to besiege it. The strength of the besiegers and the impossibility of escape was represented by the **iron pan** that Ezekiel set up in verse 3.

The **three hundred and ninety days** . . . **forty days** in verses 5 and 6 are difficult to understand. The larger figure represents the iniquity to be borne by Israel, and the smaller number, the iniquity to be borne by Judah. Each day is representative of a year. Admittedly, the problem is to correlate the figures to specific periods in the history of Israel and Judah. Three hundred ninety years from the division of the kingdom (in 931 B.C.) comes to 541 (the exiles were free to return in 538 B.C.). One hundred ninety years from the Assyrian captivity in 722 B.C. comes to 532. The forty-year siege might be reckoned from 586 B.C. (the fall of Jerusalem) to 546 B.C., when Cyrus was a threatening power to Babylon.

The significance of the defiled bread is expressed in verses 13 and 16. During the siege the dire circumstances will lead them to do many things that are abhorrent. Then, when Jerusalem falls and its inhabitants are taken captive, they will continue their way of life in a defiled manner. The case of Daniel and his three friends who requested not to eat from the king's table because of conflict with the Levitical law is an example (Dan 1:8).

5:1-2. In chapter four we saw three symbolical signs: the sign of the tile with Jerusalem sketched on it; the sign of the prophet lying three hundred and ninety days on his right side; and the sign of the polluted bread showing Israel's defilement. In chapter five we have the sign of the **sharp knife**. All of the signs show the chastisement and judgment still to come upon Israel because of her rebellion against the Lord.

With a sharp sword, using it as a barber's knife, Ezekiel is to cut off the hair from his head and face. This he is to carefully divide into three parts. One-third he shall put in the city of Jerusalem (the miniature sketched on the tile) and burn it; one-third shall be put around the city, while at the same time, cutting it to pieces; and one-third shall be scattered out to the wind. The meaning is that the sword is the king of Babylon. The hair represents the inhabitants of Jerusalem, of which one-third will be destroyed by fire in the siege, one-third killed by the sword when the siege finally breaks the city, and the remaining one-third scattered among the nations where they will continue to be afflicted.

Then the Lord reveals why Jerusalem and the nation that it represents must go through such terrible chastisement and judgment. The Lord had selected her and her people Israel (when He chose Abraham) to be a testimony in the midst of the nations of His greatness, holiness, goodness, and love. But Israel rebelled by rejecting the Lord and all that He represented and went her own way, serving idols, shedding blood, and becoming even worse than her heathen neighbors.

God's holiness must be preserved at all costs. The sinning rebels among Israel must be cut off, and the erring remnant must be subjected to chastisement in order to purify them.

The means the Lord uses for judgment are: famine, which can be brought about through siege, hail, rain, mice, locusts, and mildew; wild beasts multiplying, leaving their natural habitat and going on a carnage; bloodshed, brought by the sword of the Lord wielded in the hands of enemies; and dispersion among the nations away from Jerusalem, so they will be constantly reminded by the Lord's chastening hand to turn back to Him.

Sharp knife. The term is a sword, even though it is used as a knife. The context of the book very clearly makes the sword represent the king of Babylon. **Balances** were used for dividing the hair into three parts. This points to the justice of God. Note that one-third was not cut off, but was subjected to chastisement rather than judgment. God always remembers His remnant.

3-4. Even the few in number that escape the fire and sword will continue to be subjected to the fire of chastisement and judgment.

5. Midst of the nations. When man had failed before the Flood (and Noah and his posterity after the Flood) to walk righteously before the Lord, then God began again by choosing a man through whom He planned to make Himself and His blessings of salvation known to mankind. He chose Abraham and the nation of Israel that would issue from him. He plucked him out of the center of idolatry in Ur of Chaldea and set him in a pleasant land. There, Israel was to be a testimony of God's greatness and goodness to all the nations about her. God blessed her and raised her above the other nations of the world.

6-14. Israel forgot the Lord and became worse than the nations about her. Some would question whether this happened in actual deeds. However, in view of the greater knowledge that she had than her neighbors, she did more wickedly. Details of her wickedness will be noted in later chapters.

3 Thou shalt also take thereof a few in number, and bind them in thy skirts.
4 Then take of them again, and cast them into the midst of the fire, and burn them in the fire; *for* thereof shall a fire come forth into all the house of Israel.
5 ¶Thus saith the Lord GOD; This *is* Jerusalem: I have set it in the midst of the nations and countries *that are* round about her.

6 And she hath changed my judgments into wickedness more than the nations that *are* round about you, *and* my statutes more than the countries that *are* round about her: for they have refused my judgments and my statutes, they have not walked in them.
7 Therefore thus saith the Lord GOD; Because ye multiplied more than the nations that *are* round about you, *and* have not walked in my statutes, neither have kept my judgments, neither have done according to the judgments of the nations that *are* round about you;
8 Therefore thus saith the Lord GOD; Behold, I, even I, *am* against thee, and will execute judgments in the midst of thee in the sight of the nations.
9 And I will do in thee that which I have not done, and whereunto I will not do any more the like, because of all thine abominations.
10 Therefore the fathers shall eat the sons in the midst of thee, and the sons shall eat their fathers; and I will execute judgments in thee, and the whole remnant of thee will I scatter into all the winds.
11 Wherefore, *as* I live, saith the Lord GOD; surely, because thou hast defiled my sanctuary with all thy detestable things, and with all thine abominations, therefore will I also diminish *thee*; neither shall mine eye spare, neither will I have any pity.
12 ¶A third part of thee shall die with

the pestilence, and with famine shall they be consumed in the midst of thee: and a third part shall fall by the sword round about thee; and I will scatter a third part into all the winds, and I will draw out a sword after them.

13 Thus shall mine anger be accomplished, and I will cause my fury to rest upon them, and I will be comforted: and they shall know that I the LORD have spoken *it* in my zeal, when I have accomplished my fury in them.

14 Moreover I will make thee waste, and a reproach among the nations that *are* round about thee, in the sight of all that pass by.

15 So it shall be a reproach and a taunt, an instruction and an astonishment unto the nations that *are* round about thee, when I shall execute judgments in thee in anger and in fury and in furious rebukes. I the LORD have spoken *it*.

16 When I shall send upon them the evil arrows of famine, which shall be for *their* destruction, *and* which I will send to destroy you: and I will increase the famine upon you, and will break your staff of bread:

17 So will I send upon you famine and evil beasts, and they shall bereave thee; and pestilence and blood shall pass through thee; and I will bring the sword upon thee. I the LORD have spoken *it*.

CHAPTER 6

AND the word of the LORD came unto me, saying,

2 Son of man, set thy face toward the mountains of Israel, and prophesy against them,

3 And say, Ye mountains of Israel, hear the word of the Lord GOD; Thus saith the Lord GOD to the mountains, and to the hills, to the rivers, and to the valleys; Behold, I, even I, will bring a sword upon you, and I will destroy your high places.

4 And your altars shall be desolate, and your images shall be broken: and I will cast down your slain *men* before your idols.

5 And I will lay the dead carcases of the children of Israel before their idols; and I will scatter your bones round about your altars.

6 In all your dwellingplaces the cities shall be laid waste, and the high places shall be desolate; that your altars may be laid waste and made desolate, and your idols may be broken and cease, and your images may be cut down, and your works may be abolished.

7 And the slain shall fall in the midst of you, and ye shall know that I am the LORD.

15. Unto the nations. When Israel was young and disobedient as a nation, God did not destroy her in a great calamity. He restrained the nations, lest they say that He who had brought continuously rebelled against God and turned from Him to them out of Egypt could not preserve them. But when Israel idols, it became necessary that God demonstrate by His greatness and majesty, both to Israel and to the heathen neighbors, that He indeed is the Lord.

16-17. Through the millennia God has used famine, wild beasts, plague, and the sword to judge and chastise His people. All of these plagues would result if Israel failed to keep the Mosaic law (cf. Lev 26:14ff.; Deut 28:15ff.).

6:1-7. As an exile living in the plains of Chaldea, Ezekiel is now directed to give his attention to the mountainous country from whence he came. During the course of Israel's history, the whole land, including the mountains, hills, ravines, and valleys, was dotted with altars to false gods. Sacrifices had been offered on them, as well as sweet-smelling incense. They had even offered their sons and daughters to Molech, but now the people who had attended them are dead. Many of the altars are broken down, and many are lying before them in putrefaction. As the whole system of sacrifice and worship to idols was a stench to God and a pollution, so now these very idols themselves are polluted by the putrefying bodies of their worshipers! The cities from which the worshipers came are empty and in ruin. All of this serves as a testimony to the weakness of the false gods and the fact that God is the LORD.

But God promised that a remnant will escape the ravages upon the land. They will be taken captive and find themselves among the many nations of the world. It is here that they will remember their past ways of wickedness and idolatry and will loathe themselves for it. It is only then that they will repent and turn to the Lord. Thus, God's chastisement will have proved to turn their hearts to the Lord.

But now, with the impending calamities of sword, famine, and plague, alas, how terrible! However, this is what it will take to cause Israel to recognize that God is the LORD.

Mountains of Israel in verse 2 have a double emphasis. They are in contrast to the plains of Chaldea from whence the prophet is speaking. The mountains that God had given to Israel had become polluted with idols and altars erected to their worship in every prominent place. But these **altars** were now broken down, their worshipers lying before them dead and in putrefaction. This was mute testimony to the weakness of the false gods who could not even protect their worshipers!

8-10. Remnant. God always has preserved a remnant for Himself, and He always will. The fact that they are seen among the nations (plural) and scattered through the countries appears to call attention to days beyond their immediate captivity in Babylon. Ezekiel says they shall loathe themselves. We know this will be in the latter days, just prior to the Second Advent. During the days of His Incarnation, our Lord lamented over their rejection of Him (Mt 23:37-39). But Zechariah speaks of the time when they will mourn for the one they pierced (Zech 12:10).

11-14. Smite with thine hand, and stamp with thy foot has been variously interpreted, but the act itself is certainly associated with astonishment. The context indicates very clearly that it is about an impending calamity of sword, famine, and pestilence. However, it is this very calamity that will be the means of causing Israel to know that God is the LORD, and not the many false gods they had so obviously been serving in futility.

The term **Diblath** is found only in this reference. It is most likely identical with Riblah, situated on the northern frontier of the country (Num 34:11). The letters *d* and *r* interchange as in Deuel and Reuel (Num 1:14; 2:14). It is the same as saying from Dan to Beer-sheba. In other words, the destruction of the land would be complete, from north to south.

7:1-4. Ezekiel continues in his pronouncements of the coming doom of Jerusalem. Many of the things here stated are repeated for emphasis. Many of the exiles did not wish to accept the coming doom of their capital city, Jerusalem. And those left in the city felt that since life was continuing as usual, the doom would never come. The prophet now speaks with a voice of finality concerning the coming doom as he has not heretofore.

The chapter is as vivid as if he is speaking as an eyewitness. In a sense, this is true; for the Spirit of God sees the future as vividly as the present, unlike humans. Ezekiel, of course, spoke as the Spirit of God gave him the words (2:7; 3:27).

Ezekiel very emphatically points out the nearness of the impending judgment that will be meted out according to their own ways. Life during the time of the siege is described with its bloodshed, plague, famine, fear, anxiety, and lack of security. He even paints a picture of conditions immediately following the siege, when they are captives with no peace, no ministry of prophet, priest, and elder, and mourning by both king and people.

God has established the unalterable principle that whatsoever a man sows that shall he also reap. Here it is stated as **judge thee according to thy ways** and **recompense upon thee all thine abominations.** Violence, bloodshed, extortion, bribery, and worshiping of false gods had been the order of the day for them. Now, these very things would be exacted upon them. And as to idol worship, they would have their fill till it became nauseating to them.

8 ¶Yet will I leave a remnant, that ye may have *some* that shall escape the sword among the nations, when ye shall be scattered through the countries.

9 And they that escape of you shall remember me among the nations whither they shall be carried captives, because I am broken with their whorish heart, which hath departed from me, and with their eyes, which go a whoring after their idols: and they shall lothe themselves for the evils which they have committed in all their abominations.

10 And they shall know that I *am* the LORD, *and that* I have not said in vain that I would do this evil unto them.

11 ¶Thus saith the Lord GOD: Smite with thine hand, and stamp with thy foot, and say, Alas for all the evil abominations of the house of Israel! for they shall fall by the sword, by the famine, and by the pestilence.

12 He that is far off shall die of the pestilence; and he that is near shall fall by the sword; and he that remaineth and is besieged shall die by the famine: thus will I accomplish my fury upon them.

13 Then shall I know that I *am* the LORD, when their slain *men* shall be among their idols round about their altars, upon every high hill, in all the tops of the mountains, and under every green tree, and under every thick oak, the place where they did offer sweet savour to all their idols.

14 So will I stretch out my hand upon them, and make the land desolate, yea, more desolate than the wilderness toward Dib'lath, in all their habitations: and they shall know that I *am* the LORD.

CHAPTER 7

MOREOVER the word of the LORD came unto me, saying,

2 Also, thou son of man, thus saith the Lord GOD unto the land of Israel; An end, the end is come upon the four corners of the land.

3 Now *is* the end *come* upon thee, and I will send mine anger upon thee, and will judge thee according to thy ways, and will recompense upon thee all thine abominations.

4 And mine eye shall not spare thee, neither will I have pity: but I will recompense thy ways upon thee, and thine abominations shall be in the midst of thee: and ye shall know that I *am* the LORD.

5 Thus saith the Lord God; An evil, an only evil, behold, is come.

6 An end is come, the end is come: it watcheth for thee; behold, it is come.

7 The morning is come unto thee, O thou that dwellest in the land: the time is come, the day of trouble *is* near, and not the sounding again of the mountains.

8 Now will I shortly pour out my fury upon thee, and accomplish mine anger upon thee: and I will judge thee according to thy ways, and will recompense thee for all thine abominations.

9 And mine eye shall not spare, neither will I have pity: I will recompense thee according to thy ways and thine abominations *that* are in the midst of thee; and ye shall know that I *am* the Lord that smiteth.

10 Behold the day, behold, it is come: the morning is gone forth; the rod hath blossomed, pride hath budded.

11 Violence is risen up into a rod of wickedness: none of them *shall remain*, nor of their multitude, nor of any of theirs: neither *shall there be* wailing for them.

12 The time is come, the day draweth near: let not the buyer rejoice, nor the seller mourn: for wrath *is* upon all the multitude thereof.

13 For the seller shall not return to that which is sold, although they were yet alive: for the vision *is* touching the whole multitude thereof, *which shall* not return: neither shall any strengthen himself in the iniquity of his life.

14 They have blown the trumpet, even to make all ready: but none goeth to the battle: for my wrath *is* upon all the multitude thereof.

15 The sword *is* without, and the pestilence and the famine within: he that *is* in the field shall die with the sword; and he that *is* in the city, famine and pestilence shall devour him.

16 ¶ But they that escape of them shall escape, and shall be on the mountains like doves of the valleys, all of them mourning, every one for his iniquity.

17 All hands shall be feeble, and all knees shall be weak as water.

18 They shall also gird *themselves* with sackcloth, and horror shall cover them; and shame *shall be* upon all faces, and baldness upon all their heads.

19 They shall cast their silver in the streets, and their gold shall be removed: their silver and their gold shall not be able to deliver them in the day of the wrath of the Lord: they shall not satisfy their souls, neither fill their bowels: because it is the stumblingblock of their iniquity.

20 As for the beauty of his ornament, he set it in majesty: but they made the images of their abominations *and* of their detestable things therein: therefore have I set it far from them.

21 And I will give it into the hands of the strangers for a prey, and to the wicked of the earth for a spoil; and they shall pollute it.

22 My face will I turn also from them, and they shall pollute my secret place:

5-9. Very shortly, God will pour out His **fury** upon them and will have no **pity**. Liberals point to verses such as these and conclude that the God of the Old Testament is not the same as the God of love of the New Testament. The fact is that God is both holy and love. Without the preservation of holiness, as it would be if evil were not judged, love would be without significance. Furthermore, evil men are judged according to righteousness, especially if it follows after a warning to accept His love and mercy.

10-13. The **rod** of verse 10 is the king of Babylon (Isa 10:5). But the **rod** of verse 11 is very clearly the violence and wickedness of the people themselves. In a time of siege and captivity there is no point to **rejoice** and **mourn** concerning things bought and sold.

14-22. In those days the call to battle was by the blowing of **the trumpet**. But with people dying inside the city walls due to hunger and plague, all will to face the sword outside the walls was lost. **Gold** and **silver** cannot buy food when there is none. Idols made of gold taken from the Temple, and the gods they represented, were not delivering them from the enemy.

for the robbers shall enter into it, and defile it.

23 ¶Make a chain: for the land is full of bloody crimes, and the city is full of violence.

24 Wherefore I will bring the worst of the heathen, and they shall possess their houses: I will also make the pomp of the strong to cease; and their holy places shall be defiled.

25 Destruction cometh; and they shall seek peace, and *there shall be* none.

26 Mischief shall come upon mischief, and rumour shall be upon rumour; then shall they seek a vision of the prophet; but the law shall perish from the priest, and counsel from the ancients.

27 The king shall mourn, and the prince shall be clothed with desolation, and the hands of the people of the land shall be troubled: I will do unto them after their way, and according to their deserts will I judge them; and they shall know that I *am* the LORD.

CHAPTER 8

AND it came to pass in the sixth year, in the sixth *month,* in the fifth *day* of the month, *as* I sat in mine house, and the elders of Jūdah sat before me, that the hand of the Lord GOD fell there upon me.

2 Then I beheld, and lo a likeness as the appearance of fire: from the appearance of his loins even downward, fire; and from his loins even upward, as the appearance of brightness, as the colour of amber.

3 And he put forth the form of an hand, and took me by a lock of mine head; and the spirit lifted me up between the earth and the heaven, and brought me in the visions of God to Jerusalem, to the door of the inner gate that looketh toward the north; where *was* the seat of the image of jealousy, which provoketh to jealousy.

4 And, behold, the glory of the God of Israel *was* there, according to the vision that I saw in the plain.

5 ¶Then said he unto me, Son of man, lift up thine eyes now the way toward the north. So I lifted up mine eyes the way toward the north, and behold northward at the gate of the altar this image of jealousy in the entry.

23-27. Make a chain has reference to the captives fastened to each other when they were marched off to Babylon. The way of violence and bloodshed has brought forth this captivity as its harvest. Now, when they **seek peace,** there will be no listening ear. Now, in their calamity they will look for a **vision,** a word from God's man; but it will be too late. The fire of judgment must now do its refining work of separating the dross from the silver and gold. The end result is that the rebels will be cut off and the righteous remnant will be purified.

8:1-4. A series of visions begin in chapters 8-11, relating particularly to the evils in Jerusalem among those not yet in exile. The previous visions had dealt with the past sins of Israel and Judah.

Chapter 8 concerns itself with the abominable kinds of idolatry currently practiced in Jerusalem by those not in exile. In fact, it was happening in the very Temple built for the worship of the Lord God of heaven.

God views idolatry as the most abominable kind of sin that man can engage in. Other sins are against lower forms of creation: against his fellow man and himself. But idolatry is against the Lord God Himself. When man practices idolatry he either refuses to recognize Him at all, or at best places Him alongside the many lesser gods. When man fails to give due recognition and worship to God, he then becomes a law to himself. Whatever he wishes to do he may then have a rational reason for so doing. It is for this reason that the first and greatest of commandments is "Thou shalt have no other gods before me" (Ex 20:3).

After showing Ezekiel the various forms of idolatrous worship then being perpetrated in the Temple in Jerusalem, God says that He will deal in fury, will not pity, and will not listen to their cry.

Previously, the Lord had shown Ezekiel, by means of a vision, the abominable practices in Jerusalem. Now, He revealed Himself in His glory again. Ezekiel was thus convinced that what he was seeing, and would yet see, was of the Lord and not a mere hallucination. The whole vision described in chapters 8-11 took place while the elders of Judah were before him (8:1; 11:24-25).

This vision occurred 14 months after Ezekiel's call. This would have allowed enough time for his hair to grow back. **The image of jealousy** may perhaps have been a replacement of the image of the goddess Asherah, originally set up by King Manasseh (II Kgs 21:7) and subsequently destroyed by Josiah (II Kgs 23:6).

5-17. The **seventy men** were key leaders among the laity of Israel, perhaps similar to the seventy that Moses had appointed to assist him in his day (Num 11:16). They were seen worshiping and offering incense to various gods of a baser sort, as depicted in carved images and representations on the wall of the court.

6 He said furthermore unto me, Son of man, seest thou what they do? even the great abominations that the house of Israel committeth here, that I should go far off from my sanctuary? but turn thee yet again, and thou shalt see greater abominations.

7 ¶And he brought me to the door of the court; and when I looked, behold a hole in the wall.

8 Then said he unto me, Son of man, dig now in the wall: and when I had digged in the wall, behold a door.

9 And he said unto me, Go in, and behold the wicked abominations that they do here.

10 So I went in and saw; and behold every form of creeping things, and abominable beasts, and all the idols of the house of Israel, pourtrayed upon the wall round about.

11 And there stood before them seventy men of the ancients of the house of Israel, and in the midst of them stood Jā-az-a-nī'ah the son of Shā'phan, with every man his censer in his hand; and a thick cloud of incense went up.

12 Then said he unto me, Son of man, hast thou seen what the ancients of the house of Israel do in the dark, every man in the chambers of his imagery? for they say, The LORD seeth us not; the LORD hath forsaken the earth.

13 ¶He said also unto me, Turn thee yet again, and thou shalt see greater abominations that they do.

14 Then he brought me to the door of the gate of the LORD's house which was toward the north; and, behold, there sat women weeping for Tăm'mŭz.

15 ¶Then said he unto me, Hast thou seen this, O son of man? turn thee yet again, and thou shalt see greater abominations than these.

16 And he brought me into the inner court of the LORD's house, and, behold, at the door of the temple of the LORD, between the porch and the altar, were about five and twenty men, with their backs toward the temple of the LORD, and their faces toward the east; and they worshipped the sun toward the east.

17 ¶Then he said unto me, Hast thou seen this, O son of man? Is it a light thing to the house of Jū'dah that they commit the abominations which they commit here? for they have filled the land with violence, and have returned to provoke me to anger: and, lo, they put the branch to their nose.

18 Therefore will I also deal in fury: mine eye shall not spare, neither will I have pity: and though they cry in mine ears with a loud voice, yet will I not hear them.

CHAPTER 9

HE cried also in mine ears with a loud voice, saying, Cause them that have charge over the city to draw near, even every man with his destroying weapon in his hand.

2 And, behold, six men came from the way of the higher gate, which lieth toward the north, and every man a

B. Departure of the Glory of the Lord. 9:1-11:25.

9:1-3. Chapter nine follows through with the judgment stated in 8:18. The Lord God calls for the angelic beings in charge of Jerusalem. Six come forth with battle axes, along with another man clothed with linen who had also an inkhorn at his side. They all stand at the brazen altar waiting for further instructions.

After the glory of the Lord departed from above the mercy

18. Is it any wonder that the Lord says He will deal in wrath and not have pity? For Him to ignore open and repeated defiance of Himself and permit the worship of the wicked host of heaven cannot be tolerated. His very Name would be at stake if He did otherwise.

Women were seen worshiping **Tammuz**, a Babylonian deity, husband of Ishtar, who after his death supposedly became god of the underworld. Some have taken him to be a vegetation-deity. He was pictured as dying in the heat of the summer and rising in the spring. Base immorality was connected with his worship.

The worst act of abomination involved **five and twenty men** (priests) with their backs to the Temple of God, as if in defiance, and on their faces **worshiped the sun**. In II Kings 21:4-6 the worship of the sun and the other heavenly bodies is associated with witchcraft and divination. It is the author's conviction that when Israel practiced their idolatry, they looked upon the idols as representations of the evil hosts in the heavens. Satan is the prince of the power of the air and has under his control the angels that fell from their original estate in heaven. Thus, they were worshiping actual beings, but not the Lord, the Creator of heaven and earth.

The exact meaning of **put the branch to their nose** is not clear, but the context associates it with defiance. Any statement beyond this appears to be mere speculation, but it should be noted that historically **their nose** is traditionally held to be a scribal correction for *my nose*. This would be an attempt on the part of the scribe, or scribes, to avoid such a crude reference to God. "Early Jewish commentators translated **branch** as 'stench'. The result, 'they put forth a stench before my nose' ... falling more appropriately in the category of obscenity rather than of Tammuz-worship" (Taylor, p. 100). To say that anything stinks in God's nostrils is not a pretty phrase to employ, but it should be remembered that the forms of idolatry were not pretty either.

seat and between the two golden cherubim and moved to the entrance of the Temple, the instructions were given. First, the man with the inkhorn was asked to mark everyone that sighed over the evil being practiced, that is the righteous ones in the city. Then the six executioners went throughout the city, beginning at the sanctuary, slaying the elders and everyone else not marked as a righteous one. The Temple, which had already been defiled by idolatry, was now further defiled by dead bodies strewn over the floor.

Ezekiel, seeing all this vividly in the vision, cried out, **Ah Lord God! wilt thou destroy all the residue of Israel in thy pouring out of thy fury upon Jerusalem?** (vs. 8). It seemed to him that very nearly everyone was being slain. But the judgment was inevitable because of the bloodshed, perversion, and idolatry practiced by Israel.

A final note of mercy and grace is heard. In following through on the command to slay the city, the righteous had been spared.

The AV describes the **six men as them that have charge over the city**, and the NASB describes them as "executioners." From the root of the Hebrew term, we can say they were the ones given charge to destroy the city. Conservative scholars believe they are angelic beings, as in Daniel 4:13. Others have identified them with Nebuchadnezzar's generals (Jer 39:2). It would appear that Ezekiel saw the heavenly angels, who in the time of actual slaughter made use of the generals.

The **man clothed with linen**, having an inkhorn (or writing case) at his side, is quite clearly the Second Person of the Trinity. He is seen clothed in linen as a High Priest; He is seen manifesting omniscience in marking the righteous. Further, He is in charge of the judgment, which corresponds with the Father giving all judgment into the hand of the Son (Jn 5:22).

The glory of the God of Israel came to dwell in the midst of Israel over the mercy seat after the tabernacle was completed in the wilderness. But the Temple had seen so much defilement by idolatry that the glory of the Lord must of necessity leave His dwelling place. Here, it departs to the threshold (9:3), then to above the cherubim waiting outside (10:18), then to the mountain (Olivet) east of the city (11:23), and will return here again to abide in the millennial Temple (43:1-5).

4-7. Men that sigh and that cry over the evil taking place indicate by their actions that they are righteous ones. They are marked to be spared from destruction. We may assume that when the actual slaughter took place in 586 B.C., God providentially spared the righteous. Jeremiah would be an example of this (Jer 40:1-4).

The slaying was to begin at the **sanctuary** with the elders. Because they were the leaders in Israel's apostasy, they were the first ones to meet the sword. The Temple was not to be defiled with dead bodies by the direct command of the Lord. Israel had defiled it by her idolatry; but now, with the glory of the Lord having departed, it no longer was the Temple where He resided. In a sense, the Lord was now commanding them to **defile** the Temple because it was used for idol worship.

8-11. Great carnage had been carried out as a recompense for their shedding of blood, perversion, and idol worship; but good news was given concerning the remnant. Those marked (vss. 4) had not been touched, even as commanded (vss. 6, 11).

---

slaughter weapon in his hand; and one man among them *was* clothed with linen, with a writer's inkhorn by his side: and they went in, and stood beside the brasen altar.

3 And the glory of the God of Israel was gone up from the cherub, whereupon he was, to the threshold of the house. And he called to the man clothed with linen, which *had* the writer's inkhorn by his side;

4 And the Lord said unto him, Go through the midst of the city, through the midst of Jerusalem, and set a mark upon the foreheads of the men that sigh and that cry for all the abominations that be done in the midst thereof.

5 And to the others he said in mine hearing, Go ye after him through the city, and smite: let not your eye spare, neither have ye pity:

6 Slay utterly old *and* young, both maids, and little children, and women: but come not near any man upon whom *is* the mark; and begin at my sanctuary. Then they began at the ancient men which *were* before the house.

7 And he said unto them, Defile the house, and fill the courts with the slain: go ye forth. And they went forth, and slew in the city.

8 ¶And it came to pass, while they were slaying them, and I was left, that I fell upon my face, and cried, and said, Ah Lord God! wilt thou destroy all the residue of Israel in thy pouring out of thy fury upon Jerusalem?

9 Then said he unto me, The iniquity of the house of Israel and Ju'dah *is* exceeding great, and the land is full of blood, and the city full of perverseness: for they say, The Lord hath forsaken the earth, and the Lord seeth not.

10 And as for me also, mine eye shall not spare, neither will I have pity, but I will recompense their way upon their head.

11 And, behold, the man clothed with linen, which had the inkhorn by his side, reported the matter, saying, I have done as thou hast commanded me.

CHAPTER 10

THEN I looked, and, behold, in the firmament that was above the head of the cherubims there appeared over them as it were a sapphire stone, as the appearance of the likeness of a throne.

2 And he spake unto the man clothed with linen, and said, Go in between the wheels, even under the cherub, and fill thine hand with coals of fire from between the cherubims, and scatter them over the city. And he went in in my sight.

3 Now the cherubims stood on the right side of the house, when the man went in; and the cloud filled the inner court.

4 Then the glory of the LORD went up from the cherub, and stood over the threshold of the house; and the house was filled with the cloud, and the court was full of the brightness of the LORD'S glory.

5 And the sound of the cherubims' wings was heard even to the outer court, as the voice of the Almighty God when he speaketh.

6 And it came to pass, that when he had commanded the man clothed with linen, saying, Take fire from between the wheels, from between the cherubims; then he went in, and stood beside the wheels.

7 And one cherub stretched forth his hand from between the cherubims unto the fire that was between the cherubims; and took thereof, and put it into the hands of him that was clothed with linen; who took it, and went out.

8 ¶ And there appeared in the cherubims the form of a man's hand under their wings.

9 And when I looked, behold the four wheels by the cherubims, one wheel by one cherub, and another wheel by another cherub: and the appearance of the wheels was as the colour of a beryl stone.

10 And as for their appearances, they four had one likeness, as if a wheel had been in the midst of a wheel.

10:1. Ezekiel saw a renewed vision of the four cherubim and the Lord God in His glory as he had seen in the first vision (ch. 1). The cherubim and the Lord God are seen in connection with the departure of the glory of the Lord from the Temple and with the destruction of Jerusalem by fire.

The Father directs the Son to take fire from between the cherubim and cast it over the city. A cherub assists in giving the Son (the man clothed in linen) the coals of fire, and they were then scattered. However, this was done only after the glory had departed from the inner sanctuary over the mercy seat. With the glory of the Lord departing from His dwelling place among Israel, the divine protection from Jerusalem was lifted; and the city was destroyed by the fire from the Lord.

We see the departure of the glory of the Lord in stages, as though with hesitancy and great sorrow: from the inner sanctuary to the threshold, from the threshold to above the cherubim, from here to the east gate of the Temple and pausing there, and finally to the mountain (Olivet) east of the city.

2-6. Coals of fire from between the cherubim. Coals of fire are used in various contexts. In the case of Isaiah, it was for the purification of his lips and iniquity (Isa 6:5-7). When put on the golden altar before the mercy seat, they caused a sweet-smelling savor when the incense was put on it (Ex 30:1-10). When taken by the High Priest on the Day of Atonement from the altar of incense, along with the incense and the blood of sacrifice from the brazen altar, and then taken into the Most Holy Place, the inner sanctuary, and put on the mercy seat, it was associated with grace in covering sin for another year (Lev 16:11-16). But, here we see the coals of fire used in judgment against Jerusalem in a consuming fire (Heb 12:29). The coals of fire seen in the vision were symbolical of the fire that in 586 B.C. destroyed the city (Jer 52:12-13). Though the fire was brought about by human instrumentality, it was actually fire from the Lord (vs. 2).

7-13. The fire was put **into the hands of him that was clothed with linen** and he went out and scattered the fire. As in 9:3, 5, here also, it is the Second Person of the Trinity who is the executor of judgment.

11 When they went, they went upon their four sides; they turned not as they went, but to the place whither the head looked they followed it; they turned not as they went.

12 And their whole body, and their backs, and their hands, and their wings, and the wheels, *were* full of eyes round about, *even* the wheels that they four had.

13 As for the wheels, it was cried unto them in my hearing, O wheel.

14 And every one had four faces: the first face *was* the face of a cherub, and the second face *was* the face of a man, and the third the face of a lion, and the fourth the face of an eagle.

15 And the cherubims were lifted up. This *is* the living creature that I saw by the river of Chē'bär.

16 And when the cherubims went, the wheels went by them: and when the cherubims lifted up their wings to mount up from the earth, the same wheels also turned not from beside them.

17 When they stood, *these* stood; and when they were lifted up, *these* lifted up themselves also: for the spirit of the living creature *was* in them.

18 Then the glory of the LORD departed from off the threshold of the house, and stood over the cherubims.

19 And the cherubims lifted up their wings, and mounted up from the earth in my sight: when they went out, the wheels also *were* beside them, and *every one* stood at the door of the east gate of the LORD's house; and the glory of the God of Israel *was* over them above.

20 This *is* the living creature that I saw under the God of Israel by the river of Chē'bär; and I knew that they were the cherubims.

21 Every one had four faces apiece, and every one four wings; and the likeness of the hands of a man *was* under their wings.

22 And the likeness of their faces *was* the same faces which I saw by the river of Chē'bär, their appearances and themselves: they went every one straight forward.

CHAPTER 11

MOREOVER the spirit lifted me up, and brought me unto the east gate of the LORD's house, which looketh eastward: and behold at the door of the gate five and twenty men; among whom I saw Jā-ăz-a-nī'ah the son of Ā'zur, and Pěl-a-tī'ah the son of Be-nā'iah, princes of the people.

14-17. The listing of the **four faces** of the cherubim here, as compared with 1:10, does not fully compare, even though in verses 20 and 22 it states that the cherubim were the same. Commentators range all the way from saying there is an error to various speculative answers as to why the difference between the face of an ox and the face of a cherub. Searching the Scripture for the answer is legitimate, but saying there is an error challenges the integrity of the Author, the Holy Spirit.

18-22. **Then the glory of the LORD departed.** The glory of the Lord came and dwelt over the mercy seat between the cherubim, first of all, when the tabernacle had been completed in the wilderness (Ex 40:33-35), and later, when the Temple was built by Solomon (I Kgs 8:6, 10, 11). But now the Lord could no longer dwell in the midst of His people. They had defiled the Temple by setting up altars to other gods and had utterly turned their back to Him (8:16). In sorrow, He departed from their midst. The glory could have returned to Israel at the Lord's First Advent, but they rejected Him again (Mt 23:37-39; Lk 19:44). However, before Ezekiel's prophecy is over we see the glory of the Lord returning to the millennial Temple (43:1-12).

The time between the departure of the glory of the Lord from the Temple and the Second Advent, when He comes in glory, is the times of the Gentiles. God is working out His plan of the ages with Israel temporarily set aside. Israel is now scattered among the nations of the world until that time when she will be regathered by Him and will be ready to receive Him as King of Glory (Zech 12:10-13:1).

11:1. Ezekiel saw twenty-five men in a vision, leaders or princes in Israel, at the east gate of the Temple giving evil counsel to the people. They set the pattern by their various forms of iniquity. Also, they contradicted the warning of the prophet Jeremiah that their doom was coming. They led the people to believe that even as a caldron keeps meat from being burned by the fire, so they are safe within the walls of Jerusalem from any enemy.

Ezekiel, thereupon, gave them the Lord's answer: your dead will be secure in the city! As for the rest of you, you will be taken captive, face the sword, and be judged even up to the very borders of your land for all your wicked ways.

Ezekiel saw Pelatiah, who was one of the leaders, die. In anxiety he asked, "Lord, will all the remnant be destroyed?" The comforting answer of the Lord was that though they will be taken captive and scattered, yet they will be preserved in the countries. Then they will be regathered and given their land. In addition, they will receive a regenerated heart that will put away

2 Then said he unto me, Son of man, these *are* the men that devise mischief, and give wicked counsel in this city:

3 Which say, *It is* not near; let us build houses: this *city is* the caldron, and we *be* the flesh.

4 ¶Therefore prophesy against them, prophesy, O son of man.

5 And the Spirit of the LORD fell upon me, and said unto me, Speak; Thus saith the LORD; Thus have ye said, O house of Israel: for I know the things that come into your mind, *every* one of them.

6 Ye have multiplied your slain in this city, and ye have filled the streets thereof with the slain.

7 Therefore thus saith the Lord GOD; Your slain whom ye have laid in the midst of it, they *are* the flesh, and this city *is* the caldron: but I will bring you forth out of the midst of it.

8 Ye have feared the sword; and I will bring a sword upon you, saith the Lord GOD.

9 And I will bring you out of the midst thereof, and deliver you into the hands of strangers, and will execute judgments among you.

10 Ye shall fall by the sword; I will judge you in the border of Israel; and ye shall know that I *am* the LORD.

11 This *city* shall not be your caldron, neither shall ye be the flesh in the midst thereof; *but* I will judge you in the border of Israel:

12 And ye shall know that I *am* the LORD: for ye have not walked in my statutes, neither executed my judgments, but have done after the manners of the heathen that *are* round about you.

13 ¶And it came to pass, when I prophesied, that Pel-a-ti'ah the son of Bena-iah died. Then fell I down upon my face, and cried with a loud voice, and said, Ah Lord GOD! wilt thou make a full end of the remnant of Israel?

14 ¶Again the word of the LORD came unto me, saying,

15 Son of man, thy brethren, *even* thy brethren, the men of thy kindred, and all the house of Israel wholly, *are* they unto whom the inhabitants of Jerusalem have said, Get you far from the LORD: unto us is this land given in possession.

16 Therefore say, Thus saith the Lord GOD; Although I have cast them far off among the heathen, and although I have scattered them among the countries, yet will I be to them as a little sanctuary in the countries where they shall come.

17 Therefore say, Thus saith the Lord GOD; I will even gather you from the people, and assemble you out of the countries where ye have been scat-

evil and be in intimate relation with Him. However, any rebels will be destroyed according to their own ways.

The glory of the Lord was then hovering over the city, after which it left to the mount east of Jerusalem.

After being returned in spirit from Jerusalem to Chaldea, Ezekiel related all these visions to the elders sitting before him.

2-3. Five and twenty men. They are not the same as those in 8:16, who were within the court of the Temple where the priests alone could go. These men are lay leaders. Further, the Jaaza-niahs had different fathers (8:11; 11:1).

They were the ones whose advice was contrary to that of the prophet Jeremiah. Jeremiah had told them to submit to the king of Babylon; and, as a result, the Lord would be their protector (Jer 1:19).

4-12. Their future lot was to face the sword and captivity; and those who seem to have escaped will be overtaken and judged, even to the very border of the land. Jeremiah 52:9-10 indicates that at Riblah, Zedekiah's sons were slain before his eyes. Then he himself was blinded and bound.

13-25. Get you far from the LORD was spoken by the Jews in Jerusalem as a taunt to those already in exile. We are here because the Lord is with us, but you in exile are far from Him. Verses 16-21 include the most comforting words spoken by the Lord thus far in the prophecy. They will be taken captive, but also preserved, regathered, given the land, and converted upon their return.

Scattered them among the countries has implications of more than the captivity into Babylon. Likewise **I will ... assemble you out of the countries** has implications of a return beyond the scope or what occurred after seventy years in captivity. It has reference to the return at the close of the Tribulation at the Lord's second coming. The remnant will be regenerated at that time by the Spirit of God, as indicated by a **new spirit** and **a heart of flesh. That they may walk in my statutes** indicates that apart from this regeneration it would be impossible to do so. But even of the remnant that will be spared from the impending destruction of Jerusalem by Nebuchadnezzar, and at various times later in their history, the rebels will die in their sins. Note, **I will recompense their way upon their own heads** (see also 20:34-38).

C. Burden of the Prince and False Prophets. 12:1-15:8.

The message of chapter 12 is directed primarily to those already in captivity, but it also involves the coming captivity of those still in Jerusalem. Daniel and his associates had been taken in 606 B.C. Jehoiachin, and many others, had been taken in 597 B.C. Ezekiel was with captives taken into exile in the latter deportation. Jeremiah was left behind with those in Jerusalem who had not yet been taken captive. The ones in captivity were expecting to be released and returned to their homeland soon, though Jeremiah had predicted it would be of seventy-years' duration (Jer 25:11-12).

Ezekiel began his prophetic utterances in 593 B.C., and Jeremiah had been telling the people of a complete captivity, even those in Jerusalem. But it was now a number of years since the second deportation in 597 B.C. The people were being told by false prophets that good times were ahead. The message of gloom, predicted by both Jeremiah and Ezekiel, would never come; or if it did come, it was still many years away.

By signs he used in this message, Ezekiel endeavored to show that these hopes of a quick return were vain. He also attempted to demonstrate that the captivity of those in Jerusalem was very near, and it would certainly come to pass.

Ezekiel publicly went through the act of packing a few items for travel as a captive, digging a hole through a wall, and making his escape under cover of darkness.

The explanation of the sign is that it represents the prince (Zedekiah) and other leaders and men of war. They, however, will be caught. Some will be killed, with the prince being blinded and brought to a land that he will not see. The people will go through the terrible horrors of anxiety, sword, famine, and violence as a recompense for their own ways of violence in times past. A few will be spared alive to give testimony to the fact that God is just in his judgment, and that He is truly God.

12:1-7. The seeing and hearing, but not comprehending, constituted a spiritual problem. Israel had heard the truth and the consequences of her disobedience many times, but the unregenerate heart invariably twists the truth or rejects it.

The reason for publicly going through the act of gathering a few necessary items for travel and making an escape through a hole under cover of darkness, was to cause spiritually hardened hearts to see, if they would. It was an act of grace, God longing for them to repent.

8-20. A detailed account of the fulfillment of Ezekiel's prophecy is given in II Kings 25:1-11 and Jeremiah 52:1-11. Zedekiah and the army escaped at night, but they were overtaken in the plains of Jericho. At Riblah, Nebuchadnezzar slew Zedekiah's sons in his sight, then put out his eyes and took him

---

tered, and I will give you the land of Israel.

18 And they shall come thither, and they shall take away all the detestable things thereof and all the abominations thereof from thence.

19 And I will give them one heart, and I will put a new spirit within you; and I will take the stony heart out of their flesh, and will give them an heart of flesh:

20 That they may walk in my statutes, and keep mine ordinances, and do them: and they shall be my people, and I will be their God.

21 But *as for them* whose heart walketh after the heart of their detestable things and their abominations, I will recompense their way upon their own heads, saith the Lord GOD.

22 ¶ Then did the cherubims lift up their wings, and the wheels beside them; and the glory of the God of Israel *was* over them above.

23 And the glory of the LORD went up from the midst of the city, and stood upon the mountain which *is* on the east side of the city.

24 ¶ Afterwards the spirit took me up, and brought me in a vision by the Spirit of God into Chal-dē'a, to them of the captivity. So the vision that I had seen went up from me.

25 Then I spake unto them of the captivity all the things that the LORD had shewed me.

CHAPTER 12

THE word of the LORD also came unto me, saying,

2 Son of man, thou dwellest in the midst of a rebellious house, which have eyes to see, and see not; they have ears to hear, and hear not: for they *are* a rebellious house.

3 Therefore, thou son of man, prepare thee stuff for removing, and remove by day in their sight; and thou shalt remove from thy place to another place in their sight: it may be they will consider, though they *be* a rebellious house.

4 Then shalt thou bring forth thy stuff by day in their sight, as stuff for removing: and thou shalt go forth at even in their sight, as they that go forth into captivity.

5 Dig thou through the wall in their sight, and carry out thereby.

6 In their sight shalt thou bear *it* upon *thy* shoulders, *and* carry *it* forth in the twilight: thou shalt cover thy face, that thou see not the ground: for I have set thee *for* a sign unto the house of Israel.

7 And I did so as I was commanded: I brought forth my stuff by day, as stuff for captivity, and in the even I digged through the wall with mine hand: I brought *it* forth in the twilight, *and* I bare *it* upon *my* shoulder in their sight.

8 And in the morning came the word of the LORD unto me, saying,

9 Son of man, hath not the house of Israel, the rebellious house, said unto thee, What doest thou?

10 Say thou unto them, Thus saith the Lord GOD; This burden *concerneth* the prince in Jerusalem, and all the house of Israel that are among them.

11 Say, I *am* your sign: like as I have done, so shall it be done unto them: they shall remove *and* go into captivity.

12 And the prince that *is* among them shall bear upon *his* shoulder in the twilight, and shall go forth: they shall dig through the wall to carry out thereby: he shall cover his face, that he see not the ground with *his* eyes.

13 My net also will I spread upon him, and he shall be taken in my snare: and I will bring him to Babylon *to* the land of the Chăl-dē'ans; yet shall he not see it, though he shall die there.

14 And I will scatter toward every wind all that *are* about him to help him, and all his bands; and I will draw out the sword after them.

15 And they shall know that I *am* the LORD, when I shall scatter them among the nations, and disperse them in the countries.

16 But I will leave a few men of them from the sword, from the famine, and from the pestilence; that they may declare all their abominations among the heathen whither they come; and they shall know that I *am* the LORD.

17 ¶ Moreover the word of the LORD came to me, saying,

18 Son of man, eat thy bread with quaking, and drink thy water with trembling and with carefulness;

19 And say unto the people of the land, Thus saith the Lord GOD of the inhabitants of Jerusalem, *and* of the land of Israel; They shall eat their bread with carefulness, and drink their water with astonishment, that her land may be desolate from all that is therein, because of the violence of all them that dwell therein.

20 And the cities that are inhabited shall be laid waste, and the land shall be desolate; and ye shall know that I *am* the LORD.

21 ¶ And the word of the LORD came unto me, saying,

22 Son of man, what *is* that proverb *that* ye have in the land of Israel, saying, The days are prolonged, and every vision faileth?

23 Tell them therefore, Thus saith the Lord GOD; I will make this proverb to cease, and they shall no more use it as a proverb in Israel; but say unto them, The days are at hand, and the effect of every vision.

24 For there shall be no more any vain vision nor flattering divination within the house of Israel.

25 For I *am* the LORD: I will speak, and the word that I shall speak shall come to pass; it shall be no more prolonged: for in your days, O rebellious house, will I say the word, and will perform it, saith the Lord GOD.

26 ¶ Again the word of the LORD came to me, saying,

27 Son of man, behold, *they* of the house of Israel say, The vision that he seeth *is* for many days *to come*, and he prophesieth of the times that are far off.

captive to Babylon in utter humiliation. The army was scattered and destroyed, and the general populace in the city who were left after the toll of famine and pestilence were taken captive. The city was utterly plundered and then burnt. A few were providentially spared alive to give specific testimony: (1) that these things happened to them because of their abominations; and (2) that both they and their captors might know that **I am the LORD.**

21-28. The days are prolonged, and every vision faileth? Since the prophets had pronounced the doom over an extended period of time and the fulfillment had not occurred, many were led to believe they either would not occur for a long time, or not at all.

False prophets by **flattering divination** had told the people what they wished to hear (Jer 14:13-16). Jeremiah predicted that these very prophets who decried the idea of sword and famine would be killed in exactly that way.

Days are at hand, . . . no more prolonged, and **none of my words be prolonged any more** all speak of the very soon occurrence of the event of doom and captivity.

28 Therefore say unto them, Thus saith the Lord God; There shall none of my words be prolonged any more, but the word which I have spoken shall be done, saith the Lord God.

CHAPTER 13

AND the word of the LORD came unto me, saying,

2 Son of man, prophesy against the prophets of Israel that prophesy, and say thou unto them that prophesy out of their own hearts, Hear ye the word of the LORD;

3 Thus saith the Lord God; Woe unto the foolish prophets, that follow their own spirit, and have seen nothing!

4 O Israel, thy prophets are like the foxes in the deserts.

5 Ye have not gone up into the gaps, neither made up the hedge for the house of Israel to stand in the battle in the day of the LORD.

6 They have seen vanity and lying divination, saying, The LORD saith: and the LORD hath not sent them: and they have made others to hope that they would confirm the word.

7 Have ye not seen a vain vision, and have ye not spoken a lying divination, whereas ye say, The LORD saith it; albeit I have not spoken?

8 Therefore thus saith the Lord God; Because ye have spoken vanity, and seen lies, therefore, behold, I am against you, saith the Lord God.

9 And mine hand shall be upon the prophets that see vanity, and that divine lies: they shall not be in the assembly of my people, neither shall they be written in the writing of the house of Israel, neither shall they enter into the land of Israel; and ye shall know that I am the Lord God.

10 Because, even because they have seduced my people, saying, Peace; and there was no peace; and one built up a wall, and, lo, others daubed it with untempered morter:

11 Say unto them which daub it with untempered morter, that it shall fall: there shall be an overflowing shower; and ye, O great hailstones, shall fall; and a stormy wind shall rend it.

12 Lo, when the wall is fallen, shall it

13:1. The character, method, and judgment of the false prophets is revealed in this portion of Scripture. Satan has his counterfeit prophets. They are described as those who speak after the wisdom of men and have seen false revelations due to their close affinity to the god of this world, who works in the hearts of the disobedient. In fact, there are times when even they themselves are deceived, thinking their message is from God.

By their work they have built an insecure wall, that is, a false social and moral structure that will not stand up before God. The Lord will use the storm out of the north (Babylon) to destroy it. The false prophets will have no heritage in the glorious future of Israel. They will not be counselors; they will not even be found listed in the register of the righteous ones; and, thus, they will not have a future entrance to the land at the time of the Resurrection.

The case is similar with the false prophetesses. By their occult practices, they have led God's people astray and have been leaders in unrighteousness. Their practice in the occult will be removed from them, implying they will be slain. Thus, God's people will be delivered from them.

2-7. Foolish prophets. This is God's view of the false prophet. Man's ways are opposed to God's ways and are thus in error. He is also foolish, because he has not seen a vision or revelation from God. They are like the foxes, who only destroy. So they have done; whereas, they should have been building a strong social and moral house in Israel. They were in direct contact with Satan and his host. Apparently, this occult was so real to them that they thought their message was from God.

8-16. Written in the writing, or register, seems, from the context, to refer to a future time of blessing. John speaks of the "... book of life ..." that will be opened in the latter time (Rev 3:5; 20:15). **Neither shall they enter into the land.** The reference is to a future time when Old Testament saints will be resurrected to participate in the millennial blessings in the land (Dan 12:1-2). The **untempered mortar,** or whitewash, is the false hope given to Israel by the false prophets. The result was a social and moral structure so bad in character that it required God's destruction. This He did by means of the storm out of the north from Babylon. This is the **stormy wind, the overflowing shower and hailstones.**

not be said unto you, Where is the daubing wherewith ye have daubed it?

13 Therefore thus saith the Lord GOD; I will even rend it with a stormy wind in my fury; and there shall be an overflowing shower in mine anger, and great hailstones in my fury to consume it.

14 So will I break down the wall that ye have daubed with untempered morter, and bring it down to the ground, so that the foundation thereof shall be discovered, and it shall fall, and ye shall be consumed in the midst thereof: and ye shall know that I am the LORD.

15 Thus will I accomplish my wrath upon the wall, and upon them that have daubed it with untempered morter, and will say unto you, The wall is no more, neither they that daubed it;

16 To wit, the prophets of Israel which prophesy concerning Jerusalem, and which see visions of peace for her, and there is no peace, saith the Lord GOD.

17 ¶ Likewise, thou son of man, set thy face against the daughters of thy people, which prophesy out of their own heart; and prophesy thou against them,

18 And say, Thus saith the Lord GOD; Woe to the women that sew pillows to all armholes, and make kerchiefs upon the head of every stature to hunt souls! Will ye hunt the souls of my people, and will ye save the souls alive that come unto you?

19 And will ye pollute me among my people for handfuls of barley and for pieces of bread, to slay the souls that should not die, and to save the souls alive that should not live, by your lying to my people that hear your lies?

20 ¶ Wherefore thus saith the Lord GOD; Behold, I am against your pillows, wherewith ye there hunt the souls to make them fly, and I will tear them from your arms, and will let the souls go, even the souls that ye hunt to make them fly.

21 Your kerchiefs also will I tear, and deliver my people out of your hand, and they shall be no more in your hand to be hunted: and ye shall know that I am the LORD.

22 Because with lies ye have made the heart of the righteous sad, whom I have not made sad; and strengthened the hands of the wicked, that he should not return from his wicked way, by promising him life:

23 Therefore ye shall see no more vanity, nor divine divinations: for I will deliver my people out of your hand: and ye shall know that I am the LORD.

CHAPTER 14

THEN came certain of the elders of Israel unto me, and sat before me.

2 And the word of the LORD came unto me, saying,

3 Son of man, these men have set up their idols in their heart, and put the stumblingblock of their iniquity before their face: should I be enquired of at all by them?

17-23. The practices of these women are associated with the occult, as seen in verse 23, **Divine divinations. My people here** has reference to Israel and, perhaps particularly, the godly remnant in Israel.

14:1-3. In chapter 14 a group of the elders in exile came to Ezekiel to seek counsel of the Lord. It appears that they may have finally been convinced that judgment was going to be meted out to their brethren still at Jerusalem. The context indicates that the question in their mind was whether God would spare Jerusalem for the sake of a few righteous within it. The classic example of this principle is the promise of the Lord to spare Sodom if ten righteous were to be found in it (Gen 18:32).

But the elders were not motivated by a pure heart. They themselves, though not outwardly practicing idolatry, were still enamored with idolatry. God saw their hearts and asked them to repent and turn from their multitude of idols.

God's basic principle in dealing with an erring people is that each man must stand before Him on his own righteousness. And if an individual is not righteous before the Lord, there comes a time when judgment must come to vindicate God's holiness and righteousness. Noah, Daniel, and Job were each righteous before the Lord; but Noah could not save his generation from the Flood, Daniel could not save his nation from exile, and Job could not save his family from death.

The Bible's principle is that when a person or a nation is irreversibly set in a downward way, as was Pharaoh, and now the nation of Israel that was still in its homeland, God must bring judgment. However, God does it in grace in order that those in error will see their wicked way and turn to the Lord.

4-11. I the LORD will answer ... according to the multitude of his idols. God never turns from an individual who repents of his sin. He receives him in grace, no matter how vile his heart is. But those in Jerusalem were still openly and defiantly serving other gods. Judgment must be meted out in such a case.

Which separateth himself from men, and setteth up his idols in his heart. To turn to the Lord is to have separated from idols; to have idols is to separate himself from the Lord. God is a jealous God and will have no other gods before Him (note the principle exemplified, Kgs 18:21; I Thess 1:9). God says **I will set my face against** that man that continues in his rebellious way, but He is ever open in grace to the one who repents (vss. 6, 8, 11).

12-23. By their righteousness. The three men mentioned here—**Noah, Daniel, and Job**—were righteous, not by virtue of their own deeds, but by virtue of the imputed righteousness of God. Such was Abraham's case (Gen 15:6) and such was the blessedness of which David spoke (Ps 32:2). However, the outward life will reflect the character of the inward life. The **remnant** of verse 22 will not be righteous individuals, but will characterize the gross idolatry that prevailed in Jerusalem. When these will be brought to Babylon, the exiles already there will realize (**be comforted concerning the evil**) the justice of God in bringing His fourfold judgment upon Jerusalem.

4 Therefore speak unto them, and say unto them, Thus saith the Lord GOD; Every man of the house of Israel that setteth up his idols in his heart, and putteth the stumblingblock of his iniquity before his face, and cometh to the prophet; I the LORD will answer him that cometh according to the multitude of his idols;

5 That I may take the house of Israel in their own heart, because they are all estranged from me through their idols.

6 ¶ Therefore say unto the house of Israel, Thus saith the Lord GOD; Repent, and turn *yourselves* from your idols; and turn away your faces from all your abominations.

7 For every one of the house of Israel, or of the stranger that sojourneth in Israel, which separateth himself from me, and setteth up his idols in his heart, and putteth the stumblingblock of his iniquity before his face, and cometh to a prophet to enquire of him concerning me; I the LORD will answer him by myself:

8 And I will set my face against that man, and will make him a sign and a proverb, and I will cut him off from the midst of my people; and ye shall know that I *am* the LORD.

9 And if the prophet be deceived when he hath spoken a thing, I the LORD have deceived that prophet, and I will stretch out my hand upon him, and will destroy him from the midst of my people Israel.

10 And they shall bear the punishment of their iniquity: the punishment of the prophet shall be even as the punishment of him that seeketh *unto him*;

11 That the house of Israel may go no more astray from me, neither be polluted any more with all their transgressions; but that they may be my people, and I may be their God, saith the Lord GOD.

12 ¶ The word of the LORD came again to me, saying,

13 Son of man, when the land sinneth against me by trespassing grievously, then will I stretch out mine hand upon it, and will break the staff of the bread thereof, and will send famine upon it, and will cut off man and beast from it:

14 Though these three men, Noah, Daniel, and Job, were in it, they should deliver *but* their own souls by their righteousness, saith the Lord GOD.

15 ¶If I cause noisome beasts to pass through the land, and they spoil it, so that it be desolate, that no man may pass through because of the beasts:

16 *Though* these three men were in it, *as* I live, saith the Lord God, they shall deliver neither sons nor daughters; they only shall be delivered, but the land shall be desolate.

17 ¶Or *if* I bring a sword upon that land, and say, Sword, go through the land; so that I cut off man and beast from it:

18 Though these three men were in it, *as* I live, saith the Lord God, they shall deliver neither sons nor daughters, but they only shall be delivered them-selves.

19 ¶Or *if* I send a pestilence into that land, and pour out my fury upon it in blood, to cut off from it man and beast:

20 Though Noah, Daniel, and Job, were in it, *as* I live, saith the Lord God, they shall deliver neither son nor daughter; they shall *but* deliver their own souls by their righteousness.

21 For thus saith the Lord God: How much more when I send my four sore judgments upon Jerusalem, the sword, and the famine, and the noisome beast, and the pestilence, to cut off from it man and beast?

22 Yet, behold, therein shall be left a remnant that shall be brought forth, *both* sons and daughters: behold, they shall come forth unto you, and ye shall see their way and their doings: and ye shall be comforted concerning the evil that I have brought upon Jerusalem, even concerning all that I have brought upon it.

23 And they shall comfort you, when ye see their ways and their doings: and ye shall know that I have not done without cause all that I have done in it, saith the Lord God.

CHAPTER 15

AND the word of the Lord came unto me, saying,

2 Son of man, What is the vine tree more than any tree, or than a branch which is among the trees of the forest?

3 Shall wood be taken thereof to do any work? or will *men* take a pin of it to hang any vessel thereon?

4 Behold, it is cast into the fire for fuel; the fire devoureth both the ends of it, and the midst of it is burned. Is it meet for *any* work?

5 Behold, when it was whole, it was meet for no work: how much less shall it be meet yet for *any* work, when the fire hath devoured it, and it is burned?

6 ¶Therefore thus saith the Lord God; As the vine tree among the trees of the forest, which I have given to the fire for fuel, so will I give the inhabitants of Je-rusalem.

7 And I will set my face against them; they shall go out from one fire, and an-other fire shall devour them: and ye shall know that I am the Lord, when I set my face against them.

8 And I will make the land desolate, because they have committed a tres-pass, saith the Lord God.

15:1-8. Chapter 15 records the parable of the charred vine. As a nation, Israel was likened to a vine (Ps 80:8-16; Hos 10:1). The essential use of the vine is for fruitbearing. As lumber, it is practically useless. It is not even of great value as fuel. Whenever its fruitbearing ceases, it is pulled up and burnt. In this parable, the vine is charred at both ends and in between. It is certainly useless for fruitbearing.

Jerusalem is this charred and fruitless vine. It was not serving the Lord or bringing glory to Him. As the vine with charred ends, it had suffered burning (chastisement and judgment) on previous occasions. It must now be given up to complete de-struction because of continued fruitlessness.

A basic principle of interpretation for a parable is to look for the basic symbolical meaning that is pictured from the natural life situation. The passage clearly tells us the vine is Jerusalem in verse 6. As a charred and fruitless vine is cast into the fire for fuel, so Jerusalem is given up to the fire of God's judgment (vss. 6-8). The charred ends and middle could have reference to previous times when God dealt with her in judgment, as in the deportations of 606 B.C. and 597 B.C.

D. Adultery of Israel. 16:1-17:24.

16:1-63. In chapter 16 we have before us a parable of the spiritual adultery of Israel, likened unto the wife of the Lord. From the beginning, when God instituted marriage, it was meant that a man and woman who entered into the holy covenant of marriage would be faithful and true to each other till death separated them. Likewise, when God chose Israel to be His wife and Israel chose to accept the Lord God as her LORD, it was expected that she would ever be faithful to Him and never have intimacies with any other lovers.

But we find that Israel very soon defected from her love to the Lord, in spite of the fact that God had dealt with her in grace, first in selecting her and then in abundantly lavishing upon her His riches and protection.

Adultery and idolatry are very closely related. In idolatry, an individual gives his love, worship, adoration, and looks to some other god than the Lord God for blessing and protection. This was the way with Israel. When the heart turns from the Lord, the pattern of the world's system is quickly adopted.

Not every detail of a parable should be expected to have a particular spiritual significance. However, in this parable we do have an amazing number of details with spiritual applications for Israel.

Though Israel was actively involved in the immorality and idolatry of the land, the primary emphasis has to do with a spiritual disaffection from the Lord. As is so graphically pictured in this chapter, Israel looked to fame, riches, worldly nations, etc. to be her strength and satisfaction, rather than the Lord. Israel's wickedness is seen as greater than her neighbor's; in fact, at times it was an embarrassment even to them. The holiness and justice of God thus demanded His judgment to curb and purge Israel of these things.

But God had entered into an everlasting covenant with Israel, and she must be chastised by the ones with whom she had committed fornication. In the latter days she will be reinstated into His favor. At that time she will be ashamed of her past vileness and will be saved; and this will happen at the Lord's second advent (Zech 12:10-13:1).

CHAPTER 16

AGAIN the word of the LORD came unto me, saying,

2 Son of man, cause Jerusalem to know her abominations,

3 And say, Thus saith the Lord God unto Jerusalem; Thy birth and thy nativity *is* of the land of Canaan; thy father *was* an Amorite, and thy mother an Hittite.

4 And *as for* thy nativity, in the day thou wast born thy navel was not cut, neither wast thou washed in water to supple *thee*; thou wast not salted at all, nor swaddled at all.

5 None eye pitied thee, to do any of these unto thee, to have compassion upon thee; but thou wast cast out in the open field, to the lothing of thy person, in the day that thou wast born.

6 ¶And when I passed by thee, and saw thee polluted in thine own blood, I said unto thee *when thou wast in thy* blood, Live; yea, I said unto thee *when thou wast* in thy blood, Live.

7 I have caused thee to multiply as the bud of the field, and thou hast increased and waxen great, and thou art come to excellent ornaments: *thy* breasts are fashioned, and thine hair is grown, whereas thou *wast* naked and bare.

8 Now when I passed by thee, and looked upon thee, behold, thy time *was* the time of love; and I spread my skirt over thee, and covered thy nakedness: yea, I sware unto thee, and entered into a covenant with thee, saith the Lord God, and thou becamest mine.

9 Then washed I thee with water; yea, I throughly washed away thy blood from thee, and I anointed thee with oil.

10 I clothed thee also with broidered work, and shod thee with badgers' skin, and I girded thee about with fine linen, and I covered thee with silk.

11 I decked thee also with ornaments, and I put bracelets upon thy hands, and a chain on thy neck.

12 And I put a jewel on thy forehead, and earrings in thine ears, and a beautiful crown upon thine head.

13 Thus wast thou decked with gold and silver; and thy raiment *was of* fine linen, and silk, and broidered work; thou didst eat fine flour, and honey, and oil: and thou wast exceeding beautiful, and thou didst prosper into a kingdom.

14 And thy renown went forth among the heathen for thy beauty: for it *was* perfect through my comeliness, which I had put upon thee, saith the Lord God.

15 ¶But thou didst trust in thine own beauty, and playedst the harlot because of thy renown, and pouredst out thy fornications on every one that passed by; his it was.

16 And of thy garments thou didst take, and deckedst thy high places with divers colours, and playedst the harlot thereupon: *the like things* shall not come, neither shall it be *so*.

17 Thou hast also taken thy fair jewels of my gold and of my silver, which I had given thee, and madest to thyself images of men, and didst commit whoredom with them.

18 And tookest thy broidered garments, and coveredst them: and thou hast set mine oil and mine incense before them.

19 My meat also which I gave thee, fine flour, and oil, and honey, *wherewith* I fed thee, thou hast even set it before them for a sweet savour: and *thus* it was, saith the Lord GOD.

20 Moreover thou hast taken thy sons and thy daughters, whom thou hast borne unto me, and these hast thou sacrificed unto them to be devoured. *Is this* of thy whoredoms a small matter,

21 That thou hast slain my children, and delivered them to cause them to pass through the fire for them?

22 And in all thine abominations and thy whoredoms thou hast not remembered the days of thy youth, when thou wast naked and bare, *and* wast polluted in thy blood.

23 And it came to pass after all thy wickedness, (woe, woe unto thee! saith the Lord GOD;)

24 That thou hast also built unto thee an eminent place, and hast made thee an high place in every street.

25 Thou hast built thy high place at every head of the way, and hast made thy beauty to be abhorred, and hast opened thy feet to every one that passed by, and multiplied thy whoredoms.

26 Thou hast also committed fornication with the Egyptians thy neighbours, great of flesh; and hast increased thy whoredoms, to provoke me to anger.

27 Behold, therefore I have stretched out my hand over thee, and have diminished thine ordinary *food*, and delivered thee unto the will of them that hate thee, the daughters of the Philistines, which are ashamed of thy lewd way.

28 Thou hast played the whore also with the Assyrians, because thou wast unsatiable; yea, thou hast played the harlot with them, and yet couldest not be satisfied.

29 Thou hast moreover multiplied thy fornication in the land of Canaan unto Chăl-dē'a; and yet thou wast not satisfied herewith.

30 How weak is thine heart, saith the Lord GOD, seeing thou doest all these *things,* the work of an imperious whorish woman;

31 In that thou buildest thine eminent place in the head of every way, and makest thine high place in every street; and hast not been as an harlot, in that thou scornest hire;

32 *But* as a wife that committeth adultery, *which* taketh strangers instead of her husband!

33 They give gifts to all whores: but thou givest thy gifts to all thy lovers, and hirest them, that they may come unto thee on every side for thy whoredom.

34 And the contrary is in thee from *other* women in thy whoredoms, whereas none followeth thee to commit whoredoms: and in that thou givest a reward, and no reward is given unto thee, therefore thou art contrary.

35 ¶Wherefore, O harlot, hear the word of the LORD:

36 Thus saith the Lord GOD; Because thy filthiness was poured out, and thy nakedness discovered through thy whoredoms with thy lovers, and with all the idols of thy abominations, and by the blood of thy children, which thou didst give unto them;

37 Behold, therefore I will gather all thy lovers, with whom thou hast taken pleasure, and all *them* that thou hast loved, with all *them* that thou hast hated; I will even gather them round about against thee, and will discover thy nakedness unto them, that they may see all thy nakedness.

38 And I will judge thee, as women that break wedlock and shed blood are judged: and I will give thee blood in fury and jealousy.

39 And I will also give thee into their hand, and they shall throw down thine eminent place, and shall break down thy high places: they shall strip thee also of thy clothes, and shall take thy fair jewels, and leave thee naked and bare.

40 They shall also bring up a company against thee, and they shall stone thee with stones, and thrust thee through with their swords.

41 And they shall burn thine houses with fire, and execute judgment upon thee in the sight of many women: and I will cause thee to cease from playing the harlot, and thou also shalt give no hire any more.

42 So will I make my fury toward thee to rest, and my jealousy shall depart from thee, and I will be quiet, and will be no more angry.

43 Because thou hast not remembered the days of thy youth, but hast fretted me in all these *things*; behold, therefore I also will recompense thy way upon *thine* head, saith the Lord GOD: and thou shalt not commit this lewdness above all thine abominations.

44 ¶Behold, every one that useth proverbs shall use *this* proverb against thee, saying, As *is* the mother, *so is* her daughter.

45 Thou *art* thy mother's daughter, that lotheth her husband and her children: and thou *art* the sister of thy sisters, which lothed their husbands and their children: your mother *was* an Hittite, and your father an Amorite.

46 And thine elder sister *is* Sa-mā'-rĭ-a, she and her daughters that dwell at thy left hand: and thy younger sister, that dwelleth at thy right hand, *is* Sodom and her daughters.

47 Yet hast thou not walked after their ways, nor done after their abominations; but, as *if that were* a very little *thing*, thou wast corrupted more than they in all thy ways.

48 *As* I live, saith the Lord GOD, Sodom thy sister hath not done, she nor her daughters, as thou hast done, thou and thy daughters.

49 Behold, this was the iniquity of thy sister Sodom, pride, fulness of bread, and abundance of idleness was in her and in her daughters, neither did she

strengthen the hand of the poor and needy.

50 And they were haughty, and committed abomination before me: therefore I took them away as I saw *good*.

51 Neither hath Sa-mā'rī-a committed half of thy sins; but thou hast multiplied thine abominations more than they, and hast justified thy sisters in all thine abominations which thou hast done.

52 Thou also, which hast judged thy sisters, bear thine own shame for thy sins that thou hast committed more abominable than they: they are more righteous than thou: yea, be thou confounded also, and bear thy shame, in that thou hast justified thy sisters.

53 When I shall bring again their captivity, the captivity of Sodom and her daughters, and the captivity of Sa-mā'rī-a and her daughters, then *will I bring again* the captivity of thy captives in the midst of them:

54 That thou mayest bear thine own shame, and mayest be confounded in all that thou hast done, in that thou art a comfort unto them.

55 When thy sisters, Sodom and her daughters, shall return to their former estate, and Sa-mā'rī-a and her daughters shall return to their former estate, then thou and thy daughters shall return to your former estate.

56 For thy sister Sodom was not mentioned by thy mouth in the day of thy pride,

57 Before thy wickedness was discovered, as at the time of *thy* reproach of the daughters of Syria, and all *that* are round about her, the daughters of the Philistines, which despise thee round about.

58 Thou hast borne thy lewdness and thine abominations, saith the LORD.

59 For thus saith the Lord GOD; I will even deal with thee as thou hast done, which hast despised the oath in breaking the covenant.

60 Nevertheless I will remember my covenant with thee in the days of thy youth, and I will establish unto thee an everlasting covenant.

61 Then thou shalt remember thy ways, and be ashamed, when thou shalt receive thy sisters, thine elder and thy younger: and I will give them unto thee for daughters, but not by thy covenant.

62 And I will establish my covenant with thee; and thou shalt know that I *am* the LORD:

63 That thou mayest remember, and be confounded, and never open thy mouth any more because of thy shame, when I am pacified toward thee for all that thou hast done, saith the Lord GOD.

CHAPTER 17

AND the word of the LORD came unto me, saying,

2 Son of man, put forth a riddle, and speak a parable unto the house of Israel;

3 And say, Thus saith the Lord GOD; A great eagle with great wings, longwinged, full of feathers, which had divers colours, came unto Lebanon, and took the highest branch of the cedar:

17:1-21. In chapter 17 the ways of kings and their people are revealed to be in the hands of the Lord. The great eagle, Nebuchadnezzar, first transplants Jehoiachin and many of his people to Babylon in 597 B.C. where they prosper. He makes provision for the remainder to prosper in the land under a vassal king, Zedekiah, whom he plants there. Zedekiah had agreed under oath to a place of subservient leadership to Nebuchadnezzar. He broke this oath, and then he

vers colours, came unto Lebanon, and took the highest branch of the cedar:

4 He cropped off the top of the top of his young twigs, and carried it into a land of traffick; he set it in a city of merchants.

5 He took also of the seed of the land, and planted it in a fruitful field; he placed it by great waters, and set it as a willow tree.

6 And it grew, and became a spreading vine of low stature, whose branches turned toward him, and the roots thereof were under him: so it became a vine, and brought forth branches, and shot forth sprigs.

7 There was also another great eagle with great wings and many feathers: and, behold, this vine did bend her roots toward him, and shot forth her branches toward him, that he might water it by the furrows of her plantation.

8 It was planted in a good soil by great waters, that it might bring forth branches, and that it might bear fruit, that it might be a goodly vine.

9 Say thou, Thus saith the Lord God; Shall it prosper? shall he not pull up the roots thereof, and cut off the fruit thereof, that it wither? it shall wither in all the leaves of her spring, even without great power or many people to pluck it up by the roots thereof.

10 Yea, behold, being planted, shall it prosper? shall it not utterly wither, when the east wind toucheth it? it shall wither in the furrows where it grew.

11 ¶Moreover the word of the LORD came unto me, saying,

12 Say now to the rebellious house, Know ye not what these things mean? tell them, Behold, the king of Babylon is come to Jerusalem, and hath taken the king thereof, and the princes thereof, and led them with him to Babylon;

13 And hath taken of the king's seed, and made a covenant with him, and hath taken an oath of him: he hath also taken the mighty of the land:

14 That the kingdom might be base, that it might not lift itself up, but that by the keeping of his covenant it might stand.

15 But he rebelled against him in sending his ambassadors into Egypt, that they might give him horses and much people. Shall he prosper? shall he escape that doeth such things? or shall he break the covenant, and be delivered?

16 As I live, saith the Lord God, surely in the place where the king dwelleth that made him king, whose oath he despised, and whose covenant he brake, even with him in the midst of Babylon he shall die.

17 Neither shall Pharaoh with his mighty army and great company make for him in the war, by casting up mounts, and building forts, to cut off many persons:

18 Seeing he despised the oath by breaking the covenant, when, lo, he had given his hand, and hath done all these things, he shall not escape.

19 Therefore thus saith the Lord God;

looked to Egypt for deliverance. In the eyes of the Lord, this was the same as breaking an oath made with Him (II Chr 36:13). Therefore, the Lord used Nebuchadnezzar as His servant to be the net to subdue the rebellious and oath-breaking king. Scripture teaches that an oath must be honored, even if entered into unwisely, as the incident of the Gibeonites reveals (Josh 9:19-20; II Sam 21:1-3).

Again, we see it clearly revealed that in His providential ways God both checks and directs the ways of kings, that His will be done (Dan 4:35-37). His integrity must be maintained as it relates to the keeping of oaths; His justice must be carried out as it relates to the punishment of Zedekiah; and His glory and grace will be revealed when He plants the Lofty Cedar, the Lord Jesus Christ, upon the mountains of Israel in the latter days and brings salvation to His people.

The following are key historical incidents which help to interpret this passage: (1) the king of Babylon took King Jehoiachin from Judah to Babylon in 597 B.C. (vs. 12; cf. vss. 3-4; II Kgs 24:8-16); (2) Nebuchadnezzar made Zedekiah a puppet king in Judah (vs. 13; cf. vss. 5-6; II Kgs 24:17); (3) Egypt attracted Zedekiah (vs. 17); (4) Zedekiah broke his covenant with Nebuchadnezzar and thus with God (vss. 15-19); and (5) Zedekiah would die in Babylon and his troops would be defeated (vss. 20-21).

As I live, surely mine oath that he hath despised, and my covenant that he hath broken, even it will I recompense upon his own head.

20 And I will spread my net upon him, and he shall be taken in my snare, and I will bring him to Babylon, and will plead with him there for his trespass that he hath trespassed against me.

21 And all his fugitives with all his bands shall fall by the sword, and they that remain shall be scattered toward all winds: and ye shall know that I the LORD have spoken it.

22 ¶Thus saith the Lord GOD; I will also take of the highest branch of the high cedar, and will set it; I will crop off from the top of his young twigs a tender one, and will plant it upon an high mountain and eminent:

23 In the mountain of the height of Israel will I plant it: and it shall bring forth boughs, and bear fruit, and be a goodly cedar: and under it shall dwell all fowl of every wing; in the shadow of the branches thereof shall they dwell.

24 And all the trees of the field shall know that I the LORD have brought down the high tree, have exalted the low tree, have dried up the green tree, and have made the dry tree to flourish: I the LORD have spoken and have done it.

CHAPTER 18

THE word of the LORD came unto me again, saying,

2 What mean ye, that ye use this proverb concerning the land of Israel, saying, The fathers have eaten sour grapes, and the children's teeth are set on edge?

3 As I live, saith the Lord GOD, ye shall not have occasion any more to use this proverb in Israel.

4 Behold, all souls are mine; as the soul of the father, so also the soul of the son is mine: the soul that sinneth, it shall die.

5 But if a man be just, and do that which is lawful and right,

6 And hath not eaten upon the mountains, neither hath lifted up his eyes to the idols of the house of Israel, neither hath defiled his neighbour's wife, neither hath come near to a menstruous woman,

7 And hath not oppressed any, but hath restored to the debtor his pledge, hath spoiled none by violence, hath given his bread to the hungry, and hath covered the naked with a garment;

8 He that hath not given forth upon usury, neither hath taken any increase, that hath withdrawn his hand from iniquity, hath executed true judgment between man and man,

9 Hath walked in my statutes, and hath kept my judgments, to deal truly; he is just, he shall surely live, saith the Lord GOD.

10 ¶If he beget a son that is a robber, a shedder of blood, and that doeth the like to any one of these things,

E. Lamentation for the Princes of Israel. 18:1-19:14.

18:1-2. This proverb that the children were suffering for the sins of their fathers had been circulating in Jerusalem (Jer 31:29) and Babylon. While there are cumulative effects of sin (cf. Ex 20:5-6; Mt 23:35-36), the Lord here declares that each individual is accountable for his own sin (vs. 4). The inhabitants of Jerusalem are incorrect in saying that the judgment has taken place because of their father's sinfulness.

3-4. The **Lord God** declares that such is not the case. All individuals have an equal responsibility to Him. Therefore, He deals with everyone on the basis of his own merits. It is only the one whose life is characterized by sin that will die.

5-9. But if a man be just. This is one who is just before God by virtue of a regenerated life. From his innermost being then, such a man will seek to live a life of outward righteousness. **But if a man be just, and do that which is lawful and right . . . he shall surely live** (cf. vs. 19) is a reference to an inward righteousness received by virtue of **a new heart and a new spirit,** according to verse 31. This reflects itself by outward righteousness and observance of the Law.

22-24. The Lord makes clear that He will not permit His kingdom to be annihilated, but will fulfill His promise to the seed of David.

Nebuchadnezzar broke off a twig from the cedar and brought it to Babylon. Then, the shoot he planted died. The Lord declares that He Himself will pluck off a shoot from the top of the high cedar (the Davidic house; vss. 2-3; Isa 53:2) and plant it on a high mountain that all may see it and find protection under it (vs. 23). **A tender one** is a sprig; i.e., a clear reference to Messiah (cf. Isa 11:1; Jer 23:5; 33:15; Zech 3:8; 6:12).

10-13. This wicked son of a righteous father cannot have his life spared because of his father. His personal life is the factor that calls for his death.

14-18. This is the righteous son of the wicked father in verses 10-13. As his grandfather in verses 5-9, he will live because he is seen as righteous, not only outwardly, but issuing from an inner life that is regenerated.

19-20. The principle that a son should not suffer for the sins of his father was well established (II Kgs 14:6; Deut 24:16). Perhaps the question was raised from Exodus 20:5, referring to children of the third and fourth generation suffering for the sins of their fathers. It is true that children tend to inherit and follow the example of their fathers. But in such a case, the sin would be their own; and they would be suffering for their own sin. Thus, the principle of individual accountability is reiterated and confirmed.

21-23. A wicked man could never turn from all his transgressions without regeneration. As the root, so the fruit. The sinner is free to repent, turn from sin, and do God's will.

24-29. This passage has been used to teach that one can fall from grace. Such could not be the meaning. Rather, one who has merely an outward righteousness frequently departs into a life of wickedness because he has no inner principle to guide him. His temporal life may be cut short; but eternal life, which he never had, cannot be lost.

11 And that doeth not any of those *duties,* but even hath eaten upon the mountains, and defiled his neighbour's wife,

12 Hath oppressed the poor and needy, hath spoiled by violence, hath not restored the pledge, and hath lifted up his eyes to the idols, hath committed abomination,

13 Hath given forth upon usury, and hath taken increase: shall he then live? he shall not live; he hath done all these abominations; he shall surely die; his blood shall be upon him.

14 ¶Now, lo, *if* he beget a son, that seeth all his father's sins which he hath done, and considereth, and doeth not such like,

15 *That* hath not eaten upon the mountains, neither hath lifted up his eyes to the idols of the house of Israel, hath not defiled his neighbour's wife,

16 Neither hath oppressed any, hath not withholden the pledge, neither hath spoiled by violence, *but* hath given his bread to the hungry, and hath covered the naked with a garment,

17 *That* hath taken off his hand from the poor, *that* hath not received usury nor increase, hath executed my judgments, hath walked in my statutes; he shall not die for the iniquity of his father, he shall surely live.

18 As *for* his father, because he cruelly oppressed, spoiled his brother by violence, and did *that* which *is* not good among his people, lo, even he shall die in his iniquity.

19 ¶Yet say ye, Why? doth not the son bear the iniquity of the father? When the son hath done that which is lawful and right, *and* hath kept all my statutes, and hath done them, he shall surely live.

20 The soul that sinneth, it shall die. The son shall not bear the iniquity of the father, neither shall the father bear the iniquity of the son: the righteousness of the righteous shall be upon him, and the wickedness of the wicked shall be upon him.

21 But if the wicked will turn from all his sins that he hath committed, and keep all my statutes, and do that which is lawful and right, he shall surely live, he shall not die.

22 All his transgressions that he hath committed, they shall not be mentioned unto him: in his righteousness that he hath done he shall live.

23 Have I any pleasure at all that the wicked should die? saith the Lord God: *and* not that he should return from his ways, and live?

24 ¶But when the righteous turneth away from his righteousness, and committeth iniquity, *and* doeth according to all the abominations that the wicked *man* doeth, shall he live? All his righteousness that he hath done shall not be mentioned: in his trespass that he hath trespassed, and in his sin that he hath sinned, in them shall he die.

25 ¶Yet ye say, The way of the Lord is not equal. Hear now, O house of Israel; Is not my way equal? are not your ways unequal?

26 When a righteous *man* turneth

away from his righteousness, and committeth iniquity, and dieth in them; for his iniquity that he hath done shall he die.

27 Again, when the wicked *man* turneth away from his wickedness that he hath committed, and doeth that which is lawful and right, he shall save his soul alive.

28 Because he considereth, and turneth away from all his transgressions that he hath committed, he shall surely live, he shall not die.

29 Yet saith the house of Israel, The way of the Lord is not equal. O house of Israel, are not my ways equal? are not your ways unequal?

30 Therefore I will judge you, O house of Israel, every one according to his ways, saith the Lord God. Repent, and turn *yourselves* from all your transgressions; so iniquity shall not be your ruin.

31 ¶ Cast away from you all your transgressions, whereby ye have transgressed; and make you a new heart and a new spirit: for why will ye die, O house of Israel?

32 For I have no pleasure in the death of him that dieth, saith the Lord God: wherefore turn *yourselves*, and live ye.

CHAPTER 19

MOREOVER take thou up a lamentation for the princes of Israel,

2 And say, What *is* thy mother? A lioness: she lay down among lions, she nourished her whelps among young lions.

3 And she brought up one of her whelps: it became a young lion, and it learned to catch the prey; it devoured men.

4 The nations also heard of him; he was taken in their pit, and they brought him with chains unto the land of Egypt.

5 Now when she saw that she had waited, *and* her hope was lost, then she took another of her whelps, *and* made him a young lion.

6 And he went up and down among the lions, he became a young lion, and learned to catch the prey, *and* devoured men.

7 And he knew their desolate palaces, and he laid waste their cities; and the land was desolate, and the fulness thereof, by the noise of his roaring.

8 Then the nations set against him on every side from the provinces, and spread their net over him: he was taken in their pit.

9 And they put him in ward in chains, and brought him to the king of Babylon: they brought him into holds, that his voice should no more be heard upon the mountains of Israel.

10 ¶ Thy mother *is* like a vine in thy blood, planted by the waters: she was fruitful and full of branches by reason of many waters.

11 And she had strong rods for the sceptres of them that bare rule, and her stature was exalted among the thick branches, and she appeared in her height with the multitude of her branches.

12 But she was plucked up in fury,

30-32. The Lord's burden for His people is that they have life, not death. But life will not be forced upon anyone who wishes to remain in his sin. The individual must personally respond and repent to have life. **Every one** indicates again that each individual is judged separately. Each is to **Repent, and turn,** and thus **live.**

19:1-9. Ezekiel eulogizes in prophetic form the last declining years of Judah. First, she is likened unto a lioness that trains her young lions in the art of savagery. The two young treacherous lions are Jehoahaz and Jehoiachin. Just as they were treacherous and cruel, so were they subdued. Pharaoh Necho captured Jehoahaz and led him to Egypt as an animal where he also died. Jehoiachin was taken by Nebuchadnezzar to Babylon and imprisoned for thirty-seven years.

Second, Judah is likened to a very fruitful vine. Its strong branches are its kings. It rose to great glory, particularly in the reigns of David and Solomon. But its end came like a scorching east wind. This vine was Babylon, and its last strong branch was Zedekiah. The fire out of the branch, the wickedness of Zedekiah, led to the destruction of the vine; and it was then transplanted in the wilderness of Babylon, where it remained fruitless as a nation.

A **lamentation** is a statement of sorrow. As the book of Lamentations is poetic in form, so also is this chapter. The book of **lioness** has been believed by some to be the wife of Josiah, the father of Jehoahaz. But the lioness is related both to Jehoahaz and Jehoiachin. It appears that she is meant to refer to Judah. Jehoahaz was subdued by Pharaoh Necho, and led to prison at Riblah as an animal with a ring in his nose (II Kgs 23:33). Jehoiachin was taken captive to Babylon, along with ten thousand of the leading citizens, where he was imprisoned for thirty-seven years (II Kgs 24:14).

10-14. Judah is also likened to a fruitful **vine. In thy blood** may have reference to the red juice of a fruitful vine. But this exalted nation had a terrible end. **plucked up in fury by the east wind,** Babylon. It was replanted in the wilderness, Chaldea. The **rod** or branch, Zedekiah, who should have been Judah's benefactor, was instead the **fire** leading to its destruction. From that time until the present there has not been a **rod** or branch ruling in Israel, but we know that in due time there will be a Sceptor and Branch to rule over Israel.

she was cast down to the ground, and the east wind dried up her fruit: her strong rods were broken and withered: the fire consumed them.

13 And now she *is* planted in the wilderness, in a dry and thirsty ground.

14 And fire is gone out of a rod of her branches, *which* hath devoured her fruit, so that she hath no strong rod *to be* a sceptre to rule. This *is* a lamentation, and shall be for a lamentation.

CHAPTER 20

AND it came to pass in the seventh year, in the fifth *month*, the tenth *day* of the month, *that* certain of the elders of Israel came to enquire of the LORD, and sat before me.

2 Then came the word of the LORD unto me, saying,

3 Son of man, speak unto the elders of Israel, and say unto them, Thus saith the Lord GOD; Are ye come to enquire of me? As I live, saith the Lord GOD, I will not be enquired of by you.

4 Wilt thou judge them, son of man, wilt thou judge *them?* cause them to know the abominations of their fathers:

5 And say unto them, Thus saith the Lord GOD; In the day when I chose Israel, and lifted up mine hand unto the seed of the house of Jacob, and made myself known unto them in the land of Egypt, when I lifted up mine hand unto them, saying, I *am* the LORD your God;

6 In the day *that* I lifted up mine hand unto them, to bring them forth of the land of Egypt into a land that I had espied for them, flowing with milk and honey, which *is* the glory of all lands:

7 Then said I unto them, Cast ye away every man the abominations of his eyes, and defile not yourselves with the idols of Egypt: I *am* the LORD your God.

8 But they rebelled against me, and would not hearken unto me: they did not every man cast away the abominations of their eyes, neither did they forsake the idols of Egypt: then I said, I will pour out my fury upon them, to accomplish my anger against them in the midst of the land of Egypt.

9 But I wrought for my name's sake, that it should not be polluted before the heathen, among whom they *were,* in whose sight I made myself known unto them, in bringing them forth out of the land of Egypt.

10 Wherefore I caused them to go forth out of the land of Egypt, and brought them into the wilderness.

11 And I gave them my statutes, and shewed them my judgments, which *if* a man do, he shall even live in them.

F. History of Israel: Past and Future. 20:1-49.

The elders came before Ezekiel to inquire of the Lord, but the Lord refuses to hear them. Instead, He tells Ezekiel to speak words of judgment to them. Had the elders come in all sincerity and true repentance, the Lord would have heard them. As is seen in verses 29-31, they are still continuing in their abominable ways.

In reviewing Israel's history, Ezekiel points out that Israel was chosen by grace, and that there had been a uniform pattern of rebellion against the Lord in not observing His ordinances, statutes, sabbaths, and by continuing in idolatry. He says that because of His name's sake, God had not inflicted judgment. It was not because of any worthiness on their part. Since they are now continuing in their same ways, God is not listening to their insincere inquiries. Judgment must finally come.

But the Lord did not choose Israel in vain. After dispersion and chastisement, Israel will be regathered, not because they are worthy, but because of His grace. At that time they will repent of their sins, be saved, and enter into the promised blessings in the land.

20:1-4. The Lord refused to **be inquired of** by the leaders because of their insincerity. Had they forsaken their sins and come to Him in true repentance, He would have listened. Instead, Ezekiel was to **judge** them in the sense of pointing out their sins to them.

5-10. **The day when I chose Israel** referred to here was in Egypt (Ex 6:6-8). Even before Israel was a nation, God had chosen them when He chose Abraham. Israel had become an actual nation of people by this time. At the same time, He had **espied,** or selected, for them a land, a land belonging to Israel by sovereign choice. The frequent use of the phrase **flowing with milk and honey** is proverbial of great abundance and plenty. That Israel had already been worshiping **idols** in Egypt is explicitly stated only here, though it is intimated by such occasions as the golden calf incident in the wilderness. God first had thoughts of judgment against Israel in Egypt because of her idolatry. **Made myself known.** God very dramatically proved Himself greater than the gods of Egypt in the contest of the ten plagues. Each of them showed His superiority over a particular god of Egypt.

11-17. If any man had observed the Law perfectly, he would have had life. But no fallen man of Adam's race has ever been capable of so doing. However, it did effectively point out man's

12 Moreover also I gave them my sabbaths, to be a sign between me and them, that they might know that I am the LORD that sanctify them.

13 But the house of Israel rebelled against me in the wilderness: they walked not in my statutes, and they despised my judgments, which *if* a man do, he shall even live in them; and my sabbaths they greatly polluted: then I said, I would pour out my fury upon them in the wilderness, to consume them.

14 But I wrought for my name's sake, that it should not be polluted before the heathen, in whose sight I brought them out.

15 Yet also I lifted up my hand unto them in the wilderness, that I would not bring them into the land which I had given *them,* flowing with milk and honey, which *is* the glory of all lands;

16 Because they despised my judgments, and walked not in my statutes, but polluted my sabbaths: for their heart went after their idols.

17 Nevertheless mine eye spared them from destroying them, neither did I make an end of them in the wilderness.

18 But I said unto their children in the wilderness, Walk ye not in the statutes of your fathers, neither observe their judgments, nor defile yourselves with their idols:

19 I *am* the LORD your God; walk in my statutes, and keep my judgments, and do them;

20 And hallow my sabbaths; and they shall be a sign between me and you, that ye may know that I *am* the LORD your God.

21 Notwithstanding the children rebelled against me: they walked not in my statutes, neither kept my judgments to do them, which *if* a man do, he shall even live in them; they polluted my sabbaths: then I said, I would pour out my fury upon them, to accomplish my anger against them in the wilderness.

22 Nevertheless I withdrew mine hand, and wrought for my name's sake, that it should not be polluted in the sight of the heathen, in whose sight I brought them forth.

23 I lifted up mine hand unto them also in the wilderness, that I would scatter them among the heathen, and disperse them through the countries;

24 Because they had not executed my judgments, but had despised my statutes, and had polluted my sabbaths, and their eyes were after their fathers' idols.

25 Wherefore I gave them also statutes *that were* not good, and judgments whereby they should not live;

26 And I polluted them in their own gifts, in that they caused to pass through *the fire* all that openeth the womb, that I might make them desolate, to the end that they might know that I *am* the LORD.

27 ¶ Therefore, son of man, speak unto the house of Israel, and say unto them, Thus saith the Lord GOD;

sinfulness and demonstrate the need of salvation by a Substitute through the shedding of blood. The observance of **my sabbath** began at Sinai, and it served as a special sign between the people and the **LORD.** It showed their dependence on Him to supply their need by not working on the seventh day. In turn, God had promised to care for them. If God had had to consume or annihilate Israel, it would have given the impression that He, who had delivered them from the hand of Pharaoh, was now no longer able to care for them. Yet, because of their sin, the generation coming out of Egypt could not enter the land of milk and honey. Only their children could.

18-26. The second generation continued in the same path as their parents. Again, the Lord did not consume them because of His name before the nations. Though this generation did enter the land, the Lord predicted dispersion from it. This was, and had been, carried out several times in Israel's history. That the Lord **gave them also statutes that were not good** must be seen as God acting through secondary means. Never is the Lord to be held responsible for leading anyone into sin (Jas 1:13). However, He does allow the rebellious sinner to go his way and receive the wages of sin (Rom 1:24, 26, 28; 6:23).

27-28. Israel **blasphemed** God by taking the very things they should have offered to Him, such as blood sacrifice, incense,

them. Thus saith the Lord God: Yet in this your fathers have blasphemed me, in that they have committed a trespass against me.

28 *For* when I had brought them into the land, for the which I lifted up mine hand to give it to them, then they saw every high hill, and all the thick trees, and they offered there their sacrifices, and there they presented the provocation of their offering: there also they made their sweet savour, and poured out there their drink offerings.

29 Then I said unto them, What *is* the high place whereunto ye go? And the name thereof is called Bā'mah unto this day.

30 Wherefore say unto the house of Israel, Thus saith the Lord God; Are ye polluted after the manner of your fathers? and commit ye whoredom after their abominations?

31 For when ye offer your gifts, when ye make your sons to pass through the fire, ye pollute yourselves with all your idols, even unto this day: and shall I be enquired of by you, O house of Israel? *As* I live, saith the Lord God, I will not be enquired of by you.

32 And that which cometh into your mind shall not be at all, that ye say, We will be as the heathen, as the families of the countries, to serve wood and stone.

33 *As* I live, saith the Lord God, surely with a mighty hand, and with a stretched out arm, and with fury poured out, will I rule over you:

34 And I will bring you out from the people, and will gather you out of the countries wherein ye are scattered, with a mighty hand, and with a stretched out arm, and with fury poured out.

35 And I will bring you into the wilderness of the people, and there will I plead with you face to face.

36 Like as I pleaded with your fathers in the wilderness of the land of Egypt, so will I plead with you, saith the Lord God.

37 And I will cause you to pass under the rod, and I will bring you into the bond of the covenant:

38 And I will purge out from among you the rebels, and them that transgress against me: I will bring them forth out of the country where they sojourn, and they shall not enter into the land of Israel: and ye shall know that I *am* the Lord.

39 As for you, O house of Israel thus saith the Lord God; Go ye, serve ye every one his idols, and hereafter *also,* if ye will not hearken unto me: but pollute ye my holy name no more with your gifts, and with your idols.

40 For in mine holy mountain, in the mountain of the height of Israel, saith the Lord God, there shall all the house of Israel, all of them in the land, serve me: there will I accept them, and there will I require your offerings, and the firstfruits of your oblations, with all your holy things.

41 I will accept you with your sweet savour, when I bring you out from the people, and gather you out of the countries wherein ye have been scat-

and gifts; and instead, Israel offered them to false gods that they adopted when entering the land.

29-32. Ye pollute yourselves with all your idols, even unto this day. They were doing the very same thing their forefathers had done, and God had dealt with them. Now judgment must take place. Therefore, He is now refusing to listen to their inquiry (vs. 1).

33-44. This section describes the coming judgment of those Jews who will be living at the conclusion of the Tribulation period when Christ returns to earth. The Chief Shepherd (Christ) will then examine His flock by causing them to **pass under the rod** and thus **purge out from among you the rebels** (vs. 38). He will thus bring the faithful into the blessings of the new covenant in the kingdom.

Even in verse 32 the phrase **that which cometh into your mind shall not be at all** is an utterance that already looks into the future. First, their judgment at the hand of Babylon will be the means of stopping their idolatry. But it may also have reference to the future day when the Lord will rule with an iron hand, though equitably and in justice, not allowing idolatry of any kind.

tered; and I will be sanctified in you before the heathen.

42 And ye shall know that I am the LORD, when I shall bring you into the land of Israel, into the country for the which I lifted up mine hand to give it to your fathers.

43 And there shall ye remember your ways, and all your doings, wherein ye have been defiled; and ye shall lothe yourselves in your own sight for all your evils that ye have committed.

44 And ye shall know that I am the LORD, when I have wrought with you for my name's sake, not according to your wicked ways, nor according to your corrupt doings, O ye house of Israel, saith the Lord GOD.

45 ¶Moreover the word of the LORD came unto me, saying,

46 Son of man, set thy face toward the south, and drop thy word toward the south, and prophesy against the forest of the south field;

47 And say to the forest of the south, Hear the word of the LORD; Thus saith the Lord GOD; Behold, I will kindle a fire in thee, and it shall devour every green tree in thee, and every dry tree: the flaming flame shall not be quenched, and all faces from the south to the north shall be burned therein.

48 And all flesh shall see that I the LORD have kindled it: it shall not be quenched.

49 Then said I, Ah Lord GOD! they say of me, Doth he not speak parables?

CHAPTER 21

AND the word of the LORD came unto me, saying,

2 Son of man, set thy face toward Jerusalem, and drop thy word toward the holy places, and prophesy against the land of Israel,

3 And say to the land of Israel, Thus saith the LORD; Behold, I am against thee, and will draw forth my sword out of his sheath, and will cut off from thee the righteous and the wicked.

4 Seeing then that I will cut off from thee the righteous and the wicked, therefore shall my sword go forth out of his sheath against all flesh from the south to the north:

5 That all flesh may know that I the LORD have drawn forth my sword out of his sheath: it shall not return any more.

6 Sigh therefore, thou son of man, with the breaking of thy loins; and with bitterness sigh before their eyes.

7 And it shall be, when they say unto thee, Wherefore sighest thou? that thou shalt answer, For the tidings; because it cometh: and every heart shall melt, and all hands shall be feeble, and every spirit shall faint, and all knees shall be weak as water: behold, it cometh, and shall be brought to pass, saith the Lord GOD.

8 ¶Again the word of the LORD came unto me, saying,

8:13. The last parts of verses 10 and 13 create a problem because of the brevity in the Hebrew text. The meaning of the

The chronology of events relating to the regathering of Israel appear to be as follows: (1) Some will be in the land in unbelief, even before His return—this fact is not stated in this passage; (2) of these, only a third will survive through the Tribulation and will be saved at His return (12:10-13:1; Zech 13:9); (3) all of Israel from all lands will be returned to the land, but first to a place called the **wilderness**; (4) here the Lord pleads with them face to face to accept Him; (5) the rebels are purged out, even as two-thirds of their unbelieving brethren who were in the land; and they shall not enter the land; (6) the whole house of Israel will be restored to the land, but only after in repentance they accept Him; and (7) finally, there they will be the blessing of the Lord and will be serving Him.

45-49. Ezekiel tells the elders that the fire of judgment is about to occur. It will be clearly evident that **I the LORD have kindled it**, and not merely an earthly power. But the elders appear not to fully understand, perhaps deliberately so.

G. Sword of the Lord. 21:1-32.

The sword of the Lord is about to be wielded by Babylon against Jerusalem. It is seen as drawn from the sheath, sharpened, polished, ready for action; and it is not to be returned until the gruesome task is accomplished.

Led by divination, the king of Babylon strikes at Jerusalem prior to striking Ammon. Here, God is letting the king, who is led by a false spirit, do His will.

In the destruction, both the offices of king and prophet are removed. However, these two offices will be restored in the future to a man whose right it will be to possess them. This we know to be the Lord Jesus Christ, who will be both King and Priest in the kingdom. "The times of the Gentiles" (Lk 21:24) begins at this time when both king and priest are removed from Jerusalem.

Ammon, who rejoiced to see Jerusalem's destruction, will also be judged in the Lord's time. This occurred just a few years after Jerusalem fell to the same brutal killers of Babylon.

21:1-7. Drop thy word toward the holy places. The Temple, with its priesthood and sacrificial system, is in view in this passage. Their end has come as it is also indicated in verse 26. In a time of material calamity, both **the righteous and the wicked** suffer. Though God often providentially spares the lives of the righteous in a physical calamity, yet it is also evident that they frequently suffer as much as the wicked. But in the case of the righteous, he is removed from its evil through death (Isa 57:1).

9 Son of man, prophesy, and say, Thus saith the LORD; Say, A sword, a sword is sharpened, and also furbished:

10 It is sharpened to make a sore slaughter; it is furbished that it may glitter: should we then make mirth? it contemneth the rod of my son, *as every tree.*

11 And he hath given it to be furbished, that it may be handled: this sword is sharpened, and it is furbished, to give it into the hand of the slayer.

12 Cry and howl, son of man: for it shall be upon my people, it *shall be* upon all the princes of Israel: terrors by reason of the sword shall be upon my people: smite therefore upon *thy* thigh.

13 Because *it is* a trial, and what if *the sword* contemn even the rod? *it* shall be no *more,* saith the Lord GOD.

14 Thou therefore, son of man, prophesy, and smite *thine* hands together, and let the sword be doubled the third time, the sword of the slain: it *is* the sword of the great *men that are* slain, which entereth into their privy chambers.

15 I have set the point of the sword against all their gates, that *their* heart may faint, and *their* ruins be multiplied: ah! *it is* made bright, *it is* wrapped up for the slaughter.

16 Go thee one way or other, *either* on the right hand, *or* on the left, whithersoever thy face *is* set.

17 I will also smite mine hands together, and I will cause my fury to rest: I the LORD have said *it.*

18 ¶The word of the LORD came unto me again, saying,

19 Also, thou son of man, appoint thee two ways, that the sword of the king of Babylon may come: both twain shall come forth out of one land: and choose thou a place, choose *it* at the head of the way to the city.

20 Appoint a way, that the sword may come to Rab'bath of the Ammonites, and to Ju'dah in Jerusalem the defenced.

21 For the king of Babylon stood at the parting of the way, at the head of the two ways, to use divination: he made *his* arrows bright, he consulted with images, he looked in the liver.

22 At his right hand was the divination for Jerusalem, to appoint captains, to open the mouth in the slaughter, to lift up the voice with shouting, to appoint *battering* rams against the gates, to cast a mount, *and* to build a fort.

23 And it shall be unto them as a false divination in their sight, to them that have sworn oaths: but he will call to remembrance the iniquity, that they may be taken.

24 Therefore thus saith the Lord GOD; Because ye have made your iniquity to be remembered, in that your transgressions are discovered, so that in all your doings your sins do appear; because, *I say,* that ye are come to remembrance, ye shall be taken with the hand.

25 ¶And thou, profane wicked prince of Israel, whose day is come, when iniquity *shall have* an end,

term **rod** may be the scepter, referring either to King Zedekiah or to Judah (Gen 49:9-10). Both king and people had despised the holy things of God. The context of verse 12 supports this view. Even though Judah was ripe for judgment, yet it is no cause for **mirth;** for they are still God's people.

14-17. Both the prophet (vs. 14) and the Lord (vs. 17) **smite** their hands in grief over the judgment. Yet, it was necessary in order to appease the holy wrath of God (**cause my fury to rest**).

18-23. Ezekiel was to sketch in miniature Nebuchadnezzar coming to a fork in the road, one leading to Rabbath and the other to Jerusalem. Here at the fork the king practiced divination by three methods: using arrows, and images, and noting the color of the liver. Since the decision to take Jerusalem first was made by divination, Israel looked upon it as false. But his remembrance of their iniquity (their rebellion) caused the king of Babylon to do it.

24-27. The **diadem** had reference to part of the dress of the high priest. Some render it mitre. "Although it is elsewhere used of the headgear of the High Priest, it signifies a 'turban', and the king, as well as the High Priest, may each have worn one of a distinguishing type" (Fisch, *Ezekiel,* p. 140). Both the high priest and the king are no more. The nation has come to a sad end, but only until **he come** who can rightfully occupy the throne of David and **be the great** High Priest. The Lord Christ will be that Priest-King in the coming kingdom.

1573

26 Thus saith the Lord GOD; Remove the diadem, and take off the crown: this *shall not be the same:* exalt *him that is* low, and abase *him that is* high.

27 I will overturn, overturn, overturn, it: and it shall be no *more,* until he come whose right it is; and I will give it *him.*

28 ¶And thou, son of man, prophesy and say, Thus saith the Lord GOD concerning the Ammonites, and concerning their reproach; even say thou, The sword, the sword *is* drawn: for the slaughter *it is* furnished, to consume because of the glittering:

29 Whiles they see vanity unto thee, whiles they divine a lie unto thee, to bring thee upon the necks of *them that* are slain, of the wicked, whose day is come, when their iniquity *shall have* an end.

30 Shall I cause *it* to return into his sheath? I will judge thee in the place where thou wast created, in the land of thy nativity.

31 And I will pour out mine indignation upon thee, I will blow against thee in the fire of my wrath, and deliver thee into the hand of brutish men, *and* skilful to destroy.

32 Thou shalt be for fuel to the fire; thy blood shall be in the midst of the land; thou shalt be no *more* remembered: for I the LORD have spoken *it.*

CHAPTER 22

MOREOVER the word of the LORD came unto me, saying,

2 Now, thou son of man, wilt thou judge, wilt thou judge the bloody city? yea, thou shalt shew her all her abominations.

3 Then say thou, Thus saith the Lord GOD, The city sheddeth blood in the midst of it, that her time may come, and maketh idols against herself to defile herself.

4 Thou art become guilty in thy blood that thou hast shed; and hast defiled thyself in thine idols which thou hast made; and thou hast caused thy days to draw near, and art come even unto thy years: therefore have I made thee a reproach unto the heathen, and a mocking to all countries.

5 Those that be near, and those that be far from thee, shall mock thee, which art infamous and much vexed.

6 Behold, the princes of Israel, every one were in thee to their power to shed blood.

7 In thee have they set light by father and mother: in the midst of thee have they dealt by oppression with the stranger: in thee have they vexed the fatherless and the widow.

8 Thou hast despised mine holy things, and hast profaned my sabbaths.

9 In thee are men that carry tales to shed blood: and in thee they eat upon the mountains: in the midst of thee they commit lewdness.

10 In thee have they discovered their fathers' nakedness: in thee have they humbled her that was set apart for pollution.

11 And one hath committed abomination with his neighbour's wife; and another hath lewdly defiled his

28-32. Though Nebuchadnezzar would turn away from Ammon and toward Jerusalem, Ammon's doom would be worse; no promise of restoration is given her (vs. 32). Ammon temporarily rejoiced in Israel's judgment, but her own judgment came in due time. Whereas Israel will be restored to blessing in a future day, Ammon **shalt be no more remembered** as a nation.

H. Jerusalem Condemned and Destroyed. 22:1—24:27.

22:1-16. A stronger indictment against a city, people, and land wholly gone into moral decay could not be expressed. They have served idols instead of the Lord; by bloodshed they have despised the sanctity of life; by sexual perversion they have despised the highest form of creation, man's body; by seeking material gain at any cost, they have put the material above the spiritual. They have done all of this because they have forgotten the **Lord GOD.**

All segments of the social structure have become involved in this decay: prophet, priest, prince, and people. Therefore, the Lord must bring judgment by dispersion to a remnant, and fire, sword, and plague to the others. God's holy purpose in this is to purge out filthiness and dross, appease His wrath against sin, and bring His people back to Himself.

So terrible and widespread were the bloody crimes of Israel that they were a **Reproach unto the heathen . . . all countries.** Earlier in their history, the Lord spared them in spite of their wickedness, lest the nations say the Lord could not save. But now the order is reversed. If the Lord's name was to be upheld, He must deal with His sinful people in judgment.

daughter in law; and another in thee hath humbled his sister, his father's daughter.

12 In thee have they taken gifts to shed blood; thou hast taken usury and increase, and thou hast greedily gained of thy neighbours by extortion, and hast forgotten me, saith the Lord God.

13 Behold, therefore I have smitten mine hand at thy dishonest gain which thou hast made, and at thy blood which hath been in the midst of thee.

14 Can thine heart endure, or can thine hands be strong, in the days that I shall deal with thee? I the LORD have spoken it, and will do it.

15 And I will scatter thee among the heathen, and disperse thee in the countries, and will consume thy filthiness out of thee.

16 And thou shalt take thine inheritance in thyself in the sight of the heathen, and thou shalt know that I am the LORD.

17 ¶And the word of the LORD came unto me, saying,

18 Son of man, the house of Israel is to me become dross: all they are brass, and tin, and iron, and lead, in the midst of the furnace; they are even the dross of silver.

19 Therefore thus saith the Lord God; Because ye are all become dross, behold, therefore I will gather you into the midst of Jerusalem.

20 As they gather silver, and brass, and iron, and lead, and tin, into the midst of the furnace, to blow the fire upon it, to melt it; so will I gather you in mine anger and in my fury, and I will leave you there, and melt you.

21 Yea, I will gather you, and blow upon you in the fire of my wrath, and ye shall be melted in the midst thereof.

22 As silver is melted in the midst of the furnace, so shall ye be melted in the midst thereof; and ye shall know that I the LORD have poured out my fury upon you.

23 ¶And the word of the LORD came unto me, saying,

24 Son of man, say unto her, Thou art the land that is not cleansed, nor rained upon in the day of indignation.

25 There is a conspiracy of her prophets in the midst thereof, like a roaring lion ravening the prey; they have devoured souls; they have taken the treasure and precious things; they have made her many widows in the midst thereof.

26 Her priests have violated my law, and have profaned mine holy things: they have put no difference between the holy and profane, neither have they shewed difference between the unclean and the clean, and have hid their eyes from my sabbaths, and I am profaned among them.

27 Her princes in the midst thereof are like wolves ravening the prey, to shed blood, and to destroy souls, to get dishonest gain.

28 And her prophets have daubed them with untempered morter, seeing vanity, and divining lies unto them.

17-22. Instead of being the glory, strength, and example among the nations, Jerusalem is now likened unto a refiner's blast furnace. As the furnace is heated, the dross will rise to the top to be cast off. If any silver and gold is there, it will be purged from its filthiness.

23-31. All segments of the social structure are seen as being in utter decay. It is noteworthy that the prophet, who should get his message directly from God, tops the list. His influence is the greatest, either for good or bad. The priests are next. When worship, innate in man, is directed to Satan, rather than the Lord of Creation, the end is very near.

saying, Thus saith the Lord God, when the Lord hath not spoken.

29 The people of the land have used oppression, and exercised robbery, and have vexed the poor and needy: yea, they have oppressed the stranger wrongfully.

30 And I sought for a man among them, that should make up the hedge, and stand in the gap before me for the land, that I should not destroy it: but I found none.

31 Therefore have I poured out mine indignation upon them; I have consumed them with the fire of my wrath: their own way have I recompensed upon their heads, saith the Lord God.

CHAPTER 23

THE word of the Lord came again unto me, saying,

2 Son of man, there were two women, the daughters of one mother:

3 And they committed whoredoms in Egypt; they committed whoredoms in their youth: there were their breasts pressed, and there they bruised the teats of their virginity.

4 And the names of them were A-hō′-lah the elder, and A-hōl′ī-bah her sister: and they were mine, and they bare sons and daughters. Thus were their names; Sa-mā′rī-a is A-hō′lah, and Jerusalem A-hōl′ī-bah.

5 And A-hō′lah played the harlot when she was mine; and she doted on her lovers, on the Assyrians her neighbours,

6 Which were clothed with blue, captains and rulers, all of them desirable young men, horsemen riding upon horses.

7 Thus she committed her whoredoms with them, with all them that were the chosen men of Assyria, and with all on whom she doted: with all their idols she defiled herself.

8 Neither left she her whoredoms brought from Egypt: for in her youth they lay with her, and they bruised the breasts of her virginity, and poured their whoredom upon her.

9 Wherefore I have delivered her into

23:1. The marriage relationship was first established by God in the Garden of Eden. It is the most precious and intimate of all relationships. When such a relation is severed through death, the pain is great; but when it is broken through marital infidelity with another lover, the hurt and damage is nearly irreparable. For this one reason alone, the Lord permitted (not command) that a divorce could be granted (Mt 19:9).

Ezekiel, through inspiration of the Holy Spirit, pictures the spiritual infidelity of God's people Israel to Himself. She turned her back upon the Lord and forgot all the love that He had shown to her. She then became enamored with love of fame, pleasure, and riches. But the height of her infidelity was in giving her love to other gods in worship, taking the very children that the Lord calls His own and offering them in sacrifice to the god Molech. It is no wonder that a nation given over to such spiritual adultery would be given over to judgment by the Lord Himself, even as a jealous husband under the Old Testament law turned his wife over to judgment (Lev 20:10).

Since we have before us a parable, every detail does not need to be pressed to a literal analogy. The **one mother** only needs to refer to the two sisters having a common origin. We are not left in doubt as to who is meant by the sisters.

2-4. **Samaria is Aholah, and Jerusalem Aholibah.** Thus, Samaria represents the northern kingdom, Israel; and Jerusalem represents the southern kingdom of Judah.

5-10. When Israel was brought out of Egypt and into the land by the mighty hand of God, they were to be a people separate from the nations around them; and the tribes in the land were to be exterminated. This was because of the gross wickedness and idolatry prevailing. But Israel was enamored with the riches, fame, and power she saw in these peoples. By her courtship with them, she fell into their evil ways, which finally led to the captivity of the northern tribes to Assyria in 722 B.C.

ease *was* with her: and with the men of the common sort *were* brought Sa-bē'-anś from the wilderness, which put bracelets upon their hands, and beautiful crowns upon their heads.

43 Then said I unto her *that was* old in adulteries, Will they now commit whoredoms with her, and she *with them?*

44 Yet they went in unto her, as they go in unto a woman that playeth the harlot: so went they in unto A-hō'lah and unto A-hōl'ī-bah, the lewd women.

45 ¶And the righteous men, they shall judge them after the manner of adulteresses, and after the manner of women that shed blood; because they are adulteresses, and blood *is* in their hands.

46 For thus saith the Lord GOD; I will bring up a company upon them, and will give them to be removed and spoiled.

47 And the company shall stone them with stones, and dispatch them with their swords; they shall slay their sons and their daughters, and burn up their houses with fire.

48 Thus will I cause lewdness to cease out of the land, that all women may be taught not to do after your lewdness.

49 And they shall recompense your lewdness upon you, and ye shall bear the sins of your idols: and ye shall know that I *am* the Lord GOD.

CHAPTER 24

AGAIN in the ninth year, in the tenth month, in the tenth *day* of the month, the word of the LORD came unto me, saying,

2 Son of man, write thee the name of the day, *even* of this same day: the king of Babylon set himself against Jerusalem this same day.

3 And utter a parable unto the rebellious house, and say unto them, Thus saith the Lord GOD: Set on a pot, set *it* on, and also pour water into it:

4 Gather the pieces thereof into it, *even* every good piece, the thigh, and the shoulder; fill *it* with the choice bones.

5 Take the choice of the flock, and burn also the bones under it, *and* make it boil well, and let them seethe the bones of it therein.

6 ¶Wherefore thus saith the Lord GOD; Woe to the bloody city, to the pot

24:1-2. The parable of the boiling pot was acted out in Babylon on the very day the siege of Jerusalem began (in January 588 B.C.; cf. II Kgs 25:1) and illustrates the destruction of the city. On the very day the siege of Jerusalem by Nebuchadnezzar began, Ezekiel had full knowledge of this from the Lord, even though he was about three hundred miles away from the scene. The terrifying judgment is presented by means of a parable, and then by a sign.

Choice pieces of meat, representing the leaders, are in the pot. But they are all taken out, away from protection against the fire of judgment. Because of its wickedness, even the pot, representing Jerusalem, is consumed in the fire of judgment.

As a sign, Ezekiel was not to mourn the sudden death of his wife, though he was grief-stricken. Likewise, when they hear of the center of their delight (the Temple with its ministry) destroyed, and their sons and daughters slain, the people are not to go through the routine of loud lamentations and comforting one another, though their grief is intense.

The utterance of the siege is dated relative to the time of Jehoiachin's exile, thus nine years after 597 B.C. The utterance was not prophetic; but rather, it described what was occurring that very day some three hundred miles away.

3-14. The parable of the pot shows that there was no protection for **every good piece** in it. The pieces here most likely represent the leadership of Jerusalem. They were all taken from their place of security (11:2), and not even a **lot** was cast for the sparing of some (Joel 3:3). The **scum** could read *rust*. The red rust of the iron caldron is representative of the **bloody city**. The city is so described because of its murderous practices both in civil affairs and in the sacrifice of children to the false god Molech. **Blood**, when shed, was to be covered (Lev 17:13), thus showing the sanctity of life, which is in the blood. As they had shed blood openly and indiscriminately, so it would now be with their blood. In her past judgments Israel had nor been purged

7 For her blood is in the midst of her; she set it upon the top of a rock; she poured it not upon the ground, to cover it with dust;

8 That it might cause fury to come up to take vengeance; I have set her blood upon the top of a rock, that it should not be covered.

9 Therefore thus saith the Lord God; Woe to the bloody city! I will even make the pile for fire great.

10 Heap on wood, kindle the fire, consume the flesh, and spice it well, and let the bones be burned.

11 Then set it empty upon the coals thereof, that the brass of it may be hot, and may burn, and that the filthiness of it may be molten in it, that the scum of it may be consumed.

12 She hath wearied herself with lies, and her great scum went not forth out of her: her scum shall be in the fire.

13 In thy filthiness is lewdness: because I have purged thee, and thou wast not purged, thou shalt not be purged from thy filthiness any more, till I have caused my fury to rest upon thee.

14 I the Lord have spoken it: it shall come to pass, and I will do it; I will not go back, neither will I spare, neither will I repent; according to thy ways, and according to thy doings, shall they judge thee, saith the Lord God.

15 ¶ Also the word of the Lord came unto me, saying,

16 Son of man, behold, I take away from thee the desire of thine eyes with a stroke: yet neither shalt thou mourn nor weep, neither shall thy tears run down.

17 Forbear to cry, make no mourning for the dead, bind the tire of thine head upon thee, and put on thy shoes upon thy feet, and cover not thy lips, and eat not the bread of men.

18 So I spake unto the people in the morning: and at even my wife died; and I did in the morning as I was commanded.

19 ¶ And the people said unto me, Wilt thou not tell us what these things are to us, that thou doest so?

20 Then I answered them, The word of the Lord came unto me, saying,

21 Speak unto the house of Israel, Thus saith the Lord God; Behold, I will profane my sanctuary, the excellency of your strength, the desire of your eyes, and that which your soul pitieth; and your sons and your daughters whom ye have left shall fall by the sword.

22 And ye shall do as I have done: ye shall not cover your lips, nor eat the bread of men.

23 And your tires shall be upon your heads, and your shoes upon your feet: ye shall not mourn nor weep; but ye shall pine away for your iniquities, and mourn one toward another.

24 Thus Ez-ze'ki-el is unto you a sign: according to all that he hath done shall ye do: and when this cometh, ye shall know that I am the Lord God.

from her wickedness. The Lord now makes the declaration that His **fury** will not rest till the purging is complete. This no doubt has an implication for the future, as well as for the present. At the time of the end, at Christ's second coming, full reconciliation will be made for iniquity (Dan 9:24).

15-18. I take away from thee the desire of thine eyes is a reference to Ezekiel's wife, who was about to die **with a stroke** (i.e., a blow), possibly meaning suddenly, or by a plague, cf. Numbers 14:37. In verse 17 Ezekiel employed the normal signs of mourning. The outward manifestation of mourning was by means of having the hair tousled, no shoes on the feet, and the lips covered. Also, friends would comfort him by bringing food and eating together. Ezekiel was to forego all this as a sign.

19-27. The Temple and its ministry was the center of Jewish life; it was the place of **strength** because of the presence of the Lord. Since they continued repeatedly to **profane** this holy place by their idolatry, the Lord was now removing His presence and strength. It would now be profaned by destruction, as well as the dead bodies of their sons and daughters. All of this was ordered by the Lord Himself. When these things take place, there will be no open lamentation and comforting of one another, because all will be in the same grief-stricken situation. The exiles who believed this message were, no doubt, grief-stricken at that very moment. Others were convinced some months later, as those who **escaped** brought the message of terror, death, and destruction, both of the Temple and of their sons and daughters (33:21). On that day Ezekiel would no longer be dumb (3:26, 33:22).

25 Also, thou son of man, *shall it not be* in the day when I take from them their strength, the joy of their glory, the desire of their eyes, and that whereupon they set their minds, their sons and their daughters,

26 *That* he that escapeth in that day shall come unto thee, to cause *thee* to hear *it* with *thine* ears?

27 In that day shall thy mouth be opened to him which is escaped, and thou shalt speak, and be no more dumb: and thou shalt be a sign unto them; and they shall know that I *am* the Lord.

CHAPTER 25

THE word of the Lord came again unto me, saying,

2 Son of man, set thy face against the Ammonites, and prophesy against them;

3 And say unto the Ammonites, Hear the word of the Lord God; Thus saith the Lord God; Because thou saidst, Aha, against my sanctuary, when it was profaned; and against the land of Israel, when it was desolate; and against the house of Ju'dah, when they went into captivity;

4 Behold, therefore I will deliver thee to the men of the east for a possession, and they shall set their palaces in thee, and make their dwellings in thee: they shall eat thy fruit, and they shall drink thy milk.

5 And I will make Rab'bah a stable for camels, and the Ammonites a couching place for flocks: and ye shall know that I *am* the Lord.

6 For thus saith the Lord God; Because thou hast clapped *thine* hands, and stamped with the feet, and rejoiced

III. PROPHECIES AGAINST SEVEN FOREIGN NATIONS. 25:1-32:32.

These prophecies constitute a transition between the prophecies of judgment on Judah and Jerusalem (chs. 1-24) and the predictions of her restoration (chs. 33-39; 40-48). Other prophets group oracles against foreign nations together (cf. Isa 13-23; Jer 46-51; Amos 1-2).

Before the ideal state can be realized, enemies must be destroyed and Israel made secure in her land (28:24, 26; 34: 28, 29). "Seven nations, possibly a symbol of completeness, are destined for retribution. Five of them had formed an alliance against Chaldea (Jer 27:1-3). Babylon, the anti-God power of the Old Testament, is not included in the denunciations, perhaps because that nation was the instrument of God's justice (29:17ff.)" (Pearson, "Ezekiel," *WBC*, p. 740).

The judgment was to be carried out because of their actions and attitudes towards Israel (25: 3, 8, 12, 15; 26:2; 29:6) and because of their self-deification and ungodly pride (ch. 28-29:3). The international outlook of the Hebrew prophets is illustrated, stressing the universal sovereignty of God and the moral responsibility of all mankind. A nation's position always depends upon what it contributes to God's purpose for mankind, as well as its loyalty to His universal rule.

The nations that fall under the judgment of God are Ammon, Moab, Edom, Philistia (25:1-7, 8-11, 12-14, 15-17), Tyre (three oracles: 26; 27; 28:1-19), Sidon (28:20-26), and Egypt (seven oracles: 29:1-16, 17-21; 30:1-19, 20-26; 31:1-18; 32:1-16, 17-32). The first four oracles are short, while the pronouncements against Tyre (chs. 26-28) and Egypt (chs. 29-32) are long, as well as being magnificent poems. The dates attached to some of the oracles locate this section between 587-586 B.C. (seven months before the fall of Jerusalem, 29:1) and 571-570 B.C. (sixteen years after its fall, 29:17).

A. Judgment on Ammon. 25:1-7.

25:1-2. **Ammonites.** This people dwelt on the other side of the Jordan, northeast of Jerusalem. They were racially connected with Israel (cf. Gen 19:38). Though the Israelites had respected their territory when journeying to Canaan (Deut 2:19, 37), the Ammonites bore animosity and waged several wars against them. After the Israelite tribes on the east of the Jordan had been carried away by the Assyrians, the Ammonites seized their land (Jer 49:1). Upon the fall of Jerusalem, they instigated the treacherous murder of Gedaliah, appointed governor by the Babylonian king (Jer 40:14), and obstructed Judaea's restoration in the time of Nehemiah (Neh 4:1). Later on, they aided the Syrians in the Maccabean war (cf. I Macc 5:6).

3-7. The Ammonites took advantage of Babylon's victory over Judah and grabbed whatever they could. **Men of the east** may be a reference to the nomadic tribes of Transjordan, or possibly the Babylonians who spoiled Ammon. **Rabbah** was the chief city of Ammon (Philadelphia, cf. 21:20).

in heart with all thy despite against the land of Israel;

7 Behold, therefore I will stretch out mine hand upon thee, and will deliver thee for a spoil to the heathen; and I will cut thee off from the people, and I will cause thee to perish out of the countries: I will destroy thee; and thou shalt know that I am the LORD.

8 ¶ Thus saith the Lord GOD; Because that Moab and Sēir do say, Behold, the house of Jū́dah is like unto all the heathen;

9 Therefore, behold, I will open the side of Moab from the cities, from his cities which are on his frontiers, the glory of the country, Bĕth-jĕsh́i-mŏth, Bā́al-mé́ŏn, and Kĭr-ĭ-a-thā́im,

10 Unto the men of the east with the Ammonites, and will give them in possession, that the Ammonites may not be remembered among the nations.

11 And I will execute judgments upon Moab; and they shall know that I am the LORD.

12 ¶ Thus saith the Lord GOD; Because that Edom hath dealt against the house of Jū́dah by taking vengeance, and hath greatly offended, and revenged himself upon them;

13 Therefore thus saith the Lord GOD; I will also stretch out mine hand upon Edom, and will cut off man and beast from it; and I will make it desolate from Tḗman: and they of Dḗdan shall fall by the sword.

14 And I will lay my vengeance upon Edom by the hand of my people Israel: and they shall do in Edom according to mine anger and according to my fury; and they shall know my vengeance, saith the Lord GOD.

15 ¶ Thus saith the Lord GOD; Because the Philistines have dealt by revenge, and have taken vengeance with a despiteful heart, to destroy it for the old hatred;

16 Therefore thus saith the Lord GOD; Behold, I will stretch out mine hand upon the Philistines, and I will cut off the Chĕr-e-thĭms and destroy the remnant of the sea coast.

17 And I will execute great vengeance upon them with furious rebukes; and they shall know that I am the LORD, when I shall lay my vengeance upon them.

B. Judgment on Moab. 25:8-11.

8-10. Seir is Edom, whose judgment is described in verses 12-14. Moab denied that Judah had any special relation with the true God. Her failure was in not recognizing Israel as a special people with whom He had manifested Himself in great power and glory in Egypt, the Red Sea, the wilderness experiences, and in the conquering of the land to possess it.

11. Both Moab and Ammon were conquered by Nebuchadnezzar in the fifth year after the destruction of Jerusalem; they were then occupied by Bedouin tribes.

C. Judgment on Edom. 25:12-14.

12-14. The Edomites were descendants of Esau, Jacob's twin. They were in constant conflict with Israel, the descendants of Jacob. They rejected Moses' request to pass through their land (Num 20:14-20); they opposed King Saul (I Sam 14:47); they fought against David (I Kgs 11:14-17); they opposed Solomon (I Kgs 11:14-25) and Jehoshaphat (II Chr 20:22); and they rebelled against Jehoram (II Chr 21:8-9). "From the thirteenth to the sixth centuries B.C. they settled in Mount Seir, a mountainous region south of the Dead Sea, of which Sela (Petra) was the capital. So rugged is the terrain that the valley in which Petra is located can only be reached through a narrow canyon guarded by towering mountain walls 200-250 feet high" (Ryrie, *Study Bible*, p. 1275). Edom's hatred of Israel began when Esau selling his birthright to Jacob. **Taking vengeance** literally says, "revenging with revenge." Edom never forgave and always sought to pay back double; but God must now deal with her, erasing her as a nation.

D. Judgment on Philistia. 25:15-17.

15. They were descendants of Mizraim, the son of Ham (Gen 10:14; I Chr 1:12), and were a constant thorn in the side of Israel (cf. Ex 13:17; Jud 3:2-3; 10:6-7; I Sam 4; 13-16; 13:19-22; 17-18; II Chr 17:11; 28:18; Zech 9:1-8). The Philistines came from Caphtor, or Crete, in the Aegean basin (Jer 47:4; Amos 9:7); and as part of the sea peoples they established themselves on the southern coast of Canaan, displacing the Avim (Deut 2:23).

Their monopoly on iron implements (I Sam 18:19-23) made them particularly formidable. Their pentapolis was under the control of five lords or *serens* (cf. Gr *tyrannos*; Josh 13:3; I Sam 6:4). Their god was Dagon, the grain deity (Jud 16:23). "The great 'uncircumcised' of antiquity were mighty carousers, as their ubiquitous wine craters and beer jugs suggest (Albright, *Archaeology of Palestine*, p. 115)" (Pearson, p. 741).

Relations continued to be hostile between Judah and the Philistines until the Maccabees finally exterminated them (I Macc 5:68; 10:83-89; 11:60, 61).

16-17. Cherethim. Synonymous with the Philistines, they were Cretans; and some were even foreign mercenaries in David's bodyguard (II Sam 8:18; 15:18; 20:7). They were to experience God's **furious rebukes**, because they took vengeance with malice of **heart, to destroy it for the old hatred** (vs. 15).

when I shall lay my vengeance upon them.

CHAPTER 26

AND it came to pass in the eleventh year, in the first *day* of the month, *that* the word of the LORD came unto me, saying,

2 Son of man, because that Tyrus hath said against Jerusalem, Aha, she is broken *that was* the gates of the people: she is turned unto me: I shall be replenished, *now* she is laid waste.

3 Therefore thus saith the Lord GOD; Behold, I *am* against thee, O Tyrus, and will cause many nations to come up against thee, as the sea causeth his waves to come up.

4 And they shall destroy the walls of Tyrus, and break down her towers: I will also scrape her dust from her, and make her like the top of a rock.

5 It shall be *a place for* the spreading of nets in the midst of the sea: for I have spoken *it*, saith the Lord GOD: and it shall become a spoil to the nations.

6 And her daughters which *are* in the field shall be slain by the sword; and they shall know that I *am* the LORD.

7 ¶ For thus saith the Lord GOD; Behold, I will bring upon Tyrus Nĕb-u-chad-rĕz'zar king of Babylon, a king of kings, from the north, with horses, and with chariots, and with horsemen and companies, and much people.

8 He shall slay with the sword thy daughters in the field: and he shall make a fort against thee, and cast a mount against thee, and lift up the buckler against thee.

9 And he shall set engines of war against thy walls, and with his axes he shall break down thy towers.

10 By reason of the abundance of his horses their dust shall cover thee: thy

E. Judgment on Tyre. 26:1-28:19.

"The antiquity of Tyre is attested to by Herodotus (ii. 44) and the Amarna Letters (cf. Pritchard, ANET, 484). Forced out of Palestine and Syria in the thirteenth and twelfth centuries, the Phoenicians turned their energies seawards and became the greatest mariners and traders of all time, in relation to the known world" (Pearson, p. 741).

Ahiram I, king of Tyre (969-936 B.C.), made treaties with David and Solomon (II Sam 5:11; I Kgs 5:1-18; 9:10-14, 26, 27). Ahab's queen, Jezebel, the daughter of Ethbaal (Ittobaal I, 887-856 B.C.), king of the Sidonians, introduced the worship of the Tyrian Baal Melkart, lord of the underworld, of storm and fertility, into Israel (I Kgs 16:31; 18).

Ezekiel gives more space to Tyre than does any other Old Testament writer. In chapters 26-28 he predicts the overthrow of this major sea power at the hands of Nebuchadnezzar (ch. 26), laments the shipwreck of the gallant ship *Tyre* in a dirge (ch. 27), and in a taunting song depicts the pride and fall of the prince of Tyre (28:1-19).

The primary sins of Tyre were the making of themselves to be a god unto themselves and materialism. They were independent and self-sufficient; and they worshiped riches and all the pleasures they could supply. This materialism set a pattern for the many nations and city-states entering into commerce with her. This is indicated by the lament over her after her fall. We do not read of Tyre dealing wickedly with the house of Israel, but we can be certain her emphasis upon riches as the end in life had a negative influence upon Israel.

26:1-6. The sin of Tyre is cited in this portion. **The eleventh year** related to the reign of Zedekiah, the year in which Jerusalem was captured, 586 or 587 B.C. Verse 2 implies that the oracle came after the destruction of Jerusalem in 586 B.C., news of which Ezekiel did not hear until the twelfth year and the tenth month (33:21). Her sin was that of crying, **Aha, she is broken that was the gates of the people: she is turned unto me: I shall be replenished.** Tyre's bent toward materialism is seen in her rejoicing over the fall of Jerusalem. This meant that the caravan routes carrying trade from the north and east to Tyre, and from the south (Egypt) up to Tyre were not going to be taxed. **Gates of the people** has reference to these taxing stations. With less tax to pay, the caravan traders could do more business with Tyre. The **daughters** were the smaller, unwalled cities nearby that looked to Tyre for protection.

The **many nations** of verse 3 relates to those nations that would be involved in the destruction of Tyre. **Nebuchadrezzar** (vs. 7) besieged the mainland city for thirteen years (585-572 B.C.) and destroyed it. In 332 B.C. Alexander the Great besieged the island city for six months and finally captured it by building a causeway out to it from the debris of the destroyed mainland city. The city was later rebuilt and is mentioned in Matthew 15:21-28; Mark 3:8; Acts 21:3-6; and it was nearly destroyed by the Muslims in A.D. 1291.

7-21. Nebuchadrezzar is the form of the name Ezekiel always used for *Nabukudurri-usur*, "Nebo, protect my boundary." **Engines of war** were battering rams. He literally leveled the city to bare rock. But he conquered only the mainland city, and not the city on an island some distance out to sea. There may be an allusion to this in 29:17-20. The island fortress was subdued by Alexander in 332 B.C. He used the **stones** and rubble of the city that was demolished by Nebuchadnezzar to build a causeway to the island fortress. The mainland was **built no more** on its original location. It literally became **like the top of a rock** where fishermen spread their **nets** for drying and repair. The lamentation of the princes over Tyre would indicate that even though profit was made through the colonies, yet a happy and workable relation had existed.

walls shall shake at the noise of the horsemen, and of the wheels, and of the chariots, when he shall enter into thy gates, as men enter into a city wherein is made a breach.

11 With the hoofs of his horses shall he tread down all thy streets: he shall slay thy people by the sword, and thy strong garrisons shall go down to the ground.

12 And they shall make a spoil of thy riches, and make a prey of thy merchandise: and they shall break down thy walls, and destroy thy pleasant houses: and they shall lay thy stones and thy timber and thy dust in the midst of the water.

13 And I will cause the noise of thy songs to cease; and the sound of thy harps shall be no more heard.

14 And I will make thee like the top of a rock: thou shalt be a *place* to spread nets upon: thou shalt be built no more: for I the Lord have spoken *it*, saith the Lord God.

15 "Thus saith the Lord God to Tyrus; Shall not the isles shake at the sound of thy fall, when the wounded cry, when the slaughter is made in the midst of thee?

16 Then all the princes of the sea shall come down from their thrones, and lay away their robes, and put off their broidered garments: they shall clothe themselves with trembling; they shall sit upon the ground, and shall tremble at every moment, and be astonished at thee.

17 And they shall take up a lamentation for thee, and say to thee, How art thou destroyed, *that wast* inhabited of seafaring men, the renowned city, which wast strong in the sea, she and her inhabitants, which cause their terror *to be* on all that haunt it!

18 Now shall the isles tremble in the day of thy fall: yea, the isles that are in the sea shall be troubled at thy departure.

19 For thus saith the Lord God; When I shall make thee a desolate city, like the cities that are not inhabited; when I shall bring up the deep upon thee, and great waters shall cover thee;

20 When I shall bring thee down with them that descend into the pit, with the people of old time, and shall set thee in the low parts of the earth, in places desolate of old, with them that go down to the pit, that thou be not inhabited; and I shall set glory in the land of the living;

21 I will make thee a terror, and thou *shalt be no more:* though thou be sought for, yet shalt thou never be found again, saith the Lord God.

CHAPTER 27

THE word of the Lord came again unto me, saying,

2 Now, thou son of man, take up a lamentation for Tyrus;

3 And say unto Tyrus, O thou that art situate at the entry of the sea, *which art* a merchant of the people for many isles, Thus saith the Lord God; O Tyrus, thou hast said, I am of perfect beauty.

4 Thy borders are in the midst of the

27:1-9. Tyre is pictured as a gallant ship made from the **fir trees** of Senir (Mount Hermon, vs. 5), with **masts** from the cedars of Lebanon and **oars** from Bashan (northeast of Galilee). The **entry** in verse 3 is actually a plural, entrances of the sea, possibly a reference to its two harbors (cf. 26:4), one to the south and the other to the north. **I am of perfect beauty** relates to the sin of pride, which was Tyre's chief sin (28:2, 5, 17). **Elishah** was probably Cyprus, Alashiya (*ANET*, p. 29; Amarna Letters 33-40) or Carthage. **Zidon** and **Arvad** (an island city north of

Tripoli) furnished the **mariners** (or oarsmen) and **pilots** (lit. *rope-pullers*). The **calkers** were the ship's carpenters from ancient Byblos.

10-25. Those mentioned in 9b-11 were Tyre's mercenaries. **They of Persia** is the first mention of Persia in the Bible. From verses 12-25 different places that acted as Tyre's merchants are named. For problems involved in identifying these places, see J. Simons, *The Geographical and Topographical Texts of the Old Testament*, pp. 455ff. Commerce and trade was carried on by means of barter with actual goods; and currency, as we know it, was not used. Thus, a merchant coming from Arabia needing slaves, brought with him lambs, rams, and goats to use as payment. Perhaps the merchant from Javan did not need lambs; consequently, merchants in Tyre served as the clearing house between traders. The passage lists some twenty-three countries doing trade with about thirty-eight basic products.

seas, thy builders have perfected thy beauty.

5 They have made all thy *ship* boards of fir trees of Sě'nir: they have taken cedars from Lebanon to make masts for thee.

6 Of the oaks of Bā'shan have they made thine oars; the company of the Ăsh'urites have made thy benches of ivory, *brought* out of the isles of Chĭt'tĭm.

7 Fine linen with broidered work from Egypt was that which thou spreadest forth to be thy sail; blue and purple from the isles of E-lī'shah was that which covered thee.

8 The inhabitants of Zī'don and Ăr'văd were thy mariners: thy wise *men*, O Tyrus, *that* were in thee, were thy pilots.

9 The ancients of Gĕ'bal and the wise *men* thereof were in thee thy calkers: and all the ships of the sea with their mariners were in thee to occupy thy merchandise.

10 They of Persia and of Lud and of Phut were in thine army, thy men of war: they hanged the shield and helmet in thee; they set forth thy comeliness.

11 The men of Ăr'văd with thine army *were* upon thy walls round about, and the Găm'ma-dims were in thy towers: they hanged their shields upon thy walls round about; they have made thy beauty perfect.

12 Tar'shĭsh *was* thy merchant by reason of the multitude of all *kind of* riches; with silver, iron, tin, and lead, they traded in thy fairs.

13 Jā'van, Tū'bal, and Mĕ'shĕch, they *were* thy merchants: they traded the persons of men and vessels of brass in thy market.

14 They of the house of Tō-gär'mah traded in thy fairs with horses and horsemen and mules.

15 The men of Dĕ'dan *were* thy merchants; many isles *were* the merchandise of thine hand: they brought thee *for* a present horns of ivory and ebony.

16 Syria *was* thy merchant by reason of the multitude of the wares of thy making: they occupied in thy fairs with emeralds, purple, and broidered work, and fine linen, and coral, and agate.

17 Jū'dah, and the land of Israel, they *were* thy merchants: they traded in thy market wheat of Mĭn'nĭth, and Păn'năg, and honey, and oil, and balm.

18 Damascus *was* thy merchant in the multitude of the wares of thy making, for the multitude of all riches; in the wine of Hĕl'bŏn, and white wool.

19 Dan also and Jā'van going to and fro occupied in thy fairs: bright iron, cassia, and calamus, were in thy market.

20 Dĕ'dan *was* thy merchant in precious clothes for chariots.

21 Arabia, and all the princes of Kē'dar, they occupied with thee in lambs, and rams, and goats: in these *were they* thy merchants.

22 The merchants of Shē'ba and Rā'a-mah, they *were* thy merchants: they occupied in thy fairs with chief of

all spices, and with all precious stones, and gold.

23 Hā'ran, and Cǎn'neh, and Eden, the merchants of Shē'ba, Ǎsshur, and Chǐl'mǎd, were thy merchants.

24 These were thy merchants in all sorts *of things,* in blue clothes, and broidered work, and in chests of rich apparel, bound with cords, and made of cedar, among thy merchandise.

25 The ships of Tàr'shish did sing of thee in thy market: and thou wast replenished, and made very glorious in the midst of the seas.

26 ¶ Thy rowers have brought thee into great waters: the east wind hath broken thee in the midst of the seas.

27 Thy riches, and thy fairs, thy merchandise, thy mariners, and thy pilots, thy calkers, and the occupiers of thy merchandise, and all thy men of war, that *are* in thee, and in all thy company which *is* in the midst of thee, shall fall into the midst of the seas in the day of thy ruin.

28 The suburbs shall shake at the sound of the cry of thy pilots.

29 And all that handle the oar, the mariners, *and* all the pilots of the sea, shall come down from their ships, they shall stand upon the land;

30 And shall cause their voice to be heard against thee, and shall cry bitterly, and shall cast up dust upon their heads, they shall wallow themselves in the ashes:

31 And they shall make themselves utterly bald for thee, and gird them with sackcloth, and they shall weep for thee with bitterness of heart *and* bitter wailing.

32 And in their wailing they shall take up a lamentation for thee, and lament over thee, *saying,* What *city is* like Tyrus, like the destroyed in the midst of the sea?

33 When thy wares went forth out of the seas, thou filledst many people; thou didst enrich the kings of the earth with the multitude of thy riches and of thy merchandise.

34 In the time *when* thou shalt be broken by the seas in the depths of the waters thy merchandise and all thy company in *their* midst of thee shall fall.

35 All the inhabitants of the isles shall be astonished at thee, and their kings shall be sore afraid, they shall be troubled in *their* countenance.

36 The merchants among the people shall hiss at thee; thou shalt be a terror, and never *shalt be* any more.

CHAPTER 28

THE word of the Lord came again unto me, saying,

2 Son of man, say unto the prince of Tyrus, Thus saith the Lord God; Because thine heart *is* lifted up, and thou hast said, I *am* a God, I sit *in* the seat of God, in the midst of the seas; yet thou *art* a man, and not God, though thou set thine heart as the heart of God:

3 Behold, thou *art* wiser than Daniel; there is no secret that they can hide from thee:

4 With thy wisdom and with thine understanding thou hast gotten thee

26-36. This portion provides a picture of the shipwreck (**ruin**) of Tyre and the astonishment on the part of the seafaring men. The **east wind** is noted as an agent of destruction (cf. 17:10; 19:12; Ps 48:7; Jer 18:17; Acts 27:14). The **suburbs**, i.e., the countryside, or the common land around a town (Lev 25:34; Num 35:2-8), hear the cries of the drowning sailors. In verses 30 and 31 eight signs of grief are enumerated. The lament over Tyre is centered around the loss of material riches. Riches become a great curse when seen as the end goal in life; and to a people holding this philosophy, it is a blessing to have material wealth removed. Material riches should always be viewed as a gift from the Lord, for, as believers, we are encouraged to be good stewards of all that He entrusts to us.

28:1-10. The **prince,** or king, of Tyre at the time of its fall by Nebuchadnezzar was Ithbaal II. The prince described here should be seen as none other than the one the context demands. He is not some ideal man or central figure of a myth. Archaeology and history confirm the facts of Tyre as here stated. The prince's **heart** was **lifted up** by virtue of his wisdom and riches to the point where he declared himself to be God. Others, such as Nebuchadnezzar (Dan 2) and Herod (Acts 12:20-23), did the same. God dealt with them as He did with the Prince of Tyre. Judgment came through the instrument of Nebuchadnezzar, but because **Thus saith the Lord God.** The **Daniel** of verse 3 is undoubtedly the biblical Daniel (cf.

riches, and hast gotten gold and silver into thy treasures:

5 By thy great wisdom *and by thy* traffick hast thou increased thy riches, and thine heart is lifted up because of thy riches:

6 Therefore thus saith the Lord GOD; Because thou hast set thine heart as the heart of God;

7 Behold, therefore I will bring strangers upon thee, the terrible of the nations: and they shall draw their swords against the beauty of thy wisdom, and they shall defile thy brightness.

8 They shall bring thee down to the pit, and thou shalt die the deaths of *them that are* slain in the midst of the seas.

9 Wilt thou yet say before him that slayeth thee, I *am* God? but thou *shalt be* a man, and no God, in the hand of him that slayeth thee.

10 Thou shalt die the deaths of the uncircumcised by the hand of strangers: for I have spoken *it*, saith the Lord GOD.

11 ¶Moreover the word of the LORD came unto me, saying,

12 Son of man, take up a lamentation upon the king of Tyrus, and say unto him, Thus saith the Lord GOD; Thou sealest up the sum, full of wisdom, and perfect in beauty.

13 Thou hast been in Eden the garden of God; every precious stone *was* thy covering, the sardius, topaz, and the diamond, the beryl, the onyx, and the jasper, the sapphire, the emerald, and the carbuncle, and gold: the workmanship of thy tabrets and of thy pipes was prepared in thee in the day that thou wast created.

14 Thou *art* the anointed cherub that covereth; and I have set thee *so*: thou wast upon the holy mountain of God; thou hast walked up and down in the midst of the stones of fire.

15 Thou *wast* perfect in thy ways from the day that thou wast created, till iniquity was found in thee.

16 By the multitude of thy merchandise they have filled the midst of thee with violence, and thou hast sinned: therefore I will cast thee as profane out of the mountain of God: and I will destroy thee, O covering cherub, from the midst of the stones of fire.

17 Thine heart was lifted up because of thy beauty, thou hast corrupted thy wisdom by reason of thy brightness: I will cast thee to the ground, I will lay thee before kings, that they may behold thee.

18 Thou hast defiled thy sanctuaries by the multitude of thine iniquities, by the iniquity of thy traffick; therefore will I bring forth a fire from the midst of thee, it shall devour thee, and I will bring thee to ashes upon the earth in the sight of all them that behold thee.

19 All they that know thee among the people shall be astonished at thee: thou shalt be a terror, and never *shalt thou be* any more.

20 ¶Again the word of the LORD came unto me, saying,

14:14), rather than a patriarchal Daniel. One of these men is mentioned in the Ras Shamra tablets, *ca.* 1400 B.C.; but he could not really and truly be righteous and wise, for he was a worshiper of Baal. The strangers in verse 7 are the Babylonians (cf. 26:7). **They shall bring thee down to the pit** is a reference depicted in the second half of the verse as meaning going to Sheol, which is the pit without burial. They will be **slain in the midst of the seas.** He will die a shameful death, **the deaths of the uncircumcised by the hand of strangers.**

11-19. **The king of Tyrus** in this section has caused considerable consternation on the part of biblical scholars for many years. Who is actually being referred to? Is it the historical king? Or is it the evil personage behind him, such as Satan? Among conservative scholars, there are those who say that in this passage the king of Tyre is still the actual king described in Oriental poetic imagery. Overstatement was a common way of speaking when special attention was needed. However, we find a number of statements that go beyond the context of these three chapters on Tyre and her prince. The **sum** total of **wisdom** and **beauty** could not rightfully be stated of any earthly monarch; but it could be a reference to Lucifer, who was thus created by the **Lord GOD.** The events described go back to the time when this individual was **created.** He is spoken of as an **anointed cherub.** The Scriptures make reference to cherubim when associated with God's holiness and presence (Ex 25:18-22), **cherub** that **covereth** or guard the throne of God. The very throne, which he was set apart to protect, becomes his own desire. Satan is spoken of in other passages as the god of this world (II Cor 4:4), and as the "prince" working in the children of disobedience (Eph 2:2). Daniel speaks of a spirit being called the prince of Persia who restrained an angel from coming to him for three weeks (Dan 10:11-13). It appears that at least a number of statements in this passage have reference to the motivating power, Satan himself, behind the earthly king of Tyre.

Satan's judgment, announced in these verses (16-19), will not be consummated until he is cast forever into the lake of fire (Rev 20:10).

F. Judgment on Sidon. 28:20-26.

20-24. Tyre's neighbor, **Zidon,** will also be punished (cf. Joel 3:4-8). Zidon is located twenty-five miles north of Tyre. The

21 Son of man, set thy face against Zĭdon, and prophesy against it,

22 And say, Thus saith the Lord God; Behold, I am against thee, O Zĭdon; and I will be glorified in the midst of thee: and they shall know that I am the Lord, when I shall have executed judgments in her, and shall be sanctified in her.

23 For I will send into her pestilence, and blood into her streets; and the wounded shall be judged in the midst of her by the sword upon her on every side: and they shall know that I am the Lord.

24 ¶And there shall be no more a pricking brier unto the house of Israel, nor any grieving thorn of all that are round about them, that despised them; and they shall know that I am the Lord God.

25 Thus saith the Lord God: When I shall have gathered the house of Israel from the people among whom they are scattered, and shall be sanctified in them in the sight of the heathen, then shall they dwell in their land that I have given to my servant Jacob.

26 And they shall dwell safely therein, and shall build houses, and plant vineyards; yea, they shall dwell with confidence, when I have executed judgments upon all those that despise them round about them; and they shall know that I am the Lord their God.

CHAPTER 29

IN the tenth year, in the tenth month, in the twelfth day of the month, the word of the Lord came unto me, saying,

2 Son of man, set thy face against Pharaoh king of Egypt, and prophesy against him, and against all Egypt:

3 Speak, and say, Thus saith the Lord God; Behold, I am against thee, Pharaoh king of Egypt, the great dragon that lieth in the midst of his rivers, which hath said, My river is mine own, and I have made it for myself.

4 But I will put hooks in thy jaws, and I will cause the fish of thy rivers to stick unto thy scales, and I will bring thee up out of the midst of thy rivers, and all the fish of thy rivers shall stick unto thy scales.

5 And I will leave thee thrown into the wilderness, thee and all the fish of thy rivers: thou shalt fall upon the open fields; thou shalt not be brought together, nor gathered: I have given thee for meat to the beasts of the field and to the fowls of the heaven.

6 And all the inhabitants of Egypt shall know that I am the Lord, because they have been a staff of reed to the house of Israel.

7 When they took hold of thee by thy hand, thou didst break, and rend all their shoulder: and when they leaned upon thee, thou brakest, and madest all their loins to be at a stand.

8 ¶Therefore thus saith the Lord God; Behold, I will bring a sword upon thee, and cut off man and beast out of thee.

9 And the land of Egypt shall be desolate and waste; and they shall know that I am the Lord: because he hath

tribe of Asher did not drive out the Sidonians (Jud 1:31; 10:12), and it later became subject to Tyre. It was destroyed by Esarhaddon in 677 B.C.; then, along with Tyre, it became subject to Pharaoh Hophra in 588 B.C. and finally submitted to Cambyses in 526 B.C. It sold cedar for the rebuilding of the Jerusalem Temple (Ezr 3:7); it was destroyed by the Persians in 345 B.C.; it surrendered to Alexander the Great in 333 B.C.; and it passed into the hands of the Romans in 64 B.C. In the New Testament it is mentioned in connection with Tyre.

Zidon is singled out for judgment because of being a **pricking brier**, or a **grieving thorn**, to Israel. Her idolatry both vexed and then ensnared Israel with the worship of Baal and Ashtaroth.

25-26. In contrast to the insecurity of nations that defy God and are brought to ruin, we see another glimpse of Israel's bright future. The **land** belongs to her, and she will dwell there in safety and prosperity after her regathering from among the nations. What wars and summit conferences cannot solve, the Lord will at His coming again!

G. Judgment on Egypt. 29:1-32:32.

29:1-7. Pharaoh Hophra (Jer 44:30) had come to the aid of Jerusalem a few years earlier, when Nebuchadnezzar had besieged it. Thereupon, Nebuchadnezzar withdrew, only to come again in 588 B.C.; and finally Jerusalem collapsed in 586 B.C. This prophecy against Egypt was made when Jerusalem had been under siege one year and two days (587 B.C.). **The dragon** is used as a figure of Pharaoh and has reference to the crocodiles that were common in the Nile. The dragon and fish are seen as being cast on the land where they perish since they are water creatures. This pictures the destruction of Pharaoh and his people.

8-12. A sword is a reference to the Chaldeans (cf. vss. 8; 32:11, 12; Jer 46:13ff.). The main reason for Pharaoh's destruction was his haughty spirit that said the Nile and the glory of Egypt were his doing. To cause him and his people and surrounding nations to see that the **Lord God** is **Lord**, the land was decimated from north to south (Migdol to Syene) of both

said, The river is mine, and I have made it.

10 Behold, therefore I am against thee, and against thy rivers, and I will make the land of Egypt utterly waste and desolate, from the tower of Sy-ē'ne even unto the border of Ē-thī-ō'pī-a.

11 No foot of man shall pass through it, nor foot of beast shall pass through it, neither shall it be inhabited forty years.

12 And I will make the land of Egypt desolate in the midst of the countries that are desolate, and her cities among the cities that are laid waste shall be desolate forty years: and I will scatter the Egyptians among the nations, and will disperse them through the countries.

13 ¶Yet thus saith the Lord God: At the end of forty years will I gather the Egyptians from the people whither they were scattered:

14 And I will bring again the captivity of Egypt, and will cause them to return into the land of Păth'rŏs, into the land of their habitation; and they shall be there a base kingdom.

15 It shall be the basest of the kingdoms; neither shall it exalt itself any more above the nations: for I will diminish them, that they shall no more rule over the nations.

16 And it shall be no more the confidence of the house of Israel, which bringeth their iniquity to remembrance, when they shall look after them: but they shall know that I am the Lord God.

17 ¶And it came to pass in the seven and twentieth year, in the first month, in the first day of the month, the word of the Lord came unto me, saying,

18 Son of man, Nĕb-u-chad-rĕz'zar king of Babylon caused his army to serve a great service against Tyrus: every head was made bald, and every shoulder was peeled: yet had he no wages, nor his army, for Tyrus, for the service that he had served against it:

19 Therefore thus saith the Lord God; Behold, I will give the land of Egypt unto Nĕb-u-chad-rĕz'zar king of Babylon: and he shall take her multitude, and take her spoil, and take her prey; and it shall be the wages for his army.

20 I have given him the land of Egypt for his labour wherewith he served against it, because they wrought for me, saith the Lord God.

21 In that day will I cause the horn of the house of Israel to bud forth, and I will give thee the opening of the mouth in the midst of them; and they shall know that I am the Lord.

CHAPTER 30

THE word of the Lord came again unto me, saying,

2 Son of man, prophesy and say, Thus saith the Lord God; Howl ye, Woe worth the day!

3 For the day is near, even the day of the Lord is near, a cloudy day; it shall be the time of the heathen.

4 And the sword shall come upon man and beast. The survivors were scattered among the nations. Forty years was the period of Chaldean supremacy, anticipating verse 13. Because of the lenient policy of Persia in 539 B.C., many of the captives were allowed to go home.

13-16. Even though Egypt had been great and powerful, after their return they were never again to become a powerful nation, and they shall be there a base kingdom (cf. Jer 46:26). History has borne this out.

17-20. The date is March-April of 571 B.C. Though Nebuchadnezzar had laid siege to Tyre for thirteen years, the campaign was an economic loss. Since he had no booty with which to pay his soldiers, he invaded Egypt and got booty, the wages for his army. Thus, both Tyre and Egypt, proud because of their wealth, were humbled by God's instrument, Nebuchadnezzar.

21. The horn budding is a symbol of strength (I Sam 2:10). After Judah had been in captivity for seventy years, she was permitted to return to the land. Some think this may even be a reference to Israel's future restoration and glory at the time of the second coming of the Lord.

30:1-5. Because of her wealth, Egypt was able to hire mercenary soldiers from the countries named in this section. The day of the Lord is the day of the Lord executing His wrath upon Egypt. "Though the phrase is usually used eschatologically, here Egypt is viewed as representative of God's judgment on all godless nations" (Ryrie, p. 184). In verse 5 the allies of Egypt were to be overthrown, and the men of the land that is in league. The political and social institutions in which Egypt's

Egypt, and great pain shall be in Ē-thī-ō'pĭ-a, when the slain shall fall in Egypt, and they shall take away her multitude, and her foundations shall be broken down.

5 Ē-thī-ō'pĭ-a, and Libya, and Lydia, and all the mingled people, and Chub, and the men of the land that is in league, shall fall with them by the sword.

6 ¶ Thus saith the LORD; They also that uphold Egypt shall fall; and the pride of her power shall come down: from the tower of Sў-ē'ne shall they fall in it by the sword, saith the Lord GOD.

7 And they shall be desolate in the midst of the countries that are desolate, and her cities shall be in the midst of the cities that are wasted.

8 And they shall know that I am the LORD, when I have set a fire in Egypt, and when all her helpers shall be destroyed.

9 In that day shall messengers go forth from me in ships to make the careless Ē-thī-ō'pĭ-ans afraid, and great pain shall come upon them, as in the day of Egypt: for, lo, it cometh.

10 ¶ Thus saith the Lord GOD; I will also make the multitude of Egypt to cease by the hand of Nĕb-u-chad-rĕz'zar king of Babylon.

11 He and his people with him, the terrible of the nations, shall be brought to destroy the land: and they shall draw their swords against Egypt, and fill the land with the slain.

12 And I will make the rivers dry, and sell the land into the hand of the wicked: and I will make the land waste, and all that is therein, by the hand of strangers: I the LORD have spoken it.

13 ¶ Thus saith the Lord GOD; I will also destroy the idols, and I will cause their images to cease out of Noph; and there shall be no more a prince of the land of Egypt: and I will put a fear in the land of Egypt.

14 And I will make Păth'rŏs desolate, and will set fire in Zō'an, and will execute judgments in No.

15 And I will pour my fury upon Sin, the strength of Egypt; and I will cut off the multitude of No.

16 And I will set fire in Egypt: Sin shall have great pain, and No shall be rent asunder, and Noph shall have distresses daily.

17 The young men of Ā'ven and of Pĭ-bē'seth shall fall by the sword: and these cities shall go into captivity.

18 At Tē-hăph'ne-hēs also the day shall be darkened, when I shall break there the yokes of Egypt: and the pomp of her strength shall cease in her: as for her, a cloud shall cover her, and her daughters shall go into captivity.

19 Thus will I execute judgments in Egypt: and they shall know that I am the LORD.

20 ¶ And it came to pass in the eleventh year, in the first month, in the seventh day of the month, that the word of the LORD came unto me, saying,

21 Son of man, I have broken the arm of Pharaoh king of Egypt; and, lo, it

strength lay were to be destroyed, **and her foundations shall be broken down** (cf. vss. 6,8,13,15,17).

6-12. The **fire** may be a symbol of judgment, as in 15:5, also 30:14,16. The Lord's acts against Egypt were meant to warn the **careless Ethiopians** and the world. The wealth of Egypt was to be seized by Nebuchadnezzar, and the **multitude of Egypt** would be carried off (cf. vs. 4 and 29:17-19).

13-19. Egypt depended strongly on her idols to protect her. But they are now of no avail, as seen by her prince being removed, cities all over the land made desolate, and people taken captive.

20-26. Figuratively, Pharaoh's arm is seen as broken and not bandaged up for healing. Similarly, the strength of Pharaoh will be broken by Nebuchadnezzar, and he will not be restored to strength again. Nebuchadnezzar was the Lord's instrument to destroy Egypt.

shall not be bound up to be healed, to put a roller to bind it, to make it strong to hold the sword.

22 Therefore thus saith the Lord God; Behold, I *am* against Pharaoh king of Egypt, and will break his arms, the strong, and that which was broken; and I will cause the sword to fall out of his hand.

23 And I will scatter the Egyptians among the nations, and will disperse them through the countries.

24 And I will strengthen the arms of the king of Babylon, and put my sword in his hand: but I will break Pharaoh's arms, and he shall groan before him with the groanings of a deadly wounded *man*.

25 But I will strengthen the arms of the king of Babylon, and the arms of Pharaoh shall fall down: and they shall know that I *am* the LORD, when I shall put my sword into the hand of the king of Babylon, and he shall stretch it out upon the land of Egypt.

26 And I will scatter the Egyptians among the nations, and disperse them among the countries; and they shall know that I *am* the LORD.

CHAPTER 31

AND it came to pass in the eleventh year, in the third *month,* in the first *day* of the month, *that* the word of the LORD came unto me, saying,

2 Son of man, speak unto Pharaoh king of Egypt, and to his multitude; Whom art thou like in thy greatness?

3 Behold, the Assyrian *was* a cedar in Lebanon with fair branches, and with a shadowing shroud, and of an high stature; and his top was among the thick boughs.

4 The waters made him great, the deep set him up on high with her rivers running round about his plants, and sent out her little rivers unto all the trees of the field.

5 Therefore his height was exalted above all the trees of the field, and his boughs were multiplied, and his branches became long because of the multitude of waters, when he shot forth.

6 All the fowls of heaven made their nests in his boughs, and under his branches did all the beasts of the field bring forth their young, and under his shadow dwelt all great nations.

7 Thus was he fair in his greatness, in the length of his branches: for his root was by great waters.

8 The cedars in the garden of God could not hide him: the fir trees were not like his boughs, and the chesnut trees were not like his branches: nor any tree in the garden of God was like unto him in his beauty.

9 I have made him fair by the multitude of his branches: so that all the trees of Eden, that *were* in the garden of God, envied him.

10 ¶ Therefore thus saith the Lord God; Because thou hast lifted up thyself in height, and he hath shot up his top among the thick boughs, and his heart is lifted up in his height;

31:1-9. In this section Egypt is likened to a lofty cedar, and the greatness of Pharaoh is compared to Assyria. Assyria is presented under the figure of a beautiful and lofty cedar tree. It is greater in spendor than any other tree, even those that were in the Garden of Eden in previous days. Thus, in its day Assyria was the greatest power. Pharaoh and Egypt are compared to it. This oracle is dated to May-June of 586 B.C., about two months before the fall of Jerusalem.

10-14. The destruction of the tree is described. Pharaoh's sin was pride in verse 10, as was Satan's in 28:16-17. Therefore, God will use **the mighty one of the heathen** to fell this tree and bring it to ruin. So Nebuchadnezzar did to Pharaoh, **the terrible of the nations.**

11 I have therefore delivered him into the hand of the mighty one of the heathen; he shall surely deal with him: I have driven him out for his wickedness.

12 And strangers, the terrible of the nations, have cut him off, and have left him: upon the mountains and in all the valleys his branches are fallen, and his boughs are broken by all the rivers of the land; and all the people of the earth are gone down from his shadow, and have left him.

13 Upon his ruin shall all the fowls of the heaven remain, and all the beasts of the field shall be upon his branches:

14 To the end that none of all the trees by the waters exalt themselves for their height, neither shoot up their top among the thick boughs, neither their trees stand up in their height, all that drink water: for they are all delivered unto death, to the nether parts of the earth, in the midst of the children of men, with them that go down to the pit.

15 Thus saith the Lord GOD; In the day when he went down to the grave I caused a mourning: I covered the deep for him, and I restrained the floods thereof, and the great waters were stayed: and I caused Lebanon to mourn for him, and all the trees of the field fainted for him.

16 I made the nations to shake at the sound of his fall, when I cast him down to hell with them that descend into the pit: and all the trees of Eden, the choice and best of Lebanon, all that drink water, shall be comforted in the nether parts of the earth.

17 They also went down into hell with him unto *them that be* slain with the sword; and *they that were* his arm, *that* dwelt under his shadow in the midst of the heathen.

18 ¶ To whom art thou thus like in glory and in greatness among the trees of Eden? yet shalt thou be brought down with the trees of Eden unto the nether parts of the earth: thou shalt lie in the midst of the uncircumcised with *them that be* slain by the sword. This *is* Pharaoh and all his multitude, saith the Lord GOD.

CHAPTER 32

AND it came to pass in the twelfth year, in the twelfth month, in the first day of the month, *that* the word of the LORD came unto me, saying,

2 Son of man, take up a lamentation for Pharaoh king of Egypt, and say unto him, Thou art like a young lion of the nations, and thou *art* as a whale in the seas: and thou camest forth with thy rivers, and troubledst the waters with thy feet, and fouledst their rivers.

3 Thus saith the Lord GOD; I will therefore spread out my net over thee with a company of many people; and they shall bring thee up in my net.

4 Then will I leave thee upon the land, I will cast thee forth upon the open field, and will cause all the fowls of the heaven to remain upon thee, and I will fill the beasts of the whole earth with thee.

15-18. The trees have reference to nations, with the outstanding one being Pharaoh and his people. As the other proud nations were brought to hell or Sheol, so also will Pharaoh. A nation, as such, does not go to hell. Rather, it is individuals who go there. The point here is that Pharaoh and his people will be removed from the living on earth. "Other nations were *comforted* when Egypt fell, but they too would go down (*went down* is a prophetic perfect indicating future time) to Sheol eventually" (Ryrie, p. 1186).

32:1-8. The time is February-March of 585 B.C., one year and seven months after the fall of Jerusalem. Verses 2-8 describe Egypt's fall. As a lion is the king among animals, so Pharaoh is likening himself to the powerful one among the nations. In contrast, the Lord God is likening him to the ugly crocodile in the muddy waters of the Nile (vs. 2). A crocodile may be an animal to be feared in its own element, but not by animals on land. Furthermore, Pharaoh's destruction is likened unto the huge water creature cast upon dry land where he is helpless, perishes, and is eaten as carrion by the birds. Thus, Pharaoh is pictured as coming to his end in a despicable manner, not literally as the crocodile, but by the hand of the king of Babylon. Darkness coming over the land should in this context be considered as figurative, for the preceding verses were figurative in likening Pharaoh to the monster of the Nile. The meaning is that of intense gloom and despair coming over Egypt in this time of judgment.

9-10. These verses describe the reactions of the nations.

11-16. The instrument, Nebuchadnezzar, is pictured in these verses, **The sword of the king of Babylon shall come upon thee.** Yet, God is the ultimate devastator, **I will destroy.** So great would the judgment be that paid mourners would offer up **a lamentation.** So complete will be its destruction, that man and beast will not be left to stir up the waters of the great river and the irrigation canals.

17-32. This is related two weeks later than verse 1. It is a graphic description of Sheol (the **pit** in vss. 18, 24, 25, 29, 30). Then other nations are pictured as greeting Egypt in the **pit. Elam** was once a mighty power in the southwest. **Meshech** and **Tubal** were powers in the northwest Asia Minor. Edom is then mentioned, along with the Sidonians. **Pharaoh shall see them** indicates that he was to have the miserable comfort of knowing that he was not alone in his fate.

5 And I will lay thy flesh upon the mountains, and fill the valleys with thy height.

6 I will also water with thy blood the land wherein thou swimmest, *even to* the mountains; and the rivers shall be full of thee.

7 And when I shall put thee out, I will cover the heaven, and make the stars thereof dark; I will cover the sun with a cloud, and the moon shall not give her light.

8 All the bright lights of heaven will I make dark over thee, and set darkness upon thy land, saith the Lord God.

9 I will also vex the hearts of many people, when I shall bring thy destruction among the nations, into the countries which thou hast not known.

10 Yea, I will make many people amazed at thee, and their kings shall be horribly afraid for thee, when I shall brandish my sword before them; and they shall tremble at *every* moment, every man for his own life, in the day of thy fall.

11 ¶For thus saith the Lord God; The sword of the king of Babylon shall come upon thee.

12 By the swords of the mighty will I cause thy multitude to fall, the terrible of the nations, all of them: and they shall spoil the pomp of Egypt, and all the multitude thereof shall be destroyed.

13 I will destroy also all the beasts thereof from beside the great waters; neither shall the foot of man trouble them any more, nor the hoofs of beasts trouble them.

14 Then will I make their waters deep, and cause their rivers to run like oil, saith the Lord God.

15 When I shall make the land of Egypt desolate, and the country shall be destitute of that whereof it was full, when I shall smite all them that dwell therein, then shall they know that I *am* the Lord.

16 This *is* the lamentation wherewith they shall lament her: the daughters of the nations shall lament her: they shall lament for her, *even* for Egypt, and for all her multitude, saith the Lord God.

17 ¶It came to pass also in the twelfth year, in the fifteenth *day* of the month, *that* the word of the Lord came unto me, saying,

18 Son of man, wail for the multitude of Egypt, and cast them down, *even* her, and the daughters of the famous nations, unto the nether parts of the earth, with them that go down into the pit.

19 Whom dost thou pass in beauty? go down, and be thou laid with the uncircumcised.

20 They shall fall in the midst of *them that are* slain by the sword: she is delivered to the sword: draw her and all her multitudes.

21 The strong among the mighty shall speak to him out of the midst of hell with them that help him: they are gone down, they lie uncircumcised, slain by the sword.

22 Asshur *is* there and all her com-

1594

pany: his graves are about him: all of them slain, fallen by the sword:

23 Whose graves are set in the sides of the pit, and her company is round about her grave: all of them slain, fallen by the sword, which caused terror in the land of the living.

24 There is Eʹlam and all her multitude round about her grave, all of them slain, fallen by the sword, which are gone down uncircumcised into the nether parts of the earth, which caused their terror in the land of the living; yet have they borne their shame with them that go down to the pit.

25 They have set her a bed in the midst of the slain with all her multitude: her graves are round about him: all of them uncircumcised, slain by the sword: though their terror was caused in the land of the living, yet have they borne their shame with them that go down to the pit: he is put in the midst of them that be slain.

26 There is Meʹshĕch, Tuʹbal, and all her multitude: her graves are round about him: all of them uncircumcised, slain by the sword, though they caused their terror in the land of the living.

27 And they shall not lie with the mighty that are fallen of the uncircumcised, which are gone down to hell with their weapons of war: and they have laid their swords under their heads, but their iniquities shall be upon their bones, though they were the terror of the mighty in the land of the living.

28 Yea, thou shalt be broken in the midst of the uncircumcised, and shalt lie with them that are slain with the sword.

29 There is Edom, her kings, and all her princes, which with their might are laid by them that were slain by the sword: they shall lie with the uncircumcised, and with them that go down to the pit.

30 There be the princes of the north, all of them, and all the Zi-doʹni-ans, which are gone down with the slain; with their terror they are ashamed of their might; and they lie uncircumcised with them that be slain by the sword, and bear their shame with them that go down to the pit.

31 Pharaoh shall see them, and shall be comforted over all his multitude, even Pharaoh and all his army slain by the sword, saith the Lord God.

32 For I have caused my terror in the land of the living: and he shall be laid in the midst of the uncircumcised with them that are slain with the sword, even Pharaoh and all his multitude, saith the Lord God.

CHAPTER 33

AGAIN the word of the Lord came unto me, saying,

2 Son of man, speak to the children of thy people, and say unto them, When I bring the sword upon a land, if the people of the land take a man of their coasts, and set him for their watchman:

3 If when he seeth the sword come upon the land, he blow the trumpet, and warn the people;

IV. PROPHECIES CONCERNING ISRAEL'S FUTURE RESTORATION. 33:1-39:29.

A. Ezekiel's Appointment as a Watchman. 33:1-33.

33:1-9. Ezekiel is reminded of his call to be a watchman. In verses 1-7 the prophet's ministry is likened unto that of a watchman, or sentry, observing the danger of a coming enemy and then warning his people. In like manner, he is a watchman to his people in spiritual matters. The enemy seeking to destroy the people is their sinful way of wickedness. To point out their sin and ask them to repent and turn to the Lord is Ezekiel's mission. If, as a prophet of God, he should fail to warn his people, he should be held accountable of spiritual manslaughter.

4 Then whosoever heareth the sound of the trumpet, and taketh not warning; if the sword come, and take him away, his blood shall be upon his own head.

5 He heard the sound of the trumpet, and took not warning; his blood shall be upon him. But he that taketh warning shall deliver his soul.

6 But if the watchman see the sword come, and blow not the trumpet, and the people be not warned: if the sword come, and take *any* person from among them, he is taken away in his iniquity; but his blood will I require at the watchman's hand.

7 So thou, O son of man, I have set thee a watchman unto the house of Israel; therefore thou shalt hear the word at my mouth, and warn them from me.

8 When I say unto the wicked, O wicked *man*, thou shalt surely die; if thou dost not speak to warn the wicked from his way, that wicked *man* shall die in his iniquity; but his blood will I require at thine hand.

9 Nevertheless, if thou warn the wicked of his way to turn from it: if he do not turn from his way, he shall die in his iniquity; but thou hast delivered thy soul.

10 Therefore O thou son of man, speak unto the house of Israel; Thus ye speak, saying, If our transgressions and our sins *be* upon us, and we pine away in them, how should we then live?

11 Say unto them, *As* I live, saith the Lord God, I have no pleasure in the death of the wicked: but that the wicked turn from his way and live: turn ye, turn ye from your evil ways; for why will ye die, O house of Israel?

12 Therefore, thou son of man, say unto the children of thy people, The righteousness of the righteous shall not deliver him in the day of his transgression: as for the wickedness of the wicked, he shall not fall thereby in the day that he turneth from his wickedness; neither shall the righteous be able to live for his *righteousness* in the day that he sinneth.

13 When I shall say to the righteous, *that* he shall surely live: if he trust to his own righteousness, and commit iniquity, all his righteousnesses shall not be remembered: but for his iniquity that he hath committed, he shall die for it.

14 Again, when I say unto the wicked, Thou shalt surely die: if he turn from his sin, and do that which is lawful and right;

15 *If* the wicked restore the pledge, give again that he had robbed, walk in the statutes of life, without committing iniquity; he shall surely live, he shall not die.

16 None of his sins that he hath committed shall be mentioned unto him: he hath done that which is lawful and right; he shall surely live.

17 ¶Yet the children of thy people say, The way of the Lord is not equal: but as for them, their way is not equal.

18 When the righteous turneth from his righteousness, and committeth iniquity, he shall even die thereby.

19 But if the wicked turn from his

10-20. As in chapter 18, the emphasis is upon life gained through turning to righteousness from wickedness. His primary reference is to life after this present life. Likewise, this righteousness refers to the outward fruit of righteousness that issues forth from a regenerate heart. It is true that God has promised that His people would be spared corporately from aggression if they walked in His ways. Then, when corporate judgment became necessary, He sent enemy nations to inflict the punishment. In this process, some righteous persons suffered temporal death, and some wicked persons did not suffer temporal death. Even in this calamity that came upon Jerusalem in 586 B.C. from the hand of Nebuchadnezzar, there were wicked people spared from temporal death. Of those left in the land, idolatry and wickedness continued as the rule of life (chs. 25-26).

Ezekiel's message is to the whole house of Israel, but its application was to be made on an individual basis. This is seen in verses 12-16. The **righteousness** of the one turning to wickedness very likely has reference to the superficial righteousness of an unregenerate person.

wickedness, and do that which is lawful and right, he shall live thereby.

20 Yet ye say, The way of the Lord is not equal. O ye house of Israel, I will judge you every one after his ways.

21 ¶And it came to pass in the twelfth year of our captivity, in the tenth month, in the fifth day of the month, that one that had escaped out of Jerusalem came unto me, saying, The city is smitten.

22 Now the hand of the Lord was upon me in the evening, afore he that was escaped came; and had opened my mouth, until he came to me in the morning; and my mouth was opened, and I was no more dumb.

23 Then the word of the Lord came unto me, saying,

24 Son of man, they that inhabit those wastes of the land of Israel speak, saying, Abraham was one, and he inherited the land: but we are many; the land is given us for inheritance.

25 Wherefore say unto them, Thus saith the Lord God; Ye eat with the blood, and lift up your eyes toward your idols, and shed blood: and shall ye possess the land?

26 Ye stand upon your sword, ye work abomination, and ye defile every one his neighbour's wife: and shall ye possess the land?

27 Say thou thus unto them, Thus saith the Lord God; As I live, surely they that are in the wastes shall fall by the sword, and him that is in the open field will I give to the beasts to be devoured, and they that be in the forts and in the caves shall die of the pestilence.

28 For I will lay the land most desolate, and the pomp of her strength shall cease: and the mountains of Israel shall be desolate, that none shall pass through.

29 Then shall they know that I am the Lord, when I have laid the land most desolate because of all their abominations which they have committed.

30 ¶Also, thou son of man, the children of thy people still are talking against thee by the walls and in the doors of the houses, and speak one to another, every one to his brother, saying, Come, I pray you, and hear what is the word that cometh forth from the Lord.

31 And they come unto thee as the people cometh, and they sit before thee as my people, and they hear thy words, but they will not do them: for with their mouth they shew much love, but their heart goeth after their covetousness.

32 And, lo, thou art unto them as a very lovely song of one that hath a pleasant voice, and can play well on an instrument: for they hear thy words, but they do them not.

33 And when this cometh to pass, (lo, it will come,) then shall they know that a prophet hath been among them.

CHAPTER 34

AND the word of the Lord came unto me, saying,

2 Son of man, prophesy against the

21-22. In 3:26-27 we read of Ezekiel being dumb, except on such occasions when the Lord had a message to be delivered to Israel. This was done both as a sign and to protect the prophet from giving a compromised, or even a false, message. Now that Jerusalem was completely subdued in accordance with the prophet's many previous warnings, his speech was restored to him (24:27).

23-29. Abraham and his seed had been promised the land (Gen 13:14-16). But chastisement, taking them temporarily out of the land, was also promised (Deut 28:63-68). The few whom Nebuchadnezzar left in the land somehow felt safe and secure just because they had been left in the land. Ezekiel warns them of continued chastisement, and even destruction, in the land itself.

30-33. Now that everything the prophet had said concerning Jerusalem's destruction had taken place, the exiles were more prone to listen. They talked about him secretly (**by the walls**) and openly (**in the doors**). They even came to **hear** what the Lord would have to say at this present time; but it seemed to be more out of curiosity, than of a sincere desire to heed God's will.

B. Israel's Shepherds. 34:1-31.

34:1-10. The shepherds of Israel were her leaders, namely, the prophets, priests, and kings. Among all three there were those not true to their calling. Among the false prophets, such men as Hananiah who prophesied deliverance from Babylon (Jer 28:1-4), among the priests, such as the sons of Eli (I Sam 2:12-17), and among the kings, such as Rehoboam who over-taxed the people (II Chr 10:12-14). They did not minister to the sheep (Israel), who are described as sick, diseased, broken, scattered. The sheep wandering through the mountains and upon every high hill may have reference to the idol worship at these places led by their false shepherds. Because of this idola-try, Israel was scattered among the nations.

11-16. Beginning with verse 11, the rest of the chapter is eschatological. The Lord Himself will regather Israel from all the nations among which they are scattered. They will be brought to the land that the Lord promised to Abraham. Terms such as good pasture and cause to lie down indicate the abundant blessings in the land. The terms of verse 16 indicate a spiritual ministry.

17-24. After the regathering of Israel from among the na-

shepherds of Israel, prophesy, and say unto them, Thus saith the Lord God unto the shepherds; Woe be to the shepherds of Israel that do feed themselves! should not the shepherds feed the flocks?

3 Ye eat the fat, and ye clothe you with the wool, ye kill them that are fed: but ye feed not the flock.

4 The diseased have ye not strengthened, neither have ye healed that which was sick, neither have ye bound up that which was broken, neither have ye brought again that which was driven away, neither have ye sought that which was lost; but with force and with cruelty have ye ruled them.

5 And they were scattered, because there is no shepherd: and they became meat to all the beasts of the field, when they were scattered.

6 My sheep wandered through all the mountains, and upon every high hill: yea, my flock was scattered upon all the face of the earth, and none did search or seek after them.

7 ¶ Therefore, ye shepherds, hear the word of the Lord;

8 As I live, saith the Lord God, surely because my flock became a prey, and my flock became meat to every beast of the field, because there was no shepherd, neither did my shepherds search for my flock, but the shepherds fed themselves, and fed not my flock;

9 Therefore, O ye shepherds, hear the word of the Lord;

10 Thus saith the Lord God; Behold, I am against the shepherds; and I will require my flock at their hand, and cause them to cease from feeding the flock; neither shall the shepherds feed themselves any more; for I will deliver my flock from their mouth, that they may not be meat for them.

11 ¶ For thus saith the Lord God; Behold, I, even I, will both search my sheep, and seek them out.

12 As a shepherd seeketh out his flock in the day that he is among his sheep that are scattered; so will I seek out my sheep, and will deliver them out of all places where they have been scattered in the cloudy and dark day.

13 And I will bring them out from the people, and gather them from the countries, and will bring them to their own land, and feed them upon the mountains of Israel by the rivers, and in all the inhabited places of the country.

14 I will feed them in a good pasture, and upon the high mountains of Israel shall their fold be: there shall they lie in a good fold, and in a fat pasture shall they feed upon the mountains of Israel.

15 I will feed my flock, and I will cause them to lie down, saith the Lord God.

16 I will seek that which was lost, and bring again that which was driven away, and will bind up that which was broken, and will strengthen that which was sick: but I will destroy the fat and the strong; I will feed them with judgment.

17 And as for you, O my flock, thus

saith the Lord God; Behold, I judge between cattle and cattle, between the rams and the he-goats.

18 *Seemeth it* a small thing unto you to have eaten up the good pasture, but ye must tread down with your feet the residue of your pastures? and to have drunk of the deep waters, but ye must foul the residue with your feet?

19 And *as for* my flock, they eat that which ye have trodden with your feet; and they drink that which ye have fouled with your feet.

20 ¶ Therefore thus saith the Lord God unto them; Behold, I, even I, will judge between the fat cattle and between the lean cattle.

21 Because ye have thrust with side and with shoulder, and pushed all the diseased with your horns, till ye have scattered them abroad;

22 Therefore will I save my flock, and they shall no more be a prey; and I will judge between cattle and cattle.

23 And I will set up one shepherd over them, and he shall feed them, *even* my servant David; he shall feed them, and he shall be their shepherd.

24 And I the Lord will be their God, and my servant David a prince among them: I the Lord have spoken *it.*

25 And I will make with them a covenant of peace, and will cause the evil beasts to cease out of the land: and they shall dwell safely in the wilderness, and sleep in the woods.

26 And I will make them and the places round about my hill a blessing; and I will cause the shower to come down in his season; there shall be showers of blessing.

27 And the tree of the field shall yield her fruit, and the earth shall yield her increase, and they shall be safe in their land, and shall know that I *am* the Lord, when I have broken the bands of their yoke, and delivered them out of the hand of those that served themselves of them.

28 And they shall no more be a prey to the heathen, neither shall the beast of the land devour them: but they shall dwell safely, and none shall make *them* afraid.

29 And I will raise up for them a plant of renown, and they shall be no more consumed with hunger in the land, neither bear the shame of the heathen any more.

30 Thus shall they know that I the Lord their God *am* with them, and *that* they, *even* the house of Israel, *are* my people, saith the Lord God.

31 And ye my flock, the flock of my pasture, *are* men, *and* I *am* your God, saith the Lord God.

CHAPTER 35

MOREOVER the word of the Lord came unto me, saying,

2 Son of man, set thy face against mount Sē'ir, and prophesy against it,

3 And say unto it, Thus saith the Lord God; Behold, O mount Sē'ir, I *am* against thee, and I will stretch out mine hand against thee, and I will make thee most desolate.

4 I will lay thy cities waste, and thou

tions, a judgment of separation will take place between the sheep. In 20:38 we saw that the rebels will be cast out and not gain entrance into the land. From the context of this chapter in verse 3, the **fat** and the **strong** have reference to the false shepherds made rich at the expense of the sheep. Some expositors feel that **David** has reference to King David being resurrected. Though Old Testament saints will be resurrected to participate in the kingdom blessings, the term **my servant David** in this context is none other than the greater Son of David, the Lord Jesus Christ (Jer 23:5–6).

25.31. The blessings promised to Israel upon her return to the land are comprehensive. They will have physical security (vs. 25), blessings of weather (vs. 26), blessings of abundant fruitage (vs. 27), blessings of political peace (vss. 28–29), and spiritual blessings of a living relationship to the **Lord God** (vss. 30–31).

C. The Rebirth of the Nation. 35:1–36:38.

35:1–9. Seir means the rough or rugged place. It was the rugged and mountainous area south of the Dead Sea inhabited by Edom, the descendants of Esau. The enmity between Esau and Jacob began with the selling of his birthright for a mess of pottage. However, he had been a rebel at heart before the incident. Edom's hatred against Israel continued until Jerusalem's destruction, as indicated by **time of their calamity.** From the statement here, verse 5, and Obadiah verses 11–14, we

shalt be desolate, and thou shalt know that I *am* the LORD.

5 Because thou hast had a perpetual hatred, and hast shed *the blood of the children* of Israel by the force of the sword in the time of their calamity, in the time *that their iniquity had* an end:

6 Therefore, *as* I live, saith the Lord GOD, I will prepare thee unto blood, and blood shall pursue thee: sith thou hast not hated blood, even blood shall pursue thee.

7 Thus will I make mount Se'ir most desolate, and cut off from it him that passeth out and him that returneth.

8 And I will fill his mountains with his slain *men*: in thy hills, and in thy valleys, and in all thy rivers, shall they fall that are slain with the sword.

9 I will make thee perpetual desolations, and thy cities shall not return: and ye shall know that I *am* the LORD.

10 Because thou hast said, These two nations and these two countries shall be mine, and we will possess it; whereas the LORD was there:

11 Therefore, *as* I live, saith the Lord GOD, I will even do according to thine anger, and according to thine envy which thou hast used out of thy hatred against them; and I will make myself known among them, when I have judged thee.

12 And thou shalt know that I *am* the LORD, *and that* I have heard all thy blasphemies which thou hast spoken against the mountains of Israel, saying, They are laid desolate, they are given us to consume.

13 Thus with your mouth ye have boasted against me, and have multiplied your words against me: I have heard *them*.

14 Thus saith the Lord GOD; When the whole earth rejoiceth, I will make thee desolate.

15 As thou didst rejoice at the inheritance of the house of Israel, because it was desolate, so will I do unto thee: thou shalt be desolate, O mount Se'ir, and all I-dū-mē'a, *even* all of it: and they shall know that I *am* the LORD.

CHAPTER 36

ALSO, thou son of man, prophesy unto the mountains of Israel, and say, Ye mountains of Israel, hear the word of the LORD:

2 Thus saith the Lord GOD: Because the enemy hath said against you, Aha, even the ancient high places are ours in possession:

3 Therefore prophesy and say, Thus saith the Lord GOD; Because they have made *you* desolate, and swallowed you up on every side, that ye might be a possession unto the residue of the heathen, and ye are taken up in the lips of talkers, and *are* an infamy of the people:

4 Therefore, ye mountains of Israel, hear the word of the Lord GOD; thus saith the Lord GOD to the mountains, and to the hills, to the rivers, and to the valleys, to the desolate wastes, and to the cities that are forsaken, which be-

---

see that Edom gloated over the destruction and even assisted in cutting off survivors coming from Jerusalem. In judgment Edom shall experience **perpetual desolations.** Her main city of Petra is in ruins that are, even to this day, a tourist attraction.

10-15. When Edom had thoughts of taking the land of the two countries (Judah and Israel) after their fall, he was thereby actually challenging the Lord since He had given it to Israel. Israel has been taken out of the land in chastisement, but it still belongs to her. Israel is back in part of the land today, and in the Millennial Kingdom it will be in full possession. It appears that even in the future day of Israel's restoration, **When the whole earth rejoiceth,** Edom will continue to be a **desolate** place. Perhaps this will serve as a testimony in the future, as well as now, that he who curses Israel will be cursed of the Lord.

36:1-15. Among the nations of the world, Israel is the key nation in God's plan of the ages; for she alone was chosen to be the means of bringing God's blessings to the world. These blessings are stated in summary form in the covenant God made to Abraham (Gen 12:1-3). But when Israel apostasized, the erring nation needed to be chastised. It is at this point in Israel's history that this chapter commences and gives an outline of God's dealing with her in His plan through the future Millennial Kingdom, or age.

The mountains of Israel has reference to the whole land of Israel. Because of her wickedness, as dealt with repeatedly in earlier chapters, the land was justly made desolate by the hand of the Lord using the kings of Assyria and Babylon as the instruments. The **residue of the heathen,** the nations around her not yet brought into judgment, then occupied her. But when these nations, and particularly **Idumea** (Edom), gloated over Israel's calamity and took the land for themselves, God in jealousy speaks against them. Edom, as we saw in chapter 35

1600

came a prey and derision to the residue of the heathen that are round about:

5 Therefore thus saith the Lord GOD; Surely in the fire of my jealousy have I spoken against the residue of the heathen, and against all I-dū-mĕ'a, which have appointed my land into their possession with the joy of all *their* heart, with the despiteful minds, to cast it out for a prey.

6 Prophesy therefore concerning the land of Israel, and say unto the mountains, and to the hills, to the rivers, and to the valleys, Thus saith the Lord GOD; Behold, I have spoken in my jealousy and in my fury, because ye have borne the shame of the heathen:

7 Therefore thus saith the Lord GOD; I have lifted up mine hand, Surely the heathen that are about you, they shall bear their shame.

8 ¶But ye, O mountains of Israel, ye shall shoot forth your branches, and yield your fruit to my people of Israel; for they are at hand to come.

9 For, behold, I am for you, and I will turn unto you, and ye shall be tilled and sown:

10 And I will multiply men upon you, all the house of Israel, even all of it: and the cities shall be inhabited, and the wastes shall be builded:

11 And I will multiply upon you man and beast; and they shall increase and bring fruit: and I will settle you after your old estates, and will do better *unto you* than at your beginnings: and ye shall know that I *am* the LORD.

12 Yea, I will cause men to walk upon you, *even* my people Israel; and they shall possess thee, and thou shalt be their inheritance, and thou shalt no more henceforth bereave them *of men.*

13 Thus saith the Lord GOD; Because they say unto you, Thou *land* devourest up men, and hast bereaved thy nations;

14 Therefore thou shalt devour men no more, neither bereave thy nations any more, saith the Lord GOD.

15 Neither will I cause *men* to hear in thee the shame of the heathen any more, neither shalt thou bear the reproach of the people any more, neither shalt thou cause thy nations to fall any more, saith the Lord GOD.

16 ¶Moreover the word of the LORD came unto me, saying,

17 Son of man, when the house of Israel dwelt in their own land, they defiled it by their own way and by their doings: their way was before me as the uncleanness of a removed woman.

18 Wherefore I poured my fury upon them for the blood that they had shed upon the land, and for their idols *where- with* they had polluted it:

19 And I scattered them among the heathen, and they were dispersed through the countries: according to their way and according to their doings I judged them.

20 And when they entered unto the heathen, whither they went, they pro- faned my holy name, when they said to them, These *are* the people of the LORD, and are gone forth out of his land.

21 ¶But I had pity for mine holy name, which the house of Israel had

16-21. The Lord is concerned about the integrity of His name. When Israel **profaned** His name by her wickedness, leading to her captivity, the heathen questioned whether God could actually care for and bless the nation He had chosen to be peculiarly His.

and Obadiah, met the judgment never to exist as a nation. In contrast, Israel, though out of the land for a time for the purpose of chastening, will be regathered from among the nations. Her land will then become fruitful and her population increase. Her land **devourest** her people no longer, and she will be a nation respected rather than insulted.

22-32. As a vindication of His name, not Israel's, the Lord will regather them by His mighty power from among the nations. Those that will receive Him in true repentance will be given a **new heart** (20:33-44); but the rebels will be purged out, and only the saved will enter the land. These people will be saved and indwelt by the ministry of the **spirit**. They will be given the capacity to walk in his **statutes** and **judgments**. **Famine**, which so often plagued them in the past as an instrument of chastisement, will now be no more due to fruitfulness of the land.

33-36. In contrast to the desolation that characterized so much of her past history, her future in the Kingdom will have the beauty and splendor compared to the **garden of Eden.** What a testimony this will be to the nations of God's grace and power shown to Israel!

37-38. The **flock of Jerusalem** has reference to the sacrificial animals used. These numbered into the millions over the years. Israel's flocks of fathers, mothers, and children will become numerous.

profaned among the heathen, whither they went.

22 Therefore say unto the house of Israel, Thus saith the Lord God; I do not *this* for your sakes, O house of Israel, but for mine holy name's sake, which ye have profaned among the heathen, whither ye went.

23 And I will sanctify my great name, which was profaned among the heathen, which ye have profaned in the midst of them; and the heathen shall know that I *am* the Lord, saith the Lord God, when I shall be sanctified in you before their eyes.

24 For I will take you from among the heathen, and gather you out of all countries, and will bring you into your own land.

25 Then will I sprinkle clean water upon you, and ye shall be clean: from all your filthiness, and from all your idols, will I cleanse you.

26 A new heart also will I give you, and a new spirit will I put within you: and I will take away the stony heart out of your flesh, and I will give you an heart of flesh.

27 And I will put my spirit within you, and cause you to walk in my statutes, and ye shall keep my judgments, and do *them*.

28 And ye shall dwell in the land that I gave to your fathers; and ye shall be my people, and I will be your God.

29 I will also save you from all your uncleannesses: and I will call for the corn, and will increase it, and lay no famine upon you.

30 And I will multiply the fruit of the tree, and the increase of the field, that ye shall receive no more reproach of famine among the heathen.

31 Then shall ye remember your own evil ways, and your doings that *were* not good, and shall lothe yourselves in your own sight for your iniquities and for your abominations.

32 Not for your sakes do I *this*, saith the Lord God, be it known unto you: be ashamed and confounded for your own ways, O house of Israel.

33 Thus saith the Lord God; In the day that I shall have cleansed you from all your iniquities I will also cause *you* to dwell in the cities, and the wastes shall be builded.

34 And the desolate land shall be tilled, whereas it lay desolate in the sight of all that passed by.

35 And they shall say, This land that was desolate is become like the garden of Eden; and the waste and desolate and ruined cities *are become* fenced, *and* are inhabited.

36 Then the heathen that are left round about you shall know that I the Lord build the ruined *places, and* plant that that was desolate: I the Lord have spoken *it*, and I will do *it*.

37 Thus saith the Lord God; I will yet *for* this be enquired of by the house of Israel, to do *it* for them; I will increase them with men like a flock.

38 As the holy flock, as the flock of Jerusalem in her solemn feasts; so shall the waste cities be filled with flocks of

men: and they shall know that I am the LORD.

CHAPTER 37

THE hand of the LORD was upon me, and carried me out in the spirit of the LORD, and set me down in the midst of the valley which was full of bones,

2 And caused me to pass by them round about: and, behold, there were very many in the open valley; and, lo, they were very dry.

3 And he said unto me, Son of man, can these bones live? And I answered, O Lord GOD, thou knowest.

4 Again he said unto me, Prophesy upon these bones, and say unto them, O ye dry bones, hear the word of the LORD.

5 Thus saith the Lord GOD unto these bones; Behold, I will cause breath to enter into you, and ye shall live:

6 And I will lay sinews upon you, and will bring up flesh upon you, and cover you with skin, and put breath in you, and ye shall live; and ye shall know that I am the LORD.

7 So I prophesied as I was commanded: and as I prophesied, there was a noise, and behold a shaking, and the bones came together, bone to his bone.

8 And when I beheld, lo, the sinews and the flesh came up upon them, and the skin covered them above: but there was no breath in them.

9 Then said he unto me, Prophesy unto the wind, prophesy, son of man, and say to the wind, Thus saith the Lord GOD; Come from the four winds, O breath, and breathe upon these slain, that they may live.

10 So I prophesied as he commanded me, and the breath came into them, and they lived, and stood up upon their feet, an exceeding great army.

11 Then he said unto me, Son of man, these bones are the whole house of Israel: behold, they say, Our bones are dried, and our hope is lost: we are cut off for our parts.

12 Therefore prophesy and say unto them, Thus saith the Lord GOD; Behold, O my people, I will open your graves, and cause you to come up out of your graves, and bring you into the land of Israel.

13 And ye shall know that I am the LORD, when I have opened your graves, O my people, and brought you up out of your graves,

14 And shall put my spirit in you, and ye shall live, and I shall place you in your own land: then shall ye know that I the LORD have spoken it, and performed it, saith the LORD.

15 ¶ The word of the LORD came again unto me, saying,

16 Moreover, thou son of man, take thee one stick, and write upon it, For Judah, and for the children of Israel his companions: then take another stick, and write upon it, For Joseph, the stick of E'phra-im, and for all the house of Israel his companions:

17 And join them one to another into

D. The Resuscitation of the Nation. 37:1-14.

37:1-10. When the exiles heard of Jerusalem's fall, they were deeply distressed and had nearly given up hope for future blessings as a nation. This prophecy of the dry bones being revived was the message of hope and encouragement they needed.

That this chapter deals with resurrection is without question. Some think the primary emphasis is upon a physical resurrection of individuals, while others see a resurrection of national life following the Babylonian captivity. It appears to us that the emphasis here is upon a resurrection of national life, especially as inaugurated by the Lord Himself at His Second Coming.

The **dry bones** that come to life are figurative of the national resurrection of Israel. That this cannot refer to the physical resurrection of individuals in this context is evident by several things. These bones are all seen in one valley in Chaldea, not buried or scattered; and the remains of Israel's people were not so disposed. Furthermore, these bones are revived in stages: first bone to bone, then sinews, then flesh, then skin, and finally breath. The physical resurrection, in contrast, is instantaneous (I Cor 15).

11-14. When they heard of Jerusalem's fall to Nebuchadnezzar, the exiles responded despondently by saying **our hope is lost.** But Ezekiel gives encouragement by saying there is a time of future national life. They will rise from the **graves** and be brought into the land. The graves could here have a double meaning. First, the graves could mean the nations in which they are dispersed, from which they will be regathered as living Israelites at the Lord's return. But, secondly, it very likely refers also to actual physical resurrection. By their resurrection as individuals, they will be raised to participate in the glorious reign of Christ (Dan 12:1-2). At their return to the land, national repentance and regeneration will take place. One should note that it is still an individual matter since there will be rebels purged out who will not enter the land (20:34-38; Zech 12:10-13:1). The work of regeneration is seen to be through the agency of the **spirit.**

E. The Reuniting of the Nation. 37:15-28.

15:23. At the time of Israel's future restoration, there will be one commonwealth, not two divided kingdoms. By the time of the captivities the tribal distinctives were breaking down. Some individuals were not living in their original geographic boundaries. Thus, we read of **Judah** and **Israel his companions. Joseph** has reference to the northern kingdom. Because of their numerical greatness, the descendants of Joseph's two sons, Ephraim and Manasseh, were each allotted land as a tribe. In verses 22-23 we see a national unity of all the tribes together,

one stick; and they shall become one in thine hand.

18 And when the children of thy people shall speak unto thee, saying, Wilt thou not shew us what thou *meanest* by these?

19 Say unto them, Thus saith the Lord God; Behold, I will take the stick of Joseph, which *is* in the hand of E-phra-im, and the tribes of Israel his fellows, and will put them with him, *even* with the stick of Jū́dah, and make them one stick, and they shall be one in mine hand.

20 ¶ And the sticks whereon thou writest shall be in thine hand before their eyes.

21 ¶ And say unto them, Thus saith the Lord God; Behold, I will take the children of Israel from among the heathen, whither they be gone, and will gather them on every side, and will bring them into their own land:

22 And I will make them one nation in the land upon the mountains of Israel; and one king shall be king to them all: and they shall be no more two nations, neither shall they be divided into two kingdoms any more at all:

23 Neither shall they defile themselves any more with their idols, nor with their detestable things, nor with any of their transgressions: but I will save them out of all their dwelling-places, wherein they have sinned, and will cleanse them: so shall they be my people, and I will be their God.

24 And David my servant *shall be* king over them: and they all shall have one shepherd: they shall also walk in my judgments, and observe my statutes, and do them.

25 And they shall dwell in the land that I have given unto Jacob my servant, wherein your fathers have dwelt; and they shall dwell therein, *even* they, and their children, and their children's children for ever: and my servant Da-vid *shall be* their prince for ever.

26 Moreover I will make a covenant of peace with them; it shall be an everlasting covenant with them: and I will place them, and multiply them, and will set my sanctuary in the midst of them for evermore.

27 My tabernacle also shall be with them: yea, I will be their God, and they shall be my people.

28 And the heathen shall know that I the Lord do sanctify Israel, when my sanctuary shall be in the midst of them for evermore.

18 And when the children of thy people shall speak unto thee, saying, Wilt thou not shew us what thou *meanest* by these?—being ruled by one king and being in spiritual unity by virtue of their regeneration.

24-28. David my servant must mean the greater Son of David coming out of the loins of King David (II Sam 7:12-13). The many references dealing with the future reign speak of one king, not of a king and a vice-regent. The nature of this king and his kingdom is that it will be in the land, verse 25; it will be for **ever**, verse 25; it will be peaceful, verse 26; there will be a sanctuary or temple, verse 26; and God's presence will be with them, verse 26.

F. The Victory of the Nation over Gog and Magog. 38:1-39:29.

In the last days of Israel during the Tribulation leading up to her glory under the reign of Christ, she will yet experience the darkest days of her chastisement. Following are a series of chronological events of an eschatological nature in which Israel's dispersion among the nations, her regathering out of the nations, her role in relation to the Beast, the kings of the north, the south, and east, and the blessings of her spiritual regeneration at the inauguration of the Messianic Kingdom may be seen in their proper perspective: (1) She will be scattered among the nations without a home of her own; (2) by a mandate of the United Nations in 1948, Israel was given a home in the land west of the

1604

CHAPTER 38

AND the word of the Lord came unto me, saying,

2 Son of man, set thy face against Gog, the land of Mā′gŏg, the chief prince of Mē′shĕch and Tū′bal, and prophesy against him,

3 And say, Thus saith the Lord God; Behold, I am against thee, O Gog, the chief prince of Mē′shĕch and Tū′bal:

4 And I will turn thee back, and put hooks into thy jaws, and I will bring thee forth, and all thine army, horses and horsemen, all of them clothed with all sorts of armour, even a great company with bucklers and shields, all of them handling swords:

5 Persia, Ē-thī-ō′pĭ-a, and Libya with them; all of them with shield and helmet:

6 Gō′mer, and all his bands; the house of Tō-gär′mah of the north quarters, and all his bands: and many people with thee.

7 Be thou prepared, and prepare for thyself, thou, and all thy company that are assembled unto thee, and be thou a guard unto them.

8 After many days thou shalt be visited: in the latter years thou shalt come into the land that is brought back from the sword, and is gathered out of many people, against the mountains of Israel, which have been always waste: but it is brought forth out of the nations, and they shall dwell safely all of them.

9 Thou shalt ascend and come like a storm, thou shalt be like a cloud to cover the land, thou, and all thy bands, and many people with thee.

10 Thus saith the Lord God; It shall also come to pass, that at the same time

---

Jordan; (3) many, but not all, Jews have returned to the land while still in unbelief; (4) after the rapture of the Church, the prince (man of sin) will make a covenant with Israel for seven years to give them security (Dan 9:27; II Thess 2:3); (5) the prince will break his covenant after three and one-half years according to Daniel 9:26; (6) Israel will lose her religious liberties (Mt 24:15-16; Rev 13:1-8); (7) the false prince will impose himself as deity upon the world, including Israel (II Thess 2:4; Rev 12:13-14); (8) the false prince (the Beast) will then assume worldwide leadership through a series of political and armed conflicts (Dan 11:36-45; Rev 13:7); (9) the Beast will be opposed by a series of movements against him by the kings of the north, the south, and the east (Dan 11:40, 44); (10) a coalition of the Beast and the kings of the earth will make war against the Lord upon His return from heaven (Rev 19:19); (11) the Lord will overcome them by the sword of His mouth (Rev 19:15-21); (12) the Beast and the False Prophet are cast into the lake of fire; (13) there will be a judgment of the nations (Mt 25:31-46); (14) a regathering and consequent judgment of living Israel will take place (20:33-44; Mt 24:27-31); (15) then there will be the experience of repentance and regeneration on the part of Israel (Zech 12:10; 13:1); and (16) then the inauguration of the Messianic Kingdom will take place (Dan 2:44; Mt 25:34; Rev 20:4).

The events of Gog and his allies coming upon the mountains of Israel occur during the first half of the Tribulation while Israel is in apparent peace and safety. Nowhere do we read that the Beast entered into armed conflict with the king of the north. This did not develop because the Lord utterly annihilated him and his allies by the forces of earthquakes, storms, floods, pestilence, and confusion.

38:1-9. According to numerous scholars, the nations and peoples banded together under the leadership of **Gog** are: Rosh, being the Russian nation; Meshech, being Moscow; Tubal being Tobolsk; Persia, being today's Iran; Ethiopia or Cush, being an Arabic nation contiguous to the northern powers; Libya or Put being not the North African nation, but also an Arabic nation contiguous to the northern powers; Gomer, being modern-day Germany; and Togarmah, being what is named in modern times as Turkey or Armenia.

But it should be noted that there are several strong arguments in opposition to the above assertions. **Meshech** is to be identified with Mushke, which is located in northwest Asia Minor, not modern-day Russia's Moscow. Also, there is no linguistic affinity between the terms. The etymologies of the words are different. It should be noted that many successive Assyrian kings fought against Mushke, too. Tubal is geographically located in Asia Minor also, not in Russia. The King James version has the **chief prince of Meshech and Tubal** whereas some translators render it as "the prince of Rosh, Meshech, and Tubal." Against the latter translation, it should be noted that Meshech and Tubal are coupled together, in secular as well as biblical writings (27:13; 32:26; Gen 10:2). Thus, the popular interpretations seem to run counter to the contextual, geographical, historical, and linguistical data.

The phrases **After many days** and **in the latter years** very clearly project the events to the distant future of Israel's last days before the Second Coming.

10-13. What could possibly justify such an all-out military effort by the great northern confederacy that is described here?

shall things come into thy mind, and thou shalt think an evil thought:

11 And thou shalt say, I will go up to the land of unwalled villages; I will go to them that are at rest that dwell safely, all of them dwelling without walls, and having neither bars nor gates,

12 To take a spoil, and to take a prey; to turn thine hand upon the desolate places *that are now* inhabited, and upon the people *that are* gathered out of the nations, which have gotten cattle and goods, that dwell in the midst of the land.

13 She'ba, and De'dan, and the merchants of Tär'shïsh, with all the young lions thereof, shall say unto thee, Art thou come to take a spoil? hast thou gathered thy company to take a prey? to carry away silver and gold, to take away cattle and goods, to take a great spoil?

14 ¶Therefore, son of man, prophesy and say unto Gog, Thus saith the Lord GOD; In that day when my people of Israel dwelleth safely, shalt thou not know *it?*

15 And thou shalt come from thy place out of the north parts, thou, and many people with thee, all of them riding upon horses, a great company, and a mighty army:

16 And thou shalt come up against my people of Israel, as a cloud to cover the land; it shall be in the latter days, and I will bring thee against my land, that the heathen may know me, when I shall be sanctified in thee, O Gog, before thine eyes.

17 Thus saith the Lord GOD; *Art* thou he of whom I have spoken in old time by my servants the prophets of Israel, which prophesied in those days *many* years that I would bring thee against them?

18 And it shall come to pass at the same time when Gog shall come against the land of Israel, saith the Lord GOD, *that* my fury shall come up in my face.

19 For in my jealousy *and* in the fire of my wrath have I spoken, Surely in that day there shall be a great shaking in the land of Israel;

20 So that the fishes of the sea, and the fowls of the heaven, and the beasts of the field, and all creeping things that creep upon the earth, and all the men that are upon the face of the earth, shall shake at my presence, and the mountains shall be thrown down, and the steep places shall fall, and every wall shall fall to the ground.

21 And I will call for a sword against him throughout all my mountains, saith the Lord GOD: every man's sword shall be against his brother.

22 And I will plead against him with pestilence and with blood; and I will rain upon him, and upon his bands, and upon the many people that *are* with him, an overflowing rain, and great hailstones, fire, and brimstone.

23 Thus will I magnify myself, and sanctify myself; and I will be known in the eyes of many nations, and they shall know that I *am* the LORD.

The text says **To take a spoil.** The development of Israel since 1948 has been phenomenal. It is also a known fact that the mineral wealth in the Dead Sea is of almost incalculable value! Much of it is used for production of fertilizer. These chemicals, together with modern technology in farming by irrigation and increasing amounts of natural rainfall, could make it to be the breadbasket for a large part of the world. Israel also stands at the crossroads of world commerce. Whoever controls Israel could control much more.

14-16. The nations of the northern confederacy are communistic, or rapidly moving in that direction. As such, they are anti-God, being atheistic and materialistic. The Communist bloc of nations today represent the greatest military power in the world. It appears that the Lord will lead them to put all their military might together that by their destruction He might prove that He is God in the eyes of the world.

17-23. The greatest military power in the world will not be able to stand when God lets loose His fury by causing mountains, valleys, and buildings to be leveled. Added to this will be inundating floods, fire and brimstone through volcanic eruptions, and even confusion in the troops taking each other's lives, perhaps as an escape from the holocaust of the elements. Thus, God will be magnified, because it will be recognized that the Lord has done this.

CHAPTER 39

THEREFORE, thou son of man, prophesy against Gog, and say, Thus saith the Lord GOD; Behold, I am against thee, O Gog, the chief prince of Mē'shĕch and Tū'bal:

2 And I will turn thee back, and leave but the sixth part of thee, and will cause thee to come up from the north parts, and will bring thee upon the mountains of Israel:

3 And I will smite thy bow out of thy left hand, and will cause thine arrows to fall out of thy right hand.

4 Thou shalt fall upon the mountains of Israel, thou, and all thy bands, and the people that *is* with thee: I will give thee unto the ravenous birds of every sort, and *to* the beasts of the field to be devoured.

5 Thou shalt fall upon the open field: for I have spoken *it*, saith the Lord GOD.

6 And I will send a fire on Mā'gŏg, and among them that dwell carelessly in the isles: and they shall know that I *am* the LORD.

7 So will I make my holy name known in the midst of my people Israel; and I will not *let them* pollute my holy name any more: and the heathen shall know that I *am* the LORD, the Holy One in Israel.

8 ¶ Behold, it is come, and it is done, saith the Lord GOD; this *is* the day whereof I have spoken.

9 And they that dwell in the cities of Israel shall go forth, and shall set on fire and burn the weapons, both the shields and the bucklers, the bows and the arrows, and the handstaves, and the spears, and they shall burn them with fire seven years:

10 So that they shall take no wood out of the field, neither cut down *any* out of the forests; for they shall burn the weapons with fire: and they shall spoil those that spoiled them, and rob those that robbed them, saith the Lord GOD.

11 ¶ And it shall come to pass in that day, *that* I will give unto Gog a place there of graves in Israel, the valley of the passengers on the east of the sea: and it shall stop the *noses* of the passengers: and there shall they bury Gog and all his multitude: and they shall call *it* The valley of Hā'mon-gŏg.

12 And seven months shall the house of Israel be burying of them, that they may cleanse the land.

13 Yea, all the people of the land shall bury *them*; and it shall be to them a renown the day that I shall be glorified, saith the Lord GOD.

14 And they shall sever out men of continual employment, passing through the land to bury with the passengers those that remain upon the face of the earth, to cleanse it: after the end of seven months shall they search.

15 And the passengers *that* pass through the land, when any seeth a man's bone, then shall he set up a sign by it, till the buriers have buried it in the valley of Hā'mon-gŏg.

16 And also the name of the city *shall be* Ha-mō'nah. Thus shall they cleanse the land.

39:1-8. The decimation of the great army will be almost total. The AV states that but one-sixth will survive. However, scholars are not agreed on the meaning of the original construction. The bows and arrows may, without difficulty, be viewed as figurative of weapons of warfare of whatever kind they may be. Even the land of Magog, where many of the troops come from, will experience the wrath of fire from the Lord upon them.

9.10. The Lord turned the tables on the invaders. Instead of being the spoilers of Israel, they are now being despoiled of such wealth and equipment as can be of use to Israel.

11-20. To clean up a carnage of this magnitude, supernatural aid is required. Many, of course, will have had their permanent burial through the leveling of mountains and valleys. The ravenous beasts and birds of prey will clean off the flesh. While Israel is burying the skeletons and bones, seven months will transpire. All the people of the land will be involved in the clean-up. It has been estimated that if an individual buried two bodies a day the total may have been in the millions.

This gruesome task would appear to have a very sobering influence spiritually. No doubt it will prove to be one of the means of leading Israel, as well as the Gentiles, to repentance and faith in the Lord.

17 ¶And, thou son of man, thus saith the Lord God, Speak unto every feathered fowl, and to every beast of the field, Assemble yourselves, and come; gather yourselves on every side to my sacrifice that I do sacrifice for you, *even* a great sacrifice upon the mountains of Israel, that ye may eat flesh, and drink blood.

18 Ye shall eat the flesh of the mighty, and drink the blood of the princes of the earth, of rams, of lambs, and of goats, of bullocks, all of them fatlings of Bā´shan.

19 And ye shall eat fat till ye be full, and drink blood till ye be drunken, of my sacrifice which I have sacrificed for you.

20 Thus ye shall be filled at my table with horses and chariots, with mighty men, and with all men of war, saith the Lord God.

21 And I will set my glory among the heathen, and all the heathen shall see my judgment that I have executed, and my hand that I have laid upon them.

22 So the house of Israel shall know that I *am* the Lord their God from that day and forward.

23 And the heathen shall know that the house of Israel went into captivity for their iniquity: because they trespassed against me, therefore hid I my face from them, and gave them into the hand of their enemies: so fell they all by the sword.

24 According to their uncleanness and according to their transgressions have I done unto them, and hid my face from them.

25 Therefore thus saith the Lord God; Now will I bring again the captivity of Jacob, and have mercy upon the whole house of Israel, and will be jealous for my holy name;

26 After that they have borne their shame, and all their trespasses whereby they have trespassed against me, when they dwelt safely in their land, and none made *them* afraid.

27 When I have brought them again from the people, and gathered them out of their enemies' lands, and am sanctified in them in the sight of many nations;

28 Then shall they know that I *am* the Lord their God, which caused them to be led into captivity among the heathen: but I have gathered them unto their own land, and have left none of them any more there.

29 Neither will I hide my face any more from them: for I have poured out my spirit upon the house of Israel, saith the Lord God.

21-29. Details of God's purpose in His dealings with Israel are listed in the outline of these verses. They are: to show His glory among the nations in verse 21; a deliverance from the king of the north in verse 22; the nations observing God's purpose of chastening Israel in verses 23-24; then the nations observing Israel's regathering in verses 25-28; and the regeneration of Israel in verse 29. It should be noted that Israel will be saved by God's mercy, not by their merit; for the Lord will regather Israel for His name's sake. The regathering of Israel will be one of the great demonstrations of God's power. As Israel's deliverance from Egypt was in the past, and the resurrection of Christ from the grave is for the present, so Israel's regathering and regeneration in the future will eternally magnify the Lord.

V. PROPHECIES CONCERNING ISRAEL IN THE MILLENNIAL KINGDOM. 40:1-48:35.

A. A New Temple. 40:1-43:27.

Various views have been suggested by those who do not see this temple as a real literal temple in the future kingdom age. The first is that it was a description of Solomon's Temple. An examination of the detailed differences rejects this interpretation. The second, that it is the plan for the Temple rebuilt by Zerubbabel, is rejected for the same reasons. Third, some would say it was the ideal for the Temple to be rebuilt by the returning

1607

CHAPTER 40

1 IN the five and twentieth year of our captivity, in the beginning of the year, in the tenth *day* of the month, in the fourteenth year after that the city was smitten, in the selfsame day the hand of the LORD was upon me, and brought me thither.

2 In the visions of God brought he me into the land of Israel, and set me upon a very high mountain, by which *was* as the frame of a city on the south.

3 And he brought me thither, and, behold, *there was* a man, whose appearance *was* like the appearance of brass, with a line of flax in his hand, and a measuring reed; and he stood in the gate.

4 And the man said unto me, Son of man, behold with thine eyes, and hear with thine ears, and set thine heart upon all that I shall shew thee; for to the intent that I might shew *them* unto thee *art* thou brought hither: declare all that thou seest to the house of Israel.

5 And behold a wall on the outside of the house round about, and in the man's hand a measuring reed of six cubits *long* by the cubit and an hand breadth: so he measured the breadth of the building, one reed; and the height, one reed.

6 ¶Then came he unto the gate which looketh toward the east, and went up the stairs thereof, and measured the threshold of the gate, *which was* one reed broad; and the other threshold *of the gate, which was* one reed broad.

7 And every little chamber *was* one reed long, and one reed broad; and between the little chambers *were* five cubits; and the threshold of the gate by the porch of the gate within *was* one reed.

8 He measured also the porch of the gate within, one reed.

9 Then measured he the porch of the gate, eight cubits; and the posts thereof, two cubits; and the porch of the gate *was* inward.

10 And the little chambers of the gate eastward *were* three on this side, and three on that side; they three *were* of one measure: and the posts had one measure on this side and on that side.

11 And he measured the breadth of the entry of the gate, ten cubits; *and* the length of the gate, thirteen cubits.

12 The space also before the little chambers *was* one cubit *on this side,* and the space *was* one cubit on that side: and the little chambers *were* six

exiles. This cannot be accepted, for the Temple described by Ezekiel differs from the pattern given by God in the Old Testament. Several major changes are made, such as the elimination of the Ark of the Covenant, the Mercy Seat, the Table of Showbread, and the Golden Lampstand. Fourth, some, who allegorize, see the Temple as in some way representing the future glory of the church in heaven. The great detail of description strongly argues against this stance.

The only view that harmonizes with the grammatical-historical principle of interpretation is that Ezekiel is describing a real future Temple in great detail which in many ways differs from Solomon's Temple. This Temple will be on earth, and not in heaven, since it is described in a geographical setting that we are acquainted with historically.

40:1-4. This contains the introduction, including the date of **In the five and twentieth year of our captivity.** This is further identified as the tenth day of the fourteenth year **after that the city was smitten.** The prophet is transported in vision to the temple mountain, where a heavenly guide gives him a tour of the Temple, beginning at the east gate of the outer court. Evidently, **the man** of verse 3 is the angel of the Lord, or the Lord Himself (44:2, 5). **A line of flax** was used for long measurements **and a measuring reed** was used for short measurements.

5-27. There was a wall surrounding the whole Temple area **one reed** in thickness and **one reed** in height. The wall was severed by three gates on the east (vss. 5-16), on the north (vss. 20-23), and on the south (vss. 24-27). There were **seven steps** leading to these gateways (22, 26). The Hebrew cubit was about 17.6 inches. The long cubit was about 20.7 inches. Ezekiel's reed was about ten and one-half feet long. The **gate** in verse 6 was fifty cubits long (vs. 15) and twenty-five cubits broad (vs. 13). The **threshold of the gate** in verses 15 and 11 was six cubits deep and ten cubits wide. There was also a passageway to the gate which was thirteen cubits wide (vs. 11) with three **little chambers** (vs. 7) or side-rooms or guard-rooms on either side. Each of these were six cubits square (vs. 12), having **narrow windows** (vs. 16), and protected on the side towards the passageway by a **space** or "barrier" (NASB). This was a low wall one cubit thick (vs. 12). Thus, the outer court had three gates.

In addition to the three gates, the outer court had thirty **chambers.** In verse 17 Ezekiel and his guide pass through the east gate and enter the **outward court.** This was on the **pavement.** The thirty chambers were designed for use by the people and the Levites who worship in the outer court. The pavement is fifty cubits wide, which corresponds to the length of the outer gates (vss. 15, 18). From the **forefront of the lower gate** (outer gate) **to the forefront of the inner court without** is a hundred cubits.

The north and the south gates, which are described in verses 20-27, correspond to dimensions given for the eastern gate, with the specific mention of **seven steps** in verses 22, 26.

cubits on this side, and six cubits on that side.

13 He measured then the gate from the roof of *one* little chamber to the roof of another: the breadth *was* five and twenty cubits, door against door.

14 He made also posts of threescore cubits, even unto the post of the court round about the gate.

15 And from the face of the gate of the entrance unto the face of the porch of the inner gate *were* fifty cubits.

16 And *there were* narrow windows to the little chambers, and to their posts within the gate round about, and likewise to the arches: and windows *were* round about inward: and upon *each* post *were* palm trees.

17 Then brought he me into the outward court, and, lo, *there were* chambers, and a pavement made for the court round about: thirty chambers *were* upon the pavement.

18 And the pavement by the side of the gates over against the length of the gates *was* the lower pavement.

19 Then he measured the breadth from the forefront of the lower gate unto the forefront of the inner court without, an hundred cubits eastward and northward.

20 ¶ And the gate of the outward court that looked toward the north, he measured the length thereof, and the breadth thereof.

21 And the little chambers thereof *were* three on this side and three on that side; and the posts thereof and the arches thereof were after the measure of the first gate: the length thereof *was* fifty cubits, and the breadth five and twenty cubits.

22 And their windows, and their arches, and their palm trees, *were* after the measure of the gate that looketh toward the east; and they went up unto it by seven steps; and the arches thereof *were* before them.

23 And the gate of the inner court *was* over against the gate toward the north, and toward the east; and he measured from gate to gate an hundred cubits.

24 ¶ After that he brought me toward the south, and behold a gate toward the south: and he measured the posts thereof and the arches thereof according to these measures.

25 And *there were* windows in it and in the arches thereof round about, like those windows: the length *was* fifty cubits, and the breadth five and twenty cubits.

26 And *there were* seven steps to go up to it, and the arches thereof *were* before them: and it had palm trees, one on this side, and another on that side, upon the posts thereof.

27 And *there was* a gate in the inner court toward the south: and he measured from gate to gate toward the south an hundred cubits.

28 And he brought me to the inner court by the south gate: and he measured the south gate according to these measures;

28-47. After this Ezekiel walked through another large gateway into the inner court, which was built on a higher level. The **inner court** (vs. 28) was located one hundred cubits to the interior of the outer gates (vs. 19) on a platform that was 8 steps

29 And the little chambers thereof, and the posts thereof, and the arches thereof, according to these measures; and there were windows in it and in the arches thereof round about: it was fifty cubits long, and five and twenty cubits broad.

30 And the arches round about were five and twenty cubits long, and five cubits broad.

31 And the arches thereof were toward the utter court; and palm trees were upon the posts thereof: and the going up to it had eight steps.

32 ¶ And he brought me into the inner court toward the east: and he measured the gate according to these measures.

33 And the little chambers thereof, and the posts thereof, and the arches thereof, were according to these measures: and there were windows therein and in the arches thereof round about: it was fifty cubits long, and five and twenty cubits broad.

34 And the arches thereof were toward the outward court; and palm trees were upon the posts thereof, on this side, and on that side: and the going up to it had eight steps.

35 ¶ And he brought me to the north gate, and measured it according to these measures;

36 The little chambers thereof, the posts thereof, and the arches thereof, and the windows to it round about: the length was fifty cubits, and the breadth five and twenty cubits.

37 And the posts thereof were toward the utter court; and palm trees were upon the posts thereof, on this side, and on that side: and the going up to it had eight steps.

38 And the chambers and the entries thereof were by the posts of the gates, where they washed the burnt offering.

39 ¶ And in the porch of the gate were two tables on this side, and two tables on that side, to slay thereon the burnt offering and the sin offering and the trespass offering.

40 And at the side without as one goeth up to the entry of the north gate, were two tables; and on the other side, which was at the porch of the gate, were two tables.

41 Four tables were on this side, and four tables on that side, by the side of the gate; eight tables, whereupon they slew their sacrifices.

42 And the four tables were of hewn stone for the burnt offering, of a cubit and an half long, and a cubit and an half broad, and one cubit high: whereupon also they laid the instruments wherewith they slew the burnt offering and the sacrifice.

43 And within were hooks, an hand broad, fastened round about: and upon the tables was the flesh of the offering.

44 ¶ And without the inner gate were the chambers of the singers in the inner court, which was at the side of the north gate; and their prospect was toward the south: one at the side of the east gate having the prospect toward the north.

45 And he said unto me, This chamber, whose prospect is toward the

higher than the outer court (vss. 31, 34, 37). The inner court was accessible by gates on the south (vss. 28-31), east (vss. 32-34), and north (vss. 35-37) sides.

In the porch of the gate (east) there were arrangements for preparing sacrifices (vss. 39-43), and then there were certain rooms set apart for the priest (vss. 45, 46). The latter rooms were on the eastern sides of the inner north and south gateways.

Within the inner court was the altar (vs. 47), which was a square of one hundred cubits. It was east of the Temple. In the center of it stood the altar of burnt offering (43:13-27). The chamber . . . for the priests was situated at the western end of the inner court (42:1-14). The Temple itself was on a platform ten steps higher than the inner court (vs. 49).

The sons of Zadok were the ones charged with offering the sacrifices (43:19; 44:15; 48:11). Solomon had set aside the priesthood of the house of Eli. This was accomplished when he replaced Abiathar and put Zadok in his place (1 Kgs 2:26, 27; cf. I Sam 2:30-36).

south, *is* for the priests, the keepers of the charge of the house.

46 And the chamber whose prospect *is* toward the north *is* for the priests, the keepers of the charge of the altar: these *are* the sons of Zā'dŏk among the sons of Levi, which come near to the LORD to minister unto him.

47 So he measured the court, an hundred cubits long, and an hundred cubits broad, foursquare; and the altar *that was* before the house.

48 ¶And he brought me to the porch of the house, and measured *each* post of the porch, five cubits on this side, and five cubits on that side: and the breadth of the gate *was* three cubits on this side, and three cubits on that side.

49 The length of the porch *was* twenty cubits, and the breadth eleven cubits; and *he brought me* by the steps whereby they went up to it: and *there* were pillars by the posts, one on this side, and another on that side.

CHAPTER 41

AFTERWARD he brought me to the temple, and measured the posts, six cubits broad on the one side, and six cubits broad on the other side, *which was* the breadth of the tabernacle.

2 And the breadth of the door *was* ten cubits; and the sides of the door *were* five cubits on the one side, and five cubits on the other side: and he measured the length thereof, forty cubits: and the breadth, twenty cubits.

3 Then went he inward, and measured the post of the door, two cubits; and the door, six cubits; and the breadth of the door, seven cubits.

4 So he measured the length thereof, twenty cubits; and the breadth, twenty cubits, before the temple: and he said unto me, This *is* the most holy *place.*

5 After he measured the wall of the house, six cubits; and the breadth of *every* side chamber, four cubits, round about the house on every side.

6 And the side chambers *were* three, one over another, and thirty in order; and they entered into the wall which *was* of the house for the side chambers round about, that they might have hold, but they had not hold in the wall of the house.

7 And *there was* an enlarging, and a winding about still upward to the side chambers: for the winding about of the house went still upward round about the house: therefore the breadth of the house *was still* upward, and so increased *from* the lowest *chamber* to the highest by the midst.

8 I saw also the height of the house round about: the foundations of the side chambers *were* a full reed of six great cubits.

9 The thickness of the wall, which *was* for the side chamber without, *was* five cubits: and *that* which *was* left *was* the place of the side chambers that *were* within.

10 And between the chambers *was* the wideness of twenty cubits round about the house on every side.

11 And the doors of the side chambers *were* toward *the place that was*

48-49. This entire section (40:28–41:26) contains a description of the Temple itself. The **porch** is described first in verses 48 and 49. Some call it the "vestibule." It was twenty cubits wide from north to south and eleven cubits deep from east to west. The entrance was fourteen cubits wide and had a sidewall three cubits wide on either side; and beside the **posts** were **pillars,** two of them, called Jachin and Boaz in I Kings 7:15-22.

41:1-26. The **temple,** or "nave" (NASB) is described. It is forty cubits long from east to west and twenty cubits broad from north to south. Then in verses 3 and 4 the **most holy place** is pictured. The angel is the only one who went into the **most holy place** beyond the **temple** or "nave." It is twenty by twenty cubits.

Then the **side chambers,** which consisted of three floors of rooms, thirty per floor, are cited in verses 5-11. They were to be employed for storage purposes. There was a large building behind the Temple (vs. 12). In verses 13-17 the total measurements of the Temple and its immediate surroundings are given. Then, in verses 18-26 a description of the interior of the Temple is depicted. The three parts of the Temple were paneled with a costly black wood **from the ground up to the windows** (vs. 16).

left, one door toward the north, and another door toward the south: and the breadth of the place that was left was five cubits round about.

12 Now the building that was before the separate place at the end toward the west was seventy cubits broad; and the wall of the building was five cubits thick round about, and the length thereof ninety cubits.

13 So he measured the house, an hundred cubits long; and the separate place, and the building, with the walls thereof, an hundred cubits long;

14 Also the breadth of the face of the house, and of the separate place toward the east, an hundred cubits.

15 And he measured the length of the building over against the separate place which was behind it, and the galleries thereof on the one side and on the other side, an hundred cubits, with the inner temple, and the porches of the court;

16 The door posts, and the narrow windows, and the galleries round about on their three stories, over against the door, cieled with wood round about, and from the ground up to the windows, and the windows were covered;

17 To that above the door, even unto the inner house, and without, and by all the wall round about within and without, by measure.

18 And it was made with cherubims and palm trees, so that a palm tree was between a cherub and a cherub; and every cherub had two faces;

19 So that the face of a man was toward the palm tree on the one side, and the face of a young lion toward the palm tree on the other side: it was made through all the house round about.

20 From the ground unto above the door were cherubims and palm trees made, and on the wall of the temple.

21 The posts of the temple were squared, and the face of the sanctuary; the appearance of the one as the appearance of the other.

22 The altar of wood was three cubits high, and the length thereof two cubits; and the corners thereof, and the length thereof, and the walls thereof, were of wood: and he said unto me, This is the table that is before the LORD.

23 And the temple and the sanctuary had two doors.

24 And the doors had two leaves apiece, two turning leaves; two leaves for the one door, and two leaves for the other door.

25 And there were made on them, on the doors of the temple, cherubims and palm trees, like as were made upon the walls; and there were thick planks upon the face of the porch without.

26 And there were narrow windows and palm trees on the one side and on the other side, on the sides of the porch, and upon the side chambers of the house, and thick planks.

CHAPTER 42

THEN he brought me forth into the utter court, the way toward the north: and he brought me into the chamber

42:1-20. There are three sections to this chapter: (1) the chambers of the priests (vss. 12-14); (2) the use of these chambers by the priests (vss. 13-14); and (3) the dimensions of the temple area (vss. 15-20). The buildings containing the priests' chambers seem to be located at the west end of the inner court, between the north and south temple yards (vss. 1, 10; cf. 41:10, 12). North of the Temple, in the inner court, were two blocks of three-story buildings, one of which was twice the length of the other. This was used by the priests when eating sacrifices (46:20) and for the storage of their garments (44:19).

The overall measurements of the Temple represented a square of five hundred reeds. The purpose of the surrounding wall is to **make a separation between the sanctuary and the profane place** (vs. 20).

that *was* over against the separate place, and which *was* before the building toward the north.

2 Before the length of an hundred cubits *was* the north door, and the breadth *was* fifty cubits.

3 Over against the twenty *cubits* which *were* for the inner court, and over against the pavement which *was* for the utter court, *was* gallery against gallery in three *stories.*

4 And before the chambers *was* a walk of ten cubits breadth inward, a way of one cubit; and their doors toward the north.

5 Now the upper chambers *were* shorter: for the galleries were higher than these, than the lower, and than the middlemost of the building.

6 For they *were* in three *stories,* but had not pillars as the pillars of the courts: therefore *the building* was straitened more than the lowest and the middlemost from the ground.

7 And the wall that *was* without over against the chambers, toward the utter court on the forepart of the chambers, the length thereof *was* fifty cubits.

8 For the length of the chambers that *were* in the utter court *was* fifty cubits: and, lo, before the temple *were* an hundred cubits.

9 And from under these chambers *was* the entry on the east side, as one goeth into them from the utter court.

10 The chambers *were* in the thickness of the wall of the court toward the east, over against the separate place, and over against the building.

11 And the way before them *was* like the appearance of the chambers which *were* toward the north, as long as they, *and* as broad as they: and all their goings out *were* both according to their fashions, and according to their doors.

12 And according to the doors of the chambers that *were* toward the south *was* a door in the head of the way, *even* the way directly before the wall toward the east, as one entereth into them.

13 ¶ Then said he unto me, The north chambers *and* the south chambers, which *are* before the separate place, they *be* holy chambers, where the priests that approach unto the LORD shall eat the most holy things: there shall they lay the most holy things, and the meat offering, and the sin offering, and the trespass offering; for the place *is* holy.

14 When the priests enter therein, then shall they not go out of the holy *place* into the utter court, but there they shall lay their garments wherein they minister; for they *are* holy; and shall put on other garments, and shall approach to *those things which are* for the people.

15 ¶ Now when he had made an end of measuring the inner house, he brought me forth toward the gate whose prospect *is* toward the east, and measured it round about.

16 He measured the east side with the measuring reed, five hundred reeds, with the measuring reed round about.

17 He measured the north side, five hundred reeds, with the measuring reed round about.

18 He measured the south side, five hundred reeds, with the measuring reed.

19 He turned about to the west side, and measured five hundred reeds with the measuring reed.

20 He measured it by the four sides: it had a wall round about, five hundred reeds long, and five hundred broad, to make a separation between the sanctuary and the profane place.

CHAPTER 43

AFTERWARD he brought me to the gate, even the gate that looketh toward the east:

2 And, behold, the glory of the God of Israel came from the way of the east: and his voice was like a noise of many waters: and the earth shined with his glory.

3 And it was according to the appearance of the vision which I saw, even according to the vision that I saw when I came to destroy the city: and the visions were like the vision that I saw by the river Chê'bär: and I fell upon my face.

4 And the glory of the Lord came into the house by the way of the gate whose prospect is toward the east.

5 So the spirit took me up, and brought me into the inner court; and, behold, the glory of the Lord filled the house.

6 And I heard him speaking unto me out of the house; and the man stood by me.

7 ¶And he said unto me, Son of man, the place of my throne, and the place of the soles of my feet, where I will dwell in the midst of the children of Israel for ever, and my holy name, shall the house of Israel no more defile, neither they, nor their kings, by their whoredom, nor by the carcases of their kings in their high places.

8 In their setting of their threshold by my thresholds, and their post by my posts, and the wall between me and them, they have even defiled my holy name by their abominations that they have committed: wherefore I have consumed them in mine anger.

9 Now let them put away their whoredom, and the carcases of their kings, far from me, and I will dwell in the midst of them for ever.

10 ¶Thou son of man, shew the house to the house of Israel, that they may be ashamed of their iniquities: and let them measure the pattern.

11 And if they be ashamed of all that they have done, shew them the form of the house, and the fashion thereof, and the goings out thereof, and the comings in thereof, and all the forms thereof, and all the ordinances thereof, and all the forms thereof, and all the laws thereof: and write it in their sight, that they may keep the whole form thereof, and all the ordinances thereof, and do them.

12 This is the law of the house: Upon the top of the mountain the whole limit

43:1-12. Ezekiel saw the Lord returning through the east gate (vs. 2). This was the same gate through which He had earlier departed (10:19). He had also seen it when the Lord had come to destroy the city (vs. 3) and in the initial vision by the river Chebar.

Verses 6-12 contain God's exhortation to Israel from the inner sanctuary. He announces the Temple must be holy and free from whoredom, which means temple prostitution. The Jerusalem Temple is here pictured as the throne of God; in other places heaven is described in this manner (cf. Isa 66:1; Ps 2:4). Thus, Ezekiel pictures heaven having come down to earth (cf. 37:26-28). They are also to be separated from the graves and palaces of their kings (vss. 79), which were located on the same hill as Solomon's Temple (cf. II Kgs 23:7).

thereof round about *shall be* most holy. Behold, this *is* the law of the house.

13 ¶And these *are* the measures of the altar after the cubits: The cubit *is* a cubit and an hand breadth; even the bottom *shall be* a cubit, and the breadth a cubit, and the border thereof by the edge thereof round about *shall be* a span: and this *shall be* the higher place of the altar.

14 And from the bottom *upon* the ground *even* to the lower settle *shall be* two cubits, and the breadth one cubit; and from the lesser settle *even* to the greater settle *shall be* four cubits, and the breadth *one* cubit.

15 So the altar *shall be* four cubits; and from the altar and upward *shall be* four horns.

16 And the altar *shall be* twelve *cubits* long, twelve broad, square in the four squares thereof.

17 And the settle *shall be* fourteen *cubits* long and fourteen broad in the four squares thereof; and the border about it *shall be* half a cubit; and the bottom thereof *shall be* a cubit about; and his stairs shall look toward the east.

18 ¶And he said unto me, Son of man, thus saith the Lord God; These *are* the ordinances of the altar in the day when they shall make it, to offer burnt offerings thereon, and to sprinkle blood thereon.

19 And thou shalt give to the priests the Levites that be of the seed of Zadok, which approach unto me, to minister unto me, saith the Lord God, a young bullock for a sin offering.

20 And thou shalt take of the blood thereof, and put *it* on the four horns of it, and on the four corners of the settle, and upon the border round about: thus shalt thou cleanse and purge it.

21 Thou shalt take the bullock also of the sin offering, and he shall burn it in the appointed place of the house, without the sanctuary.

22 And on the second day thou shalt offer a kid of the goats without blemish for a sin offering; and they shall cleanse the altar, as they did cleanse *it* with the bullock.

23 When thou hast made an end of cleansing *it*, thou shalt offer a young bullock without blemish, and a ram out of the flock without blemish.

24 And thou shalt offer them before the LORD, and the priests shall cast salt upon them, and they shall offer them up *for* a burnt offering unto the LORD.

25 Seven days shalt thou prepare every day a goat *for* a sin offering: they shall also prepare a young bullock, and a ram out of the flock, without blemish.

26 Seven days shall they purge the altar and purify it; and they shall consecrate themselves.

27 And when these days are expired, it shall be, *that* upon the eighth day, and *so* forward, the priests shall make your burnt offerings upon the altar, and your peace offerings; and I will accept you, saith the Lord God.

CHAPTER 44

THEN he brought me back the way of the gate of the outward sanctuary

13-27. Verses 13-18 give a description of the altar of burnt offering (cf. 40:47). The altar is consecrated (vss. 18-27) by the application of the blood of the sin offering for seven days on its four horns (vss. 25-26), the four corners of the upper ledge, and the rim of the base. This is to **purge** and **purify** it. **And they shall consecrate themselves** literally means to fill its hand, that is, to invest it with office. The word **themselves** is rendered "it" due to the third person singular pronoun attached to the word "hand." The idiom is commonly used for the initiation or consecration of the priests. Here, it is applied to the altar. After God's regulations are carried out then and only then can it be said, **I will accept you.** He will accept their offerings because their conduct will be pleasing to Him.

B. A New Service of Worship. 44:1-46:24.

44:1-14. This section deals with those who may minister in the Temple. The **outward sanctuary** is to remain shut after the

which looketh toward the east; and it was shut.

2 Then said the LORD unto me; This gate shall be shut, it shall not be opened, and no man shall enter in by it; because the LORD, the God of Israel, hath entered in by it, therefore it shall be shut.

3 *It is* for the prince; the prince, he shall sit in it to eat bread before the LORD; he shall enter by the way of the porch of *that* gate, and shall go out by the way of the same.

4 ¶ Then brought he me the way of the north gate before the house: and I looked, and, behold, the glory of the LORD filled the house of the LORD: and I fell upon my face.

5 And the LORD said unto me, Son of man, mark well, and behold with thine eyes, and hear with thine ears all that I say unto thee concerning all the ordinances of the house of the LORD, and all the laws thereof; and mark well the entering in of the house, with every going forth of the sanctuary.

6 And thou shalt say to the rebellious, *even* to the house of Israel, Thus saith the Lord GOD; O ye house of Israel, let it suffice you of all your abominations,

7 In that ye have brought *into my sanctuary* strangers, uncircumcised in heart, and uncircumcised in flesh, to be in my sanctuary, to pollute it, *even* my house, when ye offer my bread, the fat and the blood, and they have broken my covenant because of all your abominations.

8 And ye have not kept the charge of mine holy things: but ye have set keepers of my charge in my sanctuary for yourselves.

9 ¶ Thus saith the Lord GOD; No stranger, uncircumcised in heart, nor uncircumcised in flesh, shall enter into my sanctuary, of any stranger that *is* among the children of Israel.

10 And the Levites that are gone away far from me, when Israel went astray, which went astray away from me after their idols; they shall even bear their iniquity.

11 Yet they shall be ministers in my sanctuary, *having* charge at the gates of the house, and ministering to the house: they shall slay the burnt offering and the sacrifice for the people, and they shall stand before them to minister unto them.

12 Because they ministered unto them before their idols, and caused the house of Israel to fall into iniquity; therefore have I lifted up mine hand against them, saith the Lord GOD, and they shall bear their iniquity.

13 And they shall not come near unto me, to do the office of a priest unto me, nor to come near to any of my holy things, in the most holy *place*: but they shall bear their shame, and their abominations which they have committed.

14 But I will make them keepers of the charge of the house, for all the service thereof, and for all that shall be done therein.

15 ¶ But the priests the Levites, the sons of Zā́dŏk, that kept the charge of

15-27. But the priests the Levites, the sons of Zadok, that kept the charge of my sanctuary when the children of Israel

Lord's entrance through it, lest a mortal should desecrate it (vs. 2). It may also designate the fact that the divine Presence would never again depart from the sanctuary. Even the **prince** is not to use this gate, but he is permitted to eat the sacrificial meal in its "vestibule" (vs. 3; cf. Jer 30:21).

As to the identification of the **prince,** "though some consider him to be the Messiah, this is impossible, since he needs to offer a sin offering (45:22) and he has sons (46:16). He is evidently a human representative of Messiah in the government of the kingdom" (Ryrie, p. 1208).

The glory of the LORD filled the house of the LORD (vs. 4), and then an indictment was given against **the house of Israel.** The charge was **ye have brought into my sanctuary strangers, uncircumcised in heart . . . to pollute it.** Evidently, foreign slaves or war captives had assisted in the offering of sacrifice and in performing other tasks (Deut 29:11; Josh 9:23, 27; I Sam 2:13; Ezr 8:20). They are to be replaced by Levites, who had been responsible for the religious disintegration (vs. 10) and as a result would be excluded from performing the more important priestly duties (vss. 10-14). They would only be allowed to be watchmen at the gateways (cf. 40:4), to assist the people in the outer court, and to slay their offerings and cook their sacrifices (vs. 11; 46:24).

went astray from me, they shall come near to me to minister unto me (vs. 15). Thus, God will reward the faithful priests. They will not be able to **shave their heads, nor suffer their locks to grow,** both of which were signs of mourning (Lev 21:5; 10:6). Thus, the priests were to avoid extremes and were only to **poll** (trim) their heads.

The abstinence of wine would allow for the priests to be in full control of their faculties (Lev 10:9; Hos 4:11). Their principal duty was to teach the people (Deut 33:10; Mal 2:8, 9). Mourning was forbidden to the priests, except in the cases involving the closest of relatives.

28-31. These verses deal with the maintenance of the priests. **And it shall be unto them for an inheritance: I am their inheritance** indicates the priesthood is their inheritance, and they receive no allotment in the land (cf. Deut 18:1ff.). The Lord Himself was all they would need! They are to be sustained on the offerings, things dedicated to the Lord (Lev 27:28, 29; Num 18:14ff), first fruits, and the contributions of God's people.

my sanctuary when the children of Israel went astray from me, they shall come near to me to minister unto me, and they shall stand before me to offer unto me the fat and the blood, saith the Lord GOD:

16 They shall enter into my sanctuary, and they shall come near to my table, to minister unto me, and they shall keep my charge.

17 ¶And it shall come to pass, *that* when they enter in at the gates of the inner court, they shall be clothed with linen garments; and no wool shall come upon them, whiles they minister in the gates of the inner court, and within.

18 They shall have linen bonnets upon their heads, and shall have linen breeches upon their loins; they shall not gird *themselves* with any thing that causeth sweat.

19 And when they go forth into the utter court, *even* into the utter court to the people, they shall put off their garments wherein they ministered, and lay them in the holy chambers, and they shall put on other garments; and they shall not sanctify the people with their garments.

20 Neither shall they shave their heads, nor suffer their locks to grow long; they shall only poll their heads.

21 Neither shall any priest drink wine, when they enter into the inner court.

22 Neither shall they take for their wives a widow, nor her that is put away: but they shall take maidens of the seed of the house of Israel, or a widow that had a priest before.

23 And they shall teach my people *the difference* between the holy and profane, and cause them to discern between the unclean and the clean.

24 And in controversy they shall stand in judgment: *and* they shall judge it according to my judgments: and they shall keep my laws and my statutes in all mine assemblies; and they shall hallow my sabbaths.

25 And they shall come at no dead person to defile themselves: but for father, or for mother, or for son, or for daughter, for brother, or for sister that hath had no husband, they may defile themselves.

26 And after he is cleansed, they shall reckon unto him seven days.

27 And in the day that he goeth into the sanctuary, unto the inner court, to minister in the sanctuary, he shall offer his sin offering, saith the Lord GOD.

28 And it shall be unto them for an inheritance: I *am* their inheritance: and ye shall give them no possession in Israel: I *am* their possession.

29 They shall eat the meat offering, and the sin offering, and the trespass offering; and every dedicated thing in Israel shall be theirs.

30 And the first of all the firstfruits of all *things*, and every oblation of all, of every *sort* of your oblations, shall be the priest's: ye shall also give unto the priest the first of your dough, that he may cause the blessing to rest in thine house.

31 The priests shall not eat of any

thing, that is dead of itself, or torn, whether it be fowl or beast.

CHAPTER 45

MOREOVER, when ye shall divide by lot the land for inheritance, ye shall offer an oblation unto the LORD, an holy portion of the land: the length *shall be* the length of five and twenty thousand *reeds*, and the breadth *shall be* ten thousand. This *shall be* holy in all the borders thereof round about.

2 Of this there shall be for the sanctuary five hundred *in length*, with five hundred *in breadth*, square round about; and fifty cubits round about for the suburbs thereof.

3 And of this measure shalt thou measure the length of five and twenty thousand, and the breadth of ten thousand: and in it shall be the sanctuary *and* the most holy *place*.

4 The holy *portion* of the land shall be for the priests the ministers of the sanctuary, which shall come near to minister unto the LORD: and it shall be a place for their houses, and an holy place for the sanctuary.

5 And the five and twenty thousand of length, and the ten thousand of breadth, shall also the Levites, the ministers of the house, have for themselves, for a possession for twenty chambers.

6 ¶ And ye shall appoint the possession of the city five thousand broad, and five and twenty thousand long, over against the oblation of the holy *portion*: it shall be for the whole house of Israel.

7 ¶ *And* a portion *shall be* for the prince on the one side and on the other side of the oblation of the holy *portion*, and of the possession of the city, before the oblation of the holy *portion*, and before the possession of the city, from the west side westward, and from the east side eastward: and the length *shall be* over against one of the portions, from the west border unto the east border.

8 In the land shall be his possession in Israel: and my princes shall no more oppress my people; and *the rest of* the land shall they give to the house of Israel according to their tribes.

9 ¶ Thus saith the Lord GOD; Let it suffice you, O princes of Israel: remove violence and spoil, and execute judgment and justice, take away your exactions from my people, saith the Lord GOD.

10 Ye shall have just balances, and a just ephah, and a just bath.

11 The ephah and the bath shall be of one measure, that the bath may contain the tenth part of an homer, and the ephah the tenth part of an homer: the measure thereof shall be after the homer.

12 And the shekel *shall be* twenty gerahs: twenty shekels, five and twenty shekels, fifteen shekels, shall be your maneh.

13 This *is* the oblation that ye shall offer; the sixth part of an ephah of an homer of wheat, and ye shall give the sixth part of an ephah of an homer of barley:

45:1-17. This section deals with the portions of land designated for the priests, the Levites, and the Prince. In addition to being on a high hill (40:2) and having walled courts (chs. 40-42), and in addition to being protected by the precautionary measures of 44:4ff., the Temple of Ezekiel is further guarded against desecration by its location in the midst of sacred territory surrounded by the priests' quarters (48:8-22). This sacred territory, in which the Temple was situated, was about 8 miles square.

The sacred district is called **an oblation** in verse 1, the word normally translated "heave offering" in the KJV. Here, it is more accurately designated a levy, with the idea of a compulsory contribution. This was the **city**, or the **suburbs** of verse 2 are understood to be the open spaces which surround the Temple area.

In verse 5 the Levites receive a special portion to live in, instead of the pattern proposed in Number 35:2-8. Then, in verse 6 the **city**, or the state, is also allotted an area of land adjacent to this central holy portion. The **prince** is treated likewise in verses 7-8. The rest is for the tribes to live in. "There is to be no more alienation of land by royalty in the state that is to come (cf. Isa 5:8). The story of Naboth's vineyard is to be repeated no more (vs. 8)" (Taylor, p. 274).

The duties of the princes are described in verses 9-12. They are to **remove violence and spoil, and execute judgment and justice** and to stop their **exactions.** The word **exactions** comes from the verb meaning to eject, and is used of the unjust displacement of an owner from his property (cf. Mic 2:9, "The women of my people have ye cast out from their pleasant houses"). "There is to be no revival of the kingship with the power and pomp of old. The prince's main function is to provide the offerings" (Pearson, p. 765).

In verses 13-17 the offerings of the people to the prince and the prince's offerings to the Temple are related. Specific dues are to be paid by the people of the land to the prince. He, in turn, will have the responsibility of providing the offerings and sacrifices at all the festivals. The people are to give a specified offering from the grain (vs. 13), oil (vs. 14), and sheep (vs. 15) to the prince (vs. 16). The contribution is to be proportionate: "a sixtieth in the case of wheat and barley (vs. 13), a hundredth in the case of oil (vs. 14), and one in two hundred of the flock (vs. 15)" (Taylor, p. 275).

18-25. There are three specific times for the rituals: (1) New Year's Day (vss. 18-20); (2) Passover (vss. 21-24); and (3) the Feast of Tabernacles (vs. 25).

46:1-8. The prince had the obligation of producing the offerings, not only for the major festivals, but also for the new moons and sabbaths. He was allowed to enter **by the way of the porch of that gate without,** but was only allowed to go as far as its innermost **threshold** (vs. 2). The inner court was reserved exclusively for the priests and Levites. The privilege was reserved for new moons and sabbaths; on working days the east gateway would be closed (vs. 1).

14 Concerning the ordinance of oil, the bath of oil, *ye shall offer* the tenth part of a bath out of the cor, *which is an* homer of ten baths; for ten baths *are an* homer.

15 And one lamb out of the flock, out of two hundred, out of the fat pastures of Israel; for a meat offering, and for a burnt offering, and for peace offerings, to make reconciliation for them, saith the Lord God.

16 All the people of the land shall give this oblation for the prince in Israel.

17 And it shall be the prince's part *to give* burnt offerings, and meat offerings, and drink offerings, in the feasts, and in the new moons, and in the sabbaths, in all solemnities of the house of Israel: he shall prepare the sin offering, and the meat offering, and the burnt offering, and the peace offerings, to make reconciliation for the house of Israel.

18 Thus saith the Lord God: In the first month, in the first *day* of the month, thou shalt take a young bullock without blemish, and cleanse the sanctuary:

19 And the priest shall take of the blood of the sin offering, and put *it* upon the posts of the house, and upon the four corners of the settle of the altar, and upon the posts of the gate of the inner court.

20 And so thou shalt do the seventh *day* of the month for every one that erreth, and for *him that is* simple: so shall ye reconcile the house.

21 In the first *month,* in the fourteenth day of the month, ye shall have the passover, a feast of seven days; unleavened bread shall be eaten.

22 And upon that day shall the prince prepare for himself and for all the people of the land a bullock *for* a sin offering.

23 And seven days of the feast he shall prepare a burnt offering to the Lord, seven bullocks and seven rams without blemish daily the seven days; and a kid of the goats daily *for* a sin offering.

24 And he shall prepare a meat offering of an ephah for a bullock, and an ephah for a ram, and an hin of oil for an ephah.

25 In the seventh *month,* in the fifteenth day of the month, shall he do the like in the feast of the seven days, according to the sin offering, according to the burnt offering, and according to the meat offering, and according to the oil.

CHAPTER 46

THUS saith the Lord God: The gate of the inner court that looketh toward the east shall be shut the six working days; but on the sabbath it shall be opened, and in the day of the new moon it shall be opened.

2 And the prince shall enter by the way of *that* gate without, and shall stand by the post of the gate, and the priests shall prepare his burnt offering and his peace offerings, and he shall worship at the threshold of the gate: then he shall go forth; but the gate shall not be shut until the evening.

3 Likewise the people of the land

shall worship at the door of this gate before the LORD in the sabbaths and in the new moons.

4 And the burnt offering that the prince shall offer unto the LORD in the sabbath day *shall be* six lambs without blemish, and a ram without blemish.

5 And the meat offering *shall be* an ephah for a ram, and the meat offering for the lambs as he shall be able to give, and an hin of oil to an ephah.

6 And in the day of the new moon *it shall be* a young bullock without blemish, and six lambs, and a ram: they shall be without blemish.

7 And he shall prepare a meat offering, an ephah for a bullock, and an ephah for a ram, and for the lambs according as his hand shall attain unto, and an hin of oil to an ephah.

8 And when the prince shall enter, he shall go in by the way of the porch of *that* gate, and he shall go forth by the way thereof.

9 ¶But when the people of the land shall come before the LORD in the solemn feasts, he that entereth in by the way of the north gate to worship shall go out by the way of the south gate; and he that entereth by the way of the south gate shall go forth by the way of the north gate: he shall not return by the way of the gate whereby he came in, but shall go forth over against it.

10 And the prince in the midst of them, when they go in, shall go in; and when they go forth, shall go forth.

11 And in the feasts and in the solemnities the meat offering shall be an ephah to a bullock, and an ephah to a ram, and to the lambs as he is able to give, and an hin of oil to an ephah.

12 Now when the prince shall prepare a voluntary burnt offering or peace offerings voluntarily unto the LORD, *one* shall then open him the gate that looketh toward the east, and he shall prepare his burnt offering and his peace offerings, as he did on the sabbath day: then he shall go forth; and after his going forth one shall shut the gate.

13 Thou shalt daily prepare a burnt offering unto the LORD of a lamb of the first year without blemish: thou shalt prepare it every morning.

14 And thou shalt prepare a meat offering for it every morning, the sixth part of an ephah, and the third part of an hin of oil, to temper with the fine flour: a meat offering continually by a perpetual ordinance unto the LORD.

15 Thus shall they prepare the lamb, and the meat offering, and the oil, every morning *for* a continual burnt offering.

16 ¶Thus saith the Lord GOD; If the prince give a gift unto any of his sons, the inheritance thereof shall be his sons'; it *shall be* their possession by inheritance.

17 But if he give a gift of his inheritance to one of his servants, then it shall be his to the year of liberty; after it shall return to the prince: but his inheritance shall be his sons' for them.

18 Moreover the prince shall not take

9, 10. To avoid confusion, the people coming to the feasts are to enter one gate and exit by another.

11-15. In this section further regulations are given concerning various other offerings that the prince makes on behalf of the people. Three particular incidents are dealt with: **Feasts and in the solemnities** verse 11; when the prince wishes to make a freewill offering verse 12; and the daily offering in verses 13-15.

16-18. These verses supplement 45:8-9. The prince is permitted to give gifts of land to his sons, and they may keep it by right of inheritance. But any gift to a royal servant may only be held on a lease-hold basis. The gift must be returned in **the year of liberty,** that is, the seventh year, when bondservants were to be freed (Jer 34:14). It may be that the reference is to the year of Jubilee (cf. Lev 25:10-13; 27:24). Thus, the prince's inheritance is safeguarded and kept within the family. He is not to alienate the property of others (vs. 18), and even the rights of the common person are to be protected. "After all, the land is not

of the people's inheritance by oppression, to thrust them out of their possession; *but* he shall give his sons inheritance out of his own possession: that my people be not scattered every man from his possession.

19 ¶After he brought me through the entry, which *was* at the side of the gate, into the holy chambers of the priests, which looked toward the north: and, behold, there *was* a place on the two sides westward.

20 Then said he unto me, This *is* the place where the priests shall boil the trespass offering and the sin offering, where they shall bake the meat offering; that they bear *them* not out into the utter court, to sanctify the people.

21 Then he brought me forth into the utter court, and caused me to pass by the four corners of the court; and, behold, in every corner of the court *there was* a court.

22 In the four corners of the court *there were* courts joined of forty cubits long and thirty broad: these four corners were of one measure.

23 And *there was* a row *of building* round about in them, round about them four, and *it was* made with boiling places under the rows round about.

24 Then said he unto me, these *are* the places of them that boil, where the ministers of the house shall boil the sacrifice of the people.

theirs but the Lord's, and both prince and people are His lessees" (Taylor, p. 277).

19-24. A description of the kitchens (for the priests in vss. 19-20; cf. 42:1-14, and for the people in vss. 21-24) for cooking the sacrificial meals is discussed in this section. The priests were to be very careful, so as not to bring any of the preparations into the outer court for fear that they may **sanctify the people,** or set them apart for judgment.

C. A New Holy Land. 47:1-48:35.

47:1-12. In this portion of the text Ezekiel saw a river emerging from the Temple, flowing eastward. The NASB has "trickling" (vs. 2), from a word indicating a jar, in the noun form, thus a narrow mouth. It became a deep river (vs. 5, **a river that could not be passed over**). **Trees** were growing along its sides, and it will even sweeten the waters of the Dead Sea so that fish can live in it (vss. 8-10). **En-gedi** (vs. 10) is on the middle of the western shore of the Dead Sea and **En-eglaim** is possibly near modern Ain Feshka, about two miles south of the Khirbet Qumran area, where the Dead Sea Scrolls were found. The transformation of the land will be due to God's presence (cf. 34:26-30; 36:8-15, 30-36; 37:26-28). Some salt marshes will be left unsweetened (vs. 11).

CHAPTER 47

AFTERWARD he brought me again unto the door of the house; and, behold, waters issued out from under the threshold of the house eastward: for the forefront of the house *stood toward* the east, and the waters came down from under from the right side of the house, at the south *side* of the altar.

2 Then brought he me out of the way of the gate northward, and led me about the way without unto the utter gate by the way that looketh eastward; and, behold, there ran out waters on the right side.

3 And when the man that had the line in his hand went forth eastward, he measured a thousand cubits, and he brought me through the waters; the waters *were* to the ancles.

4 Again he measured a thousand, and brought me through the waters; the waters *were* to the knees. Again he measured a thousand, and brought me through; the waters *were* to the loins.

5 Afterward he measured a thousand; *and it was* a river that I could not pass over: for the waters were risen, waters to swim in, a river that could not be passed over.

6 ¶And he said unto me, Son of man, hast thou seen *this?* Then he brought me, and caused me to return to the brink of the river.

7 Now when I had returned, behold, at the bank of the river *were* very many trees on the one side and on the other.

8 Then said he unto me, These waters issue out toward the east country, and go down into the desert, and go into the sea: *which being* brought forth into the sea, the waters shall be healed.

9 And it shall come to pass, *that* every thing that liveth, which moveth, whithersoever the rivers shall come, shall live: and there shall be a very great multitude of fish, because these waters shall come thither; for they shall be healed; and every thing shall live whither the river cometh.

10 And it shall come to pass, *that the* fishers shall stand upon it from Ĕn-gĕdi even unto Ĕn-ĕg′la-im; they shall be a *place* to spread forth nets; their fish shall be according to their kinds, as the fish of the great sea, exceeding many.

11 But the miry places thereof and the marishes thereof shall not be healed; they shall be given to salt.

12 And by the river upon the bank thereof, on this side and on that side, shall grow all trees for meat, whose leaf shall not fade, neither shall the fruit thereof be consumed: it shall bring forth new fruit according to his months, because their waters they issued out of the sanctuary: and the fruit thereof shall be for meat, and the leaf thereof for medicine.

13 ¶Thus saith the Lord GOD: This *shall* be the border, whereby ye shall inherit the land according to the twelve tribes of Israel: Joseph *shall have* two portions.

14 And ye shall inherit it, one as well as another: *concerning* the which I lifted up mine hand to give it unto your fathers: and this land shall fall unto you for inheritance.

15 And this *shall* be the border of the land toward the north side, from the great sea, the way of Hĕth′lŏn, as men go to Zĕ′dăd;

16 Hā′măth, Be-rō′thah, Sĭb′rā-im, which *is* between the border of Damascus and the border of Hā′măth: Hā′-Hau′ran, which *is* by the coast of Hau′ran.

17 And the border from the sea shall be Hā′zar-ē′nan the border of Damascus, and the border of Hā′măth. And *this is* the north side.

18 And the east side ye shall measure from Hau′ran, and from Damascus, and from Gilead, and from the land of Israel by Jordan, from the border unto the east sea. And *this is* the east side.

19 And the south side southward, from Tā′mar even to the waters of strife *in* Kā′desh, the river to the great sea. And *this is* the south side southward.

20 The west side also *shall* be the great sea from the border, till a man come over against Hā′măth. This is the west side.

21 So shall ye divide this land unto you according to the tribes of Israel.

22 And it shall come to pass, *that* ye shall divide it by lot for an inheritance unto you, and to the strangers that sojourn among you, which shall beget children among you: and they shall be unto you as born in the country among the children of Israel; they shall have inheritance with you among the tribes of Israel.

23 And it shall come to pass, *that* in what tribe the stranger sojourneth,

---

13-23. The boundaries of the land are described in this section. One can compare Numbers 34:1-12, where the north to south boundaries span about two hundred eighty miles. Each of the tribes will receive a fair allotment in accordance with God's promises to the patriarchs (vs. 14), except for the tribe of Levi. Levi had no portion (44:28); the Levites were provided for both by the offerings of the people and by the land in the central holy portion to the north of the sanctuary (45:4ff.; 48:13). This is the reason why Joseph was given two portions in the names of his two sons, Ephraim and Manasseh (47:13; 48:4, 5). Thus, the number twelve was retained for the tribes of Israel.

The northern border of Israel's land will extend from the Mediterranean Sea north of Tyre to a point near Damascus (vss. 15-17); the eastern border will be formed by the Jordan River and the Dead Sea (vs. 18); the southern boundary will extend from below the Dead Sea to the **river** (which is the brook of Egypt, vs. 19); with the western border being the Mediterranean. This will be allotted to the Israelites, even though they will apparently control all of the land from the Nile to the Euphrates (cf. Gen 15:18).

there shall ye give *him* his inheritance, saith the Lord God.

CHAPTER 48

NOW these *are* the names of the tribes. From the north end to the coast of the way of Hĕth'lŏn, as one goeth to Hā'-măth, Hā'zar-ē'nan, the border of Da-mascus northward, to the coast of Hā'-măth; for these are his sides east *and* west; *a portion for* Dan.

2 And by the border of Dan, from the east side unto the west side, *a portion for* Asher.

3 And by the border of Asher, from the east side even unto the west side, *a portion for* Năph'ta-lī.

4 And by the border of Năph'ta-lī, from the east side unto the west side, *a portion for* Ma-năs'seh.

5 And by the border of Ma-năs'seh, from the east side unto the west side, *a portion for* Ē'phra-im.

6 And by the border of Ē'phra-im, from the east side even unto the west side, *a portion for* Reuben.

7 And by the border of Reuben, from the east side unto the west side, *a portion for* Judah.

8 And by the border of Judah, from the east side unto the west side, shall be the offering which ye shall offer of five and twenty thousand *reeds in* breadth, and *in* length as one of the *other* parts, from the east side unto the west side: and the sanctuary shall be in the midst of it.

9 The oblation that ye shall offer unto the LORD *shall be* of five and twenty thousand in length, and of ten thousand in breadth.

10 And for them, *even* for the priests, shall be *this* holy oblation; toward the north five and twenty thousand *in length,* and toward the west ten thousand in breadth, and toward the east ten thousand in breadth, and toward the south five and twenty thousand in length: and the sanctuary of the LORD shall be in the midst thereof.

11 *It shall be* for the priests that are sanctified of the sons of Zā'dŏk; which have kept my charge, which went not astray when the children of Israel went astray, as the Levites went astray.

12 And *this* oblation of the land that is offered unto them a thing most holy by the border of the Levites.

13 And over against the border of the priests the Levites *shall have* five and twenty thousand in length, and ten thousand in breadth: all the length *shall be* five and twenty thousand, and the breadth ten thousand.

14 And they shall not sell of it, neither exchange, nor alienate the firstfruits of the land: for *it is* holy unto the LORD.

15 ¶ And the five thousand, that are left in the breadth over against the five and twenty thousand, shall be a profane *place* for the city, for dwelling, and for suburbs: and the city shall be in the midst thereof.

16 And these *shall be* the measures thereof; the north side four thousand and five hundred, and the south side four thousand and five hundred, and on

48:1-7. This section includes the seven northern tribes. North is determined from the Temple area. The tribes are Dan, Asher, Naphtali, Manasseh, Ephraim, Reuben, and Judah. It is interesting to note that the three tribes which are the farthest from the sanctuary are the tribes descended from sons of Jacob's concubines. Dan and Naphtali were born to Rachel's maid Bilhah, and Asher was born to Leah's maid Zilpah (Gen 30:5-13). The fourth son by concubinage is Gad, and, among the southern group of tribes, he is the farthest away from the sanctuary (vs. 27).

Judah is the closest to the sanctuary. This tribe was the inheritor of the messianic promise through the blessing of Jacob (Gen 49:8-12). He superseded Reuben, the first-born, who was in the next closest position on the north side. The other two places are held by the grandsons of Rachel, the children of Joseph.

8-22. This is another description (45:1-8) of the sacred portion of the land which included the **sanctuary** (vs. 8), the priests' portion (vss. 10-12), the Levites' portion (vss. 13-14), the city (vss. 15-20), and the prince's portion (vss. 21-22).

This strip of land was 25,000 cubits wide and reached from the eastern to the western boundaries of the land. It was set apart for sacred use, a holy district in its center (vss. 8, 9, 20).

the east side four thousand and five
hundred, and the west side four thousand and five hundred.

17 And the suburbs of the city shall
be toward the north two hundred and
fifty, and toward the south two
hundred and fifty, and toward the east
two hundred and fifty, and toward the
west two hundred and fifty.

18 And the residue in length over
against the oblation of the holy *portion
shall* be ten thousand eastward, and
ten thousand westward: and it shall
be over against the oblation of the holy
portion; and the increase thereof shall
be for food unto them that serve the
city.

19 And they that serve the city shall
serve it out of all the tribes of Israel.

20 All the oblation *shall* be five and
twenty thousand by five and twenty
thousand: ye shall offer the holy oblation foursquare, with the possession of
the city.

21 And the residue *shall* be for the
prince, on the one side and on the other
of the holy oblation, and of the possession of the city, over against the five
and twenty thousand of the oblation toward the east border, and westward
over against the five and twenty thousand toward the west border, over
against the portions for the prince: and
it shall be the holy oblation; and the
sanctuary of the house *shall* be in the
midst thereof.

22 Moreover from the possession of
the Levites, and from the possession of
the city, *being* in the midst *of that
which* is the prince's, between the border of Judah and the border of Benjamin, shall be for the prince.

23 As for the rest of the tribes, from
the east side unto the west side, Benjamin *shall have a portion.*

24 And by the border of Benjamin,
from the east side unto the west side,
Simeon *shall have a portion.*

25 And by the border of Simeon,
from the east side unto the west side,
Is'sa-char *a portion.*

26 And by the border of Is'sa-char,
from the east side unto the west side,
Zeb'u-lun *a portion.*

27 And by the border of Zeb'u-lun,
from the east side unto the west side,
Gad *a portion.*

28 And by the border of Gad, at the
south side southward, the border shall
be even from Ta'mar *unto* the waters of
strife *in* Ka'desh, *and* to the river toward the great sea.

29 This *is* the land which ye shall divide by lot unto the tribes of Israel for
inheritance, and these are their portions, saith the Lord God.

30 ¶And these are the goings out of
the city on the north side, four thousand and five hundred measures.

31 And the gates of the city *shall* be
after the names of the tribes of Israel:
three gates northward; one gate of
Reuben, one gate of Judah, one gate of
Levi.

32 And at the east side four thousand
and five hundred: and three gates; and

23-29. To the south of the holy portion are the allotted areas
for the remaining five tribes. Benjamin has the privileged position nearest to the sanctuary. He was his father's youngest son
by Rachel. Simeon, Issachar, and Zebulun come next. These
sons were all born to Leah. Then finally comes Gad, the child of
the concubine, Zilpah. "It needs little imagination to realize
that, apart from Judah and Benjamin, which adjoin the holy
portion and which always had the closest geographical interest in
Jerusalem, the other ten tribes are allotted without any regard to
their original position in the land of Israel at the time of the
conquest" (Taylor, p. 284).

30-34. There are twelve gates to the city. There are three
gates on each side, and they are named according to the twelve
tribes. It is interesting to note that **Levi** has a place (vs. 31) in
the list, as does **Joseph** (vs. 32). Joseph replaces Ephraim and
Manasseh, thus keeping the number twelve.

There is an evident arrangement in the listing of the tribes.
On the north side, the side facing the sanctuary, the gates are
named after Levi the founder of the priesthood, Judah the
Davidic ancestor, and Reuben the first-born. On the south side
are Simeon, Issachar, and Zebulun. These correspond with their

one gate of Joseph, one gate of Benjamin, one gate of Dan.

33 And at the south side four thousand and five hundred measures: and three gates; one gate of Simeon, one gate of is'sa-char, one gate of Zeb'ulun.

34 At the west side four thousand and five hundred, *with* their three gates; one gate of Gad, one gate of Asher, one gate of Naph'ta-li.

35 *It was* round about eighteen thousand *measures:* and the name of the city from *that day shall be,* The LORD *is* there.

geographical placement to the south. On the west are three concubine tribes represented, Gad, Asher, and Naphtali (vs. 34). "Perhaps the least consistent trio are those on the east side, where Joseph and Benjamin, the two children of Rachel, are linked with Dan, a child of Rachel's maid" (Taylor, p. 284).

35. The Jerusalem of the future will receive a new name symbolizing the permanence of the divine presence in the new city. In a vision Ezekiel saw the departure of God's glory from the former Temple and city (ch. 10ff.); he also beheld the return to the new Temple (ch. 43). He now concludes with the assurance that the divine glory will never again depart from the Temple and the new Jerusalem: **The LORD is there.**

BIBLIOGRAPHY

Alexander, Ralph. *Ezekiel.* Chicago: Moody Press, 1976.

Beasley-Murray, G. R. Ezekiel. In *The New Bible Commentary.* Ed. by D. Guthrie and J. A. Motyer. 3rd edition, revised. Grand Rapids: Eerdmans, 1970.

Calvin, John. *Commentaries on the First Twenty Chapters of the Book of the Prophet Ezekiel.* 2 vols. Grand Rapids: Eerdmans, reprinted, 1978.

Davidson, A. B. *The Book of the Prophet Ezekiel.* Cambridge: University Press, 1892.

Ellison, H. L. *Ezekiel: The Man and His Message.* London: Paternoster Press, 1956.

Erdman, Charles R. *The Book of Ezekiel: An Exposition.* Westwood, N.J.: Revell, 1956.

*Fairbain, Patrick. *An Exposition of Ezekiel.* Grand Rapids: Zondervan, n.d.

Fausset, A. R., David Brown, and Robert Jameison. Ezekiel. In *A Commentary Critical, Experimental and Practical on the Old and New Testaments.* Volume IV. Grand Rapids: Eerdmans, reprinted, 1945.

*Feinberg, Charles Lee. *The Prophecy of Ezekiel.* Chicago: Moody Press, 1969.

Fisch, S. *Ezekiel.* New York: The Soncino Press, 1950.

Gaebelein, A. C. *The Prophet Ezekiel: An Analytical Exposition.* New York: Our Hope, 1918.

Grant, F. W. Ezekiel. In *The Numerical Bible.* Neptune, N.J.: Loizeaux, 1903.

Henderson, E. *The Book of the Prophet Ezekiel.* London: Hamilton, Adams, 1855.

Ironside, Harry A. *Expository Notes on Ezekiel, the Prophet.* Neptune, N.J.: Loizeaux, 1959.

*Keil, Carl F. *Biblical Commentary on Ezekiel.* 2 vols. Grand Rapids: Eerdmans, n.d.

Kelly, William. *Notes on Ezekiel.* London: Moorish, 1876.

May, H. G. Ezekiel. In *The Interpreter's Bible.* Vol. VI. Nashville: Abingdon, 1956.

*Pearson, Anton T. Ezekiel. In *The Wycliffe Bible Commentary.* Ed. by Charles Pfeiffer and R. K. Harrison. Chicago: Moody Press, 1962.

Plumptre, E. H. Ezekiel. In *The Pulpit Commentary.* Ed. by Spence and Exell. Grand Rapids: Eerdmans, reprinted, 1950.

*Ryrie, Charles Caldwell. Ezekiel. In *The Ryrie Study Bible.* Chicago: Moody Press, 1976, 1978.

Schröder, F. W. J. Ezekiel. In *Lange's Commentary on the Holy Scriptures.* Grand Rapids: Zondervan, n.d.

*Taylor, John B. *Ezekiel: An Introduction and Commentary.* Downers Grove, Ill.: InterVarsity Press, 1969.

DANIEL

INTRODUCTION

Authorship. The canonical book of Daniel was written in the sixth century B.C. by Daniel, a Palestinian Jew taken captive by Nebuchadnezzar's army about 605 B.C. After his seizure as a hostage, Daniel was transported to Babylon where as a young man he became highly involved in the government of Nebuchadnezzar's kingdom (2:48). Daniel's civil service continued into the Persian period as well (1:21; 5:30-6:3), during which time he wrote the book that bears his name. Though Daniel refers to himself in the third person in the narrative of chapters 1, 2, 5, and 6, he uses the first person consistently in his visions of chapters 7-10. In 12:4 he is told to "shut up the words, and seal the book." The evidence of the book itself presents no other claim than that Daniel was God's instrument in the writing of this great book, and this opinion was universally accepted by both Jew and Christian alike. In confirmation of this, our Lord Jesus Christ clearly referred to 11:31 and 12:11 as "spoken of by Daniel the prophet" (Mt 24:15; Mk 13:14); and the unity of the book has been vigorously argued even by liberal scholars (i.e., H. H. Rowley, "The Unity of Daniel" in *The Servant of The Lord and Other Essays on the Old Testament*, 1951).

Notwithstanding, there are some critics who seek to deny Daniel's sixth-century B.C. authorship of this book. They suppose a number of errors or unexplainable qualities in Daniel's writing such as: (1) historical inaccuracies; (2) the use of a late form of Aramaic and the presence of three Greek words of musical instruments; and (3) a theology too advanced for its time in regard to the doctrine of angels, resurrection, final judgment, and the Messiah. In addition, they usually point out that Daniel: (1) concerns apocalyptic or vision literature in large measure; (2) is found in the third category of the Jewish canon, the Writings, rather than in the second—that of the Prophets; and (3) is not frequently alluded to by early external evidence. Various of these arguments have been rehearsed by such men as James A. Montgomery (*International Critical Commentary*, 1927), Robert H. Pfeiffer (*Introduction to the Old Testament*, 1951), and Norman W. Porteous (1965) in an attempt to discredit the authenticity of Daniel. Involved in this process is a redating of Daniel's writing to about 165 B.C., instead of the biblically ascertainable date of around 530 B.C. In this way Daniel's critics hope to avoid the conclusion that Daniel wrote detailed predictive prophecy. However, God is quite capable of predicting the future, as this commentary on Daniel readily points out.

These and other arguments against Daniel's authorship have been well answered time and again by many notable Old Testament scholars. See Gleason Archer, *A Survey of Old Testament Introduction* (revised, 1974); R. K. Harrison, *Introduction to the O.T.* (1964); John F. Walvoord, *Daniel* (1971); and from an earlier day, Robert D. Wilson, *Studies in the Book of Daniel* (1917), and Charles Boutflower, *In and Around the Book of Daniel* (1923).

Date and Place of Writing. As may be understood from what is stated above, the date and place of the writing of Daniel is largely connected with the arguments for or against Danielic authorship. Several ideas have been maintained. (1) Conservative scholars rightly hold that this prophecy was written by the historical Daniel who lived in Babylon in the sixth century B.C. The book abounds with the color of the Neo-Babylonian and Persian empires and was most likely composed around 530 B.C. in Babylonia. (2) Liberal critics have erroneously argued that Daniel was written by some unknown person living in Palestine around 165 B.C., implying that the book does not contain predictive prophecy. This theory is now quite difficult to maintain, due to the existence of a Daniel manuscript found in Qumran Cave 1 which many paleographic experts believe to have been copied before Maccabean days. These scholars teach that the Jews accepted this false book into their sacred canon, unaware of its pseudepigraphic character, and that Jesus either accommodated himself to their mistaken ideas or else that He was ignorant of the truth Himself (Mt 24:15). No true believer should ever countenance such heresy.

Characteristics. Because much of the contents deals with dreams and visions (chs. 2; 4; 7; 8; 10), Daniel comes under the category of vision or apocalyptic literature. This accounts for the abundance of symbolism and other imagery. Yet, on the other hand, much of Daniel is a straightforward historical narrative (chs. 1; much of 2; 3; 5; 6; 9); and the rest is predictive prophecy brought to Daniel by an angel (chs. 11-12). Though scholars sometimes differ over precise details, there are enough indications given in the visions and predictions of Daniel to chart the basic movements of future history as it concerns: (1) Nebuchadnezzar's personal history (ch. 4); (2) the fall of Babylon (ch. 5); (3) a succession of four world empires and the coming kingdom of God (chs. 2; 7); (4) the movements of the Seleucids and the Ptolemies as they would affect Israel's future (ch. 11); and (5) the coming of Messiah the Prince (ch. 9).

Purpose. Israel's failure to keep their covenant with Jehovah resulted in numerous warnings, as well as judgments from God's hand, as predicted in Leviticus 26 and Deuteronomy 28. Apt examples include the difficulties during the apostasy in the period of the Judges, the conquest of the northern capital under Shalmaneser V and Sargon II in 722/21 B.C., and the three deportations of Judah under Nebuchadnezzar beginning in 605 B.C. These latter captives are to know that God will keep His promises to Abraham and David—that the Messiah would come (9:24-27), that His kingdom would one day fill the entire earth (2:35, 44), and that the saints would rule and reign with Messiah (7:22, 27). Thus, Daniel was to encourage the Israelites living in Babylon in the sixth century B.C., as well as those of generations to come.

In addition, Daniel recorded how God made Himself respected by foreign rulers who would tend to see Jehovah as too weak to deliver His people. God demonstrated His ability to deliver out of the fiery furnace (ch. 3) and the den of lions (ch. 6). These foreign rulers then knew the absolute power of Jehovah (3:29; 6:26-27) but must also have understood God's judgment upon His people for their centuries of disobedience (cf. 9:3-19).

OUTLINE

I. The Historical Portion of Daniel. 1:1-6:28.
   A. Daniel Serves Under Nebuchadnezzar. 1:1-4:37.
      1. Daniel's removal to Babylon by Nebuchadnezzar. 1:1-21.
         a. The subjugation of Jerusalem by Nebuchadnezzar. 1:1-2.
         b. The test of Daniel's character. 1:3-7.
         c. The determination of Daniel to be true to his God. 1:8-13.
         d. The faithfulness of God to His obedient children. 1:14-21.
      2. Daniel interprets Nebuchadnezzar's image dream. 2:1-49.
         a. The astrologers' failure to tell the dream. 2:1-13.
         b. Daniel's prayer for wisdom answered. 2:14-23.
         c. Daniel brought before Nebuchadnezzar. 2:24-30.
         d. Daniel discloses the contents of the dream. 2:31-35.
         e. Daniel interprets the dream. 2:36-45.
         f. Daniel's promotion. 2:46-49.
      3. Nebuchadnezzar's fiery furnace. 3:1-30.
         a. The command to bow to the golden image. 3:1-7.
         b. The refusal of the three Hebrews to bow. 3:8-12.
         c. The three Hebrews fear only God. 3:13-18.
         d. The three Hebrews cast into the furnace, but delivered by God. 3:19-25.
         e. Nebuchadnezzar's astonishment and proclamation. 3:26-30.
      4. Daniel interprets Nebuchadnezzar's tree dream. 4:1-37.
         a. Nebuchadnezzar's proclamation of God's majesty. 4:1-3.
         b. Nebuchadnezzar recounts his tree dream. 4:4-18.
         c. Daniel interprets the dream and warns the king. 4:19-27.
         d. The fulfillment of the dream. 4:28-33.
         e. Nebuchadnezzar returns to sanity and praises God. 4:34-37.
   B. Daniel Serves Under Belshazzar. 5:1-31.
      1. Belshazzar's drunken feast. 5:1-4.
      2. The handwriting on the wall. 5:5-9.
      3. Daniel called in to help. 5:10-16.
      4. Daniel's sermon to Belshazzar. 5:17-24.
      5. Daniel's interpretation of the writing. 5:25-28.
      6. Medo-Persia conquers decadent Babylon. 5:29-31.
   C. Daniel Serves Under Darius the Mede. 6:1-28.
      1. Daniel's continued government service. 6:1-3.
      2. The conspiracy against Daniel. 6:4-9.
      3. Daniel's continued devotion to God. 6:10.
      4. Daniel accused before Darius. 6:11-15.
      5. Daniel preserved in the den of lions. 6:16-23.
      6. Daniel's accusers punished and his God praised. 6:24-28.

II. The Prophetic Portion of Daniel. 7:1-12:13.
   A. Daniel's Vision of the Four Beasts. 7:1-28.
      1. The vision received by Daniel. 7:1-14.
      2. The vision interpreted for Daniel. 7:15-28.
   B. Daniel's Vision of the Ram and the He Goat. 8:1-27.
      1. The vision received by Daniel. 8:1-14.
      2. The vision interpreted to Daniel by Gabriel. 8:15-27.
   C. Daniel's Supplication and the Seventy Weeks Prophecy. 9:1-27.
      1. Daniel repents for himself and his people. 9:1-19.
      2. God's sending of Gabriel to answer Daniel's prayer. 9:20-23.
      3. The disclosure of the Seventy Weeks prophecy. 9:24-27.
   D. Daniel's Vision of the Heavenly Messenger. 10:1-21.
   E. The Prophecy of Israel's Future to the Maccabees and Beyond. 11:1-45.
      1. Syrian and Egyptian relations foretold down to 165 B.C. 11:1-20.
      2. The career of Antiochus Epiphanes foretold. 11:21-35.
      3. The career of Antichrist foretold. 11:36-45.
   F. Daniel's Final Revelation. 12:1-13.
      1. The Great Tribulation and the resurrections. 12:1-3.
      2. Daniel told to close up the book and wait. 12:4-13.

COMMENTARY

I. THE HISTORICAL PORTION OF DANIEL, 1:1-6:28.

The book of Daniel is most commonly divided into two parts nearly equal in length—the historical and the prophetical. The historical portion begins with the historical and the prophetical. Nebuchadnezzar and his subsequent deportation to Babylon; and it ends with Daniel being freed after spending a night in a den of lions some seventy years later. The prophetical portion covers visions and prophecies received by Daniel during the years of his historical sojourn in Babylon and Persia.

A. Daniel Serves Under Nebuchadnezzar, 1:1-4:37.

The first four chapters of Daniel relate events that occurred during the reign of King Nebuchadnezzar. This king had a long and glorious reign. He was a military genius, a great builder, and a shrewd, powerful, and proud absolute monarch.

1. Daniel's removal to Babylon by Nebuchadnezzar, 1:1-21.

a. The subjugation of Jerusalem by Nebuchadnezzar, 1:1-2.

1:1. In the third year of the reign of Jehoiakim king of Judah. Jehoiakim was the eldest son of King Josiah and began ruling after his younger brother Jehoahaz had been king for a three month period. Some critics question the accuracy of Daniel's indicated third year of Jehoiakim, pointing to the apparent conflict with Jeremiah's statements in Jeremiah 25:1 and 46:2. The former says Jehoiakim's "fourth year" was the first year of Nebuchadnezzar's reign, and the latter records Nebuchadnezzar's battle at Carchemish, just prior to coming into Israel, also as being "in the fourth year" of Jehoiakim's reign. The answer lies in the fact that the Hebrew calendar reckoned time in two ways, beginning either with Nisan in April for the religious year, or with Tishri in October for the civil year. Jeremiah counts it as the fourth year since the capture occurred in the summer after passing Nisan. Daniel apparently reckons it the third year, from the standpoint that Tishri had not yet arrived. **Nebuchadnezzar king of Babylon** is called king by Daniel even though he did not become king for several more months. It is like saying King David killed Goliath, even though he was not king at that time. Nebuchadnezzar had just defeated the Assyrians and their allies, the Egyptians, at the Battle of Carchemish in 605 B.C. and was beginning to claim the territories formerly under their control. The Neo-Babylonian Empire was just beginning.

2. And the Lord gave Jehoiakim king of Judah into his hand. Nebuchadnezzar may have thought he was solely responsible for his conquest (Hab 1:11); but, in reality, God's providential dealings with His wayward children, the Jews, was simply being carried out by this great leader. God had already promised judgment to come for Judah through Huldah the prophetess (II Chr 34:22-28) and many others. Micah remarkably predicted Judah's captivity in Babylon while Babylon was still a small power (Mic 4:10) over one hundred years before the event took place. Jeremiah had also predicted this calamity (Jer 25:11), as had his contemporary, Habakkuk (Hab 1:5-11). **Part of the vessels of the house of God,** Solomon's temple, were also seized as prizes and carried away to Babylon. Nearly seventy years later these vessels were desecrated by Belshazzar at his drunken feast, and God brought his kingdom to a close. Some one hundred years earlier Isaiah had predicted that these vessels would be taken away by the king of Babylon (Isa 39:1-8).

b. The test of Daniel's character, 1:3-7.

3-4. Nebuchadnezzar brought captives from many conquered

IN the third year of the reign of Je-hoi'a-kĭm king of Judah came Nĕb-u-chad-nĕz'zar king of Babylon unto Jerusalem, and besieged it.

2 And the Lord gave Je-hoi'a-kĭm king of Judah into his hand, with part of the vessels of the house of God: which he carried into the land of Shĭ'när to the house of his god; and he brought the vessels into the treasure house of his god.

3 ¶And the king spake unto Ăsh'pe-

lands to train them for service in his government. He was accustomed to selecting the best for such training, as the text indicates. These young men were the best sons of the Hebrew nation. They would be taught the voluminous learning of the Chaldeans, as well as their language. **To stand in the king's palace** has to do with service, not just an easy life at court.

5. Three years were required to teach these lads a new language and other necessary skills. During this time they were to eat from the king's special menu of dainties and wine.

6-7. Daniel, Hananiah, Mishael, and Azariah are now introduced into the narrative as being among the captives from Judah. Their names carried meaning. Daniel meant God is judge, or my judge. Hananiah's name could be translated, Jehovah is gracious. Mishael's name, as Daniel's, contained the shortened form for God (el) and meant who is like God. Azariah's name asserted that Jehovah helps. These godly names were changed into compounds of the names of the Babylonian gods.

c. The determination of Daniel to be true to his God. 1:8-13.

8. But Daniel purposed in his heart that he would not defile himself. Daniel's resolve was also the resolve of his three friends (cf. vss. 10-17). Their determination was probably based on the dietary regulations of Leviticus 11, as well as the possibility that their food may have been dedicated to the gods of the Babylonians, the eating of which would seem defiling to them. The rich foods from the king's table also may not have been as nourishing as the menu proposed by Daniel. He desired to take care of his body. **Therefore he requested.** Daniel no doubt used tact and a pleasing manner in making his request. He did not demand something foolhardily but was a gentleman, even as we should be in this work-a-day world when our job may impose a violation of our conscience upon us.

9. God did not fail to do His part, having made the prince of the eunuchs greatly respect and admire Daniel. Compare this with the requirement that a pastor must have ". . . a good report of them which are without . . ." (I Tim 3:7).

10-11. Though their resolve was good, it could not be fulfilled without some difficulty. It is often easier to make a vow than to keep it. Nevertheless, these four lads were determined to serve God or die with clear consciences, as is apparent from chapter three. The fear of the **Melzar**, the steward in charge of Daniel and his friends, points to the absolute power of the monarch in that kingdom.

12-13. Daniel proposed a trial period of **ten days** with only **pulse to eat,** that is, vegetables, and **water to drink.** This was certainly a skimpy, but a wholesome, diet.

d. The faithfulness of God to His obedient children. 1:14-21.

14-15. During those initial ten days, Daniel and his three friends ate nutritious foods, while their comrades in slavery ate all they could of the king's dainties and wine. Naturally, God helped their cause; and the test proved successful.

16-17. The rest of their years of training passed swiftly.

---

nǎz the master of his eunuchs, that he should bring *certain* of the children of Israel, and of the king's seed, and of the princes;

4 Children in whom *was* no blemish, but well favoured, and skilful in all wisdom, and cunning in knowledge, and understanding science, and such as *had* ability in them to stand in the king's palace, and whom they might teach the learning and the tongue of the Chǎl-dē´ans.

5 And the king appointed them a daily provision of the king's meat, and of the wine which he drank: so nourishing them three years, that at the end thereof they might stand before the king.

6 Now among these were of the children of Judah, Daniel, Hǎn-a-nī´ah, Mǐsh´a-el, and Ǎz-a-rī´ah:

7 Unto whom the prince of the eunuchs gave names; for he gave unto Daniel *the name of* Bĕl-te-shǎz´zar; and to Hǎn-a-nī´ah, of Shā´drǎch; and to Mǐsh´a-el, of Mē´shǎch; and to Ǎz-a-rī´ah, of Ā-bĕd´-ne-gō.

8 ¶But Daniel purposed in his heart that he would not defile himself with the portion of the king's meat, nor with the wine which he drank: therefore he requested of the prince of the eunuchs that he might not defile himself.

9 Now God had brought Daniel into favour and tender love with the prince of the eunuchs.

10 And the prince of the eunuchs said unto Daniel, I fear my lord the king, who hath appointed your meat and your drink: for why should he see your faces worse liking than the children which *are* of your sort? then shall ye make *me* endanger my head to the king.

11 Then said Daniel to Mĕl´zär, whom the prince of the eunuchs had set over Daniel, Hǎn-a-nī´ah, Mǐsh´a-el, and Ǎz-a-rī´ah,

12 Prove thy servants, I beseech thee, ten days; and let them give us pulse to eat, and water to drink.

13 Then let our countenances be looked upon before thee, and the countenance of the children that eat of the portion of the king's meat: and as thou seest, deal with thy servants.

14 So he consented to them in this matter, and proved them ten days.

15 And at the end of ten days their countenances appeared fairer and fatter in flesh than all the children which did eat the portion of the king's meat.

16 Thus Mĕl´zär took away the portion of their meat, and the wine that

1630

they should drink; and gave them pulse.

17 ¶As for these four children, God gave them knowledge and skill in all learning and wisdom: and Daniel had understanding in all visions and dreams.

18 Now at the end of the days that the king had said he should bring them in, then the prince of the eunuchs brought them in before Nĕb-u-chad-nĕz'zar.

19 And the king communed with them; and among them all was found none like Daniel, Hăn-a-nī'ah, Mish'a-el, and Ăz-a-rī'ah: therefore stood they before the king.

20 And in all matters of wisdom and understanding, that the king enquired of them, he found them ten times better than all the magicians and astrologers that were in all his realm.

21 And Daniel continued even unto the first year of king Cyrus.

CHAPTER 2

AND in the second year of the reign of Nĕb-u-chad-nĕz'zar Nĕb-u-chad-nĕz'zar dreamed dreams, wherewith his spirit was troubled, and his sleep brake from him.

2 Then the king commanded to call the magicians, and the astrologers, and the sorcerers, and the Chăl-dē'ăns, for to shew the king his dreams. So they came and stood before the king.

3 And the king said unto them, I have dreamed a dream, and my spirit was troubled to know the dream.

4 Then spake the Chăl-dē'ăns to the king in Sÿr'ĭ-ăck, O king, live for ever: tell thy servants the dream, and we will shew the interpretation.

5 The king answered and said to the Chăl-dē'ăns, The thing is gone from me: if ye will not make known unto me the dream, with the interpretation thereof, ye shall be cut in pieces, and your houses shall be made a dunghill.

6 But if ye shew the dream, and the interpretation thereof, ye shall receive of me gifts and rewards and great

These four stood out in every aspect of knowledge and in the application of that knowledge. They also must have been well known for their obvious separation in eating habits. Daniel had **understanding in all visions and dreams.** Daniel was specially chosen of God to be entrusted with these gifts. He would use them properly and give God all the glory.

18-20. Among them all was found none like Daniel, Hananiah, Mishael, and Azariah. Nebuchadnezzar was the final judge of the accomplishments of these young men. Even though God had blessed them and had given them great abilities, they still had to study. Their reward was to be used of God in key governmental positions. God can also use true believers in government today to bring righteousness, decency, and justice before a king, or to influence legislation in that direction. **He found them ten times better.** This is a hyperbole, or exaggeration for effect.

21. Daniel continued. At this point Daniel gives his readers a glimpse into the future. Approximately seventy years would pass before Babylon was taken over by the Persian **king Cyrus.**

2. *Daniel interprets Nebuchadnezzar's image dream. 2:1-49.*

The Bible records numerous incidents where God imparted revelations to men by means of dreams and/or visions (Gen 20:6-7; 28:12-15; 37:5-11; 41:1-7; Mt 1:20; 2:12, 19). Sometimes the intent of the dream was immediately apparent, as with those of Joseph in Genesis 37:5-11; but on other occasions the recipient might be uncertain as to its meaning. This occurred with Pharaoh (Gen 41:8), and also with Nebuchadnezzar in this instance. The usual custom was to employ men who would interpret the dreams; but if a dream was sent from God, the true meaning would also have to come from Him.

a. *The astrologers' failure to tell the dream. 2:1-13.*

2:1. In the second year of the reign of Nebuchadnezzar. This probably indicates a time prior to the close of the three-year preparation period of Daniel and his friends. They were apparently still in training since they were not summoned with the other wise men in verse 2 and seemed to know nothing of the entire situation in verses 14-15.

2-3. The magicians, and the astrologers, and the sorcerers, and the Chaldeans were different groups within the general category of wise men. They were men capable of giving wise counsel and could supposedly contact supernatural powers.

4. In Syriac. The Syriac, or Aramaic, language was at that time the *lingua franca*, the most common tongue used for trading purposes throughout the world. From verse 4 until 7:28 Daniel wrote in this language rather than in Hebrew. This section basically concerns the Gentiles. **Tell thy servants the dream.** The wise men wanted to hear the dream so that they could then devise an interpretation to suit it.

5. But Nebuchadnezzar perhaps sensed that on previous occasions the wise men had deceived him with novel explanations, so he refused to tell them the dream and demanded instead that they tell him the dream so he could be sure they had the correct interpretation. **The thing is gone from me** could have referred to the dream, meaning he had forgotten it; but more likely, it referred to the edict that they produce the dream or else be killed.

6-11. The exchange that followed demonstrated the basic mistrust Nebuchadnezzar had for these wise men, as well as the ability of the wise men to use logic to their advantage.

The Kingdom of Babylon

EGYPT

ARABIA

Tema

Dumah

Brook of Egypt

Elath

Lower Sea

Ur

Larsa

Susa

Nippur

ELAM

Borsippa

Babylon

Sippar

EMPIRE

BABYLONIAN

Euphrates River

Tadmor

(Dura-Europos)

Tigris River

Hamath

Asshur

Arrapkha

Calah

ASSYRIA

Nineveh

Haran

Carchemish

Achmetha

MEDIAN

EMPIRE

Rabbath-bene-ammon

Jerusalem

Ashdod

Samaria

Damascus

Tyre

Gebal

Arvad

Great Sea

Tarsus

0   50   100 miles
0   50 100 150 Km

honour: therefore shew me the dream, and the interpretation thereof.

7 They answered again and said, Let the king tell his servants the dream, and we will shew the interpretation of it.

8 The king answered and said, I know of certainty that ye would gain the time, because ye see the thing is gone from me.

9 But if ye will not make known unto me the dream, *there is but* one decree for you: for ye have prepared lying and corrupt words to speak before me, till the time be changed: therefore tell me the dream, and I shall know that ye can shew me the interpretation thereof.

10 ¶The Chăl-dē'ans answered before the king, and said, There is not a man upon the earth that can shew the king's matter: therefore *there is* no king, lord, nor ruler, *that* asked such things at any magician, or astrologer, or Chăl-dē'an.

11 And *it is* a rare thing that the king requireth, and there is none other that can shew it before the king, except the gods, whose dwelling is not with flesh.

12 For this cause the king was angry and very furious, and commanded to destroy all the wise *men* of Babylon.

13 And the decree went forth that the wise *men* should be slain; and they sought Daniel and his fellows to be slain.

14 ¶Then Daniel answered with counsel and wisdom to A'rĭ-ŏch the captain of the king's guard, which was gone forth to slay the wise *men* of Babylon:

15 He answered and said to A'rĭ-ŏch the king's captain, Why *is* the decree *so* hasty from the king? Then A'rĭ-ŏch made the thing known to Daniel.

16 Then Daniel went in, and desired of the king that he would give him time, and that he would shew the king the interpretation.

17 Then Daniel went to his house, and made the thing known to Hăn-a-nī'ah, Mĭsh'a-el, and Ăz-a-rī'ah, his companions:

18 That they would desire mercies of the God of heaven concerning this secret; that Daniel and his fellows should not perish with the rest of the wise *men* of Babylon.

19 ¶Then was the secret revealed unto Daniel in a night vision. Then Daniel blessed the God of heaven.

20 Daniel answered and said, Blessed be the name of God for ever and ever: for wisdom and might are his:

21 And he changeth the times and the seasons: he removeth kings, and setteth up kings: he giveth wisdom unto the wise, and knowledge to them that know understanding:

22 He revealeth the deep and secret things: he knoweth what *is* in the darkness, and the light dwelleth with him.

23 I thank thee, and praise thee, O thou God of my fathers, who hast given me wisdom and might, and hast made

12-13. Nevertheless, the king had his way; and **the decree went forth that the wise men should be slain.** Sovereigns of ancient days were sometimes ruthless men who might easily abuse the powers God granted them in government (4:32b).

b. *Daniel's prayer for wisdom answered. 2:14-23.*

14-15. When they came to slay Daniel, he acted with calm courage and perfect assurance that God would meet his need of the hour. God's providential workings may be seen in Daniel's speech, the considerate reactions of Arioch, and Daniel's opportunity for an audience with the king.

16. Daniel asked for time (we are not told how much) and promised **That he would show the king the interpretation,** which of course would be connected to the dream. Daniel promised all this by faith! He knew that only God could give him what others could not produce.

17-18. That night Daniel and his three friends spent some time in prayer, and then apparently they went to bed and fell asleep still with no answer to give the king. What faith they must have had to be able to sleep calmly that night!

19. God's revelation came to Daniel **in a night vision,** proving that he had gone to sleep. Daniel immediately thanked the Lord for answering his prayer. As Daniel, we must remember to pray as the first resort, not the last, and then not forget to thank God when He graciously answers our requests.

20-23. Daniel's prayer is instructive. He first **Blessed** God for who He was. He recounted some of God's attributes and activities among men (vss. 20-22) before specifically mentioning his own thanksgiving (vs. 23). Godly prayer should include both adoration and asking. We must not be so hurried or formalistic as to omit either. God **removeth kings, and setteth up kings.** It is good to remember that God is always in control. Daniel fully realized this and, hence, was not overly-concerned about the seemingly tragic situation in which he found himself.

pletely obliterate all man-operated kingdoms and divinely and literally fulfill the Old Testament prophecies about the kingdom, even as the Jews anticipated in Christ's day (Mt 19:28; Lk 19:11; Acts 1:6-7).

f. Daniel's promotion. 2:46-49.

46 Then the king Něb-u-chad-něz'-zar fell upon his face, and worshipped Daniel, and commanded that they should offer an oblation and sweet odours unto him.

47 The king answered unto Daniel, and said, Of a truth *it is*, that your God *is* a God of gods, and a Lord of kings, and a revealer of secrets, seeing thou couldest reveal this secret.

48 Then the king made Daniel a great man, and gave him many great gifts, and made him ruler over the whole province of Babylon, and chief of the governors over all the wise *men* of Babylon.

49 Then Daniel requested of the king, and he set Shā'drăch, Mē'shăch, and A-běd'-ne-gö, over the affairs of the province of Babylon: but Daniel *sat* in the gate of the king.

CHAPTER 3

NĚB-U-CHAD-NĚZ'ZAR the king made an image of gold, whose height *was* threescore cubits, *and* the breadth thereof six cubits: he set it up in the plain of Dū'ra, in the province of Babylon.

2 Then Něb-u-chad-něz'zar the king sent to gather together the princes, the governors, and the captains, the judges, the treasurers, the counsellors, the sheriffs, and all the rulers of the provinces, to come to the dedication of the image which Něb-u-chad-něz'zar the king had set up.

3 Then the princes, the governors, and captains, the judges, the treasurers, the counsellors, the sheriffs, and all the rulers of the provinces, were gathered together unto the dedication of the image that Něb-u-chad-něz'zar the king had set up; and they stood before the image that Něb-u-chad-něz'zar had set up.

4 Then an herald cried aloud, To you it is commanded, O people, nations, and languages,

5 *That* at what time ye hear the sound of the cornet, flute, harp, sackbut, psaltery, dulcimer, and all kinds of musick, ye fall down and worship the golden image that Něb-u-chad-něz'zar the king hath set up:

46 Nebuchadnezzar's obeisance before Daniel might seem an unusual action for so great a king, but he was deeply moved by the certain revelation of the future he had just been accorded.

47 Nebuchadnezzar realized the supremacy of Daniel's God, but apparently this was not a salvation experience. It is one thing to know all about God, but it is quite another thing to actually know God, whom to know is life eternal (Jn 17:3). See, however, what may have been his salvation testimony recorded in chapter four, especially verse 37.

48 Daniel obtained two valuable appointments from Nebuchadnezzar. First, he was made **ruler over the whole province of Babylon.** But as well, he was elevated to be chief of the wise men. This gave him great authority and ability to help his people when they came as captives to Babylon later on—both from an administrative and an advisory perspective. As chief wise man, Daniel did not have to practice magic or sorcery; for he had a method far superior to any currently used in Babylon—he knew the Lord.

49 Daniel remembered his friends in his promotion and had them assigned as aides to help administer the province of Babylon. Daniel himself **sat in the gate,** indicating a strategic position of honor as a chief counselor who was near the king at all times.

3. Nebuchadnezzar's fiery furnace. 3:1-30.

a. The command to bow to the golden image. 3:1-7.

3:1. Perhaps, as a result of his dream, Nebuchadnezzar constructed a large statue approximately ninety feet tall. This imposing structure, in the figure of a man and probably made of wood, was overlaid with gold and could undoubtedly be seen for miles due to the flat nature of the area just south of Babylon.

2-3. The king called his administrators together to the dedication of the great image. They apparently came from every area of the realm and represented practically his total officialdom.

4-5. Some who claim that Daniel is a second-century forgery argue that their case is proven by the presence of three words of Greek origin in verse 5. This is because the Greek language was not widely spread and used until the conquests of Alexander the Great (c. 325 B.C.). Critics claim that a sixth-century Daniel could not have used Greek words. But the three Greek words are the names of musical instruments: (1) the **harp** (Aram *qayterôs*); (2) the **psaltery** (Aram *pesantērîn*); and (3) **dulcimer** (Aram *sûmepôneyah*). Trade and various cultural exchanges and military excursions could easily account for the passing of these names of Greek instruments into Babylonian use, and thus their Greek names also into the Aramaic language. Similar occur-

6 And whoso falleth not down and worshippeth shall the same hour be cast into the midst of a burning fiery furnace.

7 Therefore at that time, when all the people heard the sound of the cornet, flute, harp, sackbut, psaltery, and all kinds of musick, all the people, the nations, and the languages, fell down and worshipped the golden image that Něb-u-chad-něz'zar the king had set up.

8 ¶Wherefore at that time certain Chǎl-dē'anś came near, and accused the Jews.

9 They spake and said to the king Něb-u-chad-něz'zar, O king, live for ever.

10 Thou, O king, hast made a decree, that every man that shall hear the sound of the cornet, flute, harp, sackbut, psaltery, and dulcimer, and all kinds of musick, shall fall down and worship the golden image:

11 And whoso falleth not down and worshippeth, that he should be cast into the midst of a burning fiery furnace.

12 There are certain Jews whom thou hast set over the affairs of the province of Babylon, Shǎ'drǎch, Mē'shǎch, and A-běd'-ne-gŏ; these men, O king, have not regarded thee: they serve not thy gods, nor worship the golden image which thou hast set up.

13 ¶Then Něb-u-chad-něz'zar in his rage and fury commanded to bring Shǎ'drǎch, Mē'shǎch, and A-běd'-ne-gŏ. Then they brought these men before the king.

14 Něb-u-chad-něz'zar spake and said unto them, Is it true, O Shǎ'drǎch, Mē'shǎch, and A-běd'-ne-gŏ, do not ye serve my gods, nor worship the golden image which I have set up?

15 Now if ye be ready that at what time ye hear the sound of the cornet, flute, harp, sackbut, psaltery, and dulcimer, and all kinds of musick, ye fall down and worship the image which I have made; well: but if ye worship not, ye shall be cast the same hour into the midst of a burning fiery furnace; and who is that God that shall deliver you out of my hands?

16 Shǎ'drǎch, Mē'shǎch, and A-běd'-ne-gŏ, answered and said to the king, O Něb-u-chad-něz'zar, we are not careful to answer thee in this matter.

17 If it be so, our God whom we serve is able to deliver us from the burning fiery furnace, and he will deliver us out of thine hand, O king.

18 But if not, be it known unto thee, O king, that we will not serve thy gods, nor worship the golden image which thou hast set up.

rences in English are the uses of Italian words such as piano and violin, and the Hawaiian ukulele, a small guitar. If Daniel was really written around 165 B.C. the question is really why there are not many more Greek words found in the text. This actually becomes strong evidence that Daniel was written in the sixth century B.C., just as it claims. See also Boutflower, *In and Around the Book of Daniel*, pp. 246-56 for a history of early Greek influence in Persian culture.

6-7. The punishment for failure to bow and worship before the great image (in violation of God's second commandment, Ex 20:4-5) was to be cast into a **burning fiery furnace. All the people . . . fell down and worshiped the golden image**, indicating how universally and uncritically the masses generally obey when their lives are at stake. It took courage and spiritual backbone not to bend with the rest.

b. The refusal of the three Hebrews to bow. 3:8-12.

8-11. Certain Chaldeans, who were envious of the position of Shadrach, Meshach, and Abednego, came before Nebuchadnezzar after the musical invitation to bow had been sounded. They had eagerly observed that these Jews had refused to worship the image. What courage must have been in the hearts of these Hebrew lads. Instead of rationalizing their way into compromise and sin, they literally stood fast for the Lord. They disobeyed a civil law because God had clearly instructed them to do otherwise in His written Word (see above under vss. 6-7). Acts 5:29 states, '. . . We ought to obey God rather than men.'"

12. The accusation startled and enraged the king. They had disregarded the king himself, as well as his new image. This was an act of treason; and it was, of course, punishable by death.

c. The three Hebrews fear only God. 3:13-18.

13-14. When they were brought in before him, Nebuchadnezzar personally asked, half in unbelief, whether they had disobeyed his clear command. **Is it true . . . ?** was his incredulous inquiry. This renowned ruler who had recently promoted these men and offered them power and prestige could not envision the young Hebrews casting away their lives in behalf of a mere religious principle.

15. Nebuchadnezzar then offered the lads a second chance to obey, and he repeated the warning of the fiery furnace for any deviation from his orders. But in so doing he taunted God by exclaiming **who is that God that shall deliver you out of my hands?** He thought that he, not God, was omnipotent.

16. We are not careful to answer thee means they did not need to concern themselves with answering Nebuchadnezzar. They had months ago decided what their course of action would be at the image's dedication, and their refusal was permanent.

17-18. As a final tribute to God and testimony to Nebuchadnezzar, the Hebrews affirmed **our God whom we serve is able to deliver us.** Whether God did deliver them or not, they would faithfully serve Him in all events, and they would shortly be delivered, either by life or by death.

d. The three Hebrews cast into the furnace, but delivered by God. 3:19-25.

19. ¶Then was Nĕb-u-chad-nĕz′zar full of fury, and the form of his visage was changed against Sha′drăch, Mē′-shăch, and A-bĕd′-ne-gŏ: *therefore* he spake, and commanded that they should heat the furnace one seven times more than it was wont to be heated.

20. And he commanded the most mighty men that *were* in his army to bind Sha′drăch, Mē′shăch, and A-bĕd′-ne-gŏ, *and* to cast *them* into the burning fiery furnace.

21. Then these men were bound in their coats, their hosen, and their hats, and their *other* garments, and were cast into the midst of the burning fiery furnace.

22. Therefore because the king's commandment was urgent, and the furnace exceeding hot, the flame of the fire slew those men that took up Sha′drăch, Mē′shăch, and A-bĕd′-ne-gŏ.

23. And these three men, Sha′drăch, Mē′shăch, and A-bĕd′-ne-gŏ, fell down bound into the midst of the burning fiery furnace.

24. Then Nĕb-u-chad-nĕz′zar the king was astonied, and rose up in haste, *and* spake, and said unto his counsellors, Did not we cast three men bound into the midst of the fire? They answered and said unto the king, True, O king.

25. He answered and said, Lo, I see four men loose, walking in the midst of the fire, and they have no hurt; and the form of the fourth is like the Son of God.

26. ¶Then Nĕb-u-chad-nĕz′zar came near to the mouth of the burning fiery furnace, *and* spake, and said, Sha′-drăch, Mē′shăch, and A-bĕd′-ne-gŏ, ye servants of the most high God, come forth, and come *hither.* Then Sha′-drăch, Mē′shăch, and A-bĕd′-ne-gŏ, came forth of the midst of the fire.

27. And the princes, governors, and captains, and the king's counsellors, being gathered together, saw these men, upon whose bodies the fire had no power, nor was an hair of their head singed, neither were their coats changed, nor the smell of fire had passed on them.

28. *Then* Nĕb-u-chad-nĕz′zar spake, and said, Blessed *be* the God of Sha′-drăch,Mē′shăch,andA-bĕd′-ne-gŏ,who hath sent his angel, and delivered his servants that trusted in him, and have changed the king's word, and yielded their bodies, that they might not serve nor worship any god, except their own God.

29. Therefore I make a decree, That every people, nation, and language, which speak any thing amiss against the God of Sha′drăch, Mē′shăch, and

19. The heating of the furnace seven times hotter than usual for burning these wretched ingrates would, ironically, only cause them to be relieved of their misery all the sooner—if God had not intervened. **Seven times** hotter may suggest completeness, or it may be a hyperbole (an exaggeration for effect); but it does not speak of raising the temperature from 1,500° to 10,500° F. Cremations are normally run at 1,800° F.

20-22. Unfortunately, the overheated furnace had the effect of slaying the king's **most mighty men that were in his army** as they cast in the three Hebrews. The meaning of the technical words for the clothes worn by the young men was completely lost by the time the Jews translated Daniel into Greek around 150 B.C. This points to Daniel's composition as much earlier than a mere fifteen years prior (ca. 165 B.C.) as many critics seek to maintain.

23-24. Nebuchadnezzar viewed the spectacle from near the side entrance to the furnace where the three had been cast bound onto the piping-hot floor. At that point Nebuchadnezzar literally could not believe his eyes and asked for confirmation of what he saw.

25. I see four men loose, walking in the midst of the fire. Clearly, a miracle was in progress! The appearance of the fourth man was definitely distinct. Even Nebuchadnezzar could recognize that. Was it Christ who was with His servants during this trial? It certainly could have been, even though the Scriptures themselves give no confirming statement to that effect. The only other possibility would have been one of God's angels sent to minister to the lads. They often had glistening appearances, as in Matthew 28:3 and Revelation 10:1; 18:1.

e. Nebuchadnezzar's astonishment and proclamation. 3:26-30.

26. When the king called the faithful Hebrew young men to come out of the furnace he called them **servants of the most high God.** That they were indeed. There is nothing higher in God's service than to be a humble servant (Mk 10:44,45). The king apparently did not exercise personal trust in the God whose power had been demonstrated, at least not on this occasion.

27. The miracle was complete—not even a hair had been singed and not even the smell of smoke was upon their clothes. Details such as these speak of the testimony of actual eyewitnesses.

28. These men **yielded their bodies** to be true to God. If we would be willing to yield to the same degree as these men perhaps our testimonies could be used to **change** even the commandments of kings that are contrary to the gospel.

29-30. The Hebrew community advanced that day as the king prohibited anyone from speaking against the Hebrew God in a proclamation to his entire empire. The three Hebrews were

1637

A-bĕd'-ne-gō, shall be cut in pieces, and their houses shall be made a dunghill: because there is no other God that can deliver after this sort.

30 ¶Then the king promoted Shā'-drāch, Mē'shāch, and A-bĕd'-ne-gō, in the province of Babylon.

CHAPTER 4

NEB-U-CHAD-NEZ'ZAR the king, unto all people, nations, and languages, that dwell in all the earth; Peace be multiplied unto you.

2 I thought it good to shew the signs and wonders that the high God hath wrought toward me.

3 How great are his signs! and how mighty are his wonders! his kingdom is an everlasting kingdom, and his dominion is from generation to generation.

4 ¶I Neb-u-chad-nĕz'zar was at rest in mine house, and flourishing in my palace:

5 I saw a dream which made me afraid, and the thoughts upon my bed and the visions of my head troubled me.

6 Therefore made I a decree to bring in all the wise men of Babylon before me, that they might make known unto me the interpretation of the dream.

7 Then came in the magicians, the astrologers, the Chal-dē'ans, and the soothsayers: and I told the dream before them; but they did not make known unto me the interpretation thereof.

8 But at the last Daniel came in before me, whose name was Bĕl-te-shăz'-zar, according to the name of my god, and in whom is the spirit of the holy gods: and before him I told the dream, saying,

9 O Bĕl-te-shăz'zar, master of the magicians, because I know that the spirit of the holy gods is in thee, and no secret troubleth thee, tell me the visions of my dream that I have seen, and the interpretation thereof.

10 Thus were the visions of mine head in my bed; I saw, and behold a tree in the midst of the earth, and the height thereof was great.

11 The tree grew, and was strong, and the height thereof reached unto heaven, and the sight thereof to the end of all the earth:

12 The leaves thereof were fair, and the fruit thereof much, and in it was meat for all: the beasts of the field had shadow under it, and the fowls of the heaven dwelt in the boughs thereof, and all flesh was fed of it.

13 I saw in the visions of my head upon my bed, and, behold, a watcher and an holy one came down from heaven;

14 He cried aloud, and said thus, Hew down the tree, and cut off his branches, shake off his leaves, and scatter his

also advanced in the administration of the province of Babylon. Although Daniel was apparently not present for this event, he was certainly present and faithful when the lions' den was prepared in chapter 6.

4. Daniel interprets Nebuchadnezzar's tree dream. 4:1-37.

a. Nebuchadnezzar's proclamation of God's majesty. 4:1-3.

4:1-3. These verses serve as an introduction to this chapter. The words of the entire chapter are recorded from the lips of Nebuchadnezzar after the events had occurred. The occasion was that the king had been warned regarding pride, had failed to deal with it, was consequently judged by God, and then upon being restored to his throne wanted to give the glory to God by making his strange story known to all people, nations, and languages of his vast kingdom. It should not be counted strange since the words of Satan are occasionally recorded (Gen 3:1, 4, 5), as well as the utterance of Balaam's donkey (Num 22:28-30).

b. Nebuchadnezzar recounts his tree dream. 4:4-18.

4. I Nebuchadnezzar was at rest . . . flourishing in my palace. This king was not only a great warrior, but also a prolific builder; and the ruins of his kingdom are a vast archaeological storehouse today.

5-7. Nebuchadnezzar had a dream that no one could interpret, even though he **told the dream before them** this time (cf. 2:1-13). Due to the contents of the dream, the king may have surmised that it held evil in store for him.

8. But at the last Daniel came in to save the day—which amounted to announcing the king's sad fate. **The spirit of the holy gods** does not indicate any personal faith on Nebuchadnezzar's part, but merely respect for Daniel. The king still had his own **god,** which is probably a reference to Marduk, the head of all the Babylonian gods.

9-12. The description of his dream involved a great, tall tree that seemed to provide food and shelter for all. A tree is often a symbol of towering strength, providing shade, food, fuel, beauty, and the raw materials for some buildings.

13-15. But suddenly a **watcher,** that is an angel, came from heaven with the command to cut down the tree. The **band of iron and brass** around the stump would serve to preserve the life of the cut-off portion of the tree that remained in the ground. It then would retain the possibility of recovering and growing back again.

16-18. Let his heart be changed from man's, and let a beast's heart be given unto him. These were still the words of the angel in the dream and signified the human personality of the tree. It actually stood for Nebuchadnezzar. **Let seven times pass over him** had to do with the period during which the heart of a beast would pervade Nebuchadnezzar—commonly thought of as seven years. The sole purpose of this experience was declared to be that men might understand **that the most High ruleth in the kingdom of men, and giveth it to whomsoever he will.** Daniel was asked to interpret this puzzling dream that had completely baffled the other wise men.

c. Daniel interprets the dream and warns the king. 4:19-27.

19-24. Daniel at once understood the meaning of the dream and was saddened because of what it meant for King Nebuchadnezzar. Regarding the tree, Daniel told Nebuchadnezzar, **It is thou, O king** (vs. 22), as he repeated the details of the dream he had just heard, perhaps to assure the king he knew the various elements of the dream.

25-26. The message was that the king would be deposed from his throne due to a mental disorder in which he would imagine himself to be an ox. This would continue for seven years until he would learn that God really rules the earth and sets up kings as He pleases. During that interval, Daniel assured him, **thy kingdom shall be sure unto thee** (cf. vs. 36).

---

fruit: let the beasts get away from under it, and the fowls from his branches:

15 Nevertheless leave the stump of his roots in the earth, even with a band of iron and brass, in the tender grass of the field; and let it be wet with the dew of heaven, and *let* his portion *be* with the beasts in the grass of the earth:

16 Let his heart be changed from man's, and let a beast's heart be given unto him; and let seven times pass over him.

17 This matter *is* by the decree of the watchers, and the demand by the word of the holy ones: to the intent that the living may know that the most High ruleth in the kingdom of men, and giveth it to whomsoever he will, and setteth up over it the basest of men.

18 This dream I king Nĕb-u-chad-nĕz′zar have seen. Now thou, O Bĕl-te-shăz′zar, declare the interpretation thereof, forasmuch as all the wise *men* of my kingdom are not able to make known unto me the interpretation: but thou *art* able; for the spirit of the holy gods *is* in thee.

19 Then Daniel, whose name *was* Bĕl-te-shăz′zar, was astonied for one hour, and his thoughts troubled him. The king spake, and said, Bĕl-te-shăz′zar, let not the dream, or the interpretation thereof, trouble thee. Bĕl-te-shăz′zar answered and said, My lord, the dream *be* to them that hate thee, and the interpretation thereof to thine enemies.

20 The tree that thou sawest, which grew, and was strong, whose height reached unto the heaven, and the sight thereof to all the earth;

21 Whose leaves *were* fair, and the fruit thereof much, and in it *was* meat for all: under which the beasts of the field dwelt, and upon whose branches the fowls of the heaven had their habitation:

22 It *is* thou, O king, that art grown and become strong: for thy greatness is grown, and reacheth unto heaven, and thy dominion to the end of the earth.

23 And whereas the king saw a watcher and an holy one coming down from heaven, and saying, Hew the tree down, and destroy it; yet leave the stump of the roots thereof in the earth, even with a band of iron and brass, in the tender grass of the field; and let it be wet with the dew of heaven, and *let* his portion *be* with the beasts of the field, till seven times pass over him;

24 This *is* the interpretation, O king, and this *is* the decree of the most High, which is come upon my lord the king:

25 That they shall drive thee from men, and thy dwelling shall be with the beasts of the field, and they shall make thee to eat grass as oxen, and they shall wet thee with the dew of heaven, and seven times shall pass over thee, till thou know that the most High ruleth in the kingdom of men, and giveth it to whomsoever he will.

26 And whereas they commanded to leave the stump of the tree roots; thy kingdom shall be sure unto thee, after that thou shalt have known that the heavens do rule.

27 Wherefore, O king, let my counsel be acceptable unto thee, and break off thy sins by righteousness, and thine iniquities by shewing mercy to the poor; if it may be a lengthening of thy tranquility.

28 ¶All this came upon the king Nĕb-u-chad-nĕz'zar.

29 At the end of twelve months he walked in the palace of the kingdom of Babylon.

30 The king spake, and said, Is not this great Babylon, that I have built for the house of the kingdom by the might of my power, and for the honour of my majesty?

31 While the word was in the king's mouth, there fell a voice from heaven, saying, O king Nĕb-u-chad-nĕz'zar, to thee it is spoken; The kingdom is departed from thee.

32 And they shall drive thee from men, and thy dwelling shall be with the beasts of the field: they shall make thee to eat grass as oxen, and seven times shall pass over thee, until thou know that the most High ruleth in the kingdom of men, and giveth it to whomsoever he will.

33 The same hour was the thing fulfilled upon Nĕb-u-chad-nĕz'zar: and he was driven from men, and did eat grass as oxen, and his body was wet with the dew of heaven, till his hairs were grown like eagles' feathers, and his nails like birds' claws.

34 And at the end of the days I Nĕb-u-chad-nĕz'zar lifted up mine eyes unto heaven, and mine understanding returned unto me, and I blessed the most High, and I praised and honoured him that liveth for ever, whose dominion is an everlasting dominion, and his kingdom is from generation to generation:

35 And all the inhabitants of the earth are reputed as nothing: and he doeth according to his will in the army of heaven, and among the inhabitants of the earth: and none can stay his hand, or say unto him, What doest thou?

36 At the same time my reason returned unto me; and for the glory of my kingdom, mine honour and brightness returned unto me; and my counsellors and my lords sought unto me; and I was established in my kingdom, and excellent majesty was added unto me.

37 Now I Nĕb-u-chad-nĕz'zar praise and extol and honour the King of heaven, all whose works are truth, and his ways judgment: and those that walk in pride he is able to abase.

CHAPTER 5

BEL-SHAZ'ZAR the king made a great feast to a thousand of his lords, and drank wine before the thousand.

---

27. Daniel hoped that the events predicted in this God-given dream could be averted by an immediate and true repentance on the part of Nebuchadnezzar. Daniel loved the king and begged him to repent, in hope that it might provide a lengthening of thy tranquility. However, Daniel's sincere pleading could not overcome the king's pride.

d. The fulfillment of the dream. 4:28-33.

28-33. One year later, as Nebuchadnezzar walked through his tremendous palace boastful of his accomplishments, an audible voice from heaven said The kingdom is departed from thee. It may have been God's own voice, as at Christ's baptism (Mt 3:17), the Transfiguration (Mt 17:5), and the Triumphal Entry (Jn 12:28); or it may have been the voice of an angel. That very hour he was driven out into a field, but he was protected. He ate grass and acted like an ox.

e. Nebuchadnezzar returns to sanity and praises God. 4:34-37.

34-35. Mine understanding returned. This is a clear indication that Nebuchadnezzar had experienced some form of mental disorder. He immediately praised and blessed God, understanding the eternality and sovereignty of His dealings among the affairs of men.

36-37. The kingdom was sure to Nebuchadnezzar, just as Daniel had predicted (see vs. 25). In fact, all was restored in a proper manner. The lesson to learn is that those that walk in pride he is able to abase. God not only can, but He does bring down those who ignore Him. Can this happen to a Christian? Certainly. Paul cautioned us not to think of ourselves more highly than we ought to think (Rom 12:3), and that advice is just as needful today as it was then.

B. Daniel Serves Under Belshazzar. 5:1-31.

1. Belshazzar's drunken feast. 5:1-4.

5:1. Belshazzar the king. In 1850, critics doubted even the historicity of Belshazzar, claiming he was a fictitious character made up by the pseudo-Daniel who they claim composed the book around 165 B.C. With the discovery of Belshazzar's name on cuneiform tablets, his existence could no longer be questioned. Critics such as H. H. Rowley then sought to attack Daniel's statement that he was king. The recognition of two large black cylinders in a Byzantine church in Haran in the year 1956 ended that skepticism as well. The Nabonidus Chronicle, as this is called, clearly mentions Belshazzar as a coregent with Nabonidus his father. Not only that, but Belshazzar ruled at Babylon, while Nabonidus was in Teman during the final years of the Babylonian Empire. See R. P. Dougherty, *Nabonidus and Belshazzar*, and R. D. Wilson, *Studies in the Book of Daniel*, I, pp. 83-127. **A great feast.** In ancient times feasts were extremely large, and in many cases they were sensual events (cf. Est 1:9). **A thousand of his lords.** This is probably a round number. **Drank wine before the thousand.** The king apparently sat in a separate section in front of the others.

2-4. Belshazzar committed several sins during his last right on earth—drunkenness, sacrilege in the use of the sacred vessels taken from Solomon's temple, and idolatry in the worship of **the gods of gold**, etc. The references to Nebuchadnezzar as Belshazzar's father (vss. 2, 11, 13, 18, 22) are well within the bounds of Semitic usage. It need mean only that Nebuchadnezzar was a predecessor of Belshazzar on the Babylonian throne. He may also have been Nebuchadnezzar's grandson as Leupold has suggested (*Exposition of Daniel*, pp. 211-17), in which case the same terminology could be used as Pusey has explained (*Daniel the Prophet*, p. 346).

2. *The handwriting on the wall. 5:5-9.*

5-6. The supernatural occurrence of a hand suddenly appearing and writing on the light-colored plaster of the palace wall would be enough to startle any king, and Belshazzar was no exception. He may have suspected that the mysterious communication was connected in some way with his debaucherous conduct and the advances of the Persian army nearby.

7-9. Belshazzar promised whoever would decipher the message a promotion to **be the third ruler in the kingdom.** That is an accurate statement, in view of the fact that Nabonidus and his son Belshazzar were co-rulers. This confirms the historicity of Daniel and his authenticity as a sixth-century B.C. writer, since a forger of the second-century would not have had access to this long-since-buried information. The inability of **all the king's wise men** to even read the writing, let alone interpret it, contributed to make the situation even more desperate.

3. *Daniel called in to help. 5:10-16.*

10. **The queen** probably refers to the queen mother. Belshazzar's wives were already present, but this woman came in later. Her perfect acquaintance with the earlier affairs of Nebuchadnezzar's reign (when Daniel was such a leading figure) also points to this being the case.

11-12. She urged Belshazzar to call in Daniel, referring to him as the **master** of all the wise men in Nebuchadnezzar's time. She had the utmost confidence in Daniel's ability (under God) to give the answer to the strange mystery on the wall.

2 Bĕl-shăz'zar, whiles he tasted the wine, commanded to bring the golden and silver vessels which his father Nĕb-u-chad-nĕz'zar had taken out of the temple which *was* in Jerusalem; that the king, and his princes, his wives, and his concubines, might drink therein.

3 Then they brought the golden vessels that were taken out of the temple of the house of God which *was* at Jerusalem; and the king, and his princes, his wives, and his concubines, drank in them.

4 They drank wine, and praised the gods of gold, and of silver, of brass, of iron, of wood, and of stone.

5 ¶ In the same hour came forth fingers of a man's hand, and wrote over against the candlestick upon the plaister of the wall of the king's palace: and the king saw the part of the hand that wrote.

6 Then the king's countenance was changed, and his thoughts troubled him, so that the joints of his loins were loosed, and his knees smote one against another.

7 The king cried aloud to bring in the astrologers, the Chal-dē'ans, and the soothsayers. *And* the king spake, and said to the wise *men* of Babylon, Whosoever shall read this writing, and shew me the interpretation thereof, shall be clothed with scarlet, and *have* a chain of gold about his neck, and shall be the third ruler in the kingdom.

8 Then came in all the king's wise *men*: but they could not read the writing, nor make known to the king the interpretation thereof.

9 Then was king Bĕl-shăz'zar greatly troubled, and his countenance was changed in him, and his lords were astonied.

10 ¶ *Now* the queen by reason of the words of the king and his lords came into the banquet house: *and* the queen spake and said, O king, live for ever: let not thy thoughts trouble thee, nor let thy countenance be changed:

11 There is a man in thy kingdom, in whom *is* the spirit of the holy gods; and in the days of thy father light and understanding and wisdom, like the wisdom of the gods, was found in him; whom the king Nĕb-u-chad-nĕz'zar thy father, the king, *I say,* thy father, made master of the magicians, astrologers, Chal-dē'ans, *and* soothsayers;

12 Forasmuch as an excellent spirit, and knowledge, and understanding, interpreting of dreams, and shewing of hard sentences, and dissolving of doubts, were found in the same Daniel, whom the king named Bĕl-te-shăz'zar:

now let Daniel be called, and he will shew the interpretation.

13 Then was Daniel brought in before the king. *And* the king spake and said unto Daniel, *Art* thou that Daniel, which *art* of the children of the captivity of Judah, whom the king my father brought out of Jewry?

14 I have even heard of thee, that the spirit of the gods *is* in thee, and *that* light and understanding and excellent wisdom is found in thee.

15 And now the wise *men*, the astrologers, have been brought in before me, that they should read this writing, and make known unto me the interpretation thereof: but they could not shew the interpretation of the thing:

16 And I have heard of thee, that thou canst make interpretations, and dissolve doubts: now if thou canst read the writing, and make known to me the interpretation thereof, thou shalt be

clothed with scarlet, and *have* a chain of gold about thy neck, and shalt be the third ruler in the kingdom.

17 ¶Then Daniel answered and said before the king, Let thy gifts be to thyself, and give thy rewards to another; yet I will read the writing unto the king, and make known to him the interpretation.

18 O thou king, the most high God gave Nĕb-u-chad-nĕz'zar thy father a kingdom, and majesty, and glory, and honour:

19 And for the majesty that he gave him, all people, nations, and languages, trembled and feared before him: whom he would he slew, and whom he would he kept alive; and whom he would he set up; and whom he would he put down.

20 But when his heart was lifted up, and his mind hardened in pride, he was deposed from his kingly throne, and they took his glory from him:

21 And he was driven from the sons of men; and his heart was made like the beasts, and his dwelling *was* with the wild asses: they fed him with grass like oxen, and his body was wet with the dew of heaven; till he knew that the most high God ruled in the kingdom of men, and *that* he appointeth over it whomsoever he will.

22 And thou his son, O Bĕl-shăz'zar, hast not humbled thine heart, though thou knewest all this;

23 But hast lifted up thyself against the Lord of heaven; and they have brought the vessels of his house before thee, and thou, and thy lords, thy wives, and thy concubines, have drunk wine in them; and thou hast praised the gods of silver, and gold, of brass, iron, wood, and stone, which see not, nor hear, nor know: and the God in whose hand thy breath *is*, and whose *are* all thy ways, hast thou not glorified:

24 Then was the part of the hand sent from him; and this writing was written.

25 ¶And this *is* the writing that was written, MĒ'NE, MĒ'NE, TĒ'KEL, U-PHĂR'SIN.

13-16. After the usual introductory remarks, Belshazzar repeated his generous offer to the man who could make known the writing. **I have even heard of thee** (vs. 14) probably refers primarily to what the queen mother had just told him. He was anxious for an answer.

4. Daniel's sermon to Belshazzar. 5:17-24.

17-21. Daniel quickly reassured the king that he would be able to read and interpret the writing; then he began to recount some history for Belshazzar. Daniel's message was a reminder of how Nebuchadnezzar had to learn in a humbling manner about what God can do to the proud (vs. 20). Verse 21 refers to the events recorded in Daniel 4. The lesson Nebuchadnezzar learned was that **the most high God ruled in the kingdom of men, and that he appointeth over it whomsoever he will** (vs. 21). That was an apropos statement, since God was about to make someone else king in Belshazzar's place.

22-24. The application of Daniel's sermon was bold and directed at Belshazzar. Even though he knew all this, he still engaged in a proud display **against the Lord of heaven**, as demonstrated in his drunken feast using the vessels stolen from God's sacred Temple in a feeble effort to elevate his false idol gods. The result, Daniel pointed out, **was the part of the hand sent from him**, meaning from God.

5. Daniel's interpretation of the writing. 5:25-28.

25. MENE, MENE, TEKEL, UPHARSIN. The U of UPHARSIN is the word for "and" in Aramaic. In the interpretation Daniel considered each term separately, and so omitted reading the "and" that preceded PERES (vs. 28). PHARSIN is also the plural

26 This *is* the interpretation of the thing: Mᴇ′ɴᴇ; God hath numbered thy kingdom, and finished it.

27 Tᴇ′ᴋᴇʟ, Thou art weighed in the balances, and art found wanting.

28 Pᴇ′ʀᴇs, Thy kingdom is divided, and given to the Medes and Persians.

29 Then commanded Bēl-shăz′zar, and they clothed Daniel with scarlet, and *put* a chain of gold about his neck, and made a proclamation concerning him, that he should be the third ruler in the kingdom.

30 ¶In that night was Bēl-shăz′zar the king of the Chăl-dē′ans slain.

31 And Darius the Mē′dĭ-an took the kingdom, *being* about threescore and two years old.

CHAPTER 6

IT pleased Darius to set over the kingdom an hundred and twenty princes, which should be over the whole kingdom;

2 And over these three presidents; of whom Daniel *was* first: that the princes might give accounts unto them, and the king should have no damage.

3 Then this Daniel was preferred above the presidents and princes, because an excellent spirit *was* in him; and the king thought to set him over the whole realm.

4 ¶Then the presidents and princes sought to find occasion against Daniel concerning the kingdom; but they could find none occasion nor fault; forasmuch as he *was* faithful, neither was there any error or fault found in him.

5 Then said these men, We shall not find any occasion against this Daniel, except we find *it* against him concerning the law of his God.

6 Then these presidents and princes assembled together to the king, and said thus unto him, King Darius, live for ever.

form of the word **Peres** (see also Boutflower, pp. 133-141, Wood, pp. 149-150).

26. **Mene.** This word should have been easy enough for any wise man to read, it meant "numbered." The prophetic meaning was the puzzling part. Daniel informed Belshazzar that the days of his kingdom had been numbered by God, and they had expired.

27. **Tᴇᴋᴇʟ** meant "weighed." Belshazzar himself was lacking in the weighty matters of the spiritual life.

28. **Pᴇʀᴇs.** As Daniel interpreted, **Pᴇʀᴇs** signified divided, and meant that Babylon was to be given over to **the Medes and Persians,** a combined power of two nationalities, of which the Persians were the dominant force.

6. *Medo-Persia conquers decadent Babylon. 5:29-31.*

29-30. Belshazzar then rewarded Daniel as he had promised, but Daniel's polite refusal **Let thy gifts be to thyself, and give thy rewards to another** (vs. 17) was no doubt spoken with the knowledge of the meaninglessness of such rewards. In just a matter of hours, during that very night, Belshazzar would be slain; and thus, Daniel's promotion would be of no value.

31. **Darius the Median.** In the absence of positive evidence as to the identity of this man, many liberal critics claim Daniel was mistaken in some way. Daniel was not mistaken; for he knew and served Darius personally, recorded his nationality, even his age, and the name of his father Ahasuerus (9:1). No forger would be so bold as to include details of this sort. The question still remains as to whom this Darius was. Some believe Darius was another name for Cyrus, the king of all Persia; but this is unlikely, just as are the suppositions that he was Cambyses, Cyrus' son. He would appear to have been a sub-king under Cyrus. The language of 9:1, **was made king over the realm of the Chaldeans,** is in accord with this understanding. In the historical records of the period one man seemed to fit this picture. His name was Gubaru, whom the Nabonidus Chronicle says Cyrus made governor of Babylon at the time of its capture. For full discussions of all views see J. C. Whitcomb, *Darius the Mede.*

C. Daniel Serves under Darius the Mede. 6:1-28.

1. *Daniel's continued government service. 6:1-3.*

6:1-3. For discussion of the identity of **Darius,** see 5:31 above. In administering the province of Babylon, Darius appointed one hundred twenty princes over it and three overseers above them. Daniel was made chief overseer and was capable enough to be promoted **over the whole realm.** Age, experience, and complete trustworthiness are qualities that will always be in demand. Too many, however, disqualify themselves much earlier in life by some ungodly deed or foolish action.

2. *Conspiracy against Daniel. 6:4-9.*

4-5. What a remarkable testimony Daniel bore. His enemies could not find anything wrong with his conduct. Daniel's trustworthiness and godliness were so well-known, even in his own day, that Ezekiel readily classified Daniel with two ancients, Noah and Job, also known for outstanding godly living (Ezk 14:14).

6-9. Since Daniel was obeying all the laws of the kingdom, the wicked and envious Persian princes sought to establish a new law regarding worship, one that Daniel would surely break

7 All the presidents of the kingdom, the governors, and the princes, the counselors, and the captains, have consulted together to establish a royal statute, and to make a firm decree, that whosoever shall ask a petition of any God or man for thirty days, save of thee, O king, he shall be cast into the den of lions.

8 Now, O king, establish the decree, and sign the writing, that it be not changed, according to the law of the Medes and Persians, which altereth not.

9 Wherefore king Darius signed the writing and the decree.

10 ¶Now when Daniel knew that the writing was signed, he went into his house; and his windows being open in his chamber toward Jerusalem, he kneeled upon his knees three times a day, and prayed, and gave thanks before his God, as he did aforetime.

11 Then these men assembled, and found Daniel praying and making supplication before his God.

12 Then they came near, and spake before the king concerning the king's decree; Hast thou not signed a decree, that every man that shall ask a *petition* of any God or man within thirty days, save of thee, O king, shall be cast into the den of lions? The king answered and said, The thing *is* true, according to the law of the Medes and Persians, which altereth not.

13 Then answered they and said before the king, That Daniel, which *is* of the children of the captivity of Judah, regardeth not thee, O king, nor the decree that thou hast signed, but maketh his petition three times a day.

14 Then the king, when he heard *these* words, was sore displeased with himself, and set *his* heart on Daniel to deliver him: and he laboured till the going down of the sun to deliver him.

15 Then these men assembled unto the king, and said unto the king, Know, O king, that the law of the Medes and Persians *is,* That no decree nor statute which the king establisheth may be changed.

16 Then the king commanded, and they brought Daniel, and cast *him* into the den of lions. *Now* the king spake and said unto Daniel, Thy God whom thou servest continually, he will deliver thee.

17 And a stone was brought, and laid upon the mouth of the den: and the king sealed it with his own signet, and with the signet of his lords; that the purpose might not be changed concerning Daniel.

18 ¶Then the king went to his palace, and passed the night fasting: neither were instruments of musick brought

because of his solid faith in Jehovah. The new law made the king the one through whom all requests to deity had to be channeled. This flattering law would be in effect for thirty days—certainly long enough to catch Daniel directly engaging God in prayer. The king was tricked into the decree, and he later regretted it; but it was his foolish pride that caused him to sign such a decree without considering its possible effects. We must be careful to foresee the consequences of our actions before we act, especially where pride can enter in.

3. Daniel's continued devotion to God. 6:10.

10. Daniel knew he had to obey God, no matter what man might command or how much he might stand to lose personally by such actions. Just as the three Hebrew children would not disobey God in order to please a king, so Daniel purposely disobeyed a human law in order to maintain obedience to God. Later, Peter declared, ". . . We ought to obey God rather than men" (Acts 5:29). We are always to obey the laws of our government unless they obviously conflict with something God has clearly commanded us to do in His Word. In Daniel's case it involved prayer. What we may be called upon to face in the future no one knows. We need, however, to determine now to obey God if we would hope to stand then.

4. Daniel accused before Darius. 6:11-15.

11-15. Daniel was readily accused before Darius regarding the new law. There was no controversy about his guilt. He had clearly disobeyed the king's command, and no effort of the king could free Daniel. The law could not be changed, and no pardon was allowed according to Persian law. For discussion of the nature of Persian law see A. T. Olmstead, *History of the Persian Empire.*

5. Daniel preserved in the den of lions. 6:16-23.

16-18. Even though he could personally do nothing to help Daniel, Darius believed Daniel's God would intervene on his behalf. Perhaps he had heard rumors of a previous deliverance from a fiery furnace. After the den of lions was made secure, Darius went home; but he did not spend the night as he usually did. Sometimes inappropriate actions will cause us to search our hearts, as Darius must have done.

before him: and his sleep went from him.

19 Then the king arose very early in the morning, and went in haste unto the den of lions.

20 And when he came to the den, he cried with a lamentable voice unto Daniel: *and* the king spake and said to Daniel, O Daniel, servant of the living God, is thy God, whom thou servest continually, able to deliver thee from the lions?

21 Then said Daniel unto the king, O king, live for ever.

22 My God hath sent his angel, and hath shut the lions' mouths, that they have not hurt me: forasmuch as before him innocency was found in me; and also before thee, O king, have I done no hurt.

23 Then was the king exceeding glad for him, and commanded that they should take Daniel up out of the den. So Daniel was taken up out of the den, and no manner of hurt was found upon him, because he believed in his God.

24 ¶And the king commanded, and they brought those men which had accused Daniel, and they cast *them* into the den of lions, them, their children, and their wives; and the lions had the mastery of them, and brake all their bones in pieces or ever they came at the bottom of the den.

25 ¶Then king Darius wrote unto all people, nations, and languages, that dwell in all the earth; Peace be multiplied unto you.

26 I make a decree, That in every dominion of my kingdom men tremble and fear before the God of Daniel: for he *is* the living God, and stedfast for ever, and his kingdom *that* which shall not be destroyed, and his dominion *shall be even* unto the end.

27 He delivereth and rescueth, and he worketh signs and wonders in heaven and in earth, who hath delivered Daniel from the power of the lions.

28 So this Daniel prospered in the reign of Darius, and in the reign of Cyrus the Persian.

19-22. Darius hastened to the den early the next morning and called hopefully to Daniel. Daniel responded politely and announced the reason for his safety—**My God hath sent his angel, and hath shut the lions' mouths.** Why? Because God had found Daniel innocent of all wrongdoing—by divine standards. That is the only judgment that really matters. The angel, or messenger, who came may have been Christ; but it may just as well have been some created angel.

23. Daniel was taken up. The law had been kept, for Daniel had suffered the punishment for disobedience—except that the lions had not been as obliging as his enemies had hoped. Likewise, when we disobey the king's commandment in order to obey God, we may have to go "into the furnace" or "the lions' den." Let us be prepared to suffer for His Name's sake (II Tim 2:12; 3:12; I Pet 4:12-13), no matter what the results might be.

6. Daniel's accusers punished and his God praised. 6:24-28.

24. The lions got fed after all! The reason that not only the villians themselves, but also **their children, and their wives,** were fed to the lions was that they must have been blameworthy in the matter also (cf. Josh 7:24-25).

25-27. Another result of the miracle God performed in sparing Daniel was that men were pointed to the God of miracles. God's miracles are not useless displays of power, but they are calculated to turn men to Him in faith. Some great theology is contained in verses 26-27.

28. Darius is distinguished here from Cyrus the Persian. Earlier, Darius was distinctly referred to as being a Median, while Cyrus was a Persian. The statement that **Daniel prospered** has reference to far more important things than material wealth. Daniel possessed the favor of God and men, wisdom, longevity, faithfulness, godly convictions, and steadfastness in prayer. What an example.

II. THE PROPHETIC PORTION OF DANIEL. 7:1-12:13.

A. Daniel's Vision of the Four Beasts. 7:1-28.

The similarities between the general prophetic importance of this chapter and chapter 2 are numerous. Both speak of the same four successive world empires—Babylon, Persia, Greece, and Rome. Both relate events of the end time just before the second coming of Christ, and both chapters speak of the kingdom established by the Lord. However, chapter 2 views the situation from man's perspective in Nebuchadnezzar's dream—a great shining image of a man. On the other hand, God's point of view is seen in Daniel's vision where the four kingdoms are pictured as fighting beasts.

CHAPTER 7

IN the first year of Bĕl-shăz'zar king of Babylon Daniel had a dream and visions of his head upon his bed: then he wrote the dream, *and* told the sum of the matters.

2 Daniel spake and said, I saw in my vision by night, and, behold, the four winds of the heaven strove upon the great sea.

3 And four great beasts came up from the sea, diverse one from another.

4 The first *was* like a lion, and had eagle's wings: I beheld till the wings thereof were plucked, and it was lifted up from the earth, and made stand upon the feet as a man, and a man's heart was given to it.

5 And behold another beast, a second, like to a bear, and it raised up itself on one side, and *it had* three ribs in the mouth of it between the teeth of it: and they said thus unto it, Arise, devour much flesh.

6 After this I beheld, and lo another, like a leopard, which had upon the back of it four wings of a fowl; the beast had also four heads; and dominion was given to it.

7 After this I saw in the night visions, and behold a fourth beast, dreadful and terrible, and strong exceedingly; and it had great iron teeth: it devoured and brake in pieces, and stamped the residue with the feet of it: and it *was* diverse from all the beasts that *were* before it; and it had ten horns.

8 I considered the horns, and, behold, there came up among them another little horn, before whom there were three of the first horns plucked up by the roots: and, behold, in this horn *were* eyes like the eyes of man, and a mouth speaking great things.

9 ¶I beheld till the thrones were cast down, and the Ancient of days did sit, whose garment *was* white as snow, and the hair of his head like the pure wool: his throne *was like* the fiery flame, *and* his wheels *as* burning fire.

10 A fiery stream issued and came forth from before him: thousand thousands ministered unto him, and ten thousand times ten thousand stood before him: the judgment was set, and the books were opened.

11 I beheld then because of the voice of the great words which the horn spake: I beheld *even* till the beast was slain, and his body destroyed, and given to the burning flame.

12 As concerning the rest of the beasts, they had their dominion taken away: yet their lives were prolonged for a season and time.

13 I saw in the night visions, and, behold, *one* like the Son of man came with the clouds of heaven, and came to the Ancient of days, and they brought him near before him.

1. The vision received by Daniel. 7:1-14.

7:1-3. The first year of Belshazzar was the date of this vision received by Daniel during the night. Notice that this vision occurred several years prior to the events recorded in chapters 5 and 6. Those chapters were primarily history. This chapter contains the first of the revelations that came directly to Daniel and concerned prophetic events. Daniel saw **four great beasts** that **came up from the sea.**

4. The first was like a lion. The lion is the king of beasts. This one had wings, perhaps denoting swiftness of conquest. It was given a man's heart, which indicates that it was a personal being, since it represented not only Babylon, but also the nation's leader (cf. 2:36-40).

5. The second beast was **like to a bear** and devoured **much flesh.** It spoke of the Medo-Persian Empire of which the Persian element was dominant. Historically, this kingdom succeeded the Babylonian Empire when Darius the Mede, one of Cyrus' generals, conquered Babylon in 539 B.C. as recorded in 5:30-31 (cf. 6:28). The Persian kingdom is also pictured in 8:3-8, 20.

6. The third empire, Greece, was pictured as a **leopard** with four wings and four heads. The wings speak of swiftness in the conquests of Alexander the Great, and the four heads picture the fact that his empire was divided into four parts after his untimely death in 323 B.C. This kingdom is also seen in 8:5-8, 21-22, where it is a great he goat that grows four horns after its first large horn, representing Alexander the Great, is broken off. See also 11:3-4 where the same quartering of this kingdom is predicted.

7-8. The fourth beast was **dreadful and terrible, and strong exceedingly . . . and it had ten horns.** It stood for Rome, the fourth successive empire. Daniel had never seen such a strange creature in all his life. The ten horns correspond with the ten toes on Nebuchadnezzar's image (cf. 2:41) which will be ten kings. An eleventh horn suddenly appeared and destroyed three of the original ten horns and then seemed to turn into an intelligent being with eyes and speech. This eleventh horn stands for the Antichrist of Revelation 13:1-10, who is at once both a kingdom and its personal leader.

9-12. A scene of judgment came into Daniel's vision next. God the Father was pictured on the throne in all wisdom (white hair), surrounded by countless angels, preparing to judge. The only other place where God the Father is actually seen in the Bible is Revelation 5:1 and 7, but both occurrences are only visions; for God the Father is spirit. The strange horn of the fourth beast spoke (apparently reproachfully at God) and was cast into the fire. The beasts were finally put away.

13-14. The vision ended with **one like the Son of Man** coming before the **Ancient of days** to receive an eternal kingdom with those of all nations in His service. Here, the Old Testament clearly presents the Father and the Son as two separate persons within the Trinity.

14 And there was given him dominion, and glory, and a kingdom, that all people, nations, and languages, should serve him: his dominion *is* an everlasting dominion, which shall not pass away, and his kingdom *that* which shall not be destroyed.

15 ¶ I Daniel was grieved in my spirit in the midst of *my* body, and the visions of my head troubled me.

16 I came near unto one of them that stood by, and asked him the truth of all this. So he told me, and made me know the interpretation of the things.

17 These great beasts, which are four, *are* four kings, *which* shall arise out of the earth.

18 But the saints of the most High shall take the kingdom, and possess the kingdom for ever, even for ever and ever.

19 Then I would know the truth of the fourth beast, which was diverse from all the others, exceeding dreadful, whose teeth *were of* iron, and his nails *of* brass; *which* devoured, brake in pieces, and stamped the residue with his feet;

20 And of the ten horns that *were* in his head, and *of* the other which came up, and before whom three fell; even *of* that horn that had eyes, and a mouth that spake very great things, whose look *was* more stout than his fellows.

21 I beheld, and the same horn made war with the saints, and prevailed against them;

22 Until the Ancient of days came, and judgment was given to the saints of the most High; and the time came that the saints possessed the kingdom.

23 Thus he said, The fourth beast shall be the fourth kingdom upon earth, which shall be diverse from all kingdoms, and shall devour the whole earth, and shall tread it down, and break it in pieces.

24 And the ten horns out of this kingdom *are* ten kings *that* shall arise: and another shall rise after them; and he shall be diverse from the first, and he shall subdue three kings.

25 And he shall speak *great* words against the most High, and shall wear out the saints of the most High, and think to change times and laws: and they shall be given into his hand until a time and times and the dividing of time.

26 But the judgment shall sit, and they shall take away his dominion, to consume and to destroy *it* unto the end.

27 And the kingdom and dominion, and the greatness of the kingdom under the whole heaven, shall be given to the people of the saints of the most High, whose kingdom *is* an everlasting kingdom, and all dominions shall serve and obey him.

28 Hitherto *is* the end of the matter. As for me Daniel, my cogitations much

2. *The vision interpreted for Daniel. 7:15-28.*

15-17. Daniel was puzzled and desired to have the vision explained. An angel kindly obliged him. The key to the vision is contained in verse 17. The four beasts stood for **four kings,** which really represented four separate kingdoms (as NIV). Note also the clear statement of verse 23 that the fourth beast is the fourth kingdom.

18. **But the saints of the most High shall take the kingdom.** This is accomplished because of the believer's union with Christ. When Christ reigns, we shall reign with Him. This will occur at the conclusion of the Battle of Armageddon when Christ establishes his one-thousand-year reign on earth (see Rev 20:4).

19-21. Daniel's interest, however, centered in the fourth beast, and especially in that horn with the eyes and a mouth, because he **made war with the saints, and prevailed against them.** The seeming victory of the Antichrist will take place during the yet future Great Tribulation. The **saints** he overpowers are the Jews and a great multitude of Gentiles who are saved after the Church is raptured out of the world (cf. Rev 7:1-10; 12:1-6, 13-17).

22-24. But the power of the horn was overcome by **the Ancient of days** when He sat to judge. This occurs after the Tribulation period and may correspond with the judgment of the nations (the sheep and the goats) of Matthew 25:31-46. The explanation continued to disclose that the **ten horns out of this kingdom are ten kings.** These ten kings comprise the revived Holy Roman Empire. The additional horn will subdue three of these contemporary kings who will rule during the Great Tribulation as part of this European empire.

25. This horn will attempt to defeat the saints of God. He will have a measure of success until **a time and times and the dividing of time.** This is probably a reference to the final three and one half $(1 + 2 + \frac{1}{2})$ years of the Tribulation, the last half of Daniel's seventieth week (see 9:24-27). Revelation 11:2 pictures his rule as continuing for forty-two months ($3\frac{1}{2}$ years); and Revelation 12:6 speaks of the same period as being 1260 days, while Revelation 12:14 calls it a time, times, and half a time just as Daniel does.

26-28. The end of the matter was that God would sit in judgment and take over the kingdom. This kingdom is the one prophesied throughout the Old Testament. Jesus will finally sit on the throne of David and rule (Jer 23:5-6; Lk 1:32-33).

troubled me, and my countenance changed in me: but I kept the matter in my heart.

CHAPTER 8

IN the third year of the reign of king Bĕl-shăz′zar a vision appeared unto me, even unto me Daniel, after that which appeared unto me at the first.

2 And I saw in a vision; and it came to pass, when I saw, that I was at Shū′-shăn in the palace, which is in the province of Ē′lam; and I saw in a vision, and I was by the river of Ū′la-ī.

3 Then I lifted up mine eyes, and saw, and, behold, there stood before the river a ram which had two horns: and the two horns were high; but one was higher than the other, and the higher came up last.

4 I saw the ram pushing westward, and northward, and southward; so that no beasts might stand before him, neither was there any that could deliver out of his hand; but he did according to his will, and became great.

5 And as I was considering, behold, an he goat came from the west on the face of the whole earth, and touched not the ground: and the goat had a notable horn between his eyes.

6 And he came to the ram that had two horns, which I had seen standing before the river, and ran unto him in the fury of his power.

7 And I saw him come close unto the ram, and he was moved with choler against him, and smote the ram, and brake his two horns: and there was no power in the ram to stand before him, but he cast him down to the ground, and stamped upon him: and there was none that could deliver the ram out of his hand.

8 Therefore the he goat waxed very great: and when he was strong, the great horn was broken; and for it came up four notable ones toward the four winds of heaven.

9 And out of one of them came forth a little horn, which waxed exceeding great, toward the south, and toward the east, and toward the pleasant land.

10 And it waxed great, even to the host of heaven; and it cast down some of the host and of the stars to the ground, and stamped upon them.

11 Yea, he magnified himself even to the prince of the host, and by him the daily sacrifice was taken away, and the place of his sanctuary was cast down.

12 And an host was given him against the daily sacrifice by reason of transgression, and it cast down the truth to the ground; and it practised, and prospered.

13 ¶Then I heard one saint speaking, and another saint said unto that certain saint which spake, How long shall be the vision concerning the daily sacrifice, and the transgression of desola-

B. Daniel's Vision of the Ram and the He Goat. 8:1-27.

1. The vision received by Daniel. 8:1-14.

8:1-2. Daniel's second recorded vision came to him during Belshazzar's third year of reign. **I was at Shushan in the palace.** The vision placed Daniel at Susa, one of the capitals of Persia (modern Iran) since this vision concerned the Persian and Greek kingdoms. Susa was about two hundred fifty miles east of Babylon and was later a center of Jewish habitation (Est 1:2).

3-4. Two animals were prominent in this vision. Daniel first saw a ram with one horn higher than the other. This stood for **the kings of Media and Persia** (vs. 20). It moved westward in victorious conquest. Historically, the Persians conquered all the kingdoms in Asia Minor, or modern Turkey, and sought several times to take over parts of Greece. They had such famous and powerful rulers as Cyrus, Darius, Xerxes and Artaxerxes.

5-7. However, **a he goat came from the west.** It strangely had **a notable horn between his eyes.** The goat represented Greece; and the horn typified Alexander the Great, Greece's first king (vs. 21). This goat **smote the ram . . . cast him down to the ground, and stamped upon him.** Alexander's conquest of Persia was lightning fast. Beginning about 334 B.C., Alexander marched across Asia Minor, defeating the Persian armies in key battles at Granicus River and at Issus. He then captured Syria and Egypt before entering and swiftly conquering Persia itself.

8. Thereafter, the **great horn** on the goat broke off. Alexander died of a fever prematurely at age thirty-two after extending his kingdom as far as the Indus River in India. In place of the great horn (Alexander) **came up four notable ones toward the four winds.** These represent four of Alexander's powerful generals, Ptolemy, Antigonus, Lysimachus, and Cassander who each began to rule a portion of the great empire set up by Alexander.

9-10. From the horn represented by Antigonus who ruled Syria **came forth a little horn.** This little horn was Antiochus IV, called Epiphanes, who persecuted the Jews in **the pleasant land** from about 171-165 B.C. The Maccabee family led a revolt against Antiochus Epiphanes and the Jews were able to reestablish their own sovereignty in the land of Palestine by 165 B.C.

11-12. This little horn was then personified and took away **the daily sacrifice** of the Jews and desecrated their **sanctuary.** Antiochus Epiphanes actually took control of the Jewish Temple that had been rebuilt under Haggai and Zechariah. In doing so, he offered a large hog on the sacred Jewish altar and thus defiled the House of God.

13-14. The vision then turned to hear a question—**How long** should this sanctuary desolation continue with the interruption of the daily sacrifice? The answer was for 2300 days, or nearly six and one half years. Theories that transform these days into years depart radically from both literal hermeneutics and sound

tion, to give both the sanctuary and the host to be trodden under foot?

14 And he said unto me, Unto two thousand and three hundred days; then shall the sanctuary be cleansed.

15 ¶And it came to pass, when I, *even* I Daniel, had seen the vision, and sought for the meaning, then, behold, there stood before me as the appearance of a man.

16 And I heard a man's voice between *the banks of* Ū′la-ī, which called, and said, Gabriel, make this *man* to understand the vision.

17 So he came near where I stood: and when he came, I was afraid, and fell upon my face: but he said unto me, Understand, O son of man: for at the time of the end *shall be* the vision.

18 Now as he was speaking with me, I was in a deep sleep on my face toward the ground: but he touched me, and set me upright.

19 And he said, Behold, I will make thee know what shall be in the last end of the indignation: for at the time appointed the end *shall be.*

20 The ram which thou sawest having *two* horns *are* the kings of Mē′dī-a and Persia.

21 And the rough goat *is* the king of Grecia: and the great horn that *is* between his eyes *is* the first king.

22 Now that being broken, whereas four stood up for it, four kingdoms shall stand up out of the nation, but not in his power.

23 And in the latter time of their kingdom, when the transgressors are come to the full, a king of fierce countenance, and understanding dark sentences, shall stand up.

24 And his power shall be mighty, but not by his own power: and he shall destroy wonderfully, and shall prosper, and practise, and shall destroy the mighty and the holy people.

25 And through his policy also he shall cause craft to prosper in his hand; and he shall magnify *himself* in his heart, and by peace shall destroy many: he shall also stand up against the Prince of princes; but he shall be broken without hand.

26 And the vision of the evening and the morning which was told *is* true: wherefore shut thou up the vision; for it *shall be* for many days.

27 And I Daniel fainted, and was sick *certain* days; afterward I rose up, and did the king's business; and I was astonished at the vision, but none understood it.

biblical interpretation. **Then shall the sanctuary be cleansed.** This has no reference to a supposed heavenly temple, but clearly refers to the actual Jewish Temple cleansing that took place in 165 B.C. or 164 B.C. by the Maccabees. This occurred on the twenty-fifth day of Chislev, or the Jewish December. One day's supply of oil miraculously kept the golden lampstand burning for eight days. That cleansing has been celebrated ever after by the Jews as the Feast of Dedication (Jn 10:22), also called Hanukkah today. The books of I and II Maccabees in the Apocrypha contain a detailed account of all these transactions.

2. The vision interpreted to Daniel by Gabriel. 8:15-27.

15-16. As Daniel **sought for the meaning** of the vision, a voice commanded **Gabriel,** one of God's angels, to help Daniel **understand the vision.** This was Gabriel's first appearance in Scripture, though he came once again to Daniel (9:21) and also appeared to Zachariah (Lk 1:19) and Mary (Lk 1:26) over 500 years later at the beginning of the New Testament.

17-19. In general, from Daniel's perspective the vision signified events that were to occur in the future **at the time of the end,** or at **the last end of the indignation.** It would seem that the end in view in the vision is similar to that pictured in both 2:44-45 and 7:24-26, namely, the time when the Antichrist is destroyed by Christ. Antiochus Epiphanes accomplished all that was predicted of him, but he also symbolizes the final enemy of God and the Jews.

20-21. In the plainest of language, Gabriel explained that Persia would expand its kingdom westward, only to be completely decimated later by the first king of Greece. The battles that defeated Persia occurred around 331 B.C. (see comments on vss. 5-10).

22-23. But these events are only incidental to the message conveyed by the following verses. After the death of the first king of Greece, Alexander the Great, his kingdom was divided into four parts, following nearly thirty years of power struggles (see vs. 8). **The latter time of their kingdom** (vs. 23) refers to these four kingdoms rising out of the Greek dominance. One particular king was to be outstanding for his fierce opposition to God's people, Israel. This **king of fierce countenance** was Antiochus Epiphanes. He ruled Syria from 175 B.C. until his death around 165 B.C. A preview of his career is given in these verses.

24-25. Antiochus IV would seek to **destroy the mighty and the holy people.** He tried to hellenize the Jews—that is, make Greeks out of them. He introduced Greek literature, culture, plays, sports, government, and religion; and he spread the Greek language as the one means of international communication. He was a cunning man; but eventually he was **broken without hand,** that is, by God Himself. The 2300 days of vs. 14 probably refer to the primary time of his deceitful and outrageous conduct against the Jews from about 171 B.C. to 165 B.C. Antiochus IV, Epiphanes, died strangely while on an expedition to Persia.

26-27. Daniel was then told to **shut thou up the vision,** meaning he was to preserve it. Through its message the Jews of a later generation were able to recognize Antiochus Epiphanes and resist him.

CHAPTER 9

IN the first year of Darius the son of A-haś-ū-ē'rus, of the seed of the Medes, which was made king over the realm of the Chăl-dē'ans;

2 In the first year of his reign I Daniel understood by books the number of the years, whereof the word of the LORD came to Jeremiah the prophet, that he would accomplish seventy years in the desolations of Jerusalem.

3 ¶And I set my face unto the Lord God, to seek by prayer and supplications, with fasting, and sackcloth, and ashes:

4 And I prayed unto the LORD my God, and made my confession, and said, O Lord, the great and dreadful God, keeping the covenant and mercy to them that love him, and to them that keep his commandments;

5 We have sinned, and have committed iniquity, and have done wickedly, and have rebelled, even by departing from thy precepts and from thy judgments:

6 Neither have we hearkened unto thy servants the prophets, which spake in thy name to our kings, our princes, and our fathers, and to all the people of the land.

7 O Lord, righteousness *belongeth* unto thee, but unto us confusion of faces, as at this day; to the men of Judah, and to the inhabitants of Jerusalem, and unto all Israel, *that are* near, and *that are* far off, through all the countries whither thou hast driven them, because of their trespass that they have trespassed against thee.

8 O Lord, to us *belongeth* confusion of face, to our kings, to our princes, and to our fathers, because we have sinned against thee.

9 To the Lord our God *belong* mercies and forgivenesses, though we have rebelled against him;

10 Neither have we obeyed the voice of the LORD our God, to walk in his laws, which he set before us by his servants the prophets.

11 Yea, all Israel have transgressed thy law, even by departing, that they might not obey thy voice; therefore the curse is poured upon us, and the oath that *is* written in the law of Moses the servant of God, because we have sinned against him.

12 And he hath confirmed his words, which he spake against us, and against our judges that judged us, by bringing upon us a great evil: for under the whole heaven hath not been done as hath been done upon Jerusalem.

13 As *it is* written in the law of Moses, all this evil is come upon us: yet made we not our prayer before the LORD our God, that we might turn from our iniquities, and understand thy truth.

14 Therefore hath the LORD watched upon the evil, and brought it upon us: for the LORD our God *is* righteous in all his works which he doeth: for we obeyed not his voice.

C. Daniel's Supplication and the Seventy Weeks Prophecy. 9:1-27.

1. Daniel repents for himself and his people. 9:1-19.

9:1-2. After Daniel had been in captivity in Babylon for nearly seventy years, he knew that God's predictions through Jeremiah (Jer 25:11-12) were nearly fulfilled and that God might allow His people to return to Palestine (cf. Jer 29:10).

3-4. As a result, Daniel sought God by **prayer and supplications.** Daniel confessed his own sin, as well as that of his people, and begged God to be merciful in allowing them to return. Daniel's prayer began with a contemplation of some of the great attributes of Jehovah. We would do well to imitate this aspect of Daniel's prayer habit.

5-6. Confession of sin, both individual and collective, was made in these verses. **We have sinned.** Daniel associated himself with his people. He did not consider himself to be above others in righteousness. A nation's sins must be confessed by God's people if they seek God's mercy for their land.

7-9. Daniel acknowledged God's righteous activities in scattering His people Israel. They justly deserved it. All classes in Israel were involved in wickedness, but Daniel reminded God of His attributes of **mercies and forgivenesses.**

10-14. As a result of neglecting God's law, persecution came upon Israel, just as God had promised. Yet, even in the midst of all that, as Daniel noted, they refused to pray or to **turn from our iniquities, and understand thy truth** (vs. 13). The contrast was that **God is righteous;** but as Daniel had to confess, the people had **obeyed not his voice** (vs. 14).

15 And now, O Lord our God, that hast brought thy people forth out of the land of Egypt with a mighty hand, and hast gotten thee renown, as at this day; we have sinned, we have done wickedly.

16 ¶O Lord, according to all thy righteousness, I beseech thee, let thine anger and thy fury be turned away from thy city Jerusalem, thy holy mountain: because for our sins, and for the iniquities of our fathers, Jerusalem and thy people are become a reproach to all that are about us.

17 Now therefore, O our God, hear the prayer of thy servant, and his supplications, and cause thy face to shine upon thy sanctuary that is desolate, for the Lord's sake.

18 O my God, incline thine ear, and hear; open thine eyes, and behold our desolations, and the city which is called by thy name: for we do not present our supplications before thee for our righteousnesses, but for thy great mercies.

19 O Lord, hear; O Lord, forgive; O Lord, hearken and do; defer not, for thine own sake, O my God: for thy city and thy people are called by thy name.

20 ¶And whiles I was speaking, and praying, and confessing my sin and the sin of my people Israel, and presenting my supplication before the Lord my God for the holy mountain of my God;

21 Yea, whiles I was speaking in prayer, even the man Gabriel, whom I had seen in the vision at the beginning, being caused to fly swiftly, touched me about the time of the evening oblation.

22 And he informed me, and talked with me, and said, O Daniel, I am now come forth to give thee skill and understanding.

23 At the beginning of thy supplications the commandment came forth, and I am come to shew thee; for thou art greatly beloved: therefore understand the matter, and consider the vision.

24 Seventy weeks are determined upon thy people and upon thy holy city, to finish the transgression, and to make an end of sins, and to make reconciliation for iniquity, and to bring in everlasting righteousness, and to seal up the vision and prophecy, and to anoint the most Holy.

15-19. The ground of Daniel's request for forgiveness and a return to Jerusalem was not in the fact that Israel had now turned back to God, because they had not. The appeal was to God's **righteousness** (vs. 16), **for the Lord's sake** (vs. 17), **for thy great mercies** (vs. 18), **for thy city and thy people are called by thy name** (vs. 19). God's name was defamed as long as His Temple and people were a reproach. Daniel asked God to reverse that situation for the sake of God's glory alone.

2. God's sending of Gabriel to answer Daniel's prayer. 9:20-23.

20-23. Once again, the angel Gabriel was commissioned to bring Daniel revelation from God. Gabriel informed Daniel that he was **greatly beloved.** We should strive before God to be able to have the same words spoken of us. Certainly Daniel's great concern for God's honor, and for his people, must have been part of the reason he was so dearly loved of God.

3. The disclosure of the Seventy Weeks prophecy. 9:24-27.

24. Seventy weeks meant, literally, seventy units of seven, or seventy times seven. Almost all expositors, ancient and modern, have seen this as signifying seventy units, each composed of seven years, making a total of 490 years. **Are determined** indicates that these years of which God told Daniel were certain to transpire in the manner predicted. **Upon thy people and upon thy holy city.** This prophecy concerned Israel, the Hebrew nation descended through Jacob, and the city of Jerusalem. Six things dealing with sin and righteousness would be accomplished during the 490 years. The first three are negative, and the final three positive: (1) **To finish the transgression** has reference to rebellion against God; (2) **To make an end of sins** could quite naturally in this context refer to sin being put away during the Messiah's reign; (3) **To make reconciliation for iniquity** speaks of an atonement for sin on the basis of some sacrifice. This was no doubt fulfilled in Christ's own sacrificial death on the cross; (4) **To bring in everlasting righteousness.** With sin taken care of (in the first three statements), righteousness can now be a reality. This will be applied to Israel at Christ's glorious second coming at the conclusion of the Tribulation Period and will usher in the predicted righteous government of the Messiah (Isa 9:7; 11:3-5; Jer 23:5-6); (5) **To seal up the vision and prophecy.** There will come a time when all visions and prophecy will be fulfilled or consummated, and thus

25 Know therefore and understand, *that* from the going forth of the commandment to restore and to build Jerusalem unto the Messiah the Prince *shall be* seven weeks, and threescore and two weeks: the street shall be built again, and the wall, even in troublous times.

26 And after threescore and two weeks shall Messiah be cut off, but not for himself: and the people of the prince that shall come shall destroy the city and the sanctuary; and the end thereof *shall be* with a flood, and unto the end of the war desolations are determined.

27 And he shall confirm the covenant with many for one week: and in the midst of the week he shall cause the sacrifice and the oblation to cease, and for the overspreading of abominations he shall make *it* desolate, even until the consummation, and that determined shall be poured upon the desolate.

will no longer have a function. There are yet, of course, many prophecies that must still be fulfilled; and (6) **To anoint the most Holy.** This phrase has been taken at various times to refer to Zerubbabel's temple, Christ Himself, the Holy One, or the future millennial temple. The most natural usage would be a reference to the anointing of a future temple when Messiah's reign will be inaugurated with righteousness. Such a temple is predicted in Ezekiel 40-48, together with actual animal sacrifices which will commemorate Christ's death on the cross.

25. From the going forth of the commandment to restore and to build Jerusalem. These words indicate the beginning point, or *terminus a quo,* for the seventy weeks of years during which the six events specified in verse 24 are to be accomplished. It actually requires the completion of all seventy weeks, or the full 490 years, to accomplish all of the predicted events of verse 24. It is believed that this starting point can be readily identified from the Scriptures themselves. Three possibilities are found: (1) A date of 538 B.C. when Cyrus issued a command recorded in II Chronicles 36:22-23 and repeated in Ezra 1:1-4. However, this edict clearly referred only to rebuilding the Temple and not only mentioned nothing of rebuilding the city, but also accomplished nothing in that regard; (2) A date of 458 B.C. when Artaxerxes issued a decree to aid Ezra as he returned to Jerusalem. But this command, recorded in Ezra 7:11-26, also clearly had nothing to do with rebuilding the city. Ezra summarized the intent of the king's edict as being ". . . to beautify the house of the LORD which is in Jerusalem" (Ezr 7:27). (3) A date of 445 B.C. seems to be more credible, at the time when Artaxerxes gave permission to Nehemiah to go ". . . unto the city of my fathers' sepulchers, that I may build it" (Neh 2:5). The edict even mentions materials to be gathered ". . . for the wall of the city . . ." (Neh 2:8).

Unto the Messiah the Prince defines the termination point, or *terminus ad quem,* of the first sixty-nine weeks of years, meaning 483 years, as expressed by the phrase **shall be seven weeks, and threescore and two weeks.** The significance of the marking off of the initial seven weeks, or forty-nine years, is uncertain, though it may refer to the time Ezra and Nehemiah labored to firmly set up the new Jewish state in Jerusalem. Those days could certainly be described as **troublous times.**

26. The terminus of the first sixty-nine weeks was **unto the Messiah the Prince** (vs. 25), indicating some point in His life, not His birth, because of the chronology involved. This is usually seen as a reference to His baptism, earthly ministry, or, sometimes, Triumphal Entry. Sometime **after** the fulfillment of the 483-year period **shall Messiah be cut off** and "have nothing" (NASB, NIV). The crucifixion of Christ coincides with this prediction, as nearly all biblical scholars agree. The next event described is the destruction of **the city** (Jerusalem) **and the sanctuary.** This destruction occurred in A.D. 70 and was carried out by Vespasian, his son Titus, and the Roman legions. **The people of the prince that shall come** refers to the Romans, since this prince is to be distinguished from **Messiah the Prince** of verse 25. The prince of verse 26 is the Antichrist, and his people are the Roman people. It is important to note that these events happened after the first sixty-nine weeks of years, but still before the final week spoken of in verse 27. That final week is still future and awaits the fulfillment of the events of verse 27.

27. And he. He refers back to **the prince that shall come** of verse 26. It predicts the coming of the Roman Antichrist during the Tribulation Period after the Rapture of the church. **He shall confirm the covenant with many for one week.** The Antichrist will pledge protection of Israel for a seven-year period, but **in the midst of the week he shall cause the sacrifice and the oblation to cease.** After three and one half years, the Antichrist will break his covenant with Israel and defile their new Temple.

The New Testament confirms this in II Thessalonians 2:4 where Paul declares that the Antichrist, the man of sin, will sit ". . . in the temple of God, showing himself that he is God." Up until that point the Antichrist will have seemed to be Israel's protector. His true intentions will then be known. Revelation states that power was given unto him to continue forty and two months (Rev 13:5). He will have only one half of the seven-year period left after he breaks his compact with Israel. As a result, Israel will be forced to flee and to hide under God's protection ". . . for a time, and times, and half a time . . ." (Rev 12:14), again a reference to the last three and one half years of Daniel's final seventieth week of years. For a detailed treatment of this premillenarian view, see Leon Wood, *A Commentary on Daniel*, pp. 247-63, and John Walvoord, *Daniel: The Key to Prophetic Revelation*, pp. 216-37. Both adequately cover other viewpoints as well.

D. Daniel's Vision of the Heavenly Messenger. 10:1-21.

Chapter 10 is preparatory to the prophecy given in chapter 11 and contains a vision of the coming of a messenger who delivers the predictions that follow in Daniel 11.

10:1-3. Daniel had been praying, mourning, and fasting for three weeks during the third year of King Cyrus' reign. This would have been about 537 B.C. Daniel was seriously agonizing for his people.

CHAPTER 10

IN the third year of Cyrus king of Persia a thing was revealed unto Daniel, whose name was called Bĕl-te-shăz'zar; and the thing *was* true, but the time appointed *was* long: and he understood the thing, and had understanding of the vision.

2 In those days I Daniel was mourning three full weeks.

3 I ate no pleasant bread, neither came flesh nor wine in my mouth, neither did I anoint myself at all, till three whole weeks were fulfilled.

4 And in the four and twentieth day of the first month, as I was by the side of the great river, which *is* Hĭd'de-kĕl;

5 Then I lifted up mine eyes, and looked, and behold, a certain man clothed in linen, whose loins *were* girded with fine gold of Ū'phăz:

6 His body also *was* like the beryl, and his face as the appearance of lightning, and his eyes as lamps of fire, and his arms and his feet like in colour to polished brass, and the voice of his words like the voice of a multitude.

7 And I Daniel alone saw the vision: for the men that were with me saw not the vision; but a great quaking fell upon them, so that they fled to hide themselves.

8 Therefore I was left alone, and saw this great vision, and there remained no strength in me: for my comeliness was turned in me into corruption, and I retained no strength.

9 Yet heard I the voice of his words: and when I heard the voice of his words, then was I in a deep sleep on my face, and my face toward the ground.

10 ¶And, behold, an hand touched me, which set me upon my knees and *upon* the palms of my hands.

11 And he said unto me, O Daniel, a man greatly beloved, understand the words that I speak unto thee, and stand upright: for unto thee am I now sent. And when he had spoken this word unto me, I stood trembling.

12 Then said he unto me, Fear not, Daniel: for from the first day that thou didst set thine heart to understand, and to chasten thyself before thy God, thy

4-7. Standing by the **Hiddekel**, or Tigris River, Daniel received a **vision** (vs. 7) of a majestic figure. Described as a **man clothed in linen**, wearing a **gold** belt, whose **face** was like lightning, with **eyes as lamps of fire**, etc., it is easy to compare him with the similar description of Christ given in Revelation 1:13-15. Because of these similarities, many believe this was a majestic pre-incarnate appearance of Christ, perhaps similar to those of Exodus 24:9-11 or 33:18-23 with 34:5-9. This is, however, by no means certain, especially since (1) he is not so identified in the text; (2) other created angels sometimes appear in glorious splendor as in Revelation 18:1 and 10:1-7. Walvoord identifies these as created angels, though they are similar to this one in Daniel whom he believes to be Christ; and (3) the messenger here in Daniel 10 confessed his lack of omnipotence in verses 12-13

8-10. When the vision ended, Daniel was alone and felt weak. The glorious messenger he had seen in the vision then spoke to Daniel. **I heard the voice of his words**, vs. 9, must refer back to the figure in vss. 5-6; for there is no other antecedent to which the pronoun **his** may refer.

11-12. This messenger had been sent to Daniel three weeks earlier on the first day Daniel began to pray, mourn, and fast (cf. vs. 2).

words were heard, and I am come for thy words.

13 But the prince of the kingdom of Persia withstood me one and twenty days: but, lo, Michael, one of the chief princes, came to help me; and I remained there with the kings of Persia.

14 Now I am come to make thee understand what shall befall thy people in the latter days: for yet the vision *is* for *many* days.

15 And when he had spoken such words unto me, I set my face toward the ground, and I became dumb.

16 And, behold, *one* like the similitude of the sons of men touched my lips: then I opened my mouth, and spake, and said unto him that stood before me, O my lord, by the vision my sorrows are turned upon me, and I have retained no strength.

17 For how can the servant of this my lord talk with this my lord? for as for me, straightway there remained no strength in me, neither is there breath left in me.

18 Then there came again and touched me *one* like the appearance of a man, and he strengthened me.

19 And said, O man greatly beloved, fear not: peace *be* unto thee, be strong, yea, be strong. And when he had spoken unto me, I was strengthened, and said, Let my lord speak; for thou hast strengthened me.

20 Then said he, Knowest thou wherefore I come unto thee? and now will I return to fight with the prince of Persia: and when I am gone forth, lo, the prince of Grecia shall come.

21 But I will shew thee that which is noted in the scripture of truth: and *there is* none that holdeth with me in these things, but Michael your prince.

CHAPTER 11

ALSO I in the first year of Darius the Mede, *even* I, stood to confirm and to strengthen him.

2 And now will I shew thee the truth. Behold, there shall stand up yet three kings in Persia; and the fourth shall be far richer than *they* all: and by his strength through his riches he shall stir up all against the realm of Grecia.

3 And a mighty king shall stand up, that shall rule with great dominion, and do according to his will.

4 And when he shall stand up, his kingdom shall be broken, and shall be divided toward the four winds of heaven; and not to his posterity, nor according to his dominion which he ruled: for his kingdom shall be plucked up, even for others beside those.

5 ¶And the king of the south shall be

13-14. But the prince of the kingdom of Persia had detained this messenger for three weeks until **Michael, one of the chief princes** came to help him. This is the first biblical reference to Michael the Archangel. He is only found elsewhere in verse 21; 12:1; Jude 9; Revelation 12:7; and probably I Thessalonians 4:16. The messenger sent to Daniel was no doubt a supernatural being; and likewise, the prince of Persia who detained him must have been one of Satan's principalities and powers. There is a spiritual warfare going on of which we on earth know very little, and a small glimpse is afforded us in this chapter. The message he brought concerned **what shall befall thy people in the latter days.** The content of this prophecy is found in Daniel 11.

15-18. Daniel was overwhelmed with such a vision and the initial report of events outside of his understanding. The messenger strengthened him so that he could receive the revelation, but it may have taken some time for Daniel to regain his composure. Naturally, a three-week fast would have contributed to his physical weakness. Thus, this messenger still described as like **sons of men** (vs. 16), as a **man** (vs. 18, cf. vs. 5 **a certain man**) had to reawaken or refresh Daniel several different times, i.e., **came again and touched me** (vs. 18).

19-21. The messenger told Daniel that **Michael** was the **prince** for Israel (vs. 21). Most of Michael's duties do seem to relate to activity on behalf of Israel (see the references listed in the comments on vss. 13-14).

E. The Prophecy of Israel's Future to the Maccabees and Beyond. 11:1-45.

1. Syrian and Egyptian relations foretold down to 165 B.C. 11:1-20.

11:1-2. In the first year of Darius, the Mede. Daniel had been given an earlier vision in Belshazzar's reign (chs. 7; 8) that foretold of Persian and then Grecian kingdoms that would supplant the Babylonian Empire. Now that the Persians had actually taken power, God further revealed, in more detail, events that would affect the Jews for several centuries to come. He gave a foreview of the Great Tribulation. From Daniel's time, four more kings would rule over Persia, apparently fulfilled by Cambyses, Pseudo-Smerdis, Darius the Great, and Xerxes (the Ahasuerus of Esther). Xerxes did in fact **stir up all against the realm of Grecia.** This he did in fact, even capturing Athens before suffering a military defeat at Salamis in 480 B.C. Thereafter, he withdrew and stayed in Persia.

3. Upon the mention of Greece, there was predicted **a mighty king.** This could be no other than Alexander the Great.

4. His kingdom shall be broken, and shall be divided toward the four winds of heaven. After his untimely death at the young age of thirty-two, his kingdom did not pass on **to his posterity,** meaning to his own son; but it was eventually divided among four powerful Greek military leaders (see comments on 8:8).

5. The king of the south referred to Ptolemy I, Soter, who

strong, and *one* of his princes; and he shall be strong above him, and have dominion; his dominion *shall be* a great dominion.

6 And in the end of years they shall join themselves together; for the king's daughter of the south shall come to the king of the north to make an agreement: but she shall not retain the power of the arm; neither shall he stand, nor his arm: but she shall be given up, and they that brought her, and he that begat her, and he that strengthened her in *these* times.

7 But out of a branch of her roots shall *one* stand up in his estate, which shall come with an army, and shall enter into the fortress of the king of the north, and shall deal against them, and shall prevail:

8 And shall also carry captives into Egypt their gods, with their princes, *and* with their precious vessels of silver and of gold; and he shall continue *more* years than the king of the north.

9 So the king of the south shall come into *his* kingdom, and shall return into his own land.

10 But his sons shall be stirred up, and shall assemble a multitude of great forces: and *one* shall certainly come, and overflow, and pass through: then shall he return, and be stirred up, *even* to his fortress.

11 And the king of the south shall be moved with choler, and shall come forth and fight with him, *even* with the king of the north: and he shall set forth a great multitude; but the multitude shall be given into his hand.

12 *And* when he hath taken away the multitude, his heart shall be lifted up; and he shall cast down *many* ten thousands: but he shall not be strengthened *by it.*

13 For the king of the north shall return, and shall set forth a multitude greater than the former, and shall certainly come after certain years with a great army and with much riches.

14 And in those times there shall many stand up against the king of the south: also the robbers of thy people shall exalt themselves to establish the vision; but they shall fall.

15 So the king of the north shall come, and cast up a mount, and take the most fenced cities: and the arms of the south shall notwithstand, neither

ruled Egypt (cf. vs. 8) and actually began a lengthy dynasty of eleven successive Greek rulers in that ancient land. They ruled from 305 B.C. down to Cleopatra, the last of the Ptolemaic rulers, who occupied the throne from 47 B.C. (the time of Julius Caesar) to 30 B.C., one year after Octavian (Caesar Augustus) defeated her friend Mark Antony. Cleopatra then committed suicide and Rome annexed Egypt.

6. The king of the north was a reference to the Seleucid monarchy established by Seleucus I, Nicator, over Syria, Babylonia, and areas to the east. The Seleucid dynasty held sway over this territory until 65 B.C. Both the Syrian and Egyptian rulers (all of whom were of Greek origin) vied for control over the territory between them, i.e., Palestine. The returned Israelites found themselves in the midst of a severe power struggle. **They shall join themselves together.** Bernice, the daughter of Ptolemy II, Philadelphus, of Egypt married Antiochus II, Theos, in 252 B.C. to end years of war between the two powers. But Antiochus put aside his first wife, Laodice, who had a son, Seleucus II Callinius, and agreed that the progeny of Bernice should inherit the throne. However, both Ptolemy II and Antiochus II died in 246 B.C.; and Bernice and her son were murdered by Laodice just before Ptolemy Philadelphus died.

7. A branch of her roots refers to Ptolemy Philadelphus' son, Ptolemy III, called Euergates I (246-222 B.C.), the brother of Bernice. In 245 B.C. he came north **with an army** and plundered Syria, **the fortress of the king of the north**; but he did not kill the king or take over the kingdom.

8. After plundering the north, Ptolemy III returned to Egypt with great spoils and continued ruling till his death in 222 B.C. He resisted attacking the northern kingdom for some time and never lost a battle with the north.

9. So the king of the south shall come is a mistranslation of the Hebrew, which reads, literally: And he (referring to the king of the north just mentioned in vs. 8) will come into the realm of the king of the south. This refers to Seleucus Callinicus' invasion of Egypt in 240 B.C. in which he was defeated and had to **return into his own land.**

10. But his sons. The sons of Seleucus II were Seleucus III, called variously Ceraunus or Soter, and Antiochus III, the Great. Seleucus III was assassinated in 223 B.C., so Antiochus III took over, eventually running roughshod over Ptolemy IV in the land of Egypt. Later, he was defeated in the north; but he eventually captured the **fortress** of Gaza in Palestine.

11-12. And the king of the south, meaning Ptolemy IV, Philopater, **shall come forth and fight with him,** meaning Antiochus III of vs. 10. The Battle of Raphia in 217 B.C. is in view here. Ptolemy IV was victorious. **His heart shall be lifted up.** Ptolemy grew proud of his victory and was not **strengthened by** it because he did not press his victory to completion. Instead, he retired to enjoy himself in various vices.

13-15. The king of the north (Antiochus III, the Great) **shall return . . . after certain years.** Following his defeat at Raphia, Antiochus the Great strengthened his forces, solidified his eastern holdings, and returned to Egypt in 203 B.C., just after the death of Ptolemy IV who left only a four-year-old son Ptolemy V, Ephiphanes to rule. **A great army,** allied with the Macedonians, completely sacked Egypt as indicated by the words **shall come, and cast up a mount** (or siege ramp), **and take the most fenced cities.** The resistance of the south under their boy king was minimal, and they were badly defeated.

his chosen people, neither *shall there be any* strength to withstand.

16 But he that cometh against him shall do according to his own will, and none shall stand before him: and he shall stand in the glorious land, which by his hand shall be consumed.

17 He shall also set his face to enter with the strength of his whole kingdom, and upright ones with him; thus shall he do: and he shall give him the daughter of women, corrupting her: but she shall not stand *on his side,* neither be for him.

18 After this shall he turn his face unto the isles, and shall take many: but a prince for his own behalf shall cause the reproach offered by him to cease; without his own reproach he shall cause *it* to turn upon him.

19 Then he shall turn his face toward the fort of his own land: but he shall stumble and fall, and not be found.

20 Then shall stand up in his estate a raiser of taxes *in* the glory of the kingdom: but within few days he shall be destroyed, neither in anger, nor in battle.

21 And in his estate shall stand up a vile person, to whom they shall not give the honour of the kingdom: but he shall come in peaceably, and obtain the kingdom by flatteries.

22 And with the arms of a flood shall they be overflown from before him, and shall be broken; yea, also the prince of the covenant.

23 And after the league *made* with him he shall work deceitfully: for he shall come up, and shall become strong with a small people.

24 He shall enter peaceably even upon the fattest places of the province; and he shall do *that* which his fathers have not done, nor his fathers' fathers; he shall scatter among them the prey, and spoil, and riches: *yea,* and he shall forecast his devices against the strong holds, even for a time.

25 And he shall stir up his power and his courage against the king of the south with a great army; and the king of the south shall be stirred up to battle with a very great and mighty army; but he shall not stand: for they shall forecast devices against him.

16. None shall stand before him indicates the completeness of Antiochus' conquests of Egypt and the territories it controlled, even as far north as Sidon. **He shall stand in the glorious land** is a reference to Palestine (cf. vs. 41; 8:9). The Jews cooperated with Antiochus III and thus were his allies.

17. Hoping to conserve the results of his victory in a permanent manner, Antiochus III gave in marriage his daughter Cleopatra, called here **the daughter of women** (because she was so young), to the young king Ptolemy V in 197 B.C. However, Antiochus' hopes did not materialize, since his daughter Cleopatra did not **stand on his side.** She sided instead with her young husband Ptolemy V. Incidentally, the famous Rosetta Stone of Egypt, written in three languages, Greek, Demotic, and Hieroglyphic, is dated at 196 B.C., during the reign of young Ptolemy V. Discovered by Napoleon's men in A.D. 1799, it provided the information that eventually unlocked the mysterious Egyptian Hieroglyphics.

18. After this. Believing that his new marriage alliance with Ptolemy V would protect him in the south, **he,** Antiochus III, turned **his face unto the isles,** meaning some of the islands and coastlands of Asia Minor and even Greece. He was allied with Hannibal of Carthage who aided him. This created difficulties with Rome and eventuated in Antiochus' defeat by Scipio Asiaticus in 190 B.C. at the Battle of Magnesia in Asia Minor.

19. Thereafter, Antiochus III returned to Syria, **his own land: but he shall stumble and fall** is another way of predicting the death of Antiochus the Great which occurred a year after his return, around 187 B.C.

20. Then shall stand up in his estate. Antiochus' son, Seleucus IV, Philopater, took over after his father's death. Owing the Romans huge annual tribute payments, he quickly became a **raiser of taxes.** His reign lasted eleven years, only a **few days** compared with his father's thirty-seven-year regency. He was assassinated by his minister, Heliodorus, who hoped to gain the throne for himself, since Seleucus' only son was being held hostage by Rome.

2. The career of Antiochus Epiphanes foretold. 11:21-35.

21. And in his estate shall stand up a vile person. Beginning with verse 21 and continuing through verse 35, the vile person under consideration is Antiochus IV, Epiphanes. Antiochus Epiphanes was the brother of Seleucus IV, and the third son of Antiochus the Great. He quickly ousted Heliodorus and gained control for himself **by flatteries.** The kingdom was not rightfully his, but it belonged to his young nephew in Rome.

22-25. Antiochus Epiphanes began military conquests against Egypt. He worked **deceitfully** against the young Ptolemy Philopater first by posing as a friend coming only **with a small people.** But his true intentions were soon established, for he took the **fattest places of the province.** After these initial successes by Antiochus Epiphanes, **the king of the south** (Ptolemy Philometer) **shall be stirred up to battle.** The battle was fought at Pelusium east of the Nile Delta. The reason for Ptolemy's defeat was that his own men **forecast devices against him.** This simply means that there was treason among Ptolemy's men.

26 Yea, they that feed of the portion of his meat shall destroy him, and his army shall overflow: and many shall fall down slain.

27 And both these kings' hearts *shall be* to do mischief, and they shall speak lies at one table; but it shall not prosper: for yet the end *shall be* at the time appointed.

28 Then shall he return into his land with great riches; and his heart *shall be* against the holy covenant; and he shall do *exploits*, and return to his own land.

29 At the time appointed he shall return, and come toward the south; but it shall not be as the former, or as the latter.

30 For the ships of Chĭt′tĭm shall come against him: therefore he shall be grieved, and return, and have indignation against the holy covenant: so shall he do; he shall even return, and have intelligence with them that forsake the holy covenant.

31 And arms shall stand on his part, and they shall pollute the sanctuary of strength, and shall take away the daily *sacrifice*, and they shall place the abomination that maketh desolate.

32 And such as do wickedly against the covenant shall he corrupt by flatteries: but the people that do know their God shall be strong, and do *exploits*.

33 And they that understand among the people shall instruct many: yet they shall fall by the sword, and by flame, by captivity, and by spoil, *many* days.
34 Now when they shall fall, they shall be holpen with a little help: but many shall cleave to them with flatteries.

35 And *some* of them of understanding shall fall, to try them, and to purge, and to make *them* white, *even* to the time of the end: because *it is* yet for a time appointed.

36 And the king shall do according to his will; and he shall exalt himself, and magnify himself above every god, and shall speak marvellous things against the God of gods, and shall prosper till the indignation be accomplished: for that that is determined shall be done.

26-27. Antiochus' army was victorious beyond the battle at Pelusium in which he captured Ptolemy Philometer. But the Greek overlords of Egypt quickly replaced Philometer with Ptolemy Euergetes. Antiochus then assured Philometer he would reinstall him, thus courting his favor. The two spoke **lies at one table** in their efforts to gain an advantage by way of false promises. **For yet the end shall be at the appointed time** has reference to the coming death of Antiochus Epiphanes.

28. And his heart shall be against the holy covenant. In 168 B.C. Antiochus Epiphanes left Egypt, returned to Syria, and continued his policy of hellenization among the Jews. He promoted the worship of Zeus, naked participation in the Greek games, and other practices odious to the Jews.

29. He shall return, and come toward the south. Antiochus Epiphanes once again tried to recapture Egypt. **But it shall not be as the former, or as the latter** means that this latter attempt would not turn out successfully, as had the former campaign.

30. The ships of Chittim (cf. Num 24:24) are the forces of Rome who met Antiochus Epiphanes as he approached Alexandria. They forced him to return home without engaging in battle. Completely humiliated, he vented his wrath and **indignation against the holy covenant,** meaning the Jews, their sacred Temple, and the practices pertaining thereto. He joined forces with those Jews who forsook **the holy covenant,** including the Jews' apostate priest Menelaus. I and II Maccabees in the Apocrypha tell the story of those dark days.

31. Antiochus Epiphanes authorized his forces to **pollute the sanctuary . . . and . . . take away the daily sacrifice.** They sacrificed a sow, spread its remains inside the Holy Temple, and erected a large statue of Zeus for the people to worship. This was **the abomination that maketh desolate.**

32. Naturally, there were plenty of Jews who went along with Antiochus' new program, but Mattathias Maccabeus was among **the people that do know their God.** He resisted, along with his five sons; and together they engaged in guerilla warfare from 168 B.C. to 165 B.C. Their **exploits** were numerous, and they exhibited great courage. Time and again a small number of Jews would defeat Antiochus' much larger armies.

33-35. Yet, it was true that many did **fall by the sword.** After three years of fighting, they were able to restore worship to the Temple in Jerusalem. It was cleansed and purified on December 25, 165 B.C. This event has been commemorated ever since as the Feast of Hanukkah, or the Feast of Dedication as it is sometimes called (Jn 10:22). For more on the history involved in chapter 11, see the articles on Antiochus, Seleucus, and Ptolemy in *The Zondervan Pictorial Encyclopedia of the Bible* and the standard works on Daniel by Leupold, Walvoord, and Wood.

3. The career of Antichrist foretold. 11:36-45.

36. At this point the prophecy turns to describe the actions of a **king** that **shall do according to his will**—sometimes referred to as the Willful King. His actions go beyond those of Antiochus Epiphanes; and he meets death in Palestine (vs. 45), rather than in Persia as Antiochus Epiphanes did. Critics claim that pseudo Daniel here tried to go beyond the events known of Antiochus' career at 165 B.C. (when he supposedly wrote), and made these blunders; but many conservative scholars believe the career of the Antichrist of the Tribulation Period is foretold in this section. Robert Culver, "Daniel" in *The Wycliffe Bible Commentary*, p. 797, lists seven cogent reasons for seeing this Willful King as the future Antichrist, rather than as Antiochus Epiphanes; and Leon Wood, *A Commentary on Daniel*, pp. 304-305 gives eight arguments to support the same view. Their arguments will be evidenced in the following treatment. **He shall exalt himself, and magnify himself above every god.** Though Antiochus Epiphanes considered himself deity in some

37 Neither shall he regard the God of his fathers, nor the desire of women, nor regard any god: for he shall magnify himself above all.
38 But in his estate shall he honour the God of forces: and a god whom his fathers knew not shall he honour with gold, and silver, and with precious stones, and pleasant things.
39 Thus shall he do in the most strong holds with a strange god, whom he shall acknowledge *and* increase with glory: and he shall cause them to rule over many, and shall divide the land for gain.
40 And at the time of the end shall the king of the south push at him: and the king of the north shall come against him like a whirlwind, with chariots, and with horsemen, and with many ships; and he shall enter into the countries, and shall overflow and pass over.
41 He shall enter also into the glorious land, and many *countries* shall be overthrown: but these shall escape out of his hand, *even* Edom, and Moab, and the chief of the children of Ammon.
42 He shall stretch forth his hand also upon the countries: and the land of Egypt shall not escape.
43 But he shall have power over the treasures of gold and of silver, and over all the precious things of Egypt: and the Lĭb′ў-anś and the Ē-thĭ-ō′pĭ-ans *shall be* at his steps.
44 But tidings out of the east and out of the north shall trouble him: therefore he shall go forth with great fury to destroy, and utterly to make away many.
45 And he shall plant the tabernacles of his palace between the seas in the glorious holy mountain; yet he shall come to his end, and none shall help him.

CHAPTER 12

AND at that time shall Michael stand up, the great prince which standeth for the children of thy people: and there shall be a time of trouble, such as never was since there was a nation *even* to that same time: and at that time thy people shall be delivered, every one that shall be found written in the book.

2 And many of them that sleep in the dust of the earth shall awake, some to

degree, as evidenced by his coins, this will be one of the outstanding characteristics of the Roman Antichrist as seen in II Thessalonians 2:3-4. Samuel J. Andrews' *Christianity and Antichristianity in Their Final Conflict,* explains the Antichrist, and especially his claim to deity. **Shall prosper till the indignation be accomplished** refers to the Tribulation Period, as in 8:19.

37-39. Neither shall he regard the God of his fathers. This phrase does not prove that the Antichrist will be a Jew. Jew or Gentile, he has no time for the God, or gods, of his ancestors. **Nor the desire of women.** This has been taken as a reference to the Messiah, of whom Jewish women longed to be the mother; or of sexual desire. Actually, no satisfactory meaning has been found. **He shall magnify himself above all.** Paul declared that the Antichrist would enter into the Jewish Temple and declare himself to be God (II Thess 2:3-4).

40-41. **At the time of the end** refers to the end of the Tribulation period, just before Christ returns with His saints to set up His earthly kingdom. **The king of the south** speaks of a ruler from Egypt, or some other African country (perhaps the head of a confederation), who shall attack the Antichrist who **shall enter also into the glorious land**—Israel. Notice as well that **the king of the north** will also come against this endtime personage. In the previous section (vss. 21-35), Antiochus was himself called the king of the north. This distinction points to a third person— the Antichrist.

42-43. The Antichrist will strike back at **Egypt** and take the spoils of North Africa for a while. He has great power, but it is only temporary.

44-45. But tidings out of the east must refer to the great army mentioned in Revelation 16:12. **And out of the north.** Ezekiel 38 and 39 describe the advances of Gog and Magog upon the Antichrist. **Between the seas in the glorious holy mountain.** Antichrist will headquarter for the final time in Jerusalem. However, the Battle of Armageddon will transpire. **He shall come to his end** as Christ Himself returns from heaven and casts the beast, as he is called, into a lake burning with fire (Rev 19:19-20).

F. Daniel's Final Revelation. 12:1-13.

1. The Great Tribulation and the Resurrections. 12:1-3.

12:1. At that time connects these verses chronologically with what has just preceded, namely the concluding days of the Tribulation. **Shall Michael stand up.** Michael's task is to aid Israel, God's covenant people, the Jews. He does this during the time of their greatest persecution when the Antichrist and others would seek to take their lands. **There shall be a time of trouble.** This is the Great Tribulation, the time of Jacob's trouble (Jer 30:7), the final half of Daniel's seventieth week (9:27). **At that time thy people shall be delivered.** Paul declared that ". . . all Israel shall be saved . . ." (Rom 11:26; cf. Isa 59:20-21). There is coming a day of great deliverance and salvation for Israel. Christ will return (Zech 14:4); Israel will repent (Zech 12:9-10); and King Jesus will reign forever over Israel and all the earth (Zech 14:9).

2. Physical resurrection is spoken of here in a general sense, as in John 5:28-29. Yet, it specifies two separate resurrections by

everlasting life, and some to shame *and* everlasting contempt.

the unusual repetition of the word **some** (see Samuel Tregelles, *Remarks on the Prophetic Visions in the Book of Daniel*, pp. 164-169). Further revelation has more specifically shown that the resurrection of the just to **everlasting life** will occur immediately after the Great Tribulation of 12:1 (see Rev 20:4, 6). But the unjust dead will not be raised until one thousand years later, according to Revelation 20:5a. They will then be judged at the Great White Throne (Rev 20:11-15). May no one who reads these warnings fail to repent and receive Christ as personal Saviour. ". . . now is the day of salvation" (II Cor 6:2).

3 And they that be wise shall shine as the brightness of the firmament; and they that turn many to righteousness as the stars for ever and ever.

3. Having mentioned resurrection and the implied accompanying judgments, the messenger finishes his revelation to Daniel with the reminder that **they that turn many to righteousness (shall shine)** as **the stars for ever and ever.** The believer's obligation is to bear the message of Christ's saving grace to the world of lost humanity.

2. Daniel told to close up the book and wait. 12:4-13.

4 But thou, O Daniel, shut up the words, and seal the book, *even* to the time of the end: many shall run to and fro, and knowledge shall be increased.

4. Daniel was then told to protect the message received so that it could be read in later times. **The time of the end** is aptly described as a day when **knowledge shall be increased,** namely our modern computer era.

5 ¶Then I Daniel looked, and, behold, there stood other two, the one on this side of the bank of the river, and the other on that side of the bank of the river.

5-7. The messenger then swore by Almighty God that Antichrist's power would only extend until the end of the three and one half years specified earlier (see comments on 9:24-27; 11:36-45).

6 And *one* said to the man clothed in linen, which *was* upon the waters of the river, How long *shall it be to* the end of these wonders?

7 And I heard the man clothed in linen, which *was* upon the waters of the river, when he held up his right hand and his left hand unto heaven, and sware by him that liveth for ever that *it shall be* for a time, times, and an half; and when he shall have accomplished to scatter the power of the holy people, all these *things* shall be finished.

8 And I heard, but I understood not: then said I, O my Lord, what *shall be* the end of these *things?*

8-10. Daniel, even though the recipient of this revelation, did not fully comprehend it. From our perspective, 2500 years later with several Old Testament books Daniel did not have (Zechariah, for example), and the New Testament as well, we have a much better idea of what these prophecies mean and how they will transpire.

9 And he said, Go thy way, Daniel: for the words *are* closed up and sealed till the time of the end.

10 Many shall be purified, and made white, and tried; but the wicked shall do wickedly: and none of the wicked shall understand; but the wise shall understand.

11 And from the time *that* the daily *sacrifice* shall be taken away, and the abomination that maketh desolate set up, *there shall be* a thousand two hundred and ninety days.

11. The 1290 days mentioned here probably refer to the last three and one half years of the Tribulation Period, plus an additional thirty days to be used in judging the qualifications of those who will enter the Millennium (Mt 25:31-46).

12 Blessed *is* he that waiteth, and cometh to the thousand three hundred and five and thirty days.

12. The 1335 days perhaps signifies an additional forty-five days before the actual beginning of the Millennium that may be required, as Wood, pp. 228-29, suggests, for setting up the governmental machinery of the millennial period. All new governments require a transition period; and the saints who will rule and reign with Christ (7:27; Rev 20:4) must be given their assignments and instructions as to how to operate during the new age.

13 But go thou thy way till the end *be:* for thou shalt rest, and stand in thy lot at the end of the days.

13. Daniel is here personally assured he will one day be present to partake in the glorious events that follow the resurrection of believers. May all who read these words have this assurance through having trusted Christ as personal Saviour (Rom 3:23; 5:8; 6:23; 10:9-10; 13).

BIBLIOGRAPHY

Archer, Gleason. *A Survey of Old Testament Introduction*. Rev. ed. Chicago: Moody, 1974.

Baldwin, Joyce G. *Daniel: An Introduction and Commentary*. Leicester, England: InterVarsity, 1978.

Boutflower, Charles. *In and Around the Book of Daniel*. Grand Rapids: Kregel, reprinted, 1977.

Criswell, W. A. *Expository Sermons on the Book of Daniel*. Grand Rapids: Zondervan, 1976.

*Culver, Robert D. Daniel. In *The Wycliffe Bible Commentary*. Ed. by C. F. Pfeiffer and E. F. Harrison. Chicago: Moody, 1962.

———. *Daniel and the Latter Days*. Rev. ed. Chicago: Moody, 1977.

Dougherty, Raymond. *Nabonidus and Belshazzar*. New Haven: Yale University, 1929.

Gaebelein, Arno C. *The Prophet Daniel*. Grand Rapids: Kregel, reprinted, 1968.

Hall, Bert Harold. Daniel. In *The Wesleyan Bible Commentary*. Ed. by C. W. Carter. Grand Rapids: Eerdmans, 1969.

Ironside, Harry A. *Lectures on Daniel the Prophet*. 2nd ed. Neptune, N.J.: Loizeaux, 1920.

Keil, Carl F. The Book of the Prophet Daniel. In *Biblical Commentary on the Old Testament*. Trans. by M. G. Easton. Grand Rapids: Eerdmans, reprinted, 1949.

Lacocque, Andre. *The Book of Daniel*. Trans. by David Pellauer. Atlanta: John Knox, 1976.

Leupold, Herbert C. *Exposition of Daniel*. Grand Rapids: Baker, reprinted, 1973.

Montgomery, James A. A Critical and Exegetical Commentary on the Book of Daniel. In *The International Critical Commentary*. New York: Charles Scribner's Sons, 1927.

Pusey, Edward B. *Daniel the Prophet*. Minneapolis: Klock and Klock, reprinted, 1978.

Rowley, Harold H. *Darius the Mede and the Four World Empires in the Book of Daniel*. Cardiff: University of Wales, 1935.

Seiss, Joseph A. *Voices from Babylon; or, the Records of Daniel the Prophet*. Philadelphia: Muhlenberg Press, 1879.

Stuart, Moses. *A Commentary on the Book of Daniel*. Boston: Crocker and Brewster, 1859.

*Walvoord, John F. *Daniel: The Key to Prophetic Revelation*. Chicago: Moody, 1971.

Whitcomb, John C., Jr. *Darius the Mede*. Philadelphia: Presbyterian and Reformed, 1959.

*Wilson, Robert Dick. *Studies in the Book of Daniel*. 2 vols. Grand Rapids: Baker, reprinted, 1972.

*Wood, Leon. *A Commentary on Daniel*. Grand Rapids: Zondervan, 1973.

Young, Edward J. Daniel. In *The New Bible Commentary*. 2nd ed. Ed. by F. Davidson. Grand Rapids: Eerdmans, 1954.

*———. *The Prophecy of Daniel*. Grand Rapids: Eerdmans, 1949.

Zöckler, Otto. The Book of the Prophet Daniel. *Commentary on the Holy Scriptures*. Vol. VII. Ed. by J. P. Lange. Trans. by James Strong. Grand Rapids: Zondervan, reprinted, 1960.

HOSEA

INTRODUCTION

Authorship. This prophecy provides the sole source of information concerning the author, "Hosea the son of Beeri" (1:1). His name means "salvation"; and he was the son of Beeri (*expounder*), concerning whom nothing is known, though a different man by the same name is mentioned in Genesis 26:34. In the course of the prophecy he was commanded to marry Gomer (*completion* or *heat*), by whom he had two sons and a daughter (1:3b-11). Throughout the prophecy the prophet's personal history was made to be symbolic of the relationship between Jehovah and Israel. Because of the tragic details of his personal life, Hosea has been known as the brokenhearted prophet and provides a good illustration of the brokenhearted Lord in His relationship with sinful mankind.

Hosea was a contemporary of Amos who ministered in Israel and a contemporary of Isaiah and Micah who ministered in Judah (cf. Isa 1:1; Mic 1:1). Hosea was to the northern kingdom what Jeremiah was to the southern kingdom—a weeping prophet. Hosea looked forward to the Assyrian captivity of the northern kingdom, just as Jeremiah looked forward to the Babylonian captivity of the southern kingdom. Hosea's prophecy is closely related to that of Amos. Amos was very severe in his prophecy, and his ministry was somewhat like a James or John the Baptist of the Old Testament. Hosea, on the other hand, was very tender; and his ministry was something like a John of the Old Testament. Both Amos and Hosea prophesied to the northern kingdom, though Amos was a native of the southern kingdom while Hosea was a native of the northern kingdom. Hosea was the younger contemporary of Amos; and because their ministries overlap, there is much similarity in the sins that they condemn. In Amos, the prophetic discourses are very pronounced, while in Hosea, because of the intense personal involvement of the prophet, they are not very distinctly defined from one another, a fact that makes the book difficult to outline. Hosea's ministry antedated the ministries of Jeremiah, Ezekiel, and Daniel by some hundred and fifty years.

Although Hosea is the first of the minor prophets as they are arranged in our Bible, chronologically his prophecy was preceded by Obadiah, Joel, Jonah, and Amos.

Date and Place of Writing. Hosea dates his prophecy ". . . in the days of Uzziah, Jotham, Ahaz, and Hezekiah, kings of Judah, and in the days of Jeroboam the son of Joash, king of Israel" (1:1). This information informs us that Hosea had an extensive ministry of more than half a century, from about 790 B.C. to 725 B.C.; and he probably ceased his active ministry about five years before Assyria carried the northern kingdom into captivity in 722 B.C. Hosea was a citizen of the northern kingdom, and his personal experience was designed by God to be an example to the nation of which he was a citizen and to whom he prophesied.

Characteristics of the Prophecy. The prophecy is characterized by intense emotion as the prophet's personal tragedy (chs. 1-3) is transferred and applied to the nation (chs. 4-14). The prophecy abounds in figures of speech that are often intermingled with one another. The style of the prophecy is quite rhythmical, though the transitions from one topic to another are both sudden and frequent. The prophet combines severity with gentleness as he warns Israel that God's love for them includes His wrath, which must fall upon them because of their sin. Israel's sin is graphically illustrated from the prophet's personal life as he is commanded by God to take a wife who will become an adulteress, have children to whom symbolical names are given, and then bring his wife back from her adulteries to become his wife once more. Like Gomer, Israel has gone into spiritual adultery; and a promise of future restoration is given to them if they will return from their lovers unto their True Husband. Just as Hosea continues faithful towards, longs for, and will restore Gomer, so God continues faithful towards, longs for, and will ultimately bring Israel to restoration once she has been judged for her spiritual adultery and forsaken her lovers who have led her astray. In the course of the prophecy, it is often difficult to determine whether the prophet is expressing his own feelings or Jehovah's. Through it all God uses the tenderness and emotions of man to demonstrate the tenderness and emotions of God towards a people who have wandered far from Him. In spite of their spiritual infidelity, God's love continues to reign supreme!

Purpose. The purpose of Hosea's prophecy is to give Israel a tangible example of its spiritual idolatry and to portray God's love of Israel in spite of her spiritual infidelity. It becomes a national call to repentance.

Theme. God's love in spite of spiritual infidelity.

OUTLINE

I. The Introduction to the Prophecy. 1:1.
A. The Description of the Prophecy. 1:1a.
B. The Recipient of the Prophecy. 1:1b.
C. The Time of the Prophecy. 1:1c-1d.
1. As relates to the southern kingdom. 1:1c.

2. As relates to the northern kingdom. 1:1d.
II. The Messenger of the Prophecy. 1:2-3:5.
A. His Marriage to Gomer. 1:2-3a.
1. The commission to marry Gomer. 1:2a.
2. The cause for marrying Gomer. 1:2b.

COMMENTARY

I. THE INTRODUCTION TO THE PROPHECY. 1:1.

A. The Description of the Prophecy. 1:1a.

1:1a. The word of the LORD that came indicates that the prophecy is not Hosea's. It is a prophecy that originated with the Lord (Jehovah) and pre-existed in His mind. At a point of time in history it came and was delivered to Hosea for his transmission to the nation Israel. The prophecy, then, is authentic and has the power and authority of Jehovah as its basis. In dealing with the words of this prophecy, one is not dealing with the words of man, but rather with the very words of God.

THE word of the LORD that came unto Hō-sē'a, the son of Bē-ē'rī, in the days of Uz-zī'ah, Jō'tham, Ahaz, *and* Hĕz-e-kī'ah, kings of Judah, and in the days of Jĕr-o-bō'am the son of Jō'ash, king of Israel.

B. The Recipient of the Prophecy. 1:1b.

1b. Hosea, the son of Beeri. The name Hosea occurs in several forms in the Bible, including Joshua and Jesus. It means salvation, or Jehovah saves. It is interesting to note that the prophet bore the name later given to our Saviour who was the epitome of the tenderness, compassion, and love that Hosea so graphically foreshadowed. Concerning Beeri, nothing is known apart from this citation; but his chief claim to fame lay in the fact that he was Hosea's father. A man with the same name is mentioned in Genesis 26:34, but they are not to be confused or identified with one another.

C. The Time of the Prophecy. 1:1c-1d.

1. As relates to the southern kingdom. 1:1c.

1c. Hosea dates his prophecy according to the kings reigning in the southern kingdom because it was the more stable kingdom and the kingdom to whom Messiah ultimately would come.

Uzziah (Azariah) began his reign in the twenty-seventh year of Jeroboam II (II Kgs 15:1) and reigned for fifty-two years (II Kgs 15:1-2). By calculating the minimum numbers of years each king reigned, it can be seen that Hosea's ministry was extensive—from fifty to seventy years in length. It is clear that the prophet ministered until the Assyrian captivity, or nearly so; for Hezekiah began his reign in the third year of Hoshea's reign, and it was in the ninth year of Hoshea's reign that Assyria captured Samaria and took Israel into captivity (II Kgs 17:6). The period covered by Hosea's ministry, then, would be between 790 B.C. and 725 B.C.; and the prophecy itself was probably issued about 730 B.C.

2. As relates to the northern kingdom. 1:1d.

1d. Jeroboam II is the only northern king mentioned, though there were actually five kings that reigned between him and Hoshea, the last king of Israel. Two reasons can be suggested as to why only Jeroboam is mentioned: (1) his reign was the longest of the northern kings—forty-one years (II Kgs 14:23); and (2) though Israel rose to its greatest political heights during his reign, he did not depart from the way of his ancestor Jeroboam I; and subsequent kings continued to lead Israel in the idolatrous and spiritually adulterous paths that Jeroboam II forged. It is in the midst of such unparalleled political success and material wealth that God sends His prophet, Hosea, to deliver His message of judgment.

II. THE MESSENGER OF THE PROPHECY. 1:2-3:5.

It has frequently been said that the preacher should be the embodiment of his message. This was to be true of Hosea to a degree that most preachers would not care to be true of them. God was going to use the main details of the prophet's life to be representative of His dealings with and feelings for the nation Israel. There are four particulars that are relevant to God's purpose: (1) His marriage to Gomer (1:2-3a); (2) his children by Gomer (1:3b-11); (3) his contention, or problem, with Gomer (2:2-23); and (4) his care for Gomer (3:1-5).

A. His Marriage to Gomer. 1:2-3a.

1. The commission to marry Gomer. 1:2a.

2 The beginning of the word of the LORD by Hō-sē′a. And the LORD said to Hō-sē′a, Go, take unto thee a wife of whoredoms and children of whoredoms: for the land hath committed great whoredom, *departing* from the LORD.

2a. Go, take unto thee a wife of whoredoms is the first thing that Jehovah said to Hosea in initiating him early into the ministry of his prophetic office. This command has been the occasion of much investigation and speculation on the part of biblical scholars. Their conclusions generally fall into two camps: (1) Gomer was a harlot prior to her marriage with Hosea, and Hosea married her while she was in that moral state; and (2) Gomer was morally pure prior to her marriage to Hosea, but subsequently became discontented and went into harlotry, from which Hosea by his love reclaimed her. The main support for the first view is what seems to be the natural sense of the command **take unto thee a wife of whoredoms and children of whoredoms.** Against the first view, five objections can be raised: (1) this view is not required by the text; for the Hebrew language could have stated it more precisely, "take unto thee a woman who is a harlot;" (2) this view does not fit the spirit of chapter 2 in which Gomer becomes dissatisfied and leaves Hosea's home to enter harlotry; (3) this view does not fit the history of Israel who was pure before her unfaithfulness to God; (4) this view is contrary to biblical morality; and (5) chapter 1 does not describe any immoral conduct on the part of Gomer— her overt immoral conduct is not made known (except prophetically, vs. 2) until chapter 2.

It seems best, then, to hold the second view, that Gomer was a morally pure woman at the time Hosea married her and that for some reason she became discontent with her life with Hosea and went off into harlotry. It is best to regard Gomer and the events surrounding her relationship with Hosea as literal and historical. They are sovereignly superintended and used by God to portray His relationship to His people Israel. Just as Gomer has sinned, so Israel has sinned. Just as Hosea loves Gomer and will restore her in spite of her sin, so God loves Israel and will restore her in spite of her sin. As unenviable as the parallel may be from the prophet's point of view, it beautifully and graphically suits God's purpose in confronting His people with their sin, His wrath, His love, His judgment, and their ultimate restoration. Hosea certainly is an Old Testament illustration of a servant of

God who presented himself as a ". . . living sacrifice . . ." to God and ultimately proved that the will of God is ". . . good, and acceptable, and perfect . . ." (cf. Rom 12:1-2). In a way in which few would care to exchange places with Hosea, he is a graphic Old Testament illustration of the truth that ". . . all things work together for good to them that love God, to them who are the called according to his purpose" (Rom 8:28).

2. The cause for marrying Gomer. 1:2b.

2b. Hosea is advised of God's purpose in his marriage, which is to be an object lesson of the moral depths to which his nation has sunk in its departure from Jehovah. It would be interesting to know the prophet's personal thoughts over this prospect. Whatever they were, they did not hinder his obedience to God's command, in spite of the personal sacrifice involved.

3. The compliance in marrying Gomer. 1:3a.

3a. So he went and took Gomer the daughter of Diblaim. Even though, from a human prospective, the outlook for his marriage is bleak, Hosea obeyed God completely and married Gomer (completion, heat), the daughter of Diblaim (double embrace), concerning whom nothing further is known.

B. His Children by Gomer. 1:3b-11.

1. The historical citation. 1:3b-9.

3b. Which conceived, and bare him a son. To the union of Hosea and Gomer three children are born. The first is a son, Jezreel (God sows), 1:3b-5. Three things are made known concerning him: (1) his conception and birth (vs. 3b); (2) his naming, or coronation (vs. 4a); and (3) his significance for Israel (vss. 4b-5).

4. Call his name Jezreel. Jezreel is to be a reminder that God will judge the house of Jehu for the blood shed in Jezreel when the kingdom was wrested from Ahab and Jezebel and God's judgment was poured out against them (cf. II Kgs 9). Though Jehu was raised up by God to execute His judgment against Ahab, God will hold him responsible for his acts; for they stem from personal pride, rather than a desire to serve God. Jeroboam II, the king during Hosea's ministry, was a direct descendant of Jehu; hence, the house of Jehu was still reigning in the land of Israel.

5. I will break the bow of Israel in the valley of Jezreel. God pronounces judgment, not only against the house of the king, but also against the nation over which the house of Jehu reigns. The nation will be judged because it has committed spiritual adultery, having forsaken God for idols. The nation will meet its end in the valley of Jezreel, the precise location in which Ahab and Jezebel met their ends and where Naboth the Jezreelite had earlier had his vineyard (cf. I Kgs 21). The prophecy, then, is twofold, prophesying: (1) the end of Jehu's dynasty; and (2) the destruction of the northern kingdom in the valley of Jezreel (vs. 5). One must remember that this prophecy was delivered at a time when the northern kingdom was at its height and the dynasty of Jehu seemed secure. Hosea lived to see his prophecy realized, just as he foretold though the events involved transpired at least forty years apart (cf. 10:14; II Kgs 15:8-12, 18).

6-7. She conceived again, and bare a daughter . . . Lo-ruhamah. The second child born to this union was a girl, Lo-ruhamah (not pitied). Three things are made known concerning her: (1) her conception and birth (vs. 6a); (2) her naming, or coronation (vs. 6b); and (3) her significance for Israel (vss. 6c-7). Lo-ruhamah's significance is twofold: God's compassion has come to an end for Israel and her judgment is imminent (vs. 6b). For Judah, she will experience God's compassion, and judgment will not come against her at this time.

3 So he went and took Gō'mer the daughter of Dīb'lā-im; which conceived, and bare him a son.

4 And the LORD said unto him, Call his name Jĕz're-el; for yet a little while, and I will avenge the blood of Jĕz're-el upon the house of Jehu, and will cause to cease the kingdom of the house of Israel.

5 And it shall come to pass at that day, that I will break the bow of Israel in the valley of Jĕz're-el.

6 ¶And she conceived again, and bare a daughter. And God said unto him, Call her name Lō-rū-hā'mah: for I will no more have mercy upon the house of Israel; but I will utterly take them away.

7 But I will have mercy upon the house of Judah, and will save them by the LORD their God, and will not save

them by bow, nor by sword, nor by battle, by horses, nor by horsemen.

8 ¶Now when she had weaned Lō-rū-hă′mah, she conceived, and bare a son. 9 Then said *God*, Call his name Lō-ăm′mī: for ye *are* not my people, and I will not be your *God*.

10 Yet the number of the children of Israel shall be as the sand of the sea, which cannot be measured nor numbered; and it shall come to pass, *that* in the place where it was said unto them, Ye *are* not my people, *there* it shall be said unto them, Ye *are* the sons of the living God. 11 Then shall the children of Judah and the children of Israel be gathered together, and appoint themselves one head, and they shall come up out of the land: for great *shall be* the day of Jĕz′re-el.

CHAPTER 2

SAY ye unto your brethren, Ăm′-mī; and to your sisters, Rū-hă′mah.

Her deliverance will not be by military strategy or weaponry, but solely by the sovereign intervention of Jehovah in her behalf (vs. 7). This deliverance of Judah was realized near the end of the eighth century B.C. when the angel of Jehovah in one night slew 185,000 of Sennacherib's men (cf. II Kgs 19:35; Isa 37:36).

8-9. She conceived and bare a son . . . Lo-ammi. The third child born to this union was a son, Lo-ammi (not my people). Three things are made known concerning him: (1) his conception and birth (vs. 8); (2) his naming, or coronation (vs. 9a); and (3) his significance to Israel (vs. 9b). Lo-ammi was born after Lo-ruhamah. **Ye are not my people, and I will not be your God.** Lo-ammi's name indicated to the Israel of his day that they were not Jehovah's people, and Jehovah was not their God. This should in no sense be understood as a denial or mitigation of the Abrahamic covenant (cf. Gen 12:1-3), an unconditional covenant depending solely upon God for its fulfillment. That covenant continues down to the present day, unfulfilled, yet unmitigated (cf. Rom 11:1-2). The principle is the same as that proclaimed by Paul, "For they are not all Israel, which are of Israel" (Rom 9:6). As in Paul's day, when most of Israel were vessels of destruction from whom God called out a remnant to fulfill His promise, so too in Lo-ammi's day. Most of the people in Israel in Lo-ammi's day would experience the judgment of God. All of them would, if it were not for God's covenant to Abraham, in the honoring of which God would call out from Israel a remnant who were faithful to His name. By Lo-ammi's day this remnant had, for the most part, withdrawn and had moved its residence to Judah in the south. Thus, this statement is addressed to that portion of Israel which, while related to Abraham physically, was not related to him or to his God spiritually.

2. The prophetical application. 1:10-2:1.

10-2:1. Having set forth a dark picture for the Israel of his day and set before them the tangible reminders in the persons of his own children and their names, Hosea now gives a bright picture of hope. Five great national blessings are promised: (1) a national increase: **Israel shall be as the sand of the sea** (vs. 10a). Though the judgment of God will fall and many of the people of Israel will die in that judgment, a remnant will be left; and from that remnant will come a vast numberless multitude of people; (2) a national conversion: **in the place where it was said unto them, Ye are not my people, There it shall be said unto them, Ye are the sons of the living God** (vs. 10b). Though the present generation has been marked for destruction and have been told that they are not the people of God, yet in that very same place the remnant of the future will be told that they are the people of the living God; (3) a national reunion: **Then shall the children of Judah and the children of Israel be gathered together** (vs. 11a). Though in Hosea's day the nation Israel is divided into two kingdoms, the northern kingdom (Israel) and the southern kingdom (Judah), the day is coming when the nation will be united once again and the rift healed; (4) a national leadership: **and appoint themselves one head** (vs. 11b). One leader will be raised up over the reunited nation. From the complete prophetic picture we know that this leader will be none other than Jesus Christ, the Messiah, who as the Son of David will reign over the restored Israel; (5) a national restoration: **Say ye unto your brethren, Ammi; and to your sisters, Ruhamah** (2:1). The restored Israel will be the people of God (**Ammi**) and will obtain mercy in fact (**Ruhamah**). On the basis of its national conversion, the nation will be restored to favor with God. This, of course, will happen when the nation repents and receives a new heart in fulfillment of the New Covenant (cf. Jer 31:31-34).

This section began with the renumeration of the prophet's

children as signs of God's displeasure with and judgment of Israel. It concludes with a rehearsal of those names and a removal of the woes associated with them. The name Jezreel can either mean God "scatters" or "God sows". In 1:4ff. God will scatter Israel in judgment. In verse 11d God will sow Israel in righteousness, regeneration, and restoration. In verse 9 the nation is declared to be **Lo-ammi,** (not my people). In 2:1 the restored nation is proclaimed to be **Ammi,** (my people). In verse 6 God declares that He will remove His compassion from the nation; but in 2:1 that mercy is restored to the repentant, revived, and restored nation.

C. His Contention (Problem) with Gomer. 2:2-23.

1. The historical citation. 2:2-17.

The events of these verses summarize in capsule form the remainder of the prophecy—what Gomer has done, Israel has done. What happens to Gomer will happen to Israel. Three events are important: (1) her reprobation (vss. 2-5); (2) her retribution (vss. 6-13); and (3) her restitution (vss. 14-17). These events constitute the background for the messages of the prophecy that follow in the next major division: (1) concerning Israel's reprobation (4:1-7:16); (2) concerning Israel's retribution (8:1-13:16); and (3) concerning Israel's restoration (14:1-8). Detailed discussion concerning these messages will be given in the appropriate place.

2. Verses 2-5 give Gomer's reprobation. **Plead with your mother.** It is interesting to note that the Hebrew Massoritic text begins chapter 2 with what is chapter 1 verse 10 in the English text. This may help us to understand who is being addressed in this section—it is the believing remnant whom God will gather together, restore, and reign over for the thousand-year earthly Davidic millennial reign. The prophet, then, under the inspiration of the Holy Spirit, is using his personal domestic tragedy as a means of addressing, not only his own children and through them their physical mother, but beyond that the believing remnant who in turn are to plead with their mother (the nation Israel) to return to God because they, like Gomer, have defected from their true husband. **For she is not my wife, neither am I her husband** does not deal with fact (for that cannot change) but rather with the conduct of the wife and, beyond her, the nation. Neither she nor they are acting in keeping with their true relationship of being a wife. Gomer and the nation are acting contrary to fact. The address, then, is in keeping with the conduct that Gomer and the nation have adopted. Hence, the appeal, **let her therefore put away her whoredoms out of her sight, and her adulteries from between her breasts,** is for her to quit acting as though she were not properly married (vs. 2b).

3. Lest I strip her naked . . . and make her as a wilderness sets forth the extent to which the prophet (and Jehovah) is prepared to go to achieve the desired repentance on the part of Gomer (and the nation).

4. And I will not have mercy upon her children heightens the appeal, for perhaps the peril of the children will move the mother to do what she might not do if only her own future were in jeopardy.

5. For their mother hath played the harlot . . . for she said, I will go after my lovers explains the mother's action from her point of view. She had some quite natural and normal needs for the necessities of life, food (**my bread and my water**), clothing (**my wool and my flax**), and comforts (**mine oil and my drink**). The problem was not in her desires, but the source from which she sought them, **my lovers.** Gomer thought that it was men other than her husband who would provide these things for her, and Israel thought that it was gods (degrading and disgusting idols) other than Jehovah who would provide these things for

2 Plead with your mother, plead: for she *is* not my wife, neither *am* I her husband: let her therefore put away her whoredoms out of her sight, and her adulteries from between her breasts;

3 Lest I strip her naked, and set her as in the day that she was born, and make her as a wilderness, and set her like a dry land, and slay her with thirst.

4 And I will not have mercy upon her children; for they *be* the children of whoredoms.

5 For their mother hath played the harlot: she that conceived them hath done shamefully: for she said, I will go after my lovers, that give *me* my bread and my water, my wool and my flax, mine oil and my drink.

6 ¶Therefore, behold, I will hedge up thy way with thorns, and make a wall, that she shall not find her paths.

7 And she shall follow after her lovers, but she shall not overtake them; and she shall seek them, but shall not find *them:* then shall she say, I will go and return to my first husband; for then *was it* better with me than now.

8 For she did not know that I gave her corn, and wine, and oil, and multiplied her silver and gold, *which* they prepared for Bā´al.

9 Therefore will I return, and take away my corn in the time thereof, and my wine in the season thereof, and will recover my wool and my flax *given* to cover her nakedness.

10 And now will I discover her lewdness in the sight of her lovers, and none shall deliver her out of mine hand.

11 I will also cause all her mirth to cease, her feast days, her new moons, and her sabbaths, and all her solemn feasts.

12 And I will destroy her vines and her fig trees, whereof she hath said, These *are* my rewards that my lovers have given me: and I will make them a forest, and the beasts of the field shall eat them.

13 And I will visit upon her the days of Bā´al-Im, wherein she burned incense to them, and she decked herself with her earrings and her jewels, and she went after her lovers, and forgat me, saith the LORD.

14 ¶Therefore, behold, I will allure her, and bring her into the wilderness, and speak comfortably unto her.

15 And I will give her her vineyards from thence, and the valley of Ā´chôr for a door of hope: and she shall sing there, as in the days of her youth, and as in the day when she came up out of the land of Egypt.

16 And it shall be at that day, saith the LORD, *that* thou shalt call me I´shī; and shalt call me no more Bā´al-ī.

17 For I will take away the names of Bā´al-Im out of her mouth, and they shall no more be remembered by their name.

her. Such is the deception of sin! These are the causes; the effects have already been stated—both Gomer and Israel **played the harlot, hath done shamefully,** and resolved to **go after my lovers.** Such blatant disobedience demands retribution, and to that we now turn.

Verses 6-13 set forth Gomer's retribution.

6-7. I will hedge up thy way with thorns . . . then shall she say, I will go and return to my first husband. These verses set forth the gracious restraints that the loving husband sets before his wayward wife in order to cause her to resolve to return to her husband (vs. 7b).

8. For she did not know reiterates the problem lying behind Gomer's (and Israel's) defection, a misconception as to whom she was responsible and from whom she received blessings. Hosea (and Jehovah) lavished upon Gomer (and Israel) not only the necessities of life, but also the luxuries in unparalleled abundance. Effect demands a cause. Gomer (and Israel) recognized the blessing, but did not recognize the proper source or cause. Gomer must have done something similar to what Israel did with the silver and gold that God lavished upon her, for Israel took the silver and gold and **prepared** (it) **for Baal.** What Israel literally did was to take the silver and gold and make them into an idol of Baal. The error was not new; it was the same then as always and continues to be characteristic of man (cf. Rom 1:21-25).

9-13. Therefore will I return . . . take away . . . recover . . . discover . . . and none shall deliver her out of mine hand, spoken by God and addressed primarily to the nation Israel, indicates the lengths to which He is prepared to go in order to bring her to repentance and restoration. By application, these verses also indicate the extent to which Hosea is prepared to go in bringing Gomer back to her rightful place. She will be deprived of the luxuries that she sought and misused (vs. 8), and she will be deprived of the necessities that were graciously given (vs. 9). She will be exposed before her lovers (vs. 10), and every occasion of joy and false religious observance will be removed from her (vs. 11). Even the plant and animal kingdoms will be affected by her judgment (reminiscent of the suffering of creation described in Romans 8:22). There will be a harvest for sin and defection (vs. 13, cf. Rom 6:23). Instead of finding her deviation to be satisfying, as she anticipated, Israel (and Gomer) will experience only depravation, nakedness, sorrow, desolation, destruction, and retribution. All of these tragedies will befall her because there is One who loves her and desires her restoration.

14-17. I will allure her . . . bring her . . . speak comfortably unto her . . . give her . . . and she shall sing . . . thou shalt call me Ishi . . . I will take away the names of Baalim out of her mouth. These verses set forth Gomer's restoration. Once again, the primary focus is the ultimate application to the nation; but what is true of the nation in the ultimate view will also be true of Gomer in the near view. She will be wooed and brought into a private, face-to-face consultation; and she will be dealt with kindly (vs. 14). Her blessings will be restored (vs. 15a); and the occasion of her sin, rightly faced and deserted, will be the occasion of her hope (vs. 15b, cf. Rom 8:28). **I will give her . . . the valley of Achor for a door of hope.** The mention of the valley of Achor would be meaningful to the Israel of Hosea's day and to the Israel of the restoration (Millennium). It was in this valley, located near Jericho, where Achan's sin was discovered and punished. The sin that resulted in God's judgment and loss of life at the first encounter at Ai was judged and put away, which resulted in God's blessing in the second encounter at Ai. In like manner, if Israel and Gomer will deal with their sin and put it away, that very act will result in God's blessing in the second encounter at Ai. In like manner, if Israel and Gomer will deal with their sin and put it away, that very act will result in restoration and hope. Such dealings with sin will result in restoration and joy equal to that prior to the time when the sin took place (vs. 15c). She will recognize her true husband, and even the names of her false lovers will be removed from her mouth (vss. 16-17). The two names used are significant. **Ishi** (my husband) is a term of affection and represents the closest loving relationship. **Baali** (my lord or master) is a term indicating servitude and inferiority. It is the expression a servant would use of his master. It was the term commonly used by the heathen of their idol gods; and therefore, it must and will be erased from Israel's consciousness and expression because of the sin and evil connected with Baal worship.

2. The prophetical application. 2:18-23.

God continues to address the nation through His prophet. Once their sin has been faced and put away they will (1) enjoy covenant blessings (vss. 18-20) and (2) experience national regeneration (vss. 21-23).

18. And in that day will I make a covenant. Israel's restoration will result in the lifting of the curse from nature (cf. Rom 8:19-22). All of the animal kingdom will be truly in subjection to them. Not only this, but the instruments of war and warfare itself will be abolished; and peace and safety will be universal (vs. 18b).

19-20. And I will betroth thee unto me for ever . . . thou shalt know the LORD. Even more importantly, the nation will be brought into a new and more meaningful relationship with God than they had ever enjoyed previously. There will be a renewal of the wedding vows, and the nation will remain faithful to the Lord. All of this will be true because there has been a national regeneration (vss. 19-20; cf. Jer 31:31-34). This glorious restoration, of course, will be foreshadowed by Gomer's restoration to Hosea.

21-23. And it shall come to pass . . . I will hear . . . the earth shall hear . . . I will sow . . . I will have mercy . . . they shall say, Thou art my God. These verses elaborate upon the details of the national restoration. It will be accompanied by an abundant response on the part of the heavens and the earth, portrayed in verses 21 and 22 as having asked Jehovah for permission to bless the earth with bounty. **They shall hear Jezreel.** Once again, the names of the prophet's children are reiterated to confirm not only the aversion of the curse previously associated with their names, but to proclaim positive blessings that will be showered upon them. Jezreel is mentioned first (vss. 22b-23a). Jehovah will personally sow Israel in the land; thus it will remain forever. **I will have mercy upon her that had not obtained mercy.** Lo-ruhamah (cf. 1:6-8) will be changed to Ruhamah (compassion, vs. 23b). **Thou art my people.** Lo-ammi (not my people) shall be Ammi (my people, vs. 23c). **Thou art my God.** The people will once again own Jehovah as their God in full realization of the New Covenant (cf. Jer 31:31-34). Thus, the tragedy that has befallen both Gomer and the nation Israel will be completely reversed; and in some ways the latter end will be better than the former.

D. His Care for Gomer. 3:1-5.

Hosea's prophecy began in chapter 1 with primary emphasis upon his own home situation and with secondary emphasis upon application to the nation Israel. In chapter 2 the picture broadens so that there is primary emphasis on the nation Israel, with secondary emphasis on the prophet's individual family situation. From the second chapter we know that the nation will

18 And in that day will I make a covenant for them with the beasts of the field, and with the fowls of heaven, and *with* the creeping things of the ground: and I will break the bow and the sword and the battle out of the earth, and will make them to lie down safely.
19 And I will betroth thee unto me for ever; yea, I will betroth thee unto me in righteousness, and in judgment, and in lovingkindness, and in mercies.
20 I will even betroth thee unto me in faithfulness: and thou shalt know the LORD.

21 And it shall come to pass in that day, I will hear, saith the LORD, I will hear the heavens, and they shall hear the earth;
22 And the earth shall hear the corn, and the wine, and the oil; and they shall hear Jĕz're-el.
23 And I will sow her unto me in the earth; and I will have mercy upon her that had not obtained mercy; and I will say to *them which were* not my people, Thou *art* my people; and they shall say, Thou *art* my God.

be restored and, by implication, that Gomer will be restored, too. Now, in the third chapter the focus shifts back primarily to the individual relationship between Hosea and Gomer and, by application, to the nation Israel. This chapter lets us know that the prophet's individual home situation will be rectified, and Gomer will be restored.

1. The historical citation. 3:1-3.

This section divides into two parts: (1) the prophet's commission by God (vs. 1); and (2) his compliance to God (vss. 2-3).

CHAPTER 3

THEN said the LORD unto me, Go yet, love a woman beloved of *her* friend, yet an adulteress, according to the love of the LORD toward the children of Israel, who look to other gods, and love flagons of wine.

3:1. Then said the LORD unto me, Go yet, love a woman beloved of her friend, yet an adulteress, according to the love of the LORD. It is to be carefully noted that in verse 1a Jehovah directly commands the prophet to go and reclaim his wife who has lapsed into the depths of moral depravity. This command ought once and for all to lay to rest any speculation about the husband's responsibility in marriage and ought to end all speculation as to whether adultery (or anything other than the death of the marriage partner) breaks a marriage. If anyone had occasion to divorce his wife, Hosea did; and he could have done so well within the parameters of the Mosaic law (cf. Deut 24:1). It ought to be observed, however, that our Lord in commenting on Moses' provision for divorce indicated that this provision was made because of ". . . the hardness of your hearts" (Mt 19:8). Thus, whether in Moses' day, Hosea's day, or in the present day, divorce is not an alternative available to the spiritual believer to resolve marital problems—even in the case of sexual infidelity. When one does so, it is because of his own hardness of heart, that is, his spiritual insensitivity to the command and provision of God governing marriage. **Toward the children of Israel, who look to other gods.** The command delivered to Hosea is applied to Israel who, like Gomer, has been unfaithful. Whereas Gomer's sin is sexual and gives testimony to her spiritual defection, Israel's sin is spiritual and is manifested sexually and in many other ways. Gomer is described as **a woman beloved of her friend** (Heb *rēaʻ*). The Hebrew word frequently denotes a friend or companion, but it probably is best understood here as a reference to her husband (as it is also used in Jer 3:20). **Flagons of wine** (Heb *ʼashishah*) are cakes made of grapes, hence raisin cakes. They are similar to, if not identical with, the cakes mentioned in Jeremiah 7:18 and 44:19 which were prepared for and used in the idolatrous ceremonies in honor of the queen of heaven.

2 So I bought her to me for fifteen *pieces* of silver, and *for* an homer of barley, and an half homer of barley:

2. So I bought her to me for fifteen pieces of silver . . . a homer of barley, and a half homer of barley. In spite of what his personal feelings may have been (it must be remembered that Hosea was a man whose feelings undoubtedly were deeply crushed by his wife's rejection and defection), Hosea is completely obedient to Jehovah. The price that he paid to redeem Gomer is indicative of the depth to which she had sunk; thirty pieces of silver was the price commonly paid for a slave (cf. Ex 21:32). Barley was considered to be a food fit only for animals and was eaten only by the poorest people. Gomer had sunk to such depths that she was worth only half the price of a common slave and approximately ten bushels of animal food!

3 And I said unto her, Thou shalt abide for me many days; thou shalt not play the harlot, and thou shalt not be for *another* man: so *will* I also *be* for thee.

3. And I said unto her introduces Hosea's charge to Gomer. **Thou shalt not play the harlot, and thou shalt not be for another man.** While the words could be viewed as stern (and certainly they are serious), they also can be viewed with great love and assurance. Whereas in chapter 1 Gomer knew that ahead of her lay moral defection (cf. 1:2), now Gomer can be assured that her future holds permanent restoration, faithfulness, and love on the part of her husband.

2. The prophetical application. 3:4-5.

The details of Hosea and Gomer's personal lives are now applied to the nation Israel in general.

4 For the children of Israel shall abide many days without a king, and without a prince, and without a sacrifice, and without an image, and without an ephod, and *without* terephim:

4. For the children of Israel shall abide many days without a king . . . prince . . . sacrifice . . . image . . . ephod . . . teraphim portrays Israel up to the present day. She is characterized as **without** (the word occurs five times in the text). Israel actually will be without three things: (1) monarchy—she will have neither a reigning monarch nor one in line to become reigning monarch. Ultimately, a monarch must come as promised to David and Israel in II Samuel 7; (2) a sacrifice—she will not observe a God-appointed sacrificial system during this long period of time, though during it Messiah will in fact come and be the supreme Sacrifice; and (3) idolatry—even though she will not observe a true religious system, she will still forsake idolatry and all of its accoutrements. Even though Judaism falls far short of Christianity, for it deals with the picture whereas Christianity deals with the reality, still Israel will not fill its inherent void by returning to idolatry! This would not, and could not, have been accomplished if it were not for God Himself preserving Israel from returning to that degrading practice.

5 Afterward shall the children of Israel return, and seek the LORD their God, and David their king; and shall fear the LORD and his goodness in the latter days.

5. Afterward shall the children of Israel return deals with Israel's future, and glorious it is. In God's appointed time Israel will come to its senses and will have a national regeneration (cf. Jer 31:31-34). This national regeneration will cause them to seek the king that God always intended for them to have, Messiah, God's Son of the line of David, reigning over His people. It is at this time that all of God's unconditional covenant programs for Israel, summarized in the great promise given to Abraham (cf. Gen 12:1-3), will be completely and ultimately fulfilled.

III. THE MESSAGES OF THE PROPHECY. 4:1-14:8.

The subjects of these messages grow out of the historical citation in 2:2-17 and follow the cycle through which Gomer went. These messages, however, are applied to the nation and concern: (1) Israel's reprobation (4:1-7:16); (2) Israel's retribution (8:1-13:16); and (3) Israel's restoration (14:1-8).

A. Concerning Israel's Reprobation. 4:1-7:16.

In this section Israel's reprobation is demonstrated by four things: (1) her faithlessness (4:1-19); (2) God's condemnation (5:1-6:3); (3) her fickleness (6:4-11), and (4) her foolishness (7:1-16).

1. Demonstrated by her faithlessness. 4:1-19.

This section divides into three parts: (1) Israel's indictment (vss. 1-3); (2) Israel's insensitivity (vss. 4-10); and (3) Israel's idolatry (vss. 11-19).

4:1-2. Hear, together with the address **ye children of Israel** (vs. 1a), lets us know that we have moved from the personal and individual, focused upon in chapters 1 to 3, to the prophetical and national scene that comprises the remainder of the prophecy. The indictment moves from the general (vs. 1b) to the particular (vs. 2-3). The fact that **there is no truth, nor mercy** (Heb *chesed*, better, covenant loyalty), **nor knowledge of God in the land** is shown by the specific acts enumerated: **Swearing, lying, killing, stealing, committing adultery, break out** (Heb *parats*, to break out bursting through all bounds as a river bursts its banks and floods and destroys all that goes before it; hence, violence such as that shown by an unruly mob), and **blood toucheth blood** (lit., bloods touch bloods, Heb *damim*, the violence that characterizes the land is so great that it culminates in bloodshed, pictured as being so continuous and in such amount that it flows until the whole land is covered in one wide inundation of blood).

CHAPTER 4

HEAR the word of the LORD, ye children of Israel: for the LORD hath a controversy with the inhabitants of the land, because *there is* no truth, nor mercy, nor knowledge of God in the land.

2 By swearing, and lying, and killing, and stealing, and committing adultery, they break out, and blood toucheth blood.

3 Therefore shall the land mourn, and every one that dwelleth therein shall languish, with the beasts of the field, and with the fowls of heaven; yea, the

3. Therefore shall the land mourn shows the effect of man's sin. His sin affects not only himself, but animate and inanimate creation as well. The land itself is afflicted because of man's sin and every creature from the simplest that God has created to His

fishes of the sea also shall be taken away.

4 Yet let no man strive, nor reprove another: for thy people *are* as they that strive with the priest.

5 Therefore shalt thou fall in the day, and the prophet also shall fall with thee in the night, and I will destroy thy mother.

6 ¶My people are destroyed for lack of knowledge: because thou hast rejected knowledge, I will also reject thee, that thou shalt be no priest to me: seeing thou hast forgotten the law of thy God, I will also forget thy children.

7 As they were increased, so they sinned against me: *therefore* will I change their glory into shame.

8 They eat up the sin of my people, and they set their heart on their iniquity.

9 And there shall be, like people, like priest: and I will punish them for their ways, and reward them their doings.

crowning achievement, man, suffers. Not only do those dwelling on land suffer, but those who inhabit the sky and the sea suffer as well. The truth of Romans 14:7 and Romans 8:20-22 is borne out by this passage.

Verses 4-10 portray Israel's insensitivity to her sin in spite of the havoc it has wrought, not only upon man but upon beast and upon all creation. Even dumb beasts and inanimate creation are more keenly aware of the intensity and gravity of man's sin than man himself!

4. Yet let no man strive . . . with the priest reminds man of his creatureliness. The words remind one of Romans 9:20ff. Man is in no position to find fault with God, nor to condemn Him in any way; for he does not see things from God's perspective. When God sent them priests to convey His message, they argued with them. They were like the carnal man of I Corinthians 3:3b-4 whose conduct is indistinguishable from the unregenerate man's (cf. I Cor 2:14). Only a spiritual man (cf. I Cor 2:15-16) can understand things from God's perspective because he is rightfully related to God both by the Son and by the Holy Spirit. When a spiritual man is speaking, the only sensible thing that a carnal or a natural man can do is to be quiet, listen, and repent!

5. Therefore shalt thou fall gives the result of rejecting the message sent by God's messenger. They will stumble in the light of God's revelation and will contend with the priests; and the priests will become discouraged and, hence, will join these people in stumbling in the night (i.e., the time when God will withhold His revelation from priests and people alike).

6. My people are destroyed for lack of knowledge pinpoints the cause of man's problem, i.e., lack of knowledge. The lack of knowledge does not stem from a shortage of information, but rather from information rejected. The result of this will be that Israel will be removed from its place as God's representative to proclaim His revelation to the world. The **mother** (i.e., the nation Israel, cf. vs. 5) will be destroyed. All of this stems from the fact that they have forgotten God's law; they have failed to do things God's way. The results: **I will also forget thy children.** God will forget the nation from Hosea's day to our own, but ultimately He will call out a remnant; and from that remnant He will establish a new kingdom in which righteousness shall reign. The nation of Hosea's day, however, will not realize any of this. Because they are unconscious to their sin, they will not consciously experience God's blessing, but will consciously experience His judgment. This is the tragedy of sin.

7. As they were increased, so they sinned against me shows that as the nation grew in numerical strength, so their sin compounded. Fathers did not teach their children God's Law and righteousness, but rather indoctrinated their children in their sin; and children grew up worse sinners than their fathers. **Therefore will I change their glory into shame.** Their progeny, which should have been their glory, will be put into the shame of God's judgment.

8. They points out the problem, i.e., the priesthood. They have not helped the people face their sin and deal with it. Rather, they have gloried and taken pleasure in the sin of the people. What a sad commentary that the priest should compound the sin, rather than help in its confession. **Eat up the sin of my people.** Rather than look into the Law of God, they delight in the sin of the people and make that the object of their desire.

9. Like people, like priest reminds one of II Timothy 4:3; the cause in both instances is the same: a dislike and disregard for the truth of God's revelation. The result is that the priest of God is corrupted and made like the sinning people, rather than having the opposite effect. It remains true today, unfortunately, that churches still like to call pastors who will be like them,

10 For they shall eat, and not have enough: they shall commit whoredom, and shall not increase: because they have left off to take heed to the LORD.

11 Whoredom and wine and new wine take away the heart.

12 ¶My people ask counsel at their stocks, and their staff declareth unto them: for the spirit of whoredoms hath caused *them* to err, and they have gone a whoring from under their God.

13 They sacrifice upon the tops of the mountains, and burn incense upon the hills, under oaks and poplars and elms, because the shadow thereof *is* good: therefore your daughters shall commit whoredom, and your spouses shall commit adultery.

14 I will not punish your daughters when they commit whoredom, nor your spouses when they commit adultery: for themselves are separated with whores, and they sacrifice with harlots: therefore the people *that* doth not understand shall fall.

15 ¶Though thou, Israel, play the harlot, *yet* let not Judah offend; and come not ye unto Gilgal, neither go ye up to Běth-ā'ven, nor swear, The LORD liveth.

rather than will help them to be like God. **I will punish them . . . and reward them their doings.** The result of this defection is punishment. God will let them have what they want. They want to be free from Him, and to be free from Him is to be free from His blessings. Therefore, they will experience judgment.

10. They shall eat, and not have enough expresses the result. They would sink into the depths of moral corruption; but rather than finding it satisfying, they would find it made their appetite for sin insatiable. This expresses itself in defection in every way, and is similar to the action of God in Romans 1:24ff., in which God, in judgment, gives mankind over to the unbridled practice of his sin. One should note that the unchecked existence of sin is not a manifestation of God's blessing or approval; it is a manifestation of His judgment.

11. This expresses the extreme to which their sin led them, i.e., the practice of idolatry. **Whoredom and wine and new wine** are the sins that commonly accompany idolatry, i.e., moral sexual defection and drunkenness. These sins dull the sensitivity and understanding, so that the people no longer wish to retain God in their knowledge.

12. My people ask counsel at their stocks. Like the heathen of Romans 1:25, they worship and serve the creature rather than the Creator. Instead of consulting the God who made the trees and the wood, they consult the tree and the wooden idols that can be fashioned from them. Such spiritual defection leads them further from God, ultimately to the judgment in love God must exercise.

13-14. They sacrifice upon the tops of the mountains, indicates the details of their idol worship. They engage in a false sacrificial system and false religious rituals in the various sites where their religious observances were conducted. **Therefore your daughters shall commit whoredom, and your spouses shall commit adultery.** Spiritual harlotry gave way to physical harlotry, which was incorporated into the religious rituals of their idolatrous worship. Though the women of the land are involved in all forms of sexual immorality, **I will not punish your daughters . . . nor your spouses.** This indicates that God holds the men of the land primarily responsible, for no woman could be a harlot if there were not a man who would seek her services. One needs to be reminded that God constituted the man to be the head of the family and holds him primarily responsible for the safeguarding of the practice of sex, which occurs legitimately only within the marital bond. The giving of themselves to the unbridled practice of sin causes the people to be without proper understanding of God's Word and values. Hence, they come to ruin (vs. 14).

15. This constitutes a warning to Judah, the southern kingdom, who faired better morally and spiritually. This is borne out from the fact that God spared the southern kingdom one hundred thirty-five years longer than the northern kingdom, though ultimately it went the way of Israel.

Let not Judah offend. Judah is encouraged to refrain from the spiritual harlotry that has engulfed Israel, but she is also enjoined, **and come not ye unto Gilgal** (lit., circle, wheel), which during the days of Elisha had been the location of the school of the prophets (cf. II Kgs 2:1; 4:38). In the days of Hosea it had become a place of idol worship. They are also enjoined **neither go ye up to Beth-aven** (lit., house of iniquity or house of vanity). The thought is that Judah is not to go even to the places where Israel conducts its idol worship, even to observe these sinful practices, lest they become contaminated themselves. Judah is to separate itself completely from all of the God-dishonoring practices of Israel (cf. II Cor 6:17-18). The words **nor swear, The LORD liveth** indicate something that a true worshiper of God might be tempted to do when confronted with or visiting an idolatrous scene. He might be tempted to

16 For Israel slideth back as a backsliding heifer: now the LORD will feed them as a lamb in a large place.

17 É'phra-im *is* joined to idols: let him alone.

18 Their drink is sour: they have committed whoredom continually: her rulers *with* shame do love, Give ye.
19 The wind hath bound her up in her wings, and they shall be ashamed because of their sacrifices.

CHAPTER 5

HEAR ye this, O priests; and hearken, ye house of Israel; and give ye ear, O house of the king; for judgment *is* toward you, because ye have been a snare on Mizpah, and a net spread upon Tă'bor.

2 And the revolters are profound to make slaughter, though I *have been* a rebuker of them all.
3 I know É'phra-im, and Israel is not hid from me: for now, O É'phra-im, thou committest whoredom, *and* Israel is defiled.

4 They will not frame their doings to

utter an affirmation of his faith, **the LORD liveth,** in distinction to these nonexistent gods represented by these senseless idols. To issue such a proclamation in that setting would be to mingle the true God with idolatry, which He expressly forbade (cf. Zeph 1:5). The maxim is ever true: light spurned is light rejected. Israel's problem is not a lack of knowledge; it is in understanding the importance of the knowledge that they already have; and they have willfully rejected it in favor of their idolatrous practices.

16. For Israel slideth back as a backsliding heifer. The figure is more clearly understood when one realizes that the words **slideth back** and **backsliding** (Heb *sarar*) actually mean stubborn. Israel, then, is like a stubborn heifer; and Israel's problem is not knowledge, it is obedience. **Now the LORD will feed them as a lamb in a larger place** is best understood as a rhetorical question expecting a negative answer. In view of Israel's stubbornness, God cannot feed them as though they were a lamb in a large place, can He? Obviously not! This is confirmed by the statement that follows in verse 17.

17. Ephraim is joined to idols: let him alone. Ephraim (the name given to Israel because it was the largest tribe of the northern kingdom) is completely given to its idolatry and accompanying practices. He is beyond recall. The only thing to do is to leave him alone. The words are reminiscent of those expressed by Paul (cf. II Tim 3:1-5).

18-19. These verses express the futility of Israel's choice. **Their drink is sour.** They have given themselves to that which cannot satisfy and ultimately will bring them to the judgment of God. **They have committed whoredom continually.** They follow after that which they consider to be substantial and, in the final analysis, find it to be only wind. **Her rulers.** This is the only instance where the Hebrew word *magēn* is translated by the English word **rulers.** It occurs in the Old Testament more than fifty times and is usually translated by the English word "shield." The leaders who were given to the nation by God, with the express purpose of shielding the nation from sin and leading them to God, have instead led in their spiritual defection. They became enamored with the people's sins and led the people further away from God, rather than decrying their sin and leading the way back to God. Therefore, **they shall be ashamed.** God's judgment must fall.

2. Demonstrated by God's condemnation. 5:1-6:3.

In this section God's condemnation results in three things: (1) rebuke (5:1-7); (2) retribution (5:8-15); and (3) repentance (6:1-3).

5:1. Hear ye this. The rebuke is stinging and is addressed to the religious leaders (**priests**), the nation in general (**house of Israel**), and the royalty (**house of the king**), in short, to everyone in the land and especially to the religious and governmental leaders who have been prominent in leading the nation into its sin (5:1a). Rebuke comes because from the south of the land (**Mizpah**) to the north (**Tabor,** i.e., Mount Tabor), the nation has been wholly given (**snare . . . net spread**) to idolatry (vs. 1b).

2-3. Though I have been a rebuker of them all. This spiritual defection has been deliberate, in spite of God's repeated rebuke. **I know Ephraim, and Israel is not hid from me.** Though the people and their leaders have not been mindful of God, still their spiritual defection and adultery does not escape the notice of God. Though they may deny and seek to hide their true condition, God sees them for what they are, wholly given to idolatry and totally defiled. **Israel is defiled.** So given are they to their spiritual defection that they are enslaved by it and are helpless.

4. They will not frame their doings to turn to their God.

turn unto their God: for the spirit of whoredoms *is* in the midst of them, and they have not known the LORD.

5 And the pride of Israel doth testify to his face: therefore shall Israel and E'phra-im fall in their iniquity; Judah also shall fall with them.

6 They shall go with their flocks and with their herds to seek the LORD; but they shall not find *him;* he hath withdrawn himself from them.

7 They have dealt treacherously against the LORD: for they have begotten strange children: now shall a month devour them with their portions.

8 ¶Blow ye the cornet in Gĭb'e-ah, *and* the trumpet in Rā'mah: cry aloud at Bĕth-ā'ven, after thee, O Benjamin.

9 E'phra-im shall be desolate in the day of rebuke: among the tribes of Israel have I made known that which shall surely be.
10 The princes of Judah were like them that remove the bound: *therefore* I will pour out my wrath upon them like water.
11 E'phra-im *is* oppressed *and* broken in judgment, because he willingly walked after the commandment.

12 Therefore *will* I *be* unto E'phra-im as a moth, and to the house of Judah as rottenness.

13 When E'phra-im saw his sickness, and Judah *saw* his wound, then went E'phra-im to the Assyrian, and sent to king Jā'reb: yet could he not heal you, nor cure you of your wound.

14 For I *will be* unto E'phra-im as a lion, and as a young lion to the house of Judah: I, *even* I, will tear and go away; I will take away, and none shall rescue *him.*

15 I will go *and* return to my place, till they acknowledge their offence, and

Though God thoroughly and completely knows them and their condition (vs. 3), they are so completely under power of idolatry that they do not turn to Jehovah.

5. And the pride of Israel doth testify to his face. Rather than being ashamed of their sin, they flaunt it because of their perverted pride. Their sin will be their undoing and will affect not only them, but also Judah to the south. No man sins unto himself. The sin of one affects all, just as it did in the days of Joshua and Achan.

6-7. They shall go . . . to seek the LORD; but they shall not find him. Judah shares in Israel's sin and will also share in Israel's judgment. When they come to the end of themselves and finally seek Jehovah with their sacrifices and religious formality, they will not be able to find Him; for in judgment **he hath withdrawn himself from them** because **They have dealt treacherously.** They approach Him in hypocrisy and insincerity. **Now shall a month devour them.** God's judgment will fall upon them; and they, their possessions, and religious trappings will be taken away in captivity.

8. Blow ye the cornet in Gibeah, and the trumpet in Ramah: cry aloud at Beth-aven. God's retribution must fall upon Israel. The judgment heaped upon the north will be so excessive that it will endanger the tribes to the south. Gibeah, Ramah, and Beth-aven are cities belonging to the tribe of Benjamin in the south. They will be on military alert. **After thee, O Benjamin**—the battle cry used in the day of Joshua will be reactivated.

9-10. Ephraim shall be desolate. The devastation of the northern kingdom will be complete, in keeping with what God has made known prophetically.

11. Because he willingly walked after the commandment. The devastation is in just retribution because of their willful forsaking of God and wholesale turning to idols. Things will not get better, but there will be continuous decay in both the northern and southern kingdoms.

12. Therefore will I be unto Ephraim as a moth, and to the house of Judah as rottenness. The imagery God uses to portray this decay is beautiful. To the northern kingdom He will be like a moth (i.e., their demise will be more rapid), and to Judah He will be like rottenness (i.e., their decay will be slower), decaying one hundred thirty years later, but just as certain and irreparable.

13. When Ephraim saw his sickness, and Judah saw his wound. When both northern and southern kingdoms saw their sad conditions (**sickness . . . wound**), both realized that they needed help but went to the wrong source. **Then went Ephraim to the Assyrian . . . king Jareb.** Instead of going to God, the only one who could help, they went to man, the king of Assyria (here referred to by his popular name or nickname **king Jareb**) who, though powerful in man's sight, was totally helpless before God.

14. For I will be unto Ephraim as a lion . . . none shall rescue him. Though God's judgment will fall on the southern kingdom one hundred thirty years after it falls upon the northern kingdom and though the agents will be different (Babylonia for the southern and Assyria for the northern kingdom), it is equally certain for both. God will use human agencies to accomplish His purpose in judging His people, and they shall not escape (vs. 14).

15. I will go and return . . . they will seek me early. Into this dark picture of retribution shines a ray of hope. God's purpose is not punitive; it is therapeutic. He will withdraw from

seek my face: in their affliction they will seek me early.

CHAPTER 6

COME, and let us return unto the LORD: for he hath torn, and he will heal us; he hath smitten, and he will bind us up.

2 After two days will he revive us: in the third day he will raise us up, and we shall live in his sight.

3 Then shall we know, *if* we follow on to know the LORD: his going forth is prepared as the morning; and he shall come unto us as the rain, as the latter *and* former rain unto the earth.

4 ¶O Ē'phra-im, what shall I do unto thee? O Judah, what shall I do unto thee? for your goodness *is* as a morning cloud, and as the early dew it goeth away.

5 Therefore have I hewed *them* by the prophets; I have slain them by the words of my mouth: and thy judgments *are as* the light *that* goeth forth.

6 For I desired mercy, and not sacrifice; and the knowledge of God more than burnt offerings.

7 But they like men have transgressed the covenant: there have they dealt treacherously against me.

8 Gilead *is* a city of them that work iniquity, *and is* polluted with blood.

9 And as troops of robbers wait for a man, *so* the company of priests murder in the way by consent: for they commit lewdness.

10 I have seen an horrible thing in the house of Israel: there *is* the whoredom of Ē'phra-im, Israel is defiled.

11 Also, O Judah, he hath set an harvest for thee, when I returned the captivity of my people.

CHAPTER 7

WHEN I would have healed Israel, then the iniquity of Ē'phra-im was discovered, and the wickedness of Samā'rī-a: for they commit falsehood; and the thief cometh in, *and* the troop of robbers spoileth without.

2 And they consider not in their hearts *that* I remember all their wickedness: now their own doings have beset them about; they are before my face.

3 They make the king glad with their wickedness, and the princes with their lies.

His people with the purpose of causing them to seek Him; and just as certainly as the judgment will fall, so certainly will come their repentance, though the judgment is essential; for they would not seek His face without it.

6:1-2. Verses 1-3 set forth this repentance in more detail and give the very words that Israel will use to express its national repentance.

Come and let us return unto the LORD. We shall live in his sight. The prophet looks beyond both the Assyrian and Babylonian captivities down to the ultimate day when Israel as a nation will be converted (cf. Jer 31:31-34) and God will set up His millennial kingdom over His people and reign for a thousand years. In response to the Assyrian and Babylonian captivity, a remnant will come to this recognition; but in that day the entire nation will come to this realization.

3. He shall come to us as the rain. God will no longer deal with them like a **moth** and **rottenness** (cf. 5:12). Instead, He will deal with them like life-giving and refreshing **rain** (vs. 3). When given this tantalizing glimpse of the ultimate future that lies ahead for the restored nation, the prophet returns to focus upon the immediate scene.

3. Demonstrated by her fickleness (together with Judah's). 6:4-11.

4. Your goodness is as a morning cloud, and as the early dew. In spite of their blatant sin, God continues to care for Israel—both the northern and southern kingdoms. Their response is sporadic and likened to dew.

5. I hewed them by the prophets. Because of their sporadic response, God continuously has to face them with their sin through the ministries of His messengers.

6. For I desired mercy, and not sacrifice. God sends His prophets, not because He wants to afflict them, but because He wants them to respond in heartfelt reality.

7. But they . . . transgressed the covenant. Israel, however, responded not in reality, but in external religious formalism and idolatry.

8-9. Gilead is . . . polluted with blood. The religious leaders who should have led the nation by their obedience to God led the nation in its sin instead.

10. I have seen a horrible thing . . . Israel is defiled. The religious leaders led the nation into idolatry, thus defiling the entire nation. This was repugnant to God.

11. O Judah, he hath set a harvest for thee. Judah, the southern kingdom, will fare no better than Ephraim, the northern kingdom; for it committed the same sins. God's judgment will come to them some 130 years later and by a different agent, Babylon. Judah should have learned from God's dealings with Israel, but tragically did not.

4. Demonstrated by her foolishness. 7:1-16.

Israel's follies are enumerated in 7:1-7, and her floundering is portrayed in 7:8-16.

7:1-3. God's desire and will for Israel is her healing and restoration. This ultimately will be realized, but in Hosea's day the nation was not at all interested. Instead, they went about their evil deeds of lying, theft, robbery (vs. 1), blatant contempt of God (vs. 2), political corruption (vs. 3), and unbridled lust (vs. 4).

4 They *are* all adulterers, as an oven heated by the baker, *who* ceaseth from raising after he hath kneaded the dough, until it be leavened.

5 In the day of our king the princes have made *him* sick with bottles of wine; he stretched out his hand with scorners.

6 For they have made ready their heart like an oven, whiles they lie in wait: their baker sleepeth all the night; in the morning it burneth as a flaming fire.

7 They are all hot as an oven, and have devoured their judges; all their kings are fallen: *there is* none among them that calleth unto me.

8 ¶ E′phra-im, he hath mixed himself among the people; E′phra-im is a cake not turned.

9 Strangers have devoured his strength, and he knoweth *it* not: yea, gray hairs are here and there upon him, yet he knoweth not.

10 And the pride of Israel testifieth to his face: and they do not return to the LORD their God, nor seek him for all this.

11 E′phra-im also is like a silly dove without heart: they call to Egypt, they go to Assyria.

12 When they shall go, I will spread my net upon them; I will bring them down as the fowls of the heaven; I will chastise them, as their congregation hath heard.

13 Woe unto them! for they have fled from me: destruction unto them! because they have transgressed against me: though I have redeemed them, yet they have spoken lies against me.

14 And they have not cried unto me

4. They are all adulterers. This is physical adultery, which is but the outward expression of their spiritual adultery. **An oven heated by the baker.** The figure of the heated oven shows that because they have completely forgotten about God, they are consumed by their sexual passions and have no realization that He is fully acquainted with all their ways.

5. In the day of our king the princes have made him sick. So degraded is the nation that the king, who should be a leader for righteousness, is a leader in sin and debauchery. Instead of leading the nation in the ways of wisdom and God, the king plays the fool with the leaders of government who actually scorn the king.

6. Their baker sleepeth all the night. All of this transpires because there is no one to call the nation back to God. The nation is in moral degradation, completely consumed by its lust and sin.

7. They . . . have devoured their judges; all their kings are fallen. The result is anarchy. Law enforcement completely breaks down, and there is political assassination after political assassination. From the days of the division of the kingdom and the establishment of the northern kingdom, nine of its kings have been murdered! Such is the destiny of a nation that forgets God.

Verses 8-16 portray Israel's floundering. She is morally adrift; and her floundering is portrayed in three figures: (1) as **a cake not turned** (vss. 8-10); (2) as **a silly dove** (vss. 11-15); and (3) as **a deceitful bow** (vs. 16).

8. Ephraim, he hath mixed himself among the people. Israel, addressed in the name of its most prominent tribe, is reminded of the mission for which God called it into existence and the destiny that God had promised (cf. Gen 12:1-3). Instead, they mixed themselves among the people and adopted their ways. They had much religious activity, but no religious reality. The figure of the cake not turned is most appropriate. As far as religious activity is concerned, they are overdone. But so far as their attitude and reality towards God is concerned, they are raw. **Ephraim is a cake not turned.** The cake mentioned was baked on hot stones and was something like our pancake. It was easy for it to be burned on one side while yet being raw on the other. The figure fits Israel's condition perfectly.

9. Strangers have devoured his strength, and he knoweth it not. The tragedy of all of this is that Israel did not even know its own condition. Israel had been robbed of her strength and was in a state of decay, but it was totally ignorant of it all.

10. The pride of Israel testifieth to his face. The problem was the nation's pride. In all of their religious activity and consequent decay, they did not return to Jehovah or seek Him at all.

11. Ephraim also is like a silly dove without heart. Israel, again addressed as Ephraim, the most prominent tribe, is likened to **a silly dove without heart** (understanding). Instead of looking to God for protection, they made political alliances with Egypt and Assyria, seeking to play one against the other. In the end Israel was ravaged by both.

12. I will spread my net upon them. In failing to seek God's blessings, Israel becomes a candidate for God's judgment, which certainly will fall (notice the three "I wills" in this verse).

13. Woe unto them! So certain and devastating will be the destruction that God pronounces a woe upon His nation. **Though I have redeemed them.** The defection is without reason; and in spite of the fact that God has redeemed them, they still sin against the Lord and fail to seek Him in true repentance.

14-15. They have not cried unto me with their heart. When

with their heart, when they howled upon their beds: they assemble themselves for corn and wine, *and* they rebel against me.

15 Though I have bound *and* strengthened their arms, yet do they imagine mischief against me.

16 They return, *but* not to the most High: they are like a deceitful bow: their princes shall fall by the sword for the rage of their tongue: this *shall be* their derision in the land of Egypt.

CHAPTER 8

SET the trumpet to thy mouth. *He shall come* as an eagle against the house of the LORD, because they have transgressed my covenant, and trespassed against my law.

2 Israel shall cry unto me, My God, we know thee.

3 Israel hath cast off *the thing that is* good: the enemy shall pursue him.

4 They have set up kings, but not by me: they have made princes, and I knew *it* not: of their silver and their gold have they made them idols, that they may be cut off.

5 ¶Thy calf, O Sa-mã′rĭ-a, hath cast *thee* off; mine anger is kindled against them: how long *will it be* ere they attain to innocency?

6 For from Israel *was* it also: the workman made it; therefore it *is* not God: but the calf of Sa-mã′rĭ-a shall be broken in pieces.

7 For they have sown the wind, and they shall reap the whirlwind: it hath no stalk: the bud shall yield no meal: if so be it yield, the strangers shall swallow it up.

8 Israel is swallowed up: now shall

they do come together, it is not to seek the Lord, but rather to compound their sins further in drunken revelry and rebellion. **They imagine mischief against me.** In spite of God's grace, they become most creative in their expression of sin.

16. They are like a deceitful bow. Israel is likened to a **deceitful bow** that has every appearance of being good, but the arrows that it propels miss the intended target. God has intended wonderful things for Israel, but they have continuously mistaken His favor for favoritism and have misused His blessings for their own ends. **Their princes shall fall by the sword.** Their rulers shall be taken from them; and they will be ridiculed by Egypt, upon whom they depended for protection and assistance. **For the rage of their tongue.** They failed to use their tongues for God; therefore, the tongues of their enemies will be used against them.

B. Concerning Israel's Retribution. 8:1-13:16.

1. The trumpet call to retribution. 8:1-14.

Five reasons are given for the trumpet call to retribution: (1) because of her transgressions against God's covenant and Law (vss. 1-3); (2) because of her setting up kings and princes without God's direction (vs. 4a); (3) because of her idolatrous practices (vss. 4b-7); (4) because of her alliance with Assyria (vss. 8-10); and (5) because of her multiplication of sacrificial altars (vss. 11-14).

Two short figures introduce this section (vs. 1): (1) the sound of the trumpet (Heb *shōpar*), the instrument used to assemble Israel or to sound an alarm; and (2) the eagle.

8:1-2. Set the trumpet to thy mouth. This figure indicates the severity of the attack. **He shall come as an eagle.** This figure indicates the swiftness of the attack. **They have transgressed my covenant.** The judgment of God comes upon Israel because they did not take His covenant (the Abrahamic covenant, Gen 12:1-3) and Law (the whole Mosaic system) seriously. God, however, does keep His word and will send the judgment He has promised. **My God, we know thee.** When the judgment falls, Israel will plead its knowledge of God. Unfortunately, its knowledge of God has been historical and not personal.

3. Israel hath cast off the thing that is good. This is proven by their disregard of God's covenant and law; consequently, Israel shall fall into the hand of its enemy.

4. They have set up kings. The problem is not new in origin; it goes all the way back to the beginning of the northern kingdom when they set up the first king contrary to God's direction. **I knew it not.** None of the kings of the northern kingdom were God's appointed rulers of the land. All of them were usurpers. **They made them idols.** Israel's defection politically manifested itself also religiously; for the nation turned to the worship of idols.

5-6. Thy calf, O Samaria. The heart of the idolatrous worship was Samaria, and the specific form was that of a calf. **Mine anger is kindled.** God was justly angered; for they worshiped a product of their own hands, rather than worshiping the God who made them and their hands.

7. They have sown the wind, and they shall reap the whirlwind. In their defection, they have sown the seed of their defeat and undoing. However, they will not reap what they have sown but much worse, the harvest of what they have sown. They have sown a wind (Heb *rūach*), but will reap a hurricane (Heb *sūpah*). They will be swept away in the judgment of God, and any benefits that they desired would fall to the hands of the strangers to whom God would deliver them.

8-9. Israel is swallowed up. God's plan for Israel was that

1677

they be among the Gentiles as a vessel wherein *is* no pleasure.

9 For they are gone up to Assyria, a wild ass alone by himself: Ē'phra-im hath hired lovers.

10 Yea, though they have hired among the nations, now will I gather them, and they shall sorrow a little for the burden of the king of princes.

11 Because Ē'phra-im hath made many altars to sin, altars shall be unto him to sin.

12 I have written to him the great things of my law, *but* they were counted as a strange thing.

13 They sacrifice flesh *for* the sacrifices of mine offerings, and eat *it; but* the LORD accepteth them not; now will he remember their iniquity, and visit their sins: they shall return to Egypt.

14 For Israel hath forgotten his Maker, and buildeth temples; and Judah hath multiplied fenced cities: but I will send a fire upon his cities, and it shall devour the palaces thereof.

CHAPTER 9

REJOICE not, O Israel, for joy, as *other* people: for thou hast gone a whoring from thy God, thou hast loved a reward upon every cornfloor.

2 The floor and the winepress shall not feed them, and the new wine shall fail in her.

3 They shall not dwell in the LORD's land; but Ē'phra-im shall return to Egypt, and they shall eat unclean *things* in Assyria.

4 They shall not offer wine *offerings* to the LORD, neither shall they be pleasing unto him: their sacrifices *shall be* unto them as the bread of mourners; all that eat thereof shall be polluted: for their bread for their soul shall not come into the house of the LORD.

5 What will ye do in the solemn day, and in the day of the feast of the LORD?

6 For, lo, they are gone because of destruction: Egypt shall gather them up, Měm'phis shall bury them: the pleasant *places* for their silver, nettles shall possess them: thorns *shall be* in their tabernacles.

7 The days of visitation are come, the days of recompence are come; Israel shall know *it:* the prophet *is* a fool, the spiritual man *is* mad, for the multitude of thine iniquity, and the great hatred.

8 The watchman of Ē'phra-im *was* with my God: *but* the prophet *is* a snare

they should be a peculiar people for Him and that He would be their God. Israel, however, forsook God and mingled with the Gentiles (the other nations of the world). They adopted the ways of the Gentiles and ceased to depend upon God. **They are gone up to Assyria.** They turned instead to Assyria in stubborn rebellion against God. Hence, the figures of **a wild ass alone** and **hired lovers** are most appropriate. The nation did exactly as Gomer had done earlier.

10. They shall sorrow a little. This spiritual defection will result in their destruction and servitude to the king of Assyria, here described as **the king of princes.**

11-13. Ephraim hath made many altars to sin. Throughout Israel many sacrificial altars were built for the purpose of idolatrous rituals. Israel became addicted to its sin in spite of the clear and written revelation that God had given it through Moses. In spite of clear revelation (vs. 12), they went off into the practice of idolatry, which did not please Jehovah. Therefore, judgment must fall (vs. 13).

14. The root of the cause lies in the fact that Israel forgot her Maker, and their sin spread into Judah. Not only will God judge Israel, but He promises to send fire upon the cities and palaces of Judah. This promise was literally fulfilled in Sennacherib's invasion of Judah when only Jerusalem was spared (cf. II Kgs 18:13ff.).

2. The prohibition of rejoicing. 9:1-17.

There are five reasons why Israel is prohibited from rejoicing: (1) because of her immorality (vss. 1-2); (2) because of her coming captivity (vss. 3-6); (3) because of her spiritual insensitivity (vss. 7-9); (4) because of her sterility (vss. 10-16); and (5) because of her coming exile (vs. 17).

9:1-2. It was customary and right for people to rejoice at harvest time. Israel; however, was commanded not to do so, because she attributed the abundance she experienced on the **cornfloor** (Heb *gōren dagan*, threshing floor, a place where the harvest of grain was processed) to the idols she worshiped, instead of God who sent it. **The floor and the winepress shall not feed them.** Because of their spiritual defection, crops will fail; and the threshing floors and winepresses will be inactive.

3. They shall not dwell in the LORD's land. Israel will not remain **in the LORD's land.** They will go into captivity, and certainly this is no cause for rejoicing. **Ephraim shall return to Egypt.** Israel will fall victim to Egypt and Assyria.

4-6. As a result of their wholesale practice of idolatry, their worship of Jehovah in God-appointed ways will cease. They will be involved in religious activities, but they will not be pleasing to God. One must always approach God in His way and according to His terms. The price for failure to do this is captivity and humiliation before their enemies.

7. The days of visitation are come . . . the prophet is a fool. In all of this Israel remains spiritually insensitive, considering God's prophets to be fools and those who are rightly related to God to be mad. Their sin has completely warped their spiritual discernment.

8. The watchman of Ephraim. God had intended Israel to be a watchman with God, that is, to be in fellowship with Him and to experience His blessings. **But the prophet is a snare of a**

of a fowler in all his ways, *and* hatred in the house of his God.

9 They have deeply corrupted *themselves*, as in the days of Gĭb'e-ah: *therefore* he will remember their iniquity, he will visit their sins.

10 I found Israel like grapes in the wilderness; I saw your fathers as the firstripe in the fig tree at her first time: *but* they went to Bā'al-pē'ôr, and separated themselves unto *that* shame; and *their* abominations were according as they loved.

11 *As for* Ē'phra-im, their glory shall fly away like a bird, from the birth, and from the womb, and from the conception.
12 Though they bring up their children, yet will I bereave them, *that there shall* not *be* a man *left:* yea, woe also to them when I depart from them!
13 Ē'phra-im, as I saw Tyrus, *is* planted in a pleasant place: but Ē'phra-im shall bring forth his children to the murderer.

14 Give them, O Lord: what wilt thou give? give them a miscarrying womb and dry breasts.

15 All their wickedness *is* in Gilgal: for there I hated them: for the wickedness of their doings I will drive them out of mine house, I will love them no more: all their princes *are* revolters.
16 Ē'phra-im is smitten, their root is dried up, they shall bear no fruit: yea, though they bring forth, yet will I slay *even* the beloved *fruit* of their womb.

17 My God will cast them away, because they did not hearken unto him: and they shall be wanderers among the nations.

CHAPTER 10

ISRAEL *is* an empty vine, he bringeth forth fruit unto himself: according to the multitude of his fruit he hath increased the altars; according to the goodness of his land they have made goodly images.
2 Their heart is divided; now shall

fowler. The nation that God intended to be a watchman became instead a snare to the nations of the world. Instead of loving God and walking in His ways, they hated Him and departed from His ways.

9. So deep is their defection that it is likened to the **days of Gibeah** when, in outrage against Benjamin's brutal and inhumane treatment of the Levite's concubine, the nation recoiled in horror and slew all but six hundred men of Benjamin. If God had not intervened, Benjamin would have been destroyed. Like Benjamin, Israel has sunken to the depths of depravity and, like Benjamin, would be destroyed if God did not intervene and cause a remnant to be left.

10. I found Israel like grapes in the wilderness. Children were regarded as a blessing of God (cf. Ps 127:3), and barrenness was considered to be His curse. God engages in a little bit of fond reminiscing here. He looks back at Israel's founding as a nation and portrays the people like **grapes in the wilderness** and the first figs that a fig tree bears. Both figures show the tenderness with which God regarded the nation and the pleasure they were to Him in anticipation. **But they went to Baal-peor.** Israel forsook God and early went into idolatry at Baal-peor; and, having contracted the disease, they went from bad to worse.

11-12. Their glory shall fly away like a bird. Their sin is so serious that God will strike them where it will hurt the most i.e., in their offspring. The name Ephraim means "doubly fruitful," but because of its sin, Ephraim will experience both a declining birthrate (vs. 11) and an exceeding high death rate among the children that are born (vs. 12).

13. Ephraim shall bring forth his children to the murderer. Ephraim would experience every blessing of God, even as Tyre had; but in spite of all the natural blessings God gave, it would use many of its children that did survive for human sacrifice in their idolatrous worship.

14. Give them a miscarrying womb and dry breasts. The horrible prospect of human sacrifice causes the prophet to ask God to pray that they would have no more children.

15. All their wickedness is in Gilgal. Gilgal was the center where idolatrous worship was conducted. God's wrath must fall upon them because of their sin. Ultimately, He will drive them completely out of the land.

16. Ephraim is smitten, their root is dried up. Though Ephraim had a beautiful geographical situation and experienced the abundant blessing of God, barrenness of land and womb, as well as near extinction awaited them.

17. My God will cast them away . . . they shall be wanderers among the nations. All of this would come to Israel because of their sin, and they would be consigned to wandering among all the nations of the earth. Interestingly enough, the complete nation of Israel never returned from the Assyrian captivity. To this day, no one knows who comprises the ten "lost tribes"; yet they are all well-known to God (cf. Jas 1:1; Rev 7:4-8). In God's time the whole nation will be restored!

3. The portrayal of retribution. 10:1-13:16

In this section Israel's retribution is portrayed in six figures: (1) as a spreading or luxuriant vine (10:1-2); (2) as in a state of anarchy (10:3-10); (3) as a trained heifer (10:11-15); (4) as a youth (11:1-11); (5) as one who feeds on wind (11:12-12:14); and (6) as one who is spiritually dead (13:1-16).

10:1-2. Israel is an empty vine. The word **empty** (Heb *ba-qaq*) is an onomatopoetic word that means "to gush out" or "bubble out" or "pour out." However, when used in intransitive constructions, as in verse 1, it means "to be poured out" or "spread abroad" as a spreading or luxuriant vine. The remainder of the verse would harmonize better with this idea than with

they be found faulty: he shall break down their altars, he shall spoil their images.

3 For now they shall say, We have no king, because we feared not the LORD; what then should a king do to us?

4 They have spoken words, swearing falsely in making a covenant: thus judgment springeth up as hemlock in the furrows of the field.

5 The inhabitants of Sa-mâ'rĭ-a shall fear because of the calves of Bĕth-ā'ven: for the people thereof shall mourn over it, and the priests thereof *that* rejoiced on it, for the glory thereof, because it is departed from it.

6 It shall be also carried unto Assyria *for* a present to king Jâ'reb: Ē'phra-im shall receive shame, and Israel shall be ashamed of his own counsel.

7 *As for* Sa-mâ'rĭ-a, her king is cut off as the foam upon the water.

8 The high places also of Ā'ven, the sin of Israel, shall be destroyed: the thorn and the thistle shall come up on their altars; and they shall say to the mountains, Cover us; and to the hills, Fall on us.

9 O Israel, thou hast sinned from the days of Gĭb'e-ah: there they stood: the battle in Gĭb'e-ah against the children of iniquity did not overtake them.

10 *It is* in my desire that I should chastise them; and the people shall be gathered against them, when they shall bind themselves in their two furrows.

11 And Ē'phra-im *is as* an heifer *that is* taught, *and* loveth to tread out *the corn*; but I passed over upon her fair neck: I will make Ē'phra-im to ride; Judah shall plow, *and* Jacob shall break his clods.

12 Sow to yourselves in righteousness, reap in mercy; break up your fallow ground: for *it is* time to seek the LORD, till he come and rain righteousness upon you.

13 Ye have plowed wickedness, ye have reaped iniquity; ye have eaten the fruit of lies: because thou didst trust in thy way, in the multitude of thy mighty men.

the idea of being **empty.** The prophet's thought is that God has abundantly blessed Israel, but Israel did not reciprocate God's love. The more God blessed the nation, the more the nation turned to its idols in the delusion that the blessing came from the idols, not from God. In New Testament words, they did not realize that the goodness of God was designed to bring them to repentance and dependence on Him (cf. Rom 2:4). Because of this failure, Israel is found to be faulty (Heb *'asham*), or guilty. Judgment must fall. God will demonstrate His superiority in destroying not only the altars upon which Israel offered sacrifices, but also the idols to which they offered sacrifices (vs. 2).

3-10. We have no king, because we feared not the LORD. As a result of God's judgment, a state of anarchy will exist. The people will come to a realization that this judgment has come unto them because of their defection from Jehovah, and they will recognize that not even a king would help them to withstand the judgment of God. **They have spoken words, swearing falsely.** Unfaithfulness and deceit will be spread throughout the land and are set forth under the figure of poison's (**hemlock**) being sown among the crops (vs. 4). **The inhabitants of Samaria shall fear because of the calves of Beth-aven . . . It shall be also carried unto Assyria for a present to king Jareb.** The worship of idols will not give the people security and comfort. Rather, their idolatry will cause priest and people to grieve because God, in His display of sovereignty and superiority over their idols, will take those idols and send them into Assyria as a present for the king (vss. 5b-6a) who, once again, is referred to by his nickname **king Jareb** as in 5:13. **Ephraim shall receive shame, and Israel shall be ashamed.** In withstanding the judgment of God, neither king nor priest nor idol can be of assistance to the people. The nation will be brought to shame. **As for Samaria, her king is cut off.** The helplessness of the king will be demonstrated as he is swept away into captivity. **The high places also of Aven, the sin of Israel, shall be destroyed.** All the idolatrous places of worship will be removed from the land. **They shall say to the mountains, Cover us; and to the hills, Fall on us.** The judgment will be so fearful that the people will wish to die. They would rather die than repent. **O Israel, thou hast sinned from the days of Gibeah.** Israel's problem is not new. It is traced all the way back to the **days of Gibeah** (cf. 9:9ff.). At that time God used Israel to punish Benjamin for its gross sin. **The children of iniquity did not overtake them.** God protected Israel because they were right. **It is in my desire that I should chastise them.** Now, however, the tables are turned; for Israel's deeds, particularly their idolatry, demonstrate their spiritual defection. God will bring judgment upon them, and they shall not escape. The expression **in their two furrows** (Heb *'awōn*, the act of cohabiting as man and wife) is better understood as "in their adhering to their two cohabitations" and is a reference to their idolatrous connections with the two golden calves that were enshrined at Beth-el and Dan. It is because of this idolatry that God's judgment must fall.

11-15. The allusion to the calves that Israel had worshiped causes God to take up the figure referring to Ephraim (Israel) as **a heifer that is taught,** a trained heifer. This animal was used to tread out the grain. Of all the tasks that an animal could do, this probably was the most pleasant because it was permitted to eat whenever and as much as it wanted to (cf. Deut 25:4). **But I passed over upon her fair neck . . . Judah shall plow.** Israel has had it very pleasant up until the present, but that will change; for she will be put out to the field to do the hard work of plowing and will have a rider (the nation Assyria) upon its back. The same judgment awaits Judah (though it will come one hundred thirty years later) to the degree that she is a partaker of Israel's sin and likewise fails to repent (vs. 11). **Break up your fallow ground: for it is time to seek the LORD.** The only thing

14 Therefore shall a tumult arise among thy people, and all thy fortresses shall be spoiled, as Shăl′man spoiled Bĕth–är′bel in the day of battle: the mother was dashed in pieces upon *her* children.

15 So shall Bĕth-el do unto you because of your great wickedness: in a morning shall the king of Israel utterly be cut off.

CHAPTER 11

WHEN Israel *was* a child, then I loved him, and called my son out of Egypt.

2 *As* they called them, so they went from them: they sacrificed unto Bā′al-im, and burned incense to graven images.

3 I taught Ē′phra-im also to go, taking them by their arms; but they knew not that I healed them.

4 I drew them with cords of a man, with bands of love: and I was to them as they that take off the yoke on their jaws, and I laid meat unto them.

5 ¶He shall not return into the land of Egypt, but the Assyrian shall be his king, because they refused to return.

6 And the sword shall abide on his cities, and shall consume his branches, and devour *them*, because of their own counsels.

7 And my people are bent to backsliding from me: though they called them to the most High, none at all would exalt *him*.

8 How shall I give thee up, Ē′phra-im? *how* shall I deliver thee, Israel? how shall I make thee as Ăd′mah? *how* shall I set thee as Ze-bō′im? mine heart is turned within me, my repentings are kindled together.

that can prevent God's judgment from falling is repentance and a commensurate life of righteousness. The time to come to this repentance and righteousness is now, before the judgment falls (vs. 12). The expression **till he come and rain righteousness upon you** is probably better understood "till he come and teach righteousness unto you." The thought is not that God is going to come and shower righteousness upon them for their repentance, but rather, that God will come and teach (the word translated **rain**, Heb *yarah* is frequently used to indicate pointing out or showing or instructing) righteousness unto them. Their repentance will put them into a proper relationship with God, and He can then teach them His ways. **Ye have plowed wickedness, ye have reaped iniquity.** Israel, however, did not seek the Lord and consequently, reaped destruction. Rather, she went her own way, has put her trust in man rather than in God, and therefore will reap the consequent destruction (vss. 13-14a). **All thy fortresses shall be spoiled, as Shalman spoiled Beth-arbel.** It will happen unto them as happened unto Beth-arbel when Shalman (Shalmaneser) devastated it. This was an historical event that was familiar to them but is obscure to us. **The mother was dashed in pieces upon her children.** The devastation was gruesome, for mothers and children were dashed to pieces upon stone (vss. 14b). **So shall Beth-el do unto you.** Such a destruction awaits the nation and the king because of its idolatrous cancer that it practices at Beth-el (vs. 15). Actually, idolatry is spread throughout the entire land, but Beth-el was the center of its practice.

11:1-8. Portrays Israel as a youth upon whom judgment must tragically fall because of continuous faithlessness. Up to this point in the book the emphasis has been primarily upon Israel's disobedience and consequent judgment; but from this point on in the book the emphasis is upon the Lord's love for Israel, in spite of her disobedience for which judgment must fall. **When Israel was a child, then I loved him.** God's love for Israel is traced back to its very beginnings when as a child (Heb *na'ar,* lad, or better, dependent) Israel was enslaved in Egypt and God delivered them because of His eternal love for them. **I . . . called my son out of Egypt.** These words are quoted by Matthew and applied to our Lord (Mt 2:15). In such instances one must see both the points of comparison and difference in order to understand the Holy Spirit's usage of the Old Testament. Israel and Jesus were alike in that both were the objects of the love of the Father. Both were called **my son,** Israel because of its generation by the Father and Jesus because of His eternal generation by the Father. Both were in Egypt, Israel in slavery to Egypt and Jesus as a refugee from the king of Judea. Israel and Jesus were different in that Israel was an earthly people of God while Jesus was the eternal Son of God. The purpose in the Spirit's leading Matthew to apply this reference to our Lord is not to deny any historical fulfillment to the nation, but rather to show the beautiful identification of the Son of God with the historical people of God. Both had a peculiar relationship with the Father not experienced by anyone else nationally (in the case of Israel) or personally (in the case of Jesus). As a manifestation of His love to the nation, God sent His prophets to them to tell them of His will for them. **They sacrificed unto Baalim, and burned incense to graven images.** Instead of responding to the prophet's message, they rejected it and turned unto idols, offering sacrifices unto the Baalim and burning incense before the graven images, all of which was prohibited by the first commandment. **I taught Ephraim also to go, taking them by their arms.** God did not deal with Israel according to its faithlessness, but according to His love. He taught them how to walk; He healed them; He loved them with bonds of love; He lifted their burdens from them and He fed them (vss. 3-4). He dealt with them as a parent, not as an avenger. Though the nation was faithless in its love for Jehovah, still He remained faithful in His love for them.

The statement **He shall not return into the land of Egypt, but the Assyrian shall be his king** (vs. 5) at first thought seems to contradict the statement of 8:13 (**they shall return to Egypt**) and 9:3 (**but Ephraim shall return to Egypt**). It seems best to view the mentions of Egypt in 8:13 and 9:3 as being metaphorical, representing the type of bondage that they experienced while residing in the land of Egypt. Verses 8:13 and 9:3, then, are saying that the nation will return to an Egypt-like bondage; but, physically, they will be taken to the land of Assyria. Verse 5 affirms that Israel will not return to Egypt physically, but will be physically taken to Assyria, even though they might desire deliverance from Assyria by returning to Egypt. The king of Assyria will be their king, and this will happen to them because of their refusal to return to Jehovah (vs. 5). **And the sword shall abide on his cities.** Judgment will fall upon the land, and the devastation will be complete because they have done what they wanted to do, rather than what Jehovah wanted them to do (vs. 6). **My people are bent to backsliding.** Israel is bent to (Heb *tala'*, lit., hanged, in a modern idiom we would say "hooked on") her backsliding. **Though they called them to the most High, none at all would exalt him.** No matter how many prophets God sends to call her to repentance and to return to the Lord, the nation continues in its sin-hardened ways (vs. 7). **How shall I give thee up Ephraim? how shall I deliver thee, Israel?** In spite of the fact that they deserve it, God, as a true Father, is reticent to hand over His child to punishment. He makes this reticence clear by these two rhetorical questions (vs. 8a). **Admah** and **Zeboim** were two of the five cities of the plains that were destroyed along with the destruction of Sodom and Gomorrah (cf. Gen 19; Deut 29:23). Though they are guilty of the same sins, Jehovah is reticent to give them the same punishment. **Mine heart is turned within me, my repentings are kindled together.** The reason for Jehovah's dilemma is the fact that He has a covenant with Israel, which He did not have with the cities of the plains.

9-11. These verses constitute a promise of restoration following the judgment that must befall the faithless child of God. **I will not execute the fierceness of mine anger.** Though His judgment against Israel will be severe, it will not obliterate them (vs. 9); for God will keep His covenant with Israel, which necessitates the existence of the nation on into the Millennium when the entire nation will be converted and Messiah will rule and reign over them for a thousand years. **He shall roar like a lion . . . then the children shall tremble from the west.** At the time of the Millennium, Jehovah will roar like a lion against Israel's enemies; and those dispersed in the west will return (vs. 10). **They shall tremble as a bird out of Egypt, and as a dove out of the land of Assyria.** Those dispersed to the south will return, as will those from the north and east (vs. 11a). Again, God uses the figure of a trembling bird and dove (cf. 7:11-15); but the dove no longer will be silly (i.e., without understanding). At this time, Israel will in fact understand that it is Jehovah who has saved them and called them to Himself. He will place them in their land, and they shall never be removed (vs. 11b). It is important to realize that the Israel of the present day is not the Israel of the Millennium. Rather, it is the Israel of the Tribulation, for whom destruction and dispersion await (cf. Mt 24:15-28). Following this, the Son of Man will return, will summon His people from the corners of the earth, and will reign over them for a thousand years (cf. Mt 24:29-31).

9 I will not execute the fierceness of mine anger, I will not return to destroy É'phra-im: for I *am* God, and not man; the Holy One in the midst of thee: and I will not enter into the city.

10 They shall walk after the Lord: he shall roar like a lion: when he shall roar, then the children shall tremble from the west.

11 They shall tremble as a bird out of Egypt, and as a dove out of the land of Assyria: and I will place them in their houses, saith the Lord.

12. In the Hebrew text verse 12 is actually the first verse of chapter 12. **Ephraim compasseth me about with lies, and the house of Israel with deceit: but Judah yet ruleth with God, and is faithful with the saints.** This verse shifts the prophet's

12 É'phra-im compasseth me about with lies, and the house of Israel with deceit: but Judah yet ruleth with God, and is faithful with the saints.

focus back to the situation of his day. Ephraim (Israel) is ripe for judgment because of wholesale spiritual defection (manifested by lies and deceit) throughout the land. Judah, by comparison, is still in God's favor, being faithful to God, at least outwardly. With the exception of Ahaz, the kings under whom the prophet ministered (cf. 1:1) did that which was right in the sight of the Lord. The word **yet** is an indication of their decline and ultimate judgment. Because she will make the same mistakes, Judah will follow Israel in judgment some one hundred thirty years later.

12:1. Ephraim feedeth on wind, and followeth after the east wind. This is a reference to the sirocco wind, a hot dry wind coming from the eastern desert and causing great devastation in the land. The picture is graphic; for Israel has given itself to feeding on that which will not nourish it (idolatry), and the result is an increase in **lies and desolation.** Their actions stem from a heart defection from God. **They do make a covenant with the Assyrians, and oil is carried into Egypt.** Choosing not to trust in Him, they seek to make political alliances and carry on trade with the world powers of their day, Assyria and Egypt, hoping that they would be spared.

2. The LORD hath also a controversy with Judah, and will punish Jacob. Judah, too, would experience God's judgment (vs. 2a, cf. comments earlier on 11:12b). The entire nation (Jacob) will experience God's judgment, though one hundred thirty years apart, because the entire nation has forsaken God and gone after idols (vs. 2b).

3-5. These verses remind the entire nation of the patriarch from whom they have descended. Jacob always wanted God's best, even though he did not always seek it God's way. **He took his brother by the heel in the womb.** While yet in his mother's womb, he took his brother by the heel as if to displace him and thus became the first-born to inherit the promises of God (vs. 3, cf. Gen 25:24-26). **By his strength he had power with God.** In spite of Jacob's weakness, the overall testimony of his life was that he had power with God (vs. 3, cf. Gen 32:28). **Yea, he had power over the angel, and prevailed.** The illusion is to Jacob's encounter with the angel of Jehovah at Peniel (cf. vs. 4, cf. Gen 32:30). **He wept and made supplication unto him.** The outcome of that wrestling match was that the angel of Jehovah dislocated Jacob's thigh, which forever after that was a painful reminder of his weakness. As a result, Jacob no longer could depend upon himself and had to turn to God for his blessing in God's way and in God's time. What he could not accomplish of himself, he accomplished in his helpless dependence upon God; for there he met God face to face, and his name was changed from Jacob (supplanter) to Israel (prince with God). Jacob had the privilege of talking face to face with God (vs. 4), who is the **LORD** (Heb *yahweh*), the powerful God of the hosts of heaven, known to Israel by the sacred tetragrammaton, *YHWH* **LORD** (Heb *yahweh*). This is **his memorial** (Heb *zēker*) by which He is to be known by all the generations of Israel (vs. 5, cf. Ex 3:14-15). The name Yahweh (Heb *YHWH*, he is) was the name by which Israel affirmed what God had revealed about Himself when He revealed Himself to Moses as "... I AM THAT I AM ..." (Ex 3:14) and declared that he should remind Israel that it was "I AM" that had sent him. Thus, God says of Himself, "I AM" (Heb *'ehyeh*, I am); and man affirms that revelation by calling him Yahweh (Heb *YHWH*, he is). The name of God reveals His eternality and could very well be translated "the one who was", "the one who is", and "the one who is to come", or "the Eternal" (cf. Jn 8:58; Rev 1:8b, where the very name is used by and of our Lord Jesus Christ).

6-8. Therefore, turn thou to thy God. Would that Israel of the prophet's day had been like their progenitor, always seeking after God, even if in the wrong way; but they were like Him only by contrast. They sought only after false gods and were steeped

CHAPTER 12

E′PHRA-IM feedeth on wind, and followeth after the east wind: he daily increaseth lies and desolation: and they do make a covenant with the Assyrians, and oil is carried into Egypt.

2 The LORD hath also a controversy with Judah, and will punish Jacob according to his ways; according to his doings will he recompense him.

3 ¶He took his brother by the heel in the womb, and by his strength he had power with God:

4 Yea, he had power over the angel, and prevailed: he wept, and made supplication unto him: he found him in Bĕth-el, and there he spake with us;

5 Even the LORD God of hosts; the LORD is his memorial.

6 Therefore turn thou to thy God: keep mercy and judgment, and wait on thy God continually.

7 ¶He is a merchant, the balances of

deceit *are* in his hand: he loveth to oppress.

8 And Ē'phra-im said, Yet I am become rich, I have found me out substance: *in* all my labours they shall find none iniquity in me that *were* sin.

9 And I *that am* the LORD thy God from the land of Egypt will yet make thee to dwell in tabernacles, as in the days of the solemn feast.

10 I have also spoken by the prophets, and I have multiplied visions, and used similitudes, by the ministry of the prophets.

11 *Is there* iniquity *in* Gilead? surely they are vanity: they sacrifice bullocks in Gilgal; yea, their altars *are* as heaps in the furrows of the fields.

12 And Jacob fled into the country of Syria, and Israel served for a wife, and for a wife he kept *sheep*.

13 And by a prophet the LORD brought Israel out of Egypt, and by a prophet was he preserved.

14 Ē'phra-im provoked *him* to anger most bitterly: therefore shall he leave his blood upon him, and his reproach shall his Lord return unto him.

CHAPTER 13

WHEN Ē'phra-im spake trembling, he exalted himself in Israel; but when he offended in Bā'al, he died.

2 And now they sin more and more,

in idolatrous worship. **He is a merchant.** The invitation is given to the nation to turn and be like their progenitor (vs. 6); but rather than being like God, Israel is like the Canaanite and the Canaanite deities that they had adopted. The English translation, unfortunately, obscures the prophet's intent. When Jehovah says that Israel is **a merchant,** He actually says he is a Canaanite (Heb *kena'an,* Canaanite merchant). Having adopted the Canaanite deities, he also adopted the Canaanite ways of deceitful business dealings and oppression (vs. 7). **Ephraim said, yet I am become rich . . . they shall find none iniquity in me.** Ephraim (Israel) became proud in rebellion and felt that no one would discover the moral corruption and dishonesty and call them to account (vs. 8). Ephraim made the fatal mistake of thinking that their prosperity was proof that God did not care about their sin, and they failed to realize that the goodness of God was designed to bring them to repentance (cf. Rom 2:4).

9-10. And I that am the LORD thy God from the land of Egypt. In spite of their faithlessness, God still remains faithful to Himself and to the covenant which He gave to Abraham. He will extend further grace to them and will ultimately cleanse and establish and reign over them (vs. 9). **I have also spoken by the prophets . . . visions . . . and . . . similitudes.** As a sign of His continued love and faithfulness to Israel, He sends prophets to them, and they will continually call the people back to God. In addition, He will give His messengers visions and easy-to-understand illustrations (vs. 10). The point is that in no way could Israel's problem be attributed to God. He has remained faithful and has continuously sought by every possible means to turn Israel back to Himself. Yet, in spite of God's gracious dealings with them, they have departed from Him.

11. Is there iniquity in Gilead? . . . they sacrifice bullocks in Gilgal. Israel's plight is demonstrated by the fact that the entire land, both east (represented by the reference to Gilead) and west of the Jordan (represented by Gilgal), is full of idolatry. **Their altars are as heaps in the furrows of the fields.** So multitudinous are the altars to the various deities that they are likened to piles of rocks that a farmer encounters in a field (vs. 11).

12-13. Jacob fled into the country of Syria, and Israel served for a wife. Once again, Israel is reminded of the faithfulness of their progenitor, Jacob. All during the years in which he was an exile in Mesopotamia, he trusted in Jehovah, even though Laban deceived him and caused him to work twice as long as he originally intended for the wife he desired (vs. 12). **And by a prophet the LORD brought Israel out of Egypt.** In like manner, Jehovah raised up Moses (**a prophet),** brought the nation out of Egypt through him, and preserved them through the wilderness wanderings (vs. 13).

14. Ephraim provoked him to anger most bitterly. Instead of expressing gratitude to God for His preservation of their forefather and of their fledgling nation, the people of Hosea's day have completely forgotten Jehovah who has preserved them to the time of the prophecy. However, instead of seeking Jehovah who had been faithful to them, Ephraim (Israel) provoked Jehovah by his spiritual defection; and God must punish him. He will reap the harvest of the sin he has sown (vs. 14).

13:1. This passage (vss. 1-16) portrays Israel as one who is spiritually dead, and it begins by reminding Ephraim of the prominence that it once enjoyed in the nation. **When Ephraim spake trembling.** When Ephraim spoke, everyone listened to and respected him. **When he offended in Baal, he died.** Something happened. Under Ahab, the nation gave itself to the worship of Baal; and the result was spiritual death. The nation's spiritual decline also resulted in political decline (vs. 1, cf. I Kgs 16:31).

2. And now they sin more and more, and have made them

and have made them molten images of their silver, *and* idols according to their own understanding, all of it the work of the craftsmen: they say of them, Let the men that sacrifice kiss the calves.

3 Therefore they shall be as the morning cloud, and as the early dew that passeth away, as the chaff *that* is driven with the whirlwind out of the floor, and as the smoke out of the chimney.

4 Yet I *am* the LORD thy God from the land of Egypt, and thou shalt know no god but me: for *there is* no saviour beside me.

5 I did know thee in the wilderness, in the land of great drought.

6 According to their pasture, so were they filled; they were filled, and their heart was exalted; therefore have they forgotten me.

7 Therefore I will be unto them as a lion: as a leopard by the way will I observe *them:*
8 I will meet them as a bear *that is* bereaved *of her whelps*, and will rend the caul of their heart, and there will I devour them like a lion: the wild beast shall tear them.
9 ¶O Israel, thou hast destroyed thyself; but in me *is* thine help.
10 I will be thy king: where *is any other* that may save thee in all thy cities? and thy judges of whom thou saidst, Give me a king and princes?

11 I gave thee a king in mine anger, and took *him* away in my wrath.
12 The iniquity of E'phra-im *is* bound up; his sin *is* hid.

13 The sorrows of a travailing woman shall come upon him: he *is* an unwise son; for he should not stay long in *the place of* the breaking forth of children.

14 I will ransom them from the power

---

molten images. Instead of seeking the Lord, Israel turned all of its power and prestige into the worship of idols and the making of images and idols to represent their false, nonexistent deities. **Let the men that sacrifice kiss the calves.** They expressed their devotion to the idols by the kiss.

3. Therefore they shall be as the morning cloud . . . early dew . . . chaff . . . smoke. This spiritual defection sealed their doom. They would pass away just as a **morning cloud, early dew, chaff** and **smoke** does. All of these indicate that although Israel may have had the appearance of substance and prosperity, her days are numbered and she will pass away.

4. Yet I am the LORD thy God from the land of Egypt, and thou shalt know no god but me. Though the picture is dark for the Israel of Hosea's day, God will remain faithful to the nation; and there will come a day when they will know no other God but Jehovah and will in truth recognize that **there is no savior beside me.** This will be the time when the new covenant of Jeremiah 31:31-34 will be realized, and the entire nation will experience a spiritual rebirth.

5. I did know thee in the wilderness. Once again, God reminds them of His care for them during the wilderness wanderings.

6. So were they filled. Throughout all that time they were cared for, and in subsequent days they have lacked nothing. **Therefore have they forgotten me.** They were completely filled, but in their prosperity they forgot God and turned to serve vain idols.

7-8. I will be unto them as a lion . . . leopard . . . bear . . . wild beast. God, however, has not forgotten them. He likens Himself to a lion, a leopard, a bear, and a wild beast. He will track them down as a lion and a leopard track their prey. As a bereaved bear, He will tear them to pieces; and as a lionness and a wild beast, He will devour them (vs. 7-8).

9-10. O Israel, thou hast destroyed thyself; but in me is thine help. All this will befall Israel because she has brought it on herself by failing to recognize Jehovah as her God. The nation's disobedience will not frustrate the plan of God. **I will be thy king.** He will be their king in fulfillment of the Davidic Covenant (II Sam 7), and they will recognize that there is no one else capable of saving them. **Thy judges of whom thou saidst, Give me king and princes?** Once again the prophet makes a historical illusion, this time to the days of Samuel (I Sam 8:4-9) when the nation sought Samuel to give them a king ". . . like all the nations." Their sin was not in the fact that they wanted a king, but in the kind of a king that they wanted, one who would fight their battles for them so that they would no longer have to trust in God.

11-12. I gave thee a king in mine anger, and took him away in my wrath. God gave them a king like they wanted, Saul, whose chief contribution was to prepare the nation for the king like God wanted, David. Israel has continued the tradition of putting its trust in the king, and the king has led the nation in its spiritual defection. Therefore, both nation and king will be taken away in judgment. **The iniquity of Ephraim is bound up; his sin is hid.** All of the evidence necessary to show that God's judgment is righteous is in hand (vs. 12).

13. The sorrows of a travailing woman shall come upon him. The judgment of God will certainly fall; and when it does, it will be similar to the sudden pain that comes upon a woman in childbirth. **For he should not stay long in the place of the breaking forth of children.** God's purpose in bringing judgment is therapeutic. Israel should take notice of its approach and repent while there is yet time. Failure to do so can only result in death and destruction.

14. I will ransom them from the power of the grave. Into

of the grave; I will redeem them from death: O death, I will be thy plagues; O grave, I will be thy destruction: repentance shall be hid from mine eyes.

15 ¶Though he be fruitful among *his* brethren, an east wind shall come, the wind of the LORD shall come up from the wilderness, and his spring shall become dry, and his fountain shall be dried up: he shall spoil the treasure of all pleasant vessels.

16 Sa-mâ'rĭ-a shall become desolate; for she hath rebelled against her God: they shall fall by the sword: their infants shall be dashed in pieces, and their women with child shall be ripped up.

CHAPTER 14

O ISRAEL, return unto the LORD thy God; for thou hast fallen by thine iniquity.

2 Take with you words, and turn to the LORD: say unto him, Take away all iniquity, and receive *us* graciously: so will we render the calves of our lips.

3 Asshur shall not save us; we will not ride upon horses: neither will we say any more to the work of our hands, *Ye are* our gods: for in thee the fatherless findeth mercy.

4 ¶I will heal their backsliding, I will love them freely; for mine anger is turned away from him.

5 I will be as the dew unto Israel: he shall grow as the lily, and cast forth his roots as Lebanon.

6 His branches shall spread, and his beauty shall be as the olive tree, and his smell as Lebanon.

7 They that dwell under his shadow shall return; they shall revive *as* the corn, and grow as the vine: the scent thereof *shall be* as the wine of Lebanon.

8 Ė'phra-im *shall say,* What have I to do any more with idols? I have heard *him,* and observed him: I *am* like a green fir tree. From me is thy fruit found.

the midst of this dark picture, once again a ray of light shines. Instead of this whole situation resulting in the death of the nation, it will result in the death of death. Ultimately, Israel will be redeemed and will bring forth fruit of repentance.

15. Though he be fruitful . . . an east wind shall come . . . and his spring shall become dry. This national repentance and restoration will be realized in the Israel of the Millennium. Thus, the prophet returns to the Israel of his day. Though they are prosperous at the moment, judgment for their spiritual defection will come from Jehovah. This judgment is pictured as an **east wind,** a **wind of the LORD.** The reference is to Shalmaneser, the king of Assyria, whom God will bring to execute judgment upon His people and to take away all of their treasures and pleasant vessels.

16. Samaria shall become desolate. The destruction will be total and gory. The population will be slain with the **sword;** and the wrath of the Assyrians will be manifested against **infants,** whom they will dash to pieces, and pregnant **women,** whom they will rip open with their swords. Would that Israel heed this warning and repent!

C. Concerning Israel's Restoration. 14:1-8.

Of all the prophet's messages from chapter 4 to the present, this is the brightest! It divides into two parts.

1. The call to restoration. 14:1-3.

14:1-3. Hosea's message is the same as all the prophets: **return unto the LORD thy God** (vs. 1). Their sin has been their downfall (vs. 1b), but now the prophet implores them to turn to Jehovah and seek His forgiveness (vs. 2a). They are encouraged to offer to Jehovah the **calves of our lips** (vs. 2b). The word **calves** (Heb *par,* a young bull or produce) is best understood metaphorically, referring to the words that the lips produce—in this context praise to Jehovah. The nation had used its lips to praise the idolatrous calves; now it will use its lips in praise to Jehovah God. **Asshur shall not save us.** Further, they will come to the realization that Assyria (**Asshur**) will not be able to save them, nor will they find salvation in any cavalry (vs. 3a). The crowning jewel will be that they will turn from their idolatry and never more will say to an idol that they have made, **Ye are our gods: for in thee the fatherless findeth mercy.** They will recognize that only Jehovah God is their protector; and only in Him do the fatherless, who are the most helpless, find mercy and protection (vs. 3b).

2. The completion of restoration. 14:4-8.

4-8. I will heal their backsliding. God promises to heal their backsliding (on which they were hooked, cf. 11:7a). God's anger will be turned away from Israel because Israel will have repented (vs. 4). God promises to be **as the dew unto Israel;** and this will result in Israel's growth as a lily, which was noted both for its beauty and productivity. In addition, Israel will put down roots like the cedars of Lebanon, which were known for their stability and durability (vs. 5). **His branches shall spread . . . as the olive tree.** The picture is one of firm and bountiful restoration. Israel will spread throughout the land unto the cedars of Lebanon. The scar and stench of idolatry will be removed from the land, and the regenerated nation will be everything that the reprobate nation was not (vs. 6). This will be the portion of those who have dwelt under the **shadow** of Jehovah; and He will **revive** them, and they will **grow** and will give off fragrance like **the wine of Lebanon** (vs. 7). This restoration is made possible because Israel's sin has been dealt with and cured. No longer will they worship idols. In fact, they will say, **What have I to do anymore with idols?** (vs. 8a). In turning to God, Ephraim (Israel) will completely forsake its idols and will render fruit to

God like **a green fir tree** (vs. 8). Up to this time Ephraim has been a stench in the nostrils of God. Now, because its sin has been dealt with, it will be pleasing to the Lord; and the fruit will satisfy Him.

IV. THE CONCLUSION OF THE PROPHECY. 14:9.

9 Who *is* wise, and he shall understand these *things?* prudent, and he shall know them? for the ways of the LORD *are* right, and the just shall walk in them: but the transgressors shall fall therein.

9. This verse constitutes an epilogue to the entire prophecy. Those who are **wise** and **prudent** (i.e., in right relationship and fellowship with God) will understand the things written in this prophecy. Those who are **transgressors** (i.e., out of fellowship with God) will not understand them and will fall in them. The testimony of the entire prophecy is that **the ways of the LORD are right,** and those who are right with Him will heed the words of this prophecy and prosper; but those who are not right with Him will be overtaken by the words of this prophecy and perish.

(see page 1864 for Bibliography to the Minor Prophets)

JOEL

INTRODUCTION

Authorship. The author of this prophecy is noted only as "Joel the son of Pethuel." His name contains both the names Jehovah and Elohim and means, Jehovah (*Yahweh*) is God (*Elohim*), or, Jehovah is my God. Aside from this, nothing is known about him. He is one of approximately fourteen men in the Old Testament who had this name. He was a contemporary of both Hosea and Amos, though he ministered to the southern kingdom while they ministered to the northern kingdom. The frequent references throughout the prophecy to Judah and Jerusalem lend credence to the understanding that he was evidently not a priest, though he seems to have been an inhabitant of Jerusalem and was a prophet to the southern kingdom (1:13-14; 2:17).

Date and Place of Writing. Conservative Jewish and Christian scholarship has maintained a very early date for Joel. He was one of the earliest prophets of Judah, beginning his ministry shortly after the days of Elijah and Elisha. He makes no reference to Nineveh or to Babylon, but does mention the Phoenicians, Philistines, Edomites, and the Egyptians. Thus, his prophecy would date somewhere in the period 837-800 B.C. If one desires a specific date, 836 B.C. would be close enough. The critics tend to place Joel late, after the Babylonian captivity, at approximately 500 B.C. They do this because they feel that the mention of the walls of Jerusalem (2:7, 9) points to a date after Ezra and Nehemiah and that the mention of the Greeks (3:6) necessitates a late date. Concerning this last point, it can be observed that Greeks are also mentioned in an inscription of Sargon dating about 710 B.C. Thus, their mention by Joel is not necessarily an indication of its late date; it could also indicate an early date. The earlier date creates the least difficulty; and, thus, it is best to view the prophecy as having been written before the Assyrian and Chaldean world empires came to power.

The specific place from which Joel was written is not known. Since Joel was a resident of Judah and Jerusalem, it is likely that the prophecy originated from there. Frequent calls to blow a trumpet in Zion, to consecrate a fast, to proclaim a solemn assembly, and to gather the people together to come before the Lord lend credence to the view that the prophecy issued from the Temple court.

Characteristics of the Prophecy. Joel is a highly emotional prophecy, rich in imagery and vivid descriptions. In the course of the prophecy, two unique events not to be forgotten, but to be communicated to the descendants are compared: the locust plague upon Judah and the day of the Lord. The latter is by far the greater and is set forth as it is prefigured by the former. In a very real sense, Joel is the special prophet of the day of the Lord; and he mentions it five times (1:15; 2:1; 2:11; 2:31; 3:14). Joel has also been called "the Prophet of Pentecost" because of his most famous and well-known passage, 2:28-32. More than half of the book is given to the description of the locust plague, the grandest description in all literature of such a plague. Joel is also a great prophecy of repentance, both on a personal and a national scale (1:14; 2:13, 15). Joel is thought by some to have been the earliest of the prophetic writers ministering in Judah early in the reign of Joash (II Kgs 11-12), and in his youth he would have known both Elijah and Elisha. It is not certain whether Joel was the first of the writing prophets, but certainly he was the first writing prophet in Judah.

Purpose. The purpose of Joel's prophecy is to turn the nation back to God in preparation for the coming of the great Day of the Lord.

Theme. The Day of the Lord.

OUTLINE

COMMENTARY

I. THE INTRODUCTION TO THE PROPHECY. 1:1-3.

A. The Author of the Prophecy. 1:1.

THE word of the LORD that came to
Jō'el the son of Pe-thū'el.

**1:1. The word of the LORD that came to Joel the son of
Pethuel.** This verse tells us all that is known about the identity
and origin of the prophet. The prophecy about to be uttered is
so important that it is not to be obscured by trivial details such
as the identity and origin of the author. The prophecy is the
word (Heb *dabar*) that comes from the **LORD.** (Heb *Yahweh,*
Jehovah) and is therefore authoritative and of supreme importance. The prophet is content to be the agent through whom the
word of the Lord is delivered.

B. The Address of the Prophecy. 1:2-3.

2 Hear this, ye old men, and give ear,
all ye inhabitants of the land. Hath this
been in your days, or even in the days of
your fathers?

2. Hear this, ye old men . . . inhabitants of the land. The
prophecy is addressed to the elders and all the inhabitants of the
land. This address shows the importance of the prophecy, for
the elders would already have heard everything of importance;
and yet the prophecy about to be uttered is more important than
anything that has happened to this point. The address to all the
inhabitants of the land shows that the prophecy is important to
everyone who resides in the land, regardless of age, occupation,
social position, or sex. These verses emphasize the uniqueness of
this prophecy, which concerns an event the likes of which has
not happened before and will not happen again.

3 Tell ye your children of it, and *let*
your children *tell* their children, and
their children another generation.

3. Tell ye your children of it. This prophecy is not to be
forgotten, and it is to be communicated to succeeding generations. The address provides an organizational key for the
prophecy; two unique, never-to-be forgotten events are to be
remembered and communicated to their descendants: the locust
plague upon Israel and the day of the Lord. The latter is the
greater event and is prefigured by the former.

II. THE CONTENT OF THE PROPHECY. 1:4-3:17.

A. Concerning the Near View—The Locust Plague.
1:4-2:27.

1. The description of the locust plague. 1:4-7.

4 That which the palmerworm hath
left hath the locust eaten; and that
which the locust hath left hath the cankerworm eaten; and that which the
cankerworm hath left hath the caterpiller eaten.

4. This verse describes the devastation of the locust plague. It
is both progressive (going from bad to worse) and absolute. A
locust plague is perhaps the most grievous calamity that could
fall upon an agricultural people. Locusts sometimes covered the
earth for several miles; and wherever they spread, the greenness
of the land entirely disappeared. All the crops of the land were
consumed, and the trees and plants were stripped of their bark
and leaves. The Jews were familiar with locusts. It was one form
of judgment that the Lord sent upon Egypt and ultimately
caused the Egyptians to let the Israelites leave. Moses had
prophesied that God would use locusts to punish His people if
they were disobedient (Deut 28:38, 42). To make His judgments
effective, God does not need to use the great forces of nature,
such as an earthquake, a flood, lightning, or various kinds of
storms. In this case He takes one of the most insignificant
instruments, the locust, to fulfill His purpose of executing judgment against His people. God's ultimate purpose is not merely
punitive, but is for the ultimate restoration of His people and the
remedying of their faults. Some have thought that this verse
presents four separate locust plagues. The Hebrew words involved, however, do not speak of insects of different species or
of insects of different kinds within the same species. The language expresses the four stages in the development of a single
type of insect, the locust. The **palmerworm** (Heb *gazam,* to

1689

gnaw) is the stage at which the locust is first hatched and is characterized by its gnawing activity. The **locust** (Heb *'arbeh*, to be many) is the second stage of the locust's development. This is the stage in which it gets its wings and flies. This is the most common name for the locust and is given to it because of its migratory habits in this stage. The **cankerworm** (Heb *yeleq*, to lick off) is the third stage of the locust's development. It is in this stage that it does its destructive work. The **caterpillar** (Heb *chasil*, to devour or to consume) is the final stage of the locust in which it reaches its full growth and devours everything in its path. These four stages of the locust's development are often taken as prophetic of the Babylonian, Persian, Grecian, and Roman empires, which subsequently overran and controlled Judah. The parallel, however, is probably more coincidental than designed.

5 Awake, ye drunkards, and weep; and howl, all ye drinkers of wine, because of the new wine; for it is cut off from your mouth.

5. There is something unique about this calamity. **Awake, ye drunkards.** The calamity is so grievous that it affects even drunkards who are usually oblivious to everything. **The new wine; for it is cut off from your mouth.** The severity of the plague is brought to the drunkard's attention because the locusts' devastation will destroy the vine from which their wine supply comes. The most effective way to get a drunkard's attention is to deprive him of his drink.

6 For a nation is come up upon my land, strong, and without number, whose teeth *are* the teeth of a lion, and he hath the cheek teeth of a great lion.
7 He hath laid my vine waste, and barked my fig tree: he hath made it clean bare, and cast *it* away; the branches thereof are made white.

6-7. These verses describe the locust hoards and their effect on the grape vineyards in vivid figures. **For a nation is come up . . . without number.** They are like a numberless nation whose strength is irresistible. **Whose teeth are the teeth of a lion.** Their weapons are their teeth, and their teeth are as irresistible and effective as those of a great lion. **He hath laid my vine waste.** No tree or plant, or any kind of vegetation, can resist them. After they have passed through the land, it is stripped bare; and the verdant trees are left white.

2. The victims of the locust plague. 1:8-12.

8 ¶Lament like a virgin girded with sackcloth for the husband of her youth.
9 The meat offering and the drink offering is cut off from the house of the Lord; the priests, the Lord's ministers, mourn.

8-9. Lament like a virgin . . . for the husband of her youth. The prophet addresses the congregation of Israel and tells them to mourn like a virgin who on the day of her wedding was deprived of her husband by his untimely death. Instead of being dressed in her wedding garment, she is dressed in **sackcloth**, a rough garment covering her entire body and indicating the depth of her grief and penitence. **The meat offering and the drink offering is cut off from the house of the Lord.** This shows the effect of the plague upon the worship services of God's house. The grain normally used in the offering is gone. Hence, the ministers of God have nothing to offer; and the normal services of the house of God are curtailed.

10 The field is wasted, the land mourneth; for the corn is wasted: the new wine is dried up, the oil languisheth.
11 Be ye ashamed, O ye husbandmen; howl, O ye vinedressers, for the wheat and for the barley; because the harvest of the field is perished.
12 The vine is dried up, and the fig tree languisheth; the pomegranate tree, the palm tree also, and the apple tree, *even* all the trees of the field, are withered: because joy is withered away from the sons of men.

10-12. The field is wasted describes the effect of the plague upon the field and the land. They are completely devastated. To an agricultural people, this is the worst possible thing that could happen to their land. **Be ye ashamed, O ye husbandmen . . . vinedressers** shows the effect of the plague upon those who normally care for the land. The farmers and vinedressers are affected, because their fields are bare and their vineyards are gone. **Joy is withered away from the sons of men.** The entire population is affected—all rejoicing is gone from the land.

3. The instructions in the light of the locust plague's devastation. 1:13-20.

13 ¶Gird yourselves, and lament, ye priests: howl, ye ministers of the altar: come, lie all night in sackcloth, ye ministers of my God: for the meat offering and the drink offering is withholden from the house of your God.
14 Sanctify ye a fast, call a solemn assembly, gather the elders *and* all the inhabitants of the land *into* the house of

13-14. Gird yourselves, and lament. In the light of such devastation, the only thing that man can do is to repent and mourn. **Priests** are exhorted to gird themselves with **sackcloth** (the sign of mourning) and lament (vs. 13a). The **ministers** who attend the altar are likewise exhorted to spend the night wearing sackcloth and mourning (vs. 13b). **Sanctify ye a fast, call a solemn assembly.** Both the priests and the ministers are urged to consecrate a **fast** and proclaim a **solemn assembly,** thus

the LORD your God, and cry unto the LORD,

15 Alas for the day! for the day of the LORD *is* at hand, and as a destruction from the Almighty shall it come.

16 Is not the meat cut off before our eyes, *yea*, joy and gladness from the house of our God?

17 The seed is rotten under their clods, the garners are laid desolate, the barns are broken down; for the corn is withered.

18 How do the beasts groan! the herds of cattle are perplexed, because they have no pasture; yea, the flocks of sheep are made desolate.

19 O LORD, to thee will I cry: for the fire hath devoured the pastures of the wilderness, and the flame hath burned all the trees of the field.

20 The beasts of the field cry also unto thee: for the rivers of waters are dried up, and the fire hath devoured the pastures of the wilderness.

CHAPTER 2

BLOW ye the trumpet in Zion, and sound an alarm in my holy mountain: let all the inhabitants of the land tremble: for the day of the LORD cometh, for *it is* nigh at hand;

2 A day of darkness and of gloominess, a day of clouds and of thick darkness, as the morning spread upon the mountains: a great people and a strong; there hath not been ever the like, neither shall be any more after it, *even* to the years of many generations.

3 A fire devoureth before them; and behind them a flame burneth: the land *is* as the garden of Eden before them, and behind them a desolate wilderness; yea, and nothing shall escape them.

4 The appearance of them *is* as the appearance of horses; and as horsemen, so shall they run.

5 Like the noise of chariots on the tops of mountains shall they leap, like the noise of a flame of fire that devoureth the stubble, as a strong people set in battle array.

6 Before their face the people shall be much pained: all faces shall gather blackness.

7 They shall run like mighty men; they shall climb the wall like men of war; and they shall march every one on

gathering together the **elders** of the nation and all the **inhabitants** of the land to come to the house of the Lord and cry out before him.

15-20. Joel sees the present locust destruction as an adumbration of the great **day of the LORD**. The present devastation has affected man, and the animal and plant kingdoms, deeply; and they are totally helpless before it. **O LORD, to thee will I cry.** The only meaningful course of action in the light of such devastation is prayer to God. He is the only recourse. Everything else is gone; the devastation is complete. Man, beast, and nature join together in seeking God's favor for relief.

4. The nearness of the day of the Lord moves the prophet to deal with the present locust plague. 2:1-17.

2:1-2. The prophet adopts the vantage point of the ultimate day of the Lord, and from that position he looks back to the present locust plague. In the light of these dual crises there is important action to undertake. Something unique is happening; the ultimate day of the Lord is near. **Blow ye the trumpet in Zion, and sound an alarm.** Judah must hear and heed the prophet's instructions. Therefore, it is necessary to gain the people's attention by blowing the trumpet and sounding an alarm. The trumpet was used primarily for religious purposes to call the congregation together for meetings, to usher in the beginning of the month, and to note solemn days and festive occasions. In this instance, however, the trumpet is to be used to sound an alarm and alert people to the seriousness of the crises. It represents utter desperation—all human hope is gone. The Day of the Lord is described in ominous figures as a **day of darkness . . . gloominess . . . clouds and of thick darkness.** All of these figures emphasize the uniqueness of this terrible day of judgment. Truly, there has never been anything like this; and there will never be anything like it again.

3-6. A fire devoureth before them; and behind them a flame burneth. The prophet moves from the ultimate Day of the Lord to the present locust crisis, which prefigures that ultimate Day of the Lord. As bad as the present locust crisis is, it is only a taste of the worst judgment of God, which is yet to come. Verse 3 describes the general effects of the locust plague in a before and after figure. Before the locust plague, the land is as beautiful as the **garden of Eden.** After the locust plague, it is completely devastated. **The appearance of them is as the appearance of horses** describes the appearance and speed of the spoiling locusts. They are like warhorses. **Like the noise of chariots** describes the sound that the locusts make as they go about their devastation: they sound like war chariots and the crackling fire. **They leap . . . as a strong people set in battle array.** No natural barrier can contain them, and they have the appearance of a mighty people arrayed for battle. **The people shall be much pained** describes the effect of the locust plague upon their victims—the people. Their expressions are filled with terror, complexions are livid from anxiety and fear.

7-10. The prophet describes the feats of the locusts as they go about their devastation in their locust formations. They are invincible; and their number is so great that they blot out the sun, moon, and stars.

his ways, and they shall not break their ranks:

8 Neither shall one thrust another; they shall walk every one in his path: and *when* they fall upon the sword, they shall not be wounded.

9 They shall run to and fro in the city; they shall run upon the wall, they shall climb up upon the houses; they shall enter in at the windows like a thief.

10 The earth shall quake before them; the heavens shall tremble: the sun and the moon shall be dark, and the stars shall withdraw their shining:

11 And the Lord shall utter his voice before his army: for his camp *is* very great: for *he is* strong that executeth his word: for the day of the Lord *is* great and very terrible; and who can abide it?

12 ¶Therefore also now, saith the Lord, Turn ye *even* to me with all your heart, and with fasting, and with weeping, and with mourning:

13 And rend your heart, and not your garments, and turn unto the Lord your God: for he *is* gracious and merciful, slow to anger, and of great kindness, and repenteth him of the evil.

14 Who knoweth *if* he will return and repent, and leave a blessing behind him; *even* a meat offering and a drink offering unto the Lord your God?

11. And the Lord shall utter his voice before his army. This injects a new note into an already catastrophic scene. Nature has not gone awry; the locusts are not beyond God's control. In fact, the locust army is marching under God's control and at His specific command. The effect is like the great Day of the Lord, and no flesh will be able to survive.

12-13. Turn ye even to me with all your heart . . . with fasting . . . weeping . . . mourning. Man's extremities are truly God's opportunities! But why should Jehovah, who is Judah's God, bring this mighty army against His people? Here is where there is a parallel between the immediate locust plague and the ultimate Day of the Lord. God's purpose in both is therapeutic. His design is to bring restoration and healing to His people. Therefore, the invitation to repentance is extended in verses 12-13a. There is only one way to escape the judgment of God, whether it be a locust plague or in the Day of the Lord—true repentance. Repentance in and of itself is inward and intangible. It cannot be seen. However, true repentance is a root from which certain fruit will spring. This fruit will indicate the fact of the root and the quality of that root. Certain fruit will demonstrate a true repentance (**fasting, weeping, and mourning**). Fast now so that you may be filled later; weep now so that you can laugh later; mourn now so that you can be comforted later (Mt 5:4; Lk 6:21). **Rend your heart, and not your garments.** A customary way for the Jew to show his grief was to tear his outer garment. This was an external sign, which could be meaningless in and of itself. The prophet indicates that this is not a time for external ceremonies. The tearing of the outer garment is useless unless the heart is broken in repentance and contrition. These outward and inner expressions of repentance and grief are to be accompanied by positive actions of turning unto Jehovah God. Verse 13b shows what kind of a God has brought the plague and what kind of God waits for the proper response of repentance and contrition. He is a God who is **gracious and merciful, slow to anger, and of great kindness** and is repentant of the evil plague which He has sent. The plague has been sent, not in violation of the previous attributes but in consistency with them. He loves His people so much that He will cause them to face their sin and will bring them to the place of repentance, confession, and restoration.

14. The possible results of revival and repentance are set forth from man's perspective. **Who knoweth if he will return and repent, and leave a blessing behind him.** God has not changed—He is immutable. Man has changed because of God's faithfulness in causing him to face his sin. When man changes, he is unaware of the change in himself and views it as though it were a change in God. God is able to deal with man on a different basis because it is man, not God, who has changed. The change envisioned is that God will change his mind and will turn devastation into blessing. **Even a meat offering and a drink offering.** In a devastated land where there is no grain or wine, God may leave a grain offering and a libation to be used in worshiping him, not so man can consume it upon himself.

15 ¶Blow the trumpet in Zion, sanctify a fast, call a solemn assembly:
16 Gather the people, sanctify the congregation, assemble the elders, gather the children, and those that suck the breasts: let the bridegroom go forth of his chamber, and the bride out of her closet.
17 Let the priests, the ministers of the LORD, weep between the porch and the altar, and let them say, Spare thy people, O LORD, and give not thine heritage to reproach, that the heathen should rule over them: wherefore should they say among the people, Where is their God?
18 ¶Then will the LORD be jealous for his land, and pity his people.
19 Yea, the LORD will answer and say unto his people, Behold, I will send you corn, and wine, and oil, and ye shall be satisfied therewith: and I will no more make you a reproach among the heathen:
20 But I will remove far off from you the northern army, and will drive him into a land barren and desolate, with his face toward the east sea, and his hinder part toward the utmost sea, and his stink shall come up, and his ill savour shall come up, because he hath done great things.
21 Fear not, O land; be glad and rejoice: for the LORD will do great things.
22 Be not afraid, ye beasts of the field: for the pastures of the wilderness do spring, for the tree beareth her fruit, the fig tree and the vine do yield their strength.
23 Be glad then, ye children of Zion, and rejoice in the LORD your God: for he hath given you the former rain moderately, and he will cause to come down for you the rain, the former rain, and the latter rain in the first month.
24 And the floors shall be full of wheat, and the fats shall overflow with wine and oil.
25 And I will restore to you the years that the locust hath eaten, the cankerworm, and the caterpiller, and the palmerworm, my great army which I sent among you.
26 And ye shall eat in plenty, and be satisfied, and praise the name of the LORD your God, that hath dealt wondrously with you: and my people shall never be ashamed.
27 And ye shall know that I am in the midst of Israel, and that I am the LORD your God, and none else: and my people shall never be ashamed.
28 ¶And it shall come to pass afterward, that I will pour out my spirit upon all flesh; and your sons and your daughters shall prophesy, your old men shall dream dreams, your young men shall see visions:
29 And also upon the servants and upon the handmaids in those days will I pour out my spirit.
30 And I will shew wonders in the heavens and in the earth, blood, and fire, and pillars of smoke.
31 The sun shall be turned into darkness, and the moon into blood, before the great and the terrible day of the LORD come.

15-17. Blow the trumpet in Zion. This is a second invitation to blow a trumpet in Zion. This summons is primarily directed to the people and children who have been affected by the plague. The people, elders, children, nursing infants, bridegrooms, and brides are to be gathered together; and the priests and ministers are to weep and intercede for the people before God.

5. The effect of the revival upon Jehovah. 2:18-20.

18-20. The change in the people is caused by God's dealing with His people in two ways: (1) He will care for the land and have pity on His people (vs. 18) and (2) He will answer their prayers in three specific ways— (a) He will remove the devastation and restore the crops (vs. 19), (b) He will remove the people's reproach from among the nations (vs. 19b), and (c) He will remove the locust army and destroy it utterly (vs. 20).

6. Assurances to the people in the light of the locust plague. 2:21-27.

21-27. Three assurances are given: (1) to the land (vs. 21)— not to fear, but rather to rejoice and be glad because God has done great things for it, and whereas it has been completely devastated, it will be completely restored; (2) to the beasts of the field (vs. 22)—God will restore all vegetation so the beasts of the field will have ample food to eat; and (3) to the sons of Zion (vss. 23-27)—God makes five specific promises—(a) He will provide rain for crops (vs. 23); (b) He will provide abundant harvests of grain and grapes (vs. 24); (c) He will make up for the devastation suffered by the locust plague (vs. 25); (d) He will provide abundant food and end the famine (vs. 26); and (e) most of all, He will achieve His purpose and cause His people to know that He is in the midst of Israel, even during a locust plague (vs. 27a), that He is Jehovah their God (vs. 27b), that there is no other God than He (vs. 27c), and that He will protect His people and they will never again be put to shame (vs. 27d).

With these assurances of restoration from the locust plague, the prophet now turns to give attention to his ultimate concern, the Day of the Lord.

B. Concerning the Far View—The Day of the Lord. 2:28-3:17.

1. The outpouring of the Holy Spirit. 2:28-32.

28-32. It is this prophecy for which Joel has become most famous in modern days. It must be considered in the light of its context and in the light of its New Testament usage. **And it shall come to pass afterward** (vs. 28) relates this passage to the immediate restoration following the locust plague. This differentiates the locust plague from the Day of the Lord. The locust plague was preceded by nothing; the Day of the Lord follows the locust plague and will be preceded by the outpouring of the Spirit of God upon all flesh. Verse 28 reveals that the promised outpouring of the Spirit is to be universal: **Sons and daughters** will prophesy, **old men will dream dreams, young men** will **see visions.** Verse 29 indicates that the Spirit will be poured out even upon male and female servants—not even the most lowly people in society will be exempt from the outpouring

32 And it shall come to pass, *that* whosoever shall call on the name of the LORD shall be delivered: for in mount Zion and in Jerusalem shall be deliverance, as the LORD hath said, and in the remnant whom the LORD shall call.

of the Spirit. Verses 30 and 31 indicate that signs and **wonders** in nature will be manifested in conjunction with the outpouring of the Spirit. All of this will be preliminary to the coming of the **day of the LORD.** Verse 32 indicates that salvation, or deliverance, from the Day of the Lord will be possible; because of the outpouring of the Spirit, he will move men to call upon the name of the Lord. Thus, in its context Joel has compressed together, in true prophetic fashion, events separated by millennia. The crucial points of history are the events of the locust plague in Joel's day, ca. 836 B.C.; the day of Pentecost on which the Holy Spirit was indeed poured out universally and made available for all mankind, ca. A.D. 33; the event of the Great Tribulation (separated from the day of Pentecost by at least 2000 years); and the establishment of the earthly Davidic millennial kingdom that follows the events of the Great Tribulation.

In his sermon on the day of Pentecost, Peter quotes this passage in order to explain the phenomenon of speaking in tongues, which some were attributing to drunkenness. In doing so, he said, "But this is that which was spoken by the prophet Joel;" (Acts 2:16ff.). There are three ways of understanding what Peter meant: (1) this is like that, i.e., this manifestation is similar to that which was prophesied by the prophet Joel; (2) this is a partial fulfillment of that, i.e., this manifestation is a partial fulfillment of that which Joel prophesied; the ultimate and complete fulfillment will be realized at the time of the establishment of the millennial kingdom; and (3) this is that, i.e., this is the fulfillment of that which Joel prophesied would take place. The first view seems untenable because Peter is giving a metaphor, not a simile. If one adopts the second view, then he would hold that only those parts of Joel's prophecy that were prerequisites for the establishment of the church would be fulfilled, while the things pertaining to Israel would not be fulfilled until the end times—prior to the Millennium. This view has the difficulty of having the church contained, even if ever so obliquely, in Joel's prophecy. The church, however, is a mystery that was not revealed prior to the prophecy of Matthew 16 and is not contained in Old Testament prophecy even in the most oblique sense. It seems best then to view Peter as saying that the outpouring of the Spirit, prompting the phenomena observed in Acts 2, is the fulfillment of that which was prophesied by the prophet Joel. Two things were necessary for the establishment of Israel's kingdom: (1) the death of Messiah and (2) the availability of the Holy Spirit. When Peter preached his famous sermon, the death of Christ was an historic fact. All that remained, then, was the provision of the Spirit, which Peter identifies with the outpouring of the Spirit that prompted the speaking in tongues of Acts 2. With the availability of the Holy Spirit, together with the death of Messiah, all that is necessary for the establishment of Israel's kingdom has been provided. Because of unbelief, they cannot enter into these benefits; but when the time comes that they will receive their king and his kingdom, he will not need to die again, nor will the Holy Spirit have to be made available. As to the day of Pentecost, all that remains is for Israel to avail herself in belief of that which has been provided. Zechariah 13:1ff. shows that just prior to the establishment of the millennial kingdom, Israel will avail herself of the fountain that cleanses (i.e., the death of Messiah); and the prophecy of Joel 2:28-29 shows that at the same time Israel will avail herself of the availability of the Holy Spirit. Then the provision made by the fulfillment of Joel's prophecy as recorded in Acts 2:16ff. will be realized, as well as the provision made by the fulfillment of the death of Messiah.

CHAPTER 3

FOR, behold, in those days, and in that

2. The promise of restoration of Judah and Jerusalem. 3:1-8.

3:1-3. This verse is a topic sentence and tells what God's purpose is in the day of the Lord—to restore Judah and Jeru-

time, when I shall bring again the captivity of Judah and Jerusalem,

2 I will also gather all nations, and will bring them down into the valley of Je-hŏsh'a-phăt, and will plead with them there for my people and for my heritage Israel, whom they have scattered among the nations, and parted my land.

3 And they have cast lots for my people; and have given a boy for an harlot, and sold a girl for wine, that they might drink.

4 Yea, and what have ye to do with me, O Tyre, and Zī'don, and all the coasts of Palestine? will ye render me a recompence? and if ye recompense me, swiftly and speedily will I return your recompence upon your own head;

5 Because ye have taken my silver and my gold, and have carried into your temples my goodly pleasant things:

6 The children also of Judah and the children of Jerusalem have ye sold unto the Grecians, that ye might remove them far from their border.

7 Behold, I will raise them out of the place whither ye have sold them, and will return your recompence upon your own head:

8 And I will sell your sons and your daughters into the hand of the children of Judah, and they shall sell them to the Sa-bē'anṡ, to a people far off: for the Lord hath spoken it.

9 ¶Proclaim ye this among the Gentiles; Prepare war, wake up the mighty men, let all the men of war draw near; let them come up:

10 Beat your plowshares into swords, and your pruninghooks into spears: let the weak say, I am strong.

11 Assemble yourselves, and come, all ye heathen, and gather yourselves together round about: thither cause thy mighty ones to come down, O Lord.

12 Let the heathen be wakened, and come up to the valley of Je-hŏsh'a-phăt: for there will I sit to judge all the heathen round about.

13 Put ye in the sickle, for the harvest is ripe: come, get you down; for the press is full, the fats overflow; for their wickedness is great.

14 Multitudes, multitudes in the valley of decision: for the day of the Lord is near in the valley of decision.

15 The sun and the moon shall be darkened, and the stars shall withdraw their shining.

16 The Lord also shall roar out of Zion, and utter his voice from Jerusalem; and the heavens and the earth shall shake: but the Lord will be the hope of his people, and the strength of the children of Israel.

17 So shall ye know that I am the Lord your God dwelling in Zion, my holy mountain: then shall Jerusalem be holy, and there shall no strangers pass through her any more.

salem. **I will also gather all nations.** The restoration of Judah and Jerusalem will be preceded by the judgment of God on their enemies who have violated them (vs. 2a). God will bring these nations to the **valley of Jehoshaphat** (Jehoshaphat means "Jehovah judges") and will summarily judge them. **And will plead with them there for my people and for my heritage, Israel.** The basis upon which these enemies will be judged is their treatment of Judah and Jerusalem. **They have cast lots . . . given a boy . . . and sold a girl.** The offenses they have committed are enumerated. They have scattered Judah and Jerusalem among the nations; they have divided up their land; they have enslaved the people of Judah and Jerusalem; and they have sold the boys and girls of Judah and Jerusalem into slavery.

4-8. Yea, and what have ye to do with me . . . ? As might be expected, people experiencing the judgment of God will seek to make overtures to Him to ease His judgment against them. The enemies of Judah and Jerusalem will also do this (vss. 4-8). The enemies mentioned are the ancient ones of **Tyre, and Zidon, and all the coasts of Palestine** (Philistia). **Swiftly and speedily will I return your recompense upon your own head.** Their attempt to make overtures to God will fail; and their judgment will be surely executed because of what they have done in robbing God of His silver, gold, and precious treasure (vs. 5), and His people (vs. 6). What the enemies of Judah and Jerusalem have sown, they will reap. This is a divine law. God will bring back from captivity the hostages that Judah and Jerusalem's enemies have sold (vs. 7) and will, in turn, deliver their sons into slavery (vs. 8). **For the Lord hath spoken it.** The prophet guarantees the certainty of his prophecy by asserting that Jehovah has spoken this; thus, it is not wishful thinking or human hope—it is divine retribution!

3. God's taunt of His enemies. 3:9-17.

9-17. The prophet's language in this section is reminiscent of David's language in Psalm 2:4, "He that sitteth in the heavens shall laugh: the Lord shall have them in derision." **Prepare war . . . Beat your plowshares into swords, and your pruninghooks into spears.** In anticipation of the judgment that will be visited upon them, God taunts His enemies and urges them to get ready for war and to come fight Him, even though it is a hopeless cause (vs. 9); to get their armaments ready, though they will be of no avail (vs. 10); to get their allies ready, though they will be of no help (vs. 11); and to get all the nations ready to fight Him. All of their efforts and preparation will be futile, for God will judge them. Just as the land was helpless before its devastators, so they will be helpless before God who will judge them on behalf of Judah and Jerusalem. **Put ye in the sickle, for the harvest is ripe.** The judgment that will come is well-deserved; the nations are **ripe** for judgment (vs. 13). **Multitudes, multitudes in the valley of decision.** The enemies that God will judge are almost numberless; they are multitudes (vs. 14). The valley of decision in verse 14 is synonomous with the valley of Jehoshaphat in verse 2. The scene is not one where the multitudes are in the midst of making a decision in favor of Jehovah and repenting of their sin. Rather, the decision is one made by God; and it is a decision to judge the multitudes for their treatment of Judah and Jerusalem. This judgment will be meted out against them in the Day of the Lord—the Great Tribulation period that will culminate with the death of every last unbelieving human being on the face of the earth. Though they are numerous, the enemies of Judah and Jerusalem are insignificant before God who will judge them completely. **The sun and the moon shall be darkened.** The signs in nature (vs. 15) indicate that something momentous is about to transpire—the Lord is about to **roar out of Zion** (vs. 16) and will execute judgment upon His enemies and deliver. The judgment of God poured out upon their enemies has four effects upon Judah and Jerusalem (vs. 17): (1) They will know that Jehovah is God—just like after the locust plague, cf. 2:27; (2) they will know that He is in their midst; (3) Jerusalem will be holy; and (4) strangers will not violate Judah and Jerusalem anymore.

III. THE CONCLUSION OF THE PROPHECY. 3:18-21.

In the conclusion of his prophecy (vss. 18-21), Joel blends together the conclusion of the locust plague and the conclusion of the Day of the Lord.

A. The Conclusion of the Near View—The Locust Plague. 3:18.

18. **And it shall come to pass in that day.** All the effects of the devastation brought by the locust will be erased, and the land will be restored to its pristine beauty and productivity.

18 ¶And it shall come to pass in that day, *that* the mountains shall drop down new wine, and the hills shall flow with milk, and all the rivers of Judah shall flow with waters, and a fountain shall come forth of the house of the LORD, and shall water the valley of Shĭt′tĭm.

19 Egypt shall be a desolation, and Edom shall be a desolate wilderness, for the violence *against* the children of Judah, because they have shed innocent blood in their land.

20 But Judah shall dwell for ever, and Jerusalem from generation to generation.

21 For I will cleanse their blood *that* I have not cleansed: for the LORD dwelleth in Zion.

B. The Conclusion of the Far View—The Day of the Lord. 3:19-21.

19-21. The prophet sees three outcomes in his conclusion to the Day of the Lord: (1) Judah's ancient enemies will be permanently destroyed, vs. 19—Egypt and Edom are representative of all Israel's enemies (cf. vss. 2, 11, 12), for all of Judah's enemies will be made a desolation forever; (2) Judah and Jerusalem will be established forever, verse 20; and (3) national cleansing and regeneration, vs. 21. Everything promised in the New Covenant (cf. Jer 31:31-34) will be accomplished and Jehovah will dwell forever in the midst of Zion.

(see page 1864 for Bibliography to the Minor Prophets)

AMOS

INTRODUCTION

Authorship. The author of this prophecy is identified as Amos, a shepherd of Tekoa (1:1). His name means "burden" or "burden-bearer" and provides a key to the leading message of the book. The prophecy is Amos' great burden from Jehovah concerning the national sin of God's chosen people, as well as the judgment that must fall upon them unless they repent. No better testimony could be given concerning Amos than his own (7:14-15), ". . . I was no prophet, neither was I a prophet's son; but I was a herdman, and a gatherer of sycamore fruit: And the LORD took me as I followed the flock, and the LORD said unto me, Go, prophesy unto my people Israel." From this testimony we learn that Amos was not a graduate of the school of the prophets, nor had he any formal religious training or academic preparation for the mission to which God called him. Nor was he a rich owner of a choice breed of sheep and goats. Rather, he was a simple shepherd who also gathered sycamore fruit, both considered to be lowly occupations. The sycamore tree was a fig of poor quality, being a cross between a fig and a mulberry; and it was eaten for food by only the poorest of people. Tekoa, from which Amos came, was located on a hill some 2,700 feet high, overlooking the wilderness of Judea. It was one of the bleakest districts in Palestine and may have been the region in which John the Baptist was raised. In the language of today, we would consider Amos to be a poor, lower-class, formally uneducated hillbilly. And yet, in obedience to God, he was used mightily to deliver God's message of judgment against Israel, the northern kingdom. It is possible that in his youth Amos may have known both Jonah and Elijah who were passing off the scene as Amos was beginning his prophetic ministry. Amos and Hosea were co-workers and may even have gone on preaching tours through the land together, although Hosea continued his work after Amos passed off the scene. Isaiah and Micah followed Amos' ministry and may have heard him preach when they were young lads.

Date and Place of Writing. Amos provides the chronological key for his ministry as ". . . in the days of Uzziah king of Judah, and in the days of Jeroboam the son of Joash king of Israel, two years before the earthquake." (1:1) Uzziah reigned ca. 767-740 B.C. and Jeroboam II reigned ca. 782-753 B.C. Thus, the date of the prophecy is between 765-755 B.C., making Amos contemporary with Hosea, Isaiah, and Jonah, whose ministries his overlapped.

It seems from 7:10 that Amos' prophecy was issued primarily at Beth-el, the seat of idolatry in the northern kingdom.

Characteristics of the Prophecy. The prophecy is characterized by great boldness, coupled with great tact. The prophet gains the attention of his audience by pronouncing judgment upon Israel's enemies before delivering the main burden of judgment against Israel herself. In the delivery of his prophecy he is very courageous while being unusually stern and severe. He attacks Satan's stronghold, Beth-el; and when he is opposed by the idolatrous priest, Amaziah (7:10ff.), he becomes even bolder in his preaching. Throughout, the prophecy is filled with references to rural life, indicating Amos' background as a shepherd. The prophet never put on pretense. He was what he was—God's messenger for His hour to call the nation Israel to awaken to its responsibility and accountability for the national sins which it had committed against God. In the process he shows himself to be a rhetorical giant, in spite of the fact he had not had any formal training.

Purpose. The purpose of Amos' prophecy is to awaken Israel and its surrounding nations to the fact that the nation is both responsible and accountable for its sins.

Theme. National accountability for national sins.

OUTLINE

COMMENTARY

I. INTRODUCTION TO THE PROPHECY. 1:1-2.

THE words of Amos, who was among the herdmen of Te-kō′a, which he saw concerning Israel in the days of Uz-zī′ah king of Judah, and in the days of Jĕr-o-bō′am the son of Jō′ash king of Israel, two years before the earthquake.

1:1. The words of Amos, who was among the herdmen of Tekoa. In keeping with prophetic style, Amos gives us a minimum of details concerning himself, not wishing to obscure the message with relatively unimportant details concerning the messenger. **In the days of Uzziah . . . and . . . Jeroboam.** Amos does do us the favor of dating his prophecy according to the reigning monarchs—Uzziah in the southern kingdom, Judah, and Jeroboam II in the northern kingdom, Israel. **Two years before the earthquake.** While earthquakes are not uncommon in Palestine, the one to which Amos refers must have been unusualy severe; for it is mentioned again by Zechariah in his prophecy (Zech 14:4-5) more than two hundred years later. Little is certain from history about this specific earthquake; and it is not a help to the dating of the prophecy, nor is that the purpose of Amos' mention of it. Rather, it stands as a reminder of God's great power in nature and is a warning of His judgment that is about to overtake Israel.

2 And he said, The LORD will roar from Zion, and utter his voice from Jerusalem; and the habitations of the shepherds shall mourn, and the top of Carmel shall wither.

2. The LORD will roar from Zion. Both Joel (cf. Joel 3:16) and Amos describe the Lord as roaring from Zion, but there is an interesting contrast between them. In Joel Jehovah roars from Zion against Israel's enemies, whereas in Amos Jehovah roars from Zion against Israel herself. **The habitations of the shepherds shall mourn, and the top of Carmel shall wither.** The ominous nature of Jehovah's roaring is indicated by its connection with the mention of the earthquake (cf. vs. 1) and the effect it has upon the shepherd's pasture grounds and the summit of Mount Carmel (vs. 2b). The shepherd's land is in the south, whereas Mount Carmel is in the north. The mention of both comprises the limits of the entire land to be affected by Jehovah's roaring. Both will dry up completely, thus indicating that the land in general will be destroyed.

II. JUDGMENT UPON THE NATIONS. 1:3-2:16.

As he begins to deliver Jehovah's message of judgment, the prophet's style is reminiscent of a field artilleryman's. He brackets his target from north to south and from east to west until he zeroes in on his target. His order is climactic, beginning with Damascus, Syria, Gaza, and Tyre, who were raw heathen, and progressing to Edom, Ammon, and Moab, who were partly heathen and yet blood relatives. Then, he proceeds to Judah, the hated brother to the south, and finally, to Israel, his target. Thus, he gets his audience's attention by getting them to agree with God's judgment against their enemies, thus disarming them for the main message of judgment, which will be delivered against them. His tact and rhetorical skill are amazing.

A. Judgment Upon the Surrounding Nations. 1:3-2:3.

1. Judgment upon Syria. 1:3-5.

3 ¶Thus saith the LORD; For three transgressions of Damascus, and for four, I will not turn away *the punishment* thereof; because they have threshed Gilead with threshing instruments of iron:

3. Damascus is the capital city of Syria and is to be especially stricken because of the cruelties Syria had visited upon Israel. The expression **For three transgressions . . . and for four,** (which introduces the message of judgment to all of the nations, including Israel) is a rhetorical way of saying that the offender

1698

has been guilty of an incalculable number of offenses, and his cup of iniquity is filled to overflowing—judgment must fall. If understood mathematically, three transgressions fill the cup and the fourth one causes it to overflow; hence, judgment is inevitable and, once announced, irrevocable. **Because they have threshed Gilead.** The particular offense of Syria was its threshing of the people of Gilead with iron threshing instruments. Gilead was the area east of the Jordan River that had been given to the tribes of Reuben, Gad, and the half-tribe of Manasseh. Being next to Syria on the north, it was particularly vulnerable to attack.

4 But I will send a fire into the house of Hăz'a-el, which shall devour the palaces of Bĕn-hă'dăd.

4. But I will send a fire into the house of Hazael, which shall devour the palaces of Ben-hadad. These statements let us know that the particular transgression in view is that perpetrated by Hazael and his son Ben-hadad. This event occurred against Israel during the reigns of Jehu and Jehoahaz (cf. II Kgs 10:32-33; 13:3-7). Because these two were the most grievous oppressors of Israel, God will send a terrible judgment against them. The judgment is set forth in the figure of a consuming fire.

5 I will break also the bar of Damascus, and cut off the inhabitant from the plain of Ā'ven, and him that holdeth the sceptre from the house of Eden: and the people of Syria shall go into captivity unto Kir, saith the LORD.

5. I will break also the bar of Damascus indicates that God will break down the gate of the city, with the result that the enemies of Damascus will have uninhibited access to the city. The **plain of Aven** (lit., vale of vanity or iniquity) was the beautiful area between Damascus and Lebanon and was the area in which sun worship and idolatry were deeply entrenched. The inhabitants of this area were to be **cut off** (i.e., completely destroyed) because of the practice of their degrading religion. The rest of the people of Syria were simply to **go into captivity.** The **house of Eden** is a reference to Beth-Eden (house of pleasure) and is the area near the city of Haran. It apparently was a very beautiful area from which the inhabitants were to be expelled because of the participation of their king with the king of Syria in his abuse of Israel. **Kir** is probably best understood to be Kur, located in Armenia near the River Kur. It is in the area of what today is known as the Republic of Georgia in the Soviet Union on the eastern coast of the Black Sea. This predicted judgment was realized when the king of Assyria (Tiglath-pileser) came against Damascus and took the people captive (cf. II Kgs 16:9).

2. Judgment upon Philistia. 1:6-8.

6-8. Though this prophecy is addressed to the city of Gaza, the mention of **Ashdod, Ashkelon, Ekron,** and the **remnant of the Philistines** (vs. 8) lets us know that the prophecy is directed against Philistia as a whole. **They carried away captive the whole captivity, to deliver them up to Edom.** Their crime was the taking of a whole population captive and delivering it over to Edom. Joel 3:3-8 fills in the details that Amos' prophecy lacks. Philistia actually sold a portion of the prisoners to the Phoenicians, who in turn sold them to the Greeks. God had promised Abraham that He would ". . . curse him that curseth thee . . ." (Gen 12:3); and thus, Philistia will be held responsible for its treatment of God's people. The events spoken of are probably best understood as Philistia's invasion of Judah during the reign of Jehoram (cf. II Chr 21:16). Philistia devoured Judah's population; in turn, Philistia's population will be devoured by God in punishment for their crime.

6 ¶Thus saith the LORD; For three transgressions of Gă'za, and for four, I will not turn away *the punishment* thereof; because they carried away captive the whole captivity, to deliver *them* up to Edom:
7 But I will send a fire on the wall of Gă'za, which shall devour the palaces thereof:
8 And I will cut off the inhabitant from Ăsh'dŏd, and him that holdeth the sceptre from Ăsh'ke-lon, and I will turn mine hand against Ekron: and the remnant of the Philistines shall perish, saith the Lord GOD.

3. Judgment upon Phoenicia. 1:9-10.

9-10. All of Phoenicia is included in the judgment pronounced upon **Tyrus** (i.e., Tyre). **They delivered up the whole captivity to Edom.** Their sin was the same as Philistia's—the selling of captives from Judah into slavery to Edom and other nations. **And remembered not the brotherly covenant.** Phoenicia's crime was more heinous because a covenant of friendship had been made between King Hiram of Tyre and David and

9 ¶Thus saith the LORD; For three transgressions of Tyrus, and for four, I will not turn away *the punishment* thereof; because they delivered up the whole captivity to Edom, and remembered not the brotherly covenant:
10 But I will send a fire on the wall of

Tyrus, which shall devour the palaces thereof.

11 ¶Thus saith the LORD; For three transgressions of Edom, and for four, I will not turn away *the punishment* thereof; because he did pursue his brother with the sword, and did cast off all pity, and his anger did tear perpetually, and he kept his wrath for ever:
12 But I will send a fire upon Tē′man, which shall devour the palaces of Bŏz′-rah.

13 ¶Thus saith the LORD; For three transgressions of the children of Ammon, and for four, I will not turn away *the punishment* thereof; because they have ripped up the women with child of Gilead, that they might enlarge their border:
14 But I will kindle a fire in the wall of Răb′bah, and it shall devour the palaces thereof, with shouting in the day of battle, with a tempest in the day of the whirlwind:
15 And their king shall go into captivity, he and his princes together, saith the LORD.

CHAPTER 2

THUS saith the LORD; For three transgressions of Moab, and for four, I will not turn away *the punishment* thereof; because he burned the bones of the king of Edom into lime:
2 But I will send a fire upon Moab, and it shall devour the palaces of Kir′ĭ-ŏth: and Moab shall die with tumult, with shouting, *and* with the sound of the trumpet:
3 And I will cut off the judge from the midst thereof, and will slay all the princes thereof with him, saith the LORD.

Solomon. This covenant had been long-standing (cf. II Sam 5:11; I Kgs 5:2-6, 15-18; 9:11-14), and no king of Israel or Judah ever made war upon Phoenicia. Though Judah honored its side of the treaty, Phoenicia did not. Therefore, God promises to **send a fire on the wall of Tyrus, which shall devour the palaces thereof.** This prophecy was ultimately realized when Nebuchadnezzar took the city after a thirteen-year siege.

4. Judgment upon Edom. 1:11-12.

11-12. The Edomites were related to the Israelites through their kinship to Esau. **He did pursue his brother with the sword.** In spite of this kinship, Edom (probably out of jealousy) pursued his brother and sought to put him out of his God-given land. **Did cast off all pity . . . did tear perpetually . . . kept his wrath.** Not only did Edom come against his brother, but he also sought to destroy any remnant, thus casting off all pity in his seeking to obliterate Judah from the face of the earth. His anger was without bounds and was completely out of control. **Teman** was located about five miles from Petra, and it later became a Roman garrison. **Bozrah** (lit., which cuts off approach) had been known from antiquity (cf. Gen 36:11, 15) and was the seat of one of the elected kings who reigned over Edom in the days before Moses. God promises to **send a fire** upon Edom in retaliation for its treatment of his brother, Judah.

5. Judgment upon Ammon. 1:13-15.

13-15. They have ripped up the women with child . . . that they might enlarge their border. Ammon's transgression against Judah was done primarily in the name of territorial expansion. In the process, they committed terrible atrocities. They not only destroyed the inhabitants of the land, whom they sought to replace; but they also destroyed the potential life while it was yet in the mother's womb. They did this in the attempt to exterminate Israel, though Israel ultimately survived. On the other hand, Ammon ultimately perished, leaving no memorial. All this was occasioned by jealousy and covetousness on the part of Ammon. **I will kindle a fire in the wall of Rabbah.** In retaliation, God promises to visit Ammon with destruction (vs. 13) that will be like a fire, i.e., invincible and inescapable. This was fulfilled when Nebuchadnezzar subdued the Ammonites. **Rabbah** (lit., the great) was the capital city of Ammon. It was a strong city with a strong citadel, its ruins still extant. In spite of its strength it was to be utterly devoured. **Their king shall go into captivity.** The king and his princes were to go into captivity (vs. 15) and with their demise there was no one left to enable Ammon to be a threat any longer.

6. Judgment upon Moab. 2:1-3.

2:1-3. The crime of Moab was that **he burned the bones of the king of Edom into lime** (vs. 1). The specific event to which Amos refers is not known. It does give an insight into the intense wrath of Moab. They were not content with the death of the king of Edom, but had to vent their wrath upon his body, burning it into lime. This was done as an expression of their hatred and contempt. Verse 2 shows that God hates such an unreasoning and unreasonable display of wrath. As punishment, He will send **a fire upon Moab** to destroy it. **Kerioth** is thought to have been the new capital of Moab and was composed of several different towns or burroughs. Moab's death will be accomplished **with tumult, with shouting, and with the sound of the trumpet** (vs. 2). **I will cut off the judge.** The judge (vs. 3, Heb *shōpet*) is a reference to one who had the highest authority, next to the king; and in the absence of a formal king, the judges exercised supreme authority. The judges and **all the princes** of Moab will be cut off. This was accomplished with Nebuchadnezzar's subjection of Moab, at which time it passed out of existence.

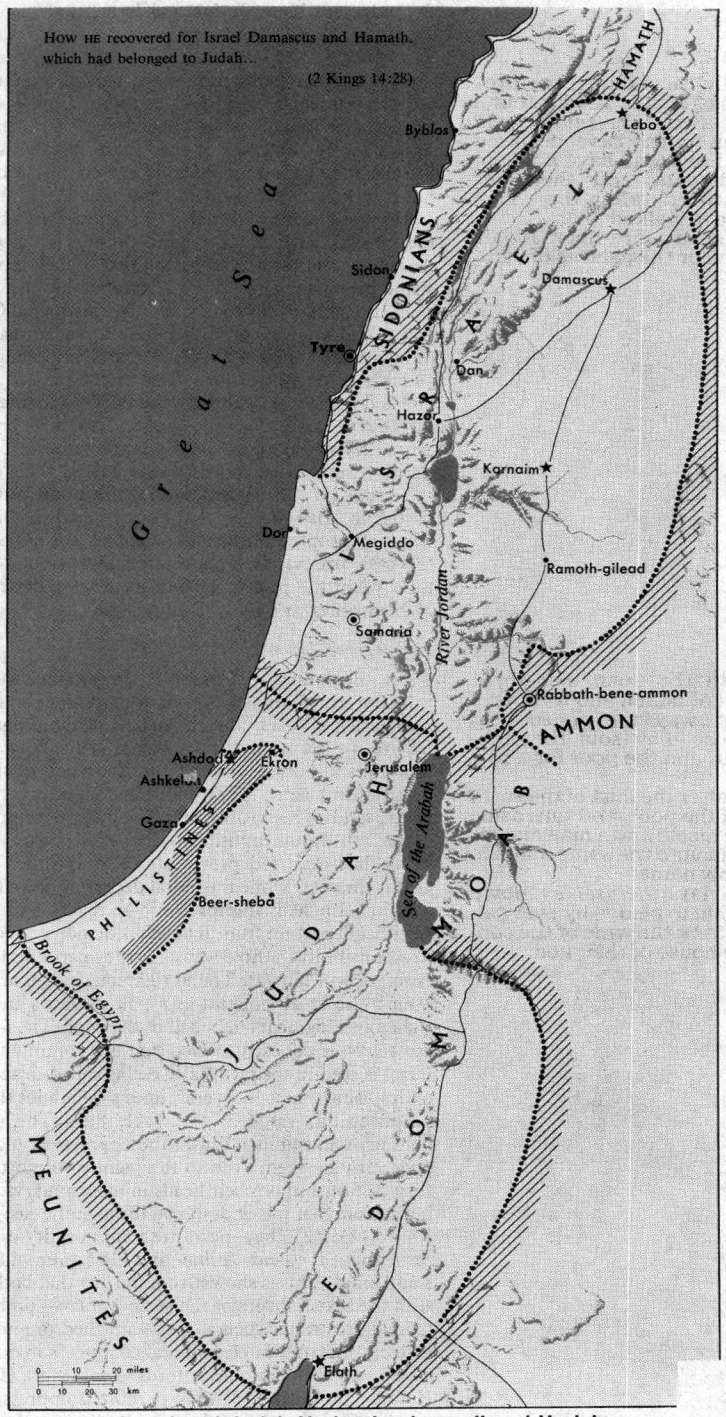

How HE recovered for Israel Damascus and Hamath,
which had belonged to Judah.
(2 Kings 14:28)

Israel and Judah Under Jeroboam II and Uzziah
Note the order in which judgment is pronounced on the
various nations—Damascus (Syria); Gaza (Philistia); Tyre
(Phoenicia); Edom; Ammon; Moab; Judah; Israel—Israel
being the object of Amos' prophecy.

B. Judgment Upon Judah and Israel. 2:4-16.

1. Judgment Upon Judah. 2:4-5.

4 ¶Thus saith the LORD; For three transgressions of Judah, and for four, I will not turn away *the punishment* thereof; because they have despised the law of the LORD, and have not kept his commandments, and their lies caused them to err, after the which their fathers have walked:

5 But I will send a fire upon Judah, and it shall devour the palaces of Jerusalem.

4-5. Though God's pronouncement of judgment grows persistently closer, it could not land with a more satisfying effect than against Judah, Israel's hated brother to the south. **They have despised the law of the LORD.** Judah's sin is similar to Israel's; they have despised and rejected the law of God and have failed to keep His commandments (vs. 4). While the judgment is directed against Judah, it should have been especially meaningful to Israel; for judgment is now falling on the family of Abraham, and particularly upon that branch to whom the Messianic promises were given. They certainly had a favored position, though they mistook it for favoritism; and God's judgment had to fall upon them. Israel should realize that if God would judge Judah, then certainly He will also judge Israel itself. Judah's sin is worse than those of the nations; for Judah has violated the law of God that was delivered to them personally by direct revelation. No other nation had such privilege, though ultimately it was to no avail; for the fathers of Judah rejected that law, embraced idolatry, and passed their evil ways on to their sons (vs. 4b). **I will send a fire upon Judah.** God is not partial in His judgment. Although Judah has been privileged above all peoples, it must likewise bear the judgment of God, in this case, fire (vs. 5). This judgment was actually realized in 586 B.C., when the palaces of Jerusalem were destroyed by fire as Nebuchadnezzar's army captured the city.

2. Judgment Upon Israel. 2:6-16.

6 ¶Thus saith the LORD; For three transgressions of Israel, and for four, I will not turn away *the punishment* thereof; because they sold the righteous for silver, and the poor for a pair of shoes;

7 That pant after the dust of the earth on the head of the poor, and turn aside the way of the meek: and a man and his father will go in unto the *same* maid, to profane my holy name:

8 And they lay *themselves* down upon clothes laid to pledge by every altar, and they drink the wine of the condemned *in* the house of their god.

6-8. Beginning with verse 6, the prophet has arrived at his primary target—Israel. Verses 6 to 16 constitute God's indictment against Israel, and the details of the judgment that must fall are spelled out in the remainder of the book. **They sold the righteous for silver, and the poor for a pair of shoes.** The main cause against Israel is that unbridled greed and lust are rampant in the land. This visible moral departure from Jehovah is the outgrowth of the invisible spiritual departure from Jehovah, which had occurred previously. The spiritual departure from God is the root, while the moral departure from God is the fruit. The indictment is impressive! The reality and gravity of their spiritual departure from Jehovah is demonstrated by their moral irresponsibility in three ways: (1) they permitted injustice to run rampant (vss. 6b-7a). The unrighteous judges are readily bribed even by so small amount as a pair of shoes and fail to render righteous judgments in behalf of the poor. The fact that the poor are always a concern to God and are continuously scorned by Israel is seen in the fact that Israel is called to account for its sin of despising the poor several times throughout the course of this prophecy (cf. vss. 6-7; 4:1; 5:11; 8:6). The unrighteous are persistent and unmerciful in the oppression and pursuit of the poor, driving them even to the point of utmost despair in that they cast dust upon their heads in mourning (vs. 7a)—a mourning custom that was widespread through the east (cf. II Sam 1:2; Job 2:12); (2) they permitted immorality to run rampant throughout the land. **A man and his father will go in unto the same maid.** This is shown from the fact that both father and son seek the sexual favors of the same woman—probably one of the temple prostitutes such as those attached to temples of the idol goddess, Astarte. Such immoral conduct is in direct violation of God's revealed law and affords comfort to His enemies (cf. II Sam 12:14); and (3) they permitted oppression of the poor (vs. 8). **They lay themselves down upon clothes laid to pledge by every altar.** The garments mentioned are the outer garments that were given as a pledge that some other obligation would be met. Moses had commanded that this garment be returned to the poor before sunset so that it could be used as a covering to

9 ¶Yet destroyed I the Amorite before them, whose height *was* like the height of the cedars, and he *was* strong as the oaks; yet I destroyed his fruit from above, and his roots from beneath.

10 Also I brought you up from the land of Egypt, and led you forty years through the wilderness, to possess the land of the Amorite.

11 And I raised up of your sons for prophets, and of your young men for Nazarites. *Is it* not even thus, O ye children of Israel? saith the LORD.

12 But ye gave the Nazarites wine to drink; and commanded the prophets, saying, Prophesy not.

13 Behold, I am pressed under you, as a cart is pressed *that is* full of sheaves.

14 Therefore the flight shall perish from the swift, and the strong shall not strengthen his force, neither shall the mighty deliver himself:

15 Neither shall he stand that handleth the bow; and *he that is* swift of foot shall not deliver *himself:* neither shall he that rideth the horse deliver himself.

16 And *he that is* courageous among the mighty shall flee away naked in that day, saith the LORD.

CHAPTER 3

HEAR this word that the LORD hath spoken against you, O children of Israel, against the whole family which I brought up from the land of Egypt, saying,

2 You only have I known of all the families of the earth: therefore I will punish you for all your iniquities.

protect against the cool night (cf. Ex 22:25-27; Deut 24:12-13). Those who had taken the garments in pledge not only refused to return them, in violation of God's law, but they used them themselves in their idol temple. **They drink the wine of the condemned.** Further, with the money that they have extorted from the poor, they buy wine to drink with their idolatrous worship. The covering up of these practices with their religious activities undoubtedly soothed their seared consciences.

9-12. God rehearses His continued faithfulness to Israel in spite of their faithlessness and disobedience. (1) He has destroyed the Amorites before them so that they could have a land in which to live (vs. 9). The Amorites, being the most powerful of all the nations that inhabited the land of Canaan, are used representatively of all the inhabitants that Israel encountered when God brought them into the land. Amos' description of the Amorites as being **like the height of the cedars, and . . . strong as the oaks,** confirms the report given earlier by the unbelieving spies who spied out the land (cf. Num 13:22, 32-33). Though their power was ominous, they were no match for God. (2) He has delivered them from **Egypt** and preserved them during the forty-year wilderness wandering so that they could come to the land God had given them (vs. 10). (3) He has raised up **prophets** and **Nazarites,** men of God, among them (vss. 11-12). **Is it not even thus . . . ?** The fact that God has done this cannot be disputed by Israel (vs. 11b). He did it so Israel might have an example of righteous and holy living among them and have those who would minister in His behalf to them. While the Nazarites' vow was taken volitionally, Israel and the Nazarites must never lose sight of the fact that it is God who placed such a desire and motivation within them. **But ye gave the Nazarites wine to drink; and commanded the prophets, saying, Prophesy not.** In view of God's gracious dealings, Israel's response is all the more appalling. They were not thankful for God's working in their midst, but rather sought to corrupt the Nazarites by making them drink wine in violation of their vow and to prohibit the prophets from proclaiming God's Word (vs. 12).

13-16. Behold, I am pressed under you, as a cart is pressed that is full of sheaves. Because of Israel's flagrant violations of God's righteous law and gracious provisions, inescapable judgment must inevitably fall, though it will fall only after God has permitted Himself to endure Israel's many and grievous sins far past what might ordinarily be considered the breaking point (vs. 13). **The flight shall perish from the swift.** Nothing will deliver Israel from God's judgment. Speed, strength, and might will be to no avail (vs. 14). Trained archers, infantry, and cavalry will be to no avail (vs. 15); and only the most courageous will barely escape with his life (vs. 16). The picture is one of abject defeat before the onslaught of the Assyrian army, which God will use as His weapon to bring judgment against the sinful nation of Israel. No one will be able to escape God's anger. Those who do live through it will be utterly stripped of their ability to resist and will be taken captive to Assyria.

III. FOUR MESSAGES OF CONDEMNATION. 3:1-6:14.

A. Concerning Certain Impending Judgments. 3:1-15.

3:1. Hear this word that the LORD hath spoken against you. Though these messages are directed primarily to Israel, the northern kingdom, they are also addressed indirectly to Judah; for He is speaking to **the whole family which I brought up from the land of Egypt.** The Exodus, of course, took place many years prior to the division of the nation into northern and southern kingdoms.

2. You only have I known of all the families of the earth. Though historically the judgment will be visited upon the northern kingdom first, it will also fall upon the southern kingdom because both have had a superior privilege—to be **known** (or, chosen) by God (vs. 2). By this expression God is not implying acquaintance, for certainly He is acquainted with all of the families of the earth. The verb to know (Heb *yada'*) in this verse should be understood in the sense of to set apart and to bring into covenant-relationship with Himself. It is used with similar meaning in Psalms 1:6; 144:3; John 10:14. That Israel as a whole enjoyed such a unique relationship to God was not new to them, nor should it seem strange to Bible students today; for passages such as Exodus 19:5; Deuteronomy 4:20; and Psalm 147:19-20 proclaim it clearly. This is the realization and out-working of the promise made to Abraham in Genesis 12:1-3. **Therefore I will punish you for all your iniquities.** The fact that Israel enjoyed such a unique relationship with God did not mean that He would overlook their sins or let them go un-punished. In fact, such privilege brings with it a greater respon-sibility (vs. 2b).

3-8. With a series of seven questions (vss. 3-8) the prophet sets forth his right to announce the judgment of God upon Israel and to show a relationship between His message and the events that are coming to pass. Underlying each of the questions is a cause-and-effect relationship. **Can two walk together, except they be agreed?** Two men do not walk together (effect) unless there has been a previous appointment (cause) (vs. 3). **Will a lion roar in the forest, when he hath no prey?** The young lion does not roar (effect) unless there is a prey to be pursued (cause) (vs. 4a). **Will a young lion cry out of his den, if he have taken nothing?** The young lion does not growl (effect) unless he has captured something (cause) (vs. 4b). **Can a bird fall in a snare upon the earth, where no gin is for him?** A bird, known for flying, does not fall into a trap on the ground (effect) unless there is a bait in the trap (cause) (vs. 5a). **Shall one take up a snare from the earth, and have taken nothing at all?** A trap does not spring up from the earth (effect) unless it has captured something (cause) (vs. 5b). **Shall the trumpet be blown in the city, and the people not be afraid?** The people in a city will not tremble, either in fear or anticipation (effect), unless a trumpet is blown (cause) (vs. 6a). **Shall there be evil in a city, and the LORD hath not done it?** A calamity does not occur (effect) unless it is caused by Jehovah (cause) (vs. 6b). With all of these questions, then, the prophet skillfully brings out the cause-and-effect relationship to heighten the calamity that is about to come upon Israel. It will not come from natural means; it will be brought by Jehovah in response to Israel's sin. **Surely the Lord GOD will do nothing, but he revealeth his secret unto his servants the prophets.** These calamities do not come without advance warning; for Jehovah reveals His intentions to those who are in fellowship with Him—His servants and prophets (vs. 7). Therefore, the prophet is a reliable and authentic wit-ness to the impending judgment of God. Verse 8 continues the cause-and-effect imagery, and the first statement is interpreted in parallel fashion by the second. **The lion hath roared** that is, **the Lord GOD hath spoken** (cause). **Who will not fear?** that is, **. . . who can but prophesy?** (effect). With this skillful state-ment, the prophet is disclaiming all originality of his message and putting behind it the complete responsibility and authority of God—he is only doing God's bidding and delivering His message.

3 Can two walk together, except they be agreed?
4 Will a lion roar in the forest, when he hath no prey? will a young lion cry out of his den, if he have taken nothing?
5 Can a bird fall in a snare upon the earth, where no gin *is* for him? shall *one* take up a snare from the earth, and have taken nothing at all?
6 Shall a trumpet be blown in the city, and the people not be afraid? shall there be evil in a city, and the LORD hath not done *it?*
7 Surely the Lord GOD will do nothing, but he revealeth his secret unto his servants the prophets.
8 The lion hath roared, who will not fear? the Lord GOD hath spoken, who can but prophesy?

9-10. Publish in the palaces at Ashdod, and . . . Egypt . . . Assemble yourselves upon the mountains of Samaria. Accord-ingly, the prophets are commissioned by God to issue an invita-tion to Ashdod (used representatively for all of Philistia) and Egypt to come to Samaria and view the unrest and oppression within it (vs. 9). God views the situation in Samaria as being so bad that even Philistia and Egypt would condemn them, and rightly so. If this be true, how much more, then, is God righ-

9 ¶Publish in the palaces at Ăsh'dŏd, and in the palaces in the land of Egypt, and say, Assemble yourselves upon the mountains of Sa-mā'rĭ-a, and behold the great tumults in the midst thereof, and the oppressed in the midst thereof.
10 For they know not to do right, saith the LORD, who store up violence and robbery in their palaces.

teous in judging them? In verse 10 Jehovah assumes the role of a prosecuting attorney pressing His case against Israel before the jury, Philistia and Egypt! In view of Israel's privilege (cf. vs. 2), the explanation **For they know not to do right** seems trite. It is, however, a sad commentary on Israel's hardened spiritual condition. Their sin has blinded their ability to discern right from wrong. They have neglected the practice of righteousness so long that they can only practice the vilest sins of greed and violence. Hence, they are guilty before God and deserve His judgment. The judgment is pronounced in verses 11-15.

11-15. An adversary . . . shall bring down thy strength from thee. This judgment was realized when Assyria invaded Israel and besieged Samaria for three years (cf. II Kgs 17:5-18). **As the shepherd taketh out of the mouth of the lion two legs, or a piece of an ear; so shall the children of Israel be taken out.** Though the judgment will be (and was) severe, still a remnant will be saved (vs. 12). The prophetic picture is one of a shepherd who is able to save only a couple of legs and piece of an ear of one of his beloved sheep from a marauding lion. In such a fashion will a small and insignificant remnant be salvaged from God's judgment, not because they deserve deliverance but because of God's future messianic plans for Israel, which cannot be allowed to be thwarted by the nation's sin. The mention of **the corner of a bed** and a **couch** shows that this judgment will overtake Israel while it is involved in careless self-indulgence. Apparently, many residents of the northern tribes moved to Damascus, which at the time of the Assyrian invasion of Samaria was under the control of Jeroboam II (cf. II Kgs 14:28).

The mention of **The house of Jacob** (vs. 13), together with the address, lets us know that God is calling the same prophets of vs. 9 to testify against all of the twelve tribes of Israel. **Saith the Lord GOD, the God of hosts.** The testimony is solemnized by the use of multiple names for God. This gives both authenticity and certainty to its fulfillment. All twelve tribes are called on to witness the fact that there will be no escape when God's judgment falls upon Israel (the ten northern tribes). Even the places of refuge (**the altars of Beth-el** and **the horns of the altar**) will be smitten by God's judgment and will offer no protection (vs. 14). **And I will smite the winter house with the summer house.** The judgment of God will also be visited upon Israel's possessions (vs. 15). The winter and summer houses of the royalty and the rich, together with all of the houses inlaid with ivory and luxuriously decorated, will be destroyed. Most of these have been gotten through ill-deserved gain and oppression of the poor. The poor could not help themselves, but God will avenge the wrong visited upon them (cf. 2:6-8).

B. Concerning the Ineffectiveness of Past Judgment.
   4:1-13.

4:1-3. Hear this word, ye kine of Bashan. The use of the feminine forms in the original, together with the reference to the **masters** (Heb *'adōn*, Lord, in this context is best understood as a reference to the husband, cf. Gen 18:12), lets us know that verses 1-3 are best understood as an indictment against the women of Samaria, though some scholars prefer to see this as a reference to the effeminate character of the wealthy rulers of the land. The **kine** (Heb *parah*, cow, heifer) **of Bashan** were noted for being well-fed and strong because of the lush pastures of the area. (Other references to the cattle of Bashan are found in Deut 32:14; Ps 22:12; and Ezk 39:18.) The region of Bashan is located east of the Jordan River near the intersection of the 36° longitude and 33° north latitude, due east of the Sea of Galilee. The women of Samaria, then, are addressed under the figure of the **kine of Bashan** because they live in luxurious wantonness. **Which oppress the poor, which crush the needy, which say to their masters, Bring, and let us drink.** They enjoy their luxury

---

11 Therefore thus saith the Lord GOD; An adversary *there shall be* even round about the land; and he shall bring down thy strength from thee, and thy palaces shall be spoiled.

12 Thus saith the LORD; As the shepherd taketh out of the mouth of the lion two legs, or a piece of an ear; so shall the children of Israel be taken out that dwell in Sa-mā′rĭ-a in the corner of a bed, and in Damascus *in* a couch.

13 Hear ye, and testify in the house of Jacob, saith the Lord GOD, the God of hosts.

14 That in the day that I shall visit the transgressions of Israel upon him I will also visit the altars of Běth-el: and the horns of the altar shall be cut off, and fall to the ground.

15 And I will smite the winter house with the summer house; and the houses of ivory shall perish, and the great houses shall have an end, saith the LORD.

CHAPTER 4

HEAR this word, ye kine of Bā′shan, that *are* in the mountain of Sa-mā′rĭ-a, which oppress the poor, which crush the needy, which say to their masters, Bring, and let us drink.

2 The Lord GOD hath sworn by his holiness, that, lo, the days shall come upon you, that he will take you away with hooks, and your posterity with fishhooks.

3 And ye shall go out at the breaches, every *cow at that which is* before her; and ye shall cast *them* into the palace, saith the LORD.

because they oppressed the poor and crushed the needy (vs. 1) through their husbands whom they urged to bring them wine for their drunken orgies—wine purchased through gain achieved by oppression of the poor. When the women of the land sink to such a low moral and degraded state, God's judgment must fall; for the entire land is degraded. **He will take you away with hooks, and your posterity with fishhooks.** The judgment that must fall is set forth under the figure of fishermen who catch fish with fishhooks (vs. 2). The picture is one of complete helplessness of the fallen victims before their captors; it will be a slaughter. **And ye shall go out at the breaches, every cow at that which is before her.** In the process, the marauding army will breach the wall at many places (vs. 3); and the women will be led out into captivity through the breaches of the wall. Such a practice is not unknown in Scripture (see such passages as I Kgs 19:28; II Chr 33:11, ASV; Jer 16:16; Ez 29:4; Hab 1:15). **And ye shall cast them into the palace.** A number of suggestions have been offered for the translation of the word **palace** (Heb *harmōn*, high place, the only occurrence of this word in the Old Testament), but about all that can be ascertained with certainty is that probably neither a particular geographical site nor a type of building is intended (vs. 3b). The context indicates that in their attempt to escape captivity the women of Samaria would flee through the breaches in the wall, seeking refuge in higher ground that would offer temporary solace, but ultimately would be to no avail.

4 ¶Come to Bĕth–el, and transgress; at Gilgal multiply transgression; and bring your sacrifices every morning, *and* your tithes after three years:

5 And offer a sacrifice of thanksgiving with leaven, and proclaim *and* publish the free offerings: for this liketh you, O ye children of Israel, saith the Lord God.

4-5. Come to Beth-el, and transgress; at Gilgal multiply transgression. These verses show that in the midst of their spiritual callousness and insensitivity the people of Israel were very religious. Their religious observance, however, was self-directed, self-serving, and self-pleasing (**for this liketh you,** lit., for so you love to do). The prophet ironically issues the invitation to come to the religious centers (**Beth-el** and **Gilgal,** vs. 4). with **sacrifices, tithes,** thank offerings, and free-will offerings in order to point out carefully that in the process of worship they compound their transgression, rather than relieve it. This is true because they have only the form of worship and no reality (cf. Ezk 33:31; Mk 7:6-7; II Tim 3:5).

6 ¶And I also have given you cleanness of teeth in all your cities, and want of bread in all your places: yet have ye not returned unto me, saith the Lord.

7 And also I have withholden the rain from you, when *there were* yet three months to the harvest: and I caused it to rain upon one city, and caused it not to rain upon another city: one piece was rained upon, and the piece whereupon it rained not withered.

8 So two *or* three cities wandered unto one city, to drink water; but they were not satisfied: yet have ye not returned unto me, saith the Lord.

9 I have smitten you with blasting and mildew: when your gardens and your vineyards and your fig trees and your olive trees increased, the palmerworm devoured *them:* yet have ye not returned unto me, saith the Lord.

10 I have sent among you the pestilence after the manner of Egypt: your young men have I slain with the sword, and have taken away your horses; and I have made the stink of your camps to come up unto your nostrils: yet have ye not returned unto me, saith the Lord.

11 I have overthrown *some* of you, as God overthrew Sodom and Gomŏr'rah, and ye were as a firebrand plucked out of the burning: yet have ye not returned unto me, saith the Lord.

6-11. These verses tell what God's response to their misdirected worship has been. Since He was not pleased, He sent various forms of punishment designed to bring them to repentance and a proper worship of Himself, but to no avail. God's chastenings have been in the form of **cleanness of teeth** (lit., famine vs. 6), drought (vs. 7), a scorching east wind with resultant **mildew** (vs. 9a), **palmerworms** (Heb *gazam*, caterpillar or creeping locust) to devour the gardens, vineyards, fig trees, and olive trees (vs. 9b), a plague such as was common to Egypt (vs. 10a), and military defeat in which many of their young men were slain and their vaunted cavalry taken captive (vss. 10b-11). Any one of these catastrophes should have had the effect of causing them to return to God; but the hardness of their heart is revealed and made the more repulsive by the recurring refrain, **yet have ye not returned unto me.**

12 Therefore thus will I do unto thee, O Israel: *and* because I will do this unto thee, prepare to meet thy God, O Israel.

13 For, lo, he that formeth the mountains, and createth the wind, and declareth unto man what *is* his thought, that maketh the morning darkness, and treadeth upon the high places of the earth, The LORD, The God of hosts, *is* his name.

CHAPTER 5

HEAR ye this word which I take up against you, *even* a lamentation, O house of Israel.

2 The virgin of Israel is fallen; she shall no more rise: she is forsaken upon her land; *there is* none to raise her up.

3 For thus saith the Lord GOD; The city that went out *by* a thousand shall leave an hundred, and that which went forth *by* an hundred shall leave ten, to the house of Israel.

4 ¶For thus saith the LORD unto the house of Israel, Seek ye me, and ye shall live:

5 But seek not Bĕth–el, nor enter into Gilgal, and pass not to Be'er–shē'ba: for Gilgal shall surely go into captivity, and Bĕth–el shall come to nought.

6 Seek the LORD, and ye shall live; lest he break out like fire in the house of Joseph, and devour *it*, and *there be* none to quench *it* in Bĕth–el.

7 Ye who turn judgment to wormwood, and leave off righteousness in the earth,

8 *Seek him* that maketh the seven stars and Ō–rī'on, and turneth the shadow of death into the morning, and maketh the day dark with night: that calleth for the waters of the sea, and poureth them out upon the face of the earth: The LORD *is* his name:

9 That strengtheneth the spoiled against the strong, so that the spoiled shall come against the fortress.

10 They hate him that rebuketh in the

12-13. Therefore thus will I do unto thee, O Israel declares God's resolve in the light of Israel's impenitent heart. Up to this point God has been content to send messengers of judgment to Israel; but now He will come Himself, and they had better prepare to meet Him in judgment. For, as they have been able to resist the messengers of judgment, they will have no hope of resisting God personally. The statement **prepare to meet thy God** (vs. 12b) is often mistakenly used by evangelists to encourage people to prepare to meet God in salvation. The context clearly indicates, however, that God is not going to visit Israel with salvation, but rather with inevitable and complete judgment. The statement is to be understood in the light of national condemnation, not personal salvation. Verse 13 describes the God whom they are to prepare to meet in judgment. The Hebrew text uses five participles to describe God's omnipotence, **he that formeth the mountains, and createth the wind** (vs. 13a); His omniscience, **declareth unto man what is his thought** (vs. 13b); and His omnipresence, **maketh the morning darkness, and treadeth upon the high places of the earth** (vs. 13c). **The LORD, The God of hosts.** He is the Jehovah God of Hosts, and Israel will be helpless before Him.

C. Concerning the Need to Seek Jehovah. 5:1-27.

5:1-3. Hear ye this word . . . even a lamentation. In the light of certain judgment pronounced in chapter 4 the lamentation, or funeral dirge, of verses 1-3 is certainly in order for Israel (cf. Isa 23:12; 47:1). Israel's devastation before Assyria is complete with only one-tenth of human life surviving. The statement, **she shall no more rise** (vs. 2), must be understood in the light of the Assyrian crisis only. God's ultimate millennial plan for the restoration and glorification of Israel will not be deterred by this calamity, as this prophecy later confirms (cf. 9:13-15).

4-7. Seek ye me, and ye shall live. Though God's judgment is imminent, it can be avoided, or at least postponed, by seeking the Lord. Three times the invitation goes forth (vss. 4, 6, 14). The invitation is stated negatively in verse 5 as Israel is urged not to continue in the idol worship of **Beth-el, Gilgal,** and **Beer-sheba** (vs. 5). Beth-el and Gilgal were well-known centers for idol worship in the north (cf. 4:4), but by this time Beer-sheba in the southern kingdom was also given to idolatry. Hence, idolatry had infected the entire land of Israel from north to south. To continue in idol worship is to seek that which will perish (vs. 5b). **Seek the LORD, and ye shall live.** The only hope is to seek Jehovah (vs. 6a) and true repentance. Any other course of action will result in His judgment, which will be like a **fire** (vs. 6b). The invitation is addressed to the **house of Joseph** (vs. 6b). Joseph had been promised a double portion in the land of Israel (cf. Gen 48:1-22); thus, a tribe was named after each of his sons, Ephraim and Manasseh. Ephraim became the most important of the ten northern tribes, hence the occasion of this address. **Ye who turn judgment to wormwood, and leave off righteousness in the earth.** The particular ones singled out for judgment on this occasion are the unrighteous judges who have made unrighteous judgments against God's righteous ones (vs. 7).

8-9. Seek him that maketh the seven stars and Orion. This reminds the people of God's ability to bring about the threatened judgment. He is the omnipotent Creator, having made the constellations, Pleiades (**the seven stars**) and Orion (which are also mentioned in Job 9:9; 38:31). He is the one who actively superintends in His creation day and night (vs. 8b); He is the one who controls all the waters of the sea (vs. 8c); in short, He is Jehovah, the Eternal One. **The LORD is his name** (vs. 8d). The God of Creation is the one who is able to bring about sudden and irreparable judgment (vs. 9).

10-13. These verses again rehearse the injustices heaped upon

1707

gate, and they abhor him that speaketh uprightly.

11 Forasmuch therefore as your treading *is* upon the poor, and ye take from him burdens of wheat: ye have built houses of hewn stone, but ye shall not dwell in them; ye have planted pleasant vineyards, but ye shall not drink wine of them.

12 For I know your manifold transgressions and your mighty sins: they afflict the just, they take a bribe, and they turn aside the poor in the gate *from their right*.

13 Therefore the prudent shall keep silence in that time: for it *is* an evil time.

14 Seek good, and not evil, that ye may live: and so the Lord, the God of hosts, shall be with you, as ye have spoken.

15 Hate the evil, and love the good, and establish judgment in the gate: it may be that the Lord God of hosts will be gracious unto the remnant of Joseph.

16 Therefore the Lord, the God of hosts, the Lord, saith thus; Wailing *shall be* in all streets; and they shall say in all the highways, Alas! alas! and they shall call the husbandman to mourning, and such as are skilful of lamentation to wailing.

17 And in all vineyards *shall be* wailing: for I will pass through thee, saith the Lord.

18 Woe unto you that desire the day of the Lord! to what end *is* it for you? the day of the Lord *is* darkness, and not light.

19 As if a man did flee from a lion, and a bear met him; or went into the house, and leaned his hand on the wall, and a serpent bit him.

20 *Shall* not the day of the Lord *be* darkness, and not light? even very dark, and no brightness in it?

21 ¶ I hate, I despise your feast days, and I will not smell in your solemn assemblies.

22 Though ye offer me burnt offerings and your meat offerings, I will not accept *them*: neither will I regard the peace offerings of your fat beasts.

the poor by the unjust judges of Samaria. They divert money exacted from the poor to their own use and have built costly homes made of hewn stone for themselves. Most homes in Israel were made of much cheaper sun-dried bricks. Their prosperity has been ill-gotten, taken from the people who can do nothing about it except suffer in silence (vs. 13). Only God can bring vengeance upon the unjust judges, and this He promises; for the unjust judges will not be able to live in their homes, or enjoy the vineyards that they had planted (vss. 11b-12).

14-15. Seek good, and not evil, that ye may live. This constitutes another call to repentance. Israel has gone insane, seeking evil in multitudinous forms. In true repentance they should seek the opposite, good; and the result will be life. The prophet recognizes, however, that in all probability Israel has gone too far; and her case is irreversible. However, God will be gracious to the remnant who repents (vs. 15; cf. vs. 3).

16-17. The prophet does not anticipate that Israel will take advantage of God's offer of life through their repentance; therefore, in verses 16 and 17 he prophetically sets forth the sorrow that will be theirs upon experiencing God's judgment. **Wailing shall be in all streets; and they shall say in all the highways, Alas! alas!** The devastation will be complete throughout the land, and sorrow will be in every street. Travelers on the highway will see it every place they go. **And in all vineyards shall be wailing.** Farmers and vineyard workers will find the burden of sorrow more pressing than the care of their crops, and this will lead them to mourn. The only ones who will profit from this judgment will be the professional mourners, **such as are skilful of lamentation to wailing,** who will have a great demand for their services. All of this will happen because Jehovah Himself will **pass through** the land in judgment as He has promised (vs. 17; cf. 4:12b).

18-20. Woe unto you that desire the day of the Lord! Amos deals with those who, perhaps with feigned piety, long for the Day of the Lord to come. They do this because they do not understand the true nature of that day. **The day of the Lord is darkness, and not light.** It is true that the Day of the Lord will result in Israel's exaltation, but they do not realize that it will involve a preparation in which all evil will be judged and evildoers destroyed. Only those in right relationship with God will survive to enjoy the benefits of the Day of the Lord. For them, then, the Day of the Lord would be worse than the judgment coming by the hand of the Assyrians, though this judgment certainly foreshadows the latter. A wicked man might conceivably be spared in this judgment, but he certainly will not escape the judgment in the Day of the Lord. Amos graphically portrays this reality (vs. 19) as he pictures a man who successfully escapes from a lion and while doing so, meets a bear from which he also successfully escapes to the supposed safety of his house (i.e., the Day of the Lord), only to be bitten (and mortally wounded) by a snake as in exhaustion he leans against the wall to recover from his escapade. **Shall not the day of the Lord be darkness, and not light? even very dark, and no brightness in it?** The summary questions (vs. 20) drive home the point: the Day of the Lord offers no hope for evildoers, only certain doom.

21-24. These verses echo a thought expressed earlier in 4:4-13. **I hate, I despise your feast days.** Religious activity without heart reality is repugnant to God! All of these forms of worship and spiritual expression were God-ordained, and they were to be expressions of a right relationship to God. Lacking that heart reality, they have become only nauseous, empty, formalism; and

23 Take thou away from me the noise of thy songs; for I will not hear the melody of thy viols.

24 But let judgment run down as waters, and righteousness as a mighty stream.

25 Have ye offered unto me sacrifices and offerings in the wilderness forty years, O house of Israel?

26 But ye have borne the tabernacle of your Moloch and Chĭ'un your images, the star of your god, which ye made to yourselves.

27 Therefore will I cause you to go into captivity beyond Damascus, saith the LORD, whose name is The God of hosts.

CHAPTER 6

WOE to them that are at ease in Zion, and trust in the mountain of Sa-mâ'rĭ-a, which are named chief of the nations, to whom the house of Israel came!

2 Pass ye unto Căl'nĕh, and see; and from thence go ye to Hā'măth the great: then go down to Gath of the Philistines: be they better than these kingdoms? or their border greater than your border?

3 Ye that put far away the evil day, and cause the seat of violence to come near;

4 That lie upon beds of ivory, and stretch themselves upon their couches, and eat the lambs out of the flock, and the calves out of the midst of the stall;

5 That chant to the sound of the viol, and invent to themselves instruments of musick, like David;

6 That drink wine in bowls, and anoint themselves with the chief ointments: but they are not grieved for the affliction of Joseph.

7 ¶Therefore now shall they go captive with the first that go captive, and the banquet of them that stretched themselves shall be removed.

they anger, rather than appease, God. **But let judgment run down as waters, and righteousness as a mighty stream.** The problem can be rectified by having a proper heart reality that expresses itself in the incorporation of justice and righteousness in all aspects of life (vs. 24).

25-27. Israel's problem is not new or recent. **But ye have borne the tabernacle of your Moloch and Chiun your images.** They were infected with idol worship from the very beginning when God brought them out of Egypt. Throughout its history, Israel made the mistake of thinking that both idols and Jehovah could be worshiped. **Therefore will I cause you to go into captivity beyond Damascus.** Israel has always had the disease; now their condition is terminal, and the only remedy is the Assyrian captivity from which they, as a nation (the ten northern tribes), will never return (vs. 27).

D. Concerning the Folly of Self-sufficiency. 6:1-14.

6:1-3. **Woe to them that are at ease in Zion, and trust in the mountain of Samaria.** The mention of both Zion and Samaria lets us know that this fourth message of condemnation is addressed both to Judah and to Israel (though primarily to the latter); for both suffer from the same ailment, i.e., spiritual insensitivity. The people of Zion mistook God's favor for favoritism, feeling that God certainly would never punish them because they were His chosen. The people of Samaria felt that even if judgment were to come, they would be delivered because of the mountains that surrounded them like a natural fortress. It is fitting, then, that God should remind them of their favored position (vss. 1b-2) in order to assure them that this is no guarantee of favored treatment. **Pass ye unto Calneh . . . Hamath . . . Gath . . . be they better than these kingdoms? or their border greater than your border?** Calneh was built by Nimrod on the east bank of the Tigris River in the land of Shinar (cf. Gen 10:10; Isa 10:9). **Hamath** was located on the Orontes River and was one of the primary cities of Syria. **Gath** was the primary city of Philistia. These cities are cited in order to remind Judah and Israel of their own superior privilege. They were favored more than the best of the gentile nations, both qualitatively and quantitatively (vs. 2b). Their problem is not due to lack of opportunity or privilege. Nor will this privilege give them immunity from judgment; in fact, it requires the greater responsibility. By the time of the prophets these gentile cities had experienced God's judgment for their sins. If God will judge the less-privileged, certainly He will not hold guiltless those who have superior privilege (vs. 3).

4-7. Verses 4 to 6 show the depth to which the people of Israel sank as they mistook God's favor for favoritism, and verse 7 shows the painful penalty that this mistake will exact. The picture is one of repugnant self-indulgence in the extreme. Instead of being grieved over the sins of their nation and seeking to turn it back to God, they turn their attention to their own self-interest. They mercilessly oppress the poor, while at the same time indulging themselves in extravagant luxuries. They gave themselves to ease, feasting, licentious music, and extravagant drinking; and they pampered themselves with the finest perfumes. All of this was done in such a way as to give the appearance of culture and refinement. **That lie upon beds of ivory.** Their beds were inlaid with ivory (vs. 4a), **and eat the lambs out of the flock, and the calves out of the midst of the stall.** Their meat was the tenderest and most costly (vs. 4b). **That chant to the sound of the viol, and invent to themselves instruments of music, like David** they invented music and musical instruments. In so doing they displayed a genius and creativity similar to that of King David, but with one great difference: David's music was inspired by God and directed man's heart to praise Him; their music turned man's heart away

8 The Lord GOD hath sworn by himself, saith the LORD the God of hosts, I abhor the excellency of Jacob, and hate his palaces: therefore will I deliver up the city with all that is therein.
9 And it shall come to pass, if there remain ten men in one house, that they shall die.
10 And a man's uncle shall take him up, and he that burneth him, to bring out the bones out of the house, and shall say unto him that *is* by the sides of the house, *Is there* yet *any* with thee? and he shall say, No. Then shall he say, Hold thy tongue: for we may not make mention of the name of the LORD.
11 For, behold, the LORD commandeth, and he will smite the great house with breaches, and the little house with clefts.

12 ¶Shall horses run upon the rock? will *one* plow *there* with oxen? for ye have turned judgment into gall, and the fruit of righteousness into hemlock:
13 Ye which rejoice in a thing of nought, which say, Have we not taken to us horns by our own strength?
14 But, behold, I will raise up against you a nation, O house of Israel, saith the LORD the God of hosts; and they shall afflict you from the entering in of Hĕ′măth unto the river of the wilderness.

from God to their own lusts. David's music made man's heart sensitive to God; theirs made man's heart insensitive to God (vs. 5). **That drink wine in bowls.** Their addiction to wine became so great that instead of using glasses they drank from bowls that were the same type as those used to catch the blood of a sacrificial victim and sprinkle it in worship services (vs. 6a, cf. Num 7:13). **And anoint themselves with the chief ointments.** All of this was given an air of pleasantness and acceptability by the perfume they lavished upon themselves (vs. 6b). **But they are not grieved for the affliction of Joseph.** All of this self-interest and self-indulgence made them spiritually insensitive to the needs of the nation (vs. 6c). The picture is one of materialism and prosperity gone awry, resulting in spiritual apathy. **Therefore now shall they go captive with the first that go captive.** The only cure for the cancer that has eaten away Israel's heart is radical surgery! Those who have had prominence in ease will have prominence in punishment. Those who have given prominence to their own self-interest will be given prominence in punishment. They have led the way in debauchery; now they will lead the way into captivity, taking the prominence in shame. **The banquet of them that stretched themselves shall be removed.** Their discordant self-directed sounds will cease, and the banqueters will pass off the scene (vs. 7).

8-11. I abhor the excellency of Jacob expresses Jehovah's revulsion at Israel's self-indulgence, and verses 9-11 convey His response. God not only loathes Jacob's arrogance; but He also hates the palaces in which the people are living, a tangible testimony of their ill-gotten gains. **Therefore will I deliver up the city with all that is therein.** The city and all that is in it will pass into oblivion. **If there remain ten men in one house . . . they shall die.** Jehovah's response is to send a judgment in which all living in a house shall die (vs. 9). **He that burneth him, to bring out the bones.** So many will die in the judgment that it will be impossible to bury their remains; so cremation will be resorted to in order to prevent the spread of disease (vs. 10a). **Hold thy tongue: for we may not make mention of the name of the LORD.** A fearful remnant will not even dare to mention the name of the Lord so that a further judgment will not come upon them (vs. 10b). They have been urged to call upon the name of the Lord for salvation, but they have refused to do so. Now that judgment has overtaken them, they continue to leave God out of their lives. Apparently even the great tragedy will not drive them to God. **He will smite the great house . . . and the little house.** The point of verse 11 is to show that the judgment of God will fall upon rich and poor alike. The problem is spiritual, not economic, status.

12-14. The section closes (vss. 12-14) with a final reminder of the futility of Israel's self-confidence. **Shall horses run upon the rock? will one plow there with oxen?** The two questions (vs. 12) are rhetorical and demand a negative answer. Horses do not run on rocks, else they will become lame; nor does one plow rocks with oxen, else the plow would be broken. To violate natural law is to reap the consequences of it. This is what Israel has done. They have violated God's justice and righteousness (vs. 12b) and make their boast in their self-perceived strength (**horns**), which, in reality, is non-existent (**a thing of nought,** lit., a non-thing, or, a thing of non-existence, vs. 13). Their confidence is bound to be shattered because it is groundless. **But, behold, I will raise up against you a nation.** God will bring a nation (which from history we know to be Assyria) against them that will ravish the land from the extreme north (**Hemath**) to the extreme south (**the river of the wilderness**) (vs. 14).

IV. FIVE SYMBOLIC VISIONS OF JUDGMENT.
7:1-9:10.
The next major division of the prophecy consists of five symbolic visions of the judgment that is to come. The first four

are introduced in a similar introductory fashion. **Thus hath the Lord God showed unto me** (cf. 7:1, 4, 7; 8:1;). It is possible to understand these visions as representative of the Assyrian invasion; but the form of the visions, together with the context, makes it better to understand these judgments as taking place in contemporary Israel during the lifetime of the prophet, similar to those already mentioned in 4:6-13. The purpose of these judgments, then, is to move Israel to return to the Lord, with the possibility that if they do, the Assyrian crisis may be averted.

CHAPTER 7

THUS hath the Lord God shewed unto me; and, behold, he formed grasshoppers in the beginning of the shooting up of the latter growth; and, lo, *it was* the latter growth after the king's mowings.

2 And it came to pass, *that* when they had made an end of eating the grass of the land, then I said, O Lord God, forgive, I beseech thee: by whom shall Jacob arise? for he *is* small.

3 The Lord repented for this: It shall not be, saith the Lord.

A. The Vision of Locusts. 7:1-3.

7:1-3. Behold, he formed grasshoppers. The prophet is privileged by God to see this plague in its formative, or anticipated, stage (vs. 1a). The grasshoppers (locusts) are better understood as literal, rather than being representative of an invading army. **It was the latter growth after the king's mowings.** As is true in most places in the world, Israel annually had two mowings of grass (hay). The first was paid to the king as tribute, and the second was kept by the people to sustain them throughout the coming year. This plague is pictured as occurring between the two mowings and, hence, would rob the people of their sustenance for the year to come (vs. 1). **Then I said, O Lord God, forgive, I beseech thee.** The tragedy moved the prophet to intercessory prayer in behalf of the people (vs. 2a). He realizes that the plague is justly deserved because of the nation's sin and asks God to pardon them (vs. 2b). The power of intercessory prayer is not just the product of New Testament revelation; it is seen in the Old Testament, too. **The Lord repented for this: It shall not be.** The prophet's concern and prayer for his people are attributed with causing God to change His mind and decide not to send the plague (vs. 3). The purpose of the vision, then, was to bring the sinful condition of his people to the prophet's attention and to move him to intercessory prayer in their behalf. Having accomplished His purpose, the Lord did not actually send the plague, though in the language of appearance it appeared as if the Lord changed His mind. In no way did the prophet's prayer modify the immutability of God.

B. The Vision of Fire (Drought). 7:4-6.

4 ¶Thus hath the Lord God shewed unto me: and, behold, the Lord God called to contend by fire, and it devoured the great deep, and did eat up a part.

5 Then said I, O Lord God, cease, I beseech thee: by whom shall Jacob arise? for he *is* small.

6 The Lord repented for this: This also shall not be, saith the Lord God.

4-6. In a second vision the prophet is privileged to see God determining to send **fire** (most likely best understood metaphorically to represent drought) against the vast bodies of water and arable land (vss. 4-6). The drought is viewed as being so severe that it consumed the **great deep** (metaphorical representation of the ocean, cf. Gen 7:11; 49:25; Isa 51:10). The ocean, of course, is the ultimate source of the arable land's water; with it gone, naturally, the land loses its fertility. The result would be total devastation, and once again this moves the prophet to intercession (vss. 5-6). **O Lord God, cease, I beseech thee: by whom shall Jacob arise? for he is small.** Again, the prophet is touched by the plight of his people; and his intercessory prayer is effective, for God decides not to send this plague. **The Lord repented for this: This also shall not be.** Once again, the primary purpose of the vision is to impress the prophet with the sad condition of his people and to move him to prayer in their behalf. The purpose having been served, there is no necessity for God to actualize the plague.

C. The Vision of the Plumb Line. 7:7-17.

1. The vision itself. 7:7-9.

7 ¶Thus he shewed me: and, behold, the Lord stood upon a wall *made* by a plumbline, with a plumbline in his hand.

7-9. Judgment has been averted twice through the prophet's intercession in behalf of his people. **Behold, the Lord stood . . . with a plumbline in his hand.** This third vision of the Lord with a plumb line in His hand lets the prophet know that all hope for

8 And the Lord said unto me, Amos, what seest thou? And I said, A plumb-line. Then said the Lord, Behold, I will set a plumbline in the midst of my people Israel: I will not again pass by them any more:

9 And the high places of Isaac shall be desolate, and the sanctuaries of Israel shall be laid waste; and I will rise against the house of Jĕr-o-bō'am with the sword.

10 ¶Then Ăm-a-zī'ah the priest of Bĕth-el sent to Jĕr-o-bō'am king of Israel, saying, Amos hath conspired against thee in the midst of the house of Israel: the land is not able to bear all his words.

11 For thus Amos saith, Jĕr-o-bō'am shall die by the sword, and Israel shall surely be led away captive out of their own land.

12 Also Ăm-a-zī'ah said unto Amos, O thou seer, go, flee thee away into the land of Judah, and there eat bread, and prophesy there:

13 But prophesy not again any more at Bĕth-el: for it is the king's chapel, and it is the king's court.

14 ¶Then answered Amos, and said to Ăm-a-zī'ah, I was no prophet, neither was I a prophet's son; but I was an herdman, and a gatherer of syco-more fruit:

15 And the Lord took me as I fol-lowed the flock, and the Lord said unto me, Go, prophesy unto my people Israel.

16 Now therefore hear thou the word of the Lord: Thou sayest, Prophesy not against Israel, and drop not thy word against the house of Isaac.

17 Therefore thus saith the Lord; Thy wife shall be an harlot in the city, and thy sons and thy daughters shall fall by the sword, and thy land shall be divided by line; and thou shalt die in a polluted land: and Israel shall surely go into cap-tivity forth of his land.

CHAPTER 8

THUS hath the Lord God shewed unto

Israel has been exhausted, and judgment must come. The pur-pose of the plumbline is to demonstrate how far Israel has strayed from God's righteousness and that it must be destroyed. The ten northern tribes are addressed by the name **Isaac** (vs. 9a), but the parallel structure leaves no doubt as to who is intended (vs. 9b). Israel's places of idol worship (**high places . . . sanctuaries**) will be destroyed, together with the kingly lines (**house of Jeroboam**) that led Israel into its spiritual defec-tion (cf. I Kgs 12:25ff.).

2. The autobiographical historical insert. 7:10-17.

10-13. Amos' message was not popularly received. He had prophesied against the religious and political corruption of the land. Amaziah, the priest of the sanctuary at Beth-el where calf worship was practiced, became the leader of the opposition. He made a threefold indictment against God's prophet and com-plained to Jeroboam the king of Israel: (1) Amos has conspired against you, i.e., he is making a personal attack against you; (2) this attack is taking place in the midst of Israel, i.e., it is a treasonous conspiracy; and (3) the land is unable to endure his words, i.e., he is upsetting what otherwise would be a peaceful land (vs. 10). **For thus Amos saith.** Amaziah seeks to support his charge by manipulating Amos' message to suit his own purpose. He tells the king that Amos had said that he would die by the sword and that Israel would be carried away captive, but his report is designed to motivate Jeroboam to take action against Amos. It is only half true, for Amos did not say that Jeroboam would die by the sword (which he did not, cf. II Kgs 14:23-29). What Amos had said was that God would bring the sword against **the house of Jeroboam** (cf. vs. 9), and this prophecy was fulfilled. Zechariah, his son, was assassinated by Shallum (cf. II Kgs 15:8-10). **Also Amaziah said unto Amos.** Apparently, Amaziah did not gain a sympathetic ear from Jero-boam; for in verses 12-13 he turned his attack to the prophet himself. He calls Amos a **seer** (in keeping with the vision related earlier, cf. vss. 1-9) and encourages him to return to his home in Judah to do his prophesying (vs. 12). **But prophesy not again any more at Beth-el: for it is the king's chapel, and it is the king's court.** Amaziah tells Amos to minister in Beth-el no longer because it is King Jeroboam's place of worship and residence, thus implying that the minister of God is not worthy of being there. Unwittingly, Amaziah has an element of truth to his message; for Beth-el is not God's place of worship. It is Jeroboam's, and it certainly isn't worthy of God's messenger.

14-17. Verses 14 through 17 give Amos' response to Ama-ziah. **I was no prophet, neither was I a prophet's son.** Amos gives a simple reference to who he was and how he came to be commissioned by God. **And the Lord took me . . . and the Lord said unto me, Go, prophesy unto my people Israel.** It is not a position that he sought (in contrast to Amaziah who had been hired by Jeroboam to fulfill his religious duties); it was a sovereign act of God who took a most unlikely person from a most unlikely place and gave him the highest privileges, i.e., to proclaim the message of God (vss. 14-15)! **Now therefore hear thou the word of the Lord.** Amos completely ignores Ama-ziah's injunction to **prophesy not again any more at Beth-el** (cf. vs. 13) and delivers a prophecy against Amaziah personally, as well as his family (vss. 16-17). His wife will become a harlot; his sons and daughters will be slain; his land would be taken from him; and he himself would die **in a polluted land** (as a captive in Assyria). Further, Israel itself will be taken captive and led away in exile (vs. 17).

D. The Vision of Summer Fruit. 8:1-14.

8:1-3. Behold a basket of summer fruit. The vision of the basket of summer fruit advances the thought given by the vision

me: and behold a basket of summer fruit.

2 And he said, Amos, what seest thou? And I said, A basket of summer fruit. Then said the LORD unto me, The end is come upon my people of Israel; I will not again pass by them any more.

3 And the songs of the temple shall be howlings in that day, saith the Lord GOD: *there shall be* many dead bodies in every place; they shall cast *them* forth with silence.

4 ¶Hear this, O ye that swallow up the needy, even to make the poor of the land to fail,

5 Saying, When will the new moon be gone, that we may sell corn? and the sabbath, that we may set forth wheat, making the ephah small, and the shekel great, and falsifying the balances by deceit?

6 That we may buy the poor for silver, and the needy for a pair of shoes; *yea*, and sell the refuse of the wheat?

7 The LORD hath sworn by the excellency of Jacob, Surely I will never forget any of their works.

8 Shall not the land tremble for this, and every one mourn that dwelleth therein? and it shall rise up wholly as a flood; and it shall be cast out and drowned, as *by* the flood of Egypt.

9 And it shall come to pass in that day, saith the Lord GOD, that I will cause the sun to go down at noon, and I will darken the earth in the clear day:

10 And I will turn your feasts into mourning, and all your songs into lamentation; and I will bring up sackcloth upon all loins, and baldness upon every head; and I will make it as the mourning of an only *son*, and the end thereof as a bitter day.

11 ¶Behold, the days come, saith the

of the plumb line in the preceding chapter. That vision set forth the certainty of God's judgment because of Israel's divergence from His standard. This vision shows that Israel is ripe for judgment, and it will come very soon. That this is the intent of the vision is made certain by the Lord's statement **The end is come upon my people of Israel; I will not again pass by them any more.** (vs. 2). The word **temple** (Heb *hēkal* palace, temple) is ambiguous. It can refer either to a palace or a temple, and the various English translations select the meaning the editors prefer. In his prophecy Amos refers both to temple songs (5:23) and palace songs (6:5). The exact identity of the songs is not important. The fact is that the songs will be turned into **howlings** and wailing because of the dead bodies that will be strewn about everywhere. In view of such death and devastation, the only fitting response will be mourning, or silence. **They shall cast them forth with silence.** So deep will be the grief that at this time words will utterly fail those whose responsibility it is to dispose of the bodies, and they will go about their work in silence (vs. 3).

4-6. Hear this, O ye that swallow up the needy. The thought of such devastation causes Amos to direct another warning to those who are obsessed with oppressing the poor (vss. 4-6). In the course of their oppression they are involved in religious observances, such as the **new moon** and **sabbath** (vs. 5), in which they were not permitted to buy or sell. Their hearts, however, are not involved in these religious observances. They can only think about when the service will be over so that they can engage in merchandising and oppressing the helpless and needy. They deal in a necessary commodity, i.e., grain and wheat. **Making the ephah small, and the shekel great, and falsifying the balances by deceit?** They defraud the poor by deflating the size of the measure, while at the same time inflating their prices. They also use scales that do not weigh honestly. **That we may buy the poor for silver.** Their whole goal is to enslave the poor and needy (vs. 6a). They even stoop to the depths of selling the **refuse of the wheat,** which an honest dealer would either throw away or give to the poor. So helpless are the poor that their only option is to meet the oppressors' demands or sell themselves into slavery.

7-10. Such oppression of the poor calls for another statement of God's judgment (vss. 7-10). The **excellency of Jacob** (vs. 7a) is his God. **I will never forget any of their works.** Hence, Jehovah swears by Himself that He will never forget the deeds of the oppressors of the poor (vs. 7b). **Shall not the land tremble for this.** To settle that score, Jehovah will pour out judgment against the land; and it will be so severe that the land will shake, and those in it will mourn (vs. 8a). **It shall rise up wholly as a flood.** The land will writhe under the impact of the judgment as though it were struck by an earthquake (vs. 8b). There will also be phenomena in the heavens (vs. 9). The sun will go down at noon, and the earth will be darkened at a time when normally it is broad daylight. The language is descriptive of more than a mere normal eclipse; for the prophet ultimately is looking down towards judgments that will fall upon the earth during the Great Tribulation (cf. Joel 2:2; 3:15; Mt 24:19-30). **I will turn your feasts into mourning.** The judgment will be so severe that there will be no occasion for joy (vs. 10). The festivals, normally times of great rejoicing, will be turned into mourning; and the songs, normally expressions of joy, will be turned into lamentations or dirges. **I will make it as the mourning of an only son.** So intense will be the mourning that it is compared to the mourning of parents for their only son (vs. 10). **I will bring up sackcloth upon all loins.** Sackcloth on everyone's loins and baldness on every head will be prevalent. These are signs of deepest mourning, and the whole day will be one of bitterness and sorrow.

11-14. Behold, the days come . . . that I will send a famine

Lord GOD, that I will send a famine in the land, not a famine of bread, nor a thirst for water, but of hearing the words of the LORD:

12 And they shall wander from sea to sea, and from the north even to the east, they shall run to and fro to seek the word of the LORD, and shall not find it.

13 In that day shall the fair virgins and young men faint for thirst.

14 They that swear by the sin of Sa-mâ′rī-a, and say, Thy God, O Dan, liveth; and, The manner of Be′er-shē′ba liveth; even they shall fall, and never rise up again.

CHAPTER 9

I SAW the Lord standing upon the altar: and he said, Smite the lintel of the door, that the posts may shake: and cut them in the head, all of them; and I will slay the last of them with the sword: he that fleeth of them shall not flee away, and he that escapeth of them shall not be delivered.

2 Though they dig into hell, thence shall mine hand take them; though they climb up to heaven, thence will I bring them down:

3 And though they hide themselves in the top of Carmel, I will search and take them out thence; and though they be hid from my sight in the bottom of the sea, thence will I command the serpent, and he shall bite them:

4 And though they go into captivity before their enemies, thence will I command the sword, and it shall slay them: and I will set mine eyes upon them for evil, and not for good.

5 And the Lord GOD of hosts is he that toucheth the land, and it shall melt, and all that dwell therein shall mourn: and

in the land . . . of hearing the words of the LORD. In verses 11-14 the prophet sets forth a new aspect of God's judgment not previously mentioned. A famine will accompany judgment, but it will not be a famine for food or one occasioned by drought. Rather, it will be a famine in which the Word of God will not be heard (vs. 11). From the beginning, Israel has expressed its contempt for God's Word by trying to mix the worship of Him with idolatry. When God sent His prophets, they were not welcomed (cf. 7:10-13). Now, God will grant Israel's desire. He will worry them no longer with His Word, but they will not find this dearth satisfying. **They shall run to and fro to seek the word of the LORD, and shall not find it.** The people will stagger like drunken men wandering in every direction, covering the land in search of the Word of the Lord; but it will not be found (vs. 12). Even the most promising (**the fair virgins**) and sturdy (**young men**) will not be successful in their quest for the Word of the Lord (vs. 13). Verse 14 gives the reason for the famine; it is because Israel is completely given to its idolatry and has no place for the only true God. Therefore, **they shall fall, and never rise up again** (vs. 14).

E. The Vision of the Lord Standing by the Altar. 9:1-10.

9:1. I saw the Lord standing upon the altar. The final vision of the prophecy portrays the destruction of the idolatrous temple at Beth-el. It is this temple that has given cohesiveness and direction to Israel in its idolatrous defection from Jehovah. Now that temple faces a showdown with Jehovah, before whom it cannot stand, demonstrating once and for all the inferiority of its idol worship to the worship of the true God. **Smite the lintel of the door, that the posts may shake.** The Lord Himself presides at the execution of judgment and directs that the blow be delivered to the top of the sanctuary. The blow is so powerful that it causes the temple to reel from top to bottom and tumble upon the heads of those gathered for an idolatrous festival. Those that are not killed in the building's collapse are slain by the sword (vs. 3). The temple and all worshiping in it are utterly destroyed. The scene is reminiscent of Samson's destruction of the temple of Dagon (cf. Jud 16:23-30).

2-4. Verses 2 to 4 amplify the impossibility of escape from God's judgment. **Though they dig into hell . . . though they climb up to heaven.** Though the idolaters might dig into hell (Heb *she'ōl*), or ascend into heaven (whether atmospheric or the abode of God is immaterial at this point), or take refuge on Mount Carmel (noted for its rough terrain, dense forests, and large caverns which offered protection for many refugees), or take refuge in the bottom of the sea, the omniscient, omnipresent God will exact judgment of them (vss. 2-3a). The reference to the **serpent** (Heb *nachash*, vs. 3b) is best understood as a sea serpent, whose venom is equal to that of any land serpent's. The prophecy of Jonah leaves ample testimony of God's ability to speak to His sea creatures for the preservation of life, and Amos' prophecy gives testimony to God's ability to speak to His sea creatures for the execution of judgment! In either case, it is beyond man's ability to escape God! Such knowledge should comfort the heart of the believer and strike fear into the heart of the unbeliever. This knowledge should comfort the hearts of the spiritual and strike terror into the hearts of the sinners. Even submission does not offer an escape from God's judgment (vs. 4). Even if Israel were to go into captivity voluntarily, they will be put to death. Such a penalty is exacted because **I will set mine eyes upon them for evil, and not for good** (vs. 4b). The long-suffering of God is over; only inescapable and complete judgment lies ahead.

5-6. Verses 5 and 6 remind Israel of God's omnipotence. He sovereignly presides over all of creation, which readily obeys His every direction. In all of God's universe, only man seems beyond

it shall rise up wholly like a flood; and shall be drowned, as *by* the flood of Egypt.

6 *It is* he that buildeth his stories in the heaven, and hath founded his troop in the earth; he that calleth for the waters of the sea, and poureth them out upon the face of the earth: The LORD *is* his name.

7 *Are* ye not as children of the Ē-thǐ-ō′pǐ-ans unto me, O children of Israel? saith the LORD. Have not I brought up Israel out of the land of Egypt? and the Philistines from Cǎph′tôr, and the Syrians from Kir?

8 Behold, the eyes of the Lord GOD *are* upon the sinful kingdom, and I will destroy it from off the face of the earth; saving that I will not utterly destroy the house of Jacob, saith the LORD.

9 For, lo, I will command, and I will sift the house of Israel among all nations, like as *corn* is sifted in a sieve, yet shall not the least grain fall upon the earth.

10 All the sinners of my people shall die by the sword, which say, The evil shall not overtake nor prevent us.

11 ¶In that day will I raise up the tabernacle of David that is fallen, and close up the breaches thereof; and I will raise up his ruins, and I will build it as in the days of old:

12 That they may possess the remnant of Edom, and of all the heathen, which are called by my name, saith the LORD that doeth this.

13 Behold, the days come, saith the LORD, that the plowman shall overtake the reaper, and the treader of grapes him that soweth seed; and the mountains shall drop sweet wine, and all the hills shall melt.

14 And I will bring again the captivity of my people of Israel, and they shall build the waste cities, and inhabit *them;* and they shall plant vineyards, and drink the wine thereof; they shall also make gardens, and eat the fruit of them.

15 And I will plant them upon their land, and they shall no more be pulled up out of their land which I have given them, saith the LORD thy God.

His control. Man, however, is re... cause he has been helplessly victm... of his finiteness because such as floods which are only fir... the forces of creation frustrated by God's fingerplay, can h... to God. If man is Himself? The answer is a resounding... stand against God God's natural forces, nor can he esc... n cannot escape

7. Are ye not as children of the E-... idolatrous practice the privileged Isr... pagans who surrounded them; hence, ... Ethiopians (vs. 7a). **Have not I brou...** reminds them that He is sovereign in H... for it was He who brought them up from ... Philistines from Caphtor (probably Cret... mainland, and who transplanted the Syr... current location in the area of Damascus...

8-10. Behold, the eyes of the Lord Go... kingdom. Certainly, a God who actively ... man will have His eye on the sinful kingd... have His way in it, too. He certainly wil... **utterly destroy the house of Jacob.** Into t... prophet now injects a ray of hope. Thoug... inevitable and inescapable, there will be a re... **will sift the house of Israel . . . yet shall not the ... upon the earth.** Even in judgment God will not lose ... individual (vs. 9). **All the sinners of my people shall ... sword.** No sinner will escape, and no righteous one ... judged. The thought is similar to that expressed by Peter (1... 2:9). Those who mistakenly think that they can escape will ... overtaken by God's judgment (vs. 10).

V. THE CONCLUSION OF THE PROPHECY: THE RESTORATION OF THE DAVIDIC KINGDOM. 9:11-15.

11-12. In that day will I raise up the tabernacle of David that is fallen. Even though Israel has sunk to an all-time low and judgment must fall, still God's plan for the house of David and His promises to Abraham have not failed and will be ultimately realized. God will repair the damage done to the **tabernacle** (Heb *sukah*, hut or booth) **of David.** The choice of this term, in contrast to the more common *house* (Heb *bayit*, house or household) of David, is indicative of the depths to which the Davidic monarchy has sunk. Though it is damaged, it is not destroyed. Though it is marred, it is not beyond God's ability to repair. **I will build it as in the days of old.** He will make it as good as new (vs. 11c). The house of David will be restored to the place of prominence and glory that it enjoyed in the days of David and Solomon. It will possess **Edom,** used representatively of all the nations of the earth, and **all the heathen** (lit., nations), **which are called by my name** (vs. 12).

13-15. The national restoration of Israel will be accompanied by unparalleled activity and abundance (vss. 13-14). At this time Israel will be permanently installed in its God-given land (vs. 15). The things promised in this remarkable restoration prophecy can be summarized as follows: (1) the Davidic dynasty will be restored, verse 11; (2) Israel will be supreme over the nations, verse 12a; (3) the nations will be converted, verse 12b; (4) the land will experience unparalleled productivity, verse 13; (5) its devastated cities will be rebuilt, verse 14; and (6) Israel will be permanently established in its own land and will never go into captivity again, verse 15.

(see page 1864 for Bibliography to the Minor Prophets)

OBADIAH

INTRODUCTION

...ing is known about Obadiah, ...nich means "servant," or "wor-..." He evidently preferred to be ...is prophetic role, rather than as an ...he chose to relate no details of his ...e' history. Twelve other men in the ...t are known by this name.

...lace of Writing. If the authorship of ...re certain, so would the date be. Esti-...by as much as six centuries. As a general ...without exception) conservatives (such as ...d Unger) tend to date the prophecy early; ...cs tend to date it late, though some con-...es (such as Feinberg) also hold for a late ...but not for the same reasons as the critics. ...s tend to date the prophecy during the Chal-...l period after the fall of Jerusalem to the Chal-...ns in 586 B.C. and also attempt to deny the ...ophecy's integrity and unity. If the prophecy is ...ated early, the events of the Philistine and Ara-bian invasion during Jehoram's reign constitute the background of the prophecy. If the prophecy is dated late, the events of the Chaldean invasion under Nebuchadnezzar (586 B.C.) constitute the background of the prophecy. While the adoption of either position is not without its problems, it seems best to hold to the prophecy's integrity and unity and, thus, to an early date while realizing that the events described are also applicable to the events of 586 B.C., perhaps as a second fulfillment of the prophecy. The prophecy is elastic enough in its fulfillment to embrace all of the times of Edom's destruction, whether by the Chaldeans who laid Edom waste (Jer 49:7ff.; Ezk 35), the Maccabees, Rome (A.D. 70), or ultimately when Christ ex-ecutes the judgment of God upon Edom and her allies (Isa 63:1-6). Unger (p. 343) suggests five evi-dences supporting the early date: (1) the historical context of 848-841 B.C. fits the demands of the prophecy. During Jehoram's reign, the Philistines and Arabians overran Judah and plundered Jeru-salem (cf. II Chr 21:16-17; Joel 3:3-6; Amos 1:6); (2) at this time Edom was a bitter enemy of Judah (cf. II Kgs 8:20-22; II Chr 21:8-20); (3) Amos, who lived later (ca. 760 B.C.), shows literary ac-quaintance and parallels with Obadiah (cf. Ob 1:4 with Amos 9:2; Ob 1:9, 10, 18 with Amos 1:11, 12; Ob 1:14 with Amos 1:6, 9; Ob 1:19 with Amos 9:12; Ob 1:20 with Amos 9:14); (4) Jeremiah (626-586 B.C.) shows literary parallels with Obadiah (cf. Ob 1:1-6 with Jer 49:7-22); and (5) Obadiah's placement in the canon following Amos suggests a pre-exilic origin. The place in which the prophecy was written is not known.

Characteristics of the prophecy. The character of the prophecy is both dark and light. For Edom, the prophecy is dark doom; for he will be utterly de-stroyed (1:5-16), though at the time of the proph-ecy's delivery they were proud and secure (1:3). For Judah/Jacob, the prophecy is light; for though things are bad for them at the time of the proph-ecy's delivery (1:10-14), a remnant will be left from them which will become a consuming fire and de-vour Edom and his allies (1:15-18). Ultimately, the kingdom will be Jehovah's (1:21). The prophecy is written in Hebrew poetry, and the interpreter needs to be mindful of Hebrew parallelism in his interpretation. The structure of the Hebrew paral-lelism portrays the intense emotion with which the prophecy was delivered.

Purpose. The purpose of prophecy is to pro-nounce God's judgment upon Edom/Esau (1:1) be-cause of his actions toward his brother Judah/Jacob (1:10ff.).

Theme. The doom of Edom.

OUTLINE

1. As relates to Edom. 15.
2. As relates to the nations. 16.
3. As relates to Judah. 17-18.

B. The Establishment of Righteousness. 19-21.
   1. The immediate realization. 19-20.
   2. The ultimate realization. 21.

COMMENTARY

I. THE INTRODUCTION TO THE PROPHECY OF EDOM'S DESTRUCTION. 1.

A. The Title of the Prophecy. 1a.

THE vision of Ō-ba-dī'ah. Thus saith the Lord GOD concerning Edom; We have heard a rumour from the LORD, and an ambassador is sent among the heathen, Arise ye, and let us rise up against her in battle.

1a. The vision of Obadiah. Obadiah's prophecy is simply called the vision of Obadiah. The title in no way suggests that the prophecy is the product of his own imagination; rather, it indicates that a **vision** (Heb *chazōn*) was presented to his mind's eye, one which he subsequently communicated to Edom and encoded for posterity by using the medium of Hebrew poetry to paint his thoughts. The prophet gives only his name, **Obadiah** (servant, or worshiper of Jehovah). He gives no other details of his personal history, apparently desiring to be known in his prophetical rather than his individual role.

B. The Authentication of the Prophecy. 1b.

1b. Thus saith the Lord. The prophet is only the intermediary agent. The prophecy comes directly from the Lord God (Heb *'Adōnay Yahweh*, lit., Lord Yahweh/Jehovah). The Jews so revered the name of God that they would not pronounce it. When they came to the sacred name of God, *Yahweh* (the Hebrew originally was written without vowels, hence the name *Yahweh* appeared in the Hebrew text simply with the four consonants *YHWH* and these four consonants were called the sacred tetragrammaton), they substituted another name of God, usually Lord (Heb *'Adōnay*). In cases such as this where *'Adōnay* already occurs in the text preceding the sacred name of God, *YHWH*, they would read *Adonai* as it occurs in the text but would substitute another name for God in the place of Yahweh (Heb *YHWH*), in this case Elohim (Heb *'Elōhīm*). Most of the English translations have followed the Hebrew custom in this matter. The follower of the English text can always tell where the sacred name of God (Heb *Yahweh*) occurs in the text by which the English name for God is entirely capitalized. The authentication of Obadiah's prophecy, then, comes from the fact that he has received it from the Lord Jehovah.

C. The Focus of the Prophecy. 1c.

1c. Concerning Edom. The prophecy is for this nation comprised of the descendants of Esau, Jacob's twin brother. The enmity between Jacob and Esau began in Genesis 27 and continued throughout the centuries. Edom was proud of its heritage and location (cf. vs. 3) and violated the bond between him and Judah (cf. vss. 10-14). The violation aroused God's displeasure, and He used Obadiah to deliver this message of doom to Edom.

D. The Summarization of the Prophecy. 1d.

1d. We have heard a rumor from the LORD. By the use of the first person plural, **We**, the prophet includes the people of Judah along with himself as having heard a **rumor** (Heb *she-mū'ah*) from the **LORD** (*Yahweh*). It is not a rumor in the English sense of that word but rather is a factual report having Jehovah as its source.

E. The Herald of the Prophecy. 1e-1g.

1e-1g. An ambassador is sent among the heathen. The report that has been heard from the Lord is to the effect that an ambassador (Heb *tsîr*, lit., envoy or messenger) has been sent among the **heathen** (Heb *gōyim*, lit., nations) for the purpose of stirring them up to come against Edom in battle.

II. THE DECLARATION OF THE PROPHECY OF EDOM'S DESTRUCTION. 2-9.

A. The Summary Declaration. 2.

1. Concerning Edom's future ruination. 2a.

2a. Behold, I have made thee small among the heathen. Though at the time of the prophecy's delivery Edom's reduction to insignificance is yet in the future, it is as certain as though it were already an accomplished fact; thus, the prophet uses the past tense, **I have made thee small among the heathen** (Heb *gōyim*, lit., nations).

2. Concerning Edom's present evaluation. 2b.

2b. Thou art greatly despised. Edom is **greatly despised** (Heb *bazah*, lit., raise the head loftily and disdainfully). Though Edom loftily lifts his head in pride against God and against the surrounding nations (cf. vs. 3), the fact is that God and the nations loftily lift their heads in disdain against Edom. Both Edom and God lift their heads against each other; Edom in pride, God in great disgust.

B. The Detailed Indictment. 3-9.

1. Against their pride. 3.

3. The pride of thine heart hath deceived thee. Edom's pride, which had the detrimental effect of deceiving them, stems from two sources: (1) the security of their location, verse 3b and (2) the inaccessibility of their location, verse 3c. Edom, whose capital city was Petra, was noted for his rock dwellings that were carved in the precipitous craigs and seemed impregnable. He literally dwelt **in the clefts of the rock.** The altitude of his dwellings gave him further self-confidence and caused him to express his pride in the vain boast, **Who shall bring me down to the ground?** Edom thought that the answer to his question was: No one! His self-exaltation leads to God's determination to bring him down (cf. vs. 4).

2. Against their location. 4.

4. God's determination to bring Edom down is prefaced by his twofold concession concerning their construction: **Though thou exalt thyself as the eagle,** and their location, **though thou set thy nest among the stars.** These figures of speech emphasize the inaccessibility and natural security of their city, which was set on the loftiest hills that seemed to reach the stars. Their natural security, however, is no match for God's determination, emphasized by three things: (1) word order, thence, (Heb *mis-ham*, lit., *even from there*, i.e., from such a remote and secure geographical setting); (2) by the use of the first person singular. **Will I** (Jehovah) **bring thee down** (Heb *hiphil* stem of *yarad*, lit., I will cause you to be brought down); and (3) the solemn declaration, **saith the Lord** (*Yahweh*). The verb **saith** is used to translate the Hebrew noun *ne'um*, which is closely bound to the name Yahweh. The resulting construction *ne'um Yahweh* indicates that the prophet is citing a divine word that has been given by Jehovah through him to Edom.

3. Against their possessions. 5-6.

5-6. If thieves came to thee, if robbers by night, . . . would they not have stolen till they had enough? The indictment against Edom's possessions is delivered by comparisons to thieves and robbers, to grape gatherers (vs. 5), and by declara-

2 ¶Behold, I have made thee small among the heathen: thou art greatly despised.

3 The pride of thine heart hath deceived thee, thou that dwellest in the clefts of the rock, whose habitation *is* high; that saith in his heart, Who shall bring me down to the ground?

4 Though thou exalt *thyself* as the eagle, and though thou set thy nest among the stars, thence will I bring thee down, saith the Lord.

5 If thieves came to thee, if robbers by night, (how art thou cut off!) would they not have stolen till they had enough? if the grapegatherers came to

thee, would they not leave *some* grapes?

6 ¶How are *the things* of Esau searched out! *how* are his hidden things sought up!

7 All the men of thy confederacy have brought thee *even* to the border: the men that were at peace with thee have deceived thee, *and* prevailed against thee; *they that eat* thy bread have laid a wound under thee: *there is* none understanding in him.

8 Shall I not in that day, saith the LORD, even destroy the wise *men* out of Edom, and understanding out of the mount of Esau?

9 And thy mighty *men*, O Tĕ′man, shall be dismayed, to the end that every one of the mount of Esau may be cut off by slaughter.

10 For *thy* violence against thy brother Jacob shame shall cover thee, and thou shalt be cut off for ever.

---

tion (vs. 6). Though devastation at the hands of thieves and robbers would be bad, still they would only plunder until they were satiated, whereas God will completely devastate them. The exclamation, **how art thou cut off!**, injected into the imagery, strongly portrays the prophet's emotion. If the grape gatherers came to thee, would they not leave some grapes? If Edom's devastation were to come at the hand of grape gatherers, that would be bad; but they would leave something behind for the gleaners. In contrast, God will leave nothing behind for looters and souvenir hunters. The import of these figures of speech is to show the extent of the devastation that Edom will experience. From the declaration of verse 6, the prophet describes the effect and the extent of Edom's devastation. The expression **How are the things of Esau searched out!** indicates that Edom will be ransacked by hostile soldiers seeking booty. **How are his hidden things sought up!** Even his most inaccessible and secure treasures will be discovered. The search will be relentless, and nothing of value will be left behind. Edom abounded in many hiding places, such as caves and clefts in the rocks; but none of them will be effective or secure.

4. Against their perpetuation. 7-9.

7-9. The agents involved in Edom's destruction are humans (vs. 7) who have been motivated and are performing their destruction under divine control (vss. 8-9). The human agents fall under three categories: (1) allies, **All the men of thy confederacy;** (2) friends, **the men that were at peace with thee;** and (3) the surrounding desert tribes, **they that eat thy bread.** Even though they have a covenant **confederacy** (*berith*, covenant) Edom's allies will turn against him. His friends, **the men that were at peace with thee,** will deceive him, overpower him, and overthrow him. The desert tribes (**they that eat thy bread**) will ambush him. The word **wound** translates the Hebrew word *mazōr* which is better understood as an ambush. None of the wisdom for which Esau was famed will be able to extricate him from his perilous position. He will be dumbfounded and unable to comprehend these events. The result will be that **there is none understanding in him.** These agents who have acted so treacherously against Edom have been motivated by a greater destructive agent, Jehovah, verses, 8-9. The prophet delivers another solemn statement (Heb *ne'um Yahweh*) which he has received from Jehovah. Edom had been known for his wise men, but they will be destroyed. Edom had been vaunted for his understanding, but at a time when he needed it most his understanding forsook him. The expression of Jehovah's destruction of the wise men and understanding from Edom is presented in a rhetorical question which emphasizes its certainty. The answer to the question is that He certainly will do it! The effect of Jehovah's destruction is set forth in verse 9. It is twofold: (1) The mighty will be **dismayed** (Heb *chatat*, lit., to shatter, to terrify, dismay) and (2) there will be a total annihilation of Edom by a vicious slaughter. Contrary to all the boasting, Edom will be totally helpless at the hand of Jehovah.

III. THE JUSTIFICATION FOR THE PROPHECY OF EDOM'S DESTRUCTION. 10-14.

A. The Summary Statement. 10.

1. The cause of Edom's destruction. 10a.

10a. For thy violence against thy brother Jacob. Edom's destruction because of the violence he did to his brother Jacob is predicted. The sin he committed is aggravated because it was against not only one who was his brother by birth and circumcision; but worse, it was against his twin brother. Edom treated Jacob exactly opposite from the way that Jacob was commanded to treat Edom in Deuteronomy 23:7. The reason Jacob was to treat Edom with kindness was that he was his brother.

2. The effects of Edom's destruction. 10b-10c.

10b-10c. The effects of Edom's destruction are described in two ways: immediately, **shame shall cover thee,** and ultimately, **thou shalt be cut off for ever.** The prophecy is that Edom as a nation will be cut off forever, though the land will be inhabited again following Edom's demise (cf. vss. 19-20).

B. The Indictment. 11.

1. The circumstances of the offense. 11a-11d.

11 In the day that thou stoodest on the other side, in the day that the strangers carried away captive his forces, and foreigners entered into his gates, and cast lots upon Jerusalem, even thou wast as one of them.

11a-11d. Two temporal clauses introduced by **In the day** (Heb beyōm) set forth the circumstances of Edom's offense. It was **In the day** when he failed to come to his brother's aid. **Thou stoodest on the other side.** The thought is that at this time Edom stood in an attitude of hostility or aloofness from Jacob's trouble, rather than exhibiting the sympathy he should have manifested as a brother. And **in the day** that strangers carried off Jacob's wealth and foreigners entered Jacob's gate and **cast lots** for the city of Jerusalem. The phrase, **carried away captive his forces** (Heb chayil), is better understood as Judah's substance or wealth being carried off, rather than his military forces being taken captive. A number of Judah's traditional enemies could adequately fulfill this prophecy. Among them are the Philistines and Arabians during the reign of Jehoram, King of Judah (cf. II Chr 21:16); the Syrians in the reign of Joash, King of Judah (cf. II Chr 24:24); and the Chaldeans under Nebuchadnezzar (cf. II Chr 36).

2. The Nature of the Offense. 11e.

11e. Even thou wast as one of them. In reality, Edom was not one of the enemies of Israel, that is, alien to Jacob or Israel. In fact, he was his twin brother! With this graphic expression the prophet magnifies the enormity of Edom's offense as one of the plunderers of Jerusalem and exclaims at this unnatural happening that the genealogical bond between Edom and Judah meant no difference to Edom, for he was **as one of them**—the aliens who plundered Judah.

C. The Admonitions. 12-14.

12 But thou shouldest not have looked on the day of thy brother in the day that he became a stranger; neither shouldest thou have rejoiced over the children of Judah in the day of their destruction; neither shouldest thou have spoken proudly in the day of distress.
13 Thou shouldest not have entered into the gate of my people in the day of their calamity; yea, thou shouldest not have looked on their affliction in the day of their calamity, nor have laid hands on their substance in the day of their calamity;
14 Neither shouldest thou have stood in the crossway, to cut off those of his that did escape; neither shouldest thou have delivered up those of his that did remain in the day of distress.

12-14. Eight admonitions are delivered to Edom in these verses. In the day of Judah's calamity, he is not to: (1) gloat over the brother's day of misfortune (vs. 12); (2) rejoice over his brother's day of destruction (vs. 12); (3) boast over his brother's day of distress (vs. 12); (4) enter the brother's gate in the day of his disaster (vs. 13); (5) gloat over his brother's calamity (vs. 13); (6) loot his brother's wealth (vs. 13); (7) harass the fugitives from Judah (vs. 14); or (8) imprison the survivors from Judah (vs. 14). The recurrent phrase **in the day,** with different descriptions, magnifies the scope of the tragedy from Judah's viewpoint and compounds the scope of the offense against Edom. **Neither shouldest thou have stood in the crossway, to cut off those of his that did escape.** Edom not only passively stood by and took pleasure in Judah's destruction, he also actively participated in hindering and imprisoning those survivors who managed to escape to their twin brother's domain for refuge. There is a progression in Edom's offense from malicious looks to malicious words to malicious deeds, deeds such as one would think totally wrong for one twin brother to do against another.

IV. THE REALIZATION OF THE PROPHECY OF EDOM'S DESTRUCTION. 15-21.

A. The Execution of Justice. 15-18.

1. As relates to Edom. 15.

15 For the day of the LORD *is* near upon all the heathen: as thou hast done, it shall be done unto thee: thy reward shall return upon thine own head.

15. We are introduced first of all to the summary statement (vs. 15a), **For the day of the LORD is near upon all the heathen.** The **For** is resumptive of the thought begun in verse 10 in which Edom was threatened with being cut off forever. In this context, **the day of the LORD** refers to the day in which Jehovah will manifest himself as the righteous punisher of all ungodly people (cf. Joel 3:14). The measure of justice will be in keeping with what Edom had done; and its harvest will be the return of his own deeds unto him with one devastating difference: Judah's wound was only temporary, for she shall recover and consume Edom (cf. vss. 17-19). Edom's wound will be permanent, and he shall never recover (vss. 10,18).

2. As relates to the nations. 16.

16 For as ye have drunk upon my holy mountain, *so* shall all the heathen drink continually, yea, they shall drink, and they shall swallow down, and they shall be as though they had not been.

16. For as ye have drunk . . . so shall all the heathen drink. The drinking referred to in this verse is the metaphorical drinking of the cup of God's wrath. Just as the heathen, with Edom's approval, caused Judah to drink of that cup and dispossessed them of their goods and national place, so shall all the heathen (Edom included) drink of the cup of God's wrath and pass out of existence (cf. Ps 60:3; Isa 51:17, 22; Jer 13:12-13; 25:15-33; 49:12; 51:7; Lam 4:21-22; Nah 3:11; Hab 2:16). A couple of other statements are worthy of special notice. The heathen will **drink continually,** differentiating between them and Judah. For as Judah's calamity will be only temporary (cf. vs. 17), Judah's foes will never regain their former position. The expression **swallow down** indicates that they will not merely **drink,** but will swallow the contents of the cup of God's wrath so as to leave nothing in it. In this, and in the preceding verse, we have put into practice the righteous principle of retribution in kind (cf. Lev 24:17; Jud 1:6, 7; 8:19; Est 7:10; Mt 7:2).

3. As relates to Judah. 17-18.

17 ¶But upon mount Zion shall be deliverance, and there shall be holiness; and the house of Jacob shall possess their possessions.
18 And the house of Jacob shall be a fire, and the house of Joseph a flame, and the house of Esau for stubble, and they shall kindle in them, and devour them; and there shall not be *any* remaining of the house of Esau; for the LORD hath spoken *it*.

17-18. But upon mount Zion shall be deliverance. Verse 17 indicates the fact that there will be a remnant from Judah. The word **deliverance** (Heb *pelētah*) is better understood as "an escaped one" or "a fugitive," hence "a remnant." In contrast to the mountains of Edom from which no one will escape, there will be survivors of the carnage of Mount Zion. The character of that remnant is holy (**holiness,** Heb *qōdesh* equals separation of person, or thing). This remnant will be set apart from Edom's purpose—destruction to Jehovah's purpose—restoration and exaltation over Edom and all enemies. The destiny of this remnant is to **possess their possessions.** All the intent of Edom and the heathen nations to strip Judah of its identity and possessions will ultimately fail. A remnant of Judah will escape when the rest of the nation has perished and **shall possess** or regain their ancient possessions (lit., shall inherit their inheritances), **And the house of Jacob shall be a fire . . . and devour them.** The future of this remnant is given in two dimensions in verse 18: (1) As relates to Judah, both Judah (Jacob) and Joseph (Ephraim) will put away their former feuds (cf. Isa 11:12-13; Jer 3:18; Ezk 37:16, 17, 19, 22; Hos 1:11) and will form one kingdom to execute God's judgment against Esau (Edom). Their power and effectiveness are set forth in the most feared figure of the day, **fire.** (2) As relates to Edom (Esau), Edom will be completely helpless against Judah. Judah will be a fire, and Edom will be stubble and will be completely consumed by Judah. **For the LORD hath spoken it.** Though this event is future with relation to the time that the prophet uttered it, it is absolutely certain because of the source from whom it comes, Jehovah. Judah can rejoice; Edom should take notice and repent.

B. The Establishment of Righteousness. 19-21.

1. The immediate realization. 19-20.

19 And *they of* the south shall possess the mount of Esau; and *they of* the plain the Philistines: and they shall possess the fields of E′phra-im, and the fields of Sa-mā′rī-a: and Benjamin *shall possess* Gilead.
20 And the captivity of this host of the children of Israel *shall possess* that of the Canaanites, *even* unto Zăr′e-phăth; and the captivity of Jerusalem, which *is* in Sĕph′a-răd, shall possess the cities of the south.

19-20. And they of the south shall possess the mount of Esau. To the Oriental mind, one of the worst things that could happen would be for land to remain uninhabited. With the destruction of Edom as a nation, others will come to inhabit the territory from which they have been dispossessed. The people of the **south** (Heb *negeb*) are the Jews who, in a time future to the prophets, will occupy the regions south of Judaea. In addition to their own territory, they will possess the adjoining mountainous regions of Edom. The people of the **plain** (Heb *shepēlah*, lit., hill country) are the Jews who in a time future to the prophet will occupy the low country along the Mediterranean Sea to the south and southwest of Israel. In addition to their territory, they will possess the land of the Philistines, which runs as a long strip between the hills and the sea. They will also possess the territory of Ephraim and the territory of Samaria. The tribe of **Benjamin** will possess the land of **Gilead**, which is the region east of the Jordan River formerly occupied by the tribes of Reuben, Gad, and the half tribe of Manasseh. In addition to his own territory, Benjamin will possess the adjoining territories eastward; and the two and one-half tribes shall occupy the adjoining territories of Moab and Ammon. The whole prophetic picture is one which necessitates the literal restoration of the ten tribes of Israel as well as the two tribes of Benjamin and Judah as foretold by the prophets. In God's economy none of the twelve original tribes of Israel will be lost. Each will be fully restored and will realize its place in God's prophetic program. The **captivity of this host** and **the captivity of Jerusalem** refer to scattered refugees who are among the Canaanites and the area of Jerusalem. These will possess the vacated cities of the south (Heb *negeb*). **Zarephath** was near Sidon and on the seacoast. It is called Sarapta in Luke 4:26 and was a place noted for smelting metals. The ". . . woman of Canaan . . ." (Mt 15:21-22) came from this area. The exact identity and location of the **Sepharad** is disputed and the subject of much conjecture. It is better understood to be a district of Lydia, thus representing the Jews' dispersion far and wide. The picture portrayed by the prophet is one of complete restoration, regardless of the extent to which one has been dispersed geographically. Not one person of the twelve tribes of Judah will miss out on God's plans for restoration and exaltation.

2. The ultimate realization. 21.

21 And saviours shall come up on mount Zion to judge the mount of Esau; and the kingdom shall be the LORD'S.

21. And saviors shall come up on mount Zion. From time to time in history God has raised up saviours, judges, and deliverers to deliver Israel from its enemies. The peace experienced under these leaders was an example, taste, of the long period of peace they would experience when Israel's Messiah reigned in person. The scope of this verse is unique. It embraces the near view, with the return of **saviors** and judges to dispense justice to the God-fearing remnant who have taken over the place vacated by the destruction of their enemies its focus. Under their administration the land would have peace. The last phrase, **and the kingdom shall be the LORD'S,** is the ultimate fulfillment of Israel's literal, earthly, Davidic kingdom under Messiah's reign (cf. Dan 2:44; 7:14, 27; Zech 14:9; Lk 1:33; Rev 11:15; 19:6). In this last phrase Obadiah is apparently quoting Psalm 22:28.

(see page 1864 for Bibliography to the Minor Prophets)

JONAH

INTRODUCTION

Authorship. Nothing is known of Jonah, except that which is learned about him through this book and through a brief historical statement made about him in II Kings 14:25. His name means "dove" and the name of his father means "truthful." Jonah came from the tribe of Zebulon, one of the twelve tribes in the northern kingdom of Israel; and he was from the village of Gath-hepher, located about two miles northeast of the city of Nazareth.

Date and Place of Writing. It is clear that Jonah prophesied at a very early date. Second Kings 14:25 indicates that Jonah gave a prophecy that was fulfilled during the reign of Jeroboam II who reigned from 824 to 783 B.C. The prophecy was given at a time when Assyria was becoming a great world power and an eminent threat to Israel. The prophecy, then, can be assigned a date in the period ranging from 825 to 782 B.C. It is likely that Jonah began his prophetic ministry at approximately the time Elisha was closing his.

There is no indication given as to where the prophecy originated. It is written in the third person and gives the record of an earlier oral ministry to Assyria. It is possible, then, that Jonah wrote the words of this prophecy from his home village of Gath-hepher after returning from the ministry to Assyria as he reflected upon the ministry's success and his own personal failure.

Characteristics of the Prophecy. Jonah is unique in that the entire prophecy is written in the third person. The fact that the prophecy ends with the prophet in discouragement and under God's reproof would leave the reader discouraged, but the fact that it is written in the third person lets the reader know that the prophet wrote it after he had returned from his mission to Assyria and had favorably responded to God's rebuke. He leaves behind the record of God's dealings with him as an individual and with Assyria as a nation, and in this unique form he magnifies the power of God and obscures himself behind his message.

What the book of Acts is to the New Testament, the prophecy of Jonah is to the Old Testament. It shows that God has always had concern for the heathen who are without hope apart from Him. It also shows God's concern for His people Israel. As a result of Jonah's ministry to Assyria, the Assyrian captivity of Israel was postponed some 130 years. While the prophecy makes no specific mention of Israel, it abounds in its clear testimony to the supernatural working of God in behalf of the prophet, whose life he preserved and whose desires he modified; the heathen Assyrians, whom he brought to national repentance; and the nation Israel, whose security he guaranteed and whose captivity he delayed for an additional 130 years.

Purpose. The purpose of the prophecy of Jonah is to show the sovereignty of God at work in the life of an individual (the prophet, Jonah) and His concern for a heathen nation. The book also shows, in oblique fashion, God's care and preservation of His own people, and that the way to avert national catastrophe is a concentrated missionary effort towards one's enemies.

Theme. The theme of the book of Jonah is: God's mercy to the individual (Jonah, a Jew), a group (the heathen sailors, Gentiles), and the heathen world power, Assyria (a gentile nation).

OUTLINE

COMMENTARY

I. JONAH IN DISOBEDIENCE: FROM THE PRESENCE OF THE LORD TO THE BELLY OF THE GREAT FISH. 1:1-17.

A. Jonah in the Presence of God. 1:1-3.

NOW the word of the LORD came unto Jonah the son of A-mǐt′ta-ī, saying,

2 Arise, go to Nǐn′e-veh, that great city, and cry against it; for their wickedness is come up before me.

3 But Jonah rose up to flee unto Tarshish from the presence of the LORD, and went down to Joppa; and he found a ship going to Tarshish: so he paid the fare thereof, and went down into it, to go with them unto Tarshish from the presence of the LORD.

1:1-3. In this section we are introduced to the prophecy, the prophet, and the problem. The prophecy is characterized as being **the word of the LORD** (Heb *debar-Yahweh*). The prophecy is characterized as a word that comes from Jehovah God; thus, the source and authority of the message are Jehovah's, which makes it important. The prophet is introduced simply as **Jonah** (dove) **the son of Amittai** (truth). In view of the importance of the prophecy, the identity of the prophet is of little consequence. Hence, nothing further is known or told of Jonah, other than the historical statement alluded to earlier (see Introduction on Jonah).

Arise, go to Nineveh . . . But Jonah rose up to flee unto Tarshish. The problem is that Jehovah has given a specific command but the prophet chose not only to ignore the commission, but to do the exact opposite. The prophet's action is understandable from a human point of view. Nineveh, first mentioned in Genesis 10:11, was the ancient capital of the Assyrian Empire and was located on the eastern bank of the Tigris River. It was the largest city in the world in that day and was a formidable threat to the existence of Israel. The prophet would have loved to go to Nineveh and declare God's judgment, but not God's grace (cf. 4:1-2). Jonah's situation is unique in two respects: (1) It is the only instance of a prophet's being sent to a heathen nation; and (2) it is the only instance in which a prophet refuses to carry out his commission. Nineveh was east of Palestine, while **Tarshish** was at the extreme western end of the then-known world. Herodotus, the Greek historian, identifies Tarshish as Tartessus in southern Spain. Later scholars have identified it as being a Phoenician smelting center, either in Spain or in Sardinia; for the name is found in both locations. There is no evidence, however, to support the view that Tarshish was what we know today as England. **Joppa** is the city of Jaffa, the Mediterranean city used today as a seaport by Israel. The phrase **from the presence of the LORD** does not indicate that Jonah thought he could escape the omnipresence of God. Rather the phrase is used to indicate the land of Israel where the Lord dwelt in His Temple. This section shows for all time that the wickedness of heathen nations does not escape the notice of God. It further shows that God is concerned about the wickedness of heathen nations, even though His own prophet is calloused against them. It further introduces the extremes to which God will go in order to get His message to those nations for the accomplishment of His purpose.

B. Jonah in the Hold of the Ship. 1:4-9.

4 ¶But the LORD sent out a great wind into the sea, and there was a mighty tempest in the sea, so that the ship was like to be broken.

5 Then the mariners were afraid, and cried every man unto his god, and cast forth the wares that *were* in the ship into the sea, to lighten *it* of them. But Jonah was gone down into the sides of the ship; and he lay, and was fast asleep.

6 So the shipmaster came to him, and said unto him, What meanest thou, O sleeper? arise, call upon thy God, if so

4-9. This section shows that when God's prophet is out of fellowship with his God, it causes problems not only for himself, but also for those around him, in this case the heathen sailors. Though God's human servant may be in disobedience to Him, God's servant in nature always obeys God's command. The servant that God calls upon in this instance is the wind. God **sent out a great wind** (Heb *tūl*, lit., hurled). The wind struck the sea with such force that it caused a great storm so fierce that the ship was endangered with breaking up (vs. 4). **Then the mariners were afraid, and cried every man unto his god, and cast forth the wares.** The sailors (vs. 5), who were familiar with storms on the Mediterranean Sea, knew that this was no ordinary storm; for they were seized with fear. They attempted to meet

be that God will think upon us, that we perish not.

7 And they said every one to his fellow, Come, and let us cast lots, that we may know for whose cause this evil *is* upon us. So they cast lots, and the lot fell upon Jonah.

8 Then said they unto him, Tell us, we pray thee, for whose cause this evil *is* upon us; What *is* thine occupation? and whence comest thou? what *is* thy country? and of what people *art* thou?

9 And he said unto them, I *am* an Hebrew; and I fear the LORD, the God of heaven, which hath made the sea and the dry *land*.

10 Then were the men exceedingly afraid, and said unto him, Why hast thou done this? For the men knew that he fled from the presence of the LORD, because he had told them.

11 Then said they unto him, What shall we do unto thee, that the sea may be calm unto us? for the sea wrought, and was tempestuous.

12 And he said unto them, Take me up, and cast me forth into the sea; so shall the sea be calm unto you: for I know that for my sake this great tempest *is* upon you.

13 Nevertheless the men rowed hard to bring *it* to the land; but they could

the crisis in two unusual ways: (1) By calling upon their individual gods; and (2) casting cargo over the side so that the ship would ride out the storm better. The first action indicates that the crew was made up of a multi-national group. Each nation had its own god, and each sailor called upon his own national god for assistance. The second action further indicates the gravity of the peril; for if the ship arrived in port without its cargo, there would be no profit for the journey. However, in an extreme instance like this, it is far better to save ship and crew without any profit than to have no future profit for anyone. **But Jonah was gone down into the sides of the ship; and he lay, and was fast asleep.** The prophet, being a paying passenger (1:3), was not required to do the work of the ship. Accordingly, he had gone down to his quarters and lay fast asleep. **So the shipmaster came to him.** The captain (vs. 6), in inspecting his ship for its seaworthiness and additional cargo to be thrown overboard, found Jonah asleep. He awakened Jonah, advised him of the situation, and commanded him to call upon his God in the hope that his God could do something that the other gods apparently were not able to do. In all likelihood, Jonah did call upon his God; but neither his prayers to his God nor the prayers of the sailors to their gods were to any avail. **Come, and let us cast lots, that we may know for whose cause this evil is upon us.** The efforts to lighten the ship and the efforts of prayer failed. The sailors then concluded that something else must be the cause of the storm. Perhaps someone aboard was guilty of personally offending the gods. The only way to find out was to cast lots, and this they did. God is not only sovereign over the wind and the storm, He is also sovereign over the lot (cf. Prov 16:33). **So they cast lots, and the lot fell upon Jonah.** Through God's sovereign intervention in the casting of lots, Jonah is identified as being the culprit. **Tell us . . . for whose cause this evil is upon us.** The sailors put Jonah through an interrogation process in order to learn the nature of his offense and to get him to confess his guilt. **I am a Hebrew; and I fear the LORD.** Jonah's confession (vs. 9) undoubtedly contained more than the brief statements in this verse (cf. vs. 10). The most important part of the confession is preserved: Jonah identifies himself nationally as being a **Hebrew** (Heb '*ibrī*, one from beyond or from the other side), a name used of Israelites to distinguish them from non-Israelites (cf. Gen 39:14, 17; 40:15). More importantly, Jonah identifies himself as one who fears (Heb *yare*, i.e., a worshiper of) the Lord (Heb *Yahweh*, Jehovah). It was important for the heathen sailors to know that Jehovah is the God (Heb '*Elōhīm*) of heaven, hence the One from whom the wind and the storm have come and who has made the sea in which they are presently in peril and the dry land for which they seek. Clearly, his God is superior to their gods. He is the God who is responsible for the present predicament, the only God who can do anything to remedy it.

C. Jonah in the Midst of Confusion. 1:10-14.

10-14. Then were the men exceedingly afraid . . . Why hast thou done this? The response of the sailors to Jonah's confession is heightened fear. Up to this point, they only feared the storm for their lives. Now, they have the fear of Jonah's God who clearly is responsible for and in control of the elements before whom they are helpless; and they show a fear and sensitivity to God that Jonah had not shown. This fear is shown by their exclamatory question, "*What* is this you do?" The disobedience that Jonah had so blatantly undertaken is beyond the comprehension of the heathen sailors. They would not dare to flaunt their disobedience in the faces of their false gods. But Jonah had dared to disobey the God of heaven whose sovereign omnipotence is being abundantly documented by the intensity of the storm. **What shall we do unto thee . . . for the sea**

not: for the sea wrought, and was tempestuous against them.

14 Wherefore they cried unto the LORD, and said, We beseech thee, O LORD, we beseech thee, let us not perish for this man's life, and lay not upon us innocent blood: for thou, O LORD, hast done as it pleased thee.

15 So they took up Jonah, and cast him forth into the sea: and the sea ceased from her raging.

16 Then the men feared the LORD exceedingly, and offered a sacrifice unto the LORD, and made vows.

17 ¶Now the LORD had prepared a great fish to swallow up Jonah. And Jonah was in the belly of the fish three days and three nights.

wrought, and was tempestuous. The increasing intensity of the storm (vs. 11) causes the sailors' consternation to turn into concern, and they ask for instructions. Why would they ask Jonah to determine his fate? Probably, because they reasoned that he knew his God best and would best know how his God could be appeased so that the sea would become calm. **Take me up, and cast me forth into the sea . . . for my sake this great tempest is upon you.** Jonah's response (vs. 12) has been interpreted by some to indicate his repentance and heroic faith. It is true that Jonah recognizes that they are all in the midst of the storm because of his disobedience and that he does not wish others to suffer on his account. However, Jonah's statement could well indicate the intensity of his disobedience; he would rather die than repent and go to Nineveh. It is difficult to know what the prophet's attitude actually was at this time, but it seems from 2:7 that his actual repentance did not come until after he was in the sea and in the stomach of the great fish. **Nevertheless the men rowed hard to bring it to the land.** Whether through kindness to the prophet or out of fear of his God, the sailors attempt an alternate solution (vs. 13); they **rowed hard** (Heb *chatar*, lit., dug their oars into the water) **to bring it** (the ship) **to the land.** The land they sought is not specifically identified. However, the storm apparently came shortly after they had put to sea (cf. 1:3ff); and thus, it is not unlikely that they sought to return to the port from which they had come, Joppa. Their reasoning may well have been that since this is the port from which this man had sought to escape the presence of God, then they should attempt to return him there so he can return to the presence of God. Regardless of their thinking or their motives, their efforts failed. **Wherefore they cried unto the LORD . . . We beseech thee, O LORD.** The sailors addressed Jehovah God (vs. 14), before whose omnipotence their efforts had been futile. Jonah had told them (vs. 9) who his God was; and it is natural that they would address their petition to his God, rather than to their gods. Their prayer demonstrates two things: (1) their basic respect for human life (they had exhausted all other efforts before having to take a measure that would result in Jonah's death); and (2) their recognition of God's sovereignty and submission to His will.

D. Jonah in the Midst of the Sea. 1:15-16.

15-16. So they took up Jonah, and cast him forth into the sea. The sailors complied with Jonah's instructions (vs. 15), which also concur with God's will in this matter. The result of their compliance is their deliverance from the peril of the sea and the storm. Verse 16, coupled with verse 14, indicates that these heathen sailors came to a true knowledge of Jehovah as their God. Their inward faith, **the men feared the LORD exceedingly,** is accompanied by overt testimony and worship. **Offered a sacrifice unto the LORD and made vows.** This whole episode illustrates the truth of the fact that God indeed works *all* things together for good (Rom 8:28). In direct disobedience, Jonah went in the opposite direction from God's commission. He sought to keep from witnessing to the Gentiles (cf. 4:2). In the process, he ends up witnessing on an even broader scope than the original commission entailed, not only to Nineveh, but also to these sailors who were brought to a knowledge of the true God!

E. Jonah in the Stomach of the Fish. 1:17.

17. Once again, God calls upon one of His servants in nature who always obey His commands. **The LORD had prepared a great fish.** Jewish tradition felt that the word **prepared** (Heb *manah*) meant that God created this particular fish at creation and kept it in reserve until the day of Jonah when it fulfilled its particular mission. As it occurs in the text, the word means "to appoint, ordain, prepare, or order." The idea is one of commission rather than creation. The fish, then, was not one that was created specially for a task, but rather was one already in existence and commissioned for a specific mission, the preservation of God's prophet.

The question has frequently been raised as to what kind of a fish this was. The Hebrew text merely says that it was a **great fish** (Heb *dag gadôl*). Jesus, in referring to this incident, says that it was a sea monster (Gr *kētos*, Mt 12:40). Jesus' citation of this event ought to lay to rest any question of its historicity once and for all. The fish has commonly been thought of as being a whale. Some men have pointed out that a whale's physical structure would not permit the swallowing of a man, though one sea captain testifies that the cavity in the throat of the sperm whale is large enough to hold a ship's jolly-boat full of men. Other commentators have suggested that the fish was a dogfish, which has a stomach so large that once the body of a man in armor was found in it. Still others suggest that the fish was a shark, some of which grow to a weight of ten thousand pounds and to a length of thirty to forty feet, and in whose stomachs full-grown horses have been found. The Smithsonian Institution has on record an incident in which one fish swallowed another fish that weighed fifteen hundred pounds. The precise identity of the fish is not important. Apparently, God has a number of fish in His repertoire capable of the feat. The important fact is that God is in control of His creature, and His creature unwittingly obeys and serves His purposes.

The text records that Jonah was **in the belly of the fish three days and three nights.** Three suggestions are made as to how this computation was accomplished: (1) this calculation was made by the sailors; (2) it represents Jonah's estimation of the elapsed time; and (3) it is Jonah's actual computation. The last view seems most likely when one recalls that the form of this prophecy is historical and occurs in the third person. Jonah certainly knew the day in which he was thrown into the water and the day in which he was vomited up on the dry land. His computation of the actual time would be a simple matter.

II. JONAH IN REPENTANCE: FROM THE BELLY OF THE GREAT FISH TO THE DRY LAND. 2:1-10.

A. Jonah in Prayer. 2:1-9.

1. The situation of the prayer. 2:1.

2:1. Then Jonah prayed unto the LORD his God out of the fish's belly. Jonah is moved to pray to God from the stomach of the fish. God has finally put His prophet in the place where he would seek His face and submit himself to Him. In His faithfulness, God has brought His prophet to the point where he can do nothing other than to submit to the will of God in prayer.

2. The content of the prayer. 2:2-9.

In this section the content of what Jonah prayed from the stomach of the fish is recorded, though it obviously was written at a time following his release from the fish. Before looking at specific passages in detail, three questions need to be considered: (1) did Jonah die? (2) why is there no request for deliverance in this prayer? and (3) why is there a close parallel between the wording of this prayer and some of the psalms?

Concerning the first question, whether Jonah actually died, scholars are predictably divided into two camps: those that say that he did die and those who say that he did not. Seven lines of proof are offered to support the view that Jonah died in the whale. They are as follows: (1) Christ used Jonah as a sign of His death and resurrection (Mt 12:40). The parallel would be incomplete if Jonah had not actually died; (2) the time in which Jonah

CHAPTER 2
THEN Jonah prayed unto the LORD his God out of the fish's belly.

prayed—if he remained alive throughout his imprisonment in the fish's stomach, then he prayed on the second or third day. If he died, then he probably prayed in the early moments of his difficulty. He probably had three to five minutes to pray in the fish's belly before death; (3) Jonah cries out of the belly of Sheol (2:2). This term has the primary meaning of being a grave (cf. Gen 42:38; Ps 88:3) thus he considered the fish to be his grave; (4) the expression **floods compassed me about** (vs. 3) describes a man who is drowning, not living; (5) the expression **I am cast out of thy sight** (vs. 4) only has adequate meaning if it indicates physical death; (6) the expression **the weeds were wrapped about my head** (vs. 5) better describes a dead man than one who simply has temporary living accommodations in a fish; (7) the word **corruption** (vs. 6) describes death and perfectly parallels Jonah's circumstances with Christ's. Those who hold this view say that the emphasis of this prayer and incident is Jonah's resurrection, not the fish or Jonah's preservation in it.

Most commentators hold the view that Jonah did not die during his three-day imprisonment in the fish's stomach. Four lines of evidence are advanced to support this position: (1) The expression **the LORD had prepared a great fish to swallow up Jonah** (1:17) implies the fish's mission is to preserve Jonah alive, not to be the agent of death; (2) the term **belly of hell** or *Sheol* (2:2) is used by David in speaking of the bands of death when, in experience, he did not die (Ps 18:5; 30:3); (3) the language of Christ in Matthew 12:40 does not require Jonah's death and resurrection. Christ's emphasis is upon the time element involved, not in the death involved; (4) the sequence of the narrative implies continuous living: (a) a prepared fish (1:17); (b) Jonah in the fish's stomach three days and nights (1:17); (c) **Then Jonah prayed** (2:1-9); and (d) Jehovah spoke to the fish and Jonah was delivered (2:10). While it is obvious that all scholars do not agree, the view that Jonah was preserved physically throughout the entire three days is simpler and probably to be preferred. Nowhere in the text is it specifically stated that he did die.

Concerning the second question, why there is no request for deliverance in this prayer, two possible suggestions have been offered. First this account of the prayer was written after the deliverance, hence no request was necessary to record. This is certainly true, but it does not adequately account for the fact that the words of the prayer are genuine expressions of Jonah's actual experience. They are not a composition concerning an experience that did not happen. Second, when Jonah was swallowed by the fish, he found that he was preserved alive in its stomach and regarded this as a pledge of his future deliverance, for which he prays to the Lord. Thus, the prophet never doubted the fact of his deliverance; it was simply a matter when it was to be realized. This latter view seems to be the more worthy.

Concerning the third question, why there is a close affinity between this prayer and the psalms, it needs only to be observed that this correlation demonstrates how well-versed in the Scriptures the prophet was. It would be normal for him to call to mind other servants of God who had found themselves in similarly hopeless situations and had looked to God for deliverance. The similarity to the psalms need not be regarded as a literary dependence impugning the character of Jonah's prophecy, but rather as a demonstration of what one could normally expect of a man of God.

2-4. Jonah's prayer is poetic in form and has three movements, each beginning with a rehearsal of the prophet's impossible situation and culminating in an expression of his faith in spite of his impossible circumstances. **I cried by reason of mine affliction . . . out of the belly of hell cried I.** The **affliction** and **the belly of hell** (Heb *she'ōl*) are synonymous descriptions of the

2 And said, I cried by reason of mine affliction unto the LORD, and he heard me; out of the belly of hell cried I, *and* thou heardest my voice.

3 For thou hadst cast me into the deep, in the midst of the seas; and the floods compassed me about: all thy billows and thy waves passed over me.

4 Then I said, I am cast out of thy sight; yet I will look again toward thy holy temple.

5 The waters compassed me about, *even* to the soul: the depth closed me round about, the weeds were wrapped about my head.

6 I went down to the bottoms of the mountains; the earth with her bars *was* about me for ever: yet hast thou brought up my life from corruption, O LORD my God.

7 When my soul fainted within me I remembered the LORD: and my prayer came in unto thee, into thine holy temple.

8 They that observe lying vanities forsake their own mercy.

9 But I will sacrifice unto thee with the voice of thanksgiving; I will pay *that* that I have vowed. Salvation *is* of the LORD.

prophet's location in the stomach of the great fish. It is fitting that the prophet should describe his condition as being in the depth of *Sheol;* for unless God did something miraculous, it would be his grave. It was his dire situation that moved him to prayer and to the reception of God's answer. **For thou hadst cast me into the deep.** The prophet recognizes that, though the mariners or seamen were the ones who had actually cast him into the sea, ultimately it was God who had placed him there. **The floods compassed me about: all thy billows and thy waves passed over me.** Even though he is in the midst of a hostile environment (the deep sea), he recognizes that even those **billows** and **waves** belong to God; hence, he is safe. **I am cast out of thy sight; yet I will look again toward thy holy temple.** This is the prophet's first expression of faith, even though he is in a hopeless situation. By faith he expresses the confidence that he will again stand and look toward God's holy temple—he will once again be in the presence of the Lord. In all of this Jonah recognized the fact that he had experienced direct divine judgment. He also, by faith, expects to experience direct divine mercy and restoration.

5-6. This is the second movement of Jonah's prayer. Once again, he begins by rehearsing his situation (vss. 5-6a). **The waters compassed me about . . . the depth closed me round about, the weeds were wrapped about my head.** The great fish descended to the depths of the sea, and everything that found its way into the fish's stomach also entwined itself around Jonah. **Yet hast thou brought up my life from corruption.** The second movement ends with this expression of faith (2:6b), in which the prophet recognizes that Jehovah delivered him safely from **corruption,** the corruption that his body would have experienced had Jehovah not delivered him.

7-9. When my soul fainted within me. The third movement begins again with a reminder of the prophet's impossible conditions (vs. 7a). When Jonah's soul was about to sink into the darkness of death, he remembered Jehovah in prayer. The fact that he prayed to Jehovah implies submission and repentance. **And my prayer came in unto thee, into thine holy temple.** The prayer reached Jehovah in His holy temple where He is enthroned as God and King of His people (2:7; cf. Ps 18:6; 88:2). In the Old Testament times, all prayers were required to come to the mercy seat, thus to the temple of Jehovah. In verses 8 and 9 the prophet contrasts those who worship **lying vanities** (Heb *hablē-shaw',* worthless or lying vanities, vain idols) with his worship of Jehovah. In their worship of the vain idols, they **forsake their own mercy,** i.e., Jehovah. Thus the worship of an idol or anything that takes the place of Jehovah is a deliberate act in which one turns from Jehovah to a false and worthless idol. Jonah had done just this. He had substituted his will and his desires for Jehovah's. Thus he, like the idolators, had forsaken Jehovah, the God of mercy. **I will pay that that I have vowed.** The experience in the fish's belly brought Jonah to his senses. He now affirms his repentance and intention to obey Jehovah with a **sacrifice, . . . the voice of thanksgiving,** and with keeping his vow (vs. 9). These expressions show that Jonah was deeply sensitive to God's merciful undertaking in his behalf. The sacrifice that he wills to offer is an expression of his gratitude, in contrast to the pagan concept of offering a sacrifice to appease a god. The sacrifice, then, is the overt expression of his complete committal to God's will. The specific kind of vow that Jonah vowed is not known. In view of the context, it was most likely a vow that expressed his unequivocal commitment to God's will. All of these resolves, though well intended, cannot be realized unless God does something. Thus, the prophet recognizes that **Salvation is of the LORD.** Salvation is in Jehovah's power, and He is the only one that can effect it. This expression forms a unique and fitting climax for this prayer.

10 ¶And the Lord spake unto the fish, and it vomited out Jonah upon the dry land.

B. Jonah in Transit. 2:10.

10. And the Lord spake unto the fish, and it vomited out Jonah upon the dry land. The faith that Jonah has shown throughout this prayer is not disappointed. God performs an act in which the deliverance prayed for is realized. Once again, the fish, in contrast to his unwilling and disobedient passenger, obeys God and vomits Jonah up upon the dry land. It is not stated precisely where the prophet was cast on shore, but in all probability it was somewhere on the coast of Palestine near the place from which he departed **from the presence of the Lord** (1:3).

III. JONAH IN OBEDIENCE: FROM THE DRY LAND TO NINEVEH. 3:1-10.

A. Jonah in Fellowship with God. 3:1-4.

3:1-4. And the word of the Lord came . . . the second time. Against the backdrop of Jonah's punishment for his disobedience and repentance, the Lord in His grace and mercy speaks to him a second time. Despite his previous unfaithfulness, Jonah is given a second opportunity to carry out his work for Jehovah. **Arise, go unto Nineveh . . . and preach unto it.** The command given to Jonah in 3:2 is essentially the same as the one given him in 1:2, except that there is an intensification of the idea of preaching; **preach unto it the preaching that I bid thee** (lit., I am about to say). **So Jonah arose, and went unto Nineveh.** Verse 3 records the obedience of the prophet—he went immediately to Nineveh in obedience to the word of Jehovah. Nineveh is described as **an exceeding great city of three days' journey.** Scholars offer differing suggestions as to what this means. Keil and Delitzsch feel that this refers to how long it would take one to go about the circumference of Nineveh on foot. They say that the diameter of Nineveh was one hundred fifty stadia (about one day's journey on foot), and that its circumference was four hundred eighty stadia. Unger, on the other hand, feels that this expression clearly indicates that an aggregate of four cities (Nineveh Proper, Rehoboth-Ir, Calah, and Resen) are meant. Nineveh and Calah were the farthest apart, being about eighteen miles distant from one another. The idea of an aggregate city might be compared to New York City, which is comprised of five boroughs. The latter view seems to have more support in view of verse 4. Whichever is correct, the point is that Nineveh was clearly the largest city of the then-known world. **And Jonah began to enter into the city . . . and he cried, and said.** Verse 4 records Jonah's compliance with God's commission. **Yet forty days, and Nineveh shall be overthrown.** The text of Jonah's sermon, as recorded in verse 4, is undoubtedly curtailed greatly. Without doubt, he preached extensively about God's displeasure at the wickedness of the people of Nineveh and elaborated on their need to repent, turn to Jehovah, and obey the true God, the Creator of heaven and earth. As he traveled into the city of Nineveh, Jonah preached all along the way. His message can be summed up in the propositional statement, **Yet forty days, and Nineveh shall be overthrown** (vs. 4).

CHAPTER 3
AND the word of the Lord came unto Jonah the second time, saying,

2 Arise, go unto Nĭn'e-veh, that great city, and preach unto it the preaching that I bid thee.

3 So Jonah arose, and went unto Nĭn'e-veh, according to the word of the Lord. Now Nĭn'e-veh was an exceeding great city of three days' journey.

4 And Jonah began to enter into the city a day's journey, and he cried, and said, Yet forty days, and Nĭn'e-veh shall be overthrown.

B. Jonah in Success. 3:5-9.

5-9. These verses record the response that Jonah's message received. **So the people of Nineveh believed God.** The people of Nineveh were ripe for Jonah's evangelistic message. They believed in the God that Jonah preached and gave testimony to their inward faith by outward actions. They **proclaimed a fast, and put on sackcloth.** The English word sackcloth is derived from the Hebrew word *sak*, which denotes a coarse cloth, dark in color, usually made of goat's hair. It was customarily worn by mourners (II Sam 3:31; II Kgs 19:1-2) and goes back in antiquity as far as the patriarchal age (Gen 37:34; Job 16:15). **From**

5 ¶So the people of Nĭn'e-veh believed God, and proclaimed a fast, and put on sackcloth, from the greatest of them even to the least of them.

6 For word came unto the king of Nĭn'e-veh, and he arose from his throne, and he laid his robe from him, and covered *him* with sackcloth, and sat in ashes.

7 And he caused *it* to be proclaimed and published through Nĭn'e-veh by

the decree of the king and his nobles, saying, Let neither man nor beast, herd nor flock, taste anything: let them not feed, nor drink water:

8 But let man and beast be covered with sackcloth, and cry mightily unto God: yea, let them turn every one from his evil way, and from the violence that *is* in their hands.

9 Who can tell *if* God will turn and repent, and turn away from his fierce anger, that we perish not?

10 And God saw their works, that they turned from their evil way; and God repented of the evil, that he had said that he would do unto them; and he did *it* not.

the greatest of them even to the least of them. It is to be noted that all classes of Ninevites were involved in this national repentance. When the matter came to his attention, even the king wrapped himself in sackcloth and sat down on ashes as a sign of deepest mourning (cf. Job 2:8). **And he caused it to be proclaimed and published through Nineveh.** Verses 7 to 9 record the fact that the king and his nobles, who had been the nation's leaders in its wickedness, now become the nation's leaders in its repentance. These verses set forth the principle that the way to effect a national repentance is to effect a repentance of the nation's leaders. The national repentance of king and people is also shared by their animals (vss. 7-8). Just as the brute beasts share in the evil effects of man's sin, and as such have been subject to vanity and yearn for deliverance (cf. Gen 3:17; Rom 8:19-23; II Pet 3:13), so symbolically the king decrees that these animals must share in man's repentance, and thus share in the benefits of that repentance, i.e., escaping the wrath of God (vs. 9). The king's decree was neither humorous nor superficial; for the king himself set the personal example, and the edict was backed by him. **Who can tell if God will turn and repent . . . that we perish not?** Verse 9 expresses faith on the part of the king and the Ninevites. They had no evidence on which to base their faith or to hope for relief, except for the fact that God had sent one to warn them instead of destroying them. Their faith was not disappointed.

C. Jonah in Awe. 3:10.

10. And God saw their works . . . and God repented of the evil. Here we have God's evaluation of the Ninevites' faith; it was genuine! The expression **God repented** should not be misunderstood. God did not change in His intentions toward the Ninevites. Rather, they changed in their attitude toward Him; and on the basis of that change, God could deal with them in grace, rather than in judgment as their failure to repent would have necessitated. The language indicates the view of God from man's viewpoint. The message had come that God intended to destroy them. This was true. But they repented, and God now can deal with them in grace. This appears to be a change in God from the viewpoint of man, who is unaware of his own change; and we know from the verses following in the next chapter that Jonah was truly in awe at this change.

IV. JONAH IN ANGER: FROM NINEVEH TO THE SHADE OF THE PLANT. 4:1-11.

A. Jonah in Discouragement/Displeasure. 4:1-4.

4:1-4. But it displeased Jonah exceedingly, and he was very angry. Instead of being pleased and praising God for His grace to Nineveh and for the success of his ministry, Jonah was **displeased exceedingly** and **very angry** (vs. 1). He lost control of himself and gave way to violent expression. His anger may have stemmed from the fact that his message did not materialize. It is possible that he feared for his reputation as a prophet. His basic problem, however, stemmed from his personal hatred of Nineveh and the Ninevites. He still is afflicted with a false Jewish nationalism and hatred of all non-Jews, especially Assyrians. This is why God corrects him as He does in 4:11. **O LORD, was not this my saying . . . ?** Jonah expresses his complaint to God in verse 2, acknowledging that his view has not changed from what it was originally and that his view of the Assyrians is drastically different from God's. **Take . . . my life from me.** The expression of despair reaches its height in verse 3 where the prophet requests God to take his life. This shows the extent and intensity of Jonah's hatred toward the Assyrians, for his life seemed to lose its meaning when he was robbed of the possibility of vengeance upon them. **Doest thou well to be angry?** The

CHAPTER 4

BUT it displeased Jonah exceedingly, and he was very angry.

2 And he prayed unto the LORD, and said, I pray thee, O LORD, *was* not this my saying, when I was yet in my country? Therefore I fled before unto Tarshish: for I knew that thou *art* a gracious God, and merciful, slow to anger, and of great kindness, and repentest thee of the evil.

3 Therefore now, O LORD, take, I beseech thee, my life from me; for *it is* better for me to die than to live.

4 ¶Then said the LORD, Doest thou well to be angry?

1731

whole situation is put into focus by God's question in verse 4. It is a rhetorical question; and the answer is, No. Jonah really has no good reason to be angry; and the rhetorical question, then, is a form of gentle reproof.

B. Jonah in Discomfort. 4:5-8.

5-8. So Jonah went out of the city. After his encounter with God, Jonah went out from the city, made a shelter for himself, and sat under it to watch to see if God would repent of His decision to have mercy upon Nineveh. **And the LORD God prepared a gourd.** Though Jonah is angry at God (vss. 1-4), God still cares for him and demonstrates His concern tangibly by preparing a **gourd** (Heb *qîqayōn*) to grow up to provide shade for Jonah's head. The exact identity of the plant is not known. Various identifications have been proposed, such as a castor oil plant or some variety of the gourd family; but its exact identity is not important. The important thing is that it grew up rapidly, and once again nature served its Creator's purpose exactly. **So Jonah was exceeding glad of the gourd.** Jonah was exceedingly happy for the provision of the plant, though he apparently does not recognize it as having come from the hand of God. **But God prepared a worm.** Verse 7 reveals that the plant was designed to serve God's purpose, not Jonah's comfort. Once again a creature of God's creation answers His Creator's call and performs His service. This time God calls on the **worm** (Heb *tōla'at*). The worm's mission is simply to attack the fast-growing plant so that it withers and Jonah is deprived of its shade. **God prepared a vehement east wind.** In verse 8 still another servant in God's arsenal of nature answers His call: this time another wind, **a vehement east wind.** This is a reference to the much-dreaded sirocco wind with its oppressive heat and its exhausting dust. **Jonah . . . fainted, and wished in himself to die.** The wind comes not for the purpose of drying up the plant or of tearing down the shelter that Jonah has built, but purely and simply for intensifying the physical distress of the prophet. It is effective in its mission, and Jonah once again wishes he were dead. The prophet is a pathetic sight! There he sits, neither praying for Nineveh or himself, nor resting to gather strength to continue his spiritual ministry, but in complete dejection and self-pity.

5 So Jonah went out of the city, and sat on the east side of the city, and there made him a booth, and sat under it in the shadow, till he might see what would become of the city.

6 And the LORD God prepared a gourd, and made *it* to come up over Jonah, that it might be a shadow over his head, to deliver him from his grief. So Jonah was exceeding glad of the gourd.

7 But God prepared a worm when the morning rose the next day, and it smote the gourd that it withered.

8 And it came to pass, when the sun did arise, that God prepared a vehement east wind; and the sun beat upon the head of Jonah, that he fainted, and wished in himself to die, and said, *It is* better for me to die than to live.

C. Jonah in Rebuke. 4:9-11.

9-11. Doest thou well to be angry for the gourd? Once again God in His faithfulness comes to the prophet with a gentle rebuke in the form of a question (vs. 9). God asks whether or not the prophet's anger over the plant's destruction was ethically justifiable. **I do well to be angry, even unto death.** Jonah, in complete self-pity and total disregard of the Ninevites, declares that he is justly angry. The phrase **even unto death** indicates that Jonah's anger had reached even to the very bottom of his soul so that he despaired even of his life. **Thou hast had pity on the gourd . . . should not I spare Nineveh . . . ?**In verses 10-11 Jehovah sharpens His rebuke of the prophet by drawing a contrast between the fast-growing plant and the city of Nineveh. Jonah was concerned over a temporary, soul-less plant; but had no concern over the great city of Nineveh, which had a population of more than 120,000 souls (vs. 11). The **sixscore thousand persons** (120,000) **that cannot discern between their right hand and their left hand** has been interpreted in various ways. The simplest understanding is to take this as referring to the number of children in the complex of cities that made up Nineveh. Chapter 3 adequately shows that the total populace could not have been incapable of moral discernment. Thus, this designation seems to speak of a distinct group of persons. In addition, God does care for the animals, though they are incapable, like this group of the populace, of moral discernment. Even animals and children benefit when leaders and adults are in a

9 And God said to Jonah, Doest thou well to be angry for the gourd? And he said, I do well to be angry, *even* unto death.

10 Then said the LORD, Thou hast had pity on the gourd, for the which thou hast not laboured, neither madest it grow; which came up in a night, and perished in a night:

11 And should not I spare Nin'e-veh, that great city, wherein are more than sixscore thousand persons that cannot discern between their right hand and their left hand; and *also* much cattle?

right relationship with God. God cares for those who are not able even to appreciate or understand that care.

The prophecy of Jonah closes as it began, with the words of Jehovah. One would be discouraged if he did not realize that the very existence of this prophecy indicates that the prophet was brought once again to repentance and restoration of his fellowship with God, or else he would not have left this prophecy for our spiritual profit. The message of Jonah rings out loud and clear. God cares for the heathen! God will spare no extreme to get His message to them. Even when the messenger would be deliberately disobedient, God will marshal His animate and inanimate creations to bring correction to His messenger and effect His purpose for the world!

(see page 1864 for Bibliography to the Minor Prophets)

MICAH

INTRODUCTION

Authorship. The author of this prophecy is identified as "Micah the Morasthite." He is called the "Morasthite" because he was a native of Moresheth-gath in Judah (he prophesied against his home town, cf. 1:14, which probably did not help his popularity with the home folks). Micah's name means, "Who is like Jehovah?" In 7:18 he apparently plays upon the meaning of his name as he asks the question, "Who is a god like unto thee, that pardoneth iniquity, and passeth by the transgression . . . ?" The author of this prophecy is not to be confused with Micaiah (cf. I Kgs 22:8, 19-23), even though there is a great similarity between the messages proclaimed by these two servants of God. Micah, along with Hosea and Amos, was a contemporary of Isaiah who had been prophesying some seventeen or eighteen years before Micah began his ministry. There are some interesting contrasts between these two prophets. Micah was a country preacher, while Isaiah was a prophet of the court and city. Micah, having come from a very poor background, spoke mostly to the poor people and always on their behalf, while Isaiah, who came from a very prominent family, spoke primarily to the leaders of the people. Micah ministered mainly in Samaria and the border sections of Judah, while Isaiah ministered mainly in Jerusalem. Micah is known simply as "Micah the Morasthite," while Isaiah was one of the most prominent prophets of Judah and occupied a very conspicuous place in Judah's history. Apparently, Micah died in peace in the days of good King Hezekiah (cf. Jer 26:16, 19).

Date and place of writing. Micah dates his prophecy according to the southern kings of "Jotham, Ahaz, and Hezekiah" (1:1). These kings of Judah reigned from about 758 B.C. to 699 B.C. Thus, it is probable that Micah's ministry lasted approximately fifty years. The reign of King Ahaz, one of the most wicked kings of all of Judah's history, is in the background of much of Micah's prophecy. It is possible that the dark picture presented by Micah's prophecy reflects the reign of King Ahaz, while the brighter aspects of Micah's prophecy reflect the godly rule under King Hezekiah.

The exact location from which the prophecy originated is not known. Though the burden of the prophecy is concerned primarily with the northern kingdom and the northern towns of Judah, the prophet conducted much of his ministry in Jerusalem; and it is likely that the prophecy originated there in the latter half of the eighth century, B.C.

Characteristics of the Prophecy. Much of Micah's prophecy is very severe in tone, though it does contain much poetic beauty similar to that of Isaiah's. In many ways the book of Micah is a "sister-book" to Isaiah, and it has been called "Isaiah in shorthand." The prophecy is filled with rapid transitions from one subject to another, i.e., from judgment to blessing. The sin of idolatry occupies an incidental place in Micah's prophecy, for he lays greater stress upon social sins with which the poor are victimized.

The most outstanding single prophecy concerns the birth of our Lord at Bethlehem (5:2). This amazing prophecy affords a wonderful demonstration of the accuracy and certainty of the fulfillment of all the prophecies in this and all the other books of prophecy. Just as this prophecy was fulfilled in complete detail by the birth of Jesus in "Bethlehem Ephratah" (5:2), so minutely will all the other prophecies of this book be fulfilled, i.e., the destruction of Israel and Judah by Assyria and Babylon and the ultimate regathering of Israel at the Millennium. With its references to the Millennial Kingdom, the book offers another proof of the truth of the premillennial approach to Scripture and demonstrates once again the sovereignty of God who is working His plan out through such an irresponsible people as Israel. His plans will not be thwarted.

Purpose. The purpose of Micah's prophecy is to face the people with their sins and to speak the word of God's judgment that must fall because of their persistent sinning. The author completes the purpose of his book by ending each discourse with a word about restoration. Though the people have sinned and Jehovah's judgment must fall, God's purposes have been fulfilled; He will regather and restore His people and will reign over them. The author pictures the restoration in two phases: (1) immediately, after the Babylonian captivity; and (2) ultimately, at the Millennium.

Theme. Sin, judgment, and restoration. This can be seen by the fact that the book consists of three discourses, each of which set forth (1) the people's sin, (2) God's judgment, and (3) God's ultimate restoration of His sinning people.

OUTLINE

2. Jehovah's sympathy for His sinning people. 1:8-16.
B. Woe Pronounced Upon Greedy Oppressors. 2:1-13.
   1. The woe pronounced. 2:1-5.
   2. The false prophets indicted. 2:6-11.
   3. A remnant to be restored. 2:12-13.
III. The Second Discourse: Rulers, Priests, and Prophets Denounced and Messianic Fore-glimpses. 3:1-5:15.
   A. Rulers, Priests, and Prophets Denounced. 3:1-12.
      1. Rebuke of the elders. 3:1-4.
      2. Rebuke of the prophets. 3:5-8.
      3. Rebuke of the rulers, priests, and prophets. 3:9-12.
   B. Messianic Fore-glimpses. 4:1-5:15.

1. Establishment of Messiah's kingdom. 4:1-5:1.
2. Messiah the King and Deliverer. 5:2-15.
IV. The Third Discourse: Jehovah's Controversy with His People and God, Israel's Only Hope. 6:1-7:20.
   A. Jehovah's Controversy. 6:1-16.
      1. God's reminder of His faithfulness. 6:1-5.
      2. The people's reply. 6:6-8.
      3. Jehovah rebukes injustice. 6:9-16.
   B. God, Israel's Only Hope. 7:1-20.
      1. Because the godly have perished. 7:1-6.
      2. Because He is the source of light in darkness. 7:7-13.
      3. Because He cares for His people. 7:14-17.
      4. Because He pardons iniquity and keeps His Word. 7:18-20.

COMMENTARY

I. INTRODUCTION. 1:1.

A. The Character of the Prophecy. 1:1a.

THE word of the LORD that came to Mī'-cah the Mō'ras-thīte in the days of Jō'-tham, Ahaz, *and* Hĕz-e-kī'ah, kings of Judah, which he saw concerning Sa-mā'rĭ-a and Jerusalem.

1:1a. The word of the LORD. At the very outset the message of this prophecy is traced to its ultimate source, i.e., Jehovah. Though it will be delivered by a human servant, the authority behind the message is Jehovah Himself; therefore, the message is authoritative, and man would do well to listen and heed.

B. The Author of the Prophecy. 1:1b.

1:1b. Micah the Morasthite. Virtually all that could be known about this prophet is gleaned from this prophecy (see Introduction above). This is fitting because the messenger is relatively unimportant, and the message is all-important. We must recognize, however, that the contemporaries of the prophet undoubtedly knew much more about him than we; and the very fact of his call to be a prophet of God would give a certain amount of empathy to him and his message.

C. The Date of the Prophecy. 1:1c.

1:1c. In the days of Jotham, Ahaz, and Hezekiah. The fact that only kings of the south are mentioned indicates that the prophet conducted his ministry in the south, though most of the prophecy is applied to the kingdom of the north. Only those prophets whose ministry was to the northern kingdom make mention of the northern kings. With this historical citation, we know that Micah ministered in the latter half of the eighth century B.C.

D. The Address of the Prophecy. 1:1d.

1:1d. Samaria and Jerusalem. The two seats of government of the northern and southern kingdoms respectively are addressed. Samaria takes prominence in the address as it will be destroyed and go into captivity one hundred thirty years before the southern kingdom. The capitals are the seats of corruption, which filtered down to and infected the entire northern and southern kingdoms. Rather than leading the people in the worship of Jehovah, the rulers of both kingdoms led the people in the worship of idols. For this, God's judgment must fall.

II. THE FIRST DISCOURSE: DESTRUCTION AND WOE TO ALL THE LAND. 1:2-2:13.

A. Destruction Pronounced Against Samaria (Israel) and Jerusalem (Judah). 1:2-16.

1. The destruction pronounced. 1:2-7.

The pronouncement of destruction divides into four parts: (1) the exhortation to the earth to hear the word of Jehovah (vs. 2); (2) the reason for listening to the exhortation (vss. 3-4); (3) the general revelation of God's grievance (vs. 5); and (4) God's judgment that is to fall (vss. 6-7).

2. Hear, all ye people; hearken, O earth, and all that therein is. All the people of the earth are summoned to hear this message from Jehovah, not because they are to experience God's judgment or because they are to be the judges that God will use to punish Israel; but rather, they are to be witnesses of God's judgment. **The Lord from his holy temple.** At the outset of the prophecy, then, Jehovah is set in the role of Judge, and from His abode in heaven (**his holy temple**) He is testifying against and pronouncing judgment upon His people.

3-4. For, behold, the LORD cometh forth out of his place. The reason why the entire earth should listen and be witnesses is given in verses 3-4. Jehovah Himself will come and wreak havoc upon the earth. **And tread upon the high places of the earth . . . the mountains shall be molten under him, and the valleys shall be cleft, as wax before the fire, and as the waters that are poured down a steep place.** His coming is set forth in language descriptive of the activity of earthquakes and volcanos. The mountains will melt, and the valleys will be torn apart; and all the earth will be ravaged like the destruction of the waters of a massive flash flood.

5. For the transgression of Jacob is all this, and for the sins of the house of Israel. The reason why this destruction will come is given in verse 5. Israel and Judah have sinned, and Jehovah is grieved. Instead of being in the forefront leading their respective nations in righteousness, the capitals of both kingdoms are leading the nation in sin, especially idolatry. In the prophet's thought **transgression, sins,** and **high places** (i.e., places in the mountains and hills in which altars were erected upon which sacrifice to idols was carried out) were all parallel. The massive moral defection from Jehovah is summed up in their having other gods before Him!

6-7. Therefore I will make Samaria as a heap of the field. Because of their defection, God's judgment must fall. Because its judgment will precede the southern kingdom's by one hundred thirty years, the prophet focuses upon the northern kingdom. Its capital, Samaria, will be leveled and become the place in which vineyards are planted. **I will pour down the stones thereof into the valley . . . and all the idols thereof will I lay desolate.** The stones of the buildings will be poured down into the valleys to clear the land for planting. All of the idols made of beaten metal will themselves be beaten to pieces, and the benefits allegedly gained from them will be destroyed. Every vestige of idolatry will be destroyed because it is spiritual idolatry. In His judgment and destruction of the idols, Jehovah will demonstrate His infinite superiority over them.

2. Jehovah's sympathy for His sinning people. 1:8-16.

8. Therefore I will wail and howl, I will go stripped and naked. Jehovah's sympathy for His sinning people is manifested in the personal grief of the prophet. The prophet's grief is real and deep, and he expresses it in the way customary in his day by lamenting and **wailing** and going about **naked**—all signs of deep mourning. He likens his wail to that of **dragons** (Heb *tanīm,* howlers or jackals) and **owls** (Heb *bat ya'anah,* daughter of

---

2 ¶Hear, all ye people; hearken, O earth, and all that therein is: and let the Lord GOD be witness against you, the Lord from his holy temple.

3 For, behold, the LORD cometh forth out of his place, and will come down, and tread upon the high places of the earth.

4 And the mountains shall be molten under him, and the valleys shall be cleft, as wax before the fire, *and* as the waters *that are* poured down a steep place.

5 For the transgression of Jacob *is* all this, and for the sins of the house of Israel. What *is* the transgression of Jacob? *is it* not Sa-mâ'rĭ-a? and what *are* the high places of Judah? *are they* not Jerusalem?

6 Therefore I will make Sa-mâ'rĭ-a as an heap of the field, *and* as plantings of a vineyard: and I will pour down the stones thereof into the valley, and I will discover the foundations thereof.

7 And all the graven images thereof shall be beaten to pieces, and all the hires thereof shall be burned with the fire, and all the idols thereof will I lay desolate: for she gathered *it* of the hire of an harlot, and they shall return to the hire of an harlot.

8 Therefore I will wail and howl, I will go stripped and naked: I will make a wailing like the dragons, and mourning as the owls.

9 For her wound *is* incurable; for it is come unto Judah; he is come unto the gate of my people, *even* to Jerusalem.

10 Declare ye *it* not at Gath, weep ye not at all: in the house of Āph'rah roll thyself in the dust.
11 Pass ye away, thou inhabitant of Sā'phir, having thy shame naked: the inhabitant of Zā'a-năn came not forth in the mourning of Bĕth-ē'zel; he shall receive of you his standing.
12 For the inhabitant of Mâ'rŏth waited carefully for good: but evil came down from the Lord unto the gate of Jerusalem.

13 O thou inhabitant of Lā'chĭsh, bind the chariot to the swift beast: she *is* the beginning of the sin to the daughter of Zion: for the transgressions of Israel were found in thee.

14 Therefore shalt thou give presents to Môr'esh-ĕth-găth: the houses of Ăch'zīb *shall be* a lie to the kings of Israel.
15 Yet will I bring an heir unto thee, O inhabitant of Ma-rē'shah: he shall come unto A-dŭl'lam the glory of Israel.

howling, or an ostrich). These animals make mournful and foreboding noises and indicate impending danger for those who hear them.

9. For her wound is incurable; for it is come unto Judah. The reason for the prophet's deep grief is set forth in verse 9. The devastation that is to come upon Samaria (vss. 6-7) will not be contained by the northern borders, for it will overflow and come into the southern kingdom up to the very gates of its capital city, Jerusalem. The enemy's thrust will be to the very heart of the southern kingdom; hence, **her wound is incurable.** Judah has been a partaker in the idolatrous sins of Israel and will likewise participate in her judgments. In fulfillment of this prophecy, the Assyrians under Sennacherib did sweep through the northern kingdom and threatened the very gates of Jerusalem. The destruction was completed 130 years later when Nebuchadnezzar took the southern kingdom captive to Babylon.

10-12. Declare ye it not at Gath, weep ye not at all. Though the wound inflicted by the Assyrians was great, the people of Judah are commanded not to relay the news to Gath, the Philistine capital; in fact, they are not to weep at all. The prophet does not want the enemies of God to have any occasion to rejoice at the affliction visited upon God's people. **Aphrah, Saphir, Zaanan, Beth-ezel,** and **Maroth** are all ancient cities of Judah that have passed into obscurity. Their sites are not known for sure; and they seem to have been mentioned by the prophet because, by playing on the meanings of their names, he is able graphically to describe the grave effects of the Assyrian invasion into Judah. **But evil came down from the Lord unto the gate of Jerusalem.** Once again, it is affirmed that he will progress to the gates of Jerusalem, but will not enter that capital; and it will not fall (cf. vs. 9).

13. O thou inhabitant of Lachish. Lachish was a well-known armed city of the prophet's day. Its inhabitants are urged to flee the city by the swiftest known means because God's judgment is coming. **She is the beginning of the sin to the daughter of Zion.** The reason God's judgment is to come is because Lachish is the site from which the sin of idolatry was introduced into Judah. **For the transgressions of Israel were found in thee.** Because Lachish is linked to Israel in a common sin, it is to be linked to Israel in a common destruction.

14-15. Therefore shalt thou give presents to Moresheth-gath. Moresheth-gath was the prophet's home town (cf. vs. 1). Of all the ways possible to understand this verse, it is probably best to understand the prophet as saying that his home town will become the possession of the Assyrians who will take its inhabitants captive. The site of this town is approximately twenty miles southwest of Jerusalem; thus, the advance of the Assyrian forces will partially surround Jerusalem, though they will not be permitted by God to enter or take it captive. **Yet will I bring an heir unto thee, O inhabitant of Mareshah.** There is a parallelism in verses 14 and 15. **Moresheth-gath** (so named because for a time it fell captive to the Philistine city of Gath) and **Mareshah** are various spellings of the same town, which also was the prophet's birthplace. **Achzib** and **Adullam** refer to the same region lying at a point between Mareshah and Jerusalem, some twenty miles to the northeast. The **heir,** or possessor, which God will bring unto Mareshah is the king of Assyria; and its inhabitants will flee from the devastation to seek safety in the area of Adullam. The **glory of Israel** is a reference to the leading citizens and nobility of Israel who have been fleeing continuously before the Assyrian invasion. Achzib **shall be a lie to the kings of Israel** because it promises safety, but even here the Assyrian invasion will overtake them. The point of the passage is that there will be no escape from the Assyrian force, and flight will be in vain. Only the staying hand of Jehovah preserves

16 Make thee bald, and poll thee for thy delicate children; enlarge thy baldness as the eagle; for they are gone into captivity from thee.

CHAPTER 2

WOE to them that devise iniquity, and work evil upon their beds! when the morning is light, they practise it, because it is in the power of their hand.

2 And they covet fields, and take *them* by violence; and houses, and take *them* away: so they oppress a man and his house, even a man and his heritage.

3 Therefore thus saith the LORD; Behold, against this family do I devise an evil, from which ye shall not remove your necks; neither shall ye go haughtily: for this time *is* evil.

4 In that day shall *one* take up a parable against you, and lament with a doleful lamentation, *and* say, We be utterly spoiled: he hath changed the portion of my people: how hath he removed *it* from me! turning away he hath divided our fields.

5 Therefore thou shalt have none that shall cast a cord by lot in the congregation of the LORD.

6 Prophesy ye not, *say they to them*

Jerusalem, and the king of Assyria will be caused to return to his own land for reasons not of his own choosing (cf. II Kgs 17-19).

16. Make thee bald, and poll thee for thy delicate children . . . they are gone into captivity from thee. Verse 16 describes the effect that this devastation will have upon the nation. The land is viewed as stripped of its children. The worst thing that could happen to land from the Jewish point of view was for it to be desolate of inhabitants. In view of this, the people are to give expression to their sorrow by shaving their heads, a practice prohibited in Deuteronomy 14:1, but done as an expression of deep mourning (cf. Isa 15:2; Jer 16:6). In this verse the prophet sees beyond the effects of Sennacherib's invasion during the days of King Hezekiah down to the day of Nebuchadnezzar when Babylon will indeed take captive all of the citizens of the land. The devastation brought about by Assyria, then, foreshadows the greater devastation that will come some one hundred thirty years later to Judah.

B. Woe Pronounced Upon Greedy Oppressors. 2:1-13.

1. The woe pronounced. 2:1-5.

This section divides in two parts: (1) the woe (vss. 1-2), and (2) Jehovah's judgment upon Israel (vss. 3-5).

2:1-5. Woe to them that devise iniquity, and work evil upon their beds! The prophet pronounces woe upon the political leaders of the land (those who have **power of their hand**) because of their unbridled lust and quest for power and possession. When they go to bed at night, they devise evil plots; and in the daylight they bring them into realization. The power that they possess enables them to bring their evil schemes to realization. Their schemes are similar to those of King Ahab of old (cf. I Kgs 2:1-16) who coveted the field of Naboth and snatched his rightful property from him. **And they covet fields, and take them by violence.** The leadership of Israel has not improved, for they continue to covet the fields and possession of their subjects and violently deprive their citizens of their rightful heritage.

Behold, against this family do I devise an evil. Jehovah's judgment must fall. Jehovah will devise evil against those doing the evil deeds of verses 1-2 against His people. The people are helpless, but Jehovah will take up their cause and will avenge the evil done upon them; and the nobility will not realize the object of their evil desires. God will humble the haughty nation by giving the land to another nation, and the people will be delivered as captives into that land.

In that day shall one take up a parable against you, and lament with a doleful lamentation. The tragedy will be so bitter that they will compose a dirge bewailing their fate. Their enemies will take it up and use it in mockery and derision against them. Because of the sins of the nation, particularly those of the nobility (cf. vss. 1-2), no one will be able to divide the land; for there will be no land to divide. **We be utterly spoiled: he hath changed the portion of my people: how hath he removed it from me!** All of the land will pass under the control of Assyria, and the rulers who have seized that which did not belong to them will in turn be dispossessed of that which they have seized; all will be losers. **Therefore thou shalt have none that shall cast a cord by lot in the congregation of the LORD.** The imagery underlying this verse is a reference to the days of Joshua when the land was originally apportioned to the people of Israel by lot and each section was measured off with a line (cf. Joshua 13-21).

2. The false prophets indicted. 2:6-11.

6-11. Prophesy ye not, say they. Micah's message is understandably unpopular, even though it is true. The nation and its

that prophesy: they shall not prophesy to them, *that* they shall not take shame.

7 O *thou that art* named the house of Jacob, is the spirit of the Lord straitened? *are* these his doings? do not my words do good to him that walketh uprightly?

8 Even of late my people is risen up as an enemy: ye pull off the robe with the garment from them that pass by securely as men averse from war.

9 The women of my people have ye cast out from their pleasant houses; from their children have ye taken away my glory for ever.

10 Arise ye, and depart; for this *is* not *your* rest: because it is polluted, it shall destroy *you*, even with a sore destruction.

11 If a man walking in the spirit and falsehood do lie, *saying*, I will prophesy unto thee of wine and of strong drink; he shall even be the prophet of this people.

rulers take issue with the prophet and contend with him not to prophesy the truth. Instead, they wish to hear false prophets who will convey messages that are pleasing to them. **O thou that art named the house of Jacob . . . do not my words do good to him that walketh uprightly?** Micah responds by pointing out that his message has no danger for those who do what God wants. Only those who are in opposition to God need fear. **Even of late my people is risen up as an enemy.** In support of the justice of God's judgment, the prophet cites current sins of the nation, particularly its leaders, which shows that the nation justly deserves the judgment of God.

Ye pull off the robe with the garment. The indictment is impressive. They robbed the poor and innocent (who posed no threat to anyone) of their robes, the only covering that they had to shelter them from the cold of night. **The women of my people have ye cast out from their pleasant houses.** They robbed helpless widows of the homes they had inherited from their deceased husbands, and which contained their precious memories. **From their children have ye taken away my glory for ever.** Even the helpless, orphaned children of the widows are deprived of their livelihood. The widows and orphans have always been the object of God's eye, and he who violates them brings destruction upon himself. One's attitude towards these helpless people is indicative of his attitude towards God (cf. Jas 1:27). **It shall destroy you, even with a sore destruction.** Because of the extent of their depravity, judgment must fall upon rulers and nations; and it will mean their utter destruction.

If a man walking in the spirit and falsehood do lie, saying, I will prophesy unto thee. The false prophet can always be identified by his message. It is always contrary to the true message of God and in keeping with what the people want to hear. This is necessary because the false prophet is a partaker of the people's sins and cannot condemn that of which he approves and in which he readily participates. The people of Micah's day did not like him or his message, and they sought those false prophets who were more acceptable. People always seek a preacher who will console them, rather than convict them of sin (cf. II Tim 4:3-4).

3. A remnant to be restored. 2:12-13.

12-13. Into the dark picture of judgment a promise of restoration is given. It is assured in verse 12 and visualized in verse 13. **I will surely assemble, O Jacob, all of thee; I will surely gather the remnant of Israel.** This restoration will be complete, for it will involve Jacob (the southern two tribes) and Israel (the northern ten tribes). Thus, the restoration envisioned is greater than that realized following the Babylon captivity when only the southern tribes were restored to their land. The restoration envisioned is that of the Millennium, when all of the nation will be restored and will experience the regeneration spoken of by Jeremiah (Jer 31:31-34). The ten tribes are lost only to man. God knows their whereabouts, and in His time will restore them completely. The restoration will be luxurious, as is indicated by the reference to the **sheep of Bozrah.** Bozrah was an area that had very rich pasture, and the sheep which grazed upon it must have been exemplary. God will ultimately restore His nation, now wracked by its sin; and great joy will be the lot of the restored and redeemed people.

The breaker is come up before them. The **breaker** of verse 13 is a reference to Israel's Messiah (Jesus, our Lord) who will break down every obstacle between the people and their God. He will restore them, forgive them of their sins, and implant within them a new heart. He will lead them to glorious restoration, and He will rule over them. No one will be able to hinder His messianic millennial work, for He is the Lord (Jehovah)!

12 ¶I will surely assemble, O Jacob, all of thee; I will surely gather the remnant of Israel; I will put them together as the sheep of Bŏz'rah, as the flock in the midst of their fold: they shall make great noise by reason of *the multitude* of men.

13 The breaker is come up before them: they have broken up, and have passed through the gate, and are gone out by it: and their king shall pass before them, and the Lord on the head of them.

To date, this promise of restoration has not been realized; but there is coming a day when it will. What a glorious future lies ahead of Israel!

III. THE SECOND DISCOURSE: RULERS, PRIESTS, AND PROPHETS DENOUNCED AND MESSIANIC FORE-GLIMPSES. 3:1-5:15.

A. Rulers, Priests, and Prophets Denounced. 3:1-12.

1. Rebuke of the elders. 3:1-4.

3:1-4. The **heads of Jacob** and **princes of the house of Israel** are those leaders in both the northern and southern kingdoms who were particularly charged with the upholding of justice in the land. They are the ones who were to protect the innocent and punish the guilty. **Is it not for you to know judgment?** They were to uphold righteousness in the land. **Who hate the good, and love the evil.** Instead, they violated their trust and persecuted the very ones that they were supposed to protect (7:2-3).

Who pluck off their skin from off them, and their flesh from off their bones; Who also eat the flesh of my people, and flay their skin from off them; and they break their bones, and chop them in pieces, as for the pot, and as flesh within the caldron. Their pursuit of the ones they were supposed to protect is so merciless and barbarous that it is portrayed in language that fits in the crudest of terms the butchery and eating of animals. So addicted are they to their pursuit of evil and persecution of the helpless and innocent that only the judgment of God can bring them to their senses. The poor, innocent, and righteous are ever the object of God's love. To do violence to them is to arouse the anger of God.

Then shall they cry unto the LORD, but he will not hear them: he will even hide his face from them at that time, as they have behaved themselves ill in their doings. This anger will fall; and judgment will overtake those to whom judgment had been entrusted, but who violated their trust. When it comes, they will not escape; and Jehovah will hide His face from them, even as they have hidden their faces from those whom they were to protect.

2. Rebuke of the prophets. 3:5-8.

5-8. Thus saith the LORD concerning the prophets that make my people err. The prophets in view in this section are those who enjoy the popularity of the people, but do not have the authority of God behind them. They are false prophets (cf. 2:11). The function of a prophet was to communicate the message of God accurately, regardless of its content. These prophets, like the rulers in 2:1-4, have violated the integrity of the office. Instead of seeking to please God, they speak to please the people and even to console the rulers in their sin. God has said that judgment will come (cf. vs. 4), but they say there shall be only peace.

Therefore night shall be unto you, that ye shall not have a vision . . . ye shall not divine. The worst thing that could happen to a prophet is to have no message to give. This is what will happen to these false prophets. They will seek to have a vision and to communicate some kind of an authoritative, authentic message; but none will come. **Then shall the seers be ashamed, and the diviners confounded.** The true nature of these false prophets will be discovered when, in their own self-interests and self-preservation, they do give forth a message that does not in fact come to pass, or worse, in which the opposite comes true. The problem stems from the fact that the God they claim to represent will in fact give no answer to them. **Yea, they shall all cover their lips; for there is no answer of God.** They will be put to shame and will show this shame openly

---

CHAPTER 3

AND I said, Hear, I pray you, O heads of Jacob, and ye princes of the house of Israel; *Is it* not for you to know judgment?

2 Who hate the good, and love the evil; who pluck off their skin from off them, and their flesh from off their bones;

3 Who also eat the flesh of my people, and flay their skin from off them; and they break their bones, and chop them in pieces, as for the pot, and as flesh within the caldron.

4 Then shall they cry unto the LORD, but he will not hear them: he will even hide his face from them at that time, as they have behaved themselves ill in their doings.

5 ¶Thus saith the LORD concerning the prophets that make my people err, that bite with their teeth, and cry, Peace; and he that putteth not into their mouths, they even prepare war against him.

6 Therefore night *shall be* unto you, that ye shall not have a vision; and it shall be dark unto you, that ye shall not divine; and the sun shall go down over the prophets, and the day shall be dark over them.

7 Then shall the seers be ashamed, and the diviners confounded: yea, they shall all cover their lips; for *there is* no answer of God.

8 But truly I am full of power by the spirit of the LORD, and of judgment, and of might, to declare unto Jacob his transgression, and to Israel his sin.

by covering their lips, which was an Oriental gesture to indicate shame and mourning.

But truly I am full of power by the spirit of the LORD, and of judgment, and of might. In verse 8, Micah sets himself forth as the true prophet of God, in contrast to all the false prophets in verses 5-7. Whereas they could get no answer from God because they had no fellowship with God, Micah is **full of power by the spirit of the LORD.** Because of this, he could declare boldly and accurately the sins of both the northern and southern kingdoms. The false prophets could only set forth a popular, perverted message. **To declare unto Jacob his transgression, and to Israel his sin.** The true prophet of God, strengthened by His Spirit, can objectively and authoritatively proclaim, not only the sin of the people, but also the judgment of God.

3. Rebuke of the rulers, priests, and prophets. 3:9-12.

9 ¶Hear this, I pray you, ye heads of the house of Jacob, and princes of the house of Israel, that abhor judgment, and pervert all equity.
10 They build up Zion with blood, and Jerusalem with iniquity.
11 The heads thereof judge for reward, and the priests thereof teach for hire, and the prophets thereof divine for money: yet will they lean upon the LORD, and say, *Is* not the LORD among us? none evil can come upon us.
12 Therefore shall Zion for your sake be plowed *as* a field, and Jerusalem shall become heaps, and the mountain of the house as the high places of the forest.

9-12. Hear this, I pray you. Emboldened by the realization of the true source of his power and the nature of his mission, Micah now confronts the rulers, priests, and false prophets with their sin and warns them of judgment to come. The rulers and princes have violated their sacred trust (cf. vss. 1-3). **They build up Zion with blood, and Jerusalem with iniquity.** Overtly, they have done this for the public good—but they have gone about it in the wrong way. They have made the nation great by making its citizens miserable, with the result that the nation is filled with sin instead of righteousness.

The proof of this is given in verse 11. Those to whom judgment is given (**The heads**) perform the function of their office for personal gain and bribery. The **priests** teach for financial gain, which was expressly forbidden by Moses (cf. Ex 23:8; Deut 16:19). The **prophets** performed their function for financial gain, which in and of itself was evidence of the fact that they were false. The problem was that they divined, which is never used in a good sense in the Old Testament, instead of prophesying for Jehovah. The tragedy is that the activity of rulers, priests, and prophets alike was carried on under the guise of religious activity. They **lean upon the LORD** and boasted of His presence among them and their peculiar national relationship to Him. **None evil can come upon us.** They made the fatal mistake of mistaking God's favor for favoritism (cf. Rom 3:17-24).

Therefore shall Zion for your sake be plowed as a field. God's judgment is impartial and must fall on all wrongdoers, whether they be rulers, priests, prophets, or whatever. The city that they have so carefully built up (vs. 10) will be utterly destroyed. It will be plowed up like the fields, and its buildings will become rock piles (**heaps**). The **mountain** on which the city sits will become desolate. The prophet Jeremiah painfully records the literalness with which this prophecy was fulfilled, and his lamentation over the desolate city is recorded in the book of Lamentations.

B. Messianic Fore-glimpses. 4:1-5:15.

1. Establishment of Messiah's kingdom. 4:1-5:1.

This section divides into two parts. In verses 1-8 the Millennium is described, in contrast to the chaos of the prophet's day in 4:9-5:1. The fact that the thoughts contained in verses 1-3 occur in almost identical form in Isaiah 2:2-4 should not lead anyone to adapt any unwarranted theory of literary dependence, either of Isaiah upon Micah or of Micah upon Isaiah. It is not beyond the power of God to lead both of His prophets to express the same thoughts in very similar terms. It is possible that there was a common core of prophetical themes set forth in some poetic form to which both could have had access and incorporated into their prophecies for their own purposes. Even if it

CHAPTER 4

BUT in the last days it shall come to pass, *that* the mountain of the house of the Lord shall be established in the top of the mountains, and it shall be exalted above the hills; and people shall flow unto it.

could be demonstrated that one did quote the other, it would not do violence to either the inspiration of the Scripture or to the integrity of either prophet. The important thing is to understand the intent of the thoughts and the context of the prophecy.

4:1. But in the last days it shall come to pass, that the mountain of the house of the Lord shall be established in the top of the mountains, and it shall be exalted above the hills. In contrast to the dark period of judgment that occupied the prophet's thought in chapter 3, Micah now turns to the bright hope for the future. It is bright because it is the word of Jehovah and depends upon Jehovah alone for its fulfillment. The phrase **in the last days** lets us know that the prophet is looking beyond the restoration from the Babylonian captivity to the days of the Millennium when every promise given to Abraham and to Israel ultimately will be fulfilled. The prophecy begins with the establishment of the kingdom of God itself upon the earth. In the prophetic writings, the word **mountain** (Heb *har*) is used symbolically to indicate a great world power (cf. Dan 2:35), while the word **hills** (Heb *gib'ah*) is used to indicate smaller world powers. Thus, the kingdom of Jehovah will be greater than any other earthly power, whether great or small from man's viewpoint. **And people shall flow unto it.** The kingdom of Jehovah will be over all earthly powers, and the people of the earth shall **flow unto it.** The expression **flow** (Heb *nahar*) indicates that all the nations of the earth will be spontaneously and irresistably drawn to Jehovah's kingdom. The thought, then, of verse 1 is that Jehovah's kingdom will be supreme in all the earth.

2 And many nations shall come, and say, Come, and let us go up to the mountain of the Lord, and to the house of the God of Jacob; and he will teach us of his ways, and we will walk in his paths: for the law shall go forth of Zion, and the word of the Lord from Jerusalem.

2. And many nations shall come, and say. The thought of verse 2 is that Messiah's kingdom will be universal in its influence. All the nations of the world will come together to Jerusalem to find out the will of God. **Come, and let us go up to the mountain of the Lord . . . he will teach us of his ways . . . for the law shall go forth of Zion.** They will seek the Messiah's personal instruction and will determine to walk in His ways. His **law** (Heb *tōrah*, direction or teaching) will go forth from the seat of His earthly government, Zion/Jerusalem.

His word will be final and binding in all matters, even to affairs between governments. Such a thought is unimaginable in the present day, considering the insignificance of modern-day Israel's nation and government. The closest this prophecy has ever come to realization was in the days of David and Solomon (cf. I Kgs 10; II Chr 9), which, of course, was already history in Micah's day. Thus, the prophet is looking forward to a day not yet realized in the history of the world, a day when David's son, Messiah, will personally reign over all the world from His throne in Jerusalem.

3 ¶And he shall judge among many people, and rebuke strong nations afar off; and they shall beat their swords into plowshares, and their spears into pruninghooks: nation shall not lift up a sword against nation, neither shall they learn war any more.

3. And he shall judge among many people . . . and they shall beat their swords into plowshares, and their spears into pruninghooks. Because Messiah's kingdom is supreme (vs. 1) and universal (vs. 2), it also will be peaceful (vs. 3). There will be no need for warfare, as earth has known in all its history. The implements of warfare will be recycled into implements of agriculture, and nations will not resort to warfare to settle their disputes. **Nation shall not lift up a sword against nation, neither shall they learn war any more.** Even the strongest and most distant nations will resort to Jerusalem and to the Messiah who will arbitrate all matters of dispute between them. His word will be binding, and any who do not obey will be dealt with summarily; for He will rule with a ". . . rod of iron . . ." (cf. Rev 2:27; 12:5).

4 But they shall sit every man under his vine and under his fig tree; and none shall make *them* afraid: for the mouth of the Lord of hosts hath spoken *it.*

4. But they shall sit every man under his vine and under his fig tree. Since there will be no need for vast financial expenditures for military hardware, Messiah's kingdom will be marked by universal prosperity, the perennial wish in the heart of man for which all schemes for redistributing wealth do not provide the answer. The answer will be provided when God's king rules

God's world from God's nation in God's time! This time will be characterized by universal prosperity and universal security, for it will depend not on the deliberations of man or upon the force that man can marshal, but upon Jehovah whose mouth has spoken it. The **vine** and **fig tree** are both native to Israel and well-established throughout their native culture. When conditions permit and they are allowed to do so, they flourish into luxuriant, natural arbors under which people can sit and enjoy fellowship while being shaded from the heat of the day. **And none shall make them afraid.** In Messiah's kingdom, men will be able to sit under their vines and fig trees in perfect safety, having no need to fear that someone will do them personal harm or seek to take their possessions.

5 For all people will walk every one in the name of his god, and we will walk in the name of the LORD our God for ever and ever.

5. For all people will walk every one in the name of his god, and we will walk in the name of the LORD our God for ever and ever. The prophet's thought is not that all people will walk after the true God in the name of their false gods, in contrast to Israel who will walk after the true God in the name of Jehovah. The text is better rendered, "Though all the peoples walk each in the name of his god, As for us, we will walk In the name of the LORD our God forever and ever" (NASB). Having set forth a beautiful picture of millennial conditions (vss. 1-4), the prophet momentarily contrasts it with what he currently observes— religious confusion among the peoples of the earth calling upon a diversity of gods (vs. 5a). This is in stark contrast to the religious unity that will characterize Israel in the Millennium. All Israel will be rightly related to Jehovah forever.

6 ¶In that day, saith the LORD, will I assemble her that halteth, and I will gather her that is driven out, and her that I have afflicted;
7 And I will make her that halted a remnant, and her that was cast far off a strong nation: and the LORD shall reign over them in mount Zion from henceforth, even for ever.

6-7. In that day . . . will I assemble her that halteth . . . her that is driven out, and her that I have afflicted. In verses 6-8 the prophet puts the whole picture into its proper historical perspective. The prophets have consistently said that God would punish Israel for her sins, scatter, and afflict her. Micah affirms that this indeed will be true; but when Jehovah's purpose has been completed, the people have repented, and Messiah establishes His millennial reign, Jehovah will regather the nation that **halteth** (is lame), **is driven out** and **afflicted** and will establish her and make her a strong nation, the most influential in all the world (cf. vs. 2). **And I will make her that halted a remnant, and her that was cast far off a strong nation: and the LORD shall reign over them in mount Zion from henceforth, even for ever.** At this time Jehovah, in the person of His Son Messiah, will reign over them in Jerusalem forever.

8 And thou, O tower of the flock, the strong hold of the daughter of Zion, unto thee shall it come, even the first dominion; the kingdom shall come to the daughter of Jerusalem.

8. The prophet addresses the **tower of the flock** (Heb *migdal-'Ēder,* tower of Eder) and **the stronghold** (Heb *'ōpel,* high place) **of the daughter of Zion.** The former was located about a mile from Beth-lehem and is indicative of King David's birthplace (and also the birthplace of his son, Messiah, cf. 5:2) and the latter is indicative of Jerusalem where David reigned and where Messiah will reign. **The kingdom shall come to the daughter of Jerusalem.** These places which have enjoyed prominence in the past, because of their connection with King David, will once again enjoy an even greater prominence under David's son, Jesus the Messiah!

9 ¶Now why dost thou cry out aloud? is there no king in thee? is thy counsellor perished? for pangs have taken thee as a woman in travail.
10 Be in pain, and labour to bring forth, O daughter of Zion, like a woman in travail: for now shalt thou go forth out of the city, and thou shalt dwell in the field, and thou shalt go even to Babylon: there shalt thou be delivered; there the LORD shall redeem thee from the hand of thine enemies.
11 ¶Now also many nations are gathered against thee, that say, Let her be defiled, and let our eye look upon Zion.

9-13. Now why dost thou cry out aloud? is there no king in thee? In contrast to the glorious days of the future Millennium, in verses 9-13 the prophet shifts his attention to the chaos of his day and to the near future that will overtake the nation. The picture is dark, for the nation will be stripped of its kingdom and taken captive into Babylon. **For pangs have taken thee as a woman in travail. Be in pain, and labor to bring forth, O daughter of Zion, like a woman in travail . . . thou shalt go even to Babylon; there shalt thou be delivered.** All of these sufferings, which the nation must endure because of its sins, are the birthpangs that will ultimately be the nation's deliverance from its enemies and its establishment under Messiah.

Now also many nations are gathered against thee. The

12 But they know not the thoughts of the LORD, neither understand they his counsel: for he shall gather them as the sheaves into the floor.

13 Arise and thresh, O daughter of Zion: for I will make thine horn iron, and I will make thy hoofs brass: and thou shalt beat in pieces many people: and I will consecrate their gain unto the LORD, and their substance unto the Lord of the whole earth.

CHAPTER 5

NOW gather thyself in troops, O daughter of troops: he hath laid siege against us: they shall smite the judge of Israel with a rod upon the cheek.

2 But thou, Bĕth–lehĕm Ĕph′ra-tăh, *though* thou be little among the thousands of Judah, *yet* out of thee shall he come forth unto me *that is* to be ruler in Israel; whose goings forth *have been* from of old, from everlasting.

mention of the birthpangs that the nation will suffer under Babylon causes the prophet to think of the greater birthpangs that the nation will suffer in the days of the Great Tribulation when all the nations of the world will lay siege against Israel. In fact, these birthpangs will issue in the establishment of Messiah's kingdom. **But they know not the thoughts of the LORD . . . and thou shalt beat in pieces many people.** The nations have come with the motive of destroying Israel; but they do not understand that they have been gathered together so that Jehovah can crush them in one massive conflagration and establish His earthly, Davidic, millennial kingdom over all the world (4:11-5:1; cf. Mt 24:15-21, 27-31; Rev 6:12-17; 13:14-18).

5:1. Now gather thyself in troops . . . he hath laid siege against us: they shall smite the judge of Israel with a rod upon the cheek. The prophet shifts his attention back to the more immediate scene, the impending Babylonian invasion. The nation is urged to prepare itself militarily because a siege is coming and the king will be stripped from them. The **judge of Israel** who will be smitten with a **rod upon the cheek** should not be misconstrued to be a reference to the humiliation of Jesus; for He was never smitten in any military siege, neither was He smitten with a rod nor by Gentiles. He was smitten by His own people. The reference is more properly to the removal of the king from Israel, particularly King Zedekiah, and his shameful treatment at the hands of Babylon (cf. II Kgs 25). Since that day, Israel has not had a king and will not have a king until Messiah sets up His kingdom and reigns over the redeemed nation.

2. Messiah the King and Deliverer. 5:2-15.

2. But thou Beth-lehem Ephratah, though thou be little among the thousands of Judah, yet out of thee shall he come forth unto me that is to be ruler in Israel; whose goings forth have been from of old, from everlasting. Given more than seven hundred years before the birth of Christ, the prophecy of verse 2 is unique for its great detail. It was this passage to which the chief priests and scribes referred when Herod demanded information from them concerning the birth of Christ. This verse reveals the exact location of Messiah's birth, His destiny, and His eternality. There were two insignificant towns in Israel that bore the name Beth-lehem. One was in the north, about six miles southeast of Mount Carmel in the area belonging to the tribe of Zebulun; and the other was approximately six miles southwest of Jerusalem in the area belonging to Judah. Thus, the town is addressed as **Beth-lehem** (house of bread) **Ephratah** (fruitful) to indicate clearly that the Beth-lehem of Judah is to be the birthplace of Messiah the king.

The fact of its obscurity, having been the birthplace of King David, is indicative of the low estate to which the Davidic dynasty had fallen and the low regard with which it was held. From this obscure village would come forth the most prominent citizen and Ruler in all the world! He will come forth in keeping with the plan of God and will fulfill His purposes as is indicated by the words **unto me.** Though there will be a specific point in time at which this Ruler will come forth, His earthly manifestation is not the beginning of His existence; for He has had many **goings forth** from **everlasting** (i.e., eternity past). He had gone forth at many times in past history and had appeared unto many people in Christophanies (i.e., pre-incarnate appearances of Christ in the form of the angel of Jehovah. Thus, in Micah verse 2 is contained in seminal form that which is revealed in fuller form in the Gospel of John chapter 1: the eternality and pre-existence of the Son of God (Jn 1:1-13) and the historical incarnation of the Son of God (Jn 1:14), though Micah treats them in the reverse order.

3 Therefore will he give them up, un-

3. Therefore will he give them up, until the time that she

til the time *that* she which travaileth hath brought forth: then the remnant of his brethren shall return unto the children of Israel.

which travaileth hath brought forth: then the remnant of his brethren shall return unto the children of Israel. Though there is great diversity of scholarly opinion concerning verse 3, it is probably best to understand it as referring to the rejection that Messiah will receive in the days of His earthly ministry. Verse 2 has shown that He transcends time in the past and, therefore, logically can be assumed to transcend time in the future. In the light of His overall eternal existence, it is nothing that He should give up a small segment of the nation's historical existence in order to fulfill the greater program of God. The Israel of Messiah's day (and the Apostle Paul's and up to the present), then, are "vessels . . . for destruction," and not redeemed Israel (cf. Rom 9-11). Had the Israel of Messiah's day not rejected Him, then this prophecy would have been frustrated, just as though He were born in some place other than Beth-lehem of Judah or not born at all.

There was a believing remnant in Messiah's day, and in Paul's day, and in the present day. In the future there will also be a believing remnant. It is over this believing remnant that Messiah will establish His kingdom and reign for a thousand years. The expression **she which travaileth** can be understood both generally and specifically. Generally, it is to the nation, which travailed until Messiah was born (cf. Rev 12), and specifically, it is to the Virgin Mary who physically travailed for the physical birth of Messiah. The import of verses 2-3 is that Messiah transcends time. His destiny is not dependent upon the Israel of the prophet's or His own day. Just as surely as God in His sovereign program has brought Messiah upon the scene historically, so He will bring the believing remnant into existence; and in His time both redeemed people and reigning Messiah will be brought together!

4 And he shall stand and feed in the strength of the LORD, in the majesty of the name of the LORD his God; and they shall abide: for now shall he be great unto the ends of the earth.

4. And he shall stand and feed in the strength of the LORD, in the majesty of the name of the LORD his God. This verse pictures the Messiah's coming to the earth to set up His Millennial Kingdom. The flow of the passage is thus: verse 2 predicts His coming; verse 3 predicts His rejection; and verse 4 predicts His exaltation. The one born in verse 2, rejected in verse 3 now becomes the Great Shepherd of Israel in verse 4. He shall meet the basic need of His people, food and security; and His provision and protection will be universal. His whole ministry will be undertaken in both the strength and authority of Jehovah.

Chapter 5 verses 5-15 enumerates what the coming of Messiah to set up His kingdom will mean for the nation over which He will rule: (1) He will establish peace (vs. 5); (2) He will deliver the nation from its enemies (vs. 6); (3) He will empower His people to be victorious over their enemies (vss. 7-9); (4) He will destroy the weapons of warfare so that there will be no more war (vs. 10); (5) He will destroy all military fortifications (vs. 11); (6) He will destroy all witchcraft and idolatry (vss. 12-14); and (7) He will destroy all of the sinful nations (vs. 15).

5 And this *man* shall be the peace, when the Assyrian shall come into our land: and when he shall tread in our palaces, then shall we raise against him seven shepherds, and eight principal men.

6 And they shall waste the land of Assyria with the sword, and the land of Nimrod in the entrances thereof: thus shall he deliver *us* from the Assyrian, when he cometh into our land, and when he treadeth within our borders.

5-6. And this man shall be the peace, when the Assyrian shall come into our land. The **Assyrian**, which was Israel's major foe in Micah's day, is probably best understood as representative of all of Israel's enemies, particularly those of the end times. This would be comprised primarily of all the forces of the king of the east and the king of the west (the kings of the north and south having been defeated in the middle of the Tribulation) drawn up in array in the vain attempt to prevent Messiah from returning to the earth to establish his kingdom. Messiah will slay them with the breath of His mouth and will institute His millennial reign of peace. The ideas conveyed by the raising up of **seven shepherds, and eight principal men** is the thought of adequate defense. The enemies of Israel cannot destroy it nor can they deter Messiah from establishing His kingdom and His reign of peace.

And they shall waste the land of Assyria . . . and the land of

Nimrod. They that would lay Israel waste will in turn be laid waste by the Messiah who will be Israel's Deliverer. The mention of **Nimrod** is fitting, for in him both Babylon and Assyria are united as a single foe (cf. Gen 10:8-13). Since in a very real way Micah is ministering to both the Babylonian and Assyrian crises (much as Isaiah also did), in Nimrod both of these crises are effectively united. **Thus shall he deliver us from the Assyrian.** Their deliverance stems from divine intervention in the person of Messiah.

7 And the remnant of Jacob shall be in the midst of many people as a dew from the Lord, as the showers upon the grass, that tarrieth not for man, nor waiteth for the sons of men.

7. The blessings that Messiah will provide for His people are set forth in the figures of **dew from the Lord** and **showers upon the grass.** What the dew and showers are to the land, Israel will be to the righteous in the nations among whom it dwells. It will refresh and provide essential nourishment to them.

8 ¶And the remnant of Jacob shall be among the Gentiles in the midst of many people as a lion among the beasts of the forest, as a young lion among the flocks of sheep: who, if he go through, both treadeth down, and teareth in pieces, and none can deliver.

8. A second figure in verse 8 sets forth what Israel will be like to the Gentiles who resist Messiah's universal reign. To them they will be like a **lion among the beasts of the forest** and as a **young lion among the flocks of sheep.** In verses 6-7, then, Israel's twofold function during the Millennium period is set forth: to believing Gentiles she will be a source of refreshment (vs. 7), but to unbelieving Gentiles she will be a source of judgment enforcing the rule of Messiah.

9 Thine hand shall be lifted up upon thine adversaries, and all thine enemies shall be cut off.

9. **Thine hand shall be lifted up upon thine adversaries, and all thine enemies shall be cut off.** This verse sets forth the victory that Israel will enjoy, her hand will be raised in victory, and every adversary will be defeated.

10 And it shall come to pass in that day, saith the Lord, that I will cut off thy horses out of the midst of thee, and I will destroy thy chariots.
11 And I will cut off the cities of thy land, and throw down all thy strong holds:
12 And I will cut off witchcrafts out of thine hand; and thou shalt have no more soothsayers.
13 Thy graven images also will I cut off, and thy standing images out of the midst of thee; and thou shalt no more worship the work of thine hands.
14 And I will pluck up thy groves out of the midst of thee: so will I destroy thy cities.

10-14. **And it shall come to pass . . . I will cut off thy horses out of the midst of thee, and I will destroy thy chariots.** All of this will come to pass because Israel will be in perfect fellowship with Jehovah. They will not be able to put their trust in the weapons of warfare, for Jehovah will remove completely all horses and chariots in which they were prone to trust. **And I will cut off the cities . . . and throw down all thy strongholds.** In addition, all of the fortified cities in which they could trust will be completely demolished. **And I will cut off witchcrafts . . . and thou shalt have no more soothsayers.** Further, all forms of false worship that had robbed the nation of its vitality will be done away. This includes witchcraft, and soothsaying (divination) will be cut off (vs. 12). **Thy graven images also will I cut off . . . I will pluck up thy groves . . . so will I destroy thy cities.** The idols and the groves (Heb *ashērah*, shrine) will be destroyed, as will the cities in which these false forms of worship are carried on. All of these had been previously outlawed in the commands God had given to Moses, but unregenerate Israel carried them on anyway. Redeemed Israel must and will have them put away, and their trust will be only in Jehovah and in His power. They will be a blessing to all who practice righteousness, and judgment to all who practice unrighteousness.

15 And I will execute vengeance in anger and fury upon the heathen, such as they have not heard.

15. **And I will execute vengeance in anger and fury upon the heathen.** This is a summary statement of the judgment God will exercise upon all the Gentiles who were the source of the evils that infected Israel. Thus not only will the evil fruit be destroyed (vss. 10-14), but also the evil root.

IV. THE THIRD DISCOURSE: JEHOVAH'S CONTROVERSY WITH HIS PEOPLE AND GOD, ISRAEL'S ONLY HOPE. 6:1-7:20.

A. Jehovah's Controversy. 6:1-16.

1. God's reminder of His faithfulness. 6:1-5.

Having focused upon the glory that will be Israel's in the future (ch. 5), the prophet now turns to look at the sins that infect Israel in the present (ch. 6).

6:1-2. **Arise, contend thou before the mountains, and let the hills hear thy voice.** Inanimate nature is called upon as

CHAPTER 6
HEAR ye now what the Lord saith:

Arise, contend thou before the mountains, and let the hills hear thy voice.

2 Hear ye, O mountains, the LORD's controversy, and ye strong foundations of the earth: for the LORD hath a controversy with his people, and he will plead with Israel.

3 O my people, what have I done unto thee? and wherein have I wearied thee? testify against me.

4 For I brought thee up out of the land of Egypt, and redeemed thee out of the house of servants; and I sent before thee Moses, Aaron, and Miriam.

5 O my people, remember now what Bā'lăk king of Moab consulted, and what Bā'laam the son of Bē'ŏr answered him from Shĭt'tĭm unto Gilgal; that ye may know the righteousness of the LORD.

6 Wherewith shall I come before the LORD, and bow myself before the high God? shall I come before him with burnt offerings, with calves of a year old?

7 Will the LORD be pleased with thousands of rams, or with ten thousands of rivers of oil? shall I give my firstborn for my transgression, the fruit of my body for the sin of my soul?

8 He hath shewed thee, O man, what is good; and what doth the LORD require of thee, but to do justly, and to love mercy, and to walk humbly with thy God?

impartial witnesses of Israel's sin. These **mountains** and **hills** were there before Israel was in the land, and they will be there when Israel is removed. They have witnessed Israel's sin and ultimately will witness Israel's glorification. The prophet exhorts the people to hear what Jehovah says and plead their cause before the **mountains** and **hills**.

Hear ye, O mountains, the LORD's controversy. Jehovah addresses the **mountains** and advises them of His controversy with His People and condescends to plead with His wayward nation.

3-5. O my people, what have I done unto thee? Jehovah addresses His people directly. In spite of their grievous sins, He still calls them **my people.** Though they have disowned Him, He remains faithful and has not disowned them. **Wherein have I wearied thee? testify against me.** Jehovah asked for an accounting for their faithlessness and invites them to testify against Him. **For I brought thee up out of the land of Egypt . . . and I sent before thee Moses, Aaron, and Miriam.** Jehovah recites the historical record to demonstrate that He has done only good to Israel, for He brought them up out of the slavery of Egypt and gave them Moses (the lawgiver who told them what God wanted), Aaron (the high priest who interceded in behalf of the people when they failed to do what God wanted) and Miriam (the prophetess who led Israel in the dance of victory after Israel had crossed the Red Sea, cf. Ex 15:20-22) to be their national leaders.

These leaders were manifestations of God's grace to them. **Remember . . . Balak . . . Balaam,** the reference to history continues. In addition to providing leaders for them, Jehovah has provided deliverance. God delivered them from Balak, the king of Moab, who hired Balaam the son of Beor (cf. Num 22-24) to curse Israel. God overruled, and the curses were turned into blessings. Such an intercession on God's part should cause Israel to know that He is righteous, and that He is their God. God cares for His people, even when they are in the enemy territory, as the citation of the place names attests. **Shittim** was the location of the first campsite where Israel paused after her encounter with Balaam. **Gilgal** was the first place where she stopped in the land of Canaan (cf. Num 25:1). It was there that they were totally disabled in the presence of their enemies, for God required Joshua to have all the males circumcised as a testimony of the fathers' belief of God's promises to Abraham (cf. Josh 4:19-5:10).

2. The people's reply. 6:6-8.

6-7. Wherewith shall I come before the LORD, and bow myself before the high God? The people, apparently convicted by Jehovah's contention (vss. 1-5), addressed their questions to the prophet. They asked what is necessary to obtain the favor of Jehovah. **Shall I come before him with burnt offerings, with calves of a year old?** Their questions indicate that they think that God will be content with external formalities (vss. 6-7). If quality will influence Jehovah, then they will offer the best of **burnt offerings.** If quantity will impress Jehovah, then they will offer **thousands of rams** and **ten thousands of rivers of oil.** If human sacrifice will secure Jehovah's favor, then they will offer their **first-born** children to atone for their sins. The fact is that none of these will secure Jehovah's favor, for all are external and stem from a wrong motive and a false understanding of Jehovah.

8. He hath showed thee, O man, what is good; and what doth the LORD require of thee, but to do justly, and to love mercy, and to walk humbly with thy God? The prophet answers the people's questions and shows that Jehovah does not wish mere external conformity, but internal reality; there must be a right inner attitude towards Him. Micah begins his answer with a bit of chiding, for they should have known what Jehovah required; He had revealed it to them through Moses. Even though the Mosaic system dealt with externals, it was not exhausted by externals. The externals were evidences of that which was true in one's heart relationship with God, which was the root while the externals were the fruit. If one's heart attitudes were right, then he would perform the externals of the Mosaic system and offer the sacrifices provided in the event of his failure to do so. Israel is addressed as **O man** to remind them that these instructions are universally applicable, and also to remind them of their finiteness before Jehovah.

Jehovah's requirements move in three dimensions: outward, inward, and upward. Outwardly, **to do justly** necessitates dealing righteously with one's fellow man. Inwardly, **to love mercy** (Heb *chesed*, covenant loyalty) necessitates having the inward commitment to God's revelation that will manifest itself in a right relationship towards man and God. Upward, **to walk humbly with thy God** necessitates having a right attitude towards God and a determination to walk in continuous fellowship with Him. This verse once again puts things in proper perspective; for the external, outward dimension is inextricably tied to the internal (the inward and upward). How one walks in relation to his fellow man is indicative of his inward resolve and relationship to God.

3. Jehovah rebukes injustice. 6:9-16.

In this section the prophet demonstrates once again that Israel does not possess the virtues enumerated in verse 8. Their dealings with their fellow men give incontrovertible evidence that this is true; therefore, God's judgment must fall upon them.

9. The LORD's voice crieth unto the city. The **city** to which the Lord's voice cries is best understood as the same city that has been addressed throughout the prophecy: Jerusalem. Although the verse is capable of other minor variations of meaning, verse 9 is probably best understood to indicate simply that when the LORD's voice speaks, the **man of wisdom** will give heed to what the voice says and will note from whom the voice comes. The **rod** (Heb *mateh*) is an instrument of punishment, and it here indicates the content of the message that the LORD's voice delivers and the man of wisdom will hear. The resultant thought, then, is that when the Lord's voice declares that judgment will fall, the man of wisdom will note that the message comes from Jehovah and, hence, will believe that judgment will in fact fall because it is a judgment appointed by God Himself. The specific forms that this judgment will take are spelled out in detail in verses 13-16.

10-12. These verses offer additional evidence, as if it were needed, of the fact that the coming judgment is well-deserved. Again, it is their dealings with their fellow men that indicate that their heart attitude and relationship with God are not right. The sins enumerated are: the unjust acquisition of treasures from their fellow men, the giving of less than true value through the use of short measures, the use of scales that do not give proper measure because they do not weigh properly, and the gaining of wealth through violence, lies, and deceit in business dealings with their fellow men. This enumeration of sins adequately shows that they do not possess the right heart attitude and relationship with God required in verse 8; therefore, they are just candidates for God's wrath, and it must fall.

13-15. These verses enumerate the forms God's judgment will take: they will experience the judgment of God and all their gains will be taken from them; they will experience famine; all of their attempts to avert God's judgment and save their ill-gotten gain will be futile; and they will not harvest the crops that they sow or use the olive oil they have made, or drink the wine which they have made; all preparations that they have made for their living in luxury will not be realized.

9 ¶The LORD's voice crieth unto the city, and *the man of* wisdom shall see thy name: hear ye the rod, and who hath appointed it.

10 Are there yet the treasures of wickedness in the house of the wicked, and the scant measure *that is* abominable?
11 Shall I count *them* pure with the wicked balances, and with the bag of deceitful weights?
12 For the rich men thereof are full of violence, and the inhabitants thereof have spoken lies, and their tongue *is* deceitful in their mouth.

13 Therefore also will I make *thee* sick in smiting thee, in making *thee* desolate because of thy sins.
14 Thou shalt eat, but not be satisfied; and thy casting down *shall be* in the midst of thee; and thou shalt take hold, but shalt not deliver; and *that* which thou deliverest will I give up to the sword.

15 Thou shalt sow, but thou shalt not reap; thou shalt tread the olives, but thou shalt not anoint thee with oil; and sweet wine, but shalt not drink wine.

16 For the statutes of Omri are kept, and all the works of the house of Ahab, and ye walk in their counsels; that I should make thee a desolation, and the inhabitants thereof an hissing: therefore ye shall bear the reproach of my people.

16. This verse gives the reason why God's judgment must fall. Instead of walking in the ways of Jehovah, they have walked in the ways of their wicked kings Omri and Ahab. These are northern kings who represented the epitome of wickedness and embodied everything that Jehovah hated. **Omri** was the founder of Samaria, which later became the capital of the northern kingdom, and instituted the idolatrous practices begun by Jeroboam in that city (cf. I Kgs 16:16-28). **Ahab** was Omri's son and followed in the wicked ways of his father, carrying them to the extreme. He instituted Baal and Asherah worship in Samaria (cf. I Kgs 16:30-33), which later spread into the southern kingdom as well. For this reason, God's judgment will fall; and those who have followed in the ways of Omri and Ahab will be made a **desolation** and an object of derision and reproach.

B. God, Israel's Only Hope. 7:1-20.

In this whole chapter the prophet speaks not only for himself, but on behalf of the godly remaining in the nation. He vividly describes the evil that is rampant in the land and points to Jehovah, who is Israel's only hope for three reasons:

1. Because the godly have perished. 7:1-6.

7:1-2. Woe is me! for I am as when they have gathered the summer fruits. The prophet pictures himself and the nation as an orchard and a vineyard after each has been harvested. **There is no cluster to eat.** There is not even so much as a cluster of grapes or a piece of ripe fruit left to eat, and the nation has been stripped of every last vestige of righteousness. This is true because the **good** (Heb *chasid*, kind, merciful, pious, godly, or better, covenant loyalty) has ceased in the land, with the result that no one walks uprightly with relation to his fellow man. Since they have thrown over their belief in God's great covenants (Abrahamic, Palestinian, Davidic, and New), they now bloodthirstily pursue one another **with a net,** which is how they caught fish and hunted animals.

3-4. These verses demonstrate the truth that covenant loyalty (the belief in the unconditional covenant God gave to Israel, cf. vs. 2), has perished in the land. Instead of seeking to do righteousness and seeking to serve Jehovah, they seek to do evil with **both hands earnestly.** The **prince** and **judge** and **great man** in the land contrive evil together and bring it to pass. They are **sharper,** but only in a harmful sense. They use their sharpness to bring hurt as a **brier** and a thorn; therefore, their judgment must come. This judgment was predicted by Israel's **watchmen,** the prophets of God. The **visitation** that they predicted was a visitation on the part of God, with a view to avenging the righteous and punishing the guilty. It was a visitation of judgment that would result in the sharp princes, judges, and notable men being punished for the evil deeds that they had performed against the godly.

5-6. Trust ye not in a friend. Because sin is so rampant throughout the land, it affects, distorts, and perverts every human relationship. A **friend** cannot be trusted; a **guide** cannot be given confidence; intimate communication cannot be entrusted to one's most intimate relationships; sons and daughters rebel against their parents; a man's wife will rebel against his mother; and household servants will turn against their masters. In short, chaos will reign throughout the land, destroying every interpersonal relationship; for it will be once again as it was in the days of the judges with each man doing that which is right in his own eyes (cf. Jud 21:25).

CHAPTER 7

WOE is me! for I am as when they have gathered the summer fruits, as the grapegleanings of the vintage: there is no cluster to eat: my soul desired the first-ripe fruit.

2 The good *man* is perished out of the earth: and *there is* none upright among men: they all lie in wait for blood; they hunt every man his brother with a net.

3 That they may do evil with both hands earnestly, the prince asketh, and the judge *asketh* for a reward; and the great *man*, he uttereth his mischievous desire: so they wrap it up.

4 The best of them *is* as a brier: the most upright *is sharper* than a thorn hedge: the day of thy watchmen *and* thy visitation cometh; now shall be their perplexity.

5 Trust ye not in a friend, put ye not confidence in a guide: keep the doors of thy mouth from her that lieth in thy bosom.

6 For the son dishonoureth the father, the daughter riseth up against her mother, the daughter in law against her mother in law; a man's enemies *are* the men of his own house.

7 Therefore I will look unto the Lord; I will wait for the God of my salvation: my God will hear me.

8 ¶Rejoice not against me, O mine enemy: when I fall, I shall arise; when I sit in darkness, the Lord *shall be* a light unto me.

9 I will bear the indignation of the Lord, because I have sinned against him, until he plead my cause, and execute judgment for me: he will bring me forth to the light, *and* I shall behold his righteousness.

10 Then *she that is* mine enemy shall see *it*, and shame shall cover her which said unto me, Where is the Lord thy God? mine eyes shall behold her: now shall she be trodden down as the mire of the streets.

11 ¶*In* the day that thy walls are to be built, *in* that day shall the decree be far removed.

12 *In* that day *also* he shall come even to thee from Assyria, and *from* the fortified cities, and from the fortress even to the river, and from sea to sea, and *from* mountain to mountain.

13 Notwithstanding the land shall be desolate because of them that dwell therein, for the fruit of their doings.

14 ¶Feed thy people with thy rod, the flock of thine heritage, which dwell solitarily *in* the wood, in the midst of Carmel: let them feed *in* Bā′shan and Gilead, as in the days of old.

1750

2. Because He is the source of light in darkness. 7:7-13.

7. Therefore I will look unto the Lord. The prophet expresses his confidence in Jehovah who alone remains faithful against the backdrop of such infidelity in every human relationship. The prophet is functioning as a spokesman for all those who are godly. In spite of the dark outlook around them, they resolutely look unto Jehovah and patiently wait for his salvation (Heb *yēsha'*, safety, ease, deliverance), confident that God will hear their prayers even though the kings, judges, and influential people of the land refuse to do so.

8. Rejoice not against me, O mine enemy. The enemy, viewed as victorious, is exhorted not to rejoice over the fallen nation because their victory was accomplished as an unwitting tool in the hand of Jehovah. **When I sit in darkness, the Lord shall be a light unto me.** The righteous, who have endured the unrighteousness of wicked princes, judges, and influential people, can also endure the indignation heaped upon them by their enemy; for Jehovah will be with them and will be light in the midst of darkness.

9. I will bear the indignation of the Lord, because I have sinned against him. The prophet expresses subjection, confession, confidence and expectation. The righteous can recognize that the judgment brought against Israel is the Lord's doing in just retribution for their sins. Further, they can have confidence in His unswerving love of them and expect the time of deliverance when He will once again restore the nation and they will be His people and He will be their God. Thus, verse 9 beautifully expresses the thought of I Peter 5:7 and the realization of the New Covenant of Jeremiah 31:31-34.

10. Then she that is mine enemy shall see it. Israel's enemies will witness this restoration and no longer will taunt asking **Where is the Lord thy God?** The restoration of Israel will result in the destruction of all of her enemies who will be **trodden down as the mire of the streets.**

11-13. Having addressed Israel's enemies in verses 8-10, the prophet now turns to address Israel itself and develops the thought of her restoration in 11-13. Verse 11 gives the thought of restoration (**thy walls are to be built**) and enlargement. The word **decree** (Heb *chōq*, statute, famed decree, or thing marked out) has been given various interpretations; but in view of the restoration, it is probably best to understand it as reference to Israel's borders or boundary lines, which will be greatly enlarged. This was to some degree realized in the restoration following the Babylonian captivity; but ultimately, it will be realized in **that day** when Israel will be established as the central nation of the world and all the nations of the world will flow unto it (cf. ch. 4). **In that day also he shall come even to thee from Assyria . . . and from mountain to mountain.** The thought of universal blessing is continued. The prophet, in the most general of language, expresses the thought that all people of all lands will prosper from Israel's blessing. Then, truly, the ultimate fulfillment of the promise to Abraham that ". . . in thee shall all families of the earth be blessed" (Gen 12:3b) will be realized. **Notwithstanding the land shall be desolate . . . for the fruit of their doings.** The prophet's view returns to the immediate problem. Before the nation can be a blessing to the world, it must be purged of its sin; hence, God's judgment must fall which will result in its intermediate desolation as just recompence for their sin.

3. Because He cares for His people. 7:14-17.

14. Verse 14 is the prophet's prayer to Jehovah, and verses 15-16 give Jehovah's response to the prophet's prayer. The prophet entreats God to meet the temporal needs of His people and protect them from every danger. The **rod** in 7:14 is not an

15 According to the days of thy coming out of the land of Egypt will I shew unto him marvellous *things*.

16 The nations shall see and be confounded at all their might: they shall lay *their* hand upon *their* mouth, their ears shall be deaf.

17 They shall lick the dust like a serpent, they shall move out of their holes like worms of the earth: they shall be afraid of the LORD our God, and shall fear because of thee.

18 ¶Who *is* a God like unto thee, that pardoneth iniquity, and passeth by the transgression of the remnant of his heritage? he retaineth not his anger for ever, because he delighteth *in* mercy.

19 He will turn again, he will have compassion upon us; he will subdue our iniquities; and thou wilt cast all their sins into the depths of the sea.

20 Thou wilt perform the truth to Jacob, *and* the mercy to Abraham, which thou hast sworn unto our fathers from the days of old.

instrument of punishment, but rather is an instrument of provision and protection as in Psalm 23:4. The geographical points of **Carmel, Bashan,** and **Gilead** are set forth as representative of the entire land. Thus, God is entreated to provide for all of the people and to protect them as He had in former days.

15-17. These verses give Jehovah's response to the prophet's prayer. God promises to do wonderful things for them as He did in delivering them from Egypt, and He will defeat the nations before them. Though the nations see Israel's deliverance and experience defeat, they refuse to believe it and vainly attempt to avoid it. Their defeat and subjection will be absolute, for **They shall lick the dust like a serpent** and **shall move out of their holes like worms.** These are figures of abject defeat and servitude, for they will crawl in the dust in unconditional surrender. The reason for their fear is not the nation or its strength, but is their God, Jehovah, who has accomplished this.

4. Because He pardons iniquity and keeps His word. 7:18-20.

18-20. The closing words of the prophecy are words of praise in which the prophet praises Jehovah for His dealings with sin (vs. 18), His compassion (vs. 19), and His fulfilling His word (vs. 20). The God whom the nations fear in terror is the God whom the prophet fears in adoration and worship. God's working for Israel in the future is possible only because He is able to pardon sin and not allow it to deter Him for His future program. He will not always be angry with His sinful people, for He delights in **mercy** (Heb *chesed*, covenant loyalty). God is occupied in fulfilling all that He covenanted to Israel in His unconditional covenant given to them; and because of His word, and for His own glory, Jehovah will have compassion upon His people, particularly in dealing with their sins and regenerating the entire nation (cf. Jer 31:31-33). The prophet's confidence rests upon the revealed word of God (which he described as **the truth to Jacob** and **the mercy to Abraham**) which God gave originally to Abraham and confirmed to all of the Patriarchs. This is a primary reference to the Abrahamic covenant of Genesis 12:1-3, which is in turn amplified in its national aspects by the Palestinian covenant of Deuteronomy 29-30, in its personal aspects by the Davidic covenant of II Samuel 7, and its universal aspects by the New Covenant of Jeremiah 31:31-34.

Thus, the prophecy concludes as it was begun, with a reference to the word of Jehovah. In the beginning it was a word that came from Jehovah concerning impending doom for Israel, and in the end it is a word that Jehovah had given to Abraham before the nation was formed and which Jehovah will unconditionally keep. The prophet and the nation can be assured of the words of this prophecy, as well as the provisions of those covenants, because they both depend upon Jehovah. Thus, both the prophet and the nation can have an assurance similar to that expressed in Romans 8:28!

(see page 1864 for Bibliography to the Minor Prophets)

NAHUM

INTRODUCTION

Authorship. The author of this prophecy is named simply "Nahum the Elkoshite" (1:1), and all that is known of the prophet is gleaned from this prophecy. Probably the identity of the prophet is obscured so that his message can be prominent. The prophet's name means consolation, which gives an indication of the purpose of the prophecy. It was Nahum's mission to comfort the kingdom of Judah following the destruction of Israel by Assyria by announcing God's coming judgment upon Nineveh, the capital of Assyria. In spite of the mission of Jonah and Nineveh's repentance some one hundred to one hundred fifty years earlier, the present generation of Assyria once again is God-rejecting and unrepentant. Under Sennacherib it invaded Judah and laid siege to Jerusalem; and the siege was lifted only by divine intervention, or Judah would have suffered Israel's fate. Nahum comes upon the scene to pronounce God's judgment against Nineveh/Assyria, thus giving consolation to Judah that Assyria will pose no further threat to them.

Nahum was a native of the city of Elkosh, but its location is not known for certain. It is possible that it is to be identified with Capernaum (lit., village of Nahum), which was renamed in honor of its most famous citizen. It is probable, then, that Nahum was born in Galilee, but during Israel's defection moved to Judah and in Jerusalem took up his ministry on behalf of Judah against Nineveh.

Nahum was a prophet contemporary with Isaiah, Hosea, Amos, and Micah.

Date and Place of Writing. Being occupied with the doom of Nineveh, Nahum does not date his prophecy according to any of the kings of Israel or Judah. It is commonly thought that he ministered during the reign of Hezekiah, and this would certainly fit if 1:9-13 is understood as a vivid description of Sennacherib's invasion of Judah and siege of Jerusalem. The only historical citation that can be identified with certainty is the reference to "No" (No-amon, i.e., Thebes), which during the period of 718 B.C. to 657 B.C. was conquered by Assyria four times (3:8-10). The prophet cites Nineveh's destruction of No-amon and points out that if God did not spare that city, then He certainly would not spare Nineveh; for Nineveh is not better than Thebes (3:11-15a). Thus, it can be ascertained with certainty that the prophecy was written after the destruction of Thebes, which destruction it records, and before the destruction of Nineveh, which destruction it predicts. Nineveh was destroyed in 612 B.C. or 606 B.C. In all probability, then, the prophet ministered about one hundred years before the event took place; thus, the date of the prophecy would be about 700 B.C.

The place from which the prophet ministered is best understood as Jerusalem which had so recently experienced near destruction by Sennacherib, king of Assyria. Its siege and divine intervention is briefly described in 1:9-13.

Characteristics of the Prophecy. The prophecy of Nahum is dominated by a single idea, the doom of Nineveh. In describing this doom, Nahum writes lyric poetry of the highest quality. It has been called the most poetical of all the prophetic writings and certainly is the most severe in tone of any of the minor prophets. The only pictures of brightness are in the beginning of the prophecy (cf. 1:7, 15), rather than at the end, as is characteristic of most of the prophets. So occupied is the prophet with the doom of Nineveh that nothing is said of either Israel's or Judah's sin, judgment, or restoration. The book contains many remarkable prophecies which were fulfilled in exact detail, and attention will be given to them later.

Purpose. The purpose of Nahum's prophecy is twofold: (1) To deliver a message of judgment and destruction against Nineveh, the capital of Assyria; and (2) to give comfort to Judah, so recently ravaged by Assyria, that Assyria is doomed and will constitute a threat no longer.

Theme. The doom of Nineveh.

OUTLINE

I. The Pronouncement of Nineveh's Doom. 1:1-15.
  A. The Prophecy of the Doom. 1:1.
    1. Its description. 1:1a.
    2. Its human author. 1:1b.
  B. The Divine Agent of the Doom. 1:2-8.
    1. He is a jealous God who takes vengeance on His enemies. 1:2.
    2. He is a long-suffering God who is slow to anger. 1:3a.
    3. He is a God of power whom none can resist. 1:3b-6.

  4. He is a good God who is a refuge to those who love Him. 1:7-8.
  C. The Verdict of the Doom. 1:9-13.
    1. Concerning the works of Nineveh in general. 1:9-10.
    2. Concerning the mission of Sennacherib. 1:11-13.
  D. The Realization of the Doom. 1:14-15.
    1. For Nineveh. 1:14.
    2. For Judah. 1:15.
II. The Description of Nineveh's Doom. 2:1-13.

A. The Warning Sounded. 2:1-2.
1. The prophet's exhortation. 2:1.
2. Jehovah's commission. 2:2.
B. The Invasion Described. 2:3-7.
1. The army. 2:3a.
2. The armor and armament. 2:3b-4.
3. The defenders. 2:5.
4. The defeat. 2:6-7.
C. The Destruction Delineated. 2:8-13.
1. The flight of her citizens. 2:8.
2. The plundering of her treasure. 2:9-10.
3. The wonder of the prophet. 2:11-12.
4. The pronouncement of Jehovah. 2:13.

III. The Vindication of Nineveh's Doom. 3:1-19.
A. Because of Her Bloody History. 3:1-7.
1. Her history reviewed. 3:1-4.
2. Her destruction determined. 3:5-7.
B. Because of God's Judgment Upon Egypt. 3:8-15a.
1. Nineveh shares Egypt's character. 3:8-10.
2. Nineveh will share Egypt's destruction. 3:11-15a.
C. Because of Their Apathy. 3:15b-19.
1. Their apathy described. 3:15b-18.
2. Their destruction to be realized. 3:19.

COMMENTARY

I. THE PRONOUNCEMENT OF NINEVEH'S DOOM. 1:1-15.

A. The Prophecy of the Doom. 1:1.

1. Its description. 1:1a.

THE burden of Nĭn'e-veh. The book of the vision of Nahum the Ĕl'kosh-īte.

1:1a. The prophecy is described as **The burden of Nineveh.** It is called a **burden** (Heb *masa'* burden, load, thing lifted up) because of its preoccupation with the judgment against Nineveh. At its outset, then, the people of Judah would be comforted; for the book deals with the destruction of Nineveh at whose hands Judah had been so recently ravaged. At the same time, Nineveh, to whom Jonah had ministered some 150 years earlier and under whose ministry Nineveh had repented of its evil ways, would be warned of its impending judgment because of its forsaking the ways of Jehovah.

2. Its human author. 1:1b.

1b. Like the book of Obadiah, Nahum is a **vision** (Heb *chazōn*) in which the realities were presented to the prophet's mind's eye; and he subsequently encoded the vision for posterity by using the medium of Hebrew poetry. The burden of Obadiah was against Edom, and he prophesied its doom, whereas the **vision of Nahum** concerned the destruction of Nineveh. The human author by which this vision is conveyed is **Nahum** of the city of Elkosh (cf. Introduction).

B. The Divine Agent of the Doom. 1:2-8.

The very mention of the name Nineveh would strike terror into the heart of every citizen of Judah. For three hundred years it had been a great city, and for the past one hundred years had been the terror of the world. It was a strongly fortified city and had engaged in many successful military campaigns. Most recently, it had taken Israel captive and had ravaged Judah, laying siege to Jerusalem itself. Only God's direct intervention caused the siege to be lifted and the city to be delivered. Thus, the prophet rightly focuses the hearer's attention on the only thing that is greater than Nineveh, i.e., the God of Judah. He describes Him in four ways.

1. He is a jealous God who takes vengeance on His enemies. 1:2.

2 God *is* jealous, and the LORD revengeth; the LORD revengeth, and *is* furious; the LORD will take vengeance on his adversaries, and he reserveth *wrath* for his enemies.

2. God is jealous, and the LORD revengeth. When the prophet describes God as being **jealous** (Heb *qanō'*, zealous, jealous), he is not ascribing a human imperfection to God. Rather, the thought is that God is one who embodies a burning zeal for righteousness and justice, quickly rises to the defense of

His own, and executes judgment on those who are not His or hurt those who are. Underlying the prophet's thought are the recent events of history in which the Assyrians have taken Israel captive and have invaded Judah, capturing its fortified cities and laying siege to Jerusalem (722 B.C.). Jehovah did not take Assyria's trespassing lightly; for three times the prophet states that the Lord will execute vengeance upon Assyria, the threefold repetition lending both solemnity and certainty to the pronouncement.

2. He is a long-suffering God who is slow to anger. 1:3a.

3 The LORD *is* slow to anger, and great in power, and will not at all acquit *the* wicked: the LORD *hath* his way in the whirlwind and in the storm, and the clouds *are* the dust of his feet.

3a. The LORD is slow to anger, and great in power. From verse 2 it might be concluded that Jehovah has a quick temper and is eager to execute judgment. Such is not the case, for Jehovah is not man; He is slow to anger. History certainly bears this out, for some one hundred fifty years earlier God had sent Jonah to Nineveh proclaiming its impending destruction. Because Nineveh repented, Jehovah spared it for one hundred fifty years, to the days of Nahum, and would not actually execute His judgment upon Nineveh for some one hundred years yet to come! Truly, Jehovah is long-suffering, slow to anger, and slow to execute judgment (cf. II Pet 3:8-9).

3. He is a God of power whom none can resist. 1:3b-6.

4 He rebuketh the sea, and maketh it dry, and drieth up all the rivers; Bā′-shan languisheth, and Carmel, and the flower of Lebanon languisheth.
5 The mountains quake at him, and the hills melt, and the earth is burned at his presence, yea, the world, and all that dwell therein.
6 Who can stand before his indignation? and who can abide in the fierceness of his anger? his fury is poured out like fire, and the rocks are thrown down by him.

3b-6. The LORD hath his way in the whirlwind. The fact that God is slow to anger and is not eager to execute judgment does not stem from His lack of power to do so, nor does it indicate that the target of His wrath will escape His judgment. On the contrary, God is great in power, as is seen in His control of the destructive **whirlwind** (Heb *sūpah,* hurricane) and the **storm.** The **clouds,** which at the time of the prophet were so far beyond the experience of man, are merely the dust of Jehovah's feet. He **rebuketh the sea, and maketh it dry.** God's power is further shown in the fact that He can cause both sea and rivers to be dry. The history of Israel readily attests to the truth of this statement, for God dried up both the Red Sea and the Jordan River so that Israel could cross (vs. 4a). Not only can God do this, but He can also control the dry lands, which under normal circumstances are rich in pasture, vineyards, and forests. **Bashan . . . Carmel, and . . . Lebanon** are cited as specific instances of each.

Further, God can cause the **mountains** to **quake,** the **hills** to **melt,** and the **earth** to be **burned** by His mere presence. Not only that, He can destroy all, both man and beast, who dwell upon the earth. **Who can stand before his indignation?** The conclusion of verse 6 is obvious. Though God is slow to anger, when the time comes for Him to execute His judgment, graphically portrayed in language in keeping with volcanic activity, not anyone or anything will be able to stand against Him. He is absolutely sovereign.

4. He is a good God who is a refuge to those who love Him. 1:7-8.

7 ¶The LORD *is* good, a strong hold in the day of trouble; and he knoweth them that trust in him.
8 But with an overrunning flood he will make an utter end of the place thereof, and darkness shall pursue his enemies.

7-8. Jehovah is intrinsically good; and His goodness is manifested in two ways: **in the day of trouble** those who trust him find Him to be a **stronghold.** He protects those who trust, but His enemies will experience destruction. The agent is said to be **an overrunning flood** that will make **an utter end** of the enemy's place. The language is applicable not only to the invading hordes of the Medes and Babylonians who overthrew Assyria but also to the Tigris River which suddenly overflowed its banks (cf. 2:6) and washed away the foundations of the palace and the city wall for twenty stadia. He also permitted the Babylonian army to enter the breach, besiege the city, burn it, and utterly destroy it. The prophet will return to this theme later in his prophecy.

C. The Verdict of the Doom. 1:9-13.

In this section the prophet directly foretells the Assyrian defeat. He addresses them directly and shows that their resistance to Jehovah is futile. In so doing, the prophet argues from the general to the specific.

1. Concerning the works of Nineveh in general. 1:9-10.

9 What do ye imagine against the LORD? he will make an utter end: affliction shall not rise up the second time.

10 For while *they be* folden together *as* thorns, and while they are drunken *as* drunkards, they shall be devoured as stubble fully dry.

9-10. What do ye imagine against the LORD? he will make an utter end. No matter what Nineveh may devise against Jehovah and His people, it will meet with utter failure. Nineveh may be successful temporarily, but ultimately she will be crushed and will not rise again. **For while they be folden together as thorns, and while they are drunken as drunkards, they shall be devoured as stubble fully dry.** In all their craftiness the Ninevites are set forth under the figure of thorns that have become hopelessly entangled and as drunkards in a drunken stupor. They are going to meet Jehovah, who is a devouring fire (cf. vs. 6); and they will be as helpless as fully-dried stubble before Him.

2. Concerning the mission of Sennacherib. 1:11-13.

11 There is *one* come out of thee, that imagineth evil against the LORD, a wicked counsellor.

12 Thus saith the LORD; Though *they be* quiet, and likewise many, yet thus shall they be cut down, when he shall pass through. Though I have afflicted thee, I will afflict thee no more.

13 For now will I break his yoke from off thee, and will burst thy bonds in sunder.

11-13. The specific example of Nineveh's evil is the mission of Sennacherib against Judah. He is the **one come out of thee, that imagineth evil against the LORD.** He has done this because of his intrinsic nature, **a wicked counselor,** i.e., he has taken counsel of wickedness (Heb *beliya'al,* worthless, belial). The plan that Sennacherib is following in his invasion of Judah and siege of Jerusalem is destined to failure. However, such is not the way things appear; for Sennacherib has come with a mighty and seemingly invincible host and has even dared to defy the God of Israel (cf. II Chr 32). **Yet thus shall they be cut down.** In spite of all of his might, his plan is destined to failure; and his mighty army will be decimated. History records the fulfillment of this prophecy in great detail (cf. II Kgs 19:35-36; II Chr 32:21). The Angel of Jehovah (the pre-incarnate Christ) went into the Assyrian camp and smote 185,000 men. This caused Sennacherib to lift the siege of Jerusalem and return home. Truly, his army was no match for Israel's God! **Though I have afflicted thee, I will afflict thee no more** is best understood as a promise to Judah. Though Assyria has caused them to suffer, it will happen no more. **For now will I break his yoke from off thee, and will burst thy bonds in sunder.** All claims of Assyria upon Judah will be broken, and all ties and obligations to that land will be done away.

D. The Realization of the Doom. 1:14-15.

1. For Nineveh. 1:14.

14 And the LORD hath given a commandment concerning thee, *that* no more of thy name be sown: out of the house of thy gods will I cut off the graven image and the molten image: I will make thy grave; for thou art vile.

14. No more of thy name be sown: out of the house of thy gods will I cut off the graven image and the molten image: I will make thy grave; for thou art vile. The prophet returns to address Sennacherib personally and to deliver the Lord's judgment concerning him: his dynasty will come to an end, and no future king will bear his name or be of his line. In addition, the worship of the gods that he worshiped will be cut off, and Sennacherib himself will be slain. The prophecy was fulfilled in detail; for as he was worshiping in the house of his god, his son slew him with a sword and escaped into the land of Armenia, and Esarhaddon acceded to the throne of Assyria (cf. II Kgs 19:36-37; II Chr 32:21).

2. For Judah. 1:15.

15 Behold upon the mountains the feet of him that bringeth good tidings, that publisheth peace! O Judah, keep

15. Behold upon the mountains the feet of him that bringeth good tidings, that publisheth peace! This verse is actually verse one of chapter two in the Hebrew text. It describes what

thy solemn feasts, perform thy vows: for the wicked shall no more pass through thee; he is utterly cut off.

CHAPTER 2
HE that dasheth in pieces is come up before thy face: keep the munition, watch the way, make *thy* loins strong, fortify *thy* power mightily.

2 For the LORD hath turned away the excellency of Jacob, as the excellency of Israel: for the emptiers have emptied them out, and marred their vine branches.

3 The shield of his mighty men is made red, the valiant men *are* in scarlet: the chariots *shall be* with flaming torches in the day of his preparation, and the fir trees shall be terribly shaken.

4 The chariots shall rage in the streets, they shall justle one against another in the broad ways: they shall seem like torches, they shall run like the lightnings.

1756

Nineveh's doom, and particularly the death of Sennacherib, will mean for Judah. It will mean good news of peace, for the arch-troubler is dead. Therefore, Judah will be able to perform the **vows** and keep the **solemn feasts**, which it has not been able to do all during Sennacherib's siege. Sennacherib (**the wicked**) will never again trouble Israel, for he will be **cut off**. It should be noted that the language in this verse is elastic enough to include both the announcement of Nineveh's destruction in 612 B.C. and the lifting of Sennacherib's siege in the days of Hezekiah (701 B.C.), though those events took place approximately 90 years apart. If a decision must be made between them, the context favors the latter.

II. THE DESCRIPTION OF NINEVEH'S DOOM. 2:1-13.

A. The Warning Sounded. 2:1-2.

1. The prophet's exhortation. 2:1.

2:1. This verse has been understood by some to be addressed to Judah, urging it to prepare for the onslaught of the Assyrians. If that were true, then **He that dasheth in pieces** would be Sennacherib, the Assyrian king. In view of the context and the purpose of the prophecy overall, it is better to view this verse as directed to Assyria itself, and particularly Nineveh. Almost as in a taunt, Nahum urges them to prepare to defend themselves against the onslaught of the Babylonian hordes. The prophet knows full-well that their destiny is sealed and that all preparations on their part will, in the final analysis, be futile. The vicious character of the Medo-Babylonian army is seen in the description **He that dasheth in pieces.** They are vicious and merciless. Almost ironically, the prophet urges them to prepare their fortifications in the vain attempt to withstand the inevitable and all-powerful foe.

2. Jehovah's commission. 2:2.

2. For the LORD hath turned away the excellency of Jacob. Turn about is fair play. Assyria has carried Israel away captive and has ravaged Judah. Now it is about to receive just recompense for its deeds. It is about to learn the truth that God promised Abraham, ". . . I will bless them that bless thee, and curse him that curseth thee . . ." (Gen 12:3a). That promise of God has never changed and still is in force today! This, then, becomes the basis of the prophet's proof that Nineveh is about to be destroyed. God has accomplished His purpose with Assyria and has sufficiently judged His people; therefore, He will now judge those who devastated them (cf. Isa 10:5-19).

B. The Invasion Described. 2:3-7.

1. The army. 2:3a.

3a. The shield of his mighty men is made red. The Medo-Babylonian army is described as **mighty men.** They were invincible. Just as today nations and institutions are represented by various colors, so it was in the day of the prophet. The favorite color of the Medo-Babylonian army was **red,** or **scarlet.** Whenever they were portrayed, it was always in colors of red (cf. Ezk 23:14). Both the shield and the cloak of the invading army were bright red and must have struck terror into the hearts of the defenders as they approached any city.

2. The armor and armament. 2:3b-4.

3b-4. The chariots shall be with flaming torches. The **chariot** was to the army of the prophet's day what the tank is to the modern army. It was an ominous weapon made even more terrifying by attaching sharp implements at right angles to the axles so they literally mowed down any who came against them.

The reference to **flaming torches** may be a reference to the speed with which they moved (cf. vs. 4), or better, their appearance as the sun was reflected off of the sharp implements protruding from the wheels as they rotated. The reference to **fir trees** being **terribly shaken** is probably best understood as a reference to the spears that the invading army brandished overhead as they advanced.

The chariots shall rage in the streets, they shall justle one against another in the broad ways: they shall seem like torches, they shall run like the lightnings. To interpret this verse as being a prediction of the modern automobile, as has sometimes been done in the past, does violence both to the nature and purpose of prophecy. The verse properly indicates the ease and access that the invading hordes and their armament have to the city. They have taken the city by surprise, and none of the defenders can restrain them at all. They have unlimited freedom and move throughout the city with such speed that they come into contact with one another, instead of the defenders; and as the sunlight reflects off of them, they seem like torches and move with such speed that to the mind of the prophet they are comparable to lightning.

3. The defenders. 2:5.

5 He shall recount his worthies: they shall stumble in their walk; they shall make haste to the wall thereof, and the defence shall be prepared.

5. This verse describes the futile attempt of the Assyrians to defend themselves. The king primarily depends upon **his worthies** (his nobles and military leaders) to defend the city. They, however, will **stumble in their walk** because, as the ancient historian Diodorus Siculus recounts, the fatal attack came when they were involved in drunken carousings. In the excavations at Nineveh, carousing scenes have been uncovered in which the king, his courtiers, and even queens are portrayed as reclining on couches or seated on thrones toasting one another with bowls of wine while being attended by court musicians. **They shall make haste to the wall.** The call to arms finds the nobles trying to make it to the wall, the city's primary defense. The wall about Nineveh was seemingly impregnable, being about 60 miles in length as it surrounded the city and having some 1500 towers, each about two hundred feet high. Under normal circumstances, given the state of military technology of the prophet's day, the defenses were more than adequate for any foe; but these were not normal circumstances!

4. The defeat. 2:6-7.

6 The gates of the rivers shall be opened, and the palace shall be dissolved.

7 And Hŭz′zab shall be led away captive, she shall be brought up, and her maids shall lead her as with the voice of doves, tabering upon their breasts.

6-7. The gates of the rivers shall be opened, and the palace shall be dissolved. The first-century Greek historian Diodorus Siculus records an old prophecy to the effect that Nineveh would not be taken until the Tigris River should become its enemy. That is precisely what happened, for the river overflowed its banks, washed away the foundations of the palace, and washed away the wall for twenty stadia. The phenomenon is exactly as described in the prophecy of verse 6. This enabled the Medo-Babylonian horde easy access into the city.

And Huzzab shall be led away captive. Some have thought Huzzab was a reference to the queen of Nineveh; but there is no proof that this is so, nor is it necessary. The word is a transliteration of a Hebrew word that means established. It fits the context best to understand this as a reference to the city of Nineveh, which for more than three hundred years had in fact been established. Now, however, the established city shall be led away captive, and her **maids** (citizens) shall mourn with voices like those of **doves** and beat upon their **breasts** because the city has been sapped of all of her wealth and utterly destroyed.

C. The Destruction Delineated. 2:8-13.

1. The flight of her citizens. 2:8.

8 But Nĭn′e-veh is of old like a pool of

8. But Nineveh is of old like a pool of water: yet they shall

water: yet they shall flee away. Stand, stand, *shall they cry;* but none shall look back.

9 Take ye the spoil of silver, take the spoil of gold: for *there is* none end of the store *and* glory out of all the pleasant furniture.
10 She is empty, and void, and waste: and the heart melteth, and the knees smite together, and much pain *is* in all loins, and the faces of them all gather blackness.

11 Where *is* the dwelling of the lions, and the feedingplace of the young lions, where the lion, *even* the old lion, walked, *and* the lion's whelp, and none made *them* afraid?
12 The lion did tear in pieces enough for his whelps, and strangled for his lionesses, and filled his holes with prey, and his dens with ravin.

13 Behold, I *am* against thee, saith the LORD of hosts, and I will burn her chariots in the smoke, and the sword shall devour thy young lions: and I will cut off thy prey from the earth, and the voice of thy messengers shall no more be heard.

CHAPTER 3
WOE to the bloody city! it *is* all full of lies *and* robbery; the prey departeth not:
2 The noise of a whip, and the noise of the rattling of the wheels, and of the pransing horses, and of the jumping chariots.
3 The horseman lifteth up both the bright sword and the glittering spear: and *there is* a multitude of slain, and a great number of carcases; and *there is* none end of *their* corpses; they stumble upon their corpses:
4 Because of the multitude of the whoredoms of the well-favoured harlot, the mistress of witchcrafts, that selleth nations through her whoredoms, and families through her witchcrafts.

flee away. Stand, stand, shall they cry; but none shall look back. Because of the flood the impregnable fortress, overcome by the water, becomes like a pool. The thing uppermost in all of the citizens' minds is escape, and so they flee. Because of the military crisis, the leaders will urge the people to stand in their places and fight against the invading hordes. However, the command will go unheeded as each flees for his own safety.

2. The plundering of her treasure. 2:9-10.

9-10. Take ye the spoil of silver . . . of gold. These verses are addressed to the invaders. Lacking defenders, the treasures of the city are theirs for the taking; and there are treasures in abundance. **She is empty, and void, and waste . . . and the faces of them all gather blackness.** When the spoilers have finished their work and have gorged themselves on Nineveh's treasure, the city will be left empty of treasure, being utterly destroyed. The people are completely smitten and are in intense grief and shock over what has transpired.

3. The wonder of the prophet. 2:11-12.

11-12. Where is the dwelling of the lions. Nahum sees the prophecy of Nineveh's destruction as already fulfilled and wonders where the mighty power of the great Nineveh is. This same wonder will be on the lips of the captors and all succeeding generations, for history records that later armies marched over the site of Nineveh without realizing that mighty Nineveh had ever been there. The figure of the **lion** and **lionesses** providing prey for the cubs is a figurative representation of the violence that characterized Assyria's history and feats in battle.

4. The pronouncement of Jehovah. 2:13.

13. Behold, I am against thee, saith the LORD of hosts, and I will burn her chariots. This verse explains why the prophet can view the destruction as already accomplished. It is because Jehovah is against Nineveh, and He will burn her war **chariots** with fire and slay her people with the **sword.** He will drive them into extinction. The truth of this is now a matter of historical record. Assyria had dared to raise itself against the people of God and would experience the wrath of God in the fulfillment of God's word originally given to Abraham (Gen 12:1-3).

III. THE VINDICATION OF NINEVEH'S DOOM. 3:1-19.

In this section three reasons that justify the doom of Nineveh are given:

A. Because of Her Bloody History. 3:1-7.

1. Her history reviewed. 3:1-4.

3:1-4. Woe to the bloody city! The history of Nineveh could not be better summed up than in the opening statement of chapter three: it was **the bloody city!** It was bloody in its dealings with others and in its dealings with itself. This was an outgrowth of its character, being **full of lies and robbery.** Its inhabitants preyed upon one another and upon other nations. They were always grabbing and grasping, and never returning. Promises made were never kept; alliances entered into were always broken; the city and nation were marked by greed and violence; it was their way of life.

The language of verses 2-3 is elastic enough to be understood both as the tactics the nation used in its conquest, as well as the tactics that were used upon it in its defeat. It is a graphic picture of the warfare of that day. One can hear the **noise of a whip** of the charioteer as he urges his horses on ever swifter and the **horses** hooves as they move faster, pulling the chariots ever more noisily through the streets and over the walls. As they ran rampant through the streets, the charioteers and horsemen brandished their swords and spears, slaying multitudes. **There is a multitude of slain, and a great number of carcases.** The city was estimated to have approximately 600,000 people. So many of them were slain that there seemed to be no end of the **corpses,** and every place those who survived moved they stumbled over corpses of fallen comrades or enemies.

Because of the multitude of the whoredoms. The reason all of this is to befall Nineveh is because of her moral defects, manifested not only in sexual license, but also in the worship of the occult. **Selleth nations through her whoredoms, and families through her witchcrafts.** She exported her sin and vices and took captive other nations, robbing them of their wealth and liberty.

2. Her destruction determined. 3:5-7.

5 Behold, I *am* against thee, saith the Lord of hosts; and I will discover thy skirts upon thy face, and I will shew the nations thy nakedness, and the kingdoms thy shame.

6 And I will cast abominable filth upon thee, and make thee vile, and will set thee as a gazingstock.

7 And it shall come to pass, *that* all they that look upon thee shall flee from thee, and say, Nĭn'e-veh is laid waste: who will bemoan her? whence shall I seek comforters for thee?

5-7. Behold, I am against thee, saith the Lord of hosts; and I will discover thy skirts upon thy face. Because of her bloody history, Jehovah takes up the unalterable position and proclaims Himself to be against her. She would be humiliated in a way in keeping with her defection, and her humiliation will be made as public as possible. All of her secrets will be known, and all of her private parts will be laid open to public gaze. In addition, **abominable filth** will be cast upon her. She will be treated as an object of contempt and disgrace.

All they that look upon thee shall flee from thee. The result of God's judgment upon Nineveh will be that all that look upon her will flee lest they partake of her judgment. No one will either mourn for her or seek to comfort her. Throughout her history she was friendly to none and cruel to all. She has shown mercy on none in the hour of their need, and she will receive none in the hour of hers.

B. Because of God's Judgment Upon Egypt. 3:8-15a.

1. Nineveh shares Egypt's character. 3:8-10.

8 Art thou better than populous No, that was situate among the rivers, *that had* the waters round about it, whose rampart *was* the sea, *and* her wall *was* from the sea?

9 Ē-thĭ-ō'pĭ-a and Egypt *were* her strength, and *it was* infinite; Put and Lū'bim were thy helpers.

10 Yet *was* she carried away, she went into captivity: her young children also were dashed in pieces at the top of all the streets: and they cast lots for her honourable men, and all her great men were bound in chains.

8-10. Art thou better than populous No . . . ? Both Jeremiah (cf. Jer 46:25) and Ezekiel (cf. Ezk 30:14-16) prophesied the doom of Egypt, and particularly the city of **No** (No-amon, i.e., Thebes) because of its wickedness and idolatry. (Jeremiah and Ezekiel ministered about one hundred years following Nahum and amplify the thought suggested here.) Thebes was located on the Nile River and was the capital city of Upper Egypt for the Pharaohs of the eighteenth, nineteenth, and twentieth Egyptian dynasties. It was a beautiful city, having many architectural wonders and cultural advantages. The city was situated among the canals of the Nile River, which acted as a natural barrier, particularly at flood time when it resembled a sea.

Ethiopia and Egypt were her strength, and it was infinite. Thebes had one great advantage over Nineveh: allies upon whom it could count in a time of trouble. Its allies were **Ethiopia,** the rest of the nation of **Egypt . . . Lubim** (probably best understood as Libya), and **Put** (probably best understood to be a country located in eastern Africa in the vicinity of Ethiopia, perhaps in the area presently known as Somaliland). These allies were militarily powerful in their day and ready to help No-amon in a time of crisis.

Yet was she carried away, she went into captivity. In spite of the strength and number of her allies, No-amon was no match for Assyria's might. God used Assyria to bring judgment on No-amon because of its sin, but Assyria was barbarously cruel in the process. She dashed children to pieces in the street, gambled over who would have the honorable men for personal slaves, and led all the notable men captive in chains, an indignity commonly heaped upon the vanquished by the victors.

11 Thou also shalt be drunken: thou shalt be hid, thou also shalt seek strength because of the enemy.

12 All thy strong holds *shall be like* fig trees with the firstripe figs: if they be shaken, they shall even fall into the mouth of the eater.

13 Behold, thy people in the midst of thee *are* women: the gates of thy land shall be set wide open unto thine enemies: the fire shall devour thy bars.

14 Draw thee waters for the siege, fortify thy strong holds: go into clay, and tread the morter, make strong the brickkiln.

15 There shall the fire devour thee; the sword shall cut thee off, it shall eat thee up like the cankerworm: make thyself many as the cankerworm, make thyself many as the locusts.

16 Thou hast multiplied thy merchants above the stars of heaven: the cankerworm spoileth, and fleeth away.

17 Thy crowned *are* as the locusts, and thy captains as the great grasshoppers, which camp in the hedges in the cold day, *but* when the sun ariseth they flee away, and their place is not known where they *are*.

18 Thy shepherds slumber, O king of Assyria: thy nobles shall dwell *in the dust*: thy people is scattered upon the mountains, and no man gathereth *them*.

19 *There is* no healing of thy bruise; thy wound is grievous: all that hear the bruit of thee shall clap the hands over thee: for upon whom hath not thy wickedness passed continually?

2. *Nineveh will share Egypt's destruction. 3:11-15a.*

11. Thou also shalt be drunken. If God will not let No-amon get by with its sin, then God, who is not partial, cannot let Nineveh get by with her sin, either. Just as Nineveh shared Egypt's character, thus also Nineveh will share Egypt's destruction. What she has done to No-amon will be done unto her. She shall **be drunken.** This may refer to the drunken orgy in which the king and his nobles were engaged the night that Nineveh fell, but probably is better understood as the drunkenness that results from having drunk the cup of God's wrath. As the result of God's wrath, she shall **be hid** (pass into extinction), which it was until archeological discoveries of the nineteenth century began to bring to light the marvels of her past. She **shalt seek strength** in the hour of her need; but in contrast to Thebes which she ravaged, she will find none.

12. This verse describes the ease with which the city will fall. It is likened unto **fig trees** that easily give up their ripe figs when shaken. So will the strongholds of Nineveh fall into the hands of the Medo-Babylonian army.

13. Behold, thy people in the midst of thee are women. Because of the terror brought on by the invading hordes, the hearts of the soldiers will faint; and they will be like **women.** There is no derogatory intention here, but the prophet is referring to the fact that women were the helpless victims of warfare of the prophet's day. That is how helpless the defenders were before the onslaught of the invaders. The result was that the gates of the city were **wide open** and the enemy had ready access through the breach in the wall and had entered at will, destroying by **fire** what the flood had not already ruined.

14-15a. Draw thee waters for the siege . . . make strong the brickkiln. Though he knows it will be in vain, the prophet urges Nineveh to prepare for a long siege. Two commodities will be the most necessary; water to sustain life and bricks to repair damage done to the wall and fortifications by the invading army.

There shall the fire devour thee; the sword shall cut thee off. All preparations will be futile, for the enemy will be victorious and will destroy the city by fire, mercilessly slaying its inhabitants. The enemy will devour Nineveh like the **cankerworm** devours a plant.

C. Because of Their Apathy. 3:15b-19.

1. *Their apathy described. 3:15b-18.*

15b-18. Make thyself many as the locusts. The population of Nineveh was about 600,000 at this time, so large a city that its population is likened to a swarm of **locusts. Thou hast multiplied thy merchants above the stars of heaven.** The city gave itself to the pursuit of wealth, and was very successful at it. The wealth acquired would become spoil for the conquerors and would flee away from them. All of the royalty (**crowned**) and military leaders (**captains**) were as apathetic and insensitive to Nineveh's need as **great grasshoppers . . . in the cold day.** They are paralyzed. However, when things heated up and they were needed, they fled away and forsook the city in its time of need. **Thy shepherds slumber, O king of Assyria.** Such apathy in the time of need results in death to the king's shepherds, his viceroy and other officials (his **nobles**), other members of his courts, and his population. The people who survive flee to the mountains, allowing capture by the invaders.

2. *Their destruction to be realized. 3:19.*

19. There is no healing of thy bruise; thy wound is grievous. The blow to be dealt Nineveh is fatal. No one can, or will, come to Nineveh's aid. In fact, when they hear the report (**bruit** Heb *shĕmaʻ*, report), it will be an occasion for rejoicing; and they will clap their hands, giving visible expression to their joy. The nations who had suffered so much at the hands of Assyria will now rejoice over the report of her suffering.

The prophecy of Nahum is a dark prophecy; and, for the most part, it is occupied with the judgment of Nineveh. However, considering the prophecy as a whole, three lessons are readily apparent: (1) God is always faithful to His own people. He sovereignly moves against Nineveh to destroy it because of His covenant relationship to His people Israel; (2) God is sovereign over all the nations of the world. He sets them up, and He puts them down. Though during the days of the prophet He was dealing primarily with Israel, He did not overlook the Gentile world powers; and they also are in the scope of His interests and direct plan; and (3) It is ever true that the nation that oppresses God's people seals its own death warrant. God promised Abraham that He would bless the one who blessed him and would curse the one who cursed him. Nineveh was a great oppressor of Israel and, therefore, was judged. So it has ever been, and so it will ever be.

(see page 1864 for Bibliography to the Minor Prophets)

HABAKKUK

INTRODUCTION

Authorship. Beyond what can be learned about him in this book, nothing is known about the author, Habakkuk. The fact that the prophet is known to us only by name once again indicates the relative unimportance of the prophet and the major importance of the prophecy and, more importantly, the God who sends the prophecy. The prophet's name means "embracer" or "a wrestler," and this provides a key to the prophecy. The prophecy is a record of the prophet's wrestling with God in behalf of his people. Further, he embraced God by faith (ch. 3) and embraces his people, giving them the message that after the judgment to come, Chaldea (Babylonia) will itself be judged. Because of the description in 3:1 and the inscription in 3:19 some have inferred that Habakkuk was a Levite who assisted in the music of the Temple. This same evidence would also make King Hezekiah a Levite, for he issued a similar direction in Isaiah 38:20. Concerning Habakkuk's identity, it has best been expressed in the truism: "Who he was, nobody knows; what he was, everybody knows."

Date and place of writing. The date of Habakkuk's prophecy is difficult to ascertain, for he does not mention the king or kings during whose reigns he prophesied. The best key that Habakkuk offers for dating his prophecy is his description of the Chaldeans in 1:5-11. Some commentators, noting that God says He is in the process of raising up the Chaldeans (1:6), would date the prophecy as early as the reign of Josiah. Habakkuk's message, then, would be that just as God raised up the Assyrians to judge Israel so He is raising up the Chaldeans (Babylonians) to judge you. This interpretation would date the prophecy before the destruction of Nineveh, which resulted in the exaltation of the Chaldeans to world prominence.

Most commentators, however, date Habakkuk's prophecy during the reign of King Jehoiakim. The fall of Nineveh occurred about 606 B.C. in fulfillment of Nahum's prophecy. It was probably after this fulfillment that Habakkuk received his vision setting forth the overthrow of the Babylonian kingdom. When Habakkuk prophesied, the southern kingdom was wallowing in its sin and tottering politically in view of the impending danger of Babylon, the current world power. It is possible that Nebuchadnezzar had already carried Daniel and many of Jerusalem's nobles into captivity (606 B.C.) and that the second deportation was soon to follow (597 B.C.). The final destruction of the city was yet to occur in 586 B.C. It is thought that Habakkuk's description of the Chaldeans and their feats alludes to all three of these events. Putting the above considerations together, Habakkuk prophesied between 635 B.C. and 598 B.C. Advocates of the former view would select 635 B.C. for the date of origin, while advocates of the latter view would select 609 B.C.

Characteristics of the prophecy. The prophecy of Habakkuk is unique among all of prophetical literature. Overall, it contains a high caliber of Hebrew poetry. The first two chapters constitute a dialogue between the prophet and Jehovah concerning the invasion of the Chaldeans (1:1-11) and the destruction of the Chaldeans (1:12-2:20). Chapter 3 is a psalm with instructions given to the musicians for its rendering (3:1,19). In the first two chapters the prophet contends with Jehovah, and in the third he submits to Jehovah.

Purpose. The purpose of Habakkuk is twofold: (1) to warn Judah of its coming judgment at the hands of Chaldea and (2) to comfort Judah concerning Chaldea's ultimate destruction.

Theme. Judgment upon Judah and Chaldea (Babylon).

OUTLINE

COMMENTARY

I. THE PROPHET'S DIALOGUE WITH JEHOVAH. 1:1-2:20.

A. The First Cycle. 1:1-11.

1. The prophet's question. 1:1-4.

THE burden which Ha-băk′kuk the prophet did see.

1:1. The burden which Habakkuk the prophet did see. The entire prophecy is introduced in verse 1. It is characterized as being a **burden** (Heb *masa'*, burden, load, or thing lifted up), as also are Nahum (cf. Nah 1:1) and Malachi (cf. Mal 1:1). This immediately lets us know that the prophecy deals with destruction, in this case the destruction of Chaldea (Babylon) after it has been used of God to bring judgment and destruction upon Judah.

The author of the prophecy is affirmed to be **Habakkuk** (cf. Introduction above), and this is a prophecy which he **did see**. This indicates that the prophecy was presented to him in a vision, a manner similar to the way that God revealed his prophecy to His other prophets (cf. Amos 1:1, Ob 1:1, Nah 1:1).

2 O LORD, how long shall I cry, and thou wilt not hear! *even* cry out unto thee *of* violence, and thou wilt not save!
3 Why dost thou shew me iniquity, and cause *me* to behold grievance? for spoiling and violence *are* before me: and there are *that* raise up strife and contention.
4 Therefore the law is slacked, and judgment doth never go forth: for the wicked doth compass about the righteous; therefore wrong judgment proceedeth.

2-4. O LORD, how long shall I cry, and thou wilt not hear! The prophet's first question is expressed in verses 2-4. Throughout his lifetime and ministry the prophet had been watching the decadence of Judah and had been bringing the matter before the Lord in prayer, asking the Lord to intervene, but seemingly to no avail (vs. 2). This naturally causes the prophet to wonder why God causes him to see this decadence when, apparently, He doesn't intend to do anything about it. Once again, the prophet rehearses the facts before the Lord. The laws of the land are not enforced; wrongdoers are never corrected; and the doers of wickedness hem in the righteous in every respect so that they are totally frustrated; and those who are given the responsibility to uphold the law are bought off and rule in favor of the wrongdoers and against the righteous at all times (vs. 4). The prophet realizes that overall, God has promised to judge sin; and He must. It is not a question of whether, but of when; and so the prophet's question is, How long will God wait before He judges His people?

2. Jehovah's response. 1:5-11.

5 ¶Behold ye among the heathen, and regard, and wonder marvellously: for *I* will work a work in your days, *which* ye will not believe, though it be told *you.*

5. Jehovah addresses the prophet and, through him, all the righteous of the nation directly, reminding them that their vision is too small. They are occupied with only a small segment of God's program and need to have their vision expanded. They are occupied only with Judah, but God is occupied with the world; and so God directs them to lift up their eyes to the **heathen** (Heb *gōyim*, nations, all non-Jews). Far from being disinterested in the events now transpiring, God is at work on a universal scale in order to bring His universal power and influence to bear on the evils that Habakkuk and the righteous of Judah are experiencing. When they get this global perspective they will **wonder marvelously** and will scarcely believe it, though they can understand it. God promises that in their days they will be witnesses to what He is doing; and when it is done, they will recognize that He is the One who has done it.

6 For, lo, I raise up the Chăl-dē′ans, *that* bitter and hasty nation, which shall march through the breadth of the land, to possess the dwellingplaces *that are* not theirs.
7 They *are* terrible and dreadful: their judgment and their dignity shall proceed of themselves.

6-7. God explains to Habakkuk what He is doing; He is raising up the Chaldeans (Babylonians). This expression, **I raise up the Chaldeans,** does not mean that He is just now in the process of founding the nation; for at this time they have already been used of God to destroy the Assyrian World Empire and defeat the Egyptians. What God is saying is that He is preparing to use this nation to answer Habakkuk's prayer and question. He is going to bring them to Judah and execute His judgment against that land in response to Habakkuk's and the other righteous peoples' prayers! God is not unacquainted with the

8 Their horses also are swifter than the leopards, and are more fierce than the evening wolves: and their horsemen shall spread themselves, and their horsemen shall come from far; they shall fly as the eagle *that* hasteth to eat.

9 They shall come all for violence: their faces shall sup up *as* the east wind, and they shall gather the captivity as the sand.

10 And they shall scoff at the kings, and the princes shall be a scorn unto them: they shall deride every strong hold; for they shall heap dust, and take it.

11 Then shall *his* mind change, and he shall pass over, and offend, *imputing* this his power unto his god.

12 ¶*Art* thou not from everlasting, O LORD my God, mine Holy One? we shall not die. O LORD, thou hast ordained them for judgment; and, O mighty God, thou hast established them for correction.

13 *Thou art* of purer eyes than to behold evil, and canst not look on iniquity: wherefore lookest thou upon them that deal treacherously, *and* holdest thy tongue when the wicked devoureth *the man that is* more righteous than he?

character of the Chaldeans; but He recognizes that they are a **bitter and hasty nation,** i.e., they are ruthless and swift in the devastation and punishment they inflict. However, God is going to allow that nation to march through and possess the land of Judah. These Chaldeans that God is going to use are **terrible and dreadful** (vs. 7); they strike terror and fear into every heart. The only law they recognize is the law of their own making, and they are a law unto themselves.

8. This verse describes their cavalry. Their horses are swift and ferocious, and their horsemen are invincible. They will pounce upon their victims as eagles do. The language is graphic!

9. The purpose for which the Chaldeans will come is now indicated. They are intent on one thing, **violence.** The prophet had complained of the violence he had seen in the land (cf. vs. 3), but the violence that he had seen will be mere child's play when compared to the violence that is to come. As Judah has sown violence; she will reap **violence.** The thought of **their faces shall sup up as the east wind** is that the faces of the invading hordes are ever set for the attack, and they are invincible in their advance. They will take so many people captive that the number of them taken will be **as the sand.**

10. So invincible is the attack and so confident are the invaders that they scoff at their enemies' **kings** and **princes** who are helpless before them. Every strong fortification will be useless before them, and they shall reduce it to be a heap of dust (just as they had done to Nineveh); and it will fall into their hands.

11. Some have seen in the language of this verse a parallel with the subsequent history of Babylon when Nebuchadnezzar was put aside and ate grass with the animals for seven years (cf. Dan 4:4-37). This is possible, but not necessary or probable. The prophet is simply indicating that Judah will not be Chaldea's last victory. He will continue and will have multiple successes, but will make one fatal mistake in that he will attribute his power and prestige to his god. He will make the same mistake that Assyria before him made in not realizing that the blessings he possesses come from the only God, Jehovah (cf. Isa 10:5-19).

Thus, in response to the prophet's complaint (vss. 2-4), God answers that He is doing something, raising up the Chaldeans whom He will bring to punish Judah for the very sins that have been observed.

B. The Second Cycle. 1:12-2:20.

1. The prophet's question. 1:12-17.

12-13. God's answer to the prophet is more perplexing than was his original complaint. He wonders, How can God use Chaldea, who is less righteous than Judah, to judge Judah? The prophet knows better than to refute Jehovah; so he remonstrates with Jehovah, reminding Him first of His character (vss. 12-13) and then of the Chaldeans' character (vss. 14-17). First, the prophet reminds God of His eternality, then His holiness, and then His power. From these attributes the prophet draws two direct conclusions: (1) the coming of the Chaldeans will not result in the annihilation of Judah so that the promises given originally to Abraham would be nullified; and (2) God's purpose in bringing the Chaldeans is for the chastisement and correction of his erring people. The prophet then reminds God of His purity and frankly cannot understand why God with seeming impunity can use a more wicked instrument to punish a less-wicked people. This, understandably, is beyond the realm of the prophet's understanding.

14 And makest men as the fishes of the sea, as the creeping things, *that have* no ruler over them?

15 They take up all of them with the angle, they catch them in their net, and gather them in their drag: therefore they rejoice and are glad.

16 Therefore they sacrifice unto their net, and burn incense unto their drag; because by them their portion *is* fat, and their meat plenteous.

17 Shall they therefore empty their net, and not spare continually to slay the nations?

CHAPTER 2

I WILL stand upon my watch, and set me upon the tower, and will watch to see what he will say unto me, and what I shall answer when I am reproved.

2 And the LORD answered me, and said, Write the vision, and make *it* plain upon tables, that he may run that readeth it.

3 For the vision *is* yet for an appointed time, but at the end it shall speak, and not lie: though it tarry, wait for it; because it will surely come, it will not tarry.

14-16. The prophet now turns to remind Jehovah of the Chaldeans' character. They were ruthless in their dealings with men and regarded human life contemptuously as though they were fish, or worms used to catch fish. In going ruthlessly about their task, the Chaldean armies operate as fishermen using nets and drag lines. With them it is a cold, calculating business; and they rejoice in the slaughter. The Chaldeans worship the implements of warfare and boast in their own strength and military powers, thinking they have made themselves successful by their own power and brilliance.

17. The prophet wonders if their success will go on continuously. Will not God do something to intervene? Will He not judge those who so ruthlessly oppress all others? The question is left with God, for all questions must ultimately be resolved by Him.

2. *Jehovah's response. 2:1-20.*

This chapter falls into two large divisions: (1) the preparations for the explanation (vss. 1-3) and (2) the giving of the explanation (vss. 4-20). There are two phases that God goes through in preparing for his explanation: (1) The prophet's resolution (vs. 1); and (2) Jehovah's commission (vss. 2-3).

2:1. The prophet has left his question with God (1:17); and he now resolves to wait and see what Jehovah will do, if anything. The language of the prophet indicates his attitude of heart, not his geographical location; he did not literally go into a watchtower, but resolved to wait on Jehovah to see what answer Jehovah would give to his question. He is to be commended in two respects: (1) his recognition of his utter dependence upon God; and (2) his willingness to wait for Jehovah to work and answer in His own time. The prophet is not expecting correction in the sense of chastisement, but rather, is indicating that when he is **reproved** (Heb *tōkachat*), he will be instructed by God and will know what he shall answer. Then he will be able to give God's answers to God's people concerning the things that presently are an enigma to them. The prophet, then, is determined to wait until God instructs him before he attempts to make any explanations at all.

2. That instruction is forthcoming, and Jehovah wants a record of it kept; so he commissions the prophet to **Write** it down and disseminate it throughout the land. The message was apparently written upon clay tablets in large, legible letters and posted in the market place where public notices were commonly placed. When one read it he was to **run,** not in fear but in joy, to disseminate the message throughout the land. The message was both bitter and sweet; for it dealt with both the coming Chaldean invasion (which would be bitter) and also the ultimate Chaldean defeat (which would be sweet).

3. The explanation of the vision is taken a step further. It pertains to **an appointed time;** and it will be fulfilled precisely on time, not a moment too late or too early. The vision will be absolutely true and absolutely certain of fulfillment, though there might be intervening circumstances or occurrences that might indicate otherwise. The **end** in view is the time at which the immediate prophecy shall be fulfilled, namely, the time at which the Chaldeans will be destroyed. The writer of Hebrews quotes the last part of this verse (cf. Heb 10:37) to apply to the coming of our Lord. We, like Habakkuk, wait for fulfillment of the Lord's Word; but the Word given to each is different. Habakkuk waited for the fulfillment of the Word of the Lord pertaining to the destruction of Chaldea, but we wait for the fulfillment of the Word of the Lord pertaining to His return. From our perspective we can see that the Lord completely fulfilled His Word to Habakkuk, and we can have assurance that He will fulfill His Word to us just as completely.

In verses 4-20 Jehovah gives a detailed explanation of the

4 ¶Behold, his soul *which* is lifted up is not upright in him: but the just shall live by his faith.

vision. His explanation involves a description of the character of the Chaldeans (vss. 4-5) and a determination of the doom of the Chaldeans; five woes are determined against them (vss. 6-20).

4. Two classes of people are contrasted: (1) the proud, haughty Chaldeans who will be the victors in the forthcoming conflict; and (2) the righteous ones of Judah who will be the vanquished in the forthcoming conflict. The Chaldean will appear to prosper and come out victorious, but his very arrogance and independence of God will be the very cause of destruction by God. The righteous Jew will appear to be defeated in the forthcoming conflict, but in reality he will be the victor because of his faith in Jehovah. Though he may die physically, he will live eternally. It is a comparison between temporal loss and eternal success. The difference between the two is the object in which they place their trust or belief—the Chaldean, in himself, and the righteous, in Jehovah. The Chaldean will die both physically and eternally; the righteous shall live!

The last part of verse 4 is one of the most popular Old Testament verses, for it is quoted three times in the New Testament (cf. Rom 1:17; Gal 3:11; Heb 10:38). It became the battle cry and the watchword of the Protestant Reformation in the days of Martin Luther. The righteous one shall live by his faith in Jehovah God.

5 Yea also, because he transgresseth by wine, *he is* a proud man, neither keepeth at home, who enlargeth his desire as hell, and *is* as death, and cannot be satisfied, but gathereth unto him all nations, and heapeth unto him all people:

5. This verse explains why the Chaldean is as he is. He is drunk with **wine** and pride. He is also drunk with power; and so he does not stay home, but rather ravages all the nations and has an appetite for destruction as insatiable as **hell** itself. He goes on these military adventures for the sheer thrill of it. **Hell** (Heb *she'ōl*, the unseen state or, the unseen world) is translated in the New Testament by the Greek word *Hades* (an English transliteration) and can be understood both as a reference to the grave and as the residence of the departed dead. Prior to the resurrection of Christ, Sheol/Hades consisted of two compartments: hell or Hades, the abode of the unrighteous dead, and paradise, the abode of the righteous dead. Between the two divisions there was a great unbridgeable gulf; and once one had arrived at either of those destinations, his eternal destiny was set (cf. Lk 16:19-31). When our Lord was resurrected from the dead, He emptied paradise and took all of the redeemed souls with Him to heaven (cf. Eph 4:9-10). Since that time hell/Hades has become the abode exclusively of the unrighteous dead while the righteous dead go immediately into the presence of God (cf. II Cor 5:1-8).

6 Shall not all these take up a parable against him, and a taunting proverb against him, and say, Woe to him that increaseth *that which is* not his! how long? and to him that ladeth himself with thick clay!

6. Though the Chaldean may be successful in his attempts and may appear to be ultimately victorious, in the end he will be vanquished; and all the nations that he has ravaged will **take up a parable** against him and will taunt him. The words they use are given in the five woes that comprise verses 6 to 20. Each woe is poetically symmetrical and is comprised of three verses. The first woe is pronounced on Chaldea because of their plundering (vss. 6b-8). **Woe to him that increaseth that which is not his!** He will not get away with it, for he will be called to account and will have to give up that which he has stolen. The word translated **thick clay** (Heb *'abtît*) does not refer to soil, but rather refers to a heavy pledge like that which Chaldea required of all of the countries it conquered. God pronounces this woe upon them because of the systematic scheme that they used for emptying the coffers of the vanquished into their own.

7 Shall they not rise up suddenly that shall bite thee, and awake that shall vex thee, and thou shalt be for booties unto them?

7. The thought of this verse is that just as the Chaldeans had placed the **bite** upon their victims and carried their wealth off to their own land, ultimately the victims would arise and put the **bite** upon the Chaldeans and take all of the ill-gotten gain from them. The biters will become the bitten, the plunderers will become the plundered, and the victors will become the vanquished.

8 Because thou hast spoiled many nations, all the remnant of the people

8. This verse sets forth the reason why all this will happen. Because they have ravaged **many nations**, they ultimately will

shall spoil thee; because of men's blood, and for the violence of the land, of the city, and of all that dwell therein.

9 ¶Woe to him that coveteth an evil covetousness to his house, that he may set his nest on high, that he may be delivered from the power of evil!

10 Thou hast consulted shame to thy house by cutting off many people, and hast sinned against thy soul.

11 For the stone shall cry out of the wall, and the beam out of the timber shall answer it.

12 ¶Woe to him that buildeth a town with blood, and stablisheth a city by iniquity!

13 Behold, is it not of the LORD of hosts that the people shall labour in the very fire, and the people shall weary themselves for very vanity?

14 For the earth shall be filled with the knowledge of the glory of the LORD, as the waters cover the sea.

15 ¶Woe unto him that giveth his neighbour drink, that puttest thy bottle to him, and makest him drunken also, that thou mayest look on their nakedness!

16 Thou art filled with shame for glory: drink thou also, and let thy foreskin be uncovered: the cup of the LORD's right hand shall be turned unto thee, and shameful spewing shall be on thy glory.

17 For the violence of Lebanon shall

be ravaged by the **remnant** of those nations. Because they have shed **men's blood,** their blood will be shed. Because they have lived in **violence, violence** will overtake them.

9. Woe to him that coveteth an evil covetousness. The second woe is pronounced upon Chaldea because of their self-exaltation (vss. 9-11). One must keep in mind that the language is poetic. The thought expressed is that the Chaldean had an insatiable covetousness; and in his quest for self-exaltation, he set about ruthlessly to satisfy it. Like Edom of old, he **set his nest on high** (cf. Ob 1:3) (Edom literally—Chaldea figuratively) to make himself as secure from attack or vengeance as possible.

10. In doing all of this, Chaldea ruthlessly annihilated **many people.** And in so doing, he not only violated the rights of others but, more importantly, he **sinned against thy soul.**

11. But who will call the Chaldean to account, or who will witness against him? The **stone** and **timber** of his own house will cry out, if necessary; for they were witnesses not only to his schemings, but also to his victorious gloatings. They would be adequate witnesses to accuse and convict the Chaldean of his wrongdoing and rightful judgment.

12-13. Woe to him that buildeth a town with blood. The third woe is pronounced upon the Chaldeans because of their violence (vss. 12-14). The Chaldeans built a mighty empire, and they had built many marvelous structures; but at what price! They gained their territory and booty with reckless bloodshed and built many of their magnificent structures with slave labor. Such doings did not go unnoticed by God, and they sealed the ultimate doom of the nation (vs. 12). The tactics the Chaldeans employed were not approved by Jehovah, and ultimately the people themselves will become weary in laboring to satisfy the Chaldean **vanity.** They will rise up and destroy the Chaldeans.

14. As magnificent as the Chaldean Empire was, it was temporal and marked for destruction. However, there is coming a kingdom founded upon righteousness; and it will be eternal. As extensive as the Chaldean kingdom was, it was local; but there is a kingdom coming that will be universal. The great kingdom to which the Chaldean Empire must give way is the kingdom of the Lord. Here the prophet views the time in which the Lord will reign over His people, the millennial reign of Christ. At that time all the **earth shall be filled with the knowledge** of the LORD, and His **glory** will cover all of the earth.

15. Woe unto him that giveth his neighbor drink. The fourth woe is pronounced upon Chaldea because of their treatment of their neighbors (vss. 15-17). It is possible to take the language of verses 15-16 literally, in which case a picture is presented of shameful drunkenness and immorality. One must keep in mind that the language is poetic imagery. The thought portrayed is that Chaldea is going forth to its conquests, enticing other nations to join in the effort. However, in the process the allies found themselves taken advantage of and all of their wealth stripped from them. The Chaldeans, then, not only took advantage of the ones they conquered, but also of the ones whom they could entice into alliance with them. The Chaldeans were invincible; one lost whether he was vanquished by them or became allied with them.

16. Such deceit on the part of the Chaldeans caused them to be held in contempt by all. To the Jews, the height of contempt was for one to be uncircumcised. When the prophet says **let thy foreskin be uncovered,** he is saying that the Chaldeans will be revealed for what they really are—contemptible, not only to their foes but also to their friends. Such treatment of friend and foe alike makes the Chaldeans candidates for retribution from the Lord's right hand, and it will come. When it does, all the glory of the Chaldeans will be spewed upon, a sign of utter contempt.

17. This verse has in view the violence which the Chaldeans

cover thee, and the spoil of beasts, *which* made them afraid, because of men's blood, and for the violence of the land, of the city, and of all that dwell therein.

18 ¶What profiteth the graven image that the maker thereof hath graven it; the molten image, and a teacher of lies, that the maker of his work trusteth therein, to make dumb idols?

19 Woe unto him that saith to the wood, Awake; to the dumb stone, Arise, it shall teach! Behold, it *is* laid over with gold and silver, and *there is* no breath at all in the midst of it.

20 But the LORD *is* in his holy temple: let all the earth keep silence before him.

CHAPTER 3

A PRAYER of Ha-băk′kuk the prophet upon Shĭ-gĭ′o-nŏth.

2 O LORD, I have heard thy speech, *and* was afraid: O LORD, revive thy work in the midst of the years, in the midst of the years make known; in wrath remember mercy.

3 ¶God came from Tē′man, and the Holy One from mount Pā′ran, Sē′lah.

wrought in the land of Judah. They cut down the forests of **Lebanon** and killed animals and men with abandon. The **land** which the prophet has in view is Judah, and the **city** is Jerusalem. Both Judah and Jerusalem will have their part in the judgment that is to be visited upon the Chaldeans.

18. The fifth woe is pronounced upon the Chaldeans because of their idolatry (vss. 18-20). This verse emphasizes the utter futility of idol worship. It is futile because it is the product of man's own hands. Man makes it, and man worships it; but the idol is dumb. Not only can it not hear or speak, it can do nothing.

19. The reason why the idol cannot hear, speak, or do anything is because it is lifeless. It is covered with gold and silver, and there is no way for it to breathe; it is smothered. It is beautiful and costly, but totally worthless!

20. In contrast to the useless idol, Jehovah God is **in his holy temple** (heaven); and He is all-powerful because He lives! One need not spend time seeking to make Jehovah talk, for He has in fact already spoken. The only sensible thing that man the creature can do is to **keep silence,** listen to Him, and heed what He says.

II. THE PROPHET'S DEFERENCE TO JEHOVAH. 3:1-19.

Having had his eyes turned to Jehovah (2:20), the prophet now responds in the only fitting way—prayer. His prayer is expressed in the form of a psalm comprised of three parts in which the prophet finds expression.

A. His Prayer to God. 3:1-2.

1. Its description. 3:1.

3:1. This description is applicable to the entire prayer (vss. 2-19, with the exception of the inscription comprised of the last sentence) and is called **A prayer** (Heb *tepilah,* prayer or song of praise). It was written to be used as a part of the public worship services of Israel. The description indicates that the song was set to **Shigionoth,** which refers to the kind of music with which the psalm was to be accompanied. It is to be a song that is sung triumphantly and in great excitement. Though the prophecy he has given is dark because it involves the judgment and destruction of Judah, the prophet is not discouraged or defeated; for he knows that ultimately Chaldea will be destroyed, Israel will be exalted, and Jehovah's glory will fill the earth (cf. 2:14, 20).

2. Its content. 3:2.

2. The prophet begins his prayer with an acknowledgment that he has heard what Jehovah has said. He has obeyed the admonition given in 2:20. When he **heard** what the Lord said, it made him **afraid;** for it involved the destruction of Judah. However, the prophet's hope goes beyond Judah to Jehovah; and in faith he urges Jehovah to go about the accomplishing of His purpose, which involves a manifestation of His wrath both upon Judah and Chaldea. The prophet beseeches Jehovah in the exercise of His **wrath** to also remember to exercise His **mercy** (Heb *racham,* to love, to pity, or to be merciful).

B. His Praise of God. 3:3-15.

In this section the prophet praises God, primarily for two of his attributes:

1. For His majesty. 3:3-7.

3a. In reflecting upon the majesty of God and what He will do in the future, the prophet turns his eyes to what God has done in the past. Just as He manifested His majesty in the past,

His glory covered the heavens, and the earth was full of his praise.

He will also manifest His majesty in the future; for God dwells in the eternal present. The prophet is not simply recalling the great deeds of the past, but is using them as sounding boards in order to project what God will do in the future. **Teman** was located in the extreme south of Edom and was probably its capital. Opposite Teman was **Paran**. The two were separated by the Valley of Ghor. In the background of the prophet's thinking is the memory of the events surrounding Israel's exodus from Egypt and their sojourn in Sinai. Just as God came and manifested Himself to the Israel of that day, God will come and manifest Himself to the Israel of the prophet's day. Just as God delivered Israel from the hands of the Egyptians after they had suffered under their cruelty, He will deliver the Israel of his day from the Chaldeans after they have suffered under their cruelty. God will deliver His people and will judge their foes. The **Selah** invites the reader/singer to stop and think about that thought. Three times the musical notation **Selah** occurs (vss. 3, 9, 13). This expression is thought to be equivalent to a musical rest in which the reader or singer was instructed to stop and think about what he just sang or read. It affords an opportunity for pause and reflection upon what has been said. When we read it, we probably should not vocalize it anymore than a singer would vocalize the rests of a musical composition.

3b-4. The **glory** and majesty of God are universal in their display. The majesty of God is seen in the brilliance of **light**; and as one views the rays emanating from the sun (which have the appearance of **horns**), one sees the visible manifestation of the invisible power and majesty of God. The sun, then, should be an ever-present reminder of the majesty of the only true God.

4 And *his* brightness was as the light; he had horns *coming* out of his hand: and there *was* the hiding of his power.

5. In their deliverance from Egypt, God visited the Egyptians with pestilence; and during their wilderness wanderings, He delivered them from all kinds of foes. As He did in the past, thus He will do in the future.

5 Before him went the pestilence, and burning coals went forth at his feet.

6. In the past God beheld the entire earth in His universal vision. He had a plan and in the process He drove **nations** apart and defeated them. Even the **mountains** and **hills** scattered in deference to their Creator. God is eternal, and His ways are everlasting; as they were in the past, so they will be in the future.

6 He stood, and measured the earth: he beheld, and drove asunder the nations: and the everlasting mountains were scattered, the perpetual hills did bow: his ways *are* everlasting.

7. In the past the majesty and power of God caused the nations to **tremble**. So it will be in the future. **Cushan** is a reference to the people of Cush who are known more familiarly as Ethiopians. The Midianites were the people located along the Red Sea opposite Ethiopia. Both of these are a nomadic people, indicated by the reference to **tents** and **curtains**. God dried up the Red Sea to enable Israel to pass through the land of Cush and into the land of Midian. This feat wrought fear into the hearts of those who beheld it. As God defended Israel in the past, thus He will do in the future.

7 I saw the tents of Cū'shăn in affliction: *and* the curtains of the land of Mĭd'ī-an did tremble.

The overriding thought of this section (vs. 3-7) is that God is majestic and powerful. It is He who protected Israel in past crises, and it is He who will defend and protect them in all future crises.

2. For His power. 3:8-15.

8 Was the Lᴏʀᴅ displeased against the rivers? *was* thine anger against the rivers? *was* thy wrath against the sea, that thou didst ride upon thine horses *and* thy chariots of salvation?

8. What God has done to the Red Sea (vs. 7), He can do to any and all **rivers**. When Israel came to the Jordan River, God dammed up the waters and caused them to pass over on dry land (cf. Josh 3:15-17). God is powerful; and what He has done for Israel in the past, He is quite capable of doing again in the future. God is in complete control of His creation. The **horses** and **chariots of salvation** are poetic references to the elements of nature. God is powerful and is in complete control of them. He has intervened for Israel in the past, and He will do so again in the future.

9 Thy bow was made quite naked, *ac-*

9. The Lord's power is open and evident to all. Poetically, it

cording to the oaths of the tribes, *even thy* word. Sē'lah. Thou didst cleave the earth with rivers.

10 The mountains saw thee, *and* they trembled: the overflowing of the water passed by: the deep uttered his voice, *and* lifted up his hands on high.

11 The sun *and* moon stood still in their habitation: at the light of thine arrows they went, *and* at the shining of thy glittering spear.

12 Thou didst march through the land in indignation, thou didst thresh the heathen in anger.

13 Thou wentest forth for the salvation of thy people, *even* for salvation with thine anointed; thou woundedst the head out of the house of the wicked, by discovering the foundation unto the neck. Sē'lah.

14 Thou didst strike through with his staves the head of his villages: they came out as a whirlwind to scatter me: their rejoicing *was* as to devour the poor secretly.

15 Thou didst walk through the sea with thine horses, *through* the heap of great waters.

is likened to an unsheathed **bow** that has ample testimony from those who have already experienced its effectiveness. None know better of its power then those who have received an arrow from it. This is in keeping with the Lord's own testimony that He would take vengeance upon His enemies. Once again, the **Selah** invites the reader/singer to stop and think about the power of God. That same power, when directed against the **earth**, caused it to part and **rivers** to gush forth.

10. This verse continues the testimony to God's power. The poetic language is in keeping with that of an earthquake in which the resultant noise is viewed as if it were the **voice** of God. That may be in view here; God is remembered as working in leveling the **mountains** and bringing the water over the entire earth during the Noahic flood. **The deep,** a reference to the sea, is pictured as lifting up its **hands on high.** The overall picture is of an omnipotent God of power capable of effecting His will anywhere in His creation. As He did it in the days of Noah, so He can do again, and will.

11. God also manifested His power in the days of Joshua when He caused **The sun and moon** to stand **still** (cf. Josh 10; 12-14). Not only is God's power manifested throughout the world, but also throughout the heavens! The God who intervened for Israel and manifested His power in the heavens in the days of Joshua can do it again in the future, and will. **Arrows** is reference to lightning which goes forth like a glittering spear (God is in complete control of His creation and all the power of nature). In the past He manipulated it for Israel's benefit, and in the future He will do so again.

12-13. These verses tell why God has manifested His power in such ways. It was for His people's sake to enable Him to **thresh** the ungodly and deliver their land into His people's possession. Further, God did it for the **salvation** of His own **people.** God is not disinterested in the concerns of His people, as the prophet had feared (cf. 1:2-4); He has brought both His majesty and power to bear on their behalf before their deliverance, and He will do so again. By **thine anointed,** it is best to understand a reference to the people of Israel who were the instrument that God used to effect the subjugation of the heathen and the accomplishments of His purpose. The **head out of the house of the wicked** who is wounded may be understood to be either a reference to one of the kings of Canaan who was slain in the deliverance of that land into Israel's hands or, better, a reference to the king of Chaldea who will be slain in the ultimate defeat of Chaldea. The language is elastic enough to include both thoughts, and certainly the historical citation of the former would be a guarantee of the historical realization of the latter. The expression **discovering the foundation unto the neck** is a poetic figure indicating the destruction of Chaldean dynasty. The head will be cut off; hence, the **neck** will be exposed. Once again, the **Selah** invites the reader/singer to stop and think about that.

14. The prophet looks at the power of God from another perspective, and he identifies himself with the people of Israel as they view God's hand of deliverance from various invaders. The invaders came intent on destroying Israel (**me** and **the poor**), but God caused them to be confused and annihilate each other.

15. The prophet views the power of God as displayed in the crossing of the Red Sea. He walked through the mighty waters of that **sea,** and the force was so great that it parted the **waters** so that Israel walked through dry land.

C. His Trust in God. 3:16-19.

Having praised God for His majesty (vss. 3-7) and His power (vss. 8-15), the prophet now moves to express his trust in such a God.

16 When I heard, my belly trembled; my lips quivered at the voice: rottenness entered into my bones, and I trembled in myself, that I might rest in the day of trouble: when he cometh up unto the people, he will invade them with his troops.

17 ¶Although the fig tree shall not blossom, neither *shall* fruit *be* in the vines; the labour of the olive shall fail, and the fields shall yield no meat; the flock shall be cut off from the fold, and *there shall be* no herd in the stalls:

18 Yet I will rejoice in the LORD, I will joy in the God of my salvation.

19 The LORD God *is* my strength, and he will make my feet like hinds' *feet,* and he will make me to walk upon mine high places. To the chief singer on my stringed instruments.

1. In spite of His work in bringing the Chaldeans. 3:16-17.

16-17. The prophet resumes and develops the thought begun in verse 2. His response is to what he knows Jehovah is going to do in bringing the Chaldeans to punish Judah for their sins (cf. 1:2-4). The enemy's invasion will be ruthless, affecting not only the population, but also the orchards, vineyards, fields, and herds. It will result in great suffering and privation, and the prophet understandably does not look forward to this prospect. However, his trust remains in God, in spite of His work in bringing the Chaldeans.

2. Because of His work in bringing salvation (deliverance). 3:18-19.

18. In spite of the testing, the prophet remains firm in his resolve to **rejoice in the LORD**; He is the **God** of **salvation**. The same God who brings judgment also brings deliverance. He will see the prophet through the trials personally and will see the nation through its crisis until all of His purposes are ultimately fulfilled.

19. The LORD God is my strength. The God who provides salvation is the God who also provides **strength**. The prophet (and all the righteous) can rise above the circumstances and stand firm in the promises of God. His joy will be their **strength**. In the midst of utter desolation they can have the consolation that only God can provide. So serene and sure will they be in the midst of the trial that, poetically, they are likened to **hinds** (gazelles) who move with great swiftness and great surety in times of danger, seemingly oblivious to it.

The instructions in the inscription at the end of the psalm indicate that this psalm was used as a part of the Temple liturgy. It is a great psalm expressing obedience to God, praise to God, and trust in God. It stands in striking contrast to the perplexity that the prophet expressed in the opening part of the book. The difference between the two is that now the prophet sees things from God's perspective and realizes that God's concern is broader and more inclusive than his. It is not until one does this that he is able to respond with such submission, praise, and trust.

(see page 1864 for Bibliography to the Minor Prophets)

ZEPHANIAH

INTRODUCTION

Authorship. Beyond the prophecy that bears his name, nothing is known about the author, Zephaniah. His name means "defended by Jehovah", "protected by Jehovah", "hidden by Jehovah". *Young's Analytical Concordance* suggests that His name means "Jah (Jehovah) is darkness." The meanings of His name do offer some clue as to the characteristics of the prophecy (see below). While other prophets gave their pedigree (cf. Isa 1:1; Jer 1:1; Joel 1:1; Zech 1:1), none goes into such great detail as Zephaniah, whose lineage shows that he was the great-great-grandson of good King Hezekiah. Zechariah traces his lineage back to his grandfather (cf. Zech 1:1). Thus, the prophet is a descendant of the royal line, which makes his rebuke of princes and nobles all the more significant (cf. 1:8, 13, 18). By giving his lineage and citing King Josiah, during whose reign he ministered, Zephaniah linked himself with the godly kings and the godly remnant of Israel's history. Zephaniah ministered about fifty years after Nahum and was a contemporary of Jeremiah.

Date and place of writing. The prophet dates his writing as "in the days of Josiah" (1:1). Josiah was the God-fearing son of Amon, who together with his father, Manasseh, were two of the most wicked kings of Israel's history (cf. II Kgs 22-23). During Josiah's reign a spiritual reformation that touched only the small remnant in Judah took place in 621 B.C. (cf. II Chr 34:3-7). Zephaniah mentions nothing of this reformation; thus, it is logical to conclude that his ministry preceded that reformation, and it is very probable that his preaching prepared the way for, greatly advanced, and furthered the power of the spiritual reformation under King Josiah. If these observations are true, then the prophecy must have been given before the reforms under Josiah, about 625 B.C.

The place from which the prophet ministered is not known with certainty. The fact that the ten northern tribes had been in captivity nearly a hundred years, together with his royal lineage (which would give him access to the king's court), makes it most likely that he ministered in Jerusalem. He may even have resided in the palace complex.

Characteristics of the prophecy. Zephaniah is a book of contrasts; for no other prophet paints a blacker picture of God's judgment, and no prophet paints a brighter picture of Israel's future glory. Zephaniah has been called "the orator" because of the oratorical style evident throughout the prophecy. Zephaniah makes mention of "the day of the LORD (Jehovah)" more than any other minor prophet and shows what that day will mean for ungodly Judah and her enemies (1:2-3:7), as well as the godly remnant of Judah (3:8-20). The prophecy is all-inclusive in its scope. One scholar has called it "the compendium" of all prophecy, and many scholars have expressed similar thoughts. Zephaniah does not make much use of historical events in the course of his prophecy, nor of happenings current in his day. Upon the dark backdrop describing the judgment of God upon Judah and the nation, Zephaniah goes further than any other of the minor prophets in emphasizing the future conversion of the Gentiles to the worship of the true God. Zephaniah has some literary affinities with Isaiah, but more with Jeremiah and Joel. Both he and Joel paint very dark pictures of the day of Jehovah, but in both books beautiful rays of light penetrate the darkness. Two recurring expressions are important: (1) "remnant," 1:4; 2:7, 9; 3:13 and (2) "day (of the LORD/Jehovah)" 1:7-10, 14-16, 18; 2:2-3; 3:8, 11, 16.

Purpose. The purpose of Zephaniah's prophecy is to set forth what the day of the Lord will mean, both to ungodly Judah and the world powers (1:2-3:7) and to the godly remnant (3:8-20). God's judgment must fall because of sin, and the nation is exhorted to repent (3:1-7). Through the prophecy the nation of the prophet's day is faced with its sin, reminded of coming judgment, and instructed concerning the ultimate glory that will come to Israel. Historically, the book was used in the providence of God to prepare the nation for the reforms and revival under King Josiah.

Theme. The Day of the LORD/Jehovah. This theme is also treated by Joel, though Joel ministered to Israel (the northern kingdom) during the Assyrian crisis. Zephaniah ministered to Judah (the southern kingdom) during the Babylonian crisis. Reference to the Day of the Lord occurs at least eighteen times in the book of Zephaniah (thirteen times in chapter one alone). The Day of the Lord destroys the false remnant of Baal (ch. 1), destroys the God-rejecting nations (ch. 2), and purifies the true remnant (3:8-20).

OUTLINE

COMMENTARY

I. THE INTRODUCTION. 1:1.

A. The Description of the Prophecy. 1:1a.

THE word of the LORD which came unto Zĕph-a-nī′ah the son of Cū′shī, the son Gĕd-a-lī′ah, the son of Ăm-a-rī′ah, the son of Hĭz-kī′ah, in the days of Jō-sī′ah the son of Amon, king of Judah.

1:1a. Even though the prophecy of Zephaniah is concerned primarily with judgment, it is still characterized as being a **word** (Heb *debar*), rather than as a "burden" (Heb *masa′*). This is probably because the prophecy does not concern the destruction of a particular nation (cf. Nah 1:1; Hab 1:1). Zephaniah, then, is an authoritative message that the prophet is going to deliver to Judah concerning the Day of the Lord, which will have ramifications both for Judah and for her enemies. The source of the message, hence its authority, is none other than **the LORD** (Jehovah). In delivering His message to man, Jehovah will use a human agent; but he is merely a channel who speaks for another—Jehovah! Hence, Judah, and all who hear or who read this prophecy, would do well to heed Him.

B. The Description of the Prophet. 1:1b.

1b. As observed earlier (cf. Introduction), the prophet's name means "defended", "protected", or "hidden by Jehovah". This not only affords a clue to the purpose of the prophecy, as noted earlier, but also gives rise to the observation that God always calls a man who is shaped exactly as the ministry to which God calls him requires; but the ministry is infinitely larger than the man. God would use Zephaniah to deliver a very dark message of judgment through which only a few rays of hope shine. In the midst of this judgment, God would defend, protect, and hide the true remnant, so that His wrath would not fall on them and they would experience the blessings the prophet announced. This principle of matching man with mission can be observed in all the other prophets, as well as in God's ministers today.

Zephaniah was **the son of Cushi**, the grandson of **Gedaliah**, the great-grandson of **Amariah**, and the great-great-grandson of King Hezekiah (**Hizkiah**). King Hezekiah was the godly king under whose reign God brought deliverance from Assyria in the days of Hosea, Micah, and Nahum almost a hundred years earlier (cf. II Kgs 18:20; II Chr 29-32). The rest of Zephaniah's ancestors are not to be confused with other men in the Old Testament who bore the same names. The purpose of giving this ancestry is to link the prophet with the house and line of royalty that he would subsequently condemn (cf. vs. 8).

The mention of King Hezekiah, under whose reign a spiritual revival was experienced (cf. II Kgs 18:3-7; II Chr 29:3-19), provides a direct link with King **Josiah**, under whose reign a revival was about to occur (cf. II Kgs 22-23:30; II Chr 34-35). Thus, the two righteous kings are linked together as contrasts to the wicked Manasseh and Amon (Josiah's father), under whose reigns Israel reached a new spiritual low. These facts enable us to date Zephaniah's prophecy at 625 B.C. and cause us to realize that Zephaniah was the last prophet God sent to Judah prior to its being carried off captive into Babylon.

II. THE PREDICTIONS OF JUDGMENT IN THE LIGHT OF THE DAY OF THE LORD. 1:2-3:7.

A. The Warnings of Judgments Delivered. 1:2-2:15.

Three warnings are delivered in verses 2-18. They are: (1) against the nation for spiritual adultery (vss. 2-6); (2) against the leaders (vss. 7-13); and (3) against the inhabitants of the land (vss. 14-18).

1. Against Judah. 1:2-2:3.

The warning against Judah for its spiritual adultery (vss. 2-6) is divided into two parts in which Jehovah tells what He will do (vss. 2-3) and why He will do it (vss. 4-6).

2-3. I will utterly consume all things. Jehovah warns that He will destroy everything in the land, air, and sea. The destruction will be universal, and it will be complete. The special focus of God's wrath includes **the stumbling blocks with the wicked,** the idols and all their trappings together with those who worship them. The warning culminates with the statement **I will cut off man from off the land.** Man is the prime offender. He offends by way of his idolatrous worship; and as a result of his sin, the creatures of land, sea, and air must also suffer (vss. 2-3, cf. Rom 8:20-22).

4-6. The general and universal judgment of verses 2-3 is particularized and focused upon Judah and Jerusalem in verses 4-6. Six groups are singled out for judgment. They are: (1) **the remnant of Baal.** Baal was the god of the Canaanites whose worship had infected Israel since the generation following Joshua, under whom the people failed to drive the Canaanites out of the land (cf. Jud 2:10-13). In the days immediately preceding Zephaniah, the worship of Baal was widespread throughout the land (during the reign of Manasseh and Amon, cf. II Kgs 21). Josiah, under whose reign Zephaniah ministered, destroyed Baal worship (cf. II Kgs 23:4-6). If Zephaniah's ministry followed the revival under Josiah, then **the remnant of Baal** is a reference to the vestiges of Baal worship that had eluded his destruction; but if Zephaniah's ministry preceded Josiah's reformation, then **the remnant of Baal** gives a recognition of the intense infection of idolatry throughout the land and an affirmation that every last trace of it will be removed. (2) **The Chemarim** (the Hebrew word is transliterated here, the Hebrew plural having an Anglicized plural 's' added, but translated as ". . . priests . . ." in Hos 10:5, and as ". . . idolatrous priests . . ." in II Kgs 23:5 where it is noted that Josiah put them down). The term has been understood to mean either "black" because, as priests, they were burners of sacrifices or wore black, or as "zealous" because of the intensity of their idolatrous worship. It is correct, then, to understand this as a reference to the idolatrous priests who make no secret of their attachment to a false worship system. They will be destroyed together **with the priests** (Heb *kohēn*) who are outwardly affiliated with the worship of Jehovah but spiritually have defected and have joined the people in their sin. (3) **Them that worship the host of heaven upon the housetops,** an individualized form of idolatry carried on from house to house throughout the land. Moses had warned against it (cf. Deut 4:19), but it was widespread. It was carried out upon the housetops because they were flat and provided an unobstructed view of the heavenly bodies. In the course of the religious observance, incense was burned on the rooftop and drink offerings were poured out (cf. Jer 19:13; 44:17-25). (4) **Them that worship and that swear by the LORD, and that swear by Malcham,** devotees of a syncretistic worship system, including elements of the worship of Jehovah with elements of the worship of **Malcham,** the tribal god of Ammon (cf. I Kgs 11:33) and variously known as Malcam, Moloch, and Milcom. (5) **Them that are turned back from the LORD,** those

---

2 I will utterly consume all *things* from off the land, saith the LORD.

3 I will consume man and beast; I will consume the fowls of the heaven, and the fishes of the sea, and the stumbling-blocks with the wicked; and I will cut off man from off the land, saith the LORD.

4 I will also stretch out mine hand upon Judah, and upon all the inhabitants of Jerusalem; and I will cut off the remnant of Bā'al from this place, *and* the name of the Chĕm'a-rĭms with the priests;

5 And them that worship the host of heaven upon the housetops; and them that worship *and* that swear by the LORD, and that swear by Măl'chăm;

6 And them that are turned back from the LORD; and *those* that have not sought the LORD, nor enquired for him.

and will make Nĭn'e-veh a desolation, *and* dry like a wilderness.

14 And flocks shall lie down in the midst of her, all the beasts of the nations: both the cormorant and the bittern shall lodge in the upper lintels of it; *their* voice shall sing in the windows; desolation *shall* be in the thresholds: for he shall uncover the cedar work.

15 This *is* the rejoicing city that dwelt carelessly, that said in her heart, I *am*, and *there is* none beside me: how is she become a desolation, a place for beasts to lie down in! every one that passeth by her shall hiss, *and* wag his hand.

CHAPTER 3
WOE to her that is filthy and polluted, to the oppressing city!

2 She obeyed not the voice; she received not correction; she trusted not in the LORD; she drew not near to her God.

3 Her princes within her *are* roaring lions; her judges *are* evening wolves; they gnaw not the bones till the morrow.

4 Her prophets *are* light *and* treacherous persons: her priests have pol-

know that the destruction of **Assyria** and **Nineveh** had not yet taken place. It was, however, soon to come. It is amplified in detail by the prophecy of Nahum. The nation, together with its capital, was to be destroyed and would become a barren waste. At its height Nineveh had a population of 600,000 people. Following its destruction, it will be inhabited only by herds of cattle and small solitary animals. The **cormorant** (Heb *qa'at*) is a pelican and the **bittern** (Heb *qipōd*) is a porcupine or hedgehog. These lonely animals will find their homes amidst the ruins of the once beautifully-appointed architecture of the city. In verse 15a the city is pictured as it was in the day of the prophet. It rejoiced in its self-sufficiency and boasted in its glory, which was renowned throughout the world. For nearly three hundred years it had been an influential and powerful city; there had been nothing like it before in the history of the world. They revelled in the glory that was theirs, completely oblivious to their obligation to God, except for the spiritual awakening under Jonah's ministry about 150 years earlier. The prophet contrasts what the city is with what it will become. So certain is the destruction to come that he views it as having already transpired. Their destruction will come suddenly, and it will be so complete that the city will be fit only for **beasts** to inhabit. It will become an object of scorn and contempt; and all who pass by will demonstrate their feelings in the customary way, hissing and wagging their hands.

B. Woe Upon Jerusalem Pronounced. 3:1-7.

1. The woe stated. 3:1.

3:1. The prophet's tactic is similar to that practiced by Amos when he pronounced judgment upon all the nations around in order to focus his judgment on Judah (cf. Amos 1-2). Thus, Zephaniah has pronounced judgment upon the nations surrounding Judah on all sides; now he focuses upon Judah herself. The **city** in verse 1 is not named, but the ensuing context lets us know that it must be Jerusalem. The sins that infect the surrounding nations also infect her; and thus, she is **filthy and polluted,** ripe for judgment. Upon such a city, woe is pronounced.

2. The woe justified. 3:2-7.

In this section two reasons why the woe is justified are presented: (1) because of their history (vss. 2-4) and (2) in spite of Jehovah's provisions (vss. 5-7).

2. In considering Judah's history, the prophet focuses upon what she has been in the past (vs. 2) and what she is in the present (vss. 3-4). Her past history has not been very commendable, for four accusations are brought against her: (1) **She obeyed not the voice.** She was disobedient to the will of God as revealed through the Law and the prophets that He sent unto them. (2) **She received not correction.** When God brought punishment upon her for her sins, she did not learn from that correction, but rather repeated the same error over and over. (3) **She trusted not in the LORD.** In time of crisis instead of trusting Jehovah who had bound her to himself by covenant relation, she trusted in herself and tried to stand in her own might, only to fail. (4) **She drew not near to her God.** In spite of all of God's provisions and blessings, Judah did not draw nigh to God; rather, she went further and further from Him until now, judgment must fall.

3-4. What Judah has been in the past is evidenced by her leaders of the present, for her leaders came from the nation that produced them. Four categories of leaders are cited and their offenses indicated: (1) **Her princes,** likened to **roaring lions** who have insatiable appetites, relentlessly oppressed those who were under them. It is interesting to note that the prophet does

luted the sanctuary, they have done violence to the law.

5 The just LORD *is* in the midst thereof; he will not do iniquity: every morning doth he bring his judgment to light, he faileth not; but the unjust knoweth no shame.

6 I have cut off the nations: their towers are desolate; I made their streets waste, that none passeth by: their cities are destroyed, so that there is no man, that there is none inhabitant.

7 I said, Surely thou wilt fear me, thou wilt receive instruction; so their dwelling should not be cut off, howsoever I punished them: but they rose early, *and* corrupted all their doings.

8 ¶Therefore wait ye upon me, saith the LORD, until the day that I rise up to the prey: for my determination *is* to gather the nations, that I may assemble the kingdoms, to pour upon them mine indignation, *even* all my fierce anger: for all the earth shall be devoured with the fire of my jealousy.

not indict King Josiah, for he was a godly king who did right in the eyes of Jehovah (cf. II Kgs 22:1-2). (2) **Her judges** are likened to **evening wolves.** They should have upheld the righteous, but instead, they devoured them mercilessly, making themselves rich in the process. (3) **Her prophets,** of course, are false prophets who distorted and repudiated the messages delivered by the true prophets of Jehovah. They are **light** in that their messages comfort the people in their sin, and they are **treacherous** in that they distort and refute the true message of God to the detriment of the people. (4) **Her priests . . . polluted the sanctuary** by sticking meticulously to the outward performance of religious deeds without the heart reality and did **violence to the law** by making it an end in itself. All of the leaders of the land, whether political, legal, or religious, were guilty of perverting their sacred trust for personal enrichment. While they prospered, the nation perished. Ultimately, they too would perish with the nation.

The second reason the woe is justified is because Judah's condition is inexcusable, for Jehovah has made ample provision for them (vss. 5-7). In His dealings with Judah, Jehovah has made three provisions: (1) His presence (vs. 5); (2) His judgment on their enemies (vs. 6); and (3) His expectation (vs. 7).

5. In spite of the nation's sin and defection, the **just** (Heb *tsadîq*, right or righteous) Jehovah is in their midst, ever ready to minister to and restore them. He remains totally separated from their sin, though every morning He faithfully makes His righteous judgment known through the ministry of His faithful prophets and servants by whom He condemns the wickedness of the leaders and nation. Though the Lord is in their midst and continuously faces the nation and leaders with their sin, the testimony goes unheeded; for **the unjust** (Heb '*awal*, perverse) **knoweth no shame.**

6. This verse describes the judgment that Jehovah executed upon Judah's enemies so that Judah could dwell in peace and come to repentance. Because Jehovah judged other nations for their sins, which were identical with Judah's, Judah should have been warned that He also would judge them; but they made the fatal error of equating God's favor with favoritism, and they did not repent.

7. The prophet makes Jehovah's motive in bringing judgment upon the surrounding nations certain in verse 6. Jehovah trusted that Judah would learn from His dealings with the nations, but they did not. Instead, **they rose early, and corrupted all their doings.** They conducted business as usual, ever weaving their sinful webs in which ultimately they would perish about them. Verses 1-7 have shown that Judah will be punished as the nations around them have been punished, for their sins are the same.

III. THE EXHORTATIONS IN THE LIGHT OF THE DAY OF THE LORD. 3:8-20.

The exhortations are twofold.

A. To Wait for Jehovah. 3:8-13.

1. The exhortation delivered. 3:8a.

8a. The godly of Judah are exhorted to **wait** upon Jehovah until his program of judgment of the nations and restoration of Israel is completed (vs. 8a).

2. The exhortation explained. 3:8b-13.

In this explanation Jehovah identifies four things He will accomplish: (1) He will gather the nations for judgment (vs. 8b); (2) He will purify His people (vss. 9-11a); (3) He will remove pride (vss. 11b-13a); and (4) He will provide for His people (vs. 13b).

8b. The day for which the righteous are to wait is a day in which all the **nations** of the world will be gathered together by Jehovah and He will execute judgment upon them. It will be a universal judgment motivated by his **jealousy**, or His holiness which the nations have violated. The judgment that the prophet pictures was adumbrated by the destruction of Assyria and Babylon, but ultimately it will be fulfilled in the judgment poured out upon all the nations of the world during the Great Tribulation.

9 For then will I turn to the people a pure language, that they may all call upon the name of the Lord, to serve him with one consent.

9. The **people** in view are the remnant of the Gentiles who survived God's judgment because of their conversion. Jehovah will give them **a pure language,** not an indication that the linguistic diversion visited upon the human race at the tower of Babel will be reversed or that they will join Israel in speaking Hebrew, but that their language will be purified from all of the oaths and prayers used in placating their idol gods. They will use a **pure language,** which is a fitting vehicle to call upon the true Jehovah. The life that follows will be consistent with their call; for they will **serve him with one consent** (Heb *shekem,* shoulder), a figure drawn from the use of a yoke whereby two animals could be linked together and serve as one. All Gentiles will be unified in their worship of Jehovah and will address Him in praise and supplication with a language purified of all heathen terminology.

10 From beyond the rivers of Ē-thǐ-ō′-pǐ-a my suppliants, *even* the daughter of my dispersed, shall bring mine offering.

10. The purification of the Gentiles will affect what they do. Those from the South (**Ethiopia**) will gather together the Jews that are dispersed among them and return them to Judah as an **offering** for Jehovah. The **suppliants** are the gentile Ethiopians, not the Jews who are dispersed among them. They are the ones who will bring **mine offering,** which is in apposition to **even the daughter of my dispersed.** Thus, the conversion of the Ethiopians is demonstrated by their deeds, returning to Jerusalem the Jews who have been dispersed among them. Because their hearts are made right with Jehovah, they returned to Jehovah that which is rightfully his.

11 In that day shalt thou not be ashamed for all thy doings, wherein thou hast transgressed against me: for then I will take away out of the midst of thee them that rejoice in thy pride, and thou shalt no more be haughty because of my holy mountain.
12 I will also leave in the midst of thee an afflicted and poor people, and they shall trust in the name of the Lord.
13 ¶The remnant of Israel shall not do iniquity, nor speak lies; neither shall a deceitful tongue be found in their mouth: for they shall feed and lie down, and none shall make *them* afraid.

11-13. The cleansing of the nations will also mean cleansing for Israel. There will be no cause for shame for Jehovah will have dealt in judgment with every ungodly person and ungodly deed. Jehovah will remove all vestiges of sinful **pride** from the nation. The **pride,** which was characteristic of the false priests and the false prophets, will be removed and will no longer infect either the worship of the Lord or the environs in which that worship is conducted. In the place of the proud, Jehovah will leave those who are truly humble and trust in Him completely. The **remnant of Israel** will be purified of their sin, whether in work or word; and they will be at peace and in fellowship with God and one another. When a nation is spiritually right, it will be physically secure. Jehovah will provide for and protect His people, and they will dwell in perfect peace and security.

B. To Rejoice in Jehovah. 3:14-20.

1. The exhortation delivered. 3:14.

14. In view of such restoration, peace, and security, Judah and Israel can confidently rejoice and praise Jehovah. The nation is exhorted to give heartfelt expression to singing, shouting, being glad, and rejoicing (vs. 14).

14 ¶Sing, O daughter of Zion; shout, O Israel; be glad and rejoice with all the heart, O daughter of Jerusalem.

2. The exhortation explained. 3:15-20.

Four causes for rejoicing are given: (1) Jehovah has removed his judgment (vss. 15-16); (2) Jehovah dwells among His people (vss. 17-18); (3) Jehovah will deal with all enemies (vs. 19); and (4) Jehovah will restore His people (vs. 20).

15 The Lord hath taken away thy judgments, he hath cast out thine enemy: the king of Israel, *even* the Lord,

15-16. Jehovah has taken away the nation's **judgments** because her sin has been punished and she has been purified. All enemies, including the spiritual enemy of idolatry which had

is in the midst of thee: thou shalt not see evil any more.

16 In that day it shall be said to Jerusalem, Fear thou not: *and to* Zion, Let not thine hands be slack.

17 The LORD thy God in the midst of thee *is* mighty; he will save, he will rejoice over thee with joy; he will rest in his love, he will joy over thee with singing.

18 I will gather *them that are* sorrowful for the solemn assembly, *who* are of thee, *to whom* the reproach of it *was* a burden.

19 Behold, at that time I will undo all that afflict thee: and I will save her that halteth, and gather her that was driven out; and I will get them praise and fame in every land where they have been put to shame.

20 At that time will I bring you *again*, even in the time that I gather you: for I will make you a name and a praise among all people of the earth, when I turn back your captivity before your eyes, saith the LORD.

infected the nation for so long, have been cast out; and Jehovah himself reigns forever within and there will never again be spiritual defection. Because of Jehovah's presence and purification, the nation need have no fear of enemies from without or within. They can give their time and effort wholly to the worship of Jehovah.

17-18. Once again, the redeemed nation is assured of the personal dwelling presence of Jehovah. He is powerful, an able Deliverer. His presence will abide upon them, not in judgment but in rejoicing. He will actually **rest in his love;** there will be no cause in Israel to elicit judgment or rebuke. Jehovah will have removed all of that from Judah, and there will now be only joy and singing. Verse 18 focuses upon the Jews of the exile who, because they were prohibited from celebrating the peace to Jehovah during their exile, sorrowed. They will be gathered, and Jehovah will rejoice over them. This restoration following the Babylonian captivity adumbrates the great restoration of the Millennium to which the prophet has eluded.

19. Before Jehovah can exalt over His people, He must destroy every enemy that has afflicted His people. This He will do. The enemies have crippled His people and have driven them out of their rightful land. They have been an object of scorn and derision; but Jehovah will deliver them, and they will be purified and restored. Instead of being objects of **shame,** they will be objects of praise; and the ones who have afflicted them will stand in awe of them and the God who has shown Himself powerful in their behalf.

20. Ultimately, Jehovah will restore His people, and all wrongs wrought against them will be righted. Their restoration will mean blessing, not only for them, but for the redeemed of all nations of the earth. This prophecy was only partially fulfilled in the restoration that followed the Babylonian captivity; but it will ultimately and fully be fulfilled in the restoration following the Great Tribulation when Jehovah returns to the earth, puts down every enemy, regathers His people, and reigns over them for a thousand years!

(see page 1864 for Bibliography to the Minor Prophets)

HAGGAI

INTRODUCTION

Authorship. The author of this prophecy is identified simply as "Haggai the prophet" or "the prophet Haggai" (cf. 1:1; 2:1, 10, 20). The meaning and etymology of the name are uncertain. Some render it "festival" or "festive" or "festal one" and have inferred that the prophet was born on a feast day. Others consider his name to be a form of feast of Jehovah and see in the name an indication of the joyous character of the predictions he delivered. Nothing is known of his personal history, though he is mentioned in Ezra 5:1 and 6:14. Once again, God obscured the origin of His prophet; it was his message that was all-important. Some have inferred from 2:3 that Haggai was born in Judah before 586 B.C. and was one of a small company who had seen the former Temple in its glory. If this is true, he must have been an old man when he prophesied. This supposition agrees with the brevity of his public ministry. Although his personal history is scarcely known, he was extremely practical in his ministry. He was a man that God raised up at a specific time for a specific mission.

Date and Place of Writing. Haggai was the first of the prophets to minister to Israel following the return from the Babylonian captivity. The period of Israel's history into which he fits is recorded in the books of Ezra, Nehemiah, and Esther; his personal historical background is recorded in Ezra 4 and 5.

Haggai dates his prophecy according to the year of the reigning Persian monarch ". . . Darius the King . . ." (Darius I, son of Darius Hystaspis who was also known as Darius the Mede, cf. 1:1) who began his reign Dec. 22, 522 B.C. His ascension to the throne was greeted with many assassinations within the kingdom and revolt on the part of satellite nations under Persian control. During his first two years as king, Darius I defeated nine kings in nineteen different battles. He became interested in law and permitted the Jews to rebuild Solomon's temple, which had been destroyed by Nebuchadnezzar in 586 B.C. The remnant of Israel had returned from Babylon, had reinstituted the feast, had laid the foundation for the new Temple, and then was interrupted in its restoration because of opposition from residents of the land. Haggai began his ministry in 520 B.C. to exhort the people to complete the task of building the Temple. The resumption of the work aroused further opposition, and a letter was sent to Darius which he did not receive until 519-518 B.C. Haggai's ministry was short, lasting only four months. His prophecy was sufficient motivation to get the people started again, and the work that he began was carried on by Zechariah and Malachi with whom he was a contemporary. The place from which the prophecy was issued is Jerusalem, the site of the Temple.

Characteristics of the Prophecy. Haggai delivered his prophecy using simple prose. The prophecy consists of four messages from God delivered to the nation after the rebuilding of the Temple had ceased for about ten years. The first message (1:1-15) reveals the low spiritual conditions of the day, for the prophet rebukes them for their indifference and urges them to build the house of the Lord. The people responded immediately to Haggai's message and began to rebuild the Temple. The prophet then issues the second message (2:1-9) in which he assures the people that Jehovah is with them even though the Temple they are rebuilding could not compare to the splendor of Solomon's temple, though the glory of the Zerubbabel's temple would be greater than the glory of Solomon's. The third message (2:10-19) assures the people of material blessing, even though at the present time there doesn't seem to be evidence of it. The final message (2:20-23) is addressed to Zerubbabel concerning the one (Messiah) who is to follow him. These four messages respectively comprise messages of motivation, consolation, affirmation, and anticipation.

Next to Obadiah, Haggai is the shortest book in the Old Testament, containing but two chapters comprised of a total of thirty-eight verses. It is the only book of the English Bible to contain two chapters. The straightforward style of the book is enhanced by the use of questions, recurring expressions, and commands.

Purpose. The four messages that comprise the prophecy let us know that the prophecy had a fourfold purpose: (1) to motivate the people to resume the building of the Temple (1:1-15); (2) to console the people that Jehovah was with them, for the Temple they were rebuilding would have a greater glory than Solomon's (2:1-9); (3) to affirm Jehovah's blessings upon them (2:10-19); and (4) to anticipate the glorious future that lies ahead (2:20-23). The immediate purpose of the book is to encourage the people to resume the building of the Temple, which had lain idle for about ten years. It is imperative that the people build the Temple, for blessing from God is dependent upon obedience. No Temple; no blessings. When the Temple is built up, then blessings from God will come down.

Theme. Rebuilding the Temple. Solomon's temple was destroyed by the Babylonians when they carried Judah captive in 586 B.C. At the end of the Captivity, 50,000 Jews returned to the land to rebuild the Temple. They had begun, but the work had lain idle for ten years. Thus, God used Haggai to rebuke the people for their apathy and procrastination and to give four messages developing the theme of rebuilding the Temple.

OUTLINE

I. The First Message: A Message of Motivation.
1:1-15.
  A. The Circumstances of the Message. 1:1.
    1. The time of the message. 1:1a.
    2. The nature of the message. 1:1b.
    3. The recipient of the message. 1:1c.
  B. The Content of the Message. 1:2-15.
    1. The need to rebuild the house of the Lord.
1:2-6.
    2. The commission to rebuild. 1:7-11.
    3. The compliance to rebuild. 1:12-15.

II. The Second Message: A Message of Consolation.
2:1-9.
  A. The Circumstances of the Message. 2:1-2.
    1. Its time. 2:1a.
    2. Its nature. 2:1b.
    3. Its address. 2:2.
  B. The Content of the Message. 2:3-9.
    1. The question. 2:3.
    2. The encouragement. 2:4-9.

III. The Third Message: A Message of Affirmation.
2:10-19.
  A. The Circumstances of the Message. 2:10-11.
    1. Its time. 2:10a.
    2. Its nature. 2:10b.
    3. Its recipients. 2:11.
  B. The Content of the Message. 2:12-19.
    1. The illustration of contamination. 2:12-
13.
    2. The application to Israel. 2:14-17.
    3. The declaration of blessing. 2:18-19.

IV. The Fourth Message: A Message of Anticipation.
2:20-23.
  A. The Circumstances of the Message. 2:20-21a.
    1. Its time. 2:20a.
    2. Its recipient. 2:20b.
    3. Its address. 2:21a.
  B. The Content of the Message. 2:21b-23.
    1. The heavens and the earth. 2:21b.
    2. The nations of the earth. 2:22.
    3. Zerubbabel. 2:23.

COMMENTARY

I. THE FIRST MESSAGE: A MESSAGE OF MOTIVATION. 1:1-15.

A. The Circumstances of the Message. 1:1.

1. The time of the message. 1:1a.

IN the second year of Darius the king, in the sixth month, in the first day of the month, came the word of the LORD by Hăg′ga-ī the prophet unto Ze-rŭb′ba-bel the son of Shē-ăl′tī-el, governor of Judah, and to Joshua the son of Jŏs′e-dĕch, the high priest, saying,

1:1a. Haggai dates his prophecy **In the second year of Darius the king, in the sixth month, in the first day of the month.** The fact that he dates his prophecy in the reign of a gentile king confirms that the ". . . times of the Gentiles . . ." (Lk 21:24) has begun. God has set Israel aside nationally and will work through the Gentiles until the times of the Gentiles is complete—at the Rapture. The time cited here coincides with that mentioned in Ezra 4:24-5:2. **The sixth month** was the month of Elul and corresponds roughly to our September. The calendar used was a lunar calendar; hence, **the first day of the month** would be a new moon. This time was always set aside for special worship observances and would be an ideal time for Haggai to deliver his message. In converting the date of the lunar calendar over to the date of the solar calendar the first message was delivered August 29, 520 B.C.

2. The nature of the message. 1:1b.

1b. The message is described as **the word of the LORD by Haggai the prophet.** Its divine and human authorship are both affirmed. The message comes from Jehovah and bears His authority and authentication. It is delivered by divine commission through Haggai the prophet.

3. The recipient of the message. 1:1c.

1c. The message is addressed to **Zerubbabel** (Heb shoot of Babylon) and **Joshua** (Heb Yahweh saves). **Zerubbabel** was a descendant of Salathiel or **Shealtiel** and was the grandson of Jehoiakim, one of the last kings of Judah prior to the Babylonian captivity. In Ezra 1:8, 11; 5:14, 16 he is called Sheshbazzar. In 536 B.C. he led the first band of exiles back to Judah and was appointed by Cyrus to serve as the governor of Judah. **Joshua was the son of Josedech** (also known as Jozadak, Ezr 3:2 and Jehozadak, I Chr 6:15, who was the high priest at the time Judah was carried captive into Babylon). **Zerubbabel**, then, was the political leader of the people; and **Joshua** was the religious leader. By giving their lineage, it is shown that their family histories antedate the Babylonian captivity and they are rightfully in their places of leadership by virtue of their line of descent, as well as by virtue of the authority of the reigning gentile monarch. If they held their positions only by virtue of the gentile monarch's decree, they would have been held in contempt by the people.

B. The Content of the Message. 1:2-15.

1. The need to rebuild the house of the Lord. 1:2-6.

The need to rebuild stems from (1) the apathy of the people—the house of God remains unbuilt (vss. 2-4) and (2) the experience of the people—the blessings of God have ceased (vss. 5-6).

2-4. Jehovah addresses His people as **this people,** not because He has cast them off, but because they are disobedient and apathetic. They had been commissioned to rebuild the Temple but had stopped when the decree of Artaxerxes had been received (cf. Ezr 4). They had begun the work under the decree of Cyrus (cf. Ezr 1), and this should not have been a deterrent to them; for one Persian king could not change the word of another, as was subsequently confirmed by Darius (cf. Ezr 6). One scholar suggests that prophecy had proved to be not a tonic or a stimulant to the people in the land but rather a sedative and narcotic. They applied Jeremiah's seventy years (cf. Jer 25:11-12) not only to the Exile, but also to the Temple. They concluded that only sixty-eight years had passed since the destruction of the Temple; and so, literally, they said, **The time is not come, the time that the Lord's house should be built.** So they let the Temple lie unfinished (vs. 2). To such an apathetic people, Jehovah sent Haggai with a message of motivation (vs. 3). The people had not passed the time in absolute idleness, for they had taken time to build themselves luxurious **ceiled houses**—houses that were paneled (not only on the walls, but also on the ceilings) with fine woods. Such a practice was common for the residences of kings (cf. I Kgs 7:7; Jer 22:14). In contrast, the Lord's house lay waste—only partially restored; and only minimal worship services could be carried on (cf. Ezr 3). The problem was not that the people had built such fine houses for themselves, but rather that they had done so to the neglect of the house of the Lord. They had gotten their priorities out of order. They had put their own self-interests above God's (vs. 4).

5-6. To such an apathetic and selfish people Jehovah issues a command of self-judgment, **Consider your ways.** This command is issued five times throughout the course of this prophecy (vss. 5, 7; 2:15, 18 (twice)). It is a plea on the part of God for the people to take note of what they are doing, compare it with what they should be doing, and amend their ways accordingly. They have been diverting all their attention to themselves and have been diverting their wealth to their own pleasure, especially the acquiring of fine houses. **Ye have sown much, and bring in little.** They had sown bountiful crops, but had reaped sparingly; they ate food, but didn't have enough; they drank, but were never satisfied; they had clothing, but it wasn't adequate; they earned money, but never could get ahead. So intent were they on achieving their own ends that they completely forgot about God. All of it was futile, because they left out Jehovah completely. They had not learned the secret that our Lord expressed so adequately many centuries later: "But seek ye first the kingdom of God, and his righteousness; and all these things shall be added unto you" (Mt 6:33). They did not realize that blessings

2 Thus speaketh the Lord of hosts, saying, This people say, The time is not come, the time that the Lord's house should be built.
3 Then came the word of the Lord by Hag′ga-ī the prophet, saying,
4 *Is it* time for you, O ye, to dwell in your cieled houses, and this house lie waste?

5 Now therefore thus saith the Lord of hosts; Consider your ways.
6 Ye have sown much, and bring in little; ye eat, but ye have not enough; ye drink, but ye are not filled with drink; ye clothe you, but there is none warm; and he that earneth wages earneth wages *to put it* into a bag with holes.

7 ¶Thus saith the LORD of hosts: Consider your ways.
8 Go up to the mountain, and bring wood, and build the house; and I will take pleasure in it, and I will be glorified, saith the LORD.

9 Ye looked for much, and, lo, *it came* to little; and when ye brought *it* home, I did blow upon it. Why? saith the LORD of hosts. Because of mine house that *is* waste, and ye run every man unto his own house.
10 Therefore the heaven over you is stayed from dew, and the earth is stayed *from* her fruit.
11 And I called for a drought upon the land, and upon the mountains, and upon the corn, and upon the new wine, and upon the oil, and upon *that* which the ground bringeth forth, and upon men, and upon cattle, and upon all the labour of the hands.

12 ¶Then Ze-rŭb′ba-bel the son of Shē-ăl′tī-el, and Joshua the son of Jŏs′e-dĕch, the high priest, with all the remnant of the people, obeyed the voice of the LORD their God, and the words of Hăg′ga-ī the prophet, as the LORD their God had sent him, and the people did fear before the LORD.
13 Then spake Hăg′ga-ī the LORD's messenger in the LORD's message unto the people, saying, I *am* with you, saith the LORD.

14 And the LORD stirred up the spirit of Ze-rŭb′ba-bel the son of Shē-ăl′tī-el, governor of Judah, and the spirit of Joshua the son of Jŏs′e-dĕch, the high priest, and the spirit of all the remnant

from God are dependent upon obedience to God. No Temple; no blessing. Perhaps some of them had wondered when they would ever get ahead; and Jehovah is saying that when the Temple is built up, His blessings will come down.

2. *The commission to rebuild. 1:7-11.*

This section divides into three parts: (1) the command to repent (vs. 7); (2) the commission to gather materials (vs. 8); and (3) the explanation of the lack of blessing (vss. 9-11).

7-8. The prophet urges the people to repent, saying: **Consider your ways.** In verse 7, he urges them to consider what they should do—get materials and get on with the building of the house of the Lord. **Go up . . . bring wood . . . build the house.** Jehovah is displeased with the present condition of His house, but He will be pleased with the obedience of His people. That obedience will be manifested by their going to the mountain, getting wood, and resuming the building. This obedience on the part of the people will indicate that Jehovah has the first place in their lives. **I will take pleasure in it, and I will be glorified.** Even though the house that they will build will not begin to measure up to the glory of Solomon's (cf. 2:3-4), still Jehovah promises to take pleasure in it and be glorified by it, because it would come from people who were rightly related to their God and consequently, rightly related to everything else.

9-11. Ye looked for much, and, lo, it came to little; and when ye brought it home, I did blow upon it. Why? . . . Because of mine house that is waste. Once again God explains why they had not been able to prosper in the land. It was because of God's judgment upon them. They had great expectations, but they came to nought. When they brought what little they were able to salvage home, God blew upon it and caused it to come to nothing. He did it because their priorities were all wrong. Instead of tending to His business, they attended to their own. Instead of building His house, they built their houses. They went about their work totally oblivious to the sad state of the house of the Lord (vs. 9). **Therefore the heaven over you is stayed from dew, and the earth is stayed from her fruit.** To get their attention, the Lord had to speak in language that they could understand. Therefore, He stopped the heavens from giving dew and stopped the earth from producing fruit. **I called for a drought upon the land.** Jehovah sent a drought upon the land which affected the crops of corn, vineyards, cattle, and all that man and cattle could produce. Once again, nature and animals suffer because of man's sin.

3. *The compliance to rebuild. 1:12-15.*

12. One good thing can be said about the leader and the people—they had enough sense to listen to the messenger of God. They **obeyed the voice of the LORD their God, and the words of Haggai the prophet.** They recognized Haggai's message to be exactly what he said it was, the Word of the Lord.

13. In response to this obedience, Jehovah sends a message of assurance to His people through his prophet: **I am with you.** Their indifference had caused the Lord to withdraw His blessing; their obedience assures His presence and blessing. All that has failed to be accomplished, and more too, will be accomplished when God's people are in obedience to and in fellowship with Him.

14. And the LORD stirred up the spirit of Zerubbabel . . . and the spirit of Joshua . . . and the spirit of all the remnant of the people. What the people did proved the genuineness of their faith and repentance. They began the work of rebuilding the house of the Lord, energized afresh by the Lord Himself.

of the people; and they came and did work in the house of the LORD of hosts, their God,

15 In the four and twentieth day of the sixth month, in the second year of Darius the king.

15. The work began on **the four and twentieth day of the sixth month**—twenty-three days after Haggai had received this message from Jehovah (cf. 1:1). We should not understand that it took them twenty-three days to obey the word of the Lord, but rather that work on the Temple began almost immediately; and the intervening time was spent in gathering new materials and preparing the building site for further construction, which began twenty-three days after the prophet delivered his message.

II. THE SECOND MESSAGE: A MESSAGE OF CONSOLATION. 2:1-9.

Work on rebuilding the Temple had gone on for nearly a month. The building was taking on shape, and it was obvious that this Temple would not come near to the glory of Solomon's. This was discouraging, for it appeared that the nation could not recapture its former glory. The people continued their task in obedience to the Word of the Lord, but there was a need for encouragement and comfort. God always meets the needs of His people at the proper time.

A. The Circumstances of the Message. 2:1-2.

1. Its time. 2:1a.

2:1a. Haggai dates his message **In the seventh month, in the one and twentieth day of the month**—about a month and a half after receipt of the first message (cf. vs. 1) and almost a month after the actual rebuilding had begun (cf. vs. 15). The seventh month was equivalent to our month of October; and the date of the message, according to the solar calendar, would be October 17, 520 B.C. Comparison with Leviticus 23:34, 36, 40-42 tells us that this was the seventh and final day of the Feast of Tabernacles. The next day was to be a sabbath of ". . . holy convocation . . ." (cf. Lev 23:36, 39). This whole period was a time of sabbath during which the people dwelt in booths and participated in the feasts commemorative of the deliverance God wrought in bringing them out of Egypt. In obedience to God, then, they were caused to remember the great deliverances of the past. They could not help but compare the past with the present, which must have seemed small and insignificant by comparison. It would only be human to become discouraged under such circumstances.

2. Its nature. 2:1b.

1b. At the proper time **came the word of the LORD by the prophet Haggai.** Again, the message is traced to its source, Jehovah, and thus bears His authority. It is communicated by His human instrument, Haggai, at the right time when the right man and the right people are in a right relationship with their God.

3. Its address. 2:2.

2. Once again the message is delivered to **Zerubbabel,** the political leader, **Joshua,** the religious leader, and to the **people.** The right message comes to the right people at the right time.

B. The Content of the Message. 2:3-9.

1. The question. 2:3.

3. **Who is left among you that saw this house in her first glory? and how do ye see it now?** It is Jehovah who asks the question and makes the comparison between the present Temple and the temple of Solomon. Undoubtedly, His question reflects a thought that was predominant in their minds. The

CHAPTER 2

IN the seventh *month,* in the one and twentieth *day* of the month, came the word of the LORD by the prophet Hăg'-ga-ī, saying,

2 Speak now to Ze-rŭb'ba-bel the son of Shē-ăl'tĭ-el, governor of Judah, and to Joshua the son of Jŏs'e-dĕch, the high priest, and to the residue of the people, saying,

3 Who *is* left among you that saw this house in her first glory? and how do ye see it now? *is it* not in your eyes in comparison of it as nothing?

question implies that there were some among them who had seen Solomon's temple. By the second year of Darius' reign, seventy years had passed since Solomon's temple was destroyed.

Ezra confirms that at the laying of the foundation of the Temple, many of the priests, Levites, and chief men that had seen Solomon's temple wept. Without doubt, a good number of those were still living; and to them it is evident that the present Temple lacked the majesty and grandeur of Solomon's. Compared to that Temple, this one was nothing (cf. Ezra 3:8-13). Feinberg cites the Babylonian Talmud, which indicated that Zerrubbabel's temple lacked five glories which were present in Solomon's temple: (1) the ark of the covenant; (2) the holy fire; (3) the shekinah glory; (4) the spirit of prophecy (The Holy Spirit); and (5) the Urim and Thummim. No wonder the older men wept! How gracious of God to recognize their deep concern and grief!

2. The encouragement. 2:4-9.

Though the difference between the two temples is evident and admitted, there is no cause for despair, nor excuse for stopping the work. The disparity between the temples ought not to discourage them but ought to cause them to rely even more heavily upon Jehovah their God. Jehovah gives them a threefold encouragement of: (1) His personal presence (vs. 4); (2) His personal commitment to keep His promise to them (vs. 5); and (3) His program of judgment which will result in His filling this insignificant house with His personal glory (vss. 6-9).

4. Yet now be strong . . . for I am with you. The important thing is not whether this house matches or exceeds the glory of Solomon's; the important thing is that Jehovah is present with them in this endeavor, and it is being carried on in obedience to Him. The important thing is heart relationship, not external trappings. Jehovah assures them of His personal presence; because they are with Him in what He is doing.

5. According to the word that I covenanted with you when ye came out of Egypt. During the preceding days Israel had ceremonially been remembering the deliverance from Egypt. God now focuses their attention upon that again and reminds them of the covenant He gave them at Mount Sinai (cf. Ex 6:7; 19:5). Throughout all the centuries from that day to the present, Jehovah has faithfully kept His covenant with Israel. His past performance is a guarantee of His future performance so long as they are rightly related to Him. He assures them that just as His spirit was with them in that day, so He is with them in the present—therefore they need not fear anything! Man is ever inclined to look at externals, whereas God is ever concerned with heart realities.

6-9. These verses lift the people's hearts from the dismal present to the glorious future that lies ahead. **Yet once, it is a little while, and I will shake the heavens, and the earth, and the sea, and the dry land.** The prophet blends together elements of the first and second comings of our Lord Jesus Christ who is also Israel's King and Messiah. The people are encouraged to continue the work of building the Temple (cf. vss. 4-5) because there is coming a day when Jehovah will shake all of the nations of the world so violently that it will topple every kingdom and result in the establishment of the kingdom of Messiah **(and I will fill this house with glory).** His thought is similar to that expressed by Daniel (cf. Dan 2:44-45) concerning the stone pulled out of the mountain without hands that will crush all the kingdoms of earth and become the eternal kingdom of God. The shaking is said to take place in **a little while.** It will involve tremendous activity on the part of God in **the heavens** and **earth,** the sea, the **dry land,** and among all the **nations** of the earth. The shaking began with the dissolution of the Babylonian

---

4 Yet now be strong, O Ze-rŭb′ba-bel, saith the Lord; and be strong, O Joshua, son of Jŏs′e-dĕch, the high priest; and be strong, all ye people of the land, saith the Lord, and work: for I *am* with you, saith the Lord of hosts:

5 *According to* the word that I covenanted with you when ye came out of Egypt, so my spirit remaineth among you: fear ye not.

6 For thus saith the Lord of hosts;Yet once, it *is* a little while, and I will shake the heavens, and the earth, and the sea, and the dry *land;*

7 And I will shake all nations, and the desire of all nations shall come: and I will fill this house with glory, saith the Lord of hosts.

8 The silver *is* mine, and the gold *is* mine, saith the Lord of hosts.

9 The glory of this latter house shall be greater than of the former, saith the Lord of hosts: and in this place will I give peace, saith the Lord of hosts.

World Empire (which they had seen), and it will continue with the dissolution of the Medo-Persian World Empire. It will continue further with the dissolution of the Grecian World Empire, and it will be concluded by the dissolution of the Roman World Empire which will ultimately issue in the establishment of the kingdom of Jehovah on earth (cf. Mt 24:27-31; Rev 6-19). The shaking of the heavens, earth, sea, dry land, and nations is figurative language indicating the personal involvement and the great extent to which Jehovah will go for the estabblishment of His kingdom on this earth. In other places in Scripture His activity is likened to the birth pains a woman suffers during the bringing forth of a child into the world (cf. Rom 8:20-23; I Thess 5:2-3). All of God's activity in the heavens and earth and among nations is moving toward one great end: **and the desire of all nations shall come.** This phrase has been given many different interpretations, but the best is probably that which understands the **desire** (Heb *chemdah*, lit., desire, desirableness) to be a reference to the Deliverer that shall come (cf. Isa 59:20-21), right all wrongs, and exalt the nation. The people of the world, and even creation itself, have had longings for this deliverance since the days of Adam (cf. Rom 8:19-23). True to prophetic format, this prophecy refers to the advent of Messiah of His first coming to earth to take on human form; but ultimately, it will be fulfilled in His second coming to earth to set up His kingdom. Both comings are blended together in the prophet's view, for the latter cannot be realized without the former. God's eternal program is applied to the people of the prophet's day by the promise **I will fill this house with glory.** The important thing was not how the house that they were building compared with the former; rather, it was the place that this house would occupy in God's overall program. The house that they were building, poor though it was, would be used by God in the ultimate fulfillment of His program, the bringing of blessings to all the peoples of the world and the ultimate establishment of the earthly, Davidic, millennial kingdom. The people could rejoice in the fact that in the accomplishment of His program they were ". . . workers together with him . . ." (cf. II Cor 6:1). Their part in God's program might be small, but it was absolutely essential (vss. 6-7).

Nor should the people be concerned over the fact that they did not have the means to overlay the Temple they were building with precious metal. The Lord reminds them that **The silver is mine, and the gold is mine.** Had He desired it, He could easily have provided it. God does not expect the people to give what they do not have; He only expects them to obey and do what He has commissioned them to do. They would not make Him any richer by adorning the Temple with precious metal, for it is all His anyway (vs. 7; cf, Ps 50:12). **The glory of this latter house shall be greater than of the former . . . and in this place will I give peace.** Though they would not live to see it, the assurance of verse 9 must have been comforting. Though the house that they were building was inferior in their sight (cf. vs. 3), God assures them that its future glory will be greater than the glory it enjoyed under Solomon. More than that, it would issue in something that Solomon's temple did not, which no amount of money and precious metals can provide—peace! In the light of subsequent history, it is interesting to note that the house that the people built was leveled and renovated by Herod in his desire to court Jewish favor. Further, Herod's temple was destroyed by the Roman invasion of A.D. 70. Ultimately, a millennial temple will be built in which the worship of Jehovah will be carried on. All of these subsequent developments are of no consequence to God, for He views His future program from the perspective of Haggai's day and views Zerubbabel's temple as being the site where God's universal glory will be manifested. Such vision would indeed be an encouragement to the prophet's generation and a motivation to continue the task immediately before them (vs. 9).

III. THE THIRD MESSAGE: A MESSAGE OF AFFIRMATION. 2:10-19.

A. The Circumstances of the Message. 2:10-11.

1. Its time. 2:10a.

10a. The message is dated **In the four and twentieth day of the ninth month, in the second year of Darius.** This message came (according to the solar calendar) on December 18, 520 B.C., about two months after the message of 2:1-9.

2. Its nature. 2:10b.

10b. Once again it is a message which comes from Jehovah through His human messenger, **Haggai the prophet.**

3. Its recipients. 2:11.

11. Ask now the priests concerning the law. The message is addressed to the people who are instructed to go to the priests for a ruling from the Law. It was the priests' function to teach and interpret the Law; and the prophet is going to give them an illustration that will show the situation to date: in the past they were disobedient, so God withheld His blessing; in the present they are obedient to God, so they can expect God's blessing.

B. The Content of the Message. 2:12-19.

1. The illustration of contamination. 2:12-13.

12-13. The people were to ask the priests two questions and, as a result, would learn that holiness is not communicable (vs. 12) while unholiness is communicable (vs. 13). A healthy person cannot communicate his health to a dying person, but a dying person can communicate his disease to a healthy one. The Mosaic system clearly taught that ceremonial cleanness was not transferrable from one person or thing to another, but ceremonial uncleanness was (cf. Lev 6:18; 22:4-6; Num 19:11).

2. The application to Israel. 2:14-17.

14-17. It is the priests' responsibility to interpret the Law to the nation and the prophet's responsibility to apply it. Haggai does this in verses 14-17 where he applies the illustration of verses 12-13 to the nation. He is addressing the people who were mentioned in 1:2, **this people . . . this nation.** All during the time that the Temple lay idle with only the foundations laid and the altar set up (cf. Ezr 3), the people continued making their offerings to God (cf. Ezr 3:4-7). All during this period their religious observances and sacrificial offerings were not pleasing to God (**unclean**) because the people were out of fellowship with God. **Unclean** people cannot offer anything that is clean to the Lord. Instead, their uncleanness is communicated to their offerings (vss. 14-15). During those lean days **when one came to a heap** of grain expecting to find twenty measures, he found only ten. When he went to the **pressfat** (Heb *yeqeb*, lit., wine or oil press or vat) expecting to get fifty measures of wine or oil, he found that there were only twenty—there was no way that he could get ahead (vs. 16, cf. 1:6-11). The reason this happened was because Jehovah was sending judgment upon them in the form of all kinds of catastrophes—**blasting** wind, **mildew,** and **hail.** Though these catastrophes took their toll on the economy, they did not achieve their purpose of causing the people to repent and obey Jehovah (vs. 17). Instead of building the house of Jehovah, for which God had brought them back to the Land, they turned to build their own houses (cf. 1:4). In

10 ¶In the four and twentieth *day* of the ninth *month,* in the second year of Darius, came the word of the LORD by Hăg′ga-ī the prophet, saying,

11 Thus saith the LORD of hosts; Ask now the priests *concerning* the law, saying,

12 If one bear holy flesh in the skirt of his garment, and with his skirt do touch bread, or pottage, or wine, or oil, or any meat, shall it be holy?And the priests answered and said, No.
13 Then said Hăg′ga-ī, If *one that is* unclean by a dead body touch any of these, shall it be unclean? And the priests answered and said, It shall be unclean.

14 Then answered Hăg′ga-ī, and said, So *is* this people, and so *is* this nation before me, saith the LORD; and so *is* every work of their hands; and that which they offer there *is* unclean.
15 And now, I pray you, consider from this day and upward, from before a stone was laid upon a stone in the temple of the LORD:
16 Since those *days* were, when *one* came to an heap of twenty *measures,* there were *but* ten: when *one* came to the pressfat for to draw out fifty *vessels* out of the press, there were *but* twenty.
17 I smote you with blasting and with mildew and with hail in all the labours of your hands; yet ye *turned* not to me, saith the LORD.

summary, their past disobedience rendered every spiritual exercise vain.

3. The declaration of blessing. 2:18-19.

18 ¶Consider now from this day and upward, from the four and twentieth day of the ninth *month, even* from the day that the foundation of the LORD's temple was laid, consider *it.*
19 Is the seed yet in the barn? yea, as yet the vine, and the fig tree, and the pomegranate, and the olive tree, hath not brought forth: from this day will I bless *you.*

18-19. The prophet points out that now that they have obeyed Jehovah and are building His Temple, they can expect His blessing. Their empty barns and their fruitless vineyards, fruitless fig, pomegranate, and olive trees bear ample testimony to Jehovah's past judgment. These selfsame messengers will give testimony to the abundant blessing of God which will begin **from this day**—immediately (vss. 18-19). In summary, obedience to God brings His blessings. As the Temple goes up, His blessings will come down.

IV. THE FOURTH MESSAGE: A MESSAGE OF ANTICIPATION. 2:20-23.

A. The Circumstances of the Message. 2:20-21a.

1. Its time. 2:20a.

20 ¶And again the word of the LORD came unto Hăg′ga-ī in the four and twentieth *day* of the month, saying,

20a. This message comes on the same date as the previous one—December 18, 520 B.C.

2. Its recipient. 2:20b.

20b. The recipient of this message is once again **Haggai.**

3. Its address. 2:21a.

21 Speak to Ze-rŭb′ba-bel, governor of Judah, saying, I will shake the heavens and the earth;

21a. This message is addressed to **Zerubbabel, governor of Judah.**

B. The Content of the Message. 2:21b-23.

1. The heavens and the earth. 2:21b.

21b. The shaking of the heavens and the earth is the same as that referred to earlier (cf. vs. 6). Once again, it is a reference to nature's preparation for the coming of the earthly, Davidic millennial kingdom of God.

2. The nations of the earth. 2:22.

22 And I will overthrow the throne of kingdoms, and I will destroy the strength of the kingdoms of the heathen; and I will overthrow the chariots, and those that ride in them; and the horses and their riders shall come down, every one by the sword of his brother.

22. This overthrow of the nations, likewise, is the same as the reference in verse 7. God is working a plan and will move all nations in order to accomplish that plan—the establishment of His kingdom upon this earth. All of the strength and weapons of the nations of all the earth will be helpless before Him. This will ultimately take place at the battle of Armageddon when the Lord shall slay all the nations of the earth with the breath of His mouth (cf. Mt 24:27-30; II Thess 2:8; Rev 14:14-20). All intervening such events are but adumbrations of this final, consummating event.

3. Zerubbabel. 2:23.

23 In that day, saith the LORD of hosts, will I take thee, O Ze-rŭb′ba-bel, my servant, the son of Shē-ăl′tī-el, saith the LORD, and will make thee as a signet: for I have chosen thee, saith the LORD of hosts.

23. Zerubbabel is brought into the middle of God's program; for it is His descendant, Jesus the Messiah, who will be the One who will accomplish this (cf. genealogy of Jesus, Mt 1:12-13—there Zerubbabel is called Zorobabel in earlier editions of the KJV). Therefore, Jehovah will make him to be **as a signet**—the ring that was used by the owner for the signing of letters and official documents. It was a mark of honor and of authority. Therefore, Zerubbabel's ministry was to bear the mark of honor and authority. He would carry with him the authority of Jehovah and would represent Him in all that he did. Truly he was one of Jehovah's prized servants, and Jehovah affirmed this to Zerubbabel as He said **for I have chosen thee.** What confidence and assurance this must have given Zerubbabel in the difficult days that lay ahead. It is the same confidence that every child of God can have today; for he, like Zerubbabel, has been chosen by God (vs. 23, cf. John 15:16).

(see page 1864 for Bibliography to the Minor Prophets)

ZECHARIAH

INTRODUCTION

Authorship. The prophet identifies himself as "Zechariah ("Jehovah remembers"), the son of Berechiah ("Jehovah blesses"), the son of Iddo ("the appointed time")" (1:1). He is not to be confused with the Zachariah mentioned in Matthew 23:35, ". . . Zacharian son of Barachias, whom ye slew between the temple and the altar." That Zechariah lived much earlier (c. 850 B.C.), and his death is recorded in II Chronicles 24:20-22. Nor should Zechariah the prophet, be confused with any of the twenty-eight other men in the Old Testament who bore this name. Zechariah the prophet was probably born in Babylon during the seventy-year Babylonian captivity. His coming to Jerusalem is recorded in Nehemiah 12:4, 16, and his ministry is mentioned in Ezra 5:1; 6:14. These historical citations confirm that Zechariah was a priest as well as a prophet. The Talmud indicates that he was a member of the Great Synagogue along with Nehemiah and Ezra. Zechariah was a younger contemporary of Haggai and continued the ministry that he began. Both Zechariah and Haggai ministered to the same people, but from different perspectives. Haggai reproved the people for their failure to rebuild the temple, while Zechariah encouraged the people by presenting to them the coming glory of Jehovah.

Because of the abrupt change in style in chapters 9-14 from chapters 1-8, some have posited a deutero-Zechariah theory. Such an extreme view is not necessary, for the difference in subject matter is ample reason to account for the difference of style. In addition, it is possible that the prophet may have recorded that part of his prophecy (chs. 9-14) at a much later time in his life. Zechariah is the most popularly quoted Old Testament book in the New Testament. All parts of it are quoted without any indication of a diversity of authorship.

Date and Place of Writing. Various scholars have estimated that Zechariah ministered at some time between 520 B.C. and 510 B.C. Comparing Zechariah 1:1 with Haggai 2:1, 10, reveals that Zechariah's first message was delivered between Haggai's second and third messages and came two months after Haggai began his ministry (cf. Hag 1:1). The message of Zechariah 7:1ff came between two and three years later. It seems safe to conclude that the prophet ministered actively for at least three years, beginning his ministry in either late October or early November of 520 B.C.

The place from which the prophecy was written was Jerusalem, near the environs of the Temple.

Characteristics of the Prophecy. The basic language and style of the prophecy is simple and direct, with the exception of the apocalyptic sections (the eight visions). Certain notable expressions recur frequently in the book, among which are "Lord (Jehovah) of hosts" (which occurs 50 times) and "thus saith the Lord (Jehovah)" (which occurs at least 62 times). Zechariah has more messianic prophecies than any other "minor" prophet, and he makes frequent mention of both the First and Second Advents of Messiah. He has been referred to as the Prophet of the Advent. The angel of the Lord (Jehovah) is more prominent in Zechariah than in any other of the prophetical writings. Zechariah is also one of the most devotional of the prophetic books. Zechariah dwells more completely on the person and work of Christ than any of the prophetic writings. Because of these qualities, it is not surprising to note that Zechariah is quoted in the New Testament more times than any other Old Testament book. The tone of the prophecy is one of encouragement. It was given to a people who were discouraged and cures that discouragement by focusing their attention on the glory of God.

Purpose. Zechariah had both primary and secondary purposes in delivering his prophecy. The primary purpose was to encourage the people to continue to rebuild the Temple and to see that task through to its completion. His secondary purposes, which serve as motivators behind the primary purpose, are to announce God's prophetic program as it concerned the Gentiles, to predict the blessings of the millennial age for Israel, and to outline the events leading up to it.

Theme. The theme of Zechariah is the glory of the Lord (Jehovah). That theme is set forth as being the motivation for completing the task of rebuilding the Temple and for the realization that the people of the prophet's day are an integral part of God's ultimate program of displaying His glory through the nation in the future.

OUTLINE

A. The Eight Night Visions. 1:7-6:8.
  1. The first vision: The man among the myrtle trees. 1:7-17.
  2. The second vision: The four horns and the four smiths. 1:18-21.
  3. The third vision: The man with the measuring line. 2:1-13.
  4. The fourth vision: Joshua the high priest standing before the angel of Jehovah. 3:1-10.
  5. The fifth vision: The golden candlestick and the two olive trees. 4:1-14.
  6. The sixth vision: The flying roll. 5:1-4.
  7. The seventh vision: The woman in the ephah. 5:5-11.
  8. The eighth vision: The vision of the four chariots. 6:1-8.
B. The Coronation of Joshua. 6:9-15.
  1. The crowning of Joshua. 6:9-11.

  2. The commissioning of Joshua. 6:12-15.
III. The Third Word (Far View). 7:1-14:21.
A. The Four Messages. 7:1-8:23.
  1. The first message: Obedience is better than fasting. 7:1-7.
  2. The second message: Disobedience leads to severe judgment. 7:8-14.
  3. The third message: God's jealousy over His people will lead to their repentance and blessing. 8:1-17.
  4. The fourth message: The fasts will become feasts. 8:18-23.
B. The Two Burdens. 9:1-14:21.
  1. The first burden: Syria, Phoenicia, and Philistia are taken as representatives of all Israel's enemies. 9:1-11:17.
  2. The second burden: God's people will be conquerors because they will experience cleansing. 12:1-14:21.

COMMENTARY

I. THE FIRST WORD. 1:1-6.

A. The Introduction to the Word. 1:1.

1. Its time. 1:1a.

IN the eighth month, in the second year of Darius, came the word of the LORD unto Zĕch-a-rī′ah, the son of Bĕr-e-chī′-ah, the son of Ĭd′dō the prophet, saying,

1:1a. Like Haggai, Zechariah dates his prophecy according to the reigning gentile monarch **Darius**. This is to be expected since: (1) Israel has no king at the time; and (2) the mission of rebuilding the Temple was being undertaken with the blessing of **Darius**, the king of Medo-Persia. The message came **In the eighth month, in the second year of Darius.** This would be in November, 520 B.C., two months after the prophet Haggai had begun his ministry (cf. Hag 1:1).

2. Its description. 1:1b.

1b. The prophecy is described simply as being **the word of the LORD.** It is the **word** (Heb *debar*, i.e., a word, matter, thing) **of the LORD** (Heb *Yahweh*, Jehovah); hence, it bears the authority of Jehovah and embodies all that He wishes to say.

3. Its agent. 1:1c.

1c. **Unto Zechariah, the son of Berechiah the prophet. Zechariah** means "Jehovah remembers"; **Berechiah** means "Jehovah blesses"; and **Iddo** means "the appointed time". Together, the three names afford a suggestion concerning the nature of the prophecy—Jehovah remembers and blesses Israel and at the appointed time sends the messages she needs. All of these men are mentioned elsewhere in the Old Testament, but little is known of them beyond what can be learned of them in this prophecy. By his lineage Zechariah identifies himself as a priest, and by the receipt of this prophecy he is established as a prophet.

B. The Content of the Word. 1:2-6a.

1. The wrath of Jehovah. 1:2.

2 The LORD hath been sore displeased with your fathers.

2. The prophet reveals the fact that Jehovah has **been sore displeased** with the **fathers.** This had been evident; for they had spent the preceding seventy years in the Babylonian captivity, and Jerusalem had been destroyed. One would have thought

that that was sufficient to satisfy Jehovah's wrath. However, He is still **displeased** with His people because: (1) they have ceased building the Temple and (2) they had turned from Jehovah to serve their own selfish interests (cf. Hag 1:2-4).

2. The invitation to turn to Jehovah. 1:3.

3. The remedy is simple—**Turn ye unto me.** The promise is sure—**And I will turn unto you.** Spiritual problems are always easily solved; just do what God wants! The turning to Jehovah will bring about a commensurate and consistent life. They will: (1) put Jehovah first in all their priorities; and (2) get on with the task of building the Temple. When God's people are in a right relationship with Him, they can enjoy His fellowship and blessings that He faithfully bestows.

3. The historical illustration of the fathers who turned from Jehovah. 1:4-6a.

4. History should be a good teacher. There is an old saying that he who will not learn from history is doomed to repeat it. The **fathers** provided a bad example; so Jehovah warns, **Be ye not as your fathers.** It was the **fathers** who were responsible for the present situation; for **they did not hear** the messages sent to them through the **former prophets,** a reference primarily to the prophets who ministered to Israel prior to the Babylonian captivity, but applicable to all of God's prophets throughout history, whether they wrote or merely spoke God's Word.

5-6a. Human beings, whether disobedient (**fathers**) or obedient (**prophets**), have one thing in common; they are mortal. They stand in stark contrast to God's **words** (prophetical messages sent through the prophets) and **statutes** (moral law). These are eternal and immutable. They were effective for the **fathers,** for they convicted the **fathers** of their sins and caused them to turn to the Lord.

C. The Response to the Word. 1:6b.

6b. To the fathers' credit, **they returned** when they experienced the judgment about which the prophets warned. Would that they had heeded earlier. One thing is abundantly clear: Jehovah is faithful and always keeps His word. The testimony of the fathers was, **Like as the LORD of hosts thought to do unto us . . . so hath he dealt with us.** While it is not specifically stated, one gets the distinct impression that Zechariah's contemporaries did not follow the bad example of their fathers, but turned to Jehovah as they were exhorted to do (cf. 1:3). Haggai's prophecy confirms this to be true (cf. Hag 1:12-15). The success of Haggai's ministry made it unnecessary for Zechariah to dwell on the subject. The point of verses 2-6 is that to experience His blessing, God's people must be in proper relationship to Him. When that is done, God's blessing can be realized. Just as Haggai gave assurance to the people once they gave testimony to their right relationship with God by resuming the building of the Temple (cf. Hag 1:13), so the remainder of Zechariah's prophecy is given to encourage the people who have truly turned to Jehovah. Zechariah focuses their attention upon the glory of Jehovah which is coming (therefore, they should build the Temple) and which will ultimately be manifested in the nation. The former emphasizes the near view (1:7-6:15), while the latter emphasizes the far view (7:1-14:21).

II. THE SECOND WORD (NEAR VIEW). 1:7-6:15.

A. The Eight Night Visions. 1:7-6:8.

All eight night visions occurred on one night and constitute a unit of revelation. The first night vision is the most important, for it provides a key for understanding all the other night visions. The night visions were not presented to the prophet in

3 Therefore say thou unto them, Thus saith the LORD of hosts; Turn ye unto me, saith the LORD of hosts, and I will turn unto you, saith the LORD of hosts.

4 Be ye not as your fathers, unto whom the former prophets have cried, saying, Thus saith the LORD of hosts; Turn ye now from your evil ways, and *from* your evil doings: but they did not hear, nor hearken unto me, saith the LORD.

5 Your fathers, where *are* they? and the prophets, do they live for ever?
6 But my words and my statutes, which I commanded my servants the prophets, did they not take hold of your fathers? and they returned and said, Like as the LORD of hosts thought to do unto us, according to our ways, and according to our doings, so hath he dealt with us.

the format of a dream, but rather with the prophet in some form of an ecstatic trance (cf. Acts 10:10; 11:15; Rev 1:10). All of the night visions have import for the immediate need and ultimate place of Israel in the economy of God. In interpreting them, primary emphasis should be given to the near view, for that is, without question, how Zechariah and the people of his day viewed them. From the perspective of God's completed revelation the student of today can appreciate what the people in the historical situation could not. At best, their understanding of the far or ultimate view was partial and amorphous. Undoubtedly, Zechariah was among the prophets who ". . . inquired and searched diligently . . ." concerning ". . . what, or what manner of time the Spirit of Christ . . . did signify, when it (he) testified beforehand the sufferings of Christ, and the glory that should follow" (I Pet 1:10-11). Many scholars since Zechariah's day have joined him in that selfsame search! The overall message of these eight night visions for the nation of Zechariah's day was: Jehovah is with you, so, build the Temple. For the Israel of the future, the eight night visions outline the prophetic program for Israel from the restoration from the Babylonian captivity to the institution of the millennial kingdom. In seeing the latter, one must not overlook the former. If he is to err, he probably would do better to err on the side of the historical import of the visions; for that is how God used them in the accomplishment of His task of that day.

1. The first vision: The man among the myrtle trees, 1:7-17.

The vision can be divided into three parts: (1) the time of the vision (vs. 7); (2) the details of the vision (vss. 8-12); and (3) the promise of the vision (vss. 13-17).

7. The time of the first vision is the time of all the visions; hence, it is spelled out with great detail. The visions occur on **the four and twentieth day of the eleventh month**—three months after the reception of the first word (cf. vs. 1), or February 24, 519 B.C.

8-11. These verses present the details of the vision. The prophet **saw** all eight of the visions **by night**. He was not dreaming, but rather was in some kind of a trance in which the information was presented to him and he remained fully alert (cf. earlier). What he **saw** was: (1) **A man riding upon a red horse;** (2) who **stood among the myrtle trees;** (3) **in the bottom;** and (4) **behind him were there red horses, speckled, and white** (vs. 8). Accompanying the scene was an interpreting **angel** whom he addresses as **my lord** and describes as **the angel that talked with me.** Other than this, the **angel** is not introduced; he is merely a functionary who describes his purpose in the words **I will show thee what these be** (vs. 9). The interpreting angel, however, does not speak further. The explanation is given by **the man that stood among the myrtle trees** who explained, **These are they whom the LORD hath sent to walk to and fro through the earth** (vs. 10). In verse 8 it was revealed that there were **horses** behind the **man riding upon a red horse.** Nothing was said about any other riders. Verse 11, however, reveals that the other horses also had riders; for they report to the **man riding upon a red horse** (here revealed to be none other than **the angel of the LORD**): **We have walked to and fro through the earth, and, behold, all the earth sitteth still, and is at rest** (vs. 11).

Before proceeding further, the following observations need to be made: (1) the **man riding upon a red horse** (vs. 8), identified as **the angel of the LORD** (vs. 11), is a Christophany—a preincarnate appearance of the Second Person of the Trinity, the Son of God; (2) the **myrtle trees** were ornamental plants or shrubs that were native to Syria—their appearance in the scene would link the vision to Israel's past exile in Babylon; (3) the **bottom** (Heb *metsulah* i.e., depth, place of shadows; hence, a

7 ¶Upon the four and twentieth day of the eleventh month, which *is* the month Sē′bat, in the second year of Darius, came the word of the LORD unto Zĕch-a-rī′ah, the son of Bĕr-e-chī′ah, the son of Ĭd′dō the prophet, saying,

8 I saw by night, and behold a man riding upon a red horse, and he stood among the myrtle trees that *were* in the bottom; and behind him *were there* red horses, speckled, and white.

9 Then said I, O my lord, what *are* these? And the angel that talked with me said unto me, I will shew thee what these *be.*

10 And the man that stood among the myrtle trees answered and said, These *are they* whom the LORD hath sent to walk to and fro through the earth.

11 And they answered the angel of the LORD that stood among the myrtle trees, and said, We have walked to and fro through the earth, and, behold, all the earth sitteth still, and is at rest.

shady place) has been suggested by some to be the Valley of Hinnom outside the Temple precinct. From the foundations of the Temple the prophet could look down and see the rider and his army coming. While this may be true, it would not exhaust the significance of the setting. The **myrtle trees** would link the vision with Israel's past in Babylon and Persia, and the **bottom** would indicate their present subjection to the world empires of the day; (4) the mission of all the riders who have **walked to and fro through the earth** indicates the activity of the **angel of the LORD** and His hosts among the affairs of men. They constantly are on patrol and are intervening to bring God's plan into reality; (5) the colors of the horses are significant. The angel of Jehovah is riding upon a **red horse,** indicative of bloodshed and warfare. He has vanquished every one of Israel's foes. The **speckled** (Heb *sarōq,* i.e., bay, speckled, fox-colored; hence, sorrel) is a mixture of the other colors, perhaps indicating their multi-purpose function. The **white** horses would be indicative of the victory that has been won (cf. Rev 6:2). The overall thought is that there has been a war and conquest over Israel; but these warriors, under the command and authority of the Son of God, have been victorious in their deliverance of Israel; (6) the inter-preting **angel** is a go-between for the Son of God and the prophet to whom the revelation is given. He is both the channel and the interpreter of revelation. His function is in many ways parallel to the Holy Spirit today who is a go-between for God and the believer. The fact that he is designated as an **angel** shows that he sustains many more things in common with the **angel of the LORD** than with the prophet in whose behalf he ministers; and (7) the report of the riders indicates that the world is currently at peace; hence, there is nothing to hinder the people in their building of the Temple.

Three results of the vision are given in verses 12-17: (1) the intercession of the angel of the LORD with the LORD (vs. 12); (2) the response of the LORD (vs. 13); and (3) the commission of the prophet (vss. 14-17).

12 ¶Then the angel of the LORD answered and said, O LORD of hosts, how long wilt thou not have mercy on Jerusalem and on the cities of Judah, against which thou hast had indignation these threescore and ten years?

12. This verse records a most wonderful truth—the interces-sion of the **angel of the LORD** (the Second Person of the Trinity) with the **LORD of hosts** (the First Person of the Trinity) on behalf of His people, Israel! The doctrine of the intercession of Christ is not the sole product of New Testament revelation (cf. Heb 7:25; I Jn 2:1) nor is the fact of the Trinity, for that matter—particularly if the parallel noted earlier concerning the ministries of the angel and the Holy Spirit is taken into consid-eration. This verse further shows the truth of I Peter 5:7—He does care about the things that concern us! The question asked by the **angel of the LORD** is most revealing: **How long wilt thou not have mercy** (Heb *racham,* viz., to love, pity, be merciful) **on Jerusalem and on the cities of Judah, against which thou hast had indignation** (a summary description of the effects of the Babylonian captivity upon Israel which has borne the wrath of God) **these threescore and ten years?** Jeremiah had revealed that the Babylonian captivity would last 70 years (cf. Jer 25:11; 29:11). Like Daniel earlier (cf. Dan 9:2), the **angel of the LORD** intercedes with the **LORD,** encouraging Him to keep His Word. He had been faithful in keeping his word of judgment against the nation; now He is encouraged to keep His word of restora-tion. From this verse three additional truths are manifest: (1) the Second Person of the Trinity (the Son) does nothing apart from the will of the First Person of the Trinity (the Father) (cf. Jn 5:19, 30; Heb 10:7); (2) while the Second Person of the Trinity is omniscient, there is some way (inscrutable to man) in which He does not know all that the First Person of the Trinity knows, except as the First Person of the Trinity reveals it to Him (cf. Mt 24:36; Mk 13:32; Jn 5:20; 8:28); and (3) the Second Person of the Trinity is the effective agent through whom the will of the

13 And the LORD answered the angel that talked with me with good words and comfortable words.

14 So the angel that communed with me said unto me, Cry thou, saying, Thus saith the LORD of hosts; I am jealous for Jerusalem and for Zion with a great jealousy.

First Person of the Trinity is accomplished (cf. Jn 5:19, 22, 26-27, 30; 6:38).

13. In response to the intercession by the **angel of the LORD** (vs. 12), the **LORD** (Jehovah, the First Person of the Trinity) answers; but He directs His answer to **the angel that talked with me** (the interpreting angel, cf. vs. 9). The message communicated is summarized as being **good words and comfortable words,** the details and implications of which are explained in verses 14-17.

14. In the process of explaining the message received from the **LORD,** the interpreting **angel** commissions the prophet to **Cry** (Heb qara', i.e., to call; translated in the NT by kērussō, lit., to be a herald, to proclaim, preach) or, better, to proclaim or preach a threefold message of: (1) God's love for Israel (vs. 14); (2) God's wrath upon the nations (vs. 15); and (3) God's blessings upon Israel (vss. 16-17).

The one delivering the commission in behalf of the **LORD** (vs. 13) is **the angel that communed with me** (referred to earlier as **the angel that talked with me,** vss. 9, 13). Parallels between his ministry to the prophet and the Holy Spirit's ministry to the believer are striking: (1) He ministers both on the behalf of the **angel of the LORD** (the Second Person of the Trinity, vss. 9, 12a) and the **LORD of hosts/LORD** (the First Person of the Trinity, vss. 12-13)—thus, he is clearly subservient to both as the Holy Spirit is to the Father and the Son; (2) he is both the channel and the interpreter of revelation—ministries which are clearly performed by the Holy Spirit; (3) he sustains a close and personal relationship with the man of God and enables him to understand what God has revealed; (4) being called an angel, he is more closely identified in his intrinsic nature with the **angel of the LORD** and the **LORD** on whose behalfs he ministers than he is with the prophet to whom he ministers; (5) he is the one to whom the man of God goes when he seeks to understand God's revelation; (6) the means by which the **angel** communicated with the prophet was by talking/communing **with me** (lit., in me; hence **the angel that talked/communed with me** has the same meaning as the angel, the one talking/communing in me). The language clearly indicates that the talking/communing was an inward talking/communing in which the message was communicated directly into the soul of the prophet without the use of vocal organs on the part of the **angel** or the use of auditory organs on the part of the prophet. This is precisely the same way in which the Holy Spirit ministers to believers today. If these parallels are allowed, then all three persons of the Godhead are present in this vision (a very important point, for where one member of the Godhead is, the others must also be, though the roles they perform are different and complementary): (1) God the Father (**LORD,** vs. 10; **LORD of hosts,** vs. 12; **LORD,** vs. 13); (2) God the Son (**a man riding upon a red horse,** vs. 8; **the man that stood among the myrtle trees,** vs. 11; **the angel of the LORD,** vs. 12); and (3) God the Holy Spirit (**my lord,** vs. 9; **the angel that talked with me,** vss. 9, 13; **the angel that communed with me,** vs. 14).

The revelation that God is love and God loves you are not exclusively New Testament revelation; for here the **LORD** reveals to His prophet through His **angel: I am jealous for Jerusalem and for Zion with a great jealousy.** One must not attribute modern-day English/American concepts to the words **jealous** (Heb qana', i.e., to be zealous, jealous) and **jealousy** (Heb qin'ah, i.e., zeal, jealousy); for God is not beset by the human frailties these words have come to imply. The words are intensive; and the emotion springs from God's intense love for His people portrayed by the mention of their capital city from two perspectives: (1) **Jerusalem,** the city in general; and (2) **Zion,** the poetical name for Jerusalem referring specifically to the

15 And I am very sore displeased with the heathen *that are* at ease: for I was but a little displeased, and they helped forward the affliction.

16 Therefore thus saith the LORD; I am returned to Jerusalem with mercies: my house shall be built in it, saith the LORD of hosts, and a line shall be stretched forth upon Jerusalem.

17 Cry yet, saying, Thus saith the LORD of hosts; My cities through prosperity shall yet be spread abroad; and the LORD shall yet comfort Zion, and shall yet choose Jerusalem.

18 ¶Then lifted I up mine eyes, and saw, and behold four horns.

southeastern hill upon which David built and to the northern hill upon which the Temple was built.

15. In contrast to His deep love for Israel, Zechariah was commissioned to preach that God is **very sore displeased** with the **heathen** (Heb, *gōyim* i.e., nations, non-Jews) because they **are at ease,** not realizing that they were tools in God's hand to help **forward the affliction** (the judgment God visited upon His people because of their sins) when He was **but a little displeased** with His people. The displeasure that God has with His people who are out of fellowship with Him is nothing compared with His displeasure with the people who do not know Him at all. Assyria and Babylon did not realize that they were raised up by God to be His instruments for punishing His people (cf. the message of Habakkuk) and that the greatness and benefits they enjoyed were not indications of His blessing upon them. They were not consciously serving God. They did what they did because of their own greed; hence, God will hold them accountable for their deeds and will judge them (cf. Isa 10; Hab 1:5-2:20).

16-17. The third facet of the message that Zechariah was commissioned to proclaim dealt with God's blessings for Israel. Four blessings are enumerated: (1) the Lord will return to Jerusalem with compassion, **I am returned to Jerusalem with mercies** (vs. 16a); (2) the Lord will build His house in Jerusalem, **my house shall be built in it** (vs. 16b); (3) the Lord will stretch a measuring line over Jerusalem, **a line shall be stretched forth upon Jerusalem** (vs. 16c); and (4) the Lord will prosper his city, comfort Zion, and choose Jerusalem—**My cities . . . shall yet be spread abroad; and the LORD shall yet comfort Zion . . . choose Jerusalem** (vs. 17). The first was indicated by the fact that the Temple was in the process of being rebuilt. The second was a guarantee that their task of building the Temple would succeed—they need not be deterred by any hostile forces. The third indicated that in addition to the Temple, the city would be rebuilt. The fourth indicated all the cities of the land would experience prosperity, and God's purpose for Zion/Jerusalem would not change—it would continue to be His earthly headquarters.

In summary, the contribution of this first and all-inclusive night vision, the Man Among the Myrtle Trees, is twofold: (1) to the Israel of Zechariah's day it assured them that Jehovah was with them and the world was at peace—therefore, they should continue the task of building the Temple until it was completed; and (2) to the Israel of the future it indicates that Israel is small and insignificant in its place among the gentile nations and is under their dominion. They could realize that, though from the perspective of the gentile nations they are as nothing, from God's perspective they are everything. The Gentiles experience their blessings and prominence because of the program God is working with Israel. They don't realize that; and, ultimately, God will punish them and exalt Israel.

2. *The second vision: The four horns and the four smiths. 1:18-21.*

The vision is divided into two parts: (1) the four horns (vss. 18-19); and (2) the four smiths (vss. 20-21).

18. The second chapter of the Hebrew text begins with this verse. Continuing in the ecstatic stance in which he saw the first vision, the prophet **saw . . . four horns.** A number of suggestions have been made concerning the significance of these four horns; but in view of the whole prophetic picture presented throughout the prophets, it seems simplest to view them as being synonymous with the four gentile world-powers earlier introduced by Daniel (cf. Dan 2, 7, 8). The horn is a well-known symbol used throughout Scripture to convey the thought of power. It is a metonymy in which the part of the bull (or other horned animal) is used to convey its power; the horn (effect) calls to mind the being to whom the horn belongs, the animal (cause). Metaphorically, the horn was applied to the strength of governments and was used representatively of nations (cf. Dan 8:3-4; Mic 4:13).

19 And I said unto the angel that talked with me, What *be* these? And he answered me, These *are* the horns which have scattered Judah, Israel, and Jerusalem.

19. The explanation of this part of the vision is given by **the angel that talked with me**, representative of the ministry of the Holy Spirit (cf. vs. 14). He explained that the horns were **the horns which have scattered Judah, Israel, and Jerusalem.** While Israel had been victimized by lesser powers, none of them fits the picture as well as the four gentile world powers of Daniel's prophecy—Babylon, Medo-Persia, Greece, and Rome. Zechariah thus sees the scattering Israel had experienced at the hands of Babylon and Medo-Persia as adumbrations of the scattering it would yet receive under Greece and Rome.

20 And the LORD shewed me four carpenters.

20. The vision is completed when **the LORD** (the First Person of the Trinity) shows the prophet **four carpenters** (Heb *charash*, viz., articifer, artisan, craftsman, or skilled worker). The Hebrew word indicates the skill of the worker, whatever his medium; in this context it would be a skilled artisan who capably shapes horns to suit his purpose.

21 Then said I, What come these to do? And he spake, saying, These *are* the horns which have scattered Judah, so that no man did lift up his head: but these are come to fray them, to cast out the horns of the Gentiles, which lifted up *their* horn over the land of Judah to scatter it.

21. In response to the prophet's query, the **angel** (vs. 19) explains that these artisans **are come to fray** (Heb *charad*, i.e., to cause to tremble, trouble) **them** (the horns), **to cast out the horns of the Gentiles, which lifted up their horn over the land of Judah to scatter it.** The purpose of the artisans, then, is to strike fear and terror into the hearts of the gentile world powers. Previously, they have operated with impunity, and **no man did lift up his head.** The gentile world powers should not come to the false conclusion that they can operate above the law and at their own whims; for God will cause them to realize that when they go as far as God intended for them to go, they will be cut off. Many years earlier God had promised Abraham that he would ". . . bless them that bless thee, and curse him that curseth thee . . ."—and those are not idle words. History is replete with nations that have been brought to naught because they dared raise up their **horn** against Israel. For every **horn** that comes into existence, God has His **carpenter** (vs. 20) who is capable of whittling the horn down to size! This is as true today as it was in the days of the prophet.

The overall significance of this vision for the Israel of the prophet's day is that the four carpenters/smiths will cut off the four nations that have troubled Israel; so they should get on with their task of building the Temple. For the Israel of the future, they can realize that though they have been kept on the bottom by the four horns, God will raise up appropriate powers to deal with the horns and will deliver Israel. God's program of horns and smiths can be charted as follows:

Horn	Smith
1. Babylon	Medo-Persia
2. Medo-Persia	Greece
3. Greece	Rome
4. Rome	Christ

3. The third vision: The man with the measuring line. 2:1-13.

The vision of the man with the measuring line in his hand is divided as follows: (1) the details of the vision (vss. 1-4a); (2) the explanation of the vision (vss. 4b-5); (3) the prophetic exhortation in the light of the vision, (vss. 6-12); and (4) the proper response to the vision (vs. 13).

2:1. Continuing in the ecstatic state in which the visions were presented to him, the prophet **looked** and saw **a man with a measuring line in his hand.** The **man** that the prophet sees is an angel in human form (cf. **another angel,** vs. 3).

2. In response to the prophet, the man with the measuring

CHAPTER 2

I LIFTED up mine eyes again, and looked, and behold a man with a measuring line in his hand.

2 Then said I, Whither goest thou?

And he said unto me, To measure Jerusalem, to see what *is* the breadth thereof, and what *is* the length thereof.

3 And, behold, the angel that talked with me went forth, and another angel went out to meet him,

4 And said unto him, Run, speak to this young man, saying, Jerusalem shall be inhabited *as* towns without walls for the multitude of men and cattle therein:

5 For I, saith the LORD, will be unto her a wall of fire round about, and will be the glory in the midst of her.

line explains that his mission is **To measure Jerusalem, to see what is the breadth thereof, and what is the length thereof.** The city that is to be measured is the Jerusalem of Zechariah's day, only partially restored at the time; and the purpose of the measuring is to ascertain what, in the economy of God, its future proportions will be.

3-4a. The language of the Hebrew text is as ambiguous as the language of the English text. The thought seems to be that the **angel that talked with me** (the interpreting angel, representative of the Holy Spirit) **went forth;** and **another angel** (whose precise identity is not given—he probably is the man with the measuring line in his hand, cf. vs. 1), stepping out of the vision, met **him** (the interpreting angel) and communicated the meaning of the vision to the interpreting angel who, in turn, communicated it to the prophet. If this understanding is correct, the resultant meaning is that the one called **another angel** was sent by the LORD (the First Person of the Trinity, vs. 5) to be the principal actor in the vision, and then to communicate the significance of the vision to the interpreting angel for communication to the prophet and through the prophet to the nation.

The interpreting angel is instructed (by authority of the LORD, vs. 5; not the authority of the actor/angel who was of inferior rank to the interpreting angel) to **Run, speak to this young man.** The thought is that the interpreting angel should communicate the meaning of the vision to the prophet quickly and completely. The term **young man** (Heb *na'ar*, i.e., young person, lit., growing) may, but does not necessarily, communicate the relative age of the prophet. The term is used of Samuel when as an infant he was presented to the Lord (cf. I Sam 1:24), and of Jeremiah when, near seventy years of age and overwhelmed with the commission of God, he protested, ". . . I cannot speak: for I am a child" (Jer 1:6). One of the most interesting (and meaningful) occurrences of the word is in Proverbs 22:6: "Train up a child in the way he should go; and when he is old, he will not depart from it." The term better indicates economic status, i.e., being a dependent, rather than a chronological age. In this context, the prophet is recognized as being a dependent—totally dependent upon the interpreting angel to reveal to him the significance of the revelation he has been given (a beautiful example of the relationship sustained between the believer and the Holy Spirit in the present).

The significance of the vision is explained in verses 4b-5. Two wonderful truths are made known: (1) the population of Jerusalem will overflow the limits imposed by the walls and will dwell in safety without walls (vs. 4b), and (2) Jehovah will personally abide in and will protect Jerusalem from all enemies (vs. 5).

4b. The first thing explained to the prophet is that **Jerusalem** is going to be **inhabited as towns without walls** because of the **multitude of men and cattle therein.** The population explosion to be experienced by the city will far exceed the number of people that can physically fit into the limits imposed by the walls. The net effect would be as though the city had no walls at all. A city without walls was secure and in danger of no peril.

5. The reason the people will dwell in safety will be because the LORD (Jehovah, the First Person of the Trinity) promises that he **will be unto her a wall of fire round about.** Israel of old had the presence of Jehovah, symbolized by the pillar of fire (cf. Ex 14:24) that provided both protection and illumination. A similar effect will be experienced by the Israel of Zechariah's day. In addition to protection, Jehovah promises that He **will be the glory in the midst of her.** The thing that will be attractive and wondrous about Israel will not be any buildings that they may build (including the Temple itself), but the personal abiding presence of Jehovah Himself!

Beginning with verse 6 and continuing throughout the rest of the chapter, the prophet delivers an exhortation in the light of the vision. He sounds four warnings: (1) all exiles remaining in Babylon should hasten to return to Jerusalem (vss. 6-7); (2) God will judge the nations that have scattered Israel (vss. 8-9); (3) God will bless Israel and through Israel will bless many nations (vss. 10-12); and (4) all mankind should be in silent obedience to the Lord (vs. 13).

6 ¶Ho, ho, *come forth,* and flee from the land of the north, saith the Lord: for I have spread you abroad as the four winds of the heaven, saith the Lord.

7 Deliver thyself, O Zion, that dwellest *with* the daughter of Babylon.

6-7. These verses are addressed to the exiles remaining behind in Babylon. They are urged to **come forth, and flee from the land of the north** (i.e., north with reference to Jerusalem viz., Babylon). The matter is urgent. The exiles have been **spread . . . abroad** by the **Lord,** though they are urged to take the initiative in returning. The responsibility for return is put upon them directly in the words **Deliver thyself, O Zion. Zion** is used here to refer not to the city but to the exiles who rightfully should be residents of Jerusalem. They can fail to heed the admonition and remain in Babylon because in Babylon they had it made. To do so, however, would cause them to be victims of the destruction that is going to overcome Babylon; and the conqueror will not distinguish between Babylonian resident and exiled Jew.

8 For thus saith the Lord of hosts; After the glory hath he sent me unto the nations which spoiled you: for he that toucheth you toucheth the apple of his eye.

9 For, behold, I will shake mine hand upon them, and they shall be a spoil to their servants: and ye shall know that the Lord of hosts hath sent me.

8-9. These verses supply the reason why it is imperative for the exiles to escape Babylon and return to Jerusalem—God is going to judge Babylon. The expression **After the glory** has been given various interpretations by commentators. Some understand it to be a reference to the **glory** mentioned in verse 5; thus, vengeance would be poured out on Israel's enemies after Jehovah takes up His residence in the midst of His people—but this is contrary to the whole testimony of God's prophetic program. Other commentators would make it parallel with the ". . . After thee, O Benjamin" (cf. Hos 5:8; Judg 5:14), the ancient battle cry used by Israel; the use of this battle cry would unite the exiles, giving them impetus to depart from Babylon and return to Jerusalem. It seems simplest and best, however, to regard it as a reference to Messiah who will personally execute Jehovah's judgment upon **the nations which spoiled** Israel, **the apple of his eye**—one of the most complex and delicate parts of the human body. Once again the promise given to Abraham is confirmed, "I will curse him that curseth you." Babylon has touched Israel with evil intent. So important is this to the **Lord** (the First Person of the Trinity) that He dispatches **the glory** (Messiah, the Second Person of the Trinity) to execute His vengeance personally upon the violaters.

In continuing to describe the judgment that will overtake the Babylonians, **the Lord of hosts** (vs. 8, Jehovah, the First Person of the Trinity) continues speaking and says **I will shake mine hand upon them** (a threatening gesture to Babylon like waving one's fist in someone's face), **and they** (the Babylonians) **shall be a spoil** (utterly defeated) **to their servants** (the Jewish exiles remaining in Babylon). In other words, Jehovah will cause (through the intervention of Messiah) the roles to be reversed; the present masters will be servants of the present servants, and the present servants will be masters of the present masters. This role reversal will be evidence **that the Lord of hosts** (First Person of the Trinity) **hath sent me** (Messiah).

In verses 10-12 Jehovah speaks and sets forth a threefold blessing that will come upon the redeemed, delivered nation: (1) He will take up His residence within them, verse 10; (2) many nations will be drawn into a close relationship to Him, and this will provide Israel with the proper authentication of His ministry, verse 11; and (3) the nation will be Jehovah's unique possession forever, verse 12.

10 ¶Sing and rejoice, O daughter of Zion: for, lo, I come, and I will dwell in the midst of thee, saith the Lord.

10. Jehovah calls upon the nation to **Sing and rejoice** because He comes and **will dwell** (Heb *shakan,* i.e., to tabernacle—here and in vs. 11) **in the midst** of the people. He will do this through the personal, visible presence of Messiah.

11 And many nations shall be joined to the LORD in that day, and shall be my people: and I will dwell in the midst of thee, and thou shalt know that the LORD of hosts hath sent me unto thee.

12 And the LORD shall inherit Judah his portion in the holy land, and shall choose Jerusalem again.

13 Be silent, O all flesh, before the LORD: for he is raised up out of his holy habitation.

CHAPTER 3

AND he shewed me Joshua the high priest standing before the angel of the LORD, and Satan standing at his right hand to resist him.

11. When Messiah is visibly present tabernacling with His people, **many nations shall be joined to the LORD . . . and shall be my people.** This will be the ultimate fulfillment of the universal aspects of the Abrahamic covenant, ". . . and in thee shall all families of the earth be blessed" (cf. Gen 12:3). Systematically, the prophets had proclaimed that the millennial kingdom would include many Gentiles with about ten Gentiles for every Israelite (cf. 8:23; Isa 10:20-21). The fact that Gentiles will have a prominent part in the millennial kingdom should not come as a surprise to Israel since the Old Testament prophets consistently predicted it. In fact, Gentile inclusion in the kingdom will enable Israel to **know that the LORD of hosts hath sent me** (Messiah) **unto thee** (Israel). If Gentiles were not included, the Word of the Lord would thereby be invalidated.

12. Gentile inclusion into the kingdom will in no way diminish Israel's prominence or peculiar relationship to Jehovah, for **the LORD shall inherit Judah his portion . . . and shall choose Jerusalem again.** Thus, Messiah will claim His people and they will sustain a peculiar (unique) relationship to Him, not as an end in itself (national blessing and restoration), but as the means to the end of making the nation to be the channel through whom universal blessing will be manifested to all. The phrase **in the holy land** confirms that Messiah will set up **his portion** (kingdom) in Israel and will speak peace from Jerusalem to all the nations of the world.

13. The proper response to such a vision is given with the prophet's exhortation: **Be silent, O all flesh, before the LORD: for he is raised up out of his holy habitation.** In view of the revelation of God's program, the only fitting response is silent subjection to the LORD. His **holy habitation** is Heaven, His dwelling place; and He is **raised up,** not in the sense of rising from sleep, but in the sense of a lion or a bear that has been aroused from its den or lair. Jehovah is **raised up,** i.e., He has embarked upon His plan, and the outcome is certain for the enemies of Israel, for Israel, and for the Gentiles who through Israel will be drawn into fellowship with Israel's God.

The overall significance of the vision of the man with the measuring line in his hand is twofold: (1) the Israel of Zechariah's day can realize that Jehovah Himself will be a protective wall around the city; and though the city will grow and overflow the area enclosed by the wall, they will be in perfect safety, for Jehovah will be a wall of fire around them. Therefore, they should get on with the task of building the Temple and let nothing deter them. (2) To the Israel of the future Jehovah promises that there will be a future regathering and rebuilding that will insure that Jerusalem will be the center of the millennial earth and Judah will be the habitation of God's people to which the Gentiles will come.

4. The fourth vision: Joshua the high priest standing before the angel of Jehovah. 3:1-10.

The vision of Joshua the high priest divides as follows: (1) the details of the vision (vss. 1-5); and (2) the explanation of the vision (vss. 6-10).

As the details of the vision are presented in verses 1-5, they can be further organized as follows: (1) the anointed—Joshua (vs. 1a); (2) the adversary—Satan (vs. 1b); (3) the advocate—the angel of Jehovah (vs. 2); and (4) the ablution (vss. 3-5).

3:1a. Continuing in the ecstatic trance through which all the visions were presented to him, Zechariah is shown **Joshua the high priest standing before the angel of the LORD. Joshua the high priest** was the son of Josedech and was the recipient, along with Zerubbabel, of Haggai's prophecy (cf. Hag 1:1; 2:2, 21) in which he is presented as being in obedience to God and faithfully serving Him (cf. Hag 1:12). The precise place where he was **standing before the angel of the LORD** is not stated, though in view of Haggai's portrayal of him it is simplest to understand that he was going about his priestly ministry in the Temple. In this capacity he was interceding for Israel and was asking God to fulfill His covenant promises.

1b. While he was going about his priestly function, Joshua had an adversary along side of him. It was none other than **Satan standing at his right hand to resist him.** It seems unthinkable—Satan in the Temple alongside God's minister in the presence of the angel of the Lord, the Second Person of the Trinity! How incongruous! Satan's mission is ominous—**to resist** (Heb *satan*, viz., to oppose, accuse, hate) Joshua in the very act of performing his spiritual duties in the presence of the Second Person of the Trinity in behalf of the people of Israel. The Hebrew text has a beautiful play on words which, if translated literally, would be something like, And Satan standing at his right hand for the purpose of satanizing him. Satan's purposes are always consistent with his intrinsic nature.

2. The angel of Jehovah, before whom Joshua was ministering, shifts his role from that of the object of worship to being the advocate for Joshua. **And the LORD** (the angel of Jehovah, the Second Person of the Trinity) **said unto Satan** (the fallen highest angelic being, confirmed in unrighteousness, dedicated to the futile attempt of frustrating the plan of God), **The LORD** (Jehovah, the First Person of the Trinity) **rebuke** (Heb *ga'ar*, to rebuke) **thee, O Satan.** Satan's purpose in being present is to bring discredit upon God's minister (who was chosen by God for this function), upon God's people Israel, and ultimately upon God Himself. If either God's minister or His people fall, then God falls in defeat. Satan's strategy is insidious, but it is immediately transparent and elementary to God; hence, the scathing rebuke. God does not question the validity of Satan's accusation or the unworthiness of His minister and people. The angel of Jehovah rebukes Satan by citing Jehovah's sovereign grace manifested in his sovereign choice of both Joshua and Israel; for the **LORD** who will rebuke **Satan** is **the LORD that hath chosen Jerusalem,** described as **a brand plucked out of the fire.** God concedes the flaw of His people—they are marred; they have been in a **fire** (the judgments God has visited upon His people because of their sins). Yet, they have not perished in the **fire,** nor did they deliver themselves from that **fire.** Someone (Jehovah Himself) **plucked** them out of the **fire** because He has a further need for them. The flaws that Satan accurately observes are the very flaws that will afford Jehovah the opportunity to manifest His sovereign grace in (1) His sovereign choice of them; and (2) in His sovereign purpose for them. How beautifully the figure tangibly illustrates Romans 8:28-30, for the nation that God has **chosen** will ultimately be glorified. God will not be deterred in the realization of His program—not even by the personal presence of Satan, the epitome of the forces of darkness and the strongest evil power. It is evident that all of this will come to pass because of God's sovereign choice. If the **LORD** had not **chosen Jerusalem,** Jerusalem (the nation Israel and all the people in it) certainly would not have chosen Jehovah; for they proved unable to do what He wanted them to do, even when they purposed to do so!

The ablution of Joshua (vss. 3-5) is set forth in three parts: (1) Joshua's condition (vs. 3); (2) Joshua's cleansing (vs. 4); and (3) Joshua's clothing and crowning (vs. 5). In this section Jehovah meets Satan's objections and removes the deficiencies in His servant.

3. In meeting needs God always begins with His servant as he is. **Joshua was clothed with filthy** (Heb *tsõ'î*, lit., excrement, dung, vomit—hence, filthy) **garments** as he **stood before the angel** of Jehovah. The garments were stained with the worst imaginable kind of filth, and one cannot help wondering whatever must have been in Joshua's mind that he would even

2 And the LORD said unto Satan, The LORD rebuke thee, O Satan; even the LORD that hath chosen Jerusalem rebuke thee: *is* not this a brand plucked out of the fire?

3 Now Joshua was clothed with filthy garments, and stood before the angel.

4 And he answered and spake unto those that stood before him, saying, Take away the filthy garments from him. And unto him he said, Behold, I have caused thine iniquity to pass from thee, and I will clothe thee with change of raiment.

5 And I said, Let them set a fair mitre upon his head. So they set a fair mitre upon his head, and clothed him with garments. And the angel of the LORD stood by.

6 And the angel of the LORD protested unto Joshua, saying,

7 Thus saith the LORD of hosts; If thou wilt walk in my ways, and if thou wilt keep my charge, then thou shalt also judge my house, and shalt also keep my courts, and I will give thee places to walk among these that stand by.

undertake such a ministry in such filthy garments. They should have been repulsive to him, to say nothing of being repulsive to the angel of Jehovah! When one is involved in sin he soon fails to see how repulsive he is in it, and worse, is so deceived that he thinks that God does not see or care either! Satan, however, is quick to see them (having led the believer into them) and to use them as an occasion against the child of God, as well as the God of the child! Joshua stands, then, morally unclean in the sight of God representing the people of God who likewise are morally unclean before God. Though outwardly delivered, they are inwardly unclean. God sees the condition of his minister and people clearly, and He takes the initiative cleansing in them.

4. God's minister is completely helpless and at the mercy of the angel of Jehovah who sovereignly undertakes Joshua's cleansing. It is not out of line at this point to suggest that this may be the purpose for which Joshua was standing in the presence of the angel of the Lord—seeking cleansing, rather than ministering in a priestly function (cf. vs. 1). The angel of the LORD speaks to **those that stood before him** (His angels or ministering spirits that perform His bidding) and commands them to **Take away the filthy garments from him.** This is what Joshua needed—to have his sins dealt with—and that is what God does. The removal of the filthy clothes signifies the forgiveness, acceptance, and restoration of the sinful prophet and the sinful people he represents. His forgiveness and cleansing are stated: **Behold, I have caused thine iniquity to pass from thee, and I will clothe thee with change of raiment.** The before and after picture is striking. In verse 3 Joshua stood before the angel of Jehovah in **filthy garments** (Heb *begadim hatsō'im* i.e., excrement-spattered common clothes); but after God has removed Joshua's sin, He has him clothed in **raiment** (Heb *machalatsah*, i.e., costly apparel). Such is the grace of God who can remove the filthy clothes of sin from His servant and clothe him in His righteousness!

5. The sight is so moving to Zechariah that as he views the vision, he responds **Let them set a fair mitre** (Heb *tsanip*, i.e., diadem, hood) **upon his head.** The **fair mitre** was the turban worn by the high priest to which a golden plate was attached on which was engraved "HOLINESS TO THE LORD" (i.e., Jehovah, cf. Ex 28:36-38). **So they set a fair mitre upon his head, and clothed him with garments.** With this Joshua's cleansing and reinstatement are complete. He now can minister unimpeded before the Lord on behalf of his people, unimpeachable before Satan. All of this transpires under the watchful and approving eye of the angel of the Lord, for **the angel of the LORD stood by.** Not even His righteousness can find fault with Joshua, for Joshua is all dressed up in the righteousness provided him by the angel of the Lord! The righteousness in which Joshua stands is equal to and identical with the righteousness that the Second Person of the Godhead (and the First, as well) possesses. This is the perfect illustration of justification—the judicial act of God whereby he declares righteous the sinner to whom the righteousness of Christ has been imputed. What a great salvation!

Verses 6-10 give the application of the vision to Israel in three parts: (1) to Israel's restoration to the service of Jehovah (vss. 6-7); (2) to the coming of Messiah (vss. 8-9); and (3) to the millennial reign (vs. 10).

6-7. To the renewed high priest comes a renewed commission. It is delivered by **the angel of the LORD** (the Second Person of the Trinity) who **protested** (Heb *'ud*, lit., to protest, i.e., cause to testify—the word conveys both the thoughts of commission and warning) **unto Joshua.**

The commission, though delivered by the **angel of the LORD** (the Second Person of the Trinity), comes from the **LORD of hosts** (the First Person of the Trinity) with two protases—(1) **If thou wilt walk in my ways** and (2) **if thou wilt keep my** charge—followed by a threefold apodosis—(1) **thou shalt also judge my house;** (2) **(thou) shalt also keep my courts;** and (3) **I will give thee places to walk among these that stand by.** In other words, if Joshua will (1) keep his personal life in conformity with the **ways** of the Lord and (2) perform his official duties in keeping with the **charge** delivered to him, then he will realize the threefold blessing of God in which he will: (1) **Judge** (Heb *Sīn*, lit., to judge, discern, i.e., make the decision whether something is clean or unclean) in God's **house** (i.e., the Temple then in the process of being rebuilt); (2) **keep** (Heb *shamar*, lit., to keep, observe, take heed, i.e., guard from any form of profanation) God's **courts** (Heb *chatsēr*, lit., enclosed place, court); and (3) will receive **places to walk** (will have unlimited access) **among these that stand by** (the angelic beings that populate the court in the presence of God). If the conditions specified are realized, the blessings are certain to follow; for they depended solely upon Him.

The coming of Messiah is portrayed in two figures: (1) His coming as the **Branch** (vs. 8); and (2) His coming as the stone with seven eyes (vs. 9).

8 Hear now, O Joshua the high priest, thou, and thy fellows that sit before thee: for they *are* men wondered at: for, behold, I will bring forth my servant the BRANCH.

8. The call, **Hear now,** together with the address, **O Joshua the high priest,** indicates something of great importance is about to be said. To Joshua it is revealed that **thou** (Joshua himself) **and thy fellows that sit before thee** (his fellow priests) **are men wondered at** (Heb *mōpēt*, a wonderful deed, miraculous sign, wonder, omen). More is involved in the priestly service than Joshua or his fellow priests realize, for they are literally men of the sign, i.e., they are a wondrous sign. In their priestly roles they themselves are prophetic and illustrative of something God will do in the future: **For, behold, I will bring forth my servant the BRANCH.** The **Branch** (Heb *tsemach*, lit., a sprout) is a proper name that is descriptive of the Messiah of whom it is used in prophecy (cf. 6:12; Isa 4:2; 11:1; Jer 23:5; 33:15) to indicate that genealogically he is a descendant of the Davidic line and is the fulfillment of the Davidic covenant (II Sam 7:8-14). This name emphasizes the humanity of Messiah who grows up out of the root of Jesse (cf. Isa 11:1). It also sets forth Messiah's function as it relates to mankind; and the name **my servant** (Heb *'ebed*, i.e., servant, doer, tiller, slave) sets forth his function as relates to the **LORD of hosts** (vs. 7). He is frequently referred to by this description (cf. Isa 42:1; 49:3; 50:10; 52:13; 53:11; Ezk 34:23-24). The parallelism is beautiful. In his ministry Joshua (lit., Jehovah saves), the high priestly servant of Jehovah, prefigures Messiah, the High Priestly Servant of Jehovah. The priests associated with Joshua in the priestly ministry prefigure those who will be drawn into fellowship with Messiah at His coming. In short, Joshua prefigures Christ; the Priests prefigure the believers. Thus, nothing Joshua and his fellow priests do is insignificant, even though the significance may not be apparent to them—a lesson we would do well to learn.

9 For behold the stone that I have laid before Joshua; upon one stone *shall be* seven eyes: behold, I will engrave the graving thereof, saith the LORD of hosts, and I will remove the iniquity of that land in one day.

9. The **stone** (Heb *'eben,*) is frequently used throughout the Old Testament to refer to Messiah (cf. Gen 49:24; Ps 118:22; Isa 28:16) and is so interpreted in the New Testament (cf. Mt 21:42; Acts 4:11; I Pet 2:6). This name relates Messiah to Israel; thus, the reference in this text is best understood to continue the reference to Messiah, and not to any other material stone, though many different suggestions are offered by commentators. The **seven eyes** that are **upon one stone** are indicative of the omniscience the **stone** possesses. The **graving** engraved upon the **stone** is ornamental, hence indicative of the beauty, desirability, and perfection of the **stone.** Through the work of the **servant-BRANCH-stone** (cf. vs. 8) the **LORD of hosts** will accomplish an amazing work, for He **will remove the iniquity of that land in one day.** This work was only adumbrated by the dedication of Zerubbabel's temple and the national Day of Atonement. This looks forward to the ultimate and complete work of Messiah (whose death on Calvary's cross made possible the regeneration not only of Israel, but of believers of all ages) when ". . . all Israel shall be saved . . ." (Rom 11:26) in the complete realization of the New Covenant (cf. Jer 31:31-34). This will literally happen in **one day!** The work that Joshua and his fellow priests are to do in the interim should remind them, and all who follow, of the coming of Messiah who will actually accomplish all that their work prefigures. In the interim, they have the greatest privilege afforded to mankind—to represent Messiah.

10 In that day, saith the LORD of hosts, shall ye call every man his neighbour under the vine and under the fig tree.

10. When Messiah is visibly present and Israel is actually and completely cleansed, the true Millennium will exist; and the peace and prosperity promised Israel will be actually realized. Such peace and prosperity is shown in the words **ye** (shall) **call every man his neighbor under the vine and under the fig tree.** There are no enemies—only neighbors. There is no danger; hence, they are safe in sitting in the open vineyards and orchards. There is no poverty, for each one has vineyards and orchards. Mankind is right in viewing warfare, violence, and poverty as enemies—for so they are. Mankind is wrong in attributing these to man's environment; for man's problems are not remedied by putting him into a perfect environment (all man does is ruin a perfect environment). The cause of man's problems are his sin. When sin is removed, and only Messiah can do it, his environment will be perfect. "O, Lord, haste the day."

The significance for the Israel of Zechariah's day of the vision of Joshua, the high priest, standing in the presence of the angel of Jehovah is that sin is not a hindrance to the realization of God's program; for He has dealt with sin. Joshua and the priests stand representatively for the work that God will accomplish ultimately when the sin of the nation is permanently put away. Therefore, they need to deal with their sin and get on with the building of the Temple. To the Israel of the future, Joshua, representing Israel, stands in a priestly ministry inviting all nations into a proper relationship with Messiah. They can stand in this ministry because they have been cleansed of sin and have been installed into this office by Messiah Himself. This raises a question: By what power will Israel be able to do this? The question is answered by the following vision.

5. The fifth vision: The golden candlestick and the two olive trees. 4:1-14.

The vision of the golden candlestick and the two olive trees can be divided as follows: (1) the details of the vision (vss. 1-5) and (2) the explanation of the vision (vss. 6-14). The details of the vision are given in four sections: (1) the introduction (vs. 1); (2) the golden candlestick with seven lamps and seven spouts (vs. 2); (3) the two olive trees by the bowl (vs. 3); and (4) the questions following (vss. 4-5).

CHAPTER 4
AND the angel that talked with me came again, and waked me, as a man that is wakened out of his sleep,

4:1. Apparently, there was a short lapse of time between the vision of Joshua and the vision of the golden candlestick during which **the angel that talked with me** (the Holy Spirit, cf. earlier) departed, perhaps to receive further instructions from the LORD **of hosts.** At any rate, Zechariah recounts that **the angel that talked with me came again, and waked me.** When the prophet was not actively engaged in receiving revelation, his ecstatic trance resembled sleep. He was a ready recipient for revelation, for the **angel** roused him as a man that is wakened out of his sleep.

2 And said unto me, What seest thou? And I said, I have looked, and behold a candlestick all of gold, with a bowl upon the top of it, and his seven lamps thereon, and seven pipes to the seven lamps, which are upon the top thereof:

2. The **angel** takes the initiative and asks the prophet **What seest thou?** The prophet responds and enumerates the details of what he sees: (1) **A candlestick all of gold;** (2) **with a bowl upon the top of it;** (3) **his seven lamps thereon;** and (4) **seven pipes to the seven lamps.** The **candlestick** (Heb *menōrah,* lit., place of light, candlestick) was familiar to Israel. Moses had given directions concerning it in Exodus 25:31-40; 37:17-24. There was such a candlestick, or, better, lampstand, in Herod's temple; and when the Romans destroyed that Temple in A.D. 70 they carried the lampstand to Rome. The record of the event is preserved in the Arch of Titus in Rome, and there the likeness of the lampstand is shown. It is the familiar seven-armed candlestick that is commonly associated with Jewish worship and is the symbol of modern Israel as well. Feinberg notes that the candlestick of Zechariah's vision differed from the candlestick described by Moses, housed in Herod's temple, and portrayed in the Arch of Titus in four ways: Zechariah's candlestick had (1) a bowl; (2) pipes; (3) olive trees; and (4) two golden spouts—features none of the other candlesticks possessed. The candlestick was **all of gold;** hence, it was representative of the purest and costliest thing imaginable to man. The **bowl upon the top of it** was an oil reservoir from which oil was supplied to each of the **seven lamps**—simple lamps mounted one upon each of the arms of the candlestick with wicks protruding from each lamp—by **seven pipes to the seven lamps.** The Hebrew text is explicit—there were seven pipes leading from the bowl to each of the seven lamps, a total of forty-nine pipes. The thought conveyed is that there was an abundant channel to convey the abundant supply of oil stored in the **bowl** to each of the **seven lamps.** It was the closest possible thing to a perpetual lamp. It did not need tending by human hands, and the abundant supply of oil would cause it to burn brightly perpetually.

3 And two olive trees by it, one upon the right *side* of the bowl, and the other upon the left *side* thereof.

3. The **two olive trees . . . upon the right side of the bowl, and . . . upon the left side thereof** are the sources from which the oil flows uninterruptedly into the **bowl** reservoir and through the forty-nine pipes channeled into the seven lampstands. The whole picture indicates an abundance of oil supplied from a never-ending source.

4 So I answered and spake to the angel that talked with me, saying, What *are* these, my lord?
5 Then the angel that talked with me answered and said unto me, Knowest thou not what these be? And I said, No, my lord.

4-5. The prophet's question, **What are these, my lord?** is answered by a question from **the angel that talked with me . . . Knowest thou not what these be?** The prophet confesses, **No, my lord.** This whole interchange underscores the fact that the application and explanation of the vision that follows is not the prophet's invention; it is revelation.

The explanation of the vision (vss. 6-14) is set forth in two parts. The **angel** makes an explanation: (1) concerning the golden candlestick (vss. 6-10); and (2) concerning the two olive trees (vss. 11-14).

6 Then he answered and spake unto me, saying, This *is* the word of the LORD unto Ze-rŭb′ba-bel, saying, Not by might, nor by power, but by my spirit, saith the LORD of hosts.

6. This part of the explanation concerning the candlestick is addressed to **Zerubbabel** and is the explanation given by **the LORD** Himself; hence, it is accurate and authoritative. For almost ten years he had been giving himself to the reconstruction of the Temple, but all efforts had failed. He is not to understand that these past failures are indications of God's disapproval of him or his efforts. Rather, he is to realize that God is his strength and will abundantly supply everything that is necessary for the accomplishment of the task to which He has called Zerubbabel. Though physical effort and objects are involved in the work, the work is spiritual and can be accomplished only through the abundant supply of the Spirit of God, which only **the LORD of hosts** (the First Person of the Trinity) can supply.

7 Who *art* thou, O great mountain? before Ze-rŭb′ba-bel *thou shalt become* a plain: and he shall bring forth the headstone *thereof with* shoutings, *crying,* Grace, grace unto it.

7. This part of the explanation concerning the candlestick is addressed primarily to Zerubbabel's problem—the unfinished Temple. His problem is addressed as though it were a **great mountain**—and such it must have seemed in Zerubbabel's eyes! Under God's enabling Spirit, which He will supply in superabundance, the **great mountain** will become **a plain.** The immediate context (cf. vss. 8-9) confirms that the problem in view is the finishing of the Temple. Hence, it is **Zerubbabel** who **shall bring forth the headstone thereof with shoutings, crying, Grace, grace unto it.** The thought is that Zerubbabel will have the joy of seeing the last stone completing the Temple put into

8 Moreover the word of the LORD came unto me, saying,

9 The hands of Ze-rŭb′ba-bel have laid the foundation of this house; his hands shall also finish it; and thou shalt know that the LORD of hosts hath sent me unto you.

10 For who hath despised the day of small things? for they shall rejoice, and shall see the plummet in the hand of Ze-rŭb′ba-bel with those seven; they are the eyes of the LORD, which run to and fro through the whole earth.

11 ¶Then answered I, and said unto him, What are these two olive trees upon the right side of the candlestick and upon the left side thereof?

12 And I answered again, and said unto him, What be these two olive branches which through the two golden pipes empty the golden oil out of themselves?

13 And he answered me and said, knowest thou not what these be? And I said, No, my lord.

14 Then said he, These are the two anointed ones, that stand by the Lord of the whole earth.

place. The finishing of the Temple would be an occasion for shoutings of joy exceeding the shouts that occurred when its foundation was laid (cf. Ezra 3:11-13), 6:15 ff.).

8-10. The last part of the explanation is additional assurance to both Zerubbabel and to Zechariah. It is **the angel that talked with me** (i.e., the Holy Spirit, cf. vss. 5 ff.) that continues His explanation: **Moreover the word of the LORD** (First Person of the Trinity) **came unto me** (the angel that spoke with me—the Third Person of the Trinity) . . . **and thou** (Zechariah/Zerubbabel) **shalt know that the LORD of hosts** (First Person of the Trinity) **hath sent me** (Third Person of the Trinity) **unto you** (Zechariah). The message is direct and tangible, hence, measurable: **Zerubbabel . . . laid the foundation of this house; his hands shall also finish it.** The man of God in the mission of God is not only indispensable, he is also indestructible. As simple as this message is, it is divine revelation. It comes from Jehovah and is conveyed by His Spirit through His prophet. Its truth will be known when it comes to pass—and come to pass it did in the sixth year of Darius' reign, four years after this prophecy came and fourteen years after the building first began (cf. Ezra 3:11-13; 6:15-18). In the immediate situation they are not to make the mistake of despising **the day of small things.** The Temple may be as nothing in their eyes, and the past ten years may seem totally wasted; but they have been the forerunners of great things to come which could not come if the **day of small things** had not taken place. They are going to have the privilege of seeing **the plummet in the hand of Zerubbabel with those seven.** The **seven** are identified for us as being **the eyes of the LORD** (the First Person of the Trinity) **which run to and fro through the whole earth.** The point of the explanation is that Jehovah has been in the starting of the reconstruction of the Temple; He has been in the delay of the reconstruction of the Temple; and He is in the resumption of the reconstruction of the Temple. The whole thing is His program. How wonderful it must have been to Zerubbabel to realize that the seemingly insignificant thing that he was doing and the years of seeming total frustration were all fitting together into God's greater program and that the omniscient and omnipotent God was not one second ahead of or behind in His program for the whole world. Truly, this is an Old Testament illustration of the truth of Romans 8:28. Nothing that the man of God is called upon to do in the will of God is unimportant or insignificant!

11-14. The second part of the explanation deals with the two olive trees. The prophet asks, **What are these two olive trees . . . What be these two olive branches which through the two golden pipes empty the golden oil out of themselves?** Again the prophet is interrogated, **Knowest thou not what these be?** and must respond, **No, my lord.** The effect again is to show that the explanation is not the prophet's invention; rather, it is God's. The explanation is short and straightforward: **These are the two anointed ones** (Heb benē-hayitshar, lit., sons of oil or shining ones) **that stand by the Lord of the whole earth.** Though others have made many different suggestions concerning the identity of these **two anointed ones,** the context clearly favors identifying them as Joshua, the high priest (concerning whom the vision of chapter 3 was primarily concerned), and Zerubbabel who in their capacities of high priest and governor will be the channels through whom God will manifest His light. Through them the Spirit of God will accomplish the work of God in the nation and in the world. What assurance to them personally and to the nation that was to follow them!

The significance of the vision of the golden candlestick and the two olive trees to the Israel of Zechariah's day was the assurance that the work of God (the building of the Temple) would be accomplished through God's leaders, Joshua and

CHAPTER 5

THEN I turned, and lifted up mine eyes, and looked, and behold a flying roll.

2 And he said unto me, What seest thou? And I answered, I see a flying roll; the length thereof *is* twenty cubits, and the breadth thereof ten cubits.

3 Then said he unto me, This *is* the curse that goeth forth over the face of the whole earth: for every one that stealeth shall be cut off *as* on this side according to it; and every one that sweareth shall be cut off *as* on that side according to it.

4 I will bring it forth, saith the LORD of hosts, and it shall enter into the house of the thief, and into the house of him that sweareth falsely by my name: and it shall remain in the midst of his house, and shall consume it with the timber thereof and the stones thereof.

5 ¶Then the angel that talked with me went forth, and said unto me, Lift up now thine eyes, and see what *is* this that goeth forth.

6 And I said, What *is* it? And he said, This *is* an ephah that goeth forth. He said moreover, This *is* their resemblance through all the earth.

7 And, behold, there was lifted up a talent of lead: and this *is* a woman that sitteth in the midst of the ephah.

Zerubbabel, who would be enabled to perform their tasks by the Spirit of God. To the Israel of the future, the vision indicates that Israel will be a blessing to all the nations of the world through an abundant supply of the Spirit of God as the result of the coming of Messiah who will unite the offices of priest and king in Himself.

6. *The sixth vision: The flying roll. 5:1-4.*

The vision of the flying roll can be divided into two parts: (1) the details of the vision (vss. 1-2); and (2) the interpretation of the vision (vss. 3-4).

5:1-2. In this vision the prophet sees **a flying roll** (Heb *megilah*, lit., a roll, volume) . . . **the length thereof is twenty cubits** (30 ft.–9 meters), **and the breadth thereof ten cubits** (15 ft–4.5 meters). While it was common for writing to be done on such rolls composed of the bark of trees and papyrus, it is probably best to understand this roll as being made of animal skins (vellum). The **roll** is seen to be **flying** because it contained news of a judgment that was swiftly going to be poured out against individuals in the land. The size of the roll indicates that the indictment is large and detailed. No small matter is involved.

3-4. The interpretation of the vision is set forth in these verses. As the roll flies over the land, the land is brought under the indictment of **the curse**—a summary description of the effect of the roll. The effect is universal, for it goes **forth over the face of the whole earth.** Two summary and representative sins are cited: stealing and swearing falsely. One side of the roll deals with the stealing, and the other side with false swearing. These sins are taken as representative of all the sins that break the Law of God—stealing violates man's duty toward man, covered by the second table of the Law; swearing falsely violates man's duty toward God, covered by the first table of the Law. Universally, man has sinned against God; the indictment is plain for all to see. It is large and grievous. What will God do with sinners like this? **Every one that stealeth shall be cut off . . . and every one that sweareth shall be cut off.** The working of the **curse** will operate very effectively; for **it shall remain in the midst of his house** (lit., spend the night, to remain permanently **and shall consume it with the timber thereof and the stones thereof.** God views sin seriously, and judgment will come upon the individual that practices it, whatever its form.

The significance of the vision of the flying roll for the Israel of Zechariah's day is to show that those who sin openly will not hinder God's work; for God's judgment is upon them, and they will not escape. For the Israel of the future the vision indicates that at the coming of Messiah God is going to pour out His judgment upon all the world and will remove every sinner from the land.

7. *The seventh vision: The woman in the ephah. 5:5-11.*

The details of this vision are set forth in verses 5-7, and its explanation is set forth in verses 8-11.

5-7. The angel that talked with me continues His revelatory activity, for He **went forth** to receive further revelation to communicate to the prophet. Attention is drawn to the fact that more revelation is about to be communicated when the **angel** says to the prophet, **Lift up now thine eyes, and see,** and then asks, **what is this that goeth forth.**

The vision presented to the prophet is something familiar to him. His question, **What is it?** is better understood to mean that he is asking for interpretation, not identification, of the things he is observing. In response to the prophet's question, the **angel** identifies (for the sake of the reader) the object that the prophet has seen and gives the interpretation of the vision. What the prophet saw was **an ephah** (the largest dry measure used by the Hebrews to measure grain, which is somewhat larger than the bushel basket that is familiar to us) **that goeth forth** (it has gone through all the land in collection of its contents and is now full to the limit). We would be at a loss to explain the statement **This is their resemblance through all the earth** if it were not for the identification made in verse 8, **This is wickedness**. This, then, is the preliminary and partial identification of that which is later fully and explicitly identified. The full **ephah** is representative of all the wickedness in all the land that has been collected together for some purpose—which we later learn to be its removal from Israel and return to Babylon (cf. vss. 8-11).

The wickedness contained in the **ephah** cannot escape from the **ephah**; there is a **talent of lead** (the heaviest weight used by the Hebrews) upon its opening. The **talent of lead** is **lifted up** (not removed) high enough to reveal that there was a **woman** sitting **in the midst of the ephah**.

8-11. The **angel** (cf. vs. 5) explains what the **woman** (vs. 7) symbolizes as he says, **This is wickedness**. Some commentators have suggested that the woman embodies a specific form of wickedness, such as idolatry (of which the Israelites were cured outwardly but not inwardly by the Babylonian captivity) or commercialism; but it is not necessary to limit the symbolism so narrowly. The best interpretative parallel is probably the reference to the man of sin (II Thess 2) who is the embodiment of all kinds of sin—including religious, for he sets himself up as God. The **woman**, likewise, is probably best viewed as the embodiment of all kinds of sin, including religious sins which may have preeminence, just as they do in the representation of the man of sin. The interpretating **angel** took the **woman of wickedness** and **cast her into the midst of the ephah**. To make sure that she could not escape from the **ephah . . . he cast the weight of lead upon the mouth thereof.** Thus, all forms of sin from all parts of the land are securely contained within the **ephah**.

The prophet does not have time to express the questions that must have been in his mind as to what the **angel** will do with the **woman** in the **ephah**; for as he lifted up his eyes **behold, there came out two women, and the wind was in their wings; for they had wings like the wings of a stork**. The women are not identified; hence, their primary function is to cause the vision to move to its completion, and their precise identity is not important. Some commentators suggest that the **women** are representations of Assyria and Babylon who were used of God to remove wickedness, particularly idolatry, from His people. This does not seem likely; for it would give the vision a historical cast looking to the past, rather than to the future. It seems better simply to view the **women** as functionaries to make the vision full and complete. Still the prophet did see something, and these were not usual women. It is possible that they were actually angels. If so, this is the only case in the Bible where angels have the appearance of women. Some commentators would not like that suggestion and would cite passages such as Matthew 22:30 to show that angels are sexless beings. However, it should be observed that when angels are seen, it is usually in the form of a man; hence, they do have sexual characteristics. Further, Matthew 22:30 does not demand that angels be sexless—it simply states that angels do not cohabit and produce baby angels. There is no reason why angels could not have the appearance of women as well as the appearance of men. That the **women** are not human is evident from the fact that they have **wings like the wings of a stork** (a migratory bird common in Palestine having long and wide wings). The **wings**, of course, are necessary to provide the **women** with mobility, speed, and ability to transport the heavy **ephah** swiftly and certainly to its distant destination. There are **two women** to divide the task between them and to demonstrate that God has at His disposal servants capable of handling this impossible task (humanly speaking) with great grace and ease. So simple is the task from God's viewpoint that

8 And he said, This *is* wickedness. And he cast it into the midst of the ephah; and he cast the weight of lead upon the mouth thereof.
9 Then lifted I up mine eyes, and looked, and, behold, there came out two women, and the wind *was* in their wings; for they had wings like the wings of a stork: and they lifted up the ephah between the earth and the heaven.
10 Then said I to the angel that talked with me, Whither do these bear the ephah?
11 And he said unto me, To build it an house in the land of Shī'när: and it shall be established, and set there upon her own base.

he can send **two women** who can discharge the task with great efficiency.

As the **two women . . . lifted up the ephah between the earth and heaven**, the prophet vocalizes his thoughts: **Whither do these bear the ephah?** The interpreting angel's answer indicates the fourfold mission upon which the **two women** have been sent: (1) **To build it a house**; (2) **in the land of Shinar**; (3) **and it shall be established**; and (4) **set there upon her own base.** The answer indicates that the wickedness thus removed from the land of Israel is going: (1) to reside permanently; (2) in the land of Babylon, from which it originated; and (3) it will be firmly entrenched there and (4) will have its base of operation there permanently. The removal of wickedness from Israel is also a judgment upon Babylon, which throughout history and Scripture is opposed to God and His righteousness. Truly, God will give them over to all forms of wickedness and uncleanness (cf. Rom 1:24-32).

The significance of the vision of the woman in the ephah for the Israel of Zechariah's day is that wickedness must be removed entirely out of the land. This is an impossible task from man's viewpoint, but from God's viewpoint it is simply and efficiently accomplished; so the people should not let any form of wickedness deter them from their task to bring the Temple to completion. To the Israel of the future the vision looks forth to the seventieth week of Daniel when God is going to remove every system and form of wickedness that manifests itself against God. The millennial kingdom will be only for the redeemed.

8. The eighth vision: The vision of the four chariots. 6:1-8.

The vision of the four chariots can be divided into two parts: (1) the details of the vision (vss. 1-3); and (2) the interpretation of the vision (vss. 4-8). The details of the vision can be further developed as follows: (a) the sight of the vision (vs. 1) and (b) the facts of the vision (vss. 2-3).

CHAPTER 6

AND I turned, and lifted up mine eyes, and looked, and, behold, there came four chariots out from between two mountains; and the mountains *were* mountains of brass.

6:1. This vision follows closely upon the preceding one; the prophet simply **turned, and lifted up** his **eyes, and looked, and, behold, there came four chariots out from between two mountains; and the mountains were mountains of brass.** The chariots (Heb *merkabah*) are war chariots of the same kind mentioned in other prophecies (cf. Joel 2:5; Mic 1:13; 5:10; Nah 3:2; Hab 3:8; Hag 2:22). The **two mountains** from between which the **four chariots** come were literal mountains known to the prophet and to Israel. This is seen from the occurrence of the Hebrew definite article occurring in the text indicating that these are the **two mountains** and that **the mountains were mountains of brass.** The article, then, indicates the definiteness of the mountains in view; and the **brass** indicates the function of the mountains in the vision—they are mountains upon which the righteous judgment of God has been manifest. The only mountains that would fit this description are Mount Moriah and the Mount of Olives; thus, the **four chariots** are seen to come through the Valley of Jehoshaphat, east of Jerusalem, the same location viewed earlier by Joel (cf. Joel 3:2, 12).

2 In the first chariot *were* red horses; and in the second chariot black horses;
3 And in the third chariot white horses; and in the fourth chariot grisled and bay horses.

2-3. These verses amplify the facts of the vision. The **first chariot** had **red horses**; the **second chariot** had **black horses**; the **third chariot** had **white horses**; and the **fourth chariot** had **grizzled** (Heb *barōd*, lit., grisled, spotted—the same word is used of the cattle that Jacob got from Laban, cf. Gen 31:10, 12) **and bay** (Heb *'amōts*, i.e., strong, deep red) **horses.** The colors of the horses are probably indicative of the missions upon which they are sent: **Red**—war and bloodshed; **black**—calamity and distress; **white**—victory and joy; and **grizzled**—plagues and pestilence.

4 Then I answered and said unto the angel that talked with me, What *are* these, my lord?

4-8. The interpretation of the vision given in these verses is introduced by the prophet's question **What are these, my lord?** The interpreting **angel** interprets the **four chariots** (vs. 1) as

5 And the angel answered and said unto me, These *are* the four spirits of the heavens, which go forth from standing before the Lord of all the earth.

6 The black horses which *are* therein go forth into the north country; and the white go forth after them; and the grisled go forth toward the south country.

7 And the bay went forth, and sought to go that they might walk to and fro through the earth: and he said, Get you hence, walk to and fro through the earth. So they walked to and fro through the earth.

8 Then cried he upon me, and spake unto me, saying, Behold, these that go toward the north country have quieted my spirit in the north country.

being **the four spirits of the heavens, which go forth from standing before the Lord of all the earth.** The four chariots (vs. 1) and their **horses,** then, are **four spirits of the heavens—**they are divine messengers of God used as His instruments in executing His judgment and pouring out His wrath upon the earth.

The mission upon which the divine messengers are sent is described in verses 6-8. The **black horses . . . go forth into the north country;** the **white** horses **go forth after them** (i.e., the black horses into the north country); the **grizzled** horses **go forth toward the south country.** The directions are given with Jerusalem as the reference point. Hence, the **black** and **white** horses go forth into the area of Babylon (reached by going north and then through the fertile crescent to the east); the **grizzled** horses go forth into the area of Egypt. Though the people of Israel had been delivered from these ancient enemies at the time of the prophet, they were in political unrest and upheaval—but God has them under control, for his ministers are on patrol.

It should be observed that the **red horses** (cf. vs. 2) seemingly are assigned no mission and that the **bay** horses are separated from the **grizzled,** whereas in verse 3 they appear to be together. While it does not solve the problem completely, it seems best to view the **black . . . white . . . and the grizzled** as being references to the second, third, and fourth chariots that are sent on specific missions and that the **bay** in verse 7 should be taken not to denote a color, but to denote a characteristic, i.e., strong (the Heb word *'amōts* can denote strength as well as a deep red color). If this understanding is correct, then the **bay** in verse 7 is a reference to the **red horses** drawing the **first chariot** of verse 2. While the second, third, and fourth chariots are off on their specific missions, the first chariot engages in a general mission of going **to and fro through the earth** (mentioned three times in vs. 7, an indication that their task is every bit as important as that undertaken by the other chariots). Their mission throughout all the earth is indicative that war and bloodshed will hold sway throughout all the world. The reference to **the earth** must be understood in a much broader sense than just to the land of Israel. It must be understood as being a reference to **the earth** universally.

The report of verse 8 indicates that all is well, especially in the **north country—**probably best understood as a reference to Babylon. The emphasis given is fitting for in the fifth year of Darius (three years after the prophet saw these visions); Babylon, which had been conquered by Cyrus, revolted against Darius and experienced devastation and depopulation in retaliation. When these things happened, Zechariah and the Israel of his day could know that truly the **spirit** (i.e., the wrath of God, cf. 1:15; Ezek 5:13; 24:13) was **quieted** (i.e., was satisfied) **in the north country.**

The significance of the vision of the four chariots to the Israel of Zechariah's day was that God's judgment has finally and fully rested upon Babylon. Even though there might be a flare up (which was realized in the fifth year of Darius' reign—just three years later); they need not let that deter them from building the Temple (which was not completed until the sixth year of Darius' reign). God has all things under complete control. The vision of the four chariots reveals to the Israel of the future why Messiah can reign universally over all the world—all enemies are judged and none can rise up against the authority of the King.

At this time it is fitting to make some general observations concerning the eight night visions as a whole. The first five night visions are conciliatory and bring comfort to Zechariah, Joshua, Zerubbabel and the people of their day. The last three deal with God's judgment that will be poured out upon sin and sinners individually (the vision of the flying roll), nationally (the vision of the woman in the ephah), and universally (the vision of the four chariots). The eight night visions are complementary to Daniel's vision, for both of them deal with the times of the Gentiles—Daniel's vision from the Gentile point of view, Zechariah's from Israel's point of view. The eight night visions, then, take us prophetically from the Babylonian captivity to the millennial kingdom, looking at that period of time from Israel's perspective.

B. The Coronation of Joshua. 6:9-15.

1. The crowning of Joshua. 6:9-11.

9 ¶And the word of the Lord came unto me, saying,
10 Take of *them of* the captivity, *even* of Hĕl′da-ī, of Tŏ-bī′jah, and of Je-dā′-iah, which are come from Babylon, and come thou the same day, and go into the house of Josiah the son of Zĕph-a-nī′ah;
11 Then take silver and gold, and make crowns, and set *them* upon the head of Joshua the son of Jŏs′e-dĕch, the high priest;

9-11. The eight symbolic visions are brought to a conclusion by a symbolic action in keeping with the instructions given by **the word of the Lord.** Zechariah was instructed to meet three men from Babylon who had come bearing gifts for the reconstruction of the Temple from the exiles remaining in Babylon. **Of Heldai, of Tobijah, and of Jedaiah.** This event happened on **the same day** in which the eight night visions were presented to the prophet (cf. 1:7). Zechariah was commanded to take the delegation with their gifts to **the house of Josiah the son of Zephaniah.** The men had brought with them gifts of **silver and gold** to assist in the reconstruction of the Temple. Zechariah is commanded to take these gifts **and make crowns, and set them upon the head of Joshua the son of Josedech, the high priest.** The word **crowns** has led some commentators to suggest that Zechariah was to make two crowns, one for Joshua and the other for Zerubbabel. This is not likely because Zerubbabel could not in any sense wear a crown; he was a descendant of Coniah (cf. Mt 1:12) whose branch of the Davidic line was cursed of God and prohibited from having a part in the Messianic line (cf. Jer 22:24-30). Zechariah was to make only one crown, but it was to be a double, or composite, crown and was to be placed **upon the head of Joshua . . . the high priest,** even though the Mosaic law made no such provisions for the Levitical priesthood. This would call attention to the fact that Joshua stood for more than the Levitical high priest—he prefigured the coming Messiah who would combine the offices of High Priest and King in Himself (cf. Ps 110) as is made known by the following verses.

2. The commissioning of Joshua. 6:12-15.

12 And speak unto him, saying, Thus speaketh the Lord of hosts, saying, Behold the man whose name *is* The BRANCH; and he shall grow up out of his place, and he shall build the temple of the Lord:
13 Even he shall build the temple of the Lord; and he shall bear the glory, and shall sit and rule upon his throne; and he shall be a priest upon his throne: and the counsel of peace shall be between them both.
14 And the crowns shall be to Hē′lĕm, and to Tŏ-bī′jah, and to Je-dā′iah, and to Hen the son of Zĕph-a-nī′ah, for a memorial in the temple of the Lord.
15 And they *that are* far off shall come and build in the temple of the Lord, and ye shall know that the Lord of hosts hath sent me unto you. And *this* shall come to pass, if ye will diligently obey the voice of the Lord your God.

12-15. The words to be spoken to Joshua in this symbolic act indicate that while the person of Joshua is not important, his position as high priest is all-important. The words to be spoken to Joshua upon his coronation are delivered by Zechariah, but they come from **the Lord of hosts** (the First Person of the Trinity). They look beyond the historical Joshua, the high priest, to the coming Messiah and give the most inclusive and complete picture of His coming reign. **Behold the man** (the very words used by Pontius Pilate in presenting Jesus to the multitude after He had been crowned with thorns; cf. Jn 19:5) **whose name is The Branch** lift the eyes of Zechariah, Joshua, and the nation of their day to the Messiah to come and unite this symbolic act with the **Branch** introduced in 3:8-10. Nine prophetic truths are set forth: (1) Messiah, the Branch, will appear as Joshua's antitype (vs. 12a). In keeping with his figure, **The Branch,** He will **grow up out of his place**—He will have a lowly origin and will grow into universal prominence (cf. Mic 5:2); (2) Messiah, the Branch, will build the millennial Temple (vss. 12b-13a). It will be His work to **build the temple of the Lord.** Four temples have a place in Israel's history: (a) Solomon's temple—destroyed by the Chaldeans; (b) Zerubbabel's temple—renovated by Herod; (c) Herod's temple—destroyed by the Romans; and (d) the millennial Temple—to be built by Messiah and never to be destroyed. The importance of the millennial Temple is shown by the repeated reference to it and the emphatic **he** in verse 13; (3) Messiah, the Branch, will bear the glory, (vs. 13b). The **glory** that He will bear is the millennial glory that is His by virtue of the fact of His fulfilling every promise made to Abraham and Israel and for His provision of righteousness and regeneration for Jew and Gentile alike; (4) Messiah, the Branch, will be King-Priest (vs. 13c, d). He **shall sit and rule upon his throne; and he shall be a priest upon his throne.** At the present He sits at the right hand of the Father's throne (cf. Ps 110:1; Heb 1:3; 8:1; 10:12; 12:2; Rev 3:21), but then He will be installed by the Father upon His own throne; and He will be a King-Priest forever, in keeping with the promise made earlier to David (cf. II Sam 7:8-16); (5) Messiah, the Branch, will combine two offices (vs. 13c). Except for Melchizedek (cf. Gen 14:18), the concept of a King-Priest was unknown in Israel and the Old Testament. The words **and the counsel of peace shall be between them both** does not refer to a supposed rift between Joshua and Zerubbabel, to a **counsel of peace** between Jehovah and Messiah, to the reconciliation of different messianic attributes, or to two characters, such as Joshua and Zerubbabel, being united in the one Person of Messiah. This description of Messiah, the Branch, develops the preceding one and shows that He will combine both offices, King and Priest, in perfect peace and harmony and thus will bring to realization God's plan from eternity past; (6) Messiah, the Branch, will be represented by the crown (vs. 14). The true purpose of **the crowns** (lit., a double or composite crown) is now made known. It was to be a **a memorial** (Heb *zikarōn*, lit., memorial, remembrance) for **Helem** (another name for **Heldai**, cf. vs. 10), **Tobijah, Jedaiah,** and **Hen** (another name for **Josiah,** cf. vs. 10) and was to be placed **in the temple of the LORD.** It was to remind Joshua and all Israel to come of the Messiah who would be King-Priest over Israel, and particularly that the dispersed of Israel and the Gentiles would have part in that kingdom. The crown was not worn by succeeding high priests. Tradition holds that it was kept in the Temple until Messiah came and then was destroyed along with the Temple by the Romans in A.D. 70. The important thing is that the crown was to serve as a reminder of God's universal purpose to use Israel as the means to reach all the world. They, however, lost sight of this and mistook God's favor for favoritism (cf. Rom 2:17-29); (7) Messiah, the Branch, will bind together both Jew and Gentile (vs. 15a). **They that are far off** is a common expression used for Gentiles who were viewed as being far off from God. Gentiles, then, **shall come and build in the temple of the LORD,** i.e., they will be united with Israel in the service of Jehovah—a theme common in prophecy (cf. Isa 60:10-11); (8) Messiah, the Branch, will corroborate the truth of God's word (vs. 15b). When Israel witnesses Gentiles being brought into fellowship with and service of Jehovah, they will **know that the LORD of hosts hath sent me** (Messiah) **unto you.** Any messianic blessing that excluded Gentiles was not genuine; God never intended for Israel to be an end in herself. He always intended to use her as a means to reach the world—gentile blessing was messianic authentication; and (9) Messiah, the Branch, will demand absolute obedience (vs. 15c). Israel missed the point of the memorial crown and did not recognize the universal ministry and mission of their Messiah. The certainty of Israel's future and the Messianic kingdom is not impaired by Israel's failure, for God's future program depends upon God Himself. However, Israel's enjoyment of blessing and benefit does depend upon their obedience; hence, the prophet concludes, **And this shall come to pass, if ye will diligently obey the voice of the LORD your God.** The Israel of Zechariah's day and our day has failed, but the Israel of the future will obey completely and will experience national regeneration and all of the blessings Messiah will bring (Jer 31:31-34).

III. THE THIRD WORD (FAR VIEW). 7:1-14:21.

Two years have passed between chapters six and seven. Two more years will yet be required to complete the rebuilding of the Temple (cf. Ezr 6:15). The people have been working hard (cf. Hag 1:14). Many exiles had returned from Babylon and had settled in Jerusalem and the other cities of Israel (cf. Ezr 2). The scars of the Babylonian invasion are slowly being erased, but the nation is still in an interim state. During the Babylonian captivity the exiles had instituted a fast day in commemoration of the destruction of Jerusalem. Now that Jerusalem is being restored, the question arises concerning the need or validity of continuing to keep the fast. A delegation is sent to Jerusalem to inquire of the Lord; and in response, God sends four messages through His prophet to the nation.

A. The Four Messages. 7:1-8:23.

1. The first message: Obedience is better than fasting. 7:1-7.

7:1. All four of the messages came **in the fourth year of king Darius**—two years after the **word** came twice from the LORD (cf. 1:1, 7) in connection with which Zechariah received the eight night visions. The precise date is **the fourth day of the ninth month, even in Chisleu**—the Babylonian name for the ninth month, corresponding roughly to the last part of our month of November and the first part of our month of December. Once again, the **word of the LORD** (Jehovah) **came unto Zechariah,** His prophet. Thus, the messages are authoritative.

2-3. The translation **When they had sent unto the house of God** is unfortunate, for it gives rise to the understanding that the delegation was sent from Jews who were yet residing in Babylon. The text is better understood to read "And Beth-el sent . . ." In the Old Testament, Beth-el always refers to a place, never to the house of God (i.e., the Temple). Two hundred and twenty-three of the exiles returning with Ezra had settled in Beth-el (cf. Ezr 2:28). The Beth-el delegation was headed by **Sherezer and Regem-melech** (their Babylonian names show that they were exiles returned from Babylon) who, together with **their men,** came **to pray** (lit., for the purpose of inquiring or entreating) **before the LORD, And to speak unto the priests** (whose responsibility it was to give interpretations and decisions concerning points pertaining to the Law, cf. Deut 17:9) **. . . and to the prophets** (Haggai and Zechariah). The question that they wanted answered was, **Should I weep in the fifth month, separating myself, as I have done these so many years?** The question is asked in the first person, showing the unity with which all the citizens of Beth-el were asking the question. Though Beth-el raised the question, the answer is applicable to all the land; and Jehovah uses Beth-el as the occasion to address the entire land (cf. vs. 5). The fast in the **fifth month** commemorated the burning of Jerusalem in 586 B.C. In their observance of the fast, the people mourned (**weep**) and abstained from food (**separating myself,** i.e., from food). This fast was observed on the tenth day of the fifth month (cf. Jer 52:12-13) throughout all the years of the Babylonian exile (**these so many years**), though God never commanded them to do so. Now that the Babylonian captivity had ended and the nation was on the way to recovery, the observance of the fast seemed pointless (though next to the Day of Atonement it is still the greatest fast day for the Jews); and its observance was becoming a chore to the people. Though the Lord had never commanded the fast, they now wished to learn from the Lord whether or not they should continue to observe it.

4-7. The answer to the delegation came directly from **the LORD of hosts** through His prophet, Zechariah (**me**), and dealt with internal realities, rather than external conformities. The message is addressed to **all the people of the land;** for all are

---

CHAPTER 7

AND it came to pass in the fourth year of king Darius, *that* the word of the LORD came unto Zĕch-a-rī'ah in the fourth *day* of the ninth month, *even* in Chĭs'leu;

2 When they had sent unto the house of God She-rē'zer and Rē'gem-mĕ'lech, and their men, to pray before the LORD,

3 *And* to speak unto the priests which *were* in the house of the LORD of hosts, and to the prophets, saying, Should I weep in the fifth month, separating myself, as I have done these so many years?

4 ¶Then came the word of the LORD of hosts unto me, saying,

5 Speak unto all the people of the land, and to the priests, saying, When

ye fasted and mourned in the fifth and seventh *month,* even those seventy years, did ye at all fast unto me, *even* to me?

6 And when ye did eat, and when ye did drink, did not ye eat *for yourselves,* and drink *for yourselves?*

7 *Should ye* not *hear* the words which the Lord hath cried by the former prophets, when Jerusalem was inhabited and in prosperity, and the cities thereof round about her, when *men* inhabited the south and the plain?

8 ¶And the word of the Lord came unto Zĕch-a-rī′ah, saying,

9 Thus speaketh the Lord of hosts, saying, Execute true judgment, and shew mercy and compassions every man to his brother.

10 And oppress not the widow, nor the fatherless, the stranger, nor the poor; and let none of you imagine evil against his brother in your heart.

11 But they refused to hearken, and pulled away the shoulder, and stopped their ears, that they should not hear.

12 Yea, they made their hearts *as* an adamant stone, lest they should hear the law, and the words which the Lord of hosts hath sent in his spirit by the former prophets: therefore came a great wrath from the Lord of hosts.

13 Therefore it is come to pass, *that* as he cried, and they would not hear; so they cried, and I would not hear, saith the Lord of hosts:

14 But I scattered them with a whirlwind among all the nations whom they knew not. Thus the land was desolate after them, that no man passed through

concerned, not just the people of Beth-el. God's answer begins with a piercing question: **When ye fasted and mourned in the fifth and seventh month, even those seventy years, did ye at all fast unto me, even to me?** The question calls for an investigation of true motive. They had asked about the fast of the **fifth month,** but God's answer anticipates that it will be but the occasion of other questions to follow; so He includes the fast of the **seventh month** (a fast that commemorated the slaying of Gedeliah, the Jewish governor of Judea—cf. II Kgs 25:23-25; Jer 41:1-3—which fast is still observed today by orthodox Jews as the Fast of Gedeliah on the third day of the seventh month). The first question is followed quickly by a second, revealing their true motivation of self-gratification in their feasts. **And when ye did eat, and when ye did drink, did not ye eat for yourselves, and drink for yourselves?** The question of verse 5 expects a strong negative answer, while the question of verse 6 expects an equally strong positive answer. Thus the Lord has revealed that in neither their fasts nor their feasts has He been pleased, for their motives were wrong. God is never pleased with mere external formalities and conformities. God is a God of realism, and He demands inward reality! They would never have had an occasion to have the fasts they were now finding burdensome if they had obeyed **the words which the Lord hath cried by the former prophets, when Jerusalem was inhabited and in prosperity, . . . when men inhabited the south** (i.e., the mountains of Judea) **and the plain** (i.e., the Shephelah, the hill country comprising the western part of Judah)—both designations make up the territory given to Judah. Had they heeded the word of the Lord, the calamities that their fasts commemorated would never have taken place. The point of the first message is: Obedience is better than fasting. God is pleased by obedience, not by self-imposed fasts!

2. The second message: Disobedience leads to severe judgment. 7:8-14.

8-10. These verses show that the requirements of Jehovah have not changed. **The word of the Lord came unto Zechariah** as it had come to the earlier prophets—Zechariah does not have a new message to proclaim to the people. God's standards of righteousness and justice have not changed. How one treats **his brother . . . the widow . . . the fatherless, the stranger,** and **the poor** is indicative of his heart attitude before God. One cannot be right with God and have wrong relationships with the people in his life. To do so is to exercise an unrighteous judgment, which the Lord hates; for it is inconsistent with His character, for He is the righteous Judge of all the earth (cf. Gen 18:25).

11-12. These verses remind the people of the nation's response in the past. **They refused to hearken, and pulled away the shoulder** (the action of an ox that refuses to accept the yoke upon its neck), **and stopped their ears. They made their hearts as an adamant stone, lest they should hear the law, and the words which the Lord of hosts hath sent in his spirit by the former prophets** (i.e., the prophets before the Babylonian captivity). The nation in the past willfully rejected God's righteous standard. **Therefore came a great wrath from the Lord of hosts.** Thus, the present generation is reminded that the Babylonian captivity through which they have just come was occasioned by disobedience to His words sent through His prophets.

13-14. These verses give the results that the nation experienced because of its disobedience. They refused to hear the word of the Lord; thus, the Lord refused to hear them when they cried unto Him as His judgment overtook them. Instead of hearing, Jehovah **scattered them with a whirlwind among all the nations whom they knew not.** This is a reference to both the Assyrian and Babylonian captivities. As a result of those captivi-

nor returned: for they laid the pleasant land desolate.

CHAPTER 8

AGAIN the word of the LORD of hosts came *to me*, saying,

2 Thus saith the LORD of hosts; I was jealous for Zion with great jealousy, and I was jealous for her with great fury.

3 Thus saith the LORD; I am returned unto Zion, and will dwell in the midst of Jerusalem: and Jerusalem shall be called a city of truth; and the mountain of the LORD of hosts the holy mountain.

ties, **the land was desolate after them.** Though God used Assyria and Babylon to punish His people, His people are held responsible; **for they laid the pleasant land** (lit., the land of desire) **desolate.** The sin of the people was the cause of the devastation visited upon the land. Had they not sinned, it would not have happened. Thus, the point of the second message is: Disobedience leads to severe judgment. This has been amply demonstrated by God's dealing with His people in the past. Do not let history repeat itself!

3. The third message: God's jealousy over his people will lead to their repentance and blessing. 8:1-17.

This section of the prophecy divides into three parts: (1) the coming of the message (vs. 1); (2) the content of the message (vss. 2-8); and (3) the application of the message (vss. 9-17).

8:1. Again lets us know that this message develops those of chapter 7. It also is **the word of the LORD of hosts** (the First Person of the Trinity) and hence is authoritative and authentic. The human messenger is the same, **me,** Zechariah.

Four wonderful truths are contained in this third message: (1) Jehovah's jealousy for Zion (vs. 2); (2) Jehovah's dwelling in Zion (vs. 3); (3) Jehovah's security for Zion (vss. 4-5); and (4) Jehovah's restoration of His people (vss. 6-8).

2. Twice **the LORD of hosts** (the First Person of the Trinity) states, **I was jealous** (Heb *qana'*, lit., to be zealous, jealous) **for Zion . . . her.** No evil connotation can be placed upon the emotion, for it is being displayed by the holy God of the universe. The root idea of the verb is to glow, or to burn, the thought being that God's heart glows or burns with the desire to pour out abundant blessings as tangible expressions of His love for His people. The revelation that ". . . God is love . . ." (cf. I Jn 4:8, 16) is not new with the New Testament! The parallelism expresses the two different manifestations that this love for Israel took: (1) toward Israel, **with great jealousy** (Heb *qin'ah,* lit., zeal, jealousy)—God is not mildly in favor of Israel; He is unalterably prejudiced (in a good sense) for Israel and never acts apart from His love for her; and (2) toward the Gentiles who have oppressed Israel, **with great fury** (Heb *chēmah,* lit., heat, fury)—His love for Israel causes Him to be unalterably opposed to those who oppress Israel. God is the infinite embodiment of consistency; and He is acting in consistency with His announced promise to Abraham: "I will bless them that bless thee, and curse him that curseth thee . . ." (Gen 12:3).

3. The Lord's future dwelling in Zion is so certain that He speaks of it as though it were an accomplished fact, **I am returned unto Zion.** In a sense this is true in the prophet's day because God is always with His people, and He has brought them back from the Babylonian Captivity. However, His return to **Zion** in the prophet's day is only an adumbration of the great day when His reign is universal over all the world and His King, Messiah, is on the throne. As an outgrowth of His return to Zion, **the LORD . . . will dwell** (Heb *shakan*, lit., to tabernacle) **in the midst of Jerusalem.** His presence with the people of the prophet's day is an adumbration of the day when He will permanently dwell in Jerusalem and Jerusalem will never again be destroyed or its people scattered. The presence of Jehovah in the city causes the city to take on His character. Thus, **Jerusalem shall be called a city of truth** (no lying or deceit can be tolerated in the Lord's presence); **and the mountain of the LORD of hosts** (Jerusalem will be universally recognized to be the peculiar possession and dwelling place) **the holy mountain** (completely set apart for the purposes of Jehovah). No other city in the world has ever been so honored with the promise and presence of the First Person of the Trinity. It should be clarified that the First Person of the Trinity will not leave His eternal throne in heaven for a throne on earth. The city will be His; and the throne will be

4 Thus saith the LORD of hosts; There shall yet old men and old women dwell in the streets of Jerusalem, and every man with his staff in his hand for very age.

5 And the streets of the city shall be full of boys and girls playing in the streets thereof.

6 Thus saith the LORD of hosts; If it be marvellous in the eyes of the remnant of this people in these days, should it also be marvellous in mine eyes? saith the LORD of hosts.

7 Thus saith the LORD of hosts; Behold, I will save my people from the east country, and from the west country;

8 And I will bring them, and they shall dwell in the midst of Jerusalem: and they shall be my people, and I will be their God, in truth and in righteousness.

9 ¶Thus saith the LORD of hosts; Let your hands be strong, ye that hear in these days these words by the mouth of the prophets, which *were* in the day *that* the foundation of the house of the LORD of hosts was laid, that the temple might be built.

His because His King, Messiah, the Son of David, will be personally present and will reign personally.

4-5. Where Jehovah is there is perfect peace and security. This is shown by the fact that **old men and old women** will **dwell in the streets of Jerusalem**—not because they do not have any houses, but because there is nothing in the streets (either war machine or evil person) that will do them harm. They will be able to enjoy the fellowship of one another's company in the open without fear. Further, there will be no warfare to shorten the lifespan, thus **every man with his staff in his hand for very age**—all mankind will be able to grow to a ripe old age in perfect peace and security. Not only will the city be safe for the elderly, but **the streets of the city shall be full of boys and girls playing in the streets thereof.** There will be an abundance of offspring—always viewed in the Bible as a blessing of God (cf. Ps 127:3). Thus, all ages, young, middle-aged, and aged, will experience perfect peace and safety as the blessing of a right relationship to Jehovah who dwells in their midst.

6-8. Such blessings as those described in the previous verses presuppose Jehovah's restoration of His people, adumbrated by the restoration in the days of the prophet. This restoration will not only be **marvellous in the eyes of the remnant of this people in these days** (the days of the prophet), but it is also . . . **marvelous in mine** (the LORD of hosts) **eyes**. That which concerns and blesses God's people also concerns and blesses God (cf. I Pet 5:7b). The restoration of the people rests upon **Thus saith the LORD of hosts** (the First Person of the Trinity). It depends solely upon Him. His sovereign determination is, **I will save my people from the east country, and from the west country.** The earth is viewed as a sphere with a line drawn around it from the north pole through the south pole and back to the north pole on the other side of the sphere. Thus, the expressions **east country** and **west country** are expressions indicating a universal restoration of His people from whatever point of the compass and whatever geographical location. This is a sovereign undertaking of Jehovah who states, **I will bring them** (they may think that they are returning at their own volition, but God is controlling all situations so that they are free of conscious compulsion to return). Jehovah's undertaking will be effective, for **they shall dwell** (Heb *shakan*, lit., to tabernacle—the same word is used of Jehovah earlier, cf. vs. 3) **in the midst of Jerusalem**—they will be just as permanent in their occupation as Jehovah is. The remnant of people will be converted, for **they shall be my people** in fulfillment of the new covenant (Jer 31:31-34). Their regeneration will be recognized by Jehovah who affirms, **I will be their God, in truth and in righteousness.** A glorious future awaits Israel. The people of the prophet's day could look at what God was accomplishing in their time and midst and realize that they are a part of the greater things that God will yet do for Israel. They should be encouraged because the greater things to follow are built upon the things that are being accomplished in their day.

The message given in verses 2-8 is applied in verses 9-17. It comes in the form of a fivefold encouragement: (1) the Temple will be rebuilt (vs. 9); (2) the land will be secure (vss. 10-11); (3) the land will be prosperous (vs. 12); (4) the nation will be a blessing (vss. 13-15); and (5) the nation will obey Jehovah (vss. 16-17).

9. Because they are part of the preparations for the glorious future presented to them in verses 6-8, **the LORD of hosts** encourages the people, **Let your hands be strong, ye that hear in these days these words by the mouth of the prophets.** Jehovah promises to strengthen their hands to accomplish the task set before them by the **prophets**. The particular **prophets** in view are the ones **which were in the day that the foundation of the house of the LORD of hosts was laid.** This refers to the

1819

ministries of Haggai and Zechariah whose ministeries were directed towards encouraging the people in the fourth year of Darius to complete the Temple whose foundations were laid during the second year of Darius. The ultimate purpose is that **the temple might be built.** The people will be enabled to complete the task already begun.

10-11. Before these days (i.e., the days in which the work of the restoration of the Temple was begun) conditions in the land were bad. **There was no hire for man, nor any hire for beast**— economic conditions were bad. **Neither was there any peace to him that went out or came in**—political and social conditions were bad; there was no security in the land. This all was **because of the affliction**, the judgment of God upon the nation because of its sin. God assumes the direct responsibility: **For I set all men every one against his neighbor.** Solomon had earlier revealed that "When a man's ways please the LORD, he maketh even his enemies to be at peace with him" (Prov 16:7). What Israel learned through bitter experience is that the reverse is also true!

Now that the nation is in obedience to Jehovah and doing His bidding—rebuilding the Temple—**the LORD of hosts** promises, **But now I will not be unto the residue** (i.e., remnant) **of this people as in the former days.** Whereas in former days there was no economic prosperity or political and social security, things will be different. The nation will be prosperous, and both the nation and individuals that comprise it will dwell in safety and in perfect security.

12. The prosperity that the land will experience is spelled out in details that would be very meaningful to the people of the prophet's day. **The seed shall be prosperous** (i.e., there would be abundant crops); **the vine shall give her fruit** (i.e., the vineyards would be luxurious and productive); **the ground shall give her increase** (the soil would be abundantly fertile); and the **heavens shall give their dew** (there would be adequate irrigation). Jehovah assumes direct responsibility for bringing these blessings to pass: **I will cause the remnant of this people to possess all these things.** These things are the indication of the people's right relationship to God. It goes without saying that whenever these things are withheld, it is a call to repentance because of a wrong relationship to God (cf. Amos 4:6ff.).

13-15. The certainty of future blessing is guaranteed by past history, which, prior to its realization, was itself the subject of prophecy. **As ye were a curse among the heathen** (Heb *gōyim*, lit., Gentiles, nations, non-Jews)—the name of Israel was used by gentile nations to utter a curse—**As I thought to punish you, when your fathers provoked me to wrath . . . and I repented not**—a reference to the Babylonian captivity through which they had passed in fulfillment of the messages sent through the pre-exilic prophets—are fulfilled prophecies which are themselves guarantees of the fulfillment of present prophecy: **Ye shall be a blessing**—the nations will use the name of Israel to utter blessings—**So again have I thought in these days to do well unto Jerusalem and to the house of Judah.** The nation's past disobedience to God brought about God's judgment. Just as surely, the nation's present obedience will bring about God's future blessing. In light of this certainty twice the people of the prophet's day are told to **fear not . . . fear ye not** and are encouraged, **but let your hands be strong**, i.e., to see the task of rebuilding the Temple to its completion.

16-17. The future blessings promised are to affect the present conduct of the people. Jehovah spells out specifically, **These are the things that ye shall do.** Their outward righteousness that is to be manifested will spring from an inward righteousness before God. What they do will give irrefutable proof as to what they are. **Speak ye every man the truth to his neighbor**—truth is to characterize all of their dealings with their fellowmen.

---

10 For before these days there was no hire for man, nor any hire for beast; neither *was there any* peace to him that went out or came in because of the affliction: for I set all men every one against his neighbour.

11 But now I *will* not *be* unto the residue of this people as in the former days, saith the LORD of hosts.

12 For the seed *shall be* prosperous; the vine shall give her fruit, and the ground shall give her increase, and the heavens shall give their dew; and I will cause the remnant of this people to possess all these *things.*

13 And it shall come to pass, *that* as ye were a curse among the heathen, O house of Judah, and house of Israel; so will I save you, and ye shall be a blessing: fear not, *but* let your hands be strong.

14 For thus saith the LORD of hosts; As I thought to punish you, when your fathers provoked me to wrath, saith the LORD of hosts, and I repented not:

15 So again have I thought in these days to do well unto Jerusalem and to the house of Judah: fear ye not.

16 ¶These *are* the things that ye shall do; Speak ye every man the truth to his neighbour; execute the judgment of truth and peace in your gates:

17 And let none of you imagine evil in your hearts against his neighbour; and love no false oath: for all these *are things* that I hate, saith the LORD.

Execute the judgment of truth and peace in your gates—the administration of justice must be characterized by truth and must make for peace **in your gates** (the place where official business was conducted in the cities of the day). **Let none of you imagine evil in your hearts against his neighbor**—this is the root from which wrong overt actions would stem. Keep the heart right, and the deeds will be right. **Love no false oath**—this deals with one of the main problems of the day (cf. 5:3-4). They are not to do these things, **for all these are things that I hate, saith the LORD.** True love of God is shown in the manifestation of the virtues that God embodies. This is all a rehearsal and practical application of that which had been given much earlier in the levitical law (cf. Lev 11:44).

The significance of the third message is that God has not abrogated His covenant program for Israel. Under the Palestinian covenant God laid down the promise of cursing for disobedience. This has been fulfilled. Now God will fulfill the promises of blessing for obedience.

4. The fourth message: The fasts will become feasts. 8:18-23.

This section of the prophecy divides into two parts: (1) the coming of the message (vs. 18); and (2) the content of the message (vss. 19-23).

18. This message is denoted to be separate from the previous three by the introductory words, **And the word of the LORD of hosts came unto me, saying.** The First Person of the Trinity continues to speak through His prophet, Zechariah.

19-23. These four messages were occasioned by the asking of the question concerning the fast of the fifth month (cf. 7:2-3). Now **the LORD of hosts** (the First Person of the Trinity) answers the question specifically, and with greater detail than they had asked. They asked about the fast of the fifth month. Jehovah answers not only concerning the **fast of the fifth** month, but also concerning the **fast of the fourth month, . . . the fast of the seventh** month, **and the fast of the tenth** month. All of these fasts were self-imposed in Israel's self-pity. God commanded none of them and was not pleased by any of them. The fasts commemorated tragic events in Israel's history. The **fast of the fourth month** commemorated the day in which the Chaldeans penetrated into the city of Jerusalem (cf. II Kgs 25:3-4; Jer 39:2). **The fast of the fifth** month commemorated the burning of the Temple by Nebuzar-adan (cf. II Kgs 25:8-9). **The fast of the seventh** month commemorated the slaying of Gedaliah, the Jewish governor of Judea, and the flight of the remnant (cf. II Kgs 25:23-25; Jer 41:1-3). **The fast of the tenth** month commemorated Nebuchadnezzar's siege of Jerusalem (cf. II Kgs 25:1). These self-imposed fasts that are so burdensome and irksome **shall be to the house of Judah joy and gladness, and cheerful feasts**—they are to discontinue these empty expressions of false piety and to replace them with demonstrations of the true joy that springs from a right relationship to God. The people are commanded, **therefore love the truth and peace**—they are to embrace the truth that these fasts have been abrogated and to enjoy the peace that their removal will bring to the individual soul and nation. In spite of the clear command of Jehovah, since A.D. 70 the Jews have kept the principal fasts observed on the seventeenth day of the fourth month, the ninth day of the fifth month, the third day of seventh month, and the tenth day of the tenth month. Their observance of these fasts is clear testimony of their false piety and lack of a proper relationship with Jehovah.

The blessings of the immediate future cause the prophet to look beyond the immediate scene to the ultimate when **It shall yet come to pass,** i.e., in the Millennium, that the **people, and the inhabitants of many cities . . . shall go to another** (city), **saying, Let us go speedily to pray before the LORD, and to**

18 ¶And the word of the LORD of hosts came unto me, saying,

19 Thus saith the LORD of hosts; The fast of the fourth *month,* and the fast of the fifth, and the fast of the seventh, and the fast of the tenth, shall be to the house of Judah joy and gladness, and cheerful feasts; therefore love the truth and peace.

20 Thus saith the LORD of hosts; *It shall* yet *come to pass,* that there shall come people, and the inhabitants of many cities:

21 And the inhabitants of one *city* shall go to another, saying, Let us go speedily to pray before the LORD, and to seek the LORD of hosts: I will go also.

22 Yea, many people and strong nations shall come to seek the LORD of hosts in Jerusalem, and to pray before the LORD.

23 Thus saith the LORD of hosts; In those days *it shall come to pass,* that ten men shall take hold out of all languages of the nations, even shall take hold of the skirt of him that is a Jew, saying, We will go with you: for we have heard *that* God *is* with you.

seek the LORD of hosts. All persecution of Israel will cease. Instead of coming against Israel with destructive intent, **many people and strong nations shall come to seek the LORD of hosts in Jerusalem, and to pray before the LORD.** Israel's right relationship to God will be so attractive that the nations of the world will also seek to be rightly related to Israel's God. All of this is absolutely certain of fulfillment because it is the message of the LORD of hosts (The First Person of the Trinity). Once again, he affirms that **In those days** (i.e., the Millennium) **it shall come to pass, that ten** (the numeral is used representatively to indicate all the peoples of the earth) **men shall take hold out of all languages of the nations, even shall take hold of the skirt** (i.e., the hem of the garment—the action is indicative of their desire to accompany him) **of him that is a Jew** (i.e., a member of the covenant nation rightly related to God), **saying, We will go with you: for we have heard that God is with you.** It is clear that the attraction is not the Jew or his nation, but the covenant keeping God who has fulfilled His every promise to the nation and has brought it to its present state of blessing.

The significance of the fourth message, then, is that the people need not keep these irksome self-imposed fasts commemorating Jehovah's chastisement of His people. Rather, they should be replaced with feasts that will look forward to all that God is going to do for His people in the future. Ultimately, God will use Israel to be the channel through which He will bring all the peoples and nations of the world to Himself.

B. The Two Burdens. 9:1-14:21.

Liberal and destructive critics, noting the difference in style in chapters 9-14 from chapters 1-8, have unnecessarily attributed the authorship of this portion of the prophecy to a Deutero-Zechariah; but the difference in subject matter is adequate to account for the difference in style. Even conservative scholars have supposed that chapters 9-14 were written at a much later date than chapters 1-8. Such suppositions are not necessary; for it is equally possible, and more in keeping with the facts, to assume that chapters 9-14 compromise a part of the revelation given at the same time the four messages (just concluded) were given (cf. 7:1). There is no manuscript evidence to support any division of the book. Further, Zechariah is the Old Testament book most frequently quoted in the New Testament with never a hint that there was more than the Zechariah indicated in 1:1. To Zechariah was given in rough outline form God's plan for the times of the Gentiles from Israel's point of view (cf. the night vision of the four horns and the four smiths, 1:18-21). These chapters contain two burdens which develop the details of that vision relating Israel to those various world powers and setting forth in great detail the glorious future of the redeemed nation.

Developing the thought of Israel's relationship to the four gentile world powers, chapters 1-8 pertain to Israel as they were under the Medo-Persian Empire; chapters 9-10 pertain to Israel as they were under the Grecian World Empire; chapter 11 pertains to Israel under the Roman World Empire; and chapters 12-14 pertain to Israel after the times of the Gentiles has come to an end, a time when God will purify the nation and Messiah will visibly reign over it.

1. The first burden: Syria, Phoenicia, and Philistia are taken as representatives of all Israel's enemies. 9:1-11:17.

This section of the prophecy divides into two parts: (1) the introduction to the burden (9:1a); and (2) the content of the burden (9:1a-11:17).

9:1a. **The burden** (Heb *masa'*, i.e., a heavy, weighty thing) **of the word** (i.e., message) **of the LORD** lets us know that a

THE burden of the word of the LORD in the land of Hā′drăch, and Damascus *shall be* the rest thereof: when the eyes of man, as of all the tribes of Israel, *shall be* toward the LORD.

2 And Hā′măth also shall border thereby; Tўrus, and Zī′don, though it be very wise.

3 And Tўrus did build herself a strong hold, and heaped up silver as the dust, and fine gold as the mire of the streets.

4 Behold, the Lord will cast her out, and he will smite her power in the sea; and she shall be devoured with fire.

message concerning the wrath of God, grievous for the prophet to deliver, follows.

The content of the **burden** concerns four subjects: (1) the destruction of the surrounding nations (vss. 1b-8); (2) the coming of Messiah (vss. 9-10); (3) Messiah's blessings upon Israel (9:11-10:12); and (4) the rejection of the true Messiah and the rule of the false Messiah (11:1-17).

1b-2. The first subject of the first **burden** concerns God's judgment of the surrounding nations (9:1b-8), beginning **in the land of Hadrach and Damascus.** The exact meaning of the reference to **Hadrach** is not certain, but its mention with **Damascus** indicates that it is best understood to have been a city in the area of **Damascus. Hadrach** will experience the judgment of God; but the prime target is **Damascus,** the capital city of Syria, for **Damascus shall be the rest** (Heb *menuchah,* lit., place of rest) **thereof.** Prophetically, the prophet is describing the events realized when Alexander the Great conquered the area. The effect of his whirlwind conquests cause **the eyes of man, as of all the tribes of Israel** to be **toward the LORD** in great wonder and amazement. **Hamath,** bordering Syria about 120 miles north of **Damascus,** would share the fate of **Damascus,** as also would the Phoenician cities of **Tyrus** (Tyre) and **Zidon** (Sidon). The fact that **Tyrus** is mentioned first indicates that it has prominence over the older **Zidon.** The appellation, **though it be very wise,** refers primarily to **Tyrus** because it is mentioned first, though **Zidon** shares in it by virtue of a family relationship. The wisdom of Tyre was renowned and was itself the subject of Ezekiel's prophecy about 100 years earlier (cf. Ex 28:3-17).

3. The wisdom of **Tyrus** is demonstrated by what she did: **And Tyrus** (Heb *tsōr,* lit., rock) **did build herself a stronghold** (Heb *matsōr,* lit., bulwark). In the Hebrew text the words **Tyrus** and "Bulwark" occur together, thus constituting an interesting play on words, lit., the rock built herself a rock-like fort. Further, **Tyrus** converted all of its assets into the most durable form known to man; for it **heaped up silver as the dust, and fine gold as the mire of the streets.** Their wealth should have been sufficient to see them through any type of crisis. If necessary, they could buy their safety from any potential foe eager to lubricate its military force with money. Economically, they should be able to weather any depression (for their wealth was as plentiful **as the dust** and as common **as the mire of the streets**) or any inflationary spiral (because the value of their wealth would rise proportionately). They were the epitome of human wisdom, prepared for anything—except the judgment of God! God is not impressed with either human wisdom or wealth.

4. Behold, the Lord will cast her out, and he will smite her power in the sea; and she shall be devoured with fire. The ancient historians, Arrian and Diodorus Siculus, describe the impregnability of the fortress that Tyre built: "The walls, 150 feet high and of breadth proportionate, compacted of large stones, embedded in gypsum . . . in order to make the wall twice as strong they built a second wall ten cubits broad, leaving a space between of five cubits, which they filled with stones and earth." History attests to the city's impregnability, for the Assyrians laid siege to it for five years and failed. King Nebuchadnezzar of Babylon laid siege to it for thirteen years and failed. From a human point of view, Tyre was justified in her great pride and confidence. Yet, Tyre had not taken into account that **the Lord will cast her out;** and the human instrument He used was Alexander the Great who is reported to have said, "Ye despise this land-army, through confidence in the place, that ye dwell in an island but soon will I shew you that ye dwell on a continent." Alexander took all of the ruins from the old city on the mainland, cast them into the sea to build a causeway out to the island, laid siege to it for seven months, and was victorious over it. Diodorus Siculus records that he massacred 6000-8000 of her men, crucified 2000 of her men and sold from 13,000-30,000 into slavery. All of her weapons of warfare and the testimonies of her wisdom were cast into the sea, and in the final humiliation fire was set to the remains of the city. The words of God's prophets Ezekiel (some one hundred years earlier) and Zechariah were abundantly fulfilled in the greatest detail.

5 Ăsh′ke-lon shall see *it,* and fear; Gă′za also *shall see it,* and be very sorrowful, and Ekron; for her expectation shall be ashamed; and the king shall perish from Gă′za, and Ăsh′ke-lon shall not be inhabited.

6 And a bastard shall dwell in Ăsh′-dŏd, and I will cut off the pride of the Philistines.

5-6. Philistia, likewise, would experience the judgment of God at the hands of Alexander the Great. **Ashkelon shall see it** (the destruction of Tyre), **and fear**—if Tyre could not escape, neither could they. **Gaza also shall see it** (the destruction of Tyre), **and be very sorrowful** (knowing that her doom would soon follow). **Ekron** (the northernmost of the Philistine cities and closest geographically to Tyre); **for her expectation** (i.e., that Tyre would be successful in resisting and ultimately would defeat Alexander the Great) **shall be ashamed** (because Tyre, in whom she placed her trust, would be utterly destroyed and she was next in line for destruction). Previous world monarchs left local governments intact, extracting tribute from them. Alexander the Great, however, changed this policy; and in his attempt to blend East and West, he removed local kings, thus **the king shall perish from Gaza.** One source states that the king of Gaza was brought alive to Alexander who had him bound to a chariot and dragged through the city until he was dead. **Ashkelon shall not be inhabited**—it was depopulated—while **a bastard** (Heb *mamzēr,* lit., mixed, spurious—one born unlawfully, whether out of marriage, or in forbidden marriage, or in adultery) **shall dwell in Ashdod**—the city lost its native population, which was replaced with a mongrel people in keeping with Alexander's policy of the exchange of populations of his conquered cities. The cumulative effect of all of this is summed up in the words, **I will cut off the pride of the Philistines**—they would lose their national identity as the result of Alexander's policy of breaking down nationalities. Philistine pride could survive the loss of cities, wealth, and possessions, but not the loss of their nationality.

7 And I will take away his blood out of his mouth, and his abominations from between his teeth: but he that re-maineth, even he, *shall be* for our God, and he shall be as a governor in Judah, and Ekron as a Jĕb′-u-sīte.

7. Philistia will not pass out of existence; for a remnant of them will remain, and they will be restored and incorporated into Israel. This will be in the Millennium; and it depends solely upon the word of Jehovah who promises, **I will take away his blood out of his mouth.** The Philistines ate their sacrifices with blood, a practice forbidden by Jehovah. God says that this practice will cease among the Philistines also. Further, God promises to remove **his abominations from between his teeth.** The **abominations** were things sacrificed to idols. Their worship of idols will cease. **He that remaineth** (the remnant of the Philistines) . . . **shall be for our God** (they will experience a spiritual conversion to the worship of Jehovah), **and he shall be as a governor** (Heb *′alōp,* i.e., a chief, captain of a thousand) **in Judah**—he shall be intimately blended on an equal basis with the people of God. **And Ekron (shall be) as a Jebusite**—the ancient inhabitants of Jerusalem but were incorporated into Israel as equal citizens in the days of Joshua (cf. Josh 15:63).

8 And I will encamp about mine house because of the army, because of him that passeth by, and because of him that returneth: and no oppressor shall pass through them any more: for now have I seen with mine eyes.

8. Jehovah, however, will spare His people from the destruction all about them. He promises, **I will encamp about mine house** a reference to the people of Israel, rather than to the land or to the Temple. **Because of the army**—none of the destruction and judgment to be visited upon Syria, Phoenicia, and Philistia will come upon Israel because God will Himself protect His people from **the army** of Alexander the Great, whether on his way to Egypt (**because of him that passeth by**) or on his return (**and because of him that returneth**). The promise of protection is reaffirmed: **No oppressor shall pass through them any more.** The prophet looks down to the time of the ultimate deliverance of Israel when the city once again will be protected against its enemies. This thought will be developed more fully in chapters 12 and 14. The promise is reliable, and the safety sure;

9 ¶Rejoice greatly, O daughter of Zion; shout, O daughter of Jerusalem: behold, thy King cometh unto thee: he *is* just, and having salvation; lowly, and riding upon an ass, and upon a colt the foal of an ass.

10 And I will cut off the chariot from E'phra-im, and the horse from Jerusalem, and the battle bow shall be cut off: and he shall speak peace unto the heathen: and his dominion *shall be* from sea *even* to sea, and from the river *even* to the ends of the earth.

for now have I seen with mine eyes—God's people are ever under the surveillance of His watchful eye, and nothing escapes His notice.

9-10. The second subject of the first **burden** concerns the coming of Messiah (9:9-10). History affirms that Alexander the Great passed by Jerusalem more than once and never harmed it, though he did vent his wrath upon the Samaritans. Alexander the Great obviously cannot be the king for whom Israel looks. Thus, the prophet turns his attention to the King for whom Israel does look—Messiah—and views His coming, first in humiliation (vs. 9) and then in exaltation (vs. 10). The coming of Messiah will be a joyous time for Israel, hence the exhortation to **Rejoice greatly**. The whole nation is addressed under the representative names **daughter of Zion** and **daughter of Jerusalem**. In contrast to the nations who feared the coming of Alexander the Great (cf. vs. 5), the coming of the King of Israel is an occasion for great joy and rejoicing. The manner in which Messiah, the King of Israel, comes is set forth in stark contrast to Alexander the Great. He is qualified for his office as King because **he is just**—His intrinsic character is righteous. He is able to effect the deliverance of His people because He is one **having salvation**, i.e., entrusted with salvation—He is able to effect a righteous salvation for His people because He is a righteous King. In contrast to Alexander the Great who was proud and haughty in his manner, Israel's king is **lowly** (Heb *'ani*, lit., lowly, humble, meek). Instead of coming riding upon a war horse to break down, destroy, and conquer, Israel's King comes **riding upon an ass, and upon a colt the foal of an ass.** The **ass** (Heb *chamōr*, i.e., ass or a donkey) was an animal of peace. Kings of the earth come to bring destruction and devastation; Israel's King comes to bring peace. The gospel writers quote this verse, applying it to our Lord's earthly life, particularly to the so-called Triumphal Entry into Jerusalem (cf. Mt 21:5; Mk 11:9; Jn 12:15).

Between the coming of verse 9 and the coming of verse 10 lie the nearly two thousand years of the church, the age of grace, completely unforeseen by the prophet. In true prophetic fashion the prophet puts the two comings of Messiah together. It takes the New Testament's perspective to separate them. The coming of verse 10 takes place when Christ will return to the earth to set up His Kingdom. The mention of **Ephraim** together with **Jerusalem** lets us know that at that time the nation will be completely restored—the ten northern lost tribes will be reunited with the two southern tribes. At that time the **chariot . . . horse . . . and the battle bow** will be completely **cut off**—all the implements of warfare will be done away—and Messiah, the King, will **speak peace unto the heathen** (Heb *gōyim*, lit., Gentiles, nations, non-Jews). **Peace** will not be an option presented to the nations of the world; it will be arbitrarily and authoritatively imposed upon them. By His spoken word Messiah will be able to accomplish in fact what mankind, in all of his millennia of inhabiting the earth, has not been able to accomplish by any means. The extent of Messiah's kingdom and rule will be **from sea even to sea, and from the river even to the ends of the earth**—it will be universal, though its center will be in Jerusalem.

The third subject of the first **burden** concerns Messiah's blessings upon Israel (9:11-10:12). The blessings which Messiah will bring upon Israel are: (1) deliverance (9:11-16); (2) a bountiful land (9:17-10:1); (3) separation from idols (10:2-3); (4) a Deliverer (10:4-7); (5) restoration (10:8-11); and (6) redemption (10:12).

11 As for thee also, by the blood of thy covenant I have sent forth thy prisoners out of the pit wherein *is* no water.

12 Turn you to the strong hold, ye pris-

11-12. The nation Israel is addressed and promised **by the blood of thy covenant** (i.e., the Abrahamic covenant which was an unconditional covenant which was ratified by blood sacrifice, hence, the most binding of covenants—cf. Gen 15:9-18) that **thy**

oners of hope: even to day do I declare *that* I will render double unto thee;

13 When I have bent Judah for me, filled the bow with Ē′phra-im, and raised up thy sons, O Zion, against thy sons, O Greece, and made thee as the sword of a mighty man.

14 And the LORD shall be seen over them, and his arrow shall go forth as the lightning: and the Lord GOD shall blow the trumpet, and shall go with whirlwinds of the south.

15 The LORD of hosts shall defend them; and they shall devour, and subdue with sling stones; and they shall drink, *and* make a noise as through wine; and they shall be filled like bowls, *and* as the corners of the altar.

16 And the LORD their God shall save them in that day as the flock of his people: for *they shall be as* the stones of a crown, lifted up as an ensign upon his land.

prisoners (i.e., Israelites still remaining in Babylon) will be **sent forth . . . out of the pit wherein is no water.** Dry cisterns were frequently used as places to detain prisoners (cf. Joseph, Gen 37:21-24; and Jeremiah, Jer 38:6). It is a graphic picture of what God considers Babylon to be.

The exiles are viewed as **prisoners of hope,** looking forward to the time when they would be free of Persia's control. They are urged to return **to the stronghold** (Zion/Israel). God promises that **even today** (i.e., the day in which they return) **do I declare that I will render double unto thee.** The double portion was the inheritance of the first-born son. They can expect that God will abundantly fulfill His promise to them—He will deliver them from their exile in Babylon and then will deliver the nation out from under Persian control. In the place of their former distress, God promises to render abundant blessing. Amid all appearances to the contrary, God will perform His word **even today.**

13-16. These verses, in the near view, refer to the deliverance Israel experienced when Greece restored a little freedom to them and later in the second century B.C. when under the Maccabees they experienced deliverance from Antiochus Epiphanes. The conflict is set forth graphically. Judah is likened to God's bow (**When I have bent Judah for me**), and Ephraim is likened to the arrow placed in the bow (**filled the bow with Ephraim**). A bow is considered to be **filled** when the arrow is placed on the string ready for release. With the mention of both **Judah** and **Ephraim** we see that the entire nation, both northern and southern kingdoms, is involved. This unification is confirmed as the entire nation is addressed in the name of its religious capital, **and raised up thy sons, O Zion.** The **sons** of **Zion** would be raised up against the **sons** of **Greece.** Though writing some 60-70 years later, Zechariah's focus is exactly the same as Daniel's (cf. Dan 8:9-14; 11:30-31). The nation would be an effective fighting force because the Lord made them **as the sword of a mighty man**—invincible. Their deliverance will be accomplished because of divine intervention. **The LORD shall be seen over them, and his arrow** (Israel) **shall go forth as the lightning** (with great speed and invincibility): **And the Lord GOD shall blow the trumpet** (calling for battle) **and shall go with whirlwinds of the south.** God's servants in nature stand ever ready to accomplish His bidding. The **whirlwinds of the south** were the most violent and frequently achieved great destruction (cf. Isa 21:1).

The sons of Zion will be invincible because the **LORD of hosts** (the First Person of the Trinity) **shall defend them.** He will make them devastating; **and they shall devour, and subdue with sling stones,** or, better, they shall tread upon the stones of the sling. The thought is that as God's arrow they are invincible. The sling stones hurled against them miss their mark and fall harmlessly upon the ground, and they tread upon them as they advance. The meaning of **they shall drink, and make a noise as through wine** is difficult; but taken in context with the preceding figure, **they shall devour,** it is apparent that the prophet is conveying the thought that Israel will be utterly victorious and their enemies will pass out of existence and will never molest them again. They will be both destroyed (**devour**) and absorbed (**drink**) by Israel. The picture of utter annihilation of Israel's enemies is continued as the nation is likened to sacrificial bowls of the Temple (**they shall be filled like bowls**) in which the blood of the sacrifice was caught and sprinkled upon the altar (**as the corners of the altar**). They would be filled with the blood of their enemies as the horns of the altar and the sacrificial bowls were filled with the blood of the sacrifice. The priestly figure is fitting because the nation is performing its task as ministers of Jehovah, doing His bidding.

The deliverance will not be of their own doing, for **the LORD their God shall save them in that day.** He will deliver them because they are **the flock of his people.** Before their enemies, they were as sheep in the midst of wolves. If **the Lord their God** had not saved them and enabled them to accomplish His bidding, they would have perished. A glorious future lies ahead for a delivered people: **They shall be as the stones of a crown** (not like fallen sling stones that have missed their mark, cf. vs. 15), **lifted up as an ensign** (Heb *nasas,* lit., to lift self up, display self, hence a display) **upon his land.** God's enemies will be trodden under foot, but His people will be raised aloft as a display of His ability to care for and protect His people and to fulfill His every promise to them.

17. Having delivered His people from every enemy, God also blesses them with a bountiful land as an expression of **how great is his goodness, and how great is his beauty!** The result is that God will receive honor and glory. The deliverance will result in great prosperity. **Corn shall make the young men cheerful, and new wine the maids.** God will give a bountiful supply of corn, so that the young men may grow and be made strong. The luxuriant vineyards will produce wine, which will enable the young women to be exhilarated and beautified.

10:1. These blessings will come because the people look only to **the Lord** for the **rain in the time of the latter rain** (March or April), so that there might be a bountiful increase in the grain fields and vineyards. They are reminded that it is **the Lord** whom they are to **Ask,** and He will supply the rain in response to their believing prayers. **So the Lord shall make bright clouds, and give them showers of rain, to every one grass in the field.**

2-3. A third blessing Messiah will bring is complete deliverance from the idolatrous practices that had plagued them in the past and had caused them to experience punishment at the hand of God. In the past they turned to idols for blessing and forsook Jehovah, but **the idols have spoken vanity** (Heb *'awen,* i.e., iniquity, vanity—their assurances and comfort were empty and useless). **The diviners** (those to whom an appeal was made concerning the future) **have seen a lie, and have told false dreams; they comfort in vain.** The very ones with whom Israel entrusted their future deceived them, with the result that **they went their way as a flock**—en masse they were led astray by those who falsely claimed to have an authoritative word from God. Instead of peace and comfort, **they were troubled**—catastrophe after catastrophe, which they sought to avert by wrong means, overtook them. All of this stemmed from the fact that **there was no shepherd**—no true messenger of God who would proclaim to them the truth of Jehovah. The nation rejected the ministries of the pre-exilic prophets and turned instead to idols and diviners who deceived them.

God did not take this spiritual defection lightly. He reminds them, **Mine anger was kindled against the shepherds** (i.e., the false shepherds who, claiming to speak for Jehovah, actually deceived the people and joined them in their sins). **And I punished the goats** (Heb *'atūd,* he goat, chief—a reference to the civic and political leaders who, in their own self-interest, led the nation in its spiritual defection). The **Lord of hosts** (the First Person of the Trinity) became personally involved as He **visited** (in mercy) **his flock,** which is **the house of Judah.** He executed judgment upon the **shepherds** and the **goats** and wrested His **flock** from further deception. To set forth His personal concern and care for **the house of Judah,** the figure is changed. He **hath made them as his goodly horse in the battle.** Just as a warrior gives primary and personal care and attention to his horse, so Jehovah gives His primary and personal care and attention to **the house of Judah.**

4-7. The fourth blessing bestowed is the Deliverer at whose hand the deliverance will be realized and the blessing bestowed. The phrase **out of him** occurs four times in verse 4. The antecedent is best understood to be **the house of Judah** (vs. 3), for this

17 For how great *is* his goodness, and how great *is* his beauty! corn shall make the young men cheerful, and new wine the maids.

CHAPTER 10

ASK ye of the Lord rain in the time of the latter rain; *so* the Lord shall make bright clouds, and give them showers of rain, to every one grass in the field.

2 For the idols have spoken vanity, and the diviners have seen a lie, and have told false dreams; they comfort in vain: therefore they went their way as a flock, they were troubled, because *there was* no shepherd.

3 Mine anger was kindled against the shepherds, and I punished the goats: for the Lord of hosts hath visited his flock the house of Judah, and hath made them as his goodly horse in the battle.

4 Out of him came forth the corner, out of him the nail, out of him the battle bow, out of him every oppressor together.

5 And they shall be as mighty *men,* which tread down *their enemies* in the mire of the streets in the battle: and they shall fight, because the LORD *is* with them, and the riders on horses shall be confounded.

6 And I will strengthen the house of Judah, and I will save the house of Joseph, and I will bring them again to place them; for I have mercy upon them: and they shall be as though I had not cast them off: for I *am* the LORD their God, and will hear them.

7 And *they of* Ē′phra-im shall be like a mighty *man,* and their heart shall rejoice as through wine: yea, their children shall see *it,* and be glad; their heart shall rejoice in the LORD.

8 I will hiss for them, and gather them; for I have redeemed them: and they shall increase as they have increased.

9 And I will sow them among the people: and they shall remember me in far countries; and they shall live with their children, and turn again.

10 I will bring them again also out of the land of Egypt, and gather them out of Assyria; and I will bring them into the land of Gilead and Lebanon; and *place* shall not be found for them.

11 And he shall pass through the sea with affliction, and shall smite the

is the source from which Messiah will come. The verb **came forth** is actually future—the passage is prophetic, not historical. Various facets of Messiah's person are set forth by the different figures used to portray Him—**corner** (Heb *pinah,* corner, front, a chief man—portrays Messiah's prominence and stability; all the government will rest upon him), **nail** (Heb *yatēd,* lit., pin, nail—reference to the large peg in tents upon which the valuables were hung; all of Israel's value will depend upon Him), and **battle bow** (Heb *qeshet,* i.e., bow—portrays His strength and reliability for defense; all of Israel's military prowess will reside in and be dependent upon Him). **Every oppressor** (Heb *nagas,* lit., to exact) **together** is not another title for Messiah, but rather indicates the outcome as the result of the previous three descriptions of Him—Messiah is the **corner,** the **nail,** and the **battle bow;** hence, everyone who would oppress or exact tribute from Israel will be removed completely.

Messiah, who is the **battle bow,** will make Israel to **be as mighty men** who will be invincible; and they will **tread down their enemies in the mire of the streets in the battle: and they shall fight, because the LORD is with them, and the riders on horses** (the cavalry, the first line of defense of Oriental armies) **shall be confounded. Because the LORD is with them,** they will be such **mighty men** that they will be more than equal to cavalrymen.

They must never think that the strength is their own; so Jehovah reminds them, **I will strengthen the house of Judah, and I will save the house of Joseph.** The mention of **Joseph** lets us know two things: (1) the northern kingdom will participate in the restoration; and (2) the restoration in view is not the restoration of the prophet's day. It looks beyond that restoration to a restoration that is still future. **Joseph** will be saved and restored by the sovereign working of God who says, **I will bring them again to place them** (they will be restored and planted in their land never to be removed again); **for I have mercy upon them: and they shall be as though I had not cast them off.** In His grace God not only will restore **Joseph,** but will abundantly bless them; it will be as though He had never visited judgment upon them. Only the grace of God could accomplish such a restoration. They will be purged of their idolatry; and Jehovah is pleased to say, **I am the LORD their God, and will hear them**—communion between them and God will be unimpeded.

The complete reunion of the nation is reemphasized by the address of **Ephraim,** the most influential tribe of the northern kingdom. **Ephraim** will share in the blessing of **the house of Judah** (cf. vs. 5), for he **shall be like a mighty man, and their heart shall rejoice as through wine.** Though their exile had been 130 years longer (actually millennia longer in view of the fact that the millennial restoration is in view) than Judah's, they will experience a victory similar to Judah's and will **rejoice as through wine,** though their joy will be genuine stemming from their right relationship to God. Their joy will be contagious, for **their children shall see it, and be glad;** and like their parents, **their heart shall rejoice in the LORD.**

8-11. The prophet turns now to develop the fifth blessing that Messiah will bring—restoration. The Lord will **hiss** (Heb *sharaq,* lit., to hiss, call) **for them, and gather them.** The return, then, is at the Lord's initiative, though they return at their own volition totally unmindful of the circumstances with which Jehovah is surrounding them, thus compelling them to return. The return is a return in belief, made possible because **I have redeemed them.** This will be the realization of the national regeneration promised in the New Covenant (cf. Jer 31:31-34). The number will be few, relatively speaking, for many of them will have perished in the judgments of the Great Tribulation, **they shall increase as they have increased.** The redeemed citizens who populate the earthly, Davidic, millennial kingdom will be

waves in the sea, and all the deeps of the river shall dry up: and the pride of Assyria shall be brought down, and the sceptre of Egypt shall depart away.

prolific. Thus, in this verse three concepts are promised: (1) restoration; (2) regeneration; and (3) repopulation.

That the prophet has more in view than the restoration of the nation following the Assyrian and Babylonian captivities is made known by what Jehovah will do with the nation. He reveals: **I will sow them among the people: and they shall remember me in far countries.** God's plan to **sow** (Heb *zara'*, lit., to sow) indicates that He will spread or multiply the influence of the nation. The figure is always used in a good sense throughout the Old Testament. The effect of the sowing is that **they shall remember me in far countries**—they will be used by God to bring Gentiles to a right relationship with Him. **They shall live with their children, and turn again**—both spiritually and politically the nation will live in conscious fellowship with God, and this right relationship with God will be shared with their **children** who will turn wholeheartedly to the Lord.

Just as in 8:7 the sphere of the earth was divided into two halves, east and west, from which God would universally regather His dispersed people, so in verse 10 **Egypt** and **Assyria** are used representatively of north and south, from which universally God will regather his dispersed people and will **bring them into the land of Gilead and Lebanon**—the areas which together formed their original territory on both sides of the Jordan River. So great will be the number of those whom the Lord regathers (cf. vs. 8) that **place shall not be found for them**—every available place in the entire land will be taken up with people that the Lord has regathered. The dimensions of this regathering dwarf any previous regathering of Israel, whether in the days of Zechariah or in modern days, and lets us know that the Israel of today cannot be the Israel of the Millennium. The Israel of today is the Israel of the Tribulation, marked for scattering and destruction. It, however, will be the forerunner of the Israel of the Millennium, which God will bring into existence and to whom He will fulfill every promise made to Abraham and to the nation.

In accomplishing His regathering, God will work in Israel's behalf in ways like He did in days of old. The Exodus from Egypt is illustrative: **He** (Israel) **shall pass through the sea with affliction, and shall smite the waves in the sea.** The crossing of the Jordan River at flood stage is also representative: **And all the deeps of the river shall dry up.** All of Israel's enemies, summarily represented by **Assyria** and **Egypt**, will be utterly defeated: **The pride of Assyria shall be brought down, and the scepter of Egypt shall depart away.** In conjunction with **Egypt**, in the light of modern days and the role it has played in world diplomacy, particularly in its dealings with Israel, it is interesting that **the scepter**, its government, will be entirely lost.

12 And I will strengthen them in the LORD; and they shall walk up and down in his name, saith the LORD.

12. The sixth and final blessing to be brought by Messiah (and really epitomizing all the others) is national redemption. This will be the realization of the New Covenant (cf. Jer 31:31-34) and will be accomplished because Jehovah promises: **I will strengthen them in the LORD.** The "I" is **the LORD of hosts** (vs. 3), the First Person of the Trinity, who has been speaking throughout the burden. He is the One who will do the regathering and the redeeming and will **strengthen them** (Israel) **in the LORD** (Messiah, the Second Person of the Trinity). The strength of Israel and the feature that is attractive about her is her Messiah—Jesus (cf. 8:20-23). The outgrowth of this is that **they** (Israel) **shall walk up and down** (i.e., conduct the whole of their life) **in his name** (i.e., the Name of Messiah, Jesus). This will take place because thus **saith the LORD**—it is the Word of God, the First Person of the Trinity, Himself. In this verse the name **LORD** occurs twice. In its first occurrence it is a reference to the First Person of the Trinity, and in the second occurrence it is a reference to the Second Person of the Trinity. A similar phenomenon is observed in Psalm 110:1 (cf. our Lord's usage of this quote in Mt 22:41-46; Mk 12:35-37; Lk 20:41-44).

CHAPTER 11

OPEN thy doors, O Lebanon, that the fire may devour thy cedars.

2 Howl, fir tree; for the cedar is fallen; because the mighty are spoiled: howl, O ye oaks of Bā'shan; for the forest of the vintage is come down.

3 ¶*There is* a voice of the howling of the shepherds; for their glory is spoiled: a voice of the roaring of young lions; for the pride of Jordan is spoiled.

4 Thus saith the LORD my God; Feed the flock of the slaughter;

5 Whose possessors slay them, and hold themselves not guilty: and they

11:1-3. The fourth subject of the first **burden** (9:1) concerns the rejection of the true Messiah and the rule of the false Messiah (cf. Dan 11; Rev 13). It contains the prophecy of what is probably the darkest chapter of Israel's history. The section divides as follows: (1) the desolation of the land (vss. 1-3); (2) the details of Messiah's rejection (11:4-14); and (3) the display and destruction of the desolator (11:15-17).

Verses 1-3 describe the desolation to be visited upon the land. There are four views as to when the desolation of the land in view in these verses takes place: (1) the destruction of the land under the Babylonians in 586 B.C.—this would necessitate the prophet's writing history, rather than giving a prophecy, and hence is to be rejected; (2) the desolation of the land by the Romans under Titus in A.D. 70; (3) the desolation of the land in the distant future (i.e., the Great Tribulation); and (4) the desolation of the land by the Romans under Titus in A.D. 70, but ultimately fulfilled in the desolation of the land in the Great Tribulation. Views two or three are both possible, but the last view best fits the nature of predictive prophecy throughout the prophets.

Open thy doors, O Lebanon has been understood by some to be a figurative reference to the Temple (because of the mention of **doors**) whose timber was furnished from the forest of Lebanon. Others understand it as a reference to the nation, with the mention of the **fir tree . . . cedar . . .** and **oaks** as being reference to the leaders of the nation or to nations that ravaged Israel. It seems better to view the address as being literally addressed to **Lebanon** which lying to the north of the land, functioned as a door through which the marauding invader would come. The prophet is predicting that the great forests of **Lebanon** will be destroyed by **fire;** for the mountain is addressed, **Open thy doors, O Lebanon, that the fire may devour thy cedars.** The **cedars,** then, are literal trees being destroyed by a literal fire set by an invading enemy intent upon the destruction of Israel.

If the enemy would destroy the cedars of Lebanon, he will follow the scorched earth policy throughout the land; hence, the other trees will experience a similar fate. Thus the address, **Howl, fir tree; for the cedar is fallen; because the mighty are spoiled: howl, O ye oaks of Bashan; for the forest of the vintage is come down.** Not only will the forests suffer, but also the pastureland will fall victim to the invader's scorched earth policy. As a result, **There is a voice of the howling of the shepherds; for their glory is spoiled.** Even the thickets along the banks of the Jordan River would not be spared; thus, there is **a voice of the roaring of young lions; for the pride of Jordan is spoiled.** The picture is one of total destruction and devastation. The mention of **Lebanon, Bashan,** and the **Jordan** indicates that the devastation will be complete throughout the length and breadth of the land; and no one or nothing would escape the judgment visited upon the land by God.

Verses 4-14 give the details of Messiah's rejection, which is the occasion for which such desolation is visited upon the land.

4. The commission comes from **the LORD my God,** the First Person of the Trinity. It is addressed to the prophet who representatively performs in the vision the actions actually performed in history by the Messiah, the Second Person of the Trinity. Thus, the Father is commissioning the Son to **Feed the flock of the slaughter.** He was to be a shepherd and **feed the flock** (Israel) whose destiny was **slaughter** at the hands of the Romans because of their sin of rejection of their Messiah. Josephus records that approximately one and a half million Jews died at the hands of Rome.

5. The treatment that Israel will experience at the hands of Rome is set forth in the figure of the treatment commonly

that sell them say, Blessed be the LORD; for I am rich: and their own shepherds pity them not.

6 For I will no more pity the inhabitants of the land, saith the LORD: but, lo, I will deliver the men every one into his neighbour's hand, and into the hand of his king: and they shall smite the land, and out of their hand I will not deliver them.

7 And I will feed the flock of slaughter, even you, O poor of the flock. And I took unto me two staves; the one I called Beauty, and the other I called Bands; and I fed the flock.

8 Three shepherds also I cut off in one month; and my soul lothed them, and their soul also abhorred me.

received by sheep: **Whose possessors slay them, and hold themselves not guilty.** The owners of sheep are not guilty of murder when they slay their sheep, because God has given them to be for food for man. This is how Rome views itself—not guilty for slaying the Jews, for God has given them into their hands. This thought is amplified in the words that follow: **And they that sell them say, Blessed be the LORD; for I am rich.** The Romans hypocritically would credit God for the gain they would realize in their abuse of Israel. As bad as the treatment Israel would receive from the Gentiles might be, it is not to be matched by the treachery of its own leaders **Their own shepherds pity them not.** The reference is to the Sanhedrin, the Pharisees, Sadduccees, Herodians and other leaders who sought their own ends and not the good of the nation (cf. Mt 12).

6. More tragic still is the fact that God says **I will no more pity the inhabitants of the land,** i.e., the inhabitants of the land of Israel. No longer will God pity them. Instead, He **will deliver the men every one into his neighbor's hand**—there will be internal strife because they have rejected Messiah, their rightful King. Further, God will deliver them **into the hand of his king,** a reference to Caesar, whom by their payment of tribute they recognized to be their king (cf. Jn 19:15). When the Romans come, **they shall smite the land** (graphically portrayed in vss. 1-3!), **and out of their hand I will not deliver them.** So devastating will be the effects of the coming judgment be that it is figured by a **fire** (vss. 1-3), a **slaughter** (vs. 4), and a plague (**smite the land,** vs. 6). The judgment of God will be complete, embracing the entire land (vss. 1-3); and it will be inescapable (vs. 6).

7. Even though **the flock** (Israel) is destined for **slaughter,** Messiah obeys the commission of Jehovah and determines, **I will feed the flock of slaughter.** In that He **will feed** them, He will do everything necessary for their health, protection, and well-being, even though from man's viewpoint His mission is destined for failure. The Son's program is important only insofar as it is the realization of the Father's! The outcome is up to the Father—the Son's lot is to obey (cf. Heb 10:5-7). The compassion with which the Messiah will go about His task is envisioned: **Even you, O poor of the flock.** He ministered to all of the flock because the Father had a future for the flock, and He had a remnant in the flock that He would call to Himself through the ministry of Messiah.

In the vision the prophet sees himself doing the things that are representative of Messiah. **And I took unto me two staves**—indicative of the office of a shepherd. The Oriental shepherd took two staves, one to protect the sheep from wild beasts and the other to assist the sheep in difficult and dangerous places. **The one I called Beauty** (Heb nō'am, lit., pleasantness, beauty, favor, graciousness), **and the other I called Bands** (Heb chabal, lit., bonds, binders)—the names given to the staves are indicative of Messiah's mission to His people. With the two staves Messiah will guide and protect the nation. The staff, called **Beauty** (or favor, or graciousness), is indicative of Messiah's attractiveness and graciousness in ministering to them. His attractiveness would draw the nation to Himself, and His graciousness would keep them safe for Himself. The staff, called **Bands** (or bonds or binders), is indicative of Messiah's ministry of binding the nation together and to Himself. In drawing the nation to Himself, protecting them, and binding them to Himself and to each other, the Messiah did the work set before Him by the Father: **I fed the flock**—He fed the entire flock so that as the result of His ministry, the remnant could be separated from the rest of the flock.

8. More than forty interpretations, covering a wide range of views, are extant as to the meaning of this verse! The possibilities concerning the identity of the **three shepherds** are appropriately limited when it is observed that they are closely related to the Messiah and are undershepherds under Him. Rather than seeing any particular Old Testament characters or gentile world powers represented by the **three shepherds,** it is probably best to understand them as being three classes of leaders given to administer the eternal theocratic kingdom for Israel—prophet, priest, and king (in the sense of rulers or civil leaders, cf. Jer 2:8; Mt 26:3). The coming of Messiah **cut off** (curtailed) the need for their services **in one month** (i.e., a very short time) because **my** (i.e., Messiah's) soul loathed them, and their soul also abhorred me (i.e., Messiah). Instead of being glad to see Messiah come and cheerfully handing over the reigns of government to Him, they sought to betray and kill Him (cf. Mt 26:3-4).

9 Then said I, I will not feed you: that that dieth, let it die; and that that is to be cut off, let it be cut off; and let the rest eat every one the flesh of another.

9. This verse contains the expression of judgment as it is uttered by Messiah (**Then said I**) again the **three shepherds** (vs. 8) and the major portion of the nation that chose to follow them (i.e., those who are not the true spiritual remnant of Israel). It is a judgmental giving over of the nation to let the effects of their rejection of Messiah be worked out in history (much like the judgmental giving over in Rom 1:24, 26, 28). **I will not feed you: that that dieth, let it die; and that that is to be cut off, let it be cut off; and let the rest eat every one the flesh of another.** Three forms of judgment are indicated: (1) famine (**I will not feed you**); (2) warfare and bloodshed (**cut off**); and (3) internal strife (**let the rest eat every one the flesh of another**). The end result is the destruction of everyone in the nation who did not receive the Messiah.

10 ¶And I took my staff, *even* Beauty, and cut it asunder, that I might break my covenant which I had made with all the people.

10. To draw attention to the dramatic change of events and to symbolize the fact that certain relationships are severed, Messiah says, **I took my staff, even Beauty, and cut it asunder, that I might break my covenant which I had made with all the people.** The **covenant** which is broken is not the Abrahamic covenant or any of Israel's unconditional covenants, but rather an indirect covenant with the nations of the earth that exists because of God's direct, unconditional covenants with Israel. The breaking of the **staff, even Beauty** indicates that in keeping Israel secure from every potential foe the grace of God will be suspended; and the nations will be permitted to come into the land to devastate and conquer Israel. During the time that Israel was in fellowship with Him, God restrained **all the people** so that none could do violence to Israel. The breaking of **Beauty** suspends that restraint, and now **all the people** may do whatever they will to Israel.

11 And it was broken in that day: and so the poor of the flock that waited upon me knew that it *was* the word of the LORD.

11. The prophet anticipates the fulfillment of the **staff, Beauty,** and writes as though it were already an accomplished fact: **And it was broken in that day,** i.e., the day in which God's long-suffering with His people should cease and His protective restraint in their behalf should be lifted. It actually occurred in the days following our Lord's earthly ministry when the Romans devastated the land (A.D. 70), and it will once again occur during the days of the Great Tribulation. As always, **the poor of the flock** (not poor economically, but humble spiritually—it is a designation for the ". . . remnant according to the election of grace" cf. Rom 11:5) **knew that it was the word of the LORD.** Those in right relationship with God always accept the Word of the Lord, regardless of its content. Their right relationship to God is indicated by their reception of His Word. This principle is ever true.

12 And I said unto them, If ye think good, give *me* my price; and if not, forbear. So they weighed for my price thirty *pieces* of silver.

12. **And I said unto them** (the unbelieving nation, not the **poor of the flock,** vs. 11)—the Messiah is speaking to the unregenerate nation in order to bring to their attention graphically the depths to which they have sunk in their rejection of Him. He asks them to evaluate Him and His ministry: **If ye think good, give me my price; and if not, forbear.** The asking for hire is indicative that the ministry is coming to an end. What

He wanted was their love, obedience, and devotion—in short, themselves. They, however, indicated their evaluation of His Person and Work; **So they weighed for my price thirty pieces of silver. Thirty pieces of silver,** according to Exodus 21:32, was the price to be paid to the master whose slave had been gored by an ox! A sound slave was considered to be worth twice that amount! This is the ultimate insult—Messiah, God's Son, worth only the price of an incapacitated, gored slave!

13 And the LORD said unto me, Cast it unto the potter: a goodly price that I was prised at of them. And I took the thirty *pieces* of silver, and cast them to the potter in the house of the LORD.

13. God's response is indicated by His instructions to the prophet: **Cast it unto the potter: a goodly price that I was prized at of them.** The **goodly price** is sharp sarcasm—the indignity of it all! The **potter** dealt with things made of earth, hence of little value. To **cast** something **unto the potter** is idiomatic for throwing away something of little value to one who deals in things that are of insignificant value.

The prophet obeys the instructions: **And I took the thirty pieces of silver, and cast them to the potter in the house of the LORD.** The whole thing is solemnized and made a matter of public record because it was carried out **in the house of the LORD.**

14 Then I cut asunder mine other staff, *even* Bands, that I might break the brotherhood between Judah and Israel.

14. The prophet executes the final action that will bring about the dissolution of the nation. **Then I cut asunder mine other staff, even Bands, that I might break the brotherhood between Judah and Israel.** With internal strife and division tearing the nation apart, it would be easy prey to any conqueror. This was realized in the Roman conquest in A.D. 70, and it will be realized again during the Great Tribulation when once again Israel will be subjugated by the King of the West!

15 ¶And the LORD said unto me, Take unto thee yet the instruments of a foolish shepherd.

16 For, lo, I will raise up a shepherd in the land, *which* shall not visit those that be cut off, neither shall seek the young one, nor heal that that is broken, nor feed that that standeth still: but he shall eat the flesh of the fat, and tear their claws in pieces.

17 Woe to the idol shepherd that leaveth the flock! the sword *shall be* upon his arm, and upon his right eye: his arm shall be clean dried up, and his right eye shall be utterly darkened.

15-17. These verses describe the display and destruction of the desolator. Having rejected the Messiah, who is the Good Shepherd, the nation is destined to be ruled by another shepherd, **a foolish shepherd.** While undoubtedly this **foolish shepherd** has been adumbrated by all the ungodly gentile rulers in Israel's history, the one in view in these verses is Satan's Messiah, the Antichrist who will rule the nation during the Great Tribulation. He is the subject of much prophetical Scripture (cf. Dan 7:20ff; 8:23ff; 11:36ff; Mt 24:15ff; II Thess 2; Rev 13:11ff). The **instruments** that the prophet is commanded to **Take** are those pertaining to a shepherd (cf. vs. 7)—they are the **instruments** by which the foolish shepherd will accomplish his evil against the nation.

Though the **shepherd** is evil, he is not beyond God's control; for He reveals to the prophet, **I will raise up a shepherd in the land, which shall not visit those that be cut off, neither shall seek the young one, nor heal that that is broken, nor feed that that standeth still.** The shepherd will be wicked and will care nothing for the flock—he will abuse, mistreat, and neglect it. He will be intent on his own interests and purposes. **He shall eat the flesh of the fat, and tear their claws in pieces.** Instead of feeding the flock, he will fleece and flay it mercilessly.

Though the **shepherd** is brought onto the scene by God and is given full sway over God's people, his mistreatment of God's people does not escape God's notice; and God's judgment will overtake him. First, an indictment is pronounced: **Woe to the idol shepherd that leaveth the flock!** The purpose of a shepherd is to care for the flock. This shepherd cares nothing for the flock and, hence, is fit only for judgment, which follows. **The sword shall be upon his arm, and upon his right eye.** The **arm** is the symbol of strength, and the **right eye** is the symbol for intelligence. Since he failed to use both in caring for the flock, they will be done away in swift judgment (i.e., **the sword**). **His arm shall be clean dried up**—failure to use it in behalf of God's people causes it to be withered in judgment. **His right eye shall be utterly darkened**—failure to use it in behalf of God's people causes it to be completely lost.

In summary, the land will be utterly desolate (vss. 1-3) because of the nation's rejection of its Messiah (vss. 4-14). In place of the true Messiah, God will raise up a false Messiah who will devastate the nation; but he, in turn, will be judged of God (vss. 15-17). Following this, Messiah will return, regather the nation, redeem it, and reign over it. Just how this will be accomplished is the subject of the second burden, which brings the prophecy to its conclusion.

2. *The second burden: God's people will be conquerors because they will experience cleansing. 12:1-14:21.*

The second burden divides into two parts: (1) the introduction to the burden (vs. 1); and (2) the content of the burden (12:2-14:21).

12:1. The final message of the prophecy is a **burden** (Heb *masa'*, lit., a heavy, weighty thing) grievous for the prophet to deliver, for it deals once again with the wrath of God. It is, however, **the word of the LORD**; hence, it is not of the prophet's invention. It is completely authentic and reliable because it comes from Jehovah. The message is grievous for the prophet to deliver because of the suffering it entails **for Israel** because of her sins. The **burden** is not only the **word** (Heb *dabar*, i.e., word, matter, thing) belonging to and issuing from **the LORD**; it is also stated directly by Him to the prophet as is indicated by the addition of **saith the LORD.** Because of the grievous nature of the content of the burden, one must be reminded of the intrinsic character of the **LORD** from whom the message comes. He is described as being **the LORD, which stretcheth forth the heavens, and layeth the foundation of the earth, and formeth the spirit of man within him. The LORD** is not only a sufficient cause to bring the heavens, earth, and man into existence, He is capable of sustaining His creation and maintaining His control of every aspect of it. In short, He is absolutely sovereign and fully capable of bringing about whatever He purposes. This is important to keep in mind as the details of the **burden** unfold. Though it will involve great suffering for Israel, it will issue in their ultimate good and eternal blessing.

The content of the **burden** is as follows: (1) the coming siege and deliverance of Jerusalem and Judah (vss. 2-9); (2) the spiritual restoration of Israel—their recognition and reception of Messiah (12:10-13:1); (3) the removal of idolatry and false religions from Israel (13:2-6); (4) the restoration of the remnant to Israel (13:7-9); (5) the return of the Lord to the earth to set up His kingdom (14:1-8); (6) the millennial reign of the Lord (14:9-11); (7) the plague on all of Judah's enemies (14:12-15); and (8) the millennial conduct (14:16-21).

The coming siege and deliverance of Jerusalem and Judah are described in verses 2-9.

2. Behold, I will make Jerusalem a cup of trembling (Heb *ra'al*, lit., a reeling). This is a work that Jehovah will do for Israel. The capital, **Jerusalem,** will be made a **cup** (a symbol of the wrath of God, cf. Isa 51:17, 22; Jer 13:13; 25:15-17, 27-28; 51:7) **of trembling** (lit., reeling) **unto all the people round about.** When the confederacy of nations comes against Jerusalem, they will find it ultimately unconquerable because of divine intervention (the details of which are spelled out later). This will be realized **when they shall be in the siege both against Judah and against Jerusalem.** The efforts of the invaders will meet with partial success. They will be able to conquer the northern part of the land and a good portion of the south, but **Jerusalem** and the environs of **Judah** will ultimately be an insurmountable obstacle because of God's intervention.

3. The expression **in that day** occurs sixteen times in the remainder of this prophecy. This lets us know that though some things similar to the things contained in this section may have occurred in Israel's past, nothing has completely fulfilled them. They deal with the ultimate consummation of Israel's history

---

CHAPTER 12

THE burden of the word of the LORD for Israel, saith the LORD, which stretcheth forth the heavens, and layeth the foundation of the earth, and formeth the spirit of man within him.

2 Behold, I will make Jerusalem a cup of trembling unto all the people round about, when they shall be in the siege both against Judah *and* against Jerusalem.

3 And in that day will I make Jerusalem a burdensome stone for all people: all that burden themselves with it shall be cut in pieces, though all the

people of the earth be gathered together against it.

and are, therefore, most important. The expression **the day of the LORD** occurs seventeen times; Jerusalem is referred to twenty-two times; and gentile nations are referred to thirteen times. Putting these facts together gives the clue to the importance of these chapters, for they portray the relationship of gentile nations to Jerusalem in the Day of the Lord. They refer primarily to the gentile invasion of Palestine and the Battle of Armageddon in the last three and one-half years of the Great Tribulation. When the great gentile invasion takes place, Jehovah will . . . **make Jerusalem a burdensome stone for all people.** Some have thought that underlying the prophet's thought is a reference to some athletic contest used to test the strength of young men. The figure of verse 2 (**cup**) indicates that that which the gentile nations experience is an outpouring of the wrath of God. The figure is changed to **a burdensome stone** in verse 3 to portray the effect of their experience. **All that burden themselves with it** (i.e., the **burdensome stone**, Jerusalem) **shall be cut in pieces.** Jehovah promises that in the final consummative struggle when the Gentile confederacy seeks to take Jerusalem (and will meet with seeming success, cf. 14:2), they will meet with a fate similar to that suffered by Sennacherib when he laid siege to Jerusalem in 701 B.C. Those who would crush God's holy city will be crushed by it instead. One sure way to seal their doom is to **burden themselves** with the intent to destroy Israel. The confederacy of the last day will be extensive, involving **all the people of the earth**; but it will be as nothing and will be totally ineffective against the divine intervention of Jehovah on behalf of His people and His city.

4 In that day, saith the LORD, I will smite every horse with astonishment, and his rider with madness: and I will open mine eyes upon the house of Judah, and will smite every horse of the people with blindness.

4. This verse gives some details about the way God will intervene for His people. The most sophisticated weapon of war in the prophet's day was the cavalry; but it will be totally ineffective against God's people, for the **LORD . . . will smite every horse with astonishment** (Heb *timahōn*, i.e., wonder, astonishment)—the horses will be totally ineffective and uncontrollable. Further, the **rider** will be smitten **with madness** (Heb *shiga'ōn*, lit., madness, erring)—the cavalrymen will be smitten with insanity and will make many errors of judgment. They will be totally ineffective as warriors; and this will happen because God says, **I will open mine eyes upon the house of Judah**—He will look with favor upon His people and will help them in the hour of their extreme need. The horses will be the more uncontrollable because God **will smite every horse of the people with blindness** and will carry their insane riders to their doom. The most effective weapon man can muster will be overpowered and rendered totally ineffective by God's intervention.

5 And the governors of Judah shall say in their heart, The inhabitants of Jerusalem *shall be* my strength in the LORD of hosts their God.

5. In addition, God will deliver His people by strengthening them and making them able to fight as never before in their history. **The governors of Judah** will realize (**say in their heart**) that **The inhabitants of Jerusalem** are effective in their efforts in support of their leaders because of the **strength in the LORD of hosts their God.** God has not only worked to rout the enemy; He has also worked to sustain and support His people.

6 In that day will I make the governors of Judah like an hearth of fire among the wood, and like a torch of fire in a sheaf; and they shall devour all the people round about, on the right hand and on the left: and Jerusalem shall be inhabited again in her own place, *even* in Jerusalem.

6. Just how effective they will be in the final conflagration is now portrayed: **In that day will I make the governors** (Heb *'alūp*, lit., a leader) **of Judah like a hearth of fire among the wood, and like a torch of fire in a sheaf.** They will be as invincible to the invaders as **fire** is invincible to **wood** and a **sheaf** of grain. **They shall devour all the people round about, on the right hand and on the left.** They will be completely victorious over the enemy on every side of them. The result is that **Jerusalem shall be inhabited again in her own place, even in Jerusalem**—the citizens, having been driven out by the invader (cf. Mt 24:15-22), will be able to return to Jerusalem and dwell in complete safety.

7 The LORD also shall save the tents of Judah first, that the glory of the house

7. The deliverance will be supernatural, for **The LORD also shall save the tents of Judah first.** Their helplessness and

of David and the glory of the inhabitants of Jerusalem do not magnify *themselves* against Judah.

8 In that day shall the LORD defend the inhabitants of Jerusalem; and he that is feeble among them at that day shall be as David; and the house of David *shall be* as God, as the angel of the LORD before them.

9 And it shall come to pass in that day, *that* I will seek to destroy all the nations that come against Jerusalem.

10 And I will pour upon the house of David, and upon the inhabitants of Jerusalem, the spirit of grace and of supplications: and they shall look upon me whom they have pierced, and they shall mourn for him, as one mourneth for *his* only *son*, and shall be in bitterness for him, as one that is in bitterness for *his* firstborn.

inability to deliver themselves is emphasized by the reference to **tents**, in contrast to a well-fortified city. So decisive and indisputable will the divine deliverance be that all human boasting will be eliminated, and there will be no attempt to divert the glory from God: **That the glory of the house of David and the glory of the inhabitants of Jerusalem do not magnify themselves against Judah.** Judah takes prominence in this deliverance, because it is the tribe from whom both David and Messiah (who effects the deliverance) come.

8. More details of the supernatural deliverance are given. **In that day shall the LORD defend the inhabitants of Jerusalem; and he that is feeble among them at that day shall be as David.** God will so strengthen the weakest inhabitant that he will be as effective a warrior as David of old. Further, **the house of David shall be as God, as the angel of the LORD before them.** The whole effect of God's strengthening the nation will make them as effective a fighting force as if they were superhuman. They will be as effective as in the days of old when the Angel of the LORD (the Second Person of the Trinity) went before them (cf. Ex 23:20; 32:34; 33:2; Josh 5:13).

9. The goal of Jehovah **in that day** will be **to destroy all the nations that come against Jerusalem.** What He seeks to do, He precisely and completely will accomplish.

The prophet now turns to the second part of the second burden—the spiritual restoration of Israel in which they will recognize and receive their Messiah (vs. 10-13:1).

10. The preceding verses have recorded what God will accomplish for Israel's enemies—destruction. Beginning with verse 10, the prophet records what God will do for Israel—regeneration. This will be brought about because God **will pour upon the house of David, and upon the inhabitants of Jerusalem, the spirit of grace and of supplications. The spirit of grace and of supplications** is a direct reference to the Holy Spirit, the Third Person of the Trinity. The Holy Spirit will accomplish the conversion of the nation; for He will cause them to become rightly related to their Messiah, the Second Person of the Trinity. As the result of the Holy Spirit's ministry, **they shall look upon me whom they have pierced** (a clear reference to the Messiah whom they rejected at His First Advent, cf. 11:8, 12-13). The Holy Spirit will move the **inhabitants of Jerusalem** to seek God's forgiveness and favor. As the result, **they shall look** (Heb *nabat*, lit., to look attentively) and come to a realization that has previously escaped them—they will realize that **they have pierced** (Heb *daqar*, i.e., to pierce through—the word cannot be taken to mean "to insult" as some would like to translate it) their Messiah. Though they did not do it personally, they will come to realize that in the rejection of their Messiah they are guilty of the same sin as their forefathers whose rejection of Messiah caused Him to be delivered to the Roman authorities to be thrust through physically. In this verse, both comings of Messiah are in view—His First Advent, in which He was rejected and slain, and His Second Advent, in which He will be looked upon and received. Any theory suggesting that there were two messiahs (one to die and one to reign) is totally without warrant and stems from unbelief. Zechariah clearly has Messiah Himself in view, and thus he prophetically declares Messiah's rejection and death at His First Advent and His reception and reigning at His Second Advent. So far as the nation is concerned, Zechariah foretells their rejection of Messiah at His First Advent but their regeneration and reception of Messiah at His Second Advent. The realization of what they have done to Messiah will cause them to **mourn for him, as one mourneth for his only son** and to **be in bitterness for him, as one that is in bitterness for his first-born.** Godly conviction, as the result of the Holy Spirit's ministry, brings about Godly sorrow. The grief expressed is so intense that it is likened to the grief one has upon the death of **his only son.**

11. The private and personal grief manifested in verse 10 now becomes public and national in its expression. **In that day shall there be a great mourning in Jerusalem, as the mourning of Hadadrimmon in the valley of Megiddon.** The public display of grief to be manifested **In that day** is likened to the public display of grief in the days when King Josiah was slain by Pharaoh Necho (cf. II Kgs 23:29-30; II Chr 35:22-27) and Jeremiah wrote special dirges for the occasion. **Hadadrimmon** was located in the valley of Megiddo in the territory belonging to the tribe of Issachar. It was not far from Jezreel and was the place where King Josiah died. It is in this area where the Battle of Armageddon will take place.

11 In that day shall there be a great mourning in Jerusalem, as the mourning of Hā-dăd-rĭm'mon in the valley of Me-gĭd'don.

12. So great will be the mourning that the prophet elaborates upon it further: **And the land shall mourn, every family apart.** The mourning will be throughout the land in general; each family group will mourn. **The family of the house of David apart, and their wives apart; the family of the house of Nathan apart, and their wives apart.** That the kingly line of David will be involved in mourning is clear. The reference to **the house of Nathan** is not certain. The reference could be to Nathan the Prophet (II Sam 7:2), in which case both kings and prophets will be involved in mourning. The reference could also be to Nathan, David's son (II Sam 5:14), in which case the most and least prominent members of the royal family will be involved in mourning.

12 And the land shall mourn, every family apart; the family of the house of David apart, and their wives apart; the family of the house of Nathan apart, and their wives apart;

13. **The family of the house of Levi apart, and their wives apart; the family of Shimei apart, and their wives apart.** The members of the priesthood will be involved in the mourning. **Shimei** was the younger son of Gershon the oldest son of Levi (cf. Num 3:17ff.). Why he is singled out of all of Levi's descendants is not known. The thought is that apparently both the main and subordinate lines of the priesthood will be involved in mourning.

13 The family of the house of Levi apart, and their wives apart; the family of Shĭm'e-ī apart, and their wives apart;

14. All the families that remain, every family apart—the families comprising the common citizens of the land will mourn each family group in its own place. **And their wives apart.** This phrase has recurred throughout the section (cf. vss. 12-13) and should not be construed to indicate any form of segregation of men from women in mourning. The thought is that the grief is so intense in all strata of society—royal, priestly, and common citizen—that even husband and wife will wish to be alone in repentant grief before God. It is a moving picture of the godly sorrow that brings repentance.

14 All the families that remain, every family apart, and their wives apart.

13:1. This gives Jehovah's response to their sorrow and repentance. **In that day there shall be a fountain opened to the house of David and to the inhabitants of Jerusalem for sin and for uncleanness.** The ones expressing their godly sorrow in 12:12-14 will experience cleansing for their sin, epitomized in the rejection of their Messiah. Just as the sorrow was general, affecting all ranks and people, so also the cleansing. They will be cleansed from all moral impurity. Once again, the realization of the New Covenant is pictured for us (cf. Jer 31:31-34); and Israel will appropriate God's provision made at Calvary (cf. Rom 11:26-27).

CHAPTER 13
IN that day there shall be a fountain opened to the house of David and to the inhabitants of Jerusalem for sin and for uncleanness.

The third part of the second burden deals with the removal of idolatry and all false religions from Israel (vss. 2-6). Following repentance and cleansing (12:12-13:1) comes the putting away of every form of false worship.

2. The LORD of hosts (the First Person of the Trinity) promises that He **will cut off the names of the idols out of the land, and they shall no more be remembered.** While it is true that Israel was cured of idolatry as the result of the Babylonian captivity, some form of idol worship will be revived as the result of the worship of the Beast (cf. Rev 13:11-18). Following the

2 And it shall come to pass in that day, saith the LORD of hosts, *that* I will cut off the names of the idols out of the land, and they shall no more be remembered: and also I will cause the prophets and the unclean spirit to pass out of the land.

regeneration and restoration of His people, the consummative blow will be dealt to idolatry as Jehovah **will cut off the names of the idols,** with the result that **they shall no more be remembered.** The power of the idols will be broken so thoroughly that they will not exercise enough power over the people to cause them to even remember their names. Every vestige will be completely removed. In addition, Jehovah **will cause the prophets and the unclean spirit to pass out of the land. The prophets** are removed because they are false prophets energized by the **unclean spirit,** in contrast to the **spirit of grace and of supplications** (cf. 12:10); and the people will no longer be led astray by any form of false religion. **The land,** mentioned twice in this verse, is a reference to Israel and should not be translated as the earth.

3. There will be subsequent attempts to gain a foothold, but whenever a member of any household attempts to become the spokesman for the unclean spirit, it is to be dealt with in accordance with the means provided by the Mosaic law. **When any shall yet prophesy, then his father and his mother that begat him shall say unto him, Thou shalt not live; for thou speakest lies in the name of the LORD: and his father and his mother that begat him shall thrust him through when he prophesieth.** Under the Mosaic law the penalty for being a false prophet was death by stoning (cf. Deut 13:6-10; 18:20), and here by being **thrust . . . through** with a weapon. The penalty is to be executed by **father** and **mother**—the love for the truth of Jehovah is to transcend even the closest natural bond.

4. The false prophets had plagued Israel throughout its history and had brazenly carried on their deceit of the people. **In that day,** however, **the prophets shall be ashamed every one of his vision, when he hath prophesied.** The false prophets will carry on their work covertly, and their brazenness will be replaced by shame. **Neither shall they wear a rough garment to deceive**—they will not wear the hairy mantle characteristic of true prophets of God in keeping with their humble estate and dire pronouncements. The false prophets wore them hypocritically to give credence to their false messages.

5. The false prophets will seek to disassociate themselves from their activity by assuming a false identity: **But he shall say, I am no prophet, I am a husbandman; for man taught me to keep cattle from my youth.** He will claim that he never has had the opportunity to follow prophetic activity because he has been a tiller of the soil from his youth.

6. This verse describes the course of events in case that his lie does not succeed in diverting suspicion and the interrogation persists. **And one shall say unto him, What are these wounds in** (Heb *bēn*, lit., between) **thine hands?** The expression **in thine hands** should literally be translated between thine hands, i.e., on the upper body—surely on the breast, for it would not be seen if it were upon the back. Some have thought that it is reference to a wound inflicted when the parents attempted to thrust him through because they suspect him to be a false prophet. The difficulty with this understanding is that the parents were to kill the false prophet, their son, not merely wound him (cf. vs. 3). His answer, **Those with which I was wounded in the house of my friends** indicates that the wounds were received as his parents disciplined him for some fault. No reference to the Antichrist should be understood here, for by the time indicated in the prophecy the Antichrist will already have received his judgment and will have been removed from the scene. Nor should a reference to Christ be understood, for the parallel between the two instances is the occurrence of wounds. Christ was not wounded between the hands, but in His hands, feet, and side—and the wounds were the occasion for His glory, not grounds for suspicion. A number of other considerations mitigate against understanding this passage as a reference to Christ:

3 And it shall come to pass, *that* when any shall yet prophesy, then his father and his mother that begat him shall say unto him, Thou shalt not live; for thou speakest lies in the name of the LORD: and his father and his mother that begat him shall thrust him through when he prophesieth.

4 And it shall come to pass in that day, *that* the prophets shall be ashamed every one of his vision, when he hath prophesied; neither shall they wear a rough garment to deceive:

5 But he shall say, I *am* no prophet, I *am* an husbandman; for man taught me to keep cattle from my youth.

6 And *one* shall say unto him, What *are* these wounds in thine hands? Then he shall answer, *Those* with which I was wounded *in* the house of my friends.

He was not wounded in the house of friends, but on a Roman cross; following His resurrection no one would dare question Christ in such a fashion; He would not say that He is not a prophet, for He was the Prophet and the Prophet of prophets; He could not say that he was a tiller of the ground, for he was a carpenter in Nazareth; He would not say that He had been a slave to keep cattle from the days of His youth. In spite of the popularity of the view that sees a reference to Christ here, it does gross disservice to Him and to accurate interpretation of the Word of God to do so.

The fourth part of the second burden deals with the restoration of the remnant to Israel (vss. 7-9). Whereas Christ was not in view in the former section, He is the central figure in this section.

7 ¶Awake, O sword, against my shepherd, and against the man *that is* **my fellow, saith the LORD of hosts: smite the shepherd, and the sheep shall be scattered: and I will turn mine hand upon the little ones.**

7. The words of this verse are spoken by **the LORD of hosts** (the First Person of the Trinity). He calls, **Awake, O sword, against my shepherd, and against the man that is my fellow.** The **sword** is the symbol of judicial power (cf. Rom 13:4) and indicates the power that God has entrusted to human government, in this case Rome. **My shepherd** is a reference to Jesus, the Messiah, the Second Person of the Godhead. He is the true Shepherd unlike the false shepherds upon whom God's wrath fell (cf. 11:8). The dual nature of Jesus the Messiah is clearly set forth: **the man** indicates that He is 100 percent man; **my fellow** (Heb 'amît, i.e., fellow, friend, companion, associate) indicates that He is 100 percent God. There is no stronger way that **the LORD of hosts** could say that His **shepherd** is His intrinsic equal—God of very God! The God-man was embodied in human form; and in the accomplishment of His eternal counsel, **the LORD of hosts** commands the **sword** to **smite the shepherd, and the sheep shall be scattered.** Jesus applied this statement to Himself (cf. Mt 26:31), but the scattering should not be limited only to the disciples following the crucifixion of our Lord. It should be understood as applying to the dispersion of Israel as a nation as the context in the prophecy makes plain. Though the **sheep shall be scattered,** they will not be forgotten; for Jehovah promises, **I will turn mine hand upon the little ones.** The Lord promises that He will intervene in behalf of the remnant, described as **little ones,** an expression of His tender affection for them.

8 And it shall come to pass, *that* **in all the land, saith the LORD, two parts therein shall be cut off** *and* **die; but the third shall be left therein.**

8. **And it shall come to pass** indicates that there is a great time lapse between the events of verse 7 and verses 8 and 9. The events of verse 7 took place with the death of our Lord and in the days immediately following (ca. A.D. 33). The events of verses 8-9 take place in the Great Tribulation, approximately 2000 years (and perhaps more) later. **In all the land** (i.e., Israel) **. . . two parts therein shall be cut off and die; but the third shall be left therein.** Two-thirds of Israel's population will die as the result of the wrath vented against them by the Antichrist. One-third of Israel's population, the remnant, will survive to go into the millennial kingdom.

9 And I will bring the third part through the fire, and will refine them as silver is refined, and will try them as gold is tried: they shall call on my name, and I will hear them: I will say, It *is* **my people: and they shall say, The LORD** *is* **my God.**

9. This verse describes the purifying process through which the Lord will bring the remnant. God says, **I will bring the third part through the fire, and will refine them as silver is refined, and will try them as gold is tried.** The Great Tribulation has two purposes from God's vantage point—to destroy the unbelieving part of Israel and to purify the believing part of Israel and cause them to come to saving faith in Him. This is precisely what shall happen; for **they shall call on my name, and I will hear them: I will say, It is my people: and they shall say, The LORD is my God.** This, once again, is a reference to national regeneration and salvation in fulfillment of the New Covenant (cf. Jer 31:31-34).

The fifth part of the second burden concerns the return of the Lord to the earth to set up His kingdom (14:1-8).

CHAPTER 14
BEHOLD, the day of the LORD cometh.

14:1. Once again the prophet returns to the same setting as in

and thy spoil shall be divided in the midst of thee.

2 For I will gather all nations against Jerusalem to battle; and the city shall be taken, and the houses rifled, and the women ravished; and half of the city shall go forth into captivity, and the residue of the people shall not be cut off from the city.

3 ¶Then shall the LORD go forth, and fight against those nations, as when he fought in the day of battle.

4 And his feet shall stand in that day upon the mount of Olives, which *is* before Jerusalem on the east, and the mount of Olives shall cleave in the midst thereof toward the east and toward the west, *and there shall be* a very great valley; and half of the mountain shall remove toward the north, and half of it toward the south.

5 And ye shall flee *to* the valley of the mountains; for the valley of the mountains shall reach unto A'zal: yea, ye shall flee, like as ye fled from before the earthquake in the days of Uz-zī'ah king of Judah: and the LORD my God shall come, *and* all the saints with thee.

12:1—the siege laid against Jerusalem by the gentile confederacy during the Great Tribulation. In no sense should it be confused with the invasion of Jerusalem by Nebuchadnezzar in 586 B.C. (for that would be history) or the Roman invasion under Titus in A.D. 70. The time is described as **the day of the LORD** and is to be understood in the same sense as the prophets Joel, Zephaniah, Malachi, and other portions of the Word of God use the term—it is the time of Jacob's trouble, the time of the great consummative battle of the end time, the Battle of Armageddon. Once again Jerusalem is advised that dark days lie ahead for her: **Thy spoil shall be divided in the midst of thee**—this will be the result of the siege; the conquerors will divide the spoil in the midst of Jerusalem.

2. Having given the effect (vs. 1), the prophet now gives the cause: **For I will gather all nations against Jerusalem to battle.** As the result, **the city shall be taken, and the houses rifled, and the women ravished; and half of the city shall go forth into captivity, and the residue of the people shall not be cut off from the city.** This victory will take place in the middle of the Great Tribulation when the king of the West moves into the land to do battle against the king of the North and the king of the South who have put a mighty pincer movement on the land. The king of the West will defeat the kings of the North and South and will set himself up in the Temple and proclaim himself to be God. He will vent his wrath upon Israel, and a deportation of people will take place; but a remnant will remain in the city.

3. The prophet moves to the culminating battle of the Great Tribulation, the Battle of Armageddon. **Then shall the LORD go forth, and fight against those nations.** The king of the East will come to do battle with the king of the West. Before they can do combat, a sign is given them in heaven (cf. Mt 24:30), indicating that Christ is about to return to the earth to set up His kingdom. Instead of doing combat with each other, the kings of East and West become confederates in the vain attempt to keep Christ from returning to earth and are slain by the breath of His mouth (cf. II Thess 2:7-8). The victory that the Lord will achieve for Israel that day will be reminiscent of the days **when he fought in the day of battle.** This will be the greatest, but not the first, deliverance that the Lord will effect for His people.

4. When the Messiah returns to earth, **his feet shall stand in that day upon the mount of Olives, which is before Jerusalem on the east**—the place was a familiar site in Israel's history. The Mount of Olives was prominent in our Lord's earthly ministry. One wonders what thoughts must have gone through His head as he walked there in the days of His humiliation. Surely he must have thought ahead to the great glory that one day would be manifested there! Our Lord returned to heaven from the Mount of Olives (cf. Acts 1:11-12), and He will return precisely to the same location; but when He does, something unusual will happen: **And the mount of Olives shall cleave in the midst thereof toward the east and toward the west, and there shall be a very great valley; and half of the mountain shall remove toward the north, and half of it toward the south.** There is no reason for not understanding this literally.

5. The reason why the Mount of Olives will divide is not only to call attention to a most significant occurrence—the return of Messiah to the earth to set up His kingdom—but also to provide an avenue of escape. **And ye shall flee to the valley of the mountains; for the valley of the mountains shall reach unto Azal** (probably located on the eastern side of the city). The prophet compares this future event to an event in past history: **Like as ye fled from before the earthquake in the days of Uzziah king of Judah.** The **earthquake** is the same one referred to by Amos more than two hundred years earlier (cf. Amos 1:1). It must have been unusually severe, for it left an indelible print

on the memories of the people of Israel. The important thing about the whole event is that **the Lord my God shall come, and all the saints with thee.** Note that the event is so striking to the prophet that he shifts to direct address. This is the great event when the Lord will return to the earth with His saints to set up His kingdom!

6-8. These verses describe the great changes that will occur in nature when the Lord returns to set up His kingdom. The most unusual phenomenon will involve light, for **the light shall not be clear, nor dark.** The precise meaning is unclear, **But it shall be one day which shall be known to the Lord**—only He will know and understand its essential character and meaning. There shall be **not day, nor night: but it shall come to pass, that at evening time it shall be light.** It will be a time when neither daylight nor night time will be normal. Further, **in that day . . . living waters shall go out from Jerusalem; half of them toward the former sea** (i.e., the Dead Sea), **and half of them toward the hinder sea** (i.e., the Mediterranean Sea). The supply of water issuing from Jerusalem will be constant, for **in summer and in winter shall it be.** Water is used symbolically throughout the Old Testament to indicate purification and refreshment. The point of the symbolism is that when Messiah returns, spiritual purification and refreshment will be ever spread throughout the land.

The sixth part of the second burden concerns the millennial reign of the Lord (vss. 9-11).

9. This verse sets forth the extent of Messiah's reign. **The Lord shall be king over all the earth**—His reign will be universal, though centered in Jerusalem. He will provide the basis for true unity; for **in that day shall there be one Lord, and his name one.** There will be no other object of worship and all the universe will be in right relationship to Him.

10. This verse shows what the land of Israel will be like during the Millennium. All **the land shall be turned as a plain from Geba to Rimmon south of Jerusalem. Geba** is modern Jeba and is located six miles north of Jerusalem. **Rimmon** is located about thirty-five miles southwest of Jerusalem. The whole area from **Geba** to **Rimmon** will be made into a level plain. **Jerusalem,** on the other hand, **shall be lifted up**—thus the waters of purification (cf. vs. 8) will be able to flow unimpeded throughout the land. **Jerusalem . . . shall be . . . inhabited in her place, from Benjamin's gate** (i.e., in the north wall of the city) **unto the place of the first gate** (the location of which is uncertain, though many identify it with the old gate), **unto the corner gate** (in the northwestern corner of the city), **and from the tower of Hananeel** (near the northeast corner of the wall close to Benjamin's Gate) **unto the king's winepresses** (probably located near the king's gardens and the Pool of Siloam on the southeast side of the city). The point of the verse is that the city will be rebuilt, just as it was in former days of its glory; and it will be repopulated. The inhabitants will dwell in safety in the city because all sin will have been removed.

11. The safety of the inhabitants is described in this verse: **And men shall dwell in it, and there shall be no more utter destruction; but Jerusalem shall be safely inhabited.** When men are rightly related to the Lord, there is no need for fear of any kind. They can dwell in perfect safety because all sin has been dealt with and done away.

The seventh part of the second burden concerns the plague to be visited upon all of Judah's enemies (vss. 12-15).

12. This verse returns to the thought begun in vss. 1-3—the destruction of the invaders of Jerusalem. There it was simply stated that the Lord would fight for Israel, but the specific means was not given. But here the means by which the Lord will execute vengeance upon Judah's enemies is given: it will be a **plague wherewith the Lord will smite all the people that have**

6 And it shall come to pass in that day, *that* the light shall not be clear, *nor* dark:

7 But it shall be one day which shall be known to the Lord, not day, nor night: but it shall come to pass, *that* at evening time it shall be light.

8 And it shall be in that day, *that* living waters shall go out from Jerusalem; half of them toward the former sea, and half of them toward the hinder sea: in summer and in winter shall it be.

9 And the Lord shall be king over all the earth: in that day shall there be one Lord, and his name one.

10 All the land shall be turned as a plain from Gē′ba to Rimmon south of Jerusalem: and it shall be lifted up, and inhabited in her place, from Benjamin's gate unto the place of the first gate, unto the corner gate, and *from* the tower of Hă-nan′ē-el unto the king's winepresses.

11 And *men* shall dwell in it, and there shall be no more utter destruction; but Jerusalem shall be safely inhabited.

12 ¶ And this shall be the plague wherewith the Lord will smite all the people that have fought against Jerusalem; Their flesh shall consume away while they stand upon their feet, and their eyes shall consume away in their

holes, and their tongue shall consume away in their mouth.

13 And it shall come to pass in that day, *that* a great tumult from the LORD shall be among them; and they shall lay hold every one on the hand of his neighbour, and his hand shall rise up against the hand of his neighbour.

14 And Judah also shall fight at Jerusalem; and the wealth of all the heathen round about shall be gathered together, gold, and silver, and apparel, in great abundance.

15 And so shall be the plague of the horse, of the mule, of the camel, and of the ass, and of all the beasts that shall be in these tents, as this plague.

16 ¶And it shall come to pass, *that* every one that is left of all the nations which came against Jerusalem shall even go up from year to year to worship the King, the LORD of hosts, and to keep the feast of tabernacles.

17 And it shall be, *that* whoso will not come up of *all* the families of the earth unto Jerusalem to worship the King, the LORD of hosts, even upon them shall be no rain.

18 And if the family of Egypt go not up, and come not, that *have* no *rain*; there shall be the plague, wherewith the LORD will smite the heathen that come not up to keep the feast of tabernacles.

fought against Jerusalem. What the plague will do is now given: **Their flesh shall consume away while they stand upon their feet, and their eyes shall consume away in their holes, and their tongue shall consume away in their mouth**—they will literally rot away!

13. In addition to the physical suffering inflicted by the plague, the Lord will send among them a supernatural confusion. **And it shall come to pass in that day, that a great tumult** (Heb *mehūmah*, lit., trouble, destruction) **from the LORD shall be among them**. This **tumult** will cause great confusion among their ranks; **And they shall lay hold every one on the hand of his neighbor, and his hand shall rise up against the hand of his neighbor.** Each will fight the other and become the other's worst enemy! Chaos will reign supreme!

14. The enemy seemed victorious at first (cf. vs. 2), but God will strengthen Judah to make them victorious at last: **And Judah also shall fight at Jerusalem.** That they are victorious over the enemy is indicated by the fact that **the wealth of all the heathen round about shall be gathered together, gold, and silver, and apparel, in great abundance.** Whereas in the first part of the battle the heathen divided up the spoil of Jerusalem (cf. vs. 1), in the end the spoil comes entirely to Judah, not only what was theirs in the beginning, but all that the invading army has brought along from its other victories.

15. The plague that fell upon the soldiers (cf. vs. 12) also falls upon the animals supporting the invading army: **And so shall be the plague of the horse, of the mule, of the camel, and of the ass, and of all the beasts that shall be in these tents, as this plague.** The animals belonging to the invaders share the fate of their masters.

The eighth and final part of the second burden concerns millennial conduct (vss. 16-21).

16. In the conflict described in the preceding verses every last unbeliever is destroyed. Only believing Israelites and believing Gentiles remain to become subjects of the millennial kingdom. At that time **every one that is left of all the nations which came against Jerusalem shall even go up from year to year to worship the King, the LORD of hosts, and to keep the feast of tabernacles.** The **feast of tabernacles** is the joyous feast of ingathering, rest, and thanksgiving. Israel had celebrated it when they returned from the exile (cf. Neh 8:14-18). No other feast will be observed because the realities they adumbrated will have been realized. The millennial reign of Messiah is the realization of the Feast of Tabernacles. Participating in it demonstrated a right relationship to Messiah.

17. But what if one did not take part in the Feast of Tabernacles? **Whoso will not come up of all the families of the earth unto Jerusalem to worship the King, the LORD of hosts, even upon them shall be no rain.** The Lord will withhold rain from the land of those who are not in right relationship with Him as punishment for their spiritual insensitivity. The withholding of rain would mean that there would be no crop the coming year. One's spiritual disobedience would be manifest to all! It is interesting to note that this verse (and the two that follow) anticipate disobedience in the millennial age. It should also be noted that the people of Israel who enter into the Millennium are regenerated—not glorified. They will still have sin natures and will have to deal with the fruit of that sin nature in the ways proscribed by the Lord.

18. The threat of withholding rain would be meaningless to the residents of Egypt, for they depended on the annual overflow of the Nile River for their water supply. If they are disobedient, they will not escape God's judgment; for He has an appropriate punishment for them. **And if the family of Egypt go not up, and come not, that have no rain; there shall be the plague, wherewith the LORD will smite the heathen that come**

not up to keep the feast of tabernacles. God has an appropriate language with which to speak to each form of disobedience!

19 This shall be the punishment of Egypt, and the punishment of all nations that come not up to keep the feast of tabernacles.

19. This shall be the punishment of Egypt, and the punishment of all nations that come not up to keep the feast of tabernacles. God intends that all peoples of the earth should participate in the Feast of Tabernacles because it commemorates the culmination of God's plan of all ages—the fulfillment of all of His promises to Abraham! To disobey is to incur His wrath. Yet, in a perfect environment, with the curse removed, with Satan chained in the bottomless pit for 1000 years, and with Jesus visibly present and reigning on His throne, there will be those who will disobey and give feigned obedience. The human heart is ever the same regardless of the dispensation!

20 ¶In that day shall there be upon the bells of the horses, HOLINESS UNTO THE LORD; and the pots in the LORD's house shall be like the bowls before the altar.
21 Yea, every pot in Jerusalem and in Judah shall be holiness unto the LORD of hosts: and all they that sacrifice shall come and take of them, and seethe therein: and in that day there shall be no more the Canaanite in the house of the LORD of hosts.

20-21. These culminating verses of the prophecy show how the righteous (the ones who do keep the Feast of Tabernacles) will conduct themselves. Holiness will pervade every aspect of their lives. **In that day shall there be upon the bells of the horses, HOLINESS UNTO THE LORD.** Bells were used for ornaments upon horses' harnesses. Even the ornamental bells will be inscribed with the same words that were engraved upon the tiara worn by the High Priest of Israel: HOLINESS UNTO THE LORD. All the vessels in the LORD's house will be equally holy, whether they are **the pots** (considered to be the lowliest vessels) or **the bowls before the altar** (which caught the blood of the sacrificial victim and were used to sprinkle the blood of the sacrifice before the Lord). Not only will all the utensils in the LORD's house be equally sacred, but **every pot in Jerusalem and in Judah shall be holiness unto the LORD of hosts.** All the vessels in private homes throughout the nation will be considered to be equally holy with the vessels used in the service of the Lord in the Lord's house! Holiness will in fact pervade the land and become the way of life.

In that day there shall be no more the Canaanite in the house of the LORD of hosts. The word **Canaanite** (Heb *kena'anî*, lit., merchant, Canaanite) is a reference to the Phoenicians in the north who were renowned mariners and merchants (cf. 9:2-3), and it is used here representatively of any unholy or ungodly person. The prophet's point is that never again will any unholy or ungodly person be in the **house of the LORD of hosts.**

The point of these two culminating verses is that in the Millennium there will no longer be a distinction between the secular and the sacred. The millennial age will be characterized by holiness, and every aspect of daily life will be a manifestation of holiness.

In conclusion, the prophecy of Zechariah makes two outstanding contributions to those who make it the topic of careful study: (1) it provides a complement to the prophecy of Daniel—Daniel gives God's program for the times of the Gentiles from the gentile perspective; Zechariah gives God's program for the times of the Gentiles from Israel's perspective; and (2) it provides encouragement to the servant of God in that the aspect of the Lord's work to which he has been called is most important and worthy of doing with wholehearted devotion. Zerubbabel and Joshua, and the nation of their day, never lived to see the glorious things promised in this prophecy; but God's program for the future was dependent upon their work. Hence, it was absolutely essential that they do their work wholeheartedly in faithful service unto the Lord.

(see page 1864 for Bibliography to the Minor Prophets)

MALACHI

INTRODUCTION

Authorship. The name Malachi means my messenger. It is a shortened form of the Hebrew name *Malakiah* (messenger of Jehovah). Keil and Delitzsch note that the Hebrews often dropped the name of God that occurred at the end of proper names. The shortened form of *Malakiah* would be simply Malachi.

Nothing is known of the personal life of the prophet. This has given rise to a number of theories concerning him. Because the Hebrew language, like the Greek language, has only one word that can mean either messenger or angel, some of the church fathers suggested that Malachi was in reality an angel incarnate. Other scholars have taken Malachi to be a pseudonym for Ezra, Nehemiah, or Zerubbabel; but there is no historical basis for this, nor is there any precedent for it in any other prophetical literature. Jewish tradition holds that Haggai, Zechariah, Ezra, and Malachi were members of the Great Synagogue of Israel. Some have supposed that since the priesthood occupies such a prominent place in the book that Malachi must have been a priest. This may or may not be so. The simplest and best view is to consider Malachi as the name of the last prophet in Israel. The fact that nothing is known of his personal lineage or history is not uncommon among the prophets. Once again, the message to be conveyed is much more important than the messenger. That the messenger is adequate for the task committed to him is evident.

Date and Place of Writing. It is certain that Malachi is later than Haggai, Ezra, and Zechariah because in those books the Temple is not finished. We know from 1:6 and 3:10 that not only was the Temple finished in Malachi's day, but it had been in operation for some time and sin was corrupting the worship that took place in it. Further, it was written after Nehemiah's first arrival in Jerusalem in the thirty-second year of Artaxerxes Longimanus in 444 B.C., probably after the walls had been rebuilt around the city. Malachi addresses the same sins noted in Nehemiah: the divorcing of Jewish wives and marrying heathen women (cf. 2:11 with Neh 13:23ff.) and the failure of the people to bring their gifts to the Temple (cf. 3:8-10 with Neh 13:10-14). Nehemiah was recalled to the Persian court in 433 B.C., and another governor who seems to have been a Persian governor was placed over Palestine (cf. Neh 13:6). Most likely, Malachi was written just before Nehemiah's second return to Jerusalem or during his presence there. Malachi ministered in support of Nehemiah's ministry, just as Haggai and Zechariah had ministered in support of Ezra and Zerubbabel approximately one hundred years earlier. Scofield, following Ussher, dates the prophecy at 397 B.C.; but this may be just a little too late. The prophecy was probably written some time between 433-425 B.C. perhaps as late as 400 B.C.

After Malachi the prophetic voice was silent for some 400 (so-called silent) years. This fact makes it necessary for even the most destructive critic to admit that the hundreds of prophecies concerning the coming of our Lord are what they claim to be—prophecy—and not the deceitful writing of history in prophetical form.

The place from which the prophecy originated was Jerusalem at a location near the Temple. This is even more certain if Malachi also was a priest (cf. earlier).

Characteristics of the Prophecy. In form, the prophecy is in continuous discourse. The dialogue of Malachi is different from the dialogue utilized in Habakkuk. In Habakkuk the questions stemmed from faith, whereas in Malachi the questions are indicative of unbelief. Malachi is very severe in tone, argumentative in style, unusually bold in his attacking the corrupt priesthood (cf. 1:6-2:9), abounding in beautiful figures of speech, and abrupt in his transitions from one thought to another. Malachi has been called "the Socrates of the prophets . . . the Hebrew Socrates" because he uses a style which rhetoricians call didactic or dialectic. It is this manner that God used to combat the false statements and to correct the misunderstandings of the Israelites. The prophecy is a testimony to the graciousness of God in condescending to answer man's foolish and childish statements. The dialectic form used in the prophecy became a popular teaching style in later Judaism.

Purpose. The purpose of Malachi is to deliver stern rebukes to people and priests, to call them to repentance, and to promise future blessing.

Theme. God's love for Israel in spite of the sins of the priests and people.

OUTLINE

COMMENTARY

I. INTRODUCTION TO THE PROPHECY. 1:1.

A. The Nature of the Prophecy. 1:1a.

THE burden of the word of the LORD to Israel by Măl'a-chī.

1:1a. The prophecy is described as being **The burden** (Heb *masa'*, i.e., burden, load, or thing lifted up), indicating that the prophecy deals with rebuke and condemnation. The same word is used to describe the prophecies of Nahum (cf. Nah 1:1), Habakkuk (cf. Hab 1:1), and the "burden" mentioned twice by Zechariah (cf. Zech 9:1; 12:1). The prophecy, then, is not one that the prophet takes delight in bringing; but he delivers it faithfully, for it is true and is what the people need, whether or not they like it.

B. The Source of the Prophecy. 1:1b.

1b. The prophecy is further introduced as being **the word of the LORD**—indicating its source. It is **the word** (Heb *dabar*, i.e., word, matter, thing) **of the LORD** (Heb *Yahweh*, i.e., Jehovah, the eternal God); hence, it embodies all that the eternal God wishes to say concerning the matters it contains. It is not the prophet's invention, but it bears the imprimatur of the eternal God and thus is both authentic and reliable.

C. The Address of the Prophecy. 1:1c.

1c. The prophecy is addressed **to Israel**, representing both northern and southern kingdoms. Representatives of all twelve tribes had returned to the land, and thus the entire nation is addressed.

D. The Agent of the Prophecy. 1:1d.

1d. The prophecy is delivered **by Malachi** (i.e., my messenger). Nothing is known of his personal lineage or history, and many theories have been advanced concerning his identity (see Introduction, above).

II. JEHOVAH'S FIRST DISPUTE WITH THE PEOPLE. 1:2-5.

A. God's Declaration of His Love. 1:2a.

2 I have loved you, saith the LORD. Yet ye say, Wherein hast thou loved us? *Was* not Esau Jacob's brother? saith the LORD: yet I loved Jacob,

2a. I have loved you, saith the LORD. Because of who He is, God in His essence is the epitome of love (cf. I Jn 4:8, 16) and cannot act apart from His love; and all of His dealings with Israel have been consistent with that love. In view of what lies ahead in the prophecy, it is important to understand all that is said against the background of His eternal love for Israel. The love God has shown for Israel ought to form the motive and model of Israel's conduct toward God; but, unfortunately, it did not.

B. Israel's Dispute of God's Love. 1:2b.

2b. Yet ye say, Wherein hast thou loved us? In all the centuries since creation the human heart has not changed—it always questions what God affirms. It began in the Garden of Eden, and it continues unchanged into the present day. This is the first of eight times in this prophecy where the people question God's affirmations (see also vss. 6-7; 2:14, 17; 3:7-8, 13).

C. God's Demonstration of His Love. 1:2c-4.

It is a testimony of God's graciousness that He condescends to answer the people's question. He offers two incontrovertible proofs of His love for Israel.

1. His sovereign choice of Israel. 1:2c-3.

3 And I hated Esau, and laid his mountains and his heritage waste for the dragons of the wilderness.

2c-3. The supreme evidence of God's love of Israel is His choice of Israel to be His peculiar people. **Was not Esau Jacob's brother? saith the LORD: yet I loved Jacob, And I hated Esau.** Jacob and Esau were twins, and the posterity of both developed into tribes and nations. Posterity would assume that God would treat Israelites and Edomites alike, but this was not the case. Even before their births Jacob was the chosen one; Esau, or Edom, was inferior and was to serve his brother (cf. Gen 25:23; Rom 9:10-13). God's love for Jacob was shown in His choice and preservation of Jacob/Israel, and his hate for Esau is shown by Edom's desolation. This expression involves the use of a Hebrew idiom. If a father had two sons and made one heir, he was said to love the one he had made his heir and to hate the one that he had not made heir. The love and hate spoken of here are not related to the emotions; they are related to the will. God, by the act of His sovereign will, chose Israel, rather than Esau.

In demonstration of His hatred for Edom, God cites the fact that He **laid his mountains and his heritage waste for the dragons** (Heb *tanōt*, i.e., howlers, jackals) **of the wilderness.** The specific reference to wasting is uncertain. It could refer to the wasting Edom experienced at the hands of the Nabateans, the Persians, the Egyptians, or the Babylonians. The reference is broad enough to refer to all of them, though the one most meaningful would be the conquest of Edom by the Babylonians who invaded Edom in 581 B.C., five years after the destruction of Jerusalem.

2. His sovereign preservation of Israel. 1:4.

4 Whereas Edom saith, We are impoverished, but we will return and build the desolate places; thus saith the LORD of hosts, They shall build, but I will throw down; and they shall call them, The border of wickedness, and, The people against whom the LORD hath indignation for ever.

4. Whereas Edom saith, We are impoverished, but we will return and build the desolate places; thus saith the LORD of hosts, They shall build, but I will throw down. Edom will recognize its sad plight and in pride will determine to rebuild and frustrate the judgment of God against them. Their attempts to rebuild will be futile, and they will meet with further defeat. **And they shall call them, The border of wickedness, and, The people against whom the LORD hath indignation for ever.** All the world will come to recognize that the desolate condition of Edom is a judgment of God upon them because of their sins.

Babylon conquered Edom and Moab as well as Israel. Edom and Moab were never restored, but Israel was rebuilt. God's preservation, together with His sovereign choice, of Israel amply demonstrated His love for Israel.

D. Israel's Recognition of His Love. 1:5.

5. God promises Israel **your eyes shall see** the futile attempts Edom makes at restoration: **and ye shall say, The LORD will be** (lit., is) **magnified from** (lit., over or above) **the border of Israel.** Israel will see Edom's superficial attempts at recovery and will then acknowledge that Jehovah is showing Himself to be great in the land. They will say, Jehovah is great over Israel, when He makes known His greatness to men by His acts of power and grace in preserving Israel and keeping Edom in desolation.

III. JEHOVAH'S DISPUTE WITH THE PRIESTS. 1:6-2:9.

A. His Causes Against the Priests. 1:6-14.

1. Concerning their failure to honor Him. 1:6-10.

This section of the prophecy divides into three parts: (1) God's interrogation (vs. 6a); (2) the priests' dispute (vs. 6b); and (3) God's demonstration of their failure to honor Him (vss. 7-10).

6. **A son honoreth his father, and a servant his master: if then I be a father, where is mine honor? and if I be a master, where is my fear? saith the LORD of hosts.** By His choice and preservation of Israel, Jehovah has acted as a Father and a Master of the nation, but His questions reveal that Israel has not reciprocated with a proper honor due a father or with the proper fear due a master (cf. Deut 32:6; Ps 100:3; Isa 63:16; Jer 31:9).

Though the questions are directed particularly to **you, O priests,** they are also applicable to the whole nation; for they followed the priests' evil example. The address describing the priests shows why they do not honor Jehovah—they are **priests, that despise my name.** This is the summation of their attitude, and later it is illustrated by specific examples.

The **priests** characteristically dispute Jehovah's contention and say, **Wherein have we despised thy name?** Rather than admit and confess their sin, they choose to respond in unbelief and ask for evidence, which God then condescends to give.

7-8. These verses give the first form that the despising took—the offering of unclean sacrifices. Evidence? **Ye offer polluted bread upon mine altar.** That the word **bread** (Heb *lechem*, food, bread, sustenance) is used metaphorically to refer to animal sacrifices offered **upon mine altar** is evident from three considerations: (1) it is used in conjunction with **mine altar** upon which animal sacrifices were offered; (2) it is further described in verse 8 as being **blind . . . lame and sick;** and (3) the identical term is used to denote animal sacrifices in Leviticus 21:6, 8, 17. Their offense, then, was the offering of polluted animal sacrifices to Jehovah, a practice specifically prohibited by Deuteronomy 15:21.

Characteristically, they dispute God's affirmation—**Wherein have we polluted thee?** Once again, Jehovah condescends to prove his point. **In that ye say, The table of the LORD is contemptible.** Whether or not they actually said these blasphemous words with their mouths is beside the point—their actions proved what they thought; and by offering polluted sacrifices, they were saying that the **table of the LORD** (here used metaphorically in parallel with the figure of **bread** earlier to denote the **altar** of sacrifice and not the table of showbread) **is contemptible** (Heb *bazah*, i.e., to be loathed, despised, condemned).

---

5 And your eyes shall see, and ye shall say, The LORD will be magnified from the border of Israel.

6 ¶A son honoureth *his* father, and a servant his master: if then I *be* a father, where *is* mine honour? and if I *be* a master, where *is* my fear? saith the LORD of hosts unto you, O priests, that despise my name. And ye say, Wherein have we despised thy name?

7 Ye offer polluted bread upon mine altar; and ye say, Wherein have we polluted thee? In that ye say, The table of the LORD *is* contemptible.

8 And if ye offer the blind for sacrifice, *is it* not evil? and if ye offer the lame and sick, *is it* not evil? offer it now unto thy governor; will he be pleased with thee, or accept thy person? saith the LORD of hosts.

The specifics of the polluted sacrifices are spelled out: **And if ye offer the blind for sacrifice, is it not evil? and if ye offer the lame and sick, is it not evil?** The answer to both questions is Yes, because the offering of such sacrifices was expressly forbidden (cf. Deut 15:21). Not only are such sacrifices unacceptable to God, they are unacceptable to the governmental officials: **Offer it now unto thy governor; will he be pleased with thee, or accept thy person? saith the LORD of hosts.** The answer to the question, of course, is No. The priests failed to honor God properly and despised His name (and hence His person) in that they offered to Jehovah the members of the flock that had no sale value at all. They should have been responding to His love by giving Him the best of everything; but they were attempting to offer to God that which even a human leader would not accept. How much more proof is needed? They were treating **the LORD of hosts** (the First Person of the Trinity) in a way that they would not dare to treat a mere human leader!

9 And now, I pray you, beseech God that he will be gracious unto us: this hath been by your means: will he regard your persons? saith the LORD of hosts.

9. And now, I pray you, beseech God that he will be gracious unto us. In light of the context it is probably best to understand this injunction as given in irony, rather than being a serious exhortation to repentance. The rest of the statement makes this evident: **This hath been by your means** (i.e., the offering of polluted sacrifices): **will he regard your persons? saith the LORD of hosts.** The thought is that their prayers will never be acceptable to God as long as they are offering unacceptable sacrifices. The repetition of **saith the LORD of hosts** is designed to remind them that they are dealing with the Eternal God, not mere man.

10 Who *is there* even among you that would shut the doors *for nought?* neither do ye kindle *fire* on mine altar for nought. I have no pleasure in you, saith the LORD of hosts, neither will I accept an offering at your hand.

10. The second form the despising took is given in this verse—they were involved in empty formalism. **Who is there even among you that would shut the doors for nought? neither do ye kindle fire on mine altar for nought.** Some have seen in this question the thought that the priests would not do even the slightest task, such as shutting the doors, without a fee. Others suggest that the question reflects the carelessness with which the priests went about their duties in that they did not close the Temple doors at the right times. It is true that **for nought** (Heb *chinam*) can have the thought of something that is for *gratis*, but the best understanding in context is that the priests were going about their duties in dull drudgery (cf. vs. 7) and empty formalism, rather than in faith. This is not pleasing to God; and He would prefer that the **doors** of the Temple be closed, rather than to have the empty formalism continue. The true sacrifice, offered in the right heart attitude, is an evidence of subjection to Jehovah and a recognition of dependence upon Him. The right heart attitude was lacking among the priests; hence, Jehovah declares; **I have no pleasure in you, saith the LORD of hosts, neither will I accept an offering at your hand.** Their whole religious activity is totally vain, empty, and useless; it is insincere and merely external. They have not honored Him; hence, He will not honor them.

2. *Concerning their profaning His Name. 1:11-14.*

This section divides into three parts: (1) God's declaration (vs. 11); (2) the priests' dispute (vs. 12); and (3) God's demonstration (vss. 13-14).

11. In contrast to the kind of worship that is not acceptable to Him, Jehovah declares the kind of worship that is acceptable.

11 For from the rising of the sun even unto the going down of the same my name *shall be* great among the Gentiles; and in every place incense *shall be* offered unto my name, and a pure offering: for my name *shall be* great among the heathen, saith the LORD of hosts.

For from the rising of the sun even unto the going down of the same my name shall be great among the Gentiles; and in every place incense shall be offered unto my name, and a pure offering: for my name shall be great among the heathen, saith the LORD of hosts. Grammatically, it is possible to understand Malachi to be talking either of events present in his day, or about some future, yet unrealized day; and scholars are divided on the question. If Malachi is understood to be talking about his own day, then he is saying that all the heathen who are offering sacrifices at that time are doing it to the true God, Jehovah. Two cogent objections argue against this view: (1) Paul's teaching (cf. Rom 1:19-20) is that the heathen can come to know the eternal God. Acts 17:22ff. gives an instance of some heathen that came to this realization and erected an altar ". . . To the Unknown God. . . ." Paul seized upon the opportunity to tell them about the God who was unknown to them, but who indeed created them, the heavens, and the earth. (2) Context—Malachi is not speaking of an unknown God. He is speaking of Jehovah and says that His name is great over all the world. At the time of Malachi, the things spoken of in this verse were not realized at all. Therefore, it is best to conclude that Malachi is speaking prophetically of a future event when the universal glory will be realized by Jehovah. This will be in the Millennium when the Temple will be rebuilt and incense and offerings will be a part of worshiping Him. In the future Jehovah will receive pure worship throughout all the world, and His name will be great among all the peoples of the world; and He is not pleased with the insincere worship and polluted sacrifices of the priesthood and people of Malachi's day.

12 ¶But ye have profaned it, in that ye say, The table of the Lord is polluted; and the fruit thereof, even his meat, is contemptible.

12. Once again the priests dispute God's affirmation, not by actual words, but by their actions by which they **profaned** Jehovah's Name and said **The table of the Lord is polluted; and the fruit thereof, even his meat, is contemptible.** Because they were insincere in what they were doing, their whole service to Jehovah became wearisome and burdensome to them; and they treated it with utmost contempt. Their actions disputed God's affirmations concerning His name and service (cf. vs. 11).

13 Ye said also, Behold, what a weariness is it! and ye have snuffed at it, saith the Lord of hosts; and ye brought that which was torn, and the lame, and the sick; thus ye brought an offering: should I accept this of your hand? saith the Lord.
14 But cursed be the deceiver, which hath in his flock a male, and voweth, and sacrificeth unto the Lord a corrupt thing: for I am a great King, saith the Lord of hosts, and my name is dreadful among the heathen.

13-14. God demonstrates that they are guilty of profaning His name using two evidences: (1) their attitude toward their offerings (vs. 13) and (2) their substitution of offerings (vs. 14). The attitude that the priests had as they went about their duties was, **what a weariness is it!** It was a tedious chore—as all empty religion is. This attitude was further indicated by what they did, **ye have snuffed at it** (they snorted and sniffed as they went about their religious service, treating it with utmost contempt). Not content with that, **ye brought that which was torn, and the lame, and the sick; thus ye brought an offering.** They made the fatal mistake of thinking that because they did not care, God did not really care, either. Jehovah asks, **should I accept this of your hand?** The answer to the question is obviously, No.

Rather than incurring God's favor, their hypocrisy incurs God's curse: **But cursed be the deceiver, which hath in his flock a male, and voweth, and sacrificeth unto the Lord a corrupt thing.** The curse is pronounced because the offerer has vowed that he is presenting his best to the Lord and then presents an inferior animal. It is a mistake similar to that made many years later by Ananias and Sapphira (cf. Acts 5:1-11). The insult is heightened by the greatness of the One upon whom it is perpetrated: **I am a great King, saith the Lord of hosts, and my name is dreadful among the heathen.** Israel was to be set apart to be a witness to the Gentiles, but Israel defiled the name of Jehovah; for the Gentiles looked at their worthless sacrifices and deduced that if their God would accept these worthless sacrifices, He must not be a very great God. Israel has failed to understand her own God. He is **a great King,** but they have despised (cf. vs. 6) and profaned (cf. vs. 12) His name; and a day is coming when His name will be exalted among the Gentiles (cf. vs. 11).

B. His Commandment to the Priests. 2:1-9.

1. The address. 2:1.

CHAPTER 2
AND now, O ye priests, this commandment is for you.

2:1. **And now, O ye priests** lets us know that the rebuke begun in 1:6 is continued in this chapter. **This commandment**

2 If ye will not hear, and if ye will not lay *it* to heart, to give glory unto my name, saith the LORD of hosts, I will even send a curse upon you, and I will curse your blessings: yea, I have cursed them already, because ye do not lay *it* to heart.

3 Behold, I will corrupt your seed, and spread dung upon your faces, *even* the dung of your solemn feasts; and *one* shall take you away with it.

4 And ye shall know that I have sent this commandment unto you, that my covenant might be with Levi, saith the LORD of hosts.

5 My covenant was with him of life and peace; and I gave them to him *for* the fear wherewith he feared me, and was afraid before my name.

(Heb *mitswah*, i.e., commandment, precept, law, ordinance) which **is for you** is the proposition spelled out in verses 2-3.

2. The indictment. 2:2-3.

2-3. If ye will not hear, and if ye will not lay it to heart, to give glory unto my name, saith the LORD of hosts, I will even send a curse upon you, and I will curse your blessings: yea, I have cursed them already, because ye do not lay it to heart. The language is reminiscent of the Palestinian covenant (cf. Deut 28-30) that operated on the principle of blessing for obedience and punishment for disobedience. The priests needed to walk right in order that they might teach the people to walk aright. If they do not observe the admonition and render to the Lord the reverence due His name as they discharge the duties of their office, they will bring punishment upon themselves.

Behold, I will corrupt your seed. Commentators, noting that the original Hebrew text contained only consonants, note that the same consonants can spell either the word seed or the word arm and are divided as to the proper reading of the text here. Those that favor the reading **seed** note that the resultant meaning is that God would cause the crops to fail. Since the priests were dependent on the increase of the harvest for their tithes, they would thus suffer if God cursed the seed. Those that favor the reading "arm" note that this improves the parallelism in the verse, for the face is mentioned in the next clause. They observe, further, that to curse the seed would not be a punishment peculiar to the priests, for they did not practice agriculture. If the word "arm" is the preferred reading, the resultant meaning is not that the lancing of the arm in any way manifests displeasure against one's arm; rather, the curse is upon the arm with which one performs his business or the duties of his calling, thus neutralizing the official duties performed at the altar and in the sanctuary. **And spread dung** (Heb *peresh*, i.e., dung, excrement) **upon your faces, even the dung of your solemn feasts.** This would be the ultimate insult that could be heaped upon a priest in the discharge of his official duties. The scene is even worse than Joshua standing in the presence of the angel of Jehovah in dung-bespattered garments (cf. Zech 3:1-7). Rather than the priest cleansing the dung, the dung would defile the priest; and he would have to be removed together with it (cf. Hag 2:11-14), hence, **and one shall take you away with it.**

3. The explanation concerning God's covenant with Levi. 2:4-7.

4. And ye shall know that I have sent this commandment unto you. In verses 2-3 God has set forth **this commandment** that He would bless the priesthood for its obedience, but would curse it for its disobedience. The cursing would take the form of disgrace and removal. When the people see the priesthood disgraced and removed, they will **know that I** (Jehovah) **have sent this commandment** (i.e., the conditions of vss. 2-3) **unto you.** The disgraceful conduct of the unfaithful priests is set forth in stark contrast to the conduct of faithful Levi: **That my covenant might be with Levi, saith the LORD of hosts.** The **covenant** referred to in this context is the ". . . covenant of an everlasting priesthood . . ." (cf. Num 25:10-13) given to Phinehas and to the covenant made with Levi and his descendants because of their faithfulness to Him in the midst of general infidelity (cf. Ex 32:25-29; Deut 33:8-11).

5. My covenant was with him of life and peace. With these words Jehovah confirms that the covenant given Levi and Phinehas and his descendants involved **life and peace** (i.e., regeneration and salvation). Jehovah continues, **I gave them to him for the fear wherewith he feared me, and was afraid before my name.** At a time when the nation defected spiritually and worshiped the golden calf (cf. Ex 32:25-29), Levi and his household remained true to Jehovah and became the executors of His judgment against the offenders. He did this because **he feared** (i.e., reverential awe stemming from faith) Jehovah and was **afraid** (i.e., jealous, zealous) for the **name** of Jehovah, which the priests of his day were profaning. Because of his wholehearted commitment to Jehovah, he was wholeheartedly against anything that in any way brought dishonor to Him.

6 The law of truth was in his mouth, and iniquity was not found in his lips: he walked with me in peace and equity, and did turn many away from iniquity.

6. Levi's record and testimony stand in stark contrast to the priests of Malachi's day. **The law of truth was in his mouth, and iniquity was not found in his lips: he walked with me in peace and equity, and did turn many away from iniquity.** Levi faithfully taught and interpreted the Law for the priests and the people, and his personal life was consistent with the teaching which he did from the Law. He walked with God in a very intimate fellowship of **peace and equity**—he did everything that he knew that God wanted, and God was pleased with his life. The result of his godly life was that, in contrast to the priests of Malachi's day, he **did turn many away from iniquity**—the purpose of the priesthood in the first place.

7 For the priest's lips should keep knowledge, and they should seek the law at his mouth: for he is the messenger of the Lord of hosts.

7. God's intentions for the priesthood are rehearsed in this verse. It is a sad commentary on the priesthood of Malachi's day that the priests needed this rebuke and reminder. **For the priest's lips should keep knowledge, and they should seek the law at his mouth: for he is the messenger of the Lord of hosts.** The priest is the God-intended means of communication between God and man. His life and message should be such that man would seek him out to find out what God says about everything. No man had a higher privilege than the priest of the Old Testament. It is matched (and perhaps exceeded) only by the minister of God in the New Testament economy. No one else has the privilege of saying, ". . . But we have the mind of Christ" (cf. I Cor 2:16)—i.e., here is what God says about the matter!

4. The failure of the priesthood. 2:8-9.

8 But ye are departed out of the way; ye have caused many to stumble at the law; ye have corrupted the covenant of Levi, saith the Lord of hosts.
9 Therefore have I also made you contemptible and base before all the people, according as ye have not kept my ways, but have been partial in the law.

8-9. These verses focus the attention on the priesthood of Malachi's day and show how far they are from the priestly model afforded by Levi (cf. vss. 4-6). **But ye are departed out of the way** (i.e., the way desired by Jehovah and exemplified by Levi); **ye have caused many to stumble at the law** (in contrast to Levi who turned many away from iniquity); **ye have corrupted the covenant of Levi, saith the Lord of hosts.** Though Malachi fearlessly delivered this message to the priests of his day, the rebuke is not of his invention; it comes from **the Lord of hosts** (the First Person of the Trinity). By their inattention to their duties the priests have neutralized the **covenant of Levi** and have forsaken the ways of their fathers, thus obligating God to deliver them up to shame and ignominy. **Therefore have I also made you contemptible and base before all the people, according as ye have not kept my ways, but have been partial in the law.** The priests had treated and regarded the service and worship of Jehovah as contemptible (cf. 1:7, 12) and thus receive retribution in kind for their offense. God humiliated them before all the people. In their exercise of duties prescribed by the Law, they were **partial,** i.e., they invented ingenious devices and methods whereby they could circumvent the intention of the Law. Outward idolatry was rendered distasteful to the people during the Exile, but it was replaced by a more refined idolatry of dead-works righteousness where the people were led to trust in outward form, rather than in inward reality. The attitudes of the priesthood in Malachi's day culminated in the Pharisaism and Sadduceeism encountered in the days of our Lord.

10 Have we not all one father? hath not one God created us? why do we deal treacherously every man against his brother, by profaning the covenant of our fathers?

IV. JEHOVAH'S SECOND DISPUTE WITH THE PEOPLE. 2:10-17.

A. The Prophet's Question. 2:10.

10. Malachi introduces the subject by asking two rhetorical questions. The answer expected to both questions is, Yes. **Have we not all one father? hath not one God created us?** The second question helps to interpret the first; for it lets us know that the **one father** of us **all** is not Abraham or Jacob, or any other human being. It is **God** who is the **father** of all mankind by creation. In addition, He is the **father** of Israel by virtue of His special covenant relationship by which He sustains them. Since the answer to the questions is Yes they admit that there is equality before God of Jew and Gentile and male and female—all mankind are equal before God. Further, they admit that they do stand in a Father-son relationship to God and thus are guilty of not giving proper filial devotion to their acknowledged father (cf. 1:6). The purpose of the two beginning clauses, then, is not to show the common descent of Israel by virtue of which they form one united family, as opposed to the heathen. It is to show that all the Israelites are the children of God and as such are spiritual brothers and sisters. Consequently, every violation of the fraternal relation, such as that of which an Israelite who married a heathen woman or put away an Israelitish wife was guilty, was also an offense against God, a desecration of His covenant.

B. The Prophet's Accusation. 2:11-17.

1. Judah has dealt treacherously with their brothers. 2:11-12.

11 ¶Judah hath dealt treacherously, and an abomination is committed in Israel and in Jerusalem; for Judah hath profaned the holiness of the LORD which he loved, and hath married the daughter of a strange god.

11. The problem is set forth in this verse: **Judah hath dealt treacherously** (Heb *bagad*, i.e., to deal treacherously, deceive) with the result that **an abomination is committed in Israel and in Jerusalem**. This indicates that the matter had consequences that were far more serious than they knew or appreciated. The particular is, **Judah hath profaned** (Heb *chalal*, i.e., to pollute, make common) **the holiness of the LORD which he loved. The holiness of the LORD** is not a reference to the attribute of God, the holy state of marriage, the sanctuary, or any holy thing. It is a reference to Israel, whom Jehovah has chosen out of all the nations of the world to be His peculiar people (Heb *'am qadôsh,* lit., holy people, i.e., a people set apart from all other peoples of the earth and set apart to the purposes of God—cf. Ex 19:5; Lev 20:24-26; Deut 7:1-6; 14:2; Ps 114:2; Jer 2:3; Ezr 9:2). **Which he loved**—the **he** is Jehovah who **loved** Israel and manifested that love in His choosing her to be in special covenant relationship to Him (cf. 1:2-3). The way in which **the holiness of the LORD** was **profaned** was, **Judah . . . hath married the daughter of a strange god**. The problem is not that God has anything against the Gentiles; it is that Israel is a set-apart nation. **The daughter of a strange god** (Heb *bat-'ēl nēchar*, lit., dependent of a strange god, cf. Ezr 9:2ff.; Neh 13:23ff.) describes a person who is an idolatress. It is true that only marriage with Canaanite women was expressly forbidden (cf. Ex 34:16; Deut 7:3); but all marriages with heathen women who did not give up their idolatry were irreconcilable with the calling of Israel (cf. Solomon, I Kgs 11:1-2). God may punish every one who commits this sin by cutting him off (cf. vs. 12).

12 The LORD will cut off the man that doeth this, the master and the scholar, out of the tabernacles of Jacob, and him that offereth an offering unto the LORD of hosts.

12. The prospect is set forth in this verse. **The LORD will cut off the man that doeth this.** The one who is guilty of this sin will experience the judgment of God. Two figures are used to show the universal application of the judgment: **The master** (Heb *'ur*, i.e., to awake, stir) is better understood as the waking one, and **the scholar** (Heb *'anah*, i.e., to answer, respond) is better understood as the answering one. No reference to Levites who kept watch in the Temple at night, should be understood, nor to the teachers or scholars of Israel. The thought of universal application throughout the land is amplified by the phrase **out of the tabernacles** (Heb *'ōhel*, lit., tent) **of Jacob**—the reference is to the houses or dwelling places in which the people lived, not to the tabernacle or holy places. The extent of the judgment includes **him that offereth an offering unto the LORD of hosts**—i.e., the one who offers an offering in behalf of the one who is guilty of committing this sin will himself incur God's judgment. Keil accurately sets forth the prophet's intent: "May God not only cut off every descendant of such a sinner out of the houses of Israel, but any one who might offer a sacrifice for him in expiation of his sin."

2. Judah has dealt treacherously with their wives. 2:13-16.

13. The problem of intermarriage with the heathen women is further complicated by the fact that some of the men of Israel were divorcing their Hebrew wives in order to do it. The prophet addresses the problem directly: **And this have ye done again, covering the altar of the LORD with tears, with weeping, and with crying out.** The **tears** were those shed by the divorced women who came to the altar of the Lord and covered it with their **tears**. The **tears** were viewed by God as a kind of effective sacrifice, for they have been so profuse **that he regardeth not the offering any more, or receiveth it with good will at your hand.** So touched is Jehovah with the plight of the divorced wives, who with their **tears** have laid their trouble before the Lord in the sanctuary, that He no longer receives the sacrifices that their erring husbands might bring.

14. Yet ye say, Wherefore? The guilty ones do not recognize their responsibility for this sin and ask God (hypocritically, with feigned innocence?) why He will no more graciously accept their sacrifices. Through His prophet, God condescends to answer their question in plainest terms: **Because the LORD hath been witness between thee and the wife of thy youth, against whom thou hast dealt treacherously.** The thought is not that Jehovah is between them as an avenging **witness**, but that God was **witness** to the marriage which took place in His presence! Jehovah affirms that though a legal divorce has taken place and another marriage has been legally consummated, that divorce did not break the marital tie. The man is still married to his Hebrew wife: **Yet is she thy companion, and the wife of thy covenant.** This verse clearly teaches that Jehovah regards marriage to be a **covenant** of God (Heb *berīt 'Elōhīm*, cf. Prov 2:17); it was concluded before the face of God, and He was a witness to that marriage. The **covenant** is not broken by divorce and a subsequent remarriage. It is clear that God regarded marriage to be a lifelong commitment broken only by the death of one of the partners.

15. And did not he make one? Yet had he the residue of the spirit. And wherefore one? That he might seek a godly seed. This verse has always been difficult to interpret. There are three major views as to the prophet's intent. The first view proposes an alternate reading and would retranslate the verse to read: And not one hath done so who had a residue of the spirit. Those holding this view understand the prophet to be saying that one possessing a residue of the Holy Spirit would not engage in the conduct of divorcing his wife and remarrying a heathen wife. While this may be true from a theological point of view, it does not fit into the context, nor does it fit smoothly with the remainder of the verse. The second view, held by early Jewish rabbis, understood the **one** to be a reference to Abraham whom the offenders might cite as one who took a second wife. This view sees the people of Malachi's day appealing to the action of Abraham as justification for their action. Further appeal is made to the fact that Abraham had **the residue of the spirit,** and under this ministry of the Spirit he took Hagar because he sought **a godly seed.** Others would use the reference to **the**

---

13 And this have ye done again, covering the altar of the LORD with tears, with weeping, and with crying out, insomuch that he regardeth not the offering any more, or receiveth *it* with good will at your hand.

14 Yet ye say, Wherefore? Because the LORD hath been witness between thee and the wife of thy youth, against whom thou hast dealt treacherously: yet *is* she thy companion, and the wife of thy covenant.

15 And did not he make one? Yet had he the residue of the spirit. And wherefore one? That he might seek a godly seed. Therefore take heed to your spirit, and let none deal treacherously against the wife of his youth.

residue of the spirit and the motive of seeking a godly seed to explain why Abraham dismissed Hagar, i.e., because God promised to give him the desired posterity not in Ishmael, but through Sarah in Isaac, so that Abraham was simply acting in obedience to the word of God (cf. Gen 21:12). In addition to being a very strained exegesis at best (it introduces a character not previously in view), the cases of Abraham and the people of Malachi's day are not parallel at all. Abraham did not divorce Sarah to marry Hagar. He took her in addition to Sarah at Sarah's suggestion (cf. Gen 16:1-4). The third view is more in keeping with the context in which the prophet is showing the reprehensible character of divorce and the fact that their Israelite wives are still their wives even though they have divorced them (cf. vs. 14). It is probably best, in view of the context, to understand did not he make one as being a reference to the establishment of marriage when He pronounced, ". . . and they shall be one (Heb 'echad, one, i.e., the one of plurality showing unity as opposed to yachīd one, viz., the only one—'echad occurs in both Gen 2:24 and in this verse) flesh." Thus, God is showing that the marital union is not broken by anything but death. Using a mathematical metaphor, marriage is not like addition $(1 + 1 = 2)$, which can be easily separated, but is rather like multiplication $(1 \times 1 = 1)$ in which the product cannot be divided and still have a whole. Had God intended it otherwise, He could have made it otherwise; for He had the residue of the spirit. This statement is difficult regardless of one's view, but it is probably best understood as a reference to the Holy Spirit who was the direct agent involved in creation. The thought is that had He so desired, Jehovah could have had the Holy Spirit create any number of wives for Adam. Polygamy is not God's design for marriage. By divorcing their wives and entering into further marital unions with heathen women, the men of Malachi's day were actually entering into polygamy; for their divorces did not break their former obligations. Had God intended polygamy, He could have created multiple wives for Adam. He did not do this; He created only one. And wherefore one? Why one man, one woman? That he (Jehovah) might seek a godly seed. Polygamy and divorce are not conducive to rearing godly children, because they spring from a union that does not take God's covenant seriously (cf. vs. 14). The effect of the first half of the verse, then, is to show that divorce is unthinkable because it is impossible to break up a union that God has put together. If one divorces, he deals treacherously with the wife of his youth (cf. vs. 14); causes her to cover the altar of the LORD with tears, with weeping, and with crying out (cf. vs. 13); and enters into a polygamous union that God never intended. Further, by doing so he teaches his children that it is not important to safeguard the sanctity of marriage.

With the previous understanding, the last part of verse 15 makes eminent sense: Therefore (since you cannot break the marital covenant with the wife of your youth) take heed to your spirit, and let none deal treacherously against the wife of his youth. When one feels the desire or need to seek a divorce from his wife, he should realize that this is a danger flag indicating that his spirit is wrong; and he must deal with whatever is producing that wrong spirit. To fail to do so will cause him to pursue a divorce and perhaps enter into a marital contract with another woman, and thus deal treacherously against the wife of his youth. He must not do this, for God is the witness between him and his wife (cf. vs. 14).

One is bound to ask how all of this squares with Deuteronomy 24:1-2. In Deuteronomy, Moses was recognizing the fact that people are going to get divorced and made provisions whereby it could be done. In giving the divine commentary on Moses' action our Lord observed that whenever one got a divorce on Mosaic (biblical) grounds, it was done ". . . because of the hardness of . . . hearts . . ." (cf. Mt 19:7-8). Not even in Moses' day did one in right relationship to God take advantage of the Mosaic provision. Rather, the fact of divorce was an admission of spiritual hardness of heart.

16 For the LORD, the God of Israel, saith that he hateth putting away: for *one* covereth violence with his garment, saith the LORD of hosts: therefore take heed to your spirit, that ye deal not treacherously.

16. That the previous understanding is correct is shown by the sweeping statement of this verse: **For the LORD, the God of Israel, saith that he hateth putting away** (i.e., divorce, the putting away of wives). If one would be like God, he will hate what God hates—divorce—and will not engage in it or anything that will hurt the wife of his youth. Rather, he will give all of his effort to the cultivating of the bond between him and the wife of his youth. **For one covereth violence with his garment, saith the LORD of hosts.** The allusion is to the custom of putting one's garment over a woman to claim her as a wife (cf. Ruth 3:9; Ezk 16:8). When one divorces his wife he fills with violence the garment that he spread over her to claim her as his wife. The garment should protect her, not violate her. One is acting most inconsistently and inconsiderately in doing this. Once again the warning comes, emphasizing its importance: **Therefore take heed to your spirit, that ye deal not treacherously.** The import is plain: at their base marital problems are spiritual problems. Marital problems are first solved spiritually, and then they are worked out practically and personally. If one's spiritual relationship with God is always correct, he will never have marital problems.

3. Judah has dealt treacherously with the Lord. 2:17.

17 ¶Ye have wearied the LORD with your words. Yet ye say, Wherein have we wearied *him*? When ye say, Every one that doeth evil *is* good in the sight of the LORD, and he delighteth in them; or, Where *is* the God of judgment?

17. First comes the Lord's statement: **Ye have wearied the LORD with your words.** Israel, characteristically, feigns impunity: **Wherein have we wearied him?** Once again, Jehovah condescends to give specific evidence. They make three complaints or charges against Jehovah: (1) **Every one that doeth evil is good in the sight of the LORD**—the Lord rewards evildoers with good so He must like them more than He does the righteous; (2) **he delighteth in them**—the Lord must approve of the evildoers or He wouldn't prosper them so abundantly; and (3) **Where is the God of judgment?**—the Lord must not exist, or He would judge the evildoers instead of prospering them. All three complaints are familiar. Jehovah graciously answers their complaint in the opening verses of the succeeding chapter by showing that One is coming who will indeed right all wrongs—including those in the priesthood and the people of Israel!

V. JEHOVAH'S DISPATCH OF THE PURIFYING MESSENGER. 3:1-6.

A. The Announcement of His Coming. 3:1.

CHAPTER 3

BEHOLD, I will send my messenger, and he shall prepare the way before me: and the Lord, whom ye seek, shall suddenly come to his temple, even the messenger of the covenant, whom ye delight in: behold, he shall come, saith the LORD of hosts.

3:1. The people have expressed themselves all too frequently (cf. 2:17). The prophet uses this occasion to present an announcement of the coming of the Day of the Lord and its true nature. He begins by showing the person who will judge. **Behold, I will send my messenger. Behold** alerts the people that something important follows. **My messenger** (Heb *malachî*, i.e., my messenger) is a play on the name of the prophet. It is not a reference to a heavenly messenger or spiritual being, nor to the angel of Jehovah, but to an earthly messenger of the Lord, the same one called Elijah in 4:4-5. **He shall prepare the way before me**—this statement relates the **messenger** to the one whom Isaiah called "the voice" (cf. Isa 40:3). This first clause is quoted a number of times in the New Testament (cf. Mt 3:3; 11:10; Mk 1:2-3; Lk 1:76; 3:4; 7:26-27; Jn 1:23) and uniformly applied to John the Baptist, the only prophet besides Jesus who was the subject of prophecy. The fact that **he shall prepare the way before me** clearly indicates that the nation was not prepared for the **God of judgment,** concerning whose whereabouts they had just inquired (cf. 2:17). The figure refers to the custom of eastern kings who would send men ahead of them to remove every barrier or obstacle to their coming. In this case, the **messenger** is going to remove the obstacles of sin through the preaching of repentance. Malachi is telling the murmurers of his day that the nation is not morally prepared for the reception of its Lord and therefore had no ground for murmuring at the delay of the manifestation of the divine glory. Rather, they should murmur at their own estrangement from God.

The next clause, **the Lord, whom ye seek, shall suddenly come to his temple,** is not quoted in the New Testament at all. This clearly shows that it has no reference to John the Baptist; but it speaks of another Messenger, Jesus. **Whom ye seek**—they had asked, **Where is the God of judgment?** (cf. 2:17). This is precisely the One who is coming. **Shall suddenly come** does not mean that He will come immediately, i.e., in Malachi's day, but that He will come unexpectedly, at a moment that they think not, i.e., ". . . as a thief in the night . . ." (I Thess 5:2; II Pet 3:10). He will come at the time appointed for His coming, but that time will be a time when they least expect it. **To his temple**—the events described in this clause and in the remainder of the verse were only partially fulfilled in the First Advent of the Lord to the earth. They will be fulfilled ultimately and completely when He returns to the earth in the appointed time and sets up His kingdom. But precisely who is **the Lord** who **shall suddenly come to his temple.** He is **even the messenger of the covenant, whom ye delight in.** In the context **the messenger of the covenant** is identified as **the Lord,** the one **whom ye seek,** the owner of **his temple**—it is clearly a reference to the Messiah. **The covenant** should not be confused with the New Covenant of Hebrews 9:15. The reference is wider than that. **The covenant** is a reference to God's whole covenant program for Israel as embodied in the Abrahamic covenant (Gen 12:1-3) alongside of which was added the Mosaic covenant (Ex 19:5; Gal 3:17-19). The Abrahamic covenant is amplified by the Palestinian covenant (Deut 29-30), the Davidic covenant (II Sam 7:4-17), and the New Covenant (Jer 31:31-34). Both the Hebrew and Greek words for **messenger** can also be translated by the English word "angel," thus the **messenger of the covenant** can also be understood to be the angel of the covenant. A careful study of Old Testament passages such as Exodus 23:20-23 and Isaiah 63:9 shows that the angel of the covenant is God's own self-revelation. He is the angel of the Lord (Jehovah), the preincarnate Christ, the Messiah, Jesus Christ. Thus, **the messenger of the covenant** is none other than Jesus Christ! Again the prophet affirms for emphasis, **behold, he shall come, saith the LORD of hosts.** There is no doubt about the fulfillment, for this is a revelation given by the **LORD of hosts** (the First Person of the Trinity). The only thing not specifically revealed is the exact time of His coming. It will be **suddenly** (i.e., unexpectedly). The prophet (unbeknownst to him) combines both the First and Second Advents of the Lord in this verse, although most of it is applicable to His Second Advent.

B. The Effects of His Coming. 3:2-6.

1. Upon Levi (priesthood). 3:2-3.

2. Once again the prophet blends together aspects of both the First and Second Advents of the Lord, as is characteristically done in prophetic writings. The people had indicated that they wanted the Lord's presence among them (cf. 2:17), in response to which the prophet reveals that He will certainly come (vs. 1) but now asks, **But who may abide the day of his coming? and who shall stand when he appeareth?** The expected answer to both rhetorical questions is no one. The questions call attention to the sinfulness of the nation; and if their request were granted,

2 But who may abide the day of his coming? and who shall stand when he appeareth? for he *is* like a refiner's fire, and like fullers' soap:

they would fall in judgment. Thus, the questions become calls for repentance. This is heightened as the nature of Messiah's coming is described: **For he is like a refiner's fire, and like fullers' soap.** The purpose of the **refiner's fire** is to purge out dross and uncleanness. This is amplified by the reference to **fullers' soap** (Heb *kabas*, i.e., to wash), which likewise is for cleansing. The import is clear: When the Lord comes, judgment will begin not on the heathen as they hoped (cf. 2:17), but on the godless members of the covenant nation.

3. If the people are to be pure, the purification must begin with the ministers of God (cf. I Pet 4:17). That process is described in this verse: **And he shall sit as a refiner and purifier of silver.** The Lord, as Judge, is set forth in the figure of a **refiner** who carefully and continuously watches over the crucible to make sure that the fire is hot enough to burn away all of the dross and impurities from the metal being refined. He keeps removing the dross until he can see his own image clearly reflected in the purified metal. The ministers of God must first be pure, so **he shall purify the sons of Levi, and purge them as gold and silver.** The priests, who should have been leaders in righteousness (cf. 2:7), have been prime leaders in sin (cf. 1:6-2:9) and thus experience cleansing judgment first. The purpose of the purification of the priests is so **that they may offer unto the LORD an offering in righteousness.** The Lord has not been pleased with their offerings (cf. 1:6ff.); but once their character conforms to the righteousness of God, they will be able to meet the requirements of the Law with a proper heart attitude, and they will be pleasing to God. The **offering** in view is the offering to be made by the priesthood of the restored nation of the Millennium. These offerings will be memorial in nature, looking backward to the sacrifice of Christ on the cross in much the same way as the Lord's Supper does for the church of the present day.

3 And he shall sit *as* a refiner and purifier of silver: and he shall purify the sons of Levi, and purge them as gold and silver, that they may offer unto the LORD an offering in righteousness.

2. Upon Judah and Jerusalem. 3:4.

4. A cleansed priesthood will be able to minister effectively to a cleansed nation: **Then shall the offering of Judah and Jerusalem be pleasant unto the LORD, as in the days of old, and as in former years.** The time indicated by **Then** is the time of the Millennium when a redeemed and cleansed people will bring an **offering** to the cleansed priesthood which will **be pleasant unto the LORD. The days of old** and the **former years** are the days of Moses and David (and may include the early days of Solomon). These were the days when the nation was at its spiritual height, and their offerings were **pleasant unto the LORD** because they came from a people who were rightly related to Him.

4 Then shall the offering of Judah and Jerusalem be pleasant unto the LORD, as in the days of old, and as in former years.

3. Upon God. 3:5-6.

5. Through His prophet God now shifts the focus from the future to the Israel of his day and promises: **And I will come near to you to judgment.** They had asked, **Where is the God of judgment** (cf. 2:17)? In answer to their insolent question the prophet states that He is imminently near. When He comes He will be **a swift witness** and will execute judgment against, not only the priesthood, but four categories of sinners: (1) **Sorcerers**—God takes the occult seriously. This evil prevailed in postexilic Israel and very likely was introduced into the nation by the heathen wives; (2) **Adulterers**—particularly in view are the men who have divorced their Israelite wives (cf. 2:16) and married heathen women. Though everything is legal, it is not right—they have entered into adulterous unions and thus are candidates for the judgment of God; (3) **False swearers**—this sin is repeatedly condemned in the Old Testament (cf. Ex 20:16; Lev 19:12; Deut 19:16-20; Prov 19:5; Jer 29:23); thus, all false witnesses will experience the judgment of God, and those to whom they have lied will be vindicated. (4) **Those that oppress**

5 And I will come near to you to judgment; and I will be a swift witness against the sorcerers, and against the adulterers, and against false swearers, and against those that oppress the hireling in *his* wages, the widow, and the fatherless, and that turn aside the stranger *from his right*, and fear not me, saith the LORD of hosts.

1857

the hireling in his wages, the widow, and the fatherless, and that turn aside the stranger from his right—these are people who generally are helpless and at the mercy of those over them. They are easily abused; but they have a very effective lawyer, and the Judge of the Universe will rule in their favor and execute judgment upon their oppressors. All of these sins, and others not specifically named, God will judge because they are performed by people who **fear me not, saith the LORD of hosts.** Their deeds are irrefutable evidence of their heart relationship that does not reverence **the LORD of hosts.** The fact that this judgment is coming is absolutely certain because it is not the prophet's invention; it is directly pronounced by **the LORD of hosts** (the First Person of the Trinity). He describes Himself further in the next verse.

6 For I am the LORD, I change not; therefore ye sons of Jacob are not consumed.

6. This is the Lord of Hosts' description of Himself: **For I am the LORD**—He is Jehovah, the Eternal, the Maker of Heaven and Earth, the One who manifested His love in His choice of Israel (cf. 1:2-3). **I change not**—He is immutable and will not go back upon the covenants given to Abraham and the nation, even though they have not conducted themselves as privileged people. **Therefore ye sons of Jacob are not consumed**—He addresses them in keeping with the name by which they enjoy covenant relationship to Him (cf. 1:2-3) and promises that they will not be destroyed because of the future that He has for them. It is not what they can do for Him that counts, but rather what He can and will do for them! If it were not for God's intervention and love, they would pass out of existence.

VI. JEHOVAH'S THIRD DISPUTE WITH THE PEOPLE. 3:7-15.

A. Concerning Keeping the Statutes of the Lord. 3:7-12.

1. God's declaration and invitation. 3:7a.

7 ¶Even from the days of your fathers ye are gone away from mine ordinances, and have not kept them. Return unto me, and I will return unto you, saith the LORD of hosts. But ye said, Wherein shall we return?

7a. The problems that the nation is experiencing are not of recent derivation. **Even from the days of your fathers ye are gone away from mine ordinances, and have not kept them.** In light of their long-standing need, God invites them to **Return unto me** (i.e., repent of your sins) and promises **I will return unto you** (i.e., in blessing instead of promised judgment).

2. The people's dispute. 3:7b.

7b. In spite of the abundant evidence of their sin and the gracious promise of blessing in response to their repentance, the people incredulously ask: **Wherein shall we return** (i.e., in what particular shall we return)?

3. God's demonstration—tithes and offerings. 3:8-12.

8 ¶Will a man rob God? Yet ye have robbed me. But ye say, Wherein have we robbed thee? In tithes and offerings.

8. The people's incredulous question gives God through His prophet the occasion once again to spell out their sin in specifics. **Will a man rob God? Yet ye have robbed me.** Is it possible that finite man could rob the infinite God? Predictably, the people dispute God's indictment: **But ye say, Wherein have we robbed thee?** Jehovah patiently and relentlessly answers: **In tithes and offerings**—they have done what no man should presume to attempt, namely, to defraud God in the tithe and heave offering. The specific nature of their offense could have taken three formats: (1) not paying their tithes and offerings at all; (2) withholding a part of their tithes and offerings because of the hard times that were upon them (cf. 3:11); or (3) not paying their tithes into the house of God as they should. The payment of tithes and offerings was a recognition of their subjection to God and a recognition that God owned them and all that they had. To withhold the tithe is to renounce the sovereign authority of God and to be guilty of the same sin as Lucifer in the beginning—a failure to recognize the sovereignty of God and be in subjection to Him.

9 Ye *are* cursed with a curse: for ye have robbed me, *even* this whole nation.

10 Bring ye all the tithes into the storehouse, that there may be meat in mine house, and prove me now herewith, saith the Lord of hosts, if I will not open you the windows of heaven, and pour you out a blessing, that *there shall* not *be room* enough *to receive it.*

9. Such a serious offense demands a commensurate punishment. That is now spelled out: **Ye are cursed with a curse: for ye have robbed me, even this whole nation.** In seeking to rob God, they actually robbed themselves of God's blessing and made themselves the recipients of a **curse.** They experienced lack of harvest and famine (cf. 3:11)—just punishment in kind. The word "robbed" occurs in participial form, indicating that they were still in the process of robbing or defrauding God. The sin was not occurring in isolated instances, for it was manifested by **even this whole nation.** The **whole nation** did not recognize its obligation incumbent upon them because of the love He had bestowed upon them in choosing them for His own (cf. 1:2-3).

10. What must be done? They must be obedient in the specific in which the disobedience lies: **Bring ye all the tithes into the storehouse.** The word **all** is emphasized, indicating that this was the primary area of fault—they were withholding that which rightly belonged to God for what seemed good reason to them, economic hard times (cf. 3:11). They are to stop withholding the tithe and bring it all . . . **into the storehouse.** Feinberg summarizes the **tithes** which were incumbent upon Israelites: "(1) the tenth of the remainder after the firstfruits were taken, this amount going to Levites for their livelihood (Leviticus 27:30-33); (2) the tenth paid by Levites to the priests (Numbers 18:26-28); (3) the second tenth paid by the congregation for the needs of the Levites and their own families at the tabernacle (Deuteronomy 12:18); and (4) another tithe every third year for the poor (Deuteronomy 14:28-29)" (*The Minor Prophets,* p. 263). These were the tithes that the people of the prophet's day were withholding from and hence robbing God (cf. Neh 13:10). The offerings were separate from the tithes. Feinberg notes: "The offerings in Israel were the firstfruits, not less than one-sixtieth of the corn, wine, and oil (Deuteronomy 18:4)" (page 265). It is interesting to note that **tithes** are never mentioned in the New Testament. Though the fact of tithing does antedate the Mosaic law (cf. Gen 14:18-20; Heb 7:9), the New Testament measure for giving is summed up in I Corinthians 16:2; "Upon the first day of the week let every one of you lay by him in store, as God hath prospered him. . . ." The New Testament teaching of giving is that it is to be regular ("Upon the first day of the week"), all-inclusive ("let every one of you"), systematic ("lay by him in store"), and proportionate ("as God hath prospered him"). Nowhere in the New Testament is it suggested that the believer is to give 10 percent of his income, though in view of the Old Testament example that is probably a good place to begin. The measure is "as God hath prospered him." It is possible that one could give 10 percent and still rob God, if God had prospered him greatly. The New Testament is more concerned with the motive in giving. "But this I say, He which soweth sparingly shall reap also sparingly; and he which soweth bountifully shall reap also bountifully. Every man according as he purposeth in his heart, so let him give; not grudgingly, or of necessity: for God loveth a cheerful giver" (II Cor 9:6-7). **The storehouse,** contrary to much popular preaching on the subject, is not the local church (which in no sense was in existence at that time or the subject of prophecy). When one understands the nature of the tithes and offerings (see earlier), he understands that **the storehouse** is a reference to the chambers in the Temple where the tithes were brought (cf. Neh 10:38; 13:12). There is the principle of bringing the tithes and offerings to the house of God to support the work of God, and in that sense believers today should bring their tithes and offerings to the local church of which they are members to support the work of the Lord in and through that local church. There is nothing in this verse, however, which would limit their giving to the local church. There is no reason why believers today cannot support with their gifts ministries of the Lord that are carried on in avenues other than their own particular local church. Each believer is independently accountable to God for the allotment of the money God entrusts to him.

The reason why the people were to bring **all the tithes into the storehouse** was so **that there may be meat in mine house.** The Levites and priests were supported by the tithes and offerings brought into the **storehouse.** These offerings primarily took the form of **meat** (food) that was used by the Levites and priests for their living. **And prove me now herewith, saith the Lord of hosts;** the First Person of the Trinity issues a challenge for the people to attempt to outgive Him by their giving. **If I will not open you the windows of heaven**—a figure denoting a copious supply of blessing so that it flows down from heaven like a pouring rain (cf. II Kgs 7:2). **And pour you out a blessing, that there shall not be room enough to receive it**—hyperbole, the thought is that God will provide a superabundance. The blessings of God would come not because God got 10 percent of their wealth, but because in giving the tithe they were in the place of obedience and subjection to God. The outward sign of their obedience and subjection to God was the giving of the tithe. The principle holds true for today. God blesses His children not because they give 10 percent (or more), but because in their cheerful giving in keeping with the measure that God has blessed, they are giving testimony of their obedience, subjection to, and dependence upon God.

11 And I will rebuke the devourer for your sakes, and he shall not destroy the fruits of your ground; neither shall your vine cast her fruit before the time in the field, saith the Lord of hosts.

11. The blessings described in a general way in verse 10 are individualized in this verse. **And I will rebuke the devourer for your sakes. The devourer** (Heb *'akal,* i.e., to eat, consume, devour) was a name given to the locust because of his insatiable appetite. God will withhold the **devourer,** with the result that **he shall not destroy the fruits of your ground; neither shall your vine cast her fruit before the time in the field, saith the Lord of hosts.** God promises that the vineyards will not **cast** (Heb *shakal,* i.e., to miscarry) or drop off their grapes before they ripen. In the prophet's day, the land was apparently experiencing a locust plague and a blight that caused the grapes of the vineyards to fall off before they ripened. No wonder they were tempted (and yielded) to withhold a part of their tithes. Tithes and offerings are a matter of faith. God promises that if His people will respond to such crises in faith and continue to give their full tithe, He will more than make it up to them. However, if they wish for God to open His storehouse, they must first open theirs in faith. God's blessing is directly proportionate to the obedience on the part of His child—that principle still holds true today.

12 And all nations shall call you blessed: for ye shall be a delightsome land, saith the Lord of hosts.

12. The sin of withholding the tithe from God had assumed national proportions (cf. vs. 9). Now, if obedience will assume national proportions, there will be national blessing and national prominence. **And all nations shall call you blessed: for ye shall be a delightsome land, saith the Lord of hosts.** If Israel will be obedient to God in the matter of the tithe, two blessings will follow: (1) all nations will call Israel blessed and (2) its land will be a pleasure to everyone (cf. Zech 7:14; 8:13, 23). These blessings are absolutely certain responses to obedience because they depend not upon man, but upon **the Lord of hosts** (the First Person of the Trinity).

B. Concerning Their Arrogance Against God. 3:13-15.

1. God's declaration. 3:13a.

13a. The second matter that God brings to the people in this third dispute with them concerns their arrogance. **Your words have been stout** (Heb *chazaq,* i.e., to be strong, hard, severe) **against me, saith the Lord.**

13 ¶Your words have been stout against me, saith the Lord. Yet ye say, What have we spoken *so much* against thee?

2. The people's dispute. 3:13b.

13b. Predictably, the people take issue with God's assertion and say, **What have we spoken so much against thee?** They ask: What have we spoken against you?

2. God's demonstration. 3:14-15.

14 Ye have said, It *is* vain to serve God: and what profit *is it* that we have kept his ordinance, and that we have walked mournfully before the LORD of hosts?

15 And now we call the proud happy; yea, they that work wickedness are set up; yea, *they that* tempt God are even delivered.

14-15. Once again, God graciously uses the people's question as an opportunity to face them directly with their sin. The same attitude that neutralized the effectiveness of the priesthood had infected the people (cf. 2:17). **Ye have said, It is vain to serve God: and what profit is it that we have kept his ordinance, and that we have walked mournfully before the LORD of hosts?** The people are saying, in essence: What good does it do to serve Jehovah? We're better off to keep the 10 percent for ourselves. They looked at the service of God from the standpoint of profit. This caused them to look at everything from a wrong perspective; hence, **now we call the proud happy; yea, they that work wickedness are set up; yea, they that tempt God are even delivered.** They made the same mistake the priests had made earlier (cf. 2:17). The view can be either of the heathen outside of Israel or the ungodly within Israel or both. The people thought that the proud and wicked were especially favored by God, for they violated God's ordinances and commandments with seeming impunity and with God's apparent blessing.

VII. THE REMNANT'S REPENTANCE. 3:16-18.

A. Their Repentance Expressed. 3:16a.

16 Then they that feared the LORD spake often one to another: and the LORD hearkened, and heard *it,* and a book of remembrance was written before him for them that feared the LORD, and that thought upon his name.

16a. As the result of the Lord's rebuke, a faithful remnant were drawn together in Israel: **Then they that feared the LORD spake often** (this word does not occur in the Hebrew text) **one to another.** In the midst of the spiritual declension that surrounded them they were drawn together by their mutual concern of manifesting obedience to the Lord. The Lord's response is beautiful: **And the LORD hearkened, and heard it.** These people realized the promise expressed in verse 7: **Return unto me, and I will return unto you.**

B. Their Repentance Accepted. 3:16b-18.

16b. Not only did the Lord incline His ear to hear their mutual fellowshiping; but also **a book of remembrance was written before him for them that feared the LORD, and that thought upon his name.** This, of course, is figurative language; for God needs no written record to keep before Him the thoughts and deeds of His people. The allusion may be to the practice of Persian kings who kept a written record of specific deeds of service performed for them by individuals (cf. Est 6:1-2), but this is not necessarily so. The Old Testament has an older idea of the names and the actions of the righteous being written in a book before God (cf. Ps 56:8; Dan 7:10; 12:1). Notice that the **book of remembrance** is **before him,** not merely in His presence—it is **before him** constantly as a reminder. The point of the figure is that God ever keeps before Himself the names of those who are His and are in proper relationship to Him.

17 And they shall be mine, saith the LORD of hosts, in that day when I make up my jewels; and I will spare them, as a man spareth his own son that serveth him.

17. God's remembrance leads to God's determination: **And they shall be mine, saith the LORD of hosts, in that day when I make up my jewels; and I will spare them, as a man spareth his own son that serveth him.** In His **book of remembrance** God has a list of all His faithful who are faithfully paying their tithes and offerings as a manifestation of their subjection to and dependence upon Him. They are His **jewels**—especially treasured by Him. **In that day,** i.e., the Great Tribulation, He will spare them and will bring them safely into His millennial kingdom. His **jewels,** then, are the faithful ones who will constitute the kingdom at the Second Advent. By contrast, He will bring inescapable judgment in which they shall perish upon the wicked (cf. 4:1).

18 Then shall ye return, and discern between the righteous and the wicked, between him that serveth God and him that serveth him not.

18. **Then shall ye return, and discern between the righteous and the wicked, between him that serveth God and him that serveth him not.** The **ye** is understood by some as a reference to the wicked in Israel who are not a part of the remnant. It is better, however, to understand the reference to be to the righteous remnant who have turned to the Lord and serve Him. They will clearly be able to realize the falseness of the objection raised in verse 16. They will realize that God does not treat the wicked and the righteous in the same way, for He will sovereignly deliver the righteous and destroy the wicked. The wicked may appear to prosper, but judgment lies ahead for them. The righteous may suffer now, but a glorious deliverance for them lies ahead.

VIII. THE COMING JUDGMENT. 4:1-6.

A. The Arrogant and Evildoer Destroyed. 4:1.

CHAPTER 4

FOR, behold, the day cometh, that shall burn as an oven; and all the proud, yea, and all that do wickedly, shall be stubble: and the day that cometh shall burn them up, saith the LORD of hosts, that it shall leave them neither root nor branch.

4:1. The people have thought that the proud and the wicked will not be called into account by God (cf. 3:15), but this verse shows that that is not so. **For, behold, the day cometh, that shall burn as an oven; and all the proud, yea, and all that do wickedly, shall be stubble.** The **day that cometh** is the day of the Lord. It is the time of Jacob's trouble, the Great Tribulation, the birth pangs for the millennial kingdom. The **day** is described as a day of burning in which the **proud** and **all that do wickedly, shall be stubble**—they will be utterly destroyed. The thought of destruction and judgment is heightened by the remainder of the verse: **And the day that cometh shall burn them up, saith the LORD of hosts, that it shall leave them neither root nor branch.** The figure of **root** and **branch** represents the two extremes of the tree—the entire tree will be destroyed. One needs to be reminded that all of this is certain because it is decreed by **the LORD of hosts** (the First Person of the Trinity). The end of the **proud** and the wicked is far different from that imagined in 3:15!

B. The Righteous Delivered. 4:2-3.

2 ¶But unto you that fear my name shall the Sun of righteousness arise with healing in his wings; and ye shall go forth, and grow up as calves of the stall.

3 And ye shall tread down the wicked; for they shall be ashes under the soles of your feet in the day that I shall do *this*, saith the LORD of hosts.

2-3. That day will be a day of destruction for the **proud** and **all that do wickedly** (cf. vs. 1), but it will be a day of deliverance for the righteous remnant. **But unto you that fear my name shall the Sun of righteousness arise with healing in his wings.** The righteous will not experience the burning wrath of God but, rather, will be gently and comfortably warmed by the **Sun of righteousness**—a figurative representation of the person of Jesus Christ, the Messiah. He will burn up the wicked (cf. vs. 1), but for the righteous there will be **healing in his wings**—a figurative representation of the rays emanating from the sun, indicating the swiftness with which the healing will be applied to the righteous that need it. As the result of the **healing . . . ye shall go forth, and grow up as calves of the stall.** The righteous will escape the judgment to be visited upon the **proud** (vs. 1) and wicked. The righteous will **go forth** (i.e., enjoy freedom) and **grow up** (Heb *pūsh*, i.e., to increase, grow fat) **as calves of the stall** (i.e., they will experience abundant blessing in an absolutely secure environment). **And ye shall tread down the wicked; for they shall be ashes under the soles of your feet in the day that I shall do this, saith the LORD of hosts.** In stark contrast, the ungodly are likened to **ashes** because they will be burned up in God's judgment. Earlier (cf. 3:14), the people had asked, **what profit is it that we have kept his ordinance . . . ?** The righteous can answer: Much in every way—not only in this life, but especially in the life to come!

C. The Exhortation to Remember Moses. 4:4.

4 ¶Remember ye the law of Moses my servant, which I commanded unto

4. **Remember ye the law of Moses my servant, which I commanded unto him in Horeb for all Israel, with the statutes**

him in Hō'rĕb for all Israel, *with* the statutes and judgments.

and judgments. One must keep in mind that these words come at the end of the Old Testament (not only physically, as in the English versions, but actually). With the end of this prophecy the voice of inspiration would be silent for four hundred years until the birth of John the Baptist was announced to Zechariah (cf. Lk 1:13). Thus, in the intervening period God was going to send no more prophets to the nation to keep calling them back to himself. It was imperative that they **Remember . . . the law of Moses,** for God gave it to **all Israel** (not to the church) to govern their lives. The Mosaic covenant is divided into three parts, all of which are mentioned in this verse: **The law of Moses**—a reference to the Commandments (cf. Ex 20:1-26) which revealed the righteous will of God; **the statutes**—a reference to the Ordinances (cf. Ex 24:12-40:38; Lev 1-7) which were given to govern the religious life of Israel; and the **judgments**—a reference to the Judgments (cf. Ex 21:1-24:11) which were given to govern the social life of Israel.

D. The Promise to Send Elijah. 4:5-6.

5 Behold, I will send you E-lī'jah the prophet before the coming of the great and dreadful day of the LORD:
6 And he shall turn the heart of the fathers to the children, and the heart of the children to their fathers, lest I come and smite the earth with a curse.

5-6. Behold, I will send you Elijah the prophet before the coming of the great and dreadful day of the LORD. Scholars and commentators are divided into two schools of thought concerning the identity of the **Elijah** who is promised in this passage. Some think that the passage refers to a second coming of Elijah the Tishbite, while others think that the reference is to the coming of John the Baptist. Both views have much to commend them. It is helpful to note that **Elijah** is to come **before the coming of the great and dreadful day of the LORD**—which is certainly the Great Tribulation. Understanding the reference here as Elisha the Tishbite necessitates understanding the **great and dreadful day of the LORD** as a reference to only the last half of the Tribulation; Elijah, together with Moses, would then be one of the two witnesses of Revelation 11. While this is possible, it seems simpler to view **the great and dreadful day of the LORD** as being the Great Tribulation, with the prophet seeing it as the next event on God's calendar—it is not uncommon for the prophets completely to overlook the church age; all of them do it. If this is correct, then the **Elijah** that is promised in this verse is John the Baptist, or Elijah representatively. The things said about Elijah in this context are applied by the Holy Spirit to John the Baptist. Note the summary effect of his ministry: **And he shall turn the heart of the fathers to the children, and the heart of the children to their fathers**—this is applied to John the Baptist in Luke 1:17, and he is identified as ". . . Elijah, which was for to come" in Matthew 11:14. It is true that John the Baptist did not accomplish this on a national scale, but he did accomplish it among the remnant of Israel of his day (much as Malachi had accomplished it among the remnant of Israel of his day). When John the Baptist was asked by the priests and Levites whether he were Elias (Elijah) or that prophet, he answered, "I am not"—meaning that he was not Elijah literally, though he was doing the work of Elijah. To summarize and approach the problem from a whole new perspective, the prophecy concerning Elijah was given through Malachi at a time when the nation was in apostasy, much like the days of Elijah when during the days of Jezebel the people had sunk to a new spiritual low. In his day, Malachi did the work of Elijah. Malachi also prophesied the coming of John the Baptist (cf. 3:1a) who also did the work of Elijah. Mention of Elijah indicates that at the time of Messiah's coming Israel will once again have sunk to a spiritual low. If it is correct to understand the **great and dreadful day of the LORD** as being the last half of the Great Tribulation, then this passsage looks beyond John the Baptist to another Elijah yet to come. The passage, however, does not predict the resurrection of Elijah, but rather God's raising up one who will do the same kind of work that Elijah had done. In regards to the Second Advent, Elijah does not have to be an individual, for this prophecy was actually fulfilled in the person of John the Baptist. All too frequently we are prone to underestimate the importance of John the Baptist and his ministry. An indication of his importance from God's point of view is given in the closing words of the prophecy: **Lest I come and smite the earth with a curse.** Had John the Baptist not come and done his work of turning the **heart of the fathers to the children, and the heart of the children to their fathers,** then the Lord would have come and smitten **the earth** universally **with a curse,** the precise nature of which is undetermined and undefined. The **curse** probably would have been something like not sending Messiah to die for our sins, thus leaving us without hope. This did not materialize, for the coming of **Elijah** was not dependent upon chance; Jehovah Himself sent **Elijah** who came and did his job. We can only thank God for Christ who came and became a curse for us that we might have eternal life, which one day will be shared with Israel nationally and the world universally.

BIBLIOGRAPHY

Allen, L. C. *The Books of Joel, Obadiah, Jonah and Micah.* Grand Rapids: Eerdmans, 1976.

Baldwin, J. G. Haggai, Zechariah, Malachi. In the *Tyndale Old Testament Commentaries.* Downers Grove, Ill.: InterVarsity Press, 1972.

Baron, David. *The Visions and Prophecies of Zechariah.* Grand Rapids: Kregel, reprinted, 1972.

Calvin, John. *Commentaries on the Twelve Minor Prophets.* Edinburgh: T. & T. Clark, 1846 ed.

Copass, B. A. and E. L. Carlson. *Study of the Prophet Micah.* Grand Rapids: Baker, 1950.

Driver, S. R. *The Books of Joel and Amos.* Cambridge: University Press, 1970.

*Feinberg, C. L. *The Minor Prophets.* Chicago: Moody Press, 1976.

Gaebelein, F. E. *Four Minor Prophets.* Chicago: Moody Press, 1970.

Ironside, H. A. *Notes on the Minor Prophets.* Neptune, N.J.: Loizeaux Brothers, 1928.

*Keil, C. F. *The Twelve Minor Prophets.* Edinburgh: T. & T. Clark, 1868.

*Laetsch, Theodore. *The Minor Prophets.* St. Louis: Concordia, 1956.

Leupold, H. C. *Exposition of Zechariah.* Grand Rapids: Baker, 1965.

Maier, W. A. *The Book of Nahum: A Commentary.* St. Louis: Concordia, 1959.

Martin, Hugh. *The Prophet Jonah.* London: Banner of Truth, 1958 reprint of 1872 ed.

*Morgan, G. C. *The Minor Prophets.* Westwood, N. J.: Revell, reprinted, 1960.

Motyer, J. A. *The Day of the Lion: The Message of Amos.* Downers Grove, Ill.: InterVarsity Press, 1974.

Orelli, C. Von. *The Twelve Minor Prophets.* Edinburgh: T. & T. Clark, 1897.

Price, W. K. *The Prophet Joel and the Day of the Lord.* Chicago: Moody Press, 1976.

*Pusey, E. B. *The Minor Prophets.* 2 vols. Grand Rapids: Baker, reprinted, 1950.

Robinson, G. L. *The Twelve Minor Prophets.* Grand Rapids: Baker, 1952.

Watts, J. D. W. *Obadiah: A Critical and Exegetical Commentary.* Grand Rapids: Eerdmans, 1967.

THE

K·J·V

PARALLEL
BIBLE
COMMENTARY

NEW
TESTAMENT

The Gospel According To
MATTHEW

INTRODUCTION

The four Gospels present a fourfold view of the life of Christ. With the exception of scant references by Tacitus and Josephus, our entire knowledge of the life of Jesus comes from these gospel accounts. Most likely, the early accounts were passed on verbally in the Aramaic language and then recorded in Greek manuscripts between A.D. 60-90. All four Gospels build upon genuine historical tradition and preserve different aspects of it.

The basic purpose of the Gospels is to present the gospel message, the good news of the Redeemer-Saviour. They present Jesus as the Messiah of Israel, the Son of God, and the Saviour of the world. The Gospels were written so that their readers would come to believe in Christ and receive eternal life (cf. Jn 20:31). They view Jesus as the Lord of Glory who is presently alive and active in heaven.

The New Testament was not given and received as a single volume, but it grew together by recognition and use. "The order in which we now read the books of the New Testament is that which on the whole, they have tended to assume; and the general internal arrangement, by which the entire collection forms for us a consecutive course of teaching, has been sufficiently recognized by the instinct and fixed by the habit of the church" (T. D. Bernard, *The Progress of Doctrine in the New Testament*, p. 23).

The order of the Gospels has been generally recognized by the church throughout its history. "The Gospel of Matthew occupies first place in all extant witnesses to the text of the four Gospels and in all early lists of the canonical books of the New Testament." (R. V. G. Tasker, *The Gospel According to St. Matthew*, Tyndale New Testament Commentary, p. 11). Matthew's emphasis upon the Old Testament preparation for the gospel makes it an ideal "bridge" from the Old to the New Testament.

The four Gospels present four portraits of Jesus, each in its own characteristic manner. "The greatness of this person could not have been captured in one picture. So we have four portraits, each bringing out its own distinctive facets of the character of Jesus" (I. H. Marshall, "The Gospels and Jesus Christ." In *Eerdman's Handbook to the Bible*, p. 470). Matthew, the Hebrew tax collector, writes for the Hebrew mind. Mark, the travel companion of Paul and Peter, writes for the Roman mind. Luke, Paul's physician-missionary, writes with the Greek mentality in view. John's gospel is different by nature from the other three. It is an interpretation of the facts of Jesus' life rather than a presentation of its facts in historical sequence.

Authorship. The book itself is anonymous, but the earliest of traditions credits it to Matthew, the disciple of Jesus. Papias, the second-century Bishop of Hierapolis, Irenaeus, the Bishop of

Lyons, Origen in the third century, and Eusebius, who wrote his *Historia Ecclesiastica* in the fourth century, all agree that Matthew was the author of this gospel and that he originally wrote it in Hebrew (probably meaning Aramaic, the common spoken language of the early Christians). However, there is no trace of this Aramaic "original" and the earliest quotations (early second century) from Matthew are in Greek.

It is difficult to determine at this time whether Matthew, as we know it today, is a Greek translation of his Aramaic original or whether it was originally written in Greek. Scholars, both conservative and liberal, are divided in their opinion on this matter. However, an examination of the Greek gospel does not substantiate the idea that it is a translation, for it has none of the characteristics of a translated work. Walvoord (*Matthew: Thy Kingdom Come*, pp. 10-12) points out that the Gospel of Matthew includes a number of untranslated Aramaic terms. He comments: "These would be intelligible to Jewish Christians, but if Matthew was translated from Aramaic into Greek for the benefit of Gentile Christians, these terms would require an explanation. The fact that the terms are not translated tends to prove that the Gospel of Matthew was originally written in Greek, even though intended for an audience that also understood Aramaic" (p. 10).

A unique statement within the book of Matthew provides internal evidence to its authorship. The account of the call of Matthew (ch. 9) is followed by that of a meal taken by Jesus in the company of "publicans and sinners." The best translation of this passage says the meal took place "at home." The parallel account in Mark 2:15 makes it clear that this feast took place in Levi's (i.e., Matthew's) house. "The phrase 'at home' means 'in my (that is, in the author's) house.' Here, therefore, is a phrase that betrays the identity of the author" (B.F.C. Atkinson, "The Gospel According to Matthew." In *The New Bible Commentary*, p. 771).

It is possible that Matthew wrote both an Aramaic "Gospel" of the sayings of Jesus, since he was bilingual. Catholic scholars (Lagrange, Chapman, Butler) have tended to uphold the idea of an Aramaic original while liberal Protestants (Allen, Albright) have favored the idea of a Greek original based on the priority of Mark as its major source. Conservative scholars (Kent, Lenski, Walvoord) have generally rejected the idea that Matthew was dependent upon Mark as a source document and hold to the view that Matthew himself wrote the Greek version of his gospel as an original apostolic witness to Christ.

Priority of Matthew. Two major critical views have been advanced in the twentieth century denying the priority of Matthew's gospel: (1) the priority of Mark as the basic source document of both Matthew and Luke; (2) the previous existence of a common source document "Q" to all the synoptics. The "Q Theory" has recently fallen on rough ground among form-critics (cf. A. M. Farrar, "On Dispensing with Q" in D. Nineham, ed. *Studies in the Gospels*). Neither view has really substantially proven its case even though many evangelicals hold to the priority of Mark (cf. Tasker, p. 17). W. R. Farmer and L. Keck are among several contemporary scholars to return to Griesbach's theory on the priority of Matthew. (For a thorough discussion of the introductory matters regarding Matthew, see D. Guthrie, *New Testament Introduction*, pp. 19-48.)

OUTLINE

B. In Judaea. 19:1-27:66.
1. His presentation as King. 19:1-25:46.
a. His journey to Jerusalem. 19:1-20:34.
(1). Jesus' teaching on divorce. 19:1-12.
(2). The rich young ruler. 19:13-30.
(3). The Parable of the Laborers. 20:1-16.
(4). The coming suffering of Christ and His disciples. 20:17-28.
(5). The healing of the two blind men. 20:29-34.
b. His joyful (triumphal) entry. 21:1-46.
(1). The messianic arrival at Jerusalem. 21:1-11.
(2). The cleansing of the Temple. 21:12-17.
(3). The cursing of the barren fig tree. 21:18-22.
(4). The question of authority. 21:23-46.
c. His jealous critics. 22:1-23:39.
(1). The Parable of the Marriage Supper. 22:1-14.
(2). The Herodians: Question of tribute. 22:15-22.
(3). The Sadducees: Question of the Resurrection. 22:23-34.

(4). The Pharisees: Question of the Law. 22:35-23:39.
d. His judgment: Olivet Discourse. 24:1-25:46.
(1). Signs of the present age. 24:5-14.
(2). Signs of the Great Tribulation. 24:15-28.
(3). Signs of the coming Son of Man. 24:29-42.
(4). The Parable of the Two Servants. 24:43-51.
(5). The Parable of the Ten Virgins. 25:1-13.
(6). The Parable of the Talents. 25:14-30.
(7). The judgment of the nations. 25:31-46.
2. His rejection as King. 26:1-27:66.
a. His denial by His disciples. 26:1-56.
b. His denunciation by the Sanhedrin. 26:57-75.
c. His deliverance to Pilate. 27:1-31.
d. His death for mankind. 27:32-66.
III. Triumph of the Messiah. 28:1-20.
A. His Resurrection. 28:1-8.
B. His Reappearance. 28:9-15.
C. His Recommission. 28:16-20.

COMMENTARY

I. COMING OF THE MESSIAH. 1:1-4:11.

A. His Ancestry. 1:1-17

THE book of the generation of Jesus Christ, the son of David, the son of Abraham.
2 Abraham begat Isaac; and Isaac begat Jacob; and Jacob begat Judas and his brethren;

1:1-2. The book of the generation. The genealogy of Christ opens with a statement similar to the various divisions of the book of Genesis (showing the unity of the Scriptures). **Jesus Christ** is the title most often used of the Saviour. Jesus (Gr *Iēsous;* Heb *Yehoshua*) is His earthly name, meaning "saviour." *Christos* is the Greek translation for "messiah" or "anointed." Technically: Jesus the Christ.

Son of David. By tracing Jesus' ancestry back to King David, through the line of Davidic kings, Matthew connects Jesus with His royal heritage. Despite six centuries of vacancy on the royal throne, the Messiah must be of royal descent. The genealogy here is that of Joseph, Jesus' legal father, whereas the genealogy of Luke 3:23-38 is that of Mary, His actual parent, showing His blood line back to David. The author's purpose is to show that the messianic promises made to David's line are fulfilled in Jesus. **Son of Abraham.** He is also the fulfillment of the covenant promises to Abraham, the forefather of the Jews (cf. Gen 12:3; 13:15; 22:18). Since Matthew is writing primarily to Jewish readers, he naturally begins by emphasizing Jesus' Jewish parentage.

3-8. Judas is the Greek form of Judah, the father of the tribe so named. The promise of Jacob was that the leadership of the twelve tribes would come through Judah (cf. Gen 49:8-12) which the Jews understood to mean that the Messiah would come from the tribe of Judah. **Thamar . . . Rachab . . . Ruth . . . wife of Uriah.** Four "questionable" women appear in this genealogy in addition to Mary, the mother of Jesus. It was not customary to list the names of women in a genealogy; therefore, the inclusion of these names must be deliberate on the part of

3 And Judas begat Phā'rĕs and Zā'ra of Thā'mar; and Phā'rĕs begat Ĕs'rŏm; and Ĕs'rŏm begat Ā'ram;
4 And Ā'ram begat A-mĭn'a-dăb; and A-mĭn'a-dăb begat Nā-ăs'son; and Nā-ăs'son begat Săl'mon;
5 And Săl'mon begat Bŏ'ŏz of Rā'chăb; and Bŏ'ŏz begat Ŏ'bed of Ruth; and Ŏ'bed begat Jesse;
6 And Jesse begat David the king;

and David the king begat Solomon of her *that had been the wife* of Ū-rī′as;

7 And Solomon begat Rō-bō′am; and Rō-bō′am begat Ā-bī′a; and Ā-bī′a begat Asa;

8 And Asa begat Jŏs′a-phăt; and Jŏs′a-phăt begat Joram; and Joram begat Ō-zī′as;

9 And Ō-zī′as begat Jŏ′a-tham; and Jŏ′a-tham begat Ā′chăz; and Ā′chăz begat Ĕz-e-kī′as;

10 And Ez-e-kī′as begat Ma-năs′sēs; and Ma-năs′sēs begat Amon; and Amon begat Jo-sī′as;

11 And Jo-sī′as begat Jĕch-o-nī′as and his brethren, about the time they were carried away to Babylon:

12 And after they were brought to Babylon, Jĕch-o-nī′as begat Sa-lā′thī-el; and Sa-lā′thī-el begat Zō-rŏb′a-bel;

13 And Zō-rŏb′a-bel begat A-bī′ud; and A-bī′ud begat E-lī′a-kĭm; and E-lī′a-kĭm begat Azor;

14 And Azor begat Sā′dŏc; and Sā′dŏc begat Ā′chĭm; and Ā′chĭm begat E-lī′ud;

15 And E-lī′ud begat Ĕ-le-ā′zar; and Ĕ-le-ā′zar begat Măt′thăn; and Măt′thăn begat Jacob;

16 And Jacob begat Joseph the husband of Mary, of whom was born Jesus, who is called Christ.

17 So all the generations from Abraham to David *are* fourteen generations; and from David until the carrying away into Babylon *are* fourteen generations; and from the carrying away into Babylon unto Christ *are* fourteen generations.

18 ¶Now the birth of Jesus Christ was on this wise: When as his mother Mary was espoused to Joseph, before they

the author. Tamar was the mother of two illegitimate sons (Pharez and Zerah) by Judah. Rahab was the converted prostitute of Jericho and the mother of Boaz. Ruth, the wife of Boaz, was a godly foreigner (Moabitess). The wife of Uriah is none other than Bathsheba whose adultery with David is infamous. However, she later became the legitimate wife of David and the mother of Solomon. The curious feature of mentioning these women in this genealogy indicates that the evangelist wished to disarm Jewish criticism about the unusual virgin birth of Jesus by showing that irregular unions were divinely blessed in the Messiah's legal ancestry. "The evangelist's argument is that Jesus, born of a virgin mother, was none the less the true lineage of David because Joseph was in fact legally married to his mother Mary" (Tasker, p. 32).

9-10. Uzziah [Ozias] is referred to as Uzziah (Isa 6:1) and Azariah (II Kgs 14:21). Three generations are omitted at this point. Matthew omits the names of Ahaziah, Joash, and Amaziah and then omits Jehoiakim after the name of Josiah. "The omissions are doubtless due to his arbitrary shortening of the list to give three groups of fourteen" (Kent, p. 3). Being familiar with rabbinical thinking, Matthew uses a symmetry of numbers. He has, accordingly, divided the generations from Abraham to Jesus into three groups of fourteen each: from Abraham to David (vss. 2-6), from David to the Babylonian exile (vss. 6-11), from the exile to the birth of Jesus (vss. 12-16). The significance of the number fourteen seems to come from the numerical values of the Hebrew consonants in the name David which add up to that number. The system of rabbinic sacred arithmetic was often based on hidden calculations. To what degree Matthew is following such a system is uncertain.

11-15. Jechoniah is also called Jehoiachin (II Kgs 24:8) and Coniah (Jer 22:24) and was cursed from having any descendant upon the throne of David according to Jeremiah 22:30. It should be noted that Jesus is not a natural descendant of his. He was recognized by the Jews of the exile as their last legitimate king. **Carried away to Babylon** refers to the seventy years' captivity of the Jews in Babylon during the days of Daniel the prophet.

Salathiel is named as the son of Jechoniah. This does not contradict Jeremiah 22:28-30 for the predicted childlessness of Jechoniah refers to reigning children, that is, that he would have no son who would rule Israel as king. The reference to Salathiel as the son of Neri in Luke 3:27 is better understood as being a totally different person, rather than the result of levirate marriage. It is assumed that the rest of this family record comes from Joseph's family annals.

16. Joseph the husband of Mary. The wording carefully inspired by the Holy Spirit avoids giving the impression that Joseph was the natural father of Jesus. As the husband of Mary, he was Jesus' legal father and the one through whom He had a right to David's throne. It is not said that Joseph "begat" Jesus, which is a deliberate change from the preceding genealogical expressions. Every emphasis of the text at this point reinforces the idea of the virgin birth of Christ. The marriage of Joseph and Mary took place after the conception but before the birth of Jesus.

17. Fourteen generations is the literary grouping used by Matthew to emphasize the three major periods of Israel's national history: theocracy, monarchy, hierarchy. The use of "so" implies this is an artificial arrangement. The translation would be "so this makes fourteen generations."

B. His Advent. 1:18-2:23.

18. Espoused means that Mary was already bound or betrothed to Joseph, although they were not yet actually married. Among the Jews, marriage vows were said at the betrothal and required a legal divorce to end them. The custom of the day

came together, she was found with child of the Holy Ghost.

19 Then Joseph her husband, being a just *man*, and not willing to make her a publick example, was minded to put her away privily.
20 But while he thought on these things, behold, the angel of the Lord appeared unto him in a dream, saying, Joseph, thou son of David, fear not to take unto thee Mary thy wife: for that which is conceived in her is of the Holy Ghost.

usually required an interval of one year of betrothal before the bride could actually take residence in her husband's house and consummate their union. It was during this interval that Mary **was found with child.** Her pregnancy naturally would have been assumed to be the result of an illegitimate union of adultery, a circumstance usually punishable by death (Deut 22:23). At this point, Mary had not yet explained her situation to Joseph. Indeed, she could hardly have expected Joseph to accept her story of the miraculous conception of the child by the Holy Spirit. **With child of the Holy Ghost** is the biblical explanation for the miraculous conception of Christ.

19-20. Because Joseph was a **just man,** he decided to divorce Mary privately (privily) but while he considered what should be done **the angel of the Lord** spoke to him in a dream. The angel is better translated as "an angel." Prior to His birth, Jesus Christ, the second person of the Trinity, often appeared to men in the form of a man. These appearances in the Old Testament are called theophanies or Christophanies. Since the Scripture clearly states that "no man hath seen God at any time" (Jn 1:18), these appearances evidently refer to Christ rather than God the Father. It is interesting to note the references to God refer to Him as Lord (cf. Gen 18:2, 13, 17). After His birth as Jesus, there were no more temporary physical appearances of God to man. After His resurrection Jesus appeared to men as Himself in a glorified body.

Put her away means literally to divorce her. The Jewish betrothal had to be legally broken. Joseph's merciful attitude gives an insight into his true nature as a man. **Thou son of David** is the address by the angel to Joseph. In spite of his humble circumstances, he was a legitimate heir to the vacant throne of David. The angel orders him to take Mary as his wife because the baby she has conceived is **of the Holy Ghost.** This divinely born miracle-Son is the fulfillment of God's miraculous

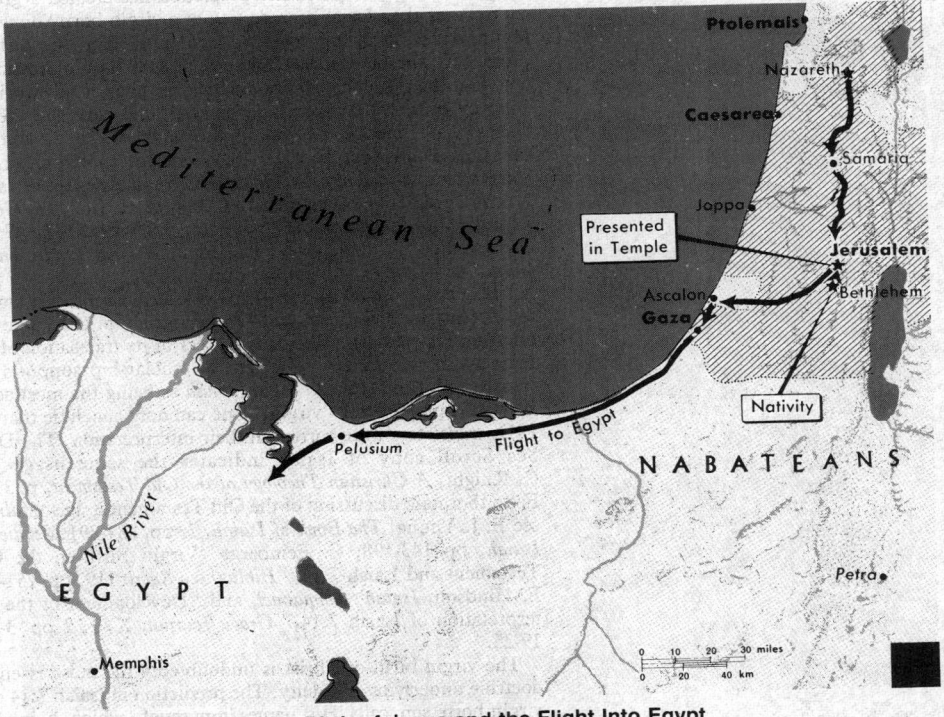

The Birth of Jesus and the Flight Into Egypt

21 And she shall bring forth a son, and thou shalt call his name JESUS: for he shall save his people from their sins.

22 Now all this was done, that it might be fulfilled which was spoken of the Lord by the prophet, saying,

23 Behold, a virgin shall be with child, and shall bring forth a son, and they shall call his name Ĕm-măn′ū-el, which being interpreted is, God with us.

24 Then Joseph being raised from sleep did as the angel of the Lord had bidden him, and took unto him his wife:

25 And knew her not till she had brought forth her firstborn son: and he called his name JESUS.

promises to the Jewish nation, which promises began in the book of Genesis with God's covenant with Abraham.

21-22. Call his name Jesus. The naming of the child Jesus (Heb *Yehoshua*) means "Jehovah saves." This points to the very purpose of Christ's coming into the world to save sinners. Placed early in the New Testament, this statement becomes the foundational concept of the gospel. Jesus, by His very name and nature, is the Saviour. **That it might be fulfilled.** This phrase (Gr *plēroō*) indicates the inevitability of the fulfillment of the words of the prophet, as well as the fact that Matthew saw Isaiah's statement as predictively fulfilled in the birth of Christ. "The verb pictures the promise or prophecy as an empty vessel which is at last filled when the event occurs" (R. Lenski, *Interpretation of St. Matthew's Gospel*, p. 52). Arndt and Gingrich list this use of the word as "the fulfillment of divine predictions or promises" (*A Greek-English Lexicon of the New Testament*, p. 677). There can be no doubt that Matthew firmly believed this reference was definitely a prediction of an event that was fulfilled in the birth of Jesus. One wishing to deny the predictive element of Isaiah or its acceptance by the early church cannot adequately do so on a philological-grammatical basis, nor on the basis of historical precedent.

23-25. A virgin relates Mary the mother of Jesus to the prediction found in Isaiah 7:14. Matthew uses the Greek word *parthenos* to translate the Hebrew word *'almah*. His contextual usage of "fulfill" is almost certainly indicative of his understanding the Isaiah passage to contain a definitely predictive element. He recognizes the prophecy as coming from God (the Greek preposition *hypo* introduces the direct agent with a passive verb, whereas *dia* introduces the mediate agent). The Lord is the source of the prophecy and the prophet is his mouthpiece. Thus, God is the cause and the prophet is the instrument which He uses. The quotation of Isaiah 7:14 follows the Septuagint (LXX) rendering where *parthenos* is also used to translate the Hebrew *'almah*. Perhaps no prophetic prediction has created a greater controversy than Isaiah's prediction of a virgin-born Son which Matthew clearly claims to have been fulfilled in the birth of Christ (cf. *The Interpreter's Bible*, V, p. 218. It is interesting to note that the exegetical and homiletical sections of this work are done by different authors, and on the same page the exegete denies that Isaiah is predicting the birth of Christ and the expositor claims that he is!). The liberal interpretation of this verse attempts to deny the validity of Matthew's use of Isaiah 7:14 as a prediction of the birth of Christ (cf. G. Cox, *The Gospel According to St. Matthew*, pp. 29-30; A. Argyle, *The Gospel According to Matthew*, p. 28; F. Filson, *A Commentary on the Gospel According to St. Matthew*, pp. 54-55).

There can be no doubt that the Greek term *parthenos* is always to be translated "virgin" (Arndt and Gingrich, p. 632). The real question is whether the LXX is correct in its translation of the Hebrew *'almah*. Since the weight of scholarship supports the translation of the Hebrew word *'almah* as being the most accurate word possible for "virgin," one can only conclude that the LXX translaters were correct in their interpretation. The Dead Sea Scroll copy of Isaiah indicates the same usage (cf. G. Knight, *A Christian Theology of the Old Testament*, p. 310). For a thorough discussion of the Old Testament usage of *'almah* see E. J. Young, *The Book of Isaiah*, I, pp. 284-291; *Studies in Isaiah*, pp. 143-198; C. Feinberg, "Virgin Birth in the Old Testament and Isaiah 7:14," *Bibliotheca Sacra* 119, pp. 251-58; E. Hindson, *Isaiah's Immanuel*, and "Development of the Interpretation of Isaiah 7:14," *Grace Journal*, X, 1, 2 pp. 3-15, 19-25.

The virgin birth of Christ is undoubtedly the most essential doctrine underlying His deity. The prediction in Isaiah 7:14 of a virgin-born son calls His name **Immanuel, which being in-**

CHAPTER 2

NOW when Jesus was born in Běth-lehěm of Judæa in the days of Herod the king, behold, there came wise men from the east to Jerusalem,

2 Saying, Where is he that is born King of the Jews? for we have seen his star in the east, and are come to worship him.

3 When Herod the king had heard *these things,* he was troubled, and all Jerusalem with him.

4 And when he had gathered all the chief priests and scribes of the people together, he demanded of them where Christ should be born.

5 And they said unto him, In Běth-lehěm of Judæa: for thus it is written by the prophet,

6 And thou Běth-lehěm, *in* the land of Juda, art not the least among the princes of Juda: for out of thee shall come a Governor, that shall rule my people Israel.

7 Then Herod, when he had privily called the wise men, enquired of them diligently what time the star appeared.

8 And he sent them to Běth-lehěm,

terpreted is, God with us. This is a title describing the deity of the person of the Son of God rather than a name actually used by him. It implies God will come to dwell among His own people. For a discussion of the significance of the virgin birth of Christ see R. Gromacki, *The Virgin Birth: Doctrine of Deity;* H. Hanke, *The Validity of the Virgin Birth;* J. G. Machen, *The Virgin Birth of Christ.*

2:1-2. Bethlehem of Judea was also called Ephrath. The town is five miles south of Jerusalem. Its name in Hebrew means "house of bread." This Judaean city was the birthplace of King David. It was the original city of Joseph's ancestors. According to Luke 2:1-7, Mary and he traveled there from Nazareth and Jesus was born in a stable after they arrived there. **Herod the king** was known as Herod the Great, and was the son of Antipater, an Edomite. He became king by Roman decree in 43 B.C. **Wise men** were originally the priestly caste among the Persians and Babylonians. These Magi from the east were experts in the study of the stars. Tradition claims there were three royal visitors who were also kings. However there is no real historical evidence to verify this. All we are told in the text is that there came wise men from the east to Jerusalem. **Born King of the Jews.** The wise men naturally came to Jerusalem, the royal capital of Israel, seeking one whom they thought was to be born a king, on the basis of their calculations of the stars. What exactly this meant to them we are not sure. Perhaps, through the science of astronomy they observed a new star and for some reason correlated that with the birth of a king. Why they would associate this star with Israel is uncertain. "It is entirely conceivable that these men had made contact with Jewish exiles, or with the prophecies and influence of Daniel, and thus were in possession of Old Testament prophecies regarding the Messiah" (Kent, p. 6). **His star.** It is unlikely that this star could only have been a natural phenomenon since it led the wise men to Jerusalem and later to Bethlehem. It almost certainly was a divine manifestation used by God to indicate the fact and place of the Messiah's birth and the place of His reign.

3-4. Naturally, such a question, seeking the birth of a new king, would upset Herod, the current ruler. He quickly gathered his scribes and demanded an explanation of them. The scribes belonged mainly to the party of the Pharisees and functioned as members of a highly honored profession. "They were professional students and defenders of the law . . . they were also referred to as lawyers because they were entrusted with the administration of law as judges in the Sanhedrin" (*Ryrie Study Bible,* p. 8). **Where Christ should be born.** This demand is highly significant in that it implies the Jews of that day were anticipating the Messiah.

5-6. When they replied that He would be born **In Bethlehem of Judea: for thus it is written by the prophet,** they clearly anticipated a literal fulfillment of the Old Testament prophecies regarding the coming of the Messiah. The quotation is from Micah 5:2 where the prophet predicts that Bethlehem of the tribe of Judah shall be the place where the governor or ruler of Israel shall originate. It is significant to note that Isaiah and Micah were contemporaries. Their prophecies of the coming of the Messiah interrelate to one another. The **Governor** who will come from Bethlehem is none other than the child-ruler predicted in Isaiah 9:6, "For unto us a child is born, unto us a son is given; and the government shall be upon his shoulder." The prophet goes on to proclaim that this ruler shall be the "mighty God" and that the increase of His government shall never end. He will sit upon the throne of David forever.

7-11. Herod's fear of a rival ruler caused him to question **what time the star appeared.** His subsequent slaughter of the children at Bethlehem from two years old and under was apparently calculated from the time given him by the wise men.

and said, Go and search diligently for the young child; and when ye have found *him*, bring me word again, that I may come and worship him also.

9 When they had heard the king, they departed; and, lo, the star, which they saw in the east, went before them, till it came and stood over where the young child was.

10 When they saw the star, they rejoiced with exceeding great joy.

11 ¶And when they were come into the house, they saw the young child with Mary his mother, and fell down, and worshipped him: and when they had opened their treasures, they presented unto him gifts; gold, and frankincense, and myrrh.

12 And being warned of God in a dream that they should not return to Herod, they departed into their own country another way.

13 ¶And when they were departed, behold, the angel of the Lord appeareth to Joseph in a dream, saying, Arise, and take the young child and his mother, and flee into Egypt, and be thou there until I bring thee word: for Herod will seek the young child to destroy him.

14 When he arose, he took the young child and his mother by night, and departed into Egypt:

15 And was there until the death of Herod: that it might be fulfilled which was spoken of the Lord by the prophet, saying, Out of Egypt have I called my son.

16 ¶Then Herod, when he saw that he was mocked of the wise men, was exceeding wroth, and sent forth, and slew all the children that were in Běth-lehěm, and in all the coasts thereof, from two years old and under, according to the time which he had diligently enquired of the wise men.

17 Then was fulfilled that which was spoken by Jeremy the prophet, saying,

18 In Rā'ma was there a voice heard, lamentation, and weeping, and great mourning, Rachel weeping *for* her children, and would not be comforted, because they are not.

19 ¶But when Herod was dead, behold, an angel of the Lord appeareth in a dream to Joseph in Egypt,

20 Saying, Arise, and take the young child and his mother, and go into the land of Israel: for they are dead which sought the young child's life.

21 And he arose, and took the young child and his mother, and came into the land of Israel.

22 But when he heard that Är-che-lā'us did reign in Judæa in the room of

The fact that the child was found in a **house** (vs. 11) and not the manger would indicate that Jesus was probably no longer a baby when the wise men found Him. They were guided to this place by the **star** which **went before them.** This again indicates the supernatural nature of this star. **The young child.** When the wise men arrived they found the child (not a baby) with His mother in a house. This would indicate that the family had now moved out of the stable into a rented home at Bethlehem. Whether the visit of the wise men occurred a few months after the birth of the child or one to two years afterwards is uncertain. Since the wise men brought three gifts, i.e., **gold, frankincense and myrrh,** it has been assumed that they were three in number (some traditions have even given them names but these are not necessarily established by fact). It has been suggested that the gifts were in recognition of Jesus as King, Son of God, and the Suffering Saviour. It is also significant that they **worshiped him,** indicating their recognition of the deity of the one whom they were worshiping. Again, Matthew has reasserted the importance of the deity of Christ. He is the virgin-born Son, "God with us," who deserves our worship.

12-15. Being warned of God. A special divine revelation in the form of a warning was given both to the wise men and to Joseph in the form of a dream. Thus instructed, the wise men did not return to Herod, and Joseph and Mary fled with the baby into Egypt. It should be remembered that there was a large Jewish population in Egypt at that time, especially in and around the city of Alexandria. The holy family would have been inconspicuous during their stay and would have been welcomed by members of their own race. **The death of Herod** occurred in 4 B.C. It should be remembered that our present calendar is off in its calculation by about six years (this would place the birth of Christ at ca. 6-5 B.C.). Herod's death is recorded in detail by Josephus (*Antiq.* xvii. 6.5). The flight to Egypt by Jesus' family is related by Matthew to the statement in Hosea 11:1 which refers historically to the deliverance of the Hebrews from Egypt. Matthew records that this was done that it **might be fulfilled.** Since the Old Testament statement is not a direct reference to Christ, it is apparent that the writer saw this prophecy as a type of Christ. (On the significance and reliability of Matthew's quotations of Old Testament prophecies see R. H. Gundry, *The Use of the Old Testament in St. Matthew's Gospel.*)

16-18. The bitter reaction of Herod when he **slew all the children** at Bethlehem was unrecorded in the history of that period. This should not surprise us because of the king's frequently outraged retaliation on people. He murdered his wife and three sons. Josephus calls him "a man of great barbarity towards all men." **Rachel weeping for her children** (vs. 18) is a quotation of Jeremiah 31:15. The calamity of Israel's mourning at the time of the exile is correlated here to this renewed calamity brought on by Herod, whose very act of ruling is a direct result of that captivity which had been caused by Israel's sin. **Rachel weeping** is a reference to Rachel, the mother of Benjamin, and thus the tribe of Benjamin. She stands as the symbol of the Benjamite mothers and their sorrow. Also, note that she died outside Bethlehem herself (Gen 35:19).

19-23. When Herod was dead refers again to the death of the king in 4 B.C. He was succeeded by his son **Archelaus,** the son of his Samaritan wife, Malthace. Archelaus was as brutal as his father. Thus, Joseph, again warned in a dream, returned to Nazareth, avoiding any further residence in Judaea. The phrase **He shall be called a Nazarene** is a reference to Christ's coming from the city of Nazareth. It should not be taken to mean that He was a Nazirite. A Nazirite was not to drink wine, touch anything unclean, or cut his hair. It was probably a misunderstanding that caused early Roman artists to depict Jesus with long hair. The proof that He was not a Nazirite is found in

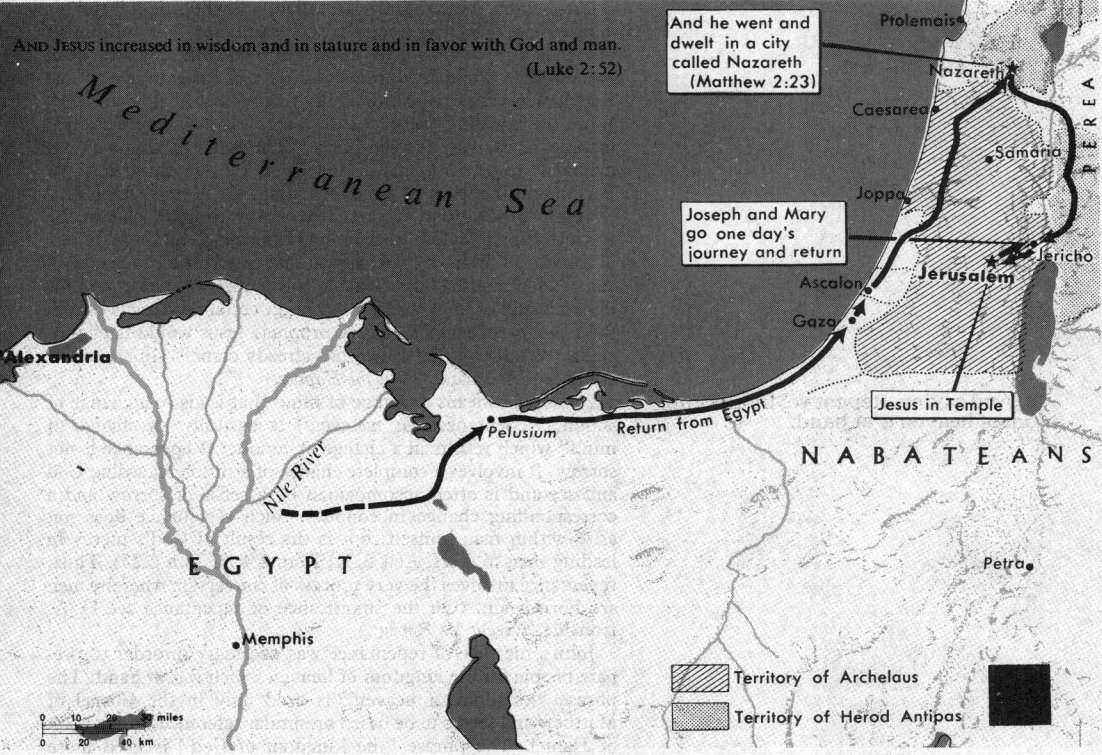

AND JESUS increased in wisdom and in stature and in favor with God and man.
(Luke 2:52)

And he went and dwelt in a city called Nazareth (Matthew 2:23)

Joseph and Mary go one day's journey and return

Jesus in Temple

Return from Egypt

Territory of Archelaus

Territory of Herod Antipas

The Return from Egypt; The Boy Jesus in the Temple

his father Herod, he was afraid to go thither: notwithstanding, being warned of God in a dream, he turned aside into the parts of Galilee:

23 And he came and dwelt in a city called Nazareth: that it might be fulfilled which was spoken by the prophets, He shall be called a Nazarene.

CHAPTER 3
IN those days came John the Baptist, preaching in the wilderness of Judæa,

the fact that He did not keep the other two provisions of the vow. Many of the very people which He came to minister to were considered "unclean" by the people of His day. Since no particular Old Testament passage is referred to, it seems best to understand this verse as referring to a fulfillment of those prophecies which indicate that the Messiah would be of insignificant origin and despised by people (e.g., Isa 53:3).

C. His Ambassador. 3:1-12.

3:1. The forerunner of Christ was **John the Baptist.** He was the son of Zacharias and Elisabeth, and a cousin of the Lord (cf. Lk 1:5-80). The significance of his preparatory ministry cannot be overestimated. Even Josephus (*Antiq.* xviii 5.2) refers to him by name. John was a child of promise whose birth had been announced by the angel Gabriel to his father who was a priest. His birth was accompanied by the promise: "He shall be great in the sight of the Lord . . . and shall be filled with the Holy Ghost" (Lk 1:15). Jesus said of him that there was none greater than John (Mt 11:11) during the Old Testament dispensation. This would imply that John the Baptist was the epitome of the message of the Old Testament itself.

Matthew's reference to John the Baptist assumes that his readers were familiar with him. There is no connection anywhere in Scripture to relate John to one of the Essene communities or to the Qumran sect (of the Dead Sea Scrolls). The real significance of John seems to be his appearance in the **wilderness of Judea,** the eastern part of the province lying beyond the mountain ridge and west of the Dead Sea. This

2 And saying, Repent ye: for the kingdom of heaven is at hand.

infertile area may rightly be called a "wilderness." John's appearance, preaching a message of repentance, is in fulfillment of Isaiah 40:3, "Prepare ye the way of the Lord." The words of the prophet originally formed the part of his message to the Babylonian exiles, who eventually returned to their own land. John, the last of the prophets of Israel, was now commissioned to prepare the way for the King. "The reign of God was immediately to be made manifest in Israel in all its fullness in the Person and the work of none other than the Messiah Himself" (Tasker, p. 47). John is presented as the prophet sent in the spirit of Elijah "before the coming of the great and dreadful day of the Lord" (Mal 4:5). His appearance (wearing a rough coat of camel's hair and having a leather belt around his waist) and his dynamic and often scathing preaching, certainly depicts him in the life-style of Israel's ancient prophet. Jesus would later proclaim, "I tell you that Elijah has already come!" (For a recent study see M. Loane, *John the Baptist*.)

2. Repent means a change of mind that leads to a change of action. Repentance (Gr *metanoia*) is basically "a change of mind" which results in a change of conduct. Repentance is not sorrow. It involves a complete change of attitude regarding God and sin and is often accompanied by a sense of sorrow and a corresponding change in conduct. Such repentance does not arise within man himself, but is the result of God's mercy in leading man to it (cf. Acts 5:31; Rom 2:4; II Tim 2:25). Thus, repentance involves the very process of conversion whereby men are born again. (On the significance of repentance see H. A. Ironside, *Except Ye Repent*.)

John's message of repentance was necessary in order to prepare people for the **kingdom of heaven** which was **at hand**. The phrase "kingdom of heaven" is used only in the Gospel of Matthew and seems to be based on similar references in the book of Daniel. The phrase "the kingdom of God" is used more frequently by Mark and Luke. The change is perhaps due to Matthew's Jewish background and outlook. Since the Jews regarded it as blasphemous to refer to God by name, it is possible that Matthew substituted the word heaven for that reason. Usually the two phrases are used interchangeably in the Gospels. The kingdom of heaven is the rule of heaven over earth. The Jews of Jesus' day were looking forward to the coming of a Messiah who would reign in a Davidic kingdom on earth. It is this kingdom which Christ proclaimed was a literal earthly kingdom, based upon spiritual principles, which would demand a right relationship with God for entrance into that kingdom. Therefore, John the Baptist's ministry is clearly seen as a time of preparation for the coming of Christ and the proclamation of His kingdom.

3 For this is he that was spoken of by the prophet E-sā′ias, saying, The voice of one crying in the wilderness, Prepare ye the way of the Lord, make his paths straight.
4 And the same John had his raiment of camel's hair, and a leathern girdle about his loins; and his meat was locusts and wild honey.
5 ¶Then went out to him Jerusalem, and all Judæa, and all the region round about Jordan,
6 And were baptized of him in Jordan, confessing their sins.
7 But when he saw many of the Pharisees and Săd′du-ceeś come to his baptism, he said unto them, O generation of vipers, who hath warned you to flee from the wrath to come?

3-7. Spoken of by the prophet Isaiah [Esaias]. All four Gospels relate this prophecy to a fulfillment in the life and ministry of John the Baptist (Mk 1:2; Lk 3:4; Jn 1:23). **Make his paths straight** refers to the straightening or preparing of one's life in a right relationship with God in order to prepare for the coming of the King. John's dress of **camel's hair, and a leathern girdle** was similar to Elijah's clothing (II Kgs 1:8) and was the usual food of prophets (Zech 13:4). **Locusts** were an allowable food (cf. Lev 11:22) and were eaten by the very poorest of people. The reference in verse 5 to **Jerusalem, and all Judea** relates to the people of those places. John's ministry was received with great enthusiasm in its early stages. So great was his success that even many of the **Pharisees and Sadducees** (vs. 7) came to this baptism.

8 Bring forth therefore fruits meet for repentance:

8-10. Fruits meet for repentance. John rebuked the Pharisees, asking them to give evidence of **fruits meet for repen-**

9 And think not to say within your-selves, We have Abraham to *our* father: for I say unto you, that God is able of these stones to raise up children unto Abraham.

10 And now also the axe is laid unto the root of the trees: therefore every tree which bringeth not forth good fruit is hewn down, and cast into the fire.

11 I indeed baptize you with water unto repentance: but he that cometh af-ter me is mightier than I, whose shoes I am not worthy to bear: he shall baptize you with the Holy Ghost, and *with* fire:

12 Whose fan *is* in his hand, and he will throughly purge his floor, and gath-er his wheat into the garner; but he will burn up the chaff with unquench-able fire.

13 ¶Then cometh Jesus from Galilee to Jordan unto John, to be baptized of him.

14 But John forbad him, saying, I have need to be baptized of thee, and comest thou to me?

15 And Jesus answering said unto him, Suffer *it to be so* now: for thus it becometh us to fulfil all righteousness. Then he suffered him.

16 And Jesus, when he was baptized, went up straightway out of the water:

tance (vs. 8). There can be no doubt that the New Testament concept of repentance grows out of its biblical usage in the Old Testament where the term (Heb *shub*) means far more than an intellectual change of mind. Genuine repentance proves itself by the fruits of a changed life. John the Baptist further rebuked them for their belief in nationalistic salvation. **Abraham to our father** means they were trusting their physical descent for salva-tion, rather than their spiritual relationship to the father of faith. **Of these stones** may be a reference to Isaiah 5:12, but is probably to be taken in the natural setting of the seashore. The **axe** about to chop the **root of the trees** is a reference to the impending judgment coming upon Israel (God's chosen tree, cf. Rom 11) if they reject the Messiah-King. Again, fruitlessness is depicted as a lack of conversion and spiritual life. No fruit means no life in the soul.

11-12. I baptize . . . with water. John's baptism in water was not Christian baptism. The death and resurrection of Christ had not yet occurred in order to be depicted by this baptism. John's baptism was similar to the Old Testament oblations (washings) that symbolized a cleansing of personal repentance on the part of a believer. Notice that Jesus submitted to this baptism to **fulfill all righteousness** (vs. 15). As God, He could not submit to baptism into the body of the church of which He is the head. **He shall baptize . . . with the Holy Ghost** refers to the spiritual rebirth of the regenerate who shall receive the baptism of the Spirit (cf. I Cor 12:13, which clearly indicates that all believers have received the baptism of the Spirit). This experience began at Pentecost (Acts 1) and was repeated upon every new group of converts: Samaritans, Gentiles, John's dis-ciples, etc. until it became normative for all Christian believers.

The term **and with fire** is better translated "or with fire." The immediate context certainly indicates that to be baptized with fire is the result of judgment (notice the reference to purging and burning in the next verse). Other than the visible tongues (bil-lows) of fire which appeared over the disciples' heads at Pente-cost, references to fire burning up unprofitable chaff refer to judgment rather than cleansing. The threshing **fan** (vs. 12) ref-ers to a wooden shovel used for tossing grain into the wind in order to blow away the lighter chaff, leaving the good grain to settle in a pile. The chaff would then be swept up and burned, **the unquenchable fire** refers to the eternal punishment of hell or the lake of fire.

D. His Approval. 3:13-4:11.

1. Baptism of Christ. 3:13-17.

13-14. All four Gospels relate this event (cf. Jn 1:31-33) with unquestioned historical verification. While this section of Mat-thew's gospel centers upon Galilee, Jesus now goes south to the Jordan River **to be baptized** (vs. 13). The word baptize (Gr *baptizo*) is an Anglicism. It means to dip or immerse in water, indicating the true form of baptism by immersion. John **forbade him** (vs. 14) for the obvious reason that Jesus needed no repen-tance of sin and John felt unworthy of this opportunity. The tense of the Greek verb emphasizes that John tried to hinder him. Thus, this was no casual hesitation on the part of the Baptist.

15. Suffer it to be so means allow it to be or let it happen. Jesus sought this outward identification with John's ministry **to fulfil all righteousness.** By identifying Himself with those whom He came to redeem, Jesus inaugurated His public minis-try as the Messiah. In regard to the Jewish religious observ-ances, Jesus always met the duties of a faithful Jew: synagogue worship, attendance at feasts, payment of the Temple tax, etc.

16-17. In the process of His baptism, Jesus **went up . . . out of the water,** the prepositions indicating that He was completely

and, lo, the heavens were opened unto him, and he saw the Spirit of God descending like a dove, and lighting upon him:

17 And lo a voice from heaven, saying, This is my beloved Son, in whom I am well pleased.

CHAPTER 4

THEN was Jesus led up of the spirit into the wilderness to be tempted of the devil.

2 And when he had fasted forty days and forty nights, he was afterward an hungred.

3 And when the tempter came to him, he said, If thou be the Son of God, command that these stones be made bread.

4 But he answered and said, It is written, Man shall not live by bread alone, but by every word that proceedeth out of the mouth of God.

in the water and came up out from it, again indicating the form of immersion. The descending of the **Spirit of God** fulfilled the predicted sign to John in order to indicate the true Messiah (cf. Jn 1:33; Isa 11:2). "As the Spirit came upon Old Testament prophets for special guidance at the start of their ministries, so now He came upon Jesus without measure" (Kent, p. 10). The **dove** was a symbol of innocence and purity (cf. Mt 10:16) and served as an ideal symbolic representation for the Holy Spirit since it is a totally defenseless animal. Jesus made it clear that the ministry of the Holy Spirit was to glorify Christ and not Himself (Jn 16:13-14). The **voice from heaven** is that of the Father (see also Mt 17:5; Jn 12:28 where He speaks at the transfiguration and just prior to the crucifixion) giving His verbal approval to the ministry of His **beloved Son**. There can be no doubt that all three persons of the Trinity are actively involved here as distinct persons of the Godhead. The Father speaks, the Spirit descends, the Son is baptized.

2. Temptation of Christ. 4:1-11.

4:1. Following His public baptism, Jesus was **led up of the Spirit into the wilderness** referring to the elevation of the Judaean wilderness. The historical setting of the temptation, which was directed against Jesus' human nature, indicates that this was a literal experience which He really conquered, not merely a mental victory over His own thoughts. The references to the work of the Holy Spirit make clear the interrelation of these two members of the Godhead. In His earthly work, Jesus depended upon the ministry of the Holy Spirit to empower Him.

That Jesus was **tempted of the devil** is clearly presented as a fact. The attack against Christ's humanity was a genuine temptation that would have overcome any normal man. However, Jesus was no ordinary man. As the virgin-born God-man, His divine nature could not sin (cf. I Sam 15:29) and thus held His human nature in check. Some have objected that the impeccability (i.e., He was not able to sin) of Christ denies the reality of Satan's temptation. Such an objection is meaningless when one remembers that Satan's rebellion against God has already been defeated in Christ's atonement, but his rebellion is nevertheless real, even though the outcome of God's victory is certain. The same is true of the temptation of Christ. One may attack a battleship with a canoe. The outcome of the attack will be certain defeat for the canoe, but the attack is nonetheless legitimate.

2-3. Jesus had **fasted forty days and forty nights,** a remarkable feat of human endurance indicating the physical strength of the former carpenter. While the three major tests followed this period, other tests evidently had occurred throughout the forty days (Lk 4:2). His real physical hunger serves as the setting for the first temptation by the **tempter** (Satan). The incident is couched in the questioning aspersion **if thou be the Son of God,** indicating Matthew's purpose for including this record of Jesus' victory: it proves that He is, in fact, the Son of God! The urgency to turn the **stones** into **bread** appealed to Jesus' most basic human need in light of the extensive fast. The natural result of using His divine power in this regard would certainly have led to the desire to eat the bread. One mistake would have led to another. However, Jesus refused to use His divine prerogative to benefit Himself. In fact, He never did a miracle to benefit Himself. His heart was always reaching out to others.

4. The victory in each aspect of the temptation is related to Jesus' use of Scripture: **It is written.** First, He quotes Deuteronomy 8:3, "Man shall not live by bread alone, but by every word that proceedeth out of the mouth of God." The source of bread is more important than the bread itself. Later, Jesus would say, "I have meat to eat that ye know not of" (Jn 4:32).

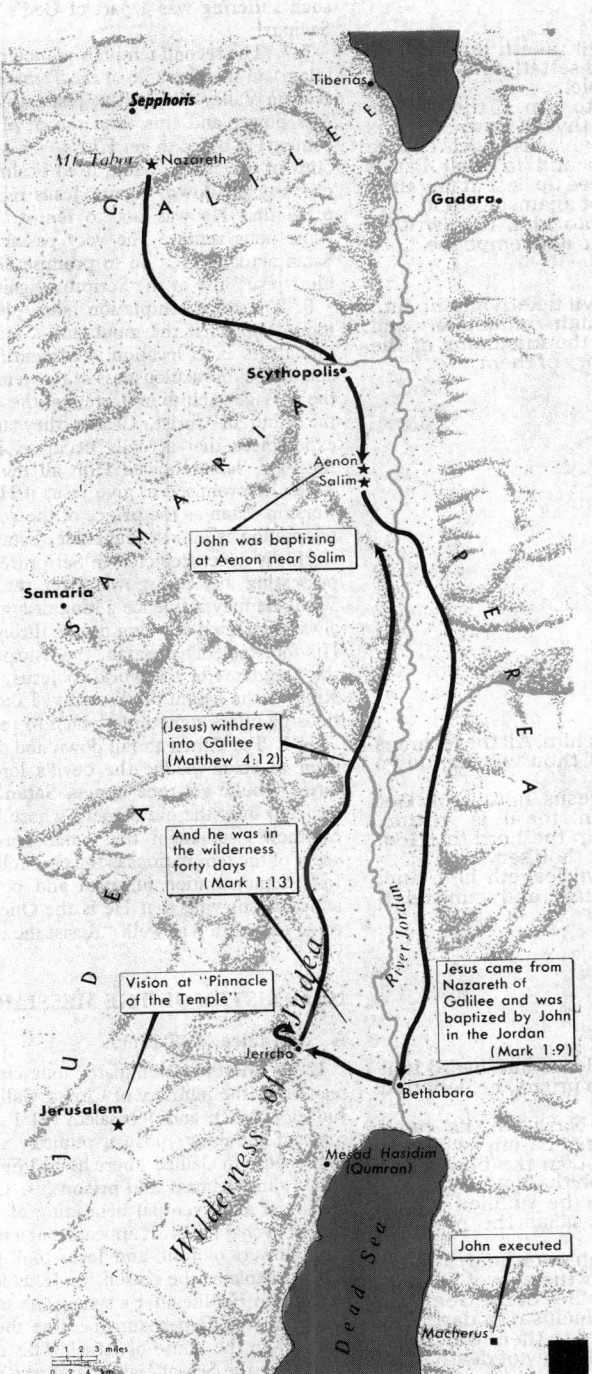

Sepphoris

Tiberias

Mt. Tabor ★ Nazareth

GALILEE

Gadara

Scythopolis

SAMARIA

Aenon
Salim ★

P E R E A

John was baptizing
at Aenon near Salim

Samaria

(Jesus) withdrew
into Galilee
(Matthew 4:12)

And he was in
the wilderness
forty days
(Mark 1:13)

J U D E A

River Jordan

Wilderness of Judea

Vision at "Pinnacle
of the Temple"

Jericho

Jesus came from
Nazareth of
Galilee and was
baptized by John
in the Jordan
(Mark 1:9)

Jerusalem ★

Bethabara

Mesad Hasidim
(Qumran)

John executed

Dead Sea

0 1 2 3 miles
0 2 4 km

Macherus

The Baptism of Jesus and The Sojourn in the Desert

His source of strength was obedience to the Father's will and He would not even work a miracle to avoid personal suffering when such suffering was a part of God's purpose for Him. What a Saviour!

5 Then the devil taketh him up into the holy city, and setteth him on a pinnacle of the temple,
6 And saith unto him, If thou be the Son of God, cast thyself down: for it is written, He shall give his angels charge concerning thee: and in *their* hands they shall bear thee up, lest at any time thou dash thy foot against a stone.
7 Jesus said unto him, It is written again, Thou shalt not tempt the Lord thy God.

5-7. The second temptation took place in the **holy city** (Jerusalem) on the **pinnacle** of the Temple, which towered above the Kidron Valley. Evidently, Jesus was transported there by Satan's power and this time the devil quoted Scripture (out of context) in order to get Him to sin and to ultimately shake His faith in the Word. Satan used Psalm 91:11-12 urging Jesus to **cast thyself down.** Again, Jesus replied with Scripture (Deut 6:16) that He was not to **tempt . . . God** by such a presumptuous action. The very passage of Scripture quoted by Satan actually goes on to promise God's ultimate victory over him! Jesus' use of the Scripture again silences the tempter.

8 Again, the devil taketh him up into an exceeding high mountain, and sheweth him all the kingdoms of the world, and the glory of them;

8. The third temptation takes place on an **exceeding high mountain.** That the mountain is real seems clear in the text, though its exact location is unidentified. Despite the grandeur and almost miraculousness of this temptation there is nothing in the passage itself to indicate that these temptations were only in the mind of Christ. Clearly they are depicted as being real experiences that actually occurred in the human life of the Messiah. Satan showed Him **all the kingdoms of the world,** which he promised to give Jesus if He would acknowledge and worship Satan as the prince of the world. The invalidity of the temptation is almost laughable. Satan, though the god of this world, is never depicted in Scripture as actually controlling or possessing any real power over the kingdoms of the world. While he may influence a king or a group of kingdoms, God is always depicted as being on the throne, over the earth which is His footstool. That Satan, the usurper, would attempt to give the kingdoms of the world to Jesus, the Messiah, the rightful King, is the height of absurdity! Like many of Satan's temptations he offers something which in reality he cannot deliver.

9 And saith unto him, All these things will I give thee, if thou wilt fall down and worship me.
10 Then saith Jesus unto him, Get thee hence, Satan: for it is written, Thou shalt worship the Lord thy God, and him only shalt thou serve.
11 Then the devil leaveth him, and, behold, angels came and ministered unto him.

9-11. For Christ to fall down and worship Satan would have been to acknowledge the devil's lordship over Him. In His direct rebuke **get thee hence, Satan,** Jesus clearly asserts His lordship over the old serpent whose head He will soon crush. Matthew's statement that Satan **leaveth him** shows that his order of the temptations is the chronological one (cf. Lk 4:1-13). In a demonstration of spirit and power, Jesus overcame the tempter, showing that He is the One who enables us to overcome temptation as well. "Resist the devil and he will flee from you."

II. MINISTRY OF THE MESSIAH. 4:12-27:66.

A. In Galilee. 4:12-18:35.

12 ¶Now when Jesus had heard that John was cast into prison, he departed into Galilee;
13 And leaving Nazareth, he came and dwelt in Ca-per'na-um, which is upon the sea coast, in the borders of Zăb'u-lon and Nĕph'tha-lĭm:
14 That it might be fulfilled which was spoken by E-śā'ias the prophet, saying,
15 The land of Zăb'u-lon, and the land of Nĕph'tha-lĭm, *by* the way of the sea, beyond Jordan, Galilee of the Gentiles;
16 The people which sat in darkness saw great light; and to them which sat in the region and shadow of death light is sprung up.

12-16. Matthew designates four clear geographical areas in relation to the ministry of Christ: Galilee (4:12), Peraea (19:1), Judaea (20:17), and Jerusalem (21:1). The author then omits some of the early Judaean ministry and begins with Jesus at Capernaum in Galilee where he had first met Christ himself (cf. 9:9). **John was cast into prison** (vs. 12). The circumstances of the arrest and eventual beheading of John the Baptist are recorded in chapter 14. It appears that a widespread persecution of the followers of John and Jesus took place at this time. Luke 4:16-31 explains the reason for Jesus **leaving Nazareth** was an attempt on His life after a synagogue service at Nazareth. From this point on, Capernaum became the headquarters of Jesus' ministry to the house of Israel. This city was a Roman settlement near the Sea of Galilee and was the center of the Roman government of the northern provinces of Israel. **That it might be fulfilled** (vss. 14-16) refers to the coming of Christ into Galilee in fulfillment of the prophecy of Isaiah 9:1-2, ". . . beyond Jordan, in Galilee of the nations. The people that walk in darkness have seen a great light . . ." Jesus Himself was that great light that now would shine forth in His earthly ministry to the people of Galilee who had so long been despised by their Judaean cousins, in the south.

17 From that time Jesus began to preach, and to say, Repent: for the kingdom of heaven is at hand.

17. Repent: for the kingdom of heaven is at hand. The message of John the Baptist is now clearly proclaimed by Jesus Christ. However, Jesus, as the Messiah, is not calling on His listeners to prepare for the coming of the kingdom but rather announces that the kingdom is here. In a very real sense the first coming of the King is an honest, straightforward presentation of the kingdom promised by the Old Testament prophets to the people of Israel. Thus, we find unusual miracles attending Jesus' presentation of this kingdom: incurable diseases and incomprehensible afflictions are cured by the power of His touch and His word. The kingdom blessings promised in Isaiah 35:5-6 to be fulfilled in a future kingdom, here become the credentials of the King in His first coming (cf. Walvoord, p. 39).

18 ¶And Jesus, walking by the sea of Galilee, saw two brethren, Simon called Peter, and Andrew his brother, casting a net into the sea: for they were fishers.
19 And he saith unto them, Follow me, and I will make you fishers of men.
20 And they straightway left *their* nets, and followed him.

18-20. Simon called Peter, and Andrew became the first two disciples called publicly by Jesus. Andrew had earlier (cf. Jn 1:40) introduced his brother to Jesus on another occasion. The invitation, **Follow me,** called these earlier believers into a permanent ministry to be shared with Christ. **I will make you fishers of men** clearly indicates the nature of this ministry. They would receive special training in bringing men into the kingdom. These former fishermen would literally become fishers of men! There can be no doubt that aggressive personal evangelism was and still is a major priority in the believer's life. Our obedience to the lordship of Christ is evidenced by our carrying forth the mission to which He has committed us. Having **left their nets** these disciples entered into a new relationship and would never again be able to fully return to the occupation they once held so dear. There can be no greater calling than to serve Christ full time with every effort of our lives.

21 And going on from thence, he saw other two brethren, James *the son of* Zĕb'e-dee, and John his brother, in a ship with Zĕb'e-dee their father, mending their nets; and he called them.
22 And they immediately left the ship and their father, and followed him.

21-22. James and **John** were also brothers and fishing partners with Simon and Andrew. Matthew and Mark agree that they were **mending their nets,** but Luke seems to differ. The two accounts can be simply harmonized. As two men were mending nets, the other two were fishing. Jesus then came upon them and called them all to follow Him. The statement in verse 22 that they **immediately** responded to His call gives us a perfect picture of true obedience to the lordship of Christ. To obey is to respond immediately in an attitude of faith.

23 ¶And Jesus went about all Galilee, teaching in their synagogues, and preaching the gospel of the kingdom, and healing all manner of sickness and all manner of disease among the people.
24 And his fame went throughout all Syria: and they brought unto him all sick people that were taken with divers diseases and torments, and those which were possessed with devils, and those which were lunatick, and those that had the palsy; and he healed them.
25 And there followed him great multitudes of people from Galilee, and *from* De-căp'o-lĭs, and *from* Jerusalem, and *from* Judæa, and *from* beyond Jordan.

23-25. The closing verses of the chapter summarize and survey the Galilean ministry of Jesus. This ministry concentrated on a presentation of the **gospel of the kingdom** to the Jews. Jesus as the Messiah (the anointed One) had arrived to set up the long-awaited kingdom. Accompanying this announcement were miracles of healing. Going from city to city throughout Galilee caused His fame to spread quickly, so that **great multitudes of people** (vs. 25) followed Him from Galilee, the Decapolis, Jerusalem, Judaea, and from beyond Jordan. Thus, followers were gleaned from virtually every geographical area of the nation of Israel as it was in the day of Christ. This is no insignificant feat when one realizes that no prophet had arisen in Israel for over four hundred years. The silence of the Intertestamental period had been broken by the proclamation of the good news of the kingdom!

1. His message: Sermon on the Mount. 5:1-7:29.

The nature of the kingdom which Jews proclaimed has long been a controversial area of interpretation among Christian scholars. While these interpretations do not divide us between orthodoxy and heresy, they nevertheless formulate our fundamental understanding of the nature and message of the church today. Liberalism taught that the keeping of the Sermon on the Mount was to be regarded as the message of the gospel. Thus it

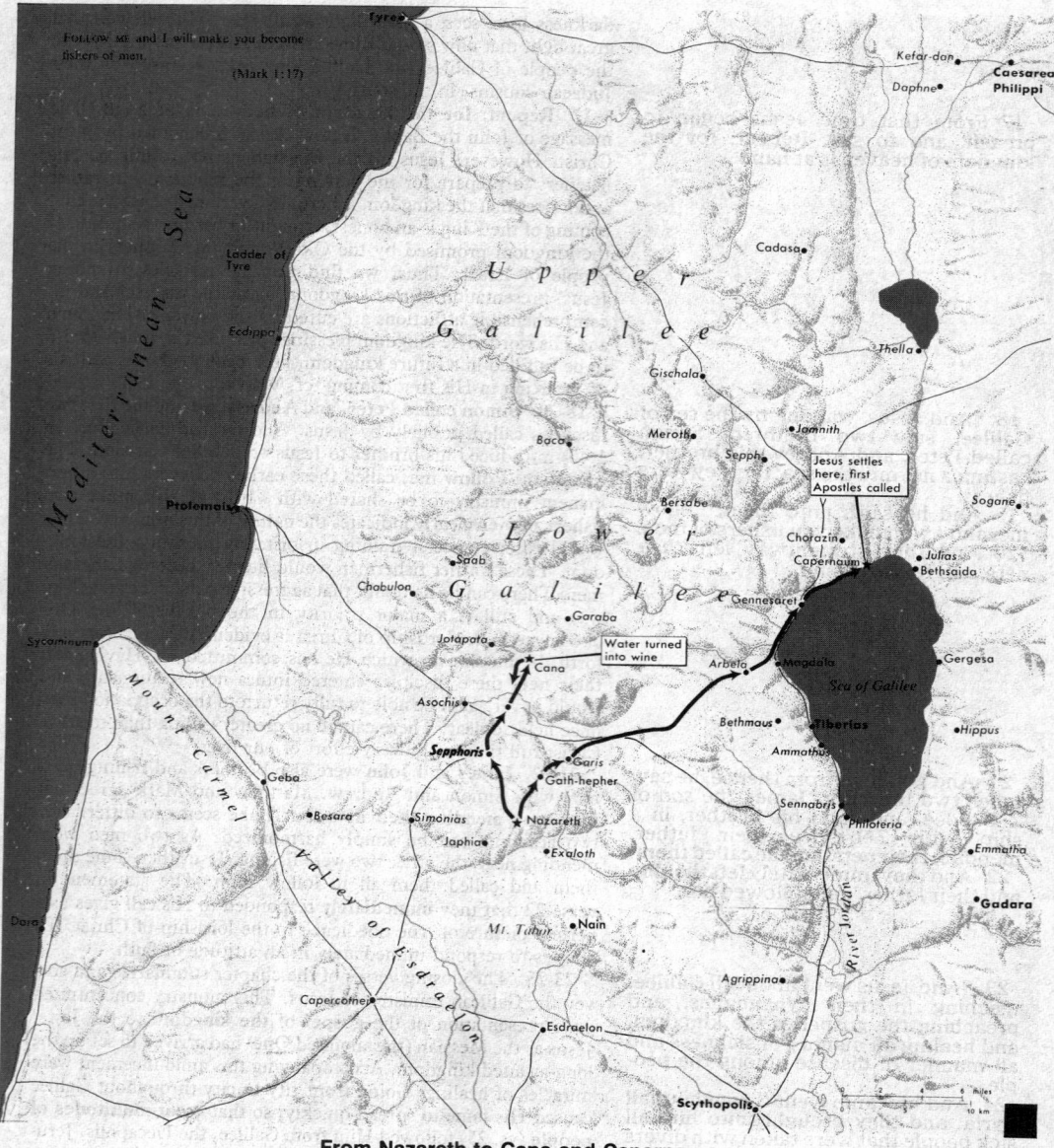

FOLLOW ME and I will make you become fishers of men.

(Mark 1:17)

Jesus settles here; first Apostles called

Water turned into wine

From Nazareth to Cana and Capernaum

predicated a system of salvation by moral works. Some dispensationalists, at times, have tended to relegate everything related to the kingdom as being under the Old Testament dispensation, thus having no significant application to the church today. Still others recognize the truths within this kingdom message, but hold that its precepts are impossible to attain, thus nullifying its significance for the Christian.

Nowhere in the presentation of the message of the kingdom does Jesus indicate that this message is significantly different from the proclamation of evangelism by the church. The difference, rather, seems to be in relation to those to whom the message is directed. During the early period of the Gospels, the message of the kingdom of heaven was directed to the nation of Israel and contained the potential fulfillment of the promised kingdom to the Jews. To the Gentile nations of the Church Age the proclamation of the message is that God will gather a people for Himself from all nations into this great kingdom. The prerequisite for entrance into this kingdom included repentance (Mt 4:17), righteousness (Mt 5:20), faith (Mt 18:3) or, in summary, being born again (Jn 3). Because the people rejected these requirements, Christ taught that His earthly reign would not be centralized in the nation of Israel but in a gathering of a people from among the nations of the earth.

5:1-2. The opening verses of the Sermon on the Mount indicate that this message deals with the inner state of mind and heart which is the indispensable absolute of true Christian discipleship. It delineates the outward manifestations of character and conduct of the true believer and genuine disciple. A dispensationalist, Lawlor writes: "We do not find basic, fundamental Law here, for law cannot produce the state of blessedness set forth herein" (cf. G. Lawlor, *The Beatitudes Are for Today*, p. 11). Rather, the quality of life herein described is the necessary product of grace alone. As Jesus states the outward legal requirements of the law and then carries His listener beyond the letter of the law to the true spirit and intent of the law, He describes a life-style which no human being could live in his own power. Thus, the life of the believer, described by Jesus in the Sermon on the Mount, is a life of grace and glory, which comes from God alone. To make this quality of life the product of man's human efforts (as does the liberal) is the height of overestimation of man's ability and underestimation of his depravity. To relegate this entire message, Jesus' longest recorded sermon, to a Jewish-only life-style, as do hyperdispensationalists, is to rob the church of her greatest statement of true Christian living!

The depth of spiritual truth proclaimed in this message of the kingdom, however, does not present the gospel of justification by faith in the death and resurrection of Christ. Pink states: "Its larger part was a most searching exposition of the spirituality of the law and the repudiation of the false teaching of the elders" (A. W. Pink, *An Exposition of the Sermon on the Mount*, p. 13). Jesus made it clear that the spirit of Christ goes beyond the outward demand of the law. The Christian, though not under the law, is to live above the law.

It has always been difficult to clearly draw the distinction between the relationship of law and grace. Dr. Martyn Lloyd-Jones has observed: "Some so emphasize the law as to turn the gospel of Jesus Christ with its glorious liberty into nothing but a collection of moral maxims. It is all law to them and there is no grace left. They so talk of the Christian, that it becomes pure legalism and there is no grace in it. Let us remember also that it is equally possible so to overemphasize grace at the expense of the law as again, to have something which is not the gospel of the New Testament" (D. Martyn Lloyd-Jones, *Studies in the Sermon on the Mount*, pp. 12-15). He goes on to note that the Sermon on the Mount and the message of the kingdom do have definite application to the Christian today. It was preached to people who were meant to practice it not only at that time but ever afterwards as well. Boice (p. 9) observes that that "World" of the Sermon on the Mount cannot be restricted to life in the future millennial kingdom, since it includes tax collectors, thieves, unjust officials, hypocrites, and false prophets.

Embodied in the Sermon on the Mount is a summation of Jesus' basic ethical teaching of the life of a born-again man. While the Sermon on the Mount is not a way of salvation, neither is it only a message to those under the law, for it obviously goes beyond the law. It is a presentation of Christian discipleship which can be wrought in the soul of an individual only by the power of God. This message does not tell one how to be saved; it tells one what it is like to be saved. It explains the

CHAPTER 5
AND seeing the multitudes, he went up into a mountain: and when he was set, his disciples came unto him:
2 And he opened his mouth, and taught them, saying,

quality of the life changed by the saving grace of God. Its basic truths are reiterated everywhere throughout the New Testament epistles. There is no fundamental contrast between this message and the message of Paul. Both are in agreement that "the just shall live by faith!"

In the Sermon on the Mount Jesus states the spiritual character and quality of the kingdom which He wished to establish. The basic qualities of this kingdom are fulfilled in the church which He would establish. Virtually every section of this message is repeated in the substance elsewhere throughout the New Testament. There is nothing here to indicate that this message is to be limited in its application only to the people of Israel. Notice in the opening verse that **his disciples** had come to Him and **he . . . taught them** the following message.

a. The Beatitudes: Character described. 5:3-20.

3 Blessed *are* the poor in spirit: for theirs is the kingdom of heaven.

3. Blessed means "happy." This is a basic description of the believers' inner condition as a result of the work of God. Kent states that it is virtually equivalent to being "saved" (H. A. Kent Jr. Matthew, in *Wycliffe Bible Commentary,* p. 15). These Beatitudes, like Psalm 1, do not show a man how to be saved, but rather describe the characteristics of one who has been saved. The **poor in spirit** are the oppositie of the proud or haughty in spirit. These are those who have been humbled by the grace of God and have acknowledged their sin and therefore their dependence upon God to save them. They are the ones who will inherit the **kingdom of heaven.** It is obvious in this usage that the kingdom of heaven is a general designation of the dwelling place of the saved.

4 Blessed *are* they that mourn: for they shall be comforted.

4. Those that **mourn . . . shall be comforted.** The depth of the promise of these statements is almost inexhaustible. Those who mourn for sin shall be comforted in confession. Those who mourn for the human anguish of the lost shall be comforted by the compassion of God.

5 Blessed *are* the meek: for they shall inherit the earth.

5. The meek . . . shall inherit the earth refers again to those who have been humbled before God and will inherit, not only the blessedness of heaven, but shall ultimately share in the kingdom of God upon the earth. Here, in the opening statements of the Sermon on the Mount, is the balance between the physical and spiritual promise of the kingdom. The kingdom of which Jesus preached is both "in you" and is yet "to come." The Christian is the spiritual citizen of the kingdom of heaven now.

6 Blessed *are* they which do hunger and thirst after righteousness: for they shall be filled.

6. These future possessors of the earth are its presently-installed rightful heirs and even now they **hunger and thirst after righteousness.** They experience a deep desire for personal righteousness which is, in itself, a proof of their spiritual re-birth. Those who are poor and empty in their own spiritual poverty recognize the depth of their need and hunger and thirst for that which only God can give them. To hunger means to be needy. It is joined with to thirst; the born-again man has a God-given hunger and thirst (inner passion) for righteousness. This hungering and thirsting continues throughout the life of the believer. He continues to hunger and to be filled and to hunger and to be filled. God supplies his every spiritual need daily. This act of hungering and thirsting after righteousness is the by-product of a regenerated life.

Lawlor (p. 60) rightly states that this is the description of a man who has already been saved. Nowhere does the Bible command unbelievers to hunger after righteousness in order to be saved. Rather, Paul clearly states "there is none that understandeth, there is none that seeketh after God" (Rom 3:11). The biblical writers make it clear that while man must come to Christ for salvation, it is not within man's normal ability and desire to want to come to God. Therefore, God is depicted throughout the New Testament as the seeking Saviour going after the lost. **They shall be filled** (Gr *chortazō*) refers to a complete filling and satisfaction. The psalmist proclaimed: "He satisfieth the longing soul, and filleth the hungry soul with goodness" (107:9). This filling comes from God, who is the total source of satisfaction of His people. It comes now and it will continue to come throughout eternity to those who hunger and thirst for it.

7 Blessed *are* the merciful: for they shall obtain mercy.

7. Those who are **merciful . . . shall obtain mercy** has reference to those who have been born again by the mercy of God. Because divine love has been extended to them, they have the work of the Holy Spirit in them producing a mercy which defies explanation by unregenerate men. Jesus Himself became the ultimate example of this when He cried from the cross, "Father, forgive them for they know not what they do" (Lk 23:34). The form of proverbial teaching should not confuse the order of these statements; for example, the believer does not show mercy in order to obtain mercy, he shows mercy because he has obtained mercy. In so continuing to show the evidence of the grace of God in his life he continues to receive that grace. In other words, he is not saved simply because he shows mercy and is kind to people. He shows mercy and is kind because he is saved.

8 Blessed *are* the pure in heart: for they shall see God.

8. Those who are truly saved shall **see God**. These are the **pure in heart**. Their lives have been transformed by the grace of God. They are not yet sinless but their position before God has been changed. They have the new birth, saving faith and holiness. The process of sanctification is ever conforming them to the image of Christ (Rom 8:29), which image consists in "righteousness and true holiness" (Eph 4:24). Purity of heart is both the end of our election and the goal of our redemption. We read in Ephesians 1:4, "He has chosen us that we should be holy" and Titus 2:14, "who gave himself for us that he might redeem us unto himself a peculiar people." To which we add Hebrews 12:14, "Follow peace with all men, and holiness, without which no man shall see the Lord."

9 Blessed *are* the peacemakers: for they shall be called the children of God.

9. The next description deals with the **peacemakers**. They are the ones who are themselves at peace with God and live in peace with all men (cf. Rom 5:1). They are called "the" peacemakers for these are not social reformers, but rather the ones reformed by the regenerating power of the gospel. They are peacemakers because they themselves are at peace with God. They have entered into the peace of Christ and thus are able ambassadors of God's message of peace to a troubled world. Hence, they shall be called **the children of God**. These only shall be called the sons of God! Throughout the Beatitudes Jesus clearly underscores that only those who have the life-changing qualities herein described are citizens of His kingdom.

10 Blessed *are* they which are persecuted for righteousness' sake: for theirs is the kingdom of heaven.

10. As Jesus develops His message He makes it clear that such a life causes His people to be in direct contrast to the world in which they live. Therefore He reminds, **Blessed are they which are persecuted for righteousness' sake**. The plural use of ye in verse 11 indicates that He foresaw this persecution as touching all His followers. Notice II Timothy 3:12, "Yea, and all that will live godly in Christ Jesus shall suffer persecution." The nature of this persecution (Gr *diōkō*) implies a driving or chasing away, a withstanding or keeping one from his goal. This does not mean that every Christian will necessarily suffer physical abuse as evidence of true salvation. While many Christians have sealed their faith with their blood, many more have had to withstand the social temptations and pressures of the world in order to live effectively for Christ.

11 Blessed are ye, when *men* shall revile you, and persecute *you*, and shall say all manner of evil against you falsely, for my sake.

11. Again, Jesus warns that men shall **revile you, and persecute you**. This became true during His own ministry, in the lives of the apostles and throughout the history of the church. But in Tertullian's words, "The blood of the martyrs became the seed of the church." The persecution spoken of here is

12 Rejoice, and be exceeding glad: for great *is* your reward in heaven: for so persecuted they the prophets which were before you.

13 ¶Ye are the salt of the earth: but if the salt have lost his savour, wherewith shall it be salted? it is thenceforth good for nothing, but to be cast out, and to be trodden under foot of men.

14 Ye are the light of the world. A city that is set on an hill cannot be hid.

15 Neither do men light a candle, and put it under a bushel, but on a candlestick; and it giveth light unto all that are in the house.

16 Let your light so shine before men, that they may see your good works, and glorify your Father which is in heaven.

17 ¶Think not that I am come to destroy the law, or the prophets: I am not come to destroy, but to fulfil.

18 For verily I say unto you, Till heaven and earth pass, one jot or one tittle shall in no wise pass from the law, till all be fulfilled.

twofold. First, it involves a physical pursuing of the persecuted and secondly a personal attack of slander against them.

12. Rejoice is the command that grows out of the blessedness of the believer. The phrase "rejoice and be exceeding glad" means rejoice, but even more exalt! The believer who is the blessed one may not only rejoice in tribulation but he may rejoice exceedingly to the point of exaltation. Therefore, he glories in tribulation even as the Apostle Paul (cf. II Cor 1:3-7; 12:7-10). **Great is your reward in heaven** focuses attention upon the eternal, spiritual destiny of all things. If God is as real as He claims, if the Bible is true, if heaven is to be gained, then there is no temporary earthly trouble or persecution that can thwart the child of God from the eternal glory that lies ahead. In Romans 8:18, Paul proclaimed, "I reckon that the sufferings of this present time are not worthy to be compared with the glory which shall be revealed in us."

13. The Beatitudes are followed by a summary statement of the basic character of the Christian's life as salt and light. **Ye are the salt of the earth;** again the phrase **ye are** indicates that only the genuinely born-again person is salt and can help meet the needs of the world. The salt adds flavoring, acts as a preservative, melts coldness and heals wounds. Thus it is a very appropriate description of the believer in his relationship to the world in which he lives. The term "lose its savor" refers to its essential saltiness. Jesus was actually saying that if the salt loses its saltiness, it is worthless. The implication of this statement is that if a Christian loses his effectiveness, his testimony will be trampled under the feet of men.

14-16. Ye are the light of the world describes the essential mission of the Christian to the world. He is the condition (salt) to meet the world's needs and he has a mission (light) to the world. His light is to clearly shine forth into the darkness of human depravity. He is to set it up on a candlestick, not hide it **under a bushel,** e.g., basket. Inconsistent living and unconfessed sin in the life of the believer will become a basket-like covering which hides the light of God. God provides the light and it continues to shine, but as believers we must keep our lives clean before the Lord in order not to cover up the light which He has placed within us. Darkness is the absence of light and darkness alone cannot dispel the light, but the smallest light can dispel the greatest darkness. Therefore, let your light shine through a clean life before the Lord and before the world in which you live.

17. Having laid the foundation of the message in the summary statements of the Beatitudes, Jesus now proceeds to show the superiority of His message to that of the law of Moses. He makes it clear that He had **not . . . come to destroy the law.** That is, the New Testament gospel is not contrary nor contradictory to the Old Testament law; rather it is the ultimate fulfillment of the spiritual intention of the law. Where the law had degenerated into legalism by the Pharisees, Jesus now takes the law beyond mere outward observance to the inner spiritual intention of God. For He had come to **fulfill** the law and its fullest implications. In his earthly life Jesus accomplished this by meeting its strictest demands and going beyond its mere outward requirements. As our Saviour, Jesus not only bore our sins, but He has also established a perfect righteousness which is given to us as a gift of God. Our sin was thus imputed to Him and His righteousness was imputed to us (cf. J. Murray, *The Imputation of Adam's Sin*).

18. Verily I say is a unique form used by Jesus throughout His preaching to draw attention to the authority of His message. Verily means truly, certainly, or amen. It is used as a designation of authoritative teaching. **One jot or one tittle** refers to the minutest marks and letters of the Hebrew alphabet. He explained that even the smallest statement in the law must be fulfilled. A jot is the smallest letter of the Hebrew alphabet, called *yodh*. It functions as a "Y" in English and looks similar to an apostrophe. A tittle is a small projection on the edge of certain Hebrew letters to distinguish them from one another. For example, the Hebrew "D" differs from the "R" only by the use of the tittle.

19 Whosoever therefore shall break one of these least commandments, and shall teach men so, he shall be called the least in the kingdom of heaven: but whosoever shall do and teach *them*, the same shall be called great in the kingdom of heaven.

19. Because of the seriousness of the law, Jesus emphasized the importance of keeping even its smallest details. However, in the ultimate plan of God, the law was not to become an extra burden on the souls of men. Rather than pointing the way to salvation, the law convinced men of the need of the Saviour. Therefore, whoever **shall teach men so** but shall not live what he teaches, he shall be made **least in the kingdom of heaven**. It is interesting to note that a person may be saved and a member of the kingdom of heaven, yet be hypocritical in his attitude toward the law. **But whosoever shall do and teach** the principles and precepts of the law shall be called **great in the kingdom of heaven**. This simply means that God will reward the faithfulness and effectiveness of our lives and there will be varying degrees of blessing and reward in the kingdom.

20 For I say unto you, That except your righteousness shall exceed *the righteousness* of the scribes and Pharisees, ye shall in no case enter into the kingdom of heaven.

20. Because of the necessity of righteousness as a requirement to enter heaven, Jesus then declared that except their righteousness should **exceed the righteousness of the scribes and Pharisees** they could not enter heaven. The significance of this is seen in the fact that the Jews of Jesus' day considered these people to be the most religious in all Israel. However, their religion was merely an outward show of self-righteousness. What the Saviour demands is a kind of righteousness that is so godly that it cannot be the product of human effort but must be the gift of God. This righteousness Christ would establish in His life and death would be made available as God's free gift. This is the righteousness that would exceed that of the scribes and Pharisees.

b. Six illustrations: Character applied. 5:21-48.

In communicating the depth of His message, Jesus used a series of contrasts between the outward demand of the law and the inner attitude of heart desired by God. In this series of contrasts we see the depth and dynamic of the teaching of Jesus Christ, the great Master Teacher. Here we discover the practical application of genuine Christian character to true spiritual living. Here we see the gospel in action. Here is piety on the pavement of life. The Christian may live above the demands of the law and the temptations of the world because he has an inner depth of character which is the product of the divine nature within him.

LAW	SPIRIT
Murder	No anger
Adultery	No lust
Divorce	Commitment
Oath-taking	Speak the truth
Retaliation	Forgiveness
Hate your enemy	Love your enemy

(1). First illustration: murder. 5:21-26.

21 ¶Ye have heard that it was said by them of old time, Thou shalt not kill; and whosoever shall kill shall be in danger of the judgment:
22 But I say unto you, That whosoever is angry with his brother without a cause shall be in danger of the judgment: and whosoever shall say to his brother, Raca, shall be in danger of the

21-22. Christ begins this series of contrasts by quoting the statement of the law, **Thou shalt not kill** (Ex 20:13). The reference to killing is clearly understood in its context in both the Old Testament and New Testament as referring to an act of murder. It must be remembered that the God who commanded the children of Israel not to murder one another, also commanded them at times to kill an enemy in order to defend their nation. Jesus goes beyond this outward demand of the law by stating that **whosoever is angry with his brother** is in just as

council; but whosoever shall say, Thou fool, shall be in danger of hell fire.

23 Therefore if thou bring thy gift to the altar, and there rememberest that thy brother hath ought against thee;
24 Leave there thy gift before the altar, and go thy way; first be reconciled to thy brother, and then come and offer thy gift.

25 Agree with thine adversary quickly, whiles thou art in the way with him; lest at any time the adversary deliver thee to the judge, and the judge deliver thee to the officer, and thou be cast into prison.
26 Verily I say unto thee, Thou shalt by no means come out thence, till thou hast paid the uttermost farthing.

27 ¶Ye have heard that it was said by them of old time, Thou shalt not commit adultery:
28 But I say unto you, That whosoever looketh on a woman to lust after her hath committed adultery with her already in his heart.

great danger of judgment as a murderer, for anger is the emotion and inner intention that leads to murder.

The term *raca* (meaning "vain fellow" or "empty head") was a Hebrew or Aramaic expression of contempt (cf. II Sam 6:20). **The council** is a reference to the Jewish religious council called the Sanhedrin. **Thou fool,** (Gr *mōros*) means "stupid." We have developed the English word *moron* from this term. Those using such a malicious expression would be in danger of **hell fire.** This statement has often caused concern and confusion in the mind of many commentators. What does it really mean? The idea clearly seems to be that if one makes light of his fellow man he will be in danger of slander. But if one makes bitter, damning statements with reference to hell toward his fellow man, he shall actually be in danger of hell himself. The concept is that one making such statements is not likely to be a born-again person. The term hell (Gr *geenna*) is Gehenna, which was the hellenized form of the name of the Valley of Hinnom at Jerusalem in which fires were constantly burning to consume the refuse of the city. This valley provided a powerful and graphic picture of the ultimate destruction of hell and the lake of fire (cf. Jer 7:31; II Chr 28:3; II Kgs 23:10). Christ locates the root of murder in the heart of the angry man and states that God's judgment will be just as swift on anger as it will be upon murder.

23-24. Having made a comparison between the command not to murder and the inner motive and heart intention of hatred, Jesus then illustrated the seriousness of this matter by referring to one who would attempt to buy off his conscience by giving something to God without clearing his conscience with his offended brother. He reminded that **if thou bring thy gift to the altar** without reconciling with the offended party, God will not receive the intended gift. Bringing a gift to the altar refers to bringing it to the Temple in order that it might be consecrated. Therefore if conflict exists between any two people, it is God's desire that they reconcile the conflict before attempting to give a gift or an act of service unto the Lord. Many people undoubtedly try to suppress the guilt of their sin by an outward act that they hope will please God in some way. Therefore, Jesus commands that we leave our gifts before the altar and **first be reconciled** to our brother before we offer them. To be reconciled means to be brought back into fellowship or favor with our fellow man. Having resolved the personal conflict, we have then but to return and perform the act of service unto the Lord. The performance of our duty to men does not free us from the obligation of direct service to God.

25-26. The Saviour then went on to remind that even if **thine adversary** (an opponent at law) disagrees with you, it is to your advantage to reconcile with him before he **deliver thee to the judge.** Many people make the foolish mistake of assuming that just because they think they are right in a given situation God will necessarily vindicate them. Jesus' exhortation here is to urge us to go out of our way to avoid legal conflicts before human judges (cf. vs. 40). The payment of debt and the **prison** referred to here simply mean the normal legal process that one would encounter in a civil suit. The term prison (Gr *phylakē*) does not refer to purgatory, as suggested by some Roman Catholic interpreters, but to the full measure of punitive justice.

(2). Second illustration: Adultery contrasted to lust. 5:27-30.

27-28. Thou shalt not commit adultery was the demand of the Old Testament law (Ex 20:14). Jesus went beyond this outward command to reveal that its act is the result of an inner attitude of lust. **Whosoever looketh** characterizes the man whose glance is not checked by holy restraint and results in an impure lusting after women. It has often been argued that there is a difference between an appreciation of beauty and a lustful, lurid look. The lustful look is the expression of a heart attitude that says in essence, "I would if I could." The act would follow if the opportunity were to occur. By taking his listener beyond the outward statement of the law to its real intention, Jesus was trying to get his attention off the physical and onto the spiritual.

29 And if thy right eye offend thee, pluck it out, and cast *it* from thee: for it is profitable for thee that one of thy members should perish, and not *that* thy whole body should be cast into hell.

30 And if thy right hand offend thee, cut it off, and cast *it* from thee: for it is profitable for thee that one of thy members should perish, and not *that* thy whole body should be cast into hell.

29-30. Most men could claim that they had not committed the sin of adultery but very few could honestly say that they had not committed the sin of lusting, which could easily turn into adultery. Thus, the statement of cutting off one's hand or plucking out one's eye definitely is not to be taken literally. What Jesus implied is that if **thy right eye offend thee** then the logical thing to do would be to **pluck it out.** His point is not that one should literally pluck out his eye but that one should recognize that the source of lust comes from within the mind and heart of man, not from the physical organ itself. The right eye is not the source of sin; the heart of man is that source. Someone who had plucked out his right eye in an attempt to deal with lust would simply become a left-eyed luster! The real source of the sin of adultery comes from within man's **heart.**

The seriousness of the sin of lusting is thus illustrated by this graphic comparison. Ultimately, it would be better for a person to be physically maimed than to enter into hell forever. However, doing physical damage to one's self does not in any way guarantee entrance into heaven. What Jesus simply taught was that man must bring the passions of his heart under control of the Spirit of God.

(3). Third illustration: Divorce as contrasted to marriage. 5:31-32.

31 ¶It hath been said, Whosoever shall put away his wife, let him give her a writing of divorcement:

32 But I say unto you, That whosoever shall put away his wife, saving for the cause of fornication, causeth her to commit adultery: and whosoever shall marry her that is divorced committeth adultery.

31-32. It hath been said is again a reference to the Old Testament commandment of the Mosaic regulation (cf. Deut 24:1). The normal custom of the ancient Near East was for a man to verbally divorce his wife. The Arab custom was to say "I divorce you" three times and the divorce was consummated without any legal protection of any kind to the wife. In contrast, the ancient law of Israel insisted on a **writing of divorcement** or certificate of divorce. This written statement gave legal protec-

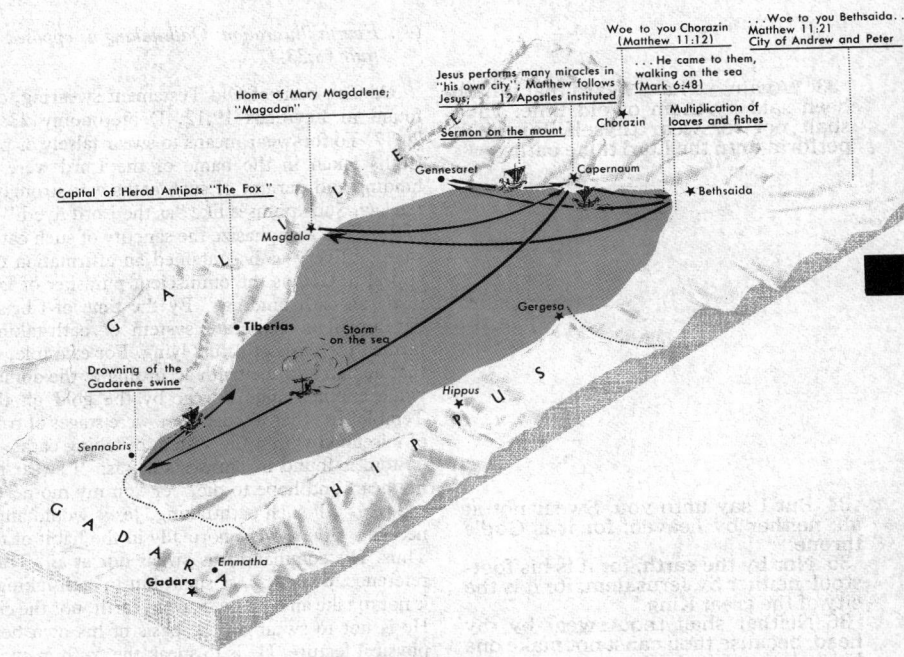

Around the Sea of Galilee

tion to both the wife and the husband. Jesus explained elsewhere (cf. Mt 19:8) that Moses' concession was not intended to be taken as license. In ancient rabbinic Judaism Moses' statement had been variously interpreted from meaning adultery (Shammai) to the trivial matters of personal preference (Hillel). The only legitimate exception for divorce allowed by Christ is possibly for **the cause of fornication** (Gr *porneia*), meaning sexual unfaithfulness. Ryrie (p. 14) notes that fornication may mean adultery prior to or after marriage, as well as unfaithfulness during the period of betrothal.

These statements make it clear that adultery or fornication is a legitimate grounds for divorce. However, the legitimacy of the divorce does not necessarily establish the legitimacy of remarriage. That one *must* divorce an unfaithful wife or husband is nowhere commanded in Scripture. To the contrary, there are many examples of extending forgiveness to the adulterous offender (cf. Hos 3:1, Gen 38:26, Jn 8:1-11). Nor does the discovery of premarital fornication on the part of the wife necessarily demand a divorce as is indicated by Atkinson (p. 780). Sexual involvement alone does not necessarily constitute a marriage in the sight of God (cf. the example of Judah and Tamar, who were both widowed at the time of their illicit sexual involvement). Though this temporary union produced twin sons, it resulted in no permanent marriage. Great care needs to be exercised when interpreting the New Testament passages regarding divorce and marriage. It should be remembered that Jesus made His statements about divorce to people who were already married, so that they might take seriously the marriage relationship. These statements were not necessarily made to add an extra burden to the already divorced person.

The responsibility of divorce is clearly laid upon the one seeking the divorce. **Whosoever shall put away his wife** without biblical basis **causeth her to commit adultery.** Lenski (pp. 230-235) translates "brings about that she is stigmatized as adulterous" and regards the sin of the divorcer as bringing about an unjust suspicion upon the divorcee.

(4). Fourth illustration: Oath-taking as opposed to speaking the truth. 5:33-37.

33. The basis of Old Testament swearing, or oath-taking, is found in Leviticus 19:12; Deuteronomy 23:21; and Exodus 20:17. To **forswear** means to swear falsely or perjure one's self. Oaths taken in the name of the Lord were looked upon as binding and perjury of such oaths was strongly condemned by the law. Such phrases like "as the Lord liveth" or "by the name of the Lord" emphasize the sanctity of such oaths. Ryrie (p. 14) states: "Every oath contained an affirmation of promise of an appeal to God as the omniscient punisher of falsehoods, which made an oath binding." By the time of Christ, the Jews had developed an elaborate system of oath-taking, which often formed the basis of actual lying. For example, one might swear that he had told the truth according to the dome of the Temple, while another might swear by the gold on the dome of the Temple! In other words, there were stages of truth and thus also of falsehood within the system of taking oaths. In our time this custom is found in phrases such as: "I swear by God," "cross my heart and hope to die," or "on my mother's grave."

34-36. All such oath-taking, Jesus would announce, was unnecessary if one were normally in the habit of telling the truth. Thus, His command was **swear not at all.** This does not have reference to cursing, as such, but to oath-taking. The Christian is not to take an oath by heaven, earth, nor the city of Jerusalem. He is not to swear on the basis of his own head or any other physical feature. He is to speak the truth in such a way that his "yes" means yes and his "no" means no.

---

33 ¶Again, ye have heard that it hath been said by them of old time, Thou shalt not forswear thyself, but shalt perform unto the Lord thine oaths:

34 But I say unto you, Swear not at all; neither by heaven; for it is God's throne:

35 Nor by the earth; for it is his footstool: neither by Jerusalem; for it is the city of the great King.

36 Neither shalt thou swear by thy head, because thou canst not make one hair white or black.

37 But let your communication be, Yea, yea; Nay, nay: for whatsoever is more than these cometh of evil.

37. Let your communication be Yea, yea; Nay, nay. When you say yes make sure that that is what you mean. When you say no, make sure that also is what you mean. Mean what you say; say what you mean. Anything that is more than a simple affirmation of the truth **cometh of evil.** When we add an oath to our regular affirmation of the truth, we either admit that our normal conversation cannot be trusted, or that we are lowering ourselves to the level of a world which normally does not tell the truth. This does not necessarily mean that it is wrong to "swear to tell the truth" in a court of law. The point is that it should be unnecessary in a genuine Christian society to have to swear to tell the truth at all!

(5). *Fifth illustration: Retaliation as opposed to forgiveness.* 5:38-42.

38 ¶Ye have heard that it hath been said, An eye for an eye, and a tooth for a tooth:

38. The principle of retaliation, *lex talionis*, is common in both Jewish and other ancient Near Eastern law codes (cf. the Code of Hammurabi). The judicial penalty of **An eye for an eye, and a tooth for a tooth** is stated in Exodus 2:24 as a means of ending feuds. However, Jesus is clearly saying this method is not a license for vengeance. Many times an offended person will overreact to the offense and retaliate in such a way as to return injury for injury. The idea here is that to the Jews of Jesus' day it was common to attempt to retaliate upon the offender through the arm of the law, especially in a nation dominated by a foreign power.

39 But I say unto you, That ye resist not evil: but whosoever shall smite thee on thy right cheek, turn to him the other also.

39. The Saviour's point is that we should **resist not evil.** Evil is seen here, not as a state, but rather as the action of the evil ones or the malicious ones. It represents the evil and sinful element in man which provokes him to an act of evil. Jesus shows how the believer should respond to personal injury. He is not discussing the government's obligation to maintain law and order. The question of nonretaliation or nonviolence is often discussed in relation to these verses. These passages alone do not mean that a man should not defend his family or his country, but rather that he should not attempt personal vengeance, even through the means of the law, to compensate for a personal injury.

Why would Jesus make such a statement? Certainly these words were spoken to remind those who would be His disciples not to expect divine justice from an unregenerate society. All justice ultimately is in the hand and heart of God. As long as human governments prevail, justice will be limited by man's finite abilities. The disciples of the kingdom are to look to the King Himself for ultimate vindication. The practical application of this truth is that the believer should not attempt to justify himself or inflict vengeance even through legal means. He is to place his total confidence in the ultimate sovereignty of God over the affairs of his life. (See Rom 12:19 where "give place unto wrath" means God's wrath.)

Jesus gives five examples of how the believer should react to unfair or unreasonable treatment. First, in retaliation to physical violence, he is to **turn to him the other** (side) **also.** Man's normal impulse is to strike back, but the disciple is not to be a normal man. He is to "overcome evil with good" (Rom 12:21). This is probably one of the most feared statements in all the Bible. People have gone to great lengths in an attempt to explain it away. Nevertheless, it remains the most pungent statement of Jesus' ethic. The life of the believer is to be lived with such a quality of spiritual verity and justice that he needs no physical retaliation in order to defend or justify his position. There is no greater example of this ethical truth than the life and death of Jesus Himself!

40 And if any man will sue thee at the law, and take away thy coat, let him have *thy* cloak also.

40. Secondly, whether robbed by personal assault or compulsory litigation, the believer is to respond with confidence in that which is eternal, rather than that which is temporal. If the believer is sued in order that the accuser may **take away thy coat,** he is to also let him have his **cloak.** The coat (Gr *chitōn*) is the undergarment or tunic. The cloak (Gr *himation*) is the more expensive outer garment worn over the tunic. Jesus taught us to have confidence in an almighty God who is completely aware of the injustices done to man and totally capable of evoking ultimate eternal justice. He must be trusted even when legal litigation goes against the believer. In our society, we would phrase Jesus' teaching, "If someone takes your suit coat, give him your overcoat as well."

41 And whosoever shall compel thee to go a mile, go with him twain.

41. Thirdly, in ancient times government agents were in a position to compel forced service upon a subjugated people. A Roman soldier, for example, could compel a Jewish native to carry his armor or materials for one mile, in order to relieve the soldier. Jesus now states that if someone compels you to walk a mile, **go with him twain.** The believer is to be willing to "go the extra mile." Doing double our duty not only proves the loyalty and faithfulness of our cooperation to human authority, but likewise proves the spiritual intention of our heart. It also provides an opportunity of conviction in order to witness effectively out of our life message. It would have been foolish for the believer of Jesus' day to reluctantly go only a mile with a Roman official and then attempt to share the gospel with him. By going the second mile he proved the innermost intention of his heart.

42 Give to him that asketh thee, and from him that would borrow of thee turn not thou away.

42. The fourth example is that of lending to **him that would borrow of thee.** Jesus made it clear that a loan should be looked upon as a potential gift. When we lend something to someone, we should not expect to receive in return. Is that not impractical? Yes it is! But that which is spiritual is not always that which is practical. There are many statements in Proverbs against borrowing, lending, and surety (cf. Prov 6:1; 11:15; 22:7; 27:13). While we are warned of the dangers of borrowing and lending, Jesus made it clear that the believer ought to be willing to lend to those in need.

Finally, even the beggar is to be ministered to through the provision of giving to **him that asketh thee.** This statement certainly forms the basis of all Christian charity and provides the proper social application of the message of the gospel to the physical needs of man as well as his spiritual needs.

(6). Sixth illustration: Love thy neighbor contrasted to love thy enemy. 5:43-48.

43 ¶Ye have heard that it hath been said, Thou shalt love thy neighbour, and hate thine enemy.

43. The law of love, sometimes called "law of Christ," summarizes the ethical principle of the Sermon on the Mount. "Love thy neighbor" summarizes the entire second table of the law (cf. Lev 19:18-34). But the unscriptural addition "hate thine enemy" was a popular concept in Jesus' day (cf. *The Qumran Manual of Discipline* 1QS 1:4, "hate all that he has rejected"). The admonition **love your enemies** is one of the greatest statements Jesus ever made. The love enjoined in this passage is that which originates from God Himself! Man is not commanded to attempt to love his enemy on the basis of mere human affection but rather on the basis of a love which comes from God. This kind of love holds a unique place in the New Testament Scripture, for it is the gift of God and the fruit of the Spirit to the believer only. It is not something that man can muster within himself. Rather, it must come from God Himself into the life of the believer (cf. Gal 5:22; I Tim 1:5).

44 But I say unto you, Love your enemies, bless them that curse you, do good to them that hate you, and pray for them which despitefully use you, and persecute you;

44. How does one love an enemy? Notice that the passage makes it clear that he does not have to attempt to work up an artificial feeling of love. The quality of love commanded here is expressed by giving. **Bless them** that curse you, **do good** to them that hate you, and **pray** for them that persecute you. Loving an enemy involves doing good toward that enemy in order to win him over to the cause that you represent. The message of the kingdom, therefore, is that we will win over those who oppose us more readily with love than with hatred. It is not in the divisiveness of contention that we win our greatest converts, but in the application of the heart of the gospel and the love of Christ.

45 That ye may be the children of your Father which is in heaven: for he maketh his sun to rise on the evil and on the good, and sendeth rain on the just and on the unjust.

46 For if ye love them which love you, what reward have ye? do not even the publicans the same?

47 And if ye salute your brethren only, what do ye more *than others?* do not even the publicans so?

45-47. In summarizing the importance of love, Jesus reminded that love was a necessary proof of salvation: "that ye may be the **children of your Father** which is in heaven." An initial reading of this text out of its context might seem to imply that loving one's neighbor automatically makes one a child of God. However, the New Testament is clear that love is an evidence of the one who is already saved by the grace of God (cf. I Jn 3:14). It is a natural tendency of human beings to love those who love them; therefore Jesus reminds that we are to love our enemies as our **brethren,** for **even the publicans** love those who love them. Publicans were public officials of Jewish nationality who worked for the Roman government as tax collectors and were generally despised by the people. The idea here is that even the most hated people of the day loved their own friends. Therefore, the true child of the kingdom is to have a quality of love that goes beyond that of the world.

48 Be ye therefore perfect, even as your Father which is in heaven is perfect.

48. This section of the Sermon on the Mount is summarized with the statement **Be ye therefore perfect.** Since the New Testament makes it clear that even the believer is capable of sin, the term perfect here (Gr *teleios*) is not to be taken as absolute sinless perfection. Rather, it is used in relation to the matter of love in this context. "As God's love is complete, not omitting any group, so must the child of God strive for maturity in this regard" (Kent, p. 19).

c. True spiritual worship: Character expressed. 6:1-7:12.

The nature of the true spiritual man previously described is not illustrated in acts of true spiritual worship as contrasted to traditional hypocritical worship. Again, Jesus goes beyond mere outward conformity to the law to the inward conviction of the spirit. The following examples are given to illustrate this point: giving, praying, fasting, serving.

(1). First example: Almsgiving. 6:1-4.

CHAPTER 6

TAKE heed that ye do not your alms before men, to be seen of them: otherwise ye have no reward of your Father which is in heaven.

6:1. Jesus warns that we do not give **alms before men** just to gain human recognition to ourselves. That practical righteousness is in view is obvious. The one who does righteousness (or gives of his possessions) to the Lord **before men** merely **to be seen of them** has **no reward** from the Father in heaven. True worship is to result from the desire to serve God, not men, since pleasing God is far more important than pleasing men. Loss of reward is incurred by gaining the reward of human recognition as an end in itself. This does not mean that all human recognition is necessarily wrong. The implication of the text simply states that we are to serve the Lord because we love Him, not just because we desire something from Him.

2 Therefore when thou doest *thine* alms, do not sound a trumpet before thee, as the hypocrites do in the synagogues and in the streets, that they may have glory of men. Verily I say unto you, They have their reward.

2. Therefore in all of our giving we are not to **sound a trumpet** before us in a hypocritical manner of gaining attention to ourselves. This metaphorical phrase means do not "publicize" your righteousness, for such performers are hypocrites (from the Greek, "play actor"). Thus, Jesus warns against "acting like the hypocrites, whose aim is to win human praise . . . whose parade and pretense are spiritually futile" (Filson, p. 92). Those who parade their righteousness through the streets receive the honor of men and **They have their reward,** meaning that God will add nothing extra to that reward. But those who are willing to serve Him **in secret,** God will reward openly.

3 But when thou doest alms, let not thy left hand know what thy right hand doeth:

3. The phrase **let not thy left hand know what thy right hand doeth** means that one's giving of finances to the work of the Lord should be done so freely and spontaneously that his right hand cannot keep up with his left hand. He literally empties his pockets as fast as he can! Such giving is to be so spontaneous as to be unplanned at times. Notice that this passage does not state that it is wrong to give systematically, nor through church envelopes, nor receiving a tax-deductible receipt. What it does teach is that one should not give by those means only. There are ample examples of systematic giving in Scripture in order to build the Temple, to provide for the needs and welfare of the underprivileged, etc. Planned giving is certainly biblical and encouraged; but all of our giving should not be limited to our predetermined plan or system.

4 That thine alms may be in secret: and thy Father which seeth in secret himself shall reward thee openly.

4. The real key to success of this kind of giving is found in the phrase: **thy Father which seeth in secret . . . shall reward** you. Giving by faith, out of a cheerful heart, depends upon our total confidence in that fact that God does indeed see us and knows our needs. The God who is there, sees in secret that which no man may observe, and that God rewards His own. The Christian is to give, not in order to receive reward, but that his love might be expressed to God who shall reward him. Our giving to the work of Christ spreads the message of the gospel throughout the world. Notice again, that these verses certainly do not condemn public giving, but rather they speak against giving out of the wrong attitude and for the wrong motive.

(2). Second example: Praying. 6:5-15.

5-6. Praying, like giving, is to be done unto the Lord, not unto man. Many professing Christians, if they were honest, would have to admit that they pray to be heard of men. Jesus said that the people of His day **love to pray standing in the synagogues.** Both a time and place for prayer were customary in the ancient Jewish synagogue (cf. Mk 11:25). Therefore, Jesus is not condemning the practice of public prayer, but rather the misuse of it! Because of the statement **enter into thy closet** some have suggested that all public prayer is wrong. This would be contrary to the rest of New Testament statements about prayer, commandments and restrictions regarding prayer, and examples of prayer meetings (cf. Acts 12:12).

5 ¶And when thou prayest, thou shalt not be as the hypocrites *are:* for they love to pray standing in the synagogues and in the corners of the streets, that they may be seen of men. Verily I say unto you, They have their reward.

6 But thou, when thou prayest, enter into thy closet, and when thou hast shut thy door, pray to thy Father which is in secret; and thy Father which seeth in secret shall reward thee openly.

The principle here is that the believer should not make a show of his prayer nor of the answers he receives to prayer in such a way as to call unnecessary attention to himself. Again, it is the God who sees in secret that rewards us openly. Here the intimate father-child relationship between God and man is clearly emphasized. It is the experience of private devotional prayer that ultimately prepares one to pray effectively in public. Most people who say they cannot pray in public, do not pray effectively in private either!

7 But when ye pray, use not vain repetitions, as the heathen *do:* for they think that they shall be heard for their much speaking.

7. Jesus warned that we **use not vain repetitions** (Gr *battalogeō* denotes babbling or speaking without thinking). Such praying was characteristic of the heathen. A good example of this is found in the ecstatic babblings of the false prophets in the Old Testament and in the prophets of Baal who confronted Elijah on Mt. Carmel (cf. I Kgs 18:26-29). Jesus condemns the use of empty repetition as an attempt to overcome the will of God by wearing Him out. It is not the length of prayer, but the strength of prayer that prevails with God. Jesus Himself prayed all night prior to His crucifixion and on most other occasions prayed very briefly. He is not condemning lengthy prayers, although there is nothing particularly spiritual about them. He is merely emphasizing that prayer must be a sincere expression of the heart, not mere accumulation of verbiage. God is not impressed with words, but with the genuine outcry of a needy heart.

8 Be not ye therefore like unto them: for your Father knoweth what things ye have need of, before ye ask him.

8. Many have questioned the meaning of the statement **your Father knoweth what things ye have need of, before ye ask him.** "Then why should we pray?" they ask. Prayer is not man's attempt to change the will of God. God's method of changing our will is to bring it into conformity with His will. More than changing things, prayer changes people. Prayer is not conquering God's reluctance to answer, but laying hold of His willingness to help! Prayer, in the life of the true believer, is an act of total confidence and assurance in the plan and purpose of God. It is not an expression of panic and desperation.

The following sample prayer is given to the disciples as an example of a suitable prayer. It is neither lengthy nor irreverent. It contains a depth of piety and a pinnacle of power. This prayer, often called the "Lord's Prayer," is in reality a disciple's prayer, for Jesus gave it to His disciples as a sample of the true principle of spiritual prayer. In no way does the prayer itself embody all of His teaching about prayer and certainly, having just warned against vain repetition, He did not intend for this particular prayer to be merely recited with empty meaninglessness. This does not mean, however, that this prayer may not be recited as an act of public worship. There are those who feel such recitation is too liturgical, while there are others who feel that the omission of ever repeating this prayer is a failure to grasp its true significance. Certainly if we are to follow its example properly we may benefit from repeating it as it was given by the Lord Himself. To place this prayer under law and eliminate it from Christian usage is to deny the great essence of what the prayer is all about.

9 After this manner therefore pray ye: Our Father which art in heaven, Hallowed be thy name.

9. The very beginning phrase, **Our Father,** is completely uncommon to the prayers of the Old Testament. Martyn Lloyd-Jones (Vol. II, p. 54) has commented: "So when our Lord says, 'Our Father,' He is obviously thinking of Christian people, and that is why I say that this is a Christian prayer." By contrast see the ultra-dispensational approach of Gaebelein who refers to the Lord's Prayer as one of the rags of popery Luther brought with him from the Catholic church. He evaluates the Lord's Prayer as "decidedly unchristian!" (A. C. Gaebelein *The Gospel of Matthew*, p. 139). The two major elements of the prayer are adoration and petition. **Hallowed be thy name** addresses the attention of the prayer toward God and reverence for His name and His person. Hallowed (Gr *hagiazō*) means to be held in reverence and awe of holiness. God's name was so sacred to the Old Testament Jew that it was never pronounced by human lips. Thus His name is the expression of His very essence. The biblical usage of the concept of a name is a characteristic description of the basic character of the person to whom the name is applied. Since the prayer is directed to our spiritual Father, only a child of God who has been born again can rightly pray this prayer.

10 Thy kingdom come. Thy will be done in earth, as *it is* in heaven.

10. The phrase **Thy kingdom come** refers to the eschatological nature of this prayer. Notice that the kingdom is to be prayed for, implying that it has not already arrived. The kingdom represents the full and effective reign of God through the mediatorial office of the Messiah. The disciples were not to think of their own convenience as their foremost expression in prayer, but the full and quick realization of the effective rule of God on earth in the hearts of men. That rule is realized through the regenerating process of the new birth in the lives of individuals. It will reach its pinnacle when the last enemy (sin and death, I Cor 15:24-28) has been destroyed at the Lord's return. The recognition of **Thy will be done** emphasizes the idea that prayer is to bring about the conformity of the will of the believer to the will of God. Prayer is an act of spiritual expression which brings us into conformity to the very nature and purpose of God.

11 Give us this day our daily bread.

11. The section of petitions begins with the request to **give us this day our daily bread.** Bread (Gr *artos*) may be applied to the provision of food in general. The term "daily" (Gr *epicusios*) denotes "indispensable" (Arndt and Gingrich, *Lexicon*, p. 296). The concept of daily provision of bread fits perfectly with the Old Testament example of the daily provision of manna to the

12 And forgive us our debts, as we forgive our debtors.

13 And lead us not into temptation, but deliver us from evil: For thine is the kingdom, and the power, and the glory, for ever. Amen.
14 For if ye forgive men their trespasses, your heavenly Father will also forgive you:
15 But if ye forgive not men their trespasses, neither will your Father forgive your trespasses.

Israelites while they were wandering in the wilderness (Ex 16:14-15). In a similar sense, while the Christian pilgrim takes his journey through a strange land that he does not yet literally possess, but which has been promised to him, it only stands to reason that God would make a similar provision to this New Testament, gospel-age wanderer.

12. The phrase **forgive us our debts** refers to sins which are our moral and spiritual debts to God's righteousness. The request for forgiveness of sin is made here by the believer. In order to be saved one need not necessarily name all of his sins, but must confess that he is a sinner. For continued spiritual growth and cleansing the believer acknowledges his sins in particular. Notice that we seek forgiveness **as we forgive**, not because we forgive. Our expression of forgiveness does not gain salvation for us. We are to seek forgiveness in the same manner as we forgive others. Forgiveness is the evidence of a regenerate heart.

13-15. Lead us not into temptation is a plea for the providential help of God in our daily confrontation with the temptation of sin. James 1:13-14 makes it clear that God does not tempt us to do evil, but rather that we are tempted of our own lusts. However, God does test us in order to give us the opportunity to prove our faithfulness to Him. It is never His desire to lead us into evil itself. Therefore if we resist the devil, we are promised that he will flee from us.

The prayer closes with a doxology of praise **for thine is the kingdom, and the power, and the glory, for ever. Amen,** which is a liturgical interpolation from I Chronicles 29:11. Though omitted in some manuscripts, these words constitute a fitting climactic affirmation of faith.

In the first three petitions of this prayer of the Lord, our soul rises directly to God; in the three following we face the hindrances of these aspirations; and in the last petition we discover the solution to all these difficulties. Stier (*The Words of the Lord Jesus,* Vol. I, p. 198) draws a unique parallel between the two tables of the Decalogue and the two sections of the Lord's Prayer. In the first petition the believer's soul is awed with the character of God, in the second petition with His grand purpose, and in the third petition with His moral condition. In the second part of the prayer the children of God humble themselves in dependence upon divine mercy in the fourth petition; they seek forgiveness in the fifth petition; gracious guidance in the sixth petition; and deliverance from the power of evil in the seventh petition. Thus, this arrangement may be readily suggested by dividing the prayer into two parts:

Relationship to God—
Hallowed be *Thy* Name;
Thy Kingdom come;
Thy will be done;

Relationship to men—
Give *us* this day our daily bread;
Forgive *us* our debts;
Lead *us* not into temptation;
Deliver *us* from evil.

Finally, the rich doxology expresses the certain hope that our prayers shall be heard and that God, in view of His great character, will bring to pass the highest good in our lives. Thus, prayer is the expression of the believer's confidence in the ultimate plan and purpose of God. In his *Commentary on the Holy Scriptures: Matthew* (p. 124), J. P. Lange has suggested the following comparison between the statements of the Beatitudes and the petitions of the Lord's Prayer:

BEATITUDES	LORD'S PRAYER
Blessed are the poor in spirit: for theirs is the kingdom of heaven	*Hallowed be thy name (the name of God which opens to us the kingdom of heaven)*
Blessed are they that mourn: for they shall be comforted	*Thy kingdom come (heavenly comfort into our hearts)*
Blessed are the meek: for they shall inherit the earth	*Thy will be done on earth as it is in heaven (this meekness, the characteristic of heaven, shall possess the new earth)*
Blessed are they that hunger and thirst after righteousness; for they shall be filled	*Give us this day our daily bread*
Blessed are the merciful for they shall obtain mercy	*Forgive us our debts as we forgive our debtors*
Blessed are the pure in heart: for they shall see God	*And lead us not into temptation*
Blessed are the peacemakers: etc.	*But deliver us from evil*

The comparison between these two pinnacles of piety is striking indeed. The inexhaustible expression of devotion and simplicity of language in both the Beatitudes and the Sermon on the Mount give them a depth of expression which goes beyond the temporal and touches the eternal.

(3). Third example: Fasting. 6:16-18.

16. **When ye fast** is a reference both to fasting prescribed under the Mosaic law in connection with the Day of Atonement (Lev 16:29) and the voluntary fast of that day. The Pharisees added two fast days, on Monday and Thursday of each week, as a case of public display and piety. The true purpose of fasting was intended, however, for deep contrition and spiritual communion. Fasting was especially emphasized as an effective means of dealing with temptation (cf. Isa 58:6). The Pharisees regarded the practice of fasting as meritorious (cf. *Taanith*, 8:3) and appeared in the synagogues negligently attired. Their sad disfigurement of face and the wearing of mourning garb gave them an opportunity to exhibit their superior ascetic sanctity before the people. The phrase **disfigure their faces** (Gr *aphanizō*) literally denotes covering their faces and is a figurative expression for mournful gestures and neglected appearance of those wanting to call attention to the fact they are enduring. This was often done with dust and ashes (cf. Isa 61:3) and is similar to the modern Roman Catholic concept of Ash Wednesday. In the original, there is a play upon two cognate words meaning, "they make their faces unappearable," that they may "appear unto men."

17-18. This passage is not to be taken as a command against fasting but rather against the misuse of the spiritual exercise of fasting. Kent (p. 21) observes: "Fasting that requires spectators is mere acting." Though Jesus Himself instituted no fast for His disciples, voluntary fasting does appear in the early churches (cf. Acts 13:2). The injunction to **anoint thine head** relates to the ancient custom of anointing one's head when going to a feast. In other words, Jesus was saying that when we fast we are to do so secretly unto the Lord, while outwardly maintaining the appearance of joy and triumph which is the end result of true fasting.

16 ¶Moreover when ye fast, be not, as the hypocrites, of a sad countenance: for they disfigure their faces, that they may appear unto men to fast. Verily I say unto you, They have their reward.

17 But thou, when thou fastest, anoint thine head, and wash thy face;
18 That thou appear not unto men to fast, but unto thy Father which is in secret: and thy Father, which seeth in secret, shall reward thee openly.

Just as we have observed the interesting parallels within this sermon, so again we discover the contrast between outward acts of worship and inward attitudes of devotion. Outward worship stresses giving; inward worship stresses possessing. Outward worship manifests praying; inward worship manifests worrying. Outward worship is characterized by fasting; inward worship is characterized by judging.

The obvious contrasts are that a proper attitude toward giving will arise from the proper inward attitude toward one's possessions. Praying will resolve all worrying. Fasting, in judging one's self, is to be preferred over judging others.

(4). 'Fourth example: Giving. 6:19-24.

The common error of Judaism was to regard material wealth as always indicating the blessing of God. While it is true that the book of Proverbs promises material blessings to those who honor God's financial principles, it does not imply that all wealth is a necessary sign of blessing. The Proverbs themselves indicate that many become temporarily wealthy because of ill-gotten gains. The contrast between these two sections of examples, both inward and outward, is directed specifically at the false spirituality of the Pharisees which arose from worldly-mindedness.

19 ¶Lay not up for yourselves trea-sures upon earth, where moth and rust doth corrupt, and where thieves break through and steal:

19. Because the false spirituality of men seeks to lay up treasures for themselves in a worldly sense, they "have their reward." Thus, their desire to be seen of men and to lay up treausre through the outward attention of men, as if some self-meritorious work could make them more acceptable to God and man, is provoked by their wrong attitude toward material possessions in the first place. Therefore, **treasures upon earth** are temporary and of short duration. These earthly possessions are at the mercy of **moth and rust . . . and . . . thieves.** Even if temporal possessions escape the clutches of the marauder, they are still likely to become moth-eaten and rusty. In other words, they do not last. Our materialistic technological society in the late twentieth century all too often has overlooked the simplicity of this truth. Our attention to wealth, possession, social status, and retirement benefits too easily causes us to trust that which man can provide rather than that which God has already provided. Our simple appreciation of the natural provisions of God are frequently overlooked in favor of the plastic provisions of our contemporary technology.

20 But lay up for yourselves trea-sures in heaven, where neither moth nor rust doth corrupt, and where thieves do not break through nor steal: 21 For where your treasure is, there will your heart be also.

20-21. The attention of the believer is directed toward **trea-sures in heaven.** The term "treasures" implies the addition or accumulation of things. The two kinds of treasures are conditioned by their place (either upon earth or in heaven). The concept of laying up treasure in heaven is not pictured as one of meritorious benefits but rather of rewards for faithful service, as is illustrated elsewhere in the teaching of Jesus. The ultimate destiny of our lives is either earthly or heavenly and the concentration of our efforts will reveal where our real treasure is. In contrast to the legalistic attempt of Judaism to establish a spiritual treasure upon earth, Jesus calls the attention of His disciples to that true and eternal treasure which is heavenly. The only way man will ever overcome his natural inclination toward materialism and wealth is to place the priority of his possessions in heaven. If one were as concerned about spiritual benefits of his life as he were about the material possessions, his motivations would be pure indeed.

22 The light of the body is the eye: if therefore thine eye be single, thy whole body shall be full of light. 23 But if thine eye be evil, thy whole body shall be full of darkness. If therefore the light that is in thee be darkness, how great is that darkness!

22-23. The **light of the body** is associated with the **eye.** The concept here is based on the ancient idea that the eyes were the windows through which light entered the body. If the eyes were in good condition the body could receive such light. Tasker (p. 75) notes that Jesus, using this language metaphorically, affirms that if a man's spiritual sight is healthy and his affections directed toward heavenly treasure, his whole personality will be without blemish. The phrase **if . . . thine eye be single** indicates devotion to one purpose. The "single eye" refers to a single, fixed vision or goal. This reminds us of the statement of James, "A double-minded man is unstable in all his ways" (Jas 1:8). The phrase **if thine eye be evil** refers to either disease or deception of vision. Though many commentators suggest the idea of disease, the context seems to imply deception. The "evil eye" is not necessarily something mysterious nor devilish, but rather a deceptive vision which causes the viewer to mistake the identity of an object. The mistake in this context is the darkening of the mind and thus **how great is that darkness!**

24. This kind of spiritual double vision causes one to believe that he can **serve two masters.** Total loyalty to God cannot be divided between Him and loyalty to one's material possessions. A master (Gr *kyrios*) is a lord or an owner. That God claims total lordship over His own is obvious in this passage. The concept of the lordship of Christ has often been greatly mistaken. Even in the face of the immediate denial of and on the part of His disciples, Jesus said to them: "Ye call me Master and Lord; and ye say well; for so I am" (Jn 13:13). There is no passage or command anywhere in the New Testament asking the believer to make Christ "Lord of his life" after salvation. The very experience of receiving Christ as Saviour is looked upon throughout the Scriptures as an acknowledgment of lordship and ownership. If perfect obedience were required in order to make Christ our Lord, He would be the Lord of no one! It is the fact that He is already Lord that makes our disobedience so serious. As Lord and Master He has the right to demand complete obedience. My disobedience as a believer is an act of sin against His lordship. The believer cannot sin away the lordship of Christ any more than he can His saviourhood.

Therefore, Jesus rightly proclaimed **Ye cannot serve God and mammon.** The term "mammon" is derived from the Aramaic term for possessions or wealth. Jesus is not condemning money or possessions in and of themselves, but the improper attitude of enslavement toward wealth. His point here cannot be overemphasized in light of the affluent society of our day. Outside the boundaries of North America the average Christian knows much more of the reality of poverty than do we. Within the depth of this message and its application we may certainly see afresh that it is the "gospel of the poor."

Double-mindedness is an attempt to sit on the fence in relation to spiritual matters. There is no halfhearted service for God. It is either all or nothing. Jesus gives the believer no option between loving God and loving the world. The regenerated heart is one which so longs for righteousness and desires the things of heaven that it lives above the temporal things of the earth.

(5). Fifth example: Worry or anxiety. 6:25-34.

24 No man can serve two masters: for either he will hate the one, and love the other; or else he will hold to the one, and despise the other. Ye cannot serve God and mammon.

25 Therefore I say unto you, Take no thought for your life, what ye shall eat, or what ye shall drink; nor yet for your body, what ye shall put on. Is not the life more than meat, and the body than raiment?

25. Adding doubt to the danger of possessions, Jesus now deals with the equally dangerous tendency of those who have no possessions: worry! **Take no thought** (Gr *merimnaō*) means do not be anxious. Filson (pp. 100-101) notes that this word means to be so disturbed about material needs that we distrust God and are distracted from faithfully doing His will. The implication of the test is that all anxiety is provoked by worrying about material and temporal things. Such anxiety causes one to avoid the responsibility of work in order to cooperate with God's provision. Anxious care is an inordinate or solicitous concern or grief beyond our immediate needs. It is the direct opposite of carefulness, cautiousness, and faith. Therefore, even the poor are not to worry needlessly about what they should eat, drink, or wear. The question, **Is not the life more than meat, and the body than raiment?** indicates that inner mental stability must come from the spirit of a man and not from outward physical provisions. To set one's heart upon material possessions or to worry

26 Behold the fowls of the air: for they sow not, neither do they reap, nor gather into barns; yet your heavenly Father feedeth them. Are ye not much better than they?

27 Which of you by taking thought can add one cubit unto his stature?

28 And why take ye thought for raiment? Consider the lilies of the field, how they grow; they toil not, neither do they spin:

29 And yet I say unto you, That even Solomon in all his glory was not arrayed like one of these.

30 Wherefore, if God so clothe the grass of the field, which to day is, and to morrow is cast into the oven, *shall he not much more clothe* you, O ye of little faith?

31 Therefore take no thought, saying, What shall we eat? or, What shall we drink? or, Wherewithal shall we be clothed?

32 (For after all these things do the Gentiles seek:) for your heavenly Father knoweth that ye have need of all these things.

33 But seek ye first the kingdom of God, and his righteousness; and all these things shall be added unto you.

34 Take therefore no thought for the morrow: for the morrow shall take thought for the things of itself. Sufficient unto the day *is* the evil thereof.

about the lack of them is to live in perpetual insecurity and to deprive one's self of the spiritual blessings of God.

26-32. Jesus illustrated His point by referring to objects in nature which were immediately at hand: the birds of the air and the flowers of the field. Though the birds which fly through the skies appeared not to labor, **your heavenly Father feedeth them.** How does God accomplish this? He does it through the normal process of nature. **Consider the lilies;** (vs. 28) they appear to do nothing for themselves and yet God, through the process of nature which He controls, does **clothe the grass of the field** (vs. 30). Even Solomon, the great and wealthy king of Israel, was not arrayed in any greater beauty than the flowers of the field which God has made.

The key point of this passage is found in the phrases **Are ye not much better than they?** (vs. 26) and **shall he not much more clothe you?** (vs. 30). The Bible makes it clear that God is the Creator and sustainer of all He has made. He is not divorced from the world which He has made. Indeed, "this is my Father's world!" Worry and anxiety are related to the length of one's life in the phrase **add one cubit unto his stature.** A cubit is a measurement of about eighteen inches. However, this reference is probably not to one's actual height but to the length of his life. The term "stature" (Gr *hēlikia*) may in this place mean "age." Thus the idea seems to be that a man cannot add the smallest measure to the span of his life by worrying. In fact, modern medicine would tell us that worry actually shortens one's life. This state of anxiety is related to having **little faith** (vs. 30). Faith is total confidence in the provision of God. Faith in salvation is a total trusting of the complete work of Christ on the cross on our behalf. The Scripture reminds: "Whatsoever is not of faith is sin" (Rom 14:23). Therefore, a lack of faith will lead to a life of psychological anxiety. Since this lack of faith is identified with sin, Adams is correct in asserting that man's emotional problems stem from his sin (J. Adams, *Christian Counselor's Manual*, p. 117 ff.). In the Sermon on the Mount we have then, not only a directive for spiritual well-being, but the model of a manual of mental health as well.

33-34. This portion of the Sermon on the Mount is summarized by the statement **seek ye first the kingdom of God.** The disciples who have pledged their allegiance to the King must continue seeking the kingdom and its righteousness. The present imperative form of the verb (Gr *zētō*) indicates a continual or constant seeking. The word **first** indicates one's first and ever dominant concern. The contrast between the spiritual and the material is again emphasized. The believer is to seek first the righteousness that is characteristic of God's kingdom and then **all these things** (i.e., material things) shall be added unto him. Seeking the kingdom of God involves a continued hunger and thirst after righteousness. We are not only to seek the kingdom of God in the sense that we set our affections on things above, we must also positively seek holiness in **righteousness**. The continual seeking here is similar to that of the seeking face of God. A true believer is never falsely content with what he has in Christ, but is continually seeking to know Him better. Thus, we could say: "Keep seeking the kingdom of God" and as you do He will continually provide your needs. When our priority is spiritual, God will take care of the material, for where God guides, He provides. We need not even worry about tomorrow for **Sufficient unto the day is the evil thereof** (vs. 34). This means that each day has its own troubles and challenges to be responsibly handled, without worrying about the hypothetical problems which could arise tomorrow. God is ever pictured in Scripture as the God of the present. Today is the day of salvation.

CHAPTER 7

JUDGE not, that ye be not judged.

2 For with what judgment ye judge, ye shall be judged: and with what measure ye mete, it shall be measured to you again.

3 And why beholdest thou the mote that is in thy brother's eye, but considerest not the beam that is in thine own eye?

4 Or how wilt thou say to thy brother, Let me pull out the mote out of thine eye; and, behold, a beam *is* in thine own eye?

5 Thou hypocrite, first cast out the beam out of thine own eye; and then shalt thou see clearly to cast out the mote out of thy brother's eye.

6 ¶Give not that which is holy unto the dogs, neither cast ye your pearls before swine, lest they trample them under their feet, and turn again and rend you.

7 ¶Ask, and it shall be given you; seek, and ye shall find; knock, and it shall be opened unto you:

8 For every one that asketh receiveth; and he that seeketh findeth; and to him that knocketh it shall be opened.

9 Or what man is there of you, whom if his son ask bread, will he give him a stone?

10 Or if he ask a fish, will he give him a serpent?

11 If ye then, being evil, know how to give good gifts unto your children, how much more shall your Father which is

(6). Sixth example: Judging others. 7:1-12.

7:1-4. Judge not refers to an unfavorable and condemnatory judgment. This does not mean that a Christian should never render judgment of any kind under any circumstances. The New Testament Scriptures are filled with exhortations to "mark those who cause divisions among you," "receive not" those who deny Christ, "exhort," "rebuke," etc. Certainly judging ourselves and those who have failed in their spiritual responsibility is a necessity of church discipline (cf. I Cor 5). The point being made here is that we are not to judge the inner motives of another. We are not to render a verdict based upon prejudiced information. Nor are we to use ourselves as the standard of judgment for **with what . . . ye mete** you shall be judged. If we were judged in eternity merely on the basis of the verbal judgments we have rendered others, we would all condemn ourselves! **That ye be not judged** seems to refer to the ultimate judgment of God rather than our own judgment. The terms **mote** (Gr *karphos*) and **beam** (Gr *dokos*) are used metaphorically for a small fault and a great fault. The mote was literally a small speck of sawdust whereas the beam was literally a rafter used in building. Thus, the idea of the text is that one cannot remove the speck from his brother's eye until he has removed the rafter from his own eye!

5-6. Thou hypocrite is the only statement that can be made for this play actor who pretends to be a physician when he himself is sick. Filson (p. 104) comments: "His concern to criticize and reform others is marred by uncritical moral complacency as to his own life." The dogs and swine refer to those who have deliberately rejected the message of truth. These particular animals were especially repulsive to Jesus' audience. The connotation in verse 6 is not that we should not present our message to those who are the outcasts of society, for Jesus Himself went to the poor sinners among His people. Rather, the idea is that it is futile to continue to present truth to those who have refused what they have already heard. A man cannot appreciate new truth until he has responded to the truth which he has already received. Since the context deals with the matter of discernment and judgment, it may rightly be assumed that there is a proper place for such activity in the Christian's life. The main difference between judgment and discernment is that a judge merely pronounces a verdict, while discernment seeks a solution.

7-10. Earlier a paralleling contrast was drawn between the outward acts of worship (giving, praying, fasting) and the inward attitudes of devotion (possessing, praying, judging). Since the opposite of judging is fasting, it seems fitting that Jesus here makes a lengthy statement on the importance of prayer. This statement is not out of place as some have assumed; rather, it is the Christian alternative to judging. If we would sincerely pray for those whom we are prone to criticize we would ultimately do them much more good. The three imperatives **Ask, seek, knock** are, in the original, in the present tense suggesting both perseverance and frequent prayer. In the English language the first letter of each word forms the acrostic A-S-K. Fervent and continual prayer is to be made on behalf of those for whom we are concerned.

God promises to answer all genuine prayer (vs. 8). Everything that we need for spiritual success has been promised to us. God leaves us no excuse for failure. **Ask, and it shall be given you; seek, and ye shall find; knock, and it shall be opened unto you,** for everyone that does such will receive an answer. You are not cut off in any way from the blessings and provisions of God for these are available to every one of His children.

11-12. Jesus illustrated His point by comparing the willingness of a human father to give his child a gift, contrasted to our heavenly Father who shall gladly give us what we need. The

in heaven give good things to them that ask him?

12 Therefore all things whatsoever ye would that men should do to you, do ye even so to them: for this is the law and the prophets.

13 ¶Enter ye in at the strait gate: for wide *is* the gate, and broad *is* the way, that leadeth to destruction, and many there be which go in thereat:

14 Because strait *is* the gate, and narrow *is* the way, which leadeth unto life, and few there be that find it.

15 ¶Beware of false prophets, which come to you in sheep's clothing, but inwardly they are ravening wolves.

16 Ye shall know them by their fruits. Do men gather grapes of thorns, or figs of thistles?

17 Even so every good tree bringeth forth good fruit; but a corrupt tree bringeth forth evil fruit.

18 A good tree cannot bring forth evil fruit, neither *can* a corrupt tree bring forth good fruit.

term **evil** (vs. 11) is used here of man's sinful nature. Even sinful men are kind unto their children; therefore, **how much more** shall your heavenly Father delight to answer your prayers. Hence, rather than judging others, we are to treat them as we would like to be treated. The statement in verse 12, **Therefore all things whatsoever ye would that men should do to you, do ye even so to them,** is the biblical injunction which has often been called "the Golden Rule." Similar statements are found in both Jewish and Gentile sources, but usually in the negative form. The phrase, **this is the law and the prophets,** indicates that the statement made here by Jesus is not intended to be unique, but rather a summarization of the second table of the law. Verse 12 is not intended to be a total summary of Jesus' teaching and in no way exhausts or explains the gospel itself. An atheist could readily accept this statement alone. However, it is when we see this statement in the context of everything that Jesus taught that we understand its true significance. Rather than judge others we ought to pray for them. If we would rather have people pray for us than criticize us, then we ought to be willing to do the same to them.

d. The two alternatives: Character established. 7:13-27.

The closing section of the Sermon on the Mount presents two choices to the listener. These are presented in a series of contrasts: two ways (vss. 13-14); two trees (vss. 15-20); two professions (vss. 21-23); and two foundations (vss. 24-29). This was a common method of teaching in both Jewish and Greco-Roman thought.

13-14. Enter ye in at the strait gate (narrow gate) means that one must come in the narrow way of the gate in order to reach the path which leads to eternal life. The order of the gate first and then the way suggests the gate is the entrance by faith in Christ into the way of the Christian life. It is interesting to recall that Christians were first called those of "the way" (cf. Acts 9:2; 19:9; 22:4; 24:14). Though the many are on the **broad . . . way that leadeth to destruction** (eternal death), the gate which leads to life is so narrow that **few there be that find it.** Christ Himself is both the gate and the way (cf. Jn 14:6), and God enables men to find that gate (cf. Jn 6:44). In the immediate context of Jesus' day it could be assumed that His way was presented as that which is narrow and the way of the Pharisees as that which is broad. The contrast here is one between the way of grace and the way of works. There are many on the broad road of life who are seeking to arrive in heaven by means of their own works, but only a few have received the grace of God which guarantees them heaven. We are reminded of Jesus' statement, **Many are called, but few are chosen** (22:14).

15. The warning of **Beware of false prophets** fits appropriately with the concept of the two ways. Since many are being misled in the wrong way, it is obvious that they are being misled by wrong ones. False prophets were prevalent in the Old Testament, whereas God's true prophets were often in the minority (as in Elijah's confrontation with the prophets of Baal). These appear in **sheep's clothing** but are in reality **ravening wolves.** This is a perfect description of those preachers who have denied or distorted the truth of the gospel. They look like a lamb but they act like a wolf. Their description is similar to that of the great false prophet in Revelation 13:11.

16-20. A true test of a prophet was the conformity of his doctrine to that of the Scripture (cf. I Cor 14:37; Deut 13:1-5). **Their fruits** not only refer to actions of their lives, for these men are very, very sheepish, but to the doctrines which they proclaim. Having warned us against falsely judging others, Jesus now must remind us to beware and know such people. We are to be discerning enough not to be taken in by their cleverness.

The two trees are contrasted in relation to the fruit which they

19 Every tree that bringeth not forth good fruit is hewn down, and cast into the fire.

20 Wherefore by their fruits ye shall know them.

21 ¶Not every one that saith unto me, Lord, Lord, shall enter into the kingdom of heaven; but he that doeth the will of my Father which is in heaven.

22 Many will say to me in that day, Lord, Lord, have we not prophesied in thy name? and in thy name have cast out devils? and in thy name done many wonderful works?

23 And then will I profess unto them, I never knew you: depart from me, ye that work iniquity.

24 ¶Therefore whosoever heareth these sayings of mine, and doeth them, I will liken him unto a wise man, which built his house upon a rock:

25 And the rain descended, and the floods came, and the winds blew, and beat upon that house; and it fell not: for it was founded upon a rock.

26 And every one that heareth these sayings of mine, and doeth them not, shall be likened unto a foolish man, which built his house upon the sand:

27 And the rain descended, and the floods came, and the winds blew, and beat upon that house; and it fell: and great was the fall of it.

produce. The searching question, **Do men gather grapes of thorns?** reminds us of the origin of spiritual life which produces spiritual fruit. Man cannot produce such fruit out of his own unregenerate nature. Because he is a sinner by nature, he is a sinner by choice. Not only must his choice be changed, but so must his nature in order for him to make the right choice. **Every good tree bringeth forth good fruit** consistently, while a **corrupt tree bringeth forth evil fruit** continually. Therefore, the normal and consistent production of fruit, whether good or evil, in a person's life will bear evidence whether or not that life is of God. Verse 19 makes it clear that the unfruitful life is a picture of the unregenerate which is **cast into the fire.** The term "fire" is used as an apparent picture of eternal punishment in hell. The evil (Gr *sapros*) trees are literally rotten and useless. While the production of fruit in the life of a Christian may vary, some thirtyfold, some one hundredfold, no true Christian has the option of producing no fruit at all. No fruit means no life. The absence of life is the absence of the regenerating power of the Holy Spirit. Thus, the fruitless life is the proof of an unregenerate heart which can only be cast into hell. Always in the New Testament the changed life is the proof of one's profession of conversion (cf. II Cor 5:17).

21-23. Not everyone professing Christ is genuinely saved. Even the outward verbal acknowledgment of His lordship is in itself not enough to save the unbeliever apart from true repentance and faith. A genuinely saved person is one **that doeth the will of my Father,** the Greek present tense meaning that he is continually living in obedience to the will of God as the normal course of his life. He may fail at times, but his general course of consistency is to obey the will of the Father. It is tragic to note that many will proclaim in that day, **Lord, Lord** and yet will be lost. On what do they base their profession? Their **many wonderful works** cause them to think that they have attained salvation and yet the response of Christ, pictured here as the Judge, will be **I never knew you: depart from me, ye that work iniquity.** Those who are continually living in sin, as the normal course of their lives, have no assurance of salvation whatever. This does not mean that one must experience basic and initial changes in one's life to validate his claim to conversion. The phase "work iniquity" is also progressive in Greek (i.e., they continue to work iniquity).

24-27. In drawing His concluding illustration of the two foundations, Jesus begins with the word **Therefore.** On the basis of all that He has taught and illustrated, He concluded that all who both hear and do His sayings shall be saved. He is not adding works to faith, but, as James reminds us, He is showing faith by its works. Faith is the root of salvation and works are its fruit. The works of man do not produce his own salvation. In fact, to the contrary, this entire message shows that man's human efforts alone are futile in gaining his salvation. Having made His point, Jesus also clearly stated that while salvation is by faith, it is by a faith which shows itself in a changed life. There is a repentant faith, a life-changing faith, a faith that works!

The contrast here is threefold: the wise man is the one who hears and practices upon a foundation of rock; the foolish man does not practice these sayings and builds upon a foundation of sand. As a great master counselor, Jesus reminded His listener that hearing this message alone will not change his life. He must both hear and do what Jesus has said. The elements of the closing illustration are drawn from the simplicity of nature itself, the **rock,** the **rain,** the **winds.** The rain (Gr *brochē*) pictured here is that of a natural storm. However, it is implied as relating to the troubles and persecutions of life. The man whose house collapsed was at fault, not because he failed to labor, but because he did not lay the proper foundation. How lively must this

28 ¶And it came to pass, when Jesus had ended these sayings, the people were astonished at his doctrine:

29 For he taught them as *one* having authority, and not as the scribes.

CHAPTER 8

WHEN he was come down from the mountain, great multitudes followed him.

2 And, behold, there came a leper and worshipped him, saying, Lord, if thou wilt, thou canst make me clean.

3 And Jesus put forth *his* hand, and touched him, saying, I will; be thou clean. And immediately his leprosy was cleansed.

4 And Jesus saith unto him, See thou tell no man; but go thy way, shew thyself to the priest, and offer the gift that Moses commanded, for a testimony unto them.

5 ¶And when Jesus was entered into Ca-per′na-um, there came unto him a centurion, beseeching him,

6 And saying, Lord, my servant lieth at home sick of the palsy, grievously tormented.

imagery have been to an audience accustomed to the fierceness of an eastern tempest and the suddenness and completeness with which it sweeps everything unsteady before it! The sand represents human opinion and the doctrines of men as opposed to **these sayings** (vs. 28).

28. The entire Sermon on the Mount is addressed to believers and presupposes faith in Jesus as Messiah. The works which are done by the believer are not based upon himself but upon the **rock** (vs. 24), who ultimately is Christ Himself (I Cor 10:4). He is the personal embodiment of all of His teachings. Thus, when He had finished the discourse, **the people were astonished.** Lenski (p. 314) notes that as Jesus spoke, crowds were in rapt attention, but when He ceased, attention relaxed and shocking amazement engulfed them.

29. The outstanding feature of His teaching was His **authority,** meaning the divine approval and authoritative constraint with which He delivered His message. Such straightforward preaching, based on the depth of one's own life, was in direct contrast to that of **the scribes.** The scribes were the copyists of the law and the theologians of their day. The scribes had to rely on tradition for their authority, whereas Christ was His own authority. This undoubtedly disturbed the Pharisees for He had no approval as an official teacher in their system. Rather than quoting the opinion of tradition, Jesus spoke as if He personally knew what He was talking about. He did!

The note of authority in the Sermon on the Mount warns the readers of Matthew's Gospel that they cannot ignore or reject Jesus' teaching without ruinous consequences. Why should we practice this sermon? Because of the beauty of its diction, its impressive pictures, its striking illustrations? No, we practice it because beyond its moral, ethical, and spiritual teaching is the person of the Preacher Himself! In the closing verses of this chapter we see that, without an ostentatious parade, our Lord calls attention to Himself as the focal point of the entire message. This is no mere restatement of the law but is the highest expression of the quality of Christian living which Christ alone can produce. The gospel is the message of the person and work of Jesus Christ. Its amazing "good news" is that He can do for us what we cannot do for ourselves. He can change a sinner into a saint!

2. His miracles: Signs of divine authority. 8:1-9:38.

a. The cleansing of a leper. 8:1-4.

8:1-4. Make me clean. According to the law of Moses, ceremonial uncleanness was attributed to leprosy (see Lev 13:45-46). **Jesus . . . touched him,** which, instead of bringing uncleanness to Jesus, caused the total cleansing of the leper! **See thou tell no man.** The purpose of Jesus in giving this command was to call attention away from the miracle itself and to appeal to the spiritual need in man. It is clear in the gospel accounts that the crowds were often attracted by Jesus' miracles, but not always by His message. **Shew thyself to the priest,** i.e., in obedience to the Mosaic law regarding cleansing. **Offer the gift that Moses commanded.** These gifts are found in Leviticus 14:2-32, where they are typical of Christ's atonement and the cleansing it provided. **For a testimony unto them,** i.e., as evidence to the priest that the leper had indeed been cleansed.

b. The healing of the centurion's servant. 8:5-13.

5-9. A centurion was a rank between that of an officer and a noncommissioned officer (somewhat equivalent to that of a modern sergeant-major). It was a position of great responsibility in the Roman occupation force (see the more complete account in Lk 7:2-10). **Servant** (Gr *pais*), meaning child or servant. **Sick of the palsy** means to be paralyzed and greatly afflicted. The

7 And Jesus saith unto him, I will come and heal him.

8 The centurion answered and said, Lord, I am not worthy that thou shouldest come under my roof: but speak the word only, and my servant shall be healed.

9 For I am a man under authority, having soldiers under me: and I say to this *man*, Go, and he goeth; and to another, Come, and he cometh; and to my servant, Do this, and he doeth *it*.

10 When Jesus heard *it*, he marvelled, and said to them that followed, Verily I say unto you, I have not found so great faith, no, not in Israel.

11 And I say unto you, That many shall come from the east and west, and shall sit down with Abraham, and Isaac, and Jacob, in the kingdom of heaven.

12 But the children of the kingdom shall be cast out into outer darkness: there shall be weeping and gnashing of teeth.

13 And Jesus said unto the centurion, Go thy way; and as thou hast believed, *so* be it done unto thee. And his servant was healed in the selfsame hour.

14 ¶And when Jesus was come into Peter's house, he saw his wife's mother laid, and sick of a fever.

15 And he touched her hand, and the fever left her: and she arose, and ministered unto them.

16 ¶When the even was come, they brought unto him many that were possessed with devils: and he cast out the spirits with *his* word, and healed all that were sick:

17 That it might be fulfilled which was spoken by E-sā′ias the prophet, saying, Himself took our infirmities, and bare *our* sicknesses.

18 ¶Now when Jesus saw great multitudes about him, he gave commandment to depart unto the other side.

19 And a certain scribe came, and said unto him, Master, I will follow thee whithersoever thou goest.

20 And Jesus saith unto him, The foxes have holes, and the birds of the air *have* nests; but the Son of man hath not where to lay *his* head.

21 And another of his disciples said unto him, Lord, suffer me first to go and bury my father.

statement does not necessarily mean that he was not personally present, but that the answer was given through messengers. For a similar use of the word **said** see 11:3. **Servant** in vs. 9 means "slave" (Gr *doulos*). The centurion was impressed with Jesus, who he likened to himself as one **under authority.** He recognized that in dealing with the realm of sickness and death Jesus had all the power of God behind Him.

10-13. The words **from the east and west,** are taken from Psalm 107 (with allusions also to Isa 49:12; 59:19; Mal 1:11). Here Christ is referring to the gathering in of the Gentiles through the preaching of the gospel, culminating in their final gathering at the time of His second coming. **Sit down,** i.e., recline (Gr *anaklinō*) to eat. It was customary in those days to recline at meals, resting on one's left elbow. There are also references to this ancient custom in the great banquet parables of the wedding feast of our Lord (see 22:1-14). **The children of the kingdom,** refers to those to whom the kingdom really belongs. The natural claim to that kingdom had been given to the Jews. Their reception of Christ as Messiah could potentially have brought in the kingdom, that had been promised by the Old Testament prophets. However, their eventual rejection of the Messiah caused the postponement of a literal kingdom on earth. **Outer darkness** refers to the condemnation of the second death. **There shall be . . . gnashing of teeth. There** is used emphatically to draw attention to the fact that such severe punishment is in fact a reality. Even though he was a Gentile, the servant was healed because of the faith of the centurion. The contrast to this incident drawn by Jesus emphasizes the foolishness of Israel's rejection of Him as Messiah.

c. The healing of Peter's mother-in-law. 8:14-17.

14-16. Laid (Gr *balō*, lit., to be laid out or sick in bed). In those days a bed was generally a mattress placed on the floor. **Ministered unto them** indicates that He attended to their needs with an immediate and complete cure. **He cast out the spirits** (i.e., evil spirits, meaning demons or devils). The gospel accounts are filled with incidents of demon activity and even resistance to the ministry of Christ. His power over their influence further vindicates His divine messiahship.

17. By Isaiah [Esaias] means that the following statement is taken from Isaiah 53:4. **Himself took our infirmities, and bare our sicknesses.** Kent (p. 943) notes that this indicates that these healings were only a partial fulfillment of what would be accomplished by Christ on the cross, when He would deal with the cause of physical sicknesses, sin itself.

d. The calming of the storm. 8:18-27.

18. He gave commandment to depart. In order to get away from the crowds and be alone with His disciples, Jesus gave the order for them to set sail.

19-27. The reference to **a certain scribe** is unusual since scribes were usually spoken in the plural. **Master, I will follow thee.** These words indicated that he was willing to follow Christ both spiritually and publicly. The word **Master** (Gr *didaskalos*) here means Teacher. Instead of making it easy to follow Him, Christ insisted that he count the cost of such commitment to discipleship. **The Son of man** is the title by which our Lord most frequently referred to Himself. The title originally came from Daniel 7:13 and had messianic significance. It must be understood that our Lord deliberately used this title of Himself in order to emphasize that He was, in fact, the Messiah. The

22 But Jesus said unto him, Follow me; and let the dead bury their dead.

23 ¶And when he was entered into a ship, his disciples followed him,

24 And, behold, there arose a great tempest in the sea, insomuch that the ship was covered with the waves: but he was asleep.

25 And his disciples came to *him*, and awoke him, saying, Lord, save us: we perish.

26 And he saith unto them, Why are ye fearful, O ye of little faith? Then he arose, and rebuked the winds and the sea; and there was a great calm.

27 But the men marvelled, saying, What manner of man is this, that even the winds and the sea obey him!

28 ¶And when he was come to the other side into the country of the Ger'ge-sēnes, there met him two possessed with devils, coming out of the tombs, exceeding fierce, so that no man might pass by that way.

29 And, behold, they cried out, saying, What have we to do with thee, Jesus, thou Son of God? art thou come hither to torment us before the time?

30 And there was a good way off from them an herd of many swine feeding.

31 So the devils besought him, saying, If thou cast us out, suffer us to go away into the herd of swine.

32 And he said unto them, Go. And when they were come out, they went into the herd of swine: and, behold, the whole herd of swine ran violently down a steep place into the sea, and perished in the waters.

33 And they that kept them fled, and went their ways into the city, and told every thing, and what was befallen to the possessed of the devils.

34 And, behold, the whole city came out to meet Jesus: and when they saw him, they besought *him* that he would depart out of their coasts.

CHAPTER 9

AND he entered into a ship, and passed over, and came into his own city.

2 And, behold, they brought to him a man sick of the palsy, lying on a bed: and Jesus seeing their faith said unto the sick of the palsy; Son, be of good cheer; thy sins be forgiven thee.

3 And, behold, certain of the scribes said within themselves, This *man* blasphemeth.

4 And Jesus knowing their thoughts

reference to **another of his disciples** must refer to a professed disciple who was unwilling to follow Him unconditionally. The request to **bury my father** probably meant he wanted to stay at home until his father had died. Jesus' strong reply, **let the dead bury their dead,** was not intended to be harsh, but rather to emphasize that the time to be about the heavenly Father's business was now. The **tempest** refers to a violent storm (Gr *seismos*). Jesus rebuked their **little faith** in light of the fact that He had commanded the trip across the Sea of Galilee. In one of His most awesome miracles, He simply **rebuked the winds and the sea,** resulting in an instantaneous miracle of total calm!

e. The healings of the Gadarene demoniacs. 8:28-34.

28. Gergesenes. The preferred reading is "Gadarenes." Gergesa was a town on the eastern slope of the Sea of Galilee and was included in the district of Gadara, one of the cities of the Decapolis. Both of these were included in the larger administrative district of Gerasa, whose center was the town of Gerasa in Gilead. **Two possessed with devils.** The description of two demoniacs is peculiar to Matthew; the parallel passages of the other synoptic writings mention only one. Instead of this being a contradiction, Mark and Luke emphasize the more predominant convert of the two, whereas Matthew gives the more complete account of both men with whom Jesus dealt.

29-34. What have we to do with thee . . . ? They reacted with resentment at Jesus' intrusion into their realm, meaning "What is there in common between us?" Their reference to Him as the **Son of God** indicates that the demons were fully aware of who Jesus was, and their question about being tormented **before the time** also indicates that they were aware of why He had come to earth. While the demons seemed to understand that they will ultimately come under the judgment of God, here their concern seems to be that of a premature suffering (Gr *basanizō*). The reference to a **herd of many swine** draws attention to the fact that they were being kept illegally by Jews who were living in this gentile region. Swine were considered unclean by the ordinances of the Mosaic law. **The whole herd . . . perished.** This is Jesus' only recorded miracle that was destructive in nature. The fact that Jesus granted the demons' request was because of His concern for the man. The spiritual principle in this incident is that those who are deliberately disobedient (as was the case of the pig-breeders) deprive themselves of divine protection and place themselves at the mercy of the forces of evil. Certainly, losing the herd of pigs, which was unlawful in the first place, was insignificant when compared to the man's gaining his spiritual health. **They besought him that he would depart.** Unfortunately this incident ends in tragedy as the people prefer their own business to the presence of the Saviour whose power they now feared.

f. The healing of the paralytic and lessons on righteousness. 9:1-17.

9:1-8. He entered into a ship, and passed over. Jesus never stayed where He was not wanted; thus, He returns to **His own city,** i.e., Capernaum (cf. 4:13). This is the incident where the paralyzed man was lowered through the roof by his four friends because of their inability to penetrate the density of the crowd (see also Mk 2:1-12; Lk 5:17-26). Jesus' statement, **Thy sins be forgiven thee,** shocked the crowds. In reality, Jesus attended to the man's spiritual needs before He dealt with his physical problem. **This man blasphemeth.** Because He claimed to forgive sins, Jesus was labeled a blasphemer by the religious leaders who were in attendance. Yet, Jesus instinctively knew the na-

said, Wherefore think ye evil in your hearts?

5 For whether is easier, to say, Thy sins be forgiven thee; or to say, Arise, and walk?

6 But that ye may know that the Son of man hath power on earth to forgive sins, (then saith he to the sick of the palsy,) Arise, take up thy bed, and go unto thine house.

7 And he arose, and departed to his house.

8 But when the multitudes saw it, they marvelled, and glorified God, which had given such power unto men.

9 ¶And as Jesus passed forth from thence, he saw a man, named Matthew, sitting at the receipt of custom: and he saith unto him, Follow me. And he arose, and followed him.

10 ¶And it came to pass, as Jesus sat at meat in the house, behold, many publicans and sinners came and sat down with him and his disciples.

11 And when the Pharisees saw it, they said unto his disciples, Why eateth your Master with publicans and sinners?

12 But when Jesus heard that, he said unto them, They that be whole need not a physician, but they that are sick.

13 But go ye and learn what that meaneth, I will have mercy, and not sacrifice: for I am not come to call the righteous, but sinners to repentance.

14 ¶Then came to him the disciples of John, saying, Why do we and the Pharisees fast oft, but thy disciples fast not?

15 And Jesus said unto them, Can the children of the bridechamber mourn, as long as the bridegroom is with them? but the days will come, when the bridegroom shall be taken from them, and then shall they fast.

16 No man putteth a piece of new cloth unto an old garment, for that which is put in to fill it up taketh from the garment, and the rent is made worse.

17 Neither do men put new wine into old bottles: else the bottles break, and the wine runneth out, and the bottles perish: but they put new wine into new bottles, and both are preserved.

18 ¶While he spake these things unto them, behold, there came a certain ruler, and worshipped him, saying, My daughter is even now dead: but come and lay thy hand upon her, and she shall live.

19 And Jesus arose, and followed him, and so did his disciples.

20 ¶And, behold, a woman, which was diseased with an issue of blood twelve years, came behind him, and touched the hem of his garment.

21 For she said within herself, If I

ture of their wicked attitude and asked them a pointed question, whether it was easier to forgive sins or heal sicknesses. He wanted them to understand that He not only had the power to deal with the symptom, but also the cause of the sickness, which was sin. The audience was stunned again when Jesus healed the man of his paralysis; and **they marveled**, (lit., they were afraid).

9-12. The receipt of custom refers to the toll booth in the street where tax collectors sat to receive various taxes. **In the house** means at home. We know from the other synoptic writers that this house was Matthew's (see Mk 2:15; Lk 5:29, where the expression is phrased as "in his house"). The usage of the phrase meaning at home in this passage indicates that Matthew was both the owner of the home and the author of this writing. This statement serves as strong internal evidence for Matthew's authorship of this gospel.

13-15. The righteous. The word is used here in an ironic sense, meaning self-righteous. Ultimately, as the Scripture tells us, "there is none righteous, no, not one" (Rom 3:10). **To repentance.** Some older manuscripts omit these words; but the principle taught by our Lord here is that fasting is not an end in itself, but is to be practiced only under appropriate circumstances. The Pharisees' fasting was part of the righteousness of men, which the Lord condemned. **The children of the bridechamber** refers to the wedding guests. **As long as the bridegroom is with them,** i.e., while the wedding festivities last, which might be for some days. **When the bridegroom shall be taken from them** is an allusion to His coming death and ascension.

16-17. The principle expressed here is that Jesus Christ has come to bring in a new dispensation altogether, which cannot be fitted into the forms of the old Jewish economy. The principle taught here by illustration is that the rule of the Law must be replaced by that of Grace, which will now have free reign in the hearts of all believers. **New cloth** means unbleached cloth. The RSV reads "unshrunk." **Bottles** (i.e., skins) were frequently used in the ancient East as liquid containers. The strength of fermentation of the new wine would be too much for the partly worn, old, or inelastic skins and would cause them to break.

g. The healing of the woman with the issue and the raising of the ruler's daughter. 9:18-26.

18-19. A certain ruler, i.e., a magistrate. The other Gospels indicate that his name was Jairus (cf. Mk 5:22-43; Lk 8:41-56). **Worshiped.** This suggests that he recognized Jesus' deity and authority. In the parallel passages we are told that she was dying when the father first came and that she died while he was en route. Matthew combines these two phrases into one, saying, **is even now dead.**

20-22. I shall be whole (lit., I shall be saved). It was customary for a rabbi to address a young girl as **daughter.** Jesus' exhortation to **be of good comfort** means to cheer up. The further statement, **thy faith hath made thee whole,** indicates that God's blessing on our behalf is usually in proportion to our willingness to trust Him.

may but touch his garment, I shall be whole.

22 But Jesus turned him about, and when he saw her, he said, Daughter, be of good comfort; thy faith hath made thee whole. And the woman was made whole from that hour.

23 And when Jesus came into the ruler's house, and saw the minstrels and the people making a noise,

24 He said unto them, Give place: for the maid is not dead, but sleepeth. And they laughed him to scorn.

25 But when the people were put forth, he went in, and took her by the hand, and the maid arose.

26 And the fame hereof went abroad into all that land.

27 ¶And when Jesus departed thence, two blind men followed him, crying, and saying, *Thou* son of David, have mercy on us.

28 And when he was come into the house, the blind men came to him: and Jesus saith unto them, Believe ye that I am able to do this? They said unto him, Yea, Lord.

29 Then touched he their eyes, saying, According to your faith be it unto you.

30 And their eyes were opened; and Jesus straitly charged them, saying, See *that* no man know *it.*

31 But they, when they were departed, spread abroad his fame in all that country.

32 ¶As they went out, behold, they brought to him a dumb man possessed with a devil.

33 And when the devil was cast out, the dumb spake: and the multitudes marvelled, saying, It was never so seen in Israel.

34 But the Pharisees said, He casteth out devils through the prince of the devils.

35 ¶And Jesus went about all the cities and villages, teaching in their synagogues, and preaching the gospel of the kingdom, and healing every sickness and every disease among the people.

36 But when he saw the multitudes, he was moved with compassion on them, because they fainted, and were scattered abroad, as sheep having no shepherd.

37 Then saith he unto his disciples, The harvest truly *is* plenteous, but the labourers *are* few;

38 Pray ye therefore the Lord of the harvest, that he will send forth labourers into his harvest.

CHAPTER 10

AND when he had called unto *him* his twelve disciples, he gave them power *against* unclean spirits, to cast them out, and to heal all manner of sickness and all manner of disease.

23-26. The scene described here is typical of a Middle Eastern home where someone lay dead. Mourners were actually hired to make noise. The **ministrels** were fluteplayers. Jesus' statement that **the maid is not dead, but sleepeth** meant that her death, though real, was ultimately going to be a temporary "sleep" in light of the fact that He would quickly raise her back to life again. On the same principle, the ". . . dead in Christ . . ." (I Thess 4:16) are said to be asleep only in view of the certainty of their resurrection. It should also be observed that those whom Jesus brought back to life during His earthly ministry later died a natural death, whereas those who are resurrected at the last day shall never die again.

h. The healing of the blind and dumb men. 9:27-38.

27-32. This incident is also peculiar to Matthew's gospel. (cf. Lk 11:14-26). Two blind men call out, **Thou son of David,** which was a messianic designation. The implication of their address seemed to indicate that they had put their faith in Jesus as the Messiah. **Into the house** probably refers to Matthew's house as in verse 10. **Believe ye . . . ?** Notice the emphasis on faith again as the catalyst to this miracle as well as the previous one. **See that no man know it** (see note on 8:4). Their disobedience does not need to be viewed as a serious violation, but rather, as an overt exuberance from the effect of the miracle itself.

33-38. The connection between spiritual evil and physical illness is clearly illustrated in this incident. The **prince of the devils** is Satan himself. **Fainted** means they were distressed. The observation that they were **as sheep having no shepherd** is taken from Numbers 27:17. The quote is taken mainly from the LXX, but with altered construction. Verses 37-38 constitute one of the great missionary passages of the New Testament. Jesus pictures the world as a great spiritual harvest in need of laborers to gather it into the fold. He urges the disciples to pray that the Lord of the harvest will send forth the workers to gather it. Kent (p. 945) observes: "As so often occurs those who prayed were themselves sent."

3. His missionaries: Sending of the Twelve. 10:1-12:50.

10:1. The **twelve disciples** had been formed as a group some time previously. Now after a time of instruction and training they were sent on their first mission. This would be no ordinary preaching mission since they were also given **power,** or "authority" over demons and disease. Their miracle-working ministry was to attest to the legitimate claim of Jesus to be the Messiah.

2 Now the names of the twelve apostles are these; The first, Simon, who is called Peter, and Andrew his brother; James *the son* of Zĕb′e-dee, and John his brother;

3 Philip, and Bartholomew; Thomas, and Matthew the publican; James *the son* of Äl-phæ′us, and Lĕb-bæ′us, whose surname was Thăd-dæ′us;

4 Simon the Canaanite, and Judas Iscariot, who also betrayed him.

5 These twelve Jesus sent forth, and commanded them, saying, Go not into the way of the Gentiles, and into *any* city of the Sa-măr′i-tanś enter ye not:

6 But go rather to the lost sheep of the house of Israel.

7 And as ye go, preach, saying, The kingdom of heaven is at hand.

8 Heal the sick, cleanse the lepers, raise the dead, cast out devils: freely ye have received, freely give.

9 Provide neither gold, nor silver, nor brass in your purses,

10 Nor scrip for *your* journey, neither two coats, neither shoes, nor yet staves: for the workman is worthy of his meat.

11 And into whatsoever city or town ye shall enter, enquire who in it is worthy; and there abide till ye go thence.

12 And when ye come into an house, salute it.

13 And if the house be worthy, let your peace come upon it: but if it be not worthy, let your peace return to you.

14 And whosoever shall not receive you, nor hear your words, when ye depart out of that house or city, shake off the dust of your feet.

15 Verily I say unto you, It shall be more tolerable for the land of Sodom

2-4. Apostles (Gr *apostolos*) is the technical term that later came to be applied to the twelve disciples. The literal meaning of the term is a "sent one." In this passage their twelve names are arranged in six pairs, which probably corresponded to the arrangement in which they were sent out on this mission. **Simon** is Peter, who heads all four lists of the Twelve (cf. Mk 3:16; Lk 6:14; Acts 1:13). Since he appears to be the most prominent disciple in the early stages of Jesus' ministry, as well as in the early period of the church, it may well be that he exercised a natural leadership over the others. It does not follow from this, however, that his leadership was necessarily passed on to successors. **Bartholomew** was generally considered to be identical with the Nathanael of John 1:45-51. **Lebbeus, whose surname was Thaddeus.** Better texts read simply "Thaddaeus." Luke gives his name as Judas (Lk 6:16). **Simon the Canaanite** actually means the Cananaean. Since he had been a member of the nationalist party known as the Zealots, who resisted Herod the Great by force, he is also at times referred to as Simon the Zealot. **Judas Iscariot** has been variously interpreted as meaning that he was a member of the tribe of Issachar, or an inhabitant of Kerioth, or the one who carried the purse (Aram *secariota*, purse), or the one who was strangled (Heb *iscara*, strangling). It has been generally recognized that he was the only disciple who was not a Galilean.

5-10. The way of the Gentiles. There were several Greek cities in Galilee which existed separately from the Jewish lifestyle. The apostles were instructed to avoid these towns and to confine themselves to the Jewish cities only. Toussaint (p. 138) observes the dispensational interpretation of this emphasis, noting the exclusiveness of their ministry to the house of Israel only. The word **Gentiles** is in the objective genitive, indicating that they were not to enter into a road even leading to the Gentiles, nor were they to enter into a city of the Samaritans. Thus, it is proper to conclude that the legitimate offer of the kingdom of Israel was still being made by the rightful King. Had Israel accepted her King, she would have had her long-awaited kingdom. Therefore, it is properly noted that the **kingdom of heaven is at hand.** The apostles were to **provide** (better "get") nothing in the way of money in their **purses** (lit., belts). The fold of the robe or the girdle served the same function as our pockets. **Scrip** refers to a wallet, actually a small bag for holding various articles. **Coats** were the outer robes or tunics that corresponded to the Roman toga. The Greek of **staves** is actually singular, meaning staff, agreeing with Luke 9:3. Some have suggested that the meaning of Mark 6:8 is that they were to have one walking stick between a pair. **The workman is worthy of his meat.** They were to rely upon the gifts and hospitality of those to whom they preached. This same concept is quoted in I Timothy 5:18, in the lucan form. The idea here is that the preacher of the gospel is to be supported by the free-will contributions of those to whom he ministers. Thus, the ministry of preaching is always viewed in the New Testament as a faith venture.

11-16. Inquire means to search out. Hospitality was a normal part of Oriental life and many offers of accommodation were probably received; however, the disciples were restricted to accepting hospitality only from those who received their message. **Shake off the dust of your feet** is a symbolic act of rejection and condemnation, the idea being that not even the dust of a wicked city was worthy of them. **Verily** (Gr *amēn*) is a transliteration from the Hebrew meaning "truly," which gives emphasis to the statement that follows. **Sodom and Gomorrha** are referred to as an example of the divine judgment against those cities that reject God (see 11:23-24 for an application of this statement to Capernaum as well). **Wise as serpents** (cf. Gen 3:1). In the ancient east the serpent was commonly regarded as

and Go-mŏr′rha in the day of judgment, than for that city.

16 ¶Behold, I send you forth as sheep in the midst of wolves: be ye therefore wise as serpents, and harmless as doves.

17 But beware of men: for they will deliver you up to the councils, and they will scourge you in their synagogues;

18 And ye shall be brought before governors and kings for my sake, for a testimony against them and the Gentiles.

19 But when they deliver you up, take no thought how or what ye shall speak: for it shall be given you in that same hour what ye shall speak.

20 For it is not ye that speak, but the Spirit of your Father which speaketh in you.

21 And the brother shall deliver up the brother to death, and the father the child: and the children shall rise up against *their* parents, and cause them to be put to death.

22 And ye shall be hated of all *men* for my name's sake: but he that endureth to the end shall be saved.

23 But when they persecute you in this city, flee ye into another: for verily I say unto you, Ye shall not have gone over the cities of Israel, till the Son of man be come.

24 The disciple is not above *his* master, nor the servant above his lord.

25 It is enough for the disciple that he be as his master, and the servant as his lord. If they have called the master of the house Bē-ĕl′ze-bŭb, how much more *shall they call* them of his household?

26 Fear them not therefore: for there is nothing covered, that shall not be revealed; and hid, that shall not be known.

27 What I tell you in darkness, *that* speak ye in light: and what ye hear in the ear, *that* preach ye upon the housetops.

28 And fear not them which kill the body, but are not able to kill the soul: but rather fear him which is able to destroy both soul and body in hell.

29 Are not two sparrows sold for a farthing? and one of them shall not fall on the ground without your Father.

30 But the very hairs of your head are all numbered.

31 Fear ye not therefore, ye are of more value than many sparrows.

32 Whosoever therefore shall confess me before men, him will I confess also before my Father which is in heaven.

33 But whosoever shall deny me before men, him will I also deny before my Father which is in heaven.

34 Think not that I am come to send peace on earth: I came not to send peace, but a sword.

35 For I am come to set a man at variance against his father, and the

---

the wisest of beasts. A cautious wisdom was necessary in order to deal with the fierce opposition that the disciples would face.

17-22. Take no thought means do not be anxious (see also Mk 13:9-13; Lk 12:11-12; 21:12-19). **It shall be given you** promises that the inner prompting of the Holy Spirit would tell them what to say in each situation they would face. **Children shall rise up against their parents** is a summary statement of Micah 7:6 (cf. Mk 13:12). **For my name's sake** (i.e., because you belong to Me). They would endure great persecution because of their identification with Jesus Christ. **But he that endureth to the end shall be saved** is a promise of perseverance, not a teaching that salvation may be lost. Rather, it indicates that those who are truly saved will indeed endure to the end.

23-24. Till the Son of man be come. Premillennialists view this passage as referring to the time of the Great Tribulation and the Second Advent, which were in the distant future. Thus, the reference to the coming of the **Son of man** in this passage is to be viewed as eschatological. To imply that at this point Jesus merely viewed Himself as a forerunner to the yet-coming Messiah is ludicrous in light of all the statements made earlier in the Gospel of Matthew. Therefore, He must have His own Second Coming in view.

25-31. Beelzebub refers to Satan himself, the ultimate evil demon. The disciples are told to **Fear . . . not.** Their enemies can only take their physical life, which cannot prevent their blessed resurrection to life everlasting. To God alone belongs the power of the second death. In other words, Jesus reminded them that it was more important to fear Him who had authority over the **soul** as well as over the **body** and who can bring both to eternal condemnation in **hell** (*Gehenna*). It should be noted that God is the One who has authority to cast men into hell, and not Satan, who will himself be ultimately cast into everlasting fire. Conversely, Jesus reminded His disciples of the Father's loving care, even for the **sparrows** (common birds in Palestine). **A farthing** (Gr *assarion*) was a copper coin worth about one-sixteenth of a denarius. **Without your Father,** i.e., without His being concerned. Here we are reminded of God's gracious providential care over His saints.

32-37. Confess me, i.e., acknowledge that you belong to Me. In reality, secret discipleship is a practical impossibility. Jesus constantly called for an open confession of Himself by His followers. We must be willing to acknowledge Jesus as Lord and Saviour, with all that those terms imply. That our confession is to be **before men** clearly indicates that a public confession of true Christian faith is a virtual necessity. The warning, **Whosoever shall deny me,** is in the aorist tense, referring not to one moment of denial (such as Peter's), but to an entire lifelong resistance to Christ which shall never cease. Therefore, it is not a single act of denial which makes one unworthy of being a

daughter against her mother, and the daughter in law against her mother in law.

36 And a man's foes *shall be* they of his own household.

37 He that loveth father or mother more than me is not worthy of me: and he that loveth son or daughter more than me is not worthy of me.

38 And he that taketh not his cross, and followeth after me, is not worthy of me.

39 He that findeth his life shall lose it: and he that loseth his life for my sake shall find it.

40 He that receiveth you receiveth me, and he that receiveth me receiveth him that sent me.

41 He that receiveth a prophet in the name of a prophet shall receive a prophet's reward; and he that receiveth a righteous man in the name of a righteous man shall receive a righteous man's reward.

42 And whosoever shall give to drink unto one of these little ones a cup of cold *water* only in the name of a disciple, verily I say unto you, he shall in no wise lose his reward.

CHAPTER 11

AND it came to pass, when Jesus had made an end of commanding his twelve disciples, he departed thence to teach and to preach in their cities.

2 ¶Now when John had heard in the prison the works of Christ, he sent two of his disciples,

3 And said unto him, Art thou he that should come, or do we look for another?

4 Jesus answered and said unto them, Go and shew John again those things which ye do hear and see:

5 The blind receive their sight, and the lame walk, the lepers are cleansed, and the deaf hear, the dead are raised up, and the poor have the gospel preached to them.

6 And blessed is *he*, whosoever shall not be offended in me.

7 ¶And as they departed, Jesus began to say unto the multitudes concerning John, What went ye out into the wilderness to see? A reed shaken with the wind?

8 But what went ye out for to see? A man clothed in soft raiment? behold, they that wear soft *clothing* are in kings' houses.

9 But what went ye out for to see? A prophet? yea, I say unto you, and more than a prophet.

10 For this is *he*, of whom it is writ-

disciple, but a refusal to confess Christ at all that eliminates one from being a true follower of Jesus Christ.

38-40. Taketh not his cross. This is the first mention of the Cross in the New Testament (for the theological significance see L. Morris, *The Cross in the New Testament* and *The Apostolic Preaching of the Cross*). It was the custom for the condemned man to carry his cross on the way to his own execution. There is plenty of evidence that our Lord anticipated the mode of His own death. These words come as the climax of His warning to the apostles that their mission would involve arrest and persecution, potentially culminating in condemnation to death. These important words also have a deep spiritual significance for every believer and constitute the basis of Paul's teaching about the identification of the believer with the cross of Christ (see Gal 2:20). **Findeth his life** means to gain something out of life for oneself. Here the word means the self-life, or natural life, as opposed to the spiritual life. **Shall find it** refers to a life emptied of self and poured out in the service of Christ in this world, and which will find full enjoyment and blessing in the world to come.

41-42. In the name of a prophet (i.e., as a prophet). The meaning of this statement is that those who are not prophets themselves may share in the labor and reward of the prophets by willingly supporting their ministry. **One of these little ones** is a reference to the fact that even the smallest service done to the most insignificant of Christ's servants shall be rewarded by the Lord Himself.

a. Excursus: John the Baptist and Christ. 11:1-30.

11:1-7. Verses 2-19 are a parallel with Luke 7:18-35. This imprisonment has already been mentioned in Matthew 4:12, but the circumstances leading up to it are not described in detail until 14:3-12, where the manner of John's death is also recounted. **The works of Christ** refers to His miracles. **He that should come** refers to the predicted Messiah of Old Testament prophecy whose coming had already been proclaimed by John. **The blind receive their sight** is an allusion to Isaiah 35:5; 61:1, where it is stated that this will be one of the works performed by the Messiah. John would certainly have understood the allusion. **The poor have the gospel preached to them** is another allusion to Isaiah 61:1. Hence, Jesus was clearly vindicating His messiahship to John who may have begun to question why Jesus had left him in prison.

8-11. But what went ye out for to see? A prophet? . . . more, i.e., much more (Gr *perissos*). The quotation in verse 10 is from Malachi 3:1. John was recognized as the foreordained forerunner of the Saviour and, technically, the last of the Old Testament prophets. Thus, he belonged to the Old Testament dispensation. This certainly emphasizes the clear distinction between the Old Testament era (i.e., before the resurrection)

ten, Behold, I send my messenger before thy face, which shall prepare thy way before thee.

11 Verily I say unto you, Among them that are born of women there hath not risen a greater than John the Baptist: notwithstanding he that is least in the kingdom of heaven is greater than he.

12 And from the days of John the Baptist until now the kingdom of heaven suffereth violence, and the violent take it by force.

13 For all the prophets and the law prophesied until John.

14 And if ye will receive it, this is E-lī′as, which was for to come.

15 He that hath ears to hear, let him hear.

16 But whereunto shall I liken this generation? It is like unto children sitting in the markets, and calling unto their fellows,

17 And saying, We have piped unto you, and ye have not danced; we have mourned unto you, and ye have not lamented.

18 For John came neither eating nor drinking, and they say, He hath a devil.

19 The Son of man came eating and drinking, and they say, Behold a man gluttonous, and a winebibber, a friend of publicans and sinners. But wisdom is justified of her children.

20 ¶Then began he to upbraid the cities wherein most of his mighty works were done, because they repented not:

21 Woe unto thee, Chō-rā′zĭn! woe unto thee, Bĕth-sā′i-da! for if the mighty works, which were done in you, had been done in Tyre and Sī′don, they would have repented long ago in sackcloth and ashes.

22 But I say unto you, It shall be more tolerable for Tyre and Sī′don at the day of judgment, than for you.

23 And thou, Ca-per′na-um, which art exalted unto heaven, shalt be brought down to hell: for if the mighty works, which have been done in thee, had been done in Sodom, it would have remained until this day.

24 But I say unto you, That it shall be more tolerable for the land of Sodom, in the day of judgment, than for thee.

25 ¶At that time Jesus answered and said, I thank thee, O Father, Lord of heaven and earth, because thou hast hid these things from the wise and prudent, and hast revealed them unto babes.

26 Even so, Father: for so it seemed good in thy sight.

27 All things are delivered unto me of my Father: and no man knoweth the

and the New Testament era (after the resurrection). The weakest believer who has the knowledge of the glory of God in the face of the risen Christ is, therefore, in a more privileged position than the greatest of the Old Testament prophets. The expression, **them that are born of women** means mortal men, the idea being that the greatest of all in this life cannot be compared with the glory of the life to come.

12-15. The kingdom of heaven suffereth violence (Gr *biazomai*). The meaning of this saying, and the connection of verses 12-14 with preceding and following contexts, indicates that John opened the kingdom of heaven to sinners and thus became the culminating point of Old Testament witness. Jesus' statement that **this is Elijah** [Elias] indicates that He saw the ministry of John as the fulfillment of the prophecy of the coming of Elijah in Malachi 4:5-6. This is a valuable hint that we are not to over-literalize Old Testament prophecy. The meaning of Malachi 4:6 seems to be that John was to form a link between the Old and New Testaments. Most commentators have taken **suffereth** to be in the passive voice, indicating that the church has been suffering from the days of John until that of the author of this gospel (cf. also the parallel passage in Lk 16:16 where the same verb is used).

16-19. This generation refused to exercise its capacity to hear, but made excuses for rejecting both John and Jesus. Some have likened the illustration of Christ to that of children playing a game of "weddings" and then a game of "funerals." The idea is that the children cannot decide which game to play, therefore, they decide to play nothing at all. The reference to the rejection of John's ascetic ministry brought the charge that he was demon-possessed. However, Jesus' open contact with sinners brought the equally untrue claim that He was **gluttonous, and a winebibber. But wisdom is justified of her children** is probably the correct reading, even though some texts read "works" for **children.** The meaning is the same in either case. The differing life-styles of John and Jesus were justified in either case by their results.

20-24. The denunciation of Galilean cities which follows is recorded also by Luke, but in a different context (see Lk 10:13-16). **Chorazin** was about an hour's journey on foot north of **Capernaum. Bethsaida** was on the west side of the Sea of Galilee, about three miles southeast of Chorazin. **Tyre and Sidon** were both on the Mediterranean coast beyond the northern boundary of Palestine. **Shalt be brought down to hell.** The statement here is an allusion to Isaiah 14:13, 15, where it is spoken of the king of Babylon and probably refers to Satan himself.

25-30. Answered. The words that follow are the response of Jesus to the circumstances just described. **Thank** (Gr *exomologeō*) is literally to acknowledge. **Babes** refers to spiritual babes who receive God's revelation in simple faith. The **yoke** refers to the teaching of Christ, which is represented as being light in comparison with the burdensome teaching of the Pharisees (see 23:4). **Ye shall find rest unto your souls.** These words are taken from Jeremiah 6:16. The LXX has "ye shall find purification unto your souls" and is corrected by Matthew to the

Son, but the Father; neither knoweth any man the Father, save the Son, and *he* to whomsoever the Son will reveal *him*.

28 ¶Come unto me, all ye that labour and are heavy laden, and I will give you rest.

29 Take my yoke upon you, and learn of me; for I am meek and lowly in heart: and ye shall find rest unto your souls.

30 For my yoke *is* easy, and my burden is light.

CHAPTER 12

AT that time Jesus went on the sabbath day through the corn; and his disciples were an hungred, and began to pluck the ears of corn, and to eat.

2 But when the Pharisees saw *it*, they said unto him, Behold, thy disciples do that which is not lawful to do upon the sabbath day.

3 But he said unto them, Have ye not read what David did, when he was an hungred, and they that were with him;

4 How he entered into the house of God, and did eat the shewbread, which was not lawful for him to eat, neither for them which were with him, but only for the priests?

5 Or have ye not read in the law, how that on the sabbath days the priests in the temple profane the sabbath, and are blameless?

6 But I say unto you, That in this place is *one* greater than the temple.

7 But if ye had known what *this* meaneth, I will have mercy, and not sacrifice, ye would not have condemned the guiltless.

8 For the Son of man is Lord even of the sabbath day.

9 ¶And when he was departed thence, he went into their synagogue:

10 And, behold, there was a man which had *his* hand withered. And they asked him, saying, Is it lawful to heal on the sabbath days? that they might accuse him.

11 And he said unto them, What man shall there be among you, that shall have one sheep, and if it fall into a pit on the sabbath day, will he not lay hold on it, and lift *it* out?

12 How much then is a man better than a sheep? Wherefore it is lawful to do well on the sabbath days.

13 Then saith he to the man, Stretch forth thine hand. And he stretched *it* forth; and it was restored whole, like as the other.

14 ¶Then the Pharisees went out, and held a council against him, how they might destroy him.

15 But when Jesus knew *it*, he withdrew himself from thence: and great multitudes followed him, and he healed them all;

16 And charged them that they should not make him known:

17 That it might be fulfilled which was spoken by E-sā′ias the prophet, saying,

18 Behold my servant, whom I have chosen; my beloved, in whom my soul is well pleased: I will put my spirit upon him, and he shall shew judgment to the Gentiles.

original meaning in the Hebrew. **Easy** means good or kind. The entire passage is peculiar to Matthew's gospel.

b. Excursus: A dispute with the Pharisees. 12:1-50.

12:1-9. The sabbath day, i.e., the seventh day of the week, corresponding to our Saturday (cf. Mk 2:23-3:6; Lk 6:1-11). However, in New Testament times it began at sunset on Friday and lasted until the following sunset. The Pharisees had burdened the Sabbath with a multitude of detailed observances which were not laid down in the Mosaic law. Correspondingly, in this incident they had objected to the manner in which Jesus' disciples had plucked grain on the Sabbath, violating the command against reaping on that sacred day (Ex 20:10). In responding to their legalistic traditions, Jesus always referred to Scripture. **Have ye not read . . . ?** The passage referred to is I Samuel 21:1-6. The point that our Lord makes is that in the case of necessity the ceremonial law might be overruled. He uses the illustration of David eating the **showbread.** These loaves were placed on the table in the holy place in the Tabernacle each Sabbath. They were to be eaten only by the priest and his family (cf. Lev 24:5-9; Num 28:9). The priests prepared the sacrifices on the Sabbath in spite of the general prohibition of work. If the necessities of temple worship permitted the priests to **profane the sabbath,** there was all the more reason why the service of Christ would allow a similar liberty. **I will have mercy, and not sacrifice.** The application of this principle is that ethics are more important than ritual. The passage clearly asserts that Jesus had the right to interpret the Mosaic ordinances in light of their spiritual intention, rather than their literal application.

10-27. Withered (i.e., paralyzed). Luke 6 shows that this incident occurred on a different Sabbath. However, the objection of the Pharisees on this occasion was ultimately the same. They were in opposition to Jesus' healing on the Sabbath. The reference to **their synagogue** indicates that in this particular synagogue the Pharisees were predominant. He asked them the searching question, **Is it lawful to heal on the sabbath days?** The Old Testament made no such prohibition, but some rabbis considered healing as work. Jesus' response was that what one would be willing to do for an unfortunate animal, in sparing its life on the Sabbath, ought to be extended as a gesture of mercy to people in physical peril as well. The miracle only enraged the Pharisees further who immediately **held a council** (lit., took counsel). The Old Testament reference to **my servant** is here applied to the person of the Messiah Himself. The statement that **he shall show judgment to the Gentiles** is a prophecy that the righteousness of God would be made known to the Gentiles through the ministry of the Messiah. **Till he send forth judgment unto victory** means until the final triumph of righteousness which shall be brought about by Christ Himself. The question **Is not this the son of David?** is definitely a messianic title (see 9:27). **Beelzebub** refers to Satan. **Jesus knew** implies that He fully understood the true meaning and intention of their thoughts. His reference to **your children** meant the disciples of the Pharisees.

19 He shall not strive, nor cry; neither shall any man hear his voice in the streets.

20 A bruised reed shall he not break, and smoking flax shall he not quench, till he send forth judgment unto victory.

21 And in his name shall the Gentiles trust.

22 ¶Then was brought unto him one possessed with a devil, blind, and dumb: and he healed him, insomuch that the blind and dumb both spake and saw.

23 And all the people were amazed, and said, Is not this the son of David?

24 But when the Pharisees heard it, they said, This fellow doth not cast out devils, but by Bē-ĕl´ze-bŭb the prince of the devils.

25 And Jesus knew their thoughts, and said unto them, Every kingdom divided against itself is brought to desolation; and every city or house divided against itself shall not stand:

26 And if Satan cast out Satan, he is divided against himself; how shall then his kingdom stand?

27 And if I by Bē-ĕl´ze-bŭb cast out devils, by whom do your children cast them out? therefore they shall be your judges.

28 But if I cast out devils by the Spirit of God, then the kingdom of God is come unto you.

29 Or else how can one enter into a strong man's house, and spoil his goods, except he first bind the strong man? and then he will spoil his house.

30 He that is not with me is against me; and he that gathereth not with me scattereth abroad.

31 Wherefore I say unto you, All manner of sin and blasphemy shall be forgiven unto men: but the blasphemy against the Holy Ghost shall not be forgiven unto men.

32 And whosoever speaketh a word against the Son of man, it shall be forgiven him: but whosoever speaketh against the Holy Ghost, it shall not be forgiven him, neither in this world, neither in the world to come.

33 Either make the tree good, and his fruit good; or else make the tree corrupt, and his fruit corrupt: for the tree is known by his fruit.

34 O generation of vipers, how can ye, being evil, speak good things? for out of the abundance of the heart the mouth speaketh.

28-30. The kingdom of God. Matthew's usual expression is the **kingdom of heaven** (e.g., 3:2). While some have attempted to distinguish between the meaning of the two, it is more likely that they mean the same thing. **Is come unto you** (lit., has come upon you unawares). The Lord's power over demons was evidence enough that He was the Messiah. Hence, **spoil his goods . . . house** refers to Satan as being defeated or ruined by the capture of souls from him for Christ by the gospel. It must be noticed that the **kingdom of God** was, in a sense, already present in the person of the King—Christ Himself! Jesus' admonition **He that is not with me is against me** clearly states that there is no middle course in relation to the authority of Christ as King and Lord. In Mark 9:40 we have the converse truth stated. The present passage applies to any person or position that is definitely anti-Christ. While the passage in Mark indicates that there may be minor differences (e.g., denominational distinctives) among genuine believers, Matthew's passage indicates that there can be no departure from the doctrine of Christ. Those who fail to affirm Him as the divine Son of God are ultimately against Him, no matter what kind of "appreciation" they claim to have for Him.

31-38. The blasphemy against the Holy Ghost. This sin is that of deliberate rejection of Christ and His salvation. It is the ultimate sin that by its very nature puts a man beyond the opportunity of salvation. The reason for this is that it is the Holy Spirit who brings the offer of salvation to the heart of man. To reject Him is to act "presumptuously" and thus to "blaspheme" God. Those who reject His offer of salvation are in reality blaspheming the very nature of God Himself and the genuineness of His grace. **The tree is known by his fruit.** The point of this verse seems to be that the good works done by Christ were evidence of His personal goodness and should have prevented any such blasphemous saying as that spoken by the Pharisees. However, this illustration is conversely applied to the Pharisees who are known by their wickedness as well. **By thy words** does not refer to justification or condemnation on the basis of what one says, but to the outward evidence of the inward attitude of the heart. While the Pharisees asked for evidence of Christ's

35 A good man out of the good treasure of the heart bringeth forth good things: and an evil man out of the evil treasure bringeth forth evil things.

36 But I say unto you, That every idle word that men shall speak, they shall give account thereof in the day of judgment.

37 For by thy words thou shalt be justified, and by thy words thou shalt be condemned.

38 ¶Then certain of the scribes and of the Pharisees answered, saying, Master, we would see a sign from thee.

39 But he answered and said unto them, An evil and adulterous generation seeketh after a sign; and there shall no sign be given to it, but the sign of the prophet Jonas:

40 For as Jonas was three days and three nights in the whale's belly; so shall the Son of man be three days and three nights in the heart of the earth.

41 The men of Nin'e-veh shall rise in judgment with this generation, and shall condemn it: because they repented at the preaching of Jonas; and, behold, a greater than Jonas is here.

42 The queen of the south shall rise up in the judgment with this generation, and shall condemn it: for she came from the uttermost parts of the earth to hear the wisdom of Solomon; and, behold, a greater than Solomon is here.

43 When the unclean spirit is gone out of a man, he walketh through dry places, seeking rest, and findeth none.

44 Then he saith, I will return into my house from whence I came out; and when he is come, he findeth it empty, swept, and garnished.

45 Then goeth he, and taketh with himself seven other spirits more wicked than himself, and they enter in and dwell there: and the last state of that man is worse than the first. Even so shall it be also unto this wicked generation.

46 ¶While he yet talked to the people, behold, his mother and his brethren stood without, desiring to speak with him.

47 Then one said unto him, Behold, thy mother and thy brethren stand without, desiring to speak with thee.

48 But he answered and said unto him that told him, Who is my mother? and who are my brethren?

49 And he stretched forth his hand toward his disciples, and said, Behold my mother and my brethren!

50 For whosoever shall do the will of my Father which is in heaven, the same is my brother, and sister, and mother.

claim, they overlooked the clear evidence that was to be seen in His miracles.

39-42. The word **adulterous** means unfaithful to God. It was a metaphor frequently used in the Old Testament for spiritual "adultery." **The prophet Jonah** [Jonas]. Here Jesus clearly refers to one of the most controversial stories in the Old Testament. Jesus uses Jonah's interment in the fish for **three days and three nights** as an illustration of the literal three days and three nights that He would spend in the grave Himself. The actual period was either, minimally, from Friday evening to Sunday morning (covering parts of three days idiomatically) or, maximally, from Wednesday evening to Sunday morning (covering seventy-two literal hours; see W. G. Scroggie, *Guide to the Gospels*, pp. 569-577). The reference to the **whale's belly** in verse 40 is unfortunate in the AV. The Greek word *ketos* means a great sea monster. The Old Testament references are to a "great fish" (e.g., Jon 1:17). It should be noted that our Lord placed this entire account on the same level of historical reality as that with which He Himself was dealing. To imply that Jesus was the "victim of the ignorance of His day" is ludicrous. He certainly did not show such victimization in dealing with other issues of life. **The queen of the south** refers to the Queen of Sheba (see I Kgs 10). Here our Lord contrasts her eagerness to hear the wisdom of a man (Solomon) with the refusal of His listeners to hear one **greater than Solomon.** Again, this statement must be taken in light of the deity of Christ, rather than as a presumptuous boast.

43-45. Jesus gives a striking parable of the precarious spiritual condition of the nation. The parable is that of a house well **swept** but unoccupied. The demon having been driven out, but finding no place to rest, returns with seven other spirits, resulting in an even greater degeneration. In using this illustration Jesus clearly indicated that though the Jews had been cleansed from their idolatry by the severity of the Babylonian exile, their unbelief and hardness of heart was in danger of producing an even worse moral condition than when they were idolaters. The moral reformation that had taken place after the captivity should have prepared Israel for the ministries of John and Jesus. Unfortunately, in most cases it fell short in that Israel's spiritual house was **empty.** Only by inviting Christ to occupy the position of Honored Guest and Head of the Home could Israel know the full blessing of God.

46-50. The chapter closes with a reference to **his mother and his brethren.** These brothers are presumably the children of Joseph and Mary born after the virgin birth of Jesus. While some have attempted to view them as cousins, this certainly is not implied in the gospel records. Kent (p. 951) believes that Jesus' preaching at Nazareth had already forced the family to move to Capernaum. By asking, **Who is my mother?** Jesus called attention away from earthly relationships to more important spiritual relationships. A believer is even closer to Christ than to a physical relative. This saying was not intended to be one of disrespect to Mary or to His brothers, for they too would come to share that spiritual relationship. It should also be noted that there is no suggestion here at all, however, that Jesus' mother had any special access to His presence or any particular influence over Him. By using this startling question, Jesus prepares the crowd to receive the precious truth that **whosoever shall do the will of my Father** was, in fact, His mother, His brother, His sister. Hendriksen (p. 542) suggests that it was to His inner circle of disciples that He gave this loving and honored designation. The beauty of this passage can be seen in the fact that while they had left all and followed Him, they were still often "of little faith" (8:26). Yet He was not ashamed to call them brothers (see Heb 2:11). Those who trust Him as their personal Saviour become adopted members of the family of God (see Rom 8:17, 29).

4. His mystery: Secret form of the kingdom. 13:1-58.

13:1-2. On one of the busiest days of Jesus' earthly ministry He gave an extended series of parables (seven in Matthew and four in Mark, including one not given in Matthew). In the overwhelming press of the crowd at a **house**, Jesus could not be reached by people, so He went **into a ship** from which **He** taught the multitude. This is the turning point in Matthew's gospel. Already sensing His impending rejection, Jesus now expresses the "mystery" form of the kingdom which will be the church. His early ministry involved a proclamation of the spiritual principles of the kingdom. The Jews, seeking a political and nationalistic kingdom, were now rejecting Jesus' concept of a kingdom of spiritual character. To bring in a political kingdom before men were born again would be a travesty. Therefore, an interval is now announced between the Messiah's original appearance and His final return. That interval is the Church Age, during which believers are citizens of the kingdom which is within them (Lk 17:21). The distinction between the church and the kingdom is not that one is more spiritual than the other. The church is the present (realized) form of the kingdom of God. The millennial kingdom, which is to come in the future (Rev 20:4) is another transitional form of the kingdom which will ultimately be presented to the Father to be the eternal kingdom of God (Rev 21).

CHAPTER 13

THE same day went Jesus out of the house, and sat by the sea side.

2 And great multitudes were gathered together unto him, so that he went into a ship, and sat; and the whole multitude stood on the shore.

3. Walvoord (p. 96) notes that this section introduces a new subject, a new approach and a new method of teaching by parables. **He spake . . . in parables**, a common method of teaching in the Near East, used to convey spiritual truth through a series of earthly comparisons. Jesus was an expert at this form of teaching. It should be noted, however, that parables did not always convert unbelievers who were often confused about their meaning. Tasker (p. 134) comments: "Jesus deliberately adopted the parabolic method of teaching at a particular stage in His ministry for the purpose of withholding further truth about Himself and the kingdom of heaven from the crowds, who had proved themselves to be deaf to His claims . . . from now onwards, when addressing the unbelieving multitude, He speaks only in parables (thirty-four in number) which He interprets to His disciples in private."

3 And he spake many things unto them in parables, saying, Behold, a sower went forth to sow;

a. The Parable of the Sower. 13:4-23.

4-10. The first parable is set in an agricultural context. **A sower went forth** refers to the ancient seed sower, planting a crop. The Greek definite article here is generic. Jesus later interpreted this parable Himself. The seed depicts the Word of God (vs. 19) and thus the sower is the gospel evangelist. The **way side** is the path trampled through the field. It was hard-packed and the seed found no root, thus the **birds** (demons? vs. 19, **wicked one**(s)) snatched it away. Here there was no response at all to the gospel. The second category is called **stony places** or the rock ledge beneath a thin, shallow layer of soil. This thin crust would warm quickly causing the seed to sprout instantly but without adequate rootage or moisture. Thus, the **sun . . . scorched** the crop and it **withered away**. The third

4 And when he sowed, some *seeds* fell by the way side, and the fowls came and devoured them up:

5 Some fell upon stony places, where they had not much earth: and forthwith they sprung up, because they had no deepness of earth:

6 And when the sun was up, they were scorched; and because they had no root, they withered away.

7 And some fell among thorns; and the thorns sprung up, and choked them:

8 But other fell into good ground, and

brought forth fruit, some an hundredfold, some sixtyfold, some thirtyfold.

9 ¶Who hath ears to hear, let him hear.

10 ¶And the disciples came, and said unto him, Why speakest thou unto them in parables?

11 He answered and said unto them, Because it is given unto you to know the mysteries of the kingdom of heaven, but to them it is not given.

12 For whosoever hath, to him shall be given, and he shall have more abundance: but whosoever hath not, from him shall be taken away even that he hath.

13 Therefore speak I to them in parables: because they seeing see not; and hearing they hear not, neither do they understand.

14 And in them is fulfilled the prophecy of E-sā'ias, which saith, By hearing ye shall hear, and shall not understand; and seeing ye shall see, and shall not perceive:

15 For this people's heart is waxed gross, and *their* ears are dull of hearing, and their eyes they have closed; lest at any time they should see with *their* eyes, and hear with *their* ears, and should understand with *their* heart, and should be converted, and I should heal them.

16 But blessed *are* your eyes, for they see: and your ears, for they hear.

17 For verily I say unto you, That many prophets and righteous *men* have desired to see *those things* which ye see, and have not seen *them*; and to hear *those things* which ye hear, and have not heard *them*.

18 ¶Hear ye therefore the parable of the sower.

19 When any one heareth the word of the kingdom, and understandeth *it* not, then cometh the wicked *one*, and catcheth away that which was sown in his heart. This is he which received seed by the way side.

20 But he that received the seed into stony places, the same is he that heareth the word, and anon with joy receiveth it;

21 Yet hath he not root in himself, but dureth for a while: for when tribulation or persecution ariseth because of the word, by and by he is offended.

22 He also that received seed among

group of seeds fell **among thorns** which had not been plowed. The thorns (wild growth) choked out the crop. The **good ground** represents well-plowed and prepared soil capable of producing a large crop. The statement, **Who hath ears to hear,** goes beyond physical hearing and implies an inner spiritual reception of truth. This prompted the disciples' question as to why He had spoken to them in **parables.** Whereas before, He had used parables to illustrate His messages, now they formed the basis of the message.

11-13. The Saviour's reply was that only the disciples were to know the **mysteries of the kingdom of heaven.** The mystery implies a secret into which one must be initiated in order to understand it. The mystery revealed would be the new form of the kingdom during the interval between the first and second advents. Kent (p. 45) notes, "These parables describe the strange form of the kingdom while the King is absent, during which time the gospel is preached and a spiritual nucleus is developed for the establishment of the messianic reign." This special revelation is given only to the apostles who will become the foundation of that church. Those to whom this revealed secret is **not given** are those who have already rejected Christ. Thus, to the unbeliever, the parable form leaves him without understanding. Their rejection of Him leads to His rejection of them.

14-17. The quotation from the **prophecy of Isaiah** [Esaias], (i.e., Isa 6:9-10) follows the LXX, emphasizing the obstinate unbelief of the people. As in Isaiah's day, the Jews had hardened themselves against God's truth and He had further hardened them in their unbelief. Their hearts had **waxed gross** (fat) and they would not, nor should not **be converted,** i.e., changed or saved. The faith of the disciples was evidence of their conversion and caused them to see and hear the truth which the **prophets** (vs. 17) had desired to know (cf. I Pet 1:10-12).

18-19. Jesus interpreted this parable Himself in verses 18-23. **The sower** is Christ working through the agency of His disciples to spread the gospel throughout the world. No longer is the message to be restricted to the house of Israel, but is to be declared to all men. The **word of the kingdom** is the gospel proclamation of Jesus the King and is not to be limited to an Old Testament Jewish-only message. Remember, these parables make it clear that the church is the present-day form of the kingdom. The key to interpreting the reception of the seed into the ground is the term **understandeth,** meaning to comprehend by believing faith (cf. vs. 23). The unsaved listener "understands" not and does not receive the seed, whereas the believer is one who both hears and "understands" the message and his life produces fruit to prove it. The reference to the **heart** in relation to the ground indicated that the quality of the soil represents man's heart response to the message.

20-23. The **stony places** are those shallow-hearted individuals who **anon,** "at once," receive (outwardly) the message with **joy,** i.e., enthusiasm or excitement. This emotional convert is not truly born again at all, for he **hath not root** and withers away. The one who is among the **thorns** (cares of this world) is the carnal, worldly convert, who never really breaks with his past. Worldliness and materialism **choke the word** in his life and he is finally **unfruitful** (unsaved). The one who received seed in the thorns is he that heareth the word; and the care of this world, and the deceitfulness of riches, choke the word, and he becometh unfruitful.

23 But he that received seed into the good ground is he that heareth the word, and understandeth *it;* which also beareth fruit, and bringeth forth, some an hundredfold, some sixty, some thirty.

the **good ground** is the one who both heard the word and understood it, **which also beareth fruit** (evidence of true conversion). While such evidence may vary in its amount, all true believers will produce some fruit. No fruit means no spiritual life.

The Parable of the Sower has been variously interpreted. Some hold that only the first one was lost, while others believe that examples two and three lost their salvation. To the contrary, only the last one was genuinely saved and produced fruit to prove it. The others fell away (not from salvation, but their profession) and were unfruitful. Jesus said that the believers' fruit would vary, but He gave no one the option of being His follower and producing no fruit at all!

b. The Parable of the Tares. 13:24-30; 36-43.

24 ¶Another parable put he forth unto them, saying, The kingdom of heaven is likened unto a man which sowed good seed in his field:

25 But while men slept, his enemy came and sowed tares among the wheat, and went his way.

26 But when the blade was sprung up, and brought forth fruit, then appeared the tares also.

27 So the servants of the householder came and said unto him, Sir, didst not thou sow good seed in thy field? from whence then hath it tares?

24-27. This parable serves as a warning to the laborers in the field (which is the world, vs. 38). Unlike the Jewish form of the kingdom in the Old Testament where citizens could be easily recognized, during the Church Age converts will be made from all over the world and received upon their profession of faith. Thus, it will be easier to slip in some counterfeits who profess what they do not possess. **The kingdom of heaven** must refer to the church, which is the subject of these parables. The **enemy** is Satan and the **tares** (Gr *zizanion*, denoting "darnel," *lolium temulentum*) are false converts. The darnel was a weed that resembled wheat but did not come to fruition. The **good seed . . . sprung up, and brought forth fruit** again, emphasizing that true converts produce fruitful lives. By contrast, false (professing) converts produce no lasting fruit. It should be noted that a "fruit" is something which God must produce in us by His power (cf. Gal 5:22ff.), whereas a "work" is something which man can do by his own effort. Singing, preaching, ushering, teaching, witnessing are all works; by contrast, loving people, having a deep-seated inner joy, being at peace with people, etc., are fruits of the Holy Spirit, as is righteousness and holiness. False converts may produce outstanding works but no real fruits.

28 He said unto them, An enemy hath done this. The servants said unto him, Wilt thou then that we go and gather them up?

29 But he said, Nay; lest while ye gather up the tares, ye root up also the wheat with them.

30 Let both grow together until the harvest: and in the time of harvest I will say to the reapers, Gather ye together first the tares, and bind them in bundles to burn them: but gather the wheat into my barn.

28-30. The servants questioned what could be done with these tares. To uproot them would be to damage the entire crop: **root up . . . the wheat with them.** The implication seems to be that too much scathing of people's genuineness of faith may damage the saved before it exposes the lost. **Let both grow together** indicates that there will always be some false professors among true Christian believers until the **time of harvest** or judgment. Note that the tares are gathered, bound, and burned first, whereas the wheat is gathered into **my barn** (heaven). The same progression of judgment, then blessing, follows in Revelation 19-22.

The Parable of the Tares is interpreted later by Jesus in verses 36-43. It should be observed that only the main details are symbolic in a parable, the minor incidents (e.g., the servants) merely give substance to the story. **The field is the world,** not the church. The sower of the good seed is the **Son of man,** or Christ Himself who will also be the final Judge who evaluates the fruit. The gospel is to be sown where lost people are and where converts need to be made in the world. As Lord of the harvest, Christ directs this sowing process, i.e., the missionary mandate of the church. The **children of the kingdom** are the saved believers of the church, who are Christ's true followers. The **harvest** is the end of the world and the **reapers** are angels who play a decisive role in the final judgment. The **fire** represents hell, or the lake of fire, the destination of all unbelievers and false professors who deny Christ. By contrast, the righteous shall enjoy the eternal **kingdom of their Father.**

31 ¶Another parable put he forth unto them, saying, The kingdom of heaven is like to a grain of mustard seed, which a man took, and sowed in his field:

32 Which indeed is the least of all seeds: but when it is grown, it is the greatest among herbs, and becometh a tree, so that the birds of the air come and lodge in the branches thereof.

33 ¶Another parable spake he unto them; The kingdom of heaven is like unto leaven, which a woman took, and hid in three measures of meal, till the whole was leavened.

34 All these things spake Jesus unto the multitude in parables; and without a parable spake he not unto them:

35 That it might be fulfilled which was spoken by the prophet, saying, I will open my mouth in parables; I will utter things which have been kept secret from the foundation of the world.

36 ¶Then Jesus sent the multitude away, and went into the house: and his disciples came unto him, saying, Declare unto us the parable of the tares of the field.

37 He answered and said unto them, He that soweth the good seed is the Son of man;

38 The field is the world; the good seed are the children of the kingdom; but the tares are the children of the wicked *one*;

39 The enemy that sowed them is the devil; the harvest is the end of the world; and the reapers are the angels.

40 As therefore the tares are gathered and burned in the fire; so shall it be in the end of this world.

41 The Son of man shall send forth his angels, and they shall gather out of his kingdom all things that offend, and them which do iniquity;

42 And shall cast them into a furnace of fire: there shall be wailing and gnashing of teeth.

43 Then shall the righteous shine forth as the sun in the kingdom of their Father. Who hath ears to hear, let him hear.

44 ¶Again, the kingdom of heaven is like unto treasure hid in a field; the which when a man hath found, he hideth, and for joy thereof goeth and selleth all that he hath, and buyeth that field.

45 ¶Again, the kingdom of heaven is like unto a merchant man, seeking goodly pearls:

c. The Parable of the Mustard Seed. 13:31-32.

31-32. See Mark 4:30-43; Luke 8:18-19. The **mustard seed** is usually small and yet grows to a great size, though not as great as described here. The idea seems to be that the tiny beginning of the church will eventually culminate in great growth. **Herbs** (Gr *lachanon*) plants or vegetables. However, such numerical growth will come to harbor the **birds** i.e., evil ones. Atkinson (p. 790) holds that, "The parable accordingly foreshadows the growth of the church into a world power . . . we have here a perfect picture of the apostasy not condemned, as such, we are reminded that outward growth is not always a true picture of spiritual depth. Again, as with the tares, false professors clutter the branches of the true tree (Rom 11) of God's fruitful people, seeking to benefit their own interest."

d. The Parable of the Leaven. 13:33-35.

33-35. Kingdom of heaven is the spiritual form of the kingdom in the church. **Leaven** is a lump of old dough in a state of fermentation which contaminates the bread. Leaven is virtually always used as a symbol of evil (cf. Mt 18:6-12; Mk 8:15; Gal 5:9). **Three measures of meal,** a common baking quantity (cf. Gen 18:6), equivalent to one and a half gallons (Gr *saton;* Heb *seah*). Kent (p. 47) sees the **woman** here as the false prophetess, Jezebel (Rev 2:20) and the great harlot (Rev 17). Thus, the leaven is not just false profession of unsaved church members but false doctrine which they will attempt to bring into the church.

36-43. See notes on verses 24-30 above.

e. The Parable of the Hidden Treasure. 13:44.

44. This tiny parable has been subject to widely diverse interpretation. Some see Christ as the **treasure hid in a field,** for which the sinner must forsake all in order to obtain (cf. H. Kee, Matthew, in the *Interpreter's Commentary on the Bible,* p. 626). However, this view smacks of self-effort in obtaining that which only grace can give. It also violates the imagery of the other parables where Christ is the man. The treasure, then, represents His treasure people whom He bought and hid with Himself in God (Col 3:3).

f. The Parable of the Pearl of Great Price. 13:45-46.

45-46. The **merchant man** is Christ who comes to purchase, through His atonement, sinners who shall become **goodly pearls.** The **one pearl of great price** is the church for whom

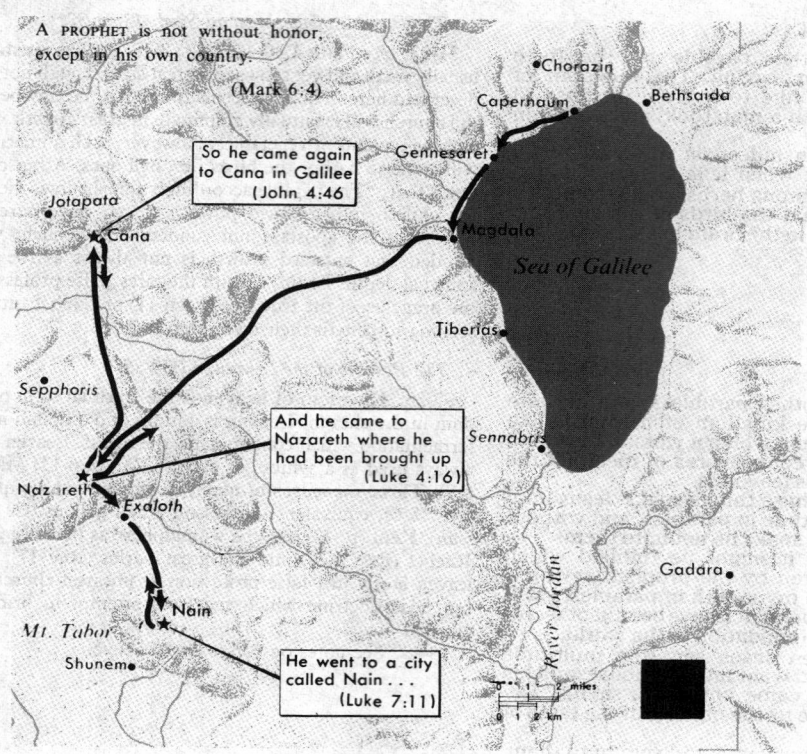

A PROPHET is not without honor, except in his own country.
(Mark 6:4)

So he came again to Cana in Galilee (John 4:46)

And he came to Nazareth where he had been brought up (Luke 4:16)

He went to a city called Nain . . . (Luke 7:11)

Chorazin
Capernaum
Bethsaida
Gennesaret
Magdala
Sea of Galilee
Tiberias
Sennabris
Gadara
Jotapata
Cana
Sepphoris
Nazareth
Exaloth
Nain
Mt. Tabor
Shunem
River Jordan

Cana and Nazareth Revisited

46 Who, when he had found one pearl of great price, went and sold all that he had, and bought it.

47 ¶Again, the kingdom of heaven is like unto a net, that was cast into the sea, and gathered of every kind:
48 Which, when it was full, they drew to shore, and sat down, and gathered the good into vessels, but cast the bad away.
49 So shall it be at the end of the world: the angels shall come forth, and sever the wicked from among the just,
50 And shall cast them into the furnace of fire: there shall be wailing and gnashing of teeth.
51 Jesus saith unto them, Have ye understood all these things? They say unto him, Yea, Lord.
52 Then said he unto them, Therefore every scribe *which is* instructed unto the kingdom of heaven is like unto a man *that is* an householder, which bringeth forth out of his treasure *things* new and old.
53 ¶And it came to pass, *that* when Jesus had finished these parables, he departed thence.
54 And when he was come into his

Christ gave His life, i.e., **all that he had.** If the pearl is Christ or the kingdom for whom a man must give all in order to obtain, then no man has ever yet given **all** that he has for Christ. While we receive Him as Saviour, we also progressively continue surrendering areas of ourselves to Him as we come to know better His will for our lives.

g. *The Parable of the Dragnet. 13:47-50.*

47-50. The dragnet. H. Staff (Matthew, in the *Broadman Bible Commentary*, p. 159) states, "It was pulled between two boats or taken out into the water by a single boat and drawn to shore by ropes." In such a process all kinds of fish and other objects would be caught together. The **good** were put into **vessels,** while the **bad** were cast away to be burned **of fire** (in hell). The imagery is similar to the Parable of the Tares.

h. *Excursus: The use of parables. 13:51-58.*

51-52. The disciples have been given the parables and the principles of interpretation. Thus, they reply **Yea, Lord,** or "yes," we understand. Since they clearly understood these parables, then obviously we are to understand them as well. An informed disciple is a true **scribe** who comprehends new and old truths and can rightly discern between them.

53-58. Jesus then gave His disciples a firsthand opportunity to witness the truth of these parables in action by teaching at the **synagogue** in His home town (Nazareth, not Capernaum). The people were **astonished,** i.e., greatly amazed or astounded.

own country, he taught them in their synagogue, insomuch that they were astonished, and said, Whence hath this *man* this wisdom, and *these* mighty works?

55 Is not this the carpenter's son? is not his mother called Mary? and his brethren, James, and Joses, and Simon, and Judas?

56 And his sisters, are they not all with us? Whence then hath this *man* all these things?

57 And they were offended in him. But Jesus said unto them, A prophet is not without honour, save in his own country, and in his own house.

58 And he did not many mighty works there because of their unbelief.

CHAPTER 14

AT that time Herod the tetrarch heard of the fame of Jesus,

2 And said unto his servants, This is John the Baptist; he is risen from the dead; and therefore mighty works do shew forth themselves in him.

3 ¶For Herod had laid hold on John, and bound him, and put *him* in prison for He-rō'dĭ-as' sake, his brother Philip's wife.

4 For John said unto him, It is not lawful for thee to have her.

5 And when he would have put him to death, he feared the multitude, because they counted him as a prophet.

6 But when Herod's birthday was kept, the daughter of He-rō'dĭ-as danced before them, and pleased Herod.

7 Whereupon he promised with an oath to give her whatsoever she would ask.

8 And she, being before instructed of her mother, said, Give me here John Baptist's head in a charger.

9 And the king was sorry: nevertheless for the oath's sake, and them which sat with him at meat, he commanded *it* to be given *her.*

10 And he sent, and beheaded John in the prison.

11 And his head was brought in a charger, and given to the damsel: and she brought *it* to her mother.

12 And his disciples came, and took up the body, and buried it, and went and told Jesus.

13 ¶When Jesus heard *of it,* he departed thence by ship into a desert place apart: and when the people had heard *thereof,* they followed him on foot out of the cities.

14 And Jesus went forth, and saw a great multitude, and was moved with

Carpenter's son refers to the family trade of Joseph, Jesus' legal guardian and earthly "father," being the husband of Mary. The word "carpenter" (Gr *tektōn*) may refer to either a carpenter or a stone mason. The indication is that Jesus had learned His family's trade. There is no valid reason for understanding **brethren and sisters** in any sense but the normal one. They are Jesus' half brothers, the children naturally generated by Joseph and Mary after Jesus' virgin birth (cf. J. Broadus, *Commentary on the Gospel of Matthew,* pp. 310-312). Two of them, James and Judas (Jude), wrote New Testament epistles and played a prominent role in the early church. Some suggest that the family had moved to Capernaum, but that the sisters had married and remained at Nazareth ("with us"). Because they were **offended** at His message He did no **mighty works** (miracles) there due to their **unbelief.** His power was not limited by man's faith, but was exercised in response to it.

5. His malediction: Seriousness of rejection. 14:1-16:28.

a. The death of John the Baptist. 14:1-12.

14:1-2. The occasion of John's death signaled a time for Jesus to retreat, lest He provoke an early death, before the appointed time. **Herod the tetrarch** is Herod Antipas, the son of Herod the Great, the ruler of Galilee and Peraea. His ignorance of Jesus prior to this time is probably due to his self-indulgent, luxurious life-style that had little contact with religious figures. His guilty conscience over John's death caused him to think Jesus was John the Baptist **risen from the dead.** His fear of the resurrection indicates its widespread belief in those days. Matthew, then, recounts the story of John's murder at Herod's hands.

3-8. John had been arrested because of challenging the illegitimacy of Herod's divorce and incestuous remarriage. **Herodias** was the daughter of Aristobolus, a half-brother of Antipas. She had been married to her uncle, Herod **Philip,** and had borne him a daughter, Salome. However, she divorced her husband and married Antipas, who was already married himself. The king's own anger was already against John, but he **feared the multitude** and kept him alive because the people believed he was a **prophet** and indeed he was the last of the Old Testament prophets. Herodias was a guilty and vindictive ungodly woman who wanted John dead and devised a plan to get rid of him. At the king's birthday party, her daughter performed a provocative and sexually enticing dance which so appealed to the drunken Herod that he **promised with an oath** that she could have whatever she wanted. Set up by her mother, she asked for **John Baptist's head in a charger,** i.e., a table platter.

9-12. The weak king complied and the forerunner of Jesus was slain. However, the vindication of the family was short-lived. Historical records confirm that the Herodian family never escaped bloodshed and violence (cf. H. Hoehner, *Herod Antipas* and S. Perowne, *The Life and Times of Herod the Great*). John's loyal **disciples** came bravely and obtained his body for burial and then informed Jesus, who departed into a **desert place apart.** We cannot fully comprehend the pressure Jesus was under at this time. Yet, in spite of His own heartache over John's death, He performs two major miracles for the multitude whom, loving, He cannot avoid healing and feeding.

b. The feeding of the five thousand. 14:13-21.

13-19. The stage was now set for the miracle of the feeding of the five thousand, which is the only miracle recorded in each of the four Gospels (see Mk 6:30-44; Lk 9:10-17; Jn 6:1-13). It became **evening** may refer to either three o'clock or sundown. Both times were used in Jewish reckoning and both may appear in the harmonization of the various accounts. While towns were nearby where food could have been purchased, it was getting

compassion toward them, and he healed their sick.

15 ¶And when it was evening, his disciples came to him, saying, This is a desert place, and the time is now past; send the multitude away, that they may go into the villages, and buy themselves victuals.

16 But Jesus said unto them, They need not depart; give ye them to eat.

17 And they say unto him, We have here but five loaves, and two fishes.

18 He said, Bring them hither to me.

19 And he commanded the multitude to sit down on the grass, and took the five loaves, and the two fishes, and looking up to heaven, he blessed, and brake, and gave the loaves to *his* disciples, and the disciples to the multitude.

20 And they did all eat, and were filled: and they took up of the fragments that remained twelve baskets full.

21 And they that had eaten were about five thousand men, beside women and children.

22 ¶And straightway Jesus constrained his disciples to get into a ship, and to go before him unto the other side, while he sent the multitudes away.

23 And when he had sent the multitudes away, he went up into a mountain apart to pray: and when the evening was come, he was there alone.

24 But the ship was now in the midst of the sea, tossed with waves: for the wind was contrary.

25 And in the fourth watch of the night Jesus went unto them, walking on the sea.

26 And when the disciples saw him walking on the sea, they were troubled, saying, It is a spirit; and they cried out for fear.

27 But straightway Jesus spake unto them, saying, Be of good cheer; it is I; be not afraid.

28 And Peter answered him and said, Lord, if it be thou, bid me come unto thee on the water.

29 And he said, Come. And when Peter was come down out of the ship, he walked on the water, to go to Jesus.

30 But when he saw the wind boisterous, he was afraid; and beginning to sink, he cried, saying, Lord, save me.

31 And immediately Jesus stretched forth *his* hand, and caught him, and said unto him, O thou of little faith, wherefore didst thou doubt?

32 And when they were come into the ship, the wind ceased.

late in the evening (cf. Lk 9:12). Jesus' suggestion to the disciples **give ye them to eat,** placed the burden of responsibility on them. According to the Gospel of John, **Andrew,** who had brought Peter to Jesus, now brought a boy's lunch consisting merely of **five loaves and two fishes,** i.e., small baked rolls and dried fish (an adequate lunch for a boy, but hardly a crumb compared to the immense crowd).

The simplicity of the story and its inclusion by all four evangelists eliminates any doubt of its true historicity. Old liberal interpretations are totally inadequate. Albert Schweitzer suggested that in actuality each person received only a small crumb or fragment and yet felt satisfied. Barclay hints that the boy's offering of his lunch convicted the crowd, so that they all got out their previously concealed lunches and shared them. None of these approaches is suggested in the text. Even Schweitzer's crumbs would add up to gigantic, unbelievable loaves in order for five to feed five thousand! The obvious miracle was the result of Jesus' divine person and power. As the Creator-God, He multiplied the bread, so that, as each piece was broken off, the original roll still remained intact. No wonder the crowd came back the next day seeking more. If the liberal interpretation of this passage was true, no one would have returned seeking more bread from Jesus (Jn 6:22-26)!

20-21. Not only is the miracle itself amazing but its result is equally stunning. **Twelve baskets full** of fragments remained over and above that which was eaten. The baskets (Gr *kophinos*) were small baskets carried on the arm and used as a satchel. These may have belonged to the disciples, who now receive a basketful of blessing as a result of their labor to feed others. Collection of the fragments emphasizes the adequacy and immensity of Christ's provision. Besides the **five thousand men** a large uncounted group of women and children were fed.

c. The walking on the water. 14:22-36.

22-27. Following the miraculous feeding, which John relates to the discourse on the Bread of Life, the disciples departed across the **sea** (of Galilee) by rented ship. Jesus dismissed the crowd and went up **into a mountain apart to pray.** That night the disciples encountered great difficulty from a **contrary wind** about three miles out in the lake (Jn 6:19). During the **fourth watch,** three o'clock to six o'clock A.M. Jesus came to them **walking on the sea** (another obvious miracle not to be explained away by His supposedly walking on stones out in the middle of the lake)! The nearly exhausted disciples, who had been rowing all night, were afraid, thinking he was a **spirit** (Gr *phantasma*), i.e., a ghost or apparition. Jesus reassured them, **It is I.**

28-32. **Peter answered him** in his characteristic impulsive manner. This part of the story is recounted only by Matthew, on whom it must have made a deep impression. Remember that he was in the boat at the time; perhaps he got wet when Peter climbed back into the ship. The incident is not presented as a parable, but an actual event involving three miracles (cf. Filson, p. 174): Jesus walks on the water, Peter temporarily does so, and the wind ceases immediately. Peter urged Jesus, **bid me come unto thee on the water,** not an unreasonable request for one who had just that day participated with the Saviour in the miracle of the feeding of the five thousand! However, Peter takes his eyes off the Saviour and fixes them on the surrounding conditions and begins to sink. With the concentration of his faith broken, Peter comes back under the control of the natural forces. The incident served as a good lesson in spiritual truth for all the disciples, to urge them not to be **of little faith** and **doubt,** i.e., doubting feeble believers.

33-36. The disciples **worshiped him** and recognized Him as **the Son of God.** Their spoken Aramaic of this phrase was a clear recognition of the deity of Jesus. No mere man deserved their worship and no mere man could do what He had done. It is no surprise, then, that the people of **Gennesaret,** on the plain to the northwest of the Sea of Galilee, were healed by simply touching **the hem of his garment.** This procedure may have been motivated by reports of the cure of hemorrhage which had previously occurred in this same region (cf. 9:20).

33 Then they that were in the ship came and worshipped him, saying, Of a truth thou art the Son of God.

34 ¶And when they were gone over, they came into the land of Gĕn-nĕs′a-ret.

35 And when the men of that place had knowledge of him, they sent out into all that country round about, and brought unto him all that were diseased;

36 And besought him that they might only touch the hem of his garment: and as many as touched were made perfectly whole.

CHAPTER 15

THEN came to Jesus scribes and Pharisees, which were of Jerusalem, saying,

2 Why do thy disciples transgress the tradition of the elders? for they wash not their hands when they eat bread.

d. The conflict with the Pharisees over ritual. 15:1-20.

15:1-2a. See Mark 7:1-23. **Of Jerusalem.** It appears that the central religious leaders came to investigate the ministry and teaching of Jesus. **The tradition of the elders.** The Jews of our Lord's time believed that, in addition to the written law of Moses, there was an oral law given to Moses on Sinai and passed down from him by word of mouth till it reached the Great Synagogue or Council of Elders which succeeded Ezra after the return from the exile. This council lasted till 291 B.C. and seems to have been the source of the many accretions to the law of God which have been found in Judaism ancient and modern.

2b-9. Wash not their hands. The washing consisted of pouring a trickle of cold water over the outstretched hands. The Jews were not concerned with cleanliness but with ritual. **Why do ye also transgress?** The Lord here shows that additions to the Word of God ultimately contradict it. **Honor thy father and mother.** This is the fifth commandment of the Decalogue (see Ex 20:12; Deut 5:16). **He that curseth . . . let him die the death** (taken from the LXX of Ex 21:17). **It is a gift.** It was possible for a Jew by a legal quibble to dedicate his property to the Temple, thus avoiding the necessity of supporting his parents, although he could continue to enjoy the proceeds himself. Notice that the Lord interprets the command to honor our parents in a practical sense. For children it means to obey them (Eph 6:1-3) and for adults to support them. Our Lord condemns this common practice based on tradition since it completely defeats the purpose of the law. **Commandments** should rather be "Word of God." Verses 8 and 9 are from Isaiah 29:13 and follow the LXX where it differs from the Hebrew.

3 But he answered and said unto them, Why do ye also transgress the commandment of God by your tradition?

4 For God commanded, saying, Honour thy father and mother: and, He that curseth father or mother, let him die the death.

5 But ye say, Whosoever shall say to *his* father or *his* mother, *It is* a gift, by whatsoever thou mightest be profited by me;

6 And honour not his father or his mother, *he shall be free.* Thus have ye made the commandment of God of none effect by your tradition.

7 *Ye* hypocrites, well did E-sā′ias prophesy of you, saying,

8 This people draweth nigh unto me with their mouth, and honoureth me with *their* lips; but their heart is far from me.

9 But in vain they do worship me, teaching *for* doctrines the commandments of men.

10 ¶And he called the multitude, and said unto them, Hear, and understand:

11 Not that which goeth into the mouth defileth a man; but that which cometh out of the mouth, this defileth a man.

12 Then came his disciples, and said unto him, Knowest thou that the Pharisees were offended, after they heard this saying?

13 But he answered and said, Every plant, which my heavenly Father hath not planted, shall be rooted up.

14 Let them alone: they be blind leaders of the blind. And if the blind lead the blind, both shall fall into the ditch.

15 Then answered Peter and said unto him, Declare unto us this parable.

10-14. Defileth, i.e., makes him profane. The term is a technical one. The idea in Judaism was that to eat the wrong sort of food deprived a man of holiness and ultimately, therefore, of acceptance with God. The Jewish leaders showed offense at this deliberate contradiction of their own teaching. In two vivid pictures (vss. 13-14) our Lord tells His disciples that the Pharisees have no real mission from God and are themselves blind. They and all that their religion stood for would be destroyed.

15-20. Peter, acting on behalf of the others, asks for an explanation of the saying which had given such offense. Our

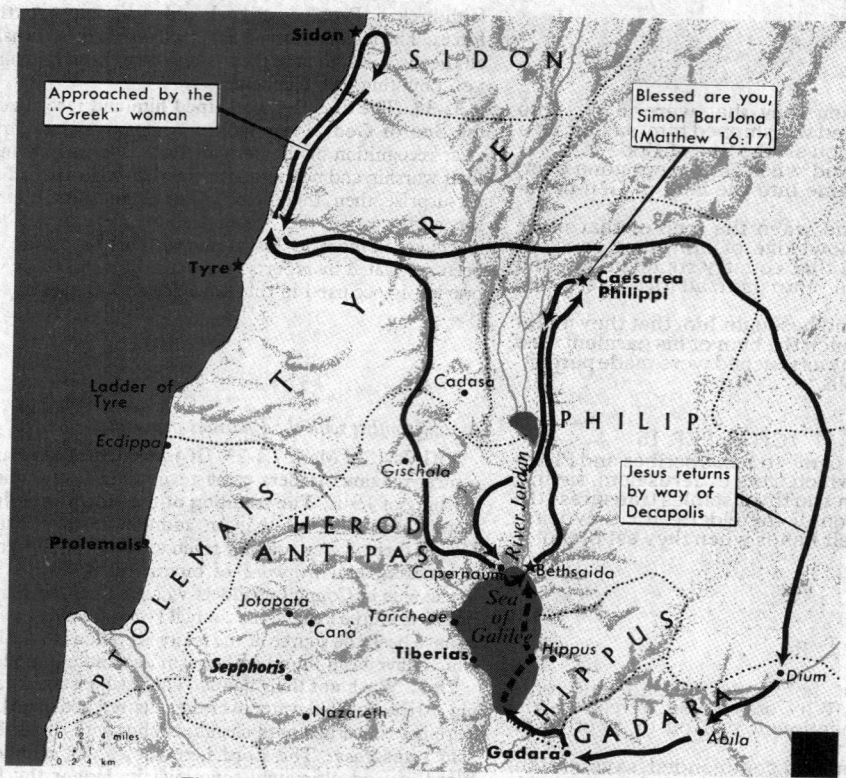

The Visit to Tyre, Sidon, and Caesarea Philippi

16 And Jesus said, Are ye also yet without understanding?

17 Do not ye yet understand, that whatsoever entereth in at the mouth goeth into the belly, and is cast out into the draught?

18 But those things which proceed out of the mouth come forth from the heart; and they defile the man.

19 For out of the heart proceed evil thoughts, murders, adulteries, fornications, thefts, false witness, blasphemies:

20 These are *the things* which defile a man: but to eat with unwashen hands defileth not a man.

21 ¶Then Jesus went thence, and departed into the coasts of Tyre and Sī'-don.

22 And, behold, a woman of Canaan came out of the same coasts, and cried unto him, saying, Have mercy on me, O Lord, *thou* son of David; my daughter is grievously vexed with a devil.

23 But he answered her not a word. And his disciples came and besought him, saying, Send her away; for she crieth after us.

24 But he answered and said, I am not sent but unto the lost sheep of the house of Israel.

25 Then came she and worshipped him, saying, Lord, help me.

26 But he answered and said, It is not

Lord proceeds to elaborate the teaching for their benefit. **Draught** (Gr *aphedrōn*) means literally "latrine." **They defile.** The "they" is emphatic. **Evil thoughts,** i.e., evil schemes. **Blasphemies,** not only blasphemy in the modern, narrow sense of the word, but also criticism or libel of others.

e. The healing of the Canaanitish woman's daughter. 15:21-28.

21-25. The second withdrawal of Jesus followed John's death and further rejection by the religious leadership of Israel. Thus, Jesus actually left the country and went into parts of **Tyre and Sidon** leaving Herod's jurisdiction to retire to Phoenicia for a time of seclusion, which was interrupted by the **woman of Canaan** (lit., Canaanitish woman). Mark 7:26 calls her a Syro-Phoenician woman. The word translated "coasts" (Gr *meros*) means districts. This is the only known occasion during His ministry that our Lord went outside the boundaries of Palestine. The woman was a Gentile and descended from the Canaanites who inhabited Syria and Palestine before the conquest of the latter by Joshua.

26-28. By **children** the Lord means Jews, and by **dogs,** Gentiles. Our Lord's attitude was intended to test the woman's

meet to take the children's bread, and to cast *it* to dogs.

27 And she said, Truth, Lord: yet the dogs eat of the crumbs which fall from their masters' table.

28 Then Jesus answered and said unto her, O woman, great *is* thy faith: be it unto thee even as thou wilt. And her daughter was made whole from that very hour.

29 ¶And Jesus departed from thence, and came nigh unto the sea of Galilee; and went up into a mountain, and sat down there.

30 And great multitudes came unto him, having with them *those that were* lame, blind, dumb, maimed, and many others, and cast them down at Jesus' feet; and he healed them:

31 Insomuch that the multitude wondered, when they saw the dumb to speak, the maimed to be whole, the lame to walk, and the blind to see: and they glorified the God of Israel.

32 ¶Then Jesus called his disciples *unto him,* and said, I have compassion on the multitude, because they continue with me now three days, and have nothing to eat: and I will not send them away fasting, lest they faint in the way.

33 And his disciples say unto him, Whence should we have so much bread in the wilderness, as to fill so great a multitude?

34 And Jesus saith unto them, How many loaves have ye? And they said, Seven, and a few little fishes.

35 And he commanded the multitude to sit down on the ground.

36 And he took the seven loaves and the fishes, and gave thanks, and brake *them,* and gave to his disciples, and the disciples to the multitude.

37 And they did all eat, and were filled: and they took up of the broken *meat* that was left seven baskets full.

38 And they that did eat were four thousand men, beside women and children.

39 And he sent away the multitude, and took ship, and came into the coasts of Măg'da-la.

CHAPTER 16

THE Pharisees also with the Săd'du-ceés came, and tempting desired him that he would shew them a sign from heaven.

2 He answered and said unto them, When it is evening, ye say, *It will be* fair weather: for the sky is red.

3 And in the morning, *It will be* foul weather to day: for the sky is red and lowring. O *ye* hypocrites, ye can discern the face of the sky; but can ye not *discern* the signs of the times?

4 A wicked and adulterous generation seeketh after a sign; and there shall no sign be given unto it, but the

faith, which was rewarded by a miraculous healing. Jesus is not angry with her, but is trying to teach the disciples a valuable lesson. Having been rejected by the Jews, He now turns to the Gentiles, a move that will later shock some of His followers. He had healed Gentiles earlier, but here in Phoenicia He does not want to give the impression that he has totally abandoned Israel. The term used for "dogs" (Gr *kynarion*) means little dogs (pets), not wild, scavenging beasts. She replied that such **dogs eat of the crumbs which fall from their master's table.** She knew what could be hers, even as a Gentile and, thus she became an illustration of millions of Gentiles who would later be blessed by the Messiah of Israel. **Great is thy faith.** Jesus again commends Gentile belief (cf. 8:10).

f. The feeding of the four thousand. 15:29-39.

29-38. See also Mark 7:31-8:10. The supposition that this is a confused duplicate account of the feeding of the five thousand must be rejected. Both Matthew and Mark include the account of the two events and do so in such a way as to indicate that they quite clearly thought of them as two separate miracles. The incident evidently took place on the southeast shore of Galilee, near the gentile Decapolis. Therefore, many Gentiles seem to be among His listeners who **glorified the God of Israel.** This feeding took place after the crowd had been with Him for **three days** and were fed with **Seven** loaves and **a few little fishes** which were then distributed in a manner similar to the other feeding. This time **seven baskets full** remained. These baskets (Gr *spyris*) were much larger than those in 14:20.

39. The lesson to the disciples seems obvious: What you accomplish among the Jews will be duplicated among the Gentiles. **Magdala** (vs. 39) is Magadan, perhaps a suburb of Tiberias. In 16:9-10 Jesus refers to both feedings as separate events, even referring to the different numbers and using the different words for the baskets.

g. The Pharisees and Sadducees rebuked. 16:1-12.

16:1-12. The unbelieving leaders came seeking a **sign from heaven,** i.e., an outward miraculous manifestation, of which Jesus had already given many. Notice that miracles alone never save anyone. They only serve to authenticate and call attention to the message, which must be believed in order for salvation to be experienced in the soul. Instead of another miracle, He points them to the **signs of the times,** eschatologically related to the sky and His second coming. He referred to their ability to discern the coming weather by the sky and implied that they should have been able to discern the time of His coming also. The **adulterous generation** is used here in a spiritual sense, unfaithful to God, though the two often interrelate. The **sign of the prophet Jonah** is one of Jesus' favorites for it relates to His resurrection (see 12:38-40; Jn 2:18-22). This sign gives hope to

sign of the prophet Jonas. And he left them, and departed.

5 ¶And when his disciples were come to the other side, they had forgotten to take bread.

6 Then Jesus said unto them, Take heed and beware of the leaven of the Pharisees and of the Săd′du-cees.

7 And they reasoned among themselves, saying, *It is* because we have taken no bread.

8 *Which* when Jesus perceived, he said unto them, O ye of little faith, why reason ye among yourselves, because ye have brought no bread?

9 Do ye not yet understand, neither remember the five loaves of the five thousand, and how many baskets ye took up?

10 Neither the seven loaves of the four thousand, and how many baskets ye took up?

11 How is it that ye do not understand that I spake *it* not to you concerning bread, that ye should beware of the leaven of the Pharisees and of the Săd′-du-cees?

12 Then understood they how that he bade *them* not beware of the leaven of bread, but of the doctrine of the Pharisees and of the Săd′du-cees.

13 ¶When Jesus came into the coasts of Cæs-a-re′a Phĭ-lip′pī, he asked his disciples, saying, Whom do men say that I the Son of man am?

14 And they said, Some *say that thou art* John the Baptist: some, E-lī′as; and others, Jeremias, or one of the prophets.

15 He saith unto them, But whom say ye that I am?

16 And Simon Peter answered and said, Thou art the Christ, the Son of the living God.

17 And Jesus answered and said unto him, Blessed art thou, Simon Băr-jō′na: for flesh and blood hath not revealed *it* unto thee, but my Father which is in heaven.

18 And I say also unto thee, That thou art Peter, and upon this rock I will build my church; and the gates of hell shall not prevail against it.

the believer but is an indication of judgment for the unbeliever, who will be judged by the risen Christ at His second coming.

h. Peter's confession. 16:13-28.

13-17. See Mark 8:27-33; Luke 9:18-21. **The coasts of Caesarea Philippi.** This was a town in the extreme northeast of Galilee, near the source of the Jordan. **Coasts** (Gr *meros*) means districts. Verse 14 shows that public opinion placed our Lord on the highest human pedestal by identifying Him with one of the national heroes of the past, i.e., **John the Baptist.** Herod himself was a victim of this particular superstition (see 14:2). From 21:26 we know that He was held in high esteem as a prophet by the people. The coming of Elijah (Elias) was prophesied by Malachi (Mal 4:5) and the Jews often linked the name of Jeremiah with the prophet foretold in Deuteronomy 18:15. **Thou art the Christ.** Simon Peter recognized and acknowledged openly our Lord's deity. He may have been speaking for all the disciples. Verse 20 suggests that it was a conviction which they all now shared. Peter further used the Greek definite article "the" to designate that Jesus was **the Son of the living God.**

18. Thou art Peter, and upon this rock I will build my church. The Greek word used for "rock" (Gr *petra*) is played against the name Peter (Gr *petros*) in the original. The Roman Catholic interpretation of this passage is that Peter was the foundation stone of the church, that he had a primacy among the apostles, that he became Bishop of Rome, and that his primacy was passed on to his successors, the popes. The verse will scarcely bear the first of these propositions and certainly none of the others. Protestant interpreters, with some patristic support (Chrysostom, Justin Martyr, and Augustine), have tended to identify the rock with Peter's faith or confession, or with our Lord Himself. The most straightforward interpretation seems to be that Peter is meant by the rock, but that he is not the exclusive foundation (J. Broadus). For the twelvefold foundation of the church see Ephesians 2:20; Revelation 21:14. This view seems borne out by the fact that the same words are spoken to all the disciples in Matthew 18:18 as are spoken to Simon Peter in 16:19. Therefore, the rock or foundation of the church is the confession (ultimately, the doctrine) of the apostles, which became normative for the true church.

The word here translated **church** (Gr *ekklēsia*) means literally "a chosen or called-out assembly." Thus the use of the word as a technical term for an assembly or group of believers in Christ was quite natural. It is not viewed as an external organization, denomination, or hierarchical system. The New Testament church, therefore, is a local, autonomous congregation or assembly of believers which is a "church" in and of itself. This is the first occurrence of the word in the New Testament and probably is used in prophetic anticipation. Jesus' prediction, **I will build** could be translated, "I shall continue to build" (Greek progressive future, see B. Chapman, *New Testament Greek Notebook*, p. 68). Since the commission in Matthew 10 sent the apostles only to the "house of Israel," and no further commission was given until chapter 28, there was no worldwide task for the disciples until the physical manifestation of the church at Pentecost. The same word was used in the LXX to translate "congregation" (Heb *kahal*) again emphasizing the local independent function of both a synagogue and a church.

Jesus promised that **the gates of hell shall not prevail** against the church (assembly). Some have viewed this as the inability of hell to overpower the church and see the church as being on the defensive against Satan. However, the phrase "shall not prevail" may be understood as meaning, "shall not stand against." The imagery would then picture the church as being on the attack against the gates of hell. Here hell (Gr *hadēs*) probably represents the kingdom of Satan, not just death and the grave. While Jesus' resurrection certainly will overcome the sting of death, it will also enable His church to aggressively and offensively attack the gates of hell (cf. usage as Satan's kingdom in Job 38:17; Isa 38:10; Ps 107:18) by snatching out victims from darkness into His glorious kingdom of light. One does not attack with gates; he defends. It is the church which is on the attack here and hell is on the defensive.

19 And I will give unto thee the keys of the kingdom of heaven: and whatsoever thou shalt bind on earth shall be bound in heaven: and whatsoever thou shalt loose on earth shall be loosed in heaven.
20 Then charged he his disciples that they should tell no man that he was Jesus the Christ.

19-20. Our Lord then promised to Peter and the other apostles **the keys of the kingdom.** This means that Peter would have the right to enter the kingdom himself, would have general authority therein, symbolized by the possession of the **keys,** and preaching the gospel would be the means of opening the kingdom of heaven to all believers and shutting it against unbelievers. The book of Acts shows us this process at work. By his sermon on the day of Pentecost (Acts 2:14-40), Peter opened the door of the kingdom for the first time. The expressions **bind** and **loose** were common in Jewish legal phraseology meaning to declare forbidden or to declare allowed. Peter and the other disciples (see 18:18) were to continue on earth the work of Christ in preaching the gospel and declaring God's will to men, and were armed with the same authority as He Himself possessed. Christ in heaven ratifies what is done in His name and in obedience to His word on earth. There is also a definite reference here to the binding and loosing of church discipline which will be further explained in chapter 18. The apostles do not usurp Christ's lordship and authority over individual believers and their eternal destiny, but they do exercise the authority to discipline and, if necessary, excommunicate disobedient church members. **They should tell no man.** The revelation was to remain the property of the disciples until after the Lord's resurrection.

21 ¶From that time forth began Jesus to shew unto his disciples, how that he must go unto Jerusalem, and suffer many things of the elders and chief priests and scribes, and be killed, and be raised again the third day.

21. Jesus then announced His coming rejection and death at Jerusalem. All this would be necessary in order to initiate the church as the spiritual form of the kingdom on earth. **From that time forth.** He would openly reveal His coming rejection since the disciples' faith was now established enough to bear it. Thus, from this point onward, our Lord's ministry takes on a somewhat different complexion as He seeks to prepare His followers for the suffering which awaited Him and which would so disappoint their hopes. **Elders,** i.e., the religious leaders. The word probably denotes members of the Sanhedrin. The words **killed** and **rise again the third day** clearly indicate the divine Messiah's awareness of His earthly mission and destiny. To predict His

22 Then Peter took him, and began to rebuke him, saying, Be it far from thee, Lord: this shall not be unto thee.

23 But he turned, and said unto Peter, Get thee behind me, Satan: thou art an offence unto me: for thou savourest not the things that be of God, but those that be of men.

24 Then said Jesus unto his disciples, If any *man* will come after me, let him deny himself, and take up his cross, and follow me.

25 For whosoever will save his life shall lose it: and whosoever will lose his life for my sake shall find it.

26 For what is a man profited, if he shall gain the whole world, and lose his own soul? or what shall a man give in exchange for his soul?

27 For the Son of man shall come in the glory of his Father with his angels; and then he shall reward every man according to his works.

28 Verily I say unto you, There be some standing here, which shall not taste of death, till they see the Son of man coming in his kingdom.

CHAPTER 17

AND after six days Jesus taketh Peter, James, and John his brother, and bringeth them up into an high mountain apart,

2 And was transfigured before them: and his face did shine as the sun, and his raiment was white as the light.

3 And, behold, there appeared unto them Moses and E-lī'as talking with him.

4 Then answered Peter, and said unto Jesus, Lord, it is good for us to be here: if thou wilt, let us make here three tabernacles; one for thee, and one for Moses, and one for E-lī'as.

5 While he yet spake, behold, a bright cloud overshadowed them: and behold a voice out of the cloud, which said, This is my beloved Son, in whom I am well pleased; hear ye him.

6 And when the disciples heard *it,* they fell on their face, and were sore afraid.

7 And Jesus came and touched them, and said, Arise, and be not afraid.

8 And when they had lifted up their eyes, they saw no man, save Jesus only.

9 ¶And as they came down from the mountain, Jesus charged them, saying, Tell the vision to no man, until the Son of man be risen again from the dead.

10 And his disciples asked him, saying, Why then say the scribes that E-lī'as must first come?

11 And Jesus answered and said unto them, E-lī'as truly shall first come, and restore all things.

12 But I say unto you, That E-lī'as is

death in view of His rejection was human, but to predict a supernatural resurrection could only be done by the God-man!

22-28. Be it far from thee. Notice the marginal readings of both AV and RV. The sentence seems to mean literally "Have mercy on yourself." Peter's instantaneous reaction to our Lord's new teaching shows how foreign to their way of thinking was this conception of His suffering. **Satan.** The Lord recognized in Peter's words a repetition of the temptations to avoid the cross which He had undergone in the wilderness. The word translated **offense** (Gr *skandalon*) means a trap or snare. **Savorest** (Gr *phroneō*) is very difficult to translate. It occurs in Romans 8:5 and Philippians 2:5, meaning to adopt and maintain an attitude of mind upon which the life and actions are based. **Deny himself,** i.e., refuse his own claims upon himself. **Take up.** The meaning is "lift up." It is a stronger word than that used in 10:38, and implies a lifting of the cross on high, so that all may see it. This is the strongest statement in the New Testament about the disciple's need to crucify himself to the claims of Christ's lordship over him. **Lose his own soul** means to lose one's life and perish. **Shall reward every man according to his works.** The words are adopted from the LXX of Psalm 62:12 and Proverbs 24:12. This great fundamental moral principle of the Old Testament is made more explicit here by our Lord in explaining that it will find its fulfillment at His return. Verse 28 has caused much difficulty and needless misunderstanding. Its fulfillment may be looked for in the transfiguration which follows immediately, an occasion on which the Apostle Peter asserts that the three disciples saw Christ's coming (cf. II Pet 1:16ff.) and also in the Lord's resurrection and subsequent glory.

6. *His manifestation: Special transfiguration. 17:1-27.*

17:1-9. See Mark 9:2-13; Luke 9:28-36. **Peter, James and John** represent the "inner circle" of leadership among the disciples (cf. Lk 8:51; Mt 26:37) and serve here as ample witnesses according to Mosaic law. They went into a **high mountain apart,** i.e., privately, by themselves. Tradition claims this took place at Mount Tabor, but a more probable location would be Mount Hermon, near Caesarea Philippi. Jesus was **transfigured** before them. The verb (Gr *metamorphoō*) indicates a transformation of essential form, proceeding from within. See Romans 12:2 and II Corinthians 3:18 where it is used of the spiritual transformation of the believer's new nature. The witness of Peter in II Peter 1:17-18 verifies the testimony that this was a real experience, not a vision. In His transfiguration, Jesus, as the personal manifestation of God's glory (cf. Jn 1:14, "we beheld his glory, even as the only begotten of the Father, full of grace and truth") reveals that glory temporarily to these key disciples. Later, in Revelation 1, His glorified resurrection form is permanently transfigured. **Moses and Elijah** were the representatives respectively of the law and the prophets (see Jude 9, where Moses' resurrection is implied, and II Kings 2:11 for the account of Elijah's being taken up into heaven). **It is good for us to be here.** Peter wished to retain the situation and so suggests building **tabernacles** or tents. **A voice,** i.e., the Father's voice (for the words spoken cf. 3:17). God the Father clearly indicated that Christ's authority completely superseded that of the Old Testament law and prophets. The warning, **tell . . . no man,** is to avoid a premature popular, but misdirected, awakening in His favor (cf. Jn 6:14-15).

10-14. The point of the disciples' question in verse 10 seems to be that, supposing that Jesus' resurrection meant the end of the world and the inauguration of the kingdom, they thought it would be necessary for Elijah, of whom they had been reminded by seeing him on the mountain, to come and appear publicly first. Our Lord's answer is a quotation from Malachi 4:5-6,

come already, and they knew him not, but have done unto him whatsoever they listed. Likewise shall also the Son of man suffer of them.

13 Then the disciples understood that he spake unto them of John the Baptist.

14 ¶And when they were come to the multitude, there came to him a *certain* man, kneeling down to him, and saying,

15 Lord, have mercy on my son: for he is lunatick, and sore vexed: for ofttimes he falleth into the fire, and oft into the water.

16 And I brought him to thy disciples, and they could not cure him.

17 Then Jesus answered and said, O faithless and perverse generation, how long shall I be with you? how long shall I suffer you? bring him hither to me.

18 And Jesus rebuked the devil; and he departed out of him: and the child was cured from that very hour.

19 Then came the disciples to Jesus apart, and said, Why could not we cast him out?

20 And Jesus said unto them, Because of your unbelief: for verily I say unto you, If ye have faith as a grain of mustard seed, ye shall say unto this mountain, Remove hence to yonder place; and it shall remove; and nothing shall be impossible unto you.

21 Howbeit this kind goeth not out but by prayer and fasting.

22 ¶And while they abode in Galilee, Jesus said unto them, The Son of man shall be betrayed into the hands of men:

23 And they shall kill him, and the third day he shall be raised again. And they were exceeding sorry.

24 ¶And when they were come to Caper'na-um, they that received tribute *money* came to Peter, and said, Doth not your master pay tribute?

25 He saith, Yes. And when he was come into the house, Jesus prevented him, saying, What thinkest thou, Simon? of whom do the kings of the earth take custom or tribute? of their own children, or of strangers?

26 Peter saith unto him, Of strangers. Jesus saith unto him, Then are the children free.

27 Notwithstanding, lest we should offend them, go thou to the sea, and cast an hook, and take up the fish that first cometh up; and when thou hast opened his mouth, thou shalt find a piece of money: that take, and give unto them for me and thee.

where the coming of Elijah was prophesied. (For the meaning of **restore all things** see Luke 1:17). He then repeats what He has told them already, i.e., that the prophecy foretelling the coming of Elijah was fulfilled in John the Baptist (see 11:14). He does not name him directly but recalls his suffering and compares with it the treatment which will be accorded to Himself (vs. 12). (On the significance of the transfiguration, see E. Harrison, *A Short Life of Christ*, pp. 150-164.)

15-23. The return down the mountain brought Jesus upon His powerless disciples who were attempting to cure a **lunatic**. The RV has "epileptic." **Sore vexed**, i.e., very ill. **How long shall I suffer you?** i.e., "can I endure you?" **Unbelief**. A better reading is "little faith," as in RV. **As a grain of mustard seed**. This seems to mean that faith, once implanted in the heart, grows naturally like a living organism. **This mountain**, i.e., any seemingly impossible obstacle or difficulty that stands in the Christian's way. Verse 21 is omitted by the more reliable texts. It seems to have been interpolated from Mark 9:29. The purpose of this incident is obvious. Since Christ alone is the glorified Saviour, the disciples' ability to work depends totally upon His empowerment. **Bring him . . . to me** clearly emphasizes this. It is never adequate to bring people to ourselves for our ideas; the true Christian evangelist must bring them to Jesus Himself. Christ emerges from this scene as totally dominant and the disciples as completely dependent upon Him, even to the point of being **exceeding sorry** or "greatly distressed" by His further announcement of His coming death, which so shocked them His prediction of His resurrection did not even register with their minds.

a. Excursus: Paying the temple tax. 17:24-27.

24-27. Jesus, as the glorified Son of God is greater than demons and also the Temple itself. The two incidents following the transfiguration clearly reassert His supremacy. **Tribute money** (lit., two drachmae) a technical term for the tax of half a shekel, which every Jew over twenty was expected to contribute to the upkeep of the Temple. The amount was about fifteen or eighteen pence. **Prevented**, used here with its seventeenth-century meaning of "anticipated." **Of strangers**. It was the subject races which were taxed first and most heavily. The **children**, i.e., the king's own race, were **free**. The Lord Jesus Christ was the Lord and owner of the Temple, and therefore it was not for Him to pay the tax. Action based on this fact might obviously be misunderstood, however, and under such circumstances our Lord would not give offense by seeming to be a lawbreaker. But note that in any matter where a fundamental principle was at stake, our Lord did not tone down His message in order not to offend (cf. 15:10-14). **A piece of money**, the silver tetradrachma, equivalent to the shekel and therefore the exact amount of the tax for two persons (cf. Atkinson, p. 794).

7. His mercy: Sanctification of forgiveness. 18:1-35.

a. Personal forgiveness. 18:1-14.

See Mark 9:33-37; Luke 9:46-48. This chapter forms Jesus' longest recorded statement regarding the principle of forgiveness. The act of forgiving one who has wronged us is one of the most responsible and spiritual activities in our lives and must be repeated continually throughout one's life. This serves as the last great discourse before the journey to Jerusalem and is given in response to the disciples' jealousy of one another and to prepare them for the crucifixion, an act they will have to learn to

CHAPTER 18

AT the same time came the disciples unto Jesus, saying, Who is the greatest in the kingdom of heaven?

2 And Jesus called a little child unto him, and set him in the midst of them,

3 And said, Verily I say unto you, Except ye be converted, and become as little children, ye shall not enter into the kingdom of heaven.

4 Whosoever therefore shall humble himself as this little child, the same is greatest in the kingdom of heaven.

5 And whoso shall receive one such little child in my name receiveth me.

6 But whoso shall offend one of these little ones which believe in me, it were better for him that a millstone were hanged about his neck, and that he were drowned in the depth of the sea.

7 ¶Woe unto the world because of offences! for it must needs be that offences come; but woe to that man by whom the offence cometh!

forgive. Mark 9:33 indicates the message was given "in a house," probably Peter's.

18:1-4. The dispute over **Who is the greatest** was settled by Jesus' emphasis that it was the one who was willing to forgive the most! Thereby, He cut down the basic human motivation of pride in order to be the greatest by calling for the "greatest" to be the one most willing to forgive, which is contrary to proud human nature. Atkinson (p. 794) suggests that the **little child** may have been a member of Peter's family. **Be converted** means a "turning" (Gr *strepho*) of one's whole life and person toward God. This is the true biblical picture of conversion. It is far more than mental acknowledgment of the truth or intellectual assent to certain ideas. He now speaks generically of man's need to turn to Him and of the evidence of that turning in an attitude of humility. Thus, He challenges the disciples' selfishness by making them examine the reality of their own conversion. To **become as little children** means to be born again (converted) as a newborn spiritual child, characterized by faith and humility.

5-7. Thus, the **little child** represents a new convert or young believer. To **receive** such a fellow believer is to welcome Christ Himself. Therefore, the basis of true Christian fellowship is established in Christ Himself. There can be no real fellowship with those who deny Him and have not been converted, but with any true believer fellowship may exist. This, of course, does not overlook the discipline of an errant believer. **Offenses** are viewed as a reality which must be accepted in the present world, but **woe** (the prophetic condemnation to death) to the one who is the source of the offense. Jesus very definitely took this matter seriously. **A millstone** is literally an "ass-stone," or a large grinding stone turned by an ass.

The Transfiguration

8 Wherefore if thy hand or thy foot offend thee, cut them off, and cast *them* from thee: it is better for thee to enter into life halt or maimed, rather than having two hands or two feet to be cast into everlasting fire.

9 And if thine eye offend thee, pluck it out, and cast *it* from thee: it is better for thee to enter into life with one eye, rather than having two eyes to be cast into hell fire.

10 ¶Take heed that ye despise not one of these little ones; for I say unto you, That in heaven their angels do always behold the face of my Father which is in heaven.

11 For the Son of man is come to save that which was lost.

12 How think ye? if a man have an hundred sheep, and one of them be gone astray, doth he not leave the ninety and nine, and goeth into the mountains, and seeketh that which is gone astray?

13 And if so be that he find it, verily I say unto you, he rejoiceth more of that *sheep*, than of the ninety and nine which went not astray.

14 Even so it is not the will of your Father which is in heaven, that one of these little ones should perish.

15 ¶Moreover if thy brother shall trespass against thee, go and tell him his fault between thee and him alone: if he shall hear thee, thou hast gained thy brother.

16 But if he will not hear *thee, then* take with thee one or two more, that in the mouth of two or three witnesses every word may be established.

17 And if he shall neglect to hear them, tell *it* unto the church: but if he neglect to hear the church, let him be unto thee as an heathen man and a publican.

18 Verily I say unto you, Whatsoever ye shall bind on earth shall be bound in heaven: and whatsoever ye shall loose on earth shall be loosed in heaven.

19 Again I say unto you, That if two of you shall agree on earth as touching any thing that they shall ask, it shall be done for them of my Father which is in heaven.

20 For where two or three are gathered together in my name, there am I in the midst of them.

21 ¶Then came Peter to him, and said, Lord, how oft shall my brother sin against me, and I forgive him? till seven times?

8-14. Verses 8-9 repeat the same ideas as in the Sermon on the Mount (see note on 5:29-30). The **hand, eye, foot** are not the real source of temptation nor are they the real cause of offending others. Just as temptation arises from within, so does offending others and being offended. It should be noted that this message is dealing with both aspects of the problem. We are most likely to offend others when we are selfish and proud. At the same time, however, we are also most likely to be offended when we are selfish and proud. The reference to **their angels** (vs. 10) supports the idea of individual guardian angels for believers (not all children, in general) (see also Heb 1:14). Verse 11, while legitimate in Luke 19:10, seems to be inserted here, since the more reliable texts omit it. The truth of the statement, however, is reinforced throughout Scripture. Salvation is not just a privilege to be enjoyed by the elect, but is also to be shared with the lost that they too may be saved. Thus, it is not the Father's **will** . . . that any of these "little ones" **should perish.** The immediate context in Matthew relates "little ones" to believers but the cross reference in Luke 15:3-7 clearly refers to lost sheep. Thus, we may conclude that it is not the ultimate wish (or desire) of God that anyone perish. While God permits man to perish in his unbelief, He does not reprobate him to such condemnation against his will. Rather, all of heaven **rejoiceth** over every lost sheep which is saved. The contrast of the imminent danger to the lost sheep and the safety of those in the fold (of faith) clearly expresses where the majority of our attention and concentration should be in the ministry and activity of the church as we fulfill our commission to the world.

b. Church discipline. 18:15-35.

The setting of these verses fits into the context of church discipline. If a church member offends someone or refuses to forgive someone, what must be done? Three basic views have been given here for the synagogue or the church (Gr *ekklēsia*). In either case the action is the same. The responsibility of action is threefold: (1) personal, "go and tell him"; (2) "two or three witnesses"; (3) corporate, "tell it to the church."

15-18. Tell him his fault means to honestly express the point of offense. This should not be done in vindictive anger, but it must be done in straightforward honesty. To fail to speak up is to be dishonest and will lead to harboring continued bitterness. The last phrase of verse 16 is taken from Deuteronomy 19:15, substantially from the LXX. This just and sensible principle of the Mosaic law is thus brought over by our Lord into the New Testament and established for the advantage of the Christian church. **Neglect,** better, "refuse," **as a heathen man and a publican,** i.e., as those who would not be admitted into the church. The obstinate sinner is to be cut off, at least temporarily, from Christian fellowship. Examples of this are to be found in I Corinthians 5:4-5 and I Timothy 1:20. The promise is here addressed to all the disciples.

19-20. Verse 19 is one of the great Gospel promises with regard to prayer. But note the close connection of the verse with those that precede and that which follows. The promise is specifically given to a gathering of disciples with Christ **in the midst** (vs. 20), called to discipline an erring brother (vs. 17). Their authority to do this is restated (vs. 18) and the promise can be claimed because they are acting on behalf of the Father, in the name of the Son. **In my name,** i.e., claiming and using My authority. Notice that the church in view here is operating in the future, in Christ's absence but by His authority.

21-22. All this teaching on forgiveness seemed overwhelming to the disciples, thus prompting Peter's question: **Lord, how oft shall my brother sin against me?** Peter wrongly assumed that **seven times** were ample to forgive anyone. Jesus responded that

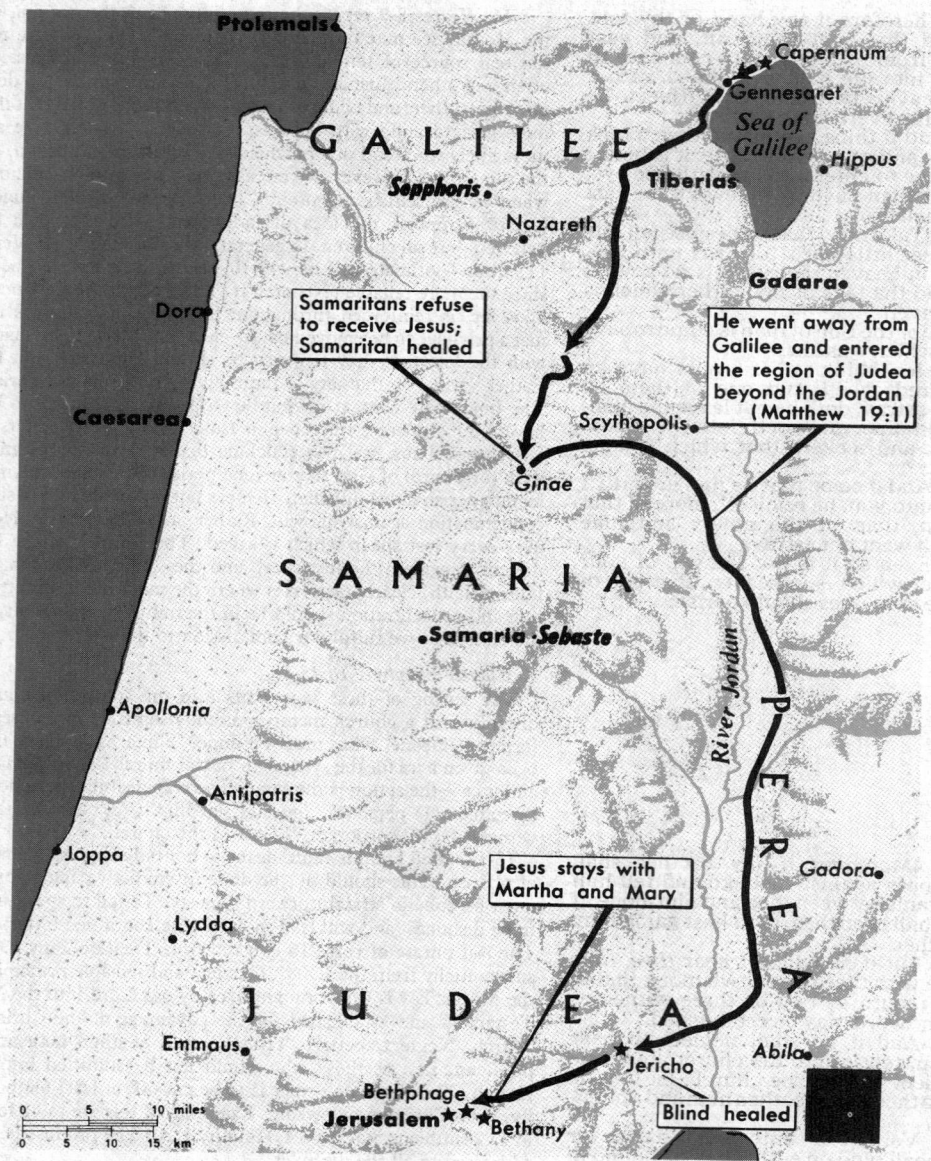

Jesus' Last Journey to Jerusalem

Map labels:
Ptolemais
Capernaum
Gennesaret
GALILEE
Sea of Galilee
Hippus
Sepphoris
Tiberias
Nazareth
Gadara
Dora
Samaritans refuse to receive Jesus; Samaritan healed
He went away from Galilee and entered the region of Judea beyond the Jordan (Matthew 19:1)
Caesarea
Scythopolis
Ginae
SAMARIA
Samaria · Sebaste
River Jordan
P E R E A
Apollonia
Antipatris
Joppa
Gadora
Jesus stays with Martha and Mary
Lydda
J U D E A
Emmaus
Abila
Jericho
Bethphage
Jerusalem
Bethany
Blind healed
0 5 10 miles
0 5 10 15 km

22 Jesus saith unto him, I say not unto thee, Until seven times: but, Until seventy times seven.

23 ¶Therefore is the kingdom of heaven likened unto a certain king, which would take account of his servants.

24 And when he had begun to reckon, one was brought unto him, which owed him ten thousand talents.

25 But forasmuch as he had not to pay, his lord commanded him to be sold, and his wife, and children, and all that he had, and payment to be made.

seven was not only insufficient but that one should forgive **seventy times seven**, in other words, unlimited forgiveness must characterize the true disciple, not retaliatory listing of others' offenses in an attitude of limited forgiveness.

23-27. The Parable of the Unforgiving Servant (vss. 23-25) was used by Jesus to reinforce the power and importance of the principle of forgiveness. **A certain king** represents God, the sovereign Father (cf. vs. 35), to whom the debt is owed. The **one** who **owed him** is a servant or satrap who had access to the king's money, and represents the individual sinner. **Ten thousand talents** was an insurmountable debt equivalent to millions of dollars in our society. It represents the debt of sin which the sinner cannot possibly pay by himself. The command that he be **sold . . . and payment to be made** indicates his being

26 The servant therefore fell down, and worshipped him, saying, Lord, have patience with me, and I will pay thee all.

27 Then the lord of that servant was moved with compassion, and loosed him, and forgave him the debt.

28 But the same servant went out, and found one of his fellowservants, which owed him an hundred pence: and he laid hands on him, and took *him* by the throat, saying, Pay me that thou owest.

29 And his fellowservant fell down at his feet, and besought him, saying, Have patience with me, and I will pay thee all.

30 And he would not: but went and cast him into prison, till he should pay the debt.

31 So when his fellowservants saw what was done, they were very sorry, and came and told unto their lord all that was done.

32 Then his lord, after that he had called him, said unto him, O thou wicked servant, I forgave thee all that debt, because thou desiredst me:

33 Shouldest not thou also have had compassion on thy fellowservant, even as I had pity on thee?

34 And his lord was wroth, and delivered him to the tormentors, till he should pay all that was due unto him.

35 So likewise shall my heavenly Father do also unto you, if ye from your hearts forgive not every one his brother their trespasses.

CHAPTER 19

AND it came to pass, *that* when Jesus had finished these sayings, he departed from Galilee, and came into the coasts of Judæa beyond Jordan;

2 And great multitudes followed him; and he healed them there.

3 ¶The Pharisees also came unto him, tempting him, and saying unto him, Is it lawful for a man to put away his wife for every cause?

4 And he answered and said unto them, Have ye not read, that he which made *them* at the beginning made them male and female,

5 And said, For this cause shall a man leave father and mother, and shall cleave to his wife: and they twain shall be one flesh?

6 Wherefore they are no more twain, but one flesh. What therefore God hath joined together, let not man put asunder.

placed in a debtor's prison. However, an entire lifetime of service could never repay such a debt. The interpreter must stick to the main point of the parable and not be sidetracked by its minor details. The **compassion** of the king releases him and forgives (cancels) the **debt.** The picture illustrates God's total forgiveness when dealing with our sins at the point of salvation. The debt has been paid by Christ and we are set free from it forever!

28-35. The contrast in verse 28, where the **same servant** is unwilling to forgive his fellow servant a debt of **a hundred pence** (about ten dollars) is deliberately presented as a hideous hypothetical situation. As unbelievable as this action would be, that is how unbelievable it would be for a Christian disciple, who has been forgiven a lifetime of sin, to be unforgiving of others. In the story, such an unforgiving servant is called a **wicked servant** because no true believer would do such. The unforgiving servant is not one who was saved and then lost his salvation. The story is merely hypothetical; no one forgiven a debt of millions would behave this way; therefore, the intention of the parable is to challenge the genuineness of the disciples' conversion. A truly saved man would never behave like the man in the story, who was delivered to the **tormentors** (Gr *basanistēs*, meaning "torturers" or "jailers"). This is certainly not a reference to purgatory. One behaving in this manner falls into the condemnation of the lost. The searching threat of verse 35 does not mean that a true believer will be lost, but if he claims to be born of God, he will act like a born-again person. True forgiveness "from the heart" of a regenerate man is one of the true signs of genuine salvation and conversion (cf. Eph 4:32). Saved people are both forgiven and forgiving. Unforgiving people prove that they have never been born of God.

B. In Judaea. 19:1-27:66.

1. His presentation as King. 19:1-25:46.

a. His journey to Jerusalem. 19:1-20:34.

(1). Jesus' teaching on divorce 19:1-12.

19:1-2. Verse 1 of chapter 19 indicates the close of another division of the gospel (see 7:28). With verse 2 it describes very briefly a journey from Galilee into the district of Judaea **beyond Jordan** (i.e., Peraea) which must have taken considerable time and into which the events of Luke 19:51-18:34 must largely be fitted. The teaching and incidents which follow in 9:3-20:34 also took place during the stay in Peraea. During the various movements on the way to Jerusalem, Matthew presents a varied series of events: Jesus' teaching on divorce, the confrontation with the rich young ruler, a parable, and a miracle.

3-6. The **Pharisees** came **tempting** him with a difficult question. They wanted to test His wisdom with one of the most controversial questions of their day and Jesus proved far superior to their expectations. **Is it lawful** they asked to challenge His interpretation of Mosaic law in Deuteronomy 24:1-5, where a "bill of divorcement" was allowed. The more strict school of Shammai held that divorce was lawful only upon a wife's shameful conduct; whereas, the more liberal school of Hillel gave the widest possible allowances for divorce. Kent (p. 67) is correct when he explains: "Thus Jesus was being asked, 'Do you agree with the most prevalent interpretation?' (Hillel's)." By asking **Have ye not read,** Jesus refers them back to God's original purpose in creation that they be **one flesh.** The passage in Genesis 2:24 indicates that being one flesh is one "person," and is not to be limited to sexual union. The Bible clearly indicates that sexual union does not itself constitute marriage, which is fundamentally a covenantal agreement between two partners for life (cf. Prov 2:17; Mal 2:14, "wife of thy covenant").

7 They say unto him, Why did Moses then command to give a writing of divorcement, and to put her away?

8 He saith unto them, Moses because of the hardness of your hearts suffered you to put away your wives: but from the beginning it was not so.

9 And I say unto you, Whosoever shall put away his wife, except it be for fornication, and shall marry another, committeth adultery: and whoso marrieth her which is put away doth commit adultery.

10 ¶His disciples say unto him, If the case of the man be so with his wife, it is not good to marry.

11 But he said unto them, All men cannot receive this saying, save they to whom it is given.

12 For there are some eunuchs, which were so born from their mother's womb: and there are some eunuchs, which were made eunuchs of men: and there be eunuchs, which have made themselves eunuchs for the kingdom of heaven's sake. He that is able to receive it, let him receive it.

13 ¶Then were there brought unto him little children, that he should put his hands on them, and pray: and the disciples rebuked them.

14 But Jesus said, Suffer little children, and forbid them not, to come unto me: for of such is the kingdom of heaven.

15 And he laid his hands on them, and departed thence.

16 ¶And, behold, one came and said unto him, Good Master, what good thing shall I do, that I may have eternal life?

17 And he said unto him, Why callest thou me good? there is none good but one, that is, God: but if thou wilt enter into life, keep the commandments.

7-9. The question **Why did Moses then command . . . ?** revealed the misuse of Deuteronomy 24 by the Jews of Jesus' day. Moses did not command, he permitted divorce. God had instituted marriage in the Garden of Eden. He is not the Author of divorce; man is its originator. However, to protect the Hebrew woman from being taken advantage of by a verbal divorce, Moses commanded that it be done with a **writing of divorcement,** i.e., official written contract, permitting remarriage. The Jews tended to take this as an excuse or license to get divorced whenever they pleased. The original provision was for the protection of the wife from an evil husband, not an authorization for him to divorce her at will. Therefore, Jesus gave one exception to the no-divorce intention of God, **for fornication** (Gr *porneia*) "sexual sins," not to be limited to premarital sex only, but it includes all types of sexual sin: adultery, homosexuality, bestiality, etc. Among the Jews only the male could divorce, so Mark 10:12 reverses the statement for His gentile audience.

10-12. Since divorce, on any grounds, was common in those days (cf. rabbinical literature) the disciples felt **it is not good to marry.** The severity of Jesus' statement was in total contrast to the society of that day and represented the true intention of God. While divorce appears to be allowed in both Testaments (cf. Deut 24:1-5; I Cor 7:15, 27-28) it is never encouraged because it always violates God's original intention in marriage. Jesus' reply, **All men cannot receive this saying,** indicates that some are called to be married and remain married; others (who cannot receive this) are called to be single (never to marry). If God calls you to be married, He will enable you to remain married. On the other hand, some are called to be single and never marry **for the kingdom of heaven's sake.** A **eunuch** was a person who never married and often served as a royal official. Some were **so born,** due to physical or mental deficiency; some were **made eunuchs of men,** either by choice or by force; some had deliberately chosen to be single for the purpose of serving God without being tied to regular family responsibilities (e.g., Origen). Unfortunately the early church began to take this statement to mean that it was more spiritual to be single than to be married, and eventually celibacy became legislation within the Roman Catholic Church. The single life is not to be forced on anyone. Those who are called to it are able to **receive it** (i.e., accept) gladly.

(2). The rich young ruler. 19:13-30

13-17. Much assimilation from the parallel accounts in Mark 10:17-31 and Luke 18:18-30 has been done in some texts; see ASV for a better rendition of Matthew's original. The **little children,** for whom Jesus cared so much, were evidently of sufficient age to repond to Him (not infants) and He bade them **come unto me** revealing that, while all childhood professions may not be genuine, a child may follow Christ. By contrast to their simple obedience came the complex young rich man with all of his "hangups," calling Jesus **Good Master,** which the Saviour challenged, not as a denial of His deity, but to impress upon this seeker the seriousness of the implication. "Are you sure you really mean that?" would be a modern paraphrase. The young man's question, **What good thing shall I do?** implies that he wanted to perform some work that might gain him **eternal life** (salvation). Jesus' challenge was intended to elevate his concept of "good." The glib comment "good master" is followed by a request for something "good" that he may do to gain heaven. Jesus' concept of good was that which is divine. Therefore, only an act of God could grant eternal life. The Master's reply, **If thou wilt enter into life,** implies that the young man was still on the outside of such life.

The idea is this, if you want to gain eternal life, you must first of all enter it! The imperative **keep the commandments** (vs. 17) was intended to hit his point of pride, i.e. self-righteousness. Jesus did not believe that mere outward keeping of the commandments of the law brought anyone salvation. He had already told Nicodemus earlier that he must be born again (cf. Rom 3:20; Gal 2:16). Why, then, did He tell this young man to keep the commandments? The rest of the story reveals the answer. Jesus will go to great lengths now to show him that he has not kept the commandments and, therefore, is in need of God's grace.

18-22. This list of commands in verse 18 centers on outward duties, rather than inward nature, which was the young man's real problem. He protested that he had kept these outward demands. Jesus then revealed his real weakness. The law had been summarized earlier by our Lord: "Love the Lord thy God, with all thy heart" and "love thy neighbor as thyself." Herein was the young man's real failure. His self-centered wealth and luxurious self-righteousness had blinded him to his real weakness. To expose this Jesus ordered, **go and sell** all your possessions **and give to the poor . . . and come . . . follow me** (vs. 21). This he would not do and went away **sorrowful** (grieved). What had Jesus done? Simply, He had shown him that he had not kept the commandments at all. He loved himself more than his neighbor (the poor) and he loved his possessions more than God (follow me). This passage teaches the seriousness of true discipleship, but it in no way teaches the average man that he must sell his possessions in order to be a Christian, or even a good one.

18 He saith unto him, Which? Jesus said, Thou shalt do no murder, Thou shalt not commit adultery, Thou shalt not steal, Thou shalt not bear false witness,
19 Honour thy father and *thy* mother: and, Thou shalt love thy neighbour as thyself.
20 The young man saith unto him, All these things have I kept from my youth up: what lack I yet?
21 Jesus said unto him, If thou wilt be perfect, go *and* sell that thou hast, and give to the poor, and thou shalt have treasure in heaven: and come *and* follow me.
22 But when the young man heard that saying, he went away sorrowful: for he had great possessions.

23-26. The further comment, **That a rich man shall hardly enter into the kingdom of heaven** shocked the disciples (note verse 25, "Who then can be saved?") who accepted the common notion of the day that the rich were blessed of God and therefore certainly saved. To correct that misunderstanding, Jesus explained the human difficulty for the rich to be converted. **Hardly** (Gr *dyskolōs*) implies with extreme difficulty, though not hopeless. The illustration of a **camel** going through the **eye of a needle** has been interpreted as a camel hair rope going through a needle; or an actual camel squeezing through a small gate, "the eye of a needle," next to the main gate at Jerusalem; or the absolute impossibility of a literal camel (Palestine's largest animal) literally going through a tiny needle's eye. The latter usage is most likely, following a similar Talmudic proverb about an elephant. Note, that they were not in Jerusalem at this time and that the first two suggestions, while very difficult, were within the realm of possibility, whereas the salvation of the rich is called humanly **impossible** (vs. 26). In fact, all human nature is incapable of saving itself and must rely on God's efficacious grace for that which is humanly impossible to become **all things . . . possible** with God. The salvation of a rich sinner is just as miraculous as the salvation of a poor sinner. Both are only possible with God!

23 ¶Then said Jesus unto his disciples, Verily I say unto you, That a rich man shall hardly enter into the kingdom of heaven.
24 And again I say unto you, It is easier for a camel to go through the eye of a needle, than for a rich man to enter into the kingdom of God.
25 When his disciples heard *it*, they were exceedingly amazed, saying, Who then can be saved?
26 But Jesus beheld *them*, and said unto them, With men this is impossible; but with God all things are possible.

27-30. Peter's response, **we have forsaken all . . . what shall we have?** was most ill-timed and certainly reflected a selfish motivation which would have to go. Nevertheless, Jesus answered the question. **In the regeneration** (Gr *palinggenesia*) refers to the renewed world of the future, the kingdom of righteousness which is yet to come: "the new heavens and the new earth." While the term is used for individual rebirth in Titus 3:5, here it looks to the future millennial kingdom where the apostles will judge **Israel** (literally). Forsaking earthly benefits will bring a **hundredfold** blessing and **everlasting life**. Yet, while rewards will be abundant, attitudes are still crucial and **many** who would be **first** shall be **last** and the **last shall be first**. On the believer's rewards see W. Kroll, *It Will Be Worth It All.*

27 ¶Then answered Peter and said unto him, Behold, we have forsaken all, and followed thee; what shall we have therefore?
28 And Jesus said unto them, Verily I say unto you, That ye which have followed me, in the regeneration when the Son of man shall sit in the throne of his glory, ye also shall sit upon twelve thrones, judging the twelve tribes of Israel.
29 And every one that hath forsaken houses, or brethren, or sisters, or father, or mother, or wife, or children, or lands, for my name's sake, shall receive an hundredfold, and shall inherit everlasting life.
30 But many *that are* first shall be last; and the last *shall be* first.

CHAPTER 20

FOR the kingdom of heaven is like unto a man *that is* an householder, which went out early in the morning to hire labourers into his vineyard.

2 And when he had agreed with the labourers for a penny a day, he sent them into his vineyard.

3 And he went out about the third hour, and saw others standing idle in the marketplace,

4 And said unto them; Go ye also into the vineyard, and whatsoever is right I will give you. And they went their way.

5 Again he went out about the sixth and ninth hour, and did likewise.

6 And about the eleventh hour he went out, and found others standing idle, and saith unto them, Why stand ye here all the day idle?

7 They say unto him, Because no man hath hired us. He saith unto them, Go ye also into the vineyard; and whatsoever is right, *that* shall ye receive.

8 So when even was come, the lord of the vineyard saith unto his steward, Call the labourers, and give them *their* hire, beginning from the last unto the first.

9 And when they came that *were hired* about the eleventh hour, they received every man a penny.

10 But when the first came, they supposed that they should have received more; and they likewise received every man a penny.

11 And when they had received *it*, they murmured against the goodman of the house,

12 Saying, These last have wrought *but* one hour, and thou hast made them equal unto us, which have borne the burden and heat of the day.

13 But he answered one of them, and said, Friend, I do thee no wrong: didst not thou agree with me for a penny?

14 Take *that* thine *is*, and go thy way: I will give unto this last, even as unto thee.

15 Is it not lawful for me to do what I will with mine own? Is thine eye evil, because I am good?

16 So the last shall be first, and the first last: for many be called, but few chosen.

17 ¶And Jesus going up to Jerusalem took the twelve disciples apart in the way, and said unto them,

18 Behold, we go up to Jerusalem: and the Son of man shall be betrayed unto the chief priests and unto the scribes, and they shall condemn him to death,

19 And shall deliver him to the Gen-

(3). The Parable of the Laborers. 20:1-16.

20:1-14. This parable reinforced Jesus' teaching regarding true Christian service and riches. The **householder** is Christ Himself, the Master of the **vineyard,** the field of labor (service to the world through His church). **Early in the morning,** the first workers were hired at dawn. **A penny** (Gr *denarion*) represents a denarius, or a common day's wage. **Others standing idle in the market place** were not lazy but were in the common place of seeking employment. From this unemployed group, the householder hired additional workers at 9 A.M., noon, 3 P.M., and 5 P.M. The pay scale will be **whatsoever is right,** indicating Christ's justice to His laborers. **When even** (evening) **was come,** i.e., at the end of the day, every man was paid the same wage. Therefore, the first hired laborers **murmured against the goodman.** However, he reminded them that he had been just in paying them that for which they bargained. The statement, **I will give unto this last even as unto thee,** is Jesus' interpretation of the "last shall be first and the first last" (vs. 16). There is here, perhaps, a sweeping view of church history, in which those working in the last hour are promised equal blessing to His original disciples. Thus, Jesus warns against jealousy and impurity of motive in serving Him.

15-16. Verse 15 shows that, everything being of grace, God has the right to give or withhold at will. We must take care that this goodness of God does not provoke us to complaint. The point of verse 16 is that all Christians receive the same, the reward being everlasting life given on the ground of Christ's death for them. By earthly standards of judgment, expressed clearly in verses 11 and 12, such action is regarded as putting the last first and the first last. **For many be called, but few chosen** refers to the general call of the gospel and the efficacious call of grace. He speaks of the difficulty that many experience in believing and obeying the gospel because their minds are fixed on what they can get for themselves, whether in this world or the next.

(4). The coming suffering of Christ and His disciples. 20:17-28.

17-28. See Mark 10:32-34; Luke 18:31-34. The journey to Jerusalem is now resumed after the stay in Peraea. As the final events of His life draw nearer, our Lord again seeks to enlighten His disciples. Again they failed to understand, as is evidenced by the request of Zebedee's sons which immediately followed. But the fulfillment of these detailed predictions would strengthen their faith when the time came. **Zebedee's children.** From Matthew 4:21 we know that the two sons were the apostles

tiles to mock, and to scourge, and to crucify *him*: and the third day he shall rise again.

20 ¶Then came to him the mother of Zĕb'e-dee's children with her sons, worshipping *him*, and desiring a certain thing of him.

21 And he said unto her, What wilt thou? She saith unto him, Grant that these my two sons may sit, the one on thy right hand, and the other on the left, in thy kingdom.

22 But Jesus answered and said, Ye know not what ye ask. Are ye able to drink of the cup that I shall drink of, and to be baptized with the baptism that I am baptized with? They say unto him, We are able.

23 And he saith unto them, Ye shall drink indeed of my cup, and be baptized with the baptism that I am baptized with: but to sit on my right hand, and on my left, is not mine to give, but *it shall be given to them* for whom it is prepared of my Father.

24 And when the ten heard *it*, they were moved with indignation against the two brethren.

25 But Jesus called them *unto him*, and said, Ye know that the princes of the Gentiles exercise dominion over them, and they that are great exercise authority upon them.

26 But it shall not be so among you: but whosoever will be great among you, let him be your minister;

27 And whosoever will be chief among you, let him be your servant:

28 Even as the Son of man came not to be ministered unto, but to minister, and to give his life a ransom for many.

29 ¶And as they departed from Jericho, a great multitude followed him.

30 And, behold, two blind men sitting by the way side, when they heard that Jesus passed by, cried out, saying, Have mercy on us, O Lord, *thou* son of David.

31 And the multitude rebuked them, because they should hold their peace: but they cried the more, saying, Have mercy on us, O Lord, *thou* son of David.

32 And Jesus stood still, and called them, and said, What will ye that I shall do unto you?

33 They say unto him, Lord, that our eyes may be opened.

34 So Jesus had compassion *on them*, and touched their eyes: and immediately their eyes received sight, and they followed him.

CHAPTER 21

AND when they drew nigh unto Jerusalem, and were come to Bĕth'pha-gē, unto the mount of Olives, then sent Jesus two disciples,

2 Saying unto them, Go into the village over against you, and straightway

James and John. **Grant,** better, "command." The request and the indignation of the others which followed show that the disciples were still thinking in terms of the setting up of an earthly kingdom, in spite of the clear prediction of suffering and death which our Lord had just made. Some texts omit the last part of our Lord's question in verse 22 and it may have been inserted from the parallel passage in Mark 10:38. The same is true of verse 23. The cup and the baptism both refer, of course, to our Lord's suffering and death. **To be ministered unto.** It is not wrong to accept ministry. Christ accepted it. But it was not the purpose of His life and should not be the purpose of ours. **His life** (Gr *psychē*) literally "his soul." **A ransom.** This important phrase provides one of the few occasions on which the doctrine of substitutionary atonement is mentioned in the Synoptic Gospels. It implies a price paid for the deliverance of captives. The price lay in the necessity for His life to be laid down. His life thus became the cost of our redemption. **Many** does not necessarily restrict the extent of His death (as contrasted to "all"), but it does indicate that not all would receive His offer of salvation.

(5). *The healing of the two blind men. 20:29-34.*

29-34. See parallel accounts in Mark 10:46-52; Luke 18:35-43. The problems of harmonization prohibit any suggestion of "collusion" (Kent, p. 71). Luke places this event on the approach to the city, whereas, Mark and Matthew state **as they departed from Jericho** (vs. 29). In actuality there were two Jerichos. The Roman city lay about a mile east of Herod's winter headquarters (also called Jericho) where the wealthy friends of the Herodian family lived near the palace and fortress. The healing of the blind man, evidently, took place while Jesus was going from one city to the other. Luke's attention would be on the Herodian city, for his next recorded event, the calling of Zacchaeus, took place there. **Two blind men** are mentioned by Matthew, while the other synoptists refer to only the more prominent Bartimaeus. Rebuked by the crowd, they cry the louder, **thou son of David,** a messianic title, earlier avoided by Jesus in public, but now accepted as He approaches Jerusalem. The miracle of restoring their sight was so total that afterwards even **they followed him.** What a contrast! The rich young ruler rejects Him for worldly possessions; His own disciples argue over who will be the greatest; the laborers in the parable murmur. Yet, now two transformed blind beggars gladly follow Him! Of such is the kingdom of heaven!

b. *His joyful (triumphal) entry. 21:1-46.*

(1). *The messianic arrival at Jerusalem. 21:1-11.*

21:1-9. This event is traditionally known as the "Triumphal Entry," in which Jesus officially offers Himself to the nation of Israel as her long-awaited Messiah. However, in many ways it is far from a triumph, for the day ends in Jesus' public prediction of His rejection by His own people (see Mk 11:1-10; Lk 19:29-

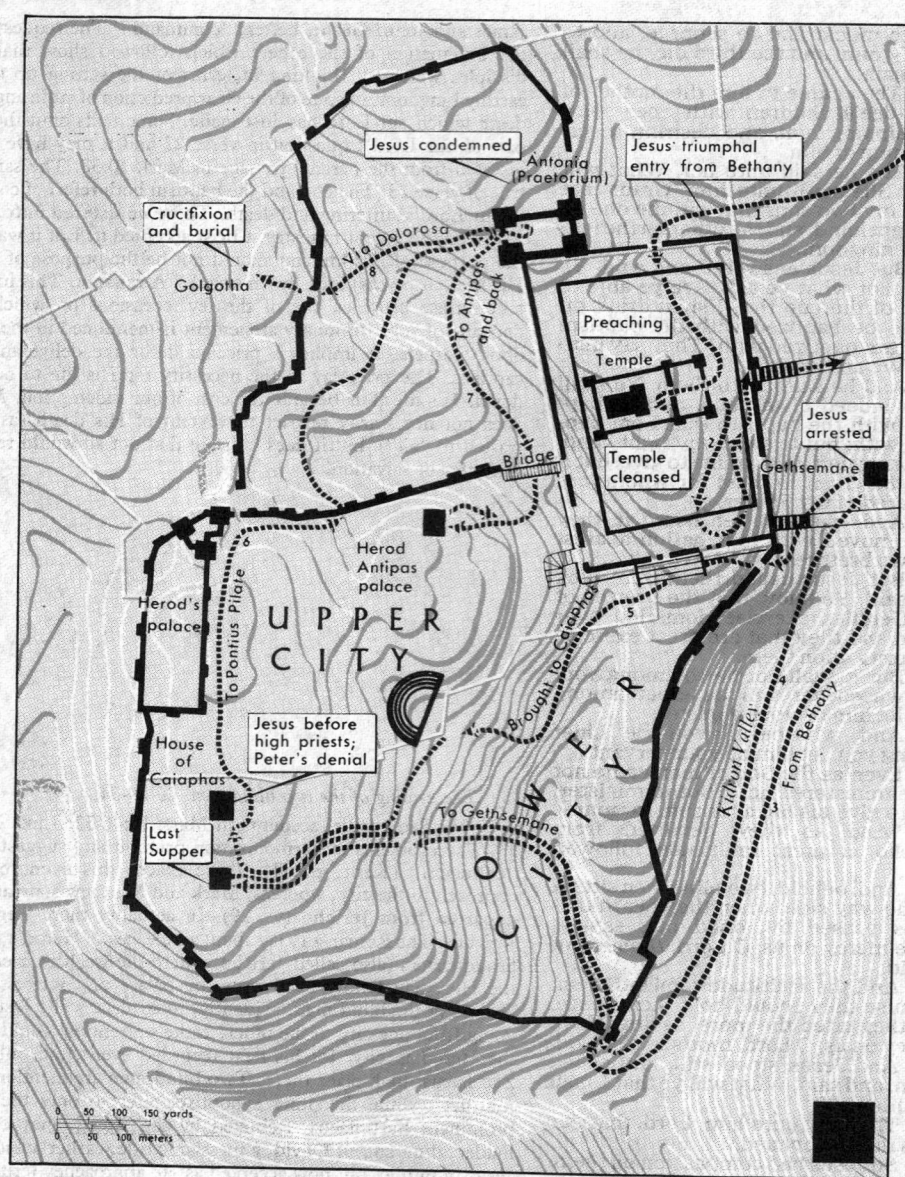

Jesus' Trial, Judgment and Crucifixion

ye shall find an ass tied, and a colt with her: loose *them*, and bring *them* unto me.

3 And if any *man* say ought unto you, ye shall say, The Lord hath need of them; and straightway he will send them.

4 All this was done, that it might be fulfilled which was spoken by the prophet, saying,

5 Tell ye the daughter of Sion, Behold, thy King cometh unto thee, meek, and sitting upon an ass, and a colt the foal of an ass.

39; Jn 12:12-15). **Bethphage** was a village near Bethany, about a mile east of Jerusalem and apparently hidden from it by the summit of the Mount of Olives, which was the hill on the east of Jerusalem. **The Lord hath need of them.** The account of these closing events in our Lord's life shows that there were men and women in Jerusalem and its neighborhood who recognized Jesus as Lord. They may have become disciples during the earlier Jerusalem ministry described by John. The quotation in verse 5 is a combination of Isaiah 62:11 and Zechariah 9:9, taken substantially from the LXX. **Thereon,** that is, on the clothes. **Hosanna** is the transliteration of a Hebrew term meaning "please save," and occurs in II Samuel 14:4 and Psalm 118:25.

6 And the disciples went, and did as Jesus commanded them,

7 And brought the ass, and the colt, and put on them their clothes, and they set *him* thereon.

8 And a very great multitude spread their garments in the way; others cut down branches from the trees, and strawed *them* in the way.

9 And the multitudes that went before, and that followed, cried, saying, Hosanna to the son of David: Blessed *is* he that cometh in the name of the Lord; Hosanna in the highest.

10 ¶And when he was come into Jerusalem, all the city was moved, saying, Who is this?

11 And the multitude said, This is Jesus the prophet of Nazareth of Galilee.

12 ¶And Jesus went into the temple of God, and cast out all them that sold and bought in the temple, and overthrew the tables of the moneychangers, and the seats of them that sold doves,

13 And said unto them, It is written, My house shall be called the house of prayer; but ye have made it a den of thieves.

14 And the blind and the lame came to him in the temple; and he healed them.

15 And when the chief priests and scribes saw the wonderful things that he did, and the children crying in the temple, and saying, Hosanna to the son of David; they were sore displeased,

16 And said unto him, Hearest thou what these say? And Jesus saith unto them, Yea; have ye never read, Out of the mouth of babes and sucklings thou hast perfected praise?

17 And he left them, and went out of the city into Bethany; and he lodged there.

18 ¶Now in the morning as he returned into the city, he hungered.

19 And when he saw a fig tree in the way, he came to it, and found nothing thereon, but leaves only, and said unto it, Let no fruit grow on thee henceforward for ever. And presently the fig tree withered away.

20 And when the disciples saw *it*, they marvelled, saying, How soon is the fig tree withered away!

21 Jesus answered and said unto them, Verily I say unto you, If ye have faith, and doubt not, ye shall not only do this which is done to the fig tree, but also if ye shall say unto this mountain,

From the following verse of this Psalm the acclamation **Blessed is he that cometh in the name of the Lord** is taken.

10-11. In verses 10 and 11 there is a contrast between the men of **the city,** who were ignorant of our Lord's identity, and the **multitude** who were able to answer their question. There were probably many Galileans in the latter who had come up for the feast and who already knew our Lord through His preaching and healing ministry in the north. In Jewish history and tradition the quoted Psalm was considered a messianic royal psalm and the riding of an ass's colt (not a horse) marked the official entry of the king (see A. Edersheim, *Life and Times of Jesus the Messiah*, II, p. 736).

(2). The cleansing of the Temple. 21:12-17.

12-17. See Mark 11:15-19; Luke 19:45-47. A similar cleansing is recorded at the beginning of Jesus' ministry (cf. Jn 2:13-22), indicating His disdain for the corruption of organized religion which lacked purity of life and the power of God. Such a violent move was not to provoke a revolution, as such, but to bring about a true spiritual conviction. In light of the seriousness of what He had come to do, Jesus could not tolerate such gross perversion of **the temple,** i.e., the whole temple area on Mount Moriah including all the precincts and courts. Note that some texts omit the words **of God. Money changers.** Temple dues could be paid only in sacred coinage, and it was necessary to change one's money. The selling of doves was, of course, for purposes of sacrifice. This exchange became a source of extortion for the High Priest's family who personally controlled it. In reality, it amounted to a public bazaar. **It is written.** In his condemnation, our Lord quotes from the LXX of Isaiah 56:7 and Jeremiah 7:11. **They were sore displeased.** It was not just our Lord's popularity that angered them; the title "Son of David" which the children kept calling out implied messiahship. The cavils of the enemy were stilled, however, by the children's praise, as is suggested by the context of the psalm from which our Lord quotes (Ps 8:2). **Bethany** was a village on the eastern shoulder of the Mount of Olives, a little more than a mile east of Jerusalem. It was the home of Lazarus and his sisters.

(3). The cursing of the barren fig tree. 21:18-22.

18-22. See also Mark 11:12-14, 20-26. **The fig tree** fruit generally appears in February, followed by leaves, which are not formed until late spring. Thus, there should normally have been some fruit on the tree. The fig tree was often used as a symbol of the nation of Israel (cf. Hos 9:10; Joel 1:7) and while Jesus literally came upon a barren fig tree, He used the incident to fully illustrate Israel's desperate condition. The curse **Let no fruit grow . . . for ever** resulted in the almost immediate withering of the entire tree. While trees are non-moral, they, like all of nature, are subject to the word of Christ. The **disciples . . . marveled** at how this could happen so fast. Notice, that none of them questioned the morality of this incident, as have misguided modern commentators (cf. Kee, p. 636). Jesus told them how to do such astounding things: **Have faith** or absolute confidence in the power of God. The removal of the **mountain** may indicate

Be thou removed, and be thou cast into the sea; it shall be done.

22 And all things, whatsoever ye shall ask in prayer, believing, ye shall receive.

23 ¶And when he was come into the temple, the chief priests and the elders of the people came unto him as he was teaching, and said, By what authority doest thou these things? and who gave thee this authority?

24 And Jesus answered and said unto them, I also will ask you one thing, which if ye tell me, I in like wise will tell you by what authority I do these things.

25 The baptism of John, whence was it? from heaven, or of men? And they reasoned with themselves, saying, If we shall say, From heaven; he will say unto us, Why did ye not then believe him?

26 But if we shall say, Of men; we fear the people; for all hold John as a prophet.

27 And they answered Jesus, and said, We cannot tell. And he said unto them, Neither tell I you by what authority I do these things.

28 ¶But what think ye? A certain man had two sons; and he came to the first, and said, Son, go work to day in my vineyard.

29 He answered and said, I will not: but afterward he repented, and went.

30 And he came to the second, and said likewise. And he answered and said, I go, sir: and went not.

31 Whether of them twain did the will of his father? They say unto him, The first. Jesus saith unto them, Verily I say unto you, That the publicans and the harlots go into the kingdom of God before you.

32 For John came unto you in the way of righteousness, and ye believed him not; but the publicans and the harlots

eliminating obstacles to giving the gospel to the Gentiles. Such appears to be the most likely meaning of the entire incident. Israel is the fruitless fig tree and the Gentiles are the mountain which shall be moved for God by the power of prayer.

(4). The question of authority. 21:23-46.

23. On Jesus' third day of successive visits to the **temple** (i.e., Herod's temple) His authority was challenged by the ever-threatened **chief priests** (Stagg, p. 201), including the High Priest, who was also president of the Sanhedrin, and **elders,** who were laymen or scribes and also served as members of the Jewish high court. In their own view, they were attempting to protect their laws and traditions against one who appeared to be a usurper who reinterpreted the law, rejected tradition and overthrew the moneychangers. Jesus had spoken with authority on matters which they considered their responsibility. Jesus did not challenge their right to question Him, but their hypocrisy and insincerity in such questioning.

They asked **By what authority** He had done these controversial things. Knowing that they would never recognize any authority but their own, He refused to answer them. Instead, He asked them about the authority of the **baptism of John,** which they had never officially sanctioned. To acknowledge that it was **from heaven** would be to condemn themselves for not receiving it and to claim it was **of men** (i.e., human origin) would upset the people. Their reply **We cannot tell** was begging the question and brought His clever response: **Neither tell I you by what authority I do these things.**

This incident forms the setting of the all-out attempt by the various religious authorities to expose and humiliate Jesus in chapter 22, which ends in their total frustration and embarrassment. The beauty and dynamics of these incidents reveal Jesus' mental prowess over the greatest minds of Israel. The divine Saviour is a genius, with no human peer. He can stump the Jews, mystify the Romans, and challenge the mind of any mortal man!

24-32. The Parable of the Two Sons (vss. 28-32) follows as an exposé of the hypocrisy of the religious leaders and as a vindication of John's ministry and the true work of God in general. The first son initially said **I will not** go (vs. 29), representing the immoral disobedience of the **publicans** and **harlots** who later **repented** under John and Jesus' preaching. Notice again, the connection between genuine repentance and changed action in verse 29 (repented, and went). No one who truly repents fails to show clear evidence of his inner heart change by his outward obedience. The **second** son promised to go but did not follow through with obedience. Jesus asked, "Which **did the will of his father?**" By answering, **The first,** the religious leaders had condemned themselves. This very effective teaching method is commonly used in the Bible as the juridical parable, whereby the answerer condemns himself by the obviously implied answer (e.g., Nathan's parable to David about the lamb; the Parable of the Good Samaritan, answering the prejudiced question, "Who is my neighbor?"). John had preached the **way of righteousness** (cf. II Pet 2:21) and the leaders had rejected him, even while claiming to be God's obedient servants. Thus, repentant sinners are more ready for the **kingdom of God** than disobedient religious leaders. The MSS support question on the variant reading in the Western Text must be decided in favor of the obvious intention of the parable (cf. discussion in Stagg, p. 202).

believed him: and ye, when ye had seen *it*, repented not afterward, that ye might believe him.

33 ¶Hear another parable: There was a certain householder, which planted a vineyard, and hedged it round about, and digged a winepress in it, and built a tower, and let it out to husbandmen, and went into a far country:

34 And when the time of the fruit drew near, he sent his servants to the husbandmen, that they might receive the fruits of it.

35 And the husbandmen took his servants, and beat one, and killed another, and stoned another.

36 Again, he sent other servants more than the first: and they did unto them likewise.

37 But last of all he sent unto them his son, saying, They will reverence my son.

38 But when the husbandmen saw the son, they said among themselves, This is the heir; come, let us kill him, and let us seize on his inheritance.

39 And they caught him, and cast *him* out of the vineyard, and slew *him*.

40 When the lord therefore of the vineyard cometh, what will he do unto those husbandmen?

41 They say unto him, He will miserably destroy those wicked men, and will let out *his* vineyard unto other husbandmen, which shall render him the fruits in their seasons.

42 Jesus saith unto them, Did ye never read in the scriptures, The stone which the builders rejected, the same is become the head of the corner: this is the Lord's doing, and it is marvellous in our eyes?

43 Therefore say I unto you, The kingdom of God shall be taken from you, and given to a nation bringing forth the fruits thereof.

44 And whosoever shall fall on this stone shall be broken: but on whomsoever it shall fall, it will grind him to powder.

45 And when the chief priests and Pharisees had heard his parables, they perceived that he spake of them.

46 But when they sought to lay hands on him, they feared the multitude, because they took him for a prophet.

CHAPTER 22

AND Jesus answered and spake unto them again by parables, and said,

2 The kingdom of heaven is like unto a certain king, which made a marriage for his son,

3 And sent forth his servants to call them that were bidden to the wedding: and they would not come.

33-39. Jesus quickly gave another parable, the Parable of the Wicked Husbandmen. Again, Jesus makes clear His divine authority by presenting Himself as the Son sent by the Father. The **householder** represents God the Father and the **vineyard** is Israel, a symbol of the theocracy which was familiar to the Jewish leaders (cf. Ps 80:8-16; Isa 5:1-7). The **husbandmen** were the priests and religious leaders and the **far country** is heaven. The anticipated **fruit** represents spiritual evidence of true conversion, which was to be the end result of the work of the husbandmen. Instead, the religion of Israel had degenerated into a formal system for the benefit of the priests who were now more concerned about perpetuating their own interests. The **servants** sent by the owner represent the Old Testament prophets who came to correct religious abuses in the nation and were also rejected by their contemporaries (though venerated by subsequent generations.) **Last of all** indicates that Jesus was God's final emissary to Israel. None has ever appeared since Him and none ever will until the Jews recognize Christ as their final Prophet and Messiah! The desire to kill the rightful heir of the Father had already been expressed by the Jewish leaders (cf. Jn 11:47-53), Jesus clearly foretold His coming rejection and death with the statement **they . . . slew him.**

40-43. Verse 40 represents the condemning question of the judicial parable, **what will he do unto those husbandmen?** Their reply again unwittingly condemned their own attitude of rejection toward Jesus. The **other husbandmen** will become the Gentiles (vs. 43). Jesus quoted Psalm 118:22-23 exactly from the LXX, relating His present rejection to His ultimate triumph (cf. Acts 4:11; I Pet 2:6-7 where the **stone which the builders rejected** is also quoted in relation to Christ). The Sanhedrinists represent the builders of Israel's religion, who rejected the real cornerstone of God, i.e., Jesus the true cornerstone of the foundation of the church, which will be that **nation bringing forth . . . fruits** (cf. I Peter 2:7-9 where the church is called a "holy nation"). Equating the vineyard with the kingdom of God, McClain (*The Greatest of the Kingdom*) notes that this clearly shows the kingdom as mediated to Israel through divinely appointed kings and now being transferred (mediated) to the church during the interval between Christ's advents.

44-46. The warning **the kingdom of God shall be taken from you** (vs. 43) was fulfilled at Pentecost when the "kingdom" was mediatorily transferred to the church (cf. Romans 9-11 which clearly promises Israel's restoration at the time of the Tribulation Period and the millennial kingdom). Yet within this warning of judgment, Jesus offers mercy by falling **on this stone,** i.e., falling upon Him in repentance and faith. But, His falling upon man in judgment will **grind him to powder.** Finally, the Pharisees and chief priests **perceived** that He was speaking **of them** and wanted to kill Him but **feared the multitude** because they looked on Him as a **prophet.**

c. His jealous critics. 22:1-23:39.

(1). The Parable of the Marriage Supper. 22:1-14.

22:1-3. In preparation for the major confrontation which was coming, Jesus gave the Parable of the Marriage Supper. While similar to the parable in Luke 14, this one differs in its occasion and details. Again, the **kingdom of heaven** must refer to the mediatorial aspect of the kingdom in the church age. The **king** is the Father and Christ is the **son.** The **marriage** must be taken in the full aspect of salvation, including union with Christ, culminating in glorification at the marriage supper which inaugurates the millennial age. Rejection of the invitation to

4 Again, he sent forth other servants, saying, Tell them which are bidden, Behold, I have prepared my dinner: my oxen and *my* fatlings *are* killed, and all things *are* ready: come unto the marriage.

5 But they made light of *it*, and went their ways, one to his farm, another to his merchandise:

6 And the remnant took his servants, and entreated *them* spitefully, and slew *them*.

7 But when the king heard *thereof*, he was wroth: and he sent forth his armies, and destroyed those murderers, and burned up their city.

8 Then saith he to his servants, The wedding is ready, but they which were bidden were not worthy.

9 Go ye therefore into the highways, and as many as ye shall find, bid to the marriage.

10 So those servants went out into the highways, and gathered together all as many as they found, both bad and good: and the wedding was furnished with guests.

11 And when the king came in to see the guests, he saw there a man which had not on a wedding garment:

12 And he saith unto him, Friend, how camest thou in hither not having a wedding garment? And he was speechless.

13 Then said the king to the servants, Bind him hand and foot, and take him away, and cast *him* into outer darkness; there shall be weeping and gnashing of teeth.

14 For many are called, but few *are* chosen.

15 ¶Then went the Pharisees, and took counsel how they might entangle him in *his* talk.

16 And they sent out unto him their disciples with the He-rō'di-ans, saying, Master, we know that thou art true, and teachest the way of God in truth, neither carest thou for any *man*: for thou regardest not the person of men.

17 Tell us therefore, What thinkest thou? Is it lawful to give tribute unto Cæsar, or not?

18 But Jesus perceived their wickedness, and said, Why tempt ye me, *ye* hypocrites?

19 Shew me the tribute money. And they brought unto him a penny.

20 And he saith unto them, Whose *is* this image and superscription?

21 They say unto him, Cæsar's. Then saith he unto them, Render therefore unto Cæsar the things which are Cæsar's; and unto God the things that are God's.

22 When they had heard *these words*, they marvelled, and left him, and went their way.

23 ¶The same day came to him the Săd'du-ceés, which say that there is no resurrection, and asked him,

24 Saying, Master, Moses said, If a man die, having no children, his brother shall marry his wife, and raise up seed unto his brother.

25 Now there were with us seven

attend constitutes disloyalty to the King, as well as discourtesy to the Son, and accounts for the severe treatment of the rebels (vss. 6-7) which included their city being **burned up,** an obvious reference to the coming destruction of Jerusalem in A.D. 70.

4-14. The **bidden** guests are the people of Israel, whereas those in the **highways** are the Gentiles. **Both bad and good** refer to moral and immoral sinners who alike need God's gracious invitation. The "highways" implies crossroads, as opposed to backroads. History has revealed the success of urban evangelization, which may be implied here. The man without the **wedding garment** came to the feast but had disregarded the propriety of the king's provision, since such garments were normally supplied by the host. The reference seems to be to the "robe of righteousness" which we must receive from the Lord in order to enter the marriage feast. Casting the unclad guest into **outer darkness** symbolizes the eternal judgment of the lost. Again the phrase is repeated, **many are called, but few are chosen,** to emphasize to the Jewish audience, who considered themselves to be God's chosen people, that the outward call of God was not sufficient for salvation apart from the efficacious call of grace.

(2). The Herodians: Question of tribute. 22:15-22.

15-22. See Mark 12:13-17; Luke 20:20-26. **The Herodians** were a party that favored the dynasty of Herod and stood for the Roman connection. They cared little or nothing for religion and normally were bitterly opposed by the Pharisees. The statements recorded in verse 16 were insincere and intended as hypocritical flattery. Their question was intended to place the Lord in a dilemma. If He said yes, He could be held up to the people as a traitor. If He said no, He could be denounced to the Roman authorities. **Caesar,** i.e., the Roman Emperor and head of the Roman state. Caesar was the family name of Julius Caesar, the first man who aspired to autocracy, and was taken over from him by his adopted son, afterwards the Emperor Augustus. It soon came to be regarded as a title. **Penny** (see 20:2). **Render therefore unto Caesar.** The Lord means that we are to give the civil magistrates all that is due to them, so long as it does not interfere with the honor due to God. Jesus had broken the Herodians' dilemma by making light of the ultimate significance of Caesar's claim. The idea is: "If the penny is his, let him have it!" Jesus' response, render **unto God the things that are God's** exposed the spiritual failure of the Herodians. In essence, Jesus made light of Caesar's temporal claim in favor of God's greater claim over men's lives.

(3). The Sadducees: Question of the Resurrection. 22:23-34.

23-29. The Sadducees made the next attempt to discredit Jesus and were even more severely humiliated. As the liberal party within first-century A.D. Judaism, they rejected belief in the supernatural, especially angels and the resurrection of the dead (see Paul's encounter in Acts 23:8ff.). **Moses said** is a reference to Deuteronomy 25:5, where the practice of levirate marriage called for an unmarried brother to take his widowed

brethren: and the first, when he had married a wife, deceased, and, having no issue, left his wife unto his brother:

26 Likewise the second also, and the third, unto the seventh.

27 And last of all the woman died also.

28 Therefore in the resurrection whose wife shall she be of the seven? for they all had her.

29 Jesus answered and said unto them, Ye do err, not knowing the scriptures, nor the power of God.

30 For in the resurrection they neither marry, nor are given in marriage, but are as the angels of God in heaven.

31 But as touching the resurrection of the dead, have ye not read that which was spoken unto you by God, saying,

32 I am the God of Abraham, and the God of Isaac, and the God of Jacob? God is not the God of the dead, but of the living.

33 And when the multitude heard this, they were astonished at his doctrine.

34 ¶But when the Pharisees had heard that he had put the Săd′du-cees to silence, they were gathered together.

35 Then one of them, which was a lawyer, asked him a question, tempting him, and saying,

36 Master, which is the great commandment in the law?

37 Jesus said unto him, Thou shalt love the Lord thy God with all thy heart, and with all thy soul, and with all thy mind.

38 This is the first and great commandment.

39 And the second is like unto it, Thou shalt love thy neighbour as thyself.

40 On these two commandments hang all the law and the prophets.

41 ¶While the Pharisees were gathered together, Jesus asked them,

42 Saying, What think ye of Christ?

brother's wife to be his own (cf. Gen 38:8). This ancient practice was recognized by the Jews but rarely followed in those days. The absurd hypothetical case which follows represents another theological dilemma, this time attempting to discredit the legitimacy of the resurrection, which the Sadducees rejected. Thus, their question: **whose wife shall she be?** This extreme example must have been thought by them to be the ultimate proof of the foolishness of this doctrine. All seven brothers had been married to her, **Therefore in the resurrection whose wife shall she be of the seven?** They must have snickered as they asked such a ridiculous question, but the smile would soon be wiped off their faces by Jesus' reply. **Ye do err, not knowing the scriptures.** Jesus had extreme contempt for the Sadducees because they made light of the Bible and the **power of God** (i.e., His resurrection power, cf. Phil 3:10). This is His strongest recorded rebuke of this Jewish party.

30. Jesus then explained that **in the resurrection** men do not **marry** but are asexual **as the angels.** The infantile illustration of the Sadducees showed that they had no confidence in the power of a glorious resurrection to a new life. They thought that a resurrection would be the same kind of life as on earth and probably "spiritualized" their rejection of such a concept. To be as the angels means that resurrected believers will have a glorified non-mortal body (capable of neither reproduction nor destruction). The reference is not intended to imply that glorified men become angels nor that all earthly family relationships are lost in heaven. All resurrected (or raptured) believers will be in a state of perfect glorification and fellowship without any clannish prejudice.

31-34. Jesus further attacked the Sadducees' major belief in no resurrection at all, by quoting Exodus 3:6, a statement from the only part of the Old Testament which the Sadducees unquestioningly accepted. He related the eternal "I am" of God to the patriarchs (Abraham, Isaac, and Jacob) to demonstrate that they were **of the living,** or immortal (a fact unlikely to be denied by the Sadducees in a public dispute). **God is not the God of the dead** does not mean that He has no relationship to those who have departed; it means that the departed are not really dead, and are thus still responsible to the living God (cf. Heb 10:31). Thus the crowd was **astonished** and the Sadducees were **put . . . to silence.**

(4). The Pharisees: Question of the Law. 22:35-23:39.

35-40. Each group came with their most difficult question, representing their expertise and their point of departure from Jesus' doctrine. In other words, each came representing his own "hangups." Remember that each of these groups normally hated each other, but were united in their rejection of Christ. A **lawyer,** i.e., an expert expounder of the Old Testament law, equivalent to a Doctor of Theology today, asked Him, **which is the great commandment in the law?** The phrase "tempting him" implies that he was trying to draw Jesus into an argument regarding the Pharisees' extensive interpretations of over six hundred laws. Instead, Christ summarized the two tables of the law: i.e., (1) responsibility to God and (2) responsibility to man, by paraphrasing Deuteronomy 6:5 and Leviticus 19:18. **Love the Lord thy God** and **love thy neighbor as thyself.** The phrase **with all thy heart,** indicates the total being of a man in Hebrew thought and is part of the "shema," the Jewish confession of faith consisting of Deuteronomy 6:4-9; 11:13-21; Numbers 15:37-41. As the greatest commandment, it was of supreme importance and priority (cf. Filson, p. 237). No Pharisee could fault such an answer.

41-46. Jesus then counterquestioned the Pharisees: **What think ye of Christ? Whose son is he?** By asking them who is the Messiah, He gave them a clear opportunity to acknowledge

whose son is he? They say unto him, *The son* of David.

43 He saith unto them, How then doth David in spirit call him Lord, saying,

44 The LORD said unto my Lord, Sit thou on my right hand, till I make thine enemies thy footstool?

45 If David then call him Lord, how is he his son?

46 And no man was able to answer him a word, neither durst any *man* from that day forth ask him any more *questions.*

CHAPTER 23

THEN spake Jesus to the multitude, and to his disciples,

2 Saying, The scribes and the Pharisees sit in Moses' seat:

3 All therefore whatsoever they bid you observe, *that* observe and do; but do not ye after their works: for they say, and do not.

4 For they bind heavy burdens and grievous to be borne, and lay *them* on men's shoulders; but they *themselves* will not move them with one of their fingers.

5 But all their works they do for to be seen of men: they make broad their phylacteries, and enlarge the borders of their garments,

6 And love the uppermost rooms at feasts, and the chief seats in the synagogues,

7 And greetings in the markets, and to be called of men, Rabbi, Rabbi.

8 But be not ye called Rabbi: for one is your Master, *even* Christ; and all ye are brethren.

9 And call no *man* your father upon the earth: for one is your Father, which is in heaven.

10 Neither be ye called masters: for one is your Master, *even* Christ.

11 But he that is greatest among you shall be your servant.

12 And whosoever shall exalt himself shall be abased; and he that shall humble himself shall be exalted.

13 ¶But woe unto you, scribes and Pharisees, hypocrites! for ye shut up the kingdom of heaven against men: for ye neither go in *yourselves,* neither

Him. Tasker (p. 213) states that Jesus "asked the all-important question 'What is your view of the Messiah?' " The question is similar to that earlier asked of the disciples in 16:15, where they gave the correct answer. The Pharisees' response, **The son of David,** was the common teaching of the scribes who accepted the Davidic lineage of the Messiah (cf. Mk 12:35). Jesus then called their attention to Psalm 110 which they already recognized as messianic (Edersheim, App IX). The psalm, whose Davidic authorship Jesus affirms, was given **in the spirit,** i.e., by inspiration of the Holy Spirit (so Atkinson, Hendricksen, Kent, Lenski) and in it David refers to the Messiah as his Lord, thus He is more than just his "son." Thus, the verse says: "The **Lord** (God) said to my Lord (the Messiah), Sit on my right hand, until I (God) put your enemies (the enemies of the Messiah) beneath your feet (the final messianic victory over all who oppose Christ)." Jesus totally stumped the Pharisees who wanted to believe in a human Messiah but not a divine Messiah. Thus, no one **was able to answer him,** i.e., defeat Him by question or debate and, therefore, no one dared ask Him **any more questions.** In one day Jesus had annihilated and humiliated the wisdom and craft of the leaders of each of Israel's religious organizations. "Hallelujah, what a Saviour!"

23:1-2. Jesus' final condemnation of the Pharisees fills the entire twenty-third chapter. This now represents His final and official rejection of them at the Temple, their very own stronghold of influence and security. Our Lord exposes the true hostility and hypocrisy of the religious leaders of Israel. See parallel passages in Mark 12:38-40; Luke 20:45-47. **Sit in Moses' seat** (Gr *kathedra* seat of authority) representing the synagogue chair which symbolized the origin and authority of their teaching.

3-6. Whatsoever they bid you observe, that . . . do. Bearing in mind the Scriptures that follow, it seems clear that this means all lawful things, i.e., it depends on the extent to which they do really sit in Moses' seat. It cannot include, for example, the traditions of the elders (see the condemnation of some of these in 15:1-20). But, as the verse goes on to show, the sin of the Pharisees lay more in their evil practices than in their teaching, for they themselves did not practice what they preached. **They make broad their phylacteries.** A phylactery was an amulet consisting of a strip of parchment on which was inscribed certain portions of the Pentateuch and which was rolled and placed in a small metal cylinder inside a square leather case. The cases were attached by the Jews with straps to their foreheads and to the back of their right hands, following a strictly literal interpretation of Deuteronomy 6:8-9. They were normally worn only during prayer, but the Pharisees appear to have worn them always and to have made them especially conspicuous. **The borders of their garments** were the fringes worn in obedience to Numbers 15:38-39. **Uppermost rooms** better, "chief place."

7-12. Rabbi is from a Hebrew word (lit., my teacher). **Master,** i.e., teacher. **Call no man your father,** i.e., in a spiritual sense. This appears to condemn the use of the word "Father" used in addressing the clergy in the unreformed churches, and to render of doubtful propriety the use of the word *Padre* (Italian for "Father") as a synonym for a chaplain. **Masters,** lit., guides or leaders, i.e., teachers. **Servant** means minister or attendant. Verses 10-12 are very typical of our Lord's teaching (cf. Lk 14:11; 18:14).

13-15. Ye shut up the kingdom of heaven against men, i.e., you put stumblingblocks in the way of the sinner coming to repentance and conversion. **Devour widows' houses,** i.e., ex-

suffer ye them that are entering to go in.

14 Woe unto you, scribes and Pharisees, hypocrites! for ye devour widows' houses, and for a pretence make long prayer: therefore ye shall receive the greater damnation.

15 Woe unto you, scribes and Pharisees, hypocrites! for ye compass sea and land to make one proselyte, and when he is made, ye make him twofold more the child of hell than yourselves.

16 Woe unto you, ye blind guides, which say, Whosoever shall swear by the temple, it is nothing; but whosoever shall swear by the gold of the temple, he is a debtor!

17 Ye fools and blind: for whether is greater, the gold, or the temple that sanctifieth the gold?

18 And, Whosoever shall swear by the altar, it is nothing; but whosoever sweareth by the gift that is upon it, he is guilty.

19 Ye fools and blind: for whether is greater, the gift, or the altar that sanctifieth the gift?

20 Whoso therefore shall swear by the altar, sweareth by it, and by all things thereon.

21 And whoso shall swear by the temple, sweareth by it, and by him that dwelleth therein.

22 And he that shall swear by heaven, sweareth by the throne of God, and by him that sitteth thereon.

23 Woe unto you, scribes and Pharisees, hypocrites! for ye pay tithe of mint and anise and cummin, and have omitted the weightier matters of the law, judgment, mercy, and faith: these ought ye to have done, and not to leave the other undone.

24 Ye blind guides, which strain at a gnat, and swallow a camel.

25 Woe unto you, scribes and Pharisees, hypocrites! for ye make clean the outside of the cup and of the platter, but within they are full of extortion and excess.

26 Thou blind Pharisee, cleanse first that which is within the cup and platter, that the outside of them may be clean also.

27 Woe unto you, scribes and Pharisees, hypocrites! for ye are like unto whited sepulchres, which indeed appear beautiful outward, but are within full of dead men's bones, and of all uncleanness.

28 Even so ye also outwardly appear righteous unto men, but within ye are full of hypocrisy and iniquity.

29 Woe unto you, scribes and Pharisees, hypocrites! because ye build the tombs of the prophets, and garnish the sepulchres of the righteous.

30 And say, If we had been in the days of our fathers, we would not have been partakers with them in the blood of the prophets.

31 Wherefore ye be witnesses unto

tort money from the helpless and bring them into debt and bondage, while making an outward show of religion. **The greater damnation,** i.e., a more severe sentence. **Proselyte.** The Jews recognized two sorts of proselytes: those who agreed to the so-called seven precepts of Noah, and those who submitted to circumcision and became full Jews by religion.

16-22. These verses give illustration of the Pharisees' casuistry with regard to oaths. **Temple** (Gr naos actually the "sanctuary"). Our Lord teaches that all oaths are equally binding, and no man can expect to escape their consequences before God by making distinctions such as these.

23. Pay tithe of. A tithe or tenth of all produce was, by the Mosaic law, to be given for the use of the priests and Levites (e.g., Lev 27:30). Several species of **mint** grow in Palestine. **Anise** (Gr anethon) is better rendered "dill." It grew both wild and cultivated, its fruits being used for medicine. The seeds of **cummin,** which resemble caraways, were used as spice in seasoning. In such little matters the Pharisees were most careful to keep the law; yet they had completely overlooked its more important precepts.

24-26. Strain at a gnat, better "strain out a gnat." The Jews strained (Gr diylizo) wine before drinking it so as to avoid touching or swallowing anything unclean. **But within they are full of extortion and excess.** For "of" read "from." The Pharisees' living was obtained by extorting wrongfully from others.

27-33. Whited sepulchers. Since contact with a dead body rendered a person unclean according to the Mosaic law, it was the custom to paint graves white in order to make them conspicuous, and so to give the opportunity of avoiding contact with them. **The children of them which killed** literally "those who murdered." **Generation** or "offspring." **The damnation of hell,** i.e., being judged worthy of Gehenna.

yourselves, that ye are the children of them which killed the prophets.

32 Fill ye up then the measure of your fathers.

33 *Ye* serpents, *ye* generation of vipers, how can ye escape the damnation of hell?

34 Wherefore, behold, I send unto you prophets, and wise men, and scribes: and *some* of them ye shall kill and crucify; and *some* of them shall ye scourge in your synagogues, and persecute *them* from city to city:

35 That upon you may come all the righteous blood shed upon the earth, from the blood of righteous Abel unto the blood of Zăch-a-rī'as son of Băr-a-chī'as, whom ye slew between the temple and the altar.

36 Verily I say unto you, All these things shall come upon this generation.

37 O Jerusalem, Jerusalem, *thou* that killest the prophets, and stonest them which are sent unto thee, how often would I have gathered thy children together, even as a hen gathereth her chickens under *her* wings, and ye would not!

38 Behold, your house is left unto you desolate.

39 For I say unto you, Ye shall not see me henceforth, till ye shall say, Blessed *is* he that cometh in the name of the Lord.

CHAPTER 24

AND Jesus went out, and departed from the temple: and his disciples came to *him* for to shew him the buildings of the temple.

2 And Jesus said unto them, See ye not all these things? verily I say unto you, There shall not be left here one stone upon another, that shall not be thrown down.

3 ¶And as he sat upon the mount of Olives, the disciples came unto him privately, saying, Tell us, when shall these things be? and what *shall be* the sign of thy coming, and of the end of the world?

4 And Jesus answered and said unto them, Take heed that no man deceive you.

34-39. That upon you may come. The generation to which these words were addressed represented the culminating point of the whole sinful history of the nation, beginning with the murder of **Abel** by his brother Cain (see Gen 4; Heb 11:4) and going on to the murder of **Zacharias son of Barachias.** In II Chronicles 24:20-21 we find the account of the murder of Zechariah son of Jehoiada "in the court of the house of the Lord." Since the books of Chronicles closed the Hebrew Old Testament canon, if this is the incident here referred to, the mention of Abel and Zacharias may be intended to cover the whole Old Testament revelation. The difficulty is that the Zechariah murdered in II Chronicles 24 was not the son of Berechiah. This Zechariah was the prophet (Zech 1:1). Though he lived after the exile and toward the close of Old Testament history there exists no tradition or record that he was murdered. Another possibility is that the Zechariah referred to here is identical with "Zechariah the son of Jeberechiah" mentioned in Isaiah 8:2, but nothing further seems to be known of him. This passage is also recorded by Luke (Lk 11:49-51) and was evidently understood by His listeners. Jesus' statement that they would **not see me henceforth** foreshadows His death, resurrection and ascension. Following His resurrection, Jesus only appeared to His followers and not to the world in general. From now on He must be received as personal Saviour by faith.

d. *His judgment: Olivet Discourse. 24:1-25:46*

24:1-4. This section forms Jesus' last major discourse and His most prophetic and apocalyptic message of the coming of the end of the world (or the present age). While the message includes a prediction of the imminent fall of Jerusalem, it also goes far beyond to point us to the distant future during which the "times of the Gentiles" will continue until the end of the Great Tribulation. **Temple** (Gr *hieron*) means the temple precincts. This prophecy of the very stones of the Temple being cast down was fulfilled in the time of the Emperor Julian who, in a futile attempt to rebuild the Temple, removed even the stones that had been left at the time of its destruction by Titus in A.D. 70. Jesus then left the city, crossed the Kidron Valley, and went east of Jerusalem to the **mount of Olives** from which He could look down on the temple courtyard. Here His disciples asked Him three questions: (1) **when shall these things be?** (i.e., the destruction of the Temple); (2) **what shall be the sign of thy coming?** (Gr *parousia*, technical term for the coming of the King); (3) **and of the end of the world?** (Gr *aion*, "the age"). Therefore, the entire discourse must be looked upon as answering all three of these questions. On the significance of the signs of the end of the age see Walvoord (pp. 179-195). He comments: "Premillenarians, accordingly, interpret the discourse as an accurate statement of end-time events, which will lead up to and climax in the second coming of Christ to set up His millennial kingdom on the earth" (p. 181).

Interpretation of the Olivet Discourse ranges widely from liberal (Allen, Moffat, McNeile, Kee, etc.) to conservative (among whom there is variation from amillennial, Hendricksen; to post-tribulational, Morgan; to pretribulational, Kent and Walvoord). Difference of interpretation may even be noted between Walvoord who views Matthew 24:4-14 as events of the Church Age leading up to the Tribulation Period and Kent (p. 85) who sees them as happening during the first part of the Tribulation Period. The key to interpreting this section rests in one's view of the "gospel of the kingdom" (vss. 13-14). Since Matthew has already shown in his selection of parables that the present form of the kingdom of heaven is the church, it seems more proper to view the events in these verses as relating to the entire Church Age and culminating especially at the end of it (thus John could say in general that he was a "companion in tribulation and in the kingdom," though he was still in the Church Age, of Revelation 1:9). Therefore, the "signs" of the end are general characteristics of the present age which shall be intensified as the age moves on to its conclusion. These are followed by more specific signs (vss. 15-26) of the Tribulation Period and the final return of Christ in judgment (vss. 27-31).

(1). Signs of the present age. 24:5-14.

5-14. Many shall come refers to the parade of false messiahs who have now spanned the centuries of church history and have led many astray into false religious cults. **Wars and rumors of wars** refer to peace being taken from the earth and the constant wars that have continually marked the "age of the Gentiles." **Famines and pestilences.** These events only mark the **beginning of sorrows** (Gr *odin*) "birthpangs." This is followed by martyrdom and the rise of **false prophets** and the abounding of **iniquity.** While Kent makes an interesting parallel of these events to the seven seals in Revelation, it still remains that the "gospel of the kingdom" refers to the missionary expansion of the church **into all the world.** It is hardly reasonable to hold that the Jews will spread the gospel throughout the entire world during the first half of the Tribulation Period of three and a half years when most conservative scholars view their coming national conversion at about the middle of the Tribulation (cf. Ez 37-39; Dan 9; Zech 12:10; 13:1-6). The gospel shall be preached in all the **world** (Gr *oikoumenē*), i.e., the inhabited world and unto **all nations** (Gr *ethnos*), "gentile nations," as contrasted with the Jews. **Then shall the end come** would then refer to the end of the church age.

(2). Signs of the Great Tribulation. 24:15-28.

15. Ye must be taken generically, since the disciples have not lived to see this take place. The **abomination of desolation** refers to Daniel 9:27; 11:31; 12:11; where Antiochus Epiphanes' profanation of the Jewish temple worship would foreshadow a similar and more severe act by the eschatological Antichrist. Whereas Antiochus offered a pig on the sacred altar of the Temple, the Antichrist will offer himself (II Thess 2:4)! The action of desecration by Antiochus, which David had predicted, will now be repeated in the future by the Antichrist as the signal of the beginning of the Great Tribulation and the breaking of the covenant "in the midst of the week" (Dan 9:27), i.e., the seventieth week of Daniel's prophecy, whose length is forty-two months (Rev 11:2), 1,260 days (Rev 12:6), or "time, and times, and half a time" (Dan 7:25; Rev 12:14). **The holy place,** i.e., Temple, which will be rebuilt. Kent (p. 86) rightly observes that this cancels limitation of Daniel's prophecy to just the days of Antiochus (Allen, p. 256) since Jesus, in His day, was still awaiting further fulfillment, and it likewise goes beyond the catastrophe of A.D. 70 (Stagg, p. 200), since it is called the greatest tribulation of all time (Mt 24:21).

16-28. The warning to **flee into the mountains** eschatologically looks beyond the first century to the Jews' flight from the persecution of the Antichrist (cf. Rev 12:6-14). Every Jew must flee and not look back. The reference to the **sabbath day** indicates these events will occur in a Jewish area, where

5 For many shall come in my name, saying, I am Christ; and shall deceive many.

6 And ye shall hear of wars and rumours of wars: see that ye be not troubled: for all *these things* must come to pass, but the end is not yet.

7 For nation shall rise against nation, and kingdom against kingdom: and there shall be famines, and pestilences, and earthquakes, in divers places.

8 All these *are* the beginning of sorrows.

9 Then shall they deliver you up to be afflicted, and shall kill you: and ye shall be hated of all nations for my name's sake.

10 And then shall many be offended, and shall betray one another, and shall hate one another.

11 And many false prophets shall rise, and shall deceive many.

12 And because iniquity shall abound, the love of many shall wax cold.

13 But he that shall endure unto the end, the same shall be saved.

14 And this gospel of the kingdom shall be preached in all the world for a witness unto all nations; and then shall the end come.

15 When ye therefore shall see the abomination of desolation, spoken of by Daniel the prophet, stand in the holy place, (whoso readeth, let him understand:)

16 Then let them which be in Judæa flee into the mountains:

17 Let him which is on the housetop not come down to take any thing out of his house:

18 Neither let him which is in the field return back to take his clothes.

19 And woe unto them that are with child, and to them that give suck in those days!

20 But pray ye that your flight be not in the winter, neither on the sabbath day:

21 For then shall be great tribulation, such as was not since the beginning of the world to this time, no, nor ever shall be.

22 And except those days should be shortened, there should no flesh be saved: but for the elect's sake those days shall be shortened.

23 Then if any man shall say unto you, Lo, here is Christ, or there; believe it not.

24 For there shall arise false Christs, and false prophets, and shall shew great signs and wonders; insomuch that, if it were possible, they shall deceive the very elect.

25 Behold, I have told you before.

26 Wherefore if they shall say unto you, Behold, he is in the desert; go not forth: behold, he is in the secret chambers; believe it not.

27 For as the lightning cometh out of the east, and shineth even unto the west; so shall also the coming of the Son of man be.

28 For wheresoever the carcase is, there will the eagles be gathered together.

29 ¶Immediately after the tribulation of those days shall the sun be darkened, and the moon shall not give her light, and the stars shall fall from heaven, and the powers of the heavens shall be shaken:

30 And then shall appear the sign of the Son of man in heaven: and then shall all the tribes of the earth mourn, and they shall see the Son of man coming in the clouds of heaven with power and great glory.

31 And he shall send his angels with a great sound of a trumpet, and they shall gather together his elect from the four winds, from one end of heaven to the other.

32 ¶Now learn a parable of the fig tree; When his branch is yet tender, and putteth forth leaves, ye know that summer is nigh:

33 So likewise ye, when ye shall see all these things, know that it is near, even at the doors.

such restrictions would be observed. **Then shall be great tribulation** makes our Lord's reference to Daniel 12:1 clearly evident as taking place just prior to the resurrection in Daniel 12:2. The terrible **days** of that time shall **be shortened** by the sudden return of Christ to destroy the Wicked One (II Thess 2:8). The **false Christs** may even refer to the False Prophet who aids the Antichrist with his miracle-working powers (Rev 13:11ff.). The phrase, **if it were possible . . . shall deceive the very elect** clearly indicates that those who have been truly saved cannot be deceived and fall away. For even if it were humanly possible, the Lord will stop it by shortening (hastening) His coming. The exclamation, **Behold, I have told you before,** indicates Jesus' belief in the predictive nature of this prophecy. The **lightning** shining from **the east . . . even unto the west** refers to the final aspect of Christ's return (not the Rapture) in judgment upon the earth. In I Thessalonians 4, He comes in the clouds for the church; in II Thessalonians 1-2, He comes to the earth with the church to judge the world.

(3). Signs of the coming Son of Man. 24:29-42.

29-31. The reference to the events **Immediately after the tribulation,** such as the sun being darkened and the stars falling, etc., refer to the cataclysmic events that will accompany Christ's return at the end of the Tribulation Period to establish His millennial kingdom on earth (see W. Price, *Jesus' Prophetic Sermon*, p. 118ff.). His return will be marked by the **sign of the Son of man in heaven** which will identify His coming to the **tribes of the earth.** What this sign (Gr *semeion*) will be is not explained here. Ancient commentators (e.g., Chrysostom) thought it to be the appearance of a cross in the sky, whereas Lange (p. 428) suggests it will be the shekinah glory of Christ Himself. It may, perhaps, even be the return of the star that marked His birth. In some way a visible manifestation will mark the gradual (cf. Acts 1:11, "in the same manner") return of Christ in judgment at the end of the Tribulation Period. As the earth revolves the various nations and tribes will be able to see this sign. Instead of repenting, though, they shall **mourn.** This indicates a severe, ritualistic mourning (cf. also Zech 12:10-12). The **clouds of heaven** indicate that Christ will come from heaven to the earth (cf. also Dan 7:13-14; II Thess 1:7-9). The **angels** are the same agents of judgment as in chapter 13. The **elect** are the saved who have come to faith in Christ by the grace of God and are gladly anticipating their Lord's return.

32-33. The illustration of the **fig tree** is referred to as a **parable.** The immediate context seems to refer to the fig tree in a natural (not symbolic) sense (see Walvoord, p. 192). While it is clear in Scripture that Israel is symbolized, at times, by the fig tree (ch. 21), the usage here simply seems to be that as these events reach the apex of their fulfillment, the actual and ultimate return of Christ follows immediately. Just as God has built into nature certain time indicators (e.g., trees budding), so He has built into history certain time indicators of coming future events. Jesus' reference to **when ye shall see all these things** has caused some to speculate that these predicted events only relate to the coming destruction of Jerusalem in A.D. 70, within the disciples' lifetime (cf. Tasker, p. 227; G. C. Morgan, p. 286, does not even attempt an explanation). Kent (p. 86) views the fig tree as Israel "budding" in the last days as a reborn nation. Walvoord (p. 192) agrees with Lenski (p. 951) that "all these things" refers to the preceding context of the Olivet Discourse.

34 Verily I say unto you, This generation shall not pass, till all these things be fulfilled.

34. Thus, the **generation** that **shall not pass** is the generation in whose lifetime all these signs occur and it is that generation that will not pass away until **all these things be fulfilled.** While some have attempted to relate "generation" (Gr *genea*) to the race of the Jews, indicating the survival of their race until Christ's return, this seems somewhat stretched. Arndt and Gingrich (p. 153) prefer "age" or "period of time." In other words, the previously listed signs will continue to multiply throughout the Church Age and reach their ultimate climax at the end of the age in the generation of those who will live to see the entire matter fulfilled in their lifetime. However, no time indication of length is clearly given so that all may anticipate the imminent return of the Master. Those who object that the "last days" began at Pentecost should also see II Timothy 3:1, where "last days" are yet coming (shall come) in the future. On the one hand, the final age began with the manifestation of the church and continues today. On the other hand, though, the final aspect of this age will be a last day of perilous times which will occur at the end of the age. Even Filson (pp. 257-258) agrees that Matthew certainly understood Jesus to be saying that "all these things" referred to the end of history in the distant future.

35 Heaven and earth shall pass away, but my words shall not pass away.
36 ¶But of that day and hour knoweth no *man,* **no, not the angels of heaven, but my Father only.**
37 But as the days of Nō'e *were,* **so shall also the coming of the Son of man be.**
38 For as in the days that were before the flood they were eating and drinking, marrying and giving in marriage, until the day that Nō'e entered into the ark,

35-38. Verse 35-36 warn against attempts to set an exact date for Christ's return at the end of the Church Age (a warning unheeded by the Adventists in 1844, the Jehovah's Witnesses in 1916, and many others). To speculate that "day" and "hour" do not eliminate "year" is a gross oversimplification. The **Father only** knows the time of Christ's return since it has been set by His authority (cf. Acts 1:7). However, we are given a comparison to the **days of Noah** (and the Flood) which illustrate and prefigure the condition of humanity at the time of Christ's return. The last generation, like the one of Noah's day, is pleasure-oriented and self-gratifying by **eating and drinking.** The reference to **marrying and giving in marriage** may refer to carrying on the normal course of life without heeding the impending judgment. However, the indication may even be stronger in that Noah's generation was judged as the result of the collapse of the godly line of Seth by spiritual intermarriage with the ungodly line of Cain's descendants (see Gen 4-6 for the setting of the Flood story). The drastic destruction of the godly families of Noah's day was due to a casual and indifferent attitude about whom one married or to whom he gave his children in marriage. Thus, Jesus' warning is that the last generation will also be so pleasure-oriented that its families will collapse (a shocking observation in view of the current failure of the American family with one million new divorces every year!).

39 And knew not until the flood came, and took them all away; so shall also the coming of the Son of man be.
40 Then shall two be in the field; the one shall be taken, and the other left.
41 Two *women shall be* **grinding at the mill; the one shall be taken, and the other left.**
42 ¶Watch therefore: for ye know not what hour your Lord doth come.

39-42. The observation that the people of Noah's day **knew not** the severity and suddenness of the coming destruction indicates that this last generation will be totally unprepared for the **coming of the Son of man** (i.e., the return of Christ to judge the world, see II Thessalonians 1:7-8). The reference to **two** being in the field or at work at the time of Christ's return implies the suddenness of His coming to separate the lost and the saved. The **one taken** and the **other left** has been variously interpreted as one being taken in the Rapture and the other left to impending judgment, or as the taken one being taken to judgment and the one left being spared (so Walvoord, p. 193 and Kent, p. 88-89). Kent notes that this separation occurs after the Tribulation (vs. 29) and correlates to "took them all away" (to judgment) in verse 39. The warning to **watch therefore** is repeated in 24:44; 25:13 and relates to the **hour** (a general period of time). **Watch**

43 But know this, that if the goodman of the house had known in what watch the thief would come, he would have watched, and would not have suffered his house to be broken up.
44 Therefore be ye also ready: for in such an hour as ye think not the Son of man cometh.
45 Who then is a faithful and wise servant, whom his lord hath made ruler over his household, to give them meat in due season?
46 Blessed *is* that servant, whom his lord when he cometh shall find so doing.
47 Verily I say unto you, That he shall make him ruler over all his goods.
48 But and if that evil servant shall say in his heart, My lord delayeth his coming;
49 And shall begin to smite *his* fellowservants, and to eat and drink with the drunken;
50 The lord of that servant shall come in a day when he looketh not for *him*, and in an hour that he is not aware of,
51 And shall cut him asunder, and appoint *him* his portion with the hypocrites: there shall be weeping and gnashing of teeth.

CHAPTER 25

THEN shall the kingdom of heaven be likened unto ten virgins, which took their lamps, and went forth to meet the bridegroom.
2 And five of them were wise, and five *were* foolish.
3 They that *were* foolish took their lamps, and took no oil with them:
4 But the wise took oil in their vessels with their lamps.
5 While the bridegroom tarried, they all slumbered and slept.
6 And at midnight there was a cry made, Behold, the bridegroom cometh; go ye out to meet him.
7 Then all those virgins arose, and trimmed their lamps.
8 And the foolish said unto the wise, Give us of your oil; for our lamps are gone out.
9 But the wise answered, saying, Not so; lest there be not enough for us and you: but go ye rather to them that sell, and buy for yourselves.
10 And while they went to buy, the bridegroom came; and they that were ready went in with him to the marriage: and the door was shut.
11 Afterward came also the other virgins, saying, Lord, Lord, open to us.
12 But he answered and said, Verily I say unto you, I know you not.
13 Watch therefore, for ye know neither the day nor the hour wherein the Son of man cometh.
14 ¶For *the kingdom of heaven is* as a man travelling into a far country, *who* called his own servants, and delivered unto them his goods.
15 And unto one he gave five talents,

(Gr *grēgoreo*) is a Greek present imperative, meaning "be continuously on guard."

(4). The Parable of the Two Servants. 24:43-51.

43-51. The Parable of the Two Servants follows to illustrate the seriousness of Christ's second coming, a fact which Jesus never allegorized or spiritualized, but spoke of in the most serious terms: **cut him asunder . . . weeping and gnashing of teeth.** Kent (p. 89) notes that the **evil servant** (a usurper and impostor) "mistakes the uncertainty of the time of coming for a certainty that it will not be soon." At Christ's return, however, all hypocrites will be suddenly exposed and judged by the Lord.

(5). The Parable of the Ten Virgins. 25:1-13.

25:1-13. The Parable of the Ten Virgins explains the place of Israel's true converts of the Tribulation Period in relation to the church. These **virgins** (Gr *parthenos*, cf. 1:23) are the attendants at the wedding, not multiple brides. The one bride of Christ is the church, John the Baptist is the best man (Jn 3:29, i.e., friend of the Bridegroom) and the prepared virgins are the saved of the Tribulation Period. While all share as the people of God, the church is accorded a unique relationship to the Master. The number **five** in each group does not necessarily indicate that half of humanity will be saved but that there are two types of people. The **lamps** seem to refer to their lives which are either prepared or unprepared. The **oil** refers to that which prepares them to give forth light and may properly be illustrative of the regeneration of the Holy Spirit. The fact that they all **slept . . . While the bridegroom tarried** implies a period of Jewish inactivity during the Church Age, while the Bride is gathered. **Foolish** (Gr *mōros*) means "stupid," and is the designation for those who are carelessly unprepared. They had no oil at all, not an insufficient amount. The refusal of the five prepared virgins to share with those unprepared must not be taken as cruelty. If the oil represents personal possession of the Holy Spirit, He cannot be shared but must regenerate each person individually. Thus, the Lord responds, **I know you not** (vs. 12), indicative of 7:23. False profession will save no one and only brings the final judgment of Christ upon the unsaved.

(6). The Parable of the Talents. 25:14-30.

14-23. The Parable of the Talents further emphasizes the need for personal preparation and faithful service to the Master (see also Lk 19:11-28). The **talents** represent monetary values and are distributed according to **ability** (vs. 15). **Far country** indicating the time between Jesus' first coming and His final

to another two, and to another one; to every man according to his several ability; and straightway took his journey.

16 Then he that had received the five talents went and traded with the same, and made *them* other five talents.

17 And likewise he that *had received* two, he also gained other two.

18 But he that had received one went and digged in the earth, and hid his lord's money.

19 After a long time the lord of those servants cometh, and reckoneth with them.

20 And so he that had received five talents came and brought other five talents, saying, Lord, thou deliveredst unto me five talents: behold, I have gained beside them five talents more.

21 His lord said unto him, Well done, *thou* good and faithful servant: thou hast been faithful over a few things, I will make thee ruler over many things: enter thou into the joy of thy lord.

22 He also that had received two talents came and said, Lord, thou deliveredst unto me two talents: behold, I have gained two other talents beside them.

23 His lord said unto him, Well done, good and faithful servant; thou hast been faithful over a few things, I will make thee ruler over many things: enter thou into the joy of thy lord.

24 Then he which had received the one talent came and said, Lord, I knew thee that thou art an hard man, reaping where thou hast not sown, and gathering where thou hast not strawed:

25 And I was afraid, and went and hid thy talent in the earth: lo, *there* thou hast *that is* thine.

26 His lord answered and said unto him, *Thou* wicked and slothful servant, thou knewest that I reap where I sowed not, and gather where I have not strawed:

27 Thou oughtest therefore to have put my money to the exchangers, and *then* at my coming I should have received mine own with usury.

28 Take therefore the talent from him, and give *it* unto him which hath ten talents.

29 For unto every one that hath shall be given, and he shall have abundance: but from him that hath not shall be taken away even that which he hath.

30 And cast ye the unprofitable servant into outer darkness: there shall be weeping and gnashing of teeth.

31 ¶When the Son of man shall come in his glory, and all the holy angels with him, then shall he sit upon the throne of his glory:

32 And before him shall be gathered all nations: and he shall separate them one from another, as a shepherd divideth *his* sheep from the goats:

33 And he shall set the sheep on his right hand, but the goats on the left.

return during which He is in heaven. The three **servants** are typical of three types who are entrusted various tasks in accordance with their own ability. Not all are expected to produce the same results, but all are to be faithful with what they have had entrusted to them. Thus, the first two double their money, while the last one hides the **one . . . in the earth.** The phrase **After a long time** gives a veiled indication of the length of Christ's departure to heaven during the present age. Each of those producing results is commended by the Master: **Well done . . . good and faithful servant** and is promised to be a **ruler over many things,** with a view to continued service in the millennial kingdom.

24-25. The great mistake of the unfaithful servant was in misjudging the character of his Master: **thou art a hard man.** He could not have known the Master well to assume him to be severe and merciless. Atkinson (p. 801) observes, "The slave seems to have thought that whatever he did his master would be unjust to him." He failed to understand the real generosity of his Master who wanted him to experience the joys of service. Whereas the Parable of the Ten Virgins emphasized personal preparation for the coming of Christ, the Parable of the Talents stresses the importance of faithful service during His present absence.

26-30. The fact that the latter man is called **wicked and slothful** and an **unprofitable servant** (vs. 30) who is cast out into **outer darkness,** certainly indicates that he was not a true disciple of the Master. The idea of this illustrative parable is that all true believers will produce results (elsewhere, "fruits") in varying degrees. Those who produce no results are not truly converted. Those who deny soul-winning, personal evangelism, and church growth will find no comfort in this story. Those who hide their treasure (probably, the life-changing message of the gospel), because of a harsh view of the Master's sovereignty over them, reveal that they do not really love people and, therefore, their own salvation is questionable!

(7). The judgment of the nations. 25:31-46.

31-46. The judgment of the nations concludes our Lord's prophetic discourse. Christ's return **in his glory** to be enthroned on the **throne of his glory** marks the great interruption of history as He brings the Tribulation Period to an end and ushers in the millennial kingdom. This judgment of **all nations** must be distinguished from the Great White Throne Judgment at the end of the Millennium. The **nations** (Gr *ethnos*) are those peoples living through the Tribulation on earth at the time of Christ's return. This is a judgment of separation: **sheep on his**

34 Then shall the King say unto them on his right hand, Come, ye blessed of my Father, inherit the kingdom prepared for you from the foundation of the world:

35 For I was an hungred, and ye gave me meat: I was thirsty, and ye gave me drink: I was a stranger, and ye took me in:

36 Naked, and ye clothed me: I was sick, and ye visited me: I was in prison, and ye came unto me.

37 Then shall the righteous answer him, saying, Lord, when saw we thee an hungred, and fed *thee?* or thirsty, and gave *thee* drink?

38 When saw we thee a stranger, and took *thee* in? or naked, and clothed *thee?*

39 Or when saw we thee sick, or in prison, and came unto thee?

40 And the King shall answer and say unto them, Verily I say unto you, Inasmuch as ye have done *it* unto one of the least of these my brethren, ye have done *it* unto me.

41 Then shall he say also unto them on the left hand, Depart from me, ye cursed, into everlasting fire, prepared for the devil and his angels:

42 For I was an hungred, and ye gave me no meat: I was thirsty, and ye gave me no drink:

43 I was a stranger, and ye took me not in: naked, and ye clothed me not: sick, and in prison, and ye visited me not.

44 Then shall they also answer him, saying, Lord, when saw we thee an hungred, or athirst, or a stranger, or naked, or sick, or in prison, and did not minister unto thee?

45 Then shall he answer them, saying, Verily I say unto you, Inasmuch as ye did *it* not to one of the least of these, ye did *it* not to me.

46 And these shall go away into everlasting punishment: but the righteous into life eternal.

CHAPTER 26

AND it came to pass, when Jesus had finished all these sayings, he said unto his disciples,

2 Ye know that after two days is *the feast* of the passover, and the Son of man is betrayed to be crucified.

3 ¶Then assembled together the chief priests, and the scribes, and the elders of the people, unto the palace of the high priest, who was called Cā'ia-phas,

right . . . goats on the left. At this judgment all nations (better, "all Gentiles") stand before Christ who then separates the sheep (the saved) from the goats (the lost) in a manner reminiscent of the wheat and tares parable. Some view this as the last general judgment (Atkinson, p. 801), whereas premillennial commentators see this as the judgment of the nations who have survived the Tribulation Period, with the saved going into the millennial kingdom. Note that these are living nations, whereas the Great White Throne Judgment is one of the wicked dead whose bodies are resurrected to face the final judgment of the lost. Thus, the saved are invited to come into and share the blessings of His Kingdom: **Come, ye blessed of my Father, inherit the kingdom.** The basis of their acceptance seems to be their treatment of the **least of these my brethren**, i.e., the saved of the Tribulation. The acts of kindness (vss. 35-38) were done by these sheep nations unto the persecuted Jewish believers and their converts during the reign of the Antichrist and now bring the blessing of God's salvation upon these nations. The acts of kindness do not themselves merit salvation apart from the atonement of Christ. Since the nations are the Gentiles and "my brethren" are neither, they must be the Jews. The goats are banished into **everlasting fire** or hell. Both the judgment and the blessed life are designated by the same adjective, "eternal" (Gr *aionios*), clearly indicating their equal duration. This eternal judgment is in keeping with Revelation 14:11; 19:15. No unsaved adults are admitted into the millennial kingdom when it is begun on earth. A natural and legitimate conclusion, then, is that the Rapture must occur before this event. Thus, the Rapture precedes the Tribulation Period, which itself precedes the millennial kingdom.

2. His rejection as King. 26:1-27:66.

These chapters describe the plot of the priests, the anointing of the Lord in Bethany, the betrayal, the institution of the Lord's Supper, the agony in the Garden, the Lord's arrest, His trial before the priests, Peter's denial, the trial before Pilate, and finally the crucifixion and resurrection.

a. His denial by His disciples. 26:1-56.

26:1 See also Mark 14:1-2, Luke 22:1-2. Jesus makes a final prediction of His death two days before Passover, which was eaten on the evening of Nisan 14. Thus the prediction was made on the twelfth of the month (April). The **feast of the passover** was the first feast on the Jewish yearly calendar and was kept in commemoration of the national deliverance from Egypt in the exodus under Moses. Passover takes its name from the Hebrew term related to the Death Angel passing over those who had applied the blood to their homes (cf. Ex 12). The Hebrew root *pesach* was transliterated into "pashcal" from which Christ's suffering is often referred to as His "passion." Passover time was a great high day among the Jews and thousands of pilgrims flocked to Jerusalem to observe it each year. Our Lord's death was the ultimate fulfillment of which the annual feast had been a shadow. It was followed by the seven-day Feast of Unleavened Bread (Nisan 15-21). Sometimes the entire period was generally referred to as Passover.

2-5. Jesus also predicted His betrayal. **Son of man** is His favorite designation of Himself. **Betrayed** (Gr *paradidomi*) is better translated here as "delivered up" or "handed over." The assemblage of the Sanhedrin takes place at the **palace**, (Gr *aule* meaning the courtyard of his residence.) **Caiaphas** was a Sadducee who had been appointed High Priest a few years earlier,

4 And consulted that they might take Jesus by subtilty, and kill *him*.

5 But they said, Not on the feast *day*, lest there be an uproar among the people.

6 ¶Now when Jesus was in Bethany, in the house of Simon the leper,

7 There came unto him a woman having an alabaster box of very precious ointment, and poured it on his head, as he sat *at meat*.

8 But when his disciples saw *it*, they had indignation, saying, To what purpose *is* this waste?

9 For this ointment might have been sold for much, and given to the poor.

10 When Jesus understood *it*, he said unto them, Why trouble ye the woman? for she hath wrought a good work upon me.

11 For ye have the poor always with you; but me ye have not always.

12 For in that she hath poured this ointment on my body, she did *it* for my burial.

13 Verily I say unto you, Wheresoever this gospel shall be preached in the whole world, *there* shall also this, that this woman hath done, be told for a memorial of her.

14 ¶Then one of the twelve, called Judas Iscariot, went unto the chief priests,

15 And said *unto them*, What will ye give me, and I will deliver him unto you? And they covenanted with him for thirty pieces of silver.

16 And from that time he sought opportunity to betray him.

17 ¶Now the first *day* of the *feast of* unleavened bread the disciples came to Jesus, saying unto him, Where wilt thou that we prepare for thee to eat the passover?

18 And he said, Go into the city to such a man, and say unto him, The Master saith, My time is at hand; I will keep the passover at thy house with my disciples.

19 And the disciples did as Jesus had appointed them; and they made ready the passover.

20 ¶Now when the even was come, he sat down with the twelve.

21 And as they did eat, he said, Verily I say unto you, that one of you shall betray me.

22 And they were exceeding sorrowful, and began every one of them to say unto him, Lord, is it I?

23 And he answered and said, He that dippeth *his* hand with me in the dish, the same shall betray me.

24 The Son of man goeth as it is writ-

about A.D. 18, just before Christ's earthly ministry began. **Not on the feast** means "not during the feast." Since many of Jesus' supporters from Galilee would be in Jerusalem during this time, the leaders did not want to upset the crowd whose emotions were at a high anyhow. Jesus ultimately foiled their plan and died at the very hour of the slaying of the Passover lambs.

6-16. The anointing at Bethany (cf. Mk 14:3-9; Jn 12:1-8) is related by John as taking place six days before Passover, indicating the one version is topical and the other chronological, since neither Matthew nor Mark dates the event. The chronological problems with the crucifixion have long been wrestled with by scholars, but the detailed accounts of factual material relating to such highly emotional material make their veracity all the more certain. These are no mere legendary accounts, embellished by Church tradition. They are highly factual and readable accounts of the most sublime narratives in Scripture. **Simon the leper** is mentioned only here and in the parallel Mark 14:3. By a comparison with John 12:1-8, it becomes a reasonable deduction that he was the father of Lazarus, Martha, and Mary. **She did it for my burial.** The point seems to be that the action was appropriate in view of His burial which was soon to take place, and that it might be regarded as symbolic or prophetic of the burial. **This gospel,** i.e., the good news of the Lord's death and resurrection (see also Mk 14:10, 11; Lk 22:3-6). **Judas Iscariot** (see Mk 3:19) . . . **And they covenanted with him for thirty pieces of silver.** Actually, they weighed the amount to him, representing about a month's wages or the price of a common slave (see Stagg, p. 231). These words are substantially from the LXX of Zechariah 11:12. **Betray him,** i.e., hand Him over. The same verb is translated "deliver" in verse 15. The Last Supper is also related in Mark 14:12-16; Luke 22:7-13; and John 13:1-29. The Synoptics agree in the basic details and seem to assert that this was the Passover meal, whereas John clearly indicates that it was eaten before the Passover, with Jesus dying at the very hour the Passover lambs were slain (Jn 18:28; cf. I Cor 5:7). Liberal interpreters see the accounts as contradictory (Kee, p. 640); others suggest that Jesus followed the Essene custom of the Qumran community in taking the Passover meal on Tuesday (J. Walther, "Chronology of Passion Week," *JBL*, 1958, pp. 116ff.). However, it seems most likely that John, writing later, is simply clarifying the ambiguous points in the chronology, as he does elsewhere in his gospel in regard to other matters. Kent's material (pp. 97-109) on the chronology of the passion week is excellent and should be thoroughly considered.

17-24. The first day . . . of unleavened bread, or the fourteenth of Nisan (cf. Mk 14:12; Lk 22:7). The day actually began at sundown on the thirteenth. While Jesus said, **I will keep the passover,** the cross reference in Luke 22:16 notes He added, "I will not eat it," implying an interruption. Perhaps He did not want Judas to be aware of His certainty of the details. Only Jesus and the Twelve were present. At this crucial time Jesus announced **one of you shall betray me.** We cannot imagine the shock with which this statement must have jolted the disciples. For the first time, Jesus had clearly indicated that the betrayer would be one of the Twelve! They were **exceeding sorrowful,** indicating their grief over such an announcement. In the original language, the question **Lord, is it I?** suggests that a negative answer was cautiously expected by each one, "It is not I, is it?" Coupled with Peter's later defensive protest and subsequent failure, it seems clear that the entire group feared the possibility of failure. What a transformation would have to take place to change these cowards into the mighty apostles of the book of Acts!

ten of him: but woe unto that man by whom the Son of man is betrayed! it had been good for that man if he had not been born.

25 Then Judas, which betrayed him, answered and said, Master, is it I? He said unto him, Thou hast said.

26 ¶And as they were eating, Jesus took bread, and blessed *it*, and brake *it*, and gave *it* to the disciples, and said, Take, eat; this is my body.

27 And he took the cup, and gave thanks, and gave *it* to them, saying, Drink ye all of it;

28 For this is my blood of the new testament, which is shed for many for the remission of sins.

29 But I say unto you, I will not drink henceforth of this fruit of the vine, until that day when I drink it new with you in my Father's kingdom.

30 ¶And when they had sung an hymn, they went out into the mount of Olives.

31 Then saith Jesus unto them, All ye shall be offended because of me this night: for it is written, I will smite the shepherd, and the sheep of the flock shall be scattered abroad.

32 But after I am risen again, I will go before you into Galilee.

33 Peter answered and said unto him, Though all *men* shall be offended because of thee, *yet* will I never be offended.

34 Jesus said unto him, Verily I say unto thee, That this night, before the cock crow, thou shalt deny me thrice.

35 Peter said unto him, Though I should die with thee, yet will I not deny thee. Likewise also said all the disciples.

36 ¶Then cometh Jesus with them unto a place called Gĕth-sĕm'a-ne, and saith unto the disciples, Sit ye here, while I go and pray yonder.

37 And he took with him Peter and the two sons of Zĕb'e-dee, and began to be sorrowful and very heavy.

38 Then saith he unto them, My soul is exceeding sorrowful, even unto death: tarry ye here, and watch with me.

25-26. Judas repeated the same question and Jesus' reply, **Thou hast said,** means "yes." The statement, **He that dippeth,** reveals the personal and intimate nature of the betrayal. **Jesus took bread.** The head of the Jewish household was accustomed to doing this during the Passover feast. Jesus gave a completely new significance to the action. **This is my body.** If the words of the Lord had intended to convey a transformation of the bread into His body they would have read "This has become my body." During the Passover feast the Jewish householder took bread in his hand and said, "This is the bread of affliction which our fathers ate in the land of Egypt," meaning, of course, that the one represented the other. By His words the Lord changed the whole significance and emphasis of the feast from looking back to the typical redemption from Egypt to faith in the redemption from sin accomplished by His death. For a clear example of the use of the word "is" as "represents" see Galatians 4:25. The bread and wine were only outward symbols of our Lord's death and a reminder to us of the cost of our redemption during our Lord's absence (cf. Lk 22:19). Nothing in the Gospels indicates that these were to be viewed as a means of grace, sacraments, or that they were physically necessary for one's salvation.

27-30. The cup. Three cups were passed around by the Jewish householder during the Passover meal; the third, which is probably that referred to here, being known as "the cup of blessing." **My blood of the new testament** taken from the LXX of Exodus 24:8 with allusions to Jeremiah 31 and Zechariah 9:11. The covenant in Exodus 24:8 was sealed with blood. The word **testament** (Gr *diathēke*) did not mean a covenant, which is an agreement between equals, but a settlement by a great or rich man for the benefit of another. As the most common form of settlement was, and still is, by testament or will, the word came to have this meaning almost exclusively. **Shed for many for the remission of sins.** Here is a clear statement that the death of Jesus was necessary to enable God to forgive sins. It, in fact, made it right or morally justifiable for Him to do so. **That day,** i.e., when He comes again in glory.

31-35. The quotation in verse 31 is taken from the LXX of Zechariah 13:7. **Go before you,** literally, lead you forth, going at your head, as an eastern shepherd leads his sheep. This does not mean that the Lord would go first to Galilee in the sense that the disciples must go there to find Him, but that He would appear to them at Jerusalem and lead them to Galilee. **Though I should,** better, "Even if I must." Peter's boast later sets the stage for his bitter denials of his Master. He promised to be more faithful than the others, thus later provoking Jesus' question, "Lovest thou me more than these?" (probably referring to the other disciples of John 21:15).

36-39. The scene in the Garden of Gethsemane is one of the most moving in all the New Testament. **Gethsemane** means "olive press" and was a lush garden east of the city near the slopes of the Mount of Olives. Jesus often resorted there for peace and quiet. He took the same inner circle as at the transfiguration (Peter, James, and John) further into the garden. **My soul is exceeding sorrowful** is found in the LXX of Psalm 43:5. The imperative **watch** means to keep awake in order to be prepared for whatever might come. The prayer for the **cup** to **pass** is not due to Jesus' fear of death. Many martyrs have faced

39 And he went a little farther, and fell on his face, and prayed, saying, O my Father, if it be possible, let this cup pass from me: nevertheless not as I will, but as thou wilt.

40 And he cometh unto the disciples, and findeth them asleep, and saith unto Peter, What, could ye not watch with me one hour?

41 Watch and pray, that ye enter not into temptation: the spirit indeed is willing, but the flesh is weak.

42 He went away again the second time, and prayed, saying, O my Father, if this cup may not pass away from me, except I drink it, thy will be done.

43 And he came and found them asleep again: for their eyes were heavy.

44 And he left them, and went away again, and prayed the third time, saying the same words.

45 Then cometh he to his disciples, and saith unto them, Sleep on now, and take your rest: behold, the hour is at hand, and the Son of man is betrayed into the hands of sinners.

46 Rise, let us be going: behold, he is at hand that doth betray me.

47 ¶And while he yet spake, lo, Judas, one of the twelve, came, and with him a great multitude with swords and staves, from the chief priests and elders of the people.

48 Now he that betrayed him gave them a sign, saying, Whomsoever I shall kiss, that same is he: hold him fast.

49 And forthwith he came to Jesus, and said, Hail, master; and kissed him.

50 And Jesus said unto him, Friend, wherefore art thou come? Then came they, and laid hands on Jesus, and took him.

51 And, behold, one of them which were with Jesus stretched out his hand, and drew his sword, and struck a servant of the high priest's, and smote off his ear.

52 Then said Jesus unto him, Put up again thy sword into his place: for all they that take the sword shall perish with the sword.

53 Thinkest thou that I cannot now pray to my Father, and he shall presently give me more than twelve legions of angels?

54 But how then shall the scriptures be fulfilled, that thus it must be?

55 In that same hour said Jesus to the multitudes, Are ye come out as against a thief with swords and staves for to take me? I sat daily with you teaching in the temple, and ye laid no hold on me.

56 But all this was done, that the scriptures of the prophets might be fulfilled. Then all the disciples forsook him, and fled.

terrible deaths without great fear. Jesus questions the **will** of the Father as to the necessity of drinking the cup. While this may refer to death ("he tasted death") it is more likely that the cup represents the wrath of God against sin, which divine wrath Christ would incur on the cross as man's sinbearer. In the awful anguish of that moment, the sin of the world was poured on Christ and He became "sin for us" (II Cor 5:21). His total submission to the will of the Father causes Him to be obedient, even unto a substitutionary death. The Innocent and Righteous One dies for the guilty. Herein is His ultimate exaltation as Lord (Phil 2).

40-46. In the meantime the **disciples** were **asleep** due to emotional fatigue and physical exhaustion. Again, He urged them to **watch and pray, that ye enter not into temptation.** Several commentators unnecessarily relate this temptation to Christ (see Atkinson, p. 803), whereas in the context, He relates it to the disciples. Because they are not prayerfully watching, they will not be prepared for the tragedy that is about to happen. He reminded them that the **spirit . . . is willing, but the flesh is weak.** Man's regenerated spirit may have good intentions, but it must control his body (cf. Rom 12:1) in order to gain spiritual victory. The Greek present imperative indicates that they were to "continually keep watching." However, their fatigue causes the remark, **Sleep on now.** The immediate interruption of the soldiers causes Him to awaken them, **let us be going.**

47-50. The arrest took place in the Garden during the middle of the night as a mixed mob arrived to take Jesus. There can be little doubt that Jesus saw them approaching as there is always a full moon at Passover, and they probably also carried lighted torches (see Filson, p. 280). The Roman soldiers carried **swords** and the Jewish temple police had **staves** (clubs). The **sign** was necessary to identify Jesus to the Romans to whom He was unknown. Judas **kissed him** as the sign of betrayal of the One he still glibly called **master** (cf. Mt 7:23ff.). In response Jesus asked, **friend wherefore art thou come?** This convicting question was far more effective than an accusation, since Judas could not answer it.

51-56. One of them was Peter (Jn 18:10) who **drew his sword,** probably one of the short swords referred to in Luke 22:38. Attempting to defend Jesus, Peter **struck a servant of the high priest's, and smote off his ear.** In a typically impetuous move Peter had struck the one person who could have embarrassed them the most at the trial. Luke, a physician (22:51) tells us that Jesus healed him by replacing the ear (His last miracle) and John (18:10) tells us his name was Malchus. Jesus' rebuke: **Put up again thy sword** clearly revealed that His kingdom would not be brought in by force at that time. The statement **they that take the sword shall perish with the sword** is a statement of fact, but cannot be taken alone to teach nonviolence in all situations. Jesus has no lack of power by which to deal with these few enemies. **Twelve legions of angels** could be called to His aid. Each Roman legion has six thousand soldiers. Christ's restraint is due to His willingness to obey the will of the Father and so fulfill **the scriptures.** Even a well-intentioned defense by one of His disciples will not deter Jesus from the cross (on the meaning of these events, see F. W. Krummacher, *The Suffering Saviour*).

57 ¶And they that had laid hold on Jesus led *him* away to Cā'ia-phas the high priest, where the scribes and the elders were assembled.

58 But Peter followed him afar off unto the high priest's palace, and went in, and sat with the servants, to see the end.

59 Now the chief priests, and elders, and all the council, sought false witness against Jesus, to put him to death;

60 But found none: yea, though many false witnesses came, *yet* found they none. At the last came two false witnesses,

61 And said, This *fellow* said, I am able to destroy the temple of God, and to build it in three days.

62 And the high priest arose, and said unto him, Answerest thou nothing? what *is it which* these witness against thee?

63 But Jesus held his peace. And the high priest answered and said unto him, I adjure thee by the living God, that thou tell us whether thou be the Christ, the Son of God.

64 Jesus saith unto him, Thou hast said: nevertheless I say unto you, Hereafter shall ye see the Son of man sitting on the right hand of power, and coming in the clouds of heaven.

65 Then the high priest rent his clothes, saying, He hath spoken blasphemy; what further need have we of witnesses? behold, now ye have heard his blasphemy.

66 What think ye? They answered and said, He is guilty of death.

67 Then did they spit in his face, and buffeted him; and others smote *him* with the palms of their hands,

68 Saying, Prophesy unto us, thou Christ, Who is he that smote thee?

69 ¶Now Peter sat without in the palace: and a damsel came unto him, saying, Thou also wast with Jesus of Galilee.

70 But he denied before *them* all, saying, I know not what thou sayest.

71 And when he was gone out into the porch, another *maid* saw him, and said unto them that were there, This *fellow* was also with Jesus of Nazareth.

72 And again he denied with an oath, I do not know the man.

73 And after a while came unto *him* they that stood by, and said to Peter, Surely thou also art *one* of them; for thy speech bewrayeth thee.

74 Then began he to curse and to swear, *saying,* I know not the man. And immediately the cock crew.

75 And Peter remembered the word of Jesus, which said unto him, Before the cock crow, thou shalt deny me thrice. And he went out, and wept bitterly.

b. His denunciation by the Sanhedrin. 26:57-75.

57-65. See Mark 14:53-72; Luke 22:54-65; John 18:13-27. **Palace,** the open court around which the main buildings were built. **Servants** (Gr *hyperetēs*, "officers"). The evidence which was eventually brought forward (vs. 61) was based upon the Lord's words recorded in John 2:19, 21, nearly three years earlier! **I adjure thee by the living God.** This statement put a man on his oath and compelled an answer. The High Priest was seeking an admission which could be the foundation of a charge of blasphemy. **Thou hast said,** this means "yes." **Hereafter,** "Henceforth." The session at God's right hand began at the ascension (even, perhaps, at the resurrection). Note the allusion in our Lord's reply to Psalm 110:1 and Daniel 7:13. The second part of the phrase may refer as much to the ascension as to the second coming. The Jewish religious leaders would be witnesses of the victories of Christ after His resurrection. **Buffeted,** i.e., punched. Verse 68 is a sarcastic demand to be told the names and identities of those who were strangers to Him as a sign of supernatural knowledge. The incident ends with the charge of **blasphemy** and the indictment that He is **guilty of death.** There can be no doubt that the Sanhedrin took Him to be claiming to be the Messiah, which claim they violently rejected.

66-72. Peter's three denials occurred during the trial proceedings. **Peter sat without in the palace** or courtyard. We know from the Synoptics that he was warming himself by a fire, prepared by servants of the priests. The first denial was prompted by a **damsel,** or young maid, and the porters who had admitted him and John. Somehow she recognized him from an earlier meeting. The form of the denial, **I know not what thou sayest,** was merely a pretense of ignorance on Peter's part (similar to, "I don't know what you mean"). Feeling the pressure of the interrogation, Peter went **into the porch,** a passageway leading to the street. Then he was confronted by **another maid,** probably the outer gatekeeper who alerted the men (thus Luke's reference to a man as the interrogator) that **This fellow was also with Jesus of Nazareth.** The terms "Galilean" and "Nazarene" were probably used in a derogatory manner by these Judaeans. This time his denial was stronger, **with an oath,** in spite of Jesus' earlier warning against oath-taking (5:34). No pretended ignorance this time either; **I do not know the man,** he exclaimed.

73-75. The third denial came **after a while** (less than an hour) when he was accused because **thy speech betrayeth thee** or "makes you evident" (ASV) or "gives you away." Under the mounting emotional pressure and fear of being condemned along with Jesus, **he began to curse and to swear.** This emotional and sinful outburst was intended to make him appear unattached with Jesus. Later, this last great outburst of denial will be corrected by an emotion-packed reaffirmation of loyalty to the Saviour (cf. Jn 21:17). **And immediately the cock crew,** probably "cockcrowing" (i.e., the end of the Roman watch from midnight to 3:00 A.M.), verifying the illegitimacy of the trial which was being conducted during the middle of the night. **And Peter remembered,** not because he heard the noise, but as Luke (22:61) records: The Lord turned and looked upon him with a convicting glance from the balcony of the High Priest's house. Then he remembered the Saviour's warning and **went out and wept bitterly**. All these events related to the betrayal, arrest, and trial of Jesus show that He was completely in control of each situation even while being in the hands of His captors! See J. Stalker, *The Trial and Death of Jesus Christ* for a devotional discussion of these matters. On the theological significance of Christ's death see J. Denney, *The Death of Christ;* L. Morris, *The Cross in the New Testament;* J. Owen, *The Death of Death;* G. Smeaton, *The Atonement According to Christ and His Apostles.*

c. His deliverance to Pilate. 27:1-31.

CHAPTER 27

WHEN the morning was come, all the chief priests and elders of the people took counsel against Jesus to put him to death:

2 And when they had bound him, they led *him* away, and delivered him to Pontius Pilate the governor.

3 ¶Then Judas, which had betrayed him, when he saw that he was condemned, repented himself, and brought again the thirty pieces of silver to the chief priests and elders,

4 Saying, I have sinned in that I have betrayed the innocent blood. And they said, What *is that* to us? see thou *to that.*

5 And he cast down the pieces of silver in the temple, and departed, and went and hanged himself.

6 And the chief priests took the silver pieces, and said, It is not lawful for to put them into the treasury, because it is the price of blood.

7 And they took counsel, and bought with them the potter's field, to bury strangers in.

8 Wherefore that field was called, The field of blood, unto this day.

9 Then was fulfilled that which was spoken by Jeremy the prophet, saying, And they took the thirty pieces of silver, the price of him that was valued, whom they of the children of Israel did value;

10 And gave them for the potter's field, as the Lord appointed me.

11 ¶And Jesus stood before the governor: and the governor asked him, saying, Art thou the King of the Jews? And Jesus said unto him, Thou sayest.

12 And when he was accused of the chief priests and elders, he answered nothing.

13 Then said Pilate unto him, Hearest thou not how many things they witness against thee?

27:1-2. See also Mark 14:1-15; Luke 23:1-25, John 18:28-19:16. **Pontius Pilate the governor.** Pontius Pilate was the Roman procurator of Judaea from A.D. 26 to 37, holding his office under the Prefect of Syria. His usual place of residence was Caesarea, but he was in Jerusalem during the festival in order to deal with any insurrection or trouble.

3-8. When he saw that he was condemned, which would be evident from seeing Jesus being taken to Pilate (a move that Judas may not have anticipated), he **repented himself** (Gr *metameleomai,* "to regret"). This word is different from the term for repentance to salvation (Gr *metanoia*). Judas shows every indication of still being unsaved: he betrays innocent blood for money, becomes guilty, returns the money, and commits suicide. These are the actions of a guilty conscience, not a forgiven and regenerate one. His admission **I have sinned** is not necessarily a true confession to faith. The reply of the priests reveals the real cruelty of their hearts: **What is that to us? See thou to that.** A. W. Tozer calls this the "great double-cross," wherein Judas betrays Christ in collusion with the priests, who in return, reject him! Judas then threw the money **in the temple** (Gr *naos* means "sanctuary") and **hanged himself.** It is generally supposed that "falling headlong" (Acts 1:18-19) happened while he was attempting to do this. Perhaps, hanging himself over the ledge, he then fell into the valley below. **Bought,** in such cases the purchase was made in the name of the man to whom the money had been paid and to whom the money by a legal fiction was supposed all the time to belong. By law, therefore, the man himself purchased the field (see Acts 1:18).

9-10. Some have expressed concern over the mention of **Jeremiah** in this passage on the basis that the quotation apparently comes from Zechariah. While there is an allusion here to Zechariah 11:12-13, the actual words do not agree with either the Hebrew or the LXX. The major difference is the addition of the word **field,** upon which the fulfillment claimed is based. This word, and the conception behind it, comes from Jeremiah 32:6-9, where the prophet refers to the purchase of a field for certain pieces of silver. It is obvious that Matthew's concept of prophetic fulfillment rests upon both passages. Thus, he combines both passages into one quotation, giving credit to Jeremiah as the older and more predominant of the two prophets. Hendricksen (p. 948) draws the same conclusion, noting that a major prophet is preferred over a minor one in a similar double reference in Mark 1:2-3. There Isaiah is credited instead of Malachi (see Mal 3:1). This is certainly to be preferred to Plummer's suggestion (p. 386) that it was a "slip of the memory."

11-31. Barabbas means the father's son in Aramaic and must be seen in contrast with Jesus, the Father's Son. Pilate's question, **Why, what evil hath he done?** comes late in the trial and represents a personal, though unofficial, acknowledgment of Jesus' innocence. Thus, Pilate attempted to shift the blame for Jesus' death to the Jews themselves. The dramatic answer, **His blood be on us,** eventually brought the wrath of God upon His own people. Certainly their subsequent suffering must be viewed in light of this self-condemnation (see comments by

14 And he answered him to never a word; insomuch that the governor marvelled greatly.

15 ¶Now at *that* feast the governor was wont to release unto the people a prisoner, whom they would.

16 And they had then a notable prisoner, called Ba-răb'bas.

17 Therefore when they were gathered together, Pilate said unto them, Whom will ye that I release unto you? Ba-răb'bas, or Jesus which is called Christ?

18 For he knew that for envy they had delivered him.

19 ¶When he was set down on the judgment seat, his wife sent unto him, saying, Have thou nothing to do with that just man: for I have suffered many things this day in a dream because of him.

20 But the chief priests and elders persuaded the multitude that they should ask Ba-răb'bas, and destroy Jesus.

21 The governor answered and said unto them, Whether of the twain will ye that I release unto you? They said, Ba-răb'bas.

22 Pilate saith unto them, What shall I do then with Jesus which is called Christ? *They* all say unto him, Let him be crucified.

23 And the governor said, Why, what evil hath he done? But they cried out the more, saying, Let him be crucified.

24 When Pilate saw that he could prevail nothing, but *that* rather a tumult was made, he took water, and washed *his* hands before the multitude, saying, I am innocent of the blood of this just person: see ye *to it*.

25 Then answered all the people, and said, His blood *be* on us, and on our children.

26 Then released he Ba-răb'bas unto them: and when he had scourged Jesus, he delivered *him* to be crucified.

27 ¶Then the soldiers of the governor took Jesus into the common hall, and gathered unto him the whole band *of soldiers*.

28 And they stripped him, and put on him a scarlet robe.

29 ¶And when they had platted a crown of thorns, they put *it* upon his head, and a reed in his right hand: and they bowed the knee before him, and mocked him, saying, Hail, King of the Jews!

30 And they spit upon him, and took the reed, and smote him on the head.

31 And after that they had mocked him, they took the robe off from him, and put his own raiment on him, and led him away to crucify *him*.

32 And as they came out, they found a man of Cy̆-rē'ne, Simon by name: him they compelled to bear his cross.

33 And when they were come unto a place called Gŏl'go-tha, that is to say, a place of a skull,

34 They gave him vinegar to drink mingled with gall: and when he had tasted *thereof*, he would not drink.

35 And they crucified him, and parted his garments, casting lots: that

McNeile, p. 413). Encouraged by their willingness to take responsibility for His death, Pilate then **scourged Jesus** in hope that a bloody beating would appease them (cf. Jn 19:1-6). It was this beating that left Jesus extremely weak and eventually caused His early death on the cross (some survived on crosses for several days). The scourging was a whipping with a leather whip with sharp pieces of bone and metal embedded in its thongs. The statement that Pilate **delivered him** means he officially turned Him over to his soldiers for execution. They took Him **into the common hall** (Gr *praitōrion* from Lat *praetorium*) or governor's quarters, probably in the castle of Antonia. They mocked His claim to be King by clothing Him with a **scarlet robe** (Gr *chlamys*). It was a military robe, usually fastened at the shoulder. The **crown of thorns** and the **reed** for a scepter added to their mockery.

d. His death for mankind. 27:32-66.

32-35. A man of Cyrene, Simon by name. Cyrene was a Roman province in North Africa where many Jews lived. They had a synagogue in Jerusalem (Acts 6:9), indicating that many of them lived there. His sons, Alexander and Rufus, later became well-known Christians (see Mk 15:21). **Compelled** (Gr *anggarevō*, a technical term for requisitioned) **to bear his cross.** The cross was generally carried by the prisoner, which John 19:17 indicates was at first the case with Christ. Evidently, the weight was more than He could bear, due to His severe scourging. The transverse piece was usually carried separately and

it might be fulfilled which was spoken by the prophet. They parted my garments among them, and upon my vesture did they cast lots.

36 And sitting down they watched him there;

37 And set up over his head his accusation written, THIS IS JESUS THE KING OF THE JEWS.

38 Then were there two thieves crucified with him, one on the right hand, and another on the left.

39 ¶And they that passed by reviled him, wagging their heads,

40 And saying, Thou that destroyest the temple, and buildest it in three days, save thyself. If thou be the Son of God, come down from the cross.

41 Likewise also the chief priests mocking him, with the scribes and elders, said,

42 He saved others; himself he cannot save. If he be the King of Israel, let him now come down from the cross, and we will believe him.

43 He trusted in God; let him deliver him now, if he will have him: for he said, I am the Son of God.

44 The thieves also, which were crucified with him, cast the same in his teeth.

45 ¶Now from the sixth hour there was darkness over all the land unto the ninth hour.

46 And about the ninth hour Jesus cried with a loud voice, saying, E'lī, E'lī, lä'ma sa-bach'tha-ni? that is to say, My God, my God, why hast thou forsaken me?

47 Some of them that stood there, when they heard that, said, This man calleth for E-lī'as.

48 And straightway one of them ran, and took a spunge, and filled it with vinegar, and put it on a reed, and gave him to drink.

49 The rest said, Let be, let us see whether E-lī'as will come to save him.

50 ¶Jesus, when he had cried again with a loud voice, yielded up the ghost.

51 And, behold, the vail of the temple was rent in twain from the top to the bottom; and the earth did quake, and the rocks rent;

52 And the graves were opened; and

attached by rope to the vertical pole at the place of execution (see Plummer, p. 393). **Golgotha . . . a place of a skull.** The name is a transliteration of the Aramaic word for **skull** and is equivalent to the Latin *calvaria*, probably due to the physical appearance of the hill. Presently two sites have been claimed as Golgotha: (1) the site of the Church of the Holy Sepulchre (which at that time was outside the wall) and (2) the hill north of Jerusalem known as "Gordon's Calvary" (which definitely resembles a skull, even until this day). **They gave him vinegar to drink mingled with gall,** an allusion to Psalm 69:21. This was customarily given to condemned prisoners to serve as a kind of anesthetic or anodyne. It was literally a drugged "wine" (Gr *oinon.*) The statement that **He would not drink** indicates that our Lord refused any mitigation of His sufferings on our behalf.

They crucified him. Crucifixion was a common means of execution.

36-44. Pilate placed a placard over Jesus' head with the accusation: **THIS IS JESUS THE KING OF THE JEWS.** Little did he realize how true this intended mockery of the Jews really was. Indeed, as Matthew shows, Jesus was the King of the Jews, whom they had rejected. The priests **wagging their heads,** an allusion to Psalm 22:7, said **Thou that destroyest the temple . . . save thyself.** However, that was the one thing Jesus could not and would not do. To save Himself would have meant the loss of the entire world. No wonder He had to have endured Satan's earlier temptation to satisfy Himself, for now He would conquer Satan's power forever by denying Himself! The further accusations, **He saved others . . . He trusted in God . . . He said I am the Son of God** were actually true in the opposite sense in which the priests intended them. **The thieves** (Gr *lēstēs*) were robbers, perhaps cohorts of Barabbas. The statement, **cast the same in his teeth,** means they repeated similar taunts to Him.

45-50. From the sixth hour . . . unto the ninth hour means from noon until 3:00 P.M. Mark (15:25) indicates Jesus had been placed on the cross at the third hour (9:00 A.M.). It is questioned whether this is Jewish or Roman time. The **darkness** was evidently supernaturally imposed since an eclipse of the sun at full noon is impossible. God's wrath was poured upon His Son during this time of darkness. At the ninth hour (3:00 P.M.) Jesus cried: **Eli, Eli, lama sabachthani** (Aramaic) for **My God, my God, why hast thou forsaken me?** Here we have the high cost of the atonement to Christ, who was accursed of God for us as our sinbearer (cf. II Cor 5:21; Gal 3:13) and suffered the agony of spiritual death for us. The sense of being forsaken was not necessarily caused by God the Father looking away from Him, but from His looking at Him in wrath, as He would look in judgment at a condemned sinner. **He . . . cried . . . with a loud voice,** as a shout of triumph, and **yielded up** His Spirit. In other words having borne the wrath of God's judgment against sin, He knew that He had triumphed over Satan and the curse of sin. His heel was "bruised," but the serpent's head had been "crushed." The yielding of His life was the result of His voluntary surrender of His life for the sake of His own.

51-53. The events immediately following Jesus' death were remarkable indeed. **The veil of the temple** refers to either the curtain over the entrance to the Holy Place (which could be viewed from the porch) or to the curtain separating the Holy Place from the Holy of Holies (cf. Ex 26:31). The latter is most

many bodies of the saints which slept arose.

53 And came out of the graves after his resurrection, and went into the holy city, and appeared unto many.

54 Now when the centurion, and they that were with him, watching Jesus, saw the earthquake, and those things that were done, they feared greatly, saying, Truly this was the Son of God.

55 And many women were there beholding afar off, which followed Jesus from Galilee, ministering unto him:

56 Among which was Mary Magdalene, and Mary the mother of James and Joses, and the mother of Zĕb'edee's children.

57 ¶When the even was come, there came a rich man of Ăr-i-ma-thæ'a, named Joseph, who also himself was Jesus' disciple:

58 He went to Pilate, and begged the body of Jesus. Then Pilate commanded the body to be delivered.

59 And when Joseph had taken the body, he wrapped it in a clean linen cloth,

60 And laid it in his own new tomb, which he had hewn out in the rock: and he rolled a great stone to the door of the sepulchre, and departed.

61 And there was Mary Magdalene, and the other Mary, sitting over against the sepulchre.

62 ¶Now the next day, that followed the day of the preparation, the chief priests and Pharisees came together unto Pilate,

63 Saying, Sir, we remember that that deceiver said, while he was yet alive, After three days I will rise again.

64 Command therefore that the sepulchre be made sure until the third day, lest his disciples come by night, and steal him away, and say unto the people, He is risen from the dead: so the last error shall be worse than the first.

65 Pilate said unto them, Ye have a

likely here and symbolizes the permanent opening of God's presence to man and man's direct access to God through the atoning death of Christ. Henceforth, all ceremonial services of priests and sacrifices would be done away for the Christian believer (cf. comments on the book of Hebrews). The **earth did quake** which was a visible manifestation of God's judgment on those who had wrongly crucified the Lord of Glory and it caused the **graves** to be **opened** and the **saints which slept** (departed Old Testament believers) **arose.** This incident is stated only by Matthew and indicates that the Old Testament believers were resurrected **after His resurrection** and **appeared unto many.** It is properly supposed that they were resurrected from "paradise," or "Abraham's bosom" and taken to heaven by the resurrected Christ (cf. Eph 4:8-9). For a discussion of a wide range of views on this see Lange (p. 528).

54-56. The **centurion and they that were with him** exclaimed: **Truly this was the Son of God** (vs. 54). Whether this was an affirmation of genuine faith (based on all they had witnessed) or merely a pagan appreciation of the awesomeness of the circumstances is not clear. However, we dare not minimize the spiritual effect these events could have had on them. Certainly the incident reveals how Jesus' life and character, even in the face of death, rose above the greatest qualities of pagan Rome. The witnesses also included several key women: **Mary Magdalene** (cf. Magdala, in Galilee. Some suggest she is the woman out of whom Jesus cast seven devils in that region. However, her identification as Mary is not clear); **Mary the mother of James and Joses** was the wife of Cleopas (Jn 19:25); the "other Mary" of verse 61; the **mother of Zebedee's children** was Salome (cf. Mk 15:40) and apparently a sister of the Virgin Mary.

57-61. The burial of Jesus' body was seen to by **a rich man of Arimathea, named Joseph.** In fulfillment of Isaiah 53:9, Jesus made His death with the rich. Joseph was a Sanhedrinist, who had become a **disciple.** His wealth enabled him to own a tomb at Jerusalem even though he lived nearly twenty miles away. Wealthy people in those days often selected their tombs while they were still living. He **begged the body** from Pilate and got it, undoubtedly not without personal risk on his part. With help from Nicodemus, a believing Pharisee (cf. Jn 3), he took the body from the cross and wrapped it in a **clean linen cloth** or shroud, in the typical burial custom of the day. On the possible legitimacy of the Shroud of Turin, see G. Habermas, *Verdict on the Shroud.* The body was then placed in Joseph's **own new tomb . . . hewn out in the rock** and covered with a **great stone,** generally rolled in a groove and into place securely over the opening of the tomb. Such a stone would be humanly impossible for one man to roll back by himself from the inside, thus nullifying the ridiculous view that Jesus had only passed out and later "revived" and got out of the tomb. All such antisupernatural compromises with the text cause more interpretive problems than they supposedly solve. According to the text only the two Marys watched the burial and no disciples were present.

62-66. The **next day . . . followed the day of the preparation.** There is some question as to whether this was Saturday (the Sabbath), following a Friday crucifixion. However, John 19:14, 31 indicates that this "preparation day" was the day before the Passover feast day. This may account for Matthew's not using the term "Sabbath" here (cf. Kent, p. 709). He favors a Wednesday crucifixion, with the burial lasting a full seventy-two hours and taking literally the terms **After three days** and **on the third day;** by contrast see Atkinson (p. 805) who favors a Friday crucifixion based on Jewish "inclusive reckoning" of any part of a day equal to a full day. In favor of the Wednesday crucifixion it should be observed that the text does not specify "Friday," and this view can harmonize all the Sabbath refer-

watch: go your way, make *it* as sure as ye can.

66 So they went, and made the sepulchre sure, sealing the stone, and setting a watch.

CHAPTER 28

IN the end of the sabbath, as it began to dawn toward the first *day* of the week, came Mary Magdalene and the other Mary to see the sepulchre.

2 And, behold, there was a great earthquake: for the angel of the Lord descended from heaven, and came and rolled back the stone from the door, and sat upon it.

3 His countenance was like lightning, and his raiment white as snow:

4 And for fear of him the keepers did shake, and became as dead *men*.

5 And the angel answered and said unto the women, Fear not ye: for I know that ye seek Jesus, which was crucified.

6 He is not here: for he is risen, as he said. Come, see the place where the Lord lay.

7 And go quickly, and tell his disciples that he is risen from the dead; and, behold, he goeth before you into Galilee; there shall ye see him: lo, I have told you.

8 And they departed quickly from the sepulchre with fear and great joy; and did run to bring his disciples word.

9 ¶And as they went to tell his disciples, behold, Jesus met them, saying, All hail. And they came and held him by the feet, and worshipped him.

10 Then said Jesus unto them, Be not afraid: go tell my brethren that they go into Galilee, and there shall they see me.

11 ¶Now when they were going, behold, some of the watch came into the city, and shewed unto the chief priests all the things that were done.

12 And when they were assembled with the elders, and had taken counsel, they gave large money unto the soldiers,

13 Saying, Say ye, His disciples came by night, and stole him *away* while we slept.

14 And if this come to the governor's ears, we will persuade him, and secure you.

15 So they took the money, and did as they were taught: and this saying is commonly reported among the Jews until this day.

16 ¶Then the eleven disciples went away into Galilee, into a mountain where Jesus had appointed them.

ences and resolve the problems of the Jewish leaders meeting with Pilate on the Sabbath and the women preparing spices on the Sabbath (see chart on "Chronology of the Crucifixion" and the detailed discussion and diagrams in W. Scroggie, *A Guide to the Gospels*, pp. 568-577).

III. TRIUMPH OF THE MESSIAH 28:1-20.

A. His Resurrection. 28:1-8.

28:1-8. See also Mark 16:1-20; Luke 24:1-12; John 20:1-31. All four Gospels essentially agree in reporting the facts of the resurrection. The variety of details in each account supplement rather than contradict each other. The empty tomb was discovered **In the end** (Gr *opse,* used as improper preposition for "after") **of the sabbath** agreeing with the other evangelists. By Jewish reckoning the day ended at sunset and the new day began at the same time. Thus, Saturday night by our reckoning was actually Sunday by their calendar. Accordingly, the resurrection actually occurred sometime during the night, for by the time the women arrived **as it began to dawn** He had already risen from the dead. The **earthquake** and the **angel** (Mark's "man in white"), who rolled the stone away, did not come to let Jesus out of the tomb, but to reveal that it was empty and that He was gone already! Evidently Mary Magdalene left immediately to tell Peter and John. The angel told the other women, **Fear not . . . He is not here: for he is risen, as he said.** The pronoun "you" is emphatic: "you women, only, do not fear me" (as the guards did, who were paralyzed with terror). "They have come to see the grave, drawn there by sorrow, love, and, perhaps, inarticulate hope. For their loyalty and persistent love they hear first the news of the resurrection" (Filson, p. 302). The angel then instructed them to go unto Galilee to meet Him.

B. His Reappearance. 28:9-15.

9-15. Running ahead with **fear and great joy** they actually met Jesus and worshipped Him. We cannot imagine their emotional attitude at this moment when fear and joy gripped them simultaneously. Again, they were instructed to go before Him into Galilee. Here Matthew's account is considerably briefer and less detailed than the other Gospels (where we have specific accounts of Peter and John running to the tomb; Mary meeting Jesus; the appearance in the upper room; the appearance to more than five hundred believers at once; and the undeniably literal incident on the seashore, Jn 21). The one addition by Matthew is the falsified report of the guards in verses 11-15. Pilate had put the soldiers at the disposal of the Jewish Sanhedrin so they reported first to them. The assemblage **gave large money** or a large bribe to the soldiers to hide the truth of the resurrection with the lie, **saying . . . His disciples came by night, and stole him away while we slept,** a ridiculous statement in view of the disciples' earlier defection in the Garden. How could this band of cowards overpower an armed Roman guard? Thus, Matthew observed that this explanation was still **commonly reported among the Jews** in his day. On the theological significance of the resurrection see G. Habermas, *The Resurrection of Jesus, An Apologetic;* J. McDowell, *The Resurrection Factor;* G. Ladd, "The Resurrection of Jesus Christ," in *Christian Faith and Modern Theology,* pp. 261-284; W. Sparrow-Simpson, *Our Lord's Resurrection;* M. Tenney, *The Reality of the Resurrection.*

C. His Recommission. 28:16-20.

16-17. Now instead of sending His disciples back to the house of Israel, they are sent into all the world. The kingdom rejected by Jews will now be offered to the Gentiles in accordance with Jesus' earlier parables. This appearance in **Galilee** is

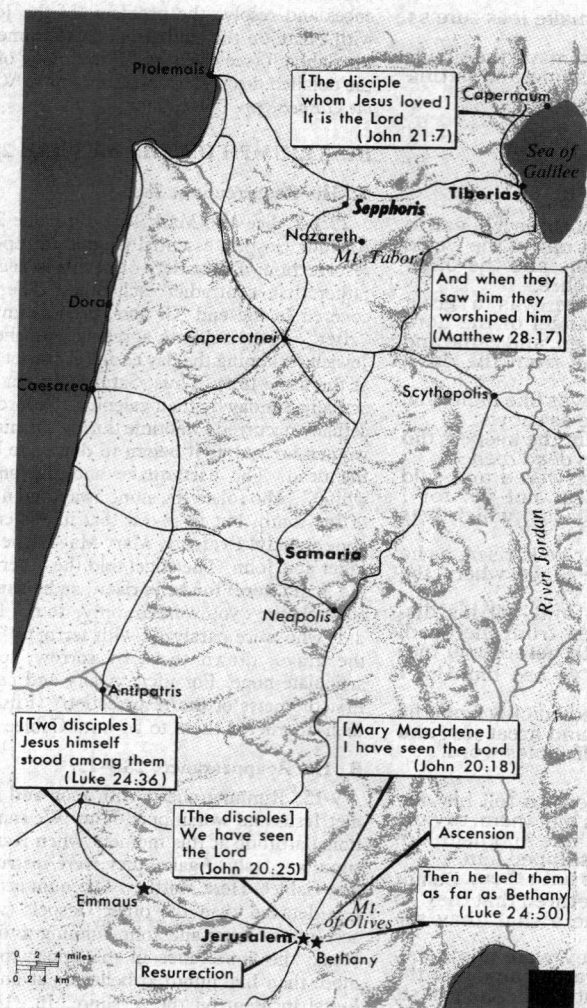

[The disciple
whom Jesus loved]
It is the Lord
(John 21:7)

And when they
saw him they
worshiped him
(Matthew 28:17)

Ptolemais

Capernaum

Sea of
Galilee

Tiberias

Sepphoris

Nazareth

Mt. Tabor

Dora

Capercotner

Caesarea

Scythopolis

River Jordan

Samaria

Neapolis

Antipatris

[Mary Magdalene]
I have seen the Lord
(John 20:18)

[Two disciples]
Jesus himself
stood among them
(Luke 24:36)

Ascension

[The disciples]
We have seen
the Lord
(John 20:25)

Then he led them
as far as Bethany
(Luke 24:50)

Emmaus

*Mt.
of Olives*

Jerusalem

Bethany

0 2 4 miles
0 2 4 km

Resurrection

The Resurrection and Ascension

17 And when they saw him, they worshiped him: but some doubted.

not to be confused with the appearances at Jerusalem and is probably the same as the appearance to "above five hundred brethren" (cf. I Cor 15:6), with the **eleven** being among them. This is further implied by the statement, **they worshiped him: but some doubted,** which would be unlikely of the eleven after the earlier appearances and the "doubting Thomas" incident (Jn 20:28). This also implies a difference in Jesus' appearance after His resurrection, as also described by John, His own beloved disciple, who barely recognizes the resurrected-glorified Christ in Revelation 1. Lange (p. 556) adds the further explanation that "doubted" (Gr *distazō*) may also be translated "hesitated," in the sense that while they obviously saw Him, they hesitated to offer Him such unbounded worship. Prior to Christ's death and resurrection, His disciples, while recognizing His divine messiahship, did not openly worship Him in the manner that would now become customary. Otherwise, why would Matthew, writing to convince the Jews of Jesus, say so close to the end of his gospel that some "doubted"? The more obvious explanation is that as he wrote to the hesitant Jewish commu-

18 And Jesus came and spake unto them, saying, All power is given unto me in heaven and in earth.

19 Go ye therefore, and teach all nations, baptizing them in the name of the Father, and of the Son, and of the Holy Ghost:

20 Teaching them to observe all things whatsoever I have commanded you: and, lo, I am with you alway, *even* unto the end of the world. Amen.

nity, he was saying he understood their hesitation for he too was a Jew who had become a Christian.

18-20. The Great Commission brings the first Gospel to its grand finale. Christianity is not represented here as the mere reverential devotion of disappointed men who honor their martyred leader. Here is a far different scene. The triumphant living Lord sends forth His ambassadors to proclaim His gospel throughout all the world. The Commission is not just an order but a pronouncement of victory (*mundus regium Christi*) by the risen Saviour through His disciples. **All power** or authority (Gr *exousia*) was now in the hands of Christ, in heaven and on the earth. On the basis of that authority and power the Christian disciple is to carry out the Great Commission of the church. **Go ye** is actually a participle and conveys not a command to go, but the assumption that the listener will automatically be going. In other words, the idea expressed is that "as you are going" make disciples, and **Teach all nations** could be translated "convert all Gentiles," or "disciple all nations." Thus the converting influence of the gospel is indicated here. Reaching the nations is not merely a matter of education but the full process of discipleship, i.e., teaching and training, beginning with conversion. The "all nations" makes it clear that the Commission to the church is a worldwide one, encompassing the entire missionary effort. The church is not to be merely "missionary-minded." The church is the vehicle of Christ's mission to the world and the two (church and mission) are inseparable. Every local church has a mission to its world. To attempt to eliminate this commission from the church age (as do the hyperdispensationalists) would be to leave the church without an assigned purpose from her Lord.

Baptizing the converted disciples is the first step of outward obedience to the Lord and brings entrance into the membership of the local congregation. "Baptize" (Gr *baptizō*) is an English transliteration, and means to "dip," or "dunk," or "immerse," thus indicating its proper mode. Nowhere does this term ever indicate "sprinkling." On baptism see A. Carson, *Baptism in the New Testament;* E. Hulse, *Baptism and Church Membership;* J. Warnes, *Baptism;* contra see J. Murray, *Christian Baptism.* These converts are to be baptized **in the name of the Father, and of the Son, and of the Holy Ghost.** The "name" is singular, followed by an elliptical clause indicating that the one name is the name of each person of the Trinity. While baptismal references in Acts refer to being baptized in Jesus' name (emphasizing His deity as Saviour) they in no way eliminate the significance of this formula given by Christ Himself. Nor do the three persons of the Godhead necessitate a trine immersion in each name. Furthermore, these baptized converts are to be taught **all things** that Jesus taught, thus the edifying and exhorting ministry of the church is seen as it develops in the book of Acts.

The closing promise, though given to the apostles, is transmitted by every generation of believers (cf. Jn 17:20). Christ's promise of His presence, **I am with you alway,** guarantees the success of the church's mission because it is really His mission carried out by His called-out disciples. The phrase **unto the end of the world** means until the end of the "age" (Gr *aiōn*). Therefore, the empowerment of Christ to the church to evangelize the world is available in every age, even unto the end of the church age. There is no excuse, then, for failing to exercise that power in our age. No time of apostasy will ever be so great as to nullify the true gospel ministry of the Bible-preaching church. In comparing the Great Commission with Jesus' promise to continually build His church (ch. 18), we must conclude that He intended His church always to be spiritually militant and evangelistically aggressive as we take His claims of lordship to the entire world of our generation. **Amen!**

BIBLIOGRAPHY

Allen, W. C. A Critical and Exegetical Commentary on the Gospel According to St. Matthew. In *International Critical Commentary*. New York: Scribners, 1925.

*Alexander, J. A. *The Gospel According to Matthew*. New York: Scribner, Armstrong & Co., 1873.

Atkinson, B.F.C. The Gospel According to Matthew. In *New Bible Commentary*. Grand Rapids: Eerdmans, 1953.

Barclay, E. *The Gospel of Matthew*. Philadelphia: Westminster Press, 1958.

*Broadus, J. A. Commentary on the Gospel of Matthew. In *American Commentary Series*. Philadelphia: American Baptist Publication Society, 1886.

Calvin, J. *Commentary on a Harmony of the Evangelists*. Trans. by A. W. Morrison, Grand Rapids: Eerdmans, 1972.

Carr, A. *The Gospel According to St. Matthew*. Cambridge: University Press, 1913.

Ellison, H. L. The Gospel According to Matthew. In *A New Testament Commentary*, Ed. by G. Howley. Grand Rapids: Eerdmans, 1969.

English, E. S. *Studies in the Gospel According to Matthew*. New York: Revell, 1935.

Filson, F. V. *Commentary on the Gospel According to St. Matthew*. New York: Harper & Brothers, 1960.

Gaebelein, A. C. *The Gospel of Matthew*. New York: Our Hope, 1910.

*Hendriksen, W. *Exposition of the Gospel According to Matthew*. Grand Rapids: Baker, 1973.

Hill, David. The Gospel of Matthew. In *The New Century Bible*. London: Marshall, Morgan & Scott, 1972.

*Kent, H. A., Jr. Matthew. In *Wycliffe Bible Commentary*. Ed. by C. Pfeiffer and E. Harrison. Chicago: Moody Press, 1962.

Lange, J. P. *Commentary on the Holy Scriptures: Matthew*. Grand Rapids: Zondervan, n.d.

Lenski, R. C. *The Interpretation of St. Matthew's Gospel*. Minneapolis: Augsburg, 1961.

McNeile, A. H. *The Gospel According to St. Matthew*. London: Macmillan, 1915.

Morgan, G. C. *The Gospel According to Matthew*. New York: Revell, 1929.

Plummer, A. *An Exegetical Commentary on the Gospel According to St. Matthew*. London: Robert Scott, 1909.

Ridderbos, H. *Matthew's Witness to Jesus Christ*. New York: Association Press, 1958.

Ryle, J. C. *Expository Thoughts on the Gospels: Matthew*. London: James Clarke, 1954.

Stonehouse, N. B. *The Witness of Matthew and Mark to Christ*. Grand Rapids: Eerdmans, 1958.

*Tasker, R.V.G. The Gospel According to St. Matthew. In *Tyndale New Testament Series*. Grand Rapids: Eerdmans, 1961.

*Toussaint, S. D. *Behold the King: A Study of Matthew*. Portland, Or.: Multnomah Press, 1980.

*Walvoord, J. *Matthew—Thy Kingdom Come*. Chicago: Moody Press, 1974.

The Gospel According To
MARK

INTRODUCTION

Authorship. Mark is commonly accepted as the author, the church fathers affirming this without controversy. In fact, they felt it necessary to explain how a seemingly improbable person like Mark came to compose this account. He became a close associate of Peter and for many years listened to his sermons and conversations about the Lord's life. Tradition says that those who observed his notes of Peter's sermons urged him to formulate them into a systematized life story of Jesus; if this were true, the source of the material would be Peter. Papias, bishop of Hierapolis, in the first half of the second century testified, "And John, the presbyter, also said this, Mark being the interpreter of Peter, whatsoever he recorded he wrote with great accuracy . . . and he was in company with Peter, who gave him such instructions as necessary, but not to give a history of our Lord's discourses" (Eusebius, *Ecclesiastical History* III, p. 39). It is probable that Papias as a young man had met the Apostle John. Ireneaus, bishop of Lyons, agrees, "Mark the disciple and interpreter of Peter, did also hand down to us in writing what has been preached by Peter." Likewise, Justin Martyr refers to Mark's work as the memoirs of Peter. Thus, we can picture the younger disciple, after hearing innumerable eyewitness accounts of the Saviour, feeling compelled to commit them to writing for the benefit of future generations.

The author's full name was John Mark (Acts 12:12). His mother, Mary, had servants, indicating the family was not ill-furnished. Besides by his mother, Mark was influenced by his cousin, Barnabas, who took him with Paul on the first missionary journey (Acts 13:5). Halfway through the journey Mark returned home (Acts 13:13). The reason for the departure must have been questionable for when Barnabas and Paul planned a second journey, Paul's insistence on excluding Mark was so intense that the two leaders parted company (Acts 15:39), Barnabas setting sail for Cyprus with Mark. Whatever Paul observed as a weakness in Mark at this point, in later years he commended Mark's efforts in the ministry (II Tim 4:11).

Little else is known of this disciple. However, his gospel does include an unusual event in connection with Christ's arrest. A young follower hurrying to escape lost his garment and sprinted away naked (Mk 14:51-52). Although it cannot be proven, most scholars understand Mark to be speaking of himself; there would be no other apparent reason for including this event.

His close association with Peter is not based on tradition alone; Peter himself mentions Mark in a manner which supports it (I Pet 5:13). It has been commonly held that Mark moved to Rome with Peter and remained there until both Peter and Paul died. He then moved to Alexandria and founded a church which later became quite influential (Eusebius, *Ecclesiastical History* II, p. 16).

Recipients. Tradition depicts Mark's work as arising from the entreaties of Roman Christians. The style and contents corroborate this belief including several "latinisms" such as those found in 4:21 (bushel), 12:14 (tribute), 6:27 (executioner), and 15:39, 44-45 (centurion). That Aramaic expressions are translated or explained (7:3-4), indicates the readers were not Jewish. Additionally, in Mark 15:21 where a man named Simon bears Jesus' cross, his sons are named, one of whom was Rufus, a resident of Rome (Rom 16:13). If the book were destined for another locality, this inclusion would seem peculiar.

Date and Place of Writing. The final composition took place after Peter's death, no earlier than A.D. 65, and before the fall of Jerusalem, A.D. 70. Papias, Clement of Alexandria, Origen, Eusebius, and Jerome all affirm or imply that the place of writing was Rome.

Purpose. If one finds specific emphases in the other Gospels (Jesus as King in Matthew, as Son of Man in Luke, and as Son of God in John), he may observe the Lord as Servant in Mark. A passage that lays stress on Christ's service says that He came "to minister" (10:45). Another factor which supports this is the growth of Roman intolerance toward Christianity, which was developing into open persecution. One author concludes, "The chief purpose of the gospel is to portray the personality of Jesus in such a way that the church in the hour of its severe trial would receive power to endure and remain faithful" (Davies, *The Abingdon Commentary*, p. 996). The design of the narrative also concurs with John who declared, "But these are written, that ye might believe . . ." (Jn 20:31).

Characteristics. Three areas of emphasis may be observed:

1. Activities, rather than teachings of Christ. The narration swiftly moves from one event to the next. In fact, the action itself is described frequently by the word "immediately" (Gr *euthus*). This style may reflect the impulsive, action-oriented personality of Peter, who furnished Mark with his information. Relatively few of Christ's teachings are included, the Olivet Discourse being the only one of substantial length (Mk 13).

2. Geography. The longest and initial location of Christ's ministry occurred in and around Galilee. A later phase describes extended trips to areas beyond. Finally, tension builds as He approaches and enters Jerusalem, where His rejection and death ensue.

3. Vividness of detail and realism. Looks, gestures and actions stand out. The author announces without hesitation that the Lord's relatives had concluded that He lost His senses (3:21) and that "all men" were looking for Him. (1:35-38). During the Crucifixion the expressions of mockery and the details of His suffering draw a graphic picture of ineffable endurance.

OUTLINE

COMMENTARY

I. THE INTRODUCTION TO CHRIST'S MINISTRY. 1:1-13.

A. The Title. 1:1.

THE beginning of the gospel of Jesus Christ, the Son of God;

1:1. The theme of Mark's book is the "Good News" (Gr *euangelion*) about Jesus Christ. The name, **Christ**, (Gr *Christos*) refers to His office (the Anointed One). His early life was only the **beginning** of this gospel, for the resurrection denies the story an ending.

B. The Preparation for His Ministry. 1:2-13.

1. John the Baptist. 1:2-8.

2 As it is written in the prophets, Behold, I send my messenger before thy face, which shall prepare thy way before thee.
3 The voice of one crying in the wilderness, Prepare ye the way of the Lord, make his paths straight.
4 John did baptize in the wilderness, and preach the baptism of repentance for the remission of sins.

2-3. The forerunner had arrived according to divine prediction: **As it is written in the prophets** (Mal 3:1 and Isa 40:3).

4. John's preparatory ministry included two basic aspects: baptizing and preaching. **Baptize** (Gr *baptizō*) literally means "to dip into" or "to immerse" and its connection with **repentance** indicates that the ordinance held no inherent virtue or merit but merely symbolized an inward change of attitude toward sin. The root problem of John's listeners parallels that of contemporary society. They not only were sinful, but were insensitive to their condition.

5 And there went out unto him all the land of Judæa, and they of Jerusalem, and were all baptized of him in the river of Jordan, confessing their sins.

5. Mark employs a hyperbole when he uses the word **all** to describe the response to his preaching. The translation "all the people of Judea were going out and were being baptized" more clearly brings out the significance of the imperfect tense used in Greek. **Confessing** stems from two Greek words which together mean "to say the same thing as." Genuine confession is not merely admitting guilt, but it places the same appraisement upon it that God does.

6 And John was clothed with camel's hair, and with a girdle of a skin about his loins; and he did eat locusts and wild honey;
7 And preached, saying, There cometh one mightier than I after me, the latchet of whose shoes I am not worthy to stoop down and unloose.
8 I indeed have baptized you with water: but he shall baptize you with the Holy Ghost.

6. A simple, if not crude, life-style marks John's priorities. His ambitions and goals pertain to the One mentioned next, not to personal convenience.

7-8. This announcement contains implications regarding Christ's person and His function. His person: to untie someone else's shoes is the task of a menial servant. So eminent is He, that to untie His is a privilege! His function: John is but a man announcing the message and baptizing those who respond; he himself cannot affect the inner person. The One whom John introduces also will baptize, but not as a physical sign. His baptism will transform the soul by "the washing of regeneration and renewing of the Holy Ghost" (Tit 3:5).

2. Christ's baptism. 1:9-11.

9 ¶And it came to pass in those days, that Jesus came from Nazareth of Galilee, and was baptized of John in Jordan.
10 And straightway coming up out of the water, he saw the heavens opened, and the Spirit like a dove descending upon him:

9. Jesus' baptism is related in surprisingly simple language. Mark recounts that He left His home town and submitted to the rite.

10. The significance of this event lies in God's public approval of Jesus. The whole Trinity is involved. The Son submits to the ordinance; the Spirit rests upon Him; and the Father voices His pleasure. The form assumed by the Spirit, **like a dove,** may be related to Genesis 1:2, which pictures Him hovering (AV, **moved**) over the waters, as a hen resides on her nest. The Spirit longs to overshadow men with His infilling power. This was accomplished perfectly in the Son, because He submitted without any reservations.

11 And there came a voice from

11. The heavenly voice both qualified and identified Jesus. Others have been called **beloved** and pleasing, but He alone can

heaven, *saying,* Thou art my beloved Son, in whom I am well pleased.

12 ¶And immediately the spirit driveth him into the wilderness.
13 And he was there in the wilderness forty days, tempted of Satan; and was with the wild beasts; and the angels ministered unto him.

14 ¶Now after that John was put in prison, Jesus came into Galilee, preaching the gospel of the kingdom of God,

15 And saying, The time is fulfilled, and the kingdom of God is at hand: repent ye, and believe the gospel.

16 ¶Now as he walked by the sea of Galilee, he saw Simon and Andrew his brother casting a net into the sea: for they were fishers.
17 And Jesus said unto them, Come ye after me, and I will make you to become fishers of men.
18 And straightway they forsook their nets, and followed him.

19 And when he had gone a little farther thence, he saw James the *son* of Zĕb′e-dee, and John his brother, who also were in the ship mending their nets.
20 And straightway he called them: and they left their father Zĕb′e-dee in the ship with the hired servants, and went after him.
21 And they went into Ca-per′na-um; and straightway on the sabbath day he entered into the synagogue, and taught.

22 And they were astonished at his doctrine: for he taught them as one that had authority, and not as the scribes.

be termed **my Son.** There are many children, but He is the unique Son of God.

3. Christ's temptation. 1:12-13.

12-13. In verse 10 Jesus' baptism resulted in the Spirit's control and here one may observe the extent of His submission. **Driveth** comes from the Greek *ekballō* which may be translated "leads." It does convey a forceful guidance, which illustrates one area of Christ's self-humiliation. Matthew and Luke include the details of the temptation (Mt 4 and Lk 4), but Mark limits his account to a general statement.

II. THE MINISTRY IN GALILEE. 1:14-7:23.

A. The Initial Stage. 1:14-3:5.

1. The opening of the Galilaean Ministry. 1:14-15.

14. In spite of all the miracles evidenced in Christ's life, the predominant characteristic of His ministry is described by the words **Jesus came . . . preaching.** In the oldest manuscripts **the gospel of the kingdom of God** is simply "the gospel of God" which may be rendered "the gospel from God," stressing its source.

15. What causes **the kingdom of God** to be **at hand?** The presence of the King! What does the King require of His servants? The answer is twofold: Negatively, **repent** (Gr *metanoéō*) change their attitudes about their sin; specifically recognize its evil and forsake it. Positively, **believe** God's Good News centered in Christ.

2. Four disciples called. 1:16-20.

16. John 1:40-42 describes the first encounter **Simon** and **Andrew** had with Jesus. The reference to them as **fishers** names their business or livelihood, not their sport.

17. Jesus frequently appealed to people on the basis of their occupation or background. Instead of catching fish, would you not rather be netting men? The prerequisite: **Come ye after me!**

18. Their response to this unusual call indicates that they had had previous contact with Him. **Forsook their nets.** Their action involved more than sacrificing a few possessions. They were giving up their trade.

19. It is interesting that James' name captures the scene. John's name joins the former as **his brother.** In spite of this, John became "the beloved disciple," penned five New Testament books, and outlived the other disciples.

20. For **Zebedee** to have had **hired servants,** employees, indicates that his business was relatively prosperous.

3. Preaching tour of Galilee. 1:21-45.

21. Capernaum. Matthew and Luke mention a visit to Jesus' home town, Nazareth, prior to this event, and Matthew 4:13 informs us that Jesus made His residence in this city. **Straightway.** The Greek word *euthus,* translated "straightway, immediately, anon," is characteristic of Mark's style. Already it has been used in verses 10, 12, 18, and 20, and it is used over forty times throughout the book. Here it signifies that Christ Jesus began teaching on the first Sabbath after He arrived.

22. The Greek imperfect tense of **they were astonished** depicts action in motion. As Jesus taught, the people were not only astonished at His sermon as a whole, but they kept reacting with amazement at every truth that crossed His lips. **Not as the scribes.** The distinction in His manner was that He ignored the normal procedure of the scribes, who consistently quoted or made reference to the Old Testament and the ancient rabbis. Jesus taught authoritatively since His word was final!

23 And there was in their synagogue a man with an unclean spirit; and he cried out,

24 Saying, Let us alone; what have we to do with thee, thou Jesus of Nazareth? art thou come to destroy us? I know thee who thou art, the Holy One of God.

25 And Jesus rebuked him, saying, Hold thy peace, and come out of him.

26 And when the unclean spirit had torn him, and cried with a loud voice, he came out of him.

27 And they were all amazed, insomuch that they questioned among themselves, saying, What thing is this? what new doctrine is this? for with authority commandeth he even the unclean spirits, and they do obey him.

28 And immediately his fame spread abroad throughout all the region round about Galilee.

29 ¶And forthwith, when they were come out of the synagogue, they entered into the house of Simon and Andrew, with James and John.

30 But Simon's wife's mother lay sick of a fever, and anon they tell him of her.

31 And he came and took her by the hand, and lifted her up; and immediately the fever left her, and she ministered unto them.

32 ¶And at even, when the sun did set, they brought unto him all that were diseased, and them that were possessed with devils.

33 And all the city was gathered together at the door.

34 And he healed many that were sick of divers diseases, and cast out many devils; and suffered not the devils to speak, because they knew him.

35 ¶And in the morning, rising up a great while before day, he went out, and departed into a solitary place, and there prayed.

36 And Simon and they that were with him followed after him.

37 And when they had found him, they said unto him, All men seek for thee.

38 And he said unto them, Let us go into the next towns, that I may preach there also: for therefore came I forth.

39 And he preached in their synagogues throughout all Galilee, and cast out devils.

40 ¶And there came a leper to him, beseeching him, and kneeling down to

23. The term **unclean** (Gr *akathartos*) bore special connotations to the Jewish mind. The Old Testament frequently distinguished between what was lawful and unlawful, accepted and rejected, and therefore may mean ungodly. "Demon" is a designation used interchangeably with **unclean spirit.**

24. When he recognized Jesus, **I know thee,** the unclean spirit questioned His presence: **let us alone; what have we to do with thee . . .?** The expression is a Greek idiom which could be translated, "What do we have in common?" It assumes that two parties have converged without a unifying bond. Therefore, he concluded, He must be here **to destroy us.**

25. Hold thy peace. Here and in verse 34 Jesus silences the demons, because they knew Him. Apparently His objection is that **unclean** persons should identify Him. Revelation would come at the proper time through pure vessels.

26. Torn. The unclean spirit caused the man to have convulsions before it left.

27. What new doctrine is this? Their question shows a basic purpose in healing. Jesus certainly was moved by physical suffering, but His eternal objectives outweighed temporal matters. Verses 14-15 named **preaching** as Jesus' primary ministry, and in this context the occasion of healing happens immediately after Jesus' authoritative lesson. At first the people responded negatively, because His method seemed bizarre, but when they witnessed Him casting out demons, they accepted His teaching on the basis of His power.

28-31. The phrase **his fame** (Gr *akoē*) commonly signified a news report or announcement. It relates to the event of the preceding verse rather than His person. **Simon's wife's mother.** Although the disciples' families are rarely mentioned in the New Testament, because of the inclusion of this incident, we learn that Peter was married, and it appears that his mother-in-law and brother lived with him.

32-34. In verse 28 it is said that the news of healing had spread **immediately,** and here the multitudes thronged after Jesus because they had heard. The same types of people were brought to Him as the ones recently healed: demon-possessed and diseased.

35-37. A great while before day. Two things may be noted regarding the time. First, He prayed very early, before other activities could distract or interfere. Second, the account comes the day after His encounter with many demons (AV, **devils** is better translated demons from the Greek *daimonion*). Ephesians 6:12 pinpoints the Christian's enemy; his actual battlefield lies in the realm of the spiritual. An even more remarkable aspect of this prayer is the lengths Jesus took to assure privacy. He went **into a solitary place.** The others, when they awoke, sought Him and finally when He was found, they complained that the multitudes were awaiting Him. He offered no apology, for what He was doing was well worth time and effort.

38-39. Jesus' stated objective in His extended ministry is to **preach** in the next towns. The miracles He performed provided the validity of His authority, and thus, His message.

40-42. Leper. In New Testament times, because of the unsanitary conditions, lepers were numerous. This one's petition

him, and saying unto him, If thou wilt, thou canst make me clean.

41 And Jesus, moved with compassion, put forth *his* hand, and touched him, and saith unto him, I will; be thou clean.

42 And as soon as he had spoken, immediately the leprosy departed from him, and he was cleansed.

43 And he straitly charged him, and forthwith sent him away;

44 And saith unto him, See thou say nothing to any man: but go thy way, shew thyself to the priest, and offer for thy cleansing those things which Moses commanded, for a testimony unto them.

45 But he went out, and began to publish *it* much, and to blaze abroad the matter, insomuch that Jesus could no more openly enter into the city, but was without in desert places: and they came to him from every quarter.

CHAPTER 2

AND again he entered into Ca·per′na-um after *some* days; and it was noised that he was in the house.

2 And straightway many were gathered together, insomuch that there was no room to receive *them*, no, not so much as about the door: and he preached the word unto them.

3 And they come unto him, bringing one sick of the palsy, which was borne of four.

4 And when they could not come nigh unto him for the press, they uncovered the roof where he was: and when they had broken *it* up, they let down the bed wherein the sick of the palsy lay.

5 When Jesus saw their faith, he said unto the sick of the palsy, Son, thy sins be forgiven thee.

6 But there were certain of the scribes sitting there, and reasoning in their hearts,

7 Why doth this *man* thus speak blasphemies? who can forgive sins but God only?

8 And immediately when Jesus per-

pertained to Jesus' desire, not His ability; he declared **thou canst**, "you are able!" The Lord's response is not routine. The healing resulted because He was **moved with compassion**. Since He is the Second Person of the Trinity, why would He need to **put forth his hand** and **touch him?** Yet the Lord typically touched when He healed. Since miracles were designed to verify Jesus as Lord, the touch would remove doubts as to the source of the healings.

43. Straitly charged . . . sent him away. Both verbs in this sentence are very strong. The first (Gr *embrimaō*) sometimes portrays a horse snorting in anger; the second (Gr *ekballō*) often was used to describe an excommunication from the synagogue. Although they are less forceful here, their presence indicates intense feelings. Jesus perceived that the man was more excited about his condition and experience than about the One who had healed him.

44-45. Verses 44 and 45 contrast the man's instructions with his actions. The first command prohibited him from telling what had happened, yet he not only disobeyed, but he became so involved in sharing his story that he apparently disregarded the other instructions also. To follow what **Moses commanded** would have affirmed that Jesus believed and fulfilled the Old Testament law.

No more openly. Jesus' fame even in this initial stage of His ministry was incredible. Crowds followed so heavily that it became impossible for Him to make His way through any city without creating a commotion.

4. The healing of a paralytic man. 2:1-12.

2:1. His entrance into **Capernaum** was unknown by the public, but **it was noised.** Someone discovered His presence and the news spread like wildfire.

2. When they heard where Jesus was, the multitudes swarmed about Him. The author lays stress on the situation by saying there was no room, **not so much as about the door,** which indicates the problem that the friends of the paralytic man faced. **Preached.** Although Jesus' fame was due to miracles, the narration more frequently has Him preaching the gospel.

3. They come unto him, bringing one sick of the palsy, which was borne of four. Why does it not simply say, "Four men came bringing their sick friend"? The wording shows that there were more than four in the group. **Sick of the palsy** (Gr *paralytikos*) refers to paralysis.

4. The crowded condition, **for the press,** prohibited an approach to the Lord. **Uncovered the roof.** Luke 5:19 identifies it as a tile roof, the tiles being made of hardened clay.

5. Perhaps many in the crowd reacted negatively to such an odd performance. A ceiling opening up, men lowering a pallet on which an invalid lay: what sort of group could this be? Jesus, however, **saw their faith,** not their deeds. His response may at first seem inappropriate. **Thy sins be forgiven.** Although their desire was physical, Christ's answer was very proper. First, the previous statement reveals Jesus' ability to discern beyond physical appearance (also Jn 2:24-25). The sin of the soul is worse than paralysis of the body. Secondly, this story testifies to Jesus' true identity as the Son of God. God alone can forgive sins, but the forgiveness of sins cannot be observed. Thus His identity was certified by a supernatural act.

6-7. The scribes immediately misinterpreted what Jesus declared. Instead of properly reasoning: He claims to forgive; only God forgives; therefore, He must be God; they conjectured on the basis of a false premise: this man cannot be God, therefore, He is blaspheming.

8-9. A proof test of His identity results from this encounter.

ceived in his spirit that they so reasoned within themselves, he said unto them, Why reason ye these things in your hearts?

9 Whether is it easier to say to the sick of the palsy, *Thy* sins be forgiven thee; or to say, Arise, and take up thy bed, and walk?

10 But that ye may know that the Son of man hath power on earth to forgive sins, (he saith to the sick of the palsy,)

11 I say unto thee, Arise, and take up thy bed, and go thy way into thine house.

12 And immediately he arose, took up the bed, and went forth before them all; insomuch that they were all amazed, and glorified God, saying, We never saw it on this fashion.

13 ¶And he went forth again by the sea side; and all the multitude resorted unto him, and he taught them.

14 And as he passed by, he saw Levi the *son* of Al-phae'us sitting at the receipt of custom, and said unto him, Follow me. And he arose and followed him.

15 And it came to pass, that, as Jesus sat at meat in his house, many publicans and sinners sat also together with Jesus and his disciples: for there were many, and they followed him.

16 And when the scribes and Pharisees saw him eat with publicans and sinners, they said unto his disciples, How is it that he eateth and drinketh with publicans and sinners?

17 When Jesus heard *it*, he saith unto them, They that are whole have no need of the physician, but they that are sick: I came not to call the righteous, but sinners to repentance.

18 ¶And the disciples of John and of the Pharisees used to fast: and they come and say unto him, Why do the disciples of John and of the Pharisees fast, but thy disciples fast not?

19 And Jesus said unto them, Can the children of the bridechamber fast, while the bridegroom is with them? as long as they have the bridegroom with them, they cannot fast.

20 But the days will come, when the bridegroom shall be taken away from them, and then shall they fast in those days.

Jesus indirectly claimed to be God, but the scribes refused to accept it. How could deity be proved while discussing forgiveness? An area which could be subjected to investigation was used, the healing.

10. The demonstration of divine power proves to sinners that He indeed can forgive sins. **Forgiven** (Gr *aphiēmi*) which means "to send away," does not merely overlook sin, but actually removes it.

11. I say. Healing is not the result of involved methodology. A word from the Son of God, whose command brought forth the universe, is sufficient.

12. Before them all. Jesus' miracles were not obscure stories developed by isolated reports; the evidence was open for examination. **We never saw it on this fashion.** Occasionally, one reads that Palestinians in the New Testament era readily accepted the supernatural in Jesus, because they **saw** it frequently elsewhere, but this statement denies that.

5. The call of Matthew. 2:13-17.

13. Resorted . . . he taught. These verbs are in the imperfect tense in Greek, emphasizing progressive or continuous action. The following translation clarifies the expression: they "were coming to Him, and He kept on teaching them."

14. Levi. Both Mark and Luke use the Aramaic name, while Matthew employs the more familiar one. **Son of Alphaeus.** Since last names are uncommon, the father's name usually was added to prevent confusion. **Sitting at the receipt of custom.** Although Mark does not use the word publican, the description refers to a tax-collector. **Follow me** may be rendered "be following me" or "continue following me." Jesus prescribed a new life-style, not a temporary errand. Matthew **followed**. He turned over his money and books to his employer and took up an occupation arranged in heaven.

15-16. Scribes. Professional interpreters of the Old Testament. **Pharisees.** An extremely strict and ritualistc religious party, who concerned themselves more with the letter than the spirit of the law. **How is it that . . .?** The question was not wrong in itself, for the Old Testament forbade wrong associations (Ps 1:1), but their attitude lacked compassion.

17. Jesus' compendious answer reveals the heart of God's Good News. Although the New Testament never condones sinful alliances, it consistently urges us to "win" sinners, for they are spiritually sick. The statement, **I came not to call the righteous,** was not given to morally segregate people; the New Testament affirms that all are depraved and under sin (Rom 3).

6. Fasting. 2:18-22.

18. Fasting means more than abstinence from food; that may be practiced for physical reasons. Scriptural fasting always involves a spiritual application, its basic purpose being to so seek God's person that temporal concerns pass unnoticed.

19-20. Christ's illustration, given as an explanation to the question in verse 18, relates to a specific purpose of fasting. It could be done because an individual hungers after a deeper knowledge of God, but more often it results from a desperate situation. Since the **bridegroom** was with His disciples, they had no need to fast. John the Baptist's disciples knew their leader remained in prison, but Jesus' disciples could rejoice with their Master. **Children of the bridechamber** refers to members of the wedding party.

21 No man also seweth a piece of new cloth on an old garment: else the new piece that filled it up taketh away from the old, and the rent is made worse.
22 And no man putteth new wine into old bottles: else the new wine doth burst the bottles, and the wine is spilled, and the bottles will be marred: but new wine must be put into new bottles.

21-22. The illustrations about the **new cloth** and the **new wine** present a principle to which fasting may be related. A patch of new cloth has not previously been shrunk, and therefore would pull the old garment apart. Conversely, new wine expands as it ages and an old wine sack would have already reached its limit. Under the context of the ancient system, the Old Testament law, limitations had been reached, but Christ brought principles that stretched these. For instance, murder in the Old Testament is physical, but Jesus said that a man can murder by hating.

7. The Lord of the Sabbath. 2:23-28.

23 ¶And it came to pass, that he went through the corn fields on the sabbath day; and his disciples began, as they went, to pluck the ears of corn.
24 And the Pharisees said unto him, Behold, why do they on the sabbath day that which is not lawful?
25 And he said unto them, Have ye never read what David did, when he had need, and was an hungred, he, and they that were with him?
26 How he went into the house of God in the days of Ă-bī′a-thar the high priest, and did eat the shewbread, which is not lawful to eat but for the priests, and gave also to them which were with him?
27 And he said unto them, The sabbath was made for man, and not man for the sabbath:
28 Therefore the Son of man is Lord also of the sabbath.

23. The word **corn** (Gr *sporimos*) actually refers to wheat or grain.

24. The Pharisees accused Jesus' disciples of breaking the **Sabbath.** Exodus 20:10 prohibits Sabbath work and Exodus 16:22 illustrates how that instruction relates to eating.

25-27. Two principles govern the uniqueness of the Sabbath. The first is illustrated in verses 25-26 and stated in 27. Jesus related David's unlawful act in I Samuel 21. David and his soldiers fleeing enemies had little time to acquire food, so they ate the showbread which was restricted for priests. Jesus' silence condoned the action, because **the sabbath was made for man,** that is, God instituted it for man's benefit.

28. The second principle is greater, because it encompasses God's nature. By definition He must be above any law which He establishes.

8. Healing on the Sabbath. 3:1-5.

CHAPTER 3

AND he entered again into the synagogue; and there was a man there which had a withered hand.

2 And they watched him, whether he would heal him on the sabbath day; that they might accuse him.
3 And he saith unto the man which had the withered hand, Stand forth.
4 And he saith unto them, Is it lawful to do good on the sabbath days, or to do evil? to save life, or to kill? But they held their peace.
5 And when he had looked round about on them with anger, being grieved for the hardness of their hearts, he saith unto the man, Stretch forth thine hand. And he stretched *it* out: and his hand was restored whole as the other.

3:1. Returning to the synagogue, He noticed a man with a **withered hand.** The condition was atrophy, the decreasing in size of a member of the body because of its lack of use.

2-5. The Pharisees, still accompanying Jesus, carefully observed Him, not hungering for spiritual food, like the crowds, but **that they might accuse him.** Earlier some of them might have had honest questions; at this point their motive became clear. The rhetorical question (vs. 4) destroys their argument by forcing a logical conclusion: would your interpretation of the law ever demand you to destroy life or do evil? No answer.

B. The Results of Popular Growth. 3:6-35.

1. Many healed by the sea. 3:6-11.

Christ's swift fame hardly could occur without affecting everyone. As the multitudes crowded after Jesus, the author relates His influence upon others also. Religious and political leaders began a conspiracy; Jesus Himself organized a team of apostles, His relatives disbelieved, and scribes publicly denounced Him as an emissary of Satan.

6-10. When they **took counsel** they did not merely share their adverse feelings in general terms. After agreeing to His death, they arranged meetings in which they could carefully plan the murder. **Herodians** refers to a political party which was loyal to Herod's family.

6 And the Pharisees went forth, and straightway took counsel with the He-rŏ′di-ans against him, how they might destroy him.
7 ¶But Jesus withdrew himself with his disciples to the sea: and a great multitude from Galilee followed him, and from Judæa,
8 And from Jerusalem, and from Ĭ-dū-mæ′a, and *from* beyond Jordan; and they about Tyre and Sī′don, a great multitude, when they had heard what great things he did, came unto him.

9 And he spake to his disciples, that a small ship should wait on him because of the multitude, lest they should throng him.

10 For he had healed many; insomuch that they pressed upon him for to touch him, as many as had plagues.

11 And unclean spirits, when they saw him, fell down before him, and cried, saying, Thou art the Son of God.

11. Two facts should be mentioned regarding the words **fell down.** First, the Greek *prospipto*, being in the imperfect tense, signifies continuous action: "they kept on falling down before Him and crying." Secondly, it may be that the reason for this action was not to worship, but to confuse the multitudes. If they heard unclean spirits announcing His title as the Son of God, they might think that good and evil in the spirit world are not totally opposite each other.

2. The Twelve chosen. 3:12-21.

12. See the discussion in 1:25.

12 And he straitly charged them that they should not make him known.

13 ¶And he goeth up into a mountain, and calleth *unto him* whom he would: and they came unto him.

14 And he ordained twelve, that they should be with him, and that he might send them forth to preach,

13. A mountain. Its identity is uncertain, but it was the same one where the Sermon on the Mount was preached (Lk 6).

14. Although Mark and Luke use different Greek words for **ordained,** both mean "appointed" or "chosen" **with him.** Their relationship to their Lord preceded their service for Him.

15 And to have power to heal sicknesses, and to cast out devils:

15. Although the power of healing is not included in some manuscripts, Matthew 10:1 clearly affirms it.

16 And Simon he surnamed Peter;

17 And James the *son* of Zĕb′e-dee, and John the brother of James; and he surnamed them Bō-a-ner′gēs, which is, The sons of thunder:

18 And Andrew, and Philip, and Bartholomew, and Matthew, and Thomas, and James the *son* of Ăl-phæ′us, and Thăd-dæ′us, and Simon the Canaanite,

19 And Judas Iscariot, which also betrayed him: and they went into an house.

20 ¶And the multitude cometh together again, so that they could not so much as eat bread.

21 And when his friends heard *of it*, they went out to lay hold on him: for they said, He is beside himself.

16-19. For more about the background of the Twelve see Matthew 10:2-4 and Luke 6:12-16.

20. Not so much as eat bread. This statement implies what their purpose was. After a full day, they were hungry, but people would not leave them alone long enough for them to eat.

21. The word **friends** may be misleading. In Greek it literally means "those near" (Gr *hoi par autou*) and is an idiom which may refer to friends or relatives. Since the apostles would be His friends and were present with Him, it speaks of members of His family. John 7:5 says His brothers had not yet believed, so one may understand how they could declare **He is beside himself.** They sought to physically restrain Him from His irrational activities.

3. The unpardonable sin. 3:22-30.

22 ¶And the scribes which came down from Jerusalem said, He hath Bē-ĕl′ze-bŭb, and by the prince of the devils casteth he out devils.

22. These **scribes** probably were more prominent than others, because of their location, **from Jerusalem.** They presented an official evaluation of this new prophet to the public. Since His supernatural powers could not be denied, they were said to have originated in **Beelzebub,** a name referring to Satan.

23 And he called them *unto him*, and said unto them in parables, How can Satan cast out Satan?

24 And if a kingdom be divided against itself, that kingdom cannot stand.

25 And if a house be divided against itself, that house cannot stand.

26 And if Satan rise up against himself, and be divided, he cannot stand, but hath an end.

27 No man can enter into a strong man's house, and spoil his goods, ex-

23-27. In answer to the question of verse 23, **How can Satan cast out Satan?,** Jesus' remarks simply, "To even think so is ridiculous!" Divided kingdoms fall (vs. 24); divided houses fall (vs. 25); therefore, Satan warring against himself would be self-destruction (vs. 26). Furthermore, complete victory must precede enjoyment of conquered territory (vs. 27). The only way to establish the kingdom of God on earth is to remove the kingdom of evil. This explains why it is only rational to view exorcism as an act of God.

cept he will first bind the strong man;
and then he will spoil his house.

28 Verily I say unto you, All sins shall
be forgiven unto the sons of men, and
blasphemies wherewith soever they
shall blaspheme:

29 But he that shall blaspheme
against the Holy Ghost hath never forgiveness, but is in danger of eternal
damnation:

30 Because they said, He hath an unclean spirit.

31 ¶There came then his brethren and
his mother, and, standing without, sent
unto him, calling him.

32 And the multitude sat about him,
and they said unto him, Behold, thy
mother and thy brethren without seek
for thee.

33 And he answered them, saying,
Who is my mother, or my brethren?

34 And he looked round about on
them which sat about him, and said,
Behold my mother and my brethren!

35 For whosoever shall do the will of
God, the same is my brother, and my
sister, and mother.

CHAPTER 4

AND he began again to teach by the sea
side: and there was gathered unto him
a great multitude, so that he entered
into a ship, and sat in the sea; and the
whole multitude was by the sea on the
land.

2 And he taught them many things by
parables, and said unto them in his
doctrine,

3 Hearken; Behold, there went out a
sower to sow:

4 And it came to pass, as he sowed,
some fell by the way side, and the fowls
of the air came and devoured it up.

5 And some fell on stony ground,
where it had not much earth; and immediately it sprang up, because it had
no depth of earth:

6 But when the sun was up, it was
scorched; and because it had no root, it
withered away.

7 And some fell among thorns, and
the thorns grew up, and choked it, and
it yielded no fruit.

8 And other fell on good ground, and
did yield fruit that sprang up and increased; and brought forth, some
thirty, and some sixty, and some an
hundred.

9 And he said unto them, He that hath
ears to hear, let him hear.

10 ¶And when he was alone, they that
were about him with the twelve asked
of him the parable.

11 And he said unto them, Unto you it
is given to know the mystery of the
kingdom of God: but unto them that

28-30. The attempt to generalize this offense to the persistence of unbelief ignores the correct definition of **blasphemies,**
which specifically means "speaking against in order to hurt" (Gr
blasphēmeō) the Holy Spirit. **In danger of eternal damnation**
would be better translated "guilty of eternal sin," sin standing in
place of "damnation" in the oldest manuscripts.

4. Family ties. 3:31-35.

31-32. His brethren and his mother (cf. vs. 21). One need
not suppose that Mary agreed with her sons' conclusion about
Jesus. She probably joined her sons to prevent them from doing
something rash.

33-35. Jesus set forth a question to advance a spiritual principle: eternal relationships surpass earthly ones. Neither religious
activities nor memberships draw the Lord's favor, but doing **the
will of God.**

C. Parables. 4:1-34.

1. Introduction. 4:1-2.

4:1-2. By parables: the Greek word *parabolē* comes from two
others (*para*, beside and *ballō*, to cast). Thus, a parable is a
rhetorical device to explain truth. Especially in His lessons on
the kingdom Jesus employed these story illustrations and with
two effects: to believers they disclose truth; to unbelievers they
hide it.

2. The Parable of the Sower. 4:3-9

3-6. Way side. Some fell, literally, "alongside the road" (Gr
hodos), the hardened surface adjacent to the road or path. **Stony
ground** (vs. 5) does not refer to a mixture of dirt and small
stones, but speaks of huge slabs of rock with only a thin layer of
soil upon them.

7. Thorns (Gr *akantha*) may be taken simply as weeds, not
just thistles, any wild plants which grow among the planted
crops.

8. Brought forth. No mention is made of the kind of produce. The purpose of the illustration centers around the type of
ground.

9. This verse contains an often used quote in the New Testament, which aims at man's tendency to ignore or make light of
truth. The statement is another way of calling the listener to pay
close attention.

3. Christ's use of parables explained. 4:10-12

10-11. Unto you. Jesus said the truth is made clear to those
who believe and follow Him. **Them that are without. Without**
(Gr *exō*) would be better translated "outside" because it refers to
those who are outside the kingdom of God.

are without, all *these* things are done in parables:

12 That seeing they may see, and not perceive; and hearing they may hear, and not understand; lest at any time they should be converted, and *their* sins should be forgiven them.

13 And he said unto them, Know ye not this parable? and how then will ye know all parables?

14 ¶The sower soweth the word.

15 And these are they by the way side, where the word is sown; but when they have heard, Satan cometh immediately, and taketh away the word that was sown in their hearts.

16 And these are they likewise which are sown on stony ground; who, when they have heard the word, immediately receive it with gladness;

17 And have no root in themselves, and so endure but for a time: afterward, when affliction or persecution ariseth for the word's sake, immediately they are offended.

18 And these are they which are sown among thorns; such as hear the word,

19 And the cares of this world, and the deceitfulness of riches, and the lusts of other things entering in, choke the word, and it becometh unfruitful.

20 And these are they which are sown on good ground; such as hear the word, and receive *it*, and bring forth fruit, some thirtyfold, some sixty, and some an hundred.

21 ¶And he said unto them, Is a candle brought to be put under a bushel, or under a bed? and not to be set on a candlestick?

22 For there is nothing hid, which shall not be manifested; neither was any thing kept secret, but that it should come abroad.

23 If any man have ears to hear, let him hear.

24 And he said unto them, Take heed what ye hear: with what measure ye mete, it shall be measured to you: and unto you that hear shall more be given.

25 For he that hath, to him shall be given: and he that hath not, from him shall be taken even that which he hath.

26 ¶And he said, So is the kingdom of God, as if a man should cast seed into the ground;

12. Lest . . . they should be converted. A superficial understanding of this quote from Isaiah 6:9-10 has confused some about the Lord's instructions regarding evangelism. Here He explains that details about God's kingdom are not to be used to "prove" God's message to anyone. Faith precedes proof, not vice versa. People are won "through the foolishness of preaching" not scientific facts. If that were the case, faith would be nothing more than the recognition of revealed evidence.

4. The Parable of the Sower explained. 4:13-20.

13-15. Because the **way side** was hardened, the seed remains on top; similarly, the word does not penetrate a hardened heart, and Satan removes it easily.

16-17. Stony ground may have enough soil to cause initial growth, but no depth is established. As weather may ruin weak plants, adversity destroys those who base their faith on emotions. A person with a solid foundation would have counted the cost, which includes hardships and sacrifices as well as benefits.

18-19. No criticism is offered regarding the ground in the third category. The dedication was genuine initially, but later they allowed "things" to affect them. Their separation to the gospel softened as new appeals and attractions gained their attention. That which began as a minor tangent ends choking the Word of God right out of their lives.

20. The virtue of the **good ground** lies in its function. Yet the amount of its produce is not the issue, for some ground brings forth more than others. Even though the fruit may appear relatively meager, the fact remains, it **brings forth fruit.**

5. The Parable of the Candle. 4:21-23.

21-23. Verse 21 raises the question of a candle's (Gr *lychnos*) primary purpose, and 22 relates that purpose to God's kingdom. Jesus was reassuring them that although there is a time of mystery, the truth will be revealed.

6. The Parable of New Standards. 4:24-25.

24-25. The two verses at first may seem unrelated, perhaps even contradictory. They relate in that they are opposite; the careful wording shows agreement. First, our world system operates on the basic premise, "regardless of the method, gain equals success." But Jesus said, the way you measure (AV, **mete**) determines how you will prosper, the verb dealing with physical materials. Secondly, when gifts are distributed among people, the poor usually receive first, but Jesus announces possessors will receive first. Obviously, these principles apply to the kingdom of God. The selfish hoarding of physical goods (vs. 24) and unwillingness to accept absolute truth (vs. 25) are indirectly rebuked.

7. The Parable about Growth. 4:26-29.

26-27. As a farmer **knoweth not how** his seed becomes mature plants which produce fruit, Christians may enjoy fruitful lives without thoroughly understanding the process.

27 And should sleep, and rise night and day, and the seed should spring and grow up, he knoweth not how.

28 For the earth bringeth forth fruit of herself; first the blade, then the ear, after that the full corn in the ear.

29 But when the fruit is brought forth, immediately he putteth in the sickle, because the harvest is come.

30 ¶And he said, Whereunto shall we liken the kingdom of God? or with what comparison shall we compare it?

31 *It is* like a grain of mustard seed, which, when it is sown in the earth, is less than all the seeds that be in the earth:

32 But when it is sown, it groweth up, and becometh greater than all herbs, and shooteth out great branches; so that the fowls of the air may lodge under the shadow of it.

33 And with many such parables spake he the word unto them, as they were able to hear *it*.

34 But without a parable spake he not unto them: and when they were alone, he expounded all things to his disciples.

35 ¶And the same day, when the even was come, he saith unto them, Let us pass over unto the other side.

36 And when they had sent away the multitude, they took him even as he was in the ship. And there were also with him other little ships.

37 And there arose a great storm of wind, and the waves beat into the ship, so that it was now full.

38 And he was in the hinder part of the ship, asleep on a pillow: and they awake him, and say unto him, Master, carest thou not that we perish?

39 And he arose, and rebuked the wind, and said unto the sea, Peace, be still. And the wind ceased, and there was a great calm.

40 And he said unto them, Why are ye so fearful? how is it that ye have no faith?

41 And they feared exceedingly, and said one to another, What manner of man is this, that even the wind and the sea obey him?

CHAPTER 5

AND they came over unto the other side of the sea, into the country of the Găd'a-rēnes.

2 And when he was come out of the ship, immediately there met him out of the tombs a man with an unclean spirit,

3 Who had *his* dwelling among the tombs; and no man could bind him, no, not with chains:

4 Because that he had been often bound with fetters and chains, and the chains had been plucked asunder by

28-29. The emphasis of this parable is found in the expression **of herself,** which in Greek means "automatically" (Gr *automatos*). God's procedure for growth does not need to be intellectually perceived to be experienced.

8. *The Parable of the Mustard Seed. 4:30-32.*

30-32. Mustard seed at the time of its sowing is extremely small compared to herbs, yet at maturity extends upward beyond any. As an illustration of the kingdom, the lesson stresses phenomenal growth; it would expand from a few to millions. That **the fowls of the air may lodge** in its suggests some impurity, since they are neither part of the plant nor permanent.

D. The Journey to Gadara. 4:33-5:20.

1. *The storm calmed. 4:33-41.*

33-36. The same day sometimes is referred to as the "busy day," because it includes everything from 3:22.

37. The **great storm of wind** was a whirlwind or cyclone. The mountainous regions surrounding the Sea of Galilee often gave rise to unusually fast and vicious weather changes.

38. Hinder part (Gr *prumna*), the stern.

39. Rebuked may be translated "commanded." The simplicity of the narrative stands out in such a dramatic scene. He sleeps; He arises; He commands; all is well!

40-41. Man is so reluctant to accept supernatural truth. Although they had seen demons cast out and diseases cured, the apostles perceived Christ as a prophet only. Witnessing His sovereignty over nature, they respond among themselves in fear, **What manner of man is this!** What emotions must have flowed as they pondered if their Master indeed was God Himself!

2. *The healing of the Gadarene demoniac. 5:1-20.*

5:1. An apparent discrepancy has been cited between Matthew's and Mark's accounts. The people are called **Gadarenes** in Mark (and Luke) but "Gergesenes" in Matthew. The discovery of the ruins of Khersa (Gerasa) on the lake shore disproved these claims because this location was in close enough proximity to the larger city of Gadara that a single event could be identified with either place.

2. Mark mentions **a man,** but Matthew reports that there were two. However, Mark does not specifically limit it to one. Probably one stood out as a leader. **With an unclean spirit** means demon-possessed.

3. His residence being **among the tombs,** the case was all the more unique. Even if a few tombs were abandoned, no rational person would choose such an environment.

4. All hope to bring this man under control had been abandoned. A few times others had tried to **bind him . . . with chains** only to see them broken and the man escape. His

him, and the fetters broken in pieces: neither could any *man* tame him.

5 And always, night and day, he was in the mountains, and in the tombs, crying, and cutting himself with stones.

6 But when he saw Jesus afar off, he ran and worshipped him,

7 And cried with a loud voice, and said, What have I to do with thee, Jesus, *thou* Son of the most high God? I adjure thee by God, that thou torment me not.

8 For he said unto him, Come out of the man, *thou* unclean spirit.

9 And he asked him, What *is* thy name? And he answered, saying, My name *is* Legion: for we are many.

10 And he besought him much that he would not send them away out of the country.

11 Now there was there nigh unto the mountains a great herd of swine feeding.

12 And all the devils besought him, saying, Send us into the swine, that we may enter into them.

13 And forthwith Jesus gave them leave. And the unclean spirits went out, and entered into the swine: and the herd ran violently down a steep place into the sea, (they were about two thousand;) and were choked in the sea.

14 And they that fed the swine fled, and told *it* in the city, and in the country. And they went out to see what it was that was done.

15 And they come to Jesus, and see him that was possessed with the devil, and had the legion, sitting, and clothed, and in his right mind: and they were afraid.

16 And they that saw *it* told them how it befell to him that was possessed with the devil, and *also* concerning the swine.

17 And they began to pray him to depart out of their coasts.

18 And when he was come into the ship, he that had been possessed with the devil prayed him that he might be with him.

19 Howbeit Jesus suffered him not, but saith unto him, Go home to thy friends, and tell them how great things the Lord hath done for thee, and hath had compassion on thee.

20 And he departed, and began to publish in De-căp'o-lĭs how great things Jesus had done for him: and all *men* did marvel.

21 ¶And when Jesus was passed over again by ship unto the other side, much people gathered unto him: and he was nigh unto the sea.

22 And, behold, there cometh one of the rulers of the synagogue, Jā-ī'rus by

strength was supernatural, which can be accounted for by demonic presence. The word **tame** (Gr *damazō*) is better translated "subdue."

5. The demon had so affected the man's mental faculties that he had been **cutting himself.** This plus his continuous outcries must have kept people away from the area.

6. Although the Greek word *proskuneō* may mean **worshiped,** here it speaks of the more literal translation, "bowed down before Him." (For more about this approach, see R. Lenski, *St. Mark's Gospel,* p. 207).

7-10. See the discussion on 1:24 regarding the demon's outcry. The demon's name, **Legion,** stresses numerous spirits involved. A Roman legion consisted of six thousand soliders, but this is used metaphorically. The New Testament often relates the seriousness of a problem to the number of demons at work (Mk 16:9; Mt 12:43; etc.).

11-13. That Jesus allowed the unclean spirits to enter the **swine** may be explained by two factors: First, it is better to have them away from their human victims, even if they do attack animals. And more importantly, pigs were unclean in the Old Testament law (Lev 11:7).

14-17. The response of the Gadarenes was typically human; they were afraid of the unknown. Fear had existed before because of the demoniac, but as long as he remained in his own domain, they could live with it. When Jesus restored the man, however, his radical change caused confusion and **they began to pray him to depart.** They preferred the status quo, where everything could be explained by natural means. Admittedly Jesus' apostles were frightened by their Master's supernatural powers (4:41), but they also believed and followed.

18-19. Naturally the liberated man wished to be **with him,** to listen at His feet, to observe every action, to express his gratitude, but even commendable desires are not always His will. The Lord sent him back to his family and relatives to testify of God's grace in his life. What greater way could the gospel reach them, for they must have known all too well of their relative's condition.

20. The former demoniac went beyond the call of duty. He undoubtedly made an immediate visit to his friends and relatives, but he was so enthusiastic about what Christ had done he shared his story with everyone he met. **Decapolis** (Gr *deka*, ten and *polis*, city) refers to an area of ten cities southeast of the Sea of Galilee.

E. Two Unique Miracles. 5:21-43.

21. Much people gathered unto him. Jesus' popularity had grown to such an extent that wherever He traveled word quickly spread and the crowds clustered.

22. Mark singles out **one of the rulers of the synagogue,**

name; and when he saw him, he fell at his feet,

23 And besought him greatly, saying, My little daughter lieth at the point of death: *I pray thee,* come and lay thy hands on her, that she may be healed; and she shall live.

24 And *Jesus* went with him; and much people followed him, and thronged him.

25 ¶And a certain woman, which had an issue of blood twelve years,

26 And had suffered many things of many physicians, and had spent all that she had, and was nothing bettered, but rather grew worse,

27 When she had heard of Jesus, came in the press behind, and touched his garment.

28 For she said, If I may touch but his clothes, I shall be whole.

29 And straightway the fountain of her blood was dried up; and she felt in *her* body that she was healed of that plague.

30 And Jesus, immediately knowing in himself that virtue had gone out of him, turned him about in the press, and said, Who touched my clothes?

31 And his disciples said unto him, Thou seest the multitude thronging thee, and sayest thou, Who touched me?

32 And he looked round about to see her that had done this thing.

33 But the woman fearing and trembling, knowing what was done in her, came and fell down before him, and told him all the truth.

34 And he said unto her, Daughter, thy faith hath made thee whole; go in peace, and be whole of thy plague.

35 ¶While he yet spake, there came from the ruler of the synagogue's *house certain* which said, Thy daughter is dead: why troublest thou the Master any further?

36 As soon as Jesus heard the word that was spoken, he saith unto the ruler of the synagogue, Be not afraid, only believe.

37 And he suffered no man to follow him, save Peter, and James, and John the brother of James.

38 And he cometh to the house of the ruler of the synagogue, and seeth the tumult, and them that wept and wailed greatly.

39 And when he was come in, he saith unto them, Why make ye this ado, and weep? the damsel is not dead, but sleepeth.

40 And they laughed him to scorn. But when he had put them all out, he taketh the father and the mother of the damsel, and them that were with him, and entereth in where the damsel was lying.

41 And he took the damsel by the hand, and said unto her, Tăl'i-tha cū'mǐ;

Jairus. The above description (Gr *archisynagōgos*) refers to a synagogue official who maintains the physical needs.

23. The despair felt by Jairus is evident in the narration. He calls his child **little daughter** (Gr *thygatrion*), connoting special endearment.

24. The scene exhibits the Lord's patience. Jesus walked away with Jairus and the people **thronged him,** continuously pressing toward Him. This word (Gr *synthlibō*) was used of a heavy load weighing upon a beast of burden.

25-29. The woman with the hemorrhage (AV, **issue of blood**) not only had the condition twelve years, but time and again endured painful treatments by many physicians. The doctors were unsuccessful, in fact the hemorrhage grew worse. The years of suffering and worry ended in a single act. **Straightway** she was healed and she knew it.

30. Jesus' power (Gr *dynamis;* AV, **virtue**) never was released without His knowledge and will. It was not a magical touch that caused healing. Many sick people had touched Him, but this particular woman was healed because Jesus permitted His power to deliver her. **Turned him about in the press** means that He turned around in the crowd.

31. The reason the Lord asked the question was to allow the woman to confess her act.

32-34. The importance of direct communication with God is accentuated, because experiencing God's power is not as vital as knowing Him. The woman could walk away not only with a restored body, but with His words of peace ringing in her heart.

35. Master (Gr *didaskalos*) means teacher.

36. To reassure Jairus after the tragic announcement Jesus said, **Be not afraid, only believe,** the Greek tense of the prohibition actually meaning, "Stop being afraid."

37. Often **Peter** and **James** and **John** are referred to as the "inner circle" because they were occasionally included in situations where no others were allowed. The phrase, **the brother of James,** suggests that John was the less prominent of the two.

38. The scene typifies an ancient Jewish wake, where outward expression was a sign of deep remorse.

39. When Jesus stated that the child only **sleepeth,** He did not mean that she was not actually dead (Lk 8:55), but that she soon would be aroused as if she had been sleeping.

40-43. They laughed him to scorn (Gr *katagelaō*): they intended to ridicule Him, but His only reaction was to dismiss them. Why did Jesus prohibit them from sharing the news of this miracle? Since opposition to Him had already grown from the religious leaders, raising a dead person might have terminated His ministry too early. Furthermore, He limited some of His greatest miracles to the witness of only a chosen few (Mk 9:2).

which is, being interpreted, Damsel, I say unto thee, arise.

42 And straightway the damsel arose, and walked; for she was *of the age* of twelve years. And they were astonished with a great astonishment.

43 And he charged them straitly that no man should know it; and commanded that something should be given her to eat.

CHAPTER 6

AND he went out from thence, and came into his own country; and his disciples follow him.

2 And when the sabbath day was come, he began to teach in the synagogue: and many hearing *him* were astonished, saying, From whence hath this *man* these things? and what wisdom *is* this which is given unto him, that even such mighty works are wrought by his hands?

3 Is not this the carpenter, the son of Mary, the brother of James, and Joses, and of Juda, and Simon? and are not his sisters here with us? And they were offended at him.

4 But Jesus said unto them, A prophet is not without honour, but in his own country, and among his own kin, and in his own house.

5 And he could there do no mighty work, save that he laid his hands upon a few sick folk, and healed *them.*

6 And he marvelled because of their unbelief. And he went round about the villages, teaching.

7 ¶And he called *unto him* the twelve, and began to send them forth by two and two; and gave them power over unclean spirits;

8 And commanded them that they should take nothing for *their* journey, save a staff only; no scrip, no bread, no money in *their* purse:

9 But *be* shod with sandals; and not put on two coats.

10 And he said unto them, In what place soever ye enter into an house, there abide till ye depart from that place.

11 And whosoever shall not receive you, nor hear you, when ye depart thence, shake off the dust under your feet for a testimony against them. Verily I say unto you, It shall be more tolerable for Sodom and Go-mŏr′rha in the day of judgment, than for that city.

12 And they went out, and preached that men should repent.

13 And they cast out many devils, and anointed with oil many that were sick, and healed *them.*

14 ¶And king Herod heard *of him;* (for his name was spread abroad:) and

F. Home Town Response. 6:1-6.

6:1. **His own country** was His home town, Nazareth.

2-3. Doubts about Jesus erupted from those who could never accept Him as more than a **carpenter.** Facts about His family seemed to confirm their judgment. Among the four half-brothers of Christ, two are well known. James presided over the Jerusalem church and wrote the book bearing His name, and Judas or Jude wrote the last New Testament epistle. The summary response, **they were offended,** is incredible. He had come to "seek and to save that which was lost" (Lk 19:10), to draw all men to Himself (Jn 12:32), and to provide abundant life (Jn 10:10), and yet those who lived near Him the longest "stumbled" (Gr *skandalizō*) before His presence.

4. The proverbial statement, **a prophet is not without honor, but in his own country,** explains why pastors often find the least acceptance as leaders among their own family and friends.

5. By definition God's omnipotence cannot be limited. When Mark said the God-man **could there do no mighty work,** the repression was self-imposed, based upon His own principles and volition. Furthermore, if God cannot work where there is no faith, then He will act when a person genuinely trusts Him.

6. **He marveled.** The Greek verb being in the imperfect tense, indicates continuous action. As His former neighbors continued to respond with questions full of doubt, He kept on marvelling at their lack of faith.

G. Activities, Pressures, and Rest. 6:7-56.

1. The Twelve sent forth. 6:7-13.

7-10. Jesus broadened His ministry by sending out teams to preach, to heal and to cast out demons. They were sent **by two and two,** a practice which was recommended in the Old Testament (Eccl 4:9).

11. Degrees of judgment parallel the measure of revelation. **It shall be more tolerable for Sodom and Gomorrah,** because they did not have the opportunity to witness any miracle-working apostle.

12-13. **And they went out, and preached that men should repent.** The same message had been preached by John the Baptist and by our Lord himself, and now it was preached by the apostles. The message was confirmed by genuine miracles.

2. Death of John the Baptist. 6:14-30.

14-19. **King Herod,** actually a tetrarch, was Herod Antipas, second son of Herod the Great (Mt 2:1; Lk 1:5). (For more

he said, That John the Baptist was risen from the dead, and therefore mighty works do shew forth themselves in him.

15 Others said, That it is E-lī'as. And others said, That it is a prophet, or as one of the prophets.

16 But when Herod heard *thereof*, he said, It is John, whom I beheaded: he is risen from the dead.

17 For Herod himself had sent forth and laid hold upon John, and bound him in prison for He-rō'dī-as' sake, his brother Philip's wife: for he had married her.

18 For John had said unto Herod, It is not lawful for thee to have thy brother's wife.

19 Therefore He-rō'dī-as had a quarrel against him, and would have killed him; but she could not:

20 For Herod feared John, knowing that he was a just man and an holy, and observed him; and when he heard him, he did many things, and heard him gladly.

21 And when a convenient day was come, that Herod on his birthday made a supper to his lords, high captains, and chief *estates* of Galilee;

22 And when the daughter of the said He-rō'dī-as came in, and danced, and pleased Herod and them that sat with him, the king said unto the damsel, Ask of me whatsoever thou wilt, and I will give *it* thee.

23 And he sware unto her, Whatsoever thou shalt ask of me, I will give *it* thee, unto the half of my kingdom.

24 And she went forth, and said unto her mother, What shall I ask? And she said, The head of John the Baptist.

25 And she came in straightway with haste unto the king, and asked, saying, I will that thou give me by and by in a charger the head of John the Baptist.

26 And the king was exceeding sorry; *yet* for his oath's sake, and for their sakes which sat with him, he would not reject her.

27 And immediately the king sent an executioner, and commanded his head to be brought: and he went and beheaded him in the prison,

28 And brought his head in a charger, and gave it to the damsel: and the damsel gave it to her mother.

29 And when his disciples heard *of it*, they came and took up his corpse, and laid it in a tomb.

30 ¶And the apostles gathered themselves together unto Jesus, and told him all things, both what they had done, and what they had taught.

31 And he said unto them, Come ye yourselves apart into a desert place, and rest a while: for there were many coming and going, and they had no leisure so much as to eat.

32 And they departed into a desert place by ship privately.

background of this family, see J. A. Alexander, *Commentary on the Gospel of Mark*, pp. 151-152.)

Since John the Baptist played such an important role in Jesus' ministry, Mark felt compelled to include the account of his death. Also, the political scene was often overlooked, but here the governing official's reaction allows the reader to view another side of the story.

20-22. The secular world during the New Testament era was filled with mysticism and superstition. Thus, even though Herod did not understand his message, he **feared John.** Recognizing his dedicated life-style, Herod was reluctant to harm John lest God be vengeful.

23. Note the absurdity of this rash promise: **Whatsoever thou shalt ask of me, I will give it thee, unto the half of my kingdom.** "Herod was not a king and did not possess a kingdom; the tetrarchy he ruled he did not rule in his own right but under the Roman Emperor. It was not in his power to give the half or any part of it to whom he pleased" (R. Lenski, *St. Mark's Gospel*, p. 255).

24. Unto her mother. Children naturally look to their parents for guidance, but this unfortunate girl had a mother who not only was ungodly herself, but who did not hesitate to involve her daughter in her depraved plan.

25-30. For the sake of an unscriptural oath (Lev 5:4) and Herod's audience, one of the greatest men who ever lived was murdered.

3. Pressures. 6:31-36.

31-33. Slipping aside from the crowds, Jesus and the apostles acquired a boat and embarked for a private place. Once they were offshore some noticed the boat and **many knew Him.** The word **knew** (Gr *epiginōskō*) means "recognized," and since **him** is not found in the better Greek manuscripts, "them" could have been supplied just as easily.

33 And the people saw them departing, and many knew him, and ran afoot thither out of all cities, and outwent them, and came together unto him.

34 And Jesus, when he came out, saw much people, and was moved with compassion toward them, because they were as sheep not having a shepherd: and he began to teach them many things.

35 And when the day was now far spent, his disciples came unto him, and said, This is a desert place, and now the time is far passed:

36 Send them away, that they may go into the country round about, and into the villages, and buy themselves bread: for they have nothing to eat.

37 He answered and said unto them, Give ye them to eat. And they say unto him, Shall we go and buy two hundred pennyworth of bread, and give them to eat?

38 He saith unto them, How many loaves have ye? go and see. And when they knew, they say, Five, and two fishes.

39 And he commanded them to make all sit down by companies upon the green grass.

40 And they sat down in ranks, by hundreds, and by fifties.

41 And when he had taken the five loaves and the two fishes, he looked up to heaven, and blessed, and brake the loaves, and gave *them* to his disciples to set before them; and the two fishes divided he among them all.

42 And they did all eat, and were filled.

43 And they took up twelve baskets full of the fragments, and of the fishes.

44 And they that did eat of the loaves were about five thousand men.

45 ¶And straightway he constrained his disciples to get into the ship, and to go to the other side before unto Bĕth-sā'i-da, while he sent away the people.

46 And when he had sent them away, he departed into a mountain to pray.

47 And when even was come, the ship was in the midst of the sea, and he alone on the land.

48 And he saw them toiling in rowing; for the wind was contrary unto them: and about the fourth watch of the night he cometh unto them, walking upon the sea, and would have passed by them.

49 But when they saw him walking upon the sea, they supposed it had been a spirit, and cried out:

50 For they all saw him, and were troubled. And immediately he talked with them, and saith unto them, Be of good cheer: it is I; be not afraid.

51 And he went up unto them into the ship; and the wind ceased: and they were sore amazed in themselves beyond measure, and wondered.

52 For they considered not *the miracle* of the loaves: for their heart was hardened.

53 And when they had passed over, they came into the land of Gĕn-nĕs'a-ret, and drew to the shore.

Verse 33 should then begin, "A great many people saw them leaving and recognized them, so that they ran on foot . . . ."

34. Tired and hungry, Jesus could easily have been disturbed by their persistence; His response is incredible! He **was moved with compassion.**

35-36. Perhaps the apostles had a selfish motive when they asked Jesus to dismiss the crowds, **for they have nothing to eat.** Verse 31 would indicate that they themselves had greater hunger.

4. Feeding the five thousand. 6:37-44.

37. Hungry and tired, Jesus appeared as other men, but suddenly the supernatural erupted. **Give ye them to eat** was a command to do the impossible.

38-44. The details remove all possibility of minimizing the event as something less than miraculous:
a. The materials: five loaves, two fish.
b. The audience: very organized (unusual stories could understandably result from a chaotic situation).
c. The leftovers: twelve baskets (no one could claim that the people ate little because the food was scarce).
d. The number of people: **five thousand men** (Gr *anēr*) definitely refers to adult males. The generic term (Gr *anthrōpos*) is not used here.

5. Walking on the sea. 6:45-52.

45-52. Verse 31 indicated that He wanted to rest, but here He feels an urgency to **pray.** Jesus demonstrated His power not simply in order to aid the disciples, for He could have uttered an effective command from shore. This miracle aimed at confirming His identity. The apostles reacted **beyond measure.** The fact that they **considered not the miracle of the loaves** points to their reluctance to accept Jesus as God. They viewed His miracles as divine interventions upon His life.

6. Reception at Gennesaret. 6:53-56.

53. Gennesaret is located on the western shore of Galilee south of Capernaum and north of Tiberias. It was well known for its fertile soil.

54 And when they were come out of the ship, straightway they knew him,

55 And ran through that whole region round about, and began to carry about in beds those that were sick, where they heard he was.

56 And whithersoever he entered, into villages, or cities, or country, they laid the sick in the streets, and besought him that they might touch if it were but the border of his garment: and as many as touched him were made whole.

CHAPTER 7

THEN came together unto him the Pharisees, and certain of the scribes, which came from Jerusalem.

2 And when they saw some of his disciples eat bread with defiled, that is to say, with unwashen, hands, they found fault.

3 For the Pharisees, and all the Jews, except they wash *their* hands oft, eat not, holding the tradition of the elders.

4 And *when they come* from the market, except they wash, they eat not. And many other things there be, which they have received to hold, *as* the washing of cups, and pots, brasen vessels, and of tables.

5 Then the Pharisees and scribes asked him, Why walk not thy disciples according to the tradition of the elders, but eat bread with unwashen hands?

6 He answered and said unto them, Well hath E-sā′ias prophesied of you hypocrites, as it is written, This people honoureth me with *their* lips, but their heart is far from me.

7 Howbeit in vain do they worship me, teaching *for* doctrines the commandments of men.

8 For laying aside the commandment of God, ye hold the tradition of men, *as* the washing of pots and cups: and many other such like things ye do.

9 And he said unto them, Full well ye reject the commandment of God, that ye may keep your own tradition.

10 For Moses said, Honour thy father and thy mother; and, Whoso curseth father or mother, let him die the death:

11 But ye say, If a man shall say to his father or mother, *It is* Corban, that is to say, a gift, by whatsoever thou mightest be profited by me; *he shall be free.*

12 And ye suffer him no more to do ought for his father or his mother;

13 Making the word of God of none effect through your tradition, which ye have delivered: and many such like things do ye.

14 ¶And when he had called all the people *unto him*, he said unto them, Hearken unto me every one *of you*, and understand:

15 There is nothing from without a man, that entering into him can defile him: but the things which come out of him, those are they that defile the man.

54-56. The enthusiasm displayed by these people was probably due to their close proximity to Capernaum, which functioned as a headquarters for the Lord. The news of miraculous healings continuously spread through their neighborhoods, and one day, unannounced, the Healer arrived. People hurried to their sick relatives and friends to bear them before His presence. So frantically was this performed that **whithersoever** He turned He met people with infirmities.

H. Pharisees and Tradition. 7:1-23.

7:1. The Pharisees, and certain of the scribes were undoubtedly sent by the nation's religious leaders **from Jerusalem** to observe and record any unlawful activity or teaching.

2. Mark 6:31 states that Jesus and His assistants were so busy that they often skipped meals. When they had time to eat, these "religious authorities" observed a breach of the law, eating with **unwashen hands.** Their fanaticism is apparent because their negative attitudes, seizing an insignificant detail of tradition, completely overlooked the laborious service that was rendered.

3-4. The apostles were characterized by their involvement in serving people, the Pharisees by their pertinacious adherence to Jewish law and custom. **Holding** is an intense expression which implies a strong, tight grasp as a hawk would seize its prey. **Tradition** (Gr *paradōsis*) comes from two words which mean "to give alongside of." Thus, Jewish tradition is men's statutes set alongside of God's law. It is not the law, but has been accepted and taught with equal authority.

5-7. Although it may appear that Jesus ignored their question, He actually strikes at the heart of the issue with such directness that they are offended. Why not keep tradition? Because **you** who practice it are just role-playing. **Hypocrites** (Gr *hypokrites*) originally referred to someone who acted in the theatre. They were merely imitating true spirituality. Their conception of religion was false because it was based upon outward conformity to a set of rules.

8-9. Usually when man affixes tradition alongside of inspired truth he centers his attention so much upon what is added that the original is neglected. **Full well** (Gr *kalōs*) is idiomatic as in "that's just great!" The Lord used sarcasm to reaffirm the folly of their conduct.

10-13. These verses present an example of how their tradition nullified the law. The precept, **Honor thy father and thy mother,** which included "honoring" by financial support, is among the Ten Commandments (Ex 20:12). It became customary for supposedly pious Jews to claim that their funds were already designated as a **gift** to God, when they were confronted with their parents' need. More than that, a Pharisee could impose a certain amount upon a layman, and if he replied, "But I am obligated to help my mother and father!" he could insist, "You are freed from this commandment, because that money is **Corban** (Greek transliteration of Hebrew *qarban*, meaning a gift for God); it is a God-appointed gift for His service."

14-19. Whatsoever . . . entereth refers to food, physical matter which contains no moral significance.

16 If any man have ears to hear, let him hear.

17 And when he was entered into the house from the people, his disciples asked him concerning the parable.

18 And he saith unto them, Are ye so without understanding also? Do ye not perceive, that whatsoever thing from without entereth into the man, it cannot defile him;

19 Because it entereth not into his heart, but into the belly, and goeth out into the draught, purging all meats?

20 And he said, That which cometh out of the man, that defileth the man.

21 For from within, out of the heart of men, proceed evil thoughts, adulteries, fornications, murders,

22 Thefts, covetousness, wickedness, deceit, lasciviousness, an evil eye, blasphemy, pride, foolishness:

23 All these evil things come from within, and defile the man.

24 ¶And from thence he arose, and went into the borders of Tyre and Sī'-don, and entered into an house, and would have no man know it, but he could not be hid.

25 For a certain woman, whose young daughter had an unclean spirit, heard of him, and came and fell at his feet:

26 The woman was a Greek, a Sȳ-rō-phe-nī'cian by nation; and she besought him that he would cast forth the devil out of her daughter.

27 But Jesus said unto her, Let the children first be filled: for it is not meet to take the children's bread, and to cast it unto the dogs.

28 And she answered and said unto him, Yes, Lord: yet the dogs under the table eat of the children's crumbs.

29 And he said unto her, For this saying go thy way; the devil is gone out of thy daughter.

30 And when she was come to her house, she found the devil gone out, and her daughter laid upon the bed.

31 ¶And again, departing from the coasts of Tyre and Sī'don, he came unto the sea of Galilee, through the midst of the coasts of De-căp'o-lĭs.

32 And they bring unto him one that was deaf, and had an impediment in his speech; and they beseech him to put his hand upon him.

33 And he took him aside from the multitude, and put his fingers into his ears, and he spit, and touched his tongue;

34 And looking up to heaven, he sighed, and saith unto him, Eph'pha-tha, that is, Be opened.

20-23. That which cometh out He interprets as non-physical, anything stemming from the mind or heart. If actions, words, or thoughts originate in an evil, rebellious heart, they certainly must be contrary to God and righteousness.

III. THE MINISTRY BEYOND GALILEE. 7:24-9:50.

At this point in the narrative a new phase in Jesus' ministry begins. Previously He had remained in Galilee or in the vicinity of the Sea of Galilee, but henceforth His travels extend farther, although He limited them to the north.

A. Tyre and Sidon. 7:24-30.

24. Tyre and Sidon were two port cities along the Mediterranean Sea northwest of Galilee, and **borders** refers to the regions or neighboring communities surrounding them. Jesus' intent on this trip was not evangelism. He **would have no man know** that He was present. Perhaps He sought to find solitude after the trying encounter with the Jerusalem delegation.

25-26. Two words identify the woman. She was **Greek** and **Syrophoenician.** The former categorized her as non-Jewish, while the latter indicates the unification of two countries, Syria and Phoenicia. The word **besought** explains the apparent reluctance of Jesus to heed a Gentile. It is a mild word (Gr *erōtaō*) which simply means "asked." He replies by testing the intent of her desire and faith.

27-28. Jesus' illustration of **dogs** is not an expression of contempt for Greeks. He is merely putting a test before her.

29. For this saying. Her words proved her heart attitude, and her request was granted. **Devil** (Gr *daimonion*) should be "demon."

30. The verb in the clause, **her daughter laid upon the bed,** does not adequately express the force involved. The Greek perfect passive may indicate she had been thrown upon the bed, the demon committing his last violent act before his departure.

B. Decapolis. 7:31-8:9.

31. From Phoenicia Christ journeyed southeast of the Sea of Galilee to **Decapolis,** the region of "ten cities."

1. A deaf-mute healed. 7:32-37.

32-34. Why did Jesus resort to this healing procedure when a word could do all that was necessary? It seems that He responded to people's attitudes and requests accordingly. Here they asked Him to touch the deaf-mute, So He obliged.

35 And straightway his ears were opened, and the string of his tongue was loosed, and he spake plain.

36 And he charged them that they should tell no man: but the more he charged them, so much the more a great deal they published *it;*

37 And were beyond measure astonished, saying, He hath done all things well: he maketh both the deaf to hear, and the dumb to speak.

CHAPTER 8

IN those days the multitude being very great, and having nothing to eat, Jesus called his disciples *unto him,* and saith unto them,

2 I have compassion on the multitude, because they have now been with me three days, and have nothing to eat:

3 And if I send them away fasting to their own houses, they will faint by the way: for divers of them came from far.

4 And his disciples answered him, From whence can a man satisfy these *men* with bread here in the wilderness?

5 And he asked them, How many loaves have ye? And they said, Seven.

6 And he commanded the people to sit down on the ground: and he took the seven loaves, and gave thanks, and brake, and gave to his disciples to set before *them;* and they did set *them* before the people.

7 And they had a few small fishes: and he blessed, and commanded to set them also before *them.*

8 So they did eat, and were filled: and they took up of the broken *meat* that was left seven baskets.

9 And they that had eaten were about four thousand: and he sent them away.

10 ¶And straightway he entered into a ship with his disciples, and came into the parts of Dăl-ma-nū′tha.

11 And the Pharisees came forth, and began to question with him, seeking of him a sign from heaven, tempting him.

12 And he sighed deeply in his spirit, and saith, Why doth this generation seek after a sign? verily I say unto you, There shall no sign be given unto this generation.

13 And he left them, and entering into the ship again departed to the other side.

14 ¶Now *the disciples* had forgotten

35. The **string** (Gr *desmos*) of his tongue is that which binds the physical member, preventing clear speech. The noun is translated "fetter" or "bond" when describing the instrument which restrains a prisoner.

36-37. Tell no man. See comments on Mark 5:43 regarding these instructions.

2. Feeding the four thousand. 8:1-9.

8:1. Notice that **Jesus called his disciples,** but prior to the previous feeding of the five thousand they had worriedly approached Him about the need for food (Mk 6:35-36). Their faith had grown.

2-3. The bulk of these followers were from Decapolis, where Jesus was ministering (7:31), although some **came from far.** The latter perhaps had followed Him from Tyre and Sidon (7:31). Their desire to be with Him surpassed their feelings of hunger, for they had fasted **three days.**

4. The contrast between the need and the location is emphasized, **From whence . . . here . . . in the wilderness.**

5. Of course the Lord could have created food out of nothing, but He chose to use what was available, even though it appeared insignificantly small.

6-7. As with the previous miraculous feeding, the distribution was highly organized (6:39-40).

8. **They . . . were filled** (Gr *chortazō*). There was enough food for each to eat until his appetite was thoroughly satisfied. In fact, leftovers filled **seven baskets** (Gr *spyris*) which at times were large enough to hold men (Acts 9:25).

9. The number four thousand does not specify men as with the five thousand, so the size of the gathering could have been significantly smaller. Since there are those who attempt to merge the two accounts into one event, the significant differences should be noted: the number of people fed, the place, the time, the numbers of fish, loaves and baskets.

C. Passing Through Galilee. 8:10-26.

1. The trip to Dalmanutha. 8:10-13.

10. The location of **Dalmanutha** is unknown, although the context implies it is on the western side of the Sea of Galilee. The parallel passage in Matthew (Mt 15:39) calls it Magdala.

11. The Pharisees' approach to Jesus had an apparent motive, **seeking of him a sign,** but they actually came **tempting him.** Their appeal implied that Jesus' previous miracles were insufficient evidence that He was of God.

12-13. Matthew 13:58 sets forth a principle which relates the Lord's response to this religious party, "He did not many mighty works there because of their unbelief."

2. The leaven of the Pharisees. 8:14-21.

14-21. Take heed, beware literally means "Continue taking heed, keep watching," because both imperatives are in the

to take bread, neither had they in the ship with them more than one loaf.

15 And he charged them, saying, Take heed, beware of the leaven of the Pharisees, and of the leaven of Herod.

16 And they reasoned among themselves, saying, It is because we have no bread.

17 And when Jesus knew it, he saith unto them, Why reason ye, because ye have no bread? perceive ye not yet, neither understand? have ye your heart yet hardened?

18 Having eyes, see ye not? and having ears, hear ye not? and do ye not remember?

19 When I brake the five loaves among five thousand, how many baskets full of fragments took ye up? They say unto him, Twelve.

20 And when the seven among four thousand, how many baskets full of fragments took ye up? And they said, Seven.

21 And he said unto them, How is it that ye do not understand?

22 ¶And he cometh to Bĕth-sā′i-da: and they bring a blind man unto him, and besought him to touch him.

23 And he took the blind man by the hand, and led him out of the town; and when he had spit on his eyes, and put his hands upon him, he asked him if he saw ought.

24 And he looked up, and said, I see men as trees, walking.

25 After that he put his hands again upon his eyes, and made him look up: and he was restored, and saw every man clearly.

26 And he sent him away to his house, saying, Neither go into the town, nor tell it to any in the town.

27 ¶And Jesus went out, and his disciples, into the towns of Cæs-a-re′a Phĭ-lip′pī: and by the way he asked his disciples, saying unto them, Whom do men say that I am?

28 And they answered, John the Baptist: but some say, E-lī′as; and others, One of the prophets.

29 And he saith unto them, But whom say ye that I am? And Peter answereth and saith unto him, Thou art the Christ.

30 And he charged them that they should tell no man of him.

31 ¶And he began to teach them, that the Son of man must suffer many things, and be rejected of the elders, and of the chief priests, and scribes, and be killed, and after three days rise again.

32 And he spake that saying openly. And Peter took him, and began to rebuke him.

33 But when he had turned about and

Greek present tense. **Leaven,** or yeast, is a substance which ferments in order to produce its effect and spreads throughout every fiber of the dough. The diffusion of this souring substance illustrates an evil equality of false teachers. The **Pharisees** and **Herod** seem to be an odd combination. Matthew unites the Pharisees and the Sadducees (Mt 16:6) with a common leaven. If Herod belonged to the Sadducee sect, as many scholars believe, the common denominator would be their attachment to a false religion.

3. The healing of a blind man. 8:22-26.

22. In **Bethsaida,** a coastal city on the northeast point of Galilee, a certain party led a blind man to Jesus.

23-25. This miracle is unique because most of Jesus' supernatural acts occurred in a single word or touch. **He put his hands again upon his eyes,** in order to bestow perfect vision.

26. Jesus wanted as little publicity as possible. Besides the direct command here, verse 23 explains that He led the blind man outside the town before He healed him.

D. Caesarea Philippi. 8:27-9:1.

27. Caesarea Philippi lay north and slightly east of the Sea of Galilee, approximately the same distance from it as from Tyre. The first half of the name, obviously referring to Caesar, was common. The latter half distinguished it from the coastal city, Caesarea, by identifying it as a part of Philip's realm. Jesus' inquiry, **Whom do men say that I am?,** introduced the more direct question which followed.

28. The response was that of the masses rather than the religious leaders, who claimed that He was a messenger of the devil (Mark 3:22).

29-30. In Greek *ye* is emphatic; it was their conclusion about His person that was the issue. Peter retorted without any hesitation, **Thou art the Christ.** The Greek *Christos* comes from the word which means "to anoint," the "Anointed One" being the Messiah (Heb *Mashiah*). Matthew adds to this title "the Son of the living God" (Mt 16:16). Although the apostles seemed to recognize His true identity, confusion remained because like other Jews they were looking for a military leader.

31. This verse marks a turning point in the book. If there had existed hopes for an earthly kingdom established by Christ, they were now dismissed, because at this point **he began to teach them** of His suffering, rejection, death, and resurrection.

32-33. Jesus' announcement was made **openly** but Peter led Him aside to **rebuke** Him. The impulsive apostle cringed in unbelief at what he heard, and he quickly let it be known that he was unwilling to accept it. The harsh statement, **Get thee**

looked on his disciples, he rebuked Peter, saying, Get thee behind me, Satan: for thou savourest not the things that be of God, but the things that be of men.

34 ¶And when he had called the people *unto him* with his disciples also, he said unto them, Whosoever will come after me, let him deny himself, and take up his cross, and follow me.

35 For whosoever will save his life shall lose it; but whosoever shall lose his life for my sake and the gospel's, the same shall save it.

36 For what shall it profit a man, if he shall gain the whole world, and lose his own soul?

37 Or what shall a man give in exchange for his soul?

38 Whosoever therefore shall be ashamed of me and of my words in this adulterous and sinful generation; of him also shall the Son of man be ashamed, when he cometh in the glory of his Father with the holy angels.

CHAPTER 9

AND he said unto them, Verily I say unto you, That there be some of them that stand here, which shall not taste of death, till they have seen the kingdom of God come with power.

2 ¶And after six days Jesus taketh *with him* Peter, and James, and John, and leadeth them up into an high mountain apart by themselves: and he was transfigured before them.

3 And his raiment became shining, exceeding white as snow; so as no fuller on earth can white them.

4 And there appeared unto them E-li'-as with Moses: and they were talking with Jesus.

5 And Peter answered and said to Jesus, Master, it is good for us to be here: and let us make three tabernacles; one for thee, and one for Moses, and one for E-li'as.

6 For he wist not what to say; for they were sore afraid.

7 And there was a cloud that overshadowed them: and a voice came out of the cloud, saying, This is my beloved Son: hear him.

8 And suddenly, when they had looked round about, they saw no man any more, save Jesus only with themselves.

9 And as they came down from the mountain, he charged them that they

behind me, Satan, arose because the attempt to sway Christ from God's plan of salvation made him a tempter of the worst sort. Peter **savorest not** (did not set his mind on) the things of God, but rather on what his finite wisdom deemed best.

34. The disciples believed and yet they misunderstood Christ's plan. Therefore, He set forth some basic principles that explain the real meaning of life. **Deny himself.** Asceticism has its end in itself, but the type of self-denial proposed here aims to give the Lord Jesus Christ the preeminence. He Himself said, "Not my will, but thine be done" (Mt 26:39). Although self-denial means giving up one's rights, God does not usually require abandonment of personal property.

35-37. What a man attempts to save or gain, he ultimately will lose. On the other hand, if one loses all for the sake of Christ and the gospel he actually is preserving his life.

38. A man may speak boldly and candidly among friends. The test of character for a Christian comes when he must stand for Christ in the midst of **adulterous** and **sinful** men. The Lord's day will come, but do our lives demonstrate that we really believe it now?

9:1. This verse belongs at the end of chapter 8; it is the final statement in Christ's lecture about self-denial. Although He had just emphasized the spiritual over the physical, men seek and need physical evidence. Thus, it is promised: **some . . . here, . . . shall not taste of death, till they have seen the kingdom of God come with power.** Various interpretations have been offered regarding this statement. Since the transfiguration occurs next in the narration, that event probably symbolizes His coming with power because of the outward glory revealed.

E. Mount of Transfiguration. 9:2-29.

2. Peter and James and John, Jesus' closest companions, consisted of what is often called the "inner circle." The high mountain perhaps refers to Mt. Hermon, the highest in the vicinity of Caesarea Philippi. The word describing His transfiguration (Gr *metamorphoō*) signifies an outward manifestation of an inward change.

3. Although Matthew and Luke's accounts mention Jesus' change in countenance, Mark restricts his comments to the Lord's apparel. A **fuller** was one who professionally cleaned clothing.

4. Elijah [Elias] and **Moses** appeared with Jesus because of their close connection with Him in prophecy. Elijah stands out as the more prominent figure because his ministry more closely correlates with the messianic advents.

5-6. Peter misjudged in his suggestion primarily because his impulsive nature responded too quickly (Jas 1:19). Although he had just exalted Christ as the Son of the living God, here he placed Him on an equal plane with the two prophets.

7-10. Jesus' uniqueness is confirmed from heaven: **This is my beloved Son: Hear him.** Jesus frequently restricted people from proclaiming His miracles in order to allow God's plan of salvation to be carried out. Had His supernatural identity been revealed, people would not have permitted His death.

should tell no man what things they
had seen, till the Son of man were risen
from the dead.
10 And they kept that saying with
themselves, questioning one with another what the rising from the dead
should mean.
11 ¶And they asked him, saying, Why
say the scribes that E-lī′as must first
come?
12 And he answered and told them,
E-lī′as verily cometh first, and restoreth all things; and how it is written
of the Son of man, that he must suffer
many things, and be set at nought.
13 But I say unto you, That E-lī′as is
indeed come, and they have done unto
him whatsoever they listed, as it is
written of him.
14 ¶And when he came to *his* disciples, he saw a great multitude about
them, and the scribes questioning with
them.
15 And straightway all the people,
when they beheld him, were greatly
amazed, and running to *him* saluted
him.
16 And he asked the scribes, What
question ye with them?
17 And one of the multitude answered and said, Master, I have
brought unto thee my son, which hath a
dumb spirit;
18 And wheresoever he taketh him,
he teareth him: and he foameth, and
gnasheth with his teeth, and pineth
away: and I spake to thy disciples that
they should cast him out; and they
could not.
19 He answereth him, and saith, O
faithless generation, how long shall I be
with you? how long shall I suffer you?
bring him unto me.
20 And they brought him unto him:
and when he saw him, straightway the
spirit tare him; and he fell on the
ground, and wallowed foaming.
21 And he asked his father, How long
is it ago since this came unto him? And
he said, Of a child.
22 And ofttimes it hath cast him into
the fire, and into the waters, to destroy
him: but if thou canst do any thing,
have compassion on us, and help us.
23 Jesus said unto him, If thou canst
believe, all things *are* possible to him
that believeth.
24 And straightway the father of the
child cried out, and said with tears,
Lord, I believe; help thou mine unbelief.
25 When Jesus saw that the people
came running together, he rebuked the
foul spirit, saying unto him, *Thou* dumb
and deaf spirit, I charge thee, come out
of him, and enter no more into him.
26 And *the* spirit cried, and rent him
sore, and came out of him: and he was
as one dead; insomuch that many said,
He is dead.
27 But Jesus took him by the hand,
and lifted him up; and he arose.

11-13. The three apostles became puzzled about Elijah's connection with the Messiah in prophecy. The scribes claimed
Elijah must first come (Mal 4:5-6), yet his recent appearance
obviously was not before Christ. Jesus agreed with the scribes,
but interpreted Elijah's coming spiritually. Verse 13 hints at
Elijah's connection with John the Baptist and Matthew 17:13
confirms it.

14-15. Evidently the crowds were unaware that Jesus was
near for when they saw Him they . . . were greatly amazed or
surprised. **Saluted** means that they "greeted" Him.

16-17. The petitioner's desperation may be seen by his boldness. Jesus directed a question to the scribes but **one of the
multitude** interrupted. **Master** means teacher. **Dumb spirit** may
be rendered "a spirit of silence" or " a mute spirit."

18. The youth's problem was more than his inability to
speak. The indwelling demon persistently gave him convulsions. Among other things, Jesus had empowered His disciples to cast out demons, but a terse indictment erupted from a
despairing father: **they could not,** they did not have the power.

19. Jesus' expression of displeasure against the **faithless
generation** was not specifically directed toward one person nor
just a small group. The word **generation** refers to a whole race.
The scribes continued to voice doubts, the disciples could not
heal, and the father of the mute son came out of despair, not in
genuine faith.

20. Tare means he caused his victim to have convulsions.

21-23. A full description is given of the condition. The length
and severity are clearly expressed to dismiss any superficial
conclusions that the ailment may have been temporary. The
healing could only be interpreted as a miracle. The brief dialogue between the petitioner and the Lord teaches a fundamental principle about obtaining supernatural aid from God.
As with this individual, human nature usually approaches God
with doubts about His ability: **if thou canst do any thing
. . . .** But Jesus clarified the issue. The prerequisite for healing
never is doubtful on God's part, only on man's. **If thou canst
believe, all things are possible.**

24-27. The man, recognizing the burden laid upon him, confessed his imperfect faith: **Lord, I believe; help thou mine
unbelief.** He longed for stronger faith, and God granted his
request, not because He saw mature faith, but because He
honored his desire for growth.

28 And when he was come into the house, his disciples asked him privately, Why could not we cast him out?

29 And he said unto them, This kind can come forth by nothing, but by prayer and fasting.

30 ¶And they departed thence, and passed through Galilee; and he would not that any man should know *it.*

31 For he taught his disciples, and said unto them, The Son of man is delivered into the hands of men, and they shall kill him; and after that he is killed, he shall rise the third day.

32 But they understood not that saying, and were afraid to ask him.

33 ¶And he came to Ca-per'na-um: and being in the house he asked them, What was it that ye disputed among yourselves by the way?

34 But they held their peace: for by the way they had disputed among themselves, who *should be* the greatest.

35 And he sat down, and called the twelve, and saith unto them, If any man desire to be first, *the same* shall be last of all, and servant of all.

36 And he took a child, and set him in the midst of them: and when he had taken him in his arms, he said unto them,

37 Whosoever shall receive one of such children in my name, receiveth me: and whosoever shall receive me, receiveth not me, but him that sent me.

38 ¶And John answered him, saying, Master, we saw one casting out devils in thy name, and he followeth not us: and we forbad him, because he followeth not us.

39 But Jesus said, Forbid him not: for there is no man which shall do a miracle in my name, that can lightly speak evil of me.

40 For he that is not against us is on our part.

41 For whosoever shall give you a cup of water to drink in my name, because ye belong to Christ, verily I say unto you, he shall not lose his reward.

42 And whosoever shall offend one of *these* little ones that believe in me, it is better for him that a millstone were hanged about his neck, and he were cast into the sea.

43 And if thy hand offend thee, cut it off: it is better for thee to enter into life maimed, than having two hands to go into hell, into the fire that never shall be quenched:

44 Where their worm dieth not, and the fire is not quenched.

45 And if thy foot offend thee, cut it off: it is better for thee to enter halt into life, than having two feet to be cast into hell, into the fire that never shall be quenched:

46 Where their worm dieth not, and the fire is not quenched.

47 And if thine eye offend thee, pluck

28-29. Jesus' answer to the question, **Why could not we cast him out?**, is written three ways: (1) Verse 29 says **by prayer and fasting;** (2) a few manuscripts, including those on which the AV is based, add **fasting;** and (3) Matthew records that the reason for failure was "unbelief," with a brief illustration about mustard-seed-type faith following (Mt 17:20). The two accounts harmonize for if a person seeks God in a season of prayer, faith will result. Mark and Matthew simply chose different emphases.

F. The Secret Trip Through Galilee. 9:30-50.

30-32. The Lord Jesus knew that soon He would depart for Jerusalem (10:1). The final phase of His earthly ministry was drawing near. Therefore, this trip through Galilee was reserved for the edification of His disciples. Again He taught them about His death and resurrection, but they **understood not.** In fact, Matthew notes, "they were exceeding sorry" (Mt 17:23).

33-34. After they entered their house in Capernaum, Jesus asked the Twelve what they had been discussing on the journey. Apparently they felt guilty, for **they held their peace.** Even though no one answered, He began a discourse on the very subject they had been disputing.

35-37. Humility characterizes those who genuinely **desire** to serve Christ and His kingdom. A disciple should esteem himself as a **servant** (Gr *diakonos*), one who willingly attends to menial tasks and eagerly receives children without recognition or reward.

38-41. John's experience occasioned an injunction against judging. The expression **He that is not against us is on our part,** often is exaggerated to opposite extremes. Second John 10-11 exhorts Christians to guard against fellowship which condones false teaching, and yet we must be careful not to distort this command so as to foster spiritual cliques.

42. To **offend** (cause to stumble) **one of these little ones** is so serious that immediate death would be better than further involvement, and thus, greater judgment. A **millstone** refers to a large stone used in a mill for grinding, this particular type being large enough to require a donkey to move it.

43-48. Jesus used a hyperbole to impress His listeners with the gravity of sin. It would be better to sever a member of the body than to keep it and go to **hell.** It is obvious, however, that the real problem lies in the heart and mind. The word translated **hell** (Gr *geennan*) is a transliteration of Hebrew, and means the "valley of Hinnom." Lying to the south of Jerusalem, it was used as a rubbish heap and gradually adopted a spiritual application. Fires burned continuously and worms multiplied throughout the debris. Thus the statement, **their worm dieth not, and the fire is not quenched,** illustrates the eternal destruction of those who have not received the Saviour.

it out: it is better for thee to enter into the kingdom of God with one eye, than having two eyes to be cast into hell fire:

48 Where their worm dieth not, and the fire is not quenched.

49 For every one shall be salted with fire, and every sacrifice shall be salted with salt.

50 Salt *is* good: but if the salt have lost his saltness, wherewith will ye season it? Have salt in yourselves, and have peace one with another.

CHAPTER 10

AND he arose from thence, and cometh into the coasts of Judæa by the farther side of Jordan: and the people resort unto him again; and, as he was wont, he taught them again.

2 ¶And the Pharisees came to him, and asked him, Is it lawful for a man to put away *his* wife? tempting him.

3 And he answered and said unto them, What did Moses command you?

4 And they said, Moses suffered to write a bill of divorcement, and to put *her* away.

5 And Jesus answered and said unto them, For the hardness of your heart he wrote you this precept.

6 But from the beginning of the creation God made them male and female.

7 For this cause shall a man leave his father and mother, and cleave to his wife;

8 And they twain shall be one flesh: so then they are no more twain, but one flesh.

9 What therefore God hath joined together, let not man put asunder.

10 And in the house his disciples asked him again of the same *matter*.

11 And he saith unto them, Whosoever shall put away his wife, and marry another, committeth adultery against her.

12 And if a woman shall put away her husband, and be married to another, she committeth adultery.

13 ¶And they brought young children to him, that he should touch them: and *his* disciples rebuked those that brought *them*.

14 But when Jesus saw *it*, he was much displeased, and said unto them, Suffer the little children to come unto me, and forbid them not: for of such is the kingdom of God.

15 Verily I say unto you, Whosoever shall not receive the kingdom of God as a little child, he shall not enter therein.

49-50. These concluding statements stand as a warning to would-be offenders. Lest one follows an unrepenting road to hell, **everyone shall be salted with fire,** that is, a certain amount of affliction befalls everyone in order to stir them toward God. This kind of fire acts as **salt.** It takes something insignificant and adds meaning. On the other hand, if salt has **lost his saltness,** it becomes ineffective and even tribulation may not turn the sinner from his way. The last clause must be related to both the ideas which preceded. **Have salt** could be paraphrased, "Receive God's providential lessons" and **have peace** refers to their dispute over who was greatest.

IV. THE CONCLUDING MINISTRY. 10:1-13:37.

A. Peraea (Beyond Jordan). 10:1-31.

1. On the way. 10:1.

10:1. Although the other gospel writers tell us that Jesus made former trips to the south, this one toward Jerusalem marks a definite break in Mark's narrative. The only other time Jesus journeyed south in Mark's account was for baptism, but at this point Jesus' departure from the north was permanent.

2. The discourse on divorce. 10:2-12.

2-9. The reference to Moses demonstrates Christ's authority over the Old Testament. Although Moses permitted divorce (Deut 24:1), it was allowed because of the people's **hardness of heart.** Jesus, however, proclaimed God's perfect and ideal plan: **they twain shall be one flesh.**

10-12. After they had left the Pharisees and had found some privacy, the disciples sought a clearer statement about divorce. Anyone who divorces his or her mate, Jesus replied, and marries another is committing adultery. Elsewhere He added an exception: "save for fornication" (Mt 5:32; 19:9).

3. Jesus' attitude toward children. 10:13-16.

13. People commonly brought their sick friends and relatives to Jesus for healing, but on this occasion some **brought young children.** The disciples failed to see the potential that their Master did. He not only observed what men were, but what by the grace of God they could be.

14-16. Of such is the kingdom of God. A child does not become distracted by all the complexities of life. When he trusts, his faith is simple and unwavering. In fact, to possess salvation one must become **as a little child.**

16 And he took them up in his arms, put *his* hands upon them, and blessed them.

17 ¶And when he was gone forth into the way, there came one running, and kneeled to him, and asked him, Good Master, what shall I do that I may inherit eternal life?

18 And Jesus said unto him, Why callest thou me good? *there is* none good but one, *that is,* God.

19 Thou knowest the commandments, Do not commit adultery, Do not kill, Do not steal, Do not bear false witness, Defraud not, Honour thy father and mother.

20 And he answered and said unto him, Master, all these have I observed from my youth.

21 Then Jesus beholding him loved him, and said unto him, One thing thou lackest: go thy way, sell whatsoever thou hast, and give to the poor, and thou shalt have treasure in heaven: and come, take up the cross, and follow me.

22 And he was sad at that saying, and went away grieved: for he had great possessions.

23 ¶And Jesus looked round about, and saith unto his disciples, How hardly shall they that have riches enter into the kingdom of God!

24 And the disciples were astonished at his words. But Jesus answereth again, and saith unto them, Children, how hard is it for them that trust in riches to enter into the kingdom of God!

25 It is easier for a camel to go through the eye of a needle, than for a rich man to enter into the kingdom of God.

26 And they were astonished out of measure, saying among themselves, Who then can be saved?

27 And Jesus looking upon them saith, With men *it is* impossible, but not with God: for with God all things are possible.

28 ¶Then Peter began to say unto him, Lo, we have left all, and have followed thee.

29 And Jesus answered and said, Verily I say unto you, There is no man that hath left house, or brethren, or sisters, or father, or mother, or wife, or children, or lands, for my sake, and the gospel's,

30 But he shall receive an hundredfold now in this time, houses, and brethren, and sisters, and mothers, and children, and lands, with persecutions; and in the world to come eternal life.

31 But many *that are* first shall be last; and the last first.

32 ¶And they were in the way going up to Jerusalem; and Jesus went before them: and they were amazed; and as

4. The rich young ruler. 10:17-22.

17-18. Jesus' reply, **Why callest thou me good,** does not deny that He is God. Many passages clearly state that He is God (Jn 1:1; Phil 2:6; Tit 2:13; Heb 1:8), and He Himself claims so (Jn 8:58; 10:30; 11:25). The response here is aimed at the young ruler's attitude toward himself. Verse 20 indicates that he considered himself to be good. Jesus wanted him to know of whom that adjective should be exclusively used.

19-21. The burden of keeping the whole law (Jas 2:10) was overbearing, yet this man claims adherence to its demands. As if those laws were not enough, Jesus adds to them, **sell whatsoever thou hast, and give . . . .**

22. This was too much; he **went away grieved.** Does this story teach that salvation is merited by good works? One must remember that prior to the acceptance of the gospel a man needs to recognize his need. Jesus was aware of the man's self-righteous attitude, trusting in his observance of rules. Therefore, his need was for Christ to point out **one thing thou lackest.** Men must be cognizant of their sin and guilt before they can be ready for "good news."

5. The perils of riches. 10:23-31.

23-24. It is almost impossible to find an extremely wealthy person who is not trusting in his riches.

25-27. Verse 25 imagines an impossible act, and verse 27 reassures the bewildered apostles: **with God all things are possible.** There is an inference of salvation by grace. The Lord will make possible through Christ's death what man cannot do in himself.

28-31. Peter's claim, **we have left all,** may have been true, but it also reveals pride. Graciously, Jesus responds with a promise; whoever forsakes his life for the gospel will receive incomparable rewards. Since the relationships refer to spiritual ones in God's family, the things mentioned may speak of new homes opened in Christian hospitality as well as personal physical blessings.

B. On the Way to Jerusalem. 10:32-52.

1. On the road. 10:32-34.

32. They were afraid. Because they were going toward Jerusalem, they sensed impending doom.

they followed, they were afraid. And he took again the twelve, and began to tell them what things should happen unto him,

33 *Saying*, Behold, we go up to Jerusalem; and the Son of man shall be delivered unto the chief priests, and unto the scribes; and they shall condemn him to death, and shall deliver him to the Gentiles:

34 And they shall mock him, and shall scourge him, and shall spit upon him, and shall kill him: and the third day he shall rise again.

35 ¶And James and John, the sons of Zĕb′e-dee, come unto him, saying, Master, we would that thou shouldest do for us whatsoever we shall desire.

36 And he said unto them, What would ye that I should do for you?

37 They said unto him, Grant unto us that we may sit, one on thy right hand, and the other on thy left hand, in thy glory.

38 But Jesus said unto them, Ye know not what ye ask: can ye drink of the cup that I drink of? and be baptized with the baptism that I am baptized with?

39 And they said unto him, We can. And Jesus said unto them, Ye shall indeed drink of the cup that I drink of; and with the baptism that I am baptized withal shall ye be baptized:

40 But to sit on my right hand and on my left hand is not mine to give; but *it shall be given to them* for whom it is prepared.

41 And when the ten heard *it*, they began to be much displeased with James and John.

42 But Jesus called them *to him*, and saith unto them, Ye know that they which are accounted to rule over the Gentiles exercise lordship over them; and their great ones exercise authority upon them.

43 But so shall it not be among you: but whosoever will be great among you, shall be your minister:

44 And whosoever of you will be the chiefest, shall be servant of all.

45 For even the Son of man came not to be ministered unto, but to minister, and to give his life a ransom for many.

46 ¶And they came to Jericho: and as he went out of Jericho with his disciples and a great number of people, blind Bär-ti-mæ′us, the son of Tī-mæ′us, sat by the highway side begging.

33-34. Knowing their feelings, Jesus predicted what would happen to Him in greater detail than ever before.

2. James' and John's request. 10:35-45.

35-37. The petition exposes the instability of the apostles. They did not understand the salvation which was about to be accomplished, nor its implication on their life-styles. Notice how contrary this desire is to Jesus' recent discourse on humility (Mk 9:33-35).

38-39. The display of ignorance continues, for instead of admitting their frailty, they claimed ability to partake of the Lord's **cup** and **baptism.** Kindly, Jesus refrains from rebuking them.

40. God will reward His servants according to faithfulness. A position in heaven is granted, not upon request, but **for whom it is prepared,** based on faithful service.

41-44. The **Gentiles'** system of success (that of the secular world) is based on "getting ahead of the other guy." The philosophy of Christ refutes this. Christians are to serve and help others, to be other-centered and not self-centered.

45. The greatest example of this philosophy is our Lord Himself. He came **not to be ministered unto, but to minister.** The verb (Gr *diakoneō*) means to serve as an attendant, to wait on tables. The greatest service the Lord Jesus Christ could ever render for man was **to give his life a ransom for many.** He had foretold His death and resurrection several times, but this occasion bore special significance, because He interpreted His death. The impending doom would lead to ultimate victory. The **ransom** would be paid; slaves of sin set free. The last three words of this phrase merit individual treatment. **Ransom** (Gr *lytron*) signifies a loosing, debtors freed. **For** (Gr *anti*) specifically means "in behalf of" indicating a substitutionary death; He died in our place. **Many** simply emphasized a contrast in number: one person died, the ransom is paid for many.

3. In Jericho. 10:46-52.

46. Jericho was the "City of Palms," located just a few miles from the Jordan River.

47 And when he heard that it was Jesus of Nazareth, he began to cry out, and say, Jesus, *thou* son of David, have mercy on me.

48 And many charged him that he should hold his peace: but he cried the more a great deal, *Thou* son of David, have mercy on me.

49 And Jesus stood still, and commanded him to be called. And they call the blind man, saying unto him, Be of good comfort, rise; he calleth thee.

50 And he, casting away his garment, rose, and came to Jesus.

51 And Jesus answered and said unto him, What wilt thou that I should do unto thee? The blind man said unto him, Lord, that I might receive my sight.

52 And Jesus said unto him, Go thy way; thy faith hath made thee whole. And immediately he received his sight, and followed Jesus in the way.

CHAPTER 11

AND when they came nigh to Jerusalem, unto Bĕth'pha-gē and Bethany, at the mount of Olives, he sendeth forth two of his disciples,

2 And saith unto them, Go your way into the village over against you: and as soon as ye be entered into it, ye shall find a colt tied, whereon never man sat; loose him, and bring *him*.

3 And if any man say unto you, Why do ye this? say ye that the Lord hath need of him; and straightway he will send him hither.

4 And they went their way, and found the colt tied by the door without in a place where two ways met; and they loose him.

5 And certain of them that stood there said unto them, What do ye, loosing the colt?

6 And they said unto them even as Jesus had commanded: and they let them go.

7 And they brought the colt to Jesus, and cast their garments on him; and he sat upon him.

8 And many spread their garments in the way: and others cut down branches off the trees, and strawed *them* in the way.

9 And they that went before, and they that followed, cried, saying, Hosanna; Blessed *is* he that cometh in the name of the Lord:

10 Blessed *be* the kingdom of our father David, that cometh in the name of the Lord: Hosanna in the highest.

11 And Jesus entered into Jerusalem, and into the temple: and when he had looked round about upon all things, and now the eventide was come, he went out unto Bethany with the twelve.

12 ¶And on the morrow, when they were come from Bethany, he was hungry:

47. Since **Jesus** was a rather common name, the phrase **of Nazareth** (lit., the Nazarene) clearly identified Him. Remarkably, Bartimaeus addressed Him as **Son of David**, aware of Jesus' ancestry and right to the Davidic throne.

48. The imperfect tense is employed in the Greek verb, stressing continuous action. They were attempting to silence this annoying cry, but he began calling even louder.

49-51. Jesus responded differently, **commanded him to be called,** because He perceived the man's need and his faith.

52. In reality it was the power of God that healed, but the man's faith was the channel by which that strength could flow.

C. Near Jerusalem. 11:1-13:37.

1. The Triumphal Entry. 11:1-11.

11:1. Bethphage and Bethany were very near Jerusalem, located on the opposite side of the Mount of Olives.

2. Jesus' knowledge of the animal's presence, **ye shall find a colt,** assumes that previous contact had been made with the owner (see the next verse). Its description, **whereon never man sat,** relates to a custom from the Old Testament (Deut 21:3; I Sam 6:7), which specifies that animals to be used for certain religious rites must not have previously been ridden, burdened, or harnessed for labor.

3-8. The statement **the Lord hath need of him** presupposes that the owners of the colt knew and wanted to obey Christ. It is possible, but very doubtful, that Jesus would have supernaturally imparted such a reaction. **Their garments** (vs. 7) refer to the long, thin outer robes. Zechariah 9:9 foresaw this event.

9-10. The jubilant exclamation exalted Jesus as "One who comes" or "the coming One," a Jewish title used for Messiah. The Hebrew equivalent of **hosanna** means "grant salvation," but here it signifies little more than an emotional expression. The people were expecting an earthly kingdom to be established, **the kingdom of our father David.** Their cry includes quotes from Psalm 118:25-26 and was chanted customarily at the Passover celebrations.

11. Mark is very brief, but Matthew informs us that Jesus healed many and had an encounter with the chief priests and scribes (Mt 21:14-15).

2. Bethany. 11:12-26.

12. The morrow would have been Monday of the passion week, the day after Palm Sunday. The expression **he was hungry** is one among many that proves Christ's humanity. The

Second Person of the Trinity was a genuine man and felt the same physical needs as we do.

13 And seeing a fig tree afar off having leaves, he came, if haply he might find anything thereon: and when he came to it, he found nothing but leaves; for the time of figs was not *yet*.

13. The normal order of growth in fig trees was that the fruit preceded the leaves. Therefore, the **leaves** presented a false picture, that fruit not only was present, but it was large and ripe.

14 And Jesus answered and said unto it, No man eat fruit of thee hereafter for ever. And his disciples heard *it*.

14. Jesus' curse upon the fruitless tree was not the result of a quick temper; He used the occasion as an object lesson against hypocrisy and misrepresenting the truth.

15 ¶And they come to Jerusalem: and Jesus went into the temple, and began to cast out them that sold and bought in the temple, and overthrew the tables of the moneychangers, and the seats of them that sold doves;
16 And would not suffer that any man should carry *any* vessel through the temple.

15-16. The close proximity of the curse and the cleansing was not accidental. Jesus displayed His feelings toward false claims through the fig tree, and those businesses in the Temple undoubtedly professed to be helping worshipers by making objects of sacrifice available. Jesus recognized that their real motive was greed.

17 And he taught, saying unto them, Is it not written, My house shall be called of all nations the house of prayer? but ye have made it a den of thieves.

17. The quote from Isaiah 56:7 significantly includes **of all nations.** God's house is revered even by Gentiles as a place of prayer. What would visitors think of the Temple with such a worldly market within its gates? Even more important, how would they view the God of such a religion?

18 And the scribes and chief priests heard *it*, and sought how they might destroy him: for they feared him, because all the people was astonished at his doctrine.
19 And when even was come, he went out of the city.

18-19. The religious leaders hated Jesus for His indictments against their hypocrisy, but here they began to conspire as a result of jealousy over His popularity as a teacher.

20 ¶And in the morning, as they passed by, they saw the fig tree dried up from the roots.

20. In the morning was Tuesday of the passion week.

21 And Peter calling to remembrance saith unto him, Master, behold, the fig tree which thou cursedst is withered away.
22 And Jesus answering saith unto them, Have faith in God.

21-22. The cursing of the fig tree is given a spiritual application. By faith this tree was destroyed; all things are possible if you **Have faith in God.**

23 For verily I say unto you, That whosoever shall say unto this mountain, Be thou removed, and be thou cast into the sea; and shall not doubt in his heart, but shall believe that those things which he saith shall come to pass; he shall have whatsoever he saith.
24 Therefore I say unto you, What things soever ye desire, when ye pray, believe that ye receive *them*, and ye shall have *them*.

23-24. The Lord's illustration is extreme so that it may dismiss all excuses which limit the faith principle. What could be more difficult than a mountain being **removed** and **cast into the sea?**

25 And when ye stand praying, forgive, if ye have ought against any: that your Father also which is in heaven may forgive you your trespasses.
26 But if ye do not forgive, neither will your Father which is in heaven forgive your trespasses.

25-26. The request for forgiveness, besides needing faith as with other petitions, requires a willingness to forgive others. **Trespasses** (Gr *paraptōma*) are offenses, false steps, or blunders.

3. Jerusalem. 11:27-12:44.

27 ¶And they come again to Jerusalem: and as he was walking in the temple, there come to him the chief priests, and the scribes, and the elders,
28 And say unto him, By what authority doest thou these things? and who gave thee this authority to do these things?
29 And Jesus answered and said unto them, I will also ask of you one question, and answer me, and I will tell you by what authority I do these things.

27-29. The chief priests and the scribes and the elders came to Christ in an official capacity putting forth the question regarding His authority, which was the paramount issue between them.

30 The baptism of John, was *it* from heaven, or of men? answer me.
31 And they reasoned with themselves, saying, If we shall say, From

30-33. These leaders were not men of principle, for they considered answering Jesus' question according to popular response and not by conviction. Since either of the possible answers would create a negative reaction, they remained silent,

heaven; he will say, Why then did ye not believe him?

32 But if we shall say, Of men; they feared the people: for all *men* counted John, that he was a prophet indeed.

33 And they answered and said unto Jesus, We cannot tell. And Jesus answering saith unto them, Neither do I tell you by what authority I do these things.

CHAPTER 12

AND he began to speak unto them by parables. A *certain* man planted a vineyard, and set an hedge about *it*, and digged *a place for* the winefat, and built a tower, and let it out to husbandmen, and went into a far country.

2 And at the season he sent to the husbandmen a servant, that he might receive from the husbandmen of the fruit of the vineyard.

3 And they caught *him*, and beat him, and sent *him* away empty.

4 And again he sent unto them another servant; and at him they cast stones, and wounded *him* in the head, and sent *him* away shamefully handled.

5 And again he sent another; and him they killed, and many others; beating some, and killing some.

6 Having yet therefore one son, his wellbeloved, he sent him also last unto them, saying, They will reverence my son.

7 But those husbandmen said among themselves, This is the heir; come, let us kill him, and the inheritance shall be ours.

8 And they took him, and killed *him*, and cast *him* out of the vineyard.

9 What shall therefore the lord of the vineyard do? he will come and destroy the husbandmen, and will give the vineyard unto others.

10 And have ye not read this scripture; The stone which the builders rejected is become the head of the corner:

11 This was the Lord's doing, and it is marvellous in our eyes?

12 And they sought to lay hold on him, but feared the people: for they knew that he had spoken the parable against them: and they left him, and went their way.

13 ¶And they send unto him certain of the Pharisees and of the He-rō'di-ans, to catch him in *his* words.

14 And when they were come, they say unto him, Master, we know that thou art true, and carest for no man: for thou regardest not the person of men, but teachest the way of God in truth: Is it lawful to give tribute to Cæsar, or not?

15 Shall we give, or shall we not give? But he, knowing their hypocrisy, said

claiming ignorance. Jesus, however, was straightforward, **Neither do I tell you.**

12:1. Christ used parables constantly in His ministry. He **began** to do so here with the prominent Jewish leaders. **Hedge** (Gr *phragmos*) means fence, probably a stone wall. The **winefat** (Gr *hypolēnion*) was a receptacle below the winepress, into which the grape juice flowed through a wooden grate. The **tower** was erected to provide a safe storage area. **Let it out** (Gr *ekdidōmi*) may be translated "rented it" or "leased it." All these details are listed to suggest the thorough business manner of the owner.

2. At the season, the time of harvest, the owner sent for the rental price which was paid not in cash, but **of the fruit.**

3-5. Many servants were sent to these vine-growers to collect the owner's share. None accomplished his mission. In fact, they were beaten, mistreated, and some even murdered. It seems hardly possible that a landowner would continue to send small parties when he could have sent a large band to forcibly take the land, or that servants would obey such dangerous orders. These facts not only are included for the purposes of the story, but they illustrate God's long-suffering with His people in the Old Testament.

6. The **son** obviously represents Jesus Christ Himself. The attitude with which the Jews should have accepted Him is expressed in the statement: **They will reverence my son.** However, God's eternal purpose was to send His Son to die for our sins (I Jn 2:2).

7-9. The ultimate act of violence, the slaying of the son, brought swift and final judgment upon those greedy men. Likewise, God endured the rebellious actions of His people for centuries. Their leaders had drifted so far from the truth that when the Son of God appeared, they rejected and murdered Him.

10-11. Psalm 118:22-23 is here fulfilled. The picture of a building parallels that of the church, of which Christ is **head.**

12-13. They (chief priests, scribes, and elders; Mk 11:27), having determined to destroy the Son, sent some **Pharisees** (2:16) and **Herodians** (3:6) to trap Him by something they might get Him to say.

14. The delegation introduced a "loaded" question, cleverly attempting to influence the way He answered. **Carest for no man** means not partial to any man (not even to the highest person in government). They wanted His answer to declare or imply disloyalty to Rome. **Teachest the way of God in truth** does not express their conviction, but hoped to appeal to Jesus' integrity. They judged that if He answered honestly, He would be "caught" by His own words.

15. Denarius (Gr *dēnarion*) was the actual name of the coin called **penny.**

unto them, Why tempt ye me? bring me a penny, that I may see it.

16 And they brought it. And he saith unto them, Whose is this image and superscription? And they said unto him, Cæsar's.

17 And Jesus answering said unto them, Render to Cæsar the things that are Caesar's, and to God the things that are God's. And they marvelled at him.

18 ¶Then come unto him the Săd'du-ceeś, which say there is no resurrection; and they asked him, saying,

19 Master, Moses wrote unto us, If a man's brother die, and leave his wife behind him, and leave no children, that his brother should take his wife, and raise up seed unto his brother.

20 Now there were seven brethren: and the first took a wife, and dying left no seed.

21 And the second took her, and died, neither left he any seed: and the third likewise.

22 And the seven had her, and left no seed: last of all the woman died also.

23 In the resurrection therefore, when they shall rise, whose wife shall she be of them? for the seven had her to wife.

24 And Jesus answering said unto them, Do ye not therefore err, because ye know not the scriptures, neither the power of God?

25 For when they shall rise from the dead, they neither marry, nor are given in marriage; but are as the angels which are in heaven.

26 And as touching the dead, that they rise: have ye not read in the book of Moses, how in the bush God spake unto him, saying, I am the God of Abraham, and the God of Isaac, and the God of Jacob?

27 He is not the God of the dead, but the God of the living: ye therefore do greatly err.

28 ¶And one of the scribes came, and having heard them reasoning together, and perceiving that he had answered them well, asked him, Which is the first commandment of all?

29 And Jesus answered him, The first of all the commandments is, Hear, O Israel; The Lord our God is one Lord:

30 And thou shalt love the Lord thy God with all thy heart, and with all thy soul, and with all thy mind, and with all thy strength: this is the first commandment.

31 And the second is like, namely

16-17. The Lord's question draws their attention to Caesar by the **image** and **superscription**. However, the principle that He sets forth calls for obedience to both the government (Rom 13) and God in their respective areas. **Render** (Gr apodidōmi) does not limit the expectation to paying tribute as in verse 14. It means "to pay back in full" whatever is owed. The word **image** suggests a further idea. Although the coin bore Caesar's image which pointed to his authority, man himself was created in God's image (Gen 1:26). Therefore, the picture was an image of Caesar immediately, but of God ultimately, implying that the emperor's authority is under divine sovereignty.

18. The **Sadducees** were a religious party, like the Pharisees, but differed from them in their liberal interpretation of the Scriptures. A foremost example of their liberal teaching is mentioned here, **they say there is no resurrection**. They recognized the fact of the doctrine of the resurrection in the Old Testament, but they refused to accept it literally.

19. Deuteronomy 25:5 is the passage referred to. **Raise up seed** (offspring) expresses a practice of levirate marriage whereby a brother of a childless, deceased man would marry the widow and rear children, designating the firstborn as the legal descendant of his brother.

20-23. The story obviously was an invention aimed at exposing the absurdity of relationships after the resurrection. If there really were a resurrection, they conjectured, seven men would be married to one woman in heaven.

24. The Sadducees' question reveals their unbelief in two fundamental areas: the Scriptures and God's power. Surprisingly, these men held prominent positions among the chosen people, yet did not recognize how foundational the resurrection was in Old Testament doctrine and living. Their problem began with the denial of the supernatural, **the power of God**.

25-27. The change which transpires in man from earth to heaven is extreme: **they neither marry nor are given in marriage; but are as the angels which are in heaven.**

28. One of the scribes. A scribe was a professional interpreter of the Old Testament.

29-30. Jesus quotes what is termed the "shema" from Deuteronomy 6:4-5; **Hear,** the first word in the Old Testament passage being shamac in Hebrew. The distinctive feature of ancient Judaism was that it held to monotheism among predominantly polytheistic cultures. In fact, "going after other gods" was one of the greatest sins. **Love the Lord thy God with all thy heart, and with all thy soul, and with all thy mind, and with all thy strength.** The multiplicity of words emphasizes the thoroughness and fervency that our love for God should embrace.

31. The second commandment (Lev 19:18) fittingly joins the

this, Thou shalt love thy neighbour as thyself. There is none other commandment greater than these.

32 And the scribe said unto him, Well, Master, thou hast said the truth: for there is one God; and there is none other but he:

33 And to love him with all the heart and with all the understanding, and with all the soul, and with all the strength, and to love *his* neighbour as himself, is more than all whole burnt offerings and sacrifices.

34 And when Jesus saw that he answered discreetly, he said unto him, Thou art not far from the kingdom of God. And no man after that durst ask him *any question.*

35 ¶And Jesus answered and said, while he taught in the temple, How say the scribes that Christ is the son of David?

36 For David himself said by the Holy Ghost, The LORD said to my Lord, Sit thou on my right hand, till I make thine enemies thy footstool.

37 David therefore himself calleth him Lord; and whence is he *then* his son? And the common people heard him gladly.

38 ¶And he said unto them in his doctrine, Beware of the scribes, which love to go in long clothing, and *love* salutations in the marketplaces,

39 And the chief seats in the synagogues, and the uppermost rooms at feasts:

40 Which devour widows' houses, and for a pretence make long prayers: these shall receive greater damnation.

41 ¶And Jesus sat over against the treasury, and beheld how the people cast money into the treasury: and many that were rich cast in much.

42 And there came a certain poor widow, and she threw in two mites, which make a farthing.

43 And he called *unto him* his disciples, and saith unto them, Verily I say unto you, That this poor widow hath cast more in, than all they which have cast into the treasury:

44 For all *they* did cast in of their abundance; but she of her want did cast in all that she had, *even* all her living.

CHAPTER 13

AND as he went out of the temple, one of his disciples saith unto him, Master, see what manner of stones and what buildings *are here!*

2 And Jesus answering said unto him, Seest thou these great buildings? there shall not be left one stone upon another, that shall not be thrown down.

first, because genuine love for God naturally results in a love for others. "On these two commandments hang all the law and the prophets" (Mt 22:40).

32-34. The scribe's response shows deep insight. **To love . . . is more than . . . .** The man recognized that loving God must be the foundation of any worthwhile service or sacrifice.

35-37. After numerous questions, Jesus reversed the situation by asking them one. It deals with David's relationship to the Messiah, **Christ.** He is both David's **Lord** and **son.** How could this be possible? The **scribes** remained silent, but the answer was not the issue anyhow. Jesus merely wanted to reveal that even the knowledgeable scribes with all their questions had their limits. The New Testament describes Christ as God-man: as incarnate God He was David's Lord; as man He was born in his line. **Son** means descendant.

38-39. Long clothing customarily was worn by distinguished persons for special occasions. **Salutations** or greetings were not simply acts of friendly courtesy; they loved recognition for their high positions.

40. Their love for praise paralleled their greed for money. **Widows** needing assistance to administer their estates often turned to "spiritual" leaders. Scribes gladly aided, managing a contrived plan for their own personal gain. **For a pretence** or "for appearance sake" declares the motive of **long prayers.** **Greater damnation** (judgment) results from this hypocrisy; it also tells us that there will be degrees of punishment.

41. The treasury speaks of an area where thirteen receptacles were placed to receive offerings and taxes for the Temple.

42. Two mites (Gr *lepton*) **which make a farthing** (Gr *kodrantēs*); approximately one fortieth of a penny (Gr *dēnarion*) (Mk 12:15). Thus, the gift was very small. Amazingly, she did not keep one coin.

43-44. The amount of an offering does not always signify the measure of love of the one who gives. Often a more important factor is what is held back. **She of her want** (poverty) **did cast in all,** everything she needed to live by.

4. Mount of Olives. 13:1-37.

13:1. The disciples' interest in the attractive stones and buildings did not arise from aesthetic appreciation only. Matthew's account of the afternoon's events includes a significant statement just prior to their exit from the Temple: "Behold your house is left unto you desolate" (Mt 23:28 as quoted from Jer 12:7). Thus, they probably wondered why such beautiful buildings would be abandoned.

2. Jesus prophesied the thorough destruction of these edifices. **There shall not be left one stone upon another.** The Greek emphatic negative construction, has the idea "by no means" or "never."

3 And as he sat upon the mount of Olives over against the temple, Peter and James and John and Andrew asked him privately,

4 Tell us, when shall these things be? and what *shall be* the sign when all these things shall be fulfilled?

5 And Jesus answering them began to say, Take heed lest any *man* deceive you:

6 For many shall come in my name, saying, I am *Christ;* and shall deceive many.

7 And when ye shall hear of wars and rumours of wars, be ye not troubled: for *such things* must needs be; but the end *shall* not *be* yet.

8 For nation shall rise against nation, and kingdom against kingdom: and there shall be earthquakes in divers places, and there shall be famines and troubles: these *are* the beginnings of sorrows.

9 ¶But take heed to yourselves: for they shall deliver you up to councils; and in the synagogues ye shall be beaten: and ye shall be brought before rulers and kings for my sake, for a testimony against them.

10 And the gospel must first be published among all nations.

11 But when they shall lead *you*, and deliver you up, take no thought beforehand what ye shall speak, neither do ye premeditate: but whatsoever shall be given you in that hour, that speak ye: for it is not ye that speak, but the Holy Ghost.

12 Now the brother shall betray the brother to death, and the father the son; and children shall rise up against *their* parents, and shall cause them to be put to death.

13 And ye shall be hated of all *men* for my name's sake: but he that shall endure unto the end, the same shall be saved.

14 ¶But when ye shall see the abomination of desolation, spoken of by Daniel the prophet, standing where it ought not, (let him that readeth understand,) then let them that be in Judæa flee to the mountains:

15 And let him that is on the housetop not go down into the house, neither enter *therein*, to take any thing out of his house:

16 And let him that is in the field not turn back again for to take up his garment.

17 But woe to them that are with child, and to them that give suck in those days!

18 And pray ye that your flight be not in the winter.

19 For *in* those days shall be afflic-

3-4. Although the city of Jerusalem and its Temple were destroyed by Titus in A.D. 70, the apostles' question initiates a discourse (called the Olivet Discourse because of its location) regarding the events of the Tribulation Period. It is common in prophetic literature to predict in a single message events with both contempoary and eschatological fulfillments (Ezk 28; Isa 7:14).

5-6. One characteristic that marks the end of this age is the rise of many impostors. Even the word **Christ** is supplied in the AV, the previous clause identifies their claim to Him, **in my name.**

7-8. **Such things must needs be,** that is, even these wars come from God's perfect plan. The word **troubles** is not found in some of the oldest manuscripts. **Beginnings** suggests that even worse judgments will follow (Rev 6-9; 16).

9-11. Verse 10 appears parenthetical; world evangelsim shall precede these afflictions. Problems in bearing witness are everywhere, but they are a necessary part of God's plan. Under the pressure, disciples may take comfort in the Holy Spirit's special guidance: **for it is not ye that speak, but the Holy Ghost.**

12-13. The extreme cruelty is illustrated not in physical terms but by the destruction of family ties. **He that shall endure unto the end . . . shall be saved** is used to support a good-works gospel. However, the New Testament teaching on this subject dismisses such an interpretation. Romans and Galatians specifically discuss this issue and clearly declare that salvation is based on faith (Rom 1:16; 3:20, 28; 4:3, 16; 5:1; Gal 3:10-14, 23-26). In this passage "one who endures" speaks of a genuine believer who perseveres to the end of his life. **Be saved** should be taken in a spiritual sense; it does not merely mean one will be delivered from earthly trials.

14. **The abomination of desolation,** meaning the abomination that desolates or appalls (Dan 12:1), has been applied to ancient events. Many Jews thought that Daniel's prophecy was fulfilled in 186 B.C. when Antiochus Epiphanes, the king of Syria, erected an idolatrous altar in the Temple of Jerusalem and sacrificed a pig thereon to the heathen god Jupiter Olympus. Others believe it referred to the entrance of Roman soldiers into the Holy Place before the destruction of Jerusalem in A.D. 70. Nonetheless, the entire discourse speaks of eschatological events, and the actions of the "man of sin" in II Thessalonians 2 corresponds to this description.

15-20. These verses vividly describe the terror involved; no other tribulation is equal to it, **neither shall be.** It, therefore, must be the Great Tribulation of the book of the Revelation.

tion, such as was not from the beginning of the creation which God created unto this time, neither shall be.

20 And except that the Lord had shortened those days, no flesh should be saved: but for the elect's sake, whom he hath chosen, he hath shortened the days.

21 And then if any man shall say to you, Lo, here *is* Christ; or, lo, *he is* there; believe *him* not:

22 For false Christs and false prophets shall rise, and shall shew signs and wonders, to seduce, if *it were* possible, even the elect.

23 But take ye heed: behold, I have foretold you all things.

24 ¶But in those days, after that tribulation, the sun shall be darkened, and the moon shall not give her light,

25 And the stars of heaven shall fall, and the powers that are in heaven shall be shaken.

26 And then shall they see the Son of man coming in the clouds with great power and glory.

27 And then shall he send his angels, and shall gather together his elect from the four winds, from the uttermost part of the earth to the uttermost part of heaven.

28 Now learn a parable of the fig tree: When her branch is yet tender, and putteth forth leaves, ye know that summer is near:

29 So ye in like manner, when ye shall see these things come to pass, know that it is nigh, *even* at the doors.

30 Verily I say unto you, that this generation shall not pass, till all these things be done.

31 Heaven and earth shall pass away: but my words shall not pass away.

32 ¶But of that day and *that* hour knoweth no man, no, not the angels which are in heaven, neither the Son, but the Father.

33 Take ye heed, watch and pray: for ye know not when the time is.

34 *For the Son of man is* as a man taking a far journey, who left his house, and gave authority to his servants, and to every man his work, and commanded the porter to watch.

35 Watch ye therefore: for ye know not when the master of the house cometh, at even, or at midnight, or at the cockcrowing, or in the morning:

36 Lest coming suddenly he find you sleeping.

37 And what I say unto you I say unto all, Watch.

CHAPTER 14

AFTER two days was *the feast of* the passover, and of unleavened bread: and the chief priests and the scribes sought how they might take him by craft, and put *him* to death.

2 But they said, Not on the feast *day*, lest there be an uproar of the people.

3 ¶And being in Bethany in the house

21-23. The **false Christs and false prophets** are so persuasive that they would deceive even God's **elect, if it were possible.**

24-27. Son of man. He who is King of Kings and Lord of Lords returns to judge men as a man.

28-29. The **parable of the fig tree** encourages readiness and alertness. As a blossoming fig tree signifies the nearness of summer, the fulfillment of Jesus' prophecy announces the end of the age.

30. During the first century, **this generation** did undergo the prophecies uttered in a general sense, but their full force awaits the Great Tribulation and Christ's coming in glory. In the latter sense the generation would be speaking of race or nation.

31-32. Jesus' divine and human natures may be observed in these verses. As God, He claimed infinite authority for His words. As man, His *kenosis* (or self-emptying) is stated regarding His knowledge: **neither the Son.**

33. Ye know not when the time is reminds the disciples of their priorities. The imminence of Christ's return should stimulate a new realization of the temporal nature of this life.

34-37. The following illustration aims at the attitudes of **servants.** They receive their orders and are to faithfully perform them until their master returns. Since they **know not when the master of the house cometh,** they must **watch** (Gr *gregoreō*), a word which specifically implies watching with alertness, staying awake. Unfortunately, disciples often conform to the world's emphasis on the temporal.

V. CHRIST'S DEATH AND RESURRECTION. 14:1—16:20.

A. The Events Preluding His Arrest. 14:1-42.

1. The chief priests plot Jesus' death. 14:1-2.

14:1-2. The two designations, **the Passover** and **unleavened bread,** refer to the same event which is described in Exodus 12:1-20.

2. Mary anoints Jesus. 14:3-9.

3-5. Although Mark spends little time introducing the occa-

of Simon the leper, as he sat at meat, there came a woman having an alabaster box of ointment of spikenard very precious; and she brake the box, and poured *it* on his head.

4 And there were some that had indignation within themselves, and said, Why was this waste of the ointment made?

5 For it might have been sold for more than three hundred pence, and have been given to the poor. And they murmured against her.

6 And Jesus said, Let her alone; why trouble ye her? she hath wrought a good work on me.

7 For ye have the poor with you always, and whensoever ye will ye may do them good: but me ye have not always.

8 She hath done what she could: she is come aforehand to anoint my body to the burying.

9 Verily I say unto you, Wheresoever this gospel shall be preached throughout the whole world, this also that she hath done shall be spoken of for a memorial of her.

10 ¶And Judas Iscariot, one of the twelve, went unto the chief priests, to betray him unto them.

11 And when they heard *it*, they were glad, and promised to give him money. And he sought how he might conveniently betray him.

12 ¶And the first day of unleavened bread, when they killed the passover, his disciples said unto him, Where wilt thou that we go and prepare that thou mayest eat the passover?

13 And he sendeth forth two of his disciples, and saith unto them, Go ye into the city, and there shall meet you a man bearing a pitcher of water: follow him.

14 And wheresoever he shall go in, say ye to the goodman of the house, The Master saith, Where is the guest-chamber, where I shall eat the passover with my disciples?

15 And he will shew you a large upper room furnished *and* prepared: there make ready for us.

16 And his disciples went forth, and came into the city, and found as he had said unto them: and they made ready the passover.

17 And in the evening he cometh with the twelve.

18 And as they sat and did eat, Jesus said, Verily I say unto you, One of you which eateth with me shall betray me.

19 And they began to be sorrowful, and to say unto him one by one, *Is* it I? and another *said*, *Is* it I?

20 And he answered and said unto them, *It is* one of the twelve, that dippeth with me in the dish.

21 The Son of man indeed goeth, as it is written of him: but woe to that man by whom the Son of man is betrayed! good were it for that man if he had never been born.

sion, John implies that it was a special celebration in honor of Jesus, with Mary, Martha, and Lazarus present. **Simon the leper** bears that title as a testimony to his healing, but that is all we know about him.

The story was included because of the manner by which Mary honored her Lord. The special significance of the anointing was its cost, around **three hundred pence**. A penny (Gr *dēnarion*) was a day's wages. The statement, **she brake the box**, refers to a jar sealed in a manner which required breakage at the neck, and therefore its contents would be used at one time. **Some** of the disciples viewed this as an unnecessary extravagance.

6-9. Jesus defended her deed. It would have been commendable to give the money to the poor, but she had a better use. **She hath done what she could** to show her love for her Lord.

3. Judas plans to betray Jesus. 14:10-11.

10-11. Judas' betrayal at least in part was a reaction to Mary's act of reverence. It was he who "held the bag" (acted as treasurer) and regularly pilfered it. His love for money provoked an indignant response when three hundred pence worth of ointment was "wasted" on Jesus. Thus, he sought to **betray,** to give Jesus over to His enemies for just thirty pieces of silver (Gr *argyrion*).

4. Preparation for the Passover. 14:12-21.

12. The question, **"Where . . ."** rather than "should we make preparations" indicates that Jesus and His apostles faithfully participated in this ritual.

13-18. Jesus' instructions are based partially upon His omnipotence. That they would encounter a **man bearing a pitcher** obviously could not have been perceived by human wisdom. On the other hand, He likely had already made arrangements with the **goodman of the house** (Gr *oikodespotēs*), the manager.

19. The translation of their question, **"Is it I?"** would be improved by "It is not I, is it?" for the Greek construction suggests that they expected a negative reply.

20-21. John's account (Jn 13:24-26) indicates that He actually did not expose Judas by this statement. It merely emphasized the close friendship that the betrayer appeared to have with Christ.

22 ¶And as they did eat, Jesus took bread, and blessed, and brake *it*, and gave to them, and said, Take, eat: this is my body.

23 And he took the cup, and when he had given thanks, he gave *it* to them: and they all drank of it.

24 And he said unto them, This is my blood of the new testament, which is shed for many.

25 Verily I say unto you, I will drink no more of the fruit of the vine, until that day that I drink it new in the kingdom of God.

26 ¶And when they had sung an hymn, they went out into the mount of Olives.

27 And Jesus saith unto them, All ye shall be offended because of me this night: for it is written, I will smite the shepherd, and the sheep shall be scattered.

28 But after that I am risen, I will go before you into Galilee.

29 But Peter said unto him, Although all shall be offended, yet *will* not I.

30 And Jesus saith unto him, Verily I say unto thee, That this day, *even* in this night, before the cock crow twice, thou shalt deny me thrice.

31 But he spake the more vehemently, If I should die with thee, I will not deny thee in any wise. Likewise also said they all.

32 ¶And they came to a place which was named Gĕth-sĕm'a-ne: and he saith to his disciples, Sit ye here, while I shall pray.

33 And he taketh with him Peter and James and John, and began to be sore amazed, and to be very heavy;

34 And saith unto them, My soul is exceeding sorrowful unto death: tarry ye here, and watch.

35 And he went forward a little, and fell on the ground, and prayed that, if it were possible, the hour might pass from him.

36 And he said, Abba, Father, all things *are* possible unto thee; take away this cup from me: nevertheless not what I will, but what thou wilt.

37 And he cometh, and findeth them sleeping, and saith unto Peter, Simon, sleepest thou? couldest not thou watch one hour?

38 Watch ye and pray, lest ye enter into temptation. The spirit truly *is* ready, but the flesh *is* weak.

39 And again he went away, and prayed, and spake the same words.

40 And when he returned, he found them asleep again, (for their eyes were heavy,) neither wist they what to answer him.

5. The Lord's Supper. 14:22-25.

22-24. **This is my body** was spoken symbolically, as when He called Himself the Door or the Vine. The **new testament**, prophesied in Jeremiah 31:31-34, is associated with regeneration (Jer 31:33), for the Mosaic law never provided the way to heaven. "All have sinned and come short of the glory of God" (Rom 3:23). Therefore, a new testament or covenant (Gr *diathēke*) was needed. Jesus' blood was **shed for many,** the word **for** meaning "in behalf of" (Gr *hyper*) which specifies a substitutionary death.

25. Indirectly Jesus informs them that His earthly life is almost over.

6. On the Mount of Olives. 14:26-31.

26. The **hymn** must have been one or more of the Hallel Psalms which were customarily included in the Passover celebrations (Alfred Edersheim, *The Temple*, p. 223).

27-28. Quoting Zechariah 13:7, the Lord predicted their disloyal flight of escape. Knowing that they would return to their home country, He speaks of His resurrection in specific terms. He would see them **into Galilee.**

29-31. Impulsively **Peter** responded to Christ's prediction in a forceful manner. Instead of defending himself, he might have obeyed the Lord's added command, "Watch ye and pray," in connection with I Corinthians 10:13. Overconfidence often precedes failure. The time, **before the cock crow twice,** refers to the third watch of the night.

7. In the Garden of Gethsemane. 14:32-41.

32. Although the Garden of **Gethsemane** was located on the same mountain, the Mount of Olives, it is mentioned separately as a special place of prayer and privacy for the Lord.

33-34. The inner circle, **Peter and James and John,** observed Jesus' agony. Significantly, it is Luke the physician who adds, "his sweat was as it were great drops of blood. . ." (Lk 22:44). Three expressions picture His inner feelings: (1) **began to be sore amazed,** (2) **to be very heavy,** and (3) **exceeding sorrowful unto death.** The first reveals His initial shock at what was to come; the second, His overwhelming sense of distress; the third describes the extent of His emotions. "Its (the agony) terrors exceeded his anticipations. His human soul received new experience—He learned upon the basis of things suffered (Heb 5:8)" (Kenneth Wuest, *Mark in the Greek New Testament*, p. 264).

35-36. Nowhere else in Scripture can one find a clearer picture of Jesus' humanity. His response to the **hour** lacks none of the emotions that other men would have felt. He, however, refused to allow inner feelings to direct Him, submitting to the Father's plan: **nevertheless not what I will, but what thou wilt.**

37-41. The command **Watch ye and pray,** may be translated "Keep watching and praying . . . ." The spirit is described as **ready** (Gr *prothymos*), willing and eager to serve. Inwardly the disciples desired to keep praying, but fatigue won over their wills.

41 And he cometh the third time, and saith unto them, Sleep on now, and take *your* rest: it is enough, the hour is come; behold, the Son of man is betrayed into the hands of sinners.

42 Rise up, let us go; lo, he that betrayeth me is at hand.

43 ¶And immediately, while he yet spake, cometh Judas, one of the twelve, and with him a great multitude with swords and staves, from the chief priests and the scribes and the elders.

44 And he that betrayed him had given them a token, saying, Whomsoever I shall kiss, that same is he; take him, and lead *him* away safely.

45 And as soon as he was come, he goeth straightway to him, and saith, Master, master; and kissed him.

46 And they laid their hands on him, and took him.

47 And one of them that stood by drew a sword, and smote a servant of the high priest, and cut off his ear.

48 And Jesus answered and said unto them, Are ye come out, as against a thief, with swords and *with* staves to take me?

49 I was daily with you in the temple teaching, and ye took me not: but the scriptures must be fulfilled.

50 And they all forsook him, and fled.

51 And there followed him a certain young man, having a linen cloth cast about *his* naked *body*; and the young men laid hold on him:

52 And he left the linen cloth, and fled from them naked.

53 ¶And they led Jesus away to the high priest: and with him were assembled all the chief priests and the elders and the scribes.

54 And Peter followed him afar off, even into the palace of the high priest: and he sat with the servants, and warmed himself at the fire.

55 And the chief priests and all the council sought for witness against Jesus to put him to death; and found none.

56 For many bare false witness against him, but their witness agreed not together.

57 And there arose certain, and bare false witness against him, saying,

58 We heard him say, I will destroy this temple that is made with hands, and within three days I will build another made without hands.

59 But neither so did their witness agree together.

60 And the high priest stood up in the midst, and asked Jesus, saying, Answerest thou nothing? what *is it which* these witness against thee?

61 But he held his peace, and answered nothing. Again the high priest asked him, and said unto him, Art thou the Christ, the Son of the Blessed?

62 And Jesus said, I am: and ye shall see the Son of man sitting on the right hand of power, and coming in the clouds of heaven.

63 Then the high priest rent his

B. The Arrest and Trials. 14:42-15:14.

1. Betrayal and arrest. 14:42-52.

42-45. Mark identifies **Judas,** not by Iscariot, but after a fashion which emphasizes how incredible the feat was; he not only was among the followers, but **one of the twelve.** The company he brought included Roman soldiers and temple police, who were sent by the Jewish leaders named. The former carried **swords,** while the latter had **staves** (stout sticks.) Judas' greeting was that customary of a disciple to his rabbi: **Master, master; and kissed him.**

46-47. John 18:10 informs us that it was Peter who drew the sword and cut off Malchus' ear.

48-49. The party came out at night with weapons as if Jesus were a violent criminal against whom cunning and force must be applied. He could have been taken easily during the day; He had been teaching in the Temple publicly for the past three days. **But the scriptures must be fulfilled** refers to general prophecies of this violent hour.

50. The prediction found in verse 27 comes true.

51-52. This incident appears in Mark's account alone, and since no other purpose for its inclusion can be found, the **young man** was probably the author himself.

2. The trial before the Jewish leaders. 14:53-65.

53-54. The three groups mentioned along with the **High Priest** comprised the Sanhedrin or **council** (vs. 55), an official group of seventy men who held religious and civil authority in Israel. However, during the last forty years before the fall of Jerusalem (A.D. 70) executions were restricted to Roman authorities. That explains why the trial before Pilate followed this one.

55-59. The fundamental purpose of a court's existence is to execute justice, but this dishonorable court only **sought for witness against Jesus to put him to death.** Not succeeding, they resorted to **false witness,** but again they failed.

60. The High Priest turned directly to the defendant in hopes of clearer "evidence." While the response to **Answerest thou nothing** causes us to admire Christ's submission, the inquirer actually was seeking a statement of self-condemnation; **he held his peace.**

61-62. Art thou the Christ? Besides His affirmative reply, **I am,** Jesus quotes two Old Testament passages which clearly are messianic (Ps 110:1 and Dan 7:13).

63-64. The verdict reveals their spiritual ignorance. Jesus'

clothes, and saith, What need we any further witnesses?

64 Ye have heard the blasphemy: what think ye? And they all condemned him to be guilty of death.

65 And some began to spit on him, and to cover his face, and to buffet him, and to say unto him, Prophesy: and the servants did strike him with the palms of their hands.

66 ¶And as Peter was beneath in the palace, there cometh one of the maids of the high priest:

67 And when she saw Peter warming himself, she looked upon him, and said, And thou also wast with Jesus of Nazareth.

68 But he denied, saying, I know not, neither understand I what thou sayest. And he went out into the porch; and the cock crew.

69 And a maid saw him again, and began to say to them that stood by, This is one of them.

70 And he denied it again. And a little after, they that stood by said again to Peter, Surely thou art one of them: for thou art a Galilæan, and thy speech agreeth thereto.

71 But he began to curse and to swear, saying, I know not this man of whom ye speak.

72 And the second time the cock crew. And Peter called to mind the word that Jesus said unto him, Before the cock crow twice, thou shalt deny me thrice. And when he thought thereon, he wept.

CHAPTER 15

AND straightway in the morning the chief priests held a consultation with the elders and scribes and the whole council, and bound Jesus, and carried him away, and delivered him to Pilate.

2 And Pilate asked him, Art thou the King of the Jews? And he answering said unto him, Thou sayest it.

3 And the chief priests accused him of many things: but he answered nothing.

4 And Pilate asked him again, saying, Answerest thou nothing? behold how many things they witness against thee.

5 But Jesus yet answered nothing; so that Pilate marvelled.

6 ¶Now at that feast he released unto them one prisoner, whomsoever they desired.

7 And there was one named Ba-răb′-bas, which lay bound with them that had made insurrection with him, who had committed murder in the insurrection.

8 And the multitude crying aloud began to desire him to do as he had ever done unto them.

9 But Pilate answered them, saying,

confession should have initiated at least some investigation, and with all the facts, its veracity. Instead, they cried blasphemy!

65. The unbelievably foul treatment against the holy Son of God seems worse in that it was commenced by national dignitaries. Isaiah 52:14 predicted hundreds of years before, "his visage was so marred more than any man."

3. Peter's denial. 14:66-72.

66-68. The scene was just outside the palace of the High Priest who was conducting the trial in the upper story. The girl, **one of the maids of the high priest,** noticed Peter and then paused to get a closer look (Gr *emblepō*). Her accusation caught Peter off guard. He who had claimed allegiance even in the face of death quickly disowned his Lord. He then retreated **out into the porch,** a vestibule between the courtyard and the street.

69-71. The pressure increased as accusations continued, and added denials only led to further accusations: **thou art a Galilean and thy speech agreeth thereto.** The Judaeans detected a Galilean accent in Peter's words perhaps as a Georgian could recognize a New Englander. **To curse and to swear** (Gr *anathematizō* and *omnyō*) means Peter took oaths in God's name and called down curses upon himself in the event he was lying.

72. The **cock crew** and its sound immediately reminded Peter of the Lord's prophetic words. Luke adds that "the Lord turned and looked upon Peter" (Lk 22:61) which must have occurred while Jesus was being transferred to a temporary cell. The apostle's reaction, **wept,** pictures an extended time of bitter weeping.

4. The trial before Pilate. 15:1-14.

15:1. The Sanhedrin regathered in the morning to make the trial official and Matthew 27:1 reiterates their singular purpose, "to put him to death." They discussed in detail the charges and how they would present them in order to gain the death sentence.

2. The insidious conspirators charged Christ with rebellion against the government (Lk 23:2), which explains Pilate's question, **Art thou the King of the Jews?** This simple affirmation does not include His detailed response (Jn 18:28-37), where He disassociates His kingdom from this physical and temporal world.

3-5. **He answered nothing,** "as a sheep before her shearers is dumb, so he openeth not his mouth" (Isa 53:7). Mark's account briefly reports that **Pilate marveled,** but in John 19:8-12 he is pictured with "fear" attempting to free Jesus.

6-7. The narration of Barabbas' release is introduced by two facts: verse 6 explains the annual custom at the Passover of freeing one prisoner of the people's choice, and verse 7 characterizes Barabbas as an insurrectionist and a murderer.

8. The crowd reminded Pilate of this precedent; they **began to desire,** or more accurately, "to ask" (Gr *aiteō*).

9-10. Pilate hoped the people would choose Jesus because he

Will ye that I release unto you the King of the Jews?

10 For he knew that the chief priests had delivered him for envy.

11 But the chief priests moved the people, that he should rather release Ba-răb′bas unto them.

12 And Pilate answered and said again unto them, What will ye then that I shall do *unto him* whom ye call the King of the Jews?

13 And they cried out again, Crucify him.

14 Then Pilate said unto them, Why, what evil hath he done? And they cried out the more exceedingly, Crucify him.

15 And *so* Pilate, willing to content the people, released Ba-răb′bas unto them, and delivered Jesus, when he had scourged *him*, to be crucified.

16 ¶And the soldiers led him away into the hall, called Præ-tō′rĭ-um; and they call together the whole band.

17 And they clothed him with purple, and platted a crown of thorns, and put it about his *head*,

18 And began to salute him, Hail, King of the Jews!

19 And they smote him on the head with a reed, and did spit upon him, and bowing *their* knees worshipped him.

20 And when they had mocked him, they took off the purple from him, and put his own clothes on him, and led him out to crucify him.

21 And they compel one Simon a Cȳ-rē′nĭ-an, who passed by, coming out of the country, the father of Alexander and Rufus, to bear his cross.

22 And they bring him unto the place Gŏl′go-tha, which is, being interpreted, The place of a skull.

23 And they gave him to drink wine mingled with myrrh: but he received *it* not.

24 And when they had crucified him, they parted his garments, casting lots upon them, what every man should take.

25 And it was the third hour, and they crucified him.

26 And the superscription of his accusation was written over, THE KING OF THE JEWS.

was beginning to discern the true source of the charges: **the chief priests had delivered him for envy.**

11. Precisely how the **chief priests moved the people** is conjecture, but it probably included special appeals for the rebel as a political and social leader and as a local resident. Conversely, they agitated the crowd against Christ, because He claimed to be God. More than factual evidence, their awesome power and position must have been the determining factors.

12-14. The extent of that influence was incredible, for less than a week before the people of this same city had honored Christ in His "Triumphal Entry."

C. The Crucifixion. 15:15-47.

15. **Scourged him** (Gr *phragelloō*). The Romans used short-handled whips with many leather lashes. On the ends of the lashes were tied small bits of metal or bone to cruelly rip the victim's flesh. They usually tied the prisoner to a low pillar so that his back was bent forward. This type of punishment would leave deep gashes, often exposing the bones.

16-20. The **hall** refers to the palace of 14:54 (Gr *aulē*), an open courtyard, which Mark identifies as **Praetorium. Band** (Gr *speira*), sometimes translated "cohort," technically included six hundred men though on occasion was used when the number was much less. The **band** was gathered to make a spectacle of their prisoner. The royal color, **purple**, and a crown of needle-like thorns served to mock the king while adding further torture. The **reed**, a royal staff, not only was painful in itself, but also drove the thorns further into His skull. Their abuse continued (imperfect tense in Greek) for some time until they wearied of their sport, and He was led away for execution.

21. The only information about **Simon** is his national origin, a **Cyrenian**, and the names of his sons. Since **Rufus** appears in Romans 16:13, and Mark's Gospel was written in Rome, the readers must have known the two brothers. Some commentators suggest that Simon's experience here eventually led to his conversion. At this time he was not a disciple for they forced (AV, **compel**) him into service.

22. Mark identifies the place of the crucifixion in Aramaic, **Golgotha**, and interprets it as the place of the skull. Two views exist regarding the location: (1) The traditional view, going back to the fourth century, places it at the Church of the Holy Sepulchre and argues that the name arose from the presence of skulls, because it was a place of execution; (2) Gordon's Calvary bases its location on the skull-like appearance of an adjacent cliff and a garden of tombs nearby. The Gospels mark it outside the city, but the location of the ancient walls cannot be conclusively determined, since Jerusalem was destroyed in A.D. 70.

23. **They gave,** or better, they were going to give (Greek imperfect tense) **wine mingled with myrrh.** The beverage acted as a stupefying drug commonly given to lessen the torture.

24. Psalm 22:18 predicted the disrespectful distribution of His clothing. Usually in Scripture **casting lots** involves religious connotations, a means to discover God's will, but here is merely gambling.

25. The **third hour** was nine o'clock in the morning according to Jewish time.

26-28. Pilate's superscription, **THE KING OF THE JEWS,** caused a harsh reaction among the Jewish leaders (Jn 19:21-22). The physical suffering in those final three hours on the cross

27 And with him they crucify two thieves; the one on his right hand, and the other on his left.

28 And the scripture was fulfilled, which saith, And he was numbered with the transgressors.

29 ¶And they that passed by railed on him, wagging their heads, and saying, Ah, thou that destroyest the temple, and buildest it in three days,

30 Save thyself, and come down from the cross.

31 Likewise also the chief priests mocking said among themselves with the scribes, He saved others; himself he cannot save.

32 Let Christ the King of Israel descend now from the cross, that we may see and believe. And they that were crucified with him reviled him.

33 ¶And when the sixth hour was come, there was darkness over the whole land until the ninth hour.

34 And at the ninth hour Jesus cried with a loud voice, saying, Ē-lō′ī, Ē-lō′ī, lä′ma sa-bach′tha-ni? which is, being interpreted, My God, my God, why hast thou forsaken me?

35 And some of them that stood by, when they heard it, said, Behold, he calleth E-lī′as.

36 And one ran and filled a spunge full of vinegar, and put it on a reed, and gave him to drink, saying, Let alone; let us see whether E-lī′as will come to take him down.

37 And Jesus cried with a loud voice, and gave up the ghost.

38 And the vail of the temple was rent in twain from the top to the bottom.

39 ¶And when the centurion, which stood over against him, saw that he so cried out, and gave up the ghost, he said, Truly this man was the Son of God.

40 There were also women looking on afar off: among whom was Mary Magdalene, and Mary the mother of James the less and of Joses, and Sa-lō′me;

41 (Who also, when he was in Galilee, followed him, and ministered unto him;) and many other women which came up with him unto Jerusalem.

42 ¶And now when the even was come, because it was the preparation, that is, the day before the sabbath,

43 Joseph of Ăr-i-ma-thæ′a, an honourable counsellor, which also waited for the kingdom of God, came, and

was bad enough, but the Lord also endured continuous insults and mockery by those who observed.

29-30. They that passed by railed on him would be better translated "kept on blaspheming" (Greek imperfect tense). When Christ prophesied about the temple He had referred to His body (Jn 2:19-21), but these accusers derided Him because they thought He spoke of the building and thus His word had failed. The claim would be fulfilled just three days later.

31-32. He saved others; himself he cannot save, though not true, indirectly emphasizes the fact that He would not save Himself because He was willing to save others. **Descend now from the cross, that we may see and believe.** Typical of fallen man, they confused the order of revelation. When a person believes in Christ, he begins to see. Spiritual understanding and discernment are results of spiritual illumination, which is accomplished by the new birth through the Holy Spirit.

33-34. The **darkness** which occurred at the sixth hour (noon until three o'clock) along with the outcry **My God, my God, why hast thou forsaken me** (Ps 22:1) bespeak of the harshest hour of human history. Although the exact meaning of the separation is debated, Bible students agree that it induced the greatest anguish.

35-36. The reaction to His outcry, **He calleth Elijah** [Elias], implies His condition; He lacked the physical strength to speak clearly.

37-38. John 19:30 informs us of Jesus' final words before He **gave up the ghost:** "It is finished." And that declaration explains why the **veil of the temple** was torn from top to bottom. Jesus had paid the penalty of sin, and thus there was no longer a barrier between God and man. He Himself had said, "I am the way, the truth, and the life" (Jn 14:6). This **veil** was a heavy curtain that separated the Holy Place from the Most Holy Place, which the book of Hebrews relates typologically to Christ (Heb 10:19-20).

39. Officially a **centurion** had one hundred men under him, but his assignment undoubtedly warranted but a small band. **Over against** means he was facing Jesus as He expired. The meaning of the confession, **Truly this man was the Son of God,** may not have come from understanding lips. The word **Son** does not have a definite article before it, so it should be translated "a" son of God. As a Roman the title he employed could have merely recognized Jesus' righteousness (Lk 23:47).

40-41. Luke 8:2 describes the former life of **Mary Magdalene.** She had been demon-possessed. The other Mary was the mother of **James the less,** one of the Twelve. **Salome** was the wife of Zebedee and the mother of James and John (Mt 27:56).

42. The time factor is mentioned to explain the necessity of hasty action. The next day, the Sabbath, would begin at 6:00 P.M. according to Jewish time, and it was already past 3:00 P.M. Since burial was unlawful on the Sabbath, both permission and the act itself required swift achievement.

43. Joseph's home, **Arimathea,** is given to distinguish him from others bearing the same name. **Honorable counselor** identifies him as a prominent member of the national religious council, the Sanhedrin. Luke 23:51 adds that he did not con-

went in boldly unto Pilate, and craved the body of Jesus.

44 And Pilate marvelled if he were already dead: and calling *unto him* the centurion, he asked him whether he had been any while dead.

45 And when he knew *it* of the centurion, he gave the body to Joseph.

46 And he bought fine linen, and took him down, and wrapped him in the linen, and laid him in a sepulchre which was hewn out of a rock, and rolled a stone unto the door of the sepulchre.

47 And Mary Magdalene and Mary *the mother* of Joses beheld where he was laid.

CHAPTER 16

AND when the sabbath was past, Mary Magdalene, and Mary the *mother* of James, and Sa-lō'me, had bought sweet spices, that they might come and anoint him.

2 And very early in the morning the first *day* of the week, they came unto the sepulchre at the rising of the sun.

3 And they said among themselves, Who shall roll us away the stone from the door of the sepulchre?

4 And when they looked, they saw that the stone was rolled away: for it was very great.

5 And entering into the sepulchre, they saw a young man sitting on the right side, clothed in a long white garment; and they were affrighted.

6 And he saith unto them, Be not affrighted: Ye seek Jesus of Nazareth, which was crucified: he is risen; he is not here: behold the place where they laid him.

7 But go your way, tell his disciples and Peter that he goeth before you into Galilee: there shall ye see him, as he said unto you.

8 And they went out quickly, and fled from the sepulchre; for they trembled and were amazed: neither said they any thing to any *man*; for they were afraid.

9 ¶Now when *Jesus* was risen early the first *day* of the week, he appeared first to Mary Magdalene, out of whom he had cast seven devils.

10 *And* she went and told them that had been with him, as they mourned and wept.

11 And they, when they had heard that he was alive, and had been seen of her, believed not.

12 ¶After that he appeared in another form unto two of them, as they walked, and went into the country.

13 And they went and told *it* unto the residue: neither believed they them.

14 ¶Afterward he appeared unto the eleven as they sat at meat, and upbraided them with their unbelief and hardness of heart, because they believed not them which had seen him after he was risen.

done the illegal trial which condemned Jesus. **Craved** (Gr *aiteō*) means "asked for" the body.

44-45. Pilate **marveled** at Joseph's request, because he was surprised that Jesus had already died. This implies how intense the Lord's suffering was. Prior to the Crucifixion, His body had been terribly and repeatedly beaten, so much so that He later was unable to bear His cross.

46-47. Matthew 27:60 says the **sepulcher** or tomb was Joseph's, and John 19:39 adds that Nicodemus helped him.

D. The Resurrection. 16:1-20.

16:1-3. The narration of the resurrection begins with an explanation of the presence of the women at the tomb. As they journeyed, they wondered how they would remove the stone which was wheel-shaped and large enough to block the entrance of the **sepulcher.** Besides its size, the area immediately in front of the entrance was lower, and thus its removal was accomplished only with extreme difficulty.

4-5. Two angels were present (Lk 24:4), but one must have been the more prominent, as in Mark's narrative.

6-8. Be not affrighted is a negative command in the present tense in Greek which is accurately translated "stop being afraid." **Neither said they anything to any man** appears to be a direct contradiction to the other Gospel accounts, which affirm that the women reported the news to the apostles. The purpose of these verses, however, centers around their immediate reaction, not the final outcome. They were afraid to tell anyone along the way, but when they found the apostles, they privately shared what had happened.

This concluding section (vss. 9-20) was not included in the two oldest manuscripts nor in other ancient reliable sources. Therefore, many Bible scholars conclude that Mark ended his Gospel with verse eight. However, the final twelve verses are discussed in this commentary. (For its inclusion in the original text see R. C. H. Lenski, *Commentary on St. Mark's Gospel,* pp. 750-755.)

9. Mary Magdalene was probably given the privilege of being first to witness the resurrected Christ because of her unreserved dedication. Having been delivered from her former condition, **out of whom he had cast seven devils** she committed herself to Christ with ineffable gratefulness.

10-13. Three times in this passage the disciples' resistance to believe is mentioned. This negative emphasis parallels the need for signs mentioned in verses 17 and 18. The **two . . . as they walked** refers to Cleopas and his companion as they journeyed to Emmaus (Lk 24:13-35.) The **residue** speaks of the rest of the disciples with the exception of Thomas who would see the Lord eight days later (Jn 20:24-29).

14-16. A striking peculiarity about this particular rendering of the Great Commission relates to baptism: **He that believeth and is baptized shall be saved.** The ordinance may appear to be a prerequisite to salvation. However, the negative statement mentions believing alone: **he that believeth not shall be**

15 And he said unto them, Go ye into all the world, and preach the gospel to every creature.

16 He that believeth and is baptized shall be saved; but he that believeth not shall be damned.

17 And these signs shall follow them that believe; In my name shall they cast out devils; they shall speak with new tongues;

18 They shall take up serpents; and if they drink any deadly thing, it shall not hurt them; they shall lay hands on the sick, and they shall recover.

19 ¶So then after the Lord had spoken unto them, he was received up into heaven, and sat on the right hand of God.

20 And they went forth, and preached every where, the Lord working with them, and confirming the word with signs following. Amen.

damned (Gr katakrinō to be condemned). In addition, baptism in the early church was the outward declaration of conversion, so even though the ordinance has no saving merit, the close connection is natural because it is the sign of genuine faith.

17-18. The distinctive emphasis of these signs causes some to conclude that the disputed ending of Mark was added to support the spiritual gifts that are listed. Since exorcism, speaking in tongues, handling snakes, and healing occurred in the books of Acts with drink any deadly thing being the single exception, one must admit that the passage could be harmonized with the New Testament on this subject.

19-20. Because of brevity, one might assume that the events occurred within a short time, as if He addressed them once and then immediately ascended. But actually He remained with them forty days (Acts 1:3). Signs following. This describes the pattern of apostolic preaching and ministry. Both leading figures in Acts, Peter and Paul, performed many miracles as a confirmation of the reality of their claims.

BIBLIOGRAPHY

Alexander, J. A. The Gospel According to Mark. London: Banner of Truth Trust, 1960.

Bruce, A. B. The Synoptic Gospels. In The Expositor's Greek Testament. Vol. 1. Grand Rapids: Eerdmans, n.d.

Cole, Robert Alan. The Gospel According to St. Mark. In the Tyndale New Testament Commentaries. Grand Rapids: Eerdmans, 1961.

*Cranfield, C. E. B. The Gospel According to St. Mark. Cambridge: Cambridge University Press, 1963.

Earle, Ralph. The Gospel According to Mark. In the Evangelical Commentary on the Bible. Grand Rapids: Zondervan, 1957.

*English, E. Schuyler. Studies in the Gospel According to Mark. New York: Our Hope, 1943.

Erdman, Charles R. The Gospel of Mark. Philadelphia: Westminster, 1917.

Hendriksen, William. Exposition of the Gospel According to Mark. In the New Testament Commentary. Grand Rapids: Baker, 1975.

*Hiebert, D. Edmond. Mark: A Portrait of the Servant. Chicago: Moody Press, 1974.

Kelly, William. An Exposition of the Gospel of Mark. Ed. by E. E. Whitfield. London: Alfred Holness, n.d.

*Lane, William L. The Gospel According to Mark. In the New International Commentary on the New Testament. Grand Rapids: Eerdmans, 1974.

Lindsay, Thomas M. The Gospel According to St. Mark. In Handbooks for Bible Classes and Private Students. Edinburgh: T. & T. Clark, 1883.

Martin, Ralph P. Mark: Evangelist and Theologian. Grand Rapids: Zondervan, 1973.

*Morgan, G. Campbell. The Gospel According to Mark. New York: Revell, 1927.

Morison, James. A Practical Commentary on the Gospel According to St. Mark. 4th revised ed. London: Hodder and Stoughton, 1882.

Plummer, A. The Gospel According to St. Mark. In the Cambridge Greek Testament for Schools and Colleges. Cambridge: Cambridge University Press, 1938.

Riddle, Matthew B. The Gospel According to Mark. In The International Revision Commentary on the New Testament. New York: Scribner, 1881.

Scroggie, W. Graham. The Gospel of Mark. London: Marshall, Morgan, and Scott, n.d.

*Swete, H. B. The Gospel According to St. Mark. Grand Rapids: Eerdmans, 1956.

*Taylor, Vincent. The Gospel According to St. Mark. London: Macmillan, 1963.

Wuest, Kenneth. Mark in the Greek New Testament for the English Reader. Grand Rapids: Eerdmans, 1950.

The Gospel According To
LUKE
INTRODUCTION

Each of the four Gospels is written from its own perspective to present Christ to a particular group of readers. Matthew, who writes primarily for the Jews, presents Christ as Messiah and King in fulfillment of prophecy. Mark stresses the servant aspects of Christ's ministry in writing for those of Roman background. John proves Christ to be the Son of God, deity incarnate. Luke's emphasis is on the humanity of Christ. In fact, the characteristic title for Christ, found in the key verse, is the "Son of man" (Lk 19:10).

As you read the book of Luke other features will also stand out. Luke includes more than the other Gospels about women, children, the home, the Holy Spirit, prayer, and praise. As the Son of Man, Jesus has experienced our griefs and sorrows, and He is able to meet these needs. Naturally, Luke, the "beloved physician," gives special touches regarding sickness and healing too. There are also more unique parables in Luke than in any other Gospel.

Authorship. From the earliest of times, believers have witnessed to the fact that Luke wrote this Gospel. Irenaeus, Tertullian, and Clement of Alexandria, who all lived circa A.D. 180, positively state that Luke was the author. From that time to this, there has been no other opinion except in the case of some more recent radical theologians.

The proof that Luke was the author must be gleaned from the book of Acts. The same author evidently wrote both books and addressed them both to a man named Theophilus (Lk 1:3 and Acts 1:1). Neither book actually states who its author is, but there are enough clues in Acts to confirm the universal testimony of history that Luke penned both volumes.

The argument may be expressed simply in several points. (1) In Acts, the writer differentiates himself from others in the account by using the pronoun "we" when he is part of the action (Acts 16:10-17; 20:5; 21:18; 27:1-28:16). Otherwise, he simply says "they." Since the author refers to Paul, Silas, and Timothy (and a few others, cf. Acts 20:4) as "they," none of them could be the author of Acts. (2) The writer's awareness of sicknesses and the use of distinct medical terminology in both Luke and Acts suggest that he may have been a doctor. (3) Luke was both a doctor and one of Paul's closest companions and fellow laborers as shown in Colossians 4:14. The latter reference, with Philemon 24, proves Luke's association with Paul in Rome after the voyage of Acts 27 and 28. In addition, in II Timothy 4:11 at the close of Paul's second Roman imprisonment, he notes that only Luke is with him. Only Luke fits all the criteria for the authorship of history found in Luke and continued in Acts.

As for Luke's personal life, he is thought by many to have been a Gentile. His name is Greek and in Colossians 4:14 Paul lists Luke with other Gentile names rather than with the Jewish believers. In any event, he was a tremendous historian, missionary, church planter, traveller, and writer, as well as being a physician.

Date. It is evident that the book of Acts is a continuation of "the former treatise" (Acts 1:1), namely, the Gospel of Luke. This means that Luke had to have been completed prior to the writing of Acts. From the abrupt ending of Acts with Paul still in custody in Rome awaiting the outcome of his case, several ideas are suggested: (1) Luke may have intended to have the book of Acts end in Rome to present the gospel as having spread from Jerusalem to the very capital of the Empire. (2) More likely, the book of Acts ends where it does because Luke had nothing more to report. Paul's trial was at a standstill. The date of Paul's first two-year Roman detainment is usually pinpointed around A.D. 60-62, on the basis of the date Porcius Festus replaced Felix (Acts 24:27). Since Luke was written prior to this time, it is most logical to place it between A.D. 58-60 when Paul was imprisoned in Caesarea. This would have given Luke ample time to consult needed eyewitnesses and examine other official Roman and Palestinian records during the two-year stay in Caesarea.

Place. The precise place where Luke penned his gospel is not known. However, since it appears to have been written prior to the book of Acts, which was published around A.D. 61 or 62, several possibilities arise: (1) Some feel it may have been written in Greece, possibly on either the first or second missionary journey. But, there does not seem to have been enough time at that point for Luke to have consulted the many "eyewitnesses" (1:2) who would necessarily have lived in Palestine. (2) Caesarea, the Roman administrative capital of Palestine, is perhaps the most ideal location that could be suggested. Luke was with Paul during Paul's two-year detainment in Caesarea awaiting trial (Acts 24:27). From that city Luke no doubt would have been able to consult various early disciples, deacons, and other believers to obtain information for the writing of his Gospel, under the superintending work of the Holy Spirit (II Pet 1:21). The two-year interval also affords Luke ample leisure time for pursuing such activities as writing. (3) A third possibility would be Rome during Paul's two-year imprisonment there from about A.D. 60-62. But, such might crowd the writing of Acts, which was accomplished during the same period. Thus, Caesarea in Palestine is perhaps the most ideal and most likely place for the Gospel to have been written, both from the chronological as well as the fact-gathering perspectives.

OUTLINE

I. The Prologue to Theophilus. 1:1-4.

II. The Preparations for the Arrival of the Son. 1:5-2:52.
  A. Gabriel's Announcement to Zechariah. 1:5-25.
  B. Gabriel's Announcement to Mary. 1:26-38.
  C. Mary's Visit to Elisabeth. 1:39-56.
  D. John's Birth in Judaea. 1:57-80.
  E. Jesus' Birth in Beth-lehem. 2:1-21.
  F. Mary's Purification in Jerusalem. 2:22-38.
  G. Jesus' Growth in Nazareth. 2:39-40.
  H. Jesus' First Passover in Jerusalem. 2:41-52.

III. The Public Presentation of the Son. 3:1-4:13.
  A. The Words and Work of John the Baptist. 3:1-20.
  B. The Baptism of Christ. 3:21-22.
  C. The Genealogy of Christ. 3:23-38.
  D. The Temptation of Christ. 4:1-13.

IV. The Preaching of the Son in Galilee. 4:14-9:50.
  A. The Preaching that Claimed Messiahship. 4:14-44.
  B. The Miracles that Supported His Messiahship. 5:1-39.
  C. The Choice of the Twelve. 6:1-49.
  D. More Miracles and Parables in Galilee. 7:1-8:56.
  E. Christ's Dealings with His Disciples. 9:1-50.

V. The Peraean Ministry of the Son. 9:51-19:27
  A. Christ's Determination to Go to Jerusalem. 9:51-62.
  B. Christ's Ministry with the Seventy. 10:1-24.
  C. Christ's Parabolic Teaching Ministry. 10:25-13:21.
  D. Christ's Growing Public Confrontation with Religious Leaders. 13:22-16:31.
  E. Christ's Instruction of His Disciples. 17:1-19:27.

VI. The Proffer of the Son's Kingdom and Its Rejection. 19:28-21:4.
  A. Christ's Entry into Jerusalem. 19:28-46.
  B. Christ's Public Teaching in Jerusalem. 19:47-21:4.

VII. The Prophecy of Tribulation to Come. 21:5-38.
  A. Prophecy About This Age. 21:5-19.
  B. Prophecy About Jerusalem. 21:20-24.
  C. Prophecy About Christ's Return. 21:25-38.

VIII. The Passion of the Son. 22:1-23:56.
  A. Christ's Final Night with His Disciples. 22:1-46.
  B. Christ's Betrayal and Trial. 22:47-23:25.
  C. Christ's Crucifixion. 23:26-56.

IX. The Power of the Son Over Death. 24:1-48.
  A. The Events Surrounding the Empty Tomb. 24:1-12.
  B. The Walk to Emmaus. 24:13-32.
  C. The Meeting in the Upper Room. 24:33-48.

X. The Promise of the Son to the Disciples. 24:49-53.

COMMENTARY

I. THE PROLOGUE TO THEOPHILUS. 1:1-4.

The first eighty-two words of the text compose just one sentence, Luke's preface. It was customary in the first century to write a formal literary prologue for most works. The purpose of such a preface was to announce the reasons for writing, the methods followed, and the dedication of the work, often to the one paying for its production. Josephus, for example, a first-century Jewish historian, follows this same pattern in his *Antiquities of the Jews*. Luke's style and vocabulary in these opening four verses comprise perhaps the best example of classical Greek in the New Testament. It is also an indication of Luke's extraordinary education and his fitness for the task God gave to him of writing such a complete biography of Christ.

1:1. Many have taken in hand to set forth in order a declaration. Apparently there were a number of early attempts to record parts of Christ's life and work, and also the beginnings of the New Testament church after His death and resurrection. These early narratives were probably written by other believers, with whom Luke seems to classify himself (vs. 3 **me also**). They may have been truthful, authentic, and genuine accounts, but they were not God-breathed (II Tim 3:16), and thus passed off the scene as they were replaced by the inspired documents penned by Matthew, Mark, Luke, and John. Luke is not referring here to the accounts drawn up by the other gospel writers.

Those things which are most surely believed among us. This is more accurately rendered "the matters which have been fulfilled or accomplished among us." The terminology Luke

FORASMUCH as many have taken in hand to set forth in order a declaration of those things which are most surely believed among us,

uses includes the material in the book of Acts as well as the Gospel, showing that at the outset he intended to pen a complete history of the events surrounding the beginnings, growth, and development of Christianity. The prologue to this gospel should also be seen as prefacing the book of Acts. In Acts 1:1-2 Luke refers to the gospel account as including "all that Jesus began to do and teach, until the day in which he was taken up." Acts simply continues the narrative of what Jesus continued to do and teach after He was taken up.

2 Even as they delivered them unto us, which from the beginning were eyewitnesses, and ministers of the word;

2. Even as they delivered them unto us, which from the beginning were eyewitnesses. Luke received information that was handed over to him from eyewitnesses who had seen the very beginnings of the gospel account he relates. Who were these early eyewitnesses? Luke may have talked with Mary, the mother of our Lord, and with James and Jude, two of Christ's brothers who were prominent enough to have written New Testament books. James was also the leading elder in the church at Jerusalem (Acts 15:13, 19; 21:18; Gal 2:9). Naturally, Luke must have met some of the twelve original disciples. Luke even tells us that he spent some time with Mnason who was a disciple of longstanding, perhaps one who knew Christ personally (Acts 21:16). Of course, there were probably hundreds if not thousands still alive who had personally heard Jesus teach and had seen Him perform miracles just thirty years previously. In addition, Paul recorded in A.D. 52 or 53 that a great number of the five hundred who all on one occasion saw Christ after His resurrection were still alive (I Cor 15:6). They apparently joined the ranks shortly after Pentecost, and were some of the original deacons, such as Philip, who conveniently lived in Caesarea, and with whom Luke lodged for a while (Acts 21:8-10).

3 It seemed good to me also, having had perfect understanding of all things from the very first, to write unto thee in order, most excellent Thē-ŏph'i-lus,

3. Having had perfect understanding of all things from the very first is more literally rendered "having traced or investigated accurately all things from the first." Luke expresses several ideas: (1) The length of his search took him back to the beginning of things. Only Luke recounts the birth announcements of Gabriel to Zacharias [Zechariah] and to Mary. (2) The breadth of his research has included "all things." He would naturally have to evalute each piece of evidence in order to retain that which would be most useful. (3) The accuracy of his investigation is declared by his use of the Greek word *akribōs* which speaks of precision and exactness.

To write unto thee in order, most excellent Theophilus. Luke's mention of "in order" perhaps hints that some of the other accounts then in existence were not only fragmentary and partial, but also somewhat disarranged. Theophilus is referred to as one would address a Greek noble. He may have had a title, or Luke may simply be honoring him in a special way as the patron who is presumably financing the writing of this work.

4 That thou mightest know the certainty of those things, wherein thou hast been instructed.

4. The purpose of Luke's Gospel, as stated here, is to certify the truthfulness of those things wherein Theophilus has been taught or "catechized" (Gr *katēchēo*), regarding the Christian faith. One's faith is no more sure than the object upon which it rests. We can thank God that our faith rests firmly upon the unshakable historical facts recorded in His matchless Word.

II. THE PREPARATIONS FOR THE ARRIVAL OF THE SON. 1:5-2:52.

A. Gabriel's Announcement to Zechariah. 1:5-25.

5 ¶THERE was in the days of Herod, the king of Judæa, a certain priest named Zăch-a-rī'as, of the course of Ā-bī'a: and his wife was of the daughters of Aaron, and her name was Elisabeth.

5. In the days of Herod, the king. Luke is very exact in giving precise historical and chronological information. This is seen in these words, as well as other references to major historical persons, events and dates as in 2:1-3; 3:1-2, 19, and 23. This Herod, known as Herod the Great, was a descendant of Esau (cf. Gen 27:39-40). Born in 73 B.C., he was appointed King of the

6 And they were both righteous before God, walking in all the commandments and ordinances of the Lord blameless.

7 And they had no child, because that Elisabeth was barren, and they both were *now* well stricken in years.

8 And it came to pass, that while he executed the priest's office before God in the order of his course,

9 According to the custom of the priest's office, his lot was to burn incense when he went into the temple of the Lord.

10 And the whole multitude of the people were praying without at the time of incense.

11 And there appeared unto him an angel of the Lord standing on the right side of the altar of incense.

12 And when Zăch-a-rī'as saw *him,* he was troubled, and fear fell upon him.

13 But the angel said unto him, Fear not, Zăch-a-rī'as: for thy prayer is heard; and thy wife Elisabeth shall bear thee a son, and thou shalt call his name John.

14 And thou shalt have joy and gladness; and many shall rejoice at his birth.

15 For he shall be great in the sight of the Lord, and shall drink neither wine nor strong drink; and he shall be filled with the Holy Ghost, even from his mother's womb.

16 And many of the children of Israel shall he turn to the Lord their God.

17 And he shall go before him in the spirit and power of E-lī'as, to turn the hearts of the fathers to the children, and the disobedient to the wisdom of the just; to make ready a people prepared for the Lord.

18 And Zăch-a-rī'as said unto the angel, Whereby shall I know this? for I am an old man and my wife well stricken in years.

19 And the angel answering said unto him, I am Gabriel, that stand in the presence of God; and am sent to speak unto thee, and to shew thee these glad tidings.

20 And, behold, thou shalt be dumb, and not able to speak, until the day that these things shall be performed, because thou believest not my words, which shall be fulfilled in their season.

21 And the people waited for Zăch-a-rī'as, and marvelled that he tarried so long in the temple.

22 And when he came out, he could not speak unto them: and they perceived that he had seen a vision in the temple: for he beckoned unto them, and remained speechless.

23 And it came to pass, that, as soon as the days of his ministration were accomplished, he departed to his own house.

24 And after those days his wife Elisabeth conceived, and hid herself five months, saying,

Jews by the Roman Senate in 40 B.C. He ruled until his death in March or April, 4 B.C. Archelaus (Mt 2:22), Philip (Lk 3:1), and Herod Antipas (Lk 23:7-12, 15) were his sons. Herod Agrippa I of Acts 12:1-6, 19-23 was his grandson, and Herod Agrippa II of Acts 25-26 was his great-grandson.

6-10. Zechariah . . . and Elisabeth were very old and childless (vs. 7), a theme repeated throughout the Old Testament, as with Sarah, Rebekah, Manoah's wife, and Hannah. Zechariah was a priest, and he was serving for about a two-week period in the Temple. This Temple was built by Zerubbabel and others in 516 B.C., but since 20 B.C. was in the process of being enlarged and redone by Herod the Great (see Jn 2:20). Zechariah had the unique opportunity of offering incense before the Holy of Holies. The people outside prayed and awaited his blessing.

11-17. At that moment the angel Gabriel (vs. 19) appeared to Zechariah, who was suddenly shaken with fear, and said his prayers had been answered. Zechariah's prayer could have been (1) his long-standing request for a son, or (2) his general petitions for the coming of the Messiah, or (3) both. Both were shortly accomplished. This Gabriel was the same angel who appeared five hundred years before to Daniel (Dan 8:15-16; 9:21). No recorded revelation from God had been given to men for over four hundred years. Naturally, Zechariah was stunned. The content of Gabriel's message was twofold. (1) Elisabeth was to bear a son and name him John. (2) John would have the spirit and power of Elijah and was to prepare the way for the Messiah.

18-20. Zechariah expressed doubt, and so as both a punishment as well as a sign, he was stricken speechless for the ensuing nine months.

21-25. When Zechariah left the Temple he had no priestly blessing to bestow upon the people. Luke contrasts this initial occasion with the final episode of this gospel as Christ, our High Priest, ascended up into heaven while giving the apostles His blessing (Lk 24:50-51).

25 Thus hath the Lord dealt with me in the days wherein he looked on *me*, to take away my reproach among men.

26 ¶And in the sixth month the angel Gabriel was sent from God unto a city of Galilee, named Nazareth,

27 To a virgin espoused to a man whose name was Joseph, of the house of David; and the virgin's name *was* Mary.

28 And the angel came in unto her, and said, Hail, *thou that art* highly favoured, the Lord *is* with thee: blessed *art* thou among women.

29 And when she saw *him*, she was troubled at his saying, and cast in her mind what manner of salutation this should be.

30 And the angel said unto her, Fear not, Mary: for thou hast found favour with God.

31 And, behold, thou shalt conceive in thy womb, and bring forth a son, and shalt call his name JESUS.

32 He shall be great, and shall be called the Son of the Highest: and the Lord God shall give unto him the throne of his father David:

33 And he shall reign over the house of Jacob for ever; and of his kingdom there shall be no end.

34 Then said Mary unto the angel, How shall this be, seeing I know not a man?

35 And the angel answered and said unto her, The Holy Ghost shall come upon thee, and the power of the Highest shall overshadow thee: therefore also that holy thing which shall be born of thee shall be called the Son of God.

36 And, behold, thy cousin Elisabeth, she hath also conceived a son in her old age: and this is the sixth month with her, who was called barren.

37 For with God nothing shall be impossible.

38 And Mary said, Behold the handmaid of the Lord; be it unto me according to thy word. And the angel departed from her.

39 ¶And Mary arose in those days, and went into the hill country with haste, into a city of Juda;

40 And entered into the house of Zăch-a-rī'as, and saluted Elisabeth.

41 And it came to pass, that, when Elisabeth heard the salutation of Mary,

B. Gabriel's Announcement to Mary. 1:26-38.

26. And in the sixth month refers to the sixth month of Elisabeth's pregnancy. Once again, Gabriel was sent to announce a special birth, this time to Mary in Nazareth.

27. To a virgin. There is no doubt according to Scripture that Christ's birth was a virgin birth, totally without parallel either before or since. This is required for several reasons: (1) to fulfill Old Testament prophecy (Gen 3:15; Isa 7:14; Jer 31:22); (2) to avoid the Old Testament curse on the seed of Jeconiah (Jer 22:24-30), yet still be able to claim the Throne of David in the kingly line; (3) to be in accord with the theological implications of the inspiration of the Scriptures and Christ's sinless humanity. Through the miraculous virgin conception, Christ avoided receiving a sinful nature; (4) to avoid receiving a human father. Christ already had a Father, and it would be unsuitable to have a second one; (5) to avoid creating a new person, as is done in all normal conceptions. Mary's conception of Christ was to be the incarnation of an already existing person.

28. Blessed art thou among women. Mary was perhaps the best female descendant of David suitable for this matchless ministry of rearing the very Son of God. We must be careful not to downgrade Mary, nor to exalt her too highly.

29-33. Mary was naturally perplexed by all this, though she accepted it. Gabriel went on to explain that the Messiah Himself was to be born to her. The importance of verses 32-33 is that of the fulfillment of the Davidic Covenant of II Samuel 7:13-16, and of the messianic reign described in Isaiah 9:6-7.

34. How shall this be, seeing I know not a man? This was a legitimate question, given Mary's present marital status. Unlike Zechariah's question in verse 18, Mary expresses no doubt, but rather a humble submission to the will of God. Note verse 38 in this regard also.

35. The Holy Ghost shall come upon thee, and the power of the Highest shall overshadow thee. These words express the completely miraculous nature of Mary's conception. It was accomplished by God alone in a unique, never-to-be-repeated way. But one asks, could not Mary transmit her sinful nature to the one conceived in her womb? Ordinarily this would be the case, but the phrase **that holy thing which shall be born of thee** declares that God supernaturally prevented this from occurring.

36-38. Gabriel's announcement to Mary concluded with the statement that Mary's elderly cousin Elisabeth had also conceived, and was in her sixth month of pregnancy. The words, **For with God nothing shall be impossible,** are applicable to what God was doing with both Mary and Elisabeth.

C. Mary's Visit to Elisabeth. 1:39-56.

39-40. Almost immediately after receiving Gabriel's message, Mary prepared to visit Elisabeth some sixty or more miles south of Nazareth in Judaean territory. She remained there about three months (vs. 56).

41-45. Elisabeth was suddenly filled with the Holy Spirit when she saw Mary. Elisabeth's words in verses 42-45 indicate

the babe leaped in her womb; and Elisabeth was filled with the Holy Ghost;

42 And she spake out with a loud voice, and said, Blessed *art* thou among women, and blessed *is* the fruit of thy womb.

43 And whence *is* this to me, that the mother of my Lord should come to me?

44 For, lo, as soon as the voice of thy salutation sounded in mine ears, the babe leaped in my womb for joy.

45 And blessed *is* she that believed: for there shall be a performance of those things which were told her from the Lord.

46 ¶And Mary said, My soul doth magnify the Lord,

47 And my spirit hath rejoiced in God my Saviour.

48 For he hath regarded the low estate of his handmaiden: for, behold, from henceforth all generations shall call me blessed.

49 For he that is mighty hath done to me great things; and holy *is* his name.

50 And his mercy *is* on them that fear him from generation to generation.

51 He hath shewed strength with his arm; he hath scattered the proud in the imagination of their hearts.

52 He hath put down the mighty from *their* seats, and exalted them of low degree.

53 He hath filled the hungry with good things; and the rich he hath sent empty away.

54 He hath holpen his servant Israel, in remembrance of *his* mercy;

55 As he spake to our fathers, to Abraham, and to his seed for ever.

56 And Mary abode with her about three months, and returned to her own house.

57 ¶Now Elisabeth's full time came that she should be delivered; and she brought forth a son.

58 And her neighbours and her cousins heard how the Lord had shewed great mercy upon her; and they rejoiced with her.

59 And it came to pass, that on the eighth day they came to circumcise the child; and they called him Zăch-a-rī′as, after the name of his father.

60 And his mother answered and said, Not *so;* but he shall be called John.

61 And they said unto her, There is none of thy kindred that is called by this name.

62 And they made signs to his father, how he would have him called.

63 And he asked for a writing table, and wrote, saying, His name is John. And they marvelled all.

64 And his mouth was opened immediately, and his tongue *loosed,* and he spake, and praised God.

65 And fear came on all that dwelt round about them: and all these

that God gave her a prophetic knowledge of Mary's condition, and filled her lips with the fruit of praise to Almighty God.

46-55. And Mary said, My soul doth magnify the Lord. This section, commonly called the Magnificat, in many ways resembles Hannah's prayer of thanksgiving and praise to God recorded in I Samuel 2:1-10. It illustrates Mary's rich acquaintance with the Old Testament Scriptures and the closeness of her fellowship with the Lord.

56. Naturally, when Mary returned home after being away for three months, and was soon obviously with child, her fiancé, Joseph, was dismayed. Only revelation from heaven could substantiate Mary's explanation regarding her condition. Matthew 1:18-25 records how God met this need.

D. John's Birth in Judaea. 1:57-80.

57-59a. Eight days after the birth of Elisabeth's baby boy, he was to be circumcised in accord with the elements enumerated in God's covenant with Abraham in Genesis 17:10-14, and made part of the Law in Leviticus 12. The idea of circumcision seems to include three truths: (1) purification of the flesh; (2) separation unto God; and (3) identification as God's very own.

59b-63. And they called him Zechariah, after the name of his father. And his mother answered and said, Not so; but he shall be called John. Zechariah, in his speechless condition had at least made known to Elisabeth the full content of the angel Gabriel's message in which the new son was to be named John. The friends and relatives were not aware of this fact; they wanted to name him after his father. They were greatly surprised to see the boy called **John,** which means in Hebrew, "Jehovah is gracious," or "Jehovah's gift." Certainly both were true regarding this gracious gift to Zechariah and Elisabeth. When the relatives questioned this new name, Zechariah confirmed the naming by writing "John" on a small wooden or wax tablet.

64-66. Immediately God miraculously ended Zechariah's long involuntary period of silence and he began praising God. These actions attracted great awe and amazement in that entire region. People began to take note of young John, and of the fact that **the hand of the Lord was with him** (cf. I Sam 2:21, 26).

sayings were noised abroad throughout all the hill country of Judæa.

66 And all they that heard *them* laid *them* up in their hearts, saying, What manner of child shall this be! And the hand of the Lord was with him.

67 ¶And his father Zăch-a-rī′as was filled with the Holy Ghost, and prophesied, saying,

68 Blessed *be* the Lord God of Israel; for he hath visited and redeemed his people,

69 And hath raised up an horn of salvation for us in the house of his servant David;

70 As he spake by the mouth of his holy prophets, which have been since the world began:

71 That we should be saved from our enemies, and from the hand of all that hate us;

72 To perform the mercy *promised* to our fathers, and to remember his holy covenant;

73 The oath which he sware to our father Abraham,

74 That he would grant unto us, that we being delivered out of the hand of our enemies might serve him without fear,

75 In holiness and righteousness before him, all the days of our life.

76 And thou, child, shalt be called the prophet of the Highest: for thou shalt go before the face of the Lord to prepare his ways;

77 To give knowledge of salvation unto his people by the remission of their sins,

78 Through the tender mercy of our God; whereby the dayspring from on high hath visited us,

79 To give light to them that sit in darkness and *in* the shadow of death, to guide our feet into the way of peace.

80 And the child grew, and waxed strong in spirit, and was in the deserts till the day of his shewing unto Israel.

CHAPTER 2

AND it came to pass in those days, that there went out a decree from Cæsar Augustus, that all the world should be taxed.

2 (*And* this taxing was first made when Cȳ-rē′nī-us was governor of Syria.)

3 And all went to be taxed, every one into his own city.

67-79. The prophecy of Zechariah, found exclusively in these verses, was spoken under the power of the Holy Spirit. His words are filled with messianic importance with references to redemption or salvation in verses 68, 69, 71, 74, and 77. That God's unchanging covenant with Abraham was being fulfilled is mentioned in verses 72-73. In fact, there are no less than sixteen direct quotations or allusions to the Old Testament contained in these few verses. Zechariah utters a remarkable prophecy which heralds the coming of the Messiah and His forerunner. It is in some ways the New Testament reiteration of the last chapter of the Old Testament.

80. As with Christ, there is but scant mention of the childhood of John the Baptist. His work was to begin some thirty years later.

E. Jesus' Birth in Beth-lehem. 2:1-21.

2:1. A decree from Caesar Augustus. Augustus was the grandnephew of Julius Caesar, and was adopted as his son. After the murder of Julius Caesar, young Octavius Augustus ruled with Mark Anthony and Lepidus in a triumvirate. Then for more than forty years, from 27 B.C. to A.D. 14, Augustus served by himself as the first emperor of the Roman Empire. It was during his reign that Christ was born.

All the world indicates only the twenty-seven provinces ruled by the Roman Senate and the emperor. **Taxed** (Gr *apographō*), better translated as enrolled, signifies a census, upon which basis perhaps a future taxation would be made.

2. When Cyrenius was governor of Syria. Syria was the most important of all the Roman provinces, and Quirinius (Cyrenius) served in several capacities there at different times. Roman censuses came every fourteen years. The first one of which we have recorded knowledge came in A.D. 6. This earlier census then may have been set in motion in Rome about 8 B.C., while Quirinius was the military governor of Syria. Several years would be required to complete such a census.

3-6. Joseph had to travel from Nazareth, where he was living, to Beth-lehem for the census, because he was a descendant of

4 And Joseph also went up from Galilee, out of the city of Nazareth, into Judæa, unto the city of David, which is called Bethlehem; (because he was of the house and lineage of David:)

5 To be taxed with Mary his espoused wife, being great with child.

6 And so it was, that, while they were there, the days were accomplished that she should be delivered.

7 And she brought forth her firstborn son, and wrapped him in swaddling clothes, and laid him in a manger; because there was no room for them in the inn.

8 ¶And there were in the same country shepherds abiding in the field, keeping watch over their flock by night.

9 And, lo, the angel of the Lord came upon them, and the glory of the Lord shone round about them: and they were sore afraid.

10 And the angel said unto them, Fear not: for, behold, I bring you good tidings of great joy, which shall be to all people.

11 For unto you is born this day in the city of David a Saviour, which is Christ the Lord.

12 And this *shall be* a sign unto you; Ye shall find the babe wrapped in swaddling clothes, lying in a manger.

13 And suddenly there was with the angel a multitude of the heavenly host praising God, and saying,

14 Glory to God in the highest, and on earth peace, good will toward men.

15 And it came to pass, as the angels were gone away from them into heaven, the shepherds said one to another, Let us now go even unto Bethlehem, and see this thing which is come to pass, which the Lord hath made known unto us.

16 And they came with haste, and found Mary, and Joseph, and the babe lying in a manger.

17 And when they had seen *it*, they made known abroad the saying which was told them concerning this child.

18 And all they that heard *it* wondered at those things which were told them by the shepherds.

19 But Mary kept all these things, and pondered *them* in her heart.

20 And the shepherds returned, glorifying and praising God for all the things that they had heard and seen, as it was told unto them.

21 ¶And when eight days were accomplished for the circumcising of the child, his name was called JESUS, which was so named of the angel before he was conceived in the womb.

22 And when the days of her purification according to the law of Moses were accomplished, they brought him to Jerusalem, to present *him* to the Lord;

23 (As it is written in the law of the

King David of Beth-lehem. Mary accompanied Joseph on the sixty-five-mile journey.

7. Wrapped him in swaddling clothes. With no midwife to help, Mary wrapped baby Jesus in long bands of cloth such as were used in wrapping the bodies of the dead. That He was born to die is perhaps intimated here and in the later gift of myrrh from the wise men (Mt 2:11). **Manger** is a cattle-feeding trough. **No room for them in the inn.** All these things suggest poverty, loneliness, and even rejection (see II Cor 8:9). The exact date and place are not recorded by Luke, perhaps to guard against the vain worship which men often attach to such information.

8-11. God sent an angel to make the first announcement of the Saviour's birth to lowly shepherds. He is called the Deliverer, the Anointed One (Messiah) promised in the Old Testament, even the Lord Himself.

12. The uniqueness of the sign was the rarity of finding a baby in a manger.

13-15. Upon completion of his announcement, this angel was immediately joined by hundreds of dazzling angels who lit up the dark sky (see vs. 9, **the glory of the Lord shone**). Nothing like that had happened for hundreds of years. It must have made the intended impression on these shepherds.

16-18. They quickly found the Christ, and then spread the news of the miraculous events associated with His coming. All who heard it marvelled.

19-20. Mary was beginning to see God's attestation of her boy who was also the Son of the Highest. This was apparently the first confirmation she had had since her visit to Elisabeth, and the dream Joseph had received some months earlier.

21. The Saviour was officially named **Jesus** upon His circumcision at eight days old.

F. Mary's Purification in Jerusalem. 2:22-38.

22-24. About five weeks later, Mary and Joseph traveled five miles north to the Temple in Jerusalem to offer the sacrifice required by the law of Moses (Lev 12:6-8). This ended Mary's period of uncleanness which had last forty days from Christ's birth. The circumcision of a male child was apparently seen as removing some of the uncleanness, because a female child would

Lord, Every male that openeth the womb shall be called holy to the Lord;)

24 And to offer a sacrifice according to that which is said in the law of the Lord, A pair of turtledoves, or two young pigeons.

25 And, behold, there was a man in Jerusalem, whose name *was* Simeon; and the same man *was* just and devout, waiting for the consolation of Israel: and the Holy Ghost was upon him.

26 And it was revealed unto him by the Holy Ghost, that he should not see death, before he had seen the Lord's Christ.

27 And he came by the Spirit into the temple: and when the parents brought in the child Jesus, to do for him after the custom of the law,

28 Then took he him up in his arms, and blessed God, and said,

29 Lord, now lettest thou thy servant depart in peace, according to thy word:

30 For mine eyes have seen thy salvation,

31 Which thou hast prepared before the face of all people;

32 A light to lighten the Gentiles, and the glory of thy people Israel.

33 And Joseph and his mother marvelled at those things which were spoken of him.

34 And Simeon blessed them, and said unto Mary his mother, Behold, this *child* is set for the fall and rising again of many in Israel; and for a sign which shall be spoken against;

35 (Yea, a sword shall pierce through thy own soul also,) that the thoughts of many hearts may be revealed.

36 And there was one Anna, a prophetess, the daughter of Pha-nu'el, of the tribe of A'ser: she was of a great age, and had lived with an husband seven years from her virginity;

37 And she *was* a widow of about fourscore and four years, which departed not from the temple, but served God with fastings and prayers night and day.

38 And she coming in that instant gave thanks likewise unto the Lord, and spake of him to all them that looked for redemption in Jerusalem.

39 And when they had performed all things according to the law of the Lord, they returned into Galilee, to their own city Nazareth.

40 And the child grew, and waxed strong in spirit, filled with wisdom: and the grace of God was upon him.

41 ¶Now his parents went to Jerusalem every year at the feast of the passover.

42 And when he was twelve years old, they went up to Jerusalem after the custom of the feast.

43 And when they had fulfilled the days, as they returned, the child Jesus tarried behind in Jerusalem; and Joseph and his mother knew not *of it.*

44 But they, supposing him to have been in the company, went a day's

cause uncleanness to remain for eighty days (Lev 12:5). The poverty of Mary and Joseph is seen in their offering a pair of doves rather than the more expensive lamb and a dove. The wise men of Matthew 2:1-12, who brought gold and other gifts, had not yet arrived. They came later after Mary and Joseph had moved from the stable into a house (Mt 2:11).

25-35. Before Christ was born, the Holy Spirit had ministered in a unique way to a man named Simeon, informing him that he would behold the long-promised Messiah before he died. Guided by the Holy Spirit, he entered the Temple at the precise moment that Mary and Joseph were there with the six-week-old child. He lifted the baby into his arms and uttered a special prophecy. He spoke of Christ as a light for the Gentiles, and as the glory of Israel. This made even Mary and Joseph take note (vs. 33). Verse 34 speaks of both the tremendous earthly and eternal difference it makes whether one trusts Christ to be his personal sin substitute. Verse 35 looks forward thirty-three years to the agony Mary will suffer while seeing her son crucified.

36-38. Anna a prophetess. Anna follows in the train of Miriam, Deborah, and Huldah in the Old Testament. Note that the tribe of Asher had not completely lost its identity. The godly of all Israelite tribes had come south to Judah prior to the 722 B.C. deportation of most in the northern tribes to Assyria. Later, James addressed all twelve tribes of Israel (Jas 1:1). Anna may have been over one hundred years old. She witnessed to the faithful remnant in Jerusalem regarding the newborn Messiah.

G. Jesus' Growth in Nazareth. 2:39-40.

39. After these Temple experiences, the wise men visited Christ in Beth-lehem, which precipitated Mary and Joseph's departure and sojourn in Egypt (Mt 2:1-14). This verse telling of the return to Nazareth corresponds with Matthew 2:19-23.

40. The boyhood of Christ was natural as far as physical growth was concerned, but extraordinary in relation to His attainment of wisdom and understanding of spiritual things.

H. Jesus' First Passover in Jerusalem. 2:41-52.

41-42. The Old Testament law required all Israelite males to appear before the Lord three times each year (Deut 16:16). Mary and Joseph were in the habit of attending Passover. At age twelve, Jesus accompanied them.

43-46. After three days they found him in the temple. Mary and Joseph had lost track of Jesus on the way back to Nazareth. They traveled a day out and a day back, and searched the city a third day before they found Jesus in the Temple. He was engaged in a profound discussion of theological topics with the

journey; and they sought him among *their* kinsfolk and acquaintance.

45 And when they found him not, they turned back again to Jerusalem, seeking him.

46 And it came to pass, that after three days they found him in the temple, sitting in the midst of the doctors, both hearing them, and asking them questions.

47 And all that heard him were astonished at his understanding and answers.

48 And when they saw him, they were amazed: and his mother said unto him, Son, why hast thou thus dealt with us? behold, thy father and I have sought thee sorrowing.

49 And he said unto them, How is it that ye sought me? wist ye not that I must be about my Father's business?

50 And they understood not the saying which he spake unto them.

51 And he went down with them, and came to Nazareth, and was subject unto them: but his mother kept all these sayings in her heart.

52 And Jesus increased in wisdom and stature, and in favour with God and man.

47. Christ's understanding astonished everyone, even as His miracles would two decades later.

48-51. At this early age, the son of Mary knew He was also the Son of God. Perhaps in the routine of daily living, Mary and Joseph's initial awareness of the true identity of this Messiah-child had faded somewhat.

52. During the so-called silent years, Jesus matured in four ways: (1) mentally, i.e., **in wisdom;** (2) physically, i.e., in **stature**; (3) spiritually, i.e., **in favor with God**; and (4) socially, i.e., in favor with **man.**

III. THE PUBLIC PRESENTATION OF THE SON. 3:1-4:13.

A. The Words and Work of John the Baptist. 3:1-20.

3:1. In the fifteenth year of the reign of Tiberius Caesar. As always, Luke gives precise historical information. Tiberius took over as Roman Emperor after Augustus (see notes on 2:1). Augustus reigned from 27 B.C. until his death in A.D. 14. However, it appears that Augustus made Tiberius co-emperor during his final two years. Thus, his fifteenth year is probably to be equated with A.D. 26 or 27. This would correspond with Jesus' being about thirty years old at that time (Lk 3:23), and with John 2:20 which says the Temple renovation began by Herod in 20 or 19 B.C. had been going on for forty-six years.

2. The word of God came unto John. John followed in the train of many other Old Testament prophets, and the same formula is used to indicate God's revelation to him as to Elijah (I Kgs 18:1), Jeremiah (Jer 1:4), Ezekiel (Ezk 1:3), and others. John's ministry was in the wilderness, a barren area between the hill country and the Jordan.

3. Preaching the baptism of repentance for the remission of sins. This should not be confused with Christian baptism, which began on Pentecost. Christian baptism, as explained by Paul in Romans 6:1-4, pictures death, burial, and resurrection in union with Christ. That meaning could only have been possible after the cross, since not even the disciples themselves understood anything about Christ having to die until after it was an accomplished fact (see Mt 16:21-23; Lk 19:11). John's baptism must have pictured a cleansing of heart and a preparedness to receive the Messiah, as evidenced by repentance. John's converts could be saved, but they were saved just as any other Old Testament saint was, such as Abraham, Job, Isaiah, or Daniel.

4-8. John's ministry was to prepare the way for the Messiah's appearance. His message was that of repentance for sin, and of a resulting change in one's life. His baptism was to picture the reality of that change, cleansing, and remission of sins. His

CHAPTER 3

NOW in the fifteenth year of the reign of Tī-be'rĭ-us Cæsar, Pontius Pilate being governor of Judæa, and Herod being tetrarch of Galilee, and his brother Philip tetrarch of Ĭ-tū-ræ'a and of the region of Trăch-o-nī'tis, and Ly-sa'ni-as the tetrarch of Ăb-i-lē'ne,

2 Ăn'nas and Cā'ia-phas being the high priests, the word of God came unto John the son of Zăch-a-rī'as in the wilderness.

3 And he came into all the country about Jordan, preaching the baptism of repentance for the remission of sins:

4 As it is written in the book of the words of E-sā'ias the prophet, saying, The voice of one crying in the wilderness, Prepare ye the way of the Lord, make his paths straight.

5 Every valley shall be filled, and

every mountain and hill shall be brought low; and the crooked shall be made straight, and the rough ways *shall be* made smooth;

6 And all flesh shall see the salvation of God.

7 Then said he to the multitude that came forth to be baptized of him, O generation of vipers, who hath warned you to flee from the wrath to come?

8 Bring forth therefore fruits worthy of repentance, and begin not to say within yourselves, We have Abraham to *our* father: for I say unto you, That God is able of these stones to raise up children unto Abraham.

9 And now also the axe is laid unto the root of the trees: every tree therefore which bringeth not forth good fruit is hewn down, and cast into the fire.

10 And the people asked him, saying, What shall we do then?

11 He answereth and saith unto them, He that hath two coats, let him impart to him that hath none; and he that hath meat, let him do likewise.

12 Then came also publicans to be baptized, and said unto him, Master, what shall we do?

13 And he said unto them, Exact no more than that which is appointed you.

14 And the soldiers likewise demanded of him, saying, And what shall we do? And he said unto them, Do violence to no man, neither accuse *any* falsely; and be content with your wages.

15 ¶And as the people were in expectation, and all men mused in their hearts of John, whether he were the Christ, or not;

16 John answered, saying unto *them* all, I indeed baptize you with water; but one mightier than I cometh, the latchet of whose shoes I am not worthy to unloose: he shall baptize you with the Holy Ghost and with fire:

17 Whose fan *is* in his hand, and he will thoroughly purge his floor, and will gather the wheat into his garner; but the chaff he will burn with fire unquenchable.

18 And many other things in his exhortation preached he unto the people.

19 ¶But Herod the tetrarch, being reproved by him for He-ro'di-as his brother Philip's wife, and for all the evils which Herod had done,

20 Added yet this above all, that he shut up John in prison.

21 ¶Now when all the people were baptized, it came to pass, that Jesus also being baptized, and praying, the heaven was opened,

message was stern (vss. 7, 9) and demanded a change in one's life (vs. 8).

9. The axe is laid unto the root. The judgment of God was imminent upon these people and their nation. Only repentance could save.

10-14. Three groups responded to John's warnings: the people or multitude (vss. 10-11), the publicans or tax collectors (vss. 12-13), and the soldiers (vs. 14). John specified appropriate actions for each class of hearers.

15. The people were wondering whether John could be the Christ (Gr *Christos*), or Messiah (Heb *Mashiach*), repeatedly promised throughout the Old Testament (see Isa 9:6-7; 11:1-9; Amos 9:11; and Mic 4:1-3; 5:2). The Baptist clearly indicated here, and in John 1:19-29, that he was not their Messiah, but only His forerunner.

16-18. He shall baptize you with the Holy Ghost and with fire. This prediction of John, which is found as well in the other Gospels (Mt 3:11; Mk 1:8; Jn 1:33), is repeated by Christ in Acts 1:5 just before His ascension into heaven. Later this baptism in (or with) the Holy Spirit occurred on the Day of Pentecost, as the Holy Spirit took up permanent residence in the bodies of the believing disciples. The baptism with fire seems to refer to a future judgment as explained in verse 17, perhaps that which purifies believers, or ultimately judges those who refuse to believe.

19. Herod the tetrarch. This Herod was one of the sons of Herod the Great who sought to kill the baby Jesus in Matthew 2. John, who was not afraid to preach against divorce, had publicly reproached this Herod for marrying Herodias, the wife of his brother Philip.

20. He shut up John in prison. Very early during Christ's public ministry (Mt 4:12; Jn 3:24), John was cast into prison at Machaerus, a fortress on the east side of the Dead Sea. As a result, he was not privileged to see many of Christ's miracles and later had personal doubts regarding Christ (Lk 7:18-23), which were soon dispelled.

B. The Baptism of Christ. 3:21-22.

21. The baptism of Christ was totally unique. It did not signify what John's baptism of repentance did, because Jesus had no sin of which to repent. Jesus' explanation was that it might "fulfill all righteousness" (Mt 3:15). It no doubt marks the beginning of Christ's public ministry and probably pictures

22 And the Holy Ghost descended in a bodily shape like a dove upon him, and a voice came from heaven, which said, Thou art my beloved Son; in thee I am well pleased.

23 ¶And Jesus himself began to be about thirty years of age, being (as was supposed) the son of Joseph, which was *the son* of Hē′lī,

24 Which was *the son* of Măt′thăt, which was *the son* of Levi, which was *the son* of Mĕl′chī, which was *the son* of Jăn′na, which was *the son* of Joseph,

25 Which was *the son* of Măt-ta-thī′-as, which was *the son* of Amos, which was *the son* of Nā′um, which was *the son* of Ĕs′lī, which was *the son* of Năg′-ge,

26 Which was *the son* of Mā′ath, which was *the son* of Măt-ta-thī′as, which was *the son* of Sĕm′e-ī, which was *the son* of Joseph, which was *the son* of Juda,

27 Which was *the son* of Jō-ăn′na, which was *the son* of Rhē′sa, which was *the son* of Zō-rŏb′a-bel, which was *the son* of Sa-lā′thī-el, which was *the son* of Ne′rī,

28 Which was *the son* of Mĕl′chī, which was *the son* of Ăd′dī, which was *the son* of Cō′sam, which was *the son* of Ĕl-mō′dăm, which was *the son* of Er,

29 Which was *the son* of Jō′se, which was *the son* of Ĕ-lī-ē′zer, which was *the son* of Jō′rīm, which was *the son* of Măt′thăt, which was *the son* of Levi,

30 Which was *the son* of Sīmeon, which was *the son* of Juda, which was *the son* of Joseph, which was *the son* of Jō′nan, which was *the son* of E-lī′a-kīm,

31 Which was *the son* of Mĕ′le-a, which was *the son* of Mĕ′năn, which was *the son* of Măt′ta-tha, which was *the son* of Nathan, which was *the son* of David,

32 Which was *the son* of Jesse, which was *the son* of Ō′bed, which was *the son* of Bō′ŏz, which was *the son* of Săl′mon, which was *the son* of Nā-ăs′son,

33 Which was *the son* of A-mĭn′a-dăb, which was *the son* of Â′ram, which was *the son* of Ĕs-rŏm, which was *the son* of Phā′rĕs, which was *the son* of Juda,

34 Which was *the son* of Jacob, which was *the son* of Isaac, which was *the son* of Abraham, which was *the son* of Thâ′ra, which was *the son* of Nā′-chôr,

35 Which was *the son* of Sâ′ruch, which was *the son* of Rā′gau, which was *the son* of Phā′lec, which was *the son* of Hē′ber, which was *the son* of Sā′la,

36 Which was *the son* of Ca-ī′nan, which was *the son* of Är-phăx′ăd, which was *the son* of Sem, which was

for Christ a pledge of His future death, burial, and resurrection for the sin of the world.

22. Here, as in other places (the Great Commission, Mt 28:19; certain benedictions, II Cor 13:14; and other passages, I Cor 6:11; I Pet 1:2), all the persons of the Godhead are mentioned together, and distinguished from one another. On two other occasions, the transfiguration (Lk 9:35), and the Triumphal Entry into Jerusalem (Jn 12:28), God the Father similarly testified audibly regarding Christ.

C. The Genealogy of Christ. 3:23-38.

23. About thirty years of age. At the time Jesus began His public ministry He was thirty years old, as were the Levitical priests when they began their service (Num 4:47). **Being (as was supposed) the son of Joseph.** Luke is careful to explain Christ's unique parentage in light of His virgin birth. Jesus had no earthly father.

24-38. This genealogy differs from that in Matthew 1 in several ways. Matthew traces the line of descent beginning with Abraham and through the line of kings who directly followed David. This line alone could claim the Davidic throne. Luke, however, apparently gives Mary's blood-line, working backward from her father Heli, who would be Joseph's father by marriage. Mary is also seen to be a descendant of King David, but her line is followed all the way back to Adam. This firmly shows Christ to be completely human, yet a true descendant of David. Jesus' genealogy through Mary avoided the curse placed on David's kingly line following Zeconiah (Jer 22:30), yet allowed Him to claim the throne legitimately as a true human descendant of David, and as the adopted heir of the kingly line of Joseph.

the son of Nō′e, which was the son of Lā′mech,

37 Which was the son of Ma-thū′sa-la, which was the son of Ē′noch, which was the son of Jā′red, which was the son of Ma-lē′le-el, which was the son of Ca-ī′nan,

38 Which was the son of Enos, which was the son of Seth, which was the son of Adam, which was the son of God.

CHAPTER 4

AND Jesus being full of the Holy Ghost returned from Jordan, and was led by the Spirit into the wilderness,

2 Being forty days tempted of the devil. And in those days he did eat nothing: and when they were ended, he afterward hungered.

3 And the devil said unto him, If thou be the Son of God, command this stone that it be made bread.

4 And Jesus answered him, saying, It is written, That man shall not live by bread alone, but by every word of God.

5 And the devil, taking him up into an high mountain, shewed unto him all the kingdoms of the world in a moment of time.

6 And the devil said unto him, All this power will I give thee, and the glory of them: for that is delivered unto me; and to whomsoever I will I give it.

7 If thou therefore wilt worship me, all shall be thine.

8 And Jesus answered and said unto him, Get thee behind me, Satan: for it is written, Thou shalt worship the Lord thy God, and him only shalt thou serve.

9 And he brought him to Jerusalem, and set him on a pinnacle of the temple, and said unto him, If thou be the Son of God, cast thyself down from hence:

10 For it is written, He shall give his angels charge over thee, to keep thee:

11 And in their hands they shall bear thee up, lest at any time thou dash thy foot against a stone.

12 And Jesus answering said unto him, It is said, Thou shalt not tempt the Lord thy God.

13 And when the devil had ended all the temptation, he departed from him for a season.

14 ¶And Jesus returned in the power of the Spirit into Galilee: and there went out a fame of him through all the region round about.

15 And he taught in their synagogues, being glorified of all.

16 ¶And he came to Nazareth, where he had been brought up: and, as his custom was, he went into the synagogue on the sabbath day, and stood up for to read.

D. The Temptation of Christ. 4:1-13.

The temptation of Christ was both a testing and a tempting. From the divine point of view, the Holy Spirit arranged a testing to show that Jesus qualified as free from sin. If He were not free from personal sin, He could not bear our sins. For Satan, it was a temptation to see if he could make Christ fall as had the first Adam. The temptation was real, yet it was impossible for God the Son to sin.

4:1. The wilderness. A barren region between the hill country and the Jordan Valley. The traditional site is northwest of Jericho.

2. Forty days. Jesus fasted during this entire period, in part as a spiritual preparation for the ministry in which He was about to engage.

3-8. If thou be the Son of God. Satan approached Christ assuming that He was God and could exercise divine power. However, for Christ to exercise His divine prerogatives at this point would be to step out of the pathway leading to the cross. Jesus met each temptation as a man. He quoted Scripture each time (Deut 8:3; 6:16; 10:20).

9-12. Pinnacle of the temple. The pinnacle is normally taken to mean the place where the southern and eastern walls of the city and temple area met. This place even today stands several hundred feet above the depths of the Kidron Valley below it.

13. For a season. These words, recorded only by Luke, indicate the fact that Satan was to similarly attack Christ again and again. Matthew and Mark record the ministry of angels to Christ at this point.

IV. THE PREACHING OF THE SON IN GALILEE. 4:14-9:50.

A. The Preaching that Claimed Messiahship. 4:14-44.

14. Jesus returned in the power of the Spirit. The Lord Jesus Christ was constantly and consciously yielded to the Holy Spirit (cf. Jn 3:34).

15. Taught in their synagogues. Practically every Jewish village had a synagogue. They were used to instruct in the Old Testament. When Jesus taught, as in the following account, He pointed to the fulfillment of the messianic Scriptures in Himself.

16. Nazareth. Nazareth is situated at the southern edge of the hill country of Galilee overlooking the beautiful Jezreel Valley. Jesus had grown up here, and everyone knew Him as the carpenter's son. **As his custom was, he went into the synagogue on the sabbath day.** Jesus set an example of regular

17 And there was delivered unto him the book of the prophet E-ŝā′ias. And when he had opened the book, he found the place where it was written,

18 The Spirit of the Lord *is* upon me, because he hath anointed me to preach the gospel to the poor; he hath sent me to heal the brokenhearted, to preach deliverance to the captives, and recovering of sight to the blind, to set at liberty them that are bruised,

19 To preach the acceptable year of the Lord.

20 And he closed the book, and he gave *it* again to the minister, and sat down. And the eyes of all them that were in the synagogue were fastened on him.

21 And he began to say unto them, This day is this scripture fulfilled in your ears.

22 And all bare him witness, and wondered at the gracious words which proceeded out of his mouth. And they said, Is not this Joseph's son?

23 And he said unto them, Ye will surely say unto me this proverb, Physician, heal thyself: whatsoever we have heard done in Ca-per′na-um, do also here in thy country.

24 And he said, Verily I say unto you, No prophet is accepted in his own country.

25 But I tell you of a truth, many widows were in Israel in the days of E-lī′as, when the heaven was shut up three years and six months, when great famine was throughout all the land;

26 But unto none of them was E-lī′as sent, save unto Sar-ĕp′ta, *a city* of Sī′don, unto a woman *that was* a widow.

27 And many lepers were in Israel in the time of Ĕl-i-sē′us the prophet; and none of them was cleansed, saving Nā′a-man the Syrian.

28 And all they in the synagogue, when they heard these things, were filled with wrath,

29 And rose up, and thrust him out of the city, and led him unto the brow of the hill whereon their city was built, that they might cast him down headlong.

30 But he passing through the midst of them went his way,

31 And came down to Ca-per′na-um, a city of Galilee, and taught them on the sabbath days.

32 And they were astonished at his doctrine: for his word was with power.

33 ¶And in the synagogue there was a man, which had a spirit of an unclean devil, and cried out with a loud voice,

attendance at the public worship services. They met on the Sabbath (Saturday), because they were still bound under the dispensation of law. After the resurrection and ascension of Christ, Christians began meeting on the first day of the week (Sunday, cf. Acts 20:7; I Cor 16:2).

17-19. Jesus participated in the service that day by opening the scroll (Gr *biblion*) and reading one and a half verses (Isa 61:1-2a). He read a portion that dealt directly with the earthly ministry of the Messiah (such as preaching and healing) and stopped just before the passage went on to describe His coming judgment in the end times.

20-22. The application was short and to the point, **This day is this scripture fulfilled in your ears.** This was a direct and full claim to be the Messiah.

23-30. Unfortunately, the people could not accept the fantastic claim of this thirty-year-old carpenter's son. Instead of believing Christ, and receiving the long-promised earthly kingdom He proclaimed, they were indignant and sought to cast Jesus over the side of the mountain into the valley far below. However, God supernaturally prevented them from carrying out their wicked intentions and Jesus went away unhindered.

31. Came down to Capernaum, a city of Galilee. Since the elevation of Capernaum is six hundred fifty feet below sea level, Jesus had to go down from the higher elevations of southern Galilee. Christ taught several Sabbaths in their synagogue on the shore of the Sea of Galilee.

32. And they were astonished at his doctrine: for his word was with power. This statement characterizes all of Christ's teaching ministry (cf. Mt 7:28-29). Such words, supported by miraculous works, should have produced faith on the part of all. Most religious leaders, however, rejected His claims, and most common people followed Him for the wrong reasons.

33-37. Demon-possession was prevalent in Christ's time, and on numerous occasions Christ cast out these fallen angels. In the synagogue at Nazareth one such demon spoke to Christ from out

34 Saying, Let *us* alone; what have we to do with thee, *thou* Jesus of Nazareth? art thou come to destroy us? I know thee who thou art; the Holy One of God.

35 And Jesus rebuked him, saying, Hold thy peace, and come out of him. And when the devil had thrown him in the midst, he came out of him, and hurt him not.

36 And they were all amazed, and spake among themselves, saying, What a word *is* this! for with authority and power he commandeth the unclean spirits, and they come out.

37 And the fame of him went out into every place of the country round about.

38 ¶And he arose out of the synagogue, and entered into Simon's house. And Simon's wife's mother was taken with a great fever; and they besought him for her.

39 And he stood over her, and rebuked the fever; and it left her: and immediately she arose and ministered unto them.

40 ¶Now when the sun was setting, all they that had any sick with divers diseases brought them unto him; and he laid his hands on every one of them, and healed them.

41 And devils also came out of many, crying out, and saying, Thou art Christ the Son of God. And he rebuking *them* suffered them not to speak: for they knew that he was Christ.

42 And when it was day, he departed and went into a desert place: and the people sought him, and came unto him, and stayed him, that he should not depart from them.

43 And he said unto them, I must preach the kingdom of God to other cities also: for therefore am I sent.

44 And he preached in the synagogues of Galilee.

CHAPTER 5

AND it came to pass, that, as the people pressed upon him to hear the word of God, he stood by the lake of Gĕn-nĕs'-a-ret.

2 And saw two ships standing by the lake: but the fishermen were gone out of them, and were washing *their* nets.

3 And he entered into one of the ships, which was Simon's, and prayed him that he would thrust out a little from the land. And he sat down, and taught the people out of the ship.

4 Now when he had left speaking, he said unto Simon, Launch out into the deep, and let down your nets for a draught.

5 And Simon answering said unto him, Master, we have toiled all the night, and have taken nothing: nevertheless at thy word I will let down the net.

6 And when they had this done, they inclosed a great multitude of fishes: and their net brake.

7 And they beckoned unto *their* partners, which were in the other ship, that they should come and help them. And

of his human captive's body. Jesus rebuked him as an improper source for proclaiming who Christ was. Jesus' fame was spreading rapidly in every direction.

38-41. That same Sabbath day, Jesus instantly and completely healed Peter's mother-in-law (cf. I Cor 9:5) of a fever. Instead of being left weak, she immediately arose and waited on her visitors. After sundown, hundreds of sick and diseased assembled at Peter's door (cf. Mk 1:33), and Christ healed them all. None were sent away unhelped, and faith is not spoken of as a condition for being healed. These miracles performed by Christ, and later by the apostles too, were for the purpose of authenticating their ministry as from God. The Bible neither offers nor requires such a ministry for today.

42-44. Went into a desert place. Mark 1:35 records the fact that Jesus went early by Himself, and for the purpose of praying. Even as constantly busy as He was in ministry, He knew the necessity of a time alone with the Father at the beginning of each day. Let us not ignore His example.

B. The Miracles that Supported His Messiahship. 5:1-39.

5:1. Lake of Gennesaret. This is the Sea of Galilee. Jesus referred to it as a "sea" but here Luke calls it a lake. It is six hundred eighty-five feet below sea level, about seven miles wide, and twelve miles long. In Christ's day, it was abundant with fish.

2-3. From Peter's boat, Jesus taught the multitudes who stood on the shore. Jesus had met Peter previously (see Jn 1:41-42) and he had followed Christ in an intermittent fashion for some time. After this experience, however (cf. Mt 4:18-19), **they forsook all, and followed him** (vs. 11).

4-9. The miracle was that Christ commanded Peter to let down his nets in the deep to take a catch of fish. This was against the common practice of fishing at night, and near the shore. However, Peter obeyed and let down the nets. The result was a magnificent catch that pointed to Christ's deity and exposed Peter's sinfulness in contrast.

they came, and filled both the ships, so that they began to sink.

8 When Simon Peter saw *it*, he fell down at Jesus' knees, saying, Depart from me; for I am a sinful man, O Lord.

9 For he was astonished, and all that were with him, at the draught of the fishes which they had taken:

10 And so *was* also James, and John, the sons of Zĕb'e-dee, which were partners with Simon. And Jesus said unto Simon, Fear not; from henceforth thou shalt catch men.

11 And when they had brought their ships to land, they forsook all, and followed him.

12 ¶And it came to pass, when he was in a certain city, behold a man full of leprosy: who seeing Jesus fell on *his* face, and besought him, saying, Lord, if thou wilt, thou canst make me clean.

13 And he put forth *his* hand, and touched him, saying, I will: be thou clean. And immediately the leprosy departed from him.

14 And he charged him to tell no man: but go, and shew thyself to the priest, and offer for thy cleansing, according as Moses commanded, for a testimony unto them.

15 But so much the more went there a fame abroad of him: and great multitudes came together to hear, and to be healed by him of their infirmities.

16 And he withdrew himself into the wilderness, and prayed.

17 ¶And it came to pass on a certain day, as he was teaching, that there were Pharisees and doctors of the law sitting by, which were come out of every town of Galilee, and Judæa, and Jerusalem: and the power of the Lord was *present* to heal them.

18 ¶And, behold, men brought in a bed a man which was taken with a palsy: and they sought *means* to bring him in, and to lay *him* before him.

19 And when they could not find by what *way* they might bring him in because of the multitude, they went upon the housetop, and let him down through the tiling with *his* couch into the midst before Jesus.

20 And when he saw their faith, he said unto him, Man, thy sins are forgiven thee.

21 And the scribes and the Pharisees began to reason, saying, Who is this which speaketh blasphemies? Who can forgive sins, but God alone?

22 But when Jesus perceived their thoughts, he answering said unto them, What reason ye in your hearts?

23 Whether is easier, to say, Thy sins be forgiven thee; or to say, Rise up and walk?

10-11. Leaving the vast catch was not a sinful waste of food, as some have supposed, because Zebedee and his servants would have been perfectly able to care for the haul. Jesus promised Peter and Andrew, and James and John that they would catch men from that time forward. The promise was certainly fulfilled.

12-13. A man full of leprosy. Leprosy is a dreadful disease that eats away the fingers, toes, ears, nose, etc. This man had an acute case, but knew Jesus could heal him if He only desired to. Jesus did, and instantly the leprosy was completely gone, not just arrested.

14. Tell no man. Jesus gave the command on several occasions, and it may seem strange to modern readers. The answer as to why Jesus said these words seems to have several aspects. (1) He was first to go to the Temple to show himself to the priest as the Law required (Lev 14). If the priest heard before his arrival that Jesus had healed him, the case might be prejudiced against him. (2) Jesus did not want to be known or sought merely as a miracle worker. His primary work was to be spiritual rather than physical.

15. Christ's fame continued to spread, nonetheless.

16. He withdrew . . . and prayed. Here is but another example Luke gives of Jesus' reliance on prayer. If Christ needed to pray much, how much greater must be the necessity with us.

17-19. Jesus' healing of the palsied man (Mk 2:1) is the backdrop for the great controversy that began to develop between Christ and the Jewish religious leaders. Luke noted (vs. 17) that some of these leaders had come from as far away as Jerusalem, some eighty miles distant.

The crowd was so great around the house where Jesus was that the palsied man had to be lowered through a makeshift hole torn in the roof by his four determined friends.

20. He saw their faith. The palsied man is probably to be included as having faith that Christ would heal him, as he was at least a consenting party to the action of his four friends. Jesus loved to see men act in faith, and thus responded: **Man, thy sins are forgiven thee.** Jesus' words were calculated to draw a particular reaction from the unbelieving Jews present.

21-24. Jesus was silently accused of blasphemy. The men rightly reasoned that only God could forgive sins. But they failed to consider the possibility that Jesus was indeed God! The omniscient Christ read their very thoughts. He pointed out that it would be easy for someone to say that another's sin was forgiven. No one could prove any differently. But the harder thing would be to heal a hopeless case of bedridden palsy. Jesus then proved He had the authority to speak the one thing by doing the other. He healed the man.

24 But that ye may know that the Son of man hath power upon earth to forgive sins, (he said unto the sick of the palsy,) I say unto thee, Arise, and take up thy couch, and go into thine house.

25 And immediately he rose up before them, and took up that whereon he lay, and departed to his own house, glorifying God.

26 And they were all amazed, and they glorified God, and were filled with fear, saying, We have seen strange things to day.

27 ¶And after these things he went forth, and saw a publican, named Levi, sitting at the receipt of custom: and he said unto him, Follow me.

28 And he left all, rose up, and followed him.

29 And Levi made him a great feast in his own house: and there was a great company of publicans and of others that sat down with them.

30 But their scribes and Pharisees murmured against his disciples, saying, Why do ye eat and drink with publicans and sinners?

31 And Jesus answering said unto them, They that are whole need not a physician; but they that are sick.

32 I came not to call the righteous, but sinners to repentance.

33 ¶And they said unto him, Why do the disciples of John fast often, and make prayers, and likewise *the disciples* of the Pharisees; but thine eat and drink?

34 And he said unto them, Can ye make the children of the bridechamber fast, while the bridegroom is with them?

35 But the days will come, when the bridegroom shall be taken away from them, and then shall they fast in those days.

36 ¶And he spake also a parable unto them; No man putteth a piece of a new garment upon an old; if otherwise, then both the new maketh a rent, and the piece that was *taken* out of the new agreeth not with the old.

37 And no man putteth new wine into old bottles; else the new wine will burst the bottles, and be spilled, and the bottles shall perish.

38 But new wine must be put into new bottles; and both are preserved.

39 No man also having drunk old *wine* straightway desireth new: for he saith, The old is better.

CHAPTER 6

AND it came to pass on the second sabbath after the first, that he went through the corn fields; and his disciples plucked the ears of corn, and did eat, rubbing *them* in *their* hands.

25-26. The reaction of the multitude was that the charge of blasphemy had been disproved. Jesus was vindicated; God was glorified.

27. **A publican, named Levi.** In Matthew and Mark, Levi is referred to as Matthew. Levi was a tax collector who worked for the Roman government, and was no doubt well off financially.

28. Upon Jesus' call of **Follow me,** Levi **left all.** He no doubt lost his job as a result. His commitment to Christ was complete and final. Levi was the writer of our first Gospel, Matthew.

29-31. Later, Levi's efforts to win his fellow tax collectors to faith in Christ was an occasion for the Pharisees to criticize Jesus and His disciples for dining with such sinners. Jesus replied that only those who are sick realize their need of a physician. The Pharisees were in need, but refused to acknowledge it.

32-35. Jesus indicated His own departure from the world in verse 32, probably for the first time. His death and resurrection had been personally foretold earlier (Jn 2:19-22). Jesus also said that fasting would become a practice of His disciples after His departure. This was fulfilled in New Testament church practice in Acts 10:30; 13:2; 14:23; and I Corinthians 7:5. The purpose for fasting is usually that one may give himself more fully to prayer and seeking the mind of the Lord in making special decisions. There may be some physical benefits to occasional fasting as well. New Testament fasting is always voluntary, never mandatory.

36-39. The two parables in this short paragraph relate the same message, only in different figures. New Testament truth cannot be bound up in the structure of the Old Testament law.

C. The Choice of the Twelve. 6:1-49.

6:1. **The second sabbath after the first.** This unique expression, which does not occur in some manuscripts, is either a manuscript error or a reference to the second of the seven Sabbaths between Passover and Pentecost (Lev 23:15-16). If it is the latter, then it helps to fully establish Christ's ministry as being about three and a half years in duration. This is easily marked by the three different Passovers mentioned in John's gospel (2:13; 6:4; and 12:1). Luke 6:1 would then refer to an additional Passover between John 2:13 and 6:4, thus accounting for three years of ministry between the four Passovers.

Plucked . . . ears of corn, and did eat. Jesus and His dis-

2 And certain of the Pharisees said unto them, Why do ye that which is not lawful to do on the sabbath days?

3 And Jesus answering them said, Have ye not read so much as this, what David did, when himself was an hungred, and they which were with him;

4 How he went into the house of God, and did take and eat the shewbread, and gave also to them that were with him; which it is not lawful to eat but for the priests alone?

5 And he said unto them, That the Son of man is Lord also of the sabbath.

6 ¶And it came to pass also on another sabbath, that he entered into the synagogue and taught: and there was a man whose right hand was withered.

7 And the scribes and Pharisees watched him, whether he would heal on the sabbath day; that they might find an accusation against him.

8 But he knew their thoughts, and said to the man which had the withered hand, Rise up, and stand forth in the midst. And he arose and stood forth.

9 Then said Jesus unto them, I will ask you one thing; Is it lawful on the sabbath days to do good, or to do evil? to save life, or to destroy it?

10 And looking round about upon them all, he said unto the man, Stretch forth thy hand. And he did so: and his hand was restored whole as the other.

11 And they were filled with madness; and communed one with another what they might do to Jesus.

12 ¶And it came to pass in those days, that he went out into a mountain to pray, and continued all night in prayer to God.

13 And when it was day, he called unto him his disciples: and of them he chose twelve, whom also he named apostles;

14 Simon, (whom he also named Peter,) and Andrew his brother, James and John, Philip and Bartholomew,

15 Matthew and Thomas, James the son of Ăl-phæ'us, and Simon called Zē-lō'tes,

16 And Judas the brother of James, and Judas Iscariot, which also was the traitor.

17 And he came down with them, and stood in the plain, and the company of his disciples, and a great multitude of people out of all Judæa and Jerusalem, and from the sea coast of Tyre and Sī'don, which came to hear him, and to be healed of their diseases;

18 And they that were vexed with unclean spirits: and they were healed.

19 And the whole multitude sought to touch him: for there went virtue out of him, and healed them all.

ciples picked some grain (probably wheat) for immediate eating as they walked along.

2. The Pharisees considered this to be harvesting and, therefore, a violation of the Sabbath. Thus, the great Sabbath controversy was continued by Christ's enemies who sought to destroy Him.

3-5. The Son of man is Lord also of the sabbath. After countering with the Old Testament example of David who once ate the sacred shewbread, Christ announced that He was Lord or supreme over the Sabbath. For one to claim personal sovereignty over an institution of God was practically to claim deity.

6-8. On another Sabbath, the Pharisees watched Christ as He was teaching in a synagogue to see if He would heal a man's withered right hand. This was clearly a test case. The scribes and Pharisees were hoping Christ would violate the law, as they saw it, in order to accuse Him. A man could be put to death for violating the Sabbath.

9-10. Jesus turned the tables by asking the rhetorical question of whether it was permitted to do good on the Sabbath. Since no one would deny this, Jesus quickly restored the man's hand.

11. The envy of the Pharisees, however, only increased as they sought means to put Jesus out of the way (cf. Jn 11:53).

12. The selection of the Twelve was made after Jesus spent a night in prayer. Much prayer is often needed before such important decisions.

13. Disciples: and of them he chose twelve, whom also he named apostles. From the larger company of learners (disciples), Jesus selected just twelve, no doubt a number with special significance (see Lk 22:30). This number was suited for group instruction and "discipling." Mark 3:14 gives the purposes of this selection as that they might be with Him, and that He might send them out to preach. These Twelve were to be special witnesses. The fact that they are called "apostles" (Gr apostellō) indicates their new position as "sent ones."

14-16. Besides this passage there are several other lists of the twelve apostles (Mt 10:2-4; Mk 3:16-19; Acts 1:13). The names sometimes vary because Bartholomew and Nathanael are the same person, Matthew is also named Levi, and Lebbaeus was sometimes called Judas (not Iscariot) and also had the last name of Thaddaeus.

17-19. Jesus' healing ministry was extensive, both in the number of people healed, the places from which they came, and the maladies of which they were relieved. Unlike modern-day healers, Jesus healed all who came to Him.

20 ¶And he lifted up his eyes on his disciples, and said, Blessed *be ye* poor: for yours is the kingdom of God.

20. He lifted up his eyes on his disciples, and said. This passage, which follows the selection of the twelve apostles, records some of their formal training from the lips of the Lord. Much of this sermon on **the plain** (vs. 17) parallels the Sermon on the Mount (Mt 5-7), but there are differences as well as similarities. Jesus no doubt spoke similar messages on various occasions, even as preachers do today.

Blessed be ye poor: for yours is the kingdom of God. Certainly no one gets to heaven simply because he is financially destitute. Matthew 5:3 adds poor "in spirit." One must realize his spiritual poverty before he will ever trust God's provision for his need, but material poverty sometimes teaches one to depend on God entirely. The phrase **kingdom of God** is here equivalent to Matthew's "kingdom of heaven."

21 Blessed *are ye* that hunger now: for ye shall be filled. Blessed *are ye* that weep now: for ye shall laugh.

21. Hunger . . . shall be filled. Certainly not a prediction of more ample food supplies, this speaks of God meeting the spiritual needs of those who are hungry for what He has to offer.

22 Blessed are ye, when men shall hate you, and when they shall separate you *from their company*, and shall reproach *you*, and cast out your name as evil, for the Son of man's sake.
23 Rejoice ye in that day, and leap for joy: for, behold, your reward *is* great in heaven: for in the like manner did their fathers unto the prophets.
24 But woe unto you that are rich! for ye have received your consolation.

22-23. Blessed are ye, when men shall hate you . . . for the Son of man's sake. There is no blessing for being hated because one is foolish, lazy, untrustworthy, inept, or unfaithful. One might deserve such treatment in these cases. But when one is hated simply because he is a good Christian, living a life of testimony for Christ, then he receives the blessing promised (cf. Jn 15:18-19; I Pet 2:19-20; I Jn 3:13).

24. Woe unto you that are rich. Money is not evil, but the love of money is (I Tim 6:10). Fortune sometimes causes one to live independently of God, and to believe in his own self-sufficiency. Wealth should be acknowledged as from God, and used in a sacred stewardship.

25 Woe unto you that are full! for ye shall hunger. Woe unto you that laugh now! for ye shall mourn and weep.
26 Woe unto you, when all men shall speak well of you! for so did their fathers to the false prophets.
27 ¶But I say unto you which hear, Love your enemies, do good to them which hate you,
28 Bless them that curse you, and pray for them which despitefully use you.
29 And unto him that smiteth thee on the *one* cheek offer also the other; and him that taketh away thy cloak forbid not *to take thy* coat also.
30 Give to every man that asketh of thee; and of him that taketh away thy goods ask *them* not again.
31 And as ye would that men should do to you, do ye also to them likewise.

25-30. Here Jesus is seeking to inculcate a godly spirit, which is exactly the opposite of how we normally react to situations around us. The point is that a man must be a Christian before he can exhibit Christian behavior.

31. This verse contains what is commonly called "The Golden Rule." Some have claimed that Buddha, Confucius, and even some rabbinical writings, all prior to Christ, contain the same teachings. This is only partly true, because their statements occur only in the negative: "Don't do to someone else what you wouldn't want him to do to you." No positive action is contemplated. Jesus, however, requires His believers to initiate helpful actions toward others.

32 For if ye love them which love you, what thank have ye? for sinners also love those that love them.
33 And if ye do good to them which do good to you, what thank have ye? for sinners also do even the same.
34 And if ye lend *to them* of whom ye hope to receive, what thank have ye? for sinners also lend to sinners, to receive as much again.
35 But love ye your enemies, and do good, and lend, hoping for nothing again; and your reward shall be great, and ye shall be the children of the

32-35. Jesus told His disciples that their actions must go far beyond even what is considered good morality by the world. The believer's standards far surpass those of the "sinner."

Highest: for he is kind unto the unthankful and *to* the evil.

36 Be ye therefore merciful, as your Father also is merciful.

37 Judge not, and ye shall not be judged: condemn not, and ye shall not be condemned: forgive, and ye shall be forgiven:

38 Give, and it shall be given unto you; good measure, pressed down, and shaken together, and running over, shall men give into your bosom. For with the same measure that ye mete withal it shall be measured to you again.

39 And he spake a parable unto them, Can the blind lead the blind? shall they not both fall into the ditch?

40 The disciple is not above his master: but every one that is perfect shall be as his master.

41 And why beholdest thou the mote that is in thy brother's eye, but perceivest not the beam that is in thine own eye?

42 Either how canst thou say to thy brother, Brother, let me pull out the mote that is in thine eye, when thou thyself beholdest not the beam that is in thine own eye? Thou hypocrite, cast out first the beam out of thine own eye, and then shalt thou see clearly to pull out the mote that is in thy brother's eye.

43 For a good tree bringeth not forth corrupt fruit; neither doth a corrupt tree bring forth good fruit.

44 For every tree is known by his own fruit. For of thorns men do not gather figs, nor of a bramble bush gather they grapes.

45 A good man out of the good treasure of his heart bringeth forth that which is good; and an evil man out of the evil treasure of his heart bringeth forth that which is evil: for of the abundance of the heart his mouth speaketh.

46 ¶And why call ye me, Lord, Lord, and do not the things which I say?

47 Whosoever cometh to me, and heareth my sayings, and doeth them, I will shew you to whom he is like:

48 He is like a man which built an house, and digged deep, and laid the foundation on a rock: and when the flood arose, the stream beat vehemently upon that house, and could not shake it: for it was founded upon a rock.

49 But he that heareth, and doeth not, is like a man that without a foundation

36. The progression of instruction has moved from an attitude of "love your enemies" (vs. 27), to the positive general action of "The Golden Rule" (vs. 31), and then to the very specific activity of leading (vs. 35). Now Jesus says to be **merciful as your Father also is merciful.** The fatherhood of God comes only by being born into His family by the new birth (Jn 3:3-7). Christ said that prior to that experience, men are naturally the children of the devil (Jn 8:44).

37. Judge not, and ye shall not be judged. This statement, and its parallel in Matthew 7:1, is often misconstrued. It means not to act as God in passing some final judgment on an individual. Because we cannot fully see motives, we often judge falsely. But we are to be discerning. We must be able to identify wolves in sheep's clothing in order to warn others and to flee ourselves. As Jesus suggests in verses 43-44, the fruit one produces is an indication of what he is like.

38-40. Give, and it shall be given unto you. Our Lord had a lot to say about money. This is because money is so important, touches every life, and is so liable to misuse. In fact, both Solomon and Jesus gave many warnings regarding wine, women and wealth. Here the principle is that we cannot outgive the Lord. Naturally, all our substance belongs to God. But as we give it back to Him, He is always more generous in returning it to us again. Every cheerful giver knows both the joy of giving and the joy of God's blessed provision. God entrusts more wealth to those who He knows will properly dispense it.

41-42. The mote that is in thy brother's eye. It is only human nature to see our brother's faults while overlooking our own. But human nature is sinful. Jesus notes that if one first takes care of his own faults, he may be able to help his brother. This correct order must be followed.

43-45. It is an unchangeable law that outward fruit resembles and reproduces the inward qualities of the tree. So with man, the mouth simply echoes the thoughts of the heart. One's speech is a good barometer of his spiritual condition. Each person must examine his own speech to see if it exhibits anger, bitterness, irritation, and gossip, or if it reflects cheerfulness, sympathy, and love.

46. Why call ye me, Lord . . . ? If one calls Christ Lord, then he had better not say what Peter said in Acts 10:14, "Not so, Lord." For he who acknowledges Christ as Lord, the only correct response is as Paul humbly said, "Lord, what wilt thou have me do?" (Acts 9:6). Jesus said, "If ye love me, keep my commandments" (Jn 14:15). Nothing less will do.

47-49. The meaning of this short parabolic saying about the house built on the rock and that built on the sand concerns the foundation of one's life. Only those who actually do Christ's will have the sure foundation of Christ beneath them. All other ways, routes, and efforts will end in destruction.

built an house upon the earth; against which the stream did beat vehemently, and immediately it fell; and the ruin of that house was great.

CHAPTER 7

NOW when he had ended all his sayings in the audience of the people, he entered into Ca-per'na-um.

2 And a certain centurion's servant, who was dear unto him, was sick, and ready to die.

3 And when he heard of Jesus, he sent unto him the elders of the Jews, beseeching him that he would come and heal his servant.

4 And when they came to Jesus, they besought him instantly, saying, That he was worthy for whom he should do this:

5 For he loveth our nation, and he hath built us a synagogue.

6 Then Jesus went with them. And when he was now not far from the house, the centurion sent friends to him, saying unto him, Lord. trouble not thyself: for I am not worthy that thou shouldest enter under my roof:

7 Wherefore neither thought I myself worthy to come unto thee: but say in a word, and my servant shall be healed.

8 For I also am a man set under authority, having under me soldiers, and I say unto one, Go, and he goeth; and to another, Come, and he cometh; and to my servant, Do this, and he doeth it.

9 When Jesus heard these things, he marvelled at him, and turned him about, and said unto the people that followed him, I say unto you, I have not found so great faith, no, not in Israel.

10 And they that were sent, returning to the house, found the servant whole that had been sick.

11 ¶And it came to pass the day after, that he went into a city called Nain; and many of his disciples went with him, and much people.

12 Now when he came nigh to the gate of the city, behold, there was a dead man carried out, the only son of his mother, and she was a widow: and much people of the city was with her.

13 And when the Lord saw her, he had compassion on her, and said unto her, Weep not.

14 And he came and touched the bier: and they that bare him stood still. And

D. More Miracles and Parables in Galilee. 7:1-8:56.

7:1. He entered into Capernaum. It seems that Capernaum, on the northwest shore of Galilee, was Jesus' primary resting place during His great Galilean ministry. Matthew 9:1 calls it "his own city." Since Jesus had no home of His own (Lk 9:58), He must have stayed with one or more of the disciples who lived there (i.e., Peter's wife's family or Matthew).

2. Centurion's servant, who was dear unto him, was sick, and ready to die. A centurion was a Roman soldier in command of at least one hundred men. There are approximately ten centurions mentioned in the New Testament, and each is presented in a good light. This centurion had numerous noble qualities.

3. He heard of Jesus. This no doubt refers to the tremendous healing miracles Jesus had done. **He sent unto him the elders of the Jews.** This centurion had great influence with the Jews, which was unusual.

4-5. These elders give two reasons as to why this Gentile was worthy of having Jesus come to heal his servant: (1) he loved the Jews though not many Romans did; and (2) he built the Jewish synagogue in Capernaum. The present synagogue ruins in Capernaum date from the fourth century A.D., and are clearly Roman in architecture, but with the Star of David, vine and branches, and other Jewish emblems quite evident. Perhaps this earlier synagogue was styled along the same lines.

6-10. Naturally, Jesus could effect healings even from a distance (Jn 4:46-53), but He went toward the centurion's house. When He had nearly arrived, the centurion sent word that he knew Jesus could simply give the command and the servant would be healed. This was said because he felt unworthy to have Jesus come under his roof. Jesus marveled at such a display of faith, and complied with the centurion's humble request.

11. The very next day Jesus journeyed about twenty-five miles into the Jezreel Valley to the city of Nain. It was a good-sized town in Christ's day. **Many . . . disciples** and **much people** were present. Luke records this event out of concern for stories about women, as well as the fact that this is one of only three recorded times Jesus raised someone from the dead. It had been approximately eight hundred years since Israel had seen someone raised from the dead. The last case was wrought by Elisha the prophet (II Kgs 4:14-37).

12. There was no doubt as to this man's condition. He was plainly dead, the funeral was over, the funeral procession was en route to the place of burial. Luke alone records that the dead man was the only son of his widowed mother.

13-15. Showing human tenderness and compassion toward the weeping mother, Jesus touched the open casket and said: **Young man, I say unto thee, Arise.** The object of recording that the young man spoke after arising was to give evidence that he was really alive.

he said, Young man, I say unto thee, Arise.

15 And he that was dead sat up, and began to speak. And he delivered him to his mother.

16 And there came a fear on all: and they glorified God, saying, That a great prophet is risen up among us; and, That God hath visited his people.

17 And this rumour of him went forth throughout all Judæa, and throughout all the region round about.

18 ¶And the disciples of John shewed him of all these things.

19 And John calling *unto him* two of his disciples sent *them* to Jesus, saying, Art thou he that should come? or look we for another?

20 When the men were come unto him, they said, John Baptist hath sent us unto thee, saying, Art thou he that should come? or look we for another?

21 And in that same hour he cured many of *their* infirmities and plagues, and of evil spirits; and unto many *that were* blind he gave sight.

22 Then Jesus answering said unto them, Go your way, and tell John what things ye have seen and heard; how that the blind see, the lame walk, the lepers are cleansed, the deaf hear, the dead are raised, to the poor the gospel is preached.

23 And blessed is *he*, whosoever shall not be offended in me.

24 ¶And when the messengers of John were departed, he began to speak unto the people concerning John, What went ye out into the wilderness for to see? A reed shaken with the wind?

25 But what went ye out for to see? A man clothed in soft raiment? Behold, they which are gorgeously apparelled, and live delicately, are in kings' courts.

26 But what went ye out for to see? A prophet? Yea, I say unto you, and much more than a prophet.

27 This is *he*, of whom it is written, Behold, I send my messenger before thy face, which shall prepare thy way before thee.

28 For I say unto you, Among those that are born of women there is not a greater prophet than John the Baptist: but he that is least in the kingdom of God is greater than he.

29 And all the people that heard *him*, and the publicans, justified God, being baptized with the baptism of John.

30 But the Pharisees and lawyers rejected the counsel of God against themselves, being not baptized of him.

31 ¶And the Lord said, Whereunto then shall I liken the men of this generation? and to what are they like?

32 They are like unto children sitting in the marketplace, and calling one to another, and saying, We have piped unto you, and ye have not danced; we have mourned to you, and ye have not wept.

33 For John the Baptist came neither eating bread nor drinking wine; and ye say, He hath a devil.

16-17. The people responded correctly by noting that Jesus was a great prophet, and the report spread throughout the surrounding region and even south into Judaea.

18-26. John the Baptist, the Old Testament's predicted forerunner of the Messiah, was cast into prison shortly after he introduced Christ to Israel. Since the kingdom had not materialized in the interim, he began to entertain doubts regarding Christ's mission (vs. 20). That very hour, Jesus performed miracles predicted of the Messiah in Isaiah 61:1-2, and told John's disciples to convey that information back to John, which must have reassured the great prophet.

27. Jesus declared that John the Baptist was more than just an ordinary prophet. He stood last in the long line of prophets and actually heralded the personal presence of the Messiah, as predicted in Malachi 3:1.

28. Though John the Baptist was the greatest of the prophets, positionally he was still in the Old Testament period, and was martyred several years before the new dispensation of grace began after Calvary. He announced the coming kingdom, but never lived to see it. Thus, even the least of those who live on into the kingdom age will be in a far more advanced period of revelation, and will enjoy more privileges than did John.

29-30. The fact that God can be **justified** proves that the term signifies "to be declared righteous," not to make righteous. The people simply acknowledged God's righteousness.

31-35. John was ascetic, while Jesus ate normally, yet their severe critics found fault with both because these critics disagreed with the message proclaimed.

34 The Son of man is come eating and drinking; and ye say, Behold a gluttonous man, and a winebibber, a friend of publicans and sinners!

35 But wisdom is justified of all her children.

36 ¶And one of the Pharisees desired him that he would eat with him. And he went into the Pharisee's house, and sat down to meat.

37 And, behold, a woman in the city, which was a sinner, when she knew that *Jesus* sat at meat in the Pharisee's house, brought an alabaster box of ointment,

38 And stood at his feet behind *him* weeping, and began to wash his feet with tears, and did wipe *them* with the hairs of her head, and kissed his feet, and anointed *them* with the ointment.

39 Now when the Pharisee which had bidden him saw *it*, he spake within himself, saying, This man, if he were a prophet, would have known who and what manner of woman *this is* that toucheth him: for she is a sinner.

40 And Jesus answering said unto him, Simon, I have somewhat to say unto thee. And he saith, Master, say on.

41 There was a certain creditor which had two debtors: the one owed five hundred pence, and the other fifty.

42 And when they had nothing to pay, he frankly forgave them both. Tell me therefore, which of them will love him most?

43 Simon answered and said, I suppose that *he*, to whom he forgave most. And he said unto him, Thou hast rightly judged.

44 And he turned to the woman, and said unto Simon, Seest thou this woman? I entered into thine house, thou gavest me no water for my feet: but she hath washed my feet with tears, and wiped *them* with the hairs of her head.

45 Thou gavest me no kiss: but this woman since the time I came in hath not ceased to kiss my feet.

46 My head with oil thou didst not anoint: but this woman hath anointed my feet with ointment.

47 Wherefore I say unto thee, Her sins, which are many, are forgiven; for she loved much: but to whom little is forgiven, *the same* loveth little.

48 And he said unto her, Thy sins are forgiven.

49 And they that sat at meat with him began to say within themselves, Who is this that forgiveth sins also?

50 And he said to the woman, Thy faith hath saved thee; go in peace.

CHAPTER 8

AND it came to pass afterward, that he went throughout every city and village, preaching and shewing the glad tidings of the kingdom of God: and the twelve *were* with him,

2 And certain women, which had been healed of evil spirits and infirmities, Mary called Magdalene, out of whom went seven devils,

36-40. Upon one occasion Jesus was invited to eat in the home of Simon, a Pharisee. When a notoriously sinful woman came in and anointed Jesus' feet with valuable perfume, Simon thought evil of Christ for not refusing her favor. Christ's omniscience told Him Simon's thoughts, and He answered with a short parable.

41-42. Jesus said that a creditor forgave two debtors, one of whom owed ten times as much as the other. Jesus then asked Simon which debtor would feel the most love toward the creditor.

43-50. The answer, of course, is the one who was forgiven the most. The application Jesus makes to Simon and the sinful woman is that both have been forgiven, but that the one who has a greater amount to have been forgiven will appreciate that forgiveness most. The more we sense the lost and hopeless condition we were in, the more we will appreciate what Christ has done for us.

8:1. He went throughout every city and village, preaching and showing the glad tidings of the kingdom of God. Jesus' ministry was very extensive in Galilee, but His message was not that He would die for the sins of the world, but that He had come to establish the kingdom prophesied in the Old Testament. The twelve disciples were gaining matchless experience by being with the Son of God during these days of teaching and healing.

2-3. Also accompanying Christ and ministering to Him were a number of formerly demon-possessed women, whose lives must have evidenced complete transformation. Joanna is only mentioned here and in 24:10 in Luke's gospel.

3 And Jō'ăn-na the wife of Chū'za Herod's steward, and Susanna, and many others, which ministered unto him of their substance.

4 ¶And when much people were gathered together, and were come to him out of every city, he spake by a parable:

5 A sower went out to sow his seed: and as he sowed, some fell by the way side; and it was trodden down, and the fowls of the air devoured it.

6 And some fell upon a rock; and as soon as it was sprung up, it withered away, because it lacked moisture.

7 And some fell among thorns; and the thorns sprang up with it, and choked it.

8 And other fell on good ground, and sprang up, and bare fruit an hundredfold. And when he had said these things, he cried, He that hath ears to hear, let him hear.

9 ¶And his disciples asked him, saying, What might this parable be?

10 And he said, Unto you it is given to know the mysteries of the kingdom of God: but to others in parables; that seeing they might not see, and hearing they might not understand.

11 Now the parable is this: The seed is the word of God.

12 Those by the way side are they that hear; then cometh the devil, and taketh away the word out of their hearts, lest they should believe and be saved.

13 They on the rock *are they*, which, when they hear, receive the word with joy; and these have no root, which for a while believe, and in time of temptation fall away.

14 And that which fell among thorns are they, which, when they have heard, go forth, and are choked with cares and riches and pleasures of *this* life, and bring no fruit to perfection.

15 But that on the good ground are they, which in an honest and good heart, having heard the word, keep *it*, and bring forth fruit with patience.

16 ¶No man, when he hath lighted a candle, covereth it with a vessel, or putteth *it* under a bed; but setteth *it* on a candlestick, that they which enter in may see the light.

17 For nothing is secret, that shall not be made manifest; neither *any thing* hid, that shall not be known and come abroad.

18 Take heed therefore how ye hear: for whosoever hath, to him shall be given; and whosoever hath not, from him shall be taken even that which he seemeth to have.

19 ¶Then came to him *his* mother and his brethren, and could not come at him for the press.

20 And it was told him *by certain* which said, Thy mother and thy brethren stand without, desiring to see thee.

21 And he answered and said unto them, My mother and my brethren are these which hear the word of God, and do it.

22 ¶Now it came to pass on a certain day, that he went into a ship with his disciples: and he said unto them, Let us

4-15. Jesus was famous for His parables. Parables are stories that are true to life and nature in every way, thus differing from allegories and fables. They are used to teach spiritual truths. Jesus used parables often, the New Testament recording about thirty separate stories. Jesus used parables for at least five reasons. (1) To attract attention. They have tremendous interest value, and everyone likes a story. (2) To prevent hearers from being repelled too quickly by normal direct statements. (3) To stimulate inquiry and to teach. These stories could easily be remembered, and were thus good vehicles for preserving the truth. (4) To reveal the truth, as some could understand a story taught in parabolic form more easily than regular teaching. (5) To conceal the truth. Often a story would protect the truth from the mockery of a scoffer who could not understand the meaning. One's spiritual condition frequently determined how much he would understand of what Jesus said. The parable of the four soils is found in every Gospel except John's. The four types of soils could easily be located within the same field. They represent the hearts (vs. 15) or minds of men. (1) The way side or pathway soil (vs. 12) is hardened and uncultivated, and the seed which represents God's Word cannot penetrate it. Note the influence of Satan in keeping this type of person from believing (cf. II Cor 4:4). (2) The rocky ground (vs. 13) has a thin layer of dirt over solid rock. This one is completely superficial and emotional, but has *no* root. (3) The thorny ground (vs. 14) is a double-minded man. He makes a profession, but it is unreal. (4) Only the good ground (vss. 8, 15) bears any fruit and represents a really saved individual. Jesus taught His disciples that they would sow much seed, but should not be distressed by seemingly poor results and some cases of apparent salvation which were in reality nothing but an outward emotional experience.

16-18. These verses contain a great principle regarding the outward indication of one's salvation: there should be no secret believers. Really saved people will grow in grace but mere professors will lose even that which they seem to possess.

19-21. His mother and his brethren. By today's standards, Mary and Joseph had a good-sized family. Four brothers and additional sisters are mentioned in Mark 6:3. Jesus was not here denying His normal family relationships or even downplaying their importance, but He was stressing the new and more important spiritual relationships resulting from belief in Himself.

22-25. Jesus stilled or walked upon the waters on several different occasions, here and again after the feeding of the five

go over unto the other side of the lake. And they launched forth.

23 But as they sailed he fell asleep: and there came down a storm of wind on the lake; and they were filled *with water*, and were in jeopardy.

24 And they came to him, and awoke him, saying, Master, master, we perish. Then he arose, and rebuked the wind and the raging of the water: and they ceased, and there was a calm.

25 And he said unto them, Where is your faith? And they being afraid wondered, saying one to another, What manner of man is this! for he commandeth even the winds and water, and they obey him.

26 ¶And they arrived at the country of the Găd′a-rēneṡ, which is over against Galilee.

27 And when he went forth to land, there met him out of the city a certain man, which had devils long time, and ware no clothes, neither abode in *any* house, but in the tombs.

28 When he saw Jesus, he cried out, and fell down before him, and with a loud voice said, What have I to do with thee, Jesus, *thou* Son of God most high? I beseech thee, torment me not.

29 (For he had commanded the unclean spirit to come out of the man. For oftentimes it had caught him: and he was kept bound with chains and in fetters; and he brake the bands, and was driven of the devil into the wilderness.)

30 And Jesus asked him, saying, What is thy name? And he said, Legion: because many devils were entered into him.

31 And they besought him that he would not command them to go out into the deep.

32 And there was there an herd of many swine feeding on the mountain: and they besought him that he would suffer them to enter into them. And he suffered them.

33 Then went the devils out of the man, and entered into the swine: and the herd ran violently down a steep place into the lake, and were choked.

34 When they that fed *them* saw what was done, they fled, and went and told *it* in the city and in the country.

35 Then they went out to see what was done; and came to Jesus, and found the man, out of whom the devils were departed, sitting at the feet of Jesus, clothed, and in his right mind: and they were afraid.

36 They also which saw *it* told them by what means he that was possessed of the devils was healed.

37 ¶Then the whole multitude of the country of the Găd′a-rēneṡ round about besought him to depart from them; for they were taken with great fear: and he went up into the ship, and returned back again.

38 Now the man out of whom the devils were departed besought him that he might be with him: but Jesus sent him away, saying,

39 Return to thine own house, and shew how great things God hath done unto thee. And he went his way and

thousand (Jn 6:17-21). By it, He demonstrated His complete and absolute sovereignty over the natural elements. Also these miracles proved Christ's deity to the disciples and to us.

26-40. The story of the maniac of Gadara took place at ruins today called Khersa in the eastern edge of the steep slopes overlooking the Sea of Galilee. The story illustrates several things about demon-possession. Some characteristics are: (1) insanity (prior to the action of verse 35). He was out of his mind, it being controlled by the demon; (2) indecency (vs. 27)—this often accompanied demonic control; (3) injury (vs. 29, cf. Mk 5:4-5)—he cut himself; and (4) infamy—his poor family must have lived in shame. That is what the devil drives man to. But this poor soul was delivered by Christ spiritually, physically, and mentally. The result was that he readily proclaimed far and wide what great things Jesus had done for him.

Many demons had controlled this man, and called themselves Legion (vs. 30). A Roman legion usually consisted of six thousand men, or ten cohorts of six hundred. They feared that Christ would send them into the deep (Gr *abyssos*). Apparently, while on earth Jesus did cast many demons into a place of confinement from which they will not be released until the Tribulation Period (cf. Rev 9:1-11). Jesus was certainly not responsible for the destruction of the herd of swine in the vicinity. The incident does reveal that demons may affect animals.

published throughout the whole city how great things Jesus had done unto him.

40 And it came to pass, that, when Jesus was returned, the people *gladly* received him: for they were all waiting for him.

41 ¶And, behold, there came a man named Jā-ī´rus, and he was a ruler of the synagogue: and he fell down at Jesus' feet, and besought him that he would come into his house:

42 For he had one only daughter, about twelve years of age, and she lay a dying. But as he went the people thronged him.

43 ¶And a woman having an issue of blood twelve years, which had spent all her living upon physicians, neither could be healed of any,

44 Came behind *him,* and touched the border of his garment: and immediately her issue of blood stanched.

45 And Jesus said, Who touched me? When all denied, Peter and they that were with him said, Master, the multitude throng thee and press *thee,* and sayest thou, Who touched me?

46 And Jesus said, Somebody hath touched me: for I perceive that virtue is gone out of me.

47 And when the woman saw that she was not hid, she came trembling, and falling down before him, she declared unto him before all the people for what cause she had touched him, and how she was healed immediately.

48 And he said unto her, Daughter, be of good comfort: thy faith hath made thee whole; go in peace.

49 ¶While he yet spake, there cometh one from the ruler of the synagogue's *house,* saying to him, Thy daughter is dead; trouble not the Master.

50 But when Jesus heard *it,* he answered him, saying, Fear not: believe only, and she shall be made whole.

51 And when he came into the house, he suffered no man to go in, save Peter, and James, and John, and the father and the mother of the maiden.

52 And all wept, and bewailed her: but he said, Weep not; she is not dead, but sleepeth.

53 And they laughed him to scorn, knowing that she was dead.

54 And he put them all out, and took her by the hand, and called, saying, Maid, arise.

55 And her spirit came again, and she arose straightway: and he commanded to give her meat.

56 And her parents were astonished: but he charged them that they should tell no man what was done.

CHAPTER 9

THEN he called his twelve disciples together, and gave them power and authority over all devils, and to cure diseases.

2032

41-42. Jairus had only had one child, a twelve-year-old daughter who was at the point of death when Jesus entered Capernaum. He came to Jesus for help, asking the Master to come quickly.

43. However, they were thronged with people, each with his own special needs, and progress toward Jairus' house was slow. In the multitude was a woman with an incurable hemorrhage. She was unclean according to Leviticus 15:19, and was not permitted to come near people, but she cared not for that if she could only be healed. She was desperate.

44-48. When she touched Jesus in faith she was healed. Jesus' omniscience caused Him to perceive her actions and He asked for the woman to identify herself, probably to reveal her publicly to the crowd and to further instruct her. Jesus said her faith had saved her.

49-50. After this incident and delay, messengers from Jairus' house came and reported the death of his daughter. Jesus knew this tried his faith, and told Jairus to continue believing and his daughter would be made well.

51. Jesus took only the parents and Peter, James, and John into the house. He preserved the sanctity of the home by not parading twelve men into this private place.

52-53. The little girl was really dead, but the death of a believer's body may outwardly be likened to sleep, which it resembles (cf. Jn 11:11-14; I Cor 11:30; I Thess 4:13-14). The Bible teaches no such doctrine as "soul sleep" as do some. At death, an individual's soul is either consciously (1) with the Lord (II Cor 5:8; Phil 1:21-23), or (2) in torment in hades awaiting the final resurrection to death (Lk 16:23).

54-56. Jesus raised the girl from the dead and her spirit reentered her body. Mark, who received much of his information from the eyewitness, Peter, records (5:42) that she arose and walked. No one could doubt this fantastic miracle.

E. Christ's Dealings with His Disciples. 9:1-50.

9:1. Christ granted His twelve disciples power and prerogatives over demons and sickness never exercised by man either before or after. The purpose of this was to place a divine

2 And he sent them to preach the kingdom of God, and to heal the sick.

3 And he said unto them, Take nothing for *your* journey, neither staves, nor scrip, neither bread, neither money; neither have two coats apiece.

4 And whatsoever house ye enter into, there abide, and thence depart.

5 And whosoever will not receive you, when ye go out of that city, shake off the very dust from your feet for a testimony against them.

6 And they departed, and went through the towns, preaching the gospel, and healing every where.

7 ¶Now Herod the tetrarch heard of all that was done by him: and he was perplexed, because that it was said of some, that John was risen from the dead;

8 And of some, that E-lī'as had appeared; and of others, that one of the old prophets was risen again.

9 And Herod said, John have I beheaded: but who is this, of whom I hear such things? And he desired to see him.

10 ¶And the apostles, when they were returned, told him all that they had done. And he took them, and went aside privately into a desert place belonging to the city called Bĕth-sā'i-da.

11 And the people, when they knew *it*, followed him: and he received them, and spake unto them of the kingdom of God, and healed them that had need of healing.

12 ¶And when the day began to wear away, then came the twelve, and said unto him, Send the multitude away, that they may go into the towns and country round about, and lodge, and get victuals: for we are here in a desert place.

13 But he said unto them, Give ye them to eat. And they said, We have no more but five loaves and two fishes; except we should go and buy meat for all this people.

14 For they were about five thousand men. And he said to his disciples, Make them sit down by fifties in a company.

15 And they did so, and made them all sit down.

16 Then he took the five loaves and the two fishes, and looking up to heaven, he blessed them, and brake, and gave to the disciples to set before the multitude.

17 And they did eat, and were all filled: and there was taken up of fragments that remained to them twelve baskets.

18 ¶And it came to pass, as he was alone praying, his disciples were with him: and he asked them, saying, Whom say the people that I am?

19 They answering said, John the Baptist; but some *say*, E-lī'as; and others *say*, that one of the old prophets is risen again.

20 He said unto them, But whom say ye that I am? Peter answering said, The Christ of God.

21 And he straitly charged them, and

seal of approval upon their message as well as to meet the needs of people.

2-6. The disciples preached the good news (vs. 6) of the kingdom of God. Spiritual birth into God's family was a requirement for entrance (Jn 3:3, 5) but the kingdom itself was to be earthly, with Jesus ruling the world from Jerusalem in fulfillment of Old Testament prophecy (Isa 2:1-4; 11:1-9; Amos 9:11-15; Mic 4:6-8).

7-9. Herod, who had beheaded John the Baptist (see Mt 14:1-12 and Mk 6:14-29), wondered if he had risen from the dead when he began to hear about the miracles Jesus was performing. His desire to see Jesus was fulfilled in Jerusalem during the mock trials prior to Christ's death (Lk 23:7-12).

10. The Twelve are called disciples prior to being sent out. They are called apostles (Gr *apostolos*), meaning "sent out ones," in this verse. The feeding of the five thousand occurred shortly after the death of John the Baptist. Jesus felt the need for privacy and for rest (Mk 6:31).

11. The plans for rest were laid aside when multitudes followed Jesus to a quiet area on the northern edge of the Sea of Galilee in the spring of the year (Jn 6:4).

12-17. All four evangelists record this great miracle, and each makes it clear that five thousand men, not counting women and children, were fed from the miraculous multiplication of five small barley loaves and two fishes. The miracle must have occurred as the disciples broke pieces from their tiny allotments and distributed them to the sitting crowds. The twelve baskets collected were like little travel bags and probably provided sustenance for the disciples as they went to the Passover which was approaching.

18-22. Peter's great confession, at Caesarea Philippi near Mount Hermon, occurred approximately six months prior to the crucifixion. It marks the beginning of any mention by Christ that He is going to be killed (vs. 22), which explains the reaction of Peter to such a prediction (see Mt 16:23). This time also marks the very first mention by Christ of the fact that He would establish His church (Mt 16:18). Jesus' use of the future tense in this initial prediction points to Pentecost when the church was first physically manifested.

commanded *them* to tell no man that thing;

22 Saying, The Son of man must suffer many things, and be rejected of the elders and chief priests and scribes, and be slain, and be raised the third day.

23 ¶And he said to *them* all, If any *man* will come after me, let him deny himself, and take up his cross daily, and follow me.

24 For whosoever will save his life shall lose it: but whosoever will lose his life for my sake, the same shall save it.

25 For what is a man advantaged, if he gain the whole world, and lose himself, or be cast away?

26 For whosoever shall be ashamed of me and of my words, of him shall the Son of man be ashamed, when he shall come in his own glory, and *in his* Father's, and of the holy angels.

27 But I tell you of a truth, there be some standing here, which shall not taste of death, till they see the kingdom of God.

28 ¶And it came to pass about an eight days after these sayings, he took Peter and John and James, and went up into a mountain to pray.

29 And as he prayed, the fashion of his countenance was altered, and his raiment *was* white *and* glistering.

30 And, behold, there talked with him two men, which were Moses and E-lī'as:

31 Who appeared in glory, and spake of his decease which he should accomplish at Jerusalem.

32 But Peter and they that were with him were heavy with sleep: and when they were awake, they saw his glory, and the two men that stood with him.

33 And it came to pass, as they departed from him, Peter said unto Jesus, Master, it is good for us to be here: and let us make three tabernacles; one for thee, and one for Moses, and one for E-lī'as: not knowing what he said.

34 While he thus spake, there came a cloud, and overshadowed them: and they feared as they entered into the cloud.

35 And there came a voice out of the cloud, saying, This is my beloved Son: hear him.

36 And when the voice was past, Jesus was found alone. And they kept *it* close, and told no man in those days any of those things which they had seen.

37 ¶And it came to pass, that on the

23-24. Jesus' challenge to His disciples was faithfulness, denial of self, and daily sacrifice. Its results are stated in paradoxical terms. If one lives merely for this life, the following life will be lost. But if one cares not about this life in order to serve Christ, only then will he secure life eternal.

25-26. For what is a man advantaged? This is still true. No amount of earthly gain can ever make up for the unutterable loss of one's soul.

27. There be some standing here, which shall not taste of death, till they see the kingdom of God. This verse has to be a prediction that some of the disciples would see Christ in all His glory during the soon-coming transfiguration.

28. Peter, James, and John made up the inner circle of disciples. At the outer perimeter was the group of five hundred who saw Christ after His resurrection (I Cor 15:6). A bit closer were the seventy disciples who were sent out two by two to preach and heal (Lk 10:1, 17). Still closer were the Twelve, of whom these three were specially selected to witness this event, the raising of Jairus' daughter, and Jesus' agony in Gethsemane. Of these three, John the beloved was closest to Christ (Jn 13:23; 21:20). The mountain of transfiguration has been thought by some to be Mount Tabor in the Jezreel Valley, but many feel that Mount Hermon's slopes above Caesarea Philippi more naturally meet the idea of "high mountain" (Mk 9:2). Hermon's highest elevation is over 10,000 feet, while Tabor only reaches to 1,843 feet, but is a majestic solitary bell-shaped hill.

29. Christ's clothing and complexion were surrounded and filled with a magnificent glory that had not been seen by mortal man since God's glory left the Temple in Ezekiel's day.

30-31. Moses and Elijah stood as representatives of the Law and the Prophets, and discussed Christ's coming death at Jerusalem. It must have been a wonderful yet an awesome experience for Christ as He was encouraged by these two fearless and faithful Old Testament saints to finish the task for which He had come.

32-33. The three disciples were fast asleep while all this was transpiring, and were surprised by what they saw when they awoke.

34-36. God the Father spoke, **This is my beloved Son: hear him.** All attention was to be directed to Christ.

37-43. Jesus and the three disciples returned from the mountain to find the other disciples unable to cast a difficult demon

next day, when they were come down from the hill, much people met him.

38 And, behold, a man of the company cried out, saying, Master, I beseech thee, look upon my son: for he is mine only child.

39 And, lo, a spirit taketh him, and he suddenly crieth out; and it teareth him that he foameth again, and bruising him hardly departeth from him.

40 And I besought thy disciples to cast him out; and they could not.

41 And Jesus answering said, O faithless and perverse generation, how long shall I be with you, and suffer you? Bring thy son hither.

42 And as he was yet a coming, the devil threw him down, and tare *him*. And Jesus rebuked the unclean spirit, and healed the child, and delivered him again to his father.

43 ¶And they were all amazed at the mighty power of God. But while they wondered every one at all things which Jesus did, he said unto his disciples,

44 Let these sayings sink down into your ears: for the Son of man shall be delivered into the hands of men.

45 But they understood not this saying, and it was hid from them, that they perceived it not: and they feared to ask him of that saying.

46 ¶Then there arose a reasoning among them, which of them should be greatest.

47 And Jesus, perceiving the thought of their heart, took a child, and set him by him,

48 And said unto them, Whosoever shall receive this child in my name receiveth me: and whosoever shall receive me receiveth him that sent me: for he that is least among you all, the same shall be great.

49 And John answered and said, Master, we saw one casting out devils in thy name; and we forbad him, because he followeth not with us.

50 And Jesus said unto him, Forbid *him* not: for he that is not against us is for us.

51 ¶And it came to pass, when the time was come that he should be received up, he stedfastly set his face to go to Jerusalem,

52 And sent messengers before his face: and they went, and entered into a village of the Sa-măr′i-tanṣ, to make ready for him.

out of a young boy. The boy's father was distraught. Apparently the disciples had not relied on God in prayer for the power they needed to cast out the demon (Mk 9:26). Jesus then immediately restored the lad. The full account is given in Mark 9:14-29.

44-45. For the second time in a month, Jesus clearly predicted His coming death in Jerusalem, but the disciples **understood not this saying.** They could not fit a crucified King into the kingdom plans which they were all so busily announcing to the people in every town and city. In fact, it was not until after the resurrection that they even began to understand how Christ's death fit into God's plan. The kingdom was to be postponed due to Jewish rejection of Christ, and the church age was to occupy the interval in between.

46-48. Jesus said that true greatness is achieved by humility. This is true, but must also be balanced with the biblical doctrine of labor, striving, pressing forward, and occupying till He comes. In all of our labors, and especially in our successes, we must not think more highly of ourselves than we ought (Rom 12:3).

49-50. Jesus was not in favor of a narrow sectarianism which looks askance at anyone not in "our group" or not approved by "our agencies." We should all serve the Lord the best we can, expose error and deceitfulness as Paul did, yet not be ruled by a spirit of divisiveness that would condemn all who do not conform to "our" way of doing things. Thus, Jesus reminded: **he that is against us, is for us.** (For the converse truth see Mt 12:30; Mk 9:40.)

V. THE PERAEAN MINISTRY OF THE SON. 9:51-19:27.

This large section of material from 9:51-19:27 is almost totally unique to Luke. Only a few isolated events are recorded in the other Gospels. This section contains an account of Christ's basic ministry in Peraea, east of the Jordan. The great majority of the parables in Luke are included here, almost all of which appear nowhere else.

A. Christ's Determination to Go to Jerusalem. 9:51-62.

51-53. Between the October Feast of the Tabernacles (Jn 7:14; 10:21) and Christ's final Passover, a period of about six months, His life was in constant danger, especially in Judaea. During this time Jesus spent most of His time in Peraea. When He ventured into Jerusalem for the Feast of Dedication or Hanukkah in December (Jn 10:22), He was practically stoned (vs. 13). Thereafter He spent some time in Peraea (Jn 10:40),

53 And they did not receive him, because his face was as though he would go to Jerusalem.

54 And when his disciples James and John saw this, they said, Lord, wilt thou that we command fire to come down from heaven, and consume them, even as E-lī'as did?

55 But he turned, and rebuked them, and said, Ye know not what manner of spirit ye are of.

56 For the Son of man is not come to destroy men's lives, but to save them. And they went to another village.

57 ¶And it came to pass, that, as they went in the way, a certain man said unto him, Lord, I will follow thee whithersoever thou goest.

58 And Jesus said unto him, Foxes have holes, and birds of the air have nests; but the Son of man hath not where to lay his head.

59 And he said unto another, Follow me. But he said, Lord, suffer me first to go and bury my father.

60 Jesus said unto him, Let the dead bury their dead: but go thou and preach the kingdom of God.

61 And another also said, Lord, I will follow thee; but let me first go bid them farewell, which are at home at my house.

62 And Jesus said unto him, No man, having put his hand to the plough, and looking back, is fit for the kingdom of God.

CHAPTER 10

AFTER these things the Lord appointed other seventy also, and sent them two and two before his face into every city and place, wither he himself would come.

2 Therefore said he unto them, The harvest truly is great, but the labourers are few: pray ye therefore the Lord of the harvest, that he would send forth labourers into his harvest.

3 Go your ways: behold, I send you forth as lambs among wolves.

4 Carry neither purse, nor scrip, nor shoes: and salute no man by the way.

5 And into whatsoever house ye enter, first say, Peace be to this house.

6 And if the son of peace be there, your peace shall rest upon it: if not, it shall turn to you again.

7 And in the same house remain, eating and drinking such things as they give: for the labourer is worthy of his hire. Go not from house to house.

8 And into whatsoever city ye enter, and they receive you, eat such things as are set before you:

9 And heal the sick that are therein, and say unto them, The kingdom of God is come nigh unto you.

10 But into whatsoever city ye enter, and they receive you not, go your ways out into the streets of the same, and say,

11 Even the very dust of your city, which cleaveth on us, we do wipe off against you: notwithstanding be ye sure of this, that the kingdom of God is come nigh unto you.

12 But I say unto you, that it shall be

interrupted only by His mission to raise Lazarus. Luke tells us that Jesus was determined to go up to Jerusalem.

54-56. The beloved disciple John, with his brother James, was not always so loving and kind, as this passage notes. They were called Boanerges, sons of thunder (Mk 3:17), and needed to be transformed just like any other sinners.

57-62. Let the dead bury their dead (vs. 60) probably means let those who are spiritually dead bury the physically dead. Doing Christ's bidding is far more important than even attendance at the funeral of one's own father.

B. Christ's Ministry with the Seventy. 10:1-24.

10:1-2. Christ was a trainer of men. He gave these seventy men a burden for the souls of men. He told them that **The harvest truly is great, but the laborers are few.** He sent them out two by two to help meet this need.

3-11. For the laborer is worthy of his hire (vs. 7) is quoted by Paul in I Timothy 5:18 as "Scripture." Even New Testament writings were counted as Scripture from the time they were written (cf. also II Pet 3:15-16 where Paul's epistles are called Scripture).

12-16. These verses definitely teach degrees of punishment,

more tolerable in that day for Sodom, than for that city.

13 Woe unto thee, Chō-rā′zĭn! woe unto thee, Bĕth-sā′i-da! for if the mighty works had been done in Tyre and Sī′don, which have been done in you, they had a great while ago repented, sitting in sackcloth and ashes.

14 But it shall be more tolerable for Tyre and Sī′don at the judgment, than for you.

15 And thou, Ca-per′na-um, which art exalted to heaven, shalt be thrust down to hell.

16 He that heareth you heareth me; and he that despiseth you despiseth me; and he that despiseth me despiseth him that sent me.

17 ¶And the seventy returned again with joy, saying, Lord, even the devils are subject unto us through thy name.

18 And he said unto them, I beheld Satan as lightning fall from heaven.

19 Behold, I give unto you power to tread on serpents and scorpions, and over all the power of the enemy: and nothing shall by any means hurt you.

20 Notwithstanding in this rejoice not, that the spirits are subject unto you; but rather rejoice, because your names are written in heaven.

21 ¶In that hour Jesus rejoiced in spirit, and said, I thank thee, O Father, Lord of heaven and earth, that thou hast hid these things from the wise and prudent, and hast revealed them unto babes: even so, Father; for so it seemed good in thy sight.

22 All things are delivered to me of my Father: and no man knoweth who the Son is, but the Father; and who the Father is, but the Son, and he to whom the Son will reveal him.

23 ¶And he turned him unto his disciples, and said privately, Blessed are the eyes which see the things that ye see:

24 For I tell you, that many prophets and kings have desired to see those things which ye see, and have not seen them; and to hear those things which ye hear, and have not heard them.

25 ¶And, behold, a certain lawyer stood up, and tempted him, saying, Master, what shall I do to inherit eternal life?

26 He said unto him, What is written in the law? how readest thou?

27 And he answering said, Thou shalt love the Lord thy God with all thy heart, and with all thy soul, and with all thy strength, and with all thy mind; and thy neighbour as thyself.

28 And he said unto him, Thou hast answered right: this do, and thou shalt live.

29 But he, willing to justify himself, said unto Jesus, And who is my neighbour?

30 And Jesus answering said, A certain man went down from Jerusalem to Jericho, and fell among thieves, which stripped him of his raiment, and wounded him, and departed, leaving him half dead.

31 And by chance there came down a

based on degrees of sin according to how much light people had. Some will be judged more severely than others, and as a result receive greater punishment in hell than others. This doctrine is also taught by Christ in each of the other Gospels (see Mt 10:15-16; 11:21-24; Mk 6:11; Jn 19:11).

17-20. The seventy are thrilled that even demons are subject to them. Jesus sees the disciples' success as a foretaste of the complete defeat of Satan. The cross would signal Satan's final downfall (Jn 12:31) and his being cast into the lake of fire only follows naturally (Rev 20:10), though separated by a larger time interval.

21-24. Christ's disciples had tremendous privileges for which countless others before them longed. Their greatest joy, however, was to be regarding their own salvation (vs. 20).

C. Christ's Parabolic Teaching Ministry. 10:25-13:21.

25-29. The parable of the Good Samaritan was told by Jesus in answer to the self-justifying question of a lawyer, **And who is my neighbor?**

30. A certain man went down from Jerusalem to Jericho. He was probably a Jew. The way down is from approximately 2600 feet above sea level to approximately 800 feet below sea level and is through a treacherous wilderness. Thieves and robbers waited for lonely travelers. This man was attacked, beaten, robbed, and stripped of clothes.

31-37. Two Jews, a priest and a Levite, passed by but did

certain priest that way: and when he saw him, he passed by on the other side.

32 And likewise a Levite, when he was at the place, came and looked *on him*, and passed by on the other side.

33 But a certain Sa-măr′i-tan, as he journeyed, came where he was: and when he saw him, he had compassion *on him*,

34 And went to *him*, and bound up his wounds, pouring in oil and wine, and set him on his own beast, and brought him to an inn, and took care of him.

35 And on the morrow when he departed, he took out two pence, and gave *them* to the host, and said unto him, Take care of him; and whatsoever thou spendest more, when I come again, I will repay thee.

36 Which now of these three, thinkest thou, was neighbour unto him that fell among the thieves?

37 And he said, He that shewed mercy on him. Then said Jesus unto him, Go, and do thou likewise.

38 ¶Now it came to pass, as they went, that he entered into a certain village: and a certain woman named Martha received him into her house.

39 And she had a sister called Mary, which also sat at Jesus′ feet, and heard his word.

40 But Martha was cumbered about much serving, and came to him, and said, Lord, dost thou not care that my sister hath left me to serve alone? bid her therefore that she help me.

41 And Jesus answered and said unto her, Martha, Martha, thou art careful and troubled about many things:

42 But one thing is needful: and Mary hath chosen that good part, which shall not be taken away from her.

CHAPTER 11

AND it came to pass, that, as he was praying in a certain place, when he ceased, one of his disciples said unto him, Lord, teach us to pray, as John also taught his disciples.

2 And he said unto them, When ye pray, say, Our Father which art in heaven, Hallowed be thy name. Thy kingdom come. Thy will be done, as in heaven, so in earth.

3 Give us day by day our daily bread.

4 And forgive us our sins; for we also forgive every one that is indebted to us. And lead us not into temptation; but deliver us from evil.

5 And he said unto them, Which of you shall have a friend, and shall go unto him at midnight, and say unto him, Friend, lend me three loaves;

6 For a friend of mine in his journey is come to me, and I have nothing to set before him?

7 And he from within shall answer and say, Trouble me not: the door is now shut, and my children are with me in bed; I cannot rise and give thee.

8 I say unto you, Though he will not rise and give him, because he is his

nothing to help the poor man. Then a Samaritan (see Jn 4:9) came along and aided the robbed victim, even seeing to his full recovery by paying for his stay at an inn. This Samaritan was a true neighbor. He had a compassionate heart, a helping hand, and unlimited concern. He gave up personal comfort, physical energy, and valuable time. As one preacher expressed it, the robbers beat him up, the priest and Levite passed him up, but the Samaritan picked him up. The thief said, "What's yours is mine, I'll take it." The priest and Levite reasoned, "What's mine is mine, I'll keep it." But the Samaritan said, "What's mine is yours, we'll share it." Let us heed Jesus' final injunction to the lawyer, **Go, and do thou likewise** (vs. 37).

38-42. Mary . . . sat at Jesus' feet, and heard his word, but Martha was cumbered about much serving. This familiar story appears only in Luke, and outside of this story Mary and Martha are only mentioned in John 11 and 12. Yet these two ladies are among the most famous of all Bible characters, and were some of our Lord's dearest friends. The lesson to be learned from this true story is that we must choose to do the best things, and not be overly concerned about ourselves through self-pity. There is nothing wrong with serving, but we must first sit at Jesus' feet and spend time with Him.

11:1. As He was praying . . . one of his disciples said unto Him, Lord, teach us to pray. Jesus set the example of prayer before His disciples (see a study of *Jesus' Habits of Prayer* by S. D. Gordon).

2-4. These verses contain what is commonly called the "Lord's Prayer," also found in Matthew 6:9-13. It is a model prayer to show us how to pray, not a pattern to be repeated in vain repetition. We are to (1) recognize God for who He is and glorify His name, (2) pray for His program and (3) His will to be accomplished, then (4) ask for daily food, (5) forgiveness of sins, and (6) deliverance from sin and evil. These points are elementary and not exhaustive. Mature prayer will not be limited to these initial requests, but should at least contain these basic points. An example of how Christ prayed is given in John 17, the second longest prayer in the Bible. The longest is found in I Kings 8 when Solomon dedicated the Temple.

5-10. The parable of the friend who came at midnight was told to reinforce an aspect about prayer. Although importunity is important in prayer, this parable is probably trying to show a contrast between God and the friend who eventually opened the door. God is more than a friend, and will certainly grant our needs much more readily than the man who had gone to bed.

friend, yet because of his importunity he will rise and give him as many as he needeth.

9 And I say unto you, Ask, and it shall be given you; seek, and ye shall find; knock, and it shall be opened unto you.

10 For every one that asketh receiveth; and he that seeketh findeth; and to him that knocketh it shall be opened.

11 If a son shall ask bread of any of you that is a father, will he give him a stone? or if *he ask* a fish, will he for a fish give him a serpent?

12 Or if he shall ask an egg, will he offer him a scorpion?

13 If ye then, being evil, know how to give good gifts unto your children: how much more shall *your* heavenly Father give the Holy Spirit to them that ask him?

14 ¶And he was casting out a devil, and it was dumb. And it came to pass, when the devil was gone out, the dumb spake; and the people wondered.

15 But some of them said, He casteth out devils through Bē-ĕl′ze-bŭb the chief of the devils.

16 And others, tempting *him*, sought of him a sign from heaven.

17 But he, knowing their thoughts, said unto them, Every kingdom divided against itself is brought to desolation; and a house *divided* against a house falleth.

18 If Satan also be divided against himself, how shall his kingdom stand? because ye say that I cast out devils through Bē-ĕl′ze-bŭb.

19 And if I by Bē-ĕl′ze-bŭb cast out devils, by whom do your sons cast *them* out? therefore shall they be your judges.

20 But if I with the finger of God cast out devils, no doubt the kingdom of God is come upon you.

21 When a strong man armed keepeth his palace, his goods are in peace:

22 But when a stronger than he shall come upon him, and overcome him, he taketh from him all his armour wherein he trusted, and divideth his spoils.

23 He that is not with me is against me: and he that gathereth not with me scattereth.

24 When the unclean spirit is gone out of a man, he walketh through dry places, seeking rest; and finding none, he saith, I will return unto my house whence I came out.

25 And when he cometh, he findeth *it* swept and garnished.

26 Then goeth he, and taketh *to him* seven other spirits more wicked than himself; and they enter in, and dwell there: and the last *state* of that man is worse than the first.

27 ¶And it came to pass, as he spake these things, a certain woman of the company lifted up her voice, and said unto him, Blessed *is* the womb that bare thee, and the paps which thou hast sucked.

28 But he said, Yea rather, blessed *are* they that hear the word of God, and keep it.

29 ¶And when the people were gathered thick together, he began to say,

11-13. In addition, God is our Father and desires to give us freely all things. One of the most precious gifts is naturally the Holy Spirit who abides with all believers today, but who was not resident in the lives of Old Testament saints.

14-23. After casting out a demon, Jesus was accused of casting out demons through the chief of demons, i.e., Satan (vs. 15). This wicked accusation on the part of some was equivalent to blasphemy against the Holy Spirit (Jn 12:10). Jesus performed His ministry through the power of the Holy Spirit, and this should have been evident to all unbiased seekers. Jesus used a piece of logic, however, to clear up the situation, noting that if Satan cast out his own demons, then he would be divided against himself, an unimaginable state of affairs.

24-28. After casting out a demon, Jesus wanted to stress the fact that a man's life must then be filled with good things, namely Christ and His salvation, or the man would be even more susceptible to the same calamity recurring than he was the first time. Mere self-reformation has no guaranteed results.

29-32. Jesus continually claimed to be God (Jn 5:17-18; 10:33), the Messiah (Jn 4:25-26), and the only way to heaven (Jn

This is an evil generation: they seek a sign; and there shall no sign be given it, but the sign of Jonas the prophet.

30 For as Jonas was a sign unto the Nĭn'e-vītes, so shall also the Son of man be to this generation.

31 The queen of the south shall rise up in the judgment with the men of this generation, and condemn them: for she came from the utmost parts of the earth to hear the wisdom of Solomon; and, behold, a greater than Solomon *is* here.

32 The men of Nĭn'e-ve shall rise up in the judgment with this generation, and shall condemn it: for they repented at the preaching of Jonas; and, behold, a greater than Jonas *is* here.

33 No man, when he hath lighted a candle, putteth *it* in a secret place, neither under a bushel, but on a candlestick, that they which come in may see the light.

34 The light of the body is the eye: therefore when thine eye is single, thy whole body also is full of light; but when *thine eye* is evil, thy body also *is* full of darkness.

35 Take heed therefore that the light which is in thee be not darkness.

36 If thy whole body therefore *be* full of light, having no part dark, the whole shall be full of light, as when the bright shining of a candle doth give thee light.

37 ¶And as he spake, a certain Pharisee besought him to dine with him: and he went in, and sat down to meat.

38 And when the Pharisee saw *it*, he marvelled that he had not first washed before dinner.

39 And the Lord said unto him, Now do ye Pharisees make clean the outside of the cup and the platter; but your inward part is full of ravening and wickedness.

40 *Ye* fools, did not he that made that which is without make that which is within also?

41 But rather give alms of such things as ye have; and, behold, all things are clean unto you.

42 But woe unto you, Pharisees! for ye tithe mint and rue and all manner of herbs, and pass over judgment and the love of God: these ought ye to have done, and not to leave the other undone.

43 Woe unto you, Pharisees! for ye love the uppermost seats in the synagogues, and greetings in the markets.

44 Woe unto you, scribes and Pharisees, hypocrites! for ye are as graves which appear not, and the men that walk over *them* are not aware of *them*.

45 Then answered one of the lawyers, and said unto him, Master, thus saying thou reproachest us also.

46 And he said, Woe unto you also, *ye* lawyers! for ye lade men with burdens grievous to be borne, and ye yourselves touch not the burdens with one of your fingers.

47 Woe unto you! for ye build the sepulchres of the prophets, and your fathers killed them.

48 Truly ye bear witness that ye al-

14:6). Here He says that failure to heed His direct plain message, supported by signs and wonders, will result in condemnation. Even the Queen of Sheba and those who repented at Jonah's preaching in Nineveh had enough light to know what to do. How much more blameworthy will these be if they fail to trust Christ! Note that Jesus fully endorsed the historicity of Jonah in these verses. Critics who deny the biblical account of Jonah degrade Christ as well.

33-36. Since the eye admits into the life that which influences it, Jesus is concerned that it be fed light, in the moral sense of the term, rather than darkness. Then one will become as a shining light himself.

37-40. The Pharisees were very careful to maintain outward cleanliness, but sometimes were unconcerned about the inside. Jesus probably ate without washing on purpose to point this out to his host.

41-54. Notice how boldly Jesus spoke in these verses. Six times he uttered woes, and once called them fools (spiritually imperceptive), and once hypocrites. Jesus was just over thirty, and this did not sit well with the older generation. Jesus rightly accused them of deceit (vss. 41-42), pride (vs. 43), inconsistency (vss. 44-46), condoning murder and conspiracy (vss. 47-51), and hindering people from being saved (vs. 53). Luke notes how heated the discussion got in verse 53 where it says the Pharisees were rudely provoking Christ to speak about many such subjects in hopes (vs. 54) of being able to accuse Jesus of something in order to put Him to death. Christ was their thorn in the flesh.

low the deeds of your fathers: for they indeed killed them, and ye build their sepulchres.

49 Therefore also said the wisdom of God, I will send them prophets and apostles, and *some* of them they shall slay and persecute:

50 That the blood of all the prophets, which was shed from the foundation of the world, may be required of this generation;

51 From the blood of Abel unto the blood of Zăch-a-rī'as, which perished between the altar and the temple: verily I say unto you, It shall be required of this generation.

52 Woe unto you, lawyers! for ye have taken away the key of knowledge: ye entered not in yourselves, and them that were entering in ye hindered.

53 And as he said these things unto them, the scribes and the Pharisees began to urge *him* vehemently, and to provoke him to speak of many things:

54 Laying wait for him, and seeking to catch something out of his mouth, that they might accuse him.

CHAPTER 12

IN the mean time, when there were gathered together an innumerable multitude of people, insomuch that they trode one upon another, he began to say unto his disciples first of all, Beware ye of the leaven of the Pharisees, which is hypocrisy.

2 For there is nothing covered, that shall not be revealed; neither hid, that shall not be known.

3 Therefore whatsoever ye have spoken in darkness shall be heard in the light; and that which ye have spoken in the ear in closets shall be proclaimed upon the housetops.

4 And I say unto you my friends, Be not afraid of them that kill the body, and after that have no more that they can do.

5 But I will forewarn you whom ye shall fear: Fear him, which after he hath killed hath power to cast into hell; yea, I say unto you, Fear him.

6 Are not five sparrows sold for two farthings, and not one of them is forgotten before God?

7 But even the very hairs of your head are all numbered. Fear not therefore: ye are of more value than many sparrows.

8 Also I say unto you, Whosoever shall confess me before men, him shall the Son of man also confess before the angels of God:

9 But he that denieth me before men shall be denied before the angels of God.

10 And whosoever shall speak a word against the Son of man, it shall be forgiven him: but unto him that blasphemeth against the Holy Ghost it shall not be forgiven.

12:1. Beware ye, of the leaven of the Pharisees which is hypocrisy. One way of teaching is to set the proper example. Jesus did that. Another way is to learn from the misconduct of others. Jesus pointed that out too.

2-3. It is sobering to think that everything we have ever spoken will one day be revealed. We must guard our hearts, minds, lips, and hands.

4-5. Jesus had much to say about hell. These verses tell us it is a place, that God has the power to cast into hell, and that this occurs after this life. The grave does not end it all.

6-9. But the child of God is secure in Christ, both now and forever. Nothing can ever harm a believer in this life, apart from the permission of God according to His perfect will.

10. The sin of blasphemy against the Holy Spirit could refer to the sin of seeing the Holy Spirit's working, and openly opposing it, such as attributing the miracles Christ performed to the power of Satan (cf. Lk 10:15). Or it could refer to an act which shows a state of sin in which there is a wilful, determined opposition to the power of the Holy Ghost. It could thus be the result of gradual progress in sin. Jesus accuses no man of such sin, but sternly warns against anyone coming to such a state of affairs. How do you avoid such a predicament? Harden not your hearts! Believe God, and trust Christ as your Saviour and Lord.

11 And when they bring you unto the synagogues, and *unto* magistrates, and powers, take ye no thought how or what thing ye shall answer, or what ye shall say:

12 For the Holy Ghost shall teach you in the same hour what ye ought to say.

13 ¶And one of the company said unto him, Master, speak to my brother, that he divide the inheritance with me.

14 And he said unto him, Man, who made me a judge or a divider over you?

15 And he said unto them, Take heed, and beware of covetousness: for a man's life consisteth not in the abundance of the things which he possesseth.

16 And he spake a parable unto them, saying, The ground of a certain rich man brought forth plentifully:

17 And he thought within himself, saying, What shall I do, because I have no room where to bestow my fruits?

18 And he said, This will I do: I will pull down my barns, and build greater; and there will I bestow all my fruits and my goods.

19 And I will say to my soul, Soul, thou hast much goods laid up for many years; take thine ease, eat, drink, *and* be merry.

20 But God said unto him, *Thou* fool, this night thy soul shall be required of thee: then whose shall those things be, which thou hast provided?

21 So *is* he that layeth up treasure for himself, and is not rich toward God.

22 ¶And he said unto his disciples, Therefore I say unto you, Take no thought for your life, what ye shall eat; neither for the body, what ye shall put on.

23 The life is more than meat, and the body *is more* than raiment.

24 Consider the ravens: for they neither sow nor reap; which neither have storehouse nor barn; and God feedeth them: how much more are ye better than the fowls?

25 And which of you with taking thought can add to his stature one cubit?

26 If ye then be not able to do that thing which is least, why take ye thought for the rest?

27 Consider the lilies how they grow: they toil not, they spin not; and yet I say unto you, that Solomon in all his glory was not arrayed like one of these.

28 If then God so clothe the grass, which is to day in the field, and to morrow is cast into the oven; how much more *will he clothe* you, O ye of little faith?

29 And seek not ye what ye shall eat, or what ye shall drink, neither be ye of doubtful mind.

30 For all these things do the nations of the world seek after: and your Father knoweth that ye have need of these things.

31 But rather seek ye the kingdom of God; and all these things shall be added unto you.

32 Fear not, little flock; for it is your Father's good pleasure to give you the kingdom.

33 Sell that ye have, and give alms;

11-12. Jesus warned that believers would be persecuted, but He also held out assurance that He would guide in that day of trouble.

13-15. A man's life consisteth not in the abundance of the things which he possesseth. What an important reminder this is in our materialistic age. Many seek after things, but all find that they do not satisfy. Jesus counselled, "Seek ye first the kingdom of God and his righteousness; and all these things shall be added unto you" (Mt 6:33).

16-21. Jesus spoke the parable of the rich fool to two young inheritance seekers (vs. 13). There are more parables dealing with money than with any other subject. This is probably because there are so many snares and temptations that beset those who possess and/or seek to acquire money. The warning contained in this story is that of providing amply for the physical aspects of life, while ignoring preparations for the life to come. Wealth cannot secure one's salvation, but it can be used for heavenly good.

22-30. In these verses the Master exhorted His disciples not to fret about securing food or clothing. He goes from the lesser to the greater by noting how God provides food for the fowl (vs. 24) and coverings for the flowers (vss. 27-28). If that is true, how much more shall God provide for His own children.

31-33. As a summary statement, Christ promised **seek ye the kingdom of God; and all these things shall be added unto you.**

provide yourselves bags which wax not old, a treasure in the heavens that faileth not, where no thief approacheth, neither moth corrupteth.

34 For where your treasure is, there will your heart be also.

35 Let your loins be girded about, and *your* lights burning;

36 And ye yourselves like unto men that wait for their lord, when he will return from the wedding; that when he cometh and knocketh, they may open unto him immediately.

37 Blessed *are* those servants, whom the lord when he cometh shall find watching: verily I say unto you, that he shall gird himself, and make them to sit down to meat, and will come forth and serve them.

38 And if he shall come in the second watch, or come in the third watch, and find *them* so, blessed are those servants.

39 And this know, that if the goodman of the house had known what hour the thief would come, he would have watched, and not have suffered his house to be broken through.

40 Be ye therefore ready also: for the Son of man cometh at an hour when ye think not.

41 ¶Then Peter said unto him, Lord, speakest thou this parable unto us, or even to all?

42 And the Lord said, Who then is that faithful and wise steward, whom *his* lord shall make ruler over his household, to give *them their* portion of meat in due season?

43 Blessed *is* that servant, whom his lord when he cometh shall find so doing.

44 Of a truth I say unto you, that he will make him ruler over all that he hath.

45 But and if that servant say in his heart, My lord delayeth his coming; and shall begin to beat the menservants and maidens, and to eat and drink, and to be drunken;

46 The lord of that servant will come in a day when he looketh not for *him*, and at an hour when he is not aware, and will cut him in sunder, and will appoint him his portion with the unbelievers.

47 And that servant, which knew his lord's will, and prepared not *himself*, neither did according to his will, shall be beaten with many *stripes*.

48 But he that knew not, and did commit things worthy of stripes, shall be beaten with few *stripes*. For unto whomsoever much is given, of him shall be much required: and to whom men have committed much, of him they will ask the more.

49 ¶I am come to send fire on the

34. For where your treasure is, there will your heart be also. One of the greatest things a pastor can ever do for his people is to get them to give tithes and offerings to the Lord. If they do, their hearts will be attuned to God. Pastors who preach on godly giving do their people a great spiritual service.

35. Let your loins be girded about, and your lights burning. Even though God will provide, the servant of Christ is to be about his Master's business until He comes. The parable that follows is drawn from the familiar Near Eastern wedding custom.

36. Men that wait for their lord, when he will return from the wedding. In the Orient, the groom returned with his bride after claiming her at her father's house. This parable could be spoken mainly for the Jews who will welcome Christ back with His bride after the Tribulation Period, but it certainly has an application for the church today.

37-40. Several things are taught: (1) Expectancy. Servants should be looking for the Master's return. (2) Preparedness. Servants should have things in order. (3) Rewards. Verse 37 indicates rewards for the faithful servants, as is taught elsewhere (vss. 43-44; Lk 19:17). The figure of the thief is also given by Paul (I Thess 5:4). The coming of Christ is never to overtake a believer as a thief. We are to be waiting and watching for His return.

41-46. This portion is vitally connected to what precedes it, and acts as a further amplification. The obedient servant will be blessed and rewarded (vss. 42-44), but that **servant** who disobeys will suffer punishment (vss. 45-46).

47-49. The fact that there will be degrees of punishment is taught here. The torment of hell will not be uniformly felt. The light one possesses helps determine how responsible one is. Some will be found more guilty than others, but no lost man can claim innocence in that day.

earth; and what will I, if it be already kindled?

50 But I have a baptism to be baptized with; and how am I straitened till it be accomplished!

51 Suppose ye that I am come to give peace on earth? I tell you, Nay; but rather division:

52 For from henceforth there shall be five in one house divided, three against two and two against three.

53 The father shall be divided against the son, and the son against the father; the mother against the daughter, and the daughter against the mother; the mother in law against her daughter in law, and the daughter in law against her mother in law.

54 ¶And he said also to the people, When ye see a cloud rise out of the west, straightway ye say, There cometh a shower; and so it is.

55 And when ye see the south wind blow, ye say, There will be heat; and it cometh to pass.

56 Ye hypocrites, ye can discern the face of the sky and of the earth; but how is it that ye do not discern this time?

57 Yea, and why even of yourselves judge ye not what is right?

58 ¶When thou goest with thine adversary to the magistrate, as thou art in the way, give diligence that thou mayest be delivered from him; lest he hale thee to the judge, and the judge deliver thee to the officer, and the officer cast thee into prison.

59 I tell thee, thou shalt not depart thence, till thou hast paid the very last mite.

CHAPTER 13

THERE were present at that season some that told him of the Galilæans, whose blood Pilate had mingled with their sacrifices.

2 And Jesus answering said unto them, Suppose ye that these Galilæans were sinners above all the Galilæans, because they suffered such things?

3 I tell you, Nay: but, except ye repent, ye shall all likewise perish.

4 Or those eighteen, upon whom the tower in Sī-lō'am fell, and slew them, think ye that they were sinners above all men that dwelt in Jerusalem?

5 I tell you, Nay: but, except ye repent, ye shall all likewise perish.

6 ¶He spake also this parable; A certain man had a fig tree planted in his vineyard; and he came and sought fruit thereon, and found none.

7 Then said he unto the dresser of his vineyard, Behold, these three years I come seeking fruit on this fig tree, and find none: cut it down; why cumbereth it the ground?

8 And he answering said unto him, Lord, let it alone this year also, till I shall dig about it, and dung it:

9 And if it bear fruit, well: and if not, then after that thou shalt cut it down.

10 ¶And he was teaching in one of the synagogues on the sabbath.

50. But I have a baptism to be baptized with. That which Jesus referred to as necessary for Him to undergo (see also Mk 10:38-39) was His own coming death which is referred to under several figures in the New Testament.

51-53. Christ is the ultimate divider. What men decide regarding Christ determines their ultimate destiny, and also draws the barrier lines between men.

54-56. Jesus declared that signs were clearly discernible relative to His ministry, yet men refused to heed these. Such men must bear the responsibility for their own destruction under such circumstances.

57-59. These verses teach that one must settle with his adversary (in this case, God) before it is too late. Verse 59 does not indicate that eventually one would get out of hell, because there no one has anything with which to "pay." It is too late.

13:1-5. Except ye repent, ye shall all likewise perish. Twice Jesus repeated identical words to reinforce the necessity of repentance (vss. 3, 5). Calamity and destruction await all who refuse to heed the warning. Jesus perhaps has reference to the events of A.D. 70, and certainly beyond to eternal punishment.

6-9. He spake also this parable; A certain man had a fig tree planted in his vineyard. This parable is found only in Luke, but both here and in the miraculous cursing of the fig tree in Matthew 21:18-21, the tree seems to stand for Israel. The lesson is that when God gives spiritual privileges, He has a right to expect fruit. One might also learn the danger of not producing fruit. Even though the Lord was merciful with Israel, He yet had to judge that nation. The three or four years in the parable are probably not meant to represent so many years of Christ's ministry, but rather an adequate time for testing fruitfulness.

10. And he was teaching in one of the synagogues on the sabbath. This was Jesus' habitual Sabbath day practice. It so happened that these occasions became times when Christ healed

11 And, behold, there was a woman which had a spirit of infirmity eighteen years, and was bowed together, and could in no wise lift up *herself.*

12 And when Jesus saw her, he called *her to him,* and said unto her, Woman, thou art loosed from thine infirmity.
13 And he laid *his* hands on her: and immediately she was made straight, and glorified God.
14 And the ruler of the synagogue answered with indignation, because that Jesus had healed on the sabbath day, and said unto the people, There are six days in which men ought to work: in them therefore come and be healed, and not on the sabbath day.
15 The Lord then answered him, and said, *Thou* hypocrite, doth not each one of you on the sabbath loose his ox or *his* ass from the stall, and lead *him* away to watering?
16 And ought not this woman, being a daughter of Abraham, whom Satan hath bound, lo, these eighteen years, be loosed from this bond on the sabbath day?
17 And when he had said these things, all his adversaries were ashamed: and all the people rejoiced for all the glorious things that were done by him.
18 ¶Then said he, Unto what is the kingdom of God like? and whereunto shall I resemble it?
19 It is like a grain of mustard seed, which a man took, and cast into his garden; and it grew, and waxed a great tree; and the fowls of the air lodged in the branches of it.
20 ¶And again he said, Whereunto shall I liken the kingdom of God?
21 It is like leaven, which a woman took and hid in three measures of meal, till the whole was leavened.

22 And he went through the cities and villages, teaching, and journeying toward Jerusalem.
23 ¶Then said one unto him, Lord, are there few that be saved? And he said unto them,
24 Strive to enter in at the strait gate: for many, I say unto you, will seek to enter in, and shall not be able.
25 When once the master of the house is risen up, and hath shut to the

some as well. The religious leaders constantly tried to convict Jesus of breaking the sabbath restrictions with such miraculous works.

11. Only Luke records this case of healing. As a physician, he has an interest in and sympathy for stories about women, of which he records more than the other gospel writers. This woman had been bent over for eighteen years by Satan (vs. 16). Though all sickness cannot be uniformly blamed on Satan, the Bible does enumerate several cases, as in Job 2:6-7; Acts 10:38; I Corinthians 5:5, and II Corinthians 12:7.

12-13. Thou art loosed. Here the Greek tense is perfect and indicates that the curse was complete and certain.

14. The speech of the synagogue ruler was a hypocritical and underhanded way of criticizing Christ. It naturally drew a severe rebuke from the Lord.

15-16. Jesus' reply was that the Sabbath was not intended to prevent works of necessity or mercy. The application of this truth is as follows: some jobs today require Sunday employment, such as hospitals, law enforcement, and fire-fighting. Most other jobs, however, can often be performed on other days, even though Sunday of itself is not to be kept as the Jewish Sabbath. As a rule, Sunday is regarded as a day of worship, and we should not needlessly violate that principle, even though we realize there are exceptions.

17. Jesus' rebuke had its proper effect. His adversaries were ashamed, while His admirers were amazed and rejoiced. Nevertheless, a polarity was developing regarding Jesus.

18-19. Jesus parabolically indicated that a mustard seed sprouting into a tree over ten feet tall represented the kingdom of God. This probably signified the large or surprising growth of Christianity from a tiny seed. The birds that sat in the branches may picture evil as in Matthew 13:4 and 19, or they may simply be an indication of the fact that this herb was large enough to hold birds on its branches.

20-21. The kingdom of God was also compared to a woman who mingled leaven into several loaves of meal until they had all risen. Perhaps a majority of older interpreters have seen this as the spreading of good throughout the world via the church. But this would seem to contradict the fact that the wheat did not take over the tares (Mt 13) and Jesus' forecast in Matthew 24:37 that the end times would be as in Noah's day. Besides, leaven is a picture of that which corrupts, and represents sin (Ex 12:15; Lk 12:1; I Cor 5:6-8). It is better to view this as a picture of the externalism, unbelief, evil doctrine, and worldliness which tend to inflate the church. Only fire ends the work of leaven!

D. Christ's Growing Public Confrontation with Religious Leaders. 13:22-16:31.

22. Journeying toward Jerusalem. Here Luke brings us back to the theme of 9:51, that Jesus was on His final preaching tour and was to keep a divine appointment in Jerusalem.

23. Lord, are there few that be saved? Ths question drew a lengthy answer from Christ that was to serve as a warning against religious presumption.

24-27. Man's time of probation ends both suddenly and surely. Naturally, death ends man's opportunity for salvation. There is no truth to some so-called second-chance theories. But apparently at the judgment some may presume upon having once seen or known Christ. But one must know Christ in the

door, and ye begin to stand without, and to knock at the door, saying, Lord, Lord, open unto us; and he shall answer and say unto you, I know you not whence ye are:

26 Then shall ye begin to say, We have eaten and drunk in thy presence, and thou hast taught in our streets.

27 But he shall say, I tell you, I know you not whence ye are; depart from me, all *ye* workers of iniquity.

28 There shall be weeping and gnashing of teeth, when ye shall see Abraham, and Isaac, and Jacob, and all the prophets, in the kingdom of God, and you *yourselves* thrust out.

29 And they shall come from the east, and *from* the west, and from the north, and *from* the south, and shall sit down in the kingdom of God.

30 And, behold, there are last which shall be first, and there are first which shall be last.

31 ¶The same day there came certain of the Pharisees, saying unto him, Get thee out, and depart hence: for Herod will kill thee.

32 And he said unto them, Go ye, and tell that fox, Behold, I cast out devils, and I do cures to day and to morrow, and the third *day* I shall be perfected.

33 Nevertheless I must walk to day, and to morrow, and the *day* following: for it cannot be that a prophet perish out of Jerusalem.

34 O Jerusalem, Jerusalem, which killest the prophets, and stonest them that are sent unto thee; how often would I have gathered thy children together, as a hen *doth gather* her brood under *her* wings, and ye would not!

35 Behold, your house is left unto you desolate: and verily I say unto you, Ye shall not see me, until *the time* come when ye shall say, Blessed *is* he that cometh in the name of the Lord.

CHAPTER 14

AND it came to pass, as he went into the house of one of the chief Pharisees to eat bread on the sabbath day, that they watched him.

2 And, behold, there was a certain man before him which had the dropsy.

3 And Jesus answering spake unto the lawyers and Pharisees, saying, Is it lawful to heal on the sabbath day?

4 And they held their peace. And he took *him,* and healed him, and let him go;

5 And answered them, saying, Which of you shall have an ass or an ox fallen into a pit, and will not straightway pull him out on the sabbath day?

6 And they could not answer him again to these things.

personal way that characterized true faith and trust in His shed blood for one's salvation from sin.

28. The kingdom of God. This phrase has several prominent usages, for which see George N. H. Peters, *The Theocratic Kingdom,* and Alva J. McClain, *The Greatness of the Kingdom.* Here it has reference to the millennial kingdom when the Old Testament patriarchs will be resurrected to join Christ and the redeemed of all the ages during His one-thousand-year earthly reign. This fulfills numerous Old Testament prophecies (Isa 11:1-9; Mic 4:1-3) as well as Revelation 20:1-6.

29. Coming from the four winds could speak either of the regathering of Israel which will take place as the kingdom age begins, or of the cosmopolitan makeup of the kingdom. Both will be true.

30. The last being first and the first turning out to be last must have been a thought of momentous proportions for any Jewish hearers who considered it. Just think, those who judged Christ and condemned Him to death will one day stand before Him who is the Almighty God of the universe. Things will be different then.

31-33. The Pharisees told Jesus that Herod Antipas (see notes on Lk 1:5) planned to kill Him. Jesus replied that He would continue His work according to schedule (the three days are not intended to be taken literally) and then His work of redemption would be completed in Jerusalem (Jn 19:30).

34-35. O Jerusalem, Jerusalem, which killest the prophets. Christ knew that Jerusalem, not Herod, was the real threat to His life. The lament for Jerusalem realizes its bloody past, but also recognizes its blessed future, which will not occur until the end of the Great Tribulation.

14:1-6. Luke the physician is the only gospel writer to record this healing. Dropsy was literally internalized or excessive water in the tissues, and this is the only mention of it in the New Testament. This Sabbath situation was apparently a trap set up by Jesus' opponents. No man with this terrible dropsy disease would be invited to supper at the house of a chief Pharisee, let alone sitting right in front of Jesus. Verse 1 also indicates that **they watched him.** The Pharisees refused to answer Jesus' question, **Is it lawful to heal on the sabbath day?** If they had answered "yes," they could not condemn Jesus for healing. But if they answered "no," they would have condemned themselves as indifferent to human suffering. Their silence was Christ's justification. If it was illegal, they should have said so. Thereafter, Christ healed the man. Christ's final question placed this Sabbath healing in its proper perspective as doing good or rendering help whenever necessary.

7 ¶And he put forth a parable to those which were bidden, when he marked how they chose out the chief rooms; saying unto them,

8 When thou art bidden of any *man* to a wedding, sit not down in the highest room; lest a more honourable man than thou be bidden of him;

9 And he that bade thee and him come and say to thee, Give this man place; and thou begin with shame to take the lowest room.

10 But when thou art bidden, go and sit down in the lowest room; that when he that bade thee cometh, he may say unto thee, Friend, go up higher: then shalt thou have worship in the presence of them that sit at meat with thee.

11 For whosoever exalteth himself shall be abased; and he that humbleth himself shall be exalted.

12 ¶Then said he also to him that bade him, When thou makest a dinner or a supper, call not thy friends, nor thy brethren, neither thy kinsmen, nor *thy* rich neighbours; lest they also bid thee again, and a recompence be made thee.

13 But when thou makest a feast, call the poor, the maimed, the lame, the blind:

14 And thou shalt be blessed; for they cannot recompense thee: for thou shalt be recompensed at the resurrection of the just.

15 ¶And when one of them that sat at meat with him heard these things, he said unto him, Blessed *is* he that shall eat bread in the kingdom of God.

16 Then said he unto him, A certain man made a great supper, and bade many:

17 And sent his servant at supper time to say to them that were bidden, Come; for all things are now ready.

18 And they all with one *consent* began to make excuse. The first said unto him, I have bought a piece of ground, and I must needs go and see it: I pray thee have me excused.

19 And another said, I have bought five yoke of oxen, and I go to prove them: I pray thee have me excused.

20 And another said, I have married a wife, and therefore I cannot come.

21 So that servant came, and shewed his lord these things. Then the master of the house being angry said to his servant, Go out quickly into the streets and lanes of the city, and bring in hither the poor, and the maimed, and the halt, and the blind.

22 And the servant said, Lord, it is done as thou hast commanded, and yet there is room.

23 And the lord said unto the servant, Go out into the highways and hedges, and compel *them* to come in, that my house may be filled.

24 For I say unto you, That none of those men which were bidden shall taste of my supper.

25 ¶And there went great multitudes with him: and he turned, and said unto them,

7-11. And he put forth a parable to those which were bidden. The conduct of the guests at this Sabbath meal was such that Jesus commented on it with a parable. The idea of lowest and highest seats refers to the almost universal custom of designating places for honored persons at meals and other functions. Jesus warned against placing oneself at the "head table" unless invited to do so. Removal could result in dishonor. Contrariwise, if the lowly seat has been selected at first, the host would thereafter assign one to the proper dignity. This thinking is against our inclination. We want the best for ourselves. But Jesus would have humility before exaltation. We must be little in our own eyes before we can be large in His eyes.

12-15. Similarly, Jesus cautioned His followers to invite guests who could provide little promise of returning the favor. This action helps one's attitude to be correct with regard to giving and receiving. When we give without hope of return, we trust God to bless and provide any reward as He may or may not see fit either here or at **the resurrection of the just** (cf. Jn 5:28-29; Rev 20:4-6).

16-17. A certain man made a great supper, and bade many. This parable paints a picture of God's abundant provision and invitation of salvation, refused by the Jews, then offered with all speed and diligence to others not previously invited.

18-20. And they all with one consent began to make excuse. Literally, they began "to beg off." Someone once defined an excuse as "the skin of a reason stuffed with a lie." There are three classes of excuses, all false on the very surface: (1) No one should buy land without previously having examined it; (2) no one would ever purchase ten oxen without knowing their condition; and (3) the excuse about marrying a wife was evidently based on Deuteronomy 24:5, but this application was certainly novel. The **I cannot come** (vs. 20) actually means, "I will not come." These invited guests rudely, ungratefully, and purposefully refused to come, even though they fully understood their deceitful practice.

21-22. After that, all classes of previously uninvited guests were asked to come, and they did come. This probably speaks in part of the command to take the gospel to the Gentiles given after the rejection, crucifixion, burial and resurrection of Christ (Mt 28:18-20; Mk 16:15).

23-25. Compel them to come in. This must be regarded as a moral persuasion, not the use of physical force. Every effort is to be made by Christ's servants to bring the lost to Him. His Word must be used diligently to overcome the sinner's despair, as well as the arrogance of the self-righteous. Jesus came to seek and to save that which was lost (Lk 19:10) and we are sent on the same task. God desires that all legitimate means be used to procure the acceptance of His gracious invitation. Many a soul has been

26 If any *man* come to me, and hate not his father, and mother, and wife, and children, and brethren, and sisters, yea, and his own life also, he cannot be my disciple.

27 And whosoever doth not bear his cross, and come after me, cannot be my disciple.

28 For which of you, intending to build a tower, sitteth not down first, and counteth the cost, whether he have *sufficient* to finish *it?*

29 Lest haply, after he hath laid the foundation, and is not able to finish *it,* all that behold *it* begin to mock him,

30 Saying, This man began to build, and was not able to finish.

31 Or what king, going to make war against another king, sitteth not down first, and consulteth whether he be able with ten thousand to meet him that cometh against him with twenty thousand?

32 Or else, while the other is yet a great way off, he sendeth an ambassage, and desireth conditions of peace.

33 So likewise, whosoever forsaketh not all that he hath, he cannot be my disciple.

34 ¶Salt *is* good: but if the salt have lost his savour, wherewith shall it be seasoned?

35 It is neither fit for the land, nor yet for the dunghill; *but* men cast it out. He that hath ears to hear, let him hear.

CHAPTER 15

THEN drew near unto him all the publicans and sinners for to hear him.

2 And the Pharisees and scribes murmured, saying, This man receiveth sinners, and eateth with them.

3 ¶And he spake this parable unto them, saying,

4 What man of you, having an hundred sheep, if he lose one of them, doth not leave the ninety and nine in the wilderness, and go after that which is lost, until he find it?

5 And when he hath found *it,* he layeth *it* on his shoulders, rejoicing.

6 And when he cometh home, he calleth together *his* friends and neigh-

led to Christ by the earnest, tearful, sincere pleading of a dedicated Christian worker yielded to the control of the Holy Spirit.

26. In the context of all other Scripture (Ex 20:12; Mt 5:44; Rom 12:10) this command must be interpreted in a comparative manner. Christ meant that one must place Him above all other relationships. To be Christ's disciple, He must be Lord. If He is not Lord of all, He may not be Lord at all!

27. Bear his cross. For one to bear a cross means to experience the shame and humiliation, as well as the toil and suffering, that this form of punishment suggests. Bearing one's cross is not an easy assignment; it is just being a true Christian with all that entails.

28-33. The short stories about considering the cost before building a tower or placing an army in the field is a picture of fully considering what it will cost before one becomes a Christian; for some, it may seemingly cost more than for others.

34-35. If the salt have lost his savor. A disciple must have certain essential qualities. If these are gone, he is useless to Christ, and as the saying goes "not worth his salt." The salt in use during Christ's time was impure, and the sodium chloride could be leached out of that common salt. This represents the type of disciple Christ does not want.

15:1-2. Publicans and sinners. Three stories with a common theme are recounted by Christ in this chapter to illustrate His love and concern for sinful men and women. **The Pharisees and scribes murmured** because Jesus showed such love and kindness to sinners.

3. And he spake this parable unto them. Both sinners and Pharisees alike were to hear and apply this parable. The word *parable* occurs only once in this chapter, perhaps pointing to one parable with three connected parts. In each story something is lost: (1) a sheep; (2) a shekel; and (3) a son. In each case, the lost object is found and produces rejoicing. The sheep is innocently lost, the coin carelessly lost, but the son willfully lost. The percentage of loss grows in each case from one out of a hundred, to one out of ten, to one out of two.

4. The **sheep** is an exceedingly dumb animal, seemingly not having much sense. As such, it is sometimes used to picture the lost spiritual condition of people (Isa 53:6; Jer 50:6; Mt 9:36; I Pet 2:25). This parable tells of a shepherd going out in search of one lost sheep while he leaves ninety-nine safely in the fold. It is almost a universal human characteristic to go after that which one loses. Jesus sees the plight of lost sinners and goes to seek and to save (Lk 19:10), while the Pharisees care little about lost sinners.

5. Layeth it on his shoulders, rejoicing. The poor sheep was probably exhausted from wandering, exposure, and hunger. The shepherd did not mind the extra burden or journey because he rejoiced.

6-7. The friends and neighbors were summoned because of the shepherd's great joy and because they may have aided in the

bours, saying unto them, Rejoice with me; for I have found my sheep which was lost.

7 I say unto you, that likewise joy shall be in heaven over one sinner that repenteth, more than over ninety and nine just persons, which need no repentance.

8 ¶Either what woman having ten pieces of silver, if she lose one piece, doth not light a candle, and sweep the house, and seek diligently till she find *it?*

9 And when she hath found *it,* she calleth *her* friends and *her* neighbours together, saying, Rejoice with me; for I have found the piece which I had lost.

10 Likewise, I say unto you there is joy in the presence of the angels of God over one sinner that repenteth.

11 ¶And he said, A certain man had two sons:

12 And the younger of them said to *his* father, Father, give me the portion of goods that falleth *to me.* And he divided unto them *his* living.

13 And not many days after the younger son gathered all together, and took his journey into a far country, and there wasted his substance with riotous living.

14 And when he had spent all, there arose a mighty famine in that land; and he began to be in want.

15 And he went and joined himself to a citizen of that country; and he sent him into his fields to feed swine.

16 And he would fain have filled his belly with the husks that the swine did eat: and no man gave unto him.

17 And when he came to himself, he said, How many hired servants of my father's have bread enough and to spare, and I perish with hunger!

18 I will arise and go to my father, and will say unto him, Father, I have sinned against heaven, and before thee,

19 And am no more worthy to be called thy son: make me as one of thy hired servants.

20 And he arose, and came to his father. But when he was yet a great way off, his father saw him, and had compassion, and ran, and fell on his neck, and kissed him.

21 And the son said unto him, Father, I have sinned against heaven, and in thy sight, and am no more worthy to be called thy son.

22 But the father said to his servants, Bring forth the best robe, and put *it* on him; and put a ring on his hand, and shoes on *his* feet:

23 And bring hither the fatted calf, and kill *it;* and let us eat, and be merry:

24 For this my son was dead, and is alive again; he was lost, and is found. And they began to be merry.

25 Now his elder son was in the field: and as he came and drew nigh to the house, he heard musick and dancing.

search. Jesus' remark that there is also joy in heaven over a sinner that repents perhaps sadly implies that not many rejoiced with Christ here on earth regarding these matters.

8-10. The story of the lost coin was perhaps told for women listeners. The coin was lost right at home. People may be members of good churches and still be lost and go to hell. The sheep may have had a vague idea it was lost, but this coin could picture those with no knowledge of being lost. We need to search for those who are lost to bring them to Christ. Joy in the presence of God's angels over repenting sinners (vs. 10) shows that they are interested in our salvation (cf. I Pet 1:10-12), though they do not aid it.

11. A certain man had two sons. In the two previous stories Jesus told how the Pharisees should act when lost sinners were found. In this longer story he pictured how they did act. They can see themselves in the person of the elder brother, who had his good and bad points. He was morally straight, a hard worker, and an obedient individual (vs. 29), but he was also proud and had no fellowship with the father. He was more willing to think of his brother's sin than of his repentance.

12-32. The younger son's conduct can be summarized in an alliterative fashion with just nine key words. His rebellion resulted in riotous living as he hit rock bottom before his realization to repent and return, where he experienced reception, reconciliation, and rejoicing. Ralph Earle sees his movements as from possessor to prodigal to pauper to penitent to pardoned. His wicked conduct was willful and inexcusable, but his repentance was complete and his forgiveness absolute. He is a picture of every man born on this earth and in need of a Saviour. It it almost ironical that everything the prodigal son sought in the far country was right at home. There was abundance, freedom, and rejoicing.

The father's part pictures God's love for lost sinners. He is kind, waits for the son, goes to meet him, perhaps to save him the deserved punishment he might have received from others for disgracing his family and village, and forgets his past life. He **was dead, and is alive again; and was lost, and is found** (vs. 32).

26 And he called one of the servants, and asked what these things meant.

27 And he said unto him, Thy brother is come; and thy father hath killed the fatted calf, because he hath received him safe and sound.

28 And he was angry, and would not go in: therefore came his father out, and intreated him.

29 And he answering said to *his* father, Lo, these many years do I serve thee, neither transgressed I at any time thy commandment: and yet thou never gavest me a kid, that I might make merry with my friends:

30 But as soon as this thy son was come, which hath devoured thy living with harlots, thou hast killed for him the fatted calf.

31 And he said unto him, Son, thou art ever with me, and all that I have is thine.

32 It was meet that we should make merry, and be glad: for this thy brother was dead, and is alive again; and was lost, and is found.

CHAPTER 16

AND he said also unto his disciples, There was a certain rich man, which had a steward; and the same was accused unto him that he had wasted his goods.

2 And he called him, and said unto him, How is it that I hear this of thee? give an account of thy stewardship; for thou mayest be no longer steward.

3 Then the steward said within himself, What shall I do? for my lord taketh away from me the stewardship: I cannot dig; to beg I am ashamed.

4 I am resolved what to do, that, when I am put out of the stewardship, they may receive me into their houses.

5 So he called every one of his lord's debtors *unto him,* and said unto the first, How much owest thou unto my lord?

6 And he said, An hundred measures of oil. And he said unto him, Take thy bill, and sit down quickly, and write fifty.

7 Then said he to another, And how much owest thou? And he said, An hundred measures of wheat. And he said unto him, Take thy bill, and write fourscore.

8 And the lord commended the unjust steward, because he had done wisely: for the children of this world are in their generation wiser than the children of light.

9 And I say unto you, Make to yourselves friends of the mammon of unrighteousness; that, when ye fail, they may receive you into everlasting habitations.

10 He that is faithful in that which is least is faithful also in much: and he that is unjust in the least is unjust also in much.

11 If therefore ye have not been faithful in the unrighteous mammon, who will commit to your trust the true *riches?*

12 And if ye have not been faithful in that which is another man's, who shall give you that which is your own?

16:1-12. The contextual connection of the story of the unjust steward with the parable of the prodigal son is perhaps that both deal with wasting and abusing wordly goods. Verse 14 also takes notice of the covetous audience. The plot is that a rich man, upon discovering wastefulness in his steward, was going to dismiss him (vs. 12). To protect his future, the steward immediately began making friends on the outside by juggling the goods in favor of those who owed the master (vss. 3-7). The story continues to have the master commend the unjust steward for his prudence (vs. 8).

Many see a problem as to why Jesus used such a character as the unjust steward, and even told of his commendation. Christ could simply be stressing the use of one's money and influence to aid others for Christ's sake (vss. 9-12), but this does not seem to be it entirely. There are, of course, some valuable character qualities in the unjust steward that are worthy of imitation, including his quick decisiveness, his self-collectedness, his energy, and his tact. But the main lesson seems to lie in the larger idea of realizing he is about to be dismissed and doing something about it. Men should realize that death comes as a certainty, and that they must prepare properly for what comes afterward.

13 No servant can serve two masters: for either he will hate the one, and love the other; or else he will hold to the one, and despise the other. Ye cannot serve God and mammon.

14 ¶And the Pharisees also, who were covetous, heard all these things: and they derided him.

15 And he said unto them, Ye are they which justify yourselves before men; but God knoweth your hearts: for that which is highly esteemed among men is abomination in the sight of God.

16 The law and the prophets were until John: since that time the kingdom of God is preached, and every man presseth into it.

13-15. Ye cannot serve God and mammon. This does not mean a man cannot be wealthy and still serve God. But the love of money is the root of all evil (I Tim 6:10). If a person desires wealth, then he ceases to please God. A man's loyalties cannot be divided, and God demands that everything be subservient to Him.

16. The law and the prophets were until John. Until the coming of John the Baptist and Jesus Christ, the only message Old Testament saints had was the law of Moses and the prophets. **Since that time the kingdom of God is preached.** John and Christ heralded a new order, the long-awaited kingdom age. John announced it as "at hand" (Mt 3:2) or as having come near. But even after John the Baptist was in jail and out of the picture, Jesus was still saying that the kingdom had not arrived, but was yet "at hand" (Mk 1:14-15). **And every man presseth into it.** Since the Jews rejected Christ's offer of the physical kingdom age and His rule over them, that dispensation and ministry was never inaugurated, though it shall be after the Great Tribulation (Mt 24:29-31; 25:31; Rev 19:11-20:6). But from the time of Christ to this day men can meet the spiritual requirements for entrance into that kingdom. In fact, the publicans and sinners often sought entrance with great earnestness and determination, while the Pharisees usually made no conscious efforts to enter. (See John 3:1-16 for the story of one who did.)

17 And it is easier for heaven and earth to pass, than one tittle of the law to fail.

18 Whosoever putteth away his wife, and marrieth another, committeth adultery: and whosoever marrieth her that is put away from *her* husband committeth adultery.

17-18. Jesus' teaching on divorce corrected the lax interpretation of the Jews based on their loose understanding of Deuteronomy 24, where Moses "permitted" divorce because of the "hardness of your hearts." While our Lord corrected and interpreted the Old Testament law, He did not eliminate it. The Law was part of God's inspired truth and therefore it will not **fail.** No exceptions are given to the matters of divorce in this passage (cf. Mk 10:11; I Cor 7:10-11ff., for further details). Some take the "exception clause" (Mt 19:9) to allow a divorce on the basis of "adultery," while others limit "fornication" (Gr *porneia*) to premarital sex. This view sees premarital unchastity as the only cause of "divorce" in breaking a Jewish engagement. A clear case of this was where Joseph suspected Mary of premarital unfaithfulness and desired to "put her away privily" (Mt 1:18-19). This interpretation allows no provision for divorce whatever. The seriousness of remarriage on non-scriptural grounds means that **whosoever marrieth her that is put away** (Gr *apolelumenen* from *apoluo* "to loose" or "divorce") also **committeth adultery.**

19 ¶There was a certain rich man, which was clothed in purple and fine linen, and fared sumptuously every day:

20 And there was a certain beggar named Lazarus, which was laid at his gate, full of sores,

21 And desiring to be fed with the crumbs which fell from the rich man's table: moreover the dogs came and licked his sores.

19-21. There was a certain rich man . . . and there was a certain beggar. This is the true account of a real history of two men, even though it is used much like a parable, i.e., to teach a particular lesson or to emphasize some principle. Some, however, contend that this is a parable saying that (1) the name Lazarus means "God helps" and is figurative or perhaps was intentionally chosen later because another Lazarus did come back from the dead; (2) it begins exactly as the preceding "parable" in Luke 16:1 (which incidentally is also not called a parable in the text); (3) it is used in parabolic fashion to prove a main point; (4) facts are presented in symbolic form; (5) it is in the context of other parables in Luke 15-18; (6) Christ would not have divulged such truths to unbelieving Pharisees; (7) the ability to see, hear, and communicate between heaven and hell after death is not possible; (8) the rich man would not have known Abraham and Lazarus by sight; and (9) in real life the names of rich men are given, while beggars' names are unknown. Some of these points are well-taken, but none prove that this account was only a parable.

There are numerous arguments for this account being a real history. (1) Parables are hypothetical illustrations and never name specific individuals. Here not only Lazarus is named, but also Abraham (vss. 22-25, 29-30) and Moses (vs. 31). (2) Jesus said "there was a certain rich man." Harry Ironside noted, "Was there, or was there not? He definitely declared that there was." (3) Moses, Abraham, and the prophets are real people, whereas parables never refer to specific Old Testament saints. (4) Luke does not call this a parable as he does in thirteen other clear cases of parable so designated. (5) It is narrated like a real history. (6) Parables deal with the commonplace of what is known to be true to illustrate moral lessons, and come from natural life. This does not. (7) Hades is a reality, not a figure of speech. (8) There is no reason why Jesus could not have had in mind a particular case. He is describing what took place after death in the cases of two men for the moral profit of His hearers. (9) The conversation between the rich man and Abraham does not seem to lend itself to parabolic format. (10) Even a case history, as this is, could be used in parabolic fashion to teach a precise moral truth.

22. Abraham's bosom. This is a designation for where Abraham was, taken variously as being heaven itself or some other intermediate place.

22 And it came to pass, that the beggar died, and was carried by the angels into Abraham's bosom: the rich man also died, and was buried;

23 And in hell he lift up his eyes, being in torments, and seeth Abraham afar off, and Lazarus in his bosom.

24 And he cried and said, Father Abraham, have mercy on me, and send Lazarus, that he may dip the tip of his finger in water, and cool my tongue; for I am tormented in this flame.

25 But Abraham said, Son, remember that thou in thy lifetime receivedst thy good things, and likewise Lazarus evil things: but now he is comforted, and thou art tormented.

26 And beside all this, between us and you there is a great gulf fixed: so that they which would pass from hence to you cannot; neither can they pass to us, that *would come* from thence.

27 Then he said, I pray thee therefore, father, that thou wouldest send him to my father's house:

28 For I have five brethren; that he may testify unto them, lest they also come into this place of torment.

29 Abraham saith unto him, They have Moses and the prophets; let them hear them.

30 And he said, Nay, father Abraham: but if one went unto them from the dead, they will repent.

31 And he said unto him, If they hear not Moses and the prophets, neither will they be persuaded, though one rose from the dead.

23-25. And in hell he lift up his eyes, being in torments. Between death and resurrection the immaterial part of man goes either to be with the Lord, if he is saved (II Cor 5:8; Phil 1:23), or into conscious torment as here. Resurrection reunites the body to the soul, and the state of existence continues to be either with Christ, or in the punishment of eternal duration (Mt 25:41, 46).

26. A great gulf fixed. Once a person passes from this life his probation is ended, and his eternal destiny is fixed. It has been appointed by God that once a man dies, then comes the judgment (Heb 9:27).

27-30. I have five brethren. The rich man's name and town are probably omitted in Christ's recounting of this history because of the embarrassment it might bring to his family that was still living.

31. If they hear not Moses and the prophets, neither will they be persuaded, though one rose from the dead. Another Lazarus did return from the dead and the religious leaders sought only to kill him, though some believed through his testimony (Jn 12:9-11). Several additional teachings about hell are contained in this brief history. Memory and personality continue there even in the midst of untold anguish, misery, and suffering. There is no returning or sending back of messages from hell; thus, no reincarnation, nor spiritism as it is thought of by those who are thereby deceived.

CHAPTER 17

THEN said he unto the disciples, It is impossible but that offences will come:

E. Christ's Instruction of His Disciples. 17:1-19:27.

17:1. At this point Jesus began to instruct His disciples more fully as the time drew near for going to the cross.

but woe *unto him*, through whom they come!

2 It were better for him that a millstone were hanged about his neck, and he cast into the sea, than that he should offend one of these little ones.

3 ¶Take heed to yourselves: If thy brother trespass against thee, rebuke him; and if he repent, forgive him.

4 And if he trespass against thee seven times in a day, and seven times in a day turn again to thee, saying, I repent: thou shalt forgive him.

5 ¶And the apostles said unto the Lord, Increase our faith.

6 And the Lord said, If ye had faith as a grain of mustard seed, ye might say unto this sycamine tree, Be thou plucked up by the root, and be thou planted in the sea; and it should obey you.

7 But which of you, having a servant plowing or feeding cattle, will say unto him by and by, when he is come from the field, Go and sit down to meat?

8 And will not rather say unto him, Make ready wherewith I may sup, and gird thyself, and serve me, till I have eaten and drunken; and afterward thou shalt eat and drink?

9 Doth he thank that servant because he did the things that were commanded him? I trow not.

10 So likewise ye, when ye shall have done all those things which are commanded you, say, We are unprofitable servants: we have done that which was our duty to do.

11 ¶And it came to pass, as he went to Jerusalem, that he passed through the midst of Sa-mā′rī-a and Galilee.

12 And as he entered into a certain village, there met him ten men that were lepers, which stood afar off:

13 And they lifted up *their* voices, and said, Jesus, Master, have mercy on us.

14 And when he saw *them*, he said unto them, Go shew yourselves unto the priests. And it came to pass, that, as they went, they were cleansed.

15 And one of them, when he saw that he was healed, turned back, and with a loud voice glorified God,

16 And fell down on *his* face at his feet, giving him thanks: and he was a Sa-mār′i-tan.

17 And Jesus answering said, Were there not ten cleansed? but where *are* the nine?

18 There are not found that returned to give glory to God, save this stranger.

19 And he said unto him, Arise, go thy way: thy faith hath made thee whole.

20 ¶And when he was demanded of the Pharisees, when the kingdom of God should come, he answered them and said, The kingdom of God cometh not with observation:

21 Neither shall they say, Lo here! or, lo there! for, behold, the kingdom of God is within you.

2. Should offend one of these little ones. The little ones could be children as in a parallel passage (Mt 18:2-6), or older believers as well (Mk 10:24). Our lives must be carefully examined to see how they affect those around us, especially our families.

3-4. The rebuking of a brother who sins against someone is to be done privately, and forgiveness toward a repentant brother is to be offered unceasingly.

5-6. Asking God for anything, even for a sycamore tree to be uprooted and cast into the sea, will be accomplished, provided it is God's will. We may never ask with assurance for anything that is outside of God's will (I Jn 5:14). To pray in the will of God we must have His Word abiding in us (Jn 15:7), because only His Word informs us with certainty regarding His will.

7-10. This short parable of service reflects upon what our attitude should be when we have done all that God has commanded. Instead of being proud we are to be humble enough to consider ourselves as useless, because we have simply done our duty. Compare what we are to say of ourselves with what Christ says to His faithful servants at the last day (Mt 25:21).

11. On His way to Jerusalem for the final Passover and his appointment with the Cross, Jesus passed between the borders of Samaria and Galilee across the Jordan and into Peraea.

12. Ten men that were lepers, which stood afar off. This group of ten men was composed of Jews and Samaritans alike, their common leprosy having erased the usual religious animosities (Jn 4:9). They stood afar off because of the command in Leviticus 13:45-46.

13-16. In response to their cry for mercy, Jesus commanded them to go show themselves to the priests (the plural perhaps referring to their respective nationalities or districts), as commanded in Leviticus 14:2-7. Only as they ventured off by faith did their healings occur. Only one of the ten, a Samaritan, returned to express thanks.

17-20. Why did the others not return to give thanks also? Perhaps it was because of superstition, ignorance, self-interest, or plain ingratitude.

21. The kingdom of God is within you. The word "within" (Gr *entos*) is used in the New Testament only twice, here and in

22 ¶And he said unto the disciples, The days will come, when ye shall desire to see one of the days of the Son of man, and ye shall not see *it.*

23 And they shall say to you, See here; or, see there: go not after *them,* nor follow *them.*

24 For as the lightning, that lighteneth out of the one *part* under heaven, shineth unto the other *part* under heaven; so shall also the Son of man be in his day.

25 But first must he suffer many things, and be rejected of this generation.

26 And as it was in the days of Nō'e, so shall it be also in the days of the Son of man.

27 They did eat, they drank, they married wives, they were given in marriage, until the day that Nō'e entered into the ark, and the flood came, and destroyed them all.

28 Likewise also as it was in the days of Lot; they did eat, they drank, they bought, they sold, they planted, they builded;

29 But the same day that Lot went out of Sodom it rained fire and brimstone from heaven, and destroyed *them* all.

30 Even thus shall it be in the day when the Son of man is revealed.

31 In that day, he which shall be upon the housetop, and his stuff in the house, let him not come down to take it away: and he that is in the field, let him likewise not return back.

32 Remember Lot's wife.

33 Whosoever shall seek to save his life shall lose it; and whosoever shall lose his life shall preserve it.

34 I tell you, in that night there shall be two *men* in one bed; the one shall be taken, and the other shall be left.

35 Two *women* shall be grinding together; the one shall be taken, and the other left.

36 Two *men* shall be in the field; the one shall be taken, and the other left.

37 And they answered and said unto him, Where, Lord? And he said unto them, Wheresoever the body *is,* thither will the eagles be gathered together.

CHAPTER 18

AND he spake a parable unto them *to this end,* that men ought always to pray, and not to faint;

2 Saying, There was in a city a judge, which feared not God, neither regarded man:

3 And there was a widow in that city; and she came unto him, saying, Avenge me of mine adversary.

4 And he would not for a while: but afterward he said within himself, Though I fear not God, nor regard man:

5 Yet because this widow troubleth me, I will avenge her, lest by her continual coming she weary me.

Matthew 23:26. Theological as well as contextual considerations suggest that it here be translated "among" meaning that the kingdom was present among the Pharisees in the person of the King, Christ Jesus.

22-24. Having spoken to the Pharisees of His messianic kingdom, Christ now turns to the disciples (vs. 22) to explain how men shall one day desire to see the kingdom, but will not be able to. Those will be the hectic days of the Great Tribulation (vs. 23, cf. Mt 24:21-31). At the conclusion of the Great Tribulation, Christ will come to set up His glorious kingdom, and His appearing will be as evident to all and as sudden as a great blinding flash of lightning (vs. 24).

25. However, before that day can come, Christ must, according to Old Testament prophecy, be rejected, suffer, and die (cf. Lk 24:25-27).

26-30. Jesus compared the days of Noah and of Lot to the time when He would return in judgment with power and glory. In those earlier days men went about their ordinary pursuits without thought of God. It will be the same when Christ comes to set up the kingdom.

31-33. In those days, Christ's judgment will center on Jerusalem, as predicted in Daniel 11:45, because that is where the Antichrist will be located. Any Jews there in that day are here warned to flee quickly away (vs. 31), remembering the tragedy that befell Lot's wife who lingered and looked back (vs. 32).

34-36. Likewise, Christ's judgment shall overtake the entire earth at once. Some shall be in bed at night, while in other places the sun will be shining. The taking is probably for judgment in this context. The Rapture which occurs seven years prior to these events will be similar in nature, though with a good end in view.

37. The saying about the vultures being gathered together to the carcass is a proverbial way of expressing the judgment that is depicted above. It corresponds with other portions of Scripture that speak of this same feast at the conclusion of the Great Tribulation (Ezk 39:4; Rev 19:17-18).

18:1-8. And he spake a parable unto them. The verses that follow are often called the parable of the unjust judge. This judge was blatantly bad, unprincipled, lawless, and void of moral fortitude to do what was right. The poor widow, on the other hand, was helpless, friendless, destitute, and with no hope. Yet through her great persistence, the wicked judge was so bothered that he finally granted her request. Although Jesus taught perseverance in prayer in other places (Mt 7:7-8), He is here using a form of logic that reasons from the lesser to the greater. Jesus said, regarding God's children, that **he will avenge them speedily** (vs. 8). The idea is this. If this poor woman with no hope received help from a wicked unscrupulous judge, how much sooner and greater will be the help a loving heavenly Father gives to His own dear children.

6 And the Lord said, Hear what the unjust judge saith.

7 And shall not God avenge his own elect, which cry day and night unto him, though he bear long with them?

8 I tell you that he will avenge them speedily. Nevertheless when the Son of man cometh, shall he find faith on the earth?

9 ¶And he spake this parable unto certain which trusted in themselves that they were righteous, and despised others:

10 Two men went up into the temple to pray; the one a Pharisee, and the other a publican.

11 The Pharisee stood and prayed thus with himself, God, I thank thee, that I am not as other men are, extortioners, unjust, adulterers, or even as this publican.

12 I fast twice in the week, I give tithes of all that I possess.

13 And the publican, standing afar off, would not lift up so much as his eyes unto heaven, but smote upon his breast, saying, God be merciful to me a sinner.

14 I tell you, this man went down to his house justified rather than the other: for every one that exalteth himself shall be abased; and he that humbleth himself shall be exalted.

15 ¶And they brought unto him also infants, that he would touch them: but when his disciples saw it, they rebuked them.

16 But Jesus called them unto him, and said, Suffer little children to come unto me, and forbid them not: for of such is the kingdom of God.

17 Verily I say unto you, Whosoever shall not receive the kingdom of God as a little child shall in no wise enter therein.

18 ¶And a certain ruler asked him, saying, Good Master, what shall I do to inherit eternal life?

19 And Jesus said unto him, Why callest thou me good? none is good, save one, that is, God.

20 Thou knowest the commandments, Do not commit adultery, Do not kill, Do not steal, Do not bear false witness, Honour thy father and thy mother.

21 And he said, All these have I kept from my youth up.

22 Now when Jesus heard these things, he said unto him, Yet lackest thou one thing: sell all that thou hast, and distribute unto the poor, and thou shalt have treasure in heaven: and come, follow me.

23 And when he heard this, he was very sorrowful: for he was very rich.

24 And when Jesus saw that he was very sorrowful, he said, How hardly shall they that have riches enter into the kingdom of God!

25 For it is easier for a camel to go through a needle's eye, than for a rich man to enter into the kingdom of God.

26 And they that heard it said, Who then can be saved?

27 And he said, The things which are impossible with men are possible with God.

When the Son of man cometh, shall he find faith on the earth? (vs. 8). The implied answer is "no." The faith spoken of is probably the body of truth, or revealed doctrine, since the word is preceded by the definite article in the original. Improvement in the worldwide spiritual climate is not here predicted.

9-14. The former parable spoke of God's part in answering prayer. This one deals with man's part, and is addressed to the self-righteous. Jesus must have stunned His audience because the outcome of the parable was the opposite of what they would expect. The Pharisee really uttered no true prayer at all. The humble publican (tax collector) was forgiven and justified solely on the basis of repentant faith.

15-17. Little children . . . of such is the kingdom of God. Jesus loved children, and declared that adults must receive His message in simple trusting childlike faith if they would be saved.

18-23. What shall I do to inherit eternal life? This story of the rich young ruler illustrates several truths. Something usually stands in the way of a person coming to Christ. It may be pride, position, family, friends, a particular sin, or even wealth. In this man's case, it was money. Jesus does not ask every wealthy individual to **sell all that thou hast, and distribute unto the poor** (vs. 22), but in this case, refusal to do so indicated unwillingness to become a disciple.

24-34. This led Jesus to remark on the difficulty of the rich coming to Christ. But with God, this practical impossibility is overcome. Verses 31-34 indicate a point in time less than two weeks before Christ's crucifixion (vss. 31, 35; 19:11, 28), when He clearly announced His coming death to the disciples. **And they understood none of these things.** (vs. 34, see also notes on 19:11).

28 ¶Then Peter said, Lo, we have left all, and followed thee.

29 And he said unto them, Verily I say unto you, There is no man that hath left house, or parents, or brethren, or wife, or children, for the kingdom of God's sake,

30 Who shall not receive manifold more in this present time, and in the world to come life everlasting.

31 ¶Then he took *unto him* the twelve, and said unto them, Behold, we go up to Jerusalem, and all things that are written by the prophets concerning the Son of man shall be accomplished.

32 For he shall be delivered unto the Gentiles, and shall be mocked, and spitefully entreated, and spitted on:

33 And they shall scourge *him,* and put him to death: and the third day he shall rise again.

34 And they understood none of these things: and this saying was hid from them, neither knew they the things which were spoken.

35 ¶And it came to pass, that as he was come nigh unto Jericho, a certain blind man sat by the way side begging:

36 And hearing the multitude pass by, he asked what it meant.

37 And they told him, that Jesus of Nazareth passeth by.

38 And he cried, saying, Jesus, *thou* son of David, have mercy on me.

39 And they which went before rebuked him, that he should hold his peace: but he cried so much the more, *Thou* son of David, have mercy on me.

40 And Jesus stood, and commanded him to be brought unto him: and when he was come near, he asked him,

41 Saying, What wilt thou that I shall do unto thee? And he said, Lord, that I may receive my sight.

42 And Jesus said unto him, Receive thy sight: thy faith hath saved thee.

43 And immediately he received his sight, and followed him, glorifying God: and all the people, when they saw *it,* gave praise unto God.

CHAPTER 19

AND *Jesus* entered and passed through Jericho.

2 And, behold, *there was* a man named Zāc-chæ′us, which was the chief among the publicans, and he was rich.

3 And he sought to see Jesus who he was; and could not for the press, because he was little of stature.

4 And he ran before, and climbed up into a sycomore tree to see him: for he was to pass that *way.*

5 And when Jesus came to the place, he looked up, and saw him, and said unto him, Zāc-chæ′us, make haste, and come down; for to day I must abide at thy house.

6 And he made haste, and came down, and received him joyfully.

7 And when they saw *it,* they all murmured, saying, That he was gone to be guest with a man that is a sinner.

8 And Zāc-chæ′us stood, and said unto the Lord; Behold, Lord, the half of my goods I give to the poor; and if I

35-43. The healing of blind Bartimaeus is recorded in all three synoptic Gospels, although he is named only in Mark, and presents several elements difficult to explain. Luke says the miracle occurred as Jesus drew nigh to Jericho (vs. 35), but Matthew says it was "as they departed" (Mt 20:29). Matthew and Mark may be referring to the old city while Luke speaks of Herod's newer city mentioned by Josephus and Eusebius. The healing may, therefore, have been performed between the two sites. **Thou son of David** (vs. 39) is a clear recognition by Bartimaeus of Jesus as Messiah. This terminology was also prominent in the Triumphal Entry into Jerusalem (Mt 21:15).

19:1-9. A man named Zacchaeus, which was the chief among the publicans, and he was rich. Zacchaeus is a good example of a man whose riches did not prevent him from coming to Christ. But like so many today, what he needed was someone to explain the way of salvation to him. This Jesus did. This story is found only in Luke.

have taken any thing from any man by false accusation, I restore *him* fourfold.

9 And Jesus said unto him, This day is salvation come to this house forsomuch as he also is a son of Abraham.

10 For the Son of man is come to seek and to save that which was lost.

11 ¶And as they heard these things, he added and spake a parable, because he was nigh to Jerusalem, and because they thought that the kingdom of God should immediately appear.

12 He said therefore, A certain nobleman went into a far country to receive for himself a kingdom, and to return.

13 And he called his ten servants, and delivered them ten pounds, and said unto them, Occupy till I come.

14 But his citizens hated him, and sent a message after him, saying, We will not have this *man* to reign over us.

15 And it came to pass, that when he was returned, having received the kingdom, then he commanded these servants to be called unto him, to whom he had given the money, that he might know how much every man had gained by trading.

16 Then came the first, saying, Lord, thy pound hath gained ten pounds.

17 And he said unto him, Well, thou good servant: because thou hast been faithful in a very little, have thou authority over ten cities.

18 And the second came, saying, Lord, thy pound hath gained five pounds.

19 And he said likewise to him, Be thou also over five cities.

20 And another came, saying, Lord, behold, *here is* thy pound, which I have kept laid up in a napkin:

21 For I feared thee, because thou art an austere man: thou takest up that thou layedst not down, and reapest that thou didst not sow.

22 And he saith unto him, Out of thine own mouth will I judge thee, *thou* wicked servant. Thou knewest that I was an austere man, taking up that I laid not down, and reaping that I did not sow:

23 Wherefore then gavest not thou my money into the bank, that at my coming I might have required mine own with usury?

24 And he said unto them that stood by, Take from him the pound, and give *it* to him that hath ten pounds.

25 (And they said unto him, Lord, he hath ten pounds.)

26 For I say unto you, That unto every one which hath shall be given; and from him that hath not, even that he hath shall be taken away from him.

27 But those mine enemies, which would not that I should reign over

10. The Son of man. This title of Christ was His favorite, and was never used by the disciples as they addressed Him. It speaks of His identification with mankind, yet it points to His uniqueness. **Is come to seek and to save that which was lost.** This is the key verse of Luke's Gospel. If this was the chief task of our Lord and Saviour Jesus Christ, it should surely loom large in our own set of priorities.

11-12. As Jesus approached Jerusalem with His disciples and others traveling to the Passover, He told a parable to show that the kingdom they had been announcing would not be established immediately as they had thought. Instead, since Jesus had been rejected by the Jewish people, the kingdom would be delayed, and during the interval something new (the church) would be set up (Mt 16:18). In this parable of the pounds, the activity of professing believers during the church age is in view. Here each servant was given one pound, speaking of equal opportunity, whereas in the parable of the talents (Mt 25:14-30), each was given according to his ability.

13. Occupy till I come. We have a dual assignment: to work, and to wait. We must do both faithfully.

14-27. Christ's first coming was as Saviour; but when He returns, it will be as Judge. False professors and Christ-rejectors will alike be cast away (vss. 26-27).

them, bring hither, and slay *them* before me.

28 And when he had thus spoken he went before, ascending up to Jerusalem.

29 ¶And it came to pass, when he was come nigh to Bĕth'pha-gē and Bethany, at the mount called *the mount* of Olives, he sent two of his disciples,

30 Saying, Go ye into the village over against *you;* in the which at your entering ye shall find a colt tied, whereon yet never man sat: loose him, and bring *him* hither.

31 And if any man ask you, Why do ye loose *him?* thus shall ye say unto him, Because the Lord hath need of him.

32 And they that were sent went their way, and found even as he had said unto them.

33 And as they were loosing the colt, the owners thereof said unto them, Why loose ye the colt?

34 And they said, The Lord hath need of him.

35 And they brought him to Jesus: and they cast their garments upon the colt, and they set Jesus thereon.

36 And as he went, they spread their clothes in the way.

37 And when he was come nigh, even now at the descent of the mount of Olives, the whole multitude of the disciples began to rejoice and praise God with a loud voice for all the mighty works that they had seen;

38 Saying, Blessed *be* the King that cometh in the name of the Lord: peace in heaven, and glory in the highest.

39 And some of the Pharisees from among the multitude said unto him, Master, rebuke thy disciples.

40 And he answered and said unto them, I tell you that, if these should hold their peace, the stones would immediately cry out.

41 ¶And when he was come near, he beheld the city, and wept over it,

42 Saying, If thou hadst known, even thou, at least in this thy day, the things *which belong* unto thy peace! but now they are hid from thine eyes.

43 For the days shall come upon thee, that thine enemies shall cast a trench about thee, and compass thee round, and keep thee in on every side,

44 And shall lay thee even with the ground, and thy children within thee; and they shall not leave in thee one stone upon another; because thou knewest not the time of thy visitation.

45 And he went into the temple, and began to cast out them that sold therein, and them that bought;

46 Saying unto them, It is written, My house is the house of prayer: but ye have made it a den of thieves.

47 And he taught daily in the temple. But the chief priests and the scribes and the chief of the people sought to destroy him,

48 And could not find what they might do: for all the people were very attentive to hear him.

VI. THE PROFFER OF THE SON'S KINGDOM AND ITS REJECTION. 19:28-21:4.

A. Christ's Entry into Jerusalem. 19:28-46.

28-40. Christ's entry into Jerusalem was in direct fulfillment of such clear messianic prophecies as Zechariah 9:9 and Psalm 118:25-26.

41-44. These verses are both a lament and a prophecy. Christ laments His rejection and, as well, predicts the city's coming destruction. What was true of this city will also be true of each individual who rejects Christ. Jesus cared for them and He cares for men today.

45-46. Christ's judgment of those who were making merchandise in the Temple was His second such action. Three years before, Jesus cast out a similar group (Jn 2:13-22).

B. Christ's Public Teaching in Jerusalem. 19:47-21:4.

47-48. Christ's final days before death were spent in public and private teaching (Jn 13-17). In contrast, the Jewish leaders spent the time in conspiracy to commit murder.

CHAPTER 20

AND it came to pass, *that* on one of those days, as he taught the people in the temple, and preached the gospel, the chief priests and the scribes came upon *him* with the elders,

2 And spake unto him, saying, Tell us, by what authority doest thou these things? or who is he that gave thee this authority?

3 And he answered and said unto them, I will also ask you one thing, and answer me:

4 The baptism of John, was it from heaven, or of men?

5 And they reasoned with themselves, saying, If we shall say, From heaven; he will say, Why then believed ye him not?

6 But and if we say, Of men; all the people will stone us: for they be persuaded that John was a prophet.

7 And they answered, that they could not tell whence *it was.*

8 And Jesus said unto them, Neither tell I you by what authority I do these things.

9 Then began he to speak to the people this parable; A certain man planted a vineyard, and let it forth to husbandmen, and went into a far country for a long time.

10 And at the season he sent a servant to the husbandmen, that they should give him of the fruit of the vineyard: but the husbandmen beat him, and sent *him* away empty.

11 And again he sent another servant: and they beat him also, and entreated *him* shamefully, and sent *him* away empty.

12 And again he sent a third: and they wounded him also, and cast *him* out.

13 Then said the lord of the vineyard, What shall I do? I will send my beloved son: it may be they will reverence *him* when they see him.

14 But when the husbandmen saw him, they reasoned among themselves, saying, This is the heir: come, let us kill him, that the inheritance may be ours.

15 So they cast him out of the vineyard, and killed *him.* What therefore shall the lord of the vineyard do unto them?

16 He shall come and destroy these husbandmen, and shall give the vineyard to others. And when they heard *it,* they said, God forbid.

17 And he beheld them, and said, What is this then that is written, The stone which the builders rejected, the same is become the head of the corner?

18 Whosoever shall fall upon that stone shall be broken; but on whomsoever it shall fall, it will grind him to powder.

19 And the chief priests and the scribes the same hour sought to lay hands on him; and they feared the people: for they perceived that he had spoken this parable against them.

20 ¶And they watched *him,* and sent forth spies, which should feign themselves just men, that they might take hold of his words, that so they might

20:1-8. The Jewish authorities (vs. 1) wanted to know what authority Jesus had to cast moneychangers out of the Temple (vs. 2). Instead of answering directly, Christ countered with a question about whether John the Baptist's ministry was of God or not. Since they refused to acknowledge or disown Jesus' forerunner (due to political expediency), they deserved no further revelation from Christ (vs. 8).

9-18. This parable is the New Testament parallel of Isaiah 5:1-7. In general terms, the householder represents God (yet not his mistaken optimism, vs. 13); the husbandmen stand for the Jewish religious leaders; the servants speak of the prophets; and the son represents Christ. In verse 15 Christ again predicted His own death. Verses 16-18 tell of future judgment and the final display of Christ's sovereignty (see also I Pet 2:6-7 and Dan 2:34).

19. The religious leaders knew instinctively that they were meant to be the wicked murderers in the parable.

20-24. As a result, they sought occasion to arrest Jesus and turn Him over to the Roman authorities for execution, since they had not the power of capital punishment (Jn 18:31).

deliver him unto the power and authority of the governor.

21 And they asked him, saying, Master, we know that thou sayest and teachest rightly, neither acceptest thou the person *of any*, but teachest the way of God truly:

22 Is it lawful for us to give tribute unto Cæsar, or no?

23 But he perceived their craftiness, and said unto them, Why tempt ye me?

24 Shew me a penny. Whose image and superscription hath it? They answered and said, Cæsar's.

25 And he said unto them, Render therefore unto Cæsar the things which be Cæsar's, and unto God the things which be God's.

26 And they could not take hold of his words before the people: and they marvelled at his answer, and held their peace.

27 ¶Then came to *him* certain of the Săd'du-ceeś, which deny that there is any resurrection: and they asked him,

28 Saying, Master, Moses wrote unto us, If any man's brother die, having a wife, and he die without children, that his brother should take his wife, and raise up seed unto his brother.

29 There were therefore seven brethren: and the first took a wife, and died without children.

30 And the second took her to wife, and he died childless.

31 And the third took her; and in like manner the seven also: and they left no children, and died.

32 Last of all the woman died also.

33 Therefore in the resurrection whose wife of them is she? for seven had her to wife.

34 And Jesus answering said unto them, The children of this world marry, and are given in marriage:

35 But they which shall be accounted worthy to obtain that world, and the resurrection from the dead, neither marry, nor are given in marriage:

36 Neither can they die any more: for they are equal unto the angels; and are the children of God, being the children of the resurrection.

37 Now that the dead are raised, even Moses shewed at the bush, when he calleth the Lord the God of Abraham, and the God of Isaac, and the God of Jacob.

38 For he is not a God of the dead, but of the living: for all live unto him.

39 Then certain of the scribes answering said, Master, thou hast well said.

40 And after that they durst not ask him any *question at all*.

41 ¶And he said unto them, How say they that Christ is David's son?

42 And David himself saith in the book of Psalms, The LORD said unto my Lord, Sit thou on my right hand,

43 Till I make thine enemies thy footstool.

44 David therefore calleth him Lord, how is he then his son?

45 ¶Then in the audience of all the people he said unto his disciples,

46 Beware of the scribes, which de-

25-26. Render therefore unto Caesar the things which be Caesar's, and unto God the things which be God's. In these few words are clearly found the basis for the doctrine of the separation of church and state. Both are to exist, and neither is to be lord over the other as supreme.

27. The Sadducees were the Jewish religious liberals of that day. They denied resurrection, angels, and spirits (Acts 23:8).

28-32. The law of levirate marriage (a man required to marry his brother's widow) is found in Deuteronomy 25:5-10. It applied in the case of Ruth (Ruth 3:13-4:10).

33-36. Angels cannot be participants of either funerals or weddings. In the resurrection we shall be like them in these two respects also.

37-38. When Moses referred to God as the God of Abraham, Isaac, and Jacob, they had already died. Jesus pointed out that **all live unto him.**

39-40. Jesus' use of Scripture and logic was so correct and devastating that His opponents stopped questioning Him.

41-47. Jesus, however, pointed out the deity of the Messiah as seen in Psalm 110:1, where God the Father called Him Lord in distinction from Himself, and promised Him rulership.

sire to walk in long robes, and love greetings in the markets, and the highest seats in the synagogues, and the chief rooms at feasts;

47 Which devour widows' houses, and for a shew make long prayers: the same shall receive greater damnation.

CHAPTER 21

AND he looked up, and saw the rich men casting their gifts into the treasury.

2 And he saw also a certain poor widow casting in thither two mites.

3 And he said, Of a truth I say unto you, that this poor widow hath cast in more than they all:

4 For all these have of their abundance cast in unto the offerings of God: but she of her penury hath cast in all the living that she had.

5 ¶And as some spake of the temple, how it was adorned with goodly stones and gifts, he said,

6 As for these things which ye behold, the days will come, in the which there shall not be left one stone upon another, that shall not be thrown down.

7 And they asked him, saying, Master, but when shall these things be? and what sign will there be when these things shall come to pass?

8 And he said, Take heed that ye be not deceived: for many shall come in my name, saying, I am Christ; and the time draweth near: go ye not therefore after them.

9 But when ye shall hear of wars and commotions, be not terrified: for these things must first come to pass; but the end is not by and by.

10 Then said he unto them, Nation shall rise against nation, and kingdom against kingdom:

11 And great earthquakes shall be in divers places, and famines, and pestilences; and fearful sights and great signs shall there be from heaven.

12 But before all these, they shall lay their hands on you, and persecute you, delivering you up to the synagogues, and into prisons, being brought before kings and rulers for my name's sake.

13 And it shall turn to you for a testimony.

14 Settle it therefore in your hearts, not to meditate before what ye shall answer:

15 For I will give you a mouth and wisdom, which all your adversaries shall not be able to gainsay nor resist.

16 And ye shall be betrayed both by parents, and brethren, and kinsfolks, and friends; and some of you shall they cause to be put to death.

17 And ye shall be hated of all men for my name's sake.

21:1. The treasury is the place where the offerings and taxes for the Temple were received. Thirteen receptacles were located there.

2. Two mites (Gr *lepton*) were worth about one fortieth of a penny (Gr *dēnarion*) (Mt 18:28). Since it was such a small amount and this was all she had, it is amazing that she did not keep one of the coins for herself.

3-4. She of her penury (poverty) **hath cast in all the living that she had.** She gave everything that she would need to buy food to sustain her life. The size of an offering is not always an indication of the measure of one's love for God. Often the amount that is held back is a better indicator of one's devotion.

VII. THE PROPHECY OF TRIBULATION TO COME. 21:5-38.

A. Prophecy About This Age. 21:5-19.

5-6. When Jesus finished teaching in the Temple area (20:1), He passed through the Temple treasury (21:1), and some commented on the splendor of the magnificent Temple reconstructed, enlarged and beautified by Herod. Jesus predicted it would be torn down (vs. 6).

7-19. Jesus' words here are descriptive of the time leading up to the destruction of Jerusalem by the Romans in A.D. 70, and also of the events preceding the Great Tribulation period when the Antichrist will enter a future Temple in Jerusalem to set himself up as God (II Thess 2:3-4).

ere shall not an hair of your
h.
our patience possess ye your

nd when ye shall see Jerusalem
assed with armies, then know
t the desolation thereof is nigh.
21 Then let them which are in Judæa
flee to the mountains; and let them
which are in the midst of it depart out;
and let not them that are in the countries enter thereinto.
22 For these be the days of vengeance,
that all things which are written
may be fulfilled.
23 But woe unto them that are with
child, and to them that give suck, in
those days! for there shall be great distress in the land, and wrath upon this
people.
24 And they shall fall by the edge of
the sword, and shall be led away captive into all nations: and Jerusalem
shall be trodden down of the Gentiles,
until the times of the Gentiles be fulfilled.

25 ¶And there shall be signs in the
sun, and in the moon, and in the stars;
and upon the earth distress of nations,
with perplexity; the sea and the waves
roaring;
26 Men's hearts failing them for fear,
and for looking after those things
which are coming on the earth: for the
powers of heaven shall be shaken.
27 And then shall they see the Son of
man coming in a cloud with power and
great glory.
28 And when these things begin to
come to pass, then look up, and lift up
your heads; for your redemption draweth nigh.
29 And he spake to them a parable;
Behold the fig tree, and all the trees;
30 When they now shoot forth, ye see
and know of your own selves that summer is now nigh at hand.
31 So likewise ye, when ye see these
things come to pass, know ye that the
kingdom of God is nigh at hand.
32 Verily I say unto you, This generation shall not pass away, till all be fulfilled.

33 Heaven and earth shall pass away:
but my words shall not pass away.

34 ¶And take heed to yourselves, lest
at any time your hearts be overcharged
with surfeiting, and drunkenness, and
cares of this life, and so that day come
upon you unawares.
35 For as a snare shall it come on all
them that dwell on the face of the
whole earth.
36 Watch ye therefore, and pray always, that ye may be accounted
worthy to escape all these things that
shall come to pass, and to stand before
the Son of man.
37 And in the day time he was teaching in the temple; and at night he went
out, and abode in the mount that is
called the mount of Olives.
38 And all the people came early in

B. Prophecy About Jerusalem. 21:20-24.

20-24. These verses graphically portray Jerusalem's destruction by Titus in A.D. 70. Titus' Arch still stands today in Rome
near the Coliseum at the entrance to the Roman Forum. It
commemorates his capture of Jerusalem. **And Jerusalem shall
be trodden down of the Gentiles.** This is taken by most to
mean Jerusalem will be under the governmental control of non-
Jews. This has been the case (with the exception of the Bar
Kochbar revolt, A.D. 123-35) until Wednesday, June 7, 1967.
Until the times of the Gentiles be fulfilled. On June 7, 1967,
the "times of the Gentiles" were completed. Jesus did not
predict what would happen after that time, but it may be
assumed that Israel would come back into God's spotlight, and
the return of Christ would be nearer. That is indeed the case.
Jerusalem is today entirely under the governmental control of
Israel, though they allow access to religious shrines for all faiths.
Israel has constantly been on page one of our newspapers from
that day to this.

C. Prophecy About Christ's Return. 21:25-38.

25-28. These verses are written for the Jews who will be
looking for Christ to return at the end of the Great Tribulation.
Satan will persecute the Jews, but God will protect them (Rev
12:13-17).

29-31. The fig tree is thought by many to be a symbol of
Israel. This is seen in Luke 13. This parable probably means
that Israel may be seen as a sign of the nearness of Christ's
return and the setting up of His kingdom (vs. 31).

32. This generation shall not pass away, till all be fulfilled.
The generation spoken of is probably the one which sees the
signs (especially those regarding the fig tree) come to pass. That
generation will see God conclude this present age prior to the
inauguration of His millennial kingdom.

33. God's Word, the Holy Bible, is more unshakable than the
universe itself. In fact, the universe shall pass away.

34-38. These verses speak of the universal extent (vs. 35) of
the Great Tribulation, and are a warning to those who will await
Christ's return in that day (Rev 7:1-16 tells of the Jews and of
the great multitude who will be saved during the Tribulation).

was wont, to the mount of Olives; and his disciples also followed him.

40 And when he was at the place, he said unto them, Pray that ye enter not into temptation.

41 And he was withdrawn from them about a stone's cast, and kneeled down, and prayed,

42 Saying, Father, if thou be willing, remove this cup from me: nevertheless not my will, but thine, be done.

2
sou
the
3 ¶
name
the tw
4 And
muned w
tains, how...ere appeared an angel unto them. ...aven, strengthening him.

5 And they...g in an agony he prayed nanted to gi...ly: and his sweat was as it

6 And he ...rops of blood falling down portunity...id.
the a...nd when he rose up from prayer,

7 ¶...as come to his disciples, he found brea...sleeping for sorrow,
kille And said unto them, Why sleep

8 And ...and pray, lest ye enter into
Go and ...on.

we may...d while he yet spake, behold a

9 An...de, and he that was called Ju-
thou th...e of the twelve, went before ...and drew near unto Jesus to kiss

...But Jesus said unto him, Judas,

10 ...yest thou the Son of man with a
wh?

sh...When they which were about him of...w what would follow, they said unto ...m, Lord, shall we smite with the word?

50 ¶And one of them smote the servant of the high priest, and cut off his right ear.

51 And Jesus answered and said, Suffer ye thus far. And he touched his ear, and healed him.

52 Then Jesus said unto the chief priests, and captains of the temple, and the elders, which were come to him, Be ye come out, as against a thief, with swords and staves?

53 When I was daily with you in the temple, ye stretched forth no hands against me: but this is your hour, and the power of darkness.

54 ¶Then took they him, and led him, and brought him into the high priest's house. And Peter followed afar off.

55 And when they had kindled a fire in the midst of the hall, and were set down together, Peter sat down among them.

56 But a certain maid beheld him as he sat by the fire, and earnestly looked upon him, and said, This man was also with him.

57 And he denied him, saying, Woman, I know him not.

mount of Olives. At the conclusion of Christ's meal and final instruction of the disciples (the Upper Room Discourse, only in John 13-17), Jesus passed over the narrow ravine of the brook Kidron (Cedron) to the Garden of Gethsemane (Mk 14:32; Jn 18:1). Peter, James, and John were selected to be near Christ during His agony of prayer (Mt 26:36-38), while the others remained some distance away.

42. Father, if thou be willing, remove this cup from me. The cup refers to Christ's coming death (Mt 20:22-23) with its accompanying physical and spiritual agonies (Mt 27:46). That event was variously referred to by Christ as His cup, baptism, and hour (Mt 20:22-23; Jn 7:30; 12:23, 27; 13:1; 17:1). Christ's human nature, though without sin, did fear death (Lk 12:50; Heb 5:7), yet more so than other men because He was to bear vicariously the sin of the entire world (Isa 53:6; Jn 1:29) and suffer the temporary loss of fellowship with God the Father (Mt 27:46). **Nevertheless not my will, but thine, be done.** Christ's human will will always completely yielded to the divine will. It was natural for Him to be perfectly obedient to the Father.

43-46. The visit of an angel to strengthen Christ in answer to His prayer is only found in Luke. Though sometimes questioned by textual critics, these two verses are attested by the overwhelming majority of manuscripts, ancient versions, and church fathers. **His sweat was as it were great drops of blood.** This does not necessarily mean that Christ actually sweat blood, though He may have.

B. Christ's Betrayal and Trial. 22:47-23:25.

47-48. Judas came to arrest Jesus with a Roman cohort (Jn 18:3), although the full cohort may not have been present. They were taking no chances.

49-53. John 18:10 identifies Peter as the one who chopped off the ear of **the servant of the high priest,** whom John also identifies as Malchus. Peter was probably aiming for the head. Only God's providence saved Peter from becoming a murderer. Luke the physician is the only one to record the healing.

54. Brought him into the high priest's house. This was the first of several illegal trials (see James Stalker, *The Trial and Death of Jesus Christ* and Simon Greenleaf, *The Testimony of the Evangelists*). **And Peter followed afar off.** How easy it is to promise (Mk 14:29-31), and so hard to fulfill.

55-60. Peter's denial was wicked and sinful; he even cursed and swore in his denial (Mk 14:71). He was no more sinful than any of us.

58 And after a little while another saw him, and said, Thou art also of them. And Peter said, Man, I am not.

59 And about the space of one hour after another confidently affirmed, saying, Of a truth this *fellow* also was with him: for he is a Galilæan.

60 And Peter said, Man, I know not what thou sayest. And immediately, while he yet spake, the cock crew.

61 And the Lord turned, and looked upon Peter. And Peter remembered the word of the Lord, how he had said unto him, Before the cock crow, thou shalt deny me thrice.

62 And Peter went out and wept bitterly.

63 ¶ And the men that held Jesus mocked him, and smote him.

64 And when they had blindfolded him, they struck him on the face, and asked him, saying, Prophesy, who is it that smote thee?

65 And many other things blasphemously spake they against him.

66 ¶ And as soon as it was day, the elders of the people and the chief priests and the scribes came together, and led him into their council, saying,

67 Art thou the Christ? tell us. And he said unto them, If I tell you, ye will not believe:

68 And if I also ask *you,* ye will not answer me, nor let *me* go.

69 Hereafter shall the Son of man sit on the right hand of the power of God.

70 Then said they all, Art thou then the Son of God? And he said unto them, Ye say that I am.

71 And they said, What need we any further witness? for we ourselves have heard of his own mouth.

CHAPTER 23

AND the whole multitude of them arose, and led him unto Pilate.

2 And they began to accuse him, saying, We found this *fellow* perverting the nation, and forbidding to give tribute to Cæsar, saying that he himself is Christ a King.

3 And Pilate asked him, saying, Art thou the King of the Jews? And he answered him and said, Thou sayest *it.*

4 Then said Pilate to the chief priests and *to* the people, I find no fault in this man.

5 And they were the more fierce, saying, He stirreth up the people, teaching throughout all Jewry, beginning from Galilee to this place.

6 When Pilate heard of Galilee, he asked whether the man were a Galilæan.

7 And as soon as he knew that he belonged unto Herod's jurisdiction, he sent him to Herod, who himself also was at Jerusalem at that time.

8 ¶ And when Herod saw Jesus, he was exceeding glad: for he was desirous to see him of a long *season,* because he had heard many things of him; and he hoped to have seen some miracle done by him.

9 Then he questioned with him in

61-62. And the Lord turned, and looked upon Peter. This was one of Peter's lowest points. He had publicly denied Christ three times. Later, Christ made Peter publicly confess three times that he loved his Lord (Jn 21:15-19).

63-71. Though Jesus was violently abused, mocked, and ridiculed, He did not return the same (I Pet 2:21-23). The only accusation they could make was Christ's positive reply to their question as to whether or not He was the Son of God. (vss. 70-71).

23:1. Led him unto Pilate. Pilate, the Roman governor of Palestine from A.D. 26-36, was in Jerusalem for the Passover feast. A stone inscription bearing his name was uncovered in A.D. 1961 in Caesarea, the ancient governmental headquarters.

2-5. Some of the charges the council (Sanhedrin) brought against Christ were manifestly false. Several times Pilate pronounced his verdict, **I find no fault in this man** (vss. 4, 14-15, 22). However, the Jewish leaders grew angry (vs. 5) and actually intimidated Pilate (Jn 19:12).

6-12. Pilate sent Jesus the Galilean to Herod Antipas, the governor of Galilee who was visiting Jerusalem for the Passover. He had earlier beheaded John the Baptist, and was desirous of seeing Jesus, but Jesus was silent before Herod and his mockers.

many words; but he answered him nothing.

10 And the chief priests and scribes stood and vehemently accused him.

11 And Herod with his men of war set him at nought, and mocked *him*, and arrayed him in a gorgeous robe, and sent him again to Pilate.

12 ¶And the same day Pilate and Herod were made friends together: for before they were at enmity between themselves.

13 ¶And Pilate, when he had called together the chief priests and the rulers and the people,

14 Said unto them, Ye have brought this man unto me, as one that perverteth the people: and, behold, I, having examined *him* before you, have found no fault in this man touching those things whereof ye accuse him:

15 No, nor yet Herod: for I sent you to him; and, lo, nothing worthy of death is done unto him.

16 I will therefore chastise him, and release *him*.

17 (For of necessity he must release one unto them at the feast.)

18 And they cried out all at once, saying, Away with this *man*, and release unto us Ba-răb′bas:

19 (Who for a certain sedition made in the city, and for murder, was cast into prison.)

20 Pilate therefore, willing to release Jesus, spake again to them.

21 But they cried, saying, Crucify *him*, crucify him.

22 And he said unto them the third time, Why, what evil hath he done? I have found no cause of death in him: I will therefore chastise him, and let *him* go.

23 And they were instant with loud voices, requiring that he might be crucified. And the voices of them and of the chief priests prevailed.

24 And Pilate gave sentence that it should be as they required.

25 And he released unto them him that for sedition and murder was cast into prison, whom they had desired; but he delivered Jesus to their will.

26 ¶And as they led him away, they laid hold upon one Simon, a Čy-rē′ni-an, coming out of the country, and on him they laid the cross, that he might bear *it* after Jesus.

27 And there followed him a great company of people, and of women, which also bewailed and lamented him.

28 But Jesus turning unto them said, Daughters of Jerusalem, weep not for me, but weep for yourselves, and for your children.

29 For, behold, the days are coming, in the which they shall say, Blessed *are* the barren, and the wombs that never bare, and the paps which never gave suck.

30 Then shall they begin to say to the mountains, Fall on us; and to the hills, Cover us.

31 For if they do these things in a green tree, what shall be done in the dry?

32 ¶And there were also two other,

13-25. And Pilate gave sentence that it should be as they required. Pilate had no backbone to stand up for justice, but instead succumbed to mob rule. Both share the immediate guilt for Christ's death, but it is also true that Christ laid down His life and that no man could take it from Him (Jn 10:17-18).

C. Christ's Crucifixion. 23:26-56.

26-33. Simon, a Cyrenian. This devout black Jew must have become a Christian. Mark records (15:21) that Simon was the father of Alexander and Rufus. **The place, which is called Calvary.** (vs. 33). No one actually knows the exact place where the crucifixion or burial occurred. The Church of the Holy Sepulchre is the traditional site but many appreciate Gordon's Calvary and the Garden Tomb because they give a better picture of what the site is presumed to be like in the early centuries.

malefactors, led with him to be put to death.

33 And when they were come to the place, which is called Calvary, there they crucified him, and the malefactors, one on the right hand, and the other on the left.

34 Then said Jesus, Father, forgive them; for they know not what they do. And they parted his raiment, and cast lots.

35 And the people stood beholding. And the rulers also with them derided *him*, saying, He saved others; let him save himself, if he be Christ, the chosen of God.

36 And the soldiers also mocked him, coming to him, and offering him vinegar,

37 And saying, If thou be the king of the Jews, save thyself.

38 And a superscription also was written over him in letters of Greek, and Latin, and Hebrew, THIS IS THE KING OF THE JEWS.

39 ¶And one of the malefactors which were hanged railed on him, saying, If thou be Christ, save thyself and us.

40 But the other answering rebuked him, saying, Dost not thou fear God, seeing thou art in the same condemnation?

41 And we indeed justly; for we receive the due reward of our deeds: but this man hath done nothing amiss.

42 And he said unto Jesus, Lord, remember me when thou comest into thy kingdom.

43 And Jesus said unto him, Verily I say unto thee, To day shalt thou be with me in paradise.

44 ¶And it was about the sixth hour, and there was a darkness over all the earth until the ninth hour.

45 And the sun was darkened, and the vail of the temple was rent in the midst.

46 And when Jesus had cried with a loud voice, he said, Father, into thy hands I commend my spirit: and having said thus, he gave up the ghost.

47 ¶Now when the centurion saw what was done, he glorified God, saying, Certainly this was a righteous man.

48 And all the people that came together to that sight, beholding the things which were done, smote their breasts, and returned.

49 And all his acquaintance, and the women that followed him from Galilee, stood afar off, beholding these things.

50 ¶And, behold, *there was* a man named Joseph, a counsellor; *and he was* a good man, and a just:

51 (The same had not consented to the counsel and deed of them;) *he was* of Ăr-i-ma-thæ′a, a city of the Jews: who also himself waited for the kingdom of God.

52 This *man* went unto Pilate, and begged the body of Jesus.

53 And he took it down, and wrapped it in linen, and laid it in a sepulchre that

34-42. Father, forgive them; for they know not what they do. As Christ and the martyr Stephen, we must be so controlled by the Spirit that in our darkest hour we will be able to speak these words and mean them.

Greek, and Latin, and Hebrew (vs. 38). These three languages were: (1) the universal tongues; (2) the official language of the Roman Empire; and (3) the official speech of the Jews. Compare all four gospel records to recover the complete reading of "This is Jesus of Nazareth the King of the Jews." This was probably written as a mockery to the Jews.

43. Today shalt thou be with me in paradise. The thief who asked Christ for salvation received it. The word **paradise** found only in two other passages (II Cor 12:4; Rev 2:7), indicates the domain of the righteous dead.

44. This darkness was supernaturally imposed.

45-49. Only the veil separated the priests from the Holy of Holies in the Temple. Its parting signified the opening to all men of the way to God. It represents Christ's flesh (Heb 10:20), the rending of which made our salvation possible.

50-53. Joseph . . . of Arimathaea (perhaps equivalent to Ramathaim, I Sam 1:1, about twenty miles northwest of Jerusalem) was a member of the council (Sanhedrin), but a devout and brave believer in Christ as Messiah. He, with Nicodemus (Jn 19:39), carefully wrapped Jesus' body in long strips of cloth, pouring in at the same time a sticky resinous mixture of myrrh and aloes. Both spices are obtained from trees. Nicodemus contributed about seventy pounds (by our weights), which was a rich amount fit for royalty.

was hewn in stone, wherein never man before was laid.

54 And that day was the preparation, and the sabbath drew on.

55 ¶And the women also, which came with him from Galilee, followed after, and beheld the sepulchre, and how his body was laid.

56 And they returned, and prepared spices and ointments; and rested the sabbath day according to the commandment.

CHAPTER 24

NOW upon the first *day* of the week, very early in the morning, they came unto the sepulchre, bringing the spices which they had prepared, and certain *others* with them.

2 And they found the stone rolled away from the sepulchre.

3 And they entered in, and found not the body of the Lord Jesus.

4 And it came to pass, as they were much perplexed thereabout, behold, two men stood by them in shining garments:

5 And as they were afraid, and bowed down *their* faces to the earth, they said unto them, Why seek ye the living among the dead?

6 He is not here, but is risen: remember how he spake unto you when he was yet in Galilee,

7 Saying, the Son of man must be delivered into the hands of sinful men, and be crucified, and the third day rise again.

8 And they remembered his words,

9 And returned from the sepulchre, and told all these things unto the eleven, and to all the rest.

10 It was Mary Magdalene, and Jō-ăn'na, and Mary *the mother* of James, and other *women that were* with them, which told these things unto the apostles.

11 And their words seemed to them as idle tales, and they believed them not.

12 Then arose Peter, and ran unto the sepulchre; and stooping down, he beheld the linen clothes laid by themselves, and departed, wondering in himself at that which was come to pass.

13 And, behold, two of them went that same day to a village called Ĕm-mā'us, which was from Jerusalem *about* threescore furlongs.

54-56. The preparation (Gr *paraskeuē*) was a common designation for Friday, though it could also refer to the day before a special feast. If we assume a Friday crucifixion (Jewish inclusive reckoning), Luke's reference to the commandment of Sabbath observance (cf. Ex 20:8-11) would identify the next day as Saturday. The women, then, rested on the Sabbath (Saturday) and returned to the tomb the following day (vs. 56; 24:1), which would be Sunday. If a Wednesday crucifixion is assumed (lit., seventy-two hours in the grave), the reference to the Sabbath would refer to the Passover itself.

IX. THE POWER OF THE SON OVER DEATH. 24:1-48.

A. The Events Surrounding the Empty Tomb. 24:1-12.

24:1. Upon the first day of the week, very early in the morning, they came. It was probably no earlier than 5 A.M. Matthew says that it was beginning to dawn (28:1), and Mark says that they arrived at the tomb as the sun was rising (16:2). They refers to the women of 23:55-56, who are identified in 24:10.

2. The stone rolled away from the sepulcher. First-century sepulchers with round stone doors may still be seen in Jerusalem at the tomb of the kings, and at Herod's tomb. The openings are from the ground to about waist-high. This explains why various persons are said to stoop down to look in (vs. 12; Jn 20:5).

3-12. These women, as well as others later, actually entered into the tomb and saw two features which proved to them the miraculous nature of Christ's bodily resurrection from the dead. (1) The body was gone. (2) The grave clothes, or strips of cloth that had encircled the body with gummy resinous spices inlaid were still intact. It must have looked like an empty mummy shell. The resurrected body of Christ had passed through the cloth wrappings, leaving them undisturbed. That was what convinced Peter and others of the truth of the resurrection (Jn 20:6-8). If the mummy-like wrapping had been disturbed in any way, no one could have been sure of what had happened. Two men stood by them (vs. 4). Naturally, these two angels confirmed the story. They looked just like other men except for their bright appearance.

B. The Walk to Emmaus. 24:13-32.

13. Two of them went that same day to a village called Emmaus. This is one of the most delightfully fascinating stories in the New Testament. One of the two was named Cleopas (vs. 18), who is mentioned elsewhere only in John 19:25, as the husband of a woman named Mary. The one returning with Cleopas may have been his wife, since both were in Jerusalem for the Passover. Emmaus was about seven or eight miles northwest of Jerusalem. It would take two to three hours to walk the distance.

14 And they talked together of all these things which had happened.

15 And it came to pass, that, while they communed *together* and reasoned, Jesus himself drew near, and went with them.

16 But their eyes were holden that they should not know him.

17 And he said unto them, What manner of communications *are* these that ye have one to another, as ye walk, and are sad?

18 And the one of them, whose name was Cle'o-pas, answering said unto him, Art thou only a stranger in Jerusalem, and hast not known the things which are come to pass there in these days?

19 And he said unto them, What things? And they said unto him, Concerning Jesus of Nazareth, which was a prophet mighty in deed and word before God and all the people:

20 And how the chief priests and our rulers delivered him to be condemned to death, and have crucified him.

21 But we trusted that it had been he which should have redeemed Israel: and beside all this, to day is the third day since these things were done.

22 Yea, and certain women also of our company made us astonished, which were early at the sepulchre;

23 And when they found not his body, they came, saying, that they had also seen a vision of angels, which said that he was alive.

24 And certain of them which were with us went to the sepulchre, and found *it* even so as the women had said: but him they saw not.

25 Then he said unto them, O fools, and slow of heart to believe all that the prophets have spoken:

26 Ought not Christ to have suffered these things, and to enter into his glory?

27 And beginning at Moses and all the prophets, he expounded unto them in all the scriptures the things concerning himself.

28 And they drew nigh unto the village, whither they went: and he made as though he would have gone further.

29 But they constrained him, saying, Abide with us: for it is toward evening, and the day is far spent. And he went in to tarry with them.

30 And it came to pass, as he sat at meat with them, he took bread, and blessed *it*, and brake, and gave to them.

31 And their eyes were opened, and they knew him; and he vanished out of their sight.

32 And they said one to another, Did not our heart burn within us, while he talked with us by the way, and while he opened to us the scriptures?

33 And they rose up the same hour, and returned to Jerusalem, and found the eleven gathered together, and them that were with them,

14-16. As they walked they were discussing the events of the past several days, including Christ's crucifixion and the reports of His resurrection. As they walked, Jesus joined them, but they were supernaturally prevented from recognizing Him.

17-18. Jesus inquired as to their evident sadness, and was asked if He were only a stranger to the area, and did not know all the things that had happened in Jerusalem that weekend.

19-24. With a great sense of drama, Jesus, the very One about whom all these events had centered, replied, **What things?** Then they unfolded the account of how they had thought Jesus was the Messiah until His crucifixion had shattered their hopes. Yet, they added seemingly incredulous reports: (1) of His resurrection and (2) of the angels at the empty tomb, who clearly said that He was alive.

25-27. At that point, Christ, still unknown to these two travelers, took the part of one familiar with the Scriptures. He pointed out from Genesis to Malachi how it was predicted that the Messiah would suffer prior to His exaltation as King. He must have quoted from Psalm 22 and Isaiah 53, and drawn from such types as the smitten rock (Ex 17:6; I Cor 10:4). What a glorious Bible lesson it must have been for them, but how it must have grieved the Saviour's heart to witness such a lack of faith and understanding in the very ones who claimed to be His followers.

28-32. When they neared Emmaus Jesus did not want to impose on His walking companions, but they had learned so much and had such sweet fellowship that they insisted He spend the evening with them. We, too, can learn from such spontaneous Christian hospitality as these manifested. Jesus consented, and as they sat to eat, they asked their new friend (still not knowing He was the risen Christ) to ask God's blessing on their meal. He did so. Then when Christ broke the bread their eyes focused on His nail-pierced hands and they immediately realized it was their Lord. Jesus disappeared from their presence, and they recalled the walk and talk they had had with Him along the way.

C. The Meeting in the Upper Room. 24:33-48.

33. Having had the privilege of being a part of one of the most unique of the post-resurrection experiences, these two hastened back the eight miles into Jerusalem. They made their way to the upper room where they knew other disciples were gathered behind locked doors for fear of the Jews (Jn 20:19). The group present consisted of only ten of the apostles, Thomas being absent (Jn 20:24), the two from Emmaus, and others who had gathered. We do not know how large the crowd was, but it could have been close to twenty or more. **The eleven** is a collective term that was used to identify the group of disciples after the death of Judas, whether all were present or not.

34 Saying, The Lord is risen indeed, and hath appeared to Simon.

34. As the two gained entrance, they were immediately told, **The Lord is risen indeed, and hath appeared to Simon.** This appearance is only mentioned here and in I Corinthians 15:5. Christ was no doubt further preparing Peter for the leadership role he would assume in the early days of the church.

35 And they told what things were done in the way, and how he was known of them in breaking of bread.

35. Then Cleopas and his companion related what had happened to them that afternoon.

36 ¶And as they thus spake, Jesus himself stood in the midst of them, and saith unto them, Peace be unto you.

36. While they were just finishing their story, Jesus miraculously appeared in their midst and said, **Peace be unto you.**

37 But they were terrified and affrighted, and supposed that they had seen a spirit.

37. Of the apostles, apparently only Peter had, up to that time, seen the resurrected Christ. The rest had only heard the stories of the appearances. Now, when confronted with the reality themselves, they were shocked by the sudden and obviously miraculous nature of this appearance. Their immediate reaction was terror, and in that first impression they must have felt they were viewing some spiritual form of their resurrected Lord.

38 And he said unto them, Why are ye troubled? and why do thoughts arise in your hearts?
39 Behold my hands and my feet, that it is I myself: handle me, and see; for a spirit hath not flesh and bones, as ye see me have.

38-39. Jesus quickly corrected their mistaken theology by drawing attention to his completely physical body. He said, **Behold my hands and my feet, that it is I myself: handle me, and see; for a spirit hath not flesh and bones, as ye see me have.** Even with these clear words, given in the context of correcting a false view of the nature of Christ's resurrected body, there still persist some false cults and "isms" who maintain the heresy of a "spiritual resurrection" of Christ. The fact that Jesus said **flesh and bones** rather than "flesh and blood" does not necessarily indicate that His body had no blood. One cannot say, but flesh and bones usually do operate with blood. However, the life principle in a resurrected body may not be in its blood, but in the spirit of God.

40 And when he had thus spoken, he shewed them his hands and his feet.
41 And while they yet believed not for joy, and wondered, he said unto them, Have ye here any meat?
42 And they gave him a piece of a broiled fish, and of an honeycomb.
43 And he took it, and did eat before them.

40-43. In order to further prove the fact of His material bodily resurrection, Jesus gave a public demonstration by eating some broiled fish and part of a honeycomb.

44 And he said unto them, These are the words which I spake unto you, while I was yet with you, that all things must be fulfilled, which were written in the law of Moses, and in the prophets, and in the psalms, concerning me.
45 Then opened he their understanding, that they might understand the scriptures.

44-45. All things must be fulfilled, which were written in the law of Moses, and in the prophets, and in the psalms, concerning me. This verse opens up the Old Testament as to its prophetic and typical import regarding Christ. We know that the Old Testament is revealed in the New, while the New is concealed in the Old. Christ then opened **their understanding, that they might understand the scriptures.**

46 And said unto them, Thus it is written, and thus it behoved Christ to suffer, and to rise from the dead the third day:

46. Our Lord continued to point out to these disciples that **it is written** that Christ should suffer and rise again the third day. This must refer to such Old Testament passages as Psalm 16:20, Isaiah 53:10, and the typology regarding Jonah. Even Genesis 3:15 may be considered as teaching the Messiah's resurrection; otherwise the "wound to the heel" would have been fatal!

47 And that repentance and remission of sins should be preached in his name among all nations, beginning at Jerusalem.
48 And ye are witnesses of these things.

47-48. These verses point to a coming change in dispensations, for whereas Christ had before strictly limited the apostles in their preaching to the Jews only (Mt 10:5-6), He now enlarges the Commission as extending to all mankind.

X. THE PROMISE OF THE SON TO THE DISCIPLES. 24:49-53.

49 ¶And, behold, I send the promise

49. In order for Christ's disciples to accomplish this task of

of my Father upon you: but tarry ye in the city of Jerusalem, until ye be endued with power from on high.

50 ¶And he led them out as far as to Bethany, and he lifted up his hands, and blessed them.

51 And it came to pass, while he blessed them, he was parted from them, and carried up into heaven.

52 And they worshipped him, and returned to Jerusalem with great joy:

53 And were continually in the temple, praising and blessing God. Amen.

the Great Commission, Jesus promised them **power from on high.** They were to remain in Jerusalem until the promised power was received. This promise involved the coming indwelling presence of the Holy Spirit mentioned the night before Christ's crucifixion (Jn 16:7-15), and previously at the Feast of Tabernacles (Jn 7:39). John the Baptist had also intimated this special ministry of the Holy Spirit for disciples after Pentecost (Lk 3:16), and Jesus reiterated this just prior to His ascension when he said, "Ye shall be baptized with the Holy Ghost not many days hence" (Acts 1:5).

50. The ascension of Christ occurred near Bethany, on the eastern side of the Mount of Olives. His ascension was in His physical bodily form, and Acts 1:11 assures us that "this same Jesus which is taken up from you into heaven shall so come in like manner as ye have seen him go into heaven." Christ's return will not be of a secret spiritual nature as some cults suppose, but He will return bodily.

51-53. He blessed them. Christ, in contrast to the speechless Zechariah in chapter 1, had a blessing to give these men. **And they worshiped him.** Jesus is entitled to worship only because He is Almighty God, the eternal, omnipotent Creator of the universe. Compare what happened to John when he mistakenly tried to worship a created being in Revelation 19:10 and 22:8-9. The text of the Authorized Version renders verses 52-53 correctly regarding Christ's deity.

The Gospel of Luke begins by announcing **good tidings of great joy, which shall be to all people** (Lk 2:10), and it ends with disciples who are filled **with great joy: And were continually in the temple, praising and blessing God.** Like those of old, we should be ready to carry this joy to others all around us. Let us imitate our Lord, who "came to seek and to save that which was lost" (Lk 19:10).

BIBLIOGRAPHY

Alford, Henry. The Gospel According to Luke. In *The New Testament for English Readers*. London: Revingtons, 1863.

Arndt, William F. *Gospel According to St. Luke*. St. Louis: Concordia, 1956.

Burnside, W. F. *The Gospel According to St. Luke*. Cambridge: Cambridge University Press, 1913.

Earle, Ralph. The Gospel According to St. Luke. In *The Wesleyan Bible Commentary*. Vol. 4. Grand Rapids: Eerdmans, 1964.

Ellis, E. E. The Gospel of Luke. In *New Century Bible*. New York: Thomas Nelson, 1966.

*Erdman, C. R. *Gospel of Luke*. Philadelphia: Westminster, 1956.

Farrar, F. W. The Gospel According to St. Luke. In *The Cambridge Bible for Schools and Colleges*. London: Clay and Sons, 1899.

Gaebelein, Arno C. *The Annotated Bible*. Vol. 3. Neptune, N. J.: Loizeaux Brothers, 1970.

*Geldenhuys, Norval. Commentary on the Gospel of Luke. In *New International Commentary on the New Testament*. Grand Rapids: Eerdmans, 1951.

*Godet, Frederick L. *Commentary on the Gospel of Luke*. Grand Rapids: Zondervan, reprinted, 1957.

Ironside, Harry A. *Addresses on the Gospel of Luke*. Neptune, N. J.: Loizeaux Brothers, 1947.

Jones, W. B. and F. C. Cook. St. Luke's Gospel. In *The Bible Commentary*. Vol. 6. Ed. by F. C. Cook. New York: Charles Scribner's Sons, n.d.

Luce, H. K. The Gospel According to St. Luke. In *The Cambridge Bible for Schools and Colleges*. Cambridge: Cambridge University Press, 1936.

*Marshall, I. H. The Gospel of Luke. In the *New International Greek New Testament Commentary*. Grand Rapids: Eerdmans, 1978.

*Morgan, G. Campbell. *The Gospel According to Luke*. New York: Revell, 1931.

*Morris, Leon. The Gospel According to St. Luke. In *The Tyndale New Testament Commentaries*. Ed. by R. V. G. Tasker. Grand Rapids: Eerdmans, 1974.

Plummer, Alfred. A Critical and Exegetical Commentary on The Gospel According to St. Luke. In *The International Critical Commentary*. New York: Charles Scribner's Sons, 1925.

Ramsay, W. M. *Luke the Physician*. Grand Rapids: Baker, 1956 reprint of 1908 ed.

Robertson, A. T. *Luke the Historian in the Light of Research*. Grand Rapids: Baker, reprinted, 1977.

Ryle, J. C. Luke. In *Expository Thoughts on the Gospels*. Vol. 2. Grand Rapids: Zondervan, reprinted, 1956.

Stonehouse, N. B. *The Witness of Luke to Christ*. Grand Rapids: Eerdmans, 1961.

Summers, R. *Commentary on Luke*. Waco: Word Books, 1972.

*Tenney, Merrill C. The Gospel According to Luke. In *The Wycliffe Bible Commentary*. Ed. by Charles F. Pfeiffer and Everett F. Harrison. Chicago: Moody Press, 1962.

The Gospel According To

JOHN

INTRODUCTION

The Gospel of John remains today a favorite among Christians. Many ministers recommend this book to new converts as a training manual for Christian development. William Hendriksen prefaces his commentary on this gospel with the words of Scripture, "Put off thy shoes from off thy feet, for the place whereon thou standest is holy ground" (William Hendriksen, *The Gospel of St. John*, p. 3). This gospel is uniquely different from the Synoptics in that ninety percent of its content is not discussed by the other gospels even though John had these gospels at his disposal when he wrote. John carefully chose, under the inspiration of the Holy Spirit, only those events, miracles, and sermons, that would supplement his literary intent. The result of his effort is a gospel that "is the most amazing book that was ever written" (Hendriksen, p. 3).

Authorship. Although the author of this book is not mentioned by name, there is ample evidence externally and internally to conclude that John the apostle was the author.

1. External evidence. The writings of early church fathers often quote from the Gospel of John and attribute this Gospel to the Apostle John. "The external evidence for the early date and Apostolic authorship of the Fourth Gospel is as great as that for any book in the New Testament" (Henry C. Thiessen, *Introduction to the New Testament*, p. 162). Irenaeus, who was a pupil of Polycarp, a friend of the Apostle John, writes, "Afterwards, John, the disciple of the Lord, who also leaned upon his breast, did himself publish a Gospel during his residence at Ephesus in Asia" (Thiessen, p. 164). The importance of this statement is that Irenaeus quotes from the Gospel (21:20, 24) and attributes the authorship to the Apostle John.

2. Internal evidence. There are certain facts about the author that can be deduced from the content. When these facts are considered collectively, they complement the external evidence and indicated johannine authorship. First, it is clearly evident from the context that the author was a Jew. He understood and quoted from the Old Testament (12:40; 13:18; 19:37) and he had a thorough knowledge of Jewish feasts and customs: wedding feasts (2:1-12), ceremonial purification (3:25), various religious feasts (2:13, 23; 6:4; 13:1; 18:28), and burial customs (11:38, 44; 19:40). Second, he must have been a resident of Palestine. Throughout the gospel he gives detailed geographical descriptions that could be given only by a Palestinian resident. He knows the exact distance between Bethany and Jerusalem (11:18), that Jacob's well is deep (4:11), that Ephraim was near the wilderness (11:54), and many other important geographical details.

Third, the author was an eyewitness to the events he describes. He saw the glory of Jesus

Christ (1:14), was at the crucifixion (19:33-35), knew the number and size of the waterpots used in Cana (2:6), knew the distance from the shore to the apostles' boat (21:8), and knew the number of fish caught (21:11). Fourth, he identifies himself with the disciple "whom Jesus loved" on five occasions (13:23; 19:26; 20:2; 21:7, 20). Since John's name is absent from the gospel, it would be logical to assume that he is its anonymous author.

Fifth, the style and vocabulary of the Gospel of John are strikingly similar to the epistles which bear his name. These five observations from the content of the fourth Gospel lead clearly to the conclusion that John the Apostle was the author.

Date and place of writing. Liberal scholars have placed the date of the book as early as A.D. 40, while other liberals have dated it around A.D. 140-170. However, conservatives agreed on a date late in the first century and between the years A.D. 85-95. This date is supported by the discovery of a papyrus fragment called P[52]. This papyrus manuscript is the earliest textual evidence of the New Testament so far discovered, and contains five verses of John (18:31-33, 37-38). Since this fragment is dated about A.D. 125, the original gospel had to be in circulation before the end of the first century (Robert G. Gromacki, *New Testament Survey*, p. 133). There is general agreement that John wrote this book from Ephesus where he spent the latter years of his life.

Purpose. John's purpose in writing this book is clearly identified in two verses (20:30-31): "And many other signs truly did Jesus in the presence of his disciples, which are not written in this book: But these are written, that ye might believe that Jesus is the Christ, the Son of God; and that believing ye might have life through his name." There are three key words in these verses: *signs, believe,* and *life.* The *signs* (Gr *sēmeion*) are the miracles which John chose to describe in proving the deity of Christ. John selected eight signs to substantiate his thesis:

1. Turning water into wine. 2:2-11.
2. Healing the nobleman's son. 4:46-54.
3. Healing the impotent man. 5:1-15.
4. Feeding the five thousand. 6:1-14.
5. Walking on the water. 6:15-21.
6. Healing the blind man. 9:1-41.
7. Raising Lazarus. 11:1-44.
8. Providing the catch of fish. 21:6-11.

The second key word in John's statement of purpose is the word *believe* (Gr *pisteuō*) which means to trust or commit. John describes the miracles to prove the deity of Christ so that the readers "might believe that Jesus is the Christ, the Son of God."

The third key word describes the results of believing the person and work of Christ—"and that believing ye might have life" (Gr *zōē*). John's gospel is not merely an intellectual exercise, but rather a historical narrative about the Son of God with the express intent of producing life in the hearts of those who believe in the Son of God. The heartbeat of the Gospel of John is evangelism—pointing men to the "Lamb of God, which taketh away the sin of the world" (1:29).

John further supplements his thesis that Christ is the Son of God by emphasizing the claims that Christ made about Himself. Christ claimed for Himself the very name of God. "Before Abraham was, I am" (8:58). In a review of familiar statements, John amplifies on the claim of Christ to be the "I AM:"

1. I am the bread of life. 6:35.
2. I am the light of the world. 8:12; 9:5.
3. I am the door. 10:7.
4. I am the good shepherd. 10:11, 14.
5. I am the resurrection and the life. 11:25.
6. I am the way, the truth, and the life. 14:6.
7. I am the true vine. 15:1.

John uses all the miracles and sermons of this gospel to develop an impeccable argument for the deity of Jesus Christ.

To those who have experienced this eternal life, a review study of this gospel will produce a deeper understanding and greater appreciation of the One who "came unto his own, and his own received him not. But as many as received him, to them gave he power to become the sons of God, even to them that believe on his name: Which were born, not of blood, nor of the will of the flesh, nor of the will of man, but of God" (1:11-13).

OUTLINE

I. Prologue. 1:1-14.
  A. The Word in the Beginning. 1:1-2.
  B. The Word in Creation. 1:3.
  C. The Word after the Fall. 1:4-5.
  D. The Word at Incarnation. 1:6-14.
II. The Public Ministry of Christ. 1:15-12:50.
  A. Christ Proclaimed by Individuals. 1:15-51.
    1. Testimony of John. 1:15-34.
    2. Testimony of disciples. 1:35-51.
  B. Christ Performs His First Miracle. 2:1-25.
    1. Wedding at Cana. 2:1-12.
    2. Cleansing of Temple. 2:13-25.
  C. Christ as Saviour. 3:1-36.
    1. Teaching of the new birth. 3:1-21.
    2. Testimony of John the Baptist. 3:22-36.
  D. Christ as the Master Soul-winner. 4:1-54.
    1. Samaritan woman's sins forgiven. 4:1-45.
    2. Nobleman's son healed. 4:46-54.
  E. Christ as the Son of God. 5:1-47.
    1. Healing of lame man. 5:1-18.
    2. Defense of His person. 5:19-47.
  F. Christ as the Bread of Life. 6:1-71.
    1. Feeding of the five thousand. 6:1-14.
    2. Walking on the water. 6:15-21.
    3. Sermon on the Bread of Life. 6:22-59.
    4. Many turn away. 6:60-71.
  G. Christ as the Master Teacher. 7:1-53.
    1. Teaching concerning His person. 7:1-36.
    2. Teaching concerning the Holy Spirit. 7:37-39.
    3. Division of people. 7:40-53.
  H. Christ as the Light of the World. 8:1-9:41.
    1. Adulterous woman forgiven. 8:1-11.
    2. Sermon on the Light of the World. 8:12-59.
    3. Application of sermon by healing blind man. 9:1-41.

  I. Christ as the Good Shepherd. 10:1-42.
    1. Sermon on the Good Shepherd. 10:1-21.
    2. Rejection of Christ's message. 10:22-42.
  J. Christ as the Resurrection and the Life. 11:1-57.
    1. Power of Christ: Raising Lazarus. 11:1-46.
    2. Plan of the Pharisees. 11:47-57.
  K. Christ as the Messiah. 12:1-50.
    1. Supper at Bethany. 12:1-11.
    2. Triumphal Entry. 12:12-19.
    3. Teaching on the cross. 12:20-50.
III. The Private Ministry of Christ. 13:1-17:26.
  A. Christ as the Servant. 13:1-38.
    1. Washing the disciples' feet. 13:1-20.
    2. Predicting His betrayal. 13:21-35.
    3. Predicting Peter's denial. 13:36-38.
  B. Christ as the Comforter. 14:1-31.
  C. Christ as the True Vine. 15:1-16:33.
    1. Christ and the disciples. 15:1-17.
    2. Disciples and the world. 15:18-27.
    3. Disciples and the Spirit. 16:1-33.
  D. Christ as the Intercessor. 17:1-26.
IV. The Passion Ministry of Christ. 18:1-21:25.
  A. Christ and the Crucifixion. 18:1-19:42.
    1. His arrest. 18:1-11.
    2. His trials. 18:12-19:16.
    3. His crucifixion. 19:17-37.
    4. His burial. 19:38-42.
  B. Christ and the Resurrection. 20:1-31.
    1. Christ revealed to Mary. 20:1-18.
    2. Christ revealed to the Ten. 20:19-23.
    3. Christ revealed to Thomas. 20:24-31.
  C. Christ and the Commission. 21:1-25.
    1. Miracle of the fish. 21:1-14.
    2. Message to Peter. 21:15-17.
    3. Conclusion. 21:18-25.

COMMENTARY

I. PROLOGUE. 1:1-14.

John begins his gospel with a series of declarative statements about the deity of Christ. In contrast to the other gospels, John begins his gospel in eternity past. Matthew, who portrays Christ as the King, begins with a genealogy to prove His Davidic lineage. Mark, who presents Christ as the Servant, begins his gospel with the public activity of Christ as a Servant. Luke, who emphasizes the humanity of Christ, begins his gospel with a lengthy description of the events that led to the birth of Christ. John, who presents Christ as the Son of God, begins his gospel in eternity.

A. The Word in the Beginning. 1:1-2.

IN the beginning was the Word, and the Word was with God, and the Word was God.

1:1. In the beginning. This opening statement is a repetition of the opening statement of the Bible (Gen 1:1). When time began, the Word was already in existence. **Was the Word.** This unique name for Christ (Gr *logos*) occurs only four times in the New Testament as a name (1:1, 14; I Jn 1:1; Rev 19:13) and is utilized only by John the apostle. Since words reveal the thoughts of one person to another, Christ as the Eternal Word is a revelation of God to man.

And the Word was with God. The words translated **with God** (Gr *pros ton theon*) could be rendered "face to face with God." Two important thoughts emerge from this statement. First, the Word is a distinct person. Second, the Word was enjoying communion and fellowship with another distinct person, God the Father. **And the Word was God.** Lest the reader assume that the Word as a distinct person is less than God, John concludes the verse with an emphatic statement that the Word was completely God. To lend the greatest possible emphasis to the importance of this statement, it literally reads "and God was the Word." The subject and predicate are reversed to underline the deity of the Word.

2 The same was in the beginning with God.

2. The same was in the beginning with God. This verse simply summarizes the deep theological truths revealed in the first verse.

B. The Word in Creation. 1:3.

Having established the eternality of the Word, John now describes His involvement in creation.

3 All things were made by him; and without him was not any thing made that was made.

3. All things were made by him; and without him was not any thing made that was made. This verse establishes Christ as the subject of creation and not the object of creation. He was the Creator, not the created. One scholar translates the latter part of this verse as follows: "and apart from him not a single thing that exists came into being" (William Hendriksen, *The Gospel of St. John*, p. 71).

C. The Word after the Fall. 1:4-5.

4 In him was life; and the life was the light of men.

4. In him was life. This verse opens with the preposition (Gr *en*), which means "in." Life is not from Him, or through Him, or by Him, but life is in Him. The life (Gr *zōē*) spoken of is not life in a physical sense but rather in a spiritual sense. John uses life fifty-four times in his gospel and first epistle to refer to the spiritual realm. **And the life was the light of men.** Christ is the Light shining in contrast to the darkness of this sinful world.

5 And the light shineth in darkness; and the darkness comprehended it not.

5. And the light shineth in darkness. In the previous verse both verbs are in the Greek imperfect tense denoting a past action. However, the tense of the verb "shineth" (Gr *phainō*) is the Greek present tense. Christ, who was the Light, continues to shine as the Light. **And the darkness comprehended it not.** The darkness referred to here is the unbelief and sin of mankind (3:19). It is the antithesis of the Light. The verb used here (Gr *katalambanō*) means to "grasp, comprehend, put out, seize with hostile intent" (W. Wilbur Gingrich, *Shorter Lexicon of the New Testament*, p. 111). This implies a hostility between the Light and the darkness with the darkness unable to put out the Light.

D. The Word at Incarnation. 1:6-14.

6 ¶There was a man sent from God, whose name *was* John.
7 The same came for a witness, to bear witness of the Light, that all *men* through him might believe.
8 He was not that Light, but *was sent* to bear witness of that Light.

6-8. These verses contrast Christ and John the Baptist. A review of the descriptive statement is given concerning John. First, He was not the *logos*, but rather a human individual. Second, he was **sent from God.** John was commissioned by God; he was not God Himself. Third, John was a **witness, to bear witness of the Light, that all men through him might believe.** John's purpose was to give testimony concerning Christ that would lead persons to a saving faith in the Light. Fourth, John **was not that Light.** The ministry of John the Baptist is similar to the ministry of Christians today. We are to give personal witness and testimony concerning the Light so that others might believe.

In the following verses John elaborates on the theme of Christ the Light. He studies the Light in a series of relationships: to the world in general (1:9-10); to the Jewish people (1:11-13); and to the disciples (1:14).

9 *That* was the true Light, which lighteth every man that cometh into the world.
10 He was in the world, and the world was made by him, and the world knew him not.

9-10. That was the true Light. Christ is the true, or genuine, or real Light. **Which lighteth every man that cometh into the world.** Christ is the one who gives to every man the light of reason and conscience. The result of this revelation was that the **world knew him not.** The verb used here (Gr *gnōskō*) means to acknowledge or recognize. The world rejected Him.

11 He came unto his own, and his own received him not.
12 But as many as received him, to them gave he power to become the sons of God, *even* to them that believe on his name:

11-12. There is a very strong play on the words **his own** (Gr *idios*). In their first occurrence, they refer to what was His own, namely His own world (see vs. 10, and compare the same expression in 19:27 where it refers to a man's home). In their second occurrence, the Greek gender has changed and the reference is to His own people, who by their rejection show Him to be truly despised (cf. Isa 53:3; Lk 19:14).

There are two actions delineated in verse 12: the action of man and the action of God. Man's action is to receive and to believe. To receive means to accept for one's self, and to believe means to place one's trust in. Both of these concepts are a part of salvation. God's action is **to them gave he power to become the sons of God.** The word power (Gr *exousia*) means the right or authority to become the sons of God.

13 Which were born, not of blood, nor of the will of the flesh, nor of the will of man, but of God.

13. The spiritual birth spoken of in the previous verse is **not of blood.** It is not on the basis of lineage or Jewish heritage. It is **nor of the will of the flesh** or a carnal desire. It is not **of the will of man** or human in its origin. It is **of God.** This birth is supernatural.

14 And the Word was made flesh, and dwelt among us, (and we beheld his glory, the glory as of the only begotten of the Father,) full of grace and truth.

14. The Word was made flesh and dwelt among us. The verb translated "dwelt" (Gr *skēnoō*) means to tabernacle or live in a tent. The author testifies that **we beheld his glory.**

II. THE PUBLIC MINISTRY OF CHRIST. 1:15-12:50.

A. Christ Proclaimed by Individuals. 1:15-51.

In the remaining verses of chapter 1, Christ is proclaimed as Messiah by several individuals including John the Baptist, Andrew, Simon, Philip, and Nathanael.

1. Testimony of John. 1:15-34.

15 ¶John bare witness of him, and cried, saying, This was he of whom I spake, He that cometh after me is preferred before me: for he was before me.

15. The writer again discusses the **witness** of John (1:7). Although Jesus comes **after** John, yet **he was before** him; He existed in eternity.

The verses are interjected into the testimony of John the Baptist and describe the personal testimony of the author.

16 And of his fulness have all we received, and grace for grace.

17 For the law was given by Moses, *but* grace and truth came by Jesus Christ.

18 No man hath seen God at any time; the only begotten Son, which is in the bosom of the Father, he hath declared *him*.

19 ¶And this is the record of John, when the Jews sent priests and Levites from Jerusalem to ask him, Who art thou?

20 And he confessed, and denied not; but confessed, I am not the Christ.
21 And they asked him, What then? Art thou E-lī′as? And he saith, I am not. Art thou that prophet? And he answered, No.

22 Then said they unto him, Who art thou? that we may give an answer to them that sent us. What sayest thou of thyself?
23 He said, I *am* the voice of one crying in the wilderness, Make straight the way of the Lord, as said the prophet E-sā′ias.
24 And they which were sent were of the Pharisees.
25 And they asked him, and said unto him, Why baptizest thou then, if thou be not that Christ, nor E-lī′as, neither that prophet?
26 John answered them, saying, I baptize with water: but there standeth one among you, whom ye know not;
27 He it is, who coming after me is preferred before me, whose shoe's latchet I am not worthy to unloose.
28 These things were done in Běth-ăb′a-ra beyond Jordan, where John was baptizing.
29 ¶The next day John seeth Jesus coming unto him, and saith, Behold the Lamb of God, which taketh away the sin of the world.

30 This is he of whom I said, After me cometh a man which is preferred before me: for he was before me.
31 And I knew him not: but that he should be made manifest to Israel, therefore am I come baptizing with water.
32 And John bare record, saying, I saw the Spirit descending from heaven like a dove, and it abode upon him.
33 And I knew him not: but he that sent me to baptize with water, the

16. Of his fulness. This **fulness** is expressed in verse 14 and the writer now claims that **of his fulness have all we received, and grace for grace** (lit., grace upon grace).

17. Continuing the thoughts of verse 14, a sharp contrast is made between the law of Moses and Jesus Christ. **The law was given by Moses.** The law had its place in revealing man's condition (Gal 3:24). However, the law did not provide **grace and truth. Grace** was to forgive and pardon the sinner and the **truth** (or the reality) was that which the sacrifices pointed to. These are found only in Jesus Christ.

18. God is a Spirit and cannot be seen by man (I Tim 6:16). The **only begotten Son . . . he hath declared him.** Christ has declared (lit., exegeted; Gr *exēgeomai*) or revealed God to man. The expression, **the only begotten Son,** has excellent manuscript evidence to support translating it, "the unique God."

19. And this is the record of John. The author now returns from a note of personal testimony to the record of John. This culminates in verse 34 with the words of John the Baptist. The Sanhedrin is alarmed at the ministry of John the Baptist, and so they send a delegation of theologians to ask him the question, **Who art thou?**

20-21. John denies that he is the Christ. He also denies being Elijah, whom the Jews expected to precede the Messiah (Mal 4:5). John did minister in the spirit of Elijah (Lk 1:17) and was even called Elijah by Christ (Mt 17:12), but he was not literally Elijah. John also denies being **that prophet** (Deut 18:15-18) or Christ Himself.

22-23. Unsatisfied with John's negation of their questions, they ask, **What sayest thou of thyself?** John answers with the words of Isaiah 40:3. He was simply a **voice** to **make straight** the paths or prepare **the way of the Lord.**

24-28. The investigating committee now becomes concerned with John's baptizing. **Why baptizest thou then?** John replies by stating that there is a vast difference between what he is doing with **water,** which is only a sign, and what the Messiah will do with the real thing, the cleansing power of the Holy Spirit (Mk 1:8). Concerning Him, John states that he is unworthy of even untying His sandal straps. These events took place in **Bethabara beyond Jordan.**

29. John seeth Jesus. The day after the committee investigates John, Jesus Himself appears on the scene. John makes the now familiar statement, **Behold the Lamb of God.** Christ is the fulfillment of the Old Testament lamb (Ex 12, 13; Num 28:4; Isa 53). **Which taketh away.** This is a Greek present participle which means "is taking away." What the Old Testament lamb could not do, the Lamb of God is doing. **The sin of the world.** The Lamb of God was not limited to the Jewish people but rather He reaches the entire world.

30-32. The message of John seemingly centered around this theme (1:15, 27). The apostle assumes that the reader is familiar with the Synoptics since **the Spirit descending like a dove** occurred at the baptism (Mt 3:13-17; Mk 1:9-10; Lk 3:21-22).

33-34. And I knew him not. The value of John's testimony to Christ is that God revealed it to him at the baptism of Jesus.

same said unto me, Upon whom thou shalt see the Spirit descending, and remaining on him, the same is he which baptizeth with the Holy Ghost.

34 And I saw, and bare record that this is the Son of God.

35 ¶Again the next day after John stood, and two of his disciples;

36 And looking upon Jesus as he walked, he saith, Behold the Lamb of God!

37 And the two disciples heard him speak, and they followed Jesus.

38 Then Jesus turned, and saw them following, and saith unto them, What seek ye? They said unto him, Rabbi, (which is to say, being interpreted, Master,) where dwellest thou?

39 He saith unto them, Come and see. They came and saw where he dwelt, and abode with him that day: for it was about the tenth hour.

40 One of the two which heard John *speak*, and followed him, was Andrew, Simon Peter's brother.

41 He first findeth his own brother Simon, and saith unto him, We have found the Mes-sī'as, which is, being interpreted, the Christ.

42 And he brought him to Jesus. And when Jesus beheld him, he said, Thou art Simon the son of Jona: thou shalt be called Cē'phas, which is by interpretation, A stone.

43 ¶The day following Jesus would go forth into Galilee, and findeth Philip, and saith unto him, Follow me.

44 Now Philip was of Bĕth-sā'i-da, the city of Andrew and Peter.

45 Philip findeth Nathanael, and saith unto him, We have found him, of whom Moses in the law, and the prophets, did write, Jesus of Nazareth, the son of Joseph.

46 And Nathanael said unto him, Can there any good thing come out of Nazareth? Philip saith unto him, Come and see.

47 Jesus saw Nathanael coming to him, and saith of him, Behold an Israelite indeed, in whom is no guile!

48 Nathanael saith unto him, Whence knowest thou me? Jesus answered and said unto him, Before that Philip called thee, when thou wast under the fig tree, I saw thee.

49 Nathanael answered and saith unto him, Rabbi, thou art the Son of God; thou art the King of Israel.

50 Jesus answered and said unto him, Because I said unto thee, I saw thee under the fig tree, believest thou? thou shalt see greater things than these.

51 And he saith unto him, Verily, verily, I say unto you, Hereafter ye shall see heaven open, and the angels of God ascending and descending upon the Son of man.

Until that time John **knew him not.** This section relating John's testimony to Christ concludes with the statement **that this is the Son of God.**

2. Testimony of disciples. 1:35-51.

35-37. In the latter portion of this chapter, Jesus is revealed to certain disciples. These verses are the transition between the ministry of John the Baptist and the ministry of Christ. John the Baptist is with two of his disciples (Andrew and John, the author), and after pointing to **the Lamb of God,** they **followed Jesus.**

38-39. Jesus then asks an important question. **What seek ye?** In response to this question, the disciples ask with another question, **where dwellest thou?** They were interested in close communion and fellowship with Christ. Christ invites them to **Come and see** and **They came and saw.**

40-41. The true response of one who has found Christ is to bring others. Andrew tells his brother Simon, **We have found the Messiah.** Messiah (Gr *Messias*) means the Anointed One; it is the transliteration of the Hebrew *Mashiach*, which is often translated by the Greek *Christos* which is then transliterated into English as "Christ."

42. Simon comes to Christ and gets a new name, **Cephas, which is by interpretation, A stone.**

43. The day following. This is the last of four successive days discussed in chapter 1. Christ now does the finding and commands Philip to **Follow** Him.

44-46. Philip immediately **findeth Nathanael** and states, **We have found him.** Nathanael responds with doubt that Nazareth could produce the Messiah. But Philip gives the invitation, **Come and see.**

47. Jesus sees Nathanael coming and addresses him as an **Israelite indeed in whom is no guile.** This is a compliment to the honesty and sincerity of Nathanael.

48-49. Nathanael responds, **Whence knowest thou me?** Then Jesus reveals the penetrating eye of deity by telling Nathanael that even before **Philip called thee, when thou wast under the fig tree, I saw thee.** In a previous moment of quiet devotion, Jesus had seen Nathanael. Nathanael then proclaims Christ **as the Son of God** and the promised Messiah.

50-51. This verse is more of a promise than a question. Because of Nathanael's faith, he would **see greater things than these.** Jesus now describes these **greater things** by referring to the Old Testament story concerning Jacob's ladder (Gen 28). Christ Himself was to be the Ladder between God and man since He was the **Son of God** (1:49) and the **Son of man** (1:51).

B. Christ Performs His First Miracle. 2:1-25.

In this chapter there are two events detailed which illustrate the emptiness and deficiency of Judaism. The empty water jars at the wedding feast describe the condition of Judaism in meeting the spiritual needs of the Jewish people. This emptiness is further described in the cleansing of the Temple, and Judaism is described as corrupt.

CHAPTER 2

AND the third day there was a marriage in Cana of Galilee; and the mother of Jesus was there:

2 And both Jesus was called, and his disciples, to the marriage.

3 And when they wanted wine, the mother of Jesus saith unto him, They have no wine.
4 Jesus saith unto her, Woman, what have I to do with thee? mine hour is not yet come.
5 His mother saith unto the servants, Whatsoever he saith unto you, do *it*.

6 And there were set there six waterpots of stone, after the manner of the purifying of the Jews, containing two or three firkins apiece.
7 Jesus saith unto them, Fill the waterpots with water. And they filled them up to the brim.
8 And he saith unto them, Draw out now, and bear unto the governor of the feast. And they bare *it*.

9 When the ruler of the feast had tasted the water that was made wine, and knew not whence it was: (but the servants which drew the water knew;) the governor of the feast called the bridegroom,
10 And saith unto him, Every man at the beginning doth set forth good wine; and when men have well drunk, then that which is worse: *but* thou hast kept the good wine until now.

11 This beginning of miracles did Jesus in Cana of Galilee, and manifested forth his glory; and his disciples believed on him.
12 ¶After this he went down to Caper′na-um, he, and his mother, and his brethren, and his disciples: and they continued there not many days.

13 ¶And the Jews' passover was at hand, and Jesus went up to Jerusalem,

14 And found in the temple those that sold oxen and sheep and doves, and the changers of money sitting:
15 And when he had made a scourge of small cords, he drove them all out of the temple, and the sheep, and the oxen; and poured out the changers' money, and overthrew the tables;
16 And said unto them that sold doves, Take these things hence; make

1. Wedding at Cana. 2:1-12.

2:1. And the third day. The third day after Jesus had attained two more disciples, Philip and Nathanael, He journeyed about eight miles north of Nazareth to Cana. **The mother of Jesus was there.** John does not mention Mary by name, which is consistent with his style, since he tends to leave himself and his close relatives anonymous (19:26-27).

2. Since the disciples had joined Christ so recently, there is the problem in resolving how they were all invited to the wedding feast. There are two possible answers: Jesus could have stopped in Nazareth on His way to Cana and accepted the invitation for His disciples; or second, Nathanael could have made the arrangements since he was from Cana.

3-5. When the wine failed, Mary came to Christ for help because she knew who Christ really was (Lk 1:26-38). Christ addressed her as **Woman** or "Lady"; no disrespect is intended. **What have I to do with thee?** Christ emphasizes that Mary should no longer think of Him as her son. **Mine hour is not yet come.** Throughout the Gospels, Christ is conscious that He is doing the will of the Father and each act has an appropriate time (7:6; 8:20; 12:23). Mary acknowledges submission to the Son of God and tells **the servants whatsoever he saith unto you, do it.**

6-8. Jesus Christ uses the **six waterpots of stone** which could each contain from 17 to 25 gallons of liquid. When they were filled with water, Christ commands the servants to **Draw out.** This refers to dipping out the water. They were told to **bear** it (Gr *pherō*) to the **governor of the feast.** The verb used here is in the Greek present tense (progressive action), and perhaps hints that the process of serving must be continued no matter how ridiculous it seemed. The total volume of water changed to wine was about 100-150 gallons.

9-10. When the wine was tasted, it was proved to be of superior quality. The governor compliments the bridegroom, **Thou hast kept the good wine until now.** The symbolism is clear. The power of Christ filled the emptiness of the waterpots and that same power is able to fill the emptiness of Judaistic religion.

11-12. This beginning of miracles. The word used here for **miracles** (Gr *sēmeion*) means signs, and the apostle gives the reason for the sign: **and manifested forth his glory.** The sign drew attention to the power and glory of the One who performed it. In this story, Christ stands as the preeminent One. The faith of the disciples was strengthened because of this sign. After this incident, Christ returned to Capernaum. This was the home of James and John.

2. Cleansing of Temple. 2:13-25.

13. The Law required every male Jew twelve years old and above to attend the **passover. Jesus went up to Jerusalem,** the political and religious capital of Israel, and because of its geographical elevation, the Jews always talked about going **up** to Jerusalem regardless of the direction they were traveling from.

14-17. Christ found in the court of the Gentiles a terrible scene. The Sanhedrin was permitting the selling of sacrificial animals at exorbitant prices and permitting the changing of foreign currency into Jewish money, which was required for the temple tax. Christ makes a whip and drives out both the animals and the wicked merchants. He overturns the tables and scatters the coins across the floor. He commands the dove owners, **Take these things hence.** Christ then justifies this striking action, **make not my Father's house an house of merchandise** (Mal 3:1-3). Again, the failure of Judaism is emphasized. The disciples recall that this is the fulfillment of prophecy (Ps 69:9).

not my Father's house an house of merchandise.

17 And his disciples remembered that it was written, The zeal of thine house hath eaten me up.

18 ¶Then answered the Jews and said unto him, What sign shewest thou unto us, seeing that thou doest these things?

19 Jesus answered and said unto them, Destroy this temple, and in three days I will raise it up.

20 Then said the Jews, Forty and six years was this temple in building, and wilt thou rear it up in three days?

21 But he spake of the temple of his body.

22 When therefore he was risen from the dead, his disciples remembered that he had said this unto them; and they believed the scripture, and the word which Jesus had said.

23 ¶Now when he was in Jerusalem at the passover, in the feast *day*, many believed in his name, when they saw the miracles which he did.

24 But Jesus did not commit himself unto them, because he knew all *men*,

25 And needed not that any should testify of man: for he knew what was in man.

CHAPTER 3

THERE was a man of the Pharisees, named Nĭc-o-dē′mus, a ruler of the Jews:

2 The same came to Jesus by night, and said unto him, Rabbi, we know that thou art a teacher come from God: for no man can do these miracles that thou doest, except God be with him.

3 Jesus answered and said unto him, Verily, verily, I say unto thee, Except a man be born again, he cannot see the kingdom of God.

4 Nĭc-o-dē′mus saith unto him, How can a man be born when he is old? can he enter the second time into his mother's womb, and be born?

5 Jesus answered, Verily, verily, I say unto thee, Except a man be born of water and *of* the Spirit, he cannot enter into the kingdom of God.

18. The Jews, who have been shocked by the action of Christ, demand a **sign** to substantiate His authority and conduct. However, this was a ridiculous request since the cleansing in itself was a sign (Mal 3:1-3).

19. Christ answers with a deep spiritual truth. **Destroy this temple, and in three days I will raise it up.** Christ was referring to the destruction of His body and to His resurrection from the dead. The physical Temple was a type of Christ's body, and when the body of Christ was destroyed, the purpose and existence of the Jewish Temple were also destroyed. Consequently, the destruction of His body also meant the destruction of the Temple.

20-22. The Jews take Christ literally, and ignore the spiritual and true meaning of His statement. The author adds these words lest his readers miss the truth of Christ's statement. Even the disciples did not fully understand until **he was risen from the dead.** They **believed the scripture,** or the Old Testament prophecies, and **the word which Jesus had said.**

23-25. Jesus remained in Jerusalem for the Passover, and **many believed in his name, when they saw the miracles.** The word used to express belief (Gr *pisteuō*) is used in the next verse. **But Jesus did not commit himself.** Christ did not entrust Himself to them because they were not true believers. He concluded this because **he knew all men.** These were nominal believers whose only interest was the miracles. He did not need their testimony **for he knew what was in man.** These people had not accepted Him with saving faith, but rather they accepted Him as a powerful miracle worker.

C. Christ as Saviour. 3:1-36.

There are two separate incidents detailed in this particular chapter: the interview with Nicodemus, and the last testimony of John the Baptist. The interview with Nicodemus is of primary importance since it reveals the doctrine of the new birth.

1. Teaching of the new birth. 3:1-21.

3:1-2. In these opening verses, Nicodemus is introduced as a **man of the Pharisees** and a **ruler of the Jews.** The Pharisees were the religious separatists and the rulers (Gr *archōn*) who predominantly formed the Sanhedrin. Nicodemus **came to Jesus by night** so that he could personally talk with Christ. **We know** seems to indicate that other influential religious leaders were convinced that Christ was a **teacher come from God** because of the miracles.

3. After Nicodemus came to Christ, Christ made a statement about the new birth. Nicodemus then asked three questions about that statement. **Except a man be born again.** The word **again** (Gr *anōthen*) means "from above." Unless a person is born from above **he cannot see the kingdom of God.** The kingdom of God is His rule over His people and refers to everlasting life.

4. Nicodemus' questions reveal that he did not grasp the spiritual meaning of the Lord's statement. Nicodemus expects a negative answer to his rhetorical question. However, Christ answers by explaining this new birth.

5. To be a part of God's kingdom, one must **be born of water and of the Spirit.** There are three interpretations as to the meaning of **water:** it refers to the washing of the water of God's Word (I Pet 1:23); it refers to baptism; or it refers to physical birth. The latter of the three seems to be the most logical.

6 That which is born of the flesh is flesh; and that which is born of the Spirit is spirit.

7 Marvel not that I said unto thee, Ye must be born again.

8 The wind bloweth where it listeth, and thou hearest the sound thereof, but canst not tell whence it cometh, and whither it goeth: so is every one that is born of the Spirit.

9 Nĭc-o-dē'mus answered and said unto him, How can these things be?
10 Jesus answered and said unto him, Art thou a master of Israel, and knowest not these things?

11 Verily, verily, I say unto thee, We speak that we do know, and testify that we have seen; and ye receive not our witness.

12 If I have told you earthly things, and ye believe not, how shall ye believe, if I tell you of heavenly things?
13 And no man hath ascended up to heaven, but he that came down from heaven, even the Son of man which is in heaven.
14 And as Moses lifted up the serpent in the wilderness, even so must the Son of man be lifted up:
15 That whosoever believeth in him should not perish, but have eternal life.

16 For God so loved the world, that he gave his only begotten Son, that whosoever believeth in him should not perish, but have everlasting life.

17 For God sent not his Son into the world to condemn the world; but that the world through him might be saved.

18 He that believeth on him is not condemned: but he that believeth not is condemned already, because he hath not believed in the name of the only begotten Son of God.

19 And this is the condemnation, that light is come into the world, and men loved darkness rather than light, because their deeds were evil.
20 For every one that doeth evil hateth the light, neither cometh to the light, lest his deeds should be reproved.
21 But he that doeth truth cometh to the light, that his deeds may be made manifest, that they are wrought in God.

22 ¶After these things came Jesus and his disciples into the land of

6. Christ continues to contrast physical birth and spiritual birth. The **flesh** produces **flesh** while the **Spirit** produces that which is spiritual.

7. Marvel not. Do not be amazed or shocked. **Ye must be born again.** To become a part of God's spiritual kingdom, one must experience a spiritual birth.

8. The wind (Gr *pneuma* which is the same word used for **spirit**) cannot be seen or explained. The wind can only be heard or observed in relation to its effect. **So is everyone that is born of the Spirit.** The new birth is inexplicable. One can only observe the results.

9-10. Nicodemus asks his third question, **How can?** He asks the same question as before (3:4). Christ rebukes him, and in doing so, brings Nicodemus to the point of submission. Both **master** (teacher) and **Israel** have a definite article in Greek. Christ rebukes Nicodemus by asking, "Are you not *the* teacher of *the* Israel and you are ignorant of those things?" Nicodemus needed a new heart (Ezk 11:19).
The conversation now becomes one-sided. Christ teaches and Nicodemus listens.

11. Verily (Gr *amēn*, truly) **I say unto thee.** In speaking for His followers, Christ reminds Nicodemus that they were saying what they knew and were testifying to what they had seen. The reality of the new birth was known to them by experience. However, the question and blindness of Nicodemus led the Lord to say, **Ye receive not our witness.**

12-13. If Nicodemus did not accept **earthly things,** matters of spiritual nature which take place on the earth, then he would not believe **heavenly things.** Firsthand knowledge must come from **the Son of man.** Knowledge of heavenly things is only possible through Him **that came down from heaven.**

14-15. Christ now illustrates, from Numbers 21, the nature of God's plan of redemption. Sin had caused God to punish the Israelites with serpents. God commanded Moses to make a brass serpent, so that when the sick looked to that serpent, they would be healed. The Son of Man must **be lifted up** (on the cross) so that man bitten by the serpent of sin might **have life eternal.**

16. The gospel in a nutshell. The love of God shown in action. (1) The source of love—**God.** (2) The extent of love—**the world.** (3) The sacrifice of love—**He gave his only begotten Son.** (4) The results of love—**whosoever believeth in him should not perish.**

17. The Jews understood that the Messiah would come to **condemn** the Gentiles (Amos 5:18-20). Against this false teaching, Christ told Nicodemus that God's plan was to save the **world.**

18. Condemnation is reserved for the one that **believeth not.** There are only two kinds of people in the world: (1) those who have everlasting life as a result of faith in Christ; and (2) those who have not believed and as a result stand **condemned already.** They are already sentenced (condemned) and await only the execution of that sentence.

19-21. Christ as the Light is rejected by a dark world **because their deeds were evil.** Those who reject the Light **also hateth** (Gr *miseō*, detest, abhor) that Light, lest their deeds be exposed. In contrast to those who abhor the Light, **he that doeth truth** gravitates toward the Light to show that his deeds are **wrought in God.** Christ concludes their interview with an invitation for Nicodemus to leave his darkness and unbelief and come to the Light.

2. Testimony of John the Baptist. 3:22-36.

22-25. After these things. Following the interview with Nicodemus, Jesus traveled to Judaea and baptized. John, who **was not yet cast into prison,** was performing a similar ministry

Judæa; and there he tarried with them, and baptized.

23 And John also was baptizing in Æ'nŏn near to Sā'lĭm, because there was much water there: and they came, and were baptized.

24 For John was not yet cast into prison.

25 ¶Then there arose a question between *some* of John's disciples and the Jews about purifying.

26 And they came unto John, and said unto him, Rabbi, he that was with thee beyond Jordan, to whom thou barest witness, behold, the same baptizeth, and all *men* come to him.

27 John answered and said, A man can receive nothing, except it be given him from heaven.

28 Ye yourselves bear me witness, that I said, I am not the Christ, but that I am sent before him.

29 He that hath the bride is the bridegroom: but the friend of the bridegroom, which standeth and heareth him, rejoiceth greatly because of the bridegroom's voice: this my joy therefore is fulfilled.

30 He must increase, but I *must* decrease.

31 He that cometh from above is above all: he that is of the earth is earthly, and speaketh of the earth: he that cometh from heaven is above all.

32 And what he hath seen and heard, that he testifieth; and no man receiveth his testimony.

33 He that hath received his testimony hath set to his seal that God is true.

34 For he whom God hath sent speaketh the words of God: for God giveth not the Spirit by measure *unto him*.

35 The Father loveth the Son, and hath given all things into his hand.

36 He that believeth on the Son hath everlasting life: and he that believeth not the Son shall not see life; but the wrath of God abideth on him.

CHAPTER 4

WHEN therefore the Lord knew how the Pharisees had heard that Jesus made and baptized more disciples than John,

2 (Though Jesus himself baptized not, but his disciples,)

near Salim. A debate erupted over the baptism of Jesus and the baptism of John as to which had greater **purifying** ability.

26-29. They came unto John. They were probably disciples of John since their statement carried a hint of jealousy toward Christ (**all men came to him**) and they refused to mention Christ by name. John's disciples were concerned about the decreasing popularity of their leader. John quickly replied that each person is given a place of service **from heaven**. John had no right to claim any importance other than what God gave him. John's position was as the forerunner of Christ. Rather than regretting his loss of popularity to Christ, John rejoices in being **the friend of the bridegroom. This my joy therefore is fulfilled.** The reports that the crowds are attracted to Christ causes John to have joy.

30. He must increase, but I must decrease. Notice the **must.** In God's plan John must diminish and Christ must continue to grow. The comparison between Christ and John the Baptist is continued and brought to conclusion in verses 31-36.

31. Christ is **from above** and is **above all**, whereas John is **of the earth** and **speaketh of the earth**. Christ, because of His origin, is above all earthly things (3:13).

32. Christ is the one spoken of here. He testifies concerning **what he hath seen and heard** (3:11, 13, 31). Again, the rejection of that testimony is discussed.

33. The one who accepts Christ's testimony concerning Himself **hath set to his seal** (lit., to certify, attest, acknowledge) **that God is true.** The antithesis of this affirmation is found in I John 1:10.

34-36. Christ is the faithful witness who **speaketh the words of God.** Christ has received the fullness of God's Spirit (**not the Spirit by measure**). It is implied that all believers receive the fullness of God's Spirit. Beyond the fullness of God's Spirit, Christ has received **all things** as a result of the love relationship between the **Father** and the **Son.**

The Baptist's last testimony to Christ is perhaps his most powerful one. It calls for a decision. Believe, and one has **everlasting life** (3:16-18). **And he that believeth not.** This second **believe** is a difficult word in the original that is used in the first part of the verse (Gr *apeitheō*, to disobey, be disobedient). Literally, the one who disobeys **shall not see life; but the wrath of God abideth on him.** Wrath (Gr *orgē*, anger, settled indignation) is abiding on the one who disobeys (Gr present tense is used to note a progressive and continual action).

D. Christ as the Master Soul-winner. 4:1-54.

There are two events described in this chapter. They are the contact with the Samaritan woman, and the healing of the nobleman's son. In the story of the woman of Samaria, we observe Christ as the personal soul-winner.

1. Samaritan woman's sins forgiven. 4:1-45.

4:1-3. The popularity of Christ was increasing to the extent that the Pharisees became alarmed. To avoid a confrontation, Jesus traveled north returning to Galilee.

3 He left Judæa, and departed again into Galilee.

4 And he must needs go through Sa-mâ′rī-a.

5 Then cometh he to a city of Sa-mâ′-rī-a, which is called Sy̆′chär, near to the parcel of ground that Jacob gave to his son Joseph.

6 Now Jacob's well was there. Jesus therefore, being wearied with *his* journey, sat thus on the well: *and* it was about the sixth hour.

7 There cometh a woman of Sa-mâ′-rī-a to draw water: Jesus saith unto her, Give me to drink.

8 (For his disciples were gone away unto the city to buy meat.)

9 Then saith the woman of Sa-mâ′rī-a unto him, How is it that thou, being a Jew, askest drink of me, which am a woman of Sa-mâ′rī-a? for the Jews have no dealings with the Sa-măr′i-tanś.

10 Jesus answered and said unto her, If thou knewest the gift of God, and who it is that saith to thee, Give me to drink; thou wouldest have asked of him, and he would have given thee living water.

11 The woman saith unto him, Sir, thou hast nothing to draw with, and the well is deep: from whence then hast thou that living water?

12 Art thou greater than our father Jacob, which gave us the well, and drank thereof himself, and his children, and his cattle?

13 Jesus answered and said unto her, Whosoever drinketh of this water shall thirst again:

14 But whosoever drinketh of the water that I shall give him shall never thirst; but the water that I shall give him shall be in him a well of water springing up into everlasting life.

15 The woman saith unto him, Sir, give me this water, that I thirst not, neither come hither to draw.

16 Jesus saith unto her, Go, call thy husband, and come hither.

17 The woman answered and said, I have no husband. Jesus said unto her, Thou hast well said, I have no husband:

18 For thou hast had five husbands; and he whom thou now hast is not thy husband: in that saidst thou truly.

19 The woman saith unto him, Sir, I perceive that thou art a prophet.

20 Our fathers worshipped in this mountain; and ye say, that in Jeru-

4-5. He must needs go through Samaria. Christ had a compelling compassion that drove Him to a woman in need. This was also the most direct route to Galilee. His journey took Him to Sychar, a city a few miles southeast of Samaria and near Mount Gerizim. According to Genesis 33:19, Jacob bought this parcel of ground and later gave it to his son Joseph (Gen 48:22).

6. Jacob's well was there. This was a well about one hundred feet deep. The writer now emphasizes the humanity of Christ in that He was travel-weary **with his journey** and consequently rested **on** (lit., **upon**) **the well.** The time of this incident was probably six o'clock in the evening.

7. A woman of Samaria. Note the contrast between chapter 3 and chapter 4. In the former, Christ deals with a man; in the latter, He deals with a woman. In the former, He deals with a Jew; in the latter, a Samaritan. In the former, he deals with a moral person; in the latter, an immoral person. Yet, He saves both. **Jesus saith unto her, Give me to drink.** In receiving this woman, Christ transcends the barriers of race (He was a Jew and she was a Samaritan), religion, and rank (He was a teacher and she was a prostitute). Soulwinning crosses any barriers.

8-9. The request for water was a logical one since the disciples had gone into **the city to buy meat.** However, the woman is amazed at this request because of the natural animosity between the Jews and the Samaritans. This hatred was caused when, after the fall of Israel, the Jews who remained in Palestine intermarried with the heathen and were called Samaritans. They were not full-blooded Jews.

10-12. Christ answers the woman's hesitancy with a spiritual riddle. The **gift of God** refers to the **living water.** The emphasis now is taken off Christ's need for physical water and placed on the woman's need for spiritual water (7:37-39). The woman understands Christ to speak of the **living water** as that which is at the deepest part of the well. **Art thou greater?** The woman realizes that if Christ can do this, He is a **greater** person than Jacob.

13-15. Christ continues by stating that if one drinks of Jacob's well, he will need to drink again, but if one drinks of Christ's well, he **shall never thirst.** This water produces a well that keeps on bubbling **into everlasting life.** With this statement, Christ appeals to the woman's craving for satisfaction. The woman is still thinking on the physical level. She wanted this **living water** so that she would not have to come all the way out to Jacob's well every day.

16. Christ commands her to call her husband. It would seem the Lord changed the subject. That is not true. In order for the woman to understand the **living water** (4:10) concept, she must be aware of her need for that **living water.** Christ now begins to arouse her conscience and sense of guilt. Before anyone can be saved, he must see his need of salvation and be convicted of his sin.

17-20. Christ reveals her sinful condition. She was morally bankrupt. She acknowledges Christ as a **prophet,** and in so doing admits her personal sin which Christ revealed. The woman now desires to be taught by the prophet. Should she worship in Mount Gerizim or in Jerusalem?

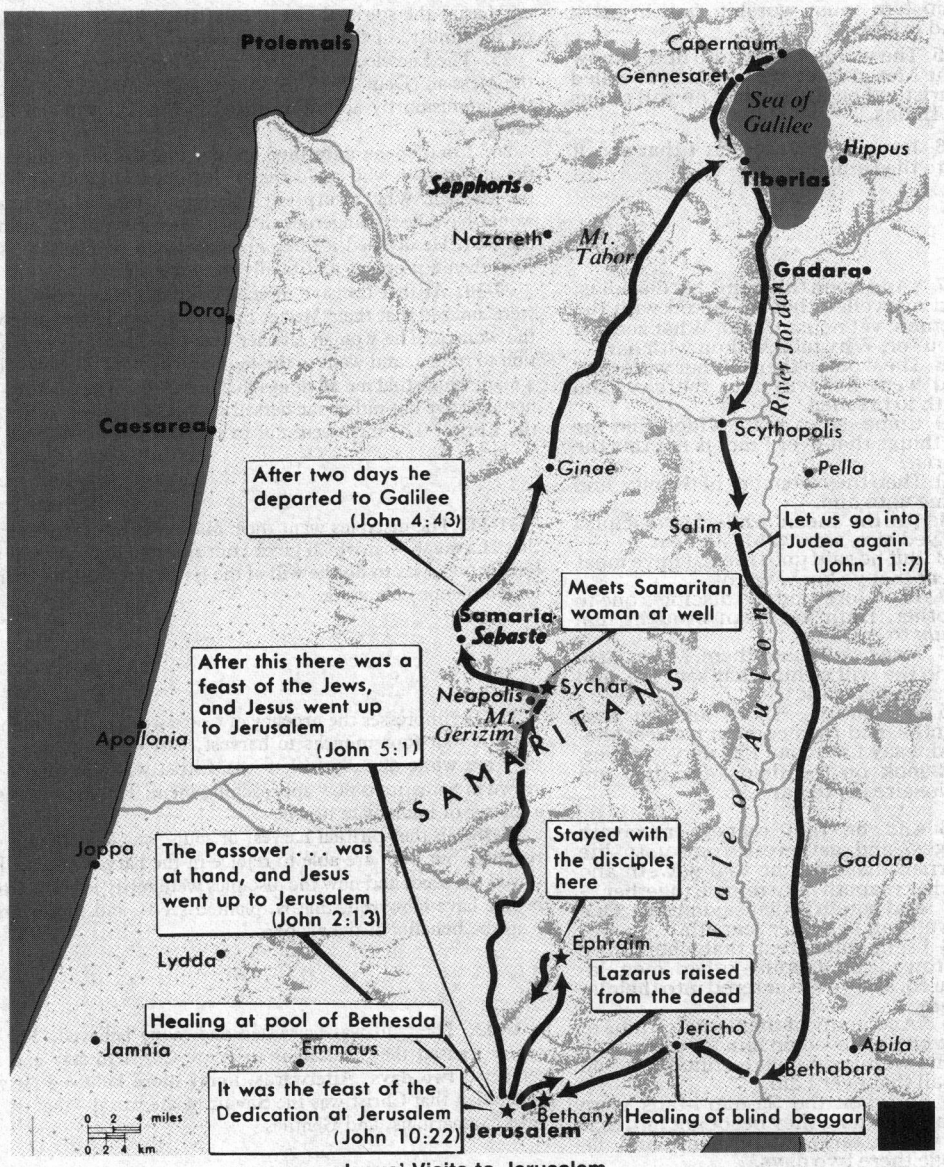

After two days he
departed to Galilee
(John 4:43)

Meets Samaritan
woman at well

Let us go into
Judea again
(John 11:7)

After this there was a
feast of the Jews,
and Jesus went up
to Jerusalem
(John 5:1)

The Passover . . . was
at hand, and Jesus
went up to Jerusalem
(John 2:13)

Stayed with
the disciples
here

Lazarus raised
from the dead

Healing at pool of Bethesda

Healing of blind beggar

It was the feast of the
Dedication at Jerusalem
(John 10:22)

0 2 4 miles
0 2 4 km

Jesus' Visits to Jerusalem

salem is the place where men ought to
worship.

21 Jesus saith unto her, Woman, believe me, the hour cometh, when ye
shall neither in this mountain, nor yet
at Jerusalem, worship the Father.

22 Ye worship ye know not what: we
know what we worship: for salvation is
of the Jews.

23 But the hour cometh, and now is,
when the true worshippers shall worship the Father in spirit and in truth: for
the Father seeketh such to worship
him.

24 God *is* a Spirit: and they that wor-

21-23. The hour cometh. Christ reveals to the woman that
where a person worships is unimportant. It is not limited to
Mount Gerizim or Jerusalem. The Samaritans worshiped what
they did not know; they had created their own religion. The
Jews had divine guidelines for worship. Nevertheless, **the hour
cometh, and now is** when God is to be worshiped in **spirit and
in truth.** Two separate concepts are implied. The worship of **the
Father** is not confined to a place but is rather an action of the
heart. Second, all worship must be in keeping with the **truth** of
God's revealed Word.

24. God is a Spirit. Spirit, the predicate, is mentioned first to

ship him must worship *him* in spirit and in truth.

25 The woman saith unto him, I know that Mes-sī'as cometh, which is called Christ: when he is come, he will tell us all things.

26 Jesus saith unto her, I that speak unto thee am *he*.

27 ¶And upon this came his disciples, and marvelled that he talked with the woman: yet no man said, What seekest thou? or, Why talkest thou with her?

28 The woman then left her waterpot, and went her way into the city, and saith to the men,

29 Come, see a man, which told me all things that ever I did: is not this the Christ?

30 Then they went out of the city, and came unto him.

31 ¶In the mean while his disciples prayed him, saying, Master, eat.

32 But he said unto them, I have meat to eat that ye know not of.

33 Therefore said the disciples one to another, Hath any man brought him *ought* to eat?

34 Jesus saith unto them, My meat is to do the will of him that sent me, and to finish his work.

35 Say not ye, There are yet four months, and *then* cometh harvest? behold, I say unto you, Lift up your eyes, and look on the fields; for they are white already to harvest.

36 And he that reapeth receiveth wages, and gathereth fruit unto life eternal: that both he that soweth and he that reapeth may rejoice together.

37 And herein is that saying true, One soweth, and another reapeth.

38 I sent you to reap that whereon ye bestowed no labour: other men laboured, and ye are entered into their labours.

39 ¶And many of the Sa-măr'i-tans of that city believed on him for the saying of the woman, which testified, He told me all that ever I did.

40 So when the Sa-măr'i-tans were come unto him, they besought him that he would tarry with them: and he abode there two days.

41 And many more believed because of his own word;

42 And said unto the woman, Now we believe, not because of thy saying: for we have heard *him* ourselves, and know that this is indeed the Christ, the Saviour of the world.

43 ¶Now after two days he departed thence, and went into Galilee.

44 For Jesus himself testified, that a prophet hath no honour in his own country.

45 Then when he was come into Galilee, the Galilæans received him, having seen all the things that he did at Jerusalem at the feast: for they also went unto the feast.

46 So Jesus came again into Cana of

emphasize the spiritual character of God. Notice the emphasis on the "must" of that type of worship.

25. The knowledge of Christ causes the woman to talk about the Messiah (Deut 18:15-16). She is still confused and resolves this confusion by admitting that the Messiah **will tell us all things.**

26. I that speak unto thee am he. The woman claimed that the only person who could answer her questions and doubt was the Messiah. What a surprise! This type of messianic revelation would have been dangerous in Jerusalem, but in this setting at the well, He deemed it safe. The Samaritan woman first saw a Jew, then a prophet, and finally the Messiah.

27-30. At that decisive moment, the disciples returned and were amazed that their Master broke tradition in speaking with the woman. The woman left her **waterpot,** showing her intention to return, and went to **the men** proclaiming the news about **a man, which told me all things that ever I did.** The question was not assertive but rather she herself wanted an answer. **Is not this the Christ?** The men went out to see.

31-34. The disciples want their Master to eat. Christ replies that His **meat,** that which gives Him spiritual nourishment and satisfaction, was **to do the will** of the Father and **finish** (or bring to completion) **his work.**

35. He impresses the urgency of God's work on the disciples. Do not wait **four months** to harvest, **Lift up your eyes, . . . they are white already to harvest.** Christ was referring to the crowd of Samaritans now approaching them. The soul-harvest is a matter of immediate urgency.

36-38. In the spiritual harvest of souls, one **soweth** and one **reapeth,** but both are able to rejoice in the harvest. Christ had sowed the seed, and now the disciples were ready to reap. **Other** people have **laboured,** that is, planted seeds, and soul-winners reap the benefits of their labors.

39-42. The fruit was harvested and **many** believed. The response caused the Samaritans to invite Christ to stay and He remained **two days.** Afterwards, **many more believed.** It was concluded that Christ was the **Savior** of the world—that is, for Jews, Samaritans, and Gentiles.

43-45. Christ returned to Galilee where He was not honored and respected like He was in Judaea. Those who had **seen all the things** in Jerusalem **received** (welcomed) Him.

2. Nobleman's son healed. 4:46-54.

46. While in Cana, a **nobleman** (Gr *basilikos*, royal officer)

Galilee, where he made the water wine. And there was a certain nobleman, whose son was sick at Ca-per'na-um.

47 When he heard that Jesus was come out of Judæa into Galilee, he went unto him, and besought him that he would come down, and heal his son: for he was at the point of death.

48 Then said Jesus unto him, Except ye see signs and wonders, ye will not believe.

49 The nobleman saith unto him, Sir, come down ere my child die.

50 Jesus saith unto him, Go thy way; thy son liveth. And the man believed the word that Jesus had spoken unto him, and he went his way.

51 And as he was now going down, his servants met him, and told *him*, saying, Thy son liveth.

52 Then enquired he of them the hour when he began to amend. And they said unto him, Yesterday at the seventh hour the fever left him.

53 So the father knew that *it was* at the same hour, in the which Jesus said unto him, Thy son liveth: and himself believed, and his whole house.

54 This *is* again the second miracle *that* Jesus did, when he was come out of Judæa into Galilee.

CHAPTER 5

AFTER this there was a feast of the Jews; and Jesus went up to Jerusalem.

2 Now there is at Jerusalem by the sheep *market* a pool, which is called in the Hebrew tongue Be-thes'da, having five porches.

3 In these lay a great multitude of impotent folk, of blind, halt, withered, waiting for the moving of the water.

4 For an angel went down at a certain season into the pool, and troubled the water: whosoever then first after the troubling of the water stepped in was made whole of whatsoever disease he had.

5 And a certain man was there, which had an infirmity thirty and eight years.

6 When Jesus saw him lie, and knew that he had been now a long time *in that case*, he saith unto him, Wilt thou be made whole?

7 The impotent man answered him, Sir, I have no man, when the water is troubled, to put me into the pool: but while I am coming, another steppeth down before me.

8 Jesus saith unto him, Rise, take up thy bed, and walk.

9 And immediately the man was

whose son was sick visited Him with a problem. It was a serious sickness at the point of death (4:47).

47-48. The royal officer was under two false impressions about the power of Christ. He thought Christ would have to travel to Capernaum to heal, and that Christ did not have power over death (ere my child die). Christ was concerned that the man's faith was based only on signs and wonders.

49-50. The nobleman compelled Christ to act, and Christ simply spoke the word. The man responded with a faith in the word of Christ and not the miracles of Christ. And he went his way. Faith is leaving our problem with Christ, accepting His Word, and going on our way.

51-53. The man returned and was met by his servants who brought news of the child's recovery. He recovered the same hour in which Christ spoke the word. The result was that the entire house believed or placed their trust and confidence in Christ.

54. This was the second miracle in Cana. The first miracle of turning the water into wine showed His power over the physical universe and His disciples believed. The second miracle proved that Christ's power was not limited by a distance of sixteen miles, and the entire house of the nobleman believed. Both miracles produced belief and life (20:30-31).

E. Christ as the Son of God. 5:1-47.

In this chapter Christ performs a miracle of healing on the Sabbath. He is questioned by the Pharisees and answers their criticism in a lengthy discussion proving Himself to be the Son of God.

1. Healing of lame man. 5:1-18.

5:1. There was a feast. Since the Greek definite article is missing, this feast was probably not the Passover. It could have been the Feast of Tabernacles.

2. Near the sheep gate there was a pool. There has been much debate over the location of this pool. In 1880 a painting depicting an angel troubling the water was discovered on the wall of the Church of St. Anne in Jerusalem. This discovery marked the site of the pool of Bethesda.

3-4. By this pool there lay a group of sick people waiting for the moving of the water. All the oldest manuscripts were copied without the latter part of verse 3 and all of verse 4.

5. Because the man had been sick for thirty-eight years does not mean that he had been at the pool for that length of time.

6. Note the three verbs: Jesus saw, Jesus knew, Jesus saith. Jesus sees each need, knows the depth of that need, and addresses Himself to meet that need. Christ's question seeks to probe the man's will to be healed.

7-8. Note the three verbs, Rise, take up, walk. The first verb symbolizes spiritual healing (salvation). The second verb symbolizes a break with the past (picking up the bed), and the last verb symbolizes Christian growth (walking on).

9. Obedience brought complete and instantaneous healing.

made whole, and took up his bed, and walked: and on the same day was the sabbath.

10 ¶The Jews therefore said unto him that was cured, It is the sabbath day: it is not lawful for thee to carry *thy* bed.

11 He answered them, He that made me whole, the same said unto me, Take up thy bed, and walk.

12 Then asked they him, What man is that which said unto thee, Take up thy bed, and walk?

13 And he that was healed wist not who it was: for Jesus had conveyed himself away, a multitude being in *that* place.

14 Afterward Jesus findeth him in the temple, and said unto him, Behold, thou art made whole: sin no more, lest a worse thing come unto thee.

15 The man departed, and told the Jews that it was Jesus, which had made him whole.

16 And therefore did the Jews persecute Jesus, and sought to slay him, because he had done these things on the sabbath day.

17 ¶But Jesus answered them, My Father worketh hitherto, and I work.

18 Therefore the Jews sought the more to kill him, because he not only had broken the sabbath, but said also that God was his Father, making himself equal with God.

19 ¶Then answered Jesus and said unto them, Verily, verily, I say unto you, The Son can do nothing of himself, but what he seeth the Father do: for what things soever he doeth, these also doeth the Son likewise.

20 For the Father loveth the Son, and sheweth him all things that himself doeth: and he will shew him greater works than these, that ye may marvel.

21 For as the Father raiseth up the dead, and quickeneth *them;* even so the Son quickeneth whom he will.

22 For the Father judgeth no man, but hath committed all judgment unto the Son:

23 That all *men* should honour the Son, even as they honour the Father. He that honoureth not the Son honoureth not the Father which hath sent him.

24 Verily, verily, I say unto you, He that heareth my word, and believeth on him that sent me, hath everlasting life, and shall not come into condemnation; but is passed from death unto life.

25 Verily, verily, I say unto you, The hour is coming, and now is, when the dead shall hear the voice of the Son of God: and they that hear shall live.

26 For as the Father hath life in himself; so hath he given to the Son to have life in himself;

27 And hath given him authority to execute judgment also, because he is the Son of man.

28 Marvel not at this: for the hour is coming, in the which all that are in the graves shall hear his voice,

29 And shall come forth; they that

The same day was the sabbath. This phrase becomes the controversial issue that upsets the Jews.

10-14. They referred to the Old Testament law (Ex 20; Jer 17:19-27). The man replied that anyone who could heal him instantaneously and completely also had the authority to tell him to carry his bed. The Jews did not ask, "Who healed you?" but rather, "Who told you to do this on the Sabbath?" The man did not know who healed him, and meanwhile, Christ had disappeared. The man goes to the Temple (probably to give thanks for healing) and meets Christ, who tells him not to continue in sin **lest a worse thing come unto thee.** Christ does not insinuate that he was sick thirty-eight years because of sin, but rather since his sins were forgiven, he must walk in a new life.

15. The man told the Jews that Jesus healed him. He did not answer their questions concerning the Sabbath.

16. Persecute Jesus. This verb (Gr *diōkō*) refers to continued hostile activity even to the point of death (**sought to slay him**).

17-18. Christ answers by establishing His authority to work on the Sabbath. He was coequal with God the Father. The Jews were angered even more by this statement and **sought the more to kill him.**

2. Defense of His person. 5:19-47.

19-24. Christ continues His claim to be equal with God. He states that whatever **he seeth the Father do,** He does also. Because of the Father's love, the Father **sheweth him all things.** Consequently, all that the Father doeth, the Son doeth. Christ claims that the Father will show Him **greater works** than the healing of the impotent man.

Two of the **greater works** are listed: the raising of the dead and the pronouncing of judgment. The raising of the dead refers both to a physical and spiritual accomplishment. The former occurs through resurrection and the latter through regeneration. Second, the Father does not set apart from the Son in pronouncing judgment, but has **committed all judgment unto the Son.** The raising of the dead and the judgment are closely related eschatological matters. One day all the dead will be raised to stand before Christ in judgment (the saved through the rapture to the Bema Judgment, and unsaved through the final resurrection to the Great White Throne Judgment, Rom 14:10; Rev 20:11-15). The father **committed all judgment unto the Son** so that the Son would be equal in **honor** with the Father. Note also that the Son is equal in character (17-18), in works (19-22), and in honor (23). If a person accepts Christ's word and believes in the Father, even now he **is passed from death unto life** (spiritual resurrection) and **shall not come into condemnation** (judgment).

25-27. These verses discuss the power of Christ to quicken the dead **now.** Because the Son **hath life in himself** (like the Father), the Son gives this life to those **dead** who **hear** His voice.

28-30. These verses discuss the future aspect (**the hour is coming**) of Christ's quickening power. Here physical resurrection is discussed, and two results are listed: the good **unto the resurrection of life** and the evil, **unto the resurrection of**

have done good, unto the resurrection of life; and they that have done evil, unto the resurrection of damnation.

30 I can of mine own self do nothing: as I hear, I judge: and my judgment is just; because I seek not mine own will, but the will of the Father which hath sent me.

31 If I bear witness of myself, my witness is not true.

32 There is another that beareth witness of me; and I know that the witness which he witnesseth of me is true.

33 Ye sent unto John, and he bare witness unto the truth.

34 But I receive not testimony from man: but these things I say, that ye might be saved.

35 He was a burning and a shining light: and ye were willing for a season to rejoice in his light.

36 But I have greater witness than that of John: for the works which the Father hath given me to finish, the same works that I do, bear witness of me, that the Father hath sent me.

37 And the Father himself, which hath sent me, hath borne witness of me. Ye have neither heard his voice at any time, nor seen his shape.

38 And ye have not his word abiding in you: for whom he hath sent, him ye believe not.

39 Search the scriptures; for in them ye think ye have eternal life: and they are they which testify of me.

40 And ye will not come to me, that ye might have life.

41 I receive not honour from men.

42 But I know you, that ye have not the love of God in you.

43 I am come in my Father's name, and ye receive me not: if another shall come in his own name, him ye will receive.

44 How can ye believe, which receive honour one of another, and seek not the honour that *cometh* from God only?

45 Do not think that I will accuse you to the Father: there is *one* that accuseth you, *even* Moses in whom ye trust.

46 For had ye believed Moses, ye would have believed me: for he wrote of me.

47 But if ye believe not his writings, how shall ye believe my words?

damnation. Again, the perfect harmony and unity of the Father and Son relationship is discussed.

31-32. Christ has made the claim to be equal with God. He recognizes that the Jews would not formally accept the claim (witness) of one person. Jewish law required two witnesses. On the basis of one witness, Christ states that the Jews would accept that witness as **not true.** In the remaining verses, Christ calls several witnesses to establish validity for His claim: John the Baptist (vss. 33-35), His works (vs. 36), the Father (vss. 37-38), the Scriptures (vss. 39-47).

33-36. John's testimony is given in 1:19-28. Christ Himself did not need John's testimony, but He mentions it because it was true and if accepted one could be **saved.** John was a **burning and shining light.** However, although people were **willing . . . to rejoice in his light,** they were not willing to accept his testimonies concerning Christ. Nevertheless, Christ had **greater witness than that of John.** His works (miracles) gave evidence to His deity. They were evidence that **the Father hath sent me** (Gr *apostellō*, to commission, send on a divine mission).

37-38. Christ continues with another testimony, that of His Father. This testimony refers both to what was said by the Father at Christ's baptism (Mk 1:11), and to what the Father had said through the Old Testament Scriptures. Christ reminds them that they had neither **heard his voice . . . nor seen his shape.** The **voice** of God and the **shape** (image, likeness) of God are Christ Himself (14:19, 24; II Cor 4:4). They did not have **His word abiding** in them (as a permanent possession).

39. Search the scriptures. This is not necessarily a command. It may be taken as the Greek present indicative and could be translated "ye are searching." The Jews were constantly searching the Scriptures because it was recognized that they contained the secret of **eternal life.** These same Scriptures bear testimony of Christ. Yet these pious Jews had missed the very key to understanding Scripture—Christ (Jn 5:46; I Pet 1:10-11).

40-43. Because of their hardness of heart, they had rejected Christ. Christ does not receive **honor** (glory or praise) **from men,** because God's love (lit., love for God) is not in them. Christ had come in the authority of His Father with mighty miracles to prove His deity. They rejected Him. If one comes in **his own name, him ye will receive.** This was proved in that the Jews accepted false messiahs such as Theudas and Judas of Galilee (Acts 5:36-37). They will also accept antichrist (II Thess 2:8-10).

44-47. The Jews could not believe because they derived praise from each other rather than praise from God. The name Jew means "praised." The Jews had the utmost confidence in Moses and his writings. They claimed to be Moses' disciples (9:28), and yet they did not accept what Moses had said (Deut 18:15-18). If they had accepted Moses' writings, they would have accepted Christ, **for he wrote of me.** Moses' writing and Christ's words are both placed on the same level, divinely inspired and inerrant.

F. Christ as the Bread of Life. 6:1-71.

In this chapter Christ reaches the height of His popularity. Because of His power to meet physical needs, the people wanted to make Him king. However, when they realized that His ministry was spiritual, they rejected Him. Such are the events of this chapter.

CHAPTER 6

AFTER these things Jesus went over the sea of Galilee, which is *the sea* of Ti-be´ri-as.

2 And a great multitude followed him, because they saw his miracles which he did on them that were diseased.

3 And Jesus went up into a mountain, and there he sat with his disciples.

4 And the passover, a feast of the Jews, was nigh.

5 When Jesus then lifted up *his* eyes, and saw a great company come unto him, he saith unto Philip, Whence shall we buy bread, that these may eat?

6 And this he said to prove him: for he himself knew what he would do.

7 Philip answered him, Two hundred pennyworth of bread is not sufficient for them, that every one of them may take a little.

8 One of his disciples, Andrew, Simon Peter's brother, saith unto him,

9 There is a lad here, which hath five barley loaves, and two small fishes: but what are they among so many?

10 And Jesus said, Make the men sit down. Now there was much grass in the place. So the men sat down, in number about five thousand.

11 And Jesus took the loaves; and when he had given thanks, he distributed to the disciples, and the disciples to them that were set down; and likewise of the fishes as much as they would.

12 When they were filled, he said unto his disciples, Gather up the fragments that remain, that nothing be lost.

13 Therefore they gathered *them* together, and filled twelve baskets with the fragments of the five barley loaves, which remained over and above unto them that had eaten.

14 ¶Then those men, when they had seen the miracle that Jesus did, said, This is of a truth that prophet that should come into the world.

15 When Jesus therefore perceived that they would come and take him by force, to make him a king, he departed again into a mountain himself alone.

16 ¶And when even was *now* come, his disciples went down unto the sea,

17 And entered into a ship, and went over the sea toward Ca-per´na-um. And it was now dark, and Jesus was not come to them.

18 And the sea arose by reason of a great wind that blew.

19 So when they had rowed about five and twenty or thirty furlongs, they see Jesus walking on the sea, and drawing nigh unto the ship: and they were afraid.

20 But he saith unto them, It is I; be not afraid.

21 Then they willingly received him into the ship: and immediately the ship was at the land whither they went.

1. Feeding of the five thousand. 6:1-14.

6:1-9. Christ went across the Sea of Galilee to the vicinity of Bethsaida (Lk 9:10). The multitudes, impressed by His miracles, followed Him. Jesus went **up into a mountain.** From His high vantage point, Christ observed the crowd approaching and asked Philip if they had bread for the people to eat. **Bread** (Gr *artos,* flat, round bread like the shape of pancakes). Christ explained why He asked this question—**to prove him** (Gr *peirazō,* to put him to the test). The Lord **knew what he would do** and is now putting Philip's faith to the test (Jas 1:2). A **pennyworth** (Gr *dēnarios*) was equivalent to one day's wages (Mt 20:2, 9, 13). Philip claims that two hundred days of wages would not be enough to give each **a little.** Andrew brings **a lad** (not necessarily a little boy) who has **five barley loaves, and two small fishes.** Andrew recognizes that this is so little to meet the need of so many. One commentator describes the problem this way: "Duty is not measured by ability, and ability is not measured by the sum-total of our resources" (J. D. Jones, *The Gospel According to St. Mark,* Scripture Truth).

10-11. Christ now takes command of the situation and has everyone sit down. The Lord gave **thanks.** Note the prayer of thanksgiving occurs before the miracle. The miracle provided **as much as they would,** whereas Philip's faith was so little.

12-14. The sufficiency of the miracle did not mean waste. All the leftovers were to be collected **that nothing be lost.** One should never waste God's blessings. The people saw the **miracle** (Gr *sēmeion,* sign) and were impressed. They proclaimed Him as **that prophet** (Deut 18:15-18) and probably thought Him to be the Messiah.

2. Walking on the water. 6:15-21.

15. Enthusiastic about this **prophet,** they are ready to make Him **king,** even to the point of kidnapping Him. But Christ's kingdom was not of this world (18:36). Thus He went **into a mountain himself alone.**

16-18. The disciples put out to sea, but were hindered by the darkness and by a **great wind that blew.** The wind would blow strongly through the narrow gorges between the hills causing severe storms.

19-21. They rowed **twenty or thirty furlongs** (Gr *stadion*), about a total of three or four miles. They saw Christ walking toward them on the water. The One who had fed five thousand was about to meet the needs of these twelve disciples. **It is I; be not afraid** (present imperative, "stop being afraid"). Matthew describes Peter's walking on the water (Mt 14:28-31). Although the disciples were far from the land when Jesus entered the boat, another miracle occurred: **immediately** (Gr *eutheōs*) **the ship was at the land.** Christ demonstrated His power over gravity (walking on the water), over the storm (stilling the winds), and over space (bringing the ship to land).

3. *Sermon on the Bread of Life. 6:22-59.*

22 ¶The day following, when the people which stood on the other side of the sea saw that there was none other boat there, save that one whereinto his disciples were entered, and that Jesus went not with his disciples into the boat, but *that* his disciples were gone away alone;

23 (Howbeit there came other boats from Ti-be′ri-as nigh unto the place where they did eat bread, after that the Lord had given thanks:)

24 When the people therefore saw that Jesus was not there, neither his disciples, they also took shipping, and came to Ca-per′na-um, seeking for Jesus.

25 And when they had found him on the other side of the sea they said unto him, Rabbi, when camest thou hither?

26 Jesus answered them and said, Verily, verily, I say unto you, Ye seek me, not because ye saw the miracles, but because ye did eat of the loaves, and were filled.

27 Labour not for the meat which perisheth, but for that meat which endureth unto everlasting life, which the Son of man shall give unto you: for him hath God the Father sealed.

28 Then said they unto him, What shall we do, that we might work the works of God?

29 Jesus answered and said unto them, This is the work of God, that ye believe on him whom he hath sent.

30 They said therefore unto him, What sign shewest thou then, that we may see, and believe thee? what dost thou work?

31 Our fathers did eat manna in the desert; as it is written, He gave them bread from heaven to eat.

32 Then Jesus said unto them, Verily, verily, I say unto you, Moses gave you not that bread from heaven; but my Father giveth you the true bread from heaven.

33 For the bread of God is he which cometh down from heaven, and giveth life unto the world.

34 Then said they unto him, Lord, evermore give us this bread.

35 And Jesus said unto them, I am the bread of life: he that cometh to me shall never hunger; and he that believeth on me shall never thirst.

36 But I said unto you, That ye also have seen me, and believe not.

37 All that the Father giveth me shall come to me; and him that cometh to me I will in no wise cast out.

38 For I came down from heaven, not to do mine own will, but the will of him that sent me.

39 And this is the Father's will which hath sent me, that of all which he hath given me I should lose nothing, but should raise it up again at the last day.

40 And this is the will of him that sent me, that every one which seeth the Son, and believeth on him, may have ever-

22-25. The day following, those who had been fed by Jesus began looking for Him. Since they knew He did not cross the lake with His disciples, they were puzzled at His disappearing. They began a search that ended in Capernaum and they asked Christ, **when camest thou hither?** These people still had the desire to make Christ king.

26. Christ rebuked their motives. He stated that although the people had seen the signs, they had not accepted them for what they were (proof of His true messiahship), and they were only interested in the physical.

27. Labor not (Gr present imperative, "stop working for") the physical bread which **perisheth.** Rather, they should work **for that meat which endureth unto everlasting life,** or work for the real food which produces everlasting life. That food is Christ Himself. His authority to give everlasting life rested in the **seal** (testimony) of the Father through His signs and miracles.

28-31. These people are confused. Christ offered to give them eternal life and they wanted to know what to **do.** Christ answered that acceptance with God or the **work of God** was to **believe on him.** The **work** is not something man does for God, but it is the act of receiving what God has done for man. The Jews ask for a sign to prove that they should **believe on him.** This shows what the Jews were thinking. They knew that Christ had made more bread out of already existing bread. Their claim was that Moses had done greater miracles than Christ; he had brought bread from heaven. Now, if Christ wanted these Jews to **believe on him,** He had better perform a greater sign than Moses.

32-35. Christ explains that the manna which Moses gave is of different character than the **true bread.** The **true bread** is a person, **he which cometh,** and is capable of giving life. The Jews want this bread, but they still think it is merely physical bread much like Moses' manna. Christ identifies Himself as the **bread of life.** The life spoken of is spiritual and not physical. To partake of this life means that one's spiritual **hunger** and **thirst** will be fully satisfied. Note the verbs **cometh** and **believeth,** indicating salvation.

36-38. They had seen Him but had not believed. **All** who were given (Gr *pas,* with participle; lit., Everything which the Father gives to me will come to me) describes God's sovereignty in salvation. **Him that cometh to me I will in no wise cast out** emphasizes human responsibility. Here Christ emphasizes the unity of the Father's will and the Son's will. To reject the Son is to reject the Father.

39-40. The Father's will revealed is the preservation of those who believe. A person cannot fall from grace. Everlasting life guarantees security because this is the Father's will. No one will be lost. Note the following references: Romans 8:29-30; Philippians 1:6; II Timothy 2:19; I Peter 1:4-5.

lasting life: and I will raise him up at the last day.

41 The Jews then murmured at him, because he said, I am the bread which came down from heaven.

42 And they said, Is not this Jesus, the son of Joseph, whose father and mother we know? how is it then that he saith, I came down from heaven?

43 Jesus therefore answered and said unto them, Murmur not among yourselves.

44 No man can come to me, except the Father which hath sent me draw him: and I will raise him up at the last day.

45 It is written in the prophets, And they shall be all taught of God. Every man therefore that hath heard, and hath learned of the Father, cometh unto me.

46 Not that any man hath seen the Father, save he which is of God, he hath seen the Father.

47 Verily, verily, I say unto you, He that believeth on me hath everlasting life.

48 I am that bread of life.

49 Your fathers did eat manna in the wilderness, and are dead.

50 This is the bread which cometh down from heaven, that a man may eat thereof, and not die.

51 I am the living bread which came down from heaven: if any man eat of this bread, he shall live for ever: and the bread that I will give is my flesh, which I will give for the life of the world.

52 The Jews therefore strove among themselves, saying, How can this man give us *his* flesh to eat?

53 Then Jesus said unto them, Verily, verily, I say unto you, Except ye eat the flesh of the Son of man, and drink his blood, ye have no life in you.

54 Whoso eateth my flesh, and drinketh my blood, hath eternal life; and I will raise him up at the last day.

55 For my flesh is meat indeed, and my blood is drink indeed.

56 He that eateth my flesh, and drinketh my blood, dwelleth in me, and I in him.

57 As the living Father hath sent me, and I live by the Father: so he that eateth me, even he shall live by me.

58 This is that bread which came down from heaven: not as your fathers did eat manna, and are dead: he that eateth of this bread shall live for ever.

59 These things said he in the synagogue, as he taught in Ca-per'na-um.

60 Many therefore of his disciples, when they had heard *this*, said, This is an hard saying; who can hear it?

61 When Jesus knew in himself that his disciples murmured at it, he said unto them, Doth this offend you?

62 *What* and if ye shall see the Son of man ascend up where he was before?

63 It is the spirit that quickeneth; the

41-42. The Jews **murmured** (Gr *songuzō,* whispered) at these unusual claims of Christ. From a human perspective, Christ could not have descended from heaven because these people knew His human heritage. The Jews are almost cynical in their attitude. "Why, we have known you from your childhood, and now you make these ridiculous claims expecting us to believe in you."

43-44. Christ returns to His message of life. In order for a person to come to the Bread of Life, the Father must **draw him.** This verb (Gr *helkuō*) is also translated *draw* in the sense of "dragged" (Acts 16:19; 21:30). People cannot be saved at all unless God through the Holy Spirit draws them.

45-47. Christ describes this drawing process. It is accomplished through the Bible. When a man hears and learns, he comes to the Father. Salvation is impossible apart from hearing the Word of God. It is through this preaching that God draws people to Himself (Isa 54:13). The learning does not mean complete knowledge of the Father; this complete knowledge is only for the Son.

48. See notes on verse 35.

49-50. Moses' manna was not eternal (see vss. 32-35). In contrast to Moses' manna, this true Bread will not let man die.

51. Christ further describes this Bread. It is His flesh. He clearly refers to His vicarious death on the cross that will provide **life** for the **world.**

52. The Jews are still thinking of eating physical food rather than spiritual food.

53-54. Christ complicates the situation further by adding **except ye . . . drink his blood.** The Jews were forbidden to drink blood (Lev 7:26-27) and this additional statement must have added insult to injury. However, the Jews misunderstood. Leviticus 17:11 clearly states that life is in the blood. Accepting the sacrifice of the body and blood of Christ is the basis for eternal life.

55-58. As food and drink are offered to meet physical needs, so the **flesh** (meat) and **blood** of Christ are offered to meet spiritual needs. To assimilate this spiritual bread and drink is to be affected both spiritually (life) and physically (raised in the last day).

59. This message was preached at the **synagogue in Capernaum.**

4. Many turn away. 6:60-71.

60. The disciples were offended by the thought of eating Christ's flesh and drinking His blood (**hard saying**). These disciples are a general group larger than the Twelve.

61-62. Christ asks them if they would accept the fact that He came from heaven when they see Him return to heaven.

63. Christ now explains. He did not intend for them to eat

flesh profiteth nothing: the words that I speak unto you, *they* are spirit, and *they* are life.

64 But there are some of you that believe not. For Jesus knew from the beginning who they were that believed not, and who should betray him.
65 And he said, Therefore said I unto you, that no man can come unto me, except it were given unto him of my Father.
66 ¶From that *time* many of his disciples went back, and walked no more with him.
67 Then said Jesus unto the twelve, Will ye also go away?

68 Then Simon Peter answered him, Lord, to whom shall we go? thou hast the words of eternal life.

69 And we believe and are sure that thou art that Christ, the Son of the living God.

70 Jesus answered them, Have not I chosen you twelve, and one of you is a devil?
71 He spake of Judas Iscariot *the son* of Simon: for he it was that should betray him, being one of the twelve.

CHAPTER 7
AFTER these things Jesus walked in Galilee: for he would not walk in Jewry, because the Jews sought to kill him.
2 ¶Now the Jews' feast of tabernacles was at hand.
3 His brethren therefore said unto him, Depart hence, and go into Judæa, that thy disciples also may see the works that thou doest.
4 For *there is* no man *that* doeth any thing in secret, and he himself seeketh to be known openly. If thou do these things, shew thyself to the world.
5 For neither did his brethren believe in him.
6 Then Jesus said unto them, My time is not yet come: but your time is alway ready.
7 The world cannot hate you; but me it hateth, because I testify of it, that the works thereof are evil.
8 Go ye up unto this feast: I go not up yet unto this feast; for my time is not yet full come.
9 When he had said these words unto them, he abode *still* in Galilee.
10 ¶But when his brethren were gone up, then went he also up unto the feast, not openly, but as it were in secret.
11 Then the Jews sought him at the feast, and said, Where is he?
12 And there was much murmuring among the people concerning him: for

physically of His flesh; that would profit **nothing**. Rather, it is His **spirit** (person) which gives life. The **words** He spoke were **spirit** and **life**. They were not dead, but they carried the potential of producing life. Accept what He said (His words) and they would have life.

64-65. Unbelief stopped people from coming to Him. They did not accept His words and, consequently, they would not draw to Him (cf. vs. 44).

66. Many of those who were impressed by the signs now left Christ because of their unbelief.

67. Christ turns to the Twelve and wants to know if they will **also go away**. This question is phrased in such a way as to expect a negative answer.

68. Peter had understood the teaching of his Master. The message of Christ was not dead words to Peter, but they were full of spirit and life and were the **words of eternal life**.

69. We believe and are sure. Peter had partaken of the Bread of Life and had assurance of that belief. Assurance always follows true salvation (I Jn 5:13). Peter proclaims Jesus as the **Christ** (the anointed, holy, and chosen One).

70-71. Jesus knows that not all the Twelve have accepted Him. One was a devil (Gr *diabolos*, slanderer, false accuser).

The chapter ends differently than it begins. It begins with the crowds wanting to make Him king and closes with Christ questioning whether His Twelve will leave Him, as everyone else. The Twelve affirm their confidence through Peter, but even one of them is a devil and will eventually betray the Bread of Life.

G. Christ as the Master Teacher. 7:1-53.

1. Teaching concerning His person. 7:1-36.

7:1-5. After these things. After many people had forsaken Him (6:66), Christ remained in Galilee because of a Jewish plot **to kill him** (5:18). The Feast of Tabernacles was a harvest feast which commemorated the years of wilderness wandering. **His brethren.** His brothers (James, Joseph, Simeon, and Judas) perceived that Christ should go to the feast and exert His influence by performing mighty works. Their desire was that Jesus would impress all the people at the feast **openly**. They gave this bad advice because they themselves had not **believed** in the spiritual ministry of the Messiah. They wanted someone who would unite the Jewish people and establish a kingdom.

6-7. Christ's **time** to go to the feast had **not yet come**. He knew that if He would go, the Jews would kill Him, and that time had not yet come. **The world** (people separated from God) could not hate Christ's brethren because they were part of that **world**. They hated Christ for His message that exposed sin.

8-9. My time is not yet fully come. Christ's time to go to Jerusalem and be crucified had not yet become full. He had no desire to gain popularity and influence people with His works.

10-13. The Lord eventually went to the feast in **secret** (that is, without public fanfare). Perhaps He traveled the back roads with only His twelve disciples. **The Jews** refers to the religious hierarchy. **Where is he?** They had hostile intentions (15:18). The people were divided in their opinion of Christ. Some thought Him a **good man** (moral, honest), while others thought He was a deceiver (interested only in leading people astray).

some said, He is a good man: others said, Nay; but he deceiveth the people.

13 Howbeit no man spake openly of him for fear of the Jews.

14 ¶Now about the midst of the feast Jesus went up into the temple, and taught.

15 And the Jews marvelled, saying, How knoweth this man letters, having never learned?

16 Jesus answered them, and said, My doctrine is not mine, but his that sent me.

17 If any man will do his will, he shall know of the doctrine, whether it be of God, or *whether* I speak of myself.

18 He that speaketh of himself seeketh his own glory: but he that seeketh his glory that sent him, the same is true, and no unrighteousness is in him.

19 Did not Moses give you the law, and *yet* none of you keepeth the law? Why go ye about to kill me?

20 The people answered and said, Thou hast a devil: who goeth about to kill thee?

21 Jesus answered and said unto them, I have done one work, and ye all marvel.

22 Moses therefore gave unto you circumcision; (not because it is of Moses, but of the fathers;) and ye on the sabbath day circumcise a man.

23 If a man on the sabbath day receive circumcision, that the law of Moses should not be broken; are ye angry at me, because I have made a man every whit whole on the sabbath day?

24 Judge not according to the appearance, but judge righteous judgment.

25 Then said some of them of Jerusalem, Is not this he, whom they seek to kill?

26 But, lo, he speaketh boldly, and they say nothing unto him. Do the rulers know indeed that this is the very Christ?

27 Howbeit we know this man whence he is: but when Christ cometh, no man knoweth whence he is.

28 Then cried Jesus in the temple as he taught, saying, Ye both know me, and ye know whence I am: and I am not come of myself, but he that sent me is true, whom ye know not.

29 But I know him: for I am from him, and he hath sent me.

30 Then they sought to take him: but no man laid hands on him, because his hour was not yet come.

31 And many of the people believed on him, and said, When Christ cometh, will he do more miracles than these which this *man* hath done?

32 ¶The Pharisees heard that the people murmured such things concerning him; and the Pharisees and the chief priests sent officers to take him.

33 Then said Jesus unto them, Yet a

Because the Jewish hierarchy had not stated their opinion, the people feared expulsion from the synagogue if their open opinion conflicted with the Sanhedrin.

14-16. Halfway through the feast, Christ went to the Temple and began to teach. The Jews were outraged at His boldness and objected to His teaching. They were amazed that He could be educated without ever having studied formally. Christ establishes a higher authority for His teaching than Jewish schools: God the Father.

17-18. To understand His teaching, one must have the desire to do the will of God. With this commitment a person could evaluate the authenticity of Christ's teaching. This person would also realize that Christ was not seeking **his own glory** but rather the glory of the One who sent Him.

19-20. To do God's will is to obey God's law. Christ is saying that these Jews had not kept the law, and consequently, they were not doing God's will. Therefore they were not in a position to properly evaluate His message. In fact, they wanted to break the sixth commandment by killing Christ. The people are unaware that the leaders have plotted to kill Christ, and they assume that Christ is insane: **Thou hast a devil.**

21. One work. The healing of the impotent man on the Sabbath, recorded in chapter 5, caused them to plot His death (5:18).

22-23. Christ appeals to the Jewish rite of circumcision which could be performed on the Sabbath. If that work of ceremonial cleansing could be performed on the Sabbath, then a work of complete healing should also be performed. The Jews had no logical answer for this convicting question.

24. Christ tells them to stop judging on the surface. **Judge righteous** (just) **judgment.**

25. The attitude of the Sanhedrin is found in verse 15, the attitude of the pilgrims in verse 20, and now the Jerusalemites who are aware of the leaders' plot react to Christ.

26. They are amazed that Christ spoke **boldly** (openly), and for a moment think that perhaps the rulers have been convinced that He is the Messiah.

27. The idea was quickly dismissed since they believed that the Messiah would appear suddenly, but everyone knew that Jesus came from Nazareth. The true Messiah, according to the leaders, would come from Bethlehem.

28-29. Christ acknowledges their opinion about his earthly home. However, they were unaware of His divine origin. The Lord thoroughly knows the Father who sent Him. The Jerusalemites did not accept Him as the true Messiah.

30-31. Because of these divine claims with regard to origin, they were anxious to arrest Him. However, His **hour** of divine appointment had **not yet come,** and all the hatred and plots of the Jews could not harm Him. Many **believed on Him** (Gr construction indicates saving faith) on the basis of His **miracles.**

32-34. The leaders have had enough. People are actually accepting this Jesus as the Messiah, and the leaders decide to apprehend Him. Christ indicates that in **a little while** (about six months or the time between the Feast of Tabernacles and the Passover) He would return to the Father. The Jewish nation

little while am I with you, and *then* I go unto him that sent me.

34 Ye shall seek me, and shall not find *me:* and where I am, *thither* ye cannot come.

35 Then said the Jews among themselves, Whither will he go, that we shall not find him? will he go unto the dispersed among the Gentiles, and teach the Gentiles?

36 What *manner of* saying is this that he said, Ye shall seek me, and shall not find *me:* and where I am, *thither* ye cannot come?

37 ¶In the last day, that great *day* of the feast, Jesus stood and cried, saying, If any man thirst, let him come unto me, and drink.

38 He that believeth on me, as the scripture hath said, out of his belly shall flow rivers of living water.

39 (But this spake he of the Spirit, which they that believe on him should receive: for the Holy Ghost was not yet *given;* because that Jesus was not yet glorified.)

40 Many of the people therefore, when they heard this saying, said, Of a truth this is the Prophet.

41 Others said, This is the Christ. But some said, Shall Christ come out of Galilee?

42 Hath not the scripture said, That Christ cometh of the seed of David, and out of the town of Bethlehem, where David was?

43 So there was a division among the people because of him.

44 And some of them would have taken him; but no man laid hands on him.

45 ¶Then came the officers to the chief priests and Pharisees; and they said unto them, Why have ye not brought him?

46 The officers answered, Never man spake like this man.

47 Then answered them the Pharisees, Are ye also deceived?

48 Have any of the rulers or of the Pharisees believed on him?

49 But this people who knoweth not the law are cursed.

50 Nĭc-o-dē'mus saith unto them, (he that came to Jesus by night, being one of them,)

51 Doth our law judge *any* man, before it hear him, and know what he doeth?

52 They answered and said unto him, Art thou also of Galilee? Search, and look: for out of Galilee ariseth no prophet.

53 And every man went unto his own house.

would then **seek** Him but their search would be in vain. They could not go to the Father, because in rejecting Him they had rejected the Father.

35-36. The Jews did not understand the spiritual meaning of Christ's statement. They thought that after Christ's failure in Judaea, He would go to the **dispersed** (Jews who lived around the world) and **teach the Gentiles** (Gr *hellēn*, Greeks). Unknowingly, these leaders had uttered a true prophecy. Christ, through His disciples, would spread His message around the world.

2. Teaching concerning the Holy Spirit. 7:37-39.

37. The last day. The seventh or eighth day of the feast. During the feast, a priest would fill a golden pitcher with water from the pool of Siloam and carry it to the altar at the Temple where he would pour it through a funnel leading to the base of the altar. Probably, after this ceremony, Christ invited those who thirsted to come to Him and drink. The emptiness of Judaism is emphasized in that it fails to satisfy.

38. The one who believes not only gets satisfied (vs. 37), but also that person becomes a channel of blessing to others; **out of his belly shall flow rivers of living water** (Isa 44:3, 4; 55:1-2).

39. This indwelling blessing would be available through the Holy Spirit after Christ was **glorified** (ascended into Heaven). The Spirit in the Old Testament came **upon** people, but Christ promised that the Spirit would come to live **in** people.

3. Division of people. 7:40-53.

40. Christ's invitation is responded to in different ways. Some thought He was a prophet.

41-42. Some thought He was the Messiah. Others said He could not be the Messiah because the Messiah was predicted to come from Beth-lehem. They were correct about this, but they were incorrect in that they assumed Christ was born in Galilee. Consequently, their conclusion that Christ was not the Messiah was also wrong.

43-44. There was division among the people.

45-46. The group whom the Pharisees sent to arrest Christ returned without Him. They were overwhelmed by the message and manner of Christ and were powerless to apprehend Him.

47-49. The Pharisees were mad and sought to instruct officers that an intellectual and spiritual leader would not believe in Christ. Only those who **knoweth not** God's law are deceived. They describe these people as **cursed,** the scum of society.

50-52. Nicodemus . . . being one of them, that is, being one of the rulers that were violating the law in judging a man without hearing him. They ignored Nicodemus' question and told him that if he would search the Scriptures, he would discover that no prophet had ever come out of Galilee. This again shows their ignorance of the Scripture, since Jonah, Nahum, and Hosea came from Galilee.

53. The Sanhedrin adjourns and the people go home.

H. Christ as the Light of the World. 8:1-9:41.

There has been debate over the authenticity of this story of the woman taken in adultery. Many older manuscripts do not include it. However, it is included in the AV and will be dealt with here.

CHAPTER 8

JESUS went unto the mount of Olives.

2 And early in the morning he came again into the temple, and all the people came unto him; and he sat down, and taught them.

3 And the scribes and Pharisees brought unto him a woman taken in adultery; and when they had set her in the midst,

4 They say unto him, Master, this woman was taken in adultery, in the very act.

5 Now Moses in the law commanded us, that such should be stoned: but what sayest thou?

6 This they said, tempting him, that they might have to accuse him. But Jesus stooped down, and with *his* finger wrote on the ground, *as though he heard them not.*

7 So when they continued asking him, he lifted up himself, and said unto them, He that is without sin among you, let him first cast a stone at her.

8 And again he stooped down, and wrote on the ground.

9 And they which heard *it*, being convicted by *their own* conscience, went out one by one, beginning at the eldest, *even* unto the last: and Jesus was left alone, and the woman standing in the midst.

10 When Jesus had lifted up himself, and saw none but the woman, he said unto her, Woman, where are those thine accusers? hath no man condemned thee?

11 She said, No man, Lord. And Jesus said unto her, Neither do I condemn thee: go, and sin no more.

12 ¶Then spake Jesus again unto them, saying, I am the light of the world: he that followeth me shall not walk in darkness, but shall have the light of life.

13 The Pharisees therefore said unto him, Thou bearest record of thyself; thy record is not true.

14 Jesus answered and said unto them, Though I bear record of myself, *yet* my record is true: for I know whence I came, and whither I go; but ye cannot tell whence I come, and whither I go.

15 Ye judge after the flesh; I judge no man.

16 And yet if I judge, my judgment is true: for I am not alone, but I and the Father that sent me.

17 It is also written in your law, that the testimony of two men is true.

18 I am one that bear witness of myself, and the Father that sent me beareth witness of me.

19 Then said they unto him, Where is thy Father? Jesus answered, Ye neither know me, nor my Father: if ye had known me, ye should have known my Father also.

20 These words spake Jesus in the treasury, as he taught in the temple: and no man laid hands on him; for his hour was not yet come.

1. Adulterous woman forgiven. 8:1-11.

8:1-6. These verses are closely connected to 7:53. When everyone went home, **Jesus went unto the mount of Olives.** Afterward He returned to the Temple to teach. The scribes and Pharisees brought to Christ a woman who had been caught in adultery. The Feast of Tabernacles had just been celebrated and acts of immorality during that festive week were not unusual. The scribes attempted to put Christ in a dilemma. If He answered that the woman should be stoned, He would be violating the Roman law which forbade such acts. If He answered that she should not be stoned, He would be violating Moses' law (Deut 22:24). They did this to **tempt** Him (Gr *peirazo*, "to entice to sin").

There are several theories about what Christ wrote on the ground. First, that He wrote the sins of the scribes and Pharisees. Second, that He wrote the Ten Commandments. Third, that He wrote a message to the Pharisees.

7-8. After pressing the issue, Christ answered the accusers. In answering, He did not abolish Moses' law; rather, He applied that law to the lives of those who had accused the woman. Again, He wrote on the ground and silence convicted the crowd.

9-11. They left, probably not out of conviction, but rather they had been defeated in their attempt to trap the Son of God. The sinner is left alone with the only person who was perfect and able to condemn her. In mercy and love, He forgave her and told her to **go, and sin no more.**

2. Sermon on the Light of the World. 8:12-59.

12. Following the incident of the adulterous woman Christ made His second "I am" statement: **I am the light of the world.** Christ shines as the Light in the world of darkness and sin. **He that followeth.** If one accepts and trusts the leading of that Light, **he . . . shall have the light of life.**

13-14. The Pharisees objected to Christ's testimony because all testimonies must be substantiated by witness. Christ knew His origin and no man could testify to that. Consequently, the Pharisees could not disprove His testimony.

15-16. Christ accused the Pharisees of judging from an external perspective. **I judge no man.** Although Christ had perfect knowledge, He came, not to judge, but to save (3:17-18). **If I judge.** Those who reject the saving ministry of Christ must be judged, and they will be judged correctly. It is judgment from both the Father and Son.

17-18. The law required two witnesses (Deut 17:6). **Two men.** Two human witnesses. If the law required two human witnesses for accuracy, how much more dependable is the witness of two divine persons, the Father and the Son.

19-20. The Jews had rejected Christ and in doing so had rejected the Father. **His hour was not yet come** (see 7:30).

4 I must work the works of him that sent me, while it is day: the night cometh, when no man can work.

5 As long as I am in the world, I am the light of the world.

6 When he had thus spoken, he spat on the ground, and made clay of the spittle, and he anointed the eyes of the blind man with the clay,

7 And said unto him, Go, wash in the pool of Sī-lō'am, (which is by interpretation, Sent.) He went his way therefore, and washed, and came seeing.

8 ¶The neighbours therefore, and they which before had seen him that he was blind, said, Is not this he that sat and begged?

9 Some said, This is he: others said, He is like him: but he said, I am he.

10 Therefore said they unto him, How were thine eyes opened?

11 He answered and said, A man that is called Jesus made clay, and anointed mine eyes, and said unto me, Go to the pool of Sī-lō'am, and wash: and I went and washed, and I received sight.

12 Then said they unto him, Where is he? He said, I know not.

13 ¶They brought to the Pharisees him that aforetime was blind.

14 And it was the sabbath day when Jesus made the clay, and opened his eyes.

15 Then again the Pharisees also asked him how he had received his sight. He said unto them, He put clay upon mine eyes, and I washed, and do see.

16 Therefore said some of the Pharisees, This man is not of God, because he keepeth not the sabbath day. Others said, How can a man that is a sinner do such miracles? And there was a division among them.

17 They say unto the blind man again, What sayest thou of him, that he hath opened thine eyes? He said, He is a prophet.

18 But the Jews did not believe concerning him, that he had been blind, and received his sight, until they called the parents of him that had received his sight.

19 And they asked them, saying, Is this your son, who ye say was born blind? how then doth he now see?

20 His parents answered them and said, We know that this is our son, and that he was born blind:

21 But by what means he now seeth, we know not; or who hath opened his eyes, we know not: he is of age; ask him: he shall speak for himself.

22 These words spake his parents, because they feared the Jews: for the Jews had agreed already, that if any man did confess that he was Christ, he should be put out of the synagogue.

23 Therefore said his parents, He is of age; ask him.

24 Then again called they the man that was blind, and said unto him, Give God the praise: we know that this man is a sinner.

25 He answered and said, Whether he be a sinner or no, I know not: one

"What?" What could be done for the man's need? This statement is the premise for the action that is about to follow. No explanation is given as to why Christ chose this method in healing the blind man. He was probably testing the blind man's faith and obedience. Christ sent him to Siloam and told him to wash. This story is similar to that of Naaman. However, the blind man responded immediately and was healed.

8-9. There is confusion over the man's identity. The miracle had changed the man's appearance. Finally, the man said, **I am he.**

10-12. Having been assured that it really is the man who was blind, the next logical question was how he had received his sight. The man related the story and the neighbors responded by wanting to know the location of Jesus.

13-14. Because the man had been healed on the Sabbath, the neighbors took him to the Pharisees. To make clay on the Sabbath was illegal.

15. Again. The second time he was asked to tell his story of healing.

16-17. The Pharisees knew Christ had broken the Sabbath. Since Christ had broken the Sabbath, He could not be **of God.** Others argued that it was impossible for a sinner to perform miracles. Since Christ did perform a miracle, maybe He was not a sinner. **There was a division among them.** They asked the man his opinion of Christ. He responded that **He is a prophet.**

18-21. The Jews refused to admit the miracle until they talked to the man's parents, who confirmed that this was their son and that he **was born blind.** However, they did not explain the means of what happened.

22-23. Because they were afraid of the Jews, they wanted their son to speak for himself. The Jews had agreed that anyone who would recognize Christ as the Messiah would be excommunicated from the synagogue.

24. They recall the blind man. **Give God the praise.** They want the blind man to attribute the miracle to God alone and to admit that Christ **is a sinner.** Rather than being objective, the Jews had already made up their minds about Christ; He was a sinner.

25. Note the **I know not** and the **I know.** The Jews said we know He is a sinner, but the man says, **I know not** if He is a

thing I know, that, whereas I was blind, now I see.

26 Then said they to him again, What did he to thee? how opened he thine eyes?

27 He answered them, I have told you already, and ye did not hear: wherefore would ye hear it again? will ye also be his disciples?

28 Then they reviled him, and said, Thou art his disciple; but we are Moses' disciples.

29 We know that God spake unto Moses: as for this fellow, we know not from whence he is.

30 The man answered and said unto them, Why herein is a marvellous thing, that ye know not from whence he is, and yet he hath opened mine eyes.

31 Now we know that God heareth not sinners: but if any man be a worshipper of God, and doeth his will, him he heareth.

32 Since the world began was it not heard that any man opened the eyes of one that was born blind.

33 If this man were not of God, he could do nothing.

34 They answered and said unto him, Thou wast altogether born in sins, and dost thou teach us? And they cast him out.

35 ¶Jesus heard that they had cast him out; and when he had found him, he said unto him, Dost thou believe on the Son of God?

36 He answered and said, Who is he, Lord, that I might believe on him?

37 And Jesus said unto him, Thou hast both seen him, and it is he that talketh with thee.

38 And he said, Lord, I believe. And he worshipped him.

39 ¶And Jesus said, For judgment I am come into this world, that they which see not might see; and that they which see might be made blind.

40 And some of the Pharisees which were with him heard these words, and said unto him, Are we blind also?

41 Jesus said unto them, If ye were blind, ye should have no sin: but now ye say, We see; therefore your sin remaineth.

CHAPTER 10

VERILY, verily, I say unto you, He that entereth not by the door into the sheepfold, but climbeth up some other way, the same is a thief and a robber.

2 But he that entereth in by the door is the shepherd of the sheep.

3 To him the porter openeth; and the sheep hear his voice: and he calleth his

sinner, but **I know, whereas I was blind, now I see.** The receiving of sight is a fact, not an opinion.

26-27. Again, the Jews ask him what happened and how it happened. The man becomes impatient with their repeated questions. **Will ye also be his disciples?** If I repeat it again, will you become Christ's disciples?

28-29. Angered by the fact that their authority has been questioned by a beggar, the Jews make a distinction between the followers of Christ who broke the Sabbath and the followers of Moses who obey the law.

30. The blind man now rubs salt in the wound. It is astonishing, he argues, that the religious leaders did not know where Christ came from when He had performed such an outstanding miracle. How could these leaders be knowledgeable and yet not know something so important?

31-33. The blind man continues his argument as follows: God only listens to those who do **his will** and not to sinners. This man performed a miracle that no one else had ever done, and God helped him do it; therefore, Christ is not a sinner, for if he were, **he could do nothing.**

34. The Pharisees had been defeated by a poor beggar and so they **cast him out** of the synagogue.

35. Christ found the outcast and began to meet his spiritual needs. **Dost thou believe on the Son of God?**

36-37. The man is ready to believe but needs some direction. Christ reveals Himself.

38-39. The man responds in faith and worships Christ. Observing the man's humble response, Christ declares that He came to judge. Those who do not see but who want to see (the blind man), will see. Those who think they see (the Pharisees) will be **made blind.**

40-41. In disdain, the Pharisees ask, **Are we blind also? If ye were blind.** If you were ignorant of God's law, Jesus responded, and yet desired to be saved, then **ye should have no sin.** You would be saved. **We see.** You are proud in your religious enlightenment, and you have rejected me. Therefore, **your sin remaineth.**

I. Christ as the Good Shepherd. 10:1-42.

This story is an allegory rather than a parable (vs. 6); this means that the details are relevant to the main idea. In this allegory Christ is referred to as the Good Shepherd and as the door into the sheepfold.

1. Sermon on the Good Shepherd. 10:1-21.

10:1. Thieves and robbers attempt to enter the **sheepfold** by climbing over the wall. The Oriental sheepfold normally consisted of four walls of stone with one door and no roof. The fold refers to Israel (vs. 16), and the thieves and robbers refer to the Jewish leaders who are trying to lead Israel while avoiding the door (Christ).

2. The true leader enters **by the door** and is the only **shepherd of the sheep.**

3-4. The true shepherd has a unique relationship with his sheep. He **calleth** them by **name.** He **leadeth them, putteth**

own sheep by name, and leadeth them out.

4 And when he putteth forth his own sheep, he goeth before them, and the sheep follow him: for they know his voice.

5 And a stranger will they not follow, but will flee from him: for they know not the voice of strangers.

6 This parable spake Jesus unto them: but they understood not what things they were which he spake unto them.

7 Then said Jesus unto them again, Verily, verily, I say unto you, I am the door of the sheep.

8 All that ever came before me are thieves and robbers: but the sheep did not hear them.

9 I am the door: by me if any man enter in, he shall be saved, and shall go in and out, and find pasture.

10 The thief cometh not, but for to steal, and to kill, and to destroy: I am come that they might have life, and that they might have *it* more abundantly.

11 I am the good shepherd: the good shepherd giveth his life for the sheep.

12 But he that is an hireling, and not the shepherd, whose own the sheep are not, seeth the wolf coming, and leaveth the sheep, and fleeth: and the wolf catcheth them, and scattereth the sheep.

13 The hireling fleeth, because he is an hireling, and careth not for the sheep.

14 I am the good shepherd, and know my *sheep*, and am known of mine.

15 As the Father knoweth me, even so know I the Father: and I lay down my life for the sheep.

16 And other sheep I have, which are not of this fold: them also I must bring, and they shall hear my voice; and there shall be one fold, *and* one shepherd.

17 Therefore doth my Father love me, because I lay down my life, that I might take it again.

18 No man taketh it from me, but I lay it down of myself. I have power to lay it down, and I have power to take it again. This commandment have I received of my Father.

19 ¶There was a division therefore again among the Jews for these sayings.

20 And many of them said, He hath a devil, and is mad; why hear ye him?

21 Others said, These are not the words of him that hath a devil. Can a devil open the eyes of the blind?

22 ¶And it was at Jerusalem the feast of the dedication, and it was winter.

23 And Jesus walked in the temple in Solomon's porch.

24 Then came the Jews round about him, and said unto him, How long dost thou make us to doubt? If thou be the Christ, tell us plainly.

25 Jesus answered them, I told you, and ye believed not: the works that I do

them forth, and **goeth before them.** The sheep respond by hearing **his voice,** knowing **his voice,** and following Him.

5-6. A stranger will they not follow (Gr emphatic negation; "never follow"). Their reaction to the **stranger** is totally opposite to that of the shepherd. They **flee.** They are not acquainted with **the voice of strangers.** They did not comprehend this story of the shepherd and the sheep.

7-8. Verily, verily. Christ begins His explanation with the same statement that He began His story. **I am the door.** Entrance into the fold is by Him and Him alone. The ones who **came before** were the scribes and Pharisees who attempted to enter the fold other than through the door.

9-10. Again, Christ emphasizes that He is **the door. If any man enter in, he shall be saved** (note vs. 10, **they might have life** refers to salvation). Also, that person will find pasture (in vs. 10, referring to abundant life) or the constant nourishment necessary to maintain life. The scribes and Pharisees **steal, kill, and destroy.** Christ gives life (salvation) and gives it **abundantly.**

11. Besides being the only door into the sheepfold, Christ is also the **good shepherd.** He is good because He **giveth his life for** (Gr *hyper*), in behalf of, for the benefit of **the sheep** (cf. Ps 23).

12-13. The scribes were merely **hirelings** (hired people) who had no true love and concern for the welfare of the sheep. In the moment of danger the hireling runs away.

14-16. The Pharisees are strangers, but Christ **knows** His sheep. The Pharisees have no love for the sheep, but Christ gives His life for them. Christ has a relationship to the sheep similar to His relationship with His Father. Christ now states that His fold will include both Jews and Gentiles (Acts 10:28).

17-18. The Lord further amplifies His statement saying that He will lay down His life in a voluntary act of sacrifice. **I lay it down of myself.** He had that **power** (right).

19-21. The Jews were divided in their opinion. Some thought He was mad and demon-possessed, while others were impressed by His miracle on behalf of the blind man.

2. Rejection of Christ's message. 10:22-42.

22-24. About two months had elapsed between the previous account and these events. **Does thou make us to doubt?** The Greek idiom means literally "lift up our soul." How long will you keep us in a state of suspense? **Tell us plainly.**

25-26. Christ had already told them (6:35; 7:37-39; 8:23-25). The problem was they had rejected what Christ had said about Himself. Christ had supplemented His claims by His works.

in my Father's name, they bear witness of me.

26 But ye believe not, because ye are not of my sheep, as I said unto you.

27 My sheep hear my voice, and I know them, and they follow me:

28 And I give unto them eternal life; and they shall never perish, neither shall any *man* pluck them out of my hand.

29 My Father, which gave *them* me, is greater than all; and no *man* is able to pluck *them* out of my Father's hand.

30 I and *my* Father are one.

31 ¶Then the Jews took up stones again to stone him.

32 Jesus answered them, Many good works have I shewed you from my Father; for which of those works do ye stone me?

33 The Jews answered him, saying, For a good work we stone thee not; but for blasphemy; and because that thou, being a man, makest thyself God.

34 Jesus answered them, Is it not written in your law, I said, Ye are gods?

35 If he called them gods, unto whom the word of God came, and the scripture cannot be broken;

36 Say ye of him, whom the Father hath sanctified, and sent into the world, Thou blasphemest; because I said, I am the Son of God?

37 If I do not the works of my Father, believe me not.

38 But if I do, though ye believe not me, believe the works: that ye may know, and believe, that the Father *is* in me, and I in him.

39 ¶Therefore they sought again to take him: but he escaped out of their hand,

40 And went away again beyond Jordan into the place where John at first baptized; and there he abode.

41 And many resorted unto him, and said, John did no miracle: but all things that John spake of this man were true.

42 And many believed on him there.

CHAPTER 11

NOW a certain *man* was sick, *named*

The cause for their unbelief is rooted in the fact that they were not His sheep.

27-28. Note the verbs used to describe Christ's sheep. They **hear** and **follow** their shepherd. This obedient response is totally opposite that of the Jews. Note the verbs used to describe the shepherd. He knows and gives **eternal life.** He promises that they **shall never perish** (Gr emphatic negation; "never perish"). To further emphasize their security, He adds the phrase, "into the ages" (Gr idiom meaning "forever") or for all eternity they shall never **perish.** No one can take these sheep out of Christ's hand.

29. Besides being in the hand of Christ, these sheep are in the hand of **the Father** and **no man is able to pluck them out of my Father's hand.**

30. I and my Father are one. God the Father and God the Son are in agreement in the matter of the believer's eternal security. On the basis of this passage, no one should ever doubt the eternal security of his salvation. Once a person is genuinely saved, he is saved forever.

31. The Jews are angered that Christ would claim equality with the Father, and took **stones** to **stone him.**

32. Christ again makes the Jews face His works, and asks them to define which **good** work deserves such cruel treatment. These **good works** reflected His supernatural origin, and should be the basis for accepting Him as Christ and not the basis for stoning Him.

33-34. The Jews ignored what Christ did, and were judging Him on what He said. Christ had made Himself **God.** In defending His claims, Christ meets the Jews on their ground and makes His appeal to the **law. Ye are gods.** This refers to Psalm 82:6, and deals with Hebrew judges because they were interpreters of divine law and justice.

35-36. Christ states that if the Jews were willing to call these judges gods because **the word of God** had come to them, why did they accuse Him of blasphemy when the Father, who had sent the **word** to the judges, sent Him and set Him apart for a divine mission?

37-39. If His works do not substantiate His claim, then do not believe Him. Christ appeals to their unbelief. **I do.** If His works agree with His message, and if they still do not believe, Christ exhorts them to consider again His **works,** so that they **may know, and believe.** Now they try to arrest Him because of these blasphemous claims.

40-41. Christ retires from the public scene. However, they find Him, and the ministry of John the Baptist is remembered. Even though John **did no miracle,** yet all that he had said about Christ was true (1:19-36).

42. Many believed. (See Merrill C. Tenney, *John the Gospel of Belief,* pp. 163-167.)

J. Christ as the Resurrection and the Life. 11:1-57.

This chapter deals with the resurrection of Lazarus and the Jewish reaction to the miracle. It is apparent that the fame of Christ had reached national prominence, and that this was of great concern to the Jews who feared that the Romans would punish them if Christ influenced the people to follow Him.

1. Power of Christ: Raising Lazarus. 11:1-46.

11:1-2. The setting for this miracle is described. Lazarus had become ill; his sisters Mary and Martha send to Christ for help.

Lazarus, of Bethany, the town of Mary and her sister Martha.

2 (It was *that* Mary which anointed the Lord with ointment, and wiped his feet with her hair, whose brother Lazarus was sick.)

3 Therefore his sisters sent unto him, saying, Lord, behold, he whom thou lovest is sick.

4 When Jesus heard *that*, he said, This sickness is not unto death, but for the glory of God, that the Son of God might be glorified thereby.

5 Now Jesus loved Martha, and her sister, and Lazarus.

6 When he had heard therefore that he was sick, he abode two days still in the same place where he was.

7 Then after that saith he to *his* disciples, Let us go into Judæa again.

8 *His* disciples say unto him, Master, the Jews of late sought to stone thee; and goest thou thither again?

9 Jesus answered, Are there not twelve hours in the day? If any man walk in the day, he stumbleth not, because he seeth the light of this world.

10 But if a man walk in the night, he stumbleth, because there is no light in him.

11 These things said he: and after that he saith unto them, Our friend Lazarus sleepeth; but I go, that I may awake him out of sleep.

12 Then said his disciples, Lord, if he sleep, he shall do well.

13 Howbeit Jesus spake of his death: but they thought that he had spoken of taking of rest in sleep.

14 Then said Jesus unto them plainly, Lazarus is dead.

15 And I am glad for your sakes that I was not there, to the intent ye may believe; nevertheless let us go unto him.

16 Then said Thomas, which is called Dĭd'y-mus, unto his fellowdisciples, Let us also go, that we may die with him.

17 Then when Jesus came, he found that he had *lain* in the grave four days already.

18 Now Bethany was nigh unto Jerusalem, about fifteen furlongs off:

19 And many of the Jews came to Martha and Mary, to comfort them concerning their brother.

20 Then Martha, as soon as she heard that Jesus was coming, went and met him: but Mary sat *still* in the house.

21 Then said Martha unto Jesus, Lord, if thou hadst been here, my brother had not died.

22 But I know, that even now, whatsoever thou wilt ask of God, God will give *it* thee.

23 Jesus saith unto her, Thy brother shall rise again.

3. Note that they do not ask Christ to do anything. They simply make Him aware of their need, and know that because He loves and cares He will respond appropriately.

4. This sickness is not unto death. This means that the final result of Lazarus' sickness will not be death. The final result will be **for the glory of God.** Sin is not the source of all sickness. Sometimes God permits sickness in order to reveal His glory. Greater glory was manifested in raising Lazarus from the dead than if Christ had simply healed him.

5-6. Jesus **loved.** In the hour of crisis and need, remember that God loves us. Christ delays His going to Bethany. This might seem strange since Lazarus had a great need; however, note again the previous verse. His waiting is based upon His love.

7-8. The disciples are alarmed when Christ wants to return to **Judaea,** because the last time He was there they tried to stone Him (10:31).

9-10. Are there not twelve hours in the day? Christ alludes to the fact that His time on the earth is a final period of time and it cannot be changed. A person who walks in the **light** of God's will cannot be harmed, but the person who does not **stumbleth.**

11. Lazarus sleepeth. Death is often referred to as sleep (Gen 47:30; Mt 27:52; I Thess 4:13). However, in no way do these passages teach a state of soul-sleep or unconsciousness. Death for the saint is restful sleep from the problems of this world, but a full consciousness of another world (Phil 1:23).

12-13. The disciples thought that Lazarus was physically asleep and assumed that sleep would be good for his illness.

14. Finally, Christ clarifies His statements by telling them **plainly, Lazarus is dead.**

15. Christ is happy that He was not with Lazarus when he died. Had He been there, He would have healed him and prevented death. Now He must perform a greater miracle that will increase the faith of the disciples.

16. Thomas, **called Didymus** (Gr "twin"), encourages the disciples to go with Christ, **that we may die with him.** The outlook for safety in Judaea is dim and Thomas feels that Christ will be killed, and as a result they will be killed as well.

17. Four days. Lazarus probably died around the same time that the messenger came to Christ (11:3).

18-19. Bethany was about two miles from Jerusalem. Many residents of Jerusalem had come to Bethany to comfort Mary and Martha.

20. Note the contrast in personalities. Martha is a woman of action, whereas Mary is a woman of quiet reflection (Lk 10:38-42).

21. This statement is not critical of Christ's action, but it is a statement of grief that if Christ could have been with Lazarus he would not have died.

22. This verse displays great hope in Christ's ability to ask from God; however, Martha did not have the resurrection of her brother in mind.

23-24. Christ assures Martha that her brother **shall rise again.** She interprets this to mean in the **last day.** Martha, like

24 Martha saith unto him, I know that he shall rise again in the resurrection at the last day.

25 Jesus said unto her. I am the resurrection, and the life: he that believeth in me, though he were dead, yet shall he live:

26 And whosoever liveth and believeth in me shall never die. Believest thou this?

27 She saith unto him, Yea, Lord: I believe that thou art the Christ, the Son of God, which should come into the world.

28 And when she had so said, she went her way, and called Mary her sister secretly, saying, The Master is come, and calleth for thee.

29 As soon as she heard that, she arose quickly, and came unto him.

30 Now Jesus was not yet come into the town, but was in that place where Martha met him.

31 The Jews then which were with her in the house, and comforted her, when they saw Mary, that she rose up hastily and went out, followed her, saying, She goeth unto the grave to weep there.

32 Then when Mary was come where Jesus was, and saw him, she fell down at his feet, saying unto him, Lord, if thou hadst been here, my brother had not died.

33 When Jesus therefore saw her weeping, and the Jews also weeping which came with her, he groaned in the spirit, and was troubled,

34 And said, Where have ye laid him? They said unto him, Lord, come and see.

35 Jesus wept.

36 Then said the Jews, Behold how he loved him!

37 And some of them said, Could not this man, which opened the eyes of the blind, have caused that even this man should not have died?

38 Jesus therefore again groaning in himself cometh to the grave. It was a cave, and a stone lay upon it.

39 Jesus said, Take ye away the stone. Martha, the sister of him that was dead, saith unto him, Lord, by this time he stinketh: for he hath been dead four days.

40 Jesus saith unto her, Said I not unto thee, that, if thou wouldest believe, thou shouldest see the glory of God?

41 Then they took away the stone from the place where the dead was laid. And Jesus lifted up his eyes, and said, Father, I thank thee that thou hast heard me.

42 And I knew that thou hearest me always: but because of the people which stand by I said it, that they may believe that thou hast sent me.

43 And when he thus had spoken, he cried with a loud voice, Lazarus, come forth.

44 And he that was dead came forth, bound hand and foot with graveclothes: and his face was bound about with a napkin. Jesus saith unto them, Loose him, and let him go.

many Christians, does not appropriate the promises of God for now. God is able to meet our needs in the present as well as in the future.

25-26. I am. This is the fifth of the seven **I am** statements (6:35; 8:12; 10:9; 10:11; 14:6; 15:5). Christ is the **resurrection** (He raises those who are dead in sin) and **the life** (He gives to them eternal life). Those who believe in Christ, though they may die physically, shall live. Beyond that, those who really have Christ's life **shall never die.**

27. Yea, Lord: I believe (Gr perfect tense; emphasizes certainty, "I *do* believe"). Martha had accepted the **I am** (vs. 25) as the Christ (Messiah), **the Son of God.**

28. Martha returns and quietly tells Mary that Christ has arrived.

29-30. Mary now goes out to meet the Master.

31-32. The Jews observing her haste, and assuming that she is going to the grave, follow her to comfort her. Note that the words of Mary were the same as Martha's (11:21). How many times they had repeated these words to each other in the last four days.

33. He groaned in the spirit. The verb used here means to become angry. Christ was probably angry at the root cause of all this sorrow and grief, i.e., sin.

34-35. Jesus wept. Jesus broke out into tears. Here we are reminded of the humanity of Christ and His love and concern for His people.

36-37. The Jews saw the love of Christ, but some of them debated whether or not He could have prevented this tragedy by healing Lazarus.

38-39. Christ came to the tomb and ordered someone to roll away the stone. Martha objected to this strange request since Lazarus' body would stink.

40. Christ reminded her of His previous statements (11:25-26).

41-42. Christ offered a prayer before He performed the miracle. The prayer was one of thanksgiving rather than requesting. He is thankful that the **Father hast heard.** Because He is in close communion with the Father, this miracle is possible. He prays so that the **people** may **believe that thou hast sent me.**

43-44. Lazarus, come forth. The voice of omnipotence speaks and the dead responds. Here is a picture of many Christians who are alive in Christ but are still bound by the **graveclothes** of the world. They cannot work because their hands are bound, they cannot walk because their feet are bound, and they cannot witness because their mouths are bound. Christ Jesus orders: **Loose him.**

45 Then many of the Jews which came to Mary, and had seen the things which Jesus did, believed on him.
46 But some of them went their ways to the Pharisees, and told them what things Jesus had done.

47 ¶Then gathered the chief priests and the Pharisees a council, and said, What do we? for this man doeth many miracles.
48 If we let him thus alone, all *men* will believe on him: and the Romans shall come and take away both our place and nation.
49 And one of them, *named* Cā′iaphas, being the high priest that same year, said unto them, Ye know nothing at all,
50 Nor consider that it is expedient for us, that one man should die for the people, and that the whole nation perish not.
51 And this spake he not of himself: but being high priest that year, he prophesied that Jesus should die for that nation;
52 And not for that nation only, but that also he should gather together in one the children of God that were scattered abroad.
53 Then from that day forth they took counsel together for to put him to death.
54 Jesus therefore walked no more openly among the Jews; but went thence unto a country near to the wilderness, into a city called E′phra-im, and there continued with his disciples.
55 ¶And the Jews' passover was nigh at hand: and many went out of the country up to Jerusalem before the passover, to purify themselves.
56 Then sought they for Jesus, and spake among themselves, as they stood in the temple, What think ye, that he will not come to the feast?
57 Now both the chief priests and the Pharisees had given a commandment, that, if any man knew where he were, he should shew *it*, that they might take him.

CHAPTER 12
THEN Jesus six days before the passover came to Bethany, where Lazarus was which had been dead, whom he raised from the dead.
2 There they made him a supper; and Martha served: but Lazarus was one of them that sat at the table with him.

3 Then took Mary a pound of ointment of spikenard, very costly, and anointed the feet of Jesus, and wiped his feet with her hair: and the house was filled with the odour of the ointment.

4 Then saith one of his disciples, Judas Iscariot, Simon's *son*, which should betray him,
5 Why was not this ointment sold for three hundred pence, and given to the poor?

45. The miracle brought results. ¹First, many **believed on him**.

46. Second, some went back to Jerusalem to report this incident to the leaders.

2. *Plan of the Pharisees. 11:47-57.*

47-48. Third, the Sanhedrin became angry and were afraid that if people continued to follow Christ, the Romans would think the Jews were planning a rebellion and would take their leaders into captivity.

49-50. Caiaphas presents a solution. He reasons that if Jesus lives, the nation will die. Therefore, in the interest of patriotism, Jesus must die so that the nation will live.

51-52. Little did Caiaphas realize the real truth of what he was saying. Christ would die to save the nation spiritually, whereas Caiaphas intended Him to die to save the nation politically. Again, the cosmopolitan nature of Christ's death is emphasized (10:16).

53-54. The Sanhedrin had formally decided to kill Christ. Knowing about their plan, Christ removed Himself from the public view.

55-57. As the pilgrims came to Jerusalem for the Passover there was much excitement and enthusiasm over the ministry of Christ. Popular opinion among the common people was in His favor. However, the leaders made it clear that anyone who saw Christ should report it, **that they might take him.**

K. Christ as the Messiah. 12:1-50.

There are four separate sections in this chapter: (1) The anointing of Jesus (vss. 1-11); (2) the Triumphal Entry (vss. 12-19); (3) the Greeks seek Christ (vss. 20-36); and (4) the Jews reject Christ (vss. 37-50). In all these events, Christ emerges as the true Messiah.

1. *Supper at Bethany. 12:1-11.*

12:1-2. Six days before the passover. Although there is debate concerning which day Christ entered Bethany, most commentators conclude that it was Saturday evening. According to Matthew 26 and Mark 14, the supper took place at the house of Simon the Leper. Martha, true to her personality, was serving (Lk 10:40). Perhaps this was a meal designed to thank the Lord for what He had done for Lazarus and Simon.

3. A pound of ointment of spikenard. Mary took twelve ounces (the weight of a Roman pound) of this perfume and **anointed the feet of Jesus.** This perfume was extracted from the root of the nard plant which is grown in India. It was a costly import. This was an act of love and devotion to the Lord. Nothing is wasted if it is given to the Lord.

4-5. Contrasted to the generosity of Mary is the selfishness of Judas. He had estimated the ointment to be worth **three hundred pence** or the amount of wages a person would receive for three hundred days' work.

6 This he said, not that he cared for the poor; but because he was a thief, and had the bag, and bare what was put therein.

7 Then said Jesus, Let her alone: against the day of my burying hath she kept this.

8 For the poor always ye have with you; but me ye have not always.

9 ¶Much people of the Jews therefore knew that he was there: and they came not for Jesus' sake only, but that they might see Lazarus also, whom he had raised from the dead.

10 But the chief priests consulted that they might put Lazarus also to death;

11 Because that by reason of him many of the Jews went away, and believed on Jesus.

12 ¶On the next day much people that were come to the feast, when they heard that Jesus was coming to Jerusalem,

13 Took branches of palm trees, and went forth to meet him, and cried, Hosanna: Blessed is the King of Israel that cometh in the name of the Lord.

14 And Jesus, when he had found a young ass, sat thereon; as it is written,

15 Fear not, daughter of Sion; behold, thy King cometh, sitting on an ass's colt.

16 These things understood not his disciples at the first: but when Jesus was glorified, then remembered they that these things were written of him, and that they had done these things unto him.

17 The people therefore that was with him when he called Lazarus out of his grave, and raised him from the dead, bare record.

18 For this cause the people also met him, for that they heard that he had done this miracle.

19 The Pharisees therefore said among themselves, Perceive ye how ye prevail nothing? behold, the world is gone after him.

20 ¶And there were certain Greeks among them that came up to worship at the feast:

21 The same came therefore to Philip, which was of Běth-să'i-da of Galilee, and desired him, saying, Sir, we would see Jesus.

22 Philip cometh and telleth Andrew: and again Andrew and Philip tell Jesus.

23 ¶And Jesus answered them, saying, The hour is come, that the Son of man should be glorified.

6-7. Judas was not concerned for the poor. He had been stealing (**he was a thief**) from the treasury (**the bag**). If the perfume had been sold, he could have stolen some of the three hundred pennies. Christ rebuked Judas. Mary, anticipating the death of her Saviour, anointed the body of Christ. In doing this prior to His death, she was expressing her complete love and devotion.

8. What Mary did was more important than feeding the poor; however, Jesus implied that Christians must minister to the poor, since **the poor always ye have with you.**

9-11. Lazarus had become a phenomenon since Christ had raised him. However, the religious leaders wanted to kill Lazarus, because **many** had believed on Christ after observing what He had done for Lazarus.

2. Triumphal Entry. 12:12-19.

12-13. **On the next day.** On Sunday, many of the people who had come to the feast took **branches of palm trees, and went forth to meet him.** It should be noted that those who sought to honor the Lord were pilgrims, not the residents of Jerusalem. **Hosanna.** The Greek is a transliteration of Hebrew meaning "Save, I beseech thee" (cf. Ps 118:25). They proclaim Christ as the **King of Israel,** and the One who comes in **the name of the Lord** (Ps 118:25-26). These people were expecting Christ to establish David's kingdom.

14-15. John now moves from the public scene to the private scene where Christ mounts a donkey. This action was in fulfillment of prophecy (Zech 9:9). The donkey was used in the Old Testament by kings who were bringing peace, while the horse was used when the kings rode into battle. **Daughter of Zion.** This symbolically represents Jerusalem and its inhabitants. Jerusalem should stop being afraid because their own King was coming.

16. The disciples understood these things after the ascension of Christ and the coming of the Holy Spirit, who called these things to their remembrance (7:39; 14:26).

17-19. The raising of Lazarus had caused great excitement in Jerusalem. Many who proclaimed Him as the **King of Israel** did so because of the miracle He performed in raising Lazarus. The Pharisees responded to this excitement by concluding that the **world** (everyone) **is gone after him.**

3. Teaching on the cross. 12:20-50.

20-21. The attention is now turned from the Jews to the Greeks. Some Greek proselytes had come **to worship at the feast.** The Greeks approached Philip and asked for an interview with Christ.

22. Philip consulted with Andrew, and they both approached Jesus. Why did Philip consult Andrew? Probably because he was wondering whether Jesus would consent to a Gentile interview since His mission was to Israel.

23. Jesus did not talk directly to the Greeks. He conveyed His message through Andrew and Philip. **The hour.** This does not refer to a sixty-minute period, but to the general time period when the **Son of man should be glorified.** This glorification is explained in the next verse.

24 Verily, verily, I say unto you, Except a corn of wheat fall into the ground and die, it abideth alone: but if it die, it bringeth forth much fruit.

25 He that loveth his life shall lose it; and he that hateth his life in this world shall keep it unto life eternal.

26 If any man serve me, let him follow me; and where I am, there shall also my servant be: if any man serve me, him will *my* Father honour.

27 Now is my soul troubled; and what shall I say? Father, save me from this hour: but for this cause came I unto this hour.

28 Father, glorify thy name. Then came there a voice from heaven, *saying*, I have both glorified *it*, and will glorify *it* again.

29 The people therefore, that stood by, and heard *it*, said that it thundered: others said, An angel spake to him.

30 Jesus answered and said, This voice came not because of me, but for your sakes.

31 Now is the judgment of this world: now shall the prince of this world be cast out.

32 And I, if I be lifted up from the earth, will draw all *men* unto me.

33 This he said, signifying what death he should die.

34 The people answered him, We have heard out of the law that Christ abideth forever: and how sayest thou, The Son of man must be lifted up? who is this Son of man?

35 Then Jesus said unto them, Yet a little while is the light with you. Walk while ye have the light, lest darkness come upon you: for he that walketh in darkness knoweth not whither he goeth.

36 While ye have light, believe in the light, that ye may be the children of light. These things spake Jesus, and departed, and did hide himself from them.

37 ¶But though he had done so many miracles before them, yet they believed not on him:

38 That the saying of E-ṣā′ias the prophet might be fulfilled, which he spake, Lord, who hath believed our report? and to whom hath the arm of the Lord been revealed?

39 Therefore they could not believe, because that E-ṣā′ias said again,

40 He hath blinded their eyes, and hardened their heart; that they should not see with *their* eyes, nor understand with *their* heart, and be converted, and I should heal them.

41 These things said E-ṣā′ias, when he saw his glory, and spake of him.

42 ¶Nevertheless among the chief rulers also many believed on him; but because of the Pharisees they did not confess *him*, lest they should be put out of the synagogue:

43 For they loved the praise of men more than the praise of God.

44 ¶Jesus cried and said, He that be-

24. Seeds which are not sown are alone. The seeds which are sown, die, and in so doing bring forth a harvest. Christ used this to illustrate His death, which will produce a rich spiritual harvest.

25-26. This principle of death producing life is applicable to the disciple as well as the Master (Mt 10:37-39; Mk 8:34-38). The reward for following Christ is honor with the **Father**.

27. The awful agony of approaching death grips Christ's emotions. **Save me.** This does not imply disobedience or weakness on the part of Christ. "A man may shrink from an experience which he, nevertheless, wants to undergo; e.g., an operation. So it is also with Christ" (Hendriksen, p. 200).

28. Christ's ultimate desire is to glorify His Father's **name**. The Father answers from heaven that His Name has been glorified (through the obedient ministry of His Son), and it will be glorified again (through the death, burial and resurrection of the Son).

29. The people **heard** but did not understand. They assumed that an angel had spoken to Him.

30-31. The voice was also for the people so that they would recognize Christ as God. Christ is referring to His judgment of sin through His death, and His defeat of Satan (I Cor 15:54-57).

32-33. Christ would **draw all men** (including the Greeks) to Himself through the cross (**be lifted up**). Christ would die on a cross lifted up.

34. The Jews were expecting **Christ** to reign forever. They were puzzled that He was talking about death. Their Messiah would not die.

35-36. Christ answered their question with a solemn warning that if they did not receive the Light, darkness would **come upon** them. The Light would soon be removed.

37-38. In spite of all the miracles, they **believed not on him**. This rejection of Christ had been prophesied by Isaiah. They rejected what they heard (**our report**) and what they saw (**the arm of the Lord** in powerful miracles).

39-41. Could not believe. God does not prevent people from being converted. In His judgment, as a result of man's unbelief, God sometimes hardens the heart.

42-43. Many leaders **believed on him** but were unwilling to confess Him for fear of the Pharisees.

44-45. The series of statements that conclude this chapter are

lieveth on me, believeth not on me, but on him that sent me.

45 And he that seeth me seeth him that sent me.

46 I am come a light into the world, that whosoever believeth on me should not abide in darkness.

47 And if any man hear my words, and believe not, I judge him not: for I came not to judge the world, but to save the world.

48 He that rejecteth me, and receiveth not my words, hath one that judgeth him: the word that I have spoken, the same shall judge him in the last day.

49 For I have not spoken of myself; but the Father which sent me, he gave me a commandment, what I should say, and what I should speak.

50 And I know that his commandment is life everlasting: whatsoever I speak therefore, even as the Father said unto me, so I speak.

CHAPTER 13

NOW before the feast of the passover, when Jesus knew that his hour was come that he should depart out of this world unto the Father, having loved his own which were in the world, he loved them unto the end.

2 And supper being ended, the devil having now put into the heart of Judas Iscariot, Simon's *son*, to betray him;

3 Jesus knowing that the Father had given all things into his hands, and that he was come from God, and went to God;

4 He riseth from supper, and laid aside his garments; and took a towel and girded himself.

5 After that he poureth water into a bason, and began to wash the disciples' feet, and to wipe *them* with the towel wherewith he was girded.

6 Then cometh he to Simon Peter: and Peter saith unto him, Lord, dost thou wash my feet?

7 Jesus answered and said unto him, What I do thou knowest not now; but thou shalt know hereafter.

8 Peter saith unto him, Thou shalt never wash my feet. Jesus answered him, If I wash thee not, thou hast no part with me.

9 Simon Peter saith unto him, Lord, not my feet only, but also *my* hands and *my* head.

10 Jesus saith to him, He that is washed needeth not save to wash *his* feet, but is clean every whit: and ye are clean, but not all.

11 For he knew who should betray him; therefore said he, Ye are not all clean.

12 So after he had washed their feet, and had taken his garments, and was set down again, he said unto them, Know ye what I have done to you?

13 Ye call me Master and Lord: and ye say well; for *so* I am.

14 If I then, *your* Lord and Master, have washed your feet; ye also ought to wash one another's feet.

Christ's final public messages to Israel. Knowing Christ means knowing the Father. Seeing Christ means seeing the Father.

46. See notes on 8:12.

47-48. Christ's purpose is not to judge, but to **save.** Those who rejected the words of Christ would be judged by those words in the **last day.**

49-50. The Father gave Christ to speak, and His words are **life everlasting.**

III. THE PRIVATE MINISTRY OF CHRIST. 13:1-17:26.

A. Christ as the Servant. 13:1-38.

The setting for chapters 13 through 17 is given in 12:36: **and did hide himself from them.** During this time prior to His death, Christ limits His ministry to His disciples.

1. Washing the disciples' feet. 13:1-20.

13:1. Christ's appointed time had come when He would leave this world. **He loved them unto the end** (or to the uttermost).

2-3. In the midst of this loving scene one can observe the work of Satan, for it was Satan who put the idea of betrayal into Judas' mind. To fully appreciate the Lord's humility, one must remember that **all things** had been given **into his hands.** The all-powerful One was about to wash His disciples' feet.

4-5. It was customary in Oriental homes for the servant to wash the feet of guests to remove the dust. However, Christ had requested privacy for His supper and, consequently, no servant was present. The disciples were too proud to perform this menial task; therefore, the Lord took the basin and washed the feet of His disciples.

6-7. Impulsive Peter strongly objected to this act of humility. Christ responded to Peter's question by implying that there is a deeper meaning in washing feet. One day Peter would understand that this was a graphic illustration of Christ's humility.

8-9. Peter responds. **Thou shalt never wash my feet.** Christ is thinking of His overall humiliation and death when He states that if Peter is not washed, he has **no part** with Christ. Peter is still thinking about physical washing.

10-11. A person who is **washed** (i.e., saved, Tit 3:5) does not need another bath. However, many times his feet may get dirty from the world, and he needs his feet washed (I Jn 1:7-9).

12. Christ now asks them if they have understood the meaning of what He has done.

13-14. If the **Master and Lord** is willing to humble Himself to the point of washing His disciples' feet, then the disciples should be willing to do the same thing.

15 For I have given you an example, that ye should do as I have done to you.

16 Verily, verily, I say unto you, The servant is not greater than his lord; neither he that is sent greater than he that sent him.

17 If ye know these things, happy are ye if ye do them.

18 ¶I speak not of you all: I know whom I have chosen: but that the scripture may be fulfilled, He that eateth bread with me hath lifted up his heel against me.

19 Now I tell you before it come, that, when it is come to pass, ye may believe that I am *he.*

20 Verily, verily, I say unto you, He that receiveth whomsoever I send receiveth me; and he that receiveth me receiveth him that sent me.

21 When Jesus had thus said, he was troubled in spirit, and testified, and said, Verily, verily, I say unto you, that one of you shall betray me.

22 Then the disciples looked one on another, doubting of whom he spake.

23 Now there was leaning on Jesus' bosom one of his disciples, whom Jesus loved.

24 Simon Peter therefore beckoned to him, that he should ask who it should be of whom he spake.

25 He then lying on Jesus' breast saith unto him, Lord, who is it?

26 Jesus answered, He it is, to whom I shall give a sop, when I have dipped *it.* And when he had dipped the sop, he gave *it* to Judas Iscariot, *the son* of Simon.

27 And after the sop Satan entered into him. Then said Jesus unto him, That thou doest, do quickly.

28 Now no man at the table knew for what intent he spake this unto him.

29 For some *of them* thought, because Judas had the bag, that Jesus had said unto him, Buy *those things* that we have need of against the feast; or, that he should give something to the poor.

30 He then having received the sop went immediately out: and it was night.

31 ¶Therefore, when he was gone out, Jesus said, Now is the Son of man glorified, and God is glorified in him.

32 If God be glorified in him, God shall also glorify him in himself, and shall straightway glorify him.

33 Little children, yet a little while I am with you. Ye shall seek me: and as I said unto the Jews, Whither I go, ye cannot come; so now I say to you.

34 A new commandment I give unto you, That ye love one another; as I have loved you, that ye also love one another.

35 By this shall all *men* know that ye are my disciples, if ye have love one to another.

15. Given you an example. Christ is not instituting an ordinance of footwashing, but is showing an example of humility. He does not command us to perform this act, but to acquire the attitude that this activity displays.

16-17. Blessing (**happy are ye**) is the result of practicing a life of humility and service.

18. I speak not of you all. Not all the disciples would have blessings on their lives because they were humble. One of the group who would eat with Christ would betray Him. Christ is speaking of Judas (cf. Ps 41:9).

19-20. Christ forewarned the disciples that this would take place. The disciples did not later question Christ's choice of Judas since this was all a part of God's plan. To accept Christ means to accept the Father.

2. Predicting His betrayal. 13:21-35.

21-22. The time had come to clearly state that one of the disciples would betray Him. This brought sorrow and grief to the Lord. The disciples were shocked, and in amazement they **looked** (kept on looking) **one on another.**

23-24. John, the beloved disciple, was leaning on Jesus. This was the customary way to recline at the table. Simon probably assumed that John knew the identity of this betrayer.

25-26. John asked, **who is it?** Christ did not identify the betrayer by name, but stated that He would give the **sop** (a piece of bread dipped in sauce) to the betrayer. Sop was usually given as a token of friendship. Even in betrayal, the Lord loved Judas.

27. Now the progress of Satan; 13:2 states, **the devil having now put into the heart.** Satan went a step further and took full possession of Judas.

28-29. The whole company of disciples did not understand this. Christ had addressed His statement about the sop to John and consequently, he was the only one who understood its implications.

30. It was night. Note the symbolism here. As Judas went out from the Saviour to betray Him, he was surrounded by darkness. This symbolizes the evil and sin surrounding the action of Judas.

31-32. With the exit of Judas the scene is now set for the death and ultimate glorification of Christ. God would glorify the Son through the Son's passion, and would show the close relationship between the two.

33. Little children. This is the only time this phrase is used in the Gospels.

34. Christ commands them to love, **as I have loved you.** The love Christians should display for each other must be a sacrificial love similar to the Lord's love.

35. Grasp the meaning of this verse. In a day of church schisms and divisions, the words of Christ have deep, significant meaning. The world should recognize us as followers of Christ because our relationship to each other is permeated with love.

36 ¶Simon Peter said unto him, Lord, whither goest thou? Jesus answered him, Whither I go, thou canst not follow me now; but thou shalt follow me afterwards.

37 Peter said unto him, Lord, why cannot I follow thee now? I will lay down my life for thy sake.

38 Jesus answered him, Wilt thou lay down thy life for my sake? Verily, verily, I say unto thee, The cock shall not crow, till thou hast denied me thrice.

CHAPTER 14

LET not your heart be troubled: ye believe in God, believe also in me.

2 In my Father's house are many mansions: if *it were* not *so,* I would have told you. I go to prepare a place for you.

3 And if I go and prepare a place for you, I will come again, and receive you unto myself; that where I am, *there* ye may be also.

4 And whither I go ye know, and the way ye know.

5 ¶Thomas saith unto him, Lord, we know not whither thou goest; and how can we know the way?

6 Jesus saith unto him, I am the way, the truth, and the life: no man cometh unto the Father, but by me.

7 If ye had known me, ye should have known my Father also: and from henceforth ye know him, and have seen him.

8 ¶Philip saith unto him, Lord, shew us the Father, and it sufficeth us.

9 Jesus saith unto him, Have I been so long time with you, and yet hast thou not known me, Philip? he that hath seen me hath seen the Father; and how sayest thou *then,* Shew us the Father?

10 Believest thou not that I am in the Father, and the Father in me? the words that I speak unto you I speak not of myself: but the Father that dwelleth in me, he doeth the works.

11 Believe me that I *am* in the Father, and the Father in me: or else believe me for the very works' sake.

12 Verily, verily, I say unto you, He that believeth on me, the works that I do shall he do also; and greater *works* than these shall he do; because I go unto my Father.

13 And whatsoever ye shall ask in my name, that will I do, that the Father may be glorified in the Son.

3. Predicting Peter's denial. 13:36-38.

36-38. Peter is still a little confused. Christ tells him that he will follow **afterwards.** Peter's time of death had not yet come (Heb 9:27). Note Peter's impulsiveness. He wants to be with Christ now. Christ predicted the exact opposite of Peter's claims. Peter said he would die, but Christ died. Peter would deny his Master.

B. Christ as the Comforter. 14:1-31.

There is a close connection between the events of chapter 13 and the promises of chapter 14. In chapter 13 the disciples had been rebuked for their lack of humility. They were instructed that Christ would soon leave them. They were told that one of their number would betray his Master, and Peter had been rebuked. To offset the depression produced by this startling revelation, Christ brought a message of hope and encouragement.

14:1. Let not your heart be troubled. This is the foundational statement of the entire chapter. To settle the emotions of the disciples, Christ lists the reasons why their hearts should not be **troubled** (Gr *trassō,* stir up, disturb, throw into confusion). **Believe.** Both times this Greek verb (*pisteliō*) can be interpreted as imperative. Christ stirs both their faith in God and their faith in Him. This settles a troubled heart.

2. The disciples should be comforted with the fact that Christ is going to **prepare** an abode for them in heaven (**my Father's house**).

3-4. I will come again. This is the promise that brings hope to troubled hearts. The emphasis of His coming is not on the dwelling places but on the prospect of being with the Saviour (Gr *pros;* lit., face to face). The **way** to heaven is through Christ Himself.

5. Overwhelmed with grief at the prospect of Christ's leaving, Thomas does not understand the meaning of Christ's statement. Thomas objects that since he does not know where Christ is going, how could he possibly know the **way** to get there?

6. Christ answers with another **I am** statement. **The way.** Christ is the only **way** to heaven (10:9). **The truth.** Christ is the embodiment of all truth (8:32). **Life** (1:4; 3:16). No man can approach the Father unless he does so through Christ.

7. From henceforth ye know him. To know Christ is to know the Father. The disciples knew Christ; therefore, they knew the Father.

8. Philip asks for a theophany (manifestation of God's glory) similar to Moses' (Ex 33:18-23).

9. So long time with you. Christ had stated this truth about seeing the Father through the Son throughout His ministry (1:18; 10:30).

10. The **words** and **works** of Christ surely must indicate a unique relationship between the Father and the Son.

11. The disciples were weak in their faith. Christ exhorts them to **Believe** what He has said, or simply to believe on the basis of His **works.**

12. What a promise this is. **Greater works.** The works of Christ were limited to a small geographical area and to a specific people. The disciples' works would be worldwide in their reach and would affect all people. In this way, they were **greater.** Christ's going away would cause Him to send the Holy Spirit.

13-14. Note the relationship of works to prayer (Acts 1:14; 2:42; 3:1; 4:31). Effective prayer is **in my name.** This is prayer in agreement with the desires of Christ. The result of prayer is the glorification of the Father, not self-glorification.

14 If ye shall ask any thing in my name, I will do *it.*

15 ¶If ye love me, keep my commandments.

16 And I will pray the Father, and he shall give you another Comforter, that he may abide with you for ever;

17 *Even* the Spirit of truth; whom the world cannot receive, because it seeth him not, neither knoweth him: but ye know him; for he dwelleth with you, and shall be in you.

18 I will not leave you comfortless: I will come to you.

19 Yet a little while, and the world seeth me no more; but ye see me: because I live, ye shall live also.

20 At that day ye shall know that I *am* in my Father, and ye in me, and I in you.

21 He that hath my commandments, and keepeth them, he it is that loveth me: and he that loveth me shall be loved of my Father, and I will love him, and will manifest myself to him.

22 Judas saith unto him, not Iscariot, Lord, how is it that thou wilt manifest thyself unto us, and not unto the world?

23 Jesus answered and said unto him, If a man love me, he will keep my words: and my Father will love him, and we will come unto him, and make our abode with him.

24 He that loveth me not keepeth not my sayings: and the word which ye hear is not mine, but the Father's which sent me.

25 These things have I spoken unto you, being *yet* present with you.

26 But the Comforter, *which is* the Holy Ghost, whom the Father will send in my name, he shall teach you all things, and bring all things to your remembrance, whatsoever I have said unto you.

27 Peace I leave with you, my peace I give unto you: not as the world giveth, give I unto you. Let not your heart be troubled, neither let it be afraid.

28 Ye have heard how I said unto you, I go away, and come *again* unto you. If ye loved me, ye would rejoice, because I said, I go unto the Father: for my Father is greater than I.

29 And now I have told you before it come to pass, that, when it is come to pass, ye might believe.

30 Hereafter I will not talk much with you: for the prince of this world cometh, and hath nothing in me.

31 But that the world may know that I love the Father; and as the Father

15. Love is not sentimental emotionalism; it is obedience to the commandments of God.

16. **Comforter** (Gr *paraklētos,* one called alongside to help). Christ would **pray the Father,** and they would receive a Helper. **Another** (Gr *allos,* another of the same kind). This would indicate that the Comforter would be of the same quality and character as Christ. The Comforter would be God. **For ever.** Christ would go away (14:2), but the Helper would remain **for ever.**

17. **Spirit of truth.** The Helper is the Holy Spirit (16:13). The world cannot **receive** the Spirit. This Spirit would have a twofold ministry. He would dwell with them (be in their midst), and He would **be in** them (dwell within).

18. **Comfortless** (Gr *orphanos,* lit., I will not leave you as orphans). **I will come.** Christ would be with them through the ministry of the Holy Spirit.

19. Very soon the world that hated Him would no longer be able to **see** Him. The disciples would **see** Him. They would see Him because they were spiritually alive, and the Holy Spirit would glorify Christ to them (16:14).

20. **At that day.** In the day of the dispensation of the Holy Spirit they would recognize the relationship between the Father and the Son and themselves: Christ in the Father, the disciples in Christ, and Christ in the disciples.

21. True love is demonstrated by obedience to the Lord's **commandments.** This love and obedience to Christ will cause the Father to love them. Christ too will love those who obey, and will reveal Himself to them through the Spirit and the Word.

22. Judas is thinking of Christ's revealing Himself to the world as the Messiah and cannot understand this limited revelation.

23-24. The answer of Christ is based on obedience. The Father and the Son will **come** only to those who love and prove their love by obedience. **Abode.** Through the Spirit, both the Father and the Son will make their home in the believer. Disobedience to the Word of Christ is also rejection of the Father's Word.

25-26. Christ had spoken **These things** while He was with the disciples, but the Holy Ghost would **teach** them **all things.** The Spirit would also cause them to remember the things that Christ had told them. The ultimate fulfillment of this promise is the completion of the canon of the New Testament.

27. **Peace.** In the hour of sorrow for the disciples, Christ promised a unique kind of **peace** that is different from the world's peace: **My peace.** This peace would calm troubled and fearful hearts.

28-29. True love would cause the disciples to **rejoice** because Christ was going away. This departure would bring glory to Christ and would enable the Holy Spirit to come. Christ foretold these events so that when they happened they would increase the faith of the disciples.

30. Christ would not continue to teach them. **The prince of this world cometh.** Satan, through the behavior of Judas, was coming. **Hath nothing in me.** Christ is the sinless Son of God, and Satan had no part in Him.

31. Christ will not resist those who come to kill Him. In obedience to the Father's commandment, He is ready and willing to die. **Arise, let us go hence.** The hour for which Jesus

gave me commandment, even so I do. Arise, let us go hence.

3 Now ye are clean through the word which I have spoken unto you.

came had arrived. He must now go to the cross, and He is ready. He voluntarily goes forward to meet His death.

C. Christ as the True Vine. 15:1-16:33.

Although there is a difference of opinion among commentators over the meaning of all that is discussed in this chapter, there is one basic truth upon which all agree. The basic truth of this chapter is that just as the branch cannot bear fruit unless it abides in the vine, Christians cannot bear fruit unless they have an abiding relationship with the True Vine, Jesus Christ.

CHAPTER 15

I AM the true vine, and my Father is the husbandman.

2 Every branch in me that beareth not fruit he taketh away: and every *branch* that beareth fruit, he purgeth it, that it may bring forth more fruit.

1. Christ and the disciples. 15:1-17.

15:1. **The true vine.** In the Old Testament, Israel is referred to as a vine. However, in this verse, we find the True or Real Vine is Christ Himself. The **husbandman.** The Father is the **husbandman,** or the One who owns the vineyard and who takes care of it.

2. **He taketh away.** Just as the husbandman disposes of branches that bear no fruit, so the Father judges those who bear no spiritual fruit. **He purgeth it.** The **husbandman** prunes (Gr *kathaireō*) the branches which bear fruit in order for them to bear **more fruit.** In like manner, God the Father cleanses Christians who are bearing fruit to bring them to bear more fruit. Fruit is the natural product of a living organism. Spiritual fruit is a spiritual product of a spiritual union (Gal 5:22-23).

3. Cleansing is produced through the Word of God.

4 Abide in me, and I in you. As the branch cannot bear fruit of itself, except it abide in the vine; no more can ye, except ye abide in me.

5 I am the vine, ye *are* the branches: He that abideth in me, and I in him, the same bringeth forth much fruit: for without me ye can do nothing.

4. **Abide in me.** In order to be a fruitful Christian, one must learn to depend on Christ and let the power and Spirit of Christ flow through him.

5. Christ now clearly states the implications of this story. He is the **vine** and we are the **branches.** Note the total dependence upon the Vine. Without that abiding relationship **ye can do nothing.** In verse 2 it refers to **more fruit,** and in verses 5 and 8 it refers to **much fruit.**

6 If a man abide not in me, he is cast forth as a branch, and is withered; and men gather them, and cast *them* into the fire, and they are burned.

6. This does not refer to everlasting punishment in hell. Note that there are results of not abiding in Christ as a branch. The man himself is not the branch; the branch represents the fruits of his relationship with Christ. When the Christian fails to abide in Christ, he withers, dries up, and his fruit or works will be judged by fire (I Cor 3:12-15).

7 If ye abide in me, and my words abide in you, ye shall ask what ye will, and it shall be done unto you.

8 Herein is my Father glorified, that ye bear much fruit; so shall ye be my disciples.

7-8. Those who abide in Christ, and who permit His **words** to abide in them, have a blessed promise that Christ will perform whatever they ask. This is a blessed promise of the **Father.**

9 As the Father hath loved me, so have I loved you: continue ye in my love.

10 If ye keep my commandments, ye shall abide in my love; even as I have kept my Father's commandments, and abide in his love.

11 These things have I spoken unto you, that my joy might remain in you, and *that* your joy might be full.

12 This is my commandment, That ye love one another, as I have loved you.

9-10. In the center of this unique abiding relationship is the love of God. Christ exhorts His disciples to continue in **my love.** It is interesting to note that this is the first fruit of the Spirit mentioned in Galatians 5:22. Christ remained in the Father's love because He obeyed Him. We remain in Christ's love because we obey His commandments (14:21, 23-24).

11. The second fruit of the Spirit is joy. The abiding relationship also gives us Christ's joy. Christ promises them fruit, answered prayer, love, and joy as the result of abiding in Him.

12. This is the second commandment found in chapter 15. The first is **abide in me** (vs. 7), and now Christ commands them to **love one another.** He defines the extent of that love in the phrase, **as I have loved you.**

13 Greater love hath no man than this, that a man lay down his life for his friends.

14 Ye are my friends, if ye do whatsoever I command you.

15 Henceforth I call you not servants;

13-14. Love is giving sacrificially for others. Love is not an emotional feeling, but it is the act of giving (3:16). To be a friend of Christ means to obey Him.

15. Because of their obedience, Christ could now call them

Whatsoever ye shall ask the Father in my name, he will give *it* you.

24 Hitherto have ye asked nothing in my name: ask, and ye shall receive, that your joy may be full.

25 These things have I spoken unto you in proverbs: but the time cometh, when I shall no more speak unto you in proverbs, but I shall shew you plainly of the Father.

26 At that day ye shall ask in my name: and I say not unto you, that I will pray the Father for you:

27 For the Father himself loveth you, because ye have loved me, and have believed that I came out from God.

28 I came forth from the Father, and am come into the world: again, I leave the world, and go to the Father.

29 ¶His disciples said unto him, Lo, now speakest thou plainly, and speakest no proverb.

30 Now are we sure that thou knowest all things, and needest not that any man should ask thee: by this we believe that thou camest forth from God.

31 Jesus answered them, Do ye now believe?

32 Behold, the hour cometh, yea, is now come, that ye shall be scattered, every man to his own, and shall leave me alone: and yet I am not alone, because the Father is with me.

33 These things I have spoken unto you, that in me ye might have peace. In the world ye shall have tribulation: but be of good cheer; I have overcome the world.

CHAPTER 17

THESE words spake Jesus, and lifted up his eyes to heaven, and said, Father, the hour is come; glorify thy Son, that thy Son also may glorify thee:

2 As thou hast given him power over all flesh, that he should give eternal life to as many as thou hast given him.

3 And this is life eternal, that they might know thee the only true God, and Jesus Christ, whom thou hast sent.

4 I have glorified thee on the earth: I have finished the work which thou gavest me to do.

5 And now, O Father, glorify thou me with thine own self with the glory which I had with thee before the world was.

6 I have manifested thy name unto the men which thou gavest me out of the world: thine they were, and thou gavest them me; and they have kept thy word.

requested the Father in Christ's **name, he will give it you.** Since Christ has returned to the Father, the prayers of Christians must be made to the Father in the name of the Son.

24. Until then, prayer had been made directly to God. Now they were to pray in the merits of the finished work of Christ. Note the order: **ask, . . . receive, . . . joy may be full.**

25. Proverbs (Gr *paromoids*, veiled sayings). Christ had not spoken openly because the disciples would not understand. However, when the Spirit came, Christ would reveal the Father **plainly.** This occurred through the inspiration and writing of the epistles.

26-27. Prayer made in Christ's name was not so that Christ could somehow convince the Father to answer the prayers. The Father will answer prayer because of His love for the disciples.

28. Here is the entire purpose of Christ. His eternity, His humiliation, and His exaltation are all implied in this verse.

29-30. The disciples now realize that Christ is speaking to them openly. They realize that Christ knows all things, and would reveal them without the disciples asking questions. Their conclusion is faith, that Christ came **forth from God.**

31-32. Thrilled with these revelations, the disciples are quickly reminded that soon they would scatter at the arrest of their Master. Christ would be **alone,** and yet in that hour the **Father is with me.**

33. Note the origin of **in me . . . peace.** They had peace in Christ, but in the **world** they would have **tribulation. Be of good cheer** (be courageous). Even though they would be opposed by the world, they should remember that Christ had overcome the world.

D. Christ as the Intercessor. 17:1-26.

This chapter contains the prayer of Christ for His disciples. In many aspects, it is a model prayer for all Christians.

17:1. Lifted up his eyes to heaven. This was a common practice when one prayed, since He was addressing Himself to God. **Father.** Christ uses this term six times in His prayer. **The hour.** The moment of crisis had come when Christ would consummate His earthly ministry. **Glorify thy Son.** The hour that Christ referred to was not only the hour of death, but also His resurrection and exaltation.

2-3. Christ had been given **power** (authority) **over all flesh** (all mankind). This authority extended to the giving of **eternal life. As many as thou hast given.** This refers specifically to the disciples and generally to those of **all flesh** whom God has given to Christ. Eternal life results in a true knowledge of both God and Jesus Christ.

4. I have glorified thee. Christ has brought glory to the Father by fulfilling His will and completing His task (4:34; 6:38). Note that Christ views His death as having been completed. He is so certain and sure of His atonement that He can speak as if it had already been completed.

5. Christ again asks the Father to glorify Him. He desires that glory which He had in eternity past, but which He voluntarily laid aside to redeem mankind (1:1-3, 14).

6. Christ made known (**manifested**) the Father's name to those who followed Him. These disciples had been given to Christ by the Father. Note the results of Christ's revelation of the Father: **they have kept thy word.** An evidence of true conversion is obedience to the Word of God.

7 Now they have known that all things whatsoever thou hast given me are of thee.

8 For I have given unto them the words which thou gavest me; and they have received *them*, and have known surely that I came out from thee, and they have believed that thou didst send me.

9 I pray for them: I pray not for the world, but for them which thou hast given me; for they are thine.

10 And all mine are thine, and thine are mine; and I am glorified in them.

11 And now I am no more in the world, but these are in the world, and I come to thee. Holy Father, keep through thine own name those whom thou hast given me, that they may be one, as we *are*.

12 While I was with them in the world, I kept them in thy name: those that thou gavest me I have kept, and none of them is lost, but the son of perdition; that the scripture might be fulfilled.

13 And now come I to thee; and these things I speak in the world, that they might have my joy fulfilled in themselves.

14 I have given them thy word; and the world hath hated them, because they are not of the world, even as I am not of the world.

15 I pray not that thou shouldest take them out of the world, but that thou shouldest keep them from the evil.

16 They are not of the world, even as I am not of the world.

17 Sanctify them through thy truth: thy word is truth.

18 As thou hast sent me into the world, even so have I also sent them into the world.

19 And for their sakes I sanctify myself, that they also might be sanctified through the truth.

20 Neither pray I for these alone, but for them also which shall believe on me through their word;

21 That they all may be one; as thou, Father, *art* in me, and I in thee, that they also may be one in us: that the world may believe that thou hast sent me.

22 And the glory which thou gavest me I have given them; that they may be one, even as we are one:

23 I in them, and thou in me, that they may be made perfect in one; and that

7-8. The disciples had come to understand that **all things** (the message and the mission of Christ) which Christ had were ultimately from the Father. Christ was faithful in giving the Father's **words** to the disciples. The disciples accepted the message, and obtained a twofold knowledge: they understood that Christ had come from God, and that God had sent Him.

9. I pray for them. Christ's concern was for His own (Rom 8:34; Heb 7:25). **I pray not for the world.** This does not mean that Christ is unconcerned about the unsaved (Lk 23:34). However, His prayer for sanctification, glorification, and protection is only applicable to those who belong to Him.

10. Christ is praying to the Father in behalf of the disciples, and is confident that His prayers will be answered, since the disciples belong to the Father as well as the Son.

11. Note that Christ is again speaking as if His death had already occurred (17:4). **Keep** (Gr *tēreō*, keep watch over, guard, or preserve). Christ prays for the Father to stand guard over the disciples in the wicked world. **That they may be as one.** This does not mean that Christ wants all denominations to be as one; He is praying that the disciples would be united in their stand against the wickedness of the world.

12. Christ states that during His earthly ministry, He guarded the disciples. None of them perished (compromised with the wicked world). **The son of perdition.** The word **perdition** means the lost one. Note the synthesis of human responsibility and God's purpose. Judas was lost by his own volition, but his behavior was a fulfillment of divine prophecy (Ps 41:9).

13-14. Christ was about to leave the earth, and He was conscious of the void that He would leave with His disciples. He requests that His **joy** would fill them. It was the disciples' acceptance of Christ's **word** that caused the world to hate them.

15. Christ did not want the disciples taken out of the world because He would fulfill His purpose in their lives while they were in the world. He wanted them to be delivered from the evil one (Satan himself, Mt 6:13; I Pet 5:8).

16. The disciples did not belong to the world, they belonged to Christ (17:9-10).

17-18. Sanctify (Gr *hagiazō*, make holy, consecrate, dedicate, purify, set apart). This is the positive aspect of being delivered from the world. This process of becoming holy could only be accomplished through the Word of God. The disciples had been commissioned to go into the world.

19. I sanctify myself. Christ does not state that He is in the process of becoming holy; He is referring to His self-sacrifice and total commitment. It is His example that should stir His followers to that same type of surrender.

20. Beginning in this verse and continuing through the remainder of the prayer, Christ now prays for His entire church. The first part of the prayer was for the disciples; this part includes believers today. He prays for everyone who will **believe** on Him.

21. May be one (see notes on 17:11).

22. The Father had manifested Himself through the Son, and now the Son manifests Himself through His followers. This is **glory**.

23. Made perfect. The idea here is that of completeness, not

the world may know that thou hast sent me, and hast loved them, as thou hast loved me.

24 Father, I will that they also, whom thou hast given me, be with me where I am; that they may behold my glory, which thou hast given me: for thou lovedst me before the foundation of the world.

25 O righteous Father, the world hath not known thee: but I have known thee, and these have known that thou hast sent me.

26 And I have declared unto them thy name, and will declare it: that the love wherewith thou hast loved me may be in them, and I in them.

CHAPTER 18

WHEN Jesus had spoken these words, he went forth with his disciples over the brook Cĕ'dron, where was a garden, into the which he entered, and his disciples.

2 And Judas also, which betrayed him, knew the place: for Jesus ofttimes resorted thither with his disciples.

3 Judas then, having received a band of men and officers from the chief priests and Pharisees, cometh thither with lanterns and torches and weapons.

4 Jesus therefore, knowing all things that should come upon him, went forth, and said unto them, Whom seek ye?

5 They answered him, Jesus of Nazareth. Jesus saith unto them, I am he. And Judas also, which betrayed him, stood with them.

6 As soon then as he had said unto them, I am he, they went backward, and fell to the ground.

7 Then asked he them again, Whom seek ye? And they said, Jesus of Nazareth.

8 Jesus answered, I have told you that I am he: if therefore ye seek me, let these go their way:

9 That the saying might be fulfilled, which he spake, Of them which thou gavest me have I lost none.

10 Then Simon Peter having a sword drew it, and smote the high priest's servant, and cut off his right ear. The servant's name was Măl'chus.

11 Then said Jesus unto Peter, Put up thy sword into the sheath: the cup which my Father hath given me, shall I not drink it?

12 Then the band and the captain and officers of the Jews took Jesus, and bound him,

13 And led him away to Ăn'nas first; for he was father in law to Cā'ia-phas, which was the high priest that same year.

14 Now Cā'ia-phas was he, which gave counsel to the Jews, that it was expedient that one man should die for the people.

15 ¶And Simon Peter followed Jesus, and so did another disciple: that dis-

sinless perfection. The ultimate result of that unity will be that the world will see God's love revealed through the believers.

24. This is Christ's final request. He desires that all who believe on Him would see His **glory** (Rev 1:12-18).

25-26. Righteous Father. Because the Father is righteous, He will fulfill all that the Son has requested for His followers. To **declare** God's name is to declare God's love, for God is love.

In this prayer, Christ prays for Himself (vss. 1-5); for His disciples (vss. 6-19); and for His entire church (vss. 20-26).

IV. THE PASSION MINISTRY OF CHRIST. 18:1-21:25.

A. Christ and the Crucifixion. 18:1-19:42.

1. His arrest. 18:1-11.

18:1. After the prayer of chapter 17, Jesus takes His eleven disciples to a **garden** (Gethsemane). The **brook** mentioned refers to a stream that flows only during the winter season.

2-3. Ofttimes. Frequently Christ had taken His disciples to this place of seclusion. Judas came to the garden with a large crowd. **Band** (Gr *speira*) refers to a Roman cohort of six hundred soldiers. John, however, is using the term in its more general sense of " a detachment." Note the paradox: they came with **torches** to take the Light of the world, and they came with weapons to arrest the Prince of Peace.

4. Christ was completely aware of Judas' plan. **Went forth.** Probably Christ went from the garden to meet the crowd as they approached the gate. It was at this point that Judas kissed the Master (Mt 26:49).

5. Jesus of Nazareth. This was the name that appeared on the official arrest warrant issued by the Sanhedrin and the Roman government. **I am.** Again, Jesus states His deity (8:58).

6. The crowd was caught off guard by the unusual behavior of Christ. He calmly faced the crowd, identified Himself, and made no effort to escape.

7-8. Again He asked the crowd whom they sought. He requested that the disciples be left alone. In the moment of personal crisis, the Shepherd's concern was not for Himself, but for His sheep.

9. The Scripture mentioned deals with spiritual preservation rather than physical protection. Perhaps the disciples had already been arrested, and Christ knew that "it would have been too severe a test for their faith" (Hendriksen, p. 380).

10-11. Impulsive Peter proceeded to cut off a slave's ear with his **sword** (Gr *machaira*, denotes any long knife). Christ rebuked him by stating that He will drink of the **cup** which the **Father hath given me.** This **cup** refers to the suffering and agony of the cross.

2. His trials. 18:12-19:16.

12. The cohort and the temple guard take Jesus (arrest Him). They **bound** the One who had come to set them free (8:36).

13-14. They took Him to Annas. Although he was not at this time the high priest, nevertheless Annas had a great influence over the Sanhedrin. Christ was taken there for a preliminary examination. Annas would then give his advice to Caiaphas. Caiaphas had already drawn a conclusion regarding Christ's destiny.

15-16. Another disciple. This probably refers to John.

ciple was known unto the high priest, and went in with Jesus into the palace of the high priest.

16 But Peter stood at the door without. Then went out that other disciple, which was known unto the high priest, and spake unto her that kept the door, and brought in Peter.

17 Then saith the damsel that kept the door unto Peter, Art not thou also *one* of this man's disciples? He saith, I am not.

18 And the servants and officers stood there, who had made a fire of coals; for it was cold: and they warmed themselves: and Peter stood with them, and warmed himself.

19 ¶The high priest then asked Jesus of his disciples, and of his doctrine.

20 Jesus answered him, I spake openly to the world; I ever taught in the synagogue, and in the temple, whither the Jews always resort; and in secret have I said nothing.

21 Why askest thou me? ask them which heard me, what I have said unto them: behold, they know what I said.

22 And when he had thus spoken, one of the officers which stood by struck Jesus with the palm of his hand, saying, Answerest thou the high priest so?

23 Jesus answered him, If I have spoken evil, bear witness of the evil: but if well, why smitest thou me?

24 Now Ăn'nas had sent him bound unto Cā'ia-phas the high priest.

25 ¶And Simon Peter stood and warmed himself. They said therefore unto him, Art not thou also *one* of his disciples? He denied *it*, and said, I am not.

26 One of the servants of the high priest, being *his* kinsman whose ear Peter cut off, saith, Did not I see thee in the garden with him?

27 Peter then denied again: and immediately the cock crew.

28 ¶Then led they Jesus from Cā'ia-phas unto the hall of judgment: and it was early; and they themselves went not into the judgment hall, lest they should be defiled; but that they might eat the passover.

29 Pilate then went out unto them, and said, What accusation bring ye against this man?

30 They answered and said unto him, If he were not a malefactor, we would not have delivered him up unto thee.

31 Then said Pilate unto them, Take ye him, and judge him according to your law. The Jews therefore said unto him, It is not lawful for us to put any man to death:

32 That the saying of Jesus might be fulfilled, which he spake, signifying what death he should die.

33 Then Pilate entered into the judgment hall again, and called Jesus, and said unto him, Art thou the King of the Jews?

Palace. Here was the courtyard located in the center of the building. Peter could not enter the courtyard. John talked to the woman who controlled the entrance, and Peter was finally admitted.

17-18. John records only one of Peter's three denials. He was aware, however, that three were predicted by Christ (13:36-38). Here is a picture of a defeated man who had denied the Lord. He was warming himself by the fires of those who had arrested his Master.

19. The high priest. This refers to Annas (cf. 18:13). This was not a true trial since the Sanhedrin had not been assembled. The purpose of this inquisition was probably to gather evidence. Annas was interested in Christ's **disciples** and His **doctrine.** He was interested in the number of followers that Christ had gained.

20-21. Openly. Christ does not answer the question directly. He appeals to the fact that He taught His doctrine **openly. Why askest thou me?** Christ refused to be a witness for Himself. He asked Annas instead to produce witnesses who could testify about His teaching. Failure to produce reliable witnesses (those who **heard me**) would make the trial illegal.

22-24. One of the **officers** hit Christ in order to make Him answer the high priest. Again Christ appealed to them to produce witnesses who could testify that He had done **evil.** If they could not, then the behavior of the officer and the arrest itself were wrong. Annas could not answer the Lord, and he sent Him to Caiaphas.

25-27. Prior to describing the trial before Caiaphas, John interjects Peter's last two denials of the Lord. The crowd around the fire asks Peter if he is one of Christ's disciples, and he denies it. Then one of the relatives of Malchus states that he saw Peter in the **garden.** Again, he denies the Lord. **Immediately the cock crew.** This refers to "the third of four watches into which the night was divided" (*Wycliff Bible Commentary*, p. 363).

28. The trial before Caiaphas is not mentioned in John's narrative (Mt 26:57-68). **Hall of judgment.** They took Him to the governor's place of residence. Note that the Jews did not enter their gentile quarters. They were more interested in ceremonial purity than justice.

29-30. Pilate asks for the formal **accusation** that they were bringing **against** Christ. This was a logical question. The Jews had not prepared a formal indictment. They wanted Pilate to accept the fact that they would not bring a person to him if he were not a **malefactor** (evildoer).

31. Pilate, unaware that the Jews want to kill Christ, tells them to judge the case and pass sentence **according to your law.** The Jews could not legally execute anyone. They wanted Pilate to pass the death sentence on Christ.

32. The Jews used the method of stoning to execute criminals. If Pilate were to authorize death, it would mean crucifixion. This Roman method of execution had been predicted by Christ (Mt 20:17-19).

33. John does not describe all the details of the trial. It is assumed that the reader knows from the other gospels that a charge has been brought against Christ because He claimed to be the King of Israel. Pilate now questions Christ about this accusa-

34 Jesus answered him, Sayest thou this thing of thyself, or did others tell it thee of me?

35 Pilate answered, Am I a Jew? Thine own nation and the chief priests have delivered thee unto me: what hast thou done?

36 Jesus answered, My kingdom is not of this world: if my kingdom were of this world, then would my servants fight, that I should not be delivered to the Jews: but now is my kingdom not from hence.

37 Pilate therefore said unto him, Art thou a king then? Jesus answered, Thou sayest that I am a king. To this end was I born, and for this cause came I into the world, that I should bear witness unto the truth. Every one that is of the truth heareth my voice.

38 Pilate saith unto him, What is truth? And when he had said this, he went out again unto the Jews, and saith unto them, I find in him no fault at all.

39 But ye have a custom, that I should release unto you one at the passover: will ye therefore that I release unto you the King of the Jews?

40 Then cried they all again, saying, Not this man, but Ba-răb'bas. Now Ba-răb'bas was a robber.

CHAPTER 19

THEN Pilate therefore took Jesus, and scourged him.

2 And the soldiers platted a crown of thorns, and put it on his head, and they put on him a purple robe,

3 And said, Hail, King of the Jews! and they smote him with their hands.

4 Pilate therefore went forth again, and saith unto them, Behold, I bring him forth to you, that ye may know that I find no fault in him.

5 Then came Jesus forth, wearing the crown of thorns, and the purple robe. And Pilate saith unto them, Behold the man!

6 When the chief priests therefore and officers saw him, they cried out, saying, Crucify him, crucify him. Pilate saith unto them, Take ye him, and crucify him: for I find no fault in him.

7 The Jews answered him, We have a law, and by our law he ought to die, because he made himself the Son of God.

8 ¶When Pilate therefore heard that saying, he was the more afraid;

9 And went again into the judgment hall, and saith unto Jesus, Whence art thou? But Jesus gave him no answer.

tion. He may have asked this question with irony. It was ridiculous that this seemingly helpless prisoner would think Himself to be the King.

34-35. Christ desired to know whether Pilate was asking this question for the Jews or for himself. The Jews were looking for a political king and He was not at that moment their king. Pilate dismissed any prior conversation with the Jews. He simply wanted to know, what hast thou done?

36. Christ then explains the nature of His kingdom. He has no political motives in mind. His kingdom is a spiritual one which is not expanded or defended by military force.

37. Pilate wants to know if Christ is really a king. He was still confused about Christ's concept of a king and a kingdom. Pilate assumed Christ to be a political king. To this end. The purpose for which Christ was born of royal inheritance (as King of kings) was to bring truth to mankind. Those who are born again of that truth hear His voice (10:4).

38. Still confused about the spiritual purposes of Christ, Pilate asks the question, What is truth? The answer was standing before him (14:6). Satisfied that Christ is not a political threat to the Roman authorities, Pilate declares Christ to be innocent.

39-40. Pilate, although declaring the innocence of Christ, was fearful of the angry Jewish leaders. Since it was customary to release a prisoner at the Passover, Pilate attempted to place the responsibility of Christ's destiny in the hands of the Jews. It must be remembered, however, that each man is personally responsible for his relationship and actions to Christ. Pilate probably assumed that the majority would want Christ released since He was a popular person. Instead, the crowd asked for a robber (Mt 27:19-21).

19:1. Pilate orders Jesus to be scourged, hoping that the Jews would accept this rather than execution. The scourge was made of thongs to which were attached sharp pieces of metal and pieces of bone. The prisoners were beaten across the back, having the flesh and sometimes the organs torn. Many prisoners died from this cruel punishment.

2-3. The soldiers mock and torture Christ by their actions. They force a crown of thorns on His head, causing blood to flow down His face. They hit Him and dress Him like a king.

4-5. Pilate presents Christ dressed in a purple robe, with a crown and a reed. The robe is drenched with blood from the gaping wounds received from the scourging. Behold the man. Pilate clearly states that Christ is no king. He is simply a man. It is interesting to note that Pilate declares Christ innocent, yet subjects Him to a terrible beating.

6. Rather than being appeased, the angry multitude chants, Crucify, . . . Crucify . . . Frustrated, Pilate tells them that if Christ is to be crucified, they will have to do it. No fault. This is the third time that Pilate declares the innocence of Christ.

7. According to Roman law, Christ was innocent. The Jews now appeal to their law. Christ had claimed to be God, and by Jewish law, He should die (Lev 24:16).

8-9. When Pilate hears that Christ claimed to be the Son of God, he is more afraid. Superstitious Pilate had already been warned by his wife about Christ (Mt 27:19) and now he realizes that he may be dealing with the Son of God. Pilate immediately attempts to discover the origin of this person standing before him. An answer would be useless, since Pilate was spiritually blind.

10 Then saith Pilate unto him, Speakest thou not unto me? knowest thou not that I have power to crucify thee, and have power to release thee?

11 Jesus answered, Thou couldest have no power *at all* against me, except it were given thee from above: therefore he that delivered me unto thee hath the greater sin.

12 And from thenceforth Pilate sought to release him: but the Jews cried out, saying, If thou let this man go, thou art not Cæsar's friend: whosoever maketh himself a king speaketh against Cæsar.

13 ¶When Pilate therefore heard that saying, he brought Jesus forth, and sat down in the judgment seat in a place that is called the Pavement, but in the Hebrew, Găb'ba-tha.

14 And it was the preparation of the passover, and about the sixth hour: and he saith unto the Jews, Behold your King!

15 But they cried out, Away with *him,* away with *him,* crucify him. Pilate saith unto them, Shall I crucify your King? The chief priests answered, We have no king but Cæsar.

16 Then delivered he him therefore unto them to be crucified. And they took Jesus, and led *him* away.

17 And he bearing his cross went forth into a place called *the place* of a skull, which is called in the Hebrew Gŏl'go-tha:

18 Where they crucified him, and two other with him, on either side one, and Jesus in the midst.

19 ¶And Pilate wrote a title, and put *it* on the cross. And the writing was, JESUS OF NAZARETH THE KING OF THE JEWS.

20 This title then read many of the Jews: for the place where Jesus was crucified was nigh to the city: and it was written in Hebrew, *and* Greek, *and* Latin.

21 Then said the chief priests of the Jews to Pilate, Write not, The King of the Jews; but that he said, I am King of the Jews.

22 Pilate answered, What I have written I have written.

23 ¶Then the soldiers, when they had crucified Jesus, took his garments, and made four parts, to every soldier a part; and also *his* coat: now the coat was without seam, woven from the top throughout.

24 They said therefore among themselves, Let us not rend it, but cast lots for it, whose it shall be: that the scripture might be fulfilled, which saith, They parted my raiment among them, and for my vesture they did cast lots. These things therefore the soldiers did.

25 ¶Now there stood by the cross of Jesus his mother, and his mother's sister, Mary the *wife* of Clē'o-phas, and Mary Magdalene.

26 When Jesus therefore saw his mother, and the disciple standing by,

10-11. Fearful and confused, Pilate attempts to hide his weaknesses by the statement, **I have power.** Christ reminds him that the only authority he has is that which has been given to him by a higher source. **Greater sin.** Although Pilate was responsible for his actions to Christ, Caiaphas, who had planned the entire plot to kill Christ, had committed a greater sin and would be more accountable to God.

12. Fearful of Christ, and knowing that He was innocent, Pilate again attempted to release Him. The Jews made their final argument, **thou art not Caesar's friend.** If the Jews contacted Caesar, and explained that Pilate released a king who threatened Roman authority, Pilate would be guilty of treason against Rome.

13-14. Pilate was ready to make his decision. (For a discussion of the chronology of the events of the crucifixion see notes on Mt 26.) **Behold your king.** It was apparent that Pilate hated the Jews and in scorn he gives them their king, poor, miserable, and beaten.

15-16. Driven by the crowd and not his conscience, Pilate succumbs to the wishes of the Jews.

3. His crucifixion. 19:17-37.

17. Christ was already weakened by the treatment of the soldiers, and now they make Him carry His cross. **Golgotha.** Called a **place of a skull** probably because its physical appearance resembles a skull, this place was also called Calvary (Lk 23:33).

18. They crucify Him between two criminals.

19-20. Since Christ had not been found guilty of a crime, Pilate placed a title above the cross. It was written in Aramaic, the language of the Jews; Greek, the language of culture; and Latin, the official language of Rome.

21-22. The **chief priest** was furious, and demanded that the title be changed from a statement to a claim. Pilate, vacillating in his character, now refused to change under pressure.

23-24. Four soldiers normally carried out the crucifixion sentence. Each soldier took one garment, and because of the value of the seamless inner coat, they **cast lots for it.** Unknowingly, the soldiers were actually fulfilling Old Testament Scripture (Ps 22:18). **These things therefore the soldiers did.** Bruised, beaten, mocked, tortured, compelled to carry His cross, Christ is now left hanging naked before the angry mob.

25. Contrasted to the soldiers and the crowd, John mentions three woman who loved the Lord: Mary, His mother; Mary, **the wife of Cleophas;** and Mary Magdalene.

26-27. Woman. Although Mary was His earthly mother, Christ as her Redeemer and Saviour refers to her in that redemp-

whom he loved, he saith unto his mother, Woman, behold thy son!
27 Then saith he to the disciple, Behold thy mother! And from that hour that disciple took her unto his own *home*.
28 ¶After this, Jesus knowing that all things were now accomplished, that the scripture might be fulfilled, saith, I thirst.
29 Now there was set a vessel full of vinegar: and they filled a spunge with vinegar, and put *it* upon hyssop, and put *it* to his mouth.
30 When Jesus therefore had received the vinegar, he said, It is finished: and he bowed his head, and gave up the ghost.
31 ¶The Jews therefore, because it was the preparation, that the bodies should not remain upon the cross on the sabbath day, (for that sabbath day was an high day,) besought Pilate that their legs might be broken, and *that* they might be taken away.
32 Then came the soldiers, and brake the legs of the first, and of the other which was crucified with him.
33 But when they came to Jesus, and saw that he was dead already, they brake not his legs:
34 But one of the soldiers with a spear pierced his side, and forthwith came there out blood and water.
35 And he that saw *it* bare record, and his record is true: and he knoweth that he saith true, that ye might believe.
36 For these things were done, that the scripture should be fulfilled, A bone of him shall not be broken.
37 And again another scripture saith, They shall look on him whom they pierced.

38 ¶And after this Joseph of Ăr-i-ma-thæ'a, being a disciple of Jesus, but secretly for fear of the Jews, besought Pilate that he might take away the body of Jesus: and Pilate gave *him* leave. He came therefore, and took the body of Jesus.
39 And there came also Nĭc-o-dē'-mus, which at the first came to Jesus by night, and brought a mixture of myrrh and aloes, about an hundred pound *weight*.
40 Then took they the body of Jesus, and wound it in linen clothes with the spices, as the manner of the Jews is to bury.
41 Now in the place where he was crucified there was a garden; and in the garden a new sepulchre, wherein was never man yet laid.
42 There laid they Jesus therefore because of the Jews' preparation *day*; for the sepulchre was nigh at hand.

CHAPTER 20

THE first *day* of the week cometh Mary Magdalene early, when it was yet dark, unto the sepulchre, and seeth the stone taken away from the sepulchre.

2 Then she runneth, and cometh to Simon Peter, and to the other disciple,

tive relationship. Here is love again. Christ tells John to take care of His mother. This teaches that everyone has a responsibility to provide for and take care of his parents.

28. The life and death of Christ was a constant fulfillment of prophecy (Ps 22:15). This statement was another evidence of His physical suffering.

29. Vinegar (Gr *unuo*). This was a very strong wine.

30. It is finished. (The Gr perfect tense denotes the certainty of the fact.) **Gave up the ghost.** He died and gave His Spirit to God.

31. To permit a body to remain on the cross until the next day was a violation of Jewish law (Deut 21:22-23). **Legs might be broken.** Since the victim would press on his legs to lift his chest enough to breathe, if the legs were broken, this would hasten death. The victim would not be able to breathe.

32-33. When they came to Christ, they did not break His legs.

34. One of the soldiers took a **spear** and **pierced his side.**

35. John adds that he personally witnessed the events he has just described.

36-37. The importance of the piercing, and the fact that they did not break Jesus' legs, is given in that it fulfilled prophecy (Ps 34:20; Zech 12:10). Even these wicked soldiers in their duties were completing the plan of God.

4. His burial. 19:38-42.

38-40. Joseph and Nicodemus, who were secret disciples, now came into the open, and prepared the body of Christ for burial. Both men were wealthy, and they were members of the Sanhedrin (Lk 23:51; Jn 3:1).

41-42. They quickly prepared the body for burial, and put it in a **new sepulcher** near the place of the crucifixion. They intended to finish their preparations after the Sabbath (Lk 24:1).

B. Christ and the Resurrection. 20:1-31.

1. Christ revealed to Mary. 20:1-18.

20:1. On Sunday, **Mary Magdalene** came to the tomb with spices to anoint the body of Christ (Mk 16:1; Lk 24:1). **Seeth the stone taken away.** Mary would have had trouble removing the stone; now her problem is worse. The body is missing.

2. Mary runs to tell startling news to Peter and John (**the other disciple, whom Jesus loved**). These two were considered

whom Jesus loved, and saith unto them, They have taken away the LORD out of the sepulchre, and we know not where they have laid him.

3 Peter therefore went forth, and that other disciple, and came to the sepulchre.

4 So they ran both together: and the other disciple did outrun Peter, and came first to the sepulchre.

5 And he stooping down, *and looking in,* saw the linen clothes lying; yet went he not in.

6 Then cometh Simon Peter following him, and went into the sepulchre, and seeth the linen clothes lie,

7 And the napkin, that was about his head, not lying with the linen clothes, but wrapped together in a place by itself.

8 Then went in also that other disciple, which came first to the sepulchre, and he saw, and believed.

9 For as yet they knew not the scripture, that he must rise again from the dead.

10 Then the disciples went away again unto their own home.

11 ¶But Mary stood without at the sepulchre weeping: and as she wept, she stooped down, *and looked* into the sepulchre,

12 And seeth two angels in white sitting, the one at the head, and the other at the feet, where the body of Jesus had lain.

13 And they say unto her, Woman, why weepest thou? She saith unto them, Because they have taken away my LORD, and I know not where they have laid him.

14 And when she had thus said, she turned herself back, and saw Jesus standing, and knew not that it was Jesus.

15 Jesus saith unto her, Woman, why weepest thou? whom seekest thou? She, supposing him to be the gardener, saith unto him, Sir, if thou have borne him hence, tell me where thou hast laid him, and I will take him away.

16 Jesus saith unto her, Mary. She turned herself, and saith unto him, Rab-bō'nī; which is to say, Master.

17 Jesus saith unto her, Touch me not; for I am not yet ascended to my Father: but go to my brethren, and say unto them, I ascend unto my Father, and your Father; and *to* my God, and your God.

18 Mary Magdalene came and told the disciples that she had seen the LORD, and *that* he had spoken these things unto her.

19 ¶Then the same day at evening, being the first *day* of the week, when the doors were shut where the disciples were assembled for fear of the Jews, came Jesus and stood in the midst, and saith unto them, Peace *be* unto you.

20 And when he had so said, he shewed unto them *his* hands and his

to be the leading disciples and were a part of Christ's inner circle (Lk 9:27-29).

3-4. Peter and John immediately made their way to the tomb, first walking together, and then running together. Perhaps John was younger than Peter, since he arrived there first.

5. John, **stooping down,** looks in, and observes the **linen clothes** lying there. However, the resurrection does not explain this phenomenon in the disciple's mind (20:9).

6-7. Impulsive Peter does not stop outside the tomb, but goes inside. What Peter saw was strange. Everything was neat and orderly in the tomb, except that the body of the Lord was no longer there. The headband was folded and lying in a separate place from the rest of the grave clothes. It was now obvious that the body had not been stolen.

8-9. John entered the tomb, and **saw** and **believed.** The teaching of Christ's resurrection now began to dawn on them, and their sight now turned to faith as they realized that Christ had risen **again from the dead.**

10. Overwhelmed with their observations and the faith it produced, they returned home.

11. It is logical to assume that Mary returned to the tomb after Peter and John have returned home. She has no knowledge of the Lord's resurrection. She too stoops down and looks into the tomb.

12. **Two angels.** No explanation is given for the appearance of the angels to Mary and not to the two disciples. It is interesting to note that heaven is interested in the resurrection.

13-15. **Why weepest thou?** This is a time of joy and triumph; therefore, the angels want to know why Mary is weeping. Mary wants to know where the Lord's body is lying so that she can complete the embalming process. Mary is so overcome with sorrow and grief that she does not even recognize Jesus. He asks the same question that the angels asked, and He receives the same answer.

16. **Mary.** She now recognizes the person to whom she is speaking and calls him. **Rabboni (Master).**

17. **Touch me not** (Gr *haptomai,* to cling to or to take hold of). Christ told Mary to stop (Greek prohibition with present tense) clinging to Him because, by doing so, she could not keep the Lord there with her. His destination was to go **to the Father.** Note the warm and close terminology used: **my brethren, your Father, your God.** This is the new relationship between the disciples, the Son, and the Father.

18. The command given to Mary is the command given to all Christians: go and tell that Jesus is risen.

2. Christ revealed to the Ten. 20:19-23.

19. **First day of the week.** The Sabbath commemorates the creation of the world, but Sunday, the first day of the week, commemorates the redemption of the world. Fearful and confused, the disciples meet in secret. Christ appears to them apparently by coming through the wall. **Peace.** To the troubled disciples, Christ brings a message of peace.

20. Several important concepts emerge from this action: Jesus had a real body; His body had been resurrected (not just

side. Then were the disciples glad, when they saw the Lord.

21 Then said Jesus to them again, Peace be unto you: as my Father hath sent me, even so send I you.

22 And when he had said this, he breathed on them, and saith unto them, Receive ye the Holy Ghost:

23 Whose soever sins ye remit, they are remitted unto them; and whose soever sins ye retain, they are retained.

24 ¶But Thomas, one of the twelve, called Dĭd'y-mus, was not with them when Jesus came.

25 The other disciples therefore said unto him, We have seen the Lord. But he said unto them, Except I shall see in his hands the print of the nails, and put my finger into the print of the nails, and thrust my hand into his side, I will not believe.

26 ¶And after eight days again his disciples were within, and Thomas with them: then came Jesus, the doors being shut, and stood in the midst, and said, Peace be unto you.

27 Then saith he to Thomas, Reach hither thy finger, and behold my hands; and reach hither thy hand, and thrust it into my side: and be not faithless, but believing.

28 And Thomas answered and said unto him, My Lord and my God.

29 Jesus saith unto him, Thomas, because thou hast seen me, thou hast believed: blessed are they that have not seen, and yet have believed.

30 ¶And many other signs truly did Jesus in the presence of his disciples, which are not written in this book:

31 But these are written, that ye might believe that Jesus is the Christ, the Son of God; and that believing ye might have life through his name.

CHAPTER 21

AFTER these things Jesus shewed himself again to the disciples at the sea of Ti-be'ri-as; and on this wise shewed he himself.

2 There were together Simon Peter, and Thomas called Dĭd'y-mus, and Nathanael of Cana in Galilee, and the sons of Zĕb'e-dee, and two other of his disciples.

3 Simon Peter saith unto them, I go a fishing. They say unto him, We also go with thee. They went forth, and entered into a ship immediately; and that night they caught nothing.

4 But when the morning was now come, Jesus stood on the shore: but the disciples knew not that it was Jesus.

5 Then Jesus saith unto them, Children, have ye any meat? They answered him, No.

6 And he said unto them, Cast the net on the right side of the ship, and ye shall find. They cast therefore, and now

His spirit), and the nail prints proved that He was Jesus and not someone else.

21. The resurrection had certain implications for the disciples. It gave them **Peace,** and it implied a commission: **So send I you.**

22-23. He breathed. This gift of the Holy Spirit is connected with the action of forgiving or retaining sins. It was not the work of the disciples to forgive sins, but the work of the Holy Spirit through the disciples as they fulfilled the Great Commission (Mt 28:18-20). Christ gave the disciples authority to state that forgiveness of sins was possible.

3. Christ revealed to Thomas. 20:24-31.

24-25. No explanation is given for Thomas' not being with the other disciples. Perhaps he was alone mourning the death of his Master. When the other disciples tried to comfrot him with the news of the resurrection, he refused to accept it until he had actually touched the hands, feet, and side of the Saviour.

26. One week later, Christ appears again to the disciples (including Thomas), and gives the same message of **Peace.**

27. Compare this verse with verse 25. Christ answers all of Thomas' requests. Christ commands him to do what he said was necessary for him to believe.

28-29. My Lord and my God. Thomas now recognizes both the resurrection and the deity of Christ. Thomas based his faith on sight. Christ promises a blessing for those who believe upon hearing instead of upon seeing.

30. Many other signs. The greatest sign found in the writings of John is the sign of the resurrection (For a detailed description of the importance of this event see Josh McDowell's *Evidence that Demands a Verdict.*)

31. A detailed analysis of this verse is given in the Introduction to this Commentary.

C. Christ and the Commission. 21:1-25.

1. Miracle of the fish. 21:1-14.

21:1. Showed he himself (Gr *phaneroō*, to reveal or make known; show or manifest). Jesus now reveals His glory to the disciples at the **sea of Tiberias** (Galilee).

2. Peter, Nathanael, James, John, and two other unnamed disciples were together.

3-4. Again Peter is the man of action. **I go a fishing.** Although the Greek present tense (I am going to fish) is used here and normally denotes continual action, this does not necessarily mean that Peter intended to return permanently to his former occupation. As they arrive at the shore after a frustrating night, they see Jesus, but for some providential reason, they do not recognize Him.

5-6. Children (lit., lads). This question and negative answer was a blow to these fishermen's egos. Fishermen would not usually respond immediately to this unusual request by a stranger on the shore. However, there was something compelling about this Stranger that caused them to obey without an objection.

they were not able to draw it for the multitude of fishes.

7 Therefore that disciple whom Jesus loved saith unto Peter, It is the Lord. Now when Simon Peter heard that it was the Lord, he girt *his* fisher's coat *unto him,* (for he was naked,) and did cast himself into the sea.

8 And the other disciples came in a little ship; (for they were not far from land, but as it were two hundred cubits,) dragging the net with fishes.

9 As soon then as they were come to land, they saw a fire of coals there, and fish laid thereon, and bread.

10 Jesus saith unto them, Bring of the fish which ye have now caught.

11 Simon Peter went up, and drew the net to land full of great fishes, an hundred and fifty and three: and for all there were so many, yet was not the net broken.

12 Jesus saith unto them, Come *and* dine. And none of the disciples durst ask him, Who art thou? knowing that it was the Lord.

13 Jesus then cometh, and taketh bread, and giveth them, and fish likewise.

14 This is now the third time that Jesus shewed himself to his disciples, after that he was risen from the dead.

15 ¶So when they had dined, Jesus saith to Simon Peter, Simon, *son* of Jonas, lovest thou me more than these? He saith unto him, Yea, Lord; thou knowest that I love thee. He saith unto him, Feed my lambs.

16 He saith to him again the second time, Simon, *son* of Jonas, lovest thou me? He saith unto him, Yea, Lord; thou knowest that I love thee. He saith unto him, Feed my sheep.

17 He saith unto him the third time, Simon, *son* of Jonas, lovest thou me? Peter was grieved because he said unto him the third time, Lovest thou me? And he said unto him, Lord, thou knowest all things; thou knowest that I love thee. Jesus saith unto him, Feed my sheep.

18 Verily, verily, I say unto thee, When thou wast young, thou girdedst thyself, and walkedst whither thou wouldest: but when thou shalt be old,

7-8. It is the Lord. John finally recognizes that this Stranger is the Lord. Peter again is the first in action; he puts on his coat, for he **was naked** (lit., "stripped" of his overcoat). Peter's enthusiasm to be with the Lord would indicate that he was not fishing in disobedience to the Lord's command. The rest of the disciples now join the Lord and Peter.

9-11. Christ had already prepared a meal when they arrived. It consisted of **fish** and **bread. Bring of the fish.** They count the number of fish and discover that although there were one hundred fifty-three fish, **yet was not the net broken.**

12-13. Come and dine. Christ invites them to breakfast. The disciples are speechless in the presence of their risen Lord.

14. Shewed himself (see notes on 21:1).

2. Message to Peter. 21:15-17.

15. After breakfast, the attention of the Lord is upon Peter. Peter had denied his Lord three times, and now the Lord asks Peter three times, **Lovest thou me?** Two Greek words for "love" are played against each other in the original: *Agapaō,* when used in distinction from the other, connotes love as an emotion of deep appreciation based upon careful consideration. It means to recognize the worth of someone and esteem him highly. The synonym *phileō,* when used in distinction as here, connotes "love" as a pure, intense "feeling of love." It is a personal, warm, intimate relationship like that between family members. It is a love that is more spontaneous than philosophical. Jesus asks Peter, **lovest thou me more than these?** This refers to the other disciples. Peter had boasted of his loyalty, and yet had denied his Lord. The other disciples had not denied the Lord. Consequently, the Lord is really probing the sincerity of Peter's love. Peter answers, using a different word (Gr *phileō*). "I have a deep affection for You." **Feed** (Gr *boskō,* feed, graze, or tend to) **my lambs.** Christ is commissioning Peter to a pastoral office of caring for His sheep.

16. Jesus asks, **lovest thou me** (Gr *agapaō*)? Peter responds, **I love thee** (Gr *phileō*). **Feed** (Gr *poimainō,* shepherd) **my sheep.**

17. Jesus asks a third time, and the third question is the most convicting. The first two times, Jesus was asking Peter if he loved Him (using *agapaō*). Now the third time Jesus changes the verb to *phileō.* Peter is **grieved,** and he appeals to the omniscience of his Master. **Thou knowest all things; thou knowest that I love thee** (Gr *phileō*). It is interesting to note that in Christ's commissioning Peter to tend to the sheep, the first time He tells Peter to feed His lambs, the second and third times to feed His sheep (using two different Greek words).

3. Conclusion. 21:18-25.

18-19. Christ now prophesies that one day Peter's freedom would cease. **Old.** This indicates that Peter will have a long, useful life of service. **Thou shall stretch forth thy hands.** This language could refer to crucifixion, and church tradition concurs

thou shalt stretch forth thy hands, and another shall gird thee, and carry *thee* whither thou wouldest not.

19 This spake he, signifying by what death he should glorify God. And when he had spoken this, he saith unto him, Follow me.

20 Then Peter, turning about, seeth the disciple whom Jesus loved following; which also leaned on his breast at supper, and said, Lord, which is he that betrayeth thee?

21 Peter seeing him saith to Jesus, Lord, and what *shall* this man *do?*

22 Jesus saith unto him, If I will that he tarry till I come, what *is that* to thee? follow thou me.

23 Then went this saying abroad among the brethren, that that disciple should not die: yet Jesus said not unto him, He shall not die; but, If I will that he tarry till I come, what *is that* to thee?

24 This is the disciple which testifieth of these things, and wrote these things: and we know that his testimony is true.

25 And there are also many other things which Jesus did, the which, if they should be written every one, I suppose that even the world itself could not contain the books that should be written. Amen.

that this is how Peter died. **Glorify God.** What confidence the Lord gives to the one who had denied Him. Peter would be faithful to the end, and would bring glory to God through his death. **Follow me.** The Lord calls Peter to a life of total commitment to Him.

20-23. Jesus begins to leave, and as Peter follows Him, he turns around and sees John following. Having been told about his future, Peter wants to know about John's future. The emphasis of Christ's rebuke is that Peter should not be concerned about John, but about the job which he must do. The disciples misunderstand the rebuke. They had forgotten the **if.** The future of John was not their business.

24. The disciple. This refers to John. **Testifieth.** The entire book of John is a testimony to the deity of Jesus Christ. **We know.** The we probably refers to the elders in the church of Ephesus. They are not identified by name.

25. John concludes by reminding his readers that he has described only a small portion of all that **Jesus did.**

BIBLIOGRAPHY

Barclay, William. The Gospel of John. In *The Daily Study Bible.* 2 Vols. 2nd ed. Philadelphia: Westminster, 1956.

Barrett, C. K. *The Gospel According to St. John.* London: S.P.C.K., 1962.

Gaebelein, A. C. *The Gospel of John.* Wheaton: Van Kampen Press, 1936.

Godet, Frederic. *Commentary on the Gospel of John.* Trans. by Timothy Dwight. 2 Vols. Grand Rapids: Zondervan, reprinted, n.d.

*Hendriksen, William. *A Commentary on the Gospel of John.* Grand Rapids: Baker, 1953.

Ironside, Harry. *Addresses on the Gospel of John.* New York: Loizeaux Brothers, 1942.

Kelly, William. *An Exposition of the Gospel of John.* Denver: Wilson Foundation, reprinted, 1966.

*Kent, Homer A., Jr. *Light in the Darkness: Studies in the Gospel of John.* Grand Rapids: Baker, 1974.

Lange, John P. The Gospel According to John. In *Lange's Commentary on the Holy Scriptures.* Trans. and ed. by Philip Schaff. Grand Rapids: Zondervan, reprinted, n.d.

Lenski, R. C. H. *The Interpretation of St. John's Gospel.* Columbus: Lutheran Book Concern, 1942.

Lightfoot, R. H. *St. John's Gospel: A Commentary.* Ed. by C. F. Evans. Oxford: Clarendon, 1956.

Luthardt, Christoph Ernst. *St. John's Gospel, Described and Explained According to Its Peculiar Character.* Trans. by C. R. Gregory. 3 Vols. Edinburgh: T. and T. Clark, 1876-78.

Morgan, G. Campbell. *The Gospel According to John.* Westwood, N. J.: Revell, 1933.

*Morris, Leon. The Gospel According to John. In the *International Commentary on the New Testament.* Grand Rapids: Eerdmans, 1971.

*Pink, Arthur W. *Exposition of the Gospel of John.* 3 Vols. Grand Rapids: Zondervan, 1945.

Plummer, Alfred. The Gospel According to St. John. In *Cambridge Greek Testament for Schools and Colleges.* Cambridge: Cambridge University Press, 1905.

Scroggie, W. Graham. St. John, Introduction and Notes. In *Study Hours Series.* New York: Harper and Brothers, 1931.

*Tasker, R. V. G. The Gospel According to St. John. In *The Tyndale New Testament Commentaries.* Grand Rapids: Eerdmans, 1960.

*Tenney, Merrill C. *John: The Gospel of Belief.* Grand Rapids: Eerdmans, 1960.

Vine, W. E. *John: His Record of Christ.* Grand Rapids: Zondervan, 1957.

Westcott, B. F. *The Gospel According to St. John: The Authorized Version with Introduction and Notes.* Grand Rapids: Eerdmans, 1950.

THE ACTS
Of The Apostles

INTRODUCTION

The Acts of the Apostles is unique among the books of the New Testament. One of the most influential books of all time, it forms the essential link between the gospel accounts of Jesus and the only account of the beginning of His church. The book of Acts is our chief source of information about the first century. As Matthew, Mark, Luke, and John record the gospel as evidenced in the life of Jesus Christ, Acts records the gospel as evidenced in the lives of those who followed Him. Luke writes his first letter (the Gospel according to Luke) to tell what Christ did while on earth through His physical body (see Lk 1:1-4). His second letter (the Acts) was written to tell what Christ was doing while in heaven through His spiritual body, the church.

The story in Acts moves rapidly from one episode to another. It records the birth and the growing pains of the fledgling church. It reveals the vitality of the first-century faith. It maps out the master plan for world evangelization. The first half of the book essentially records the ministry of Peter, the second half the ministry of Paul. Subthemes in the lives of Stephen, Philip, and others are also revealed. But essentially the book of Acts records the working of the Holy Spirit in the lives of the New Testament church.

Authorship. Although the book of Acts is anonymous, and not even its title indicates authorship, yet a nearly universal tradition ascribes this writing to Paul's physician-friend, Luke. In the prologues to both Luke and Acts the author refers to himself by the first person pronoun. Theophilus, the recipient of both writings (Lk 1:4; Acts 1:1), obviously knew the identity of the author.

1. External evidence. The uniform tradition of the early church ascribes this work to Luke. The oldest extant list of New Testament writings, known as the Muratorian Fragment, which dates from the later half of the second century A.D., lists both the third Gospel and the Acts of the Apostles as the work of Luke. The so-called antimarcionite prologue to Luke (ca. A.D. 150-180), in discussing the third Gospel comments, "and afterwards this same Luke wrote the Acts of the Apostles." In his *Against Heresies* (A.D. 185), Ireneaus takes for granted that Luke is the author of Acts. Clement of Alexandria (ca. A.D. 155-215) quotes from the Acts in *Stromata* and says, "As Luke in the Acts of the Apostles relates that Paul said, 'Men of Athens, I perceive that in all things ye are too superstitious.'" In his work *On Fasting*, Tertullian (ca. A.D. 150-220) frequently quotes from or alludes to Acts naming Luke as the author. And Eusebius, in his *Ecclesiastical History*, published in A.D. 324, explicitly mentions Luke as the author of two books, the Gospel and the Acts. Origen (ca. A.D. 185-254) and others add their voices to the testimony of scholars that spans a hundred years attesting that Luke is the author of the Acts of the Apostles.

2. Internal evidence. Likewise, there is an overwhelming abundance of internal evidence to the authorship of Acts by Luke. First, an analysis of the style and language of both the third Gospel and the Acts of the Apostles makes it clear that whoever wrote the first also wrote the second. If Lucan authorship can be proved for the Gospel which bears his name, it can also be proved for the Acts. Secondly, the medical terminology which is characteristic of the vocabulary of the Acts necessitates that the author either be a physician or one well versed in that discipline. Since the traditional author is known to have been a physician (Col 4:14), it seems conclusive that Luke authored the Acts. Thirdly, there is a great deal of archaeological and epigraphal evidence which points to the fact that the author of Acts was well familiar with the first-century world. As an educated man, Luke would have been well traveled and would have personally known the Mediterranean world of the first century. Finally, a reading of the book makes it clear that the writer was a companion of Paul in many of the adventures recorded in Acts. In the so-called "we" passages the author describes the situation in the first person (16:10-17; 20:5-15; 21:1-18; 27:1-28:16). A survey of Paul's close associates produces only one individual who could have authored the passages which record these experiences. Timothy was in the presence of those awaiting Paul's arrival at Troas. Neither Titus nor Silas was with Paul on the journey to Rome or in Rome. The only close associate who fits the facts is Luke.

Date and place of writing. There is strong evidence to date the Acts of the Apostles in the first century. The style and vocabulary of the writer are certainly that of this era. He has a command of facts that is best explained by his being an eyewitness to them. The tone of the writing seems to rule out the possibility that it was written after the organized attack on the church by the Roman emperor Domitian (A.D. 81-96).

Apparently Acts could not have been written beyond the turn of the second century, for there are possible references to the text of Acts in the *Epistle of Barnabas* (ca. A.D. 100) and in Justin Martyr (ca. A.D. 150). Likewise, the earliest possible date for the completion of Acts is two years after Paul's arrival in Rome as a prisoner (Acts 28:30-31). Thus the book must have been composed sometime between A.D. 61-62 and approximately A.D. 95.

Although most conservative scholars place the date of writing between A.D. 62 and A.D. 68, a very good case can be made for the early 60's. First, there is an apparent excitement in the record of the "we passages" which most likely existed shortly after the events occurred. Secondly, the lack of any discussion of the fall of Jerusalem in A.D. 70 would seem to preclude a date of writing beyond that date. Thirdly, the abrupt ending of Acts is best explained by a drawing to a close of Paul's two-year imprisonment in Rome. Luke had to finish his writing in order to once again sail with Paul.

Although arguments can be advanced for other early dates, there seem to be no facts prohibiting a date of A.D. 62-63 for the writing of Acts. Even though the place of writing is not mentioned by name, it is reasonable to assume that if the A.D. 62-63 date is correct, then the place of writing is Rome. As attending physician to the Apostle, Luke would certainly have had time to write the historical account of Acts during that two-year house arrest of Paul at Rome.

Purpose. Although the book of Acts does not contain any indication of the author's purpose, it nevertheless cannot be divorced from the Gospel of Luke. Since these two works are an integral whole, with coherent purpose running throughout, it is safe to assume that the purpose stated clearly in the initial verses of Luke is still the purpose for the writing of the Acts. In the words of the author

himself: "Forasmuch as many have taken in hand to set forth in order a declaration of those things which are most surely believed among us, Even as they delivered them unto us, which from the beginning were eyewitnesses, and ministers of the word; It seemed good to me also, having had perfect understanding of all things from the very first, to write unto thee in order, most excellent Theophilus, That thou mightest know the certainty of those things, wherein thou hast been instructed" (Lk 1:1-4).

Since the church was growing so rapidly in the Roman world, those who joined its ranks needed an authoritative account of its birth and early history. Thus Luke sets himself to the task of giving a coherent account of the life of Jesus Christ as it was lived through those closest to Him. Thus the birth and development of the church, the preaching of Peter, and the missionary activity of Paul became the motifs of the most accurate history of the first century, i.e., the Acts of the Apostles (see the discussion of Sir William Ramsey, *St. Paul the Traveller and the Roman Citizen*, p. 7ff.).

OUTLINE

COMMENTARY

I. THE BIRTH OF THE CHURCH AT JERUSALEM. 1:1-3:26.

A. From Resurrection to Ascension. 1:1-14.

THE former treatise have I made, O Thē-ŏph'i-lus, of all that Jesus began both to do and teach,

2 Until the day in which he was taken up, after that he through the Holy Ghost had given commandments unto the apostles whom he had chosen:

1:1-2. The former treatise have I made, O Theophilus. The relationship between Luke and Acts has already been discussed. It is obvious that the Gospel of Luke is the former treatise mentioned here. There is no reason to suppose that Theophilus was not a real person, although some would translate literally as "dear to God." In that event, Luke would be addressing those Christian readers in general. However, the title of respect, "most excellent" as found in Luke 1:3, makes it most improbable that the author is addressing a company of individuals. Whether Theophilus is a Jew or Greek cannot be absolutely determined. The absence of the honorific title here in Acts 1:1 may not mean a loss of affection but rather a deepening friendship between Luke and Theophilus.

3 To whom also he shewed himself alive after his passion by many infallible proofs, being seen of them forty days, and speaking of the things pertaining to the kingdom of God:

3. Many infallible proofs. The resurrection ministry of the Lord was accompanied by unmistakable signs. Over a period of forty days between His passion and ascension Jesus appeared at frequent intervals to His apostles. No one could seriously doubt that He was alive. The adjective "infallible" (Gr *tekmērion*) is employed in the AV in order to extract the complete meaning. So infallible were the "proofs" of Christ's resurrection that the author does not feel it necessary to list them for his first-century readers.

4 And, being assembled together with *them*, commanded them that they should not depart from Jerusalem, but wait for the promise of the Father, which, *saith he*, ye have heard of me.

5 For John truly baptized with water; but ye shall be baptized with the Holy Ghost not many days hence.

4-5. Wait for the promise of the Father. Much ink has been used attempting to explain these five words, **the promise of the Father.** Various passages of Scripture make it clear that the promise of the Father (Joel 2:28; Acts 2:16) and also the promise of the Son (Jn 14:16, 26; 15:26; 16:7) were references to the arrival of the Holy Spirit of God.

6 When they therefore were come together, they asked of him, saying, Lord, wilt thou at this time restore again the kingdom to Israel?

7 And he said unto them, It is not for you to know the times or the seasons, which the Father hath put in his own power.

6-7. Lord, wilt thou at this time restore again the kingdom of Israel? Even after the resurrection ministry of our Lord, the disciples were yet confused about His true purpose in coming to live among them. Jesus did not answer the apostles' question concerning the precise time when God would restore the kingdom of Israel, but He did promise them something far more important in those seconds prior to the ascension.

8 But ye shall receive power, after that the Holy Ghost is come upon you: and ye shall be witnesses unto me both in Jerusalem, and in all Judaea, and in Sa-mā'rĭ-a, and unto the uttermost part of the earth.

8. But ye shall receive power, after that the Holy Ghost is come upon you. The power to which He referred was not political, but spiritual. When the Holy Ghost came upon the disciples they would be clothed with heavenly power. As Jesus had been anointed at His baptism with the Holy Spirit and power, so now His disciples will share in that anointing. The Holy Ghost will come upon them in power. **Ye shall be witnesses unto me.** Jesus came to bear witness of the Father and His love for mankind. The apostles would bear witness of Jesus' death and resurrection, proving God's love for mankind. The references to **Jerusalem, Judea,** and **Samaria,** and **the uttermost part of the earth,** give the widening circles of the witness to God's love. Actually this verse provides a table of contents and divine outline for the entire book of Acts: (1) witnessing in Jerusalem (chs. 1-7); (2) witnessing in Judaea and Samaria (chs. 8-12); and (3) witnessing unto the uttermost part of the earth (chs. 13-28).

9 And when he had spoken these things, while they beheld, he was taken up; and a cloud received him out of their sight.

10 And while they looked stedfastly toward heaven as he went up, behold, two men stood by them in white apparel;

9-11. Having commissioned His disciples, the Lord was now prepared to disappear from their sight and make no further resurrection appearances. As the cloud received Him out of their sight, the Lord was once again restored to the glory which He had with the Father before the world began (Jn 17:4-5). As those gathered looked stedfastly toward heaven, two men in white appeared, whom Luke obviously intends his readers to un-

11 Which also said, Ye men of Galilee, why stand ye gazing up into heaven? this same Jesus, which is taken up from you into heaven, shall so come in like manner as ye have seen him go into heaven.

12 ¶Then returned they unto Jerusalem from the mount called Olivet, which is from Jerusalem a sabbath day's journey.
13 And when they were come in, they went up into an upper room, where abode both Peter, and James, and John, and Andrew, Philip, and Thomas, Bartholomew, and Matthew, James the son of Ăl-phae͞'us, and Simon Ze-lo͞'teš, and Judas the brother of James.
14 These all continued with one accord in prayer and supplication, with the women, and Mary the mother of Jesus, and with his brethren.
15 ¶And in those days Peter stood up in the midst of the disciples, and said, (the number of names together were about an hundred and twenty,)
16 Men and brethren, this scripture must needs have been fulfilled, which the Holy Ghost by the mouth of David spake before concerning Judas, which was guide to them that took Jesus.
17 For he was numbered with us, and had obtained part of this ministry.

18 Now this man purchased a field with the reward of iniquity; and falling headlong, he burst asunder in the midst, and all his bowels gushed out.
19 And it was known unto all the dwellers at Jerusalem; insomuch as that field is called in their proper tongue, Acĕl'da-ma, that is to say, The field of blood.
20 For it is written in the book of Psalms, Let his habitation be desolate, and let no man dwell therein: and his bishoprick let another take.

21 Wherefore of these men which have companied with us all the time that the Lord Jesus went in and out among us,
22 Beginning from the baptism of John, unto that same day that he was taken up from us, must one be ordained to be a witness with us of his resurrection.
23 And they appointed two, Joseph called Bär'să-bas, who was surnamed Justus, and Mat-thi'as.
24 And they prayed, and said, Thou, Lord, which knowest the hearts of all men, shew whether of these two thou hast chosen,
25 That he may take part of this ministry and apostleship, from which Ju-

derstand as angelic messengers (cf. Mt 28:3; Jn 20:12). They gave to the followers of the Lord Jesus the tremendous promise, **this same Jesus . . . shall so come in like manner.** Not another and in a different way, but this same Jesus in the same way, would descend for believers as they had seen Him ascend from them. Between ascension and His return for them, however, would be an interval of time in which the Holy Spirit would empower His church to carry on the ministry of worldwide evangelization.

12-14. To the disciples their duty was clear. They were to return to Jerusalem and wait there for the empowerment of the Spirit of God. Thus they came to the upper room where the Eleven **continued with one accord in prayer and supplication.**

B. Twelfth Apostle Chosen. 1:15-26.

15-17. Peter stood up in the midst of the disciples. It is clear that the Apostle Peter has now become the undisputed leader of the apostolic band. The bumbling, denying Peter has now become the rock and is the principal preacher of Christianity following the ascension of the Lord. Peter clearly understands that the defection of Judas and his subsequent replacement are both fulfillments of Old Testament prophecies. The Lord also applied Psalm 41:9 to the defection of Judas (Jn 13:18). Peter here adduces further "testimonies" from the Psalter indicating that they must continue following the plan of God, as they understand it to be.

18-20. Now this man purchased a field . . . insomuch as that field is called in their proper tongue, Aceldama, that is to say, The field of blood. "The account of Judas' faith (vss. 18-20) is not inconsistent with that set forth by Matthew (27:3-10). The field was probably bought by the legally-minded priests in Judas' name. Amid the crazed inconsistencies of despair he may have laid claim to it in consequence, and in bitter irony made it the scene of suicide. The two accounts preserve different but equally true details from the rest of the shocking story, and the field won its sombre name on more than one count" (E. M. Blaiklock, Acts of the Apostles, p. 53).

Further evidence confirming the prophetic character of Judas' death is given by Luke in Peter's quotation from the Psalms. The former, from Psalm 69:25, is a prayer that the final resting place of the foes of the psalmist will be a place of desolation. The latter, from Psalm 109:8, is a prayer to the enemy of the psalmist that a possible replacement will be found for the psalmist.

21-23. The essential criteria for the replacement for the apostolic band were twofold: this person must have been with the Lord from His baptism by John unto His ascension; and, more importantly, he must have been a witness of the resurrection, as the others were. **Joseph called Barsabas . . . and Matthias.** Of either man we know nothing. We even hear no more of Matthias in the New Testament, although a legend of Ethiopian martyrdom is known.

24-26. A momentous decision was about to be made. Immediately the disciples set themselves to praying, seeking the will of the Lord. Specifically, they asked that the Father would make known unto them which of the two candidates had already been chosen by God. **And they gave forth their lots.** The disciples did not now engage in a bit of gambling. We must

das by transgression fell, that he might go to his own place.

26 And they gave forth their lots; and the lot fell upon Mat-thī'as; and he was numbered with the eleven apostles.

CHAPTER 2

AND when the day of Pentecost was fully come, they were all with one accord in one place.

2 And suddenly there came a sound from heaven as of a rushing mighty wind, and it filled all the house where they were sitting.

3 And there appeared unto them cloven tongues like as of fire, and it sat upon each of them.

4 And they were all filled with the Holy Ghost, and began to speak with other tongues, as the Spirit gave them utterance.

5 And there were dwelling at Jerusalem Jews, devout men, out of every nation under heaven.

6 Now when this was noised abroad, the multitude came together, and were confounded, because that every man heard them speak in his own language.

7 And they were all amazed and marvelled, saying one to another, Behold, are not all these which speak Galilæ-ans?

8 And how hear we every man in our own tongue, wherein we were born?

9 Pär'thĭ-ans, and Medes, and Ē'lam-ītes, and the dwellers in Mĕs-o-po-tā'-

remember that before lots were cast they selected two men whom they judged most worthy to fill Judas' vacancy. Having passed that difficult screening test, they were now prepared to receive the will of God. Casting lots to discern God's will was a very respectable Hebrew custom. The disciples believed in God's providence and perhaps even remembered, "The lot is cast into the lap; but the whole disposing thereof is of the Lord" (Prov 16:33). Divine will is now known; the lot fell to Matthias, and he was numbered with the eleven apostles.

C. Pentecost, 2:1-13.

Pentecost was the third great Israelite feast mentioned in Leviticus 23. It was a harvest festival fifty days after the Passover week. This particular Pentecost, however, was to have greater significance than those which had preceded it. Old Testament Pentecost occurred fifty days after Israel left Egypt and the Passover lamb was slain. New Testament Pentecost occurred fifty days after Christ rose from the dead, the Lord being our Passover Lamb. Old Testament Pentecost celebrated the birth of the nation Israel (Ex 19:5). New Testament Pentecost celebrated the birth of the church (2:41-47). Old Testament Pentecost witnessed the slaying of some three thousand souls (Ex 32:28). New Testament Pentecost witnessed the saving of some three thousand souls (2:41). The former pointed typologically to the latter.

2:1-3. They were all with one accord in one place. The word translated **with one accord** (Gr *homothymadon*), meaning likemindedness, occurs twelve times in the New Testament, eleven of which are found in the book of Acts. This shows the unity of purpose among these early disciples.

The coming of the Holy Spirit of God with power was accompanied by two manifestations. The first was the sound of a **rushing mighty wind,** and the second was **cloven tongues like as of fire.** The wind is symbolic of the Spirit of God. In Ezekiel 37, Ezekiel prophesies that the wind would blow upon the dead bones in the valley of his vision. He was actually prophesying the coming of the Spirit of God upon Israel. Here that same wind is used to symbolize the Spirit's presence. In addition to the audible appeal, an appeal was made to their eyes as the cloven tongues of fire appeared. Again, Matthew and Luke both report that John the Baptist foretold of One who would baptize "with the Holy Ghost, and with fire" (Mt 3:11; Lk 3:16). Together the fire and wind make a graphic picture of the coming of the Spirit of God.

4. And they were all filled with the Holy Ghost, and began to speak with other tongues. Although glossolalia is not always a proof of the presence of the Spirit of God, for many pagans practiced speaking in other tongues, nevertheless here, as the Spirit gave them utterance, these men at Pentecost were given an unnatural ability to speak in tongues that were not their own. The word translated tongue (Gr *dialektos*) can mean language as well as dialect. The various languages being spoken corresponded to the nationalities of those present (cf. 2:8).

5-11. And there were dwelling at Jerusalem, devout men, out of every nation under heaven. From farflung lands and many languages, Jews had come from the Diaspora to celebrate the Feast of Weeks in Jerusalem. This was because only at the Jerusalem Temple could they attend these special sacrificial services (Num 28:26 ff.). News of the strange events taking place on Pentecost quickly spread throughout the city. **And they were all amazed and marvelled.** It was not immediately evident how these Galilean Jews could be speaking in the tongues of each of the listeners. A lengthy and impressive list of the nationalities of those present is now given. They were all there: Parthians to Phrygians; Cretans to Cappadocians; Elamites to Egyp-

mǐ-a, and in Judǽa, and Cǎp-pa-dō'-čĭ-a, in Pontus, and Asia,

10 Phrȳǵ'ǐ-a, and Pǎm-phȳl'ǐ-a, in Egypt, and in the parts of Lǐb'ȳ-a about Čy-rē'ne, and strangers of Rome, Jews and proselytes,

11 Cretes and Arabians, we do hear them speak in our tongues the wonderful works of God.

12 And they were all amazed, and were in doubt, saying one to another, What meaneth this?

13 Others mocking said, These men are full of new wine.

14 ¶But Peter, standing up with the eleven, lifted up his voice, and said unto them, Ye men of Judǽa, and all ye that dwell at Jerusalem, be this known unto you, and hearken to my words:

15 For these are not drunken, as ye suppose, seeing it is but the third hour of the day.

16 But this is that which was spoken by the prophet Jō'el:

17 And it shall come to pass in the last days, saith God, I will pour out of my Spirit upon all flesh: and your sons and your daughters shall prophesy, and your young men shall see visions, and your old men shall dream dreams:

18 And on my servants and on my handmaidens I will pour out in those days of my Spirit; and they shall prophesy:

19 And I will shew wonders in heaven above, and signs in the earth beneath; blood, and fire, and vapour of smoke:

20 The sun shall be turned into darkness, and the moon into blood, before that great and notable day of the Lord come:

21 And it shall come to pass, that whosoever shall call on the name of the Lord shall be saved.

22 Ye men of Israel, hear these words; Jesus of Nazareth, a man approved of God among you by miracles and wonders and signs, which God did by him in the midst of you, as ye yourselves also know:

23 Him, being delivered by the determinate counsel and foreknowledge of God, ye have taken, and by wicked hands have crucified and slain:

24 Whom God hath raised up, having loosed the pains of death: because it was not possible that he should be holden of it.

25 For David speaketh concerning him, I foresaw the Lord always before my face, for he is on my right hand, that I should not be moved:

26 Therefore did my heart rejoice, and my tongue was glad; moreover also my flesh shall rest in hope:

27 Because thou wilt not leave my soul in hell, neither wilt thou suffer thine Holy One to see corruption.

28 Thou hast made known to me the

tians. The astounding testimony of each one was, **we do hear them speak in our tongues the wonderful works of God.**

12-13. Although all were amazed, **others mocking said, These men are full of new wine.** The new wine (Gr *gleukos*) is "sweet wine." Pentecost is too early for new vintage wine, August being the next vintage. So different were these disciples at Pentecost that those who looked on mocked them as if they were drunk.

D. Peter's Preaching. 2:14-3:26.

14-16. But Peter, standing up with the eleven, lifted up his voice. Having been a disciple of the Lord, and a follower, Peter is now ready to assume a role of leadership. Even though he is the principal preacher of Christianity after the ascension, nevertheless, we must notice that the Eleven stand behind him giving their full support to his message. Peter warns the onlookers that the one hundred and twenty are not drunken as everyone thought, but what they are viewing is in actuality a fulfillment of prophecy. They should not be surprised at what they see, for it was predicted hundreds of years before by the prophet Joel.

17-21. These verses are a quotation of Joel 2:28-32 in which the prophet announces the coming day of the Lord. Joel's prophecy was given in the midst of a call for repentance from the nation Israel (Joel 2:12-14). Peter quotes that prophecy in the same context.

"The wonders and signs to be revealed in the world of nature, as described in verses 19 and 20, may have more relevance in the present context than is sometimes realized: it was little more than seven weeks since the people in Jerusalem had indeed seen the sun turned into darkness, during the early afternoon of the day of our Lord's crucifixion. And on the same afternoon, the paschal full moon may well have appeared blood-red in the sky in consequence of that preternatural gloom. These were to be understood as tokens of the advent of the day of the Lord, 'that great and notable day,' a day of judgment, to be sure, but more immediately the day of God's salvation to all who invoked His name" (F. F. Bruce, *The Book of Acts*, p. 69).

22-24. Jesus of Nazareth . . . being delivered by the determinate counsel and foreknowledge of God, ye have . . . crucified and slain: Whom God hath raised up. Peter now gets to the main theme of his message. In the ears of his hearers, he rehearses the death, burial, and resurrection of the Lord Jesus Christ. One who accomplished mighty works and signs and wonders through the power of God had been taken and crucified and slain. It was the howling mob that cried, "Crucify Him!" However, all who participated in putting the Lord to death were unconsciously fulfilling the determinate counsel and foreknowledge of God. It was God's purpose that the Messiah should suffer death for us (cf. Lk 24:25, 46; Acts 17:3; 26:23). But if the Messiah's suffering and death were ordained by the determinate counsel of God, so was His resurrection and glory.

25-28. As support for his message, Peter appeals to the Old Testament. His quotation comes from Psalm 16:8-11. These prophetic words, so Peter argues, were fulfilled in Jesus of Nazareth and in no one else. Therefore, the Messiah whom David promised was in fact Jesus of Nazareth.

ways of life; thou shalt make me full of joy with thy countenance.

29 Men *and* brethren, let me freely speak unto you of the patriarch David, that he is both dead and buried, and his sepulchre is with us unto this day.

30 Therefore being a prophet, and knowing that God had sworn with an oath to him, that of the fruit of his loins, according to the flesh, he would raise up Christ to sit on his throne;

31 He seeing this before spake of the resurrection of Christ, that his soul was not left in hell, neither his flesh did see corruption.

32 This Jesus hath God raised up, whereof we all are witnesses.

33 Therefore being by the right hand of God exalted, and having received of the Father the promise of the Holy Ghost, he hath shed forth this, which ye now see and hear.

34 For David is not ascended into the heavens: but he saith himself, The Lord said unto my Lord, Sit thou on my right hand,

35 Until I make thy foes thy footstool.

36 Therefore let all the house of Israel know assuredly, that God hath made that same Jesus, whom ye have crucified, both Lord and Christ.

37 ¶Now when they heard *this*, they were pricked in their heart, and said unto Peter and to the rest of the apostles, Men *and* brethren, what shall we do?

38 Then Peter said unto them, Repent, and be baptized every one of you in the name of Jesus Christ for the remission of sins, and ye shall receive the gift of the Holy Ghost.

39 For the promise is unto you, and to your children, and to all that are afar off, *even* as many as the Lord our God shall call.

40 And with many other words did he testify and exhort, saying, Save yourselves from this untoward generation.

41 ¶Then they that gladly received his word were baptized: and the same day there were added *unto them* about three thousand souls.

42 And they continued stedfastly in the apostles' doctrine and fellowship, and in breaking of bread, and in prayers.

43 And fear came upon every soul: and many wonders and signs were done by the apostles.

44 And all that believed were together, and had all things common;

45 And sold their possessions and goods, and parted them to all *men*, as every man had need.

46 And they, continuing daily with one accord in the temple, and breaking bread from house to house, did eat their meat with gladness and singleness of heart,

47 Praising God, and having favour with all the people. And the Lord added to the church daily such as should be saved.

29-32. Men and brethren, let me freely speak unto you of the patriarch David. Peter now clarifies the prophecy which he has just quoted. It is evident that prophecy did not literally find its fulfillment in David, for the patriarch died and is buried and is in a sepulchre that very day. But Jesus Christ's triumph over death in the resurrection confirms the veracity of this Old Testament prophecy. Therefore the prophecy was not made of David himself, but of his descendant, Jesus of Nazareth. They are all witnesses of the resurrected Lord and could attest to the veracity of the prophecy.

33-36. Peter continues to illustrate that the patriarch David is not the Messiah, **For David is not ascended into the heavens.** The exaltation of Christ allows Him to sit at the right hand of the Father and thus send the Holy Spirit of God on His believers. This David could not do, for he had not ascended into the heavens. In proof of this, Peter appealed to Psalms 110:1 which he quotes as evidence that David addressed the Lord Jesus as One on high. Peter's conclusion: **that God hath made that same Jesus, whom ye have crucified, both Lord and Christ.**

37-40. Peter's preaching was tremendously effective, for those who heard **were pricked in their heart.** Those listening asked, **what shall we do?** Peter's answer to them was, **Repent, and be baptized every one of you in the name of Jesus Christ.** This is one of the most controversial verses in the New Testament. In understanding it we must remember that it was originally stated as a message to Israel concerning their national crime of murdering their Messiah. It is unwise to link baptism with the remission of sins for nowhere do the Scriptures teach that salvation is dependent on baptism (see I Cor 1:17; cf. I Cor 15:1-4, where Paul clearly states what the gospel is and baptism is not included). Those who insist upon baptismal regeneration literally "rob Paul to pay Peter" (see II Pet 3:15-16).

41-47. And they continued steadfastly in the apostles' doctrine and fellowship, and in breaking of bread, and in prayers. By the Holy Spirit of God, so effective was Peter's first sermon that three thousand souls were added unto the church that day. Not only is evangelism evident here, but growth in the church is evident as well. Each one saved was then nurtured in the faith as he continued to learn the doctrine of the apostles, to fellowship with the believers, to sit in equality at the Lord's table, to pray and share his burdens with others of like precious faith.

And not only that; **all that believed were together, and had all things common.** The enjoying of all things in common among those of the early church should not be interpreted as communism. This was an early system of mutual ownership (2:45) which is distinct from communism. Communism says, "what is yours, is mine." "Common-ism" says, "what is mine is yours also." At the birth of the church, this system was absolutely necessary for many who came to know the Lord were repudiated by society and disinherited by family. This system was temporary, and had its problems (cf. Acts 5:1; 6:1). It is a system which gave rise to laziness (II Thess 3:7-10) and had to be clarified by the Apostle Paul.

Nevertheless, in the harmony of the early church, the people continued likeminded, **Praising God, and having favor with all the people.** This unity of purpose produced much fruit and daily the Lord added to His church.

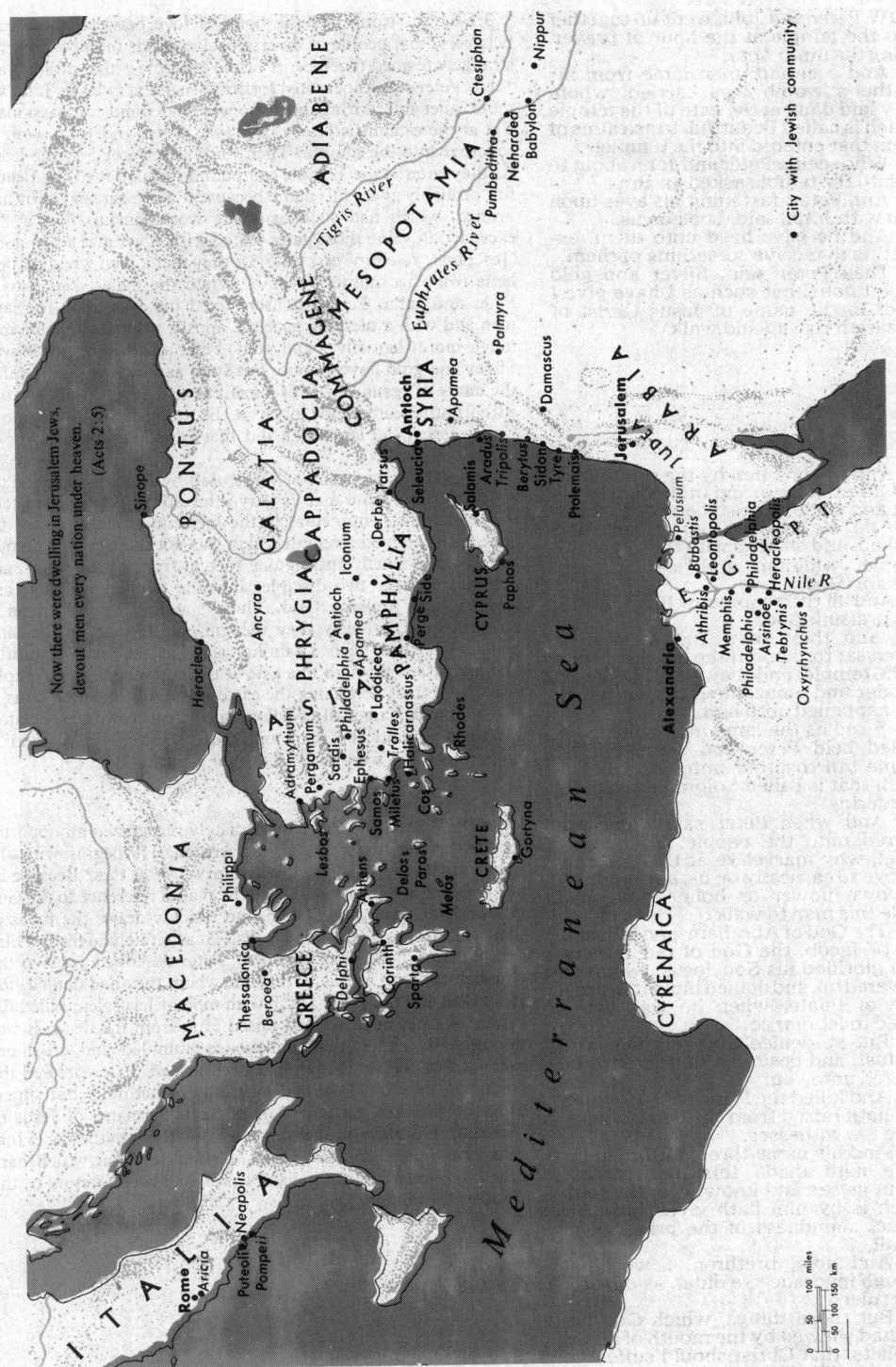

Now there were dwelling in Jerusalem Jews, devout men every nation under heaven. (Acts 2:5)

● City with Jewish community

The Jewish Diaspora in the Times of Jesus

CHAPTER 3

NOW Peter and John went up together into the temple at the hour of prayer, *being* the ninth *hour*.

2 And a certain man lame from his mother's womb was carried, whom they laid daily at the gate of the temple which is called Beautiful, to ask alms of them that entered into the temple;

3 Who seeing Peter and John about to go into the temple asked an alms.

4 And Peter, fastening his eyes upon him with John, said, Look on us.

5 And he gave heed unto them, expecting to receive something of them.

6 Then Peter said, Silver and gold have I none; but such as I have give I thee: In the name of Jesus Christ of Nazareth rise up and walk.

7 And he took him by the right hand, and lifted *him* up: and immediately his feet and ancle bones received strength.

8 And he leaping up stood, and walked, and entered with them into the temple, walking, and leaping, and praising God.

9 And all the people saw him walking and praising God:

10 And they knew that it was he which sat for alms at the Beautiful gate of the temple: and they were filled with wonder and amazement at that which had happened unto him.

11 ¶And as the lame man which was healed held Peter and John, all the people ran together unto them in the porch that is called Solomon's, greatly wondering.

12 And when Peter saw *it*, he answered unto the people, Ye men of Israel, why marvel ye at this? or why look ye so earnestly on us, as though by our own power or holiness we had made this man to walk?

13 The God of Abraham, and of Isaac, and of Jacob, the God of our fathers, hath glorified his Son Jesus; whom ye delivered up, and denied him in the presence of Pilate, when he was determined to let *him* go.

14 But ye denied the Holy One and the Just, and desired a murderer to be granted unto you;

15 And killed the Prince of life, whom God hath raised from the dead; whereof we are witnesses.

16 And his name through faith in his name hath made this man strong, whom ye see and know: yea, the faith which is by him hath given him this perfect soundness in the presence of you all.

17 And now, brethren, I wot that through ignorance ye did *it*, as *did* also your rulers.

18 But those things, which God before had shewed by the mouth of all his prophets, that Christ should suffer, he hath so fulfilled.

19 Repent ye therefore, and be converted, that your sins may be blotted

3:1-6. So strong was the bond of love between these early believers, that people of diverse backgrounds found themselves strangely teamed together. A prime example is that of Peter and John. Peter was impetuous, forthright, and very bold. John was more quiet and retiring, one who was tender and compassionate. Yet at the established hour of prayer, Peter and John **went up together into the temple.** Their unity is rewarded by the Lord. As they entered the Temple compound through the Gate Beautiful, probably given this name because it was a gate of Corinthian bronze, which had such exquisite workmanship that it "far exceeded in value those gates plated with silver and set in gold" (Josephus, *Jewish Wars*, vs. 5:3), they met a man who had been lame from his mother's womb. When the man asked alms of Peter and John, Peter intensely fixed his eyes upon the lame man and with a piercing gaze the apostle offered the lame man much more than silver and gold. Peter's classic response was, **Silver and gold have I none; but such as I have give I thee: In the name of Jesus Christ of Nazareth rise up and walk.** At that authoritative command, given in the authority of the name of Christ Jesus, the lame man did that which he could never do before.

7-11. The progression of verbs used by Luke to describe the activity of this lame man is very interesting. When Peter took the man's hand, immediately the feet and ankle bones of the lame man received strength which was not their own. The man leaped up, walked, putting one foot in front of the other, and accompanied the two disciples into the temple, **walking, and leaping, and praising God.** Those standing by looked on in amazement. Obviously they recognized the man as the lame beggar who had been a familiar sight at the Gate Beautiful. Having passed through this gate at the entrance to the Temple, they made their way along the eastern wall of the outer court to the colonnade named after Solomon. Here a crowd of spectators thronged around the man and the disciples. They stood in amazement and were ready for some explanation.

12-18. The astute Peter immediately recognized an opportunity to preach his second great sermon. He begins with the question, **Ye men of Israel, why marvel ye at this?** Because he is appealing to a Jewish audience, he makes reference to the God of Abraham, Isaac, and Jacob, but quickly draws the focus of that reference to God's Son, Jesus. To accurately identify Him, and to cause them to feel remorse, Peter described Jesus as the One delivered up to Pilate, the One whom they had denied, **the Holy One and the Just.** The Jewish mob of Jerusalem killed the Prince of Life, but God had raised Him from the dead. It was through His name, that name once humbled and cried out against, that this lame man had been healed. Peter pressed the point that he was not healed magically or naturally but supernaturally through the power invested in the name of Jesus of Nazareth. His purpose again was to bring them to the belief that Jesus was indeed the predicted Messiah and that which happened to Him, His suffering and death, had been foretold by the mouths of the prophets.

19-21. Repent ye therefore, and be converted, that your sins may be blotted out. Peter's second sermon follows the lines

out, when the times of refreshing shall come from the presence of the Lord:

20 And he shall send Jesus Christ, which before was preached unto you:

21 Whom the heaven must receive until the times of restitution of all things, which God hath spoken by the mouth of all his holy prophets since the world began.

22 For Moses truly said unto the fathers, A prophet shall the Lord your God raise up unto you of your brethren, like unto me; him shall ye hear in all things whatsoever he shall say unto you.

23 And it shall come to pass, that every soul, which will not hear that prophet, shall be destroyed from among the people.

24 Yea, and all the prophets from Samuel and those that follow after, as many as have spoken, have likewise foretold of these days.

25 Ye are the children of the prophets, and of the covenant which God made with our fathers, saying unto Abraham, And in thy seed shall all the kindreds of the earth be blessed.

26 Unto you first God, having raised up his Son Jesus, sent him to bless you, in turning away every one of you from his iniquities.

CHAPTER 4

AND as they spake unto the people, the priests, and the captain of the temple, and the Săd'du-ceeś, came upon them,

2 Being grieved that they taught the people, and preached through Jesus the resurrection from the dead.

3 And they laid hands on them, and put them in hold unto the next day: for it was now eventide.

4 Howbeit many of them which heard the word believed; and the number of the men was about five thousand.

5 ¶And it came to pass on the morrow, that their rulers, and elders, and scribes,

6 And Ăn'nas the high priest, and Că'ia-phas, and John, and Alexander, and as many as were of the kindred of the high priest, were gathered together at Jerusalem.

7 And when they had set them in the midst, they asked, By what power, or by what name, have ye done this?

8 Then Peter, filled with the Holy

of his first. He makes reference to the Lord Jesus and His messiahship and then calls for repentance on the part of those who crucified the Lord of Glory. Interestingly, the gift of the Holy Spirit is not mentioned in this sermon, for he is speaking nationally to Israel and not individually to the Israelites. It is in the context of this national message that he mentions the **times of refreshing** and the **times of restitution of all things.** The word rendered "refreshing" (Gr *anapsyxis*) is and may be translated "respite" (cf. Ex 8:15). Prior to the time when God shall send Jesus Christ again, He who has now ascended into heaven, the believing remnant of Israel will repent and turn to God in preparation for the Millennium which is to follow (cf. Deut 30:1-3; Zech 12:10-14). Peter implores national Israel to repent of their sins so that they may be part of that remnant when the "times of refreshing" come.

The word rendered "restitution" (Gr *apokatastasis*, vs. 21) should perhaps be rendered "fulfillment" or "establishment." It is a restoration to the former state in the program of God. Although at the time of writing things looked very bleak for national Israel, nevertheless Peter assures the Israelites that God will once again deal with Israel in a blessed and bountiful way (cf. Rom 11:26-27).

22-26. The apostle introduces the testimony of Moses to support his case in a call for national repentance. The words that follow are from Deuteronomy 18:15ff. Moses is there warning the children of Israel not to follow after the practices of the Canaanites, but to trust God to raise up a prophet like Moses from among their brethren. Peter contends that that prophet was indeed the Lord Jesus Christ, whom the Jews had crucified.

The prophetic testimonies of Samuel and the subsequent prophets are added to that of Moses. The whole of Old Testament prophetic testimony is to show that Jesus was indeed the expected Messiah, but in the plan of God, was crucified, buried, and raised from the dead. In addressing the **children of the prophets,** Moses makes reference to the fact that the Israelites are the heirs to the covenants made to Abraham and others. Hence God is vitally interested in having the Israelites repent and receive Jesus Christ as Messiah and Saviour so that He may turn **away every one of you from his iniquities.**

II. PERSECUTION AND THE EXPANSION OF THE CHURCH. 4:1-9:31.

A. Persecution Before the Sanhedrin. 4:1-22.

4:1-4. Such a crowd had gathered around Peter and John at Solomon's colonnade that the priest, the captain of the Temple (an official referred to in literature as the chief *sagan*) and the Sadducees seized them. Traditionally the priests and High Priests came from the ranks of the aristocratic Sadducees. These three groups were angered at the fact that Peter and John **taught the people, and preached through Jesus the resurrection from the dead,** a doctrine to which the Sadducees were violently opposed. The end result was that Peter and John were bodily thrown into prison and incarcerated until the next day. However, from Peter's second sermon five thousand men believed, another great victory for the faith.

5-7. The next morning the Sanhedrin met to discuss this problem. Their meeting probably took place just west of the temple area, across the Tyropoeon Valley, in the open-air gathering place known as the Xystos (i.e., "polished floor"). Present were Annas, the senior ex-High Priest, his son-in-law Caiaphas, the present High Priest, John, Alexander, and other kinsmen of the High Priest who cannot be identified with certainty. They were not at all concerned that a man was healed or that a sermon was preached, but in **what power, or by what name, have ye done this?**

8-12. Always boldly ready to preach, and having been suc-

Ghost, said unto them, Ye rulers of the people, and elders of Israel,

9 If we this day be examined of the good deed done to the impotent man, by what means he is made whole;

10 Be it known unto you all, and to all the people of Israel, that by the name of Jesus Christ of Nazareth, whom ye crucified, whom God raised from the dead, *even* by him doth this man stand here before you whole.

11 This is the stone which was set at nought of you builders which is become the head of the corner.

12 Neither is there salvation in any other: for there is none other name under heaven given among men, whereby we must be saved.

13 ¶Now when they saw the boldness of Peter and John, and perceived that they were unlearned and ignorant men, they marvelled; and they took knowledge of them, that they had been with Jesus.

14 And beholding the man which was healed standing with them, they could say nothing against it.

15 But when they had commanded them to go aside out of the council, they conferred among themselves,

16 Saying, What shall we do to these men? for that indeed a notable miracle hath been done by them *is* manifest to all them that dwell in Jerusalem; and we cannot deny *it.*

17 But that it spread no further among the people, let us straitly threaten them, that they speak henceforth to no man in this name.

18 And they called them, and commanded them not to speak at all nor teach in the name of Jesus.

19 But Peter and John answered and said unto them, Whether it be right in the sight of God to hearken unto you more than unto God, judge ye.

20 For we cannot but speak the things which we have seen and heard.

21 So when they had further threatened them, they let them go, finding nothing how they might punish them, because of the people: for all *men* glorified God for that which was done.

22 For the man was above forty years old, on whom this miracle of healing was shewed.

23 ¶And being let go, they went to their own company, and reported all that the chief priests and elders had said unto them.

24 And when they heard that, they lifted up their voice to God with one accord, and said, Lord, thou *art* God, which hast made heaven, and earth, and the sea, and all that in them is:

25 Who by the mouth of thy servant David hast said, Why did the heathen rage, and the people imagine vain things?

26 The kings of the earth stood up, and the rulers were gathered together against the Lord, and against his Christ.

27 For of a truth against thy holy child Jesus, whom thou hast anointed, both Herod, and Pontius Pilate, with

cessful in his first two endeavors, Peter, **filled with the Holy Ghost,** now begins his third sermon. He boldly asserts that the man was healed in the power, by the authority of, and in the name of Jesus of Nazareth. Then, as has now become his practice, he preaches the death, burial, and resurrection of the Lord Jesus and links that to the well-known Old Testament Scripture, "The stone which the builders rejected is become the head of the corner" (Ps 118:22). The once-despised Jesus of Nazareth, now glorified and at the right hand of the Father, was the One by whose authority this man was healed. If the Sanhedrin insists on repudiating the name and power of Jesus, they must also insist in repudiating the possibility of salvation, **for there is none other name under heaven given, whereby we must be saved.** Healing, tongues, the church, the Spirit of God, even God the Father Himself is not the point of contact with sinful man. Jesus Christ alone is the One by whom salvation comes to mankind.

13-22. These highly educated and sophisticated members of the Sanhedrin were completely astonished at the boldness of Peter and John. Obviously they had no formal training in the rabbinical schools, yet they ably defended their actions and sustained a theological disputation with the Supreme Court of the nation. There was but one answer: **they had been with Jesus.** Their only recourse was to release Peter and John.

After they had done so, the Sanhedrin then attempted to deal with their dilemma. A miracle had been performed in their midst and all of Jerusalem knew it. They could not deny the miracle. However, they could attempt to keep the news of that miracle from spreading to other communities. The decision: **let us straitly threaten them, that they speak henceforth to no man in this name.**

Peter and John were recalled to the chambers of the Sanhedrin and advised that they could never again speak or teach in the name of Jesus of Nazareth. Actually, the Sanhedrin had little hope that they would obey this command. There was only one course of action for Peter and John: **we cannot but speak the things which we have seen and heard.** This open defiance only provoked an additional threat by the Sanhedrin. Their arrest and release were only to increase the number of believers in Jesus of Nazareth. The New Testament church had been born, was expanding rapidly, and had two eloquent spokesmen in the persons of Peter and John. Nothing could stand in the way of its development. Persecution only hastened the inevitable growth of the church.

B. Character of the Persecuted Church. 4:23-5:16.

23-30. Having been finally released by the Sanhedrin, Peter and John returned to where the other disciples were gathered and recounted for them what had just taken place. It was an occasion for rejoicing and together, with one accord, they made their prayer unto God. It was a prayer of thanksgiving.

They addressed God as Sovereign Lord (Gr *despotēs*, cf. Lk 2:29; Rev 6:10). God is the Sovereign Creator of all, and as such was in complete control of the Sanhedrin situation. After addressing the Lord in typical Hebrew language, the disciples then quoted the opening words of Psalm 2 (vs. 25). Next came a rehearsing of Satan's attempts to thwart the purpose of God as represented by Herod Antipas, Tetrarch of Galilee and Peraea (cf. Lk 23:7ff.), and Pontius Pilate. They are not concerned, however, with Satan's attempts for they are convinced that what happened to the Lord Jesus (and now to them) was foreordained by the counsel of God. The Sanhedrin and others may threaten them, but they can never defeat them. "If God be for us, who

the Gentiles, and the people of Israel, were gathered together,

28 For to do whatsoever thy hand and thy counsel determined before to be done.

29 And now, Lord, behold their threatenings: and grant unto thy servants, that with all boldness they may speak thy word,

30 By stretching forth thine hand to heal; and that signs and wonders may be done by the name of thy holy child Jesus.

31 And when they had prayed, the place was shaken where they were assembled together; and they were all filled with the Holy Ghost, and they spake the word of God with boldness.

32 ¶And the multitude of them that believed were of one heart and of one soul: neither said any of them that ought of the things which he possessed was his own; but they had all things common.

33 And with great power gave the apostles witness of the resurrection of the Lord Jesus: and great grace was upon them all.

34 Neither was there any among them that lacked: for as many as were possessors of lands or houses sold them, and brought the prices of the things that were sold,

35 And laid them down at the apostles' feet: and distribution was made unto every man according as he had need.

36 And Joses, who by the apostles was surnamed Barnabas, (which is, being interpreted, The son of consolation,) a Levite, and of the country of Cyprus,

37 Having land, sold it, and brought the money, and laid it at the apostles' feet.

CHAPTER 5

BUT a certain man named Ăn-a-nī′as, with Sap-phī′ra his wife, sold a possession,

2 And kept back part of the price, his wife also being privy to it, and brought a certain part, and laid it at the apostles' feet.

3 But Peter said, Ăn-a-nī′as, why hath Satan filled thine heart to lie to the Holy Ghost, and to keep back part of the price of the land?

4 Whiles it remained, was it not thine own? and after it was sold, was it not in thine own power? why hast thou conceived this thing in thine heart? thou hast not lied unto men, but unto God.

5 And Ăn-a-nī′as hearing these words fell down, and gave up the ghost: and great fear came on all them that heard these things.

6 And the young men arose, wound

can be against us?" (Rom 8:31). In the midst of persecutions and threats, the disciples pray that with all boldness **they may speak thy word, By stretching forth thine hand to heal.** Here the medical language of Luke comes to the fore. The word translated "heal" (Gr *iasis*) is used elsewhere twice by Luke and by no one else in the New Testament. This offers good evidence for the authorship of Luke. The disciples' prayer closes with a petition that signs and wonders may be done **by the name of thy holy child Jesus.**

31. And when they had prayed, the place was shaken. This first-century fledgling church was not only a persecuted church, and a Spirit-filled church, and a powerful church, it was also a praying church. They had found that prayer was the ground of power. So evident was the Spirit of God that the place in which they were assembled shook as with an earthquake when their prayer was offered up. Again, **they were all filled with the Holy Ghost.** While this was a fresh filling of the Spirit, it cannot be considered a fresh baptism. The only baptism by the Spirit of God they would experience had already occurred at Pentecost. With increased filling came increased boldness to speak the Word of God.

32-37. Characteristic of a praying church is its lack of selfishness. Each member of this Jerusalem church was interested in the welfare of each other member. The expression, **of one heart and of one soul,** shows the remarkable unanimity of this Spirit-filled community. Richer members of the church made provision for those who were poor. No one was in want or hunger. Those who had houses or land sold them in order to see to the welfare of others. Money was brought and laid at the apostles' feet and distribution was made to everyone **according as he had need.** No one made windfall profits; no one was impoverished. **Joses . . . surnamed Barnabas . . . Having land, sold it.** The exact etymology of Joses' name **Barnabas** is not clear, but he does show himself to be a true "son of consolation [encouragement]." As a Levite from the island of Cyprus, he was not unfamiliar with Jerusalem, for he had relatives there (see 12:12; Col 4:10). The land which Barnabas sold may have been great or little, but whichever, he brought the money and willingly laid it at the apostles' feet to be distributed to every man according as he had need. Here is a fine example of Christian commitment that goes beyond mere words.

5:1-6. The account of Ananias and Sapphira occurs within the context of, and right on the heels of, the account of the generosity of Barnabas in sharing with other believers. As Barnabas has sold a possession and brought the money and laid it at the apostles' feet, so too this husband-and-wife team, Ananias and Sapphira, **sold a possession.** The difference between Barnabas and them, however, is seen in the second verse, **And kept back part of the price.** Ananias and Sapphira had apparently not learned the lesson that there is no such thing as secret sin. The psalmist David had to exclaim, "O God, thou knowest my foolishness; and my sins are not hid from thee" (Ps 69:5; see also Moses, Ex 2:11-14; and Achan, Josh 7:21-22).

When Peter confronted Ananias with whether or not Satan had filled his heart to lie to the Holy Ghost, the apostle made it abundantly clear that the practice of "common-ism" was definitely not communism. Peter asserted, **While it remained, was it not thine own?** What belonged to Ananias was indeed his and did not belong to the church, unless he gave it to them. Like-

him up, and carried *him* out, and buried *him.*

7 And it was about the space of three hours after, when his wife, not knowing what was done, came in.

8 And Peter answered unto her, Tell me whether ye sold the land for so much? And she said, Yea, for so much.

9 Then Peter said unto her, How is it that ye have agreed together to tempt the Spirit of the Lord? behold, the feet of them which have buried thy husband *are* at the door, and shall carry thee out.

10 Then fell she down straightway at his feet, and yielded up the ghost: and the young men came in, and found her dead, and, carrying *her* forth, buried *her* by her husband.

11 And great fear came upon all the church, and upon as many as heard these things.

12 ¶And by the hands of the apostles were many signs and wonders wrought among the people; (and they were all with one accord in Solomon's porch.

13 And of the rest durst no man join himself to them: but the people magnified them.

14 And believers were the more added to the Lord, multitudes both of men and women.)

15 Insomuch that they brought forth the sick into the streets, and laid *them* on beds and couches, that at the least the shadow of Peter passing by might overshadow some of them.

16 There came also a multitude *out* of the cities round about unto Jerusalem, bringing sick folks, and them which were vexed with unclean spirits: and they were healed every one.

17 ¶Then the high priest rose up, and all they that were with him, (which is the sect of the Săd'du-ceeś,) and were filled with indignation,

18 And laid their hands on the apostles, and put them in the common prison.

19 But the angel of the Lord by night opened the prison doors, and brought them forth, and said,

20 Go, stand and speak in the temple to the people all the words of this life.

21 And when they heard *that* they entered into the temple early in the morning, and taught. But the high priest came, and they that were with him, and called the council together, and all the senate of the children of Israel, and sent to the prison to have them brought.

22 But when the officers came, and

wise, after he sold the land, Ananias could do with the money whatever he wished. If he shared it with the believers of Jerusalem who were less fortunate than he, it would be out of concern and love for them, not out of requirement. Since he chose to give it to the church in the same manner that Barnabas had given, he should not have attempted to lie to God and His servants by claiming that he had given his all. A lie to the servant of God was tantamount to lying to the Spirit of God Himself.

When Ananias learned that he had lied unto God, he fell down, **and gave up the ghost.** Ananias was struck dead for his sin against God, and the young men bound him in grave linen, carried him out, and buried him.

7-11. Unaware of what had happened to her husband, about three hours later Sapphira came before Peter and the other disciples. A similar question was asked her concerning the selling of her possession. Because she had conspired with her husband to lie to the Spirit of God, and attempted to increase her image in the eyes of the other believers, Peter predicted that the feet of those that carried out her husband would also carry out Sapphira.

Then fell she down straightway at his feet, and yielded up the ghost. As predicted, the men quickly came and bore her body away to be buried alongside her husband. Satan first attacked the church from without, persecuting it as a roaring lion. Now he has attacked the church from within, persecuting it as a serpent. But the end result is still the same: **And great fear came upon all the church.** All who had assembled as believers in Jerusalem were brought into a right relationship with God because of persecution. This not altogether unhealthy effect of persecution must have caused havoc in the dominions of darkness.

12-16. The shock of the double death of Ananias and Sapphira apparently sparked the apostles to double their efforts in behalf of the Lord. **Many signs and wonders wrought among the people.** This paragraph is a summary of the great things that have been accomplished through the Spirit of God (cf. 2:43-47; 4:32-35). The sick were brought into the streets on beds and couches and so evident was the presence of the Spirit of God on these men that even the very shadow of Peter passing over someone might cause the healing of that person. For miles around the news spread, and the sick and those possessed by unclean spirits were brought to the disciples. The end result was a record of performance that should cause distrust of modern-day healing campaigns: **and they were healed every one.**

C. Persecution before the Sadducees. 5:17-42.

17-28. Not long before this Peter and John had been released from the court of the Sanhedrin with a stern warning. But the additional healings and the multitudes which crowded around the disciples caused the High Priests and the Sadducees to become very indignant. They ordered that the disciples should be seized and thrown into the common prison. It was there that another miracle occurred. Their escape from the common prison was not accomplished by a *deus ex machina,* as in the Greek tragedies, but by a real angel or "messenger" from the Lord. They were released from prison and were told, **Go, stand and speak in the temple.** Having been warned and imprisoned, the disciples could not be deterred from this heavenly command.

Early the next morning they entered the Temple and did as they had been commanded by the angel. When the Sanhedrin convened to discuss the matter of the disciples, whom they thought were in prison, they felt it necessary to bring the disciples before them once again. Thus an officer was sent to the prison to retrieve them, but returned with the news that the

found them not in the prison, they returned, and told.

23 Saying, The prison truly found we shut with all safety, and the keepers standing without before the doors: but when we had opened, we found no man within.

24 Now when the high priest and the captain of the temple and the chief priests heard these things, they doubted of them whereunto this would grow.

25 Then came one and told them, saying, Behold, the men whom ye put in prison are standing in the temple, and teaching the people.

26 Then went the captain with the officers, and brought them without violence: for they feared the people, lest they should have been stoned.

27 And when they had brought them, they set *them* before the council: and the high priest asked them,

28 Saying, Did not we straitly command you that ye should not teach in this name? and, behold, ye have filled Jerusalem with your doctrine, and intend to bring this man's blood upon us.

29 Then Peter and the *other* apostles answered and said, We ought to obey God rather than men.

30 The God of our fathers raised up Jesus, whom ye slew and hanged on a tree.

31 Him hath God exalted with his right hand *to be* a Prince and a Saviour, for to give repentance to Israel, and forgiveness of sins.

32 And we are his witnesses of these things; and *so is* also the Holy Ghost, whom God hath given to them that obey him.

33 ¶When they heard *that,* they were cut *to the heart,* and took counsel to slay them.

34 Then stood there up one in the council, a Pharisee, named Ga-mā′li-el, a doctor of the law, had in reputation among all the people, and commanded to put the apostles forth a little space;

35 And said unto them, Ye men of Israel, take heed to yourselves what ye intend to do as touching these men.

36 For before these days rose up Theū′das, boasting himself to be somebody; to whom a number of men, about four hundred, joined themselves: who was slain; and all, as many as obeyed him, were scattered, and brought to nought.

37 After this man rose up Judas of Galilee in the days of the taxing, and drew away much people after him: he also perished; and all, *even* as many as obeyed him, were dispersed.

38 And now I say unto you, Refrain from these men, and let them alone: for if this counsel or this work be of men, it will come to nought:

39 But if it be of God, ye cannot overthrow it; lest haply ye be found even to fight against God.

40 And to him they agreed: and when they had called the apostles, and beaten *them,* they commanded that they should not speak in the name of Jesus, and let them go.

prison doors were securely shut and the keepers were on duty outside the doors, but no one was to be found in the prison. The immediate concern of the High Priest, the captains of the Temple, and the chief priests was that the miraculous release of the disciples would be yet another story that would grow, causing even greater popularity for the followers of the Lord Jesus. Thus the officers were commanded to bring Peter and the others from the Temple, but without violence for fear of the people.

When they took their place before the Sanhedrin, the president of the court (the High Priest) reminded them that they had previously been warned about preaching in the name of Jesus. They thought the disciples were attempting to place responsibility for the death of Jesus on the leaders of the Sanhedrin. In questioning Peter, the High Priest attested to a fact that is truly miraculous in light of the great persecution the early church had received. In just a short time, due to the indwelling presence of the Holy Spirit of God, the High Priest exclaimed to the disciples, **ye have filled Jerusalem with your doctrine.** This remains as an example and a challenge to every church of every age to do likewise.

29-32. We ought to obey God rather than men. Peter is not so much advocating open defiance against the state as he is absolute dependence upon God. Having yet another golden opportunity to preach Christ and Him crucified, Peter falls back upon his pattern of making reference to the slaying of Jesus and the cursed hanging upon a tree (Deut 21:23; Gal 3:13). Also his message contains a note of repentance and forgiveness of sin, as well as his repeated claims to be among the witnesses of these things.

33-40. So enraged at the defiance of the believers in Christ were the Sadducees that they were about to pass judgment on the disciples and sentence them to death. However, the pharisaic members of the court, although in the minority, still had a very powerful and persuasive voice in the judgments of that court. Perhaps the most respected man of the entire Sanhedrin was the renowned Pharisee named Gamaliel. This *rabban,* a doctor of the law, was the leader of the famous school of Hillel. He had many illustrious disciples, among them Saul of Tarsus (cf. 22:3). When this prestigious elder rose to speak, everyone listened.

With calmer heads now prevailing, Gamaliel cautioned the Sanhedrin conecerning thir intentions to put the disciples to death. First he reminded them of an insurgent named Theudas, **boasting himself to be somebody.** It is obvious that Gamaliel did not believe Theudas was anyone of importance, but his following grew to four hundred persons before he was slain and his patriots scattered. Nothing for certain is known of this man except that he was probably one of many insurgents who arose in Palestine about the time of Herod the Great in 4 B.C.

Again, Gamaliel reminded the Sanhedrin of a more successful insurgent, Judas of Galilee. This man had a larger following in his revolt of A.D. 6, when he incited a nationalist revolt against paying tribute to Caesar when God alone was Israel's true King (see Josephus, *Jewish War* ii. 8.1; *Antiq.* xviii. 1.1). The taxing for census referred to was that of Publius Sulpicius Quirinius when he was the imperial legate of Syria for the second time (A.D. 6-7).

Gamaliel's counsel and advice to the Sanhedrin is classic. It is this. If the movement which involves these disciples of Jesus of

Nazareth is not of God, it will come to nothing. But, on the other hand, if it is of God, the Sanhedrin certainly would not want to fight against it. This put the Sanhedrin on the horns of a dilemma. They hated the movement, but the reasoning of Gamaliel and his "wait and see" policy had to be adopted. The end result was that **when they had called the apostles, and beaten them, they commanded that they should not speak in the name of Jesus, and let them go.** A now common procedure, releasing the disciples and forbidding them to preach in the name of Jesus, took on one additional feature. This time the disciples were beaten before they were released.

41-42. Having received the harshest punishment to date, the disciples were in no way disheartened. On the contrary they were **rejoicing that they were counted worthy to suffer shame for His name.** Increased persecution simply evoked increased dedication. So much so that **daily in the temple, and in every house, they ceased not to teach and preach Jesus Christ.**

41 And they departed from the presence of the council, rejoicing that they were counted worthy to suffer shame for his name.
42 And daily in the temple, and in every house, they ceased not to teach and preach Jesus Christ.

CHAPTER 6

AND in those days, when the number of the disciples was multiplied, there arose a murmuring of the Grecians against the Hebrews, because their widows were neglected in the daily ministration.
2 Then the twelve called the multitude of the disciples *unto them*, and said, It is not reason that we should leave the word of God, and serve tables.
3 Wherefore, brethren, look ye out among you seven men of honest report, full of the Holy Ghost and wisdom, whom we may appoint over this business.
4 But we will give ourselves continually to prayer, and to the ministry of the word.

D. Persecution of Stephen. 6:1-8:4.

6:1-4. And in those days. This passage may be regarded as an epilogue to what has preceded. The time has now come for an important advance in organization in the New Testament church. This organizational advance arose out of a rift between the **Grecians** and the **Hebrews.** Both of these groups were Jews, the Grecians were Greek-speaking Jews and the Hebrews were Aramaic-speaking Jews. As is so frequently the case, a conflict arose over a minute concern. Since the wealthy of the Christian community had sold their goods to provide for the poor, some of the Grecian Jews felt their poor and widows were being neglected in favor of the more traditional Hebrew-speaking Jews.

Thus the Twelve called the disciples together and asked them to seek out seven men of good reputation, men who would be responsible for administering the charitable allocations. Upon the appointment of such men, the Twelve could give themselves to the ministry to which they were called: **prayer, and to the ministry of the word.** The twentieth century church would do well to take this advice given by the Twelve. Many church leaders today are not free to devote themselves to the two prime aspects of their ministry, prayer and the preaching of the word. Members of the local assembly must assume positions of responsibility in order to free the pastor to do the job for which he has been called.

5-8. And they chose Stephen . . . and Philip and Prochorus, and Nicanor, and Timon, and Parmenas, and Nicolas. The suggestion of the Twelve was readily accepted by the church of Jerusalem. Seven men were chosen to fulfill the obligation of deacon. The first named is Stephen, who is a **man full of faith and the Holy Ghost.** This description is not without substance as the next chapters of Acts portray. Philip is also mentioned and he too will figure heavily in the next chapters. Of the others, less is known. A later tradition suggests that Prochorus was an amanuensis of John the evangelist and became Bishop of Nicomedia and was subsequently martyred at Antioch. The last-named man, Nicolas, is mentioned as not a Jew but a proselyte from Antioch. Some have speculated that he was the founder of the Nicolaitans in Revelation 2:6, 15. This, however, cannot be said with great certainty.

And the word of God increased. At this point Luke interprets the narrative of this organizational advance to give a progress report on the church's activities. Five other such reports punctuate this history of Acts (see also 9:31; 12:24; 16:5; 19:20; 28:31). Perhaps the interjection here is to indicate that the church need not choose between evangelistic zeal and the social and physical concerns of its constituency. Both advanced together.

9-15. Then there arose certain of the synagogue . . . dis-

5 And the saying pleased the whole multitude: and they chose Stephen, a man full of faith and of the Holy Ghost, and Philip, and Prŏch′o-rus, and Nĭ-cā′nor, and Tī′mon, and Pär′me-nas, and Nicolas a proselyte of Antioch:
6 Whom they set before the apostles: and when they had prayed, they laid *their* hands on them.
7 And the word of God increased; and the number of the disciples multiplied in Jerusalem greatly; and a great company of the priests were obedient to the faith.
8 ¶And Stephen, full of faith and power, did great wonders and miracles among the people.

9 Then there arose certain of the syna-

gogue, which is called *the synagogue* of the Lib'er-tines, and C̄y-rē'nĭ-anṣ, and Alexandrians, and of them of Cĭ-lĭ'-ćia and of Asia, disputing with Stephen.

10 And they were not able to resist the wisdom and the spirit by which he spake.

11 Then they suborned men, which said, We have heard him speak blasphemous words against Moses, and *against* God.

12 And they stirred up the people, and the elders, and the scribes, and came upon *him*, and caught him, and brought *him* to the council,

13 And set up false witnesses, which said, This man ceaseth not to speak blasphemous words against this holy place, and the law:

14 For we have heard him say, that this Jesus of Nazareth shall destroy this place, and shall change the customs which Moses delivered us.

15 And all that sat in the council, looking stedfastly on him, saw his face as it had been the face of an angel.

CHAPTER 7
THEN said the high priest, Are these things so?

2 And he said, Men, brethren, and fathers, hearken; The God of glory appeared unto our father Abraham, when he was in Mĕs-o-po-tā'mi-a, before he dwelt in Châr'ran,

3 And said unto him, Get thee out of thy country, and from thy kindred, and come into the land which I shall shew thee.

4 Then came he out of the land of the Chăl-dē'anṣ, and dwelt in Châr'ran: and from thence, when his father was dead, he removed him into this land, wherein ye now dwell.

5 And he gave him none inheritance in it, no, not *so much as* to set his foot on: yet he promised that he would give it to him for a possession, and to his seed after him, when *as yet* he had no child.

6 And God spake on this wise, That his seed should sojourn in a strange land; and that they should bring them

puting with Stephen. The ministry of Stephen is the link between the establishment of the church in Jerusalem and the conversion of the Apostle Paul. As Stephen entered the synagogue to preach in the name of Jesus Christ, he encountered opposition. Apparently this synagogue was one which catered to those who were either from the dispersion or descendants of those from areas outside of Palestine. Specifically, this synagogue of the Libertines was made up of those who were Cyrenians, Alexandrians, and Cilicians. The dispute with Stephen brought little success to the Jews. **They were not able to resist the wisdom and the spirit by which he spake.**

These stubborn men, however, did not give up when they were beaten philosophically. They simply resorted to baser tactics, slanderous charges of blasphemy against Moses and God. Apparently in the first century the charge of blasphemy included more than a profane use of the ineffable name of the God of Israel (*Mishnah, Sanhedrin* vii. 5). Since Stephen had said nothing against Moses or God, they had to introduce false witnesses, a common practice among the Jews (see also Mt 26:59-61; Mk 14:55-59). These false witnesses stirred up the people by saying that Stephen spoke **blasphemous words against this holy place, and the law.** The false witnesses then alluded to a portion of Stephen's message in which he quoted Jesus' statement about destroying the body, and it being raised again in three days (cf. Mt 26:61; Mk 14:58). As this statement was misinterpreted when Jesus uttered it, now it is misinterpreted when Stephen reported it. Thus the persecution of Stephen began and he was dragged before the council. There they looked upon him and saw **his face as it had been the face of an angel.** This is not to intimate that he had the gentle, effeminate face often portrayed in medieval paintings of angels. Rather his face was aglow with the love of the Lord Jesus for these his persecutors.

7:1. Then said the high priest, Are these things so? In response to the question of the High Priest concerning the false allegations leveled against Stephen, this Spirit-filled deacon replied with what amounts to an early apology for the Christian faith. It is a general historical account of the moving of God in the lives of Abraham and his descendants. But when Stephen makes his application to this historical account (vss. 51-53) it is evident that he shows Christianity to be the natural fulfillment of the promises made to Abraham and the Patriarchs. He does not divorce his heritage from his newfound belief in the Messiah. Instead, he shows that Jesus of Nazareth is the fulfillment of Jewish heritage and those who have not recognized Him as Messiah are indeed traitors to their forefathers.

2-5. Men, brethren, and fathers, hearken. As Stephen begins his apology, he addresses them in a polite manner, not what one would expect of false witnesses. In these verses he addresses himself to the call of Abraham (Gen 12) and to his removal by faith from Ur of the Chaldees to Haran. Also mentioned is the possession of the Promised Land and Abraham's faith that this land would be retained forever, **when as yet he had no child.**

6-10. His seed should sojourn in a strange land. This section records the rite of circumcision given to Abraham as a sign of God's covenant with him and the birth of Isaac, Jacob, and

into bondage, and entreat *them* evil four hundred years.

7 And the nation to whom they shall be in bondage will I judge, said God: and after that shall they come forth, and serve me in this place.

8 And he gave him the covenant of circumcision: and so *Abraham* begat Isaac, and circumcised him the eighth day; and Isaac *begat* Jacob; and Jacob *begat* the twelve patriarchs.

9 And the patriarchs, moved with envy, sold Joseph into Egypt: but God was with him,

10 And delivered him out of all his afflictions, and gave him favour and wisdom in the sight of Pharaoh king of Egypt; and he made him governor over Egypt and all his house.

11 Now there came a dearth over all the land of Egypt and Chā′naan, and great affliction: and our fathers found no sustenance.

12 But when Jacob heard that there was corn in Egypt, he sent out our fathers first.

13 And at the second *time* Joseph was made known to his brethren; and Joseph's kindred was made known unto Pharaoh.

14 Then sent Joseph, and called his father Jacob to *him*, and all his kindred, threescore and fifteen souls.

15 So Jacob went down into Egypt, and died, he, and our fathers,

16 And were carried over into Sȳ′chem, and laid in the sepulchre that Abraham bought for a sum of money of the sons of Ēm′môr *the father* of Sȳ′chem.

17 But when the time of the promise drew nigh, which God had sworn to Abraham, the people grew and multiplied in Egypt.

18 Till another king arose, which knew not Joseph.

19 The same dealt subtilly with our kindred, and evil entreated our fathers, so that they cast out their young children, to the end they might not live.

20 In which time Moses was born, and was exceeding fair, and nourished up in his father's house three months:

21 And when he was cast out, Pharaoh's daughter took him up, and nourished him for her own son.

22 And Moses was learned in all the wisdom of the Egyptians, and was mighty in words and in deeds.

23 And when he was full forty years old, it came into his heart to visit his brethren the children of Israel.

24 And seeing one *of them* suffer wrong, he defended *him*, and avenged him that was oppressed, and smote the Egyptian:

25 For he supposed his brethren would have understood how that God by his hand would deliver them: but they understood not.

26 And the next day he shewed himself unto them as they strove, and would have set them at one again, saying, Sirs, ye are brethren; why do ye wrong one to another?

27 But he that did his neighbour wrong thrust him away, saying, Who made thee a ruler and a judge over us?

the twelve Patriarchs. Also the deliverance into Egyptian bondage is addressed here.

11-16. Joseph was made known to his brethren. In these verses the touching story of Joseph, sold into slavery and risen to power, is recorded. When Jacob learns that his beloved son is still alive, he migrates to Egypt where there is corn and food for all his family. Here the Patriarch dies and his body is taken to Shechem for burial.

17-22. Till another king arose, which knew not Joseph. Stephen now relates the birth and early life of Moses. His learning and wisdom in the sciences of the Egyptians is noted, and that he was **mighty in word and in deed.**

23-29. It came into his heart to visit his brethren the children of Israel. Now when Moses was forty years old and he spied an Egyptian beating one of his brethren. Moses' anger brought him to commit murder and he slew the Egyptian and hid him in the sand. When this atrocity was made known, Moses had to flee to the land of Midian **where he begat two sons.**

28 Wilt thou kill me, as thou diddest the Egyptian yesterday?

29 Then fled Moses at this saying, and was a stranger in the land of Mā'di-an, where he begat two sons.

30 And when forty years were expired, there appeared to him in the wilderness of mount Sī'na an angel of the Lord in a flame of fire in a bush.

31 When Moses saw it, he wondered at the sight: and as he drew near to behold it, the voice of the Lord came unto him,

32 Saying, I am the God of thy fathers, the God of Abraham, and the God of Isaac, and the God of Jacob. Then Moses trembled, and durst not behold.

33 Then said the Lord to him, Put off thy shoes from thy feet: for the place where thou standest is holy ground.

34 I have seen, I have seen the affliction of my people which is in Egypt, and I have heard their groaning, and am come down to deliver them. And now come, I will send thee into Egypt.

35 This Moses whom they refused, saying, Who made thee a ruler and a judge? the same did God send to be a ruler and a deliverer by the hand of the angel which appeared to him in the bush.

36 He brought them out, after that he had shewed wonders and signs in the land of Egypt, and in the Red sea, and in the wilderness forty years.

37 This is that Moses, which said unto the children of Israel, A prophet shall the Lord your God raise up unto you of your brethren, like unto me; him shall ye hear.

38 This is he, that was in the church in the wilderness with the angel which spake to him in the mount Sī'na, and with our fathers: who received the lively oracles to give unto us:

39 To whom our fathers would not obey, but thrust him from them, and in their hearts turned back again into Egypt,

40 Saying unto Aaron, Make us gods to go before us: for as for this Moses, which brought us out of the land of Egypt, we wot not what is become of him.

41 And they made a calf in those days, and offered sacrifice unto the idol, and rejoiced in the works of their own hands.

42 Then God turned, and gave them up to worship the host of heaven; as it is written in the book of the prophets, O ye house of Israel, have ye offered to me slain beasts and sacrifices by the space of forty years in the wilderness?

43 Yea, ye took up the tabernacle of Mō'lŏch, and the star of your god Rĕm'phan, figures which ye made to worship them: and I will carry you away beyond Băb'y-lon.

44 Our fathers had the tabernacle of witness in the wilderness, as he had appointed, speaking unto Moses, that he should make it according to the fashion that he had seen.

45 Which also our fathers that came after brought in with Jesus into the possession of the Gentiles, whom God

30-36. Next in order in Stephen's historical account of Israel is the call of Moses **in a flame of fire in a bush.** The speaker is obviously the God of Abraham, Isaac, and Jacob and the place where Moses stood was holy ground. Moses was commissioned to return to Egypt and to stand in the court of Pharaoh demanding that God's people be released from bondage. After showing the Egyptians great wonders, Moses would lead the children out of the land across the Red Sea and into the wilderness for forty years.

37-43. A prophet shall the Lord your God raise up unto you of your brethren. Although Stephen is yet a great distance from the conclusion of his apology, he begins to lay the groundwork for his contention that the New Testament church is a natural result from those who have received Jesus as Messiah. Even Moses proclaimed that God would raise a prophet up from among the Israelites, whom they should hear and obey. That prophet was Jesus Christ.

The church (Gr ekklēsia) **in the wilderness** is a reference to the assembly of the people of God at the foot of Mount Sinai. Here Stephen makes reference to the idolatry of his forefathers and the worship of the golden calf. In addition the Israelites worship **the host of heaven,** represented specifically by the planetary deities **Moloch** and **Remphan.** His purpose is to show that the nation Israel has the history of needing prophets like unto Moses and Jesus Christ. They also have a history, however, of not receiving those prophets. Interestingly, Stephen had just been charged by the false witnesses with speaking blasphemous words against Moses. But now his purpose is to show that those guilty of disrespect to Moses are his heirs, the Israelites, and not his new companions, the Christians.

44-50. Our fathers had the tabernacle of witness in the wilderness. The attention of the deacon is focused on the building of both the tabernacle and the Temple. He makes reference to the tabernacle in the wilderness and the fact that it was brought in **with Joshua into the possession of the Gentiles.** The Greek form of Joshua, which is translated "Jesus" (AV) in Hebrews 4:8, may be a purposeful allusion to the fact that the one who led Israel into the land of inheritance bears the same

drave out before the face of our fathers, unto the days of David;

46 Who found favour before God, and desired to find a tabernacle for the God of Jacob.

47 But Solomon built him an house.

48 Howbeit the most High dwelleth not in temples made with hands; as saith the prophet,

49 Heaven *is* my throne, and earth *is* my footstool: what house will ye build me? saith the Lord: or what *is* the place of my rest?

50 Hath not my hand made all these things?

51 ¶Ye stiffnecked and uncircumcised in heart and ears, ye do always resist the Holy Ghost: as your fathers *did,* so *do* ye.

52 Which of the prophets have not your fathers persecuted? and they have slain them which shewed before of the coming of the Just One; of whom ye have been now the betrayers and murderers:

53 Who have received the law by the disposition of angels, and have not kept *it.*

54 ¶When they heard these things, they were cut to the heart, and they gnashed on him with *their* teeth.

55 But he, being full of the Holy Ghost, looked up stedfastly into heaven, and saw the glory of God, and Jesus standing on the right hand of God,

56 And said, Behold, I see the heavens opened, and the Son of man standing on the right hand of God.

57 Then they cried out with a loud voice, and stopped their ears, and ran upon him with one accord,

58 And cast *him* out of the city, and stoned *him:* and the witnesses laid down their clothes at a young man's feet, whose name was Saul.

name as the One who can lead Israel into the land of eternal life.

Next, reference is made to the days of David and the fact that it was his desire to build the house of the God of Jacob. This his son Solomon was permitted to do. **Howbeit the most High dwelleth not in temples made with hands.** Stephen quickly draws his apologetic to the person of Jesus Christ. At His trial, the Lord said, "I will destroy this temple that is made with hands, and in three days I will build another made without hands" (Mk 14:58). This reference is obviously to clarify the charge which the false witnesses brought against him (cf. 6:14). Stephen has shown that the Temple, as well as the tabernacle, which preceded it, was never intended to be the permanent dwelling place of God. Jesus of Nazareth gave a correct perspective to the Temple of Jerusalem and its relationship to the God who dwells in the hearts of believers.

Stephen's argument has now been concluded. However, he must yet convince his hearers that what he says is legitimate. Therefore, he has to undertake concluding remarks which will make the application of this historical argument.

51-53. Ye stiffnecked and uncircumcised in heart and ears. In making his conclusion Stephen appeals to a descriptive term which had been used many times of the Jews. God Himself complained that His people were "stiffnecked" (Ex 33:5). That they were "uncircumcised in heart and ears" meant that while they were circumcised in the physical sense, nevertheless their disobedience in not receiving the message of the prophets caused them to be ungodly in their hearts and lives. The resistance of the present generation of Jews to the work of the Holy Spirit is something that their forefathers also exhibited.

The coming of the Just One. Stephen now addresses himself to the present hardness of this stiffnecked people. Characteristic of being a prophet of God in the nation Israel was undergoing extreme persecution and, more often than not, martyrdom. Stephen depicts the Lord Jesus as one in a long line of such prophets whom the Jews betrayed and murdered. Again the tie with Christianity is made in the history of Judaism. The forefathers had killed the messengers who foretold of the coming of the Just One; but they themselves had gone even further in bringing the Just One Himself to a violent death.

54-56. When they heard these things, they were cut to the heart. The testimony of Stephen in his application to the council did more to increase their ire than anything imaginable. The verb used here, and in Acts 5:33 (Gr *diaprio*) expresses the cutting done by a saw. It is designed to show how deep their feelings were, and the similar expression, **they gnashed on him with their teeth,** although not literally done, was always an expression of rage.

Saw the glory of God, and Jesus. Stephen makes no retaliation to the irritated council. Instead he fastens his attention on the heavens, which, during this transition period of Acts, are said to have opened so that Stephen could see the **glory of God, and** (or "even") **Jesus** standing on the right hand of God.

Although the **glory of God** usually represents the shekinah glory of the Old Testament, Jesus is nevertheless the Glory of God. Now ascended into heaven, Jesus has again received the glory which He had with the Father before the world began (Jn 17:5). It is that glory that all men have come short of, and in essence, it is that glory that shows each of us to be sinners (Rom 3:23). Stephen was given the unique opportunity to view Jesus as the Glory of God in heaven.

57-60. Again incensed by the calm, quiet attitude of Stephen, the crowd rushed upon him, crying for his death. Dragging him out of the city, they **stoned him.** Since this is the Jewish form of death, it would indicate that the Sanhedrin and the members of the council provided the oversight for the murder of Stephen. Although this was not legal, and apparently Pilate either turned

59 And they stoned Stephen, calling upon *God*, and saying, Lord Jesus, receive my spirit.

60 And he kneeled down, and cried with a loud voice, Lord, lay not this sin to their charge. And when he had said this, he fell asleep.

CHAPTER 8

AND Saul was consenting unto his death. And at that time there was a great persecution against the church which was at Jerusalem; and they were all scattered abroad throughout the regions of Judæa and Sa-mâ′rĭ-a, except the apostles.

2 And devout men carried Stephen *to his burial*, and made great lamentation over him.

3 As for Saul, he made havock of the church, entering into every house, and haling men and women committed *them* to prison.

4 Therefore they that were scattered abroad went every where preaching the word.

5 ¶Then Philip went down to the city of Sa-mâ′rĭ-a, and preached Christ unto them.

6 And the people with one accord gave heed unto those things which Philip spake, hearing and seeing the miracles which he did.

7 For unclean spirits, crying with loud voice, came out of many that were

a deaf ear to the situation or was not apprised of it, nevertheless the action was carried out in the rage of the Jews.

As was customary, the witnesses cast the first stones. This duty was prescribed both in the Mishnah and also in the Law itself (cf. Lev 24:24; Deut 17:7). In order to throw the first stone the witnesses would divest themselves of their outer garments. These garments were placed **at a young man's feet, whose name was Saul.** At this first introduction to the man Saul, one very important element is frequently overlooked. Nowhere is it stated or even intimated that Saul, later the Apostle Paul, actually participated in the death of Stephen. Saul consented to his death, guarded the garments of those who first stoned him, but is not said to have actually cast a stone himself.

Lord Jesus, receive my spirit. This utterance of Stephen, and the one to follow, echoes the Lord's utterances from the cross. On his knees and being constantly bombarded with stones, Stephen's one concern was not for himself but for those who were his persecutors. As the Lord cried unto the Father, "Father, forgive them; for they know not what they do" (Lk 23:24), so too, Stephen cries unto the Lord in a loud voice, **Lord, lay not this sin to their charge.** When the men of Israel were at their worst, the man Stephen was at his best. He interceded to the Lord God of heaven for those who persecuted him. Even in death his concern was for their eternal life.

8:1-4. There was a great persecution against the church which was at Jerusalem. The murder of Stephen precipitated a persecution unlike any seen heretofore. This time the target was not just the individual, Stephen, but the church as a whole. The most severe persecution must have fallen upon the Hellenistic Jews, for from this time onward the church at Jerusalem appears to have consisted almost entirely of Hebrew or Aramaic-speaking Jews. Although the persecution was deadly, nevertheless it accomplished the direct will of God. This persecution caused the dispersion of the Jews of the Jerusalem church throughout the regions of Judaea and Samaria, except for the apostles who remained in Jerusalem. Thus the Lord's command in chapter 1, verse 8 was fulfilled by the persecution of chapter 8, verse 1.

It was directly against the Jewish law to make lamentations at the funeral of an executed person (see *Mishnah, Sanhedrin* vi. 6). However, certain devout men gave Stephen the burial that was due this first Christian martyr. And what is the "young man" Saul doing while this is going on? He has become the prime mover in the campaign against the church. With papers of permission from the authority of the Sanhedrin and high priest, Paul harassed the church, smashing down doors and arresting men and women in their homes, sending them off to prison. He did so as a zealous Pharisee, fully believing that he was keeping the Law pure from those of this new Christian sect whom he considered to have prostituted the Law. Then what was the result of Saul's and the others' harassment? **They that were scattered abroad went every where preaching the word.** Not only was persecution the means by which the gospel spread to other regions in Palestine, but also it caused the gospel to go to much further fields as well (cf. 11:19ff).

E. The Ministry of Philip. 8:5-40.

5-7. Then Philip . . . preached Christ unto them. It is difficult to say whether "the city of Samaria" was actually the city that bore that name in the Old Testament. At this period of history it had been rebuilt by Herod the Great as a great city and given the name Sebaste in honor of the Roman Emperor (Gr *sebastos;* Lat equivalent *augustus*). It may be that he went to a city in the region of Samaria and may even have been Gutta, which Justin Martyr (*Apology* i, 26) designates as the birthplace

possessed *with them:* and many taken with palsies, and that were lame, were healed.

8 And there was great joy in that city.
9 But there was a certain man, called Simon, which beforetime in the same city used sorcery, and bewitched the people of Sa-mā′rĭ-a, giving out that himself was some great one:
10 To whom they all gave heed, from the least to the greatest, saying, This man is the great power of God.
11 And to him they had regard, because that of long time he had bewitched them with sorceries.
12 But when they believed Philip preaching the things concerning the kingdom of God, and the name of Jesus Christ, they were baptized, both men and women.
13 Then Simon himself believed also: and when he was baptized, he continued with Philip, and wondered, beholding the miracles and signs which were done.

14 ¶Now when the apostles which were at Jerusalem heard that Sa-mā′-rĭ-a had received the word of God, they sent unto them Peter and John:
15 Who, when they were come down, prayed for them, that they might receive the Holy Ghost:
16 (For as yet he was fallen upon none of them: only they were baptized in the name of the Lord Jesus.)
17 Then laid they *their* hands on them, and they received the Holy Ghost.
18 And when Simon saw that through laying on of the apostles' hands the Holy Ghost was given, he offered them money,
19 Saying, Give me also this power, that on whomsoever I lay hands, he may receive the Holy Ghost.
20 But Peter said unto him, Thy money perish with thee, because thou hast thought that the gift of God may be purchased with money.
21 Thou hast neither part nor lot in this matter: for thy heart is not right in the sight of God.
22 Repent therefore of this thy wickedness, and pray God, if perhaps the thought of thine heart may be forgiven thee.
23 For I perceive that thou art in the gall of bitterness, and *in* the bond of iniquity.
24 Then answered Simon, and said, Pray ye to the Lord for me, that none of these things which ye have spoken come upon me.

of Simon the Sorcerer. Whatever the case, Philip had great success in his preaching efforts there. These efforts were accompanied by healing, casting out of unclean spirits, and other signs of the presence of the Holy Spirit in him.

8-13. In the midst of the joy over those who had believed in Jesus of Nazareth as Saviour and those who had been healed, Luke introduces the infamous Simon the Sorcerer. Frequently known as Simon Magus, this man has been the subject of much of early Christian literature. Ireneaus (*Against Heresies* i.) names Simon as the founder of gnosticism. Justin Martyr (*Apology* i, 26) mistakenly ascribes an ancient inscription in the city of Rome to Simon. In the pseudo-Clementine *Recognitions* and *Homilies* the legend about Simon's becoming the nemesis of Peter is greatly elaborated. Also the apocryphal *Acts of Peter* tell how the Christians of Rome were corrupted by this man's false teaching. Whether any of this is historical or not is presently beside the point. What is known is that this sorcerer had great sway over the people of Samaria. So bewitching was his sorcery that it was said of him, **This man is the great power of God.**

When those who had been bewitched by Simon came to know the Lord as Saviour, through the preaching of Philip, and were baptized, **Then Simon himself believed also.** There seems to be some little doubt about the legitimacy of Simon's conversion. There is no sign of repentance. There is no confession of sin. But there is the statement that he continued with Philip **and wondered, beholding the miracles and signs which were done.** Apparently Simon wanted the secret of Philip's power. His only concern was not for his own soul but for the ability to get close to Philip and learn the secret of his ability to heal the sick and perform miracles.

14-24. They sent unto them Peter and John. When the news of Philip's preaching and the subsequent conversion of the Samaritans reached Jerusalem, it was necessary for the Jewish church there to send their two key representatives in order to investigate these "conversions." The church at Jerusalem had been all Jewish; this assembly was all Samaritan. Thus Peter and John descended the heights of Jerusalem into Samaria and prayed that these believers would receive the Holy Spirit. The Samaritan believers had been baptized in water in the name of the Lord Jesus, but as yet the Holy Spirit had fallen on none of them. Therefore, Peter and John placed their hands upon them and **they received the Holy Ghost.**

This special function of Peter and John was not to be repeated. The first instance of the Holy Spirit's coming upon a group of individuals was in the upper room with the one hundred twenty. They were Jews; these Samaritans were not present. Thus Peter and John bring the power of Pentecost to another group of people. This will occur twice again in this transition period of Acts: at the household of Cornelius when Gentiles receive the Holy Spirit (ch. 10) and when the disciples of John the Baptist receive the Holy Spirit (ch. 19). The baptism of the Holy Spirit, as it occurred in each of these groups, was never to be repeated again. Every believer is baptized into the body of Christ the instant he believes (I Cor 12:12-13). Subsequent baptisms of the individual by the Holy Spirit are unknown in Scripture.

He offered them money, Saying, Give me also this power. In further proof of the spurious character of Simon's so-called conversion, one can see his materialistic view of God. He attempted to buy that which is God's prerogative alone to give.

Simon was quite taken back by the stern rebuke he received from Peter. Peter sized up the situation and immediately diagnosed the problem: **for thy heart is not right in the sight of God.** A call for repentance was accompanied by Peter's perception that Simon was yet caught up in the bitter gall-root of superstition and his fascination with magic, and sorcery was still

25 And they, when they had testified and preached the word of the Lord, returned to Jerusalem, and preached the gospel in many villages of the Sa-măr′i-tans.
26 ¶And the angel of the Lord spake unto Philip, saying, Arise, and go toward the south unto the way that goeth down from Jerusalem unto Gā′za, which is desert.
27 And he arose and went: and, behold, a man of Ē-thĭ-ō′pĭ-a, an eunuch of great authority under Căn′da-ce queen of the Ē-thĭ-ō′pĭ-ans, who had the charge of all her treasure, and had come to Jerusalem for to worship,
28 Was returning, and sitting in his chariot read E-sā′ias the prophet.
29 Then the Spirit said unto Philip, Go near, and join thyself to this chariot.

30 And Philip ran thither to *him*, and heard him read the prophet E-sā′ias, and said, Understandest thou what thou readest?
31 And he said, How can I, except some man should guide me? And he desired Philip that he would come up and sit with him.
32 The place of the scripture which he read was this, He was led as a sheep to the slaughter; and like a lamb dumb before his shearer, so opened he not his mouth:
33 In his humiliation his judgment was taken away: and who shall declare his generation? for his life is taken from the earth.
34 And the eunuch answered Philip, and said, I pray thee, of whom speaketh the prophet this? of himself, or of some other man?
35 Then Philip opened his mouth, and began at the same scripture, and preached unto him Jesus.

36 And as they went on *their* way, they came unto a certain water: and the eunuch said, See, *here is* water; what doth hinder me to be baptized?
37 And Philip said, If thou believest with all thine heart, thou mayest. And he answered and said, I believe that Jesus Christ is the Son of God.
38 And he commanded the chariot to stand still: and they went down both into the water, both Philip and the eunuch; and he baptized him.
39 And when they were come up out of the water, the Spirit of the Lord caught away Philip, that the eunuch saw him no more: and he went on his way rejoicing.
40 But Philip was found at A-zō′tus: and passing through he preached in all the cities, till he came to Cæs-a-re′a.

for him a bond of iniquity. Terror-stricken, Simon begged Peter to pray for him, **that none of these things which ye have spoken come upon me.**

25-29. With the conclusion of the matter concerning Simon Magus, Peter and John returned to Jerusalem, apparently accompanied by Philip. Their evangelistic efforts among the Samaritans continued along the road. However, an angel of the Lord spoke unto Philip, advising him, **Arise, and go toward the south.** Philip was specifically instructed to go into the region of Gaza, a narrow desert strip which provided access along the sea to the great Sinai Peninsula. Philip obeyed and, in consequence of that, encountered a man of Ethiopia.

This man had apparently come to Jerusalem to worship, which may mean that he was a God-fearing Gentile. As a eunuch he was the chamberlain to the Queen of Ethiopia. **Candace** was not the name of the queen but rather a title given to the mother of each Ethiopian king (see Bion of Soli, *Aethiopica* 1). This Ethiopian eunuch had come to a position of great trust under the authority of the queen. Upon his return from Jerusalem, while sitting in his chariot reading from the prophet Isaiah, the Spirit of the Lord moved upon Philip, telling him, **Go near, and join thyself to this chariot.** This expression shows the definite moving of the Spirit of God in evangelism. What the Spirit of God commanded, Philip could not fail to do.

30-35. Understandest thou what thou readest? Having been moved by the Spirit of God to speak to this man, and recognizing the exact portion of Isaiah that the eunuch was reading, Philip received his cue to initiate conversation. The question concerning his ability to understand what he read was natural enough since this man was Ethiopian and not Jewish. The eunuch's response also indicates this, **How can I, except some man should guide me?** The Ethiopian's need and Philip's apparent ability to meet it precipitated the invitation for Philip to come and sit in the chariot with the man. The actual passage which the man was reading was Isaiah 53:7ff. This event recorded in the New Testament sets the New Testament seal of approval on the interpretation of Isaiah 53 and the Servant passages as pertaining to Jesus Christ. When the eunuch asked Philip whether or not the prophet was speaking of himself as the sheep before the slaughter and the lamb dumb before his shearer, Philip boldly opened his mouth **and began at the same scripture, and preached unto him Jesus.** There was no question in the mind of Philip that the Suffering Servant of Isaiah 53 was Jesus of Nazareth. Luke recorded this as fact. We must accept it in the spirit in which it was recorded, i.e., as a prophecy concerning the sacrificial death of Jesus Christ.

36-40. Here is water; what doth hinder me to be baptized? We don't know how far or to what spot Philip and the Ethiopian had traveled. Perhaps it was the Wadi el-Hesi northeast of Gaza, which is the traditional sight. Wherever the spot was, there was sufficient water to perform baptism. Although some manuscripts do not include verse 37, it does fit perfectly into the story and gives the sense of what Philip must have told the Ethiopian eunuch. **If thou believest with all thine heart, thou mayest.** Apparently this whole discussion concerning baptism was precipitated by Philip's instruction to the eunuch subsequent to salvation. He must have told the eunuch that the next step in a believer's life is a physical sign of baptism which outwardly speaks of the believer's death to the world and resurrection to new life in Christ. The confession of faith and the lordship of Christ made by the eunuch was absolutely sincere: **I believe that Jesus Christ is the Son of God.** Such public confession of new faith was a common practice when a convert was formally admitted to the Christian fellowship by baptism. Because of the evidence in the eunuch's life, and his sincere confession of the deity of Christ, Philip and the eunuch descended into the water and the eunuch was baptized.

Immediately another miracle occurs. After coming up out of the water the Spirit of the Lord caught Philip away so that he was no more seen by the eunuch. Philip next appeared at Azotus, the old Philistine city of Ashdod, some twenty miles north of Gaza. From there he proceeded along the coastal highway to Caesarea preaching in all the cities along the way. The ministry of Philip is a refreshing interlude in the great persecutions endured by the early church. It is as if Luke, guided by the Spirit of God, knew just when to put a note of encouragement into his history, for the next chapter deals again with the persecutions engineered by Saul of Tarsus.

F. Conversion of Saul. 9:1-31.

9:1-2. And Saul, yet breathing out threatenings and slaughter. This phrase (Gr *empneonapeiles*) is a difficult one to translate. Literally, Saul "breathed in" threatening and slaughter. Perhaps this is just designed to mean that with every breath he took, he became more adamant against the Christian believers.

As the narrative now returns to Saul of Tarsus, we may note that he pushes his campaign against the Christians far beyond the reaches of Jerusalem. Thus this zealous Pharisee procures extradition papers from the High Priest in Jerusalem to bring back **any of this way** who have fled to Damascus. For Christianity to be described as "The Way" is a common occurrence (cf. 19:9-23; 22:4; 24:14, 22). It was Saul's desire to bind the disciples and drag them back to Jerusalem for trial by the council of the Sanhedrin, of which the High Priest was president.

3-9. Suddenly there shined round about him a light from heaven. Armed with official papers from the High Priest, Saul set out for Damascus to bring back the refugees from Jerusalem and Judaea who had fled by dint of persecution. He almost made it to the captital of the Syrian Empire when one of the most phenomenal events recorded anywhere on the pages of history occurred. Although it was midday (cf. 22:6; 26:13), a light shined out of heaven that completely engulfed the light of the sun. So awesome was this light that Saul fell to the ground recognizing his inferiority to the One generating the light. In addition, he heard a voice, a phenomenon the rabbis call "the daughter of the voice (of God)." The voice of One far superior to him said, **Saul, Saul, why persecutest thou me?**

Here a great truth is seen. Although Saul had set out to Damascus to continue his persecution of Christians, it is the Lord who speaks to him and says, "Saul, Saul, why persecutest thou me?" All sin, regardless of its character, is ultimately directed against the Lord God. There is no such thing as private or personal sin. Every sin that is committed affects others, but in its terminal point, every sin affects God. Saul thought he was persecuting meaningless Christians; instead he was persecuting the Lord God of heaven. This is the same reaction given by the young Joseph when Potiphar's wife attempted to seduce him. He responded to her, "How then can I do this great wickedness, and sin against God?" (Gen 39:9). Even the prodigal son recognized this, for when he came to himself, he determined to return to his father and say, "I have sinned against heaven, and before thee" (Lk 15:18). In anger, sin must be directed against an object. In lust, sin may be directed against a person. But in actuality, all sin is directed against God.

Who art thou, Lord? Immediately the Pharisee recognized that he was dealing with someone superior to himself. The reply which he received was undoubtedly the least expected, **I am Jesus whom thou persecutest.** Naturally, this caused Saul to tremble in amazement, but his response was the only one possible when one meets his superior and is vanquished: **Lord, what wilt thou have me to do?** Saul was commanded to arise and

CHAPTER 9

AND Saul, yet breathing out threatenings and slaughter against the disciples of the Lord, went unto the high priest, 2 And desired of him letters to Damascus to the synagogues, that if he found any of this way, whether they were men or women, he might bring them bound unto Jerusalem.

3 And as he journeyed, he came near Damascus: and suddenly there shined round about him a light from heaven: 4 And he fell to the earth, and heard a voice saying unto him, Saul, Saul, why persecutest thou me? 5 And he said, Who art thou, Lord? And the Lord said, I am Jesus whom thou persecutest: *it is* hard for thee to kick against the pricks. 6 And he trembling and astonished said, Lord, what wilt thou have me to do? And the Lord *said* unto him, Arise, and go into the city, and it shall be told thee what thou must do. 7 And the men which journeyed with him stood speechless, hearing a voice, but seeing no man. 8 And Saul arose from the earth; and when his eyes were opened, he saw no man: but they led him by the hand, and brought *him* into Damascus. 9 And he was three days without sight, and neither did eat nor drink.

enter the city, while those who journeyed with him stood speechless, hearing a voice, but seeing no man.

"On the surface this statement appears to conflict with Luke's own statement in chapter 22:9, 'That what were with me beheld indeed the light, but they heard not the voice of him that spake to me.' This does not contradict 22:9. The verb 'to hear' (Gr *akouō*) in Greek governs an accusative (22:9; or a genitive, 9:7). The genitive is partitive and in itself conveys the idea that they did not apprehend the sound in its entirety. Hence, the genitive at 9:7. It was correct to use the accusative in the second context. The accusative signifies the complete domination of the object, and the company did not understand the purport of the words. Admittedly this distinction is often blurred, but Luke is a careful writer" (E. M. Blaiklock, *The Acts of the Apostles*, pp. 92-93).

When his eyes were opened, he saw no man. When Paul finally arose from the Damascus road he was unable to see. Thus, his companions led him by the hand to Damascus and **he was three days without sight.** It is not beyond the realm of possibility that the events recorded in II Corinthians 12:1-4 occurred during this three-day period.

10 ¶And there was a certain disciple at Damascus, named Ăn-a-nī′as; and to him said the Lord in a vision, Ăn-a-nī′-as. And he said, Behold, I *am here,* Lord.

11 And the Lord *said* unto him, Arise, and go into the street which is called Straight, and enquire in the house of Judas for *one* called Saul of Tarsus: for, behold, he prayeth,

12 And hath seen in a vision a man named Ăn-a-nī′as coming in, and putting *his* hand on him, that he might receive his sight.

10-12. And there was a certain disciple at Damascus, named Ananias. Ananias was apparently a Damascene Jew who believed in Jesus as the Messiah. The Lord appeared unto him in a vision, calling his name, and he answered, **I am here, Lord.** The request of the Lord to Ananias was probably the strangest request this man would ever receive. It was, **go into the street which is called Straight, and inquire . . . for one called Saul, of Tarsus.** The escapades of the zealous Saul were well-known in Damascus. For Ananias to receive a vision from the Lord asking him to seek out a man who made it his religious practice to throw Christian men and women into prison must have been almost too much for Ananias to take. Nevertheless, it was explained to him in the vision that Saul himself had had a vision in which he saw a man named Ananias coming toward him, placing his hand upon him, and causing him to receive sight.

13 Then Ăn-a-nī′as answered, Lord, I have heard by many of this man, how much evil he hath done to thy saints at Jerusalem:

14 And here he hath authority from the chief priests to bind all that call on thy name.

15 But the Lord said unto him, Go thy way: for he is a chosen vessel unto me, to bear my name before the Gentiles, and kings, and the children of Israel:

16 For I will shew him how great things he must suffer for my name's sake.

13-16. As expected, Ananias was quick to object to this request. In explaining that he had heard of the evil this man had done to the saints in Jerusalem, Ananias is simply being cautious in living his Christian testimony and is not guilty of cowardice. His objections are overruled, however, and his concerns alleviated by the Lord who said, **for he is a chosen vessel unto me, to bear my name before the Gentiles.** Paul later would make frequent references to the fact that he was called of God to be the apostle to the Gentiles (see Gal 1:15-16). As Saul had been the minister of suffering to many believers, he himself would now be the recipient of much suffering, both at the hands of believers, and especially at the hands of his own kinsmen, the Jews.

17 And Ăn-a-nī′as went his way, and entered into the house; and putting his hands on him said, Brother Saul, the Lord, *even* Jesus, that appeared unto thee in the way as thou camest, hath sent me, that thou mightest receive thy sight, and be filled with the Holy Ghost.

18 And immediately there fell from his eyes as it had been scales: and he received sight forthwith, and arose, and was baptized.

19 And when he had received meat, he was strengthened. Then was Saul certain days with the disciples which were at Damascus.

20 And straightway he preached Christ in the synagogues, that he is the Son of God.

21 But all that heard *him* were amazed, and said; Is not this he that

17-22. And Ananias . . . putting his hands on him said, Brother Saul. What a difference three days can make in a man's life. Seventy-two hours earlier the chances of a Jewish believer addressing the threatening Saul as "brother" would have been nil. But now Saul and Ananias are all part of the same family. Ananias understands that Saul has come to him so that he might receive his sight and be filled with the Holy Ghost. **Immediately there fell from his eyes as it had been scales.** Probably speaking metaphorically, Luke here records that finally after three days of temporary blindness Saul has now regained his sight. After being baptized, presumably at the hands of Ananias, Saul received strength and remained a number of days with the disciples at Damascus.

During those days Saul was not idle. **He preached Christ in the synagogues, that he is the Son of God.** This is the only reference to Jesus Christ as **the Son of God** in the book of the Acts. It is significant that it occurs very early in the preaching of

destroyed them which called on this name in Jerusalem, and came hither for that intent, that he might bring them bound unto the chief priests?

22 But Saul increased the more in strength, and confounded the Jews which dwelt at Damascus, proving that this is very Christ.

23 ¶And after that many days were fulfilled, the Jews took counsel to kill him:

24 But their laying await was known of Saul. And they watched the gates day and night to kill him.

25 Then the disciples took him by night, and let *him* down by the wall in a basket.

26 And when Saul was come to Jerusalem, he assayed to join himself to the disciples: but they were all afraid of him, and believed not that he was a disciple.

27 But Barnabas took him, and brought *him* to the apostles, and declared unto them how he had seen the Lord in the way, and that he had spoken to him, and how he had preached boldly at Damascus in the name of Jesus.

28 And he was with them coming in and going out at Jerusalem.

29 And he spake boldly in the name of the Lord Jesus, and disputed against the Grecians: but they went about to slay him.

30 *Which* when the brethren knew, they brought him down to Cæs-a-re′a, and sent him forth to Tarsus.

31 Then had the churches rest throughout all Judæa and Galilee and Sa-mâ′rĭ-a, and were edified; and walking in the fear of the Lord, and in the comfort of the Holy Ghost, were multiplied.

32 ¶And it came to pass, as Peter passed throughout all *quarters*, he

Paul, indicating that he immediately recognized not only the messiahship of Christ Jesus, but also His deity as well.

One can imagine the astonishment of those Jews in the synagogue at Damascus when they heard the man, whom they all respected and to whom they looked for leadership in quenching the spreading flame of Christianity, stand up in their midst and proclaim Jesus of Nazareth as God. The Damascus Jews were completely taken back; they could not believe their eyes or ears. But Paul proved that his conversion was real, in that he **confounded the Jews which dwelt at Damascus.**

23-25. And after that many days were fulfilled. In these verses the account of Paul's escape from Damascus is recorded. II Corinthians 11:32-33 adds even greater detail to the account of this escape. We know that it occurred during the reign of Aretas IV (9 B.C.-A.D. 40), the leader of the Nabataean Kingdom who extended his influence as far north as Damascus. The expression "many days" may lead us to the impression that his escape from the city occurred only a few days after his conversion. Such is not the case, for Galatians 1:17-18 clearly indicates to us that upon salvation Paul did not go to Jerusalem or confer with other of the apostles but once receiving his sight went to Arabia (the Nabataean Arabia), returned again unto Damascus, and apparently there communed with the Lord and preached for the space of about three years. His preaching was so successful that the Jews and Nabataeans **watched the gates day and night to kill him.** Their plans were foiled, however, when one of those who came to know the Lord through the ministry of Paul, who had a house built upon the wall, enabled Paul to escape by night by letting him down over the wall in a basket. From here Paul journeyed south to Jerusalem.

26-31. Paul spent the bulk of his life as a loner. He was one solitary man on a dedicated mission to the Gentiles. But when a friend was needed, God always saw to it that a friend was there. In Damascus that friend was Ananias. Now it is Barnabas' turn. **And when Saul was come to Jerusalem . . . But Barnabas took him, and brought him to the apostles.** Like that of Ananias, the initial reaction of the disciples in Jerusalem to the presence of Saul was one of fear. Thus Barnabas presented Paul as one who had been genuinely saved by the grace of God and who had spoken boldly of the Lord Jesus in Damascus. Now that he was in the great Jewish city of Jerusalem, Paul did not change his tactics. Back in Jerusalem for the first time since he left there with extradition papers from the High Priest, Paul is not warmly received as he would have been had he not had the Damascus road experience. However, Paul again speaks out boldly against the Grecian Jews. Quite a little stir followed and they sought to slay Paul. Thus some of the brethren whisked him away to Caesarea, the Mediterranean seaport city built by Herod the Great, and from there he took a ship to his native Tarsus.

With Saul of Tarsus now safely entrenched on their side, and his defection to the ranks of Christianity so sudden that a replacement was not readily available, **Then had the churches rest throughout all Judaea and Galilee and Samaria, and were edified.** One great period of persecution has ended; others will follow; but for now the church has weathered its first great storm, withstood its first great critics, and won its first great adversary, Saul of Tarsus. Thus the local assembly of God's people, walking in the fear of the Lord, and in the comfort of the Holy Ghost, was multiplied.

III. PETER AND THE BEGINNING OF GENTILE CHRISTIANITY. 9:32-12:25.

A. Peter's Healing Ministry. 9:32-43.

32-35. The last time Peter was mentioned in the narrative of Acts was in 8:25 when he returned with John from their visit to

came down also to the saints which dwelt at Lyd'da.

33 And there he found a certain man named Æ'nē-as, which had kept his bed eight years, and was sick of the palsy.

34 And Peter said unto him, Æ'nē-as, Jesus Christ maketh thee whole: arise, and make thy bed. And he arose immediately.

35 And all that dwelt at Lyd'da and Sâ'ron saw him, and turned to the Lord.

36 ¶Now there was at Joppa a certain disciple named Tabitha, which by interpretation is called Dorcas: this woman was full of good works and almsdeeds which she did.

37 And it came to pass in those days, that she was sick, and died: whom when they had washed, they laid her in an upper chamber.

38 And forasmuch as Lyd'da was nigh to Joppa, and the disciples had heard that Peter was there, they sent unto him two men, desiring him that he would not delay to come to them.

39 Then Peter arose and went with them. When he was come, they brought him into the upper chamber: and all the widows stood by him weeping, and shewing the coats and garments which Dorcas made, while she was with them.

40 But Peter put them all forth, and kneeled down, and prayed; and turning him to the body said, Tabitha, arise. And she opened her eyes: and when she saw Peter, she sat up.

41 And he gave her his hand, and lifted her up, and when he had called the saints and widows, presented her alive.

42 And it was known throughout all Joppa; and many believed in the Lord.

43 And it came to pass, that he tarried many days in Joppa with one Simon a tanner.

CHAPTER 10

THERE was a certain man in Cæs-a-re'a called Cornelius, a centurion of the band called the Italian band,

2 A devout man, and one that feared God with all his house, which gave much alms to the people, and prayed to God alway.

3 He saw in a vision evidently about the ninth hour of the day an angel of God coming in to him, and saying unto him, Cornelius.

4 And when he looked on him, he was afraid, and said, What is it, Lord? And he said unto him, Thy prayers and thine alms are come up for a memorial before God.

5 And now send men to Joppa, and call for one Simon, whose surname is Peter:

6 He lodgeth with one Simon a tanner, whose house is by the sea side: he shall tell thee what thou oughtest to do.

7 And when the angel which spake unto Cornelius was departed, he called

Samaria. During this period Peter appears to be carrying on an itinerate ministry among those Christian communities of Judaea. Thus he comes to a stronghold of Jewry, the city of Lydda (Lod in the Old Testament). This city, in the ancient Philistine territory, had a Christian assembly. One of the believers in the church at Lydda was **a certain man named Aeneas, which had kept his bed eight years.** When Peter encountered this man, immediately he said unto him, **Aeneas, Jesus Christ maketh thee whole: arise, and make thy bed.** This command probably meant to get up and begin carrying on a normal life. This miracle caused many of the city of Lydda and the surrounding plain of Sharon to turn to the Lord.

36-38. Now there was at Joppa a certain disciple named Tabitha. Today known as Jaffa, Joppa was a Mediterranean coastal city about ten miles northwest of Lydda. There also was a Christian community in which a certain disciple was named Tabitha or **Dorcas** (Gr dorkas, meaning gazelle), who had endeared herself to that Christian community because she **was full of good works and almsdeeds.** However, Dorcas had fallen ill, died. She was prepared for burial and placed in the upper chamber. Apparently having heard of the healing of Aeneas by Peter, some disciples from Joppa sent to Lydda to fetch Peter, hoping that he could come and perform an even greater miracle on the behalf of their beloved Tabitha.

39-43. Peter quickly removed himself from Lydda and arrived in Joppa. There he saw the lifeless body of Tabitha already washed, in accordance with the Jewish custom of "purification of the dead," and prepared in the upper room. She was surrounded by weeping widows who had come to display the coats and garments which Tabitha had made for them. "But Peter sent them and the other mourners out of the room, as he had seen his Master do before he raised Jairus' daughter from her deathbed; and then he uttered a short sentence differing only in one letter from the word of Jesus to Jairus' daughter. Whereas Jesus had said Talitha cumi (Mk 5:41), Peter now said Tabitha qumi (Tabitha arise)" (F. F. Bruce, The Book of the Acts, p. 212). The result of the mighty power of the Spirit of God in Peter was that Tabitha opened her eyes, sat up, gave her hand to Peter, and he presented her alive to all the saints and widows who waited outside. Again, due to this miracle, many throughout the region round about Joppa believed in the Lord. Peter had a fruitful ministry there, being accommodated by the hospitality of one Simon a tanner.

B. Cornelius Receives the Gospel. 10:1-48.

10:1-8. The city of Caesarea, the major seaport city of New Testament Palestine, was located some distance up the coast from Joppa. Here a man named Cornelius lived. He was a **centurion of the band called the Italian band.** The word translated "band" (Gr speira) is equivalent to the Latin word cohors (cohort). A cohort, or tenth part of a legion, may have consisted of up to six hundred men, and was divided into centuries each commanded by a centurion. But when used in reference to auxiliary provincial troops, it meant a regiment of a full thousand men. Thus Cornelius would have been one of the leaders of a rather sizable group of Roman soliders.

In addition to Luke's information that this man was a Roman soldier, we also learn that he was a devout man, and one who feared God. This would place Cornelius among the "God-fearers" who were so prevalent in the first century. These were Gentiles who were not prepared to enter into the Jewish community as proselytes but were attracted to the morality and ethical standards of the monotheistic Jewish religion. Therefore some of them attended the synagogue services and were greatly knowledgeable in the practices of the Jewish religion. Hence, Cornelius gave much alms and prayed to God.

two of his household servants, and a devout soldier of them that waited on him continually;

8 And when he had declared all *these* things unto them, he sent them to Joppa.

9 ¶On the morrow, as they went on their journey, and drew nigh unto the city, Peter went up upon the housetop to pray about the sixth hour:

10 And he became very hungry, and would have eaten: but while they made ready, he fell into a trance,

11 And saw heaven opened, and a certain vessel descending unto him, as it had been a great sheet knit at the four corners, and let down to the earth:

12 Wherein were all manner of four-footed beasts of the earth, and wild beasts, and creeping things, and fowls of the air.

13 And there came a voice to him, Rise, Peter; kill, and eat.

14 But Peter said, Not so, Lord; for I have never eaten any thing that is common or unclean.

15 And the voice *spake* unto him again the second time, What God hath cleansed, *that* call not thou common.

16 This was done thrice: and the vessel was received up again into heaven.

17 Now while Peter doubted in himself what this vision which he had seen should mean, behold, the men which were sent from Cornelius had made enquiry for Simon's house, and stood before the gate,

18 And called, and asked whether Simon, which was surnamed Peter, were lodged there.

19 While Peter thought on the vision, the Spirit said unto him, Behold, three men seek thee.

20 Arise therefore, and get thee down, and go with them, doubting nothing: for I have sent them.

21 Then Peter went down to the men which were sent unto him from Cornelius; and said, Behold, I am he whom ye seek: what *is* the cause wherefore ye are come?

22 And they said, Cornelius the centurion, a just man, and one that feareth God, and of good report among all the nation of the Jews, was warned from God by an holy angel to send for thee into his house, and to hear words of thee.

One day Cornelius had a vision of an angel of God coming to him with a vital message. At first he was afraid; but then was assured that his alms-giving and prayers had been looked upon by God with favor. The language of verse 4 is couched in sacrificial terms similar to those found in the book of Leviticus.

The message which the angel had for Cornelius was that he should call for one named Simon, whose surname was Peter, and who lodged with one Simon the tanner in the city of Joppa. Cornelius was assured that Simon Peter would be able to tell Cornelius why the Lord had appeared unto him in such an unusual way. The centurion wasted no time in dispatching two of his household servants, and a soldier as devout as himself, south to the city of Joppa.

9-18. Peter went up upon the housetop to pray. The forthcoming meeting between Cornelius and Peter was well prepared by the Lord. Both Cornelius and Simon Peter had a vision paving the way for their meeting. Peter's vision came the day after that of Cornelius. The representatives of the Roman centurion were almost to Caesarea when Peter went to the top of Simon's house to pray. The quietest and most retiring spot in an Eastern house is the housetop (cf. I Sam 9:25-26). At about noon, as was the Jewish custom, Peter entered into a period known as "the midday prayer." While praying, and waiting for lunch to be prepared, **he fell into a trance.** In this trance Peter saw the heavens open and a vessel descending unto him that appeared to be **a great sheet knit at the four corners.** This huge sheet was being lowered from heaven and inside were **all manner of fourfooted beasts . . . and wild beasts, and creeping things, and fowls of the air.** The distinction between clean and unclean was very sharply drawn in the Levitical law (Lev 11:41-44; 20:25; see also Deut 14:3-20).

To the complete amazement and astonishment of Peter, a voice came to him, **Rise, Peter; kill, and eat.** Peter's ancestral sensitivities at this point must have been at the breaking point. His Jewish conscience would never permit him to eat that which was prohibited by Levitical law; and thus his answer was, **Not so, Lord,** claiming that he had never eaten anything that was unclean. But Peter was about to learn his first major lesson in the new covenant. The abolition of Jewish ceremonial laws was about to be graphically illustrated to the apostle. Since the Lord Jesus' original command and commission to the disciples was "go not into the way of the Gentiles, and into any city of the Samaritans enter ye not. But go rather to the lost sheep of the house of Israel" (Mt 10:5-6). Peter could not readily accept the commission he was receiving now. But on the cross of Calvary God had already broken down the middle wall of partition (Eph 2:14-18) between the Jews and Gentiles, and thus the voice from heaven spoke to Peter a second time saying, **What God hath cleansed, that call not thou common** (unclean). Three times this interchange of conversation took place.

19-21. And while Peter doubted what he had seen in the vision, nevertheless he had no time to dwell on that doubt. Immediately the representatives of Cornelius appeared at Simon's house, standing before the gate and inquiring whether or not Peter lodged there. The apostle was still on the roof in a trance, but what he had learned was soon to be practiced. God is not looking for a debate from Peter, just obedience.

22-29. Upon hearing that the men from Cornelius had arrived, Peter immediately made his way down to greet them. This could have been a very tense moment, Jew meeting Gentiles, but in fact it appears to be one filled with great hospitality. The men informed Peter that Cornelius was a centurion, a God-fearer, a man who was well respected among the Jews.

23 Then called he them in, and lodged *them*. And on the morrow Peter went away with them, and certain brethren from Joppa accompanied him.

24 And the morrow after they entered into Cæs-a-re′a. And Cornelius waited for them, and had called together his kinsmen and near friends.

25 And as Peter was coming in, Cornelius met him, and fell down at his feet, and worshipped *him*.

26 But Peter took him up, saying, Stand up; I myself also am a man.

27 And as he talked with him, he went in, and found many that were come together.

28 And he said unto them, Ye know how that it is an unlawful thing for a man that is a Jew to keep company, or come unto one of another nation; but God hath shewed me that I should not call any man common or unclean.

29 Therefore came I *unto you* without gainsaying, as soon as I was sent for: I ask therefore for what intent ye have sent for me?

30 And Cornelius said, Four days ago I was fasting until this hour; and at the ninth hour I prayed in my house, and, behold, a man stood before me in bright clothing,

31 And said, Cornelius, thy prayer is heard, and thine alms are had in remembrance in the sight of God.

32 Send therefore to Joppa, and call hither Simon, whose surname is Peter; he is lodged in the house of *one* Simon a tanner by the sea side: who, when he cometh, shall speak unto thee.

33 Immediately therefore I sent to thee; and thou hast well done that thou art come. Now therefore are we all here present before God, to hear all things that are commanded thee of God.

34 ¶Then Peter opened *his* mouth, and said, Of a truth I perceive that God is no respecter of persons:

35 But in every nation he that feareth him, and worketh righteousness, is accepted with him.

36 The word which *God* sent unto the

Immediately Peter invited them in, undoubtedly to share the meal for which he had been waiting, and to give them lodging. It was now close to evening and the journey of more than thirty miles back to Caesarea could not have been undertaken immediately. Thus, the next day, Peter, accompanied by six other Christians from Joppa, went with the men to Caesarea.

The day after that they entered the city and found Cornelius anxiously awaiting their arrival. When Peter approached, **Cornelius met him, and fell down at his feet, and worshipped him.** Probably this reaction was evoked from the unusual character of the vision which instructed Cornelius to seek Peter's counsel. The word "worshipped" (Gr *proskyneō*) is one that is commonly used for any act of reverence or respect. But being a strict Jew, Peter could not allow Cornelius to behave in such a manner, and commanded him, **Stand up; I myself also am a man.**

When Peter was invited into Cornelius' house he undoubtedly did not expect to find the great company of kinsmen and friends of the centurion. His immediate thought was to justify his presence among them and give adequate explanation for this apparent breech of Jewish law. Jews and Gentiles had no ordinary social intercourse between each other. Thus it would be highly unlikely for Peter to enter the home of a Roman centurion. Because of the Levitical dietary restrictions, the least likely practice Peter, as a Jew, would find himself engaging in was eating at the table of a Gentile. Nevertheless this was about to take place. In explaining how uncommon it was for a Jew to keep company with a Gentile, **or come unto one of another nation,** Luke uses a word (Gr *allophylos* "one of another nation") which is found only here in the New Testament. However, it is a common expression like "Philistines" (see Jud 3:3). Thus Peter is saying that it is highly unlikely that he would dine in the household of an "uncircumcised Philistine."

What then was his reason for doing so? **God hath showed me that I should not call any man common or unclean.** Hence, Peter immediately began to inquire of Cornelius the reason for which he requested Peter's presence.

30-33. In answer to the apostle's question, Cornelius explains that four days ago he was fasting when he received a vision from the Lord. He saw a man standing before him in bright clothing. This angel of the Lord instructed him to send to the house of Simon the tanner in Joppa and request a man named Simon, whose surname is Peter, to come to Caesarea and speak with him. Cornelius did not hesitate but immediately dispatched his representatives to bring Peter to this house. Cornelius still does not understand exactly why this has happened, but he shows a complete readiness to receive whatever Peter has to say. He says, **Now therefore are we all here present before God, to hear all things that are commanded thee of God.** On that occasion Peter had a captive audience, those who received willingly what the Holy Spirit of God impressed upon him to say. God has led both Peter and Cornelius to this hour. It is evident in this transitional book of Acts that He has also led both the Jews and Gentiles to this hour. It is evident that the Gentile writer Luke recognized the importance of this hour because of the space he dedicated to it in his narrative. The program of God stands sure, but in the eyes of Peter and Cornelius, and those who witnessed these events, this program appears to be undergoing fundamental changes. For the first time Jew and Gentile could sit down with some measure of commonality.

34-43. Then Peter opened his mouth. This expression is a unique one which is generally used to introduce something of extreme importance. The weighty material which follows is perfectly in keeping with the expression. What Peter has to say in the next verses will run counter to centuries of racial prejudice between Jews and Gentiles.

children of Israel, preaching peace by Jesus Christ: (he is Lord of all:)

37 That word, *I say*, ye know, which was published throughout all Judæa, and began from Galilee, after the baptism which John preached;

38 How God anointed Jesus of Nazareth with the Holy Ghost and with power: who went about doing good, and healing all that were oppressed of the devil; for God was with him.

39 And we are witnesses of all things which he did both in the land of the Jews, and in Jerusalem; whom they slew and hanged on a tree:

40 Him God raised up the third day, and shewed him openly;

41 Not to all the people, but unto witnesses chosen before of God, *even* to us, who did eat and drink with him after he rose from the dead.

42 And he commanded us to preach unto the people, and to testify that it is he which was ordained of God *to be* the Judge of quick and dead.

43 To him give all the prophets witness, that through his name whosoever believeth in him shall receive remission of sins.

44 ¶While Peter yet spake these words, the Holy Ghost fell on all them which heard the word.

45 And they of the circumcision which believed were astonished, as many as came with Peter, because that on the Gentiles also was poured out the gift of the Holy Ghost.

46 For they heard them speak with tongues, and magnify God. Then answered Peter,

47 Can any man forbid water, that these should not be baptized, which have received the Holy Ghost as well as we?

48 And he commanded them to be baptized in the name of the Lord. Then prayed they him to tarry certain days.

The great lesson which Peter has learned is that God does not play favorites. **God is no respecter of persons.** Anyone from any nation may be saved, all on the same basis of faith. Any man who does justly and loves mercy and walks humbly before God may receive the salvation provided by God (Mic 6:8). The animosity toward Gentiles and the unbelievability that Gentiles could even be saved, doesn't appear at all to enter into Peter's speech. What was once impossible, is now possible. What was once unacceptable is now, by the grace of God, acceptable. What was once unheard of is now being boldly spoken by Peter. Gentiles may actually be saved in the same way that Jews have been saved.

At this point, Peter summarizes the life and teaching of the Lord Jesus, and the disciples' relationship to Him. He makes reference to the fact that Jesus' ministry was in both Judaea and Galilee after His baptism by John (vs. 37) and that the ministry of the Lord Jesus was not only approved by God the Father and God the Spirit, but was accompanied by signs of their approval (vs. 38). The disciples were witnesses to the death of the Lord Jesus (vs. 39) but many were witnesses to the fact that He was raised from the dead on the third day (vs. 40). Those who witnessed the post-resurrection activity of the Lord Jesus were chosen by God to do so and were commanded to testify to the world that Jesus Christ was indeed alive (vss. 41-42). The end result of the life and death of the Lord Jesus was not only predicted by the prophets but has proved to be the only entrance into salvation. **Through his name whosoever believeth in him shall receive remission of sins.** It is now obvious to Peter that "whosoever" included both Jews and Gentiles.

44-48. The Holy Ghost fell on all them which heard the word. Here is the second incident of a special, nonrepeated, transitional baptism of the Spirit of God. The first was the descending of the Spirit to the Samaritans who believed (8:17). Like that incident, this too was the baptism of a group of believers, not an individual. Like that event, this baptism occurred to open a new field of evangelistic ministry and give validity to that new field. So unusual was this event that even those Jews who accompanied Peter were astonished **because that on the Gentiles also was poured out the gift of the Holy Ghost.** The baptism of the Spirit of God, and the subsequent speaking with tongues magnifying God, is clearly not in the context of everyday salvation experience. As the restrictive preaching of the original Twelve was broadened to the Samaritans and now to the Gentiles, it was necessary for them to have a similar experience to the Jews at Pentecost. This event, however, has been incorrectly called "the Pentecost of the Gentile World" This is not a Pentecost for non-Jews. It is a unique, one-time-only occurrence which was designed to show the Jews the validity of Gentile salvation. There would have been good reason to doubt whether Cornelius and his household were actually saved or not, had not his salvation experience been accompanied by the baptism of the Spirit and speaking in tongues. During that age these were characteristic evidences of salvation. The fact that this occurs in historical context should be reason enough not to assume that this will become a normative or continuing practice.

Can any man forbid water, that these should not be baptized. . . ? Peter recognizes that as they have received the outward manifestation of the Spirit of God in their hearts, it is also necessary for them to show the world that they have identified with the death, burial, and resurrection of the Lord Jesus; thus, **he commanded them to be baptized in the name of the Lord.** Peter does not appear to have baptized these converts himself, anymore than Paul did his converts (I Cor 1:13-17).

CHAPTER 11

AND the apostles and brethren that were in Judæa heard that the Gentiles had also received the word of God.

2 And when Peter was come up to Jerusalem, they that were of the circumcision contended with him,

3 Saying, Thou wentest in to men uncircumcised, and didst eat with them.

4 But Peter rehearsed *the matter* from the beginning, and expounded *it* by order unto them, saying,

5 I was in the city of Joppa praying: and in a trance I saw a vision, A certain vessel descend, as it had been a great sheet, let down from heaven by four corners; and it came even to me:

6 Upon the which when I had fastened mine eyes, I considered, and saw fourfooted beasts of the earth, and wild beasts, and creeping things, and fowls of the air.

7 And I heard a voice saying unto me, Arise, Peter; slay and eat.

8 But I said, Not so, Lord: for nothing common or unclean hath at any time entered into my mouth.

9 But the voice answered me again from heaven, What God hath cleansed, *that* call not thou common.

10 And this was done three times: and all were drawn up again into heaven.

11 And, behold, immediately there were three men already come unto the house where I was, sent from Cæs-a-re'a unto me.

12 And the spirit bade me go with them, nothing doubting. Moreover these six brethren accompanied me, and we entered into the man's house:

13 And he shewed us how he had seen an angel in his house, which stood and said unto him, Send men to Joppa, and call for Simon, whose surname is Peter;

14 Who shall tell thee words, whereby thou and all thy house shall be saved.

15 And as I began to speak, the Holy Ghost fell on them, as on us at the beginning.

16 Then remembered I the word of the Lord, how that he said, John indeed baptized with water; but ye shall be baptized with the Holy Ghost.

17 Forasmuch then as God gave them the like gift as *he did* unto us, who believed on the Lord Jesus Christ; what was I, that I could withstand God?

18 When they heard these things, they held their peace, and glorified God, saying, Then hath God also to the Gentiles granted repentance unto life.

C. Peter Defends His Ministry. 11:1-18.

11:1-3. Long before Peter returned to Jerusalem, the news of the conversion of Cornelius preceded him. Although the text makes specific reference to **the apostles and brethren that were in Judaea**, undoubtedly the character of Peter's revolutionary activities in Judaism must have come to the attention of the High Priest and others of more traditional Judaism. Thus both the more zealous Jewish believers and the greatly zealous Jewish unbelievers were waiting for Peter's arrival and explanation as to why he entered the house and ate with the heathen.

It is unnatural for Luke, a Gentile himself, to make reference to these Jews as **the circumcision**. The distinction is again seen in the record of what the Jews inquired of Peter, **Thou wentest in to men uncircumcised**. It is clear that the harmony which existed in Caesarea did not exist yet in Jerusalem.

4-17. Peter apparently understood his best defense to be a straightforward offense. Thus, **Peter rehearsed the matter from the beginning and expounded it.** In no way did Peter shrink away from giving complete details of what had happened at both Joppa and Caesarea. Quickly and completely he related to them the trance into which he fell in Joppa (vs. 5) and the great sheet which he saw coming down out of heaven. Fastening his eyes on this unbelievable object, and noticing the content, Peter was shaken by a voice from heaven saying, **Arise, Peter; slay and eat** (vs. 7). As one would expect in rehearsing these events for the circumcision, Peter makes direct reference to his initial opposition to this proposition (vs. 8) but also makes sure that they understand that it is God who is speaking to him (vs. 9).

Again when he was approached by the representatives of Cornelius, Peter alludes to the fact that **the Spirit bade me go with them, nothing doubting** (vs. 12). Then too there was the account that Cornelius had been prepared by his own vision from the Lord to receive Peter. Cornelius was told that Peter would tell him words **whereby thou and all thy house shall be saved** (vs. 14).

Now Peter reaches the climax of his account. He makes reference to the fact that the Holy Ghost fell on them at Caesarea, in the same manner **as on us at the beginning.** In concluding the defense of his actions, he makes reference to the teaching of the Lord Jesus concerning baptism and, in accordance with that teaching, these Gentile believers were baptized with water. Finally, and most forcefully, Peter informs the circumcision that these Gentiles have **believed on the Lord Jesus Christ**, even as the Jews had done. Peter's terminal statement is phrased in the form of a question, to which there is no obvious answer, and from which there is no retreat: **What was I, that I could withstand God?** If the Jewish believers of the church at Jerusalem are to question Peter's action, they must first question the direct leading of God the Father, provision of salvation by God the Son, and verifying signs of God the Spirit. Absolutely no one was ready to do that.

18. They held their peace, and glorified God. No rebuttal was made to Peter's argument; none could be. It has now become evident to the Jewish believers of Jerusalem that Gentiles may indeed become believers as well. It was also within the plan of God to grant **repentance unto life** to those with whom the Jews would not associate. In the minds of Jewish Christians, the evangelization of Gentiles would mean a drastic reappraisal of their own position before God. With this initial foray into previously untapped Gentile territory, the door has been opened for a flood of salvational activity on behalf of non-Jews throughout the world. The door which was cracked by Peter was crashed by Paul. Most who read these words must do so out of thankfulness and gratitude toward God for the event that occurred on that day centuries ago in Caesarea.

D. Continued Persecution. 11:19-12:25.

19-21. After a brief interlude in which the ministry of Philip, the conversion of Saul of Tarsus, and the varied ministry of Peter are elaborated upon, Luke now returns in his narrative to the point of the story at which he departed in 8:1. Under the dint of fierce persecution which arose when Stephen was stoned, the believing Jews of Jerusalem were scattered as far away as Phoenicia, Cyprus, and Antioch. Phoenicia is a narrow strip of coastline in northern Palestine, one hundred twenty miles long and only about twelve miles wide. It extends from the river Eleutherus southward to approximately the region of Mount Carmel. Cyprus is an island just off the coast of, and in sight of, Phoenicia. The historians Philo and Josephus both speak of a Jewish colony on this island. Antioch, some fifteen miles from the mouth of the Orontes River, was the capital of the Greek kingdom of Syria. It was founded by Seleucus Nicator in 300 B.C. in honor of his father Antiochus, one of Alexander the Great's generals. Antioch was made a free city in 64 B.C. when Syria was incorporated into the Roman Empire. The ministry of persecuted Jews who fled north and westward to these areas was characterized by **preaching the word to none but unto the Jews only.**

However, there were some bold men of Cyprus and Cyrene (a city in the province of Libya in Africa) who dared to speak **unto the Grecians, preaching the Lord Jesus.** These Grecians are not to be thought of as those Greek-speaking Jews mentioned earlier. There is good manuscript evidence that the rendering here ought to be "Greeks," instead of "Hellenists" (Grecian Jews). If this rendering is followed, it would more greatly substantiate the reason for the statement **unto the Jews only** in the preceding verse. Men of Cyprus and Cyrene had actually begun to preach the gospel to Greeks at Antioch. Also the reference to **preaching the Lord Jesus** tends to make an understanding of the Grecians being actually non-Jews all the more probable. If they were actually Jews, the evangelist would refer to Jesus as Messiah, the fulfillment of the hope of Israel. Instead, however, he refers to him in Greek terms, "Lord" (Gr *kyrios*), and "Saviour" (Gr *sōtēr*). Since the hand of the Lord was on these efforts, **a great number believed, and turned unto the Lord.** Although an Ethiopian eunuch and a Roman centurion have already been saved, this preaching of the gospel of Jesus Christ to the Gentiles is on a far broader scale than the Jews had ever seen before.

19 ¶Now they which were scattered abroad upon the persecution that arose about Stephen travelled as far as Pheni̇́ce, and Cyprus, and Antioch, preaching the word to none but unto the Jews only.
20 And some of them were men of Cyprus and Cy̆-rē′ne, which, when they were come to Antioch, spake unto the Grecians, preaching the Lord Jesus.
21 And the hand of the Lord was with them: and a great number believed, and turned unto the Lord.

22-26. These things came unto the ears of the church which was in Jerusalem. It was only a short time until the events which had taken place in Antioch were made known unto the church at Jerusalem. As had been the situation when Peter and John were dispatched to Samaria to investigate the missionary activity of Philip there, so too now the Jerusalem church must send someone to Antioch to do the same. Who better to investigate the activities of Jews from Cyprus than a Jew from Cyprus? Thus Barnabas was sent forth by the Jerusalem church. Whatever report Barnabas returned with could be trusted, for Barnabas **was a good man, and full of the Holy Ghost and faith.** Thus, upon arrival at Antioch, when Barnabas viewed the situation there and saw that at Antioch a great number of Gentiles had been saved by the grace of God, he **was glad, and exhorted them all.**

22 ¶Then tidings of these things came unto the ears of the church which was in Jerusalem: and they sent forth Barnabas, that he should go as far as Antioch.
23 Who, when he came, and had seen the grace of God, was glad, and exhorted them all, that with purpose of heart they would cleave unto the Lord.
24 For he was a good man, and full of the Holy Ghost and of faith: and much people was added unto the Lord.
25 Then departed Barnabas to Tarsus, for to seek Saul:
26 And when he had found him, he brought him unto Antioch. And it came to pass, that a whole year they as-

sembled themselves with the church, and taught much people. And the disciples were called Christians first in Antioch.

27 ¶And in these days came prophets from Jerusalem unto Antioch.
28 And there stood up one of them named Ăg′a-bus, and signified by the spirit that there should be great dearth throughout all the world: which came to pass in the days of Claudius Cæsar.
29 Then the disciples, every man according to his ability, determined to send relief unto the brethren which dwelt in Judæa:
30 Which also they did, and sent it to the elders by the hands of Barnabas and Saul.

CHAPTER 12
NOW about that time Herod the king stretched forth his hands to vex certain of the church.

Apparently Barnabas was to do more than just observe the activities of the Antiochene Christians. He must have become the advisor to them from the mother church in Jerusalem. But Barnabas quickly realized that the job was too big for one man, for Antioch was a large city, with a population at this time of perhaps five hundred thousand or more. Therefore he began to consider those who might assist him in this task. He needed someone who was of stellar quality and character, and yet someone who could sympathize with both the Jews and the Gentiles who were being saved. There was no question in the mind of Barnabas; there was only one man. **Then departed Barnabas to Tarsus for to seek Saul.**

Some years earlier Saul of Tarsus had been escorted to Caesarea by the Christians of Jerusalem, and from there he took a ship to his native Tarsus of Cilicia. Now Barnabas travels to Tarsus in order to seek out Saul, who probably had been disinherited for his commitment to Christ (Phil 3:8) and was undoubtedly buried in the mass of humanity at Tarsus, engaged in tentmaking. All this time Saul was being prepared by the Lord for a greater work and he was patiently waiting for the time of the initiation of that work to come. Apparently Barnabas did not immediately locate Saul, for the verb "to seek" (Gr anazēteō) implies a searching with great difficulty. But **when he had found him, he brought him unto Antioch.** The next year in Antioch proved to be one of great accomplishment. Under the ministry of Barnabas and Saul, the Christians of Antioch grew both in depth and number. **And the disciples were called Christians first in Antioch.** This refers to a practice with which the nimble wits of Antioch prided themselves. They are known to have coined words to describe persons and events. Perhaps as a derogatory term originally, Antiochenes called those who had claimed Jesus as Messiah the "Christ-ones." Thus, as an accurate historian, Luke did not hesitate to record that the followers of the Lord first came to be popularly known as Christians at Antioch.

27-30. And in these days came prophets from Jerusalem unto Antioch. In the first-century church, a prophet belonged to a recognized order in the church (cf. 2:17-18; 13:1; 20:23; 21:9-10; I Cor 12:28-29; Eph 4:11). One of these prophets was a man named Agabus who indicated, prophesying under the influence of the Spirit of God, **that there should be great dearth throughout all the world.** Luke is interested in pinpointing the exact time of this famine. Thus he goes one step further in identifying it by saying that the famine occurred in the days of Claudius Caesar (41-54 A.D.). Many extrabiblical sources make note of a succession of bad harvests and extreme famine throughout the entire Roman Empire, especially Palestine, during the reign of Claudius.

In response to this prophetic announcement, the believers at the church of Antioch **determined to send relief unto the brethren** who lived in Jerusalem and its environs. Thus, they set aside a certain percentage of their income to collect a contribution to be sent to the believers of Judaea. This relief fund was to be sent to the elders **by the hands of Barnabas and Saul.** This social and communal interest the church at Antioch had for the church at Jerusalem is not only a pleasing expression of the love of the Lord Jesus for the brethren (Jn 10:35), but it marks the beginning of the Pauline practice of accepting the responsibility for caring not only for the souls of those to whom he ministered but for the bodies as well. The church at the end of the twentieth century could well take a lesson from the church at the end of the first century.

12:1-2. Herod the king. The Herod mentioned in this chapter is Herod Agrippa I. Agrippa I was the grandson of Herod the Great and his first wife named Mariamne. This Mariamne was a Hasmonean princess and therefore provided the tie between

2 And he killed James the brother of John with the sword.

3 And because he saw it pleased the Jews, he proceeded further to take Peter also. (Then were the days of unleavened bread.)

4 And when he had apprehended him, he put *him* in prison, and delivered *him* to four quaternions of soldiers to keep him; intending after Easter to bring him forth to the people.

5 Peter therefore was kept in prison: but prayer was made without ceasing of the church unto God for him.

6 And when Herod would have brought him forth, the same night Peter was sleeping between two soldiers, bound with two chains: and the keepers before the door kept the prison.

7 And, behold, the angel of the Lord came upon *him*, and a light shined in the prison: and he smote Peter on the side, and raised him up, saying, Arise up quickly. And his chains fell off from *his* hands.

8 And the angel said unto him, Gird thyself, and bind on thy sandals. And so he did. And he saith unto him, Cast thy garment about thee, and follow me.

9 And he went out, and followed him; and wist not that it was true which was done by the angel; but thought he saw a vision.

10 When they were past the first and the second ward, they came unto the iron gate that leadeth unto the city; which opened to them of his own accord: and they went out, and passed on through one street; and forthwith the angel departed from him.

Herod and the Jews. Born in 11 B.C., Agrippa I was sent to Rome to live upon the execution of his father, Aristobulus, in 7 B.C. While a young lad in Rome he became intimate friends with members of the imperial family, especially with Gaius, who was the grandnephew of the emperor Tiberius. In A.D. 37, Gaius succeeded Tiberius as emperor and, in consequence of their long friendship, he awarded the tetrarchies of Philip and Lysanias in southern Syria to his friend Agrippa. It was at this point that Agrippa took the title "king." Some two years later, Galilee and Peraea were added to Agrippa's kingdom when his uncle Herod Antipas was deposed by emperor Gaius. However, Agrippa's kingdom was even further enhanced by the addition of Judaea in A.D. 41 when, upon the assassination of Gaius, Claudius became the Roman emperor. In the fact that he was a descendant of the Hasmonean royal family, Agrippa enjoyed unusual popularity among the Jews. He went out of his way to win their support. Thus it is not surprising to find a notation in Luke's historical account concerning Agrippa's persecution of the nemesis of the Jews, the early church.

And he killed James . . . with the sword. The first of the apostles to fall victim to martyrdom, and the only one recorded on the pages of the Sacred Text, was James, the son of Zebedee. His death fulfills the promise of Jesus that he would drink of His cup and be baptized with His baptism (Mk 10:39). Although this promise was made to both James and John, John outlived all the other apostles, but nevertheless suffered "for the Word of God and the testimony of Jesus" (Rev 1:9). In his *Ecclesiastical History* (ii. 9) Eusebius preserves a tradition, which was first found in Clement of Alexandria, that the officer who was attached to James and commissioned with guarding him, was so impressed with the apostle's witness, that before James was martyred, this officer confessed Christ as Saviour and was beheaded with the apostle.

3-7. He saw it pleased the Jews. Agrippa's policy to maintain a spirit of goodwill with the Jews got a real boost in the death of James. So elated were they that this apostle was martyred, Agrippa next attempted to take the life of Peter. Peter was apprehended and put into prison on the first day of the Festival of Unleavened Bread. He was therefore incarcerated throughout the entire festival with the intent to bring him to public trial after this period had ended.

The apprehension of Peter did not discourage the Jerusalem church. Rather it set them to praying (Jas 5:16). On the night preceding the day Herod Agrippa I would have brought Peter forth for trial and execution, a very strange phenomenon occurred in that prison. Sleeping between two soldiers, and bound with two sturdy chains, with the keepers of the prison standing guard just outside the door, the angel of the Lord came upon him, and a light shined in the prison. The light apparently emanated from the angel and Peter was quickly roused, probably unaware of what was happening to him. When the angel struck Peter on the side to awaken him, his chains, the passports to his execution, fell from his hands.

8-11. Gird thyself . . . Cast thy garment about thee, and follow me. The instruction of the angel to Peter was to prepare himself for leaving the prison. Peter was still in a daze, not fully knowing what was happening to him. He wasn't quite aware whether this was indeed a vision or in fact someone leading him from the depths of the prison. After leaving his cell, Peter successfully, by the leading of the angel, made his way through the first and second wards, the two guarded checkpoints before the gate that led to the city. Apparently with his garment cast about him, and in the obvious power of the Spirit of God, Peter and the angel were permitted to pass through these two wards. There would be no hope, however, of passing through the iron gate, for it was securely shut. However, this miraculous escape

11 And when Peter was come to himself, he said, Now I know of a surety, that the Lord hath sent his angel, and hath delivered me out of the hand of Herod, and *from* all the expectation of the people of the Jews.

12 And when he had considered *the thing,* he came to the house of Mary the mother of John, whose surname was Mark; where many were gathered together praying.
13 And as Peter knocked at the door of the gate, a damsel came to hearken, named Rhoda.
14 And when she knew Peter's voice, she opened not the gate for gladness, but ran in, and told how Peter stood before the gate.
15 And they said unto her, Thou art mad. But she constantly affirmed that it was even so. Then said they, It is his angel.

16 But Peter continued knocking: and when they had opened *the door,* and saw him, they were astonished.
17 But he, beckoning unto them with the hand to hold their peace, declared unto them how the Lord had brought him out of the prison. And he said, Go shew these things unto James, and to the brethren. And he departed, and went into another place.
18 Now as soon as it was day, there was no small stir among the soldiers, what was become of Peter.
19 And when Herod had sought for him, and found him not, he examined the keepers, and commanded that *they* should be put to death. And he went down from Judæa to Cæs-a-re'a, and *there* abode.

would not be prevented by a locked gate **which opened to them of his own accord.** With the gate opening unaided by anyone, the angel and Peter passed on through one street, and at that point the angel departed from him. Once Peter found himself alone, he had opportunity for the first time to appraise his situation. **And when Peter was come to himself.** With the cool night air in his face, and the immediate danger of the prison behind him, Peter could now fully appreciate **that the Lord hath sent his angel** to deliver Peter out of the hand of Herod and spoil the anticipation of the Jews the next morning. Peter sized up the situation correctly: this indeed was a miracle of God effected by the prayers of righteous saints.

12-15. Once Peter had come to his senses, his first reaction was to apprise the other disciples of his release. Therefore he made his way to a well-known meeting place for believers; **he came to the house of Mary the mother of John.** This is the first introduction to a man who will play a vital role in the transmission and recording of the gospel over the next thirty years. John Mark is the son of Mary and it is to their house that Peter made his way. As Peter knocked on the gate, his knock was answered by a young girl perhaps standing guard to warn the praying disciples of approaching Roman soldiers. The door upon which Peter knocked was the street door. This would give entrance to a courtyard or a long hallway from the street to the sanctuary of the home. When the young girl heard Peter's voice and recognized it, **she opened not the gate for gladness.** So excited was Rhoda to hear the voice of the imprisoned apostle that in her excitement she neglected to let him in. Rather she ran and told the others that Peter was at the street gate. Their immediate response was one of disbelief. **Thou art mad.** So insistent was Rhoda that she had actually heard the voice of Peter, that those who prayed inside amended their assessment of Rhoda by assuming that perhaps she had heard a voice, although certainly not Peter's voice. Perhaps this was the voice of his angel who had come in Peter's stead.

16-19. But Peter continued knocking. Just as persistent as Rhoda was in insisting that Peter was outside the door, so persistent was Peter in knocking upon the door. There was but one way to solve this puzzle; those inside must answer the door. When they did, and they saw Peter standing there, **they were astonished.** Peter made a gesture which told them not to say a word, for he was yet unaware that his escape had not been discovered. His immediate thought was for the others and he said, **Go show these things unto James, and to the brethren.** James, the brother of the Lord Jesus and a pillar of the Jerusalem church, and the brethren or elders (11:30) would have to be warned because, with the escape of Peter, their lives would be in danger as well.

Now as soon as it was day, there was no small stir among the soldiers. One can imagine the consternation that would have occurred in the minds of the two soldiers on either side of Peter, chained now to no one, the soldiers who stood guard outside the cell, now with no one to guard, and those who guarded the first two wards leading to the outside of the prison. No one had an explanation as to what happened to their prisoner. When Herod looked for him and the report came that he was not to be found, **he examined the keepers, and commanded that they should be put to death.** The penalty for losing a prisoner was severe in the Roman Empire, and these men took very seriously their responsibility in keeping prisoners secure. But now nothing could be done; the prisoner was gone. Because of this, Herod Agrippa I departed from Jerusalem and went to reside at Caesarea, his other capital.

Although these verses do not advance the narrative, they do provide great insight into the death of Herod Agrippa I. Luke is

20 ¶And Herod was highly displeased with them of Tyre and Sī'don: but they came with one accord to him, and, having made Blăs'tus the king's chamberlain their friend, desired peace; because their country was nourished by the king's *country.*

21 And upon a set day Herod, arrayed in royal apparel, sat upon his throne, and made an oration unto them.

22 And the people gave a shout, *saying, It is* the voice of a god, and not of a man.

23 And immediately the angel of the Lord smote him, because he gave not God the glory: and he was eaten of worms, and gave up the ghost.

24 ¶But the word of God grew and multiplied.

25 And Barnabas and Saul returned from Jerusalem, when they had fulfilled *their* ministry, and took with them John, whose surname was Mark.

CHAPTER 13

NOW there were in the church that was at Antioch certain prophets and teachers; as Barnabas, and Simeon that was called Nī'ger, and Lucius of Cȳ-rē'ne, and Măn'a-en, which had been brought up with Herod the tetrarch, and Saul.

2 As they ministered to the Lord, and fasted, the Holy Ghost said, Separate me Barnabas and Saul for the work whereunto I have called them.

3 And when they had fasted and prayed, and laid *their* hands on them, they sent *them* away.

always interested in keeping a historical perspective in the book of Acts. Thus he includes these verses.

20-23. For an unknown reason, the people of Tyre and Sidon have fallen out of favor in the eyes of Agrippa. This was a very precarious situation for them since the seaboard Phoenician cities of Tyre and Sidon depended entirely on the green fields of Galilee for their food supply. This had been the case for centuries (cf. I Kgs 5:9 ff.). Realizing that they must again be restored to the good graces of the king, residents of this town befriended the king's chamberlain, Blastus.

At this point Luke's account is paralleled by an extrabiblical account which provided confirmation of the accuracy and validity of Acts. Josephus (*Antiquities* xix. 8.2) records that on the birthday of the emperor (**upon a set day**), Agrippa held a large festival in which he donned a robe made of silver throughout. As he entered the theater of Caesarea at day break, the silver glittered in the morning sunlight and was so resplendent that all who looked upon it were immediately enamored with the king. Luke records that **the people gave a shout, saying, It is the voice of a god and not of a man.** Josephus says the cry invoked by the crowd was, "Be gracious unto us! Hitherto we have reverenced thee as a man, but henceforth we acknowledge thee to be of more than mortal nature." Agrippa relished and revelled in the plaudits that had been thrown his way. He was claimed to be a god; and he did not deny the claim. Therefore, **the Lord smote him, because he gave not God the glory.** Herod's receiving the praise due only to Jehovah, and his subsequent death, are not without precedent. But his own particular species of blasphemy is recorded by Luke to be the single cause of his death.

24-25. But the word of God grew and multiplied represents another of Luke's progress reports periodically seen in this historical account (cf. 6:7; 9:31). At this point Barnabas and Saul set out from Jerusalem taking with them John Mark. They apparently had just come to the city with the relief offering collected from the Antiochene believers and are now returning to Antioch. The death of Herod Agrippa I probably occurred prior to their departure from Antioch.

IV. PAUL'S FIRST MISSIONARY JOURNEY: ITS EFFECT. 13:1-15:35.

A. Commissioning of Barnabas and Saul. 13:1-13.

13:1-3. The first official gentile mission was carried by Paul and Barnabas, who were sent by the **church at Antioch to** Cyprus and the cities in the southern part of the Roman province of **Galatia.** This church was characterized by many outstanding Christians and **prophets and teachers. Simeon . . . called Niger,** the Latin word meaning "black," was apparently a nickname for his dark complexion and suggests that he was perhaps of African origin. Some have suggested that he may have been Simon of Cyrene (cf. Mk 15:21) who carried Jesus' cross. The designation for **Manaen . . . brought up with Herod** means that he was a "foster brother." This term was generally used of children who were brought up in the royal court, and later the phrase was retained as an actual title. **Herod** is Herod Antipas who ruled Galilee and Peraea between 4 В.C. and A.D. 39. The relationship between them is one of the remarkable apologetic notices of the book of Acts. Ladd (*Wycliffe Bible Commentary*, p. 427) suggests that the **prophets** gave or were given direct revelation from God by the Holy Spirit and the **teachers** were gifted in the interpretation of that revelation. Thus, the utterance of the **Holy Ghost** probably came through a prophet. During a time of fasting and prayer, which was always especially significant for the early church, the Holy Spirit designated the two most eminent and gifted leaders among the entire group to become the first actual missionaries. While it is true that every Christian was to carry on the mission of the church (cf. Mt 28:20, notes), these men became the first actual "sent-ones." It should be noted that **they . . . laid their hands on them** refers to the church at Antioch as the sending agency. Thus in its purest form, the New Testament local church sent forth missionary representatives from the midst of its own congregation. In the book of Acts we find no reference to mission boards or organizations as such. Nor do we find single individuals sending forth missionaries apart from the commission of the church. In other words, as the Great Commission was given to the apostles who were to become the foundation of the church, it was, therefore, given to the church, not to individuals. The laying on of hands did not impart any special power nor qualification to the missionaries, but "expressed its fellowship with Barnabas and Paul and recognized them as its delegates or 'apostles'" (F. F. Bruce, p. 261).

4-7. Seleucia (vs. 4) was the port of Antioch from which they sailed for **Cyprus,** the large island off the shore in the Mediterranean Sea. It was formally annexed by Rome in 57 B.C. and later became a province governed by an imperial legate. After 22 B.C. Augustus gave its control to the Roman Senate and it was thereafter administered by a proconsul. Thus, Luke accurately indicates the magistrate's title as "governor." **Salamis** (vs. 5) was the eastern port of Cyprus and was its largest city. There were several synagogues there because of the large Jewish population. **John** Mark accompanied the apostles. He was the cousin of Barnabas whom they had recently taken with them from Jerusalem to Antioch (cf. 12:25). He was to serve as their **minister,** or "attendant." Some have suggested that his responsibility was that of instructing new converts in the gospel. He later would write the Gospel of Mark. **Paphos** was the official capital of the province in those days. **Elymas** (vs. 8) is referred to as a **sorcerer** (Gr *magos*) and a **false prophet.** In essence he was a magician or astrologer attached to the political entourage as an "advisor" to the governor **Sergius Paulus.** Some have suggested that he is to be identified with Lucius Sergius Paulus who is known to have been one of the curators of the Tiber during the reign of Claudius.

8-12. Elymas was an alternate name for Bar-Jesus whose original Aramaic name means "Son of Salvation" but was in fact a "magician" and "false prophet." As he sensed the governor was accepting the message of Barnabas and Saul, he realized his own position would be endangered. Therefore, he attempted to sway Sergius Paulus **from the faith.** While this passage uses interchangeable names, it very interestingly shifts at this point from **Saul** to **Paul.** Paul is the Greek form of the Semitic name, Saul. Because of the correlation to the governor's name, and the fact that they are now in distinctly Greek-influenced territory, Paul changes the outward usage of his name as a matter of cultural identification with the people whom he is trying to reach with the gospel. Paul's rebuke of this false prophet is stern and straightforward. He calls him a **child of the devil** and **enemy of all righteousness.** He rebukes his perversion of the truth and strikes him with temporary blindness. Amazed and stunned by the power of these servants of the Lord over his resident magician, the proconsul **believed . . . the doctrine of the Lord** (vs. 12). W. Ramsay (*The Bearing of Recent Discovery on the Trustworthiness of the New Testament*, p. 165) argues that there is evidence that the next two generations of his family were known as Christians.

13. Leaving Barnabas' native land of Cyprus, they sailed to the country bordering Paul's homeland. **Pamphylia** was a district on the coast of Asia Minor which included the city of **Perga,** some twenty miles inland. For some unexplained reason John Mark forsook them and **returned to Jerusalem.** Specula-

---

4 ¶So they, being sent forth by the Holy Ghost, departed unto Se-leu′ci-a; and from thence they sailed to Cyprus.

5 And when they were at Săl′a-mĭs, they preached the word of God in the synagogues of the Jews: and they had also John to *their* minister.

6 And when they had gone through the isle unto Pā′phŏs, they found a certain sorcerer, a false prophet, a Jew, whose name *was* Bär-jē′śus:

7 Which was with the deputy of the country, Sergius Paulus, a prudent man; who called for Barnabas and Saul, and desired to hear the word of God.

8 But Ĕl′y-mas the sorcerer (for so is his name by interpretation) withstood them, seeking to turn away the deputy from the faith.

9 Then Saul, (who also *is called* Paul,) filled with the Holy Ghost, set his eyes on him,

10 And said, O full of all subtilty and all mischief, *thou* child of the devil, *thou* enemy of all righteousness, wilt thou not cease to pervert the right ways of the Lord?

11 And now, behold, the hand of the Lord *is* upon thee, and thou shalt be blind, not seeing the sun for a season. And immediately there fell on him a mist and a darkness; and he went about seeking some to lead him by the hand.

12 Then the deputy, when he saw what was done, believed, being astonished at the doctrine of the Lord.

13 ¶Now when Paul and his company loosed from Pā′phŏs, they came to Per′ga in Păm-phy̆l′ĭ-a: and John departing from them returned to Jerusalem.

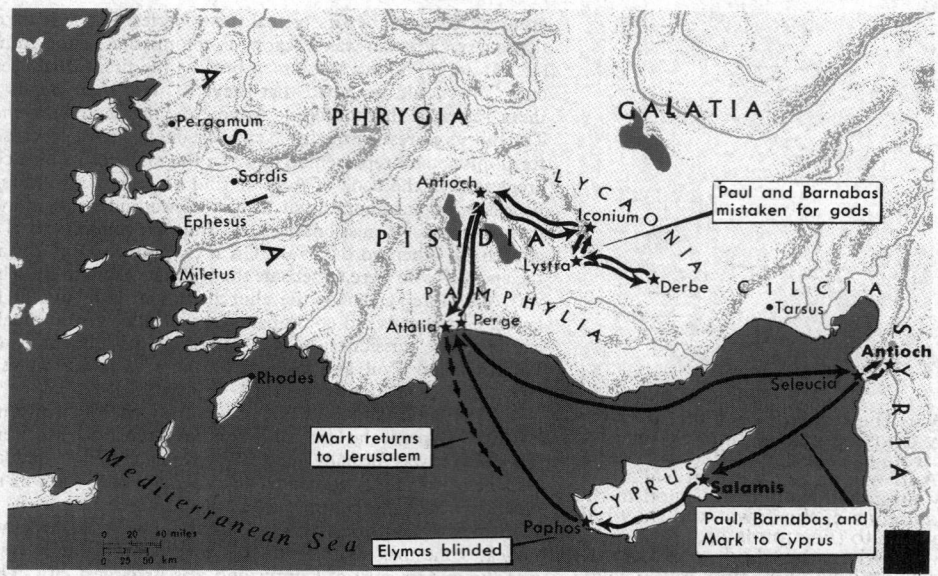

Paul and Barnabas mistaken for gods

Mark returns to Jerusalem

Elymas blinded

Paul, Barnabas, and Mark to Cyprus

The First Missionary Journey of Paul

tion at this point needs to be contained since we are not told why he left. It could have been due to news of an emergency, fear of strange territory, or uncertainty as to the new change of direction in their mission. It seems obvious later that Paul looked upon his action as inexcusable desertion and refused to give him a second chance (cf. 15:37). On the other hand, Barnabas reconciled with Mark and restored him for effective ministry in the future.

A number of important and practical observations can be made from this incident. Paul, standing for the truth and the severity of their mission, demanded total allegiance which later led him to a new partner. Barnabas, however, equally a servant of the Lord, was able to restore one who had fallen as his new partner. An objective look at this incident makes it difficult to judge which was right or wrong, if indeed either were. The unavoidable "split" is ultimately overruled by the Lord to accomplish a double ministry.

B. The First Foray into Asia Minor. 13:14-52.

14-16. The phrase **Antioch in Pisidia** is mistranslated in the AV. Actually Antioch was not in Pisidia but near the region of Pisidia and thus came to be known as Pisidian Antioch. The so-called "South Galatian" theory and the "North Galatian" theory arise from the designation of this province. Most conservative commentators hold to Ramsay's view that the Epistle to the Galatians was written to these cities of southern Galatia (cf. Ladd, Tenney, etc.). Others (Bruce) hold the opposite. Ramsay (*St. Paul the Traveller,* pp. 94 ff.) infers from Galatians 4:13 that Paul caught malaria in the low-lying territory around Perga and went to recuperate in the higher altitudes of southern Galatia. Following their normal custom, Paul and Barnabas went to the synagogue of the Jewish community on the Sabbath day. Paul seemed to give great importance to the evangelization of Roman colonies (such as this one) which were stationed at strategic points along the imperial roads within the empire. The **rulers of the synagogue** were not clergymen but lay leaders or officers who were given the authority to invite anyone from the audience to give a word of exhortation. Notice that **Paul stood up** and that he beckoned **with his hand.** Thus, we observe

14 ¶But when they departed from Per′ga, they came to Antioch in Pĭ-sĭd′-ĭ-a, and went into the synagogue on the sabbath day, and sat down.

15 And after the reading of the law and the prophets the rulers of the synagogue sent unto them, saying, Ye men *and* brethren, if ye have any word of exhortation for the people, say on.

16 Then Paul stood up, and beckoning with *his* hand said, Men of Israel, and ye that fear God, give audience.

17 The God of this people of Israel chose our fathers, and exalted the people when they dwelt as strangers in the land of Egypt, and with an high arm brought he them out of it.

18 And about the time of forty years suffered he their manners in the wilderness.

19 And when he had destroyed seven nations in the land of Chā'naan, he divided their land to them by lot.

20 And after that he gave *unto them* judges about the space of four hundred and fifty years, until Samuel the prophet.

21 And afterward they desired a king: and God gave unto them Saul the son of Cis, a man of the tribe of Benjamin, by the space of forty years.

22 And when he had removed him, he raised up unto them David to be their king; to whom also he gave testimony, and said, I have found David the *son* of Jesse, a man after mine own heart, which shall fulfil all my will.

23 Of this man's seed hath God according to *his* promise raised unto Israel a Saviour, Jesus:

24 When John had first preached before his coming the baptism of repentance to all the people of Israel.

25 And as John fulfilled his course, he said, Whom think ye that I am? I am not *he*. But, behold, there cometh one after me, whose shoes of *his* feet I am not worthy to loose.

26 Men *and* brethren, children of the stock of Abraham, and whosoever among you feareth God, to you is the word of this salvation sent.

27 For they that dwell at Jerusalem, and their rulers, because they knew him not, nor yet the voices of the prophets which are read every sabbath day, they have fulfilled *them* in condemning *him*.

28 And though they found no cause of death *in him*, yet desired they Pilate that he should be slain.

29 And when they had fulfilled all that was written of him, they took *him* down from the tree, and laid *him* in a sepulchre.

30 But God raised him from the dead:

31 And he was seen many days of them which came up with him from Galilee to Jerusalem, who are his witnesses unto the people.

32 And we declare unto you glad tidings, how that the promise which was made unto the fathers,

33 God hath fulfilled the same unto us their children, in that he hath raised up Jesus again; as it is also written in the second psalm, Thou art my Son, this day have I begotten thee.

34 And as concerning that he raised him up from the dead, *now* no more to return to corruption, he said on this wise, I will give you the sure mercies of David.

35 Wherefore he saith also in another

something of the authoritative presentation of his message as he both stands to speak and gestures to the audience. The **Men of Israel** were Jews and **ye that fear God** were Gentiles who worshiped the God of the Jews and accepted the demands of the Law (cf. 10:2).

17-41. Paul's sermon in the synagogue in Pisidian Antioch recounted the history of God's deliverance of the Jewish nation from the time of Moses through the reign of David. Several important dates are given within this message. The **forty years . . . in the wilderness** (vs. 18) and the **four hundred and fifty years** (vs. 20) **in the land of Canaan** (vs. 19). The **seven nations** conquered **in the land of Canaan** are listed in Deuteronomy 7:1: "the Hittite, the Girgashite, the Amorite, the Canaanite, the Perizzite, the Hivite, and the Jebusite." The **four hundred and fifty years** may be intended to cover the period up to David's reign or the entire four hundred year period of sojourn in Egypt, along with the forty years of wandering in the wilderness and ten years of the initial period of conquest until the actual distribution of the land (cf. Josh 14). Paul especially identifies the line of God's promised Messiah through **David . . . their king** (vs. 22). God's **promise** has been kept to Israel in providing a **Saviour, Jesus** (vs. 23). The reference to John the Baptist (vs. 24), his preaching, and **the baptism of repentance** seems to provide very early authoritative reference to the historicity of John's ministry as it is quoted here by the Apostle Paul. One should also note the connection between John's "baptism of repentance" and the people of "Israel," indicating, as do the Gospels, that John's ministry was not that of initiating the church but bringing to a conclusion the ministry of the Old Testament prophets.

The resurrection of Christ is the central theme of victory in Paul's sermon as it was in the majority of New Testament evangelistic messages. Notice that the gospel centers in the death, burial, and resurrection of Christ in this sermon. It should be observed that true gospel preaching does not really occur until this central theme of the person and work of Christ in relation to salvation has been declared. The agents of His message are called **witnesses** (Gr *martys*, from which we derive "martyr"). These messengers of God were declaring the **glad tidings** (vs. 32) of the promise which God has made to their fathers and was now fulfilled in their lifetimes.

In verse 35 Paul quotes Psalm 16:10 as referring to Christ since it could not refer to David who had died and remained dead. Therefore it must refer to his promised descendant, the Messiah, whom Paul was now declaring to be Jesus Christ. The fact that Christ rose from the dead literally and physically is emphasized by the statement that he **saw no corruption** (vs. 37). On the basis of his triumphal death and resurrection, **forgiveness of sins** could now be offered to Paul's hearers. The key to receiving these benefits is faith. So **all that believe are justified** (vs. 39). Justification (Gr *dikaioō*) involves the declaring of one righteous. This, then, is the good news or glad tidings of the gospel.

psalm, Thou shalt not suffer thine Holy One to see corruption.

36 For David, after he had served his own generation by the will of God, fell on sleep, and was laid unto his fathers, and saw corruption:

37 But he, whom God raised again, saw no corruption.

38 ¶Be it known unto you therefore, men *and* brethren, that through this man is preached unto you the forgiveness of sins:

39 And by him all that believe are justified from all things, from which ye could not be justified by the law of Moses.

40 Beware therefore, lest that come upon you, which is spoken of in the prophets;

41 Behold, ye despisers, and wonder, and perish: for I work a work in your days, a work which ye shall in no wise believe, though a man declare it unto you.

42 ¶And when the Jews were gone out of the synagogue, the Gentiles besought that these words might be preached to them the next sabbath.

43 Now when the congregation was broken up, many of the Jews and religious proselytes followed Paul and Barnabas: who, speaking to them, persuaded them to continue in the grace of God.

44 ¶And the next sabbath day came almost the whole city together to hear the word of God.

45 But when the Jews saw the multitudes, they were filled with envy, and spake against those things which were spoken by Paul, contradicting and blaspheming.

46 Then Paul and Barnabas waxed bold, and said, It was necessary that the word of God should first have been spoken to you: but seeing ye put it from you, and judge yourselves unworthy of everlasting life, lo, we turn to the Gentiles.

47 For so hath the Lord commanded us, *saying,* I have set thee to be a light of the Gentiles, that thou shouldest be for salvation unto the ends of the earth.

48 And when the Gentiles heard this, they were glad, and glorified the word of the Lord: and as many as were ordained to eternal life believed.

49 And the word of the Lord was published throughout all the region.

50 But the Jews stirred up the devout and honourable women, and the chief men of the city, and raised persecution against Paul and Barnabas, and expelled them out of their coasts.

51 But they shook off the dust of their feet against them, and came unto Ī-cō′-nǐ-um.

52 And the disciples were filled with joy, and with the Holy Ghost.

42-45. The excitement of this new message of forgiveness of sin and impartation of righteousness created a great deal of excitement. After the synagogue service, many indicated their readiness to accept the message. This reception seems to have been the greatest among the **religious proselytes** (vs. 43). During the week the report of the impact of this service was so great that by the next Sabbath the synagogue was filled with Gentiles desiring to hear Paul's message. Unfortunately, such a crowd of Gentiles provoked the Jews to envy, and they began **contradicting and blaspheming** Paul's message.

46-52. In the face of this rejection by his Jewish listeners, Paul reminded them that it was **necessary that the word of God should first have been spoken to** them and if they **judge** themselves **unworthy of everlasting life,** then he will **turn to the Gentiles** (vs. 46). This rejection on the part of the Jews at the synagogue, however, did not stop the influence upon the Gentiles, who **were glad, and glorified the word of the Lord.** Thus the response by the Gentile "God-fearers" seems to have been outstanding. Without a doubt this incident serves as the great turning point in Paul's missionary strategy. While he will continue to offer the gospel to the Jew first, he will concentrate his major attention on the most responsive element of society to whom he is preaching: the Gentiles. Thus, it is said that as **many as were ordained to eternal life believed** (vs. 48). At this point the primary significance of this reference to predestination is more historical than it is theological, though the one does not detract from the other. That God is sovereign in sending His messengers to carry His message wherever He will, is obvious from both Scripture and the history of the church. It is the living Lord of heaven, Jesus Himself, who directs the activities of His messengers and opens and closes the doors of opportunity which He sets before them! There can be no doubt that the apostles were to be personally responsible for carrying the message of Christ to the hearts of men.

Again we notice that the "Acts of the Apostles" are really the Acts of Christ carried on through His apostles. Not only was the gospel rejected here by the majority of the Jews, but they in turn **stirred up** the "devout and honorable women," or those of high and influential standing. The **persecution against Paul and Barnabas** is the first such action recorded against the missionary enterprise of the early church. The shaking of the **dust off their** feet implied their recognition of the rejection of their message and their rejection in turn of those who had refused Christ's salvation. Notice that the **disciples** were not discouraged by this incident but were **filled with joy and with the Holy Ghost** (vs. 52).

CHAPTER 14

AND it came to pass in Ĭ-cō'nĭ-um, that they went both together into the synagogue of the Jews, and so spake, that a great multitude both of the Jews and also of the Greeks believed.

2 But the unbelieving Jews stirred up the Gentiles, and made their minds evil affected against the brethren.

3 Long time therefore abode they speaking boldly in the Lord, which gave testimony unto the word of his grace, and granted signs and wonders to be done by their hands.

4 But the multitude of the city was divided: and part held with the Jews, and part with the apostles.

5 And when there was an assault made both of the Gentiles, and also of the Jews with their rulers, to use *them* despitefully, and to stone them,

6 They were ware of *it*, and fled unto Lys'tra and Der'be, cities of Lyc-a-o'ni-a, and unto the region that lieth round about:

7 And there they preached the gospel.

8 ¶And there sat a certain man at Lys'tra, impotent in his feet, being a cripple from his mother's womb, who never had walked:

9 The same heard Paul speak: who stedfastly beholding him, and perceiving that he had faith to be healed,

10 Said with a loud voice, Stand upright on thy feet. And he leaped and walked.

11 And when the people saw what Paul had done, they lifted up their voices, saying in the speech of Lyc-a-o'ni-a, The gods are come down to us in the likeness of men.

12 And they called Barnabas, Jupiter; and Paul, Mer-cū'rĭ-us, because he was the chief speaker.

13 Then the priest of Jupiter, which was before their city, brought oxen and garlands unto the gates, and would have done sacrifice with the people.

14 *Which* when the apostles, Barnabas and Paul, heard *of*, they rent their clothes, and ran in among the people, crying out,

15 And saying, Sirs, why do ye these things? We also are men of like passions with you, and preach unto you that ye should turn from these vanities unto the living God, which made heaven, and earth, and the sea, and all things that are therein:

16 Who in times past suffered all nations to walk in their own ways.

C. Iconium, Derbe, and Lystra. 14:1-28.

14:1-5. Following their previously established pattern, Paul and Barnabas went first to the **synagogue of the Jews** which was located in **Iconium**, in the eastern district of **Phrygia**. The text indicates that a **great multitude** (vs. 1) of both Jews and Greeks believed. However, the **unbelieving Jews** began to stir up opposition again to the message of the apostles. Since it took a while for the opposition to become effective, Paul and his team were able to remain there preaching for a **long time**. In Luke's typically historical fashion, he does not indicate how long a period of time this actually was, making an exact chronology of Paul's travels almost impossible. Finally, the hostile Jews succeeded in inciting a riot which caused Paul and Barnabas to have to leave Iconium. Verse 3 indicates that the message of the gospel was the **word of His grace** and that their ministry was also accompanied by **signs and wonders,** or miracles.

6. The missionary team **fled into Lystra and Derbe** which are described as **cities of Lycaonia.** Luke's ancient contemporaries seemed to refer to these cities as being outside the district of Lycaonia, leading many scholars to challenge his accuracy. The investigation of this matter was the great turning point in archaeologist Sir William Ramsay's life as this reference caught his attention and careful examination of the matter proved Luke to be correct. Beginning as a critic of the veracity of the book of Acts, Ramsay became one of its strongest defenders (see *Bearing of Recent Discovery on the Trustworthiness of the New Testament*, ch. 3).

7-15. The missionary-apostles **preached the gospel** (Gr *euangelizomai*), or the "good news" of Christ's death and resurrection. The preaching was followed by the healing of a crippled man **who never had walked** (vs. 8). The miracle was based upon the man's **faith** and was total and instantaneous, for he immediately leaped and walked (vs. 10). The people became ecstatically overwhelmed and began to speak in their native dialect indicating that these men were **gods,** thinking that they were **Jupiter** and **Mercurius** (Mercury). Therefore, the **priest** of **Jupiter** brought a sacrifice unto them which resulted in their rebuking the people and reminding them that they were human beings who had come to turn them from **these vanities** unto the **living God.** Paul's usage of his term in pagan cities seems to be deliberate to distinguish God the Creator as the only God whom he represented. The names "Jupiter" and "Mercury" are the Latin equivalents for the Greek names of these gods, Zeus, the father of gods, and Hermes, the messenger of the gods. Greek mythological literature is filled with references to these deities.

16-18. Paul's apologetic speech reminded them that **in times past** God had allowed the nations to go their own ways but had

17 Nevertheless he left not himself without witness, in that he did good, and gave us rain from heaven, and fruitful seasons, filling our hearts with food and gladness.

18 And with these sayings scarce restrained they the people, that they had not done sacrifice unto them.

19 ¶And there came thither *certain* Jews from Antioch and I-cŏ′nĭ-um, who persuaded the people, and, having stoned Paul, drew *him* out of the city, supposing he had been dead.

20 Howbeit, as the disciples stood round about him, he rose up, and came into the city: and the next day he departed with Barnabas to Der′be.

21 And when they had preached the gospel to that city, and had taught many, they returned again to Lys′tra, and *to* I-cŏ′nĭ-um, and Antioch,

22 Confirming the souls of the disciples, *and* exhorting them to continue in the faith, and that we must through much tribulation enter into the kingdom of God.

23 And when they had ordained them elders in every church, and had prayed with fasting, they commended them to the Lord, on whom they believed.

24 And after they had passed throughout Pĭ-sĭd′ĭ-a, they came to Păm-phȳl′ĭ-a.

25 And when they had preached the word in Per′ga, they went down into Ăt-ta′lĭ-a:

26 And thence sailed to Antioch, from whence they had been recommended to the grace of God for the work which they fulfilled.

not left Himself **without witness.** The concept of this message was to show them that the great Creator-God was revealing Himself to them through nature, a message which Paul indicates in Romans 1-2 was sufficient to make men responsible to God, but not sufficient to bring them to salvation. The Lord had allowed the nations to go their own way, because they had previously rejected His way (cf. Gen 10-11, which forms the great turning point in God's dealing with man). The effect of the sermon was to restrain the people from honoring them as gods. There can be no doubt that the early Christian disciples did not consider themselves worthy of worship or sainthood. They rejected any special place of spiritual authority or recognition. They clearly saw themselves as men simply doing God's work by carrying out the commission which Christ had left to His church.

19-20. No reference is actually made to a Jewish synagogue in Lystra, but probably such a synagogue existed, for when the Jews from Antioch and Iconium came there they were able to raise up strong opposition against Paul. He was eventually **stoned** and left for **dead** (vs. 19). Paul evidently refers to this event in II Corinthians 11:24-25, where he mentions being caught up into the "third heaven." The abrupt nature of the narrative at this point seems to indicate a miraculous deliverance of some sort. Any man stoned in such a manner without receiving severe physical injuries, both externally and internally, would be a miracle indeed! The reference in Galatians 6:17 to the "marks of Jesus" may well refer to the scars received from this stoning. There can be no underestimation of the shock which must have come upon the people of the city when Paul **rose up** (vs. 20) and came back into the city probably to continue his preaching. Note that the **disciples** were present at this "resurrection." The next day they left and went to **Derbe,** a frontier city of the province of Galatia. No opposition is recorded in this city, where it is said they made many disciples.

21-25. Having completed this initial tour, they returned to each city in reverse order, **Confirming the souls of the disciples** (vs. 22). This sets the pattern for the concept of "follow-up" work among new converts, whom they exhorted to **continue in the faith.** This does not mean that a born-again believer might stop believing and thus lose his salvation, but rather, emphasizes the importance of continued growth in the Christian life. This process of growth will bring us through **much tribulation** to enter **the kingdom of God,** which here must refer to heaven. The reference to "tribulation" is not to the Tribulation itself, but to the continued troubles and sufferings of the church throughout all ages. The fact that they **ordained them elders** in each church indicates that the leadership of each local congregation rested in the authority of its own men. While the leaders of the church at Jerusalem had spiritual influence over the local congregations, nowhere do we find any hierarchical structure in the early church. One predominant church did not overrule the affairs of another. Certainly the church at Jerusalem remained the spiritual standard during these early years because of its geographical proximity to the origin of the Christian faith. But even there great latitude was permitted toward the individual local congregations. The "elders" (Gr *presbuteros*) were spiritual leaders who shared the oversight of the church and from among whom a "bishop" or pastor was chosen as their leader. The elders were similar to the pastoral staff of most of our churches today. They engaged in the spiritual oversight of the church, whereas the deacons were designated as servants of the congregation.

26-28. The missionary team then **sailed to Antioch** from the seaport **Attalia.** Upon their return to their sending church they gathered them together and **rehearsed all that God had done.** Certainly this experience sets the pattern of sent missionaries

27 And when they were come, and had gathered the church together, they rehearsed all that God had done with them, and how he had opened the door of faith unto the Gentiles.
28 And there they abode long time with the disciples.

CHAPTER 15

AND certain men which came down from Judæa taught the brethren, *and said*, Except ye be circumcised after the manner of Moses, ye cannot be saved.
2 When therefore Paul and Barnabas had no small dissension and disputation with them, they determined that Paul and Barnabas, and certain other of them, should go up to Jerusalem unto the apostles and elders about this question.

returning to the sending church with a report of their evangelistic activities. Note that **God . . . opened the door of faith unto the Gentiles** (vs. 27). Again we observe that Christ, the Lord of the church, is sovereignly directing her affairs from heaven. The church in Antioch had now become independent of the "mother church" in Jerusalem. Thus they remained there a **long time**. This again is one of Luke's characteristically indefinite references to time. It is generally assumed that this first missionary journey took about one year and was followed by another year of recuperation and preparation in Antioch.

D. The Council of Jerusalem. 15:1-35.

15:1-2. The Council of Jerusalem is one of the great turning points of the book of Acts, as are the conversions of Paul and Cornelius. The relation between the Jewish and Gentile believers in terms of admission to membership in the church was the issue of this discussion. In the beginning, the church consisted almost entirely of converted Jews who had automatically been circumcised as Old Testament believers. Even Peter, earlier, had great difficulty making the transition to full fellowship with the Gentiles. The establishment of a predominantly Gentile church in Antioch and now the success of the Gentile mission in Galatia refocused attention upon fellowship with these growing churches. Church growth certainly underlies the basic themes represented by Luke in the book of Acts. The power of the message of the gospel is demonstrated by the fact that it gains reception and response almost everywhere. When the Jewish converts from Judaea arrived in Antioch, they insisted that **ye be circumcised** in order to **be saved** (vs. 1). The text later (vs. 5) indicates that these converts were from among the Pharisees, the strictest of the sects of the Jews. The disputations would also seem to indicate that some of the early believers still looked upon Christianity as a movement within Judaism at this point (cf. Ladd, p. 435).

It should be noted that a substantial difference of opinion exists among commentators as to whether or not this visit to Jerusalem is represented in Galatians 2 or not. Harrison (*Wycliffe Bible Commentary,* pp. 698-699) argues for this (cf. also Lightfoot, *Galatians,* pp. 125ff. and Ladd, pp. 435ff.), and others argue that the Epistle to the Galatians was written shortly before the Council of Jerusalem, which would adequately explain why that epistle makes no allusion to that Council. Since the discussions and decisions of the Council were distinctly relevant to the issue at hand in the Epistle to the Galatians, it would seem highly unlikely that Paul would not have made reference to this decision. Thus, Paul's visit to Jerusalem in Galatians 2 seems to be equated with the famine-relief visit of Acts 11. No matter how important that interview was when Paul wrote to the Galatians, its importance was erased by that of the Jerusalem Council which took place soon afterwards. According to the text of Acts the visit that Paul paid to Jerusalem at the time of the Council was his third visit after his conversion (cf. 9:26; 11:30; 12:25). In the Epistle to the Galatians Paul tells of two visits which he paid to Jerusalem after his conversion, the first being identified with that of Acts 9 and the second with that of Acts 11, rather than with this visit in Acts 15. Bruce argues that a "reasonable and satisfying sequence of events" can be reconstructed by accepting the view that the Epistle to the Galatians was written to the young churches founded by Paul and Barnabas during their first missionary tour and that it was written at Antioch shortly before the Jerusalem Council. The rapid progress of Gentile evangelization in Antioch, Cyprus, and Asia Minor posed a serious threat to the Jewish Christians at Jerusalem. It was this issue which was settled by the epochal conference at Jerusalem.

3 And being brought on their way by

3-6. The Jerusalem church welcomed the delegation from

2167

the church, they passed through Phe-nĭ́ce and Sa-mấrĭ-a, declaring the conversion of the Gentiles: and they caused great joy unto all the brethren.

4 And when they were come to Jerusalem, they were received of the church, and *of* the apostles and elders, and they declared all things that God had done with them.

5 ¶But there rose up certain of the sect of the Pharisees which believed, saying, That it was needful to circumcise them, and to command *them* to keep the law of Moses.

6 And the apostles and elders came together for to consider of this matter.

7 And when there had been much disputing, Peter rose up, and said unto them, Men *and* brethren, ye know how that a good while ago God made choice among us, that the Gentiles by my mouth should hear the word of the gospel, and believe.

8 And God, which knoweth the hearts, bare them witness, giving them the Holy Ghost, even as *he did* unto us;

9 And put no difference between us and them, purifying their hearts by faith.

10 Now therefore why tempt ye God, to put a yoke upon the neck of the disciples, which neither our fathers nor we were able to bear?

11 But we believe that through the grace of the Lord Jesus Christ we shall be saved, even as they.

12 ¶Then all the multitude kept silence, and gave audience to Barnabas and Paul, declaring what miracles and wonders God had wrought among the Gentiles by them.

13 ¶And after they had held their peace, James answered, saying, Men *and* brethren, hearken unto me:

14 Simeon hath declared how God at the first did visit the Gentiles, to take out of them a people for his name.

15 And to this agree the words of the prophets; as it is written,

16 After this I will return, and will build again the tabernacle of David, which is fallen down; and I will build again the ruins thereof, and I will set it up:

17 That the residue of men might seek after the Lord, and all the Gentiles, upon whom my name is called, saith the Lord, who doeth all these things.

18 Known unto God are all his works from the beginning of the world.

19 Wherefore my sentence is, that we trouble not them, which from among the Gentiles are turned to God:

20 But that we write unto them, that they abstain from pollutions of idols, and *from* fornication, and *from* things strangled, and *from* blood.

21 For Moses of old time hath in every city them that preach him, being read in the synagogues every sabbath day.

22 ¶Then pleased it the apostles and elders, with the whole church, to send chosen men of their own company to Antioch with Paul and Barnabas; *name-*

Antioch and listened eagerly to the story of their successful evangelization of the Gentiles in Galatia, which caused **great joy unto all the brethren.** Objections by the **Pharisees which believed** (or Christian converts from among the Pharisees) led to a formal conference of the **apostles and elders** with the delegation from Antioch. While the leaders were involved in the discussion, verses 12 and 22 show that the whole church participated in the ultimate decision. The wrong decision at this point would have thrown the church back under Jewish bondage to the law and would have stalled the expansion of the church as designed by her Lord.

7-11. Paul's earlier rebuke of Peter in Antioch (cf. Gal 2:11) had taken effect. Now, as the leader of the apostles, Peter reinforced his original position on the Gentile mission as he had with Cornelius. He reminded them that God had accepted the Gentiles by faith alone and not on Jewish terms. Peter emphasized that it was God's **choice** to give the gospel to the Gentiles and that He who directed this mission had given them **the Holy Ghost** even as He had done unto the Jewish believers. Therefore, there exists **no difference** (vs. 9) between Jewish and Gentile believers, for both have their hearts purified **by faith.** The entire discussion of this matter and its final conclusion should have guarded the church over the centuries against any concept of salvation by works or faith plus works. Each speaker in this conference made it clear that salvation is by faith alone. Peter emphasized that salvation was **through the grace of the Lord.** Thus, the book of Acts is consistent throughout in emphasizing that salvation is of God and does not originate with man.

12-21. The impact upon the congregation was such that the **multitude kept silence,** giving Barnabas and Paul an opportunity to review the results of the Gentile missionary enterprise. Then the turning point came when **James,** the brother of our Lord, spoke decisively in regard to this matter. While all of the apostles appeared to be actively involved in this discussion, it seems clear from this passage that James, the pastor of the church at Jerusalem, was the ultimate leader and his decision was accepted by the others. Rather than Peter or Paul being in the leadership role at this point, James alone assumes that responsibility. This incident gives great understanding of the authority of the pastor's leadership in the church. Even the leader of the apostles, Peter, and the church's outstanding missionary spokesman, Paul, could not overrule his decision. It should also be observed that all of these men essentially agreed in how to handle this matter. Spirit-directed ministry will always reflect harmony and fellowship in vital matters of this nature. The reference to the **tabernacle of David** which is **fallen down** (vs. 16) seems to be a reference to the spiritual leadership of the Jewish nation, not a literal reference to the Temple as such. Therefore, the rebuilding referred to here may not necessarily be to the reconstruction of the Tribulation or millennial Temple, but rather to the ultimate rebuilding of the nation of Israel itself at the time. James' decision was that they no longer **trouble** the Gentiles who had **turned to God** (vs. 19), referring to the drastic nature of their conversion. However, he suggested that they **write unto them** that they abstain from **idols,** from **fornication,** from things **strangled,** and from **blood** (vs. 20). Each of these prohibitions related to particular pagan offenses which were especially objectionable to orthodox Jews.

22-29. The final decision was reached with such unanimity that it **pleased . . . the apostles and elders, with the whole church.** Thus, we find the first major ecumenical council ending with total harmony. Messengers were then chosen to take a

ly, Judas surnamed Bär′să-bas, and Silas, chief men among the brethren:

23 And they wrote *letters* by them after this manner; The apostles and elders and brethren *send* greeting unto the brethren which are of the Gentiles in Antioch and Syria and Çĭ-lĭ′çia.

24 Forasmuch as we have heard, that certain which went out from us have troubled you with words, subverting your souls, saying, *Ye must* be circumcised, and keep the law: to whom we gave no *such* commandment:

25 It seemed good unto us, being assembled with one accord, to send chosen men unto you with our beloved Barnabas and Paul,

26 Men that have hazarded their lives for the name of our Lord Jesus Christ.

27 We have sent therefore Judas and Silas, who shall also tell *you* the same things by mouth.

28 For it seemed good to the Holy Ghost, and to us, to lay upon you no greater burden than these necessary things;

29 That ye abstain from meats offered to idols, and from blood, and from things strangled, and from fornication: from which if ye keep yourselves, ye shall do well. Fare ye well.

30 So when they were dismissed, they came to Antioch: and when they had gathered the multitude together, they delivered the epistle:

31 *Which* when they had read, they rejoiced for the consolation.

32 And Judas and Silas, being prophets also themselves, exhorted the brethren with many words, and confirmed *them*.

33 And after they had tarried *there* a space, they were let go in peace from the brethren unto the apostles.

34 Notwithstanding it pleased Silas to abide there still.

35 Paul also and Barnabas continued in Antioch, teaching and preaching the word of the Lord, with many others also.

36 ¶And some days after Paul said unto Barnabas, Let us go again and visit our brethren in every city where we have preached the word of the Lord, *and see* how they do.

37 And Barnabas determined to take with them John, whose surname was Mark.

38 But Paul thought not good to take him with them, who departed from them from Păm-phylĭ-a, and went not with them to the work.

39 And the contention was so sharp between them, that they departed asunder one from the other: and so Barnabas took Mark, and sailed unto Cyprus;

40 And Paul chose Silas, and departed, being recommended by the brethren unto the grace of God.

41 And he went through Syria and Çĭ-lĭ′çia, confirming the churches.

letter to Antioch explaining the decision. Judas and Silas (who appears later as Paul's companion) were to communicate the Council's findings by word of mouth and also by carrying a letter from the apostles and elders at Jerusalem to the church at Antioch. Paul and Barnabas returned to Antioch where they remained and were accompanied by Judas and Silas as representatives from the Jerusalem church to which they returned. The letter is quoted in its entirety in verses 23-29. It is clear, direct, uncomplicated, and simple. It is neither artificially "spiritual," nor unnecessarily lengthy. The letter is referred to as **the epistle** (vs. 30).

30-35. The reception at Antioch was joyous and the issue was permanently settled in that church. Judas and Silas are referred to as **being prophets** (vs. 32). Paul and Barnabas were engaged in the activity of **teaching and preaching** (vs. 35). The reference seems to indicate that several men were involved in the teaching and preaching ministry of this congregation and that the entire membership was mobilized in the task of evangelism. The reference to "prophets" clearly seems to be that of the task of preaching or proclaiming the Word of God.

V. PAUL'S SECOND JOURNEY: CHRISTIANITY SPREADS WESTWARD. 15:36-18:22.

A. A New Team. 15:36-16:5.

36-41. After some time passed (again the amount of time is vaguely stated), Paul initiated to Barnabas the idea of returning to the cities where they had established churches. It should be noted that they did not merely establish believers who were unattached from each other in the cities to which they had gone, but rather they established churches, or local assemblies of believers, in each city.

The disagreement over **John, whose surname was Mark,** brought about the division of the first missionary team. Paul objected to taking Mark, who had **departed from them from Pamphylia** earlier. The difference was so **sharp** that each took a new assistant and traveled in a different direction—Barnabas taking Mark and sailing to **Cyprus;** Paul choosing Silas and departing into Cilicia. Much speculation has been done over the nature of this division; however, it is presented by Luke in a matter-of-fact tone. Evidently each man had a preference for his native land in his missionary work. Barnabas returned to Cyprus; Paul returned to his native Anatolia. As a missionary handbook, Acts indicates that immediate evangelization is most effective in a context where one is most familiar with the people and their needs. This does not mitigate against cross-cultural evangelism, for Paul would be engaged in such throughout most of his career. However, as a training model, the immediate implication seems to be that one receives his best early training for evangelism within his own cultural context. The new teams evidently were both very effective. Barnabas was able to recover and rebuild the life of Mark whom Paul later referred to as one whom he appreciated (cf. Col 4:10; II Tim 4:11). In the meantime, Paul was able to develop the qualities which he had observed in Silas. In either case God's work was extended, and again the Lord of the church must be seen as sovereignly operating over and above the affairs, and even the disputes, of men.

16:1-5. Paul returned to Derbe and Lystra where he selected **Timothy,** the son of a **Jewess** who was a believer. This outstanding young man would become his travel companion and later would be one of the leaders of the early church. He is the same Timothy to whom the epistles bearing his name were sent. The cultural barrier to evangelism of the Jews centered on the issue of circumcision. Therefore, since Timothy was a half-Jew, Paul **circumcised him** so that he would be acceptable to the Jews in their forthcoming Jewish ministry. This action can hardly be looked upon as a compromise of conviction in relation to chapter 15, since Paul had spoken so strongly in favor of the Gentile mission. It should be remembered, however, that Paul was not giving up on the Jews, though he must have experienced a growing awareness of the Gentile thrust of his mission. He would continue to go "to the Jew first" and then to the Gentiles. This incident teaches us that cultural accommodation in relation to missionary evangelism is often vital to the furtherance of the gospel. It should be observed, though, that such accommodation is made in matters of external preference and should not be made in matters considered morally sinful (see this principle expressed in I Cor 9:20). Ladd notes that it was probably at this time that Timothy was set aside by the elders in Lystra for missionary activity, referred to in I Timothy 4:14 (p. 441). The initial stage of the second missionary journey took them back to the churches which had been established on the first journey and were now **increased in number daily** (vs. 5), emphasizing again Luke's apologetic approach to church growth as proof of the power of the gospel. As in the earlier reference to the church at Jerusalem (2:42ff), these churches are said to have been growing in number daily. This would certainly mean that conversion was occurring as a result of every-member evangelism, not just evangelistic preaching on Sundays. While such preaching is never mitigated against in the New Testament, daily personal evangelism seems to have been the strength of the early church. Thus, the pattern of aggressively evangelistic, soul-winning church ministries is modeled for us in these early New Testament churches.

CHAPTER 16

THEN came he to Der′be and Lys′tra: and, behold, a certain disciple was there, named Ti-mō′the-us, the son of a certain woman, which was a Jewess, and believed; but his father *was* a Greek:

2 Which was well reported of by the brethren that were at Lys′tra and I-cō′-ni-um.

3 Him would Paul have to go forth with him; and took and circumcised him because of the Jews which were in those quarters: for they knew all that his father was a Greek.

4 And as they went through the cities, they delivered them the decrees for to keep, that were ordained of the apostles and elders which were at Jerusalem.

5 And so were the churches established in the faith, and increased in number daily.

B. A New Direction. 16:6-40.

6-8. The geographical movement which ultimately led the missionary leader to Troas is viewed differently in relation to the "North Galatian theory" or the "South Galatian theory." The latter seems the most reasonable; that they came to **Phrygia and the region of Galatia,** not as separate regions but as a single area: Phrygian Galatia. Thus their journey would have taken them from Derbe and Lystra through this part of Galatia directly westward to the great cities of the province of Asia. It hardly needs to be mentioned that this is not a reference to the continent of Asia, but to the province of that name within a peninsula of Asia Minor. Nevertheless, a great deal of allegorical interpretation and preaching has often been done by those misunderstanding this reference. Traveling through this area they then turned northward toward **Mysia** and **Bithynia** and again were restrained by the Holy Spirit. Consequently, they came to the seaport of Troas (ancient Troy). From this spot on the edge of the geographical continent of Asia, their attention would be turned across the straits to Greece and the continent of Europe.

6 Now when they had gone throughout Phrȳg-ĭ-a and the region of Ga-lā′tia, and were forbidden of the Holy Ghost to preach the word in Asia,

7 After they were come to Mȳs′ĭa, they assayed to go into Bĭ-thȳn′ĭ-a: but the Spirit suffered them not.

8 And they passing by Mȳs′ĭa came down to Troas.

9 ¶And a vision appeared to Paul in the night; there stood a man of Macedonia, and prayed him, saying, Come over into Macedonia, and help us.

10 And after he had seen the vision, immediately we endeavoured to go into Macedonia, assuredly gathering that the Lord had called us for to preach the gospel unto them.

11 Therefore loosing from Troas, we came with a straight course to Săm-o-thrā′cia, and the next *day* to Nē-ăp′o-lĭs:

12 And from thence to Phĭ-lip′pĭ, which is the chief city of that part of Macedonia, *and* a colony: and we were in that city abiding certain days.

13 And on the sabbath we went out of the city by a river side, where prayer was wont to be made; and we sat down, and spake unto the women which resorted *thither.*

14 ¶And a certain woman named Lyd′i-a, a seller of purple, of the city of Thȳ-a-tī′ra, which worshipped God, heard *us:* whose heart the Lord opened, that she attended unto the things which were spoken of Paul.

15 And when she was baptized, and her household, she besought *us,* saying, If ye have judged me to be faithful to the Lord, come into my house, and abide *there.* And she constrained us.

16 ¶And it came to pass, as we went to prayer, a certain damsel possessed with a spirit of divination met us, which brought her masters much gain by soothsaying:

17 The same followed Paul and us, and cried, saying, These men are the servants of the most high God, which shew unto us the way of salvation.

18 And this did she many days. But Paul, being grieved, turned and said to the spirit, I command thee in the name of Jesus Christ to come out of her. And he came out the same hour.

9-12. The famous Macedonian vision takes place at this point. Paul had been postponed by the Holy Spirit from preaching in Asia Minor (a mission which would be engaged in later). At this point, certainly some sense of concern, perhaps even confusion, must have gone through the apostle's mind. Why had they traveled all the way to the seaport of Troas? It was here that **a vision appeared to Paul**, evidently sent by God and not merely the product of his own imagination. In the vision a **man of Macedonia** (northern Greece) called to them to **Come over . . . and help us.** We note the need to preach the gospel in each of these areas. It may be also said that they did not attempt to second-guess God. They had just come from the east, they had been forbidden to go south or north, so they waited. God's ultimate will is not always the easiest thing to find, but once found, it becomes the most blessed! In the vision at Troas Paul saw the man of Macedonia and prepared a team of evangelists to enter Europe. Evidently, at this point, the author, Luke, joined the team. The reference to "we came" indicates that the story is now autobiographical. Luke was a physician, an intellectual, an author, and Greek by background. Thus, by adding an educated Greek doctor to the evangelistic team, they would only enhance their effectiveness in the new mission. Whether Luke was a practicing physician in Troas at the time, or whether he was there for some other purpose, or whether he joined them along the way, is difficult to tell. Nevertheless from this point it is obvious that he continues in Paul's company to Philippi. Thus, the evangelistic team now consists of Paul the leader, Silas his assistant, Timothy the young man, and Luke the intellectual. While this four-man team is in no way designed to set a necessary precedent, it is interesting that the variety of their backgrounds added balance and flexibility to the team. (On the "we" sections see also 20:5; 21:18; 27:1.) The group took ship from Troas and sailed to the island of **Samothracia** and on to **Neapolis.**

13-15. They arrived at **Philippi**, a Roman **colony**, made up of transplanted Roman citizens. Colonies were usually located at strategic points throughout the empire and enjoyed such privileges as self-government. Evidently, there was no Jewish synagogue there, since Paul and his team went to the **riverside** seeking the Jewish "place of prayer." There they met **Lydia** (perhaps a proper name, "the Lydian") designating the region in which **Thyatira** was located. She was a **seller of purple,** indicating that she had learned the dye and textile business of her hometown, and had brought it to Philippi. (On the significance of this industry in Thyatira, see E. M. Blaiklock, *Cities of the New Testament,* pp. 107-111.) She seems to have been a Gentile "God-fearer" (or Jewish proselyte). She was saved and baptized and **her household** followed her example. A woman of wealth and great position, she undoubtedly had a number of servants and attendants. The reference to her "household" does not necessarily refer to small children. Conversions in the book of Acts seem to be limited to adults or older young people.

16-18. The demoniac girl who followed Paul and disturbed his preaching services was miraculously healed. **Spirit of divination** (Gr *pythōn*). The priestess of Delphi was called "the python" after the serpent that had guarded the oracle, and the word was also used of soothsayers. Such a person was thought to be inspired by the god Apollo who was associated with the giving of oracles. This girl was demon-possessed and her uncontrolled utterances were considered to be the utterances of a god. Paul exorcised a demon from this slave girl and set her free. She had previously followed them around chanting, **These men are the servants of the most high God** (vs. 17). Just as a demon had recognized Jesus as the "Holy One" (Mk 1:24), so this demon recognized the divine power upon Paul and his companions. The demon was cast out of her **in the name of Jesus**

Christ. Only by His personal power and authority resident in the one who uses His name can such be accomplished.

19 ¶And when her masters saw that the hope of their gains was gone, they caught Paul and Silas, and drew *them* into the marketplace unto the rulers,

20 And brought them to the magistrates, saying, These men, being Jews, do exceedingly trouble our city,

21 And teach customs, which are not lawful for us to receive, neither to observe, being Romans.

22 And the multitude rose up together against them: and the magistrates rent off their clothes, and commanded to beat *them.*

23 And when they had laid many stripes upon them, they cast *them* into prison, charging the jailor to keep them safely:

24 Who, having received such a charge, thrust them into the inner prison, and made their feet fast in the stocks.

19-24. This miracle led to their being cast into jail, because of the complaint of **her masters.** Having delivered her from demon power, they had rendered the girl incapable of "soothsaying." Thus she was now a financial liability to those who owned her. Paul and his companions were taken to the **magistrates,** equivalent to the Latin *praetor.* They were especially criticized for **being Jews** (vs. 20). The objections against them were increased by the citizens of Philippi because of their being **Romans.** This later explains Paul's action in demanding a proper apology since he was also a Roman! The mob was incited to near riot and Paul and Silas were beaten, probably by "lictors," who attended the magistrates. Each lictor carried a bundle of rods and an axe, symbolizing the power to inflict capital punishment. This symbol was later popularized by the Fascists in Italy in the twentieth century. Paul and Silas were then jailed as anarchists. The personal touches of the stories of Philippi had led Ramsay and Blaiklock (p. 124) to assume that Luke may have been a Philippian himself. On the other hand, Rackham (*Acts of the Apostles,* pp. 278-281) strongly rejects this. Most others are undecided. Bruce notes that the "double discomforts of the lictors' rods and the stocks was not calculated to fill Paul and Silas with joy" (p. 337).

25 ¶And at midnight Paul and Silas prayed, and sang praises unto God: and the prisoners heard them.

26 And suddenly there was a great earthquake, so that the foundations of the prison were shaken: and immediately all the doors were opened, and every one's bands were loosed.

27 And the keeper of the prison

25-34. However, **at midnight** Paul and Silas **prayed, and sang.** Such singing must have startled and surprised both the jailor and the prisoners. We thus have here the first "sacred concert" ever held in Europe and one that eventually "brought down the house"! The **great earthquake** shook the prison foundations to the point that the doors were opened and everyone's bands were loosed. While this may seem strange, modern-day earthquake phenomena certainly verify the actual possibility of

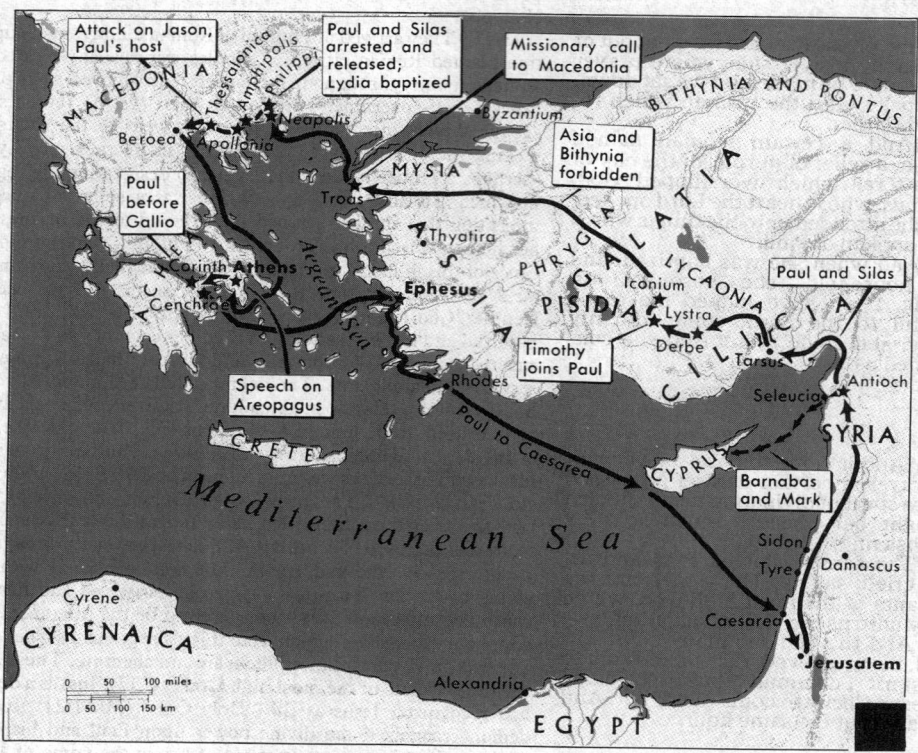

The Second Missionary Journey of Paul

awaking out of his sleep, and seeing the prison doors open, he drew out his sword, and would have killed himself, supposing that the prisoners had been fled.

28 But Paul cried with a loud voice, saying, Do thyself no harm: for we are all here.

29 Then he called for a light, and sprang in, and came trembling, and fell down before Paul and Silas,

30 And brought them out, and said, Sirs, what must I do to be saved?

31 And they said, Believe on the Lord Jesus Christ, and thou shalt be saved, and thy house.

32 And they spake unto him the word of the Lord, and to all that were in his house.

33 And he took them the same hour of the night, and washed *their* stripes; and was baptized, he and all his, straightway.

34 And when he had brought them into his house, he set meat before them, and rejoiced, believing in God with all his house.

35 And when it was day, the magistrates sent the serjeants, saying, Let those men go.

36 And the keeper of the prison told this saying to Paul, The magistrates have sent to let you go: now therefore depart, and go in peace.

37 But Paul said unto them, They have beaten us openly uncondemned, being Romans, and have cast *us* into prison; and now do they thrust us out privily? nay verily; but let them come themselves and fetch us out.

38 And the serjeants told these words unto the magistrates: and they feared, when they heard that they were Romans.

39 And they came and besought them, and brought *them* out, and desired *them* to depart out of the city.

40 And they went out of the prison, and entered into *the house of* Lyd'i-a: and when they had seen the brethren, they comforted them, and departed.

CHAPTER 17

NOW when they had passed through Ăm-phĭp'o-lĭs and Ăp-ol-lō'nĭ-a, they came to Thĕs-sa-lo-nī'ca, where was a synagogue of the Jews:

2 And Paul, as his manner was, went in unto them, and three sabbath days reasoned with them out of the scriptures,

3 Opening and alleging, that Christ must needs have suffered, and risen again from the dead; and that this Jesus, whom I preach unto you, is Christ.

4 And some of them believed, and consorted with Paul and Silas; and of the devout Greeks a great multitude, and of the chief women not a few.

such an incident. The jailor, hearing that all the prisoners had escaped and that he had failed his responsibility, prepared to kill himself. Then Paul cried out, **Do thyself no harm.** The fact that he came in **trembling** and **fell down before** them implies that he was shaken not only by the incident but by the evident power of God which had been demonstrated in the earthquake. His question, **Sirs, what must I do to be saved?** appears to be genuine and Paul's answer is really the gospel in a nutshell: **Believe on the Lord Jesus Christ.** Using the tragedy of the moment as an opportunity to present the truth of the gospel, the two missionaries told him that faith in Jesus as Lord was the way of salvation for himself and his family. The jailor and his entire household believed their message and were baptized that very night. This evidence of "household conversion" does not imply that the family was saved simply because the father believed, but rather because each one in particular believed. Nor does it imply that infants were baptized along with the rest of the family. We are told nothing of the ages of the family members. The jailor's first Christian act of mercy was to wash the stripes of Paul and Silas, which before apparently had been left unattended.

35-40. After receiving apologies from the terrified city officials, who now learned that they had shamelessly beaten two Roman citizens, the team left Philippi and moved on to Thessalonica. Notice that Paul used his Roman citizenship as an opportunity to bring credibility upon the new believers in the community. Upon leaving the prison they returned to Lydia's house and comforted . . . **the brethren.** Apparently Luke stayed behind to oversee the new work and to add leadership to its direction. The use of "we" is not mentioned again until 20:5, when Paul returns to Philippi on his third journey, when Luke evidently rejoins the missionary team.

C. Flight from Thessalonica to Athens. 17:1-34.

17:1-4. Paul, Silas, and Timothy journeyed westward along the great military road, *Via Egnatia.* They passed through **Amphipolis** and **Apollonia.** Why they passed by these cities we are not told. However, it should be observed that Paul followed definite missionary strategy in establishing churches in key centers which could form evangelistic outreach centers around their location. Thus, he moved on to **Thessalonica** the chief city and capital of the province of Macedonia. In his epistle to this church (I Thess 1:8) Paul indicated that the gospel had gone forth from them into Macedonia and Achaia. The cities bypassed were not small towns, for Amphipolis was itself a major community, though it declined in significance after this time. In Thessalonica Paul discovered a **synagogue of the Jews,** and went there three consecutive **sabbath days.** Paul spent at least these three weeks in the home of Jason organizing a church from the Jewish converts, while working as a tentmaker that he might not be a burden to the believers (cf. I Thess 2:9; II Thess 3:7-12). However the three weeks only refers to the time Paul was allowed to present his case in the Jewish synagogue. Again Luke's chronological references are vague and it is possible that they spent a great deal of time in this community establishing an

5 ¶But the Jews which believed not, moved with envy, took unto them certain lewd fellows of the baser sort, and gathered a company, and set all the city on an uproar, and assaulted the house of Jason, and sought to bring them out to the people.

6 And when they found them not, they drew Jason and certain brethren unto the rulers of the city, crying, These that have turned the world upside down are come hither also;

7 Whom Jason hath received: and these all do contrary to the decrees of Cæsar, saying that there is another king, *one* Jesus.

8 And they troubled the people and the rulers of the city, when they heard these things.

9 And when they had taken security of Jason, and of the other, they let them go.

10 ¶And the brethren immediately sent away Paul and Silas by night unto Be-rē′a: who coming *thither* went into the synagogue of the Jews.

11 These were more noble than those in Thĕs-sa-lo-nī′ca, in that they received the word with all readiness of mind, and searched the scriptures daily, whether those things were so.

12 Therefore many of them believed; also of honourable women which were Greeks, and of men, not a few.

13 But when the Jews of Thĕs-sa-lo-nī′ca had knowledge that the word of God was preached of Paul at Be-rē′a, they came thither also, and stirred up the people.

14 And then immediately the brethren sent away Paul to go as it were to the sea: but Silas and Tī-mō′the-us abode there still.

15 And they that conducted Paul brought him unto Athens: and receiving a commandment unto Silas and Tī-mō′the-us for to come to him with all speed, they departed.

16 ¶Now while Paul waited for them at Athens, his spirit was stirred in him, when he saw the city wholly given to idolatry.

17 Therefore disputed he in the synagogue with the Jews, and with the devout persons, and in the market daily with them that met with him.

18 Then certain philosophers of the Ĕp-i-cū-rē′ans, and of the Stō′ĭcks, encountered him. And some said, What

outstanding local church. Paul's method of evangelism was to "reason" with them **out of the scripture.** This does not mean that he merely used philosophic arguments, which he attempted to tie to the Old Testament, but rather that he presented prophecies that related to Christ, His death and resurrection, to prove to them that **this Jesus, whom I preach is . . . Christ.**

5-10. Some of the Jews believed and **a great multitude of the Greeks.** The gospel was once again opposed, however, by the unbelieving Jews who dragged Jason into court and unsuccessfully attempted to put him in jail. The **rulers of the city,** literally "politarchs," were responsible for reviewing the case. Since the term "politarch" was unknown in Greek literature until recent archaeological discoveries, some commentators wrongly accuse Luke of being inaccurate in his designation. The disciples were referred to as those who had **turned the world upside down** (vs. 6) referring to the impact of their ministry in the previous places. One needs to be careful not to allegorize this statement too strongly. They had obviously not yet won the world to Christ but they were in the process of bringing about a confrontation with the wills of men which left no doubt as to the clarity and definiteness of their message. They were literally shaking communities with the gospel! They were also accused of claiming to have **another king, . . . Jesus.** Ladd (p. 446) very vividly notes that this may explain why there is such little reference to Christ as king or to the "kingdom" in the epistles, since the term "king" was the common Greek designation for the Roman emperor and could be easily misunderstood. Rome was tolerant of many things but not rebellion against the emperor. This may explain Paul's preferred usage in the Gentile epistles of the term "Lord." The designation also helps us understand the concept of Christ's lordship; it is recognizing him to be King of one's life. Jason had to put up a **security** (or bond) which would be forfeited if there were any further disturbances. In the meantime, Paul and Silas slipped away at night unto Berea and went to the Jewish synagogue which was there.

11-14. In Beroea Paul found the people more open-minded than at Thessalonica for they received the word with all **readiness of mind.** This open reception to the gospel message caused them to spend a considerable amount of time establishing the church in this community where the people **searched the scriptures daily.** This would imply that the method of Jewish evangelism was again basically the same, concentrating on the fulfillment of Old Testament predictions of the Messiah as related to Jesus. We are told that **many of them believed.** It should be observed again that Luke continually emphasizes the numerical growth of the early church as proof of the power of its message. Eventually Paul had to escape because of the hostility of the Jews of Thessalonica who came to Beroea and stirred up opposition to his message. Thus, Paul departed for **Athens.** In the meantime Silas and Timothy remain in Beroea to minister to the believers, while awaiting the opportunity to rejoin Paul as soon as possible.

15-34. Athens was no longer a city of great political or commercial influence but had remained the world's most famous intellectual center of thinking. Even Roman students desired to go to Athens for their university training. It should be noted that Paul's original strategy did not include the evangelizing of this city. But as he waited there for Silas and Timothy, he was greatly disturbed by the **idolatry** in which he saw the city engulfed. Again, he went to the synagogue daily to preach to the Jews and to the open marketplace to preach to the Gentiles. He was invited to explain his message at the open forum on Mars Hill by the **Epicureans** and **Stoics** who were the leading schools of thought among the Greek **philosophers.** The former group had been founded by Epicurus in about 300 B.C., believing in the existence of gods but never their interference in the affairs of

will this babbler say? other some, He seemeth to be a setter forth of strange gods: because he preached unto them Jesus, and the resurrection.

19 And they took him, and brought him unto Ār-ē-ŏp′a-gus, saying, May we know what this new doctrine, whereof thou speakest, is?

20 For thou bringest certain strange things to our ears: we would know therefore what these things mean.

21 (For all the Athenians and strangers which were there spent their time in nothing else, but either to tell, or to hear some new thing.)

22 ¶Then Paul stood in the midst of Mars' hill, and said, Ye men of Athens, I perceive that in all things ye are too superstitious.

23 For as I passed by, and beheld your devotions, I found an altar with this inscription, TO THE UNKNOWN GOD. Whom therefore ye ignorantly worship, him declare I unto you.

24 God that made the world and all things therein, seeing that he is LORD of heaven and earth, dwelleth not in temples made with hands;

25 Neither is worshipped with men's hands, as though he needed any thing, seeing he giveth to all life, and breath, and all things;

26 And hath made of one blood all nations of men for to dwell on all the face of the earth, and hath determined the times before appointed, and the bounds of their habitation;

27 That they should seek the LORD, if haply they might feel after him, and find him, though he be not far from every one of us:

28 For in him we live, and move, and have our being; as certain also of your own poets have said, For we are also his offspring.

29 Forasmuch then as we are the offspring of God, we ought not to think that the Godhead is like unto gold, or silver, or stone, graven by art and man's device.

30 And the times of this ignorance God winked at; but now commandeth all men every where to repent:

31 Because he hath appointed a day, in the which he will judge the world in righteousness by that man whom he hath ordained; whereof he hath given assurance unto all men, in that he hath raised him from the dead.

32 ¶And when they heard of the resurrection of the dead, some mocked: and others said, We will hear thee again of this matter.

33 So Paul departed from among them.

34 Howbeit certain men clave unto him, and believed: among the which was Dī-o-nȳs′i-us the Ār-ē-ŏp′a-gīte, and a woman named Dăm′a-rĭs, and others with them.

CHAPTER 18

AFTER these things Paul departed from Athens and came to Corinth;

2 And found a certain Jew named Āq′ui-la, born in Pontus, lately come from Italy, with his wife Priscilla; (because that Claudius had commanded

men. Their philosophy of life was one of pleasure and freedom from fear of death. "Eat, drink, and be merry," was their motto. On the other hand, the Stoics founded by Zeno at approximately the same time believed in the brotherhood of all men and held to the high moral principles of a life of self-denial. To these men Paul certainly must have seemed to be a babbler (Gr *spermologus*), literally a "seed-picker."

Gaining the opportunity to share his personal philosophy with these **Athenians,** Paul used the immediate surroundings as an opportunity in which to present his message. Observing the numerous temples, statues, and idols of their religious mythology, Paul began by announcing that he believed that they were too **superstitious** and, so much so, that he had even found an inscription **To the Unknown God** (vs. 23). This **Unknown God** Paul then declared to them to be the Creator, Governor, Saviour, and Judge of the world. In essence, he was announcing to them that he knew the real God, who was unknown to them in spite of their extreme religiosity. Standing on the Areopagus and facing the crowd, Paul had his back to the great temples of the city, which would be instantly observed by his audience to whom he announced that God **dwelleth not in temples.** Certainly his point would be vividly made to his listeners. It should be observed that in addressing these pagan philosophers Paul did not quote extensively from the Old Testament which would have related only to a Jewish audience. Nothing in the text itself indicates that Paul used the wrong approach with his audience. In fact, he actually quoted from two Greek poets: Epimenides of Crete and Aratus of Cilicia. By referring to men as the **offspring of God** Paul is not implying by any means that all men are saved, but rather, that they are all God's creatures and, therefore, responsible to Him. The ignorance of their past may have been overlooked (not "winked at," AV), but God was now calling **all men everywhere to repent.** This makes it clear that the message of repentance was not limited only to believers, nor to the Jews, but was issued to all men everywhere as the passage clearly says. On the nature and significance of the doctrine of repentance see H. Ironside, *Except Ye Repent.* It is foolish to argue, as do some dispensationalists, that repentance is not necessary for salvation, when the New Testament Scriptures clearly say that it is. (On this matter see also E. Hindson, *Glory in the Church,* pp. 75-83.) The central biblical theme of Paul's message was the resurrection of Christ from the dead. This was the crucial content of the gospel as proclaimed by the early evangelists and caused a mixed reaction in the audience: **some mocked . . . Howbeit certain men . . . believed.** Among these converts were Dionysius the **Areopagite,** meaning that he was a member of the Areopagus itself. A woman named **Damaris, and others** also **believed.** Little is said in the New Testament of the converts at Athens. While a church does appear there later in history, there is no reference to a local church at Athens as such at this time. This does not mean that such a church was not organized there at this point, but that we have no record of it. Paul apparently stayed only a brief time in this city and moved on to Corinth where he would eventually spend a great deal of time and effort, and to whose church he would write two major epistles.

D. The Corinthian Ministry. 18:1-22.

18:1-17. Here Paul met a Christian Jew named **Aquila** and his **wife Priscilla,** who had recently been driven from Rome by the anti-Semitic activities of the empire at that time. There are inscriptions in the catacombs which hint that Priscilla was of a distinguished family of high standing in Rome. Later, in Ephe-

all Jews to depart from Rome:) and came unto them.

3 And because he was of the same craft, he abode with them, and wrought: for by their occupation they were tentmakers.

4 And he reasoned in the synagogue every sabbath, and persuaded the Jews and the Greeks.

5 And when Silas and Tī-mō'the-us were come from Macedonia, Paul was pressed in the spirit, and testified to the Jews that Jesus was Christ.

6 And when they opposed themselves, and blasphemed, he shook his raiment, and said unto them, Your blood be upon your own heads; I am clean: from henceforth I will go unto the Gentiles.

7 And he departed thence, and entered into a certain man's house, named Justus, one that worshipped God, whose house joined hard to the synagogue.

8 And Crispus, the chief ruler of the synagogue, believed on the LORD with all his house; and many of the Co-rĭn'-thĭ-ans hearing believed, and were baptized.

9 Then spake the LORD to Paul in the night by a vision, Be not afraid, but speak, and hold not thy peace:

10 For I am with thee, and no man shall set on thee to hurt thee: for I have much people in this city.

11 And he continued there a year and six months, teaching the word of God among them.

12 ¶And when Găl'lĭ-ō was the deputy of A-chā'ia, the Jews made insurrection with one accord against Paul, and brought him to the judgment seat,

13 Saying, This fellow persuadeth men to worship God contrary to the law.

14 And when Paul was now about to open his mouth, Găl'lĭ-ō said unto the Jews, If it were a matter of wrong or wicked lewdness, O ye Jews, reason would that I should bear with you:

15 But if it be a question of words and names, and of your law, look ye to it; for I will be no judge of such matters.

16 And he drave them from the judgment seat.

17 Then all the Greeks took Sŏs'the-nĕs, the chief ruler of the synagogue, and beat him before the judgment seat. And Găl'lĭ-ō cared for none of those things.

18 ¶And Paul after this tarried there yet a good while, and then took his leave of the brethren, and sailed thence into Syria, and with him Priscilla and Āq'ui-la; having shorn his head in Cĕn'chre-a: for he had a vow.

19 And he came to Ĕph'e-sus, and left them there: but he himself entered into the synagogue, and reasoned with the Jews.

20 When they desired him to tarry longer time with them, he consented not;

21 But bade them farewell, saying, I must by all means keep this feast that cometh in Jerusalem: but I will return

sus, a church met in their home (cf. I Cor 16:19). In later years they apparently moved back to Rome (cf. Rom 16:3-5). At this time Silas and Timothy caught up with Paul. They had been left behind at Beroea with instructions to meet Paul in Athens, but this had evidently not worked out. Silas had left Beroea for Philippi to help Luke with the new church there (cf. 18:5). Timothy, at Paul's request, had gone back to Thessalonica to oversee the work there (cf. I Thess 3:1). Both men now meet Paul in Corinth. Silas brought a financial gift for Paul from the Philippian church for his missionary support, which is referred to in II Corinthians 11:8 and Philippians 4:15, and Timothy brought a good report concerning the work in Thessalonica. **Crispus** (vs. 8) was the chief ruler of the synagogue and was gloriously converted along with many other Corinthians, all of whom were baptized. So great was the response in this city that Paul remained there **a year and six months.** The conversion of **Crispus** and his family must have been a tremendous defeat for the Jews and a great incentive to Paul's continued mission. However, the success of the ministry caused Paul to remain here for a full eighteen months, during which period he wrote I and II Thessalonians. In time, however, the unbelieving Jews dragged Paul into court before the governor Gallio accusing him of blasphemy. Because of the religious nature of the case, Gallio quickly dismissed it. **Gallio** (vs. 12) was the brother of the philosopher Seneca. Since proconsuls (**deputy**) served a two-year term it is relatively certain that this incident must be dated in A.D. 51 or 52. The Jews evidently thought to put pressure on the new Roman governor by instigating a riot and bringing Paul before the **judgment seat,** accusing the evangelist of propagating a religion that was contrary to the Roman law, which recognized Judaism as a legitimate religion, but had not officially recognized Christianity as such. It was technically *illicita* as a religion in the eyes of the Roman government. Therefore, Gallio's decision would have been epoch-making for the fate of Christians in the province of **Achaia.** Not to be denied, an unruly Greek mob (doubtless organized by the Jews to harm Paul) grabbed **Sosthenes,** who had succeeded Crispus as **ruler of the synagogue,** and severely **beat him** in the presence of **Gallio.** It has been suggested that this experience may have later led to his conversion to Christ (cf. I Cor 1:1)!

18-22. After remaining in Corinth **yet a good while** beyond the year and a half, he took Aquila and Priscilla and left for Ephesus. At this time we are told that he **had shorn his head . . . for he had** vowed **a vow** (vs. 18). Evidently, before leaving Corinth, he assumed a Nazarite vow and during the period of the vow allowed his hair to grow uncut and at the end of the period, cut his hair. While Paul strongly refused to allow the demand of the Old Testament law to be imposed upon Gentiles, he himself, as a Jew, continued to practice many of its demands in order to increase his effectiveness in Jewish evangelism. Arriving at **Ephesus** he left Aquila and Priscilla and there remaining only a short time himself and refusing their invitation to stay longer, he **bade them farewell** (vs. 21), or bid their leave. He was determined to return to Jerusalem to **keep this feast.** While this phrase is lacking in the majority of texts, there

again unto you, if God will. And he sailed from Ĕph′e-sus.

22 And when he had landed at Cæs-a-re′a, and gone up, and saluted the church, he went down to Antioch.

23 And after he had spent some time there, he departed, and went over all the country of Ga-lā′tia and Phrўg′i-a in order, strengthening all the disciples.

24 ¶And a certain Jew named Apollos, born at Alexandria, an eloquent man, and mighty in the scriptures, came to Ĕph′e-sus.

25 This man was instructed in the way of the LORD; and being fervent in the spirit, he spake and taught diligently the things of the LORD, knowing only the baptism of John.

26 And he began to speak boldly in the synagogue: whom when Ăq′ui-la and Priscilla had heard, they took him unto them, and expounded unto him the way of God more perfectly.

27 And when he was disposed to pass into A-chā′ia, the brethren wrote, exhorting the disciples to receive him: who, when he was come, helped them much which had believed through grace:

28 For he mightily convinced the Jews, and that publickly, shewing by the scriptures that Jesus was Christ.

CHAPTER 19

AND it came to pass, that, while Apollos was at Corinth, Paul having passed through the upper coasts came to Ĕph′e-sus: and finding certain disciples,

2 He said unto them, Have ye received the Holy Ghost since ye believed? And they said unto him, We have not so much as heard whether there be any Holy Ghost.

3 And he said unto them, Unto what then were ye baptized? And they said, Unto John's baptism.

4 Then said Paul, John verily baptized with the baptism of repentance, saying unto the people, that they should believe on him which should come after him, that is, on Christ Jesus.

is no other explanation for his hasty return to Palestine. He promised to return again to Ephesus **if God will** (vs. 21). Such an attitude should condition all of our plans in relation to the work of God (cf. Heb 6:3; Jas 4:15). Paul **landed at Caesarea,** went from there and **saluted the church,** and from there went **down to Antioch** (vs. 22). **The church** must be the one at Jerusalem to whom he reported and then returned to Antioch, his sponsoring church. Again we notice a great deal about missionary strategy in the activities of the Apostle Paul.

VI. PAUL'S THIRD JOURNEY: REINFORCEMENT. 18:23-21:14.

A. The Prolonged Ephesian Ministry. 18:23-19:41.

23-28. Paul left again for Asia Minor (modern Turkey) visiting and encouraging the churches there. He covered the country of **Galatia** and **Phrygia** where he strengthened the **disciples.** About this time an eloquent Bible teacher named **Apollos** (born in Alexandria, Egypt) arrived in Ephesus on a preaching tour. Apollos had learned of the ministry and message of John the Baptist from Jewish pilgrims while still in Egypt but knew nothing beyond that point. He came to Jerusalem during the days of our Lord's earthly ministry. He had heard of the message of John the Baptist that the Messiah was soon to come and that this coming was fulfilled in the life of Jesus. Armed with these limited facts, he traveled afar faithfully proclaiming what he knew. Apollos is described as an **eloquent man** being **mighty in the scriptures,** meaning that he was an effective speaker and especially able to present the messiahship of Jesus to the Jews. He is described as being **fervent in the spirit** (vs. 25). This is an interesting statement in regard to the fact that his followers in chapter 19 are unaware of the Holy Spirit, giving us insight into the Old Testament believers who, though they were regenerated and probably indwelt by the Holy Spirit, were unaware of a full understanding of the nature of His work in them. Aquila and Priscilla were impressed with his ability and took him in **and expounded the way of God more perfectly,** implying that they brought him to a full understanding of the Christian gospel. Eventually he felt called to Corinth and departed, carrying with him the written recommendations of fellow believers in Ephesus. In Corinth he was greatly used of God in the apologetic ministry of convincing the Jews **by the scriptures that Jesus was Christ** (or Messiah). Notice that he used the Word of God as the focal point for his apologetic approach which resulted in a great number of conversions.

19:1-3. Paul's two-year stay at Ephesus was marked by three noteworthy events. The first was his confrontation with the disciples of John who had not **heard whether there be any Holy Ghost** (vs. 2). These followers of John's preaching had believed the truth that John had proclaimed but had not yet been informed of the full message of the gospel including the coming of the Holy Spirit at Pentecost. Several questions arise in relation to this incident. The Greek participle should be translated "when you believed" rather than "since ye believed" (AV). This passage does not imply that one receives the Holy Spirit *after* salvation, since the rest of the New Testament makes it clear that the Holy Spirit is received at the time of salvation and that every true believer has received the Holy Spirit, or been a partaker of the Holy Spirit (cf. I Cor 12:3, 7, 11, 13). Paul then asks them unto what they had been baptized, and they replied **Unto John's baptism** (vs. 3).

4-7. John's **baptism of repentance** in verse 4 clearly distinguishes the baptism of John from Christian baptism. His was a baptism of repentance in preparation for the coming of Jesus Christ. It was not a baptism of identification with the death, burial, and resurrection of Christ, for at that point He had not

5 When they heard *this*, they were baptized in the name of the LORD Jesus.

6 And when Paul had laid *his* hands upon them, the Holy Ghost came on them; and they spake with tongues, and prophesied.

7 And all the men were about twelve.

8 And he went into the synagogue, and spake boldly for the space of three months, disputing and persuading the things concerning the kingdom of God.

9 But when divers were hardened, and believed not, but spake evil of that way before the multitude, he departed from them, and separated the disciples, disputing daily in the school of one Tў-răn'nus.

10 And this continued by the space of two years; so that all they which dwelt in Asia heard the word of the LORD Jesus, both Jews and Greeks.

11 And God wrought special miracles by the hands of Paul:

12 So that from his body were brought unto the sick handkerchiefs or aprons, and the diseases departed from them, and the evil spirits went out of them.

13 ¶Then certain of the vagabond Jews, exorcists, took upon them to call

yet died. Baptisms or "washings" were frequently employed in Jewish spiritual matters. Therefore, it is a mistake to regard John the Baptist as beginning a Christian ministry of baptism. Certainly, he was not the founder of the "Baptist" church! Upon hearing Paul's explanation, these disciples of John who were caught in a dispensational overlap from the Old Testament era were **baptized** (Gr *baptizō*) **in the name of the Lord Jesus.** Again, the use of **baptized** indicates the form of baptism as immersion, or dipping or dunking into water (to symbolize death and resurrection). The identification with the name of Jesus was to emphasize the significance of this baptism as distinctly Christian as opposed to that of John in preparing the Jews for the first coming of the Messiah. The references to being baptized in the name of Jesus in the book of Acts do not necessarily imply that the baptismal formula given in Matthew 28 was not used, but that the emphasis was especially upon identification with the person of Christ. Paul then **laid hands** upon them, and **the Holy Ghost came on them** and as a result they spoke with **tongues, and prophesied.** This experience is designated to illustrate the oneness and unity of the church. Since believers are baptized by one Spirit into one body (cf. I Cor 12:13), there can be no offshoot groups of disciples outside the church. Ladd (p. 454) correctly observes, "It is beside the point to debate whether or not these disciples were Christians before Paul met them, even as it is futile to question whether the apostles were saved before Pentecost. They were disciples of the Lord Jesus but with an incomplete knowledge of the Gospel." Like the believers in Samaria (cf. 8:16-17), these followers of John, who believed in the Lord to the point which they had truth revealed to them, now experienced an extension of Pentecost to include all believers. Like the other transitional groups in Acts, the original disciples, the Samaritan believers, the Gentile converts, and now these wandering followers of John the Baptist, each new group receives the baptism of the Holy Spirit in a dramatic outward manner, resulting in speaking in tongues. This is never intended to be normative for all believers and certainly not for all time. In writing to the Corinthian church which was completely overbalanced in regard to the gift of tongues, Paul had to remind them that they all had received the baptism of the Spirit, but all of them were not intended in the first place to receive the gift of tongues (cf. I Cor 12:13; and 12:29-31).

8-12. For the next three months Paul continued his synagogue ministry and, upon being opposed there, rented a public hall and carried on the work. He probably taught from 11 A.M. to 4 P.M. and worked as a tentmaker both before and after this time period. God performed several unusual miracles through Paul at this time so that even **handkerchiefs or aprons** taken from his body caused healing of disease and the exorcism of evil spirits. The total ministry in Ephesus lasted for about **two years** and centered in the **school of one Tyrannus** (vs. 9). As a result of this concentrated ministry virtually all of the province of Asia (in Asia Minor) heard the Word of the Lord Jesus (vs. 10). The unique position of the ministry of the apostles, as the foundation of the early church, was attended by a series of unusual miracles. While the dynamic of their preaching and their gospel message was to be repeated in every age, it has become obvious throughout church history that direct revelation from God ceased with the closing of the canon of New Testament Scripture as did other revelational gifts, such as tongues and predictive prophecy. While God still heals as a result of answered prayer, healing by means of a handkerchief is no longer legitimate for the church any more than raising the dead, which was also done by the early disciples.

13-20. A family of **vagabond Jews** composed of Sceva, a priest, and his seven sons had been watching Paul do his mighty

over them which had evil spirits the name of the LORD Jesus, saying, We adjure you by Jesus whom Paul preacheth.

14 And there were seven sons of *one* Scē′va, a Jew, *and* chief of the priests, which did so.

15 And the evil spirit answered and said, Jesus I know, and Paul I know; but who are ye?

16 And the man in whom the evil spirit was leaped on them, and overcame them, and prevailed against them, so that they fled out of that house naked and wounded.

17 And this was known to all the Jews and Greeks also dwelling at Ēph′e-sus; and fear fell on them all, and the name of the LORD Jesus was magnified.

18 And many that believed came, and confessed, and shewed their deeds.

19 Many of them also which used curious arts brought their books together, and burned them before all *men:* and they counted the price of them, and found *it* fifty thousand *pieces* of silver.

20 So mightily grew the word of God and prevailed.

21 ¶After these things were ended, Paul purposed in the spirit, when he had passed through Macedonia and A-chā′ia, to go to Jerusalem, saying, After I have been there, I must also see Rome.

22 So he sent into Macedonia two of them that ministered unto him, Tī-mō′the-us and E-răs′tus; but he himself stayed in Asia for a season.

23 ¶And the same time there arose no small stir about that way.

24 For a certain *man* named De-mē′-trī-us, a silversmith which made silver shrines for Diana, brought no small gain unto the craftsmen;

25 Whom he called together with the workmen of like occupation, and said, Sirs, ye know that by this craft we have our wealth.

26 Moreover ye see and hear, that not alone at Ēph′e-sus, but almost throughout all Asia, this Paul hath persuaded and turned away much people, saying that they be no gods, which are made with hands:

27 So that not only this our craft is in danger to be set at nought; but also that the temple of the great goddess Diana should be despised, and her magnifi-

miracles and decided to attempt an exorcism of their own. Traveling Jewish exorcists were common in the ancient world. Listening to the name of Jesus, which Paul used to command evil spirits to come out of people, they attempted to use the same name as a sort of magical charm. However the **evil spirit** replied: **Jesus I know, and Paul I know; but who are ye?** Then the man who was demon-possessed jumped upon them, beat them up, and stripped them **naked.** Exorcism is dangerous unless the exorcist is anointed by the Holy Spirit and is dealing genuinely with real demon powers. The story of the incident spread quickly and resulted in a great revival in which many people came to believe in the **name of the Lord Jesus** (vs. 17) and forsook their former practice of black magic. Over $10,000 worth of occult scrolls and magic charms were burned at a public bonfire. It was normally thought by magicians that if their magical secrets were made public, they would lose their potency. Therefore, a public discrediting of their practice was seen as a genuine conversion of turning from evil to Christ. It is often noted, even today, by missionaries in such places as Haiti where voodoo is still practiced, that a private confession of faith is almost worthless until the individual is willing to go to his home, bring out his occult objects, and openly and publicly destroy them.

21-22. Paul's ultimate plan for his future ministry is revealed in his statement that he would **go to Jerusalem** and afterwards must **also see Rome.** He planned to revisit the churches in Macedonia and Achaia in order to collect money for the needy saints at Jerusalem, and after taking this collection to the church he intended to visit Rome itself. Romans 15:24-28 seems to imply that he did not intend to stay in Rome for an extended period of time but merely stop there on his way to Spain. It was his normal policy to preach the gospel where it had never been preached and to avoid building on another man's foundation. The personal motivational drive and dynamic of this man is almost incomprehensible to the modern reader. Having already extended himself throughout Asia Minor and the peninsula of Greece, he now reveals his plan to move westward into Italy and ultimately to Spain, which was the western extremity of the Roman Empire of that day. The extensive nature of his travels has rarely been repeated by missionaries even in the modern era. However, the next verse indicates that he **stayed in Asia** and sent Timothy and Erastus to Macedonia. Luke does not mention Timothy between the time he rejoined Paul at Corinth (cf. 18:5) and this point, but he obviously had continued with the Apostle Paul in Ephesus. Nor does Luke record the fact that Paul had previously sent Timothy to Corinth to deal with certain problems in the church (cf. I Cor 4:17; 16:10).

23-41. In the meantime a riot was instigated in Ephesus by a silversmith named **Demetrius** whose business of selling silver shrines of the Greek goddess Diana had been severely threatened by Paul's preaching. The statement that there arose a stir about **that way** (vs. 23) refers to the way of Christ or the Christian faith. Demetrius was able to rally several **workmen of like occupation** (vs. 25) with the objection that Paul's preaching was destroying their income. The statement: **This Paul hath persuaded and turned away much people** reveals the dynamic and extensive nature of the success of Paul's ministry in Ephesus. The New Testament later makes it clear that the church at Ephesus was one of the outstanding churches of the apostolic period. A church which, though she had left her first love in Revelation 2, nevertheless was an outstanding, warmhearted church, was one of the greatest examples of the New Testament. It is amazing that the spiritual growth of the Ephesian church was contemporary to the spiritual confusion and carnality of the

cence should be destroyed, whom all Asia and the world worshippeth.

28 And when they heard *these sayings*, they were full of wrath, and cried out, saying, Great *is* Diana of the E-phē'şians.

29 And the whole city was filled with confusion: and having caught Gaius and Ăr-Iṣ-tär'chus, men of Macedonia, Paul's companions in travel, they rushed with one accord into the theatre.

30 And when Paul would have entered in unto the people, the disciples suffered him not.

31 And certain of the chief of Asia, which were his friends, sent unto him, desiring *him* that he would not adventure himself into the theatre.

32 Some therefore cried one thing, and some another: for the assembly was confused; and the more part knew not wherefore they were come together.

33 And they drew Alexander out of the multitude, the Jews putting him forward. And Alexander beckoned with the hand, and would have made his defence unto the people.

34 But when they knew that he was a Jew, all with one voice about the space of two hours cried out, Great *is* Diana of the E-phē'şians.

35 And when the townclerk had appeased the people, he said, Ye men of Ĕph'e-sus, what man is there that knoweth not how that the city of the E-phē'şians is a worshipper of the great goddess Diana, and of the *image* which fell down from Jupiter?

36 Seeing then that these things cannot be spoken against, ye ought to be quiet, and to do nothing rashly.

37 For ye have brought hither these men, which are neither robbers of churches, nor yet blasphemers of your goddess.

38 Wherefore if De-mē'tri-us, and the craftsmen which are with him, have a matter against any man, the law is open, and there are deputies: let them implead one another.

39 But if ye enquire any thing concerning other matters, it shall be determined in a lawful assembly.

40 For we are in danger to be called in question for this day's uproar, there being no cause whereby we may give an account of this concourse.

41 And when he had thus spoken, he dismissed the assembly.

CHAPTER 20

AND after the uproar was ceased, Paul called unto *him* the disciples, and embraced *them*, and departed for to go into Macedonia.

2 And when he had gone over those parts, and had given them much exhortation, he came into Greece,

3 And *there* abode three months. And when the Jews laid wait for him, as he was about to sail into Syria, he purposed to return through Macedonia.

4 And there accompanied him into Asia Sōp'a-ter of Be-rē'a; and of the Thĕs-sa-lō'nĭ-anṣ, Ăr-Iṣ-tär'chus and

Corinthian church. Notice that Luke continually emphasizes the principle of church growth and numerical evaluation of evangelism throughout the book of Acts. Not only is Paul preaching the truth, but the truth is producing results! Obviously, Paul must have had more than just a handful of believers to cause the silversmiths to riot in the fashion in which they did. In many cities throughout the world today, people are not opposed to the church because they are not even aware of the threat which she poses to their life-style!

Soon the huge city amphitheater, capable of seating twenty-five thousand, was packed with a howling mob that chanted hysterically for two uninterrupted hours: **Great is Diana of the Ephesians** (vs. 34)! The temple of Diana, whose Greek name was Artemis, was one of the seven wonders of the ancient world. The image within the temple was of a woman carved with many breasts to signify the fertility of nature. The original stone from which the image had been carved was reported to have "fallen from heaven," leading many historians to believe that it may have been a meteorite. Paul determined to appear in the arena along with some of the believers who had been dragged there by the mob, but was persuaded at the last minute by the Christians not to go there. It is very likely that, had he appeared before the mob as the leader of the Christian movement, he would have occasioned his death long before his arrival in Rome. The text indicates that the crowd was in such a state of hysteria that they were **confused** and many did not even understand why they were there. Apparently some of the Jews feared being condemned along with the Christians and put forth a man named **Alexander** to make a speech in defense of them, but he was shouted down by the crowd and chaos prevailed. Finally order was restored by the **townclerk** (vs. 35) who reminded them that the city was not in danger of being destroyed by these Christians since Ephesus was known throughout the world of her day as the **worshipper** (actually "temple keeper") of Diana. He also reminded them that the Christians in question were not sacrilegious men nor **robbers of churches** (lit., robbers of temples). He then challenged the legitimacy of the procedure since the silversmiths had not gone to the **deputies** (proconsuls) to bring formal charges against these people through proper channels. Anything other than that, he reminded them, would be determined in **lawful assembly** (Gr *ekklēsia*, "congregation," and the same word used to designate the "church"). This reference shows us that not all assemblies referred to in Scripture are church assemblies. The reference here is simply to the legal gathering of Roman citizens, which was a democratic local organization.

B. From Macedonia to Miletus. 20:1-16.

20:1-6. After the riot had ceased, Paul was convinced of the stability of the church at Ephesus and was now free to depart **into Macedonia** to revisit and strengthen the churches there. The apostle's departure from Ephesus is recorded in II Corinthians in relation to his visit to Troas to await the arrival of Titus, whom he had previously sent to Corinth to deal with the serious problems among the believers there. Titus' delayed arrival eventually brought news of improved conditions in the church and occasioned the writing of Paul's second letter to the Corinthians, which he sent to them by the hand of Titus and another brother. After spending three months in **Greece**, Paul was preparing to sail for Syria when he discovered a plot by the

The Third Missionary Journey of Paul

Se-cŭn'dus; and Gaius of Der'be, and Tī-mō'the-us; and of Asia, Tych'ī-cus and Trŏph'i-mus.

5 These going before tarried for us at Troas.

6 And we sailed away from Phĭ-lip'pĭ after the days of unleavened bread, and came unto them to Troas in five days; where we abode seven days.

Jews against his life and decided to **return through Macedonia** instead. It is probably during this time that he wrote the Epistle to the Romans. Several people **accompanied him** including **Sopater, Aristarchus, Secundus, Gaius, Timothy, Tychicus, and Trophimus.** Again we note that Paul rarely worked alone and usually carried a team of evangelists and ministers with him. Many of these men are referred to elsewhere in the New Testament. Upon their arrival in Philippi, Luke also rejoined the team; the second "we" section of Acts begins at verse 5, runs through verse 15 of chapter 20, and is resumed again in 21:1. The reference to the keeping of the **days of unleavened bread** (vs. 6) shows Paul's adherence to his Jewish past, and yet the reference to the gathering of believers at Troas **upon the first day of the week** to preach and celebrate the Lord's Supper clearly emphasizes the distinct non-Jewish nature of the New Testament church. Although Paul was in Troas for seven days (vs. 6), he apparently did not meet with the local church for the purpose of breaking bread until the first day of the week (vs. 7). The *New Scofield Bible* states: "The fact that Paul and others sometimes attended Sabbath services in Jewish synagogues (17:1-3) does not prove that the apostolic church kept the seventh day as a special day of worship. It only shows that the early missionaries took the gospel message wherever and whenever they found people gathered together (5:19-20; 13:5;

16:13, 25-33; 17:17, 19, 22; 18:7; 19:9; 25:6, 23). This witness was carried on daily (2:47; 17:17; 19:9) in every possible way (I Cor 9:19-22). The early churches were specifically warned against submitting themselves to the bondage of any legalistic observance of Sabbath days (cf. Col 2:16; Gal 4:9-11). On the other hand, in the exercise of their Christian liberty (Rom 14:5-6), these same churches voluntarily chose the first day of the week as an appropriate time for fellowship and worship (Acts 20:7; I Cor 16:2), the day on which the Lord arose and repeatedly appeared to His disciples (Jn 20:19-24, 25-29). It was a new day for a new people belonging to a new creation (II Cor 5:17), a day of commemoration and joy (Mt 28:9 margin, "service" Mt 28:10), and spiritual rest (Heb 4:9-10). This observance of the first day of the week is corroborated by the early fathers in the writings of Barnabas (A.D. 100), Ignatius (A.D. 107), Justin Martyr (A.D. 145-150), and Irenaeus (A.D. 155-202). The Edict of Laodicea (fourth century A.D.) did not change the day of worship from the seventh day to the first day of the week, as sometimes alleged, but rather put the stamp of official approval upon an observance already long established in the early churches" (pp. 1194-1195).

7-16. The meeting at Troas **continued . . . until midnight.** The service was held in an upper room on the **third** floor, with illumination provided by many smoky lamps which would have made the air thick and stuffy. Tragically, a young man named **Eutychus** fell asleep and fell from the **third loft** and was **taken up dead** (vs. 9). It seems clear from early custom that the Christians often met on Saturday night as well as Sunday morning. Early Jewish reckoning observed the beginning of the new day at sunset, continuing through the night and the next day until sunset again. Rackham (p. 379) notes that the meeting was held in a private house in the uppermost room which was the most removed from any possibility of interruption. Either Eutychus fell out of the upper window and landed on the ground outside the house or he fell down through the house to the bottom floor of an open area. Paul came and embraced him after the manner of Elijah and Elisha and bade them **Trouble not yourselves** because **his life is in him.** This would seem to indicate that even though he had every outward appearance of being dead, his spirit had not yet departed from his body. This would also explain modern instances where people are pronounced legally dead for a few moments and yet are still brought back to life. Once the spirit leaves the body there is no possibility of life returning, except by direct miraculous resurrection from God Himself. Paul raised the young man **alive** to the thrill and amazement of the congregation. The next day Luke and the other members of the party sailed from Troas to **Assos,** while Paul traveled **afoot** (by land). Again we notice the reference to "we" in verse 14. The rest of the missionary party met the apostle at Assos and sailed to **Mitylene,** the chief town of the island of Lesbos, from which the myth of the homosexual girls (lesbians) originated. From there they sailed between the mainland and the islands of **Chios** and **Samos,** until they came to **Miletus,** on the mainland of Asia Minor. Paul wanted to take time to go inland from there to visit the church at **Ephesus,** but could not arrive in time for the **day of Pentecost,** so he arranged for the **elders of the church** to meet him at the seaport of Miletus a few hours away.

C. Farewell to the Ephesians. 20:17-38.

17-21. Paul's sermon to the Ephesian elders is important in revealing the simple structure of the early church, the nature of apostolic authority, and the content of apostolic preaching. Paul sent for the Ephesian elders, who hurried to meet him at Miletus during a layover in his ship's schedule. On this occasion the apostle delivered his third main recorded discourse. He began

7 ¶And upon the first *day* of the week, when the disciples came together to break bread, Paul preached unto them, ready to depart on the morrow; and continued his speech until midnight.

8 And there were many lights in the upper chamber, where they were gathered together.

9 And there sat in a window a certain young man named Eū'ty-chus, being fallen into a deep sleep: and as Paul was long preaching, he sunk down with sleep, and fell down from the third loft, and was taken up dead.

10 And Paul went down, and fell on him, and embracing *him* said, Trouble not yourselves; for his life is in him.

11 When he therefore was come up again, and had broken bread, and eaten, and talked a long while, even till break of day, so he departed.

12 And they brought the young man alive, and were not a little comforted.

13 ¶And we went before to ship, and sailed unto Ăs'sŏs, there intending to take in Paul: for so had he appointed, minding himself to go afoot.

14 And when he met with us at Ăs'sŏs, we took him in, and came to Mĭt-y-lē'ne.

15 And we sailed thence, and came the next *day* over against Chī'ŏs; and the next *day* we arrived at Sā'mŏs, and tarried at Trō-ġȳl'lĭ-um; and the next *day* we came to Mī-lē'tus.

16 For Paul had determined to sail by Ĕph'e-sus, because he would not spend the time in Asia: for he hasted, if it were possible for him, to be at Jerusalem the day of Pentecost.

17 ¶And from Mī-lē'tus he sent to Ĕph'e-sus, and called the elders of the church.

18 And when they were come to him, he said unto them, Ye know, from the first day that I came into Asia, after

what manner I have been with you at all seasons,

19 Serving the Lord with all humility of mind, and with many tears, and temptations, which befell me by the lying in wait of the Jews:

20 *And* how I kept back nothing that was profitable *unto you,* but have shewed you, and have taught you publickly, and from house to house,

21 Testifying both to the Jews, and also to the Greeks, repentance toward God, and faith toward our Lord Jesus Christ.

22 And now, behold, I go bound in the spirit unto Jerusalem, not knowing the things that shall befall me there:

23 Save that the Holy Ghost witnesseth in every city, saying that bonds and afflictions abide me.

24 But none of these things move me, neither count I my life dear unto myself, so that I might finish my course with joy, and the ministry, which I have received of the Lord Jesus, to testify the gospel of the grace of God.

25 And now, behold, I know that ye all, among whom I have gone preaching the kingdom of God, shall see my face no more.

26 Wherefore I take you to record this day, that I *am* pure from the blood of all *men.*

27 For I have not shunned to declare unto you all the counsel of God.

28 Take heed therefore unto yourselves, and to all the flock, over the which the Holy Ghost hath made you overseers, to feed the church of God, which he hath purchased with his own blood.

his message by reviewing the past two years and the tears and toils he had while serving the Lord in Ephesus. The church leaders or elders (Gr *presbyteros*) were the **overseers** (vs. 28, Gr *episcopos*) or guardians of the church and "bishops." It becomes obvious from Paul's interchangeable usage of the two terms that a bishop was also an elder. It is also clear that there was a plurality of elders in the church. It seems that early church custom was for one of the elders to eventually become the bishop or pastor of the church. This would parallel the modern situation in most evangelical churches which are led by a pastoral staff (elders) who in turn are led by the pastor himself (the bishop). Paul's statement about his preaching clearly reveals the nature and content of early New Testament preaching of the gospel. The message which was **profitable** unto them which he had taught both **publicly** and **from house to house** (i.e., privately) was the same message for both **Jews and Greeks** (vs. 21). That message had a twofold thrust: **Repentance toward God, and faith toward our Lord Jesus Christ.** This verse along with several others in the book of Acts makes it clear that repentance was an essential ingredient in the preaching of the gospel. Those who have argued that repentance is not to be preached to the unsaved, but only to the saved, or only to the Jews, certainly do not develop such a view from this passage of Scripture! Paul makes it clear that part of his essential message to both Jews and Greeks was that they repent and believe. Ironside (*Except Ye Repent*) emphasizes that one must repent in his overall attitude toward God in order to have genuine saving faith in Christ. Therefore, both repentance and faith are essential to salvation and inseparable from salvation.

22-28. Paul exclaimed that he was going **bound in the spirit unto Jerusalem,** emphasizing the sense of divine compulsion which he felt. The **spirit** here must be identified with the Holy Spirit who is referred to in verse 23. Paul was determined to **finish my course with joy** and to **testify the gospel of the grace of God** to as many men as possible. This preaching he refers to as **preaching the kingdom of God** (vs. 25), which must refer to the gospel proclamation of the church which he was establishing. Again, we see that the present-day form of the kingdom is the church. This in no way denies the literal nature of the coming millennial kingdom, but clearly indicates that the church is the mediatorial form of the kingdom at the present. Otherwise, this reference would have to be looked upon as if Paul were still preaching a Jewish kingdom message (so, hyper-dispensationalists). Paul could claim that he was **pure from the blood of all men,** meaning he had fully preached and testified to as many men as possible and had a clear conscience toward all men with whom he had contact regarding the nature of their soul. The book of Acts makes it very clear that Paul was an intense soul-winner and gospel evangelist. One should note, however, that being **pure from the blood of all men** does not mean that he had witnessed to every single person he had ever seen, or every single person in the world, which would obviously be a human impossibility. The point is that Paul had a clear conscience before God and man, knowing that he had used every occasion and opportunity to witness to those that he had come in contact with in his extensive travels. He was also pure of the blood of all men because he had fully declared unto them **all the counsel of God.**

He then reminded the elders to **Take heed . . . unto yourselves** and unto all the **flock** over which the Holy Spirit had made them **overseers.** The nature of pastoral care in the church is clearly placed in the hands of leadership. It should be observed that Paul did not call for the entire church to come to meet him in Miletus, which also would have been a human impossibility. Rather, he called for the designated and ordained leaders of that church. The New Testament throughout clearly emphasizes the importance of pastoral leadership in the local church. While that church is an independent, local congregation, its authority has been invested, nevertheless, in certain designated leaders. These leaders are the representatives of the congregation, not its dictators. The church is the Lord's and not man's to begin with. Thus, Christ, the Lord of the church, invests His authority in men who are to lead and oversee the direction of His church. They are His undershepherds and thus carry His authority as revealed in the Scriptures. However, it should equally be observed that they are not dictators who rule after the whim of their own wills, apart from the will of God. Their responsibility is to **feed the church of God** (vs. 28) which has been **purchased with his own blood.** This passage has varying manuscript support, and a problem has arisen centering on the idea of God purchasing the church with His blood, rather than the blood of Christ. Therefore some ancient texts read "the church of the Lord." However, the more favorable reading (followed by the AV) is **church of God.** Bruce (p. 16) suggests the translation, "which he hath purchased with the blood of his Own." The actual rendering is definitely to the blood of Christ which was shed for the church, which is ultimately the church of God. His blood was shed as an atoning death for all men. Christ's atonement is efficacious only for those who by faith receive Him as Saviour and become part of His church.

29-38. Paul then previewed the future and warned them that after his departing, **grievous wolves** would enter in among them not sparing the flock. He further reminded them that some of these men would arise from among **your own selves.** Paul later wrote to Timothy who was in Ephesus concerning these **grievous wolves** (see I Tim 1:3-7). His warning was later fulfilled in the apostasy of such men as Hymenaeus, Alexander, and Philetus. In general, however, the church at Ephesus was an outstanding example of the early New Testament church, and Paul finished his interview and last farewell to these Ephesian elders **with tears.** He knew that he could leave them because he was leaving them in the hand of God, so he commended them to God and **to the word of his grace.** Here Paul seems definitely to express confidence in the inspired Scriptures which were now becoming more and more available to the early church. This sure word of prophecy is that which is able to **build you up.** Paul was "warning" the leaders of the church by admonishing them (Gr *noutheteō*) and by "confronting" them with their responsibilities in this matter. (On the significance of "nouthetic confrontation" see J. Adams, *Competent to Counsel.*) The touching farewell gives us a keen insight into the warm fellowship of the early church. **Paul kneeled down and prayed with** his converts and they all **wept . . . and kissed him** (following the common early Christian greeting of the "kiss of peace"). It is also interesting to note that they sorrowed most because they would not have the opportunity to hear him speak again, more so than sorrowing over missing his presence. The implication here is clearly that their loyalty to Paul was based on his message of truth rather than on his personality.

29 For I know this, that after my departing shall grievous wolves enter in among you, not sparing the flock.

30 Also of your own selves shall men arise, speaking perverse things, to draw away disciples after them.

31 Therefore watch, and remember, that by the space of three years I ceased not to warn every one night and day with tears.

32 And now, brethren, I commend you to God, and to the word of his grace, which is able to build you up, and to give you an inheritance among all them which are sanctified.

33 I have coveted no man's silver, or gold, or apparel.

34 Yea, ye yourselves know, that these hands have ministered unto my necessities, and to them that were with me.

35 I have shewed you all things, how that so labouring ye ought to support the weak, and to remember the words of the Lord Jesus, how he said, It is more blessed to give than to receive.

36 ¶And when he had thus spoken, he kneeled down, and prayed with them all.

37 And they all wept sore, and fell on Paul's neck, and kissed him,

38 Sorrowing most of all for the words which he spake, that they should see his face no more. And they accompanied him unto the ship.

CHAPTER 21

AND it came to pass, that after we were gotten from them, and had launched, we came with a straight course unto Cō'ōs, and the *day* following unto Rhodes, and from thence unto Păt'a-ra:

2 And finding a ship sailing over unto Phe-nĭ'ċia, we went aboard, and set forth.

3 Now when we had discovered Cyprus, we left it on the left hand, and sailed into Syria, and landed at Tyre:

D. Return to Palestine. 21:1-14.

21:1-7. Paul and his party resumed their trip by boat sailing between the islands of **Coos** and **Rhodes,** where they apparently anchored overnight. From there, they reached **Patara,** a city on the mainland, where they found shipping that would take them directly across the sea to **Syria** (or **Phoenicia**) on the near eastern mainland, just north of Israel. Landing at **Tyre,** Paul spent seven days with a group of disciples while the ship apparently unloaded its cargo (vs. 3). It was here that Paul was warned by a group of prophets in the church who disclosed **through the Spirit** that he should not go to Jerusalem. It would

for there the ship was to unlade her burden.

4 And finding disciples, we tarried there seven days: who said to Paul through the Spirit, that he should not go up to Jerusalem.

5 And when we had accomplished those days, we departed and went our way; and they all brought us on our way, with wives and children, till *we were* out of the city: and we kneeled down on the shore, and prayed.

6 And when we had taken our leave one of another, we took ship; and they returned home again.

7 And when we had finished *our* course from Tyre, we came to Ptŏl-e-mā′is, and saluted the brethren, and abode with them one day.

8 And the next *day* we that were of Paul's company departed, and came unto Cæs-a-re′a: and we entered into the house of Philip the evangelist, which was *one* of the seven; and abode with him.

9 And the same man had four daughters, virgins, which did prophesy.

10 And as we tarried *there* many days, there came down from Judæa a certain prophet, named Ăg′a-bus.

11 And when he was come unto us, he took Paul's girdle, and bound his own hands and feet, and said, Thus saith the Holy Ghost, So shall the Jews at Jerusalem bind the man that owneth this girdle, and shall deliver *him* into the hands of the Gentiles.

12 And when we heard these things, both we, and they of that place, besought him not to go up to Jerusalem.

13 Then Paul answered, What mean ye to weep and to break mine heart? for I am ready not to be bound only, but also to die at Jerusalem for the name of the Lord Jesus.

14 And when he would not be persuaded, we ceased, saying, The will of the Lord be done.

15 And after those days we took up our carriages, and went up to Jerusalem.

16 There went with us also *certain* of the disciples of Cæs-a-re′a, and brought with them one Mnā′son of Cyprus, an old disciple, with whom we should lodge.

17 And when we were come to Jerusalem, the brethren received us gladly.

18 And the *day* following Paul went in with us unto James; and all the elders were present.

19 And when he had saluted them, he declared particularly what things God had wrought among the Gentiles by his ministry.

20 And when they heard *it*, they glori-

seem that the apostle made a mistake here, though this is a highly debated issue. He had already been warned during the beginning of his ministry to: **Make haste and get thee quickly out of Jerusalem: for they will not receive thy testimony concerning me** (22:18). Paul's motive for going to Jerusalem at this time seems to have been his great love for his people and his hope that the gifts of the Gentile churches, sent by him to the poor saints at Jerusalem, would open the hearts of the law-bound Jewish believers to the gospel. of God's grace. At any rate, it is significant that his stop at Jerusalem was one of the very few where absolutely no fruit whatsoever was recorded. Whether he had a constraint of the Spirit which was stronger than that of the disciples at Tyre, or whether this must be seen as an act of disobedience to the will of God, since we are told that the men at Tyre spoke **through the Spirit,** is difficult to discern. Nevertheless, Paul did go to Jerusalem and ultimately did go "bound unto Rome."

8-14. Paul next went to **Caesarea** where he visited the home of **Philip the evangelist,** previously one of the deacons of the Jerusalem church, who had engaged in evangelism in Samaria and on the coastal plain. He is the same fellow who led the Ethiopian eunuch to Christ. He last appeared in Caesarea (8:40) and apparently made his permanent home there. His **four daughters, virgins,** are referred to as "prophetesses." These girls are the last ones mentioned in the Bible who had this gift (others were Miriam, Ex 15:20; Deborah, Jud 4:4; Isaiah's wife, Is 8:3; Huldah, II Kgs 22:14; and Anna, Lk 2:36). While he was there, a **prophet named Agabus** came from Jerusalem and symbolically acted out the fate that he foresaw for the apostle in Jerusalem and predicted that he would be delivered **into the hands of the Gentiles.** He bound his hands and feet with the apostle's belt ("girdle") and was joined by the other believers in pleading with Paul not to go on to Jerusalem. Luke indicates again by using "we" that he joined the appeal to Paul. Paul, fighting back the tears, told them not to weep for him because he was ready if necessary **to die at Jerusalem** for his Lord. No one could prevail over him. They committed him to **the will of the Lord** (vs. 14). Paul next stayed with **Mnason of Cyprus,** who is referred to as an **old disciple,** referring to the fact that he was a disciple from the earliest days (rather than being a reference to his age). With such a person Paul would feel most comfortable. On Paul's arrival in Jerusalem he was **gladly received** by the brethren and went unto **James,** the pastor of the church, who met him with **all the elders.** It would appear that there were no other "apostles" residing in Jerusalem at this time.

VII. PAUL'S JOURNEY TO ROME. 21:15-28:31.

A. The Apprehension of Paul. 21:15-22:30.

15-26. Paul met with the leaders of the church at Jerusalem and reported to them what **God had wrought among the Gentiles.** They were thrilled with the report and **glorified the Lord.** They reported to him that a rumor was making its rounds among the Christian Jews in Jerusalem (of whom vs. 20 says there were "many thousands," indicating the gigantic size of the church there at the time) to the effect that he was telling all Jews who were among the Gentiles to **forsake Moses,** not to circumcise their children, neither to walk after the customs of their forefathers. In order to avoid misunderstanding and such a misrepresentation, Paul submitted himself to a **vow** (vs. 23) to show them that the charges were **nothing** and that he himself walked **orderly** in his own personal life. The leaders then reminded him that, as **touching the Gentiles which believed,** they would abide by their original decision. Therefore, it becomes obvious that while the church was large and the number

fied the Lord, and said unto him, Thou seest, brother, how many thousands of Jews there are which believe; and they are all zealous of the law:

21 And they are informed of thee, that thou teachest all the Jews which are among the Gentiles to forsake Moses, saying that they ought not to circumcise *their* children, neither to walk after the customs.

22 What is it therefore? the multitude must needs come together: for they will hear that thou art come.

23 Do therefore this that we say to thee: We have four men which have a vow on them;

24 Them take, and purify thyself with them, and be at charges with them, that they may shave *their* heads: and all may know that those things, whereof they were informed concerning thee, are nothing; but *that* thou thyself also walkest orderly, and keepest the law.

25 As touching the Gentiles which believe, we have written *and* concluded that they observe no such thing, save only that they keep themselves from *things* offered to idols, and from blood, and from strangled, and from fornication.

26 Then Paul took the men, and the next day purifying himself with them entered into the temple, to signify the accomplishment of the days of purification, until that an offering should be offered for every one of them.

27 And when the seven days were almost ended, the Jews which were of Asia, when they saw him in the temple, stirred up all the people, and laid hands on him,

28 Crying out, Men of Israel, help: This is the man, that teacheth all *men* every where against the people, and the law, and this place: and further brought Greeks also into the temple, and hath polluted this holy place.

29 (For they had seen before with him in the city Trŏph'i-mus an E-phē'sian, whom they supposed that Paul had brought into the temple.)

30 And all the city was moved, and the people ran together: and they took Paul, and drew him out of the temple: and forthwith the doors were shut.

31 And as they went about to kill him, tidings came unto the chief captain of the band, that all Jerusalem was in an uproar.

32 Who immediately took soldiers and centurions, and ran down unto them: and when they saw the chief captain and the soldiers, they left beating of Paul.

33 Then the chief captain came near, and took him, and commanded *him* to be bound with two chains; and demanded who he was, and what he had done.

34 And some cried one thing, some another, among the multitude: and when he could not know the certainty for the tumult, he commanded him to be carried into the castle.

35 And when he came upon the stairs, so it was, that he was borne of the soldiers for the violence of the people.

of Christian disciples was great at this time in Jerusalem, there was still not yet a clear-cut break with their Jewish heritage. It should be observed, however, that the law is not evil in and of itself, but that it is insufficient to bring a man to salvation. By retaining allegiance to the moral aspects of the law, these Christian Jews were retaining the good part of their cultural and spiritual heritage, while acknowledging Christ as Lord. After the destruction of the Temple and the subsequent dispersion these Jewish Christians eventually discarded the Jewish distinctions. The believing Jews would later come to understand that it was unnecessary to retain outward observance of the ceremonies of Judaism, when the Temple no longer existed. The future nature of the church in general was already being developed in the Gentile churches where Paul's missionary efforts were bringing about the most significant results. This should also be a reminder to us that many times the original mission station may eventually become a mission field. We in America need to remember that the gospel came to us from Europe, which today is desperately in need of the same gospel! We should also remember that the gospel has gone forth from us to Latin America, Africa, and Asia and that missionary statistics now claim that the greatest church growth of this century is actually going on outside of North America! The pattern of the expansion of the church throughout its history seems to indicate that God continues to move and bless where the gospel seed is being planted in fresh ground.

27-40. In spite of his submission to the vow, Paul was set upon by a mob of unbelieving Jews who saw him in the Temple and mistakenly concluded that he had brought a Gentile in with him. A riot was stirred up by **Jews which were of Asia,** where Paul had just completed his most extensive evangelism. These would appear to be related to the same people who had so violently opposed him during his missionary journeys. The **uproar** that resulted nearly brought about Paul's death, and he was spared only by the commander of the Roman garrison stationed there. Soldiers were normally housed in the Tower of Antonia, northwest of the temple area, having easy access to the temple courtyard by two flights of stairs. During the time of trouble these soldiers could run into the courtyard to restore order. The **chief captain** (Gr *chiliarchos*) brought a band of **soldiers** and **centurions,** numbering at least two hundred men, and intervened just in time to save Paul's life so that the Jews **left beating of Paul** (i.e., they stopped beating him). He was then arrested by the chief captain, chained and carried by the soldiers to the top of the stairs and **into the castle** (i.e., "barracks"). The **violence of the people** (vs. 35) was so extreme that the soldiers literally had to fight off the crowd in order for the captain to speak personally to Paul. Upon arriving in the barracks Paul asked if he could speak to the captain, who was surprised to find that he could **speak Greek** (note that there can be no doubt that Greek was freely spoken as the common language of that day as the form of communication between both Romans and Jews). The Roman chiliarch was surprised because he thought Paul was **that Egyptian** who had earlier rallied **four thousand men** in an attempt to overthrow the government. History records that this revolt was led by an Egyptian Jew who rallied supporters called in Latin, *sicarii*, "dagger men," because each carried a dagger (Lat *sica*), with which he might assassinate military and political leaders. The revolt had been crushed by the Roman procurator, Felix, but the Egyptian had escaped. Paul assured the tribune that he was a Jew and that he had the

36 For the multitude of the people followed after, crying, Away with him.

37 And as Paul was to be led into the castle, he said unto the chief captain, May I speak unto thee? Who said, Canst thou speak Greek?

38 Art not thou that Ē-gўp′tian, which before these days madest an uproar, and leddest out into the wilderness four thousand men that were murderers?

39 But Paul said, I am a man *which am* a Jew of Tarsus, *a city* in Çĭ-lĭ′çia, a citizen of no mean city: and, I beseech thee, suffer me to speak unto the people.

40 And when he had given him licence, Paul stood on the stairs, and beckoned with the hand unto the people. And when there was made a great silence, he spake unto *them* in the Hebrew tongue, saying,

CHAPTER 22

MEN, brethren, and fathers, hear ye my defence *which I make* now unto you.

2 (And when they heard that he spake in the Hebrew tongue to them, they kept the more silence: and he saith.)

3 I am verily a man *which am* a Jew, born in Tarsus, *a city* in Çĭ-lĭ′çia, yet brought up in this city at the feet of Gamā′lĭ-el, *and* taught according to the perfect manner of the law of the fathers, and was zealous toward God, as ye all are this day.

4 And I persecuted this way unto the death, binding and delivering into prisons both men and women.

5 As also the high priest doth bear me witness, and all the estate of the elders: from whom also I received letters unto the brethren, and went to Damascus, to bring them which were there bound unto Jerusalem, for to be punished.

6 And it came to pass, that as I made my journey, and was come nigh unto Damascus about noon, suddenly there shone from heaven a great light round about me.

7 And I fell unto the ground, and heard a voice saying unto me, Saul, Saul, why persecutest thou me?

8 And I answered, Who art thou, Lord? And he said unto me, I am Jesus of Nazareth, whom thou persecutest.

9 And they that were with me saw indeed the light, and were afraid; but they heard not the voice of him that spake to me.

10 And I said, What shall I do, Lord? And the Lord said unto me, Arise, and go into Damascus; and there it shall be told thee of all things which are appointed for thee to do.

11 And when I could not see for the glory of that light, being led by the hand of them that were with me, I came into Damascus.

12 And one Ăn-a-nī′as, a devout man according to the law, having a good report of all the Jews which dwelt *there*,

13 Came unto me, and stood, and said unto me, Brother Saul, receive thy sight. And the same hour I looked up upon him.

right to enter the temple precincts and that he was also a citizen of the important city of Tarsus; and it is also likely that he asserted his Roman citizenship in order to receive fair treatment from the Roman soldiers. It is interesting to note that Paul's citizenship was a protection to him which his Master Jesus did not have. Standing on the stairs he **beckoned with the hand** (an interesting reference to the use of gestures in speaking) and addressed the people **in the Hebrew tongue** (certainly a reference to the native Aramaic dialect which was the common Jewish language of both Palestine and western Asia at that time. Since many of the Jews of the Diaspora could speak only Greek, the apostle captured the attention of the native crowd by speaking in their own dialect. The New Testament makes it clear that the apostle was certainly trilingual, if not quadrilingual, speaking Hebrew, Greek, Aramaic, and probably to some degree Latin).

22:1-21. In the latter chapters of Acts we find the most extensive personal references to Paul's life and experiences. From these an extensive biography may be gleaned of this important early church leader. On his life see Conybeare and Howson, *The Life and Epistles of Paul*, and Lenski, *St. Paul;* on the significance of his theology see Bruce, *Paul and Jesus*, Ridderbos, *Paul: An Outline of His Theology*. It is interesting to note that Paul made his defense on the same Roman stairway where Pilate had condemned Christ to death some twenty-six years earlier. The attitude of the Jewish mob also reflects a similar treatment of the Lord's servant who had returned, in one last desperate appeal for the Jews to come to Christ. Paul used the opportunity to relate his conversion on the Damascus road. He also emphasized his Jewish heritage as one **brought up in this city** (i.e., Jerusalem) and educated by the outstanding rabbi of that time, **Gamaliel,** and being a Pharisee in his zeal for the law. Then he reminded the Jews that he himself had originally **persecuted this way,** referring to the "way of Christ." Paul went on to explain the Damascus vision, the voice that cried to him, and his resulting question, **Who art thou, Lord?** and the response: **I am Jesus of Nazareth** (vs. 8). The statement in verse 9 that those that were with him saw the light but **heard not the voice** has been wrestled with by some commentators in comparing the statement in 9:7 where the soldiers also heard the voice of Christ. Kent, *From Jerusalem to Rome* (p. 166), observes, "it may be significant that the verb 'to hear' uses different grammatical cases for its object in these two instances. Perhaps in 9:7 the use of the genitive case implies that they heard a sound coming from some identified source, whereas the accusative case in 22:9 indicates that they did not hear it as intelligible speech." Paul further emphasized that he then was instructed to go into Damascus where he would meet a man who would tell him what to do. He then explained that man was **Ananias** who was a **devout man according to the law** (an obvious apologetic appeal), who then told them that the **God of our fathers had chosen** him to **know his will** and see that **Just One** (referring to Christ) and that he should be a **witness unto all men** of what he had seen and heard. Paul further referred to the incident of the **martyr Stephen** and his part in his death and how he had hoped originally to bring the message of Christ only to the Jews, but instead the Lord said, **I will send thee far hence unto the Gentiles** (vs. 21).

14 And he said, The God of our fathers hath chosen thee, that thou shouldest know his will, and see that Just One, and shouldest hear the voice of his mouth.

15 For thou shalt be his witness unto all men of what thou hast seen and heard.

16 And now why tarriest thou? arise, and be baptised, and wash away thy sins, calling on the name of the Lord.

17 And it came to pass, that, when I was come again to Jerusalem, even while I prayed in the temple, I was in a trance;

18 And saw him saying unto me, Make haste, and get thee quickly out of Jerusalem: for they will not receive thy testimony concerning me.

19 And I said, Lord, they know that I imprisoned and beat in every synagogue them that believed on thee:

20 And when the blood of thy martyr Stephen was shed, I also was standing by, and consenting unto his death, and kept the raiment of them that slew him.

21 And he said unto me, Depart: for I will send thee far hence unto the Gentiles.

22 ¶And they gave him audience unto this word, and then lifted up their voices, and said, Away with such a *fellow* from the earth: for it is not fit that he should live.

23 And as they cried out, and cast off *their* clothes, and threw dust into the air,

24 The chief captain commanded him to be brought into the castle, and bade that he should be examined by scourging; that he might know wherefore they cried so against him.

25 And as they bound him with thongs, Paul said unto the centurion that stood by, Is it lawful for you to scourge a man that is a Roman, and uncondemned?

26 When the centurion heard *that*, he went and told the chief captain, saying, Take heed what thou doest: for this man is a Roman.

27 Then the chief captain came, and said unto him, Tell me, art thou a Roman? He said, Yea.

28 And the chief captain answered, With a great sum obtained I this freedom. And Paul said, But I was *free* born.

29 Then straightway they departed from him which should have examined him: and the chief captain also was afraid, after he knew that he was a Roman, and because he had bound him.

30 On the morrow, because he would have known the certainty wherefore he was accused of the Jews, he loosed him from *his* bands, and commanded the chief priests and all their council to appear, and brought Paul down, and set him before them.

CHAPTER 23

AND Paul, earnestly beholding the council, said, Men *and* brethren, I have lived in all good conscience before God until this day.

2 And the high priest Ăn-a-nī′as com-

22-30. Until this point the crowd had retained a hostile silence, but with the mention of Paul's divine call to the Gentiles, they burst into rage, demanding that he be taken **away . . . from the earth** because he was **not fit to live.** The hostile Jewish mob tore their clothes, and threw dust in the air and made such a tumult that the chief captain brought him into the barracks. They then prepared to scourge him. At this point Paul reminded the man with the whip that it was unlawful to scourge a **Roman** who was uncondemned by lawful trial (vs. 25). The chief captain was amazed to discover that Paul was a Roman citizen and assumed that he had obtained **this freedom** with a **great sum** of money. To which Paul replied that he was **free born** (vs. 28), by virtue of having been born in the colony city of Tarsus. In fact, the chief captain was now even fearful of the fact that he had bound Paul in the first place, so he decided to allow him to appear before the **chief priests and all their council** (i.e., the Sanhedrin), to determine **wherefore he was accused of the Jews** and whether any adequate grounds existed for a legal proceeding against Paul.

B. Paul's Defense before the Sanhedrin and Pharisees. 23:1-22.

23:1-10. Paul began by protesting his innocence before the council, stating that he had **lived in all good conscience before God.** Throughout his epistles and recorded sermons, there are numerous references by Paul to the importance of having a clear conscience with God and man. **Ananias** was the high priest of

manded them that stood by him to smite him on the mouth.

3 Then said Paul unto him, God shall smite thee, *thou* whited wall: for sittest thou to judge me after the law, and commandest me to be smitten contrary to the law?

4 And they that stood by said, Revilest thou God's high priest?

5 Then said Paul, I wist not, brethren, that he was the high priest: for it is written, Thou shalt not speak evil of the ruler of thy people.

6 But when Paul perceived that the one part were Săd'du-ceĕś, and the other Pharisees, he cried out in the council, Men *and* brethren, I am a Pharisee, the son of a Pharisee: of the hope and resurrection of the dead I am called in question.

7 And when he had so said, there arose a dissension between the Pharisees and the Săd'du-ceĕś: and the multitude was divided.

8 For the Săd'du-ceĕś say that there is no resurrection, neither angel, nor spirit: but the Pharisees confess both.

9 And there arose a great cry: and the scribes *that were* of the Pharisees' part arose, and strove, saying, We find no evil in this man: but if a spirit or an angel hath spoken to him, let us not fight against God.

10 And when there arose a great dissension, the chief captain, fearing lest Paul should have been pulled in pieces of them, commanded the soldiers to go down, and to take him by force from among them, and to bring *him* into the castle.

11 And the night following the Lord stood by him, and said, Be of good cheer, Paul: for as thou hast testified of me in Jerusalem, so must thou bear witness also at Rome.

12 And when it was day, certain of the Jews banded together, and bound themselves under a curse, saying that they would neither eat nor drink till they had killed Paul.

13 And they were more than forty which had made this conspiracy.

14 And they came to the chief priests and elders, and said, We have bound ourselves under a great curse, that we will eat nothing until we have slain Paul.

15 Now therefore ye with the council signify to the chief captain that he bring him down unto you to morrow, as though ye would enquire something more perfectly concerning him: and we, or ever he come near, are ready to kill him.

16 And when Paul's sister's son heard of their lying in wait, he went and entered into the castle, and told Paul.

17 Then Paul called one of the centurions unto *him,* and said, Bring this young man unto the chief captain: for he hath a certain thing to tell him.

18 So he took him, and brought *him* to the chief captain, and said, Paul the prisoner called me unto *him,* and prayed me to bring this young man unto thee, who hath something to say unto thee.

Israel from about A.D. 48-58. A crude and overbearing man, he was angered by Paul's claim and commanded someone who stood by him to **smite him on the mouth.** Jesus similarly had been struck during His trial (see Jn 18:22). In response to the action of the high priest, Paul replied: **God shall smite thee, thou whited wall** (vs. 3). The term "whited wall" suggests a whitewashed coating over a precarious, tottering wall (cf. Bruce, p. 451). Paul's outburst might seem strong to some, until one realizes the tremendous pressure that he was under and the tension of the moment in which his life was literally at stake! Also note that the action of the high priest was **contrary to the law.** The crowd, however, was shocked by Paul's response in "reviling" the high priest. Paul then seemed to change the tactic of his defense. Realizing that the situation was "stacked" against him, Paul replied that he did not know that he was the high priest, probably the result of the action and character which he displayed, for certainly he would have been dressed in some manner to indicate who he was. Instead, Paul recognized that the Sanhedrin, of which many feel he was himself originally a member (cf. Blaiklock, p. 176), as the ruling body of the Jews was composed of both **Pharisees** and **Sadducees.** They held the majority, and differed with each other on important matters of doctrine, such as, the Resurrection, angels, and the nature of supernatural intervention. Paul used their difference to gain an opportunity to save his own life. He openly identified himself as a Pharisee and a believer in the resurrection of the dead, thus causing an immediate split between the assembled Pharisees and the resurrection-denying Sadducees. The clamor became so intense that Paul was removed by the Roman commander and the interview before the Sanhedrin came to a close. Paul's statement that he had been called into question because of the **hope and resurrection of the dead** (vs. 6) was true in light of the fact that he believed in the resurrection as the hope of the dead! The Pharisees naively arose to Paul's defense, but the **dissension** became so intense that Paul was returned to the barracks.

11-22. One of the heartwarming and encouraging statements of Paul's entire life occurred at this point when that night **the Lord stood by him,** referring to a literal appearance of Christ who came to tell Paul to **be of good cheer** for he must bear witness also at Rome. Paul had often hoped to get to Rome, and at Ephesus he even made plans to go to Rome, but at this point he was not even sure he would get out of Jerusalem alive. But now, for the first time, God had confirmed his original plan. It is difficult to state honestly these many centuries later whether Paul made a mistake in going to Jerusalem, or whether the Lord knew all along that he would go to Jerusalem, and warned him so that he would be prepared for the ultimate consequences, and used his arrest as the opportunity to get him to the place where he ultimately wanted to go. Certainly Paul's life shows us time and again that God can overrule the most difficult of human circumstances in order to accomplish His will. He may even overrule our own will so that His ultimate will may be done. The next day **certain of the Jews banded together . . . under a curse** in a unified effort to kill Paul. The extent of their fanaticism can be understood when we realize that the execution of this plot certainly would have meant the death of many of them at the hands of the Roman guard who protected Paul. Such intense religious fanaticism was common among the Jews of that day. **Paul's sister's son** (a nephew) learned of their **lying in wait** (ambush) and came to warn Paul. This is the only reference in the New Testament to Paul's family, and we have no clear indication as to who this person was. The Roman commander quickly removed Paul that night to **Caesarea** (vs. 23), protected by four hundred seventy armed soldiers. He sent a letter on ahead to Felix in Caesarea, explaining why Paul was being transferred to his authority.

19 Then the chief captain took him by the hand, and went *with him* aside privately, and asked *him*, What is that thou hast to tell me?

20 And he said, The Jews have agreed to desire thee that thou wouldest bring down Paul to morrow into the council, as though they would enquire somewhat of him more perfectly.

21 But do not thou yield unto them: for there lie in wait for him of them more than forty men, which have bound themselves with an oath, that they will neither eat nor drink till they have killed him: and now are they ready, looking for a promise from thee.

22 So the chief captain *then* let the young man depart, and charged *him*, See thou tell no man that thou hast shewed these things to me.

23 And he called unto *him* two centurions, saying, Make ready two hundred soldiers to go to Cæs-a-re′a, and horsemen threescore and ten, and spearmen two hundred, at the third hour of the night;

24 And provide *them* beasts, that they may set Paul on, and bring *him* safe unto Felix the governor.

25 And he wrote a letter after this manner:

26 Claudius Ly′si-as unto the most excellent governor Felix *sendeth* greeting.

27 This man was taken of the Jews, and should have been killed of them: then came I with an army, and rescued him, having understood that he was a Roman.

28 And when I would have known the cause wherefore they accused him, I brought him forth into their council:

29 Whom I perceived to be accused of questions of their law, but to have nothing laid to his charge worthy of death or of bonds.

30 And when it was told me how that the Jews laid wait for the man, I sent straightway to thee, and gave commandment to his accusers also to say before thee what *they had* against him. Farewell.

31 Then the soldiers, as it was commanded them, took Paul, and brought *him* by night to Ăn-tĭp′a-trĭs.

32 On the morrow they left the horsemen to go with him, and returned to the castle:

33 Who, when they came to Cæs-a-re′a, and delivered the epistle to the governor, presented Paul also before him.

34 And when the governor had read *the letter*, he asked of what province he was. And when he understood that *he was* of Cĭ-lĭ′cia;

35 I will hear thee, said he, when thine accusers are also come. And he commanded him to be kept in Herod's judgment hall.

CHAPTER 24

AND after five days Ăn-a-nī′as the high priest descended with the elders, and *with* a certain orator *named* Ter-tŭl′lus, who informed the governor against Paul.

C. Paul's Defense Before Felix and Festus. 23:23-25:12.

23-35. Paul was transferred under heavily armed guard to **Felix the governor** (or procurator). The troop departed during the **third hour of the night**, between nine and ten P.M., and brought him safely unto Caesarea. The transcript of the official letter sent by the tribune, **Claudius Lysias**, unto Felix is given in length, verses 26-30. The nature of the letter seems to indicate that the tribune was afraid that he might have accorded some improper treatment to this Roman citizen, and therefore, wanted to make sure that the situation was properly handled. In the morning they arrived at **Antipatris**, some forty miles from Jerusalem and well on the way to Caesarea. Being out of immediate danger of the Jews, the majority of the guard returned and seventy **horsemen** (cavalrymen) accompanied Paul the remaining distance. Learning that Paul was a citizen of **Cilicia**, the governor agreed to hear the case when the **accusers** arrived to bring formal charges against him.

24:1-9. Antonius Felix was the governor of Judaea from A.D. 52-59 and was a man of servile origin who owed his unprecedented advancement to the influence of his brother at the imperial court of Claudius. His governorship was marked by a period of unrest and several Jewish uprisings which resulted in

2 And when he was called forth, Tertŭl'lus began to accuse *him*, saying, Seeing that by thee we enjoy great quietness, and that very worthy deeds are done unto this nation by thy providence,

3 We accept *it* always, and in all places, most noble Felix, with all thankfulness.

4 Notwithstanding, that I be not further tedious unto thee, I pray thee that thou wouldest hear us of thy clemency a few words.

5 For we have found this man *a* pestilent *fellow*, and a mover of sedition among all the Jews throughout the world, and a ringleader of the sect of the Nazarenes:

6 Who also hath gone about to profane the temple: whom we took, and would have judged according to our law.

7 But the chief captain Ly'si-as came *upon us*, and with great violence took *him* away out of our hands,

8 Commanding his accusers to come unto thee: by examining of whom thyself mayest take knowledge of all these things, whereof we accuse him.

9 And the Jews also assented, saying that these things were so.

10 ¶Then Paul, after that the governor had beckoned unto him to speak, answered, Forasmuch as I know that thou hast been of many years a judge unto this nation, I do the more cheerfully answer for myself:

11 Because that thou mayest understand, that there are yet but twelve days since I went up to Jerusalem for to worship.

12 And they neither found me in the temple disputing with any man, neither raising up the people, neither in the synagogues, nor in the city:

13 Neither can they prove the things whereof they now accuse me.

14 But this I confess unto thee, that after the way which they call heresy, so worship I the God of my fathers, believing all things which are written in the law and in the prophets:

15 And have hope toward God, which they themselves also allow, that there shall be a resurrection of the dead, both of the just and unjust.

16 And herein do I exercise myself, to have always a conscience void of offence toward God, and *toward* men.

17 Now after many years I came to bring alms to my nation, and offerings.

18 Whereupon certain Jews from Asia found me purified in the temple, neither with multitude, nor with tumult.

ruthless response by Felix, which in turn alienated more Jews and led to further revolts. Tacitus, the Roman historian, wrote of him: "Felix indulging in every kind of barbarity and lust, exercised the power of a king in the Spirit of a slave" (*Histories* V, 9). He had three successful marriages to princesses, which elevated his status among the Romans. The first of the three was the granddaughter of Antony and Cleopatra; the third was Drusilla, the daughter of Agrippa. After five days, **Ananias** arrived with the **elders** and a professional **orator named Tertullus** to present a formal case against Paul. As the official representative of his client, he **began to accuse** (i.e., made his charges) to the governor against Paul. Years after this incident Ananias was assassinated and his son Jonathan became the high priest and was later assassinated by Felix! Paul was accused of treason, religious heresy, and desecration of the Temple. Since Tertullus' name is a common Roman designation, it may be that he was a Hellenistic Jew or that he was a hired attorney on behalf of the Jews. The reference to **our law** would seem to indicate the former to be true. The flattering speech was in fact the exact opposite of the truth; instead of **great quietness** (vs. 2) and **clemency** (vs. 4), Felix was noted for his ferocious temper and prevailing discontent throughout his realm. The charges brought against Paul claimed that he was a troublemaker among **all the Jews throughout the world** and that he was the **ringleader of the sect of the Nazarenes** (vs. 5). The term "sect" was used by Josephus to designate the various parties and divisions within Judaism, indicating that the opposition still considered the Christians as an unorthodox break within Judaism. This is the only place in the New Testament where the followers of Jesus are called **Nazarenes**. The term continued to be used as a derisive designation for Christians in Hebrew and Arabic. It is certainly not wrong to call the followers of Jesus "Nazarenes," but there is no precedent within the Scriptures for churches ever to call themselves by this term. "Nazarene" was at times a term of derision used by Judaeans against the Galileans within the Jewish nation and, therefore, did not necessarily carry any spiritual connotation.

10-21. Paul waited until the governor **beckoned unto him to speak.** Beginning with a modest compliment, he openly denied the charge of stirring up rebellion. To the first charge, he pointed out that he had only been in Jerusalem for twelve days and could not have possibly created all the alleged trouble in that brief time. In regard to the second charge, he showed that he was actually more orthodox than some members of the Sanhedrin who denied the doctrine of the resurrection. Concerning the third charge, he reminded the court that the Jews in Jerusalem itself could not make that indictment stick, which was the only legitimate charge that could have occasioned his death according to the law. Felix wisely decided to defer any action until he received the official testimony of Lysias, the arresting Roman commander. The only charge which Paul accepted was to **confess . . . the way which they call heresy** (vs. 14). Notice again that Christianity is referred to as "the way" (of Christ). Paul emphasized the importance of having a **conscience void of offense** toward God and man (vs. 16). Having a clear conscience was vital to the preparation for spiritual warfare. He proceeded to explain that the **Jews from Asia** (vs. 18) who had originally accused him were not even there to bring formal charges against him (since they had by now returned to their homeland). Paul ended his defense by pointing out that he was really called into question in regard to his view of the **resurrection of the dead** (vs. 21).

19 Who ought to have been here before thee, and object, if they had ought against me.

20 Or else let these same *here* say, if they have found any evil doing in me, while I stood before the council,

21 Except it be for this one voice, that I cried standing among them, Touching the resurrection of the dead I am called in question by you this day.

22 ¶And when Felix heard these things, having more perfect knowledge of *that* way, he deferred them, and said, When Ly'si-as the chief captain shall come down, I will know the uttermost of your matter.

23 And he commanded a centurion to keep Paul, and to let *him* have liberty, and that he should forbid none of his acquaintance to minister or come unto him.

24 And after certain days, when Felix came with his wife Drŭ-sĭl′la, which was a Jewess, he sent for Paul, and heard him concerning the faith in Christ.

25 And as he reasoned of righteousness, temperance, and judgment to come, Felix trembled, and answered, Go thy way for this time; when I have a convenient season, I will call for thee.

26 He hoped also that money should have been given him of Paul, that he might loose him: wherefore he sent for him the oftener, and communed with him.

27 But after two years Pôr′ci-us Fĕs′tus came into Felix′ room: and Felix, willing to shew the Jews a pleasure, left Paul bound.

CHAPTER 25

NOW when Fĕs′tus was come into the province, after three days he ascended from Cæs-a-re′a to Jerusalem.

2 Then the high priest and the chief of the Jews informed him against Paul, and besought him,

3 And desired favour against him, that he would send for him to Jerusalem, laying wait in the way to kill him.

4 But Fĕs′tus answered, that Paul should be kept at Cæs-a-re′a, and that he himself would depart shortly *thither*.

5 Let them therefore, said he, which among you are able, go down with *me*, and accuse this man, if there be any wickedness in him.

6 And when he had tarried among them more than ten days, he went down unto Cæs-a-re′a; and the next day sitting on the judgment seat commanded Paul to be brought.

7 And when he was come, the Jews which came down from Jerusalem stood round about, and laid many and grievous complaints against Paul, which they could not prove.

8 While he answered for himself, Neither against the law of the Jews, neither against the temple, nor yet against Cæsar, have I offended any thing at all.

9 But Fĕs′tus, willing to do the Jews a pleasure, answered Paul, and said, Wilt

22-27. When Paul's defense was finished, Felix had a **more perfect knowledge of that way,** meaning that he had a more accurate understanding of the Christian faith. Eventually Paul had the opportunity to speak to both Felix and his wife Drusilla. This girl was the youngest daughter of Herod Agrippa I (the murderer of James, ch. 12) and the sister of Agrippa II and Bernice (25:13). She was not yet twenty years old and had already left an Assyrian king to marry Felix. She was a **Jewess** and died twenty-one years later in the eruption of Mount Vesuvius! The passage says that he sent for Paul to explain to him **the faith in Christ** (vs. 24); and as Paul preached **righteousness, temperance, and judgment to come,** the message was brought home with such conviction that **Felix trembled.** Obviously disturbed by what he heard, he responded with his now infamous statement, **Go thy way for this time; when I have a convenient season, I will call for thee** (vs. 25). The closing verses of the chapter indicate that he had hoped for a bribe from Paul in order to release him; however, the bribe was never forthcoming and **after two years** Felix was recalled to Rome by the emperor Nero under an accusation of bad administration by the Jews of his dominion. **Porcius Festus** succeeded him as procurator of Judaea, and Felix left Paul in prison for his successor to decide his fate. Thereby, he hoped to pacify the Jews who were now bringing the accusations against him.

25:1-12. In A.D. 58 Felix's soldiers put down a riot of Jews in Caesarea with such violence that he was replaced by Festus, a more fair and honorable ruler, but one who was unable to control the situation in Palestine which had now become a hotbed of revolution and within twelve years would come under the wrath of the emperor himself. Upon his arrival in the province, Festus went from **Caesarea to Jerusalem** (vs. 1). There, the **high priest** and the **Jews** again brought charges against Paul, requesting that he be sent to Jerusalem, in hope that they might ambush him on the way. Instead, Festus resisted their pressure and returned to Caesarea where the Jews were forced to come and make formal charges against the apostle before the **judgment seat** (Gr *bēma*). When Festus suggested that Paul return to Jerusalem to be tried, the apostle then appealed to **Caesar's judgment seat** (vs. 10). It is clear that Paul was willing to accept the penalty of death if he had done anything **worthy of death** (vs. 11). Festus, seeing an immediate way out, honored the appeal to Caesar (who was Nero, having begun his reign in A.D. 54). The early years of his rule were gentle in nature and gave no hint of the awful cruelties which would soon follow.

thou go up to Jerusalem, and there be judged of these things before me?

10 Then said Paul, I stand at Cæsar's judgment seat, where I ought to be judged: to the Jews have I done no wrong, as thou very well knowest.

11 For if I be an offender, or have committed any thing worthy of death, I refuse not to die: but if there be none of these things whereof these accuse me, no man may deliver me unto them. I appeal unto Cæsar.

12 Then Fĕs′tus, when he had conferred with the council, answered, Hast thou appealed unto Cæsar? unto Cæsar shalt thou go.

13 ¶And after certain days king A-grĭp′pa and Bernice came unto Cæs-a-re′a to salute Fĕs′tus.

14 And when they had been there many days, Fĕs′tus declared Paul's cause unto the king, saying, There is a certain man left in bonds by Felix:

15 About whom, when I was at Jerusalem, the chief priests and the elders of the Jews informed *me*, desiring *to have* judgment against him.

16 To whom I answered, It is not the manner of the Romans to deliver any man to die, before that he which is accused have the accusers face to face, and have licence to answer for himself concerning the crime laid against him.

17 Therefore, when they were come hither, without any delay on the morrow I sat on the judgment seat, and commanded the man to be brought forth.

18 Against whom when the accusers stood up, they brought none accusation of such things as I supposed:

19 But had certain questions against him of their own superstition, and of one Jesus, which was dead, whom Paul affirmed to be alive.

20 And because I doubted of such manner of questions, I asked *him* whether he would go to Jerusalem, and there be judged of these matters.

21 But when Paul had appealed to be reserved unto the hearing of Augustus, I commanded him to be kept till I might send him to Cæsar.

22 Then A-grĭp′pa said unto Fĕs′tus, I would also hear the man myself. To morrow, said he, thou shalt hear him.

23 And on the morrow, when A-grĭp′-pa was come, and Bernice, with great pomp, and was entered into the place of hearing, with the chief captains, and principal men of the city, at Fĕs′tus' commandment Paul was brought forth.

24 And Fĕs′tus said, King A-grĭp′pa, and all men which are here present with us, ye see this man, about whom all the multitude of the Jews have dealt with me, both at Jerusalem, and *also* here, crying that he ought not to live any longer.

25 But when I found that he had committed nothing worthy of death, and that he himself hath appealed to Augustus, I have determined to send him.

26 Of whom I have no certain thing to write unto my lord. Wherefore I have brought him forth before you, and specially before thee, O king A-grĭp′pa,

D. Paul's Defense Before Agrippa. 25:13-26:32.

13-21. Agrippa II was the son of Herod Agrippa (12:1) and Bernice, who was the sister of both Drusilla and Agrippa. She had previously been married to her uncle until his death, and was now living with her brother in a relationship widely rumored to be incestuous. She later left him for another pagan king, then deserted him and finally became the mistress of both the Roman emperor Vespasian and his son Titus, who later destroyed Jerusalem in A.D. 70. Upon hearing about Paul from Festus, **Agrippa** requested an audience with the famous prisoner. Paul was brought into the palace court and in chains preached Christ to his royal guests. It is interesting to note that **Agrippa,** who had come to power in A.D. 53, controlled most of Palestine at the time and supervised the appointment of the high priest in Jerusalem. His powerful influence in Jewish affairs certainly made Paul's interview with him one of extreme importance. Festus related how Paul had been left there from the time of Felix and how he **doubted of such manner of questions** (vs. 20) because of his lack of understanding of the nature of Jewish matters, since he was new to that territory. The term **Augustus** (vs. 21) is misleading since the word is a translation of the Latin *Augustus*, meaning the "revered" or "august one." This term was applied to all Roman emperors, of whom Augustus Caesar had been the first. Again note that the emperor at this time was Nero. The modern equivalent for this term would be similar to "his majesty" (Gr *sebastos*). Because of Paul's appeal to Caesar, no further action could be taken by these royal rulers.

22-27. A further hearing was set up before Festus, Agrippa, Bernice, and an advisory council consisting of the **chief captains** (or military tribunes) and **principal men of the city.** Luke's purpose in including these appearances before public officials in such lengthy detail seems to be of an apologetic nature in defense of Christianity. Such statements as that he had committed **nothing worthy of death** (vs. 25) are used to verify the credibility of this great Christian leader. While the book of Acts first centered on the ministry of James and Peter, it has now shifted totally to that of Paul, undoubtedly due to Luke's close relationship to him. Festus went on to explain that the entire process **seemeth to me unreasonable,** since no proven charge had ever been established against Paul.

that, after examination had, I might have somewhat to write.

27 For it seemeth to me unreasonable to send a prisoner, and not withal to signify the crimes *laid* against him.

CHAPTER 26

THEN A-grĭp'pa said unto Paul, Thou art permitted to speak for thyself. Then Paul stretched forth the hand, and answered for himself:

2 I think myself happy, king A-grĭp'-pa, because I shall answer for myself this day before thee touching all the things whereof I am accused of the Jews:

3 Especially *because I know* thee to be expert in all customs and questions which are among the Jews: wherefore I beseech thee to hear me patiently.

4 My manner of life from my youth, which was at the first among mine own nation at Jerusalem, know all the Jews;

5 Which knew me from the beginning, if they would testify, that after the most straitest sect of our religion I lived a Pharisee.

6 And now I stand and am judged for the hope of the promise made of God unto our fathers:

7 Unto which *promise* our twelve tribes, instantly serving *God* day and night, hope to come. For which hope's sake, king A-grĭp'pa, I am accused of the Jews.

8 Why should it be thought a thing incredible with you, that God should raise the dead?

9 I verily thought with myself, that I ought to do many things contrary to the name of Jesus of Nazareth.

10 Which thing I also did in Jerusalem: and many of the saints did I shut up in prison, having received authority from the chief priests; and when they were put to death, I gave my voice against *them.*

11 And I punished them oft in every synagogue, and compelled *them* to blaspheme; and being exceedingly mad against them, I persecuted *them* even unto strange cities.

12 Whereupon as I went to Damascus with authority and commission from the chief priests,

13 At midday, O king, I saw in the way a light from heaven, above the brightness of the sun, shining round about me and them which journeyed with me.

14 And when we were all fallen to the earth, I heard a voice speaking unto me, and saying in the Hebrew tongue, Saul, Saul, why persecutest thou me? *it is* hard for thee to kick against the pricks.

15 And I said, Who art thou, Lord? And he said, I am Jesus whom thou persecutest.

16 But rise, and stand upon thy feet: for I have appeared unto thee for this purpose, to make thee a minister and a witness both of these things which thou hast seen, and of those things in the which I will appear unto thee;

17 Delivering thee from the people, and *from* the Gentiles, unto whom now I send thee,

26:1-12. Paul's defense before Agrippa began again with a gesture of salutation as he **stretched forth the hand.** Paul expressed his gratitude that he was able to make his defense before Agrippa since he was an expert in Jewish customs and affairs. Paul's approach, notes Ladd (p. 478), was to convince him that faith in Christ was the ultimate fulfillment of Jewish belief. Therefore, the apostle outlined his upbringing as a Jew in the **straitest sect** of the Jewish religion as a **Pharisee** (vs. 5). Paul centered his appeal on the question of the resurrection and God's power to **raise the dead** (vs. 8). He went on to explain that he himself had thought and done many things **contrary to the name of Jesus of Nazareth.** Notice that the early Christian movement always identified itself closely with Jesus' name. He explained how he imprisoned believers ("saints," Gr *hagios*). He went on to explain that he even **compelled them to blaspheme.** A better translation would be "tried to make them blaspheme." The tense of the Greek word indicates that Paul failed in his attempt to bring them to blasphemy, an experience which certainly would have left a marked impression upon the young Jewish inquisitor!

13-23. This account gives more details into Paul's experiences as a persecutor than any other passage in the New Testament. Having laid this background, the apostle now began to explain the Damascus vision which occurred at **midday,** in which Christ appeared to him and called to him **in the Hebrew tongue** (vs. 14). The phrase **it is hard for thee to kick against the pricks** means that it was "painful" to kick back against the "goads," used to prod beasts of burden. This was a proverbial saying in Latin and Greek, but is unknown to us in Hebrew or Aramaic. Paul's terminology is such that it would be most understandable to his Gentile listeners. Then, Paul clearly recounted the voice as identifying himself as **Jesus whom thou persecutest** (vs. 15). He went on to explain that Jesus was sending him to the **Gentiles . . . to open their eyes.** Paul was making it clear that his very defense before these earthly kings was a fulfillment of the mission upon which his Lord had sent him! Thus, he could offer **forgiveness of sins** (vs. 18) unto his Gentile listeners. He drew the story of his conversion to a close by announcing: **Whereupon O king Agrippa, I was not dis-**

18 To open their eyes, *and* to turn *them* from darkness to light, and *from* the power of Satan unto God, that they may receive forgiveness of sins, and inheritance among them which are sanctified by faith that is in me.

19 Whereupon, O king A-grĭp′pa, I was not disobedient unto the heavenly vision:

20 But shewed first unto them of Damascus, and at Jerusalem, and throughout all the coasts of Judæa, and *then* to the Gentiles, that they should repent and turn to God, and do works meet for repentance.

21 For these causes the Jews caught me in the temple, and went about to kill *me.*

22 Having therefore obtained help of God, I continue unto this day, witnessing both to small and great, saying none other things than those which the prophets and Moses did say should come:

23 That Christ should suffer, *and* that he should be the first that should rise from the dead, and should shew light unto the people, and to the Gentiles.

24 ¶And as he thus spake for himself, Fĕs′tus said with a loud voice, Paul, thou art beside thyself; much learning doth make thee mad.

25 But he said, I am not mad, most noble Fĕs′tus; but speak forth the words of truth and soberness.

26 For the king knoweth of these things, before whom also I speak freely: for I am persuaded that none of these things are hidden from him; for this thing was not done in a corner.

27 King A-grĭp′pa, believest thou the prophets? I know that thou believest.

28 Then A-grĭp′pa said unto Paul, Almost thou persuadest me to be a Christian.

29 And Paul said, I would to God, that not only thou, but also all that hear me this day, were both almost, and altogether such as I am, except these bonds.

30 And when he had thus spoken, the king rose up, and the governor, and Bernice, and they that sat with them:

31 And when they were gone aside, they talked between themselves, saying, This man doeth nothing worthy of death or of bonds.

32 Then said A-grĭp′pa unto Fĕs′tus, This man might have been set at liberty, if he had not appealed unto Cæsar.

CHAPTER 27

AND when it was determined that we

obedient unto the heavenly vision (vs. 19). He then quickly summarized his entire ministry preaching to them of **Damascus . . . Jerusalem . . . Judaea . . . and then to the Gentiles** (vs. 20). In each case, and to each group, he had preached that **they should repent and turn to God.** Again, there can be no doubt that repentance was an essential ingredient to salvation and was a vital part of Paul's apostolic preaching! He went on to explain that it was for **these causes** (those of his evangelistic mission) that the Jews had taken him and wanted to kill him. However, he explained that he had obtained the **help of God** (vs. 22) and that God had kept him alive until that day **witnessing both to small and great** of what Christ had suffered and that He had risen from the dead **to show light unto the people, and to the Gentiles** (vs. 23).

24-32. Festus, a Gentile who was unaware of Jewish thinking and Old Testament teaching, was shocked and uttered with a loud voice: **Paul, thou art beside thyself** (or insane). Reference to his **much learning** which had made him **mad** indicates that it was obvious that Paul was a man of unusual intelligence but must have gone crazy from all of these religious investigations. While the point is not made directly by the story, it seems obvious that Luke recounts this incident to show that Christianity could be no mere invention of the mind of man but only the revelation of the truth. Only the life-changing experience of conversion could drive a person like the Apostle Paul for so many years to remain faithful to what had happened in his life on one given day so many years before. Paul protested that he was **not mad** but was speaking the **truth** in **soberness** (Gr *sōphrosynē,* "temperate," "self-control," of "balanced mind"). He also appealed to Agrippa, that as an expert in Jewish affairs, he understood the things of which he had spoken because these things were not **done in a corner.** He was reminding him that the events of the death and resurrection of Christ were hardly a secret and were openly known to anyone who had any knowledge of Jewish affairs at all. Paul's final appeal, **Believest thou the prophets? I know that thou believest,** must be seen as an appeal to the king who evidently showed some outward indication of conviction and concern at that point. However, Agrippa, evidently embarrassed by the presence of Festus, was not about to make such an admission, and his response, **Almost thou persuadest me to be a Christian,** is probably best understood as a parody on Paul's appeal: "In short, you are trying to make me play the Christian." Paul, however, went on to say that he wished they were **both almost, and altogether** true believers! After dismissing him, they conferred among themselves and decided that he had done **nothing worthy of death or of bonds** (vs. 31). Again, Paul's innocence was verified by Roman officials who agreed that he **might have been set at liberty** had he not **appealed unto Caesar.** Because of the formality of such an appeal, the legal process had to be carried through. It is most likely that Festus and Agrippa sent some kind of letter of explanation to the emperor along with their unusual prisoner who was now finally on his way to Rome!

E. The Journey to Rome. 27:1-28:10.

27:1-14. Paul never seemed to be able to do anything half-

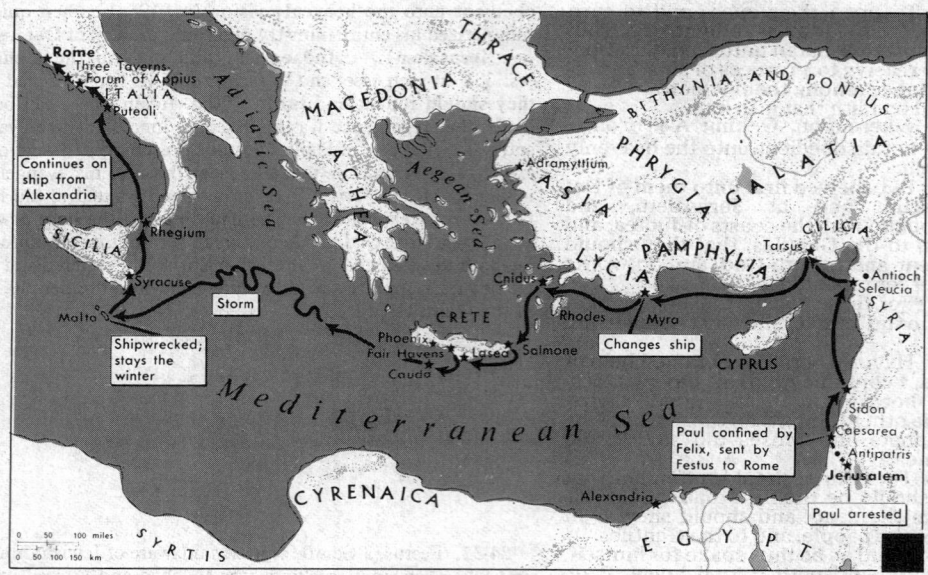

Paul's Voyage to Rome

should sail into Italy, they delivered Paul and certain other prisoners unto *one* named Julius a centurion of Augustus' band.

2 And entering into a ship of Ăd-ra-mўt'tĬ-um, we launched, meaning to sail by the coasts of Asia; *one* Ăr-ĭs-tär'chus, a Macedonian of Thĕs-sa-lo-nĭ'ca, being with us.

3 And the next *day* we touched at Sĭ'don. And Julius courteously entreated Paul, and gave *him* liberty to go unto his friends to refresh himself.

4 And when we had launched from thence, we sailed under Cyprus, because the winds were contrary.

5 And when we had sailed over the sea of Cĭ-lĭ'ćia and Păm-phўl'Ĭ-a, we came to Mў'ra, *a city* of Lў'cia.

6 And there the centurion found a ship of Alexandria sailing into Italy; and he put us therein.

7 And when we had sailed slowly many days, and scarce were come over against Cnĭ'dus, the wind not suffering us, we sailed under Crete, over against Săl-mō'ne;

8 And, hardly passing it, came unto a place which is called The fair havens; nigh whereunto was the city *of* La-sē'a.

9 ¶ Now when much time was spent, and when sailing was now dangerous, because the fast was now already past, Paul admonished *them*,

10 And said unto them, Sirs, I perceive that this voyage will be with hurt and much damage, not only of the lading and ship, but also of our lives.

11 Nevertheless the centurion believed the master and the owner of the ship, more than those things which were spoken by Paul.

12 And because the haven was not commodious to winter in, the more part advised to depart thence also, if by any means they might attain to Phe-

heartedly and the journey to Rome is itself an exciting and unusual story. A group of prisoners had collected at the headquarters of the Roman officials in Caesarea, and Paul was sent with them to Rome under the charge of a centurion and the cohort of **Augustus' band** (an unidentified military formation). The final "we" section of the book picks up again with verse 1. Thus Paul was accompanied by Luke, who had originally arrived with him at Jerusalem, and is assumed to have remained nearby during the two-year imprisonment in Caesarea. The obscure but faithful Aristarchus (as Blaiklock calls him, p. 189) also accompanied them. References to him appear in Colossians 4:10 and Philemon 24. The ship of **Adramyttium** refers to a seaport on the Aegean opposite the island of Lesbos. They went north along the Palestinian coast to **Sidon,** where **Julius,** the centurion, allowed Paul to go ashore briefly to visit his friends. Because the prevailing winds blow from the west, the ship sailed between **Cyprus** and the mainland, rather than going directly into the winds which were **contrary.** Eventually they had to head out into the open sea below **Cilicia** and **Pamphylia** and finally came to **Myra,** a Lycian port, where larger ships could be found. There they transferred to an Alexandrian grain ship and headed for Rome. Sailing against the wind, they finally arrived with difficulty at **Cnidus,** on a promontory point at the southwest tip of Asia Minor. From this point they had to choose whether they would wait for a more favorable wind moving westerly, or whether they would sail southward to Crete itself. The statement, **the wind not suffering us,** means the wind did not allow them to go on. Therefore, they chose the alternate route and sailed southward around **Salome** at the eastern end of Crete and coasted along westward on the leeward side of the island. Eventually they came to the port called **Fair Havens** which was, and still is, about halfway along the coast and beyond which the land slopes downward, exposing ships to the open wind. By the early fall the winter winds become fierce, and by mid-November all sailing was an impossibility in the Mediterranean in those ancient times because the ships were not large enough to withstand the winter storms. **Paul admonished** his superiors not to attempt the journey under such dangerous circumstances. The **fast** (vs. 9) to which Luke refers is the Day

nī́ċe, *and there* to winter; *which is* an haven of Crete, and lieth toward the south west and north west.

13 And when the south wind blew softly, supposing that they had obtained *their* purpose, loosing *thence*, they sailed close by Crete.

14 But not long after there arose against it a tempestuous wind, called Eū-rŏc′lȳ-dŏn.

15 And when the ship was caught, and could not bear up into the wind, we let *her* drive.

16 And running under a certain island which is called Clau′da, we had much work to come by the boat:

17 Which when they had taken up, they used helps, undergirding the ship; and, fearing lest they should fall into the quicksands, strake sail, and so were driven.

18 And we being exceedingly tossed with a tempest, the next *day* they lightened the ship;

19 And the third *day* we cast out with our own hands the tackling of the ship.

20 And when neither sun nor stars in many days appeared, and no small tempest lay on *us*, all hope that we should be saved was then taken away.

21 ¶But after long abstinence Paul stood forth in the midst of them, and said, Sirs, ye should have hearkened unto me, and not have loosed from Crete, and to have gained this harm and loss.

22 And now I exhort you to be of good cheer: for there shall be no loss of *any man's* life among you, but of the ship.

23 For there stood by me this night the angel of God, whose I am, and whom I serve,

24 Saying, Fear not, Paul; thou must be brought before Cæsar: and, lo, God hath given thee all them that sail with thee.

25 Wherefore, sirs, be of good cheer: for I believe God, that it shall be even as it was told me.

26 Howbeit we must be cast upon a certain island.

27 But when the fourteenth night was come, as we were driven up and down in Ā′drĭ-a, about midnight the shipmen deemed that they drew near to some country;

28 And sounded, and found *it* twenty fathoms: and when they had gone a little further, and they sounded again, and found *it* fifteen fathoms.

29 Then fearing lest we should have fallen upon rocks, they cast four anchors out of the stern, and wished for the day.

30 And as the shipmen were about to flee out of the ship, when they had let down the boat into the sea, under colour as though they would have cast anchors out of the foreship,

31 Paul said to the centurion and to the soldiers, Except these abide in the ship, ye cannot be saved.

32 Then the soldiers cut off the ropes of the boat, and let her fall off.

33 And while the day was coming on, Paul besought *them* all to take meat,

of Atonement which generally falls at the end of September. Through the influence of the **master and owner** of the ship, they attempted to sail to the more commodious port of **Phoenix** on Crete. Leaving the **Fair Havens** they were able to follow close along the shore of the island because the **south wind blew softly.** Thinking they had made the right decision, they got away from the safety of the port and were caught on the open seas by a **tempestuous wind** called **Euroclydon** (a hybrid word meaning "northeaster").

15-26. Luke then vividly recounts the story of the treacherous voyage which drove them twenty-three miles across the turbulent sea to the offshore island of **Clauda.** During this time the passengers had to aid the crew and struggled desperately to haul aboard the ship's boat, which was towing, water-logged, behind. Fearing the **quicksands** (*Syrtis*, the graveyard of many ships off the north African coast), they **struck sail** (probably meaning they set storm sails) and were driven by the wind. When the storm did not abate the next day, they were forced to "lighten" the ship by throwing the cargo overboard; and when it did not calm the following day, they threw over all the extra **tackling** and gear. The storm then continued for many days and the ancient sailors lost all hope of navigation because they could not see the stars. The reference to being **saved** (vs. 20) refers to the salvation of their lives from the storm. Paul's unusual leadership now arose to the forefront as he stood up in the midst of the storm and rebuked the sailors for not listening to his original advice and then reassured them that no man would die, in spite of the loss of the ship. He announced that the **angel of God** had appeared unto him in the storm to assure him that he would be **brought before Caesar** (vs. 24). There can be little doubt that Paul's unique experience on the road to Damascus was not limited by a one-time event in his life. Time and again God continued to put His miraculous mark of approval on His unusual servant. In the midst of our greatest personal dangers we can have the confidence that God is with us.

27-44. Blaiklock's (pp. 190ff.) vivid description states: "They were, indeed, at the end of human resource. They had looped and tautened cables precariously round the hull, to bind the straining timbers against the stress of the violent seas, and the leverage of the mast; they cut loose all dispensable tackling and gear to lighten the vessel." As they drifted across the sea of **Adria** (a reference to the entire eastern Mediterranean, not the Adriatic Sea), they could tell they were approaching land, probably due to the sound of breakers crashing against the shore or the rock. As the depth soundings revealed that the water was becoming more shallow, they **cast four anchors** (vs. 29) in an attempt to secure the ship before drifting into the shore. The alert apostle frustrated an attempt by the **shipmen** (crew) to escape in the boat launch, leaving the rest on board. Therefore, the soldiers cut the ropes and let the smaller boat drift off. Toward daybreak, Paul then urged them all to have something to eat, a suggestion that paid off later. In unique Christian style he **gave thanks to God in presence of them all** (vs. 35). Certainly a true believer can never become reluctant or embarrassed to ask God's blessing over his meal in a public situation in light of the example of the Apostle Paul. The total number of people

saying, This day is the fourteenth day that ye have tarried and continued fasting, having taken nothing.

34 Wherefore I pray you to take *some* meat: for this is for your health: for there shall not an hair fall from the head of any of you.

35 And when he had thus spoken, he took bread, and gave thanks to God in presence of them all: and when he had broken *it*, he began to eat.

36 Then were they all of good cheer, and they also took *some* meat.

37 And we were in all in the ship two hundred threescore and sixteen souls.

38 And when they had eaten enough, they lightened the ship, and cast out the wheat into the sea.

39 And when it was day, they knew not the land: but they discovered a certain creek with a shore, into the which they were minded, if it were possible, to thrust in the ship.

40 And when they had taken up the anchors, they committed *themselves* unto the sea, and loosed the rudder bands, and hoised up the mainsail to the wind, and made toward shore.

41 And falling into a place where two seas met, they ran the ship aground; and the forepart stuck fast, and remained unmoveable, but the hinder part was broken with the violence of the waves.

42 And the soldiers' counsel was to kill the prisoners, lest any of them should swim out, and escape.

43 But the centurion, willing to save Paul, kept them from *their* purpose; and commanded that they which could swim should cast *themselves* first *into the sea*, and get to land:

44 And the rest, some on boards, and some on *broken pieces* of the ship. And so it came to pass, that they escaped all safe to land.

CHAPTER 28

AND when they were escaped, then they knew that the island was called Mĕl'ĭ-ta.

2 And the barbarous people shewed us no little kindness: for they kindled a fire, and received us every one, because of the present rain, and because of the cold.

3 And when Paul had gathered a bundle of sticks, and laid *them* on the fire, there came a viper out of the heat, and fastened on his hand.

4 And when the barbarians saw the *venomous* beast hang on his hand, they said among themselves, No doubt this man is a murderer, whom, though he hath escaped the sea, yet vengeance suffereth not to live.

5 And he shook off the beast into the fire, and felt no harm.

6 Howbeit they looked when he should have swollen, or fallen down dead suddenly: but after they had looked a great while, and saw no harm come to him, they changed their minds, and said that he was a god.

7 ¶In the same quarters were possessions of the chief man of the island, whose name was Publius; who re-

on the ship was two hundred seventy-six. Finally, they cast even the remaining **wheat into the sea.** Therefore the ship owner's attempt to get his cargo to Rome in time to get the best price had now totally failed. At daybreak they attempted to run the ship aground in a creek which parted the shore. They cast off the anchors and, using the **rudder bands** (two large steering oars on either side of the ship), they attempted to make the shore with a small "foresail." However, they did not make it and **ran the ship aground.** The bow of the ship was stuck on the shoal, while the force of the waves against the stern began breaking the ship in two. Had Paul not stepped to the forefront as he had and won the confidence of the centurion, all the prisoners would have been put to death by the **soldiers' counsel** (vs. 42). This action would have followed traditional Roman discipline to kill their charges rather than risk escape. The centurion, however, **willing to save Paul** and many of those who could swim did so and the rest floated in on **boards,** and some even on the **pieces of the ship.** Nevertheless, they all were able to reach land safely from the sandbar. The incident reveals the outstanding faith and character of the Apostle Paul, who emerged as the hero of the story in spite of being a prisoner on the ship!

28:1-10. Again the reader is amazed that Paul's spiritual determination does not quit even under such difficult circumstances. In spite of his imprisonment, the series of trials, and now the traumatic shipwreck, Paul dominated the scene on the island of Melita (modern Malta) lying about a hundred miles south of Sicily. **Melita** is related to the Canaanite word "refuge" and was at one time part of the territory of Carthage, and the peasantry still spoke the Phoenician language. The term **barbarous** does not refer to primitive people, but rather those who spoke an unintelligible language. A better rendering would be "foreigner." A fire was kindled to warm them from the cold winter rain and Paul helped gather sticks for the fire, when a **viper** (snake, which had hibernated in the wood pile) **fastened on his hand** (i.e., bit him). The Melitians assumed that the snakebite had been inflicted in punishment of Paul's misdeeds. The common concept was that the goddess of justice, *Dike*, would use tragedy to catch up with her victims. When Paul shook off the snake unharmed, they **changed their minds** and decided that he was a **god** (vs. 6). Note that the verb **changed their minds** (Gr *metaballō*), meaning to change their "opinion," is a completely different word from the theological term "to repent" (Gr *metanoeō*). As a result, the **chief man of the island** (the leading official), named **Publius,** lodged them for three days in his villa estate. His father **lay sick of a fever** and **bloody flux** (hemorrhage). Dysentery and fever were common on the island

ceived us, and lodged us three days courteously.

8 And it came to pass, that the father of Publius lay sick of a fever and of a bloody flux: to whom Paul entered in, and prayed, and laid his hands on him, and healed him.

9 So when this was done, others also, which had diseases in the island, came, and were healed:

10 Who also honoured us with many honours; and when we departed, they laded *us* with such things as were necessary.

11 ¶And after three months we departed in a ship of Alexandria, which had wintered in the isle, whose sign was Castor and Pollux.

12 And landing at Syracuse, we tarried *there* three days.

13 And from thence we fetched a compass, and came to Rhḗ′gi-um: and after one day the south wind blew, and we came the next day to Pū-tē′o-lī:

14 Where we found brethren, and were desired to tarry with them seven days: and so we went toward Rome.

15 And from thence, when the brethren heard of us, they came to meet us as far as Ăp′pĭ-ī fô′rŭm, and The three taverns: whom when Paul saw, he thanked God, and took courage.

16 And when we came to Rome, the centurion delivered the prisoners to the captain of the guard: but Paul was suffered to dwell by himself with a soldier that kept him.

17 And it came to pass, that after three days Paul called the chief of the Jews together: and when they were come together, he said unto them, Men *and* brethren, though I have committed nothing against the people, or customs of our fathers, yet was I delivered prisoner from Jerusalem into the hands of the Romans.

18 Who, when they had examined me, would have let *me* go, because there was no cause of death in me.

19 But when the Jews spake against *it*, I was constrained to appeal unto Cæsar; not that I had ought to accuse my nation of.

20 For this cause therefore have I called for you, to see *you*, and to speak with *you*: because that for the hope of Israel I am bound with this chain.

21 And they said unto him, We neither received letters out of Judæa concerning thee, neither any of the brethren that came shewed or spake any harm of thee.

22 But we desire to hear of thee what thou thinkest: for as concerning this

of Malta and often took many lives. Paul came to the man and **prayed, and laid his hands on him, and healed him.** These unusual miracles completely dominate the story of their three-month winter sojourn on this island. Afterwards they continued "healing" the people of the island. Because of the change of the verbs for "healing" some have suggested that the subsequent "cures" may have been wrought by Luke the physician as well as by Paul. However, note the same use of the latter verb for the healing done by Peter in Acts 5:16. The ultimate concept seems to be that even in the presence of a medical doctor, miraculous healing was being done by the Apostle Paul!

F. Conclusion. 28:11-31.

11-16. Since the shipwreck had taken place during the early part of November, three **months** later would have put them near the end of February. Again they departed in a **ship of Alexandria** (vs. 11) which had wintered at Melita and which bore the sign of **Castor and Pollux.** Ancient sailing vessels often took their names from their figureheads, these being the *dioscuri*, meaning "the sons of Zeus," who were regarded as the patron deities of sailors. Sailing directly north they came to **Syracuse,** the most important city on Sicily at that time. The quaint archaism of the AV, **fetched a compass,** means they "made a circuit," or had to tack back and forth in order to reach **Rhegium** on the southern toe of Italy. They reached **Puteoli** on the bay of Naples, the regular port of arrival for grain ships coming from Alexandria. Here they spent seven days with **brethren.** By this time in the history of the early church Christian believers could be found almost anywhere throughout the entire empire. From **Puteoli** the land route was taken to Rome which normally included a barge passage through the Pontine Marshes and reached its terminus at the **Appii Forum,** some forty-three miles from Rome. **Three Taverns** was about ten miles closer and both were stopping places where travelers might lodge for the night. The reference in verse 16 is the last of the "we" statements in Acts. But since Luke is mentioned in Paul's letters which were written from Rome (cf. Phm 24; Col 4:14), it must be understood that he remained with Paul throughout this Roman imprisonment. It is not likely that Paul was actually put in jail or prison at this time, but was actually under personal attachment to a soldier whose responsibility was to bring him before the authorities at the proper time. Paul was able to dwell in a home.

17-31. The two-year imprisonment is briefly recorded by Luke in which Paul spent the greater amount of the time in a **hired house** (vs. 30), where he was allowed to receive visitors including many of the Jews and the Christians of the community. Very interestingly Paul put forth an aggressive attempt to evangelize the Jews at Rome who were totally ignorant of his disastrous encounters back in Palestine. To them he **expounded and testified the kingdom of God** (vs. 23) and **some believed . . . and some believed not.** Luke records the apostle's tireless effort to carry on his mission but then records the statement of **Isaiah,** quoting 6:9-10, which describes the spiritual dullness of the Jews. Luke, himself a Gentile, seems convinced that only a minority of the people of Israel would be converted to the true gospel; therefore the statement is made again that **the salvation of God is sent unto the Gentiles** (vs. 28), reaffirming the ultimate Gentile mission of Paul. During the two-year wait for his court trial, Paul continued **Preaching the kingdom of God** and teaching the doctrine of **the Lord Jesus Christ.** Again the reference to the **kingdom of God** must refer to the church and not to continued Jewish preaching at so late a time in the apostle's ministry. His preaching was continued **with all confidence, no man forbidding.** The book obviously ends abruptly, which has caused most commentators to believe that Luke wrote right up until the present time and closed the book at the point

sect, we know that every where it is spoken against.

23 And when they had appointed him a day, there came many to him into *his* lodging; to whom he expounded and testified the kingdom of God, persuading them concerning Jesus, both out of the law of Moses, and *out of* the prophets, from morning till evening.

24 And some believed the things which were spoken, and some believed not.

25 And when they agreed not among themselves, they departed, after that Paul had spoken one word, Well spake the Holy Ghost by E-ṣā′ias the prophet unto our fathers,

26 Saying, Go unto this people, and say, Hearing ye shall hear, and shall not understand; and seeing ye shall see, and not perceive:

27 For the heart of this people is waxed gross, and their ears are dull of hearing, and their eyes have they closed; lest they should see with *their* eyes, and hear with *their* ears, and understand with *their* heart, and should be converted, and I should heal them.

28 Be it known therefore unto you, that the salvation of God is sent unto the Gentiles, and *that* they will hear it.

29 And when he had said these words, the Jews departed, and had great reasoning among themselves.

30 ¶And Paul dwelt two whole years in his own hired house, and received all that came in unto him,

31 Preaching the kingdom of God, and teaching those things which concern the Lord Jesus Christ, with all confidence, no man forbidding him.

at which they had now arrived. No statement is made of Paul actually going to trial before Caesar, nor of his traditional release and a two- or three-year interval, finally ending in his reimprisonment and death in A.D. 68. The two pastoral epistles (I Tim and Tit) seem to reflect a continued traveling and preaching ministry of Paul which cannot be properly fitted into the narrative of the book of Acts, whereas II Timothy reflects the atmosphere of imprisonment awaiting final execution. In the early stages of these last events Paul seems confident of his release and looks forward to a continued ministry, whereas, in his last letter to Timothy he accepts the fact that he has "finished his course" and inevitable execution awaits him. Most writers agree that during the Roman imprisonment Paul penned the letters of Ephesians, Colossians, Philemon, and Philippians, and that he was eventually released and once more traveled throughout the empire preaching Christ, perhaps as far west as Spain, before his final arrest and martyrdom in Rome. It is not likely that Luke, who so carefully narrates the exciting experiences of Paul's encounter with worldly kings, would have omitted his appearance before Caesar had such already taken place at the time of the writing of this book. It would appear then that the narrative ends as it does because it had caught up with history. Luke has brought us up to the most contemporary point in the apostle's life at this time. The narrative is closed and the message is sent off to the church, who shall forever be grateful, that a sovereign God was pleased to send into Paul's company one so capable and prepared under the hand of grace to recount in such accurate historic detail the events of the greatest servant of Christ in the history of the church. The unfinished ending of the Acts of the Apostles does not conclude beside the Tiber River, but in reality continues on in our own day and time as the living Lord of the church continues to build His church, against which the gates of hell shall not prevail! Hallelujah!

BIBLIOGRAPHY

*Alexander, J. A. *A Commentary on the Acts of the Apostles.* London: Banner of Truth, reprint of 1857 ed.

Baumgarten, M. *The Acts of the Apostles or the History of the Church in the Apostolic Age.* Edinburgh: T. & T. Clark, 1854.

*Blaiklock, E. Acts of the Apostles. In *Tyndale New Testament Commentary.* Grand Rapids: Eerdmans, 1959.

*Bruce, F. F. *The Acts of the Apostles.* Grand Rapids: Eerdmans, 1951. (Based on Greek text.)

*————Commentary on the Book of Acts. In *New International Commentary.* Grand Rapids: Eerdmans, 1954.

*Carter, C. and R. Earle. *The Acts of the Apostles.* Grand Rapids: Zondervan, 1959.

Erdman, C. *The Acts.* Philadelphia: Westminster Press, 1919.

Foakes-Jackson, F. J. and K. Lake. *The Beginnings of Christianity.* 5 vols. London: Macmillan, 1920-1933.

Gloag, P. *A Critical and Exegetical Commentary on the Acts of the Apostles.* Edinburgh: T. & T. Clark, 1870.

Hackett, H. B. *A Commentary on the Acts of the Apostles.* Philadelphia: American Baptist Publication Society, 1851.

*Jensen, I. *Acts: An Inductive Study.* Chicago: Moody Press, 1968.

Kent, H. A. *From Jerusalem to Rome: Studies in the Book of Acts.* Grand Rapids: Baker, 1972.

Ladd, G. E. Acts In *Wycliffe Bible Commentary.* Chicago: Moody Press, 1962.

Lindsay, T. *The Acts of the Apostles.* 2 vols. Edinburgh: T. & T. Clark, 1884.

Lumby, J. The Acts of the Apostles. In *Cambridge Greek Testament.* Cambridge: University Press, 1899.

*Morgan, G. C. *The Acts of the Apostles.* New York: Revell, 1924.

Rackham, R. The Acts of the Apostles. In the *Westminster Commentaries.* New York: Macmillan, 1901.

Ramsay, W. *Pictures of the Apostolic Church: Studies in the Book of Acts.* Grand Rapids: Baker, reprint of 1910 ed.

Ridderbos, H. *The Speeches of Peter in the Acts of the Apostles.* London: Tyndale Press, 1962.

*Scroggie, W. G. *The Acts of the Apostles.* London: Marshall, Morgan, Scott, 1931.

Thomas, W. H. G. *Outline Studies in the Acts of the Apostles.* Grand Rapids: Eerdmans, 1956.

The Epistle To The
ROMANS

INTRODUCTION

No other portion of Holy Scripture so completely sets forth the great doctrines of the Christian faith as does Paul's Epistle to the Romans. No other product of the pen has ever more powerfully confronted the mind of man with the great truths of God. All of man's alibis, all of his pretenses, all of his attempts at self-justification are mightily struck down by the truths of this book. In this, his *magnum opus*, every argument which man can muster against the claims of God are thoroughly demolished with unanswerable logic by the Apostle Paul.

Romans has rightly been called "the Constitution of Christianity," "the Christian Manifesto," "the Cathedral of the Christian Faith." There is nowhere to be found a more complete compendium of Christian doctrine. Herein are recorded the doctrines of justification, sanctification, divine election, condemnation, the perseverance of the saints, total depravity, the last judgment, the fall of man, the revelation of God in nature, the final restoration of the Jews, and many more. This epistle stands at the head of Paul's epistles as the brazen altar did before the Holy Place. You could not enter the tabernacle until you passed the brazen altar. Likewise, you cannot enter the great doctrinal portions of the New Testament without first passing Romans. It is the gateway to New Testament truth. It is basic training for the Christian. By the Holy Spirit of God, it is the masterpiece of Paul.

The Church at Rome. As the capital of the empire, Rome was the largest and most important city in the first-century world. Located about fifteen miles from the Mediterranean Sea, Rome was a teeming metropolis. In 1941 an inscription was discovered at Ostia which indicated that in A.D. 14 the city had a population of 4,100,000 (see Jack Finegan, *Light From the Ancient Past*, p. 288).

It is impossible to determine with great certainty who founded the church of this great metropolis. There are, however, several contenders for this honor who can be eliminated. First, it is evident that Paul did not establish the Roman church. Romans 1:10-11, 13, 15 all make reference to the fact that Paul had never been to Rome at the writing of this epistle. He obviously could not have founded the church there. Secondly, Peter must be ruled out as well. The view of the present Roman church, which adamantly holds to Petrine founding of the church in Rome, is based on an erroneous statement of Eusebius in his *Ecclesiastical History*, Book II, Chapter 14. This church historian inaccurately records that Peter went to Rome during the second year of the reign of the Roman Emperor Claudius to encounter the impostor Simon Magus, the sorcerer who tried to buy the power of the Holy Spirit (Acts 8:18-19). The second year of the reign of Claudius would have been A.D. 42. However, Peter was a pillar in the church of Jerusalem, not

Rome (Gal 2:9). He is frequently mentioned as being active in Jerusalem (Acts 9). He was certainly in Jerusalem up until and through the Council of Jerusalem (Acts 15). Since the Council of Jerusalem can be dated A.D. 49, it would have been highly unlikely for Peter to be in residence in Rome earlier than that.

Besides, in the salutation of the last chapter of Romans, Paul salutes twenty-seven individuals by name. If Peter was bishop of the church by that time, why did Paul not mention his name as well? Also, Luke has been demonstrated to be the most accurate historian of the first century A.D. (see Sir Wm. Ramsay, *St. Paul the Traveller and the Roman Citizen*, pp. 1-10). If Peter, as prominent as he was, had founded the church at Rome, how could Luke have overlooked such an important fact in recording the history of the early church in Acts? In addition, in Romans 15:20 Paul writes, "Yea, so have I strived to preach the gospel, not where Christ was named, lest I should build upon another man's foundation." If Peter had founded the church at Rome, why was Paul so anxious to preach there? (Rom 1:15). These considerations would make it appear impossible that Peter established the Roman church.

If neither Paul nor Peter established this church, then who did? Two possibilities exist. The first arises from those present at the Day of Pentecost. Acts 2:9-11 mentions that among those in Jerusalem on that eventful day were "strangers of Rome, Jews and proselytes." It is quite possible that believing Jews carried their new faith and the message of the gospel back to the imperial city and founded the church there. Another possibility is that families from Pauline churches in the East settled in Rome and, discovering the faith of each other, gathered together to worship independently of the Jewish synagogues. Either way, the church at Rome apparently owed its origin to the migration of Christians from the eastern part of the empire who were converted through their contact with the gospel there.

It is generally accepted that when Paul wrote Romans there was a church of considerable size at Rome. The contents of this epistle make it evident that the Roman church was comprised of both Jews and Gentiles. There was a Jewish community in Rome as early as the second century B.C. It was greatly enlarged by Pompey's conquest of Judaea in 63 B.C. when Jewish prisoners-of-war marched in his grand procession. Cicero makes reference to the size and influence of the Jewish colony in Rome in 59 B.C. (*Pro Flacco* 66). In A.D. 19 the Jews of Rome were expelled from the city by a decree of Emperor Tiberius. Another mass expulsion took place in the reign of Emperor Claudius (A.D. 41-54). This expulsion caused Aquila and Priscilla to migrate to Corinth where they encountered Paul

(Acts 18:2). But the effects of this expulsion order were temporary, for less than three years after the death of Claudius, Paul wrote of the Jewish Christians in Rome, speaking of their faith as a matter of common knowledge. The original nucleus of the church must have been Jewish.

However, the Gentile element in the Roman church was predominant at the time of writing. Even though Paul addressed the Jews in 4:1 when he spoke of Abraham as "our father, as pertaining to the flesh," there are many direct references to the Gentiles. In his introduction Paul spoke of "obedience to the faith among all nations" (1:5). Paul desired fruit among the Romans, "even as among other Gentiles" (1:13). After he reviewed God's dealings with Israel in chapters 9-11, it is to the Gentiles that Paul gives concluding admonitions (11:13). Later when he wrote to the Philippians from Rome, Paul intimated that it was among the Gentiles that the gospel had chiefly taken hold in Rome (Phil 1:13; 4:22). The church which had begun in Jewish hearts had taken on a decidedly Gentile tone.

Place of writing. The contents of the Epistle to the Romans indicate that it was written from Corinth on Paul's third missionary journey. The events of this epistle fit perfectly into the chronology of Acts 20:1-5. Paul's eastern journeys were over; his face was set toward the West (Rom 15:23-24; Acts 19:21). At this time Paul was heading to Jerusalem with the collection for the poor (Rom 15:24-27). This he did at the close of his three months' visit to Corinth (Acts 24:17). This collection was emphasized in his Epistles to the Corinthians (I Cor 16:1-4; II Cor 8:9). Romans must have been written about the same time as the Corinthian epistles, only a bit later. When he wrote the epistle, Paul mentioned that with him were Timothy, Sosipater, Gaius, and Erastus (Rom 16:21-23). Timothy, Sosipater (Sopater), and Gaius were all mentioned as being with Paul in Corinth during his three months' visit (Acts 20:4). By cross-referencing we note that those mentioned in Romans were the same men who were with Paul at Corinth and it was from there that he wrote the Epistle to the Romans.

Date of writing. It is possible to pinpoint the date of writing even further than simply Paul's three-month stay at Corinth. The absence of defensive tactics by Paul and the tranquil tone of the epistle suggest that it was written toward the end of his stay in Corinth, after the troubles at Corinth had been quieted. Since all navigation on the Mediterranean ceased between the middle of November and the middle of March, the plans of Phoebe to travel to Rome would hardly have been made before the spring. Thus it is likely that the date of the Roman epistle was the spring of A.D. 57, although estimations range from A.D. 56-58.

Purpose of writing. During the decade A.D. 47-57 Paul had spent most of his time intensively evangelizing the territories which border the Aegean Sea and planting churches throughout Asia Minor and Greece. His eastern campaign was now concluded, but his task was by no means complete. During the winter of A.D. 56-57, which he spent at

the house of his Corinthian friend Gaius, he apprehensively looked forward to an immediate journey to Jerusalem where he hoped the gift he bore from the gentile churches to the poor Jewish saints at Jerusalem would help salve the wounds of controversy and strengthen the bonds between the mother church and the churches of the Gentiles. Once this mission was complete, Paul could continue his dream to labor where no man had labored and build where no man had built. His choice was Spain, the oldest Roman colony in the West. But a journey to Spain would afford opportunity to realize another lifelong ambition, to visit Rome and spend some time with the believers there.

The purpose of his epistle to these Roman believers was as follows: (1) To enlist the cooperation and support of the church at Rome for the inauguration of his missionary campaign in the West. Paul realized the strategic and political importance of this city. He needed the assistance of the believers of Rome to launch him into missionary activity in the West as the church at Antioch had done in the East. (2) Paul also wanted to enlist the prayer support of the Roman Christians for his forthcoming venture at Jerusalem (15:30-33). He was concerned about the outcome of his journey there and rightly so. (3) Paul was emphatic in his claim to be the apostle to the Gentiles. Since Rome was the capital of the gentile world it was entirely appropriate that he visit the church there. (4) Paul knew that the Roman church had come into existence without the authoritative leadership of an apostle of the Lord. Thus Paul wanted to add validity to their existence by instructing them in the faith through his epistle. (5) Paul desired to deposit a compendium of theological truth and the capital city of the empire was the natural place for him to do so. Besides, Paul was apprehensive about the immediate trip to Jerusalem and perhaps the Epistle to the Romans would be his final opportunity to draft a theology of the Christian faith in a written, changeless form. As Adam W. Miller says, "He bequeaths to them in the form of the Epistle the gospel that he would preach to them, should he be permitted to reach there, and if not, they have his letter to read and refer to again and again" (Adam W. Miller, *An Introduction to the New Testament*, p. 209). Paul certainly fulfilled these purposes. This epistle has proved to be one of the bulwarks of evangelical Christianity.

Authorship. That Paul was the author of the Epistle to the Romans is indisputable and universally acknowledged. On internal grounds, Paul claims to be the author (1:1). The writer makes personal references which can only apply to Paul (cf. 11:13; 15:15-20). The style, argument, and theology are all Pauline. On external grounds quotations from this epistle are found in Clement of Rome, Ignatius, Justin Martyr, Polycarp, Hippolytus, Marcion, the Muratorian Canon, and the Old Latin and Syriac Versions. Romans was recognized as Pauline and a canonical writing since the time of Irenaeus, A.D. 130-202.

Although Pauline authorship is indisputable, some critics have questioned the authenticity of chapters 15 and 16. It seems certain that Marcion did not include the last two chapters in his canon. There is also evidence that the early Latin Version ended the epistle with chapter 14 and the doxology of 16:25-27. However, there is no extant Greek manuscript which omits these chapters.

These two chapters have been assaulted basically on three grounds. Critics charge: (1) The large number of personal greetings in chapter 16 is improbable if Paul had never visited Rome; (2) the commendation of Phoebe was not appropriate to a church Paul had never met; and (3) the suitability of 15:33 as an ending to the epistle makes the addition of chapter 16 unlikely. These criticisms, however, are weak and can be otherwise explained. The great Roman system of roads would have made it easy for Paul to have met the people mentioned in chapter 16 or to have known them before they moved to Rome. Since Paul was well enough known to the church at Rome to have written an epistle to them, he was well enough known to have commended Phoebe to them. And, although 15:33 does make an appropriate ending, nevertheless its style is unparalleled in all the Pauline Epistles. The word "grace" occurs in each of Paul's benedictions except 15:33 (cf. Rom 16:24; I Cor 16:23; II Cor 13:14; Gal 6:18; Eph 6:24; Phil 4:23; Col 4:18; I Thess 5:28; II Thess 3:18; I Tim 6:21; II Tim 4:22; Tit 3:15; Phm 25). Hence, there is no reason not to accept all sixteen chapters of the Epistle to the Romans as authentically Pauline.

The importance of Romans. It is likely that the importance of the Epistle to the Romans cannot be overstated. In the summer of A.D. 386 Aurelius Augustinus, a native of Tagaste in North Africa and Professor of Rhetoric at Milan, was on the brink of beginning a new life. Taking up his scroll he read, "Not in rioting and drunkenness, not in chambering and wantonness, not in strife and envying. But put ye on the Lord Jesus Christ, and make not provision for the flesh, to fulfil the lusts thereof" (Rom 13:13-14). "No further would I read," he said, "nor had I any need; instantly, at the end of this sentence, a clear light flooded my heart and all the darkness of doubt vanished away" (*Confessions* viii. 29). Such was the conversion experience of St. Augustine.

In November, 1515, an Augustinian monk and Professor of Sacred Theology at the University of Wittenberg, Germany, began to expound this epistle to his students. As he prepared his lectures, he became more and more convinced that the just shall live by faith. "I greatly longed to understand Paul's Epistle to the Romans," he wrote, "and nothing stood in the way but that one expression, 'the righteousness of God.' . . . Night and day I pondered until . . . I grasped the truth that the righteousness of God is that righteousness whereby, through grace and sheer mercy, he justifies us by faith. Thereupon I felt myself to be reborn . . ." (*Luther's Works*, Weimar edition, Vol. 54, pp. 179 ff.). Through the reading of this epistle, Martin Luther was born into the family of God.

On the evening of May 24, 1738, John Wesley unwillingly attended a society meeting at Aldersgate Street where someone was reading Luther's Preface to the Epistle to the Romans. Wesley wrote in his journal, "About a quarter before nine, while he was describing the change which God works in the heart through faith in Christ, I felt my heart strangely warmed. I felt I did trust in Christ, Christ alone, for my salvation; and an assurance was given me that he had taken my sins away, even mine; and saved me from the law of sin and death" (*Works*, 1872, Vol. I, p. 103). This event, more than any other, launched the Evangelical Revival of the eighteenth century.

The great Swiss Reformer John Calvin said of this epistle, "When any one understands this Epistle, he has a passage opened to him to the understanding of the whole Scriptures." James I. Packer, twentieth-century theologian, comments that "there is one book in the New Testament which links up with almost everything that the Bible contains: that is the Epistle to the Romans. . . . From the vantage-point given by Romans, the whole landscape of the Bible is open to view, and the broad relation of the parts to the whole becomes plain. The study of Romans is the fittest starting-point for biblical interpretation and theology" (James I. Packer, *Fundamentalism and the Word of God*, pp. 106ff.).

In his commentary on Romans the well-known Greek scholar Frederic Godet observed that "The Reformation was undoubtedly the work of the Epistle to the Romans, as well as of that to the Galatians; and the probability is that every great spiritual revival in the church will be connected as effect and cause with a deeper understanding of this book." One cannot say what might happen if Christians undertake an intensive study of this epistle. What happened to Augustine, Luther, Calvin, and Wesley, which left a mark on the world, could happen to us today. So, let the reader beware. Do not begin a serious study of this epistle unless you are willing to bear the consequences. Reading through Romans repeatedly results in revival.

OUTLINE

B. The Need of the Moralist. 2:1-16.
1. Condemned by his own judgment. 2:1.
2. Condemned according to truth. 2:2-5.
3. Condemned according to works. 2:6-10.
4. Condemned without respect of persons. 2:11-16.
C. The Need of the Jew. 2:17-3:8.
1. His law cannot make him righteous. 2:17-24.
2. His circumcision cannot make him righteous. 2:25-27.
3. His birth cannot make him righteous. 2:28-29.
4. His arguments cannot make him righteous. 3:1-8.
D. The Need of the Whole World. 3:9-20.
1. The charge against the whole world. 3:9.
2. The indictment against the whole world. 3:10-18.
3. The defense on behalf of the whole world. 3:19a.
4. The verdict against the whole world. 3:19b-20.
III. The Righteousness of God Provided. 3:21-8:39.
A. The Provision for Justification. 3:21-5:21.
1. Justification is by faith alone. 3:21-31.
2. Justification is illustrated in the Old Testament. 4:1-25.
3. Justification brings blessings to its recipients. 5:1-11.
4. Justification is imputed to us as was sin. 5:12-21.
B. The Provision for Sanctification. 6:1-7:25.
1. Sanctification and the principle of sin. 6:1-14.
2. Sanctification and the practice of sin. 6:15-23.
3. Sanctification and the law. 7:1-14.
4. Sanctification and the conflict within. 7:15-25.
C. The Provision for Assurance. 8:1-39.
1. The assurance of the righteousness of God. 8:1-4.
2. The assurance of the indwelling Spirit of God. 8:5-13.
3. The assurance of eternal heirship. 8:14-25.
4. The assurance of present intercession. 8:26-27.
5. The assurance of the eternal purpose of God. 8:28-34.
6. The assurance of the eternal presence of God. 8:35-39.
IV. The Righteousness of God Exemplified. 9:1-11:36.
A. Righteousness Exemplified in Divine Sovereignty. 9:1-33.
1. Sovereignty exhibited in Israel's identity. 9:1-8.
2. Sovereignty exhibited in God's personal choices. 9:9-13.
3. Sovereignty exhibited in God's powerful will. 9:14-24.

4. Sovereignty exhibited in Israel's partial blindness. 9:25-33.
B. Righteousness Exemplified in Human Responsibility. 10:1-21.
1. Nearness of the gospel: opportunity for responsibility. 10:1-10.
2. Offer of the gospel: ground for responsibility. 10:11-15.
3. Disobedience to the gospel: failure of responsibility. 10:16-21.
C. Righteousness Exemplified in Israel's Future. 11:1-36.
1. Israel's rejection leaves a remnant. 11:1-10.
2. Israel's rejection is not permanent. 11:11-24.
3. Israel's restoration is prophesied. 11:25-32.
4. Israel's restoration evokes praise. 11:33-36.
V. The Righteousness of God Enacted. 12:1-15:13.
A. Righteousness Produces a Life of Transformation. 12:1-21.
1. Transformation exhibited in humility. 12:1-8.
2. Transformation exhibited in love of the brethren. 12:9-16.
3. Transformation exhibited in honor before the world. 12:17-21.
B. Righteousness Produces a Life of Subjection. 13:1-14.
1. Subjection to the state. 13:1-7.
2. Subjection to the citizens of the state. 13:8-10.
3. Subjection to the timetable of God. 13:11-14.
C. Righteousness Produces a Life of Consideration. 14:1-15:13.
1. Consideration for a brother weak in the faith. 14:1-13.
2. Consideration for our neighbor. 14:14-23.
3. Consideration as we have Christ as example. 15:1-13.
VI. Conclusion. 15:14-16:27.
A. The Presentation of Personal Feelings. 15:14-33.
1. Explanation for writing. 15:14-16.
2. Vindication for writing. 15:17-21.
3. Paul's plans following the writing. 15:22-29.
4. Paul's plea for prayers on his behalf. 15:30-33.
B. The Presentation of Personal Greetings. 16:1-23.
1. Commendation of Phoebe. 16:1-2.
2. Greetings for friends in Rome. 16:3-16.
3. Warnings to friends in Rome. 16:17-20.
4. Greetings from friends with Paul. 16:21-23.
C. The Concluding Doxology. 16:24-27.
1. The worthy recipient of praise. 16:24.
2. The ascription of praise. 16:25-26.
3. The benediction. 16:27.

COMMENTARY

I. INTRODUCTION. 1:1-17.

A. Salutation to the Romans. 1:1-7.

The epistolary form which Paul uses is thoroughly consistent with other authors of the New Testament era. Paul begins each of his epistles with his own name, gives his salutation, adds a note of thanksgiving for his readers (Galatians is the only exception) and then, in epistles dealing with theological problems, he launches into a doctrinal section followed by a practical section. Finally, personal greetings and an autograph conclude his letters. The basic form does not essentially vary from epistle to epistle.

PAUL, a servant of Jesus Christ, called *to be* **an apostle, separated unto the gospel of God,**

1:1. Paul, a servant of Jesus Christ, called to be an apostle. Paul calls himself **a servant** (Gr *doulos*, bondslave) **of Jesus Christ.** In his mind, since a Roman slave was answerable only to his master, Paul was not just servant to the Lord but slave as well and answerable only to Him (I Cor 4:1-4). In addition, he was a "called" apostle. Paul claimed apostleship on at least four grounds: (1) he was a chosen vessel of God (Acts 9:15); (2) he was personally commissioned by Christ (Acts 9:6); (3) he had actually seen the risen Lord (I Cor 9:1-2); and (4) he was the recipient of divine revelation (Gal 1:10-12, 16-17).

Separated unto the gospel of God. Paul was set apart for the ministry of the gospel long before the Damascus road experience (Gal 1:15). With the pedigree of Paul (Phil 3:5-6), he would have made an excellent minister to his people, the Jews. But in the providence of God, Paul was separated unto the gospel of God as an apostle to the Gentiles (Acts 9:15). Thus a disastrous schism between the Jewish and gentile factions of the early church was avoided through the unique ministry of Paul.

2 (Which he had promised afore by his prophets in the holy scriptures,)
3 Concerning his Son Jesus Christ our Lord, which was made of the seed of David according to the flesh;

2-3. With the mention of the gospel (Gr *euangelion*) of God, the apostle begins an explanation of the person of that gospel, Jesus Christ. In the AV the first sentence of Romans includes one hundred twenty-six words and encompasses seven verses. We can proceed directly from verse 1 to verse 7 without losing Paul's train of thought. But the mere mention of the gospel of God prompts him to include the interlude of verses 2 through 6 in which he describes this gospel as that **Which he had promised afore by his prophets in the holy scriptures.** The gospel was not an innovation but had been preannounced by the Old Testament prophets from Genesis 3:15 to Malachi 4:2. By quoting sixty-one times from the Old Testament, Paul indicated to the Jews that their Scriptures were really speaking of Jesus Christ. **Concerning his Son Jesus Christ our Lord** expresses the subject of the gospel. The gospel is not about Jesus Christ, the gospel *is* Jesus Christ. **Which was made of the seed of David according to the flesh.** The Davidic descent of Jesus Christ was the fulfillment of the promise that one from the chosen line would sit on the throne of David forever (II Sam 7:13; Jer 33:17).

4 And declared *to be* **the Son of God with power, according to the spirit of holiness, by the resurrection from the dead:**

4. And declared to be the Son of God with power. Notice that although Jesus Christ was *made* of the seed of David according to the flesh, He was not *made* the Son of God. The word rendered **declared** (Gr *horizō*) has the meaning of "appointed" or "marked out by unmistakable signs." It is used in Acts 10:42; 17:31 of Christ's appointment as Judge. Christ was not *made* but eternally is the Son of God. This fact graphically and unmistakably was revealed to the world **according to the spirit of holiness, by the resurrection from the dead.** There is an obvious antithesis between **according to the flesh** and **according to the spirit.** Here is a distinction between the two states of Christ's humiliation and His exaltation. Christ's humiliation came when He voluntarily was made in the likeness of men (Phil 2:7) and

His exaltation when He was resurrected by the Holy Spirit of God.

5-6. Grace and apostleship. Probably better translated "grace of apostleship," Paul regards his calling as a heavenly gift. The purpose of his apostleship is **for obedience to the faith among all nations, for his name.** Paul wants to bring the nations of the world, both Jew and Gentile, into obedience to the faith (i.e., the body of doctrine which he teaches). **Among whom are ye also the called of Jesus Christ.** The expression **the called** is a favorite one of the apostle to indicate those who have trusted the Lord Jesus as Saviour (cf. 8:28).

5 By whom we have received grace and apostleship, for obedience to the faith among all nations, for his name:
6 Among whom are ye also the called of Jesus Christ:

7 To all that be in Rome, beloved of God, called to be saints: Grace to you and peace from God our Father, and the Lord Jesus Christ.

7. To all that be in Rome, beloved of God, called to be saints. Sainthood is not to be identified with the practice of canonization which later arose out of the Roman church. The saint is one called of God and "holy," that is (Heb *quadosh*) set apart to God. The saints of Rome were **beloved of God,** which marks them out as the undeserving yet grateful recipients of God's love, **Grace to you and peace.** One of the interesting features of the Pauline style is that in every one of the Pauline Epistles these two words appear together. Grace and peace are never separated by Paul (cf. Rom 1:7; I Cor 1:2; I Cor 1:2; Gal 1:3; Eph 1:2; Phil 1:2; Col 1:2; I Thess 1:1; II Thess 1:2; I Tim 1:2; II Tim 1:2; Tit 1:4; and Phm 3). The reason is that Paul, a Hebrew of the Hebrews but the apostle to the Gentiles, was the bridge between the Jews and Gentiles of the first-century church. **Grace** is the typical Greek greeting (*charis*) whereas **peace** is the usual Hebrew greeting (*shalom*). Paul always uses both to bind Jews and Gentiles together in the Lord.

B. Expression of Personal Feelings. 1:8-15.

8 First, I thank my God through Jesus Christ for you all, that your faith is spoken of throughout the whole world.

8. Your faith is spoken of throughout the whole world. So strong was the faith of these Roman believers that, as the church of the Thessalonians (I Thess 1:8), Paul speaks of it in world-wide terms. The expression **throughout the whole world** is the common one for "everywhere."

9 For God is my witness, whom I serve with my spirit in the gospel of his Son, that without ceasing I make mention of you always in my prayers;

9. Whom I serve with my spirit. Without ceasing I make mention of you always in my prayers. Paul's prayer life is intertwined with his life of service. The word the apostle uses for service (Gr *latruō*) is that of the function of a priest in the Temple and is very frequently used by Paul to mean worship (cf. Phil 3:3; II Tim 1:3). A great deal of Paul's priestly service to the Lord was his regular program of intercessory prayer on the behalf of other believers (cf. Eph 1:16; Phil 1:3; Col 1:3; I Thess 1:2; II Tim 1:3; Phm 4).

10 Making request, if by any means now at length I might have a prosperous journey by the will of God to come unto you.
11 For I long to see you, that I may impart unto you some spiritual gift, to the end ye may be established;
12 That is, that I may be comforted together with you by the mutual faith both of you and me.
13 Now I would not have you ignorant, brethren, that oftentimes I purposed to come unto you, (but was let hitherto,) that I might have some fruit among you also, even as among other Gentiles.

10-13. Paul now states his purpose in wanting to come to Rome. He says, **For I long to see you** (in current idiom, "I am homesick for you"). This deep longing of Paul to be with the Roman believers arises out of three reasons. First, **that I may impart unto you some spiritual gift.** Paul wants to be more than a blessing to them, he wants to build them up in the most holy faith and explain to them more fully what it means to be "in Christ Jesus." Knowing that this local church had not had the apostolic stamp of approval placed on it, Paul wishes to visit them to do so. Secondly, Paul desires the Romans to reciprocate, **that I may be comforted together with you.** It has been the lifelong desire of the apostle to preach the gospel in Spain where no man had laid a foundation. Rome was to be a stopover for that journey. Paul would need lodging, food, and Christian fellowship. He desires the Roman believers to provide these for him. Finally, verse 13 indicates that Paul's desire is not only to evangelize Spain but also the capital of the Gentile world. He says, **that I might have some fruit among you also.** An evangelist at heart, Paul does not look to Rome simply as a launching pad for further evangelistic effort but as a needy field itself.

Even as among other Gentiles would seem to indicate that although the nucleus of the Roman church was originally Jewish, it is now predominantly a Gentile church.

14 I am debtor both to the Greeks, and to the Barbarians; both to the wise, and to the unwise.

14. I am debtor. Paul views himself as a debtor to the whole world. He has been placed in debt by the love of Jesus Christ (II Cor 5:14). The Pauline concept of Christian service is that each believer is deeply in debt. It is probably this same concept that inspired Isaac Watts to pen the words of the hymn "At the Cross" when he said, "But drops of grief can ne'er repay the debt of love I owe. Here, Lord, I give myself away, 'tis all that I can do." Paul felt he had a responsibility to give nothing less than himself to the propagation of the gospel by which he was saved.

To the Greeks, and to the Barbarians. In the Jewish mind, there were but Jews and heathen; in the Greek mind there were Greeks and barbarians; but in God's mind there are but the saved and the lost (I Jn 5:12). From the golden age of Athens under Pericles in the fifth century B.C. until the decline of the empire, Greece was more highly civilized and educated than any other society of its time. However, when Paul contrasted the Greek with the barbarian, it is evident that he included the Romans with the Greeks. Rome was heir to Greek culture and learning. Most people looked upon Rome as a militarized extension of the Grecian Empire. This is not to say that the Romans had no culture of their own, but that it was successfully synthesized with the Grecian so as to form a new culture, the Graeco-Roman. The Roman orator-author Cicero (106-43 B.C.) places Greece and Rome in the same category in his treatise *De Finis, On Ends.* He says, "not only Greece and Italy, but also every foreign country." Therefore, Paul can readily say to the Romans that he is debtor both to the Greeks (Gr *Hellenes*), including the Romans, and the less civilized barbarians (Gr *barbaroi*).

15 So, as much as in me is, I am ready to preach the gospel to you that are at Rome also.

15. I am ready to preach. This expression appears to be the middle statement of a trilogy of three first-person statements concerning Paul's preaching of the gospel of Christ. The first segment is **I am debtor.** The third statement is **I am not ashamed.**

All of us are debtors to Christ. All of us should be unashamed of the gospel of Christ. But not all are ready to preach that gospel. Paul was not only able and willing, but he was ready to preach as well. He was a clean vessel, not just a chosen vessel. He was ready to be used of God. Paul was like the old country preacher who, when asked how he prepared his Sunday sermon, said, "I read myself full, think myself clear, pray myself hot, and let myself go." Many believers are not ready to be let go because they are not read full, clear-minded about Christian doctrine, or prayed up. Paul was ready to be "let go" and sent to Rome by any means.

C. Statement of the Theme. 1:16-17.

16 For I am not ashamed of the gospel of Christ: for it is the power of God unto salvation to every one that believeth; to the Jew first, and also to the Greek.

16. For I am not ashamed of the gospel. In stating the theme of the gospel as the good news that Christ died for our sins, Paul makes a bold claim that he is not ashamed of that news. He may have had our Lord's warning in the back of his mind (Lk 9:26). Someone might well ask why Paul could have been ashamed of the gospel. Perhaps he would be ashamed to spread the gospel because of the fierce persecution for those who had come to believe in this message. As a Jew, Paul could have been ashamed of the gospel because the Jews abhorred it as subverting the law. As an educated man he might have been ashamed because to the wise Greek the gospel was sheer foolishness. He may have been ashamed of the gospel of Christ because, by the pagans, Christians were branded as atheists, a brand no Pharisee could tolerate. This atheism was not a theoretical denial of the existence of the gods (Gr *asebeia*), but was a practical refusal to recognize pagan deities as truly God (Gr *atheos*). For those whom the Romans considered to be "Christian atheists," the consequences were severe, perhaps forced labor in mines or even capital punishment.

Although for these and other reasons Paul could have been ashamed of the gospel of Christ, there is never a hint in the Pauline corpus that he ever was ashamed. Quite the contrary (cf. Rom 9:33; 10:11; II Tim 1:8, 11-12, 16). **It is the power of God unto salvation.** Paul now gives the reason why he is not ashamed of the gospel of Christ. It is the power of God, the great and admirable mystery which has been hidden with God from before the foundation of the world. The gospel, through the agency of the Holy Spirit of God, does what no amount of mere human reasoning or argumentation can do. The gospel compels men to face the reality of their own sin and guilt, the inevitability of divine judgment, and the need for a perfect substitute to make atonement for sin, if man is to survive at all. The gospel is the dynamite (Gr *dinamis*) which blasts away self-complacency, self-delusion, and sinful self-reliance. This nothing else can do, for nothing else is in itself the **power of God unto salvation to every one that believeth.**

To the Jew first. Paul has deliberately proclaimed that the gospel is for everyone. He did so because there were many Jewish believers who thought the gospel was not for the heathen, the Gentile. Paul says no. The gospel is for all, it is the power of God unto salvation to everyone, without distinction of age, sex, race, or condition. But faith is the key to receiving the gospel and the gospel is to be proclaimed first to the Jew.

From the days of Abraham the Jews have always been highly distinguished from all the rest of the world in many and great divine privileges. They are the royal family of the human race. They are the rightful heirs to the Promised Land. They are the chosen nation of God. They were given the oracles of God. They had a covenant with Jehovah God. It was through the Jews that Christ Jesus came. Originally the preaching of the gospel was addressed to them exclusively (Mt 10:5-6). During His ministry on earth Jesus Christ was a minister to the circumcision only (Rom 15:8). The spread of the gospel was to begin in Jerusalem, the center of Judaism (Acts 1:8). Paul did not forget that the gospel was to be first directed toward God's chosen nation, Israel, but the words **and also to the Greek** indicate that Paul was well aware that the message of the gospel is a universal message, for everyone needs it. It is not for just the Jew or the Roman citizen, it is not just for the wise, but it is for the heathen and the Roman slave as well. The gospel is open to all, it is for everyone, but there is a condition or restriction put on that everyone. That restriction is faith. The gospel is for all who believe. It is efficacious to everyone **that believeth.**

17 For therein is the righteousness of God revealed from faith to faith: as it is written, The just shall live by faith.

17. For therein links verse 17 with verse 16; "for in it," that is in the gospel, is the rightness of God revealed. This explains why the gospel is the power of God.

The gospel is "dynamite" because through it the righteousness of God is revealed. Righteousness is that aspect of God's holiness which is seen in His treatment of His creatures. Simply, righteousness is how God treats us. Jesus Christ is our righteousness. He is how God treats us. We are unrighteous, unholy, and unlovely. Yet Christ died for our sins (I Cor 1:30).

How is righteousness obtained? **From faith to faith.** Righteousness is received by faith in Christ Jesus and is in turn revealed in faithful living. Thus, in answer to the question, "How are the righteous to live?" Paul quotes Habakkuk 2:4, **"The just shall live by faith."** This faith implies more than mere acceptance of Christ's righteousness for salvation. It implies a life style that is characterized by faith and righteous living. It was this truth that excited Martin Luther and initiated the Protestant Reformation (1:18).

II. THE RIGHTEOUSNESS OF GOD NEEDED. 1:18-3:20.

A. The Need of the Heathen. 1:18-32.

With the introduction complete, thanksgiving made, and the theme of his epistle stated, Paul now turns to the heart of the doctrinal teaching in Romans. Paul has both good news and bad news for the world. The good news, which will shortly follow, is that God has provided an atonement for our sins. The bad news, which he explores first, is that all men need atonement for their sins. Before you can appreciate the good news, you must know that there is bad news. Before Paul tells us that the gift of God is eternal life, he tells us that the wages of sin is death. Verse 18 begins the groundwork which Paul lays for his case against man's self-righteousness. His aim is to show that the whole world is morally bankrupt, unable to receive a favorable verdict at the judgment bar of God, and desperately in need of divine mercy and pardon.

1. The heathen have clearly seen God. 1:18-20.

18 For the wrath of God is revealed from heaven against all ungodliness and unrighteousness of men, who hold the truth in unrighteousness;

18. For the wrath of God is revealed. God's attitude toward the sin of mankind is not one of tolerance. He does not simply hold man accountable for what may be reasonably expected of him in view of man's nature as a sinner. If God did, His holiness and purity would be soiled by complicity with our guilt. God hates man's sin. His wrath is a holy aversion to all that is evil. Wrath is as essential to divine righteousness as love and mercy are. God could not be free from wrath unless He were also free from all concern about His moral universe.

Against all ungodliness and unrighteousness of men. Ungodliness has to do with religion, our relation to a sovereign God. Unrighteousness has to do with morality, our relation to our fellowman. Ungodliness is sin against the being of God. Unrighteousness is sin against the will of God. Man is both a religious sinner (he is ungodly) and a moral sinner (he is unrighteous). The unrighteous man lives as if there were no will of God revealed. The ungodly man lives as if there were no God at all. God's wrath is against both.

Who hold the truth in unrighteousness. The word **hold** (Gr *katechō*), carries the meaning of "hold down," "keep back," or "suppress." Those who are unrighteous and ungodly restrain the truth of God's righteousness. The meaning of this word is clearly seen in the way it is used in Luke 4:42, "And when it was day, he (Christ) departed and went into a desert place: and the people sought him, and came unto him, and stayed him, that he should not depart from them." Paul contends that the heathen have had the righteousness of God revealed to them, yet they suppress the truth of His righteousness for they are ungodly and unrighteous.

19 Because that which may be known of God is manifest in them; for God hath shewed it unto them.
20 For the invisible things of him from the creation of the world are clearly seen, being understood by the things that are made, even his eternal power and Godhead; so that they are without excuse:

19-20. The apostle now anticipates the question: "If these ungodly men do not have full knowledge of God, are they then really lost?" The key word in Paul's answer is the first word of verse 19, **Because.** Paul will now present two lines of argument which will prove that the condemnation of the sinner does not rest upon the depth of his knowledge of God but upon what use he makes of that knowledge. **That which may be known of God is manifest in them.** Paul's first reason that the heathen are lost (or any man who willingly suppresses the knowledge of God) is because of the revelation of God in nature. Man has a sufficient knowledge of God to make him responsible to God. That knowledge arises from the fact that **the invisible things of him from the creation of the world are clearly seen** (cf. Ps 19:1). Man's mind is capable of drawing obvious conclusions from effect to cause. To the animals below us the phenomena of nature may just be a spectacle before their eyes, but make no impression on their minds. But to man, they have a language, a communication. They awake wonder, awe, a basic idea of God and His righteousness. **Even his eternal power and Godhead.** Nature does not simply give the impression that God is an abstract principle but a real person, the Supreme Person, transcendent above His creation and not part of it. The testimony of nature alone is sufficient to lead man to an understanding of the personal, righteous nature of God, **so that they are without excuse.**

2. The heathen have clearly rejected God. 1:21-23.

21 Because that, when they knew God, they glorified *him* **not as God, neither were thankful; but became vain in their imaginations, and their foolish heart was darkened.**
22 Professing themselves to be wise, they became fools,
23 And changed the glory of the uncorruptible God into an image made like to corruptible man, and to birds, and fourfooted beasts, and creeping things.

21-23. Paul's second line of argument is that the heathen are lost because of the revelation of God to the conscience. **They glorified him not as God.** As if the natural world around us isn't enough, God has planted in the heart of every man the knowledge that there is a righteous God. Though the heathen knew that He was God and deserved to be glorified, they willfully chose not to glorify Him as God. They did not ascribe to His person the holiness, perfection, and sovereignty which are His alone. **Neither were thankful.** To add injury to insult, the heathen accepted the good things of nature from the hand of God, but were not thankful for them. **But became vain in their imaginations.** In order to suppress the witness of the ordered structure of the universe, and the innate testimony of the conscience, fallen man had to develop a reasoning process of imagination. This reasoning is described by God as vain because the whole structure of man-made philosophy is devoid of divine truth and therefore invalid. Thus, by suppressing the truth of God and believing their man-made falsehood, they plunged their foolish heart deeper into darkness. When they exalted their human reasoning and paraded their wisdom before their peers, they acted as fools. The foolish heart is not one deficient in intelligence but one deficient in the moral understanding of who God is.

Laboring under the handicap of this extreme deficiency, the heathen **changed the glory of the uncorruptible God into an image.** By creating a god suitable to their own fallen conception of deity the heathen have violated the first commandment. They have devised their own concept of divinity and placed it above the one true God. **Made like corruptible man, and to birds, and fourfooted beasts, and creeping things.** More than just conceptualizing what they thought God ought to be, the heathen actually created animal-like images of their concept of God. In so doing they violated the second commandment.

The apostle has thus given two reasons why the man without God is lost and deserving of condemnation: (1) because of the revelation of God in nature (vss. 19-20); and (2) because of the revelation of God in their conscience (vss. 21-23). The wrath of God is revealed from heaven against all who suppress the truth of these two witnesses. To the heathen who does not suppress this fundamental light, the Lord Jehovah grants additional enlightenment of His person. But whoever is guilty of suppressing the available truth about God does not receive light unto salvation.

3. The heathen have clearly become reprobate. 1:24-32.

24 Wherefore God also gave them up to uncleanness through the lusts of their own hearts, to dishonour their own bodies between themselves:

24. Wherefore God also gave them up to uncleanness. Ungodliness and unrighteousness have a definite terminal point and that is idolatry. The word **wherefore** indicates that the retribution to follow finds its ground in the antecedent sins and is therefore justifiable. Because the heathen participated in idolatry, God gave them up to uncleanness. As seen by Paul's usage of this term elsewhere (cf. II Cor 12:21; Gal 5:19; Eph 5:3; Col 3:5; I Thess 4:7), **uncleanness** means sexual aberration by which they would **dishonor their own bodies between themselves.**

25 Who changed the truth of God into

25. Who changed the truth of God into a lie. Suppression of

a lie, and worshipped and served the creature more than the Creator, who is blessed for ever. Amen.

26 For this cause God gave them up unto vile affections: for even their women did change the natural use into that which is against nature:

27 And likewise also the men, leaving the natural use of the woman, burned in their lust one toward another; men with men working that which is unseemly, and receiving in themselves that recompence of their error which was meet.

28 And even as they did not like to retain God in *their* knowledge, God gave them over to a reprobate mind, to do those things which are not convenient;

29 Being filled with all unrighteousness, fornication, wickedness, covetousness, maliciousness; full of envy, murder, debate, deceit, malignity; whisperers,

30 Backbiters, haters of God, despiteful, proud, boasters, inventors of evil things, disobedient to parents,

31 Without understanding, covenant breakers, without natural affection, implacable, unmerciful:

32 Who knowing the judgment of God, that they which commit such things are worthy of death, not only do the same, but have pleasure in them that do them.

CHAPTER 2

THEREFORE thou art inexcusable, O man, whosoever thou art that judgest:

the truth which God gave to the heathen became the basis for their idolatry and thus they **worshipped and served the creature more than the Creator.** They degraded themselves in that which they worshiped and exalted those things created to a higher position than the One who created them.

26-27. For this cause God gave them up unto vile affections. These **vile affections** (Gr *pathē atimias*) were passions of infamy. The apostle goes on to explain that **their women did change the natural use into that which is against nature.** Sexual perversion always accompanies idolatry. **And likewise also the men . . . burned in their lust one toward another; men with men.** Homosexuality is likewise the result of idolatry. Although today the world seeks to popularize and legitimize homosexuality, nevertheless it is despicable to God and condemned by Him. Increased homosexuality is a sign of the soon return of the Lord (II Tim 3:2). God never overlooks this blatant misuse of the body and consequently those who have engaged in this perversion receive **in themselves that recompense of their error which was meet.**

28. God gave them over to a reprobate mind. The word **reprobate** means "unapproving" or "undiscerning." Since they had suppressed the truth of God revealed to them, the heathen did not retain God in their knowledge and consequently, for the third time in almost as many verses, the apostle records that God gave them up (or over) to what they wanted all along. When He did so, the results were disastrous. The effects of their abandonment result solely from the corruption of the human heart; this cannot be blamed on God.

29-31. Being filled expresses (by the Greek perfect tense) that the heathen were not simply tainted by the catalogue of sins that follow but were in fact saturated with them. Thus the ugly character traits listed as the result of abandonment by God include: **unrighteousness,** or injustice (Gr *adika*) **fornication, wickedness** (Gr *poneria*), **covetousness** (Gr *pleonexia*, grasping for more than is needed), **maliciousness** (Gr *kakia*, intending evil toward others), . . . **whisperers, Backbiters, haters of God, despiteful, proud, boasters, inventors of evil things, disobedient to parents, Without understanding, covenant-breakers, without natural affection . . . unmerciful.** This gallery of iniquity was not only true of the first-century heathen world but reads much like our newspapers today.

32. Who knowing the judgment of God . . . do the same, . . . have pleasure in them that do them. The heathen world is not unaware of God's displeasure with these activities. Therefore, fully cognizant of the consequences of their sin, they continue to defy the Lord God of heaven and take great pleasure in keeping company with those who do the same.

Paul's conclusion is that the heathen are never without a witness to the presence and personality of God. They have the witness of nature and the witness of their own conscience. However, the heathen have deliberately suppressed these witnesses to the truth and have consistently opted for a lie in place of the truth. They have chosen the course of idolatry, which is always accompanied by debauchery. Thus, God has revealed His wrath from heaven against all ungodliness and unrighteousness of men who suppress the truth of God. In addition, God has given them up to idolatry, to passions of infamy, and to an undiscerning and unapproving mind. Are the heathen lost? Yes, the entire heathen world is lost, deserving condemnation, desiring evil, and desperately wicked.

B. The Need of the Moralist. 2:1-16.

1. *Condemned by his own judgment. 2:1.*

2:1. Therefore thou art inexcusable, O man, whosoever thou art that judgest. In the last chapter Paul painted a picture

for wherein thou judgest another, thou condemnest thyself; for thou that judgest doest the same things.

of the deplorable condition of the heathen. The apostle knew, however, that there would be a whole class of men who would say "amen" to what he had said about the heathen. These were the self-righteous moralists. So Paul expands his argument to show that **all ungodliness and unrighteousness of men** (1:18) includes the moralist as well as the debauched heathen. The moralist is inexcusable when he judges the heathen for sin but is blind to his own sin. He only condemns himself when he condemns another. **For thou that judgest doest the same things.** It is obvious that the moral man was not involved in the sexual deviations of the heathen, else Paul could not call him a moral man. But he was inwardly living in an identical manner as the heathen was living outwardly. Perhaps the moral man did not commit adultery, but did he lust? Our Lord put them in the same category (Mt 5:27-28). Maybe the moral man did not steal, but did he covet? Stealing and covetousness are listed together in Mark 7:22. Perchance the moral man did not commit murder, but did he hate? The Bible says if you hate your brother you are guilty of murder (I Jn 3:15). No one dares judge another while he is doing the same thing because he is then condemned by his own judgment.

2. Condemned according to truth. 2:2-5.

2 But we are sure that the judgment of God is according to truth against them which commit such things.

2. The judgment of God is according to truth. When God judges it is always according to truth or in accordance with the facts. The moralist may attempt to hide the facts, but God always exposes them. The searching eye of God always ferrets out the truth.

3 And thinkest thou this, O man, that judgest them which do such things, and doest the same, that thou shalt escape the judgment of God?
4 Or despisest thou the riches of his goodness and forbearance and longsuffering; not knowing that the goodness of God leadeth thee to repentance?

3-4. And thinkest thou this, O man . . . that thou shalt escape the judgment of God? Or despisest thou the riches of his goodness and forbearance and long-suffering. Since the judgment of God is according to truth, it is foolhardy for the moralist to believe that God will judge the heathen and not him. Since he does in his heart what the heathen does in his life, the moralist must withstand the same judgment as the man he condemned. To put ourselves in the position of the moralist would mean to despise God's **goodness** (Gr *khrēstotēs*, lit., kindness), **forbearance** (Gr *anochē*, the willingness to tolerate the intolerance of others), and **long-suffering** (Gr *makrothymia*, patience which forgives until there is no more hope of repentance). **The goodness of God leadeth thee to repentance.** In judging others, the moralist has completely missed the truth that the purpose of God's goodness is to lead to repentance. It never occurs to the moralist that he personally needs the goodness of God just as the heathen does. He is unaware of his need for repentance.

5 But after thy hardness and impenitent heart treasurest up unto thyself wrath against the day of wrath and revelation of the righteous judgment of God;

5. But after thy hardness and impenitent heart. After years of glossing over his personal sin and guilt, the pride of the moralist will not allow him to have a change of mind (Gr *metanoia*) which is repentance. Thus his pride and sinful heart stockpile the wrath of God so that in the day of wrath, the day of God's righteous judgment, the Lord God will deal as justly with the moral man as he does with the heathen.

3. Condemned according to works. 2:6-10.

6 Who will render to every man according to his deeds:

6. Who will render to every man according to his deeds. When unsaved men appear before the final judgment bar of God, the Great White Throne Judgment, salvation will not be the issue there. This is a judgment to determine the degree of punishment. Thus God will mete out punishment in relation to the evil deeds of the individual. By the same token, at the judgment seat of Christ, where only believers appear, God will reward us according to our deeds.

7 To them who by patient continuance in well doing seek for glory and honour and immortality, eternal life:

7. To them who by patient continuance in well doing. Patient continuance in well doing does not mean that we are saved by doing good. Paul is expressing an eternal truth. Obedience to God does well in every dispensation. When Cain brought his fruit as an offering and God rejected it, God said, "If thou doest well, shalt thou not be accepted?" (Gen 4:7). Obedience to God in bringing the proper sacrifice would have been doing well. Today, in the age of grace, we do well by placing our faith in Christ Jesus as Saviour. Thus faith in Christ is patient continuance in well doing in this age. This is what will bring **glory and honor and immortality, eternal life.**

8 But unto them that are contentious, and do not obey the truth, but obey unrighteousness, indignation and wrath,
9 Tribulation and anguish, upon every soul of man that doeth evil, of the Jew first, and also of the Gentile;

8-9. But unto them that are contentious, and do not obey the truth. The moralist is likened to "those who are of contention." This formula is similar to other such expressions as "those who are of the circumcision" (4:12; Tit 1:10); "they which are of faith" (Gal 3:7); "they which are of the law" (4:14). Those who create a spirit of rivalry or factionalism have promised to them, **indignation** (Gr *orgē*), **wrath** (Gr *thymos*, a sudden outburst of anger), **tribulation** (Gr *thlipsis*, affliction), and **anguish** (Gr *stenochōria*, distress). As the gospel was promised to the Jew first and also to the Greek, so likewise these fruits of unrighteousness are **of the Jew first, and also of the Gentile.**

10 But glory, honour, and peace, to every man that worketh good, to the Jew first, and also to the Gentile:

10. But glory, honor, and peace to every man that worketh good. Opposed to the reward of the unrighteous, Paul now indicates that the reward of the righteous is glory, honor, and, instead of immortality as in verse 7, peace. The formula of impartiality is then the same, **to the Jew first, and also to the Gentile.**

4. Condemned without respect of persons. 2:11-16.

11 For there is no respect of persons with God.

11. For there is no respect of persons with God. An eternal truth is that as God deals in condemnation without favoritism, likewise He deals in salvation without favoritism. **Respect of persons** (Gr *prosōpolēmpsia*, lit., "lifting the face") simply means partiality (cf. Deut 10:17; II Chr 19:7; Acts 10:34; Gal 2:6; Eph 6:9; Col 3:25; I Pet 1:17). God is impartial because He does not change His pattern "to the Jew first," whether righteousness or unrighteousness is involved.

12 For as many as have sinned without law shall also perish without law: and as many as have sinned in the law shall be judged by the law;
13 (For not the hearers of the law *are* just before God, but the doers of the law shall be justified.

12-13. Unchecked and unatoned sin leads to perdition whether we are in the law or without the law. If the moralist is to live by the law then **not the hearers of the law are just before God, but the doers of the law shall be justified.** The antithesis between merely hearing the law and doing it is elaborated in James 1:22-25. **The doers of the law** is an expression also found in the literature of the Dead Sea Scrolls. The moralist (now identified with the Jews, vs. 9) is no better off than the heathen if the moralist has the law but does not keep it. The reason follows in the next verses.

14 For when the Gentiles, which have not the law, do by nature the things contained in the law, these, having not the law, are a law unto themselves:
15 Which shew the work of the law written in their hearts, their conscience also bearing witness, and *their* thoughts the mean while accusing or else excusing one another;)
16 In the day when God shall judge the secrets of men by Jesus Christ according to my gospel.

14-16. For when the Gentiles, which have not the law, do by nature the things contained in the law, these . . . are a law unto themselves. Although the Gentiles do not possess the Old Testament law, nevertheless they do those things which are contained in the law. This is because of **the law written in their hearts, their conscience also bearing witness.** The Gentiles manifested a moral principle at work in their hearts, because when they broke their own ethical code, their conscience (Gr *syneidēsis*) would prick them and cause them to feel guilt. The result of their guilt, however, was they would excuse themselves by making a defense for their actions. But Jew and Gentile alike must face a day of judgment with God when the **secrets of men** (Gr *ta krypta*) are judged by the Lord Jesus Christ according to the truth of the gospel preached by Paul.

C. The Need of the Jew. 2:17-3:8.

1. His law cannot make him righteous. 2:17-24.

17 Behold, thou art called a Jew, and restest in the law, and makest thy boast of God,

17. Behold, thou art called a Jew, and restest in the law. Israelites who remained in Palestine, or who returned to it after the Babylonian captivity, were designated as "Jews," even though tribes other than Judah were included. Paul calls himself a "Jew" in Acts 21:39 but "an Israelite" in Romans 11:1 and "a Hebrew" in Philippians 3:5. All three names refer to the same people; but in a technical sense "Hebrew" is the racial name, "Israel" is the national name, and "Jew" is the religious name of the sons of Jacob. The Jews rested in the law because it was described as "wisdom and . . . understanding in the sight of the nations" (Deut 4:6). The Jew did not have to travel around the world to study in a distant university. He did not have to rely on the philosophy of the Gentiles. The Jew trusted his law to be all that he needed and the best education he could get. Thus he boasted in the God who gave that law.

18 And knowest *his* will, and approvest the things that are more excellent, being instructed out of the law;

18. And knowest his will, and approvest the things that are more excellent, being instructed out of the law. Because he had received catechetical training in the law as a youth, and rabbinical teaching as a man, the Jew felt confident that he could prove (Gr *dokimazō*) or discern those things that are more excellent.

19 And art confident that thou thyself art a guide of the blind, a light of them which are in darkness,
20 An instructor of the foolish, a teacher of babes, which hast the form of knowledge and of the truth in the law.

19-20. Confident that he would be saved by his law, the Jew was convinced that he had been made righteous and therefore was able to assume four roles: **a guide of the blind** (the blind being the Gentile in his unjewish darkness); **a light of them which are in darkness** (the Gentile needs to be enlightened by the Jew who was enlightened by the law); **an instructor of the foolish** (because he did not know the law, the Gentile was a fool); **a teacher of babes** (the Gentile was immature, an object of Jewish disgust).

21 Thou therefore which teachest another, teachest thou not thyself? thou that preachest a man should not steal, dost thou steal?
22 Thou that sayest a man should not commit adultery, dost thou commit adultery? thou that abhorrest idols, dost thou commit sacrilege?
23 Thou that makest thy boast of the law, through breaking the law dishonourest thou God?

21-23. There is a touch of sarcasm in Paul's question, **Thou therefore which teachest another, teachest thou not thyself?** The Jews were prepared to teach the heathen Gentiles the commandments of the law, but were themselves breaking these commandments. **Dost thou steal?** (the eighth commandment), **dost thou commit adultery?** (the seventh commandment), **dost thou commit sacrilege?** (lit., "Do you rob temples"), (the second commandment). The Jews were ready to preach morality but their lives did not back up their message. They were stealing from one another, perhaps by collecting an extreme interest; they were committing adultery; they were profaning the house of God by commercialism; and thus Paul asked the biting question, **Thou that makest thy boast of the law, through breaking the law dishonorest thou God?** Transgression of the law brings dishonor to God. The Jews claim to have known the law but were silent in claims to have kept it.

24 For the name of God is blasphemed among the Gentiles through you, as it is written.

24. For the name of God is blasphemed among the Gentiles through you. This quotation from Isaiah 52:5 confirms that the inadequacies in the life-styles of the Jews caused the Gentiles to speak lightly of the God of Israel. The Word of God was actually being blasphemed among the Gentiles because of the inconsistency of the Jews. Much the same thing could be said today about hearers of the Word but not doers. The Jews rested in his law, but since he did not keep it, his law could not make him righteous.

2. His circumcision cannot make him righteous. 2:25-27.

25 For circumcision verily profiteth, if thou keep the law: but if thou be a breaker of the law, thy circumcision is made uncircumcision.

25. For circumcision verily profiteth, if thou keep the law. Notice that the apostle did not say "Circumcision verily justifieth." That has never been true. But circumcision is not a meaningless rite if it aids in keeping the law. However, when the Jew does not keep the law, **thy circumcision is made uncircumcision.** If the Jew trusts in his circumcision for salvation, *and does not keep the law*, his circumcision is made void.

26 Therefore if the uncircumcision keep the righteousness of the law, shall not his uncircumcision be counted for circumcision?
27 And shall not uncircumcision

26-27. If the uncircumcision keep the righteousness of the law. Now the tables are turned completely. If an uncircumcised Gentile gives his heart to God, and lives in a righteous relationship to the law, he is more pleasing to God than the circumcised Jew who does not. **And shall not uncircumcision . . . if it fulfill**

which is by nature, if it fulfil the law, judge thee, who by the letter and circumcision dost transgress the law?

the law, judge thee . . . ? The sin of the circumcised but unworthy Jew will be graphically demonstrated by the example of the Gentile who, though uncircumcised, nevertheless pleases God. Lack of circumcision would not condemn a Gentile, just as the possession of circumcision would not save the Jew. The key is the law. If the law was broken then the Jew became as helpless as the Gentile. Therefore, the circumcised Jew is in the same pitiful state as the uncircumcised heathen if the Jew has broken the law. Since all the Jews have, Paul's conclusion is that his circumcision cannot save the Jew, for he has broken the law.

3. His birth cannot make him righteous. 2:28-29.

28 For he is not a Jew, which is one outwardly; neither is that circumcision, which is outward in the flesh:

29 But he is a Jew, which is one inwardly; and circumcision is that of the heart, in the spirit, and not in the letter; whose praise is not of men, but of God.

28-29. For he is not a Jew, which is one outwardly . . . But he is a Jew, which is one inwardly. Here we see the double sense in which the term "Jew" is used. Frequently people speak of "Christians" as a term in opposition to heathen. In another sense, true believers in the Lord are called Christians. Paul is making the case that not all who are called Jews are truly Jewish. Possession of the law does not make one Jewish. Circumcision does not make one Jewish. Even birth in a Jewish family does not make one Jewish. Paul says that two things are necessary to be truly Jewish: (1) to be born of Abraham through Isaac (**that circumcision, which is outward in the flesh**); and (2) to be spiritually in tune with Abraham's God (**circumcision is that of the heart, in the spirit**). No one can claim to be Jewish who is not born of Abraham through his son Isaac. But to the requirement of outward circumcision (ancestry from Abraham), Paul adds the requirement of the circumcision of the heart. This spiritual or ethical circumcision is seen throughout the Scriptures, e.g., "uncircumcised lips" (Ex 6:12); "uncircumcised ear" (Jer 6:10); "uncircumcised heart" (Lev 26:41). The Jew who is born after the seed of Abraham through Isaac, yet does not have his heart circumcised in the way that Abraham did, that is, "to love the Lord thy God with all thine heart" (Deut 30:6; see also Jer 4:4), is not truly a Jew. He is a Jew outwardly, but not inwardly. He is born of Abraham, but not born again by the Spirit of God. The only true Jew is one who is a Jew by race, and a believer by God's grace. Thus, birth alone cannot make a Jew righteous.

4. His arguments cannot make him righteous. 3:1-8.

At the beginning of chapter 3 Paul anticipates arguments in rebuttal to his conclusion that neither Israel's law, her circumcision, nor her birth could save her. These theoretical objections are stated in the even-numbered verses and Paul's answer to each objection is stated in the odd-numbered verses.

CHAPTER 3
WHAT advantage then hath the Jew? or what profit is there of circumcision?

3:1. What advantage then hath the Jew? If the Jews are condemned along with the heathen, what advantage is there in being the chosen nation of God? **Or what profit is there of circumcision?** Since circumcision is the sign of Israel's covenant relationship with God, what advantage is that relationship if being Jewish will not save?

2 Much every way: chiefly, because that unto them were committed the oracles of God.

2. Much every way. Paul contends that there are many privileges which God has granted to Israel. A list of them is given in chapter 11; it is not necessary for Paul to enumerate them here. Rather, he simply points out one as example of the others. **Unto them were committed the oracles of God.** One of the chief ancestral privileges of Israel is that they were the custodians of the oracles of God. Acts 7:38 and Hebrews 5:12 mention these oracles, the Old Testament Scriptures. It was a great advantage to the Jew to be singled out by God and entrusted with the reception, inscription, and transmission of the Old Testament Scriptures.

3 For what if some did not believe? shall their unbelief make the faith of God without effect?

3. Now a second argument is anticipated. **Shall their unbelief make the faith of God without effect?** As keepers of the Old Testament, the Jews had in fact failed to comprehend the message of the Old Testament, especially the prophetic and messianic passages. The unbelief of the Jews is seen in their rejection of Jesus as Messiah, and consequently they did not believe the oracles of God which they so carefully guarded. The question is, "Shall the unfaithfulness of Israel in this respect alter God's faithfulness?" Paul's answer is a classic.

4 God forbid: yea, let God be true, but every man a liar; as it is written, That thou mightest be justified in thy sayings, and mightest overcome when thou art judged.

4. God forbid. This expression (Gr *mē genoito*) corresponds to the Hebrew *chalilah* which is translated the same in the KJV of Genesis 44:17; Joshua 22:29; 24:16; I Kings 21:3; et al. It is an expression which indicates a recoiling abhorrence, utter shock, and disgust. It has been variously translated as "good heavens, no," "may it not prove to be so," "perish the thought," etc.

Let God be true, but every man a liar establishes a principle which is found throughout this epistle. God does not purpose or will according to extraneous influences but according to what He Himself is. If men prove unfaithful to God's oracles, He is nevertheless faithful in His promises to them. The quotation which follows is from Psalm 51:4 where King David had broken the covenant of God and had found in himself no righteousness or integrity of any kind. Paul quotes this verse in order that his readers may clearly see the difference between the faithfulness and integrity of God and the lack of the same in man.

5 But if our unrighteousness commend the righteousness of God, what shall we say? *Is* God unrighteous who taketh vengeance? (I speak as a man)
6 God forbid: for then how shall God judge the world?

5-6. A third objection is now theoretically advanced. **But if our unrighteousness commend the righteousness of God, what shall we say?** This is a clever but illogical argument. It is twisting Scripture to make what is inherently evil appear to be ultimately good. Paul anticipates someone saying, "If my unfaithfulness causes God's faithfulness to be more apparent, is not my sin by contrast enhancing the world's concept of the absolute holiness and faithfulness of God?" And a second question is: **Is God unrighteous who taketh vengeance?** Would it not be unjust of God to punish me for contributing to a more pristine picture of His true character?

The expression **I speak as a man** should not be understood as an absence of divine inspiration in recording these questions, but rather that Paul is using the form of human reasoning to express this inspired truth about God. Since God's justice is not something that may be called into question, Paul indicates that only foolish human reasoning would attempt to do so.

The answer to these questions is an emphatic **God forbid.** The consequence of this line of reasoning would be to deny God the divine right to judge any man. If God cannot judge men, then who can?

7 For if the truth of God hath more abounded through my lie unto his glory; why yet am I also judged as a sinner?

7. For if the truth of God hath more abounded through my lie; . . . why yet am I also judged as a sinner? Paul had been slandered by the Jews for teaching salvation by grace apart from works. Therefore he uses that situation to theorize a final argument from the Jews. If the doctrine of salvation which Paul preaches is a lie, and the truth is seen in contrast to Paul's teaching, then why is Paul also judged as a sinner? Should not he be considered a saint if his alleged false doctrine more clearly indicated what was true? Paul has turned the tables on the Jews by using their own logic and putting them in an untenable situation. They could not admit that Paul's teachings were true. But if they claimed them to be false, by their own logic, they would have to say that divine good arose out of Paul's doctrine.

8 And not *rather*, (as we be slanderously reported, and as some affirm that we say,) Let us do evil, that good may come? whose damnation is just.

8. We be slanderously reported. It was the Jewish argument that Paul was teaching the lie, **Let us do evil, that good may come.** For those who regarded the practice of religion as merely a matter of keeping the law, Paul's emphasis on justification by faith indeed seemed to make the law and its keeping superfluous. But justification by faith never meant believers could blatantly disregard the precepts of the law. If they did, it is theirs **whose damnation is just.** Damnation, or better condemnation, is executed on all those who, in light of their unfaithfulness, turn God's faithfulness into lasciviousness and license. This Antinomian philosophy is further condemned in chapter 6:2ff.

God is just in condemning the Jews for they have sinned against Him and that their sin enhances His own righteousness is but a diversion from their own culpability as sinners. The justified man, whether heathen, moralist, or Jew, must never do evil. Arguments to the contrary can never save anyone.

D. The Need of the Whole World. 3:9-20.

Paul has shown that the heathen are lost because, even though they had the witness of both nature and conscience, they suppressed God's truth to them. He has shown also that the moral man is lost because even though he outwardly put on a facade to judge the heathen, inwardly he was guilty of the same sins. Likewise the Jew is lost because he has not kept the law, and neither his circumcision, ancestry, nor arguments can save him from the condemnation of disobedience. Now Paul wraps up his argument and the summation assumes the terminology of the courtroom.

1. The charge against the whole world. 3:9

9. The Jews enjoyed certain privileges as the elect nation of God, but these privileges did not include special treatment at the judgment bar of God. So to the question, **are we better than they?**, Paul's answer is **No, in no wise.** His reason is simple. **For we have before proved both Jews and Gentiles, that they are all under sin.**

The first step in the judicial procedure is to make an accusation or charge against the offender. This Paul does when he says **they are all under sin.** The word **prove** (Gr *proaitiaomai*) is a combination of two Greek words, *pro* meaning "before" and *altiaomai* meaning "to bring an accusation against" or "press formal charges." Paul has charged the entire world with being innately sinful. If the evidence is sufficient and the charge can be proved, the whole world will be judged guilty before God. Notice he does not say "all have sinned" but that all are **under sin.** This means they are all under the penalty as well as the power of sin. The apostle has in mind here a very definite contrast between being "under sin" and being "under grace." Romans 6:14-15 speaks of being "under grace" with our sins pardoned and ourselves justified.

2. The indictment against the whole world. 3:10-18.

10. Next in the judicial procedure is an indictment. Webster defines indictment as " a charge; accusation; specifically, a formal written accusation charging one or more persons with the commission of a crime" (*Webster's New World Dictionary*). An indictment is then a formal, written charge and every indictment must have at least one count, one specific charge to it. The more serious the crime, the more counts to the indictment. Paul immediately follows this pattern by quoting from a series of Old Testament passages which demonstrate, in no less than fourteen counts, the perversity and depravity of the entire world. **As it is written, There is none righteous, no, not one.** This same theme is seen throughout the Old Testament and is summarized in Psalm 14:1-3. Righteousness is not only the key word in this epistle, it is also the criterion by which sin is judged.

11. There is none that understandeth. Not a verbatim quote, this charge is derived from Psalm 14:2; 53:3. Here understanding is not mental but spiritual. The world is totally lacking in spiritual discernment (Eph 4:18). The natural man may not be mentally deranged, but he is certainly spiritually deranged and incapable of spiritual understanding (I Cor 2:14).

There is none that seeketh after God. In Psalm 53:2-3 David remarked that there is no man who innately seeks after God

---

9 What then? are we better *than they?* No, in no wise: for we have before proved both Jews and Gentiles, that they are all under sin:

10 As it is written, There is none righteous, no, not one:

11 There is none that understandeth, there is none that seeketh after God.

12 They are all gone out of the way, they are together become unprofitable; there is none that doeth good, no, not one.

13 Their throat is an open sepulchre; with their tongues they have used deceit; the poison of asps is under their lips:

14 Whose mouth is full of cursing and bitterness:

15 Their feet are swift to shed blood:

16 Destruction and misery are in their ways:

17 And the way of peace have they not known:

2218

because man is sinful. When the sinner is drawn by God, he then seeks the Lord Jesus Christ in repentance and confession (Jn 6:44). Because he naturally does not seek the Lord, man gives evidence of being guilty of unrighteousness.

12. They are all gone out of the way. Man has not only "missed the mark," he has also "perverted his path." In this quote from the LXX of Psalms 14:3; 53:4, the picture is of a camel caravan crossing the desert which has strayed from the route and cannot return to the proper path. Likewise man has lost his way by deviating from God's prescribed route of righteousness. **They are together become unprofitable** is the fifth count of the indictment. Man is unuseful, of no benefit. Like salt that has lost its savor or fruit that hast become rotten, so all men are viewed as useless, rotten, corrupted when compared to the righteousness of Christ.

There is none that doeth good, no, not one. Again the written indictment comes from Psalm 14. This means that he can do nothing of spiritual or eternal value. No matter what he does, as far as righteousness is concerned, it is nothing but filthy rags (Isa 64:6).

13. Their throat is an open sepulcher. This seventh count of the indictment is the first one that is specific. Paul addresses himself to the chief outlets through which the sinner can display his sin. He will speak to the sinners' throats, tongues, lips, and mouths. Paul shows his familiarity with the Old Testament by drawing on King David's prayer for protection in Psalm 5.

Nothing is more abominable than the stench rising from an open sepulcher. The apostle graphically portrays the conversation of the wicked by likening the filth that arises from their mouths with the stench of the open sepulcher.

With their tongues they have used deceit. The sugared tongue, which is used to butter up the boss, is next listed by Paul as characteristic of sinful men. He indicts the world for the Madison Avenue approach to life which makes something out of nothing and promises what cannot be performed.

The poison of asps is under their lips. This ninth indictment is reminiscent of the final speech of Zophar, one of Job's critical friends (Job 20:14-16). The poison of the asp was stored in a bag under the lips of the serpent. When he spoke of this deadly poison Paul probably had in mind the Egyptian cobra, *naja haje*, the reptile used by Pharaoh Tutankhamen as his imperial symbol. Of the evil and violent man David says, "They have sharpened their tongues like a serpent; adders' poison is under their lips" (Ps 140:3). The natural man's human speech is likened to this poison.

14. Whose mouth is full of cursing and bitterness. Psalm 10:7 indicates that man's mouth, which was created to speak the truth of God and praise Him continually, has been perverted to speaking of Satan and praising him through cursing and bitterness. You do not have to teach a man to curse; it is the common expression of the bitterness within him that is rooted in personal sin.

15. Their feet are swift to shed blood. Paul now turns his attention, not to man's words, but to his deeds. Quoting from Isaiah 59:7ff., the feet which were created to carry the gospel to the ends of the earth have in every era of history readily carried men violently to commit injustice and war with their fellowman (cf. Prov 1:7-19).

16. Destruction and misery are in their ways. This twelfth charge in the apostle's indictment lists not only what man is seeking but what he shall certainly receive if he continues in his unrighteous path. Calamity and misery always follow the sinner's futile search for happiness apart from Jesus Christ (cf. Jas 4:2).

17. And the way of peace have they not known. Unregenerated man can never find peace with his fellowman until peace has been made with his Creator. The United Nations and other peace-oriented agencies are doomed to failure because man is a ferocious animal. The most savage of animals does not destroy his own species to appease his hunger, but man destroys his fellowman for much less. The world is filled with animosity, hatred, terrorists, and murderers. Man will never be at peace with himself until he is at peace with God (Isa 59:8).

18 There is no fear of God before their eyes.

18. There is no fear of God before their eyes. Quoted from Psalm 36:1, this final charge is the fountain from which all the others spring. All the characteristics of man, his lack of understanding, his unprofitableness, his lack of peace, etc. stem from the fact that man does not fear God (Ps 36:2). Since man has no spiritual understanding, and the fear of the Lord is the beginning of wisdom, man is caught in a vicious circle. Only the external force of the Holy Spirit of God can break the circle of man's ignorance, arrogance, and guilt. Paul presents these fourteen specific, written counts in his indictment against the whole world.

3. The defense on behalf of the whole world. 3:19a.

19 Now we know that what things soever the law saith, it saith to them who are under the law: that every mouth may be stopped, and all the world may become guilty before God.

19a. Having charged the whole world with being under sin, and having listed fourteen counts to his indictment, Paul now moves in the judicial procedure to the defense on behalf of the world. He quickly anticipates the line of argument the Jew will use in his defense. The Jew will say that Paul's description of mankind in the preceding verses does not describe him but the heathen. So Paul makes it clear, **what things soever the law saith, it saith to them who are under the law.** Using law as the entire Old Testament Scriptures, the apostle presses that he was in fact speaking of Jews as well as the heathen for they had received the oracles of God and were bound by them.

Ordinarily, in a civil court, the time of the defense is usually given to flowery speeches, insinuation, discrediting of witnesses, muddling of the issues, etc. But this will not be the case at the judgment bar of God. When the evidence against the universal sinfulness and guilt of man is presented and the opportunity for defense comes, there will be no defense. **That every mouth may be stopped.** The mouth of the heathen will be stopped. The mouth of the moral man and religious man will be stopped. Even the mouth of the cursing and bitter man will be stopped. A silent world will stand in judgment before the bar of God and neither clever lawyers, plea bargaining, bribing the judge, nor an impassioned appeal will get the sinner off. The famous French infidel, Jean Jacques Rousseau, who refused to marry and sent his illegitimate children to an orphanage, exclaimed: "I will stand before God and defend my conduct!" Bad news for Rousseau. No one will utter a word in his defense, for no one will have a defense before the righteous God.

4. The verdict against the whole world. 3:19b-20.

19b. All that remains in the judicial procedure is the verdict. The charge has been made. The indictment has been read. No defense can be made for there is no supporting case for mankind. The verdict is now ready to be heard. **All the world may become guilty before God.** The verdict is guilty, the only thing it can be. The word guilty (Gr hypodikos) means to come under judgment. It does not presuppose guilt, but denotes the state of a man who has been justly charged with a crime and is both legally responsible for it and worthy of blame.

20 Therefore by the deeds of the law there shall no flesh be justified in his sight: for by the law is the knowledge of sin.

20. Therefore. Anytime we see the word "therefore" we ought to ask ourselves what is "therefore" there for, better translated "because." Paul is now coming to the summation of his argument and is about to make an application and draw a conclusion. He began back in chapter 1, verse 18, by proposing that the wrath of God is revealed from heaven against all ungodliness and unrighteousness of men. He has shown that the righteousness of God is sadly needed in the world. It is needed by the heathen, the moralist, the Jew. The righteousness of God is needed by the whole world. Having given his proposition, and the facts assembled from the Old Testament and present experience, Paul is now ready to draw a conclusion. He begins with **therefore** or "because."

By the deeds of the law there shall no flesh be justified in his sight. This free rendering of Psalm 143:2 (cf. Gal 2:16; 3:11) does not have the definite article "the" before law in the original language and thus Paul concludes that there is no law anywhere that can justify any man. The law of the heathen, the law of nature, the law of morality, the law of conscience, the law of Moses, none can justify a man and make him righteous in the sight of God. Even the law of Christ, laid down in the Sermon on the Mount, cannot justify a man. It is by the law that the knowledge of sin comes, a point expanded in 5:20; 7:7ff., but no law can save a man. The law can convict men of sin, it can define sin, but it cannot emancipate man from sin. Only the grace of God can do that. The whole world is sinful and desperately in need of the righteousness of God. But if that righteousness is to come to the individual, it must come through the agency of grace, sovereign grace, not human works.

III. THE RIGHTEOUSNESS OF GOD PROVIDED. 3:21-8:39.

Having clearly established that the righteousness of God is needed by man, Paul now proceeds to indicate that the righteousness of God is provided by God. Thus, the second major division of the Epistle to the Romans begins at 3:21 with reference to divine provision for human need.

A. The Provision for Justification. 3:21-5:21.

The apostle begins this section with the Greek phrase *nyni de* which is usually translated "but now." This phrase is used in the Pauline Epistles eighteen times and twice in Hebrews. It does not occur anywhere else in the New Testament. *Nyni de* is an adverb of time. It is a favorite expression of Paul when he makes a transition from a dark, gloomy picture to something wonderful that God does for us. Man has gotten himself in so deep that only God can get him out. God must enter man's world or else man will never enter God's world. In establishing guidelines for writers of tragedies in his day, the Roman poet Horace said, "Do not bring a god onto the stage, unless the problem is one that deserves a god to solve it" (Horace, *Ars Poetica*, 191ff.). The predicament of man is not one that Horace's gods can solve, but one that only Abraham's God can solve.

There are two very important words which pervade this passage. They are **righteousness** and **justify**. Although quite different in English, these two words are practically identical in Greek (*dikaios*, to be righteous; *dikaioō*, to justify). Justification is a legal declaration issued by God in which He pronounces the person free from any fault or guilt and acceptable in His sight. "To justify means 'to pronounce and treat as righteous.' It is vastly more than being pardoned; it is a thousand times more than forgiveness. You may wrong me and then come to me; and I may say, I forgive you. But I have not justified you. I cannot justify you. But when God justifies a man, He says, 'I pronounce you a righteous man. Henceforth I am going to treat you as if you never committed any sin'" (Alva J. McClain, *Romans the Gospel of God's Grace*, p. 107).

1. Justification is by faith alone. 3:21-31.

21. The righteousness of God. The righteousness of God is neither an attribute of God nor the changed character of the believer. As defined in Romans 1:17, the righteousness of God is Christ Himself, who met every demand of the law for us in our

21 But now the righteousness of God without the law is manifested, being witnessed by the law and the prophets;

stead, and is "made unto us . . . righteousness" (I Cor 1:30). God's righteousness is demonstrated and communicated to us through the cross.

This righteousness is **without the law.** This expression, which is literally "apart from the law" (Gr *chōris nomou*) is a strong expression categorically stating that righteousness is given totally apart from any law. See the same use of this word in Hebrews 4:15 where the Lord Jesus was tempted in all points as we are "yet totally apart from sin." Just as sin and Jesus Christ have nothing in common, so too the righteousness was not manifested in keeping the law but it was manifested at the cross when "he (God the Father) hath made him (God the Son) to be sin for us, who knew no sin; that we might be made the righteousness of God in him" (II Cor 5:21).

Being witnessed by the law and the prophets. Every time a man took his sacrifice to the Temple for a sin offering, confessed his sin, and killed the animal, he was testifying that he had faith in a righteousness that was not his own. Thus, the law bears witness to an external righteousness that God provides, but the law itself cannot provide. Likewise the prophets witness to this righteousness (cf. Isa 53:6; the same thought that is expressed in II Cor 5:21 and in I Pet 2:21-25).

22 Even the righteousness of God *which is* by faith of Jesus Christ unto all and upon all them that believe: for there is no difference:

22. The righteousness of God which is by faith of Jesus Christ. Since the genitive case is objective here, a more understandable rendering is that we are justified when the righteousness of God is applied to us "through faith in Jesus Christ." The righteousness of God then does not come to one who simply has faith in God but to those who by faith claim the name of Jesus Christ. Saving faith in Christ is a necessary part of the righteousness God provides (Acts 4:12). **Unto all and upon all them that believe.** Although the words **upon all** are not included in some manuscripts (S, A, B, D, and some other versions), nevertheless the meaning is still the same. God's righteousness is provided unto all men. We therefore go into all the world and preach the gospel to every creature (Mk 16:15). However, even though this righteousness is provided unto all, it is nevertheless applied upon only those who believe in Jesus Christ as Saviour. This is the only conditional element of the gospel. This righteousness is placed upon us as a cloak when by faith we receive Jesus Christ as Saviour. Righteousness is from God, through Jesus Christ, to all who receive Him by faith.

For there is no difference. This phrase **no difference** occurs in only one other place in the Epistle to the Romans. In this verse there is no difference between the need of the Jew and the Gentile. That need is explained in the expression **For all have sinned.** But just as there is no difference in human need likewise there is no difference in divine provision (Rom 10:12-13), the other place the expression occurs.

23 For all have sinned, and come short of the glory of God;

23. And come short of the glory of God. The brief but all-encompassing statement that **all have sinned** is further enhanced by the fact that both Jew and Gentile have come short of God's glory. What is the glory of God? The Bible frequently speaks of the glory of God appearing in the pillar of the cloud leading Israel (Ex 16:7-10); the tabernacle of the congregation at Kadesh (Num 14:10); the temple of Solomon (I Kgs 8:11); the Mount of Olives at Jerusalem (Ezk 11:23); etc. The glory of God now, however, rests in the person of Jesus Christ (Jn 1:14). The glory of God is the person of Jesus Christ.

When Stephen was stoned he looked steadfastly to heaven and saw the glory of God and (or even) Jesus standing at the right hand of God (Acts 7:55). The knowledge of the glory of God is said to be in the face of Jesus Christ (II Cor 4:6). When Paul says that we have come short of the glory of God he means that we do not measure up to the sinlessness of Jesus Christ. The Mosaic law served as God's standard of righteousness until the coming of Christ. But when the Lord Jesus was made a curse for

24 Being justified freely by his grace through the redemption that is in Christ Jesus:

us, He redeemed us from the curse of the law (Gal 3:19; Rom 10:4). Thus, the standard of God's holiness today is not the Old Testament law but the person of Jesus Christ.

24. Paul makes three observations about the righteousness of God which brings justification. He says that the righteous man is **justified freely** and that this justification is **by his grace and** provided **through the redemption that is in Christ Jesus.** Being justified freely means being justified without any prior conditions being met. Being justified by God's grace (in the Greek this expression is in the dative of means or instrumental case) indicates that not only is our justification without prior conditions being met but, on the other hand, it is graciously given. We do not merit justification, but we enjoy it. You cannot have both merit and grace. Our justification was by the grace of God. Beyond this, it was through the redemption that is in Christ Jesus. Since the word redemption signifies a buying back, it must have been accomplished by the payment of a price. The price of our redemption was the blood of Jesus Christ (Mt 20:28; I Cor 6:20; I Pet 1:18-19). Therefore, we are justified in the sight of God when the righteousness of Christ is placed upon us by the grace of God, freely and without cause. Only then God views us as ransomed by the blood of Christ.

25 Whom God hath set forth *to be* a propitiation through faith in his blood, to declare his righteousness for the remission of sins that are past, through the forbearance of God;
26 To declare, *I say*, at this time his righteousness: that he might be just, and the justifier of him which believeth in Jesus.

25-26. The main points of these two verses are: (1) God presented Jesus Christ as an atoning sacrifice, a propitiation. (2) This sacrifice was one of Christ's blood. (3) It is appropriated to the sinner by faith. (4) The sacrifice was necessary because in the past God had not fully punished sin. (5) It was also necessary to validate the justice of God. (6) This sacrifice demonstrated that it is God who justifies those who have faith in Jesus Christ.

God hath set forth to be a propitiation. The Bible is filled with types, which foreshadow future persons or events, and antitypes, which are the real person or events foreshadowed. The type is the arrow; the antitype is the target.

One of the most unique types in the Old Testament is the mercy seat. This was the lid on the ark of the covenant and was covered with gold. At each end was a golden cherub, whose wings stretched toward the center of the lid. The ark was the meeting place between God and man. It contained the tablets of the Mosaic law (Ex 25:16-22). Therefore, the mercy seat was that which covered the law of God.

When the translation of the Hebrew Old Testament was made into Greek, which is called the Septuagint, the Greek word chosen to translate "mercy seat" (Heb *kaphorah*) was *hilastērion* which means "the place of propitiation." To propitiate means to appease an offended party and the *hilastērion* (mercy seat) was the place where, by blood, the sins of Israel were atoned, the penalty paid, and wrath of God (the offended party) was appeased. It is certainly no coincidence that the word Paul uses here to describe Jesus Christ is the same word used for "mercy seat," the *hilastērion*. Jesus Christ is our mercy seat. He is the person by whom our sins were atoned, our penalty paid, and the offended party appeased. Jesus Christ is where God meets man.

Why did Jesus Christ become our propitiation? The answer is **to declare . . . his righteousness.** This is done by atoning for sins, which prior to Calvary were not permanently dealt with (Ps 50:16-23; Acts 17:30). God made His statement about sin at the cross. He not only said something about it, He did something about it. The righteousness of God is declared by atoning for present and future sins as well as past sins. Therefore God is the justifier of any man, past, present, or future, who places his faith in the blood of Jesus Christ.

27 Where *is* boasting then? It is excluded. By what law? of works? Nay: but by the law of faith.

27. These verses represent some final questions concerning justification and the conclusion Paul draws. **Where is boasting then?** In view of the fact that it is God who justifies us by providing Christ Jesus as our propitiation, what does this do to boasting? Paul's answer is **It is excluded.** Boasting is shut out, there is no room for man's boasting in the plan of God. **By what law? of works?** What is it that caused boasting to be inappropriate? Is it the law of works? Paul's answer, **Nay: but by the law of faith.** If man could work to be justified, then he would have reason to boast. But we are saved by God's grace through faith, not of works. And why? "Lest any man should boast (Eph 2:8-9).

28 Therefore we conclude that a man is justified by faith without the deeds of the law.

28. Paul now comes to a conclusion which is central to Pauline theology. He concludes **that a man is justified by faith without the deeds of the law.** This is the same conclusion which came to the heart of Martin Luther and spawned the Protestant Reformation. When this concept grasps our hearts we too come to the conclusion that salvation is *sola gratia, sola fide, soli Deo gloria* (by grace alone, through faith alone; to God alone be the glory).

29 *Is he* the God of the Jews only? *is he* not also of the Gentiles? Yes, of the Gentiles also:
30 Seeing *it is* one God, which shall justify the circumcision by faith, and uncircumcision through faith.

29-30. Is he the God of the Jews only? This question naturally arises in the Jewish mind, which still cannot conceive of the heathen being loved and justified by faith alone. Paul's answer to the question is **Yes, of the Gentiles also.** The reason is, **it is one God.** There is not a god of the Jews and another god of the Gentiles. There is but one God of Jews and Gentiles. Paul is not here simply teaching monotheism as opposed to heathen polytheism. As a Jew, a Hebrew of the Hebrews, but the called apostle to the Gentiles, Paul is the bridge between the Jew and the Gentile. But his message has made both one in Christ (Gal 3:28). The law of faith is the universal law of salvation by God.

31 Do we then make void the law through faith? God forbid: yea, we establish the law.

31. Do we then make void the law through faith? Because God saves through faith and not the deeds of the law, does this make the law useless? Paul gives his characteristic answer, **God forbid: yea, we establish the law.** Faith in Christ is the proper response to the law, for what the law could not do, Christ alone can do. The teaching that justification is by faith alone does not destroy the law. It completes the law, fulfills it, makes it meaningful. Justification by faith alone honors the law, because prior to Jesus Christ no one ever honored the law by perfectly keeping it. Since the Lord Jesus did, faith in the finished work of Christ on Calvary brings the ultimate respect to the law.

2. Justification is illustrated in the Old Testament. 4:1-25.

Paul has just firmly established that the righteousness of God is apart from the law (3:21) and that man is justified by faith apart from the deeds of the law (3:28). He is aware, however, that the Jew will offer the case of Abraham as rebuttal to this teaching. Paul's own people were still engrossed with the idea that being Jewish ought to afford them certain judicial privileges in the eyes of God. Thus, in this chapter, Paul analyzes the principle by which God saved Abraham. The father of Israel is an illustration of God's message of salvation in the Old Testament.

CHAPTER 4
WHAT shall we say then that Abraham our father, as pertaining to the flesh, hath found?
2 For if Abraham were justified by works, he hath *whereof* to glory; but not before God.

4:1-2. Abraham our father, as pertaining to the flesh. Paul's use of the possessive pronoun "our" and the qualifying phrase "as pertaining to the flesh" indicates that he is identifying himself with his people, the Jews. The question is, was Abraham saved by his acts of good work and obedience or was he saved by the faith of which Paul spoke in the preceding chapter?

3 For what saith the scripture? Abraham believed God, and it was counted unto him for righteousness.

3. As a Hebrew, a rabbi, a Sanhedrinist and a Pharisee, Paul knew exactly how to settle a Jewish argument. He could have debated the point, but instead he says, **For what saith the scripture?** This is a lesson we all should learn well. Whenever we are asked for a moral, ethical, or eternal answer, we should always ask ourselves, "What do the Scriptures say?" The apostle answers his own question by quoting what Moses records in Genesis 15:6. **Abraham believed God, and it was counted unto him for righteousness.** What do we mean when we say that faith was counted unto Abraham for righteousness? The word translated "counted" (Gr *logizomai*) is a commercial term which is

4 Now to him that worketh is the reward not reckoned of grace, but of debt.

5 But to him that worketh not, but believeth on him that justifieth the ungodly, his faith is counted for righteousness.

6 Even as David also describeth the blessedness of the man, unto whom God imputeth righteousness without works,

7 *Saying,* Blessed *are* they whose iniquities are forgiven, and whose sins are covered.

8 Blessed *is* the man to whom the Lord will not impute sin.

9 *Cometh* this blessedness then upon the circumcision *only,* or upon the uncircumcision also? for we say that faith was reckoned to Abraham for righteousness.

10 How was it then reckoned? when he was in circumcision, or in uncircumcision? Not in circumcision, but in uncircumcision.

11 And he received the sign of circumcision, a seal of the righteousness of the faith which *he had yet* being uncircumcised: that he might be the father of all them that believe, though they be not circumcised; that righteousness might be imputed unto them also:

12 And the father of circumcision to them who are not of the circumcision only, but who also walk in the steps of that faith of our father Abraham, which *he had* being *yet* uncircumcised.

used with regard to credits or debits. It means to set to one's credit or lay to one's charge. If you authorize your lawyer to write checks on your bank account, and he does so, although the check is written by him and money received by him, nevertheless the amount of the check is charged to you. This one word *logizomai,* occurs eleven times in this chapter and is translated by various words such as "count," "reckon," and "impute." Abraham was not righteous. Justification never means to make a man righteous. It only means that God reckons and treats a man as if he were righteous.

4-5. This principle is now further explained. Paul reasons that justification by works rests on the principle that men may earn their salvation by doing good. If this principle were true, good men would be saved by their good works and salvation would not be a gift at all. But justification by faith rests on the principle that God imputes righteousness to the ungodly as a free gift. Salvation is not, therefore, earned by the sinner but is freely given to him when he puts his faith in the blood of Jesus Christ.

6-8. Paul has made a case for Abraham's justification apart from works; now he strengthens that case with another Old Testament illustration. The purpose of introducing David's testimony is twofold: (1) The Jews' law regarding two witnesses (Deut 19:15; referred to by Jesus in Mt 18:16 and by Paul in II Cor 13:1 and I Tim 5:19). David corroborated what is said about Abraham and further illustrates salvation apart from works; (2) David gives witness that the same principle of justification was operative even for those living under the Mosaic law.

David also describeth the blessedness of the man, unto whom God imputeth righteousness without works. Even King David, the type of the Messianic King, knew the truth of the words he penned in Psalm 32:1-2, which Paul quotes in verses 7 and 8. As believers, our iniquities are forgiven and our sins are covered. The reason the believer's sins are not reckoned to him is that they have been imputed to Christ Jesus (cf. Isa 53; I Pet 2:24-25).

9-12. Paul has well argued that justification is by faith alone. He has illustrated, by the lives of Abraham and David, that God has never worked on a principle of justification by works. Yet it is difficult for the Jews, the sons of Abraham, to accept that they may be justified in exactly the same way as the heathen Gentiles. Thus, these verses introduce another potential argument against justification by faith.

It is true that both pre-law Abraham and under-law David received righteousness. But, so the Jew would argue, both of them were also circumcised. Since circumcision is the sign of the covenant between God and His chosen people (Gen 17:9-14), is it not possible that this was the ground of their justification? **Cometh this blessedness then upon the circumcision only, or upon the uncircumcision also?** Paul answers, **faith was reckoned to Abraham for righteousness.** This immediately prompts the question as to the timing of the reckoning of righteousness. **How was it then reckoned? when he was in circumcision, or in uncircumcision?** The answer is clear. Faith was reckoned to Abraham while he was yet uncircumcised.

The facts are these. (1) Genesis 15:6 records the event of Abraham receiving righteousness from God. (2) Sometime after that, Abraham had a son by Hagar when he was eighty-six years old (Gen 16:16). (3) At least one year had to elapse between the two events so that at the outside Abraham was eighty-five years old when righteousness was imputed to him. (4) Ishmael was thirteen years old when both he and Abraham were circumcised (Gen 17:25-26). (5) Abraham had righteousness imputed to him at least fourteen years before he was circumcised. Paul concludes that circumcision had nothing whatever to do with the imputation of righteousness to Abraham.

This does not mean circumcision was unimportant. Abraham received **the sign of circumcision, a seal of the righteousness of the faith.** Circumcision did not bring righteousness, but was the visible sign to Abraham's descendants of the righteousness that was imputed to him by faith. Also, circumcision was God's seal of righteousness. Once righteousness has been imputed to the individual, it is sealed there forever. This is true also of Christian baptism. It does not bring about salvation but is an outward sign declaring salvation and is God's seal of approval on the finished work of Christ in behalf of the believer. Abraham received righteousness before he was circumcised that he might be the father of all them that believe, whether circumcised or not, who also **walk in the steps of that faith of our father Abraham.** Abraham, therefore, not only bears a physical relationship with the nation Israel but also bears a spiritual relationship with all who believe by faith, whether Jew or Gentile.

13 For the promise, that he should be the heir of the world, *was* not to Abraham, or to his seed, through the law, but through the righteousness of faith.

14 For if they which are of the law *be* heirs, faith is made void, and the promise made of none effect:

15 Because the law worketh wrath: for where no law is, *there is* no transgression.

16 Therefore *it is* of faith, that *it might be* by grace; to the end the promise might be sure to all the seed; not to that only which is of the law, but to that also which is of the faith of Abraham; who is the father of us all,

13-16. Each of Abraham's descendants expected to receive the inheritance of Abraham. That inheritance was no less than the world. **For the promise, that he should be the heir of the world.** Although not directly stated, this promise is drawn from Genesis 12:3 and the correlative promises given in Genesis 18:18; 22:18, etc. Abraham's heritage was limited in geographical terms to the land between Egypt and the Euphrates (Gen 15:18; cf. 13:14ff.). But the promise was made to Abraham and **to his seed.** In Galatians 3:16 the "seed" is obviously Jesus Christ. The promise of inheriting the world must be understood then in relationship to the Messiah's future domination of this earth as "KING OF KINGS, AND LORD OF LORDS" (Rev 19:16). This promise will come to reality when the seed of Abraham, Jesus Christ, sits on the throne of David during the Millennium and rules the entire world with a rod of iron. Because of this, it is impossible that Abraham's inheritance can be obtained by law. No heir of Abraham, save Jesus Christ, has ever been able to entirely keep the law. If fulfillment of this promise depended on law-keeping, man's inability to keep the law would insure that the promise would never be fulfilled and thus would be **the promise made of none effect.**

The law worketh wrath. Eventually failure to keep the law imposes penalties which bring to the law-breaker the wrath of God. **For where no law is, there is no transgression.** Paul appears to be drawing on a current legal maxim in the Roman Empire ("no penalty without law"), when here, as in 5:13, he claims that sin is not imputed where there is no law. The law simply declares what is right, and requires conformity to it. But the law does not give either power to obey it or atonement when it is not obeyed.

Therefore it is of faith, that it might be by grace. Since the promise of salvation is dependent upon faith, the blessings of salvation are afforded by the means of God's grace. Therefore they come **not to that only which is of the law, but to that also which is of the faith of Abraham.** Paul is insistent that only those who possess the faith of Abraham are the seed of Abraham and whether we be Jew or Gentile, if we have placed our faith in the salvation provided by Abraham's God, then Abraham is the **father of us all.**

17 (As it is written, I have made thee a father of many nations,) before him whom he believed, *even* God, who quickeneth the dead, and calleth those things which be not as though they were.

17. As it is written, I have made thee a father of many nations. Again Paul quotes from the Old Testament, this time from Genesis 17:5. Throughout this next series of verses it is noticed that in giving and confirming the covenant to Abraham, God interchangeably uses the words "I will" and "I have." The reason is that God is above time; He has no future nor past, only an eternal present. When in Genesis 17:5 God said, "A father of many nations have I made thee," Abraham was yet childless.

But it didn't matter, the promises of God are better than money in the bank. They always come true. We can count God's "wills" as God's "haves." The same thing was true before the battle of Jericho when the Lord appeared unto Joshua and said, "See, I have given into thy hand Jericho, and its king thereof, and the mighty men of valor" (Josh 6:2). What was for Joshua yet to happen, was for God an accomplished fact.

God, who quickeneth the dead. Although this is a general designation for God in Judaism, it is used here with reference to Abraham's own body, now as good as dead, and to the deadness of Sarah's womb (vs. 19).

18 Who against hope believed in hope, that he might become the father of many nations, according to that which was spoken, So shall thy seed be.

18. Who against hope believed in hope. Grammatically this is known as an oxymoron, a figure of speech in which contradictory ideas are combined (e.g., thunderous silence, sweet sorrow, etc.). Abraham against hope, or beyond hope, nevertheless believed in hope. When the promise was given that Abraham would become the father of many nations, there was no human ground for hope with regard to Abraham's wife Sarah bearing a child. Although beyond hope, Abraham believed God anyway and his faith generated hope.

19 And being not weak in faith, he considered not his own body now dead, when he was about an hundred years old, neither yet the deadness of Sarah's womb:

19. And being not weak in faith. Abraham believed God in spite of the circumstances. He did not consider his lack of virility at one hundred years old. Neither did he consider the inability of his ninety-year-old wife to conceive and withstand the pain of childbirth. Adverse circumstances did not stand in the way of Abraham's faith.

20 He staggered not at the promise of God through unbelief; but was strong in faith, giving glory to God;

20. He staggered not at the promise of God. The word translated staggered (Gr *diakrinomai*), means to separate, distinguish, and as a deponent means "dispute." In regard to faith in God, Abraham was not of a divided mind. How can we reconcile this with Abraham's laughter in Genesis 17:17? We need not understand Abraham's laughter as mocking. Jerome translated laughter as "marveled." Calvin and Augustine both translated it as "laughed for joy." Abraham's questioning how a child could be born of him at one hundred years of age was more an exclamation of holy wonder which was immediately overcome by holy faith. Therefore, he was **strong in faith,** as opposed to being weak in faith (vs. 19). Above all, Abraham gave God the glory, for great things He had done.

21 And being fully persuaded that, what he had promised, he was able also to perform.

21. Abraham was not just wistfully hoping that God would make him the father of many nations, but was **fully persuaded that, what he had promised, he was able also to perform.** History teaches us that what God promises, He also performs.

22 And therefore it was imputed to him for righteousness.

22. This verse begins **And therefore** which means what is to be said is linked closely with what has just been said. Because Abraham had faith, because he believed God in the face of adverse circumstances, therefore, that faith **was imputed to him for righteousness.** All that Abraham had, his righteousness, his inheritance, and his posterity, he gained not by works, but by faith.

23 Now it was not written for his sake alone, that it was imputed to him;
24 But for us also, to whom it shall be imputed, if we believe on him that raised up Jesus our Lord from the dead;
25 Who was delivered for our offences, and was raised again for our justification.

23-25. This illustration of the way in which Abraham received righteousness is not recorded for his sake alone, or applicable to him only. The expression, **But for us also,** indicates that all believers are justified by faith in the promises of God. **If we believe on him that raised up Jesus our Lord from the dead.** The reviving of Abraham's generative power, and his faith that God could do so, foreshadows the faith that we must have in the resurrection of Jesus Christ.

Who was delivered for our offenses. God the Father delivered Jesus Christ to the cross of Calvary, not as an example, but to make atonement for our sins (II Cor 5:21). God the Father also raised Jesus Christ again **for our justification.** The meaning of the resurrection for us today is that Christ Jesus died on account of our sins, and was raised from the dead in order to render us righteous in the eyes of God. The righteousness that

Abraham had, and David had, and which we enjoy, is the righteousness of the risen Lord.

What can we learn from this chapter? The noun **faith** occurs ten times in this chapter and the corresponding verb **believe** occurs six times. Together the idea of believing faith is found no less than sixteen times in Romans 4. The words **count, reckon,** or **impute,** all of which mean to charge to one's account, occur eleven times in Romans 4. The word **righteousness** occurs in one of its forms eight times in this chapter and the corresponding verb **justified** occurs in one of its forms three times. Together the idea of righteousness is found no less than eleven times in Romans 4. It is significant that, apart from the common words of our language, these three words occur so frequently. The application of Romans 4 is simple: *faith imputes righteousness.* There isn't a thing anyone can do to become clothed with God's righteousness except have faith in Jesus Christ as his Saviour from sin.

3. Justification brings blessings to its recipients. 5:1-11.

Having established God's method of justifying sinners, and having provided an Old Testament example of that method, Paul now demonstrates that not only are there benefits derived from justification at the moment of salvation, but there are blessings that accompany justification throughout the believer's life.

Therefore indicates that there is a close link between chapter 4 and chapter 5. It is unfortunate that there is a chapter break here for there is no break in Paul's logical pattern of thought. "Therefore" is a bridge between the two chapters and the ideas of past justification and present blessings.

5:1. Therefore being justified by faith. The word translated **being justified** (Gr *dikaioō*) is an aorist passive participle in Greek. The time of action is in the past. The voice is obviously passive which means that the subject received and did not initiate the action. So Paul says that at some point in the past, without our help, God justified us, that is, He declared us and began to treat us as if we were righteous. Thus, we should understand this verse today "having been justified by faith" we have . . . .

Paul will now list the benefits of having been justified by God. The first is **we have peace with God.** This is not the peace of God, but peace with (Gr *pros*) God. This is not a feeling of peace but a state of peace. Between the sinner and God exists a state of enmity, hostility, and antagonism. Sinners are the enemies of God (Isa 48:22; Jas 4:4; Col 1:21). The state of war that exists between the unbeliever and God continues until a state of peace is declared. Therefore, having been justified by faith, we have a peace treaty with God **through our Lord Jesus Christ.** He is the Mediator between the two parties at war (I Tim 2:5-6). As our Mediator, Jesus Christ has worked out our peace treaty with God. But since He made peace through His blood, He is our peace with God (Eph 2:13-18).

2. By whom also we have access. If you have ever attempted to call the President of the United States, you know how relatively inaccessible he is. To the unbeliever, God the Father is even more inaccessible than the President. He cannot be reached for there is no common ground, no mediator between the unbeliever and God. To the believer, there is access to God because He has justified us. Jesus Christ provides immediate and consistent access to God for all those whom God has declared and treats as righteousness.

Wherein we stand. An age-old problem is this, "How can a sinner stand in the presence of a holy God?" The psalmist wrestled with this question (Ps 130:3). Men and women shall wrestle with this problem at the opening of the sixth seal in Revelation 6:16-17 (see also Ps 1:5). We do not have a leg to

---

CHAPTER 5
THEREFORE being justified by faith, we have peace with God through our Lord Jesus Christ:

2 By whom also we have access by faith into this grace wherein we stand, and rejoice in hope of the glory of God.

stand on when it comes to a defense of our sinful actions. How is it possible for a sinner to stand before God? The Swiss reformer Robert Haldane said, "And it is by Him (Jesus Christ) they enter into the state of grace, so by Him they stand in it, accepted before God; secured, according to His everlasting covenant, that they shall not be cast down" (Robert Haldane, *Romans*, p. 186). The only possible way we can stand before God is by His grace.

And rejoice in hope of the glory of God. The word "hope" confuses many new Christians. Of the one hundred forty-one times this word occurs in the authorized version, in all of its forms, only twenty-one times does it occur as a verb (excluding the Psalms). Hope is not nebulous, it is concrete. We have joy in hope. The glory of God, of which we have fallen short, is the perfect standard of Christ's righteousness (Jn 1:14; 17:22-23; Heb 1:3). We can rejoice in the fact that whatever we are like today, one of the benefits of having been justified is the hope that one day we shall be like Him (Rom 8:29; I Jn 3:2-3).

3 And not only so, but we glory in tribulations also: knowing that tribulation worketh patience;
4 And patience, experience; and experience, hope:

3-4. We glory in tribulations also. He who has been justified rejoices, not in spite of his tribulations, but in or because of his tribulations. In delineating the progression from tribulation to hope, Paul shows that there is a natural, logical connection between the four: tribulations—patience—experience—hope. The tribulations of which Paul speaks (I Cor 5:9-13; II Cor 1:4-10; 11:23-30; Phil 4:12; II Tim 3:11-12; etc.), result in patience (Gr *hypomonē*). This is not a passive quality but the ability to remain strong while bearing the burden of tribulation. The test of endurance in turn results in experience (Gr *dokimē*) or proof of the presence of the Spirit of God which makes patience possible. The end result of this proof proceeds to hope, the certain knowledge that we will one day be glorified as the Son of God and be "heirs of God, and joint-heirs with Christ" (8:17). Here is a perfect circle: we began with hope of the glory of God, passed through tribulation which caused us to be steadfast; this endurance proved that we are indeed a child of God and this proof encourages us in the hope of the glory of God.

5 And hope maketh not ashamed; because the love of God is shed abroad in our hearts by the Holy Ghost which is given unto us.

5. And hope maketh not ashamed. Having already been justified we have a hope that cannot be humiliated. The hope we have is in the glory of God and even though it is tested in the caldron of fiery tribulation, it will be proved genuine **because the love of God is shed abroad in our hearts.** This passage began by speaking of faith, moved to hope, and now has come to the end of the trilogy with charity or love. Our hearts are flooded with God's love for us because we have been justified. But more than that, there is another benefit which accompanies justification and that is **the Holy Ghost which is given unto us.** It is the Holy Spirit who pours into the heart of the believer a sense of God's love for him. Not only did the Holy Spirit come to us at salvation communicating God's love for us, but the Scripture says He **is given unto us.** The verb **is given** (Gr *didōmi*) means to grant, impart, or put into the heart. The clear implication is that at the moment of salvation we received the gift of the Holy Spirit Himself. A justified man need not anxiously look to a future time when he will be baptized with the Holy Spirit. The Holy Spirit is God's gift to us at the moment of justification. Then Christ's righteousness is ours, God's love is ours, and the Holy Spirit's presence is ours. They are inextricably bound together in a package we call salvation.

6 For when we were yet without strength, in due time Christ died for the ungodly.
7 For scarcely for a righteous man will one die: yet peradventure for a good man some would even dare to die.
8 But God commendeth his love toward us, in that, while we were yet sinners, Christ died for us.

6-8. The distinctive quality of God's love is that it operates irrespective of merit. Human love is given to those who are lovable; but God's love embraces even the unlovely. **When we were yet without strength.** This expression is parallel to the expression in verse 8, **while we were yet sinners.** Paul uses it to show man's utter helplessness in the face of his all-encompassing sin. In due time Christ died for the ungodly. This means that circumstances did not bring Christ to the cross, the divine plan of God did (Gal 4:1-5). At the time of man's greatest need, nothing but the blood of Jesus would satisfy that need.

Verses 7 and 8 expand what is implicit in verse 6. When Paul said that Christ died for the ungodly, he was indicating that the Lord did not die for those who were simply void of morality but for those who were actively opposed to God. **For scarcely for a righteous man will one die.** Here the just or righteous man is distinguished from the good or benevolent man. The just man is approved by God, and hardly anyone would think of dying for him. The good man is loved by men, and most would not think of dying for him, although some may be tempted. Paul's argument is that while you will rarely find anyone who will lay down his life for a righteous or good man, God demonstrated His love by sending Christ Jesus to die for us while we were yet sinners, something no one else would even consider doing. The sacrifice of Christ on the cross of Calvary arose out of the heart of God filled with the love of God. All these blessings are ours because at some point in the past, without our help, we have been justified by God and are now being treated as if we were righteous.

9 Much more then, being now justified by his blood, we shall be saved from wrath through him.

9. In addition to the blessings we presently enjoy because we are justified, there is yet the promise that **we shall be saved from wrath through him.** All men are by nature the children of wrath (Jn 3:36). The prophet Nahum warns that the Lord has reserved wrath for His enemies (Nah 1:2). It is comforting for the believer to note, however, that "God hath not appointed us to wrath, but to obtain salvation by our Lord Jesus Christ" (I Thess 5:9). One of the future benefits of the fact that we have been justified is that we shall be preserved from the day of God's fierce wrath.

10 For if, when we were enemies, we were reconciled to God by the death of his Son, much more, being reconciled, we shall be saved by his life.

10. **We shall be saved by his life.** Paul makes reference to us who were once enemies of God, but now are reconciled to Him by the death of His Son. It is the death of Christ and His shed blood which provide our atonement and redemption (Eph 1:7; 2:13; Col 1:14; Heb 9:12-15). It is the death of Christ which effects our salvation; but it is the life of Christ which sustains it. Christ died for our sins and was raised for our justification to make continual intercession for us (Heb 7:25). The life of Jesus Christ did not take away the penalty of our sins, His death did. But Christ ever lives to take away the dominion of sin over us. This is how we are continually kept saved by His intercessory life.

11 And not only so, but we also joy in God through our Lord Jesus Christ, by whom we have now received the atonement.

11. Not only shall the justified man escape the wrath of God by the death of Christ, but also he shall obtain joy in God because of Christ's life. The word translated **joy** is the same as is translated **rejoice** in verse 2 and **glory** in verse 3. The blessings which justification brings to its recipients terminate in joy **through our Lord Jesus Christ.** This last expression is identical to that found in verse 1 of this chapter. All that we have we owe to Him, the Lord Jesus Christ.

4. Justification is imputed to us as was sin. 5:12-21.

Thus far in the Epistle to the Romans, Paul has dealt with two great doctrinal subjects: condemnation and justification. Before the apostle leaves the subjects he enhances our understanding of them by contrasting the two. The contrasts which he draws are: a contrast between Adam and Christ (vss. 14-15); between condemnation and justification (vs. 16); between disobedience and obedience (vs. 19); between law and grace (vs. 20); between sin and righteousness (vs. 21); and between death and life (vs. 21). Since these verses are so doctrinal in nature, it will be helpful to keep in mind three very important truths established in Romans 5:12-21. They are: (1) one offense, by one man, made all the world guilty of sin; (2) the resultant guilt of Adam's original sin is imputed to each of us; and (3) Adam acted as our official representative when he cast his vote against God.

12 Wherefore, as by one man sin entered into the world, and death by sin; and so death passed upon all men, for that all have sinned:

13 (For until the law sin was in the world: but sin is not imputed when there is no law.

14 Nevertheless death reigned from Adam to Moses, even over them that had not sinned after the similitude of Adam's transgression, who is the figure of him that was to come.

15 But not as the offence, so also *is* the free gift. For if through the offence of one many be dead, much more the grace of God, and the gift by grace, *which is* by one man, Jesus Christ, hath abounded unto many.

16 And not as *it was* by one that sinned, *so is* the gift: for the judgment *was* by one to condemnation, but the free gift *is* of many offences unto justification.

17 For if by one man's offence death reigned by one; much more they which receive abundance of grace and of the gift of righteousness shall reign in life by one, Jesus Christ.)

18 Therefore as by the offence of one *judgment came* upon all men to condemnation; even so by the righteousness of one *the free gift came* upon all men unto justification of life.

19 For as by one man's disobedience many were made sinners, so by the obedience of one shall many be made righteous.

12. By one man sin entered into the world. Genesis 3 makes it abundantly clear that this one man, Adam, brought sin to the human race by disobedience. It was not the sins of Adam's lifetime, but the one original sin which allowed death, sin's close ally, to enter the world with it. On no less than five occasions in verses 15-19 the principle of one sin by one man is asserted. One act of disobedience to God was sufficient to allow sin to enter and permeate the entire realm of humanity, **for that all have sinned.**

13-14. Sin immediately inundated the whole world and had a mortal effect on its inhabitants. **Sin is not imputed when there is no law,** but even before the law of Moses was given, physical death attested to the presence of sin in Adam and his posterity. So universal was this sin that its deadly effects were seen over them that had not sinned after the similitude of Adam's transgression. Adam is here contrasted with Christ and said to be a "figure" (Gr *typos*) or "type" of Him that was to come. The only Old Testament character to be called explicitly a type of Christ is Adam. Here the contrast between the first Adam and the Last Adam begins.

15. But not as the offense, so also is the free gift. The continued contrast between Adam and Christ shows a correspondence both in similarity and dissimilarity. Through the offense of Adam the many (i.e., all of Adam's descendants) incurred the penalty of death. Similarly, the many (i.e., all the redeemed) have incurred the free gift of eternal life through the Last Adam, Jesus Christ. The dissimilarity is seen in the phrase, **much more the grace of God.** The grace of God, which is the ground of our justification, is contrasted with the sin of Adam, because it is greater in quality and greater in degree than Adam's sin. In Adam we got what we deserved, condemnation and guilt. In Christ we have received much more of what we do not deserve, mercy and grace.

16. Now the contrast turns to condemnation in Adam and justification in Christ. **For the judgment was by one to condemnation.** Not only is our guilt derived from one man's sin, but it is derived from only one sin of that man. Notice that Paul never refers to the "offenses" of one man, but to the **offense** (singular) of one man (vss. 14-15, 17-20). It is not the sins of Adam's lifetime that have been imputed to us, but only his original sin. That one sin brought condemnation. However, the righteousness which is imputed to us by Christ, through the free gift of God's grace, covers not just that one offense but **many offenses.**

17-18. As the representative head of the human race, Adam's offense dethroned him as the ruler of God's creation. Consequently, death became the ruler of nature. Adam became the representative of a death-destined society. As long as we are born into that society, death is our destiny as well. The Last Adam, Jesus Christ, is also the representative of a society. Through the gift of righteousness, He **shall reign in life.** Since all are born into the society of death, the only way to enter Christ's society, in which men are born unto justification of life, is to be born again. By the new birth experience we pass from our old relationship to Adam into a new and living relationship with Christ.

19. One man's disobedience . . . the obedience of one. Here the contrast drawn is between blatant disobedience and willful obedience. God's command to our representative Adam concerning the Tree of Knowledge of Good and Evil was, "thou shall not eat of it" (Gen 2:17). Almost immediately the head of the human race disobeyed that divine command. However, Christ Jesus, the Last Adam and Head of the heavenly race, totally obeyed the will of God and testified to that when He said, "I have glorified thee on the earth: I have finished the work which thou gavest me to do" (Jn 17:4). The difference between obedience and disobedience is the difference between life and death.

20 Moreover the law entered, that the offence might abound. But where sin abounded, grace did much more abound:

20. Moreover the law entered, that the offense might abound. At this point the Jew might ask, "Well, what is the law for?" The law is "the necessary yardstick of God's holiness which served to bring out into sharp relief the guilt of man in revolt against God, showing him the hopelessness of attempting to earn salvation by good works" (Gleason L. Archer, Jr., *The Epistle to the Romans*, p. 32). The law came not to make a man a sinner, but to show him how great a sinner he is. **But where sin abounded, grace did much more abound.** Grace did not set aside the law, but rather completely satisfied it. As deep as sin goes, God's grace goes deeper. As wide as sin is, God's grace is wider. When sin abounded, grace super-abounded. God's grace is greater than all our sin.

21 That as sin hath reigned unto death, even so might grace reign through righteousness unto eternal life by Jesus Christ our Lord.

21. This verse contains the double contrast between sin and righteousness and between death and life. From the very moment sin entered the universe it has reigned, bringing about physical and spiritual death. Its principle of rulership has been to separate mankind from his Creator and to cause his end to be a mortal one. But through the blood of Jesus Christ, sin has been dethroned and righteousness now rules in its stead. Whereas death was the order of the day in Adam's society, now life eternal is the order of the day for those who have believed in Jesus Christ. The contrast is a great one. It is a contrast between man's sin and Christ's obedience, between the wages of sin and the gift of God.

Some have thought that universal salvation is taught in this passage, thinking that just because all were condemned, now all will be saved. Such is not the case. New birth is mandatory for eternal life and the qualifying expression, **they which receive** in verse 17, teaches that faith in Jesus Christ is absolutely essential for salvation.

B. The Provision for Sanctification. 6:1-7:25.

Having established in 3:21-5:21 that justification is provided by faith alone, Paul now turns his attention to the provision for sanctification. In the preceding chapter he has drawn some conclusions concerning the contrasts between Adam and Christ. In chapters 6 and 7, however, the contrast is between justification and sanctification. There is noticeable smoothness in the transition between the discussion of justification in chapter 5 and that of sanctification in chapter 6. Although there is a sharp contrast between the two, nevertheless the intimacy of the relationship between justification and sanctification is clearly seen in the way they are connected in these chapters.

Basically the contrast between the two is this: justification deals with the penalty for sin; sanctification deals with the power of sin. As was seen in 5:1, justification is a declarative act of God. As will be seen in chapter 6, sanctification is a progressive act of God. Both works of God deal with the sinner: justification with the unsaved sinner; sanctification with the saved sinner. The end result of justification is salvation; the end result of sanctification is obedience. Although distinctly different, justification and sanctification are two aspects of the one work of God in saving men.

1. Sanctification and the principle of sin. 6:1-14.

CHAPTER 6
WHAT shall we say then? Shall we continue in sin, that grace may abound?
2 God forbid. How shall we, that are dead to sin, live any longer therein?

6:1-2. Shall we continue in sin, that grace may abound? God forbid. In every age there have been those who have denounced the doctrine of justification by faith on the incorrect supposition that this doctrine logically leads to sin. "If the believer is treated as righteous by God, and if good works will not save him, then evil works will not condemn him either. Why then should he be concerned about his sin or attempt to live a godly life?" Paul anticipated this very attitude in 6:1-2. Theo-

3 Know ye not, that so many of us as were baptized into Jesus Christ were baptized into his death?

4 Therefore we are buried with him by baptism into death: that like as Christ was raised up from the dead by the glory of the Father, even so we also should walk in newness of life.

5 For if we have been planted together in the likeness of his death, we shall be also *in the likeness* of *his* resurrection:

6 Knowing this, that our old man is crucified with *him*, that the body of sin might be destroyed, that henceforth we should not serve sin.

7 For he that is dead is freed from sin.

8 Now if we be dead with Christ, we believe that we shall also live with him:

logically, this belief is known as antinomianism. Paul's answer is crystal clear. Just because where sin abounded grace super-abounded, the believer is not automatically drawn to license in his life-style. On the contrary, a mature understanding of justification by faith leads the believer to appreciate God's grace, so that the end result is obedience to God out of a heart filled with gratitude. Paul's characteristic expression **God forbid,** shows how appalled he is at the mere suggestion of continuing in sin once we have experienced the grace of God. We cannot continue in sin because through our identification with Jesus Christ we are dead to sin. To die unto sin means that we are dead to the guilt of sin. Sin can no longer make any legal claim on the believer because we are viewed by God as if we ourselves had died that fateful day at Calvary.

3-5. At this point Paul begins to relate the secret of living a holy and sanctified life, a life which is characterized by being dead to sin. The secret of sanctification is not found in some sanctimonious formula or some deeper or mystical experience with the Lord. The secret is found in three words: (1) **know** (vs. 3); (2) **reckon** (vs. 11); and (3) **yield** (vs. 13). We must be vitally aware of these words as we seek to understand the relationship between justification and sanctification.

To show the immaturity of those who would continue in sin after justification so that grace may abound, Paul introduces the subject of baptism as evidence that life in sin cannot coexist with death to sin. **So many of us as were baptized into Jesus Christ.** Baptism into Christ means to be incorporated into Him, to become a member of His body (I Cor 12:13), and to share with Him those experiences which, although were historically His, are vicariously ours (i.e., His crucifixion, death, burial, and resurrection). **Therefore we are buried with him by baptism into death.** Burial with Christ Jesus signifies that sin no longer judicially has a hold upon us. The ordinance of Christian baptism beautifully portrays this burial into Christ in which the old order of a death-controlled life comes to an end and the new order of a Christ-controlled life begins. Therefore, having already been justified, a believer tells that fact to the world by submitting to the ordinance of water baptism. When he has been symbolically **raised up from the dead,** even as Christ was physically, the purpose of his resurrection is that he **should walk in newness of life.** This should entirely preclude the foolish idea of continued sin so that a display may be made of the grace of God. Just as we were buried into Him **in the likeness of his death, we shall be also in the likeness of his resurrection.** Hence we enter into His life and become a part of Him spiritually, yielding to Him our desires, our wishes, ourselves.

6-8. Paul is still expounding the first principle of true sanctification. Hence, as in verse 3, he repeats the word that is characteristic of this first principle. **Knowing this, that our old man is crucified with him.** The old man referred to here is our old self, the man we once were before we were crucified with Christ. This crucifixion is not a present, daily experience but is rather a past event, expressed by the aorist tense in Greek. I Corinthians 15:31 was spoken by Paul in the context of physical not spiritual death. Our old man is not constantly being crucified, day by day, but has been crucified at the cross of Calvary. The reason is **that the body of sin might be destroyed.** A better rendering of **might be destroyed** (Gr *katargeō*), is "might be rendered inoperative." At the cross of Calvary a victory was won which provided the believer with the power not to live as he once did, serving his old master, i.e., sin, but to live eternally serving his new master, i.e., Christ.

For he that is dead is freed from sin. All who have died to sin are no longer debtor to it. Death wipes the slate clean. The death of our Lord has completely removed the guilt and penalty of our sin. Consequently, because we have died with Christ, we shall also live with Him. Living with Christ precludes the possibility of carnally continuing in sin so that grace may abound.

9 Knowing that Christ being raised from the dead dieth no more; death hath no more dominion over him.

10 For in that he died, he died unto sin once: but in that he liveth, he liveth unto God.

9-10. Knowing that Christ being raised from the dead dieth no more. This is the third time Paul has used the word **know** or **knowing.** These three instances teach that we have been baptized into Jesus Christ, that our old man is crucified with Christ, and that because Jesus died unto sin once, He never shall die again. Death is a completed transaction by which we have once and for all passed into the resurrection life of our Lord. Jesus Christ can never die again. When we died with Him to sin, we never die to sin again. **Death hath no more dominion over him.** When He went to the cross and paid the debt in full for our sin, death could no longer claim Him or those who died with Him. Therefore, sanctification is knowing what Christ has already accomplished for us through His death. It is not primarily a matter of striving to live holy, but of knowing that we are holy in Him.

11 Likewise reckon ye also yourselves to be dead indeed unto sin, but alive unto God through Jesus Christ our Lord.

12 Let not sin therefore reign in your mortal body, that ye should obey it in the lusts thereof.

11-12. Knowing what has been accomplished on our behalf at Calvary is not in itself sanctification. It is but the first principle in the process of sanctification. Paul couples to that principle a second one. **Likewise reckon ye also yourselves to be dead indeed unto sin, but alive unto God.** The word reckon (Gr *logizomai*) means that we know something is true and then, moment by moment, day by day, consider it to be true. We take as a solid reality that which God has promised. Therefore, not only do we know what has been accomplished in our justification, but we continue to live as though we had already entered into the resurrection presence of our Lord. We do not die daily, we live daily unto the glory of God.

"This 'reckoning' is no vain experience but one which is morally fruitful, because the Holy Spirit has come to make effective in believers what Christ has done for them, and to enable them to become in daily experience, as far as may be in the present conditions of mortality, what they already are 'in Christ' and what they will fully be in the resurrection life" (F. F. Bruce, *The Epistle of Paul to the Romans,* p. 139). When we daily count ourselves to be dead to the penalty of sin and alive unto God, there will be no temptation to continue in sin for we will refuse that temptation out of thankfulness to God for counting us and treating us as if we were righteous.

13 Neither yield ye your members *as* instruments of unrighteousness unto sin: but yield yourselves unto God, as those that are alive from the dead, and your members *as* instruments of righteousness unto God.

13. The third and final principle in living a sanctified life is the negative principle, **Neither yield ye your members as instruments of unrighteousness unto sin,** and a corresponding positive principle, **but yield yourselves unto God.** As those who have been justified, we are not to allow our members (i.e., our hands, our feet, our tongues, etc.) to become the instruments or weapons of unrighteousness. In the original language, the words "neither yield" carry the idea of a continuous yielding. Knowing of our justification and reckoning ourselves dead to the penalty of sin, we are to continually keep ourselves from yielding to sin. But, on the other hand, we are to once for all, as the Greek implies, yield to God. Although we will yet sin, by yielding ourselves to God we will never again be caught in the trap of continuing in sin. Our life and all that we have will be given over to the One who has spiritually raised us from the dead.

14 For sin shall not have dominion over you: for ye are not under the law, but under grace.

14. Paul's concept of sanctification, then, is not a daily dying to one's self. It is rather being mature enough to rest wholly on the finished work of Calvary, knowing that we have been justified there, daily reckoning that work to be finished, and constantly yielding ourselves to be used of God. When one is obedient to these commands, the believer finds himself on a road climbing progressively toward the resurrection life of the Lord. For those who seek santification in this manner, the Lord has a definite promise: **For sin shall not have dominion over you.**

15 What then? shall we sin, because we are not under the law, but under grace? God forbid.

16 Know ye not, that to whom ye yield yourselves servants to obey, his servants ye are to whom ye obey; whether of sin unto death, or of obedience unto righteousness?

17 But God be thanked, that ye were the servants of sin, but ye have obeyed from the heart that form of doctrine which was delivered you.
18 Being then made free from sin, ye became the servants of righteousness.

19 I speak after the manner of men because of the infirmity of your flesh: for as ye have yielded your members servants to uncleanness and to iniquity unto iniquity; even so now yield your members servants to righteousness unto holiness.
20 For when ye were the servants of sin, ye were free from righteousness.

21 What fruit had ye then in those things whereof ye are now ashamed? for the end of those things is death.
22 But now being made free from sin, and become servants to God, ye have your fruit unto holiness, and the end everlasting life.

23 For the wages of sin is death; but the gift of God is eternal life through Jesus Christ our Lord.

2. Sanctification and the practice of sin. 6:15-23.

15. What then? shall we sin? The antinomian argument of verse 1 is now repeated but with a significant difference. In verse 1 the question was, **Shall we continue in sin?** This dealt with the principle of continuation in sin after the believer recognizes he is dead to it. But now the question is, "Shall we sin?" Here he does not speak of a life-style of sin, but rather an occasional excursion into iniquity. "Because we are not under law but under grace, is it not permissible to fall into sin once in a while?" Paul's abhorrence is seen in his typical answer, **God forbid.**

16. To whom ye yield yourselves servants to obey, his servants ye are. Paul uses the analogy of the slave market to illustrate that the sanctified believer dare not even occasionally fall into sin. His point is that if you start to obey sin, you are thereby admitting the mastery of sin in your life. Paul develops our Lord's words, "No man can serve two masters" (Mt 6:24). Yielding to the mastery of sin brings death; yielding to obedience to Christ brings righteousness.

17-18. But God be thanked, that ye were the servants of sin, . . . ye became the servants of righteousness. Paul was ever mindful that God is to be thanked that these Roman believers obeyed from their hearts the traditions or "patterns of teaching" which were embodied in Christ Jesus. Because of Him they have been made free from service to sin and, in turn, have become the servants of righteousness. Freedom from service to Satan is, by definition, bondage to the Lord, who loved us and gave Himself for us.

19-20. I speak after the manner of men because of the infirmity of your flesh. Paul uses the human analogy of a slave in order that the weakest flesh may understand. He now counsels them to yield themselves to holiness with the same gusto they once yielded themselves to uncleanness. When they were servants of sin, it was their master. Now that they are servants of Christ, righteousness must be their master. They cannot serve the master of righteousness and dabble in sin at the same time.

21-22. What fruit had ye then in those things whereof ye are now ashamed? Paul now addresses a biting question to those who would dare to practice sin. He asks what fruit has been yielded from that sin. Paul knows well that sin always promises more than it can deliver. None of sin's fruit is worth having, and the final result of being a slave to sin is the ghastly horror of death. But for those who are freed from the bondage of habitual sin and who are servants of God, **ye have your fruit unto holiness, and the end everlasting life.** There is a drastic contrast between the outcome of the two bondages. Bondage to sin has shame as its by-product. Bondage to Christ has as its by-product the status of being positionally holy and in the process of becoming conformed to the image of Christ. This is biblical sanctification. Bondage to sin has as its end death. Bondage to Christ has as its end everlasting life.

23. For the wages of sin is death; but the gift of God is eternal life through Jesus Christ our Lord. The outcome of enslavement to sin is quite different from that of obedience to Christ. Remuneration is the principle by which we become heirs of death. Sin always pays a wage, and that wage is a drastic one. But just as remuneration is the principle by which we become heirs to death, unmerited favor is the principle by which we become heirs to eternal life. Death is earned, eternal life is purely gratuitous.

3. Sanctification and the law. 7:1-14.

Paul now continues his teaching on the sanctified life, but thoroughly changes his analogy. Although the slave market is an appropriate analogy for our former relationship to the Mosaic law, an even better analogy to depict the justified man's relationship to Christ is that of the bonds of marriage. This is because the marriage relationship involves a response of the heart and emotion. Paul draws upon it to show the proper correspondence between our sanctified lives as believers and that of a wife to her husband. The believer's life in Christ is likened to widowhood and a second marriage.

7:1. The law hath dominion over a man as long as he liveth. Paul speaks of the law of God (Mosaic law) and the law of the state (Roman law). Both divine and civil law maintain a hold on mankind as long as he lives.

2-3. For the woman which hath a husband is bound by the law to her husband so long as he liveth. Both the Jewish and Roman law required that a woman remain with her husband until his death. Should a woman join herself to another man prior to the death of her husband, she was considered an adulteress (Mk 10:12). The Greek verb used here is *chrēmatizō* which means "to be publicly known as" (cf. Acts 11:26 where this verb was used in giving the name "Christians" to the followers of Jesus Christ). Only if her husband should die was a woman free to marry another without publicly being branded an adulteress.

4-6. Ye also are become dead to the law by the body of Christ. Having given the analogy of marriage, Paul now draws this conclusion. The law confirms and seals our bondage to sin. As long as we are governed by the law, there is no possibility of being released from that bondage. The only alternative is death. But when Christ died at Calvary, we died to the law. Sin has no more dominion over us, neither does the law. **That we should bring forth fruit unto God.** The purpose of our being free from the law and married to another, the risen Lord, is that we may produce fruit unto God. Although this may be an extension of the marriage analogy, and the fruit mentioned is the progeny which is the result of marriage (i.e., the winning of others to the Lord), it is most likely that the fruit unto God is a righteous life which is characterized by those "good works, which God hath before ordained that we should walk in them" (Eph 2:10).

Having been justified by faith, we are now set free from that which held us in bondage. Since we are now free, we are also expected to produce the fruit of freedom, i.e., the sanctified life. Hence, we serve in newness of spirit, and not in the oldness of the letter. The holy law of God is not an external code of "do's" and "don'ts." Rather it is a law of love written on our hearts. We do not obey that law because we fear the Lord, but because we love Him. In our former marriage to sin and the law we attempted to do only that which would meet the minimum standard of God. Now in our marriage to Christ, we seek to be all that we can be and to do for Him all that we can do to please Him and demonstrate our love for Him.

7. What shall we say then? Is the law sin? God forbid. Still another series of pauline questions concerns the relationship of the law to sin. Characteristic abhorrence is shown to the question, **Is the law sin? . . . Nay, I had not known sin, but by the law.** Paul claims that the function of the law is to reveal what sin truly is. Man would not have known what covetousness was if the law had not commanded, **Thou shalt not covet.** A fifty-five-mile-per-hour speed sign is not sin, but teaches us the parameters of sin. This too is the function of the law.

8. But sin, taking occasion by the commandment, wrought in me all manner of concupiscence. Not only does the law reveal sin, but it provokes it as well. Law does not cause sin, but sin takes occasion by the commandment. The word rendered **occasion** (Gr *aphormē*) has the meaning of a base for military operation. The moment Paul attempted to keep the law, (abstaining from covetousness, e.g.) the very commandments which he attempted to keep (and could not) provoked him to acts of sin. Thus he says, **For without the law sin was dead.** Sin has no existence apart from God's law, since by definition **sin** is the violation of God's law.

CHAPTER 7

KNOW ye not, brethren, (for I speak to them that know the law,) how that the law hath dominion over a man as long as he liveth?

2 For the woman which hath an husband is bound by the law to her husband so long as he liveth; but if the husband be dead, she is loosed from the law of her husband.

3 So then if, while her husband liveth, she be married to another man, she shall be called an adulteress: but if her husband be dead, she is free from that law; so that she is no adulteress, though she be married to another man.

4 Wherefore, my brethren, ye also are become dead to the law by the body of Christ; that ye should be married to another, even to him who is raised from the dead, that we should bring forth fruit unto God.

5 For when we were in the flesh, the motions of sins, which were by the law, did work in our members to bring forth fruit unto death.

6 But now we are delivered from the law, that being dead wherein we were held; that we should serve in newness of spirit, and not in the oldness of the letter.

7 What shall we say then? Is the law sin? God forbid. Nay, I had not known sin, but by the law: for I had not known lust, except the law had said, Thou shalt not covet.

8 But sin, taking occasion by the commandment, wrought in me all manner of concupiscence. For without the law sin was dead.

9 For I was alive without the law once: but when the commandment came, sin revived, and I died.

10 And the commandment, which *was ordained* to life, I found *to be* unto death.
11 For sin, taking occasion by the commandment, deceived me, and by it slew *me*.

12 Wherefore the law *is* holy, and the commandment holy, and just, and good.
13 Was then that which is good made death unto me? God forbid. But sin, that it might appear sin, working death in me by that which is good; that sin by the commandment might become exceeding sinful.
14 For we know that the law is spiritual: but I am carnal, sold under sin.

9. For I was alive without the law once: but when the commandment came, sin revived, and I died. This verse records the dawn of conscience in the life of Apostle Paul. He had lived a self-complacent, self-righteous life in which he was free from conviction of sin. It is difficult to say exactly when this period existed in Paul's life. Some have suggested that it was the first thirteen years of Paul's life, before his bar mitzvah ceremony (the ceremony in which a Jewish boy becomes a "son of the commandment" and assumes personal responsibility to keep the commandments of the law). But it may not be necessary to restrict Paul's complacency to those early, unreflecting years of childhood. When the commandment came to him, an apparent reference to **thou shalt not covet** in verse 7, for the first time, Paul became conscious of his lack of ability to keep the law. At that point sin sprang back to life and, says Paul, **I died.** This must be put in contrast with **I was alive without the law** and therefore should be understood as death to his complacent attitude toward sin.

10-11. And the commandment, which was ordained to life, I found to be unto death. This is a reference to the original purpose of the law. God had declared, "This do, and thou shalt live!" The law was intended to guard and promote life but man could not keep the law. Paul found that unheeded law produced death. The more law of which Paul became aware the more sin he found himself committing. The more sin Paul committed the more convinced he was that one day he would have to pay for that sin. Since "the wages of sin is death," we learn that the law not only reveals sin but also produces death.

For sin, taking occasion by the commandment, deceived me. The deception to which Paul referred was this. Since the commandment was intended unto life, Paul expected the commandment to yield life as a result. But instead it became the occasion for sin and consequent death. Since the commandment yielded the opposite of what Paul expected, he felt deceived. But the perpetrator of this deception was not the commandment itself, but sin. The commandment was merely the instrument by which sin deceived him.

12-14. Wherefore the law is holy. From what Paul has just said in verses 7 through 11, we might expect a totally different conclusion. But since the law intrinsically and originally was intended to guide men to life, it is therefore a holy law, just and good. Paul then expands on the principle that it is sin which is the deceiver and not the law. **Was then that which is good made death unto me?** His vigorous denial is again, **God forbid.** It is sin that works death using the instrument of the law and the purpose is that sin might be shown to be sin. Death is brought by sin, even though the instrumentality of the law is good.

Paul's conclusion concerning the law then is this: **For we know that the law is spiritual.** The apostle is convinced that the Mosaic law is holy and just and good because it is derived from the Holy Spirit. The word **spiritual** (Gr *pneumatikos*) is not used in contradistinction to corporeal, but is used to intimate that the law finds its roots in the Holy Spirit. (See this same use of spiritual words, I Cor 2:13; the spiritual man, I Cor 2:15; spiritual songs, Col 3:16; etc.).

4. Sanctification and the conflict within. 7:15-25.

Paul has exclaimed that the Mosaic law is spiritual. If it is holy and good, why cannot the law bring holiness? Paul immediately gives the answer, **I am carnal, sold under sin.** In this section the apostle continues to speak in the first person singular. He uses the present tense. Here, there is inward tension evident that was not evident in his discussion of the law (7:1-13). Autobiographically Paul points out that even the believer is constantly beset by the tugs and pulls of a self-seeking and self-centered ego. Paul designates this ego "the flesh." This is no straw man which he sets up, but in fact pictures the anguish of Paul's own soul. He knows to do right and to obey the law, but in himself he cannot do either.

This passage presents the tension between Paul's knowledge and his ability in three phrases: (1) **We know that the law is spiritual** (vs. 14); (2) **I know that in me (that is, in my flesh,) dwelleth no good thing** (vs. 18); (3) **I find then a law, that, when I would do good, evil is present.** (vs. 21). Each of these phases presents significant knowledge by Paul. Each of them is immediately followed by proof that, even though he knows what is right, he cannot do what is right. The conclusion of the whole matter, which he draws in verse 25, should be an encouragement to all believers.

15-17. For that which I do I allow not: for what I would, that do I not. While recognizing that the law is spiritual because it is God's law, Paul also must admit that he is carnal (Gr *sarkinos*). As a slave to the power of sin, Paul recognizes that those things he wishes he could do, he cannot do; and conversely, those things he knows he must not do, he finds himself doing. A historical parallel to this is Horace's statement, "I pursue the things that have done me harm; I shun the things I believe will do me good" (*Epistle* 1.8.11). Paul differs from Horace, however, in his conclusion. **Now then it is no more I that do it, but sin that dwelleth in me.** Paul is not attempting to rid himself of responsibility for his sin. He is aware that in the Christian there are two wills, that of the fleshly, sinful nature which causes him to sin, and that which is born of God which does not commit sin (I Jn 3:9).

18-20. For I know that in me (that is, in my flesh,) dwelleth no good thing. In the second phase of Paul's knowledge he recognizes that in himself there is not the ability to do good. He wills to do good, but how to accomplish his will is not known. He cannot do the will of God for sin holds dominion over him. Sin is his master, his lord, his king. By himself he cannot break it. He is a defeated Christian when he is controlled by sin. "It is not the new man in Christ who carries on this life of defeat, but it is the sin-principle in him, engendered by the unyielded flesh and occupying the Lord's temple as a trespassing squatter like the Tobiah whom Nehemiah expelled" (cf. Neh 13:7-9) (Gleason L. Archer, Jr., *The Epistle to the Romans*, p. 43).

21-23. I find then a law. The law which is referred to here has been variously interpreted as the law of God (vs. 22) and the law of sin (vs. 23). Either interpretation is plausible. It seems likely, however, that the law to which he refers prohibits him from doing good and therefore is the law of sin. **For I delight in the law of God after the inward man.** It is the desire of Paul, as it should be with every believer, to love and obey the law of God. However, opposed to the law of God is the law of sin, which brings his members (i.e., his body, his hands, his tongue, etc.) into captivity.

The law which he finds is the third phase of his knowledge. Paul has come to the conclusion that as long as the believer is alive there will be a constant warfare between the old sinful nature and his delight in the law of God. Unfortunately, when the believer attempts to win that battle in himself, he is always defeated. Self-attempts to rid our members of the tyranny of indwelling sin cause the frustration which underlies this passage.

24. O wretched man that I am! who shall deliver me from the body of this death? Helplessly, Paul throws up his hands and exclaims what a wretched individual a believer is when he has not gained mastery over sin. **O wretched man** (Gr *talaiporos*) is an expression used in pagan Greek drama to express tragic misfortune and woe. Paul recognizes that he is in a helpless state of despair because he cannot rid himself of his bent toward sinning. **The body of this death** (lit., this body of death)

15 For that which I do I allow not: for what I would, that do I not; but what I hate, that do I.
16 If then I do that which I would not, I consent unto the law that *it is* good.
17 Now then it is no more I that do it, but sin that dwelleth in me.

18 For I know that in me (that is, in my flesh,) dwelleth no good thing: for to will is present with me; but *how* to perform that which is good I find not.
19 For the good that I would I do not: but the evil which I would not, that I do.
20 Now if I do that I would not, it is no more I that do it, but sin that dwelleth in me.

21 I find then a law, that, when I would do good, evil is present with me.
22 For I delight in the law of God after the inward man:
23 But I see another law in my members, warring against the law of my mind, and bringing me into captivity to the law of sin which is in my members.

24 O wretched man that I am! who shall deliver me from the body of this death?

probably does not refer to a physical body. Sin is much more deeply rooted than the body. Paul is speaking of human nature which has inherited guilt and sin from Adam. Paul knows there hangs over his life a cloud of guilt and death which is imputed with sin.

The main purpose of this statement, however, is in the question **Who shall deliver me . . . ?** Paul indicates that if he is to be delivered from the mastery of sin, that deliverance must come from without. He is unable to live the Christian life in himself. He is incapable of gaining mastery over sin. If Paul is to live a mature and godly life, and to delight in the law of God after the inward man, the strength to do so must come from outside himself.

25 I thank God through Jesus Christ our Lord. So then with the mind I myself serve the law of God; but with the flesh the law of sin.

25. I thank God through Jesus Christ our Lord. Paul inescapably comes to the conclusion that only Jesus Christ can enable us to live a sanctified life. He would like to serve the law of God, but his flesh causes him to serve the law of sin. The Lord Jesus turns that around.

Romans 7 is not a hypothetical case. It is an actual picture of the internal strife caused by the law of sin against the law of the Spirit in the Apostle Paul. This need not be the normal Christian experience, for Paul has already instructed us how to avert this internal strife. The preceding chapter presents the proper way to sanctification; this chapter presents the improper way (cf. D. M. Lloyd-Jones, *Romans*, pp. 1-13). To live a sanctified life we must know well what Christ has accomplished for us in our justification, daily reckon that we have died with Him and are alive unto righteousness, and yield ourselves completely to Him.

C. The Provision for Assurance. 8:1-39.

1. The assurance of the righteousness of God. 8:1-4.

8:1. There is therefore now no condemnation to them which are in Christ Jesus. The word **condemnation** (Gr *katakrima*) means more than just the opposite of justification; it indicates that we are not servants to the penalty for our sin, but that guilt and penalty have been removed at the cross. Therefore, for those who are **in Christ Jesus,** we do not live under the constant threat of judicial punishment by God. In many ways this chapter is the consummation of Paul's argument concerning the depravity of man and the righteousness God provided to meet man's need. The expression, **who walk not after the flesh, but after the Spirit** is not in the original. There should be an exclamation point after the expression **therefore now no condemnation to them which are in Christ Jesus!**

CHAPTER 8

THERE is therefore now no condemnation to them which are in Christ Jesus, who walk not after the flesh, but after the Spirit.

2-4. The law of the Spirit of life in Christ Jesus hath made me free from the law of sin and death. This expression is reminiscent of II Corinthians 3:17, "Where the Spirit of the Lord is, there is liberty." We should understand the law of the Spirit of Life here to be the principle upon which the Holy Spirit works. The reference to the Spirit of Life is the first time (with the exception of Romans 1:4 and 5:5), that the Spirit of God is mentioned in this epistle. However, during this chapter, the Spirit and His operation will be mentioned nineteen times. Even a casual reading of Romans 8 will leave us with the impression that the Spirit of God and the absence of an attitude of defeat go hand in hand. Life in the Spirit enables us to live free from the law or principle of sin and death. This does not mean that the believer is free from sin or free from the prospect of death, but that the principle of sin and death does not have dominion over him. It is possible for those for whom there is no condemnation to live a life that is not inundated with sin, a life which will not end in death.

2 For the law of the Spirit of life in Christ Jesus hath made me free from the law of sin and death.
3 For what the law could not do, in that it was weak through the flesh, God sending his own Son in the likeness of sinful flesh, and for sin, condemned sin in the flesh:
4 That the righteousness of the law might be fulfilled in us, who walk not after the flesh, but after the Spirit.

For what the law could not do. The law of Moses could not justify us; it could not sanctify us because it was **weak through the flesh.** The Mosaic law is good and holy, but our flesh is

weak and we are unable to keep the law; therefore, the law does
not have the power to justify. However, God sending his own
**Son in the likeness of sinful flesh, and for sin, condemned sin
in the flesh.** What the law could do, the Lord could. Paul
chose his words carefully when he that God sent His Son in
the likeness of sinful flesh. Had that Jesus came "in
sinful flesh" he would be guilty of the heresy. However,
he says that Jesus Christ came in the likeness of a
man, but was not Himself in sinful "knew no sin"
(II Cor 5:21). **And for sin.** The word (hamartia) is the
equivalent of the Old Testament "si Heb chattah).
This indicates that Jesus Christ came fering for us
and, since the law could not be that of vided our
atonement by offering the person of J e reason.
**That the righteousness of the law mig us. We
do not fulfill the law by walking in the S flesh,
but God fulfills the law in us when we ... it of
God. Thus we are assured of the righteou
law could not provide but the atonement o

2. The assurance of the indwelling Spirit of the

5-6. For they that are after the flesh do
the flesh. The verb **mind** (Gr *phroneo*) mean
as the habit of your thought; something in
total interest. Those who place their total int
of the flesh cannot have their interest in the t
to be carnally minded is death. If the mi
centered and our interest is constantly on ca
results are the symptoms of spiritual death.
interests of the mind are placed on the things
God, there is a peace in life that passes all underst

7-8. The carnal mind is enmity against God. Th
carnality is that which is placed in the mind. If our mi
an interest in carnal things, they cause us to be the enem
God. This is why James counsels, "Ye adulterers and ad
teresses, know ye not that friendship with the world is enmity
with God? Whosoever therefore will be a friend of the world is
the enemy of God" (Jas 4:4). The carnal mind **is not subject to
the law of God, neither indeed can be,** because it is natural.
Paul is not speaking here of two types of Christians, one spiritual
and one unspiritual. He is speaking of believers and unbelievers,
as verse 9 plainly indicates. Therefore, **they that are in the flesh
cannot please God.** Until faith is placed in Jesus Christ, a man
in no spiritual way can be pleasing to God the Father (Heb
11:6).

**9-10. But ye are not in the flesh, but in the Spirit, if so be
that the Spirit of God dwell in you.** The Holy Spirit of God is
the decisive factor in salvation. If a man does not have the Spirit,
he does not have Christ, and he is **none of his.** Paul clearly
teaches that no one can receive Christ's atonement for salvation
unless the Spirit of God dwells within him. It is therefore
irrational to say that there are Christians who have not fully
received the blessing of the Spirit of God. There is no scriptural
basis for a second work of grace or a baptism of the Holy Spirit
subsequent to salvation. At salvation either we have all of the
Spirit of God or we have none of Him. There may be a time
subsequent to salvation in which the Spirit of God gets more of
us, but there is never a time when we get more of Him. **And if
Christ be in you, the body is dead because of sin.** This does
not mean that we have already died physically, but that the
energizing Spirit of God within us has given us new life, a life of
righteousness. The body is yet mortal (i.e., subject to physical
death).

**11-13. He that raised up Christ from the dead shall also
quicken your mortal bodies by his Spirit that dwelleth in you.**
The resurrection of believers is always made dependent upon

---

5 For they that are after the flesh do
mind the things of the flesh; but they
that are after the Spirit the things of the
Spirit.
6 For to be carnally minded *is* death;
but to be spiritually minded *is* life and
peace.

7 Because the carnal mind *is* enmity
against God: for it is not subject to the
law of God, neither indeed can be.
8 So then they that are in the flesh
cannot please God.

9 But ye are not in the flesh, but in the
Spirit, if so be that the Spirit of God
dwell in you. Now if any man have not
the Spirit of Christ, he is none of his.
10 And if Christ *be* in you, the body *is*
dead because of sin; but the Spirit *is* life
because of righteousness.

11 But if the Spirit of him that raised
up Jesus from the dead dwell in you, he
that raised up Christ from the dead

...ortal bodies
shall also quicken you...in you.
by his Spirit that dwell...'we are debt-
12 Therefore, bret... live after the
ors, not to the fle...
flesh.
13 For if ye ...ugh the Spirit do
shall die: but ... he body, ye shall
mortify the ...
live.

the resurrection of Christ (see II Cor 6:14; II Cor 4:14; I Thess 4:14; etc.). The same Spirit that raised Jesus Christ from the dead will energize our mortal bodies as well when we are "in Christ Jesus." Consequently, we are not debtors to the flesh for we have not received new life by the flesh. When the Spirit of God comes to us at salvation we are under new management and therefore we are debtors to that management. All things are new in Christ for **there is therefore now no condemnation to them that are in Christ Jesus.** We must not give ourselves to life-styles that are characterized by the flesh, for we no longer owe allegiance to it. If we continually serve the flesh our life is characterized by a state of death. However, **if ye through the Spirit do mortify the deeds of the body, ye shall live.** The deeds of the body are those fleshly activities which characterize one who is not alive in Christ Jesus. Paul exhorts us to mortify or reckon as dead (cf. 6:11) these deeds and no longer engage in them. When that is the case, and our thoughts and deeds are energized by the presence of the Spirit of God, we will truly have a born-again behavioral pattern. Because of the fruit borne by our life, men shall know that the Spirit of God resides in us.

3. The assurance of eternal heirship. 8:14-25.

14. For as many as are led by the Spirit of God, they are the sons of God. There is one characteristic quality of all who are truly born again. That quality is that in their thoughts, behavioral patterns, and life-styles they are constantly and habitually led by the Spirit of God (Mt 7:20; Jn 13:35).

15. For ye have not received the spirit of bondage again to fear. There is a contrast to be drawn here between the life of a servant and the life of a son. When Paul says that we have not received the spirit of bondage he is saying that when the Spirit of God dwells in us we are not treated by God as servants but as sons (cf. I Cor 2:12; II Tim 1:7). We do not fear God as the slave fears his master. Rather we love Him as a son loves his father. The slave does his master's bidding because he knows he will be punished if he does not. But to him in whom the Spirit of God dwells, to him there is no element of fear that can intrude into his service for the Lord. He serves the Lord as a son lovingly serves his loving father. **Ye have received the Spirit of adoption, whereby we cry, Abba, Father.** The son is on entirely different footing than the servant. The spirit of adoption, (Gr *huiothesia*) or sonship, enables us to enter into a relationship with God the Father that the unbeliever can never experience. In the first century A.D. the adopted son was one who was deliberately chosen to perpetuate the name of his father and inherit his estate. He was not at all inferior to a son born after the course of nature. Thus we are enabled to cry **Abba, Father.** The word *abba* is an Aramaic word which was never used by the Jews in addressing God. But when the Holy Spirit dwells within us, our relationship to God the Father is such that we may address Him as freely as we would our own father.

16. The Spirit itself beareth witness with our spirit, that we are the children of God. How can we be sure that we are the children of God? Because we take God at His Word and we have the ever-present Spirit of God dwelling within us to give assurance that we are indeed the sons of God. As His children we look at the world a bit differently when our lives are responsive to His commands.

17. And if children, then heirs; heirs of God, and joint-heirs with Christ. Because we are no longer servants but sons (Gal 4:7), we then are rightfully the heirs of God. But more than that, we share in the inheritance of Christ Jesus because we will inherit by grace the glory which is His by right (Jn 17:22-24). The status of sonship, however, involves not only the privileges of inheritance, but the responsibilities of suffering.

18-19. For I reckon that the sufferings of this present time

...r as many as are led by the ... of God, they are the sons of God.

...5 For ye have not received the spirit ... bondage again to fear; but ye have ...eceived the Spirit of adoption, where-...y we cry, Abba, Father.

16 The Spirit itself beareth witness with our spirit, that we are the children of God:

17 And if children, then heirs; heirs of God, and joint-heirs with Christ; if so be that we suffer with *him*, that we may be also glorified together.

18 For I reckon that the sufferings of

this present time *are* not worthy *to be compared* with the glory which shall be revealed in us.

19 For the earnest expectation of the creature waiteth for the manifestation of the sons of God.

20 For the creature was made subject to vanity, not willingly, but by reason of him who hath subjected *the same* in hope,

21 Because the creature itself also shall be delivered from the bondage of corruption into the glorious liberty of the children of God.

22 For we know that the whole creation groaneth and travaileth in pain together until now.

23 And not only *they*, but ourselves also, which have the firstfruits of the Spirit, even we ourselves groan within ourselves, waiting for the adoption, *to wit*, the redemption of our body.

24 For we are saved by hope: but hope that is seen is not hope: for what a man seeth, why doth he yet hope for?

25 But if we hope for that we see not, *then* do we with patience wait for *it*.

26 Likewise the Spirit also helpeth our infirmities: for we know not what we should pray for as we ought: but the Spirit itself maketh intercession for us with groanings which cannot be uttered.

27 And he that searcheth the hearts

are not worthy to be compared with the glory which shall be revealed in us. If the suffering we presently endure brings great hardship, cruel and unusual punishment, severe persecution or even death itself, none of these evils can compare with the heavenly bliss that is awaiting those who are in Christ Jesus.

20-23. For the creature was made subject to vanity. As the preacher of Ecclesiastes observed, there is nothing in this life (apart from Jesus Christ) which provides lasting significance to life. If the hand of God were today removed from His creation, all that existed would be found pursuing a course of ultimate frustration. Creation is not subject to vanity by its own desire, but **by reason of him who hath subjected the same in hope.** This can only mean God, for only God can subject His creation in hope. **Because the creature itself also shall be delivered from the bondage of corruption.** The word **because** could be instead translated "that." It tells of the connection between bondage and vanity. Apart from God, creation is meaningless; it is plunging headlong into decay and death. However, God promises that even creation will one day be delivered from bondage to liberty. **The whole creation groaneth and travaileth in pain together until now.** The pain with which the whole creation groans is not death pains but birth pains. Paul has in mind the Jewish expectation of a coming Messiah, but he knows that a time of distress will precede that messianic age. Both mankind and the rest of God's creation will share in these birth pains as they together anticipate the joy that follows the pain of birth. **And not only they, but ourselves also, which have the first fruits of the Spirit.** As the creation groans for the coming of the Messiah, so too the believer groans. We are said to have the first fruits of the Spirit. That is, the indwelling Spirit is the first installment or down payment on the eternal glory that awaits both the believer and God's creation. This provides the assurance of our eternal heirship. As believers we await the adoption, that is, **the redemption of our body.** Though we may today be attacked by physical pain, surrounded by financial distress, discouraged by failing health, nevertheless we know that because we possess the Holy Spirit as our down payment, God will certainly redeem our bodies as He has already redeemed our souls. As the sons of God we will one day be clothed with immortal and incorruptible bodies (I Cor 15:5-55; II Cor 5:2-3; Phil 3:21).

24-25. For we are saved by hope. This expression does not imply that salvation comes through the instrumentality of hope. The uniform teaching of Paul, as well as Scripture in general, is that we are saved by faith (cf. 1:16-17; Eph 2:8). The words **by hope** refer to that ingredient which is inseparable from salvation and a natural accompaniment to it. Hope can never be divorced from salvation because salvation is the ground of our hope. **But hope that is seen is not hope.** Once we have realized the heirship that has been promised to us and the redemption of our bodies, we will no longer hope in them. Therefore, **if we hope for that we see not, then do we with patience wait for it.** This expression of patience is a fitting conclusion to the chapter which deals with the provision of assurance. Looking to a future adoption of the body provides opportunity for our faith to grow and mature. Consequently the virtue of patience is developed in addition to hope and faith. Therefore, although we are assured of eternal heirship, nevertheless we develop patience in waiting for the coming of the Lord.

4. The assurance of present intercession. 8:26-27.

26-27. Likewise the Spirit also helpeth our infirmities. The great consolation we have during this period of waiting for the Lord's return is the presence of the Holy Spirit. He is the One who helps our **infirmities** (Gr *astheneia*) which is better translated in the singular. We have one great infirmity while waiting for the Lord to return to us, and that is **we know not what we**

knoweth what *is* the mind of the Spirit, because he maketh intercession for the saints according to *the will of* God.

should pray for as we ought. The only thing our Lord's disciples asked Him to teach them was how to pray. Each believer encounters that same difficulty in knowing how to pray and for what to pray. Consequently, God has given His Holy Spirit to make intercession for us **with groanings which cannot be uttered.** Even when we do not know what to say to God, the Holy Spirit interprets our innermost feelings and intercedes in our behalf. These inarticulate sounds are heard by God when intercession is made for us by the Holy Spirit. **And he that searcheth the hearts knoweth what is the mind of the Spirit.** The Scriptures frequently speak of God as One who searches the heart (cf. I Chr 28:9; Ps 139:1, 23; Jer 17:10; I Cor 4:5; Heb 4:12-13). As the omniscient eye of God searches even the inarticulate groanings of our hearts, the Spirit of God makes intercession for the saint of God. Thus, intercession is made for us not only by God the Son, who sits at the right hand of God the Father, but also by God the Spirit who dwells within the believer.

5. The assurance of the eternal purpose of God. 8:28-34.

28 And we know that all things work together for good to them that love God, to them who are the called according to *his* purpose.

28. And we know that all things work together for good to them that love God, to them who are the called according to his purpose. In the midst of the distress of this world, Paul has presented the future adoption of our bodies at the coming of the Lord as a source of strength and hope. The Spirit of God within us is also given as a source of strength. Now the apostle lists a third source of encouragement for the believer. In the midst of the sufferings of this life, God has given us knowledge that He is working every detail of life to the end established in His eternal purpose. Grammatically, **all things** may be either subject or object of the verb. Therefore, it is God who works things out according to His will. **To them who are the called according to his purpose. The called** is not in the general sense of "many are called but few are chosen" but in the specific sense of those who comprise the family of God. Therefore, the promise of all things working together for good is given to a specific group, **the called** (i.e., those who are in Christ Jesus and justified by His blood). The world in general does not have this promise.

29 For whom he did foreknow, he also did predestinate *to be* conformed to the image of his Son, that he might be the firstborn among many brethren. 30 Moreover whom he did predestinate, them he also called: and whom he called, them he also justified: and whom he justified, them he also glorified.

29-30. For whom he did foreknow, he also did predestinate to be conformed to the image of his Son. The last word of the preceding verse is the **purpose** of God. Paul now expands on that purpose in verses 29 and 30 by means of a "sorites," a construction in which the predicate of one clause becomes the subject of the next clause. In the salvation provided by God, there is a link from eternity past, through the present, to eternity future. That link includes foreknowledge, predestination, calling, justification, and glorification. However, we must understand that the key word in this passage is the word **purpose.** All the others arise out of the purpose of God and our understanding of them must be in consort with God's eternal purpose.

Probably no doctrine has evoked a greater variety of interpretations than that of God's foreknowledge. Although it is true that foreknowledge means to know beforehand, in the context of God's purpose, to interpret the expression in this way would be an oversimplification. For God to preview history in order to discern our response to the gospel, and then act accordingly, would make the creature sovereign over the Creator. The word **foreknow** occurs infrequently in the New Testament, and therefore a clear understanding of its import must be seen from the way it is used in both Old and New Testament Scriptures. When God takes knowledge of His people it is more than just a basic understanding of them (cf. Amos 3:2; Hos 13:5; I Cor 8:3; Gal 4:3; etc.). It is the knowledge a father has of his child. God knows and loves the world, but His foreknowledge of His own is an intimate knowledge which results in an abiding love (5:8) for us that draws us to Him in salvation.

He also did predestinate to be conformed to the image of his Son. God's foreordination or predestination must not be equated with fatalism. Fatalism says that the world is plunging headlong toward an indeterminate end. Paul teaches that there is a very determinate end for those who are **the called.** Their end or goal is to be conformed to the image of God's Son, Jesus Christ. We are not plunging downward but are progressing upward in being sanctified toward the Son of Righteousness. As believers, we should become more and more like the Master every day. But God has planned for us a final and complete conformity to the resurrection glory of the Lord for He is the **firstborn among many brethren** (I Cor 15:49; II Cor 3:18; Phil 3:21; I Jn 3:2). Since the term firstborn always implies a position of supremecy, it is the eternal purpose of God that we become increasingly more conformed to the image of Him who is the Supreme Being in the universe. **Them he also called.** As believers, we were foreknown and foreordained prior to our birth. Yet God does not manipulate us like puppets. Rather He calls us, He beseeches us to receive His offer of salvation. When we are quickened by the Spirit of God (Eph 2:2), and respond to His call in faith, we are then justified in His sight by faith.

Them he also justified. Justification is a vital doctrine in Pauline thinking. When God justifies us, He reckons us as if we are righteous because of the atoning death of Jesus Christ. He imputes the righteousness of Christ to our account. Therefore, **whom he justified, them he also glorified.** The final step in the purpose of God is the glorification of His people. We will ultimately be completely conformed to "the image of His Son." "When Christ, who is our life, shall appear, then shall ye also appear with him in glory" (Col 3:4; cf. I Jn 3:2). This is God's view of salvation. Foreknowledge and foreordination belong to the eternal past, in the eternal counsel of the Godhead; calling and justification take place in the believer's present experience; the glory which begins now will not ultimately and completely be known until the future. Although salvation from our viewpoint is an instantaneous act, it has in fact stretched from eternity past to eternity future and finds its basis, not in our merit or in the works of the law, but in the purpose of God. In the depression and turmoil of these days, nothing can be of greater encouragement to believers than to know that God is working all things together for our good and His glory.

31 What shall we then say to these things? If God *be* for us, who *can be* against us?

31. Paul now asks a series of four rhetorical questions in relation to the eternal purpose of God. **What shall we then say to these things?** In essence, this verse is the conclusion Paul draws to the first eight chapters of Romans. What will our response be to what has been said? **If God be for us, who can be against us?** This is not one of the four rhetorical questions but rather the answer to the first question. Paul's only response is he has complete assurance that the eternal purpose of God will come to fruition because God is God. **Who can be against us?** does not mean that we have no adversaries. Verses 35 and 36 list a great number of adversaries. By this Paul means that there is no adversary too great to thwart the eternal purpose of God.

32 He that spared not his own Son, but delivered him up for us all, how shall he not with him also freely give us all things?

32. As evidence of the fact that God will bring His eternal purpose to its proper conclusion, Paul argues that God **spared not his own Son, but delivered him up for us all.** These words are reminiscent of the classic example of the redemptive efficacy of martyrdom which is given in Genesis 22:12. There God says to Abraham, "Thou hast not withheld (Gr *pheidomai*, as here) thy son, thine only son from me." So much did God love us that He did not spare His own Son in providing atonement for us. Paul then argues from the greater to the lesser in the rhetorical question, **how shall he not with him also freely give us all things?** If God did not spare His own Son, but delivered Him up to the cross of Calvary, it isn't logical that He would fail to bring to its completed end the purpose for which Christ was sacrificed.

33 Who shall lay any thing to the charge of God's elect? *It is* God that justifieth.

34 Who *is* he that condemneth? *It is* Christ that died, yea rather, that is risen again, who is even at the right hand of God, who also maketh intercession for us.

35 Who shall separate us from the love of Christ? *shall* tribulation, or distress, or persecution, or famine, or nakedness, or peril, or sword?

36 As it is written, For thy sake we are killed all the day long; we are accounted as sheep for the slaughter.

37 Nay, in all these things we are more than conquerors through him that loved us.

38 For I am persuaded, that neither

Hence, all the gifts and blessings which accompany salvation are promised to us even as salvation is ours.

33. Paul's third rhetorical question is, **Who shall lay anything to the charge of God's elect?** This question is along the same line as that in verse 31, **Who can be against us?** Paul is issuing a challenge to the universe that if there is any man, any angel, any demon, anyone who can bring forth a charge and lay it at the doorstep of God's elect, let him do so now. In answer to this question Paul says, **It is God that justifieth.** Since the **called** are justified by God, therefore no one will be able to appeal God's verdict of justification. Every tongue that attempts to do so will be silenced (cf. Isa 50:8-9; 54:17).

34. Who is he that condemneth? This fourth rhetorical question belongs with the preceding statement, **It is God that justifieth.** Paul is saying that anyone can issue a charge, but only One has the authority to condemn and that authority is committed into the hands of God the Son (Jn 5:22). In answer to this question he says, **It is Christ that died.** Only the Lord God could devise a plan in which the only person in the universe who can condemn us, is the very person who died for us. But more than His death is that He **is risen again, who is even at the right hand of God, who also maketh intercession for us.** The death of the Lord Jesus on our behalf would avail little apart from His resurrection. It is the living Lord that insures the security of God's eternal purpose. Consequently, He is now sitting at the right hand of God where He is highly exalted in glory and sovereignty. By the authority which is innate to His deity, the Lord Jesus makes intercession for us to God the Father. By His victorious death, His victorious resurrection, His victorious ascension into heaven, and His victorious intercession for us, the Lord Jesus has sealed the eternal purpose of God. In the whole universe there is nothing which can provide greater assurance than the finished work of Christ.

6. The assurance of the eternal presence of God. 8:35-39.

35. Who shall separate us from the love of Christ? Our assurance in the eternal presence of God is based upon the unfailing love of God. Again Paul asks a rhetorical question. The love of God keeps us in the palm of His hand and has been demonstrated to us through the atoning sacrifice of His son, Jesus Christ (5:8). Paul then amplifies the question by asking if it is possible that tribulation, distress, persecution, famine, nakedness, peril, or the sword can enter our lives and undo what Christ has accomplished on our behalf at the cross.

36. As it is written. Before Paul answers his question, there is a verbatim quote from Psalm 44:22. This quote is introduced to indicate that God's people shall endure affliction even as the faithful did in the Old Testament. However, the persecution and tribulation that enter our lives, which have featured so prominently in this chapter, are not sufficient to separate us from God's love, demonstrated at the cross of Christ.

37. Now for Paul's answer. **Nay, in all these things we are more than conquerors through him that loved us.** In the midst of illness, suffering, and myriad of life's afflictions, we have God's assurance of His eternal presence and therefore are said to be **more than conquerors.** The word used here in the original language is *hypernikaō* which literally means that we are "super-conquerors." We do not merely hold our own in the face of testing, but through suffering we are drawn closer to Christ and become more conformed to His image. Notice, however, the means by which we are super-conquerors, **through him that loved us.** Personal heroism and inner strength are not contributors to success in the Christian life. As we owe our justification to Him and our sanctification to Him, we also owe our assurance to Him. All we have we owe to Him.

38-39. For I am persuaded . . . shall be able to separate us

death, nor life, nor angels, nor principalities, nor powers, nor things present, nor things to come,

39 Nor height, nor depth, nor any other creature, shall be able to separate us from the love of God, which is in Christ Jesus our Lord.

from the love of God, which is in Christ Jesus our Lord. Paul searches the entire universe to see if there is anything that can possibly separate us from the eternal presence of God. He goes first to the realm of death and finds nothing there. Then he turns to the realm of life and again finds nothing. He looks to the angels and they have no power to separate us. He turns to principalities which, in this case, may refer to the angelic hosts representing Satan. There is nothing there. He proceeds to examine **things present** and finds nothing. He explores the future and in the **things to come** there is nothing which can separate us. Nothing can happen now nor in the future which can remove the love of God from us or us from His eternal security.

Paul does not stop here for next he searches the entire universe and nothing in the expanses of space, **height, nor depth** can be found to prohibit the presence of God from us. But just in case he has missed something, Paul then says that there is no other creature or creation of God that is able to separate us from the love of God in Christ Jesus. Nowhere can the apostle find anything in the whole universe of God which can sever the relationship that the children of God have with their Father's love. This great assurance comes to those who are "the called" in Christ Jesus our Lord.

"Blessed assurance, Jesus is mine! Oh what a foretaste of glory divine! Heir of salvation, purchase of God, born of His Spirit, washed in His blood." Paul has completed this great chapter in the same way he began it. **There is therefore now no comdemnation to them which are in Christ Jesus** (8:1). Paul is persuaded that nothing **shall be able to separate us from the love of God, which is in Christ Jesus our Lord.** All these wonderful promises belong to us because we belong to Him.

IV. THE RIGHTEOUSNESS OF GOD EXEMPLIFIED. 9:1-11:36.

Although in many ways Romans 9-11 is parenthetical, nevertheless it is an integral part of Paul's argument for justification by faith alone. Paul may have been accused of being so dedicated as the apostle to the Gentiles that he had completely forgotten about his Jewish kith and kin. Therefore he addresses the problem of Israel before proceeding to the practical section of this epistle. Also, the original believers in Rome appear to have been Jews; but in Paul's day the church was predominantly Gentiles. Those Jewish believers at Rome needed Paul's reassurance of their place in the kingdom of God. But above all, the many messianic promises to the Jews of old necessitated an understanding that God would yet honor those promises. If Paul's message of salvation by faith is true, then why did not Paul's own people receive that message? Paul must deal with the problem of Jewish unbelief before he can proceed to a conclusion concerning the life we live in Christ Jesus.

Paul's treatment of the problem is daring. He readily admits that the Jewish nation has rejected the gospel, and yet he takes a firm stand in declaring that God is not finished with the Jew. Paul views everything that happens as part of the eternal purpose of God and therefore moving toward God's desired end.

A. Righteousness Exemplified in Divine Sovereignty. 9:1-33.

1. Sovereignty exhibited in Israel's identity. 9:1-8.

CHAPTER 9

I SAY the truth in Christ, I lie not, my conscience also bearing me witness in the Holy Ghost,

2 That I have great heaviness and continual sorrow in my heart.

3 For I could wish that myself were accursed from Christ for my brethren, my kinsmen according to the flesh:

9:1-3. I say the truth in Christ, I lie not. Paul arrests the attention of his readers by certifying the truthfulness of what he is about to say. He adds the negative **I lie not** to emphasize the veracity of his statement (cf. II Cor 11:31; Gal 1:20; I Tim 2:7). To this he adds **my conscience also bearing me witness in the Holy Ghost.** This indicates that to what his tongue will speak, his conscience will attest.

In the midst of Paul's expression of joy and great assurance, he also bears witness **That I have great heaviness and continual sorrow in my heart.** This unceasing pain and sorrow which Paul bears is for his kinsmen, the Jews. **For I could wish that myself were accursed from Christ for my brethren.** This statement about being anathema from Christ is reminiscent of Moses' statement made upon returning from Mount Sinai. As the great leader viewed the children of Israel involved in the wicked worship of the golden calf, he desired to have his name blotted out of God's book in return for the salvation of Israel (Ex 32:30-33). The understanding of Paul, however, in relation to justification by faith, does not allow him to actually wish himself accursed from Christ (i.e., separate from Christ for everlasting destruction). Paul knows that his life is not his own. Therefore he is not the master of his own life and does not have the power to cast away the eternal life that was purchased for him by the blood of Christ. The verb is in the imperfect tense ("I could wish"), meaning that Paul would accept everlasting destruction in return for the salvation of Israel, but God will not allow him to do so.

4 Who are Israelites; to whom *pertaineth* the adoption, and the glory, and the covenants, and the giving of the law, and the service *of God,* and the promises;
5 Whose *are* the fathers, and of whom as concerning the flesh Christ *came,* who is over all, God blessed for ever. Amen.

4-5. Who are Israelites; to whom pertaineth . . . Paul does not address his kinsmen according to the flesh by their racial name, but as "Israelites," their theocratic name. Unto them pertain **the adoption** (i.e., sonship; cf. Ex 4:22-23; Deut 14:1-2; Hos 11:1; Mal 1:6); **the glory** (which appeared on Mount Sinai, Ex 24:16-17 and filled the tabernacle, Ex 40:34-38); **the covenants** (made to Abraham, Moses, and David); **the giving of the law** (the Mosaic constitution); **the service of God** (the ordinance of worship and sacrifice in the sanctuary, Heb 9:1-6); and **the promises** (that of forgiveness of sins, the inheritance of the Promised Land, but most especially the promise of the Messiah, Gal 3:16).

Whose are the fathers, and of whom as concerning the flesh Christ came. All of these privileges pertain to the Patriarchs and their seed. Notice that Paul does not say that Christ belongs to them but that He came from their flesh. This is to indicate that the culmination of all the promises given to the Patriarchs is seen in the person of Jesus Christ. Each of these privileges finds its focus in Him, **who is over all, God blessed for ever.**

6 Not as though the word of God hath taken none effect. For they *are* not all Israel, which are of Israel:
7 Neither, because they are the seed of Abraham, *are they* all children: but, In Isaac shall thy seed be called.
8 That is, They which are the children of the flesh, these *are* not the children of God: but the children of the promise are counted for the seed.

6-8. For they are not all Israel, which are of Israel. Paul now repeats the distinction he made in 2:28-29 between Israel of natural destiny and the true Jew. Often distinctions have been made between Israel and those who are truly of Israel (cf. Jn 8:30-32). The Lord Jesus spoke of Nathanael as "an Israelite indeed, in whom is no guile" (Jn 1:47). Paul speaks of the Israelites as being true Israel when they are "born after the Spirit" (Gal 4:29). Being of the seed of Abraham does not make one an Israelite, for Abraham had two sons, Ishmael and Isaac. "In Israel shall thy seed be called" (Gen 21:12). **But the children of the promise are counted for the seed.** In Paul's understanding, the children of promise are those who believe in the God of Abraham and their faith is imputed to them for righteousness, as was his. Since not all of Abraham's descendants through Isaac have experienced this type of faith, not all of Israel are truly of Israel.

2. Sovereignty exhibited in God's personal choices. 9:9-13.

9 For this *is* the word of promise, At this time will I come, and Sarah shall have a son.

9. For this is the word of promise, At this time will I come and Sarah shall have a son. This quotation from Genesis 18:10 is in accordance with the promise that Isaac would be born, a promise which seemed so unlikely that it provoked Sarah to laughter (Gen 18:12). Nevertheless, Isaac was born and, although not the firstborn of Abraham, he was God's choice as the son through whom the promises of God would be manifested. God chose Isaac. It was His purpose that in **Isaac shall**

10 And not only *this;* but when Rebecca also had conceived by one, *even* by our father Isaac:

11 (For *the children* being not yet born, neither having done any good or evil, that the purpose of God according to election might stand, not of works, but of him that calleth;)

12 It was said unto her, The elder shall serve the younger.

13 As it is written, Jacob have I loved, but Esau have I hated.

14 What shall we say then? *Is there* unrighteousness with God? God forbid.

15 For he saith to Moses, I will have mercy on whom I will have mercy, and I will have compassion on whom I will have compassion.

16 So then *it is* not of him that willeth, nor of him that runneth, but of God that sheweth mercy.

17 For the scripture saith unto Pharaoh, Even for this same purpose have I raised thee up, that I might shew my power in thee, and that my name might be declared throughout all the earth.

thy seed be called. Paul advances Isaac as an illustration that God deals on the principle of His sovereignty.

10-13. And not only this. Paul concedes that someone might say that the example of Isaac is inappropriate because Ishmael was the son of the bondwoman and therefore not truly legitimate. Consequently, Paul introduces a second example of God's election of grace. This time the example is Jacob. Had the principle of sovereign election been seen only in the life of Isaac, it would not have produced a biblical pattern. But this principle is seen as well in God's choice of Isaac's sons.

Rebecca also had conceived by one, even by our father Isaac. There is no question that the sons Jacob and Esau are both legitimately in the line of Isaac, the promised child. Yet Paul advances that God, in His sovereignty, supersedes the process of natural primogenitureship and chooses Jacob the younger to be served by Esau the elder. The reason for this choice is that **the purpose of God according to election might stand.** Every action of God arises out of His eternal purpose (8:28). The selection of Jacob to be the heir of the promise instead of his older brother Esau is a perfect example of the sovereignty of God exhibited in God's personal choices. Jacob was chosen **being not yet born, neither having done any good or evil.** Salvation is never upon the basis of human merit, **not of works, but of him that calleth.** Salvation is always upon the basis of divine grace which arises out of the eternal purpose of the sovereign God.

As it is written, Jacob have I loved, but Esau have I hated. The expression **Esau have I hated** cannot simply mean to love less but must mean, in the context of Malachi 1:1-5, that God has actually directed his wrath toward Esau and his descendants. The judgments upon Edom are positive judgments and not merely the absence of blessing. God displays His wrath upon the sins of Edom not in unholy rancor but in righteous judgment. He does the same with individuals.

3. Sovereignty exhibited in God's powerful will. 9:14-24.

14. What shall we say then? When Paul asserted this teaching on the election of God's grace, he was well aware that many would object. Their objection was embodied in the question, **Is there unrighteousness with God?** Would not God be unrighteous if He chose one man and not another? To the human observer the choice of Jacob in preference to Esau, prior to their birth, must appear to be arbitrary and unjust. This is because the human observer is acting on the basis of his limited knowledge. Paul's response to the thought that God is unrighteous in choosing one over another is the strongest negative he can express, his characteristic, **God forbid.**

15-16. I will have mercy on whom I will have mercy. This statement is a quote from Exodus 33:19 and is God's response to Moses' request, "I beseech thee, show me thy glory" (Ex 33:18). Paul quotes this verse without commentary. He intends to show that even Moses had no particular claim to any favor before God. God operates on the just principle of His eternal purpose. **So then it is not of him that willeth, nor of him that runneth, but of God that showeth mercy.** Again it is emphasized that God's mercy finds its cause in Himself and not in any activity of man. As in Galatians 2:2 and Philippians 2:16, "running" is symbolic of human activity and has no effect whatsoever on the mercy or purpose of God.

17. For the scripture saith unto Pharaoh. The case of the Pharaoh of the Exodus strikingly illustrates this principle of divine mercy. Pharaoh is said to have been raised up by God. **That I might show my power in thee, and that my name might be declared throughout all the earth.** Not even the power of the great Egyptian Pharaoh was sufficient to thwart the eternal purpose of God or to prohibit Him from blessing and delivering

His people. The Scripture which Paul quotes is Exodus 9:16 where the Hebrew verb *amadth* meaning "stand" is used for the expression "have I raised thee up." God put Pharaoh in a position of being the Egyptian king. He also preserved him there in spite of his disobedience, so that the purpose of God may be fulfilled. The purpose was that His name might be declared throughout the earth (cf. Ex 15:14; Josh 2:10; 9:9; I Sam 4:7-9).

18 Therefore hath he will *have mercy*, and whom he will he hardeneth.

18. Therefore hath he mercy on whom he will have mercy, and whom he will he hardeneth. The initial phrase of this verse echoes Exodus 33:19 but the later phrase refers to the occasions on which the heart of Pharaoh was hardened. It must be recognized that Pharaoh hardened his own heart (cf. Ex 5:2; 7:3, 13) by his deliberate opposition to the will of the God of Israel. However, a time came when he was judicially bound over in hardness by God, and the initial indifference of Pharaoh's heart was cemented by God into a permanent hardness (cf. Ex 5:21; 7:23; 9:12; 10:1, 20, 27; 11:10; 14:4, 8).

19 Thou wilt say then unto me, Why doth he yet find fault? For who hath resisted his will?
20 Nay but, O man, who art thou that repliest against God? Shall the thing formed say to him that formed *it*, Why hast thou made me thus?

19-20. Why doth he yet find fault? For who hath resisted his will? Paul knows that the unbeliever will object to his teaching, saying that God cannot find fault with him because it is the way God made him. If God is sovereign, it is impossible to resist His will and therefore man is not accountable for his lost condition. Although there is a fallacy in this type of reasoning (God did not make man the way he is; He created him in His own image and man is what he is today because of his own sin), Paul does not argue that point. Rather his reply is, **Nay but, O man, who art thou that replieth against God?** Paul maintains that the creature is not competent to sit in judgment on his Creator. To judge the validity of God's actions is to imply that man is more righteous than God; to judge the wisdom of God's movements is to imply that man is wiser than God. Thus Paul sternly rebukes any type of reasoning which inverts the divine order of creature to Creator. **Shall the thing formed say to him that formed it, Why hast thou made me thus?** God is not answerable to man for what He does, but He must act consistent with His character. Divine sovereignty does not permit God to do what divine character will not allow. If we can trust the character of God, we can trust the wisdom of His sovereignty as well.

21 Hath not the potter power over the clay, of the same lump to make one vessel unto honour, and another unto dishonour?
22 *What* if God, willing to shew *his* wrath, and to make his power known, endured with much longsuffering the vessels of wrath fitted to destruction:
23 And that he might make known the riches of his glory on the vessels of mercy, which he had afore prepared unto glory,
24 Even us, whom he hath called, not of the Jews only, but also of the Gentiles?

21-24. The apostle now engages in a bit of philosophical argumentation. **Hath not the potter power over the clay? . . . What if God, willing to show his wrath, and to make his power known, endured with much long-suffering the vessels of wrath fitted to destruction.** Here Paul argues that man displays the justice and grace of God, both through the persistent unbeliever (whom he calls a vessel fitted for wrath), and through the believer, (a vessel of mercy). We must remember Paul does not say that God created one vessel to wrath and another to mercy. He endured the vessels of wrath which were fitted to destruction and made known the riches to His glory on the vessels of mercy **which he had afore prepared unto glory.** As the potter does not take one lump of clay and make it a good lump, and another lump and make it bad, so too God does not make one person evil and another one good. We must notice that the expression **fitted to destruction** is in the Greek middle voice, and should be interpreted that man fits himself for destruction. God never does that. On the other hand, are those who were prepared by the grace of God through faith in His Son and are fitted by God for eternal life. With a thankful heart Paul notes that God has sovereignly called to glory both those of the Jews and also those of the Gentiles. As believers, whether Jew or Gentile, we have been the recipients of God's mercy and have been prepared for the glory of His presence. For this we should be intensely thankful.

4. Sovereignty exhibited in Israel's partial blindness. 9:25-33.

25 As he saith also in Ō′see, I will call them my people, which were not my people; and her beloved, which was not beloved.
26 And it shall come to pass, *that* in the place where it was said unto them, Ye *are* not my people; there shall they be called the children of the living God.

25-26. As he saith also in Osee. Paul now appeals to a number of Old Testament prophecies concerning God's people and the principle of election. He paraphrases Hosea 2:23, **I will call them my people, which were not my people; and her beloved, which was not beloved.** In the tragedy of his domestic life, this Old Testament man of God saw a parable of the relationship between God and Israel. Hosea took Gomer to be his wife and a child was born which he named Jezreel. But when Gomer's second and third children were born, of whom Hosea was not convinced he was the father, names were given which expressed his dismay, They were named in Hebrew, Lo-ammi (no kin of mine) and Loruhamah (one for whom no natural affection is felt). These names strikingly indicate God's attitude toward His people Israel when they broke their covenant with Him and forsook His commands. **And it shall come to pass, that in the place where it was said unto them, Ye are not my people; there shall they be called the children of the living God.** Paul does not make an application here to the prophecy of Hosea but it is evident that he is extracting from this prophecy the principle of divine election. He shows that great numbers of Gentiles, who had never been "the people of God," could now lay claim to the same relationship with God which Israel had.

27 E-ŝā′ias also crieth concerning Israel, Though the number of the children of Israel be as the sand of the sea, a remnant shall be saved:
28 For he will finish the work, and cut *it* short in righteousness: because a short work will the Lord make upon the earth.

27-28. Next Paul appeals to the prophecy of Isaiah 10:22-23. The meaning of Isaiah's prophecy is that although Israel is numerous as a people, nevertheless only a small minority will survive the judgment of God by the Assyrian Empire. **A remnant shall be saved.** If only a remnant of Israel will survive, there will be at least a remnant. God has always had a people. Paul applies Isaiah's teaching of the remnant to his own day. Although Israel has rejected God, nevertheless there are some who, through the grace of God, have received the salvation of God. The teaching of verse 28 is that the punitive judgment of God will exhibit both thoroughness and great dispatch. God will cut short His working upon the earth to prevent Israel from spiritually destroying herself. In His eternal purpose a remnant, at least, will be saved.

29 And as E-ŝā′ias said before, Except the Lord of Săb′a-ŏth had left us a seed, we had been as Sŏd′o-ma, and been made like unto Go-mŏr′rha.

29. Except the Lord of Sabaoth had left us a seed, we had been as Sodom, and been made like unto Gomorrah. This quote from Isaiah 1:9 reveals that Isaiah placed squarely on the grace of God the fact that a seed (i.e., a remnant, the very germ of the nation) had been saved and they had not been obliterated like Sodom and Gomorrah. To the Lord of Hosts alone belongs the praise for the salvation of any of the wicked Israelites.

30 What shall we say then? That the Gentiles, which followed not after righteousness, have attained to righteousness, even the righteousness which is of faith.
31 But Israel, which followed after the law of righteousness, hath not attained to the law of righteousness.

30-31. What shall we say then? Paul's summary question in this chapter follows the same form as we have seen elsewhere in this epistle (cf. 3:5; 4:1; 6:1; 7:7; 8:31; 9:14). **The Gentiles . . . have attained to righteousness . . . But Israel . . . hath not attained to the law of righteousness.** God has always saved on the basis of faith and never on the basis of good works. Therefore Gentiles can come to the Saviour and follow after the righteousness which is of faith, even without the privileges of the Jew, and with no prior knowledge of the Scriptures. The Jews, on the other hand, who had great privileges and knew well the Old Testament Scriptures, tragically attempted to establish their own righteousness by adherence to the works of the Mosaic law. Consequently Paul concludes that the partial blindness of Israel exhibits God's sovereignty in allowing those who were most distant from Himself (the Gentiles) to come unto Him by faith.

32 Wherefore? Because *they sought it* not by faith, but as it were by the works of the law. For they stumbled at that stumblingstone;
33 As it is written, Behold, I lay in

32-33. How can such as has just been described possibly happen to Paul's kinsmen according to the flesh? **Because they sought it not by faith, but as it were by the works of the law. For they stumbled at that stumbling stone; As it is written, Behold, I lay in Zion a stumbling stone and rock of offense.**

Sion a stumblingstone and rock of offence: and whosoever believeth on him shall not be ashamed.

The great tragedy of the Jewish nation was that the Messiah they so long awaited became to them a stumbling stone rather than a shelter in which to hide. The quotation here is from Isaiah 28:16, which is set in the context of Israel trusting Egypt for deliverance from the Assyrians instead of trusting in the power of God. Those who trust in God need never fear that their trust has been ill-placed or is ill-founded. **Whosoever believeth on him shall not be ashamed.** Had Israel trusted in her God rather than her law and her neighbors, she would not have been confounded and dispersed throughout the world. But the partial blindness of Israel, in the eternal purpose of God, has wrought good to the Gentiles and to the world in general. God is now calling out a people unto His name from both Jews and the Gentiles.

B. Righteousness Exemplified in Human Responsibility. 10:1-21.

The groundwork for chapter 10 has already been laid in 9:30-33. The emphasis here is on righteousness and why Israel lacks it. Paul will lay the responsibility for the lack of righteousness squarely on the shoulders of the individual. He knows that when sinners are brought into the presence of divine sovereignty their frequent response is to justify themselves by placing the responsibility for their sin on God. Paul does not apologize in any way for what he has said about God's sovereignty in chapter 9. He does not retreat at all from his strong belief that God has always worked by the principle of election. However he does demonstrate that God is not responsible for the unbeliever's lost condition. Man alone is responsible and it is futile to try to hide behind divine sovereignty and the doctrine of election as an excuse for personal sin.

1. Nearness of the gospel: opportunity for responsibility. 10:1-10.

10:1-3. Brethren, my heart's desire and prayer to God for Israel is, that they might be saved. In the first three verses of chapter 10, Paul reiterates his feeling for his kinsmen the Jews. He has already expressed this in the first three verses of chapter 9. Even though he is the apostle to the Gentiles, Paul takes no satisfaction in Israel's rejection of God. He bears witness to the fact that the Jews have a definite zeal for God, **but not according to knowledge.** The problem with Israel is that her improper motives have caused her to have a zeal for keeping the Law, but not for being the nation God would have her be. They have read the Law and memorized the Law, but have never internalized the truth of the Law about God's righteousness and consequently they are **going about to establish their own righteousness,** and in so doing they **have not submitted themselves unto the righteousness of God.** To earn righteousness is to gain spurious righteousness. Any attempt to establish one's own righteousness is open rebellion against God and His method of establishing righteousness in us.

4. For Christ is the end of the law for righteousness to everyone that believeth. In what respect is Christ the end (Gr *telos*) of the law? The word may mean, on the one hand, that Christ is the goal or purpose for which the law was given. In this respect it would mean that the law was aimed at bringing us to Christ and that He came to fulfill the law and thus give it validity (cf. Isa 42:21; Mt 5:17). But on the other hand, this word may properly mean that Christ is the terminal point of the law. With the advent of the Lord Jesus, the old order, of which the law was a significant part, has been done away and the new order of the Holy Spirit of God has been instituted.

There is one qualification to Christ being the end of the law for righteousness. He is only the end, **to everyone that believeth.** Those who yet attempt to establish their own righteousness do not find Christ as the end of the law and consequently do not discover true righteousness.

CHAPTER 10

BRETHREN, my heart's desire and prayer to God for Israel is, that they might be saved.

2 For I bear them record that they have a zeal of God, but not according to knowledge.

3 For they being ignorant of God's righteousness, and going about to establish their own righteousness, have not submitted themselves unto the righteousness of God.

4 For Christ *is* the end of the law for righteousness to every one that believeth.

The antithesis seen in verses 3 and 4 between self-established righteousness and God-established righteousness is now alluded to as recorded by Moses. Moses speaks both of the righteousness which is of the law and of the righteousness which is of faith. For the righteousness of the law he quotes Leviticus 18:5.

5 For Moses describeth the righteousness which is of the law, That the man which doeth those things shall live by them.

6 But the righteousness which is of faith speaketh on this wise, Say not in thine heart, Who shall ascend into heaven? (that is, to bring Christ down from above:)

7 Or, Who shall descend into the deep? (that is, to bring up Christ again from the dead.)

8 But what saith it? The word is nigh thee, even in thy mouth, and in thy heart: that is, the word of faith, which we preach;

5-8. That the man which doeth those things shall live by them. In reference to Moses' teaching concerning the righteousness which is of faith, the apostle quotes Deuteronomy 30:12, 14, **Say not in thine heart, Who shall ascend into heaven?** The righteousness which is of the law taught men to do and live. But the righteousness which is by faith teaches men to believe and live (10:6). The Pentateuch clearly shows that the law is to be written upon the hearts of men. It was not to be an external means of external justification. Unfortunately, the Jews mistakenly perverted the law and were attempting to keep the law outwardly without the right inward heart attitude.

Throughout this passage Paul is interested in establishing the accessibility of the message of God's righteousness. To that end he counseled the Jew, **Say not in thine heart, who shall ascend into heaven? (that is, to bring Christ down from above).** This appears to be a taunt. The Jew feels the righteousness of God is inaccessible because no one can ascend into heaven to inquire about it. Paul teaches, however, that we do not have to ascend into heaven for God came and tabernacled among us in the person of Jesus Christ, to show us the righteousness of God. Similarly he asks, **Who shall descend into the deep? (that is, to bring up Christ again from the dead).** Again, a taunt of unbelief. This smacks of a denial of the resurrection of Christ. We do not need to descend into the abyss to learn of God's righteousness for Christ is alive and is living proof of that righteousness.

In putting an end to these foolish questions the apostle quotes Deuteronomy 30:12-14, "The word is nigh unto thee, even in thy mouth, and thy heart; that is, the word of faith which we preach." Paul maintains that the true word concerning the righteousness of God is near the Jews. He even goes so far as to say that it is in their mouths and in their hearts. How can this be? The answer is that when entering a town to preach, Paul immediately proceeded to the synagogue. Whether the Jews believed his message or not, when he left, they remained behind to discuss what Paul had taught. The very message of the gospel of Christ had been in their mouths and in their hearts, but they did not believe. The truth of righteousness was as close to them as it could possibly be, but they failed in their responsibility to receive that truth.

9 That if thou shalt confess with thy mouth the Lord Jesus, and shalt believe in thine heart that God hath raised him from the dead, thou shalt be saved.

10 For with the heart man believeth unto righteousness; and with the mouth confession is made unto salvation.

9-10. That if thou shalt confess with thy mouth the Lord Jesus. Paul has just made reference that the gospel has been in the mouths of the Jews. Now he builds on that thought. He explains that the confession "Jesus is Lord" refers to the lordship which Jesus exercises as the exalted Christ. Salvation must entail faith in One who is Lord. Confession of the lordship of Christ presupposes the incarnation, death, and resurrection of the Lord. The apostle goes on to say that in order to be saved one must **believe in thine heart that God has raised him from the dead.** Necessary belief in the resurrection is mentioned because new life to the believer is contingent upon a living Lord.

Token assent that Jesus is Lord and the fact of His resurrection is not sufficient for salvation. **For with the heart man believeth unto righteousness.** Belief in the saving power of the risen Christ must come from the innermost part of man's being. This is described as man's heart. But more than that, **with the mouth confession is made unto salvation.** Confession with the mouth is evidence of genuine faith in the heart. Frequently both our Lord and the Apostle Paul indicate the coordination of faith and a confession (cf. Mt 10:22; Lk 12:8; I Tim 6:12). The natural response of the lordship and resurrection of Jesus Christ believed is the lordship and resurrection of Jesus Christ confessed. Confession with the mouth does not bring about genuineness of belief in the heart, but it gives evidence to it.

2. Offer of the gospel: ground for responsibility. 10:11-15.

11 For the scripture saith, Whosoever believeth on him shall not be ashamed.

12 For there is no difference between the Jew and the Greek: for the same Lord over all is rich unto all that call upon him.

13 For whosoever shall call upon the name of the Lord shall be saved.

11-13. For the scripture saith. As is Paul's customary habit, he always appeals to Scripture to validate his teaching. **Whosoever believeth on him shall not be ashamed.** The key element in salvation is again seen to be faith. Salvation is not appropriated to the sinner's life until there is a heartfelt belief in the Lord Jesus. But just as the gospel is near all, likewise it is offered to all. The word **whosoever** is used to indicate the universality of God's offer of salvation. **For there is no difference between the Jew and the Greek.** The immediate purpose of the universal offer of salvation is to show the Jew that it is possible for the heathen Gentile to be saved. God's prerequisite to salvation is faith, not racial distinction. Therefore the call to salvation is to whoever will believe, whether Jew or Gentile. The reason is that **the same Lord over all is rich unto all that call upon him.** The Lord God is rich in His attitude toward all sinners and ready to receive anyone who calls on Him for salvation.

For whosoever shall call upon the name of the Lord shall be saved. Paul restates his belief that the gospel is offered to all by quoting the prophet Joel (Joel 2:32). The expression **call upon the name of the Lord** is a common Old Testament expression of worship to God (cf. Gen 4:26; 12:8; I Kgs 18:24; Ps 79:6; Isa 6:47). Paul's application of this formula to Christ is another example of his practice of taking Old Testament passages which refer to God the Father and, without any qualification whatsoever, applying them to Christ. Thus, in the New Testament, sinners are advised to call upon the name of the Lord Jesus Christ (cf. Acts 9:14, 21; 22:16; I Cor 1:2; II Tim 2:22). The ground for human responsibility in salvation arises out of the fact that the gospel is offered to all, irrespective of national heritage. Both Jew and Gentile may be saved by the grace of God.

14 How then shall they call on him in whom they have not believed? and how shall they believe in him of whom they have not heard? and how shall they hear without a preacher?

15 And how shall they preach, except they be sent? as it is written, How beautiful are the feet of them that preach the gospel of peace, and bring glad tidings of good things!

14-15. Paul now gives a rationale for his responsibility to present the gospel worldwide. Men are told that they must call upon the name of the Lord to be saved. However, they will not call unless they have been moved to believe in Him, and they cannot believe in Him unless they hear about Him. Furthermore, they cannot hear about Him unless the good news of the gospel is brought to them. The gospel message will not be taken to the unbeliever until someone is sent to him. Consequently salvation begins with God's sending process. Isaiah was asked the double question, "Whom shall I send?" and "Who will go for us?" Isaiah's answer was, "Here am I; send me" (Isa 6:8). Isaiah was willing to go with the message, but he could not go until he was sent by God. Consequently, Paul indicates that each of us has been sent by the Lord Jesus (Jn 20:21) and the success of getting the gospel message to those who need it is now dependent upon our obedience as servants of the Lord. We must proclaim the gospel message in every nook and cranny of the globe, because we are commissioned to do so; for unless they hear they cannot be saved.

How beautiful are the feet of them that preach the gospel of peace. Probably these words were originally intended to describe those who carried the good news home to Jerusalem that the days of Babylonian exile were passed. But in the context of the New Testament, these words indicate that the feet of a gospel messenger are beautiful things to those who believe the message and place their faith in the Lord Jesus. They become new creations in Christ Jesus. This may happen to any man who hears the gospel and believes.

16 But they have not all obeyed the gospel. For E-sā'ias saith, Lord, who hath believed our report?

17 So then faith *cometh* by hearing, and hearing by the word of God.

18 But I say, Have they not heard? Yes verily, their sound went into all the earth, and their words unto the ends of the world.

19 But I say, Did not Israel know? First Moses saith, I will provoke you to jealousy by *them that are* no people, *and* by a foolish nation I will anger you.

20 But E-sā'ias is very bold, and saith, I was found of them that sought me not; I was made manifest unto them that asked not after me.

21 But to Israel he saith, All day long I have stretched forth my hands unto a disobedient and gainsaying people.

CHAPTER 11

I SAY then, Hath God cast away his people? God forbid. For I also am an Israelite, of the seed of Abraham, *of* the tribe of Benjamin.

2 God hath not cast away his people which he foreknew. Wot ye not what

3. Disobedience to the gospel: failure of responsibility. 10:16-21.

16-17. Paul now comes to the crux of his argument concerning human responsibility and the righteousness of God. He claims that God takes the responsibility for Jewish unbelief and places it squarely upon the shoulders of the Jews. The gospel has been near unto them, it's been offered unto them, but it has not been believed by them. As proof of this he again quotes from the Jews' own Scripture as recorded in Isaiah 53:1, **Lord, who hath believed our report?** The report was Isaiah's message of the gospel concerning the Messiah. It was brought to the mouths of the Jews and offered to them, but that message was not obeyed. **So then faith cometh by hearing, and hearing by the word of God.** The word translated **report** (Gr *akoē*) in verse 16 is the same word in the original language as that translated **hearing** in verse 17. We must understand that hearing alone does not bring salvation, but faith in the message heard does. The heathen is not saved by looking at a tree and conceptualizing a god-form represented in that tree. The moralist is not saved by leading a moral life-style. Salvation comes when the message of the gospel is preached, believed, and then confessed by men. That message must come from the Word of God.

18-19. But I say, Have they not heard? In typical pauline style the apostle anticipates an objection from his Jewish readers. Is it not possible that some of his Jewish brethren have not heard the message of the gospel? Paul uses the language of Psalm 19 to remind them of the testimony of the stars and the heavens. The gospel had gone out through the entire Jewish world and therefore there was no excuse for ignorance of its claims.

20. But Isaiah is very bold, and saith, I was found of them that sought me not. Now Paul very convincingly turns to the greatest of the Jewish prophets and quotes Isaiah 65:1. The prophet's statement is very bold because he utterly ruled out any merit or privilege on the part of the Jews, and said that the Gentiles, who had been indifferent to God, would someday have the gospel preached to them and would come to a knowledge of God. Paul proclaims that this is that day and that the gospel is open to anyone who believes on Jesus Christ.

21. Paul now brings to a conclusion the exemplification of righteousness and human responsibility. He places the blame on men and not on God. **All day long I have stretched forth my hands unto a disobedient and gainsaying people.** The Lord God has patiently dealt with Israel throughout history (**all day long**) but she has been disobedient to His love. She is therefore guilty of spurning the love of God, and the responsibility for her future is clearly her own.

C. Righteousness Exemplified in Israel's Future. 11:1-36.

1. Israel's rejection leaves a remnant. 11:1-10.

11:1. I say then, Hath God cast away his people? God forbid. The problem of the unbelief of Israel as a **disobedient and gainsaying people** was prevalent in chapters 9 and 10. Paul now anticipates this theme will cause the Jews to wonder if God is finished with Israel as a nation. Thus he frames his question in Greek in such a way as to require the answer "no." The answer to the question is **God forbid.** He will give several lines of proof.

As exhibit A, Paul offers himself. **For I also am an Israelite, of the seed of Abraham, of the tribe of Benjamin.** There are two views why he offers this biographical material but the most probable one (which may boast exponents in Luther, Calvin, Hodge, Godet, etc.) is that Paul is appealing to his own salvation as proof that God has not completely abandoned Israel. Paul was enjoying the promises of God and as long as he did, he offered a living example of God's continuing relationship to Israel.

2. God hath not cast away his people which he foreknew. As exhibit B, Paul now offers the faithfulness of God. God's

the scripture saith of E-lī'as? how he maketh intercession to God against Israel, saying,

3 Lord, they have killed thy prophets, and digged down thine altars; and I am left alone, and they seek my life.
4 But what saith the answer of God unto him? I have reserved to myself seven thousand men, who have not bowed the knee to *the image of* Bā'al.

5 Even so then at this present time also there is a remnant according to the election of grace.
6 And if by grace, then *is it* no more of works: otherwise grace is no more grace. But if *it be* of works, then is it no more grace: otherwise work is no more work.

7 What then? Israel hath not obtained that which he seeketh for; but the election hath obtained it, and the rest were blinded

8 (According as it is written, God hath given them the spirit of slumber, eyes that they should not see, and ears that they should not hear;) unto this day.

9 And David saith, Let their table be

foreknowledge is the guarantee that He has not cast off His people. Had He done so, it would mean a revocation of God's promises to Abraham, Moses, David, and others which guaranteed to them an ultimate restoration of the seed of Abraham.

As exhibit C, Paul offers an Old Testament quotation. The reference is to I Kings 19:10, 14 where Elijah is the speaker. **Wot ye no what the scripture saith of Elijah? How he maketh intercession to God against Israel, saying.**

3-4. Although apostasy has been present many times in the life of Israel, yet God has always preserved a remnant of true believers out of that apostasy. The Northern Kingdom in Elijah's day had grossly violated her covenant relationship with God and had slain His prophets. So bleak was the situation that Elijah felt he was the only believer left. **But what saith the answer of God unto him?** The Greek expression for **the answer** is *chrēmatismos* which is used of a divine response. To his question, Elijah received a divine and therefore certain reply, **I have reserved to myself seven thousand men, who have not bowed the knee to the image of Baal.** The presence of a remnant of believers in the Northern Kingdom meant that God would preserve that kingdom. He did so for another one hundred thirty years. Even after the Assyrian captivity, there were a few of believing Israel from the ten tribes who returned to form the nucleus of the Hebrew population in Galilee during the days of Paul.

5-6. Having presented three lines of evidence to support his answer to the question **Hath God cast away His people?**, Paul now draws a conclusion. It is utterly ridiculous to think that the nation Israel has been entirely rejected of God, for even at the present time, **there is a remnant according to the election of grace.** This remnant of Israel is not saved by her line of descent, nor by personal righteousness, but upon the same ground that Gentiles are saved—the grace of God. No claim to special merit can be made even by this remnant. **And if by grace, then is it no more of works: otherwise grace is no more grace.** *A priori* grace cannot include works. They are mutually exclusive. If works are to be added to grace, as the Jews thought, then grace is completely cancelled out. Salvation is a free gift and no payment at all can be made, else it would cease to be free.

7. What then? Israel hath not obtained that which he seeketh for. What was Israel seeking for? Righteousness. Chapter 10 indicates that while seeking to establish their own righteousness, the Jews did not recognize the divine method of imputed righteousness. It was their own fault that they did not receive what they sought, for they sought it by works and not by faith. However the remnant did obtain the righteousness of God through the grace of God. The rest of national Israel has been blinded. The Greek verb *pōroō* which is used for **blinded,** means to render insensitive. Because they sought not the righteousness of God, the rest of Israel became insensitive to God. Such moral insensitivity was the judicial penalty inflicted on them for their refusal to heed the Word of God.

8. God hath given them the spirit of slumber. This quote from Deuteronomy 29:4 and Isaiah 29:10 gives reference to the unseeing eyes and unhearing ears of those who refuse to recognize the truth of God. Each of the gospel writers used this expression to indicate the Jews' failure to recognize Jesus as the Messiah (cf. Mt 13:14; Mk 4:12; Lk 8:10; Jn 12:40). The spirit of **slumber** (stupor or torpor) literally means "the spirit of stinging." The word (Gr *katanyxis*) is used for the numbness which is the result of a bite or poisonous sting. Israel had refused to seek righteousness after the manner of God and had attempted to establish her own righteousness. Thus God gave them to a blinding stupor and poisoning insensitivity toward the truth of God.

9-10. And David saith, Let their table be made a snare. The

made a snare, and a trap, and a stumblingblock, and a recompence unto them:

10 Let their eyes be darkened, that they may not see, and bow down their back alway.

11 I say then, Have they stumbled that they should fall? God forbid: but *rather* through their fall salvation *is come* unto the Gentiles, for to provoke them to jealousy.

12 Now if the fall of them *be* the riches of the world, and the diminishing of them the riches of the Gentiles; how much more their fulness?

13 For I speak to you Gentiles, inasmuch as I am the apostle of the Gentiles, I magnify mine office:

14 If by any means I may provoke to emulation *them which are* my flesh, and might save some of them.

15 For if the casting away of them *be* the reconciling of the world, what *shall* the receiving *of them be*, but life from the dead?

16 For if the firstfruit *be* holy, the lump *is* also *holy*: and if the root *be* holy, so *are* the branches.

17 And if some of the branches be broken off, and thou, being a wild olive tree, wert graffed in among them, and with them partakest of the root and fatness of the olive tree;

words **snare, trap,** and **stumblingblock** are closely related. Their combination serves to enforce the turning of the table to its opposite intent. The table is indicative of the bountiful mercy and blessing of God to Israel. Israel has not partaken of the good things of God's table. The recurring motif of the unseeing eyes indicates the principle that the temporary blindness has overtaken all of Israel, with the exception of the believing remnant. Thus the application is clear. Those who seek their own righteousness must **bow down their back always** to the bondage of sin. But those who seek the righteousness of Christ receive it by grace and are the believing remnant of God.

2. Israel's rejection is not permanent. 11:11-24.

11-12. I say then, Have they stumbled that they should fall? God forbid. Again Paul introduces his thought with a question and his reply of abhorrence. **But rather through their fall salvation is come unto the Gentiles, for to provoke them to jealousy** . . . One of the purposes of the fall of the Jewish nations, in the eyes of God, is that the Gentile nations may come to Him in salvation. In return this will provoke the Jews to jealousy, as was suggested in Romans 10:19 where Deuteronomy 32:21 was quoted. When the Jews see the Gentiles feasting on bread from the banquet table of God and enjoying the salvation which could have been theirs, they will be convinced of their apostasy and foolish rejection of Jesus as their Messiah. However, if the fall of the Jews brings the riches of salvation to the world, **how much more their fullness,** or large-scale conversion, will bring riches to the Gentile nations and glory to God. Thus Paul begins to lay the groundwork for the proof that Israel's rejection is not permanent. She will be restored to God.

13-14. For I speak to you Gentiles . . . I magnify mine office. The apostle now addresses the Gentiles directly in response to their anticipated question, "Paul, as the apostle to the Gentiles why are you concerned about the salvation of Jews?" Paul's answer reflects both his conviction concerning his divine calling and the compassion he has for his own people. He magnifies his office in that the salvation of the Gentiles will provoke to jealousy the Jews and bring them to salvation as well. The swelling of the ranks of true believers among Paul's own countrymen will also cause the swelling of the ranks among the Gentiles and the ministry of the apostle will then be a greater ministry.

15. For if the casting away of them be the reconciling of the world, what shall the receiving of them be, but life from the dead? Here we have an *a fortiori* argument. The **receiving** is being contrasted with the **casting away.** The rejected Messiah of Israel was taken by her to the cross and there He reconciled the world to Himself. But if Israel's blindness brought salvation to the Gentile world, what will her reception by God bring? The ultimate reception of a repentant Israel will bring revival on an unprecedented scale. We may expect to see a mighty evangelistic movement in the last days which will be characterized by large numbers of Jews coming to receive Jesus Christ as their Messiah and Saviour.

16-17. If some of the branches be broken off, and thou, being a wild olive tree, were grafted in among them. In preparing to warn the Gentiles, Paul introduces the principle of dedication of firstfruits to God (cf. Num 15:20-21) and the organic relationship between the root of a tree and its branches. These two metaphors illustrate one central truth: Israel is not only the firstfruits in God's program of salvation, but also the nation in which that salvation is rooted. However, some of the branches of Israel have been broken off through unbelief. The Gentiles, being wild olive trees, have been grafted into the life of the Abrahamic root in place of those dead Jewish branches which have been discarded. Gentiles must remember, however, that

18 Boast not against the branches. But if thou boast, thou bearest not the root, but the root thee.

19 Thou wilt say then, The branches were broken off, that I might be graffed in.

20 Well; because of unbelief they were broken off, and thou standest by faith. Be not highminded, but fear:

21 For if God spared not the natural branches, *take heed* lest he also spare not thee.

22 Behold therefore the goodness and severity of God: on them which fell, severity; but toward thee, goodness, if thou continue in *his* goodness: otherwise thou also shalt be cut off.

23 And they also, if they abide not still in unbelief, shall be graffed in: for God is able to graff them in again.

24 For if thou wert cut out of the olive tree which is wild by nature, and wert graffed contrary to nature into a good olive tree: how much more shall these, which be the natural *branches*, be graffed into their own olive tree?

25 For I would not, brethren, that ye should be ignorant of this mystery, lest ye should be wise in your own conceits; that blindness in part is happened to Israel, until the fulness of the Gentiles be come in.

26 And so all Israel shall be saved: as it is written, There shall come out of Sion the Deliverer, and shall turn away ungodliness from Jacob:

not all branches of Israel have been discarded. Just unrepentant Israel is broken off. The life of the tree of Abraham has not been removed. The wild branches gain sustenance from the root which still bears a remnant of Jewish believers.

18-24. The apostle issues a strong warning to the Gentiles about their understanding of what has happened to unbelieving Jews. **Boast not against the branches . . . because of unbelief they were broken off, and thou standest by faith . . . For if God spared not the natural branches, take heed lest he also spare not thee . . . And they also, if they abide not still in unbelief, shall be grafted in: for God is able to graft them in again.** The great lesson of this passage is certainly that just as the Jews of the Old Testament became proud, assuming that they alone knew God, the same thing may happen to Gentiles in the New Testament era. Gentile believers must not yield to the temptation to disrespect the Jews. If it had not been for the grace of God, Gentiles would never have been grafted into the life of God which the Jews enjoyed. The new life which enables them to produce fruit grows from the same root that the old stock of Israel grows. New Testament believers must not assume that they are better than the Jews because they were cut off for their unbelief. The Gentile church must never forget its reliance upon the divine grace of God, else her end will be the same as that of the old branches. The process of being grafted into the life of God finds its basis in the grace of God. We must never lord the grace of God over those who have been cut from the tree, for it is much easier to put the natural branches back, than to graft different branches in their place. We therefore must rest totally on the grace of God for our salvation, as the remnant does.

3. Israel's restoration is prophesied. 11:25-32.

25. The expression **For I would not, brethren, that ye should be ignorant** (cf. 1:13; I Cor 10:1; 12:1; II Cor 1:8; I Thess 4:13) indicates that what Paul is about to say is of extreme importance. He is in the process of revealing a mystery **lest ye should be wise in your own conceits.** The Gentiles dare not fall into the trap, as those in Rome apparently had done, of disparaging the Jews as a nation lest they become self-complacent in their newfound position. Paul reveals to them a mystery, not in the sense of a secret, but in the sense of a divine truth previously unknown. The mystery is that **blindness in part is happened to Israel, until the fullness of the Gentiles be come in.** The spiritual blindness of Israel is not only to be understood as partial and not total, but also as temporal and not eternal. This blindness holds sway over the nation Israel until the **fullness of the Gentiles** is come. According to Acts 15:14, God is visiting the Gentiles today to call out a people for His name. Luke 21:24 says, "Jerusalem shall be trodden down of the Gentiles, until the times of the Gentiles be fulfilled." This means that when the complete number of Gentiles has entered the kingdom of God, the spiritual blindness on the nation Israel shall be removed.

26. And so all Israel shall be saved. The Greek *houtōs* (**and so**) is important and must not be missed. It shows the relationship of what has preceded to what follows and can be translated "and accordingly." Throughout this passage Israel has been taken to mean a nation in contradistinction to the Gentiles. It must mean the same here. However, this may not be interpreted as implying that, in the time of fulfillment, every Israelite will be converted simply on the basis of his inheritance. The German theologian Adolph Harnach (*The Date of the Acts and of the Synoptic Gospels,* pp. 40-66) attacked Paul for this statement saying that he allowed his patriotism to override his logic. But when Paul says **all Israel shall be saved** he is not repudiating the doctrines he expounded in chapter 2 (that the Jews' law, circumcision, birth, or arguments could not make him righteous). We must understand the **all** (Gr *pas*) to be taken in the proper meaning of the word, i.e., Israel as a whole or Israel as a nation and not necessarily including every individual Israelite. This clearly is the way the Jews used the phrase "all Israel." The Mishnah tractate *Sanhedrin* X.I. says, "All Israel has a portion in the age to come" and then proceeds immediately to name the Israelites who have no portion in that age. Thus we must understand this expression to mean Israel as a company, rather than every Jew without single exception. No one is ever saved without a personal relationship with the Saviour.

Paul seals the restoration of Israel with a prophecy from Isaiah 59:20, **There shall come out of Zion the Deliverer, and shall turn away ungodliness from Jacob.** This reference is to a manifestation to Israel of her Redeemer and Messiah. When He comes, Israel shall be restored to the root of God.

27 For this *is* my covenant unto them, when I shall take away their sins.

27. For this is my covenant unto them, when I shall take away their sins. Paul continues the quotation of Isaiah 59:21, but then passes into the promise of Jeremiah 31:33 to indicate that God will not fail to keep His covenant with Israel.

28 As concerning the gospel, *they are* enemies for your sakes: but as touching the election, *they are* beloved for the fathers' sakes.
29 For the gifts and calling of God *are* without repentance.

28-29. They are enemies for your sakes . . . they are beloved for the fathers' sakes. The Jews have been alienated from God's favor and blessing, and thus are said to be enemies concerning the gospel. At the same time they are beloved as the election of God. Israel is still God's chosen people, regardless of her present condition. This proves that **the gifts and calling of God are without repentance.** Those privileges and prerogatives in 9:4-5 have never been abrogated. What God promises, He also performs. Israel will one day be restored to the favor and blessing of God. Her restoration is prophesied; it will happen.

30 For as ye in times past have not believed God, yet have now obtained mercy through their unbelief:
31 Even so have these also now not believed, that through your mercy they also may obtain mercy.
32 For God hath concluded them all in unbelief, that he might have mercy upon all.

30-32. For God hath concluded them all in unbelief, that he might have mercy upon all. The apostle is still addressing the Gentiles. Verse 30 is a repetition of what he has stated in verses 11, 12, 15, 28, that the Gentiles have received God's mercy by way of the unbelief of Israel. Verse 31 indicates the relationship which the salvation of the Gentiles has to the restoration of Israel. Verse 32 shows the relationship of God's mercy to all. Jew and Gentile alike must realize that both are undeserving sinners and the expression of the love of God on their behalf is an act both of mercy and grace.

4. Israel's restoration evokes praise. 11:33-36.

33. In the first eleven chapters of this epistle Paul shows that the human race is split into two segments: Jew and Gentile. The promises of God came to the Jews but they failed to receive those promises and crucified the Lord of Glory. This resulted in the expansion of those promises to the Gentiles. The day is prophesied, however, when Israel will once again be restored to the Father and God will have mercy upon all, both Jew and Gentile. This plan of God calls forth transcendent praise.

33 O the depth of the riches both of the wisdom and knowledge of God! how unsearchable *are* his judgments, and his ways past finding out!

O the depth of the riches both of the wisdom and knowledge of God! Paul exclaims in this final doxology that the wisdom and knowledge of God are much greater than that of humanity, for the human mind could never conceive of a solution to the problem of how God could punish sin and still justly save the sinner. God's wisdom provided that solution. The depths of that wisdom are far beyond man's power to comprehend them.

How unsearchable are his judgments, and his ways past finding out! Paul employs two emphatic words in describing God's wisdom. They are **unsearchable** and untrackable (cf. Eph 3:8). So unfathomable are the wisdom and knowledge of God that man can never descend to the bottom of that wisdom to search it out nor can he trace it through history, because it is beyond possibility to follow it completely.

34 For who hath known the mind of

34. For who hath known the mind of the Lord? or who hath been his counselor? The expression **Who hath known the**

the Lord? or who hath been his counsellor?

35 Or who hath first given to him, and it shall be recompensed unto him again?

36 For of him, and through him, and to him, *are* all things: to whom *be* glory for ever. Amen.

CHAPTER 12

I BESEECH you therefore, brethren, by the mercies of God, that ye present your bodies a living sacrifice, holy, acceptable unto God, *which is* your reasonable service.

2 And be not conformed to this world: but be ye transformed by the renewing of your mind, that ye may prove what *is* that good, and acceptable, and perfect, will of God.

mind of the Lord? tells of the unsearchable depth of God's knowledge. No one can completely know it. The expression **Who hath been his counselor?** implies that God, without dependence on any creature for counsel, devised the plan of our salvation (Eph 1:9-11).

35-36. Or who hath first given to him, and it shall be recompensed unto him again? In echoing Job 41:11, Paul cannot resist going back to the principle of grace. The salvation that both Jew and the Gentile enjoy is based, not on what God must give back to them for what they have first given to Him, but on the basis of the grace of God alone. **For of him, and through him . . . are all things.** God is the very reason for our existence. Out of God all things have come: He is their origin. Through God all things exist: He is their sustainer. Unto God all things repair: He is their goal. In the circle of eternity, past, present, and future, God is all and to Him all the praise for salvation must go. **To whom be glory for ever. Amen.**

V. THE RIGHTEOUSNESS OF GOD ENACTED. 12:1-15:13.

A. Righteousness Produces a Life of Transformation. 12:1-21.

1. Transformation exhibited in humility. 12:1-8.

In the last eleven chapters Paul has taken his readers through quite heavy doctrine. But doctrine is never taught in the Bible as an end in itself. It is always taught in order that doctrine may be translated into practice. John 13:17 declares, "If ye know these things, happy are ye if ye do them." Consequently, it is the Pauline practice to follow a doctrinal section of Scripture with a practical section, and usually these two are linked together with the word **therefore** (cf. Eph 4:1; Col 3:5).

This section begins with the third and final **therefore** in the Epistle to the Romans. Each of these "therefore's" marks a great division in the book. **Therefore being justified by faith, we have peace with God through our Lord Jesus Christ** (5:1). **There is therefore now no condemnation to them which are in Christ Jesus** (8:1). **I beseech you therefore** (12:1). It is now Paul's purpose to tie together all the doctrinal material he has presented. Hence, the rest of this epistle will be as intensely practical as what has preceded was intensely doctrinal.

12:1-2. I beseech you therefore, brethren, by the mercies of God. The word **brethren** identifies the group to whom these words are addressed. Paul is speaking to Christians, whether Jews or Gentiles. The **mercies of God** are all those good things we have because we are in Christ Jesus. Most especially he is referring to those mercies enumerated in 8:35-39. The progression of Pauline thought moves very easily from the end of chapter 8 to the beginning of chapter 12. He is now dealing again with what our responsibility is to those who have received the righteousness of God.

That ye present your bodies a living sacrifice, holy, acceptable unto God, which is your reasonable service. This request is eminently linked to his discussion of sanctification in chapters 6 and 7. In fact, the word rendered **present** here (Gr *partisēmi*) is the same as translated **yield** in 6:13, 19. Paul now deals in greater detail with what it means to present ourselves to God.

The Lord God wants the sacrifice of our life, not our death. Consequently, the sacrifice we are to make of our bodies (representing our whole person) is a **living** sacrifice. This is in contrast with the Old Testament sacrifices which were put to death on the altar. Since we know that we have died with Christ Jesus, we are in a position to present Him with our lives that are hidden with Him. Not only is the presentation of our bodies a **living** sacrifice but it is also a **holy** and **acceptable** sacrifice.

Holiness is contrasted with the defilement which is the usual characteristic of the sinful man. When the sacrifice of ourselves to God is holy it is inherently acceptable to God and well-pleasing to Him. More than this, says the apostle, the sacrifice of ourselves to God is our **reasonable** service. The word **service** (Gr *latreia*) is a term used for the function of priests in the tabernacle. The adjective (Gr *logikos*) which precedes it may be translated either reasonable (i.e., rational) or spiritual. But our worshipful service can only be spiritual in the biblical sense when it is characterized by our conscious, intelligent, rational service to the Lord God. In Paul's theology, spirituality is not some mindless flittering of the heart but is the presentation of an entire life to the Lord.

Not only is the presentation of our bodies the subject of Paul's request, it is the pattern of our behavior as well. **And be not conformed to this world.** Paul cautions the believer not to be fashioned after this world or age (Gr *aiōn*). The world system of this age is an evil one (Gal 1:4), and is dominated by "the god of this world" (II Cor 4:4). The new creation in Christ is to live with the understanding that "old things are passed away; behold, all things are become new" (II Cor 5:17). We are therefore not to have our lives governed by the thought patterns and dictates of this evil world system.

But how can we prevent that? **Be ye transformed by the renewing of your mind.** The only possible way for the believer not to be fashioned (Gr *syschēmatizō*) after this world is to be transformed in mind. The word **transformed** (Gr *metamorphoō*) reaches far deeper than conformity to the world. This implies a fundamental change in the Christian's inward nature and a following pattern of character which corresponds to that new nature. Thus the **mind** (Gr *nous*, the center of logical reasoning, ethical judgment, and moral awareness) must be completely changed if we are to live a life that is holy and acceptable unto God. The reason this change must be undertaken is **that ye may prove what is that good, and acceptable, and perfect, will of God.** To prove (Gr *dokimazein*) something is to test, scrutinize, or examine it. When we put the will of God to the test of actual experience we will find that it is **good, acceptable** (Gr *euarestos*) and **perfect** (Gr *teleios*). God's will is good in that, even when we cannot conceive it to be so, it is never mistaken. It is acceptable in that when you recognize it as good, it will be heartily endorsed by the believer. It is perfect in that it achieves the desired end that God has in mind. When the righteousness of Christ is placed upon us like a cloak, a life of transformation is produced that conceives of God's will in these ways.

3 For I say, through the grace given unto me, to every man that is among you, not to think *of himself* **more highly than he ought to think; but to think soberly, according as God hath dealt to every man the measure of faith.**

4 For as we have many members in one body, and all members have not the same office:

5 So we, *being* **many, are one body in Christ, and every one members one of another.**

3. For I say, through the grace given unto me. Paul now expands the biblical idea of the transformed life. His authority to speak in the way he does comes from the **grace** which is given unto him. That grace is the spiritual gift of apostleship (cf. 1:5; 15:15). From his position as an apostle Paul counsels, **every man that is among you, not to think of himself more highly than he ought to think; but to think soberly.** The transformation which comes through imputed righteousness is first exhibited in humility. The believer must be careful of being above-minded (Gr *hyperphroneo*), having an attitude of superiority. Rather we are to have a sober assessment of ourselves. This assessment is properly based in Galatians 2:20 where we recognize that we have been crucified with Christ and He lives through us.

4-5. Paul uses the metaphor of the body to indicate that the life of humility must be lived in relationship to other believers. Each of us must recognize that we possess a special **gift** (Gr *charisma*) as an outgrowth of our salvation and the indwelling gift of the Holy Spirit. There are many members in the body of Christ, and each of us, regardless of how humble our station in life or how deficient in education or how expert we may be, has a

6 Having then gifts differing according to the grace that is given to us, whether prophecy, *let us prophesy* according to the proportion of faith;

7 Or ministry, *let us wait* on *our* ministering: or he that teacheth, on teaching;

8 Or he that exhorteth, on exhortation: he that giveth, *let him do it* with simplicity; he that ruleth, with diligence; he that sheweth mercy, with cheerfulness.

gift from God to contribute to the whole body. In His sovereignty, God has just the proper place for each of us.

6-8. What is the believer to do with his gift? Since the members of the body of Christ have gifts which differ, each of us is to use his gift in the way that God intends. **Whether prophecy, let us prophesy.** Prophecy is the gift of inspired utterance (I Cor 14:1). This activity is to be done **according to the proportion of faith** or in harmony with that which has already been spoken by God. **Or ministry, let us wait on our ministering.** Ministry (Gr *diakonia*) is the general work of deaconing. This denotes a very broad office that may cover almost any kind of service in the local church. **Or he that teacheth, on teaching.** Teaching is the art of making the unchanging message of God understandable to the unlearned. Teaching is a gift of God; those who have that gift must not neglect to give attention to teaching. **Or he that exhorteth, on exhortation.** Unlike the teacher who appeals to the mind, the exhorter takes his brother aside and appeals to his heart in order to console or encourage him. Exhortation (Gr *paraklēsis*) is a specific and highly necessary ministry in the local church, especially in times like these. **He that giveth, let him do it with simplicity.** Each member of the church has the opportunity to give. The term **simplicity** (Gr *haplotēs*) sometimes means liberally (cf. II Cor 8:2; 9:11-13), and sometimes it means in singleness of heart or motive (cf. II Cor 11:3; Eph 6:5; Col 3:22). Essentially when we give, whatever we give, we are to do it with all our heart. **He that ruleth, with diligence.** The exercise of leadership in the church is as much a spiritual gift as any of the others. He who presides (Gr *proistēmi*) is not to do so sluggishly but responsibly and diligently. **He that showeth mercy, with cheerfulness.** This is the Christian gift of engaging in practical deeds of kindness. There is a place in the local church for those who cannot teach or cannot minister. Many there are within the church who go about their business in an unspectacular way doing a much-needed work in showing kindness and helpfulness to their fellow believers. Each of these gifts is necessary for the proper functioning of the body of Christ. Since that is the case, one gift cannot be exalted over another and therefore the transformed life exhibits humility in its relationship to others in the local church.

2. Transformation exhibited in love of the brethren. 12:9-16.

9 *Let* love be without dissimulation. Abhor that which is evil; cleave to that which is good.

9. The injunctions in this section are a practical outworking of the Sermon on the Mount. The brotherhood of believers is expected to have a mutual love toward one another. Thus the apostle says, **Let love be without dissimulation.** Dissimulation (Gr *anypokritos*) literally means without hypocrisy or insincerity. We must genuinely love one another. **Abhor that which is evil; cleave to that which is good.** We should not expect God to remove sin from us until we actually hate it and have rooted out of our transformed lives any secret love that we still hold for that which is evil.

10 *Be* kindly affectioned one to another with brotherly love; in honour preferring one another;

10. Be kindly affectioned one to another with brotherly love. We must have a tender regard for those who are our brothers in the Lord. **Brotherly love** (Gr *philadelphia*) is a love for all members of the local assembly, regardless of their heritage or financial status. **In honor preferring one another.** Since the root of all "above-mindedness" is taken away by the basis of our salvation, which is grace, therefore we must not count ourselves better than our brother (Phil 2:3). We need a devalued opinion of our own worth before the Lord, but a greatly inflated opinion of what He can do through a devalued person who is yielded to Him.

11 Not slothful in business; fervent in spirit; serving the Lord;

11. Not slothful in business. The local church must be run in just as businesslike fashion as any secular corporation. We dare not to be sluggish or unenthusiastic about the business of the church. **Fervent in spirit; serving the Lord.** This expression, which was used of Apollos in Acts 18:25, means to be boiling or bubbling up (Gr *zeō*) or aflame with the Spirit of God. Not only must we serve the Lord as a slave would serve his master, but we must do so in an energetic and enthusiastic manner (cf. Eccl 9:10; Col 3:23).

12 Rejoicing in hope; patient in tribulation; continuing instant in prayer;

12. Rejoicing in hope; patient in tribulation; continuing instant in prayer. The life of love among the brethren never allows adverse circumstances to restrain the joy of the local congregation. The believer must bear up steadfastly under the great weight of tribulation which the church will sustain and the only possible way to do that is to be steadfastly given to prayer, seeking the comfort and aid of the Lord.

13 Distributing to the necessity of saints; given to hospitality.

13. Distributing to the necessity of saints; given to hospitality. The transformed life exhibits love among other believers in such a way as to be tangibly moved by those of the brethren who have a financial lack. We need a genuine concern for those who are poor and needy and our hospitality must extend to them as automatically as did Abraham's extend to the three strangers (Gen 18:2-3).

14 Bless them which persecute you: bless, and curse not.
15 Rejoice with them that do rejoice, and weep with them that weep.

14-15. Bless them which persecute you. Paul is a good example of one who lived up to this admonition (cf. I Cor 4:12-13; Acts 28:19). **Rejoice with them that do rejoice, and weep with them that weep.** That this practice can be found in the life of Christ proves that this is not just a Stoic philosophy. Jesus Christ rejoiced at the marriage feast with those who rejoiced (Jn 2:1-12) and wept at the graveside of Lazarus with those who wept (Jn 11:1-44). We need to be so intimately involved with the lives of other believers that we know of their joys and their sorrows, and can identify with each.

16 *Be* of the same mind one toward another. Mind not high things, but condescend to men of low estate. Be not wise in your own conceits.

16. Be of the same mind one toward another. Although we may not always see eye to eye with other believers, nevertheless we must preserve the unity of belief and practice which characterized the early church. When we are told to **Mind not high things, but condescend to men of low estate,** the apostle brings us right back to the base of humility. The believer who is concerned about exhibiting his transformation in an attitude of love for the brethren will not attempt to cultivate friendships only among the attractive or wealthy of the church, but will especially befriend those who are not befriended by others. **Be not wise in your own conceits** is a quotation from Proverbs 3:7 and summarizes the teaching of this section.

3. Transformation exhibited in honor before the world. 12:17-21.

17 Recompense to no man evil for evil. Provide things honest in the sight of all men.

17. Not only is the life transformed by the righteousness of Christ to be lived in love toward the brethren, but it is to be lived in honor toward those who are outside the church as well. **Recompense to no man evil for evil.** When we are wronged our natural instinct is to fight to assert ourselves and right the wrong. But in the believer's life there is no place for retaliation. **Provide things honest in the sight of all men.** Because retaliation can mean a complete loss of our Christian testimony, we are advised to let our aims be such as men consider honorable. The quotation from Proverbs 3:4 (LXX) means that we have to live honorably and righteously before the world just as we must live godly before the Lord.

18 If it be possible, as much as lieth in you, live peaceably with all men.

18. If it be possible, as much as lieth in you, live peaceably with all men. Insofar as it is consistent with our obedience to God, the Christian is to labor in the utmost harmony with men of the world. We must live in good will toward men and attempt not to be offensive or obnoxious toward them, unless our offense comes through loyalty to God and our refusal to participate in those activities which are prohibited by God.

19 Dearly beloved, avenge not yourselves, but *rather* give place unto wrath: for it is written, Vengeance *is* mine; I will repay, saith the Lord.

19-21. Dearly beloved, avenge not yourselves, but rather give place unto wrath. Self-vengeance has no place in the Christian life. We are told to make room for divine retribution to operate and therefore to **give place unto wrath** means to allow

20 Therefore if thine enemy hunger, feed him; if he thirst, give him drink: for in so doing thou shalt heap coals of fire on his head.

21 Be not overcome of evil, but overcome evil with good.

God to bring His vengeance to bear on those of the world, rather than taking revenge ourselves. We are not to give a place for wrath in our dealings with men, but rather to give that place to God's wrath. Thus the apostle introduces the quotation from Deuteronomy 32:35 that **Vengeance is mine; I will repay, saith the Lord.** In light of this, and quoting from Proverbs 25:21, we are to treat our enemy kindly and not vengefully. If he is hungry, we are to give him food; if he is thirsty, we are to give him drink. **For in so doing thou shalt heap coals of fire on his head.** There are two main lines of interpretation to this phrase. One is that this quotation from Proverbs 25:22 reflects an Egyptian ritual in which a man showed his repentance by carrying a pan of burning charcoal on his head. This was a dynamic symbol of the change of mind which had taken place in his life. The meaning would then be that our act of love in giving him food or drink would bring about a change of attitude toward us. The prevailing view, however, is that heaping coals of fire on the head refers to the sense of shame, punishment, or remorse which is engendered in the mind of our enemy when we show kindness to him. Whichever meaning is to be held, it is obvious that verse 21 is closely linked with it. **Be not overcome of evil, but overcome evil with good.** As believers we must resist the impulse to retaliate but rather we promote our sanctification by doing good to those who do evil to us. Therefore we exhibit our life of transformation before a watching world.

B. Righteousness Produces a Life of Subjection. 13:1-14.

1. Subjection to the state. 13:1-7.

When one receives the righteousness of Christ and begins to live out that righteousness, it not only produces a life of transformation but also a life of subjection. It was inevitable that Paul would have to say something with regard to the believer's relationship to the state. The men and women of the first century were vitally interested in their position before the Roman Empire. Jesus was questioned in Mark 12 by the Jewish leaders concerning His attitude toward the Roman government. The Corinthian Jews dragged Paul before Gallio, the proconsul of Achaia, and charged him with propagating a religion that was illegal in the empire (Acts 18:12-13). Paul's opponents at Thessalonica went to the civil magistrates and accused the Christians of subversion to the state (Acts 17:6-7). The question of religion versus state was very much on the minds of those of the first century.

13:1. Let every soul be subject unto the higher powers. Even though governments are generally carried on by nonbelievers, the teaching of the Lord Jesus (Mk 12:17), the teaching here of the Apostle Paul, and historic position of the church (cf. the *Westminster Confession of Faith*, Chapter XXIII, Section IV) has always been that the believer must live under the law, governed by a magistrate. The reason, **For there is no power but of God: the powers that be are ordained of God.** There is no governmental authority except that which is ordained of God. It is God who establishes kings and dethrones kings (cf. Dan 4; see also Prov 21:1). This truth was strikingly illustrated of Pilate by the Lord Jesus. In his anger Pilate said, "Speakest thou not unto me? knowest thou not that I have power to crucify thee, and have power to release thee?" Jesus put this magistrate in his place when He answered, "Thou couldst have no power at all against me, except it were given thee from above" (Jn 19:10-11). Since all power comes from God, the believer is to be subject to that power.

2. Whosoever therefore resisteth the power, resisteth the ordinance of God. As a general rule, God condemns civil disobedience toward the lawfully-existent government. Those who would riot and rebel must know that opposition to govern-

CHAPTER 13

LET every soul be subject unto the higher powers. For there is no power but of God: the powers that be are ordained of God.

2 Whosoever therefore resisteth the power, resisteth the ordinance of God: and they that resist shall receive to themselves damnation.

ment is opposition to God. However, the obedience which the Christian owes to the government is never absolute and must be carefully weighed in light of his subjection to God. To unlawfully and unethically resist government brings the judgment (not **damnation**) of God upon the believer.

3 For rulers are not a terror to good works, but to the evil. Wilt thou then not be afraid of the power? do that which is good, and thou shalt have praise of the same:

3. For rulers are not a terror to good works, but to the evil. Since God's purpose in ordaining government in the days of Noah was to restrain wickedness and promote virtue, we are to be in subjection to any government which fulfills this purpose. However, the Declaration of Independence was composed to rebuke George III's government for punishing virtue while at the same time rewarding wickedness. Christians are never under subjection to injustice or a government of wickedness. Rulers are to be established to be a terror to evil and to promote the good. That is the basic principle of good government. Consequently, we are to respect any government which does so and reject any government which does not.

4 For he is the minister of God to thee for good. But if thou do that which is evil, be afraid: for he beareth not the sword in vain: for he is the minister of God, a revenger to *execute* wrath upon him that doeth evil.

4. For he is the minister of God to thee for good. The officer of the state is ordained of God to minister that which is good. Therefore the town mayor is as much a minister of God as the local pastor, but in a very different way. We ought to have as much respect for a good mayor as we do for a good minister. **For he beareth not the sword in vain: for he is the minister of God.** God has granted human government the power of enforcing itself and therefore this verse unquestionably provides New Testament justification for capital punishment. The divine directive was established in Genesis 9:6, "Whoso sheddeth man's blood, by man shall his blood be shed." The hands of good government should never be so tied that they cannot execute good judgment and the wrath of God upon those who do evil.

5 Wherefore *ye* must needs be subject, not only for wrath, but also for conscience sake.

5. Wherefore ye must needs be subject . . . but also for conscience sake. At this point Paul reiterates God's general rule that we need to be subject to the higher powers, but he introduces the question of the conscience as well. The Christian always lives in a tension between the two competing claims of obedience to the state and obedience to God. The state has a right to demand our respect and conformity. Thus, we are to be in subjection to those in authority over us, not only out of fear and respect, but also out of a good conscience before God. However, the believer dare not blindly bow to the state if his conscience is offended by the wickedness of the state. There may be times when "we ought to obey God rather than men" (Acts 5:29; cf. 4:19). Since the state and its magistrate are not infallible, the believer may at times have to conscientiously object to what the state requires that is in direct contradiction to the law of God.

6 For for this cause pay ye tribute also: for they are God's ministers, attending continually upon this very thing.
7 Render therefore to all their dues: tribute to whom tribute *is due*; custom to whom custom; fear to whom fear; honour to whom honour.

6-7. For this cause pay ye tribute also . . . Render therefore to all their dues: tribute to whom tribute is due; custom to whom custom; fear to whom fear; honor to whom honor. To be a good citizen of the state we must **render . . . to all their dues,** that is, to discharge our obligation to all men. Tribute is today called tax, that which is levied on persons and property (cf. Lk 20:22; 23:2). Custom refers to the tax levied on goods and corresponds to the tax paid on those things we import or export. **Fear** (Gr *phobos*) is the same word that is rendered **terror** in verse 3. This word means both concern and reverence. If we disobey the state, we are to fear those who have been charged with the responsibility of punishing disobedience. At the same time we are to respect the laws of the state and those who make the laws. Honor means that it is not right for a Christian to speak in a disrespectful way of the state or officers of the state. For the sake of the Lord Jesus we are to give honor to those who are His ministers as evidence that we give honor to Him.

Frequently twentieth-century Christians try to rationalize their infidelity to the state by saying that Paul simply could not understand what it meant to live in such a corrupt society as we do. We must remember, however, that as Paul wrote these words he was living under the reign of the wicked Emperor Nero. Nero's mother, Agrippina (sister of Emperor Caligula, who killed and tortured thousands for pleasure), had Nero's stepfather assassinated with a dish of poisoned mushrooms. Nero himself killed his stepbrother, Britannicus, when the boy was just fourteen years old. Later when he feared that his mother would attempt to exercise the power of the throne, Nero killed her as well. He banished his first wife, Octavia, to an island and had her killed. Still later he slew his second wife, Poppaea. In light of these facts, if Paul can so tenaciously hold that the believer should be subject to the higher powers, the twentieth-century believer must be very careful not to jump to the conclusion that he should not be subject to the present-day powers.

2. Subjection to the citizens of the state. 13:8-10.

8-10. Owe no man any thing, but to love one another. The key word in determining that the believer's relationship should be to other citizens of the state is **love**. Love enables us to perfectly fulfill all our obligations, whether to the state, to the citizens, or to God. More than anyone, Christians ought to pay their debts and honor their obligations. To be ever-increasingly in debt is to show a lack of regard and love for the one to whom you are indebted. We should not buy what we cannot reasonably afford.

Good citizenship in financial matters brings Paul to quote the seventh, sixth, eighth, ninth, and tenth commandments of the Mosaic law (cf. Ex 20:13-17; Deut 5:17-21). To these he adds the chief commandment in which the law is fulfilled in one word, **Thou shalt love thy neighbor as thyself** (Gal 5:14). Love adds to the complete performance of the law, because it shows that we do not conform to the law out of duty but out of a right heart attitude. No man will commit adultery, murder, or theft if the love of Christ motivates his heart. No man will cause ill to his neighbor if the seat of his action is love. **Therefore love is the fulfilling of the law** (lit., "the fulfillment of the law"). If the law is filled to the brim with love, it is a law which can easily be obeyed. The believer will have no difficulty in subjection to the citizens of the state if his heart is filled with love toward them.

3. Subjection to the timetable of God. 13:11-14.

11. It is high time to awake out of sleep. The duty of spiritual vigilance with relation to the timetable of God was constantly enjoined by the Apostle Paul (cf. I Thess 5:4). The urgent nature of these days in the end time necessitates that the Christian awake out of his lethargy and fervently pursue his calling as an evangelist. It is time for believers to stand up and be counted and to make a mark for God. **For now is our salvation nearer than when we believed.** The salvation of which the apostle speaks is **the adoption, to wit, the redemption of our body** for which believers wait (8:23). We are now much closer to that day than the day we first believed. This behooves us to be the transformed believers we ought to be and to be more actively engaged in the process of transforming others.

12. Let us therefore cast off the works of darkness, and let us put on the armor of light. The Christian must recognize that he is engaged in a warfare with the powers of darkness. It is therefore absolutely necessary that we discard the works and values of that darkness and replace them with the armor of light. A detailed description of this armor is given in Ephesians 6:14-17. We constantly live in subjection to the timetable of God and time is running out.

13. Let us walk honestly as in the day. Those who have received the light, must walk in the light. The manner of life which spawns riotous living, drunken bouts, sexual orgies, and

8 Owe no man any thing, but to love one another: for he that loveth another hath fulfilled the law.
9 For this, Thou shalt not commit adultery, Thou shalt not kill, Thou shalt not steal, Thou shalt not bear false witness, Thou shalt not covet; and if *there be* any other commandment, it is briefly comprehended in this saying, namely, Thou shalt love thy neighbour as thyself.
10 Love worketh no ill to his neighbour: therefore love *is* the fulfilling of the law.

11 And that, knowing the time, that now *it is* high time to awake out of sleep: for now *is* our salvation nearer than when we believed.

12 The night is far spent, the day is at hand: let us therefore cast off the works of darkness, and let us put on the armour of light.

13 Let us walk honestly, as in the day; not in rioting and drunkenness, not in

chambering and wantonness, not in strife and envying.

14 But put ye on the Lord Jesus Christ, and make not provision for the flesh, to *fulfil* the lusts *thereof.*

CHAPTER 14

HIM that is weak in the faith receive ye, *but* not to doubtful disputations.

2 For one believeth that he may eat all things: another, who is weak, eateth herbs.
3 Let not him that eateth despise him that eateth not; and let not him which eateth not judge him that eateth: for God hath received him.

4 Who art thou that judgest another man's servant? to his own master he standeth or falleth. Yea, he shall be holden up: for God is able to make him stand.

all forms of wanton revelry cannot be that of those who walk honestly or honorably. When a person claims to be a Christian, if he cannot change his life-style, he had better change his name.

14. But put ye on the Lord Jesus Christ. Paul urges his Christian converts to **put on** Christian virtues in the same manner that they would put on their clothes (Col 3:12). When they had "put on the new man" (Eph 4:24) they had in fact been baptized into Christ and had "put on Christ" (Gal 3:27). Putting on Christ means to allow Him to envelop us so that when others view us they see His righteousness. He therefore not only lives in us and through us, but on us as well. When that is the case, we need not take thought of satisfying our bodily lusts or carnal desires, but our prime concern will be to live in honor to the Lord. When Christ is on us and in us, we will not feed our fleshly desires but will feed a soul striving to be more like Him, and much more so realizing our subjection to the timetable of God.

C. Righteousness Produces a Life of Consideration. 14:1-15:13.

1. Consideration for a brother weak in the faith. 14:1-13.

14:1. Him that is weak in the faith receive ye. What was the nature of the weakness? Scholars differ dramatically on the root of the weakness in the lives of the Roman believers. But whatever were the particular religious scruples which caused differences between them, the basic problem was that some of the believers had not grasped the great truths Paul has just expounded in his epistle. Those who are weak in the faith were Christians who did not have full understanding that salvation is the free gift of God and that the believer faces no condemnation whatever because of the atonement of Christ. Paul enjoyed his Christian liberty to the fullest and was totally emancipated from foolish superstitions and unbiblical taboos. Some of the Romans, however, were yet clinging to these taboos for they did not fully accept the doctrine of justification by faith alone. In relation to this, Paul addresses both those living freely in Christ and those in Christ who are still bound by fleshly legalism. The strong who had internalized Bible doctrine, were to receive the weak, those who did not fully rest in the grace of God. But they were not to argue with them over secondary points of difference.

2-3. For one believeth that he may eat all things: another, who is weak, eateth herbs. Let not him that eateth despise him . . . and let not him which eateth not judge him. So that he may be easily understood, Paul immediately advances two concrete examples of the weak in the faith versus the strong in the faith. What is the proper diet for the separated Christian? Some believers (whom Paul characterizes as the weak in faith), in order to avoid eating the flesh of animals that had been consecrated to pagan gods (cf. Dan 1:8), refused to eat anything but vegetables. Converts from heathenism would be especially sensitive to the eating of such meat. Paul's contention is that the meat itself is not destroyed of nutritional value because it was offered to idols. Since these idols have no validity before God, there is no reason not to partake of this meat. However, he counsels those who do eat, not to despise those who do not. Those who feel no compelling reason not to eat are to refrain from ridiculing those who have definite scruples against meat. The reason is God has received this brother who is weak in the faith and we must as well.

4. Who art thou that judgest another man's servant? Essentially addressing the weak in faith, Paul draws a principle which is found many times in Scripture (cf. Mt 7:1; Lk 6:37; I Cor 4:3ff). Each Christian is the property of God and we are not in a position to see the inner motives of others. God's jurisdiction over all believers is not to be infringed upon by

5 One man esteemeth one day above another: another esteemeth every day *alike.* Let every man be fully persuaded in his own mind.

6 He that regardeth the day, regardeth *it* unto the Lord; and he that regardeth not the day, to the Lord he doth not regard *it.* He that eateth, eateth to the Lord, for he giveth God thanks; and he that eateth not, to the Lord he eateth not, and giveth God thanks.

7 For none of us liveth to himself, and no man dieth to himself.

8 For whether we live, we live unto the Lord; and whether we die, we die unto the Lord: whether we live therefore, or die, we are the Lord's.

9 For to this end Christ both died, and rose, and revived, that he might be Lord both of the dead and living.

10 But why dost thou judge thy brother? or why dost thou set at nought thy brother? for we shall all stand before the judgment seat of Christ.

11 For it is written, *As* I live, saith the Lord, every knee shall bow to me, and every tongue shall confess to God.

12 So then every one of us shall give account of himself to God.

13 Let us not therefore judge one another any more: but judge this rather, that no man put a stumblingblock or an occasion to fall in *his* brother's way.

14 I know, and am persuaded by the Lord Jesus, that *there is* nothing unclean of itself: but to him that esteemeth any thing to be unclean, to him *it is* unclean.

15 But if thy brother be grieved with *thy* meat, now walkest thou not charitably. Destroy not him with thy meat, for whom Christ died.

either those who are weak or those who are strong. God is judge and not we ourselves.

5-6. A second concrete example is now given of the differences between those who have laid hold on the truths of God's Word and those who tenaciously cling to some legalistic practice. It is the keeping or honoring of certain days. **One man esteemeth one day above another: another esteemeth every day.** Some of the brethren, those who are weak, pick out a certain day and proclaim it holy, more holy than other days. Those who, like Paul, understand the liberty we have in Christ Jesus, do not observe days but rather serve and worship Him consistently seven days a week. Paul clearly aligns himself with those who are seven-day-a-week Christians, those who view one hundred percent of their income as holy to the Lord, not just one-tenth. But he says that even though believers disagree with regard to this issue, they must respect the opinion of others for the motive of both the weak and the strong is to honor God with thanksgiving.

7-9. For none of us liveth to himself . . . whether we live therefore, or die, we are the Lord's. For to this end Christ both died, and rose. The adage "no man is an island unto himself" is the modern outgrowth of these verses, but that is not the central truth taught here. The basic teaching is that each Christian must live his life in the full view of the Lord Jesus Christ. We do so as servant to Master and therefore our relationship to Him will affect our relationship to the brethren. We must interact with others in a method pleasing to the Lord and not in judging the strong or demeaning the weak. The ground of our actions toward one another is the absolute lordship of Christ Jesus as established in His death, burial, and resurrection. From His authority as resurrected Lord He bids us live in harmony with one another.

10-13. But why dost thou judge thy brother? Paul addresses this question to the weak in faith. **Or why dost thou set at nought thy brother?** This question is addressed to the strong. **For we shall all stand before the judgment seat of Christ.** As Paul, each believer must live with the Judgment Seat of Christ in view. All that we do will be judged at that heavenly *bēma* or judgment seat (cf. II Cor 5:10). On that day all meaningless differences between Christians will fade away and we will not be concerned about the validity of what others have done for **every one of us shall give account of himself to God** (see Woodrow Michael Kroll, *It Will Be Worth It All*). The weaker brother does not have to defend the actions of the strong. The stronger brother will not have to answer for the actions of those weak in the faith. We must give an account of our life and activities for the Lord, individually, one-on-one, with the Lord of Glory. To indicate the certainty of this event, Paul quotes from Isaiah 49:18 and Isaiah 45:23, a passage he also applies to Christ in Philippians 2:10ff. Under the lordship of Christ we must live with the convictions we have and not those of others. This responsibility naturally drives us to constantly take inventory of our religious scruples and convictions to make sure that they are based in the infallible Word and not in the traditions or whims of men.

2. Consideration for our neighbor. 14:14-23.

14-15. Martin Luther, in his treatise *On the Freedom of a Christian Man,* wrote, "A Christian man is a most free lord of all, subject to none. A Christian man is a most dutiful servant of all, subject to all." By this he meant that even though our liberty in Christ may permit us to engage in a certain activity, we nevertheless may not be wise in doing so. **I know, and am persuaded by the Lord Jesus, that there is nothing unclean of itself.** Paul casts his lot with the strong in faith who are not given to the legalism of the weak. However he is well aware that he may become a **stumbling block** (Gr *proskomma*) to the weaker brother for the conscience of the weak will not allow him to engage in the activities of Paul. There is no virtue in flaunting Christian liberty. **But if thy brother be grieved with thy meat, now walkest thou not charitably.** Believers must not insist on their liberty in the presence of those whose consciences would be offended. To do so is not to walk in love under the lordship of Christ. To the strong in faith Paul admonishes, **Destroy not him with thy meat, for whom Christ died.** If we are to live a life of consideration for our neighbor then we must learn that even though there are things we feel we biblically may do, many of those same things, for the sake of others, we should not do.

16-19. Let not then your good be evil spoken of. Paul reaffirms that the position of the strong is right and good, but advises them not to let what is good become the object of misunderstanding. **For the kingdom of God is not meat and drink; but righteousness, and peace, and joy.** The kingdom of God does not consist in observing or not observing days, eating or not eating meats, or any other secondary issues of religious scruples, but in **righteousness** (perfect uprightness in our daily walk), **peace** (perfect peace with God and a consistent attempt to be a peacemaker of the brethren), and **joy** (perfect union and intimate love through the Holy Spirit, cf. Mt 6:31; 5:6, 9, 10, 12). **Let us therefore follow after the things which make for peace, and things wherewith one may edify another.** Paul cautions the Romans not to ride moral or theological hobby-horses but to pursue those issues which will tend toward building the common bond of faith between the weak and the strong. The basis of fellowship is not peripheral matters of eating or drinking but the salvation which both enjoy in Christ.

20-21. For meat destroy not the work of God. Convictions are fine, says the apostle, but not at the expense of the work of God. The reason is simple. All foods are clean in themselves but they become unclean to the one who eats them when his conscience tells him otherwise. For conscience' sake that man should avoid them. To the strong Paul advises, **It is good neither to eat flesh, nor to drink wine, nor any thing whereby thy brother stumbleth, or is offended, or is made weak.** What a beautiful picture: a Christian that knows he is at liberty to do something but does not for the sake of another. That is living under the lordship of Christ. The best thing one who is strong in the faith can do is to assist one who is weak in the faith to become strong. This will never be accomplished if we parade our liberty in the face of the weak and offend him.

22-23. Hast thou faith? have it to thyself before God. Faith here means a firm conviction before God that what you believe is right. Paul remarks that it is proper to have and cherish a conviction, but we must not force our convictions upon others. We do not have the prerogative to do so. We must hold that conviction before God. **And he that doubteth is damned if he eat.** For the translators of the AV the word **damned** did not have the force it has today. It did not mean that if someone violates his conscience by eating that which he feels is wrong he will be damned to irrevocable perdition. Rather the meaning is that he is condemned in his conscience for doing that which it will not allow. If he does not eat in faith believing that it is acceptable to God, he eats in sin **for whatsoever is not of faith is sin.** If our actions do not arise from our convictions then they are sinful actions and unacceptable to God.

3. Consideration as we have Christ as example. 15:1-13.

15:1-3. We then that are strong ought to bear the infirmities of the weak. Again, Paul casts himself as one of the strong, one who has grasped the principle of Christian liberty and freedom from man-made taboos. But note that he does not merely relish his strength of understanding doctrine but rather uses his

16 Let not then your good be evil spoken of:

17 For the kingdom of God is not meat and drink; but righteousness, and peace, and joy in the Holy Ghost.

18 For he that in these things serveth Christ *is* acceptable to God, and approved of men.

19 Let us therefore follow after the things which make for peace, and things wherewith one may edify another.

20 For meat destroy not the work of God. All things indeed *are* pure; but *it is* evil for that man who eateth with offence.

21 *It is* good neither to eat flesh, nor to drink wine, nor *any thing* whereby thy brother stumbleth, or is offended, or is made weak.

22 Hast thou faith? have *it* to thyself before God. Happy *is* he that condemneth not himself in that thing which he alloweth.

23 And he that doubteth is damned if he eat, because *he eateth* not of faith: for whatsoever *is* not of faith is sin.

CHAPTER 15
WE then that are strong ought to bear the infirmities of the weak, and not to please ourselves.

2 Let every one of us please *his* neighbour for *his* good to edification.

3 For even Christ pleased not himself: but, as it is written, The reproaches of them that reproached thee fell on me.

4 For whatsoever things were written aforetime were written for our learning, that we through patience and comfort of the scriptures might have hope.

5 Now the God of patience and consolation grant you to be likeminded one toward another according to Christ Jesus:

6 That ye may with one mind *and* one mouth glorify God, even the Father of our Lord Jesus Christ.

7 Wherefore receive ye one another, as Christ also received us to the glory of God.

8 Now I say that Jesus Christ was a minister of the circumcision for the truth of God, to confirm the promises *made* unto the fathers:

9 And that the Gentiles might glorify God for *his* mercy; as it is written, For this cause I will confess to thee among the Gentiles, and sing unto thy name.

10 And again he saith, Rejoice, ye Gentiles, with his people.

11 And again, Praise the Lord, all ye Gentiles; and laud him, all ye people.

12 And again, E-sā'ias saith, There shall be a root of Jesse, and he that shall rise to reign over the Gentiles; in him shall the Gentiles trust.

13 Now the God of hope fill you with all joy and peace in believing, that ye may abound in hope, through the power of the Holy Ghost.

strength to assist the weak in doctrine. His desire is that the strong bear with those whose scruples he regards as weaknesses or sicknesses (Gr *asthenēma*). **For even Christ pleased not himself.** As the prime example of one strong in the faith, living in light of those weak in the faith, the apostle proposes the Lord Himself. The Lord Jesus had every right to please Himself for what He would do of necessity would be right. Yet He was willing to set aside His own desires and follow the Father's directives. The quote from Psalm 69:9, **The reproaches of them that reproached thee fell on me,** is applied to the life of the Lord in that He obeyed the will of the Father even when He Himself might have chosen an easier path. He did not exercise His perfect freedom, in order that the ultimate task of salvation could be accomplished.

4. For whatsoever things were written aforetime were written for our learning. This is akin to the apostle's statement in II Timothy 3:16 about the profitableness of Scripture. An earnest study of the Word of God will not only make the weak strong but will enable us to bear the burdens and weaknesses of others. The instruction which the Scriptures impart is directed to patience and comfort. Patience is steadfastness or endurance, and comfort (Gr *paraklēsis*) is more properly understood as encouragement or consolation. These culminate in hope, not some wistful desire that everything will turn out all right, but in the confidence that **all things work together for good** (8:28).

5-7. Now the God of patience and consolation grant you to be likeminded one toward another. The reference to the God of patience and consolation indicates that behind the patience and comfort that the Scriptures bring is a God who energizes them through the Scriptures. Paul appeals to this God to bring the strong and weak together and advises, **Receive ye one another, as Christ also received us to the glory of God.** In the same manner in which we were received of Christ the Lord, we are encouraged to receive each other as believers. Paul's point is that if the Lord can receive us with the great chasm that existed between Him and us, should we not also be able to accept one another even if there are minor differences between us? The result of such acceptance of one another will be the harmonious praise **That ye may with one mind and one mouth glorify God.** Since the Lord Jesus found it possible to embrace us and reconcile sinners to Himself, it should be an easy task to **receive ye another, as Christ also received us to the glory of God.**

8-13. Paul turns his apostolic guns squarely on Jew/Gentile acceptance of each other. As we have Christ our example, the Jew must receive the Gentile and the Gentile the Jew. Jesus Christ came to be a **minister of the circumcision.** This word **minister** is the word *diakonos* in Greek. Paul's assessment of the Lord's ministry squares with the Lord's own assessment. "The Son of man came not to be ministered unto, but to minister" (Gr *diakoneō* Mk 10:45). The truthfulness of God's Word is seen in the fulfillment of His promises to the Patriarchs. **And that the Gentiles might glorify God for his mercy.** The fulfillment of promises to the Jews devotes praise to God from the Gentiles. Paul also appeals to Psalm 18:49 where David included Gentile nations in the heritage of God to Israel, **as it is written, For this cause I will confess to thee among the Gentiles, and sing unto thy name.**

Not content with that, the apostle begins a series of quotations from the Old Testament. From the Song of Moses, **Rejoice, ye Gentiles, with his people** (Deut 32:43). Then, from Psalm 117:1, **Praise the Lord, all ye Gentiles, and laud him, all ye people.** Next a quote from Isaiah 11:10, **There shall be a root of Jesse, and he that shall rise to reign over the Gentiles; in him shall the Gentiles trust.** Paul's purpose is to indicate that Gentiles as well as Jews will be included in the family of God. The *goyim* (Heb for **Gentiles**) will put their trust in the Root of

Jesse (the Lord Jesus) the same as believing Jews will. Although there are many differences between these two groups of believers, nevertheless their common bond is faith in Christ. As a result, Paul's prayer is, **Now the God of hope fill you with all joy and peace in believing, that ye may abound in hope, through the power of the Holy Ghost.**

VI. CONCLUSION. 15:14-16:27.

The Apostle Paul begins to conclude this letter long before he actually does so. The change from doctrine to practice has made it difficult for him to say goodby to these Roman saints for they were apparently weak in both. He has intense personal feelings for them even though he has never been to Rome. Since he has met many of them in other areas of the Mediterranean world, he must express personal greetings. A lengthy list of final greetings is capped by a final note of praise to the Lord.

A. The Presentation of Personal Feelings. 15:14-33.

1. Explanation for writing. 15:14-16.

14 And I myself also am persuaded of you, my brethren, that ye also are full of goodness, filled with all knowledge, able also to admonish one another.

15 Nevertheless, brethren, I have written the more boldly unto you in some sort, as putting you in mind, because of the grace that is given to me of God,

16 That I should be the minister of Jesus Christ to the Gentiles, ministering the gospel of God, that the offering up of the Gentiles might be acceptable, being sanctified by the Holy Ghost.

14-16. And I myself also am persuaded of you . . . Nevertheless, brethren, I have written the more boldly unto you . . . That I should be the minister of Jesus Christ to the Gentiles. Paul did not want the Roman believers to think that he considered them spiritually immature. Thus the admonitions which he gives in this epistle are not to be received by them alone but by every reader of the Epistle to the Romans, in every country, in every age. Paul knew that the Roman believers were full of goodness and kindness and that they were adept enough in doctrine to be able to admonish one another. Nevertheless the apostle has spoken boldly **in some sort** (Gr idiom; "in part," or "on some points," e.g., 6:12; 8:9; 11:17; 12:3; 13:3; 14:3, 10, 15). Clothed in the vocabulary of worship, Paul asserts that the reason for his writing the way he has is the grace of God has made him an officiating-priest (Gr *leitourgos*) to preach the gospel as a priestly service (Gr *hierourgeo*). This is done to present the Gentiles as an acceptable thank offering (Gr *prosphora*) to the Lord God. They are sanctified, not by circumcision, but by something much better, the Holy Spirit. He wants to include the Gentiles of the church at Rome in that offering.

2. Vindication for writing. 15:17-21.

17 I have therefore whereof I may glory through Jesus Christ in those things which pertain to God.

18 For I will not dare to speak of any of those things which Christ hath not wrought by me, to make the Gentiles obedient, by word and deed,

19 Through mighty signs and wonders, by the power of the Spirit of God; so that from Jerusalem, and round about unto ĭ-lўr'i-cum, I have fully preached the gospel of Christ.

17-19. I have therefore whereof I may glory through Jesus Christ . . . so that from Jerusalem, and round about unto Illyricum, I have fully preached the gospel of Christ. Though there were many triumphs already in the life of the apostle about which he may boast, Paul is careful to give the praise to the Lord Jesus. His only glory is **through Jesus Christ.** Through the grace of God Paul has preached the gospel of God with mighty signs and wonders in a wide radius from Jerusalem through Macedonia to the area round about Illyricum, the Roman province bordering the eastern shore of the Adriatic Sea. What God has chosen to do through Paul gives him vindication for writing to a church he has never visited.

20 Yea, so have I strived to preach the gospel, not where Christ was named, lest I should build upon another man's foundation:

21 But as it is written, To whom he was not spoken of, they shall see: and they that have not heard shall understand.

20-21. Yea, so have I strived to preach the gospel, not where Christ was named, lest I should build upon another man's foundation. Paul made it his ministerial ambition to break up fallow ground with the gospel. He wanted to be missionary as well as theologian, scholar, and soul-winner. His intent was to lay a foundation where other men had not labored and for this the Lord drew him to various metropolitan centers such as Ephesus, Philippi, and Corinth. Each time Paul encountered first-time hearers of the message he bore.

3. Paul's plans following the writing. 15:22-29.

22 For which cause also I have been much hindered from coming to you.

22-24. For which cause also I have been much hindered from coming to you. The pioneering spirit of Paul to spread the

23 But now having no more place in these parts, and having a great desire these many years to come unto you;

24 Whensoever I take my journey into Spain, I will come to you: for I trust to see you in my journey, and to be brought on my way thitherward by you, if first I be somewhat filled with your *company*.

25 But now I go unto Jerusalem to minister unto the saints.

26 For it hath pleased them of Macedonia and A-chā'ia to make a certain contribution for the poor saints which are at Jerusalem.

27 It hath pleased them verily; and their debtors they are. For if the Gentiles have been made partakers of their spiritual things, their duty is also to minister unto them in carnal things.

28 When therefore I have performed this, and have sealed to them this fruit, I will come by you into Spain.

29 And I am sure that, when I come unto you, I shall come in the fulness of the blessing of the gospel of Christ.

30 Now I beseech you, brethren, for the Lord Jesus Christ's sake, and for the love of the Spirit, that ye strive together with me in *your* prayers to God for me;

31 That I may be delivered from them that do not believe in Judæa; and that my service which I have for Jerusalem may be accepted of the saints;

32 That I may come unto you with joy by the will of God, and may with you be refreshed.

33 Now the God of peace *be* with you all. Amen.

CHAPTER 16

I COMMEND unto you Phebe our sister, which is a servant of the church which is at Čĕn'chre-a:

2 That ye receive her in the Lord, as becometh saints, and that ye assist her in whatsoever business she hath need of you: for she hath been a succourer of many, and of myself also.

gospel where no man had done so has thus far prohibited the apostle from coming to Rome. However, years of desire are about to give way to an actual journey to Spain which will necessitate a stopover in the capital city of the Empire. The activity in Spain will likewise be cultivating virgin soil but before he arrives there he wants his visit to Rome to be one of mutual benefit for both the Romans and himself. He has spiritual benefit to impart to them as a teacher of the Word and they have comfort, fellowship, and lodging to give to him. He desires to be filled with their company.

25-29. But now I go unto Jerusalem . . . to make a certain contribution for the poor saints which are at Jerusalem. Paul cannot immediately embark on his way to Rome for he must travel first to Jerusalem. He must deliver to the poor saints there an offering which the apostle had collected from the Christians of Macedonia and Achaia. This was not only an act of Christian love but a way of cementing the relationship between the Jewish and Gentile factions of the early church, since the Christians of Macedonia and Achaia were predominantly Gentile. The **contribution** (Gr *koinōnia* or sharing of their wealth) was a voluntary gesture on the part of the Gentile churches, yet it also recognized the moral debt they owed to the mother church which had first disseminated the gospel.

When therefore I have performed this . . . I will come by you into Spain . . . in the fullness of the blessing of the gospel of Christ. Paul again returns to the thought of his arrival in Rome en route to Spain. He is convinced that his coming to them will be more than a blessing. It will be **the fullness of the blessing of the gospel of Christ** (cf. Eph 3:8, 19). At the time he was unaware that when he finally arrived in Rome, he would be in chains. Even so it was in the fullness of the blessing of the gospel. This is exhibited in the fact that Colossians, Philemon, Ephesians, and Philippians were all written from Rome during his first imprisonment there.

4. Paul's plea for prayers on his behalf. 15:30-33.

30-33. Paul appeals for the support of Roman prayers in the face of the imminent dangers he must face before he comes to them. His requests are: **that ye strive together with me in your prayers . . . That I may be delivered . . . that my service which I have for Jerusalem may be accepted . . . That I may come unto you with joy . . . and may . . . be refreshed.** Paul knows that dangers threaten him in Judaea, for there are many that mark him as a traitor to the Jewish cause. Coupled with the hatred of unbelieving Jews is the danger that the church at Jerusalem might misread his intentions in bringing a monetary gift. Perhaps they might not receive it because it was given by the Gentiles. Also, he desires to come to Rome **with joy by the will of God,** that is, only if it be the will of God. He desires to be refreshed both physically and spiritually there. Since these requests are couched in the language of prayer, it is appropriate for him to close with a doxology. The beautiful benediction, addressed to the weak as well as the strong, to the Jew as well as to the Gentile, is, **Now the God of peace be with you all. Amen.**

B. The Presentation of Personal Greetings. 16:1-23.

1. Commendation of Phoebe. 16:1-2.

16:1-2. I commend unto you Phoebe our sister, which is a servant of the church which is at Cenchrea. Phoebe, whose name means radiant, was apparently a businesswoman from the city of Cenchrea, the seaport city of Corinth on the Saronic Gulf (cf. Acts 18:18). She was a servant (Gr *diakonos*) of the church in that location. Paul designates her **our sister,** as a term of Christian endearment. Likewise she is said to be a succorer (Gr *prostatis*) or befriender of many including Paul. Apparently Phoebe was a widow, else she would not have been able to travel so freely in the Roman Empire. This woman was preparing for a business trip to Rome and Paul seizes that opportunity, since as a private citizen he was not permitted to use the official Roman postal system, to send his epistle to Rome. Thus he advises the Romans **That ye receive her in the Lord . . . and that ye assist her in whatsoever business she hath need of you.**

2. Greetings for friends in Rome. 16:3-16.

3 Greet Priscilla and Ăq'ui-la my helpers in Christ Jesus:
4 Who have for my life laid down their own necks: unto whom not only I give thanks, but also all the churches of the Gentiles.

3-4. Greet Priscilla and Aquila my helpers in Christ Jesus. This Jewish couple moved, under the dint of persecution and in their quest for souls, from Rome to Corinth, to Ephesus and back to Rome again. They supplied lay leadership in various evangelistic endeavors. **Who have for my life laid down their own necks.** Just when these two risked their lives for Paul is not known, but their friendship with the apostle was so intense that he mentions them in the salutations of two other epistles (cf. I Cor. 16:19; II Tim 4:19).

5 Likewise *greet* the church that is in their house. Salute my well beloved E-pæn'e-tus, who is the first fruits of A-chā'ia unto Christ.

5. Salute my well-beloved Epaenetus, who is the first fruits of Achaia unto Christ. The translation here should undoubtedly be "Asia" not **Achaia** and such rendering is supported by manuscripts P^{46}, A, B, D*, G and others. According to I Corinthians 16:15, "the household of Stephanas" was the first fruits of Achaia. As a convert, and especially among the first in Asia Minor, Paul had a special love for Epaenetus.

6 Greet Mary, who bestowed much labour on us.

6. Greet Mary, who bestowed much labor on us. The labor which this woman bestowed probably refers to her association with Priscilla and Aquila from the inception of the Roman church. We know nothing of her but that she bore the name Mary, one of the six persons so named in the New Testament.

7 Salute Ăn-drŏ-ni'cus and Junia, my kinsmen, and my fellowprisoners, who are of note among the apostles, who also were in Christ before me.

7. Salute Andronicus and Junia, my kinsmen, and my fellow prisoners. It is impossible to know for sure if the second of the names is the feminine, Junia, or masculine, Junias. When Paul says they are his **kinsmen,** he need not be referring to a close family relationship for all Jews were his kinsmen (cf. 9:3). Since the apostle's imprisonments were many (cf. II Cor 6:5; 11:23), it is difficult to say in which of these they shared. They were of note among the apostles (using this term in the general sense of messenger, cf. II Cor 8:23; Phil 2:25) and came to know the Lord as Saviour even before the Apostle Paul.

8 Greet Ăm'plĭ-as my beloved in the Lord.

8. Greet Amplias my beloved in the Lord. Amplias is an abbreviated form of Ampliatus, a common name in the Empire. "A branch of the *gens Aurelia* bore this cognomen. Christian members of this branch of the family are buried in one of the oldest Christian burying-places in Rome, the Cemetery of Domitilla, the beginnings of which go back to the end of the first century. One tomb in that cemetery, decorated with paintings in a very early style, bears the inscription AMPLIAT in uncials of the first or early second century" (F. F. Bruce, *The Epistle of Paul to the Romans*, p. 272).

9 Salute Ûr'bāne, our helper in Christ, and Stā'chÿs my beloved.

9. Salute Urbane, our helper in Christ, and Stachys my beloved. Urbane, or Urbanus, by his very name, must have been a native of Rome. He is said to be a helper in Christ but not a fellow worker as Priscilla and Aquila. **Stachys,** a name meaning ear (of grain), is not a common name and occurs with no further amplification other than **my beloved.**

10 Salute A-pĕl'lĕs approved in Christ. Salute them which are of Ăr-ĭs-tŏ-bū'lus' *household.*

10. Salute Apelles approved in Christ. Apelles is distinguished as **approved in Christ** but we are not left with a clue as to why. His is a common name, found in Roman inscriptions, sometimes related to the imperial household. **Salute them which are of Aristobulus' household.** Although it cannot be said with certainty, J. B. Lightfoot suggests that this Aristobulus was the grandson of Herod the Great and the brother of Herod Agrippa I. If so, he lived in Rome as a private citizen and

11 Salute He-rō'dĭ-on my kinsman. Greet them that be of the *household* of När-cĭs'sus, which are in the Lord.

12 Salute Trȳ-phē'na and Trȳ-phō'sa, who labour in the Lord. Salute the beloved Persis, which laboured much in the Lord.

13 Salute Rufus chosen in the Lord, and his mother and mine.

14 Salute A-sȳn'crī-tus, Phlĕ'gŏn, Her'mas, Păt'ro-bas, Her'mēs, and the brethren which are with them.

15 Salute Phĭ-lŏl'o-gus, and Julia, Ne're-us, and his sister, and Ō-lȳm'pas, and all the saints which are with them.

16 Salute one another with an holy kiss. The churches of Christ salute you.

enjoyed a close friendship with the Emperor Claudius. He is not saluted himself, but the slaves of his household are being greeted as Christians.

11. Salute Herodion my kinsman. This name, and the context of the preceding verse, would suggest that this man was one of Herod's household. He was a kinsman of Paul and therefore Jewish. **Greet them that be of the household of Narcissus, which are in the Lord.** It may be possible to identify this man with Tiberius Claudius Narcissus, a wealthy freedman of the Emperor Tiberius. Narcissus was executed by order of Agrippina, Nero's mother, shortly after her son's accession to the throne in A.D. 54. If his possessions were at this time confiscated, his slaves would become imperial property and would be known as the *Narcissiani* or **household of Narcissus.**

12. Salute Tryphaena and Tryphosa, who labor in the Lord. Tryphaena and Tryphosa were probably sisters and possibly even twins. It was a common practice to name twins of the same root word. The name means those who live voluptuously. Although these names stem from a pagan, Anatolian root, Paul nevertheless associates them with labor in the Lord. **Salute the beloved Persis, which labored much in the Lord.** Persis (the name means Persian woman) is said to be **beloved** but with a woman Paul delicately avoids using the phrase "my beloved." Her name appears on Greek and Latin inscriptions as that of a slave or freedwoman.

13. Salute Rufus chosen in the Lord, and his mother and mine. It may be possible to make an identification between this Rufus and the man of the same name who Mark records was the son of Simon of Cyrene (cf. Mk 15:21). Mark says, "And they compel one Simon a Cyrenian, who passed by, coming out of the country, the father of Alexander and Rufus, to bear his cross." That Simon would be identifiable by the name of his son Rufus must mean that the son was a man of some reknown. F. F. Bruce, in addressing how Rufus' mother could act as mother to Paul, hazards the guess that when Barnabas brought Paul from Tarsus to become his missionary colleague, one of the teachers of the church at Antioch permitted Paul to lodge with him, a certain Simon surnamed Niger, (cf. Acts 13:1) whom Bruce identifies with Simon of Cyrene. In the course of Paul's lodging there, Simon's mother cared for or mothered the apostle. Although interesting, this must be considered speculation.

14. Salute Asyncritus, Phlegon, Hermas, Patrobas, Hermes. Little is known of these believers other than that they were apparently of one community and were all men. Hermas is an abbreviation of some names such as Hermogenes or Hermodorus and very common (cf. *The Shepherd of Hermas* is apocryphal literature). Patrobas was abbreviated from Patrobius. Hermes was the name of the god of good luck and became a common slave name.

15. Salute Philologus, and Julia, Nereus, and his sister, and Olympas. Philologus and Julia were perhaps husband and wife. Both names occur several times in connection with the imperial household of Rome. Nereus, according to a tradition which goes back to the fourth century, is associated with Flavia Domitilla, a Christian woman who was banished to the Island of Pandateria by her uncle Emperor Domitian in A.D. 95. She was released after his death the following year. Olympas is an abbreviated form of Olympiodorus. These all appear to have been a community of faith.

16. Salute one another with a holy kiss. The holy kiss was a common feature of Christian greeting (cf. I Cor 16:20; II Cor 13:12; I Thess 5:26; I Pet 5:14). Justin Martyr mentions that it was a common feature in early Christian worship (*First Apology*, 66). It was "holy" as opposed to that in the question, "betrayest thou the Son of man with a kiss?" (Lk 22:48). Although a feature in the liturgy of the Eastern Church to this day, the holy kiss is noticeably absent in the Western Church.

3. Warnings to friends in Rome. 16:17-20.

17 Now I beseech you, brethren, mark them which cause divisions and offences contrary to the doctrine which ye have learned; and avoid them.

17. Now I beseech you, brethren, mark them which cause divisions . . . and avoid them. Paul's admonition and warning to his friends at Rome concerns those who would cause divisions among the brethren. He commands two things; **mark** (Gr *skopeō*) them as to who they are, and then **avoid them** (Gr *ekklinō*). Those who cause divisions may have been antinomians who pushed their liberty in Christ to the "nth" degree. They may have been the ubiquitous Judaizers who seemed to incessantly plague Paul. But Paul characterizes them as those **which cause divisions and offenses contrary to the doctrine which ye have learned.** This may mean any group which denied the teachings of the apostle.

18 For they that are such serve not our Lord Jesus Christ, but their own belly; and by good words and fair speeches deceive the hearts of the simple.

18. They . . . serve not our Lord Jesus Christ, but their own belly. In further description of these divisive teachers, Paul describes them, not as servants of the Lord, but in service to their own carnal desires and self-interests. This is characterized by the symbol of their belly. In Philippians 3:19 the apostle warns the Philippian Christians against people "whose God is their belly." **And by good words and fair speeches deceive the hearts of the simple.** These smooth-talking teachers have ensnared innocent (**simple**) believers in their doctrinal trap.

19 For your obedience is come abroad unto all *men.* I am glad therefore on your behalf: but yet I would have you wise unto that which is good, and simple concerning evil.

19. I would have you wise unto that which is good, and simple concerning evil. In Matthew 10:16 we are counseled to "be ye therefore wise as serpents, and harmless as doves." The Greek adjectives, *sophos* and *akeraios*, are used both in Matthew and here. Paul cautions the Roman Christians to be alert and discerning in relation to false doctrine (cf. I Cor 14:20).

20 And the God of peace shall bruise Satan under your feet shortly. The grace of our Lord Jesus Christ *be* with you. Amen.

20. And the God of peace shall bruise Satan under your feet shortly. In echoing Genesis 3:15, Paul reminds the believers at Rome that God has promised ultimate victory to His church and shortly, despite Satan's crafty attacks, the enemy will be defeated as promised. God will crush Satan, under the feet of the faithful, and that right speedily.

4. Greetings from friends with Paul. 16:21-23.

21 Tī-mō'the-us my workfellow, and Lucius, and Jason, and Sō-sīp'a-ter, my kinsmen, salute you.

21. Timothy my workfellow, and Lucius, and Jason, and Sosipater, my kinsmen, salute you. Timothy, Paul's convert from Lystra and subsequent colleague, was of particular affection to Paul. Of him Paul said to the church at Philippi, "For I have no man like-minded, who will naturally care for your state . . . But ye know the proof of him, that, as a son with the father, he hath served with me in the gospel." (Phil 2:20, 22). Lucius, Jason, and Sosipater are mentioned as Paul's kinsmen and therefore as Jewish Christians. Jason may have been Paul's host on his first visit to Thessalonica (Acts 17:6-7, 9). Sosipater is probably Sopater of Beroea, the son of Pyrrhus, according to Acts 20:4.

22 I Ter'tĭus, who wrote *this* epistle, salute you in the Lord.

22. I Tertius, who wrote this epistle, salute you in the Lord. Tertius, probably a native Italian, was the stenographer or amanuensis of the apostle. Paul's practice of using an amanuensis is attested in other epistles (cf. I Cor 16:21; Gal 6:11; Col 4:18; II Thess 3:17). Apparently Tertius interjects his own greeting into Paul's narration because he too knows and loves the believers at Rome.

23 Gaius mine host, and of the whole church, saluteth you. E-răs'tus the chamberlain of the city saluteth you, and Quartus a brother.

23. Gaius mine host . . . Erastus the chamberlain of the city saluteth you, and Quartus a brother. Gaius is to be identified with the man whom Paul baptized at Corinth (I Cor 1:14) and may be identified as well with Titus Justus of Acts 18:7 who extended the hospitality of his house to Paul when the fledgling church of Corinth was expelled from the synagogue next door. The Roman system of naming a citizen was by the use of three names (*praenomen, nomen,* and *cognomen*) and Gaius was a common *praenomen*. His full name would then have been Gaius Titus Justus. Erastus the chamberlain of the city was in fact the city treasurer of Corinth. Quartus, of whom we know nothing, is simply mentioned as **a brother.**

C. The Concluding Doxology. 16:24-27.

1. The worthy recipient of praise. 16:24.

24 The grace of our Lord Jesus Christ *be* with you all. Amen.

24. The grace of our Lord Jesus Christ be with you all. Amen. Some older manuscripts do not include this phrase in the doxology. Its truth is evident from similar language in II Thessalonians 3:18.

2. The ascription of praise. 16:25-26.

25 Now to him that is of power to stablish you according to my gospel, and the preaching of Jesus Christ, according to the revelation of the mystery, which was kept secret since the world began,

25. To him that is of power to stablish you according to my gospel. Paul's readers are commended to the only God who has the power to establish them and keep them from falling. When Paul says **my gospel** (cf. 2:16) he is referring to the gospel of Christ which he preaches. Equivalent to that is **the preaching of Jesus Christ** for that was the apostle's calling. **According to the revelation of the mystery.** The preaching of Christ was not an innovation in the plan of God, but the fulfillment of the Old Testament prophecies. This, Paul explains, is a mystery, for the Old Testament prophets did not fully appreciate the new life which we have in Christ.

26 But now is made manifest, and by the scriptures of the prophets, according to the commandment of the everlasting God, made known to all nations for the obedience of faith:

26. But now is made manifest. That which was not clearly known in the Old Testament is now clearly known **by the scriptures of the prophets,** i.e., the fulfillment of the Old Testament prophecies concerning the Messiahship of Christ (cf. Isa 9:6; 53:1-2; Jer 23; Mic 5; Zech 9; etc.). The purpose of manifesting God's plan in Christ Jesus is that He may be **made known to all nations for the obedience of faith.** The preaching of the gospel is not just for intellectual acceptance but that nations may come to place their faith in the Christ of the gospel.

3. The benediction. 16:27.

27 To God only wise, *be* glory through Jesus Christ for ever. Amen.

27. To God only wise, be glory through Jesus Christ for ever. Amen. This great hymn of praise ends with the glory for man's salvation being directed toward God, exactly where it belongs. But inherent to Paul's theme throughout the epistle is that it is **through Jesus Christ** that praise and glory are channelled toward God. Thus, **To God only wise, be glory through Jesus Christ for ever. Amen.**

BIBLIOGRAPHY

Barnhouse, Donald Grey. *Exposition of Bible Doctrine Taking the Epistle to the Romans as the Point of Departure*. 10 vols. Grand Rapids: Eerdmans, 1952-1963.

Barth, Karl. *The Epistle to the Romans*. Trans. by E. C. Hoskyns. London: Oxford University Press, 1933.

*Bruce, F. F. The Epistle of Paul to the Romans. In the *Tyndale New Testament Commentaries*. Grand Rapids: Eerdmans, 1963.

Calvin, John. *Commentaries on the Epistle of Paul the Apostle to the Romans*. (Published 1539). Trans. and ed. by John Owen. Grand Rapids: Eerdmans, 1947.

Denny, James. St. Paul's Epistle to the Romans. In the *Expositor's Greek New Testament*. Grand Rapids: Eerdmans, reprinted, n.d.

Erdman, Charles. *The Epistle to the Romans*. Philadelphia: Westminster Press, 1925.

Godet, Frederic. *Commentary on St. Paul's Epistle to the Romans*. Grand Rapids: Zondervan, n.d.

*Haldane, Robert. *Exposition of the Epistle of the Romans*. London: Banner of Truth Trust, reprinted, n.d.

*Hodge, Charles. *Commentary on the Epistle to the Romans*. Grand Rapids: Eerdmans, reprinted, 1950.

Ironside, Harry. *Lectures on the Epistle to the Romans*. New York: Loizeaux Brothers, 1951.

Liddon, H. P. *Explanatory Analysis of St. Paul's Epistle to the Romans*. London: Longmans, Green & Co., 1899.

*Lloyd-Jones, D. Martyn. *Romans*. 6 vols. Grand Rapids: Zondervan, 1970.

Luther, Martin. *Lectures on Romans*. Trans. by Wilhelm Pauck. Philadelphia: Westminster, 1961.

*McClain, A. J. *Romans: Gospel of God's Grace*. Chicago: Moody Press, 1973.

Moule, H. G. G. Romans. In *The Expositor's Bible*. Grand Rapids: Zondervan, n.d.

*Murray, John. The Epistle to the Romans. 2 vols. In the *New International Commentary on the New Testament*. Grand Rapids: Eerdmans, 1959-1965.

Newell, William R. *Romans Verse by Verse*. Chicago: Moody Press, 1938.

Plumer, W. S. *Commentary on St. Paul's Epistle to the Romans*. New York: Randolph & Co., 1870.

*Shedd, W. G. T. *A Critical and Doctrinal Commentary on the Epistle of St. Paul to the Romans*. Grand Rapids: Zondervan, 1967.

Steele, David N. and Curtis C. Thomas. *Romans: An Interpretive Outline*. Philadelphia: Presbyterian and Reformed, 1963.

Stifler, James M. *The Epistle to the Romans*. Chicago: Moody Press, 1960.

Thomas, W. H. Griffith. *St. Paul's Epistle to the Romans*. Grand Rapids: Eerdmans, 1946.

Vine, W. E. *The Epistle to the Romans: Doctrine, Precept, Practice*. London: Oliphants Ltd., 1948.

Wuest, Kenneth. Romans, In *The Greek New Testament*. Grand Rapids: Eerdmans, 1956.

The First Epistle To The
CORINTHIANS
INTRODUCTION

Falling second in the corpus of pauline litera-ture, I Corinthians both complements and con-trasts the great doctrinal epistle which precedes it. Where Romans emphasizes matters of biblical theology, I Corinthians is concerned with practical theology and its application to a particular local assembly.

Yet, this is not to say that Romans is not a practical epistle (as chs. 12-15 demonstrate). Nor is this to suggest that Paul does not give attention to doctrine in I Corinthians (note especially chs. 7-15). But, the predominant thrust here is that of a pastor concerned with the spiritual welfare of a wayward assembly. And that concern does not ap-pear to be misplaced, as a closer look at the city of Corinth will show.

The city of Corinth. Corinth was a wealthy com-mercial center located on a narrow neck of land (four miles wide) that connected the Peloponnesus and northern Greece. Situated as it was, it became a crossroads for travel and commerce both north and south, east and west. It had two harbors, one (Lechaeum) facing toward Italy, and the other (Cenchrea) facing toward Asia. The wealth of Corinth was acquired by hauling freight and smaller vessels across the isthmus, and by politi-cians who would levy tolls on the commerce.

The history of the city may be divided into two periods—the old and the new. The old city (which gave to the world the classic Corinthian pillar) was founded ca. 1500 B.C. and was destroyed in 146 B.C. by the Roman general, Lucius Mummius. A century later, the new city was built on the same location. The old city of Corinth rose to wealth and fame during the period of the Greek city-states. It was known for its cosmopolitan culture and luxurious temples. On the gray, rocky hill to the south of the city (called Acrocorinth), the shining sanctuary to Aphrodite was located. Visible far out to sea, this temple was serviced by a thousand slave girls who doubled both as temple prostitutes and as entertainers for the city's night life (E. F. Harri-son, *Introduction to the New Testament*, p. 267). The destruction of the old city (together with the sack-ing of Carthage) largely became the means by which Rome rose to wealth and power.

The new city was built by Julius Caesar in 46 B.C. and elevated to the status of a Roman colony with the title *Colonia Laus Julia Corinthiensis.* When Paul came to Corinth in A.D. 51, it was again a thriving metropolis, the capital of Achaia, and ruled by a Roman proconsul. Its population, vastly different from the old city (a mixture of Roman, Greek, and Oriental), was nearly half slaves. This rich cosmopolitan city boasted that it was heir to the glories of ancient Greece.

The city knew every type of religion its plu-ralistic society could bring to it. There was also a synagogue and a sizable contingency of Jews.

Corinth was known for the Isthmian Games held in the stadium on alternate years. These were second in popularity only to the Olympics. An outdoor theater, accommodating twenty thousand people, was the arena for the gladiatorial games and contests with wild beasts. There was also a smaller indoor theater (capacity of three thousand) for those interested in plays and music.

From such a cultural hub, a strong gospel wit-ness might well be heard all over the world. It was no wonder that Paul felt constrained to bear a testimony to such a city.

But the moral depravity most vividly reflects the spiritual need of Corinth. The vile character of the old city carried over into the city of New Testament times. The Greek word *korinthiazomai* (lit., "to act the Corinthian"), came to mean, "to commit fornication." Corinth was a seaman's paradise and a moral cesspool. Divorce was rampant. Prostitu-tion plagued the streets, and the moral air was polluted with the luring aroma of sin. It was fam-ous for all that is debauched. It was, no doubt, the inspiration for the catalogue of man's sins in Ro-mans 1:18-32 (written by Paul while a guest of Gaius in this wicked city)!

Inebriated by the swaggering pride of supposed Greek wisdom, they had even reduced their reli-gion to a quagmire of gross sensualism. And it was from this filthy slough of sin that Paul's converts were extracted (cf. 6:9-11).

The founding of the church. Luke records the ori-gin of the Corinthian church in Acts 18:1-17. Paul came to Corinth in A.D. 51 after a very unfruitful evangelistic effort at Athens (Acts 17:16-34). His experience at Athens, no doubt, influenced Paul's methodology when he moved on to Corinth. When he came to Corinth, Paul determined (the Greek suggests the idea of "predetermined") to preach nothing but "Jesus Christ, and him crucified" (I Cor 2:2). It was not with human wisdom but the gospel with which God built a thriving assembly in this heathen city.

Upon arrival in the city Paul accepted the hospitality of Aquila and his wife Priscilla, exiled Jews from Rome. During the week, he worked with them making tents (Acts 18:1-4). On the Sab-bath he would go to the synagogue where he reasoned with the Jews concerning Christ.

After the arrival of Silas and Timothy, Paul no longer required secular employment, and thus de-voted himself entirely to an aggressive evangelistic effort. One of his earliest converts was Crispus, the leader of the synagogue. Subsequently, the man's entire household believed, along with many Corin-thians (Acts 18:8). Incurring opposition from the Jews, he was forced to find another meeting place. Providentially, he was led to the home of Titus Justus (probably the "Gaius" of I Cor 1:14) next door to the synagogue!

Later, the Jews had Paul arraigned before Gallio, where the proconsul dismissed their charges and demonstrated his contempt for the Jews by looking the other way as their new leader, Sosthenes, was flogged in the street.

Paul ministered in Corinth eighteen months (Acts 18:11), during which time he also wrote I and II Thessalonians. It is noteworthy that another church was started in the eastern port of Corinth in Cenchrea (cf. Rom 16:1). Whether Paul initiated this during his first visit or at a later time is not known for certain. The leadership of the assembly was assumed by Apollos, an eloquent preacher from Alexandria, at the conclusion of Paul's first visit (Acts 18:24-19:1). Paul then moved on to Ephesus where he enjoyed the longest ministry that he was ever to have in any one place.

Paul's relations with the church. In order to understand the occasion for the writing of I Corinthians, it is necessary to outline Paul's involvements with the church subsequent to going to Ephesus. While it is true that much of this is open to debate, the best that can be done here is to outline the most conspicuous details.

1. Those of Chloe's household reported a lack of harmony (I Cor 1:11).

2. Although Paul promised a second visit (I Cor 4:19), he did not have occasion to see them again before writing I Corinthians.

3. After his initial visit described above, Paul wrote the church a letter, known as the "previous letter," in which he warned the Corinthians not to associate with immoral persons (I Cor 5:9). This letter was misconstrued by the people and required further explanation in I Corinthians 5:10-11. It is doubtful that this "previous letter" is incorporated in any way into the text of the canonical book of I Corinthians, as suggested by some (Moffatt, *Introduction to the Literature of the New Testament*, p. 109).

4. A letter was sent to Paul containing several questions (note the recurring phrase "now concerning" or the similar "as concerning" or "as touching." I Cor 7:1; 25; 8:1; 12:1; 16:1, 12). This letter may well have been delivered to Paul by the three men mentioned in I Corinthians 16:17.

5. After writing I Corinthians, Paul sent Timothy to check into conditions in the church, with the promise that he would come in person to deal with their carnality (I Cor 4:17-19; 16:10, 11; Acts 19:22). It is not known whether Timothy ever made it. He may have also requested Apollos to take time out to help with the situation (I Cor 1:12).

6. With the problems apparently unresolved, Paul was forced to pay a brief but "painful" visit (II Cor 2:1-4; 12:14; 13:1-2).

7. Upon his return, Paul sent a third letter to Corinth which was of such a severe nature that he later regretted having sent it (II Cor 2:4). This letter was carried by Titus, who was to meet Paul at Troas to give him a status report. This letter (along with the "previous letter") has been lost, and may well have been destroyed after Paul's final visit with them.

8. When Paul failed to meet Titus at Troas, his anxiety was so great that he was unable to even preach, though he had the opportunity (II Cor 2:12-13). He hurried on to Macedonia where he met Titus en route. Titus' report was very encouraging. Paul immediately sat down and penned II Corinthians to express his great relief at improved conditions (II Cor 2:13-14; 7:5-16), and to deal with some of the remaining problems in anticipation of another visit.

9. He followed this letter with his last recorded visit when he spent the winter in Corinth on his way to Jerusalem with the collection for the poor (Acts 20:1-4).

Purpose. From the foregoing data, it is discerned that Paul's letter was occasioned by at least two factors. First, he had received word from two sources of divisions in the church (I Cor 1:11; 16:17). This sectarianism probably rose more out of the sophist spirit in Corinth than from Judaistic tendencies (as at Galatia). The tendency to faction had long characterized the Greek race (D. Stanley, *Epistles of St. Paul to the Corinthians,* p. 8). They split on politics, sports, and philosophy. Thus it is not surprising to see them carry this habit over into the church. Paul was to show them that this was totally incompatible with the gospel of Christ (I Cor 1:18-25).

Secondly, Paul had received a letter from the assembly requesting answers to a series of questions. Paul felt obliged to respond.

In addition to these factors, there were apparently other reports not recorded (such as that mentioned in 5:1) that concerned the apostle. Thus, with pen in hand, Paul purposes to: (1) rebuke the party spirit in the assembly; (2) encourage them to moral purity; (3) instruct them regarding specific doctrinal problems; (4) urge their participation in the collection for Jerusalem; and (5) inform them of his immediate plans.

Authorship. The authorship of I Corinthians is so well attested that only a brief sketch is necessary here. External evidence derives from references to the epistle from the first century onward. Clement of Rome, the *Epistle of Barnabas* (3:1, 16), the *Didache* (ch. 10), Polycarp, Hermas, Justin Martyr, Athanagoras, Irenaeus, Clement of Alexandria, Tertullian, the Muratorian Canon, Marcion, the Old Syriac and Old Latin texts all attest to the authority and Pauline authorship of I Corinthians.

Internal evidence is equally strong. The writer calls himself Paul (1:1; 3:4, 6, 22; 16:21). The epistle harmonizes well with Acts and other pauline letters. Frequent mention is made of contemporaries of the mid-first century (thus eliminating a second-century forgery). This, without doubt, is a genuine product of the apostle.

Date and place of writing. Paul himself tells us that I Corinthians was written from Ephesus (I Cor 16:8-9, 19). The subscription in the TR and the AV is probably due to a misunderstanding of I Corinthians 16:5. If it were written toward the end of Paul's stay at Ephesus, the time would be spring of A.D. 55. This is suggested since he says he planned to stay in Ephesus till Pentecost (I Cor 16:8) and he was in Jerusalem on or about Pentecost in A.D. 56 (Acts 20:16). In the interim, he visited Corinth briefly (II Cor 2:1-4), spent some time in Macedonia (Acts 20:1-6), wrote II Corinthians (fall, A.D. 55), came to Corinth a few weeks later and stayed about three months. He spent the Passover season of A.D. 56 in Philippi on his way to Jerusalem (Acts 20:6).

Argument. Particular problems as they are brought under the gaze of the apostle actually form the outline of the book. However, his discussion falls basically into two categories; unsolicited advice (chs. 1-6; 15), and solicited advice (chs. 7-14). They have requested his counsel on some problems they knew about. Paul responds to these, but not until he directs their attention to a few problems they didn't know about. Hence, he opens the epistle with a rebuke: (1) The disorders in the assembly, viz., misconceptions regarding the na-

ture of the body of Christ, the message of the gospel, and the nature of the ministry (chs. 1-4). (2) Then he deals with the matter of discipline as it was necessary in the cases of lust, lawsuits, and license (chs. 5-6). Having taken care of these matters, Paul (3) answers the specific questions addressed to him on matters of doctrine and church polity. Here he focuses his attention on Christian marriage, Christian liberty, worship, and spiritual gifts (chs. 7-14). (4) His chapter on the resurrection is directed to an additional problem of certain Greeks in the assembly who had problems with the concept of the bodily resurrection (ch. 15). This is the only doctrinal "error," as such, that Paul has to deal with in the epistle, and it does not appear to have been one of the questions asked of him.

OUTLINE

a. The indivisibility of the members in the body. 12:12-19.
b. The interdependence of the members in the body. 12:20-26.
c. The induction of the members into the body. 12:27-31.
3. The primacy of love. 13:1-13.
a. Contrast of love. 13:1-3.
b. Character of love. 13:4-7.
c. Constancy of love. 13:8-13.
4. The prominence of prophecy. 14:1-40.
a. In the edification of the assembly. 14:1-17.
b. In the example of Paul. 14:18-19.
c. In the essential purpose. 14:20-25.
d. In the exercise in the assembly. 14:26-40.
E. Doctrine of the Resurrection. 15:1-58.
1. A defense of the doctrine of the Resurrection (based on known truth). 15:1-34.

a. Resurrection is vital to the historical preaching of the gospel. 15:1-19.
b. Resurrection is vital to the prophetic preaching of the gospel. 15:20-28.
c. Resurrection is vital in suffering persecution for the gospel. 15:29-34.
2. A development of the doctrine of the Resurrection (based on revelation). 15:35-58.
a. The nature of resurrection for the dead. 15:35-49.
b. The nature of resurrection for the living. 15:50-58.
V. Conclusion. 16:1-24.
A. The Contribution. 16:1-9.
1. Its instruction. 16:1-4.
2. Its collection. 16:5-9.
B. The Collector. 16:10-12.
C. The Close. 16:13-24.

COMMENTARY

I. INTRODUCTION. 1:1-9

Paul's introduction to I Corinthians consists of (a) the salutation, where he introduces himself and the recipients of his letter; and (b) the setting of the epistle, where he introduces the direction he intends to take in his writing.

A. The Salutation of the Apostle. 1:1-3.

1. Addresser: Paul and Sosthenes. 1:1.

PAUL, called *to be* **an apostle of Jesus Christ through the will of God, and Sŏs'the-nĕs** *our* **brother.**

1:1 Paul. The addresser of this letter is Paul, the great apostle, the one whom God used to establish this young assembly. **Called to be an apostle.** There is particular stress on Paul's authority as an apostle through divine call. This, together with the expression **through the will of God,** answers at the outset those who had questioned Paul's right to speak (cf. 9:1-2; II Cor 10:10). **Sosthenes our brother.** Rather than exalt himself unduly, Paul joins with him in writing the well-known brother Sosthenes. This man was not a fellow apostle, but certainly a fellow minister of the gospel. He was probably the ruler of the Jewish synagogue mentioned in Acts 18:17, although this cannot be established beyond question. However, if this is the case, it is noteworthy that the Jewish synagogue in Corinth had no little trouble retaining their leaders! Acts 18 also mentions Crispus, the synagogue ruler when Paul first arrived, as one of the first converts (Acts 18:8). Sosthenes is the man who had been elected to take his place, and subsequently, in a display of anti-Semitism in Corinth, had been beaten. Now he appears as a fellow Christian and minister of the gospel. In light of the opposition facing Paul at the Corinthian church, it is no doubt possible that he uses Sosthenes, probably a native Corinthian, to help ingratiate himself with his readers.

2. Addressees: Church in Corinth. 1:2.

2 Unto the church of God which is at Corinth, to them that are sanctified in Christ Jesus, called *to be* **saints, with all that in every place call upon the name of Jesus Christ our Lord, both theirs and ours:**

2. Unto the church of God which is at Corinth. Humanly speaking, Paul could have taken some credit here. But, for purposes of the epistle, he identifies the church as **of God.** And to add additional force to this, he adds the phrase **to them that are sanctified** (lit., "having been sanctified") **in Christ Jesus.** Here Paul has special reference to the Corinthians' correct standing before God. That is, they were set apart for God's special use. His aim in the epistle is to bring the Corinthians' "state" into closer alignment with their positional "standing." **Called to be saints, with all that in every place call upon the name of Jesus Christ our Lord, both theirs and ours.** Since the Corinthians are claiming the family name, Paul expects that they will live in conformity to the family way. The emphasis, of course, is upon the unity of all who call upon the name of the Lord.

3. Address. 1:3.

3 Grace *be* unto you, and peace, from God our Father, and *from* the Lord Jesus Christ.

3. Grace . . . and peace. In the former, Paul contemplates all that is understood in God's love as it is exercised toward sinners. The latter has in mind those benefits which fall from the exercise of God's love. Note that this grace and peace come from God, who is identified as **our Father and . . . the Lord Jesus Christ.** Here the Father and the Son are shown to be of equal status, yet clearly distinguished (cf. Phil 2:6).

B. The Setting of the Epistle. 1:4-9.

This takes the form of genuine thanksgiving to God for specific benefits enjoyed by the Corinthian assembly.

1. The regularity of Paul's thanks—always. 1:4.

4 I thank my God always on your behalf, for the grace of God which is given you by Jesus Christ;

4. I thank my God. The direction of Paul's thanks is to God. The very fact that a church should have been brought into existence at all in so wicked a place as Corinth was evidence of God's grace and power. The regularity of Paul's prayer is expressed in the term **always.** The concern of Paul's prayer was **on your behalf.** This is a good illustration of what the theologians like to call the "communion of the saints"; that is, to give thanks to God for the mutual benefits that he extends to all believers. In this case, it is for **the grace of God which is given you.** Here Paul hints on that important subject which he mentions in the next verse and will enlarge upon later in chapters 12-14.

2. The cause of Paul's thanks—enrichment. 1:5-8.

5 That in every thing ye are enriched by him, in all utterance, and *in* **all knowledge;**

5. That in every thing ye are enriched by him, in all utterance, and in all knowledge. The cause of Paul's thanks was that the Corinthians had been enriched, and that this enrichment was "in all utterance and knowledge." The extent of this enrichment is expressed in verse 7 that they **come behind in no gift.** While the term **gift** (Gr *charisma*) has a wide variety of meanings, here it probably has reference to spiritual gifts later developed in the epistle.

6 Even as the testimony of Christ was confirmed in you:

6. Testimony of Christ was confirmed in you. Here is the most significant result of their enrichment. This is that message of the gospel concerning Jesus Christ that Paul faithfully preached at Corinth (cf. I Cor 2:2).

7 So that ye come behind in no gift; waiting for the coming of our Lord Jesus Christ:
8 Who shall also confirm you unto the end, *that ye may be* **blameless in the day of our Lord Jesus Christ.**

7-8. Waiting for the coming of our Lord Jesus Christ. Since the gospel had been faithfully preached and responded to by the Corinthian believers, they are now privileged to wait upon the Second Coming of Jesus Christ, who in turn **shall also confirm you.** Historically, the gospel had been confirmed in them. Now they anticipate the prospect of that blessed event when Jesus Christ shall also confirm them blameless before the throne of God.

4. The ground of Paul's thanks—God. 1:9.

9 God *is* **faithful, by whom ye were called unto the fellowship of his Son Jesus Christ our Lord.**

9. God is faithful. Just as Paul directed his thanksgiving toward God, so the ground of his thanksgiving is that same God. For it is God who **is faithful.** And it is also that same God by whom **ye were called unto the fellowship of his Son.** The term **fellowship** (Gr *koinonia*) includes both union and communion. The Corinthian believers had been brought into union with the Lord Jesus Christ. Accordingly, this great truth implies that they had been brought into communion with one another. It will be upon this basis that Paul attacks their sectarianism.

II. DISORDER IN THE FELLOWSHIP. 1:10-4:21.

A. Denunciation of Division. 1:10-31.

The first major concern of the Apostle Paul has to do with the divisive spirit in Corinth. He approaches the problem by first denouncing their factional spirit (1:10-31), then by demonstrating the quality of divine wisdom as contrasted with human wisdom (ch. 2). In chapter 3, he develops those qualities that make for mature Christian service. And finally, in chapter 4, he defends his own ministry, and that of Apollos and the apostles, contrasting personal discomfort which he himself endured, with the arrogance of the Corinthians who are now criticizing him.

1. Paul's exhortation. 1:10-17.

10. Now is adversative. With this, Paul introduces his appeal for unity. **I beseech you, brethren, by the name of our Lord Jesus Christ.** Paul does two things here. First of all, notice the significant way in which he addresses them as brethren. He is about to exhort them to unity, which is characteristic of brethren in Christ. Paul establishes his authority when he says, **I beseech you . . . by the name of our Lord** (cf. Rom 12:1; II Thess 3:12). Their reverence and love for Christ should induce them to yield obedience to the apostle. Since Paul's own integrity has been called into question, he appeals to the authority of Christ. **That ye all speak the same thing, and that there be no divisions among you.** Quarrels had split the congregation into factions. The appeal is to unity in speech, and fellowship. **But that ye be perfectly joined together** (this is translated "mending" in Mark 1:19). The force of this term (Gr *katartizō*) is that they be adjusted to one another in **mind and . . . judgment** (lit., "thought" or "opinion").

11. Word had come to the apostle concerning the condition of the assembly at Corinth by **them . . . of Chloe** (probably slaves of Chloe's household who were in Ephesus on business). The report was that there were **contentions among you.**

12. There appear to have been four rival parties. Those who professed to follow **Paul;** perhaps as the most sublime teacher. Then there were those who professed to follow **Apollos,** the gifted orator from Alexandria. Others claimed to follow Peter, or **Cephas** as it is given in the text. These may have been Judaists or, more likely, they were those who preferred Peter as representing more authority, as he was with Christ in His earthly ministry. Then there were those who renounced all the others, and claimed only **Christ.** What special advantage this last party claimed is not certain. But they were as much sectarian as the others since they degraded the Lord to the level of a party leader (also notice II Cor 5:15; 10:7; and 11:23).

13. Is Christ divided? The implied answer is "no." There is but one Christ. **Was Paul crucified for you?** Paul asks, "was I ever your saviour, or did I ever pretend to be?" **Were ye baptized in the name of Paul?** "You never swore loyalty to me."

14-16. In view of the divisions in the assembly, Paul is thankful that very few in Corinth were even baptized by him. No one could ever accuse him of trying to gather a following in this way. The implication of this is rather significant. Baptism is not necessary to salvation, else the apostle would have been giving thanks to God that he saved so few.

17. The point is that baptism was not part of the apostle's commission; rather, he asserts **Christ sent me . . . to preach the gospel.** Paul concludes his exhortation regarding the divisions in the assembly with a call to evangelize. **Not with wisdom of words.** This looks ahead to the next segment of the apostle's argument when he deals with the problems of human

10 Now I beseech you, brethren, by the name of our Lord Jesus Christ, that ye all speak the same thing, and *that* there be no divisions among you; but *that* ye be perfectly joined together in the same mind and in the same judgment.

11 For it hath been declared unto me of you, my brethren, by them *which are of the house* of Chlō'e, that there are contentions among you.

12 Now this I say, that every one of you saith, I am of Paul; and I of Apollos; and I of Cē'phas; and I of Christ.

13 Is Christ divided? was Paul crucified for you? or were ye baptized in the name of Paul?

14 I thank God that I baptized none of you, but Crispus and Gaius;
15 Lest any should say that I had baptized in mine own name.
16 And I baptized also the household of Stĕph'a-nas: besides, I know not whether I baptized any other.

17 For Christ sent me not to baptize, but to preach the gospel: not with wisdom of words, lest the cross of Christ should be made of none effect.

wisdom as opposed to divine. **Lest the cross of Christ should be made of none effect** (Gr *kenoō* means "to empty or deprive of substance"). The success of the gospel lies in the plain doctrine of a crucified Lord. Paul was not about to ascribe its power to the flourish of oratory, or the intricacies of Greek philosophy. In spite of his learning at the feet of Gamaliel, the Apostle Paul lays his learning aside when he preaches the simple gospel of Christ. This truth needs no artificial dress. It alone carries with it the "power of God unto salvation" (Rom 1:16). Having exhorted the people to unity, the apostle now goes on to correct a misconception that they have regarding the nature of the gospel.

2. Paul's proclamation. 1:18-25.

18 For the preaching of the cross is to them that perish foolishness; but unto us which are saved it is the power of God.

18. Paul directs his attention first to the word of the Cross (vss. 18-20). **For** introduces the reason he did not come in wisdom of words. **The preaching** (Gr *logos*) **of the cross.** The content of Paul's message was the Cross, not wisdom. **To them that perish foolishness.** In its effect on man, Paul singles out two groups. Those that perish deem the word of the Cross foolishness. For men of wit and learning, and of the cultivated arts and sciences, the word of the Cross was met with scorn and contempt. As those who cried out on Golgotha's hill, "He saved others, himself he cannot save." Another group Paul identifies with the words **unto us which are saved.** The language here is strongly reminiscent of our Lord's instructions regarding the broad way that leads to destruction, and the many that enter by it, and the narrow way that leads to life, while there are few who find it (Mt 7:13-14). To the saved, the pure, simple message of the Cross is the power of God.

19 For it is written, I will destroy the wisdom of the wise, and will bring to nothing the understanding of the prudent.
20 Where *is* the wise? where *is* the scribe? where *is* the disputer of this world? hath not God made foolish the wisdom of this world?

19-20. Paul further buttresses his argument by the appeal from inspired Scripture (Isa 29:14; 19:12; 33:18). The "wise" of Corinth are no more effectual to the saving of souls than the "wise" of Judah in staving the threat against Sennacherib. The great stress in these verses is upon the activity of God. God will **destroy** human wisdom, and make the wisdom of the world **foolish.** But where is the wisdom of God, and how is it demonstrated? Paul's answer to this question is given in verses 21-25. It is the wisdom of the Cross.

21 For after that in the wisdom of God the world by wisdom knew not God, it pleased God by the foolishness of preaching to save them that believe.

21. The world by wisdom knew not God. By leaving man to his own wisdom, God demonstrates man's folly. For he is not only incapable of knowing God, but in fact, has degraded Him to the level of the creature (cf. Rom 1). Why are these Corinthian believers taken up with sophistry when history affirms that through wisdom, the knowledge of God is impossible? By way of contrast, Paul says that the knowledge of God is possible to **them that believe.** Here is the wisdom of God. Salvation comes through the foolishness of **preaching** (Gr *kērygma*). The emphasis of the apostle here is not upon the act of preaching, but upon the content of preaching (viz., the message of the Cross, cf. vs. 18 above).

22 For the Jews require a sign, and the Greeks seek after wisdom:
23 But we preach Christ crucified, unto the Jews a stumblingblock, and unto the Greeks foolishness;
24 But unto them which are called, both Jews and Greeks, Christ the power of God, and the wisdom of God.
25 Because the foolishness of God is wiser than men; and the weakness of God is stronger than men.

22-25. Verse 22 deals with the matter of man's curiosity. **Jews require a sign, and the Greeks seek after wisdom.** For the Jew, it was necessary that the message be accredited by physical wonders. For the Greeks, they required intellectual splendor. Both found it equally difficult to accept a dead man on a cross as an eternal Saviour. **But unto . . . (the) called . . . Christ (is) the power . . . and the wisdom of God.** The superiority of the Cross is seen in that it is both a sign and wisdom. But only to the **called** (these are to be identified with those above who **believed,** vs. 21).

3. Paul's evaluation. 1:26-31.

The factional spirit at Corinth was wrong because it represented an attitude that was incompatible with the gospel of Christ. It was also wrong because it represented a misunderstanding of the nature of the gospel. Paul goes on, now, to show it is wrong because their own experience belies such a haughty spirit.

26 For ye see your calling, brethren, how that not many wise men after the flesh, not many mighty, not many noble, *are called*:

26. For introduces the negative side of Paul's argument. **Ye see . . . not many wise . . . mighty . . . noble.** Look around you, the apostle says, and tell me the kind of men God is calling. Are they the wise, mighty, or noble? Obviously not. The nature of Paul's argument here tells us that most of the Corinthian congregation was poor and of the lower element of society. They certainly had very little to offer in themselves.

27 But God hath chosen the foolish things of the world to confound the wise; and God hath chosen the weak things of the world to confound the things which are mighty;
28 And base things of the world, and things which are despised, hath God chosen, *yea*, and things which are not, to bring to nought things that are:
29 That no flesh should glory in his presence.
30 But of him are ye in Christ Jesus, who of God is made unto us wisdom, and righteousness, and sanctification, and redemption:

27-29. God hath chosen . . . the foolish, . . . the weak, . . . and things which are not. The selection of God is designed to bring to silence the wisdom of man. He selects the foolish to shame the wise; the weak to shame the strong; and the "no-bodys" to shame the "somebodys."

30. But introduces the positive side of Paul's argument. Paul concludes that all the riches of salvation are lodged in Jesus Christ. All that the Corinthian believers are, they owe to Him. Thus, it is not in oneself, or in party alignment, or in supposed human ability, that any believer ought to glory, but **of him are ye in Christ Jesus.** To answer the implied question, "What am I in Christ?", Paul tabulates those qualities which belong to the believer. **Wisdom.** This is positional. It does not contemplate the acquisition of cognitive skills, but the wisdom of God as demonstrated in the Cross. **Righteousness** is a legal concept, and has in mind that righteousness that is registered to the believer's account the moment he believes (Rom 5). **Sanctification** has in mind that which Paul has already introduced in 1:2 in the words: "sanctified in Christ Jesus." This contemplates the work of Christ "in" the believer. It has in mind both a positional and a progressive truth. In justification, there is the idea of righteousness applied to one's account. In sanctification, the idea is that of righteousness activated in the believer's life, equipping him for service to the Lord. **Redemption.** If the order of these terms is logical, this would have in mind more the eschatological prospect of the resurrected body. However, the apostle is more emotional than logical in this passage, and it is more likely that he has injected this as a factor which underlines all the above. As the twenty-four elders put it, "Thou art worthy . . . for thou wast slain, and hast redeemed us to God by thy blood out of every kindred, and tongue, and people, and nation" (Rev 5:9). It was the atonement which opened the way for God to extend His grace to sinful man, and pour out upon him such benefits as wisdom, righteousness, sanctification, etc.

31 That, according as it is written, He that glorieth, let him glory in the Lord.

31. That indicates purpose. If there is to be boasting, it is to be properly directed. That is, to **the Lord.** If the gospel were shackled with human contingencies, this would not be possible. But because salvation is of Jehovah, to Him alone must be the praise.

B. Demonstration of Divine Wisdom. 2:1-16.

Having denounced the divisive spirit which characterized the Corinthian assembly, the Apostle Paul in chapter 1 has shown that the real genius of the Christian assembly is unity, not controversy. Chapter 2 is related to the preceding in that while the former deals with a worldly attitude, the latter deals with a worldly mentality. Paul's message was in demonstration of divine wisdom. He is about to show the Corinthians that divine wisdom is unlike any they had ever seen before. Paul characterizes it as: (1) wisdom of divine power (2:1-5); (2) wisdom of divine origin (2:6-9); and (3) wisdom of divine perception (2:10-16).

CHAPTER 2

AND I, brethren, when I came to you, came not with excellency of speech or of wisdom, declaring unto you the testimony of God.

2 For I determined not to know any thing among you, save Jesus Christ, and him crucified.

3 And I was with you in weakness, and in fear, and in much trembling.

4 And my speech and my preaching *was* not with enticing words of man's wisdom, but in demonstration of the Spirit and of power:

5 That your faith should not stand in the wisdom of men, but in the power of God.

6 Howbeit we speak wisdom among them that are perfect: yet not the wisdom of this world, nor of the princes of this world, that come to nought:

7 But we speak the wisdom of God in a mystery, *even* the hidden *wisdom*, which God ordained before the world unto our glory:

8 Which none of the princes of this world knew: for had they known *it*, they would not have crucified the Lord of glory.

9 But as it is written, Eye hath not seen, nor ear heard, neither have entered into the heart of man, the things which God hath prepared for them that love him.

---

1. Wisdom of divine power. 2:1-5.

2:1-2. In pursuing his argument, Paul reflects upon his initial ministry with the Corinthians. His message was not characterized by eloquence (although he certainly was capable of it). Rather, it was a declaration of the **testimony of God.** This was not Paul's testimony of God, but God's testimony of Himself (viz., "the cross").

I determined (lit., "I decided not"). The implication is that Paul gave careful thought to his approach, and resolved to lay aside the ornaments of speech and philosophical skill to announce **Jesus Christ, and him crucified.** Not only was Paul's message of divine wisdom, but his method also reflected the same.

3. Weakness . . . fear . . . trembling. To some of Paul's enemies, this approach was a stumbling block (cf. II Cor 10:10).

4. But Paul resolved to come **not with enticing words . . . but in demonstration of the Spirit and of power.** With a deep sense of his own insufficiency, Paul carried on a ministry characterized by modesty and humility. Paul was determined, as John the Baptist, that "he must increase, but I must decrease." Instead, his ministry demonstrated the Spirit and power. Obviously, the power was not in respect to any human agency, but the power of divine wisdom. Paul's mention of the Spirit here is significant. The Corinthians thought they knew much about the Holy Spirit, for as no other church in apostolic times, they had experienced the gifts of the Spirit. But they still had a lot to learn, and Paul will have many things to say about this important subject.

5. That your faith should . . . stand . . . in the power of God. Paul has a motive. Paul knows that his clever speech and polished oratory can save no one. Furthermore, he knows that if they are merely drawn by the logic of his arguments, their faith will be at the mercy of the next man that comes with a more clever presentation. Paul's motive is that their faith should "stand," and that it should stand in the "power of God."

2. Wisdom of divine origin. 2:6-9.

6. Paul does not depreciate wisdom as some anti-intellectuals do today. On the contrary, what Paul proclaims is the only true wisdom. **We speak** (lit., "go on speaking"). Contrast the historical aorist in Greek in verses 1-3. Paul wants them to know that his message has not changed.

But this wisdom could only be fully appreciated by **them that are perfect** (mature, Gr *teleios;* cf. I Cor 14:20; Phil 3:15; and Heb 6:1). Paul cannot resist the use of irony here. **That come to nought** (Greek present passive participle, "who are being made ineffective").

7-9. This wisdom is also a hidden wisdom. This is the **wisdom of God.** In contrast to the groping speculation of fallen men, Paul's message is the unchanging truth of God. **In a mystery. In** has an instrumental force. **Mystery** (Gr *mystērion*) refers to some work or purpose of God hitherto unrevealed (Rom 16:25-26). In this case, the reference is to the **hidden wisdom, which God ordained . . . unto our glory.** The counsels of God concerning our salvation are from eternity, and directed toward the same everlasting glory (cf. Rom 8:28-32; Phil 1:10). That this wisdom was hidden from men has the horrible consequence that the **Lord of glory** was crucified (on the expression "Lord of glory," meaning perhaps "the Lord whose attribute was glory," see Ps 29:1; Acts 7:2; Eph 1:17; Jas 2:1). **Eye hath not seen . . .** Paul employs the language of Isaiah 64:4 in order to demonstrate that the wisdom of God is not of human origin, and also to contrast the thought of verse 10.

This wisdom which is of divine power, and of divine origin, is also shown by the apostle to be of divine perception (vss. 10-16).

3. *Wisdom of divine perception. 2:10-16.*

Paul develops his thought here by showing, first of all, that this perception is through the Spirit, then by contrasting the perception of **natural man** in verse 14 with the perception of the spiritual man in verse 15.

10 But God hath revealed *them* **unto us by his Spirit: for the Spirit searcheth all things, yea, the deep things of God.**
11 For what man knoweth the things of a man, save the spirit of man which is in him? even so the things of God knoweth no man, but the Spirit of God.

10-11. The truth of which the apostle is speaking is not truth that remains hidden to every human heart; on the contrary, it is **revealed . . . unto us** (**unto us** is in the emphatic position in the original). For the mature believer, all that God has revealed is open unto him. In verses 10-13 the apostle deals with three vital doctrines. In verse 10 he deals with the doctrine of revelation. For the believer today, the truth which Paul is talking about is contained in that record which God has given to us, the Bible. This is eternally and unchangingly the truth of God. Verse 11 deals with the doctrine of illumination, which has to do with human perception of divine truth. **The Spirit** (see Rom 8:4). The things of God can only be recognized by the highest element of human personality. They have not entered into the heart (vs. 9) but into the spirit, which is the principal point of contact with God. Since the truth of God is of divine origin, it requires divine enablement to properly understand it.

12 Now we have received, not the spirit of the world, but the spirit which is of God; that we might know the things that are freely given to us of God.
13 Which things also we speak, not in the words which man's wisdom teacheth, but which the Holy Ghost teacheth; comparing spiritual things with spiritual.

12-13. The subject of verses 12 and 13 is the doctrine of inspiration. In verse 12 Paul talks about the content of inspiration. **That we might know the things that are freely given to us of God.** In verse 13 his concern is with the communication of inspiration **which things** (the things freely given) **also we speak.** Paul's message was not of human contrivance. He was a channel, simply communicating God's truth. The faithful minister of the gospel today does the same thing. He takes of that truth, God's Word, and communicates it to man. **Comparing spiritual things with spiritual.** The term **comparing** (Gr *synekrinō*) occurs only here and in II Corinthians 10:12 where the meaning is clearly "compare." However, in classical Greek, the term was always used in a sense of "to compound" or "to interpret" (cf. LXX Gen 40:8). Probably the most satisfactory interpretation is "combining spiritual things with spiritual words," or "doing spiritual things by spiritual means." After speaking of spiritual things (11-13), Paul now speaks of the forms in which they are conveyed. In other words, spiritual truth is conveyed in language that is given by God's Spirit. This would not be the case if he uttered the revelations of the Spirit in the speech of human wisdom (cf. Vincent, *Word Studies in the New Testament*, Vol. II, p. 197). Having established the principle by which God's truth is made known, the apostle contrasts two kinds of men to whom the truth comes, i.e., the natural and the spiritual man.

14 But the natural man receiveth not the things of the Spirit of God: for they are foolishness unto him: neither can he know *them,* **because they are spiritually discerned.**

14. Natural man (lit., "soulish man"). Paul contrasts the soulish man (the soul as the organ of human cognition) with the "spiritual" (the spirit as the organ of spiritual cognition). The former, when confronted with spiritual truth, **receiveth not.** He is unreceptive. He does not admit the truth into his heart (cf. Lk 8:13; Acts 8:14; 11:1; I Thess 1:6; Jas 1:21). **They are foolishness.** He passes it off with scorn. **Neither can he know** (lit., "he cannot know"). As spiritual discernment is generated only by the Holy Spirit, the capacity to know spiritual truth is beyond the innate powers of the natural man.

Because they are spiritually discerned shows that the natural man is incompetent. The fundamental idea of **discerned** (Gr *anakrinomai*) is that of examination or scrutiny. It is used only by Paul and Luke, and mostly of judicial examination (cf. Luke 23:14; Acts 4:9; I Cor 9:3; 10:25, 27). It speaks of the impatient human spirit which prejudges the truth and wants to anticipate the full judgment. On the spiritual plain, the natural man does not even have the ability to sift the facts.

15 But he that is spiritual judgeth all

15. But introduces the contrast with **he that is spiritual** (he who is dominated by the Spirit). Such a man **judgeth** (Gr

things, yet he himself is judged of no man.

16 For who hath known the mind of the Lord, that he may instruct him? But we have the mind of Christ.

CHAPTER 3
AND I, brethren, could not speak unto you as unto spiritual, but as unto carnal, *even* as unto babes in Christ.
2 I have fed you with milk, and not with meat: for hitherto ye were not able *to bear it*, neither yet now are ye able.
3 For ye are yet carnal: for whereas *there is* among you envying, and strife, and divisions, are ye not carnal, and walk as men?

anakrino, discerns) **all things.** The difference between the natural man and the spiritual man is primarily that the spiritual man has been exposed to God's revelation, has received it, and founded his faith upon it. He can judge now both earthly and heavenly things. He can discern what is and what is not of the gospel and salvation, and whether a man truly preaches the truth of God. It is important to observe that the spiritual man does not lose his power of reasoning. Nor does Paul renounce the concepts of reason and logic. Rather, he elevates revelation above reason, and subjects the imaginations of human reason to the objective truth of God. The natural man operates in reverse. Discerning all things, the spiritual man is **judged of no man** who is not spiritual.

16. But we have the mind of Christ. This answers the question that Paul puts in the same verse, "who has known the mind of the Lord?" The answer is, "we do!" The term **we** no doubt includes the Apostle Paul and all true believers.

C. Development of Mature Service. 3:1-23.

In chapter 1 Paul has denounced their divisive spirit. In chapter 2 he has shown that they have totally misunderstood the message of the gospel. The burden of chapter 3 is the development of mature service. Paul develops his thought by, first, citing the fleshliness in Corinth (vss. 1-3), then by showing that he, Apollos, and others who assisted with the ministry in Corinth were not party leaders, but rather, fellow workers in the gospel (vss. 4-17). Then, in verses 18-23, he shows the utter folly in human wisdom.

1. Fleshliness in Corinth. 3:1-3.

3:1-3. In the opening verses, Paul notes that the fleshliness in Corinth had hindered his ministry. **And I, brethren, could not speak.** The pronoun **I** is emphatic. Paul calls them brethren not simply to ingratiate himself with them. But, it is important to observe that they cannot be robbed of their relationship to Jesus Christ in spite of their immaturity and sin. The apostle observes that even on his first encounter with them, he was unable to speak as to spiritual men. Paul recalls this to mind briefly in order to compare the present state of the Corinthians with their beginnings in the faith, a comparison that must have filled them with shame. They still are acting like spiritual babes (cf. Lenski, *The Interpretation of I and II Corinthians,* p. 120). **I have fed you with milk, and not with meat.** As newborn babes, this would be natural and to be expected (I Pet 2:2). But, at this stage in their development, it is embarrassing. Their problem was that they were still **carnal** (lit., "fleshly"). The warfare between the flesh and the Spirit receives continual emphasis in Paul's writings (cf. Gal 5:17; Rom 7:14-8:13). The factions which have destroyed the unity in Corinth indicate that these believers were not walking by the Spirit, but were allowing the flesh to direct their behavior. They were acting just like fleshly men, with no uplifting power of the Holy Spirit. They were soldiers of the Lord's army trying to march to the beat of Lucifer's drums.

Such an attitude also hindered the spiritual maturity and development of these people. They are still **babes** ("nonspeakers" or "infants"). This strongly contrasts with the "perfect" in 2:6. **Milk,** the drink suitable for babies, suggests their undeveloped spiritual state. **Envying, and strife, and divisions,** all works of the flesh, are symptomatic of their carnality. **Walk as men.** Paul does not say that they "are" men, but they are as men (the inference is "natural" men, cf. 2:14). Having finally labeled the wranglings at Corinth for what they were (carnality), Paul goes on to show the absurdity of such party alliances, since he and Apollos and the other apostles were actually fellow workers in the gospel (3:4-17).

2. Fellow workers in the gospel. 3:4-17.

4 For while one saith, I am of Paul; and another, I *am* of Apollos; are ye not carnal?

5 Who then is Paul, and who *is* Apollos, but ministers by whom ye believed, even as the Lord gave to every man?

6 I have planted, Apollos watered; but God gave the increase.

7 So then neither is he that planteth any thing, neither he that watereth; but God that giveth the increase.

8 Now he that planteth and he that watereth are one: and every man shall receive his own reward according to his own labour.

9 For we are labourers together with God: ye are God's husbandry, *ye are* God's building.

10 According to the grace of God which is given unto me, as a wise masterbuilder, I have laid the foundation, and another buildeth thereon. But let every man take heed how he buildeth thereupon.

11 For other foundation can no man lay than that is laid, which is Jesus Christ.

12 Now if any man build upon this foundation gold, silver, precious stones, wood, hay, stubble;

13 Every man's work shall be made manifest: for the day shall declare it, because it shall be revealed by fire; and

4-5. In verses 4 and 5, the Apostle Paul shows that he and Apollos were united in service. **Another** (Gr *heteros*, another of a different kind). **Carnal.** The better texts read "men." In other words, Paul is saying, "Are you not mere men?" Who (Gr *ti* "what"). . .? Function is emphasized in this expression. What then are Paul and Apollos? **Ministers by whom ye believed, even as the Lord gave.** Paul comes now to the crucial question, "What are these men around whom the Corinthians had built their little coteries?" They are simply ministers (Gr *diakonos*) serving the Lord. The apostle was not there to extend his own influence and popularity; rather, he was in Corinth in obedience to God (note especially Acts 18:9-10).

6. These ministers were also united in sowing (vss. 6-8). **I have planted, Apollos watered; but God gave** (Greek imperfect tense, "was giving") **the increase.** Men are used to accomplish specific tasks in the economy of God, but in the process, God is giving the increase. While men can be used to plant and cultivate things, only God can make things grow.

7. Neither is he that planteth any thing. The point is that men are unimportant when compared to God who makes our efforts effectual.

8. Are one (of one purpose). **Every man shall receive his own reward.** Just as there are differences in quality of workmanship among craftsmen, even so among God's ministers. The quality of one's work and service will be directly related to the rewards he receives. We each have a responsibility to serve God faithfully, knowing that our best results are but the work of His grace.

Paul's servants are also united in structure. This is the essence of Paul's argument in verses 9-17.

9. Here is the key to this chapter. The principle is expressed in the words, **we are laborers together with God** (lit., "fellow workers of God"). This, in effect, restates the phrase in verse 8, **he that planteth and he that watereth are one.** Then Paul employs two illustrations to explicate this principle. The first looks back to verses 6-8, **ye are God's husbandry.** The second he introduces by saying **ye are God's building.** This is the imagery which dominates the remainder of the chapter. The use of the architectural metaphor is best understood if one remembers the magnificent temples and buildings common in Corinth. The important thrust of this metaphor applies to the believer's works.

10-11. First a reminder. **I have laid the foundation.** The foundation is always the least noticed and the most important part of any building. Paul had laid the foundation of the church among them in that he had "begotten (them) through the gospel" (cf. 4:15). **Another buildeth thereon** corresponds to the phrase **Apollos watered,** above. **Let every man take heed how he buildeth thereupon.** We are urged to examine *how* we build, not *what* we build. The warning is necessitated by the nature of the foundation which is **Jesus Christ** (cf. Acts 4:12; Lk 6:46-49). The second factor which is important to the apostle is that there is to be a time of reckoning. Verse 12 deals with the materials employed in the building. Verses 13-15 deal with manifestations of every man's work.

12. Gold, silver, precious stones. There are two kinds of material that can be employed in the superstructure of the building. The first are eternal. These are consistent with the quality of the foundation. A second kind of material is temporal. **Wood, hay, stubble.** In contrast to the above, these will not withstand the trial by fire.

13. Every man's work shall be made manifest. While it is possible to hide the true quality of one's service for Christ in this life, there is coming a time when it will be openly displayed for

the fire shall try every man's work of what sort it is.

14 If any man's work abide which he hath built thereupon, he shall receive a reward.
15 If any man's work shall be burned, he shall suffer loss: but he himself shall be saved; yet so as by fire.

16 Know ye not that ye are the temple of God, and *that* the Spirit of God dwelleth in you?

17 If any man defile the temple of God, him shall God destroy; for the temple of God is holy, which *temple* ye are.

18 Let no man deceive himself. If any man among you seemeth to be wise in this world, let him become a fool, that he may be wise.

19 For the wisdom of this world is foolishness with God. For it is written, He taketh the wise in their own craftiness.
20 And again, The Lord knoweth the thoughts of the wise, that they are vain.

21 Therefore let no man glory in men. For all things are yours;

22 Whether Paul, or Apollos, or Cē′-phas, or the world, or life, or death, or things present, or things to come; all are yours;

what it is. The time is given in the words **the day.** This is the day of the Judgment Seat of Christ (cf. 4:5; II Cor 5:10). **Fire.** This is figurative for judgment. More specifically, it speaks of the absolutely righteous judgment of God. Fire is used here, not for its enlightening power, but its consuming power. Of the six types of material mentioned, three are combustible and three are incombustible. (see also Deut 4:24; Mal 3:2; II Thess 1:8; Heb 12:29).

14-15. Abide . . . reward . . . burned . . . loss. The results of the judgment are broken into two categories. If a man's work remains undamaged by the fire, accordingly, he receives rewards (Gr *misthos*, "wages," cf. 3:8). Of course, it goes without saying that even the "wages" mentioned here are entirely a gift of grace (cf. Dan 12:3; I Cor 9:17; II Jn 8; Rev 4:4; 11-18). If a man's work does not endure, and is consumed in the fire, then he shall "suffer loss." Everything he has devoted himself to in this life shall be suddenly swept away. **But he himself shall be saved; yet so as by fire.** It is important to notice that such a man does not suffer the loss of his salvation, but the loss of reward. The stress in this entire passage is not upon a man's relationship to Christ, but upon service to Christ. (On the believer's rewards see, W. Kroll, *It Will Be Worth It All.*)

Then Paul directs his attention to the fact that the building being erected is a residence of Almighty God (vss. 16-17).

16. Ye are the temple of God. Here the temple is the local church, not the individual believer (cf. Eph 2:21; II Cor 6:16). **The Spirit of God dwelleth in you.** This expression does not vitiate the doctrine of the omnipresence of the Holy Spirit. Indeed, the Holy Spirit is everywhere, but He does not "dwell" everywhere. He dwells in the local church because He has taken up residence in every believer (cf. Jn 14:16).

17. Defile . . . destroy (Gr *phtheirō*, has the idea of dishonoring or destroying). **Him shall God destroy.** This is a much stronger expression than "suffer loss" above. Paul seems to have in mind unsaved people who may or may not be in the assembly, but who, in fact, are false believers. The prospect for such a one is a fearful one. **The temple of God is holy, which temple ye are.** Paul has built a syllogism here. In verse 16 he has said, "you are a shrine of God." Now he says, "the shrine of God is holy." Therefore, the conclusion is, "you are holy."

3. Folly in worldly wisdom. 3:18-23.

18. Here the apostle gives the formula for godly wisdom. **Let no man deceive himself.** Do not be led away from the truth and simplicity of the gospel by having too high an opinion of human wisdom. **If any . . . seemeth to be wise in this world, let him become a fool.** Do not have too high an opinion of yourself. Learn to resign your own understanding to follow the instruction of God. This is the way to truth and everlasting wisdom. In order that **he may be wise.** One must learn to prefer the infallible revelation of God to his own shallow reasonings.

19-20. There can be no comparison between God's wisdom and man's. **He taketh the wise in their own craftiness** (cf. Job 5:13; Ps 94:11).

The conclusion to chapter three is very much like the conclusion to chapter 2. If you must boast, then by all means, do not boast within yourself or man, but in Christ.

21. For all things are yours. The man who belongs to Christ is a child of God, and his Father will do anything for him. Nothing of the Father's resources shall be begrudged to the believer (cf. Rom 8:32).

22. Whether Paul, or Apollos, or Cephas. The absurdity of their dividing over allegiances to any of these men is that God gave them "all" to the Corinthians. **Or the world,** a rebuke to the legalists of Paul's day. **Or life, or death,** the former denoting

23 And ye are Christ's; and Christ *is* God's.

CHAPTER 4

LET a man so account of us, as of the ministers of Christ, and stewards of the mysteries of God.

2 Moreover it is required in stewards, that a man be found faithful.

3 But with me it is a very small thing that I should be judged of you, or of man's judgment: yea, I judge not mine own self.

4 For I know nothing by myself; yet am I not hereby justified: but he that judgeth me is the Lord.

5 Therefore judge nothing before the time, until the Lord come, who both will bring to light the hidden things of darkness, and will make manifest the counsels of the hearts: and then shall every man have praise of God.

---

things present, the latter, **things to come.** The believer in Christ "shall want no good thing" (Ps 84:11).

23. But it must be remembered that **Ye are Christ's.** It is only because of our relationship to Christ who is Lord of all, that all of these benefits accrue. **Christ is God's.** Christ is not subordinate to God, as the believer is to Christ; rather, He is the Anointed One of God. He is God in the flesh, "reconciling the world unto himself" (II Cor 5:19).

D. Defense of a Faithful Steward. 4:1-21.

Since all who ministered at Corinth were servants of God (cf. 3:5), and since the church belongs to God and was His temple (cf. 3:16-17), then the Corinthians were not justified in qualifying these ministers by some arbitrary standard. It is God whom these men serve, and He must be their Judge. Paul, Apollos, and Peter were simply faithful ministers of Christ, and along with the other apostles, were simply obeying God in extending the gospel around the world. In this chapter, Paul shows that the wranglings in Corinth were inappropriate, unfair, and intolerable.

1. Execution of faithfulness. 4:1-5.

4:1-3. The character of a faithful steward of God is that his ministry is centered in Christ and he is committed to Him. **Ministers** (Gr *hypēretēs*, "under rower," "a subordinate," or "servant," J. H. Thayer, *Greek-English Lexicon of the New Testament*, p. 641). This term is used only here in Paul's epistles. It differs from the word translated "ministers" in 3:5 in that it has the idea of an attendant or helper that assists a master. The apostle and minister of Christ is simply an underling, or an attendant of Christ. He takes orders and executes them. **Stewards,** (Gr *oikonomos*). Generally, a slave in the master's household who is entrusted with property. Both of these terms emphasize subordination to the master. However, in the latter, there is particular stress on accountability. He must render account for the manner in which he carries out his master's orders. **That a man be found faithful.** In verse 2, Paul moves from the plural to the singular ("stewards"—"a man"). This is characteristic of Paul. He moves from principle to particular: i.e., it is sought for in all stewards, that each one be found reliable and trustworthy. The subject of verse three is the criticism of a faithful steward. **A very small thing.** It amounts to very little that the apostle finds himself subject to the judicial examination of the Corinthians. **Man's judgment** (lit., "man's day"). This is an implied contrast with the day of the Lord (cf. vs. 5). **I judge not mine own self.** If Paul were to resort to introspective critical examination of himself, then he too would be guilty of usurping a responsibility which belongs only to God.

4. Verses 4 and 5 deal with the manner by which this faithful steward is certified. **I know nothing by myself** ("I know nothing against myself"). It was this sort of total commitment that gave Paul the authority to make such a statement as "be ye followers of me" (cf. I Cor 4:16; 11:1). **Yet am I not hereby justified.** Paul recognized that even he himself was not competent to adequately examine himself. Arthur Custance observes, "Man is totally irrational in his attitude and assessment of his own nature. He is a fallen creature with a heart that is desperately wicked above all else (Jer 17:9), and a mind that has to be renewed (Rom 12:2)" (A. C. Custance, *Man in Adam and in Christ*, p. 17).

5. The Lord alone is the Judge. Therefore the examination must await His time, that is, "when He comes" (cf. 1:7). Then He will shed light on the **hidden things,** which Paul defines as **the counsels of the hearts: and then shall every man have praise of God** (lit., "praise from God"). God who knows the mind and the hearts will apportion to each his due praise.

2. Example of faithfulness. 4:6-13.

Paul goes on in verse 6-13 to use himself, Apollos, and the other apostles as examples of faithfulness. In an effort to shame the Corinthians into recognizing the nature of their behavior, Paul first contrasts the efforts of Apollos and himself to accommodate the Corinthians (vs. 6) with their continued arrogance (vss. 7-8). Then in verses 9-13, he attacks their haughty spirit by citing the continued abuse of all the apostles.

6 And these things, brethren, I have in a figure transferred to myself and *to* Apollos for your sakes; that ye might learn in us not to think *of men* above that which is written, that no one of you be puffed up for one against another.

6. I have in a figure transferred (Gr *metaschēmatizō*, exchanged the outward fashion). Paul adapted himself for the purpose **that no one of you be puffed up for one against another.** The expression, **not to think . . . above that which is written,** is a proverbial expression. The Apostle Paul is enjoining the Corinthians not to go beyond Scripture. In other words, learn to live by the Book, and stop following men.

7 For who maketh thee to differ *from another?* and what hast thou that thou didst not receive? now if thou didst receive *it,* why dost thou glory, as if thou hadst not received *it?*

8 Now ye are full, now ye are rich, ye have reigned as kings without us: and I would to God ye did reign, that we also might reign with you.

7-8. Three pointed questions puncture the bubble of the Corinthian pride. **For who maketh thee to differ . . .?** There is no room for pride and self-conceit, when all the distinction made among them is owing to God. **What hast thou . . . received?** Everything they had, including their gifts in the ministry were given them by God. To take personal pride in them was tantamount to insulting God. Irony exudes from the apostle in verses 7 and 8 in the words, **Now ye are full, now ye are rich, ye have reigned as kings without us.** These are three blessings promised in the coming messianic kingdom. The Corinthians were boasting each with his own party as if he had already arrived in that kingdom. And so Paul says, **I would to God ye did reign, that we also might reign with you.** The Corinthians had already arrived while the apostle was still waiting (vs. 5)!

9 For I think that God hath set forth us the apostles last, as it were appointed to death: for we are made a spectacle unto the world, and to angels, and to men.

9. For I think. The apostle is about to level the arrogance of the Corinthians. With the consideration of my own suffering and the abuse of the apostles, since you are already reigning, God must have placed **the apostles last.** We have not come into the kingdom yet! To the world, we are a **spectacle** (Gr *theatron*, a theater). The apostles were like exhibits in a sideshow. Notice the verb form of this term in Hebrews 10:33.

10 We *are* fools for Christ's sake, but ye *are* wise in Christ; we *are* weak, but ye *are* strong; ye *are* honourable, but we *are* despised.

11 Even unto this present hour we both hunger, and thirst, and are naked, and are buffeted, and have no certain dwellingplace;

12 And labour, working with our own hands: being reviled, we bless; being persecuted, we suffer it:

13 Being defamed, we intreat: we are made as the filth of the world, *and are* the offscouring of all things unto this day.

10-13. The series of growing distinctions between Paul and the Corinthians must have been nothing short of embarrassing to his readers. **We are fools for Christ's sake, but ye are wise.** The apostles were considered fools because they knew and preached nothing but Christ. On the other hand, the Corinthians used their Christianity as another philosophy to extend their reputation as wise and enlightened people. **We are made . . . the offscouring of all things unto this day.** Some find an illusion to an ancient Athenian custom of throwing certain worthless persons into the sea in case of plague or famine, saying "be our offscouring" in the belief that they would wash away the nation's guilt (Vincent, *Word Studies in the New Testament,* vol. II, p. 208).

3. Exhortation to faithfulness. 4:14-21.

Here Paul's tone changes. He lays aside the irony which characterizes so much of this chapter, and he entreats them as a loving father his wayward children.

14 I write not these things to shame you, but as my beloved sons I warn *you.*

14. I write not . . . to shame you. Paul realized that if all he does is expose his readers to open shame, he will only provoke them to obstinacy. And so, while wishing to expose their sin, he does not wish to exasperate them. **As my beloved sons I warn.** With great love and affection, the apostle admonishes his children in the faith. He was not interested in making them cringe before him, but in correcting them, and offering them a chance to respond and be restored.

15 For though ye have ten thousand instructors in Christ, yet *have ye* not

15. Though ye have ten thousand instructors (Gr *paidagōgos,* slave guardians). The guardians to which Paul refers are not strictly instructors, or even tutors, but they were guardians that

many fathers: for in Christ Jesus I have begotten you through the gospel.

16 Wherefore I beseech you, be ye followers of me.
17 For this cause have I sent unto you Tĭ-mō′the-us, who is my beloved son, and faithful in the Lord, who shall bring you into remembrance of my ways which be in Christ, as I teach every where in every church.
18 Now some are puffed up, as though I would not come to you.
19 But I will come to you shortly, if the Lord will, and will know, not the speech of them which are puffed up, but the power.
20 For the kingdom of God is not in word, but in power.
21 What will ye? shall I come unto you with a rod, or in love, and in the spirit of meekness?

CHAPTER 5
IT is reported commonly that there is fornication among you, and such fornication as is not so much as named among the Gentiles, that one should have his father's wife.

were common in wealthy families to oversee the children. **Yet have ye not many fathers.** No matter how many guardians a man may have had to assist him through his early life, there is only one person who brought him into this life, and that is his father. If Paul was just a stranger, he could not have spoken so freely. But he was their father. Hence, he was probably the only one who could speak to them in this way. Not only that, he was under obligation to do so. **I have begotten you** ("I" is emphatic). Paul alone was responsible for the beginning of the Corinthian assembly. The term "begot" does not have in mind so much the conversion of these people, but the fact that it was Paul who laid the foundation (3:10). **Through the gospel.** Not through the power of Paul's personality, or through the sagacity of his wisdom, but the gospel of Christ and Him crucified (cf. 2:1-5).

16-17. Be ye followers of me (cf. 11:1, lit., "continue to imitate me"). No doubt Paul has in mind those characteristics which are common to him and the other apostles, listed in verses 11-13. But his thinking goes further to include his doctrine and his teaching, as shown in the expression: **my ways.** If they have any questions as to how to follow the apostle, Timothy was on his way, and would clarify any problems they had.

18-20. The Apostle Paul assures them that he is coming to see them. He warns that when he comes he will know **not the speech of them which are puffed up, but the power.** Paul was well known for confronting trouble head-on (cf. Gal 2:11). **The kingdom of God is not in word, but in power.** We will see if the Millennium has come to Corinth!

21. Finally an alternative is extended to them. **Shall I come unto you with a rod or in love?** It is all up to them. The **rod** introduces the note of discipline which is Paul's primary concern in the next section.

III. DISCIPLINE FOR THE FELLOWSHIP. 5:1-6:20

In coming to this, Paul's second major division of the epistle, it is well to remember the vile surroundings out of which the Corinthian converts had come. They had been truly won to Christ. They had broken from their idolatries, and formed a local church. They had indeed come out of the corruption of Corinth to form a community of saints. But the question was now, could they get Corinth out of the assembly? It is imperative that they learn that the gospel does not tolerate compromise. There must be a clean break. This is the thrust of I Corinthians 5-6. "The Holy Spirit is grieved and thwarted in the assembly where sin is allowed a footing" (J. S. Baxter, *Explore the Book*, Vol. 5, p. 109). Here Paul confronts successively: the problem of lust (5:1-33), the problem of lawsuits (6:1-11), and the problem of license (6:12-20).

A. Relating to Lust. 5:1-13.

1. A common report. 5:1.

5:1. It is reported commonly. "It is a fact" that the report had come to Paul's hearing of fornication existing in the Corinthian assembly. The word **fornication** (Gr *porneia*) is used in a comprehensive way ("sexual sins"). Perhaps implying that the offense in different forms more or less prevailed in the Corinthian assembly. But one case in particular is so gross that it is **not so much as named among the Gentiles.** Cicero (*Oratio Pro Cluent.* 5, 6) refers to this sin as "*scelus incredibile, et praeter unum in omni vita inauditum*" ("incredible wickedness, such I never heard of in all my life besides"). The crime was **that one should have his father's wife.** One of the members of the church had taken his stepmother (cf. Lev 18:8) and had married her (the expression "to have a woman" always means "to marry," cf. Mt 14:4; 22:28; I Cor 7:2, 29). Hence, this man's crime is worse

2 And ye are puffed up, and have not rather mourned, that he that hath done this deed might be taken away from among you.

**3 For I verily, as absent in body, but present in spirit, have judged already, as though I were present, concerning him that hath so done this deed,
4 In the name of our Lord Jesus Christ, when ye are gathered together, and my spirit, with the power of our Lord Jesus Christ,
5 To deliver such an one unto Satan for the destruction of the flesh, that the spirit may be saved in the day of the Lord Jesus.**

6 Your glorying is not good. Know ye not that a little leaven leaveneth the whole lump?

7 Purge out therefore the old leaven, that ye may be a new lump, as ye are unleavened. For even Christ our passover is sacrificed for us:

than adultery. It is incest. Otherwise, the apostle would not have spoken of it in such terms.

2. A critical rebuke. 5:2

2. And ye are puffed up, and have not rather mourned. The problem with the assembly was that they were laden with pride and lacking in discipline. Such an outrageous and detestable sin should have provoked the strongest response from the congregation. But because of their pride and carnality, they were immobilized when it came to dealing with a real problem in their midst.

3. A corrective remedy. 5:3-8.

3-5. "In verses 3-5 we have an interesting indication of the manner in which discipline was administered in the early church. The congregation would be called together, with an apostle presiding if available, and the person accused would be arraigned before them. After the evidence had been heard, and the accused had said what he had to say in defense of himself, the judgment of the congregation would be pronounced by the president. Paul, though absent in person, yet pictures himself present and presiding in spirit, and he leaves them in no doubt concerning the verdict which ought to be pronounced: the offense should be condemned and the offender excommunicated" (P. E. Hughes, "I Corinthians," *The Biblical Expositor*, Vol. 3, p. 267).

To deliver . . . unto Satan. Concerning this difficult and obscure passage, several observations must be made. (1) It involved excommunication from the church (vs. 2). (2) It involved the chastisement of the man (it was the **body** which was to be handed over). Paul elsewhere conceives affliction, disease, or loss as Satan's work (I Thess 2:18; II Cor 12:7, cf. I Tim 1:20). **Destruction** nowhere means annihilation. The reference seems to be to the destruction of the physical appetites which prompted this gross immorality. (3) Paul has the restoration of this man ultimately in view. **That the spirit may be saved.** This last purpose shows that the phrase "destruction of the flesh" cannot mean that the person could be brought to death. This is asserted for several reasons: (a) because nowhere in Scripture is Satan asserted as God's executioner, (b) because restoration would be impossible if the man were put to death. God does not want him killed, He wants him restored (cf. Mt 18:15; Gal 6:1; II Cor 2:1-11). The implications of Paul's instruction are given in verses 6-8.

6. A little leaven leaveneth the whole. No sin can be considered an isolated event. Just as with the sin of Achan (Josh 7:11), the sin had to be purged out or else it would contaminate the whole "lump" (on this see Rom 12:21). The stress is on the church as a singular unity.

7. Cleansing is essential. Purge out therefore the old leaven. Here the leaven does not signify the sinful man, *per se*, but evil of any kind in accordance with the more general statement of the leavening power of evil in verse 6. The background for this metaphor is Exodus 12:19 and 13:7. The larger scope of the apostle's imagery here is that he sees Christ as the fulfillment of the Old Testament Passover Feast of Unleavened Bread. The Passover depicted, typically, Christ's vicarious death on behalf of His own. That is, "the Lamb of God, which taketh away the sin of the world" (Jn 1:29). The Feast of Unleavened Bread accompanied the Passover. It involved a period of seven days during which no leaven was to be found in the homes of the Israelites. This was typical of the holy life that was to accompany partaking of the paschal lamb. The expression, **ye are unleavened** denotes a positional truth. Paul is interested that their practice match up to their position. **Christ our passover is**

8 Therefore let us keep the feast, not with old leaven, neither with the leaven of malice and wickedness; but with the unleavened *bread* of sincerity and truth.

sacrificed for us. Since sin required the sacrifice of the Lamb of God, it is inconceivable that it would ever be tolerated in the assembly of believers.

8. Therefore let us keep the feast (Greek present subjunctive; "go on keeping"). By purging out **malice and wickedness** let us go on to celebrate holiness of living. **Sincerity and truth** are those qualities on which the believer is to feed.

It is not surprising that the apostle uses the Passover as an illustration here. I Corinthians was written just before the Passover (cf. I Cor. 16:8) and the celebration of the feast is on Paul's mind. This is a good example of how God used the experiences of the biblical authors in the writing of Scripture.

4. A commanding regulation. 5:9-13.

9 I wrote unto you in an epistle not to company with fornicators:

9. I wrote unto you in an epistle. This is the "previous epistle" discussed in the introduction. This letter is now lost but we know that at least one subject discussed in this letter was that they were **not to company with fornicators.** The intent of the apostle in this epistle was misunderstood, and so he finds it necessary to clarify himself in verses 10 and 11.

10 Yet not altogether with the fornicators of this world, or with the covetous, or extortioners, or with idolaters; for then must ye needs go out of the world.

10. Yet not altogether. Of course Paul does not intend to say that they are not to have any association with vile and sinful men. In order to do this, one would have to **go out of the world.** As long as the believer is "in" the world, it will be necessary to rub shoulders with sinners. A parallel idea is contained in the words of our Lord in John 17:15-18.

11 But now I have written unto you not to keep company, if any man that is called a brother be a fornicator, or covetous, or an idolater, or a railer, or a drunkard, or an extortioner; with such an one no not to eat.

11. Not to keep company. The key to Paul's thought is here. The term translated "to keep company" (Gr *synanameignymi*) is found only here and in II Thessalonians 3:14. It is a compound of three Greek terms, and means "to mingle together with." It has the idea of close, habitual intercourse. **If any man that is called a brother.** Paul's instruction relates to those who are in the assembly calling themselves brethren in Christ. If such a person is a **fornicator, or covetous,** etc., then this person is not to be included in fellowship. **With such a one, no, not to eat.**

12 For what have I to do to judge them also that are without? do not ye judge them that are within?

12. Them . . . that are without. Those outside of the church (cf. Col 4:5; I Thess 4:12). The command of the apostle had reference only to those who were in the church, but it was not his prerogative to judge those outside of the church. The Corinthians should have understood this.

13 But them that are without God judgeth. Therefore put away from among yourselves that wicked person.

13. Them that are without God judgeth. The Greek present tense of this verb fits well with Paul's thought in Romans 1:18, "For the wrath of God is being revealed (presently) from heaven against all ungodliness." There is a vitally important truth to be observed here. It is true, as the Apostle John said, that "the whole world lieth in wickedness" (I Jn 5:19). But it will not do to simply curse the darkness. It is the task of the believer to proclaim the positive truth of the gospel. The saints are obligated to be faithful stewards; as for the world, God will take care of it.

Paul summarizes: **Therefore put away . . . that wicked person.** As for this person who is committing open sin, remove him from the assembly, and have no further fellowship with him.

B. Relating to Lawsuits. 6:1-11.

Paul has already introduced the subject of judging in the previous chapter. Accordingly, he has shown that the responsibility for judging sin lies with the assembly. Now he goes on to show that even in matters of civil dispute, the responsibility for settling such matters lies with the leadership of the local church. Paul develops this matter by first introducing the problem (vs. 1). Then in verses 2 and 3 he shows the absurdity of stooping to a pagan judge to adjudicate some matter between two brethren in Christ. Finally, in verses 4-11, he traces the biblical principles underlying his instructions.

CHAPTER 6

DARE any of you, having a matter against another, go to law before the unjust, and not before the saints?

2 Do ye not know that the saints shall judge the world? and if the world shall be judged by you, are ye unworthy to judge the smallest matters?

3 Know ye not that we shall judge angels? how much more things that pertain to this life?

4 If then ye have judgments of things pertaining to this life, set them to judge who are least esteemed in the church.

5 I speak to your shame. Is it so, that there is not a wise man among you? no, not one that shall be able to judge between his brethren?

6 But brother goeth to law with brother, and that before the unbelievers.

7 Now therefore there is utterly a fault among you, because ye go to law one with another. Why do ye not rather take wrong? why do ye not rather *suffer yourselves to* be defrauded?

8 Nay, ye do wrong, and defraud, and that *your* brethren.

9 Know ye not that the unrighteous shall not inherit the kingdom of God? Be not deceived: neither fornicators, nor idolaters, nor adulterers, nor effeminate, nor abusers of themselves with mankind,

10 Nor thieves, nor covetous, nor drunkards, nor revilers, nor extortioners, shall inherit the kingdom of God.

1. An inquiry. 6:1.

6:1. Dare any of you (this is very emphatic). "Is anyone so bold as to shock the Christian sense of propriety?" (Hodge, *Commentary on the First Epistle to the Corinthians*, p. 93). **Go to law before the unjust, and not before the saints?** The terms "unjust" and "saints" are generic, referring to all unbelievers as opposed to all believers. How incredible that the just should go before the unjust for justice!

2. An inference. 6:2-3.

2-3. Here the apostle argues *a majori ad minus*. That is, he cites a major premise in order to contrast and establish a minor premise. The first is that **the saints shall judge the world.** Certainly the Corinthians must have known this elementary truth (cf. Dan 7:22; Mt 19:28; Rev 2:26; 3:21; 20:4). Now, if this be the case, Paul goes on, **are ye unworthy to judge the smallest matters?** (lit., "on the lowest tribunals"). You who shall comprise the Supreme Court of the world, do you not feel qualified to sit on some tiny local court? But Paul goes on with another major premise. **We shall judge angels** (Isa 24:21; II Pet 2:4; Jude 6). The contrast now borders on the ridiculous. **How much more things that pertain to this life** (lit., "to say nothing of common life affairs"). Here is the minor premise.

3. An inconsistency. 6:4-11.

4. Things pertaining to this life (Gr *biōtikos*, common life affairs). Paul connects what is to follow with the above. **Then** is inferential. **Judgments** may mean "legal causes," or it may simply mean "trials." The former is more consistent with the normal usage of the term. **Set them to judge who are least esteemed.** In the original, this may either be taken as indicative or interrogative. If the latter, then Paul is being sarcastic. That is, if you are going to go to a civil court, you might just as well put your least qualified members as jurors. If it is a question, then it is emphatic, "Are you setting them to judge who are least esteemed in the church" (i.e., "the heathen")? This would render a statement of shock and surprise that they were doing such a thing. The latter seems more in keeping with the context.

5-6. I speak to your shame (i.e., "to move you to shame"). This suggests Paul's purpose in speaking as he does. **Is it so, that there is not a wise man among you?** This is a rather ironic question to be asking the Corinthians who boasted in their wisdom. Apparently this is the case, since in verse 6 Paul says **brother goeth to law with brother, and that before the unbelievers.** The apostle is incensed for at least two reasons: (1) that they went to law; and (2) that they went to law before heathen judges. In verses 7-11, the apostle probes some of the underlying causes for this situation existing in Corinth.

7. They have a defect. **There is utterly a fault among you.** They were defective in that they would even consider taking a problem between each other before a heathen judge. Before doing this, the apostle says it would be better to **take wrong** (and) . . . **be defrauded.**

8. Instead of following the correct course when they were wronged, they were defrauding one another. The very opposite of what they should have done. It would be better to accept the wrong committed than to pursue it and inflict further injury on anyone else.

9-10. They are also deceived. Those who would accuse the Apostle Paul of bifurcating works and faith should take a closer look at these verses. **The unrighteous shall not inherit the kingdom of God.** It would seem that there were some in the Corinthian assembly who have professed Christianity as a system of doctrine, but not as a rule of life. The apostle warns that this is a fatal mistake. **Be not deceived.** No one who can allow himself the indulgence of known sin in his life can be saved. This passage proves that "Paul and James are in basic agreement. Both affirm that genuine faith produces good works (cf. Eph 2:8-10), and that the absence of good works indicates the lack of faith (cf. James 2:14-26)." (S. L. Jackson, "I Corinthians," *The Wycliffe Bible Commentary*, p. 1238).

11 And such were some of you: but ye are washed, but ye are sanctified, but ye are justified in the name of the Lord Jesus, and by the Spirit of our God.

11. Then Paul concludes this section with a positive appeal. He assures them that they have been delivered. **Such were some of you.** Here Paul cites the fact that there were some in the assembly who were formerly characterized in the catalogue of sins listed in verse 10. **But ye are washed . . . sanctified . . . justified.** Logically, one would expect to find these words in inverse order. That is, they are first justified, then they are sanctified, then they experience daily cleansing. Paul placed them in this order for emphasis. Now you are washed, indeed you have been sanctified or set apart to do God's special service. Indeed, you stand before God declared righteous. In such an exalted position, it seems incredible that such people would find it necessary to go before an inferior human court to arbitrate their dispute.

C. Relating to License. 6:12-20.

Paul now goes on to distinguish between proper Christian liberty and the problem of unbridled license. Some were presuming that all physical passions and appetites were as lawful as eating and drinking, and were to be freely gratified. In the pagan society of Corinth, prostitution was accepted as a normal thing. It was not difficult for some of the Christians to justify themselves with the argument that such behavior only involved the body and not the soul (cf. Acts 15:20, where the prohibition of certain foods was also joined with the prohibition against fornication). The teaching regarding this important subject is given in verses 12-14, and the thrust of it is applied in verses 15-20.

1. The teaching. 6:12-14.

12 All things are lawful unto me, but all things are not expedient: all things are lawful for me, but I will not be brought under the power of any.

12. Paul's principles may be summarized in three words. **Lawful . . . expedient . . . power.** The first is the principle of liberty. When Paul says "all things," we cannot understand this in an absolute sense. Obviously, what God forbids can never be allowed. Rather, it seems to have in mind those things about which the Scriptures are non-explicit. These matters are left to the Christian's own judgment. The apostle is careful not to vitiate the important doctrine of Christian liberty by leading these people back under Judaistic legalism. Rather, his intent is to circumscribe its application through proper restrictions. These are expressed, first of all, in the principle of "expediency." Not everything is of benefit. Whether a law of prohibition exists or not, it is wrong to do something to ourselves or others simply because it is beneficial (cf. Rom 14:15-23; I Cor 8:7-13; 10:23-33). A second restriction is expressed in the words, **I will not be brought under the power of any.** This is the principle of control. Certain forms of indulgence become wrong when they bring the person into bondage. One of the character qualities of the believer is self-control (cf. Gal 5:22-23). The spiritual man of I Corinthians 2:15 is not in subjection to any appetite or habit.

13 Meats for the belly, and the belly for meats: but God shall destroy both it and them. Now the body *is* not for fornication, but for the Lord; and the Lord for the body.
14 And God hath both raised up the Lord, and will also raise up us by his own power.

13-14. Meats for the belly. Nature demonstrates the law of mutual adaptation. This is illustrated by meat and the digestive system. **God shall destroy both.** The present bodily constitution is only temporary. **Now,** a mild adversative, better "but," **the body is not for fornication.** Contrary to the natural law of adaptation, the body is not designed for fornication, **but for the Lord.** The body is intended to be a member of Christ (vs. 15), and the dwelling place of His Holy Spirit (vs. 19).

Whereas God is to destroy the belly and meats, the ultimate purpose of the body is fulfilled in the resurrection. **And God** hath both raised up the Lord, and will also raise up us by his own power. With this argument, Paul dismisses the notion that the sexual drives are the same as all of the other physical appetites. Where the latter are considered temporary, the former are permanent. The one touches matters of indifference, the other tampers with the very nature of the design for which we were created.

Paul's usage of the pronoun us, shows that his use of the term body goes beyond its normal usage to signify the whole man. Note also its connection with the second-person pronoun in verse 19, below. (On the destiny of the body, see also I Cor 15:15, 20 and 35-56; Phil 3:21; Rom 8:11; II Cor 4:14; and I Thess 4:14). Paul's argument runs something like this. It was an uncommon honor that God should raise up the body of Jesus Christ. It will be an undue honor that our bodies will also be raised by His own power. Therefore, let us not abuse those bodies through fleshly lusts.

2. The thrust. 6:15-20.

15 Know ye not that your bodies are the members of Christ? shall I then take the members of Christ, and make *them* the members of an harlot? God forbid.
16 What? know ye not that he which is joined to an harlot is one body? for two, saith he, shall be one flesh.

15-16. The real thrust of Paul's concern is now taken into account. In the first place, your bodies are the members of Christ. The body is not only for the Lord (vs. 13), but they belong to Him by virtue of His redemptive work, and because they are united with Him. This union pertains not only to the soul, but also to the body (cf. I Cor 12:12-27; Rom 8:6-11; Eph 2:6-7; 5:30). It is this fact, above all else, that makes fornication such a wicked and malicious sin. It takes what belongs to Christ and makes them the members of a harlot. To this Paul recoils with God forbid. He then goes on to enlarge on this point to say that he which is joined to a harlot is one body. The verb joined (Gr *kollaō*) is used in Genesis 2:24 (Gr *proskallaō*) of the relationship of husband and wife. It is also used of man's relationship to God (Deut 10:20; 11:22; Jer 13:11). When fornication is committed, the parties involved share a common life. In the same sense, one cannot serve God and mammon, or share in the life of Christ and in the life of Belial. It is inconceivable that one can be simultaneously joined to Christ and to the body of a harlot. On the phrase shall be one flesh, compare Ephesians 2:15.

17 But he that is joined unto the Lord is one spirit.

17. But he that is joined unto the Lord is one spirit. As if Paul's mundane analogies were not enough, he lays them aside to express, in eleven short words, a concept that "suggests to us the highest possible unity between the believer and the Lord. Many other forms are used to express this identification, but none approach this in the conception of inseparable oneness. The sheep may wander from the shepherd, the branch may be cut off from the vine, the member may be severed from the body, the child alienated from the father, and even the wife from the husband, but when two spirits blend in one, what shall part them? No outward connection of unity, even of wedlock, is so emphatically expressive of the perfect merging of two lives in one" (A. T. Pierson, *Knowing the Scriptures*, p. 108). This imposes the highest conceivable obligation to refrain from fornication.

18 Flee fornication. Every sin that a man doeth is without the body; but he that committeth fornication sinneth against his own body.

18. Flee ("Make it your habit to flee"). Compare Joseph's response (Gen 39:1-12). Without the body. The body is not the instrument, but the subject. But when man commits fornication, then he sinneth against his own body. Here the body becomes the instrument of the sin.

19 What? know ye not that your body is the temple of the Holy Ghost *which is* in you, which ye have of God, and ye are not your own?

19. Your body is a temple of the Holy Ghost. Not only is the local church a temple of the Holy Spirit (cf. I Cor 3:16), but the individual believer's body itself also is a temple of the Holy Spirit, which ye have of God. Notice, the thought here is indicative, not imperative. Paul is not telling them that they can become more spiritual by receiving the Holy Spirit. The fact is, they already received the Holy Spirit. He dwells within them. This fact, instead, introduces the imperative of verse 20.

20 For ye are bought with a price: therefore glorify God in your body, and in your spirit, which are God's.

20. The blessed fact that our body is the temple of the Holy Spirit has two sides. One, that He is ours, the other, that we are His. **For ye are bought with a price** (lit., "were bought"). The believer was purchased on Golgotha's hill. The price paid was the blood of God's only Son (Acts 20:28). While it is true that this is applicable to all men, even those who deny the Lord (II Pet 2:1), it has a very unique and special significance for the believer (cf. I Pet 2:9; I Tim 4:10). Paul concludes with the imperative **therefore, glorify God in your body.** In other words, use your bodies in order that other men may see that you belong to God.

IV. DOCTRINE FOR THE FELLOWSHIP. 7:1-15:58.

A. Doctrine of Christian Marriage. 7:1-40.

Up until now, the main thrust of the epistle has been on reproof and correction. Paul now turns his attention to matters of instruction. The Corinthians had written to Paul concerning several matters that perplexed them. Paul deals with each of these in order. The first concerns Christian marriage. It is not surprising, in light of the preceding, that there were evident problems in this area. Paul's advice may be broken into four broad categories: (1) concerning the precept of marriage (vss. 1-7); (2) concerning the permanence of marriage (vss. 8-16); (3) concerning the place of marriage (vss. 17-24); (4) concerning the priorities of marriage (vss. 25-40).

1. Concerning the precept of marriage. 7:1-7.

a. A prevention of sin through the marriage relationship. 7:1-2.

CHAPTER 7
NOW concerning the things whereof ye wrote unto me: *It is* good for a man not to touch a woman.
2 Nevertheless, *to avoid* fornication, let every man have his own wife, and let every woman have her own husband.

7:1-2. Now concerning. (Gr *peri de,* see also 7:25; 8:1; 12:1; 16:1, 12). This recurring formula indicates that Paul is dealing in turn with the points the Corinthians had raised in their letter. **It is good for a man not to touch a woman.** The manner in which the apostle introduces this subject suggests that there was a reactionary element in the church to the libertines dealt with in chapter 6. It is likely that they were recommending celibacy as desirable if not obligatory on all believers. Paul says, such a practice is **good** ("expedient" or "profitable," cf. Mt 17:4; I Cor 9:15). That the apostle does not intend to teach that marriage is morally wrong as compared with celibacy is clear from verses 2, 7, 9, and 26 (see also Gen 2:18; II Cor 11:2; Rom 7:4; Eph 5:28-33; I Tim 4:3; Heb 13:4). **Nevertheless.** Here and throughout this passage, Paul demonstrates balance. On the one hand, there is a principle established to be applied in extenuating circumstances (such as those in which the apostle finds himself). But, on the other hand, there is the more general rule to be applied to the majority of cases. **To avoid fornication.** Paul overrides his principle of expedience (vs. 1) with the principle of necessity. Because of the prevalence of immorality in Corinth, Paul's advice to these believers is that every man is to have his own wife, and every wife her own husband.

b. A pledge of persons in the marriage relationship. 7:3-4.

3 Let the husband render unto the wife due benevolence: and likewise also the wife unto the husband.
4 The wife hath not power of her own body, but the husband: and likewise also the husband hath not power of his own body, but the wife.

3-4. Persons are to, first, **render . . . due benevolence** (lit., "fulfill (their) duty"). Paul clarifies what he means by this in the next verse when he says, **The wife hath not power of her own body, but the husband: and likewise also the husband hath not power of his own body, but the wife.** Partners in a marriage no longer have the right to autonomous existence (cf. vss. 32-33). Thus, it is sin to sexually reject one's partner!

5 Defraud ye not one the other, except *it be* with consent for a time, that ye may give yourselves to fasting and prayer; and come together again, that Satan tempt you not for your incontinency.

6 But I speak this by permission, *and* not of commandment.

7 For I would that all men were even as I myself. But every man hath his proper gift of God, one after this manner, and another after that.

8 I say therefore to the unmarried and widows, It is good for them if they abide even as I.

9 But if they cannot contain, let them marry: for it is better to marry than to burn.

10 And unto the married I command, *yet* not I, but the Lord, Let not the wife depart from *her* husband:

11 But and if she depart, let her remain unmarried, or be reconciled to *her* husband: and let not the husband put away *his* wife.

12 But to the rest speak I, not the Lord: If any brother hath a wife that believeth not, and she be pleased to dwell with him, let him not put her away.

13 And the woman which hath an husband that believeth not, and if he be

c. A parenthesis in the marriage relationship. 7:5-7.

5. Defraud ye not one the other ("stop depriving one another"). The biblical precept of marriage implies that conjugal rights will be regularly exercised. The only exception to this rule will be **for a time.** And then only for **fasting and prayer.** Again the apostle's advice is practical in nature. It is given in order that **Satan tempt you not.**

6-7. I speak this by permission . . . not of commandment. The apostle does not take sides with the extreme Jewish view that held that it was a sin if a man reached twenty years of age without being married. Instead, he regards the matter as optional. **Even as I myself.** Content, not necessarily single. As to Paul's marital status, he was probably a widower (cf. Vincent, *Word Studies in the New Testament,* Vol. 2, p. 217). But that is not the point here. The point is that **every man hath his proper gift of God** (cf. vss. 17, 20, 24, and 27). Both marriage and celibacy are considered as gifts of the Holy Spirit.

2. Concerning the permanence of marriage. 7:8-16.

Here the apostle develops guidelines for three categories of individuals: the unmarried and widows (vss. 8-9), the married believers (vss. 10-11), and mixed marriages (vss. 12-16).

a. For the unmarried and widows. 7:8-9.

8-9. I say therefore to the unmarried and widows. The apostle is not being redundant when he singles out widows for special mention along with the unmarried. No doubt they would have special cause to consider their situation a sad one, and therefore desire to have it changed. **Abide even as I.** The personal reference here is not identical with that given in verse 7. The point of verse 7 has to do with being content with the gift God gives you. This verse merely points to the matter of remaining unmarried. **It is better to marry than to burn.** This expression is not to be taken to indicate that the apostle conceives of marriage in mere physical, brute terms. Rather, it is to be taken in light of the preceding. That is, if a person's gift is to be married, then let him not try to exercise a gift he does not possess by remaining unmarried.

b. For the married believers. 7:10-11.

10-11. And unto the married I command. Notice Paul's advice to the unmarried is given as optional; his advice to the married is given as a command. In case his readers miss this point, he reinforces it with the words, **not I, but the Lord.** No doubt, the apostle has in mind explicit instruction of our Lord recorded in Matthew 5:32; 19:3-9; Mark 10:2-12; Luke 16:18. **Let not the wife depart.** Paul's command here is in opposition to Greek and Roman law which permitted a woman to divorce her husband. The command is unequivocal; let her not depart. **And if she depart, let her remain unmarried, or be reconciled.** While Paul disapproves of separation on any grounds, he recognizes that there will be cases of unapproved separation. In these cases, they are to "remain unmarried." The Greek present tense emphasizes a permanent state. The only other option is reconciliation. **And let not the husband put away his wife.** This is tantamount to saying, "and the same thing goes for husbands."

c. For the mixed marriages. 7:12-16.

12-13. Now the apostle turns his attention to the special case of mixed marriages. **But to the rest speak I, not the Lord.** This is not to be taken as marking a contrast between inspired Scripture and what Paul is about to say. On the contrary, while on the earth, the Lord explicitly gave instructions about marriage and divorce. However, He did not make any special reference to the

pleased to dwell with her, let her not leave him.

14 For the unbelieving husband is sanctified by the wife, and the unbelieving wife is sanctified by the husband: else were your children unclean; but now are they holy.

15 But if the unbelieving depart, let him depart. A brother or a sister is not under bondage in such *cases:* but God hath called us to peace.

16 For what knowest thou, O wife, whether thou shalt save *thy* husband? or how knowest thou, O man, whether thou shalt save *thy* wife?

17 But as God hath distributed to every man, as the Lord hath called every one, so let him walk. And so ordain I in all churches.
18 Is any man called being circumcised? let him not become uncircumcised. Is any called in uncircumcision? let him not be circumcised.
19 Circumcision is nothing, and uncircumcision is nothing, but the keeping of the commandments of God.
20 Let every man abide in the same calling wherein he was called.

case of a mixed marriage. Thus, it is incumbent on the Apostle Paul, under inspiration of the Holy Spirit, to give additional instructions regarding this kind of situation. The instruction is essentially the same. If a Christian person is married to an unbelieving spouse, and the unbeliever is **pleased to dwell** with the believer, then divorce or separation is prohibited. Paul's advice here is intended to answer any of his Jewish converts who might be inclined to make an unwarranted application of the situation recorded in Ezra 10:3.

14. In the event that his readers should have any misgivings, the apostle shows why his advice is sound. **The unbelieving . . . is sanctified.** And the children are **holy.** This is not to indicate that the children or the spouse of a believer are automatically born into the family of God. The words "holy" and "unclean" in this text are equivalent to "sacred" and "profane." Again, the apostle's thought has Old Testament antecedents (cf. Hag 2:11-13). The unbeliever and the children are considered holy in a positional sense. Hence, the principle of the communication of uncleanness given in the Old Testament does not apply here (cf. also Rom 11-16). Together with the believer, they share in God's blessing, and are more likely to become converted by the presence and influence of the saved partner.

15. But if the unbelieving depart (Gr *chōrizō*, in the middle voice, almost a technical term for divorce, Moulton & Milligan, *The Vocabulary of the Greek New Testament*, pp. 695-696). In the foregoing instruction, the apostle presumes that the unbeliever is content to remain with the believer. But what of the situation where the unbeliever takes the initiative in dissolving the marriage? In such a case, Paul's advice is that the believer is **not under bondage.** There is no conflict here between Paul's advice and that of our Lord in Matthew 5:32. The point is that the divine standard cannot be imposed upon the unregenerate. There is nothing the believer can do but submit to the divorce. The overriding principle is that **God hath called us to peace.** The mild adversative clues us as to Paul's meaning in the use of this principle. He does not herein justify the divorce, even though the believing partner is free. Rather, there should be every effort on the part of the believer to avoid the separation if possible. This understanding fits well with the previous context, and also helps us understand the intent of the next verse.

16. For what knowest thou, O wife, whether thou shalt save thy husband? The reason why every means should be taken to induce the unbeliever to fulfill his marriage covenant is that the unbeliever might be saved. To give up too soon on an unsaved partner may mean that he will never come to Christ.

3. Concerning the place of marriage. 7:17-24.

Marriage, like everything else, is determined by the selection of God (vss. 17-20), and directed to the service of God (vss. 21-24).

a. The selection of God. 7:17-20.

17-20. But as God has distributed to every man . . . so let him walk. The apostle now builds on the principle stated in verse 7, that is, **every man hath his proper gift of God, one after this manner, and another after that.** There is no special reason why a believer should change his occupation or position in life subsequent to being saved. When applied to marriage, this simply means that there is no reason why a believer should put away his unbelieving spouse. Paul illustrates his point with the rite of circumcision. There is no need for a Gentile convert to be circumcised. On the other hand, there is no obligation incumbent upon a Jewish convert to be uncircumcised. In the New Testament, this rite had no direct reference on the life of faith (cf. Rom 2:25, 29; Gal 5:6). Therefore, even though it means living with an unbeliever, Paul is able to say, **Let every man abide in the same calling wherein he was called.**

b. The service for God. 7:21-24.

21 Art thou called *being* a servant? care not for it: but if thou mayest be made free, use *it* rather.
22 For he that is called in the Lord, *being* a servant, is the Lord's freeman: likewise also he that is called, *being* free, is Christ's servant.
23 Ye are bought with a price; be not ye the servants of men.
24 Brethren, let every man, wherein he is called, therein abide with God.

21-24. Here, the apostle employs another illustration to show that, properly understood, marriage should be viewed as directed to the service of God. **For he that is called in the Lord, being a servant, is the Lord's freeman: likewise also he that is called, being free, is Christ's servant.** As to one's social status at salvation, it matters little whether he was a slave or free. In reality, he has been set free from the bond of sin to serve the living and true God. Thus, the horizontal relationships have little significance when compared to the vertical. Again, when applied to the question of marriage, there is no reason why the believer cannot remain faithful to his obligation to God, whether he be single, widowed, married in the Lord, or married to an unbeliever. The overriding principle is again repeated **Let every man, wherein he is called, therein abide with God.** The prescription for peace and holiness is to remain in communion with God.

4. Concerning the priorities of marriage. 7:25-40.

Here the problem centers around how to advise young people contemplating marriage, and how to instruct the parents of young people who are of marriageable age. Without being dogmatic, the apostle begins the subject by giving his personal judgment (vss. 25, 26). Then he reminds them of the prospect of tribulation (vss. 27, 28), the passing away of worldly fashions (vss. 29-31), and the problem of divided allegiance (vss. 32-35). Then he suggests to parents a pattern for advising virgin daughters (vss. 36-38). And finally (vss. 39, 40), Paul gives his personal preference.

a. The personal judgment of Paul. 7:25-26.

25 Now concerning virgins I have no commandment of the Lord: yet I give my judgment, as one that hath obtained mercy of the Lord to be faithful.
26 I suppose therefore that this is good for the present distress, *I say,* that *it is* good for a man so to be.

25-26. Now concerning (Gr *peri de*). Paul is now about to deal with another subject about which the Corinthians had written him (cf. 7:1). **I have no commandment of the Lord.** In our Lord's instruction regarding marriage and divorce recorded in the Gospels, there is no record of His speaking directly to this issue. And so, the apostle says, **yet I give my judgment.** This again is not to say his advice is less inspired than something he may or may not quote from our Lord. Rather, Paul gives advice under the inspiration of the Holy Spirit in order to fulfill this obligation to the Lord **to be faithful.**

It is good for a man so to be. That is, it is good for a man to remain single. In Paul's judgment, celibacy is to be preferred. Why? His answer is **for the present distress.** This expression is probably best understood in light of I Corinthians 15:30-31; and II Corinthians 11:21-33. The Apostle Paul had already experienced intense persecution, and no doubt anticipated it would get worse. History records all too well that he was right.

b. The prospect of tribulation. 7:27-28.

27 Art thou bound unto a wife? seek not to be loosed. Art thou loosed from a wife? seek not a wife.
28 But and if thou marry, thou hast not sinned; and if a virgin marry, she hath not sinned. Nevertheless such shall have trouble in the flesh: but I spare you.

27-28. Because of this prospect of tribulation, Paul's advice is **Art thou bound unto a wife? Seek not to be loosed. Art thou loosed from a wife? Seek not a wife.** Although what Paul has said can never justify the dissolution of a marriage, hopefully it will discourage some from getting married. Notice that "bound" refers to marriage and "loosed" to divorce. This verse warns the divorced not to remarry, but also states that it is not a sin to do so. If married, Paul says, **thou hast not sinned.** There is nothing morally wrong with getting married. **Nevertheless, such shall have trouble in the flesh: but I spare you.** The term **trouble** (Gr *thlipsis*) indicates that Paul understands this trouble will not come from within, as though marriage would necessarily be accompanied by turmoil and distress; rather, this trouble would come from without. This fits well with his emphasis on the persecution and trouble confronting the church at that time.

c. The passing away of worldly fashions. 7:29-31.

29 But this I say, brethren, the time *is* short: it remaineth, that both they that have wives be as though they had none;
30 And they that weep, as though they wept not; and they that rejoice, as though they rejoiced not; and they that buy, as though they possessed not;
31 And they that use this world, as not abusing *it:* for the fashion of this world passeth away.

29-31. The essence of all worldly relationships constitutes an additional reason why one should not marry. **Brethren, the time is short: it remaineth** (or, "brethren, the time henceforth is short"). Life, at best, is exceedingly brief. Furthermore, the relationships contracted during this life are only transient. Indeed, it will be all too soon for all of us that marrying and weeping and rejoicing and buying (and every other earthly activity) will be all over and it will be as though they never occurred. Paul is not asking his readers to give up anything of eternal value, only temporal things: **the fashion of this world** (which) **passeth away.**

d. The problem of divided allegiance. 7:32-35.

32 But I would have you without carefulness. He that is unmarried careth for the things that belong to the Lord, how he may please the Lord:
33 But he that is married careth for the things that are of the world, how he may please *his* wife.
34 There is difference *also* between a wife and a virgin. The unmarried woman careth for the things of the Lord, that she may be holy both in body and in spirit: but she that is married careth for the things of the world, how she may please *her* husband.
35 And this I speak for your own profit; not that I may cast a snare upon you, but for that which is comely, and that ye may attend upon the Lord without distraction.

32-35. In the light of the above, Paul notes that a person who is married has a problem with divided allegiance. As for the men, the unmarried **careth for the things that belong to the Lord,** but the married man **careth for the things that are of the world.** It is only natural for the married man to be concerned about the welfare of his wife and family. But as noted above, these are only of passing value. The same problem also exists for the woman. If the woman is a virgin, she is unencumbered by worldly necessities, and her only concern is **for the things of the Lord.** On the other hand, **she that is married careth for the things of the world, how she may please her husband.** One must take care not to misconstrue the force of Paul's argument here. It is not that he views the married life as less spiritual than the celibate life, but that the celibate life is less distracted by worldly cares. Hence, the single man or woman enjoying greater freedom, also enjoys greater potential in terms of service. And so Paul is able to say, **and this I speak for your own profit.** It is not that the apostle is trying to ensnare them, nor much less that he is trying to mislead them. Nor is he impugning a divine ordinance. Rather, he is concerned about the distress which will surely accompany them should they be married, and **that ye may attend upon the Lord without distraction.** The focal point of Paul's advice is the promotion of faithful, undistracted devotion to the Lord.

e. The pattern for advising virgin daughters. 7:36-38.

36 But if any man think that he behaveth himself uncomely toward his virgin, if she pass the flower of *her* age, and need so require, let him do what he will, he sinneth not: let them marry.
37 Nevertheless he that standeth stedfast in his heart, having no necessity, but hath power over his own will, and hath so decreed in his heart that he will keep his virgin, doeth well.
38 So then he that giveth *her* in marriage doeth well; but he that giveth *her* not in marriage doeth better.

36-38. If what Paul says is correct, then how does a parent advise his single daughter? It will help in understanding this passage to remember the control which the father had over the marriage of his daughter in ancient times. The apostle's advice is first to the man who thinks **he behaveth himself uncomely toward his virgin.** In other words, the father who thinks that he is being unreasonable. In this case, his daughter is past **the flower of her age.** This is a euphemism for "full sexual maturity." And **need so require.** There seems to be some reason why marriage is necessary. Perhaps the daughter's happiness is involved. Paul does not elaborate. His advice is **let him do what he will, he sinneth not: let them marry.** In other words, in spite of Paul's foregoing advice, he does not intend to discourage marriage, especially in situations where it becomes necessary for the happiness of the individuals involved. Then he deals with the situation where there is no **necessity,** and the father **hath so decreed in his heart that he will keep his virgin.** Again, there is no hard, fast rule. And so Paul is able to say to this man, he **doeth well.** But all things being equal, the one who **giveth her not in marriage doeth better.** While there is no sin in marriage and no superior virtue in celibacy, in light of the "present distress," Paul still maintains that the single life is better.

39 The wife is bound by the law as long as her husband liveth; but if her husband be dead, she is at liberty to be married to whom she will; only in the Lord.

40 But she is happier if she so abide, after my judgment: and I think also that I have the Spirit of God.

f. The preference of Paul. 7:39-40.

39-40. To summarize, marriage is for life, broken only by death. In that event, a woman **is at liberty to be married to whom she will; only in the Lord.** But in Paul's personal judgment, **she is happier if she so abide.** The expression **I think also that I have the Spirit of God,** has been taken to suggest that Paul did not know for sure if he were writing under inspiration. This is not the case at all. The verb **think** (Gr *dokeō*) does not suggest doubt in any way (cf. Gal 2:6; I Cor 12:22). The phrase is better translated, "and I consider also that I have the Spirit of God."

B. Doctrine of Christian Liberty. 8:1-11:1.

The next matter concerning which the Corinthian believers had solicited Paul's advice had to do with the question of meats sacrificed to idols. The question was a serious one for these believers. There were many pagan temple rituals, state occasions, and festivals of various kinds which obligated them to participate. Generally, a part of an animal was burned at the sacrifice, and the rest was prepared for the feast that followed. Sometimes portions were taken home and eaten there. Meat unused at such feasts also found its way into the marketplace and the butcher shops. It had been determined earlier at the Council at Jerusalem that the Gentile converts should "abstain from meat offered to idols" (cf. Acts 15:29). Although the apostle does not allude to this decision in this text, it is very likely that this constituted a legal precedence for the Jewish converts in the assembly. Paul's approach is to state the principle of liberty (8:1-13), then to cite himself as a picture of Christian liberty (9:1-27), and finally, to demonstrate to the Corinthians how they should put into practice their Christian liberty (10:1-11:1).

1. The principle of liberty. 8:1-13.

CHAPTER 8

NOW as touching things offered unto idols, we know that we all have knowledge. Knowledge puffeth up, but charity edifieth.

8:1. We know that we all have knowledge. To paraphrase this: "We both know that you consider yourself to be thoroughly informed about this matter." Apparently in their question to Paul, they implied that they felt adequate to deal with the problem. Perhaps some in the assembly were disputing their approach. One should recall that it was this arrogance in regard to their knowledge that constituted one of their major problems. But knowledge alone will not suffice when dealing with Christian liberty. Paul is about to introduce a much higher principle. **Knowledge puffeth up, but charity edifieth.** Mere theoretical or speculative knowledge acquired in a vacuum has the effect of inflating a person and rendering him vain and conceited. On the other hand, love (Gr *agapē*) edifies. That is, it does not terminate upon itself as knowledge does, but goes beyond to seek the well-being and benevolence of others. And it is this incomparably higher principle which the apostle applies to this case.

2 And if any man think that he knoweth any thing, he knoweth nothing yet as he ought to know.

2. If any man think that he knoweth any thing. If knowledge is simply a cognitive process, then Paul says, **he knoweth nothing yet as he ought to know.** If, in a person's life, he simply acquires knowledge components, he is a seriously defective person.

3 But if any man love God, the same is known of him.

3. In true knowledge, the intellect and the emotions go hand in hand. **If any man love God, the same is known of him.** The true knowledge of God does not come about through the acquisition of cognitive data concerning Him. It comes through loving Him.

4 As concerning therefore the eating of those things that are offered in sacrifice unto idols, we know that an idol *is* nothing in the world, and that *there is* none other God but one.

5 For though there be that are called

4-8. As concerning therefore. Paul returns now to the main subject, which is **eating of those things which are offered in sacrifice unto idols.** The first thing Paul establishes is that **an idol is nothing.** Any thinking person knows that since there is **none other God but one,** if a person offers a sacrifice to an idol, he is, in fact, sacrificing to a nonentity. For, while we know that

gods, whether in heaven or in earth, (as there be gods many, and lords many,)

6 But to us *there is but* one God, the Father, of whom *are* all things, and we in him; and one Lord Jesus Christ, by whom *are* all things, and we by him.

7 Howbeit *there is* not in every man that knowledge: for some with conscience of the idol unto this hour eat *it* as a thing offered unto an idol; and their conscience being weak is defiled.

8 But meat commendeth us not to God: for neither, if we eat, are we the better; neither, if we eat not, are we the worse.

9 But take heed lest by any means this liberty of yours become a stumblingblock to them that are weak.

10 For if any man see thee which hast knowledge sit at meat in the idol's temple, shall not the conscience of him which is weak be emboldened to eat those things which are offered to idols;

11 And through thy knowledge shall the weak brother perish, for whom Christ died?

12 But when ye sin so against the brethren, and wound their weak conscience, ye sin against Christ.

13 Wherefore, if meat make my brother to offend, I will eat no flesh while the world standeth, lest I make my brother to offend.

in the pagan world there are those **that are called gods,** we who are Christians know **there is but one God, the Father . . . and one Lord Jesus Christ.** And, of course, all things owe their existence to Him. **Howbeit there is not in every man that knowledge.** As irrational as it may seem, there are some who are still under the apprehension that heathen gods are real beings. For such a person to eat meat sacrificed to idols, **their conscience being weak is defiled.**

9-10. Since we know that our relationship with God is not necessarily affected by whether or not we eat meat, then, it ought not to be offensive to the stronger Christian to limit himself for the sake of the weaker. Here is where the principle of love is most conspicuously applied. **Take heed lest by any means this liberty of yours becomes a stumbling block to them that are weak.** The term **liberty** (Gr *exousia*) may be translated, "authority" or "lawful right." The availability of an option does not necessitate its exercise, especially when love and concern for someone else becomes a factor. The most serious danger to an unbridled latitudinarian approach to Christian liberty is the possibility of causing sin in the weaker brother. **For if any man see thee which hast knowledge sit at meat in the idol's temple.** If the stronger brother publicly exercises his right to eat meat sacrificed to idols, he, in effect, encourages **him which is weak . . . to eat those things which are offered.** But the problem in the latter case is that he has violated his conscience, and has sinned. The expression **be emboldened** is literally, "be edified." The sense is ironic; edification should build up to righteousness. Here, one is edified or built up to sin.

11-12. And through thy knowledge shall the weak brother perish (lit., "for because of your knowledge, the weak one is destroyed"). Is Paul implying that this weak brother could lose his salvation? No. This is tantamount to what he says in Romans 14:23, "he that doubteth is damned if he eat." In other words, he is to be brought under the sure judgment of God for his sin. In the most extreme application of this principle, it would involve sinning unto death (cf. I Cor 5:5; 11:30; I Jn 5:16-17). **For whom Christ died?** The force of this expression here is practical, not soteriological. It is true that Christ died to secure this man's salvation, but speaking more to the point, He did so to put away his sin. Hence, if you, being a "stronger brother" should entice another brother to sin, then in effect, **Ye sin against Christ.** This truth is derived from two facts. First, and most immediate, the stronger brother has enticed a weaker brother to sin against the Saviour who died for him. Secondly, Jesus said in Matthew 25:40, "inasmuch as ye have done it unto one of the least of these my brethren, ye have done it unto me."

13. Wherefore directs us to the conclusion of the matter. It is not knowledge which forms the basis of the conclusion, but love. Hence, Paul says, **I will eat no flesh while the world standeth.** The latter half of this phrase is intended for emphasis. The apostle does not qualify this. He does not say he will refrain in public and exercise his liberty in private. In order to avoid offending a brother, he would permanently exclude the eating of meat from his diet. An additional comment that needs to be made on this subject has been very succinctly stated by S. L. Johnson. "In the first place the passage does not refer to legalists desirous of imposing their narrow-minded scruples on others. Such are not weak brethren, but willful brethren desirous of glorying in the subjection of others to their tenets (cf. Gal 6:11-13). This is tyranny, and Christianity must always be on guard against this. In the second place, it should be noted in this

CHAPTER 9

AM I not an apostle? am I not free? have I not seen Jesus Christ our Lord? are not ye my work in the Lord?

2 If I be not an apostle unto others, yet doubtless I am to you: for the seal of mine apostleship are ye in the Lord.

3 Mine answer to them that do examine me is this,

4 Have we not power to eat and to drink?

5 Have we not power to lead about a sister, a wife, as well as other apostles, and *as* the brethren of the Lord, and Cē′phas?

6 Or I only and Barnabas, have not we power to forbear working?

7 Who goeth a warfare any time at his own charges? who planteth a vineyard, and eateth not of the fruit thereof? or who feedeth a flock, and eateth not of the milk of the flock?

8 Say I these things as a man? or saith not the law the same also?

9 For it is written in the law of Moses, Thou shalt not muzzle the mouth of the ox that treadeth out the corn. Doth God take care for oxen?

verse that the decision to follow the path of love rests with Paul, not with the weak. The strong are to yield to love's appeal voluntarily, not because the weak demand it, legalists always demand subjection to their laws." (*Wycliffe Bible Commentary*, p. 1242).

2. The picture of liberty. 9:1-27.

Having established the principle of Christian liberty, Paul is concerned that his readers understand that this principle does not just apply to meat sacrificed to idols. Rather, it cuts across every aspect of the Christian's life. The apostle appeals to his own experience to show how multifaceted the problem is. He does this by defending his right to exercise Christian liberty (vss. 1-14), then by citing his own deportment in the exercise of his ministry (vss. 15-22), and finally by expressing his desire to run the race well, to keep his eyes on target, and to win the prize (vss. 23-27).

9:1-2. The seal of Paul's authority is the very existence of the Corinthian church. Whenever he speaks, he can do so with authority because of his relationship to the Corinthian assembly. **Am I not an apostle? Am I not free?** (In the original, these questions appear in reverse order.) The first question has to do with his freedom and liberty in Christ. He says, in effect, "am I not just as free as any other believer to regulate my conduct according to my own convictions? Yet more, I am an apostle as well." **Have I not seen Jesus Christ our Lord?** This follows to substantiate his claim to apostleship (cf. Acts 1:21-22; 9:3-9, 17). **Are not ye my work in the Lord?** Again if Paul is an apostle, then one would expect to see evidence of his ministry. The Corinthian assembly itself was that evidence. Hence, whether anyone else considered Paul an apostle, there was certainly no ground for doubt among the Corinthians. Conversion of men is a divine work performed through the agency of God's ministers. The fact that people were saved at Corinth and formed an assembly of believers, validates Paul's commission.

3-5. Mine answer to them that do examine me is this. As for those who are questioning Paul's authority, he answers, **Have we not the power to eat and drink? Power** here has the force of "right," or "authority" (and so throughout this context). **To lead about a sister,** that is, a sister in Christ; **a wife,** in other words. Paul had the authority to take a wife, and bring her on his journeys with him as **other apostles.** The inclusion of **the brethren of the Lord, and Cephas** shows the fallacy of those who promote celibacy among the clergy by citing the example of the apostles (cf. Mt 8:14).

6. Or I only and Barnabas, have we not power to forbear working? To paraphrase, "Are Barnabas and I the only exceptions to the rule that ministers should be supported by their respective churches?" At the beginning of his ministry in Corinth, the apostle supported himself. Then, when financial aid did come, it did not come from the Corinthian assembly. This issue was no doubt an embarrassment to the Corinthians, and appears to have been an annoyance to the apostle.

7. That Paul has the right to expect remuneration for his labors is supported by natural law. Whoever heard of a soldier who went to war at **any time at his own charges?** The same is true of the owner of a vineyard, or a flock of sheep. They have the right to expect to be supported by the vocation to which they devote themselves.

8-9. What Paul says is further supported by the Mosaic law. **Say I these things as a man? Or saith not the law the same also?** Is this simply a secular principle, or can we expect to find biblical precedence? **For** introduces Paul's quotation of Deuteronomy 25:4. **Thou shalt not muzzle the mouth of the ox that treadeth out the corn.** Even the ox has the right to expect to be fed for his labors. **Doth God take care for oxen?** This question is not to be understood as irony, nor as a contemptuous question. Rather, the implied answer to the question is "yes." God cares for His entire creation (cf. Job 38:41; Ps 147:9; Mt 6:26; Lk 12:24).

10 Or saith he it altogether for our sakes? For our sakes, no doubt, this is written: that he that ploweth should plow in hope; and that he that thresheth in hope should be partaker of his hope.

10. For our sakes, no doubt, this is written. Certainly if this principle should apply to the brute beast, much more should it apply to mankind in general. **That he that ploweth should plow in hope; and that he that thresheth in hope should be partaker of his hope.** That is, of being rewarded. It is only natural and right, but more than that, it is scriptural that one should expect profit from his labors.

11 If we have sown unto you spiritual things, is it a great thing if we shall reap your carnal things?
12 If others be partakers of this power over you, are not we rather? Nevertheless we have not used this power; but suffer all things, lest we should hinder the gospel of Christ.

11-12. Spiritual things . . . we shall reap your carnal things. The contrast here is not of a moral sense, but a qualitative sense. Paul, as their minister and teacher, imparted to them spiritual things. Was it any great thing if he should expect remuneration to sustain the body? The former connoted things of infinite value, the latter, only of temporal value. Paul is not through with this argument yet, but he pauses here to interject a reminder, **Nevertheless we have not used this power.** In order not to **hinder the gospel of Christ,** the Apostle Paul continues to **suffer all things.** Paul is not justifying something he did, but only something that he has the right to do—a right which he did not exercise. He continues.

13 Do ye not know that they which minister about holy things live of the things of the temple? and they which wait at the altar are partakers with the altar?

13. Not only is Paul's position supported by natural law, and by Scripture, but it is also supported by the temple law. **They which wait at the altar are partakers with the altar.** The point here is that with every sacrifice made at the altar, the priest would receive a portion. This was an institution ordained by God Himself in the Old Testament.

14 Even so hath the Lord ordained that they which preach the gospel should live of the gospel.

14. Even so, Paul concludes, **hath the Lord ordained that they which preach the gospel should live of the gospel.** The ministers of the gospel in the New Testament have no less holy a vocation than the priests of the Old Testament. So Paul establishes beyond question that he has the authority to receive financial support from the Corinthian assembly. But the bottom line of this entire discussion is not given until the next verse.

15 But I have used none of these things: neither have I written these things, that it should be so done unto me: for it were better for me to die, than that any man should make my glorying void.

15. But I have used none of these things. "I never exercised that right," And the apostle is quick to add that he is not mentioning these things now in order to receive a remuneration belatedly. He would rather die **than that any man should make my glorying void,** or "that any man should pay me now for my labors in Corinth." The reason for this is simply because this policy of self-denial enabled the apostle to face his enemies squarely. He could never be accused of self-interest, nor could his integrity ever be questioned.

16 For though I preach the gospel, I have nothing to glory of: for necessity is laid upon me; yea, woe is unto me, if I preach not the gospel!

16. For though I preach the gospel, I have nothing to glory of. Paul is ironically answering now the questions he asked to begin with. "Am I not free, am I not an apostle?" The implied answer to the first is "no"; as for the second, "yes, but that is no cause for glorying." **For necessity is laid upon me; yea, woe is unto me, if I preach not the gospel!**

17 For if I do this thing willingly, I have a reward: but if against my will, a dispensation of the gospel is committed unto me.

17. As proof of the fact that Paul had no grounds for boasting, he adds, **For if I do this thing willingly, I have a reward.** If it was optional for him to preach the gospel, then he would deserve remuneration. **But if against my will, a dispensation of the gospel is committed unto me.** By this, the apostle is not implying that he was an unwilling servant of the Lord (cf. Rom 1:5; 11:13; 15:15-16; I Cor 15:9; Gal 1:15-16; Eph 3:8). He is simply drawing a distinction between what was optional for him, and what was obligatory upon him. Paul was given a stewardship to preach. That was enough (cf. 4:1-2; Lk 17:10). A steward received no pay. He was merely a slave doing his assigned task faithfully.

18 What is my reward then? Verily that, when I preach the gospel, I may make the gospel of Christ without

18. What is my reward then? The answer to this question is twofold. **That . . . I may make the gospel of Christ without charge.** And secondly, **that I abuse not my power in the**

charge, that I abuse not my power in the gospel.

19 For though I be free from all *men*, yet have I made myself servant unto all, that I might gain the more.

20 And unto the Jews I became as a Jew, that I might gain the Jews; to them that are under the law, as under the law, that I might gain them that are under the law;
21 To them that are without law, as without law, (being not without law to God, but under the law to Christ,) that I might gain them that are without law.
22 To the weak became I as weak, that I might gain the weak: I am made all things to all *men*, that I might by all means save some.

23 And this I do for the gospel's sake, that I might be partaker thereof with *you*.

24 Know ye not that they which run in a race run all, but one receiveth the prize? So run, that ye may obtain.

25 And every man that striveth for the mastery is temperate in all things. Now they *do it* to obtain a corruptible crown; but we an incorruptible.

gospel. The former discharges his obligation to God. The latter discharges his obligation to man. In the context, it is important to note that Paul is not laying this down as a general principle for all ministers of the gospel to follow. The point is that it was a voluntary necessity. He had the authority to do many things, yet, he did not **abuse** (Gr *katachraomai*, "use to the full") that authority. The historical, social, and cultural context were the criteria by which Paul made this determination, as it is shown by what follows.

19. I be free from all men. When understood in the context of his Christian liberty, Paul was indeed free. But when understood in the light of his Christian responsibility, **yet have I made myself servant unto all.** With all the freedom in the world open to him, why did the apostle restrict himself so severely? The answer is **that I might gain the more.** His foremost interest was to preach the gospel and win men to Jesus Christ. Whatever it took in terms of personal freedom, he was prepared to pay the price. It is only fair to point out here that the apostle is not teaching that the end justifies the means. Or that compromise is in order. Certainly if there was anyone who was prepared to stand rigidly upon matters of principle, it was the Apostle Paul (cf. Gal 2:5). But as for matters of indifference, they are luxuries, and therefore, dispensable.

20-22. Unto the Jews I became as a Jew. How far Paul was willing to go in this regard is recorded in Acts 21:18-27. Again, he did not accommodate himself to sin, or to error, but to social custom. Likewise, **To them that are without law, as without law.** He goes on to explain that he does not intend to say that he was antinomian. He was certainly **under the law of Christ.** What he has in mind are the Gentiles. And the extent to which he is willing to go to win the Gentiles is clearly reflected in this entire chapter. He summarizes his guiding principle in the words, **I am made all things to all men, that I might by all means save some.** "I am willing to concede Christian liberties at all points if in the process, the gospel is preached, and the lost are won to Christ." This implies a willingness to do more, not less than the law required. It certainly does not condone sinful activity and compromise in order to "win" some.

Paul's paramount interest is expressed in the closing verses of this chapter.

23. And this I do (better manuscripts have "I do all things"), viz. all the things mentioned above, I do **for the gospel's sake.** His ultimate criterion is not the prejudices of men, but the gospel. Notice, this is so much more than simply preaching the gospel. It is living the gospel.

24. Paul draws upon a scene very familiar to his Corinthian readers in order to drive home his point. The Isthmian games were an athletic event known to all of his readers, held on alternate summers within the vicinity of Corinth. It was an event not to be missed by anyone of importance in all parts of Greece. As a national institution, it was as familiar to his readers as football is in Texas. And so he says, **Know ye not.** He takes for granted that his readers understand the rules of the game. The most important rule is that while all participants run, only one **receiveth the prize.** And this is Paul's desire for his readers. **So run, that ye may obtain.** There was no legal compulsion which demanded that the runners strive to attain the crown. Why then do they run? They run because they're athletes. And that is what they are there for. To achieve their final objective, it took great sacrifice on the part of all.

25. And every man that striveth for the mastery is temperate in all things. During the long days of preparation, the athlete is free to do as he pleases. He still has personal liberty. But if his intent is to win the crown, he restricts himself in all things: his diet, his activities, his associations, and probably even his friendships. He "laid aside every weight." And all for temporal glory. **But,** counters the apostle, the crown for which we strive is **incorruptible.** If temperance and self-discipline are so important in the temporal realm, much more in the spiritual.

26 I therefore so run, not as uncertainly; so fight I, not as one that beateth the air:

26. I therefore so run. That is, like the athletes in verse 25. **Not as uncertainly** (this term, Gr *adēlōs*, appears only here in the New Testament). Paul does not run as one who has no specific objective. **So fight I.** Paul changes his metaphor to that of the boxer. **Not as one that beateth the air.** Paul does not swing wildly without hitting his target, but to reach his level of proficiency in the gospel ministry.

27 But I keep under my body, and bring it into subjection: lest that by any means, when I have preached to others, I myself should be a castaway.

27. I keep under my body, and bring it into subjection. The expression, **I keep under** (Gr *hypōpiazō*), loses much of the original sense. It has the idea of "to give one a black eye," "buffet," or "bruise." Paul's Corinthian readers knew that in the Isthmian games, the boxers wore gloves consisting of ox-hide bands covered with knots and nails and loaded with lead and iron. To prepare for such an event, a man would have to steel himself against all forms of physical abuse. **Lest . . . when I have preached to others, I myself should be a castaway.** It is unlikely in these words that the apostle intends to associate himself with the herald at the Grecian games whose task was to proclaim the rules, and to summon the competitors to their places. It is more likely that he drops the metaphor now, and applies it to the main subject at hand. The reason he, in effect, restrains himself so, sacrificing even his essential Christian liberties, is that he might never reach the point where he is no longer qualified to run the race. Again, this expression must not be construed to suggest that Paul was afraid of losing his salvation. His subject is still Christian liberty, and his point is that sometimes the mature Christian will have to restrict himself in order to accomplish the ultimate task.

3. The practice of liberty. 10:1-11:1.

Paul concludes his discussion of Christian liberty with an admonition to beware of temptation and unbelief (vss. 1-13), to be conscious of the association of tables with demons and idolatry (vss. 14-22), and to be guided by the principles of thankfulness and expediency (vss. 23-11:1).

In his opening section, Paul begins by illustrating his point (vss. 1-5), and then by applying it (vss. 6-13).

CHAPTER 10
MOREOVER, brethren, I would not that ye should be ignorant, how that all our fathers were under the cloud, and all passed through the sea;

10:1. Moreover (Gr *gar*, for). He concludes chapter 9 with a discussion of the need for self-discipline. A classic case of what happens when self-control is absent is seen in the experience of Israel in the wilderness. The immediate connection is with the word, "castaway." Israel refused to deny self, and demanded the fleshpots of Egypt, and so became a castaway in the desert. **I would not that ye should be ignorant.** Here is one of Paul's favorite expressions introducing a matter of great importance (cf. Rom 1:13; 11:25). **How that all.** The five "alls" in verses 1-4 emphasize the five downward moral steps of verses 5-10. The very same people who enjoyed great privilege from God, also fell into serious apostasy from God. This also ties with 9:24, "all the runners run." Historically, in the case of Israel, all ran, but only Caleb and Joshua received the prize. The five privileges are enumerated as follows. **Under the cloud.** This speaks of divine guidance and protection (cf. Num 9:15, 23; 14:15; Deut 1:33; Ps 78:14; Mt 28:20). **Passed through the sea.** This has reference to divine deliverance (cf. Ex 14:15-22; I Pet 1:18-20).

2 And were all baptized unto Moses in the cloud and in the sea;

2. All baptized unto Moses. This has neither a sacerdotal nor a soteriological import. Rather, it is a nontechnical use of the term "baptism." The people were immersed in Moses' authority. Thus, the expression speaks of divine leadership (cf. Ex 14:31). Therefore, they came under the influence of his authority. The reference is not to water baptism.

3 And did all eat the same spiritual meat;

3-4. Their fourth privilege was that they all ate of **the same spiritual meat.** The reference here is obviously to manna,

4 And did all drink the same spiritual drink: for they drank of that spiritual Rock that followed them: and that Rock was Christ.

5 But with many of them God was not well pleased: for they were overthrown in the wilderness.

6 Now these things were our examples, to the intent we should not lust after evil things, as they also lusted.

7 Neither be ye idolaters, as *were* some of them; as it is written, The people sat down to eat and drink, and rose up to play.

8 Neither let us commit fornication, as some of them committed, and fell in one day three and twenty thousand.

spoken of in Psalm 78:25 as "angels' food." This speaks of divine provision. By employing the term "spiritual," Paul does not intend to imply that the manna was not literal food. It was clearly designed for ordinary nourishment (cf. Neh 9:15; Jn 6:49). It was spiritual in the sense that it was supernaturally provided by the Spirit of God. Likewise, **And did all drink the same spiritual drink.** The water that was received from the rock was real water. It was spiritual in the sense that it was given through the divine intervention of God. They drank of the spiritual rock that followed them, and **that Rock was Christ.** Here, Paul does not intend to advance an old Jewish fable that the rock that Moses smote actually was not part of the mountain, but rolled after them during their journeys. The rock was not a theophany. Rather, it was a "type" of Christ. It prefigured the character and provision that Christ would ultimately make for His people. But also, it is intended to mean that the ultimate supply was Christ and not the rock. This spiritual Rock, even Christ, remained with them and followed them.

This passage is an impressive affirmation of the pre-existence of Jesus Christ (cf. also vs. 9; Jn 8:58; 12:41; Heb 11:25; and Jude 5). In light of what follows, it is most probable that the expression, "spiritual meat" and "spiritual drink" are intended to be parallel with the elements employed in the Lord's Supper.

5. But. In spite of their great privilege, **God was not well pleased.** Divine privilege does not guarantee divine success. The evidence of this is that **they were overthrown in the wilderness** (lit., "their bodies were strewn about the wilderness"). Paul draws a pathetic picture of people, sated with providential privilege, paving the wilderness trail with their dead bodies (cf. Num 14:29).

The five successive backward steps are now enumerated.

6. Now introduces Paul's application of the preceding to the experience of his readers. **Examples** (Gr *typos*, type or example). The AV rendering here is no doubt correct. Unless we are careful, the history of Israel will be duplicated in our own experience. The first step was that they lusted **after evil things.** Not satisfied with the manna supplied by the Lord, the people lusted after the fleshpots of Egypt. Because of their inordinate desire, while the meat was yet in their mouths, God struck them with a plague (cf. Num 11:4-34). The specific application to the Corinthians' situation is hard to miss. The pot roasts of Egypt were no more unclean than the prime ribs of Corinth. But what a terrible consequence that they should become an obstacle between God and His people.

7. Neither be ye idolators, as were some of them. The second step down is to substitute a graven image for the Holy God. The allusion is to Exodus 32. What is significant here is that the Israelites considered that their golden calf was made in honor of Jehovah. Likewise, for Paul's readers, the inordinate exercise of Christian liberty was considered a celebration of their freedom in Christ. The evidence of idolatry was seen in that **The people sat down to eat and drink, and rose up to play.** Sensual amusement was always associated in the pagan world with their feasts and idolatrous practices.

8. The third step is to **commit fornication.** Spiritual defection always leads to moral defection. If this was symptomatic of the spiritual decay in Israel, how much more in Corinth (cf. 5:1-5). Allowing immorality to persist in their assembly, they were no different from their neighbors who worshiped at the temple of Venus. Again, the same truth holds today. When men, even Christians, substitute anything for the God of the Bible, the results are the same. **In one day three and twenty thousand** is not a mistake. In Numbers 25:9, the total people who died is given as twenty-four thousand. The discrepancy may be accounted for in at least two ways. The actual figure may be midway between twenty-three and twenty-four thousand,

and hence, in each case the figure is rounded off. Furthermore, it will be noted that Paul refers to the number slain in one day. Numbers refers to the total number that died. In any case, the precise number is only given in approximate terms.

9 Neither let us tempt Christ, as some of them also tempted, and were destroyed of serpents.

9. The fourth step is to **tempt Christ** (cf. Num 21:4-9; Ps 78:19). This, in effect, reflects skepticism over whether or not God will discipline them for their sins. The exhortation is that one should not provoke the forbearance of God. If it comes as especially obnoxious that some of the Corinthians had to give up some of their better cuts of meat for the cause of the gospel of Christ, let them remember from whence they were delivered. To become overly concerned about temporal desires is to forget the great spiritual privilege they enjoy. Anyone who doubts that God can and will exercise His option to punish sin should remember Israel and the fiery serpents.

10 Neither murmur ye, as some of them also murmured, and were destroyed of the destroyer.

10. The fifth step down is **murmur.** This implies a total rejection of divine leadership. The reference is to Numbers 16:41-50. But the spirit which prompted that situation is expressed in Numbers 14:4. The results are that they **were destroyed.** The parallel situation and obvious admonition is seen in the Corinthians' attitude toward their leadership (viz., Paul). Nothing provokes the anger of God more than to chafe under the yoke that we share with Christ (cf. Mt 11:29-30; I Cor 3:9).

11 Now all these things happened unto them for ensamples: and they are written for our admonition, upon whom the ends of the world are come.

11. Paul summarizes with both an admonition and an encouragement. **Now all these things happened . . . for examples** (lit., "now these things happened to them typically"). The expression emphasizes God's providential control over all the affairs of men (cf. Gen 50:20; Prov 21:1). Although the Israelites rebelled against God and received subsequent judgment because of it, God intended to use their experience for His own good. **And they are written for our admonition.** The reason God had Moses to record the experiences of the children of Israel was because He had Paul and his Corinthian believers in mind. He knew that the Corinthians were going to face a similar crisis situation. When that time came, the example of the children of Israel would provide the deterrent to guide them from sin, and to lead them to spiritual victory. **Ends of the world.** That is, "for us who are living in the end times." Paul considered the second coming of Christ to be imminent. Thus, as far as he knew, he and his generation constituted the end times.

12 Wherefore let him that thinketh he standeth take heed lest he fall.

12. Him that thinketh he standeth. The one who thinks himself to be the strong Christian, who can exercise his Christian liberty at the expense of the weaker brethren, **take heed lest he fall.** Not from salvation, nor yet from his position of strength to that of weakness, but that he should suffer the judgment of God, as the Israelites, and "fall in the wilderness."

13 There hath no temptation taken you but such as is common to man: but God *is* faithful, who will not suffer you to be tempted above that ye are able; but will with the temptation also make a way to escape, that ye may be able to bear *it.*

13. Temptation. Paul is about to show that trials and temptations will be proportionate to our strength. **Common to man** (Gr *anthrōpinos*). This term occurs mostly in this epistle. The trials you face are only normal problems (cf. also Rom 4:19; Jas 3:7; I Pet 2:13; I Cor 2:4, 13; and I Cor 4:3). **But.** A mild adversative. In the context of those temptations **God is faithful.** What great comfort Paul provides for his readers. Though men and the world about be false, God is true, God is faithful, and our strength and security are in Him. **Above that ye are able.** God knows our frame, and He knows exactly what we can take. Sometimes when the exigencies of life seem to overwhelm us, we think we can take no more. But take heart. If God did not know that you could take it, He would not have allowed you to suffer it. **Make a way to escape.** In early Greek usage, this term (Gr *ekbasis*) had the sense of a landing place. It was a nautical term. The idea is not that He will enable us to escape temptation, but that He will enable us to land safely on the other side victoriously. **To bear.** Often the only escape is to endure (cf. Jas 1:12). Having shown the seriousness of abusing one's Christian lib-

14 Wherefore, my dearly beloved, flee from idolatry.

erty, the apostle now goes on to inform his readers that there is a direct relationship between heathen feasts and demonic activity.

14. Wherefore (Gr *dioper*, a strengthened form of *dio*, lit., "for which very reason"). This term appears only here and I Corinthians 8:13 (14:13 in some MSS). In light of God's judgment upon Israel, **flee idolatry.** These words have a triple significance. They contain a concern because they are addressed to people whom Paul loved. They express a command, they are given in the imperative mode. And they express a consequence. Because of the expression of their Christian liberty, the Corinthians are edging dangerously close to idolatry.

15 I speak as to wise men; judge ye what I say.

15. Wise men. This is not irony. Not wishing to be authoritarian or dogmatic on this issue, he appeals to their sense of wisdom. **Judge ye what I say.** "Consider for a moment the logic of my argument."

16 The cup of blessing which we bless, is it not the communion of the blood of Christ? The bread which we break, is it not the communion of the body of Christ?

17 For we *being* many are one bread, *and* one body: for we are all partakers of that one bread.

16-17. The cup . . . communion of the blood of Christ? The bread . . . communion of the body of Christ? Consider the Lord's table. When a believer participates, he partakes of Christ's blood and His body. This means to share and to participate in the benefits of Christ's saving work on Calvary. This being the case, all those who come to the Lord's Supper enter into communion with one another. They form one body in virtue of their joint participation of Christ. **For we being many are one bread, and one body: for we are all partakers of that one bread.**

18 Behold Israel after the flesh: are not they which eat of the sacrifices partakers of the altar?

18. This argument is further substantiated by the example of the altar of Israel. **Are not they which eat of the sacrifices partakers of the altar?** When a sacrifice was brought to the altar, it was not entirely consumed. Rather, the residue was divided between the priest and the offerer (cf. Lev 7:15; 8:31; Deut 12:18). Thus, it became an act of mutual sharing and worshiping of God. It is for this reason that non-Jews were forbidden to attend the sacrificial feasts of the Jews since it involved mutual sharing and joint worship of Jehovah. This passage must not be construed to indicate that the Lord's Supper is a sacrifice. The point of correspondence was not sacrifice, but communion.

19 What say I then? that the idol is any thing, or that which is offered in sacrifice to idols is any thing?

19. What say I then? That the idol is any thing? The writer anticipates the obvious question. "But, Paul, you just said an idol was, in reality, nothing. Therefore, to worship an idol is to worship nothing. If one participate in fellowship with an idol, he would, in fact participate in nothing."

20 But *I say*, that the things which the Gentiles sacrifice, they sacrifice to devils, and not to God: and I would not that ye should have fellowship with devils.

20. It is very true, the idol is nothing. But the ones behind the idol are very real. **The things which the Gentiles sacrifice, they sacrifice to devils** (lit., demons) **and not to God.** What is of grave concern to the apostle is that behind the idols are fallen angels; evil spirits. This is in keeping with Deuteronomy 32:17 and Psalm 106:37. Since Paul has already established that these religious feasts involved fellowship with the altar, should they attend a heathen feast, they will be having **fellowship with devils** ("demons"). And this was the last thing Paul hoped for his young converts at Corinth.

21 Ye cannot drink the cup of the Lord, and the cup of devils: ye cannot be partakers of the Lord's table, and of the table of devils.

21. Ye cannot drink of the cup of the Lord, and the cup of devils. It is not possible to be simultaneously related to the Lord and to demons. Paul does not merely indicate that this is an inconsistency, but an impossibility. We cannot expect that the Lord will allow this to continue. The consequences of such behavior have already been amply illustrated in the case of Israel. Thus, it is not necessary at this point for the apostle to do more than ask the simple question.

22 Do we provoke the Lord to jealousy? are we stronger than he?

22. Do we provoke the Lord to jealousy? Unless they intend to provoke the greatest displeasure from the Lord, the Corinthians must be careful not to attend the heathen feasts.

So Paul has answered two questions. Question one, what about exercising my right to eat meat sacrificed to idols? Question two, what about my attendance at heathen feasts? The

23 All things are lawful for me, but all things are not expedient: all things are lawful for me, but all things edify not.

24 Let no man seek his own, but every man another's *wealth*.

25 Whatsoever is sold in the shambles, *that* eat, asking no question for conscience sake:
26 For the earth *is* the Lord's, and the fulness thereof.
27 If any of them that believe not bid you *to a feast*, and ye be disposed to go; whatsoever is set before you, eat, asking no question for conscience sake.
28 But if any man say unto you, This is offered in sacrifice unto idols, eat not for his sake that shewed it, and for conscience sake: for the earth *is* the Lord's, and the fulness thereof:

29 Conscience, I say, not thine own, but of the other: for why is my liberty judged of another *man's* conscience?
30 For if I by grace be a partaker, why am I evil spoken of for that for which I give thanks?
31 Whether therefore ye eat, or drink, or whatsoever ye do, do all to the glory of God.

32 Give none offence, neither to the Jews, nor to the Gentiles, nor to the church of God:
33 Even as I please all *men* in all *things*, not seeking mine own profit, but the *profit* of many, that they may be saved.

CHAPTER 11
BE ye followers of me, even as I also *am* of Christ.

remaining question is, what about meat purchased in the market place. In answer, he returns to the original issue of Christian liberty, and the principles which govern it.

23. First, there is the principle of expedience. **All things are lawful for me, but all things are not expedient.** Two observations must be made on this point. When Paul says, **all things,** he is speaking in an obviously restricted sense (cf. 6:12). He intends to mean all matters of indifference. The second observation has to do with the significance of his advice. While on such matters all options are open to the believer, there is only one choice that is best. And there are some choices that will be of no help at all. Then, there is the principle of edification. **All things are lawful . . . but all things edify not.** Here he enlarges on his original statement of this principle in 6:12. If what I do subjects me rather than serves me, I must avoid it.

24. Wealth (better translated "welfare"). The principle of edification will please the concerns and needs of others first.

25-28. Then there is the principle of conscience. **The shambles** (Gr *makellō*, a Latin term used only here in the New Testament, refers to the market). In the sacrifices, usually only a part of the victim was consumed. The rest was given to the priest or sold again in the market. Anyone might therefore unknowingly purchase meat offered to idols. Concerning such purchases, Paul's advice is **Whatsoever is sold . . . that eat, asking no question for conscience sake.** Your conscience need not be activated on this issue. Going back to the original discussion, the idol is nothing; therefore, it can have no intrinsic effect upon the meat. While it is wrong to go to the heathen feast and to participate with demons in idolatrous worship, once the meat has been disassociated from that gathering, there is no reason why it cannot be eaten without scruple. Likewise, if you have been invited to a feast at the home of an unbeliever, and it is your desire to go, **whatsoever is set before you, eat, asking no questions for conscience sake.** On the other hand, if another brother in Christ (apparently a weaker brother) should turn to you and say **this is offered in sacrifice unto idols,** then the stronger brother is to **eat not for his sake that showed it.** The principle here is to bow to the weaker conscience.

29-31. Then there is the principle of thanksgiving. The question naturally arises, **why is my liberty judged of another man's conscience?** This is a legitimate question. The answer is: **I by grace be a partaker.** The word **grace** (Gr *charis*) is used here in the sense of thanksgiving. We use it today when we speak of "saying grace" before a meal. It is illogical to give thanks to God for something that will cause me to be **evil spoken of.** Whence the admonition in verse 31. **Whatsoever ye do, do all to the glory of God.** I fail in the proper exercise of my Christian liberty, if in the process I do not bring glory to God (see also I Pet 4:11; and Col 3:17).

32-33. Then there is the principle of evangelism. Care must be taken to **give none offense,** whether to **Jews . . . Gentiles** (or) **the church of God.** Thus, whatever we do in our public ministries or our personal lives should not deliberately bring offense to the church. **That they may be saved.** "Why should I go about offending people in the name of Christian liberty, and unnecessarily causing them to repudiate the gospel?" (cf. also 9:22).

11:1. The bottom line on the discussion of Christian liberty is the example of Christ as He is reflected in the Apostle Paul. The ultimate standard is Christ, and insofar as Paul is following Him, he is able to say to the Corinthian believers, **Be ye followers of me.**

To summarize then, in this section on Christian liberty, Paul is anxious to lead his assembly to maturity under grace. The Christian life is not governed by legalism. Yet on the other hand, this does not justify license. The best example of how it works is

Jesus Christ. In Him we see ultimate sacrifice and supernatural love. And by these standards, every act is to be judged.

C. Doctrine of Worship. 11:2-34.

In this chapter, Paul is concerned with two vital matters. First, the order of authority (vss. 2-16), then the ordinance of communion (vss. 17-34). Since Paul does not begin with his characteristic expression, "now concerning" (Gr *peri de*), it is possible that this chapter falls into the category of unsolicited advice. Perhaps in their letter to Paul there was allusion to some of their public worship practices. Or perhaps his discussion of worship practices in the previous chapter prompted him to speak directly to this issue.

1. The order of authority. 11:2-16.

Paul develops this subject in two ways. First, he states the principle of headship (vss. 2-6). Then he defends this principle from Scripture and nature (vss. 7-16).

2. Now indicates the transition to a new subject. **I praise you, brethren.** It is always a good practice to compliment someone before you rebuke him. **That ye . . . keep the ordinances, as I delivered them to you.** There is a play on the two words **ordinances** and **delivered**. Both are derived from the Greek term *paradidōmi*, meaning "to give over." It is best rendered "oral teaching," or "tradition." Paul will have more to say about this in verses 17-34.

3. But is adversative. **I would have you know** is probably not intended as ironic, but it is difficult not to miss the irony of the situation. The Corinthians prided themselves in their knowledge, yet it is their knowledge that the apostle repeatedly finds deficient. **That** indicates purport. **The head of every man is Christ.** This is established by the fact that Christ is the head of the body, which is the church (Col 1:18; Eph 1:22-23). Whether "man" is taken generically (mankind), or "man" as opposed to "woman," the truth still stands. However, the latter sense seems to be dictated by the context. **The head of the woman is the man.** This constitutes the fundamental order in the race in the sense that **the head of Christ is God.** It is important here to note that the concept of headship does not connote qualitative or essential difference. It connotes a functional subordination. The prototype is seen in the persons of the Trinity. The Father and Christ are co-equal, yet the Son is answerable to the Father (cf. Jn 6:38-40 10:29-30; 14:9; I Cor 15:28; and Phil 2:6). It is unfortunate that Paul has been so misunderstood on this point. He is not a male chauvinist. On the contrary, he argues here for the equality of the sexes. Any other sense leads to Sabellianism, which is heresy.

4. Since this constitutes the order of authority, it is inappropriate for a man to participate in public worship of God with something on his head. The covering would seem to indicate another authority coming between the man and Christ.

5. On the other hand, when a woman **prayeth or prophesieth with her head uncovered,** this is equally wrong. It is wrong for the same reason the opposite is wrong for the man. The covering is symbolic, indicating the authority that exists above the woman, yet still under Christ. A further teaching of this verse is that women did prophesy and pray in public worship. This, no doubt, involved edifying, exhorting, and comforting. And apparently this did not constitute a point of contention, since the apostle does not feel obligated to speak directly to it. Yet this is not a contradiction with I Corinthians 14:34-37. Here the context has reference to orderly participation. Chapter 14 refers to disorderly participation.

6. For if the woman be not covered, let her also be shorn: but if it be a shame for a woman to be shorn . . . let her be covered. In Corinth, it was not uncommon for prostitutes to

---

2 Now I praise you, brethren, that ye remember me in all things, and keep the ordinances, as I delivered *them* to you.

3 But I would have you know, that the head of every man is Christ; and the head of the woman *is* the man; and the head of Christ *is* God.

4 Every man praying or prophesying, having *his* head covered, dishonoureth his head.

5 But every woman that prayeth or prophesieth with *her* head uncovered dishonoureth her head: for that is even all one as if she were shaven.

6 For if the woman be not covered, let her also be shorn: but if it be a shame for a woman to be shorn or shaven, let her be covered.

7 For a man indeed ought not to cover *his* head, forasmuch as he is the image and glory of God: but the woman is the glory of the man.

8 For the man is not of the woman; but the woman of the man.

9 Neither was the man created for the woman; but the woman for the man.

10 For this cause ought the woman to have power on *her* head because of the angels.

11 Nevertheless neither is the man without the woman, neither the woman without the man, in the Lord.

12 For as the woman *is* of the man, even so *is* the man also by the woman; but all things of God.

13 Judge in yourselves: is it comely that a woman pray unto God uncovered?

14 Doth not even nature itself teach you, that, if a man have long hair, it is a shame unto him?

15 But if a woman have long hair, it is a glory to her: for *her* hair is given her for a covering.

shave their heads and don blonde wigs, thus signifying their availability to the men in the streets. This is not a point of indifference to the apostle. It is a serious matter. An unsubmissive woman standing before the congregation is tantamount to going out in public improperly attired (e.g., with her head shaven). But the force of Paul's words here is poignant. Just as no respectable Christian woman would go out in public dressed as a prostitute, it is equally important that she not participate in public worship without proper dress.

Having established the principle of headship, Paul goes on to validate his position from Scripture (vss. 7-12) and from nature (vss. 13-16).

7. The image and glory of God. It must not be inferred from this that only the man is in the image of God. In Genesis 1:26-27 it is said that God created man in His own image, "male and female created he them." But, Paul uses the term "image" in a restrictive sense. The only sense in which the man is uniquely in the image of God is that to him was given dominion over the earth. This was done before the creation of the woman. Thus, in the same sense, **the woman is the glory of the man.** That is, whatever dominion and authority she has is delegated.

8-9. The order of creation also supports Paul's position. **Neither was the man created for the woman; but the woman for the man.** Chronologically, she came *after*. Constitutionally, she was made *for* the man (cf. Gen 2:21-25).

10. Power signifies here the symbol of authority **on her head.** A further reason is **because of the angels.** The reference is to the holy angels who elsewhere are spoken of as "worshiping spirits" (cf. Heb 1:4). The keynote of Paul's thought is submission to the divine order of things. Women should demonstrate the same sense of submission to God in recognizing their true position, and fulfilling its claims, as do the angels who know nothing of insubordination among their ranks. Since the angels have their very existence in the presence of God, they are also present whenever the congregation meets together to worship the Lord (cf. I Cor 4:9; Eph 3:10; I Tim 5:21).

11. Lest his readers understand this distinction in a qualitative sense, Paul hastens to add, **neither is the man without the woman, neither the woman without the man, in the Lord.** Both are mutually dependent upon each other. The expression "in the Lord" has the sense of "according to the will and purpose of the Lord." Neither can exist without the other.

12. Even so is the man also by the woman. Just as the principle of submission is supported by the order of creation, the principle of mutual dependency is supported by the order of procreation. In Genesis 2, the woman came out of the man. In Genesis 4:1, the man came out of the woman. So have all men since. In the final analysis, **all things** (are) **of God.**

13-15. Nature itself ("the recognized constitution of things"). **If a man have long hair, it is a shame.** This is a difficult passage, especially in a culture where nature does not seem to be dictating it. It cannot mean that nature naturally grows short hair on men and long hair on women, since biologically we know this is not the case. Several factors must be considered. First, the context: Paul is talking about differentiating between the sexes. **Have long hair** (Gr *komaō*) means to wear long hair like that of a woman. It cannot be said that he has in mind a specific kind of haircut. He is simply saying that it is shameful for a man to wear his hair in an effeminate way. Another factor has to do with culture. In Paul's experience, he knew of no culture, whether Hebrew, Greek, or Roman, that did not consider long hair a disgrace to man. The only exception to this rule was the Nazarite (Num 6:5; and Ezek 44:20). Thus, to Paul it was significant that just naturally, worldwide cultures emerged with the same sense of propriety regarding long hair on men. The same principle holds true today. The vast majority of cultures regard effeminacy of hair and dress as distasteful and shameful to a man. **But if a woman have long hair, it is a glory to her.** The logic is obvious. In the natural order of things, it only seems appropriate to cover a woman's head and here her ultimate covering is her hair. The Scripture does not dictate "spirituality" by the length of one's hair. The real issue here is submission to divine authority. Therefore, every aspect of the believer's life should reflect his obedience and submission to the Lord Jesus Christ and divinely established authority. Some suggest the long hair constitutes the "covering" of verses 5-6. However, it may be argued that the shorn head in verse 5 is equated only hypothetically with the absence of the covering.

16 But if any man seem to be contentious, we have no such custom, neither the churches of God.

16. If any man seem to be contentious. If someone desires to dispute me, then, **we have no such custom.** In other words, there is no other precedent. To violate this principle is to go against a standard that is maintained in every church of which Paul is knowledgeable. Having appealed to their sense of wisdom, and their sense of propriety, here Paul ultimately appeals to his own authority as an apostle. But he does so only last, and inserts it almost as a footnote. In keeping with his approach to Christian liberty, he hopes there will be a voluntary submission to the principles he has laid out in this chapter.

2. The ordinance of communion. 11:17-34.

The Corinthians were to be commended for keeping the ordinances (vs. 2). But they deserved sharp criticism for the manner in which they did so. In the observance of the Lord's Supper, they have been guilty of carnality (vss. 17-22). They are desperately in need of correction (vss. 23-26), and they are in danger of chastisement from the Lord (vss. 27-34).

17 Now in this that I declare *unto you* I praise *you* not, that ye come together not for the better, but for the worse.

17. Now in this. The reference is to what follows. **Declare,** better rendered, "command." **I praise you not.** An obvious contrast with verse 2. **Ye come together not for the better, but for the worse.** Your congregational gatherings are more debilitating than edifying. Sometimes one may be worse for attending services if he goes out of the wrong motivation.

18 For first of all, when ye come together in the church, I hear that there be divisions among you; and I partly believe it.

18. First . . . I hear that there be divisions among you (cf. 1:10). The expression is intended as irony to contrast with **when ye come together.** What is described is a party spirit in the assembly. It is evident in what follows that the factions were largely divided between the rich and the poor. **I partly believe it.** What Paul knew of the Corinthian assembly compelled him to accept part of what he had heard. What Paul aspired of the Corinthian assembly compelled him to reject the rest.

19 For there must be also heresies among you, that they which are approved may be made manifest among you.

19. For there must be also heresies (Gr *hairesis*, factions, the term is used in a nonecclesiastical sense. Note Acts 5:17 and 15:5, translated, "the sect"). Paul was certain that some divisions would occur in the assembly, if only to bring to light those who defend the truth. It is significant that God in His sovereign purpose might even use dissension and disorders in the assembly to put His people to the test.

20 When ye come together therefore into one place, *this* is not to eat the Lord's supper.

20. When ye come together . . . this is not to eat the Lord's supper. It is a supper, but not the Lord's. It is a disorderly gathering of people going through the motions.

21 For in eating every one taketh before *other* his own supper: and one is hungry, and another is drunken.

21. For in eating . . . one is hungry, and another is drunken. In the early church, the Lord's Supper was commonly preceded by a fellowship meal, later known as the Agape Feast. Eventually, so many problems accompanied these feasts that at the Council of Carthage (A.D. 397), they were strictly forbidden. And such was the case at Corinth. In their coming together, they were not eating together; hence it could not be called communion, and their behavior was so dishonoring to the Lord, it could hardly be called the Lord's Supper. Some were actually getting drunk.

22 What? have ye not houses to eat and to drink in? or despise ye the

22. Despise ye the church of God, and shame them that have not? Paul's indictment is twofold. They disgraced the

church of God, and shame them that have not? What shall I say to you? shall I praise you in this? I praise *you* not.

23 For I have received of the Lord that which also I delivered unto you, That the Lord Jesus the *same* night in which he was betrayed took bread:

24 And when he had given thanks, he brake *it*, and said, Take, eat: this is my body, which is broken for you: this do in remembrance of me.

25 After the same manner also *he took* the cup, when he had supped, saying, This cup is the new testament in my blood: this do ye, as oft as ye drink *it*, in remembrance of me.

26 For as often as ye eat this bread, and drink this cup, ye do shew the Lord's death till he come.

27 Wherefore whosoever shall eat this bread, and drink *this* cup of the Lord, unworthily, shall be guilty of the body and blood of the Lord.

28 But let a man examine himself, and so let him eat of *that* bread, and drink of *that* cup.

Lord's house, and they embarrassed the poor in their midst who were not invited to participate in the fellowship dinner. This being the case, they could just as well do this at home. The apostle is writing to correct these abuses in the church. His statement should not be taken as a prohibition against eating any food at all in the church.

23. Having given ample expression of his sentiments about how not to come to the Lord's Supper, Paul now goes on to give instruction as to how it ought to be done. **I have received of the Lord.** Paul traces his authority to the Lord Himself. He does not indicate how the Lord gave him the instruction. It is likely that he received it through the apostles. **That which also I delivered unto you.** Evidently, this was not the first time Paul had been through this with the Corinthians. Paul's method here is to take his readers back to the Upper Room to trace the events of the Last Supper. This says several things. In the first place, it bases what he has to say in history, not dogmatism. In the second place, it forces his readers to think back with him to Calvary, which, of course, is what the Lord's Supper is all about. Thirdly, he delineates precisely what the Lord said and did so that his readers cannot escape the significance of it.

24. Take, eat: . . . broken, are all omitted in the best manuscripts. **This is my body.** Certainly not literally, but figuratively. He was there in the midst participating with the disciples in the element of the bread which signifies His incarnation. **Which is . . . for you.** This signifies the sacrificial and vicarious character of the death of Christ. Christ is memorialized at this table, not as a great example, or teacher, or even prophet, but as the Lamb of God that takes away the sin of the world. **This do in remembrance of me.** In contrast to the often thoughtless and reckless gathering of Corinthian believers at their so-called love feast, Jesus asked of His disciples, "remember me."

25. This cup is the New Testament in my blood. Christ is the Mediator of the New Covenant who ". . . by his own blood . . . entered in once into the holy place, having obtained eternal redemption for us" (Heb 9:12-15). Notice the emphasis on the blood. This signifies our Lord's death which in turn signifies the grounds on which an eternal salvation is applied to the heart of the believing sinner. **This do ye, as oft as ye drink it.** The observance is commanded. The frequency is not. In the apostolic church, it was generally a weekly occurrence.

26. Ye do show the Lord's death till he come. The service at the Lord's table looks both back and ahead. It recalls the accomplishments of Calvary, and anticipates our Lord's glorious return. Incidentally, the fact that this is observed "till he come" indicates that our Lord intended this ordinance to be observed throughout the present age. Certain hyper-dispensationalists are inclined to see this as no longer applicable to the present age. Such a view does serious injustice to our Lord's stated purpose in the ordinance. Nor should this memorial ordinance be viewed as a sacrament ("means of grace").

27-28. Paul concludes his discussion of the Lord's Supper with a warning to his readers that they may be facing the sure chastisement of the Lord unless they correct their abuse of the Lord's Supper. **Wherefore whosoever shall eat . . . unworthily.** This is defined in verse 29 as "not discerning the Lord's body." In other words, there is an irreverent and careless attitude displayed at the table of the Lord. Such a one **shall be guilty of the body and blood of the Lord.** This expression is not to be taken to prove the doctrine of consubstantiation (cf., Lenski, pp. 477-479). Rather, the intent is to show that when one violates this sacred institution, he is, in effect, despising the body and blood of our Lord. In the same sense as it is expressed in Hebrews 9:26, they profane the institution and crucify the Saviour all over again. Instead of being cleansed by His blood, they are guilty of His blood. For this reason, it is imperative that

29 For he that eateth and drinketh unworthily, eateth and drinketh damnation to himself, not discerning the Lord's body.

30 For this cause many *are* weak and sickly among you, and many sleep.
31 For if we would judge ourselves, we should not be judged.

32 But when we are judged, we are chastened of the Lord, that we should not be condemned with the world.

33 Wherefore, my brethren, when ye come together to eat, tarry one for another.
34 And if any man hunger, let him eat at home; that ye come not together unto condemnation. And the rest will I set in order when I come.

a man examine himself. Before one partakes of the Lord's Supper, it is essential that he take stock of himself as he takes stock of our Lord. There is no room here for callousness of heart or carelessness of mind.

29. Coming to the table with the wrong attitude and the wrong approach may cause a man to eat and drink **damnation to himself, not discerning the Lord's body. Damnation** (Gr *krima*) is best rendered "judgment." The kinds of judgment the apostle has in mind are enumerated in the following verse.

30-31. For this cause, many are weak and sickly among you, and many sleep. Paul knows that the judgments of God many times take the form of physical illness and even death (cf. Acts 5:1-10). It is his conviction that such judgment has already occurred in their midst. The verb (Gr *koimao*) **sleep** when referring to death, always refers to the death of believers (cf., Jn 11:11-12; Acts 7:60; I Cor 15:6, 18, 20, 51; I Thess 4:13-15; II Pet 3:4). Judgment here is physical and temporal, not eternal. The exhortation of verse 31 goes back to verse 28. **If we would judge ourselves** corresponds to self-examination. The benefit of such examination is that **we should not be judged.** Paul gives his readers a choice. They may either exercise their own judgment upon themselves, or they may await God's judgment.

32. Lest his readers misunderstand what he means by judgment, Paul adds, **But when we are judged, we are chastened of the Lord.** Chastening itself is evidence of sonship (cf., Heb 12:6). The purpose is **that we should not be condemned with the world.** The sin of which the Corinthians were guilty was worthy of the certain judgment of God. But it was certainly not unpardonable. And true to his previous exhortation to the church, Paul's primary interest is not reprobation, but restoration.

33-34. Tarry one for another. Paul concludes his discussion of the Lord's Supper with a practical exhortation that the Corinthian believers show proper concern for one another. He implies his disapprobation of the common love feast in the words **eat at home.** And he demonstrates again pastoral concern when he expresses the thought **that ye come not together to condemnation.** Paul takes no delight in the chastening hand of the Lord. **Will I set in order** (Gr *diatassō*) refers to outward practical arrangement, (cf. Mt 11:1; I Cor 9:14; 16:1; and Gal 3:19). Any other details pertaining to the Lord's Supper, Paul will clarify upon his visit to the city.

D. Doctrine of Spiritual Gifts. 12:1-14:40.

In the eleventh chapter, Paul introduced the general subject of Christian worship. There he dealt a much needed corrective regarding authority as it is now demonstrated in public worship and the practice of the ordinances. He now turns his attention to a related subject concerning which the Corinthians had solicited his advice. This is without a doubt the most difficult section of I Corinthians to interpret. The comment made by Robertson and Plummer more than fifty years ago is as pertinent today, "The difficulty of this passage lies in our ignorance of the condition of things to which it refers" (*International Critical Commentary*, p. 257). This will be noted as we progress through the text. In this section Paul strives to achieve four objectives: (1) to show that the partitioning of the gifts is under the control of the Holy Spirit (12:1-11); (2) to show that the proportion of the gifts in the church is as diverse as the members of the human body (12:12-31); (3) to establish the primacy of love (13:1-13); (4) to show the prominence of the gift of prophecy over all other manifestations of the Holy Spirit (14:1-40).

1. The partitioning of gifts. 12:1-11.

Paul begins by dealing with the assignment of the gifts (vss. 1-6). He then treats the allotment of the gifts (vss. 7-10), and finally, the administration of the gifts (vs. 11).

CHAPTER 12

NOW concerning spiritual *gifts*, brethren, I would not have you ignorant.

2 Ye know that ye were Gentiles, carried away unto these dumb idols, even as ye were led.

3 Wherefore I give you to understand, that no man speaking by the Spirit of God calleth Jesus accursed: and *that* no man can say that Jesus is the Lord, but by the Holy Ghost.

4 Now there are diversities of gifts, but the same Spirit.

5 And there are differences of administrations, but the same Lord.

6 And there are diversities of operations, but it is the same God which worketh all in all.

7 But the manifestation of the Spirit is given to every man to profit withal.

8 For to one is given by the Spirit the word of wisdom; to another the word of knowledge by the same Spirit;

9 To another faith by the same Spirit; to another the gifts of healing by the same Spirit;

10 To another the working of miracles; to another prophecy; to another discerning of spirits; to another *divers* kinds of tongues; to another the interpretation of tongues:

a. The assignment of the gifts. 12:1-6.

12:1. Spiritual gifts (Gr *pneumatikos*, **spiritual**). This term may be either masculine or neuter, referring to either "men" or "gifts." The context is determinative. Here it is best understood as neuter, denoting "spiritual gifts" (cf. vss. 4, 5, 31; 14:1 where the neuter is used). **I would not have you to be ignorant.** This is a common pauline expression to denote a subject of importance (cf. 10:1; 14:38; II Cor 1:8; 2:11; Rom 1:13; 11:25; I Thess 4:13).

2. Ye were Gentiles, carried away. Herein lie both a statement of fact and an insinuation. They need to face the fact that before they were saved they were led about into all forms of superstition and blind impulse. The pagan worship at Corinth not only involved the worship of **dumb idols** and temple prostitution, but it also involved a pagan exercise of "tongues." The practice of "ecstatic utterances" was very common in the cults and in the worship of various Greek gods and goddesses (Kittel, *Theological Dictionary of the New Testament*, I, p. 722). The insinuation is that they are still being **carried away.** This expression has the force of being controlled by an influence they could not resist (cf. Gal 2:13; II Pet 3:17).

3. While Paul is about to deal with the entire subject of spiritual gifts, it is clear from the start that emphasis will be on only one of them, tongues. **Wherefore** ties with verse 2 and indicates they are in need of instruction. In evaluating spiritual gifts there are two criteria to be employed. The first is negative. **No man speaking by the Spirit of God calleth Jesus accursed.** The second is positive. **No man can say that Jesus is the Lord, but by the Holy Ghost.** How a person speaks determines the nature of the spirit that is within him. His very recognition and reception of Christ is by the Holy Spirit.

4-6. In the first three verses Paul's burden is to show that the Spirit is in control. This says something of the quality of what is done in the exercise of them. In verses 4-6 he shows that the Spirit is central and this says something about the consistency of what is done in the exercise of them. **Diversities of gifts . . . differences of administration . . . diversities of operations.** Paul is not necessarily classifying the gifts into three categories, but their relationship to **Spirit . . . Lord . . . God.** They are the gifts given by the Spirit, used in ministry by the Son, and energized by the Father.

b. The allotment of the gifts. 12:7-10.

7. Manifestation of the Spirit. It is improper to equate this expression with "diversities of gifts" in verse 4. Neither is Paul about to tabulate the gifts *per se*, but the manner in which they are demonstrated. **Given to every man,** may refer to every man in the body of Christ or every man with a spiritual gift. If the stress is on **given,** the former is preferred. If the stress is on **profit,** the latter is preferred.

8-10. Given by the Spirit. This is the Holy Spirit not just the spirit of unity (cf. vss. 3, 11, 13). **The word of wisdom.** This has to do with the exposition of wisdom. It is speech that has wisdom as its content (Grosheide, *Commentary on I Corinthians*, p. 285). **The word of knowledge.** This relates to the previous gift in that both are gifts of the Spirit. They are distinguished in that the former has in mind the exposition of truths dealing with the being and nature of God and the latter, the experiential and personal knowledge of God. Where the one promotes sound theology, the other promotes sound living. **Faith.** This is not saving faith but the wonder-working faith to "move mountains." **Gifts of healing.** This has in mind gifts whereby the healing of the sick was effected (cf. Acts 4:30). Two important facts should be noted here. First, the use of the plural ("gifts," "healings"). This indicates that a special gift is necessary every time a healing occurs. Second, the stress is on the results, not on the process. The gift does not produce divine "healers" but divine "healing" (cf. Jas 5:14-15). **The working of miracles.** This gift is more comprehensive than the gift of healings. It has in mind such manifestations as are recorded in Acts 5:1-12; 9:32-43; and 13:8-12. **Prophecy.** This is the communication of special revelation from God. It could have been in the sense of "foretelling" (Acts 11:28) or simply "forthtelling." Most of the New Testament epistles fall into this category. The gift was temporary, no longer needed after the canon of the New Testament was completed. **Discerning of spirits.** During the period of time when Scripture was still being formulated a class of individuals gifted with discerning true prophets from false prophets was necessary. This seems to be what John has in mind in I John 4:1 (cf. 14:29; I Thess 5:20-21). **Tongues . . . interpretation.** The gift of speaking in tongues in the book of Acts appears to have been limited to speaking in "known languages" (cf. Acts 2:4; 10:46; and 19:6). In the Acts 2 passage it does not appear that the gift of interpretation was necessary, since "every man heard in his own dialect" (Acts 10 and 19 are not as clear). However at Corinth it seems that the exercise of tongues involved more than just speaking with "known" languages. This being the case, the gift of interpretation was vital in every instance. For a fuller discussion of the nature and exercise of these gifts see the exposition of 13:1 and 14:1-40.

c. The administration of the gifts. 12:11.

11. But all these worketh that one and the selfsame Spirit, dividing to every man severally as he will.

11. But all these. All the above mentioned gifts. **Worketh . . . one . . . Spirit.** While the gifts are diverse, the source is a common one. **Dividing to every man severally as he will.** The Holy Spirit not only produces these gifts but distributes them, and that according to His own will, not according to the wishes or merits of men. Notice here that the Apostle Paul attributes to the Third Person of the Trinity one of the qualities of personality (viz., **will**). The Holy Spirit is not a force but a Person.

2. The proportion in the body. 12:12-31.

Paul uses the illustration of the human body in order to explain and illustrate the unity of Christ's body (vss. 12-19); the interdependence of each of its members (vss. 20-26); and the importance of each integral part (vss. 27-31).

a. The indivisibility of the members in the body. 12:12-19.

12 For as the body is one, and hath many members, and all the members of that one body, being many, are one body: so also *is* Christ.

12. The body is one, and hath many members. The church is viewed as an organism. Like the human body it reflects both unity and diversity. **One body.** While there are many members, there is only one body. This truth is further emphasized in Romans 12:4-5; Ephesians 1:23; and 4:4, 16. **So also is Christ.** That is, the body of Christ, which is the church. This expression is appropriate since Christ is the Head of that body.

13 For by one Spirit are we all baptized into one body, whether *we be* Jews or Gentiles, whether *we be* bond or free; and have been all made to drink into one Spirit.

13. One Spirit are we all baptized into one body. This is not the baptism of water but the baptism of the Spirit. This has the same force as the expression **and have been all made to drink into one Spirit.** This fulfills Matthew 3:11; John 1:33; and Acts 1:5. That this baptism is common to all believers at Corinth is implied by the fact that Paul does not further exhort them to be baptized by the Spirit. Rather he assumes that they have all been baptized. The believer does not tarry or pray for this baptism. It occurs at the moment of regeneration. While speaking in tongues occurred in conjunction with the baptism of the Spirit at Pentecost, this outward manifestation was not always repeated as the only proof of such baptism.

14 For the body is not one member, but many.
15 If the foot shall say, Because I am not the hand, I am not of the body; is it therefore not of the body?

14-19. Here the illustration of the body is further developed with the emphasis on the diversity and placement of each member. One cannot escape the force of Paul's argument: for a body to be a body it must have diverse members. It is absurd to expect everyone to have the same gift. **God set the members every one**

16 And if the ear shall say, Because I am not the eye, I am not of the body; is it therefore not of the body?

17 If the whole body *were* an eye, where *were* the hearing? If the whole *were* hearing, where *were* the smelling?

18 But now hath God set the members every one of them in the body, as it hath pleased him.

19 And if they were all one member, where *were* the body?

20 But now *are they* many members, yet but one body.

21 And the eye cannot say unto the hand, I have no need of thee: nor again the head to the feet, I have no need of you.

22 Nay, much more those members of the body, which seem to be more feeble, are necessary:

23 And those *members* of the body, which we think to be less honourable, upon these we bestow more abundant honour; and our uncomely *parts* have more abundant comeliness.

24 For our comely *parts* have no need: but God hath tempered the body together, having given more abundant honour to that *part* which lacked:

25 That there should be no schism in the body; but *that* the members should have the same care one for another.

26 And whether one member suffer, all the members suffer with it; or one member be honoured, all the members rejoice with it.

27 Now ye are the body of Christ, and members in particular.

28 And God hath set some in the church, first apostles, secondarily prophets, thirdly teachers, after that miracles, then gifts of healings, helps, governments, diversities of tongues.

29 *Are* all apostles? *are* all prophets? *are* all teachers? *are* all workers of miracles?

30 Have all the gifts of healing? do all speak with tongues? do all interpret?

31 But covet earnestly the best gifts: and yet shew I unto you a more excellent way.

of them in the body, as it hath pleased him. Paul stresses the sovereignty of God in this process. It is not only foolish but disobedient to covet another man's gift. The place and gifts of each member are determined by the Lord.

b. The interdependence of the members in the body. 12:20-26.

20. And now are they many members, yet but one body. Based upon the theological fact of organic unity, Paul is now going to show that each member is interdependent upon the others.

21. I have no need of thee. There is no such thing as a freelance Christian. No part of the body can take leave of the other members as though they were not necessary.

22-23. Those members of the body, which seem to be more feeble, are necessary. Like the human body some members are weaker than others. Likewise, there are some we think to be less honorable. Some parts of the body seemingly receive more attention and exposure than others, while there are other parts of the body that are never noticed at all.

24. But God hath tempered the body together. As God views the body He does not see it in part but in the whole. Tempered was used to speak of mingling two elements to form a compound.

25-26. That there should be no schism in the body. Divisions and alienation of feelings should find no place in the body of Christ. Rather, the members should have the same care one for another. The body is one and it has a common life and consciousness, therefore, whether one member suffer, all the members suffer. Likewise, if one be honored, all the members rejoice with it.

c. The induction of the members into the body. 12:27-31.

27. Now ye are the body of Christ, and members in particular. In one succinct statement the apostle expresses both the unity and the diversity of the body of Christ. In the original the definite article does not appear before body. The thought is not that this particular local assembly constituted the body of Christ. The stress is on quality. Since they are of the body of Christ their actions and their attitudes toward one another should reflect His character.

28. Paul gives a further listing of the gifts with some additions to those included in verses 4-11. Here the stress is twofold. First on the source, God hath set. And secondly on priority. The list is so arranged as to put the most important first and the least important last. In this arrangement apostles are first, tongues are last. It is doubtful that the apostle ever intended that this list be exhaustive.

29-30. Are all apostles? Just as a body possesses many different members, even so the members of the church possess a variety of gifts. It is both absurd and sinful to expect otherwise. Compare the assumption that all believers have the baptism of the Spirit (vs. 13) with the rhetorical question: Do all speak with tongues? The implied answer is no! If all these had the baptism of the Spirit and not all had spoken in tongues, then tongues cannot be the confirming factor of Spirit baptism!

31. But covet earnestly the best gifts. This expression explains why the apostle has arranged the list in verse 28 in order of priority. He wants his readers to be clear in their own minds as to which gifts are the best. Obviously, his intent is to steer them away from the more spectacular gifts, such as tongues. Covet here is not to be construed negatively but has the idea of

"earnestly desire." **Yet I show unto you a more excellent way.** The import of this statement is to be seen in chapter 13. Paul will show that a better way is not through striving but through loving.

3. *The primacy of love. 13:1-13.*

Johnson is correct when he notes, "The last clause of chapter 12 has been misunderstood. Many feel that Paul is here showing how the gifts are to be administered, i.e., in love. However, the use of 'way' (Gr *hodos*) in the sense of 'a road' instead of the 'way' (Gr *tropos*) in the sense of 'manner,' and the statement of 14:1 indicate that Paul was, rather, pointing out a path of life superior to a life spent seeking and displaying of spiritual gifts." (S. L. Johnson, *Wycliffe Bible Commentary*, p. 1251). Paul's interest here is not to instruct his readers how they may best use their gifts, but how to have their priorities straight. It is love for which they should strive, not spiritual gifts. The chapter breaks quite naturally into three sections: the contrast of love, verses 1-3; the character of love, verses 4-7; and the constancy of love, verses 8-13.

a. *Contrast of love. 13:1-3.*

13:1. Tongues of men and of angels. This expression is important in two ways. First, it shows that the content of chapter thirteen is directed foremost against the abuse of the gift of tongues (contrast 12:28 where tongues is listed last). Secondly, it shows that in the apostle's mind the gift of tongues involved both known and unknown languages. The Corinthians considered these tongues to be languages of the angels. Such was the association of tongues—speaking in pagan worship at Corinth. When a priest or devotee spoke in tongues it was considered that he spoke in the language of the gods (see J. Dillow, *Speaking in Tongues*, pp. 12, 13). The apostle is not so lacking in tact as to accuse his readers of actually incorporating a pagan activity into their worship. His approach in the next two chapters is to so circumscribe the exercise of the gift that the inordinate exercise of it will be eliminated.

2. And have not charity. (Gr *agapē*, love). The AV translation derives from the Latin and unfortunately does a serious injustice to the force of the Greek term. This is ultimately that which acts in conformity to the character and nature of God. It is not benevolence, yet produces it. It is not motivated or moved by external circumstances, yet always acts appropriately in response to them. It is no wonder that the apostle considered that though a man possessed any or all of the gifts but be destitute of love he was nothing.

3. Love has been shown to be superior to the very best of the spiritual gifts. It is also superior to philanthropy, **though I bestow all my goods to feed the poor,** and personal dedication, **though I give my body to be burned,** without love this **profiteth me nothing.**

b. *Character of love. 13:4-7.*

4-7. What is the character of love? Paul now proceeds to show the reader the character qualities of love. **Suffereth long.** It is not easily roused to resentment (cf. Jas 5:7). **Is kind** (Gr *chrēsteuomai*). This term appears only here in the New Testament in the finite verb form. It has the idea of "useful," i.e., inclined to be of good service to others. **Vaunteth not itself.** It does not sound its own praises. **Not puffed up.** It is not swelled with pride (cf. 4:6; 8:1). **Not easily provoked** (lit., "is not provoked or exasperated," Acts 17:16). **Thinketh no evil** ("does not reckon evil"). This expression of love does not keep track of the offenses committed against it. **Rejoiceth not in iniquity.** It does not take delight in that which is offensive to God. **But rejoiceth in the truth.** This may be taken in an instrumental sense "re-

---

CHAPTER 13

THOUGH I speak with the tongues of men and of angels, and have not charity, I am become *as* sounding brass, or a tinkling cymbal.

2 And though I have *the gift of* prophecy, and understand all mysteries, and all knowledge; and though I have all faith, so that I could remove mountains, and have not charity, I am nothing.

3 And though I bestow all my goods to feed *the poor,* and though I give my body to be burned, and have not charity, it profiteth me nothing.

4 Charity suffereth long, *and* is kind; charity envieth not; charity vaunteth not itself, is not puffed up,
5 Doth not behave itself unseemly, seeketh not her own, is not easily provoked, thinketh no evil;
6 Rejoiceth not in iniquity, but rejoiceth in the truth;
7 Beareth all things, believeth all things, hopeth all things, endureth all things.

joiceth together with truth" (cf. Vincent, *Word Studies*, II, p. 265), or it may be taken in the locative sense as is reflected in the AV. The latter is probably more consistent with Paul's thought in the context (cf. also Rom 1:8; Jn 3:21; I Jn 1:6). **Beareth all things** (lit., "covers all things," cf. I Pet 4:8). **Believeth all things.** This does not suggest that it is gullible, but that it will believe well of others unless convinced otherwise. In any case, it always **hopeth all things.** Rather than having a negative and critical spirit, it is always positive and hopeful. **Endureth all things.** This is a military term; it means to sustain the assaults of an enemy (cf. also II Tim 2:10; Heb 10:32; 12:2).

c. Constancy of love. 13:8-13.

Unlike many of the spiritual gifts, love will never be outmoded, unnecessary, or eliminated.

8 Charity never faileth: but whether there be prophecies, they shall fail; whether there be tongues, they shall cease; whether there be knowledge, it shall vanish away.

8. Charity never faileth (Gr *ekpiptō*, falls off, cf. Lk 16:17). Unlike the leaf or the flower, love never fades and falls off (cf. Jas 1:11; I Pet 1:24). **Prophecies, they shall fail** (lit., "be abolished"). **Tongues, they shall cease.** The significance of the Greek word (*pauō*) indicates that tongues would soon be "cut off" as their necessity in the process of New Testament revelation ceased. It is important to note that tongues are never mentioned again in the New Testament after this warning. **Knowledge, it shall vanish away** ("be abolished"). This is the same word used in reference to prophecy above. This is not knowledge in general but the "gift" of knowledge by direct revelation (cf. 12:8; 13:2).

9 For we know in part, and we prophesy in part.
10 But when that which is perfect is come, then that which is in part shall be done away.

9-10. For suggests reason. **We know in part, and we prophesy in part.** Knowledge and prophecy as we now know it are suited only to an imperfect state of existence. **That which is perfect.** This is best understood in light of I Corinthians 2:6, in the sense of "mature" or "complete" (cf. also Col 3:14; Heb 6:1). Conservative biblical scholars have proposed two main interpretations of **perfect.** It may be a reference to the completion of the canon of Scripture, with which partial revelation (by knowledge, prophecy, or tongues) came to an end, culminating in a complete revelation of God's Scripture or it may refer to the maturation of the body of Christ (in the sense of Ephesians 4:11-16). Paul employs the neuter because he does not contemplate an individual. Thus, **that which is perfect** cannot refer to the coming of Christ Himself. **Then that which is in part will be done away.** Once the **perfect** has been achieved, there will be no need for that which is immature. It will not be needed or accepted and should not be desired.

11 When I was a child, I spake as a child, I understood as a child, I thought as a child: but when I became a man, I put away childish things.

11. The apostle illustrates his point by likening it to the maturation of a person from infancy to manhood. A child speaks, reasons, and assimilates knowledge at the level of his maturity. Paul's use of **spake . . . understood . . . thought** seem to correspond respectively to "tongues," "prophecy," and "knowledge" above. If this is the case, it is reasonable to expect changes to occur. The apostle goes on to say **when I became a man, I put away childish things.** A child's speech is undeveloped, his understanding crude, and knowledge incomplete. At that time his attention is focused upon developing the skill of speech, coming to terms with truth and assimilating knowledge. But when the child becomes a man his speech becomes subject to his mind, his understanding is tempered, and his knowledge complete. Paul is not implying that they had reached or attained that level of maturity but, akin to Philippians 3:7-15, that is the end toward which they should be striving.

12 For now we see through a glass, darkly; but then face to face: now I know in part; but then shall I know even as also I am known.

12. Now we see through a glass, darkly (lit., "for yet we see through a mirror in a riddle"). Paul seems to be alluding to the incident in Num 12:8. On another occasion Paul says the writings were an enigma compared to the revelations contained in the gospel (cf. II Cor 3:12-13). **But then face to face.** The apostle understands that complete maturity will not be achieved until we see the Lord face to face. At that time we will not only achieve complete maturity but perfect knowledge. As Paul puts it, **but then shall I know even as also I am known.** The gifts are fragmentary and only a means to an end. Paul's advice is keep your eyes on the goal and not on the means towards achieving that goal.

13 And now abideth faith, hope, charity, these three; but the greatest of these *is* charity.

13. And now abideth faith, hope, charity. Now is best understood in a temporal sense (cf. Rom 8:24; II Cor 5:7; Heb 11:1). If the present Christian experience were to be reduced to three essential qualities they would be faith, hope, and love. **The greatest of these is charity.** Faith and hope will one day vanish from sight. Love alone abides. Its clearest expression is to be seen on Golgotha's hill. Thus Paul's approach is not to decry the possible abuses at Corinth but to challenge them to something much better.

4. The prominence of prophecy 14:1-40.

While the acquisition and exercise of spiritual gifts in general constituted a problem at Corinth, it appears that the most serious difficulty was centered on the gift of tongues. Earlier (12:10) in Paul's tabulation, he listed tongues among the least of the spiritual gifts. In this chapter he is going to compare it with the greatest of the gifts, i.e., prophecy.

a. In the edification of the assembly. 14:1-17.

Comparing the gift of tongues with prophecy as they are used in the edification of the assembly, Paul, first of all, cites a contrast in usefulness (vss. 1-6); then he notes a contrast in understanding (vss. 7-17).

CHAPTER 14
FOLLOW after charity, and desire spiritual *gifts*, but rather that ye may prophesy.

14:1. Follow after charity (lit., "pursue love"). This ties the preceding thought to what follows (cf. 12:31; 13:13). **And desire spiritual gifts.** Paul is anxious that his readers do not misunderstand him. He does not intend to mean by what he says in chapter 13 that spiritual gifts have no value at all; his concern is only that they keep the gifts in the proper perspective. **But rather that ye may prophesy** (Gr *prophēteuo*, proclaim a divine revelation). Now, as for desiring spiritual gifts, it is only proper to seek after those gifts which will best fulfill the mandate of love. Since prophecy issues in the greatest benefit to the greatest number of people then it is only appropriate that one seeks that gift above all others.

2 For he that speaketh in an *unknown* tongue speaketh not unto men, but unto God: for no man understandeth *him;* howbeit in the spirit he speaketh mysteries.

2. Unknown tongue (lit., "tongue"). Omit **unknown** throughout this chapter whenever it occurs with tongues as it has no support in the Greek text. **For no man understandeth him.** That is, apart from an interpreter. **Howbeit in the spirit he speaketh mysteries.** Even though he may be speaking spiritual mysteries, the benefit to the hearers is nil because they cannot understand. This, of course, is in contrast to the gift of prophecy.

3 But he that prophesieth speaketh unto men *to* edification, and exhortation, and comfort.

3. But he that prophesieth. Continuing his contrast, Paul returns to prophecy. **Speaketh unto men.** Communication is taking place. The results are **edification, and exhortation, and comfort.**

4 He that speaketh in an *unknown* tongue edifieth himself; but he that prophesieth edifieth the church.

4. On the other hand, **He that speaketh in an unknown tongue edifieth himself.** When a person speaks in tongues only one person is benefited. By way of continuing contrast, **he that prophesieth edifieth the church.**

5 I would that ye all spake with tongues, but rather that ye prophesied: for greater *is* he that prophesieth than he that speaketh with tongues, except he interpret, that the church may receive edifying.

5. I would that ye all spake with tongues. It must not be misconstrued with Paul's argument that he undervalued the gift of tongues. He did admit its importance. **But rather that ye prophesied.** Admitting the value of tongues, it would still be better if you prophesied. The reason, of course, is that the **church may receive edifying.**

6 Now, brethren, if I come unto you speaking with tongues, what shall I

6. If I come to you speaking with tongues, what shall I profit you? The question is, what benefit is it to you if I come

profit you, except I shall speak to you either by revelation, or by knowledge, or by prophesying, or by doctrine?

7 And even things without life giving sound, whether pipe or harp, except they give a distinction in the sounds, how shall it be known what is piped or harped?
8 For if the trumpet give an uncertain sound, who shall prepare himself to the battle?
9 So likewise ye, except ye utter by the tongue words easy to be understood, how shall it be known what is spoken? for ye shall speak into the air.
10 There are, it may be, so many kinds of voices in the world, and none of them is without signification.
11 Therefore if I know not the meaning of the voice, I shall be unto him that speaketh a barbarian, and he that speaketh *shall be* a barbarian unto me.

12 Even so ye, forasmuch as ye are zealous of spiritual *gifts*, seek that ye may excel to the edifying of the church.

13 Wherefore let him that speaketh in an *unknown* tongue pray that he may interpret.

14 For if I pray in an *unknown* tongue, my spirit prayeth, but my understanding is unfruitful.

15 What is it then? I will pray with the spirit, and I will pray with the understanding also: I will sing with the spirit, and I will sing with the understanding also.

16 Else when thou shalt bless with the spirit, how shall he that occupieth the room of the unlearned say Amen at thy giving of thanks, seeing he understandeth not what thou sayest?
17 For thou verily givest thanks well, but the other is not edified.

18 I thank my God, I speak with tongues more than ye all:
19 Yet in the church I had rather speak five words with my understanding, that *by my voice* I might teach others also, than ten thousand words in an *unknown* tongue.

20 Brethren, be not children in understanding: howbeit in malice be ye

speaking in tongues. Paul really doesn't answer the question except by way of contrast. **Except I shall speak to you.** If you are benefited I must speak **either by revelation** (apostolic gift), **or by knowledge** (the gift of knowledge) **or by prophesying** (the gift of prophecy), **or by doctrine** (the gift of teaching). Any of the above gifts are far superior to the gift of tongues because they communicate and they edify and they profit.

7-8. Even things without life. Paul goes on to add additional examples to prove his point. An instrument **giving sound** must also be distinctive to be understood **whether pipe or harp.** This is clearly understood by the soldier who follows the sound of a trumpet. How could he **prepare himself to the battle** if the signal is **uncertain?**

9-10. So many kinds of voices in the world. That is, so many kinds of languages. **And none of them is without signification.** They are all intelligible to those who understand them.

11. On the other hand if I do not know a specific language **I shall be unto him that speaketh a barbarian.** Paul's use of "barbarian" here simply has the general sense of "foreigner" (cf. Rom 1:14; Acts 28:24; Col 3:11).

12. Seek that ye may excel to the edifying of the church. If you must be zealous of spiritual gifts then seek after one that will benefit the church.

13. Pray that he may interpret (pray in order that he may interpret). Paul is not saying that speaking in a tongue and praying are coterminous, but that if one is seeking to speak in a tongue it would be well to ask God for the gift of interpretation also. Notice that the tongues-speaker was to provide his own interpretation.

14. For indicates the reason for Paul's advice in verse 13. **My spirit prayeth.** This is a difficult expression but probably means "the Holy Spirit in me" in the sense that my spiritual gift is being exercised. **But my understanding is unfruitful.** I do not understand what I am saying. This further evidences that "unknown languages" are in view here, else the apostle would have knowledge of what he was saying (cf. Acts 2).

15. What is it then? What is the conclusion to all this discussion? **Pray with the spirit . . . sing with the spirit.** These expressions must be defined by verse 14. Paul, no doubt, has in mind praying and singing in tongues. **Pray with the understanding also . . . and . . . sing with the understanding.** If I should pray or sing in tongues then it will also be accompanied with intelligible praying and singing (viz., the tongues interpreted).

16-17. How shall he . . . say Amen at the giving of thanks. Even if a person should bless the Lord in tongues it would be impossible for anyone else to join in because no one would know it. **For thou verily givest thanks well, but the other is not edified.** What has been said may be well and good but no one has been edified.

b. In the example of Paul. 18-19.

18-19. I speak with tongues more than ye all. Paul possessed the gift of tongues. It is interesting that this is the only place that he makes mention of it. **Yet in the church** (emphatic) **I had rather speak five words with my understanding . . . than ten thousand words in an unknown tongue.** Words have meaning only as they are understood and it is Paul's intent that he might **teach others.**

c. In the essential purpose. 14:20-25.

20. Continuing his contrast with prophecy Paul goes on to show that in the essential purpose of spiritual gifts, prophecy

children, but in understanding be men.

21 In the law it is written, With *men* of other tongues and other lips will I speak unto this people; and yet for all that will they not hear me, saith the Lord.

22 Wherefore tongues are for a sign, not to them that believe, but to them that believe not: but prophesying *serveth* not for them that believe not, but for them which believe.

23 If therefore the whole church be come together into one place, and all speak with tongues, and there come in *those that are* unlearned, or unbelievers, will they not say that ye are mad?

24 But if all prophesy, and there come in one that believeth not, or *one* unlearned, he is convinced of all, he is judged of all:

25 And thus are the secrets of his heart made manifest; and so falling down on *his* face he will worship God, and report that God is in you of a truth.

26 How is it then, brethren? when ye come together, every one of you hath a psalm, hath a doctrine, hath a tongue, hath a revelation, hath an interpretation. Let all things be done unto edifying.

27 If any man speak in an *unknown* tongue, *let it be* by two, or at the most *by* three, and *that* by course; and let one interpret.

28 But if there be no interpreter, let him keep silence in the church; and let him speak to himself, and to God.

29 Let the prophets speak two or three, and let the other judge.

30 If *any thing* be revealed to another

was to be preferred. **Be not children.** This is the second time the apostle has measured their spiritual maturity by this term (cf. 13:11). **In understanding be men.** Paul associates the gift of tongues with spiritual immaturity. He anticipates that as the church matures her concerns will be less in the arena of the spectacular and more in the stimulation of understanding.

21. In the law it is written. Law has in mind the entire Old Testament Scriptures. In this case he has in mind Isaiah 28:11-12 (cf. Jn 10:34; Rom 3:20).

22-23. Wherefore tongues are for a sign. This is best understood as a general reference to divine power evidenced in the exercise of the gift. It does not profit the believer but **them that believe not.** Its purpose was to demonstrate divine power to the unbeliever. **But prophesying serveth not for them that believe not, but for them which believe.** Insofar as the assembly is the gathering of saints and not of unbelievers, prophecy is, by far, the more appropriate gift. Yet Paul's concern goes even beyond this. He asserts that the main purpose of the gift was as a sign. However, if an unbeliever should visit the congregation where gifts are being exercised without regard for order or understanding, the results will be just the opposite. Paul asks, **will they not say that ye are mad?** In other words, the very purpose of the gift is mitigated by the unbridled exercise of it.

24-25. On the other hand, it is almost impossible to misuse the gift of prophecy. Should an unbeliever wander into the assembly and be exposed to the truth of God being taught through prophecy **he is convinced of all, he is judged of all.** Thus, instead of being repelled by the service, **falling down on his face he will worship God.** He will be convinced of his sin, of God's righteousness, and repentance and faith in God. And, so far as Paul is concerned, it is far more important that the unbeliever hear each message and testimony clearly in his own language.

d. In the exercise in the assembly. 14: 26-40.

In the concluding verses Paul circumscribes how these gifts are to be utilized in the assembly. He deals, first of all, with rules regulating the gift of tongues (vss. 26-29) and then rules regulating the gift of prophecy (vss. 30-35). He concludes the chapter with a challenge (vss. 36-40).

26. The key in the exercise of any gift is **Let all things be done unto edifying.** Throughout this chapter this has been the overriding principle and continues to dominate the apostle's thinking as he regulates the proper exercise of these gifts. Incidentally, this paragraph is also significant because it gives "us the most intimate glimpse we have of the early church at worship. Here we are able to see something of what the early Christians actually did when they assembled to worship God" (L. Morris, *The First Epistle of Paul to the Corinthians*, pp. 198-199).

27. If any man speak. The worship services of the early church do not seem to have been dominated by one individual, rather there seems to be the open and free participation in the worship service by all who would choose to participate. Thus, in this situation if a man should speak in a tongue, Paul says, **let it be by two, or at the most by three.** It is permissible for as many as three to speak in tongues and **that by course.** That is, one at a time, not all together. **And let one interpret.**

28. But if there be no interpreter, let him keep silence. To speak in tongues without an interpreter is forbidden in the church.

29-30. Let the prophets speak two or three, and let the other judge. Likewise, those who would share a special truth revealed to them by God were to do so in order and no more than two or three. The only exception to this would be in the event

that sitteth by, let the first hold his peace.

31 For ye may all prophesy one by one, that all may learn, and all may be comforted.

32 And the spirits of the prophets are subject to the prophets.
33 For God is not *the author* of confusion, but of peace, as in all churches of the saints.
34 Let your women keep silence in the churches: for it is not permitted unto them to speak; but *they are commanded* to be under obedience, as also saith the law.
35 And if they will learn any thing, let them ask their husbands at home: for it is a shame for women to speak in the church.

36 What? came the word of God out from you? or came it unto you only?
37 If any man think himself to be a prophet, or spiritual, let him acknowledge that the things that I write unto you are the commandments of the Lord.
38 But if any man be ignorant, let him be ignorant.

39 Wherefore, brethren, covet to prophesy, and forbid not to speak with tongues.

40 Let all things be done decently and in order.

that a person felt unusually constrained, while someone was speaking, to inject a thought and in this situation **let the first hold his peace.** In other words, the new communication was entitled to be heard at once.

31. Ye may all prophesy one by one. Again this is to be understood in the light of verse 29. Paul is not now saying that any number of people may prophesy but that the two or three will prophesy one at a time. And in the case of possible interruption the two are not to prophesy simultaneously, but one at a time.

32-35. And the spirits of the prophets are subject to the prophets. In contrast to tongues where it appears that the spirit of an individual is out of control, in the exercise of the prophetic gift, all is done decently and in order. **God is not the author of confusion.** The service that is disorderly, confusing, and disruptive is not of God, for God is the author of **peace. Let your women keep silence in the churches.** Obviously, this must be interpreted in light of 11:5 where it is clear that Paul understood that women were permitted to prophesy and to pray in public worship so long as they were properly dressed. The expression may have reference to speaking in tongues. That is, they were denied the privilege of exercising the gift of tongues in the assembly. Alternatively, it may have reference to what follows. **And if they will learn any thing, let them ask their husbands at home.** They were not allowed to disrupt the service by asking questions and talking while the service was going on. Certainly, they were not to speak out in tongues either.

36-38. Paul asks a sarcastic question. **What? Came the word of God out from you? or came it unto you only?** Are you the only repository of God's truth? If there is anyone in the assembly that considers himself a prophet or spiritual he must acknowledge that **the things I write unto you are the commandments of the Lord.** Here Paul unequivocally asserts his apostolic authority. **If any man be ignorant, let him be ignorant.** If there was anyone who would refuse to acknowledge divine authority he was not going to waste his time trying to convince him.

39. Covet to prophesy . . . not to speak with tongues. Again, Paul compares the two gifts and in so doing asserts the legitimacy of the gift of tongues and the primacy of the gift of prophecy.

40. Let all things be done decently and in order. Public worship was to be reflective of the one to whom it was directed, thus it was to be beautiful and harmonious. While the revelational gift of tongues was still being given, they were to **forbid not to speak with tongues.** Today, however, this original apostolic gift has ceased and forbidding its misuse by modern day "Corinthian" churches is valid.

E. Doctrine of the Resurrection. 15:1-58.

The only doctrinal "error" to which the apostle addresses himself in this epistle is contained in this chapter. What were the historical factors behind this problem? One possibility is that the individuals to whom Paul addresses himself constituted one of the parties mentioned in 1:12. By process of elimination the party of Apollos is usually suggested. However, this does not agree with what we know of Apollos and of his ministry (cf. also Acts 18:27-28; I Cor 16:12). Another possibility is that they were the moral libertines mentioned in chapter 6 and against whom the apostle urges the resurrection in 6:14. The problem with this is if they doubted the resurrection, Paul could hardly have used this as an argument for moral purity. Another view is that the problem came from converted Sadducees (cf., also Acts 24:6-9; 26:6-8). However, there is no evidence of any such maverick breed at Corinth. Others suggest that the opponents of the doctrine were Epicureans (note the reference to material indulgence in 15:32). However, again there is no indication that such a party existed in the Corinthian assembly. Furthermore, the reference in 15:32 argues that the careless life-style is a consequence and not a cause of the denial of the resurrection. Probably the best view understands this problem in light of Acts 17:32. The tenets of Greek platonic philosophy had generally pervaded the Hellenistic world. Generally it was considered that the material universe was unsuited to a spiritual existence. The Gnostics, for example, even went so far as to suggest that the body was intrinsically evil. It is this kind of skepticism that formed the background for both I Corinthians 15 and Colossians 2:8-23. See also II Timothy 2:17-18.

Paul develops his thought first, by defending the doctrine of the resurrection (15:1-34) and second, by developing the doctrine of the Resurrection (15:35-58). In the opening section he shows that: (a) Resurrection is vital to the historical preaching of the gospel (vss. 1-19); (b) Resurrection is vital to the prophetic preaching of the gospel (vss. 20-28); and (c) Resurrection is vital in suffering persecution for the gospel (vss. 29-34).

1. A defense of the doctrine of the Resurrection (based on known truth). 15:1-34.

a. Resurrection is vital to the historical preaching of the gospel. 15:1-19.

CHAPTER 15

MOREOVER, brethren, I declare unto you the gospel which I preached unto you, which also ye have received, and wherein ye stand;

2 By which also ye are saved, if ye keep in memory what I preached unto you, unless ye have believed in vain.

15:1-2. Moreover, tells us that Paul has finished his answers to the Corinthians' questions and he now goes on to a new subject. **I declare unto you,** primarily looks ahead to verses 3 and 4. **The gospel which I preached unto you.** The good news which the Corinthians **have received . . . stand . . . are saved.** Paul is now at the very heart of the gospel message. **Unless ye have believed in vain. In vain** may mean "without cause," i.e., blind faith (cf. Gal 2:21). Or it may mean "without effect," i.e., to no purpose (cf. Gal 3:4; 4:11). The latter idea seems to be best. If, as some are saying in Corinth, there is no resurrection, then faith is vain and worthless (cf. vs. 14).

3 For I delivered unto you first of all that which I also received, how that Christ died for our sins according to the scriptures;

4 And that he was buried, and that he rose again the third day according to the scriptures:

3-4. First of all, that is, in order of priority. **I also received.** Paul is not speaking of his personal salvation experience but the fact that the gospel which he preached was from direct revelation of God (cf. 11:23; Gal 1:12). Four vital truths are asserted here, identified by the word **that. That Christ died for our sins.** This is a substitutionary and propitiatory sacrifice (cf. Rom 3:23-26). **That he was buried.** This evidences the reality and totality of his death. **That he rose again.** The Greek perfect tense stresses the certainty of the fact. **According to the scriptures.** The facts of the gospel are not only important historically, but prophetically as well. They occurred as had been predicted (cf. Jn 20:9; Acts 26:23; Ps 16:10).

5 And that he was seen of Cē′phas, then of the twelve:

6 After that he was seen of above five hundred brethren at once; of whom the greater part remain unto this present, but some are fallen asleep.

7 After that, he was seen of James; then of all the apostles.

5-7. That he was seen of Cephas. The fourth vital truth of the gospel is that Christ appeared after the resurrection, not to a few but to **Cephas, then of the twelve: After that . . . of above five hundred brethren at once.** It is not certain when this last event occurred. The most likely possibility is Matthew 28:16-20. Since Jesus had previously announced this meeting (cf. Mt 26:32; 28:10, 16) it is unlikely that anyone would have intentionally missed it. **Seen of James.** Probably the Lord's brother (Mt 13:55). He was earlier mentioned as an unbeliever (cf. Jn 7:5) and later with the assembly of believers (cf. Acts 1:14; 12:17; 15:13; 21:18). One wonders if this was not the turning point of his life.

8 And last of all he was seen of me also, as of one born out of due time.

9 For I am the least of the apostles, that am not meet to be called an apostle, because I persecuted the church of God.

8-9. Last of all he was seen of me also. In Paul's characteristically self-effacing way, he cites the fact that he too had the honor of seeing the risen Lord (cf. Acts 9:1-6). **For I am least of the apostles.** Not simply because he was the last to see the risen Lord but because he was **not meet** (unworthy). Paul has not yet recovered from the "wonder of it all" that he should be elevated to the honor and office of apostleship, **because I persecuted the church of God.**

10-11. But by the grace of God I am what I am. Paul does not magnify his personal credentials but only the sovereign grace of God. Yet this least of the apostles **labored more abundantly than they all.** Whether this is taken to mean any of the apostles individually or all of them collectively the intent of the apostle is not to boast but to magnify **the grace of God which was with me . . . so we preach.** Paul's message and that of the other apostles is the same. Furthermore, both included the message of the resurrection. **And so ye believed.** If some of the Corinthians are now questioning the resurrection they are departing from their initial starting point. If they believed the message of the gospel they believed in the resurrection.

10 But by the grace of God I am what I am: and his grace which *was bestowed* upon me was not in vain; but I laboured more abundantly than they all: yet not I, but the grace of God which was with me.

11 Therefore whether *it were* I or they, so we preach, and so ye believed.

12. This verse stands as a focal point around which the first nineteen verses revolve. **Now if Christ be preached that he rose from the dead** directs our attention to the first eleven verses. **How say some among you that there is no resurrection?** This question looks ahead to verses thirteen through nineteen. Paul has established first of all that resurrection is an essential fact of the gospel. He now tabulates the logical consequences of denying the resurrection.

12 Now if Christ be preached that he rose from the dead, how say some among you that there is no resurrection of the dead?

13. Then is Christ not risen. The first consequence of denying the resurrection is that Christ is still in the grave. The nature of Paul's argument here does not suggest that his objectors admitted the resurrection of Christ, only that it led to an unthinkable conclusion for any genuine believer.

13 But if there be no resurrection of the dead, then is Christ not risen:

14-19. The logic is inescapable. **If Christ be not risen, then is our preaching vain.** The proclamation of the gospel as outlined in verses 1-11 is hollow. Not only that, but **your faith is also vain,** i.e., "groundless." Faith in a dead Saviour is both preposterous and pathetic. And not only so, but **we are found false witnesses of God** (lit., false witnesses against God). If Paul's preaching affirms something that God did not really accomplish, his message and ministry are opposed to God. They perpetrate a lie about Him. Paul summarizes his logic here and goes on to suggest yet another consequence. **Ye are yet in your sins.** Since the resurrection of Christ is essential to our justification (Rom 4:25), then the denial of it vitiates the forgiveness of sins. Not only that, but **they also which are fallen asleep in Christ are perished.** "Fall asleep in Christ" is used to speak of those who die in Christ (cf. I Thess 4:14 and Rev 14:13). "Perish" is tantamount to "perdition." **Only** is to be taken with the entire opening clause. If our hope in Christ does not take us beyond this present life, then **we are of all men most miserable.** Indeed, we are both deceived and unwitting deceivers. What a sad lot among men the Christian becomes.

14 And if Christ be not risen, then *is* our preaching vain, and your faith *is* also vain.

15 Yea, and we are found false witnesses of God; because we have testified of God that he raised up Christ: whom he raised not up, if so be that the dead rise not.

16 For if the dead rise not, then is not Christ raised:

17 And if Christ be not raised, your faith *is* vain; ye are yet in your sins.

18 Then they also which are fallen asleep in Christ are perished.

19 If in this life only we have hope in Christ, we are of all men most miserable.

Having shown the relationship of the doctrine of resurrection to biblical soteriology, Paul now goes on to show its vital link to biblical eschatology.

b. Resurrection is vital to the prophetic preaching of the gospel. 15:20-28.

20. The first important truth is that Christ has **become the first fruits of them that slept** (cf. Lev 23:9-14). The "first fruits" in Israel always anticipated a harvest.

20 But now is Christ risen from the dead, *and* become the firstfruits of them that slept.

21 For since by man *came* death, by man *came* also the resurrection of the dead.

21. For since by man came death is to be understood in the light of the parallel idea in verse 22. **By man came also the resurrection of the dead.** If the death which Adam brought is physical death then the life which Christ brings also includes physical life.

22 For as in Adam all die, even so in Christ shall all be made alive.

22. As in Adam all die. The plight of all the descendants of Adam is that they must pay the consequences of his sin. **Even so in Christ shall all be made alive.** The two occurrences of **all** are to be understood in a restricted sense. In the first instance it is qualified **in Adam.** In the second instance it is qualified "in

23 But every man in his own order: Christ the firstfruits; afterward they that are Christ's at his coming.

24 Then *cometh* the end, when he shall have delivered up the kingdom to God, even the Father; when he shall have put down all rule and all authority and power.

25 For he must reign, till he hath put all enemies under his feet.

26 The last enemy *that* shall be destroyed *is* death.

27 For he hath put all things under his feet. But when he saith all things are put under *him, it is* manifest that he is excepted, which did put all things under him.

28 And when all things shall be subdued unto him, then shall the Son also himself be subject unto him that put all things under him, that God may be all in all.

29 Else what shall they do which are baptized for the dead, if the dead rise not at all? why are they then baptized for the dead?

30 And why stand we in jeopardy every hour?

31 I protest by your rejoicing which I have in Christ Jesus our Lord, I die daily.

Christ." Paul does not subscribe to universalism, i.e., that all are saved, as some liberal theologians aver: it is only in Christ that the sinner receives life.

23-26. Order (lit., rank). **Christ the first fruits.** He was the first to experience the resurrection of the body from the dead. **Afterward they that are Christ's at his coming.** When Christ comes for the church at the Rapture, then the believers will also experience the resurrection (cf. I Thess 3:13; 4:14-19). **Then** suggests an interval in the same way **afterward** (cf. vs. 23) suggests an interval of an indeterminate length of time. **The end** refers to the end of the **kingdom of God.** At that time he will have **put down all rule.**

27-28. Then shall the Son also himself be subject unto him. This is a difficult expression and has often been misunderstood to suggest that the apostle subordinated the Son to the Father. However, two facts must be accounted for here. First, when Paul says that the Son is subject to the Father he is not speaking of the Son in terms of his essence, but in terms of his function, or ministry, as the incarnate Son. Second, the force of Paul's statement is best understood dispensationally. At this present time the administration of the messianic kingdom is given to the Son (cf. Mt 28:18). However, at the conclusion of the messianic kingdom this function will be returned to the triune God **that God may be all in all.**

c. Resurrection is vital in suffering persecution for the gospel. 15:29-34.

Not only is the resurrection vital to both the content and the implications of the gospel but such a hope is also vital to the enduring of suffering for the gospel.

29. The expression **they . . . which are baptized for the dead** is obscure. The practice of vicarious baptism such as that which is practiced by Mormons today, appeared as early as the second century (Leon Morris, *The First Epistle of Paul to the Corinthians,* p. 219). Some suppose that this custom had already been introduced into Corinth (Hodge, *Commentary on the First Epistle to the Corinthians,* p. 337). It is extremely doubtful that the apostle would have made reference to this heretical practice without, in the same breath, condemning it. The context clearly indicates a different concept. Two more satisfactory views are as follows. First, the expression may refer to young converts who took the place of the older brethren in the church who had died so that it would be properly rendered "baptized in the place of" (Gr *hyper*) which has this sense (cf. II Cor 5:15; Phm 13).

Since the context centers on the reality of the resurrection, it seems that Paul would be questioning why they are continuing to baptize new converts "over" or "in place of" the dead ones, if there is no resurrection, since baptism symbolizes our death and resurrection. To continue to baptize new converts, then, in place of the dead ones, would be meaningless if there were to be no real resurrection of the dead.

A second alternative is that the expression is to be taken synonymously with verse 30, thus being rendered "baptized with reference to the dead." This would be a nonsacerdotal use of the term "baptism." That is, the people of whom Paul was speaking were being literally immersed in such severe persecution that they were dying for their faith.

30. Why stand we in jeopardy every hour? Certainly if there is no resurrection, there is no sense in suffering persecution for Christ. On the contrary, it is only logical that one would do whatever is necessary to prolong life on earth.

31. I die daily. This does not teach that Paul mortified the flesh every day. The context tells us that he, in effect, faced the wild beasts every day. Paul's life was in such constant jeopardy that he never knew when he might be called upon to give his life for the gospel.

32 If after the manner of men I have fought with beasts at Ĕph'e-sus, what advantageth it me, if the dead rise not? let us eat and drink; for to morrow we die.
33 Be not deceived: evil communications corrupt good manners.

32-33. What advantageth it me? If one's existence is terminated in the arena for the sake of a gospel which can only provide empty hopes we may as well **eat and drink; for tomorrow we die.** Borrowing a proverb from the Greek poet Menander, Paul warns **evil communications corrupt good manners.** Evil is contagious. By this the apostle implies that those who are denying the resurrection are in fact false teachers.

34 Awake to righteousness, and sin not; for some have not the knowledge of God: I speak *this* to your shame.

34. Awake to righteousness and sin not. Wake up to righteousness, open your eyes to the delusion of your spiritual superiority. **For some have not the knowledge of God.** The denial of the resurrection suggests that those who hold to such a view are literally "ignorant of God" (cf. Mt 28:22). **I speak this to your shame.** It is both incredible and shameful that such a church so gifted to God could have allowed persons in their assembly to have called such a cardinal truth into question.

2. A development of the doctrine of the Resurrection (based on revelation). 15:35-38.

In the first half of this chapter Paul argues on the basis of known truth and thereby commends the preaching of the resurrection. In the remaining part of the chapter he develops the doctrine, based on new revelation, to provide his readers with insights into the blessed hope of the believer.

a. The nature of resurrection for the dead. 15:35-49.

35 But some *man* will say, How are the dead raised up? and with what body do they come?
36 *Thou* fool, that which thou sowest is not quickened, except it die:

35-36. The first question Paul answers is **How are the dead raised up? and with what body do they come?** While both questions are distinct they must be taken together. The first deals with how life can come from death and the second deals with the nature of the resurrection body. The first question is answered with an analogy from common life. **That which thou sowest is not quickened, except it die.** Whenever a seed is sown in the ground it must first die before it can germinate (cf. Jn 12:24). As to the second question the apostle requires more explanation.

37 And that which thou sowest, thou sowest not that body that shall be, but bare grain, it may chance of wheat, or of some other grain:
38 But God giveth it a body as it hath pleased him, and to every seed his own body.

37-38. Thou sowest not that body that shall be, but bare grain. That which is produced is very different from that which is planted. A grain is sown, a plant is the result. **God giveth it a body.** All of nature illustrates the providential control of God. The precise nature of the body of every living thing is determined by the good pleasure of God.

39 All flesh *is* not the same flesh: but *there is* one *kind of* flesh of men, another flesh of beasts, another of fishes, *and* another of birds.
40 *There are* also celestial bodies, and bodies terrestrial: but the glory of the celestial *is* one, and the *glory* of the terrestrial *is* another.
41 *There is* one glory of the sun, and another glory of the moon, and another glory of the stars: for *one* star differeth from *another* star in glory.

39-41. All flesh is not the same flesh. Furthermore, it is clear in nature that diversity exists among all living beings. Such diversity is not only reflected in the earthly sphere but also in the heavenly.

42 So also *is* the resurrection of the dead. It is sown in corruption; it is raised in incorruption:

42. So also is the resurrection of the dead. It is to be understood in the context of reaping and sowing. It thus reflects the same principle of unity and diversity. The resurrection body is related to the earthly body in the same sense that the plant is related to the seed. Yet, it will be different. **It is sown in corruption; it is raised in incorruption.**

43 It is sown in dishonour; it is raised in glory: it is sown in weakness; it is raised in power:
44 It is sown a natural body; it is raised a spiritual body. There is a natural body, and there is a spiritual body.
45 And so it is written, The first man

43-44. Paul enlarges upon the contrast between the two. The one is **sown in dishonor . . . weakness . . . a natural body.** It is **raised in glory . . . power . . . spiritual.**

45. So it is written. Tantamount to saying, "and this agrees with Scripture." **Adam was made a living soul** seems to have in

Adam was made a living soul; the last Adam *was made* a quickening spirit.

mind the earthly animal nature given to Adam in the original creation. This seems to suit the parallel ideas in verses 46 through 49. **The last Adam was made a quickening spirit** (lit., "the last Adam became a quickening spirit"). The expression **last Adam** was coined by the Apostle Paul as a reference to Christ (cf. also Rom. 5:14). The contrast here is not so much between the soul and the spirit as it is between "living" (Gr *zao*) and "life-giving" (Gr *zōopoieō*). The principle of life is common with all men. The last Adam is infinitely more than that (Jn 5:26). The one partakes of temporality, the other of eternality.

46-48. However, it was the **natural** which came first; it was the **spiritual** which came afterward. Adam is **of the earth,** Christ is **the Lord from heaven.** The former is thus earthly, the latter is heavenly.

46 Howbeit that *was* not first which is spiritual, but that which is natural; and afterward that which is spiritual.

47 The first man *is* of the earth, earthy: the second man *is* the Lord from heaven.

48 As *is* the earthy, such *are* they also that are earthy: and as *is* the heavenly, such *are* they also that are heavenly.

49 And as we have borne the image of the earthy, we shall also bear the image of the heavenly.

49. The certainty of the resurrection is verified by the reality of human, earthly existence. **As we have borne the image of the earthly, we shall also bear the image of the heavenly.** Thus the human body, instead of becoming an argument against the resurrection becomes an argument in its favor.

b. The nature of resurrection for the living. 15:50-58.

But what of those who are alive at the coming of Christ? How shall they be distinguished from those who have died? Paul's final statement in the chapter is to turn his attention upon the nature of the Resurrection for those who are still living at the time of the second coming of Christ.

50 Now this I say, brethren, that flesh and blood cannot inherit the kingdom of God; neither doth corruption inherit incorruption.

50. First the statement of a principle, **flesh and blood cannot inherit the kingdom of God.** A change is mandatory if the believer is ever to realize his promised blessings.

51 Behold, I shew you a mystery; We shall not all sleep, but we shall all be changed,

51. I show you a mystery (cf. 2:7). Not all believers will sleep ("die") but we can all be assured of one thing. **We shall all be changed.** How will that occur?

52 In a moment, in the twinkling of an eye, at the last trump: for the trumpet shall sound, and the dead shall be raised incorruptible, and we shall be changed.

52. In a moment, in the twinkling of an eye, expresses the suddenness with which it will occur. The time is indicated **at the last trump.** This is not the last trump of Revelation 11:15 but the last trump of I Thessalonians 4:16. It is so designated because it signals the end of the present age. Two groups are distinguished. **The dead shall be raised incorruptible, and we shall be changed.** The term **dead** refers to those who have died in Christ. The term **we** refers to those who are still living at the time of the Rapture.

53-54. Both groups are alike in that they are **corruptible** and **mortal.** That to which both groups are changed is likewise the same, designated as **incorruption** and **immortality. Death is swallowed up in victory** is taken from Isaiah 25:8.

53 For this corruptible must put on incorruption, and this mortal *must* put on immortality.

54 So when this corruptible shall have put on incorruption, and this mortal shall have put on immortality, then shall be brought to pass the saying that is written, Death is swallowed up in victory.

55 O death, where *is* thy sting? O grave, where *is* thy victory?

55. Such hope and assurance issues in a great song of triumph. **O death, where is thy sting? O grave, where is thy victory?**

56 The sting of death *is* sin; and the strength of sin *is* the law.

56. The sting of death is sin and Paul would answer "and yet am I forgiven." **The strength of sin is the law,** and Paul would exclaim "and yet I am pardoned."

57 But thanks *be* to God, which giveth us the victory through our Lord Jesus Christ.

58 Therefore, my beloved brethren, be ye stedfast, unmoveable, always abounding in the work of the Lord, for-

57-58. No man can take credit for this victory. It comes **through our Lord Jesus Christ.** And this blessed hope, this blessed assurance, issued forth in a challenge in verse 58. **Be ye steadfast, unmovable, always abounding.** How does this relate to the doctrine of resurrection? Paul answers **ye know that your labor is not in vain.** For Paul it was more than faith. It was

asmuch as ye know that your labour is not in vain in the Lord.

knowledge. It was the sure conviction that one day he would share in the glory of the resurrection.

V. CONCLUSION. 16:1-24.

The concluding chapter is taken up with practical and personal matters concerning: (a) The contribution for the support of the Jerusalem church (vss. 1-9); (b) Paul's personal efforts on behalf of the Corinthian assembly (vss. 10-12). And then a concluding challenge (vss. 13-24). It is here that the apostle reiterates the theme of the epistle, i.e., **called unto the fellowship of his Son Jesus Christ our Lord** (1:9) in the most practical of terms.

A. The Contribution. 16:1-9.

1. Its instruction. 16:1-4.

CHAPTER 16
NOW concerning the collection for the saints, as I have given order to the churches of Ga-lā′tia, even so do ye.

16:1. Now concerning. The common formula used in this epistle to introduce matters about which the Corinthians had queried the apostle. In this case it had to do with **the collection for the saints.** The believers at Corinth were aware that the apostle was gathering funds for the Jerusalem church, and apparently they had written to inquire to what extent they could participate in this collection. **I have given order** suggests that this was not an optional matter for the Corinthian believers any more than it was for the **churches of Galatia.**

2 Upon the first *day* of the week let every one of you lay by him in store, as *God* hath prospered him, that there be no gatherings when I come.

2. The procedure by which they were to gather these funds was **Upon the first day of the week.** Their giving was to be systematic and planned. **Let every one of you lay by him in store.** This obligation extended to everyone. **As God hath prospered him.** The amount of each gift was proportionate to the giver's income. **That there be no gatherings when I come.** The apostle was desirous that the collection be taken before he came. This was for two reasons. First, through systematic and planned giving he knew that the amount would be more. Second, he did not want to apply pressure when he came.

3 And when I come, whomsoever ye shall approve by *your* letters, them will I send to bring your liberality unto Jerusalem.
4 And if it be meet that I go also, they shall go with me.

3-4. And when I come. While his arrival in Corinth was yet indefinite, Paul is stressing here that they be prepared with the collection at any time. **Whomsoever you shall approve by your letters.** Placing himself above suspicion, the apostle shows that he is not so much interested in handling their money as in assuring that it got to Jerusalem. He suggests that they appoint stewards to carry their money. **And if it be meet.** If it be substantial enough **that I go also,** then they would all go together. Paul was willing, if their contribution was especially large, to rearrange his schedule and go with the group to Jerusalem.

2. Its collection. 16:5-9.

5 Now I will come unto you, when I shall pass through Macedonia: for I do pass through Macedonia.

5. Now I will come unto you, when I shall pass through Macedonia. Paul here changes his original itinerary and subsequently came under the charge of being fickle (cf. II Cor 1:15-17).

6 And it may be that I will abide, yea, and winter with you, that ye may bring me on my journey whithersoever I go.
7 For I will not see you now by the way; but I trust to tarry a while with you, if the Lord permit.
8 But I will tarry at Ĕph′e-sus until Pentecost.

6-7. Paul's plans at this time are to spend the winter at Corinth. **If the Lord permit.** The apostle was always subject to the will of God above his own.

8. I will tarry at Ephesus till Pentecost. The time is near the close of Paul's three-year stay at Ephesus and the season is early spring.

9 For a great door and effectual is opened unto me, and *there are* many adversaries.

9. A great door. Door is used here metaphorically for "opportunity." **Many adversaries.** This is best taken with the previous expression. The apostle seems to have in mind his pending trip through Macedonia and is accounting for why he is staying a little longer in Ephesus (cf. 15:32; Acts 19:1-4).

B. The Collector. 16:10-12.

10 Now if Tĭ-mō'the-us come, see that he may be with you without fear: for he worketh the work of the Lord, as I also *do*.

10. Now if Timothy come (cf. Acts 19:22). At this time Timothy was traveling through Macedonia and the apostle anticipated that he would be reaching Corinth eventually (cf. 4:17). **See that he may be with you without fear.** The apostle hoped that the Corinthians would not intimidate Timothy, being a somewhat young and timid individual (cf. I Tim 4:12; 5:21-23; II Tim 1:6-8; 2:1, 3, 15; 4:1-2). Paul commends his ministry to them for **he worketh the work of the Lord, as I also do.**

11 Let no man therefore despise him: but conduct him forth in peace, that he may come unto me: for I look for him with the brethren.
12 As touching *our* brother Apollos, I greatly desired him to come unto you with the brethren: but his will was not at all to come at this time; but he will come when he shall have convenient time.

11. Let no man therefore despise him. This advice is reminiscent of the advice given to Timothy in I Timothy 4:12.

12. As touching our brother Apollos. Paul had asked Apollos if he would be willing to go to Corinth in order to adjudicate some of their problems. Apparently, at that time he was not able but **he will come when he shall have convenient time.** Now, Paul begins a series of closing remarks, exhortations, challenges, and greetings.

C. The Close. 16:13-24.

13 Watch ye, stand fast in the faith, quit you like men, be strong.

13. As a military leader he exhorts the brethren to **Watch ye,** i.e., be wakeful and alert to your spiritual enemies. **Stand fast in the faith.** Don't be unsettled in your mind. Don't be afraid to be firm in your convictions. Don't be as the Sophists who called everything into question. **Quit you like men.** Be courageous. Be strong. Characteristic of Paul, he sees the Christian life as though he were in the arena. Faith, conviction, and courage are the essential ingredients for success and victory.

14 Let all your things be done with charity.

14. So that his readers do not understand his words to legitimize a careless and uncaring attitude, Paul moderates his advice with **Let all your things be done with charity.** This, of course, calls to mind all that he said in chapter thirteen.

15 I beseech you, brethren, (ye know the house of Stĕph'a-nas, that it is the firstfruits of A-chā'ia, and *that* they have addicted themselves to the ministry of the saints,)
16 That ye submit yourselves unto such, and to every one that helpeth with *us*, and laboureth.

15-16. The house of Stephanas (cf. 1:16) **Addicted themselves,** i.e., they devoted themselves in a self-imposed duty to the believers. This was the very first family to receive Christ in Paul's ministry in Achaia. This does not conflict with Romans 16:5, which in the better texts do not read "Achaia" but "Asia."

17 I am glad of the coming of Stĕph'a-nas and Fôr-tu-nā'tus and A-chā'i-cus: for that which was lacking on your part they have supplied.

17. Stephanas and Fortunatus and Achaicus were three members of the Corinthian assembly who ministered to Paul's needs in Ephesus. Note the Latin names. This is not surprising since the new city of Corinth was largely composed of Romans.

18 For they have refreshed my spirit and yours: therefore acknowledge ye them that are such.

18. They . . . refreshed my spirit and yours. Here Paul has in mind both their ministry to him, in terms of reporting the progress of the Corinthian assembly, and their ministry to the Corinthians in terms of sharing the ministry Paul had with them in Ephesus.

19 The churches of Asia salute you. Āq'ui-la and Priscilla salute you much in the Lord, with the church that is in their house.

19. Aquila and Priscilla. This couple, having been exiled from Rome (Acts 18:2), first met Paul in Corinth. They have since moved on to Ephesus (cf. also Rom 16:3-5). **The church that is in their house.** Apparently, wherever this couple went, they made their home a sanctuary where Christ was honored and believers gathered to share the Word together and worship.

20 All the brethren greet you. Greet ye one another with an holy kiss.
21 The salutation of *me* Paul with mine own hand.
22 If any man love not the Lord Jesus Christ, let him be A-nǎth'e-ma Mǎr'an-ǎ'tha.
23 The grace of our Lord Jesus Christ *be* with you.

20-24. Greet ye one another with a holy kiss (cf. Rom 16:16; II Cor 13:12; I Thess 5:26; I Pet 5:14). In the custom of the day, this was an expression of mutual affection and friendship. In other words, they were to put away their divisive spirit and unite in the bonds of love. **With mine own hand** has reference to the salutation, not the entire epistle. In Galatians 6:11, Paul remarks that his writing of that epistle with his own hand was something unusual due to his poor sight. Ordinarily, he used a secretary to whom he would dictate his letters and then

24 My love *be* with you all in Christ Jesus. Amen.

he would write the salutation with his own hand to authenticate it (Col 4:18; II Thess 3:17). **Anathema,** "devoted to destruction" (cf. Rom 9:3; I Cor 12:3: Gal 1:18-19). **Maranatha.** Properly, two words in the Aramaic. It expresses one of two possible ideas. It may be taken in the sense of "our Lord is come," signifying the incarnation. Or it may mean "our Lord cometh," signifying the Second Coming. The latter seems to be in view here. It is much like John's concluding remarks in Revelation: "Even so, come, Lord Jesus" (Rev 22:20). **My love be with you all.** Only their spiritual father could speak to them in this way. His love is extended not only to those who agree with him, but to all in the assembly, even his enemies. The greatest example these Christians have of how to live the Christian life is the great apostle himself.

BIBLIOGRAPHY

Alford, H. *The Greek Testament.* Vol. II. Revised by E. F. Harrison. Chicago: Moody Press, 1968.

Barclay, W. *Letters to the Corinthians.* Philadelphia: Westminster Press, 1956.

Barrett, C. K. The First Epistle to the Corinthians. In *Harper's New Testament Commentaries.* New York: Harper and Row, 1968.

Boyer, J. B. *For a World Like Ours.* Grand Rapids: Baker, 1971.

Erdman, C. R. *The First Epistle of Paul to the Corinthians.* Philadelphia: Westminster Press, 1928.

Findlay, G. G. Saint Paul's First Epistle to the Corinthians. In *The Expositor's Greek New Testament.* Vol. 2. Grand Rapids: Eerdmans, n.d.

*Godet, F. *Commentary on Saint Paul's Epistle to the Corinthians.* 2 vols. Edinburgh: T. & T. Clark, 1957.

*Gromacki, R. G. *Called to Be Saints, An Exposition of I Corinthians.* Grand Rapids: Baker, 1977.

*Grosheide, F. W. Commentary on the First Epistle to the Corinthians. In *The New International Commentary.* Grand Rapids: Eerdmans, 1953.

*Hodge, C. *An Exposition of the First Epistle to the Corinthians.* Grand Rapids: Eerdmans, reprinted, 1974.

Ironside. H. A. *Addresses on the First Epistle to the Corinthians.* New York: Loizeaux Brothers, 1938.

*Johnson, S. L. The First Epistle to the Corinthians. In *The Wycliffe Bible Commentary.* Ed. by C. F. Pfeiffer and E. F. Harrison. Chicago: Moody Press, 1963.

Kling, C. W. The First Epistle of Paul to the Corinthians. In *A Commentary on the Holy Scriptures.* Ed. by J. P. Lange. Trans. by P. Schaff. New York: Scribner's, 1889.

Lenski, R. C. H. *The Interpretation of Paul's First and Second Epistle to the Corinthians.* Columbus: Wartburg Press. 1957.

Morgan, G. C. *The Corinthian Letters of Paul.* Old Tappan, N. J.: Revell, 1946.

*Morris, L. The First Epistle of Paul to the Corinthians. In *Tyndale New Testament Commentary.* Grand Rapids: Eerdmans, 1976.

Redpath, A. *The Royal Route to Heaven.* Westwood: Revell, 1960.

Rice, J. R. *The Church of God at Corinth.* Murfreesboro: Sword of the Lord, 1973.

Robertson, A. and A. A. Plummer. Critical and Exegetical Commentary on the Epistle of Paul to the Corinthians. In *The International Critical Commentary.* New York: Scribner's, 1911.

Zodhiates, S. *Conquering the Fear of Death. A Commentary on I Corinthians 15.* Grand Rapids: Eerdmans, 1970.

The Second Epistle To The

CORINTHIANS

INTRODUCTION

II Corinthians is actually the fourth letter that Paul wrote to Corinth (see Introduction to I Cor). A "previous epistle" was written prior to I Corinthians, and then another "sorrowful letter" was written between I Corinthians and II Corinthians. The second canonical epistle has several features which distinguish it. His first epistle is both practical and instructional but this epistle is intensely personal and autobiographical. In fact, its style appears so spontaneous and emotional that some have questioned its internal unity. For this reason a word needs to be said about the integrity of the epistle.

Authorship. Although the historical evidence is not as early as that of I Corinthians, it is almost equally as strong. External evidence suggests that the second epistle to the Corinthians had not yet reached Rome by the end of the first century (A.D. 96) since it is not quoted by Clement of Rome. However, it was known to Polycarp who quotes 4:14. II Corinthians is further attested in the letter to Diognetus, Athanagoras, Theophilus of Antioch, Tertullian, Clement of Alexandria, Irenaeus, the Muratorian Canon, and Marcion's *Apostolocon.* It is also found in the Old Syriac and the Old Latin, along with the first epistle. By the end of the second century the attestation is replete.

The internal evidence is also very strong. The writer calls himself Paul (1:1; 10:1). Likewise, conservative scholarship is unanimous in its agreement that the pauline authorship of this epistle is unmistakable, not only in content but in style and vocabulary.

Background. II Corinthians is written to the assembly which was founded on Paul's first visit to that city. Since his departure and subsequent ministry in Ephesus, the apostle has learned a great deal about the problems fomenting in this little assembly. Problems with worldliness, internal wranglings, and doctrinal defections continue to fester in spite of Paul's efforts in the first epistle.

Opposition to Paul's ministry continues to mount, especially coming from the party which associated itself with "Christ" (cf. 10:7; 11:13). The leader of this group seems to have been especially obnoxious to the apostle (10:7-11). When the news of these conditions reached Paul at Ephesus he made a brief visit to Corinth in order to deal with them (cf. 2:1; 12:14, 21; 13:1-2). At this time the personal vendetta against the Apostle Paul himself was shown. Upon his return to Ephesus the apostle was so distressed he penned a letter to the church of such a severe nature that he later regretted having written it. This he sent to them by Titus (2:3-4, 9;7:8-12). It is probable that this letter was lost in its entirety. While some have suggested that this letter is preserved in II Corinthians 10-13 (Plummer, *Commentary on Second Corinthians,* p. xviii), this theory is quite unlikely (Bernard,

Expositor's Greek Testament, vs. 3, pp. 21-27). The charges leveled against the apostle by this group are indicated in a number of passages in the epistle. For example, he was accused of being fickle (1:17), authoritarian (1:24), ministering without proper credentials (3:1), cowardice (10:1, 10), failure to maintain proper clerical dignity (11:7), presumption (10:13-17), and fleshliness (10:2). Likewise, the apostle has a few things to say about his accusers. For example, they corrupted the Word (2:17), they were deceptive (3:1), they were Jews masquerading as ministers of Christ (11:23-27), they were domineering (11:20), and bold (11:21), they lacked the spiritual courage to step out on their own and start their own ministry (11:23-27). Thus it was no small wonder that the apostle was seriously concerned about the spiritual well-being of the church at Corinth.

Titus was to deliver the "sorrowful letter," then return to Paul with a report of the response of the Corinthians and subsequent development. However, Paul had to leave Ephesus earlier than scheduled because of the uprising of the silversmiths (cf. Acts 20:1). He stopped at Troas and apparently was engaging in a very fruitful evangelistic effort in that city. However, Titus tarried much longer than the overstrained and impetuous apostle could stand. He discontinued his ministry in Troas and crossed over to Macedonia, expecting to meet him somewhere along the *Via Egnatia,* the great highway which connected the chief Macedonian towns along the coast. It was therefore with great relief that the apostle received Titus' report that they had been genuinely grieved by the painful letter (7:9), the offending person had been dealt with (2:6-8), the great majority of the Corinthians were really loyal to the apostle as he had suspected all along (7:14), and Titus himself had developed a new appreciation for this assembly (7:15). Thus it is not surprising in the first seven chapters of II Corinthians to see the apostle pour out his thanksgiving to God in encouragement at the progress this assembly was making. Thus, he sat down immediately and penned II Corinthians from Macedonia (2:3; 7:5-7; 8:1; 9:2-4), probably from the city of Philippi.

Purpose. Thiessen has ably summarized Paul's reasons for writing II Corinthians. He did so in order: (1) to explain his sufferings in Asia (1:3-11); (2) to justify himself in his change of plans about returning to Corinth (1:12-2:4); (3) to instruct them as to the treatment of the offender (2:5-11); (4) to express his joy at the good news of their progress (2:12-13); (5) to attain full reconciliation with himself (6:11-7:16); (6) to urge the Corinthians to participate in the collection for the church at Jerusalem (chs. 8-9); and (7) to establish his authority as an apostle (10:1-13:10).

The unity of II Corinthians has frequently been

called into question (cf. Alford, Zahn, Lake, Moffatt, Kummel, and Plummer). However, there is absolutely no external evidence to support the contention that II Corinthians was ever more than one unit. The arguments rest entirely upon internal evidence such as the change of tone in chapters 10-13, certain supposed inconsistencies in 1-9 compared with 10-13, and the reconciling of some statements with Paul's geographical location at the time of writing (10:16). None of these objections bears a great deal of weight. The basic tenor of the epistle is less formal than others of Paul's epistles. It is much more emotional, and therefore, there are

more abrupt changes in his thought. Yet the main divisions are clearly visible. Thiessen is probably correct to suggest that the changes in tone between chapters 1-9 and 10-13 are likely due to the particular group Paul is addressing in each of these sections (Thiessen, *Introduction to the New Testament*, p. 210). This peculiarity in style can be demonstrated, not only in other biblical literature, but in secular literature as well.

(**Editor's note.** The author acknowledges much indebtedness throughout this study to notes originally compiled by his late father, Burton C. Mitchell, noted Bible lecturer.)

OUTLINE

I. Introduction. 1:1-11.
  A. Salutation. 1:1-2.
  B. Thanksgiving 1:3-11.
II. Apology for Paul's Ministry. 1:12-7:16.
  A. The Conduct of Paul. 1:12-2:17.
    1. Paul's change of plans. 1:12-2:4.
      a. His concern. 1:12-14.
      b. His plan. 1:15-22.
      c. His explanation. 1:23-2:4.
    2. Paul's charge concerning the offender. 2:5-11.
    3. Paul's confidence in the Corinthians. 2:12-17.
  B. The Calling of Paul. 3:1-6:10.
    1. The superiority of his ministry. 3:1-4:6.
      a. The credentials of his ministry. 3:1-5.
      b. The quality of his ministry. 3:6-4:6.
        (1). The glory of the New Covenant. 3:6-11.
        (2). The permanence of the New Covenant. 3:12-18.
        (3). The ministry of the New Covenant. 4:1-6.
    2. The suffering in his ministry. 4:7-12.
    3. The goal of his ministry. 4:13-5:10.
      a. Hope of the Resurrection. 4:13-15.
      b. Confidence in ministry. 4:16-18.
      c. Contemplation of new life. 5:1-10.
    4. The service in his ministry. 5:11-6:10.
      a. Paul's motives. 5:11-15.
      b. Paul's message. 5:16-21.
      c. Paul's methods. 6:1-10.
  C. The Challenge of Paul. 6:11-7:16.
    1. The entreaty for reconciliation. 6:11-7:4.

      a. Sympathy towards Paul. 6:11-13.
      b. Separation from the world. 6:14-7:4.
    2. The encouragement from their response. 7:5-16.
      a. Comfort of Titus. 7:5-7.
      b. Correction of the letter. 7:8-12.
      c. Consolation. 7:13-16.
III. Appeal of Paul's Ministry. 8:1-9:15.
  A. Faithfulness Illustrated. 8:1-5.
  B. Faithfulness Exhorted. 8:6-15.
  C. Faithfulness Delegated. 8:16-9:5.
  D. Faithfulness Directed. 9:6-15.
IV. Authority of Paul's Ministry. 10:1-13:10.
  A. The Defense of the Apostle. 10:1-18.
    1. By his attitudes. 10:1-6.
    2. By his authority. 10:7-11.
    3. By divine commendation. 10:12-18.
  B. The Boast of the Apostle. 11:1-12:10.
    1. The basis for his boast. 11:1-15.
    2. The proof of his boast. 11:16-33.
    3. The consequences of his boast. 12:1-10.
      a. The revelation. 12:1-6.
      b. The thorn in the flesh. 12:7-10.
  C. The Credentials of the Apostle. 12:11-18.
    1. His position among the other apostles. 12:11.
    2. His performance as a true apostle. 12:12-13.
    3. His behavior as an apostle. 12:14-18.
  D. The Charge of the Apostle. 12:19-13:10.
    1. The charge to repent. 12:19-13:4.
    2. The charge to self-examination. 13:5-10.
V. Conclusion. 13:11-14.

COMMENTARY

I. INTRODUCTION. 1:1-11.

A. Salutation. 1:1-2.

PAUL, an apostle of Jesus Christ by the will of God, and Timothy *our* brother, unto the church of God which is at Corinth, with all the saints which are in all A-chā'ia:

1:1. Paul, an apostle. Paul characteristically begins, as in his other epistles, by establishing his authority and his commission (cf. Eph 1:1; Col 1:1; I Tim 1:1; II Tim 1:1; Gal 1:1). This ministry was commissioned him of **Jesus Christ by the will of**

God. Paul takes for granted that he fulfills any requisites for the office of apostleship. His is no usurpation of power, but obedience to the call of God. **And Timothy.** This companion of Paul is not mentioned in the introduction to I Corinthians, presumably because Timothy had already been sent to Corinth (I Cor 4:17; 16:10). That he appears here indicates that he has since rejoined the apostle, given his report concerning the affairs at Corinth, and traveled with him to Macedonia. The epistle is primarily addressed to **the church of God which is at Corinth.** That is, the local assembly. But, that it was intended also as a circular letter to be read by other churches is implied by the fact that he also addresses **all the saints that are in all Achaia.** This would embrace at least the Christians that were in Athens (cf. Acts 17:34) and in Cenchreae, the eastern port of Corinth (cf. Rom 16:1). **Saints** calls to mind all who have been set apart by God and walk in newness of life (cf. Rom 1:7; I Cor 1:2; 6:11; II Cor 5:17).

2 Grace be to you and peace from God our Father, and from the Lord Jesus Christ.

2. Grace be to you and peace. For Paul, grace always precedes peace. Until one has received the grace of God he can know nothing of His peace. **Grace** (Gr *charis*) is the infinite love of God that enables Him to pour out infinite favor on the object loved without receiving anything in return. It demands no merit and incurs no obligation. It has been extended to all of humanity by the cross work of Jesus Christ which alone makes God's love available to mankind (I Jn 2:2). Anything that we might place between the provision of God's grace and the power of God's grace has been received by faith. There is nothing that brings this peace so much as the undiluted gospel of God's grace (cf. Eph 2:14; Phil 4:7; Col 1:20; 3:15). **From God our Father and from the Lord Jesus Christ.** The single preposition (Gr *apo*) links the Father and the Son, thus affirming unequivocally the deity of Christ. The reference is to the eternal Father and the incarnate Son (cf. also 13:14).

B. Thanksgiving. 1:3-11.

3-4. Blessed (Gr *eulogētos,* "well spoken of"). This term is used in the New Testament of God and so here. It is a term of adoration and praise. In consideration of God's grace and peace (vs. 2) and in anticipation of His mercies and comforts (vs. 3b) such a pronouncement from the apostle is understood. For he contemplates both who God is and what God does. **Even the Father of our Lord Jesus Christ, the Father of mercies, and the God of all comfort.** The mercies in view here, no doubt, include such great verities as deliverance from the world, sin, and Satan to participation in sonship, light, and life. But the force is even more than this. The stress is that the Father is "characterized" by mercy (cf. Ps 86:5; Dan 9:9; Mic 7:18). **Comfort** (Gr *paraklēsis*) is cognate to "the Comforter" of John 16:7. This term does not connote "sympathy" as much as "empathy" or "encouragement." It has the idea of someone coming alongside to provide support. Since the Comforter abides within (cf. Jn 14:16-17) a twofold process is implied: strength for the inner man and encouragement for the outer man. Paul now turns his thoughts to the everyday problems of life and he does so in the context of the **God of all comfort; who comforteth us in all our tribulation.** In the general scope of life, God's comfort extends to every area. But the purpose emphasized here is not just for our own good, but **that we may be able to comfort them which are in any trouble.** God's comfort is transferable and intended to be shared.

3 Blessed be God, even the Father of our Lord Jesus Christ, the Father of mercies, and the God of all comfort;
4 Who comforteth us in all our tribulation, that we may be able to comfort them which are in any trouble, by the comfort wherewith we ourselves are comforted of God.

5 For as the sufferings of Christ abound in us, so our consolation also aboundeth by Christ.

5. For as the sufferings of Christ abound in us, so our consolation also aboundeth by Christ. As the problems increase so does the consolation. Both, in this case, are measured by the experience of Christ (cf. Lk 24:26, 46; Phil 3:10; Col 1:24; I Pet 1:11). Paul's use of the term "abound" is significant throughout this epistle (cf. II Cor 4:15; 8:2, 7-8, 12).

6 And whether we be afflicted, *it is* for your consolation and salvation, which is effectual in the enduring of the same sufferings which we also suffer: or whether we be comforted, *it is* for your consolation and salvation.

7 And our hope of you *is* stedfast, knowing, that as ye are partakers of the sufferings, so *shall ye be* also of the consolation.

6-7. Many ancient manuscripts differ in the order of the clauses in these verses. But the sense in every case is basically the same: "if we are afflicted, it is for your good, or if we are comforted, it is for your good." Everything else, in these verses, is subordinated to these two main ideas. Paul does not glory in suffering, per se. But, he knows that the fact of suffering identifies us with Christ and with His church (cf. also Rom 8:17). He also knows that **as ye are partakers of the sufferings, so shall ye be also of the consolation.** If we should suffer together, then we know that we shall also rejoice together. Those who share mutual suffering and affliction share also in the joy of consolation. This relationship of intimacy implied by the apostle's terminology stands in stark contrast to the divisive spirit that persisted in Corinth. His readers could not help but compare their own situation against the feelings and experiences expressed by Paul.

8 For we would not, brethren, have you ignorant of our trouble which came to us in Asia, that we were pressed out of measure, above strength, insomuch that we despaired even of life:

9 But we had the sentence of death in ourselves, that we should not trust in ourselves, but in God which raiseth the dead:

10 Who delivered us from so great a death, and doth deliver: in whom we trust that he will yet deliver *us;*

8-10. Paul draws upon his recent experience to do two things: to share with his readers his needs and concerns, and also, to explain his change in plans. **We despaired even of life** and the expression, **we had the sentence of death in ourselves** are parallel concepts. Paul's condition, due to external pressures and physical limitations, reached the point where the only way out, visible to him, was death (cf. Acts 14:19). Yet God's purpose, even in this, was being fulfilled so that Paul would come to the end of himself and trust in **God which raiseth the dead.** For Paul has initiated a process of faith that is viewed in a threefold sense, **Who delivered us** (past) . . . **and doth deliver** (present) . . . **he will yet deliver** (future). Faith liberated Paul from bondage to his circumstances and the fear of death (cf. Heb 2:14-15).

11 Ye also helping together by prayer for us, that for the gift *bestowed* upon us by the means of many persons thanks may be given by many on our behalf.

11. Helping together probably has reference to their cooperation in interceding on his behalf with the other churches. Paul's thinking in this verse is very much like that in verses 6-7. Since there were many who where sharing together in **prayer for us,** then the fact of Paul's deliverance may also elicit **thanks . . . by many on our behalf.** The preposition **by** (Gr *dia*) is best rendered "by means of." Thus the sense of the verse is: as health was rendered by means of prayer so also thanksgiving to God is rendered by means of many who shared in that prayer.

II. APOLOGY FOR PAUL'S MINISTRY. 1:12-7:16.

A. The Conduct of Paul. 1:12-2:17.

In this opening section the Apostle Paul has three concerns: (1) his change of plans (1:22-2:4); (2) his charge concerning the offender (2:5-11); and (3) his confidence in the Corinthians to do what is right (2:12-17). In the opening section he alludes to his desire to come again to Corinth. It was on this score that he had been criticized by his enemies in the church. They accused him of promising them a visit with no intention of ever coming. It is this allegation that the apostle answers here.

I. Paul's change of plans. 1:12-2:4.

a. His concern. 1:12-14.

12 For our rejoicing is this, the testimony of our conscience, that in simplicity and godly sincerity, not with fleshly wisdom, but by the grace of God, we have had our conversation in the world, and more abundantly to you-ward.

12. The testimony of our conscience may suggest the "ground" of his rejoicing, or the "substance" of his rejoicing. The latter idea seems to fit best with what follows. Paul was able to rejoice in a ministry of **simplicity and godly sincerity.**

13 For we write none other things unto you, than what ye read or acknowledge; and I trust ye shall acknowledge even to the end;

14 As also ye have acknowledged us

13-14. For we write none other things unto you, than what ye read or acknowledge. Paul's epistles are characterized by the same degree of honesty and integrity that characterize his life. **Ye have acknowledged us in part.** Most in Corinth stood with the apostles in affirming his integrity. On the other hand, there

in part, that we are your rejoicing, even as ye also *are* ours in the day of the Lord Jesus.

15 And in this confidence I was minded to come unto you before, that ye might have a second benefit:
16 And to pass by you into Macedonia, and to come again out of Macedonia unto you, and of you to be brought on my way toward Judæa.

17 When I therefore was thus minded, did I use lightness? or the things that I purpose, do I purpose according to the flesh, that with me there should be yea yea, and nay nay?
18 But *as* God *is* true, our word toward you was not yea and nay.

19 For the Son of God, Jesus Christ, who was preached among you by us, *even* by me and Sīl-vā′nus and Tī-mō′the-us, was not yea and nay, but in him was yea.

20 For all the promises of God in him *are* yea, and in him Amen, unto the glory of God by us.
21 Now he which stablisheth us with you in Christ, and hath anointed us, *is* God;
22 Who hath also sealed us, and given the earnest of the Spirit in our hearts.

23 Moreover I call God for a record upon my soul, that to spare you I came not as yet unto Corinth.

was a small contingency of individuals who did not. **We.** This is an editorial use of the pronoun to refer to the apostle himself. **Your rejoicing.** Those who appreciated the apostle's ministry. **Ye are also ours.** Likewise, the apostle rejoiced in those who received his ministry. **In the day of the Lord Jesus.** In the day when all the secrets of men are revealed, Paul was confident that these believers would have the assurance that their faith in him was not misplaced.

b. His plan. 1:15-22.

15-16. In this confidence refers to the confidence which elicited their rejoicing in the previous verse. **I was minded to come unto you.** In Paul's initial itinerary he intended to go immediately from Ephesus to Corinth. **Second benefit** must not be misconstrued as Paul's second visit to them, since he had already visited them twice (cf. 12:14). But, that in his trip he would be seeing them twice: as he explains, **to pass by you into Macedonia, and to come again out of Macedonia unto you.** Thus he would be visiting with them twice before he went on his way to Judaea. **And of you to be brought on my way** (Gr *propempō*, "to be aided in my journey"). Following the custom of ancient times, since Paul would be traveling immediately to Judaea from Corinth, it would be appropriate for the assembly to assist him financially.

17-18. When I therefore was thus minded, did I use lightness? Here Paul avers the sincerity of his purpose. Nor did he intend any secular advantages to himself **according to the flesh . . . there should be yea, yea, and nay, nay?** The apostle cannot be charged with inconsistency. That which he affirmed he affirms still. That which he denies, he denies still. Hence, **as God is true, our word toward you was not yea and nay.** As the truth of God stands so does the word of the apostle (cf. also Gal 1:8; I Jn 5:10). The trustworthiness of Paul's words are seen in the nature of his gospel.

19. Jesus Christ, who was preached among you by us . . . was not yea and nay. Those who truly knew the Lord as Saviour in the Corinthian assembly could hardly doubt the veracity of this statement. They had received and experienced the reality of saving faith and knew that Paul's words were true.

20-22. For all the promises of God in him are yea (lit., "as many promises of God"). The thrust of this expression is that the promises of God find their affirmation and fulfillment in Christ. **Amen** is equivalent to "yea." Whether one is a Gentile (yea) or a Hebrew (amen) the promises of God are sure. But the force of Paul's analogy is that his word is as good as the gospel because **he which stablisheth us with you in Christ . . . is God.** The same God who conceived and consummated the redemption of lost humanity energized the apostolic ministry. **Who hath also sealed us.** The sealing of the Holy Spirit has a threefold significance in the New Testament: (1) to indicate ownership; (2) to indicate genuineness; and (3) to preserve and keep safe (cf. Eph 1:3; 4:30; II Tim 2:19; Rev 7:2). This last idea is amplified with **the earnest of the Spirit.** The Holy Spirit Himself is the down payment, or pledge, or redemption. The indwelling Spirit is the surety and the "security" of all that is to follow in the final salvation of the believer (cf. Rom 8:9-11, 23; Eph 1:14; II Cor 5:5).

c. His explanation. 1:23-2:4.

In 1:23-2:4 Paul explains the reason he has waited before coming to Corinth. He said he was not desirous of causing any more sorrow among them. His desire was that he would come with joy instead of anguish.

23. To spare you I came not as yet. The apostle was eagerly desirous of seeing the Corinthian assembly again, but even more than that he was concerned that when he got there he would have a positive ministry among them.

24 Not for that we have dominion over your faith, but are helpers of your joy: for by faith ye stand.

24. Not that we have dominion over your faith. Paul does not want to "pull rank." He does not wish to dictate to them in an authoritarian way, as he goes on to express, **we . . . are helpers of your joy.** In light of the present state of affairs this could hardly be enhanced if Paul came immediately. **By faith ye stand.** Our strength and stability are grounded in our faith, not our acquiescence to some human authority, whence also must flow our comfort and joy.

CHAPTER 2

BUT I determined this with myself, that I would not come again to you in heaviness.

2:1. But I determined this with myself. Over and above Paul's commitment to visit the Corinthian assembly according to his original itinerary was a commitment to himself that **I would not come again to you in heaviness.** While there is no mention of it in the book of Acts it is clear from 12:14 21 and 13:1 of this epistle that Paul had already visited the Corinthian church after writing I Corinthians for the purpose of correcting abuses and dealing directly with those who were challenging his ministry and authority. Paul had vowed within himself that he would not allow this to happen again.

2 For if I make you sorry, who is he then that maketh me glad, but the same which is made sorry by me?

2. If there are those in the assembly who think Paul derived any degree of satisfaction from his previous visit Paul assures them that it inflicted no small amount of hurt to his own heart. **If I make you sorry, who is he then that maketh me glad?** The greatest joy the minister of the gospel can experience is to see that his spiritual children are walking in the truth (cf. III Jn 4). Conversely, nothing is more painful than to have to employ the rod of correction. Paul derived no joy from that last encounter and the anxiety is still with him, as reflected in these verses.

3 And I wrote this same unto you, lest, when I came, I should have sorrow from them of whom I ought to rejoice; having confidence in you all, that my joy is the joy of you all.

3. And I wrote this same unto you. That is, I gave instructions regarding disciplinary measures that were necessary in the assembly (cf. I Cor 5-6). **Lest, when I came, I should have sorrow from them of whom I ought to rejoice.** His desire is that they would take care of these measures themselves so that when he came he would be able to rejoice in a congregation that acted obediently and he would see that it had elicited repentant hearts and the restoration of those who had been disciplined.

4 For out of much affliction and anguish of heart I wrote unto you with many tears; not that ye should be grieved, but that ye might know the love which I have more abundantly unto you.

4. For. Connects with the preceding verse to show why he wrote. **Affliction . . . anguish . . . tears.** All characterize Paul's emotional condition as he penned the letter to the Corinthians. **I wrote unto you.** Doubtless, this refers to a letter now lost. It could not refer to I Corinthians because, while he did have to deal with some difficulties in that epistle, it could have hardly been characterized as he describes here. **That ye might know the love which I have.** It is not frustration which motivates the apostle but deep concern and love for a group of people whom he considers to be his spiritual children.

2. *Paul's charge concerning the offender. 2:5-11.*

Since by this time the apostle has heard the report from Titus (cf. vss. 12-14) he now knows that they have, indeed, followed his advice. They have disciplined one offender at least in the assembly and it has produced such radical results the apostle now finds it necessary to give some additional counsel regarding this particular matter (vss. 5-11).

5 But if any have caused grief, he hath not grieved me, but in part: that I may not overcharge you all.

5. If any have caused grief (lit., if there is anyone in the assembly who has caused sorrow). Paul is generalizing in order to state a principle. At the same time he is speaking specifically to the situation recorded in I Corinthians 5:1-13. **He hath not grieved me, but in part: that I may not overcharge you all.** The sentence structure is awkward here and the sense is difficult to derive from the AV. Here Paul is saying, to paraphrase, "if someone has caused grief in the assembly, his offense is not so much against the apostle as it is against the local assembly, to put it mildly." For this reason the obligation of discipline lies not on the shoulders of the apostle but on the leadership of the

6 Sufficient to such a man *is* this punishment, which *was inflicted* of many.

7 So that contrariwise ye *ought* rather to forgive *him*, and comfort *him*, lest perhaps such a one should be swallowed up with overmuch sorrow.

8 Wherefore I beseech you that ye would confirm *your* love toward him.

9 For to this end also did I write, that I might know the proof of you, whether ye be obedient in all things.

10 To whom ye forgive any thing, I *forgive* also: for if I forgave any thing, to whom I forgave *it*, for your sakes *forgave I it* in the person of Christ;

11 Lest Satan should get an advantage of us: for we are not ignorant of his devices.

12 Furthermore, when I came to Troas to *preach* Christ's gospel, and a door was opened unto me of the Lord,

13 I had no rest in my spirit, because I found not Titus my brother: but taking my leave of them, I went from thence into Macedonia.

14 Now thanks *be* unto God, which

local church, and Paul is prepared to go along with their decision (cf. vs. 10). Tasker follows Menzies in suggesting that the offender in view is not the one mentioned in I Corinthians 5:1. On the contrary, he suggests that the person is not guilty of immoral conduct but rude and disagreeable conduct. It is asserted that it is quite contrary to the moral position of Paul to say that he could have ever tolerated the presence of the incestuous person in the church (R. V. G. Tasker, *The Second Epistle of Paul to the Corinthians*, p. 52). To this two things need to be said. First, while this view commends itself, Tasker fails to show how it is concluded without question that the person involved had been guilty of rude and disagreeable conduct. Secondly, Paul has already cited the fact that his forgiveness, and certainly that of the Lord, has been extended to persons guilty of grossly immoral conduct (cf. I Cor 6:9-11). Therefore, the view favored by the majority of the older commentators is to be preferred here; that is, that the offender involved is the incestuous person mentioned in chapter 5 of I Corinthians.

6-8. Sufficient to such a man is this punishment. Your discipline of this individual is enough. Paul sensed that they had gone far enough in bringing this person to repentance. His advice now is to, **forgive . . . and comfort . . . lest perhaps such a one should be swallowed up with overmuch sorrow.** The purpose of discipline is not to destroy but to edify and restore. Therefore, when true repentance is evidenced the proper response is to **Confirm your love toward him.** Paul goes on to express why he instructed the church to administer discipline.

9. That I might know the proof of you. Paul needed to know that the Corinthian assembly possessed the maturity and character to deal with sin in their midst. It is now clear to him that they did. In 1:3-4 Paul indicated that God's comfort was designed to be shared. Here is Paul's application of this principle in the context of church discipline. As they had received God's forgiveness they are to forgive.

10. To whom ye forgive any thing, I forgive also. Paul awaits the church's decision. He was prepared to sanction their ruling on the matter. Notice here that there is no hierarchical structure dictating to the local church. The ruling authority was the local church.

11. Lest Satan should get an advantage of us. Such an advantage could be gained by Satan either by the despair of an individual Christian, or the disunity of the local assembly through the incident in view. **For we are not ignorant of his devices.** Paul knows that Satan can and will use this incident to distract and diminish the work of God in the Corinthian assembly unless it is properly handled. Satan's first attack is against the gospel (cf. II Cor 4:4). If he can bring disunity to the church, which is the agent of propagating the gospel, then he will also bring dishonor upon the gospel. The church which God can best use is the church which exudes God's forgiveness and consolation (on Satan's devices see also 10:3-4; 11:3, 12-14).

3. Paul's confidence in the Corinthians. 2:12-17.

12-13. When I came to Troas . . . a door was opened unto me of the Lord. The connection of this verse is with verse 4: "that ye might know the love which I have." Further evidence of this love is Paul's behavior while engaged in a very fruitful ministry in Troas: **I had no rest in my spirit.** Paul's concern for the evangelization of the lost was overridden by his concern for the Corinthian assembly, and that was saying something (cf. I Cor 9:16)! It is not love for the lost nor love for the world which distinguishes the believer. It is love for one another (Jn 13:35). **But taking leave of them I went . . . into Macedonia.** This was in hopes of meeting Titus on the way. On Titus' report to Paul about the condition of things in Corinth, see 7:5-6.

14-17. Triumph (cf. Col 2:9-15). The imagery conveyed in

always causeth us to triumph in Christ, and maketh manifest the savour of his knowledge by us in every place.

15 For we are unto God a sweet savour of Christ, in them that are saved, and in them that perish:

16 To the one we are the savour of death unto death; and to the other the savour of life unto life. And who is sufficient for these things?

17 For we are not as many, which corrupt the word of God: but as of sincerity, but as of God, in the sight of God speak we in Christ.

CHAPTER 3

DO we begin again to commend ourselves? or need we, as some others, epistles of commendation to you, or letters of commendation from you?

2 Ye are our epistle written in our hearts, known and read of all men:

3 Forasmuch as ye are manifestly declared to be the epistle of Christ ministered by us, written not with ink, but with the Spirit of the living God; not in tables of stone, but in fleshy tables of the heart.

4 And such trust have we through Christ to God-ward:

5 Not that we are sufficient of ourselves to think any thing as of ourselves; but our sufficiency is of God;

6 Who also hath made us able minis-

the use of this term is of the Roman general who marched in victory with his entourage, consisting of two groups: **Them that are saved, and . . . them that perish.** The former group consisted of those allowed to live as slaves of the Empire. They were being led into a new life. The latter group were the condemned. They were being led to their death. Each group carried a burning incense. The one was a **savor of death unto death,** the other was a fragrance of **life unto life.** Calvary was the mighty display of the infinite power of a sovereign God. The human race was divided into two categories: those of life unto life and those of death unto death. The practical lesson here is that the believer is a "savor" of God's infinite power and unspeakable love wherever he goes. Also, as the believer proclaims this truth, he divides men. This is not a "method" of evangelism, but a proclamation of the triumph of Christ at Calvary. **Who is sufficient for these things?** The implied answer to Paul's question is "I am." Paul's credentials are given in the words **as . . . in the sight of God speak we in Christ** (lit., "but as from sincerity, but as from God, we speak in Christ in the sight of God"). The apostle's adequacy is not within himself, but God (cf. 3:5). This is in contrast to those who merely **corrupt the word of God** (Gr kapēleuō, should read, "are peddling the Word of God").

B. The Calling of Paul. 3:1-6:10.

1. The superiority of his ministry. 3:1-4:6.

a. The credentials of his ministry. 3:1-5.

3:1. Do we begin again to commend ourselves? The apostle is incredulous that a formal introduction to a church he founded should be necessary. **Epistles of commendation to you.** Such letters of introduction constituted a common practice in New Testament times (cf. Acts 9:1-2; 18:27). Due to the prevailing social, political, and religious climate, such letters were both advisable and necessary. Paul here does not disparage their use. He can only be amazed that the Corinthian believers require it of him.

2-3. Ye are our epistle. Paul's converts at Corinth were living testimonials to the genuineness of his ministry. **Our hearts.** Paul employs the plural in agreement with the use of the editorial "we" throughout this passage. **Known and read of all men.** To any who would "take up and read" Paul's ministry was authenticated (cf. I Cor 9:2). **The epistle of Christ ministered by us.** The apostle is always careful to show that the enabling power of his ministry did not reside in himself but in Christ (cf. I Cor 15:9-10). This epistle is distinguished in two ways. First, it is **not written with ink, but with the Spirit of the living God.** It was supernaturally composed. Second, it was written **not in tables of stone, but in the fleshy tables of the heart.** The contrast is with the law of Moses. The force of the comparison is that Moses' law is external. The law of the Spirit is internal.

4-5. Such trust (lit., "such confidence"). Not only in the genuineness of the Corinthians' conversion experience but also, in a general sense, **to God-ward.** Paul was not "self-confident" but "God-confident." **Not that we are sufficient of ourselves** ("not that we are competent from ourselves"). "Sufficient" occurs three times in verses 5 and 6. **To think anything** (Gr logizomai, "to think out," "to judge," "to reckon"). Paul's competency to give account of what God did at Corinth in the hearts of his converts does not reside in himself, but his **sufficiency is of God.**

b. The quality of his ministry. 3:6-4:6.

(1) The glory of the New Covenant. 3:6-11.

6. Who also. The relative pronoun here does two things.

ters of the new testament; not of the letter, but of the spirit: for the letter killeth, but the spirit giveth life.

7 But if the ministration of death, written *and* engraven in stones, was glorious, so that the children of Israel could not stedfastly behold the face of Moses for the glory of his countenance; which *glory* was to be done away:
8 How shall not the ministration of the spirit be rather glorious?

9 For if the ministration of condemnation *be* glory, much more doth the ministration of righteousness exceed in glory.
10 For even that which was made glorious had no glory in this respect, by reason of the glory that excelleth.
11 For if that which is done away *was* glorious, much more that which remaineth *is* glorious.

12 Seeing then that we have such hope, we use great plainness of speech:

13 And not as Moses, *which* put a vail over his face, that the children of Israel could not stedfastly look to the end of that which is abolished:

14 But their minds were blinded: for until this day remaineth the same vail untaken away in the reading of the old testament; which *vail* is done away in Christ.

15 But even unto this day, when Moses is read, the vail is upon their heart.

First, it points us back to God and, second, it suggests cause or reason (see its use in Lk 8:13). **Hath made us able ministers** (lit., "made us competent ministers"). Here is the third instance of the term translated "sufficient" and "sufficiency" in verse 5. Having established his credentials for the ministry Paul is now elaborating on the distinctive qualities of his ministry. The first is that it was energized by God and not himself or any human agency. The second is that it was of the new testament ("new covenant"). **New** because it was not inaugurated until Christ (cf. Mt 26:28; Lk 22:7-23; I Cor 11:25; Heb 8:8;9:15). **Not of the letter, but of the spirit.** This expression corresponds with the thought of verse 3 contrasting "ink" with the "Spirit." The contrast is with the externalism inherent in the old covenant and the internalism inherent in the New Covenant. **The letter killeth, but the spirit giveth life.** Paul explains his thought here more fully in Romans 7:6-11. Since there were certain Judaists in the assembly at Corinth who were concerned with Paul's defection from Moses' law, Paul here explains. The best the law could do was condemn the sinner but the **spirit giveth life.** It is not here implied that the law of Moses was evil. On the contrary, it is holy, just, and good (cf. Rom 7:21). This can be asserted because it brought men to the end of themselves, to Christ (cf. Gal 3:24).

7-8. Yet this contrast has even further implications. The old covenant **was glorious.** Paul alludes to the incident in Exodus 34:29-35. The old covenant, limited as it was, nevertheless, was so glorious that it caused the face of Moses to radiate. Now if this **ministration of death,** which was only a transient and temporary measure, so manifested the glory of God **How shall not the ministration of the spirit be rather glorious?** Not only is Paul's message "new," it is also "better" (cf. Heb 9:11-28; 10:11-22).

9-11. The ministry of the gospel of grace in Christ surpasses the old covenant so much that **that which is made glorious had no glory.** The import of this is again reiterated in the word **if that which is done away was glorious, much more that which remaineth is glorious.**

The Apostle Paul's ministration of the new covenant is justified not only by its surpassing glory (vss. 1-11), but also, its surpassing permanence (vss. 12-18).

(2). The permanence of the New Covenant. 3:12-18.

12. Seeing then that we have such hope. The "confidence" of verse 4 has now issued in "hope." This hope originates in the expectation that if the old covenant was accompanied by the unsurpassed glory of God how much more can we anticipate the new covenant to be accompanied by glory. **We use great plainness of speech.** Paul now becomes very explicit.

13. And not as Moses. What follows is an allegorization of the account given in Exodus 34:29-35. **Put a veil over his face.** The veil was not to hide the glory but to obscure it. The people saw his brightness but not directly). Not only did this veil actually conceal the brightness of the glory but it also concealed the **end of that which was abolished.** The transience of the glory which accompanied the old covenant was not manifestly evident to the children of Israel. And for Paul this has typical significance.

14. Their minds were blinded: for until this day remaineth the same veil. For Israel the same obscurity obtains. Their minds are still blinded to the truth as though the veil upon Moses' face were thrown upon their hearts. **Which veil is done away in Christ.** Only the gospel of God's grace exposes the truth to full view.

15. But even unto this day, when Moses is read, the veil is upon their heart. Unfortunately, as far as the Jews are concerned, Christ is still a stumbling block they cannot see (cf.

I Cor 1:23). For the apostle this is no light matter but a concern which caused him great anxiety (cf. Rom 9:1-4). But now the veil is not so much upon the revelation of the glory but upon their own hearts (cf. Lk 24:25; Acts 13:27-29).

16 Nevertheless when it shall turn to the Lord, the vail shall be taken away.

16. Nevertheless, when it shall turn to the Lord, the veil shall be taken away. The practice of Moses of removing the veil when he turned to the Lord to speak with Him directly is in view here (Ex 34:29-35). In the same sense, when Israel turns once again to the Lord, she will see and understand—the veil will be removed.

17 Now the Lord is that Spirit: and where the Spirit of the Lord is, there is liberty.

17. Now connects the reference to "the Lord" in the previous verse with the reference to **the Lord** in the present verse. This Lord is Christ (cf. vs. 14). **Is that Spirit.** While the article does not appear in the original text the AV has properly rendered the sense when it includes "that" before Spirit. Paul is not saying "the Lord is Spirit" (in the same sense that is indicated in Jn 4:24) but "the Lord is the Holy Spirit, the Third Person of the Godhead." It is also important to note here that Paul is not confusing the two Persons. Jesus said earlier, "I and my Father are one" (Jn 10:30). He bears the same relationship to the Holy Spirit. Here is the ineffable mystery of the Trinity, one in essence yet three distinct personalities. **And where the Spirit of the Lord is, there is liberty.** Indeed, when Israel turns once again to the Lord and the veil is removed, there is glorious liberty that comes with the confrontation with the truth (cf. Jn 8:32; 14:6, 17; 15:26). For further insight into the relationship of the Holy Spirit to the ministry of Christ see Jn 14:16-17,26;15:26-27; and 16:7.

18 But we all, with open face beholding as in a glass the glory of the Lord, are changed into the same image from glory to glory, even as by the Spirit of the Lord.

18. But we all. Reaching a climax, based upon the experience of Moses and Israel. Paul now applies the truth to all his readers. **With open face beholding as in a glass.** As though looking at a clear reflection in a mirror. **The glory of the Lord.** As Moses' face reflected God's glory at Sinai the face of every believer radiates the glory of Christ. That which was reserved for only the highest under the old covenant is made available to all in the new. Some commentaries have attempted to identify the mirror in this text with Christ, the Word, or the believer's heart. This, however, is difficult to justify from the context. What the apostle has in mind, specifically, is difficult to say. The term "beholding" can have the sense of "reflecting." Thus, in agreement with Lenski (*The Interpretation of I and II Corinthians*, pp. 947-948), the believer himself "reflects" the glory of the Lord just as the face of Moses reflected the glory of the Lord. This view fits most favorably with Paul's imagery.

Yet there is more. For Moses the glory eventually faded away, but under the New Covenant the believer is **changed into the same image.** Paul has already established that, ". . . as we have borne the image of the earthy, we shall also bear the image of the heavenly" (I Cor 15:49). The Apostle John says that ultimately we will be just like Christ because ". . . we shall see him as he is" (I Jn 3:2). (see also I Pet 1:4; Gal 4:19; and Jn 17:17). **Even as by the Spirit of the Lord** (lit., "as from the Lord the Spirit"). This transformation takes place by the abiding presence of the Spirit of God.

(3). The ministry of the New Covenant. 4:1-6.

CHAPTER 4
THEREFORE seeing we have this ministry, as we have received mercy, we faint not;

4:1. Therefore, seeing we have this ministry, as we have received mercy, we faint not. In light of the superiority and character of the gospel of Jesus Christ under the new covenant, the Apostle Paul vigorously and enthusiastically assumes the task of proclaiming its message everywhere. The expression **we faint not** has the sense that Paul was not derelict in discharging his responsibilities to this ministry.

2 But have renounced the hidden things of dishonesty, not walking in craftiness, nor handling the word of

2. But (the strong adversative). What follows stands in sharp contrast to the last statement of verse 1. What Paul denies of himself he affirms of the false teachers at Corinth (C. Hodge,

God deceitfully; but by manifestation of the truth commending ourselves to every man's conscience in the sight of God.

3 But if our gospel be hid, it is hid to them that are lost:

4 In whom the god of this world hath blinded the minds of them which believe not, lest the light of the glorious gospel of Christ, who is the image of God, should shine unto them.

5 For we preach not ourselves, but Christ Jesus the Lord; and ourselves your servants for Jesus' sake.

6 For God, who commanded the light to shine out of darkness, hath shined in our hearts, to give the light of the knowledge of the glory of God in the face of Jesus Christ.

Commentary on the Second Epistle to the Corinthians, p. 82). In that regard, Paul demonstrates that he has **renounced the hidden things of dishonesty**. This may have reference to either disgraceful conduct or secret motives. The latter idea is best since the emphasis is upon "hidden things." The apostle's ministry was one of openness and honesty. He was **not walking in craftiness**. The apostle was not an opportunist nor shrewdly and unscrupulously seeking to achieve his desired aims. **Nor handling the word of God deceitfully** (cf. 2:17). Paul was not "peddling the Word of God" or adulterating it with false doctrine. Paul could say "I have received of the Lord that which also I delivered unto you" (I Cor 11:23). That which Paul preached was exactly as God revealed it to him. It was **the manifestation of the truth**. In contrast to those in the Corinthian assembly who were giving undue stress to human credentials Paul's message commended itself to **every man's conscience in the sight of God**.

3. **But if our gospel be hid.** Carrying over the analogy of the veil in the preceding chapter, such a veil conceals the truth only from **them that are lost**.

4. **In whom the God of this world hath blinded the minds of them which believe not.** On Satan's control of the world system see Matthew 4:8-9; John 12:31; 14:30; I Corinthians 10:20; Ephesians 2:2; 6:12; II Timothy 2:26. The "lost" of verse 3 are the "unbelievers" of this verse. Such ones are so controlled by Satan that he effectively shields them from the **light of the glorious gospel of Christ**. There are two vital inferences that must be drawn from this passage. The first is contextual. The apostle effectively categorizes those who find his message difficult to accept. In effect, he is saying that the person who is criticizing his ministry at Corinth is not even saved. He is lost, unbelieving, and has been blinded by Satan. The second inference is theological. For those who inordinately stress human freedom it must be observed here and elsewhere that the unregenerate man is in bondage. He is under satanic control and is, therefore, incompetent to evaluate the truth of God.

5. **For** connects with the preceding verse. **We preach not ourselves but Christ Jesus the Lord.** Paul's message was clear and simple and could be summed up in a word, or even better, in a name, i.e., Christ Jesus. The singular object of Paul's preaching was to confront men with the person of Christ. **And ourselves your servants for Jesus' sake.** As a minister of the gospel, Paul is not his own man. He is a slave of his constituents and compelled by his Master.

6. **For.** The particle connects with the preceding verse and forms the basis for it. **God, who commanded the light to shine out of darkness.** This contemplates the old creation. Genesis 1:3. **Hath shined in our hearts.** This contemplates the new creation. Some suggest that "our" is used editorially to speak of the apostle himself. The reference would thus connect primarily with such passages as Acts 9:3-6; 26:15-16; Galatians 1:15-16. However, the plural "hearts" seems to lend more support to the notion that Paul here has in mind all believers, not just himself. Thus, the miracle of the new birth while not always accompanied by an outward manifestation of lights such as the experience of Paul, nevertheless involves a spiritual illumination concomitant with Paul's experience on the road to Damascus. **To give the light** (lit., "for illumination"). Just as the comfort of God is to be shared (cf. 1:3-4) even so the light which penetrates the darkness and regenerates the soul is to be reflected to others, and for Paul that constituted the essence of the gospel ministry. Specifically, for Paul this light was **the knowledge of the glory of God in the face of Jesus Christ**. This calls to mind Acts 9:3-6. Yet the experience is nonetheless glorious for all who have seen the light (cf. Jn 1:1-14; 9:24-25, 35-41; I Cor 2:10-14).

2. The suffering in his ministry. 4:7-12.

Having discussed his credentials for the ministry (3:1-5), and then in much more detail the specific quality of his ministry (3:6-4:6), Paul now gives attention to his personal suffering in the ministry (4:7-12).

7. We have this treasure in earthen vessels. In the wilderness under the old covenant God dwelt in a tent; today He dwells in the believer's heart. This is unspeakable truth and forms the theological rationale for holy living (cf. I Cor 6:19-20). But the stress here is upon "earthen." An earthenware jar is a brittle one. It depicts humanity in its weakness. The gospel is not a product of human genius or clever intellect (humanity in its strength). Yet it resides in men of clay, **that the excellency of the power may be of God, and not of us.** The quality of the gospel ministry is calibrated by the degree to which it points attention to the God of glory.

8-9. We are troubled on every side, yet not distressed. The believer may be hard pressed but never crushed. He may be **perplexed** but he need never **despair.** Though he be **persecuted** he will never be abandoned. He may be **cast down** but he'll never be cast out.

10-12. Always bearing about in the body the dying of the Lord Jesus. The persecution and suffering and the trial which confronts the believer are to be understood as the "fellowship of his suffering" (cf. Phil 3:10; I Cor 15:31; 4:9; II Cor 11:23; Rom 8:36; Gal 6:17). **That the life also of Jesus might be made manifest in our body.** This same thought occurs in Romans 8:17. If we share in His suffering we will also share in His glory (cf. II Tim 2:11; I Pet 4:13-14; Rom 6:8-9; Jn 14:19).

We which live (lit., "the living"). **That the life also of Jesus might be made manifest in our mortal flesh.** A diamond is best seen against a black background. The brilliance of the life that is in Christ Jesus is best seen against the background of death. **So then death worketh in us.** Paul relates this to his own personal ministry. **Us** is used editorially to refer to the apostle himself. **But life in you.** Through a ministry of weakness and suffering Paul was able to accomplish a very positive ministry in Corinth (cf. I Cor 2:1-4). The tone is not ironic such as that in I Corinthians 4:8-10.

The Apostle Paul was able to endure suffering in his ministry not only because he knew that his message was vastly superior to anything offered in the old covenant but also because the gospel of Christ assured him of the glorious prospect of going far beyond the present exigencies of life. This subject he deals with in 4:13-5:10.

3. The goal of his ministry. 4:13-5:10.

a. Hope of the Resurrection. 4:13-15.

13. We having the same spirit of faith. That is, the same Spirit of 3:17, who is the Holy Spirit, often designated by the effects which He produces (e.g., He is called the Spirit of adoption, Rom 8:15; the Spirit of wisdom, Eph 1:17; the Spirit of grace, Heb 10:29; the Spirit of glory, I Pet 4:14). Here He is so called because He is the Spirit who produces faith. Thus, in much the same way that David expressed himself in Psalm 116:10, Paul extolls the goodness of God. **We also believe, and therefore speak.** The assurance in Paul's heart because of faith caused him to proclaim the gospel with utter confidence in its truth.

14. Knowing. This indicates the basis for the confidence expressed in the preceding verse. **He which raised up the Lord Jesus** refers to the literal, bodily resurrection of Jesus Christ. **Shall raise up us also by Jesus.** Personal affliction and death become of little consequence when measured against the pros-

---

7 But we have this treasure in earthen vessels, that the excellency of the power may be of God, and not of us.

8 *We are* troubled on every side, yet not distressed; *we are* perplexed, but not in despair;

9 Persecuted, but not forsaken; cast down, but not destroyed;

10 Always bearing about in the body the dying of the Lord Jesus, that the life also of Jesus might be made manifest in our body.

11 For we which live are alway delivered unto death for Jesus' sake, that the life also of Jesus might be made manifest in our mortal flesh.

12 So then death worketh in us, but life in you.

13 We having the same spirit of faith, according as it is written, I believed, and therefore have I spoken; we also believe, and therefore speak;

14 Knowing that he which raised up the Lord Jesus shall raise up us also by Jesus, and shall present *us* with you.

pect of resurrection. **And shall present us with you.** This prospect was expressed by Jude, who said, Thanks be "... unto him that is able to ... present you faultless before the presence of his glory with exceeding joy" (Jude 24; cf. II Cor 11:2 and Col 1:22). The thought is similar to that of I Corinthians 15:19-22 in the idea of "the first fruits." Throughout pauline literature the resurrection of Christ is seen as evidence of the resurrection of the believer (Rom 8:11; I Cor 6:14; Eph 2:6; Col 2:12; I Thess 4:14).

15 For all things *are* for your sakes, that the abundant grace might through the thanksgiving of many redound to the glory of God.

15. For all things are for your sakes. Everything the apostle endured to carry the gospel to Corinth was for their benefit. **That** ("in order that"). The ultimate purpose was **the glory of God** and this Paul envisions as being directly proportional to the sum of gratitude offered in thanksgiving to God for His grace.

b. Confidence in ministry. 4:16-18.

16 For which cause we faint not; but though our outward man perish, yet the inward *man* is renewed day by day.

16. For which cause. The certainty of the glorious resurrection. **We faint not.** In 4:1 the Apostle Paul uses this expression in response to the superiority of the New Covenant. Now he does so in anticipation of the glory of the New Covenant in the resurrection. **Though our outward man perish, yet the inward man is renewed day by day.** The physical body is temporal and passing away. It is subject to decay and, through affliction and suffering, is utterly worn out. Yet, the believer can rejoice that he has a life within that is increasing in vitality with every passing day. "The inward man" does not have reference to man's soul or immaterial nature but to a new life imparted to the believer (cf. Rom 7:22).

17 For our light affliction, which is but for a moment, worketh for us a far more exceeding *and* eternal weight of glory;
18 While we look not at the things which are seen, but at the things which are not seen: for the things which are seen *are* temporal; but the things which are not seen *are* eternal.

17-18. For our light affliction. Paul is being modest (see 11:16-33). The reader would hardly suspect how intense the affliction was for him. Yet Paul does not patronize his readers here, nor does he use irony. For the afflictions of life are **but for a moment.** And they work **a far more exceeding . . . weight of glory; while we look not at the things which are seen, but at the things which are not seen.** In the sufferings of life the power of God transforms the experience of the faithful Christian into glorious expectation.

Paul's confidence in the ministry expressed in the preceding verse is justified in 5:1-10. In 4:18 Paul says his eyes are not upon temporal things but heavenly. In the next section he explains what he means by that.

c. Contemplation of new life. 5:1-10.

CHAPTER 5
FOR we know that if our earthly house of *this* tabernacle were dissolved, we have a building of God, an house not made with hands, eternal in the heavens.

5:1. For we know. This knowledge is based on 4:13-14. It is the knowledge of faith which has already been ratified in the experience of Jesus Christ. **If our earthly house of this tabernacle were dissolved. Earthly** here has the sense of "terrestrial," i.e., that which is upon the earth (cf. I Cor 15:40). **Tabernacle** (Gr *skēnos*) is best rendered as "tent." The figure has reference to the physical body and the transient character of it. **Were dissolved** (Gr *katalyo*, "take down"). Appropriately used to signify "taking down a tent." Here it signifies physical death. **We have a building of God.** The tense shows that Paul reckons himself to be already in possession of this new building. This expresses certainty (Rom 8:30). In contrast to the old body the new body is pictured as a permanent dwelling: **A building of God, a house not made with hands, eternal in the heavens.** There are, generally, three views taken on this passage: (a) that the "house" is heaven itself; (b) that it has reference to an intermediate body provided at death; and (c) that it has reference to the resurrection body.

The first view fits well with John 14:2, but does not adequately account for the language of verses 1 and 2. The second view would seem to fit best with verses 6-9 and Philippians 1:23. However, it fails to account for Paul's clear teaching in I Corinthians 15 and I Thessalonians 4. The third view, that Paul contemplates the resurrection body, is supported by the following arguments. (1) To say that this transformation occurs at the time of death contradicts I Corinthians 15:51-52, that this occurs at the time of the Rapture of the church, not at death. (2) None of the churches established by Paul, or the early church fathers held to an intermediate body, as far as we know. (3) Paul, ordinarily, passes over the intermediate state in discussing the glorified body. (see Rom 8:23, 30; Col 3:4; Phil 3:20-21.) (4) Other New Testament writers also support this view (I Pet 1:7, 13; 4:13; I Jn 3:2; Mt 25:31-34; 16:27). (For further arguments see G. Peters, *The Theocratic Kingdom*, II, pp. 240, 41; 394-403).

Thus, the third view is to be preferred primarily for two reasons: the sheer weight of the evidence and its faithfulness to all the biblical data. It is incumbent on any student of the Word to speak where Scripture speaks and to remain silent where Scripture is silent. While it would be a worthy goal to be able to explain the intermediate state, such a noble objective does not justify the fabrication of a doctrine to do so. Thus the contrast in verse 1 is between the physical body and the resurrection body. The one is earthly and destined to be dismantled. The other is heavenly, designed and made by God, not human hands, and is eternal.

2 For in this we groan, earnestly desiring to be clothed upon with our house which is from heaven:

2. For in this we groan. In this earthly body. **Earnestly desiring to be clothed upon.** Not uncharacteristically Paul changes the metaphor. It is a house in verse 1, it is a garment in verse 2. **With our house which is from heaven.** The resurrection body.

3 If so be that being clothed we shall not be found naked.

3. If so be that being clothed we shall not be found naked. After the resurrection we will not be found without a body. Paul argues as he does in I Corinthians, for a "bodily resurrection" not merely a "spiritual resurrection."

4 For we that are in this tabernacle do groan, being burdened: not for that we would be unclothed, but clothed upon, that mortality might be swallowed up of life.

4. For we . . . do groan. Here again, due to the burdens of life (cf. Rom 8:23). **That mortality might be swallowed up of life.** The pressures and trials of life notwithstanding, Paul is further motivated by a much more positive motive. He anxiously awaits the day when he participates fully in the abundant life promised in heaven.

5 Now he that hath wrought us for the selfsame thing is God, who also hath given unto us the earnest of the Spirit.

5. The assurance of all this is **the earnest of the Spirit** (Gr *arrabōn*), meaning "the guarantee" or "pledge which is the Spirit." Paul views this in a twofold sense. First, the abiding presence of the Spirit Himself is a continual reminder of the certainty of Jesus' promises. Second, the Spirit Himself generates those inner longings, within the beast of the believer, that will only be satisfied when he sees Him face to face (cf. Rom 8:23).

6 Therefore we are always confident, knowing that, whilst we are at home in the body, we are absent from the Lord:

6. Therefore we are always confident. Paul's confidence is not a temporary feeling but a permanent state of mind. **Knowing that, whilst we are at home in the body, we are absent from the Lord.** So long as this earthly tent is our home our realization of heaven is detained.

7 (For we walk by faith, not by sight:)
8 We are confident, I say, and willing rather to be absent from the body, and to be present with the Lord.

7-8. (For we walk by faith, not by sight:) The AV correctly renders this as a parenthesis in Paul's thought for it answers to his confidence in verse 6 and again in verse 8. **We are confident, I say, and willing rather to be absent from the body, and to be present with the Lord.** All things being equal, Paul would just as soon take leave of this tabernacle and take up his residence with the Lord in glory.

9 Wherefore we labour, that, whether present or absent, we may be accepted of him.

9. Wherefore we labor, that, whether present or absent, we may be accepted of him. Paul lived every day with eternity's values in view.

10 For we must all appear before the judgment seat of Christ; that every one may receive the things done in his body, according to that he hath done, whether it be good or bad.

10. For we must all appear before the judgment seat of Christ. The **judgment seat** (Gr *bema*) was an elevated seat in the square at Corinth where Roman magistrates sat to administer justice and where the athletes who distinguished themselves in the arena received their reward. The judgment in view here is not of the unbeliever but of the believer (cf. I Cor 4:5; Col 3:4).

That every one may receive the things done in his body. That is, be rewarded for the deeds done in this life **whether it be good or bad.** While it is true that for the Christian there is "no condemnation" (Rom 8:1), it is not correct to assume that God will not hold him responsible for the deeds done in the body. Paul has already explicated this truth in I Corinthians 3:10-15.

4. The service in his ministry. 5:11-6:10.

Now Paul turns his attention to the import of all this in terms of his personal ministry. He discusses his motives (vss. 11-15), his message (vss. 16-21), and his methods (6:1-10).

a. Paul's motives. 5:11-15.

11. Knowing therefore indicates that what follows is inferred from that which precedes it. **The terror of the Lord.** This is best understood in the general sense of "the fear of the Lord" as it is found throughout the Scriptures (cf. Acts 7:1; 9:31; Rom 3:18; Eph 5:21). It denotes a deep reverence for God. Here it is particularly in view of the judgment seat, before which we all must stand. **We persuade men.** That is, of his own personal integrity as is also verified by the fact that **we are made manifest unto God; and I trust also are made manifest in your consciences.** "My character is known to God and I trust it is known to you as well."

11 Knowing therefore the terror of the Lord, we persuade men; but we are made manifest unto God; and I trust also are made manifest in your consciences.

12. We commend not ourselves again to you. Paul's object was not to glory in his credentials nor to prove his character to the Corinthians, but simply to authenticate his personal integrity. For the most part the Corinthian assembly by this time was convinced of Paul's genuineness but Paul was also aware that he still had enemies in the assembly and the purpose here is to give his followers **somewhat to answer them.**

12 For we commend not ourselves again unto you, but give you occasion to glory on our behalf, that ye may have somewhat to *answer* them which glory in appearance, and not in heart.

13. Paul's ministry was never motivated by or directed to self-interest. **Whether we be beside ourselves,** (to paraphrase, "if I appear out of my senses") **it is to God.** Paul may be introducing irony here. Some may well have thought he was insane to waste his time with an assembly that demonstrated so little appreciation for his ministry. Nevertheless, if his actions seemed to betray sound logic, he was only acting in obedience to God. **Or whether we be sober, it is for your cause.** The suggestion is that Paul's enthusiasm and spontaneity is held in check in order not to offend the Corinthian believers.

13 For whether we be beside ourselves, *it is* to God: or whether we be sober, *it is* for your cause.

14. For the love of Christ constraineth us. Whether Paul appeared to be out of control or under control, Christ's love for Paul held him in such a grip, that it constituted the compelling force in everything he did. **Because we thus judge.** We have thus concluded. **That if one died for all, then were all dead:** the first conviction to which Paul comes has to do with the total depravity of man. If the atoning death of Christ was for all, then it must follow that all are dead.

14 For the love of Christ constraineth us; because we thus judge, that if one died for all, then were all dead:

15. They which live should not henceforth live unto themselves. The second conviction to which Paul comes has to do with God's purpose in the redemption of man. He does not thereby release the shackled sinner to live henceforth unto himself but unto the One who **died for them** (cf. Rom 5:12-21; 6:1-8; I Cor 15:21-22; Gal 2:20; Eph 2:5-6). **And rose again.** The resurrection of Christ is as essential to the salvation of the sinner as the death of Christ (Rom 4:24-25). It also provides incentive to holy living.

15 And *that* he died for all, that they which live should not henceforth live unto themselves, but unto him which died for them, and rose again.

b. Paul's message. 5:16-21.

16. Now Paul turns his attention to his message (vss. 16-21). **Wherefore** (Gr *hoste,* "so that") is inferential. **Henceforth know we no man after the flesh:** For the Apostle Paul the death and resurrection of Jesus Christ has forever destroyed all human distinctions. **Yea, though we have known Christ after the flesh. We** is used editorially for Paul himself. He admits that

16 Wherefore henceforth know we no man after the flesh: yea, though we have known Christ after the flesh, yet now henceforth know we *him* no more.

there was a time when all he knew of Christ was what other men said about Him. **Yet now henceforth know we him no more.** Since the day he was saved, Paul could no longer think of Christ as just another man.

17 Therefore if any man *be* in Christ, *he is* a new creature: old things are passed away; behold, all things are become new.

17. Therefore. Paul infers, **if any man be in Christ, he is a new creature.** What Paul particularizes in verse 16 he generalizes in verse 17. The reason Paul could no longer think of Christ in carnal terms is because of the universal truth that has been applied to Him personally. When a man comes into vital union with the risen Lord he is a "new creation" (cf. Jn 3:3; 15:5; 8:1-9; Gal 6:14-15). **Old things are passed away.** The aorist tense indicates a decisive break with the old life at the moment of salvation. **Behold, all things are become new** (literally, "new things have come to be"). Paul changes to the perfect tense to stress the abiding results of the Christian's union with Christ (cf. Isa 43:18-19; 65:17; Rev 21:4-5; Eph 4:24).

18 And all things *are* of God, who hath reconciled us to himself by Jesus Christ, and hath given to us the ministry of reconciliation;
19 To wit, that God was in Christ, reconciling the world unto himself, not imputing their trespasses unto them; and hath committed unto us the word of reconciliation.

18-19. And all things are of God. All the "new things" introduced to the experience of those who are in Christ Jesus. **Who hath reconciled us to himself by Jesus Christ.** To "reconcile" (Gr *katallassō*) is to remove enmity between two enemy parties. In the strictest sense it involves "a change of mind." Since the sinner cannot do this for himself God does it through Jesus Christ in His sacrificial death (cf. Rom 5:9-10). **And hath given to us the ministry of reconciliation.** This is identical to the "word of reconciliation" in the next verse. This is announcing the good news **that God was in Christ, reconciling the world unto himself.** The great message of the apostle was that here was not just another man ("now we know no man after the flesh"). But here at the "end of the age" Christ, on Calvary's tree, put away sin forever (cf. Heb 10:5-12). **Not imputing their trespasses unto them.** Not to impute is to forgive (cf. Rom 4:5; Col 2:13; II Tim 4:16). The Greek present tense here emphasizes a continuous action (cf. I Jn 1:9).

20 Now then we are ambassadors for Christ, as though God did beseech *you* by us: we pray *you* in Christ's stead, be ye reconciled to God.

20. This ministry of reconciliation involves calling upon men to demonstrate a changed life and so Paul considered himself, and all who are truly born again, to be **ambassadors for Christ.** Paul did not usurp authority to himself. His ministry at Corinth was representative. His appeal to them is as though **God did beseech you by us** and his desire is, for the sake of Christ, for them to be **reconciled to God.** The verb is not active but passive. He does not call upon them to change themselves for he has already established that it is God who does the reconciling (vs. 18). Rather he is asking them to submit to the reconciling work of God.

21 For he hath made him *to be* sin for us, who knew no sin; that we might be made the righteousness of God in him.

21. For he hath made him to be sin for us, who knew no sin. Three aspects of Paul's concept of imputation are seen in this passage. In verse 19 God imputes not iniquity (cf. Ps 32:2). Here he imputes sin to Christ, the spotless Lamb of God (cf. Jn 1:29; I Pet 1:19). This imputation helps us understand Christ's struggle in the garden of Gethsemane with the cup of sin which would be poured upon Him on the cross. **That we might be made the righteousness of God in him.** Then the righteousness of Christ is imputed to the sinner's account. This truth may be viewed from the side of justification, whereby the sinner is declared righteous upon the merits of Jesus Christ (cf. Rom 3:24-25), or it may be viewed from the side of sanctification, wherein the righteousness of Christ is daily applied. This is the sense enjoined here and is best understood in conjunction with 3:18.

c. Paul's methods. 6:1-10.

CHAPTER 6

WE then, *as* workers together *with him*, beseech *you* also that ye receive not the grace of God in vain.

6:1. What follows is based upon Paul's teaching in 5:17-21. **As workers together with him** (lit., "working together"). The AV adds "with him." The addition is appropriate since Paul seems to be enlarging on the thought of 5:19. **Beseech you also.** In 5:20 the exhortation was "to be reconciled." Now Paul has an additional exhortation. **That ye receive not the grace of God in vain** ("not receive the grace of God to no purpose"). There is no hint here that the salvation of the Corinthian believers is in jeopardy. The grace of which he speaks has reference to 5:21. That they have received this grace denotes clearly that the people to which he is speaking are genuinely born again. But a judicial pardon does not guarantee practical Christian living and it is the application of the "righteousness of God in him" on a practical level, that Paul has in mind (cf. I Pet 1:22; 2:9).

2 (For he saith, I have heard thee in a time accepted, and in the day of salvation have I succoured thee: behold, now is the accepted time; behold, now is the day of salvation.)

2. For he saith. Prompted by **receive** (Gr *dechomai*), the apostle recalls to mind the **accepted** (Gr *dektos*) of the LXX translation of Isaiah 49:8. **I have heard thee in a time accepted** (in the Hebrew, "in the time of grace I answer thee"). **In the day of salvation have I succored thee.** Consistent with Hebrew parallelism, in poetic writings, this is intended as parallel to the previous expression. In Isaiah both expressions constituted a promise to the Servant of Jehovah to sustain him in the time of his ministry. However, the passage not only has messianic implications but is addressed also to Messiah's people, who represent Him. Since his readers have put their faith in the Messiah of whom Isaiah wrote, Paul is justified in making the specific application here. So they do not miss it, he underscores it with the words **behold, now is the accepted time; behold, now is the day of salvation.** Using an intensified form (Gr *euprosdektos*, "well received"), Paul emphasizes that the time is now. The force of his statement is that God conveys His grace and salvation to men in the day and time suited to Him and it is incumbent upon men to appropriate that grace in the time appointed by God. This is a good example of an analogical use of Scripture not uncommon to Paul (cf. Rom 10:18).

3 Giving no offence in any thing, that the ministry be not blamed:

3. That which Paul asked of others he demanded of himself. Thus at this time, his thoughts were upon his own ministry and the demands he made upon it based on the principle he had just stated. **Giving no offense in any thing.** The apostle scrupulously avoided doing anything that would cause someone to reject the gospel on his account. **That the ministry be not blamed** (lit., "that the ministry be not discredited").

4 But in all things approving ourselves as the ministers of God, in much patience, in afflictions, in necessities, in distresses,

5 In stripes, in imprisonments, in tumults, in labours, in watchings, in fastings;

4-5. But in all things approving ourselves as the ministers of God, in much patience. A careless reading of verses 4-10 might lead one to think that the apostle is spontaneously tabulating disjointed thoughts as they come to his mind. A closer look, however, will reveal a very careful and logical arrangement. There are twenty-seven categories divided into three groups of nine each. In verses 4-5 his thoughts are upon his trials, verses 6-7 upon divine provision, and verses 8-10 upon his resultant victory over circumstances. **In afflictions, in necessities, in distresses** (lit., "in troubles, in hardships, in difficulties") intends to convey the idea of pressures in general from every side. **In stripes, in imprisonments, in tumults.** These are the kinds of external pressures he endured. **In labors, in watchings, in fastings** denote the internal pressures faced by the apostle in his ministry (by this time quite evident in his ministry to the Corinthians, cf. 2:1-13).

6 By pureness, by knowledge, by longsuffering, by kindness, by the Holy Ghost, by love unfeigned,

7 By the word of truth, by the power of God, by the armour of righteousness on the right hand and on the left,

6-7. Appropriately placed between a tabulation of the trials encountered by Paul and the varied circumstances in which he found himself, Paul tabulates those spiritual graces with which God enabled him to carry on victoriously. The connection is with **heard thee** and **succored thee** of verse 2 and the entire section together demonstrates, from the experience of Paul, that he did not receive **the grace of God in vain** (vs. 1). **By pureness** may have a moral sense or a constitutional sense. That is, it may refer to freedom from immorality or singleness of motive and purpose. It is not unlikely that Paul has both in view. **By knowledge.** The context here implies insight to cope with difficult situations. **By longsuffering, by kindness.** The former is a passive idea the latter is active. In the one there is patient

8 By honour and dishonour, by evil report and good report: as deceivers, and yet true;

9 As unknown, and yet well known; as dying, and, behold, we live; as chastened, and not killed;

10 As sorrowful, yet alway rejoicing; as poor, yet making many rich; as having nothing, and yet possessing all things.

11 O ye Co-rĭnthʹĭ-anŝ, our mouth is open unto you, our heart is enlarged.

12 Ye are not straitened in us, but ye are straitened in your own bowels.

13 Now for a recompence in the same, (I speak as unto my children,) be ye also enlarged.

14 Be ye not unequally yoked togeth-

submission to injustice, in the other there is the kind disposition to do good to others, providing enabling gifts, comfort, and assurance (cf. I Cor 12:7-11; Jn 14:16-17; II Cor 1:3-4, 22). **By love unfeigned** (cf. I Cor 13), **By the word of truth** refers to the "preaching" of the truth (cf. 4:2). **By the power of God** has relation to his apostolic ministry (cf. Rom 15:14-21; I Cor 15:10). **By the armor of righteousness on the right hand and on the left.** This has in mind, primarily, the righteousness of God in justification (cf. Rom 5:1-2). Hence the expression is equivalent to "armor of God" (Eph 6:11) and does not denote one piece of armor, but all of it. By this means Paul was protected on every side.

8-10. Prompted by the expression **on the right hand and on the left** in the previous verse, the apostle now analyzes the extremes of life and here shows that regardless of the situation, whether ridding the wave of popularity or digging in against the onslaughts of opposition he was always approved a faithful minister of God. As he does in verses 4-5, here too he arranges his thoughts in three groups of triplets. **By honor and dishonor, by evil report and good report: as deceivers, and yet true.** Regardless of the reputation or report that precedes him, Paul never compromised on the integrity of his message. **As unknown, and yet well known; as dying, and, behold, we live; as chastened, and not killed.** In the front lines of the spiritual warfare Paul can be seen weary but undaunted, beaten but not broken, bruised but unbowed. **As sorrowful, yet always rejoicing; as poor, yet making many rich; as having nothing, and yet possessing all things.** Paul had learned to abound and be abased, he had learned to have much, and nothing. For he had learned, on a practical level, the lesson of our Lord in Luke 12:15. ". . . a man's life consisteth not in the abundance of the things which he possesseth."

C. The Challenge of Paul. 6:11-7:16.

1. The entreaty for reconciliation. 6:11-7:4.

This section turns on three imperatives. **Be ye also enlarged** (vs. 13), **be ye not unequally yoked together** (vs. 14), and **receive us** (7:2). Thus Paul deals successively with: (a) sympathy toward himself (6:11-13); (b) separation from the world (6:14-7:1); and (c) surety of reconciliation (7:2-4).

a. Sympathy towards Paul. 6:11-13.

11. O ye Corinthians. Paul addresses his readers by name in only two other places (Gal 3:1; Phil 4:15). In each case it reflects deep emotion. **Our mouth is opened unto you** (lit., "our mouth has spoken freely"). On the use of this expression see also Matthew 5:2; Acts 8:32, 35; and Ephesians 6:19. On its significance in this context compare 3:12. **Our heart is enlarged** (Gr *platynō*, "widen"). This is a common expression from the LXX (cf. Gen 9:27; Ps 4:1; 119:32). To enlarge the heart gives the idea of increasing its capacity for sympathy and understanding.

12. Ye are not straitened in us. This is the antithesis of **enlarged.** Paul is saying that there is no want of room in his heart for the Corinthians. **But ye are straitened in your own bowels.** That is, the problem lies with Paul's readers and their ability to receive him.

13. Be ye also enlarged. If the Corinthians would but open themselves to the apostle the problem could be resolved. In the "ministry of reconciliation" there is no room for bickering between the brethren.

On the other hand, Paul's principle of openness does not justify compromise.

b. Separation from the world. 6:14-7:4.

14. Be ye not unequally yoked together with unbelievers. In

2351

er with unbelievers: for what fellowship hath righteousness with unrighteousness? and what communion hath light with darkness?

15 And what concord hath Christ with Bē'lĭ-al? or what part hath he that believeth with an infidel?

16 And what agreement hath the temple of God with idols? for ye are the temple of the living God; as God hath said, I will dwell in them, and walk in *them;* and I will be their God, and they shall be my people.

17 Wherefore come out from among them, and be ye separate, saith the Lord, and touch not the unclean *thing;* and I will receive you,
18 And will be a Father unto you, and ye shall be my sons and daughters, saith the Lord Almighty.

CHAPTER 7

HAVING therefore these promises, dearly beloved, let us cleanse ourselves from all filthiness of the flesh and spirit, perfecting holiness in the fear of God.

2 Receive us; we have wronged no man, we have corrupted no man, we have defrauded no man.

3 I speak not *this* to condemn *you:* for I have said before, that ye are in our hearts to die and live with *you.*

enlarging one's capacity to receive others the apostle is careful to insist that he has only believers in mind. There is no doubt that he makes special reference to the situation in Corinth with all of its vice and pagan associations (cf. I Cor 6:6-20; 8:1-13; 10:14-33).

15. **Belial** ("worthlessness" or "wickedness"). The expression may also be used in the sense of "wicked one" (cf. II Sam 23:6; Job 34:18). Here it is used as a reference to Satan, ("the wicked one" in I Jn 5:19). **Infidel** is the same term used in the previous verse rendered "unbeliever."

16. **Temple of God.** In Scripture this expression has a variety of meanings: (a) It may have reference to heaven as God's dwelling place (cf. Ps 11:2; Hab 2:20); (b) It may refer to the church as God's temple (Eph 2:20; I Cor 3:16); or (c) It may have reference to the individual believer as a temple of God (I Cor 6:19). The plural pronouns in the Old Testament quotation suggest that Paul had the second idea in mind in this passage. That is, collectively, they constitute the temple of God. Accordingly, the promise of God in Exodus 29:45 and Leviticus 26:11, 12 applies to their situation as well. **I will dwell in them, and walk in them** ("in" is best best rendered "among"). Paul does not quote directly from the Old Testament here, but seems to be employing the language of the Old Testament. **I will be their God, and they shall be my people.** This great promise to Abraham and to his natural seed, is now applicable to all who are sons of Abraham by faith (Gal 3:6-16).

17-18. **Wherefore come out from among them, and be ye separate** (cf. Isa 52:11-12). **And I will receive you** (Ezk 20:34). **And will be a Father unto you, and ye shall be my sons and daughters** (cf. Isa 43:6; Hos 1:10). Separation from the ungodly and those who compromise their Christian standards is a basic biblical doctrine related to church discipline. This ultimate connection of Paul's thought here is with the **ministry of reconciliation** (5:18). He has shown that it was motivated by **the terror of the Lord** (5:11), energized by the **love of Christ** (5:14), exemplified by the experience of Paul (6:1-10), and qualified by the promise of God (6:16-18). In what follows, he shows that it provides incentive to holy living. The Apostle Paul always roots practical Christianity in sound Bible doctrine. The exhortation is to holiness before God and ultimately, to reconciliation with the apostle.

7:1. **Having therefore these promises, dearly beloved, let us cleanse ourselves from all filthiness of the flesh and spirit, perfecting holiness in the fear of God.** The promises of God demand a purity of heart and life on the part of those who receive them.

2. The apostle now turns back upon his previous concern, that is, their relationship to him. Here is the third imperative, **Receive us.** Since they are the temple of God and since their relationship ought to be with God and His people rather than unbelievers and wickedness, their hearts should be open to Paul. For he has **wronged no man . . . corrupted no man . . . defrauded no man.** The biblical definition of separation has both a negative and a positive side. The negative, expressed in 6:14-17, is that the believer abstains from fellowship with all who are opposed to God. But the positive side is that the believer is open to all that are truly the children of God and such individuals will be evidenced by the quality of their lives. In this category Paul places himself.

3. **I speak not this to condemn you:** The apostle does not insinuate that the Corinthian church was reprobate, or that they were not genuine believers. For, Paul practiced what he preached. He says, **ye are in our heart.** This could not be true if they were not believers. Thus, he conveys his unfeigned love to this wayward assembly. **To die and live with you.** Neither death

nor any other circumstance of life could destroy Paul's deep affection for the Corinthian believers.

4 Great *is* my boldness of speech toward you, great *is* my glorying of you: I am filled with comfort, I am exceeding joyful in all our tribulation.

4. Great is my boldness of speech toward you, great is my glorying of you. This expresses joyful confidence. **I am filled with comfort, I am exceedinging joyful in all our tribulation.** And rightly so. He has just received word from Titus that the Corinthians were actively seeking to rectify the evils and abuse in the assembly.

2. The encouragement from their response. 7:5-16.

In this passage Paul discusses: (a) the comfort of his friend Titus (vss. 5-7); (b) the correction of his letter (vss. 8-12); and (c) the consolation of his spirit (vss. 13-16).

a. Comfort of Titus. 7:5-7.

5 For, when we were come into Macedonia, our flesh had no rest, but we were troubled on every side; without *were* fightings, within *were* fears.
6 Nevertheless God, that comforteth those that are cast down, comforted us by the coming of Titus;

5-6. Upon leaving Troas and coming **into Macedonia** Paul's anxiety over the Corinthian believers was evident (2:12). **Without were fightings.** There were external wranglings all about. **Within were fears.** Not the least bit assuaged by the situation at Corinth. **God, that comforteth** (cf. 1:3-4). **Comforted us by the coming of Titus,** (i.e., his arrival from Corinth) with the news that the church had accepted Paul's letter (the "severe letter," 2:3-4).

7 And not by his coming only, but by the consolation wherewith he was comforted in you, when he told us your earnest desire, your mourning, your fervent mind toward me; so that I rejoiced the more.

7. Your earnest desire, your mourning, your fervent mind toward me. The Corinthians had evidenced toward Titus a repentant spirit and a desire to be reconciled to Paul.

b. Correction of the letter. 7:8-12.

8 For though I made you sorry with a letter, I do not repent, though I did repent: for I perceive that the same epistle hath made you sorry, though *it were* but for a season.
9 Now I rejoice, not that ye were made sorry, but that ye sorrowed to repentance: for ye were made sorry after a godly manner, that ye might receive damage by us in nothing.
10 For godly sorrow worketh repentance to salvation not to be repented of: but the sorrow of the world worketh death.
11 For behold this selfsame thing, that ye sorrowed after a godly sort, what carefulness it wrought in you, yea, *what* clearing of yourselves, yea, *what* indignation, yea, *what* fear, yea, *what* vehement desire, yea, *what* zeal, yea, *what* revenge! In all *things* ye have approved yourselves to be clear in this matter.
12 Wherefore, though I wrote unto you, *I did it* not for his cause that had done the wrong, nor for his cause that suffered wrong, but that our care for you in the sight of God might appear unto you.

8-10. For though I made you sorry with a letter, I do not repent. Although for a while Paul was sorry that he had written as he did, he is now thankful. **Not that ye were made sorry, but that ye sorrowed to repentance** (on "repentance" cf. Mt 3:8; Lk 5:32; Acts 5:31; Heb 12:17). The criminal may feel sorry that he is caught, but that is not sorrow **after a godly manner.** What happened at Corinth agitated the believers to realignment with the will and purpose of God. This made all of Paul's efforts worthwhile.

11-12. Revenge. The apostle is not gloating that circumstances have turned out in his favor, but rejoicing that a sense of justice (Gr *ekdikēsis*) had been aroused in them to the extent that they felt a moral obligation to discipline sin in the assembly. **Not for his cause that had done the wrong, nor for his cause that suffered wrong** refers to the individuals involved in I Corinthians 5. This indicates that the offender's father is still alive, thus making his sin all the more heinous.

13 Therefore we were comforted in your comfort: yea, and exceedingly the more joyed we for the joy of Titus, because his spirit was refreshed by you all.
14 For if I have boasted any thing to him of you, I am not ashamed; but as we spake all things to you in truth, even so our boasting, which *I made* before Titus, is found a truth.

c. Consolation. 7:13-16.

13. Therefore we were comforted in your comfort. The comfort Paul could not find (vs. 5), is supplied by the report of the spiritual progress at Corinth.

14. I have boasted. In Paul's discussions with Titus, previously, he was convinced that the opposition in Corinth was coming from only a small group of dissenters. But the vast majority of the congregation wanted to do what was right. This conviction is confirmed by Titus' report so that Paul is able to say, **even so our boasting, which I made before Titus, is found a truth.**

15 And his inward affection is more abundant toward you, whilst he

15-16. With fear and trembling ye received him. Not that they cower before him but they treat him with respect and honor

remembereth the obedience of you all, how with fear and trembling ye received him.

16 I rejoice therefore that I have confidence in you in all *things*.

(Eph 6:5). **I have confidence in you in all things.** Paul concludes this section fully assured that the Corinthian believers will take whatever steps are necessary to restore unity in the church, to enforce discipline, and to be restored to fellowship with himself.

III. APPEAL OF PAUL'S MINISTRY. 8:1-9:15.

Paul is commonly credited with being a great theologian and missionary. But what is often not known of him is that he was also a great financial genius of the early church. Chapters 8 and 9 of this epistle concern the offering for the poor saints at Jerusalem. Concerning this offering several factors may be noted.

It took eight years to accomplish (from the Council of Jerusalem in ca. A.D. 49, to Paul's arrest in A.D. 57). It involved thousands of miles of travel, covering four Roman provinces and including most of the Gentile churches. There were at least ten collectors involved. Since it is here that Titus is first introduced to the New Testament narrative, it is likely that this constituted one of his first responsibilities. The full amount collected was apparently significant since it excited the attention of the Roman governor, Porcius Festus, who hoped to get his hands on some of it (Acts 24:17-26). It nearly cost Paul his life and it did cost him much of his freedom.

Pentecost and poverty have long distinguished the Christian church (Acts 2:45). But the problem facing the church at this time was especially acute. On March 23, A.D. 37, in the reign of Caligula, there occurred a great earthquake. It was followed by another in the reign of Claudius, accompanied by widespread crop failures. The Christians, the poorest of all, had their source of help in the church of Antioch. Agabus, the prophet, had announced a famine at hand (Acts 11:28), and the fellowship determined to send relief. Saul and Barnabas were chosen to take the contribution to the elders at Jerusalem (Acts 11:30). They, most likely, were the initiators of its collection. So Paul was quite well trained in famine relief and in the art of taking collections. God is preparing him for something greater. A few years later, at the Council of Jerusalem (A.D. 49), when Paul and Barnabas, again in Jerusalem, were defending themselves and the liberty of the Gentile converts, a special plea was added to the decree. The Diaspora and the Christians were to remember the suffering and poverty of the Judaean Christians (Acts 15:23-29). And this, Paul later says, he was very anxious to do (Gal 2:10). From here on a definite plan of missionary giving becomes a primary part of every church Paul establishes (I Cor 16:1 ff.), and he urges it upon all those to whom he writes (Rom 15:26-27).

The peculiar difficulties at Corinth opened up the whole picture of the offering. They demonstrated a special willingness to pledge (II Cor 8:10), and their pledging inspired the Galatians, the Macedonians, and the Romans. Verbal instructions were followed by questions and written instructions regarding how they were to give and how it was to be handled (I Cor 16:1ff.; II Cor 9:1). There was careful, businesslike handling of all the finances. Each was to vote their own financial representative (II Cor 8:23). We know who some of these were. From Beroea there was Sopater, from Thessalonica there were Aristarchus and Secundus, from Asia there were Tychicus and Trophimus, from Galatia there were Gaius of Derbe and possibly Timothy (Acts 20:4). Since no one is specifically mentioned as coming from Achaia, it is likely that Luke or Titus or perhaps even the apostle himself represented them.

The spiritual nature of this offering is evident in the terms Paul uses. He never calls it "money" because he never seems to think of it as such. Instead, he calls it "grace" or "generosity" or "blessing" or "partnership." Thus, Paul speaks of the "grace of giving" as one of the highest Christian virtues. It would seem that such explicit directions for the offering would be adequate and apparently this was the case in Galatia and Macedonia. But Corinth had failed, though she had been first to pledge. Now special action and instructions are necessary. Hence, there is the special attention devoted to the subject in these chapters.

The section turns on the concept of "faithfulness." As this is exemplified in the apostle, in the previous section, it is now exhorted upon the Corinthian believers. His argument is structured as follows: faithfulness illustrated (8:1-5), faithfulness exhorted (8:6-15); faithfulness delegated (8:16-9:5); and faithfulness directed (9:6-15).

A. Faithfulness Illustrated. 8:1-5.

8:1. Moreover indicates a new subject. **We do you to wit of the grace of God bestowed on the churches of Macedonia** (lit., "we want to make known to you the grace of God given in the churches of Macedonia"). The Macedonian churches of Philippi, Thessalonica, and Beroea had demonstrated extreme liberality in their giving (cf. 11:9; Phil 2:25; 4:15, 18).

2. Trial of affliction . . . deep poverty. Both expressions stand in sharp relief against the **abundance of their joy . . . the riches of their liberality.** Instead of allowing circumstances to inhibit their giving, the churches of Macedonia turned personal and financial distress into a unique opportunity to demonstrate the riches of God's grace.

3. For to their power, I bear record, yea, and beyond their power (lit., "according to their ability and beyond their ability"). Their giving was not measured inversely according to their own needs, but proportionately to the need of others. **They were willing of themselves.** They did not need to be coerced; their giving was strictly voluntary.

4-5. Praying . . . with much entreaty that we would receive the gift. More is to be seen here by what is omitted than what is expressed. That they found it necessary to beg the apostle to participate in the collection for Jerusalem suggests that the apostle must have considered their own needs to be sufficiently extreme to exempt them from participation. **The fellowship of the ministering to the saints.** Giving is a form of fellowship (note, theme of the previous epistle, I Cor 1:9). **And this they did, not as we hoped** (lit., "not as we had expected"). Such giving on the part of these believers was totally unexpected by the apostle in light of their own needs. **But first gave their own selves to the Lord, and unto us by the will of God.** The proper order of New Testament giving is expressed here. "First" is understood in order of priority, not chronology. The gift is first to God and then to the saints.

B. Faithfulness Exhorted. 8:6-15.

6. We desired Titus, that as he had begun. In Titus' previous visit he, no doubt, had already begun discussing the collection (cf. I Cor 16:1). **So he would also finish in you the same grace also.** At Paul's suggestion Titus is delegated the responsibility of overseeing the offering at Corinth.

7. See that ye abound in this grace also. As the previous verse explained Titus' commission, here Paul expresses his expectations on the part of the Corinthian church. **As ye abound in every thing** (cf. I Cor 1:5, 7). This expression does two things. First, it stands in contrast to the poverty of the Macedonian church with obvious implications. Second, at the outset, it expresses to the Corinthians exactly what Paul expects of them.

8. I speak not by commandment. No legal stipulation regulates the believer's giving, but on account of **the forwardness of others.** By calling to mind the zeal demonstrated by others, Paul intends to **prove the sincerity of your love** (this is best understood in light of 9:2).

9. For ye know the grace of our Lord Jesus Christ, that,

CHAPTER 8

MOREOVER, brethren, we do you to wit of the grace of God bestowed on the churches of Macedonia;

2 How that in a great trial of affliction the abundance of their joy and their deep poverty abounded unto the riches of their liberality.

3 For to *their* power, I bear record, yea, and beyond *their* power *they were* willing of themselves;

4 Praying us with much intreaty that we would receive the gift, and *take upon us* the fellowship of the ministering to the saints.

5 And *this they did*, not as we hoped, but first gave their own selves to the Lord, and unto us by the will of God.

6 Insomuch that we desired Titus, that as he had begun, so he would also finish in you the same grace also.

7 Therefore, as ye abound in every *thing*, *in* faith, and utterance, and knowledge, and *in* all diligence, and *in* your love to us, *see* that ye abound in this grace also.

8 I speak not by commandment, but by occasion of the forwardness of others, and to prove the sincerity of your love.

9 For ye know the grace of our Lord

Jesus Christ, that, though he was rich, yet for your sakes he became poor, that ye through his poverty might be rich.

10 And herein I give *my* advice: for this is expedient for you, who have begun before, not only to do, but also to be forward a year ago.

11 Now therefore perform the doing *of it;* that as *there was* a readiness to will, so *there may be* a performance also out of that which ye have.

12 For if there be first a willing mind, *it is* accepted according to that a man hath, *and* not according to that he hath not.

13 For *I mean* not that other men be eased, and ye burdened:

14 But by an equality, *that* now at this time your abundance *may be a supply* for their want, that their abundance also may be *a supply* for your want: that there may be equality:

15 As it is written, He that *had gathered* much had nothing over; and he that *had gathered* little had no lack.

16 But thanks *be* to God, which put the same earnest care into the heart of Titus for you.

17 For indeed he accepted the exhortation; but being more forward, of his own accord he went unto you.

18 And we have sent with him the brother, whose praise *is* in the gospel throughout all the churches;

19 And not *that* only, but who was also chosen of the churches to travel with us with this grace, which is administered by us to the glory of the same Lord, and *declaration of* your ready mind:

20 Avoiding this, that no man should blame us in this abundance which is administered by us:

21 Providing for honest things, not only in the sight of the Lord, but also in the sight of men.

22 And we have sent with them our brother, whom we have oftentimes proved diligent in many things, but now much more diligent, upon the great confidence which *I have* in you.

23 Whether *any do enquire* of Titus, *he is* my partner and fellowhelper concerning you: or our brethren *be enquired of, they are* the messengers of the churches, *and* the glory of Christ.

24 Wherefore shew ye to them, and before the churches, the proof of your love, and of our boasting on your behalf.

though he was rich, yet for your sakes he became poor. There is no need to read into this verse any more than is warranted by the context. On the self-emptying of Christ, see Philippians 2:7 and Hebrews 1:2. The intent of Paul's argument is not unlike that of verse 8. Sacrificial love was exemplified by the Macedonian churches. But the supreme example of such love is our Lord.

10-11. And herein I give my advice ("here is my opinion on the matter"). For this is expedient for you, who have begun before, not only to do, but also to be forward a year ago (see 9:2). It is only right for Paul to expect the Corinthian church to participate. This was their expressed desire more than a year ago. Now therefore perform the doing of it. Paul asks only that they follow through with their original commitment.

12. For if there be first a willing mind. In the ministry of giving, God is concerned first with the attitude of the individual, not the precise amount that he gives. That, of course, varies according to that a man hath.

13-14. Paul does not intend to merely transfer the burden from one group to another. But by an equality, that now at this time your abundance may be a supply for their want. He wants to equalize matters.

15. As the Scripture has it, He that had gathered much had nothing over; and he that had gathered little had no lack (cf. Ex 16:18). Hodge (p. 206) observes "property is like manna, it will not bear hoarding."

C. Faithfulness Delegated. 8:16-9:5.

16-17. Titus illustrates the reciprocity implied in verse 14. But thanks be to God, which put the same earnest care into the heart of Titus for you. What Paul is asking of the Corinthians in terms of spontaneous loving concern for brethren in need, is reflected in the attitude of Titus toward them. Notice here that Paul understands the character qualities distinctive of a spiritual life are not intrinsic to human nature, but given by God.

18. We have sent with him the brother. All that is known of this individual is what is indicated here. Since his name is not given, it is useless to conjecture who he was. At any rate, he was known throughout all the churches.

19. Like Titus, he was chosen of the churches to travel with us with this grace. He was selected by the churches to assist the apostles in overseeing the collection for Jerusalem. Most likely, he was one of the men cited in Acts 20:4.

20-21. Such men were selected so that no one would question how the funds were acquired or what was done with them subsequently. Providing for honest things, not only in the sight of the Lord, but also in the sight of men. Especially in financial matters, the apostle is scrupulously aware of his vulnerability to criticism.

22-24. And we have sent with them our brother. Along with the previously unnamed individual (vs. 18), there will be one other who will be accompanying Titus when he arrives.

CHAPTER 9

FOR as touching the ministering to the saints, it is superfluous for me to write to you:

2 For I know the forwardness of your mind, for which I boast of you to them of Macedonia, that A-chā'ia was ready a year ago; and your zeal hath provoked very many.

3 Yet have I sent the brethren, lest our boasting of you should be in vain in this behalf; that, as I said, ye may be ready:

4 Lest haply if they of Macedonia come with me, and find you unprepared, we (that we say not, ye) should be ashamed in this same confident boasting.

5 Therefore I thought it necessary to exhort the brethren, that they would go before unto you, and make up beforehand your bounty, whereof ye had notice before, that the same might be ready, as *a matter of* bounty, and not as *of* covetousness.

6 But this *I say*, He which soweth sparingly shall reap also sparingly; and he which soweth bountifully shall reap also bountifully.

7 Every man according as he purposeth in his heart, *so let him give;* not grudgingly, or of necessity: for God loveth a cheerful giver.

8 And God *is* able to make all grace abound toward you; that ye, always having all sufficiency in all *things,* may abound to every good work:

9 (As it is written, He hath dispersed abroad; he hath given to the poor: his righteousness remaineth for ever.

10 Now he that ministereth seed to

9:1-2. It is superfluous for me to write. Paul rendered this exhortation, and his earlier one, unnecessary. In fact, it was Paul's understanding that the offering in **Achaia was ready a year ago** and he had cited their **zeal** as an example of sacrificial giving and willingness to give.

3-4. Yet have I sent the brethren, lest our boasting of you should be in vain in this behalf. Of course, Paul knows that the Corinthian church has been derelict in discharging its original commitment in this regard. Thus, while he applies pressure he tactfully suggests that he is only concerned that they be on schedule. **That, as I said, ye may be ready.** In the event they were **unprepared,** it would not only be an embarassment to the apostle but a disgrace to themselves.

5. Lest those of the assembly at Corinth should interpret the ministry of Paul's three companions in the wrong way, he assures them that they are there only to oversee and to expedite the offering. His desire is only that those who wish to give and who are able to give have the opportunity to do so.

D. Faithfulness Directed. 9:6-15.

6. But this (lit., "as to this, however"). Paul now turns his attention to some positive instruction and encouragement regarding giving. In so doing he provides the church with the clearest and most comprehensive treatment of the subject to be found in the New Testament. His approach is to extract principles from both the Old Testament and experience to demonstrate why and how they are to give. **He which soweth sparingly shall reap also sparingly; and he which soweth bountifully shall reap also bountifully** (cf. Prov 11:24; Lk 6:38; Gal 6:7). One's return is determined by his investment. The Greek expression *ep eulogiais* ordinarily translated "with blessings," here has the sense of "freely." While it does not suggest "undiscriminating" giving, it does denote "unrestrained" giving.

7. Every man according as he purposeth in his heart, so let him give. The apostle does not have a minimum quota, nor yet a minimum percentage figure in mind. For each individual it is an amount to be determined before the Lord. **Not grudgingly, or of necessity: for God loveth a cheerful giver.** There is to be a willing heart and a sincere desire on the part of the one giving in order to participate. Paul is not so much interested in their money, nor is God, for that matter, as the passage from Proverbs 22:9 indicates. The Greek term *hilaron* from which the English term "hilarious" derives, is best rendered as the AV suggests, "cheerful." Giving is not a joke; it is serious business, but it is also a delightful experience.

8. And God is able to make all grace abound toward you. Paul's logic is identical to that of our Lord in Matthew 6:33. When the temporal concerns of life are placed first, God is usually excluded. But when the kingdom of God is placed first, God sees to it that the temporal needs are included. **That ye, always having all sufficiency in all things, may abound to every good work.** Giving is a grace that has reciprocal benefits.

9. As it is written (cf. Ps 112:9), **He hath dispersed abroad; he hath given to the poor: his righteousness remaineth for ever.** Of course, neither Paul nor the psalmist intended to mean that every believer will always be wealthy, nor yet that the believer who gives regularly and faithfully will always be wealthy. Both experience and the context (cf. 8:2) deny this. He only intends to say that the abundance of God's riches are available to those who are rightly related to Him. **His righteousness remaineth for ever.** The righteous acts of the man who readily gives and supplies the needs of others have eternal value.

10. This should best be rendered "now he that ministereth

2357

the sower both minister bread for *your* food, and multiply your seed sown, and increase the fruits of your righteousness;)

11 Being enriched in every thing to all bountifulness, which causeth through us thanksgiving to God.

12 For the administration of this service not only supplieth the want of the saints, but is abundant also by many thanksgivings unto God;

13 Whiles by the experiment of this ministration they glorify God for your professed subjection unto the gospel of Christ, and for *your* liberal distribution unto them, and unto all *men;*

14 And by their prayer for you, which long after you for the exceeding grace of God in you.

15 Thanks *be* unto God for his unspeakable gift.

seed to the sower and bread for your food will supply you seed sown and increase fruits of your righteousness." The AV renders it as a prayer to God. Actually it is an affirmation of the surety of God's supply.

11. Being enriched in every thing to all bountifulness, which causeth through us thanksgiving to God (lit., "you shall be enriched"). This unusual use of the participle is not foreign to the New Testament, nor yet to the Apostle Paul (cf. Acts 15:22; Eph 3:17; 4:2; Col 2:2; 3:16).

12-13. Giving consummates in a twofold grace. It **supplieth the want of the saints,** and it is **abundant** ("overflowing") by means of **many thanksgivings unto God.** The final result is that God is glorified. It will be noted that this process is cyclical. Out of the riches of God's grace He supplies the needs of the believer. The believer, in an expression of gratitude and liberality, shares of his abundance with others. They, in turn, direct their expressions of thanksgiving ("grace") to God from whom the supply originated. Thus, the cycle is complete. And so Paul says **they glorify God for your professed subjection unto the gospel of Christ, and for your liberal distribution unto them.** The act of giving is evidence of obedience to the gospel.

14. And by their prayer for you. The connection is with "abundant" in verse 12. Another positive result of faithful giving is that the recipients are induced to extend the giver before the Throne of Grace. It is in this way that the giver is compensated by the recipient of the gift. This further explains the thought of 8:14.

15. Thanks be unto God for his unspeakable gift. The reference is to the gift of God's Son, but the verse is more than a spontaneous outburst of the writer. It is the supreme illustration of the principles Paul has just enumerated. As the example of Christ is applied to the experience of suffering in I Peter 2:21, so Paul applies the example of Christ to the grace of giving.

IV. AUTHORITY OF PAUL'S MINISTRY. 10:1-13:10.

In the next three chapters Paul's tone changes drastically. It is for this reason that some suggest that this section constitutes the text of the "severe letter" of 7:8. However, as has been noted earlier, it is more likely that the change in approach may be more readily accounted for by a change in the direction of Paul's words. In the first nine chapters he is writing to the majority of the congregation who love and appreciate him. In the remaining chapters he turns his attention to that small pocket of resistance which continues to voice opposition to his ministry. Apparently these are former Jews professing faith in Christ (11:22), but who are actually "false apostles" (11:13). Since the apostle is now certain that the majority of the believers are with him, he is emboldened to deal more forcefully and directly with this group. And so he will defend his apostleship (10:1-18), he will boast of his experiences (11:1-12:10), he will demonstrate his credentials (12:11-18), and he will charge them to repentance (12:19-13:10).

A. The Defense of the Apostle. 10:1-18.

Paul defends his apostleship here in terms of his attitude (vss. 1-6), his authority (vss. 7-11), and his divine commendation (vss. 12-18).

CHAPTER 10

NOW I Paul myself beseech you by the meekness and gentleness of Christ, who in presence *am* base among you, but being absent am bold toward you:

1. By his attitudes. 10:1-6.

10:1. Now indicates the change of subject. **Myself** is emphatic. **I Paul.** The change in Paul's tone is immediately evident. Like the boxer squaring off in the ring, his stance is clearly visible. **By the meekness and gentleness of Christ** (cf. the parallel "mercies of God" in Rom 12:1). The apostle not only understands that his authority comes from Christ, but even the accompanying grace with which that authority is exercised. In

2 But I beseech *you*, that I may not be bold when I am present with that confidence, wherewith I think to be bold against some, which think of us as if we walked according to the flesh.

3 For though we walk in the flesh, we do not war after the flesh:

4 (For the weapons of our warfare *are* not carnal, but mighty through God to the pulling down of strong holds;)

5 Casting down imaginations, and every high thing that exalteth itself against the knowledge of God, and bringing into captivity every thought to the obedience of Christ;

6 And having in a readiness to revenge all disobedience, when your obedience is fulfilled.

7 Do ye look on things after the outward appearance? If any man trust to himself that he is Christ's, let him of himself think this again, that, as he *is* Christ's, even so *are* we Christ's.

8 For though I should boast somewhat more of our authority, which the Lord hath given us for edification, and not for your destruction, I should not be ashamed:

9 That I may not seem as if I would terrify you by letters.

10 For *his* letters, say they, *are* weighty and powerful; but *his* bodily presence *is* weak, and *his* speech contemptible.

11 Let such an one think this, that,

---

this case, it has a particularly ironic tone in the words: **who in presence am base among you, but being absent am bold toward you.** Paul had been charged with demonstrating undue boldness in his letters without the strength of character to back what he had to say in person (10:10).

2. But I beseech you, that I may not be bold ("please do not force me to prove this allegation to be false"). **Some, which think of us as if we walked according to the flesh.** The charge is not that he is carnal, but that he is lacking divine unction in his ministry and has usurped the apostolic office to himself.

3. To this Paul replies: **we walk in the flesh,** that is, we are just human beings, but **we do not war after the flesh.** To paraphrase: "you see me as a person and perhaps that is not convincing. But if you walk with me awhile and see what my work requires me to do, then you will be convinced."

4. For the weapons of our warfare are not carnal. If Paul did not possess divine authority, he could not possess divine power. But Paul's strength was **mighty through God to the pulling down of strongholds.**

5. Casting down imaginations, and every high thing that exalteth itself against the knowledge of God. The AV properly renders the previous verse as a parenthesis. This is correct since the Greek participle *kathairountes* ("pulling down") connects with "war" at the end of verse 3. Paul continues with the military metaphor in the use of "strongholds." These were high military battlements thrown up in battle. Here, they denote opposition to Paul's work in the gospel. They are literally, "pulled down" and **every thought** is brought **into captivity . . . to the obedience of Christ.** One cannot help but reflect on I Corinthians 1. The apostle subsumes all human wisdom, philosophy, and authority under the divine. Paul acted on the assumption that any of the devices brought against him at the contrivance of men would fall before the power of God and the wisdom of God.

6. And having in a readiness to revenge all disobedience. Continuing the metaphor, Paul is still at war. He is casting down strongholds. He is leading captives. Now he is prepared to punish all disobedience. **When your obedience is fulfilled.** Paul does not intend to deal with them quite so severely until he has given them ample time to repent and fall into submission both to the Lord and to himself.

2. By his authority. 10:7-11.

7. Paul's attitude is fully justified by his delegated authority, as will be shown in what follows. **Do ye look on things after the outward appearance?** This connects with **those which think of us as if we walked according to the flesh** (vs. 2). If such an individual should **trust to himself that he is Christ's,** let him know that **even so are we.** The opposition indicated here may have derived from the faction within the assembly that identified itself with the name of Christ (I Cor 1:12). At any rate they were giving out that they were from Christ and Paul was not. The apostle was quick to assert that they had no authority or advantage which did not apply equally to him.

8-10. For though ("even if") **I should boast somewhat more of our authority** implies that Paul is showing restraint. **Which the Lord hath given us for edification, and not for your destruction.** His restraint is due to an overriding desire to help them, not hinder them. **I should not be ashamed** (lit., "I shall not be ashamed"). He contains himself so as to provide no opportunity for criticism. It has been on this account that they have brought charge against him, **For his letters, say they, are weighty and powerful; but his bodily presence is weak, and his speech contemptible.** Paul does not wish to give any cause for them to point the finger again.

11. On the contrary, he intends to demonstrate that his ac-

such as we are in word by letters when we are absent, such *will we be* also in deed when we are present.

12 For we dare not make ourselves of the number, or compare ourselves with some that commend themselves: but they measuring themselves by themselves, and comparing themselves among themselves, are not wise.

13 But we will not boast of things without *our* measure, but according to the measure of the rule which God hath distributed to us, a measure to reach even unto you.

14 For we stretch not ourselves beyond *our* measure, as though we reached not unto you: for we are come as far as to you also in *preaching* the gospel of Christ:

15 Not boasting of things without *our* measure, *that is,* of other men's labours; but having hope, when your faith is increased, that we shall be enlarged by you according to our rule abundantly,

16 To preach the gospel in the *regions* beyond you, *and* not to boast in another man's line of things made ready to our hand.

17 But he that glorieth, let him glory in the Lord.

18 For not he that commendeth himself is approved, but whom the Lord commendeth.

CHAPTER 11

WOULD to God ye could bear with me a little in *my* folly: and indeed bear with me.

2 For I am jealous over you with godly jealousy: for I have espoused you to one husband, that I may present *you as* a chaste virgin to Christ.

3 But I fear, lest by any means, as the serpent beguiled Eve through his subtilty, so your minds should be corrupted from the simplicity that is in Christ.

4 For if he that cometh preacheth another Jesus, whom we have not preached, or *if* ye receive another spirit, which ye have not received, or another gospel, which ye have not accepted, ye might well bear with *him.*

tions will correspond to his words. **Such will we be also in deed when we are present.** He does not give empty threats.

3. By divine commendation. 10:12-18.

12-15. Paul does not measure his credentials as his enemies do, **measuring themselves by themselves.** Such an approach Paul says is **not wise.** Rather he will measure his credentials by an objective standard, **a measure to reach even unto you.** What he has in mind is his "track record." Where Paul's enemies cited their authority, he cites his accomplishments. **For we are come as far as to you also in preaching the gospel of Christ.** Paul's critics were not responsible for founding the church at Corinth; he was. Paul is not riding on another's coattails. He is **not boasting of things without our measure,** i.e., another man's labors. He is an original. Accordingly, he is prepared to take credit even for their spiritual growth; as he puts it: **when your faith is increased, that we shall be enlarged by you.** The principle of 9:10 not only applies to one's material possessions, but also to the investments of one's energies.

16-18. Paul does not intend to allow this situation or any other to inhibit him from going even further. **To preach the gospel in the regions beyond you.** He had no intention of lowering himself to **boast in another man's line of things.** Lest they interpret what he has to say as expressions of self-conceit, Paul shows that in the final analysis, his commendation comes from Christ. Paul was always careful to show that any success he enjoyed in the ministry was not due to his own innate ability but Christ working in him (cf. Rom 15:17-18). Thus, his boast is not in himself, but **in the Lord.**

B. The Boast of the Apostle. 11:1-12:10.

The boasting that Paul is about to engage in stands as an apparent contradiction to what he has said in 10:17-18. Thus, at the outset, he must present the basis for his boast (11:1-15). This he follows with the proof of his boast (vss. 16-33). Then he relates the consequences of his boast (12:1-10).

1. The basis for his boast. 11:1-15.

11:1. Bear with me a little in my folly. Already the apostle is uneasy about what he has to do. For him it is "foolishness." And yet, as repugnant as it is to him, it is necessary.

2. For indicates "reason." What follows answers why they must bear with him. Paul has their own well-being in mind. **I have espoused you to one husband, that I may present you as a chaste virgin to Christ.** They were in danger of being turned from Christ by being turned away from the ministry of the apostle. As an "ambassador for Christ," he realizes he must win them back to himself in order to win them back to Christ.

3. What is implied in the previous verse is expressed here. **I fear, lest by any means, as the serpent beguiled Eve through his subtilty, so your minds should be corrupted from the simplicity that is in Christ.** His deepest concern is that the Corinthians are being seduced from their faithfulness to Christ.

4. Paul could understand **if he that cometh preacheth another Jesus, whom we have not preached.** Or another **spirit** or **another gospel.** If such were the case, **ye might well bear with him.** Paul is being ironic here. The Corinthians would be justified in listening to the false teachers if what they had to say introduced them to a genuine gospel which they had not yet received. The irony of the passage cannot be escaped. That which Paul finds necessary to beg of them in verse 1 they had willingly offered to false teachers.

5 For I suppose I was not a whit behind the very chiefest apostles.
6 But though *I be* rude in speech, yet not in knowledge; but we have been throughly made manifest among you in all things.

7 Have I committed an offence in abasing myself that ye might be exalted, because I have preached to you the gospel of God freely?

8 I robbed other churches, taking wages *of them*, to do you service.

9 And when I was present with you, and wanted, I was chargeable to no man: for that which was lacking to me the brethren which came from Macedonia supplied: and in all *things* I have kept myself from being burdensome unto you, and *so* will I keep *myself*.
10 As the truth of Christ is in me, no man shall stop me of this boasting in the regions of A-chā'ia.

11 Wherefore? because I love you not? God knoweth.
12 But what I do, that I will do, that I may cut off occasion from them which desire occasion; that wherein they glory, they may be found even as we.

13 For such *are* false apostles, deceitful workers, transforming themselves into the apostles of Christ.

14 And no marvel; for Satan himself is transformed into an angel of light.

15 Therefore *it is* no great thing if his ministers also be transformed as the ministers of righteousness; whose end shall be according to their works.

16 I say again, Let no man think me a fool; if otherwise, yet as a fool receive me, that I may boast myself a little.

17 That which I speak, I speak *it* not after the Lord, but as it were foolishly, in this confidence of boasting.

18 Seeing that many glory after the flesh, I will glory also.

5-6. Although Paul was **not a whit behind the very chiefest apostles** it was not immediately evident in his personal ministry. He was **rude in speech** and this was apparently offensive to some. Yet he could not have been criticized **in knowledge.** And, as for the message that he preached, the Corinthians had been **thoroughly made manifest . . . in all things.** The AV is misleading here. He has in mind making manifest the things of the gospel. The tone is clearly ironic and the contrast is with verse 4. They may have criticized his style, but they could add nothing to his sermon.

7. Have I committed an offense in abasing myself? (I Cor 9:1-18). Irony fairly drips from his pen. Their only legitimate criticism was his self-effacing manner. **I have preached to you the gospel of God freely.** In eighteen months of ministry he never once extracted from them a living wage.

8. I robbed other churches is hyperbolic, and intended to shame them. **Taking wages of them, to do you service.** Paul, no doubt, has the Philippian church primarily in mind (Phil 4:15-16). He could have mentioned the fact that he worked with his own hands to sustain a living on his first arrival in Corinth. It is suggestive of his restraint that he does not.

9. And so will I keep myself. Paul's behavior at Corinth was unimpeachable. And he was not going to start now allowing his readers to force him to compromise his principles (cf. Acts 18:3; 20:34-35; I Thess 2:9; II Thess 3:8; I Cor 9:15-18).

10. This is an oath. **No man shall stop me of this boasting in the regions of Achaia.** It is significant that Paul readily receives aid from the Macedonian churches and refuses it from those at Corinth.

11-12. Why? Because he has no interest in them and no desire for their help? No, but **that I may cut off occasion from them which desire occasion.** Those who are looking for things to criticize will find no help from Paul. **That wherein they glory, they may be found even as we.** There is method in Paul's madness. He knows that if they are to bring accusation against his character, theirs had better, at least, match his; i.e., they will be forced to stop merchandising the gospel.

13. For such are false apostles, deceitful workers, transforming themselves into the apostles of Christ. Until now Paul has been dealing gratuitously with his enemies. He now lays his cards on the table and says what he really thinks of them (cf. Phil 3:2).

14. And no marvel. It is no surprise that they have been able to deceive the Corinthian believers **for Satan himself is transformed into an angel of light.** The passage calls to mind the culmination of our Lord's discussion with the Pharisees in John 8. The specific allusion Paul makes is not altogether clear. Perhaps it is to Job 1:6.

15. Therefore it is no great thing. They were acting only according to their nature. **Whose end shall be according to their works.** Their judgment will not be according to the role they have assumed. One day their true character will be revealed for "that day shall declare it."

2. The proof of his boast. 11:16-33.

16. What Paul is about to do he considers foolishness. It runs crossgrain to every fiber of his being. But the spiritual welfare of a congregation in danger of being led astray is at stake, and it becomes necessary to **boast myself a little.**

17. I speak it not after the Lord. Paul is not here disclaiming inspiration. But, what he is about to do, is out of character with his mission from the Lord.

18. Seeing that many glory after the flesh (lit., "since many glory after fleshly standards"), **I will glory also.** If the Corin-

19 For ye suffer fools gladly, seeing ye *yourselves* are wise.
20 For ye suffer, if a man bring you into bondage, if a man devour *you*, if a man take *of you*, if a man exalt himself, if a man smite you on the face.

21 I speak as concerning reproach, as though we had been weak. Howbeit whereinsoever any is bold, (I speak foolishly,) I am bold also.
22 Are they Hebrews? so *am* I. Are they Israelites? so *am* I. Are they the seed of Abraham? so *am* I.

23 Are they ministers of Christ? (I speak as a fool) I *am* more; in labours more abundant, in stripes above measure, in prisons more frequent, in deaths oft.
24 Of the Jews five times received I forty *stripes* save one.
25 Thrice was I beaten with rods, once was I stoned, thrice I suffered shipwreck, a night and a day I have been in the deep;
26 *In* journeyings often, *in* perils of waters, *in* perils of robbers, *in* perils by *mine own* countrymen, *in* perils by the heathen, *in* perils in the city, *in* perils in the wilderness, *in* perils in the sea, *in* perils among false brethren;
27 In weariness and painfulness, in watchings often, in hunger and thirst, in fastings often, in cold and nakedness.

thians wish to qualify Paul on strictly human standards he will give them a *curriculum vitae.*

19-20. Paul seems to have a hard time getting into his task, i.e., to boast about himself. However the irony continues to drip from his pen. **Ye suffer fools gladly.** Since you so readily receive fools I shall attempt to qualify myself as one. **Seeing ye yourselves are wise** (cf. I Cor 4:8). This trait seems to be characteristic of their brand of wisdom. Their faulty sense of values also ties in with their warped sense of discrimination. **Ye suffer.** As in verse 19, "ye tolerate." **If a man bring you into bondage, if a man devour you, if a man take of you, if a man exalt himself, if a man smite you on the face** (cf. Gal 1:7; I Pet 5:3). In this strange turn of events these believers had forsaken their own loving father in the faith and had subjected themselves to spiritual tyrants who were self-seeking and destructive of true spirituality.

21-22. I speak as concerning reproach (lit., "by way of disparagement"), **as though we had been weak.** Such tolerance had hardly been extended to the apostle. **Howbeit whereinsoever any is bold (I speak foolishly,) I am bold also.** While in reality it amounts to nothing, if one wishes to discuss personal qualifications, Paul will advance his own. Here Paul boasts about his nationality. **Hebrews . . . Israelites . . . seed of Abraham** indicate that Paul's enemies were primarily Jewish. On Paul's claim see also Philippians 3:5.

23-27. Then Paul boasts of the cost of his commitment to Christ. **Are they ministers of Christ? (I speak as a fool).** The expression is hypothetical. If they are ministers of Christ as they claim to be, then **I am more.** Discipleship cannot be purchased at bargain prices (Lk 9:23). The cost exacted of the Apostle Paul is measured by the tabulation which follows.

What Paul does here is demonstrate the depth of his commitment by delineating the sufferings and trials he endured because of it. **In deaths oft** (lit., "in many deaths"). This is tantamount to saying "I die daily" (I Cor 15:31). **Forty stripes save one.** Deuteronomy 25:3 forbids the Jews to inflict more than forty stripes upon an offender. Scrupulous in their observance of Moses' law, they were in the habit of giving no more than 39 (so as not to go over the limit of the law). **Once was I stoned** (Acts 14:19). **Thrice I suffered shipwreck, a night and a day I have been in the deep.** Since Paul penned this letter long before the shipwreck recorded in Acts 27, it must be reckoned that the incidents of which he speaks find their mention in Scripture only here. There are numerous occasions recorded in Acts 13:1-20:5 when Paul traveled by sea. Since Luke, the author of the book of Acts, did not accompany Paul much of that time (apparently only in Acts 16:10-17), it is not surprising that some of the incidentals have been omitted from his account. **Perils of waters** ("perils of rivers"). Along the roads traversed by Paul there were numerous rivers which seasonally swell with flood waters, and which to this day, are legendary for the perils they pose for the traveler. This, especially along the Appian Way, road extending through Lebanon from Jerusalem to Antioch. **Perils of robbers.** The area from Perga to Antioch in Pisidia was especially known for this (Acts 13:14). **Perils among false brethren.** Halfway through the list of Paul's perils from "outside" he includes his enemies at Corinth. What is implied by this is explicitly stated in 11:13. **In fastings often.** The context does not view this as a ritualistic observance practiced by the Pharisees. Rather it is an "involuntary abstinence." While it is admitted that *nesteia* is ordinarily used of ritualistic fastings (cf. Lk 2:37; Acts 14:23), it is unlikely that such is the sense here. From its connection with **hunger and thirst** it is not unlikely that there is a touch of irony here. No doubt Paul's Jewish adversaries at Corinth made a practice of ritualistic fasting and

28 Beside those things that are without, that which cometh upon me daily, the care of all the churches.

29 Who is weak, and I am not weak? who is offended, and I burn not?

30 If I must needs glory, I will glory of the things which concern mine infirmities.

31 The God and Father of our Lord Jesus Christ, which is blessed for evermore, knoweth that I lie not.

32 In Damascus the governor under Ăr'e-tas the king kept the city of the Dăm'as-cēnes with a garrison, desirous to apprehend me:

33 And through a window in a basket was I let down by the wall, and escaped his hands.

CHAPTER 12
IT is not expedient for me doubtless to glory. I will come to visions and revelations of the Lord.

2 I knew a man in Christ above fourteen years ago, (whether in the body, I cannot tell; or whether out of the body, I cannot tell: God knoweth;) such an one caught up to the third heaven.

took pride in it. On the other hand, Paul fasted because the pressures of a faithful ministry required it of him.

28. Besides those things that are without (lit., "not to mention those things which are besides"). To enumerate the things that came upon him **daily** in the **care of all the churches,** Paul could go on. But he chooses not to.

29-30. Instead he chooses to boast, not in his ability to endure hardness, but in his weakness. **Who is weak, and I am not weak?** (cf. I Cor 9:22). **Who is offended, and I burn not?** ("Who is caused to stumble, and I am not indignant?") The apostle is deeply concerned about the weaker brethren and he "burned" with indignation when he thought of those who would lead them astray. On the relation of his weakness to the evidences of God's strength see also 12:10; 13:9; I Corinthians 4:10.

31-33. Paul's thought here is difficult to connect with either what precedes or what follows. It sounds as though he is about to introduce a discussion of his experiences shortly after his conversion. In this regard he asserts **I lie not.** What he says is in essential agreement with Acts 9:24-25. The only addition is **Aretas the king.** When one correlates this with Acts it must be inferred that Aretas was acting at the behest of the Jews. Why Paul does not continue at this point to pursue this discussion can only be speculated. Perhaps he was interrupted or distracted. At any rate, this is all he says and when he begins chapter twelve, his mind is on a matter of much greater moment.

3. The consequences of his boast. 12:1-10.

This section turns on the concept of **glory** (*Kauchaomai,* "boast"). Paul's adversaries were boasting after the flesh (11:18). Paul's boasting is of another sort.

In coming to this passage, one almost senses an attitude of frustration in the apostle. He has entered into something that is especially obnoxious to him, i.e., boasting of himself. In the previous chapter his focus of attention has been on earthly, physical experiences in the gospel. Yet, there is something even more significant on his mind and one senses that it is a matter he had hoped he could avoid. But, two factors converge to force him to say what he does here. The first is the contempt of Paul's adversaries for his personal appearance and delivery (10:10; I Cor 2:1-4). The second is that the nature of Paul's boasting in chapter 11 requires explanation. Left as it is, one might suspect that Paul derived some sort of warped pleasure from physical suffering. As to the first he will stop their mouths forever. As to the second he will demonstrate that his attitude was fully justified in consequence of his unparalleled spiritual privilege.

a. The revelation. 12:1-6.

12:1. It is not expedient for me doubtless to glory. What Paul does he is forced to do, but from his perspective, it hardly seems appropriate. **I will come to visions and revelations of the Lord.** The connection is with "infirmities" of 11:30. How is it that Paul takes pleasure in his infirmities? The answer is that they constitute a reminder of something that, no doubt, stands out as the most incredible experience of his life. **Of the Lord.** Visions of which the Lord is the Author, not the object. He may very well have seen the Lord at this time, although if he did, he does not say. But that is not the point. What follows is not intended to point attention to the one who received the vision, but to God who gave it.

2. I knew (Gr *oida,* "know") **a man in Christ,** i.e., "a Christian" (Rom 16:7). Although this person is not mentioned by name, it is clear that Paul is speaking of himself. This is said because the context demands it. The personal pronouns (below) demand it. His application to himself demands it (cf. vss. 6-10). **Above fourteen years ago** connects with "know" not "in

Christ." The date is not precise enough to pinpoint the exact time or event to which the apostle alludes. Some suggest that this occurred when he was stoned in Acts 14:19. Others date it to the time when he was at Tarsus, waiting for the Lord to point out his work, somewhere between Acts 9:30 and 11:25. (Alford, *The Greek Testament*, v. II, p. 710). (**Whether in the body, I cannot tell; or whether out of the body, I cannot tell: God knoweth;**). This does not connect with "vision" but "man." It is not that he is unsure as to whether it was a dream or a vision (internal or external) but uncertainty as to whether he was in a bodily or disembodied state. At any rate **such a one** was **caught up** (Gr *harpazo*, "to snatch away"). The term is used in regard to Philip in Acts 8:39 and the Rapture, in I Thessalonians 4:17. **To the third heaven.** The exact sense of this expression is not clear. Later rabbis were accustomed to dividing the heavens into seven strata. However, it is not certain if this notion dates back to the Apostolic Age. In any case, if this were the sense, it would indicate an assumption only to the area of the clouds. Some who take this view see the reference to "paradise" in the next verse to be a yet further assumption. Other commentaries suggest that a threefold division was often employed among the Jews: the air (*nubiferum*), the sky (*astriferum*), and heaven (*angeliferum*). However, there is absolutely no evidence in rabbinical sources to substantiate the existence of this idea among the Jews. Thus, the best that can be offered is that Paul's precise intent here cannot be established with absolute certainty. At any rate what follows makes the question merely academic.

3 And I knew such a man, (whether in the body, or out of the body, I cannot tell: God knoweth;)
4 How that he was caught up into paradise, and heard unspeakable words, which it is not lawful for a man to utter.

3-4. He was caught up into paradise. This term is used in the LXX in Genesis 2:8 in describing the Garden of Eden. In Paul's day it was used commonly by Jewish writers to speak of heaven (Lk 23:43; Rev 2:7). Thus, whether the **third heaven** is viewed on the way to heaven or synonymous with it, Paul's celestial journey eventually took him to heaven. **And heard unspeakable words.** Not words which "could" not be uttered, but which "may" not be uttered. As Paul renders it **Not lawful for a man to utter.** What Paul saw and heard were forbidden to be communicated to anyone.

5 Of such an one will I glory: yet of myself I will not glory, but in mine infirmities.

5. Of such a one (Gr *hyper tou toioutou*, "regarding such a one"). Again, the direction of Paul's boast is not toward himself but in regard to the experience the Lord afforded him. **Will I glory.** Such a divine favor and privilege justifies his response. **Yet of myself I will not glory, but in mine infirmities.** Paul is careful to keep the attention of his readers upon the true object of his boast.

6 For though I would desire to glory, I shall not be a fool; for I will say the truth: but *now* I forbear, lest any man should think of me above that which he seeth me *to be,* or *that* he heareth of me.

6. For though I would desire to glory. The connection is more with what is implied in the preceding verse than in what is stated. The inference is that, in the flesh, Paul had a natural inclination to want to exalt himself because of this privilege, as though he warranted God's favor in some way. **I shall not be a fool.** Paul will boast, but not in an empty claim. **For I will say the truth: but now I forbear.** What Paul says is absolutely true, yet even now he is reluctant to share it with his readers with the fear that they might **think of me above that which he seeth me to be.** Paul does not even wish to share his glory vicariously. His only interest is to exalt the Lord.

b. The thorn in the flesh. 12:7-10.

7 And lest I should be exalted above measure through the abundance of the revelations, there was given to me a thorn in the flesh, the messenger of Satan to buffet me, lest I should be exalted above measure.

7. What follows explains Paul's attitude, **lest I should be exalted above measure through the abundance of the revelations** (lit., "in order that I might not, by the abundant excess of the revelation, be uplifted"). **There was given me a thorn in the flesh** (cf. Gal 4:14). The next expression **the messenger of Satan** is appositional. Just what Paul means by this has excited no small amount of conjecture. Among the views suggested are: (a) temptations from the devil; (b) Paul's opposition from his adversaries; (c) some intense bodily pain; and (d) some recurring physical affliction such as eye trouble, epilepsy, or malaria. What is known of it is that it was a tool of Satan, it was painful ("thorn"), and it was accompanied by shame and/or embarrassment to the apostle. A fairly strong argument can be sustained in favor of the view that it was eye trouble (ophthalmia). See also Acts 13:9; 23:1; Gal 4:14-15; 6:11. However, as Alford has observed, "it may also have been something else besides this, and to such an inference, probability would lead us; disorders in the eyes, however sad in their consequences, not being usually of a very painful or distressing nature in themselves" (*Ibid*, p. 713). W. Ramsey makes a strong case for epilepsy (*St Paul the Traveller*) as does S. Asch (*The Apostle*).

8 For this thing I besought the Lord thrice, that it might depart from me.

9 And he said unto me, My grace is sufficient for thee: for my strength is made perfect in weakness. Most gladly therefore will I rather glory in my infirmities, that the power of Christ may rest upon me.

10 Therefore I take pleasure in infirmities, in reproaches, in necessities, in persecutions, in distresses for Christ's sake: for when I am weak, then am I strong.

8-9. So troublesome was this affliction that Paul **besought the Lord thrice, that it might depart** from him. Subsequently to his third request, God gives him an answer: **My grace is sufficient for thee: for my strength is made perfect in weakness.** The trial will remain but accompanied always by the enduring grace of God. And thus for Paul, this and every affliction reminded him **that the power of Christ may rest upon** him.

10. Paul concludes, this is the reason I have such an attitude, i.e., **I take pleasure in infirmities.** Not that I should suffer, but **for Christ's sake.** The thrill of suffering for the sake of Christ is that **when I am weak, then am I strong.** And so Paul concludes his "foolishness," stopping the mouths of his adversaries and establishing once and for all his right to speak as he does.

C. The Credentials of the Apostle. 12:11-18.

Paul has at length concluded a task which has been manifestly repugnant to him. He now goes on to review his credentials as an apostle and to demonstrate why 11:1-12:10 need never to have been written, especially to his own children in the faith. This he discusses in terms of his position (vs. 11), his performance (vss. 12-14) and his integrity (vss. 15-18).

1. His position among the other apostles. 12:11.

11 I am become a fool in glorying; ye have compelled me: for I ought to have been commended of you: for in nothing am I behind the very chiefest apostles, though I be nothing.

11. I am become a fool in glorifying. One can almost visualize the flush of embarrassment. **Ye have compelled me** ("Ye" is emphatic). The sincerity of Paul's affection for these people is measured by the pain he is willing to endure to secure theirs. **For I** (also emphatic) **ought to have been commended of you.** That these people whom Paul loved so much failed to take the initiative in defending him against his critics inflicted a crushing blow to the apostle. **For in nothing am I behind the very chiefest apostles.** His personal and official credentials were as clear as if Peter, James and John visited them. **Though I be nothing.** Not that Paul considered himself, personally, to be on a par with any of the other apostles; only that his credentials were equally as good (cf. also I Cor 4:7; 15:5-8).

2. His performance as a true apostle. 12:12-13.

12 Truly the signs of an apostle were wrought among you in all patience, in signs, and wonders, and mighty deeds.

13 For what is it wherein ye were inferior to other churches, except it be that I myself was not burdensome to you? forgive me this wrong.

12. Truly the signs of an apostle were wrought among you. The expression here is elliptical, suppressing a negative reaction, i.e., signs, indeed, were truly demonstrated, but never recognized.

13. For what is it wherein ye were inferior to other churches. In what respect do you find your church handicapped, for not having been founded by one of the other apostles (see I Cor 1:6-7)? **Except it be that I myself was not burdensome to you?** The only fault of his ministry was that he showed them preferential treatment. Against such ingratitude Paul's irony deals a mortal blow. Then, as though the blade did not penetrate enough, he gives it an additional twist with the words **forgive me this wrong.**

3. His behavior as an apostle. 12:14-18.

14 Behold, the third time I am ready

14-15. Finally, Paul cites his own behavior as reflective of his

to come to you; and I will not be burdensome to you: for I seek not yours, but you: for the children ought not to lay up for the parents, but the parents for the children.

15 And I will very gladly spend and be spent for you; though the more abundantly I love you, the less I be loved.

16 But be it so, I did not burden you: nevertheless, being crafty, I caught you with guile.

17 Did I make a gain of you by any of them whom I sent unto you?

18 I desired Titus, and with *him* I sent a brother. Did Titus make a gain of you? walked we not in the same spirit? *walked we* not in the same steps?

19 Again, think ye that we excuse ourselves unto you? we speak before God in Christ: but *we do* all things, dearly beloved, for your edifying.

20 For I fear, lest when I come, I shall not find you such as I would, and *that* I shall be found unto you such as ye would not: lest *there be* debates, envyings, wraths, strifes, backbitings, whisperings, swellings, tumults:

21 *And* lest, when I come again, my God will humble me among you, and *that* I shall bewail many which have sinned already, and have not repented of the uncleanness and fornication and lasciviousness which they have committed.

CHAPTER 13

THIS *is* the third *time* I am coming to you. In the mouth of two or three witnesses shall every word be established.

2 I told you before, and foretell you, as if I were present, the second time; and being absent now I write to them which heretofore have sinned, and to all other, that, if I come again, I will not spare:

integrity. **Behold, the third time I am ready to come to you.** Paul anticipates his third visit (on the chronology see 13:1 and the Introductions to both I and II Cor). **And I will not be burdensome to you.** Again he still expects nothing in terms of personal remuneration from them. **For I see not yours, but you.** His intentions were benevolent, not selfish. **Children . . . parents.** Paul was the spiritual father of the Corinthian assembly. Thus, he maintained a parental concern for them. **And I will very gladly spend and be spent.** The apostle considered himself expendable in the interests of the Corinthian assembly. **For you** (lit., "in the service of your souls"). **Though the more abundantly I love you, the less I be loved.** This is not a statement of fact, but a condition he was prepared to accept, i.e., to spend himself totally, even if it meant without a return of his affection.

16. **But be it so** ("but be that as it may") **I did not burden you,** i.e., it must be admitted that I posed no financial burden upon your church. **Nevertheless, being crafty, I caught you with guile.** This is ironic, intended as an additional objection Paul's enemies might propose.

17-18. Not only in terms of Paul's personal ministry there, but also in terms of the ministry of **Titus** and the other **brother,** the **same spirit** was evidenced, and it was clear that they walked in the **same steps.** No devious tactics could be seen in Paul or any of his companions.

D. The Charge of the Apostle. 12:19-13:10.

1. The charge to repent. 12:19-13:10.

19. **Again, think ye that we excuse ourselves upon you?** (lit., "you have been some time imagining that it is to you that I am defending myself"). If they are under the delusion that Paul has gone through all of this only on their behalf, Paul's answer is: **we speak before God in Christ.** The apostle was not accountable to the Corinthians, only to God. As for them his only concern was their **edifying.** It was not necessary for Paul to defend himself before anyone, much less qualify his apostolic authority. On the other hand it was imperative that the Corinthian believers be brought back into line and into submission to their father in the faith.

20. **For I fear, lest, when I come, I shall not find you such as I would.** His only fear is that when he arrives in Corinth he will discover, still neglected, all the same problems that he has been dealing with in these two epistles. **And that I shall be found unto you such as ye would not.** Indeed that his dark side should be exposed. And such would be the case if he should arrive to find the abuses and sins reputed of them still persisting.

21. **My God will humble me among you,** i.e., "that I should be humiliated in your midst." And such would be the case if he arrived and discovered the **uncleanness and fornication and lasciviousness which they have committed.**

13:1-2. This is the third time I am coming to you (cf. 12:14). On the "third visit" see Acts 18:1; 20:2-3; II Corinthians 2:1; and the Introduction. **In the mouth of two or three witnesses** (cf. Num 35:30; Deut 17:6; 19:15; Mt 18:16; Jn 8:17; and I Tim 5:19). Paul would leave no stone unturned upon his arrival. As he promised the last time he visited them, if he should be required to come again he **will not spare.** Should there be evidence of disobedience and sin in the assembly Paul's authority as an apostle would be witnessed, not by "signs" but in the exercise of discipline.

3 Since ye seek a proof of Christ speaking in me, which to you-ward is not weak, but is mighty in you.
4 For though he was crucified through weakness, yet he liveth by the power of God. For we also are weak in him, but we shall live with him by the power of God toward you.

5 Examine yourselves, whether ye be in the faith; prove your own selves. Know ye not your own selves, how that Jesus Christ is in you, except ye be reprobates?

6 But I trust that ye shall know that we are not reprobates.

7 Now I pray to God that ye do no evil; not that we should appear approved, but that ye should do that which is honest, though we be as reprobates.
8 For we can do nothing against the truth, but for the truth.

9 For we are glad, when we are weak, and ye are strong: and this also we wish, *even* your perfection.
10 Therefore I write these things being absent, lest being present I should use sharpness, according to the power which the Lord hath given me to edification, and not to destruction.

11 Finally, brethren, farewell. Be perfect, be of good comfort, be of one mind, live in peace; and the God of love and peace shall be with you.

12 Greet one another with an holy kiss.

13 All the saints salute you.

3. Since ye seek a proof of Christ speaking in me, i.e., they seek a proof that the apostle spoke with divine authority.

4. For though he was crucified through weakness, yet he liveth by the power of God. Paul's experience was much like that of our Lord, not only in that "He came unto his own and his own received him not." But especially here, that as Christ endured suffering and weakness, He thereby demonstrated the power of God and the wisdom of God. Even so, the weakness of the apostle would serve as a catalyst to demonstrate **the power of God toward you.**

2. The charge to self-examination. 13:5-10.

5. Thus Paul charges his readers, **Examine yourselves, whether ye be in the faith.** Paul's critics were prepared to examine him, to see if he was rightly related to Christ. He asks them to subject themselves to the same scrutiny. **Know ye not your own selves, how that Jesus Christ is in you,** ("Do you know yourselves if Christ is in you?") **except ye be reprobates?** ("unless you are counterfeits"). The challenge is to ascertain if they be genuine believers or fakes.

6. But I trust that ye shall know that we are not reprobates. Regardless of how the Corinthians came out in the test, they are to be assured that the apostle was genuine (notice the play on the term *dokimen*, "evidence" in vs. 3 and here, and *adokimen*, "counterfeit").

7-8. Now I pray to God that ye do no evil. He is not encouraging them to give occasion to show evidence of his authority through continued disobedience. **Though we be as reprobates,** i.e., "even though it means you will still look on us as reprobates." It was more important that the Corinthian believers do that which was right in the eyes of God than that they should be provided with an opportunity to see the "evidence" of Paul's apostolic authority in terms of discipline. Indeed such evidence would not be forthcoming because **we can do nothing against the truth, but for the truth.**

9-10. For we are glad. The confirmation of Paul's joy is that **when we are weak** (afforded no opportunity to display apostolic authority through punishment) **ye are strong** (by virtue of their spiritual maturity they do not need such a demonstration): **and this also we wish, even your perfection.** Their spiritual well-being was, of course, Paul's paramount interest. That is why **being absent** he **should use sharpness.** His intent under the Lord was to **edification, and not to destruction.** If in his absence they can be induced to obedience, so much the better.

V. CONCLUSION. 13:11-14.

11. Finally, brethren, farewell. In the first nine chapters Paul addressed the majority of the faithful brethren in the Corinthian assembly. In 10:1-13:10 his words have been directed primarily to those who questioned his integrity. Paul is not even certain if these are true believers. But in his farewell address the apostle turns his attention once again to those who really love and appreciate him. Thus he calls them "brethren." To these he exhorts **Be perfect, be of good comfort, be of one mind, live in peace; and the God of love and peace shall be with you.** Maturity, contentment, unity, and harmony, reflected in these terms, answer to the immaturity, unrest, division, and quarreling so evident in the Corinthian assembly.

12. Greet one another with a holy kiss. This denoted affection and kinship. It was and continues to be common, especially in the East. It was practiced even in the West till the thirteenth century.

13. All the saints salute you. This should be properly restricted to Paul's companions at the time. However, the more general truth also finds appropriate emphasis in the apostle. That is, that all the saints everywhere enjoy a common fel-

14 The grace of the Lord Jesus Christ, and the love of God, and the communion of the Holy Ghost, *be* with you all. Amen.

lowship and, therefore, a mutual interest in the spiritual welfare of one another.

14. The grace of the Lord Jesus Christ, and the love of God, and the communion of the Holy Ghost, be with you all. Amen. In his concluding benediction, Paul not only invokes the fullness of God's provision on behalf of the Corinthian believers, but also in passing, provides one of the clearest expressions in the New Testament on the doctrine of the Trinity. The deity of the Son, of the Father, and of the Holy Spirit are affirmed by virtue of their relation to one another. The distinctive personality of each is implied by the independent activity denoted in the threefold operation of grace, love, and communion.

BIBLIOGRAPHY

Barclay, W. *The Letters to the Corinthians.* Philadelphia: Westminster Press, 1956.

Darby, J. N. *Notes of a Reading on I and II Corinthians.* London: G. Morrish, n.d.

Denny, J. The Second Epistle to the Corinthians. In *The Expositor's Bible.* Ed. by W. R. Nicoll. Cincinnati: Jennings and Graham, n.d.

Erdman, C. R. *The Second Epistle of Paul to the Corinthians.* Philadelphia: Westminster Press, 1929.

Gouge, H. L. *The Mind of St. Paul.* London: Edward Arnold, 1911.

Hering, J. *The Second Epistle of St. Paul to the Corinthians.* Trans. by P. J. Allcock and A. W. Heathcote. London: The Epworth Press, 1967.

*Hodge, C. *Commentary on the Second Epistle to the Corinthians.* Grand Rapids: Eerdmans, n.d.

*Hughes, P. E. Paul's Second Epistle to the Corinthians. In *The New International Commentary.* Grand Rapids: Eerdmans, 1975.

Ironside, H. A. *Addresses on the Second Epistle to the Corinthians.* New York: Loizeaux Brothers, 1939.

Kelly, W. *Notes on the Second Epistle to the Corinthians.* Oak Park, Ill.: Bible Truth, 1975.

McPheeters, J. C. The Epistles to the Corinthians. In *Proclaiming the New Testament.* Vol. 6. Grand Rapids: Baker, 1964.

Menzies, A. *The Second Epistle of Paul to the Corinthians.* New York: Macmillan, 1912.

Ockenga, H. J. *The Comfort of God.* New York: Revell, 1944.

Plummer, A. The Second Epistle of St. Paul to the Corinthians. In *International Critical Commentary.* Edinburgh: T. & T. Clark, 1915.

Rendall, G. H. *The Epistles of St. Paul to the Corinthians.* New York: Macmillan, 1909.

Strachan, R. H. The Second Epistle of Paul to the Corinthians. In *Moffatt Commentary.* London: Hodder and Stoughton, 1935.

*Tasker, R. V. G. The Second Epistle of Paul to the Corinthians. In *Tyndale New Testament Commentaries.* Grand Rapids: Eerdmans, 1975.

The Epistle To The

GALATIANS

INTRODUCTION

Authorship. The authorship of Galatians never has been seriously doubted and it has been well said that "whoever is prepared to deny the genuineness of the epistle, would pronounce on himself the sentence of incapacity to distinguish true from false." Findlay says, "No breath of suspicion as to the authorship, integrity, or apostolic authority of the Epistle to the Galatians has reached us from ancient times" (*International Standard Bible Encyclopaedia*, Vol. 2, p. 1156). Lightfoot adds, "Its every sentence so completely reflects the life and character of the apostle to the Gentiles that its genuineness has not been seriously questioned" (*St. Paul's Epistle to the Galatians*, p. 57). Even Baur, father of the radical school of critics in Germany, and the radical Dutch scholars concede that Paul wrote Galatians. Both the internal and the external evidences of Galatians are strong, and it is not necessary to produce extensive proof of its early existence or of its pauline authorship.

Destination. The letter is addressed to the churches of Galatia. Galatia is the name that was given originally to the territory in North Central Asia Minor, where the invading Gauls settled in the third century before Christ. Gradually the Gallic population was absorbed into other peoples living there, and after a number of political changes, the territory became the property of Rome in 25 B.C. The Romans incorporated this northern section into a larger division of the land which they made a province and called it Galatia. Politically, Galatia was the Roman province which included Isauria, Lycaonia, and parts of Phrygia and Pisidia. Geographically, it was the center of Celtic tribes and included Derbe, Lystra, Iconium, and Antioch of Pisidia. The question is did Paul write to the ethnic Galatia of the north or the geographical Galatia of the south? Paul and Barnabas evangelized the southern section of the Roman Galatia during their first missionary journey (Acts 13:14-14:26). The Epistle to the Galatians agrees with everything that we know about the churches Paul founded on this journey in southern Galatia. Whereas, the existence of churches in northern Galatia is hypothetical. No churches are mentioned in the North Galatia territory, only disciples. "While the evidence for either view is not conclusive, it seems to us that the balance of probability is in favor of the South Galatian theory. While this position is steadily growing in popularity it must be admitted that the North Galatian theory is arguable and has its able defenders. Fortunately, neither the value of the epistle or its interpretation is seriously affected by the question" (D. Edmond Hiebert, *An Introduction to the Pauline Epistles*, p. 83).

Date. The date depends on whether Paul wrote to churches in the North or the South Galatian territory. The North Galatian theory would require A.D. 57, but the South Galatian theory would place it about A.D. 49. Most of the older commentators follow Lightfoot in favor of the North Galatian theory and the later date. Most contemporary commentators follow Ramsay in favor of the South Galatian theory and an early date, A.D. 49 from Antioch just before the Council of Jerusalem.

Occasion of the epistle. This epistle was called forth by the activities of the unscrupulous Judaizers. These legalists had vigorously discredited and denounced Paul and his gospel and had persuaded many to turn away from Christianity to Judaism. They claimed that the Jewish law was binding upon Christians and that salvation must be attained by the works of the law. They especially urged the Galatians to submit to circumcision. The purpose of Galatians was to root out the errors of the legalists, to win back the converts to allegiance to Christ, and to expound the doctrine of justification by faith. Paul sets forth grace as opposed to law, faith as opposed to works, and spirit as opposed to flesh.

Permanent value of Galatians. Some look upon this epistle as having little value for our times. But the perverted gospel, which is so severely condemned in this epistle, is the very message so prevalent in our days. Christendom is so thoroughly permeated by the leaven of legalism, Judaism, ritualism, Romanism, materialism, and every form of externalism. "A little leaven leaveneth the whole lump" (5:9). The Epistle to the Galatians has a contemporary relevance in its message of justification by faith for modern man, with all his cults and religious systems that seek to gain heaven by human merit, rather than by divine mercy. Erdman says, "Wherever religion has lost its reality, wherever ritual is more regarded than right living, wherever subscription to a creed is substituted for submission to Christ, wherever loud claims of orthodoxy are accompanied by conduct devoid of charity, wherever deeds of self-righteousness are obscuring the glory of the cross, there this epistle should be made to sound out its clarion call to a new dependence upon justifying grace, to a faith that is shown by works, to a walk that is by the Spirit, to a life inspired by love" (Charles R. Erdman, *The Epistle of Paul to the Galatians*, p. 5).

OUTLINE

I. Personal: The Apostle of Liberty. 1:1-2:21.
A. Introduction. 1:1-9.
B. Paul's Apostleship. 1:10-2:21.
   1. Paul's revelation from Christ. 1:10-17.
   2. Paul's acceptance by the churches. 1:18-24.
   3. Paul's approval by the apostles. 2:1-10.
   4. Paul's rebuke of Peter. 2:11-21.
II. Polemical: The Doctrine of Liberty. 3:1-4:31.
A. Paul's Appeal to Liberty. 3:1-7.
   1. Rebuke of the Galatians. 3:1-4.
   2. Reception of the Spirit. 3:5-7.
B. Paul's Argument for Liberty. 3:8-29.

   1. The promise to Abraham. 3:8-14.
   2. The purpose of the law. 3:15-29.
C. Paul's Amplification of Liberty. 4:1-31.
   1. The coming of God's Son. 4:1-7.
   2. The conduct of the Galatians. 4:8-21.
   3. The comparison of Hagar and Sarah. 4:22-31.
III. Practical: The Life of Liberty. 5:1-6:18.
A. Liberty Is Imperiled by Legalism. 5:1-12.
B. Liberty Is Perverted by Lawlessness. 5:13-26.
C. Liberty Is Perfected by Love. 6:1-10.
D. Conclusion. 6:11-18.

COMMENTARY

I. PERSONAL: THE APOSTLE OF LIBERTY. 1:1-2:21.

A. Introduction. 1:1-9.

PAUL, an apostle, (not of men, neither by man, but by Jesus Christ, and God the Father, who raised him from the dead;)

1:1. Paul. Paul was his Latin name; Saul was his Hebrew name. He was born in Tarsus in Cilicia (Acts 9:11; 22:3) of Jewish parents (Phil 3:5). His father was a Pharisee and a Roman citizen (Acts 23:6), so Paul was a Roman citizen by birth (Acts 22:27-28). He studied under the renowned Gamaliel (Acts 5:34; 22:3). **An apostle.** An apostle is one who is sent with authority to represent and speak for another. He is accredited with special delegated authority and entrusted with a special divine message. Paul claims to be a messenger, an envoy, an ambassador for Christ. He was endowed with all the credentials of his office. He was owned by Christ, commissioned by Christ, and empowered by Christ. **Not of men.** Not from men. The bluntness of Paul's denial is due to the charge of the legalists that he was not one of the Twelve and not a genuine apostle. The preposition (Gr *apo*) signifies origin and separation. Paul already states that the source of his apostleship is not from men, not emanating from men. **Neither by man.** The preposition here (Gr *dia*) implies means, medium, instrument. Paul declares decisively that the means of receiving his apostleship was not a man. "The first preposition denotes the fountain-head whence the apostle's authority springs, the second the channel through which it is conveyed" (J. B. Lightfoot, *The Epistle of St. Paul to the Galatians*, p. 71). Paul was not an ambassador of men, and his gospel was not the word and wisdom of man. Paul's "mission to the Gentiles had apparently been disparaged on the plea that it had been emanated from men, i.e., from the church of Antioch only. Again, the validity of his commission was impugned on the ground that he originally had received the Spirit through a man, i.e., through the agency of Ananias, who had been deputed to lay his hands upon him at Damascus" (Frederic Rendall, *The Epistle to the Galatians*, p. 149). Paul knew nothing about apostolic succession, but he experienced an abundant measure of apostolic success. **But by Jesus Christ, and God the Father.** When the preposition (Gr *dia*) is used of a personal agent sometimes it expresses the author of the action as well as its instrument. Here Jesus Christ is both the ultimate source and the mediate agency. Both Christ and God are governed by one preposition and joined by one conjunction, indicating that they are coequal and coeternal. There was no one higher to commission Paul and no lower through whom he was commissioned. He had a divine commission to expose false teaching, to exclaim the gospel, to establish churches, to exhort Christians, and to exalt

Christ. **Who raised him from the dead.** Paul had seen the risen Christ (I Cor 9:1; 15:8) and was qualified to be an apostle. The resurrection was God's "Amen" to Christ's "It is finished." Paul emphasized the resurrection because some were saying that he had not seen the Lord Jesus Christ and could not be an apostle. It was the risen, glorified Son of God whom Paul had seen on the road to Damascus (Acts 9:3-9). Paul's mission and message were divine, not human.

2 And all the brethren which are with me, unto the churches of Ga-lā′tia:

2. And all the brethren which are with me. Paul implies that there were with him a goodly number of Christian believers, members of the household of faith. Paul associates these unnamed fellow workers with him in sending greetings. **Unto the churches of Galatia.** Not to the church of Galatia. To Paul there was no state or national church. The word church (Gr *ekklēsia*) occurs over one hundred times in the New Testament. Once it refers to the assembly of saints in heaven (Heb 12:23), several times it is used in a wide sense (mostly in Ephesians and Colossians), but the vast majority of times it refers to a local assembly of called-out, born-again Christians bonded together for worship and work. Paul addresses this epistle to a group of churches that were relinquishing the essential truths of the gospel of grace and were going back to the works of the law as a means of justification. "The omission of any expression of praise in addressing the Galatians shows the extent of their apostasy" (J. B. Lightfoot, *The Epistle of St. Paul to the Galatians*, p. 73).

3 Grace *be* to you and peace from God the Father, and *from* our Lord Jesus Christ,

3. Grace be to you and peace. Grace was the usual Greek greeting, and peace was the usual Hebrew greeting. By these two words, Paul sums up all the blessing his heart would desire for them. In Christ, God revealed His grace, and through Christ He bestowed His peace. Grace is the sum of all the blessings extended by God; peace is the sum of all the blessings experienced by man. This customary salutation is not a perfunctory thing with Paul. He uses it here even when he has so much fault to find. He does not withhold the wish for divine grace and peace even for those whom he is about to upbraid. **From God the Father, and from our Lord Jesus Christ.** The Father and the Son cooperate fully in the salvation of sinful man.

4 Who gave himself for our sins, that he might deliver us from this present evil world, according to the will of God and our Father:

4. Who gave himself for our sins. Christ voluntarily and vicariously offered Himself on account of our sins. The preposition (Gr *hyper*) speaks of substitution, instead of, in behalf of. Christ who knew no sin, made sin for us that we might be made the righteousness of God in Him (II Cor 5:21). He exchanged places with us; He took all of our sins and gave us all of His righteousness. He was both the purchaser and the price of our redemption. There was no other good enough to pay the price of sin. At Calvary Jesus Christ once for all settled the sin question. Just before He bowed His head and gave up the ghost, He said, "It is finished" (Jn 19:30). Our sins made His sacrifice necessary, and His sacrifice is the only ground of our acceptance with God. **That he might deliver us from this present evil world.** The purpose of His sacrifice was to deliver us, rescue us, and set us free from this present evil age. It is "out of" (Gr *ek*) rather than from this pernicious age; those delivered had been within the grasp of an enemy. Christ not only delivers the believer from the penalty of sin, but also from the power of sin. Salvation is an emancipation out from a state of bondage. This is the keynote of the epistle. The word "rescued" (Gr *exaireō*) is used in Acts 23:27 to speak of Paul's rescue from the mob, and in Acts 7:34 to speak of Israel being taken out of Egypt. Here it has the connotation of rescue from danger and deliverance from bondage. Sin had endangered and enslaved us; Christ delivered us and set us free. All is due to His atoning death. This age is evil, corrupt and corrupting, deceived and deceiving. The word **evil** (Gr *ponēros*) means not only evil in its nature but actively and viciously evil in its influence. It is used to describe Satan, the god of this age, who is corrupting man and dragging him to

5 To whom *be* glory for ever and ever. Amen.

6 I marvel that ye are so soon removed from him that called you into the grace of Christ unto another gospel:

7 Which is not another; but there be some that trouble you, and would pervert the gospel of Christ.

destruction. The substitutional sacrifice of Christ alone can liberate man from Satan. **According to the will of God.** This was all in accordance with God's determinate counsel and foreknowledge (Acts 2:23).

5. To whom be glory for ever and ever. Amen. Paul ascribes praise unto God unto the ages of the ages, in contrast to the present transitory age. This doxology in the salutation takes the place of Paul's usual thanksgiving for his readers.

6. I marvel. This word (Gr *thaumazō*) was used often by Greek orators of surprise at something reprehensible and can be translated "amazed," "astonished," "bewildered." Norley translates it "dumbfounded." Paul is painfully surprised and alarmed at the instability of the Galatians. **That ye are so soon removed.** Not referring to the brevity of time since Paul's visit, but "so quickly" referring to the rapidity of their apostasy. Instead of ushering the legalists out the door (II Jn 10), these churches gullibly listened to their false teaching. The Galatians were very fickle and easily induced to change. False teaching issued in spiritual delinquency. Corrupt teaching always leads to corrupt living. In classical Greek, this word **removed** (Gr *metatithēmi*) was used of a turncoat. The Galatians were deserting Christ and turning renegade. The present tense indicates: (1) that the transfer had begun; (2) that it was in progress; and (3) that it was not yet complete. Paul does not despair because there is some hope of spiritual recovery and restoration. All is not lost, but time is of a premium. The middle voice of the verb implies that the Galatians were transferring themselves from grace to law and from liberty to bondage. They were responsible and accountable for their own defection. **From him that called you.** Their defection was not only from the gospel of God, but from God Himself. This assertion should have startled the Galatians who probably thought they were honoring God by trying to keep His law. Their departure from God was dangerous and dreadful. They were abandoning God and His grace by putting themselves under the law and its curse. **Into the grace of Christ.** God calls in and by Christ's grace. This suggests the permanency of the divine favor in which God calls and through which the blessings of Christ are given. God called the Galatians to salvation which was: (1) purchased at Calvary; (2) offered in and by grace; and (3) to be accepted by faith. All that God requires of man, He has already provided by grace in Christ. **Unto another gospel.** There are two Greek words which mean **another**. One (Gr *allos*) means another of the same kind, a numerical difference; and the other (Gr *heteros*) means another of a different kind, a qualitative difference. Here the meaning is that there is no other gospel, although the legalists had brought them a different kind of teaching, which they claimed to be the gospel. There is an essential difference between the true gospel and a man-made, spurious gospel (cf. II Cor 11:4). There is but one, and only one gospel concerning the eternal Son of God who became incarnate in order to become the propitiation for the sins of the whole world (I Jn 2:2). Christ's finished work at Calvary enables God to be just and the justifier of him who believes in Christ (Rom 3:26). God has no other gospel, and He cannot and will not tolerate the perversion of His gospel.

7. Which is not another. It was different and therefore no gospel at all. A message of salvation by works is not good news to lost sinners. The message of the legalists was diametrically opposed to the gospel of God's grace. When the works of the law are added to grace, you no longer have grace. "If the clause be rendered, whereas there is no other gospel (i.e., than the true), the sense becomes perfectly clear, and it forms an appropriate introduction to the succeeding anathemas by its emphatic testimony to the one true gospel" (Frederic Rendall, *The Epistle to the Galatians*, p. 152). There is no other gospel, only a spurious semblance. **Some that trouble you.** This word (Gr *tarassō*) means to agitate, to trouble, to cause inward commotion, to disturb mentally with fear, excitement, and perplexity. The present tense means that the legalists were in Galatia at the time Paul wrote, and they were confusing the Galatians and shaking their allegiance to Christ. **And would.** The legalists are determined to pervert the gospel, and Paul writes to hinder their success. **Pervert the gospel of Christ.** This word **pervert** (Gr *metastrephō*) is used only three times in the New Testament, and it means to completely change into something of the opposite nature as in Acts 2:20 where the sun is turned into darkness and in James 4:9 where laughter is turned into mourning. The legalists were determined to pervert the gospel by substituting law for grace, circumcision for the cross, works for faith, bondage for liberty, and self for Christ. Any change in the gospel of Christ is a corruption, interfering with its simplicity, its purity, and its effectiveness. Even the thought of this stirs Paul to the very depths of his being. Note how vehement is his language now, and how he repeated it for greater emphasis.

8 But though we, or an angel from heaven, preach any other gospel unto you than that which we have preached unto you, let him be accursed.

8. But though we, or an angel from heaven, preach any other gospel. Paul does not say that he or a messenger from heaven was likely to preach any other gospel. He merely uses a future hypothetical possibility to illustrate the case. This passage directly speaks against such claims as that of the Mormons, whose *Book of Mormon* claims angelic authority as delivered by the Angel Moroni and "translated" by their founder Joseph Smith. **Let him be accursed.** An "anathema" on anyone who would proclaim a gospel contrary to that which Paul delivered and had received from God (I Cor 15:3-4). God does not want His Word twisted by unlearned and unstable men unto the destruction of souls (II Pet 3:17). God said what He meant, and He meant what He said. God can do nothing less than put an awful curse on all who reject, pervert and falsify the gospel of His Son. It was the Holy Spirit who moved Paul to pen these serious words. We must never forget that the awful day of doom and destruction is coming when the divine "anathema" pronounced here will be executed (II Thess 1:7-9). May God's people everywhere stand with Paul in opposition to false teaching. May God help us to believe the gospel, to behave the gospel, and to become living epistles of the gospel.

9 As we said before, so say I now again, if any man preach any other gospel unto you than that ye have received, let him be accursed.

9. As we said before. The language is too emphatic to refer to the verse lightly. Paul no doubt had warned them of the dangers of false teachers as he did the Ephesian elders (Acts 20:29-32). The perfect tense of **said** (Gr *prolegō*) means that it was a certain and clear pronouncement. The Galatians still remember Paul's warning, and therefore their defection is inexcusable. The plural number **(we)** shows that the previous warning was given by others in addition to Paul. **If any man.** The particle (Gr *ei*) speaks of a fulfilled condition. Paul is not speaking of a future probability (vs. 8), but of an actual, current fact, and he hurls the anathema directly at the legalists. Note the omission in verse 9 of "we or an angel."

B. Paul's Apostleship. 1:10-2:21.

1. Paul's revelation from Christ. 1:10-17.

10 For do I now persuade men, or God? or do I seek to please men? for if I yet pleased men, I should not be the servant of Christ.

10. For. This introduces a justification of the severe language just used. **Do I now persuade men. . . ?** This means to win over, to conciliate, to render friendly to one's self. These rhetorical questions indicate that an attack has been made on Paul for the purpose of discrediting both him and his ministry. He denies the charges. Paul was not softening down unwelcome truths to men, that he might by some means win them over to his way of thinking. Neither was he trying to persuade God to tone down His message. Paul's loyalty to Christ and his sufferings for Christ were evidences that he was not seeking man's approval,

11 But I certify you, brethren, that the gospel which was preached of me is not after man.

11. But I certify you. I make known, inform, tell you plainly, assure you. This word (Gr *gnorizō*) is used to introduce matters of great importance (I Cor 12:3; 15:1; II Cor 8:1). Paul uses a strong word to leave no doubt as to the truth of the statement he is about to make. **Brethren.** Paul addresses them as brethren in Christ, sons of the same heavenly Father. They are deceived, disturbed, and defecting in their devotion and duty to Christ. But they are still regarded as brethren, brethren needing Paul's Spirit-inspired counsel. **That the gospel which was preached of me.** Literally, the gospel gospelled by me. **Is not after man.** Not according to man. Paul sets the record straight. He affirms the divine origin of his message in terms similar to those used to declare the divine origin of his apostleship. Both his mission and his message are independent of man, both received by direct divine revelation.

12 For I neither received it of man, neither was I taught *it*, but by the revelation of Jesus Christ.

12. For I neither received it of man. Man had absolutely nothing to do with Paul's gospel. His message was not received from man as a source or through man as a channel. The preposition (Gr *para*) translated of emphasizes the idea of transmission and connects the giver with the receiver. Paul did not receive the gospel "from" man. **Neither was I taught it.** Paul was taught the precepts of Judaism at the feet of Gamaliel (Acts 5:34; 22:3), but he received no human instruction or human interpretation of the gospel. But, on the contrary, **by the revelation.** Therefore there was nothing human about it. It was a direct divine communication of previously unknown truth. The word "revelation" is used of the unveiling of divine persons or things, never of one human revealing a secret to another man. Paul refers to his experience on the road to Damascus (Acts 9), which was supplemented during his seclusion in Arabia. **Of Jesus Christ.** This can mean either Christ is revealing or Christ is revealed; both interpretations make good sense. This is a subjective genitive. Christ revealed Himself to Paul. Christ was the subject, sum, and substance of that revelation with the result that Paul became a new man with a new message to proclaim. Paul was not a man-made apostle. He received his commission and his message from Christ.

13 For ye have heard of my conversation in time past in the Jews' religion, how that beyond measure I persecuted the church of God, and wasted it:

13. For ye have heard. Paul refers to the time he spent with them. He often related his personal testimony as part of his ministry (Acts 22 and 26). **Of my conversation.** Originally the word (Gr *anastrophē*) meant "upturning" and then came to mean that thing which would keep on turning up, and means the custom, conduct, or manner of one's life. It refers to Paul's everyday life. **In time past in the Jews' religion.** This was Judaism as a religion of faith and custom, with human traditions superimposed upon it; an apostate Judaism as an ethical, unspiritual cult. **How that beyond measure.** Transliterated hyperbole and means according to excess, immeasurable. **I persecuted.** This word (Gr *diōkō*) means put to flight, drive away, harass, trouble, molest, persecute. The imperfect tense denotes continuous action (I kept on persecuting). Paul constantly and relentlessly persecuted the church. **The church of God.** The whole body (Gr *ekklēsia*) of born-again believers. It is God's church; redeemed by God's Son and regenerated by God's Holy Spirit. It is the body of Christ, in whom the Holy Spirit lives and through whom the Holy Spirit ministers. **And wasted it.** This word (Gr *portheō*) means to overthrow, destroy, make havoc, lay waste. The original idea is that of rooting up and leaving devastation behind. The imperfect tense implies that Paul continually, persistently, and violently kept on ravaging the church (Acts 9:13; 26:10-11). Paul had been the supreme Judaistic fanatic of his time.

14 And profited in the Jews' religion above many my equals in mine own na-

14. And profited. Literally (Gr *prokoptō*) "to cut forward," hence to blaze a trail or cut a pioneer path. Paul was advancing,

tion, being more exceedingly zealous of the traditions of my fathers.

15 But when it pleased God, who separated me from my mother's womb, and called *me* by his grace,
16 To reveal his Son in me, that I might preach him among the heathen; immediately I conferred not with flesh and blood:

pushing forward, and outstripping all others in power and prestige. **In the Jews' religion.** Traditional Judaism was not much like Mosaism in its pristine purity. Paul was a zealous, law-loving Pharisee. **Above many my equals.** He started out with his fellow classmates but soon far surpassed them in his zeal and activities for the traditions of Judaism. **In mine own nation.** My race. **Being more exceedingly zealous.** Paul was an uncompromising partisan, a zealot burning with superabundant zeal. **Of the traditions of my fathers.** Traditions played a large part in the precepts and practices of the Pharisees. By traditions Paul means those hundreds of human commandments built around the Old Testament law and which must be maintained at any cost. Our Lord Jesus distinguished between the written law and man-made traditions and clearly proclaimed that the traditions of man caused the Word of God to be of none effect (Mt 15:1-6; Mk 7:3-13). But for the grace of God, Paul would have lived and died a profound protagonist of Judaism.

15-16. But. Very strong here, in contrast to the traditions. **When it pleased God.** God's good pleasure in His gracious purpose. **Who separated me.** Refers to God's setting Paul apart for special service. The word (Gr *aphorizō*) means to work off from a boundary, to limit, to separate, to designate, to set apart, to appoint. The Pharisees were the separatists who held themselves off from others. Paul conceives himself a spiritual separatist, separated unto the gospel of God (Rom 1:1). **From my mother's womb.** The preposition (Gr *ek*) makes the temporal starting point. Only God could define the limits of one's life while yet in the womb of his mother. God's plan for Paul's life was determined before he was born (cf. Jer 1:5). **And called me by his grace.** It was by means of grace that God called Paul out of darkness into His marvelous light (I Pet 2:9) and made him a chosen vessel (Acts 9:15), "a vessel unto honor, sanctified, and meet for the master's use, and prepared unto every good work" (II Tim 2:21). **To reveal his Son in me.** Paul was inwardly enlightened. After his vision of Christ, Paul spent three days in solitary communion (Acts 9:9). There "was an inward and spiritual revelation which followed that appeal to eye and ear" (Frederic Rendall, *The Epistle to the Galatians*, p. 154). "The whole subject of discourse in this paragraph is not how Paul made known his gospel, but how he received it" (Ernest DeWitt Burton, *A Critical and Exegetical Commentary on the Epistle to the Galatians*, p. 51). There was altogether a threefold revelation: (1) to Paul; (2) in Paul; and (3) through Paul, and in that order. **That.** In order that, (Gr *hina*). Now the purpose of the revelation is made known. It was not for salvation alone, but for service. We are saved to serve. Salvation is a means to an end, not an end in itself. **I might preach him.** The final object of God's revelation to Paul was that he should go on proclaiming Christ to others. The present tense (Gr *euagglizomai*) speaks of continued effort, and the accusative case (Gr *auton*), **him**, the person preached. Christ was the sum total of Paul's message, not the law or ceremonies. Paul was not proclaiming a plan of salvation but the person of the Saviour. It is not a matter of one religion against another. Paul has a divine commission to preach Christ. **Among the heathen.** God not only told Paul **whom** to preach, but where to preach, among the Gentiles (Acts 9:15; 22:15; 26:16-19). **Immediately I conferred not.** Paul received his commission from God, and there was no need to consult man. The double compound (Gr *prosanatilhēmi*) means "to place over and toward," hence to put one's self in communion with another. The real purpose of a conference is to get advice from someone more knowledgeable than yourself. Paul already had been made an apostle and already knew God's plan for his life (Acts 26:14-19); he had no need of man's advice. Paul is establishing his dependence upon God and his independence from man. **With flesh and blood.** Apparently a reminiscence of "flesh and blood hath not revealed it unto thee, but my Father" (Mt 16:17). Flesh and blood suggests human weakness and ignorance and represents human as opposed to divine wisdom. Man could not add anything to God's revelation.

17 Neither went I up to Jerusalem to them which were apostles before me; but I went into Arabia, and returned again unto Damascus.

17. Neither. Literally, not even **apostles before me.** The Jerusalem apostles were genuine apostles, but so was Paul. Before in order of time, but not in rank; they had more seniority, but not more authority. Paul's call and commission did not come from them nor did he receive confirmation by them. Paul's apostleship was firsthand. There was no human instrumentality in his apostleship. **But.** On the contrary, Paul took the opposite course, **I went into Arabia, and returned again unto Damascus.** Paul avoided Jerusalem and emphasizes his independence of the other apostles. The Holy Spirit has not revealed all we would like to know, but Paul spent considerable time alone with God (cf. Moses and Elijah).

2. Paul's acceptance by the churches. 1:18-24.

18 Then after three years I went up to Jerusalem to see Peter, and abode with him fifteen days.

18. Then after three years. Paul dates the time from his conversion. During these three years, he had no contact with any of the apostles. **I went up to Jerusalem.** His first visit is recorded in Acts 9:26-30. **To see Peter.** See (Gr *historeō*), used only here in the New Testament, is the word from which we get our word "history." It was used to express either: (1) to learn facts from personal inquiry or observation or; (2) to relate facts as a historian would. There was an interchange of facts between Paul and Peter. The purpose of this visit was to become personally acquainted with Peter, not to gain official sanction or recognition. They met on common ground. Peter did not install Paul into the apostleship nor confer anything upon him. Paul uses the old Aramaic name "Cephas." **And abode with him.** The preposition (Gr *pros*) means "toward" him. Paul was facing Cephas in a most personal, intimate, and friendly manner, but not subordinating himself in any way. Paul visited Peter as an equal. **Fifteen days.** Paul's visit was interrupted because the Grecians were seeking his life (Acts 9:29) and the Lord appeared to him while he was praying in the Temple and told him to leave quickly (Acts 22:17-18).

19 But other of the apostles saw I none, save James the Lord's brother.

19. James. The half-brother of our Lord Jesus Christ. This distinguishes him from James the brother of John. He was a leader in the Jerusalem church (Acts 15).

20 Now the things which I write unto you, behold, before God, I lie not.

20. Before God, I lie not. Paul's enemies had accused him of being a slick talker. He asserts his integrity by a solemn affirmation, made as if in the very presence of God. His word was as good as his oath, as Christ taught every man's word should be (Mt 5:33-37).

21 Afterwards I came into the regions of Syria and Cī-lī′cia;

21. Regions of Syria and Cilicia. Regions (Gr *klema*) is the source of our word "climate" and refers to the coastal plains of the countries named. Paul does not describe his ministry here, but it lasted for about six years. During this time Paul was out of contact with Jerusalem. Syria is named first because of its prominence in the Roman Empire and because of the greater significance of Paul's ministry here.

22 And was unknown by face unto the churches of Judæa which were in Christ:

22. And was unknown by face. They did not recognize Paul when they saw him. **Into the churches of Judea.** There were other local churches in Judea besides the church at Jerusalem. **Which were in Christ.** True churches are in Christ as branches are in the True Vine (Jn 15:5).

23 But they had heard only, That he which persecuted us in times past now preacheth the faith which once he destroyed.

23. But they had heard only. The members of the Judaean churches kept on hearing from time to time, as the Greek present tense implies. **Now preacheth the faith.** The saving faith in Christ based on the truth of the gospel which was once for all delivered unto the saints (Jude 3). **Which once he destroyed.** Same word (Gr *portheō*) translated as "wasted" in verse 13. The imperfect tense speaks of continuous action. Before his

24 And they glorified God in me.

24. And they glorified God in me. They recognized God's handiwork (Eph 2:10) in Paul and kept on glorifying God for saving, transforming, and using Paul. How different from the reaction of the legalists who were seeking to destroy Paul's ministry. Paul has displayed the divine origin of his apostleship and his independence from the apostolic band.

3. Paul's approval by the apostles. 2:1-10.

CHAPTER 2
THEN fourteen years after I went up again to Jerusalem with Barnabas, and took Titus with *me* also.

2:1. Then fourteen years after. If fourteen years after his conversion, it could be his visit recorded in Acts 11:30; but if fourteen after his first visit, it would be the one recorded in Acts 15:2. Scholars are divided. J. B. Lightfoot and others hold to the traditional view (Acts 15:2) but Sir William Ramsay and many contemporary scholars hold to the other view (11:30). The evidence is not conclusive, so we must be tolerant, and not dogmatic. The exact date is important in establishing the chronology of Paul's mission but not in the exposition of his message. **I went up again to Jerusalem.** The preposition (Gr *ana*) may be used because of the geographical position of Jerusalem, or more probably because of its religious superiority. Paul's contacts with Jerusalem were few and brief. **With Barnabas.** A wealthy Levite of Cyprus. He had keen insight into the character of man and clear understanding of Christianity. He was a philanthropist and had the confidence of the whole church. **And took.** This double compound (Gr *sumparalambanō*) means to take along with as a companion. **Titus.** A Gentile convert. He is not mentioned in the book of Acts, and little is known of him.

2 And I went up by revelation, and communicated unto them that gospel which I preach among the Gentiles, but privately to them which were of reputation, lest by any means I should run, or had run, in vain.

2. And I went up by revelation. The Holy Spirit revealed His will to Paul, and Paul was obedient to His divine guidance. Paul did not go merely because of any doubt or difficulty he was experiencing, and neither on his own initiative, nor at the direction of the church of Antioch. **And communicated.** Literally "set up" (Gr *anatithēmi*) for the consideration of others. The real purpose of his visit is to place before the apostles the gospel he is preaching among the peoples in the Gentile lands. **Privately.** To the recognized spiritual leaders, rather than to the whole church body. This does not imply secrecy. **Of reputation.** The apostolic leaders (cf. vss. 6 and 9), were men of eminence, those looked upon as authorities and held in high regard. **Run in vain.** Lest I should be running in vain, thwarted by misunderstanding and opposition. Paul is not expressing any doubt. He desires to maintain unity and fellowship with the apostles in Jerusalem and avoid a split. A schism would have caused division in every church. But he did not go to Jerusalem to determine whether he was preaching the one true gospel but whether they were. But Paul would be running a fruitless race and to no purpose if the message of the legalists was the true gospel. There was so much at stake: Is salvation by law or by grace, a matter of human attainment or of divine atonement, by works or by faith?

3 But neither Titus, who was with me, being a Greek, was compelled to be circumcised:

3. But neither. Not even. **Titus.** This Gentile was accepted as a real Christian just as he was. (Not) **compelled to be circumcised.** Titus was a test case. The legalists failed completely in their demands and position. It is evident that the apostles at Jerusalem did not sanction their teaching that circumcision is necessary for salvation. Paul prevailed against all the pressure brought by the legalists to force the issue. Paul stood firmly and successfully and won the full approval of the apostles. Paul resisted, rejected, and refused the demands of the legalists. Concession was not expedient; it was impossible, and it would have been fatal to Christianity. Paul could not and would not surrender on this vital issue. The gospel of grace would have disintegrated if Paul had circumcised Titus on the demands of the legalists. "Once the Judaizers made their demand regarding Titus, they destroyed all reason for his ever being circumcised"

(R. C. H. Lenski, *Interpretation of Paul's Epistles to the Galatians, to the Ephesians, and to the Philippians*, p. 76). Thank God for the undaunted, uncompromising apostle who "kept the faith" (II Tim 4:7), and may He raise multitudes to follow his steps.

4 And that because of false brethren unawares brought in, who came in privily to spy out our liberty which we have in Christ Jesus, that they might bring us into bondage:

4. False brethren. Those who ostentatiously profess to be Christians, but who are destitute of spiritual life. They may have regarded Christ as Messiah, but they knew nothing of salvation through His atoning blood. They were clinging to a salvation-by-works system. **Unawares brought in.** Literally, brought in by the side or on the sly (Gr *pareiserchomai*). These traitors were foisted in unexpectedly, smuggled in surreptitiously and insidiously. **Came in privily.** Further describing the secret infiltration of these enemies who "crept in unawares" (Jude 4). The verb means to come in secretly or by stealth, to creep or steal in. **To spy out.** This infinitive of purpose (Gr *kataskopeō*) means to reconnoiter, to make a treacherous investigation, to examine carefully with hostile intent. **Our liberty which we have in Christ Jesus.** Our emancipation from legalism and ceremonialism. **That they might bring us into bondage.** Expressing the ultimate result they hoped to attain. Their object was to reduce Christians to abject spiritual slavery, completely enslave them by rites, rules, and regulations. These spies operating under false colors were trying to undermine our liberty in Christ.

5 To whom we gave place by subjection, no, not for an hour; that the truth of the gospel might continue with you.

5. To whom we gave place. Paul refused to yield for a single moment. He held his ground firmly and did not give in an inch. He refused to compromise the truth of God. **By subjection.** The article (Gr *tē*) identifies the submission as that demanded by the legalists. **That the truth of the gospel.** The gospel in its integrity as opposed to the pseudo-gospel of the enemies of the cross. This denotes salvation by faith. This was the reason for Paul's adamant stand in earnestly contending for the faith. He would not let the Gentiles be deprived of the true gospel. The future of Christianity was bound up in this test case, and by God's grace Paul gained the victory. **Might continue with you.** For you and your spiritual welfare. "The idea of firm possession is enforced by the compound verb, by the present tense, and by the preposition" (J. B. Lightfoot, *The Epistle of Paul to the Galatians*, p. 107). Many weak-kneed, jellyfish preachers would have yielded and then justified themselves on the basis of love and expediency, but not the champion Paul.

6 But of these who seemed to be somewhat, (whatsoever they were, it maketh no matter to me: God accepteth no man's person:) for they who seemed *to be somewhat* in conference added nothing to me:

6. Whatsoever they were. Referring to the Jerusalem apostles, their past privileges and their present position. They had sojourned with Christ and had been appointed to Him. It **maketh no matter to me.** Paul does not say "that the standing and repute of the apostles were matters of indifference to him, but that he was indifferent about receiving his commission from them as recognized dignitaries of the church" (M. R. Vincent, *Word Studies in the New Testament*, Vol. IV, pp. 97-98). Paul received his apostleship directly from Christ and was independent on the other apostles. **God accepteth no man's person.** Literally, God does not receive the face of man. God looks on the heart and is no respecter of persons. Phillips translates, "God is not impressed with a man's office." **Added nothing to me.** They imparted no new information, no new interpretation, and no new application. There was no correction of, deletion from, or addition to Paul's message. There was no deficiency in Paul's gospel. He preached the truth, the whole truth, and nothing but the truth (Acts 20:27).

7 But contrariwise, when they saw that the gospel of the uncircumcision was committed unto me, as *the gospel* of the circumcision *was* unto Peter;

7. But contrariwise. Those in repute not only set nothing before Paul, but they heartily approved him and his mission. **Saw.** Perceived the divine source of Paul's apostleship. **The gospel.** There is only one gospel. There is no difference in content, only in recipients. The same gospel is for all men. **Committed unto me.** Entrusted. The perfect tense speaks of Paul's certain commission. **Uncircumcision . . . circumcision.**

Gentiles and Jews respectively. **Peter.** Mentioned not with the idea of excluding the other apostles, but as representing them. The ministry of Paul was primarily, but not exclusively, to the Gentiles. That of Peter was primarily, but not exclusively, to the Jews. Both men were divinely appointed to proclaim a divine message by divine power.

8 (For he that wrought effectually in Peter to the apostleship of the circumcision, the same was mighty in me toward the Gentiles:)

8. Wrought effectually. Energized (Gr *energeō*) by the inward power of the Holy Spirit for the furtherance of the gospel. God gets all the glory for what He accomplished through Peter and Paul. There was material acknowledgement of each other's equal apostleship.

9 And when James, Cē′phas, and John, who seemed to be pillars, perceived the grace that was given unto me, they gave to me and Barnabas the right hands of fellowship; that we *should go* unto the heathen, and they unto the circumcision.

9. James, Cephas, and John. James is named first because of the prominence of his leadership in Jerusalem and because of his strict legal tendencies. His support of Gentile freedom was of great importance. **Who seemed to be pillars.** The Jews used this metaphor to refer to their great teachers. The church was looked upon as the temple of God, and these men were regarded as supporters. **Perceived the grace.** As they reflected on the manifestation of God's grace in Paul, they recognized his equality with them, his official status and prerogative, and his independent mission to the Gentiles. **The right hands of fellowship.** Fellowship speaks of cooperation and joint participation. The right hand of fellowship was given to equals and indicated a token of approval and a pledge of fidelity and agreement to work in their respective fields, so that all men would be evangelized by the same gospel. This was the dramatic conclusion of the pact for cooperation in independent spheres of evangelism. The legalists were brushed aside when these five men shook hands as equals in the work of Christ.

10 Only *they would* that we should remember the poor; the same which I also was forward to do.

10. Only. One stipulation was emphasized. **Remember the poor.** Judaea often experienced famine, and the Christians there suffered most because of social ostracism and religious hatred. **I also was forward to do.** Paul was zealous to keep on remembering the poor and needed no prompting. Such generosity would foster a sense of unity in both Jewish recipients and Gentile givers.

4. Paul's rebuke of Peter. 2:11-21.

11 But when Peter was come to Antioch, I withstood him to the face, because he was to be blamed.

11. But when Peter was come to Antioch. The exact time is not stated. Certainly it was after Peter's vision at Joppa (Acts 10:10-16) and his experience in the home of Cornelius (Acts 11:1-8). Peter knew that God is no respecter of persons and that ceremonial uncleanness is a thing of the past. **I withstood him to the face.** This was face to face confrontation between two apostles. Paul set himself against Peter, resisting and reprimanding him. There is no hint of Peter's so-called "primacy." The false teachers attributed superiority to Peter, whose words and actions were regarded as next to infallible. Peter had no authority over Paul. Paul is not belittling Peter in the eyes of the Galatians; he is proving his own divine commission. How could anyone claim that Paul received his apostleship from any man after he rebuked Peter? **Because he was to be blamed.** Peter incurred reproach by his own inconsistent conduct, and he stood self-condemned without any defense. In this verse Paul introduces an incident which not only proves that he had not received his apostleship from the apostles, but that he actually was so independent of them that he openly rebukes Peter for a course of action wholly inconsistent with the gospel.

12 For before that certain came from James, he did eat with the Gentiles: but when they were come, he withdrew and separated himself, fearing them which were of the circumcision.

12. For before that certain came from James. Certain certified members in good standing in Jerusalem; no doubt they were of the circumcision party who assailed Peter once before (Acts 11:1-3). At that time he successfully defended his actions. It does not say that James sent these men with any special authority or for the purpose of bringing believers under the bondage of law. However, their presence in Antioch exerted a tremendous influence on Peter. **He did eat with the Gentiles.** The Greek imperfect tense shows that Peter was in the habit of eating with Gentiles; his habit was to publicly fraternize with them. God had revealed to Peter that the Levitical legislation regarding certain foods had been set aside. In obedience to God's revelation, Peter laid aside the obsolete Jewish custom and was eating with Gentiles. **He withdrew and separated himself.** He began to draw back in isolation, holding himself aloof, and having nothing to do with the Gentiles, as if he was afraid of defilement. Peter gradually discontinued his former practice of eating with the Gentiles when the circumcision party arrived. He was trying to change his conduct without letting them know what he had been doing and without breaking off so abruptly that the Gentile brethren would notice it. **Fearing them.** Peter had his eyes on man instead of looking unto Christ, and he was afraid of losing his prestige in Jerusalem and of facing the arrogant attitude of the circumcision party. He concluded that it was more important to keep his Jerusalem friends happy than to avoid the possible risk of estranging Gentile believers. His breach of fellowship with the Gentiles brought about misunderstanding and division in Antioch. Paul recognized that Peter's conduct practically exhibited to the Gentiles that they were not fit company for the circumcised apostle, and was in effect a summons for them to become Jews.

13 And the other Jews dissembled likewise with him; insomuch that Barnabas also was carried away with their dissimulation.

13. And the other Jews dissembled. Other Jews followed the example of Peter, who was trying unsuccessfully to play both ends against the middle without letting either the Gentiles or the Jews know exactly what he was doing. **Barnabas.** Paul's co-laborer in proclaiming grace and liberty was also carried away. The legalists claimed that the law could do something that faith in Christ could not do. They were not only trying to supplement the gospel Paul preached, but to supplant it. **Carried away.** Followed their example. Barnabas was swept off his feet and shaped his conduct by that of others. **Their dissimulation** (Gr *hypocrisis*). The source of our word "hypocrite." It is pretense, playing a part, believing one thing and practicing another. Their inconsistent conduct was hypocrisy because it concealed their true convictions. It was a surrender of Christian liberty, a denial of Christian unity, and an impeachment of the Christian message. Thank God Paul saw the gravity of the situation and did something about it.

14 But when I saw that they walked not uprightly according to the truth of the gospel, I said unto Peter before *them* all, If thou, being a Jew, livest after the manner of Gentiles, and not as do the Jews, why compellest thou the Gentiles to live as do the Jews?

14. Walked not uprightly. Literally, straight-footed, forward, unwavering (Gr *orthopodeō*). Peter and company were walking in a crooked path, a path that was likely to lead others astray. They were guilty of appearing to walk one way, but turning aside whenever it was convenient to give another impression. **According to the truth of the gospel.** Their compromising conduct was contrary to the gospel. They had deviated from the standard of God's Word. **I said unto Peter before them all.** Paul severely and publicly rebukes Peter for his inconsistency and his insincerity. The rebuke was as wide as the relapse. Paul, vested with divine authority, took Peter to task. Paul's unsparing, but tactful, rebuke of Peter reveals his apostolic independence of all human authority. Peter did not try to defend himself, but graciously accepted the well-deserved rebuke and later referred to "our beloved brother Paul" (II Pet 3:15-16). **Livest after the manner of Gentiles.** Not under the customs and restrictions of the Jews. Peter's habit had been to live according to Gentile ways, although he was a Jew by birth. With this as a condition, Paul asks Peter a pointed question. **Why compellest. . . ?** Indirect compulsion by his example, not by false preaching. He was guilty of compromising conduct by which he was obliging the Gentiles to Judaize, to adopt Jewish customs and observe Jewish statutes.

15 We *who are* Jews by nature, and not sinners of the Gentiles,

15. We. Paul includes Peter in holding the doctrine of justification by faith. **Jews by nature.** Born Jews with special privileges and prerogatives, not Jews by proselytism. **Sinners of the**

Gentiles. Jews regarded all Gentiles as unclean dogs, sinners without the restraint of the law.

16 Knowing that a man is not justified by the works of the law, but by the faith of Jesus Christ, even we have believed in Jesus Christ, that we might be justified by the faith of Christ, and not by the works of the law: for by the works of the law shall no flesh be justified.

16. Knowing that a man, any man, Jew or Gentile, **is not justified by the works of the law.** Justification is the judicial act of God whereby He declares righteous those who trust in Christ. It is the reversal of His attitude toward the sinner because of the sinner's new relationship to Christ. God did condemn, now He acquits. This means that all the guilt and penalty of the believer is removed forever (Rom 8:1) and that the perfect righteousness of Christ is imputed to him from (Gr *ek*) the works of the law, not resulting from man's deeds of obedience. The standard of the law was so exacting that no one (except Christ) ever kept it, and so the broken law could only condemn (Rom 3:19-20). **But by the faith of Jesus Christ.** Not on account of faith but only by means of faith. Faith is not the ground of justification: grace is. It is not faith in our faith, but faith in Jesus Christ. No one is justified except through faith in Christ. Salvation is wholly by divine mercy (Tit 3:5) and not by human merit. **Even as we have believed in Jesus Christ.** Even the Jews with all their privileges are no better than the Gentiles. Their law was inadequate and insufficient to bring them into a right relationship with God. Therefore it was necessary for Jews to believe in Christ in order to be justified. Since no flesh, Jew or Gentile, could ever be justified by the works of the law, how ridiculous it is to bind the burden of law-works on the Gentiles who were already justified by faith in Christ. Note the progressive order in this verse: knowing, believing, justified.

17 But if, while we seek to be justified by Christ, we ourselves also are found sinners, *is* therefore Christ the minister of sin? God forbid.

17. Is therefore Christ the minister of sin? An illogical inference. They were sinners already in spite of being Jews. Christ simply revealed to them the fact of their sin. Since grace does not encourage men to sin (Rom 6:1-2), Christ is not a minister or promoter of sin by causing us to abandon the law as a means of justification. This is a rebuttal to the argument of the legalists that salvation in Christ is insufficient.

18 For if I build again the things which I destroyed, I make myself a transgressor.

18. For if I build again. Return to the law. After Paul had preached that justification is only by faith in Christ plus nothing, it would be folly to seek righteousness by keeping the law. This would be building again that which he destroyed. **Destroyed.** This word means to demolish, dissolve, disunite, pull down. Paul destroyed the teaching that salvation was by works of merit by proclaiming that salvation was by grace through faith in Christ. When Peter lived as a Gentile he tore down the ceremonial law; when he lived as a Jew he tore down the doctrine of salvation by grace. **A transgressor.** If he denied the absolute sufficiency of Christ. Jewish believers were right when they abandoned law-works as a means of salvation and were justified by faith in Christ; it would be wrong for them to return to law-works now.

19 For I through the law am dead to the law, that I might live unto God.

19. For I through the law. Through the agency of the law. Paul relates his own experience. The Old Testament law is powerless to give life; it only condemns the guilty. Under the law, Paul was brought to despair; his only hope was to find salvation elsewhere. The condemnation of the law drove Paul to Christ for salvation. **Am dead to the law.** Better, died to the law. To die to anything is to cease to have any relation to it so that it has no claim or control over one. The law condemned Paul to death, but Christ, his substitute, died for him. Paul died in Christ and is now united with Him in resurrection life. The sentence of death was executed on Paul in the person of the Lord Jesus Christ. Once the law has executed the death penalty it has no more jurisdiction over the one executed, for the law has dominion over a man only as long as he lives (Rom 7:1). Having died with Christ, Paul is dead to the law, and so is every true believer. When Christ died, we died. **That I might live unto God.** Identification with Christ enabled Paul to die unto the law

20 I am crucified with Christ: nevertheless I live; yet not I, but Christ liveth in me: and the life which I now live in the flesh I live by the faith of the Son of God, who loved me, and gave himself for me.

as a means of obtaining righteousness and to live unto God, the source of his righteousness and the object of his new life.

20. I am crucified with Christ. This is Paul's personal testimony, which may be repeated by every believer in Christ (Rom 6:3-11). The Greek perfect tense speaks of completed action in time past and present certainty of results. Having been crucified with Christ when He died on Calvary, Paul is truly dead to everything else except Christ and what He represents. Paul's faith united him to Christ in such a way that Christ's death was his death, and Christ's resurrection was his resurrection. In Christ, Paul found a perfect sacrifice for sin and a perfect righteousness forever. **Christ liveth in me.** This is the union of the vine and the branches. A Christian is one in whom Christ lives. Christ is our life (Col 1:27; 3:4). The old self-righteous, self-centered Saul died, and the new Christ-centered Paul lives. Paul's new life is really Christ living His life in and through Paul. It is not a matter of imitation, but of realization. A Christian is not an unregenerate, religious sinner trying to attain salvation by works, but a regenerated saint manifesting the life of Christ through the presence and power of the indwelling Holy Spirit. **In the flesh.** This new life must be lived in the flesh, but not by the flesh. **By the faith.** Not by works. **The Son of God.** Paul specifically states that Christ is the Son of God. **Who loved me and gave himself for me.** Note how personally Paul appropriates to himself the love and sacrifice of Christ, which belong equally to the whole world. Christ is our sovereign, sufficient sacrifice.

21 I do not frustrate the grace of God: for if righteousness *come* by the law, then Christ is dead in vain.

21. I do not frustrate the grace of God. Lest someone should misunderstand, Paul says he does not set aside, reject, nullify, or invalidate the grace of God. **For if righteousness come by the law.** Through the agency of the law. False teachers were trying to make of no effect the gospel by adding something (law-works) one must "do" instead of trusting and being united to Christ who has already "done" everything necessary for time and eternity. **Then Christ is dead in vain.** A logical conclusion if righteousness is through the agency of the law. The choice must be made between works and grace, between law and Christ. If salvation is of works, it is not of grace; if it is of grace, it is not of works (Rom 11:6). If salvation is by works, then the atonement of Christ was in vain, a blunder, a useless tragedy, without a cause. But the purpose of the cross has not failed; the message of the cross is not vanity. Salvation must be either by the works of the law or through the atoning death of Christ. It cannot be a combination of both. There are two mutually exclusive teachings prevalent in the world: (1) salvation is by human merit; and (2) salvation is by divine mercy (Tit 3:5). Christ is not a part Saviour, either He must be all (Col 3:11) or He is nothing at all.

II. POLEMICAL: THE DOCTRINE OF LIBERTY. 3:1-4:31.

A. Paul's Appeal to Liberty. 3:1-7.

1. Rebuke of the Galatians. 3:1-4.

3:1. O foolish Galatians. Paul jolts them with this exclamation of surprise and indignation. The Galatians were not naturally stupid or unintelligent, but were acting as if they were bereft of reason when they questioned the sufficiency of Christ. They did not stop to think how senseless it is to mix lawkeeping with faith in Christ, and they were swept along with this false doctrine (cf. Eph 4:14). **Bewitched you** (Gr *baskainō*). The Galatians acted as if subject to some weird occult influence or under the spell of an evil eye. The false teachers had so fascinated them and confused their minds that they seemed to be groping around in a spiritual fog. **That ye should not obey the**

CHAPTER 3

O FOOLISH Ga-lā′tians, who hath bewitched you, that ye should not obey the truth, before whose eyes Jesus Christ hath been evidently set forth, crucified among you?

truth. These words are not found in the best manuscripts, but they present the fact of the Galatians' defection. **Set forth.** This word was used of public pronouncements and means to present vividly, displaying graphically, post clearly, placard (as on a sign board). **Crucified.** As having been crucified. The Greek perfect tense emphasizes a past completed action resulting in certain and positive present effects. Paul is not speaking of the figure of a dead Christ on a crucifix, but of a risen, ascended Christ who had been crucified and is now alive forever more (Rev 1:18). Paul preached Christ crucified (I Cor 2:2) as man's only and sufficient Saviour. Paul and Barnabas had lifted up Christ before the Galatians, who should have kept their eyes on Him and not heeded the errors of the legalists.

2 This only would I learn of you, Received ye the Spirit by the works of the law, or by the hearing of faith?

2. Learn of you. Ascertain from your personal testimony, not from hearsay. The mere asking of the question gives the answer and is a decisive argument. **Receive ye the Spirit.** The Galatians heard the gospel of grace, believed, and received the Holy Spirit. All believers receive the Holy Spirit at the time of salvation. The indwelling of the Holy Spirit is the unmistakable evidence of salvation (Rom 8:9; I Cor 3:16; 6:19-20). **By the works of the law.** Definitely not. **By the hearing of faith.** From what source (Gr *ek*). By hearing and believing God's message of grace (Rom 10:17; I Thess 2:13). What the law could not do, grace has done. The works of the law and the hearing of faith are exclusive opposites and cannot tolerate each other. It must be one or the other, not a combination of both.

3 Are ye so foolish? having begun in the Spirit, are ye now made perfect by the flesh?

3. Having begun in the Spirit. Whom ye received at the time of your salvation. The Holy Spirit is the author of the new birth; He is the creator of the new creation in Christ (II Cor 5:17). **Are ye now made perfect by the flesh.** The word **perfect** (Gr *epiteleō*) most certainly does not mean sinless, but complete, spiritual maturity. The middle voice implies "making yourselves perfect" by means of self-effort. The present tense indicates that the action is in progress and that there is still time to correct the error. Spirit and flesh indicate the two spheres of moral and spiritual influence, one divine and one human. Turning from the divine to the human is not the way to spiritual maturity. No man can ever do the work of the Holy Spirit. There is a double contrast between having begun and finished, and between Spirit and flesh. There is irony in this thrust. The flesh denotes the unregenerate, depraved self, all that a person is apart from the transforming power of the Holy Spirit. The flesh is incurably evil, it is corrupt, and cannot produce a holy influence. It may be educated, cultivated, reformed, and refined; but it is still flesh (Jn 3:6), still at enmity against God (Rom 8:7-8), and at war against the Spirit (Gal 5:17). It would be the height of folly to descend from the high plane of the Spirit to the low level of the flesh and expect ceremonial circumcision and ritual observance to accomplish what only the Holy Spirit can do. The natural can never produce the supernatural. The old nature can never improve the new nature. Salvation is what God does for man and not what man does for himself. Christ is the Author and the Finisher of our faith (Heb 12:2). What God begins, He finishes (Phil 1:6).

4 Have ye suffered so many things in vain? if *it be* yet in vain.

4. Suffered so many things. Because of their identification with Christ, they experienced many hardships. Indications of these persecutions are recorded in Acts 13:45, 50; 14:2, 5; 14:19, 22. Paul refers to them in his second letter to Timothy and then adds, "Yea, and all that will live godly in Christ Jesus shall suffer persecution" (II Tim 3:10-12). **If it be yet in vain.** Paul is unwilling to believe that they will completely and finally abandon Christ for Judaism; he hopes for better results. It would be vain, useless, and of no purpose for them to forsake grace for law.

5 He therefore that ministereth to you the Spirit, and worketh miracles among you, *doeth he it* by the works of the law, or by the hearing of faith?

2. Reception of the Spirit. 3:5-7.

5. Ministereth (Gr *epichorēgeō*). Furnish, lavish, bestow liberally, supply abundantly. God bestows His Spirit abundantly. **Worketh miracles among you.** We read of miracles at Iconium and Lystra (Acts 14:3, 9-10). **Doeth he it.** The Greek present tense shows that the work still goes on. **Works . . . faith.** Once again Paul points to this contrast. Faith in Christ is the means of their new life and the channel of all their spiritual blessings. The gift of the Holy Spirit to them and His mighty works in and among them were dependent absolutely on their faith, not by the works of the law. Divine, supernatural power is not received from a human, natural source. Spiritual power is not produced by fleshly efforts. The Galatians had irrefutable evidence that grace is the way of salvation. The legalists had no evidence that their message was from God. The question raised here has only one answer.

6 Even as Abraham believed God, and it was accounted to him for righteousness.

6. Even as. Paul appeals to the witness of the Word of God, and he implies that the experience of the Galatians and that of Abraham are essentially the same. **Abraham believed God.** Abraham put his trust in God (Gen 15:4-6; Rom 4:3; Jas 2:23) to do for him what he could not do for himself. Abraham's faith was not a meritorious action that deserved a reward. That would have made salvation by works. Works were not involved in obtaining justification. Abraham was justified by faith when he was an uncircumcised Gentile and before he performed any good works. **Accounted to him for righteousness.** Accounted (Gr *logizō*) is common to Greek accounting. It is to reckon, put down on the ledger, credit to one's account. God imputed righteousness to Abraham on the basis of faith, not works. God's accounting changed Abraham's status. The moment Abraham believed, he was justified. Abraham believed God's promise. He had nothing to add, and God required nothing. Abraham committed himself completely and unreservedly to God. Paul shuts the Galatians up to faith alone, not faith plus circumcision and the keeping of the law, as the false teachers would have them do.

7 Know ye therefore that they which are of faith, the same are the children of Abraham.

7. Know ye. Realize, perceive. **Therefore;** a logical deduction from the previous verse. **Of faith.** Believes. Abraham was accepted on the basis of faith. God deals with all men on the same terms. **The same.** These and no others. **Children of Abraham.** Sons with all rights, privileges, and responsibilities. The legalists taught that only the natural descendants of Abraham and those circumcised were his sons. But God says men of faith become his spiritual children. Those who trust in works are aliens, not sons (Rom 2:28-29). Abraham is the father of all believers, Jews and Gentiles.

B. Paul's Argument for Liberty. 3:8-29.

1. The Promise to Abraham. 3:8-14.

8 And the scripture, foreseeing that God would justify the heathen through faith, preached before the gospel unto Abraham, *saying*, In thee shall all nations be blessed.

8. The scripture. This points to divine inspiration (II Tim 3:16). The word spoken to Abraham was recorded by Moses much later. **Foreseeing** (Gr *prooraō*). Anticipating beforehand, seeing a long distance off. God foresaw that Abraham would become a channel of blessing to the Gentiles; God knows the end from the beginning (Acts 15:18). **Justify the brother through faith.** Not the Jews only. Abraham is an example of how Jew and Gentile alike must appropriate salvation, through faith alone, not through faith plus works. How can anyone believe God's Word and entertain the idea that salvation is by human merit? Salvation must be altogether by grace or altogether by works; it cannot be a combination of both (Rom 11:6). The present tense of the word justify signifies that God is justifying now in exactly the same manner He has always done. **Preached before the gospel.** He announced the "good news" beforehand, before the blessing came to the Gentiles. **In thee.** In union with thee as spiritual progenitor. From Abraham would flow blessings to all nations. This speaks of the Messiah and messianic blessings. These blessings are wider than justification by faith, without which no other spiritual blessing could be bestowed.

9 So then they which be of faith are blessed with faithful Abraham.

9. So then. Consequently. Adducing the result in conclusion of the argument just presented. **Blessed.** The Greek present tense shows the blessing to be axiomatic, and the passive voice shows that God is the blesser. **With.** In association and fellowship with (Gr *syn*) Abraham. **Faithful Abraham.** Believing Abraham or Abraham the believer. Abraham was a man of faith. The emphasis is on his faith, not his faithfulness.

10 For as many as are of the works of the law are under the curse: for it is written, Cursed *is* every one that continueth not in all things which are written in the book of the law to do them.

10. Of the works of the law. All those who are resting upon their works and counting on justification by their obedience to the law. Two classes of men stand out in opposition: those of faith and those of works. **Are under the curse.** The wrath of God is hanging over them. This curse includes both their present alienation from God and their future, eternal separation from God (Jn 3:18, 36). Those under the law stand condemned, not justified; cursed, not blessed. **Written.** The Greek perfect tense indicates that God's Word is a permanent record (Ps 119:89) and shall never be altered, amended, or annulled. Jesus said, "Heaven and earth shall pass away: but my words shall not pass away" (Mk 13:31). **Every one.** Jew and Gentile. **Continueth not in all things.** All, not just a majority; both small and great in their sum total with no exception. **To do them.** The infinitive expresses purpose. To do them fully, precisely, entirely. Who could be saved on those terms? No one except our Lord Jesus Christ ever perfectly kept the law all the time. To fail in just one point, one time, puts one under the curse (Deut 27:26; Jas 2:10). Men put themselves under the curse by putting themselves under the law.

11 But that no man is justified by the law in the sight of God, *it is* evident: for, The just shall live by faith.

11. No man is justified by the law. No man ever kept it. A broken law can only curse, not bless. **The just shall live by faith.** God did not design the law to be the means of justification; He designed faith for that purpose. Righteousness and faith are inseparable. Law and righteousness are total strangers. Faith is not a substitute for righteousness; it is that heart trust that brings one into a new relation with God, that of being accepted in Christ (Eph 1:6) and which results in faithfulness, integrity, and steadfastness. The just shall live by faith. This Old Testament verse (Heb 2:4) is quoted three times in the New Testament (Rom 1:17; Gal 3:11; Heb 10:38). The righteous live by faith, not works.

12 And the law is not of faith: but, The man that doeth them shall live in them.

12. The law is not of faith. The two principles of legalism and faith are diametrically opposed to each other and are mutually exclusive of each other as a means of justification. Man can be in only one of two conditions; he is either under the law or he is under grace (Rom 6:14-15). **The man that doeth them shall live in them.** This expresses the principle of the law. Men are not commanded to believe the Old Testament law, but to do it. Failure to render absolute obedience is fatal.

13 Christ hath redeemed us from the curse of the law, being made a curse for us: for it is written, Cursed *is* every one that hangeth on a tree:

13. Christ hath redeemed us. What the law could not do, God did (Rom 8:3-4). **Redeemed** (Gr *exagorazō*) means "to buy out from" the slave market so that the liberated slave shall never be put on sale again. Christ paid the ransom price, His precious blood (I Pet 1:18-19), to deliver us from slavery to liberty. The Bible knows nothing of partial redemption. Christ redeemed us completely, freely, and irreversibly. Once acquitted, acquitted forever (Jn 5:24; Rom 8:1). **From the curse of the law.** Out from (Gr *ek*) the curse of a violated law, i.e., from its condemnation. The curse was the effect of sin in separating us from God. We were sentenced to die (Rom 6:23), but Christ died as our Substitute (Rom 5:8). The curse of the law was: universal (Rom 3:23), fearful (Ps 9:17), and present (Jn 3:18, 36). The law was of divine origin, holy and heavenly. But it was just as cold, hard, and irresistible as the tablets of stone on which the Mosaic law was written with the finger of God (Ex 31:18). **Being made a curse for us.** The method by which Christ redeemed us. He suffered the just for the unjust that He might bring us to God (I Pet 3:18). He was our only Mediator (I Tim 2:5). He became a curse for us (I Pet 2:24) and was made sin for us (II Cor 5:21). He did it for us voluntarily (Jn 10:17-18). This preposition (Gr *hyper*) implies substitution. **For it is written, Cursed.** Deuteronomy 21:23 does not refer to crucifixion, but rather to the ignominious hanging of a body of an executed criminal on a post or stake. God wants Christ to be seen as what He actually became, a curse. Three prepositions give us a vivid picture of redemption. We were under (Gr *hypo*) the curse of the law (vs. 10). Christ came above (Gr *hyper*) us, between us and the curse, and took us out from (Gr *ex*) under the curse having become a curse for us. He took our place; He took all of our sins and gave us all of His righteousness. God was satisfied forever; the law was silenced forever; and the believer is saved forever.

14 That the blessing of Abraham might come on the Gentiles through Jesus Christ; that we might receive the promise of the Spirit through faith.

14. That . . . that. Two purpose clauses. The blessing of Abraham is justification by faith. There is no room for the law. This blessing is intended for the whole world, but it is only in and through (Gr *en*) Christ. No man is saved apart from Christ and any man may be saved by Christ (Jn 6:37). The promise of the Spirit, the gift which comes to all who accept Christ, is through (Gr *dia*) faith. It is folly indeed to seek for higher or holier blessings by deeds of merit.

2. The purpose of the law. 3:15-29.

15 Brethren, I speak after the manner of men; Though it be but a man's covenant, yet if it be confirmed, no man disannulleth, or addeth thereto.

15. Brethren. Denoting affection. **Manner of men.** Paul takes an analogy from human affairs of everyday life and illustrates his point so clearly that all can understand. **Man's covenant.** Better, human testament. This word (Gr *diathēkē*) strictly speaking is not a contract between two parties (Gr *synthēkē*), but a binding will or testament instituted by the first party. **Confirmed.** Ratified. The Greek perfect tense means that the ratification is complete and in force. The matter stands settled. **Disannulleth,** annul, abrogate, make void. **Or addeth thereto.** No new condition may be imposed, no codicil allowed. Since no one can alter, amplify, or annul a man's testament after it has been duly executed, surely no one can add to God's unconditional promise to Abraham, as the legalists were trying to do. God's promise was not a matter of mutual arrangement and it remains inviolate.

16 Now to Abraham and his seed were the promises made. He saith not, And to seeds, as of many; but as of one, And to thy seed, which is Christ.

16. To Abraham and his seed. The beneficiaries of the promise were not limited to Abraham. Some may have objected that God's promise to Abraham was only temporary, so Paul adds "and his seed." **The promises.** Plural because frequently repeated (Gen 13:15; 17:8; 18:18; 22:18). **Thy seed, which is Christ.** The promise looked forward to the one descendant of Abraham in whom all the promises were to be fulfilled.

17 And this I say, that the covenant, that was confirmed before of God in Christ, the law, which was four hundred and thirty years after, cannot disannul, that it should make the promise of none effect.

17. Confirmed before God. By repeated ratifications and sealed with God's own oath (Gen 22:16-17; Heb 6:13). The perfect participle indicates the certainty of prior ratification. Unbelief here charges God with perjury. **Four hundred and thirty years after.** God's ratified promise of long standing certainly could not be rendered inoperative by the law. The law, which was not given for centuries after God's gracious promise, had nothing to do with that promise or with Abraham's justification. If the law had nothing to do with Abraham's justification, how can it have anything to do with anyone's justification? **Cannot disannul.** Does not repeal. The law cannot unconfirm God's confirmed testament. **None effect.** Cancel, render inoperative. The law cannot invalidate the promise which God has validated; it cannot nullify the promise.

18 For if the inheritance be of the law, it is no more of promise: but God gave it to Abraham by promise.

18. Inheritance. The messianic blessing. **Of the law.** Derived from the law as its source. **God gave it.** God graciously granted it as a free gift without reserve, with no strings attached.

God's promised gift did not contain even one legal stipulation. The perfect tense emphasizes its permanence; it still holds good after the law has come. Note that God gave it, not merely promised it. **By promise.** By promise alone, plus nothing. This excludes all self-effort. A new law may repeal or replace a previous law, but the law cannot affect in any way God's promise. Faith is not superseded by the works of the law. The legalists' stipulation of works meant not merely modification, but cancellation of God's confirmed promise. Grace and faith precede law and works. Grace and faith supersede law and works.

19 Wherefore then *serveth* the law? It was added because of transgressions, till the seed should come to whom the promise was made; *and it was* ordained by angels in the hand of a mediator.

19. Wherefore. Why then the law? What is the meaning and purpose of the law? **It was added.** Not as a codicil. The law was not part of God's original and confirmed testament, and it was not added to it later. The law was not added to grace; it did not become another ingredient of salvation. It was brought in alongside of the promise. It was supplemental and subordinate. **Because of transgressions. Because** (Gr *charin*) means for this cause and denotes the aim of the law. **Transgressions** (Gr *parabasis*) mean a step beyond a fixed limit into forbidden territory. It is a willful act of violating an explicit law, overstepping what is right into the realm of what is wrong. The law was added much later to make men conscious of the existence and the extent of sin (Rom 3:19; 5:20). The law was added to reveal sin, not remove it. To show men the need of righteousness, not to be a means of securing righteousness. The law drives men to despair and to cry out for deliverance (Rom 7:24-25). The law declares man to be a helpless, hopeless sinner. **Till the seed should come.** The law was temporary and preparatory, from Moses to Christ; it was not of permanent duration. It was a temporary institution between the original promise and its fulfillment in Christ. After Christ came, the law was abolished (Rom 10:4) as a means of securing righteousness. **Ordained by angels.** Put in force or promulgated through angels as a channel (Deut 33:2; Acts 7:53; Heb 2:2). God used angels to communicate with Moses. The angels represented God and Moses represented Israel. **Hand of a mediator.** Moses stood between God and Israel (Deut 5:5) and received the tablets of stone (Ex 32:15-16).

20 Now a mediator is not *a mediator* of one, but God is one.

20. Mediator. A mediator is a middleman between two parties: He does not act on behalf of one person alone. The presence of Moses implies two other parties, God and Israel. The law was a contract to which both parties agreed to the condition. God said, "If ye will obey," and Israel said, "We will do" (Ex 19:5, 8). Israel was obligated to obey, and God was obligated to bless if they did obey. The law was valid so long as both parties fulfilled the terms of the contract. Israel defaulted and did not live up to her part of the bargain. So then God was no longer obligated to keep His part. The conditions were not kept, and the blessings were not received. Israel therefore had no hope on the basis of keeping the law. **God is one.** The immutable God acted alone when He graciously gave Abraham the promise. He dealt personally and directly with Abraham, not through a mediator. The promise was unconditional, with no stipulation. Its fulfillment depended upon God's faithfulness, not upon Abraham's obedience to a set of rules (Rom 4:13-16).

21 *Is* the law then against the promises of God? God forbid: for if there had been a law given which could have given life, verily righteousness should have been by the law.

21. Against the promises. The law has its own specific function; it is different in nature and purpose. It is not opposed to the promise; it is not competitive, but complementary. The law operates in a different area. The law has a ministration of condemnation. Grace has a ministration of righteousness (II Cor 3:9). **If there had been a law.** This premise is assumed to be contrary to fact. There never was such a law. The law was given through Moses (Jn 1:17), but not to be a source or means of justification. **Could have given life.** Capable of imparting life. The very impossibility of such a law is evident, and yet the legalists were urging the Galatians to abandon the righteousness of Christ which was theirs by faith alone and go back to the law. Man by nature is dead in trespasses and sin (Eph 2:1, 5), and he needs a new life. It was not God's plan to make men alive by the law, but by the new birth (Jn 1:12-13). The broken law demands satisfaction and will not accept good works in lieu of the death penalty. The law demands death. It cannot give life. The law demands righteousness, but it cannot provide it. **Verily.** Indeed, in reality as opposed to the mere pretense. **Righteousness should have been by the law.** Better, it would have been by the law.

22 But the scripture hath concluded all under sin, that the promise by faith of Jesus Christ might be given to them that believe.

22. But. In contradiction to the hypothesis of the preceding verse. **The scripture.** The inspired writing (II Tim 3:16; II Pet 1:21). God's recorded will. **Hath concluded all under sin.** Hath confined, shut up, locked up in prison, for care and constraint. This is a universal arraignment (Deut 27:26; Rom 3:9, 19, 22-23), with no exception. All men are prisoners of sin. The law shows that man does not attain justification by human works, but obtains it by divine mercy (Tit 3:5). **That the promise by faith.** This states the reason for the law and the intention of God. The law paves the way for salvation by grace and justification by faith in Jesus Christ. Consciousness of sin is a necessary step to justification. Until a man realizes that he is lost, he will have little or no interest in being saved. The words faith and believe state clearly how God's gift of eternal life is bestowed. Faith always has an object, here the object is our Lord Jesus Christ. A promise is received by faith only. How can legalists, Galatians or anyone else, say that God's promise is received by the works of the law?

23 But before faith came, we were kept under the law, shut up unto the faith which should afterwards be revealed.

23. Before faith came. The personal faith mentioned in the preceding verse. **Kept under the law.** The Greek imperfect tense indicates that we were continually guarded, by a stern and strict jailer to prevent our escape. It was really for protection rather than incarceration for punishment. **Shut up unto the faith.** This expresses the object of being held in custody. It shuts men up to faith in Christ as their only means of freedom. The law imprisoned men so that they might find true liberty in Christ; it cuts off every other way of escape. The purpose of the law was to prepare men for faith in Christ. **Which should afterwards be revealed.** The about-to-be-revealed faith. The law was a preparation for faith in Christ, not a substitute for it or a supplement to it. The law sentry was relieved of its duty when Christ came. The legalists claim the law is still on duty and even assign it an unscriptural function. They would place God's liberated sons back in slavery under a terrible taskmaster.

24 Wherefore the law was our schoolmaster to bring us unto Christ, that we might be justified by faith.

24. Wherefore. So that. **The law was our schoolmaster.** A schoolmaster (Gr *paidagōgos*) is really the trusted boy-leader or child-escort employed to attend a boy from six to sixteen and who watched over his morals and manners. He was not the teacher and he had no authority to punish. His business was to see that the child went to the right place and did the right thing. Such was the purpose of the law, to prescribe right conduct and impose certain checks. The law convicts of sin, restrains from sin, and condemns for sin; but the law cannot save from sin. **Bring us to Christ.** The God-given purpose of the law has led us to Christ; its work is finished. **That we might be justified by faith.** The ultimate purpose of the law.

25 But after that faith is come, we are no longer under a schoolmaster.

25. Faith. The faith in Christ. **No longer under a schoolmaster.** The born-again believer is no longer under the boy-leader, who has been discharged from service. We are not under the law, but under grace (Rom 6:15).

26 For ye are all the children of God by faith in Christ Jesus.

26. Ye are. Paul changes from "we" to "ye" to apply the truth to the Galatians. **All.** Jews and Gentiles. **Children of God.** There is a distinction between the term **children** (Gr *teknon*) and the term sons (Gr *huios*). All Christians are God's children, having been born again and sharing God's nature (II Pet 1:4).

The term "son" denotes a legal status, that of a liberated, mature person in possession of the inheritance (fulfilled promise). **By faith in Christ Jesus.** The Word of God knows nothing of the so-called universal Fatherhood of God and the universal brotherhood of man. Only those who exercise faith in Christ are sons of God (Acts 4:12). Faith in our Lord Jesus Christ is the only human condition of salvation (Eph 2:8-10).

27 For as many of you as have been baptized into Christ have put on Christ.

27. Baptized into Christ. This is how one becomes united to Christ. This is not baptismal regeneration and does not refer to water baptism, for that never put anyone into Christ. Paul speaks of the baptism of the Holy Spirit which places all true believers into a living union with Christ (I Cor 12:12-13), and with each other (Eph 4:15-16). The Greek passive voice means that this was done for them and not by them. Baptism in water symbolizes, but does not effect, this glorious experience. **Have put on Christ.** Clothed yourself with Christ (Rom 13:14). This implies family likeness to Christ. The Greek aorist middle infers their own deed, with reflexive action, and refers to the custom of investiture. When a boy became of age, he put on a garment which signified the full privilege of a grown-up son enjoying full citizenship.

28 There is neither Jew nor Greek, there is neither bond nor free, there is neither male nor female: for ye are all one in Christ Jesus.

28. Ye are all one in Christ. This is a statement of fact, rather than a mere possibility. The point is that "in Christ Jesus" race or national distinction does not exist; class differences vanish, and sex rivalry disappears. These things are not barriers to Christian fellowship. At the foot of the cross all men are equal, and no one enjoys special privileges.

29 And if ye be Christ's, then are ye Abraham's seed, and heirs according to the promise.

29. If ye be Christ's. Since you Galatians are His, it follows that you are Abraham's seed and heirs according to promise. Christ is heir to all things (Heb 1:2) and you are joint-heirs with Him (Rom 8:17).

C. Paul's Amplification of Liberty. 4:1-31.

1. The coming of God's Son. 4:1-7.

4:1. Child. One of tender years (Gr *nepios*) in contrast to (Gr *teleios*), one full grown. He is illustrating the spiritual immaturity of those living under the law and who are being prepared for faith in Christ. **Differeth nothing from a servant.** He has no more freedom than a slave and is no better off than a slave. **Lord of all.** He is an heir *de jure*, but not *de facto*. He is not enjoying the actual possession of his promised inheritance. He is Lord of all by birthright and by title. Paul's meaning is clear and his purpose is plain. He is warning the Galatians against becoming entangled in the bondage of the law, and he is encouraging them to enjoy the spiritual liberty they have by faith in Christ.

CHAPTER 4
NOW I say, *That* the heir, as long as he is a child, differeth nothing from a servant, though he be lord of all;

2 But is under tutors and governors until the time appointed of the father.

2. Under tutors. Guardians who have the supervision of the person. **Governors.** Stewards who have the supervision of the property. They are the trustees who manage the estate. During his minority, the heir is controlled and restrained by guardians and stewards. **Until the time appointed.** The time appointed beforehand for the termination of his minority status when he attains his inheritance. Under the law men were minors and enjoyed little of the inheritance because they were under tutelage and in servile condition.

3 Even so we, when we were children, were in bondage under the elements of the world:

3. Even so we. Paul makes the application. **When we were children.** In our minority. **Were in bondage.** The Greek perfect tense implies that we were in a real state of servitude under the legalistic system and not free sons under grace. **Under the elements of the world.** The word elements (Gr *stoicheion*) denotes things placed in a row, thus the letters of the alphabet. Hence, the ABC's or first principles of non-Christian humanity, the elemental lesson in simple symbols of outward things (Col 2:8, 20). The kindergarten department of instruction in religious observances which are external and temporal as contrasted

4 But when the fulness of the time was come, God sent forth his Son, made of a woman, made under the law.

5 To redeem them that were under the law, that we might receive the adoption of sons.

6 And because ye are sons, God hath sent forth the Spirit of his Son into your hearts, crying, Abba, Father.

7 Wherefore thou art no more a servant, but a son; and if a son, then an heir of God through Christ.

with the permanent spiritual principles of faith in Christ. Under law men were in the process of preparatory training.

4. But when. Marks the beginning of a remarkable change in the state of affairs. **The fullness of the time.** The proper time had arrived for both God and man. The time appointed by the Father and foretold by the prophets. It was a time of outward prosperity and inward corruption. The religions of the world were spiritually bankrupt, devoid of power to change men's lives, and had degenerated into feeble superstitions and meaningless rituals. The pre-messianic period ended right on schedule. **God sent forth his Son.** There was no other way to save man (Acts 4:12). With Christ there is an endless hope; without Christ there is a hopeless end. God sent forth Christ from Himself, from heaven's majesty to earth's misery, to execute His plan and purpose. This reveals Christ's pre-existence, His deity, and His authority. It was the Second Person of the Trinity who was commissioned. **Made of a woman.** The Son of God became out of (Gr *ex*) a woman, became incarnate and dwelt among us (Jn 1:14). The fact of the miraculous virgin birth agrees perfectly with the language here. Christ did not cease to be God when He became man, the God-man, one person with two natures. **Made under the law.** Not only a human birth but a Jewish birth, subject to all the ordinances of the law.

5. To redeem. Buy out of the slave market (3:13). This means both purchase and liberation. The purpose of the incarnation was redemption, to deliver us from the curse of the law and make us sons under grace. Christ came not to explain the law, but to expiate sin, to obliterate a guilty past and initiate a glorious future. **Them that were under the law. The law** is not preceded by the definite article, so *law* in general. Even Gentiles are not without law to God (Rom 2:14). Christ came to redeem all men (I Tim 2:4-6). **That we might receive.** Receive from the giver for the first time, not recover something we once possessed. It means to get from, not to get back. **The adoption of sons.** Placed and recognized as adult sons. This means full deliverance from the child-servant status. This is based on redemption and implies family likeness with its position, privilege, and prestige. Regeneration gives us the relationship; adoption gives us the position.

6. Because ye are sons. God could not do this while men were still minors under guardians and stewards. As a consequence of sonship and as a proof of sonship (Rom 8:14-16). **God hath sent forth the Spirit of his Son.** Commissioned Him, as He had His Son. Note the parallels: Son and Spirit. The Holy Spirit is called here the Spirit of His Son (Rom 8:9; Phil 1:19; Jn 15:26). **Into your hearts.** Every child of God is indwelt by the Holy Spirit (I Cor 3:16; 6:19-20). He is the earnest of our inheritance (Eph 1:13-14). All guardians and stewards have been discharged; their supervision is no longer needed because believers are full-grown sons indwelt by the Holy Spirit. **Crying Abba, Father.** This cry of deep emotion comes from the indwelling of the Holy Spirit. While an immature child is under supervision, he doesn't fully appreciate his Father; but when he reaches his maturity, he begins to realize who and what his Father is, and so cries out Abba, Father (Rom 8:15). These words were used by Christ in the Garden of Gethsemane (Mk 14:36). Wherever the Aramaic "Abba" occurs in the New Testament, it has the Greek interpretation added. This combination may suggest the impartiality of the Holy Spirit's ministry in all believers, whether they are Jews or Gentiles.

7. Wherefore. On the basis of what has gone before, after God sent His Son for you and His Holy Spirit in you. We are what we are because God sent forth His Son; we have what we have because God sent forth His Spirit—God's work external and internal. The whole Trinity has been involved in making the believer a son and an heir. **Thou art no more a servant.** Paul addresses each one individually and tells him what he is by the grace of God. Though you were once a slave (Gr *doulos*) to the law, you are no longer. **But a son.** How foolish to abandon this high position and privilege for the low state of a slave under the bondage of the law. **And if a son.** This is a Greek first-class condition of logic, meaning "since" you are a son. There is no doubt about it. **Then an heir.** Enjoying a new spiritual heritage, not through works of personal merit, but through grace. It is not by placing themselves under the law, but by remaining free from it, that they will obtain the blessing of Abraham.

2. The conduct of the Galatians. 4:8-21.

8 Howbeit then, when ye knew not God, ye did service unto them which by nature are no gods.

8. Howbeit then. In your former pagan state. **Ye knew not God.** Ignorant of God, not acquainted with Him. They lived in utter spiritual darkness. Paul is not excusing them, merely stating the fact of their wretched condition. **Ye did service.** Ye slaved and were in bondage. The Galatians had been pagans and had worshiped idols before they were saved. **Which by nature are no gods.** Paul is not denying their existence, but their deity. Paul refers to them as so-called gods (I Cor 8:4-6) and demons (I Cor 10:19-20).

9 But now, after that ye have known God, or rather are known of God, how turn ye again to the weak and beggarly elements, whereunto ye desire again to be in bondage?

9. But now. Since your salvation. **After that ye have known God.** Having come to God by personal experience, and enjoying fellowship with Him. **Or rather are known of God.** This explains how the Galatians came to know God. The initiative was not theirs. Paul emphasizes the fact that it is all of grace. God recognizes them as His sons and heirs. The word for "know" (Gr *ginōskō*) often implies a personal relationship between the knower and the known. God knows them in a saving relationship (Mt 7:23; I Cor 8:3). The Greek aorist tense (ingressive) emphasizes the beginning of the action and leaves room for the question about the present. **How turn ye again. . . ?** The Greek present tense signifies that they were in the act of turning from grace and liberty to law and bondage. Their defection was just beginning and still in progress, not yet complete. **To the weak and beggarly elements.** These two adjectives express the utter impotence of these elements to do and bestow what was done and given by God sending His Son. These elements are without strength and without resources; they are spiritually powerless and spiritually poverty-stricken. **Ye desire again to be in bondage.** The combination of these words (Gr *palin* and *anōthen*) describes the completeness of their proposed relapse into second childhood. Paul's question shows the absurdity of their desire to be slaves again. They were in the process of leaving the light and liberty of Christianity for the shadow and slavery of legalism. Ritualistic observances are heathenish in principle. They are a system of bondage opposed to God's grace. How can anyone want to exchange the robe of Christ's righteousness for the filthy rags of heathenism, Judaism, or any other "ism"?

10 Ye observe days, and months, and times, and years.

10. Ye observe. The Greek present middle implies that they are continually observing for themselves, for their own benefit, some of the requirements of Judaism. They were in the process of launching into legalism and were scrupulously observing with meticulous care certain rules with the belief that such practice would gain merit. This shows the partial success of the legalists.

11 I am afraid of you, lest I have bestowed upon you labour in vain.

11. I am afraid of you. He is afraid about or concerning them. **Lest.** Denotes the reason for Paul's fear. **I have bestowed upon you labor.** The perfect tense indicates the finished work of Paul in placarding Christ as the crucified One. **Labor** (Gr *kopiaō*) means to labor to the point of exhaustion. **In vain.** It is placed before the verb for emphasis and means to no purpose, without effect, without due result. Could it be possible that Paul's labor was merely a mirage and not a miracle? Paul's labor would have been in vain if all that was accomplished was for the

Galatians to exchange their pagan religion for the old abrogated legalism of the Jews. Turning to legalism is equivalent to rejecting the gospel and renouncing Christ. Paul's admonition to the Galatians should be a solemn warning to Christians not to sacrifice their spiritual liberty in Christ for the slavery of forms and ceremonies.

12 Brethren, I beseech you, be as I am; for I am as ye are; ye have not injured me at all.

12. Brethren. Paul identifies himself with them, and though fearful, he will not give them up. **I beseech you.** I beg you, suggesting the intensity of his appeal. **Be as I am.** The Greek present middle imperative means keep on becoming as I am. Don't give up grace for law, but get all the way out from under the law and come all the way under grace. Paul had been liberated from legalism; he gave it up. Paul laid aside the pedigree, privileges, and prejudices of Judaism for Christ (Phil 3:4-8). He abandoned his own righteousness of the law for the righteousness of God in Christ, and he asks the Galatians to do the same. **For I am as ye are.** Since being saved by grace and being liberated from legalism, Paul is living like a Gentile, in order to be more effective in winning Gentiles to Christ (I Cor 9:21). The bondage of the law does not promote spiritual life, but it endangers Christian liberty. **Ye have not injured me at all.** Ye did me no wrong, no injustice.

13 Ye know how through infirmity of the flesh I preached the gospel unto you at the first.

13. Ye know. In what unfavorable light his infirmity placed him when he first came among them. **How through infirmity.** Because of illness. An attack of some malady detained Paul and made it necessary to spend more time than he had planned to spend in their region. Some think it may have been an attack of malaria or epilepsy, or perhaps ophthalmia, an Oriental eye disease prevalent in the lowlands of Pamphylia. But whatever it was, it occasioned Paul's preaching the gospel to them. **At the first.** Paul's first visit. Some believe this implies a second visit on a subsequent missionary journey. But on Paul's first missionary journey, he retraced his steps after preaching in Derbe (Acts 14:20-25), so he actually visited most of these cities twice on his first tour.

14 And my temptation which was in my flesh ye despised not, nor rejected; but received me as an angel of God, even as Christ Jesus.

14. My temptation. The best Greek texts have "your" temptation. The trial to which you were subjected by my bodily infirmity and which might have caused you to treat me with indifference. **Ye despised not.** This word (Gr *exoutheneō*) means despise utterly, set at nought, scorn, treat with contempt. **Nor rejected.** Literally, "spit out" (Gr *ekptuō*). Hence to disdain, spurn, loathe. Spitting was a sign of disgust. The ancients expectorated when they saw a person having an epileptic seizure. This may have even been Paul's malady. **But.** On the contrary. **Received me.** In spite of Paul's illness and repulsive appearance, they treated him with great kindness. **As an angel of God.** With veneration (Acts 14:11-18). **As Christ Jesus.** The highest honor.

15 Where is then the blessedness ye spake of? for I bear you record, that, if it had been possible, ye would have plucked out your own eyes, and have given them to me.

15. Where is then. What became of the congratulatory spirit? **Blessedness.** The blessedness of being in a state of prosperity resulting from having Paul as their apostle. **I bear you record.** I testify or bear witness. **Plucked out your own eyes.** Literally, dug out, gouged out (Gr *exorussō*). Some infer from these words that Paul had a disease of the eyes and that he needed a new pair of eyes, but there is no conclusive evidence that such was the case. It is a graphic description of their attitude and expresses supreme love and devotion. Paul lamented their changed attitude toward him.

16 Am I therefore become your enemy, because I tell you the truth?

16. Therefore. And so, seeing your love has waned. **Am I . . . become.** The Greek perfect tense signifies permanence of the action. **Your enemy.** Your personal enemy (Gr *echthros*) in a hostile, active sense. Paul has not changed, and the gospel has not changed. Why do they regard him as an enemy? He chides them for their fickle disloyalty. Paul is not their enemy. **Because I tell you the truth.** The legalists accused Paul of not telling the truth and of keeping the Galatians in a retarded spiritual condition by his adamant stand against circumcision as a means of salvation.

17 They zealously affect you, *but* not well; yea, they would exclude you, that ye might affect them.

17. They zealously affect you. Affect has its root in (Gr *zeō*) a word meaning to boil with heat and is used of intense passions. The legalists were courting, taking a warm interest in, striving after, and earnestly desiring the Galatians. **But not well.** Not honorably. They were zealous for their own cause. Their ulterior motive was to promote Judaism and steal their hearts from Christ. Their great proselyting zeal was condemned by Christ (Mt 23:15). **They would exclude you.** They would separate, isolate, and shut you out from other teachers and from the liberating gospel of Christ. They would exclude you from salvation unless you observed the law. **That ye might affect them.** The purpose of the legalists in excluding the Galatians from salvation was that they, having no hope elsewhere, would court the legalists and seek affiliation with them. With their fawning fallacies they were seeking to monopolize the affections of the Galatians and make them a prey for their false teachings.

18 But *it is* good to be zealously affected always in *a* good *thing*, and not only when I am present with you.

18. It is good. It is good to be courted in a good way. It is good for someone to take a warm interest in you in an honorable manner. Paul zealously sought the Galatians for Christ, and he welcomes all such efforts in relation to the gospel of Christ. The motive behind the courting is very important. Paul did not desire a monopoly in serving them, but he did not want them seduced from Christ. **In a good thing.** Paul is speaking primarily of preaching Christ and Him crucified. All true Christians are fervent in their evangelistic zeal and persistent and consistent in seeking the lost for Christ. This differs vastly from the selfish proselytism of legalists, both ancient and modern.

19 My little children, of whom I travail in birth again until Christ be formed in you,

19. My little children (Gr *teknion*). The usual word for maternal endearment. It expresses the tenderness of Paul and the immaturity of the Galatians. **Of whom I travail in birth again.** For whom I am undergoing the birth pangs (I Cor 4:15; Phm 10). Paul is again experiencing the same painful anguish as when he brought them to Christ. **Until Christ be formed in you.** This word (Gr *morphoō*) means to give outward expression to one's inward nature. Paul wants Christ to be seen in the lives of the Galatians. A living Christ on the inside will manifest Himself on the outside (Gal 2:20; Rom 8:29). As a result of the legalists' propaganda, the Galatians were beginning to trust "self" in their efforts to obey the law, instead of depending on the Holy Spirit to produce a Christlike life in them and through them.

20 I desire to be present with you now, and to change my voice; for I stand in doubt of you.

20. I desire. Greek imperfect tense. I was desiring to be present with you. **Change my voice.** Paul was under the handicap of having to write, which is never as effective as the spoken word. If Paul could speak to them, he could straighten matters out in a very short time. **I stand in doubt of you.** Literally, I am perplexed in you. Paul was at his wits' end, not knowing the best way to prevent them from the error into which they were drifting.

21 Tell me, ye that desire to be under the law, do ye not hear the law?

21. Tell me. A direct appeal. **Ye that desire to be under the law.** On the verge of adopting law and of becoming subject to all its demands and condemnation. **Do ye not hear the law?** Are you hearing what it really says and heeding what it really means? Paul wants them to learn a very important lesson.

3. The comparison of Hagar and Sarah. 4:22-31.

22 For it is written, that Abraham had two sons, the one by a bondmaid, the other by a freewoman.

22. It is written. Not a direct quotation, but a summation of the historical facts. **Abraham had two sons.** Those who claim to be Abraham's sons by their submission to the law forget that Abraham had two sons. Abraham had other sons, but it is clear that Paul is speaking of Ishmael and Isaac (Rom 9:6-9). The status of the mother determined the status of the son. Natural birth is no guarantee of spiritual privilege. The son of the slave

23 But he *who was* of the bondwoman was born after the flesh; but he of the freewoman *was* by promise.

24 Which things are an allegory: for these are the two covenants; the one from the mount Sī′naī, which gendereth to bondage, which is Ā′gär.

25 For this Ā′gär is mount Sī′naī in Arabia, and answereth to Jerusalem which now is, and is in bondage with her children.

26 But Jerusalem which is above is free, which is the mother of us all.

27 For it is written, Rejoice, *thou* barren that bearest not; break forth and cry, thou that travailest not: for the desolate hath many more children than she which hath an husband.

28 Now we, brethren, as Isaac was, are the children of promise.

29 But as then he that was born after the flesh persecuted him *that was born* after the Spirit, even so *it is* now.

girl, Hagar, was rejected; the son of the free woman, Sarah, obtained the inheritance.

23. But. Although sons of the same father. **Was born.** The Greek perfect tense, "has been born," emphasizes the certainty of the distinction between these two births. Ishmael's descendants do not belong to the covenant people; Isaac's descendants have the promise. Slave girls were customarily given by a barren wife, but could not be taken by a husband voluntarily. Sarah, losing hope that the promise would be fulfilled, substituted Hagar for herself and sought to get an heir by proxy. But God had a better idea and later carried out His plan and fulfilled His promise. Ishmael's birth was natural; Isaac's birth was supernatural, through a miraculous intervention of God (Rom 4:18-21).

24. An allegory. Speaking allegorically. Paul uses the historical narrative to illustrate his point for the benefit of the Galatians who were tempted to place themselves under the burden of the law. Paul illustrates the deep distinction and distance between grace and law, between the children of promise and the subject of legalism. An allegory is a veiled presentation of a meaning, metaphorically implied but not expressly stated. The superficial reader sees only the surface, but there is more to see, the facts in their full reality. Paul gives these historical facts a symbolic meaning and uses them to illustrate the already established doctrine of justification by faith. **These are the two covenants.** These two women symbolize the two covenants, law and grace. Hagar represents the Mosaic covenant of law and bondage and is the mother of the child of the flesh. Sarah represents the Abrahamic covenant of grace and liberty and is the mother of the child of promise.

25. Mount Sinai. Hagar represents Mount Sinai. **Answereth to.** Belongs to the same or corresponds to. **Jerusalem which now is.** The earthly Jerusalem stands for Judaism and represents the Jewish nation. Jerusalem was the center of apostate Judaism. **Is in bondage with her children.** Jerusalem is a slaving mother of slaving children. A severe condemnation of the legalists from Jerusalem who were trying to seduce the Galatians, and of all who would supplant grace with law.

26. But. Opposes the preceding verse. **Jerusalem which is above.** The heavenly Jerusalem (Heb 12:22-24) is the spiritual city of which all Christians are children. **Free.** Independent of the Mosaic law. The heavenly Jerusalem is a free mother with free children.

27. Written. We have here a quotation from the Septuagint of Isaiah 54:1 which is applied to unfruitful Sarah, who answers to the heavenly Jerusalem. Abraham's spiritual seed shall be more numerous than his natural seed. Isaiah closes the fifty-third chapter with these words, "He bare the sins of many, and made intercession for the transgressors." The next word is "sing." Paul translates it **Rejoice.** The grace of God gives men something to sing about. Israel will some day realize the full meaning of Isaiah 53 and experience glorious deliverance and restoration through God's grace.

28. Now. Paul applies the truth to the Galatians. **We brethren.** The best texts have "ye" instead of "we," Paul assures the Galatians that they, like Isaac, are born according to promise, not of mere fleshly descent, as Ishmael. The sons of promise are free.

29. But as then. As then, so now. **Born after the flesh.** Born naturally and are enslaved sinners. **Born after the Spirit.** Born supernaturally and are liberated saints. **Persecuted.** The word (Gr *diōkō*) means drive away, put to flight, harass, molest. The presence of Isaac causes Ishmael to manifest his true character (Gen 21:9). From Isaac, came the Hebrews; from Ishmael, came the Arabs. From the beginning these two sons of Abraham were unfriendly, and so have been their descendants. The presence of

30 Nevertheless what saith the scripture? Cast out the bondwoman and her son: for the son of the bondwoman shall not be heir with the son of the freewoman.

31 So then, brethren, we are not children of the bondwoman, but of the free.

CHAPTER 5

STAND fast therefore in the liberty wherewith Christ hath made us free, and be not entangled again with the yoke of bondage.

2 Behold, I Paul say unto you, that if ye be circumcised, Christ shall profit you nothing.

3 For I testify again to every man that is circumcised, that he is a debtor to do the whole law.

the new nature makes known what the old nature really is. The legalists were persecuting Paul and all who would not abandon grace for law. There are two types of men in the world: those who have been born only of the flesh, and those who in addition have been born of the Spirit. It would be better not to have been born at all than not to be born again. Men of the flesh detest men of the Spirit. No one despises grace like the man who is trying to save himself by his own merit.

30. Cast out. Abraham by divine direction sent Hagar and Ishmael away (Gen 21:10-12). This is an encouragement to all who have been born of the Spirit and a solemn warning to all who are born only of the flesh. Grace, not law, brings the inheritance in the family of God. **Shall not be heir.** The son of the slave girl shall not, no never, by any means share the inheritance with the son of the free woman. Those who seek acceptance with God through obedience to the law, and are destitute of true sonship, have no inheritance. This verdict stands for all who have no higher birth than Ishmael.

31. So then. A deduction from the preceding verse. **Bondwoman.** The absence of the Greek definite article emphasizes Hagar's lower status. God says that His children are the children of promise, saved by grace. It is impossible to be children of both the slave girl and the free woman. It is impossible to be under law and under grace. We belong to Christ and are therefore liberated from the bondage of the law. Christendom is critically infected with the deadly doctrine of the legalists. The crying need of the hour is for uncompromising men to proclaim the liberty in Christ which is the birthright of every believer.

III. PRACTICAL: THE LIFE OF LIBERTY. 5:1-6:18.

A. Liberty Is Imperiled by Legalism. 5:1-12.

5:1. Stand fast therefore. Take a tenacious stand and do not be moved from this position. Keep on standing, and do not bow your neck to the yoke of slavery. **In the liberty.** For the purpose of freedom which belongs to the children of the free woman (4:31). Legalism destroys liberty. **Christ hath made us free.** Christ, the great Liberator, definitely, deliberately, and decisively liberated us. The emphasis is on the completeness of our freedom. **And be not entangled again.** Stop being held in the yoke of bondage. Having escaped the slavery of heathenism, they were in danger of the slavery of Judaism. The legalists were trying to yoke the Galatians with Judaism. Yoke is a symbol of slavery.

2. Behold, I Paul. The stalwart champion of liberty asserts all his personal and apostolic authority. **If ye be circumcised.** A hypothetical case, but with awful consequences. If implies that they had not yielded yet to the demands of the legalists. The present tense indicates, not one act, but a practice they were considering as necessary for salvation. If they should receive circumcision under such conviction, they would obligate themselves to keep the whole law, because circumcision is a pledge to live by the law, and it is a badge of Judaism. **Christ shall profit you nothing.** Grace and law are diametrically opposed to each other and mutually exclusive of each other. Christ is of advantage only to the one who trusts Him exclusively. There can be no compromise between grace and law and no combination of faith and works.

3. For I testify again. Paul's emphatic protest and warning addressed to all who were contemplating circumcision. **That he is a debtor to do the whole law.** A debtor is one who assumes an obligation. To accept circumcision as a condition of salvation is to abandon the liberty for which Christ liberated us and to bind one's self to the slavery of legalism. Submission to circumcision commits one to perfect obedience to the whole law; he takes

4 Christ is become of no effect unto you, whosoever of you are justified by the law; ye are fallen from grace.

5 For we through the Spirit wait for the hope of righteousness by faith.

6 For in Jesus Christ neither circumcision availeth any thing, nor uncircumcision; but faith which worketh by love.

7 Ye did run well; who did hinder you that ye should not obey the truth?

8 This persuasion *cometh* not of him that calleth you.

upon himself both the requirements of the law and its curse (Jas 2:10; Gal 3:10).

4. Christ is become of no effect unto you. Literally, ye were brought to nought from Christ. Your relation to Christ is finished, rendered null and void. Without an effective relation to Christ, one deprives himself of spiritual blessing. **Whosoever of you are justified by the law.** Justified as you think, but not really. You who are trying to be justified in the law, trying to seek a right standing with God on the basis of works or merit. One either attains salvation by his own works or he attains it as a free gift of God (Rom 11:6). **Ye are fallen from grace.** The only time this phrase is used in the Bible. Having been saved by grace, the Galatians, who were reverting to the law for Christian living, were actually falling short of the standard of grace by which they were saved. The frustrating result would have been similar to the believer in Romans 7 who was struggling to live under the law (see the discussion on that passage). This does not teach that children of God can lose their salvation by falling out of grace. Paul is contrasting grace and law. Depending on circumcision, or any other work, means renouncing justification by grace through faith and takes one out of the spirit of grace and puts him under the dominion of the law. There cannot be two grounds of salvation, two means of justification, two ways of life. To accept the one means to reject the other. It is either law or grace, either works or faith, either self-righteousness, or the righteousness of God, either circumcision or Christ. The Galatians were in danger of substituting law for Christ as a means of salvation.

5. For we. True born-again believers, who cling to the covenant of grace. **Through the Spirit.** Not through the flesh; not through the law. **Wait.** This compound verb means literally, receive-away-from-out of. It means more than mere waiting passively. It suggests earnest, constant expectancy. This verb occurs eight times in the New Testament each time with eschatological significance. **For the hope of righteousness by faith.** The realization of perfect righteousness.

6. For in Jesus Christ. In vital union with Him, the true sphere of salvation. **Neither circumcision availeth anything.** Circumcision is not strong to effect (Gr *ischuō*) anything; it conveys no spiritual blessing in return for its binding pledge to keep the whole law. **But faith which worketh by love.** Faith is a vital heart trust and personal commitment to Christ (Rom 10:9-10) which identifies the believer with Christ in the sphere of grace. A living faith expresses itself in love. Love does not add anything to faith; it gives it a place to operate. This coincides with the familiar statement, "Faith alone justifies, but the faith which justifies is not alone."

7. Ye did run well. You were running nobly, gallantly, and bravely with every prospect of reaching the goal. You were making good progress on the right course. **Who.** Probably refers to some ringleader of the legalists. **Did hinder you.** A military term (Gr *enkoptō*) which pictures an enemy impeding one's progress and preventing him from reaching his goal by cutting off his way and setting up a roadblock. Since Paul is using the figure of a race, this word suggests the "cutting in" of one runner on another and thus slowing up his progress and throwing him off course. **That ye should not obey the truth.** The Galatians were turned aside from obedience to the truth by false teaching.

8. This persuasion. The flattering fallacies of the legalist; their sedulous attempts to persuade the Galatians to turn from the course they were already pursuing. **Cometh not of him that calleth you.** This counsel toward ritualism and legalism was not of God, who calls men to liberty. The legalists were not God's servants, and the Galatians should not have heeded them (Jn 10:45).

9 A little leaven leaveneth the whole lump.

9. A little leaven. The false doctrine which appeared so slight and harmless. **Leaveneth the whole lump.** Goes on working slowly, silently, and satanically until the whole lump is corrupted. Leaven is corrupt and produces corruption; its nature is never altered. Doctrinal differences are dangerous. The process of doctrinal fermentation was going on but all the assemblies had not been permeated yet. Paul expresses confidence that they will deal with this doctrinal error summarily.

10 I have confidence in you through the Lord, that ye will be none otherwise minded: but he that troubleth you shall bear his judgment, whosoever he be.

10. I have confidence in you through the Lord. Paul has been persuaded that the Galatians will share his loyalty to Christ, but he doesn't trust them apart from the Lord. **That ye will be none otherwise minded.** Let us say through the influence of false teachers. **He that troubleth you.** The one continually agitating, disquieting, and disturbing your faith. **Shall bear his judgment.** He cannot escape; God will judge him. **Whosoever he be.** It seems unlikely that Paul knew precisely who the leader was.

11 And I, brethren, if I yet preach circumcision? then is the offence of the cross ceased.

11. And I, brethren. Paul contrasts himself with the legalists. **If I yet preach circumcision.** As Paul's enemies accused. **Why do I yet suffer persecution?** If Paul preached legalism, he would not be persecuted. The legalists charged Paul with inconsistency and duplicity. They had misconstrued Paul's act of having Timothy circumcised (Acts 16:3). Paul could not be preaching both circumcision and the cross, for they are contradictory. **Then is the offense of the cross ceased.** The offense is the stumbling block of the Cross (I Cor 1:23). The Cross uproots the doctrine of salvation by human merit. Salvation is by grace alone, and justification is by faith alone; there can be no compromise. The offensiveness of the Cross to the legalists is that salvation is by grace without circumcision and obedience to the law.

12 I would they were even cut off which trouble you.

12. I would. I could wish. That **they were even cut off.** That they will cut themselves off. All the ancient Greek interpreters and most modern scholars apply this to the self-mutilation practiced by the heathen priests of Cybele. Paul speaks with satire. **Which trouble you.** Causing so much disturbance and throwing you into confusion.

B. Liberty Is Perverted by Lawlessness. 5:13-26.

13 For, brethren, ye have been called unto liberty; only *use* not liberty for an occasion to the flesh, but by love serve one another.

13. For brethren. A tender title. **Ye.** Emphatic contrast to the false teachers. **Have been called unto liberty.** Ye were called unto liberty, not slavery. Liberty is not an excuse for license. License destroys liberty. **Only use not liberty for an occasion to the flesh.** Some of the Galatians may have already done this, and others were tempted. Liberty must be maintained, not abused. It is abused when it is made the occasion of turning liberty into license. **Occasion** (Gr *aphorme*) is a military term signifying a camping place which becomes a launching pad to capture the opposing army. It is the base of operations for giving way to carnal passions. The flesh is the sinful nature to man, which has been crucified with Christ (2:20), but which seems to possess possibilities of revival. Therefore do not let your liberty become the impulse which will start the old nature to assert itself again. **But.** On the contrary. **By love.** True Christian love is the motive of true Christian conduct. **Serve one another.** Constantly and voluntarily enslave yourselves to one another.

14 For all the law is fulfilled in one word, *even* in this; Thou shalt love thy neighbour as thyself.

14. For all the law is fulfilled in one word. The whole moral law stands fully accomplished and completed in one precept. **Thou shalt love thy neighbor as thyself.** Such love is produced by the Holy Spirit. Love is the real fulfillment of the law which the legalists were wanting to serve. It was said of the early Christians, "Behold how they love one another," not how they quarrel, criticize, and backbite. Christ did not come to destroy the law . . . but to fulfill (Mt 5:17). Grace does not make one free to sin; it makes him free to serve.

15 But if ye bite and devour one another, take heed that ye be not consumed one of another.

15. But if. Setting in contrast what they were doing with what they should do. **Bite and devour.** Continually biting and devouring like wild animals in deadly combat, i.e., a picture of church strifes. **Take heed.** Watch out. **That ye be not consumed one of another.** Mutual destruction by slander and criticism.

16 *This* I say then, Walk in the Spirit, and ye shall not fulfil the lust of the flesh.

16. Walk in the Spirit. Have the habit of continually walking by the energizing power and under the divine direction of the Holy Spirit. This is the only way of deliverance from selfish lusts. **And ye shall not fulfill the lust of the flesh.** The double negative with the aorist subjunctive means you will never gratify the sinful desires originating in and overflowing from the lower nature. When God saved us, He did not eradicate the old nature, neither did He reform the old life; He gave us an absolutely new life (Jn 3:6). The old nature is "not subject to the law of God, neither indeed can be" (Rom 8:7). The Christian can conquer the self-life and have continual victory by walking by the Holy Spirit.

17 For the flesh lusteth against the Spirit, and the Spirit against the flesh: and these are contrary the one to the other: so that ye cannot do the things that ye would.

17. For the flesh lusteth against the Spirit. There is a constant deadly feud being waged. Bunyan shows that both Christ and Satan long for the possession of the city of Man Soul. Romans 7:15-25 is an inspired commentary on this verse. The flesh opposes the Spirit in an effort to prevent the believer from a life of obedience, surrender, and victory. **The Spirit against the flesh.** The Holy Spirit opposes the flesh and gives the believer victory over it. **And these are contrary.** Lined up in hostile, face-to-face conflict. There is mutual antagonism. **So that ye cannot do the things that ye would.** So that you may not keep on doing whatever you may want to do.

18 But if ye be led of the Spirit, ye are not under the law.

18. But if ye be led of the Spirit. If you are being led continually by the Holy Spirit, then it follows that **ye are not under the law.** Christians have a live-in divine Person to keep them in line, and they do not need an external curb.

19 Now the works of the flesh are manifest, which are *these;* Adultery, fornication, uncleanness, lasciviousness,

19. Now the works of the flesh. Note the plural, **works,** the complex mixture of evil desires and deeds. The flesh is always active; it never takes a vacation. **Are manifest.** Plainly evident to everyone. These works all issue from a heart in rebellion against God and insisting upon doing as it wills (Mt 15:19; Mk 7:21-22). **Adultery.** Illicit sexual intercourse between married partners. **Fornication.** Illicit sexual intercourse between unmarried partners. **Uncleanness.** Moral impurity. **Lasciviousness.** Wantonness, debauchery, lewdness. This word (Gr *aselgeia*) was used to describe an attitude of utter disregard for the opinions and conventions which governed others.

20 Idolatry, witchcraft, hatred, variance, emulations, wrath, strife, seditions, heresies,

20. Idolatry. Worship of idols, putting anything in the place of God. **Witchcraft.** Sorcery, the profession of magical arts which used various combinations of chemicals (drugs) to deceive and get control of their victims (cf. Rev 21:8). **Hatred.** Enmities, personal animosities (cf. I Jn 3:15). **Variance.** Strife, rivalry, discord, factions, quarrelsomeness. **Emulations.** Jealousies, sedition, constant desire to excel other people and secure their admiration. **Wrath.** Passionate anger, stirring up the emotions of temper resulting in an explosion. **Strife.** Factions, intrigues manifested in party spirit. **Seditions.** Splits, divisions. **Heresies.** Choices based on preferences, sectarian parties.

21 Envyings, murders, drunkenness, revellings, and such like: of the which I tell you before, as I have also told *you* in time past, that they which do such things shall not inherit the kingdom of God.

21. Envyings. Feelings of ill-will. **Drunkenness.** Excessive indulgence in strong drink. **Revellings.** Carousals such as the outrageous feasts to the god Dionysus associated with horrible orgies, not unlike many riotous, wild parties of today. **And such like.** The list is representative, not exhaustive. **They which do such things.** Those whose lives are charactericized by the habit of continually doing such things. Such life-style is proof positive that one has not become a new creature in Christ (II Cor 5:17), that he is not in the kingdom of God, and that he shall have no share in it. A Christian may fall temporarily into these sins, but he will be miserable until he confesses and forsakes them (Prov 28:13).

22 But the fruit of the Spirit is love, joy, peace, longsuffering, gentleness, goodness, faith,

22. But the fruit. Singular in number; not nine fruits, but one fruit composed of nine elements. The first three are in relation to God; the next three are in relation to man; and the last three are in relation to one's own inner life. **Of the Spirit.** The Holy Spirit produces this fruit through the believer who is in vital union with Christ (Jn 15:1-8). **Love.** The self-denying, self-sacrificing, Christlike love which is the foundation of all other graces. A divine exposition of this kind of love is found in I Corinthians 13. **Joy.** The joy of the Holy Spirit (I Thess 1:6), that deep abiding, inner rejoicing in the Lord (Phil 4:4). **Peace.** Tranquillity of soul (Phil 4:7), the peace that Christ gives (Jn 14:27), and which the world cannot take away. **Longsuffering.** Patient endurance and steadfastness under provocation; forbearance under ill-will, with no thought of retaliation. **Gentleness.** Graciousness, kindly disposition. **Goodness.** Beneficence, ready to do good, love in action. **Faith.** Fidelity which makes one true to his promise and faithful to his task.

23 Meekness, temperance: against such there is no law.

23. Meekness. Not weakness, but controlled strength. This word conveys the idea of a listening ear to hear what God has to say. It is submission to God and unselfishness to our fellowmen. **Temperance.** Rational restraint of the natural impulses, self-control. **Against such there is no law.** No law forbids the possession and the practice of these virtues. No law is needed to require a man who is bearing much fruit in his life to do right to his fellowman.

24 And they that are Christ's have crucified the flesh with the affections and lusts.

24. And they that are Christ's. Belong to Christ by purchase. **Have crucified the flesh.** This is a settled matter (2:20), but the very fact that the flesh and the Spirit are in constant conflict shows that the flesh is very active. When one puts his trust in Christ, he receives the actual benefits of identification with Christ, resulting in breaking the power of cancelled sin and in setting the prisoner free. The Christian is to daily give outward expression of his inward experience and in order to do this, he must constantly reckon himself "to be dead indeed unto sin, but alive unto God through our Lord Jesus Christ" (Rom 6:11). **With the affections and lust.** Emphasizes the completeness of the transaction.

25 If we live in the Spirit, let us also walk in the Spirit.

25. If we live in the Spirit. Since we live by the Spirit we derive our life from Him. **Let us also walk in the Spirit.** Let us go on walking, making progress toward spiritual maturity, by the Holy Spirit's indwelling presence and power. The word **walk** (Gr *stoicheō*) means to walk in a line, keep in rank and file, march in battle order. We need to keep in step with the Holy Spirit.

26 Let us not be desirous of vain glory, provoking one another, envying one another.

26. Let us not be desirous of vain glory. Let us cease becoming self-conceited. **Provoking one another.** Challenging one another to combat. **Envying one another.** Pining away with feelings of jealousy over the other's undeserved praise. Such actions toward one another are not consistent with a life of faith, lived by one who has been crucified with Christ and who is keeping step with the Holy Spirit.

C. Liberty Is Perfected by Love. 6:1-10.

6:1. Brethren. Members of the same spiritual family. **If a man be overtaken.** Literally, to take before. Sudden temptation seized him unawares before he could escape. This is a probable contingency. **In a fault.** A falling beside, a trespass, a lapse or deviation from truth and uprightness. It is important to distinguish between willful, deliberate sin and sudden, unexpected failure because of overwhelming temptation taking one off guard. **Ye which are spiritual.** Those who are constantly walking by the Spirit and living by the Spirit (5:16, 25), and who are exhibiting the fruit of the Spirit (5:22-23). These are experts in

CHAPTER 6
BRETHREN, if a man be overtaken in a fault, ye which are spiritual, restore such an one in the spirit of meekness; considering thyself, lest thou also be tempted.

2399

2 Bear ye one another's burdens, and so fulfil the law of Christ.

3 For if a man think himself to be something, when he is nothing, he deceiveth himself.

4 But let every man prove his own work, and then shall he have rejoicing in himself alone, and not in another.

5 For every man shall bear his own burden.

6 Let him that is taught in the word communicate unto him that teacheth in all good things.

7 Be not deceived; God is not mocked: for whatsoever a man soweth, that shall he also reap.

mending souls. **Restore such an one.** This word (Gr *katartizō*) is used as a surgical term, of setting a bone or dislocated joint. It is the same word used in Matthew 4:21 of mending nets. The present imperative signifies to keep on having the habit of restoring the offender to his former condition. Bring him into line. It takes skill to bring one who has slipped off the road of grace and is struggling in the quicksand of legalism back into his former manner of life and rightful place of unbroken fellowship with Christ. **In the spirit of meekness.** A fruit of the Spirit. This is the opposite of arrogance and harshness; it is tender consideration and forbearance. There must be no self-complacency, no scolding, and no "better-than-thou" attitude. **Considering thyself.** Constantly looking with fixed attention on thyself. **Lest thou also be tempted.** All need this warning; no one is immune from temptation.

2. **Bear ye one another's burdens.** Have the habit of mutual burden-bearing. Lend a helping hand by lifting heavy loads. **Burdens** (Gr *baros*) is an overload which we can lighten, a weight too heavy for the individual and capable of being shared with others of the fellowship. **And so.** In this manner. **Fulfil the law of Christ.** Satisfy the requirements of the law and fill it to overflowing.

3. **For if a man think himself to be something, when he is nothing.** If he has the habit of accounting himself a big number, when he is a zero, he is conceited without a cause. Self-esteem is vanity, and vanity is nothing. The very fact of thinking more highly of himself than he ought to think (Rom 12:3) condemns him; he is weighed in the balances and found wanting (Dan 5:27). **He deceiveth himself.** He is constantly leading his own mind to stray; he deceives no one else. Self-conceit results in self-deception.

4. **But let every man prove his own work.** Let each one continually and carefully test his own actual accomplishments by objective scrutiny. Such testing is for the purpose of approving. **Then.** After he has done this. **Shall he have rejoicing.** A ground of glorying. **In himself alone.** With regard to himself. **And not in another.** He will not arrive at a wrong conclusion by comparing himself with the other person and decide that he is better than the other person.

5. **For every man shall bear his own burden.** Each one shall carry his own responsibility, shoulder his own pack, bear his own private load. There is no contradiction between verses 2 and 5; different Greek words are translated "burden." In verse 2 the word is the Greek *baros* and denotes a heavy, crushing, overtaxing weight; our extra load, which can and must be relieved. Here in verse 5 the word is the Greek *phortion* and is used to designate a pack carried by a soldier. It is the word used by Christ to describe the burden He lays on His disciples (Mt 11:30), which He says is light. This word is the diminutive form of the Greek *phortos* which is used of the lading or cargo of a ship (Acts 27:10).

6. **Let him that is taught in the word.** Let him that is being taught in the word. In the early church, there were those whose full-time duty it was to give instruction in the Word of God. **Communicate.** Be a partner with, share with, enter into fellowship with financially. **Unto him that teacheth in all good things.** In all material and spiritual things (cf. I Cor 9:10-11). The Christian community was expected to support these gifted teachers.

7. **Be not deceived.** Stop being led astray into error. **God is not mocked.** God is not ignored, sneered at, ridiculed, treated with contempt by cynical gestures. There can be no double-dealing with God; He is not deceived by hypocrites. **For whatsoever a man soweth.** Keeps on sowing. **That.** Not something different. There is an identity of what is sown and what is harvested. **Shall he also reap.** Eventually there will be a har-

vest, and the immutable law of sowing and reaping applies (Mt 7:16-19).

8 For he that soweth to his flesh shall of the flesh reap corruption; but he that soweth to the Spirit shall of the Spirit reap life everlasting.

8. For he that soweth to his flesh. The one who is constantly (Greek present tense) sowing with a view to the promotion of his own corrupt, sinful nature; that nature which is opposed to God and unrenewed by the Holy Spirit. **Shall of the flesh reap corruption.** Physical, moral, and spiritual rottenness and ruin. **But he that soweth to the Spirit.** Our life here is a sowing of one kind or another. **Shall of the Spirit reap life everlasting.** In opposition to corruption. Eternal life is produced by the Holy Spirit in those who put their trust in Christ. Paul has shown (5:19-25) the intermediate products of the flesh and the Spirit; here he mentions the two final harvests. "For if ye live after the flesh, ye shall die: but if ye through the Spirit do mortify the deeds of the body, ye shall live" (Rom 8:13).

9 And let us not be weary in well doing: for in due season we shall reap, if we faint not.

9. And let us not be weary in well doing. Stop (Greek present imperative) getting discouraged and tired of doing good, i.e., sowing to the Spirit. This word **weary** means to retreat in battle, to give up the fight, to flag in one's efforts. The idea is that one may get tired on the job and slacken up his work, or even stop, before the field is plowed and planted. **For in due season.** At its proper season, i.e., harvest time. **We shall reap, if we faint not.** If we do not relax, let down, become exhausted, and faint.

10 As we have therefore opportunity, let us do good unto all *men*, especially unto them who are of the household of faith.

10. As we have therefore opportunity. Occasion, appropriate season. **Let us do good unto all men.** Let us keep on working the good to everyone. **Especially unto them who are of the household of faith.** All born-again believers belong to the same spiritual family. For these we are under special obligation to work good, whenever we have an opportunity.

D. Conclusion. 6:11-18.

11 Ye see how large a letter I have written unto you with mine own hand.

11. Ye see how large a letter. Better, with how large letters. **I have written unto you with mine own hand.** I wrote (Greek epistolary aorist). Paul now takes the pen from the amanuensis and writes the rest of the letter.

12 As many as desire to make a fair shew in the flesh, they constrain you to be circumcised; only lest they should suffer persecution for the cross of Christ.

12. As many as desire to make a fair show. Make a pretentious display of religion, i.e., put on a good front, present a good-looking face to win favor of men and avoid the loss of popularity, position, and prominence. **In the flesh.** In external rites and ritual. **They constrain you to be circumcised.** They are trying to compel you by saying it is absolutely necessary. **Only lest they should suffer persecution.** The legalists were not concerned for the Galatians, or for God, but only about their own comfort and reputation. **For the cross of Christ.** Because of the cross of Christ. The symbol of suffering and shame, which came to those identified with the cross of Christ.

13 For neither they themselves who are circumcised keep the law; but desire to have you circumcised, that they may glory in your flesh.

13. For neither. Not even. **They themselves who are circumcised.** Those who are submitting to circumcision, the legalistic circumcision party. **Keep the law.** The legalists were insincere and inconsistent, pretending to be zealous for the law. They felt that merely observing circumcision would compensate for not observing the rest of the law. **But desire to have you circumcised.** They had a twofold selfish purpose in mind: (1) to escape persecution which comes with the cross of Christ; and (2) to brag and boast over the Galatians. **That they may glory in your flesh.** Get credit for proselytizing Gentiles or persuading Gentiles to be circumcised and adopt the legalistic system.

14 But God forbid that I should glory, save in the cross of our Lord Jesus Christ, by whom the world is crucified unto me, and I unto the world.

14. But God forbid that I should glory. May it not come to pass to me so that I continue glorying. This is a wish for the future. **Save in the cross of our Lord Jesus Christ.** What was a shame to the legalists was the object of glorying to Paul. The cross represents the sacrificial sufferings of Christ; not Paul's sufferings for Christ (II Cor 12:9-10), but Christ's sufferings for Paul (Phil 3:3). **By whom.** Our Lord Jesus Christ. **The world.** The satanic world system which is opposed to God and Christ, both the religious and the irreligious world. **Is crucified unto me, and I unto the world.** The perfect tense emphasizes the present, permanent results of this double crucifixion. Crucifixion means a death of shame. The world has no more power over Paul because it is dead as far as he is concerned and Paul is also dead so far as the world is concerned. This was accomplished by means of the cross of our Lord Jesus Christ. Paul was crucified to the world when he was crucified with Christ (2:20). The old Saul died and was buried with Christ; the new Paul lives.

15 For in Christ Jesus neither circumcision availeth any thing, nor uncircumcision, but a new creature.

15. For in Christ Jesus. In living union with Him. **Neither circumcision availeth anything, nor uncircumcision.** Circumcision affects only the body, not the soul. A surgical operation can have absolutely no effect on the old nature. Nothing short of death and the creation of a new nature can be effective, and this comes only when one is identified with the crucified, risen Christ. **But a new creature.** The only thing that is important is to be a new creation in Christ (II Cor 5:17). "He that hath the Son hath life; and he that hath not the Son hath not life" (I Jn 5:12).

16 And as many as walk according to this rule, peace *be* on them, and mercy, and upon the Israel of God.

16. And as many as walk according to this rule. Man needs a standard or a measuring rod to guide his steps. The law was a failure, so God has given us another standard, placing all our hopes of salvation in the crucified, buried, risen, and coming again Christ. **Peace be on them, and mercy, and upon the Israel of God.** Not a different class of believers. Israel of God is in contrast to Israel after the flesh. Those who received the Saviour who came through Israel are true Israelites, spiritual descendants of Abraham.

17 From henceforth let no man trouble me: for I bear in my body the marks of the Lord Jesus.

17. From henceforth let no man trouble me. Paul's apostleship, authority, and gospel had all been questioned. He successfully answered all the criticism, and now he says, "Let's hear no more of such disturbing, distracting attacks." **For I bear in my body the marks of the Lord Jesus.** Let anyone show the like if he wants to qualify to speak. There were devotees who stamped upon their bodies the names of the gods whom they worshiped; some slaves had the names or marks of their owners on their bodies; and sometimes soldiers were thus identified. Paul glorified in being a slave of Jesus Christ. The brandmarks, his badge of lifelong, faithful service, were the scars left by scourgings, stones at Lystra, and rods at Philippi (cf. II Cor 11:24-27). Paul had endured hardness as a good soldier of Jesus Christ (II Tim 2:3).

18 Brethren, the grace of our Lord Jesus Christ *be* with your spirit. Amen.

18. Brethren. They remained brethren by the grace of God. This final touch of affection, in spite of the sharp things he said to them. **The grace of our Lord Jesus Christ be with your spirit.** What more fitting benediction could have been given at the close of a letter emphasizing grace instead of law, and spirit rather than flesh. **Amen.**

BIBLIOGRAPHY

Burton, E. de Witt. A Critical and Exegetical Commentary on the Epistle to the Galatians. In *The International Critical Commentary*. Edinburgh: T. & T. Clark, 1921.

Calvin, John. *Commentaries on the Epistles of Paul to the Galatians and Ephesians*. Trans. by William Pringle. Grand Rapids: Eerdmans, 1948.

DeHaan, Martin R. *Galatians*. Grand Rapids: Zondervan, 1960.

*Eadie, John. *Commentary on the Epistle of Paul to the Galatians*. Grand Rapids: Zondervan, n.d.

Erdman, Charles R. *The Epistle of Paul to the Galatians*. Philadelphia: Westminster Press, 1930.

Findlay, George G. Galatians. In *The Expositor's Bible*. New York: Hodder and Stoughton, n.d.

Hendriksen, William. Exposition of Galatians. In *New Testament Commentary*. Grand Rapids: Baker, 1968.

Hiebert, D. Edmond. *An Introduction to the Pauline Epistles*. Chicago: Moody Press, 1954.

Ironside, H. A. *Expository Messages on the Epistle to the Galatians*. Neptune, N.J.: Loizeaux Brothers, 1941.

*Kent, H. A. *Freedom of God's Sons: Studies in Galatians*. Grand Rapids: Baker, 1976.

Lenski, R. C. H. *The Interpretation of St. Paul's Epistles to the Galatians, to the Ephesians, and to the Philippians*. Columbus, Ohio: The Wartburg Press, 1937.

*Lightfoot, J. B. *The Epistle of St. Paul to the Galatians*. Grand Rapids: Zondervan, second reprinted edition, 1957.

Luther, Martin. *A Commentary on St. Paul's Epistle to the Galatians*. Westwood, N.J.: Revell, reprinted, n.d.

*Ramsay, Sir William M. *A Historical Commentary on St. Paul's Epistle to the Galatians*. New York: G. P. Putnam's Sons, 1900.

*Rendall, Frederic. The Epistle to the Galatians. In *The Expositor's Greek Testament*. Grand Rapids: Eerdmans, n.d.

*Ridderbos, H. B. The Epistle of Paul to the Churches of Galatia. In *The New International Commentary on the New Testament*. Grand Rapids: Eerdmans, 1954.

Stott, John R. W. *The Message of Galatians*. London: InterVarsity Press, 1968.

Strauss, Lehman. *Devotional Studies in Galatians and Ephesians*. Neptune, N.J.: Loizeaux Brothers, 1957.

Tenney, Merrill C. *Galatians: The Charter of Christian Liberty*. Grand Rapids: Eerdmans, 1951.

Wuest, Kenneth S. *Galatians in the Greek New Testament for the English Reader*. Grand Rapids: Eerdmans, 1944.

The Epistle To The

EPHESIANS

INTRODUCTION

The Church of Ephesus. Ephesus was the queen city of Asia Minor, situated about three miles from the Aegean Sea on the Cayster River, and had a population of about 340,000. It was the capital of the proconsular province of Asia and was one of the most important cities visited by the Apostle Paul. Ephesus was noted for the Great Temple of Diana (Artemis), an open-air theatre seating 25,000, a magnificent stadium, and the shrine of Serapis (an Egyptian divinity). Ephesus was famous for its rich culture: Oriental religion, Greek philosophy, Roman government, and worldwide commerce.

At the close of his second missionary journey, Paul made a brief visit to Ephesus, left Priscilla and Aquila there to work in his absence, and promised to return (Acts 18:19-21). Apollos spent some time there (Acts 18:24-28). On his third missionary journey, Paul remained in Ephesus for about three years evangelizing the city and the surrounding region. On his last voyage to Jerusalem, Paul met the elders of Ephesus at Miletus (Acts 20:17-38). Others who labored at Ephesus were Timothy (I Tim 1:3), Onesiphorus (II Tim 1:16), Tychicus (II Tim 4:12), and the Apostle John after A.D. 70.

Authorship. The writer identifies himself as Paul (1:1; 3:1). Both the internal and the external evidences are strong for the pauline authorship.

Date and place of writing. This is one of the Prison Epistles. Paul states that he was a prisoner (3:1; 4:1; 6:20). Paul was in prison three times: (1) at Caesarea for about two years, A.D. 58-60; (2) once in Rome for about two years, A.D. 61-63; and (3) again in Rome about A.D. 67. He probably wrote the Prison Epistles during his first Roman imprisonment, A.D. 61-63. Ephesians was composed about the same time as Colossians. Tychicus was the bearer of both letters (Col 4:7-8; Eph 6:21-22).

Destination. Scholars are divided as to the destination of this epistle: (1) that it was written for and sent directly to Ephesus; (2) that it was a circular letter sent to the churches of Asia Minor, of which Ephesus was the chief; or (3) that it was addressed to Gentile Christians. The oldest and most reliable Greek manuscripts do not have the words "which are at Ephesus" (Gr *en Ephesoi*) in 1:1. Lightfoot maintains that wherever these manuscripts agree, they almost always represent the original text. However, the great majority of Greek manuscripts do include the words "in Ephesus," and there are no Greek manuscripts which include the name of any other city. In Colossians 4:16, Paul mentions "the epistle from Laodicea." Perhaps the autograph copy had a blank space in 1:1, and since most of the manuscripts were copies of the letter sent to Ephesus, it came to be known as the Epistle to the Ephesians. No doubt it was a general or circular letter for the churches of Asia Minor. The letter lacks a personal tone; there are no personal greetings and no personal references. After all is said, the value of the epistle is not affected by the problem of its destination.

Purpose. This epistle magnifies the church as a divine institution, sets forth God's purpose of heading up all things in Christ (1:9-10), emphasizes that salvation is only in Christ, and shows that a well-rounded life issues out of salvation by grace through faith.

This epistle is not personal, but general. It is not polemic: Paul is not defending his apostleship as in I Corinthians, not rebuking fickleness as in II Corinthians, not controverting Judaizers as in Galatians, and not battling Gnosticism as in Colossians.

Theme. Ephesians has been called "The Heavenly Epistle" and "The Alps of the New Testament." In it Paul takes us from "the depths of ruin to the heights of redemption." The church is one with Christ: it is the body of which He is the Head (1:22-23); it is the building of which He is the Chief Corner Stone (2:20-22); and she is the bride of whom Christ is the Bridegroom (5:25-32).

Comparison with Colossians. In Ephesians the emphasis is on the dignity of the church, which is the body of Christ. In Colossians the emphasis is on the deity of Christ, who is the Head of that body. Ephesians considers the church's oneness with Christ; Colossians considers the church's completeness in Christ. Ephesians speaks of the Christian being in Christ; Colossians speaks of Christ being in the Christian.

OUTLINE

COMMENTARY

I. INTRODUCTION. 1:1-2.

PAUL, an apostle of Jesus Christ by the will of God, to the saints which are at Ĕph'e-sus, and to the faithful in Christ Jesus:

1:1. Paul. Designated as the human author. **An apostle.** One fully equipped and sent on a mission. Paul claims to be directly commissioned by Christ to represent Him. He was an envoy, an ambassador for Christ. **Of Jesus Christ.** He was owned by Christ and sent from Him; both possessed and commissioned. **By the will of God.** Paul is always conscious of the divine origin and authority of his commission. This assurance sustained him throughout all of his trials. His ministry was not of his own choosing. He could ever say, "By the grace of God I am what I am." **To the saints.** The separated and holy ones (Ps. 4:3). Saints are sinners saved by the grace of God, separated from sin, and set apart for God. They are not sinless, have not attained to certain heights of sanctity, and do not belong to some special religious group. **At Ephesus.** Geographically. **And to the faithful.** Even those who are distinguished for their faithfulness and loyalty to Christ. This is one way to describe Christians. The word means that they are "believers" in Christ. **In Christ.** Spiritually they are in vital union with Christ enjoying blessed fellowship with Him.

2 Grace *be* to you, and peace, from God our Father, and *from* the Lord Jesus Christ.

2. Grace. That divine, free, and unmerited favor of God. **And peace.** Not only the absence of all strife but the blessing of tranquility. It is the result of reconciliation between God and man based on faith in and union with the Lord Jesus Christ. Here both words are used as a greeting. **From God . . . and . . . the Lord Jesus Christ.** The source of spiritual blessings, our gracious heavenly Father and our lovely Lord.

II. THE CALLING OF THE CHURCH. 1:3-3:21.

A. The Origin of the Church. 1:3-14.

3 Blessed *be* the God and Father of our Lord Jesus Christ, who hath blessed us with all spiritual blessings in heavenly *places* in Christ:

3. Blessed. This doxology is composed of three stanzas, each of which closes with a similar refrain (vss. 6, 12, 14). This word **blessed** is always used of God in the New Testament, and it means praised or eulogized. **Who hath blessed us.** God is the great giver, and the blessings are already ours. **With all spiritual blessings.** With every kind of spiritual blessing. They are spiritual in nature as opposed to temporal and material, and they are the products of the Holy Spirit. **In heavenly places.** In the realm and sphere of heavenly things as contrasted with earthly things. The adjective expresses quality rather than place. This expression is found several times in this epistle and refers to that exalted sphere of activities to which the believer has been lifted in Christ. **In Christ.** In vital union with Him. Note how often these words are found in this epistle. **In Christ** is the key to this wonderful passage. Since the saints are in Him, nothing is too good or too great for God to bestow upon them.

4 According as he hath chosen us in him before the foundation of the world, that we should be holy and without blame before him in love:

4. He hath chosen us. This word (Gr *eklegomai*) means to pick out, to choose. This is a definite statement of God's elective grace concerning believers in Christ. **In him.** In union with Christ. Apart from Christ, there would have been no election and no salvation. God always deals with man in Christ, who is the one and only Mediator between God and men (I Tim 2:5). Paul traces man's salvation back to the plan of God's will. **Before the foundation of the world.** Before the projection of the world order. God's choice was eternal; His plan is timeless. The fall of man was no surprise to God, and redemption was no afterthought. God provided for our salvation before one star glittered in infinite expanse. We must be careful not to draw false conclusions from this sublime truth. God is not stating a fatalistic doctrine in which He arbitrarily elects some to heaven and consigns all others to hell. There is no scriptural doctrine of election to damnation. God's election provides for the means as well as the ends. God's infallible Word plainly states, "For whosoever shall call upon the name of the Lord shall be saved" (Rom 10:13). Man either receives or disbelieves God's provisions in Christ. "So far as the human race is concerned, every man may not only accept Christ as Saviour but is urged and invited to do so. The ground of this invitation is the work of the incarnate Son . . . Divine foreordination and human freedom are humanly irreconcilable, but like two parallel lines that meet in infinity, they have their solution in God" (Merrill F. Unger, *Unger's Bible Handbook*, pp. 672-674). "To explain an apparent difficulty by denying one or the other of these tenets is to explain away the truth" (W. Curtis Vaughn, *The Letter to the Ephesians*, p. 13). **That we should be holy and without blame before him in love.** This is the purpose of God's election. The real purpose of God's elective grace is not "pie in the sky by and by," but has to do with a separated life here and now (cf. Rom 8:29). Holiness is the positive side of a Christlike life (Heb 12:14), separated from all evil courses and connections. Blamelessness in character is the negative side of the Christlike life: not sinless, but stainless, without blemish and without defect. God's expectation is for His saints to live on a high spiritual plane.

5 Having predestinated us unto the adoption of children by Jesus Christ to himself, according to the good pleasure of his will,

5. Having predestinated us. Having decided beforehand by marking off the boundaries of His possession in His saints. **Unto the adoption of children.** With a view to our being placed as adult sons (Gal 4:5; Rom 8:15; 9:4). The purpose of His predestination was that we should experience sonship. **By Jesus Christ to himself.** By means of Christ's mediation and for His very own to serve Him and glorify Him. **According to the good pleasure of his will.** It was right for Him to do this.

6 To the praise of the glory of his grace, wherein he hath made us accepted in the beloved.

6. To the praise of the glory of his grace. Literally, the glory, the splendor, of His unmerited favor. The purpose was for God's glory and intended to issue forth in praise. **He hath made us accepted in the beloved.** God accepts us into His family because of our vital relationship with Christ and on no other grounds.

7 In whom we have redemption through his blood, the forgiveness of sins, according to the riches of his grace;

7. In whom we have. A present possession, not a future prospect. **Redemption.** Redemption is deliverance from bondage by means of a price paid. Saints have been liberated from the slavery of self, sin and Satan, having been bought out of the slave market. "If the Son therefore shall make you free, ye shall be free indeed" (Jn 8:36). **Through his blood.** His blood is the ransom price paid for our salvation. Redemption is effected by the precious blood of Christ (I Pet 1:18-20). Salvation is not a matter of human attainment, but of divine atonement. God makes everything of the blood of Christ: we are redeemed by His blood (Eph 1:7); justified by His blood (Rom 5:9); purged as to conscience by His blood (Heb 9:14); forgiven by His blood (Col 1:14); cleansed by His blood (Rev 7:14); have peace through His blood (Col 1:20); enter the Holiest by His blood (Heb 10:19). **The forgiveness of sins.** Remission rests on ransoming. Forgiveness means the bearing away of all our shortcomings. God's remission is unqualified and unchanging. His Word is very specific in telling us what He has done with our sins; He has blotted them out (Isa 43:25; 44:22), He has removed them (Ps 103:11-12), He has cast them behind His back (Isa 38:17), He has cast them into the depths of the sea (Mic 7:19), and He remembers them no more (Heb 8:12). God's forgiveness is free, full, and final. When He forgives, He forgets. **According to the riches of his grace.** Our redemption is measured by the boundless resources of His marvelous, infinite grace. This is a very rich epistle which reveals our riches in Christ; the riches of His grace (1:7), the riches of the glory of His inheritance in the saints (1:18), the riches in mercy (2:7), the unsearchable riches of Christ (3:8), and the riches of His glory (3:16).

8 Wherein he hath abounded toward us in all wisdom and prudence;

9 Having made known unto us the mystery of his will, according to his good pleasure which he hath purposed in himself:

10 That in the dispensation of the fulness of times he might gather together in one all things in Christ, both which are in heaven, and which are on earth; *even* in him:

11 In whom also we have obtained an inheritance, being predestinated according to the purpose of him who worketh all things after the counsel of his own will:

12 That we should be to the praise of his glory, who first trusted in Christ.

13 In whom ye also *trusted*, after that ye heard the word of truth, the gospel of your salvation: in whom also after that ye believed, ye were sealed with that holy Spirit of promise,

14 Which is the earnest of our inheritance until the redemption of the purchased possession, unto the praise of his glory.

8. Wherein he hath abounded toward us. Which He lavished on us to overflowing. God's grace enriches believers (cf. Rom 5:20). **In all wisdom.** Wise insight and spiritual perception which come from above (Jas 1:5; 3:17). **Prudence.** This is the practical use of wisdom and spiritual discernment.

9. The mystery of his will. God has a plan which was once hidden from human reason for ages (Rom 16:25) but now is divinely revealed (Col 1:26-27). **Which he hath purposed in himself.** Which He set forth in Christ.

10. That in the dispensation. A stewardship or administration to carry out His plan and purpose. **The fullness of times.** The appointed time of the historical ages. **He might gather together in one all things in Christ.** To sum up, to head up all things in Christ in orderly and harmonious completion. Christ is the center of the universe, which some day will be integrated into one harmonious whole.

11. In whom . . . we have obtained an inheritance. Better, we were made the inheritance, we became God's heritage, and became the Lord's portion (Deut 32:9). Zephaniah 3:17 records a remarkable expression, "He will save, he will rejoice over thee with joy; he will rest in his love, he will joy over thee with singing." This is applicable to Gentile saints, as well as to Hebrew saints.

12. That we should be to the praise of his glory. This second refrain praises God the Son.

13. In whom ye also trusted. Faith is the connecting link between man and Christ. **After that ye heard.** They first heard God's good news, called the Word of truth and further described as the gospel of your salvation. Notice the order here. They first heard God's good news and then they put their trust in Christ. ". . . faith cometh by hearing, and hearing by the word of God" (Rom 10:17). **After that ye believed, ye were sealed with that holy Spirit of promise.** They were sealed, not in order to be redeemed, but because they were already redeemed. They had trusted in Christ and now they are sealed in Him. The word seal means to set a seal on one as a mark of ownership. The Holy Spirit ratified God's ownership of believers by fixing His seal on them in a supernatural manner. They were sealed at the same time they believed, not at some later time. The sealing was not something apart from salvation, not something in addition to salvation, and not something subsequent to salvation. All who believe in Christ are sealed then and there. The seal is: (1) a sign of a finished transaction (Jer 32:9-10; Jn 17:4; 19:30); (2) a sign of ownership (I Cor 16:19-20; II Tim 2:19); and (3) a sign of security (Dan 6:17; Eph 4:30). The Holy Spirit is called the Spirit of promise because Christ promised to send Him (Jn 14:16).

14. Which is the earnest of our inheritance. An earnest (Gr *arrabōn*) is a partial down payment in the first installment and a pledge guaranteeing a complete transaction and payment of the total obligation. Since God has graciously given us the Holy Spirit and we now have a foretaste of heaven, we have His guarantee that He will perform all that He has promised (Phil 1:6). **Unto the praise of his glory.** Paul uses similar, though not identical, terms in ascribing these wonderful blessings to the grace of God. In verse 6, God the Father is praised for selecting us by His mercies; in verse 12, God the Son is praised for securing us by His mediation; and in verse 14, God the Holy Spirit is praised for sealing us by His ministry. We see in each stage of salvation grace, marvelous grace, and nothing but grace. In its past inception, in its present possession, and in its future glory, grace is supreme.

B. The Prayer for the Church. 1:15-23.

There are two prayers in Ephesians. God is both light and love. Paul's first prayer (1:15-23) is for light, and his second

15 Wherefore I also, after I heard of your faith in the Lord Jesus, and love unto all the saints,

16 Cease not to give thanks for you, making mention of you in my prayers,

17 That the God of our Lord Jesus Christ, the Father of glory, may give unto you the spirit of wisdom and revelation in the knowledge of him:

18 The eyes of your understanding being enlightened; that ye may know what is the hope of his calling, and what the riches of the glory of his inheritance in the saints,

19 And what *is* the exceeding greatness of his power to usward who believe, according to the working of his mighty power,
20 Which he wrought in Christ, when he raised him from the dead, and set *him* at his own right hand in the heavenly *places*,

21 Far above all principality, and power, and might, and dominion, and every name that is named, not only in

prayer (3:14-21) is for love. It is as natural for a regenerate man to pray as it is for an unregenerate man to breathe.

15. Wherefore, on this account, for this cause. This looks back to verses 3-14, and Paul adds prayer to praise. **Faith** and **love** are two great words. Love is the outgrowth of faith, and faith manifests itself by love. Faith works by love (Gal 5:6), and love is the proof of discipleship (Jn 13:35; 15:12; I Jn 3:14).

16. Cease not to give thanks for you. A vital part of Paul's ministry was his intercession for the saints. This was his constant and continual fixed habit. Prayer and thanksgiving go together.

17. That (Gr *hina*). In order that. This introduces the definite purpose and object of Paul's prayer for them. He makes specific requests. **The God of our Lord Jesus Christ.** Paul addresses the throne of grace, the source of all blessings. **The Father of glory.** The one who is all glorious and the source of all that is glorious. **May give unto you the spirit of wisdom and revelation.** Revelation has to do with new truths. The Ephesians were the recipients of God's revelation, and they had knowledge of spiritual truths. The Holy Spirit knows the deep things of God (I Cor 2:11), and He is our teacher (Jn 14:26). Man needs much more than reason and research; he needs a revelation from God. Wisdom is general illumination, the know-how to apply the revealed spiritual truths. **In the knowledge of him.** This is that deep and wide, growing, experimental knowledge (II Pet 3:18). We all need a fuller knowledge of Christ (Phil 3:10).

18. The eyes of your understanding being enlightened. Better, that the eyes of your heart having been enlightened. The heart refers to the whole inner man. The soul has eyes that need to be and can be enlightened, i.e., flooded with divine light. The Holy Spirit opens the eyes and hearts in order that the believer may see the great truths mentioned here. The purpose of spiritual illumination and spiritual perception is that believers may know and experience God's grace, inheritance, and power. **The hope of his calling.** The call from Him and a summons to Him. It is a call to new life in Christ, through Christ, for Christ, and with Christ. It involves perfect deliverance and perfect fellowship. God's calling is a high calling (Phil 3:13-14) to be like Christ and with Christ. **The riches of the glory of his inheritance in the saints.** God owns the universe, but His most precious possession is the pearl of great price, the church. The saints are the trophies of His grace.

19-20. The exceeding greatness of his power. The transcendent, immeasurable, more-than-sufficient greatness of His dynamic power. Paul heaps up terms that defy description in speaking of God's power. **To us-ward who believe.** We can depend on God's power. It is divine, inexhaustible, irresistible, and available. No one need ever complain of insufficient power to meet temptations, to overcome sinful habits, or to live and witness for Christ. Little power is an indisputable evidence of little fellowship with Christ. Paul prays that we may know: the hope to which He calls us, the riches He possesses in us, and the power He extends toward us. **Which he wrought in Christ.** A demonstration of God's omnipotence; putting forth energetically His infinite power. **When he raised him from the dead.** Resurrection power is available to us. The resurrection of Christ is the attestation of God's acceptance of Christ's sacrifice and the pattern and pledge of the believer's resurrection. **And set him at his own right hand.** This refers to the ascension, exaltation, and enthronement of Christ. God's right hand is the place of honor, privilege, and power. The same omnipotence which seated our Lord amid ineffable glory is pledged to seat the church with Him in the same glory.

21-22. Far above all. The primacy of Christ far above all angelic and celestial beings, His sovereign dominion; He is superior to and authoritatively over all. He is "KING OF KINGS,

this world, but also in that which is to come:

22 And hath put all *things* under his feet, and gave him *to be* the head over all *things* to the church,

23 Which is his body, the fulness of him that filleth all in all.

CHAPTER 2

AND you *hath he quickened*, who were dead in trespasses and sins;

2 Wherein in time past ye walked according to the course of this world, according to the prince of the power of the air, the spirit that now worketh in the children of disobedience:

3 Among whom also we all had our conversation in times past in the lusts of our flesh, fulfilling the desires of the flesh and of the mind; and were by nature the children of wrath, even as others.

4 But God, who is rich in mercy, for his great love wherewith he loved us,

5 Even when we were dead in sins,

AND LORD OF LORDS" (Rev 19:16). **Head over all things to the church.** The word church (Gr *ekklēsia*) is used over one hundred times in the New Testament and in most cases refers to a local assembly of believers. In Ephesians it is used in a comprehensive sense referring to all the redeemed, the body of Christ. Christ has sovereign authority over the church, and He will rule and reign supreme.

23. Which is his body. Paul states that the relationship between Christ and His church is similar to that between the head and the body of a human organism. The church is a living organism, not a dead organization. The union of Christ and His church is a real, mystical, perfect, and permanent union. The head directs the body's activities. The church is a living expression of Christ; it is the means by which He effects His plan and purpose; it is the agent through which He accomplishes His work. Believers are not only members of His body, they are members one of another in that body (cf. Rom 12:4-5). **The fullness of him that filleth all in all.** Christ is the full expression of God (Col 1:19; 2:9), and the church is the expression of Christ. The church is filled with His presence, animated with His life, and endowed with His gifts. In Christ the church has everything needed to fulfill its mission.

C. The Character of the Church. 2:1-10.

2:1. And you hath he quickened. The main verb in Greek does not occur until verse 5. **Who were dead.** Scripture paints man as he really is. Lost men are spiritually dead, not merely weakened, incapacitated, disabled, or sick. **In trespasses and sins.** Trespasses (Gr *paraptōma*) refer to stepping out of line of true conduct, a deviation from truth and uprightness. Sins (Gr *hamartia*) are missing the mark of life's divine aim, as an archer misses the "bull's eye." These lead to guilt, and man's need of forgiveness; they lead to death, and man's need of new life. This truth is denied in these days. Men speak of "the better self" and "the good spark." Man needs a new heart, not just a new start; a new life, not just turning over a new leaf; a resurrection, not just reformation. Signing a pledge card will not suffice. No one can live a life for God until he first receives life from God.

2. Wherein in time past. Paul describes the past manifestation of a man devoid of spiritual life. **Ye walked according to the course of this world.** Before conversion, you walked habitually in a wrong path of conduct conforming to the world's low standard of morality, doing what comes naturally. Life was determined by the spirit and practice of the age in its unregenerate state. **According to the prince of the power of the air.** Dominated by the devil, who administers the corrupt power of unholy spirits. The devil is a real person, whose many aliases reveal his true character. **The spirit that now worketh in the children of disobedience.** Satan exerts himself effectively in the society of unregenerate men (Jn 8:44; I Jn 3:8). The conduct of lost men mark them as children of disobedience.

3. Among whom also we all. We Jews, as well as Gentiles. **Our conversation.** (Gr *anastrephō*), Literally, to turn back and forth, hence to live (II Cor 1:12). **Lusts of our flesh.** Dominated by the desires of the fallen, unregenerate nature. **Fulfilling the desires of the flesh.** Following the evil inclinations of the desires of fleshly appetites. **And were by nature the children of wrath.** Worthy of and subject to wrath (Jn 3:36). The only hope for men in this condition is to experience the grace of God in Christ.

4. But God. God alone can meet man's needs. **Who is rich in mercy.** Wealthy in mercy by His very nature. This is much more than being merciful. Instead of dealing with us as deserving wrath and judgment, He deals with us in compassionate mercy. **His great love.** The source of our salvation (Jn 3:16).

5. When we were dead. Spiritually dead and needing new

hath quickened us together with Christ, (by grace ye are saved;)

6 And hath raised *us* up together, and made *us* sit together in heavenly *places* in Christ Jesus:

7 That in the ages to come he might shew the exceeding riches of his grace in *his* kindness toward us through Christ Jesus.

8 For by grace are ye saved through faith; and that not of yourselves: *it is* the gift of God:

9 Not of works, lest any man should boast.

10 For we are his workmanship, created in Christ Jesus unto good works, which God hath before ordained that we should walk in them.

life in Christ (Jn 1:12-13; I Jn 5:11-12). **Quickened us together with Christ.** He made us alive spiritually by imparting the life of Christ in us. This is what is meant by the new birth. **With Christ** refers to resurrection; literal in His case and spiritual in our case. What God did for Christ, He did for all who put their trust in Him. Note that God did it. We were born from above instantly and once for all. God may have used a powerful preacher, a praying parent, or a tearful teacher; but He did it. He did it when we trusted Christ, not because we prayed so earnestly, repented so bitterly, or resolved so thoroughly. Salvation is by grace plus nothing.

6. And hath raised us up together. Christ was raised in a physical resurrection and we in a past spiritual resurrection. On the basis of that, a future physical resurrection or transformation will occur for all living at the time of Rapture. **Made us sit together.** God set us down alongside of Christ in the heavenly realms and relations. God has already accomplished this. He dealt with us in Christ and sees us in Christ.

7. That in the ages to come. The end in view of God's gracious salvation in Christ. **He might show the exceeding riches of his grace.** God delights to show great grace to great sinners. God will display the trophies of His grace throughout the endless ages of eternity. Saints will be concrete demonstrations of the overflowing wealth of His grace.

8. For by grace are ye saved. The grace mentioned in verse 5. Grace is what God does for man, not what man does for God or for himself. Salvation is God's greatest gift and man's greatest need. The Greek perfect tense denotes the certainty of this God-given salvation; we have been saved in the past, and are just as thoroughly saved in the present. We have a perfect salvation. God gives; man receives. **Through faith.** Grace is God's provision; faith is man's appropriation. Faith is not a meritorious act, but the indispensable channel through which man receives God's free gift (Heb 11:6). **And that.** The word that (Gr *houtos*) is neuter and does not refer to faith (which is feminine) or to grace (also feminine), but to the fact of being saved by grace on God's part and conditioned on faith on man's part. **Not of yourselves.** Not through your merits or efforts. **It is the gift of God.** The free gift of God.

9. Not of works. Not based upon or produced by the works of man. **Lest any man should boast.** "He that glorieth, let him glory in the Lord" (I Cor 1:31). Calvin sums up Paul's meaning as follows: "In these three phrases,—not of yourselves,—it is the gift of God,—not of works,—he [Paul] embraces the substance of his long argument in the Epistles to the Romans and to the Galatians, that righteousness comes to us from the mercy of God alone,—is offered to us in Christ by the gospel,—and is received by faith alone, without the merit of works" (John Calvin, *Commentaries on the Epistles of Paul to the Galatians and Ephesians*, Trans. William Pringle, p. 228).

10. For we are his workmanship. We are God's poem (Gr *poiēma*). His masterpiece. In the matter of salvation, we are the product of the will and work of God. **Created in Christ Jesus.** The new birth, in living union with Christ. **Unto good works.** For good works, destined to good works. The purpose of the new creation in Christ. Christ in us still goes "about doing good" (Acts 10:38). We are saved apart from good works, but saved unto good works. Good works are the aim of our salvation and the evidence of our faith (Jas 2:17-18). Works never produce salvation, but salvation always produces good works. A man is not justified by works, but a justified man works. Works are the consequences, not the causes of salvation. They are the fruit, not the root of salvation. One must be a Christian before he can live as a Christian; he must be good before he can do good. One must be **created in Christ Jesus unto good works** before he can walk in them (Phil 1:6; 2:12-13). God is still working. **By grace** (vs. 8), it was Christ for us; **through faith** (vs. 8), it was Christ in us; and **unto good works,** it is Christ through us.

D. The Progress of the Church. 2:11-22.

11 Wherefore remember, that ye *being* **in time past Gentiles in the flesh, who are called Uncircumcision by that which is called the Circumcision in the flesh made by hands;**

11. Wherefore remember. Keep constantly in mind the precious truth just stated. **Gentiles.** All peoples who are not born Jews, as they are classified on the flesh basis and **are called Uncircumcision. Called the Circumcision in the flesh.** The Jews who proudly claim a religious sanction for racial exclusiveness and exaltation, even though the distinction is quite superficial. **Made by hands.** Handmade and limited to the flesh. Paul tactfully points out that the rite once used as a sign for spiritual promises is used now as a mere superficial thing of little or no value.

12 That at that time ye were without Christ, being aliens from the commonwealth of Israel, and strangers from the covenants of promise, having no hope, and without God in the world:

12. That at that time. Before your salvation experience. **Ye were without Christ.** Paul speaks of the destitution and desolation of the unregenerate, lost and undone. Being Christless we were: without rest (Mt 11:28); without life (Jn 14:6), without light (Jn 8:12); without salvation (Acts 4:12); and without peace (Col 1:20). **Alien from the commonwealth of Israel.** We were friendless, estranged and separated from Israel and the theocracy of God's chosen people. **Strangers from the covenants of promise.** We were homeless, not having any share in the messianic promises. God's Word has thousands of promises, but very few apply to the lost. God's promises are exceeding great and precious, but Christless souls see no value in them. **Having no hope.** We were hopeless. We had aspirations for the present, but cherished no hope for the future. Being Christless, we had no faith, no hope, and no love. **And without God.** We were atheists (Gr *atheos*) in the sense of being without God and in hostility to Him. A terrible picture, but a true one. We had gods many and lords many, but not the true God. We had no knowledge of God and no saving relationship to Him.

13 But now in Christ Jesus ye who sometimes were far off are made nigh by the blood of Christ.

13. But now. A strong, glorious contrast to **at that time** of verse 12. **In Christ.** Our new position in union with Him in contrast to being **without Christ** in verse 12. **Are made nigh by the blood of Christ.** This is what God has done. We are made nigh by the blood of Christ; not by becoming a proselyte of Judaism, not by the sincerity of our repentance, not by the strength of our faith, not by the depth of our devotion, not by the joy of our spiritual experience. A new relationship has been established in a new covenant sealed with the sacrificial blood of Christ, who suffered the just for the unjust, that He might bring us to God (I Pet 3:18).

14 For he is our peace, who hath made both one, and hath broken down the middle wall of partition *between* **us;**

14. For he is our peace. He Himself, not just what He did. He is our peace with God and with each other without distinction. **Who hath made both one.** Jews and Gentiles united in position and in privilege. A new unity has been established where race and national distinctions disappear in Christ (Gal 3:28). **Hath broken down the middle wall of partition.** The dividing wall of racial and religious enmity has been destroyed once for all. In the Temple courts a partition wall divided the court of the Gentiles from the court of Israel with an inscription forbidding a Gentile from going further on pain of death (cf. Acts 21:28). No such division exists in the church.

15 Having abolished in his flesh the enmity, *even* **the law of commandments** *contained* **in ordinances; for to make in himself of twain one new man,** *so* **making peace;**

15. Having abolished. This modifies **hath broken down** and means to make ineffective, null and void. **In his flesh.** In His incarnate state. **The enmity.** The old enmity of personal and national prejudice and exclusiveness between Jews and Gentiles was slain at Calvary. Only Christ crucified can effect so great a task as to reconcile and reunite hostile members of the human family. Christ is the world's only hope. **For to make in himself.** There was no other way to accomplish this except by taking two separate and antagonistic groups and making **one new man.** God's purpose is one new people. Christ's body, the church, is

16 And that he might reconcile both unto God in one body by the cross, having slain the enmity thereby:

17 And came and preached peace to you which were afar off, and to them that were nigh.

18 For through him we both have access by one Spirit unto the Father.

19 Now therefore ye are no more strangers and foreigners, but fellowcitizens with the saints, and of the household of God;

20 And are built upon the foundation of the apostles and prophets, Jesus Christ himself being the chief corner stone;

21 In whom all the building fitly framed together groweth unto an holy temple in the Lord:

22 In whom ye also are builded together for an habitation of God through the Spirit.

CHAPTER 3

FOR this cause I Paul, the prisoner of Jesus Christ for you Gentiles,

the one new man made up of new men (II Cor 5:17). **So making peace.** He is our peace (vs. 14) and our peacemaker (Col 1:20). He puts an end to the hostility between God and man and between man and man.

16. And that he might reconcile. Previously there had been a state of alienation, estrangement, and enmity, but there has been a change of relations both Godward and manward. Christ has harmonized both the factional and the fractional divisions of mankind. **In one body.** The church, Christ's spiritual body. **By the cross.** "God was in Christ, reconciling the world unto himself" (II Cor 5:19). **Having slain the enmity thereby.** God utterly put an end to the enmity that separated men into antagonistic groups.

17. Preached peace. By His vicarious death He procured peace, and by His servants He proclaims peace. Peace was the first word Christ spoke to His disciples in the upper room on the night of His resurrection (Jn 20:19). **To you which were afar off.** Gentiles were far away from God. **To them that were nigh.** Jews were regarded as near, but just as needy and just as dead in sin.

18. For through him. And only through Him. **We both have access.** A continuous, common, and unhindered approach to God. Through Christ all believers can "come boldly unto the throne of grace" (Heb 4:16). **By one Spirit.** Our access to the Father is through the Son and by the Holy Spirit. All three persons of the Trinity share in the total work of salvation.

19. Now therefore. So then, in the light of all this, because all hostility and enmity are past. **Ye are no more strangers.** Sojourners dwelling nearby, but not in the family of God. **Foreigners.** Without full rights and privileges of citizenship. **But fellow-citizens.** Having been born into the family of God, with citizenship in heaven (Phil 3:20). **And of the household of God.** Suggests the fellowship enjoyed by members of God's family.

20. And are built. Paul changes the figure of speech from a family to a spiritual temple in setting forth the unifying character of the church. **The foundation of the apostles and prophets.** The eternal foundation of God's purpose as proclaimed by the apostles and prophets. **Jesus Christ himself being the chief corner stone.** Christ is the stone rejected by the Jewish builders but chosen of God as the Head of the corner (Mt 21:42). He is not only the Chief Corner Stone, He is also the foundation (I Cor 3:11).

21. In whom. In present, precious, and permanent union with Him. **All the building fitly framed together.** As architectural metaphor. God places each one exactly where He wants him. We would be misfits anywhere else. **Groweth unto an holy temple.** The church is a growing temple in the process of construction. It is holy in the sense of being sanctified in Christ for God's glory. **In the Lord.** He is the center of its unity.

22. Ye also. Gentiles are included. **Builded together.** The Greek present tense implies continuous and contemporaneous building together with varied materials (I Pet 2:3-7). **For a habitation of God through the Spirit.** The great objective is to provide a place of habitation for God, who by the Spirit dwells permanently in His holy temple (Jn 14:16-17; I Cor 3:16; 6:19-20). In Old Testament times, God dwelt *with* His people; in New Testament times, God dwells *in* His people. Note the work of the Trinity: in Christ all believers are fitted and formed into one building by the Holy Spirit who regenerates and indwells them so that we are a dwelling place for God.

E. The Function of the Church. 3:1-13.

3:1. For this cause. Refers to the preceding exposition of God's elective grace and for the sake of the holy temple of redeemed men which God is building. **Prisoner of Jesus Christ**

for you Gentiles. On behalf of you Gentiles whom the Jews are not willing to accept freely.

2 If ye have heard of the dispensation of the grace of God which is given me to you-ward:

2. If ye have heard. Since ye have heard with the understanding. **Dispensation.** Paul refers to his high privilege and sacred trust of the administration of stewardship of God's universal grace to all men. This was given to Paul, and not of his own choosing. **Of the grace of God.** The grace of God is to be shared with others; it is not a personal luxury (Col 1:25; I Pet 4:10). Paul was merely a channel of blessing to the Gentiles.

3 How that by revelation he made known unto me the mystery; (as I wrote afore in few words,

3. How that by revelation he made known unto me the mystery. The mystery was not unintelligent or mysterious, but merely God's secret until He revealed it. It was unknown and unknowable apart from divine revelation. It did not come to Paul by research or by rationalization, but by revelation (Gal 1:11-12).

4 Whereby, when ye read, ye may understand my knowledge in the mystery of Christ)

4. When ye read. This epistle was to be read in public. **My knowledge.** Having this information you are able to comprehend my God-given insight in the mystery of Christ, God's eternal purpose in Christ.

5 Which in other ages was not made known unto the sons of men, as it is now revealed unto his holy apostles and prophets by the Spirit;

5. In other ages. Preceding generations. **As it is now revealed.** Up until that time, God's revelation was frequent and partial, now it is full and final. Then there were faint gleams of light in types and symbols, now there is a clear and complete revelation. **By the Spirit.** The Holy Spirit is the agent of inspiration and illumination (Jn 14:26; 16:12-15).

6 That the Gentiles should be fellow-heirs, and of the same body, and partakers of his promise in Christ by the gospel:

6. That the Gentiles. As truly as the Jews and along with them and on the same terms. The Gentiles are not second-class citizens of heaven. Paul gives a clear statement of the mystery. **Fellow heirs.** Because they are in the same body and the same family by regeneration, they are joint-heirs with Christ (Rom 8:17) and co-heirs with the Jews. **Of the same body.** Fellow-members of the same unitary, corporate body the church (2:15). The church is one body with one head. Anything else would be a spiritual monstrosity. In Christ there is perfect amalgamation of each and every member. **Partakers of his promise.** Gentiles are fellow-partakers and equal sharers of the same promise. **In Christ by the gospel.** The Old Testament is not silent as to blessings for Gentiles, but it says nothing of a union of all believers of every nationality in the Lord Jesus Christ, so as to form one body of which Christ Himself is the glorified Head. It is all made actual by means of the gospel of the grace of God in its marvelous comprehension and its glorious contents.

7 Whereof I was made a minister, according to the gift of the grace of God given unto me by the effectual working of his power.

7. Whereof I was made a minister. A God-appointed minister. **The gift of grace.** It took divine grace to transform Paul from a blasphemer into a saint, from a Pharisee into an apostle, and from a persecutor of Christians into a preacher of Christ. Then it took divine power and authority to enable Paul to function as a minister of God.

8 Unto me, who am less than the least of all saints, is this grace given, that I should preach among the Gentiles the unsearchable riches of Christ;

8. Less than the least of all saints. Paul's sense of unworthiness is progressive: (1) the least of the apostles (I Cor 15:9); (2) **less than the least of all saints;** and (3) chief of sinners (I Tim 1:15). Paul's high calling humbled him, and he never got over his own unworthiness. He is ever conscious of his demerit and never thinks of himself more highly than he ought to think (Rom 12:3). **The unsearchable riches of Christ.** The contents of message, the wealth beyond description which God provides for all men in the person and work of Christ. It is a vast and measureless resource, this love and grace of God. If Christ were not too big for our mental comprehension, He would be too little for our spiritual need.

9 And to make all *men* see what *is* the fellowship of the mystery, which from the beginning of the world hath been hid in God, who created all things by Jesus Christ:

9. And to make all men see. This is Paul's purpose in preaching the unsearchable riches of Christ. He would cause all men to see by turning the light on. Paul was aiming at spiritual enlightenment and spiritual apprehension. **Fellowship of the mystery.** The stewardship of worldwide proclamation of Christ

10 To the intent that now unto the principalities and powers in heavenly *places* might be known by the church the manifold wisdom of God,

11 According to the eternal purpose which he purposed in Christ Jesus our Lord:

12 In whom we have boldness and access with confidence by the faith of him.

13 Wherefore I desire that ye faint not at my tribulations for you, which is your glory.

14 For this cause I bow my knees unto the Father of our Lord Jesus Christ,

15 Of whom the whole family in heaven and earth is named,

16 That he would grant you, according to the riches of his glory, to be strengthened with might by his Spirit in the inner man;

17 That Christ may dwell in your hearts by faith; that ye, being rooted and grounded in love,

18 May be able to comprehend with all saints what *is* the breadth, and length, and depth, and height;

and His gospel. **Hid in God.** The mystery of God's eternal plan and purpose had been concealed from the beginning.

10. To the intent. In order that now. **Might be known.** The mystery had been made known to Paul, and now he wants to make it known. Our great mission in this life is to know Christ and to make Him known. **By the church.** Through the church. The church is God's instrument to make known the grace of God in Christ. **The manifold wisdom of God.** The much-variegated and many-sided wisdom of God. This speaks of the beauty and diversity of God's grace.

11. The eternal purpose. God's purpose runs through the ages, not arbitrarily or capriciously, but according to a definite course and consummation, which He projected in Christ Jesus our Lord.

12. In whom we have boldness. Free speech. It speaks of the absence of fear and restraint and the liberty believers enjoy (Heb 4:16). **And access.** This is our approach to God. **With confidence.** Assurance of acceptance (I Jn 5:14-15). **By the faith of him.** Through faith in Him.

13. That ye faint not. Don't lose heart and give in to evil or behave badly. **At my tribulations for you.** In the thought of my afflictions in behalf of you (II Cor 11:23-28). Paul's imprisonment did not mean that the Word of God was bound, that the purpose of God had failed, or that the servant of God was out of the path of duty (Phil 1:12). Opposition and difficulty are not reasons for abandoning a divinely-appointed task. **Which is for your glory.** Even this experience is your glory.

F. The Fullness of the Church. 3:14-21.

14. For this cause. In view of God's plan in Christ and my relation to it. **I bow my knees.** The usual bodily posture in prayer. The position of the body reflects the condition of the soul. Bow in humiliation, in lowly supplication, in special solemnity, and in unusual urgency. **Unto the Father.** The preposition (Gr *pros*) implies face to face communication.

15. The whole family. God has only one family. Some of the members are already in heaven, and others are here on earth representing and interpreting Christ to the world.

16. That. The purpose of Paul's petition. Grant you. Born-again believers. **According to.** Not out of. **The riches of his glory.** God's endowment, His infinite wealth and resources. You can't possibly ask too much. **To be strengthened.** Paul prays that they will be made mightily strong with spiritual power. The nature of this endowment is divine, dynamic power that comes from God. **In the inner man.** In contrast to the outer man (Rom 7:22), the spiritual man as opposed to the fleshly man. **By his Spirit.** This dynamic power is communicated to us by the Holy Spirit. He is our dynamo, our powerhouse. He resides in us and works through us.

17. That Christ may dwell in your hearts. Christ should be enthroned; He must have first place. It is God's purpose that He dwell in our hearts personally, permanently, and powerfully (2:22). Christ is not a guest or an occasional visitor; He is the rightful owner and lives here (Gal 2:20). **By faith.** Faith is the medium of appropriating Christ. Faith opens the door and receives Him. In some Christ is just present, in others He is prominent, and in still others He is preeminent. **Rooted.** Established and settled securely in the love of Christ. Rooted like a tree growing strong and massive. **And grounded.** Deeply and firmly founded, like a building rising higher and larger.

18. May be able to comprehend. May be strong to comprehend, lay hold of effectually (spiritual enlightenment). **With all saints.** This is not an isolated privilege. Each one comprehends a little; all together we fathom the unfathomable. Our comprehension is partial and progressive. **What is the breadth, and length, and depth, and height.** The love of Christ is immeasurable. The breadth extends to all people; its length extends to all time; its depth extends to the lowest condition of human need; and its height extends to the highest heavens. Truly Christ is "able also to save them to the uttermost that come unto God by him" (Heb 7:25).

19 And to know the love of Christ, which passeth knowledge, that ye might be filled with all the fulness of God.

19. And to know by experience the unknowable, the love of Christ in all its dimensions mentioned above. The love of Christ is knowledge-transcending. **That ye might be filled with all the fullness of God.** Filled with His presence and power, the fullness which God imparts.

20 Now unto him that is able to do exceeding abundantly above all that we ask or think, according to the power that worketh in us,

20. Now unto him. This ascription of praise to God's ability expresses our assurance of answered prayer. Why should we hesitate to offer our deepest petitions? Note the expressive and exhaustive language. **Is able.** The strength of our confidence is the fact that He is vastly able above and beyond all that we might ask. **To do exceeding abundantly.** Superabundantly, overwhelming, over and above, more than enough. David said, "my cup runneth over" (Ps 23:5), and we can say, "He brought me to the banqueting house, and his banner over me was love" (Song 2:4). **That we ask or think.** Our highest aspirations are not beyond God's power to grant. **According to the power that worketh in us.** This is that omnipotence that raised Christ from the dead and quickened us when we were dead in sins.

21 Unto him be glory in the church by Christ Jesus throughout all ages, world without end. Amen.

21. Unto him be glory in the church by Christ Jesus. Christ and His church constitute one living organism. The church is His body, and He is the Head of that one body. **Throughout all ages.** The duration of our praise and thanksgiving. **Amen.** Paul sealed the doxology.

III. THE CONDUCT OF THE CHURCH. 4:1-6:9.

A. The Undivided Conduct of the Church. 4:1-16.

CHAPTER 4
I THEREFORE, the prisoner of the Lord, beseech you that ye walk worthy of the vocation wherewith ye are called,

4:1. Therefore. In view of grace revealed, new life imparted, and your high and heavenly calling. **The prisoner of the Lord.** Paul was not seeking sympathy, but declaring his acceptance of his circumstances. He was a prisoner because of his relationship to Christ, his faithfulness to Christ, and his service for Christ. **Walk worthy.** Walk indicates activity and advance step by step. Paul is beseeching the saints to order their lives in a worthy manner. **Of the vocation wherewith ye are called.** A vocation (Gr *klēsis*) is a calling or life's work. It behooves Christians to walk worthy of the source, the substance, and the sequence of their high and holy calling of God in Christ. Christians are called to live for Christ (Phil 1:21) and walk "even as he walked" (I Jn 2:6).

2 With all lowliness and meekness, with longsuffering, forbearing one another in love;

2. With all lowliness. Your high calling should not lead to pride or self-exaltation, but on the contrary to all lowliness of mind and modest opinion of yourself. This means unfailing humility, an utter lack of self-assertiveness, and a deep sense of unworthiness, in every experience and in every relationship. **And meekness.** This is not timidity, cowardice, or servile fear, but self-suppression for the purpose of serving others. It is the spirit that never takes offense and which manifests itself in submission to God's will and gentleness toward men. **With longsuffering.** This is the opposite to short-tempered. The old nature is so quick to take offense that we need longer fuses. The new life in Christ enables one to endure with unruffled temper any wrong suffered without retaliation and to turn the other cheek (I Pet 2:21-23). **Forbearing one another.** Forbearance is restraint under just provocation with a liberal allowance for the faults and failures of others. It is that mutual and enduring putting up with one another, and making allowances for one another (Col 3:13). **In love.** Love beareth all things and endureth all things (I Cor 13:7).

3 Endeavouring to keep the unity of the Spirit in the bond of peace.

3. Endeavoring. This means to give diligence to do your best in persistent effort, fixed determination, and heroic perseverance. It combines the ideas of haste, eagerness, and zeal. **To keep.** Not produce; it already exists as a reality. **The unity of the Spirit.** Not external, ecclesiastical union, but internal, spiritual unity (Jn 17:21-23). Such unity cannot be legislated or produced by the mechanics of an organization. It is produced and maintained by the Holy Spirit. **In the bond of peace.** Peace with God and with one another is the unifying bond that holds all together.

4 *There is* one body, and one Spirit, even as ye are called in one hope of your calling;

4. There is one body. The church is a living organism composed only of living members, i.e., blood-bought, born-again, Bible-believing saints. This one body has one Head and many members (I Cor 12:12-13). **One Spirit.** The Holy Spirit who is the life and breath of that body, who was instrumental in the regeneration of each member, and who now maintains a vital connection of each member with the other members and with the head. **One hope of your calling.** The same ultimate, glorious reality for both Jews and Gentiles.

5 One Lord, one faith, one baptism,

5. One Lord. The Lord Jesus Christ, not a series of aeons. "If He is not Lord of all, He is not Lord at all." **One faith.** Not a creed, but a commitment to Christ. One saving experience of trust in Christ, one way of salvation (Rom 10:9-10). **One baptism.** One result of baptizing (Gr *baptisma*), not the act of baptizing (Gr *baptismos*). Scriptural baptism is the outward expression of an inward experience; a public confession of Christ. Men are not made disciples by baptism, but merely profess to be disciples. Water baptism presupposes and pictures the baptism of the Holy Spirit (I Cor 12:12-13). The one baptism is the expression of the one faith in the one Lord which resulted in the baptism of the one Spirit into the one body.

6 One God and Father of all, who *is* above all, and through all, and in you all.

6. One God and Father of all. For all; not a separate God for each nation. **Who is above all.** This speaks of His transcendence and His unshared sovereign power. **And through all.** This speaks of His immanence, His pervading action. **And in you all.** This speaks of His indwelling presence of believers, His personal relationship. The one God rules over all, works through all, and dwells in all.

7 But unto every one of us is given grace according to the measure of the gift of Christ.

7. But unto every one of us is given grace. Each member of the body receives from the Sovereign Lord his own integral value, place, responsibility, opportunity, and duty. No one should be idle for each one has a place to fill, which no one else can fill. **According to the . . . gift of Christ.** There is a wide variety of gifts. Each Christian has some gift; no one has all the gifts; and not all have the same gifts. These gifts are not just natural endowments, but specific graces and capacities for service. Since God deems these gifts important, man should not despise them. We should be content with our own gifts and not envy or look down on the gifts of others.

8 Wherefore he saith, When he ascended up on high, he led captivity captive, and gave gifts unto men.

8. Wherefore. Because the living Lord distributes His grace by sovereign love to each member of the body and thus makes them fit to be His gifts for service to men. **When he ascended up on high.** This is a quotation from Psalm 68:18, a messianic psalm of victory in which God is praised for deliverance. **He led captivity captive.** The inferences drawn from the triumphal return of the King are: (1) the thought of victory; and (2) the bestowal of gifts. The captives are most probably the Old Testament saints in sheol (hades).

9 (Now that he ascended, what is it but that he also descended first into the lower parts of the earth?

9. Ascended . . . descended. Christ's ascension back to heaven after accomplishing the purpose of His incarnation. **The lower parts of the earth.** Probably hades (Mt 12:40; Acts 2:25-35; II Cor 12:2-4).

10 He that descended is the same also that ascended up far above all heavens, that he might fill all things.)

10. That he might fill all things. The purpose and plan of Christ is to fill all with His presence and His Spirit.

11 And he gave some, apostles; and some, prophets; and some, evangelists; and some, pastors and teachers;

11. He gave. He gave gifts to men, and He gave gifted men to the church, in which and through which they function. **Apostles.** The official title of the Twelve, including Paul. This was a temporary office. Nowhere does God's Word teach apostolic succession. To the contrary, God's Word indicts those who lay claim to the title of apostle as deceivers (Rev 2:2). **Prophets.** These men were both foretellers and forthtellers. They received their message from God and delivered it for God and to man. They had deep insight into spiritual truths as they interpreted God's message under the power of the Holy Spirit. **Evangelists.** These were the itinerant missionaries who preached the gospel to the unconverted in new areas (Acts 21:8; II Tim 4:5). **Pastors and teachers.** This refers to one office with two functions, i.e., teaching pastors. The word "pastor" is used by Christ referring to Peter (Jn 21:16); by Peter referring to ministers (I Pet 5:2); and by Paul referring to elders (bishops) of Ephesus (Acts 20:28). They were to shepherd the sheep and train the saints.

12 For the perfecting of the saints, for the work of the ministry, for the edifying of the body of Christ:

12. For the perfecting of the saints. With a view to equipping them for service. The purpose of Christ's gifts is not making saints sinlessly perfect, but of completely outfitting them to be vessels unto honor, sanctified and meet for the Master's use (II Tim 2:21). **For the work of the ministry.** Unto spiritual service. Not doing their work for them, but preparing them for their work. D. L. Moody said, "It is better to put ten men to work than to do the work of ten men." The church is not a spiritual rest home, but a barracks for training soldiers of the cross. **For the edifying of the body of Christ.** With the end in view of building up spiritually the whole body of Christ. Our Lord is interested in quantity, but He is more concerned about quality. All the saints are to be equipped for the work of edification and then be engaged in work of edification.

13 Till we all come in the unity of the faith, and of the knowledge of the Son of God, unto a perfect man, unto the measure of the stature of the fulness of Christ:

13. Till we all come in the unity of the faith. This has reference to the whole body of Christ. We should not neglect anyone. The goal is that we attain unity, not uniformity; and our essential work is far from being accomplished. **And of the knowledge of the Son of God.** Paul speaks of true, accurate, and full knowledge which enables saints to cooperate with one another in working out God's plan and purpose. **Unto a perfect man.** As long as our faith in Christ is imperfect we cannot be full-grown, mature Christians. **Unto the measure of the stature of the fullness of Christ.** No under-shepherd has finished his work while the sheep fall short of this goal, a full-grown man in Christ. This fullness, this Christlikeness, is that which belongs to Christ and that which is imparted by Christ. God predestined His saints "to be conformed to the image of his Son" (Rom 8:29). It would be wise for all of us to cry out with John, "He must increase, but I must decrease" (Jn 3:30). As long as we have a factious, contentious, immature church, we will not make much headway in evangelizing the world.

14 That we henceforth be no more children, tossed to and fro, and carried about with every wind of doctrine, by the sleight of men, and cunning craftiness, whereby they lie in wait to deceive;

14. That we henceforth be no more children. In this verse Paul sets forth the negative results of spiritual unity and maturity. God desires that we be stalwart Christians with doctrinal stability, spiritual perception, responsibility, and direction toward the goal. Too many are content to remain in weakness and immaturity, spiritual infancy. **Tossed to and fro.** Cast about as driftwood on the waves of the sea. This is a picture of instability, helplessness, and restlessness. **Carried about with every wind of doctrine.** Christians should not be whirled around in circles by every shifting wind of false doctrine. If not anchored in Christ, Christians are at the mercy of these ever-changing winds which blow unstable souls in every direction. **By the sleight of men.** By the deceit and dishonesty of the religious quacks. The word (Gr *kubeia*) means "dice-throwing," and the dice are loaded. **And cunning craftiness.** These unscrupulous, scheming frauds stop at nothing to ensnare fickle souls by their clever deceit and treacherous trickery. **Whereby they lie in wait to deceive.** By deliberate planning and scheming deceit, they wrestle, twist, and pervert the Word of God (Acts 13:10; Gal 1:7;

15 But speaking the truth in love, may grow up into him in all things, which is the head, *even* Christ:

16 From whom the whole body fitly joined together and compacted by that which every joint supplieth, according to the effectual working in the measure of every part, maketh increase of the body unto the edifying of itself in love.

17 This I say therefore, and testify in the Lord, that ye henceforth walk not as other Gentiles walk, in the vanity of their mind,

18 Having the understanding darkened, being alienated from the life of God through the ignorance that is in them, because of the blindness of their heart:

19 Who being past feeling have given themselves over unto lasciviousness, to work all uncleanness with greediness.

20 But ye have not so learned Christ;

21 If so be that ye have heard him,

II Pet 3:16). The Christian's only hope is to "search the scriptures daily, whether those things were so" (Acts 17:11).

15. But speaking the truth in love. Paul now turns to the positive results of spiritual unity and maturity. The truth should always be spoken in love without any tricks or gimmicks. **May grow up into him in all things, which is the head, even Christ.** Ever growing up in all ways, in all respects, and in fellowship with Him and with each other.

16. From whom the whole body. Christ is the source and sustainer of the body. **Fitly joined together.** Harmoniously and closely fitted together, with no one out of place, and with each one contributing his share for the good of the whole body. **And compacted.** Firm and solid adhesion to Christ and to other Christians. **Maketh increase of the body.** When all the members of the body perform faithfully their several functions, it results in the growth and maturity of the whole body. The church is a living organism united to Christ and indwelt by the Holy Spirit so that every member helps and is helped, strengthens and is strengthened, whereby the whole body grows and "increaseth with the increase of God" (Col 2:19). The result is a unified and an edified church.

B. The Unblemished Conduct of the Church. 4:17-5:16.

17. This I say therefore. Paul bears his testimony as to the Christian calling and conduct. **In the Lord.** Speaking in His name as His servant and clothed with divine authority as His apostle. **That ye henceforth walk not as other Gentiles.** Let the daily conduct of your lives conform with your new life in Christ. Make a clean break with your old life and stop living by the standards of behavior of the pagan people. The low standards of the world must be abandoned and repudiated, and the Christian must live ethically and morally in segregation from the world (II Cor 6:14). The church is a colony of heaven living here on earth. **In the vanity of their minds.** Their intellect is empty of truth and filled with false delusions and things that lead to nothing. This implies: aimlessness, uselessness, and futility.

18. Having the understanding darkened. Their beclouded intellect and their emotions have been darkened permanently so that they are without the faculty of discernment and are unable to distinguish clearly between right and wrong. **Being alienated from the life of God.** Having alienated themselves completely, they are held in the grips of spiritual death. The cause of their alienation is twofold. **Through the ignorance that is in them.** They were born in moral, ethical, and spiritual stupidity. **Because of the blindness of their heart** (Gr *pōrōsis*). Literally "hardness," covered with a callus (Mk 3:5; Rom 11:25). The heart lost its capacity to feel, and they became insensible, indifferent, and unresponsive to all moral principles and practices.

19. Who being past feeling. Insensible to moral and spiritual impressions and to the appeal of truth. Conscience is not functioning, and there is no hatred of sin and no love for Christ. **Have given themselves over unto lasciviousness.** They abandoned and delivered themselves over once for all to moral degradation, unbridled lusts, excessive immorality, and dissipating debauchery, with no sense of shame or decency and with scorn for all moral restraint. **To work all uncleanness.** Committing themselves to active indulgence in every form of impurity, outrageous sensuality, indecency and lewd conduct, such that shocks the public. **With greediness.** With insatiable desires to have more, with no regard for the person or property of others. He gets what he wants no matter whom he hurts and no matter what methods he uses.

20. But ye have not so learned Christ. In sharp contrast to the pagan life. Christ teaches men to renounce sin and vice and to cultivate holiness and virtue.

21. If so be that ye have heard him. Since you did hear.

and have been taught by him, as the truth is in Jesus:

Have been taught by him. Instructed as to the standards, meaning, and behavior of Christian living. **As the truth is in Jesus.** Embodied in Him and exemplified in His character and conduct, as He lived the truth on the plane of human experience.

22 That ye put off concerning the mer conversation the old man, which is corrupt according to the deceitful lusts;

22. That ye put off concerning the former conversation the old man. Put off definitely, deliberately, quickly, and permanently, once for all the old man as a filthy and repulsive garment. The old man is the unregenerated self, a slave to sin, and headed for judgment. It is the old "I" that has been crucified with Christ (Gal 2:20) and must be so reckoned (Rom 6:9-14). **Which is corrupt according to the deceitful lusts.** The old man is decaying day by day, like a decomposing corpse, and inevitably grows more and more corrupt. The old man is not renewed (Jn 3:6); he must be denounced and replaced.

23 And be renewed in the spirit of your mind;

23. And be renewed. The Greek present tense means continual and progressive renewal. This is the antithesis of the growing corruptness of the old man. **In the spirit of your mind.** That attitude and disposition which determines behavior and conduct. Being renewed with spiritual food, constantly and continually grasping and appropriating new truth.

24 And that ye put on the new man, which after God is created in righteousness and true holiness.

24. And . . . put on the new man. Clothe yourself once for all. The old man is stripped off and the new man is put on. These two acts are inseparable. The new man is the new life we receive in Christ (II Cor 5:17; Gal 6:17; Col 3:10). **Which after God is created in righteousness and true holiness.** This is not the reformation or renovation of the old man; this is the product of the new birth and results in a new creation. The new man is created after God and in the family likeness of God. The brand new man is known by the Christlikeness exhibited day by day in living out the new life. Righteousness refers to his new conduct toward his fellowmen. Holiness refers to his new conduct towards God. These two are the essential qualities and the evidence of the new man in Christ.

25 Wherefore putting away lying, speak every man truth with his neighbour: for we are members one of another.

25. Wherefore putting away lying. Paul now describes the old, obsolete, filthy rags of the old man which are to be discarded. Lying is to be put away definitely and deliberately. The Greek middle voice indicates that you will personally receive some benefit from this action. Lying speaks of everything false: deception of every kind, dishonesty in personal relations, unscrupulous practices in public relations, and corruption in the government. **Speak every man truth with his neighbor.** Speaking the truth habitually is the only intelligent and consistent way to deal with our neighbors, or those who are members of the body and of one another, where deceit and dishonesty in any form is unthinkable. We must guard our tongue.

26 Be ye angry, and sin not: let not the sun go down upon your wrath:

26. Be ye angry, and sin not. This is a permissive imperative, rather than a direct command to be angry. There is a righteous indignation which is not sin (Mk 3:5), but "the wrath of man worketh not the righteousness of God" (Jas 1:20). Do not go on being angry and let it not take root in your heart and degenerate into wrath. **Let not the sun go down upon your wrath.** There is a grave danger in cherished, prolonged anger. We must get cooled off quickly and maintain such control and restraint of our temper that we make a Christlike adjustment to the irritating circumstances.

27 Neither give place to the devil.

27. Neither give place to the devil. Satan waits for opportunity to get his foot in the door. The Greek present imperative means: Do not have the habit of giving place to Satan. Uncontrolled anger is an open door and an invitation for Satan to enter in to disrupt and corrupt the body. He can only hurt and harm as he finds a place in some life to do his evil work.

28 Let him that stole steal no more: but rather let him labour, working with *his* hands the thing which is good, that

28. Let him that stole steal no more. Let the one who has the habit of stealing stop stealing. There is no place for dishonesty in Christian dealings. **But rather let him labor.** Let him adopt the higher Christian standard and ideals of manly inde-

he may have to give to him that need-eth.

29 Let no corrupt communication proceed out of your mouth, but that which is good to the use of edifying, that it may minister grace unto the hearers.

30 And grieve not the holy Spirit of God, whereby ye are sealed unto the day of redemption.

31 Let all bitterness, and wrath, and anger, and clamour, and evil speaking, be put away from you, with all malice:

32 And be ye kind one to another, tenderhearted, forgiving one another, even as God for Christ's sake hath forgiven you.

pendence and brotherly helpfulness. Let him toil honestly rather than subsist by the labor of others. Instead of robbing others, let him bring forth fruits fit for repentance. **The thing which is good.** As opposed to stealing, honest work is rich and rewarding. **That he may have to give to him that needeth.** That he may accumulate and contribute to the needy.

29. Let no corrupt communication proceed out of your mouth. Corrupt speech comes from a corrupt heart, and pure speech comes from a pure heart. Corrupt speech is like rotten fruit (Mt 7:16-20) or a fish (Mt 13:48) and tainted with moral decay. Corrupt speech will contaminate the thoughts of others. **But that which is good to the use of edifying.** Our speech should be suitable to building up where the need for constructive help exists. We must watch our words (Ps 141:3) and be careful that our speech is "always with grace, seasoned with salt" (Col 4:6). **That it may minister grace unto the hearers.** Our speech should impart a blessing, not a blight. If a rotten word is found in the mind, shut it off at the mouth.

30. And grieve not the holy Spirit of God. The Holy Spirit is a very sensitive person. Paul says stop having the habit of offending the Holy Spirit by rebellious deeds and grievous words (vss. 25-31). **Whereby ye are sealed unto the day of redemption.** Sealed with God's stamp, marking you as God's purchased possession and destined unto the day of complete redemption, when final redemption is realized and we are transformed into His likeness (Phil 3:20-21; I Jn 3:2).

31. Let all bitterness. Let every form of irritability, every inward resentful disposition against others, and hardness of spirit be put away from everyone of you. **And wrath.** This is the rapid boiling up and furious outburst of temper into passionate expression. **And anger.** Anger is the settled disposition of indignation. **And clamor.** Clamor is the loud, railing outburst in a storm of anger. **And evil speaking.** This is the reviling, deliberate insult with abusive words. **With all malice.** This refers to a vicious disposition of character. Each of these vices is to be put away once and for all. God wants us to make a clean sweep of these unchristian characteristics.

32. Be ye kind. Paul summarized Christian character. Keep on becoming kind towards one another—well disposed, useful, benevolent, gracious and gentle mannered, as opposed to being harsh, hard, bitter, and sharp. The person who is kind is full of benign courtesy, is distinguished by gracious deeds, and is desirous of promoting common interests and conferring reciprocal obligations. This kindness is the outward expression of love in the heart and applies to all contacts and situations. **Tenderhearted.** Merciful, compassionate, pitiful. There is a willingness to be understanding of and patient with the faults and failures of others, ready to put kindness into action. **Forgiving one another.** The word "forgive" (Gr *charizomai*) is built on the same root as the word "grace" and means to bestow favor unconditionally. This means that a Christian will always treat the offending party graciously, letting the wrong go without any claim for punishment or reparation. It means pardoning the guilty person instead of displaying resentment or exercising retaliation. Forgiveness is not probation, i.e., merely suspending the sentence under supervision and specific conditions. Forgiveness is not a reprieve, i.e., temporarily postponing the punishment. Forgiveness results in complete reconciliation and restored fellowship. **Even as God for Christ's sake hath forgiven you.** We are to forgive others just as God forgave us. We are to exhibit the life of Christ in and through us, thus giving evidence of having been made partakers of the divine nature ((II Pet 1:4). God's forgiveness is the model, the motive, and the measure of our forgiving others. God's forgiveness is free, full, and final. When God forgives, He forgets; so must we.

prayerful that we do not walk in perilous places, in the pitfalls of perdition, and in the snares of Satan.

16 Redeeming the time, because the days are evil.

16. Redeeming the time. Buy up the opportunity. The Greek present tense denotes keep on buying. There is a price to be paid or we will forgo the bargain. The price is self-denial and strenuous work. There is also opportunity, i.e., to serve the Lord, to witness for Christ, to be a channel of blessing, and to advance the cause of Christ. We must recognize the opportunity, appreciate it, and take hold of it for God's glory. **Because the days are evil.** There are many obstacles in the way, much opposition to God, and much corruption in the world. The days are full of difficulty, danger, darkness, and death. We dare not lose one opportunity by letting things drift aimlessly and carelessly.

C. The Unblamable Conduct of the Church. 5:17-6:9.

17 Wherefore be ye not unwise, but understanding what the will of the Lord is.

17. Be ye not unwise. Stop becoming foolish, senseless, without intelligence, and lacking in wisdom; and start exercising good judgment and reason. **But understanding.** Divinely enlightened by prayer and meditation. **What the will of the Lord is.** Be a Bible Christian; give God's Word the place it deserves, then you will understand what He wants you to be and do. The entrance of God's Word gives light (Ps 119:130). God's will is revealed in God's Word. Our first concern is God's will; it is not what is most profitable, what is most pleasurable, or what is most honorable.

18 And be not drunk with wine, wherein is excess; but be filled with the Spirit;

18. And be not drunk with wine. Stop the habit of getting drunk. **Wherein is excess.** Drunkenness leads to riot and ruin. It corrupts character, debauches life, brooks no restraint, defies efforts to reform it, and sinks its victim lower and lower into helplessness and hopelessness. **But.** A strong contrast from the physical to the spiritual, from the debasing to the ennobling. In days of drab routine, disappointment, and depression, men need stimulation and inspiration. The Christian's resource is the Holy Spirit. **Be filled with the Spirit.** Although all Christians have been baptized by the Spirit at salvation, all Christians are not filled with the Spirit, which is their heritage. The fullness of the Holy Spirit was the normal experience of the early Christians. The natural man has not the Spirit (Jude 19; Rom 8:9); the carnal man has the Spirit, but lives by the power and dictates of the flesh; the spiritual man has the Spirit, and the Spirit has him, and he lives by the power and dictates of the Holy Spirit. **Be filled** (Gr *plēroō*) is full of meaning. The second person plural means "you all," everyone without exception. It is in the imperative mood, which means it is a positive command, a distinct duty. Just as surely as God commanded all men everywhere to repent (Acts 17:30), so He has commanded every born-again believer to be filled with the Spirit. This verb is in the Greek present tense and means keep on being filled moment by moment. God speaks of an abiding reality; yesterday's filling will not do for today. The early Christians were repeatedly filled with the Spirit. This verb is in the passive voice, the voice that presents the subject as receiving the action, rather than doing the action. The filling is what God does. When we are willing to let the Holy Spirit saturate us He will pervade our entire being with His presence and with His power. The filling is not a question of having more of the Holy Spirit, but a question of the Holy Spirit having all of us. Our only choice is to obey or to disobey this divine direction.

19 Speaking to yourselves in psalms and hymns and spiritual songs, singing and making melody in your heart to the Lord;

19. Making melody. Playing by means of an instrument. This word means to make or let a string twang and signifies to play an instrument as an accompaniment to the voice. **In your heart to the Lord.** Not merely with the lips and the fingers for man, but with the heart for the glory of the Lord.

20 Giving thanks always for all

20. Giving thanks always for all things. See Philippians 4:6.

things unto God and the Father in the name of our Lord Jesus Christ;

21 Submitting yourselves one to another in the fear of God.

22 Wives, submit yourselves unto your own husbands, as unto the Lord.

23 For the husband is the head of the wife, even as Christ is the head of the church: and he is the saviour of the body.

24 Therefore as the church is subject unto Christ, so *let* the wives *be* to their own husbands in every thing.
25 Husbands, love your wives, even as Christ also loved the church, and gave himself for it;

26 That he might sanctify and cleanse it with the washing of water by the word,

27 That he might present it to himself a glorious church, not having spot, or wrinkle, or any such thing; but that it should be holy and without blemish.

In the name of our Lord Jesus Christ. Jesus taught His disciples to use His name in prayer.

21. Submitting yourselves one to another. The way to have happy harmony. This submission is reciprocal, mutual, voluntary, and personal. It is opposed to rudeness, haughtiness, and selfish preference of one's own opinions.

22. Wives, submit yourselves unto your own husbands, as unto the Lord. The duty and manner of submission. The Christian home is a symbol of Christianity, and should be a "little bit of heaven" on earth. The word **submit** (Gr *hypotassō*) is an old military figure to line up under (Col 3:18) and means to subject yourselves in line in a specialized way. Christian wives will be ordering their lives in proper subjection to their own husbands as required in this relation in the Lord, for subjection to the Lord includes loyal living in the home. Submission is not slavish fear, neither is it forced upon her by a demanding domestic despot, but it is voluntary. There is no hint of inferiority, but a matter of authority and responsibility in the home. Husbands and wives are parts of a unit. The question arises, what if the husband is not a born-again believer? The Word of God gives definite instructions covering such a case (I Pet 3:1-7).

23. For the husband is the head of the wife. The reason of submission. Authority and government are lodged in the husband. The home has its center and unity in the husband. The truest unity is conjugal duality. **Even as Christ is the head of the church.** Headship in a living union where Christ and His church become one. **And he is the saviour of the body.** No husband can ever be saviour, but he represents Christ symbolically as good provider and protector.

24. As . . . so. This description of the submissive obedience of wives is clear, concise, complete, and correct.

25. Husbands, love your wives. The plain duty of husbands is now set forth. Husbands are to love their wives, not treat them as inferior subjects. Such love will lift a husband out of a state of arbitrary self-indulgence and capricious self-satisfaction. **Even as Christ also loved the church.** Christ is the husband's ideal example. The measure of Christ's love for the church is to be the measure of the husband's love for his wife. Husbands owe their wives the same kind of love and loyalty as Christ has for His bride; supreme, self-forgetting, self-sacrificing love. In the economy of the family and after the manner of Christ, husbands are to reign in love. The church is called the body of Christ (1:22-23). **Gave himself for it.** The measure and manifestation of Christ's love for the church. Christ gave Himself both in life and in death on behalf of the church.

26. That he might sanctify. The purpose of His death is set forth in the words sanctify, cleanse, and present. Sanctify means to consecrate, set apart for sacred service. **And cleanse.** The tense of this participle indicates antecedent action to sanctify. First there was the cleansing and then the sanctifying. **With the washing of water by the word.** The washing of water refers to "the washing of regeneration" (I Cor 6:11; Tit 3:5). **By the word.** God the Holy Spirit uses the Word of God to accomplish God's purpose in redemption (Ps 119:9; Jn 15:3; 17:17; I Pet 1:23).

27. That he might present it to himself a glorious church. He Himself as loving, saving, and sanctifying Lord. The Bridegroom presents His bride to Himself. It will then be a glorious church arrayed in glory, with nothing to mar her beauty. **Not having spot, or wrinkle, or any such thing.** In perfect purity. Spots are from without, wrinkles from within. "The world about the church causes the stains, the flesh still in her causes the wrinkles" (R. C. H. Lenski, *The Interpretation of Saint Paul's Epistles to the Galatians, to the Ephesians, and to the Philippians*, p. 635). **But that it should be holy.** Morally pure and wholly consecrated. **Without blemish.** Immaculate, just like the heavenly Bridegroom.

28 So ought men to love their wives as their own bodies. He that loveth his wife loveth himself.

28. So ought men to love their wives. In the same manner and same measure as Christ loved the church, assumed all responsibility for her, and spared nothing that contributes toward His purpose for her. Husbands are under similar obligations to devote themselves, all they are and have, to their own (individual) wives. **As their own bodies.** Treat them as constituting their own personal bodies. The two have become one in marriage. **He that loveth his wife loveth himself.** For he is completed and perfected in her, with whom he has become one flesh (Mk 10:8).

29 For no man ever yet hated his own flesh; but nourisheth and cherisheth it, even as the Lord the church:

29. Nourisheth. That it may develop to maturity. **Cherisheth.** To foster with tender care, concern, and comfort. The best and highest interest of the husband is to recognize his complete identity with his wife.

30 For we are members of his body, of his flesh, and of his bones.

30. For we are members of his body. Consequently we should understand and adopt His principle in our relationships with each other within His church (Rom 12:4-5; I Cor 12:12-27).

31 For this cause shall a man leave his father and mother, and shall be joined unto his wife, and they two shall be one flesh.

31. For this cause shall a man leave his father and mother. In response to this divinely given ideal. **And shall be joined unto his wife.** Once for all glued to his wife. Marriage is a picture of the union of Christ and His church. Paul insists on the sanctity of the family and treats marriage as an inseparable union between a husband and wife. **And they two shall be one flesh.** One unit of flesh by assimilation (Gen 2:24; Mk 10:2-12). God is insisting that both husband and wife joined in perfect union live up to the standard of Christ and His church. They are joined together in body, soul, and spirit and should be set apart to each other in a holy union of sinless human relationship.

32 This is a great mystery: but I speak concerning Christ and the church.

32. Great mystery. This holy secret revealed in the Word of God is great. The comparison of the marriage union with the union of Christ and His church is the mystery.

33 Nevertheless let every one of you in particular so love his wife even as himself; and the wife *see* that she reverence *her* husband.

33. Nevertheless let every one of you in particular so love his wife. Husbands measure up to the ideal of Christ in His love for the church. **And the wife see that she reverence her husband.** Wives measure up to the church in its devotion to Christ.

CHAPTER 6

CHILDREN, obey your parents in the Lord: for this is right.

6:1. Children. We come to the duties of children and parents. **Obey your parents.** The word (Gr *hypakouō*) means to hear as under another with listening and attentive ears, to give obedient heed. This duty has been recognized among all people, in all lands, and in all ages. The neglect of this duty is lamented. Disobedience to parents is a sin (Rom 1:30; II Tim 3:2). **In the Lord.** God commands it. It is a Christian duty for children to obey their parents promptly, habitually, and cheerfully. **For this is right.** It is a moral duty, not merely becoming or an accepted custom (Col 3:20).

2 Honour thy father and mother; which is the first commandment with promise;

2. Honour thy father and mother. Honor is the attitude of love, respect, and disposition of heart that produces obedience. **First commandment with promise.** The second commandment has a general promise, but the fifth has a specific promise (Ex 20:12; Deut 5:16).

3 That it may be well with thee, and thou mayest live long on the earth.

3. That it may be well with thee. Both temporal and spiritual prosperity.

4 And, ye fathers, provoke not your children to wrath: but bring them up in the nurture and admonition of the Lord.

4. And, ye fathers. Mothers are included in this exhortation. **Provoke not your children to wrath.** The word provoke means do not irritate, exasperate, rub the wrong way, incite. This is done by a wrong spirit and by wrong methods, i.e., severity, unreasonableness, sternness, harshness, cruel demands, needless restrictions, and selfish insistence upon authority. Such provocation would produce adverse reactions, deaden his affection, check his desire for holiness, and make him feel that he can't possibly please his parents. A wise parent seeks to make obedience desirable and attainable by love and gentleness. Parents must not be godless tyrants. Luther said, "Keep an apple beside the rod to give the child when he does well." **But bring them up in the nurture.** Discipline in general education and culture must be exercised with watchful care and constant training. **And admonition.** Chastening, disciplining, and counsel by the Word of God, giving both reproof and encouragement whenever needed. **Of the Lord.** Proceeding from the Lord, learned in the school of Christian experience, and administered by the parents. Christian discipline is needed to prevent children from growing up without reverence for God, respect for parental authority, knowledge of Christian standards, and habits of self-control.

5 Servants, be obedient to them that are *your* masters according to the flesh, with fear and trembling, in singleness of your heart, as unto Christ;

5. Servants. Bondslave, yet free men in Christ. The Bible does not condone slavery nor does it advocate its violent overthrow. Slavery must ultimately disappear where the gospel is proclaimed, with its implications of human equality, Christian brotherhood, and the lordship of Christ. **Be obedient.** Servants are to be obedient and loyal. **Masters.** Either owners or employers, who have control of the body, but not of the spirit. **With fear and trembling.** Not dread of the master, but respect for authority and anxious to leave no duty undone. **In singleness of your heart.** With genuine readiness of heart and undivided purpose, not with pretense or an ulterior motive, not half-hearted, but sincere. **As unto Christ.** Your Christian duty.

6 Not with eyeservice, as menpleasers; but as the servants of Christ, doing the will of God from the heart;

6. Not with eyeservice. Working only while being under the watchful eye of an exacting employer and to make a show and gain human praise. **As menpleasers.** Who have no higher motive than to please their human masters and curry their favor. **But as the servants of Christ.** Rather meet the demands of your station as bondslaves of Christ. **Doing the will of God from the heart.** Even while the servants of men, view your tasks as doing God's will from the heart (lit., "out of the soul").

7 With good will doing service, as to the Lord, and not to men:

7. With good will doing service. And not with resentment. This implies enthusiasm and a generous spirit.

8 Knowing that whatsoever good thing any man doeth, the same shall he receive of the Lord, whether *he be* bond or free.

8. Knowing that whatsoever . . . any man doeth, the same shall he receive of the Lord. Get back in compensation from the Lord. The Lord remembers and rewards. **Bond or free.** The law of spiritual equity operates without regard to social class or economic status.

9 And, ye masters, do the same things unto them, forbearing threatening: knowing that your Master also is in heaven; neither is there respect of persons with him.

9. Ye masters, do the same things unto them. Accept the same Christian principles, with the same attitude, and the same spirit with regard to the will of God and to the authority of Christ. **Forbearing threatening.** Leave off the evil practice of threatening shorter hours, lower wages, and loss of employment by using harsh compulsions and treating them like chattels. **Your Master also is in heaven.** He is ruling and reigning. He keeps accurate records, and we will be judged by the perfect standards of heaven. **Neither is there respect of persons with him.** God does not have a double standard. He weighs the unfaithfulness in servants and the unkindness in masters in the same scales of divine equity and justice.

IV. THE CONFLICT OF THE CHURCH. 6:10-20.

10 Finally, my brethren, be strong in the Lord, and in the power of his might.

10. Finally. In respect of the rest. Paul has already spoken of the church's heavenly calling and her earthly conduct, now he is revealing her spiritual conflict. **Be strong in the Lord.** Be continuously empowered in union with Him. He is the source of spiritual power. Spiritual battles require spiritual strength.

11 Put on the whole armour of God, that ye may be able to stand against the wiles of the devil.

11. Put on the whole armor of God. God supplied the panoply, the complete armor, but He expects the Christian warrior to put it on. **That ye may be able to stand.** A purpose clause. In order that you may stand your ground and not retreat or fall in the struggle (cf. Jas 4:7). **Against the wiles of the devil.** The devil's wiles are attractive, deceptive, and ensnaring. Satan is a personal enemy, a great adversary, a slanderous accuser, and a malignant foe. He uses clever and crafty methods to deceive. Men dream of a devil that is a hideous, horned, and hoofed monster who haunts the vice dens of the world; but God says he fashions himself into an angel of light and fashions his ministers as ministers of righteousness (II Cor 11:14-15). He is the champion of liberalism, ritualism, rationalism, and every other "ism" that seeks to displace Christ. His aim is to substitute something else and something different for the grace and truth of Christ. Never underestimate the enemy.

12 For we wrestle not against flesh and blood, but against principalities, against powers, against the rulers of the darkness of this world, against spiritual wickedness in high *places*.

12. For we wrestle not against flesh and blood. We are not engaged in a human, physical warfare. Wrestle means to throw or swing. It is a contest between two opponents that continues until one hurls the other one down and holds him down. The word **against** presents the idea of a personal foe, face-to-face and hand-to-hand conflict to the finish, a life and death struggle. Paul is not describing a Sunday school picnic. **But against principalities.** Principalities refer to the high-ranking hierarchy of demonic authority. **Powers.** Invested with authority. **Rulers of the darkness of this world.** The world rulers in revolt against God and limited to "this darkness" here on earth. **Spiritual wickedness.** The army of invisible wicked spirits. **In high places.** The sphere of this conflict is in the heavenlies, where life in Christ is lived (2:5-6).

13 Wherefore take unto you the whole armour of God, that ye may be able to withstand in the evil day, and having done all, to stand.

13. Wherefore take unto you the whole armor of God. Appropriate promptly, for there is no time to lose. No ordinary weapons will do (II Cor 10:4). Confronted by the old subtle serpent out of the pit, we need the panoply of God, which is fully provided and freely given. **Withstand . . . stand.** The purpose of the armor is that we may hold our ground firmly, completely, gloriously, and victoriously.

14 Stand therefore, having your loins girt about with truth, and having on the breastplate of righteousness;

14. Stand therefore. Take your stand therefore, bent on victory. **Having your loins girt about with truth.** This Greek aorist participle indicates antecedent action to the standing; it means belted around your thighs with the military band of true integrity and sincerity. This band holds the tunic in place and holds the scabbard. It is not an ornament, but an armament. Truth is revealed in the Word of God; it is light from heaven and dispels darkness. **Having on the breastplate of righteousness.** Clothed with the breastplate of righteousness both in character and conduct. The breastplate protects the vital organs in the chest area from the assaults of the enemy. Without it we would be vulnerable, disgraced, and defeated.

15 And your feet shod with the preparation of the gospel of peace;

15. And your feet shod with the preparation of the gospel of peace. Having bound under (cf. Mk 6:9; Acts 12:8) for firm footing, for sure steps, and for protection. Preparation indicates readiness; prepared to see duty, prepared to do God's will, and prepared to proclaim the gospel of peace.

16 Above all, taking the shield of faith, wherewith ye shall be able to quench all the fiery darts of the wicked.

16. Above all. In addition to all. **Taking the shield of faith.** The shield is the large oblong shield for full protection. Note it is to be taken. Faith is utter dependence on God, upon His presence and His power. Faith puts God between you and the enemy. **Wherewith ye shall be able to quench all the fiery darts of the wicked.** The fire-tipped darts are the arrows dipped in combustible material and set on fire in Satan's malignant efforts to destroy you. The shield will quench every one of them without exception. It will stop the missiles and put out the fire.

17 And take the helmet of salvation, and the sword of the Spirit, which is the word of God:

17. And take the helmet of salvation. Take means receive or accept it from God. It is the assurance of salvation (II Tim 1:12; I Jn 5:11-13). Salvation is a present possession. The helmet protects the head, the citadel of intelligence, from false teachings and gives confidence and boldness in the conflict. **And the sword of the Spirit, which is the word of God.** This sword is the sharp one used in hand-to-hand conflict. It is the only offensive weapon. It is provided by the Spirit. When the church, or the Christian, used the rotten sticks of culture, science, theories, traditions, or commands of men, defeat is inevitable. God has promised to bless His Word (Isa 55:8-11). Our Lord used this powerful source in the wilderness and met the devil with, "It is written" (Mt 4:4-10). The sword must be unsheathed; the Bible must not lie idle.

18 Praying always with all prayer and supplication in the Spirit, and watching thereunto with all perseverance and supplication for all saints;

18. Praying always. Pray without ceasing (I Thess 5:17) as you engage in battle. Keep the lines of communication open with the Captain of our salvation (Josh 5:13-15; Heb 2:10). Prayer and the Word should never be separated. The searching of the Word must be done with prayer, and prayer will be effectual through knowing the Word. **With all prayer.** Confession, adoration, thanksgiving, petition, intercession, supplication. **In the Spirit.** Not for the Spirit. It is the Holy Spirit who prays in us, through us, and for us (Rom 8:26-27; Jude 20). **Watching.** Be on guard, vigilant, wide awake (Mt 26:41). **Perseverance.** Persistence and importunity (Lk 11:5-8). **Supplication.** Specific requests. **For all saints.** In behalf of all believers. Christians should fight shoulder-to-shoulder and knee-to-knee.

19 And for me, that utterance may be given unto me, that I may open my mouth boldly, to make known the mystery of the gospel,

19. And for me. Paul requests prayer for himself. **That utterance.** Freedom of speech. Paul was not trusting in education or experience. **Make known.** With clear fullness and boldness. **The mystery of the gospel.** The divine meaning of the gospel in its universal application to all races on equal terms and conditions. Paul had a message from God, and desired the means to deliver that message.

20 For which I am an ambassador in bonds: that therein I may speak boldly, as I ought to speak.

20. An ambassador in bonds. An ambassador (II Cor 5:20) of the risen Lord, in chains and in prison.

V. CONCLUSION. 6:21-24.

21-22. Tychicus (Acts 20:4; Col 4:7; II Tim 4:12; Tit 3:12), the bearer of this epistle, will inform the recipients of Paul's circumstances and encourage their troubled hearts.

21 But that ye also may know my affairs, and how I do, Tych'ĭ-cus, a beloved brother and faithful minister in the Lord, shall make known to you all things:
22 Whom I have sent unto you for the same purpose, that ye might know our affairs, and that he might comfort your hearts.
23 Peace be to the brethren, and love with faith, from God the Father and the Lord Jesus Christ.

23. Peace. Christ's gift. **Brethren.** In the Lord and in the Lord's work. **Love with faith.** Love of the saints and faith in Christ.

24 Grace be with all them that love our Lord Jesus Christ in sincerity. Amen.

24. Grace will be with all them that love our Lord Jesus Christ. Lord speaks of His deity, Jesus speaks of His humanity, and Christ speaks of His Saviourhood. **In sincerity.** Incapable of being corrupted (I Cor 9:25; 15:52; I Tim 1:17). **Amen.** So let it be. Amen.

BIBLIOGRAPHY

Abbott, T. K. A Critical and Exegetical Commentary on the Epistles to the Ephesians and the Colossians. In the *International Critical Commentary*. Edinburgh: T. & T. Clark, 1964.

Bruce, F. F. *The Epistle to the Ephesians*. Westwood, N.J.: Revell, 1961.

*Eadie, John. *Commentary on the Epistle to the Ephesians*. Grand Rapids: Zondervan, n.d.

Erdman, Charles R. *The Epistle to the Ephesians*. Philadelphia: Westminster Press, 1931.

Gerstner, John H. *The Epistle to the Ephesians*. Grand Rapids: Baker, 1967.

Hendriksen, William. Exposition of Ephesians. In *New Testament Commentary*. Grand Rapids: Baker, 1967.

*Hodge, Charles. *A Commentary on the Epistle to the Ephesians*. Grand Rapids: Eerdmans, 1950.

Ironside, H. A. *In the Heavenlies*. New York: Loizeaux Brothers, 1937.

Kent, Homer A., Jr. *Ephesians: The Glory of the Church*. Chicago: Moody Press, 1971.

*Lenski, R. C. H. *The Interpretation of St. Paul's Epistles to the Galatians, to the Ephesians, and to the Philippians*. Columbus, Ohio: Lutheran Book Concern, 1937.

Miller, H. S. *The Book of Ephesians*. Houghton, N.Y.: Word-Bearer Press, 1931.

*Moule, H. C. G. *The Epistle of Paul the Apostle to the Ephesians*. Cambridge: Cambridge University Press, 1937.

Paxson, Ruth. *The Wealth, Walk and Warfare of the Christian*. Westwood, N.J.: Revell, 1939.

The Epistle To The
PHILIPPIANS

INTRODUCTION

The city of Philippi. The city of Philippi anciently bore the name of Krenides meaning "The Little Fountains" because numerous springs surrounded it. When Philip of Macedon, father of Alexander the Great, seized it, he enlarged the site and named it after himself. It was the eastern military outpost of Philip's empire, protecting it from the wild Thracians.

We know little of the history of Philippi from then on until it was made a Roman colony by Augustus, as a memorial of his victory over Brutus and Cassius. A colony was a planned outpost of Rome, a portion of Rome transplanted to the province. The members of the colony were Roman citizens in a place of danger to defend the homeland and its borders. The colony was to Romanize the district in which it was placed. It is interesting and suggestive that Paul refers to the church at Philippi as a colony of heaven (3:20). The city is seldom mentioned in Roman history, but it is spoken of as an important city. It was destroyed or ceased to exist sometime during the Turkish domination. Today it lies in ruins. Archaeologists have uncovered a colonial archway, a marketplace, and an amphitheater. The population of Philippi was dominantly Roman with a large percentage of Greek and Oriental.

Philippi was the center of the old licentious Bacchus worship, the newer mystery religions, and the Roman Emperor worship. It also became the center of Christianity.

The church at Philippi. In obedience to the Macedonian call, Paul and his co-laborers, on the second missionary journey, took the gospel into Europe for the first time. There was no synagogue there, so Paul met with the Jews at the riverside. Paul's labors were crowned with success, and a church was established.

Luke remained in Philippi (Acts 19:10-40). After leaving Ephesus on his third missionary journey, Paul went into Macedonia (Acts 20:1-2; II Cor 2:12-13; 7:5-6), and it is reasonable to think he spent some time in Philippi. Three or four months later, on his return from Greece, he evidently spent the Passover at Philippi (Acts 20:6). Luke rejoins Paul here.

The church membership was largely Gentiles, and women occupied a prominent place (Acts 16:12-15; Phil 4:2-3). The church was loyal to Paul and grateful and generous to Paul (Acts 18:5; II Cor 8:1-5; 11:8-9; Phil 4:15-18). The Philippians had not been affected by the false Judaizing teachers, yet Paul warns them of this danger (3:14).

Authorship. The majority of scholars and a preponderance of both internal and external evidence favor the pauline authorship. There is no reason to question either the authorship or the integrity of Philippians.

Date and place of writing. Philippians was written from Rome during Paul's imprisonment. The references to the "palace" (1:13) and to "Caesar's household" (4:22) confirm this. Paul was a prisoner (1:7, 13-14) and expected a speedy release (1:19-20, 26; 2:24).

Occasion of the epistle. Epaphroditus had brought a contribution from the church in Philippi (4:18), and became sick nigh unto death (2:27). He was grieved over the sorrow which this sickness caused the Philippians (2:26). When he was well enough, Paul sent him back with this letter of thanks and explanation of Epaphroditus' long absence.

Contents. This "Hymn of Joy" has as its theme the adequacy of Christ for life and for death. The whole atmosphere of this epistle is that of joy. When Paul penned this letter, he was in a Roman prison. Years before in the jail in Philippi, Silas and he "prayed and sang praises to God" (Acts 16:25). Joy, the fruit of the Spirit (Gal 5:22), does not depend on and is not affected by outward circumstances.

The words "sin" and "sins" are not found in this epistle. The words "joy" and "rejoicing" are used eighteen times. We find no murmuring or complaining. Paul counts "it all joy" (Jas 1:2) and is glorying "in tribulation" (Rom 5:3).

Philippians shows us what true Christian experience is, the outward expression of the Christ-life within the believer in the power of the Holy Spirit, apprehending our position in Christ and manifesting Christ in our daily walk.

OUTLINE

COMMENTARY

I. REJOICING IN CHRIST AS THE PRINCIPLE OF LIFE. 1:1-30.

A. Introduction. 1:1-11.

1. Salutation. 1:1-2.

PAUL and Tĭ-mō'the-us, the servants of Jesus Christ, to all the saints in Christ Jesus which are at Phĭ-lip'pī, with the bishops and deacons:

1:1. Paul. Paul does not mention his apostleship in this epistle. He is not insisting on his apostolic authority; he is not defending some doctrine; he is not enforcing some command. **And Timothy.** Timothy is not the co-author of the epistle, but the co-laborer of the apostle. He was with Paul when the church at Philippi was founded (Acts 16:1) and had been there since (Acts 19:19-22; 20:4). **Servants of Christ Jesus.** A servant is one who gives himself up wholly to another's will, a bondservant, a man of servile condition, one devoted to another to the disregard of his own interest. Paul and Timothy were the property of our Lord Jesus Christ. They were His slaves and of no one else. No man can serve two masters (Mt 6:24). Paul and Timothy had been servants of sin by the first birth, now they are servants of Christ by the second birth. They have been purchased by the blood of Christ and they are owned by Christ. Therefore, they have no will of their own, no business of their own, no time of their own. They are acting for Christ; they are dependent upon Christ; they are obedient to Christ. **To all the saints.** Saints are holy ones both in character and conduct. They are set apart for God to be exclusively His, dedicated to God, holy (holiness of heart and conduct in contrast to the impurity of unbelievers). Saints are set aside for sacred use. **In Christ Jesus.** This is the position of the saints. This is Paul's summation of the Christian life, the most intimate and living union between the believer and his Lord. **Which are at Philippi.** This is the place of their residence, the place of their discipline, the place of their experience, and the place of their service. **With the bishops.** The bishops were the overseers, guardians, those who had a care for them. The word is synonymous with presbyter and elder; they were the spiritual leaders. They were not dictators, but godly examples and undershepherds (I Pet 5:1-4). **And deacons.** Deacons are servants (in their activities for the work and not in their relationship to any other person). "The etymology (Gr *dia, konis*) suggests raising a dust by hastening" (A. T. Robertson, *Word Pictures of the New Testament*, Vol. IV, p. 435). Both bishops and deacons were the recognized officers of the church at this time. There was simple organization in the early church. We must never violate the scriptural principals of (1) the priesthood of all believers and (2) the lordship of Christ.

2 Grace *be* unto you, and peace, from God our Father, and *from* the Lord Jesus Christ.

2. Grace be unto you, and peace. Grace and peace, always in that order. Grace is the foundation and peace is the result. Where there is no grace, there can be no peace. Grace denotes unmerited favor and expresses God's sacrificial love to men. Peace expresses "the tranquil state of a soul assured of its salvation through Christ, a soul fearing nothing from God and content with its earthly lot, of whatsoever sort that is." Peace is that harmony and health of the one who has been reconciled to

God through the grace of our Lord Jesus Christ (Rom 5:1-2). **From God our Father, and from the Lord Jesus Christ.** The preposition (Gr *apo*) governs both objects, God and Christ, who form one unit and are placed on a level of equality. A definite affirmation of Christ's deity. God is called our Father because we are His children by the new birth; Christ is called our Lord because we live under Him and serve Him in righteousness.

2. Thanksgiving. 1:3-8.

3 I thank my God upon every remembrance of you,

3. I thank my God. Paul expresses his personal relationship to God. He says in effect, God is mine, and I am His. **Upon every remembrance of you.** This is Paul's basis and the stimulus for his thanksgiving. Paul remembers their acceptance of the gospel, their consistency of faith, their growth in grace, and their burden for lost souls.

4 Always in every prayer of mine for you all making request with joy,

4. Always in every prayer of mine for you all. The word **prayer** (Gr *deēsis*) means supplication, petition, entreaty. Paul was a great prayer warrior. In a day when programs, publicity, and promotion characterize much of the Lord's work, it should be emphasized that without prayer no lasting work will be accomplished for God. **Making request with joy.** Joy is the keynote of this epistle. Paul had been a happy prisoner in Philippi (Acts 16:25).

5 For your fellowship in the gospel from the first day until now;

5. For your fellowship in the gospel. Fellowship is joint participation and cooperation in a common interest and activity. Not fellowship primarily with Paul or with each other, but fellowship in the furtherance of the gospel by their living, loyalty, love, and liberality. They were fellow laborers with Paul to take the whole Word to the whole world.

6 Being confident of this very thing, that he which hath begun a good work in you will perform *it* until the day of Jesus Christ:

6. Being confident of this very thing. Paul has been persuaded. The Greek perfect tense signifies past completed action with present existing results. Paul is still firmly confident and will continue to be so. He has no doubts about their salvation or their security. **That he which hath begun a good work in you will perform it until the day of Jesus Christ.** God's beginning the work is a pledge of its completion. What God begins, He will finish (I Sam 3:12). The good work has its initiation in regeneration (past); has its continuation in sanctification (present); and will have its consummation in glorification (future). In the past there was God's unchangeable purpose; in the present there is God's unlimited power; and in the future there is God's unbreakable promise. This is God's guarantee for the final preservation and perseverance of the saints. Salvation is all of God.

7 Even as it is meet for me to think this of you all, because I have you in my heart; inasmuch as both in my bonds, and in the defence and confirmation of the gospel, ye all are partakers of my grace.

7. Even as it is meet for me to think this of you all. Paul gives the reason for his settled persuasion. It was right for him to feel this way concerning them. **Because I have you in my heart.** Paul loved them as his own soul. Paul's heart beats in unison with Christ's heart, for Christ lives in and loves through Paul. Paul's love for them was the fruit of the Holy Spirit. **Inasmuch as both in my bonds.** Paul's bonds refer to his present imprisonment. **And in the defense and confirmation of the gospel.** Defense is our word apology, but not with the idea of apologizing (Acts 22:1; 25:16). Defense is the negative side and confirmation (verification) is the positive side of establishing the gospel. Defense means clearing away the objections and removing the obstacles; confirmation means the aggressive advancement in proclaiming the good news. Both words are connected by the same definite article in Greek, and combined to form one complete idea. It is the defense and confirmation of the gospel, not Paul's self-defense. The fate of the apostle was of little concern; the fate of the gospel was then and still is everything. **Ye all are partakers of my grace.** Literally, my co-sharers or fellow-participants in grace.

8 For God is my record, how greatly I long after you all in the bowels of Jesus Christ.

8. For God is my record. Literally, God is my witness (Gr *martys*). Our word martyr is derived from this word. **How greatly I long after you all.** The word means to long for, desire earnestly, pursue with love. **In the bowels of Jesus Christ**. The word (Gr *splangchnos*) means heart, viscera (lit., vital organs), the seat of the affections. We translate, "with the heart of Jesus Christ with the tender affections and yearnings of Christ."

3. Prayer. 1:9-11.

9 And this I pray, that your love may abound yet more and more in knowledge and *in* all judgment;

9. And this I pray. Keep on praying. **That your love may abound yet more and more.** Their love was already in existence and that in no small degree to God, to one another, and to all men. The word **abound** (Gr *perisseuō*) means to exceed a fixed number or measure, to be over, to abound, to overflow. The Greek present active subjunctive means to keep on overflowing in a perpetual flood of love. **In knowledge and in all judgment.** The word knowledge means whole, complete, precise, and correct knowledge, knowledge gained by experience. Judgment means perception, delicate discernment, and spiritual understanding. It is keen, intelligent, spiritual insight that selects, classifies, and applies that which knowledge furnishes. Knowledge deals with the general principles; judgment deals with the discriminating of those principles.

10 That ye may approve things that are excellent; that ye may be sincere and without offence till the day of Christ;

10. That ye may approve things that are excellent. The word **approve** (Gr *dokimazō*) means to test, scrutinize, prove, recognize as genuine after examination, to sanction after testing. Some translate "approve things that are excellent" and others, "try the things that differ." The meaning is very similar. For by testing things that differ, we approve the things that are excellent. The Greek present participle means literally to carry different ways to different places. Thus to test things that differ, sift truth from error, discriminate the higher spiritual blessings from the lower material blessings. The criterion is always the Word of God as taught by the Holy Spirit. **That ye may be sincere.** The word sincere means unmixed, unalloyed, pure, free from falsehood, sincere. God wants sterling Christians, not those who are merely "plated" with outward religion. God wants men and women of transparent character, clear as crystal, so that the world will see Christ in their character and in their conduct. **And without offense.** Having nothing for one to strike against, not causing to stumble, without offense. Here the word conveys both ideas of not stumbling and of not causing others to stumble. Stepping-stones not stumbling blocks. **Till the day of Christ.** With a view to His glorious appearance.

11 Being filled with the fruits of righteousness, which are by Jesus Christ, unto the glory and praise of God.

11. Being filled. The word (Gr *plēroō*) means to make full, cause to abound, filled to the full. This Greek perfect participle expresses the present results of a past action. They have been filled and are still filled. There is no room for anything else; there is no room for any other fruit. **With the fruits of righteousness.** Righteousness fruit. **Which are by Jesus Christ.** This fruit cannot be produced by human power but only by the Holy Spirit as the believer is in vital union with Christ (Jn 15:4-5). **Unto the glory and praise of God.** This is the spiritual purpose of all Christian endeavor.

B. Rejoicing in the Christian Ministry. 1:12-26.

1. Proclaiming the gospel. 1:12-20.

12 But I would ye should understand, brethren, that the things *which happened* unto me have fallen out rather unto the furtherance of the gospel;

12. But I would ye should understand. Paul wants the Philippians to be informed that his bonds led to a wider witness. Paul turned his prison cell into a gospel chapel. His chain did not curtail the gospel, but advanced it. **The things which happened unto me.** Paul refers to being mobbed in Jerusalem, unjustly imprisoned, shipwrecked, chained to guards, etc. These things happened not for crimes, but for Christ. **Have fallen out rather unto the furtherance of the gospel.** Paul's affairs turned out just the reverse of what might have been expected. Progress means advancement. This word pictures the

13 So that my bonds in Christ are manifest in all the palace, and in all other *places;*

14 And many of the brethren in the Lord, waxing confident by my bonds, are much more bold to speak the word without fear.

15 Some indeed preach Christ even of envy and strife; and some also of good will:

16 The one preach Christ of contention, not sincerely, supposing to add affliction to my bonds:

17 But the other of love, knowing that I am set for the defence of the gospel.

18 What then? notwithstanding, every way, whether in pretence, or in truth, Christ is preached; and I therein do rejoice, yea, and will rejoice.

pioneer cutting a way before an army and thus furthering its advance. Paul's imprisonment did not hinder his ministry of intercession, his ministry of evangelism, his ministry of writing.

13. So that my bonds in Christ. Paul's bonds were in connection with Christ and His cause. Paul is imprisoned for Christ's sake, and his chains are seen in relation to Christ and thus bear witness for Christ. **Are manifest in all the palace.** The palace of the provincial governor, probably including the barracks of the praetorian guard. The imperial guard was made up of noble soldiers appointed to keep guard over the emperor and the palace. These men had been reached with the gospel. **In all other places.** To all the rest.

14. And many of the brethren in the Lord. The majority of the brethren. **Waxing confident by my bonds.** Paul's courage was contagious. His confinement did not intimidate these brethren. Paul's brave and fearless example brought confidence to them. **Are much more bold.** In a greater degree and with increased zeal. **To speak.** The word denotes the fact of speaking, rather than the substance of speaking. **The word without fear.** The brethren dared fearlessly to proclaim God's Word.

15. Some indeed preach Christ even of envy and strife. Envy and strife are very low motives for preaching the gospel. On account of their jealousy of Paul, they sought to undermine his influence. These men are in contrast to the brethren of verse 14. Strife means rivalry, contention, wrangling. These men were motivated by malice. They had the right message, but they had the wrong motive. **And some also of good will.** These brethren found pleasure and satisfaction in Paul's work. These have the right message and the right motive.

16. The one preach Christ of contention. The word **contention** (Gr *eritheia*) means self-seeking, the desire to put one's self forward, selfish ambition, a partisan and factious spirit. Their motives were rivalry and ambition. **Not sincerely.** The word (Gr *hagnōs*) means not purely, not chaste, not modest, not immaculate. They are not preaching Christ from pure motives; not from unalloyed love for Christ; but insincerely. **Supposing to add affliction to my bonds.** Their aim was unchristian. Their purpose was to stir up vexation for Paul and to aggravate his sufferings. Their purpose was to triumph over Paul, not to triumph over pagans. They were concerned about promoting a sect, not saving souls.

17. But the other of love. Love both for Christ and for Paul knowing that **I am set for the defense of the gospel.** The same defense that is mentioned in verse 7. The word **set** (Gr *keimai*) means appointed, placed, destined. We see in these last two verses two types of preachers. They differ in their hearts: in one contention rules, and in the other love reigns. They differ in spirit: in one there is envy and strife; in the other good will. They differ in the source of their strength: in one there is merely the love of party; in the other there is confidence in the Lord. They differ in their aim: in one the aim is to advance a branch of the church; in the other the aim is to advance the cause of Christ. They differ in conviction: one aims to add affliction to Paul; the other knows that Paul is set for the defense of the gospel.

18. What then? Notwithstanding, every way, whether in pretense. Pretense means an excuse, a pretext, that which is put forward to hide the true state of things. It has the idea of an ulterior motive. **Or in truth.** In sincerity. Paul could not and would not condone false teaching, but he graciously could and would tolerate wrong motives. We find no resentment in Paul's part and no rebuke in his actions. Paul rose above petty jealousy and animosity. Christ was in control, and Paul was out of sight. **Christ is preached.** Paul was bound, but the Word of God was not bound (II Tim 2:9). **And I therein do rejoice, yea, and will rejoice.** Paul rejoiced because Christ was being openly pro-

19 For I know that this shall turn to my salvation through your prayer, and the supply of the Spirit of Jesus Christ,

claimed; not because of the wrong motive of some, but in spite of the wrong motive.

19. For I know that this shall turn to my salvation. Paul speaks of his deliverance and his preservation. He was being delivered from discouragement and spurred on to greater endeavors for Christ. He was experiencing victory and blessings in the midst of and in spite of his trials and his tribulations. It was Paul whom the Holy Spirit used to write, "tribulation worketh patience" (Rom 5:3). **Through your prayer.** Through your petition. Paul depended much on the intercession of God's people. **And the supply of the Spirit of Jesus Christ.** The ample supply comes as a result of the supplication. Note the cooperation of the human (petition) and the divine (ample supply). The Holy Spirit is both the gift and the giver.

20 According to my earnest expectation and *my* hope, that in nothing I shall be ashamed, but *that* with all boldness, as always, *so* now also Christ shall be magnified in my body, whether *it be* by life, or by death.

20. According to my earnest expectation. The word translated **earnest expectation** (Gr *apokaradokia*) means to watch with the head erect and outstretched, to direct attention to anything, to wait for in suspense, anxious anticipation, intense desire, persistent expectation. The word is used only here and in Romans 8:19. It comes from the Greek terms *apo* (away from), *kara* (head), and *dokeō* (to watch closely). The idea of eagerness is intensified by (the Greek term *apo*), which implies abstraction. Paul's attention is drawn away from all other things and concentrated on one thing in order to see its very first appearance. **That in nothing I shall be ashamed.** Put to shame, disgraced. **But that with all boldness.** Boldness means freedom in speaking, fearless, confidence, cheerful courage, assurance, boldness. The absence of fear in speaking boldly was Paul's privilege as a slave of Jesus Christ. **As always, so now also Christ shall be magnified in my body.** Paul shrinks from using the first person (I will magnify Christ) lest he should seem to magnify himself. The Holy Spirit will use Paul as an instrument to glorify Christ. The idea is that the glory of Christ will be manifest to others through Paul. Paul desires to be a magnifying glass through whom others could more clearly see Christ in all His glory. **Whether it be by life, or by death.** Through life or through death. Paul's utter committal to magnify Christ is seen in his willingness to accomplish it through life or through death. The Holy Spirit will determine which means best suits His purpose.

2. Surrendering to Christ. 1:21-26.

21 For to me to live *is* Christ, and to die *is* gain.

21. For me to live is Christ. Christ lives in Paul (Gal 2:20) and is the source and sustainer of Paul's spiritual life (Col 3:4). Paul is in vital union with Christ and lives in devotion to Christ. **And to die is gain.** The Greek aorist tense implies the state after death; not the act of dying, but the consequences of dying. Death does not interrupt our conscious fellowship with Christ. The moment of absence here is the moment of presence there (II Cor 5:8). One of the martyrs said to his persecutors as they led him to death, "You take a life from me that I cannot keep, and bestow a life upon me that I cannot lose." The idea of gain is a precious thought on dying. After death Christians will collect the profits of their life's investments for Christ, and God pays rich dividends. It will be gain both in what we lose (sinful body, temptation, sorrow, sufferings, enemies, etc.) and in what we gain (glorified body, personal presence with Christ, joy, reunion with departed saints, etc.). Not all share Paul's view. Some would say to live is wealth, or knowledge, or fame, or fortune, or pleasure, or prestige, or power. But for Paul living in Christ: the commencement of life was being identified with Christ; the continuation of life was daily revelation of Christ; the conduct of life was self-renunciation for Christ; and the consummation of life will be transformation into the likeness of Christ.

22 But if I live in the flesh, this *is* the

22. But if I live in the flesh, this is the fruit of my labour. Paul speaks of life in the flesh because when he moves out of the

fruit of my labour: yet what I shall choose I wot not,

23 For I am in a strait betwixt two, having a desire to depart, and to be with Christ; which is far better:

24 Nevertheless to abide in the flesh *is* more needful for you.

25 And having this confidence, I know that I shall abide and continue with you all for your furtherance and joy of faith;

26 That your rejoicing may be more abundant in Jesus Christ for me by my coming to you again.

27 Only let your conversation be as it becometh the gospel of Christ: that whether I come and see you, or else be absent, I may hear of your affairs, that ye stand fast in one spirit, with one

body, he will still be living. If to go on living in the flesh be Paul's lot, this will issue in more fruit from his work. **Yet what I shall choose I wot not.** This word **wot** or know (Gr *gnōrizō*) has two distinct meanings: transitive, to make known; intransitive, to know, to become acquainted with, to discover. Paul was in a dilemma concerning which to choose between life and death.

23. For I am in a strait betwixt two. The expression means to hold together, compress, constrain. Paul was hard-pressed. He was hemmed in on both sides and prevented from inclining either way because of the pressing in upon him from the two considerations. There is a desire to depart; there is a necessity to abide. There is a very strong reason for either choice; he is being pulled in both directions. Paul is in a dilemma and is held back from a decision. **Having a desire to depart.** This word (Gr *analyō*) means to unloose, to undo again, to depart. This word pictures the loosing of the tent pins for breaking up camp (cf. II Cor 5:1) or the loosing of the ship from its moorings, to lift anchor and sail away, sail away from earth to heaven, from time to eternity. **And to be with Christ.** The destination for which Paul yearns. There is no soul-sleeping; there is no intermediary probation. **Which is far better.** Very much better. By far the preferable. This is a double comparative and means literally by much more better. Labor for Christ is sweet, but rest with Christ will be sweeter. Whitfield said, "I am often weary *in* the work, but never weary *of* it." Paul was ready to go and willing to wait. Life has its attractions; death has its advantages. Paul desires to live and labor, preferring Christ's purpose.

24. Nevertheless to abide in the flesh is more needful for you. It was necessary and indispensable for Paul to continue abiding in the flesh. Paul's eagerness to be a channel of blessing to the Philippians outweighs his desire for personal gain. He wants to finish the work God gave him to do (II Tim 4:6-8).

25. And having this confidence. Here the Greek perfect tense implies that Paul has been persuaded in time past, and presently thoroughly convinced with this settled conviction. **I know that I shall abide and continue with you all.** The preposition (Gr *para*) stresses the place of Paul's abiding, by the side of you all, denoting continuance in a certain place, or with certain persons, or in certain relations. **For your furtherance and joy of faith.** This states the purpose for which Paul will continue and remain with them. The word furtherance is the same word found in 1:12. Paul will continue abiding with them for the purpose of promoting the progressive advancement of their faith. Paul's purpose is twofold: progress of their faith and joy of their faith. Both words are connected by one definite article in Greek. It is the joy of the faith. Their progress will result in their joy.

26. That your rejoicing may be more abundant in Jesus Christ for me. The word **rejoicing** (Gr *kauchēma*) is exultation, that of which one glories or can glory, a matter or ground of glorying, reason for boasting. The word does not mean the act of glorying. Their exultation is the natural result of their joy. Paul desires that their exaltation may constantly overflow, exceed a fixed number or measure, exist in abundance, be over and above, overflow. The sphere in which this blessing is enjoyed is in Christ Jesus, the only legitimate realm for glorying (I Cor 1:31). **By my coming to you again.** Paul refers to his own personal presence with them.

C. Rejoicing in Christian Living. 1:27-30.

27. Only. The emphatic position states Paul's purpose for which he desires to remain alive. Whatever may happen, make this your chief business. **Let your conversation be.** Keep on conducting yourselves. The word (Gr *politeuō*) means to be a citizen, behave as a citizen. Here the present imperative middle

2435

mind striving together for the faith of
the gospel;

describes the subject as acting in reference to himself and for his
own benefit, participating in the results of the action. This word
is taken from the political life. The church at Philippi was a
colony of heaven, and the members are commanded to walk as
citizens of heaven, not by outward regulations, but by the power
of the indwelling Holy Spirit. Their conduct is to reflect what
Christ has done in them. They are to recognize their responsibilities and perform their obligations. God wants all of His children
to be holy in character and conduct so that spiritual unity and
power may be achieved. Our daily deportment should betray us
as pilgrims and strangers down here and as citizens of that "city
which hath foundations, whose builder and maker is God" (Heb
11:10). A life worthy of the gospel is a life lived in the power of
the Holy Spirit. It is the earthly walk of a heavenly man. Such
consistency is: (1) the result of gospel disposition; (2) maintained by gospel principles; (3) conformable to gospel precepts;
(4) resembles gospel patterns; and (5) possible through gospel
power. **That ye stand fast in one spirit.** The idea is to keep
one's ground in battle, and in order to do this, one must be
settled on the firm foundation of the Rock of Ages. In one spirit
means in the spirit of unity and harmony; for bickering, contention, and self-seeking hinder and mar the gospel witness. One
spirit refers to that unity into which the church is fused by the
presence and the power of the Holy Spirit (Eph 4:3-4). **With one
mind striving together for the faith of the gospel.** To strive at
the same time (Gr *synathleō*) with one another, to contend along
with, share, or take part in a contest. There is to be a mutual
striving together: side by side, shoulder to shoulder, and heart
to heart. We get our word "athlete" from this word. The
preposition (Gr *syn*) implies cooperation and coordination
against common opposition. The Philippians are already contending with united effort, working as a team for the faith once
for all delivered unto the saints (Jude 3). Every Christian is an
important member of the team, an important link in an important chain extending the gospel of Christ. Christians are friends,
not foes; co-workers, not competitors. Since the church has a
common objective and a common adversary, Paul pleads for a
consistent church, a united church, and a zealous church to
resist the adversary, develop Christian graces, establish the true
faith, and advance the gospel of Christ.

28 And in nothing terrified by your
adversaries: which is to them an evident token of perdition, but to you of
salvation, and that of God.

28. And in nothing terrified by your adversaries. The word
terrified (Gr *ptyrō*) means to frighten, scare, alarm. This word
was used of horses being scared and startled and turning about
or springing aside. God wants fearless fighters with undaunted
courage, who will not be startled or intimidated by anything.
Such holy boldness is produced by the Holy Spirit. **Your adversaries.** Better, by those opposing you. Christians have adversaries. There is no middle ground; a person is either for Christ or
against Him (Mt 12:30). **Which is to them an evident token of
perdition.** This is a legal term denoting proof obtained by an
appeal to the facts. The opposition of the adversaries was in fact
strong evidence that they were rushing headlong into perdition.
Perdition never means annihilation. Too bad they didn't realize
their final destiny and flee from the wrath to come. **But to you
of salvation.** The same evidence was a positive pledge of salvation to the Philippians. **And that of God.** Their salvation was
from God. God is the source and origin of salvation.

29 For unto you it is given in the behalf of Christ, not only to believe on
him, but also to suffer for his sake;

29. For unto you. To you who are striving and struggling. **It
is given.** It is graciously granted. **In the behalf of Christ.** For
His sake. **Not only to believe on him, but also to suffer for his
sake.** The Christian's privileges are to believe on Him and to
suffer for Him, and always in that order. God confers upon us
the high honor of suffering with Christ and for Christ (II Tim
2:12; 3:12). Christ suffered to provide salvation. God crowns the
believing in His Son with the suffering for His Son (Mt 5:11-12).
A glorious reward awaits all who suffer (II Cor 4:17).

30 Having the same conflict which ye saw in me, and now hear *to be* in me.

30. Having the same conflict. The **conflict** (Gr *agōn*) signifies a contest of athletes or the inner conflict of the soul. The inner conflict is often the result of an outward conflict of struggle. Our word agony is derived from this word. **Which ye saw in me.** The Philippians saw Paul beaten and thrown into prison (Acts 16). **And now hear to be in me.** Paul was an example and an encouragement to the Philippians.

II. REJOICING IN CHRIST AS THE PATTERN OF LIFE. 2:1-30.

A. The Need of a Pattern. 2:1-4.

2:1. If. Since. Here we have a first-class conditional sentence expressing the condition as a fact in Greek. Since these things are blessed realities, how incongruous it would be for any saint to act as if they were nonexistent. **There be therefore.** Paul is expanding the exhortation of 1:28. All the terms used in this verse get their coloring from that connection. **Any consolation in Christ.** Any exhortation. The word is always modified by the context. Paul is pleading for unity. Surely an exhortation in Christ must be heeded. **If any comfort of love.** Any consolation. The idea is to make things easier by speaking to a person in trouble. This is the encouragement of tender persuasiveness which love gives, an incentive to action (II Cor 5:14). Love is that unselfish, self-sacrificing love of John 3:16. **If any fellowship of the Spirit.** Any intimate partnership or joint participation. Such common interests and mutual, active participation are the results of the Holy Spirit's work. The fellowship of the Spirit is a blessed reality, not merely a beautiful idea. **If any bowels and mercies.** Bowels is the same word as we find in 1:8 and means tenderheartedness, tender mercies. Mercies means compassionate yearnings and action. These graces present in the lives of the Philippians will result in peace and in power. Unity will prevail, differences will be dissolved, bickerings will cease, and estrangements will be completely healed.

CHAPTER 2

IF *there be* therefore any consolation in Christ, if any comfort of love, if any fellowship of the Spirit, if any bowels and mercies,

2 Fulfil ye my joy, that ye be likeminded, having the same love, *being* of one accord, of one mind.

2. Fulfill ye my joy. Fill up to the full. Paul wants his cup of joy full and running over. The Philippians can accomplish this by heeding Paul's admonitions and exhibiting the virtues to which he exhorts them. **That ye be likeminded.** That you all may keep on thinking the same thing. They are to be intent on one thing, one purpose. **Having the same love.** This unity of affection is the fruit of the Holy Spirit. Equally loving and being loved. **Being of one accord.** Literally, souls together. Souls knit together in love by the Holy Spirit, hearts beating in unison, unity in sentiment. **Of one mind.** Thinking one thing. Unity of thought and purpose. Unity is defined as something far deeper than: (1) consent to a common creed; (2) union in a form of worship; and (3) participation in a common task. It is unity of heart, soul, and mind. This is what Christ can and will do.

3 *Let* nothing *be done* through strife or vainglory; but in lowliness of mind let each esteem other better than themselves.

3. Let nothing be done through strife. Factious strife, intriguing for office, a desire to put one's self forward, a partisan and factious spirit, self-seeking. **Or vainglory.** Empty, proud, or groundless self-esteem. Ambition and vanity will destroy the unity and harmony of a church. Paul's prohibitions are indicators of what is wrong, which he wishes to correct. Christians should seek the approval of God, not the applause of men. **But in lowliness of mind.** Humility of mind and deportment, a deep sense of one's littleness. This indicates self-forgetfulness in serving others, the spirit which most resembles Christ. The pathway to unity is lowly and lonely. **Let each esteem other better than themselves.** Go on regarding others above themselves. This is that Christlike spirit of humility which fixes its eyes on the excellency of others and judges them from that standpoint.

4 Look not every man on his own things, but every man also on the things of others.

4. Look not every man on his own things. Keep an eye for the good of others. Have respect for, fix your attention upon with a desire for an interest in others. They were to be attentive to the interests of others as well as their own. Every member of the church should practice unselfishness and due consideration for all the others. **But every man also on the things of others.** Others is the keynote of these verses. This was the dominant feature in the life of our Lord who "came not to be ministered unto, but to minister, and to give his life a ransom for many" (Mk 10:45). A man of the flesh "looks out for number one," but a man of the Spirit lives in submission to Christ and in service to his fellowman.

B. Christ the Pattern. 2:5-11.

1. Preexistence of Christ. 2:5-6.

5 Let this mind be in you, which was also in Christ Jesus:

5. Let this mind be in you, which was also in Christ Jesus. Keep on thinking this in you which was also in Christ Jesus. Paul says in I Corinthians 2:16, "We have the mind of Christ," and here he exhorts the saints at Philippi to allow that mind to dominate and control their lives. When this is done, saints will not: (1) assert their own virtues; (2) defend their own rights; (3) promote their own selfish interests; or (4) live for themselves. Verse 5 introduces one of the most sublime and wonderful mysteries of the Scriptures, what is called the doctrine of the *kenosis*. This doctrine of our Lord's self-emptying is used as an example and as an illustration of that lowliness of mind which should be the pattern for all the followers of Christ. Paul is stating accepted facts to enforce the obvious duties of humility and unselfish consideration of others.

6 Who, being in the form of God, thought it not robbery to be equal with God:

6. Who, being in the form of God. The word **being** (Gr *hyparchō*) is better translated existing or subsisting. This word is much stronger than the verb to be; it does not simply mean being but existing. Christ ever was, is, and ever shall be God. This word denotes prior existence (cf. Jn 1:1; Col 1:17). From all eternity the Son was co-existent, co-equal, and co-eternal with the Father. Christ existed in the form of God. This is the strongest Greek word (Gr *morphē*) to denote the exact image, the image of being and essence. It has no reference to the shape of a physical object, but refers to the expression of being. Christ is the brightness of God's glory, "and the express image of his person" (Heb 1:3). Christ is not merely like God; He is God (Jn 1:1; Col 2:9). **Form** signifies the mode in which He expresses His divine essence. **Form** (Gr *morphē*) "always signifies a form which truly and fully expresses the being which underlines it" (H. A. A. Kennedy, *The Epistle to the Philippians*, p. 436). No creature could exist in **the form of God,** but Lucifer aspired to this (Isa 14:12-14). To give expression to the essence of deity implies the possession of deity. What Peter, James, and John witnessed on the Mount of Transfiguration was a glimpse of the outward expression of His deity (Mt 17:1-2). Christ's own eternal self-manifesting characteristics were shining forth from His divine essence. **Thought it not robbery.** This word (Gr *harpagmos*) has two distinct meanings. One, a thing unlawfully seized, and two, a treasure to be clutched and retained. Christ did not cling to His prerogatives of His divine majesty, did not ambitiously display His equality with God. Christ waived His rights to: (1) express His deity; (2) display His divine attributes; and (3) demonstrate His equality with God. He did not regard His position as equal with God as something to be held onto, but as something to be relinquished for the redemption of man. He gave up His throne in glory for a cross of shame and suffering. **To be equal with God.** This confirms the meaning of **form.** Christ was on an equality with God. He laid aside His divine glory, but He did not and could not lay aside His divine nature. He laid aside the expression of deity, but He did not and could not lay aside His possession of deity. He laid aside His rights as the Son and took His place as a servant. He put aside the insignia of deity and put on the robes of humanity.

2. Incarnation of Christ. 2:7-8.

7 But made himself of no reputation, and took upon him the form of a servant, and was made in the likeness of men:

7. But made himself of no reputation. He emptied Himself. He divested Himself of His prerogatives. We have an incomplete thought which leaves us with the question "of what?" Certainly not His deity, but only His divine prerogatives and privileges. He did not and could not cease to be God when He was made flesh (Jn 1:14). His deity remained throughout the whole course of His self-imposed humiliation. He gave up something that was His. **Himself** is accusative in Greek. He did not empty something from Himself, but He emptied Himself from something, i.e., the form of God. The figure presented is similar to pouring water from a pitcher into a glass. The form is different, but the substance remains the same. "Jesus Christ the same yesterday, and to day, and for ever" (Heb 13:8). Christ emptied Himself of His divine glory (Jn 17:3), but not of His divine nature. He emptied Himself of the self-manifestation of His divine essence. "He was not *unable to assert* equality with God. He was able *not to assert it*" (M. R. Vincent, *Word Studies in the New Testament.* p. 433). He stripped Himself of His expression of deity, but not His possession of deity. He restricted the outward manifestation of His deity. In His incarnation, He clothed Himself with humanity. He was like a king temporarily clothing himself in the garb of a peasant while still remaining king, even though it was not apparent. When Christ became incarnate, He was one person with two natures, divine and human, "each in its completeness and integrity, and that these two natures are organically and indissolubly united, yet so that no third nature is formed thereby. In brief, to use the antiquated dictum, orthodox doctrine forbids us either to divide the person or to confound the natures" (A. H. Strong, *Systematic Theology*, p. 673). Christ emptied Himself in order that He might fill us (II Cor 5:21; 8:9). **And took upon him the form of a servant.** The form of a slave refers to His mode of expression. He veiled Himself with humanity (Heb 2:14-18). The same divine person who existed in the form of God took on Himself the form of a slave. He who was the Sovereign manifested Himself as a slave. When He did this, His person did not change, only the mode of His expression. God refutes all claims of modernism that the Lord Jesus Christ emptied Himself of His deity. **And was made in the likeness of men.** Becoming in the likeness of men. The verb forms emptied, taking, and becoming are punctiliar aorists, expressing simultaneous, but not identical action. Becoming, as opposed to what He was by nature; entering into a new state. Likeness denies identity. It refers to an outward expression that is assumed from the outside and does not come from within. Likeness means similarity, but not sameness. Christ was not identical with man (not merely a man, and nothing else); He was the sinless Son of God, the God-man. Adam aspired to be like God; Christ condescended to be like man. His humanity was the vehicle through which he manifested Himself as a slave.

8 And being found in fashion as a man, he humbled himself, and became obedient unto death, even the death of the cross.

8. And being found. Men discovered Him to appear as man. Men recognized Him as a true man. **In fashion as a man.** In appearance. The word form (Gr *morphē*) differs from fashion (Gr *schēma*) as that which is intrinsic from that which is outward. The contrast is between what He is in Himself (God) and what He appears to be in the eyes of men (man). Christ had all the qualities which Adam had before he sinned, but not the sinful nature which came through Adam's fall. **He humbled himself.** This is not the same as "He emptied Himself," but shows how the self-emptying manifested itself. His love for us prompted Him to voluntarily do this. **And became obedient unto death.** The mark of a slave is obedience. When slaves were executed they were crucified. Christ placed Himself on the same plane as the worst of criminals. The cross was a horrible death of shame and suffering. Christ's obedience was **unto death** and not to death. He never was death's slave, but death's master and conqueror. Adam was disobedient unto death; Christ was obedient unto death (Rom 5:19). Christ's death was voluntary, vicarious, and victorious. **Even the death of the cross.** The most despised death of a condemned criminal on an accursed cross.

3. Exaltation of Christ. 2:9-11.

9 Wherefore God also hath highly exalted him, and given him a name which is above every name:

9. Wherefore. Because of His voluntary renunciation, obedience, and death (cf. Mt 23:12). **God also hath highly exalted him.** God exalted him supremely. Christ's exaltation is not only God's attestation of satisfaction in Christ's work, but also God's recognition of Christ's equality with God. Christ emptied Himself; God exalted Him. On earth Christ was God, but appeared as man, back in heaven. He retained His humanity, but He manifests His prerogatives of deity. God graciously granted to Him the name. On earth Christ was crowned with thorns (Mt 27:29), back in heaven He is crowned with glory and honor (Rev 5:12-14). **And given him a name which is above every name.** Probably "KING OF KINGS, AND LORD OF LORDS" (Rev 19:16).

10 That at the name of Jesus every knee should bow, of *things* in heaven, and *things* in earth, and *things* under the earth;

10. That at the name of Jesus every knee should bow. Every created rational and moral being will bow in submission to Christ's lordship. **Of things in heaven, and things in earth, and things under the earth.** Heavenly ones, earthly ones, and subterranean ones. They refer to personal beings, not to impersonal things existing in heaven, existing upon the earth, and existing under the earth.

11 And *that* every tongue should confess that Jesus Christ *is* Lord, to the glory of God the Father.

11. And that every tongue should confess that Jesus Christ is Lord. Every tongue shall profess openly that Christ is Lord. The word Lord is equivalent to the Old Testament word *Jehovah*. God made Him "both Lord and Christ" (Acts 2:36). Men may flaunt Christ's lordship here, but they will be compelled to acknowledge it hereafter. This will not result in their salvation. Subjugation is not reconciliation. When reconciliation is under consideration, only two spheres are mentioned, on earth and in the heavens (Col 1:20), but the things under the earth are omitted. This passage does not teach that ultimately all the lost will be saved, as taught by many cults. No future reconciliation for the lost is anywhere promised in the Word of God. **To the glory of God the Father.** God is glorified when men openly acknowledge Christ as Lord.

C. Example of Paul. 2:12-18.

12 Wherefore, my beloved, as ye have always obeyed, not as in my presence only, but now much more in my absence, work out your own salvation with fear and trembling.

12. Wherefore. So then. This refers to what precedes. Having the example of Christ's humility to guide us and the exaltation of Christ to encourage us. **My beloved, as ye have always obeyed, not as in my presence only, but now much more in my absence.** There is always a tendency to relax obedience when the spiritual leader is absent, but the Philippians obeyed "much more" in Paul's absence. **Work out.** Keep on working out thoroughly in your own interests so as to achieve the desired results. Both freedom and responsibility are implied. In verses 12 and 13 we see divine sovereignty and human freedom in blessed cooperation. Our salvation is **worked in** by the Holy Spirit in answer to faith in God's promises and it is *worked out* by the Holy Spirit by our obedience to God's precepts. It is always a matter of trust and obey. The verse does not say "work for" your salvation. The Philippians had already been saved. Salvation is all of grace (Eph 2:8-10), but it is to be manifested in the daily life by glorifying Christ in everything. One must possess salvation first, and then work it out to its ultimate conclusion, namely, Christlikeness. No one can live the Christian life until he has Christ. It is not a matter of the imitation of Christ but the manifestation of Christ, the Holy Spirit reproducing the life of Christ in and through the believer. **Your own salvation.** Salvation is a personal relationship; it is a divine work accomplished at Calvary. Salvation should be viewed in three tenses: past, justification; present, sanctification; and future, glorification. **With fear and trembling.** These two words describe the anxiety of the person who distrusts his own ability to meet all the requirements, but nevertheless does his best to discharge his duty. This is not slavish fear, but wholesome, serious caution. It is the constant apprehension of the deceitfulness of the heart, taking heed lest we fall (I Cor 10:12); or stop short of the final goal (II Pet 1:1-11). It is that desirable distrust of our own self-sufficiency and the consciousness that all depends on the grace of God. It is not fear of being lost, but fear of the failure of not walking in lowliness of mind, in true humility, and in unfailing obedience. It is fear of all that would rob us of our spiritual vitality and spiritual victory and of shrinking from all carelessness in matters of faith and life.

13 For it is God which worketh in you both to will and to do of *his* good pleasure.

13. For it is God which worketh in you. For God is the one continually working effectually in you. This word is used in Galatians 2:8 (wrought effectually) and in I Thessalonians 2:13 (effectually worketh). We are God's workmanship (Eph 2:10). **Both to will and to do.** To keep on willing and to keep on working. God is the source of all we need. The Holy Spirit dwelling within makes the abundant life a reality (not merely a possibility). The energy of God enables a Christian to desire God's will and replace the Christian's weakness with the needed power. "Paul has no sympathy with a cold and dead orthodoxy of formalism that knows nothing of struggling and growth. He exhorts as if he were an Arminian in addressing men. He prays as if he were a Calvinist in addressing God, and feels no inconsistency in the two attitudes. Paul makes no attempt to reconcile divine sovereignty and human free agency, but boldly proclaims both" (A. T. Robertson, *Word Pictures in the New Testament*, Vol. IV, p. 446). **Of his good pleasure.** For the sake of His good pleasure—His sovereign and gracious purpose.

14 Do all things without murmurings and disputings:

14. Do all things without murmurings. Keep on doing all things apart from murmuring. Murmurings mean to mutter, to murmur, an expression of secret and solemn discontent. This word (Gr *gongysmos*) appears many times in the LXX (Septuagint) of the children of Israel in the wilderness and refers to their stubborn spirit. **And disputings.** Disputings refer to the thinking of a man deliberately with himself, rationalizing and calculating. This word is translated "imagination" in Romans 1:21. It has two distinct meanings: (1) inward questionings; and (2) outward disputings or discussions. Used here in the first sense it implies a doubtful spirit. We get our word dialogue from this word. The Christian is called to unquestioned submission to God's will.

15 That ye may be blameless and harmless, the sons of God, without rebuke, in the midst of a crooked and perverse nation, among whom ye shine as lights in the world;

15. That ye may be blameless and harmless. That ye may become blameless, faultless, without defect, deserving no censure. This refers to outward conduct, and presents the idea of a person in whom no grace is defective. It is that moral integrity as expressing itself outwardly. The word harmless means sincere, unmixed, pure, unadulterated. It refers to the inward, intrinsic character. This word is used of unalloyed metal. It describes the saint with not one thing in his heart or motives which ought not to be there. **The sons of God.** Better, the children of God. This stresses the dignity and character of the relationship. Children of God are expected to resemble their Father. **Without rebuke.** Better, without blemish. **In the midst of a crooked and perverse nation.** Crooked means forward, perverse, wicked (in the sense of departing from the truth). This describes the outward perverted conduct of their generation, crooked in mind, heart, and action, bent in all directions. The word **perverse** (Gr *diastrephō*) is a perfect passive participle and can be translated having been turned out of the way. The Greek perfect tense expresses the existence of a completed action. The word means to warp, twist, corrupt, distort, pervert, turn out of the way.

Among whom ye shine. Among whom ye are appearing. This refers not to the act of shining, but to the fact of appearing, being recognized as God's children. **As lights in the world.** As luminaries. Christ is the light of the world (Jn 8:12) and His followers are luminaries (Mt 5:14-16; Eph 5:8), light-bearers, reflecting His light (II Cor 4:6). The picture is that of a procession at night, in a crooked and distorted age, in which torchbearers are going and holding high the blazing torches, so that those following can see how to walk in this sin-darkened world.

16 Holding forth the word of life; that I may rejoice in the day of Christ, that I have not run in vain, neither laboured in vain.

16. Holding forth the word of life. The world does not have this Word of Life. Apart from the Word of God, all are spiritually dead (Jn 6:63; I Pet 1:23). There is a connection between life and light. Christ is both the light (Jn 8:16) and the life (Jn 14:6). Christians are to be continually holding forth the Word of Life; they are to offer God's salvation to a lost and dying world. This explains how the saints at Philippi are luminaries. **That I may rejoice in the day of Christ.** That I may have cause of glorying or a ground of boasting and exultation. **That I have not run in vain, neither labored in vain.** The word run means to progress freely and advance rapidly. The idea is to spend one's strength in performing or attaining something. The word labored means toil with wearisome effort. It refers to laboring to the point of exhaustion. Paul did not want his life to be without fruit or an empty failure.

17 Yea, and if I be offered upon the sacrifice and service of your faith, I joy, and rejoice with you all.

17. Yea, and if I be offered. But even if I am being poured out as a libation. In the passive, this word (Gr *spendō*) means to be in the act of being sacrificed. "The Philippians are the priests; their faith (or their good works springing from their faith) is a sacrifice: St. Paul's life-blood the accompanying libation" (J. B. Lightfoot, *St. Paul's Epistle to the Philippians*, p. 119). **And service of your faith.** Ministration of your faith. This word (Gr *leitourgia*) is used of a priest's ministration of a sacrifice. **I joy, and rejoice with you all.** I am going on rejoicing together with you all.

18 For the same cause also do ye joy, and rejoice with me.

18. For the same cause also do ye joy, and rejoice with me. Keep on rejoicing together with me.

D. Example of Timothy. 2:19-24.

19 But I trust in the Lord Jesus to send Ti-mo'the-us shortly unto you, that I also may be of good comfort, when I know your state.

19. But I trust in the Lord Jesus. Paul was hoping to send Timothy, and his hope is founded on faith in the Lord Jesus Christ, and all of his plans and purposes center in Christ. **To send Timothy shortly unto you.** Paul was hoping to send Timothy to be a channel of blessing for the personal benefit of the Philippians, and to learn firsthand just how they were getting along. **That I also may be of good comfort, when I know your state.** Paul is facing possible death and yet he is more concerned over the affairs of the Philippian saints than over his own affairs. He longs for news from his Christian friends which will encourage him.

20 For I have no man likeminded, who will naturally care for your state.

20. For I have no man likeminded. Not even one was available at this time. There were some of Paul's fellow workers who were not with him in Rome. The word likeminded means equal in soul. Timothy's pastoral concern (shepherd-heart) was a gift from the Holy Spirit, and no one with Paul was so competent or so willing to serve Christ and His church. **Who will naturally care for your state.** Or who genuinely will care for your state. The word care for (Gr *merimnaō*) means to be anxious, solicitous, be troubled with care, extend careful thought, feel an interest in, concern one's self, seek to promote someone's interest. Timothy was spiritually qualified to promote the interest of Christ and His church and is an example for all Christians.

21 For all seek their own, not the things which are Jesus Christ's.

21. For all seek their own. They are constantly seeking after their own affairs. All without exception were striving after, looking for, and searching for their own things. Paul does not say they are not saved, but they are not so self-sacrificing as

Timothy. Some will help only when Christ's gain is compatible with their own. So few have a genuine dedication to Christ and an unselfish devotion to His church. **Not the things which are Jesus Christ's.** It is possible to be an admired and eloquent speaker and yet be a self-seeker, using God's gifts for personal aggrandizement, and not sincerely. These were not pursuing Christ's interest and glory, but allowing their own interests to interfere. Therefore the Philippians should appreciate Timothy all the more.

22 But ye know the proof of him, that, as a son with the father, he hath served with me in the gospel.

22. But ye know the proof of him. The proven worth, that by which something is tried or proved, a specimen of tried worth. It refers to that which has met the test and has been approved, the sterling life, love, and loyalty of Timothy. **That as a son with the father.** This refers to the personal relationship, the reciprocal affection, and the closest companionship between Paul and Timothy. **He hath served with me in the gospel.** Better, he has discharged the duties of a slave.

23 Him therefore I hope to send presently, so soon as I shall see how it will go with me.

23. Him therefore I hope to send presently, so soon as I shall see how it will go with me. As soon as Paul gets a clear view of his own circumstances relative to his trial, he plans to send Timothy.

24 But I trust in the Lord that I also myself shall come shortly.

24. But I trust in the Lord. I have been persuaded. Paul reached this settled conviction through communion with Christ. Paul's confidence and hope are in Christ. **That I also myself shall come shortly.** Paul was confident that he also would soon come to Philippi.

E. Example of Epaphroditus. 2:25-30.

25 Yet I supposed it necessary to send to you E-păph-ro-dī′tus, my brother, and companion in labour, and fellowsoldier, but your messenger, and he that ministered to my wants.

25. Yet I supposed it necessary to send to you Epaphroditus. Suppose (Gr *hēgeomai*) means to consider, regard, think. This is a word that refers to the decision made after weighing all the facts. **My brother** speaks of common origin and parenthood. **And companion in labor.** Fellow worker, cooperator. **And fellow soldier.** Paul emphasized Christian brotherhood and regards the Christian life as that of a soldier of Jesus Christ (II Tim 2:3-4). **But your messenger, and he that ministered to my wants.** Your apostle and your minister. The word apostle has a dignified tone. Epaphroditus was sent on a mission with a specific commission to minister to Paul's needs on behalf of the church. The word minister means a servant, one who ministers, acts as an official, public servant, or engages in a priestly service. Epaphroditus was duly commissioned and officially appointed by the church.

26 For he longed after you all, and was full of heaviness, because that ye had heard that he had been sick.

26. For he longed after you all, and was full of heaviness. Because he was desiring earnestly to see you all and being depressed. The word translated **full of heaviness** (Gr *adēmoneō*) means to be depressed or rejected, be troubled, distressed, full of anguish or sorrow. This word is used of Jesus in the Garden of Gethsemane (Mt 26:37; Mk 14:33). The word does not refer to homesickness, but to the discomfort and distress of not being at home. Epaphroditus was aggravated and full of heaviness because the Philippians heard that he fell sick. **Because that ye had heard that he had been sick.** Epaphroditus became ill, but he did not quit working.

27 For indeed he was sick nigh unto death: but God had mercy on him; and not on him only, but on me also, lest I should have sorrow upon sorrow.

27. For indeed he was sick nigh unto death. His illness nearly proved fatal. **But God had mercy on him.** God had compassion and intervened and granted recovery no doubt in answer to prayer. **And not on him only, but on me also, lest I should have sorrow upon sorrow.** The word **sorrow** (Gr *lypē*) means pain, distress, grief, afflictions. The heaping up of one thing upon another, with the idea of accumulation. This would have been true if to Paul's bonds and trials had been added the death of his friend and benefactor.

28 I sent him therefore the more carefully, that, when ye see him again, ye

28. I sent him therefore the more carefully. Or the more earnestly, diligently, hastily. Sooner than might otherwise have been expected. **That, when ye see him again, ye may rejoice.**

may rejoice, and that I may be the less sorrowful.

29 Receive him therefore in the Lord with all gladness; and hold such in reputation:

30 Because for the work of Christ he was nigh unto death, not regarding his life, to supply your lack of service toward me.

CHAPTER 3

FINALLY, my brethren, rejoice in the Lord. To write the same things to you, to me indeed *is* not grievous, but for you *it is* safe.

2 Beware of dogs, beware of evil workers, beware of the concision.

3 For we are the circumcision, which

That ye may recover your cheerfulness, which had been marred by the news of Epaphroditus' illness. **That I may be the less sorrowful.** More free from sorrow. Paul would be more relieved than he would otherwise be. He would have one burden lifted from his heart. If the Philippians have the joy of seeing Epaphroditus again, Paul's own troubles will be lessened, but his prior sorrow (prison, trial) will remain for the present.

29. Receive him therefore in the Lord with all gladness. Receive him to yourselves. **And hold such in reputation.** Keep on holding him in high honor.

30. Because for the work of Christ he was nigh unto death. He drew near, approached death. This means that Epaphroditus was at the point of death. **Not regarding his life.** Having thrown by the side his life. This (Gr *paraboleuomai*) is a gambling term and was used when a person placed all his money on one throw of the dice. Epaphroditus threw down a stake and gambled his life recklessly in the service of Christ and in his devotion to the Apostle Paul. **To supply your lack of service toward me.** That he might fill up to the full the deficiency of your sacred ministration to me. The Philippians were unavoidably absent, so Epaphroditus, as their personal representative, did what they would have done if they had been with Paul. There is no reproach. They lacked the opportunity, not the will. All that was wanting was their ministration in person, which distance prevented them from rendering.

III. REJOICING IN CHRIST AS THE PRIZE OF LIFE. 3:1-21.

A. True Goal of Life. 3:1.

3:1. Finally. Literally, for the rest. **My brethren, rejoice in the Lord.** Keep on constantly rejoicing in the Lord. Paul exhorts them to be joyful Christians. Rejoicing in the Lord is much more than rejoicing in His grace and in His gifts, much more than rejoicing in our salvation and in our service. **To write the same things to you.** To go on writing the same counsel. **To me indeed is not grievous.** Not irksome, not troublesome. It was not wearisome for Paul to repeat his warnings of lurking dangers. **But for you it is safe.** It means your safety.

B. False Goal of Legalism. 3:2-14.

2. Beware. Keep a watchful eye always, constantly look out for. **Dogs** (Gr *kuōn*). The word used here is not that of a household pet (Mt 15:26), but the prowling wild dogs, without a home and without an owner. They were scavengers which ate garbage; they were vicious, attacking every passerby; they were unclean, mangy, flea-ridden dogs. Paul is referring to the false teachers who boasted in their religion, trusted in human attainment rather than divine atonement, trusted in the works of man rather than in the grace of God. They perverted the gospel and substituted something else for the blood of Christ. These false teachers dogged Paul's footsteps, snapping and snarling, biting and barking. **Beware of evil workers.** Deceitful workers (II Cor 11:13). They were mischief-makers who disturbed both the faith and the peace of believers. They were wolves in sheep's clothing, deceiving, deluding, and destroying the flock. **Beware of the concision.** Beware of the mutilation (Gr *katatomē*) in contrast to circumcision (Gr *peritomē*). Paul refers to those who are not of the true circumcision (Rom 2:28-29; Col 2:11; Eph 2:11) as merely mutilated. Circumcision has no spiritual value in itself. There were those who followed the law, but had no heart for God. They substituted circumcision for the new birth, and rested in the rite without the reality, and trusted in the sign without having the substance. Thus Paul gives a warning against false teachers.

3. For we are the circumcision. Paul presents the true posi-

worship God in the spirit, and rejoice in Christ Jesus, and have no confidence in the flesh.

4 Though I might also have confidence in the flesh. If any other man thinketh that he hath whereof he might trust in the flesh, I more:

5 Circumcised the eighth day, of the stock of Israel, of the tribe of Benjamin, an Hebrew of the Hebrews; as touching the law, a Pharisee;

6 Concerning zeal, persecuting the church; touching the righteousness which is in the law, blameless.

7 But what things were gain to me, those I counted loss for Christ.

8 Yea doubtless, and I count all things but loss for the excellency of the knowledge of Christ Jesus my Lord: for whom I have suffered the loss of all

tion of the Christian. We who believe in Christ have the true spiritual circumcision of the heart. True circumcision is spiritual, not physical; inward, not outward; reality, not a rite. **Which worship God in the spirit.** Worship by, or render sacred service by, the Holy Spirit. Christians practice priestly service in a spiritual ministry. Their service is inspired by the Holy Spirit, guided by the Holy Spirit, and supported by the Holy Spirit. Sacred service is of the heart, not by ordinances and traditions. **And rejoice in Christ Jesus.** Better, glory or exalt in Christ Jesus, not in external ceremonies or legal observances. Let him that glorieth, glory in the Lord (I Cor 1:31). **And have no confidence in the flesh.** Have no settled persuasion in trusting in the flesh or of relying upon external ceremonies. We have not placed confidence in anything of a fleshly nature. Christians expect nothing from the flesh. The flesh is always flesh; it is always corrupt; it is never improved; it is never changed. One may educate it, or reform it, or give it religion, but it is still flesh. "They that are in the flesh cannot please God" (Rom 8:8).

4. Though I might also have confidence in the flesh. Paul now presents his pedigree. **If any other man thinketh that he hath whereof he might trust in the flesh, I more.** Paul claims to have more ground for boasting than anyone else.

5. Circumcised the eighth day. Ishmaelites were circumcised in the thirteenth year, proselytes from Gentiles in mature age, but Jews on the eighth day (Lev 12:3). **Of the stock of Israel.** Paul was not a proselyte; he was not grafted into the covenant race. Paul's parents were Jews. **Of the tribe of Benjamin.** Not one of the so-called lost tribes, but the tribe that gave Israel their first king, and the tribe that remained true to the Davidic throne when other tribes rebelled. **A Hebrew of the Hebrews.** A full-blooded Jew of Hebrew parents, who retained Hebrew customs and characteristics, as distinct from the Hellenistic Jews (Acts 6:1). Paul was educated at the feet of Gamaliel in Jerusalem and was proficient in the Hebrew language and the Hebrew Scriptures. **As touching the law, a Pharisee.** In distinction from the Sadducees. Paul was of the straightest and strictest sect.

6. Concerning zeal, persecuting the church. Paul was a zealot of Judaism and against Christianity. He was the ringleader from the death of Stephen until his own conversion (Acts 8:1-9:9). Paul was a conscientious, relentless, persistent persecutor of the Christians. **Touching the righteousness which is in the law, blameless.** Paul observed the fine points of the law. He was blameless, faultless, and beyond reproach. He knew and practiced the rules of the rabbi. He scored one hundred percent in Judaism.

7. But what things were gain to me. Gains (plural), assets, profits, anything that would be an advantage. Paul had natural pride in his Jewish attainment. But all these assets did not save him, justify him, give him peace, nor bring him into fellowship with God. **Those I counted loss for Christ.** All those things were on the wrong side of the ledger. They were as worthless stock, and Paul renounced and relinquished them all for Christ. Paul did not exchange one religion for another; he did not exchange one creed for another; he did not exchange one system of rites for another. The word counted (Gr *hēgeomai*) is in the perfect tense and means that Paul had counted, and at the moment of writing, he still counted all things lost for Christ, not for Christianity, but for Christ crucified, buried, risen, and glorified. Christ alone meets the needs of a soul; Christ alone meets the demands of God's righteous judgment. Paul had no reserve, no retreat, no regrets.

8. Yea doubtless, and I count all things but loss. The word count here is in the present tense. Paul says I am still counting all things but loss. **For the excellency of the knowledge of Christ Jesus my Lord.** Literally, the surpassing superiority of

things, and do count them *but* dung,
that I may win Christ.

9 And be found in him, not having
mine own righteousness, which is of
the law, but that which is through the
faith of Christ, the righteousness which
is of God by faith:

10 That I may know him, and the power of his resurrection, and the fellowship of his sufferings, being made conformable unto his death;

11 If by any means I might attain
unto the resurrection of the dead.

12 Not as though I had already attained, either were already perfect: but
I follow after, if that I may apprehend
that for which also I am apprehended
of Christ Jesus.

13 Brethren, I count not myself to
have apprehended: but *this* one thing *I
do*, forgetting those things which are
behind, and reaching forth unto those
things which are before,

14 I press toward the mark for the
prize of the high calling of God in
Christ Jesus.

the personal experiential knowledge of Christ, the personal relationship with Him. Excellency is the priceless privilege and the
exceeding value of knowing Christ. **For whom I suffered the
loss of all things.** Paul was willing to count everything else as a
liability and as a disadvantage. **And do count them but dung.**
Refuse of any kind, useless, worthless, and harmful. **That I may
win Christ.** Better, gain Christ. Christ is the only item on the
credit side of Paul's ledger.

9. And be found in him. Discovered to be united to Him and
in union with Him. Such union with Christ is real, vital, and
fruit-bearing. One is either in Christ or out of Christ. The first
question God ever asked man was, "Adam, where art thou?"
Not having mine own righteousness, which is of the law. A
righteousness of mine own, by works, by strict observance of the
law, a righteousness that is self-achieved by a series of "do's"
and "don't's." Such self-righteousness is worthless. It is the
opposite of the righteousness which is of God by faith. This
righteousness is derived from God, obtained by faith, and is of
infinite value.

10. That I may know him. Not speculate about Him, but
know Him. Paul desires a fuller and a richer experience in the
knowledge of Christ. Everything else fades into worthlessness
before this knowledge which makes Christ Jesus one's Lord.
And the power of his resurrection. That power exercised when
God raised Christ from the dead. Such power is available (Eph
1:19-20) and imparted by the indwelling, risen Christ. **And the
fellowship of his sufferings.** Or the joint-partnership in His
sufferings. **Being made conformable unto his death.** Christians
are to live as those who died with Christ (Rom 6:6-8) and who
have been raised to a newness of life (Rom 6:4).

11. If by any means I might attain. Not implying uncertainty; there is no doubt about the realization. The only uncertainty is as to how Paul is going to attain unto the resurrection of
the dead: by a martyr's death, by a nonviolent death, or by the
Rapture. Sufferings cannot daunt Paul; death cannot terrorize
him. These are just opportunities for a fuller and a richer
fellowship with Christ.

**12. Not as though I had already attained, either were
already perfect.** Paul disclaims perfection; he had made great
progress in Christlikeness, but the goal is still before him and
not behind him. **But I follow after.** I am pressing on. Paul is
encouraged, not discouraged, as he keeps up the chase in pursuit
of the goal. **If that I may apprehend that for which also I am
apprehended of Christ Jesus.** If I may lay hold of that for which
I was laid hold of by Christ Jesus. Christ laid hold of Paul on the
road to Damascus, and Paul's desire is to lay hold of Christ's
purpose for his life. God desires to reveal His Son in Paul (Gal
1:16). Paul desires a fuller apprehension of Christ, a fuller
appropriation of Christ, and a fuller appreciation of Christ.

13. Brethren, I count not myself to have apprehended. To
have grasped completely. **But this one thing I do.** Paul had a
singleness of purpose. Paul's life was summed up in 1:21 where
he said, "for me to live is Christ." Nothing could distract Paul
and nothing could divert Paul from this one thing. **Forgetting
those things which are behind.** Both his old pre-Christian life
and his previous progress as a Christian. Paul had no time for
the past and scant attention for the present. The future goal
claims all of his attention and all his efforts. It is good to forget
all that hinders and to remember all that helps. **And reaching
forth unto those things which are before.** Paul was stretching
himself out toward the goal, as a runner as he breaks down to the
finish line, straining every nerve and muscle.

14. I press toward the mark. Paul was constantly bearing
down upon the goal. **For the prize of the high calling of God in
Christ Jesus.** Paul found no time to relax; he found someone
worth living for. Everything else was a waste of time and energy.

Note it is the high calling of God or the upward calling. It was a call from heaven and a call to heaven. It was a call to be like Christ and some day to be with Christ. Paul is in hot pursuit of Christlikeness.

C. False Goal of Antinomianism. 3:15-21.

15 Let us therefore, as many as be perfect, be thus minded: and if in any thing ye be otherwise minded, God shall reveal even this unto you.

15. Let us therefore, as many as be perfect, be thus minded. As many as are spiritually mature, full grown. This does not mean sinless perfection. We have not attained perfection. **If in anything ye be otherwise minded.** If ye think that ye are perfect. **God shall reveal even this unto you.** Such cases are turned over to God. There are three stages of perfection: First, there is positional perfection or justification (Heb 10:14; Col 2:10). Secondly, there is progressive perfection, or sanctification (II Cor 7:1; Eph 4:11-12; Gal 3:3). Thirdly, there is ultimate perfection in heaven or glorification (Eph 5:27; I Jn 3:1-2). The Philippians were not all mature; some were satisfied with low attainment and others with a medium attainment. But Paul says God will reveal this to them.

16 Nevertheless, whereto we have already attained, let us walk by the same rule, let us mind the same thing.

16. Nevertheless, whereto we have already attained, let us walk by the same rule. We need to continue in the same straight path in which we have been walking, guided by the same divine truths and the unchanging principles of faith. We need to hold on to what we have and then strive to go higher.

17 Brethren, be followers together of me, and mark them which walk so as ye have us for an ensample.

17. Brethren, be followers together of me. Keep on becoming imitators together of me. Paul is asking them to mimic his good example. Paul lived Christ and Paul preached Christ. It was on this basis that Paul told the Philippians to imitate him (I Cor 11:1). **And mark them which walk so as ye have us for an example.** Observe attentively and follow them as a pattern or model. Paul says keep your eye on your guide.

18 (For many walk, of whom I have told you often, and now tell you even weeping, *that they are* the enemies of the cross of Christ:

18. For many walk, of whom I have told you often, and now tell you even weeping. Paul had warned them repeatedly even weeping in deep emotion as he warned them of the enemy. **That they are the enemies of the cross of Christ.** Paul was not talking about erring Christians, but non-Christians. He referred to the anti-legalists, those who were a law unto themselves. They confessed Christ with their lips, but denied Christ with their lives. They taught and practiced loose living; they confused liberty with license. They taught freedom from sin, but really meant freedom to sin. They were religious and made a pretense of piety, but they denied the cross, loved the world, and lived after the flesh.

19 Whose end *is* destruction, whose God *is their* belly, and *whose* glory *is* in their shame, who mind earthly things.)

19. Whose end is destruction. Paul now gives us a description of the enemies of the cross. Paul states the plain, terrible fact that their end is doom and destruction, eternal ruin from the presence of God (II Thess 1:9). They do not realize that they are on the road to hell. **Whose God is their belly.** They admit of no one higher than themselves, and they worship themselves. They live for self-indulgence, for comfort, and for convenience. **And whose glory is in their shame.** Their glory is their shameless conduct. They boast of liberty, yet are slaves to Satan, sin, and self. **Who mind earthly things.** They are living for this world only. They are completely occupied with the material, not the spiritual; with the earthly, not the heavenly.

20 For our conversation is in heaven; from whence also we look for the Saviour, the Lord Jesus Christ:

20. For our conversation is in heaven. Our citizenship is in heaven. Heaven is the Christian's home; he is only temporarily in this world. The church is really a colony of heaven: our names are enrolled in heaven; we are under heaven's government; we share heaven's glory; we enjoy heaven's honor. Heavenly conduct should mark the Christian. Our allegiance is to Jesus Christ. **From whence also we look for the Saviour, the Lord Jesus Christ.** We wait with eager expectation for the Second Coming of Christ. This is the normal attitude of a citizen of heaven. This expectancy of His coming should spur us on to higher and holier giving and living. The greatest event in a

21 Who shall change our vile body, that it may be fashioned like unto his glorious body, according to the working whereby he is able even to subdue all things unto himself.

CHAPTER 4

THEREFORE, my brethren dearly beloved and longed for, my joy and crown, so stand fast in the Lord, *my* dearly beloved.

2 I beseech Eū-ō′dǐ-as, and beseech Sŷn′tŷ-che, that they be of the same mind in the Lord.

3 And I intreat thee also, true yokefellow, help those women which laboured with me in the gospel, with Clement also, and *with* other my fellowlabourers, whose names *are* in the book of life.

4 Rejoice in the Lord alway: *and* again I say, Rejoice.

colony was the visit of the emperor. Our blessed hope is in the coming of Christ: it is our daily delight; it is our earnest expectation; it is our eager longing. The blessed hope motivates heavenly living (I Jn 3:1-3).

21. Who shall change our vile body. Who shall fashion anew our body of humiliation, the body suited for this world, but not for the next. These earthly bodies are subject to disease, death, and decay. **That it may be fashioned like unto his glorious body.** Conformed to the body of His glory, the body in which He appears in His present glorified state. **According to the working whereby he is able even to subdue all things unto himself.** Better subject, not merely subdue, all things unto Himself.

IV. REJOICING IN CHRIST AS THE POWER OF LIFE. 4:1-23.

A. Steadfastness in Christ. 4:1-3.

4:1. Therefore. For this reason. **My brethren dearly beloved.** This is the same word used when God spoke of Christ at His baptism (Mt 3:17). **And longed for.** These brethren were loved and longed for. Paul had a strong yearning to see them face to face. **My joy and crown.** They were his joy because he had won them to Christ; they will be his crown of reward or wreath of victory at the Second Coming (I Thess 2:19). **So stand fast in the Lord.** Keep on standing firm and hold on to your present possession and your heavenly hopes. They were tempted to defection, and standing firm is difficult when a panic starts.

2. I beseech Euodias, and beseech Syntyche. Euodias means "prosperous journey" and Syntyche means "pleasant acquaintance." These two were women of prominence, leadership, and capability. But they had had a quarrel which is the fruit of the flesh. Paul beseeches or better exhorts or admonishes these two women. He does not use his apostolic authority. Pride, stubbornness, and ambition for prominence usually get in the way of reconciliation. These two women had not been pulling together, and both were equally at fault and were not good examples. **That they be of the same mind in the Lord.** That they agree in the Lord. No doubt they had minds of their own. Paul admonishes them to be of the same mind in the Lord, to think the same thing. Peace and unity must be preserved. It is inconsistent for two Christians to be at variance when they are in Christ; but stubborn pride and selfish ambition get in the way. Christians should be able to resolve their differences, for the scriptural cure is natural, simple, and easy.

3. And I entreat thee also, true yokefellow. It is not known who this peacemaker was. A yokefellow is one who pulls well in double harness. **Help those women which labored with me in the gospel.** Take hold with and lend a helping hand to those women in their efforts to settle their differences and to be reconciled. Paul states that they had labored with him in the gospel. They had earnestly contended in cooperation by the side of Paul. They did not usurp the place of man (I Tim 2:12), but they supplemented Paul's ministry (Tit 2:3-4). Women have access that men do not have, and they have abilities that men do not have, especially in reaching other women and children for Christ. **With Clement also, and with other my fellow-laborers, whose names are in the book of life.** Hence they are real Christians in spite of their bickerings.

B. Rejoicing in Christ's Peace. 4:4-9.

4. Rejoice in the Lord always: and again I say, Rejoice. The Christian is not gloomy, but glorious. The keynote of this book is joy. Paul exhorts them to keep on rejoicing. Paul kept on rejoicing whether he were in prison or in the palace; in prosperity or in adversity; in health or in sickness. Joy is a fruit of the

Spirit and is the result of peace with God (Rom 5:1-2). Joy drives out discord and is contagious. Christians rejoice because they are in living union with Christ.

5 Let your moderation be known unto all men. The Lord *is* at hand.

5. Let your moderation. Your forbearance, considerateness, graciousness, gentleness, sweet reasonableness; overlooking the faults and failures of others. This is the opposite of stubbornness and thoughtlessness. **The Lord is at hand.** Christ may come at any moment (Jas 5:7-9).

6 Be careful for nothing; but in every thing by prayer and supplication with thanksgiving let your requests be made known unto God.

6. Be careful for nothing. Stop being anxious and do not have the habit of worrying. In days of tension and trouble, in days of frustration and failure, instead of worrying, take it to the Lord in prayer. **But in everything by prayer and supplication with thanksgiving let your requests be made known unto God.** Prayer is the essence of worship and devotion. Supplication is entreating, earnest pleading for personal needs. Prayer is a general term; supplication is definite and detailed. Thanksgiving should always accompany a prayer or a petition. Thanksgiving for past blessings is good preparation for successful supplications. Care and prayer are mutually opposed. We should be anxious for nothing, prayerful for everything, and thankful for anything. "Casting all your care upon him; for he careth for you" (I Pet 5:7).

7 And the peace of God, which passeth all understanding, shall keep your hearts and minds through Christ Jesus.

7. And the peace of God. This is more than peace with God (Rom 5:1); it is a peace which God has and which Christ gives (Jn 14:27). The peace of God comes to a child of God who trusts and prays. All Christians have peace with God, and all Christians may have the peace of God, i.e., that inward tranquility of soul grounded in God's presence, God's promise, and God's power. One may have peace with God without having the peace of God. Peace with God is dependent upon faith, and peace of God is dependent upon prayer. Peace with God describes the state between God and the Christian, and the peace of God describes the condition within the Christian. **Which passeth all understanding.** Which surpasses all power of human reason or comprehension (Eph 3:20). The peace of God in the Christian will keep peace in the church. "Thou wilt keep him in perfect peace, whose mind is stayed on thee: because he trusteth in thee" (Isa 26:3). The Christian can put everything into God's hand and let the peace of God rule in his heart (Col 3:15). **Shall keep your hearts and minds through Christ Jesus.** Shall keep safely and continually, garrison, stand guard as an armed sentinel.

8 Finally, brethren, whatsoever things are true, whatsoever things *are* honest, whatsoever things *are* just, whatsoever things *are* pure, whatsoever things *are* lovely, whatsoever things *are* of good report; if *there be* any virtue, and if *there be* any praise, think on these things.

8. Finally. In conclusion. **Whatsoever.** Whatsoever introduced six adjectives picturing old-fashioned Christian ideas. **True.** Resting on reality and aiming at reality. **Honest.** Honorable, dignified, worthy of reverence, the combination of gravity and dignity. **Just.** Righteous relations between man and man, and man and God. **Pure.** Stainless, chaste, unsullied. **Lovely.** Lovable, endearing, amiable, gracious, charming, pleasing, winsome. **Of good report.** Attractive, fair speaking. **If there be any virtue.** Mental, moral, and physical excellence. **If there be any praise.** Anything praiseworthy, deemed worthy of praise. **Think on these things.** Meditate on them with careful reflection, not casually and superficially, but constantly and logically. "For as he thinketh in his heart, so is he" (Prov 23:7). Noble thinking produces noble living; high thinking produces high living; and holy thinking produces holy living. All these noble qualities were exemplified in Christ and are produced by the Holy Spirit.

9 Those things, which ye have both learned, and received, and heard, and seen in me, do: and the God of peace shall be with you.

9. Those things . . . do. Paul was the interpreter of the spiritual life, and his life at Philippi was an illustration of this high and holy thinking. Paul lived what he preached, and he preached by his living. His life spoke more eloquently than his lips. The Philippians can safely follow Paul's example and exhortation. He urges them to keep on doing and practicing those things; converting creed into conduct and profession into performance. **And the God of peace shall be with you.** God will be with you in this turbulent, tempestuous world and bring unity and harmony to you and through you to the church.

C. Rejoicing in Christ's Provisions. 4:10-19.

10. But I rejoice in the Lord greatly. The Philippians had sent a love offering and Paul's cup of joy overflowed. But Paul rejoiced in the Lord, not their gift. **Your care of me hath flourished again.** Literally, you caused your thinking of me to bloom afresh. Their care not only blossomed again, but it bore fruit. **Wherein ye were also careful, but ye lacked opportunity.** Ye were continually taking thought, but, through no fault of your own, you lacked opportunity. Paul traveled far and communication was slow. The Philippians did not lack love, but the opportunity to express it. They had not forgotten Paul; they had not failed Paul.

11. Not that I speak of respect of want. Paul's commendation was not a complaint in disguise; he was not hinting for another gift. Paul does not need gifts to rejoice. Joy is not dependent on outward circumstances, but on the indwelling Christ. Paul's joy bubbles from within, not from without. **For I have learned.** He did not always know this precious truth; he learned it through long, hard experience. **In whatsoever state I am.** In prison and in chains; in want and in hunger. **Therewith to be content.** Self-sufficient, not needing outside help, able to make ends meet. Paul was totally independent of man because he was totally dependent upon God. Paul's satisfaction and sufficiency were in Christ (II Cor 12:9).

12. I know both how to be abased. Humbled, having very little, and running low as a river in a drought, facing poverty. **And I know how to abound.** Overflow in an abundance, having more than enough, facing prosperity. **I am instructed both to be full.** Well-fed with a seven-course dinner. **And to be hungry.** Suffer need. Paul had been in God's school of discipline, and earned his advance degree by taking post-graduate courses in difficulty. Paul was a victor over every circumstance, not a victim to any circumstance. He adjusted well to the will of God.

13. I can do all things through Christ which strengtheneth me. In all things I continue to be strong by the One who infuses the power into me. Paul has such strength as long as Christ keeps pouring the power (Gr *dynamis*) into him. A living Christ on the inside is more than sufficient to endure the circumstances on the outside. What Christ wants Paul to do, Christ enables Paul to do. Where the finger of God points, the hand of God provides the way.

14. Notwithstanding ye have well done. Paul commends the Philippians for their loving care in relieving his sufferings. They had avoided such dangers as: (1) the deceitfulness of riches, which choked the Word; (2) contentment in their own circumstances; (3) carelessness about the needs of others; and (4) unfaithfulness in their obligations in stewardship. **That ye did communicate with my affliction.** They became fellow partakers in common with Paul in the furtherance of the gospel. Paul's needs were real and his appreciation was sincere.

15. In the beginning of the gospel. In the early days of Paul's missionary work he left Philippi. **No church communicated with me.** No other church had partnership with Paul or supported him. Paul depended upon God, and God depended upon faithful stewards. Only the church at Philippi was thoughtful in sharing and generous in giving. **Concerning giving and receiving.** Paul uses bookkeeping terms to express their dealings with him. Paul did not have to keep books with any other church at that time. Later Thessalonica and Berea joined in supporting Paul (II Cor 11:8). Not even Antioch contributed anything other than prayers and good wishes.

10 But I rejoiced in the Lord greatly, that now at the last your care of me hath flourished again; wherein ye were also careful, but ye lacked opportunity.

11 Not that I speak in respect of want: for I have learned, in whatsoever state I am, *therewith* to be content.

12 I know both how to be abased, and I know how to abound: every where and in all things I am instructed both to be full and to be hungry, both to abound and to suffer need.

13 I can do all things through Christ which strengtheneth me.

14 Notwithstanding ye have well done, that ye did communicate with my affliction.

15 Now ye Phi-lip′pi-ans know also, that in the beginning of the gospel, when I departed from Macedonia, no church communicated with me as concerning giving and receiving, but ye only.

16 For even in Thĕs-sa-lo-nī′ca ye sent once and again unto my necessity.

17 Not because I desire a gift: but I desire fruit that may abound to your account.

18 But I have all, and abound: I am full, having received of E-păph-ro-dī′-tus the things *which were sent* from you, an odour of a sweet smell, a sacrifice acceptable, wellpleasing to God.

19 But my God shall supply all your need according to his riches in glory by Christ Jesus.

20 Now unto God and our Father *be* glory for ever and ever. Amen.

21 Salute every saint in Christ Jesus. The brethren which are with me greet you.

22 All the saints salute you, chiefly they that are of Cæsar's household.

23 The grace of our Lord Jesus Christ *be* with you all. Amen.

16. For even in Thessalonica ye sent once and again unto my necessity. Twice while Paul was in Thessalonica the Philippians contributed toward his needs.

17. Not because I desire a gift. This is delicate courtesy; Paul is not seeking another gift. **But I desire fruit that may abound to your account.** The fruit is the returns on their investments. God is a good bookkeeper; He will settle all accounts, and He pays big dividends.

18. But I have all, and abound. More than enough. You have paid me in full. **I am full.** I have been filled and am still full, supplied and satisfied. **Having received of Epaphroditus the things which were sent from you.** The Philippians' stewardship was a barometer of their spiritual condition. One can give without loving, but he cannot love without giving. Love takes the *stew* out of stewardship. The love gift pleased God, relieved Paul, and enriched the Philippians. **An odor of a sweet smell, a sacrifice acceptable, well-pleasing to God.** Their generosity was like a sweet fragrance (cf. Gen 8:20-21; Ex 29:18).

19. But my God shall supply all your need according to his riches in glory by Christ Jesus. The Philippians had met Paul's need of their poverty by Epaphroditus; God will meet their need out of His riches by Christ Jesus. We see first of all in this verse a great need. God promises to meet all of their need, not all of their wishes, wants, or whims. Men have physical needs, mental needs, social needs, economic needs. Men have not only temporal needs, but spiritual and eternal needs. Men need perpetual pardon, perpetual peace, and perpetual power. Secondly, we see in this verse a great helper. Paul says **But my God.** Paul could not repay the Philippians, but God could and would. Paul does not say my God *can* supply all your needs, but my God *shall* supply all your needs. This was Paul's personal testimony and confession of faith. We see next a great Supplier. There is a total supply for a total need. God's supply is infinite, abundant, inexhaustible, limitless, boundless. God many times uses the agencies of men to meet our needs. Next we see great resources. God's riches in glory. Paul says **according to his riches,** not *out of* His riches, not off the top. God's supply is not according to our deserts, but according to His mercy; not out of debt, but out of grace; not according to our emptiness, but according to His fullness; not according to our poverty, but according to His wealth. God has great riches. Lastly, look at the great and glorious channel by Christ Jesus. "For there is one God, and one mediator between God and men, the man Christ Jesus; Who gave himself a ransom for all, to be testified in due time" (I Tim 2:5-6). There is no other Mediator; there is no other channel. With such precious truth before us there can only be concurrence with the past, contentment with the present, and confidence for the future.

D. Benediction. 4:20-23.

20. Now unto God and our Father be glory for ever and ever. Amen. This doxology flows out of the joy of the epistle. For ever and ever means unto the ages of the ages.

21. Salute every saint. No partiality here. **In Christ.** Every saint is in vital union with Christ. **The brethren.** Paul's companions.

22. All the saints salute you. All of God's children join in sending greetings. **Chiefly they that are of Caesar's household.** Not necessarily members of the imperial family, but those connected with the imperial household. Paul had personally won many of them to faith in Christ, and they send greetings.

23. The grace of our Lord Jesus Christ be with you all. Paul closes with this short, simple, sublime benediction, **Amen.**

BIBLIOGRAPHY

Barth, Karl. *The Epistle to the Philippians.* Richmond: John Knox Press, 1962.

Beet, J. A. *A Commentary on St. Paul's Epistles to the Ephesians, Philippians, Colossians, and to Philemon.* London: Hodder & Stoughton, 1890.

*Boice, J. M. *Philippians: An Expositional Commentary.* Grand Rapids: Zondervan, 1971.

Calvin, John. *Commentaries on the Epistles of Paul the Apostle to the Philippians, Colossians, and Thessalonians.* Trans. by John Pringle. Edinburgh: Calvin Translation Society, 1951.

Eadie, John. *Commentary on the Greek Text of the Epistle of Paul to the Philippians.* Grand Rapids: Zondervan, n.d.

Erdman, Charles R. *The Epistle of Paul to the Philippians.* Philadelphia: The Westminster Press, 1932.

*Hendriksen, William. A Commentary on the Epistle to the Philippians. In *New Testament Commentary.* Grand Rapids: Baker, 1962.

Herklots, H. G. G. *The Epistle of St. Paul to the Philippians. A Devotional Commentary.* London: Lutterworth Press, 1946.

Ironside, H. A. *Notes on Philippians.* New York: Loizeaux Brothers, 1922.

Johnstone, R. *Lectures on the Book of Philippians.* Edinburgh: T. & T. Clark, 1875.

Kennedy, H. A. A. The Epistle to the Philippians. In *The Expositor's Greek Testament.* Grand Rapids: Eerdmans, n.d.

Lenski, R. C. H. *The Interpretation of St. Paul's Epistles to the Galatians, to the Ephesians, and to the Philippians.* Columbus, Ohio: The Wartburg Press, 1937.

*Lightfoot, J. B. *Saint Paul's Epistle to the Philippians.* Grand Rapids: Zondervan, 1953.

Martin, Ralph P. The Epistle of Paul to the Philippians. In *Tyndale New Testament Commentaries.* Grand Rapids: Eerdmans, 1959.

Meyer, F. B. *The Epistle to the Philippians.* Grand Rapids: Baker, 1952.

*Moule, H. C. G. *Philippian Studies: Lessons in Faith and Love.* Grand Rapids: Zondervan, n.d.

Plummer, Alfred. *A Commentary on St. Paul's Epistle to the Philippians.* London: Robert Scott, 1919.

*Robertson, A. T. *Paul's Joy in Christ.* New York: Revell, 1917.

Strauss, Lehman. *Devotional Studies in Philippians.* New York: Loizeaux Brothers, 1959.

Tenney, Merrill C. *Philippians: The Gospel at Work.* Grand Rapids: Eerdmans, 1956.

Vincent, M. R. A Critical and Exegetical Commentary on the Epistles to the Philippians and to Philemon. In the *International Critical Commentary.* New York: Scribner's, 1897.

*Wuest, K. S. *Philippians in the Greek New Testament for the English Reader.* Grand Rapids: Eerdmans, 1944.

The Epistle To The
COLOSSIANS

INTRODUCTION

The church of Colossae. Colossae was located in Asia Minor in the Lycus Valley, about one hundred miles east of Ephesus on the main east-west highway. The population was heterogeneous, i.e., native Phrygians, Greek colonists, and Jews. The city was deserted completely about A.D. 700 and today is a place of ruins. The church at Colossae was not mentioned in the book of Acts, and it was not directly founded by the Apostle Paul (2:1). Probably during Paul's stay at Ephesus when "all they which dwelt in Asia heard the word of the Lord Jesus" (Acts 19:23; see also 18:23 and 19:26). Philemon, Aphia, Archippus, Epaphras, and other natives were converted and became effective witnesses in this area (Phm 2, 13, 19, 23; Col 1:6-8; 4:12-13). The membership was composed largely of Gentiles (1:21, 27; 2:13). Its size is not indicated; it attained no prominence in history, and it soon faded from view.

Authorship. The author claims to be Paul (1:1, 23; 4:8), and there is no evidence that anyone else used Paul's name to palm off this powerful polemic.

Date and place of writing. This is one of the Prison Epistles and was written from Rome 61-63 A.D. Tychicus was the bearer of Colossians and Ephesians (Col 4:7-8; Eph 6:21-22).

Occasion of the epistle. Epaphras, who helped evangelize the Lycus Valley, arrived with greetings and with disturbing news from Colossae (1:7-9; 4:12). After Paul's departure from Ephesus, the "grievous wolves" (Acts 20:29 ff.) had entered into the church, playing havoc and leading many away from the truth. The Phrygians had a mystic tendency in their worship of Cybele and were susceptible to incipient Gnosticism, which later developed into strange heresies. This threatening danger was both doctrinal and ethical. There was a false conception of theology characterized by mysticism regarding the person of Christ and the origin and nature of the universe. There was also a false basis of morals characterized by ritualism and formalism. At Colossae there was a strict asceticism, attempting to purify lives by a code of strict prohibitions (2:20-23), and also a wild unrestrained license, antinomianism (3:5-7).

Purpose. Paul writes to express his personal interest in the Colossians and to warn them against reverting to their old vices. He refutes false doctrine and proclaims the truth. He presents a full-length portrait of Christ as supreme, sufficient (2:9-10), Son of Man (humanity), and Son of God (deity).

Relation to the Epistle to the Ephesians. In Ephesians the emphasis is on the dignity of church, which is the body of Christ; in Colossians the emphasis is on the deity of Christ, who is the Head of that body. Ephesians considers the church's oneness with Christ; Colossians considers the church's completeness in Christ. Ephesians speaks of the Christian being in Christ; Colossians speaks of Christ being in the Christian.

OUTLINE

COMMENTARY

I. INTRODUCTION. 1:1-14.

A. Salutation. 1:1-2.

PAUL, an apostle of Jesus Christ by the will of God, and Ti-mō'the-us *our* brother,

1:1. Paul, an apostle. Paul refers to his apostleship because he is unknown to the Colossians. This refers to his authoritative title, signifying equality with the Twelve, because he has seen the risen Christ (I Cor 15:8). It refers to the dignity of his office; he is clothed with authority and endued with power. In his official capacity, he is writing to combat error. **Of Jesus Christ.** Paul is our Lord's ambassador. He bore His commission, and did His work, and sought His acceptance. Paul's life and work were ordered by Christ. **By the will of God.** This speaks of his divine appointment. His appointment was not by the Twelve, by religious leaders, by his family, nor by himself. This is an assertion of his divine authority, a declaration of his independence of all human authority, and he disclaims any individual merit or personal power. **And Timothy our brother.** Timothy was not an apostle; he was a brother. This trusted companion was with Paul in Rome. As an act of courtesy, Paul includes Timothy in the salutation. Timothy was Paul's spiritual son (I Tim 1:2, 18; II Tim 1:2; I Cor 4:17).

2 To the saints and faithful brethren in Christ which are at Co-lŏs'se: Grace *be* unto you, and peace, from God our Father and the Lord Jesus Christ.

2. To the saints (Gr *hagios*). This speaks of their divine relationship. It means "holy ones," born-again believers, not some special group. It also means "separated ones": separated to God, separated by God, and separated from the world. The main idea is not excellence of character, but separation to God, for His purpose and for His service. **And faithful brethren.** Believing brethren. This refers to their human relationship. They were full of faith, trustful, and trustworthy. They were loyal to Christ. Paul refers to them as brethren. There is no spiritual nobility. God has one spiritual family, and all are equal, despite difference of cultural background, social status, or racial origin. **In Christ.** This speaks of the spiritual position of believers in union with Christ. This is a real, mystical union. There is not only filial relation to God, but also brotherly relation to believers. Paul speaks of their faith, fraternity, and fellowship. **Grace.** God's unmerited favor. Grace gives us what we do not deserve; mercy withholds from us what we do deserve. Grace always precedes peace. **And peace.** Peace with God and the peace of God. Peace speaks of the calm tranquility of heart amidst disturbing circumstances. **From God.** The source of grace and peace.

B. Thanksgiving. 1:3-8.

3 We give thanks to God and the Father of our Lord Jesus Christ, praying always for you,

3. We give thanks. Paul begins with thanksgiving because there is much for which to be thankful. Thanksgiving precedes intercession; praise precedes prayer. Paul calls God the Father of our Lord Jesus Christ. **Praying always for you.** Continually, Paul practices what he preached (Eph 6:18).

4 Since we heard of your faith in Christ Jesus, and of the love *which ye have* to all the saints,

4. Since we heard of your faith in Christ Jesus. Having heard, because we heard. There were no secret believers. Paul simply refers to your faith; not your great faith, abounding faith, or extraordinary faith. Their faith was in Christ. They trusted Christ; committed themselves to Christ, and had a vital spiritual connection with Christ. Their faith was Christ-centered; they rested in Christ, and they were anchored in Christ. **And of the love.** Love is a fruit of the Spirit (Gal 5:22; Rom 5:5). Love is the evidence of faith (Jn 13:35; 15:12; Gal 5:6; Jas 2:14-20; I Jn 3:14). Love is the characteristic mark of Christianity; it is not superficial friendliness. **To all the saints.** They were not isolationists; there were no sectarian limitations. They loved everyone of whatever position or disposition. This speaks of the depth of brotherly fellowship and the breadth of brotherly concern.

They were not indifferent to the needs of others, nor disapproving of the deeds of others, nor critical of the motives of others.

5 For the hope which is laid up for you in heaven, whereof ye heard before in the word of the truth of the gospel;

5. For the hope. Because of the hope, not on account of the hope. This states the cause or reason of their love. **Laid up for you in heaven.** Stored up like a treasure, reserved (II Tim 4:8; I Pet 1:3-5). The hope Paul speaks of is still future, and its nature is still unknown, but its possession is absolutely certain. **Whereof ye heard before.** They heard the gospel from Epaphras before Gnosticism crept in. **The word of the truth of the gospel.** Knowledge of this hope came through the Word. Truth is the very essence of the gospel. Paul speaks of faith; the beginning of the Christian life, which lays hold of Christ. Faith rests in the past. Paul speaks of love; love lives in the present and links together faith and hope. Hope looks toward the future and anticipates the crown (I Jn 3:1-3).

6 Which is come unto you, as *it is* in all the world; and bringeth forth fruit, as *it doth* also in you, since the day ye heard *of it*, and knew the grace of God in truth:

6. Which is come unto you. Present with you. **In all the world.** The gospel was spreading all over the Roman Empire. **Bringeth forth fruit.** Is bearing fruit, keeps on bearing fruit. The gospel is dynamic, and this speaks of its inner energy and transforming power. It is folly to look for fruit before there is life. "By their fruits ye shall know them" (Mt 7:20). **Increasing.** Growing and fruit-bearing are simultaneous. There is inward growth and outward expression. The outward extension of the gospel never stops. We read in John 12:24, "Verily, verily, I say unto you, Except a corn of wheat fall into the ground and die, it abideth alone: but if it die, it bringeth forth much fruit." The church must germinate or terminate; it will either evangelize or fossilize. **Since the day ye heard.** This fruit-bearing and growing began and it continues. **Knew the grace of God in truth.** The grace of God was fully apprehended and should have made them immune from Gnosticism.

7 As ye also learned of Ĕp'a-phrăs our dear fellowservant, who is for you a faithful minister of Christ;

7. As ye also learned of Epaphras. Epaphras was their teacher; a native of Colosse; Paul's fellowservant; and a faithful minister of Christ.

8 Who also declared unto us your love in the Spirit.

8. Who also declared. Made manifest. **Your love.** This is the supernatural of John 3:16 and produced by the Holy Spirit.

C. Intercession. 1:9-14.

9 For this cause we also, since the day we heard *it*, do not cease to pray for you, and to desire that ye might be filled with the knowledge of his will in all wisdom and spiritual understanding;

9. For this cause. The reason for Paul's intercession. **Do not cease to pray.** Daily and definitely. **Filled with the knowledge of his will.** This is available to all, not for a privileged few. The thoughts, feelings, and emotions are to be saturated with this knowledge of God's will. The word knowledge here is in contrast with the knowledge of the Gnostics. It is full knowledge, super-knowledge, thorough knowledge gained by experience, and deep accurate comprehension. It is not theoretical, but experimental and practical. Notice it is a knowledge of His will, not of His nature. We are not expected to understand and explain the Trinity, but we are expected to understand His plan and His purpose for our lives. This is the foundation of all Christian character and conduct. The cure for Gnosticism is more knowledge of, and obedience to, God's will. **In all wisdom.** This is practical good sense, the ability to use knowledge. **And spiritual understanding.** This is spiritual insight, correct apprehension, inner perception, and clear discernment.

10 That ye might walk worthy of the Lord unto all pleasing, being fruitful in every good work, and increasing in the knowledge of God;

10. That ye might walk worthy. To the end that ye should walk worthy. This is the aim and the result of knowing God's will. Knowledge is not an end in itself, and is not given to satisfy curiosity. Walk refers to the total conduct and course of life. Right knowledge issues in right conduct; right conduct is never the product of wrong knowledge. God wants His children to walk worthy; to be a credit to Christ, to live in conformity with our union with Christ, and in conformity with His purpose for our lives. Our lives should be Christ-centered (Gal 2:20). **Unto all pleasing.** Not pleasing everybody, but pleasing God in everything, in every way, and all the time. **Being fruitful.** This modifies the word walk. Continually bearing fruit. Christians are to be perennial fruit-bearers. **In every good work.** Fruit of right relationship to Christ. This is an evidence of discipleship (Jn 15:8). **Increasing in the knowledge of God.** This speaks of both the sphere where spiritual growth takes place and also the means of that spiritual growth (II Pet 3:18). A fruit-bearing tree grows; one that does not grow ceases to bear fruit.

11 Strengthened with all might, according to his glorious power, unto all patience and longsuffering with joyfulness;

11. Strengthened with all might. Empowered with all power. We are engaged in a spiritual conflict (Eph 6:10ff.), and we need spiritual power from God. The word strengthened is in the Greek present tense and indicates that God keeps continuously and progressively filling us with dynamic power. **According to his glorious power.** His limitless omnipotence. This strengthening is not proportioned simply to our need, but according to His abundant supply. **Unto all.** The threefold results of such empowerment: not working miracles, not outburst of eloquence, but producing homely virtues. **Patience.** Literally, "remaining under." This is the opposite of cowardice and despondency. It is forbearance, steadfast endurance, fortitude, and the capacity to see things through. It means remaining under difficulties without succumbing to them. **Long-suffering.** This is the opposite of wrath and revenge. It is self-restraint, even-temperedness, holding out long. Long-suffering does not retaliate in spite of injury or insult (cf. Jas 5:7-11). **With joyfulness.** Not with a long face, not with a sickly smile, but with psalms in the night. "The joy of the Lord is your strength" (Neh 8:10).

12 Giving thanks unto the Father, which hath made us meet to be partakers of the inheritance of the saints in light:

12. Giving thanks. Not striving for, not praying for, but giving thanks for three things. **Made us meet.** Made us fit, adequate; not worthy. He qualified us, made us competent and sufficient. This is true of every Christian. There are no degrees of fitness. Fitness depends on privilege and position, not character or experience. The Greek aorist tense points to the instantaneous act of conversion, not a progressive process. It is a present reality. **To be made partakers of the inheritance.** Not purchasers. We have a portion and share of the inheritance as an unearned gift. **In light.** This marks the inheritance as future and as heavenly. Light speaks of the realm where there is no night and no sin.

13 Who hath delivered us from the power of darkness, and hath translated us into the kingdom of his dear Son:

13. Delivered us from the power of darkness. God rescued and liberated us from the power, dominion, authority, and tyranny of darkness. Darkness speaks of a miserable, horrible state of being held captive by Satan. Darkness is a symbol of ignorance, falsehood, and sin. **Translated us.** This is an accomplished fact. God transported, transplanted, and transferred us from the devil's dominion to Christ's control. **Into the kingdom of his dear son.** The Son is the object of the Father's love. Paul rules out the system of aeons which the Gnostics placed above Christ. It is Christ's kingdom in which He is sovereign. God removed us from the realm of darkness and He established us as colonists and as citizens in the realm of light (I Pet 2:9).

14 In whom we have redemption through his blood, *even* **the forgiveness of sins:**

14. In whom we have redemption. This is a present possession. We have redemption because of our vital union with Christ. Redemption means deliverance, ransom, release, emancipation. Redemption speaks of our release on the payment of a ransom (Mk 10:45; Acts 20:28; Gal 3:13; Tit 2:14). **Through his blood.** The best texts do not contain these words; however this truth is taught elsewhere (Eph 1:7; I Pet 1:18; I Jn 1:7). This deliverance is exhibited by **the forgiveness of sins.** This is the logical result of redemption, the real consequences of salvation. Forgiveness is remission, the sending away and removal of our sins (Ps 103:12; Mic 7:18; Isa 43:25; 44:22).

II. PERSONAL: THE CHRIST. 1:15-2:3.

A. The Person of Christ. 1:15-19.

1. His relation to God. 1:15a.

15 Who is the image of the invisible God, the firstborn of every creature:

15a. Who is the image of the invisible God. The image expresses Christ's deity in relation to the Father; it is the very stamp of God as He was before the incarnation (Jn 17:5). The word is not *form* (Phil 2:6), but **image**. This is more than a resemblance, more than a representation. It is a manifestation, a revelation. The "Word" of John 1:1 is a divine person, not a philosophical abstraction. In the incarnation, the invisible God became visible in Christ: deity was clothed with humanity (Mt 17:2), deity under some human limitations. Christ in God: visible, audible, approachable, knowable, and available. All that God is, Christ is.

2. His relation to creation. 1:15b-17.

15b. The first-born of every creature. This expresses Christ's deity and sovereignty in relation to creation. Christ was the first-born, not the first created. First-born signifies priority in time. First, this speaks of His preexistence, what He was from eternity. He was before all creation; not a part of creation, but apart from creation. He is not a creature, but the Creator. Secondly, this speaks of the supremacy of His position. He is the self-existent, acknowledged Head of creation. Thirdly, this also speaks of being recognized as the Messiah (Ps 89:27). So we have here declared the eternity, the sovereignty, and the lordship of Christ.

16 For by him were all things created, that are in heaven, and that are in earth, visible and invisible, whether *they be* thrones, or dominions, or principalities, or powers: all things were created by him, and for him:

16. For by him were all things created. Three prepositions tell the story: (1) *In* Him, sovereign source; (2) *by* Him, divine agent; (3) *unto* Him, for His use and for His glory. The first word **created** (Gr *ktizō*) is in the Greek aorist tense and views creation as a definite, historical act. Creation is a past, perfect work. The second word **created** is in the Greek perfect tense and speaks of the resulting state. Creation stands created, a permanent work. We have a Christo-centric universe, and this is complete denial of the Gnostic philosophy.

17 And he is before all things, and by him all things consist.

17. And he is before all things. Christ existed prior to all creation. He is the great "I am" (Jn 8:58). The Jehovah of the Old Testament is the Jesus of the New Testament. **And by him all things consist.** Through Christ all things hold together, cohere, are sustained, and united. Christ is the personal sustainer and preserver. He maintains harmony and order. All things are created by Him and are controlled by Him. Apart from Christ all things would disintegrate: He holds the stars in their courses, He directs the planets in their orbits, and He controls the laws of the universe. We have a cosmos, not a chaos.

3. His relation to the church. 1:18-19.

18 And he is the head of the body, the church: who is the beginning, the firstborn from the dead; that in all *things* he might have the preeminence.

18. And he is the head of the body, the church. He is emphatic; He alone, and no one else. He directs, controls, guides, and governs the church. The church is His body; He is its source and its life. He unites the members into one organism. The church is a living organism, composed of living members joined together; an organism through which Christ works, carries out His purposes; and an organism in which Christ lives. **Who is the beginning, the first-born from the dead.** The Prince of Life (Acts 3:15). The church is also a family, composed of those who share in His resurrection life. The word **beginning** is used in three senses: (1) prior in time; (2) supremacy in rank; (3) creative initiative. Christ is not the first of a series, but the source. Christ is the source of new creation and the sovereign Head of that new creation. **That in all things he might have the pre-eminence.** He is emphatic; He alone, not angels or men. Christ has unshared supremacy; He has first place; He is in a class by Himself; He is eminent above all others. It is not enough for Christ to be present, nor prominent; He must be pre-eminent.

19 For it pleased *the Father* that in him should all fulness dwell;

19. For it pleased the Father. His good pleasure and purpose. **That in him should all fullness dwell.** Christ is a manifestation of God, the Sovereign Creator, and the Head of the church. The sum total of all the power and attributes are in Christ. The Gnostics distributed the divine powers among various aeons. Paul gathers them all up in Christ. In Christ there is divine perfection: not just a part, nor just almost all, but all divine nature in all its fullness (Eph 1:23; 3:19; 4:13; Col 2:9; 3:11). The word **dwell** indicates permanent residence, not just a temporary visit. Only a divine person could create a world, be the Head of the church, and reconcile a world to God.

B. The Work of Christ. 1:20-23.

20 And, having made peace through the blood of his cross, by him to reconcile all things unto himself; by him, *I say*, whether *they be* things in earth, or things in heaven.

20. And, having made peace through the blood of his cross. This for the special benefit of the Docetic Gnostics, who denied the real humanity of Christ. The blood speaks of Christ's redemptive work and the sacrificial aspect of His death. **By him to reconcile . . . unto himself.** Reconcile (Gr *apokatallassō*) means to change completely (Rom 5:6-10). Christ is the chosen and sufficient agent in reconciliation; nothing else is needed. Divine harmony has been restored; all barriers and obstacles have been removed. God took the initiative. Religion is man seeking God; Christianity is God seeking and saving man (II Cor 5:18-20; Eph 1:10; 2:14-16).

21 And you, that were sometime alienated and enemies in *your* mind by wicked works, yet now hath he reconciled

21. And you . . . alienated . . . enemies. Alienated means that we were estranged from God. Enemies means we were hostile and at war with God (Rom 1:30; 8:7; Eph 2:1-2, 12, 19). **In your mind.** The seat of antagonism was the thoughts, attitude, and disposition of their minds. **By wicked works.** The evidence and manifestation of alienation. This indicates willful opposition and personal animosity.

22 In the body of his flesh through death, to present you holy and unblameable and unreproveable in his sight:

22. In the body of his flesh through death. This emphasizes the reality of His incarnation and humanity. Death speaks of real suffering, not mere appearance. There was an actual atonement; not through His birth, His baptism, His miracles, His teaching; but through His death (Eph 2:15-16; Heb 9:22; 10:19-20). **To present you.** The ultimate purpose of reconciliation (Eph 5:27). **Holy.** The positive side. Christians are consecrated, dedicated, and set apart for God. Christ's righteousness becomes our righteousness. **Unblameable.** This is the negative side. Unblameable is a technical, sacrificial term and means "without flaw, free from defects, without blemish, and stainless in character and conduct." **Unreprovable.** There is no charge and no accusation either here or hereafter. All of this through His precious blood.

23 If ye continue in the faith grounded and settled, and *be* not moved away from the hope of the gospel, which ye have heard, *and* which was preached to every creature which is under heaven; whereof I Paul am made a minister;

23. If ye continue in the faith. Provided that and assuming that there is a continuance in a firm position of faith. The test of reality is steadfastness in faith. There is no doubt insinuated, no threatening danger implied, but a certain necessary condition. Paul is sure that they will continue in the faith. **Grounded.** A firm foundation. The church is built on the rock and there is no shifting (Eph 3:17). **Settled.** Referring to the superstructure or the firm building in a solid fashion. The church is immovably fixed. **And be not moved away.** Not continually shifting away. The church has a stable position and shall never be dislodged. **From the hope of the gospel.** The hope given in the gospel. We read of: the hope of righteousness (Gal 5:5); the hope of His calling (Eph 1:18); the hope of eternal life (Tit 3:7); the living hope (I Pet 1:3-4); and the hope that we have (Heb 6:19). **Whereof I Paul am made a minister.** One who serves.

C. The Servant of Christ. 1:24-2:3.

1. Paul's solemn charge. 1:24-27.

24 Who now rejoice in my sufferings for you, and fill up that which is behind of the afflictions of Christ in my flesh for his body's sake, which is the church:

24. Who now rejoice in my sufferings. Paul was in prison and in chains. **For you.** Not in your place, but in your interest, on your behalf, for your benefit, and for your advantage. Afflictions of Christ. These were sufficient for the finished atonement (Jn 1:29; I Jn 2:1-2). The sufferings of Christ provided the gospel and salvation. The afflictions of Paul proclaimed the gospel, and referred to servants. The afflictions of Paul are identified with the afflictions of Christ but are on a different plane. Paul's afflictions could add nothing to the finished work of Christ. The proclamation of the gospel transforms sinners into saints, and saints into martyrs. **For his body's sake.** Not in the sense of atonement, but the announcing of that atonement (Phil 4:11).

25 Whereof I am made a minister, according to the dispensation of God which is given to me for you, to fulfil the word of God;

25. I am made a minister. Become a servant. Paul's appointment made him a minister of the gospel (Eph 3:7; Col 1:23) a minister of God (II Cor 6:4); a minister of Christ (I Cor 4:1); and a minister of the New Covenant (II Cor 3:6). **Dispensation.** Divine ordering (Gr *oikonomia*), administration, stewardship, trusteeship. This was Paul's high privilege and sacred trust. Paul was a steward in God's economy; a trustee in God's household; and an administrator of God's business. Paul was on business for the King. **Given.** Not usurped. **For you.** For your benefit and for your blessing. **To fulfill the word of God.** God's purpose was Paul's purpose, and God's Word was Paul's message. Therefore Paul's message was pure and uncorrupted by false teaching (Rom 15:19; II Tim 4:2-5).

26 *Even* the mystery which hath been hid from ages and from generations, but now is made manifest to his saints:

26. Even the mystery. Sacred secret. There is no connection here with mystery religions. **Hid.** Unknown in ages past; once concealed, now revealed by the Holy Spirit. **Manifest.** Clear as day. **To his saints.** To all born-again Christians.

27 To whom God would make known what *is* the riches of the glory of this mystery among the Gentiles; which is Christ in you, the hope of glory:

27. To whom. God was pleased to make this mystery known (Eph 1:17-18). God willed this change from hidden mystery to manifestation. **Riches.** Glorious wealth. **Christ in you.** The indwelling Christ (Jn 15:5; Gal 2:20; Eph 3:17). Christ is the answer: not the law, not circumcision, not ceremony, not philosophy, not science, not social reform. **Hope of glory.** Pledge of the future.

2. Paul's loving care. 1:28-2:3.

28 Whom we preach, warning every man, and teaching every man in all wisdom; that we may present every man perfect in Christ Jesus:

28. Whom we preach. Paul did not proclaim precepts, a creed, a code of ethics, rules or regulations, not a plan, not a program, but a Person (II Tim 1:12). **Warning.** Addressing, admonishing the heart; reproving and convincing of error. This refers to conduct and leads to repentance. **Teaching.** Addressing the intellect; informing, and instructing in faith and morals. This refers to doctrine. **May present.** Paul's aim and purpose. **Every man.** This is repeated three times for emphasis. Paul has no narrow exclusiveness such as the Gnostics. **Perfect in Christ Jesus.** Not sinless, but perfect, complete, full-grown, mature.

29 Whereunto I also labour, striving according to his working, which worketh in me mightily.

29. Whereunto. Paul's goal. **I also labor.** Exerting all my strength in weariness and exhaustion. **Striving.** Intense struggling (like an athlete), agonizing in strenuous effort. **His working.** Divine energy and supernatural power in Paul and through Paul. Paul was God's instrument to do God's work, through God's power, and for God's glory.

CHAPTER 2

FOR I would that ye knew what great conflict I have for you, and *for* them at La-od-i-ce'a, and *for* as many as have not seen my face in the flesh;

2:1. Knew. The seriousness of the situation and perils in which Paul stood. Paul desires them to know this so that they will appreciate him, pray for him, and share with him in this great conflict. **Great conflict.** The strain of Paul's soul in his pastoral concern (II Cor 11:28; I Thess 2:2). **For you.** The Colossians, Laodiceans and for others. Paul prayed earnestly for the converts and for the churches.

2 That their hearts might be comforted, being knit together in love, and unto all riches of the full assurance of understanding, to the acknowledgement of the mystery of God, and of the Father, and of Christ;

2. Hearts . . . comforted. Confirmed, strengthened, encouraged. Not consoled, but strengthened; not relief, but reinforcements. They were in danger of being shaken. **Being knit together in love.** A closer unity, a vital helpful relationship, being welded together, a unibody. This will safeguard against the corruption and the disruption of false teaching. **All riches.** Complete abundance of inward wealth. **Full assurance.** Confidence, deep convictions, full knowledge of Christ (I Cor 2:12; Eph 3:17-20). **To the acknowledgement.** Personal knowledge of the sacred secret.

3 In whom are hid all the treasures of wisdom and knowledge.

3. In whom are hid. Don't look anywhere else. **Treasures.** Our thesaurus or storehouse. These treasures are available and accessible to every believer. Paul confronts the Gnostics with the fact that Christ sums up all wisdom and knowledge.

III. POLEMICAL: THE CHURCH. 2:4-3:4.

A. The Position of the Church. 2:4-15.

1. The threatening danger: false philosophy. 2:4-7.

4 And this I say, lest any man should beguile you with enticing words.

4. Beguile. Literally, "reason alongside." This means to elude, deceive by false reasoning, and lead astray (Mt 24:4; Acts 20:30; II Cor 11:13; Eph 4:14; I Jn 4:1). **Enticing words.** Attractive arguments, persuasive rhetoric, plausible speech, fast talk, and a smooth line.

5 For though I be absent in the flesh, yet am I with you in the spirit, joying and beholding your order, and the stedfastness of your faith in Christ.

5. Your order. This is a military term (Gr *taxis*) indicating an orderly array of disciplined soldiers. The Colossians' ranks had not been broken yet; but the Gnostics were attacking, and Paul was concerned for them. **Steadfastness of your faith in Christ.** Another military word (Gr *stereōma*) signifying solidity. With unbroken ranks, every man was in his place, presenting a solid front. This speaks of the unyielding nature of their faith which was firm and true to Christ.

6 As ye have therefore received Christ Jesus the Lord, *so* walk ye in him:

6. As . . . received Christ Jesus the Lord. This refers to a personal appropriation of Christ, not just believing a truth about Him. By using this unique phrase, Paul discharged both barrels at the same time to lay low the two forms of Gnostic heresy about the person of Christ: (1) the recognition of the historical Jesus in His actual humanity (Docetic Gnostics); and (2) the identity of Christ with this historical Jesus (Cerinthian Gnostics). **So walk.** Live accordingly, keep on walking. Our walk must match our talk.

7 Rooted and built up in him, and stablished in the faith, as ye have been taught, abounding therein with thanksgiving.

7. Rooted. Permanently rooted in Christ and firmly anchored in Him. This is what God has done. **Built up.** This is a continual process, being built up constantly like an ever-expanding building. **Stablished in the faith.** This means to make firm or stable. **Abounding.** The natural consequence.

2. The saving doctrine: person and work of Christ. 2:8-15.

8 Beware lest any man spoil you through philosophy and vain deceit, after the tradition of men, after the rudiments of the world, and not after Christ.

8. Beware. Take heed, see to it, be on your guard, keep a watchful eye ever open, be alert to the imminent danger because the enemy is lurking in darkness. **Spoil you.** Carry away captive, carry you off as booty. The picture here is of kidnapping you for the purpose of seducing you from faith in Christ. It is not robbing you of some blessing, but taking you captive; a picture of a long line of prisoners of war, leading them away into slavery. The false teachers were men-stealers, entrapping and dragging men into spiritual slavery. **Through philosophy.** Love of wisdom. Paul does not condemn knowledge and wisdom, but only this false philosophy, knowledge falsely named (I Tim 6:20). **And vain deceit.** An explanation of this philosophy: empty delusions, vain speculations, hollow sham, devoid of truth, high-sounding nonsense. This all amounts to nothing, and cannot meet the needs of the soul. **After the tradition of men.** That which is handed down. Here it refers to foolish theories of the Gnostics. We see here a contrast between human reason and divine revelation (Mk 7:6-9); man's theories versus God's truth; fables versus facts. **After the rudiments of the world.** Anything in a row or series (Gr *stoicheion*) like the letters of the alphabet; elementary, preparatory, and immature. Paul is speaking of the ritualistic and materialistic elements of Gnosticism. This is a contrast between the outward and the material as opposed to the inward and the spiritual. **And not after Christ.** In contradiction to Christ, and to God's Word. Gnosticism stood in the way of Christ, weakened faith in Christ, and took men away from Christ. Such heresy is best met, not by detailed discussion, nor by bitter denunciation, but by the declaration of truth.

9 For in him dwelleth all the fulness of the Godhead bodily.

9. For in him. This is emphatic, and means nowhere else. **Dwelleth.** Permanent residence. **All the fullness of the Godhead.** The godhood. All attributes and the essence of deity are in Christ; not just divinity, but deity; not Godlike, but God; not a nature like God's, but a nature the same as God's. **Bodily.** The incarnation was real. Here our Lord Jesus Christ was one person with two natures: the God-man. Paul disposes of the Docetic theory that Jesus had no human body as well as the Cerinthian separation between the man Jesus and aeon Christ. Paul declares the deity and the humanity of Jesus Christ in corporeal form.

10 And ye are complete in him, which is the head of all principality and power:

10. And ye are complete in him. God did this in connection with Christ. This is both complete and permanent. Having been completely filled in the past, we are in a state of fullness now. All we need is in Christ (I Cor 1:30). We do not need the emptiness of the Gnostics, since we have the fullness of Christ. We seek no other source of grace and truth; we show no allegiance to anyone else; and we submit to no other authority. Christ is the Head; He is the source of life; and He is sovereign over life.

11 In whom also ye are circumcised with the circumcision made without hands, in putting off the body of the sins of the flesh by the circumcision of Christ:

11. Circumcised. This points to conversion (Rom 4:1; 2:28-29; Phil 3:3). The character of this circumcision is spiritual and not physical. It is without hands; inward and not outward. The extent of this circumcision is the whole body, not just one organ. The author of this circumcision is Christ, not Moses. This circumcision that Paul speaks of is not a rite, but a reality. **Putting off the body . . . the flesh.** Stripping and casting aside as a filthy garment. The flesh is removed from the throne, and the Christian is set free from his sinful nature. The evil nature is not eradicated (I Jn 1:8), but its power is broken. Christ is now on the throne; but the flesh lurks about and tries to usurp the throne. Our physical members are to be instruments not of unrighteousness unto sin, but of righteousness unto God (Rom 6:11-14).

12 Buried with him in baptism, wherein also ye are risen with *him* through the faith of the operation of God, who hath raised him from the dead.

12. Buried with him in baptism. Jointly entombed with Christ; sharing in His experience. Baptism is not a magic rite, but an act of obedience in confessing our faith. Baptism symbolizes our experience of death to the old life and resurrection to the new life (Rom 6:3-5). Baptism is an outward expression of an inward experience. **Through the faith.** Without saving faith, baptism is an empty, meaningless ceremony. Through faith we receive Christ (Jn 1:12-13) and experience the new birth.

13 And you, being dead in your sins and the uncircumcision of your flesh, hath he quickened together with him, having forgiven you all trespasses;

13. And you, being dead. Devoid of the life of God, a totally depraved nature (Eph 2:1; 5:6, 11). **Hath he quickened.** Made alive in union with Christ. **Having forgiven you all trespasses.** Graciously pardoning and cancelling the debt (cf. Lk 7:42).

14 Blotting out the handwriting of ordinances that was against us, which was contrary to us, and took it out of the way, nailing it to his cross;

14. Blotting out. Erased, wiped away, obliterated, cancelled the note. This explains the forgiveness. **The handwriting of ordinances.** The handwritten document consisting of ordinances. The bond here is the certification of debt, the instrument of condemnation, the indictment drawn up against a prisoner, and a signed confession of indebtedness. Three expressions describe the law: (1) it is written in ordinances, expressed in decrees and commandments; (2) it was against us, had a valid claim on us; (3) it was contrary to us, because we couldn't meet the claim. Paul states that bond was: (1) blotted out; (2) taken out of the way; (3) and nailed to His cross. This was once-for-all removal (II Cor 5:21; Eph 2:15-16; Gal 3:13). In the East, a bond is cancelled by nailing it to the post. Our bond of guilt was nailed to His cross.

15 *And* having spoiled principalities and powers, he made a shew of them openly, triumphing over them in it.

15. Having spoiled principalities and powers. Stripped off and away from. The principalities and powers are conquered antagonists stripped of their weapons, disarmed (Mt 12:29; Lk 11:21-22; Jn 16:11; Rom 8:37-39; I Cor 15:55-57; Heb 2:4). By His death, Christ conquered His enemies, stripped them of their power, exposed them to public disgrace, held them up in contempt, and led them captives in His triumph.

B. The Responsibility of the Church. 2:16-3:4.

1. Negatively. 2:16-19.

a. There must be no submission to former legalism. 2:16-17.

16 Let no man therefore judge you in meat, or in drink, or in respect of an holyday, or of the new moon, or of the sabbath *days:*

16. Let no man therefore judge you. Sit in judgment, take you to task, deciding for you, criticizing and condemning. Paul is encouraging the Colossians not to be enslaved by legalism, ritualism, rites, and ceremonies.

17 Which are a shadow of things to come; but the body *is* of Christ.

17. Which are a shadow. A shadow is not the real thing. There is a difference between the shadow and the substance. Symbols and types may stimulate thought, may awaken emotions, may convey divine truth, and may even strengthen faith; but beyond this they are meaningless and dangerous, and may replace the Living Christ. Mosaic institutions are of value, setting forth man's need for pardon, purity, and holiness; and setting forth God's provision of a great high priest, an atonement, and fellowship with God. Why look at the shadow when we can look to Christ, the Author and the Finisher of our faith? These ceremonies are shadows, superseded, and should be abandoned. Since Christ has come, we no longer need the symbols (Heb 8:13; 10:1).

b. There must be no subservience to false philosophy. 2:18-19.

18 Let no man beguile you of your reward in a voluntary humility and worshipping of angels, intruding into those things which he hath not seen, vainly puffed up by his fleshly mind,

18. Let no man beguile you of your reward. Rob you of your prize. The word means to act as an umpire, denying your claim, defrauding you, and declaring you as unworthy. **Voluntary humility.** This is self-imposed, mock humility which is expressed in **worshiping of angels. Intruding . . . not seen.** This refers to alleged visions, imagined and invented revelations, and the living in a world of hallucinations. **Vainly puffed up.** Inflated with conceit, senseless pride, like a big bag of wind. **Fleshly mind.** Literally, the mind of the flesh. He is dominated by his unregenerate nature and devoid of spiritual enlightenment.

19 And not holding the Head, from which all the body by joints and bands having nourishment ministered, and knit together, increaseth with the increase of God.

19. And not holding the Head. This one lacks a vital connection with Christ, and has never been a part of the body. **The body.** The figure of the body emphasizes both its unity and its diversity. Christ supplies: (1) nourishment, i.e., life and energy; (2) unity, i.e., knitted together; and (3) growth, i.e., the increase of God.

2. Positively. 2:20-3:4.

a. Dead with Christ, we are free from earthly ordinances. 2:20-23.

20 Wherefore if ye be dead with Christ from the rudiments of the world, why, as though living in the world, are ye subject to ordinances,

20. Wherefore if ye be dead with Christ. Since ye died at the time of your conversion (Rom 6:2-4, 6, 11; 7:4; II Cor 5:15; Gal 6:14). Death means separation: the Colossians were separated from the **rudiments of the world.** This refers to the first principle, the childish lessons, and the ABC's of elementary spiritual instructions. **Subject to ordinances.** Pestered by rules and regulations. These are outward forms: outworn, annulled, and superseded.

21 (Touch not; taste not; handle not;

21. Touch not; taste not; handle not. Specimens of Gnostic rules, of which the Christian stands liberated, but which are still a test of holiness in certain religious groups.

22 Which all are to perish with the using;) after the commandments and doctrines of men?

22. Perish with the using. Destined for corruption in their consumption. **After . . . of men.** Human origin, based on the will and the word of men (Mt 15:8-9).

23 Which things have indeed a shew of wisdom in will worship, and humility, and neglecting of the body; not in any honour to the satisfying of the flesh.

23. A shew of wisdom in will-worship. An appearance, a masquerading. Will-worship is self-imposed worship, prescribed for one's self. **Humility.** Spurious, hypocritical, mock humility. **Neglecting of the body.** Ascetic discipline, severe, harsh, torturing. **Not in any honor.** Not of any value, impotent; not a remedy, it can't deliver. **Satisfying of the flesh.** The indulgence of the flesh.

CHAPTER 3
IF ye then be risen with Christ, seek those things which are above, where Christ sitteth on the right hand of God.

b. Risen with Christ, we are bound to heavenly principles. 3:1-4.

3:1. If ye then be risen with Christ. Since you are jointly raised up and new life has begun. **Seek.** Keep on seeking, an outward active. **Things.** Real, heavenly, spiritual things (II Cor 4:18). **Above.** The upward things (Phil 3:14), treasures of heaven (Mt 6:20). Our Head is there; our home is there. **Where Christ sitteth.** The place of exaltation, power, and authority. Paul gives heavenly motives for earthly duties.

2 Set your affection on things above, not on things on the earth.

2. Set your affection. This is inward active. Keep on thinking about and directing your mind toward heavenly things. We should seek everything in the light of eternity. The Christian must be heavenly-minded, not worrying about earthly things.

3 For ye are dead, and your life is hid with Christ in God.

3. For ye are dead. Literally, you died. **Your life . . . hid.** Permanently hidden. We are locked together with Christ in security, and Satan can't break the lock.

4 When Christ, *who is* our life, shall appear, then shall ye also appear with him in glory.

4. Christ . . . our life, shall appear (Jn 14:6; Phil 1:21; I Jn 5:11-12). **Shall ye also appear.** Be made manifest (I Jn 3:1-3).

IV. PRACTICAL: THE CHRISTIAN. 3:5-4:6.

A. Principles for the Inner Life. 3:5-17.

1. Vices to put off. 3:5-11.

5 Mortify therefore your members which are upon the earth; fornication, uncleanness, inordinate affection, evil concupiscence, and covetousness, which is idolatry:

5. Mortify. Put to death quickly. The flesh must be kept in the place of death; it must be nailed to a cross. **Members.** Not yourselves. **Fornication.** A perilous, prevalent, perverse sin, which is lightly regarded by many and committed without scruples and without shame. It is illicit sexual intercourse between unmarried partners; similar to, but not identical with, adultery (Mt 5:32; 15:19; Mk 7:21). **Uncleanness.** Impurity in thought and speech, dirty mindedness, indecency. **Inordinate affection.** Depraved passion, uncontrolled lust, an evil desire. **Evil concupiscence.** Wicked craving and sensualness beyond natural expression. **Covetousness.** Greedy desire to have more; entire disregard for the right of others. **Which is idolatry.** The worship of false gods, putting things in place of God.

6 For which things' sake the wrath of God cometh on the children of disobedience:

6. For which things' sake. God does not regard sin with indifference. **The wrath of God.** God's vengeance and dreadful judgment. **Cometh.** Denotes certainty and imminence (Jn 3:18, 36). **Children of disobedience.** Unbelievers.

7 In the which ye also walked some time, when ye lived in them.

7. In which ye also walked. These vices characterized their past, pagan, pre-Christian experience. They were addicted to and practiced these vices (Eph 2:2; I Pet 4:3). **Lived in them.** The Greek imperfect tense implies constant conduct, the habit of existence.

8 But now ye also put off all these; anger, wrath, malice, blasphemy, filthy communication out of your mouth.

8. But . . . put off all these. Put aside and rid yourselves completely of all these. **Anger.** Uncontrolled temper, a deep-seated emotion of ill will, a settled feeling of habitual hate, revengeful resentment. **Wrath.** Boiling agitation, fiery outburst of temper, violent fit of rage, passionate outbreak of exasperation. **Malice.** Vicious disposition, depraved spite, willful desire to injure, cruel malignity, which rejoices in evil to others. **Blas-**

9 Lie not one to another, seeing that ye have put off the old man with his deeds;

10 And have put on the new *man*, which is renewed in knowledge after the image of him that created him:

11 Where there is neither Greek nor Jew, circumcision nor uncircumcision, Barbarian, Scӯth'ϊ-an, bond *nor* free: but Christ *is* all, and in all.

12 Put on therefore, as the elect of God, holy and beloved, bowels of mercies, kindness, humbleness of mind, meekness, longsuffering;

13 Forbearing one another, and forgiving one another, if any man have a quarrel against any: even as Christ forgave you, so also *do* ye.

14 And above all these things *put on* charity, which is the bond of perfectness.

15 And let the peace of God rule in

phemy. Slanderous talk, reviling, evil speaking, railing insults, reckless and bitter abuse. **Filthy communication out of your mouth.** Obscene speech, shameful speaking, foul-mouthed abuse, dirty epithets, unclean stories (Eph 4:29; 5:4).

9. Lie not one to another. The Greek present imperative forbids a continuation of action that is going on. Stop lying (Eph 4:25); there is no such thing as "a little white lie." All lies are big and black. **Seeing that ye have put off the old man.** The old man is the old unregenerated nature derived from Adam and received by the first birth. The old man has not been converted, has not been renewed, and has not been improved; he is corrupt, useless, and must be put off. The word **put off** means to strip off and discard like a filthy, worn-out garment, tossed on the rubbish heap.

10. And have put on the new man. Have clothed yourselves with the new man. The new man is the person you are after having been saved. The new man is received from Christ at the time of the second birth, and is the regenerated man, the new nature. **Renewed.** This present passive participle (Gr *anakaineō*) indicates constantly being renewed. This is a continuous process; the new man has not yet matured and is ever in the state of development.

11. Where there is neither Greek nor Jew. In the new man there is an obliteration of distinctions. National privilege has been obliterated; ceremonial standings have been obliterated; cultural standings have been obliterated; and social castes have been obliterated. **Christ is all, and in all.** Christ is absolutely everything.

2. Virtues to put on. 3:12-17.

12. Put on therefore. Clothe yourselves with. This Greek aorist imperative implies a sense of urgency; this command is to be obeyed at once. We now have a characterization of believers: (1) elect of God, i.e., chosen of God; (2) holy, i.e., set apart by God and for God; and (3) beloved, i.e., loved by God. These are the attire of the new man; his spiritual wardrobe of practical righteousness. **Bowels of mercies.** A heart of compassion, mercy in action, and heartfelt sympathy for the less fortunate. **Kindness.** Thoughtfulness of others, unselfishness, sweetness of disposition, gentleness, and graciousness. This is the fruit of the Holy Spirit and refers to the inner attitude. **Humbleness of mind.** This refers to the outward expression of that inner attitude. Humbleness is modesty, it places self last, and regards self as least (Eph 3:8). **Meekness.** Not weakness, but lowliness; delicate consideration for others. It is the opposite of arrogance and self-assertion. Pride has no place in the Christian's life. **Long-suffering.** Patient under provocation. This denotes restraint which enables one to bear injury and insult without resorting to retaliation. It accepts the wrong without complaint. Long-suffering is an attribute of God (Rom 2:4) and a fruit of the Holy Spirit (Gal 5:22).

13. Forbearing one another. Put up with things we dislike and get along with those who disagree. Christians can disagree without being disagreeable. **Forgiving one another.** The word **forgiving** (Gr *charizomai*) is built on the same root as the word grace and means to bestow favor unconditionally. This means that the Christian will always treat the offending party graciously. The Christian not only forgives, he forgets. **Quarrel.** A quarrel is a cause of blame, a ground for complaint. He thinks himself aggrieved.

14. And above all these things. On top of all these things, like an outer garment. **Put on charity.** Love is the basis and cloak of all the graces (I Cor 13:13) **bond.** The bond that binds the others together. **Perfectness.** This means completeness, full grown, mature.

15. Let the peace of God. Better, the peace of Christ. This is

your hearts, to the which also ye are called in one body; and be ye thankful.

16 Let the word of Christ dwell in you richly in all wisdom; teaching and admonishing one another in psalms and hymns and spiritual songs, singing with grace in your hearts to the Lord.

17 And whatsoever ye do in word or deed, do all in the name of the Lord Jesus, giving thanks to God and the Father by him.

18 Wives, submit yourselves unto your own husbands, as it is fit in the Lord.

19 Husbands, love your wives, and be not bitter against them.

20 Children, obey your parents in all things: for this is well pleasing unto the Lord.

21 Fathers, provoke not your children to anger, lest they be discouraged.

22 Servants, obey in all things your masters according to the flesh: not

that heart-peace which Christ demonstrated. It is a tranquility of soul which is not ruffled by adversity nor disturbed by fear. This peace passeth all understanding (Phil 4:7) and is given by Christ (Jn 14:27). **Rule.** Sit as umpire, arbitrate, decide all doubts, settle all questions, and make the final decision. **Hearts.** Thoughts, feelings, desires. **Thankful.** Grateful.

16. Let the word of Christ dwell in you richly in all wisdom. Be at home and dwell permanently (Josh 1:8; Jn 15:7). Let the Word of Christ saturate you and remain in you as a rich treasure.

17. Do all in the name of the Lord Jesus. In all relations of life, act as His representative; obeying His word, trusting in His power, and devoted to His service. We should like Christ-centered lives. All of life must be Christian; belief relates to behavior; creed issues in conduct; and doctrine relates to duty.

B. Precepts for the Outer Life. 3:18-4:6.

1. Relation to the domestic life. 3:18-4:1.

a. Helpmeets and husbands. 3:18-19.

18. Wives, submit. This is an old military figure (Gr *hypotassō*) meaning to line up under (Eph 5:22) or to subject yourselves in a specialized way. There is no hint of inferiority, but a matter of authority and responsibility in the home. Wives are to be in habitual subjection with implicit trust. This is voluntary, not forced on her by a demanding despot. The wife is a helpmeet (a help suitable to the husband), not a slave. The family is held together by authority and obedience. The wife's submission is prompted by the husband's love. **As it is fit in the Lord.** As it should be, becoming, and proper. All of life is to be lived in fellowship with Christ. God is emphasizing responsibilities, not rights (Eph 5:22-24).

19. Husbands, love your wives. Keep on loving your wives. This is more than human affection; it is produced by the Holy Spirit. The dominant trait of the Christian husband is self-devotion, not self-satisfaction (Eph 5:25-28). **Be not bitter against them.** Stop being bitter and do not have the habit of being bitter against them. This sin wrecks many marriages.

b. Families and fathers. 3:20-21.

20. Children, obey your parents in all things. This is an old verb and means to listen under, harken, to hear and heed, to obey. Children are to have the habit of hearing and heeding instructions (Eph 6:1-3). **In all things.** Continual, not just occasional obedience. **This is well-pleasing.** Your commendable Christian duty.

21. Fathers, provoke not. Do not have the habit of exasperating your children. This is an old word (Gr *erethizō*) and means to excite, to nag, to vex, to rouse to resentment (Eph 6:2-4). Fathers exasperate their children by: being inconsiderate, being too demanding, being over-corrective, and being unjust and severe. Parents also provoke their children by continual fault-finding, always frowning, never smiling, and holding other children up as examples. The twig is to be bent with caution, not broken. **Lest they be discouraged.** This negative purpose with the Greek present subjunctive (Gr *athymeo*) implies the forbidding of beginning an act. Discouraged means disheartened, depressed, frustrated. Such children are broken in spirit, give up, and feel it is impossible to please. Could this not be the source of the sorrow of so many runaway children?

c. Servants and the served. 3:22-4:1.

22. Servants, obey in all things your masters. Paul does not denounce slavery nor demand its violent overthrow. The slaves

with eyeservice, as menpleasers; but in singleness of heart, fearing God:

are part of a household, and they are without rights. They are to constantly obey and give service, not demand freedom. **Not with eyeservice as menpleasers.** Working only while being under the watchful eye of an exacting master and for the purpose of making a show or gaining human praise. Menpleasers are those who have no higher motives than to please their human masters and curry their favor. **In singleness of heart.** Literally, without a fold in the heart, under which to hide a false motive. Christians are to have a genuine readiness of heart and undivided purpose, not with pretense or ulterior motive, not half-hearted, but sincere. **Fearing God.** Rather than the masters according to the flesh. The real motive of service is dreading God's displeasure.

23 And whatsoever ye do, do *it* heartily, as to the Lord, and not unto men;

23. Heartily. Literally, out of the soul. Christians are to throw their souls into their work, and labor cheerfully and diligently. **As to the Lord.** This is the real test of Christian service.

24 Knowing that of the Lord ye shall receive the reward of the inheritance: for ye serve the Lord Christ.

24. Knowing . . . inheritance. The heavenly inheritances are full recompense in return for faithful service. **For ye serve the Lord Christ.** Christians are actually employed by Christ. This verb could either be an indicative or an imperative, in which case it would mean, keep on slaving for the Lord.

25 But he that doeth wrong shall receive for the wrong which he hath done: and there is no respect of persons.

25. But he that doeth wrong. Slave or master, God will pay either one. **There is no respect of persons.** Literally, receiving of face, judging on the basis of outward appearance. There is respect of persons with man, but not with God. God does not have a double standard; He weighs the unfaithfulness in servants and the unkindness in masters in the same scale of divine equity and justice. There are no partialities, no favorites, and no exceptions with God (I Pet 1:17).

4:1. Masters, give . . . just and equal. Render on your part that which is right and fair; deal equitably. This would solve a lot of problems between management and labor. **Knowing . . . a Master in heaven.** A reminder that God keeps His eye on the character and the conduct of all men, and that "every one of us shall give account of himself to God" (Rom 14:12).

CHAPTER 4

MASTERS, give unto *your* servants that which is just and equal; knowing that ye also have a Master in heaven.

2. Relation to the world. 4:2-6.

a. Duty of prayer. 4:2-4.

2 Continue in prayer, and watch in the same with thanksgiving;

2. Continue in prayer. This is an appeal to give constant attention to prayer. The Christian should persevere steadfastly in intercession (Eph 6:18; Phil 4:6). **Watch in the same.** Literally, keep awake, give strict attention to and be spiritually alert. You must guard against wandering thoughts, and beware of indifferences (Mt 26:41). **With thanksgiving.** The heart is to be thankful.

3 Withal praying also for us, that God would open unto us a door of utterance, to speak the mystery of Christ, for which I am also in bonds:

3. Withal. At the same time (Eph 6:18-19). **That God would open.** Only God can open (I Cor 16:7-9; Rev 3:7). **A door.** A door for the Word, not the door of the prison. Paul is asking them to pray that he will have the opportunity to proclaim the Word of God (I Cor 16:9; II Cor 2:12). **The mystery of Christ.** As opposed to the senseless mysteries of the Gnostics. **For which I am also in bonds.** Paul is conscious that his chains are the result of preaching Christ. Paul is kept in prison, but yet he has opportunities to witness (Phil 1:12).

4 That I may make it manifest, as I ought to speak.

4. That I may make it manifest. Paul's chief concern is to make the message clear and plain. **As I ought to speak.** As it is my duty; as it is necessary for me to speak (I Cor 2:4; II Cor 2:14, 17).

b. Duty of propriety. 4:5-6.

5 Walk in wisdom toward them that are without, redeeming the time.

5. Walk in wisdom . . . are without. It takes wise walking as well as wise talking to win the lost to Christ. The walk refers to one's behavior. Christians are to conduct themselves wisely, to be prudent in their behavior, and to be discreet in their conduct.

In order to advance the cause of Christ, we must walk consistently and avoid everything that would turn the unsaved off, and do everything that would turn the unsaved on. **Redeeming the time.** Buying up (Gr *exagorazomai*) the opportunity for one's self; making wise and sacred use of every opportunity; using the time to the best possible advantage. There is the price of self-denial and strenuous work to be paid or we will forego the bargain.

6. Let your speech be always with grace. Christ was full of grace and truth (Jn 1:14). Christians are to be gracious, pleasant, attractive, winsome, and courteous. **Seasoned with salt.** Not insipid, not flat, not dull, not tasteless. Christians are to have an edge of liveliness, and to be marked by purity, wholesomeness, and hallowed pungency. **That ye may know . . . answer every man.** In order that we can adapt the message to the situation and speak appropriately to each and every man.

6 Let your speech *be* alway with grace, seasoned with salt, that ye may know how ye ought to answer every man.

V. CONCLUSION. 4:7-18.

7. All my state. My affairs, the things relating to me. **Tychicus.** The bearer of this letter (cf. Eph 6:21).

7 All my state shall Tych'ĭ-cus declare unto you, *who is* a beloved brother, and a faithful minister and fellowservant in the Lord:

8 Whom I have sent unto you for the same purpose, that he might know your estate, and comfort your hearts;

8. Whom I have sent unto you for the same purpose. Paul has a twofold purpose in sending Tychicus. **That he might know your estate.** Better, that ye may know our estate, the things concerning us. **Comfort your hearts.** Give encouragement, rather than consolation.

9 With O-nĕs'ĭ-mus, a faithful and beloved brother, who is *one* of you. They shall make known unto you all things which *are done* here.

9. With Onesimus. The co-bearer of the letter, and Philemon's runaway slave. **Who is one of you.** Now a brother in Christ.

10 Ăr-Ĭs-tär'chus my fellowprisoner saluteth you, and Marcus, sister's son to Barnabas, (touching whom ye received commandments: if he come unto you, receive him;)

10. Aristarchus my fellow prisoner. From Thessalonica, he accompanied Paul to Jerusalem (Acts 19:29; 20:4). Now in Rome with Paul. **Marcus.** John Mark who was once rejected by Paul (Acts 15:36-39) but now commended (II Tim 4:11). He was a nephew or cousin of Barnabas.

11 And Jesus, which is called Justus, who are of the circumcision. These only *are my* fellowworkers unto the kingdom of God, which have been a comfort unto me.

11. And Jesus, which is called Justus. Joshua, a common name. **Who are of the circumcision.** Jewish Christians. **These only.** Not many of Paul's Jewish friends were sympathetic to his mission to the Gentiles. **A comfort.** Our word paregoric comes from this word.

12 Ĕp'a-phrăs, who is *one* of you, a servant of Christ, saluteth you, always labouring fervently for you in prayers, that ye may stand perfect and complete in all the will of God.

12. Epaphras, who is one of you. Probably one of the founders of the church at Colossae. He brought Paul news of the conditions in the church. **Always laboring fervently for you in prayers.** Strenuous intercession, wrestling with God on their behalf. **That ye may stand.** Stand firm, mature in all the will of God.

13 For I bear him record, that he hath a great zeal for you, and them *that are* in La-od-i-ce'a, and them in Hī-e-răp'o-lis.

13. Great zeal for you. Expending painful toil.

14 Luke, the beloved physician, and Demas, greet you.

14. Luke, the beloved physician. Luke, the dear and trusted friend, was now with Paul. **Demas.** In II Timothy 4:10-11, he is mentioned as one who deserted Paul for this present world.

15 Salute the brethren which are in La-od-i-ce'a, and Nўm'phas, and the church which is in his house.

15. Nymphas. This Greek word could either be masculine or feminine, depending on the position of the accent. Then some texts read "his" house and others read "her" house. Scholars are divided as to whether this is a man's name or a woman's name. **The church.** Christians did not have church buildings until the third century.

16 And when this epistle is read among you, cause that it be read also in the church of the Lă-ŏd-i-cē'ans; and that ye likewise read the *epistle* from La-od-i-ce'a

16. And when this epistle is read among you. Read in public to the church. **The epistle from Laodicea.** "The most likely meaning is that the so-called Epistle to the Ephesians was a circular letter to various churches in the province of Asia, one copy going to Laodicea and to be passed on to Colossae as the Colossian letter was to be sent to Laodicea. This was done by

17 And say to Är-chĭp′pus. Take heed to the ministry which thou hast received in the Lord, that thou fulfil it.

copying and keeping the original" (A. T. Robertson, *Word Pictures of the New Testament*, Vol. IV, p. 513).

17. And say to Archippus. He is mentioned in Philemon 2 in such a way as to suggest that he was a member of Philemon's household, probably his son. **Take heed.** Keep an eye on. **Thou hast received in the Lord.** Archippus was called of the Lord, and most probably had some ministerial responsibility in the church at Colossae. **That thou fulfill it.** That you keep on filling to the full, discharge fully. This is a lifetime job. God does not discharge His servants.

18 The salutation by the hand of me Paul. Remember my bonds. Grace *be* with you. Amen.

18. The salutation by the hand of me Paul. Paul adds this salutation in his own handwriting. **Remember my bonds.** The chain probably clanked as Paul penned the salutation. This is an indirect appeal to pray for his release. **Grace be with you. Amen.**

BIBLIOGRAPHY

Abbott, T. K. A Critical and Exegetical Commentary of the Epistles to the Ephesians and to the Colossians. In the *International Critical Commentary*. Edinburgh: T. & T. Clark, n.d.

Barnes, Albert. *Notes on the New Testament, Explanatory and Practical—Ephesians, Philippians and Colossians*. Ed. by Robert Frew. Grand Rapids: Baker, 1950.

*Bruce, F. F. Commentary on the Epistles to the Ephesians and the Colossians. In *The New International Commentary on the New Testament*. Grand Rapids: Eerdmans, 1957.

Calvin, John. *Commentaries on the Epistles to the Philippians, Colossians and Thessalonians*. Trans. and ed. by John Pringle. Grand Rapids: Eerdmans, 1948.

Carson, H. M. The Epistles of Paul to the Colossians and Philemon. In *Tyndale New Testament Commentaries*. Grand Rapids: Eerdmans, 1960.

*Eadie, John. *Commentary on the Epistles of Paul to the Colossians*. Grand Rapids: Zondervan, 1957.

English, E. Schuyler. *Studies in the Epistle to the Colossians*. New York: Our Hope, 1944.

Erdman, Charles R. *The Epistles of Paul to the Colossians and to Philemon*. Philadelphia: The Westminster Press, 1933.

Findlay, G. G. The Epistle of Paul to the Colossians. In *The Pulpit Commentary*. Grand Rapids: Eerdmans, 1950.

*Harrison, Everett F. *Colossians: Christ All-Sufficient*. Chicago: Moody Press, 1971.

*Hendriksen, William. Exposition of Colossians and Philemon. *New Testament Commentary*. Grand Rapids: Baker, 1964.

Ironside, Harry A. *Lectures on the Epistle to the Colossians*. Neptune, N.J.: Loizeaux Brothers, 1955.

Lenski, R. C. H. *The Interpretation of St. Paul's Epistles to the Colossians, to the Thessalonians, to Timothy, to Titus and to Philemon*. Columbus, Ohio: The Wartburg Press, 1937.

*Lightfoot, J. B. *Saint Paul's Epistles to the Colossians and to Philemon*. London: MacMillan, 1927.

Maclaren, Alexander. The Epistles of St. Paul to the Colossians and to Philemon. In *The Expositor's Bible*. Grand Rapids: Eerdmans, 1943.

*McDonald, H. D. *Commentary on Colossians and Philemon*. Waco: Word Books, 1980.

*Moule, H. C. G. The Epistle of Paul the Apostle to the Colossians and to Philemon. In the *Cambridge Bible for Schools and Colleges*. Cambridge: Cambridge University Press, reprinted, 1932.

Nicholson, William R. *Popular Studies in Colossians*. Ed. by James M. Gray. Grand Rapids: Kregel, n.d.

Peake, A. S. The Epistle to the Colossians. In *The Expositor's Greek Testament*. Grand Rapids: Eerdmans, n.d.

Thomas, W. H. Griffith. *Christ Pre-Eminent, Studies in the Epistle to the Colossians*. Chicago: Moody Press, 1923.

Wuest, Kenneth S. Ephesians and Colossians. In *The Greek New Testament for the English Reader*. Grand Rapids: Eerdmans, 1953.

The First Epistle To The
THESSALONIANS

INTRODUCTION

Historical background. Paul was personally acquainted with the city of Thessalonica and its inhabitants since he founded the church there on his second missionary journey. It had been a Roman free city, in fact the capital of the province of Macedonia, before Paul arrived there. It had a strong city government which was accurately described by Luke (Acts 17: 6-7). Thessalonica was also an important city because it was on the Egnatian Way, the main East-West Roman highway.

In the western spread of the gospel, Paul was led by the Spirit all the way. After his first missionary journey with Barnabas, Paul reported his successes as he made his deputation tour of the home churches in Palestine. He began to realize the meaning and power of God's calling him to be the apostle of the Gentiles (Acts 14:27; 15:4). Anxious to return to the work, Paul chose a new companion, Silas, and started out again intending to strengthen the churches and establish new ones (Acts 15:36-41). Very soon, Paul and Silas were joined by Timothy (Acts 16:1-4). It is interesting to note how sensitive to the leading of the Spirit these three missionaries were; in Acts 16:6-9 they followed the Holy Spirit through three changes of course. As they crossed the Galatia-Phrygia border, they intended to go west to Ephesus, the leading city of Asia Minor. They were, however, in some unknown way prevented from doing this, and so followed the Spirit to the north. At the latitude of Mysia, they were again led by the Spirit of the Lord not to go into Bithynia, but instead to turn west once more toward the city of Troas on the Aegean coast. From Troas the Spirit led Paul and the others across the Aegean to Neapolis, Philippi, and then Thessalonica by means of a vision in which Paul saw a man of Macedonia calling for help. This is how the gospel got started on its way westward.

In Europe, Paul and his companions went first to Neapolis, and then founded the Philippian church, and after their miraculous deliverance from the Philippian jail (Acts 16:11-40), went on through Amphipolis and Apollonia to Thessalonica. The Bible mentions that there was a synagogue there (Acts 17:2); this synagogue was the base of operations for Paul's intensive campaign in founding the Thessalonian church (Acts 17:4). "To the Jew first" was Paul's usual method; it was effective here also, but the Jewish believers were far from a majority of those early believers. We also gather from I Thessalonians 1:9, that most of Paul's success was among Gentiles and that the Thessalonian church became a mainly Gentile church. The majority of the Jews at Thessalonica were opposed to Paul from the very beginning and became vehement enemies of the gospel not only there but throughout the area. They even followed Paul to Beroea to incite riots against him. Paul

escaped, in fact, only with his life to go on to Athens where he waited for his companions Timothy and Silas.

It is evident from both Acts and Thessalonians that Silas and Timothy were active fellow workers with Paul throughout the Thessalonian campaign (see the introductory words of each of the Thessalonian epistles). When Paul, throughout these two epistles, reminds the Thessalonians of things which had been taught or spoken among them, he is probably not using the editorial "we" but referring quite literally to the work of his companions as well as to his own personal accomplishments.

It seems unnecessary to make Paul the only one who could preach and teach the message of the Word of God. Furthermore, Timothy could have continued to establish the young church on his return visit as Paul's delegate. Paul's primary ministry in Thessalonica was probably not much more than a month (Acts 17:2). In that time he and his companions worked night and day not only in the gospel but also supporting themselves with their own hands so that no false accusations could be brought against the gospel.

Occasion of the epistle. At any rate, a beginning had been made for the Thessalonian church in the early part of Paul's second missionary journey, and Paul now had occasion in that same journey to write back to this church which he had established. Silas and Timothy had gotten separated from Paul at Beroea. They were to meet Paul in Athens. It was while Paul was waiting at Athens for his companions that he gave his famous Mars Hill sermon and started another church (Acts 17:16-34). Paul used every opportunity to reach the world for Christ. Paul went from Athens to Corinth where he stayed and worked with Priscilla and Aquila (Acts 18:1-4) and where Silas and Timothy also worked (Acts 18:5).

Paul worked for a time in Corinth with the synagogue as his base, but soon made the decision to put all his efforts into working among the Gentiles, where he seemed to be more successful. For a year and a half, Paul taught the Word of God at Corinth. It appears that this long stay provided the opportunity to write the Thessalonian epistles. While he was still in Athens, Paul had sent Timothy to help the rapidly growing Thessalonian church (I Thess 3:1-6). It was evidently in response to Timothy's reports that Paul wrote I Thessalonians.

Date and place of writing. In light of the above discussion, it appears that the city of Corinth is the only acceptable site for the place of writing of I Thessalonians. The subscription in the AV which reads, "The first epistle unto the Thessalonians was written from Athens" is an addition to the text which is not to be accepted in light of the facts.

The date of the epistle is quite easily discerned

from the fact that it was written during Paul's long stay at Corinth on his second missionary journey (see Acts 18:5; I Thess 3:6). This period itself can be dated by the reference to the proconsulate of Gallio which, according to a mutilated fragment discovered at Delphi, dated from the summer of A.D. 52. Paul arrived in Corinth before the proconsulate of Gallio, perhaps a year earlier, and thus the writing of I Thessalonians must have taken place in the summer or fall of A.D. 51.

Purpose. There seem to be multiple purposes for the writing of this epistle. First, Paul wanted to commend the Thessalonians that they had withstood the temptations of the devil (3:6). They were, too, examples to other believers in the area of steadfastness of faith (1:7). In addition, he writes to admonish them to keep themselves from the immoral practices of the heathen (4:1-8). But the most pressing reason for writing was apparently to reveal information to them about the coming of Christ for His church. Thus, he presents the great doctrine of the Rapture of the church in chapter 4. This would correct any erroneous ideas concerning the relation between the resurrection of the dead and the coming of Christ. It was a source of great comfort to the Thessalonians, as it is for us today.

OUTLINE

I. Introduction. 1:1.
II. Personal Relations with the Thessalonians. 1:2-3:13.
    A. Thanksgiving and Praise. 1:2-10.
    B. Defense of Paul's Motives. 2:1-12.
    C. Reception of the Word of God. 2:13-16.
    D. Timothy's Service There. 2:17-3:5.
    E. Response to Timothy's Report. 3:6-13.

III. Practical Exhortations. 4:1-5:28.
    A. Sanctification. 4:1-8.
    B. Love. 4:9-12.
    C. Comfort for the Bereaved. 4:13-18.
    D. Apocalyptic Encouragement. 5:1-11.
    E. Summary Exhortations. 5:12-22.
IV. Conclusion. 5:23-28.

COMMENTARY

I. INTRODUCTION. 1:1.

PAUL, and Sīl-vā'nus, and Tī-mō'the-us, unto the church of the Thĕs-sa-lō'nĭ-anś *which is* in God the Father and *in* the Lord Jesus Christ: Grace *be* unto you, and peace, from God our Father, and the Lord Jesus Christ.

1:1. Paul, and Silvanus, and Timothy. I Thessalonians may well be the earliest written epistle of the New Testament. Paul is writing from Corinth to encourage and strengthen these new Christians (3:1-6). Timothy had just arrived with the news from the Thessalonians of their splendid growth and Paul makes immediate reply (3:6). The salutation here is in form like that of any everyday Greek letter of the Hellenistic world; it includes the names of Paul's fellow ministers, Silvanus (Acts uses the Semitic form of his name, Silas, rather than the Latin form used here) and Timothy, because they were involved like Paul in the preaching at Thessalonica, and because they too have an interest in this letter and its encouragement to the believers.

The letter is addressed to **the church of the Thessalonians which is in God the Father and in the Lord Jesus Christ.** A new entity had come into existence, and the name **church** (Gr *ekklēsia*) is applied to it. The word was common, and originally meant simply an "assembly." Jesus had used the term (Mt 16:18) to refer to the Christian community and from that time on the word began to take on a specialized and exclusive meaning. The special group at Thessalonica to which Paul now wrote were those who had believed in Christ in response to the preaching of the gospel there (Acts 17:2-4). These people were probably immediately baptized like those in Philippi (Acts 16:33-34), and became the nucleus of the Christian community there. The word "church" is used over one hundred times in the New Testament, and nearly always has the same technical meaning as here: a local group of baptized believers in Christ. The church is said to be in God the Father and in the Lord Jesus Christ, which limits the word "church" to its new technical meaning. In the New Testament, the word "church" never refers to a building. The people of Thessalonica believe in God and have committed themselves to Christ as the promised Old Testament Messiah (cf. Acts 17:1-4; II Thess 1:1).

Grace be unto you, and peace. This is the normal greeting in an everyday letter except that it has been adapted for Christian use.

II. PERSONAL RELATIONS WITH THE THESSALONIANS. 1:2-3:13.

A. Thanksgiving and Praise. 1:2-10.

2 We give thanks to God always for you all, making mention of you in our prayers;

2. We give thanks to God always for you. The "we" in these epistles is probably not editorial. Paul and his colleagues in the ministry are honestly thankful for their eager response to the Word of God.

3 Remembering without ceasing your work of faith, and labour of love, and patience of hope in our Lord Jesus Christ, in the sight of God and our Father;

3. The reason for thanksgiving is specifically named: they gave thanks because they remembered the **faith . . . love and . . . hope** of these new Christians. This is Paul's famous trilogy, "Faith, hope, and love live on" (I Cor 13:13)! See also Paul's commendation of the Colossians for the same spiritual qualities (Col 1:4-5), and observe the similar words of the Lord to the pastor of the Ephesian church (Rev 2:2).

It is interesting to note that the word **patience** (Gr *hypmonē*) might be better translated "steadfastness," since it refers to their specific endurance of evil treatment and opposition by the Thessalonian Jews, during which these new Christians had their hopes in the return of Christ and drew their comfort from that alone. The hope of His coming has given strength to endure to Christians of all ages since that time.

4 Knowing, brethren beloved, your election of God.

4. Knowing, brethren beloved, your election of God. A less vague translation here would be, "We know, brethren beloved by God, that He has chosen you." The fact of election cannot be known until after a person has been saved. Paul explains how he was able to recognize it in the Thessalonians: it was their positive response to the gospel (1:5-9).

5 For our gospel came not unto you in word only, but also in power, and in the Holy Ghost, and in much assurance; as ye know what manner of men we were among you for your sake.

5. For our gospel came not unto you in word only. The word **gospel** (Gr *euangelion*) means "good news." This word was adopted as a technical term for the Christian message which is succinctly stated by Paul in I Corinthians 15:1-4 and finds complete expression in the four Gospels. **In word only** refers to the effect of the gospel. It was not mere human words; the words contained a mysterious power, the power of the Holy Spirit to change their lives. Paul describes the power of the message in a similar way when he writes to the Corinthians (I Cor 2:3-4).

6 And ye became followers of us, and of the Lord, having received the word in much affliction, with joy of the Holy Ghost:

6. And ye became followers of us, and of the Lord, having received the word. It was because of their "reception" (Gr *dechomai*) of the Word (which means to receive in a respectful, obedient, and favorable way) that they became **followers.** A more literal translation would be, "You became imitators." The **joy of the Holy Ghost** is to be interpreted as a Greek subjective genitive: it is joy inspired by the Holy Spirit. Receiving the Word is receiving Christ, receiving Christ is receiving the Holy Spirit, and He brings joy and gladness. He inspires confidence and liberty in our lives.

7 So that ye were ensamples to all that believe in Macedonia and A-chã'-ia.

7. The effect of the gospel was so powerful that Thessalonians became examples to the whole province of Macedonia, of which their town was the capital. The word **examples** (Gr *typos*) is singular in the original and refers not to a number of individual examples of Christian living, but rather to the single pattern of response to the Word. It was this willingness to obey the good news and believe in Christ as the Messiah promised in the Old Testament that Paul praised.

8 For from you sounded out the word of the Lord not only in Macedonia and A-chã'ia, but also in every place your faith to God-ward is spread abroad; so that we need not to speak any thing.

8. For from you sounded out the word of the Lord. It should be observed here that the word **sounded out** (Gr *exēcheō*) means to "bounce off" and is the word from which we get the English "echo." The Thessalonians became a sounding-board from which the gospel would echo across the world. Paul states hyperbolically that he hardly needed to preach where people had heard of the faith of the Thessalonians; he had only to ask,

9 For they themselves shew of us what manner of entering in we had unto you, and how ye turned to God from idols to serve the living and true God;

"Have you heard what happened?" The fantastic story of the conversion from idols to God was known everywhere.

9. Ye turned to God from idols to serve the living and true God. The word **turned** (Gr *epistrephō*) corresponds more precisely to our English word "conversion." The Thessalonians were a classic example of Christian conversion. Conversion involves both positive and negative elements; one turns from one thing to something else. Here the positive element is stressed: they turned to God. This was a complete reversal in their religious philosophy. It was not that they "got religion" so much as that they changed religions. They turned from a pagan religion to the Christian God to worship Him through Jesus Christ. Idols were an integral part of life for pagans. I Corinthians 12:2 shows that, whatever the moving force, non-Christians are drawn to idols or false religions. It takes the reality of the true God to draw people away from the power of superstition. In the Christian religion God must be first. The Ten Commandments (Ex 20:1-17) show how that we must worship God alone. It is interesting that the word **serve** (Gr *douleuō*) means literally to be a slave to, and alludes to the Old Testament bondslave who was the personal property of another. So complete is real conversion to Christianity that one is "sold out" completely to God. We belong to Him: it is bondage, but it is a bondage of love. We love Him and want to do only His will. This is, in fact, the very heart of Christianity. God is the living God in contrast to idols which have no life, and the true God in contrast to all the false gods of the pagan world.

10 And to wait for his Son from heaven, whom he raised from the dead, *even* Jesus, which delivered us from the wrath to come.

10. And to wait for his Son from heaven, whom he raised from the dead, even Jesus, which delivered us from the wrath to come. Wait (Gr *anamenō*) means more than just wait; it emphasizes an expectant and active attempt to live for His glory in the meantime. It is an attitude of faith toward the complete fulfillment of the messianic promises of the Old Testament in the second coming of Christ. These last two verses contain the basic tenets of Christianity: conversion, worship of God, hope in the Second Coming, belief in the resurrection of Jesus, complete faith in salvation from the wrath of God which will surely come upon all those who do not accept Christ.

B. Defense of Paul's Motives. 2:1-12.

CHAPTER 2

FOR yourselves, brethren, know our entrance in unto you, that it was not in vain:
2 But even after that we had suffered before, and were shamefully entreated, as ye know, at Phĭ-lip'pī, we were bold in our God to speak unto you the gospel of God with much contention.

2:1-2. For yourselves, brethren, know our entrance in unto you, that it was not in vain. Verses 1-12 imply that there had been slanderous accusations against Paul's work and motives. Part of the purpose of the letter is to show that the allegations were far from the truth. This is important, not just for Paul personally, but for the growth and development of the Thessalonians themselves. If they had begun to believe that Paul's **gospel** was just another philosophical dream, and that Paul was just "in it for the money," they could not have continued to grow in Christ. It was not that Paul's reputation alone was at stake, but that their Christian faith was in danger. Paul's coming to the Thessalonians was not in **vain** (Gr *kenos*). The word denotes what is empty of real meaning and purpose. Paul had come to them because he believed the gospel himself, and truly felt that the people of Thessalonica were eternally lost without that message. The argument is that Paul would have quit at Philippi (vs. 2), and would never have gotten to Thessalonica in the first place, had he been there for the money or for anything less than the call of God. He had no other choice but to go on to Thessalonica, "although" (Greek circumstantial participle of concession) he had already suffered shamefully (Acts 16:20-24), and although he knew that it would happen again (Acts 17:5). Paul and his companions were driven by the purest motives. They were completely committed to their own message and concerned for the welfare of the Thessalonians.

3 For our exhortation *was* not of deceit, nor of uncleanness, nor in guile:
4 But as we were allowed of God to be put in trust with the gospel, even so we speak; not as pleasing men, but God, which trieth our hearts.

5 For neither at any time used we flattering words, as ye know, nor a cloak of covetousness; God *is* witness:
6 Nor of men sought we glory, neither of you, nor *yet* of others, when we might have been burdensome, as the apostles of Christ.

7 But we were gentle among you, even as a nurse cherisheth her children:

8 So being affectionately desirous of you, we were willing to have imparted unto you, not the gospel of God only, but also our own souls, because ye were dear unto us.
9 For ye remember, brethren, our labour and travail: for labouring night and day, because we would not be chargeable unto any of you, we preached unto you the gospel of God.

3-4. For our exhortation was not of deceit, nor of uncleanness, nor in guile. Paul appealed to the impartial judgment of his readers. Could they honestly say that Paul and his companions had ever acted like someone trying to deceive? Had there been any hint of impure motives? Had they not rather spoken like men who had been entrusted with the gospel message? Twice in verse 4 Paul uses the word "approved" (Gr *dokimazō*) by God, which means that God has "checked them out" by His own standards and has put His stamp of approval on them. Paul derived a great deal of personal confidence from the fact that God had "entrusted" (Gr *pisteuō*) him with the gospel (see also I Tim 1:11-12). His goal in life was not to "please" men but God (Gal 1:10). Had he not outwardly seemed true to this inner motivation?

5-6. For neither at any time used we flattering words . . . nor a cloak of covetousness. Paul calls upon God as his witness that none of their activities had been **a cloak of covetousness.** The word **cloak** (Gr *prophasis*) means an "excuse," "cover-up," or "front" for an impure motive of greed. We were not after **glory** (Gr *doxa*) says Paul, using the word from which we get our word "doxology." It is interesting that in John 12:43 this same word is used to condemn the Pharisees who "loved the praise of men more than the praise of God." Paul could have claimed that glory, in fact he had been a Pharisee before his own conversion. Now, he could have claimed similar glory as an **apostle** (Gr *apostolos*). He refers to himself and to his companions as **apostles,** since he considers them to be representatives of Christ with a commission, like his own. This word obviously is not limited in its use in the New Testament to the Twelve. That they **might have been burdensome** should rather be translated, "we might have made great demands." It is an idiom requiring this meaning. Elsewhere (e.g., II Cor 11:9) Paul shows that he believes that ministers of the gospel should be supported financially by the gifts of God's people. The thought of this passage is obvious: they did not even take what they had a right to because they were so motivated to get the gospel out. How could anyone accuse them of impure motives?

7. But we were gentle among you, even as a nurse cherisheth her children. It seems probable, although there is little certainty about the matter, that the text in verse 7 should read, "we came like infants," rather than, "we were gentle among you." If this reading is taken, the meaning would go with the previous verse. Far from coming like authoritative apostles, Paul and the others claimed no more prestige than mere infants. Paul next applies the metaphor of a **nurse** (Gr *trophos*) to himself and his companions. This word comes from a root meaning to "feed," "nourish," "support," and "provide with food." The word can also refer to a "mother," and that translation would probably make better sense here. The word **cherisheth** means to "take warm and tender care of." It is found also in Ephesians 5:29, where a man "takes care of" his own body. The portrait Paul intends to paint in this verse is that of a mother tenderly caring for all the needs of her own children. A few verses later in verse 11 Paul changes the figure to a father, and again it is the father taking care of his own children. It was mother-father love that motivated Paul and his companions, rather than greed as someone must have suggested.

8-9. Also our own souls. According to verse 8, they had made up their minds to share not only the gospel, but also their own lives. In verse 9, Paul asks his readers simply to recall the fact that Paul and his companions worked hard with their own hands to support themselves while they were in Thessalonica in order that they might not be a burden to the people. It was customary in Palestine for rabbis to have a secular trade with which they supported themselves. We learn from Acts 18:3 that Paul's trade was tentmaking. The two words **labor and travail**

are also used in the same context in II Corinthians 11:27 and II Thessalonians 3:8. They denote work which is very tiring and very difficult. Paul did not consider it wrong to receive help from preaching the gospel, in fact he received a gift from the Philippian church while he was at Thessalonica (Phil 4:16). His point here was that he had not made any demands on these people even though he had a right to do so. The word translated **preached** (Gr *kēryssō*) means to "proclaim." Note that in verse 8 the gospel is **imparted**, and in verse 9 it is **preached**. Also note that it is the gospel of God here, meaning that God has given it to Paul to preach.

10 Ye *are* witnesses, and God *also*, how holily and justly and unblameably we behaved ourselves among you that believe:

10. Ye are witnesses, and God also, how holily and justly and unblamably we behaved ourselves among you that believe. Here Paul stresses qualities of conduct which could have been denied by the Thessalonians if they were not true. Their conduct was holy, just, and blameless. It is obvious that these things were true and known by all readers. In this verse the Thessalonians are called "believers" which is synonymous with "Christians" and shows again that the church is made up of believers in Christ.

11 As ye know how we exhorted and comforted and charged every one of you, as a father *doth* his children,

12 That ye would walk worthy of God, who hath called you unto his kingdom and glory.

11-12. Paul again refers to the father figure to sum up and justify their apostolic activities as they founded the church. They **exhorted** (Gr *parakaleō*) the believers, which means literally to "encourage." The noun form of this word is used as a name for the Holy Spirit (Comforter). The second word used here, **comforted** (Gr *paramytheō*) can be used of physical comforting as well as giving mental assurance. We can only guess as to the kind of comfort Paul and his companions may have given, but obviously some kind of consolation was needed in the face of the opposition of these Jews who had almost killed Paul. The third summary word here, **charged** (Gr *martyreō*), means to "witness" or "testify." It is the word from which we get our English word "martyr." The result toward which all this apostolic activity was directed is again stated by Paul, **That ye would walk worthy of God.** All through the New Testament, the Christian life and conduct are referred to as a **walk**. Here also, Paul is referring to proper Christian conduct which, of course, was quite different from the generally accepted conduct of the day.

C. Reception of the Word of God. 2:13-16.

13 For this cause also thank we God without ceasing, because, when ye received the word of God which ye heard of us, ye received *it* not *as* the word of men, but as it is in truth, the word of God, which effectually worketh also in you that believe.

13. For this cause also thank we God without ceasing, because, when ye received the word of God which ye heard of us, ye received it not as the word of men, but as it is in truth, the word of God, which effectually worketh also in you that believe. Verse 13 is a very important verse because of its implications for inspiration and for the Christian attitude toward the Scriptures. There are several distinctions intended by Paul which do not come across in the translations of this verse. The first is the distinction between the words here translated **received**. The first occurrence (Gr *paralambanō*) is a word which means to "take to oneself." In this context it means to listen to and apply the words that were spoken. It could have been used of the teaching of any philosopher of the day. The second occurrence (Gr *dechomai*) is a word which means primarily "to receive" in the sense of receiving a guest, entertaining someone, or welcoming with open arms a true friend; this word involves much more commitment. This is the word that shows the responsive attitude of all true believers for God's Word.

It is also important in this verse to distinguish between the three occurrences of **word** (Gr *logos*). The first occurrence would be literally "word of hearing" and is a technical term for the "preached word" of the prophets and apostles. This same expression translates Isaiah 53:1, "Who hath believed our report?" It is alluded to several times in the New Testament (Jn 12:38; Rom 10:16). Hebrews 4:2 uses this technical term to allude to the promise made to the Israelites that they would enter the Promised Land. Paul also used the term of his own preaching to the Galatians (Gal 3:2, 5). The meaning in Thessalonians is that the people not only listened to and applied the preaching of the apostles, and gladly recognized this message as something more than a merely human message (**word of men**), but welcomed it for what it really was, the **word of God.** This kind of response to the Word of God is characteristic of every true believer. **Effectually worketh** (Gr *energeō*) means simply to be "effective." It is interesting that this same word is found in the same connection in Galatians 3:2, 5 and that it is the Spirit of God in both passages who causes believers to recognize the Word of God. Although Paul does not refer to the written Word of God in I Thessalonians 2:13, the implications are the same, and the oral message was just as inspired and just as authoritative. It was a word spoken by God (Greek subjective genitive) so that this verse is, in effect, parallel to II Timothy 3:16.

14 For ye, brethren, became followers of the churches of God which in Judæa are in Christ Jesus: for ye also have suffered like things of your own countrymen, even as they *have* of the Jews:

14. For ye, brethren, became followers of the churches of God which in Judea are in Christ Jesus. Paul once more refers to the Thessalonians as **followers** or "imitators" (1:6). This is another reference to the persecution which these people suffered when they became Christians, at the hands of their own fellow citizens. Paul himself had been guilty of persecuting Christian churches prior to his conversion. There were already at that early date many churches (plural) in Palestine, and persecution must have been a part of their lives from the very beginning. The persecution in Thessalonica was different only in that it was carried out by Gentiles rather than by Jews.

15 Who both killed the Lord Jesus, and their own prophets, and have persecuted us; and they please not God, and are contrary to all men:

15. Who both killed the Lord Jesus, and their own prophets, and have persecuted us. Paul's sentence structure in the original emphasizes that the one whom they murdered was Jesus the Lord. Jesus Himself had reminded the Pharisees and the leaders of the Jews that prophets and wise men and scribes had been subjected to murder and beating by their ancestors (Mt 23:34). Peter denounced the Jews of Jerusalem for the murder of Jesus, even though His death was a part of the determinate counsel and foreknowledge of God (Acts 2:23). Paul now justly charges the Jews of Thessalonica with their recent persecution of himself.

16 Forbidding us to speak to the Gentiles that they might be saved, to fill up their sins alway: for the wrath is come upon them to the uttermost.

16. Forbidding us to speak to the Gentiles. Not only did the Jews persecute Paul and his companions at Thessalonica, but time after time in his life they have tried to prevent him from preaching to the Gentiles, thus hindering them from being saved. Jesus had strongly condemned those who would hinder people from believing and being saved (Mark 9:42), and Paul now reinforces that condemnation.

D. Timothy's Service There. 2:17-3:5.

17-20. Being taken from you. The word used here (Gr *aporphanizō*) is colorful and intensely passionate. It is related to our word "orphan," and might be translated "since we have been torn apart." It shows the characteristically strong emotional involvement of Paul with his converts everywhere; they were his children, his relatives, his joy and crown. His heart, he said, was still with them even though they had been separated. Paul had also been unable to get back and visit them personally, but in spite of his strong desire Satan somehow blocked his efforts. Paul assures them of his great love for them, and points forward to the hope of the Second Coming (Gr *parousia*). This is the first use of this term in the New Testament, although it was common in the Hellenistic world for the formal visits of royalty. This word became a technical term for the Second Coming of Christ. It is so used eighteen times in the New Testament and seven of these are in the Thessalonian epistles.

17 But we, brethren, being taken from you for a short time in presence, not in heart, endeavoured the more abundantly to see your face with great desire.
18 Wherefore we would have come unto you, even I Paul, once and again; but Satan hindered us.
19 For what *is* our hope, or joy, or crown of rejoicing? *Are* not even ye in the presence of our Lord Jesus Christ at his coming?
20 For ye are our glory and joy.

CHAPTER 3
WHEREFORE when we could no long-

3:1-2. Wherefore when we could no longer forbear, we thought it good to be left at Athens alone. Finally, Paul

er forbear, we thought it good to be left at Athens alone;

2 And sent TÍ-mŏ'the-us, our brother, and minister of God, and our fellow-labourer in the gospel of Christ, to establish you, and to comfort you concerning your faith:

decided to send Timothy to help the Thessalonians while he himself continued the work in Athens. The **we** seems to be editorial here; he probably really intends "I sent" since he speaks of being left **alone**. It is not possible to know the whereabouts of Silas at this time. **Minister of God** is a variant reading which was probably substituted for the more prestigious "God's fellowworker" (Gr *synergos*). Paul had used this term when he wrote to the Corinthians to refer to himself and Apollos as "laborers together with God" (I Cor 3:9), in distinction to the Corinthian believers themselves who were "God's field," or "God's building" in the metaphor.

The reason Paul sends Timothy to the Thessalonians is, first, **to establish** (Gr *stērizō*). The word means "to stabilize," or to support an already existing structure. In the New Testament this word is used in the figurative sense of stabilizing believers. The other reason is to **comfort** (Gr *parakleō*), which should be translated "encourage" rather than **comfort**. It is the word from which we get the name of the Holy Spirit in John, namely "the Comforter." The same word is used of Christ in I John 2:1, where it means a legal advocate. A better translation might be, "to support and help you in your faith."

3 That no man should be moved by these afflictions: for yourselves know that we are appointed thereunto.

4 For verily, when we were with you, we told you before that we should suffer tribulation; even as it came to pass, and ye know.

3-4. That no man should be moved by these afflictions. Paul explains Timothy's mission: **moved** (Gr *sainō*) means usually "wave," "wag the tail." Perhaps here it means "wobble," and thus collapse. This would carry on the figure of Timothy's stabilizing or "buttressing" their faith like a wall. The **afflictions** (Gr *thlipsis*) are those which had just been experienced as reported by Timothy. Paul had warned that they would come.

5 For this cause, when I could no longer forbear, I sent to know your faith, lest by some means the tempter have tempted you, and our labour be in vain.

5. For this cause. Paul again states his reason for sending Timothy: he had to know that the Thessalonians were surviving the temptations of Satan and that Paul's work in Thessalonica had not been in vain.

E. Response to Timothy's Report. 3:6-13.

6 But now when TÍ-mŏ'the-us came from you unto us, and brought us good tidings of your faith and charity, and that ye have good remembrance of us always, desiring greatly to see us, as we also *to see* you:

6. But now when Timothy came from you unto us. The sense of the original here is that Timothy has just now arrived with the news when Paul sat down to write. This clearly shows the occasion and purpose of the letter. When Timothy arrived, his news was good; so good in fact, that **brought us good tidings** is the same word (Gr *euangelizomai*) often translated "preach the gospel." Paul was glad to hear of their faith and love, and the fact that they had wanted to see him just as much as he had wanted to see them.

7 Therefore, brethren, we were comforted over you in all our affliction and distress by your faith:

7. Therefore, brethren, we were comforted (Gr *parakaleō*). This is again the word which means "help" or "encourage." Another translation has, "we have been encouraged about you." The encouragement was badly needed. Paul was himself in **affliction and distress.** Both of these words are strong. The first (Gr *anangkē*) is related to the word from which we get "anxiety," while the second (Gr *thlipsis*) means "rubbing" or "pressure," and is the word often translated in the New Testament "tribulation." The thing that gave Paul the needed encouragement was the faith of these converts.

8 For now we live, if ye stand fast in the Lord.

8. For now we live, if ye stand fast in the Lord. The idea is that we can now carry on, since we know that you are holding your ground in the faith. The word **stand fast** is not the usual word for stand; it meant rather "to take a stand." This gives Paul the courage to go on, now that he knows that he has made some real converts.

9 For what thanks can we render to God again for you, for all the joy wherewith we joy for your sakes before our God;

10 Night and day praying exceeding-

9-10. For what thanks can we render to God again for you . . .? A better translation would be, "for what thanksgiving" (Gr *eucharistia*); it is the word from which we get the English word "eucharist." **Render** (Gr *antapodidōmi*) has the sense of paying back something owed. The meaning is that we as Christ-

ly that we might see your face, and might perfect that which is lacking in your faith?

11 Now God himself and our Father, and our Lord Jesus Christ, direct our way unto you.

12 And the Lord make you to increase and abound in love one toward another, and toward all *men*, even as we *do* toward you:

13 To the end he may stablish your hearts unblameable in holiness before God, even our Father, at the coming of our Lord Jesus Christ with all his saints.

CHAPTER 4

FURTHERMORE then we beseech you, brethren, and exhort *you* by the Lord Jesus, that as ye have received of us how ye ought to walk and to please God, *so* ye would abound more and more.

2 For ye know what commandments we gave you by the Lord Jesus.

3 For this is the will of God, *even* your sanctification, that ye should abstain from fornication:

4 That every one of you should know

ians owe to God joyful thanksgiving and praise for what He has done.

11-12. Now God himself and our Father. Another order is possible: "Now may our God and Father Himself, and our Lord Jesus direct our way to you." The Greek verb is optative (to express a wish), as are the two in verse 12. Paul has a threefold desire, or really a "prayer," since it calls upon God. He asks for himself, that God would direct his path back to the people of Thessalonica. He must, however, leave this desire in the hands of the Heavenly Father. He also asks for them, that the Lord may cause their love to continue to grow beyond all limits both among themselves and toward others outside the church.

13. To the end he may stablish. This is the purpose to which Paul's prayers are directed. **Stablish** (Gr *sterizō*) means to "buttress" or "support" an existing structure; here the personal faith of the Thessalonians is in view. The desire is that they will be strengthened in holiness as they wait for the coming Saviour. **At the coming** (Gr *parousia*), Paul again uses what has become a Christian technical term for the Second Coming. It is qualified here by the words **with all his saints.** The adjective **saints** (Gr *hagios*) is used here in the masculine plural, and may refer to holy persons, namely believers (Eph 1:1), or to holy beings like angels (Mk 8:38). It is possible that both are in view.

III. PRACTICAL EXHORTATIONS. 4:1-5:28.

A. Sanctification. 4:1-8.

4:1. Furthermore then we beseech you, brethren. Vss. 1-12 comprise a key section in the book, perhaps the main point of the letter. The word **furthermore** (Gr *loipos*) may be an indication of this. At any rate, Paul now gets down to business and tells how we should live. This section on practical theology was especially important for the Thessalonians as **Gentiles** (vs. 5), since they had no customary moral traditions like the Jews. The words **beseech** and **exhort** are ordinary words meaning "ask" and "encourage" but here they are tempered with **by the Lord Jesus.** This becomes then an authoritative expression of Christian living. Paul has already passed on this Christian traditional information to the Thessalonians by word of mouth in his preaching. Now, he gives it to them in writing. The topic is very clearly labeled, **how ye ought to walk,** and means precisely, "how you must live and please God." These two verbs are in the present tense in Greek, implying that Christianity is a way of life which characterizes all our activities and not just a few of the things we do. It is also interesting to note from verse 1, that Paul acknowledges the fact that his readers are already living according to Christian standards; he is merely encouraging them to continue to grow as they already have.

2. For ye know what commandments we gave you by the Lord Jesus. Again the word **commandments** shows that these exhortations to purity are Christian moral standards. That these are not to be taken lightly is further indicated in this verse by the reference to Paul's apostolic authority; he is acting through the Lord Jesus, or we might say as His representative.

3. For this is the will of God. Verses 1 and 2 were quite general, while verses 3-8 are specific. In this passage Paul has in mind **sanctification** or "holiness" (Gr *hagiasmos*) as it relates specifically to sexual purity. He says in verse 3 that sanctification means to **abstain from fornication** (Gr *porneia*). This is the general word for any kind of illicit sexual intercourse, prostitution, premarital sex, or adultery. Paul is here emphasizing the negative side of sanctification when he tells his readers to abstain (the Greek word means to keep oneself entirely away from).

4-5. Every one of you should know how to possess. This is the positive side of sanctification in this same matter. A better

how to possess his vessel in sanctification and honour;

5 Not in the lust of concupiscence, even as the Gentiles which know not God:

6 That no *man* go beyond and defraud his brother in *any* matter: because that the Lord *is* the avenger of all such, as we also have forewarned you and testified.

7 For God hath not called us unto uncleanness, but unto holiness.

8 He therefore that despiseth, despiseth not man, but God, who hath also given unto us his holy Spirit.

9 But as touching brotherly love ye need not that I write unto you: for ye yourselves are taught of God to love one another.

10 And indeed ye do it toward all the brethren which are in all Macedonia: but we beseech you, brethren, that ye increase more and more;

11 And that ye study to be quiet, and to do your own business, and to work with your own hands, as we commanded you;

12 That ye may walk honestly toward them that are without, and *that* ye may have lack of nothing.

translation of verse 4, "that each of you know how to take a wife for himself in holiness and honor." The word **vessel** (Gr *skeuos*) is used of the wife as the "weaker vessel" in I Peter 3:7. Sanctity in marriage was something brand-new for the Thessalonians who had come from obviously corrupt Gentile culture. They grew up not knowing God, and now that they had turned to God they needed to know and conform to Christian standards.

6-7. That no man go beyond and defraud his brother in any matter. Several words need explanation here. First, **go beyond** (Gr *hyperbainō*) means quite literally "to overstep" or "break laws." In this context it obviously means to break this moral law. Secondly, if he does break this moral law, a man will, by that very fact, **defraud** (Gr *pleonekteō*) his brother. This word denotes "taking advantage of," "robbing," or "cheating someone" through greed. A comment is also needed on the phrase **in any matter.** The construction in the original language of the New Testament (an article of previous reference) allows only one meaning here. It is not just **any matter** that is in view, but specifically this matter which has just been mentioned, that is unethical sexual activity. The sense of the passage is then that when a man does not live with his own wife as he should, but instead commits adultery with someone else's, he must know that he has violated, or "robbed" his brother by so doing, and that he deserves the vengeance of God. To show the seriousness of his sin, Paul alludes to Psalm 94:1 where God is called the "God of vengeance." Note that according to verse 7, this kind of conduct is the opposite of **holiness** and is called **uncleanness.** To be sanctified according to God's will must mean to be pure or clean in this matter.

8. He therefore that despiseth. Paul here seems to allude to a saying of Jesus recorded in Luke 10:16, where Jesus gives authority to the apostles, and literally explains, "whoever obeys me, and whoever rejects you rejects me; the person who rejects me, rejects the one who sent me." Note that "despise" and "reject" translate the same Greek word.

B. Love. 4:9-12.

9. But as touching brotherly love ye need not that I write unto you. This is a way of reminding the Thessalonians about the importance of **brotherly love** (Gr *philadelphia*) without sounding too harsh. **Taught of God** is one word in the original and implies that they should automatically know that God expects them to **love** (Gr *agapaō*) one another.

10-12. And that ye study (Gr *philotimeomai*). This word does not refer to **study** in the sense of opening books or reading; it means "to desire," or "to determine." A possibly clearer translation would be, "aspire to live quietly and take care of your own affairs while you work with your hands as we instructed you." We gather from this passage, and from II Thessalonians 3:11, that some of the believers in this church believed that the Second Coming of Christ was very near, and in their zeal, abandoned their jobs. Paul gets into the social implications of the gospel when he tells them to look after their families and continue their secular work. According to verse 12 it would be wrong and harmful to their testimonies to depend upon the church to feed their families. Furthermore this might cause actual poverty and economic recession. These verses are then significant for the Christian work ethic.

C. Comfort for the Bereaved. 4:13-18.

There are several indications in these letters that Paul had given considerable emphasis to the Second Coming when he preached to the Thessalonians. One problem, as we have seen, was that some of the Thessalonians quit work to wait for Jesus to come back. In this section of the letter Paul replies to those who had lost loved ones in death since Paul had left. They wondered about the spiritual welfare of those who had died. What a tragedy, they must have thought, for their friends to have died before the return of the Lord. Would they now miss all the blessings of believers at the Second Coming? Would they still be saved even though they died before the *Parousia?*

13 But I would not have you to be ignorant, brethren, concerning them which are asleep, that ye sorrow not, even as others which have no hope.

13. But I would not have you to be ignorant. Although this sounds insulting to our ears, it was a formula Paul used often to mean simply, "I have something I want to tell you." The same introductory clause is used in Romans 1:13; 11:25; I Corinthians 10:1; II Corinthians 1:8. **Concerning them which are asleep.** This, of course, is not to be taken literally. Paul is not talking about those who are asleep, but about those who are dead. This euphemistic metaphor is common to all languages and religions and is used often in the New Testament (Mt 27:52). The word is also used in the same metaphorical sense in verses 14 and 15. **That ye sorrow not.** This is Paul's purpose for wanting to tell them about the dead. The Greek verb is in the present tense, making possible the translation, "so that you will not continue to grieve as others do." Paul intends to impart knowledge which they may find comforting. **Others which have no hope.** The word **hope** (Gr *elpis*) is the key to this passage. In the New Testament this word refers to a "certain expectation," rather than something one wishes might happen. The Christian's **hope** is resurrection. It is the doctrine of the resurrection which here provides **hope** concerning the loved ones who have died; we know for certain that they will rise. The certainty of the resurrection for the Christian is based upon the resurrection of Jesus Christ our Lord. An obvious parallel is I Corinthians 15. Christ arose according to the Scriptures and appeared to many as indisputable truth. Paul shows the relationship between the resurrection of Christ and that of Christians in I Corinthians 15:20; the fact is, however, that "now is Christ risen from the dead, and become the first fruits of them that slept." So the argument runs that since Christ rose from the dead, so we shall rise at His coming (cf. I Cor 15:23).

14 For if we believe that Jesus died and rose again, even so them also which sleep in Jesus will God bring with him.

14. Them also which sleep in Jesus will God bring with him. Again, it is the resurrection of departed saints which is based on the resurrection of Christ. We believe that Jesus died and rose again (as the first fruits), so we have the "sure expectation" that God will raise the saints as He raised Jesus. **Bring** (Gr *agō*) could mean that God will bring saints back to the earth with him in the *Parousia*, but that does not seem to follow in the context. Since the first part of verse 14 refers to the death and resurrection of Christ, the last part of the verse should have a corresponding death and resurrection of believers. The death of believers is obvious from **them also which sleep in Jesus,** but the resurrection must be implied in the word **bring.** At the very least, the word must imply a resurrection in order for God to bring them back with Jesus at His Coming.

15 For this we say unto you by the word of the Lord, that we which are alive and remain unto the coming of the Lord shall not prevent them which are asleep.

15. For this we say unto you by the word of the Lord. By this Paul intends to make an authoritative announcement (cf. I Cor 7:10). **Shall not prevent them which are asleep.** The word **prevent** (Gr *phthanō*) has the meaning "precede." A better translation would be, "we who are alive, who are left until the coming of the Lord, shall not precede those who have fallen asleep." The construction in the original language (the subjunctive of emphatic future negation) emphasizes the fact that the living have no advantage over the dead at the coming of the Lord. This is clearly demonstrated in the next two verses, where Paul gives the order of events step by step.

16 For the Lord himself shall descend from heaven with a shout, with the voice of the archangel, and with the trump of God: and the dead in Christ shall rise first:
17 Then we which are alive and re-

16-18. First, **the Lord himself shall descend.** This is qualified by three attendant circumstances each introduced with the same preposition in the original: a command, an archangel's voice, and a trumpet blast. Second, **the dead in Christ shall rise first.** The word **rise** denotes the resurrection of the body, and not "rising" into the air. Likewise **first,** means that this resur-

main shall be caught up together with them in the clouds to meet the Lord in the air: and so shall we ever be with the Lord.

18 Wherefore comfort one another with these words.

CHAPTER 5

BUT of the times and the seasons, brethren, ye have no need that I write unto you.

2 For yourselves know perfectly that the day of the Lord so cometh as a thief in the night.

3 For when they shall say, Peace and safety; then sudden destruction cometh upon them, as travail upon a woman with child; and they shall not escape.

4 But ye, brethren, are not in darkness, that that day should overtake you as a thief.

5 Ye are all the children of light, and the children of the day: we are not of the night, nor of darkness.

6 Therefore let us not sleep, as do others; but let us watch and be sober.

7 For they that sleep sleep in the night; and they that be drunken are drunken in the night.

rection occurs before the Rapture. Verse 17 indicates the third item in order; "then" means the next thing in order after their resurrection. **We which are alive and remain shall be caught up together with them.** It is important to note that the whole church, including those who have died prior to this event, as well as those who are still alive, is caught up together. There is no advantage either way. It is from the word **caught up** (Gr *harpazō*) in the Latin translation we get our word "rapture." The word in the original means "snatch," or "seize," and denotes a sudden violent taking away. The word pictures being "swept off" into the air as by a tornado. The result of this sweeping away, of course, is that we meet the Lord. Paul points out that these words are to be used by the Thessalonians to comfort one another concerning the welfare of their loved ones who have passed on. They will be reunited at His Coming!

D. Apocalyptic Encouragement. 5:1-11.

5:1-2. But of the times and the seasons. Two synonyms for **time** are used; the first (Gr *chronos*) denotes chronological extension or "periods of time." The second (Gr *kairos*) denotes "specific points" in time when designated events occur. Paul states that the Thessalonians have no need for him to write about either "periods of time" which must elapse or "designated points in time" when something, like the *Parousia*, might occur.

The reason that Paul would not need to write is introduced in 5:2. They know perfectly well **that the day of the Lord so cometh as a thief in the night.** Paul here identifies the Old Testament "Day of the Lord" with the *Parousia*. The prominent idea associated with that Day in the Old Testament, and in this passage as well, is that of "judgment" and destruction upon the enemies of God. This stands in striking contrast to the previous passage (4:13-18), where the emphasis was **hope** and resurrection. The difference of course is one of focus; it depends upon whether believers or unbelievers are in view. The simile of the **thief in the night** heightens the element of surprise for unbelievers in the day of the Lord. Paul had perhaps taught the Thessalonians the words of the Lord Jesus himself concerning that day; Jesus had also called it "the coming of the Son of man" (Mt 24:37), and had said that the time was unknown to the angels of heaven and to Himself. Jesus had alluded to the flood in the time of Noah and the fact that the people were completely surprised and swept away by the flood.

3. Peace and safety. These were slogans of the Roman Empire. The suddenness of the event is portrayed by yet another simile, that of a pregnant woman's labor pains. Just that quickly **destruction** will be **upon** (Gr *ephistēmi*) them. The fact that this verb is in the perfect tense in Greek emphasizes the certainty or reality of the destruction. People in catastrophic situations have wondered, "Can this really be happening?" Paul is saying that the destruction of the Day of the Lord will not only be sudden, but it will be certain, and those upon whom it comes will definitely **not escape** (emphasized in Greek by the subjunctive of emphatic future negation)!

4-7. But ye. Paul, having focused briefly on the negative aspects of the *Parousia*, now moves to its positive aspects. This contrast is marked in the Greek text by the use of the emphatic personal pronoun with the adversative conjunction. Paul now makes full use of the symbols, **day** and **night**. His readers, since they have been saved, are **children of light,** which is an Old Testament figure meaning to be characterized by light, as opposed to darkness. Therefore, the negative aspects of his former simile of the thief do not apply to them. He is not trying to scare them with the Second Coming. Instead, he gives several exhortations (the Greek hortatory subjunctive corresponds to the occurrence of "let us" in the English text). The exhortations about not sleeping, and being sober correspond exactly to Paul's

8 But let us, who are of the day, be sober, putting on the breastplate of faith and love; and for an helmet, the hope of salvation.

9 For God hath not appointed us to wrath, but to obtain salvation by our Lord Jesus Christ,

10 Who died for us, that, whether we wake or sleep, we should live together with him.

11 Wherefore comfort yourselves together, and edify one another, even as also ye do.

12 And we beseech you, brethren, to know which labour among you, and are over you in the Lord, and admonish you;

13 And to esteem them very highly in love for their work's sake. *And* be at peace among yourselves.

14 Now we exhort you, brethren, warn them that are unruly, comfort the feebleminded, support the weak, be patient toward all *men.*

15 See that none render evil for evil unto any *man;* but ever follow that which is good, both among yourselves, and to all *men.*

16 Rejoice evermore.

17 Pray without ceasing.

18 In every thing give thanks: for this is the will of God in Christ Jesus concerning you.

19 Quench not the Spirit.

20 Despise not prophesyings.

21 Prove all things; hold fast that which is good.

exhortation elsewhere to "redeem the time." The idea is that we must take advantage of every opportunity to serve Jesus Christ (Eph 5:16).

8. The metaphors of **faith . . . love and . . . hope** as pieces of armor are given more fully in Ephesians 6:14-17, but originally came from the Old Testament (Isa 59:17).

9. For God hath not appointed us to wrath. This again shows the intended contrast between believers and unbelievers at the time of the Second Coming. God has designed for us as believers that we should **obtain** (Gr *peripoiēsis*) **salvation by our Lord Jesus Christ** at His coming.

10. Who died for us. These words explain how salvation is by Jesus Christ. His accomplishment of salvation is through His death for us. The purpose for which He died, to put it another way, was in order that we might live together with Him. Again in this verse, it is the resurrection of Jesus Christ which is the basis of our new life in Christ and our hope of the resurrection.

11. Comfort yourselves together, and edify one another. The two verbs are in the present tense in Greek implying a continuing obligation of believers to "encourage" and "build" one another. This is, of course, one of the reasons for fellowship together in the church.

E. Summary Exhortations. 5:12-22.

12. The first exhortation concerns the leaders of the Thessalonian church who **labor among you, and are over you in the Lord, and admonish you.** The words who **are over you** (Gr *proistēmi*) obviously indicate a governing leadership, and refer to spiritual leaders like pastors, elders, or bishops. Since the church was very young, its leaders must have been appointed by the apostolic missionaries in a manner similar to that mentioned in Acts 14:23. Paul asks his readers **to know** or recognize and appreciate the spiritual leaders. The spiritual nature of their leadership is indicated by **in the Lord.**

13. Esteem them very highly in love. The adverb here (Gr *hyperekperissōs*) is a double compound with a very intensive meaning which is probably quite adequately translated by **very highly** in the English text. The means of this high regard is suggested by **in love.** The reason for the high regard is that they have earned respect by their work. Paul in fact used the same word to describe their labor as he had used earlier for his own.

14. This verse sums up the responsibilities of Christians one toward another in three areas of ministry. A different imperative verb is used with each distinct group, implying that one's method must change according to the type of ministry. The first imperative (Gr *noutheteō*), **warn,** denotes a rather firm reminder to be used with the **unruly** (Gr *ataktos*, meaning, "incorrigible"). The second imperative (Gr *paramytheō*), **comfort** indicates soothing and comforting words for those who are "depressed" or discouraged (**feeble-minded** has other connotations not found in this verse). The third imperative (Gr *antechomai*), **support** calls for a supportive ministry for those who are weak or sick. The fourth exhortation in the verse is general, **be patient,** and encourages true patience **toward all men.**

15-18. Paying back evil with evil, in a manner similar to the Old Testament "eye for an eye," is not a part of the Christian philosophy; we must pursue what is good in our relationships to all men. Paul encourages other positive attitudes: a continual joy, or looking for the positive possibilities in every situation, persistent prayer, and thanksgiving. These are the things which are in accord with God's will for the Christian.

19-22. **Quench** (Gr *sbennymi*) means in this context to "suppress." It is, in fact, a synonym of the word **despise** in verse 20. The work of the **Spirit** should never be quenched, stifled, or suppressed. Verse 20 is parallel to verse 19; a gift like prophesy-

22 Abstain from all appearance of evil.

23 And the very God of peace sanctify you wholly; and *I pray God* your whole spirit and soul and body be preserved blameless unto the coming of our Lord Jesus Christ.
24 Faithful *is* he that calleth you, who also will do *it*.

25 Brethren, pray for us.
26 Greet all the brethren with an holy kiss.
27 I charge you by the Lord that this epistle be read unto all the holy brethren.
28 The grace of our Lord Jesus Christ *be* with you. Amen.

ing is not to be despised or belittled. Yet, in spite of the fact that the Thessalonians are quite literally called upon to stop these kinds of activities, they are encouraged to continue "testing" all things, that is, applying Christian principles to all situations, and to continue holding fast to that which is good. The idea is that, while they should not hinder someone who is genuinely working for God, neither should they be gullible and accept anyone who claims to be religious. Paul also reminds them that they should continue to **abstain** (Gr *apechō*) from every possible kind of evil. What Paul is calling for here is balance; Christians should neither be overcritical nor gullible.

IV. CONCLUSION. 5:23-28.

23-24. And the very God of peace sanctify you wholly. Paul's prayer for the Thessalonians here is put in the form of a wish (optative of wish) and might better be translated as, "may the God of peace himself sanctify you completely." The word **sanctify** (Gr *hagiazō*) is related to the word "holiness" and implies that God himself is the ultimate influence in changing a man's life. Holiness is more than a set of rules which can be legally imposed. Holiness or sanctification is the work of God's Holy Spirit who indwells us. Paul, having done all that is within his power to teach the Thessalonians to be holy, now commits them to God who alone can make them holy. **I pray God your whole spirit and soul and body be preserved blameless,** should rather be translated "may your spirit, soul, and body be kept sound and blameless at the coming of our Lord Jesus Christ." Paul is not here giving us a list of the separable parts of man, but is simply asking God to preserve the whole man in safety and holiness so that there will be no reason for shame or punishment at the coming of Christ (cf. Phil 1:10). Again, verse 25 emphasizes that, as it is God who saves, so it is God who keeps; God called them in the first place, and He will preserve them.

25-28. In his close, Paul asks for their continued prayers for him. The affection intended is indicated by the use of the term **Brethren,** the intimate **pray for us,** and the issuing of **a holy kiss** by mail. Prior to the words of benediction, Paul solemnly gives a **charge** (Gr *enorkizō*), by an oath to the Lord, that this letter be **read** aloud (Gr *anaginōskō*) to all the brethren. **The grace of our Lord Jesus Christ be with you. Amen.**

(see page 625 for Bibliography to I and II Thessalonians)

The Second Epistle To The
THESSALONIANS

INTRODUCTION

Authenticity. Although the authenticity of I Thessalonians has never been seriously questioned, being supported by internal evidence and the external support of Marcion, the Muratorian Canon, Irenaeus, Clement of Alexandria, Tertullian, and others, nevertheless the authenticity of II Thessalonians has received serious objection from the more radical schools of theology.

Opponents of the authenticity of II Thessalonians have objected to the difference in tone between this and the first epistle, to the doctrine of the man of sin, in chapter 2, and, oddly enough, to the similarities between the two epistles. However, both internal and external evidence favor pauline authorship of this epistle as well.

Twice the writer refers to himself as Paul (1:1; 3:17). The general contents, style, vocabulary, theological concepts, etc. are all pauline in nature. In addition, this epistle is quoted more frequently by the church fathers as pauline than is the first epistle. Polycarp appears to quote from it; Justin Martyr alludes to it. Irenaeus mentions it directly by name. Both Clement of Alexandria and Tertullian attribute it to the Apostle Paul. It is found in the Muratorian Canon, the Syriac, Old Latin and Vulgate versions, as well as Marcion's Canon. Thus the authenticity of the epistle is only questioned by the extremely biased, and then not forcefully.

Authorship. There can be little question that, like I Thessalonians, this epistle was written by Paul. See the discussion above and that of the introduction to I Thessalonians.

Date and Place of Writing. Like the first epistle, II Thessalonians was written in Corinth. Again the names of Paul, Silas, and Timothy are associated in the salutation (1:1; cf. I Thess 1:1). Acts 18:5 indicates that these three were together in Corinth but shortly thereafter Silas drops out of sight, according to the book of Acts.

The date of this epistle must have been only months after the writing of the first. Circumstances at Thessalonica had not materially changed, yet enough time had elapsed in order to allow the believers there to fall into idleness as a result of Paul's teaching in I Thessalonians. Thus, we may date II Thessalonians during late A.D. 51 or early A.D. 52.

Purpose. As in the pauline practice, Paul never writes a church but what he commends them. This is his purpose here as well. But the overriding purpose is the correction of errors.

The Thessalonians had misread Paul's intentions in the first letter. They interpreted the coming of the Lord to be upon them in such a way as to require them to sell their houses and lands, give up their jobs, and move to the hilltops in order to wait for the coming of Christ. This attitude had created idleness in the church and was a reproach on the name of the Lord Jesus. Paul had to give them additional instruction concerning the coming of the Lord, the Man of Sin who will be revealed before the *Parousia,* and the order of events preceding the second coming of Christ.

This epistle, written to Gentile believers, is especially helpful to new converts to Christianity. New Christians need to understand God's prophetic program and the work ethic of serving until the Lord comes.

OUTLINE

I. Introduction. 1:1-2.
II. Personal Responses. 1:3-12.
   A. Thanksgiving and Praise. 1:3-4.
   B. Apocalyptic Encouragement. 1:5-12.
III. The Day of the Lord. 2:1-12.
   A. Plea for Stability. 2:1-2.
   B. The Man of Sin. 2:3-12.

IV. God's Grace. 2:13-17.
   A. The Means of Salvation. 2:13-14.
   B. The Manifestations of Salvation. 2:15-17.
V. Practical Exhortations. 3:1-18.
   A. Mutual Prayer. 3:1-5.
   B. The Work Ethic. 3:6-15.
VI. Conclusion. 3:16-18.

COMMENTARY

I. INTRODUCTION. 1:1-2.

PAUL, and Sĭl-vā′nus, and Tĭ-mō′theus, unto the church of the Thĕs-sa-lō′nĭ-anś in God our Father and the Lord Jesus Christ:

1:1-2. Paul, and Silvanus, and Timothy. The salutation of II Thessalonians is almost the same as that of I Thessalonians (see the comments there). II Thessalonians adds **our** in verse 1, and **from God our Father and the Lord Jesus Christ** in verse 2.

2 Grace unto you, and peace, from God our Father and the Lord Jesus Christ.

3 We are bound to thank God always for you, brethren, as it is meet, because that your faith groweth exceedingly, and the charity of every one of you all toward each other aboundeth;

4 So that we ourselves glory in you in the churches of God for your patience and faith in all your persecutions and tribulations that ye endure:

5 *Which is* a manifest token of the righteous judgment of God, that ye may be counted worthy of the kingdom of God, for which ye also suffer:

6 Seeing *it is* a righteous thing with God to recompense tribulation to them that trouble you;

7 And to you who are troubled rest with us, when the Lord Jesus shall be revealed from heaven with his mighty angels,

II. PERSONAL RESPONSES. 1:3-12.

A. Thanksgiving and Praise. 1:3-4.

3-4. We are bound to thank God always for you. Although the language is slightly different, Paul begins II Thessalonians in the same way that he begins I Thessalonians, by thanking God for the faith and love of the believers. "Hope" is not mentioned in these introductory remarks; perhaps it is taken for granted. This passage seems to be more direct than the parallel passage in I Thessalonians, in that there is no need to "remember." There is, however, the same warm praise and thanksgiving for the progress and growth of the Christians.

B. Apocalyptic Encouragement. 1:5-12.

5. Which is a manifest token. The word **token** (Gr *endeigma*) refers to the result of a demonstration and thus means "a sign," "proof," or "evidence." Paul says that this is a demonstration of the righteous judgment of God, but the problem comes when we ask, "What is a demonstration?" If we take this to refer back to the "afflictions" of the Thessalonians, then Paul must mean to say that God judges righteously and gives the Thessalonians what they deserve. This hardly seems fair and does not fit the context either, since verse 6 shows that God will in fact bring rest to the Thessalonians when Christ comes. Most commentators take the word **token** to refer back to the whole of verse 4, so that it is the way in which the Thessalonians endured their persecutions which is a sign that God judges righteously. It is not the suffering, but their faith which proves God's righteous judgment. It would seem, however, that the main verbal idea in verse 4 is the "praise," or **glory** which Paul and the apostles give to the Thessalonians; this could certainly be understood as a "sign" of the way God would look upon endurance of the Thessalonians in his righteous judgment at the coming of Christ. **That ye may be counted worthy of the kingdom of God,** is an indication of the purpose of Paul's boasting about the Thessalonians and their faith to other churches. Paul wants them to be **counted worthy** which does not mean "made worthy" but simply recognized as being worthy. Paul does not consider it out of character to praise the Thessalonians for their faithfulness; in fact, that is his main means of encouraging them. Paul praises them for patience, faith, enduring persecutions, and suffering for the sake of the **kingdom of God.**

6. Seeing it is a righteous thing with God to recompense. The word **recompense** (Gr *antapodidōmi*) means to "reward" or "pay back." Paul emphasizes both the negative and the positive aspects of the Second Coming. The enemies of the gospel, those who are now troubling the Thessalonians, will be paid back by God for the suffering they caused; they will suffer themselves. It is interesting that the noun and the verb here are cognate forms, so that the literal translation would be, "God will repay those who trouble you with trouble." In other words, they will get a dose of their own medicine. The theme of God punishing sinners is a primary characteristic of all apocalyptic literature.

7. And to you who are troubled rest. This is the positive side of the second coming of Christ, that God will bring comfort and reward to His saints. The reward for those who are troubled by the troublers is **rest** (Gr *thlibō* is the common New Testament word for **tribulation**). The word **rest** (Gr *anesis*) means primarily "release" or "relaxation." This is the word from which we get our common trademark, "Anacin." Real comfort and relaxation in the future, in spite of temporary affliction here, are the rewards of all those who serve the living and true God. According to this verse, Christ comes with His **mighty angels**, which may parallel the meaning of the original in I Thessalonians 3:13, where the angels are called His "Holy Ones." Note that the same expression in the original recurs in this chapter (1:10). **The**

8 In flaming fire taking vengeance on them that know not God, and that obey not the gospel of our Lord Jesus Christ:

9 Who shall be punished with everlasting destruction from the presence of the Lord, and from the glory of his power;

10 When he shall come to be glorified in his saints, and to be admired in all them that believe (because our testimony among you was believed) in that day.

11 Wherefore also we pray always for you, that our God would count you worthy of *this* calling, and fulfil all the good pleasure of *his* goodness, and the work of faith with power:

12 That the name of our Lord Jesus Christ may be glorified in you, and ye in him, according to the grace of our God and the Lord Jesus Christ.

CHAPTER 2

NOW we beseech you, brethren, by the coming of our Lord Jesus Christ, and *by* our gathering together unto him,

2 That ye be not soon shaken in mind, or be troubled, neither by spirit, nor by word, nor by letter as from us, as that the day of Christ is at hand.

Lord Jesus shall be revealed could be more literally translated "in the revelation of the Lord Jesus." This is a new word for the second coming of Christ which emphasizes the manifestation of the person of Jesus Christ as a powerful Judge.

8. Flaming fire taking vengeance. In flaming fire should probably be taken as a part of verse 7; almost the same apocalyptic imagery is found in Revelation 1:13-14, as well as in Daniel 7:13. The emphasis seems to be upon His manifestation as the Son of Man. He comes with the sword of God's vengeance to destroy those who do not know God. Not "knowing" God may be an extension of the Old Testament idiom of not loving God or serving Him rather than a simple lack of knowledge. Another important concept in Old Testament theology was obedience as we see, for example, in Isaiah 66:4, "I also will choose their delusions, and will bring their fears upon them; because when I called, none did answer; when I spake, they did not hear: but they did evil before mine eyes, and chose that in which I delighted not." In Thessalonians, their disobedience is to the gospel of our Lord Jesus (an objective genitive).

9-10. Who shall be punished. The literal translation here would be, "who shall pay the penalty of eternal destruction from the face of the Lord." Again, this is the uniform theme of apocalyptic literature in general (cf. Isa 2:11, 17; Rev 9:6). **In that day** alludes again to the Old Testament Day of Jehovah which has now been identified with the revelation of Jesus Christ. Here Paul mentions once more the positive purpose for the Second Coming, namely that the Lord should receive glory from those who believe because of the apostolic witness.

11-12. Wherefore should rather be translated "unto this end." Paul's prayer is the encouragement he desires to impart to them. Only God can accomplish His will in the lives of the believers, so Paul prayed that God would first count them worthy, and then fulfill His good pleasure in their lives. The result of the answer to this prayer will be that God will be **glorified in** the believers (by their good lives), and that the believers will be glorified in God. All this is accomplished by God's wonderful grace.

III. THE DAY OF THE LORD. 2:1-12.

A. Plea for Stability. 2:1-2.

2:1. Now we beseech you, is simply the word (Gr *erōtaō*) "ask," but it is used with considerable authority by Paul in this epistle (see 4:1; 5:12). Another misunderstanding about the Second Coming needs correction, and although oral instruction had been given before, Paul uses this opportunity to underscore it in writing. **By the coming,** is better translated, "concerning the coming of our Lord Jesus Christ and our being gathered to meet Him." Paul is not making some kind of oath, but simply introducing this next aspect of the subject at hand. Several aspects had needed comment in these letters: worshiping God involves waiting for His Son (1:10), ultimate joy and reward comes later at His coming (I Thess 2:17-20), His coming encourages us to holiness now (I Thess 3:13), those who die before His coming will not be cheated out of the Rapture, but will be raised first (I Thess 4:13-18), and now it must be shown that however they had gotten the impression that the Day of the Lord events had already started, it simply was not true.

2. That ye be not soon shaken in mind. This clause indicates the purpose of Paul's authoritative statement. He does not want them to be so easily swayed from the position they had already accepted as the Word of God. Nor should they be **troubled** (Gr *throeō*), a word denoting great inward pain and anxiety, which is used elsewhere in the New Testament only twice and both times it is in the same eschatological context of the Second Coming. Their tendency to believe that they were in the midst of the very last days had caused other problems too (see I Thess 4:11; II Thess 3:12). **By spirit** evidently refers to a supposed prophetic utterance which might have come from some non-apostolic source; **nor by word,** which again would be a false message but pretending to be authoritative like the Word that Paul had given (I Thess 2:13). **Letter** (Gr *epistolē*) means a forged letter; in 3:17 he tells them that his letters can afterward be recognized by the sign of a closing greeting in his own handwriting. **That the day of Christ is at hand** (Gr *enistēmi*) should rather be translated, "to the effect that the day of the Lord has come." The word means "to be present"; Paul wants to assure them that the Day of the Lord is not already in progress when he writes. Paul taught that the Lord was "near" (Phil 4:5), and that the era of fulfillment (the last days) was inaugurated with the first coming of Christ, but never implied that the apocalyptic Day of the Lord had already begun.

B. The Man of Sin. 2:3-12.

3 Let no man deceive you by any means: for *that day shall not come,* except there come a falling away first, and that man of sin be revealed, the son of perdition;

3. Let no man deceive you by any means: for that day shall not come, except there come a falling away. Part of the sentence is implied in the original, and must be supplied in the translation; the Day of the Lord will not begin without the **falling away** (Gr *apostasia*). Our English word "apostasy" comes, of course, directly from this Greek word, which means literally a "standing away from" or "departure." In the religious sense it is a departure from the faith, and what we have in this passage is called the final apostasy which is to be led by the man of lawlessness. Some have taken the words **falling away** to refer to the Rapture of the church in order to prove a point; there is no historical support for that translation, however. The religious meaning is illustrated by Paul in I Timothy 1:4, and by the author of Hebrews in 3:12. At any rate, an apostasy must precede the Day of the Lord.

Simultaneously with the great apostasy, or at least another prerequisite to the beginning of the events of the Second Coming, is appearance of the **man of sin.** The better manuscripts read here, "man of lawlessness," but there is no important difference in the name, for the Bible tells us that "sin is lawlessness" (I Jn 3:4). That the Man of Sin is **revealed** (Gr *apokalyptō*) shows that he exists prior to the time of this revelation or appearance. I John 2:18 states that there were already many antichrists, in the sense of people who are against Christ, existing in that day. It is not certain exactly who this person will be; but the identification of the Man of Sin with the coming Antichrist of Revelation is the most logical conclusion. He is the "beast out of the sea" (Rev 13:1), the "little horn" of Daniel 7:8. He is the Antichrist, i.e., the false christ who will force himself and his kingdom upon the world one day hence (Rev 13:15-17).

4 Who opposeth and exalteth himself above all that is called God, or that is worshipped; so that he as God sitteth in the temple of God, shewing himself that he is God.

4. Who opposeth and exalteth himself. Because of Paul's familiarity with the language of the Old Testament, there are many similarities to Daniel (especially 11:36). This is, however, a new description of the leader of the forces of evil in the final apocalyptic battle against God. **Opposeth** (Gr *antikeimai*) is present tense in Greek and implies continued, determined, and planned opposition to God. It is a common word for the opposing sides in a battle. **Exalteth himself** shows his extreme pride; he puts himself over everything considered as a god or an object of worship and as it were, seats himself in the Temple of God. **As God** was not a part of the original text, although it is certainly implied that this rebellious person acts as if he were God and sits in the Temple personally, unlike Gaius who in A.D. 40 attempted to have his statue placed in the sanctuary at Jerusalem (see Mk 13:14). **Showing himself** (Gr *apodeiknymi*) has the sense of "attempting to demonstrate" that he is God.

5 Remember ye not, that, when I was yet with you, I told you these things?

5. Remember ye not. Paul must have put great emphasis upon the second coming of Christ and related apocalyptic events when he was with the Thessalonians in order to refer back to that preaching so often. Two grammatical items in the Greek make the meaning clear, "You surely recall, do you not, that during my stay, I told you this repeatedly."

6 And now ye know what withholdeth that he might be revealed in his time.

6. And now ye know what withholdeth (Gr *katechō*) is literally, "the thing which holds down." Paul seems to say that for the present (**now**), there is something (a Greek neuter participle) which is holding back the appearance of the lawless leader of the final rebellion. What that "something" meant to the Thessalonian readers is impossible for us to know with any degree of certainty. It may have been the Roman Empire, or perhaps more generally the social structures of law and order manifested in the Roman Empire. This meaning would explain the shift to the masculine participle (**he who now letteth**; same word) in verse 7. However, there is some good reason to assume that it is the ministry of the Holy Spirit which now hinders the work of the Man of Sin. The work of the Spirit is exhibited in the church and when the church is **taken out of the way** (vs. 7), the Antichrist will manifest his plan of world domination. This rebel will be revealed in his time (Gr *kairos*). This statement is very strong; and the entire section supports it, namely, that the Day has not yet begun. The "time" is a divinely predetermined time; no one knows when it will be, but Paul shows that it could not have happened already.

7 For the mystery of iniquity doth already work: only he who now letteth *will let*, **until he be taken out of the way.**

7. The mystery of iniquity. If this is translated, "the mystery of lawlessness," it is easier to see the connection with the man of lawlessness (vs. 3), and the "lawless one" (vs. 8). The idea is that there is already rebellion and lawlessness going on in their day, but that up to that time (**now**) "someone" was restraining it. Obviously, the principle of rebellion to the gospel had been at work in the opposition Paul himself experienced at Thessalonica and other places, but it was not as bad as it might have been. **He who now letteth** (Gr *katechō*) corresponds to **what withholdeth** in verse 6, except that the gender is changed from a restraining thing to a restraining person.

8 And then shall that Wicked be revealed, whom the Lord shall consume with the spirit of his mouth, and shall destroy with the brightness of his coming:

8. That Wicked is the same word translated **man of sin** in verse 3, and **mystery of iniquity** in verse 7; a more consistent translation would be "the lawless one." **Whom the Lord.** Better manuscripts have "the Lord Jesus." **Shall consume.** Again, this is a variant which should read "execute" (Gr *anaireō*). The Lord Jesus will execute this wicked rebel **with the spirit of his mouth.** This last phrase should rather be translated, "with the breath of his mouth" and means, of course, "with a word." This expression occurs only here in the New Testament, but corresponds exactly in meaning with the adjective translated "inspired by God" in II Timothy 3:16, and is related idiom. The Scriptures are the "Word" of God because they are "breathed out" or spoken by Him; in the same sense this "word" to execute the lawless one will be breathed out by the Lord Jesus. It is His word, and only a word from Him will **destroy** (Gr *katargeō*) this archenemy of the gospel. This last word means "to make ineffective"; none of his work through the ages will have any effect on the final accomplishments of the gospel. God and the Lord Jesus will have the final victory.

9 Even him, whose coming is after the working of Satan with all power and signs and lying wonders,

9. Even him, whose coming. The word **coming** (Gr *parousia*) is used for the coming or presence of various people in the New Testament; in Thessalonians it is used seven times, and except for this last time refers to the second coming of Christ. This is the *Parousia* of the Antichrist, corresponding to the *Parousia* of the Lord Jesus mentioned in verse 8; the events concomitant to each coming are supernatural and roughly concurrent. **After the working of Satan.** The distinction of this coming is that all the activities are satanic; they are the signs of an apostle (see II Cor 12:12), but are perverted and false.

10 And with all deceivableness of unrighteousness in them that perish; be-

10. In that Day, as in Paul's day, there will be followers on both sides; the Antichrist will have his "believers" too. They are

cause they received not the love of the truth, that they might be saved.

11 And for this cause God shall send them strong delusion, that they should believe a lie:
12 That they all might be damned who believed not the truth, but had pleasure in unrighteousness.

13 But we are bound to give thanks alway to God for you, brethren beloved of the Lord, because God hath from the beginning chosen you to salvation through sanctification of the Spirit and belief of the truth:

14 Whereunto he called you by our gospel, to the obtaining of the glory of our Lord Jesus Christ.

called here **them that perish** (Gr *apollymi*) meaning "the lost" or "those who are perishing." The reason these people are lost is **because they received not** the gospel. Note that the word **received** (Gr *dechomai*) is a vivid attitude indicator; it means "to welcome" as one welcomes a guest he wishes to entertain. This is an opposite attitude to that of the Thessalonians themselves who **received** the gospel message for what it was, the Word of God (see I Thess 2:13). These people will not be able to blame God for being lost; they refused to believe the Word of God and be saved. A better translation of the verse has "because they refused to love the truth and so be saved."

11-12. Since they will not believe the truth, God allows them to believe the great lie. Although God is the sovereign agent behind all that happens, it is clear in this passage that a voluntary, rational choice is made by these people of every age who have **pleasure in unrighteousness.** The word used here (Gr *eudokeō*) means to "make a decision about what is right." The decision was theirs; they decided for unrighteousness rather than for righteousness and God. The result is that they are condemned, i.e., lost!

IV. GOD'S GRACE. 2:13-17.

A. The Means of Salvation. 2:13-14.

13. Paul now moves into a more positive description of how God saved the Thessalonians by His grace through the preaching of the gospel there earlier (I Thess 1:20). Paul puts his obligation for thanksgiving in the plural, indicating that Silas and Timothy join him in feeling the obligation to give thanks to God concerning the believers. As in I Thessalonians 1:4, Paul addresses the Thessalonians as **brethren beloved of the Lord.** The word **beloved** (Gr *agapaō*) is in the perfect tense in Greek, emphasizing the certainty of the fact that God loves them; the passive voice also stresses once again the point that in salvation God always takes the initiative. The reason for the obligation to give thanks follows, **because God hath from the beginning chosen you to salvation.** Paul gives thanks because God has **chosen** (Gr *haireomai*) the believers to salvation. It is interesting that this word, in the active voice, means "to pick out" as one picks fruit, while in the passive it is a regular word for "making a choice." This is also the word used in the Greek Old Testament for God's choice of Israel rather than the Gentiles; it is now applied here to Gentile believers. God has chosen them from among the Gentiles and has washed them, sanctified them, and justified them, in the name of Jesus (I Cor 6:11). **From the beginning** should probably be instead, "as the first converts to salvation." The word for "first converts" (Gr *aparchē*) is used in six other places in Paul's epistles as a favorite expression to show the continuity between the people of God in the Old Testament and the people of God in the New Testament. Verses 13 and 14 comprise a compendium of the doctrine of salvation where several significant redemptive concepts are given. Note the concepts of obligation, thanksgiving, brotherly love, the love of God, God's choosing the Thessalonians for salvation, first fruits, salvation, sanctification by the Holy Spirit, faith, truth, God's calling, the apostolic preaching of the gospel, the attainment of glory, and Jesus Christ as our Lord. **Through sanctification of the Spirit** shows the agency of the Holy Spirit in "setting apart" these believers to salvation, while **belief of the truth** shows the means of salvation is by faith in the gospel.

14. Whereunto he called you by our gospel. Here the **calling** of God corresponds to the "choosing" of God in verse 13. Note that God's call comes through the preaching of the gospel, and that it results in **obtaining of the glory.** The word **obtaining** (Gr *peripoiēsis*) refers generally to "obtaining" or "attaining" to something but more specifically and more technically in the

Bible it can refer to God's creation of a people for himself. In the Old Testament God made Israel a "people for his own possession." That same idea in the New Testament has been applied to both Jews and Gentiles as they are brought into the church which becomes a "people for God's own possession" (see also I Thess 5:9; I Pet 2:9; and cf. Mal 3:17). The interpretation of the special use of this word may be supported by the fact that the next word, **glory**, does not have an article in Greek so that the phrase might be translated, "to the glorious obtaining." This would mean that the Lord Jesus is accomplishing God's intended salvation by His death on the cross.

B. The Manifestations of Salvation. 2:15-17.

15 Therefore, brethren, stand fast, and hold the traditions which ye have been taught, whether by word, or our epistle.

15. Therefore, brethren, stand fast, and hold the traditions which ye have been taught, whether by word, or our epistle. Another interesting technical term is the word **traditions**, which comes from a verb meaning "to hand down by tradition." These **traditions** were the gospel itself which had been preached among the Thessalonians. Paul uses the word **taught** here for what was often called "preaching." Actually there is little difference between "teaching" and "preaching" according to the New Testament; the content of the teaching and preaching of the apostles was the gospel, and Paul is saying here that it makes no difference whether these traditions were given orally (**by word**) or in written form (**our epistle**). Either way, this teaching, preaching, or tradition, is the Word of God and is authoritative.

16 Now our Lord Jesus Christ himself, and God, even our Father, which hath loved us, and hath given us everlasting consolation and good hope through grace,

17 Comfort your hearts, and stablish you in every good word and work.

16-17. Now our Lord Jesus Christ himself, and God, even our Father. Paul inserted a similar doxological prayer in I Thessalonians 3:11 where he also used the Greek optative mood to make his prayer concerning his readers. In both passages the prayer is directed to God the Father as well as to the Lord Jesus Christ. It is also interesting that this prayer emphasizes encouragement (**consolation** and **Comfort** are cognate) as well as support. One should note also that the word **finally** (3:1) marks the beginning of the conclusion of the letter after the prayer here, just as it does in I Thessalonians 4:1.

V. PRACTICAL EXHORTATIONS. 3:1-18.

A. Mutual Prayer. 3:1-5.

CHAPTER 3

FINALLY, brethren, pray for us, that the word of the Lord may have *free* course, and be glorified, even as *it is* with you:

2 And that we may be delivered from unreasonable and wicked men: for all *men* have not faith.

3:1-2. Finally, brethren, pray for us, that the word of the Lord may have free course. Paul again refers to the gospel as **the word of the Lord**, meaning the Lord Jesus. In I Thessalonians 2:13 Paul praised the believers for welcoming their preaching as the Word of God. Paul wants the Word of God to be successful and accomplish its purpose, and so **be glorified** as it was among the Thessalonian believers themselves when they recognized it was the Word of God, believed it, and were saved. When Paul asked for prayer for Silas, Timothy, and himself, it is the same as asking prayer for the Word of the Lord. They are stewards of the Lord who preach His Word as their primary occupation in life. He also wishes them to pray for their safety in the work, and that they might be protected from evil men who oppose them.

3 But the Lord is faithful, who shall stablish you, and keep *you* from evil.

4 And we have confidence in the Lord touching you, that ye both do and will do the things which we command you.

5 And the Lord direct your hearts into the love of God, and into the patient waiting for Christ.

3-5. But the Lord is faithful, who shall stablish you, and keep you from evil. Paul's statement at the end of verse 2 that all men are not of the faith is a classic understatement. Jesus had put it much more strongly, saying that the world hated them (Jn 17:14), and Paul himself had been often badly misused. The unfaithfulness of men, however, provides a transition to the faithfulness of God, which is a favorite subject of Paul's (I Cor 10:13; I Thess 5:24; II Tim 2:13). The faithfulness of God means here that He will support and keep from evil. The word **keep** (Gr *phylassō*) means rather "guard." **From evil**, should rather be translated, "from the evil ONE," since the gender is masculine in the original (cf. Jn 17:15). In verse 4, Paul expresses his emphatic (the perfect tense in Greek stresses the certainty of a fact) confidence in his readers that they will continue to obey the Word of God, just as they have been doing. To that end he again expresses his prayer that the Lord will direct their hearts into the love of God and true courage for Christ. The word translated **patient waiting for** (Gr *hypomonē*) has the idea of steadfastness or endurance rather than patience, and is a different word from the one Paul uses in I Thessalonians 1:10 as an example of **waiting for** Christ to return in the Second Coming. What Paul has in mind here is courage on the part of the Thessalonians to continue to live for God in spite of the problems.

B. The Work Ethic. 3:6-15.

6-9. Now we command (Gr *parangellō*). This is a very strong and authoritative word; it denotes standing beside someone like a drill sergeant and telling him what to do. Paul uses it seldom, and only when he wants to be very serious and very authoritative. Neither the verb nor the noun form is used in I or II Thessalonians except in connection with the so-called "work ethic" (I Thess 4; II Thess 3). To make this commandment even more authoritative it is given **in the name of our Lord Jesus Christ.** This important, indirect command is completed by the infinitive of another unusual word for Paul, **that ye withdraw yourselves** (Gr *stellomai*) which denotes disassociation. The word is used only one other time in the New Testament, and even there it does not have this sense of ecclesiastical separation or censure. Other strong words are also used in this commandment; **walketh disorderly** (Gr *atakios*) indicates a continual pattern of life which is "not subjected" to and cannot be subjected to the authority of Christ. It is also noteworthy that the synonymous descriptive clause uses the cognate noun and verb for the authoritative "traditions" of the gospel. The obvious implications are that the message that was preached by the apostles was the Word of God; it was authoritative, inspired, and canonical. If a person refuses to submit to the authority of the Word of God, he is "walking disorderly." In this Paul reminds them that they must follow the apostolic pattern; **for we behaved not ourselves disorderly** (a cognate form is used). While the apostles were in Thessalonica they supported themselves, working hard day and night so that their demands upon the community would not be too great. Paul states again that as apostles, they had the authority to have both their wages and expenses paid by the community. They had purposely avoided using this privilege for the benefit of the Thessalonians.

6 Now we command you, brethren, in the name of our Lord Jesus Christ, that ye withdraw yourselves from every brother that walketh disorderly, and not after the tradition which he received of us.

7 For yourselves know how ye ought to follow us: for we behaved not ourselves disorderly among you;

8 Neither did we eat any man's bread for nought; but wrought with labour and travail night and day, that we might not be chargeable to any of you:

9 Not because we have not power, but to make ourselves an ensample unto you to follow us.

10-12. For even when we were with you, this we commanded you, that if any would not work, neither should he eat. Again, the word **commanded** refers back to the problem that arose while the apostles were still present in Thessalonica, namely that some people got so excited about the second coming of Christ they decided to quit work and just wait. It should be noted that Paul does not say that if they could not work they should not "be allowed" to eat, but rather that if anyone did not want to continue working he should decide to stop eating also. Paul has heard that some people have disobeyed his former injunction against that sort of attitude and that they have become **busybodies.** They seem to have been the ancestors of some today who are so heavenly-minded that they are of no earthly good.

According to verse 11, this sort of super-spirituality is really pride and a refusal to submit to the authority of God's Word; the same word **disorderly** is used again (vs. 11), along with the word for a "strict command" which is given in the name of the Lord Jesus Christ (vs. 12). The opposite of that sort of conduct is to eat one's own bread, which he earns by means of working at an occupation while he quietly serves the Lord.

10 For even when we were with you, this we commanded you, that if any would not work, neither should he eat.

11 For we hear that there are some which walk among you disorderly, working not at all, but are busybodies.

12 Now them that are such we command and exhort by our Lord Jesus Christ, that with quietness they work, and eat their own bread.

13 But ye, brethren, be not weary in well doing.

13. But ye. The pronoun is emphatic showing that Paul here speaks to those who are really most spiritual, and whom he has often praised in these epistles. **Be not weary in well doing.** This statement is almost identical with that in Galatians 6:9, except that here Paul uses a Greek construction for the prohibition which implies that these believers are already doing what is noble and right, and that they have not yet begun to despair. The translation might be accurately expanded to "don't ever get depressed; just keep on doing good."

14 And if any man obey not our word by this epistle, note that man, and have no company with him, that he may be ashamed.
15 Yet count *him* not as an enemy, but admonish *him* as a brother.

14-15. Note that man. The word **note** (Gr *sēmeioō*) implies that the person who refuses to obey the Word of the Lord while professing to be a "Christian" should be marked out and distinguished in some way from normal believers so that he is disassociated from them. He is not to be treated as an enemy, however, but as a brother. It must be made clear to that person and to the others as well that he is a disobedient Christian, and that if he wishes to associate with believers he must be willing to submit to and obey the Word of God (cf. Mt 18:17).

VI. CONCLUSION. 3:16-18.

16 Now the Lord of peace himself give you peace always by all means. The Lord *be* with you all.

16. Now the Lord of peace himself give you peace always by all means. In his closing benediction Paul again reminds the Thessalonians that in the end it is not their own efforts but the Lord Himself who must accomplish His salvation and His peace within them. The **Lord of peace** is probably intended by Paul specifically as a name for Jesus Christ.

17 The salutation of Paul with mine own hand, which is the token in every epistle: so I write.

17. The salutation of Paul in his own hand is the mark of genuineness for his letter. The Thessalonians need not wonder whether another letter they might get would be authentic. It was implied in II Thessalonians 2:2 that some doubt had been present in their minds when they received a letter purporting to be from Paul. Now they would know his letters by this token.

18 The grace of our Lord Jesus Christ *be* with you all. Amen.

18. The grace of our Lord Jesus Christ be with you all. Amen. This is the identical conclusion as given in I Thessalonians, the substance of which would come to form a pauline pattern.

BIBLIOGRAPHY

Askwith, Edward H. *An Introduction to the Thessalonian Epistles.* London: Macmillan, 1902.

Bruce, F. F. I and II Thessalonians. In *New Bible Commentary.* Grand Rapids: Eerdmans, 1953.

Denney, James. The Epistles to the Thessalonians. In *Expositor's Bible.* New York: Armstrong & Son, 1903.

*Eadie, John. *A Commentary on the Greek Text of the Epistles of Paul to the Thessalonians.* Ed. by William Young. London: Macmillan, 1877.

*Ellicott, Charles J. *Commentary on the Epistle of St. Paul to the Thessalonians.* Grand Rapids: Zondervan, 1957.

Erdman, Charles R. *The Epistles of Paul to the Thessalonians.* Philadelphia: Westminster Press, 1935.

Findlay, George C. The Epistles of Paul the Apostle to the Thessalonians. In the *Cambridge Greek Testament.* Cambridge: Cambridge University Press, 1911.

Hendriksen, William. Exposition of I and II Thessalonians. In *New Testament Commentary.* Grand Rapids: Baker, 1964.

*Hiebert, D. Edmond. *The Thessalonian Epistles.* Chicago: Moody Press, 1971.

Hogg, Charles and William Vine. *The Epistles to the Thessalonians.* London: Pickering and Inglis, 1959.

Horne, Charles. The Epistles to the Thessalonians: A Study Manual. In the *Shield Bible Study Studies.* Grand Rapids: Baker, 1961.

Hubbard, David A. I and II Thessalonians. In *Wycliffe Bible Commentary.* Chicago: Moody Press, 1962.

Lenski, R. C. H. *The Interpretation of St. Paul's Epistles to the Colossians, to the Thessalonians, to Timothy, to Titus, and to Philemon.* Columbus, Ohio: Lutheran Book Concern, 1937.

MacDonald, William. *Letters to the Thessalonians.* Kansas City, Kansas: Walterick Publishers, 1969.

Milligan, George. *St. Paul's Epistles to the Thessalonians.* London: Macmillan, 1908.

II THESSALONIANS

Morris, Leon. The Epistles of Paul to the Thessalonians. In *The Tyndale New Testament Commentaries*. Grand Rapids: Eerdmans, 1957.

_____. The First and Second Epistles to the Thessalonians. In *The New International Commentary on the New Testament*. Grand Rapids: Eerdmans, 1959.

Plummer, Alfred. *A Commentary on St. Paul's First Epistle to the Thessalonians*. London: Robert Scott, 1918.

_____. *A Commentary on St. Paul's Second Epistle to the Thessalonians*. London: Robert Scott, 1918.

*Ryrie, Charles Caldwell. First and Second Thessalonians. In *Everyman's Bible Commentary*. Chicago: Moody Press, 1959.

Stevens, William Arnold. Commentary on the Epistles to the Thessalonians. In *An American Commentary*. Philadelphia: The American Baptist Publication Society, 1890.

*Walvoord, John F. *The Thessalonian Epistles*. Grand Rapids: Zondervan, 1956.

Ward, Ronald A. *A Commentary on First and Second Thessalonians*. Waco, Texas: Word, 1973.

The First Epistle To
TIMOTHY

INTRODUCTION

The three letters addressed to Timothy and Titus (I Timothy, II Timothy, and Titus) constitute what is known as the Pastoral Epistles. It is said that this term was used by Thomas Aquinas. Polycarp, bishop of Smyrna early in the second century, is known to have been aware of this corpus (see C. K. Barrett, *The Pastoral Epistles*, p. 1). But it was not until 1703 that D. N. Berdot, followed later by Paul Anton in 1726, popularized the term "pastoral" to describe these letters.

Authorship. The authorship of the Pastoral Epistles came slowly to be suspected as being non-pauline. In fact, it was not until the last century that these three little epistles became a battleground of biblical criticism. In 1807 Schleiermacher denied the genuineness of I Timothy. His criticisms quickly spread to the other two as well. Today scholars are divided into three camps around the question of authorship: (1) those who hold to pauline authorship (Godet, Lightfoot, Alford, Lange, Schaff, Ramsay, etc.); (2) those who believe that these epistles should be placed in the second century and consequently are not to be considered pauline in any sense of the word (Baur, Hatch, Goodspeed, etc.); and (3) those who take a mediating position claiming that while these letters were not written by Paul, they do contain some genuine pauline fragments (Ewald, Harnack, Moffatt, etc.).

1. *External evidence.* Although these epistles were rejected by Marcion and perhaps Tatian, the early church as a whole received them as wholly authoritative. They were accepted as canonical by Irenaeus (cf. *Adversus Haereses* I, Preface, I); Tertullian (cf. *De Praescriptione Haereticorum* 7); and were included in the Muratorian Canon (ca. A.D. 200). Perhaps the most notable concern over the canonicity of these epistles arises out of their absence from the Chester Beatty Papyrus (P[46]). Yet the church at large supported their inclusion into the canon.

2. *Internal evidence.* Personal references to Paul seem to necessitate pauline authorship. It is highly unlikely that anyone but Paul would have referred to Paul as "injurious" (1:13) or the "chief" of sinners (1:15). Paul identifies himself as author (1:1) and the author exhibits the same sense of divine call that Paul exhibits (1:12; 2:7; II Tim 1:11). The doctrine of the epistles is Paul's doctrine. Like other epistles (e.g., Romans or Philemon), a large number of personal names is introduced into this epistle. This was a pauline practice. Down through the centuries the church has been identifying elements of each of these epistles as pauline. Thus, if we are to reject pauline authorship, the objections of the critics must first be proven (which has not been successfully done) and the direct claim of authorship by Paul must be deleted from each epistle (which will never be done). For an excellent discussion of the problems and positions on pauline authorship see Donald Guthrie, The Pastoral Epistles, in the *Tyndale New Testament Commentaries*.

Recipient. The recipient of I Timothy was a young resident of Lystra named Timothy (Acts 16:1-3). He was the son of a Greek father (Acts 16:2) and a Jewish mother, Eunice (II Tim 1:5). He had been taught the Scriptures from his youth (II Tim 1:5; 3:15) which is a testimony to the faithfulness of his godly mother and grandmother.

Timothy came to know the Lord as Saviour through the ministry of Paul on his first missionary journey (Acts 14:8-20). When Paul revisited the Lycaonian city of Lystra on his second missionary journey he decided to take young Timothy with him as a fellow laborer. Timothy was ordained to the ministry by the presbytery, Paul being a party to that ordination (4:14; II Tim 1:6). This "beloved child" in the faith periodically spent his next years laboring with or in behalf of the apostle. In Paul's last epistle, II Timothy, the apostle summons his friend to Rome, hoping to see him once more before he dies (II Tim 4:9, 21).

That Paul loved Timothy dearly is evident from the two epistles addressed to him and the character of those epistles. Once the apostle made reference to the closeness of Timothy to his heart by saying that he had "no man likeminded" (literally, "of equal soul") as Timothy. To Paul, Timothy was a brother, a likeminded or soul brother.

Date and place of writing. On the likely assumption that there were two imprisonments of Paul in Rome, the Pastoral Epistles must be dated after Paul's first release from prison in the spring of A.D. 63. The exact date will depend on the order of activity which Paul followed between the two imprisonments. However, we will not severely stray if we place the date of I Timothy in the fall of A.D. 63 or early A.D. 64.

"This epistle was addressed to Timothy, stationed at Ephesus, some time after Paul had left for Macedonia (1:3). He appears to be in Macedonia at the time of writing (perhaps at Philippi), but it is possible that he may have gone on to Greece when he wrote" (D. E. Hiebert, *An Introduction to the Pauline Epistles*, p. 329).

Purpose. Although not the pastor at Ephesus, Timothy was Paul's personal envoy to that city and later became his representative there. Being a "young man," Paul felt Timothy would need encouragement for the task which faced him at Ephesus. This epistle is designed to provide such encouragement. In addition, an epistle from the respected, once-imprisoned apostle would add validity to the credentials of Timothy in the eyes of the Ephesians.

However, it appears that false teachers, perhaps Gnostic Jews, men who sought to be known as "teachers of the law" (1:7), had invaded Ephesus and were spreading their poisonous doctrine. The pernicious effects of this teaching (1:4; 6:4-5) had to be halted. Paul advises Timothy on the exhortation needed to quell this tide of heresy (4:11, 16; 6:2).

Many of the problems that Timothy faced, the young pastor of the twentieth century also faces. Thus the Pastoral Epistles continue to be the young pastor's best manual for church leadership.

OUTLINE

COMMENTARY

I. INTRODUCTION. 1:1-2.

A. Paul the Author. 1:1.

PAUL, an apostle of Jesus Christ by the commandment of God our Saviour, and Lord Jesus Christ, *which is* our hope;

1:1. Paul. The founder of churches who was once the fighter of churches as Saul before meeting Jesus. The preacher who was the persecutor. His name (Gr *Paulos*) means "little." He was "in his own sight" little (I Sam 15:17) and God highly exalted him too (cf. Phil 2:5-11)! Note his evaluation of himself as "the least of all saints" (Eph 3:8) and finally "the chief of sinners" (I Tim 1:15). He exemplified John 3:30, "I must decrease." That's maturing. I Peter 5:6 works today too. No wonder he could say, "Be ye followers of me" (I Cor 11:1). An **apostle.** His official position. An apostle was appointed by the Holy Spirit (I Cor 12:8-11), he had to have seen the risen Christ (Acts 1:22; II Cor 15:8-9), and he must be endued with miraculous powers (II Cor 12:12). There are no apostles in this sense today. **By the commandment of God,** his authority, "No man takes this honor to himself" (Heb 5:4). He makes it plain God "called" him (Gal 1:15-16). There is a divine call. Happy is the church who has a God-called preacher and not a man-made preacher. **God . . . our Saviour . . . Jesus . . . our hope.** Our Saviour speaks of His past ministry, **our hope** of His future coming. It is a "blessed hope" (Tit 2:11-13), "a purifying hope" (I Jn 3:1-3), a "comforting" hope (I Thess 4:13-18).

2 Unto Timothy, *my* own son in the faith: Grace, mercy, *and* peace, from God our Father and Jesus Christ our Lord.

3 As I besought thee to abide still at Ĕph'e-sus, when I went into Mac-e-do'-ni-a, that thou mightest charge some that they teach no other doctrine,

4 Neither give heed to fables and end-less genealogies, which minister ques-tions, rather than godly edifying which is in faith: *so do.*

5 Now the end of the commandment is charity out of a pure heart, and *of* a good conscience, and *of* faith un-feigned:

6 From which some having swerved have turned aside unto vain jangling;

7 Desiring to be teachers of the law; understanding neither what they say, nor whereof they affirm.

8 But we know that the law *is* good, if a man use it lawfully;

9 Knowing this, that the law is not made for a righteous man, but for the lawless and disobedient, for the un-godly and for sinners, for unholy and

B. Timothy the Recipient. 1:2.

2. Timothy. This name means "he who honors God." **My own son. Son** (Gr *teknon*), is "a child, a born one" and **own** (Gr *gnēsios*) indicates "legitimately born, genuine." He was for real and proved it. Every young preacher needs a spiritual father. Every church should produce preachers! What an honor to both pastor and people to have someone they can call **my own son in the faith.**

The salutation is **Grace** (Gr *charis*), the Greeks' "hello." It means to get what you don't deserve. Salvation is by grace (Eph 2:8-9). **Mercy** (Gr *eleos*) means you don't get what you do deserve. It is only in the Pastoral Epistles that Paul breaks from his usual pattern of saying "grace and peace" and includes "mercy." Preachers need mercy. **Peace** (Gr *eirēnē*) means "to bind together that which has been separated." Christ is our peace (Eph 2:14) and binds us to God.

II. THE CHARGE CONCERNING DOCTRINE. 1:3-11.

Paul begins immediately with his course in pastoral theology on how to "behave in the house of God" (3:15) which is the theme for his whole letter. The basis for correct behavior is correct belief. But correct belief should always issue in correct behavior.

A. Purity of Doctrine (Life). 1:3-4.

3. Besought (Gr *parakaleō*) the same word as Romans 12:1. It is a strong word and suggests Timothy had other plans. **Abide** means "stay put" and **charge some** that is "take a strong stand." To build a strong church the pastor has to take a strong stand! There must be purity of doctrine maintained. **No other doctrine,** "other" meaning doctrine of a "different kind" from what he had taught (cf. Gal 1:6-7).

4. Fables or "myths." These and **endless genealogies** were so prevalent among the Jews **desiring to be teachers of the law** (vs. 7). These countless legends led to questions and doubts. Beware of any teacher or teaching which generates doubts and questions, rather than building godliness.

B. Purpose of Doctrine (Love). 1:5.

5. The **end** or purpose of his charge is "charity" or "love" and not divisions. Some claiming to contend for the faith are contentious about the faith and bring divisions. God is never the author of confusion in churches (I Cor 14:33). This love can only come from a **pure heart** which has been redeemed and cleansed in the blood of Christ. **A good conscience.** There should be "nothing between" not only us and the Saviour but saints as well. Confessing our faults and forgiving others' faults gives a clear conscience. **Faith unfeigned** (Gr *anypokritos*). The Greek word here is the one from which we get "hypocrite." It was a term used of actors, one who pretends to be what he is not!

C. Perversion of Doctrine (Law). 1:6-11.

6. Having swerved (Gr *ektrepō*) is a medical term which means "to twist out of joint" like an arm out of socket. This causes great pain to the whole body.

7-8. Teachers of the law. The law is good and meant to be used even today, but it must be used for its intended purpose, i.e., "that every mouth may be stopped, and all the world may become guilty before God" (Rom 3:19), so that man turns toward Christ for righteousness (Rom 10:1-4; Gal 2:21; 3:24-25).

9-11. A righteous man, "a saved person" is not under the law but grace. He is not lawless but the controlling force is the Holy Spirit and the grace of God (Gal 3:1-5; Tit 2:11ff.). The list of sins parallels the Ten Commandments which condemn each sin

profane, for murderers of fathers and murderers of mothers, for manslayers,

10 For whoremongers, for them that defile themselves with mankind, for menstealers, for liars, for perjured persons, and if there be any other thing that is contrary to sound doctrine;

11 According to the glorious gospel of the blessed God, which was committed to my trust.

12 And I thank Christ Jesus our Lord, who hath enabled me, for that he counted me faithful, putting me into the ministry;

13 Who was before a blasphemer, and a persecutor, and injurious: but I obtained mercy, because I did it ignorantly in unbelief.

14 And the grace of our Lord was exceeding abundant with faith and love which is in Christ Jesus.

15 This is a faithful saying, and worthy of all acceptation, that Christ Jesus came into the world to save sinners; of whom I am chief.

16 Howbeit for this cause I obtained mercy, that in me first Jesus Christ might shew forth all longsuffering, for a pattern to them which should hereafter believe on him to life everlasting.

17 Now unto the King eternal, immortal, invisible, the only wise God, be honour and glory for ever and ever. Amen.

18 This charge I commit unto thee, son Tĭm'o-thÿ, according to the prophecies which went before on thee, that thou by them mightest war a good warfare;

and bring guilt. **Sound doctrine** can be judged by whether it is a "gospel of the glory of the blessed God," which is the sense here. People are transformed in the church by "beholding . . . the glory of the Lord" (II Cor 3:18) and not a constant bombardment of legalistic preaching or teaching. Paul felt keenly this ministry was a trust.

III. THE CHARGE CONCERNING DUTY. 1:12-20.

A. The Challenge from His Own Ministry. 1:12-17.

Doctrine demands duty. These verses share the extreme gratefulness and humility in Paul. What a contrast to the Pharisaic legalities of his day. Correct behavior by the people begins with the behavior of the pastor. Paul, who greeted Timothy with grace and mercy, realized his salvation and ministry was obtained through grace and mercy.

12. I thank Christ Jesus our Lord. There was no arrogance in Paul. The world is "unthankful." He did not take his privilege for granted. **Enabled me** (literally, "put strength"). Paul knew well his "strength is made perfect in weakness" (II Cor 19:9). **Faithful.** This is required of stewards with a trust (I Cor 4:1-2). **Ministry.** No man takes this honor to himself (Heb 4:5) and Paul did not "handle the Word of God deceitfully" (II Cor 4:2), as did the legalizers.

13. Blasphemer. Formerly, Paul was a blasphemer of Jesus, not knowing He was God. A Pharisee couldn't slander God. He "did it ignorantly in unbelief" (Acts 26:9), and thus obtained mercy. **Persecutor,** with the idea of pursuing as one chasing an animal. **Injurious** means one whose contempt breaks forth into outrageous acts of harm. The same gospel that transformed men like this works today as well.

14. Grace . . . was . . . abundant. Regardless of what a man was before he was saved, "where sin abounded, grace did much more abound" (Rom 5:20). Paul appreciated the grace which became the main theme of his ministry. Great churches are built with great emphasis on grace. "Amazing Grace" is the theme song and a favorite of those who believe and behave in the house of God as they should.

15. This is a faithful saying or "faithful is the word," as was the familiar formula in Paul's day. He uses it five times. **To save sinners.** The prime purpose of Christ's coming was not to teach nor to heal nor to be an example, but to save sinners. To the self-righteous Pharisees and legalizers, as Paul himself once was, it would be repugnant to say that among sinners, **I am chief.** Someone said, "The beginning of greatness is to be little; it increases as we become less and is perfect when we become nothing."

16. Long-suffering. Paul was the supreme example of II Peter 3:9. We must not wonder why God does not strike down blasphemers today. He is still long-suffering and some are still being saved today. Paul was the pattern and proof of that.

17. Now unto the King eternal, immortal, invisible, the only wise God, be honor and glory for ever and ever. Amen. Sharing his testimony and remembering what manner of man he had been causes Paul to break out with this great doxology. The Lord's Supper should remind us of the long-suffering of God and suffering of the Saviour and cause heartfelt praises today.

B. The Charge to Timothy's Ministry. 1:18-20.

18. Commit (Gr *paratithēmi*) means "to deposit." It is a banking term. With Paul was deposited the responsibility to warn about false teaching. Every preacher would rather preach positive truth, but God's people need warnings as well. **War.** War has been declared by our enemy and we are constantly engaged in **warfare**. It means wounds and bruises, but there are also the medals of honor.

19 Holding faith, and a good conscience; which some having put away concerning faith have made shipwreck:

19. Holding (the) **faith.** The definite article is here speaking of "the faith" once delivered (Jude 3). "Stay true to the Word" is the meaning today. **Good conscience.** Six times in the Pastoral Epistles Paul speaks concerning the conscience. Some people need an amplifier for that still small voice. It can only be kept clear by judging oneself and confessing sin (I Cor 11:30 ff.; I Jn 1:9). Once the conscience is seared (4:2), even a preacher is capable of committing gross sin. David's conscience wasn't cleared, his sin was ever before him (Ps 51:3), until he confessed it. **Shipwreck.** Many a shipwreck began with unconfessed small sins.

20 Of whom is Hў-me-næ′us and Alexander; whom I have delivered unto Satan, that they may learn not to blaspheme.

20. Two examples are named. **Hymeneus and Alexander** are mentioned again in II Timothy 2:17, but positive identifications are impossible. The seas are filled with shipwrecked preachers. **Delivered unto Satan.** Probably means excommunication as I Corinthians 5:3-5 indicates. It is scriptural. It certainly was effective and would be today, if done correctly (Mt 18:15 ff.).

IV. THE CHARGE CONCERNING PUBLIC WORSHIP. 2:1-15.

Keep in mind these instructions are concerning how to behave in the house of God.

A. Prayer in the Church. 2:1-7.

In Acts 6:4 the early pastors gave themselves to prayer. Prayer was very prominent and should be used properly in the church today.

1. The prescription for prayer. 2:1a.

2:1a. Prayer should include more than asking for needs. **Prayers** (Gr *proseuchē*), the common word for talking to God, should include worship and praise. **Intercessions.** Not in behalf of others, as the English word means, but has the idea of coming to God in boldness and confidence (Heb 10:19). **Giving of thanks.** This should be for specific things, not a phrase tacked on at the close of prayer (I Thess 5:18).

CHAPTER 2
I EXHORT therefore, that, first of all, supplications, prayers, intercessions, *and* giving of thanks, be made for all men;

2. The people for prayer. 2:1b-2a.

1b. All men. This is certainly intercession and is connected with the "all men" of verse 4.

2a. Kings. Respect for authority runs throughout Scripture. Responsibility to pray for those in authority is also the Christian's obligation.

2 For kings, and *for* all that are in authority; that we may lead a quiet and peaceable life in all godliness and honesty.

3. The purpose of prayer. 2:2b-4.

2b. The purpose of prayer for our life here is to live a **quiet** life. **Quiet** means free from outward disturbances, and **peaceable** means inward tranquility. This was especially significant since this was the era of terrible persecution by the Roman emperors such as Nero.

3 For this *is* good and acceptable in the sight of God our Saviour;

4 Who will have all men to be saved, and to come unto the knowledge of the truth.

3. This. Refers to praying for all men. It's the right thing to do!

4. Who will have all men to be saved. God certainly doesn't want anyone in hell (II Pet 3:9). But no one will ever go to hell who ought not be there! He doesn't say He "wishes to save all men" for men could then say, "Why doesn't He save all of them?" **Knowledge of the truth.** What truth they have known, the unsaved have rejected (Rom 1:19-23) or God would have given them more truth (Jn 7:17).

4. The provisions of prayer. 2:5-7.

5 For *there is* one God, and one mediator between God and men, the man Christ Jesus;

5. One God. Emphatically God declares there is no other God beside Him (Isa 43:10 ff.; 44:6-8; 45:5, 21-22; 46:9-10). **One mediator.** God is not one among many but the only one, even as only one God. **The man Christ Jesus.** He spells it out

6 Who gave himself a ransom for all, to be testified in due time.

7 Whereunto I am ordained a preacher, and an apostle, (I speak the truth in Christ, *and* lie not;) a teacher of the Gentiles in faith and verity.

8 I will therefore that men pray every where, lifting up holy hands, without wrath and doubting.

9 In like manner also, that women adorn themselves in modest apparel, with shamefacedness and sobriety; not with broided hair, or gold, or pearls, or costly array.
10 But (which becometh women professing godliness) with good works.

11 Let the woman learn in silence with all subjection.
12 But I suffer not a woman to teach, nor to usurp authority over the man, but to be in silence.

13 For Adam was first formed, then Eve.
14 And Adam was not deceived, but the woman being deceived was in the transgression.

plainly. In Paul's day the Gnostics had a vast system of mediators made up of angels but God declares, not so. The Virgin Mary, Joseph Smith, nor anyone else is such a mediator. He is the Mediator for prayer as well (Heb 4:10; 10:19-20).

6. Gave himself. Calvary was no accident, no failure! (Jn 10:17-18). **A ransom.** He paid for man's sins in full, not just a down payment (Rom 5:8; I Pet 3:18). **Testified.** The Lord Jesus did His part and now it is up to man to get this good news to every creature (Mk 16:15). Christ was obedient in testifying the gospel to man; now men must be obedient in testifying the gospel to other men (Jn 20:21).

7. Whereunto I am ordained a preacher. The primary purpose of any preacher is to preach the gospel to every creature (Mk 16:15). Christ did the work of reconciliation, now man has the word of reconciliation (II Cor 5:18 ff.).

B. People in the Church. 2:8-15.

Paul now deals with issues concerning the place and performance of men and women in the church. He tells how they should behave in the house of God.

1. The men. 2:8.

8. Therefore. Since "men ought always to pray" (Lk 18:1) and since there is a mediator through whom man can pray, Paul now gives some instructions of how men should pray. **Men.** This is the word for man (Gr *anēr*) in contrast to women; not the word mankind (Gr *anthrōpos*). Men should pray, not just the ladies' missionary circles or prayer groups. Some take this specifically to mean public prayer in a church and believe it indicates men should do the public praying. The emphasis, however, is that men should pray **every where** as opposed to infrequently or not at all. **Holy hands.** Paul stresses the "holy" or "unpolluted" and not the posture of "lifting up" hands, though there is nothing wrong with the raising of hands in prayer. Men who expect to get prayers answered must be men of God, godly men, or God won't hear them (Isa 59:1; Ps 66:18). Toward others there must be no **wrath,** even against the evil rulers of the day. Toward God there must be faith **without . . . doubting** (Mt 13:58; 21:22).

2. The women. 2:9-15.

9-10. In like manner also. He now turns to women and worship. To say Paul was a woman-hater and wrote this as a personal feeling is to misunderstand the teaching of the apostle or to deny the inspiration of Scripture (II Pet 1:21). He is simply admonishing women to perform and function as God designed them to. Women are not in any way inferior to men in pauline thought. In Christ women are equal to men (Gal 3:28). **Modest.** This is a natural trait of women until they are taught differently. A beautiful and innate quality of womanhood is an emotional need for attention. God designed this quality but says this need should be fulfilled not by clothes but by conduct. **Good works.** She can win her husband to Christ by her behavior (I Pet 3:1-2).

11-12. The home is the woman's castle. In the church the situation is different (I Cor 14:34 ff.). This is God's order and chain of command "in the house of God." Proverbs 31 gives details of a wise woman's place and function: properly performed, her children "call her blessed" and "her husband . . . praiseth her" (vs. 28).

13-14. The precedent for this order in function is in creation of mankind itself. **Adam was first formed.** He was designed for headship by God. Woman was taken from his side to rule creation by his side (Gen 2:21-22). Of all God's creations, only woman could meet the innermost needs of a man for only woman was designed to meet those needs (Gen 2:20ff.). As man is the crown of God's creation, so woman is the prized jewel in that crown. The **woman being deceived** or beguiled by Satan indicates a fundamental tendency which shows the woman should not be the leader in the home or the church. Paul speaks later (II Tim 3:6) how women are susceptible to be "led away."

15 Notwithstanding she shall be saved in childbearing, if they continue in faith and charity and holiness with sobriety.

15. Childbearing. Uniquely the woman's body is wondrously designed for childbearing. The "barren womb" is "never satisfied" (Prov 30:16). Unless psychologically scarred somewhere along the way, every woman has an inner craving to be a mother. God designed her so. **Saved in childbearing.** Every mother is not going to heaven simply because she is a mother. The most acceptable meaning of this passage is that it refers to the incarnation of Christ as promised to Eve (Gen 3:15) and the woman who believes in this One, the Lord Jesus, shall be saved.

V. THE CHARGE CONCERNING LEADERS. 3:1-16.

In discussing how to behave in the house of God, Paul now turns to the leader. There are two scriptural officers of the church: the bishop (Gr *episkopos*), the pastor or overseer today, and the deacon (Gr *diakonos*). The overseer, the pastor or preacher of the gospel, is to live by the gospel (I Cor 9:14). This is his calling. The deacon serves in the church but does not live by this service. He is nowhere told he is called to this as a living. There are no double standards of Christian living. What *ought* to be true of every believer *must* be true of leaders in the house of God. It is very proper to have standards of conduct for leaders in a local church. Here is a good list to go by.

A. The Pastors. 3:1-7.

3:1. Desireth. What is the call to preach, to pastor God's people? Philippians 2:13 says, "For it is God which worketh in you both to will and to do of his good pleasure." God works from within. He "draws" men to salvation from within and does the same for service, through placing a desire "to do His good pleasure." This is not to be equated with "burden" for some people or particular field. You may have a burden for India and pray for those people every day; but if God has never placed a desire deep in your being to go there and minister to them, you do not have the call of God to India. One has to be sure any desire for a particular field of service is not a selfish desire of the flesh! The word "desire" is a very strong and intense word. Paul said "woe is unto me, if I preach not the gospel" (I Cor 9:16). The call to preach or pastor ("to do His good pleasure") is an intense burning desire for this ministry planted in one's heart by God. **Bishop** means overseer or pastor; I Peter 5:12, "taking the oversight" of God's flock. Hebrews 13:17 says he is to "watch for your souls." This is not to be entered into lightly. Just as there were some disqualifications for soldiers (Deut 20:5-8) and priests (Lev 21:16 ff.) so there are for pastors. Some of the qualifications are absolute and some are relative, but one must not change nor lower the standard, only do all to measure up to God's standard. **Good work.** Pastoring is a good work. It must be approached with that attitude. It is a tragedy to see disillusioned and defeated ex-pastors decrying the ministry.

CHAPTER 3

THIS *is* a true saying, If a man desire the office of a bishop, he desireth a good work.

2 A bishop then must be blameless, the husband of one wife, vigilant, sober, of good behaviour, given to hospitality, apt to teach;

2. Blameless. It does not mean sinless. There is to be no just cause to blame him. Pastors will never be sinless this side of glory, but they must be blameless. **Husband of one wife.** The traditional and most widely accepted view of Bible-believing, soul-winning preachers has been that a pastor must not be divorced and remarried. History has shown it almost never works for a pastor to be divorced. If he cannot rule his own house how can he rule the church?

Vigilant or "temperate" is the idea; watchful as he oversees the flock. **Sober** or serious-minded about a serious business. It doesn't mean a long-faced person with no humor. A sense of humor is essential and the strain could be too much for any man. **Good behavior** means orderly. It is the outward result of a sober mind. **Hospitality.** He must love people. He must be given to this! A pastor once said, "I don't like people, they bother me." He loved to preach, but he had no business being a pastor. He failed in the pastorate and later became an evangelist. **Apt to teach.** The construction of Ephesians 4:12 indicates definitely a pastor is also a teacher. A God-called pastor most assuredly has the gift of teaching. A pastor must reach the sinner and teach the saint. To not do both is unscriptural and unbalanced.

3 Not given to wine, no striker, not greedy of filthy lucre; but patient, not a brawler, not covetous;

3. Not given to wine or "not a drinker." **No striker.** This refers to physical acts of violence while **brawler** means a quarrelsome person, i.e., argumentative. He must keep his cool! **Greedy.** The love of money will certainly ruin a pastor. **Patient** or gentle with the wisdom from above which is peaceable (Jas 3:17). **Covetous** (Gr *aphilargyros*), the literal meaning is no lover of money. He must "be content with such things as he has" (Heb 13:5). The Levites had no inheritance in the land, God was their inheritance (Deut 18:2; Num 18:20). A pastor must set his affections on things above (Col 3:1).

4 One that ruleth well his own house, having his children in subjection with all gravity;
5 (For if a man know not how to rule his own house, how shall he take care of the church of God?)
6 Not a novice, lest being lifted up with pride he fall into the condemnation of the devil.

4-5. Ruleth. It must be done by a loving leadership and not a dominating dictatorship. The test of his calling and his success can be measured by the success in his home. His sons in the faith will turn out like the sons of his family!

6. Not a novice (Gr *neophytos*). The Septuagint (LXX) uses this word of newly planted trees. **Let these also first be proved** (vs. 10) and **lay hands suddenly on no man** (5:22) fits here as well.

7 Moreover he must have a good report of them which are without; lest he fall into reproach and the snare of the devil.

7. Good report. He must deal with them that are "without" (the secular world) and so must have a good report of them to reach them. **Reproach.** Satan is the accuser. He will see to it that every flaw is seen by the world and do all to ruin God's servant's testimony and effectiveness.

B. The Deacons. 3:8-13.

8 Likewise *must* the deacons *be* grave, not doubletongued, not given to much wine, not greedy of filthy lucre;

8. Likewise. Just as a pastor lives in a glass house and represents all a Christian should be, so does the deacon. He must be chosen for what he is and not what he has or who he is in the world's eyes. There are musts for him as well as the pastor or overseer. **Deacon** means servant. They were initially chosen to wait on tables and minister to particular situations in the church (Acts 6:1 ff.). They are not to "run the church." They are to relieve the pastor from tasks that would hinder him from giving himself to prayer and ministering the Word (Acts 6:4). **Grave.** On the positive side, the deacon must be worthy of respect. **Not double-tongued.** It simply means not saying one thing and meaning another. **Not given to much wine.** The biblical testimony is consistently against the use of strong drink. The practical application of the principle in modern society is total abstinence for all concerned. **Not greedy of filthy lucre.** The temptation is there even to the most godly deacon. It cannot be tolerated as it is the root of all other evil.

9 Holding the mystery of the faith in a pure conscience.

9. The faith. To be a deacon a man must be grounded in the faith. Belief is the basis of behavior. **Pure conscience.** His behavior must conform to his belief so that his conscience is pure.

10 And let these also first be proved; then let them use the office of a deacon, being *found* blameless.
11 Even so *must their* wives *be* grave, not slanderers, sober, faithful in all things.

10. Proved. By his belief and behavior. A new convert cannot be grounded and must not be thrust into prominence.

11. Wives. The construction and context seems to indicate "deaconesses" as Phoebe (Rom 16:1). To be sure these qualities must be in the wives of deacons as well or the deacon's ministry would be blemished and hindered for not ruling his own house well. **Grave.** Same as the deacon (vs. 8). **Not slanderers** (Gr *diabolos*), the word for the devil. A slanderer is a devil indeed. **Sober.** Same as in 3:2. **Faithful in all things.** This covers a multitude of areas in practical matters of the church.

12 Let the deacons be the husbands of one wife, ruling their children and their own houses well.

13 For they that have used the office of a deacon well purchase to themselves a good degree, and great boldness in the faith which is in Christ Jesus.

14 These things write I unto thee, hoping to come unto thee shortly:

15 But if I tarry long, that thou mayest know how thou oughtest to behave thyself in the house of God, which is the church of the living God, the pillar and ground of the truth.

16 And without controversy great is the mystery of godliness: God was manifest in the flesh, justified in the Spirit, seen of angels, preached unto the Gentiles, believed on in the world, received up into glory.

CHAPTER 4

NOW the Spirit speaketh expressly, that in the latter times some shall depart from the faith, giving heed to seducing spirits, and doctrines of devils;

2 Speaking lies in hypocrisy; having their conscience seared with a hot iron;

3 Forbidding to marry, *and commanding* to abstain from meats, which

---

12. See verses 4 and 5 above.

13. **Used the office . . . well.** The motivation to do so is a positive promise. **Purchase.** Obtain or acquire is the sense. **Good degree.** It means standing or respect in the church. Not a promotion, for that would make the motives wrong. **Great boldness.** Confidence and assurance to speak with authority. This was sought after in the early church (Acts 4:13; 29ff.).

C. The Purpose of This Charge. 3:14-16.

14. **Hoping to come unto thee shortly.** Paul planned to come shortly with his apostolic authority to set things in order there, but the problems could not wait and so he writes his instructions.

15. **The house of God . . . the church.** This most assuredly refers to the local church in Ephesus. The emphasis here is in order and structure in a local church. There has to be order, or organization, a chain of command and a policy of correct behavior for God's work to function properly. No Christian is an island unto himself, nor is anyone to do that which is right in his own sight.

16. Now comes one of the greatest, most profound statements of Scripture. The depths of the truths of verse 15 he calls **the mystery of godliness. Mystery** (Gr *mystērion*) does not mean mysterious but a "secret," now being made known. It was used of Greek rites which were secret. **Godliness.** Godliness is "profitable" (4:8) and "great gain" (6:6). The doctrine which follows will produce this highly treasured godliness. Notice the couplets: "flesh" and "spirit"; "angels" and "nations"; and "world" and "glory." **Was manifest in the flesh.** Christ the eternal Son became flesh (Jn 1:14), to provide salvation which was to be both preached and believed. No wonder it is called "so great salvation" (Heb 2:3). **Justified in the Spirit.** The flesh refers to His humanity and Spirit refers to His deity. He proved to be all He claimed. **Seen of angels.** The holy angels witnessed His every move, such as His birth (Lk 2:9), temptation (Mt 1:13), Gethsemane (Mt 26:53), resurrection (Mt 28:2), and ascension (Acts 1:10). **Preached unto the Gentiles.** This good news is to go to all the world (Mt 28:19). This is the Christian's responsibility after Christ performed the work of reconciliation (II Cor 5:29 ff.). **Believed.** Man's responsibility is to respond to these great truths and believe. **Received up into glory.**

VI. THE CHARGE CONCERNING FALSE TEACHING. 4:1-16.

Chapter 1 dealt with the false teaching of Judaizers. Now Paul deals with the late false teachers such as the Gnostics. They are identifiable even today, as they were then.

A. The False Teaching. 4:1-5.

4:1. The Spirit speaketh expressly or distinctly. There is no uncertainty but that these **depart from the faith.** This faith is that "which was once delivered unto the saints" (Jude 3) and the "one faith" of Ephesians 4:5. **Giving heed to seducing spirits.** They are active. There are the "deep things of Satan" (Rev 2:24). **The doctrines of devils.** To some it seems harsh to attribute false teaching as coming from Satan, and one must be careful not to attribute everything with which he disagrees to Satan. The doctrine of devils probably means doctrines taught by demons.

2. **Conscience seared.** How can they believe such things? As your finger is numb when it has been burned with a hot iron, so too their consciences are numbed by the searing of sin.

3-5. **Forbidding to marry . . . meats.** The Essenes of the first century felt marriage was only necessary for the preserva-

God hath created to be received with thanksgiving of them which believe and know the truth.

4 For every creature of God *is* good, and nothing to be refused, if it be received with thanksgiving:

5 For it is sanctified by the word of God and prayer.

6 If thou put the brethren in remembrance of these things, thou shalt be a good minister of Jesus Christ, nourished up in the words of faith and of good doctrine, whereunto thou hast attained.

7 But refuse profane and old wives' fables, and exercise thyself *rather* unto godliness.

8 For bodily exercise profiteth little: but godliness is profitable unto all things, having promise of the life that now is, and of that which is to come.

9 This *is* a faithful saying and worthy of all acceptation.

10 For therefore we both labour and suffer reproach, because we trust in the living God, who is the Saviour of all men, specially of those that believe.

11 These things command and teach.

12 Let no man despise thy youth; but be thou an example of the believers, in word, in conversation, in charity, in spirit, in faith, in purity.

13 Till I come, give attendance to reading, to exhortation, to doctrine.

14 Neglect not the gift that is in thee, which was given thee by prophecy, with the laying on of the hands of the presbytery.

tion of the human race and thus forbade it to their followers. The Bible does not teach such a drastic policy. Forced celibacy is not scriptural. **Meats** (Gr *brōma*) means solid food in general and not simply animal meat. All types of ascetic teachings have promoted this error even to the present day. The Bible says "marriage" and "meats" were created by God and are not to be refused. **Thanksgiving.** The blessing at the table is not simply a ritual but is scriptural. Vincent says, "Not declared holy but made holy. Thanksgiving to God has a sanctifying effect. The food itself has no moral quality (Rom 14:14), but acquires a holy quality by its consecration to God; by being acknowledged as God's gift, and partaken of as nourishing the life for God's service" (*Word Studies in the New Testament*, p. 246).

B. The Faithful Teacher. 4:6-16.

6. Remembrance. It is so easy to forget. Thus the need for the Lord's Supper to "remember" His death for sins (I Cor 11:24-25), and to "stir up your pure minds by way of remembrance" (II Pet 3:1). **A good minister** will warn of false teaching (**these things**) as well, though not always a popular thing to do.

7-8. But, in contrast, Paul says, **refuse profane and old wives fables.** Don't get detoured by profitless trivia. **Exercise** about things that lead unto **godliness. Exercise** (Gr *gumuazo*) is the word from which we get gymnasium. Exercise takes determination and discipline. Godliness comes at a price but it is **profitable . . . now,** here and hereafter. If half the effort that goes into **bodily exercise** were put into spiritual exercise, God's people would be much healthier and stronger spiritually, and much better off.

9. This is . . . worthy of all acceptation and that no one can deny. The wise become doers of the Word.

10. We . . . labor (Gr *kopiaō*) means to work at it to the point of exhaustion as athletes do. Did you ever watch football players practice and exercise like this? To pay such a price for godliness is done because **we trust in the living God. The Saviour of all men.** When Christ died He made atonement sufficient for the whole world. He is the Deliverer, the preserver of all mankind, but the Saviour from sin of those who believe. This does not teach universalism, that all will be saved. When you compare Scripture with Scripture you find Him saying to some, "Depart from me, I never knew you" (Mt 7:23).

11. To timid Timothy, Paul says emphatically, **command** and **teach** these things.

12. Then follows the great verse to encourage youth. Timothy was somewhere between thirty and forty years of age. He was but a youth to the "elders" at Ephesus. The wise elder will not "look down" on those younger than he. The wise youth will be an example of believers so as to earn the respect of his elders. **Example** (Gr *typos*) is a pattern, type or model. He is to be a model in **word** or speech, in **conversation** or behavior, in **charity** or love, the fruit of the Spirit, in **faith** or faithfulness and in **purity** in motives as well as acts.

13. For a balanced ministry Paul admonishes Timothy concerning three things. **Give attendance to reading** (Gr *anaginōskō*), public reading of Scripture since all did not possess Bibles as we do. **Exhortation** or encouragement, the application of teaching. It is the grounding in the truth for belief that affects behavior. **Doctrine.** This is the basis of Christian belief. "Experience" is quick and easily gotten, but doctrine takes time and a great deal of effort. Yet doctrinally weak believers are immature believers and the pastor who does not give attention to doctrine does not exhibit a love for his people.

14. Neglect not. There is difference of opinion as to whether this meant stop neglecting or don't start neglecting the gift. An entrusted spiritual gift is not to be put under a bushel (Mt 5:15) nor hid in the earth (Mt 25:25) but to be put to use. Every

15 Meditate upon these things; give thyself wholly to them; that thy profiting may appear to all.

16 Take heed unto thyself, and unto the doctrine; continue in them: for in doing this thou shalt both save thyself, and them that hear thee.

CHAPTER 5

REBUKE not an elder, but intreat *him* as a father; *and* the younger men as brethren;

2 The elder women as mothers; the younger as sisters, with all purity.

3 Honour widows that are widows indeed.

4 But if any widow have children or nephews, let them learn first to shew piety at home, and to requite their parents: for that is good and acceptable before God.
5 Now she that is a widow indeed, and desolate, trusteth in God, and continueth in supplications and prayers night and day.

6 But she that liveth in pleasure is dead while she liveth.

7 And these things give in charge, that they may be blameless.
8 But if any provide not for his own, and specially for those of his own house, he hath denied the faith, and is worse than an infidel.
9 Let not a widow be taken into the number under threescore years old, having been the wife of one man,
10 Well reported of for good works; if she have brought up children, if she have lodged strangers, if she have washed the saints' feet, if she have relieved the afflicted, if she have diligently followed every good work.

Christian is gifted (I Pet 4:10; I Cor 12:7, 11) and needs to heed this admonition. "The gift to Timothy was through prophecy; that is, it was made known to him by an inspired prophet. The imposition of hands was a symbolic action accompanying the reception of the gift" (H. Kent, *The Pastor's Epistle*, p. 164).

15. Meditate here means "to care for" these things he has just mentioned. Paul then emphasizes the importance of this by saying, **give thyself wholly to them.** To do so will have an effect (**profiting**) that is apparent to all!

16. Take heed . . . unto the doctrine of God and you will not be "giving heed . . . to doctrines of devils" (vs. 1). This seems to be the contextual meaning of "save thyself." The hearers also will be saved from "giving heed to seducing spirits."

VII. THE CHARGE CONCERNING THE LAITY. 5:1-6:2.

A. The Older. 5:1-2.

5:1. Rebuke not an elder. Timothy is not to let any man reject his youth, but he is not to rebuke an elder or older person, which is what elder here means and not an official office. There must be respect on the part of each. He should not rebuke with harsh words but entreat or beseech as a member of the family.

2. Treatment of women must be **with all purity.** God's servants must be so discreet. Any impropriety (especially with women) can and has ruined many a pastor's ministry.

B. The Widows. 5:3-16.

3. Widows indeed. There were almost certainly no public "widowages" as there are orphanages in the first century. Those widows, cared for by the church, had to fall into certain guidelines and have certain responsibilities.

4. Nephews (Gr *ekgonos*) is a word which meant descendant, usually a grandson. If widows had descendants it was their obligation to care for these widows. The widows must **show piety** or proper respect toward their family.

5. Now, in contrast widows without relatives to care for them, . . . **a widow indeed, and desolate** has some guidelines to meet before being the responsibility of the church. **Trusteth in God.** She must be a Christian. She should be giving herself to spiritual matters. **Supplication and prayers.** With the hardships and perhaps tragedies she has faced, she can have a heart for others and truly intercede on their behalf. Only eternity will reveal the enormous importance godly widows have played in the ministries of God around the world.

6. Liveth in pleasure. Her way of life is one of pleasure. **Is dead** is a present participle meaning now she is already useless to God and others while she still lives physically.

7-8. Women who are blameless in meeting the spiritual requirements are first to be cared for by **his own,** that is, the children or descendants of verse 4. For a believer not to **provide** for his own house is worse than an infidel, for even they recognize their obligations to widows. Believers must as well.

9-10. The widow with no descendants is not to be **taken into the number,** or "added to the list" to be cared for by the church, unless they meet the following conditions: they must be over sixty years of age and must not be married more than once. **Good works.** To qualify for receiving the good works of others a widow must have performed good works herself.

These good works follow. (1) **Brought up children.** The grand duty and privilege of the homemaker (Tit 2:4-5) is the bearing and rearing of children (I Tim 2:15). Women given to good works are not deceived by the clever but satanic furor of the twentieth century of the role of women in modern life. (2)

11 But the younger widows refuse: for when they have begun to wax wanton against Christ, they will marry;

12 Having damnation, because they have cast off their first faith.

13 And withal they learn *to be* idle, wandering about from house to house; and not only idle, but tattlers also and busybodies, speaking things which they ought not.
14 I will therefore that the younger women marry, bear children, guide the house, give none occasion to the adversary to speak reproachfully.
15 For some are already turned aside after Satan.

16 If any man or woman that believeth have widows, let them relieve them, and let not the church be charged; that it may relieve them that are widows indeed.
17 Let the elders that rule well be counted worthy of double honour, especially they who labour in the word and doctrine.

18 For the scripture saith, Thou shalt not muzzle the ox that treadeth out the corn. And, The labourer *is* worthy of his reward.

19 Against an elder receive not an accusation, but before two or three witnesses.

20 Them that sin rebuke before all, that others also may fear.
21 I charge *thee* before God, and the Lord Jesus Christ, and the elect angels, that thou observe these things without preferring one before another, doing nothing by partiality.
22 Lay hands suddenly on no man, neither be partaker of other men's sins: keep thyself pure.

23 Drink no longer water, but use a little wine for thy stomach's sake and thine often infirmities.

2504

Lodged strangers. The widow should be hospitable if she wants others' hospitality now. **Washed . . . saints' feet.** The whole context is of good works done by women primarily in the home and not religious duties. This does not mean footwashing as an ordinance in the church. **Relieved.** The women should care for those neighbors or fellow Christians who are afflicted.

11. Younger widows refuse. Those under sixty years of age (vs. 9). They are not to be the responsibility of the church for they will usually **wax wanton** Gr *katastrēniaō*). This word carries the idea of having sexual desires to which she yields and marries again.

12. Having damnation. The idea here seems to be that she marries an unbeliever, setting aside her **first faith.** Paul approves remarriage "in the Lord" (Rom 7:7; I Cor 7:39). The damnation has to be taken as chastening according to I Corinthians 11:30-32 and Hebrews 12:4-11.

13. Under divine inspiration Paul foretells that the tendency of young widows is to be **idle, wandering, . . . tattlers, busybodies.** This fits with I Timothy 3:6. It should be noted that this is not always the case, but too frequently is the case.

14-15. Because of this, Paul reasons that the **younger women marry, bear children.** This is the design of the Creator for their bodies and personalities. The "barren womb" is never satisfied (Prov 30:16). Under normal conditions this is fulfilling and totally rewarding to a woman. To denigrate this divine desire, as some modern liberationists have done, is to cause women to question God's wisdom. Thus they exhibit that they **are already turned aside after Satan.**

16. Believers are to care for their own relatives so the church can care for those who have no one to care for them.

C. The Elders. 5:17-25.

17. Elders. These are not the same as those in verse 1, but are the pastors of the church who **rule** (cf. Heb 13:7, 17, 24). They **labor in the word,** that is, teach or preach. The word **labor** (Gr *kopos*) is strong word meaning "to work hard to the point of exhaustion." The ministry is hard work and not to be taken lightly. Those who rule **well,** for not all do, are to have **double honor.** This seems best to mean honor for their works' sake as in I Thessalonians 5:12-13, and to receive remuneration as indicated in verse 18.

18. The laborer is worthy of his reward. Men called of God would preach whether they are paid or not, but God ordained they are to live by their ministry (I Cor 9:7-11). Paul says that even the animals reaped from their toils as was told they should in Deuteronomy 25:4.

19. Accusation (Gr *katēgoria*). This word is used of formal charges before a court. A minister has one solemn possession, i.e., his character. An accusation against him, therefore, is serious and must be witnessed before two or three persons or not at all. This would stop many rumors and save many of God's servants, if heeded.

20-21. It must be done decently and in order (I Cor 14:40). When an elder is found guilty God says, **rebuke before all** and it is to be done without **partiality.** If God's people expect Congress and public officials to police themselves, so must God's servants.

22. The charging of God's servants is important. Thus ordination must not be an impulsive act. **Lay hands suddenly on no man** or hastily. Many have been ordained too young or too soon. This could save having to discipline a man later if he is first proved (3:10).

23. Use a little wine, for thy stomach's sake. Obviously he did not advocate drinking, but to take the wine for medicinal use

24 Some men's sins are open beforehand, going before to judgment; and some *men* they follow after.

25 Likewise also the good works *of some* are manifest beforehand; and they that are otherwise cannot be hid.

CHAPTER 6

LET as many servants as are under the yoke count their own masters worthy of all honour, that the name of God and *his* doctrine be not blasphemed.

2 And they that have believing masters, let them not despise *them,* because they are brethren; but rather do *them* service, because they are faithful and beloved, partakers of the benefit. These things teach and exhort.

3 If any man teach otherwise, and consent not to wholesome words, *even* the words of our Lord Jesus Christ, and to the doctrine which is according to godliness;

4 He is proud, knowing nothing, but doting about questions and strifes of words, whereof cometh envy, strife, railings, evil surmisings,

5 Perverse disputings of men of corrupt minds, and destitute of the truth, supposing that gain is godliness: from such withdraw thyself.

6 But godliness with contentment is great gain.

7 For we brought nothing into *this* world, *and it is* certain we can carry nothing out.

8 And having food and raiment let us be therewith content.

9 But they that will be rich fall into temptation and a snare, and *into* many foolish and hurtful lusts, which drown men in destruction and perdition.

was common. With highly effective, prescribed medicines today there is no justification for believers to hide behind this verse to imbibe!

24-25. Cannot be hid. Time will tell! It is not always evident what is inside a man. Therefore don't rush into ordaining a man until it is quite evident by his works as to his character. Poor character qualities will always surface in a man, given enough time.

D. The Slaves. 6:1-2.

6:1. Slavery is nothing new. Paul faced it. God doesn't advocate revolution here but a resolution through proper attitudes and treatment. **Servants.** Addressed here are believing slaves (Gr *doulos*) under unbelieving masters. The Christian attitude is to **honor** those over you whether they are in public office (Rom 13:1 ff.), or parents in the home (Eph 6:1 ff.), or a boss on the job. God is totally against anarchy. For a Christian not to obey those in authority can cause the name of God to be **blasphemed** or "slandered."

2. Let them not despise believing masters either. Despise here means "to look down on." The believing master was not under any obligation to free a slave (cf. Philemon). Though equal in Christ, all men are not created equal. Some will never be leaders. Some will always have more than others by virtue of inheritance or harder work. **These things** refers back to the doctrine and duty presented by Paul so that one might behave in the house of God, the church. The believer is to seek godliness and not gain of worldly goods or glory. The rest of this chapter elaborates on this.

VIII. THE CHARGE CONCERNING THE PASTOR. 6:3-19.

A. His Teaching. 6:3-5.

3. If is an "if" of a fulfilled condition and could be translated, "if, as the case is." It was being done. **Teach otherwise** (Gr *heterodidaskaleō*), to teach heresy. **Wholesome** (Gr *hygiainō*, from which we get hygiene or healthy. Any other teaching is unhealthy and doesn't lead to **godliness.**

4. He is proud, "puffed up" or "in a fog." **Knowing nothing** and doesn't even know that he knows nothing. **Doting** (Gr *noseō*) means "to be sick" as opposed to "wholesome" in verse 3. Unhealthy **questions** and **strifes** bring on the diseases of **envy, strife,** etc. and should be avoided in the house of God.

5. Perverse disputings (Gr *diaparatribē*) means "rubbing against" or friction. These false teachers are a continuous friction and destitute of the truth. **Supposing that gain is godliness.**

The Greek construction is really saying that godliness, which is the subject in the original language, is the way or source of gain. There are those today who openly advocate riches and material gain for those who follow their brand of Christianity. They promise you will ride in the biggest car and wear the most expensive clothes.

B. His Living. 6:6-10.

6-8. Conversely the believer is to be "content" which is **great gain.** Too many marriages have gone on the rocks because this principle was violated. Many couples are strained financially, putting enormous pressure on their marriage. **Contentment,** when coupled with **godliness,** brings great pleasure and harmony.

9-10. They that will be rich. The word **will** (Gr *boulomai*), is not just an emotional fancy but indicates a calculated and planned procedure to get rich. It causes a **temptation . . . snare, and hurtful . . . lusts.** Money doesn't do this, it is the **love of**

10 For the love of money is the root of all evil: which while some coveted after, they have erred from the faith, and pierced themselves through with many sorrows.

11 But thou, O man of God, flee these things; and follow after righteousness, godliness, faith, love, patience, meekness.

12 Fight the good fight of faith, lay hold on eternal life, whereunto thou art also called, and hast professed a good profession before many witnesses.

13 I give thee charge in the sight of God, who quickeneth all things, and before Christ Jesus, who before Pontius Pilate witnessed a good confession;

14 That thou keep this commandment without spot, unrebukeable, until the appearing of our Lord Jesus Christ:

15 Which in his times he shall shew, who is the blessed and only Potentate, the King of kings, and Lord of lords;

16 Who only hath immortality, dwelling in the light which no man can approach unto; whom no man hath seen, nor can see: to whom be honour and power everlasting. Amen.

17 Charge them that are rich in this world, that they be not highminded, nor trust in uncertain riches, but in the living God, who giveth us richly all things to enjoy;

18 That they do good, that they be rich in good works, ready to distribute, willing to communicate;

money. Riches are neither good nor bad. It is the attitude toward them that is good or bad. Some very wealthy love money far less than poorer people who say they can't afford to tithe!

Coveted (Gr *oregomai*) means "to stretch one's self out to grasp." It causes to err from the faith. Rather one should "set his affections on things above" (Col 3:1).

C. His Goals. 6:11-16.

11-12. But, in striking contrast, the man of God should **flee, follow,** and **fight. Flee** is in the Greek present imperative and denotes a continuous action. The temptation for riches is ever present and Timothy was to constantly run from this desire. Instead he was to **follow** (Gr *diōkō*) or "to run" after **righteousness.** This is not the imputed righteousness which every believer has by faith (Rom 10:1-9), but is personal and practical righteous living which brings usefulness and rewards. Not defeated by the snares which he flees, but clothed with this fruit of the Spirit (righteousness, godliness, faith, etc.) he is to **Fight the good fight of faith.** The word **Fight** (Gr *agōnizomai*) is an athletic term meaning "to engage in a contest." This contest is the whole life of the believer striving to win "the prize of the high calling of God in Christ Jesus" (Phil 4:13). It is a **good** fight whereas the fight for money is **evil** (vs. 10).

Lay hold on eternal life. Timothy was already saved and possessed eternal life. The idea here seems to be "get hold" of this eternal life that you have until "the things of earth grow strangely dim." Let it grip you until you get into this race and win the prize. **Called.** This is a "high calling" and every believer has this same calling in life. Timothy had already professed a **good profession** before many witnesses, as every believer should.

13. Charge or command. Once again Paul presents the seriousness of what he had said. Timothy is to keep this charge, not for Paul's sake, but before God who **quickeneth** or "preserves life" and Christ Jesus who gave a good witness before **Pontius Pilate.** Pilate said, "I find in him no fault at all" (Jn 18:38).

14. Commandment probably refers to the initial command of 1:3-5. The whole book is a charge to be alert to the false teachers and their doctrine. **Until the appearing.** The coming of Christ is the great motivation for godly living (I Jn 3:2-3). What happened to Israel was for our admonition (I Cor 10:6, 11) and what was written to Timothy is for our admonition as well, even until the appearing of our Lord Jesus Christ. God never changes (Heb 13:8). Standards and mores may change in men's minds, but God's standards and qualifications are the same until Jesus comes.

15. In his times. He shall show this old world who is boss, who is the **only Potentate, the King of kings,** and **Lord of lords.** We may often wonder why He doesn't quiet some of the wicked rulers today but "the fullness of time" (Gal 4:4) hasn't come yet for that great moment.

16. Who only (Gr *monos*); the word for "only" expresses uniqueness. Jesus uniquely has immortality. In no uncertain terms Jesus is equated fully with God Himself in this verse.

D. His Duty. 6:17-19.

17-18. With this in mind, Paul says, **Charge them that are rich** to trust only in the living God and not in uncertain riches. There is nothing wrong with being rich, if those who are rich are "rich toward God" (Lk 12:21) and are willing to communicate or give of what they have to those in need. Then God will give "richly all things to enjoy." This is the path to true happiness and contentment. It is the summation of Matthew 6:33 and Psalm 37:4. There is nothing wrong with making money if the motive is "that he may have to give to him that needeth" (Eph 4:28).

19 Laying up in store for themselves a good foundation against the time to come, that they may lay hold on eternal life.

19. Laying up in store. The proper attitude toward riches and the use of money lays up treasure for the future. The age-old expression, "You can't take it with you," is still true. But the believer can send it on ahead of him in the form of rewards. To do this is what it means to **lay hold on eternal life.**

IX. CONCLUSION. 6:20-21.

A. Plea for Faithfulness. 6:20a.

20 O Tim'o-thy, keep that which is committed to thy trust, avoiding profane and vain babblings, and oppositions of science falsely so called:

20a. O Timothy. What a pleading this is. Paul's love for Timothy comes through loud and clear. **Keep** (Gr *phylassō*) means to "guard" in the military sense. Guard that which was committed to thy trust. Paul pleads for Timothy's faithfulness as the requirement of a steward (I Cor 4:2). To each of us are given "gifts and callings" (Rom 11:33). They are sacred; they must not be taken lightly. None of us dares let up his guard for one minute. We must all be found faithful.

B. Plea for Separation. 6:20b-21a.

20b. To not be found faithful is a sin. But, in order to be found faithful, one must avoid the detours of **profane and vain babblings** and **science falsely so called.** This is not to intimate that science is innately evil and to be avoided at all costs. The **science** (Gr *gnōsis*) here means any falsely named wisdom, any wisdom which does not begin with the fear of the Lord.

21 Which some professing have erred concerning the faith. Grace be with thee. Amen.

21a. Failure to avoid this type of so-called wisdom caused some to err, **concerning the faith.** Err (Gr *astocheō*) means to miss the mark. They miss the mark of God's purpose for them now and they miss the mark of God's prize for them in heaven (Phil 4:13). Believers must separate themselves from those who are drunken with worldly wisdom.

C. Benediction. 6:21b.

21b. Grace be with thee. What a fitting conclusion to a letter to the young pastor, Timothy. It takes the grace of God to shepherd the flock, but thank God His grace is sufficient and available. All of Paul's advice is of no avail unless the grace of God be present in the ministry of Timothy. The same is true today. **Amen.** So let it be, in every place, in every age.

(see page 663 for Bibliography to the Pastoral Epistles)

The Second Epistle To
TIMOTHY

INTRODUCTION

Recorded in II Timothy are the final words of the great apostle. Sometimes referred to as the Apostle Paul's "swan song," this second epistle to his own son in the faith is an exhortation for Timothy to stand strong in the face of insurmountable difficulties. As the final writing of Paul, it is tender, sympathetic, tearful, and yet heroic and stately. It is an exciting and fitting conclusion to the pauline corpus.

Authorship. As with I Timothy, the internal and external evidences for pauline authorship are strong. Paul again claims to be the author (1:1) and the style and tone are such as you would expect from the soon-to-be-martyred apostle. Everything about the epistle is typically pauline and there is little reason to question Paul's claimed authorship.

Date and place of writing. The epistle must be dated shortly before Paul's death. If Paul was arrested somewhere in the East, upon his return from Spain, and from there was taken to prison, then the date of the epistle can be fixed in dependence on the date of his arrest. Since it appears that the apostle was released from his first Roman imprisonment about A.D. 63, and since he appears to have traveled immediately to the churches he had established and loved so much in Greece and Asia Minor, we must allow a year or more for traveling from Rome to the eastern Mediterranean world and visits to the beloved churches. But in addition to this, it is implied that he also accomplished his lifelong desire to preach the gospel where no man had laid a foundation, i.e., in Spain. Another year must be allowed for this task. Thus, with time given for a return to the East and a return voyage to Rome, the earliest conceivable date for the writing of II Timothy would have been sometime in A.D. 66. Navigation on the Mediterranean comes to a halt during the winter months and thus his arrival in Rome for a second imprisonment can be safely concluded to have taken place in late summer. The writing of this epistle must have then occurred in autumn of A.D. 66.

It is evident that Paul was again a prisoner when he penned II Timothy (1:8, 16). He makes reference to the fact that he is suffering "hardship unto

bonds, as a malefactor" (2:9). He is in Rome again. This imprisonment, however, cannot be the one mentioned in Acts 28, for he is no longer permitted to live in a hired dwelling under house arrest (Acts 28:30). Now he is closely guarded in strict confinement. During his first imprisonment he was readily accessible to his close friends and had many visitors (Acts 28:17-31; Col 4:10-14; Phil 1:13-14). But now he is virtually all alone (4:11).

Tradition is strong that Paul died in the Neronian persecution which began at the great fire of Rome on July 19, A.D. 64. This persecution continued until Nero's death in A.D. 68. Apparently Paul died in the heat of that persecution, in the city of Rome, about A.D. 66.

Purpose. It appears that Paul's primary purpose in writing II Timothy was to encourage the young minister. This epistle reads like a coach's halftime pep-talk to a discouraged team. Three times in II Timothy the note of suffering hardship is mentioned (1:8; 2:3; 4:5), indicating the need for Timothy's encouragement. Paul instructs Timothy to be a "good soldier of Christ Jesus" (2:3). The whole tenor of the epistle is a note of encouragement and who better to encourage Timothy than an aged warrior who was about to die.

But a secondary purpose is also seen. Paul wants Timothy to come to Rome as soon as possible (4:9, 21) for the apostle is now convinced that he will never be free again. He longs to see his young son in the faith once more before he dies. Yet with a full and rich life of service to the Lord behind him, Paul can look confidently in the face of death, whether Timothy arrives in time or not. This request, a dying request, and the letter in which it was contained must have had a devastating effect on Timothy. In the midst of Paul's strength and encouragement comes the pathetic appeal for his cloak, left at Troas (perhaps at his arrest), the books, and especially the parchments (4:13). The only worldly possessions the great apostle has left are these, the friendship of the faithful brethren, and the certain knowledge that he has fought a good fight (4:7).

OUTLINE

A. Unfaithfulness of the World. 3:1-9.
B. Faithfulness through His Word. 3:10-17.
V. The Call to the Ministry. 4:1-7.
A. Purpose of the Ministry. 4:1-2.
B. Perversion of the Ministry. 4:3-4.

C. Priority of the Ministry. 4:5-7.
VI. Conclusion. 4:8-22.
A. Wanting of Timothy. 4:8-13.
B. Warning of Alexander. 4:14-15.
C. Witness of Paul. 4:16-22.

COMMENTARY

I. INTRODUCTION. 1:1-5.

PAUL, an apostle of Jesus Christ by the will of God, according to the promise of life which is in Christ Jesus,

1:1. Paul, an apostle of Jesus Christ. See comments on I Timothy 1:1. **By the will of God.** It is great to know the will of God for one's life. God has a **will** (Gr *thelēma*) "desire" for each one's life. **Promise of life.** An apostle was sent with a message of the promise of life in Christ Jesus. This is the preacher's message and the people's hope today.

2 To Tim'o-thy, *my* dearly beloved son: Grace, mercy, *and* peace, from God the Father and Christ Jesus our Lord.

2. My dearly beloved son. Here the aged apostle shows his deep affection for his son in the ministry. The older any preacher gets the more he appreciates his "sons" in the ministry, as should teachers and parents.

3 I thank God, whom I serve from *my* forefathers with pure conscience, that without ceasing I have remembrance of thee in my prayers night and day;

3. I thank God. What a comely trait, to be thankful. It is so characteristic of Paul and should be of any pastor (I Thess 5:18). It surely is not characteristic of the world (II Tim 3:2). **Serve.** What a great dividend there was to serve God, as we see in Acts 26:23ff. **Pure conscience.** The five references to conscience in I and II Timothy emphasize its importance. A pastor must have a clear conscience, with no unconfessed, hidden sins, to be effective like Paul. **Without ceasing.** "Pray without ceasing" (I Thess 5:17). Paul practiced it. What an encouragement to Timothy. Paul prayed for young Timothy daily. He prayed for Timothy for years. Much of Timothy's "success" in the ministry must be attributed to Paul's prayers for his son in the faith.

4 Greatly desiring to see thee, being mindful of thy tears, that I may be filled with joy;

4. Greatly desiring to see thee. This again shows Paul's deep love for Timothy. Every pastor knows this feeling for some pastor who has gone out under his ministry. What an honor for Timothy. What joy for Paul.

5 When I call to remembrance the unfeigned faith that is in thee, which dwelt first in thy grandmother Lois, and thy mother Eunice; and I am persuaded that in thee also.

5. Call to remembrance. Precious memories. **Unfeigned faith** (Gr *anhypokritos*), unhypocritical faith. He was no fake. What a powerful influence godly parents are. How fulfilling to any woman to influence the world so mightily through her children.

II. THE CALL TO COURAGE. 1:6-18.

A. Exhortation to Courage. 1:6-11.

6 Wherefore I put thee in remembrance that thou stir up the gift of God, which is in thee by the putting on of my hands.

6. Stir up. This is in the present tense and should be "keep stirring up." The gifts of God are without repentance (Rom 11:33), but they must be used and exercised (see note on I Tim 4:14).

7 For God hath not given us the spirit of fear; but of power, and of love, and of a sound mind.

7. Fear. It was probably part of Timothy's nature to be fearful. All of God's people need to fear fear itself. God can't use fearful servants (Jud 7:3). To the preacher of old God says, "Be not afraid of their faces" (Jer 1:8). This fear is not of God! Satan must be resisted and rebuked by faith (Jas 5:7; Mt 16:23). **Power** (Acts 1:8; I Cor 2:3, 4). Paul could identify with Timothy for he knew fear naturally, but also power supernaturally. **Sound mind** (Gr *sōphronismos*). The word here means "disciplined" or "self-control."

8 Be not thou therefore ashamed of the testimony of our Lord, nor of me his prisoner: but be thou partaker of the afflictions of the gospel according to the power of God;

8. Therefore. There is no excuse to ever be ashamed of the testimony of our Lord. Paul wasn't (Rom 1:16). **Be not.** This is the Greek subjunctive and means "don't start." Paul had not been guilty of being ashamed of the testimony of the Lord. **Nor of me.** Many were ashamed of Paul and had forsaken him

2509

9 Who hath saved us, and called *us* with an holy calling, not according to our works, but according to his own purpose and grace, which was given us in Christ Jesus before the world began,

10 But is now made manifest by the appearing of our Saviour Jesus Christ, who hath abolished death, and hath brought life and immortality to light through the gospel:

11 Whereunto I am appointed a preacher, and an apostle, and a teacher of the Gentiles.

12 For the which cause I also suffer these things: nevertheless I am not ashamed: for I know whom I have believed, and am persuaded that he is able to keep that which I have committed unto him against that day.

13 Hold fast the form of sound words, which thou hast heard of me, in faith and love which is in Christ Jesus.

14 That good thing which was committed unto thee keep by the Holy Ghost which dwelleth in us.

15 This thou knowest, that all they which are in Asia be turned away from me; of whom are Phȳ-ġel'lus and Her-mŏġ'e-nĕs.

16 The Lord give mercy unto the house of Ŏn-e-sĭph'o-rus; for he oft refreshed me, and was not ashamed of my chain:

17 But, when he was in Rome, he sought me out very diligently, and found *me*.

(4:10). **Afflictions.** This is par for the course. One wonders where such afflictions are today!

9. Called. Salvation and service are all by grace, not in human power (Zech 4:6). **Us.** Paul puts Timothy's calling on the same par with his own. This must have added courage to Timothy. **Before the world began** (cf. Gal 1:15). How humbling and awesome the responsibility.

10. The "purpose" of God (vs. 9) is **now made manifest by the appearing.** This refers to His incarnation including His whole life, death, and resurrection. Eternal life, immortality, comes through the gospel (Rom 1:16).

11. Preacher. How shall anyone believe this gospel without a preacher! (Rom 10:14). Men were once glad to be known as "gospel preachers." Paul was. Pastors should be known above all for their "preaching" (Acts 6:4; I Cor 1:18-21). **Teacher.** A pastor must also teach. He must be "apt to teach" (I Tim 3:2).

B. Example of Courage. 1:12-14.

12. Suffer. (Phil 1:29; I Pet 4:12). Paul knew it would cost him to serve as a preacher **nevertheless I am not ashamed** and so Timothy should not be either. The basis is knowing a person, the Lord Jesus, and His power to keep (Phil 3:10). Here the word **know** (Gr *oida*) means "absolute knowledge," beyond a shadow of a doubt. **Keep** (Gr *phylassō*) is a military term meaning "guard." **That which.** What is Paul committing, his salvation or his service? Both could be included in his mind, as it seems in verse 9. **Committed** (Gr *parathēkē*) is a banking term meaning "to deposit." **That day** no doubt refers to the day of Christ and the Judgment Seat of Christ, where believers' service and works will be judged (I Cor 3:11 ff.; 4:5).

13. Paul must have had in mind the near end of his ministry and that Timothy was to carry on in his place and so exhorts him, **Hold fast.** What was committed unto him, by Paul, **which thou hast heard of me. Form** (Gr *hypotypōsis*) means "pattern" of sound words.

14. Good thing refers to pattern of sound words which was committed or deposited with Timothy. He is to "keep on guard" (same word as in verse 12) even as God keeps what we commit to Him. What an awesome responsibility. What a tragedy that the truth, the faith, or the gospel has not been guarded by churches, denominations, and schools so that eventually Ichabod has been written over many. Paul did what he exhorted Timothy to do in 2:2, i.e., pass on gospel to faithful men. He is to accomplish this by the power of the Holy Spirit. There must be that conscious dependence on His anointing and teaching (Jn 2:27).

C. Experience of Courage. 1:15-18.

15. Here is one of the saddest verses of the New Testament. **Asia** refers to the Roman province of which Ephesus was the capital and would include what was known as Asia Minor or Turkey today. **All . . . turned away.** As you read the letter to the Ephesians it is obvious they were greatly instructed. The indictment of Revelation 2, that they had "left their first love" and were in danger of their church (candlestick) being removed, was solemn. The turning away was not personal but positional from the truth which Paul was charging Timothy to beware of doing or allowing. No doubt **Phygellus** and **Hermogenes** were well-known for their apostasy.

16-17. God, in His wisdom, provided the house of Onesiphorus who **oft refreshed** Paul. Who encourages a pastor? Who is his pastor? It is ones like Onesiphorus and his house who Paul says were **not ashamed of my chain** and who, when in Rome, **sought me out.** He looked Paul up when in Rome. No doubt it wasn't easy, but he would not be denied, he **found** him.

18 The Lord grant unto him that he may find mercy of the Lord in that day: and in how many things he ministered unto me at Ĕph'e-sus, thou knowest very well.

CHAPTER 2

THOU therefore, my son, be strong in the grace that is in Christ Jesus.

2 And the things that thou hast heard of me among many witnesses, the same commit thou to faithful men, who shall be able to teach others also.

3 Thou therefore endure hardness, as a good soldier of Jesus Christ.
4 No man that warreth entangleth himself with the affairs of *this* life; that he may please him who hath chosen him to be a soldier.

5 And if a man also strive for masteries, *yet* is he not crowned, except he strive lawfully.

6 The husbandman that laboureth must be first partaker of the fruits.

7 Consider what I say; and the Lord give thee understanding in all things.

8 Remember that Jesus Christ of the seed of David was raised from the dead according to my gospel:

18. How many things he ministered unto me. Without complaining Paul seems to cover a multitude of problems and the help Onesiphorus gave. Few people ever realize the enormous pressures and problems a pastor faces as included in the daily "care of all the churches" (II Cor 11:28). What reward there will be **in that day** for those who minister to the ministers!

III. THE CALL TO SERVICE. 2:1-26.

The Lord Jesus used familiar pictures and subjects to bring out great truths and now Paul does the same with seven powerful portraits of the Christian life.

A. As a Son. 2:1-2.

2:1. Thou, in the emphatic position in the Greek sentence. Though others falter and fail, he expects more of Timothy. **My son** (Gr *teknon*), child, used even of adults, is a very affectionate term. How Paul dearly loved him as a son. **Be strong.** This is in the present imperative and indicates the continued growth in strength and stamina one can muster to go on and not turn away (cf. Eph 6:10 ff.). **Grace.** This grace is available for living as well as salvation (Heb 4:16).
2. The same commit thou. Here is the ultimate goal of the ministry: pass it on. Paul is saying, what I have committed to you, you commit to faithful men who then will pass it on and commit it to others also. The buck may stop with you, but truth must never stop.

B. As a Soldier. 2:3-4.

3-4. As a son he is to be strong; as a soldier he is to endure hardness. A soldier is at war. It may mean wounds and suffering. Remember God didn't start the war, Satan did. See Isaiah 28 and Ezekiel 14. **Endure hardness** (Gr *syngkakopatheo*) has a prefix in Greek. **With.** Paul did not ask Timothy to do something he hadn't done. He says, "I have endured hardness, now you endure it with me." Pastors must lead the way (I Cor 11:1). **Entangleth.** Deuteronomy 20:5-8 warns a man not to go to war if there are unsettled affairs in his life. The battle is serious and a soldier cannot be distracted by entanglements of business or family affairs.

C. As an Athlete. 2:5.

5. Paul now speaks of one of his favorite subjects, that of athletics. **Strive** (Gr *athleō*) means to engage in athletic contests. To win the prize, he must **strive lawfully** (Gr *nominos*) or actually keep the rules of the game. To run the race of life one does not break God's rules and get away with it. As the umpire of the game of life, God calls the fouls real close!

D. As a Farmer. 2:6-13.

6. The husbandman. Now comes the sower or farmer. The athlete gets the crown only at the end of the race. The farmer reaps of his labors before the final harvest. He must be partaker of the first fruit. Those who labor for the Lord are blessed and rewarded here and hereafter. It does pay to serve Jesus.
7. Consider. "Let this sink in." It would do well to meditate much on these things (Josh 1:8). There are many more lessons and parallels. The seed sown must be understood and bring forth fruit! (Mt 13:23).
8. Lest he become weary or fainthearted, Paul begins to elaborate on the hardness and suffering that must be endured. **Remember.** The death, burial, and resurrection of Christ are always to be remembered (I Cor 11:23ff.). **Of the seed of David.** Speaking of His humanity, He was of the lineage of David and rightful heir to the throne of David. **Was raised from the dead.** The Greek perfect tense denotes the certainty of the

9 Wherein I suffer trouble, as an evil doer, *even* unto bonds; but the word of God is not bound.

10 Therefore I endure all things for the elect's sakes, that they may also obtain the salvation which is in Christ Jesus with eternal glory.

11 *It is* a faithful saying: For if we be dead with *him*, we shall also live with *him:*

12 If we suffer, we shall also reign with *him:* if we deny *him*, he also will deny us:

13 If we believe not, *yet* he abideth faithful: he cannot deny himself.

14 Of these things put *them* in remembrance, charging *them* before the Lord that they strive not about words to no profit, *but* to the subverting of the hearers.

15 Study to shew thyself approved unto God, a workman that needeth not to be ashamed, rightly dividing the word of truth.

fact. **My gospel** means the gospel which Paul preached and if anyone preaches any other, he is to be accursed (Gal 1:8, 9).

9-10. Preaching this gospel of the resurrection of Christ brought about Paul's persecution. **Suffer trouble.** God doesn't protect His servants from trouble, but preserves them through trouble. Sufferings or troubles are not always the chastening of God or the result of sins. A good soldier should expect suffering while in an enemy's country (Phil 1:29). This world is not our home. Paul suffered for the gospel's sake, even as an **evildoer.** The Greek word is a technical word meaning malefactor. Persecuting Christians and consenting to their death didn't make him a criminal, but preaching the gospel did, in the eyes of the Jews! How often someone who curses, drinks, and carouses gets saved and stops all that, and then receives persecution from loved ones for trying to live right. "Think it not strange!" (I Pet 4:12ff.). Paul was bound, but the Word of God wasn't bound, he still witnessed! The facts were that these things were to the "furtherance of the gospel" (Phil 1:12ff.). The reverse is often true today. People are free but their tongue is bound! **Endure all things.** He said it beautifully in Acts 20:24 when he said, "None of these things move me, neither count I my life dear unto myself. . . ." **For the elect's sake.** It was a joy for Paul to suffer for the gospel because when he did so he was actually suffering on behalf of the elect. The persecution which Paul endured would most certainly be a tremendous source of encouragement for other believers. He did not suffer vicariously for believers, as Christ did, but his strength in suffering incited them to action. He would endure anything to see them saved, and now would endure anything to encourage them.

11. Faithful saying or "trustworthy." You can count on it. **For** connects what he has been saying and the conclusions he now draws from his statements. He is talking about the great doctrine of the substitutionary death of Christ and our identification with Him in His death and resurrection as a fact. **We shall also live with him.** The basis of our eternal life is our personal identification with Christ and acceptance of Him. Because we shall live with Him we should endure hardness gladly.

12. If we suffer, and again you can count on it, we will. **We shall also reign.** The rewards are worth it all. Paul is encouraging Timothy with this great hope of the believer and we should be encouraged as well. **Deny him.** The Greek verb here is future, "if we shall deny him." Two things to remember here. First, Peter denied Christ three times, even though he was saved, but his reaction was conviction and contrition. Secondly, I John 2:19 tells of those who "went out from us, but they were not of us; for if they had been of us, they would no doubt have continued with us: but they went out, that they might be made manifest that they were not all of us." These were apostate. It must be remembered man only sees the outward, God sees the heart (I Sam 16:7).

13. Believe not (Gr *apisteuō*) refers to unfaithfulness. There is an obvious play on words with **he abideth faithful** (Gk *pistos*). God has to remain true to His character. He cannot be unfaithful or deny Himself.

E. As a Workman. 2:14-19.

14. These things. The momentous facts of verses 11-13 are of such importance that it is foolish to get involved and strive about insignificant words to no profit. A faithful pastor will keep off the side issues. Paul told Timothy to keep reminding those he teaches to do the same.

15. Study (Gr *spoudazō*) is not the normal word you think of as a student but a word used of a workman meaning "give diligence," "endeavor," or "exert oneself." A workman is to give diligence or endeavor to show himself **approved** unto God. Approval means one has been put to the test and measures up, thus winning the approval of the person testing him. The workman here is one who is handling the Word of God and thus the conclusion of studying. It certainly takes diligent study of the Word to **rightly divide it** (Gr *orthotomeō*) meaning "to cut a straight course," or "lay out a road," or "correctly interpret." All of the Word of God is true. There are no contradictions when rightly laid out. You cannot add to nor take away any of it (Rev 22:19).

16 But shun profane *and* vain babblings: for they will increase unto more ungodliness.

16. But, in sharp contrast, **shun** or avoid **profane and vain babblings.** As in I Timothy 6:20, this includes false and empty talk. It just leads to more ungodliness. False belief produces foolish behavior.

17 And their word will eat as doth a canker: of whom is Hȳ-me-næ′us and Phī-lē′tus;

17. The tragedy is it spreads like a **canker** (Gr *ganggraina*), gangrene! **Hymeneus and Philetus** were prime examples of how it happens.

18 Who concerning the truth have erred, saying that the resurrection is past already; and overthrow the faith of some.

18. Erred (Gr *astocheō*) means to deviate or "miss the mark." To get bogged down debating such vain babblings only harms and pollutes and must be avoided. "If any man be ignorant, let him be ignorant" (I Cor 14:28). There are some things and some people you just don't debate. **Resurrection is past.** They probably spiritualized the resurrection of the future as the gnostics of the day taught.

19 Nevertheless the foundation of God standeth sure, having this seal, The Lord knoweth them that are his. And, Let every one that nameth the name of Christ depart from iniquity.

19. Nevertheless. In spite of all the failures of men, **the foundation of God standeth sure.** This foundation is referred to in I Corinthians 3:11. It is Christ. Build on Him and there will be no defection, no apostasy. Remember, "they went out because they weren't of us" (I Jn 2:19). **Knoweth.** He surely does. About His sheep He said, "I know them . . . and they shall never perish" (Jn 10:27-28). To the lost He said, "I never knew you: depart from me . . ." (Mt 7:23). These were not sheep who once had departed. **Depart from iniquity.** This security never means one can live like the devil. In fact, one who appreciates his salvation never attempts to take advantage of it.

F. As a Vessel. 2:20-22.

20 But in a great house there are not only vessels of gold and of silver, but also of wood and of earth; and some to honour, and some to dishonour.

20. House. The believer is now part of the great house of God being paralleled here. **Vessels of gold . . . also of wood.** Every family has their special and valued dishes as well as everyday inexpensive ones.

21 If a man therefore purge himself from these, he shall be a vessel unto honour, sanctified, and meet for the master's use, *and* prepared unto every good work.

21. In God's house if a man **purge himself** from the vessels of dishonor, **he shall be a vessel unto honor.** A long time before Paul said, "Come out from among them, and be ye separate . . ." (II Cor 6:17). God doesn't play favorites, but He is holy and cannot use unholy vessels. God is constantly on a talent hunt "for them whose heart is perfect toward him" (II Chr 16:2). **Meet** means "usable" or "fit" for His use. **Master** (Gr *despotes*) from which we get despot or lord. He is Lord and must be acknowledged as such to be used. **Prepared** means "equipped."

22 Flee also youthful lusts: but follow righteousness, faith, charity, peace, with them that call on the Lord out of a pure heart.

22. Flee also youthful lusts. The youthful desires for fame, fortune and fun are to be run from, **but to follow** (Gr *diōkō*) which means "to pursue" and not just meekly follow. That which the believer is to pursue is a catalogue of Christian graces, i.e., **righteousness, faith, charity, peace.**

G. As a Servant. 2:23-26.

23 But foolish and unlearned questions avoid, knowing that they do gender strifes.
24 And the servant of the Lord must not strive; but be gentle unto all *men,* apt to teach, patient,
25 In meekness instructing those that oppose themselves; if God peradventure will give them repentance to the acknowledging of the truth;

23-25. Once again Paul warns about foolish questions for they lead to strife. **The servant** here refers primarily to a pastor. A true servant obeys his master. **Must not strive** (Gr *machomai*). The word here means "quarrel" or "argue" with emotions heated. Usually there will be more heat than light. It is a sin for anyone to lose patience and especially a minister. **Gentle** in one's manner and **meek** in one's disposition. **Instructing.** Giving the truth from God's Word which shows the need for verse 15 and being "apt to teach" (I Tim 3:2). **If God peradventure will give them repentance.** Notice God must give repentance. Re-

26 And *that* they may recover themselves out of the snare of the devil, who are taken captive by him at his will.

CHAPTER 3

THIS know also, that in the last days perilous times shall come.

2 For men shall be lovers of their own selves, covetous, boasters, proud, blasphemers, disobedient to parents, unthankful, unholy,

3 Without natural affection, trucebreakers, false accusers, incontinent, fierce, despisers of those that are good,

4 Traitors, heady, highminded, lovers of pleasures more than lovers of God;

5 Having a form of godliness, but denying the power thereof: from such turn away.

6 For of this sort are they which creep into houses, and lead captive silly women laden with sins, led away with divers lusts,

7 Ever learning, and never able to come to the knowledge of the truth.

8 Now as Jăn′nĕś and Jăm′brĕś

pentance (Gr *metanoia*). Repentance is not sorrow for sin, that is, contrition. Sorrow leads to repentance (II Cor 7:9-10). Repentance is not changing direction or your ways of living; that's a result of salvation. Repentance is changing one's mind from false ideas to the **acknowledging of the truth**. A sinner must be willing to change directions and turn from sin, but that's not a condition of salvation, else we have salvation as a result of works or deeds and not of faith (Eph 2:8-9).

26. Here Paul is talking primarily about those accepting false teaching that they may recover themselves out of the snare of the devil. Satan is behind all false teaching. There is nothing innocent about any of it. Pastors must be good shepherds to lead their flocks and protect them from such wolves.

IV. THE CALL TO FAITHFULNESS. 3:1-17.

A. Unfaithfulness of the World. 3:1-9.

3:1. The last days. This includes the whole church age. Paul stated these conditions would be prevalent in Timothy's day, for he said to him, "from such turn away" (vs. 5). **Perilous times** are evident today as well.

2-3. Lovers of their own selves. Everyone does that which is right in his own eyes. Selfishness abounds. **Covetous.** People must keep up with the Joneses. Few are content with such things as they have. **Disobedient to parents.** Juvenile delinquency is the term in this generation, but now more common and rampant. **Unthankful.** There is no loyalty or thankfulness for anything but only wanting more. **Unholy, Without natural affection.** Romans 1:26 ff. is accepted as a way of life. The gay crowd, sex out of bounds from God's limits, is accepted by much of society. **Trucebreakers.** One only has to look at Korea and Vietnam to see blatant trucebreaking. **Incontinent** (Gr *akratēs*) meaning "no power" or "restraint" over oneself. Senseless killings and atrocious sex crimes give evidence to this today. **Fierce,** meaning "not tame" or "savage." **Despisers of those that are good.** The all-American boy is not emulated, but the radicals and immoral celebrities are. The honest, wholesome teenager is so often ridiculed! Those who do good and act good are greatly in the minority.

4. Lovers of pleasures. One would have to be blind not to see that pleasure-seeking is skyrocketing today. The cry of first-century Rome was, "Give us bread and the circus." The two "necessities" of life were welfare and entertainment. The situation hasn't changed a bit.

5. Form of godliness. Church attendance is at an all-time high, **but** powerless. No longer are God and His teaching considered in matters of divorce, sex, or abortion. Most Christians and churches are powerless in the community. They only appear to be godly. Inwardly they are impotent because of sin.

6. Lead captive silly women. Eve was the first deceived (I Tim 2:14). A sad fact of life is that Satan consistently attacks the women in the area of discernment. Christian women must be especially dependent upon God to give them doctrinal direction and understanding. Many cults today are directed and dominated by women who have had their discernment taken captive by Satan. A Christian woman must be wise enough to seek the counsel and advice of the pastor and church leaders lest in the areas of doctrine and practice she fall prey to the snares of the devil.

7. Ever learning. This refers to the women led astray. One of the strange phenomena of our day is the great number of women going to all kinds of Bible studies and religious meetings, who seem to gravitate to strange doctrines and unorthodox ideas. They never come for the **truth**, that faith once delivered unto the saints, the old-fashioned fundamentals of the Bible.

8. Withstood (Gr *anthistēmi*) is forceful and means "to set

withstood Moses, so do these also resist the truth: men of corrupt minds, reprobate concerning the faith.

9 But they shall proceed no further: for their folly shall be manifest unto all *men*, as theirs also was.

10 But thou hast fully known my doctrine, manner of life, purpose, faith, longsuffering, charity, patience,

11 Persecutions, afflictions, which came unto me at Antioch, at I-cō'nĭ-um, at Lȳs'tra; what persecutions I endured: but out of *them* all the Lord delivered me.

12 Yea, and all that will live godly in Christ Jesus shall suffer persecution.

13 But evil men and seducers shall wax worse and worse, deceiving, and being deceived.

14 But continue thou in the things which thou hast learned and hast been assured of, knowing of whom thou hast learned *them;*

15 And that from a child thou hast known the holy scriptures, which are able to make thee wise unto salvation through faith which is in Christ Jesus.

16 All scripture *is* given by inspiration of God, and *is* profitable for doctrine, for reproof, for correction, for instruction in righteousness:

17 That the man of God may be perfect, throughly furnished unto all good works.

CHAPTER 4

I CHARGE *thee* therefore before God, and the Lord Jesus Christ, who shall judge the quick and the dead at his appearing and his kingdom;

2 Preach the word; be instant in sea-

oneself against." The boldness of **Jannes and Jambres** to set themselves against Moses is manifest today in multitudes who adamantly "resist" the truth.

9. Their folly shall be manifest. Apostate individuals and groups have come and gone throughout the ages. They are finally exposed for what they really are. In our day many so-called faith healers and charlatans have faded out or died with their followers disillusioned and dispersed.

B. Faithfulness through His Word. 3:10-17.

10. Fully known (Gr *parakoloutheō*) is translated in Luke 1:3 as "perfect understanding." **My doctrine.** Doctrine is foundational and must be the basis of discipleship. Experiences can never be the basis. Paul invites close scrutiny of his whole life and ministry. This should be done with anyone who would be followed.

11. Paul endured much persecution of apostates but God delivered him. **Antioch . . . Iconium . . . Lystra** are but three of the places where Paul suffered persecution.

12. Then he assures that persecutions await all who will live godly. **Shall suffer persecution** is a promise with great prospect (I Pet 3:14).

13. This situation will continue to worsen. **Evil men . . . seducers.** This is an age of evil men and deception. The irony is that evil men are deceiving one another and being deceived. They must learn the truth that whatever a man sows, he also reaps.

14. Continue. Others "swerved" (I Tim 1:6). "Made shipwreck" (1:19). "Erred" (6:20). Stewards must be faithful (I Cor 4:2).

15. Holy scriptures refers to the Old Testament Scriptures taught Timothy by his mother and grandmother (1:5). It is so important to teach the Word of God to children in order to bring them to salvation. Salvation comes through faith (Eph 2:8-9) and faith comes by the Word of God (Rom 10:17).

16. All scripture refers not to the Old Testament as a whole but to every part of the Old Testament. **Inspiration** (Gr *theopneustos*) means "God breathed out" the Scriptures and not that God breathed into the human authors. The authors themselves were controlled by God so that they were not left to their human limitations (II Pet 1:21). **Doctrine . . . reproof . . . correction . . . instruction.** The Scriptures are not only profitable for salvation but for sanctification and Christian growth as well. They are not only the road map to heaven, but the road map of the Christian life. They are all we need for faith and doctrine.

17. When sanctification takes place in the man of God and he is **perfect** or mature, the Scriptures are for service "furnished unto all good works." Doctrine always should emanate in good works.

V. THE CALL TO THE MINISTRY. 4:1-7.

A. Purpose of the Ministry. 4:1-2.

4:1. Charge thee. Paul's final charge to Timothy. A **charge** is more than a command for a charge carries with it the moral obligation to be carried out. **Judge.** In the light of what has been said in chapter 3 about the last days, Paul reminds Timothy of a day of reckoning. **The quick,** the living, those who are alive and remain (I Thess 4:17) **and the dead,** "for the dead in Christ shall rise first" (I Thess 4:16). Pastors and people alike shall stand at the Judgment Seat of Christ (II Cor 5:10), **at his appearing.** "To whom much is given much is required" (Jas 3:1).

2. Preach the word. This means to herald as the emperor's

son, out of season; reprove, rebuke, exhort with all longsuffering and doctrine.

3 For the time will come when they will not endure sound doctrine; but after their own lusts shall they heap to themselves teachers, having itching ears;

4 And they shall turn away *their* ears from the truth, and shall be turned unto fables.

5 But watch thou in all things, endure afflictions, do the work of an evangelist, make full proof of thy ministry.

6 For I am now ready to be offered, and the time of my departure is at hand.

7 I have fought a good fight, I have finished *my* course, I have kept the faith:

8 Henceforth there is laid up for me a crown of righteousness, which the Lord, the righteous judge, shall give me at that day: and not to me only, but

herald gave a formal message in an authoritative way. Be consistent, he says, always at it. Don't be afraid to **reprove** or **rebuke** but do it with **long-suffering** and **doctrine**. The minister's personal feelings are not the ground for reproof: doctrine alone is that ground.

B. Perversion of the Ministry. 4:3-4.

3. **The time will come** and most believe it is here today. **Itching ears** will be "tickled" by preachers who do not preach the Bible. Many pastors bow to the wishes of ungodly congregations who only want to hear what pleases them.

4. **Turn away** (Gr *apostrephō*) is in the Greek active voice and has the idea of deliberate action by themselves. **Shall be turned** (Gr *ektrepō*) means they are acted upon; it is a medical term meaning "to twist out of place."

C. Priority of the Ministry. 4:5-7.

5. **But,** in contrast to these, Timothy is to **watch,** which has the idea of being sober and alert. **Endure afflictions.** Satan doesn't play games. He puts up a fight. The preacher must not get discouraged and run. **Do the work of an evangelist.** Every pastor must evangelize, he must be a soul-winner. He cannot simply pray and preach. He cannot expect his people to witness if he doesn't. He must preach "Be ye followers of me . . ." (I Cor 11:1). To **make full proof** of his ministry the pastor must be faithful in all the above admonitions.

6. **For.** Paul's exhortation to Timothy to make full proof of his ministry was given because Paul knew his own ministry was almost over and he knew the deep satisfaction of having done the same himself. What a horrible feeling it must be to come to the end of one's life and have nothing but regrets at a wasted life. **I.** The "I" here is emphatic. Paul is saying "as for myself." How important to be honest with ourselves. **I am now ready to be offered.** Only one who had finished his course (vs. 7) could say this. **Offered** (Gr *spendomai*). This is a word used of pouring out a drink offering. Paul used it of himself in Philippians 2:17, of pouring out himself for the Philippians. **The time of my departure is at hand.** God's servants are indestructible until their work is done. **Departure** (Gr *analyseos*) was used by the military meaning to take down one's tent. The idea is like the old saying of the Arab who took up his tent and silently stole away. As servants we must silently steal away and soon be forgotten so that only what's done for Christ will last!

7. What a power-packed verse. There are three great statements. **A good fight.** The definite article is in the Greek. Paul is not boasting of what he had done but that he had spent his life in the good fight or contest. **Fight** (Gr *agōn*) was used of the Greek athletic contests. **Fought** (*agōnizomai*) in the perfect tense speaks of completed action and expresses Paul's confidence. We get our word "agonize" from this. It does cost. There aren't many who agonize in their labors for Christ today. **I have finished my course.** Course refers to a race track. He had crossed the finish line. He didn't quit. The Christian's life is not a hundred-yard dash; it is a marathon and most often an obstacle course. **I have kept the faith.** The faith is not personal faith in Christ but the whole body of Christian truth, i.e., doctrine. Paul never was detoured by some new wind of doctrine.

VI. CONCLUSION. 4:8-22.

A. Wanting of Timothy. 4:8-13.

8. **Henceforth.** The tragedy of life is what people miss here and hereafter. Only those who have borne their cross will win the crown. **Crown** (Gr *stephonos*) referred to the laurel wreath placed on the winner of the athletic contests. There are five

unto all them also that love his appearing.

9 Do thy diligence to come shortly unto me:

10 For Demas hath forsaken me, having loved this present world, and is departed unto Thĕs-sa-lo-nī'ca; Crĕs'cenś to Ga-lā'tia, Titus unto Dăl-mā'ti-a.

11 Only Luke is with me. Take Mark, and bring him with thee: for he is profitable to me for the ministry.

12 And Tӯch'ĭ-cus have I sent to Ĕph'e-sus.

13 The cloak that I left at Troas with Carpus, when thou comest, bring with thee, and the books, but especially the parchments.

14 Alexander the coppersmith did me much evil: the Lord reward him according to his works:
15 Of whom be thou ware also; for he hath greatly withstood our words.

16 At my first answer no man stood with me, but all men forsook me: I pray God that it may not be laid to their charge.

17 Notwithstanding the Lord stood

crowns spoken of in Scripture, all of which we will cast at Jesus' feet in adoration one day (Rev 4:10-11). This **crown of righteousness** is available to **all them also that love his appearing.** How tragic that multitudes are not taught about the Second Coming of Christ and therefore are cheated out of gaining this crown! No preacher should say the preaching of the Second Coming and all that surrounds it is unimportant!

Like the great crescendo of a symphony, Paul has concluded his message in verse 8 and now adds a few final remarks. Some of these give personal insights to this great man who is in a Roman dungeon awaiting his final appearance before the Roman ruler.

9. Do thy diligence. This is from the same Greek word for "study" in 2:15 and it means here "do your best," to come quickly to me.

10. Forsaken here means literally "let me down." Demas was standing with Paul in Colossians 4:14 and Philemon 24. What a disappointment. Even Paul had those moments too! **Having loved this present world.** No matter how much disciplining, one can still turn from faithfulness to this world. Every pastor needs to know this so that he does not falter when someone he has spent many years training turns away. They did it to Jesus too, "And they all forsook him and fled" (Mk 14:50).

11. Only Luke is with me. What a man is this beloved physician. Paul is not seeking pity here, but gives insight for pastors to know how that when he came to the end of his ministry he was fortified against discouragement during those lonesome hours. **Take Mark, and bring him.** In the accounts of Acts 13:13 and 15:36-41 Mark seems to have deserted Paul and later Paul and Barnabas had a strong disagreement over Mark. Mark has now proven himself and, whatever happened in Acts 13:13, Paul has years before forgiven and forgotten. This is as it should be. Too many pout today over trivial things and never are reconciled.

12. And (or but) **Tychicus have I sent to Ephesus.** This implies the others left on their own. Probably Tychicus was the bearer of this letter to Timothy who was in Ephesus (I Tim 1:3).

13. The cloak. This was a long heavy cape with a hole in the middle to slip over one's head. It hung down to the knees. It was now needed in this cold damp dungeon. **The books** or scrolls were made from papyrus and the **parchments** were much better quality made from sheep or goat skins. These parchments may well have been copies of the Old Testament Scriptures. To the very end Paul kept his mind sharp and his heart full by reading. What an example to this young preacher and us today.

B. Warning of Alexander. 4:14-15.

14-15. Alexander the coppersmith did me much evil. Alexander was a common name, so he is identified as "the coppersmith" and no doubt Timothy knew who he was. Paul did not do this to harm Alexander but to prevent Timothy from being hurt by this man. Too often, in our mobile society one of God's servants causes trouble in one place and then travels across the country to cause harm there also. There needs to be honesty about such a person and a warning of others, lest they be hurt too (I Tim 5:24).

C. Witness of Paul. 4:16-22.

16. Answer Gr apologia). From this we get our word apology or defense. He is referring to his trial. **Stood with me** (Gr paraginomai). This is a technical word and would refer to a defense lawyer or advocate. **All men forsook me.** The same word used of Demas in verse 10, but he did not let it make him bitter. No matter how it hurts, no root of bitterness can be allowed lest many others be hurt (Heb 12:15).

17. The Lord stood with me and He always will (Heb 13:5).

with me, and strengthened me; that by me the preaching might be fully known, and that all the Gentiles might hear: and I was delivered out of the mouth of the lion.

18 And the Lord shall deliver me from every evil work, and will preserve me unto his heavenly kingdom: to whom be glory for ever and ever. Amen.
19 Salute Prĭs'ca and Ăq'ui-la, and the household of Ŏn-e-sĭph'o-rus.
20 E-răs'tus abode at Corinth: but Trŏph'i-mus have I left at Mī-lē'tum sick.
21 Do thy diligence to come before winter. Eū-bū'lus greeteth thee and Pū'děns, and Li'nus, and Clau'dĭ-a, and all the brethren.

22 The Lord Jesus Christ be with thy spirit. Grace be with you. Amen.

He is all one needs. **Strengthened me** (Gr *endynamoō*) means to pour in strength. It is always available. There is no need to give in or give up. **That by me the preaching might be fully known.** From this one must conclude that at Paul's trial before Nero he preached the gospel, even as he did before Felix! **I was delivered out of the mouth of the lion.** This referred back to Psalm 22:21. It simply means here he was not immediately executed after his trial and thus he could write this letter. We are much richer for it today.

18. Deliver me . . . preserve me. What security! He was sure of being delivered from evil work here and preserved to the glory up there! Preservation from the wicked one is a certainty for the believer (Eph 1:13; 4:30).

19-21. These last greetings show Paul's deep concern for people. It shows God's concern for people and even the smallest detail. Imagine the wonder that God included these items in the eternal Word of God.

Prisca and Aquila are the close friends of Paul (cf. Acts 18:2, 18, 26; Rom 16:3; I Cor 16:19); **Onesiphorus** is the Ephesian Christian mentioned in 1:18; **Erastus** was the "chamberlain" or treasurer of the city of Corinth, where at the time of this writing he again resides; **Trophimus**, a native Ephesian, had been left sick at **Miletus** (Miletum), on the coast south of Ephesus. For **Eubulus . . . Pudens . . . Linus . . . and Claudia** no positive identification can be made.
22. Grace be with you. You here is plural, not to Timothy alone but even to us also. With Paul we may exclaim, "to whom be glory forever and ever." **Amen.**

(see page 663 for Bibliography to the Pastoral Epistles)

The Epistle To
TITUS

INTRODUCTION

As a companion of Paul, Titus did not enjoy the fame of Barnabas, Silas, or Timothy. He is only mentioned thirteen times in the New Testament. Yet this young Greek (Gal 2:3), converted to Christ directly from heathenism, was one of the most faithful of Paul's own converts.

His home was apparently Syrian Antioch. His name does not come to our attention in a ministerial relation until Paul's third missionary journey. Then the mention of Titus is checkered throughout the latter years of Paul's life.

Authorship. Again, as in I and II Timothy, and all the recognized pauline epistles, Paul claims to be the author of this epistle (1:1). The discussion on authorship in the introduction to I Timothy is pertinent here.

Date and place of writing. It is impossible to date the writing of Titus with pinpoint accuracy. If it was written after Paul's visit to Spain, it would then be dated only shortly before II Timothy. If it was written before this western visit it would have been written during Paul's first year of freedom from house arrest in Rome. On the assumption that it is more likely that Paul would have written the letter as soon after his release as possible, and probably visited the churches of Greece and Asia Minor directly upon being released from prison, we can suggest a date of the fall of A.D. 63 or a bit later.

Establishing the place of writing is equally difficult. At first this may not appear to be the case for the subscription to Titus in the AV reads, "It was written to Titus, ordained the first bishop of the church of the Cretians, from Nicopolis of Macedonia." This statement, which is not part of the inspired writing of Paul, is in error. It was made on the mistaken assumption that Paul was already in Nicopolis at the time of the penning of Titus. It is evident from 3:12, however, that Paul's intention is to winter at Nicopolis and he has not yet reached that point.

Thus the writing of the Epistle to Titus must have taken place somewhere en route to Nicopolis. The prime suggestion is that it was written at Corinth, following Paul's arrival there from Crete. Although this cannot be maintained dogmatically, there is nothing to suggest that this is not an accurate assumption.

Purpose. Perhaps the chief aim of Paul in writing to Titus was to authenticate the work of Titus on Crete. Titus was Paul's representative there. He would undoubtedly encounter opposition to his leadership there since he was not a native. Paul's epistle to him would add authority to his presence.

In addition, Paul found it necessary to advise Titus of specific instructions which he was to convey to the churches of Crete, the Mediterranean island. The believers of Crete had banded together to worship and pray but had not been organized into proper local assemblies. They were ignorant of church polity or structure. They had no indigenous leadership. Thus Titus was to instruct them in the basic structure of authority in the local church. He would appoint elders in the various churches and dictate the qualifications of those in leadership positions. Paul's instruction to Titus would add validity to the very existence of these churches on Crete. The Epistle to Titus was that instruction.

I Timothy and Titus are quite similar and cover a great deal of the same material. Yet Titus is less personal than I Timothy and much more brief. Also, Titus is characterized by a series of doctrinal summaries, brief capsules of what is most certainly to be believed among the churches.

OUTLINE

COMMENTARY

I. INTRODUCTION. 1:1-4.

PAUL, a servant of God, and an apostle of Jesus Christ, according to the faith of God's elect, and the acknowledging of the truth which is after godliness;

1:1. Paul. The common way to begin a letter in Paul's day was with an identification of the author by name and title. Paul did not vary from this form. **Servant** (Gr *doulos*). This is not just a worker but one who is born into slavery and one who gives himself wholly to another's will. This was Paul's view of himself in relation to God and ought to be that of every Christian. On the other hand, he was chosen of God to be an apostle. What a humble and high position he held at the same time. He was an apostle **according** to "or in accord with" **the faith,** the whole body of revealed truth. The church had to try those who "say they are apostles" (Rev 2:2). Paul could stand the test.

2 In hope of eternal life, which God, that cannot lie, promised before the world began;

2. In hope of eternal life. (Gr *epi*) "upon the basis of" a hope or expectation of eternal life. **Promised before the world began.** God's plan of salvation was not an afterthought (Rev 13:8).

3 But hath in due times manifested his word through preaching, which is committed unto me according to the commandment of God our Saviour;

3. In due times. God has a schedule and is always on time. God's plan is revealed in **his word** and His Word is manifested through preaching. On the importance of preaching see Romans 10:13-15 and I Corinthians 1:17-21.

4 To Titus, *mine* own son after the common faith: Grace, mercy, *and* peace, from God the Father and the Lord Jesus Christ our Saviour.

4. Own son (Gr *gnēsios*) means "legitimate born." Titus was another of Paul's converts. What a blessed event. **Common faith** or faith held in common. **Grace, mercy, and peace.** Paul's usual greeting in the Pastoral Epistles.

II. ORDER IN THE CHURCH. 1:5-16.

A. Order in the Church by the Elders. 1:5-9.

5 For this cause left I thee in Crete, that thou shouldest set in order the things that are wanting, and ordain elders in every city, as I had appointed thee:

5. Crete, one of the largest islands of the Mediterranean where Paul ministered with Titus, probably between his imprisonments. Paul's ministry must have been fantastic. He left a church and converts wherever he went and they needed to **set in order** a church and **ordain elders in every city.**

The qualifications of elders in the church:

6 If any be blameless, the husband of one wife, having faithful children not accused of riot or unruly.

6. For the **husband of one wife** and other phrases not dealt with here, see notes on I Timothy 3:2 ff. **Faithful** or "believing" children. Not only believing children but ones **not accused of riot or unruly.** If Proverbs 22:6 is true and it is, "Train up a child in the way he should go; and when he is old, he will not depart from it," then there is no excuse for a Christian's son being accused of "riot" or "dissolute."

7 For a bishop must be blameless, as the steward of God; not selfwilled, not soon angry, not given to wine, no striker, not given to filthy lucre;

7. Bishop or overseer as **the steward of God.** A steward has charge of or governs another's affairs (cf. Heb 13:17). He must not be **self-willed** or "self-pleasing," as the Greek indicates, not arrogant. Then, **not soon angry** or prone to anger. The fruit of the Spirit is temperance, the opposite of this.

8 But a lover of hospitality, a lover of good men, sober, just, holy, temperate;

8. A lover of good men, really "a lover of all that is good" and not just men. **Temperate.** It means one who is held in check and this is done by the Holy Spirit, for it is a fruit of the Spirit (Gal 5:23).

9 Holding fast the faithful word as he hath been taught, that he may be able by sound doctrine both to exhort and to convince the gainsayers.

9. Holding fast or "firmly to" the **word** which is faithful and trustworthy. **As he hath been taught,** meaning "according to the teaching" of the Lord Himself and the inspired apostles (Isa 8:20; Acts 2:42). This is necessary in order to **exhort,** encourage, and help believers and **convince** or convict the **gainsayers,** those who "oppose" or "speak against," as the Greek indicates, by means of **sound doctrine.**

B. Disorder in the Church by False Teachers. 1:10-16.

The need for elders arose because of false teachers.

10 For there are many unruly and vain talkers and deceivers, specially they of the circumcision:

10. These false teachers, **teaching things which they ought not** (vs. 11) are first of all **unruly** or uncontrolled as the children of verse 6. The same word occurs in both places. They balk at and reject any authority over them. And so we see it today. **Vain**

11 Whose mouths must be stopped, who subvert whole houses, teaching things which they ought not, for filthy lucre's sake.

12 One of themselves, *even* a prophet of their own, said, The Cretians *are* alway liars, evil beasts, slow bellies.

13 This witness is true. Wherefore rebuke them sharply, that they may be sound in the faith;

14 Not giving heed to Jewish fables, and commandments of men, that turn from the truth.

15 Unto the pure all things *are* pure: but unto them that are defiled and unbelieving *is* nothing pure; but even their mind and conscience is defiled.

16 They profess that they know God; but in works they deny *him*, being abominable, and disobedient, and unto every good work reprobate.

CHAPTER 2
BUT speak thou the things which become sound doctrine:

2 That the aged men be sober, grave, temperate, sound in faith, in charity, in patience.

3 The aged women likewise, that *they* be in behaviour as becometh holiness, not false accusers, not given to much wine, teachers of good things;

4 That they may teach the young women to be sober, to love their husbands, to love their children,

talkers, in the sense of "empty" or "useless." **Deceivers** are really "mind" deceivers. **Of the circumcision,** i.e., the Jews.

11. Whose mouths must be stopped (Gr *epistomizō*) originally meant to put something in the mouth as a gag. Why? Because **whole houses** or families were being overthrown by them. There was much at stake. They taught for **filthy lucre** or "shameful gain," which God's true servants must not do (vs. 7).

12. A prophet of their own probably refers to the famed Cretan poet Epimenides, born around 600 B.C. Just as sodomy refers to an infamous sin of which Sodomites were guilty, so "Cretan" became almost synonymous with a liar. They were also **slow bellies.** The Greek here really means "idle gluttons." About such a one God says he should put a knife to his throat (Prov 23:2).

13. This witness is true. Paul confirms these as facts and says **rebuke them sharply.** There was no place for timidity here. **Sharply** (Gr *apotomōs*) meant "to cut off abruptly." **That** meant the purpose of the rebuke was that they may be **sound** or "healthy" in the faith. **Rebuke** was not vindictive but curative, as it should be always.

14. These things, **Jewish fables,** they taught (cf. I Tim 1:4-11) and the **commandments of men** that turn away from the truth of God. This was an ever-present danger of the Jews (cf. Mk 7:7-13).

15. Unto the pure . . . defiled. This is a fascinating verse and much needed today. Paul is referring to the Jewish legalists who were extremists about Old Testament Jewish ceremonial washings. These insisted on the ceremonial washings and were still calling some meats unclean, showing the need for the teaching of Matthew 15:1-20. People today can go to extremes and see something wrong in everything and every person until they separate themselves into total isolation.

16. They profess . . . but. Profession and performance should not contradict. Faith and works go together. True faith produces true works. **Reprobate** has the idea of being tested but disapproved.

III. OBEDIENCE IN THE CHURCH. 2:1-15.

A. Obedience of Older Men. 2:1-2.

2:1. But. In decided contrast to these false teachers Titus is exhorted. The word **become** has the idea of conspicuously becoming to sound doctrine. There would be no question about it.

2. The **aged men** are not the official elders but older men in years. **Sober** means sober-minded, sincere. **Grave** means dignified as opposed to frivolous and was used of deacons (I Tim 3:8). **Temperate** means "to curb one's desires and impulses." **Sound,** the familiar word meaning healthy.

B. Obedience of Older Women. 2:3.

3. Healthy doctrine shows up in the **aged women . . . in behavior** or "demeanor." **As becometh** means as is fitting and not out of place with **holiness.** Every believer's body is the temple of the Holy Spirit and everything done should be fitting the temple of God. **Not false accusers** (Gr *diabolos*) rendered devil in some places and meaning "slanderer." **Not given to much wine.** This is a translation of the Greek perfect participle *douloō*, "to make a slave of." The Greek tense speaks here of a confirmed drunkard. Women are not to be false accusers but **teachers of good things.**

C. Obedience of Young Women. 2:4-5.

4. They should teach the **young women.** Christian matrons have a responsibility to give their years of experience to the younger women. They are the best teachers of younger women. **To love their husbands . . . their children.** This is a friendly

5 *To be* discreet, chaste, keepers at home, good, obedient to their own husbands, that the word of God be not blasphemed.

companionship in which you do things together. Most homes could use a lot of this teaching.

5. Discreet is the same word as in verse 2, translated "temperate," and can mean sound-minded. **Chaste** or pure. **Keepers at home** (Gr *oikourgos*) means "working at home." Again, Paul is no male chauvinist. God-ordained women are to work at home, but not as a maid or slave. Being a good homekeeper is not demeaning. There is no higher calling. Every man knows the transforming power in the home of a lovely, godly wife. Her power is felt in a much greater institute than a bank or political office when she influences the home and children for God. **Obedient to their . . . husbands.** What an awesome responsibility this puts on the husband to be a man of God and represent Christ in the home! Why are wives to live like this? **That the word of God be not blasphemed.** What an awful result when wives are out of place and unsubmissive.

D. Obedience of Young Men. 2:6-8.

6 Young men likewise exhort to be sober minded.

6. The other side of this coin is for **young men** to be **soberminded.** This is the same word (Gr *sophroneō*) as in verses 2 and 5, translated "temperate" and "discreet," and has the idea of "curbing one's desires and impulses," or "self-controlled."

7 In all things shewing thyself a pattern of good works: in doctrine *shewing* uncorruptness, gravity, sincerity,

7. Showing thyself. He now turns to Titus. **A pattern of good works, pattern** (Gr *typos*) meaning model or type. It is common for young men to have a hero and pastors should be the best human models for them to pattern themselves after. Then, **in doctrine showing uncorruptness,** that is, no taint of heresy. **Gravity** here means "dignity" and a man of God must have such and then he will win the respect of older men and women as well.

8 Sound speech, that cannot be condemned; that he that is of the contrary part may be ashamed, having no evil thing to say of you.

8. Sound speech, that cannot be condemned. Besides being a good pattern as a leader, the pastor must exhibit the wisdom to speak only that which is well-thought-out and not that which is rash or reprehensible. He should say nothing that will bring blame to his ministry (I Tim 5:14).

E. Obedience of Slaves. 2:9-10.

9 *Exhort* servants to be obedient unto their own masters, *and* to please *them* well in all *things;* not answering again;

9. Servants (Gr *doulos*) were slaves in a pagan society. Paul did not get side-tracked into social reform. One cannot reform a lost society. The gospel will transform individuals in society and this is the minister's calling. The trend today is to go around passing out aspirins, in the form of a so-called social gospel, to a sick society when it needs the work of a doctor "delivering" new babes into the kingdom of God. This is a much harder work and is opposed by every demon of hell, but it is the only lasting work and must be done by the man of God. Servants are **to be obedient unto their . . . masters,** not liberated! The context indicates that the obedient lives of Christian slaves should **adorn the doctrine of God.** (vs. 10). **Not answering again** (Gr *antilego*), not "contradicting."

10 Not purloining, but shewing all good fidelity; that they may adorn the doctrine of God our Saviour in all things.

10. Not purloining (Gr *nosphizomai*). The root of this word really means to embezzle or pilfer. Petty thievery was common among slaves and they felt no compunction against it. Too many workers today fall into this same error. Businesses lose millions annually to employees who see nothing wrong with such thievery. Of a Christian this must not be, but he must show **fidelity.**

F. The Basis of Obedience. 2:11-15.

11 For the grace of God that bringeth salvation hath appeared to all men,

11. Why such restraining of oneself? Why demand obedience and submission of men and women? The **grace of God.** Let no one say grace gives license to sin or to be rude or crude. It would take volumes just to delve into the depths of God's grace but II Corinthians 8:9 sums it up by saying, "For ye know the grace of our Lord Jesus Christ, that, though he was rich, yet for your sakes he became poor, that ye through his poverty might be rich." Oh, how rich He was in glory, and how poor He became as He took our sins upon Himself! Then how rich we became as the "sons of God" and "heirs of God" (Rom 8:16). This is the salvation grace brings. See Ephesians 2:8-10. **Hath appeared** refers to the past act of Christ's first coming to give **himself for us, that he might redeem us** (vs. 14).

12. Our initial response to God's grace must be **denying ungodliness.** Some very blindly accuse those who believe salvation is solely by grace of turning grace into a license to sin. Not so, for grace teaches to deny ungodliness and **worldly lusts.** While in the world the believer is not of the world and his desires are not to be set on this world system and its values. Rather, **we should live soberly.** This same word in different forms is in verses 2, 4, 5, 6 of this chapter. **Righteously,** or in simple terms, just do right no matter what others may do! **Godly** means in a godly manner, not "holier than thou" but with true piety. **In this present world.** The gospel is not a pie in the sky, but it is for the here and now, and it teaches how to really live and not just exist, as the world does.

13. There is a great future as well and grace teaches to look for **that blessed hope.** "If in this life only we have hope in Christ, we are of all men most miserable" (I Cor 15:19). There is much more to come. Jesus is coming again and it will be **the glorious appearing of the great God and our Savior Jesus Christ.** The Greek construction here is fantastic for the construction makes the **blessed hope** and **glorious appearing** to be one and the same thing. The one true hope and expectation of the believer is seeing Jesus as He is and being like Him (I Jn 3:2). How the heart of the believer longs for that day (II Tim 4:8). Then the same rule of construction makes **the great God** and **our Savior Jesus Christ** to be one and the same thing as well. This is a strong statement of the deity of Christ. "Let God be true but every man a liar" but Jesus is **God,** not simply like God or godly, but He is God, for indeed, "the Word was God" (Jn 1:1).

14. Who gave himself. This is why He humbled Himself (Phil 2:5-8) and became a man so He, the God-man, might suffer and die for our sins and **redeem us from all iniquity.** The word **redeem** (Gr *lutroō*) means "to set free by the payment of a ransom." The believer is now set free from sin to become **zealous of good works.** He is "created in Christ Jesus unto good works" (Eph 2:10), not because of good works which would be contrary to salvation by grace.

15. These things speak . . . with all authority. God's man must be authoritative. Jesus was (Mt 7:29). The scribes weren't!

IV. OBEDIENCE IN THE WORLD. 3:1-11.

A. Obedience in Relationship to Rulers. 3:1.

3:1. Put them in mind or simply remind them **to be subject.** This is in the middle voice and means "put oneself" with the idea of doing it willingly and not being made to do it. **To principalities.** This refers to the principal person or first in authority, such as the king. Then **powers** refer to those of delegated authority under them. **Obey magistrates** reminds us there is a chain of command in the civil realm and believers are to be obedient in civil matters. To do away with this principal would lead to anarchy and chaos. **Every good work.** This seems to indicate the believer's sphere of influence for good ought to be felt in every realm. Joseph, Daniel, and Moses are good examples of this.

B. Obedience in Relationship to People. 3:2-7.

2. To speak evil of no man, from which we get blaspheme (Gr *blasphēmeō*). Usually this is used with reference to God but here it is to men also. How tragic to hear so much of this done among Christians today, even of one another. While this refers

---

12 Teaching us that, denying ungodliness and worldly lusts, we should live soberly, righteously, and godly, in this present world;

13 Looking for that blessed hope, and the glorious appearing of the great God and our Saviour Jesus Christ;

14 Who gave himself for us, that he might redeem us from all iniquity, and purify unto himself a peculiar people, zealous of good works.

15 These things speak, and exhort, and rebuke with all authority. Let no man despise thee.

CHAPTER 3
PUT them in mind to be subject to principalities and powers, to obey magistrates, to be ready to every good work,

2 To speak evil of no man, to be no brawlers, *but* gentle, shewing all meekness unto all men.

3 For we ourselves also were sometimes foolish, disobedient, deceived, serving divers lusts and pleasures, living in malice and envy, hateful, *and* hating one another.

4 But after that the kindness and love of God our Saviour toward man appeared,
5 Not by works of righteousness which we have done, but according to his mercy he saved us, by the washing of regeneration, and renewing of the Holy Ghost;

6 Which he shed on us abundantly through Jesus Christ our Saviour;

7 That being justified by his grace, we should be made heirs according to the hope of eternal life.

8 *This is* a faithful saying, and these things I will that thou affirm constantly, that they which have believed in God might be careful to maintain good works. These things are good and profitable unto men.
9 But avoid foolish questions, and genealogies, and contentions, and strivings about the law; for they are unprofitable and vain.
10 A man that is an heretick after the first and second admonition reject;

11 Knowing that he that is such is subverted, and sinneth, being condemned of himself.

12 When I shall send Artemas unto thee, or Tych'i-cus, be diligent to come unto me to Nī-cŏp'o-lĭs: for I have determined there to winter.

2524

to the world primarily, name-calling is not a Christian's prerogative and especially of a brother in the Lord. **Brawler** means "not a contentious person." It is usually the contentious who speak evil of others. **Gentle** usually refers to our outward conduct while **meekness** to inward attitude. Both are Christlike characteristics.

3. We . . . were . . . foolish. It is so easy to forget what manner of men we once were. **Foolish** means "without understanding" which is true of the natural man (I Cor 2:14). **Disobedient.** Romans 1:18ff. shows just how far the unbeliever will go to be disobedient to God. He is **deceived** by the deceiver himself and will believe a lie rather than the truth. **Serving** (Gr *douleuō*) or slaving to **divers lusts.** "Whosoever committeth sin is the servant of sin" (Jn 8:34). **Living** (Gr *diagō*) meaning "to pass the time" in **malice** or **envy.** Then, as unbelievers, we were **hateful, and hating one another.** What a history. Who dares write his true autobiography before he knew Christ.

4-5. But, thank God for the "buts" in Scripture. But for the grace of God we would all still be in the same wretched condition as the unbeliever in the world, therefore, beware how you speak against even them! **The kindness . . . of God . . . appeared** showing that **Not by works of righteousness which we have done, but according to his mercy he saved us.** We are not saved because we do not do the above things anymore, but are saved **according to his mercy.** Salvation comes not by trusting our works of righteousness, but His work of redemption on the cross. Salvation then includes **the washing of regeneration.** (Gr *palinggenesia*) is a compound of "again" and "to become." Jesus spoke of it as being born again. It is the act of the **Holy Ghost** (Jn 3:5-8).

6. It also comes **through Jesus Christ our Savior.** God thought it, Christ bought it, and the Spirit wrought it.

7. Salvation is not just a narrow escape from hell. What was shed on us abundantly was that **we should be made heirs,** heirs of God and joint-heirs with Christ (Rom 8:16-17). What a "great salvation" (Heb 2:3).

C. Obedience and Our Relationship to Heretics. 3:8-11.

8. I will that thou affirm constantly. The word "affirm" is the same word used of the false teachers in I Timothy 1:7. It means to strongly affirm. Affirm that believers are **to maintain good works.** Sometimes this is neglected and believers can take a "who cares" attitude. This must not be so.

9. But avoid foolish questions. These admonitions were given over and over to Timothy as well. See I Timothy 1:4; II Timothy 2:23ff.

10. Heretick (Gr *hairetikos*) means "to choose, prefer, or take for oneself." It has the idea of choosing to believe what one wants, in spite of what God says. The Word of God must be the final authority for what we believe. Those who accept so-called "further revelations" which are contrary to the Word of God are heretics and should be rejected.

11. This one is **subverted** (Gr *ektrepō*), meaning twisted. It is a medical term used of such as an ankle that has been sprained. Being condemned of himself (Gr *autokatakritos*) means self-condemned. By his own contentions, the subverted one condemns himself and shows whose camp he is in.

V. CONCLUSION. 3:12-15.

Now comes a number of personal notes which conclude the epistle. This is typical of the apostle.

12. Evidently **Artemas** or **Tychicus** was to replace Titus on the island of Crete. Artemas is unknown to us but Tychicus is well attested in Pauline literature being the bearer from Rome to Asia Minor of the epistles to the Colossians, Ephesians, and to

Philemon. Also Tychicus was to be sent by Paul to relieve Timothy in Ephesus (II Tim 4:12). He was the trusted companion of Paul. Both here and in II Timothy 4:21 there is a reference to Paul's plan to winter in **Nicopolis** and in each case he urges his associates to **be diligent to come** to him.

13 Bring Zenas the lawyer and Apollos on their journey diligently, that nothing be wanting unto them.

13. Zenas the lawyer and Apollos. Zenas the "lawyer" (Gr *nomikos*) is otherwise unknown but Apollos is the eloquent evangelist mentioned frequently in Acts and I Corinthians. Assistance is to be provided to them so **that nothing be wanting unto them.**

14 And let ours also learn to maintain good works for necessary uses, that they be not unfruitful.

14. Learn to maintain good works. The Cretan Christians are not only to conduct themselves properly, but are to engage only in honorable occupations and to make themselves practically useful to all the other believers. "The practical side of Christianity is here brought into vivid focus. The words **for necessary uses** can be understood either as necessitous cases or as wants. The more probable interpretation is the former, as RSV 'so as to help cases of urgent need.' All who engage in such works of mercy need never fear that they will be unfruitful" (Donald Guthrie, *The Pastoral Epistles*, p. 210).

15 All that are with me salute thee. Greet them that love us in the faith. Grace *be* with you all. Amen.

15. Grace be with you all. Amen. This final benediction is identical with those of I and II Timothy, except for the "all" at the end. In characteristic shortness, yet tenderness, Paul has completed his letter to another son in the faith, Titus.

(see page 663 for Bibliography to the Pastoral Epistles)

The Epistle To
PHILEMON

INTRODUCTION

Paul's letter to Philemon is the shortest of his thirteen canonical books (only 430 words in the AV), and is thus placed last in the collection of Pauline Epistles in our Bible. It was written and sent at the same time as Colossians, about A.D. 62, while Paul was under guard in Rome awaiting trial before Caesar (Acts 25:12; 28:16, 30).

This little letter in Paul's own handwriting (vs. 19) is to Philemon, a well-to-do Christian who resided in Colossae (cf. vss. 2, 23 and Col 4:12, 17) in the Roman province of Asia. Paul had been the principal human agent responsible for the salvation of Philemon (vs. 19), accomplished some five or six years prior through Paul's ministry in Ephesus (Acts 19:10, 26). Paul's purpose in writing is to ask Philemon to reinstate Onesimus, a slave who had run away from Philemon, and who apparently had stolen some valuables (vs. 18).

The backdrop of the whole story is, of course, the first-century Roman Empire. There were millions of slaves throughout the empire. Many slaveholders had ten or more, and not a few owned hundreds. These slaves were not of any particular race or nationality, but were composed of the people of Rome's many conquered territories from the East to the West. Roman law governing slavery was quite severe toward the slave. They were considered nothing more than pieces of property to be bought, sold, and used for any purpose whatsoever. Life was not easy for slaves. They could be beaten for minor offenses and even crucified for running away.

In contrast to Roman law was the Old Testament law about slaves. They were treated like household members (Lev 25:53) and became partakers of the covenant (Gen 17:27). They were freed during the sabbatical year (Ex 21:2). Harming a slave resulted in his freedom (Ex 21:26-27), and if someone killed a slave he would be severely punished (Ex 21:20). An escaped slave was to be neither hunted nor returned to his master (Deut 23:15-16). For more on slavery, both Jewish and Roman, see J. B. Lightfoot's introduction to Philemon, and W. Alexander's eight-page section in the introduction to Philemon in *The Bible Commentary*, edited by F. C. Cook.

With this contrast between the Jewish law and the Roman practice of slavery in mind, we see how masterfully Paul sought to bring mercy into the Roman system where Christians were concerned. Paul must also have had the slave Onesimus in mind when he addressed Christian slaveholders in Ephesians 6:5-8 and Colossians 3:22-25, both near the time he wrote this letter to Philemon.

OUTLINE

I. Paul's Prologue. 1-3.
II. Paul's Prayer and Praise for Philemon. 4-7.
III. Paul's Plea for Profitable Onesimus. 8-21.

IV. Paul's Personal Prospects. 22.
V. Paul's Postscript. 23-25.

COMMENTARY

I. PAUL'S PROLOGUE. 1-3.

PAUL, a prisoner of Jesus Christ, and Tĭm'o-thỹ *our* brother, unto Phĭ-lē'mon our dearly beloved, and fellowlabourer,

1. Paul, a prisoner of Jesus Christ. As was customary, Paul first identifies himself to his readers. But here, instead of calling himself an apostle, he reminds Philemon that he is a prisoner for Christ's sake (cf. vs. 9; Eph 3:1; 4:1 and II Tim 1:8). **And Timothy, our brother.** All true believers in Christ are brothers. Timothy was no doubt visiting Paul in Rome, and was not being detained. **Unto Philemon.** All we know about Philemon is contained in this short letter. Residing at Colossae, Philemon was apparently a model Christian. He was an active worker for Christ and also the owner of the slave Onesimus, who had run away.

2 And to *our* beloved Ăp'phĭ-a, and Är-chĭp'pus our fellowsoldier, and to the church in thy house:

2. Apphia was no doubt Philemon's wife, and is thus warmly greeted, along with **Archippus,** who may be their son, and who apparently has certain responsibilities in the local congregation of believers at Colossae (Col 4:17). **And to the church in thy**

house. The word church (Gr *ekklēsia*), as it is used here, refers to a local group of immersed believers who would gather together for worship, prayer, edification, exhortation, fellowship, and the commemoration of Christ's death (the Lord's Supper), and then go forth to serve Christ and to tell others about Him. Since believers did not build meeting houses, they frequently met in homes (Acts 2:4-6; Rom 16:5).

3 Grace to you, and peace, from God our Father and the Lord Jesus Christ.

3. Grace to you, and peace. Grace (Gr *charis*) was the common Greek greeting, just as peace (Heb *shalōm*) was the ordinary Hebrew salutation. Paul combines both of these terms, heightened with the full Christian meaning of all the blessings of salvation that freely come to us through Christ, and the peace of God that we have because Christ has made peace with God on our behalf. The fact that God the Father and the Lord Jesus Christ together send this grace and peace illustrates their equality in the Godhead.

II. PAUL'S PRAYER AND PRAISE FOR PHILEMON. 4-7.

4 I thank my God, making mention of thee always in my prayers,

4. Paul perpetually set a proper example in his prayer life. We should be thankful for other believers and bear them up before the Lord. Paul had a long prayer list which he remembered daily (see Eph 1:15-16; Phil 1:3-4; Col 1:9; I Thess 1:2; and II Tim 1:3). We should follow his example.

5 Hearing of thy love and faith, which thou hast toward the Lord Jesus, and toward all saints;

5. Hearing. Paul continually heard of Philemon's love and faith from others around him. Philemon was a model believer, both before the Lord, and with regard to other believers. This naturally has a bearing on the request Paul makes of Philemon.

6 That the communication of thy faith may become effectual by the acknowledging of every good thing which is in you in Christ Jesus.
7 For we have great joy and consolation in thy love, because the bowels of the saints are refreshed by thee, brother.

6. This verse expresses the content of Paul's prayer for Philemon. He prays that Philemon might generously share with others, the results of which would glorify God.

7. This was in fact what Paul had been hearing about Philemon. Paul was encouraged because Philemon was such a rest and refreshment to the saints (other believers) in Colosse. **Brother.** Paul refers both to Philemon and to Onesimus (vs. 16) as his brothers. Such ties in the Lord are often more meaningful than even blood relations with those who are unsaved.

III. PAUL'S PLEA FOR PROFITABLE ONESIMUS. 8-21.

8 Wherefore, though I might be much bold in Christ to enjoin thee that which is convenient,

8. Wherefore. Because Philemon's heart was so gracious, kind, and loving (vss. 4-7), Paul knows that he does not need to command Philemon with the authority of an apostle to perform his request.

9 Yet for love's sake I rather beseech *thee*, being such an one as Paul the aged, and now also a prisoner of Jesus Christ.

9. Instead, Paul makes a forthright appeal to Philemon to act on a higher plane, that of love. Paul's mention that he is aged, and also a prisoner, is calculated to gain the approval sought from Philemon. Paul must have been nearly sixty years old at that time, and he was a missionary statesman by anyone's standards. Not a young inexperienced preacher, Paul was an elder apostle who knew the mind of Christ. His status as a "helpless" prisoner made his appeal all the more weighty upon Philemon. He was trusting God to speak to Philemon concerning his plea.

10 I beseech thee for my son Ō-nĕs′i-mus, whom I have begotten in my bonds:

10. My son Onesimus. Paul's plea is for Onesimus, Philemon's runaway slave. After Onesimus fled from Colossae he made his way to Rome, and somehow came into contact with Paul, who led him to a saving knowledge of Christ. This is why Paul refers to Onesimus as his son whom he has begotten (in the faith). Paul elsewhere refers to Timothy and Titus in similar fashion (I Tim 1:2; Tit 1:4). It is possible that Onesimus, who willingly returned to Philemon with Paul's letter, stood in the very presence of Philemon as the letter was read.

11 Which in time past was to thee unprofitable, but now profitable to thee and to me:

11. This verse contains a play on words. The name Onesimus (Gr *onēsimos*) means "useful" or "profitable." Paul is saying that Onesimus had previously not lived up to his name, but now

12 Whom I have sent again: thou therefore receive him, that is, mine own bowels:

13 Whom I would have retained with me, that in thy stead he might have ministered unto me in the bonds of the gospel:

14 But without thy mind would I do nothing; that thy benefit should not be as it were of necessity, but willingly.

15 For perhaps he therefore departed for a season, that thou shouldest receive him for ever;

16 Not now as a servant, but above a servant, a brother beloved, specially to me, but how much more unto thee, both in the flesh, and in the Lord?

17 If thou count me therefore a partner, receive him as myself.

18 If he hath wronged thee, or oweth thee ought, put that on mine account;

19 I Paul have written it with mine own hand, I will repay it: albeit I do not say to thee how thou owest unto me even thine own self besides.

20 Yea, brother, let me have joy of thee in the Lord: refresh my bowels in the Lord.

21 Having confidence in thy obe-

(since his salvation) he will not only be useful to Philemon, but already has proven himself such to Paul. True salvation changes one's attitude and his actions (II Cor 5:17).

12. Mine own bowels. Paul's deep affection and admiration for Onesimus must have been evident to Philemon, as he refers to Onesimus as his own heart. Paul multiplies the terms in calling Onesimus his son (vs. 10), his own heart (vs. 12), his brother (vs. 16), and even exhorts Philemon to receive him as he would Paul himself (vs. 17).

13. Paul longed to keep Onesimus with him because he ministered to him in his difficult situation in Rome. Paul lovingly mentions that if Onesimus were in Rome he would only be doing what Philemon himself would do if he could. Certainly, Philemon must have been in tears as he read these affectionate words of his beloved friend and apostle.

14. Paul refused to keep Onesimus because to have done so and then to have sought Philemon's approval may have forced Philemon to grudgingly approve of the situation. But Paul knows that if kindness or helpfulness is in any way forced, it becomes insincere. Philemon's goodness always proceeded willingly from a heart of compassion. We must constantly examine our own lives to insure that proper actions are produced by proper motives.

15. The marvelous providence of God is in view in this verse. Onesimus' departure eventuated in his salvation in Christ. Now he returns to Philemon for the duration of this life, with the happy prospect of spending eternity in heaven with Philemon and all other believers. This does not mean that Onesimus never would have been saved if he had not run away. But God in His providence did turn his evil around for good.

16. Though Onesimus was still Philemon's slave, and as far as we know remained such, in Christ he was the Lord's freeman (I Cor 7:21), and a brother and a joint heir with Paul and Philemon (Gal 3:28; Rom 8:17). Christian bonds transcend human barriers and exceed mere earthly relationships.

17. Paul had already asked Philemon to receive Onesimus back (vs. 12), but now he put the request in terminology that could scarcely be ignored. He stated that if Philemon regarded him as an associate, a partner in spiritual matters, then he should receive Onesimus as he would Paul himself. There is, of course, no question as to how Philemon would receive Paul! This is also a perfect picture of how God receives sinners who trust Christ as Lord and Saviour. How is that? Just as He receives Christ.

18. Put that on mine account. Paul wants all of Onesimus' wrongs placed on his own account as if they were his. In the same way, Christ takes all the believer's sins on Himself and pays for all completely by His shed blood (I Pet 2:24). Christ is our substitute. He suffered our punishment. No wonder Luther could so aptly say, "We are all the Lord's Onesimi."

19. When Paul wrote his various epistles, he often used a stenographer to do the writing; but here, perhaps because of his great personal concern, he points out that he has written the letter in his own handwriting. Paul's offer to pay all that Onesimus owed must have moved Philemon, as well as the reminder that with regard to eternal values Philemon owed everything to Paul's concern for him (humanly speaking).

20. The apostle makes his final appeal to Philemon, calling him brother, and asking him, as it were, for a personal favor. The language expressing Paul's desire is very heightened. He yearns for that which will bring to his own heart abundant joy in Christ. His final challenge is that Philemon might refresh his heart, even as Philemon has refreshed the hearts of others (cf. vs. 7 where the same expression occurs).

21. Thy obedience refers to the obedience that proceeds from a heart of love, not from the compulsion of Paul's authority

dience I wrote unto thee, knowing that thou wilt also do more than I say.

as an apostle. **Thou wilt also do more than I say.** The extreme confidence Paul has in Philemon's response is noted here. There is even a hint at possible emancipation, i.e., "more than I say," which was merely to receive Onesimus back.

IV. PAUL'S PERSONAL PROSPECTS. 22.

22 But withal prepare me also a lodging: for I trust that through your prayers I shall be given unto you.

22. With the plea for Onesimus ended, Paul presents his personal plan of visiting Philemon once his case in Rome is decided. He expects to be released soon (Phil 2:24). He is confident that Philemon will provide some hospitality, and that Philemon's prayers will move God to intervene on his behalf. Prayer does move God. One can also imagine how Paul's intention to visit Philemon must have encouraged him to grant Paul's initial request for Onesimus.

V. PAUL'S POSTSCRIPT. 23-25.

23 There salute thee Ĕp'a-phrăs, my fellowprisoner in Christ Jesus;

23. Epaphras, my fellow prisoner. Epaphras was well known to the Colossians (Col 1:7; 4:12-13). To call him a fellow prisoner (as he did Aristarchus, Col 4:10) must mean that these men were so constantly with Paul that it seemed they were prisoners too.

24 Marcus, Ăr-Ĭs-tär'chus, Demas, Lucas, my fellowlabourers.

24. Marcus [John Mark] had recovered from his failure on the first missionary journey (Acts 13:13; 15:36-41) and was now with Paul again (cf. II Tim 4:11). **Aristarchus** was one of Paul's converts from Thessalonica who accompanied Paul on much of the third missionary journey (Acts 20:4) and on the trip to Rome (Acts 27:2; Col 4:10). **Demas,** sad to say, later turned back from following Christ (II Tim 4:10). **Lucas** [Luke], the beloved physician, the author of Luke and Acts, was faithful to the very end (II Tim 4:11). These all sent their greetings to Philemon. Of the eleven persons mentioned in this short letter, Onesimus is precisely in the middle, and is the central character.

25 The grace of our Lord Jesus Christ be with your spirit. Amen.

25. Paul ends this letter as he began it, with **the grace of our Lord Jesus Christ** directed toward Philemon's entire household. All grace resides in Him who freely gave all He had for us. "Thanks be unto God for his unspeakable gift" (II Cor 9:15).

BIBLIOGRAPHY

Barnes, Albert. *Notes on the New Testament, Explanatory and Practical—Thessalonians, Timothy, Titus, and Philemon.* Ed. by Robert Frew. Grand Rapids: Baker, 1951.

Barrett, C. K. The Pastoral Epistles. In *The New Clarendon Bible.* Oxford: Clarendon Press, 1963.

Bernard, J. H. The Pastoral Epistles. In the *Cambridge Greek Testament.* Cambridge: Cambridge University Press, 1922.

Erdman, Charles R. *The Pastoral Epistles of Paul.* Philadelphia: Westminster Press, 1923.

*Fairbairn, Patrick. *Commentary on the Pastoral Epistles.* Grand Rapids: Zondervan, 1956.

*Guthrie, Donald. The Pastoral Epistles. In *Tyndale New Testament Commentaries.* Grand Rapids: Eerdmans, 1957.

*Hendriksen, William. Exposition of the Pastoral Epistles. In *New Testament Commentary.* Grand Rapids: Zondervan, 1956.

*Hiebert, D. Edmond. *First Timothy.* Chicago: Moody Press, 1957.

*_____. *Second Timothy.* Chicago: Moody Press, 1958.

*_____. *Titus and Philemon.* Chicago: Moody Press, 1957.

Humphreys, A. E. The Epistles to Timothy and Titus. In *Cambridge Bible for Schools and Colleges.* Cambridge: Cambridge University Press, 1925.

Ironside, Harry, *Timothy, Titus and Philemon.* Neptune, New Jersey: Loizeaux Brothers, 1955.

Kelly, William. *An Exposition of the Two Epistles to Timothy.* Third edition. London: C. A. Hammond, 1948.

*Kelly, J. N. D. The Pastoral Epistles. In *Harper's New Testament Commentaries.* New York: Harper and Row, 1963.

*Kent, H. A. *The Pastoral Epistles.* Chicago: Moody Press, 1958.

Lenski, R. C. H. *The Interpretation of St. Paul's Epistles to the Colossians, to the Thessalonians, to Timothy, to Titus, and to Philemon.* Columbus, Ohio: Lutheran Book Concern, 1937.

PHILEMON

Liddon, Henry P. *Explanatory Analysis of St. Paul's First Epistle to Timothy*. London: Longmans, Green and Co., 1897.

*Lilley, J. P. The Pastoral Epistles. A New Translation with Introduction, Commentary, and Appendix. In *Handbooks for Bible Classes*. Edinburgh: T. & T. Clark, 1901.

Moule, H. C. G. *The Second Epistle to Timothy*. London: Religious Tract Society, 1905.

Plummer, Alfred. The Pastoral Epistles. In *The Expositor's Bible*. New York: A. C. Armstrong and Son, 1908.

Simpson, E. K. *The Pastoral Epistles*. London: Tyndale Press, 1954.

Vine, W. E. *The Epistles to Timothy and Titus: Faith and Conduct*. Grand Rapids: Zondervan, 1965.

Ward, R. A. *Commentary on First and Second Timothy and Titus*. Waco: Word Books, 1972.

Wuest, Kenneth S. *The Pastoral Epistles in the Greek New Testament for the English Reader*. Grand Rapids: Eerdmans, 1952.

The Epistle To The
HEBREWS

INTRODUCTION

First century Jewish Christians were involved in a traumatic identity struggle. Persecuted by both the Romans and their fellow Jews, they were involved in the always difficult conflict of trying to interpret new thoughts in contrast to long-held tradition. Further, the eschatology of Christ remained unfulfilled. There were no indications that Christ's return and the restoration of Israel would ever occur. The first generation of Christians had passed, and Israel was still unsaved. Outwardly, Christ remained unvindicated before many of these Jewish Christians (Westcott, p. V), and the purpose of the Epistle to the Hebrews seems clearly to be one of exhorting them to hold fast to their faith in Christ.

Throughout the epistle the author stresses the continuity and flow between the Old Testament revelation and the new faith in Christ, emphasizing the superiority of both Christ and the new covenant which He initiated. In doing so he assures the Jewish Christians of the biblical heritage of the new covenant. He challenges them to run with endurance the race that is set before them (12:1), even as their Jewish ancestors had done in Old Testament times. In the exhortative style of the epistle we find encouragement, comfort, and warning.

Authorship. The most intriguing mystery surrounding the book of Hebrews is that of its authorship. For one reason or another, the author remains anonymous to us, though he was known to his original readers (13:23). Discussion concerning the author's identity dates back to the second century. We are not told whether the writer was Gentile or Hebrew (see the Commentary on 13:10). He did have a superb knowledge of Jewish tradition and levitical thought. His Greek syntax and style are so outstanding that many feel that his are the finest in the New Testament. We know also that he was well acquainted with Timothy (13:23). While these facts serve to give us clues regarding the writer's identity, they also may confuse the issue. The following is a survey of the arguments, both positive and negative, regarding those who are most popularly thought to have written the epistle.

Paul. The strongest argument for pauline authorship of the epistle involves the ancient historical tradition of the church. As early as the second century, Paul was regarded in the East as the author; during the third century the eastern churches commonly accepted his authorship. In the West, where the epistle was known from earliest times, pauline authorship was rejected and did not gain general acceptance until the fourth century (Gardiner, *The Nicene and Post-Nicene Fathers*, First Series, Vol. XIV, p. 341). Even in the East, Clement of Alexandria had difficulty reconciling the literary character of Hebrews with Paul's style and thus proposed that "it was written by Paul for Hebrews

in the Hebrew language, but that Luke translated it and published it for the Greeks; thus he endeavored to account for the similarity in style between Hebrews and the Lucan writings." (F. F. Bruce, p. XXXVI). Though the literary style of Hebrews in no way allows it to be a translation, the proposal by Clement does reveal the disparity some early Greek-speaking scholars saw between Paul's style and that of the Epistle to the Hebrews.

Conversely, the argument commonly raised against pauline authorship, which is based upon Paul's usual practice of identifying himself at the beginning of his epistles, lacks substance. In his epistles that are written to churches in gentile cities, Paul has good reason to immediately identify himself. But if Paul were writing to Jewish believers, it may have been to his advantage not to identify himself so readily. Also in favor of pauline authorship is the comment in chapter thirteen regarding Timothy "our brother." Further, Paul was very familiar with the Hebrew tradition and levitical ritual presented so often in the epistle. He was born a Pharisee, a son of Pharisees (Acts 23:6 NASB), and had an excellent background in the Jewish law.

The strongest argument against pauline authorship is found within the epistle itself. In 2:3 the author regards himself as one whose knowledge of Christ was secondhand. By contrast, Paul vehemently declares that his apostleship and message were directly from Jesus Christ (Gal 1:1, 12).

Luke. Those arguments which speak against pauline authorship speak for lucan authorship: the Greek literary form, the author's secondhand knowledge of Jesus, and even the witness of ancient church tradition. Also, the author's common practice of quoting from the Greek Old Testament, the Septuagint, parallels Luke's pattern while going counter to Paul's.

The argument that no Gentile could write this book is not insurmountable. Luke demonstrates himself to be a careful student of the Word of God. If a Jew could appeal to a gentile world, it is possible that a gentile Christian could admonish Jewish Christians. This could also account for the anonymous character of the epistle. One factor, however, that speaks against lucan authorship is the author's apparent identification of himself with his Jewish readers when he says "Let *us* go forth therefore unto him without the camp" (13:13), and, "We have an altar" (13:10). Such scholars as Calvin and Delitzsch have supported the lucan authorship.

Barnabas. The viewpoint that Barnabas was the author of the Epistle to the Hebrews was put forth as early as the second century by Tertullian. Barnabas was a Levite from Cyprus. As such, he would have been familiar with levitical ritual.

2507

The arguments against Barnabas' authorship stem more from the fact that little positive evidence exists for it. Since Barnabas was well known in the early church, if indeed he wrote the book, more evidence should exist supporting his authorship.

Apollos. The view that Apollos was the author of Hebrews apparently was first suggested by Luther. Today the view is a popular one. Most of the evidence cited for Apollos stems from information contained in Acts 18:24-28. There we learn that Apollos was an Alexandrian Jew and, so, was most likely familiar with the philosophical thinking commonly seen in the development of the Epistle to the Hebrews. We further read that he was an eloquent man and "mighty in the scriptures." Apparently, Apollos had an effective ministry in reaching the Jews by means of the Scriptures, showing that Jesus was indeed the Christ. This same thought development is basic to the book of Hebrews; many quotes from the Old Testament Scriptures are used to illustrate the excellency of Christ.

The greatest weakness in the argument for Apollos' authorship is the lack of early historical evidence. It seems logical that if Apollos had indeed written such a remarkable epistle, one of the second-century Alexandrian fathers, such as Clement or Origen, would have laid claim to one of their own as the author.

It seems best to conclude the whole subject of authorship with the words of Origen from the second century: "Who the author of the Epistle is, God truly knows" (Eusebius 6.25). Whoever the author may be, the crucial thing seems to be that he encourages us to be "Looking unto Jesus the author and finisher of our faith" (12:2). The author asks that we look to Jesus for everything, drawing from Him the strength and encouragement to live the Christian life that is set before us.

Recipients. The earliest extant manuscripts of Hebrews contain the heading "To Hebrews." From every indication in the epistle, it would appear that these Hebrews are Jewish Christians. The various warnings throughout the book indicate that some of them were in danger of returning to Judaism. By so doing, these early Christians could avoid persecution. Judaism was a legal religion, sanctioned and protected under Roman law; Christianity was not. Apparently, many of the recipients had undergone suffering (10:32).

Many cities have been suggested as the locality of these believers (cf. F. F. Bruce, pp. XXXI-XXXV). The situation favors two: Jerusalem and Rome. The Jewish Christians had often received persecution in both cities. In Jerusalem, it was at the hand of Jews for being Christians. In Rome, at times they were persecuted for being Jews (Acts 18:2), and at other times for being Christians.

Though Jerusalem would provide an appealing setting, some scholars find the internal evidence to be problematic (cf. Kent, pp. 23-24). The most significant problem involves the author's statement that the readers had not heard the Lord for themselves but that the message had been passed on by those who had heard Him (2:3). Thus, it would seem easier to imagine that the readers did not live in Jerusalem.

One piece of evidence that makes Rome attractive is the author's closing statement that "They of Italy salute you" (13:24). Since the word "of" (Gr *apo*) is more commonly translated "from," the author may be relaying to those in Rome greetings from those who had formerly lived there. The epistle seems to have been written either by an author in Rome or to recipients in Rome.

Date. The question of date remains somewhat unresolved since the authorship and destination of the epistle escape complete analysis. The evidence clearly places Hebrews within the first century. The allusions to Hebrews by Clement of Rome demand a date prior to A.D. 96 (Bruce, p. XLII). The reference to Timothy as still living (13:23) likewise demands a date within the first century. Yet, the date cannot be early within the church age; for the readers are described as second-generation Christians (2:3). Evidently the date precedes A.D. 70; for throughout all the discourses on the tabernacle ritual, not once is any allusion made regarding the destruction of the Temple by the Romans. The Jewish sacrificial system still appears to be in effect (8:4; 10:8,11). Further, since these Christians had not undergone persecution unto death (12:4), the epistle apparently predates the last days of Nero in the late sixties. A date within the mid-sixties conforms to the known data.

OUTLINE

a. The consequences of Israel's unbelief. 3:7-11.
b. The warning against unbelief. 3:12-19.
c. The warning against missing God's rest. 4:1-13.

D. Christ Is Superior to the Levitical Priesthood Because of the Intercession Provided. 4:14-7:28.
1. The confidence provided through Christ's priesthood. 4:14-16.
2. The qualifications of a priest. 5:1-10.
3. The third warning passage: Do not be spiritually immature. 5:11-6:20.
a. The rebuke of immaturity. 5:11-14.
b. The exhortation to maturity. 6:1-3.
c. The warning of apostasy. 6:4-8.
d. The encouragement to go on. 6:9-12.
e. The certainty of God's promises. 6:13-20.
4. The priestly order of Melchizedek. 7:1-28.
a. A royal priest. 7:1-3.
b. A priest greater than Aaron. 7:4-10.
c. A priestly order which is unending. 7:11-25.
d. A priestly character which is superior. 7:26-28.

E. Christ's Ministry Through the New Covenant Is Superior to the Old System. 8:1-10:30.
1. The better sanctuary in which Christ ministers. 8:1-6.
2. The promise of the New Covenant proclaimed in the Old Covenant. 8:7-13.
3. The operation of the Old Covenant. 9:1-10.
a. The contents of its tabernacle. 9:1-5.
b. The closed chamber of its tabernacle. 9:6-10.
4. The operation of the New Covenant. 9:11-10:18.

a. Christ has opened its inner sanctuary. 9:11-14.
b. Christ is the mediator of the New Covenant. 9:15-22.
c. Christ is the perfect sacrifice. 9:23-28.
d. Christ's offering is once-for-all. 10:1-18.
5. The fourth warning passage: Do not turn back. 10:19-39.
a. Exhortations to use the new access. 10:19-25.
b. The warning. 10:26-31.
c. Exhortations to recall former victories. 10:32-39.

II. Exhortations Based upon Example. 11:1-13:25.
A. Past Triumphs Through Faith. 11:1-40.
1. Necessity of faith. 11:1-3.
2. Prepatriarchal examples. 11:4-7.
3. Patriarchal examples. 11:8-22.
4. Examples from Moses and at Jericho. 11:23-31.
5. Examples from the judges, kings, and prophets. 11:32-38.
6. The conclusion. 11:39-40.

B. Exhortation to Perseverance and Holiness. 12:1-29.
1. The supreme example of endurance. 12:1-4.
2. The example of fatherly discipline. 12:5-13.
3. Exhortation to holiness. 12:14-17.
4. The fifth warning: Do not refuse warning from heaven. 12:18-29.

C. General Admonitions for Service. 13:1-25.
1. Involving love. 13:1-6.
2. Involving leaders and living. 13:7-17.
3. Involving author and recipients. 13:18-25.

COMMENTARY

I. EXHORTATION BASED UPON DOCTRINE—THE PERSON AND WORK OF CHRIST. 1:1-10:39.

A. Christ Is the Finality of Revelation. 1:1-3.

The epistle begins without any greeting or address, demonstrating that it is not a personal letter but a **Word of exhortation** (13:22). Immediately, the author proclaims his theme: The work of Jesus Christ is God's final work and is superior to all that which preceded it.

1. The former revelation in the prophets. 1:1.

GOD, who at sundry times and in divers manners spake in time past unto the fathers by the prophets,

1:1. God, who at sundry times and in divers manners. Although as the subject of the sentence, **God** is placed first, in the Greek it is neither first nor the thought that is emphasized. **At sundry times** (lit., in many parts) and **in divers manners** (lit., in many ways) open the message of this epistle. By putting these words first the author fixes our attention upon the variations and imperfection of the Old Testament revelation (Wescott, p. 4). That revelation came bit by bit, as men were ready and able to receive it. God used visions, dreams, events, and

2 Hath in these last days spoken unto us by *his* Son, whom he hath appointed heir of all things, by whom also he made the worlds;

direct communication to reveal His message **by the prophets.** This fragmentary and varied method demonstrates God's graciousness and versatility in matching His message to the capability of man to understand it (Kent, p. 34).

2. The final revelation in the Son. 1:2-3.

2. Hath in these last days spoken unto us by his Son. These first two verses contrast the former revelation with the revelation which has been given through the Son. The latter revelation is not fragmentary, but complete. It has been reserved for and is now committed to the One **whom he hath appointed heir of all things.** Within verses 2 and 3, seven statements are made concerning the person and work of the Son. Though they are difficult to see in the English translation, these statements gather around three relative clauses, two located in verse 2 and the last in verse 3. First, the One through whom God's final revelation came to man is the One whom God has made heir of all. This language is reminiscent of Psalm 2, to which the author shortly refers (vs. 5). "In that psalm, God places His Anointed One (i.e., Messiah) upon the messianic throne, and grants Him the earth and its people for His inheritance (Ps 2:2-8). The Son's messianic office is thus fully assured" (Kent, p. 36). The One through whom God has given His final message is also the heir of God's final program for this earth. Second, the Son is described as the One **by whom also he made the worlds.** This work infinitely surpasses the mighty works performed by the Old Testament prophets. It is a work of deity.

3 Who being the brightness of *his* glory, and the express image of his person, and upholding all things by the word of his power, when he had by himself purged our sins, sat down on the right hand of the Majesty on high;

3. Who . . . sat down on the right hand of the Majesty on high completes the three relative clauses. Other phrases within verse 3 describe the Son, but this is the last idea that parallels those of verse 2. When He had made purification for sin, He sat down on high. This sitting does not imply present inactivity; rather, it suggests the completion of His redemptive work. This is in direct contrast to the Old Testament priest whose work was never completed.

Who being introduces the phrases which now describe Christ. The use of **being** (Gr *ōn*) "guards against the idea of mere 'adoption' in the Sonship, and affirms the permanence of the divine essence of the Son during His historic work" (Westcott, p. 9). He did not become deity; He always was like the Father. The attributes ascribed to Jesus Christ make up His very nature. They were neither added to, nor taken from, Him during His earthly life. He is **the brightness of his glory, and the express image of his person.** The **brightness** (Gr *apaugasma*) spoken of here refers to a radiance or a shining forth of the divine glory through the Son. "As the rays of light are related to the sun, and neither exists without the other, so Christ is the effulgence of the divine glory. They are essentially one; that is, both are God" (Kent, p. 37). Further, the Son is the **express image** (Gr *charaktēr*) or "imprint," as of a die perfectly representing the original design. The radiant light implies the oneness of the Son with the Father; the imprint of His person implies the distinctness of the Son from the Father. Yet, oneness and distinctness are implicit in both; so the two figures serve to enhance and balance each other (Hughes, p. 41).

The Son is further described as the One who is **upholding all things.** More precisely, the Son is described as carrying (Gr *pherōn*) all things. Christ is not viewed simply as an Atlas supporting the dead weight of the world, but as One sustaining and bringing it to its goal (Westcott, pp. 13-14). Compare the similar teaching of Colossians 1:17.

B. Christ Is Superior to the Angels Because of the Work Accomplished. 1:4-2:18.

After declaring the superiority of the Son and the finality of the revelation which came through Him, the author demonstrates Christ's superiority to the angels. It was necessary that he prove Christ's superiority over the angels to his readers, for in the first-century world pagans and Christians alike accorded great significance and power to angels. Some had possibly taught that Christ Himself was an angel, and for that reason He was able to perform miracles. There is evidence from Scripture (Col 2:18) that some even worshiped angels. Further, angels were involved in the giving of the Mosaic law (2:2; Acts 7:53; Gal 3:19). Thus, if the author wishes to prove the overall superiority of Christ, he must prove that Christ is superior to angels.

1. The Proof of Christ's superiority. 1:4-14.

4. The first proof that Christ is superior to the angels is manifested through the name which He has received, as the Old Testament Scriptures themselves declare. **Being made** (Gr *genomenos*) indicates that the incarnation of Christ is in view here. Progress or development is involved. The author will later show (2:9) that for a short time Christ became lower than the angels by becoming man and dying for him. Still, He is **better** (Gr *kreittōn*) than they are. Thirteen times the author uses this word to develop his theme that Christ is better than any person, being, or institution. He is better than the angels, for **he hath by inheritance obtained a more excellent name than they.** Indeed, His is the "name which is above every name" (Phil 2:9). This includes angels.

5. For unto which of the angels said he at any time. The author here begins a series of Old Testament quotations. No other writer quotes so extensively or develops the Old Testament in the New so exegetically. No other New Testament writer quotes extended passages and then analyzes the many points more thoroughly. In verse 5 the author quotes two passages to demonstrate that Jesus Christ is the **Son** and is therefore superior to the angels; for they are never so designated (Ps 2:7; II Sam 7:14). Though angels have been called "sons of God" in the sense that they are of a direct creation of God, no individual angel has ever been addressed as "son of God" in all of Scripture (Kent, p. 40). By contrast, the preincarnate Christ was often designated as "the Angel of the Lord." Thus, it becomes important that the readers understand that, though He was the Messenger of the Lord, He was not in any sense an angelic being. He is superior, first, because of the name the Father attributes to Him and, second, because of His position which the author now develops in the next nine verses.

6-7. The Old Testament Scriptures abundantly demonstrate the superiority of the Son to the angels from His superior position. Five passages are cited from these few verses. **And again, when he bringeth** (Gr *hotan de palin eisafafē*) suggests that verse 6 is a third quotation parallel to the two in verse 5. However, this does not seem to be the case. The phrase **and again** that connects the two quotes in verse 5 is different from the Greek form in verse 6. The word *de* in verse 6 is the word translated **but** in verses 8, 12, and 13. In each of these verses the Son is contrasted with the angels and Creation. Since verse 6 does not express a similar contrast between Christ and the angels, many translators use "and again." But verses 5 and 6 do express a contrast, not another contrast between the Son and the angels; but a change in thought development. In verses 4 and 5 the author has established that Christ alone is the Son. Starting with verse 6, he reveals the position of the angels in relation to Him. The earlier verses showed the relation of the Son to the Father; verses 6 and following show the relation of the angels to the Son (Westcott, p. 21).

Thus, how does **again** fit into the sentence? It can be taken as a particle of connection, "but again," or as qualifying **he bringeth** (Westcott, pp. 21-23, proposes the latter view). The Greek

4 Being made so much better than the angels, as he hath by inheritance obtained a more excellent name than they.

5 For unto which of the angels said he at any time, Thou art my son, this day have I begotten thee? And again, I will be to him a Father, and he shall be to me a Son?

6 And again, when he bringeth in the firstbegotten into the world, he saith, And let all the angels of God worship him.
7 And of the angels he saith, Who maketh his angels spirits, and his ministers a flame of fire.

could literally be rendered, "But whenever He again should bring the first-born into the world." The verse would then be stating that the angels will worship the Son at His second coming, rather than as a babe at his first. Angels did worship Him at His incarnation (Lk 2:13f.), and they will at His second coming (Mt 16:27; 24:30ff.; 25:31; Mk 13:27; Rev 5:11ff.; see Hughes, pp. 57-59, for various arguments).

The reference to Christ as the **first begotten** (*prōtotokon*) is unusual; for in all other usages the word is modified, whereas here it is absolute. Elsewhere, He is spoken of as the first-born of his earthly brothers and sisters (Mt 1:25; Lk 2:7), of the dead (Rev 1:5), of other men (Rom 8:29; Col 1:18), and of creation (Col 1:15). In each case His preeminence with some group is expressed. Here His preeminence is absolute, receiving no restriction. Bruce declares that Jesus is the first-born because He exists before all creation and because it is His heritage (p. 15), while Kent refers to it as position and dignity (p. 42).

Verses 6 and 7 cite two Old Testament texts (Ps 97:7; Ps 104:4) to demonstrate that the Son is superior to the angels. He is worshiped by them; they were created to serve.

8 But unto the Son *he saith,* **Thy throne, O God,** *is* **for ever and ever: a sceptre of righteousness** *is* **the sceptre of thy kingdom.**
9 Thou hast loved righteousness, and hated iniquity; therefore God, *even* **thy God, hath anointed thee with the oil of gladness above thy fellows.**

8-9. The author continues to quote from the Psalms (45:6-7) to reveal the superior nature of the Son. He is declared to be God Himself, One whose throne is righteous and eternal. Because of His righteousness, He is anointed above His **fellows** (Gr *metochous*). Because of the context, we may first imagine that the **fellows** are angels in that He is superior to them. Yet, it is that very fact, the contextual development, which would seem to disqualify angels from being His peers or companions. The better interpretation seems to be to regard these **fellows** as the **brethren** of Christ (2:11), even the **many sons** (2:10). It is with man that Christ has chosen to be identified since He has taken man's nature and not that of the angels (2:16).

10 And, Thou, Lord, in the beginning hast laid the foundation of the earth; and the heavens are the works of thine hands:
11 They shall perish; but thou remainest; and they all shall wax old as doth a garment;
12 And as a vesture shalt thou fold them up, and they shall be changed: but thou art the same, and thy years shall not fail.

10-12. And, Thou, Lord, in the beginning hast laid the foundation. The quotations from Psalms continue (Ps 102:25-27). The Son as Creator is emphasized in these verses. As Creator, He possesses a superior position. The realm of His creation that is stressed is the heavens, which by metonymy could include the angels. The heavens will pass, but the Son will stand. **Thou art the same.** All creation will change, but not the Son. He is **the same yesterday, and today, and for ever** (13:8).

13 But to which of the angels said he at any time, Sit on my right hand, until I make thine enemies thy footstool?
14 Are they not all ministering spirits, sent forth to minister for them who shall be heirs of salvation?

13-14. The last of the seven proofs from the Old Testament which demonstrate the superiority of the Son over the angels involves the ultimate position of each. The Son sits, whereas the angels are sent. The angels are not asked by the Father to sit at His right hand, the position of privilege. They are sent to serve the brethren of the Son.

Some might argue that Christ must be inferior to the angels since He died for and ministered to man (the problem confronted in 2:5-18). Still, the angels would be no better than He is; for they, too, minister to man. Indeed, the ministry of the Son is self-initiated (Gal 1:4); the angels are sent. They were created to minister to God (including the Son) and to us who believe. **Sent forth to minister.** The use of the present participle here, "being sent forth," emphasizes the continuance of angelic ministry. By contrast, the aorist tense is used in 13:2, implying that though in the past some have entertained angels unknowingly, it need not happen anymore. The ministering of the angels, however, continues today without end (cf. Ps 91).

As chapter 1 ends and chapter 2 begins, one prominent thought continues: "As God had no greater messenger than His Son, he had no further message beyond the gospel" (Bruce, p. 26). The author will now warn his readers with that thought in chapter 2.

2. The first warning passage: Do not neglect Christ's message. 2:1-4.

The Epistle to the Hebrews contains five warning passages. The uniqueness of these passages to Hebrews lies in the rhetorical method of this author. Other New Testament writers place warnings and exhortations within the development of their message. However, our author, due to his strict, logical, grammatical development "avoided all irrelevant digression" (Marcus Dods, p. 224). He places his warnings and exhortations parenthetically, after his arguments, at opportune times. There is no grammatical formula by which any of these warnings is introduced. They must be isolated by means of context alone. Though the passage may contain exhortations, it is not merely exhortation. It must contain some explicit warning—a danger sign. Usually, the warning itself will involve only one or several verses. Such is the case with this first warning.

CHAPTER 2

THEREFORE we ought to give the more earnest heed to the things which we have heard, lest at any time we should let *them* slip.

2:1. Therefore (Gr *dia touto*). This word does two things. Obviously it ties the previous message to that which is at hand. The superior Son has proclaimed a superior message which must be heeded. But it further points to the vital connection between doctrine and practice (Hughes, p. 72). Practice must follow the hearing of the truth (cf. Jas 1:22-25). The warning begins in verse 1 with the statement that **we ought to give the more earnest . . . lest at any time we should let them slip.** The word **slip** (Gr *pararreō*) means to slip away as a ring from a finger or as a ship from a harbor. Kent (p. 47) suggests that this term possesses a nautical connotation here, since the verb **give . . . heed to** (Gr *prosechō*) is also used nautically of bringing a ship to land. He concludes that the verse is not speaking of something drifting from us, but that we might drift from something (p. 47). The author is not warning the Hebrews to grasp the gospel more intently, lest they lose their salvation. Rather, he warns them not to drift beyond the gospel; for there is no other harbor. From the human side, there certainly is need of warning and examination to be sure that we are in the faith. From God's side, the work is accomplished and secure. One who is genuinely born again does not lose that life; yet, however, his life will manifest or demonstrate this regeneration.

2 For if the word spoken by angels was stedfast, and every transgression and disobedience received a just recompence of reward;

2. If the word spoken by angels was steadfast. As was stated earlier (1:4), the New Testament writers regarded the angels as intermediaries associated with the giving of the Law (Acts 7:53; Gal 3:19). Now, if the message delivered through the angels was so fixed that its sentences were carried out, how much more so the message given by the Son. The word **steadfast** (Gr *bebaios*) is common in Hebrews (5 of 9 NT occurrences), expressing the idea of that which is sure, steadfast, and fixed. Our author also uses it of our hope (3:6), our confidence (3:14), our anchor in Jesus (6:19), and a human covenant after its maker is dead (9:17).

3 How shall we escape, if we neglect so great salvation; which at the first began to be spoken by the Lord, and was confirmed unto us by them that heard *him*;
4 God also bearing *them* witness, both with signs and wonders, and with divers miracles, and gifts of the Holy Ghost, according to his own will?

3-4. How shall we escape, if we neglect so great salvation. . . ? The warning reaches its climax with these words. The word **neglect** (Gr *ameleō*) does not mean to deny or to reject. It is to recognize but to ignore, to know but to fail to do, to admit but not to administer. Our author uses this word once elsewhere to express that which God did to Israel when they forsook the Mosaic covenant He "regarded them not"; He neglected them (8:9).

The author further produces three statements which emphasize the importance of this salvation. First, it was **spoken by the Lord.** Second, it **was confirmed unto us by them that heard him.** Evidently, the author had not heard the message directly from the Son, which is a strong argument against Paul's authorship of this epistle (see "*Authorship*" within the Introduction). Also, the readers had not heard directly from Christ—an argument against Palestinian recipients. The third statement is that God verified this salvation **with signs and wonders . . . miracles, and gifts of the Holy Ghost.** The author states that these sign gifts were given to the first-century witnesses. He does not suggest that his readers possessed these same miraculous gifts. If the phrase **gifts of the Holy Ghost** is a subjective genitive, then it has reference to those **gifts** given by the Holy Spirit to all believers for the profiting of the body of Christ (Rom 12; I Cor 12). Otherwise, and less likely, it refers to God's bestowal of the Holy Spirit Himself (cf. Gal 3:5) upon every believer (Kent, p. 50).

3. The reasonableness of Christ's humiliation. 2:5-18.

Following the Old Testament proof that Christ is superior to the angels and following the warning not to neglect His superior message, our author faces the problem of Christ's humanity. If Christ became a man and partook of death, how can He be superior to the angels? This apparent antinomy is presently answered as being reasonable and logical. The author demonstrates, first, that Christ's humanity does not conflict with His superiority over angels, and then demonstrates the same regarding His suffering and death.

a. Christ's humanity does not abnegate His superiority over angels. 2:5-9.

5. The author begins to develop his thesis by stating that **unto the angels hath he not put in subjection the world to come.** The angels will not be in positions of authority when Christ establishes His kingdom. Throughout the past and present ages, angels have ministered judgment upon man: at Sodom (Gen 19:13), upon Israel (II Sam 24:15-17), upon kings (Acts 12:23), during the Great Tribulation (Rev 8-9). Angels have had power over the nations (Dan 10:13, 20; Eph 6:11-12). But in the age to come angels will have no authority over the saints. In fact, the saints will judge angels (I Cor 6:3). The verse does not specify who will have that authority; it only states that the angels will not have it. The author reveals the answer in the next verses.

6-8. Quoting Psalm 8, the author shows God's intended ruler: **What is man . . . or the son of man.** This Psalm does not speak both of man and Christ; it is not messianic. The **son of man** is not to be distinguished from **man.** The phrases are merely an example of the common synonymous parallelism in Hebrew poetry. "Hence this passage was not regarded as a messianic prediction by Jewish teachers, but as a description of what God intended man to be" (Kent, p. 53). God made man **a little lower than the angels.** A **little** (Gr *brachu ti*) has two possible interpretations. It can refer to time (a little while) or degree (a small degree). The Hebrew word (*me'at*) from the Psalm likewise provides both possibilities. But this is not to our detriment since the context already incorporates both concepts. Obviously, man possesses a lower status than the angels; and obviously, it is temporary. Since the time of this lower status exists until the kingdom, it seems better to understand the word as connoting degree—a small degree lower than the angels.

Although God has made man slightly lower than the angels for the present, He also has crowned him **with glory and honor** and set him over His creation. Thus Psalm 8 does not minimize man, but exalts him. Man is the capstone and the crown of God's creation. It is into man's hands that He will ultimately place His creation. God proclaimed this from the moment of man's creation (Gen 1:26,28). Our author further interprets **all things** to mean that **he left nothing** excluded. The intent is to show that in the coming age even the angels will be subject to **man**—and if to man, how much more to Christ, as verse 9 promptly declares.

9. But we see Jesus. Verse 8 ended by confessing that man's present status does not suggest (surely it does not prove) that he

5 For unto the angels hath he not put in subjection the world to come, whereof we speak.

6 But one in a certain place testified, saying, What is man, that thou art mindful of him? or the son of man, that thou visitest him?
7 Thou madest him a little lower than the angels; thou crownedst him with glory and honour, and didst set him over the works of thy hands:
8 Thou hast put all things in subjection under his feet. For in that he put all in subjection under him, he left nothing that is not put under him. But now we see not yet all things put under him.

9 But we see Jesus, who was made a little lower than the angels for the suffering of death, crowned with glory and honour; that he by the grace of God should taste death for every man.

10 For it became him, for whom *are* all things, and by whom *are* all things, in bringing many sons unto glory, to make the captain of their salvation perfect through sufferings.
11 For both he that sanctifieth and they who are sanctified *are* all of one: for which cause he is not ashamed to call them brethren.
12 Saying, I will declare thy name unto my brethren, in the midst of the church will I sing praise unto thee.
13 And again, I will put my trust in him. And again, Behold I and the children which God hath given me.

14 Forasmuch then as the children are partakers of flesh and blood, he also himself likewise took part of the same; that through death he might destroy him that had the power of death, that is, the devil;
15 And deliver them who through fear of death were all their lifetime subject to bondage.
16 For verily he took not on *him the nature of* angels; but he took on *him* the seed of Abraham.
17 Wherefore in all things it behoved him to be made like unto *his* brethren, that he might be a merciful and faithful high priest in things *pertaining* to God, to make reconciliation for the sins of the people.
18 For in that he himself hath suf-

will someday be over all creation. But Christ's status does. He too **was made a little lower than the angels.** However, unlike man, He already has been **crowned;** and because of His identity with and victory for man, He makes Psalm 8 an eschatological (future) reality for man. Death is one significant quality that makes man lower than the angels (Lk 20:36). But Christ has conquered death for man.

b. *Christ's suffering does not abnegate His superiority over angels. 2:10-18.*

Christ's humanity does not make Christ inferior to the angels; for humanity is innately superior to angelic nature, and someday men will rule over the angels. Likewise, Christ's suffering does not make Him inferior to angels, who have never suffered. This concept of a suffering Messiah was a stumbling block to the Jews. The author tackles this problem by declaring that the suffering of the cross was an integral part of the plan of salvation.

10-13. It became him. The first of three reasons why Christ must suffer is contained in these verses. It was necessary for His identification with humanity. For God to become truly human, He must suffer and even **taste death** (vs. 9). **In bringing.** The participle (Gr *agagonta*, bringing in) is aorist but appears to be timeless, merely stating an event, as our English translation suggests—**In bringing many sons.** It would be incorrect to restrict this to a past occurrence, referring only to Old Testament saints (Kent, p. 56).

Christ is identified here as the **captain** (Gr *archēgos*) of our salvation. The word is also used of Christ in Acts 5:31 (as a leader) and in Hebrews 12:2 (as a founder or originator). Since both ideas fit this text, the thought might be that Christ is both the Author and Captain of our salvation. Our Captain is described as made **perfect through sufferings.** Can the Son who was presented as the very essence of deity (1:3) and called God (1:8) somehow fall short of perfection? Surely He cannot in His deity, but in His relation to humanity He could. "The perfect Son of God has become His people's perfect Savior, opening up their way to God; and in order to become that, He must endure suffering and death" (Bruce, p. 43).

Christ's absolute identity with humanity is stressed several times in verses 11-13. First, Christ as the sanctifier and we as those sanctified are identified as **all of one.** This does not suggest that we are out of the same source, but that we are of the same nature or stock. We possess a common humanity. Second, we are called **brethren.** And He is not ashamed to call us brothers. He does not regard us as "poor relations," nor was His becoming a man a patronizing condescension (Kent, p. 57). He is not ashamed to be identified with us. How could we ever be ashamed of Him?

14-15. The second reason given as to why it was necessary for Christ to suffer is now provided. He must suffer even to death in order to destroy the power and fear of death. The word translated **destroy** (Gr *katargeō*) does not convey the thought of annihilation, nor has Satan been destroyed in that sense. The word means "to make inoperative" or "ineffective." Through His resurrection from death, Christ broke the hold which Satan possessed over man.

16-18. The third reason suggested by the author regarding the necessity of Christ's suffering is that He might become an intercessory high priest for His brothers. **He took . . . on him.** This verb (Gr *epilambanomai*) in verse 16 generally means to lay hold of, but in many contexts it takes on the added idea of "helping." It can at times mean simply "to help." Most likely, therefore, the idea of verse 16 is that Christ has taken hold of Abraham's seed in order to help them, whereas He has not chosen to help angelic beings. The verse probably does not have

fered being tempted, he is able to succour them that are tempted.

reference to a *nature* taken and one not taken, but to a *help*
provided and not provided (cf. Westcott, pp. 54-55).

That he might be a merciful and faithful high priest. In
verses 17 and 18 the author introduces a key thought of this
epistle for the first time, i.e., the high priestly nature of Christ.
As a man He can compassionately serve as our High Priest. His
primary role as High Priest is **to make reconciliation for the
sins of the people.** The verb (Gr *hilaskomai*) means "to propitiate" or "expiate" sin. As our High Priest, He does not merely
make atonement (a covering) for our sins; He satisfactorily and
actually takes sin away.

The word **succor** (Gr *boetheō*) means "to come to the aid of"
or "to help" someone. How much easier it is to come to the aid
of someone when we ourselves have gone through similar trials.
How good it is to know that Christ was fully man, experiencing
what we experience and so was able to provide the comfort we
need (cf. II Cor 1:3-5). These Christian Jews needed to hear that
Christ had suffered as they were suffering.

C. Christ Is Superior to Moses and Joshua Because of the Rest Provided. 3:1-4:13.

The thought of the epistle shifts from angels to Old Testament leaders. Moses and Joshua were faithful and godly leaders;
yet, their works were incomplete. The household wherein
Moses labored did not bring security and rest to his people
(3:1-6). The land into which Joshua led his people similarly did
not produce rest for them (4:1-13). As the Builder of the house
and as the Sabbath Rest, Jesus has placed us into the household
of God and has provided an eternal rest for our souls.

1. Christ is superior to Moses. 3:1-6.

In order to reveal the truth of Christ's superiority over Moses,
three points are developed within these verses. First, both
Moses and Christ have faithfully fulfilled their assigned works
(vss. 1-2). Second, whereas Moses was a part of God's house
(program), Christ is the Builder (vss. 3-4). And lastly, whereas
Moses was a servant in the house, Christ is the Son over it
(vss. 5-6).

CHAPTER 3
WHEREFORE, holy brethren, partakers of the heavenly calling, consider the
Apostle and High Priest of our profession, Christ Jesus;
2 Who was faithful to him that appointed him, as also Moses *was faithful*
in all his house.

3:1-2. The author makes it clear that he regards his Jewish
readers as believers by addressing them as **holy brethren, partakers of the heavenly calling.** He admonishes them not in his
usual hortative, "Let us," but with the imperative, **consider.**
They are to consider Jesus as the **Apostle and High Priest.**
These titles do not involve His divine essence; they speak in
regard to His superior ministry. Moses was very highly regarded
by the first-century Jews. The author of Hebrews now attempts
to make his argument for the superiority of Christ without
casting aspersion on the ministry of Moses. He presents nothing
negatively. Rather, he simply elevates Christ. The two
appellations given to Christ speak of His superior ministry. The
author's use of the word Apostle (used of Christ only here)
expresses the superiority of His commission, being sent directly
from God. As High Priest He is man's direct intercessor with
God.

The emphasis of verse 2 is that both Moses and Christ have
faithfully fulfilled their work (cf. Num 12:7). Positioning the
word **faithful** first in the Greek text demonstrates this. The word
appointed (Gr *poieō*) could be translated "made." Indeed, centuries ago the Arians used this text to support their teaching that
God "made" Christ. Likewise, centuries ago Chrysostom properly responded by asking what God made Him. The context is
clear; God made or appointed Him an Apostle and High Priest
(see Hughes, pp. 129-130). God did not create Christ (Jn 1:1-3).

3 For this *man* was counted worthy
of more glory than Moses, inasmuch as

3-4. More glory than Moses. Christ's superiority and greater
glory are not based upon His faithfulness, but upon his superior
position. Christ is described as the one who **hath builded the**

he who hath builded the house hath more honour than the house.

4 For every house is builded by some *man;* but he that built all things *is* God.

5 And Moses verily *was* faithful in all his house, as a servant, for a testimony of those things which were to be spoken after;

6 But Christ as a son over his own house; whose house are we, if we hold fast the confidence and the rejoicing of the hope firm unto the end.

7 Wherefore (as the Holy Ghost saith, To day if ye will hear his voice,

8 Harden not your hearts, as in the provocation, in the day of temptation in the wilderness:

house (cf. vs. 6). In contrast, Moses is spoken of as part of the house itself (cf. vs. 5). The Builder is, of necessity, superior to his house. The author takes his argument one step farther. In verse 4 he logically proposes that every house must have a builder and that surely God's house was built by God. The conclusion is unexpressed but obvious. Christ, the Builder, is God (see A. W. Pink, *An Exposition of Hebrews,* pp. 160-161, regarding the implicit teaching of Christ's deity here).

5-6. Moses . . . a servant. In these verses the analogy of a house is continued. The contrast, however, is now between a servant *in* and a son *over* the house. The description of Moses as a servant (Gr *therapōn*) is not demeaning. This verse is a citation from Numbers 12:7, which uses the same word in the Septuagint to describe Moses. This word, used only here in the New Testament, connotes the idea of a free servant of honorable position (Dods, p. 273). Moses is described as a faithful servant in that he bore witness **of those things which were to be spoken after.** Moses has faithfully testified concerning the Son.

Christ is identified **as a son over his own house.** The translation, **his own,** is stronger than the Greek (*auton*). It is **his** house. But His house is the same as God's house (vs. 3). There is only one house involved in these verses. It is not Moses' house; it is not ours. It is God's. Moses was a part of this one house. It is what Paul calls the household of God (Eph 2:19; cf. I Pet 4:17) or the household of faith (Gal 6:10). It includes all believers of all time. We are included—**whose house are we.** It continues as a present reality, of which we are part.

If we hold fast. Bruce writes: "Nowhere in the New Testament more than here do we find such repeated insistence on the fact that continuance in the Christian life is the test of reality" (p. 59). The life of a saint is the evidence of a new life in the saint. Just as his life cannot produce new life, neither can his life remove God's new life. Moreover, God's new life will manifest itself in his life (Rom 6; 8:1-11; II Cor 5:17). In the author's thinking, new life results in continuance. With this statement the author prepares his readers for the next warning passage.

2. The second warning passage: Do not doubt God's promise. 3:7-4:13.

As is common with the other warning passages, exhortations and illustrations are incorporated into the warning. Israel's disbelief and hardness of heart, under the godly leadership of Moses and then Joshua, serve as examples.

a. The consequences of Israel's unbelief. 3:7-11.

7. Wherefore. The admonition of verse 6 is now connected to the warning that starts at verse 12. Verses 7 through 11 serve as an introduction to this warning, as the parentheses surrounding verses 7 through 11 in our AV show. These verses cite Israel's experiences in the wilderness as an example. **As the Holy Ghost saith.** The words that follow from Psalm 95:7-11 are attributed to the Holy Spirit. Three times (3:7-8,15; 4:7) this Psalm is quoted within this warning passage, and in 4:7 David is implicitly regarded as its author. Also, the Holy Spirit is the speaker, demonstrating that the words and message are God's, though recorded by means of a man's words. **Today.** The emphasis our author picks up here is the same point stressed by David to the people of his time—do not commit the same sin that Israel committed in the wilderness.

8. As in the provocation, in the day of temptation. The terms **provocation** (Gr *parapikrasmos*) and **temptation** (Gr *peirasmos*) are taken from the Septuagint reading of the Psalm, which is an etymological translation of the Hebrew words, *Meribah* and *Massah,* respectively. These Hebrew terms are likewise descriptive translations, rather than the rendering of proper names. Both terms originate with Moses' smiting the rock for water while in Rephidim (Ex 17:1-7). Following that experience, Exodus 17:7 says concerning Moses, "And he called the name of the place Massah, and Meribah, because of the chiding of the children of Israel, and because they tempted the LORD, saying, Is the LORD among us, or not?" At this time, Israel had been out of Egypt only one month. Within that one month they had repeatedly witnessed God's miraculous deliverance and provision. They had witnessed the last of the plagues (Ex 12), God's leading by cloud and fire (Ex 13), the Red Sea divided (Ex 14), the bitter water of Marah purified (Ex 15), and the provision of manna and quail (Ex 16). Yet, almost immediately they murmur and harden their hearts against both Moses and God. This incident with the water at Rephidim became symbolic of Israel's temptation (Massah) of God (cf. Deut 6:16). David uses it to speak of Israel's continuous rebellion throughout the 40 years in the wilderness. See the discussion of the subject by F. F. Bruce (p. 64) and Homer Kent, Jr. (p. 70).

9 When your fathers tempted me, proved me, and saw my works forty years.

9. Saw my works forty years. The unexpected placing of the **forty years** with the seeing of God's works, rather than with God's grieving as it is in Psalm 95 and as our author later uses it (3:17), is unusual in the light of his careful exegesis. Kent suggests, as one good possibility, that "the writer was conscious of a parallel in years between the forty years of Israel's rebellion in the wilderness and approximately the same period that had now elapsed since the rejection of Christ in A.D. 30" (p. 71). As Israel saw God's work forty years in the wilderness, so the present readers have had almost forty years since A.D. 30 to observe the evidence regarding Christ.

10 Wherefore I was grieved with that generation, and said, They do alway err in *their* heart; and they have not known my ways.
11 So I sware in my wrath, They shall not enter into my rest.)

10-11. The psalmist records God's estimation of Israel and His resultant action. The people **do always err** and **have not known my ways.** Therefore, they would not enter into God's **rest.**

b. The warning against unbelief. 3:12-19.

12 Take heed, brethren, lest there be in any of you an evil heart of unbelief, in departing from the living God.
13 But exhort one another daily, while it is called To day; lest any of you be hardened through the deceitfulness of sin.
14 For we are made partakers of Christ, if we hold the beginning of our confidence stedfast unto the end;

12-14. This warning is addressed to the **brethren** the professing believers, lest any have unbelief in his heart and thus depart from God. This **departing** (Gr *apostēnai*) is the source of our word apostasy, which is a deliberate departure from God's full revelation. These Jewish brethren were being tempted by an "evil heart of unbelief" to return to Judaism. To do so meant they would have to reject that fuller revelation which they have received and return to the incomplete revelation of Judaism. Thus, they are admonished to **exhort one another daily** with the truths that will strengthen their faith in Christ, such as the truths in this epistle.

For we are made partakers. The verb uses the perfect tense (Gr *gegonamen*) and might be better understood if it were translated, "we have become." With it is placed the condition, **if we hold . . . steadfast unto the end.** Because of this condition, some propose that one cannot become, or at least be sure of becoming, a partaker until the end. If the verb were future, that would surely fit—we will be partakers if we hold fast. The verb, however, is perfect, expressing a completed action with existing results—we have become and remain partakers, if we should hold steadfast. If the verb were future, then the partaking would be based upon one's ability or determination to hold on. As it is, the condition is a test by which one can know if he has faith—the test of continuance. The author proposes that Israel's fickle faith did not manifest itself as true faith, nor will such faith today. As Jesus taught, true faith is the implanting of the Word into a receptive, believing heart (Lk 8:4-15). Although **partakers** (Gr *metochoi*) could also be translated "partners," neither the context nor its usage in 3:1 favor it. We have become partakers in Christ, not partners with Him.

15 While it is said, To day if ye will

15-19. The author develops the last portion of chapter three by looking back again at Israel's history and asking three ques-

hear his voice, harden not your hearts, as in the provocation.

16 For some, when they had heard, did provoke: howbeit not all that came out of Egypt by Moses.

17 But with whom was he grieved forty years? *was it* not with them that had sinned, whose carcases fell in the wilderness?

18 And to whom sware he that they should not enter into his rest, but to them that believed not?

19 So we see that they could not enter in because of unbelief.

CHAPTER 4

LET us therefore fear, lest, a promise being left *us* of entering into his rest, any of you should seem to come short of it.

2 For unto us was the gospel preached, as well as unto them: but the word preached did not profit them, not being mixed with faith in them that heard *it.*

3 For we which have believed do enter into rest, as he said, As I have sworn in my wrath, if they shall enter into my rest: although the works were finished from the foundation of the world.

4 For he spake in a certain place of the seventh *day* on this wise, And God did rest the seventh day from all his works.

5 And in this *place* again, If they shall enter into my rest.

6 Seeing therefore it remaineth that some must enter therein, and they to whom it was first preached entered not in because of unbelief:

7 Again, he limiteth a certain day, saying in David, To day, after so long a time; as it is said, To day if ye will hear his voice, harden not your hearts.

8 For if Jesus had given them rest, then would he not afterward have spoken of another day.

tions. **For some.** The Greek pronoun (Gr *tines*) can either be indefinite ("some") or interrogative ("who?"), depending on the accent. Since the oldest Greek manuscripts do not contain accents, the context must determine the appropriate usage. The context favors the interrogative usage in verse 16, for the same word is used interrogatively in both verses 17 and 18. Since the form of those two interrogatives is the same (Gr *tisin de*), each appears to be a continuation of the interrogation. Thus the questions begin in verse 16, not 17. Likewise, the thought development favors the interrogative idea. The idea of the passage is that all, not some, provoked God. Though two spies brought back a good report, it was 600,000 men who rejected it. Verse 16 might better be translated as: "For who after they heard, did embitter (God)? Yea, did not all who came out of Egypt through Moses?"

The second question is found in verse 17. **With whom was he grieved forty years?** It was those who sinned. The use of the aorist participle puts the emphasis on the nature of the action, rather than an idea involving continuation or a single act. He was grieved because that which Israel did was sin. The third question asks, **to whom sware he that they should not enter into his rest?** (vs. 18). Those who deliberately disobeyed through unbelief did not enter. They doubted God's promise.

c. The warning against missing God's rest. 4:1-13.

4:1-2. The author continues his warning: **Let us therefore fear** lest we think we have missed God's promise. **Seem** (Gr *dokeō*) might here be translated "to think." The readers may have imagined that since they had left the Jewish temple and its ritual, they may lack something and end up short of God's promise in lack of faith (vs. 2).

3-5. These verses attest that a rest has definitely been provided. Evidently, the idea supposes that since Israel never knew it, some Jews might challenge the actual existence of the promised rest. The author offers two logical arguments for the existence of this rest and accents each argument by explaining Israel's lack—God swore it would not happen to Israel. The first argument states that **we which have believed do enter into rest.** Presently, God is providing a rest.

If they shall enter into my rest. As it is translated here, this clause, found in both verses 3 and 5, is confusing. If the translators had followed the same grammatical principles here that they used in 3:11, there would be no problem. Each of these passages has exactly the same Greek clause; in fact, each is precisely the same quotation from Psalm 95:11. It is an elliptical form of a Hebrew negative oath, of which the complete form might be, "May I be judged more, if they shall enter into my rest." In its shorter, elliptical form it is better translated, as in 3:11, "They shall not enter into my rest" (see Kent, p. 72). They who believe have rest, but unbelieving Israel shall not enter God's rest.

The second argument for the existence of a genuine rest states that rest has existed ever since the seventh day of creation week (vss. 3-4). God rests; but unbelieving Israel will not rest, as He has sworn.

6-8. Not only has God provided a rest, but the promise that some should enter it must be fulfilled (vs. 6). **Today.** Long after Israel's failure, David was still looking for a rest in his own day. Likewise, the author of Hebrews uses that word repeatedly in this passage to declare that a rest can still be known. The reference to Jesus (Gr *Iēsous*) in verse 8 involves Joshua of the Old Testament. The two names are identical, both in Hebrew and Greek. The context certainly involves Joshua, the son of Nun. Joshua brought the second generation (those under twenty

9 There remaineth therefore a rest to the people of God.

10 For he that is entered into his rest, he also hath ceased from his own works, as God *did* from his.

11 Let us labour therefore to enter into that rest, lest any man fall after the same example of unbelief.

12 For the word of God *is* quick, and powerful, and sharper than any twoedged sword, piercing even to the dividing asunder of soul and spirit, and of the joints and marrow, and *is* a discerner of the thoughts and intents of the heart.

13 Neither is there any creature that is not manifest in his sight: but all things *are* naked and opened unto the eyes of him with whom we have to do.

when the spies were sent) into Canaan, and they did enter into a rest as the Scriptures record (Deut 12:9-10; Josh 21:44; 22:4; 23:1). Yet, the author suggests that there must be a permanent, better rest for the people of God; or David would not have still been looking forward to it in his day.

9. There remaineth therefore a rest to the people of God. We must come to this conclusion from a study of Old Testament revelation, even as our author has done. This rest is greater than that realized through Joshua. The author stresses that fact by introducing a new word into the text (Gr *sabbatismos*, sabbath rest), which is used only here in the entire New Testament. It is a word that suggests a rest like God's own rest following creation (vs. 4). On the theological significance of **rest** as referring to the present blessing of God, cf. F. F. Bruce, *The Epistle to the Hebrews*, pp. 73-79; *contra*, as the Millennium, see G. H. Lang, *The Epistle to the Hebrews*, pp. 73ff.

10. For he that is entered into his rest. Several views exist as to whom the **he** might be (see Kent, pp. 86-87). It could represent the believer who has experienced spiritual rest, either in salvation or by consecration. With this interpretation, however, the verse lacks unity; for the one who experiences this rest has ceased from **his own works, as God did from his.** Since God has ceased from good labor, parallelism would favor the cessation of good works on the part of the other. The works given up in salvation or consecration, however, are evil works of self. A better view would be to understand this as describing the Christian at death. At that point he ceases from his good works and enters into heaven's rest (cf. Rev 14:13). The third, and most likely view, is that this refers to Christ, who has finished His work of redemption and so, like the Father, has entered into His rest. The theme of this book would surely favor this view, as does the personal pronoun **he.** In this passage the believers have continually been referred to in the plural and in the first or second persons as we or you.

11. Let us labor or be diligent to enter into God's rest. Rest involves more than mere inactivity. It is that which follows the satisfactory completion of a task. Salvation rest is the gift reckoned to the believer resulting from Christ's finished work. Heaven and millennial rest is the reward of the believer's labors for the Lord (Rev 14:13). Verse 11 records the warning one more time: Do not miss through unbelief what God has promised.

12-13. For the word of God. The reason given for our careful scrutiny of our lives involves the reality that God is intently scrutinizing us. His Word exposes us; His eye sees through us. His Word is **quick** (living). This is the first word of the verse and is, no doubt, the emphasis. God's Word is not old or archaic; it is living. It is not inept or inactive; it is **powerful** (active). God's Word is **sharper than any two-edged sword.** It has no blunt side; it cuts both ways. It penetrates so deeply that it divides the **soul and spirit** and the **joints and marrow.** These phrases suggest that there is no part of man which God's Word cannot penetrate—immaterial or physical. In fact, it reaches into the inner secrets of man's mind to discern his **thoughts and intents.** Likewise, God's eye sees man as though he were naked, unable to hide behind any excuse or pretense. Let us be careful not to reject His Word through unbelief.

D. Christ Is Superior to the Levitical Priesthood Because of the Intercession Provided. 4:14-7:28.

The central and extended theme of Hebrews involves Christ's priestly ministry and the levitical priesthood. In the author's mind Christ's superiority to the prophets, the angels, Moses, and Joshua is seemingly secondary to the absolute superiority of Christ to the Old Testament priests. Even the following section

(Chs. 8-10), which contrasts the Old Covenant with the New, focuses upon the high priestly work of Christ.

1. The confidence provided through Christ's priesthood. 4:14-16.

The author both begins and ends this unit about Christ's priesthood by showing the confident access we possess through Christ's intercession. The present verses provide a comfort that is in vivid contrast to the fear pronounced in 4:1.

14 Seeing then that we have a great high priest, that is passed into the heavens, Jesus the Son of God, let us hold fast *our* profession.

14. We have a great high priest, that is passed into the heavens. The first evidence of Christ's superiority is that He has passed into the heavens into God's very presence to intercede for us (cf. 9:24). Conversely, the Aaronic priests only passed through an earthly tabernacle. At best, one man (the high priest) once a year (the Day of Atonement) was allowed to pass through the earthly veil to enter the Holy of Holies in order to gain access to the mercy seat (cf. Lev 16). Jesus is described here as **the Son of God** and so is not to be confused with the Jesus (Joshua) of 4:8. Because of the Son's great priestly work, we are admonished to hold fast our **profession** (Gr *homologia*). This word, which is also translated "confession," involves both the inward confession of the heart and the outward profession before men (Hughes, p. 171).

15 For we have not an high priest which cannot be touched with the feeling of our infirmities; but was in all points tempted like as *we are, yet* without sin.

15. Tempted like as we are, yet without sin. Christ is able to understand our weaknesses and miseries, for He Himself has experienced these very things. To imagine that since Jesus could not sin, He could not suffer is to miss the point of the passage. First, this passage only explicitly states that He did not sin, not that He could not. Second, temptation can be, and is, a reality apart from sin. God cannot be **tempted** (Gr *apeirastos*) with evil (Jas 1:13), yet God is tempted (Gr *peirazō*) by men (3:9; Acts 15:10). Christ was tempted; He did not sin; He can understand and intercede. Yet, beyond the explicit statements of this passage, He who is God was made like sinful man (Rom 8:3). But He could not sin (impeccable); and, indeed, He need not sin to be human. Before he sinned, Adam was human, and probably "more" human than after his fall; for that was not how God had created him. One needs not sin to be human, nor does one even need to possess the potential to sin. The glorified saint will never again be able to sin, yet he remains human. Christ's temptation was real, for temptation exists apart from yielding to it through sin. Indeed, the temptation is greater in duration and intensity when one does not take the "easy" way out by sinning. If man's temptation is greater when he endures it, surely Christ's was great since He had no alternative but to endure it. He has suffered, or endured, the temptation (2:18).

16 Let us therefore come boldly unto the throne of grace, that we may obtain mercy, and find grace to help in time of need.

16. Because of our tried and proven High Priest, we can come **boldly** to God's throne. In the Old Testament everyone who looked upon the Ark of the Covenant faced the fear of death, including the high priest, unless he met all of the conditions, and then only on the Day of Atonement. Now we, including these Jewish saints, are encouraged to come before the Lord at any time, especially when we truly need help. Only Christianity provides such boldness by sinful men before a holy God, and that boldness is only possible because of our great Intercessor, Jesus Christ.

2. The qualifications of a priest. 5:1-10.

This section breaks naturally between verses 4 and 5. The first four verses describe the qualifications of the levitical priests, the other six verses demonstrate Christ's qualifications.

5:1. Sacrifices for sins. The discussion of the priestly office focuses first upon the function or goal of that office. Men were placed in the office to minister on behalf of (Gr *huper*) other men by offering sacrifices and offerings for their sins.

CHAPTER 5
FOR every high priest taken from among men is ordained for men in things *pertaining* to God, that he may offer both gifts and sacrifices for sins:

2 Who can have compassion on the ignorant, and on them that are out of

2-3. The second qualification of a human priest involved his character. He must have **compassion** upon those who inadver-

the way; for that he himself also is compassed with infirmity.

3 And by reason hereof he ought, as for the people, so also for himself, to offer for sins.

4 And no man taketh this honour unto himself, but he that is called of God, as was Aaron.

5 So also Christ glorified not himself to be made an high priest; but he that said unto him, Thou art my Son, to day have I begotten thee.

6 As he saith also in another place, Thou art a priest for ever after the order of Mĕl-chĭs'e-dĕc.

7 Who in the days of his flesh, when he had offered up prayers and supplications with strong crying and tears unto him that was able to save him from death, and was heard in that he feared;

8 Though he were a Son, yet learned he obedience by the things which he suffered;

9 And being made perfect, he became the author of eternal salvation unto all them that obey him;

10 Called of God an high priest after the order of Mĕl-chĭs'e-dĕc.

---

tently sin out of ignorance. This **compassion** (Gr *metriopatheō*) is a controlled compassion, meaning "to be gentle with." Etymologically, it involved a measured, or balanced, feeling. This unusual word (found nowhere else in the New Testament) was used "in the Aristotelian philosophical tradition in the sense of to moderate one's feelings or passions and so to avoid excesses either of enthusiasm or impassivity" (Hughes, p. 176). It involves caring without undue harshness or weepy sentiment. It was a necessary quality of character for all priests. It stemmed from the patience learned by the priest's own **infirmity** and out of his own need of a priest for his sins.

4. The third qualification of the priest concerned his appointment. He must be appointed by or **called of God.** These qualifications are listed here, not because God is looking today for those who aspire to be priests, as He is for pastors (Gr *episkopos*, I Tim 3:1). Just the opposite—the priests were appointed by God's decree. Those who took the office to themselves suffered severe consequences (Korah in Num 16:1-35; Saul in I Sam 13:9-11; Uzziah in II Chr 26:16-23).

5-6. Starting with verse 5, Christ's qualifications are shown to parallel those of the levitical priests. They are, however, presented in reverse order. The author's first point, therefore, is that **Christ glorified not himself to be made a high priest;** rather, God the Father appointed Him, as the Scriptures declare. The first of the two passages cited, **Thou art my Son,** is from Psalm 2:7 and was previously cited in Hebrews 1:5. Even though a reference to Christ's Sonship may seem irrelevant here, Christ's position as Son, and hence sovereign King, is important in light of the priesthood He possesses. He has been appointed a **priest for ever after the order of Melchizedek.** Since Melchizedek was a king-priest (cf. 7:1-3), so Christ, who is of that order, must be a king-priest.

7-8. Christ also meets the qualification of being a compassionate priest due to those things which He has suffered. **Who in the days of his flesh** speaks of the thirty years during which the Son became flesh and dwelt among men (Jn 1:14), suffering many things in behalf of His people. After this brief phrase concerning His life, the author focuses upon one trying event— Gethsemane. **Offered up prayers and supplications with strong crying and tears.** These words are even more intense and descriptive than those that are recorded in the Gospels. The tone compares to that of Psalm 22, in which Christ's thoughts upon the cross are expressed. In Gethsemane, Jesus reveals that His soul is ". . . exceeding sorrowful unto death . . ." (Mk 14:34). He prays to the Father, asking if this cup might be taken away, referring to His suffering on the cross. Though it may involve the ignominy and anguish of the physical death, its quintessence is the horror of the Son's separation from the Father, bearing the wrath and curse of God's holiness against man's sin. For the first time in eternity, the fellowship between Father and Son will be broken; God will forsake Him.

And was heard in that he feared. How the Father heard or answered Christ's prayer is not answered here since it is not the point of the author's discourse. God may have answered by removing Christ's fear of the imminent cross experience. More likely, in harmony with the statements of Psalm 22, He answered by reaffirming the promise of the Resurrection (see Bruce, pp. 100-102).

9-10. He became the author of eternal salvation. That which had been described first in relation to the levitical priests has been reserved until last in relation to Christ. His offering for sin was complete and final, providing eternal salvation for **all them that obey him.** It is eternal, but not universal. Only those who come to God claiming the sacrifice of Christ receive this eternal life (7:25; 9:26 ,28; 10:10-14).

3. *The third warning passage: Do not be spiritually immature.*
5:11-6:20.

a. *The rebuke of immaturity. 5:11-14.*

11 Of whom we have many things to say, and hard to be uttered, seeing ye are dull of hearing.

12 For when for the time ye ought to be teachers, ye have need that one teach you again which *be* the first principles of the oracles of God; and are become such as have need of milk, and not of strong meat.

11-12. Of whom we have many things to say. This parenthetical passage of warning is placed where one would expect the author to develop his discourse on the priesthood of Melchizedek. He has just brought the Old Testament prophecies that predicted Christ's priesthood according to the order of Melchizedek to light. Obviously, his intent is to develop this theme as quickly as possible; for he begins to do so in chapter 7, immediately after this rebuke. The author wishes to present many things concerning Melchizedek; but he knows they are not ready to receive them, for they are **dull of hearing.** This adjective (Gr *nōthroi*) means to be lazy or sluggish. In Proverbs 22:29 (LXX) it is translated "slothful." The only other New Testament occurrence is in the next chapter (6:12). In verse 11 the rebuke concerns the slothfulness of their hearing. They have not been listening; they have not, therefore, been growing. Shortly, he will warn them, lest their whole life becomes sluggish (6:12).

In verses 11-12 he describes their condition as due to poor, lazy hearing. They are immature. Whereas they should now be teachers, they still need to be taught. Whereas they should be ready to understand new and difficult teachings from God's Word, they can only handle the **milk.** They have not advanced beyond the **first principles of the oracles of God.** Most likely, these first principles involve the "principles of the doctrine of Christ" that are enumerated in 6:1-3.

13 For every one that useth milk *is* unskilful in the word of righteousness: for he is a babe.

14 But strong meat belongeth to them that are of full age, *even* those who by reason of use have their senses exercised to discern both good and evil.

13-14. The author has used the second person to present the condition of his readers; now he changes to the third person to teach the nature of immaturity in general. Those who are immature are as babies who can only digest milk. They are **unskillful** (Gr *apeiros*), inexperienced in or unacquainted with the **word** that instructs them in how to live a life of righteousness. By contrast, the strong Christian is the one who by constant application of God's Word to his life has his spiritual senses **exercised** (Gr *gegymnasmena*) as an athlete exercises or trains his body. Thus, the strong Christian can discern truth from error.

b. *The exhortation to maturity. 6:1-3.*

CHAPTER 6

THEREFORE leaving the principles of the doctrine of Christ, let us go on unto perfection; not laying again the foundation of repentance from dead works, and of faith toward God,

6:1. Therefore leaving the principles. The author is not content to allow his readers to remain in their immature state (5:11-14). Unlike Paul's capitulation to his Corinthian hearers, in that he feeds them as the babes they are (I Cor 3:2), our author admonishes his readers to "grow up." Such words sting, but they are sometimes necessary. **Let us go on** (Gr *pherōmetha*). The verb is unusual in that it is not active as the translation would imply; rather, it is passive. It does not involve going as much as "being carried" or "being moved." Westcott (p. 143) suggests the translation, "Let us be moved along." Maturity will not be attained by personal effort as much as by personal surrender to God, who alone can accomplish the needed perfection (cf. vs. 3). **The principles of the doctrine of Christ** involve the same elementary principles that were mentioned in 5:12. The six doctrines now cited are probably representative, rather than inclusive, of all elementary teachings. They can be easily gathered into three sets. The first set involves conversion itself: **of repentance from dead works, and of faith toward God.** Both the negative (repentance) and the positive (faith) aspects of conversion are cited. The dead works refer to one's former sinful ways, which are ways of death. These works might include either the sinner's unholy deeds of the flesh or his ungodly deeds of self-righteousness. Both produce death and must be renounced. The positive aspect, faith, must always be directed toward God alone. Paul's witness regarding the Thessalonian believers, that they turned ". . . to God from idols . . ."

2 Of the doctrine of baptisms, and of laying on of hands, and of resurrection of the dead, and of eternal judgment.

(I Thess 1:9), likewise expresses these two aspects of conversion.

2. The second set of elementary doctrines represents post-conversion experiences: **Doctrine of baptisms, and of laying on of hands.** The word **baptisms** (Gr *baptismoi*) creates several difficulties. First, the other uncontested usages of this word involve ceremonial washings (9:10; Mk 7:4), rather than Christian baptism. The usual word for baptism (Gr *baptisma*) is not used here. Nevertheless, baptism may be the correct usage; for *baptismos* appears to be the proper reading for the contested passage (Col 2:12), which does refer to Christian baptism. Second, the fact that the word is plural suggests to some that the reference must be to ceremonial washings. Yet, there are several baptisms to which the author could be referring—John's baptism (with which these Jewish readers should be acquainted), Christian baptism, and Spirit baptism. The third set of elementary teachings are eschatological, involving last things. Some eschatological teachings are closely associated with the salvation message, such as **resurrection** and **eternal judgment**; for they involve the hope of salvation. Eschatology is included here among the first truths, not as part of the deeper truths. The mere study of last things does not demonstrate spiritual maturity. The practical changes which these eschatological truths produce within our lives are what manifest maturity.

3 And this will we do, if God permit.

3. **And this will we do.** The author now uses chapter 6 as a warning and admonition to move his readers on to maturity in order that they might receive and understand the difficult doctrine which they are about to hear (chs. 7ff.). **If God permit.** We must acknowledge that when a man is going in the wrong direction, only God can change his life.

c. The warning of apostasy. 6:4-8.

4 For *it is* impossible for those who were once enlightened, and have tasted of the heavenly gift, and were made partakers of the Holy Ghost,
5 And have tasted the good word of God, and the powers of the world to come,
6 If they shall fall away, to renew them again unto repentance; seeing they crucify to themselves the Son of God afresh, and put *him* to an open shame.

4-6. For it is impossible . . . to renew them again unto repentance. For centuries Hebrews 6 has been a battleground. That fact alone ought to warn us to study carefully and to conclude slowly concerning the teaching of these verses. The crux of the issue is whether or not a born-again believer can lose his salvation. Though many interpretations of these verses have been proposed, four common, contemporary views merit listing.

Some propose that these verses refer to the saved who have fallen from salvation (cf. Lenski, *Interpretation of Hebrews*, pp. 185-187). Others teach that these are professing Christians, though unsaved, who apostatize and so are forever unable to be brought to repentance and true saving faith (cf. Bruce, *The Epistle to the Hebrews*, pp. 118-125). A third group proposes that these are indeed saved people who do not fall from salvation, but who fall into sin—they backslide. This view understands the statement of something being **impossible** as the impossibility of starting over again in the Christian life. These have fallen in regard to Christian growth, or concerning the perfection spoken of in 6:1. They have become castaways from God's service (cf. G. H. Lang, *The Epistle to the Hebrews*, pp. 93-107; M. F. Unger, *Unger's Bible Handbook,* pp. 95-101). The fourth popular view states that these verses refer to a hypothetical situation whereby the author stresses what would happen to a saved person if he could fall away (cf. Kent, *The Epistle to the Hebrews*, pp. 107-115; and, T. Hewitt, *The Epistle to the Hebrews*, TNTC, pp. 108-111). The author does not believe one can lose his salvation, or that his readers had (6:9); but he speaks to demonstrate the folly some might have in imagining that they can turn back to Judaism without suffering loss. "The warning was directed to those who claimed to be saved, and took them at their own estimate of themselves to show the folly of their viewpoint" (Kent, p. 113). True believers would also be warned of the severity of excluding Christ from their lives. Though the author is not writing about his readers (vs. 4, **those**), he is still writing for their sakes (vs. 9, **you**). This writer sees the fourth interpretation as harmonizing best with the grammatical and doctrinal data in the passage.

Though much uncertainty exists regarding the interpretation of these verses, six facts stand forth. First, verses 4-6 contain no regular, finite verbs. The verbal forms are participles, an infinitive, and an implied verb. This structure makes interpretation difficult. Second, those who are described within these verses have received profound spiritual blessings (whether saved or not). Third, it is impossible to bring those who fall away back again to repentance. So if this passage teaches that a person can lose his salvation, it also must teach that he can never be saved a second or third time. Fourth, whatever these verses might teach, such is not true of those believers to whom the author writes (vs. 9). Fifth, though these things are not true of the recipients, yet they are warned to be diligent **to the full assurance of hope** (vs. 11). They need to know the security which they possess, so as to gain assurance. Sixth, verses 13-20 emphatically teach the certainty of God's promise of redemption. Despite the negative tone with which the warning began (5:11-14), it ends positively. In fact, it speaks against insecurity regarding the believer's salvation. Actually, the problem of the passage is immaturity, not insecurity.

Hebrews 6 agrees with the general tenor of Scripture concerning the security of the born-again believer. Security is objective and depends upon God. Assurance of salvation, however, is subjective, depending upon the believer's acceptance of God's promise. Although a believer's spiritual life is secure, he may not think or feel so; and thus, he lacks assurance. We cannot mature in the Christian life if we are uncertain about God's promise of eternal life, for it is the first step of trust. One basis for the security of the believer involves the promises that are recorded in God's Word (6:18-20; 7:24-25; 8:12; 10:10-14; Jn 10:28-30; Rom 8:28-39; Phil 1:6; I Jn 5:13). Yet, an even stronger basis for our security is found within the nature of the new life that God gives. Though conversion involves man's will, it is God's will that produces regeneration (Jn 1:13). Thus, salvation is infinitely more than a decision that man can make and then break. It is the work of God that transforms us from darkness to light (Col 1:13; II Cor 4:4), from death to life (Jn 5:24), from a child of the devil to a son of God. God makes us His sons (Rom 8:14-17). It is a completed, regenerating work (10:14; Eph 2:8—"Ye are saved" or "You have been and stand saved," perfect tense). And through His saving grace He makes us holy (II Cor 5:21; Rom 4:8—"Blessed is the man concerning whom the Lord will never reckon sin," Gr *ou mē*).

Several participles within these verses describe those who cannot be renewed. One should not base any doctrine upon these descriptive terms, since none absolutely imply regeneration; yet, they do suggest the salvation experience. The author refers to these persons first as **those who were once enlightened** (vs. 4). Even though this phrase could refer to something short of regeneration, two facts favor the idea that it is. It is used in the parallel fourth warning (10:32). There the author seems to describe their salvation experience: "But call to remembrance the former days, in which, after ye were illuminated, ye endured a great fight of afflictions." Second, the use of **once** (Gr *hapax*, once-for-all) suggests finality. The second participle describes these people as having **tasted of the heavenly gift**. The word **tasted** (Gr *geuomai*, taste) often carries a broader meaning (to partake of something in its entirety). In Acts 10:10 it refers to partaking of a meal, not merely tasting the food. In Chapter 2 verse 9, Christ tasted death; He fully partook of it. In the same sense these people have partaken of the heavenly gift and of the Holy Spirit. Further, they have fully experienced the Word of God and powers of the coming age.

If they shall fall away. The interpretation of the fifth participle has created much controversy. This participle (Gr *parapesontas*) has the same basic form as the first four, which have been translated substantivally (**those who were**). Our version translates it circumstantially (adverbially) as a condition: **if they shall fall away.** This is a legitimate usage and even a common practice by our author as witnessed in 2:3 and 10:26, but especially in 6:8 (if it bear thorns). The context does allow a difference between the fifth participle and the first four, in that the first four refer to blessings which they have experienced, whereas this one and the following two do not. The very last two are commonly treated as circumstantial with a causal idea, as in our Authorized Version (**seeing they crucify**). It should not be assumed that the fifth participle cannot also be circumstantial. Nevertheless, extreme caution should be taken in developing any doctrine or even an interpretation based upon these participles alone. The utter impossibility of the next phrase would indicate that this "falling away" is hypothetical and not actual.

They crucify to themselves the Son of God afresh. The author's thought is that once they have experienced all that Christ has to offer and then deliberately turn back, they are as those who first crucified Christ. By their rejection of Christ's ministry on their behalf, they **put him to an open shame.** The last two participles use the present tense (the first five are aorist), expressing a continuous act, so that they keep on crucifying Christ and exposing Him to shame. Anyone who would do such things can never be brought to repentance, for there is no other gospel. There is no other Saviour. Since this epistle makes it clear that Christ can only be crucified once, this situation must be viewed hypothetically. The writer's argument is that "if" one could "fall away," he would, thereby, "crucify afresh" his Lord. Since that cannot happen (for Christ died once for all sin), then the one falling away could not be renewed to faith and repentance. Such is never the case, for Christ is always available to the repentant sinner.

7-8. For the earth. To enhance the blessing of maturity and the ultimate destruction of that which is barren, the author provides an illustration from nature. Much effort or work must be placed into the earth in order for it to produce. This is also true in the hearts of men if they are to produce perfection (6:1). That upon which no effort is expended becomes worthless. It should also be noticed that the illustration does not speak of a parcel of land that first produces and later becomes void of life; so it does not illustrate someone saved then lost. It speaks of two kinds of fields, one maturing unto **blessing** and the other degenerating unto **cursing.**

d. The encouragement to go on. 6:9-12.

9-10. We are persuaded better things of you. Following this severe warning, the author consoles his readers with his confidence concerning them. He was not speaking about them; he does not even suggest that he was speaking of some of them who were merely professing Christians. He is persuaded that his readers possess better qualities and **things that accompany salvation,** or literally "things having salvation" (Gr *echomena*). This warning was hypothetical, showing the awesomeness of apostasy if one could actually renounce Christ after being born again. The fourth warning (ch. 10) demonstrates the hypothetical nature of these warnings more clearly than chapter 6 does. In chapter 10 the author includes himself within the warning (10:26) and further states that neither he nor his readers were on the road to apostasy (10:39). He pronounces the fearful punishment upon one who would trample the Son of God under foot and would count the blood by which he was sanctified as unholy (see the commentary on 10:29). He is describing what would happen to him and to them, not what has happened to anyone.

7 For the earth which drinketh in the rain that cometh oft upon it, and bringeth forth herbs meet for them by whom it is dressed, receiveth blessing from God:

8 But that which beareth thorns and briers *is* rejected, and *is* nigh unto cursing; whose end *is* to be burned.

9 But, beloved, we are persuaded better things of you, and things that accompany salvation, though we thus speak.

10 For God *is* not unrighteous to forget your work and labour of love, which ye have shewed toward his name, in that ye have ministered to the saints, and do minister.

11 And we desire that every one of you do shew the same diligence to the full assurance of hope unto the end:

12 That ye be not slothful, but followers of them who through faith and patience inherit the promises.

11-12. Show the same diligence to the full assurance of hope. The author is desirous that, as they were diligent in the past, so now in the present they might grow and mature in order to know the full assurance of their eternal life, or "so as to realize the full assurance of hope until the end" (NASB). They must not become slothful (Gr *nōthroi*) or sluggish. They had already become sluggish in their hearing (5:11); they must now be diligent, lest such sluggishness characterize their whole life. They need to become **followers** of those saints who demonstrate **faith and patience.** To follow (Gr *mimētēs*) involves much more than trailing after another. The word used here refers to an imitator, or to one who follows another's example. One such example was Abraham.

e. The certainty of God's promises. 6:13-20.

13 For when God made promise to Abraham, because he could swear by no greater, he sware by himself,

14 Saying, Surely blessing I will bless thee, and multiplying I will multiply thee.

15 And so, after he had patiently endured, he obtained the promise.

13-15. For when God made promise to Abraham. The greatest encouragement to faith and patience is the confidence that God's promises are trustworthy. So the author uses Abraham as an example of one who practiced the diligence of a fruitful life. In so doing, he cites God's promise to Abraham in Genesis 22:16-17, which is a restatement of His promise in Genesis 12:2-3. God backed up His promise with His integrity. He signed His name to the promise. "Thus both God's authority and His integrity were at stake" (Ross, *Wycliffe Bible Commentary*, p. 918).

The interpretation of **he obtained the promise** (vs. 15) must consider the significance of 11:13, which states that Abraham died **not having received the promises.** The ultimate fulfillment of the Abrahamic Covenant involved the coming and ministry of the Christ Himself, which Abraham did not see during his lifetime. Yet, the promise to which our author refers in chapter 6 concerns the receiving of Isaac. And though the quote is taken from the statement made to Abraham when he offered Isaac to God on Mount Moriah, it is only the reaffirmation of a promise made before Isaac was born. Of course, this promise was simply the first step of the ultimate fulfillment, but in no way does it contradict the promises referred to in 11:13 (see Kent, p. 119).

16 For men verily swear by the greater: and an oath for confirmation *is* to them an end of all strife.

17 Wherein God, willing more abundantly to shew unto the heirs of promise the immutability of his counsel, confirmed *it* by an oath:

18 That by two immutable things, in which *it was* impossible for God to lie, we might have a strong consolation, who have fled for refuge to lay hold upon the hope set before us:

16-18. An oath . . . is to them an end of all strife. Since God accompanied His promise with an oath, the author seeks to show the value of an oath. Even when men take an oath, swearing by someone greater than themselves, others regard it as a **confirmation** (Gr *bebaiōsin*) of the promise. This is a technical usage involving a legal guarantee. **God . . . confirmed it by an oath.** God desired that His people should fully understand the certainty of His promises, and so He established them by His oath.

That by two immutable things. God's covenant to Abraham was based on two immutable (unchangeable) elements. First, God's promise was based upon His own unchanging word. He cannot lie; He will not allow His word to fail (Mt 5:28; Jn 10:35; 17:17). What He says, He will do. Further, His word was confirmed by His oath. And since He can swear by none greater, He swears by Himself. If in any way His word would not be sufficient, He bases His promise upon His own holy character. **We might have a strong consolation.** God's covenant to Abraham is irreversible. It is as immutable as God Himself. That truth did not provide assurance for Abraham alone, but it applies equally to us who have received the salvation provided in the Abrahamic covenant. The author has focused upon the appropriate text to prove the security of salvation which he desires his readers to have.

19 Which *hope* we have as an anchor of the soul, both sure and stedfast, and which entereth into that within the vail;

20 Whither the forerunner is for us

19-20. Which hope we have as an anchor. Starting at the end of verse 18, the author uses three illustrative pictures to demonstrate the security of being in Christ. First, it is described as being a safe protection to the believer, as the six cities of refuge in the Old Testament were to those allowed their protec-

entered, *even* Jesus, made an high priest for ever after the order of Mĕl-chĭs'e-dĕc.

CHAPTER 7

FOR this Mĕl-chĭs'e-dĕc, king of Salem, priest of the most high God, who met Abraham returning from the slaughter of the kings, and blessed him;

2 To whom also Abraham gave a tenth part of all; first being by interpretation King of righteousness, and after that also King of Salem, which is, King of peace;

3 Without father, without mother, without descent, having neither beginning of days, nor end of life; but made like unto the Son of God; abideth a priest continually.

tion (Num 35:6-32). Second, our hope is **sure** and **steadfast** as a well-placed, unbending anchor. Our anchor is not located in the deepest sea, but in the highest heaven. It is fixed in the surest of all places—in the sanctuary of heaven itself. The third figure is that of a **forerunner.** Though the figure changes, the location does not. Our forerunner is likewise positioned in the sanctuary of heaven. As our forerunner, Jesus is far different from the Old Testament priests. The Old Testament high priest could represent and intercede for the people within the sanctuary, the Holy of Holies; but he could not take the people into it. As our forerunner, Jesus has opened the way before us, that eventually (but certainly) we might enter in with Him.

The warning passage ends where it began, speaking of Jesus as a priest according to the priesthood of Melchizedek. It is the author's hope that his readers would no longer be sluggish in hearing (5:11) but would be ready to grapple with this new and difficult doctrine.

4. The priestly order of Melchizedek. 7:1-28.

The thesis that Christ is superior to the levitical high priest began at 4:14. Due to the immaturity of the readers, our author has not yet presented the main part of his argument. He now does this in chapter 7. Christ's ministry is superior, for his priesthood is after the order of Melchizedek.

a. A royal priest. 7:1-3.

7:1. For this Melchizedek. Melchizedek appears only briefly in the Old Testament (Gen 14:18-20; Ps 110:4), but our author minutely scrutinizes him in his epistle. The preliminary discussion presented in these verses is taken from the historical account in Genesis. **Who met Abraham returning from the slaughter of the kings.** The capture of Lot during the battle at Sodom between four northern kings and five southern kings caused Abraham, with 318 men, to pursue them. After defeating them near Damascus, he turned south with the people and goods which had been plundered. Melchizedek, **King of Salem** (later called Jerusalem) and **priest of the most high God,** brought out food to feed them and blessed Abraham. Abraham acknowledged Melchizedek's priestly status by giving him a tenth of all the spoils.

2-3. Being by interpretation. The writer sees in Melchizedek a type or figure of Christ and begins to express the parallels which he sees between the two. The word **interpretation** (Gr *hermēneuomenos*) might better be rendered, "by the translation of his name" (NASB). His name means **King of righteousness.** His position as king of the ancient city-state of Salem made him also "king of peace," since Salem means peace. Thus, by name and location he is king of both righteousness and peace, two attributes that link him in type to Christ. By emphasizing the silence of the passage, the author is able to establish many parallels within the typology. **Without father, without mother.** What is true of Melchizedek (the type) only because of silence is intrinsically true of Christ (the reality). Melchizedek is without parents only in that they are unknown. He is **without descent** in that his genealogy has not been preserved, as verse 6 implicitly states. Genealogy was essential to a priest, for under the levitical system one could not serve if he could not prove his pedigree (cf. Ezr 2:62; Neh 7:64). Melchizedek had no papers. Similarly, in His divine person Christ was indeed without father or mother, without genealogy. Melchizedek is without beginning and ending due to silence; so is Christ due to His eternal nature. The author explicitly states his point when he declares that Melchizedek is **made like** (Gr *aphōmoiōmenos*), or resembles, the Son of God. Has the author taken too great a liberty with his typology? No, for it is God Himself who first made the similar connection in Psalm 110:4, ". . . Thou art a priest for ever after the order of

Melchizedek." It is God who decrees that Melchizedek's priesthood is everlasting. **Abideth a priest continually.** Our author concludes exactly that which God had proclaimed earlier—Melchizedek's priesthood continues. The present tense indicates that Melchizedek is a priest, not that he was a priest.

Some have understood these verses in Hebrews to suggest that Melchizedek was a theophany, an appearance of Christ Himself, rather than a historical king at Salem. Neither Hebrews nor Genesis, however, supports that view. Even in Hebrews, such phrases as **made like unto the Son of God** (7:20) and **after the order of Melchizedek** (vs. 20) seem to indicate a clear distinction between Melchizedek and Christ. The Genesis account provides sufficient historical data to disallow the idea that this is a temporary manifestation. This Melchizedek was a king of a literal city in Canaan. The setting of Genesis 14 is unlike any of the settings involving a theophany. In those settings the theophany is recognized as the Lord or is declared within the text to be the Lord (Gen 16:7ff.; 18:1ff.; 22:11ff.; Ex 3:2ff.). Further, to argue from etymology that since the name means "king of righteousness," Melchizedek is not historical, lacks substance. Both historical and archaeological evidence demonstrate that the Jebusite kings of that area used compound names including "-zedek" for their titles. For example, Adoni-zedek was the Jebusite king of the same city several centuries later (Josh 10:1). For an extensive treatment of this subject, see James Borland, *Christ in the Old Testament*, pp. 164-174.

b. A priest greater than Aaron. 7:4-10.

4 Now consider how great this man was, unto whom even the patriarch Abraham gave the tenth of the spoils.

5 And verily they that are of the sons of Levi, who receive the office of the priesthood, have a commandment to take tithes of the people according to the law, that is, of their brethren, though they come out of the loins of Abraham:

6 But he whose descent is not counted from them received tithes of Abraham, and blessed him that had the promises.

7 And without all contradiction the less is blessed of the better.

4-7. Consider how great this man was. The point being made now is quite obvious. Even Abraham, the patriarch, or father, of the Jewish people, considered Melchizedek superior enough to tithe willingly and humbly of his spoils. **Spoils** (Gr *akrothinion*) means literally the top of the heap or the best of the spoils, which were usually reserved for deity. The point of verse 5 is not as clear, but it seems to focus around two factors that distinguish Melchizedek from the levitical priests. First, the levitical system was **according to the law,** so that tithing to them was the result of mere legal consignment. Second, they received the tithes from those who were **brethren.** Therefore, Dods concludes, "Paying tithes is in their case no acknowledgement of personal inferiority, but mere compliance with law. But Abraham was under no such law to Melchizedek, and the payment of tithes to him was a tribute to his personal greatness" (p. 309). Verses 6 and 7 add the further point that Melchizedek **blessed him that had the promises.** Even though the great Abraham was the recipient of the Covenant, he is the receiver, rather than the bestower, of the blessing. Thus, Melchizedek is his better and is certainly superior to Abraham's offspring.

8 And here men that die receive tithes; but there he *receiveth them*, of whom it is witnessed that he liveth.

9 And as I may so say, Levi also, who receiveth tithes, payed tithes in Abraham.

10 For he was yet in the loins of his father, when Mĕl-chĭs′e-dĕc met him.

8-10. Here men that die receive tithes. In these verses the author marshals two ideas that will not allow any to think that the more recent levitical order was a replacement of the earlier system. First, the levitical system is weakened by the continual death of its priests. The Melchizedecian order, however, has the witness of God (vs. 3; Ps 110:4) that its priest lives on. Second, **Levi, also . . . paid tithes in Abraham.** The levitical system was neither a better nor a later replacement, for in a corporate sense even Levi was present at the Genesis 14 event. The author is cautious in his assertion, as his introductory words indicate: **As I may so say.** The phrase might more clearly be expressed by "I might almost say" (Dods, p. 310) or "so to speak" (NASB). The author suggests that there is a sense in which even Levi paid tithes to Melchizedek. He cannot be Melchizedek's superior.

c. A priestly order which is unending. 7:11-25.

Though the author has repeatedly referred to the unending nature of the Melchizedecian order, this now becomes the cen-

11 If therefore perfection were by the Le-vit'i-cal priesthood, (for under it the people received the law,) what further need *was there* that another priest should rise after the order of Měl-chĭs'e-děc, and not be called after the order of Aaron?

12 For the priesthood being changed, there is made of necessity a change also of the law.

13 For he of whom these things are spoken pertaineth to another tribe, of which no man gave attendance at the altar.

14 For *it is* evident that our Lord sprang out of Juda: of which tribe Moses spake nothing concerning priesthood.

15 And it is yet far more evident: for that after the similitude of Měl-chĭs'e-děc there ariseth another priest,

16 Who is made, not after the law of a carnal commandment, but after the power of an endless life.

17 For he testifieth, Thou *art* a priest for ever after the order of Měl-chĭs'e-děc.

18 For there is verily a disannulling of the commandment going before for the weakness and unprofitableness thereof.

19 For the law made nothing perfect, but the bringing in of a better hope *did*; by the which we draw nigh unto God.

20 And inasmuch as not without an oath *he was made priest:*

21 (For those priests were made without an oath; but this with an oath by him that said unto him, The Lord sware and will not repent, Thou *art* a priest for ever after the order of Měl-chĭs'e-děc:)

22 By so much was Jesus made a surety of a better testament.

tral point. But before developing the positive aspects of this, he addresses the weaknesses of the levitical system. The Old Testament bears witness within itself to the provisional nature of its priesthood.

11-12. What further need was there that another priest should rise. . . ? The author raises the questions as to why the Old Testament should make reference to **another** (Gr *heteros*), a different priesthood. If the levitical priesthood was producing **perfection** (Gr *teleiōsis*), meaning completion or fulfillment of its role, why is another needed? The old system pronounced its own doom by speaking of another. Further, the author teaches that the passing of the levitical priesthood necessitates the removal of the Mosaic law, for they are inextricably united. According to verses 11-12, the Law did not produce the levitical priesthood; but the priesthood required the Law. Both Moses and Aaron were chosen of God before the Law was given. The Law was given at Sinai to provide the procedures and ordinances for the functioning of the priesthood He had already established. So our author accurately acknowledges that the passing of the levitical priesthood demands the passing of the Mosaic system (cf. Kent, pp. 132-133).

13-14. Another tribe. As long as the Mosaic law was operative, the fact that Jesus was of the tribe of Judah created an insurmountable obstacle. The Law never honored or allowed one from that tribe to function as priest. Conversely, when King Uzziah, a Judahite, took that role to himself, God judged him with leprosy (II Chr 26:16-21). As long as the Law was functional, Jesus could not serve as priest. But the Law promised another priest, one after the order of Melchizedek, who would replace the insufficient levitical priesthood and its law.

15-19. After the power of an endless life. One has arisen who is qualified to serve after the order of Melchizedek, for He has an endless life. As in verse 11, the word **another** (Gr *heteros*) in verse 15 means another who is different rather than a similar one (Gr *allos*) Verse 16 indicates how He is different in His qualification. Under the levitical system, men were appointed on the basis of physical descent. The word **carnal** (Gr *sarkinēs*) does not mean fleshly, implying sinful characteristics (as *sarkikēs* would); rather, it means "fleshly," implying that which pertains to the physical. Christ was not appointed because of physical descent, but because of His spiritual fitness. He possesses endless life. He possesses divine qualities that no levitical priest ever possessed. Thus, though their priesthood was weak and ineffective, His is able to present men before God forever.

20-22. Not without an oath he was made priest. The oath with which God established the Melchizedecian order certifies it as unending. The levitical system received no such certification. God did not swear that it would endure, but this one will. There will never be a third system. There are no new, latter-day priesthoods. God's oath will allow no other.

With the new priesthood, God has also established a new and **better testament,** or covenant, just as the levitical priesthood contained the Old Covenant, the Mosaic. The Greek word translated **testament** (Gr *diathēkē*) is used seventeen times in Hebrews, the first being here. During the New Testament era this was the exclusive word for a will or testament (a one-sided promise involving the death of the testator). The Greek word uniformly used to express a compact, or covenant (a two-sided agreement), was *synthēkē*. Yet, the Old Testament word for covenant (Heb *berīt*) consistently uses *diathēkē*, though one might expect to see *synthēkē*. The reason for this word usage arises from the fact that God's covenants were not compacts or agreements made between equal parties. Thus *diathēkē* more aptly expresses the one-sided nature of God's covenants (Moulton and Milligan, *The Vocabulary of the Greek Testament*, pp. 148-149). This better covenant is a promise, not an agreement. It was established solely by God and confirmed with His oath. No one can annul it or the eternal salvation which it promises. Jesus Himself is the **surety** (Gr *eggyos*) of the covenant. He is not here presented as the mediator, but as the guarantor, of this better covenant. A mediator is one who gathers the two parties to devise an agreement. A guarantor is one who sees that the obligations of the covenant are carried out (Kent, pp. 137-138).

23-25. An unchangeable priesthood. The levitical high priest possessed an inherent instability due to the death of its priests. Each generation faced this change. By contrast, the New Covenant possesses a priesthood that is unchanging (Gr *aparabaton*). This word has the connotation of that which is not passed along. This new priesthood needs no successor. Therefore, He is able **to save them to the uttermost** (Gr *eis to panteles*). The possibilities for this Greek phrase are twofold, completely or forever. The context allows both ideas; and so the broader meaning, completely, seems the more appropriate usage. The one other occurrence of this Greek phrase also suggests completeness (Lk 13:11—of a woman completely stooped over). Christ has saved us to the uttermost; our salvation is complete in every respect. It is complete in regard to time; so it is secure to the end of time. It is complete in that it can perfect regeneration in any life. Christ is a better high priest because His intercession is unending and complete, providing access into God's presence (cf. 4:14-16).

d. A priestly character which is superior. 7:26-28.

26. Much has been said previously concerning Christ's priestly character, coming bit by bit and in various ways; but here the message reaches its climax. **For such a high priest became us.** The passage might be rendered more forcefully, as, "such a high priest meets our need" (NIV) or, "such a high priest does indeed fit our condition" (NEB). He meets our needs so well because of His qualities. He is **holy, harmless, undefiled, separate from sinners.** Westcott cleverly arranges these attributes as follows: "Christ is personally in Himself *holy,* in relation to men *guileless,* in spite of contact with a sinful world *undefiled.* By the issue of His life He has been *separated from sinners* in regard to the visible order, and, in regard to the invisible world, He has *risen above the heavens*" (Westcott, p. 193). It seems simpler and more congruous with the context to regard these as qualities which merely distinguish His priestly role from that represented by the levitical priests. He is holy in His personal piety; He is harmless or guileless morally. He is undefiled, similar to the cleanness required of levitical priests (Lev 21:1-21:16ff.). But whereas theirs only involved physical contacts, His undefilement is total. Outwardly, they were separated from sinners; His separation is total, for He is sinless. They interceded to the God in heaven; He is the God of heaven. Though He intercedes daily, He has no need to sacrifice daily.

27-28. The levitical priest offered sacrifices **first for his own sins** day after day (see Lev 4:2-3; 16:6). Christ offered Himself as the sacrifice for the sin of man (II Cor 5:21; I Pet 2:24). The beautiful aspect of this passage is that it reveals Christ as both high priest and sacrifice (cf. Gal 1:4). Christ has both all the authority and holiness of a superior high priest and all the love necessary to become the very sacrifice for our sin. Verse 28 states the contrasts once again. They whom the Law appointed have **infirmity** (Gr *astheneia*) or "weaknesses." The Son, who has been perfected (Gr *teleiōmenon*) forever, was appointed after (Gr *meta*) the Law by God's oath.

E. Christ's Ministry Through the New Covenant Is Superior to the Old System. 8:1-10:30.

Whereas the former chapters have highlighted Christ's superiority due to His personal character or work, chapters 8-10 lay

23 And they truly were many priests, because they were not suffered to continue by reason of death:
24 But this *man,* because he continueth ever, hath an unchangeable priesthood.
25 Wherefore he is able also to save them to the uttermost that come unto God by him, seeing he ever liveth to make intercession for them.

26 For such an high priest became us, *who is* holy, harmless, undefiled, separate from sinners, and made higher than the heavens;

27 Who needeth not daily, as those high priests, to offer up sacrifice, first for his own sins, and then for the people's: for this he did once, when he offered up himself.
28 For the law maketh men high priests which have infirmity; but the word of the oath, which was since the law, *maketh* the Son, who is consecrated for evermore.

CHAPTER 8

NOW of the things which we have spoken *this is* the sum: We have such an high priest, who is set on the right hand of the throne of the Majesty in the heavens;

2 A minister of the sanctuary, and of the true tabernacle, which the Lord pitched, and not man.

3 For every high priest is ordained to offer gifts and sacrifices: wherefore *it is* of necessity that this man have somewhat also to offer.

4 For if he were on earth, he should not be a priest, seeing that there are priests that offer gifts according to the law:

5 Who serve unto the example and shadow of heavenly things, as Moses was admonished of God when he was about to make the tabernacle: for, See, saith he, *that* thou make all things according to the pattern shewed to thee in the mount.

6 But now hath he obtained a more excellent ministry, by how much also he is the mediator of a better covenant, which was established upon better promises.

7 For if that first *covenant* had been faultless, then should no place have been sought for the second.

stress upon the superiority of the new system with its heavenly tabernacle, its New Covenant, and its totally efficacious, once-for-all sacrifice.

1. The better sanctuary in which Christ ministers. 8:1-6.

8:1-3. Of the things which we have spoken this is the sum. Although this translation of verse 1 suggests that chapter 8 provides a summary of the preceding discourse, this does not seem to be the case. The word translated **sum** (Gr *kephalaion*) equally means main point. In view of the fact that the participle used here is present tense rather than a past tense, the author appears to be emphasizing that which he is about to speak, rather than what he has said. A fitting translation would be, "The point of what we are saying is this" (NIV). The point is that Jesus has His ministry in the heavenly sanctuary, even the **true tabernacle.**

Just as any credible earthly priest, Jesus must have **somewhat also to offer.** The author makes the statement, but does not provide any proof. One reason for the omission of a response at this point could be that he has mentioned Christ's offering only several verses earlier (7:27), stating that he gave **himself.** Another reason for the omission might be the fact that he will develop shortly that very truth regarding Christ's sacrifice (cf. 9:12ff.). The contrast between the continual offering of the priests and Christ's one-time offering is demonstrated in verse 3 by the tenses of the infinitives, being first present (to continue offering) and then aorist (**to offer**).

4-5. He should not be a priest. The author seems to desire to squelch any notion that if Christ did not have a priestly office on earth, how could He have one in heaven. The author's point is that another levitical priest was not needed. They have enough. In fact, He would not qualify according to that order. Jesus is part of God's new, heavenly order.

The example and shadow of heavenly things. Verse 5 sets forth three words that demonstrate the relation between the earthly and heavenly tabernacles. First, the earthly is called an **example** (Gr *hypodeigma*), implying that it is a copy or model of the heavenly. This word is used again to express the relationship of the tabernacle furniture to the heavenly elements (9:23). It is an imitation of the heavenly. Second, the earthly is a **shadow** (Gr *skia*). This word suggests several further facts. A shadow requires the existence of the real thing from the beginning. The heavenly tabernacle has existed at least as long as its shadow—the earthly. A shadow also adds depth and perspective to the real. The levitical priesthood with its Mosaic ritual is a shadow, but the reality is Christ (cf. Col 2:16-17). The third word, **pattern** (Gr *typos*), speaks to the opposite relationship—that of the heavenly to the earthly. The heavenly provided the stamp or imprint from which the earthly came. The pattern, or archetype, which Moses was to follow when building his tabernacle was that of the true tabernacle, spoken of in verse 2. Due to their presentation in the Old Testament, biblical types, such as the Mosaic tabernacle, are revealed before their antitype, which is found in the New. Their existence, however, is preceded by the antitype, as here with the heavenly tabernacle.

6. The superiority of Christ's ministry to that of the levitical priests is parallel to the superiority of the New Covenant, of which He is the Mediator, to that which Moses mediated (Gal 3:19). Furthermore, the New Covenant is superior because it possesses **better promises.**

2. The promise of the New Covenant proclaimed in the Old Covenant. 8:7-13.

7. For if that first covenant had been faultless. The author again takes up the point which he had mentioned in 7:11, that the Law and the corresponding levitical priesthood could not bring men to the necessary perfection. Its fault was that it could not save (Rom 3:20), nor could it sanctify (Rom 7:12-24; 8:2-3). Yet, we must not assume that the Law has failed to do its work; for its work was not to save, but to reveal sin (Rom 3:19-20), making men aware of their sin and condemnation (Rom 4:15; Deut 27:26). The Law manifests sin's terrible nature (Rom 7:7-13) and extent (Rom 5:20). Furthermore, the Law was given to actively restrain sin (Gal 3:23; I Tim 1:9-10).

But the Law was never intended to be God's final program, or even His first. It was not first, for Paul says "it was added"; nor was it final, for it was only given ". . . till the seed should come to whom the promise was made . . ." (Gal 3:19, cf. Gal 3:23-25). God first made the promise (the Old Covenant) with Abraham. During the interval, before the promise was fulfilled, the Law was added until Christ should come. He has now come, and the Mosaic law has passed away. Scriptural proof is abundant (Rom 6:14; 7:1-6; Gal 3:10,13,19-25; I Cor 9:20; II Cor 3:11-13). Its removal, however, did not involve its destruction (Mt 5:17-18), but its fulfillment. Christ has attained the righteous goal toward which the Law was directed (Rom 10:4). He has paid its penalty on behalf of others, and so He has fulfilled its demand (Gal 3:10-13). Thus, the believer is now free from the Law and united with Christ (Rom 7:1-6; Gal 2:19-20; 3:19-25). The unsaved man, however, still lives under its convicting and condemning work (I Tim 1:8-11).

8-12. For finding fault with them. The fault lay not so much in the Law as it did in those who were to live by it. Despite Israel's failure, God promises that the day will come when He will **make a new covenant**. The content of verses 8-12 involves the quotation of one extended Old Testament passage (Jer 31:31-34). Many important truths can be gleaned from this passage regarding the New Covenant. First, during Jeremiah's day it was future and was something **new**. Second, it will be established **with the house of Israel and with the house of Judah**. The statement concerning those with whom this covenant is made is very precise. It involves the Jewish people at a time when they will again be united. When Jeremiah revealed this prophecy, Israel was scattered throughout the Middle East and Judah had just recently begun its exile in Babylon. This New Covenant made with the Jewish people would come after they were regathered to Israel (Jer 30:1-3) and after a time of severe tribulation identified as "the time of Jacob's trouble" (Jer 30:7). Third, it is unlike the covenant God made with Israel at Sinai (vs. 9). It is different in that the Old Covenant had been conditional. When Israel abandoned it, God also abandoned it and them.

Fourth, this New Covenant is based upon an inner, spiritual change within people. This covenant is not written upon stone, but **in their hearts** (cf. Ezk 36:26-27; II Cor 3:6-18). The next two principles of the covenant also involve its spiritual superiority over the Old Covenant. All who are involved in the New Covenant will personally **Know the Lord**. It is unlike the old, Mosaic covenant which included all according to a physical, national qualification. Further, this covenant involves a complete forgiveness for its people (vs. 12). The once-for-all sacrifice of its High Priest will remove the remembrance of sins. The daily sacrifices made it difficult for the Old Testament saint to forget his sins.

13. He hath made the first old. In that God calls this one **new**, the author concludes that God is also calling the former one **old**. And if it is old, it **decayeth** and is **ready to vanish away**. Even in Jeremiah's day (ca. 600 B.C.) the Law was already regarded as old. Yet, most amazingly, the Old Covenant prophesies the new and, thus, foretells its own demise.

The relation of the New Covenant to the gentile, church-age believer is commonly viewed in several ways. First, the amillen-

8 For finding fault with them, he saith, Behold, the days come, saith the Lord, when I will make a new covenant with the house of Israel and with the house of Judah:
9 Not according to the covenant that I made with their fathers in the day when I took them by the hand to lead them out of the land of Egypt; because they continued not in my covenant, and I regarded them not, saith the Lord.
10 For this is the covenant that I will make with the house of Israel after those days, saith the Lord; I will put my laws into their mind, and write them in their hearts: and I will be to them a God, and they shall be to me a people:
11 And they shall not teach every man his neighbour, and every man his brother, saying, Know the Lord: for all shall know me, from the least to the greatest.
12 For I will be merciful to their unrighteousness, and their sins and their iniquities will I remember no more.

13 In that he saith, A new covenant, he hath made the first old. Now that which decayeth and waxeth old is ready to vanish away.

nialists believe that the church replaces Israel; and so this covenant is fulfilled by the church. A second view proposes that this covenant, like Jeremiah 31 suggests, is for the nation of Israel alone. The third view suggests that two new covenants exist: one for Israel and one for the church. In the understanding of this writer, the best view is that there is one New Covenant, which God will one day fulfill with Israel and in which the church participates soteriologically today. In other words, though the covenant is not fulfilled, Christ's death has initiated its benefits for today for those who will some day share in its ultimate blessings when it is fulfilled with Israel. This view allows the witness of both the Old and New Testament to stand. Further, nowhere does Scripture speak of two new covenants, any more than it speaks of two old covenants. Paul was a minister to the churches of this New Covenant (II Cor 3:6). The ordinance of the Lord's Supper that has been given to the church is based upon the sacrifice of the New Covenant—Christ's death. Many references to the New Covenant within the New Testament clearly relate it to the church (12:23-24; I Cor 11:25; II Cor 3:6), and others also relate it to Israel (8:10; 12:23-24; Rom 11:27). As heirs of Christ's kingdom, we partake of the New Covenant's spiritual blessings today and in the future will share in its fulfillment with Israel. See Homer Kent, Jr., in *The Epistle to the Hebrews,* for a concise summary of these views (pp. 156-160).

3. The operation of the Old Covenant. 9:1-10.

Chapter 9 continues the theme of the superiority of Christ's ministry to the levitical priesthood and its Mosaic covenant. In chapter 8 Christ's tabernacle was declared to be the true tabernacle in heaven and its covenant to be the New Covenant that would replace the Mosaic. Now chapter 9 pronounces another fault (cf. 8:7; 7:11) within the Old Covenant, that is, its tabernacle involved a physical ritual which could not make men perfect (righteous). The old tabernacle would stand only until the true tabernacle would come. The first part of the chapter (vss. 1-10) describes the operation of the Old Covenant through its tabernacle; the second part (vss. 11-28) reveals the operation of the New.

a. The contents of its tabernacle. 9:1-5.

9:1-2. The first covenant had also ordinances. The author does not speak derogatorily of the Old Testament tabernacle. He gives it its rightful dignity, for it had been ordained by God and was a type of the heavenly tabernacle. God very precisely established its physical features and service. The fact that it was a **worldly** (Gr *kosmikon*) sanctuary does not reveal anything regarding its spiritual status, but rather its role in this world. It had been made by man's hands from earthly elements (cf. 8:2; 9:11).

The author then proceeds to describe its structure and furniture. Within its **sanctuary** (Gr *hagia*) were placed the **candlestick** and the **table** of **showbread**. Into this area, often called the Holy Place, the priests entered daily to minister before the Lord. The candlestick was a lampstand holding seven lamps (Ex 25:31-39; 37:17-24), which were trimmed daily (Ex 30:7-8). The table of showbread contained twelve loaves or cakes of bread that were replaced each Sabbath.

3-5. The tabernacle which is called the Holiest of all. Within the holy place behind the **second veil,** the Holy of Holies (Gr *hagia hagiōn*) was located. It was a fifteen-foot cube into which only the high priest was allowed to enter, and that only on the Day of Atonement.

Which had the golden censer. Two difficulties arise when seeking to interpret this phrase. First, what was the censer (Gr *thumiātērion*)? Second, could it have been located in the Holy of Holies? The word translated **censer** properly refers to a vessel

CHAPTER 9

THEN verily the first *covenant* had also ordinances of divine service, and a worldly sanctuary.

2 For there was a tabernacle made; the first, wherein *was* the candlestick, and the table, and the shewbread; which is called the sanctuary.

3 And after the second vail, the tabernacle which is called the Holiest of all;

4 Which had the golden censer, and the ark of the covenant overlaid round about with gold, wherein *was* the golden pot that had manna, and Aaron's rod that budded, and the tables of the covenant;

5 And over it the cherubims of glory

shadowing the mercyseat; of which we
cannot now speak particularly.

used for burning incense. It might properly describe either the
shovel (**censer**) for carrying the coals or the altar upon which the
coals were placed. Two factors support the usage of this word as
censer. First, the Septuagint uses this word to translate censer,
but never uses it for the incense altar (II Chr 26:19; Ezk 8:11).
Second, this translation avoids the difficulty of placing the
incense altar within the Holy of Holies. Several problems,
however, exist with this view. First, no mention is ever made in
the Scriptures of such a censer within the Holy of Holies.
Second, the censers are never described as golden. The third,
and biggest, problem with this view is that it only makes the
problem of the incense altar greater. For if this word refers to a
censer, then the golden incense altar is totally overlooked by our
author. The second view, which regards this as the incense altar,
presents fewer problems and has significant supporting factors.
First, this word (Gr *thumiatērion*) is used for the incense altar by
both early Jewish (Philo and Josephus) and Christian writers
(Clement of Alexandria and Origen). Second, the incense altar
was golden, even as this is (Ex 30:1-10). Third, as versed as he is
regarding the Old Testament and the tabernacle, our author
would not have overlooked the incense altar when describing the
tabernacle.

Since the *thumiatērion* properly refers to the golden incense
altar, how could the author locate it in the Holy of Holies? Quite
the contrary, the author does not explicitly say the altar was in
the Holy of Holies. When he refers to the incense altar, he
changes his language from **wherein was** in verse 2 to **which had**
in verse 4. The author's intent seems to be that while the Holy
Place had the candlestick and table within it, the Holy of Holies
only had the incense altar related to it. Exodus 30:6 similarly
stresses the close relation of the incense altar to the Holy of
Holies, even though it was not in it physically: ". . . thou shalt
put it before the veil that is by the ark of the testimony . . . ."
(see also Ex 40:5). The altar was located in the Holy Place so
incense could be placed upon fresh coals morning and evening.
It was located immediately in front of the Holy of Holies so that
its fragrance might enter into the Holy of Holies. Thus, its
physical location was in the Holy Place, but its liturgical function was with the Holy of Holies.

Within the Holy of Holies proper was the **ark of the covenant**
and the things stored within it. The **golden pot** of manna and
Aaron's rod were missing as early as Solomon's day (I Kgs 8:9).
The stone **tables** of the Law and the ark itself probably vanished
during the Babylonian captivity. Our author, however, is de-

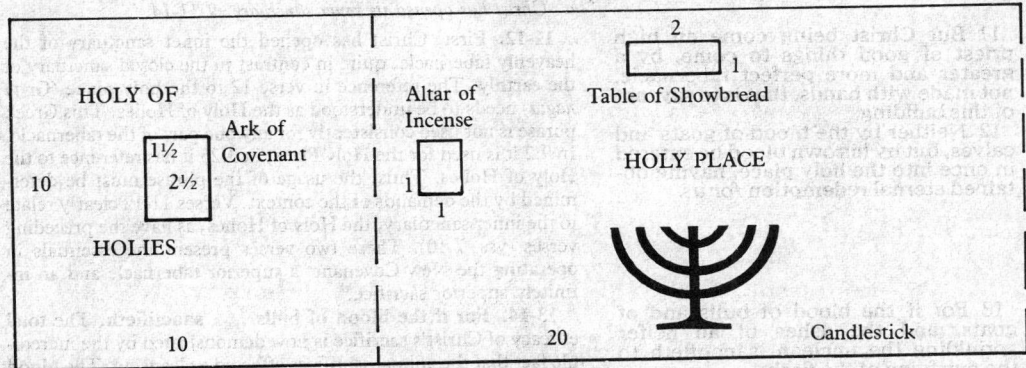

THE LAYOUT OF THE OLD TESTAMENT
TABERNACLE

Measurements are in cubits; a cubit = ca. 18 inches

scribing the tabernacle as it existed in Moses' day. Upon the ark or chest was a cover called the **mercy seat** which was overshadowed by cherubim. The Greek word used to translate **mercy seat** (Gr *hilastērion*) is used in the Septuagint to translate the Hebrew word (Heb *kapporet*, meaning covering). On the Day of Atonement the high priest would sprinkle blood upon the mercy seat, first for himself and then for the nation (Lev 16:14-15). The mercy seat was a covering for more than the ark alone. It became a place of covering for the sins of the people.

b. The closed chamber of its tabernacle. 9:6-10.

6-7. Accomplishing the service of God. The priests entered daily into the Holy Place to fulfill their continuous tasks. Morning and evening the lamps were trimmed and the coals with incense were placed upon the golden altar. The showbread was replaced weekly. But the Holy of Holies was a closed chamber into which the high priest ventured alone once a year with blood to sprinkle for his sins first, and then for the **errors of the people.** These errors (Gr *agnoēmatōn*) involved sins of ignorance and weakness in the flesh, such as lying, stealing, and adultery. There was no atonement for sins of defiance or deliberate rebellion against God (see Num 15:27-31 and Commentary notes on 10:26).

6 Now when these things were thus ordained, the priests went always into the first tabernacle, accomplishing the service *of God.*

7 But into the second *went* the high priest alone once every year, not without blood, which he offered for himself, and *for* the errors of the people:

8-10. The Holy Ghost this signifying. Through this typological picture of the tabernacle the Holy Spirit was showing that man did not possess direct and complete access to God (and would not) while the tabernacle and its law still stood. The tabernacle further served as a **figure** (Gr *parabolē*), a physical picture or symbol, for all to see that, just as access was not open into the Holy of Holies, access to God was not complete. Man's **conscience** was always left unsatisfied. Since he must return repeatedly and since he never knew what happened within the closed chambers, he could never feel he had been completely and permanently cleansed. These outward rituals could not meet the deep spiritual need of man, nor would they remain after the **time of reformation.** This **reformation** (Gr *diorthōsis*—used only here in the New Testament) involved a reconstruction, a reshaping of all that existed within Israel's religious structure. It might be called a "New Order" (Bruce, p. 197).

8 The Holy Ghost this signifying, that the way into the holiest of all was not yet made manifest, while as the first tabernacle was yet standing:

9 Which *was* a figure for the time then present, in which were offered both gifts and sacrifices, that could not make him that did the service perfect, as pertaining to the conscience;

10 *Which stood* only in meats and drinks, and divers washings, and carnal ordinances, imposed *on them* until the time of reformation.

4. The operation of the New Covenant. 9:11-10:18.

In chapter 9 the author declares the superiority of the New Covenant to the Old by focusing upon their respective tabernacles. The tabernacle of the Old was earthly and symbolic; but, most importantly, its inner sanctuary was a closed chamber (vss. 1-10). Beginning at verse 11, the author demonstrates the superiority of the New Covenant by expressing four things which Christ has done so as to make it superior.

a. Christ has opened its inner sanctuary. 9:11-14.

11-12. First, Christ has opened the inner sanctuary of the heavenly tabernacle, quite in contrast to the closed sanctuary of the earthly. The reference in verse 12 to **the holy place** (Gr *ta hagia*) needs to be understood as the Holy of Holies. This Greek phrase is not used consistently for any one part of the tabernacle. In 9:2 it is used for the Holy Place; in 9:25 it has reference to the Holy of Holies. Thus, the usage of the phrase must be determined by the demands of the context. Verses 11-12 clearly relate to the inner sanctuary, the Holy of Holies, as have the preceding verses (vss. 7-10). These two verses present the essentials in operating the New Covenant: a superior tabernacle and an infinitely superior sacrifice.

11 But Christ being come an high priest of good things to come, by a greater and more perfect tabernacle, not made with hands, that is to say, not of this building;

12 Neither by the blood of goats and calves, but by his own blood he entered in once into the holy place, having obtained eternal redemption *for us.*

13-14. For if the blood of bulls . . . sanctifieth. The total efficacy of Christ's sacrifice is now demonstrated by the incredible fact that the animal sacrifices effected a cleansing. The **blood of bulls and of goats** obviously makes reference to the activities

13 For if the blood of bulls and of goats, and the ashes of an heifer sprinkling the unclean, sanctifieth to the purifying of the flesh:

14 How much more shall the blood of Christ, who through the eternal Spirit offered himself without spot to God, purge your conscience from dead works to serve the living God?

within the Holy of Holies on the Day of Atonement (Lev 16:5ff.), when the high priest sprinkled first the blood of a bull for his sins and then the blood of a goat for the sins of the people. **The ashes of a heifer** refers to the ceremony involving the red heifer (Num 19). A heifer would be taken outside the camp, killed, and then burned. As it was burning, the priest would throw cedar, hyssop, and scarlet wool upon it. Afterwards, the ashes would be gathered and stored outside the city. Whenever anyone became ceremonially unclean because of contact with a dead body, these ashes would be mixed with water to constitute a "water of separation" or "water for impurity" (NASB) and sprinkled upon this one **to the purifying of the flesh.** "Perhaps this particular practice was selected because it illustrates so clearly the largely ceremonial nature of the purity provided by Old Testament sacrifices" (Kent, p. 172).

How much more shall the blood of Christ . . . purge your conscience. If the rituals of the Old Testament tabernacle possessed merit, even as an outward, ceremonial cleansing, how much superior the merit of Christ's shed blood will be! If God accepted the former ritual as a purifying of the flesh, how much more will God be satisfied by the sacrifice of His Son! He accepts it so completely that it inwardly regenerates the individual and purifies his conscience (cf. 9:9). There exists a peace of conscience because there is now peace with God (cf. Rom 5:1). Access to God within the Holy of Holies through Christ's sacrifice brings peace with God.

b. Christ is the Mediator of the New Covenant. 9:15-22.

15 And for this cause he is the mediator of the new testament, that by means of death, for the redemption of the transgressions *that were* under the first testament, they which are called might receive the promise of eternal inheritance.

15. For this cause he is the mediator of the new testament. Because of His blood, His death, Christ has accomplished what the Old Covenant could not. Therefore, He has been set as the Mediator for a New Covenant. His sacrifice has achieved what the many sacrifices of the Old Testament could not, for He effectuated **the redemption of the transgressions that were under the first testament.** The Old Testament sacrifices could not take away sin (10:4); they merely made an atonement, a covering for sin. Christ's sacrifice expiated all those past sins that had received atonement. The Old Testament sacrifices might be compared to the writing of a check. The paper upon which it is written is practically worthless. Yet, it is used and accepted in place of money, since it is backed by what has been deposited in the bank. Christ's death was deposited from the foundation of the world as that which backed the Old Testament sacrifices. With Christ's death upon the cross, the deposit was released and all the past checks were honored and paid.

16 For where a testament *is*, there must also of necessity be the death of the testator.
17 For a testament *is* of force after men are dead: otherwise it is of no strength at all while the testator liveth.

16-17. The author now avails himself of the natural realm to provide an illustration of a will or **testament.** The word is the same as that used in 8:6-7, for a covenant (Gr *diathēkē*), but its usage here is obviously different (see the discussion at 7:22). The usual Greek usage of this word (rare in New Testament usage, however) is that of a will. Such is its usage here, for this testament required the death of its maker. The Old Testament covenant may or may not require a sacrifice. A will, however, requires the death of its own maker. Indeed, a will can be changed many times, so long as its maker lives; but his death sets it in force. The nature of Christ's death satisfies the requirements of both a will and a covenant, and it may thus be described as both (ch. 8—a covenant; here—a will).

18 Whereupon neither the first *testament* was dedicated without blood.
19 For when Moses had spoken every precept to all the people according to the law, he took the blood of calves and of goats, with water, and scarlet wool, and hyssop, and sprinkled both the book, and all the people,
20 Saying, This *is* the blood of the tes-

18-22. Whereupon neither the first testament was dedicated without blood. Verse 18 establishes the thought for the next several verses. Even the Old Covenant was activated by death and the shedding of blood. At the confirmation of the Law, Moses ratified it by sprinkling both the Book of the Covenant and the people with blood, saying, **This is the blood of the testament** (cf. Ex 24:8; and Christ's words in establishing the New Testament, Mt 26:28). Likewise, when the **tabernacle**

tament which God hath enjoined unto you.

21 Moreover he sprinkled with blood both the tabernacle, and all the vessels of the ministry.

22 And almost all things are by the law purged with blood; and without shedding of blood is no remission.

23 It was therefore necessary that the patterns of things in the heavens should be purified with these; but the heavenly things themselves with better sacrifices than these.

24 For Christ is not entered into the holy places made with hands, which are the figures of the true; but into heaven itself, now to appear in the presence of God for us:

25 Nor yet that he should offer himself often, as the high priest entereth into the holy place every year with blood of others;

26 For then must he often have suffered since the foundation of the world: but now once in the end of the world hath he appeared to put away sin by the sacrifice of himself.

27 And as it is appointed unto men once to die, but after this the judgment:

28 So Christ was once offered to bear the sins of many; and unto them that look for him shall he appear the second time without sin unto salvation.

was finished, both it and its **vessels** were dedicated by the sprinkling of blood. No explicit record of this sprinkling is recorded in the Old Testament, but Exodus 40:9 does speak of a complete anointing of its parts with oil. Later, in Numbers 7:1, reference is made to Moses' act of anointing and sanctifying it. This latter passage may be the source of our author's seeing the anointing with oil and the sanctifying with blood. On the basis of the preceding verses, the author concludes two things in verse 22. The law seems to require that everything be purged with blood. And there is no **remission** (Gr *aphesis*), forgiveness, without the shedding of blood.

c. Christ is the perfect sacrifice. 9:23-28.

23-24. The perfect nature of Christ's sacrifice is observed first from the fact that he purified heavenly things by means of His sacrifice. As the lesser tabernacle needed lesser sacrifices, so the heavenly tabernacle needed a perfect sacrifice. Since the **patterns** (Gr *hypodeigmata*) or examples of the heavenly things need purification, it might be easy to imagine that the heavenly tabernacle is tainted and needs cleansing. To suppose that satanic defilement, or even God's wrath, necessitated a purification of the heavens is to miss the point of the context. Even the earthly tabernacle itself did *not* need cleansing. It was those who approached it who needed the cleansing. Further, the comparison which our author has just presented involved the consecration of the tabernacle when it was instituted. For a comprehensive presentation of this heavenly purification, see Philip E. Hughes, *A Commentary on the Epistle to the Hebrews*, pp. 379-382.

Verse 24 identifies the true **holy places** as **heaven itself**. This would dispute the notion that heaven contains a tabernacle corresponding in appearance to that which Moses was commanded to build. Heaven itself is the fulfillment, or archetype, of that pattern.

On behalf of those Jewish Christians who had difficulty relinquishing the ceremony and ritual of Judaism from their past, Christ has provided a superior ritual. Though the physical embellishments of the church are plain and simple, the symbolism of our Saviour is superior to all. The priest of Christianity is the Son of God Himself. The sacrifice is the Lamb of God. The tabernacle into which the shed blood has been taken is heaven itself. And beyond any parallelism, we, the people, have been taken into the Holy of Holies itself, possessing complete access to God.

25-26. A second quality that makes Christ's sacrifice perfect is that which has often been stated and will extensively be treated in the first half of chapter 10—it is once-for-all. If Christ's sacrifice, of which the animal sacrifices were a type, had to be repeated, it could not be perfect. And if a continuation of His sacrifice was necessary, then His sacrifice would have had to start at the **foundation of the world** (e.g., Gen 3:21).

27-28. As it is appointed unto men once to die. The relation of verse 27 to its context is often dismissed in order to stress the certainty of man's future judgment. It is axiomatic that man dies once. Exceptions do exist: Enoch and Elijah of the Old Testament, the New Testament saints who will be alive at Christ's return who will never die, or Lazarus and others who have been raised from the dead and died twice. But no exceptions concerning God's judgment can be cited. There is no reincarnation; every person gets one chance to prepare for God's judgment.

Yet the full significance of verse 27 cannot be seen apart from verse 28. **As it is appointed unto men once to die. . . . So Christ was once offered to bear the sins of many** (cf. Isa 53:12). The author is clearly presenting a comparison. As it is with man, so it was with Christ. As man can only die once, so the man Christ could only die once as a sacrifice. His relation to humanity would be marred if he would have to die more than once. Similarly, a second comparison seems evident. Beyond death there exists another reality. For man it is the reality of appearing for judgment; for Christ it is the certainty of appearing with deliverance from condemnation **unto them that look for him.**

Three "appearings" of Christ are noted in this paragraph. Verse 24 states that he now appears in heaven and on our behalf. Verse 26 speaks of His former appearance on earth to bear sin. His next appearing is that future coming when our salvation is brought to its complete realization. (The Greek verbs used for the "appearings" are, however, three different words.) This last appearing is **without sin** in the sense that He will not need to deal with sin again (Hughes, p. 387).

d. Christ's offering is once-for-all. 10:1-18.

The fourth feature of the New Covenant to be emphasized is Christ's once-for-all offering. The author has frequently stated this feature in the preceding chapters (cf. 7:27; 9:12, 26, 28), but now it becomes the focal point of the discussion.

10:1-4. The truth of Christ's one-time sacrifice is emphasized by means of relief—a distinct contrast with the Mosaic system. The Mosaic system is first described as a **shadow** and not **the very image.** This figure was used earlier at 8:5. There, however, the tabernacle itself was described as a shadow of the heavenly tabernacle; here the levitical sacrifices are designated as a shadow of Christ's one-time offering. The two are not of the same essence or **image** (Gr eikōn); the later sacrifice is the reality of which the former was a mere shadow (cf. Col 2:16-17). The sacrificial system of the Old Testament was planned and ordained of God; and it fulfilled its temporary, imperfect role. Its role, nevertheless, was that of a picture and prophecy of Christ's later, totally efficacious, sacrifice.

The repetitious nature of the Mosaic system serves as another means for highlighting the once-for-all sacrifice of Christ. Those sacrifices had to be offered **year by year continually.** They served as a reminder that sin needed continued cleansing. If the levitical system had cleansed the Old Testament people, then, according to verse 2, they would have had **no more conscience of sins** and would have ceased to sacrifice. This must not be misconstrued to suggest that once one has been born again he will have no remembrance or consciousness of sin in his life. What is true is that the Christian knows peace with God (Rom 5:1) and peace from the guilt of sin. He must still deal with daily sin (I Jn 1:6-10). As Dods aptly states: "The sinner once cleansed may, no doubt, be again defiled and experience a renewed consciousness of guilt. But in the writer's view this consciousness is at once absorbed in the consciousness of his original cleansing" (Dods, p. 342). Thus, the guilt of sin is removed for all time for the New Testament saint. For the Old Testament saint that guilt had to be removed yearly.

Yet, one must not imagine that there was no forgiveness possible for the Old Testament sinner. The Scriptures clearly state otherwise (Lev 4:20,26,31,35). What the sinner did lack was a full and final cleansing; he did not know the assurance of permanent forgiveness. As Kent says: "Day of Atonement offerings brought forgiveness 'up to date,' but subsequent sins required further sacrifices and the passing of another year necessitated the cycle to begin again" (p. 185).

5-10. When he cometh into the world. The author sees further proof of the superiority of Christ's one-time sacrifice to the many sacrifices of the levitical system within a prophecy from Psalm 40:6-7. The words of David are used typologically of Christ as a conversation between Himself and the Father. When Christ came (referring to His entire incarnation, rather than

CHAPTER 10

FOR the law having a shadow of good things to come, and not the very image of the things, can never with those sacrifices which they offered year by year continually make the comers thereunto perfect.

2 For then would they not have ceased to be offered? because that the worshippers once purged should have had no more conscience of sins.

3 But in those sacrifices there is a remembrance again made of sins every year.

4 For it is not possible that the blood of bulls and of goats should take away sins.

5 Wherefore when he cometh into the world, he saith, Sacrifice and offering thou wouldest not, but a body hast thou prepared me:

6 In burnt offerings and sacrifices for sin thou hast had no pleasure.

7 Then said I, Lo, I come (in the vol-

2563

ume of the book it is written of me,) to do thy will, O God.

8 Above when he said, Sacrifice and offering and burnt offerings and *offering* for sin thou wouldest not, neither hadst pleasure *therein;* which are offered by the law;

9 Then said he, Lo, I come to do thy will, O God. He taketh away the first, that he may establish the second.

10 By the which will we are sanctified through the offering of the body of Jesus Christ once *for all.*

11 And every priest standeth daily ministering and offering oftentimes the same sacrifices, which can never take away sins:

12 But this man, after he had offered one sacrifice for sins for ever, sat down on the right hand of God;

13 From henceforth expecting till his enemies be made his footstool.

14 For by one offering he hath perfected for ever them that are sanctified.

15 *Whereof* the Holy Ghost also is a witness to us: for after that he had said before,

16 This *is* the covenant that I will make with them after those days, saith the Lord, I will put my laws into their hearts, and in their minds will I write them;

17 And their sins and iniquities will I remember no more.

18 Now where remission of these *is,* *there is* no more offering for sin.

merely His birth) he said, **Sacrifice and offering thou wouldest not, but a body hast thou prepared me.** The quotation is taken from the Septuagint and, at first sight, appears to fail to express the Hebrew. In Hebrew the last clause reads: "mine ears has thou opened." Though "body" is used here instead of "ears," neither the Septuagint nor the author of Hebrews should be regarded as corrupting or even weakening the meaning of the Hebrew. Rather, they heighten its meaning. And, as Owens suggests, synecdoche is being used, that is, the substitution of a part for the whole. The use of the ears for the body is fitting here, since the context involves the hearing of and obedience to the will of the Father. Ears require the reality of a body (John Owen, *Hebrews: The Epistle of Warning,* p. 189). God prepared a body for Christ, inasmuch as levitical sacrifices could not ultimately fulfill God's **will.** His will was to sanctify men through the once-for-all offering of the **body** of Christ (vs. 10).

11-14. Every priest standeth daily ministering. The levitical priest never finished his work. The symbolism of the tabernacle involves no element that suggests rest or completion. These priests never sat in the tabernacle. They stood and offered the same sacrifices day after day. But after the Son had offered His one sacrifice, He **sat down** and is now waiting at God's right hand. His work as a priest offering sacrifices is accomplished by His one offering. He now awaits to function as King. Verses 12 and 13 are a quotation of Ps 110:1 (the author's third from that passage; cf. 1:3,13).

Christ's once-for-all sacrifice has **perfected for ever them that are sanctified.** The use of **perfected** (Gr *teteleiōken*) involves the completed cleansing of regeneration (Tit 3:5). This verse (vs. 14) reveals the twofold nature of salvation. The believer possesses a positional, judicial standing of righteousness and, second, a remaining need for practical, progressive holiness. Three factors within this verse make **perfected** absolute, suggesting the eternal security of the believer. The word itself (Gr *teleioō*) involves completion, the bringing of something to its end. Second, the use of the Greek perfect tense suggests that the perfection has been accomplished and its effects are continuing. Third, the modifier, **for ever,** expresses security for the believer.

The need, however, of a progressive sanctification is expressed by the word **sanctified** (Gr *hagiazomenous*). The use of the present participle implies the thought of a sanctification that is continuing, rather than completed. There is an initial, or positional, sanctification involved in regeneration (I Cor 1:2; 6:1). Equally, there is a progressive sanctification by which the Holy Spirit continually maintains and strengthens the holiness imparted in regeneration (Rom 6:19; II Cor 7:1; I Thess 4:3). Finally, there exists for the people of God an ultimate or completed sanctification whereby we will be freed from even the very presence of sin within our lives (I Thess 5:23). Even though the believer's sanctification is still in progress, yet because of Christ's once-for-all sacrifice, he stands eternally secure and perfect because of Christ's righteousness (II Cor 5:21).

15-18. The Holy Ghost also is a witness to us. The Holy Spirit adds His testimony to what Christ has just said. Jeremiah 31:33-34 is quoted again (cf. 8:8-12). The institution of the New Covenant promises the removal of sins. Christ's one-time sacrifice has fulfilled that promise. **Their sins . . . will I remember no more.** This does not suggest that part of God's omniscience is lacking. Rather, He no longer remembers it against us. Christ has taken our sin upon Himself; thus, the Father will not hold it against us who have turned to Christ's redemption (I Pet 2:24). See J. Brown, *An Exposition of the Epistle to the Hebrews,* pp. 458-461, for an excellent discussion on the "assurance of faith."

5. *The fourth warning passage: Do not turn back. 10:19-39.*

In light of Christ's superiority to every aspect of the Old Testament system (its covenant, its tabernacle, its priesthood and sacrifices), the readers are warned not to turn back to the former ways. In this fourth warning (see 2:1-4; 3:7-4:13; 5:11-6:20 for earlier warnings) the critical danger of turning from Christ's once-for-all, perfect sacrifice is emphatically proclaimed. The warning consists of three parts. First, exhortations involving the new access through Christ are pronounced; then the warning is sounded, followed by a second series of exhortations.

a. *Exhortations to use the new access. 10:19-25.*

19-23. The author begins his practical exhortations on the basis of Christ's priestly work, as the inferential conjunction, **therefore,** indicates. Before he pronounces the three explicit exhortations of this passage, he restates in summary fashion that which Christ has accomplished for the believer (vss. 19-21). We have direct access into the very holy place of God by means of **the blood of Jesus** taken within the veil by our priest, Jesus Himself. This access is **living;** for, unlike the lifeless animal which made the access of the high priest in behalf of the people possible, this access is made possible by the resurrected and living Lamb of God. And the imagery connecting Christ's **flesh** with the **veil** is fitting, when we remember that the veil into the earthly sanctuary was rent in two by God, simultaneously with the breaking of Christ's flesh (Mt 27:50-51). Christ's sacrificial death removed the barrier of the veil, making access possible.

Verse 22 contains the first exhortation: **Let us draw near.** This verb (Gr *proserchomai*) can simply mean to come to. Yet, in this chapter its meaning is semitechnical and refers to the approach of the worshiper to God, which is a common usage in the Septuagint (Moulton and Milligan, *The Vocabulary of the Greek New Testament,* p. 547). No doubt, the author is contrasting this use with his usage in verse 1: **For the law . . . can never with those sacrifices which they offered year by year continually make the comers thereunto** (Gr *proserchomai*) **perfect.** What the law could not do, Christ has now accomplished. Therefore, **Let us draw near.**

The author next proceeds to tell the readers how they are to approach God. He first uses two prepositions to show the present, subjective qualities that God expects: **with a true heart** and **in full assurance of faith.** He then uses two perfect passive participles that manifest the completed, objective work which God has provided: **having our hearts sprinkled from an evil conscience and our bodies washed with pure water.** As the sprinkling of blood and the washing with sacrificial ashes (cf. 9:13-14) ceremonially cleansed those under the old system, so Christ's sacrifice has sprinkled us in regard to our hearts and washed us in regard to our bodies.

The second exhortation is contained in verse 23. **Let us hold fast the profession of our faith without wavering.** This is an exhortation for endurance. First come; now stay. The reason, God is faithful in regard to His promise.

24-25. The third exhortation presents the greatest problems and also has the closest relationship to the warning which follows. The exhortation itself reads: **And let us consider one another to provoke unto love and to good works.** The word translated **provoke** (Gr *paroxysmos*) usually has a negative sense as is witnessed by its only other New Testament usage at Acts 15:39. The bad relationship between Paul and Barnabas occasioned by John Mark is expressed by this word: "And the contention was so sharp between them, that they departed asunder one from the other . . .". The positive connotation that this word possesses means to stir up, as our present context de-

19 Having therefore, brethren, boldness to enter into the holiest by the blood of Jesus,
20 By a new and living way, which he hath consecrated for us, through the vail, that is to say, his flesh;
21 And *having* an high priest over the house of God;
22 Let us draw near with a true heart in full assurance of faith, having our hearts sprinkled from an evil conscience, and our bodies washed with pure water.
23 Let us hold fast the profession of *our* faith without wavering; (for he *is* faithful that promised;)

24 And let us consider one another to provoke unto love and to good works:
25 Not forsaking the assembling of ourselves together, as the manner of some *is;* but exhorting *one another:* and so much the more, as ye see the day approaching.

mands. It is easy to stir up hate and godless deeds; it takes much more to stir up another to love and good works.

Verse 25 continues to develop the exhortation by the use of two participles: **Not forsaking the assembling of ourselves together** and **exhorting one another.** These two participles seem to function modally, showing that the manner in which one is to consider others is his "stirring up." One is negative; the other is positive. The positive manner involves encouraging (Gr *parakaleō*) one another. The negative to be avoided concerns **forsaking the assembling.** One very important reason Christians are to assemble is for reciprocal encouragement, strengthening, and stirring up that they can gain from one another (cf. Col 3:12-16). Without such assembling all this is impossible.

But the author has more than mere erratic attendance in mind. Complete separation from the assembly of the believers is involved. Several elements clearly demonstrate this point. First, the word used in verse 25 is severe (*egkataleipō*). It is an intensified form, meaning to leave behind, forsake, abandon, or desert. This is more than just an inconsistency. Second, the close positioning of this action with the warning of no more sacrifice (vs. 26) demands some severe negative action. The use of **for** in verse 26 indicates that the warning served as the basis for one or more of the preceding exhortations. This third and closest exhortation would certainly be one that related to the warning. Third, the historical situation of these Jewish Christians, which has already been described, involved something severe.

Exactly what is involved in the expression **forsaking the assembling** may be difficult to state precisely. Arthur Pink, following John Owen's understanding, states that "there is a synecdoche (a part put for the whole) in the word 'assembling,' and it is put for the whole worship of Christ" (p. 607). The assembling of the believers is often an outward indication of the inner condition. If a man's faith will not get him to church, it is doubtful if it will get him to heaven. Further, the importance of assembling is both subjective and objective. It benefits the individual with spiritual stability and growth. It benefits objectively by its positive effect on others. The church meeting is far more than a place for one to be entertained or to hear, for these can be accomplished through radio or television. The purpose for the assembling is for participation in worship and fellowship and with one another. Attendance is necessary. The church is a body interacting (I Cor 12:14-27), not merely a granary for dispensing food. The assembling of the believers is one measure that indicates the condition of the heart. Thus, the author encourages the readers not to desert the assembly.

And so much the more, as ye see the day approaching. For these Jewish readers this day may have involved either the day wherein the Jewish nation would be destroyed (A.D. 70) or the second coming of Jesus. In fact, they may have viewed them as two phases of one event. For us, it involves obedience in the light of Christ's second coming.

Lenski aptly summarizes these three exhortations in the following words: "The first admonition deals with the heart, the second with the mouth (confession), the third with conduct. The first with God, the second with the world, the third with the church" (p. 352).

b. The warning. 10:26-31.

These verses, which pronounce the fourth warning of this epistle, contain no promises or exhortations, but only the severity and meaning of the warning. The contents seem better fitted for topical analysis, rather than strict chronological presentation; and so they will be presented under the following three topics: the nature of the sin, the content of the warning, and the judgment of the sin. Verses 26, 28-29 will aid in describing the sin to which the author is referring.

26 For if we sin wilfully after that we have received the knowledge of the truth, there remaineth no more sacrifice for sins,

27 But a certain fearful looking for of judgment and fiery indignation, which shall devour the adversaries.

28 He that despised Moses' law died without mercy under two or three witnesses:

29 Of how much sorer punishment, suppose ye, shall he be thought worthy, who hath trodden under foot the Son of God, and hath counted the blood of the covenant, wherewith he was sanctified, an unholy thing, and hath done despite unto the Spirit of grace?

26-29. In verse 26 we read the statement: **For if we sin willfully.** Westcott notes two distinct elements within this phrase: voluntariness, that is, a realized consciousness of the sin, and the habitual practice of the sin (pp. 327-328). The verbal expression employed in this clause is a circumstantial participle used conditionally inasmuch as that form best fits the context, as was true in several earlier warning passages (2:3; 6:6-8). The participle is in the present tense, implying that the act is habitual, as Westcott noted. The use of the adverb **willfully** reveals that this sin is deliberate and intentional. This is not a sin of ignorance or weakness; it is by choice.

The nature of this sin fits perfectly with the illustration given in verse 28: **He that despised Moses' law died without mercy under two or three witnesses.** The indefinite pronoun (Gr *tis*), translated **he** in our version, indicates that what is to follow applies to every one. Thus, the use of **despised** (Gr *atheteō*) for the one who rejects the law of Moses is "plainly not every violator of that Law; since for many of its violations there were expiatory sacrifices" (Brown, p. 471). The author seems to be alluding to a particular rejection of the Law, which is recorded in Deuteronomy 17:2-7. These verses record that upon the evidence of two or three witnesses, death by stoning was the punishment for rejection (Deut 17:5-6). The sin of rejection in this passage is apostasy—going after and serving false gods (Deut 17:2).

On the basis of the description of the sin of apostasy in verse 28, the word **willfully** in verse 26 could hark back to Numbers 15:22-31. Numbers 15:30-31 easily parallel the situation in Hebrews. Numbers 15:27-31 reads: "And if any soul sin through ignorance, then he shall bring a she goat . . . . And the priest shall make an atonement for the soul that sinneth ignorantly . . . . But the soul that doeth aught presumptuously . . . that soul shall be cut off from among his people. Because he hath despised the word of the LORD . . . that soul shall utterly be cut off; his iniquity shall be upon him."

When one willingly or defiantly (lit., with a high hand—Heb *beyad ramad*) disobeyed God, there was no sacrifice for such apostasy. He must die. This is the nature of the sin of Hebrews 10:26.

Verse 29 further pictures this sin as parallel with the apostasy of Numbers 15. This sinner would tread **under foot the Son of God,** consider his shed blood as **unholy,** and insult **the Spirit of grace.** He is equal with the one who would raise his hand in defiance of God. This one despises both the person of Jesus and His ministry as priest. He will not allow the Spirit to work within him. Brown aptly describes the sin of this one: "He treats with the greatest conceivable indignity two divine Persons—the Son and the Spirit of God; he 'tramples under foot' Him whom angels adore; he counts polluted and polluting that which is the sole source of sanctification" (p. 475).

The grammatical forms of verse 29 are very significant. The three particular, defiant sins are expressed by three aorist participles used adjectivally. All three relate to the phrase, **shall he be thought worthy.** The fact that this sin is described by aorist participles does not suggest that it has already been committed. Aorist participles normally express antecedent, and possibly even simultaneous, time. Since the main verb is in the future tense, the aorist participles can appropriately be translated with the word "would." Verse 29 might fittingly be rendered, "By how much worse punishment do you think he will be deemed worthy who would tread under foot the Son of God, and would reckon the blood of the covenant as common by which he was sanctified, and would insult the Spirit of grace?" The one who would commit such sin would be guilty of apostasy—nothing less.

After expressing the nature of this sin, verses 26-27 describe the twofold nature of the warning. They set forth the negative condition that **there remaineth no more sacrifice for sins,** and the positive prospect of **a certain fearful looking for of judgment and fiery indignation.** The one who would commit this sin of apostasy can know no more sacrifice for his sin.

One element that demands our attention at this point concerns the possibility and reality of this sin. Had some born-again believers apostatized and thus been removed from God's saving grace? Is the author implying that one can lose his salvation? Several facts disallow that supposition. First, as has already been stated, the participles in verse 29 by no means imply that some believer has indeed trampled **under foot the Son of God,** etc. Rather, if one would do this, then certain judgment would fall. The author does not say believers have apostatized, nor does he say they would (Pink, p. 612). Second, the author includes himself in the warning—**For if we sin willfully.** Surely the author was not on the road to apostasy when he wrote this epistle. He makes that clear in verse 39: **But we are not of them who draw back unto perdition; but of them that believe to the saving of the soul.** He describes his readers as saved. Even his description of the apostate concerns one who has a genuine knowledge of Christ. Maybe the author includes himself to soften the blow and also at the same time to broaden the scope. All must beware. By placing himself under the warning, as he has done in all of the preceding warnings, he demonstrates that they are for the saved, not the unsaved. Yet, here, as in chapter 6, the author clearly does not say that anyone has committed this sin. He always describes what would happen, not what has happened. He is describing a hypothetical situation. The severe admonition of this warning, and all others in Scripture, is God's means to ensure our perseverance.

The final topic within the warning is the judgment that would be poured out. This judgment occupies the majority of these verses, and its emphasis is upon the severity and certainty of the judgment.

The severity of the judgment is demonstrated in verses 27-29. The author describes it as **a certain fearful looking for of judgment.** The author's carefully chosen words (Gr *tis phobera edochē*) suggest an indescribable, terrifying expectation (Brown, p. 469). In verses 28-29 the author uses comparison to describe the degree of its severity. Under the law of Moses, everyone who rejected the law by apostatizing died without pity. In verse 29 the comparison which expresses the severity here is stated: **Of how much sorer punishment, suppose ye, shall he be thought worthy, who hath trodden under foot the son of God. . . ?**

At times some express the idea that God's punishment ought to be milder during this age of grace. They entertain the notion that under law judgment was more severe. This verse should shatter that impression. It harmonizes with what Jesus Christ often taught. The man who has greater revelation will receive greater judgment (Mt 11:20-24); and to whom much is given, much is required (Lk 12:48).

30-31. The certainty of this judgment is expressed in verses 30-31. The author first states that one's knowledge of God ought to strengthen, not weaken, his awareness of God's inevitable judgment. His divine character demands justice and holiness; His divine attributes can perform punishment. To emphasize this certainty, he quotes two statements from Deuteronomy 32:35-36: **Vengeance belongeth unto me, I will recompense, saith the Lord** and **The Lord shall judge his people.** The most significant fact concerning these two quotations from Deuteronomy involves their historical setting. This was Moses' final warning to the Israelites before he died and they entered the Promised Land. Our author pronounces this same warning of God's certain judgment for his Jewish readers. He then concludes this fourth warning of the epistle by stating, **It is a fearful**

30 For we know him that hath said, Vengeance *belongeth* unto me, I will recompense, saith the Lord. And again, The Lord shall judge his people.
31 *It is* a fearful thing to fall into the hands of the living God.

thing to fall into the hands of the living God. God is still living and active; His judgment is certain and severe. For believers, our God is a God of love and mercy; for the defiant, He is a God to be dreaded and feared.

c. Exhortations to recall former victories. 10:32-39.

The connection between the following exhortations and the warning itself is not as close as it was between the preceding exhortations and warning. The **for** of verse 26 attests to this. Those exhortations were based upon the warning. Now the author makes two final exhortations and concludes with a note of confidence in his readers.

32-34. The first of these two exhortations enjoins the readers to remember the sufferings they endured shortly after they were saved: **call to remembrance.** They had been made a **gazing-stock** (Gr *theatizō*), and they had lost their possessions. They had sympathized and associated with others who had experienced even greater trials. The textual support for the reading of verse 34 as **me in my bonds** is very weak. The verse probably refers to their companions who were put in bonds or in prison, rather than to an imprisonment of the author. Through all this they had **endured** with joy and with a knowledge that they possessed something far greater than that which they had lost. They had done it before; they must do it now.

35-38. In the second exhortation the author encourages them to hang on to the boldness they have known: **Cast not away therefore your confidence.** A just man must **live by faith** (cf. Hab 2:4; Rom 1:17; Gal 3:11). God will reward that endurance, but the reward cannot come without the perseverance.

32 But call to remembrance the former days, in which, after ye were illuminated, ye endured a great fight of afflictions;
33 Partly, whilst ye were made a gazingstock both by reproaches and afflictions; and partly, whilst ye became companions of them that were so used.
34 For ye had compassion of me in my bonds, and took joyfully the spoiling of your goods, knowing in yourselves that ye have in heaven a better and an enduring substance.
35 Cast not away therefore your confidence, which hath great recompence of reward.
36 For ye have need of patience, that, after ye have done the will of God, ye might receive the promise.
37 For yet a little while, and he that shall come will come, and will not tarry.
38 Now the just shall live by faith: but if *any man* draw back, my soul shall have no pleasure in him.
39 But we are not of them who draw back unto perdition; but of them that believe to the saving of the soul.

39. Verse 39 expresses the author's confidence and assurance concerning the recipients. **But we are not of them who draw back unto perdition; but of them that believe to the saving of the soul.** They had been disillusioned and were indifferent, but, due to their former action, the author expresses confidence, just as he had done in the third warning (6:9-10). Nairne notes: "As in chapter six so here, a severe warning is followed by encouragement based on the remembrance of former faithfulness" (Alexander Nairne, *The Epistle of Priesthood*, p. 384). The form and content of the warnings of chapters 6 and 10 are so similar that each must be understood in the light of the other.

In both the preceding and the following contexts, the author has spoken of the recipients as true believers. In the former he exhorted his readers to claim and continue in what they possess. All three former exhortations employ the present tense, suggesting a continuation of action. In the following context the author speaks of them as believers who have already severely suffered for Christ. In both he identified himself with his readers (vss. 19 and 39). Therefore, it would be strange if the warning passage between them would not somehow involve these same believers also. The warning is spoken to believers. Yet, the sin described and the judgment pronounced could only involve an unsaved person. Thus, the warning is hypothetical and is designed to stress the severity of sin and the need for perseverance to believers.

II. EXHORTATIONS BASED UPON EXAMPLE. 11:1-13:25.

The first 10 chapters contained exhortation based upon the person and ministry of Christ. In chapters 1-7 He was portrayed as better than the prophets (1:1-3), than the angels (chs. 1-2), than Moses and Joshua (chs. 3-4), and the Levitical priests (chs. 5-7). In chapters 8-10 his ministry was described as better than the old system because of His New Covenant, His heavenly tabernacle, and His once-for-all sacrifice. Starting at chapter 11, the motif shifts from doctrinal themes to practical examples. The exhortations which follow are not so much to teach doctrine as they are from the example and practice of others.

A. Past Triumphs Through Faith. 11:1-40.

The first examples for living which our author sets forth demonstrate faith—the faith needed to please God during Old Testament times. The author has just finished exhorting his readers to patience and faith (10:36-38). He now provides abundant examples. This chapter might rightly be called "The Hall of Faith." By faith, those under the old system gained approval from God (vs. 2). They all died, not experiencing the fulfillment of God's promises (vs. 13), never seeing the better, heavenly city (vs. 16). The final testimony concerning these saints is that they all gained approval through their faith, though they did not receive the promises during their lifetime (vs. 39).

1. Necessity of faith. 11:1-3.

CHAPTER 11

NOW faith is the substance of things hoped for, the evidence of things not seen.
2 For by it the elders obtained a good report.

11:1-2. Now faith is the substance of things hoped for, the evidence of things not seen. Verse 1 is not so much a definition of what faith is as it is a description of what faith does. Two truths concerning its activity are stated here. First, faith provides **substance** (Gr *hypostasis*). Precisely what this word means here is difficult to determine. The word *hypostasis* occurs twenty times in the Septuagint and translates twelve different Hebrew words. It is used five times in the New Testament. Four main connotations must guide us as we determine its usage here. (See Hughes for a comprehensive treatment of this subject, pp. 438-440). The first connotation is that of **substance** as an essence of something. This is its sense in Hebrews 1:3, where Christ is described as the *hypostasis* of God, the essence or express image of God. But since faith is not really the substance or essence of something else (if this connotation were to be used), it would have to be construed in a subjective sense as lending substance to. The second connotation is that of **substance** as the foundation of something. Faith then would be regarded as the foundation upon which hope is built. The third connotation is that of assurance. This concept has the support of all other New Testament usages (3:14; II Cor 9:4; 11:17), except Hebrews 1:3. This concept is simpler; it also is more fitting and parallels the concept of the last half of verse 1. The fourth connotation, that of a guarantee, finds some support from Greek papyri documents. Thus, faith might be looked upon as the "title deed" of things hoped for (Moulton and Milligan, *The Vocabulary of the Greek Testament*, pp. 659-60). Moulton and Milligan conclude that within all the connotations "there is the same central idea of something that *underlies* visible conditions and guarantees a future possession" (p. 660). "Assurance" may be the best translation for Hebrews 11:1.

Second, faith provides **evidence** (Gr *elegchos*). It is evidence in the sense of proof which results in conviction. Now, the difference between the substance or assurance of the first part of the verse and the evidence or conviction of the last part may seem minimal; but the contrast within the verse focuses upon the qualifying phrases: **of things hoped for** and **of things not seen.** The first involves future hopes; the second involves present realities, which are unseen. The first includes the hope of the resurrection, the return of Christ, and the glorification of the saints. The second involves unseen realities, such as the forgiveness of sin through Christ's sacrifice and the present intercession of Christ in heaven. Hope is faith relating to the future; conviction is faith relating to the present.

Because of faith, objective reality is not required. Faith is the affirmative response to God's will and Word. Man possesses faith when He takes God at His Word. One does not need to see something to believe it. Faith is the acceptance of something merely because God has said it. ". . . blessed are they that have not seen, and yet have believed" said Jesus (Jn 20:29). For these Jewish readers (and us as well), faith must involve Jesus; for as the Son of God, He is the Revelation and Redemption for man. Therefore, our author later concludes this treatise on faith with these words: **Looking unto Jesus the author and finisher of our faith** (12:2).

Faith is necessary, for it underlies both our future hopes and present spiritual blessings (vs. 1). It is faith alone that makes the lives of these Old Testament individuals worth noting (vs. 2). In fact, "faith is absolutely necessary if we are to understand even the first pages of Scripture" (Kent, p. 217). Verse 3 begins our study of faith at the right place, not with the history of Moses or Abraham, but with the Creation as revealed in Genesis 1. No man was present to witness the Creation; it must be accepted by faith.

3 Through faith we understand that the worlds were framed by the word of God, so that things which are seen were not made of things which do appear.

3. Through faith we understand that the worlds were framed by the word of God. The word translated **worlds** (Gr *aiōnas*) refers to "the vast eons of time and all that fills them" (Kent, p. 218). Though the word has mainly a temporal idea, it involves the physical world that is united with time. God is the framer of time and space. His word (Gr *rhēma*) was the creative fiat; He spoke, and it came into being. He created *ex nihilo*, "out of nothing," **so that things which are seen were not made of things which do appear.** The book of Genesis explains the events of this creation, and that explanation must be accepted **through faith.**

2. Prepatriarchal examples. 11:4-7.

4 By faith Abel offered unto God a more excellent sacrifice than Cain, by which he obtained witness that he was righteous, God testifying of his gifts: and by it he being dead yet speaketh.

4. By faith Abel. The author begins his cavalcade of the faithful by focusing upon the first man in the biblical record to demonstrate faith. Abel's faith was demonstrated in that he **offered unto God a more excellent sacrifice than Cain.** In what way was his sacrifice better? Was it because his was animal and Cain's vegetable? or his a firstling and Cain's not the first-fruit? or his with blood and Cain's without? Genesis 4:1-15 helps us understand our text. Genesis states that God ". . . had respect unto Abel and to his offering," and that God did not receive ". . . Cain and . . . his offering" (Gen 4:4-5). In other words, it was not the offering that made one acceptable and the other unacceptable, since God accepted both grain and animal offerings according to their purposes. But it was the character of the person that made one offering acceptable and the other not. Both Hebrews and Genesis stress that point. In Hebrews it is witnessed that Abel offered **By faith;** obviously Cain did not. Genesis records that even before the rejection of his offering Cain's heart was not right with God (Gen 4:7). God's acceptance of Abel's offering was a **witness that he was righteous** (cf. Mt 23:35). **He being dead yet speaketh.** This statement may suggest an allusion to Abel's blood speaking from the ground (Gen 4:10); more likely, Abel's testimony of faith, given so long ago, still speaks to us.

5 By faith E'noch was translated that he should not see death; and was not found, because God had translated him: for before his translation he had this testimony, that he pleased God.
6 But without faith *it is* impossible to please *him:* for he that cometh to God must believe that he is, and *that* he is a rewarder of them that diligently seek him.
7 By faith Noah, being warned of God

5-6. The second example of a pre-Jewish saint is Enoch. Genesis 5:21-24 briefly records the life of this saint. By faith he was translated, never experiencing death, because **he pleased God.** The verb **pleased** (Gr *euaresteō*) is the Septuagint rendering of the Hebrew phrase "to walk with." Enoch pleased God in that he walked with God. Thus, our author concludes that without faith it is impossible to **please** God. One cannot please God without walking in the light of truth and in righteousness before God (cf. I Jn 1:5-7).

7. By faith Noah. Noah was asked by God to do things in

of things not seen as yet, moved with fear, prepared an ark to the saving of his house; by the which he condemned the world, and became heir of the righteousness which is by faith.

8 By faith Abraham, when he was called to go out into a place which he should after receive for an inheritance, obeyed; and he went out, not knowing whither he went.

9 By faith he sojourned in the land of promise, as in a strange country, dwelling in tabernacles with Isaac and Jacob, the heirs with him of the same promise:
10 For he looked for a city which hath foundations, whose builder and maker is God.

11 Through faith also Sara herself received strength to conceive seed, and was delivered of a child when she was past age, because she judged him faithful who had promised.
12 Therefore sprang there even of one, and him as good as dead, so many as the stars of the sky in multitude, and as the sand which is by the sea shore innumerable.

13 These all died in faith, not having received the promises, but having seen them afar off, and were persuaded of them, and embraced them, and confessed that they were strangers and pilgrims on the earth.
14 For they that say such things declare plainly that they seek a country.
15 And truly, if they had been mindful of that country from whence they came out, they might have had opportunity to have returned.
16 But now they desire a better country, that is, an heavenly: wherefore God is not ashamed to be called their God: for he hath prepared for them a city.
17 By faith Abraham, when he was tried, offered up Isaac: and he that had received the promises offered up his only begotten son,
18 Of whom it was said, That in Isaac shall thy seed be called:
19 Accounting that God was able to raise him up, even from the dead; from

faith which were incongruous with what he had formerly experienced. He had never seen rain (Gen 2:5), and yet God told him to build an ark because of a coming flood (Gen 6:13-17). **By the which he condemned the world.** The word **which** allows either **faith** or **ark** as its antecedent. The better idea is that in sharp contrast to the godlessness of the world, Noah's faith condemned it (cf. Gen 6:5-12).

3. Patriarchal examples. 11:8-22.

8. By faith Abraham. Extended portions of this chapter are allotted for the faith of the two prominent Old Testament fathers—Abraham and Moses. The first recorded incident involving Abraham's faith was when he left Ur of the Chaldees (Gen 11:31; 12:1). That act involved great faith, for he left family and friends to go to a place he had never seen, not knowing what it was like or how to get there. He went merely because God had told him to go, and he obeyed. Likewise, at times God asks us to take a step of faith to leave home for school, to leave friends in order to serve Him somewhere else, or to leave our country to serve in another.

9-10. By faith he sojourned. Yet, even after Abraham received the promise of this land, he never possessed it. The only property he owned in Canaan was the burial plot at Machpelah (Gen 23:1-20). The verb **sojourned** (Gr *paroikeō*) means to migrate. He was a transient. An interesting contrast is found in the verb **dwelling** (Gr *katoikeō*), which means to dwell permanently or to settle down. The only thing permanent about Abraham's dwelling was that he always lived in a tent. Still, he continued to look **for a city** that God would build (cf. 12:22; Ps 87; Rev 21). By faith, he expected that city; so he never returned to Ur, not even to Haran.

11-12. Sarah's faith in the birth of Isaac may seem out of place here. When she first heard the announcement she laughed in unbelief (Gen 18:10-15). Still, she did have faith and cooperated in carrying out God's promise. This necessitated considerable faith, for she was a woman who had been barren all her life; and she was now ninety years old. God's promise came to pass, and he who was **as good as dead** became the father of a great nation. The whole Jewish nation is the product of a miracle birth. The Messiah, of whom Isaac was a type, would also be the product of a miraculous birth (Isa 7:14; Mt 1:18-25). More than anyone else, a Jew ought to be able to accept the supernatural birth of Jesus; for he himself is the result of Isaac's miraculous birth.

13-16. These all died in faith is obviously a summary of only verses 8-12, for **these** refers to the patriarch and his seed who had received the promises but never possessed the land. Enoch is no contradiction to this statement since he was not one of **these** who were **pilgrims**. These had enough faith to recognize the promises of God from **afar off**.

17-19. The point of these verses is that Abraham, after he had finally received the son of God's promise, now **when he was tried, offered up Isaac** (cf. Gen 22:1-19). This was his **only begotten son** (Gr *monogenē*) which must be understood as his unique or one-of-a-kind son. Abraham had other sons, but Isaac was the miraculous son through whom God would fulfill His promises (cf. Abraham's other unique descendant, Jn 3:16).

whence also he received him in a figure.

20 By faith Isaac blessed Jacob and Esau concerning things to come.
21 By faith Jacob, when he was a dying, blessed both the sons of Joseph; and worshipped, *leaning* upon the top of his staff.
22 By faith Joseph, when he died, made mention of the departing of the children of Israel; and gave commandment concerning his bones.

23 By faith Moses, when he was born, was hid three months of his parents, because they saw *he was* a proper child; and they were not afraid of the king's commandment.
24 By faith Moses, when he was come to years, refused to be called the son of Pharaoh's daughter;
25 Choosing rather to suffer affliction with the people of God, than to enjoy the pleasures of sin for a season;
26 Esteeming the reproach of Christ greater riches than the treasures in Egypt: for he had respect unto the recompence of the reward.

27 By faith he forsook Egypt, not fearing the wrath of the king: for he endured, as seeing him who is invisible.
28 Through faith he kept the passover, and the sprinkling of blood, lest he that destroyed the firstborn should touch them.
29 By faith they passed through the Red sea as by dry *land:* which the Egyptians assaying to do were drowned.

30 By faith the walls of Jericho fell down, after they were compassed about seven days.
31 By faith the harlot Rahab perished not with them that believed not, when she had received the spies with peace.

By this time in life Abraham's faith was so strong that he could believe that God would raise Isaac **from the dead,** though he had never seen such a miracle. He totally trusted God to do all things well. **From whence also he received him in a figure.** Though Abraham was stopped before the actual slaying of his son, Isaac was as good as dead; here he serves as a parable (Gr *parabolē*) of a literal resurrection. This incident prefigured the resurrection of Abraham's ultimate Seed, Jesus Christ.

20-22. The author briefly expresses the faith of the other patriarchs. **By faith Isaac blessed Jacob and Esau.** Even though these events of the Book of Genesis 27:1-28:5 seem to involve deceit rather than faith, Isaac's part was in faith in that He was accomplishing God's will. Likewise, Jacob's blessing of both sons of Joseph involved faith, for it also involved the carrying out of God's promise. The choice of these particular events from the lives of Isaac and Jacob to serve as the one demonstration of this faith surely demonstrates the intimacy between faith and God's will and Word. Yet, even more amazing is the accompanying statement that Jacob did this **leaning upon the top of his staff.** The reason for this statement probably lies in the fact that nothing depicted Jacob's dedication and faith more dramatically than his staff. Evidently, Jacob's life of surrender and faith began the night he wrestled with the Lord at Peniel (Gen 32:24-32). God permanently put Jacob's thigh out of joint that night as a reminder of their encounter. Jacob's staff was a daily reminder of God's promises, and his life of faith was best symbolized by his staff.

Similarly, Joseph's faith is also united with the promise God made with the patriarchs. For though he spent most of his life in Egypt, Joseph **gave commandment concerning his bones** that they should be carried back to the Promised Land.

4. Examples from Moses and at Jericho. 11:23-31.

23-26. By faith Moses . . . was hid. This of course is not the faith of Moses, but that faith which was exercised by his parents at his birth (Ex 2:1-10). How much his parents understood concerning the imminent completion of Israel's four hundred years in Egyptian bondage (see Gen 15:13) or the part Moses would play in Israel's deliverance is impossible to imagine. Yet, somehow, through faith they responded to God's leading.

By faith Moses made his break with the world and was willing to suffer with the people of God (the same thing our author is anxious to see his readers do). Moses knew that the pleasure of sin lasts only **for a season,** and he reckoned the **reproach of Christ** greater than the treasures of Egypt. Moses did know of the coming Messiah (Deut 18:15) and was willing to bear reproach on His behalf.

27-29. By faith he forsook Egypt, not fearing the wrath of the king. Moses left Egypt twice, first for Midia, and forty years later at the Exodus. His first departure was a hasty flight because of his fear. Forty years later he had learned to walk by faith and did not fear the entire Egyptian nation. The second departure must be understood as the correct one, even though it puts the next event of faith out of order. By faith, Moses **kept the passover,** which is mentioned in verse 28 before his departure spoken of in verse 27.

The last example of Moses' faith demonstrates that faith is not a daring leap in the dark. Faith is man's response to God's command. Thus, by faith Israel **passed through the Red Sea;** but when the Egyptians mustered enough audacity to try it, they **were drowned.**

30-31. By faith the walls of Jericho fell. Surely, neither the marching nor the trumpets brought the walls down. Likewise, a doubting heart would cause one to stop such marching long before the seventh day. But by faith they persisted in obedience to God's command. Similarly, within the city, faith also deliv-

32 And what shall I more say? for the time would fail me to tell of Gĕd'e-on, and of Bā'rak, and of Samson, and of Jĕph'tha-ē: of David also, and Samuel, and of the prophets:

33 Who through faith subdued kingdoms, wrought righteousness, obtained promises, stopped the mouths of lions,

34 Quenched the violence of fire, escaped the edge of the sword, out of weakness were made strong, waxed valiant in fight, turned to flight the armies of the aliens.

35 Women received their dead raised to life again: and others were tortured, not accepting deliverance; that they might obtain a better resurrection:

36 And others had trial of cruel mockings and scourgings, yea, moreover of bonds and imprisonment:

37 They were stoned, they were sawn asunder, were tempted, were slain with the sword: they wandered about in sheepskins and goatskins; being destitute, afflicted, tormented;

38 (Of whom the world was not worthy:) they wandered in deserts, and in mountains, and in dens and caves of the earth.

39 And these all, having obtained a good report through faith, received not the promise:

40 God having provided some better thing for us, that they without us should not be made perfect.

CHAPTER 12

WHEREFORE seeing we also are compassed about with so great a cloud of witnesses, let us lay aside every weight, and the sin which doth so easily beset us, and let us run with patience the race that is set before us,

---

ered the life of Rahab, the harlot. And though Rahab's faith delivered her, it was her works, James says, that demonstrated her to be righteous (justified her). Although her epithet as a harlot lingered, her life changed (Jas 2:25).

5. Examples from the judges, kings, and prophets. 11:32-38.

32-38. And what shall I more say? The author wants to go on, but time constrains him. So many more deserve recognition. Verses 33-38 list mighty deeds of **faith** done by those of biblical history. Surely David is an example of one who **subdued kingdoms** (II Sam 8:1-14) and **wrought righteousness,** in that he ". . . executed judgment and justice unto all his people" (II Sam 8:15). Daniel **stopped the mouths of lions** (Dan 6:16-23), although in a lesser sense so did Samson (Jud 14:5-6) and David (I Sam 17:34-36). Shadrach, Meshach, and Abednego **Quenched the violence of fire** (Dan 3:19-30). Zechariah, the son of Jehoiada, was **stoned** (II Chr 24:20-22); according to tradition Isaiah was **sawn asunder.** These are but a few examples of those who endured because of faith.

6. The conclusion. 11:39-40.

39-40. The important thing is that **these all** persisted in their faith even though they **received not the promise.** Genuine faith persists unto the end; emotional decisions do not. True faith continues to believe the truth. Once again, the author shows the superiority of the New Covenant. God saved this **better thing,** or fulfillment of **the promise,** for this age. In fact, **without** those of the New Covenant, even the mightiest champion of **faith** in the Old Testament could **not be made perfect.**

B. Exhortation to Perseverance and Holiness. 12:1-29.

Chapter 12, probably more than any other, sets forth the practical aspect of this book of exhortation (cf. 13:22). Prior to chapter 11, the primary emphasis was doctrinal, with a lesser place given to exhortation. Chapter 11 began the practical section of the book by parading many Old Testament examples of faith and patience. Now chapter 12, building upon those examples, begins the extensive exhortations of this epistle. Chapter 13 also contains many exhortations, but they are general admonitions which are not directly based upon the thought developed in the earlier chapters.

1. The supreme example of endurance. 12:1-4.

12:1. Wherefore . . . let us run expresses the exhortation and, hence, the main idea of verse 1. The exhortation finds its ground, or basis, within the examples of the champions mentioned in chapter 11. These heroes of the faith are like a **cloud of witnesses.** These **witnesses** (Gr *martyrōn*) could easily be imagined as spectators (Gr *theatai*) or as martyrs; yet this Greek word should be understood as referring simply to those who testify. During the terrible days of martyrdom following the New Testament era, this word became the common term for identifying those who testified through their death. In our verse these witnesses testified to the need for a persistent faith through their lives. These saints may also be spectators, and some were surely martyrs; yet the emphasis of this verse (in harmony with the choice of *martyrōn*) is upon the witness their lives demonstrated.

We also need to run as they. The author is emphatic about this point. What they have done, we must do. **Let us run.** Whereas the Christian's position involves a sitting in the heavenlies with Christ (Eph 2:6) and his conduct is as a walk (Eph 4:1,17; 5:2,15), his activity or service is described as the running of a race (12:1; I Cor 9:24-27). **Let us run** is the only cohortative or hortatory form in the Greek text. **Let us lay aside every weight** is an aorist participle used circumstantially, probably telling us how we are to run—by laying aside every weight. The participle may also be attendant and so translated like the main verb, as in our translation; but nevertheless, it is subordinate to the main idea of **let us run.** We are to run by laying aside every **weight** and the **sin** which does **beset us.** The **weight** (Gr *ogkos*—used only here) refers to that which impedes or burdens by weighing one down. For a runner it could either refer to clothing or his own excessive body weight (Hughes, pp. 519-520). Obviously, for the Christian it would involve not wicked but weighty things. It would include anything that could hinder his effectiveness for service. These are not things which are inherently wrong, but for the diligent runner or the faithful Christian they are an impediment that must be removed. The Christian is not allowed to be selective regarding these weights; he will remove them. He must put off **every weight.** Whatever does not aid in the race is a weight and must be cast aside.

The second thing which must be put off is of itself morally wrong, for it is **sin.** The adjective that describes this sin is difficult to interpret; it is found nowhere else in the New Testament. It is translated **easily beset** or "easily entangles" (NASB and NIV). Kent believes that this does not refer "to some specific sin, but to the peculiar character of all sin as continually surrounding men and so easily getting hold of them" (p. 258). Truly this is the nature of all sin; yet, the use of the Greek article would certainly support the notion that individual sins are in mind. This probably does not refer to some universal sin. Yet, it may refer to one sin above all others that defeats one's Christian life. This may be a different sin for each Christian. For one person it may be sensual lust; for another it may be money, greed, gossip, or lying. That sin must be put off in order to run the race which God has placed before us.

The casting off of **every weight** and the entangling **sin** refer to what one must do before he can seriously run the race. The use of the aorist participle also supports that understanding; they might even have been translated "having put off every weight . . . ." Now, after the race has begun, we are encouraged to run **with patience** (Gr *hypomonēs*). Since patience is not an attribute commonly associated with running, this word would be better translated as endurance. Endurance is a quality that every distance runner must develop. It is amazing that this translation was not used since the cognate verb used in verses 2-3 is translated **endured.** Endurance and persistence have been upon the mind of the author since the end of chapter 10 (cf. 10:32, 36-38; 11:13). We must run with endurance, for a race has no rest stops; it knows no vacations.

2. Just as verse 1 establishes some qualities for the entrance and actual running of the race, so verse 2 directs our eyes to the finish line. **Looking** (Gr *aphoraō*) is an uncommon word that literally means to look away or to fix one's eyes, and so to gaze. Our gaze or attention is to be focused upon **Jesus the author and finisher of our faith.** He is our pioneer and perfecter (Hughes, p. 522). He has "blazed the trail for us and has completed the course" (Kent, p. 258). Though chapter 11 has provided us with many champions to emulate, the supreme example of endurance is Jesus Himself. So the Christian is to run the course that has been placed before him with endurance,

2 Looking unto Jesus the author and finisher of *our* faith; who for the joy that was set before him endured the cross, despising the shame, and is set down at the right hand of the throne of God.

as Christ endured the cross **for the joy that was set before him.** The usual translation of the preposition **for** (Gr *anti*) is instead of. Thus, some (e.g., Goodspeed, Delitzsch) would understand this to say that Christ took the difficult course, rather than the course that led directly to joy, an idea parallel to Philippians 2:6-8. However, the context favors the less common idea, for the sake of. As Jesus fixed His gaze upon the joy which lay at the end of the course, so we must fix our gaze upon Jesus; for as the finisher of our faith, He is **set down at the right hand of the throne of God.**

3 For consider him that endured such contradiction of sinners against himself, lest ye be wearied and faint in your minds.
4 Ye have not yet resisted unto blood, striving against sin.

3-4. For consider him. Jesus provides a far better example of persistent endurance than any Old Testament saint, and He is a better example of endurance than the readers are. They had been mocked and afflicted (10:32-34), but they had not paid with their lives for their opposition to sin. If they had, and if we would look to Christ's example instead of looking at our own afflictions, we would not become so weary or fainthearted. Are you unhappy over your sacrifice? Take a new look at His!

2. The example of fatherly discipline. 12:5-13.

5 And ye have forgotten the exhortation which speaketh unto you as unto children, My son, despise not thou the chastening of the Lord, nor faint when thou art rebuked of him:
6 For whom the Lord loveth he chasteneth, and scourgeth every son whom he receiveth.
7 If ye endure chastening, God dealeth with you as with sons; for what son is he whom the father chasteneth not?
8 But if ye be without chastisement, whereof all are partakers, then are ye bastards, and not sons.

5-8. Several concepts unite this section with the preceding—endurance, affliction, and fainting. In the preceding context they were told to endure the opposition of sinners and not faint. Now they are told to endure the chastening of God and not faint (vss. 5,7), for the former may be the means to the latter. God may be using the opposition of sinners to accomplish His good work within the believer. **Ye have forgotten.** They had forgotten God's earlier exhortation of Proverbs 3:11-12. The afflictions of life are for our good, so we must endure them whether it is God scourging (Gr *mastigoō*, flogging with a whip) or the world persecuting (Jas 1:2-12). **Whom the Lord loveth he chasteneth.** God's principle of disciplining His own people is completely congruous with human practices. This quotation from Proverbs 3:12 stating God's practice, corresponds to the commands God gave in Proverbs to fathers. "He that spareth his rod hateth his son: but he that loveth him chasteneth him betimes (promptly)" (Prov 13:24; cf. 22:15; 23:13). Love and corporal punishment are not incongruous; they are two complementary and necessary aspects of training. Indeed, **If ye be without chastisement,** then you are not a true son. Somehow, this one got among the sons, but he was not one. God's discipline is universal, **whereof all are partakers.** Every father who loves his son disciplines him; and, likewise, it is true that the father does not discipline the boys of the neighborhood. They understand that they are not sons.

9 Furthermore we have had fathers of our flesh which corrected *us*, and we gave *them* reverence: shall we not much rather be in subjection unto the Father of spirits, and live?
10 For they verily for a few days chastened *us* after their own pleasure; but he for *our* profit, that *we* might be partakers of his holiness.
11 Now no chastening for the present seemeth to be joyous, but grievous: nevertheless afterward it yieldeth the peaceable fruit of righteousness unto them which are exercised thereby.

9-11. Fathers of our flesh. Our physical fathers have corrected us and we have called them blessed. Should not the **Father of spirits,** our spiritual Father, receive like reverence when He disciplines us? Our earthly fathers corrected us **after their own pleasure.** Sometimes they were severe, other times mild. Sometimes they showed favoritism; sometimes they were concerned only for their own interest. But our heavenly Father always corrects us **for our profit** (Gen 50:20; Ps 119:71; Rom 8:28), that we might share in **his holiness.** The persistent endurance which God desires of His people is not to weaken but to strengthen them. It is to produce maturity and holiness (Rom 5:3-5; II Pet 1:4-8). When passing through affliction, one must also remember that it is brief. With our human fathers it was **for a few days,** and with God there is an **afterward** during which the benefit of our training is enjoyed.

12 Wherefore lift up the hands which hang down, and the feeble knees;
13 And make straight paths for your feet, lest that which is lame be turned out of the way; but let it rather be healed.

12-13. Wherefore lift up the hands which hang down, and the feeble knees. The inferential conjunction, **Wherefore,** suggests that the following exhortations develop logically from the preceding statements. Verses 12-13 revert to the athletic figure of speech. The description of weakened hands and feeble (Gr *paralyō*), even disabled, knees depicts those who were too weak or weary to run with endurance the course which lay before them. The verb **lift up** (Gr *anorthoō*) literally means to straighten up, as with the crippled woman who was healed (Lk 13:13) and once more stood erect. Likewise, some of the runners of verse 1 have grown so weary that they have become stooped and need the spiritual strength to be straightened up again. A cognate of this verb is used in verse 13 for making the paths **straight** (Gr *orthos*). The path must be simple for those who are weak. This is not to suggest that we must make the Christian life easy or compromise its principles. It is the weak one who is commanded to keep his path straight: You **make straight paths for your feet.** He must keep the obstacles which would trip him up spiritually out of his path. **Lest that which is lame be turned out of the way** has two possible interpretations. Bruce believes that **turned out of the way** (Gr *ektrapē*) possesses its medical connotation of to put out of joint in this context, for it next exhorts them to **be healed.** Thus, "dislocation and not deviation" would be implied (Bruce, p. 363). Hughes is equally convinced that the connotation is "to turn aside," for this is its usage in all other New Testament locations (I Tim 1:6; 5:15; II Tim 4:4). And since the concept of apostasy is involved in each of those texts (except I Tim 6:20), this ought to be its usage here, inasmuch as apostasy has been prominent in the thought of the author of Hebrews (Hughes, p. 535).

3. Exhortation to holiness. 12:14-17.

14 Follow peace with all *men*, and holiness, without which no man shall see the Lord:

14. The athletic motif is now dropped. Likewise, the primary exhortation is no longer one of endurance, but that of holiness. **Follow peace . . . and holiness.** To **follow** (Gr *diōkō*) more precisely means to pursue. This is not a passive role that one just lets happen; it is an active concept that one must strive for. They must pray for a life of peace with both other believers and the world (I Tim 2:1-2); they must labor for it, too (Ps 34:14; Rom 12:18). Yet this must not be peace at any cost. We are to strive for peace **and holiness,** for without holiness no man can **see the Lord.** This holiness has been imputed through Christ to those who have made Him their Saviour and Lord (10:10-14; II Cor 5:21; I Pet 2:24). Man's righteous acts can never attain to this holiness (Isa 64:6; Mt 5:20). **Without which** must not be construed as meaning that without peace no one will see the Lord, or even to mean without peace and holiness. The relative pronoun, **which,** is singular and in the masculine gender. Thus, being singular it cannot refer to both and must refer to the noun, which is masculine. Holiness is masculine; peace is not.

Holiness, like faith, is a crucial element in the Christian's life. Without the former one cannot see God; without the latter one cannot please God (11:6). At salvation, God changes man's spiritual nature. Before salvation we are free from righteousness (holiness) and slavery to sin (Rom 6:17,20). At salvation we become free from sin and a slave to holiness (Rom 6:18). This radical change should become apparent shortly after salvation, for one is not and cannot be a slave to two masters. Even a spy who appears to serve two masters serves only one. Even if he is a double agent, he has one true master.

15 Looking diligently lest any man *fail of the grace of God; lest any root of* bitterness springing up trouble *you,* and thereby many be defiled;
16 Lest there *be* any fornicator, or profane person, as Esau, who for one morsel of meat sold his birthright.
17 For ye know how that afterward, when he would have inherited the blessing, he was rejected: for he found no place of repentance, though he sought it carefully with tears.

15-17. The author continues this exhortation with a series of subordinate admonitions. **Looking diligently.** With this participle the author cautions his readers in four areas. First, he cautions lest anyone **fail of the grace of God.** He reminds them that some of them may have entered into close contact with Christians, but might stop short of salvation itself and so fail to experience the grace of God. Second, he cautions lest **any root of bitterness springing up trouble you.** Probably the Old Testament source to which our author is alluding is Deuteronomy 29:18: "Lest there should be among you man, or woman . . . whose heart turneth away this day from the LORD our God, to go and serve the gods of these nations; lest there should be among you a root that beareth gall and wormwood." This one who possesses the root of bitterness is, also like the first, one who continues among the believers but was never born again. He is like a **root**. At first his bitterness is hidden; but when it is discovered, its noxious roots have spread and it springs up as something much bigger and more destructive. Beware! Live peacefully, but require holiness to govern your life and the life of the church.

The third and fourth cautions are located in verse 16. The third briefly warns against the unholy practice of fornication. The fourth occupies the remainder of verses 16-17. Beware of the **profane person**. This profanity (Gr *bebēlos*) involves far more than one's speech. It is a quality of one's life. The author sees that quality exemplified within Esau, even though Esau was not a vile man. In fact, he was less of a crook than his brother Jacob. The author accurately focuses upon the one area that revealed Esau as profane—the selling of his birthright. To **profane** is to regard something as unhallowed, to make something sacred to be common. Esau took that which God considered sacred and made it common. Being so totally concerned with his temporary and material needs, he gave them priority over his rights as the first-born son and his responsibilities as heir to the blessing of the Abrahamic covenant (Gen 25:29-34). Every Christian must beware lest he count as unimportant what God considers sacred. The result in Esau's life was that **afterward**, when he wanted that blessing, he was **rejected**. He repented with tears, but the situation was irrevocable.

4. The fifth warning: Do not refuse warning from heaven. 12:18-29.

This is the fifth and final warning passage of Hebrews. Within each of these passages a particular area of danger is revealed. This fifth warning is similar to the second (3:7-4:13). Likewise, there is a parallel between the third (5:11-6:20) and the fourth (10:19-39). But, whereas the parallelism of numbers three and four involved teaching and doctrine, the parallel between two and five concerns form. Both the second and fifth warnings begin by exhibiting Israel's failures and disobedience while journeying to the Promised Land of Canaan. In the second Israel's sin was unbelief concerning God's promise to care for them; in the fifth their sin is the refusal to hear God's warning at Sinai.

18-21. For ye are not come unto the mount that might be touched. The author describes the day at Sinai when God spoke to the whole congregation of Israel (Ex 19:9-25; 20:18-21; Deut 4:10-24). Though our author depicts it as a physical mountain that could be **touched**, on that day (ironically) they were not allowed to touch it as the author later stresses. Normally, God spoke only to Moses; but on this one day God spoke to all. When God spoke, His presence was accompanied with **fire . . . blackness . . . darkness** and **tempest**. God's purpose for that day is expressly recorded in the Old Testament: ". . . I will make them hear my words, that they may learn to fear me all the days that they shall live upon the earth . . ." (Deut 4:10; cf. Ex 20:20). God was warning them from heaven with an awesome demonstration in order that they might fear and obey Him.

They that heard entreated that the word should not be spoken to them any more. The word they requested not to hear did not involve the Ten Commandments; but, as verse 20 demonstrates, it was the command that not so much as a **beast touch the mountain.** God had been very severe in His restrictions regarding even the slightest touching of Mount Sinai (Ex 20:18-21). If even a beast should touch the mountain, they were forbidden to touch the beast, but must rather immediately stone it or shoot it with an arrow. Such stringent regulations did not produce a proper, positive response in the hearts of the Israelites. Rather, they **entreated** God to call the whole thing

18 For ye are not come unto the mount that might be touched, and that burned with fire, nor unto blackness, and darkness, and tempest,
19 And the sound of a trumpet, and the voice of words; which *voice* they that heard intreated that the word should not be spoken to them any more:
20 (For they could not endure that which was commanded, And if so much as a beast touch the mountain, it shall be stoned, or thrust through with a dart:
21 And so terrible was the sight, *that* Moses said, I exceedingly fear and quake:)

off; and instead, they spoke to Moses privately. The verb (Gr *paraiteomai*) could also be translated to require or to beg. More significantly, it can also mean to refuse, which is its translation only several verses later: **See that ye refuse not him that speaketh** (vs. 25). Since this whole warning involves the drawing of a comparison between then and now, the author's use of this verb for both parties should suggest approximately the same idea for both uses of the verb. At Sinai the Israelites refused to hear God's awesome voice from heaven; now we must not do the same. They preferred that He did not speak (cf. Ex 20:19); they rejected His voice of warning from heaven. Truly, the presence of our holy God is awesome, as Moses himself testifies (vs. 21). Since no Old Testament passage explicitly expresses Moses' fear, the author may be inferring it from Exodus 19:16 by including Moses among the congregation.

22-24. But ye are come unto Mount Zion. How much better the relationship between God and His people is under the New Covenant. We have come unto the **city of the living God, the heavenly Jerusalem.** This city is not part of the Old Covenant, nor even of this present earth. It is that city for which Abraham looked, but never saw (11:16); it is the one called the New Jerusalem (Rev 21:2). We have an inheritance in this city wherein God Himself will live (Rev 21:22-23).

Several groups of inhabitants are identified within these verses. First, there is an **innumerable company of angels.** The next phrase, **to the general assembly,** is ambiguous. This word (Gr *panēgyris*), which is used nowhere else in the New Testament, refers to a festal assembly, as at one of the Jewish feasts. This certainly does not refer to a second group of inhabitants; but whether it refers to the angels or has reference to the church is difficult to ascertain. Kent prefers to regard this assembly as a festal gathering of angels. "This is somewhat similar to the presence of angels at Sinai . . . , although here the emphasis is on festive celebration rather than awesome majesty" (Kent, p. 273).

The second group of inhabitants is described as the **church of the firstborn.** Obviously, the word **church** (Gr *ekklēsia*) suggests that they are the saints of the church age; but it may refer only to the living saints since these have their names enrolled in heaven, suggesting that they are still upon the earth. We are described as the **church of the firstborn** because of our privileged position with Christ "the first-born" (Col 1:15,18). A third group involves the **spirits of just men made perfect.** Since they are **spirits,** they are those who have died but have not yet been resurrected. Since they are **just men made perfect,** certainly they refer to the Old Testament saints who could not be made perfect before Christ's time (11:40); but now, they have been made perfect through His one sacrifice (10:14; Bruce, p. 378).

This heavenly Jerusalem is also the abode of God, the **Judge of all,** and of **Jesus the mediator of the new covenant** (cf. Rev 21:22-23). It is the shedding of His blood in the New Covenant that makes this assembly possible. **That speaketh better things than that of Abel.** Abel's blood, being the first blood shed by another man, speaks from the earth, crying for vengeance (Gen 4:10). Christ's blood, which alone has been shed for His brothers, speaks better things; for it speaks of blessing instead of cursing. "Abel's blood cried out for judgment; but Christ's blood cries out for mercy and pardon" (Hughes, p. 552).

25-27. See that ye refuse not him that speaketh. Verse 25 contains the heart of this warning. The danger lies in refusing to hear the warning of Him who speaks from heaven; for if those at Mount Sinai did not escape God's wrath, **much more shall not we escape.** One may escape God's warnings now, but God will not be escaped then.

Exodus 19:18 tells us that God's **voice then shook the earth.** Haggai 2:6 states that God will again shake both **earth** and

22 But ye are come unto mount Sion, and unto the city of the living God, the heavenly Jerusalem, and to an innumerable company of angels,
23 To the general assembly and church of the firstborn, which are written in heaven, and to God the Judge of all, and to the spirits of just men made perfect,
24 And to Jesus the mediator of the new covenant, and to the blood of sprinkling, that speaketh better things than *that of* Abel.

25 See that ye refuse not him that speaketh. For if they escaped not who refused him that spake on earth, much more *shall not* we *escape*, if we turn away from him that *speaketh* from heaven:
26 Whose voice then shook the earth: but now he hath promised, saying, Yet

once more I shake not the earth only, but also heaven.

27 And this *word,* Yet once more, signifieth the removing of those things that are shaken, as of things that are made, that those things which cannot be shaken may remain.

28 Wherefore we receiving a kingdom which cannot be moved, let us have grace, whereby we may serve God acceptably with reverence and godly fear:

29 For our God *is* a consuming fire.

heaven. This shaking will occur only **once more;** so this probably refers to the occasion of Christ's second coming. Most likely this is not a metaphorical shaking, referring to political or social upheavals; rather, it is physical. The shaking at Sinai was physical; and since this is God's final shaking of heaven and earth, it relates well to the physical calamity at Christ's second coming, prophesied by Old and New Testaments (Joel 3:14-16; Isa 34:1-8; Mt 24:27-30; Rev 16:16-21). Further, the author says that it is the things which are **made,** the physical things, that will be shaken.

28-29. Let us have grace. We who are of God's kingdom, which cannot be shaken, are exhorted to **have grace** (Gr *echomen charin*). This phrase might more meaningfully be translated, "Let us be grateful." "As ingratitude lies at the very root of all sin and rebellion against God (Rom 1:21), so gratitude is the pulsating heartbeat of every positive response to the gospel, gratitude which spontaneously bursts forth in the apostle's exclamation: 'Thanks be to God for his inexpressible gift!'" (Hughes, p. 559). Our service for God involves love and gratitude, but also **reverence and godly fear;** for **our God is a consuming fire.** Inasmuch as our author quotes Deuteronomy 4:24 and identifies the Old Testament "God of fear" (the epithet given by some) as **our** God, we ought to worship Him with love and godly fear.

C. General Admonitions for Service. 13:1-25.

This final chapter is a composite of admonitions which covers a wide range of topics. The author has finished the main thrust of the epistle. In chapter 13 he focuses upon the particular needs and problems of those to whom he is writing. These admonitions cluster around the basic topics of love, leadership, and last words.

1. Involving love. 13:1-6.

The author's admonitions involving love contain cautions against selfishness in regard to people (vss. 1-3), lust in physical love, (vs. 4), and greed for things (vss. 5-6).

13:1-3. Let brotherly love continue. This exhortation applies to all of God's people and must be proclaimed constantly (Rom 12:10; I Thess 4:9; I Pet 1:22; II Pet 1:7). One incentive for showing such love and hospitality is that some have **entertained angels unawares.** For example, Abraham (Gen 18:1-3) and Lot (Gen 19:1-2) were unaware that their guests were angels at the time they received them. Care must be taken so as not to read too much into this statement. The verse says that **some have entertained** (aorist tense). The use of the present tense, meaning that some do entertain angels, would provide grounds for expecting this will still happen. This is not correct teaching. Nevertheless, we should show hospitality to the needy; for indeed, it will benefit us as well as them, when it is done in the name of the Lord and as to the Lord (cf. Mt 25:35-40).

Remember them that are in bonds, as bound with them. These Jewish believers had gone through severe persecution (10:32-34) and had possessed a camaraderie, rallying to the needs of others (10:33). Now they have begun to grow indifferent to those who suffered and may even have avoided them, trying to escape such suffering themselves. They must remember to help their fellows, for they are **in the body.** This should not be construed to mean that they are in the body of Christ, since the Greek article is missing and simply says, "in body." The point our author is making is that his readers need to be concerned about those who are suffering; for since they possess the same physical body as others, it could happen just as easily to them.

CHAPTER 13

LET brotherly love continue.

2 Be not forgetful to entertain strangers: for thereby some have entertained angels unawares.

3 Remember them that are in bonds, as bound with them; *and* them which suffer adversity, as being yourselves also in the body.

4 Marriage *is* honourable in all, and

4. Marriage is honorable in all. The author now turns to some problems regarding physical love. To determine the full

the bed undefiled: but whoremongers and adulterers God will judge.

intent of this verse, one grammatical point must be resolved. In the Greek clause, the verb is omitted and must be supplied by the reader, as is common in both Hebrew and Greek. One may supply an indicative verb, **marriage is,** and make it a declarative sentence (KJV). Or one may supply a subjunctive verb, "let marriage be," and make it an exhortation (NASB). The latter seems preferable since the context is hortatorical and the author is bringing up a new subject for exhortation. Also, if the first half is exhortation, the second half of the verse fits better. Thus, this is a command to purity, rather than a declaration against the ascetic teaching which regarded the marriage relation itself as unwholesome. Ascetic teaching was a problem at this time (cf. I Tim 4:3). But this does not seem to be the intent of our author. Marriage is honorable and the marriage bed undefiled. It must be kept that way. **But** (Gr *gar*) could better be translated for. Keep marriage relationships, for God will judge those who do not. The **whoremongers** (Gr *pornos*) are the fornicators, that is, those who indulge in sexual relationships, heterosexual and homosexual, outside of marriage bonds. The **adulterers** are those who are unfaithful to their marriage vows.

5 *Let your* conversation *be* without covetousness; *and be* content with such things as ye have: for he hath said, I will never leave thee, nor forsake thee.

6 So that we may boldly say, The Lord *is* my helper, and I will not fear what man shall do unto me.

5-6. Let your conversation be without covetousness. The problem touched upon here is the love of things—greed. The phrase **without covetousness** is one word (Gr *aphilargyros*) literally means without money-love. The admonition is to be **content with such things as ye have.** These Jewish Christians to whom this epistle was written had been spoiled financially by their persecutors, and they had accepted it joyfully at first (10:34). But, as is often true, it grew more difficult to live with the condition as it continued. The author then bases his admonition to contentment upon two Old Testament promises. The first is positional in concept: **for . . . I will never leave thee, nor forsake thee.** This is God's encouraging promise to Joshua, recorded in Deuteronomy 31:6 and 8 (cf. also I Chr 28:20). The second promise is provisional: **The Lord is my helper** (Ps 118:6). God's presence and provision will produce contentment. When trust is placed in money, it will only produce covetousness and contention (cf. I Tim 6:9-10).

2. Involving leaders and living. 13:7-17.

7 Remember them which have the rule over you, who have spoken unto you the word of God: whose faith follow, considering the end of *their* conversation.

8 Jesus Christ the same yesterday, and to day, and for ever.

9 Be not carried about with divers and strange doctrines. For *it is* a good thing that the heart be established with grace; not with meats, which have not profited them that have been occupied therein.

7-9. Remember them which have the rule over you. Time often brings changes, and apparently these Jewish Christians falsely believed that things had now changed from when they first believed. In light of such possible changes, several admonitions regarding their leaders and their own lives are necessary. First, they must **remember** their spiritual fathers. These first leaders had probably died already, considering the use of the word **end** (Gr *ekbasis*), which suggests the end and outcome of one's life. The word **remember** and the reference to the present leaders in verse 17 further support this interpretation. These Christians are to remember the godly character of these fathers, for such character gives credence to one's message. They are to **follow** (Gr *mimeomai*) or imitate, not merely the men, but their faith. Second, they must understand that the program and person of Jesus Christ have not changed from when they first believed. He is **the same yesterday, and today, and for ever.** Third, they must not be **carried about with divers** (various) **and strange doctrines.** They must rather mature in the **grace** which they received when they first believed. The reference to seeking spiritual profit from **meats** would suggest that some of these Jewish Christians were being tempted to return to the ritual of the Jewish system. Meat was a vital element of Jewish ritual, for it was that which established the greatest barrier between Jew and Gentile. The distinction of what was clean or unclean for eating was largely based upon that which was clean or unclean upon the altar. Thus, for a Jew to eat any or all meats meant that he was implicitly setting aside the distinction of clean and un-

10 We have an altar, whereof they have no right to eat which serve the tabernacle.
11 For the bodies of those beasts, whose blood is brought into the sanctuary by the high priest for sin, are burned without the camp.
12 Wherefore Jesus also, that he might sanctify the people with his own blood, suffered without the gate.
13 Let us go forth therefore unto him without the camp, bearing his reproach.
14 For here have we no continuing city, but we seek one to come.

clean sacrificial meats (Owen, p. 274); and for a Jew to return to a doctrine involving clean and unclean meats was a tacit return to the Jewish sacrificial system (cf. 9:9-10; Acts 10:9-16,28; 11:1-13; I Cor 8:8; Col 2:16-17).

10-14. We have an altar. The precise meaning of **we** is significant. Does the author mean "we Christians" or "we Jews"? If he is referring to Christians, then our **altar** should be understood either as the cross, which was the place where Christ was crucified, or as Christ, the sacrifice itself. If this interpretation is true, then the Jewish priesthood would have no part in that altar (vs. 10) and verse 11 would explain why that was so. For example, verse 11 might state that because they have not partaken of Christ they have no right. But verse 11 does not state any such thought. Therefore, it is much easier to understand the **we** as Jews. The argument, then, would be, that there were times within the Jewish ritual when even the priests could not eat of the sacrifice. One such time was the Day of Atonement, when the priest took the blood of a goat and sprinkled it upon the ark in the Holy of Holies. However, the flesh would be taken outside the camp and burned (Lev 16:27; for other sin offerings which were burned rather than eaten see Lev 4:3-21). Verse 11 does fit with this view, for it expresses the very thing that was just explained—the events on the Day of Atonement.

Wherefore Jesus also. Jesus is presented as the fulfillment of that picture. He suffered outside the gate upon Golgotha. The Gospels do not place stress upon the fact that Golgotha lay outside the city; but each does imply this fact, and John is sufficiently clear: ". . . the place where Jesus was crucified was nigh to the city . . ." (Jn 19:20). **Let us go . . . without the camp.** The admonition is clear. As our sin offering, Christ has been separated from the Jewish camp. Those who have turned to Him for redemption must also join Him outside the camp. "Jesus had been rejected by Judaism, both literally by crucifixion at the demand of Jewish leaders and symbolically by suffering outside the gate analogous to the sin offering" (Kent, p. 286). **For here have we no continuing city.** Here is a foreboding of Jerusalem's imminent destruction. Even if there was no prophetic intent within the author's statement, God is about to remove the temptation for Jewish Christians to return to the sacrificial ritual of the Jerusalem temple. Though the city of Jerusalem would continue but briefly, we seek **one to come** (10:16; 12:22).

15 By him therefore let us offer the sacrifice of praise to God continually, that is, the fruit of *our* lips giving thanks to his name.
16 But to do good and to communicate forget not: for with such sacrifices God is well pleased.

15-16. Let us offer the sacrifice of praise. Our sacrifice is not to involve blood or an animal, for that sacrifice has seen its fulfillment in the once-for-all sacrifice of Christ. Our sacrifice, therefore, ought to be one of **praise** on behalf of Christ's perfect offering. Though Christ's perfect sacrifice was onetime, ours is to be **continually.** Whereas the Levitical system required yearly and daily outward ritual, God desires from us an unending offering out of our hearts. Our second sacrifice, involved with our daily living under the new system, is **to do good;** and the third is **to communicate.** This word (Gr *koinōnia*) can mean fellowship; or, in a more restricted sense, it may mean generosity, sharing, contribution or gift. Due to the exhortations regarding hospitality and the love of money in the early part of this chapter, it seems that the idea of sharing of goods is apropos. Our sacrifices to God, then, involve our tongue, our actions, and our finances. Surely such teaching is harmonious with Paul's exhortation to present our bodies as a living sacrifice (Rom 12:1).

17 Obey them that have the rule over you, and submit yourselves: for they watch for your souls, as they that must give account, that they may do it with joy, and not with grief: for that *is* unprofitable for you.

17. Obey them that have the rule over you. Our author began this section with an exhortation for his readers to remember their former leaders (vs. 7). Now he speaks in regard to the present leaders. **Obey** (Gr *peithesthe*) is passive and more simply means be persuaded; but it can also mean trust, believe, obey, or follow. In fact, in the very next verse this word is translated trust: for we trust we have a good conscience. Our author seems to suggest that we ought to believe, trust, or *be persuaded* by our leaders. The next command is to submit (Gr *hypeikete*), or yield. Kent sees the first verb as denoting an assent to another's direction, whereas the latter denotes a yeilding of one's contrary opinions in favor of another's opinion (p. 288). The leader must not imagine that this passage authorizes him to dictate. God has given to the leaders the work of overseeing, not by being an overlord but by being an example (I Pet 5:1-3). We must follow our spiritual leaders and submit to them; for they watch over our lives, knowing that they, as well as we, will give an accounting of our lives. We ought to make their ministry over us joyful rather than miserable.

3. Involving author and recipients. 13:18-25.

18-19. Pray for us. Surely this request on the part of the author implies an acquaintance between the author and his readers. They knew who he was, even though we today can only guess. Greater still, that for which they were to pray, **that I may be restored to you the sooner,** suggests a former association with them. Whether it was imprisonment (see Commentary on 10:34), illness, or some mission that had prevented an earlier restoration is impossible to know (see Introduction at the beginning of this commentary for views regarding authorship).

20-21. Now the God of peace. The benediction of these verses provides the formal conclusion to this epistle; they serve as a postscript. Following the extended and severe admonition contained in this epistle, this benediction, involving **the God of peace,** is comforting. Likewise, the appellation of Jesus as the **great shepherd of the sheep** is a consolation to God's people. The application of the Shepherd motif to the Messiah is common in Old and New Testaments (Ps 23; Isa 40:11; Ezk 34:23; Jn 10:11; I Pet 2:25; 5:4). The description of Jesus as **brought again from the dead** is the only explicit statement of Christ's resurrection within the epistle, which is surprising since so much is taught concerning Christ and His death. References to His present position in heaven, however, are abundant (e.g., 1:3; 5:7; 6:20; 12:2). Thus, the doctrine is sufficiently taught.

The purpose of this blessing is that God may **Make you perfect.** This is not the same perfection which the author earlier stated to be the result of Christ's once-for-all sacrifice (10:14; 11:40). That word (Gr *teleioō*) involves the positional sanctification of the redeemed. Our word in 13:21 (Gr *katartizō*) has more the idea of to mend or to equip for a task. The equipping needed here is to do **every good work.**

22. Suffer the word of exhortation. Obviously, as the author now attests, the primary nature and purpose of this epistle has been for exhortation. And his last admonition is that they might bear with it. The author regards his letter as brief, inasmuch as he would like to have said more (cf. 9:5; 11:32).

23-25. In his last few personal notes he wants them to know that **Timothy is set at liberty.** Apparently, Timothy was well-known to both the author and readers and was the Timothy common to the New Testament since he is only given the appellation **brother Timothy.** He had recently been released from an imprisonment, and the author hopes to meet him and his readers at the same time.

Second, he wants them to salute all their leaders. They need to submit to and have respect for every one of them. And, finally, he extends greetings from **They of Italy.** The preposition (Gr *apo*) might better be translated from Italy. At first sight this phrase seems to imply those in **Italy;** but it can equally mean those who presently are in Italy, or those who formerly were from Italy. Acts 10:23 provides an example of the former interpretation of this construction for it speaks of those still living in Joppa (cf. also Acts 17:13). On the other hand, Acts 21:27 uses

18 Pray for us: for we trust we have a good conscience, in all things willing to live honestly.
19 But I beseech *you* the rather to do this, that I may be restored to you the sooner.

20 Now the God of peace, that brought again from the dead our Lord Jesus, that great shepherd of the sheep, through the blood of the everlasting covenant,
21 Make you perfect in every good work to do his will, working in you that which is wellpleasing in his sight, through Jesus Christ; to whom *be* glory for ever and ever. Amen.

22 And I beseech you, brethren, suffer the word of exhortation: for I have written a letter unto you in few words.

23 Know ye that *our* brother Tim'o-thy is set at liberty; with whom, if he come shortly, I will see you.
24 Salute all them that have the rule over you, and all the saints. They of It-aly salute you.
25 Grace *be* with you all. Amen.

this same construction to identify those from Asia who were then in Jerusalem. Thus, **They of Italy** may refer to those in Italy or those from Italy. The phrase only identifies their origin; they were Italians. It does seem safe, though, to conclude that either the writer or the recipients were living in Rome (see Introduction for further discussion).

May God's **Grace be with you all. Amen.**

BIBLIOGRAPHY

Archer, G. *The Epistle to the Hebrews: A Study Manual.* Grand Rapids: Baker, 1961.

Brown, J. *An Exposition of the Epistle to the Hebrews.* London: Banner of Truth, reprint of 1862 ed.

*Bruce, F. F. The Epistle to the Hebrews. In the *New International Commentary.* Grand Rapids: Eerdmans, 1964.

Davidson, A. B. *The Epistle to the Hebrews.* Edinburgh: T. & T. Clark, 1870.

Delitzsch, F. *Commentary on the Epistle to the Hebrews.* 2 vols. Edinburgh: T. & T. Clark, 1870.

Dods, M. The Epistle to the Hebrews. In the *Expositors Greek Testament.* Vol 4. Grand Rapids: Eerdmans, n.d.

English, E. Schuyler. *Studies in the Epistle to the Hebrews.* Findlay: Dunham, 1955.

Hewitt, T. The Epistle to the Hebrews. In the *Tyndale New Testament Commentary.* Grand Rapids: Eerdmans, 1960.

*Hughes, P. E. *A Commentary on the Epistle to the Hebrews.* Grand Rapids: Eerdmans, 1977.

*Kent, H. A. *The Epistle to the Hebrews: A Commentary.* Grand Rapids: Baker, 1972.

Lenski, R. C. H. *Interpretation of the Epistle to the Hebrews and the Epistle of James.* Minneapolis: Augsburg Publishing House, 1966.

Manson, W. *The Epistle to the Hebrews.* London: Hodder & Stoughton, 1951.

Moffatt, J. Epistle to the Hebrews. In the *International Critical Commentary.* New York: Scribner's, 1924.

Murray, Andrew. *The Holiest of All.* Westwood: Revell, 1960.

Newell, W. R. *Hebrews Verse by Verse.* Chicago: Moody Press, 1947.

*Owen, J. *Hebrews: The Epistle of Warning.* Abridged ed. Grand Rapids: Kregel, 1968.

Pink, A. W. *An Exposition of Hebrews.* Grand Rapids: Baker, 1963.

Ross, R. W. Hebrews. In the *Wycliffe Bible Commentary.* Chicago: Moody Press, 1962.

Thomas, W. H. Griffith. *Let Us Go On.* Grand Rapids: Eerdmans, 1966.

Vine, W. E. *The Epistle to the Hebrews.* London: Oliphants, 1952.

*Westcott, B. F. *The Epistle to the Hebrews.* Grand Rapids: Eerdmans, reprinted, 1974.

The Epistle Of
JAMES

INTRODUCTION

The Epistle of James was one of the last books of the New Testament to be accepted into the canon. One of the earliest lists of authoritative books, the Muratorian Canon (A.D. 170-200), omitted it, but general agreement of its canonicity solidified at the Council of Carthage (A.D. 397). Some early Christian writings did allude to it, and Origen definitely accepted it (A.D. 250). Although Eusebius categorized it among the disputed books, he affirmed that it was received by most churches. The primary cause for reluctance to recognize the epistle lies in a misunderstanding of James' soteriology (2:14-16). However, a close examination of his "justification by works" discussion reveals no disagreement between himself and Paul.

Authorship. The author identifies himself as "James, a servant of God and of the Lord Jesus Christ" (1:1). Four men in the New Testament bore that name: First, the father of Judas (the apostle) not Judas Iscariot (Lk 6:16); second, James, the son of Alphaeus, another apostle (Mt 10:3); third, James, the brother of John and the son of Zebedee (Mt 4:21); and last, the brother of the Lord Jesus (Mt 13:55). Since the first two are rather obscure, neither has been postulated as the author, and the brother of John was martyred too early to receive serious consideration. The Lord's brother not only has overwhelming traditional support, but his prominent position in the Jerusalem assembly makes him the most likely choice (cf. Acts 12:17; 15:13; Gal 1:19; 2:9). Prior to Jesus' death and resurrection, James, along with his brothers did not believe (Jn 7:5). Perhaps it was Christ's post-resurrection appearance to him that brought about his conversion (I Cor 15:7).

Recipients. The salutation labels the addressees as "the twelve tribes which are scattered abroad," which could have been translated "the twelve tribes of the diaspora (dispersion)." Because the expression was typically applied to Israel, some conclude that James was addressing all Jews. Others interpret the phrase metaphorically, referring to Christians in general. In its content and style the letter concedes partial truth in both views. He wrote to Christian Jews. "Brethren" of James 1:2 and 2:1 addresses fellow Christians, while the style and content anticipate a Jewish reader.

Occasion and date. The date of writing proposed is either early or late and, ironically, for the same reason, i.e., the epistle's apparent contrast to pauline theology. To those who argue for a late date, Paul's "justification by faith" had been abused and exaggerated resulting in the neglect of Christian service. Accordingly, James refutes perversions of this doctrine. Others, contending that he wrote before Paul, explain that his aim centered around the practical, works being emphasized. That being the case, a salient need still existed for a clear exposition of justification, which, of course, was accomplished by Paul. Another indication of an early date is found in James 2:2, where the "assembly" mentioned is actually "synagogue," the place commonly used for worship in the earliest years of Christianity. The epistle probably was written in the middle forties, prior to the Council at Jerusalem, which dates to A.D. 49.

The author's subject matter also implies that he wrote early. New Testament epistles notably involve doctrinal issues, because sufficient time had elapsed for perversions to arise. Nevertheless, James disregards such discussion, which implies that significant heresies had not yet developed. Since the initial church consisted of Jews only, the prevailing Jewish style also suits this period.

Characteristics. Many view the Epistle of James as the foremost Jewish book in the New Testament. Christ's name is found only twice (1:1; 2:1), and the author resorts to the Old Testament freely. Illustrations, such as, Abraham, Rahab, and Elijah, and peculiar expressions, as "your synagogue" and "the Lord of Sabaoth" attest to this.

The author's approach is pragmatic. Wielding warnings and reproofs (there are over fifty imperatives), James resembles the prophets of old.

Contents. Admittedly the book's structure is somewhat loose, but it is an exaggeration to characterize it as a series of independent admonitions. An outline within the epistle offers general advice to those under adverse circumstances (1:19): they should be "swift to hear, slow to speak, and slow to wrath." The first point is modified to "obedience" (1:22), the crowning purpose of hearing. Details may be examined in the separate outline.

OUTLINE

2. True wisdom is expressed through daily living. 3:13-18.
D. "Slow to Wrath." 4:1-5:6.
 1. Wrath stems from a worldly attitude. 4:1-5.

2. Wrath stems from a proud attitude. 4:6-17.
3. Extreme wrath often comes from the rich. 5:1-6.
IV. Conclusion. 5:7-20.

COMMENTARY

JAMES, a servant of God and of the Lord Jesus Christ, to the twelve tribes which are scattered abroad, greeting.

I. INTRODUCTION. 1:1.

1:1. The author identifies himself as **James, a servant of God and of the Lord Jesus Christ.** He, as well as Jude, was a brother of the Lord. For further discussion about him see the introduction. The designation **servant** (Gr *doulos*) means "bond-slave," and is to be distinguished from an employee. He affirms his life, and therefore what he writes, to be under the direction of the One who owns him.

The twelve tribes which are scattered abroad refers to Christians who were by persecution driven out of and scattered from Jerusalem (Acts 8:1). Since James was the leader of the Jerusalem congregation, it was only natural that he write to them regarding their faith.

II. THE TESTS OF LIFE. 1:2-18.

A. Joy Under Temptations. 1:2-11.

2. The trials which befall Christians should not cause alarm or sorrow. In fact, James urges his readers to **count it all joy.** The child of God may rejoice victoriously in the darkest hour. The following verse explains why. **My brethren:** the recipients are Christians. **When ye fall into divers temptations:** the trials (Gr *peirasmos*) refer to internal and external adversities which would misdirect the servant of God. The verb and adjective join to underline a predominant characteristic of trials; they cannot be anticipated in type or time.

2 My brethren, count it all joy when ye fall into divers temptations;

3 Knowing *this*, that the trying of your faith worketh patience.

3. Joy amid hardship springs up from an illumined heart. The Christian perceives purpose among persecution and problems. **Knowing** (Gr *ginōskō*) involves experiential knowledge, not merely the accumulation of known facts. **That the trying of your faith worketh patience:** the word for **trying** (Gr *dokimion*) implies victory over trial, and may be better rendered "the proving of your faith. . . ." **Patience** (Gr *hypomonē*) does not mean waiting without anxiety, but to endure adverse circumstances without letting them sour the attitude.

4 But let patience have *her* perfect work, that ye may be perfect and entire, wanting nothing.

4. Endurance is a virtue which very few people experience fully. Too often we grasp relief from trouble so eagerly that we fail to receive the entire lesson that God intended for us. **Let patience have her perfect work** cautions us to observe our attitudes more than our circumstances. If one does this, he will realize the road to Christian maturity. Perfection in the absolute sense, however, will be reserved for the life to come (I Jn 1:8).

5 If any of you lack wisdom, let him ask of God, that giveth to all *men* liberally, and upbraideth not; and it shall be given him.

5. The close connection between verses 4 and 5 is marked in the AV by translating a single Greek word in two ways. **Wanting** (vs. 4) and **lack** (vs. 5) stem from the same word (Gr *leipō*) which implies that the reader might ask after verse 4, "How can I find purpose in this predicament?" **If any of you lack wisdom** (specifically in what God is accomplishing through the trials), **let him ask.** Two characteristics of God's attitude toward giving become apparent; **God that giveth to all men liberally, and upbraideth not.** Both contrast to man's style of bestowing. He neither displays reluctance to release His gifts, nor humiliates the needy petitioners.

6 But let him ask in faith, nothing wa-

6. The restriction involves the receiver, not the Giver. To **ask**

vering. For he that wavereth is like a wave of the sea driven with the wind and tossed.

7 For let not that man think that he shall receive any thing of the Lord.
8 A double minded man *is* unstable in all his ways.

9 Let the brother of low degree rejoice in that he is exalted:
10 But the rich, in that he is made low: because as the flower of the grass he shall pass away.
11 For the sun is no sooner risen with a burning heat, but it withereth the grass, and the flower thereof falleth, and the grace of the fashion of it perisheth: so also shall the rich man fade away in his ways.

12 Blessed *is* the man that endureth temptation: for when he is tried, he shall receive the crown of life, which the Lord hath promised to them that love him.
13 Let no man say when he is tempted, I am tempted of God: for God cannot be tempted with evil, neither tempteth he any man:
14 But every man is tempted, when he is drawn away of his own lust, and enticed.
15 Then when lust hath conceived, it bringeth forth sin: and sin, when it is finished, bringeth forth death.
16 Do not err, my beloved brethren.

17 Every good gift and every perfect gift is from above, and cometh down from the Father of lights, with whom is no variableness, neither shadow of turning.

18 Of his own will begat he us with the word of truth, that we should be a kind of firstfruits of his creatures.

19 Wherefore, my beloved brethren, let every man be swift to hear, slow to speak, slow to wrath:
20 For the wrath of man worketh not the righteousness of God.

in faith denotes the absence of **wavering** (Gr *diakrinomai*), which suggests an anxious reevaluation, "second thoughts" about one's prayer. This type of person compares to a **wave** which is **driven** and **tossed** by circumstances. Christians, by faith, should persistently avow under any circumstances that God is all He claims to be.

7-8. A "waverer" may expect nothing. He lives in two philosophical worlds, the natural and the supernatural; and while he rejects the natural intellectually, he will not wholly commit himself to God. The Lord covets servants who will be "one hundred percenters."

9-11. These three verses underscore the urgency of submitting to God's perspective. We are to **rejoice** not because of earthly circumstances but by reason of spiritual realities. A **brother** may be **of low degree** (Gr *tapeinos*), of a "lowly" economic or social status, but there is reason for joy. In God's esteem **he is exalted.** Through the grace of God he has been lifted out of the miry clay (Ps 40:2) and claims a heavenly position in Christ (Eph 1:3). Conversely, the **rich** may rejoice because temporal possessions are not all they have. When they humble themselves, repenting of sin, they become children of God and joint-heirs with Christ (Rom 8:17). The illustration of the short-lived flower reminds us how ephemeral this life really is.

B. The Source of Temptations. 1:12-18.

12. Endureth. (Gr *hypomenō*) is the verb form of the word "patience" (see 1:3 for its etymology). The **crown of life** is not a tangible wreath as in the Greek games, but the reward is life itself.

13. Since temptation may have beneficial results, some might conclude that God Himself sends it. The author categorically denies that; God is never the source of temptation.

14. The actual source of temptation lies within man, **his own lust** (Gr *epithymia*), his inherent longings.

15-16. The process of evil compares to a life cycle. **Lust** may seem insignificantly small, but it produces sin, which, when it is **finished** (Gr *apoteleō*), literally, has matured enough to bear children, **bringeth forth death.** Lust, so to speak, is the grandmother of death.

17. Not only are God's gifts **good** (useful, practical) and **perfect** (nothing lacking in them), but His liberality is wholly consistent. Fickle man may succumb to "lusts," but He, **the Father of lights,** does not embrace the faintest shadow of change.

18. If "justification by works" (2:24) causes one to question James' soteriology, he should note here the basis of salvation: **Of his own will begat he.** The verb, **begat** (Gr *apokyeō*), stems from the same root as "bringeth forth" of verse 15. Sin kills, but God regenerates.

III. THE CHRISTIAN LIFE THROUGH TESTING. 1:19-5:6.

A. The Author's Structure. 1:19-20.

19-20. From this point, the practical Epistle of James follows the three categories listed here: (1) **swift to hear** (1:21-2:26), regarding hearing as doing; (2) **slow to speak** (3:1-18), including the vulnerability of excessive talking and the comparison of conduct and speech; and (3) **slow to wrath** (4:1-17), identifying the sources of bitterness. The threefold admonition explains the proper response to the trials of life discussed in 1:2-18.

21 Wherefore lay apart all filthiness and superfluity of naughtiness, and receive with meekness the engrafted word, which is able to save your souls.

22 But be ye doers of the word, and not hearers only, deceiving your own selves.

23 For if any be a hearer of the word, and not a doer, he is like unto a man beholding his natural face in a glass:
24 For he beholdeth himself, and goeth his way, and straightway forgetteth what manner of man he was.
25 But whoso looketh into the perfect law of liberty, and continueth *therein*, he being not a forgetful hearer, but a doer of the work, this man shall be blessed in his deed.

26 If any man among you seem to be religious, and bridleth not his tongue, but deceiveth his own heart, this man's religion *is* vain.
27 Pure religion and undefiled before God and the Father is this, To visit the fatherless and widows in their affliction, *and* to keep himself unspotted from the world.

CHAPTER 2

MY brethren, have not the faith of our Lord Jesus Christ, *the Lord* of glory, with respect of persons.

2 For if there come unto your assembly a man with a gold ring, in goodly apparel, and there come in also a poor man in vile raiment;
3 And ye have respect to him that weareth the gay clothing, and say unto him, Sit thou here in a good place; and say to the poor, Stand thou there, or sit here under my footstool:
4 Are ye not then partial in yourselves, and are become judges of evil thoughts?

5 Hearken, my beloved brethren, Hath not God chosen the poor of this world rich in faith, and heirs of the kingdom which he hath promised to them that love him?
6 But ye have despised the poor. Do not rich men oppress you, and draw you before the judgment seats?

B. "Quick to Hear." 1:21-2:26.

1. Real hearing involves doing. 1:21-25.

21. The command to **lay aside all filthiness and superfluity of naughtiness** employs expressions of coarseness rather than immorality. To overcome trials one must shun vulgarity as well as wickedness. **The engrafted word,** the implanted message of the gospel (1:18), should be **received** by Christians (cf. "brethren," 1:19) with unqualified submissiveness. The phrase, **able to save your souls,** points out the inherent efficacy of the gospel which they have already accepted.

22. The Greek present tense in **be ye doers of the word** may be rendered "Continue being doers. . . ." However, the word **be** (Gr *ginomai*), often translated "become," views their obedience as a constant struggle. Hearing profits when it generates a transformed life, but **hearers** only merely soothe their consciences temporarily, deceiving themselves.

23-24. He who follows this form of irrational thinking sees **his natural face in a glass** (mirror) . . . and goeth his way. He observes, becomes entirely cognizant of the flaws, and promptly **forgetteth.**

25. The **perfect law of liberty** parallels the **glass** of verse 23. James chose two words which contradict each other. **Law** signifies restrictions; **liberty** the absence of them. The apparent misnomer sets forth a momentous teaching. Although God embraces inflexible standards and laws, He freely pardons anyone who trusts in Christ. **Whoso looketh** (Gr *parakyptō*) implies much more than a glance (vs. 24), for the word involves bending over for closer inspection. It pictures a person before a mirror noticing a blemish, then leaning forward to examine and attend to it.

2. Doing involves mercy. 1:26-2:13.

26-27. The word **religion** (Gr *thrēskeia*), has to do with worship in the outward sense, religious service. An uncontrolled **tongue** exposes a spiritual problem. **This man's religion is vain** (Gr *mataios*); it yields no results. **Pure religion and undefiled** involves visiting the forsaken and relinquishing worldly enticements. Without governmental-aid programs **widows** and orphans face hunger and cold alone. Their welfare was the responsibility of Christians. It still is.

2:1. The AV's chapter division here is misleading, for the two previous verses relate closely to this passage. If true religion entails visiting the destitute, it leaves no room for **respect of persons** (Gr *prosōpolēmpsia*), which connotes "receiving because of one's face or appearance."

2-4. A clear illustration dismisses all excuses and exceptions. One might imagine two visitors arriving at a church on a Sunday morning. A chauffeured limousine exhibits a man arrayed in expensive clothing. Another man approaches in an old jalopy, and his cheap suit has almost worn through. When the usher favors the wealthy man, he becomes **partial** and a **judge of evil thoughts.** **Partial** comes from the same verb (Gr *diakrinomai*) as a word used in 1:6 ("wandering"). By their partiality the offenders have "wavered" in their faith. "Judges with evil thoughts" (RSV) explains that their evaluation was based on sinful attitudes.

5. In contrast to these inequitable religionists, God chose **the poor of this world.** Christian paupers possess secret riches both in their present **faith** and in His eternal **kingdom.**

6. Despised. (Gr *atimazō*), involves not only attitudes but shameful treatment, as when Jesus was "dishonored" by the

Jewish leaders (Jn 8:49). **Oppress** refers to the arrogant flaunting of governmental authority over Christians, as tyrants over helpless peasants. James has Jewish officials in mind when he says they **draw you before the judgment seats** (Gr *kritēria*). Acts 9:2, where Saul traveled to Damascus with official letters to arrest Christians, testifies to the authority which Rome handed over to the Jews. The **judgment seat** speaks of the local court.

7. Not only do they despise the poor and oppress Christians, but the rich direct their assaults against the Lord Himself. **They blaspheme** (Gr *blasphēmeō*) or "speak evil against" **that worthy name by the which ye are called,** i.e., Christians (Acts 11:26).

8. **The royal law** means "law that is truly royal in its quality" (R. C. H. Lenski, *The Epistle of Hebrews and James*, p. 570), because the definite article is absent in Greek, indicating that quality is emphasized. It is royal or kingly in its relation to other laws. Jesus said that this and the first commandment are so fundamental that on them "hang all the law and the prophets" (Mt 22:40). An individual "loves" himself irrespective of financial or social status. We should love others in the same manner. When we practice the law, we **do well;** it's beautiful!

9. The secular view of success assumes that favoritism must be employed, if one is to "climb the ladder" of accomplishment. Nonetheless, James warns that if one adopts this method, **have respect to persons** (2:1), what he "accomplishes" (AV is **commit,** but the Greek is *ergazomai*) in God's eyes is **sin.** Singular in form, the word **sin** points to quality. **Convinced of the law as transgressors** may be better translated "convicted by." The word for "convinced" (Gr *elenchō*) means to point out the guilt or fault in someone. **The law** is not the Mosaic code, but the "royal law," the law of love. Partiality represses genuine love.

10. **Offend** (Gr *ptaiō*) literally means to stumble or trip. Thus, James, for the sake of argument, awards the party pure motives, granting that the sin appears accidental. The result, **guilty of all,** contradicts salvation by works. Since all men are "guilty before God" (Rom 3:19), salvation necessarily is by grace through faith (Eph 3:8-9).

11. A basketball, whether it misses the hoop by an inch or a yard, still fails to score. Likewise, he who shows partiality **becomes a transgressor** just as readily as if he had murdered or committed adultery.

12. **So speak ye, and so do.** Both of these verbs being in the Greek present tense, which connotes continuous action, this phrase would be better translated, "Continue speaking and continue doing." How may we be motivated to do so? **As they that shall be judged.** The AV phraseology, however, implies a too distant judgment. The verb (Gr *mellō*) means "about to be," denoting imminent retribution. Christians ought to conduct themselves as if judgment may come at any moment. The constraining stimulus should not be a harsh, merciless court, but the **law of liberty,** which assures us we are free from the bondage of sin.

13. Mercy is so basic to Christian living that it is impossible for a true believer not to have it. Of course, the extent may vary, but he that shows none will find **judgment without mercy.**

3. Doing demonstrates faith. 2:14-26.

The last thirteen verses of the second chapter of James have been among the most controversial passages in Scripture. The statements in this chapter may appear to oppose pauline doctrine, but a careful analysis demonstrates indissoluble harmony between the two inspired writers. The difference in expression arises from their distinct purposes. Paul wrote to explain the gospel; James had in view its practical implications.

14. If one regards the author's purpose, the discussion will be less difficult to interpret. Many misunderstand this verse be-

---

7 Do not they blaspheme that worthy name by the which ye are called?

8 If ye fulfil the royal law according to the scripture, Thou shalt love thy neighbour as thyself, ye do well:

9 But if ye have respect to persons, ye commit sin, and are convinced of the law as transgressors.

10 For whosoever shall keep the whole law, and yet offend in one *point,* he is guilty of all.

11 For he that said, Do not commit adultery, said also, Do not kill. Now if thou commit no adultery, yet if thou kill, thou art become a transgressor of the law.

12 So speak ye, and so do, as they that shall be judged by the law of liberty.

13 For he shall have judgment without mercy, that hath shewed no mercy; and mercy rejoiceth against judgment.

14 What *doth it* profit, my brethren,

though a man say he hath faith, and have not works? can faith save him?

15 If a brother or sister be naked, and destitute of daily food,
16 And one of you say unto them, Depart in peace, be ye warmed and filled; notwithstanding ye give them not those things which are needful to the body; what *doth it* profit?
17 Even so faith, if it hath not works, is dead, being alone.

18 Yea, a man may say, Thou hast faith, and I have works: shew me thy faith without thy works, and I will shew thee my faith by my works.

19 Thou believest that there is one God; thou doest well: the devils also believe, and tremble.

20 But wilt thou know, O vain man, that faith without works is dead?

21 Was not Abraham our father justified by works, when he had offered Isaac his son upon the altar?

22 Seest thou how faith wrought with his works, and by works was faith made perfect?

23 And the scripture was fulfilled which saith, Abraham believed God,

cause they fail to observe two significant facts. First, James does not state that the hypothetical person "has" faith, but merely a man **say he hath faith.** It distinguishes the one who "possesses" from the one who merely "professes." Secondly, conclusions are based on the question, **can faith save him?** The AV unfortunately gives a wrong impression, for he is not asking about faith in general, but that type of faith which one has who makes claims without producing fruit. This is affirmed by the presence of the definite article in Greek meaning "the faith." "Can that faith save him?" would be a proper translation. Which faith? That which the man claims to have. That being the case, James does not contradict Paul. Both affirm that true saving faith results in a changed life as evidenced by works (Eph 2:8-10).

15-16. When Christians **say** empty platitudes without actually helping those in physical need, **what doth it profit?** How many words fill a hungry stomach?

17. Even so. As the worthlessness of well-wishers reveal their selfishness, so barrenness in a professing believer's life exposes his insincerity. Significantly, the Greek text states with the article, that "the **faith . . . is dead, being alone.** James refers specifically to the faith which is claimed, not the genuine brand.

18. A man may say. The author communicates his accusation through an assumed third person, allowing his remarks to be received more objectively. The matter of contention is not works *per se*, but the evidence of faith. Pious expressions may **seem to be religious** (1:26), but actions are what people hear.

19. One fixed tenet of these Jewish readers was monotheism, **Thou believest that there is one God;** but doctrine alone does not save. **Thou doest well** inserts a measure of sarcasm, for he quickly points out that **the devils** (Gr *daimonion*, "demons") also affirm that truth. Demonic faith, far from effecting service, exists in terror.

20. Wilt thou know is rhetorical. Having developed his argument to this point, James expects the recognition of truth. The address, **O vain man,** extends beyond empty faith to a person void of reality. As in verse 17, the word **faith** occurs with the Greek definite article meaning "the faith" or "that faith."

21. Abraham is the father of all believers (Rom 4:16), but the reference here, **our father,** links him with his nation, the Jews. That he was **justified by works** appears to contradict Paul's "justification by faith" (Rom 3:28; 4:2; 5:1). Romans 3:20 conclusively declares, "Therefore by the deeds of the law there shall no flesh be justified in his sight." Observe Paul's references to God: "in His sight" plus "before God" in Romans 4:2 (cf. Thomas Manton, *An Exposition of the Epistle of James,* p. 244). Most frequently, the word for justify (Gr *dikaioō*) in the New Testament speaks of God's positive verdict, the opposite of condemnation. The unjustified man, according to Romans, is a condemned sinner; but in the Epistle of James he is a hypocrite. Consequently, Abraham's justification in this passage consisted of man's verdict. Christians, Jews, and Arabs have "declared righteous" this man of God, because of the faith demonstrated when he offered his only son.

22. A more accurate translation of **faith wrought with his works** would be "faith operated by means of his works." Salvation is not accomplished through the cooperation of faith and works, but faith finds its channel of expression in works. **By works was faith made perfect** may be rendered "out of works was faith completed." James 1:3-4 embraces the same thought: the development of inner character parallels the extent of testing endured (I Pet 1:7).

23. The author never impugns faith *per se,* but he candidly denounces that brand of self-acclaimed faith which finds no

and it was imputed unto him for righteousness: and he was called the Friend of God.

24 Ye see then how that by works a man is justified, and not by faith only.

25 Likewise also was not Rahab the harlot justified by works, when she had received the messengers, and had sent *them* out another way?

26 For as the body without the spirit is dead, so faith without works is dead also.

CHAPTER 3
MY brethren, be not many masters, knowing that we shall receive the greater condemnation.

2 For in many things we offend all. If any man offend not in word, the same *is* a perfect man, *and* able also to bridle the whole body.

3 Behold, we put bits in the horses' mouths, that they may obey us; and we turn about their whole body.
4 Behold also the ships, which though *they be* so great, and *are* driven of fierce winds, yet are they turned about with a very small helm, whithersoever the governor listeth.

5 Even so the tongue is a little member, and boasteth great things. Behold, how great a matter a little fire kindleth!

6 And the tongue *is* a fire, a world of iniquity: so is the tongue among our members, that it defileth the whole body, and setteth on fire the course of nature; and it is set on fire of hell.

7 For every kind of beasts, and of birds, and of serpents, and of things in

profitable service. Genesis 15:6 was spoken years before Isaac was offered, but it was then that Abraham's faith became evident. His fame resulted from works, the corollary of real faith (Rom 4:19-22); but his relationship with the Lord had been settled years before. He has been **called the Friend of God** for centuries by Jews, Arabs, and Christians.

24. In a court, if a man's motive comes in question, the only means to justify or vindicate his motive is to examine his acts. Genuine faith is conscious of others. "Pure religion" involves a life of ministry, not introspective qualities.

25. Rahab's works were done by faith (Heb 11:31), but actions were necessary to affirm her inner change. Had she remained in sin while acclaiming faith, she would never have been "declared righteous" (justified).

26. The comparison of the human spirit and faith converges around their modes of operation. The spirit (Gr *pneuma*) may also be translated "breath." As a breathless body emits no indication of life, so fruitless faith exhibits nothing more than hypocrisy.

C. "Slow to Speak." 3:1-18.

1. The tongue is destructive. 3:1-12.

3:1. According to the structure provided in James 1:19, the second directive is "slow to speak." The problem is rather obvious: too much talking. Its root cause lies in a proud attitude, which thrives in pretentious self-expression. Being **masters** or teachers (Gr *didaskalos*) could become the means for releasing it. Having too many teachers is like having more foremen than laborers. The Bible clearly commends submissiveness, "a contrite spirit" (Isa 66:2), but humility must not be equated with position. James cautions those who would be leaders to examine their motives. Is the Lord Himself directing you, or are you gratifying desires for self-promotion? **Greater condemnation** or judgment (Gr *krino*) parallels greater responsibility (Lk 12:48).

2. The verb **offend** (Gr *ptaiō*) means to trip or stumble, and thus, the clause may be rendered, "We all are stumbling in many areas." None of us has reached perfection. **Perfect** (Gr *teleios*) describes the man who has reached his goal, the man who is self-controlled. That being the case in speech, he is **able also to bridle the whole body,** because the tongue resists control more than any other area of behavior. **Bridle** pictures restrained guidance.

3-4. Two illustrations emphasize that often what holds the greatest influence may appear insignificant, size having nothing to do with importance. In comparison to the total dimensions of a horse, a **bit** in the mouth appears trivial, yet the animal obeys it. **Ships,** enormous and **driven** by awesome winds, may be steered by a **very small helm** (Gr *pēdalion*), rudder. **Whithersoever the governor listeth** in contemporary language may be translated, "Wherever the pilot wants it to go."

5. Behold, how great a matter a little fire kindleth! The tongue may be compared to a match in size, but its effect is like a raging forest fire.

6. Nowhere else in Scripture is the tongue pictured with such pungent language. It is a **world of iniquity** (Gr *adikia*, literally, unrighteousness), and it spreads throughout the body like a devouring cancer. The **course of nature** (Gr *genesis*) refers to the pattern of history; a sharp tongue may instigate war or prevent an election. The source accounts for its character; **hell,** (Gr *geenna*) originally referred to the Valley of Hinnom, south and west of Jerusalem, where a perpetual fire blazed on its garbage heaps. It became an awesome symbol of the eternal abode of the lost.

7-8. Every is obviously restricted to creatures of sufficient intelligence to be **tamed.** The wildest stallion may be broken,

the sea, is tamed, and hath been tamed of mankind:

8 But the tongue can no man tame; *it is* an unruly evil, full of deadly poison.

9 Therewith bless we God, even the Father; and therewith curse we men, which are made after the similitude of God.

10 Out of the same mouth proceedeth blessing and cursing. My brethren, these things ought not so to be.

11 Doth a fountain send forth at the same place sweet *water* and bitter?

12 Can the fig tree, my brethren, bear olive berries? either a vine, figs? so *can* no fountain both yield salt water and fresh.

13 Who *is* a wise man and endued with knowledge among you? let him shew out of a good conversation his works with meekness of wisdom.

14 But if ye have bitter envying and strife in your hearts, glory not, and lie not against the truth.

15 This wisdom descendeth not from above, but *is* earthly, sensual, devilish.

16 For where envying and strife *is*, there *is* confusion and every evil work.

17 But the wisdom that is from above is first pure, then peaceable, gentle, *and* easy to be intreated, full of mercy and good fruits, without partiality, and without hypocrisy.

but the tongue continually erupts in outbursts of uncontrolled emotion. This does not necessarily mean that everyone unceasingly makes unintended comments, but it does mean that even the most respected, gracious people have their own seasons of regretful words. **Full of deadly poison** speaks of the death blows words may deliver to good relationships. A single sentence uttered in heated discussion may sever a long friendship.

9-10. Contrasting the actions of the tongue unveils its inconsistency: **bless . . . curse.** Although the offender may excuse his contradictory expressions on the basis of depravity, men **are made after the similitude of God.** In spite of man's fall and resulting wickedness, he still bears God's image (Gen 1:26; 5:1, 3; 9:6; I Cor 11:7; Eph 4:24; and Col 3:10). Although there is an infinite qualitative difference between them, man resembles God in a way which distinguishes him from the rest of God's creation. The Bible does not clearly specify the nature of the image, and therefore, scholars differ as to the meaning. The main views are: (1) bodily form; (2) dominion over the animal world; (3) moral nature; and (4) personality. Stephen Barabas synthesizes three of these. Man is a "rational, self-conscious, self-determining creature, capable of obedience to moral law, and intended by God for fellowship with Himself." (Merrill C. Tenney, Ed. *Zondervan Pictorial Bible Dictionary*, p. 371). **These things ought not so to be.** A distinction may be seen in Scripture between carnal judging and spiritual discernment. Care must be practiced to aim denunciations against sin and not the sinner. The Lord can forgive the worst offender; thus Christians should hope for God's regenerating power even in unlikely persons.

11-12. Fountain (Gr *pēgē* would be a "spring" in modern terminology. Just as it would be absurd to think that it produces both **sweet water** and **bitter,** or **salt walter** and **fresh,** or that a grape **vine** yields **figs,** so a mouth which condemns men while praising God lacks credibility. That sort of person would have a shallow Christian experience, if one at all.

2. True wisdom is expressed through daily living. 3:13-18.

13. A **wise** man may desire to manifest his knowledge through teaching, but James says **let him show** a changed life through **works. Conversation** (Gr *anastrophe*) means behavior or conduct.

14. The verse correlates the tongue and wisdom. The former, as an outward sign, may reveal a heart of **bitter envying and strife,** which is founded on pride. To bless and curse **out of the same mouth** (vs. 10) is to elevate oneself above God's truth. A man may judge others for wrongdoing, yet overlook his own failure of the **royal law** (2:8). **Glory not, and lie not,** both present tense verbs, may be translated "stop glorying and stop lying."

15. If wisdom displays itself apart from good conduct and meekness, it is **not from above.** In fact, it is characterized as **earthly,** wise by the world's standards, **sensual** (Gr *psychikos*), meaning natural as distinguished from spiritual, and **devilish** (Gr *daimoniōdēs*), of demonic influence.

16. The author leaves no doubt about the effects of **envying and strife** of verse 14. **Confusion** (Gr *akatastasis*) opposes that which is established. **Every evil work** specifically means "every foul practice." **Strife** usually begins with gossip and climaxes in direct confrontation.

17. Pure contrasts with **evil** of the previous verse. **Peaceable, gentle, and easy to be entreated** join as opposites of **confusion** (vs. 16). **Full of mercy and good fruits** reminds one that faith apart from works is unprofitable (2:14-26). **Without hypocrisy.** Practicing **partiality** (2:4), **faith without works** (2:17), and **boasting** (2:14) all involve hypocrisy, which originally referred to the "acting" that was performed in theaters.

18 And the fruit of righteousness is sown in peace of them that make peace.

18. This section, "slow to speak" (1:19), has focused around the uncontrolled tongue. Inner qualities are what season one's speech, and here **peace** is emphasized in two ways: (1) **righteousness is sown**, that is, it has its beginnings in peaceful conditions, not **envying and strife** (vs. 16); and (2) righteousness appears in those who practice peace. The glaring blemish of evangelical churches is inner turmoil and bickering, yet Christian living depends upon **peace**.

D. "Slow to Wrath." 4:1-5:6.

1. Wrath stems from a worldly attitude. 4:1-5.

CHAPTER 4

FROM whence *come* wars and fightings among you? *come they* not hence, *even* of your lusts that war in your members?

4:1. James addresses church members who are infected by materialism, given to partiality, and jealous of each other. **War in your members** sounds like Peter (I Pet 2:11) or Paul (Rom 7:23) who agree that carnal desires rage within the believer or thwart his spiritual progress. Since self-control is a fruit of the Spirit (Gal 5:22), His filling is the means of victory.

2 Ye lust, and have not: ye kill, and desire to have, and cannot obtain: ye fight and war, yet ye have not, because ye ask not.

2. Kill, along with **wars and fightings** of the previous verse, is best taken figuratively. It seems inconceivable that Christians were involved in actual combat and murder without any mention of any governmental intervention. These strong words were chosen to stress the seriousness of their acts.

3 Ye ask, and receive not, because ye ask amiss, that ye may consume *it* upon your lusts.

3. Even when they did **ask,** their prayers went unanswered, because they sought personal gratification, disregarding God's will. "What a picture of the lustful heart tossed about and buffeted on the sea of his own selfish desires, committing murder in his heart attitude, jealous and contentious, forgetting to pray except only to pray amiss, always and ever unrestful and unsatisfied" (Zane Hodges, Lectures on James, unpublished).

4 Ye adulterers and adulteresses, know ye not that the friendship of the world is enmity with God? whosoever therefore will be a friend of the world is the enemy of God.

4. Ye adulterers and adulteresses. Spiritual adultery was mentioned often in the Old Testament (Isa 57:3-9; Jer 3:20; Ezk 16:32, 35, 38; and Hos 2). It is no more right for a Christian to love both God and the world, than for a man to have two wives. Unfaithfulness would repulse the offended party in either case. **Know ye not. . . ?** A common characteristic of backsliding is the voluntary blindness toward the seriousness of sin. **Enmity with God** is something the Christian was delivered from (Rom 5:10), and therefore, his "affair" with the world should cause shame and remorse.

5 Do ye think that the scripture saith in vain, The spirit that dwelleth in us lusteth to envy?

5. Do ye think that the scripture saith in vain expects a negative reply. Could we imagine God's Word going forth without purpose, direction, or power? Since this quote cannot be found in the Old Testament, it appears that James alludes to a principle. In the original, **to envy** (Gr *phthonos*) receives prominence by its position. This expression, when taken adverbially, "the Spirit that dwells in us lusts jealously," speaks of divine jealousy, a familiar doctrine to these Jews (Ex 20:5; 34:14; Zech 8:2). **Dwelleth** (Gr *katoikeō*) differs from the word which signifies a temporary dwelling. The Holy Spirit's indwelling in the believer is not transient, but He, as it were, makes His residence within us. **Lusteth** (Gr *epipotheō*) speaks of intense desires, which explains why the charge of spiritual adultery was made in the previous verse. Its counterpart, spiritual faithfulness, measures the believer's love for the Lord. Friendship with the world exposes the shallowness of one's spirituality.

2. Wrath stems from a proud attitude. 4:6-17.

6 But he giveth more grace. Wherefore he saith, God resisteth the proud, but giveth grace unto the humble.

6. A sharp contrast exists between worldly and divine jealousy; men want revenge, but **he giveth more grace.** That statement, plus the quote (Prov 3:34), assure the repenting sinner that no offense is too great for God's forgiveness.

7 Submit yourselves therefore to God. Resist the devil, and he will flee from you.

7. Verses 7 through 10 contain a group of imperatives, the first and the last being almost identical: **Submit . . . Humble yourselves. Submit** (Gr *hypotassō*), a combination of two words, literally means "to place under," hence, subjection or submis-

8 Draw nigh to God, and he will draw nigh to you. Cleanse *your* hands, *ye* sinners; and purify *your* hearts, *ye* double minded.

9 Be afflicted, and mourn, and weep: let your laughter be turned to mourning, and *your* joy to heaviness.

10 Humble yourselves in the sight of the Lord, and he shall lift you up.

11 Speak not evil one of another, brethren. He that speaketh evil of *his* brother, and judgeth his brother, speaketh evil of the law, and judgeth the law: but if thou judge the law, thou art not a doer of the law, but a judge.

12 There is one lawgiver, who is able to save and to destroy: who art thou that judgest another?

13 Go to now, ye that say, To day or to morrow we will go into such a city, and continue there a year, and buy and sell, and get gain:

14 Whereas ye know not what *shall be* on the morrow. For what *is* your life? It is even a vapour, that appeareth for a little time, and then vanisheth away.

15 For that ye *ought* to say, If the Lord will, we shall live, and do this, or that.

16 But now ye rejoice in your boastings: all such rejoicing is evil.

sion. Because of God's never-ending grace, the Christian's logical behavior is total submission to Him, rather than enslavement to the world's allurements (Rom 12:1-2). Two factors should be mentioned regarding **Resist the devil.** First, we should stand against outward opposition, even though we are instructed to flee inner cravings (II Tim 2:22). Secondly, **devil** (Gr *diabolos*), a word meaning "accuser," portrays our enemy scrutinizing the intimate details of one's personal life to expose any fault. Thus the believer must walk in the Spirit with the utmost caution. He must walk worthy (Col 1:9-10).

8-9. The tense of **Draw nigh** implores the listeners to complete a single, definite act. **Cleanse** and **purify** differ in what they affect. The former, along with **hands** and **sinners,** speaks of actions which may be observed. The latter, addressed to the internal insecurities of the "double-minded" (1:8), is aimed against improper motives and wicked thoughts. Spirituality involves regeneration and revival, not just reformation; a new heart precedes a changed life.

10. Humble yourselves. The man who submits himself to the Lord will be exalted in ways which he himself could never accomplish. This primarily refers to one's spiritual relationship with God.

11. With the **wars and fighting among you** (4:1), James discussed humility in order to advance a principle. True humility cannot be achieved by one who slanders his brothers. As an appeal to spiritual unity, the word **brother** is mentioned three times. When a man impugns his Christian brother, he proudly sets himself above the law that God has established.

12. The word, **one** is placed first in the original to extol Him above all others. In many older manuscripts He is called **lawgiver** (Gr *nomothetēs*), the one **who is able . . . . to destroy,** and also **judge.** These designate God as author, interpreter, and executor of the law. If He alone holds these functions, then **who art thou that judgest another?** Yet, in spite of its haughty character, Christians, through various attempts to rationalize, condone its presence in each other.

13. Go to now, used as an interjection, compares to our expression, "Come now!" James attacks another area where pride frequently erupts: the world of business. God has gifted His chosen people with unusual ability in commercial ventures, and these Christian Jews erred because of wrong attitudes toward it. Careful planning must be included in successful business methods, but sound principles of management are insufficient. Before making an expensive investment a wise executive considers all factors in painful detail. The folly exposed is disregarding the preeminent fact of life, i.e., God! Carnal men assume extended life without knowing "the Life" (Jn 14:6), taking for granted each day as if they had earned it.

14. Ye know not. In spite of human frailty and ignorance of tomorrow, man arrogantly predicts his life's course. **For what is your life?** The question hopes to shake someone out of apathy and cause him to reassess his priorities. **Vapor** (Gr *atmis*) is used of smoke (Acts 2:19), incense (Ezk 8:11), and of steam. It makes no difference which one is chosen, for all are transient and gone in a moment. Compared to eternity, the span of our lives appears insignificant.

15. The command does not mean to keep adding the phrase, **If the Lord will,** to everything one says. To do such could become another form of pride. At the same time one's behavior and plans should consistently demonstrate dependence upon the Lord. He may determine that at the present time patience through tribulation (Rom 5:3) is a greater need than attaining our goals.

16. Rejoice (Gr *kauchaomai*) could be translated "boast." The noun, **boastings** (Gr *alazoneia*), connotes vain pretensions. A man who brags about future plans while ignoring God's

17 Therefore to him that knoweth to do good, and doeth *it* not, to him it is sin.

CHAPTER 5

GO to now, *ye* rich men, weep and howl for your miseries that shall come upon *you.*

2 Your riches are corrupted, and your garments are motheaten.

3 Your gold and silver is cankered; and the rust of them shall be a witness against you, and shall eat your flesh as it were fire. Ye have heaped treasure together for the last days.

4 Behold, the hire of the labourers who have reaped down your fields, which is of you kept back by fraud, crieth: and the cries of them which have reaped are entered into the ears of the Lord of Săb'a-ŏth.

5 Ye have lived in pleasure on the earth, and been wanton; ye have nourished your hearts, as in a day of slaughter.

6 Ye have condemned *and* killed the just; *and* he doth not resist you.

7 Be patient therefore, brethren, unto the coming of the Lord. Behold, the husbandman waiteth for the precious

sovereignty is foolish, but more than that his attitude is **evil.** The extent of this marks the depravity of contemporary society.

17. Not only does pride condemn others and boast in its potential, but it overlooks its own failure, and those failures which go unnoticed longest are omissions. It is easier to detect wrong than the absence of right. **To him that knoweth to do good** specifically addresses their lack of submission to God's will, which is called **sin** (Gr *hamartia*), missing the mark.

3. Extreme wrath often comes from the rich. 5:1-6.

5:1. The author censored pride in the previous chapter, and here, in phraseology similar to the prophetic tones of certain Old Testament literature, he repudiates the **rich. Go to now** appeared in 4:13 where it also was used as an interjection. **Weep and howl for your miseries that shall come upon you** reminds one of ancient apocalyptic outcries (Isa 13:6; 14:31; 15:3; Jer 4:8; Joel 1:5, 13). Audible crying is heightened by outbursts of wailing. **Miseries . . . shall come** contrasts to present Christian suffering under trials. When the Lord comes, the experience will be reversed (5:8) in greater proportions. Who are these **rich men?** This social class receives attention neither as a tangent nor because his recipients were such, but James is indirectly warning his double-minded Christian readers of the life-styles they approach.

2. One characteristic of prophetic literature is to view the future as though it were present. The perfect tense of **are corrupted** and **are moth-eaten** pictures the effects of **riches** as already having occurred.

3. The destructive results of **rust** upon **gold and silver** testify to the vanity of riches. It is difficult to affirm conclusively the meaning of **eat your flesh as it were fire,** but perhaps James uses this dramatic phrase to contrast the array of mortal bodies to their final state. Analogous to quotes of Jesus (Mt 6:10-20 and Lk 12:21), **the last days** should be a time for securing heavenly treasure, not earthly wealth ("in" the last days would be a more accurate translation than **for).**

4. Uncontrolled appetites for worldly accumulations have carried them to the worst extremes. Not only did they strive for the greatest profits, but they cheated employees in order to do so. **By fraud** they tricked the laborers out of their wages. The resulting desperate **cries** seemed to be in vain, but eternity reveals them to have **entered into the ears of the Lord of Sabaoth.** That title, often translated "Lord of Hosts," emphasizes His omnipotence; in spite of how things may appear, He is sovereign!

5. In a day of slaughter may be taken in two ways. Some explain the slaughter as the excess killing of animals to prepare for a great feast. Thus, preparations for further indulgence seem to be in order. Others find eschatological significance to the phrase (Jer 12:3), making it refer to their self-fattening process for their own slaughter. Perhaps, the author had both ideas in mind. They anxiously make ready for another "day of slaughter" and feasting, while being ignorant of their own ensuing judgment.

6. The just does not refer to Christ (in favor of this interpretation, see Thomas Manton, *An Exposition of the Epistle of James,* p. 416). It is a common Old Testament expression which emphasizes a believer's faithful life. **Resist** has nothing to do with the good man's opposition to the oppressor's wickedness. It deals with the victim's mute response toward the tyrant abuse.

IV. CONCLUSION. 5:7-20.

7. Be patient (Gr *makrothymeō*) may be translated "endure" or "be long-tempered," as opposed to short-tempered. **The coming of the Lord** will dismiss present inequities, while be-

fruit of the earth, and hath long patience for it, until he receive the early and latter rain.

8 Be ye also patient; stablish your hearts: for the coming of the Lord draweth nigh.

9 Grudge not one against another, brethren, lest ye be condemned: behold, the judge standeth before the door.

10 Take, my brethren, the prophets, who have spoken in the name of the Lord, for an example of suffering affliction, and of patience.

11 Behold, we count them happy which endure. Ye have heard of the patience of Job, and have seen the end of the Lord; that the Lord is very pitiful, and of tender mercy.

12 But above all things, my brethren, swear not, neither by heaven, neither by the earth, neither by any other oath: but let your yea be yea; and your nay, nay; lest ye fall into condemnation.

13 Is any among you afflicted? let him pray. Is any merry? let him sing psalms.
14 Is any sick among you? let him call for the elders of the church; and let them pray over him, anointing him with oil in the name of the Lord:

coming a special goal for oppressed believers. **The husbandman,** farmer, illustrates the type of patience believers should possess. Plowing, planting, and caring for his crop are all means to an end, i.e., the harvest. He labors because he believes a day of reaping will be enjoyed. Christians likewise should view current trials and hardships as a preparation process that helps conform them to the image of Christ.

8. The command of the previous verse here becomes personal: **ye also. The coming** (Gr *parousia*), often translated "appearance," implies the suddenness of His arrival, and thus urges constant readiness. **Stablish** (Gr *stērizō*) may be translated "fix firmly" or "set fast" and is another indication of the double-mindedness of a certain element among the recipients.

9. The foremost unbefitting response to testing is bitterness; but since Christians are reluctant to assault God for their problems, their bitter attitudes erupt against others. The command, **grudge not,** is appropriate here. As when a judge enters a courtroom, a reverent hush moves over the audience, so the **judge** who is **before the door** should quell slanderous remarks among His people.

10. A man undergoing trying circumstances may be comforted to learn that others have endured worse situations. The word **example** (Gr *hypodeigma*) is positioned first in Greek to receive emphasis. A man's outspoken testimony for the Lord, not only attributes a positive stand for the gospel, it frequently occasions harsh opposition from its enemies. **Of suffering affliction, and of patience** both have definite articles in the original, which signifies "an example of the suffering affliction and the patience" which James has been discussing. **The prophets** stood loyal to their Lord, suffered for it, and now their experience encourages us.

11. We count them happy holds somewhat of a paradox, although it may not have been intended. Objectively as we observe suffering in others, we urge them to endure, because victory will eventually arrive. Yet when we ourselves **fall into divers temptations** (1:2), our immediate human response often is negative. Job, who endured loss of property, family and health, stands out as a specimen (see J. Moulton and G. Milligan, *The Vocabulary of the Greek New Testament*) of enduring faith. His case not only asserts his patience but demonstrates the purpose and character of his Lord. **The end of the Lord** (Gr *telos*) may be better rendered "the Lord's goal." Our Lord permits suffering, because it leads to His excellent purposes (Rom 8:28; Phil 1:6). Moreover, while critics blaspheme God because of human suffering, Job's record shows the Lord to be "full of pity" (this translation is more accurate than the AV's **very pitiful,** which suggests a negative idea) **and of tender mercy.** Suffering, then, must be attributed either to the means for God's ultimate purposes or (more often) man's own doing through corrupt leaders or personal sin.

12. Swear not, etc., is the clearest allusion in this epistle to the Sermon on the Mount (Mt 5:34-37). The importance of this command, **above all things,** has two views: **above** (Gr *pro*) may signify superiority (A. T. Robertson, *A Grammar of the New Testament in the Light of Historical Research*, p. 622), but commonly it means "before." The latter view makes better sense, for the absence of oath-taking could hardly be superior, but speech should be the first notable change when the Spirit receives control.

13-14. God honors unity in prayer (Mt 18:19), but the healing process here specifically involves **the elders** (Gr *presbyteros*), mature spiritual leaders of the church. No inference can be found of the gift of healing. Moreover, it is the sick who must take the initiative: **let him call.** The **oil** carries no supernatural powers, but often was used in anointing to symbolize the outpouring of God's Spirit. The phrase, **in the name of the Lord,**

15 And the prayer of faith shall save the sick, and the Lord shall raise him up; and if he have committed sins, they shall be forgiven him.

16 Confess *your* faults one to another, and pray one for another, that ye may be healed. The effectual fervent prayer of a righteous man availeth much.

17 E-lī′as was a man subject to like passions as we are, and he prayed earnestly that it might not rain: and it rained not on the earth by the space of three years and six months.
18 And he prayed again, and the heaven gave rain, and the earth brought forth her fruit.

19 Brethren, if any of you do err from the truth, and one convert him;
20 Let him know, that he which converteth the sinner from the error of his way shall save a soul from death, and shall hide a multitude of sins.

points to the real source of healing. Also, the service is to take place in the privacy of the home, since the needy person summoned the elders to him.

15. All too often prayer bears little fruit, but **the prayer of faith,** of unqualified trust, will deliver. Nothing about the passage requires instantaneous healing, nor is there any restriction of medical treatment. The presence of **sins** may be the cause for the sickness, but not necessarily. We must reserve judgment for God alone. **They shall be forgiven** assumes that the one who seeks help from the church also recognizes his personal shortcomings.

16. The two imperatives, **Confess** and **pray,** both in the Greek present tense, call for the habitual practice of openness in two activities. Caution should be observed though; confession should be made only to the extent that the sin is open. Lest anyone regard the prayer of faith to be an impulsive expression of desire, James describes its involvement as **The effectual fervent prayer** with only one adjective in Greek, not two as in the AV. One may observe that our English word "energy" is akin to this modifier (Gr *energeō*), which stresses hard labor. If one becomes desperate about a critical situation, he will not be satisfied uttering a few pious sentences.

17-18. The adverb **much** (vs. 16) leaves the effects of prayer ambiguous. The example of Elijah's answered petition responds to the assumed question by the reader, "How much?" Even the forces of nature may be altered, for three and one-half years! But a doubter may react, "That's fine for a prophet, but what about an average man like me?" Only two qualities are ascribed to this man: (1) **a man subject to like passions as we are:** he fled Jezebel's fury immediately after God sent fire on Mount Carmel (I Kgs 19:1-4); (2) he **prayed earnestly.** His greatness did not lie in special gifts or a superhuman character, but he is distinguished by the way he prayed. One may imagine **earnestly** to hold special significance of a unique manner, but not so. He prayed with all superficial distractions removed. **And he prayed again.** The simplistic wording, in fact, seems to ignore the manner. Prayer is communicating with God, and genuine communication results in visible response. Most public "prayers" are ineffective, because in reality they are intended for man's ears.

19-20. The author speaks to **Brethren** who are in doctrinal error. **Err from the truth** may be rendered "misled from the truth," but the passive voice in no way excuses the sin. **And one convert him** means return or persuade him back to the truth. **Save a soul from death.** Since the word **soul** (Gr *psychē*) may mean "life," the clause may be taken as a warning that backsliding may end in physical death (I Cor 11:30). **Shall hide a multitude of sins** along with the former clause attributes supernatural accomplishments to the one who converts the sinner; God alone can save life or forgive sin. The human connection relates to I Corinthians 3:9, "For we are laborers together with God."

BIBLIOGRAPHY

Adamson, James. The Epistle of James. In *The New International Commentary on the New Testament*. Ed. by F. F. Bruce. Grand Rapids: Eerdmans, 1976.

Alford, Henry. *The Greek Testament*. Vol. 4. Rev. by E. E. Harrison. Chicago: Moody Press, 1958.

Carr, Arthur, The General Epistle of St. James. In the *Cambridge Greek Testament*. Cambridge: Cambridge University Press, reprinted, 1930.

Gaebelein, Frank E. *Practical Epistle of James: Studies in Applied Christianity*. Greatneck, N.Y.: Doniger and Raughley, 1955.

Gibson, E. C. S. The General Epistle of James. In *The Pulpit Commentary*. Grand Rapids: Eerdmans, 1950.

*Johnstone, Robert. *Lectures, Exegetical and Practical, on the Epistle of James*. Grand Rapids: Baker, 1954.

*_____. *Lectures on the Epistle of James*. London: Oliphants, 1871.

Knowling, Richard J. The Epistle of James. In the *Westminster Commentaries*. London: Methuen and Co., 1904.

Lenski, R. C. H. *The Interpretation of the Epistle to the Hebrews and the Epistle of James*. Minneapolis: Augsburg, 1943.

*Manton, Thomas. *An Exposition of the Epistle of James*. London: Banner of Truth Trust, 1962.

Mayor, Joseph B. *The Epistle of James*. Grand Rapids: Zondervan, 1954.

Mitton, C. Leslie. *The Epistle of James*. Grand Rapids: Eerdmans, 1966.

Oesterley, W. E. *The Expositors Greek New Testament*. Vol. 4. Ed by W. R. Nicoll. Grand Rapids: Eerdmans, 1961.

Plummer, Alfred. The General Epistles of St. James and St. Jude. In *The Expositors Bible*. New York: A. C. Armstrong and Son, 1908.

Plumptre, E. H. The General Epistle of St. James. In the *Cambridge Bible for Schools and Colleges*. Cambridge: Cambridge University Press, reprinted, 1915.

*Robertson, A. T. *Studies in the Epistle of James*. Nashville: Broadman Press, 1959.

Ross, Alexander. The Epistles of James and John. In the *New International Commentary on the New Testament*. Grand Rapids: Eerdmans, 1954.

Strauss, Lehman. *James. Your Brother: Studies in the Epistle James*. New York: Loizeaux Brothers, 1956.

*Tasker, R. V. G. The General Epistle of James. In *The Tyndale New Testament Commentaries*. Grand Rapids: Eerdmans, 1960.

*Zodhiates, Spiros. *The Behavior of Belief*. Grand Rapids: Eerdmans, 1970.

The First Epistle Of
PETER

INTRODUCTION

Authorship. Peter identifies himself as the apostle of Jesus Christ in the salutation to his first epistle (1:1). This identity has never been seriously questioned among evangelical scholars. The book was received and used as the authentic and authoritative Word of God by Peter from earliest times in Christian churches. I Peter is quoted by Clement of Rome, Polycarp, and other early Fathers of the Christian church.

It is interesting that Peter mentions in the close of his letter that he is writing "through Sylvanus," who was a companion of Paul on his second missionary journey (I Pet 5:12). This probably means that for I Peter, Silas (which is the name used in Acts) was the amanuensis or secretary for Peter. Paul also wrote most of his letters in the same manner.

We should mention that the objections to apostolic authorship have been mainly based on language and style. Could Peter the fisherman have written such a polished book with its many allusions to the Septuagint? We might briefly answer that some "polish" would be assumed with the passing of time between Peter's introduction to Jesus and the writing of the book. Peter's lack of education has often been misunderstood or overemphasized. An important factor to note is that Acts 4:13 does not mean to teach that Peter was stupid or even that he was less educated than his peers. It was confidence and authority that priests detected in Peter and John, but could not discern where they had gotten it since they were not priests but laymen. Their "field was not religion," we might say today. The clause might be better translated, "they saw that they were laymen rather than formally educated priests." It is ridiculous prejudice which supposes that Peter could not have written such a good book. Furthermore, even if Peter had been incompetent to write the book himself, he might have done quite well with the help of his secretary, Silas. Often, in ancient times, style and precision of expression were attributed more to the amanuensis than to the author of a letter. Sylvanus (or Silas as he is called in Acts) does not appear to be less competent than Paul himself as a preacher of the apostolic message; Paul includes him in all the "we" references in the Thessalonian epistles.

A third authenticating figure is Mark who was with Peter (5:13) in Rome. Since Peter calls him "my son," we assume a very close working relationship. Mark is, of course, John Mark who also wrote the Gospel.

Purpose. Peter wrote to the Christians who lived in the Roman provinces of Pontus, Galatia, Cappadocia, Asia, and Bithynia (1:1). From the tone of the book and its vocabulary we gather that it was a time of persecution and suffering (1:6; 2:12, 15; 4:12, 14-16; 5:8-9). It is not necessary to assume any specific historical period; in fact, we do not have much information about persecution in individual localities throughout the Roman Empire. It is not certain how far and fast official government persecution spread when it did begin. Perhaps persecution started earlier in various communities. No specific information about this is given in the book itself either. It is obvious that Peter writes to encourage faithfulness and praise to God in spite of some assumed persecution. The important thing in this book is the attitude a person takes toward the suffering, persecution, and circumstances of life. Encouragement to praise God in spite of the circumstances seems to recur throughout the book along with the exhortations to holy living and hope.

Characteristics. Peter is a book of praise as much as the Psalms. The salutation itself is an abbreviated Christian psalm of praise for God's grace in Christ. The book mentions suffering and persecution but is not at all pessimistic. 1:3 praises God for the new birth. The Christian life is to be a life of hope, and the greatest hope is the return of Christ and the resurrection. Peter is a real positive thinker; note 3:13-14, "who is he that will harm you . . . and if ye suffer for righteousness' sake, happy are ye." This attitude of praise in spite of persecution is probably not peculiar to Peter but seems to be a part of the apostolic pattern of early Christian preaching. The readers are also encouraged to live lives of purity as God's people (2:9) and God's servants (2:16). They must submit to and live in accordance with God's will for their lives in this world (2:13-3:12). Peter exhorts his readers to true humility and unity as well (5:1-6), and asks them to follow the example of Christ (2:21).

Date and place of writing. Peter wrote from "Babylon" (5:13), which is an esoteric symbol of Rome. The same symbolism is used in Revelation 17 and 18. Although persecution is mentioned often in the book, no specific persecution is mentioned, and the fact applies only generally to the latter part of the first century for a date. The most probable time seems to be between A.D. 62 and 64. Besides the references to suffering and persecution, the primitive state of the development of the church in the epistle, and the still high regard for the authority of the state (I Pet 2:13-17) support a date before A.D. 64. It was, in fact, during the notorious bloodbath begun in A.D. 64 that both Peter and Paul laid down their lives in martyrdom.

OUTLINE

COMMENTARY

I. INTRODUCTION. 1:1-2.

PETER, an apostle of Jesus Christ, to the strangers scattered throughout Pontus, Ga-lā′tia, Căp-pa-dō′ĉi-a, Asia, and Bī-thўn′ĭ-a,
2 Elect according to the foreknowledge of God the Father, through sanctification of the Spirit, unto obedience and sprinkling of the blood of Jesus Christ: Grace unto you, and peace, be multiplied.

1:1-2. Peter, an apostle of Jesus Christ. This letter opens in the usual manner for New Testament epistles and for all letters of the Hellenistic world, with the name of the writer, the address, and a greeting. Peter names himself as an **apostle** of Jesus Christ, which means that he is sent by the Lord with a commission. With this statement Peter claims a certain authority; his letter must then be received and recognized by the churches as the Word of God. The name **Peter** is the Greek form of the Aramaic "Cephas" and means "a stone." The name was given to Peter by the Lord Jesus; compare John 1:42 and Matthew 16:18. **To the strangers scattered.** The Greek word for **scattered** (Gr *diaspora*) means literally "to sow through," and was a technical term for Jews who lived outside of Palestine. Here it is applied to Gentile Christians who figuratively were sown throughout the world by God to be a witness for Him. Although they live in these various Roman provinces, Peter looked upon these Christians as **strangers,** a word that means something like "landed immigrants," and indicates that they are foreigners to the native residents, and that their permanent homeland and citizenship is in heaven. **Elect** (Gr *eklektos*) is in verse 1 in the original, and means "chosen." The implication is that God has purposely placed these Christians in their respective communities to serve Him; they are selected temporary residents who are representatives of God.

Peter now summarizes his theology within his greeting by referring to the Trinity and their cooperative work in accomplishing our great salvation. **According to the foreknowledge** (Gr *prognosis*) which means more than to merely "know about ahead of time." It is a term emphasizing the biblical idea of foreordination. Compare the use of this word in Acts 2:23 and I Peter 1:20 with reference to Christ, and in Romans 8:29 and Romans 11:2 with reference to God's people. It is especially significant here that Peter uses this word with reference to Gentiles, although he had been a devout Jew himself. Foreordination, with reference to these Christians, was accomplished by God the Father through the agency of the Holy Spirit in **sanctification.** This word (Gr *hagiasmos*) means literally "to set apart" or "make holy." The purpose toward which this activity of the Father and the Holy Spirit is directed is the **obedience and sprinkling of the blood of Jesus Christ.** In other words, the activity of the Father and the **Spirit** is directed toward salvation.

II. THE GLORY OF SALVATION. 1:3-12.

A. Salvation of Hope. 1:3-4.

3 Blessed *be* the God and Father of our Lord Jesus Christ, which according to his abundant mercy hath begotten us again unto a lively hope by the resurrection of Jesus Christ from the dead.

3. Blessed be the God and Father. The word **blessed** (Gr *eulogēios*) is the word from which we get "eulogy," and means "to be well spoken of" or "to be praised." Peter is expressing a desire that God should be praised by all believers everywhere. Although it would be frowned upon in some churches where gravity is a visible virtue, Peter says in effect "Praise God!" The thing for which Peter wishes to praise God is the very foundation or beginning of our salvation, the new birth. If for no other reason, every Christian should praise God for being born again. It is entirely of God's initiative that we have been included in His family. He **hath begotten us again** by His great mercy and for this reason is worthy of all our praise. The words **begotten again** (Gr *anagennaō*) is used only here and in verse 23 in the New Testament and means "to give new life to." In other literature outside the New Testament this word is used in a botanical sense, as when the trees, plants, and flowers come to life in the spring. Peter pictures the heart of man as dry, shriveled, and dead in sin until God implants the principles of the new life. When this happens, we sprout into life, leaf out, and grow in the grace and knowledge of our Lord and Saviour Jesus Christ.

Note the ideas of the "sprouting seed" and "new life" which recur in verse 23 where this same word is used. The results of the new birth for which Christians are obligated to praise God are indicated by three words in the original each preceded by the same Greek preposition: observe the words **lively hope** in verse 3, **inheritance** in verse 4, and **salvation** in verse 5. Because of the new birth we have a **lively hope,** which should probably be understood as the hope of the resurrection. We should note that the word **hope** is used in the Bible with the distinctive meaning "confident expectation." Today, of course, hope means merely to "want" something to happen, without having any real assurance that it will happen, as in the sentence, "I hope tomorrow will be a sunny day." The resurrection is the central hope of Christianity; it is not merely something that we want to happen, but an assurance we have. We know we shall rise!

Furthermore, Peter tells us that this living hope is built upon the resurrection of Jesus Christ Himself. This is the core of the gospel and all Christian creeds through the ages. To prove a point, Paul, in I Corinthians 15:16, reasoned negatively, "For if the dead rise not, then is not Christ raised." He went on to say, in I Corinthians 15:20, that Christ had in fact risen from the dead, and as Peter points out here, we shall rise also.

4 To an inheritance incorruptible, and undefiled, and that fadeth not away, reserved in heaven for you,

4. To an inheritance. The second result of the new birth for which we should praise God is called our **inheritance** (cf. Col 1:5, 12). The idea of an inheritance was much more important to a New Testament Jew than it is to us today. For some of us this spiritual inheritance is the only one we will ever have, but its description as incorruptible, undefiled, and unfading, evokes from us the greatest possible praise to God. This inheritance is more lasting than any earthly inheritance could be. Every stone of earth will crumble, every column will fall, every arch will collapse. Diamonds chip, gold wears away, but this inheritance of ours is a truly "imperishable" commodity. This inheritance is also described as **undefiled,** which means that it has no spot of dirt or pollution on it; it is pure as the driven snow (cf. Jas 1:27). **Fadeth not away.** Furthermore, this inheritance is "unfading," which alludes to the inheritance or "crown" of an athlete which, although considered very valuable, would very quickly fade and lose its beauty. This inheritance is said to be **reserved in heaven for you.** The perfect tense is used in Greek to show the confirmed nature of the reservation; it will not be given to someone else by mistake, it cannot be devalued by taxes, and title insurance is provided.

B. Salvation of Power. 1:5.

5. Who are kept by the power of God through faith. Believers themselves are now declared to be **kept** (Gr *phroureō*) by the power of God. This is a military term for the protection of a city by means of a military garrison. In the picture here, the power of God corresponds to an army base with the sole function of protecting believers. The soldiers of God, His angels, surround us to protect us from the bombardment of various trials and temptations so that we do not become crushed by depression and despair. The soldiers are visible only through the eyes of faith.

Unto salvation. The third result of God's grace in giving us new life in Christ is called **salvation.** This, of course, does not refer to the initial experience of accepting Jesus Christ as Saviour, but to the final, inclusive result of salvation; eternal bliss in the presence and service of God. What does the consummation of salvation include? No one knows, for as Paul said, "Eye hath not seen, nor ear heard" what "God hath prepared for them that love him" (I Cor 2:9). We have not yet seen this full and final manifestation, but Peter tells us that it is **ready to be revealed.** The implication here is that everything is fully prepared and accomplished, but remains to be unveiled. The moment of revelation is called **the last time.** The word **time** (Gr *kairos*) does not denote extension of time but designated time when something is to happen. This corresponds to the day of the Lord in Paul's writings, or the second coming of Jesus Christ. The upshot of all this is that, although a person is truly saved when he gives his life to Jesus Christ, and although he experiences the blessings of salvation every day, these are only the pledges of that glorious salvation to which he looks forward in the Day of Christ.

C. Salvation of Trial. 1:6-9.

6. Wherein ye greatly rejoice. The two words **greatly rejoice** (Gr *agalliaō*) are one word in the original which conveys the idea of a strong, deep, supporting exultation; this verb form in the original may be taken as indicative or imperative, depending on the context. The context of exhortation here seems to favor taking it as imperative. The translation would then be, "Always rejoice in this!" The thought here is parallel to the beginning of verse 3, where Peter implies the imperative "Praise God!" Although you would never realize it to look at the faces of some Christians, God wants us to be happy, and to enjoy all the physical and spiritual blessings which He gives to us. **Though now for a season.** These words indicate a concession in spite of which Christians are commanded to praise God. Another translation puts verse 6 this way, "Continue to praise God for this, even though now for a little while you may have had to suffer various trials." We shall have to learn to live more positive, happy, and praise-filled lives in obedience to this commandment if we want to hear His "Well done" on that day.

7. That the trial of your faith. The purpose toward which this command of praise is directed is that the approved character of our faith might result in praise, glory, and honor for us in that day in which Christ is revealed. Verse 7 is better translated, "So that the genuineness of their faith, more precious than gold which though perishable is tested by fire, may redound to praise and glory and honor at the revelation of Jesus Christ." It is interesting that the three words for the "approval" that God will give to those of true faith on that day are found elsewhere in Scripture with the same sense, for example I Corinthians 4:5, where Paul expresses his disinterest in the praise of men because

5 Who are kept by the power of God through faith unto salvation ready to be revealed in the last time.

6 Wherein ye greatly rejoice, though now for a season, if need be, ye are in heaviness through manifold temptations:

7 That the trial of your faith, being much more precious than of gold that perisheth, though it be tried with fire, might be found unto praise and honour and glory at the appearing of Jesus Christ:

of his forward look at the future and says, "then shall every man have praise of God."

8 Whom having not seen, ye love; in whom, though now ye see *him* not, yet believing, ye rejoice with joy unspeakable and full of glory:

9 Receiving the end of your faith, *even* the salvation of *your* souls.

8-9. Whom having not seen, ye love; in whom, though now ye see him not, yet believing, ye rejoice with joy unspeakable and full of glory:

Receiving the end of your faith, even the salvation of your souls. The mention of the name of Jesus Christ in verse 7 causes Peter to insert here a doxological creed concerning the One who is the center of our faith. In this passage two central concepts of Christianity, love and continual joy, revolve around the central person in Christianity by means of two relative pronouns in the original language, of which the antecedent is "Jesus Christ." It does seem strange that the recurrent theme of praise for our great salvation which pervades this passage is so often absent from our preaching today. Likewise, the two concepts of **love** and **joy**, which according to these verses should characterize all those who possess this great salvation, seem now to be in rather short supply.

D. Salvation of Revelation. 1:10-12.

10 Of which salvation the prophets have enquired and searched diligently, who prophesied of the grace *that should come* unto you:

11 Searching what, or what manner of time the Spirit of Christ which was in them did signify, when it testified beforehand the sufferings of Christ, and the glory that should follow.

12 Unto whom it was revealed, that not unto themselves, but unto us they did minister the things, which are now reported unto you by them that have preached the gospel unto you with the Holy Ghost sent down from heaven; which things the angels desire to look into.

10-12. Of which salvation the prophets have inquired and searched diligently. To show how great a privilege it is to possess this glorious salvation, Peter refers first to the Old Testament prophets. To describe the excitement and wonder of the prophets concerning salvation and grace, verse 10 uses two emphatic compound words. The objects of this industrious research on the part of the prophets were first, the person specifically in whom all these messianic prophecies would be fulfilled, and second the precise moment of fulfillment (Gr *kairos*). The prophets knew a great deal about the coming salvation and the coming Saviour. They knew that their prophecies reached far beyond their own times, and even beyond the bounds of their own nation. These things were supernaturally revealed to them. There were certain aspects of the glorious salvation which they prophesied which continually escaped them, and Peter's point is that the glorious objects of prophetic inquiry have now been openly proclaimed and fulfilled in the preaching of the apostles.

The privilege of living in the age of fulfillment should overwhelm us. This privilege is further emphasized by Peter as he refers in verse 12 to the angels; **which things the angels desired to look into.** The last word in the verse, **look into,** means graphically "stooping down close to get a peek at." The picture is that this is something the angels had always wanted to do (Greek present tense) but have never been able to accomplish. This stresses the point that although prophets and angels have been unable to satisfy themselves as to precisely what salvation is all about, we have the privilege not only of full exposition, but of real possession.

III. THE EXHORTATION TO SANCTIFICATION. 1:13-25.

A. Admonition to Sanctification. 1:13-16.

13 Wherefore gird up the loins of your mind, be sober, and hope to the end for the grace that is to be brought unto you at the revelation of Jesus Christ:

13. The main verb in verse 13 is an imperative **hope** with a participle in attendant circumstance, **gird up** (Gr *anazōnnymi*) which is a metaphor referring to the ancient Oriental custom of tying up one's loose flowing robes in the process of getting ready for hard work. An equivalent contemporary metaphor would be, "let's roll up our sleeves and get right to work on the business of holiness." Observe that the main command is **hope,** which means to assume a confident attitude of expectation toward the **grace** (Gr *charis*). Into this one word **grace** Peter has put all the glorious content of our salvation previously given in 3-12; this "package," he says, is now being brought to us (Greek present tense), and we should live with our expectations fixed

14 As obedient children, not fashioning yourselves according to the former lusts in your ignorance:

15 But as he which hath called you is holy, so be ye holy in all manner of conversation;

16 Because it is written, Be ye holy; for I am holy.

17 And if ye call on the Father, who without respect of persons judgeth according to every man's work, pass the time of your sojourning *here* in fear:

18 Forasmuch as ye know that ye were not redeemed with corruptible things, *as* silver and gold, from your vain conversation *received* by tradition from your fathers;

19 But with the precious blood of Christ, as of a lamb without blemish and without spot:

20 Who verily was foreordained before the foundation of the world, but was manifest in these last times for you,

21 Who by him do believe in God, that raised him up from the dead, and gave him glory; that your faith and hope might be in God.

upon it. The package, **grace,** is on its way now, and will arrive in the revelation of Jesus Christ.

14-16. Not fashioning yourselves. Again, the main verb is imperative: **be ye holy.** Holiness is the emphatic demand put upon believers. Here it is to involve, as a better translation has it, "all your conduct." The participle of attendant circumstance **not fashioning yourselves** (Gr *syschematizo*) means "to assume the same visible form," and likewise assumes the imperative character of the main word. Holiness has both a positive side, patterning oneself after God, and a negative side, nonconformity to one's former, sinful life. Pagan standards are to be abandoned; the new model is God Himself (see Isa 40:25; 41:16, 20).

B. Basis for Sanctification. 1:17-21.

17. And if ye call on the Father. This clause is the protasis of a logical premise, and might better be translated "since you invoke as Father Him who judges each person impartially according to his deeds, conduct yourselves with fear." The thought is that since these Gentiles have named the name of God, and since He is the one who will judge all men as a truly just Judge, conduct here is important. **Pass the time of your sojourning here in fear. Pass the time** (Gr *anastrephō*) might be misunderstood as "twiddle your thumbs" and tremble. Once again, this is the main verb in the imperative, and means "conduct yourself in godly reverence." Holiness is to pervade every secret corner of one's life. When we name the name of God we must abandon all to Him.

18. Forasmuch as ye know. The participle here implies cause, and gives reason for conducting oneself with godly reverence; it is because we know that we have been redeemed. The word **redeemed** (Gr *lytroō*) refers to the payment of a required price to release one from an obligation. This is one of the most important words in the Bible since it succinctly describes the atonement of Jesus Christ and the reason for His death on the cross. Peter refers to the fact that his readers, like all Christians, have been released from empty and meaningless lives by a payment made on their behalf. The value of the payment that was made was far greater than silver or gold in any amount; it was the blood of Christ, meaning His death on the cross, which paid the price of release from traditional, pagan conduct. The command to live holy lives for our brief sojourn on the earth, in the interim, as we wait for the consummation of our salvation, is based upon the great price paid by Jesus Christ.

19. But with the precious blood of Christ, as of a lamb without blemish and without spot. Note the continuity that Peter assumes between the Old and New Testaments in the phrase like that **of a lamb without blemish or spot.** This metaphor of Jesus as the sacrificial lamb may have been the first thing that Peter himself learned about Jesus (see Jn 1:29-42).

20-21. Who verily was foreordained before the foundation of the world. The word **foreordained** is the verb form of the noun in 1:2 translated "foreknowledge." Here in this verse it refers to the prior determination on the part of the Father, to send the Son as the Saviour of the world. Although He was predestined before the foundation of the world, He was not made known or manifested until **these last times.** The **last times** (Gr *chronos*) translates the idea of "extension of time." According to the overall schema of the Bible, there are two extended periods of time called "the former times" in which the prophecies and promises were made, and the "latter times" in which the prophecies and promises were fulfilled. This is, of course, another reference to the fulfillment of prophecy in Jesus Christ. The believers of Peter's day and the New Testament were the first generation to have these things preached and made known to them as fulfilled. In verse 21 Peter again refers to the privilege and blessing of belief and hope in God.

22 Seeing ye have purified your souls in obeying the truth through the Spirit unto unfeigned love of the brethren, *see that ye* love one another with a pure heart fervently:

23 Being born again, not of corruptible seed, but of incorruptible, by the word of God, which liveth and abideth for ever.

24 For all flesh *is* as grass, and all the glory of man as the flower of grass. The grass withereth, and the flower thereof falleth away:

25 But the word of the Lord endureth for ever. And this is the word which by the gospel is preached unto you.

CHAPTER 2

WHEREFORE laying aside all malice, and all guile, and hypocrisies, and envies, and all evil speakings,

2 As newborn babes, desire the sincere milk of the word, that ye may grow thereby:

3 If so be ye have tasted that the Lord *is* gracious.

4 To whom coming, *as unto* a living stone, disallowed indeed of men, but chosen of God, *and* precious,

C. Results of Sanctification. 1:22-25.

22-25. The appeal now goes back to the important ingredient of love mentioned in 1:8. The main verb in these four verses is **love one another**; this is the fourth in a series of imperative main verbs which are all based on the primary description of our glorious salvation in verses three through twelve. The call to holiness in verses 13-25 then involves: hope (vs. 13), holiness (vs. 15), reverence (vs. 17), and now love (vs. 22). Love, not bitterness and separation, is the outcome of holiness. If we have really **purified** (perfect tense in Greek) our lives by obeying the truth, Peter says it will result in unhypocritical brotherly love. This is possible because of our new life in Christ (again the participle in Greek is the perfect tense and implies the reality or certainty of the fact of life in Christ). Here, in verse 23, the living Word of God is the instrument used by the Spirit of God to impart principles of the new life (cf. Hebrews 4:12). Peter now quotes from Isaiah 46 and following in praise of the Word of God, which unlike any human or created thing continues its beauty, effectiveness, and life forever. Everything else in the world is like grass; its beauty is only temporary. The grass dies, and its beauty fails. God's Word, however, is living and effective. Note the synonyms for the **Word**: in verse 23 it is the **word of God**, in verse 25 it is first, **the word of the Lord,** and then **the word which by the gospel is preached unto you.** It is interesting that four different expressions are used here in the Greek.

IV. THE COMMITMENT TO THE LORD. 2:1-8.

A. The Exhortations. 2:1-3.

2:1-3. Another vivid word picture is painted by Peter as he refers to Christians as needing milk to grow. The metaphorical allusions are mixed, since Peter goes from "putting on new clothes," to "fussing for milk," to "growing like a plant" unto salvation, to "tasting" the goodness of the Lord, to "stones," and "spiritual houses." One thing is common to all these metaphors, however, and that is the idea of growing to maturity, or becoming what God wants us to be in the world. Again, Peter introduces his thought with a subordinate clause and a participle of attendant circumstance, **laying aside.** This is an everyday word which means "to change clothes"; it is the word used by Paul in Ephesians 4:22 where he speaks of putting off the old man and putting on the new man like a suit of clothes. As Christians, we must take off the ragged and filthy clothes of sin: malice, hypocrisy, deceit, envy, and slander.

In verse 2, the figure changes to a hungry, fussing, sucking baby who wants to be fed. The **milk** with which we long to be fed in the figure is, of course, **the word** (Gr *logikos*). This adjective really means "reasonable" or "rational," and intends to interpret the figure. Peter intends the reader to understand "milk for the mind," rather than for the mouth. We are to **desire** this milk; the word used here denotes a very strong emotion or passion fixed upon something. The figure is again changed to plant growth, where the resulting mature plant or tree is salvation (see 1:3-12). The idea of a tree, perhaps with fruit, may have suggested Peter's next figure of "tasting" to see if the Lord is good (quoted from Ps 34:8).

B. The Stone of Stumbling. 2:4-8.

4. **As unto a living stone.** Since Peter had become very familiar with the Greek Old Testament and the striking continuity between its prophecies of the Messiah and their fulfillment in Jesus Christ on the one hand, and between the people of God in the Old Testament and believers in his own era on the other hand, he is here taken up completely with the beauty of

metaphor and allusion. He is thinking now of God's people as a building and of Jesus Christ as the **living stone,** fulfilling the prophecy of Isaiah 28:16, "Behold, I lay in Zion for a foundation a stone, a tried stone, a precious corner stone, a sure foundation." Christ is called a **living stone** because, although He is a part of the figure, He is also a real person. Likewise, those who have come to Christ and have received life through Him are called **living stones.** Since Christ had been rejected by the chief priests and leaders of the Jews, Matthew (21:42) saw this as a fulfillment of the Old Testament. Paul also (I Cor 3:11) looked upon his preaching of Christ as laying a foundation upon which others might build. For Paul too, the church was a "building" (I Cor 3:9).

5. Peter uses the same figure that Paul had used and says, **ye also, as lively stones** or "and like living stones you are yourselves being built into a spiritual house so that you may be a holy priesthood." The preposition used in the original language here implies that the purpose for which these Gentile Christian **stones** are being selected, trimmed, and built into a structure is that they might function as a **holy priesthood.** With this, Peter again changes the figure momentarily from buildings and stones to the priesthood. Since the priesthood in the Old Testament had the function of offering animal sacrifices acceptable to God, in the metaphor the church as the new **priesthood** offers sacrifices through Jesus Christ, but they are **spiritual sacrifices.** The author of Hebrews (13:15) also uses the same figures but more specifically names the sacrifices as those of praise and confessing His name.

6. Another reference to the chosen and valuable cornerstone, Jesus Christ applies this statement also, **he that believeth on him shall not be confounded.** The word **confounded** (Gr *kataischynō*) comes from a textual variation in the Septuagint translation of Isaiah 28:16 which is quoted by the New Testament writers. Paul, in Romans 9:33 and 10:11, seems to define quite well the meaning of being **confounded,** or being "put to shame"; it means to "fail to be saved." Whatever the meaning in the Old Testament, the meaning of the quotation in the New Testament and here is, "the person who believes in Him will certainly not fail to be saved."

7-8. Christianity is a matter of one's attitude toward Jesus Christ. He uses the quotations from Isaiah to show that while believers consider this choice stone to be valuable in that they honor, respect, and worship Him, to the unbelievers and disobedient on the other hand Christ has become a **stone of stumbling and a rock of offense.** According to the Old Testament prophecy and Peter's view of its fulfillment, the "chief cornerstone" and foundation of salvation for some, has become the cause of destruction for others who refuse to believe in Him.

V. THE IMPLICATIONS OF HUMILITY. 2:9-3:12.

A. The Believer's Life in General. 2:9-21a.

9-10. But ye shows a strong contrast between unbelievers and Peter's readers who are Christians. The figure is changed again, and the focus is on the church (New Testament believers) to which are applied the words **ye are a chosen generation, a royal priesthood, a holy nation, a peculiar people; that ye should show forth the praises of him.** These words are from two Old Testament passages (Ex 19:6; Isa 43:21) and show that Peter considers that the privileges and responsibilities of Israel in the Old Testament are now being transferred to the church as the people of God in his own day. This same continuity is recognized by the other New Testament writers as well (see II Cor 4:6; Col 3:12; Rev 1:6). Along with the great blessings of being the heirs of God's salvation, however, there are great responsibilities.

---

5 Ye also, as lively stones, are built up a spiritual house, an holy priesthood, to offer up spiritual sacrifices, acceptable to God by Jesus Christ.

6 Wherefore also it is contained in the scripture, Behold, I lay in Sion a chief corner stone, elect, precious: and he that believeth on him shall not be confounded.

7 Unto you therefore which believe *he is* precious: but unto them which be disobedient, the stone which the builders disallowed, the same is made the head of the corner,
8 And a stone of stumbling, and a rock of offence, *even to them* which stumble at the word, being disobedient: whereunto also they were appointed.

9 But ye *are* a chosen generation, a royal priesthood, an holy nation, a peculiar people; that ye should shew forth the praises of him who hath called you out of darkness into his marvellous light:
10 Which in time past *were* not a people, but *are* now the people of God: which had not obtained mercy, but now have obtained mercy.

Peter sums up these in the words **that ye should show forth the praises of him.** The word **show forth** (Gr *exangellō*) means literally "to tell out," and refers to the "preaching" of the gospel, the good news, or **praises** of God. **His marvelous light** (see II Cor 4:6) is probably a reference to Isaiah 9:1, and Christ as the "Light of the World." See also II Peter 1:3. Another amazing proof of the continuity between the Old Testament and Peter's age of fulfillment, and between Israel and the church, is the application of the Hosea passages (1:6, 9; 2:3, 23) directly to his readers and therefore to the church.

11 Dearly beloved, I beseech *you* as strangers and pilgrims, abstain from fleshly lusts, which war against the soul;

12 Having your conversation honest among the Gentiles: that, whereas they speak against you as evildoers, they may by *your* good works, which they shall behold, glorify God in the day of visitation.

11-12. Dearly beloved, I beseech you. The word **beseech** (Gr *parakaleō*) actually denotes encouragement, and might better be translated, "My dear people, let me encourage you. . . ." Although this is the main verb in these two verses, it is completed by two others which comprise the content of the exhortation to these who are **strangers and pilgrims** (that is, they are in the world of the Gentiles, but no longer of the world.) The first exhortation is to **abstain from fleshly lusts,** and the reason given is that they are in constant battle against the soul or the spirit (cf. Gal 5:24). The second exhortation is to maintain good conduct **among the Gentiles.** It should be noted that **conversation,** as usual in the New Testament, does not refer to talking but to conduct. Note further that the word **honest,** with reference to conduct, does not mean merely the virtue we today call honesty; Peter means rather to say that one's whole life is to be good, in the sense of being "Christian." The purpose toward which all this care in conduct is directed is the glory of God. Even though some people might slander the believers as if they were evildoers, they would in the long run, as they observed their Christian conduct, be forced to glorify God in the **day of visitation.** This phrase comes from Isaiah 10:3 where it is the name for the day of punishment or judgment; since that eschatological **day** is for some a day of judgment and for others a day of vindication and salvation, the term can have either connotation (cf. Lk 1:68 and 19:44).

13 Submit yourselves to every ordinance of man for the Lord's sake: whether it be to the king, as supreme;

13. Submit yourselves to every ordinance of man for the Lord's sake. The word **submit** (Gr *hypotassō*) is the key to the whole section 2:11-3:12; it means literally "to arrange under," and is used in various contexts to indicate subjection or subordination. In military contexts it was used for the idea of rank. In various New Testament contexts it is used for the relationship between children and their parents, servants and their masters, or wives and their husbands. Here, Peter seems to command the believers, "fit into your place in the social structure with Christian humility." This idea of subordination to the system controls the whole passage. Notice that the word is used in verse 18 for servants, in 3:1 for wives, and implied in 3:7 for husbands (not subjection to their wives but to the social structure as Christians).

In this passage as well as in Ephesians 5, this word for "submit" is very closely related to the word for "humility" which is found in 3:8 as a summary of this whole passage. The implications of Christian humility for Christian living are first given generally in 2:13-17, and then specifically as they relate to servants, wives, and husbands. **To every ordinance of man** is a difficult phrase to translate; perhaps, "Be subject for the Lord's sake to every human institution." Peter writes that they are to be subject to the king because he is supreme; the king or ruler at this time was the Roman Emperor Nero. Christians respected the office regardless of the personal ethics of the man because they believed he had been appointed by God to rule.

14 Or unto governors, as unto them that are sent by him for the punishment of evildoers, and for the praise of them that do well.

15 For so is the will of God, that with

14-17. Or unto governors. Since they are authorized by the king, the reasoning behind this philosophy is that we are all the servants of God (vs. 16) and so are obligated to submit to those whom He allows to be in office. The passage seems to be assuming a good government which recognizes, at least in gen-

well doing ye may put to silence the ignorance of foolish men:

16 As free, and not using *your* liberty for a cloak of maliciousness, but as the servants of God.

17 Honour all *men*. Love the brotherhood. Fear God. Honour the king.

18 Servants, *be* subject to *your* masters with all fear; not only to the good and gentle, but also to the froward.

19 For this *is* thankworthy, if a man for conscience toward God endure grief, suffering wrongfully.

20 For what glory *is it*, if, when ye be buffeted for your faults, ye shall take it patiently? but if, when ye do well, and suffer *for it*, ye take it patiently, this *is* acceptable with God.

21 For even hereunto were ye called: because Christ also suffered for us, leaving us an example, that ye should follow his steps:

eral, the laws of God according to the Scripture. Government is supposed to punish those who do evil (vs. 14), and reward those who do good. There are times when government is itself in violation of the power and authority given by God and contrary to Scripture, when the Christian must not submit (Acts 5:29). Peter himself on one occasion boldly refused to submit to authority on the grounds that it was contrary to the will of God (Acts 4:19). The general introduction to the subject of humility is summarized by four brief commandments in verse 17: **Honor all men. Love the brotherhood. Fear God. Honor the king.**

18-21a. Peter now approaches the subject of the implications of humility for specific groups, and deals first with **Servants.** The word used here for **servants** is used of household servants or domestics who received wages for what they did in the household. Out of respect for their **masters** they are to submit or conduct themselves properly under the circumstances of this social institution. This is Christian humility. Their conduct is not to be determined by whether their masters are good and gentle, but by Christian ethics; they must also submit to those who are "crooked" and difficult, since there are some people who are hard to get along with. **For this is thankworthy.** The word **thankworthy** (Gr *charis*) is idiomatic for "what pleases God"; the literal translation would be "grace," which in the New Testament usually has the underlying connotation of something which is acceptable to God. Here, what pleases God is that a man can endure pain while suffering unjustly for the sake of his godly conscience.

A similar idiom is found in verse 20, **For what glory is it.** Here, the word "glory" is likewise idiomatic. It is not the punishment, or even enduring punishment which is creditable, but doing good, continuing to be humble, and continuing to submit even though your goodness is not recognized. **For even hereunto were ye called.** Peter indicates by this that the humility or submission that is advocated is the will of God for all Christians. At this point Peter introduces the example of Christ.

B. The Atonement of Christ. 2:21b-25.

21b. Christ also suffered for us. That the suffering of Christ was vicarious is indicated by the preposition **for** (Gr *hyper*), which means "in behalf of" or "instead of." The passion of Christ was the most prominent aspect of the preaching of Christ, and was very familiar to all Christians. No mere human being could ever suffer as He suffered.

Leaving us an example. This, of course, is not the main purpose of the suffering of Christ (a participle of attendant circumstance in Greek) but it does so happen that His conduct even in His passion provides us with a perfect pattern of Christian humility, and this is what Peter offers here. **Example** (Gr *hypogrammos*) was literally something to "write under." Originally a line of writing at the top of a tablet written by the teacher so that the child could write under it and make his letters like the master. Our Lord and Master suffered more than any other, and we are called upon to follow His humility. The figure is emphatic, here, since the word **follow** really means "follow exactly" and there are clear "footprints." The mention of the suffering of Christ leads Peter into a recitation of the essentials of the messianic nature of the suffering experienced; He suffered, but more important than that, He suffered as the Servant of Jehovah, and as it was predicted of Him in the Old Testament. This was too important to Peter to be left unsaid; he had been rebuked as "Satan" for missing it before (Mk 8:31-33.)

22 Who did no sin, neither was guile found in his mouth:

23 Who, when he was reviled, reviled not again; when he suffered, he threat-

22-23. Who did no sin, neither was guile found in his mouth is a quotation from Isaiah 53:9 and was part of the apostolic preaching identifying Jesus as the Messiah. The silence of Christ in the fact of His extreme suffering is also a prominent idea

ened not; but committed *himself* to him that judgeth righteously:

24 Who his own self bare our sins in his own body on the tree, that we, being dead to sins, should live unto righteousness: by whose stripes ye were healed.

25 For ye were as sheep going astray; but are now returned unto the Shepherd and Bishop of your souls.

CHAPTER 3

LIKEWISE, ye wives, *be* in subjection to your own husbands; that, if any obey not the word, they also may without the word be won by the conversation of the wives;

2 While they behold your chaste conversation *coupled* with fear.

3 Whose adorning let it not be that outward *adorning* of plaiting the hair,

found in Isaiah 53:7. He as our example in humility left the vindication with God the Father.

24. Who his own self bare our sins in his own body is from Isaiah 53:4-5, and is used to show the vivid and detailed way in which Jesus fulfilled the prophecies and accomplished our redemption. He had no sins of His own (vs. 22); He suffered and died vicariously. He gave His body in death on the cross for the purpose (Greek final clause) that we **being dead to sins, should live unto righteousness. Being dead** (Gr *apoginomai*) means literally to "move away from," and might be better translated, "that we might die to sin and live to righteousness." The thought is that the life of Christian humility which is being exhorted here is a basic part of the reason for Christ's death on the cross. **By whose stripes** (wounds) is another supporting quotation from Isaiah 53:6.

25. For ye were as sheep going astray. Healing is one primary figure for redemption; coming home is another, probably suggested by it. Ezekiel 34:5-6 refers to the people of God as scattered sheep; Peter sees that the church has now been brought back, and since it is Christ who has accomplished this, He is the Shepherd. The word **Bishop** (Gr *episkopos*) meaning "manager" is used in the New Testament as synonymous with "elder" or "pastor," but is here applied to Christ as the ultimate Bishop of souls.

C. The Believer's Life at Home. 3:1-12.

3:1. Likewise, ye wives, be in subjection to your own husbands. This section (3:1-6) is grammatically related to the general statement on humility (2:13-17) by **likewise** (Gr *homoiōs*), and by the general dependent participial clause translated **be in subjection.** The word **subjection** (see on 2:13) says to the women readers, "Your part in applying humility to Christian living is to be a living testimony to your own husbands by the way you fit into the social structure; take your place in marriage seriously and be a good wife." It is obvious that the attitude encouraged here can only be expected from a Christian person; Peter does not imply that women are inferior, and therefore should submit to their husbands. A person who is born again has already submitted to God through Christ. If he wants to live Christian humility, he will also submit to government for God's sake, to his masters or employers, and now in this institution of marriage, the wife will submit to her husband (a good or bad husband) in the same spirit.

Does this mean that the husband is the boss in the institution of marriage? How can it mean anything else? The king is the boss, the employer is the boss, and now in the same context the husband is the boss. Keep in mind that in verse 7 Peter has a word to the husband concerning his part in submitting to the system. This does not mean, of course, that wives must obey their husbands if their husbands command something that will violate the law of God; here, the principle of Acts 4:19 would once more apply. The purpose toward which this unbearable humility is directed is that **they also may without the word be won** (Gr *kerdainō*). This is a business word and means "to make a profit" as opposed to experiencing a loss; it vividly portrays the credit and debit sides of the ledger. In the New Testament, the "business" of the church is "winning" the lost (Mt 28:19); the converts are in the sense of this word, "gains." In this verse Christian wives can win their husbands to the Lord just by applying humility and by being a good wife.

2. Conversation in the Bible means "conduct" or "behavior," and the kind of behavior suggested here is further described by **chaste,** and **coupled with fear,** fear meaning respect or reverence, and implying true humility.

3-4. Whose adorning (Gr *kosmos*) means to refer to the beauty or attractiveness which these husbands will see in their

and of wearing of gold, or of putting on of apparel;

4 But *let it be* the hidden man of the heart, in that which is not corruptible, *even the ornament* of a meek and quiet spirit, which is in the sight of God of great price.

5 For after this manner in the old time the holy women also, who trusted in God, adorned themselves, being in subjection unto their own husbands:

6 Even as Sara obeyed Abraham, calling him lord: whose daughters ye are, as long as ye do well, and are not afraid with any amazement.

7 Likewise, ye husbands, dwell with *them* according to knowledge, giving honour unto the wife, as unto the weaker vessel, and as being heirs together of the grace of life; that your prayers be not hindered.

8 Finally, *be ye* all of one mind, having compassion one of another, love as brethren, *be* pitiful, *be* courteous:

9 Not rendering evil for evil, or railing for railing: but contrariwise blessing; knowing that ye are thereunto called, that ye should inherit a blessing.

10 For he that will love life, and see good days, let him refrain his tongue from evil, and his lips that they speak no guile:

11 Let him eschew evil, and do good; let him seek peace, and ensue it.

12 For the eyes of the Lord *are* over the righteous, and his ears *are* open

wives. The sense is, "Make sure your primary beauty is found in your heart and not merely in your clothes and jewelry." These verses should not be twisted to condemn the use of cosmetics or jewelry; they merely emphasize that, as far as God is concerned, it is more important to have a **meek and quiet spirit.**

5-6. For after this manner. Peter again turns to the Old Testament for illustrations to support his exhortation to humility. This is the way **holy women . . . who trusted in God adorned themselves.** Trusted (Gr *elpizō*) means literally "hoped" in God, and pictures a life of calm assurance and certainty about the fact that God will reward such humility. These women made themselves beautiful to God by **being in subjection unto their own husbands.** Sarah is the prime example. As Abraham was the father of the faithful, so Sarah is the mother of the faithful. Peter's readers should want to be her **daughters;** this can be accomplished by doing **well.** Doing well in this passage can only mean humbling oneself to submit to one's husband. The meaning of humility for wives becomes terribly clear with the concrete example of Sarah: she obeyed her husband and called him **lord.**

7. Likewise. This is the same word which was used in 3:1 to refer back to 3:18 and 3:13; by it Peter introduces the third specific group to which he applies the principle of humility. The use of this word implies that the husbands are also to be "subject" in the social institution of marriage which is in view here; the Greek word for subjection is not used but the idea is understood as now applying to husbands, just as it did to servants and wives. In what sense can husbands "be subject" in marriage? Certainly, they cannot be subject to their wives for that would contradict 3:1-6. In a marriage, someone has to be the head of the home; it cannot be a fifty-fifty split of authority, and democracy will not work here since the vote would be tied. The husband is the leader, and yet he must also submit in humility, not to his wife, but to the good of the marriage.

Ye husbands, is now addressing Christian husbands who may or may not have unsaved wives to win to the Lord. **Dwell with them according to knowledge.** The husband has a much greater responsibility than the wife; all the decisions of living together are his. **Giving honor unto the wife** may imply a great deal of humility and self-sacrifice in order to show this honor. In this way the husband can submit without neglecting leadership. **As unto the weaker vessel** does not imply inferiority, but probably does refer to physical strength. **As being heirs together of the grace of life.** The grace of life is the inheritance which has been received together; part of that grace is the wife's, and the husband is to see that she gets it. If the husband does not give honor to the wife, prayers will be hindered. All the responsibility in this verse is with the husband; all the blessing and honor belongs to the wife.

8-9. Finally. This does not signal the end of the letter, but the end of the section (2:11-3:12); this is to introduce another summary or general statement like that at the beginning. Again, the central idea is humility, and the same main verb is implied, namely, "submit" to one another, each one humbly filling his place in the Christian community by being or doing the things listed here. **Be pitiful, be courteous** should rather be translated, "have a tender heart and a humble mind."

10-12. For he that will love life. Although the arrangement of the text does not show it, verses 10-12 are a poem quoted from Psalm 34:13-17 of the Septuagint, the Greek version of the Old Testament. The poem sums up the implications of humility for all the aspects of life in general; it is the epitome of the Christian life. The person who wants a truly happy life, enjoying all God's blessings, must first turn away from evil in both word and deed. On the positive side, he must pursue or "run after" peace. This

unto their prayers: but the face of the Lord *is* against them that do evil.

13 And who *is* he that will harm you, if ye be followers of that which is good?

14 But and if ye suffer for righteousness' sake, happy *are ye:* and be not afraid of their terror, neither be troubled;

15 But sanctify the Lord God in your hearts: and *be* ready always to *give* an answer to every man that asketh you a reason of the hope that is in you with meekness and fear:

16 Having a good conscience; that, whereas they speak evil of you, as of evildoers, they may be ashamed that falsely accuse your good conversation in Christ.

17 For *it is* better, if the will of God be so, that ye suffer for well doing, than for evil doing.

18 For Christ also hath once suffered for sins, the just for the unjust, that he might bring us to God, being put to death in the flesh, but quickened by the Spirit:

kind of person can be happy because God's eye is on him for protection, God's ear is open to his prayer.

VI. THE CHRISTIAN ATTITUDE TOWARD SUFFERING. 3:13-4:19.

A. Christians and the World. 3:13-17.

13. And who is he that will harm you. . . ? Paul had asked (Rom 8:34) a similar question, "Who can condemn you?" Peter seems to take the view that is highly unlikely that anyone would deliberately bring harm to someone who is a **follower** (Gr *zēlōtēs*) or "zealot" **of that which is good.**

14. But and if ye suffer for righteousness' sake, happy are ye. This is a future condition with the Greek optative mood indicating the possibility that some of them could suffer in the future, but even if they should suffer, they would in fact be **happy. Happy** does not mean they will be singing about it, but rather that they would in fact be privileged to suffer for the sake of Christ. This is exactly what Jesus had taught in the Beatitudes (Mt 5:10), and what Peter had reminded his readers of in 2:20.

15. But sanctify the Lord God. Following another text, a better translation has, "Have no fear of them, nor be troubled, but in your hearts reverence Christ as Lord." **Be ready always to give an answer** (Gr *apologia*), that is not just a reply, but a defense **of the hope that is in you.** What Peter is suggesting is that suffering may be another opportunity to testify of the saving power of Christ and so win some of the persecutors. The word **hope** refers to the whole system or philosophy of Christianity in general, as well as specifically to the attitude of certainty and assurance about the resurrection and the coming of Christ. **With meekness and fear.** These indicate an attitude of humility toward men, and not fear but reverence and worship toward God.

16-17. Having a good conscience. Again, Peter emphasizes that it is better to suffer for doing good than for doing evil. (On these verses, see 2:20.)

B. Christ's Ministry on Earth. 3:18-22.

18. For Christ also hath once suffered for sins. Some texts have "died for sins," but most interpreters opt for **suffered** because it fits the context better and is a very common word in this epistle. The word **for** translates three different Greek words in the verse; some translations have four "for's." The reason for the advice in verse 17 is, "Because Christ suffered" (Gr *hoti*). Christ suffered "concerning" (Gr *peri*) sins, and He suffered on our behalf, the Just One "in place of" (Gr *hyper*) unjust sinners. It is made very clear that His suffering was not just an exemplary suffering; it was vicarious, and it was an atonement for our sins. Its purpose was to **bring us to God.**

Peter now moves into the illustrative and hortatory part of his citation of the suffering of Christ. He is writing to those who may very soon have to suffer at the hands of wicked men, and so refers to the fact that Christ had also suffered at the hands of wicked men. This is apparently the meaning of the cryptic **being put to death in the flesh.** The word **flesh** is used by Peter to refer to mankind in 1:24, and this seems here to be the obvious opposite to the **Spirit** who raised Christ to life again. At any rate, it would seem that **flesh** and **Spirit** have a parallel but opposite meaning; if Jesus' flesh and spirit are meant rather than the Holy Spirit, it is difficult to view the resurrection as pertaining to only the spirit and not the body. Furthermore, the "in-his-flesh, in-his-spirit" interpretation says nothing as to the agents of the passive verbs, and gives no example or encouragement for Peter's readers.

19 By which also he went and preached unto the spirits in prison;

19. By which also he went and preached connotes the agency of the Holy Spirit if we retain the AV translation, **by the Spirit** (vs. 18). In this view, maintaining the continuity between verse 18 and verse 19, the same Holy Spirit who raised Christ from the dead had enabled him to preach to the men of Noah's day through Noah himself. While this interpretation fits the context and is legitimate by twentieth-century standards, it does require some juggling of one's natural understanding of the original text. The alternative interpretation is to understand that before the resurrection someone "made alive" the human spirit of Jesus so that in this form He preached to the spirits in Hades. This interpretation has problems too; for example, the content of the preaching is supposed to be an announcement of victory rather than the preaching of the gospel message, but the wrong word is used (Gr *kēryssō*). Also, according to 4:6, the gospel is preached to the dead, and the word there definitely means "preach the gospel" or "evangelize" (Gr *euangelizomai*).

20 Which sometime were disobedient, when once the longsuffering of God waited in the days of Noah, while the ark was a preparing, wherein few, that is, eight souls were saved by water.
21 The like figure whereunto *even* baptism doth also now save us (not the putting away of the filth of the flesh, but the answer of a good conscience toward God,) by the resurrection of Jesus Christ:

20-21. The ark . . . wherein few, that is, eight souls were saved by water. The mention of Noah and the ark provides the perfect opportunity to expound on the figurative correspondence between the **ark** and **baptism**, which **doth also now save us.** Technically, of course, it is not true that baptism saves; the merely mechanical performance of the religious rite would only make a sinner into a very wet sinner. Peter means to explain this with **not the putting away of the filth of the flesh.** What it means is just as the ark had something to do with the deliverance of those people from the judgment of the Flood, so baptism, assuming that a person has accepted Christ as Saviour and desires to obey in this ordinance, has something to do with deliverance from sin. It's only a picture, a type, and the correspondence is very close.

22 Who is gone into heaven, and is on the right hand of God; angels and authorities and powers being made subject unto him.

22. Angels and authorities and powers being made subject unto him. The mention of the resurrection and ascension calls for the declaration of Christ's victory over the powers; they have all been subjected to Him (Gr *hypotassō*). Just as Christians must submit to human social structures (2:13-3:12) to live in true humility, so the structures themselves together with all supernatural powers must submit to Jesus Christ who is over all (cf. Eph 1:21; Col 2:15; Heb 2:5).

CHAPTER 4

FORASMUCH then as Christ hath suffered for us in the flesh, arm yourselves likewise with the same mind: for he that hath suffered in the flesh hath ceased from sin;
2 That he no longer should live the rest of *his* time in the flesh to the lusts of men, but to the will of God.

C. Christ's Example in Suffering. 4:1-6.

4:1-2. Peter now goes back to the thought of the suffering of Jesus mentioned in verse 18, in order to encourage these believers who might very shortly have to suffer themselves. **Forasmuch then as Christ hath suffered for us in the flesh.** No article or preposition occurs before either use of **flesh** in verse 1 or the use in 3:18; the contexts alone must determine the meaning. **Arm yourselves likewise with the same mind.** Arm (Gr *hoplizomai*) means to "equip" or "outfit" as one would outfit an army unit with the best possible weapons for a particular battle. The best "weapon" here would be the same **mind** (Gr *ennoia*) or view toward the suffering that Christ Himself had. It was not that Christ enjoyed suffering, but He endured it in order to accomplish our salvation (3:18). **For** (Gr *hoti*) may indicate the content of the proper view toward suffering at the hands of sinful men, namely that **he that hath suffered . . . hath ceased from sin** (Greek perfect tense, meaning "to have truly stopped"). **That** (Gr *eis*) indicates the reason or purpose for so equipping oneself, that is, so that he need no longer **live the rest of his time in the flesh to the lusts of men, but to the will of God.** "In the flesh" in verse 2 has a preposition which may mean "among."

3 For the time past of *our* life may suffice us to have wrought the will of the Gentiles, when we walked in lasciv-

3. For the time past of our life may suffice us to have wrought the will of the Gentiles. This might better be translated, "You have already spent too much time thinking like

iousness, lusts, excess of wine, revellings, banquetings, and abominable idolatries:

4 Wherein they think it strange that ye run not with *them* to the same excess of riot, speaking evil of *you:*

Gentiles, living in licentiousness, passion, parties, carousing, drinking, and meaningless idolatry."

4. Wherein they think it strange that ye run not with them. Peter's readers were, of course, Gentiles, and had lived like Gentiles all their lives. Their salvation and conversion to Christianity was much more profound than we can imagine today. It is no wonder that the companions of these people were surprised when they no longer continued to live in sin. **Speaking evil of you** (Gr *blasphēmeo*). Since they were unable to understand the Christians, they abused them.

5 Who shall give account to him that is ready to judge the quick and the dead.
6 For for this cause was the gospel preached also to them that are dead, that they might be judged according to men in the flesh, but live according to God in the spirit.

5-6. Who shall give account. There will come a time when they shall have to settle up with God who is **ready to judge the quick** (living) **and the dead. For this cause was the gospel preached also to them that are dead.** The idea here parallels 3:19, although the word **preached** (Gr *euangelizomai*) here is different and means specifically to "evangelize." It is probably impossible to be sure, but to **the dead** could mean that they are dead when Peter writes, but were alive when the gospel was preached to them. At least we know that the Bible does not teach that men have a second chance to be saved after death. **That they might be judged according to men in the flesh, but live according to God in the spirit.** If this refers to the opportunity these Gentiles had to be saved while they were still alive, we might rephrase it, "They had a choice between human condemnation by wicked men, or divine life by the Spirit." This interpretation at least allows a consistent meaning throughout the passage for "flesh" and "Spirit."

D. Christian's Conduct through Suffering. 4:7-19.

7 But the end of all things is at hand: be ye therefore sober, and watch unto prayer.

7. But the end of all things is at hand. As he continues to develop the theme of the Christian attitude toward suffering, Peter wishes now to reemphasize the positive elements of the Christian life in light of the consummation of all things. **At hand** (Gr *enggizō*) is in the perfect tense in Greek and emphasizes the certainty of the nearness of the end. Although this word is used only once in Peter, it was a frequent topic in the apostolic preaching and in the preaching of Jesus and John the Baptist. An equivalent statement in James 5:8 says that the *Parousia* of the Lord is very near.

8 And above all things have fervent charity among yourselves: for charity shall cover the multitude of sins.

8. Have fervent charity means, of course, "warm love" toward each other as Christian brothers; it has nothing to do with either giving money as a contribution or the slippery, formal, outward courtesy of good culture. **Charity shall cover the multitude of sins.** Peter draws support from the Greek Old Testament with the quotation of Proverbs 10:12, which simply means that if a person has true love for others, his shortcomings will not be obvious.

9 Use hospitality one to another without grudging.
10 As every man hath received the gift, *even so* minister the same one to another, as good stewards of the manifold grace of God.
11 If any man speak, *let him speak* as the oracles of God; if any man minister, *let him do it* as of the ability which God giveth: that God in all things may be glorified through Jesus Christ, to whom be praise and dominion for ever and ever. Amen.

9-11. Hospitality . . . without grudging (Gr *gonggysmos*) is easily understood if difficult to perform; hospitality, again, should not be confused with courtesy which is far less costly. Because of the separation of verses in our Bible, it is easy to overlook the fact that verses 10 and 11 are an exposition of "love" and "hospitality" in verses 8 and 9. **As every man hath received the gift** (Gr *charisma*) does not refer to talents, nor does the word have the article in the original. Not "the gift," but "any gift" (meaning something one gets for nothing) is to be given in the same way that it is received, without grudging. This is the thing that makes us **good stewards** of God's **grace. Minister the same one to another** in this context means being hospitable to one another. In the early church, apostles and preachers were constantly travelling from one town to another spreading the gospel. In this type of ministry, they needed someone to minister to them in return by providing the physical necessities of life. The gospel came as a free gift, so should the support of the gospel preachers. In this passage, both the

12 Beloved, think it not strange concerning the fiery trial which is to try you, as though some strange thing happened unto you:
13 But rejoice, inasmuch as ye are partakers of Christ's sufferings; that, when his glory shall be revealed, ye may be glad also with exceeding joy.

14 If ye be reproached for the name of Christ, happy are ye; for the spirit of glory and of God resteth upon you: on their part he is evil spoken of, but on your part he is glorified.

15 But let none of you suffer as a murderer, or as a thief, or as an evildoer, or as a busybody in other men's matters.
16 Yet if any man suffer as a Christian, let him not be ashamed; but let him glorify God on this behalf.

17 For the time is come that judgment must begin at the house of God: and if it first begin at us, what shall the end be of them that obey not the gospel of God?
18 And if the righteous scarcely be saved, where shall the ungodly and the sinner appear?

preaching of the message of the gospel, and ministering to the physical needs of the preachers through genuine Christian hospitality, are to be done to glorify God in the name of Jesus Christ.

12-13. Beloved, think it not strange concerning the fiery trial which is to try you. It is possible that the **Amen** of verse 11 was an attempt to close the letter and Peter may have just now heard of some new development in which some of his readers are involved. If not, then he feels that he needs to say a bit more about the attitude of a Christian toward suffering. Either way **fiery trial** need not refer to literal fire like that of Rome in A.D. 64. The important thing here is to note how they are to look upon whatever trial it is; they are not to consider it **strange** (Why me, Lord?), but to rejoice (consider themselves privileged) that they can share in the sufferings of Christ. Then, in the Revelation of Christ, they will be able to be **glad also with exceeding joy.** Three words for joy are used to emphasize true happiness at His coming, and the translations are necessarily awkward at expressing this.

14. If ye be reproached (Gr *oneidizō*) is present tense and literally, "if you are being reproached"; the word denotes heaping insults upon a person. The reproach here is caused by confessing **the name.** The apodosis of the sentence implies "you are" really fortunate, that is, according to the teachings of Christ (Mt 5:10) and Christianity. **Happy are ye.** The reason they should consider themselves fortunate is because of the presence of the Spirit which is a sign of the approval, blessing, and protection of God. **The spirit of glory and of God. Glory** may be an allusion to the "Shekinah" glory cloud of the Old Testament (Ex 33:9-10; 40:34-35).

15-16. But let none of you suffer as a murderer, or as a thief, or as an evildoer, or as a busybody. Peter again returns to this truth mentioned before in 2:20 and 3:17, to show that it is not suffering in itself which is virtuous, but suffering for the name of the Lord, or **as a Christian,** which counts. None of his readers should suppose that just punishment for sin by the government would bring the praise of God. The name "Christian" was applied in New Testament times as a term of derision (Acts 11:26; 26:28). Just being a Christian was at times punishable by death, or lesser penalties. History indicates that many have been killed for admitting to being Christians in these times of persecution by the government. **Let him not be ashamed,** that is, of this name of being a "Christian." Let him rather be proud of it, and use this derogatory name as a means and instrument for bringing glory to God.

17-18. For the time is come. The word **time** (Gr *kairos*) refers to a specific, designated, or predicted time when something is supposed to happen. Peter is again making reference to the end time; these verses are an apocalyptic pronouncement with application from the persecution which is beginning to come upon believers. One of the elements of apocalyptic discourse is **judgment** (Gr *krima*); the meaning here would be rather general, the same as "suffering" or "punishment." The application runs that if in the end time judgment and punishment are to come, and we are now beginning to see suffering and punishment (for being a Christian) of the people of God (this is the meaning of **house of God**), this must mean that the end of time is here, or at least very close. **What shall the end be,** that is, what will happen most certainly before this is all over, to **them that obey not the gospel of God?** There is obviously no doubt at all about what will happen to them; they will be judged, and all the apocalyptic predictions about God's wrath upon His enemies will be fulfilled. Peter is attempting to encourage the believers to gladly face any dangers or suffering for Christ by appealing to the apocalyptic comfort that God will punish the ungodly in that day. He draws support from his deep knowledge

19 Wherefore let them that suffer according to the will of God commit the keeping of their souls *to him* in well doing, as unto a faithful Creator.

CHAPTER 5

THE elders which are among you I exhort, who am also an elder, and a witness of the sufferings of Christ, and also a partaker of the glory that shall be revealed:

2 Feed the flock of God which is among you, taking the oversight *thereof*, not by constraint, but willingly; not for filthy lucre, but of a ready mind;

of the Old Testament and quotes Proverbs 11:31, **if the righteous scarcely be saved, where shall the ungodly and the sinner appear?**

19. In summary of this section, Peter exhorts, **let them that suffer** (the Greek present tense implies the suffering may already have begun) . . . **commit** (Gr *paradidōmi*). It is interesting that this is the same word Peter used in 2:23 to describe what Jesus did in His suffering for our sins on the Cross; He committed Himself "to him that judgeth righteously." Compare Luke 23:46, where Jesus committed His spirit to God, and Acts 7:59, where Stephen prayed in his martyrdom for the Lord Jesus to receive his spirit. This may be an encouragement to bravery in martyrdom if it becomes inevitable, rather than telling Christians to pray for deliverance.

VII. THE CHRISTIAN AND THE COMING OF THE LORD. 5:1-9.

A. Exhortation to the Elders. 5:1-4.

5:1. The elders which are among you I exhort. The **elders** (Gr *presbyteros*) are not a group in any one place, since this is a circular letter intended for several different congregations, but probably individuals who have been appointed by the apostles in various cities (see 1:1; Acts 14:23). **Elder** as the title for an office has not to do with age, but respect (which originally came from age). Peter has a special exhortation for these spiritual leaders, and to make it more effective, he briefly lists his superior qualifications. **Who am also an elder.** The original has the compound word (Gr *sympresbyteros*) which means an elder serving along with you who are elders.

Peter is also a **witness of the sufferings of Christ.** The word "witness" (Gr *martys*) is the word from which we get the English word "martyr," but denotes here a person who testifies to the truth of something. A **witness** of the sufferings of Christ, then, does not mean someone who has necessarily seen the sufferings, but someone who testifies to the truth and meaning of what happened. The apostles were all witnesses in the sense that they affirmed Jesus to be the Suffering Servant of Jehovah, who according to the Old Testament, was to accomplish the salvation of God's people. Peter learned this himself (cf. Mk 8:31-33) and was now an authoritative proclaimer of the sufferings of Christ. It should be noted that the prophets (1:11) had the Spirit's **witness** of the sufferings of Christ, long before anyone had "seen" these sufferings.

And also a partaker of the glory that shall be revealed. A **partaker** (Gr *koinonos*) is one who shares in something, or is a partner in it. It is not likely that Peter would call himself a "partner" in something that was not yet revealed; it may be that he means to say that he is a partner in the great glory of salvation which was revealed (partially) to the prophets and now had already been fulfilled in his time. See again 1:3-12, and note especially verse 1:11 concerning the **glory** that was to follow the sufferings of Christ according to the prophets. **Shall be** (Gr *mello*) is a present participle in the original which might be better translated, "the glory that was to be revealed," meaning the prophesied blessing of salvation to the Gentiles. Note in this connection, Acts 2:39 from the preaching of Peter at Jerusalem.

2. The content of Peter's exhortation to the elders is expressed in the first word of verse 2, **Feed the flock of God.** This one word sums up the total pastoral responsibility to the flock, or congregation. The word **feed** (Gr *poimainō*) is a cognate of **flock** (Gr *poimnion*), and is especially important because of the biblical metaphor of the people of God as a flock, and their spiritual leaders as shepherds (Gr *poimēn*). The responsibilities of the shepherds (or elders, the terms are synonymous) are many, but are quite obvious from this metaphor of "tending the flock." Compare Jn 21:16; Acts 20:28; I Tim 3:2-7; Tit 1:11; Phm 14; I Pet 2:25. The shepherd has the total responsibility for the care and welfare of the flock; he does not just **feed**. This basic concept has come down to the present day in the word "pastor" (from the Latin *pascere*, "feed"); it is the key concept in seminary training.

Peter defines his exhortation to the elders with three sets of negative and positive words; two sets of words deal with how to pastor as far as the pastor's attitude is concerned, while the third set deals with how to pastor as far as the method is concerned. **Not by constraint, but willingly** means that the pastor or elder is "called" to this vocation; he does not need to be pressed into it, for he feels called, he wants to do it. This is the proper attitude for the pastor today as well; he should enjoy his work. **Not for filthy lucre, but of a ready mind.** Filthy lucre (Gr *aischrokerdōs*) is an adverb from two words meaning "shameful gain." Since the word is used only one time in all Christian literature, it is difficult to determine its precise meaning, but we know that its opposite here is **of a ready mind** (Gr *prothymōs*) which means "eagerly." The passage does not say that there is something wrong with money, or with the pastor getting paid. The Bible clearly teaches that pastors should be paid at least as well as other professional people. The pastor or elder should not choose this vocation just because it is such a lucrative occupation (fortunately, there is no danger of this today!), however, but should be eager to do it.

3 Neither as being lords over *God's* heritage, but being ensamples to the flock.

3. The third set of words, **Neither as being lords over God's heritage, but being examples to the flock,** has to do with method of ministry. Another translation has, "not as domineering over those in your charge." The idea is that there is to be no "browbeating," "whipcracking," or "intimidation."

4 And when the chief Shepherd shall appear, ye shall receive a crown of glory that fadeth not away.

4. Peter refers to the second coming of Christ as the manifestation of the **chief Shepherd,** when the shepherds will be rewarded with a glorious and unfading crown.

B. Exhortation to the Younger. 5:5-9.

5 Likewise, ye younger, submit yourselves unto the elder. Yea, all *of you* be subject one to another, and be clothed with humility: for God resisteth the proud, and giveth grace to the humble.

5. **Likewise, ye younger, submit yourselves unto the elder.** Both words are in the plural; the younger men likewise have an exhortation from Peter. It is to **submit** (Gr *hypotassō*) to the elders. See 2:13-17 for the meaning of this word which here implies that the younger men, the elders or pastors, as well as all Christians in general (in this text, the congregation) must fit themselves into the social structure (here the church) and do their part. The elders are not told to submit because they are the leaders, but it is implied that they submit to the "Chief Shepherd." **Be clothed with humility.** The word **be clothed** (Gr *engkomboomai*) means literally to "tie on" an apron; here the thing to be tied on is **humility,** which is the same word used by Peter in 3:8 in the same close connection with the word "submit." Humility is simply assuming the proper role in relationship to others. Again Peter draws upon the Old Testament to prove his point by quoting Proverbs 3:34.

6 Humble yourselves therefore under the mighty hand of God, that he may exalt you in due time:

6. **Humble yourselves therefore under the mighty hand of God, that he may exalt you in due time. Due time** (Gr *kairos*) sounds like "by and by" or "after sufficient time has passed," but the word really means a specific and designated time; here it refers to God's time, namely the second coming of Christ, and more precisely, at the Revelation. **Humble** (synonymous with humility and submit above) is the opposite of **exalt;** it means literally "think low," but in actual usage in the Bible it does not gender a lack of self-confidence or a low self-image. Humility in the Bible, in fact, is an attitude that will bolster and support self-confidence, for it simply means assuming the role that God has assigned to us in life. True humility does not say, "I'm no good; I can't.". It says, "This is what God wants me to do; I shall."

7 Casting all your care upon him; for he careth for you.

8 Be sober, be vigilant; because your adversary the devil, as a roaring lion, walketh about, seeking whom he may devour:

9 Whom resist stedfast in the faith, knowing that the same afflictions are accomplished in your brethren that are in the world.

10 But the God of all grace, who hath called us unto his eternal glory by Christ Jesus, after that ye have suffered a while, make you perfect, stablish, strengthen, settle you.

11 To him be glory and dominion for ever and ever. Amen.

12 By Sīl-vā'nus, a faithful brother unto you, as I suppose, I have written briefly, exhorting, and testifying that this is the true grace of God wherein ye stand.

13 The church that is at Babylon, elected together with you, saluteth you; and so doth Marcus my son.

14 Greet ye one another with a kiss of charity. Peace be with you all that are in Christ Jesus. Amen.

(see page 762 for Bibliography to I and II Peter)

7. Casting all your care. Humility means that we do not have to bear our anxieties; we are told to "toss them over to him" (**casting** is a participle of attendant circumstance which assumes the imperative character of the main verb here). The two words for "care" in verse 7 must be distinguished: the first means anxieties, the second refers to the meticulous, personal concern God has about us. He is interested in us and willing to carry all our anxieties if we are willing to do what He wants us to do.

8-9. Several summary exhortations are now given: **Be sober** is nearly the same in meaning as **be vigilant.** The devil is pictured as a prowling lion who is seeking someone to devour. The mention of suffering twice in the context indicates that the devil is to be blamed for it, but is to be resisted with strong faith.

VIII. CONCLUSION. 5:10-14.

10-11. Verses 10 and 11 are more than a doxology and close; they are a great encouragement to these suffering saints. They promise that God will Himself **make you perfect, stablish, strengthen, and settle** the faithful.

12-14. By Silvanus probably indicates the amanuensis or secretary who assisted Peter. Note that he is a faithful brother (a preacher in his own right, and apostolic companion of Paul for some time). The purpose is restated: to encourage, and testify (solemnly affirm) **that this is the true grace** (note that he means by **grace** the whole system of Christianity). Greetings are included from the **church** (implied by the feminine form of **elected together**) at Rome (which here has the symbolic name of Babylon).

The Second Epistle Of
PETER

INTRODUCTION

Authorship. Peter identifies himself as the "apostle of Jesus Christ" in 1:1 and maintains this claim by implication in 1:14 with reference to the Lord's statement about his death. The claim is assumed in 1:18 when he recalls the Mount of Transfiguration experience, and again in his mention of Paul in 3:15. In 3:1 the author mentions by the way that this is the second epistle to these same general readers.

Although there is little certain external evidence (Origen, A.D. 250 is the first to definitely mention it by name) for the book in the earliest times, it was finally and formally recognized as canonical in A.D. 397 at the Council of Carthage. Origen and Eusebius show that there was dispute about its authenticity at first among some of the churches, but it cannot be denied that quotations and allusions of it occur in Irenaeus, Justin Martyr, the Shepherd of Hermas, the Didache, and Clement of Rome.

In modern times some scholars have questioned the authenticity of the book because of the great dissimilarity in style and content between I and II Peter. Other scholars, however, have demonstrated convincingly that there are definitely similarities in style and content between the two books, as well as between II Peter and the sermons of Peter in Acts. Arguments from style and content seem to cancel each other out; but no one has ever disproved the apparently direct and honest claims of the book itself.

Jude seems to be slightly later in date than II Peter, and attests to the apostolic authorship of the latter by his apparent use of it. There is, in short, no reason to doubt the author's statement in 1:1 that he is the Apostle Peter.

Purpose. Reports on the activity of false teachers among the churches of Asia must have come to Peter shortly after the writing of the first epistle. He seems very concerned about the effect these false teachers might have on his readers, who may have already been depressed by suffering and persecution according to I Peter. The book, then, intends to remind the believers of the importance of supplementing their faith with virtue, knowledge, and steadfastness (1:5-7, 12). Peter also turns to the Old Testament again in this letter to find illustrations for the dangers of listening to the false teachers (ch. 2), and reminds the believers of the approaching day in which the ungodly false teachers will be destroyed (3:1-10). In the light of these facts, Peter encourages his readers to holy lives as they wait for the coming of the Day of God (3:11-13).

Date. This second epistle must have been written quite close to the end of the Apostle Peter's life. He sensed (1:15) that the end was near for him, and wanted to provide written reminders for his readers. The *terminus a quo* would be, according to 3:16, the circulation of several of the epistles of Paul; the *terminus ad quem*, the martyrdom of Peter in about A.D. 67.

OUTLINE

COMMENTARY

I. INTRODUCTION. 1:1-2.

SIMON Peter, a servant and an apostle of Jesus Christ, to them that have obtained like precious faith with us through the righteousness of God and our Saviour Jesus Christ:

2 Grace and peace be multiplied unto

1:1-2. Simon Peter includes both his given Jewish name and the symbolic Christian name given to him by the Lord Jesus (Mt 16:18). **A servant and an apostle.** Apostle claims the authority to be heard in the name of the Lord, but **servant** (Gr *doulos*) is a word of deep humility meaning literally "slave" and implying total and permanent ownership by a master. Paul also used this

you through the knowledge of God, and of Jesus our Lord,

word to describe his relationship to the Lord (e.g., Rom 1:1) as did Jude the brother of the Lord. It is difficult to see why, if the author here had been an impostor, a false author would have changed the introductory formula in this way and made it different from I Peter. This seems then to be an open and direct claim to acceptance. Here, believers are called those who have **obtained like precious faith with us. Obtained** (Gr *langchanō*) means "to be chosen to a position by divine will or by lot," and suggests exactly the same theology as **elect** in I Peter 1:2. Christians are those who are saved only by the grace of God; they do not **obtain** it by their own initiative or works. The word **like precious** expresses the same theme as I Peter 1:3-12, namely, the glory of salvation. We have been chosen to the **faith . . . through** (Gr *en*), literally "in" **the righteousness of God and our Savior Jesus Christ.** In order to show that the titles **God** and **Savior** both refer to the same person, the translation should be, ". . . in the righteousness of our God and Savior Jesus Christ." Peter clearly calls Jesus **God.**

II. SUPPLEMENTING OUR FAITH. 1:3-21.

A. Christian Virtues. 1:3-14.

3 According as his divine power hath given unto us all things that *pertain* unto life and godliness, through the knowledge of him that hath called us to glory and virtue:

3. According as his divine power hath given unto us all things that pertain unto life and godliness. There is no main verb in verse 3, and we must assume that the whole of verses 3 and 4 is preparatory in some way for the major exhortation of the chapter in verse 5, "supplement your faith." Verses 3-4 are perhaps a review for his readers of what was started in I Peter 1:3-9. **Hath given** (Gr *dōreomai*) means "to freely give," the stress is on "freeness" of the gift. The names Dorothy and Theodore come from this word and mean "God's gift." In the original, the perfect tense also stresses the certainty of the fact and possession of this gift.

The context of the gift is expressed in the words **all things that pertain unto life and godliness.** Everything that has to do with life or serving God has been freely given so that we lack nothing. **Through the knowledge of him** expresses the means through which He gives us these things; it is through knowing Him (objective genitive in Greek). **Him that hath called us to glory and virtue** does not refer to our glory and virtue, but that of Jesus Christ. A better translation would be, ". . . through the knowledge of him who called us by his own glory and excellence." Compare I Peter 2:9, which uses both "called," and "virtue" in the same sense as here.

4 Whereby are given unto us exceeding great and precious promises: that by these ye might be partakers of the divine nature, having escaped the corruption that is in the world through lust.

4. Whereby are given unto us (Gr *dōreomai*). Once more, as in verse 3, the perfect tense is used in Greek to imply the certainty of the unmerited gift of his **great and precious promises.** The word **promises** (Gr *epanggelma*) really is not the promise, but the result of the promise, namely its "fulfillment." Peter proposes in both epistles that we no longer live in the age of prophecy and promise, but in the new age, the age of fulfillment. Taken together, these two words stress that God has in fact freely given to us the very things that He had promised in the Old Testament. The verse corresponds to I Peter 1:12, and emphasizes the privilege of living at a time when through the preaching of the gospel the promises were fulfilled. **That by these ye might be partakers.** The final clause shows the reason that the promises were fulfilled: that they might become partakers of the divine nature. That is, God intended by accomplishing salvation in Christ that believers would share a common quality of life. Peter is not making new promises for the future, he is proclaiming fulfillment and present reality for his readers; he is a preacher and a witness, not a prophet. That this is true is seen also in his use of the word **partakers** which he had used in the same sense in I Peter 5:1 where he stated that he *was* a partner, not that he would be.

Having escaped (Gr *apopheugō*) is a participle of attendant circumstance and must be translated according to the mood of the main verb; the vague translation **having escaped** implies that we can become partakers of the divine life only in the far-off future after we have safely escaped the corruption of the world. Peter's point is totally different from this: God has made it possible for us to share this new quality of life now by having accomplished the promised salvation in Christ. A more accurate translation would be, ". . . so that through these you might escape from lustful, worldly corruption and share a new divine life." This is the same general idea that was expressed in I Peter 1:3 and 23 where he called it a new birth and used the same word for "corrupt seed" from which we are born.

5 And beside this, giving all diligence, add to your faith virtue; and to virtue knowledge;

5. And beside this, giving all diligence, add to your faith. A translation may read, "For this very reason, make every effort to supplement your faith with virtue. . . ." The word **add to** (Gr *epichorēgeō*) originally in the Athenian drama festivals meant "to finance, support, or back a chorus," and financial support is primary to most usage of the word in Christian literature; in 1:11 it means "provide." Here Peter calls upon believers to put everything they have into supporting their faith with virtue, etc. **Faith** is not something the believers could "provide" in this verse (cf. 1:1); faith has been given to them or rather they have been chosen to it. What they are called upon to do here is to "provide" certain items of support for faith. Each item is, in turn, to be supported or supplemented with another. Seven items are needed to support perfect faith; each of them is a philosophical abstraction of an aspect of the Christian life or divine nature that we share.

6 And to knowledge temperance; and to temperance patience; and to patience godliness;
7 And to godliness brotherly kindness; and to brotherly kindness charity.

6-7. To read the list one must understand the main verb "support" with each quality named. The most important item of support to each quality will be the quality which follows in the list. At the end of the list is the quality which supports all the others and is most needed in the Christian life, love (cf. I Cor 13). **Temperance** means "self-control," and this is the item that is most needed to support knowledge. An ancient Greek saying put it briefly, "Know yourself." Self-control requires more than anything else **patience**, which should rather be translated "endurance," or "strength of character" (Gr *hypomonē*).

8 For if these things be in you, and abound, they make *you that ye shall* neither *be* barren nor unfruitful in the knowledge of our Lord Jesus Christ.

8. For if these things be in you, and abound. Peter now points out how important these items of support to faith really are. If they exist in you and if they abound you will be effective and fruitful. These are the elements of success in the Christian life. **They make you** (Gr *kathistēmi*) has the connotation of "distinguishing as" and could be translated, ". . . they keep you from being ineffective or unfruitful." **In the knowledge of our Lord Jesus Christ.** The word **knowledge** (Gr *epignōsis*) is the same one which recurs in 1:2, 3, 8, and 2:10; it means "knowledge" or "recognition of," and may be equal to the simplex form used in 1:5-6; 3:18. There is an emphasis on knowledge in this chapter: grace and peace are in the knowledge or recognition of God (1:2), all things are in the knowledge or recognition of God (1:2), all things are given through this knowledge (1:3), and knowledge must support virtue (1:5).

9 But he that lacketh these things is blind, and cannot see afar off, and hath forgotten that he was purged from his old sins.

9. He that lacketh these things is blind, and cannot see afar off, and hath forgotten that he was purged from his old sins. Verse 9 is a conditional sentence corresponding to the one in verse 8; they are positive and negative reinforcements of the importance of the seven indispensable qualities of the Christian life listed in verses 5-7. The protasis here establishes that the person does not possess these qualities; the apodosis is a metaphor: he is blind. The two circumstantial participles explain first the meaning of the metaphor (**cannot see afar**, Gr *myōpazō*, from which we get "myopia"), and then the application of the metaphor: he has spiritual myopia. He never got close enough to Christianity to focus on the fact that he needed to be

cleansed from his sins! It should be obvious that the object of the
forgetting here is *not* that he was purged, since he had never
been cleansed in the first place. What escaped him was "the
cleansing"; he never saw that his sins had to be cleansed or
washed away before he could live the Christian life.

**10 Wherefore the rather, brethren,
give diligence to make your calling and
election sure: for if ye do these things,
ye shall never fall:**

10. In verse 10, Peter urges his readers to confirm **calling and
election**, not memory. It does not seem likely that a person
could forget it if his sins had been washed away by the atoning
death of Christ, but the whole matter could escape his notice if
he were not urged to make sure about it. We cannot be sure of
calling and election if we have not been **purged** (vs. 9) from our
former sin. On the other hand, if these are confirmed by the fact
that we have been cleansed from our old sins, it is certain that we
shall never fall (Greek subjunctive of emphatic future negation)!

**11 For so an entrance shall be minis-
tered unto you abundantly into the everlasting kingdom of our Lord and Saviour Jesus Christ.**

11. For so (meaning "in this way") **an entrance** (Gr *eisodos*,
with the article, "the way into," and there is only one Way; see
Jn 14:6) **shall be ministered** (Gr *epichorēgeō*, see 1:5) unto us.
This means that if we make sure our sins are washed away by
Christ, God, the richest supporter possible, will back us and
provide everything else that is needed on our road to heaven.

**12 Wherefore I will not be negligent
to put you always in remembrance of
these things, though ye know** *them,*
**and be established in the present truth.
13 Yea, I think it meet, as long as I am
in this tabernacle, to stir you up by putting** *you* **in remembrance;
14 Knowing that shortly I must put
off** *this* **my tabernacle, even as our Lord
Jesus Christ hath shewed me.**

12-14. Wherefore refers back to **According as** (1:3) and now
introduces a new paragraph based on the propositions of the
previous one. Since we share a new nature, and have a new
quality of life in Christ, Peter says, **I will not be negligent to put
you always in remembrance of these things.** A more accurate
translation has, "I intend always to remind you of these things."
What is given here is the purpose for the writing of the letter.
**Though ye know them, and be established in the present
truth,** is a tactful concession. **As long as I am in this tabernacle.**
Tabernacle (Gr *skēnōma*), meaning "tent," is a Christian
metaphor for the body or this earthly life as a temporary quarters for the real person which lives on after death.

To stir you up by putting you in remembrance. Stir (Gr
diegeirō) is the word for "wake up" from sleep. Peter's purpose
is to remind them and wake them up because he feels that
suddenly and unexpectedly he will be taken from them (alluding
to Jn 21:18). He wants them to have a reminder for reference
after his death.

B. Christian Doctrine. 1:15-18.

15-18. The two key verbs in this paragraph of the letter are
made known (16) and **We have** (19). In the light of the work of
false teachers, these are the things Peter wants them to remember. **For we have not followed** is not a main verb in the original,
but a circumstantial participle of cause; the reason Peter and the
other apostles preached was not because they had researched
(**followed,** Gr *exakoloutheō*) and believed in sophisticated fables
(Gr *mythos*) but because they were eyewitnesses of the greatness
of Jesus Christ. The main verb is **we made known unto you the
power and coming of our Lord Jesus Christ.** What is referred
to here is the preaching of the apostles. Peter says that they (the
apostles) preached Christ because they were eyewitnesses of the
gospel events; the implication is that the false teachers were not,
and therefore should not be listened to. To further corroborate
the apostolic authority of his message, Peter vividly recalls
actually hearing the voice of God who proclaimed on that holy
mountain. "This is my beloved Son." Peter and the apostles
knew what they were talking about when they preached; this is
the meaning of the reminder here. Could the false teachers come
up with this kind of authority?

**15 Moreover I will endeavour that ye
may be able after my decease to have
these things always in remembrance.
16 For we have not followed cunningly devised fables, when we made
known unto you the power and coming
of our Lord Jesus Christ, but were eyewitnesses of his majesty.
17 For he received from God the
Father honour and glory, when there
came such a voice to him from the excellent glory, This is my beloved Son, in
whom I am well pleased.
18 And this voice which came from
heaven we heard, when we were with
him in the holy mount.**

C. Christian Scriptures. 1:19-21.

**19 We have also a more sure word of
prophecy; whereunto ye do well that ye
take heed, as unto a light that shineth in**

19. The other key verb in the passage is **We have also a more
sure word of prophecy.** The meaning here is clearer in the
translation, "We also have the confirmed, prophetic Word."

a dark place, until the day dawn, and
the day star arise in your hearts:

20 Knowing this first, that no
prophecy of the scripture is of any private interpretation.

21 For the prophecy came not in old
time by the will of man: but holy men of
God spake *as they were* moved by the
Holy Ghost.

CHAPTER 2

BUT there were false prophets also
among the people, even as there shall
be false teachers among you, who privily shall bring in damnable heresies,
even denying the Lord that bought
them, and bring upon themselves swift
destruction.

2 And many shall follow their pernicious ways; by reason of whom the way
of truth shall be evil spoken of.

3 And through covetousness shall
they with feigned words make merchandise of you: whose judgment now

Peter is appealing not only to the apostolic preaching of Christ,
but to the Old Testament prophetic Word, that is, the promises
and prophecies about Christ which have now been fulfilled.
More sure (Gr *bebaios*) is a predicate adjective here. It means
"confirmed," "well-established," and often used with the promises or prophecies which have been fulfilled in Christ (cf. I Pet
1:12, "which in the Gospel have been declared as fulfilled").
They must, at least, believe the Old Testament. Peter insists in
fact, that they must **take heed** to the Old Testament; it is like a
light. This is of course another simile: they are in the dark
dungeon of sin, they need a lamp to find their way out; they
need it until dawn. They have, of course, already seen the light
and believed the Old Testament prophecies about Christ. Both
the verbs are progressive present in the original; they are "doing
well," and they are already "paying attention" to the light. This
figure suggests the metaphor of Christ as the light: like the
dawn, He shines into their hearts (cf. Lk 1:78-79, Jn 8:12).

20. Knowing this first, that no prophecy of the scripture.
The word **scripture** (Gr *graphē*) is obviously the Old Testament
Scripture and is synonymous here with the prophetic Word.
Peter uses the same word with the same meaning in 3:16 to refer
to the "other Scriptures" which the false teachers pervert. It is
also used in I Peter 2:6 to refer to the Old Testament. Paul used
it as well in II Timothy 3:16 when he said, "All Scripture is
given by inspiration of God." **Is of any private interpretation.**
This verse needs to be retranslated. First note that it is not
interpretation (Gr *epilysis*) really tended here (Gr *ginomai* means
"become," "originate"); origin is implied in the word **came** in
verse 21 as well as in the process of inspiration described there.
The word translated as **interpretation** (Gr *epilysis*) really means
"ingenuity." Secondly, note that **private** does not mean the
opposite of "public" but means "pertaining to a particular
individual" which in this case is the prophet. Thirdly, note that
specific reference is made to the Old Testament prophecies, the
same prophetic Word mentioned in verse 19. The implied question is "How can you recognize a real prophetic Word?" The
reply given is, "No prophecy of Scripture ever arises from
human ingenuity, for never did a single Old Testament prophecy come at the impulse of a man; what those men spoke was the
Word of God because they were being influenced by the Holy
Spirit" (II Pet 1:20-21). In these verses then Peter has made it
possible on the basis of his reminder of the apostolic preaching,
as well as on the basis of the Old Testament, for his readers to
recognize a false prophet when they see one. Now in chapter two
he will become more blunt.

21. Prophecy refers to the total revelation of God which did
not originate by human invention but as the writers of scripture
were **moved by the Holy Ghost**, meaning they were "borne
along" by the Holy Spirit. Thus, He moved upon them in such a
way that their words were indeed the very Word of God!

III. SECURING OUR FAITH. 2:1-22.

A. Warning Against False Prophets. 2:1-14.

2:1-3. There were false prophets among the people. The
people here means the people of Israel, God's chosen people,
and Peter believes, like Paul, that ". . . these things happened
unto them for examples: and they are written for our admonition" (I Cor 10:11). See also I Peter 2:9 where **people** is applied
to the church. Deuteronomy 13:1-5 warned the people that if a
false prophet came and tried to draw them away from the
worship of God, they should not listen. It was a test to see if they
loved God with all their hearts. Peter is telling his readers the
same thing; he draws upon all the apocalyptic passages he knows
to show that the false teachers are despicable to God and doomed
to destruction as His enemies. Peter warns that **there shall be**

of a long time lingereth not, and their damnation slumbereth not.

4 For if God spared not the angels that sinned, but cast *them* down to hell, and delivered *them* into chains of darkness, to be reserved unto judgment;

5 And spared not the old world, but saved Noah the eighth *person*, a preacher of righteousness, bringing in the flood upon the world of the ungodly;

6 And turning the cities of Sodom and Go-mŏr'rha into ashes condemned *them* with an overthrow, making *them* an ensample unto those that after should live ungodly;
7 And delivered just Lot, vexed with the filthy conversation of the wicked:
8 (For that righteous man dwelling among them, in seeing and hearing, vexed *his* righteous soul from day to day with *their* unlawful deeds);

9 The Lord knoweth how to deliver the godly out of temptations, and to reserve the unjust unto the day of judgment to be punished:

10 But chiefly them that walk after the flesh in the lust of uncleanness, and despise government. Presumptuous *are they*, selfwilled, they are not afraid to speak evil of dignities.

false teachers among you, who privily shall bring in (that is smuggle into the church false doctrine without the people knowing it) **damnable heresies** (literally heresies of destruction, which means that the faith will be destroyed if people believe these things). The reason the false teachers sneak in heresy is because they deny the **Lord that bought them.** This does not mean that Christ is their Lord (master, despot) or ever was, but He could have been since He had paid the price for their release from sin. They denied Him (renounced) and would not have anything to do with Him when they could have been saved, and so will **bring upon themselves swift destruction.**

The problem for Peter and the church is that **many shall follow** them. Paul mentions the great apostasy of the end times in II Thessalonians 2:3 as well as in II Timothy 4:1. This is harmful to the testimony of the **way of truth** (another name for the church). **Make merchandise of you.** The word (Gr *emporeuomai*) means "exploit." The false teachers are in it only for the money (cf. I Pet 5:2). Their **judgment** and destruction are sure since they have made it obvious that they are the enemies of God, and God's enemies will be judged.

4. Peter again draws from the Old Testament to make it very obvious that the false teachers who are exploiting (or soon will be) his Christians readers will certainly be punished in the day of judgment by our Righteous God. This is the implied apodosis to the "if" clause begun in verse 4 but never completed; verse 9 could be translated, ". . . then the Lord knows how to. . . ." Three terrible examples of God's judgment are given. **For if God spared not the angels that sinned.** In Jude 6 they are called "the angels which kept not their first estate, but left their own habitation." Compare Genesis 6:1-4. These are said to be chained in darkness until the judgment.

5. The second example is the **old world,** meaning the people who lived in the time of Noah before the Flood. God destroyed the whole world by the **flood** (Gr *kataklysmos*), the great cataclysm, and saved only eight people. The word **saved** here (Gr *phylassō*) means literally "guard" or "protect," and this is exactly what God did for Noah and his family (**eighth** is an idiom which includes the other seven).

6-8. The third classic example (Gr *hypodeigma*) is the destruction of **Sodom and Gomorrah** from which only Lot was **delivered** (Gr *hruomai*, meaning "rescue"). It strikes us very strange that Lot, of all people, should be used as an example of the **righteous.** You will remember, however, that in this instance he is the only person who could be used since he was probably the only one delivered (except for his daughters who were probably more immoral than he). Perhaps in contrast to the totally wicked population of the cities, he was righteous, or perhaps we do not have as much information as we need to judge. At any rate, we are told that he vexed his **righteous soul** (Peter uses the word "just" or "righteous" of Lot three times here) **from day to day with their unlawful deeds.** It is interesting that the Flood and Sodom and Gomorrah were used by Jesus as examples of judgment (Lk 17:25-30).

9. These examples were cited by Peter to show that **The Lord knoweth how to deliver the godly . . . and to reserve the unjust unto the day of judgment to be punished.** To be **punished** is a present participle in the original, and might better be rendered, ". . . and to keep the unrighteous under punishment until the day of judgment." The Lord will deliver the godly, but He will punish the ungodly, and especially these false teachers to whom Peter applies this whole section (vs. 10a).

10-14. Peter now describes them as bold and willful, slandering even the angels of God (cf. Eph 1:21; Col 1:16). But even the angels do not bring a slanderous word against them. **But these, as natural brute beasts** (i.e., "dumb animals," Gr *zōon*). So deserving are these false teachers of judgment, that Peter says

11 Whereas angels, which are greater in power and might, bring not railing accusation against them before the Lord.

12 But these, as natural brute beasts, made to be taken and destroyed, speak evil of the things that they understand not; and shall utterly perish in their own corruption;

13 And shall receive the reward of unrighteousness, *as* they that count it pleasure to riot in the day time. Spots *they are* and blemishes, sporting themselves with their own deceivings while they feast with you;

14 Having eyes full of adultery, and that cannot cease from sin; beguiling unstable souls: an heart they have exercised with covetous practices; cursed children:

15 Which have forsaken the right way, and are gone astray, following the way of Balaam *the son* of Bō'sôr, who loved the wages of unrighteousness;

16 But was rebuked for his iniquity: the dumb ass speaking with man's voice forbad the madness of the prophet.

17 These are wells without water, clouds that are carried with a tempest: to whom the mist of darkness is reserved for ever.

18 For when they speak great swelling *words* of vanity, they allure through the lusts of the flesh, *through much* wantonness, those that were clean escaped from them who live in error.

19 While they promise them liberty, they themselves are the servants of corruption: for of whom a man is overcome, of the same is he brought in bondage.

20 For if after they have escaped the pollutions of the world through the knowledge of the Lord and Saviour Jesus Christ, they are again entangled therein, and overcome, the latter end is worse with them than the beginning.

21 For it had been better for them not to have known the way of righteousness, than, after they have known *it,* to turn from the holy commandment delivered unto them.

22 But it is happened unto them according to the true proverb, The dog *is* turned to his own vomit again; and the sow that was washed to her wallowing in the mire.

they ought to be caught and killed like animals, they will be in fact. As a reward for their wrongdoing, they will themselves be wronged in the judgment. **They shall utterly perish in their own corruption,** should rather be translated, ". . . they will be destroyed like them" (i.e., as if they were dumb animals). They revel in the daytime; they are like blots and blemishes, and have an insatiable appetite for sin.

B. Characteristics of False Prophets. 2:15-22.

15-16. They **have forsaken the right way** and the point of the whole description is that they will get what they deserve.

17. These are wells without water. More properly "springs" (Gr *pēgē*); either way they are quite worthless without water. **Clouds** (or mists) are not much help for watering a crop. For these worthless false teachers, the gloom of darkness is reserved.

18-19. For when they speak. Probably this is a participle of means; it is by their well-modulated, authoritative, bloated vanities that they are able to lure (Gr *deleazō*, a fishing term) **those that were clean escaped** (rather, those who are just now barely escaping). New converts are easy prey for these slick-talking pseudo-Christians who are really false teachers. Although they promise freedom (vs. 19), they are themselves slaves of corruption and sin. Here the principle of Romans 6:16 is stated: if anyone is in fact conquered by something, he is actually a slave to it.

20-22. Verse 20 begins with an **if** which must not be overlooked. Peter does not say that these false teachers have escaped from the pollutions of the world. The main verb is **overcome** (Gr *hētaomai*) which is in the Greek present tense, implying that they are now being overcome or conquered by the terrible sins depicted in this chapter; the construction in the original has the effect of a present contrary-to-fact protasis. The writer, Peter, views the statement as a premise which is contrary to fact. He says, "If it were true that these false prophets were just now being conquered by sin and had already escaped the pollutions of the world (it is not true, but if it were), then they would actually be in worse condition now than when they started." These false teachers, of course, had never really escaped **the pollutions of the world** like true believers (cf. 1:4); if they had, and were now as **entangled** (Gr *emplekō*, meaning "hopelessly trapped" like a fish in a net) as they are in sin, they would be better off if they had never heard of Christianity. According to their pretense, they claim to have been saved; according to fact, they have returned to the most despicable sins. This would be, obviously, like a dog eating its vomit, or a pig which has just been washed going back to wallow in the mire.

The whole chapter warns the believers to secure the faith which had been preached to them by the apostles against the barbarous attack by obvious frauds who have shown themselves to be worthy of the certain judgment of God which will come upon them.

IV. SERVING IN FAITH. 3:1-13.

A. Purpose of the Epistle. 3:1-2.

CHAPTER 3
THIS second epistle, beloved, I now write unto you; in *both* which I stir up your pure minds by way of remembrance:

2 That ye may be mindful of the words which were spoken before by the holy prophets, and of the commandment of us the apostles of the Lord and Saviour:

3:1-2. This second epistle, beloved, I now write unto you . . . to stir up . . . in remembrance. Another allusion to the purpose of writing the letter (see 1:12-13, where the same words are used) as being hortatory and didactic, and, of course, an implied claim to apostolic authorship. The reminder is that, although there are false teachers among them who claim to be also representing God, believers must recognize, accept, and obey only the true word of God as found in the Old Testament (**the holy prophets**) and in the preaching of **the apostles** (meaning himself and the others). This is parallel to 1:16-18, and shows the aspects of continuity between the Old Testament and the new age, and the promise and fulfillment theme of the apostolic preaching.

B. Unbelief of Scoffers. 3:3-9.

3 Knowing this first, that there shall come in the last days scoffers, walking after their own lusts,

3. Knowing this first. This is an emphatic reminder of a primary fact (Gr *prōtos*); Peter had used these exact words in 1:20 to stress the primary fact that their preaching did not arise from their own ingenuity but was the Word of God as much as was the Old Testament. The fact here is that **scoffers** will come. Although the great apostasy was a generally known fact from all apocalyptic literature (see I Tim 4:1; II Thess 2:3 which also assume this), Peter now applies it to his own time and specifically to the reports of the false teachers, giving us a hint of the occasion of the letter. For Peter, as well as for Paul (I Tim 4:1), the days in which he lived were the **last days.** In biblical terminology, these were not the former days of promise and prophecy, but the latter days of fulfillment and blessing in Jesus Christ. By calling the false teachers **scoffers** (Gr *empaiktēs*), denoting one who ridicules or scorns, a "satirist"), Peter is in turn ridiculing them and coming to the aid of the truth of the Second Coming.

4 And saying, Where is the promise of his coming? for since the fathers fell asleep, all things continue as *they were* from the beginning of the creation.

4. Before coming to the message of the scoffers Peter stresses their false character and corruption. They heap scorn and ridicule on the message of the gospel (lit., "scorners with their scorn") and yet they themselves live (Greek present tense) in lust. Talk about the pot and the kettle—how ludicrous can one get? Once again, it is obvious that these false teachers will be destroyed as the enemies of God in the day of judgment! The ridiculous implication of their question (vs. 4) is: "There is no Second Coming, we can live any way we want. God will never judge us." This was, of course, in direct opposition to the apostolic preaching which always included the second coming of Christ as the ultimate fulfillment of the prophecies of the Old Testament. **All things continue as they were,** they said, God won't bring judgment upon the living and the dead.

5 For this they willingly are ignorant of, that by the word of God the heavens were of old, and the earth standing out of the water and in the water:

5. But this they willingly are ignorant of. A more precise translation would be, "They persistently (Greek progressive present) ignore one obvious fact." The fact is, all things are not the same; God destroyed the world in judgment once, and this confirms rather than disproves the warning that He will do it again (vss. 5-6). **By the word of God** (vs. 5) is emphatic in the original. Creation was by the Word of God; the sky, the dry land, and the water were distinguished by the Word of God (Gen 1:6-7, 9), and the world continues to exist by the Word of God (cf. Col 1:17 where the same word is used for Jesus Christ as the Living Word of God in exactly the same sense of sustaining the world).

6 Whereby the world that then was, being overflowed with water, perished:
7 But the heavens and the earth, which are now, by the same word are kept in store, reserved unto fire against

6-7. According to Peter's analogy here, water and the Word were involved in the destruction of the world by the Flood according to verse 6 (**Whereby** is plural and means "by these two things"). With pungent success comes the reply to those satirists who dared to suggest that God would not keep His

the day of judgment and perdition of ungodly men.

8 But, beloved, be not ignorant of this one thing, that one day *is* with the Lord as a thousand years, and a thousand years as one day.

9 The Lord is not slack concerning his promise, as some men count slackness; but is longsuffering to us-ward, not willing that any should perish, but that all should come to repentance.

10 But the day of the Lord will come as a thief in the night; in the which the heavens shall pass away with a great noise, and the elements shall melt with fervent heat, the earth also and the works that are therein shall be burned up.

promise of the Second Coming: **by the same word** of God, this world is **kept in store**. Both ideas, **kept in store**, and **reserved** are certified as fact by the use of the perfect tense in the original. It is as clear as Peter can make it that God's Word will certainly be fulfilled in this matter as it has been in others, the second coming and the day of judgment will transpire exactly as promised, and these ungodly men will be destroyed!

8. Be not ignorant of this one thing. Be not ignorant (Gr *lanthanō*) is the same word used in verse 5 but here there are no condemning insinuations; we might translate, "Don't allow this fact to escape your notice any longer," or, "You are overlooking something, my friends." **This one thing.** Several things are brought up here, but the one idea supported by them all is that "the day of the Lord will come." This part of the apostolic preaching is the main point that had been challenged by these immoral false teachers, and this is the main reason Peter had written this second letter. His readers needed this encouragement to be true to Christ and the gospel as they waited for the glorious appearing of the Lord. First, God does not count time in the same way that we do. To Him **a thousand years** may count **as one day** (cf. Ps 90:4).

9. Secondly, the reason for the delay in the return of Christ is not that the Lord is **slack concerning his promise.** This means that it is not one of God's attributes to be slow about keeping promises, although some (like these false teachers) might consider that to be true. The thought is probably parallel to Habakkuk 2:3 (quoted also by Heb 10:37 in another connection), where the writer says, "The prophecy awaits its time; if it seems to be slow, wait for it. It will surely come." **But** (a strong adversative emphasizing that the reason for the delay is a different matter entirely) **is long-suffering. Long-suffering** (Gr *makrothymeō*) is the regular word for "patience," and has the idea deep concern and feeling for someone over an extended period of time. The reason God has delayed that final day is His patience and concern for men that they might be saved. This same word is used again in verse 15 where God's patience is to be considered as salvation; it is made very plain in the passage that the reason for the delay is not negligence on God's part but concern for salvation. This is also stated in a negative way: **not willing that any should perish.** The word **willing** (Gr *boulomai*) means the same as "want" in English; God does not want men to be lost (He does not elect them to damnation but to salvation). The main verb in this sentence is translated by "God is patient"; the word "want" is a circumstantial participle expressing the reason for God's patience. The reason is both negative and positive as shown in the two complementary infinitives; He is patient because He does not want any to be lost, but wants all to **come to repentance. Come** (Gr *chōreō*) to repentance or "make room" for repentance (as one would make room at home for a welcomed guest) expresses the same thought as I Timothy 2:4, but with different words.

C. Looking for the Day of the Lord. 3:10-14.

10. These facts make it clear that **the day of the Lord will come.** Peter uses the same figure as Paul (I Thess 5:2) to express the imminency of the coming, **as a thief in the night.** The description of the judgment of that Day is given in the most vivid apocalyptic terms: weird **noise** (Gr *hroizēdon*, meaning a "rushing" and "sizzling" sound; the Greek, like the English word is onomatopoetic), destruction of all the elements by means of burning, and the leveling of all earthly constructions. The last of these descriptions, **the earth also and the works that are therein shall be burned up,** involves a textual variant; instead of **burned** we should read "discovered," which is difficult to understand, but evidently means that everything which has been constructed upon the earth is razed or pushed away so that the earth itself is exposed and nothing else remains. After the noise and the burning, the bulldozer of God's wrath will level the site in preparation for the new city.

11 *Seeing* then *that* all these things shall be dissolved, what manner *of persons* ought ye to be in *all* holy conversation and godliness,

11. Peter now, having reminded his readers of the certainty of the coming Day, encourages them to **holy conversation** (always means conduct in the Bible) **and godliness.** The beginning of verse 11 in this version is a bit misleading because of some textual variations and peculiarities of translation. First, note that Peter is not talking about the dissolution of **things** *per se,* but about the judgment and destruction of ungodly "people," and particularly about "these" ungodly people described in chapter two. He speaks about the coming of Christ as a **day of judgment and perdition of ungodly men** (3:7). Although verse 10 mentions **works** being burned up, it is for the punishment of the ungodly false teachers. Peter begins in verse 11, "In the light of the fact that all these ungodly men are to be destroyed (present tense to make it vivid) in this way, shouldn't you live your lives in holiness and godliness as you eagerly anticipate the coming of the day of God?" Note the contrast between "these" ungodly false teachers, and the emphatic "you" in verse 11. These ungodly false teachers have been trying to lure the Christians into immorality; it should be plain now that, since they will be judged and destroyed, their way is not the way to live.

12 Looking for and hasting unto the coming of the day of God, wherein the heavens being on fire shall be dissolved, and the elements shall melt with fervent heat?
13 Nevertheless we, according to his promise, look for new heavens and a new earth, wherein dwelleth righteousness.
14 Wherefore, beloved, seeing that ye look for such things, be diligent that ye may be found of him in peace, without spot, and blameless.

12-14. Verse 12 continues to mark the contrast in the way the Day is viewed by the ungodly and the godly; they tremble because it means punishment and destruction, while the Christian is **Looking for and hasting unto the coming of the day.** **Looking for** (Gr *prosdokaō*) is used in this context with the sense of "anticipation" with the word **hasting** (Gr *pseudō*) which means "hurry," or "get busy," and is translated **be diligent** in verse 14. The hope or expectation of the Christian, **new heavens and a new earth, wherein dwelleth righteousness,** is the basis for the exhortation to blamelessness and purity of conduct. There will be no false teachers in heaven.

D. Exhortation Against the Unstable. 3:15-16.

15 And account *that* the longsuffering of our Lord *is* salvation; even as our beloved brother Paul also according to the wisdom given unto him hath written unto you;
16 As also in all *his* epistles, speaking in them of these things; in which are some things hard to be understood, which they that are unlearned and unstable wrest, as *they do* also the other scriptures, unto their own destruction.

15-16. The imperative of verse 15, **account that the longsuffering of our Lord is salvation,** encourages believers to recognize the fact that just because God's day hasn't come yet, they shouldn't follow the false teachers in believing that it's not going to come; they should think of it in God's way: the longer He delays it, the more people can be saved. Peter draws support from Paul, saying that he taught the same thing; this is perhaps a reference to Romans 2:4 where God's patience is twice called "kindness," and "leads" to repentance. It is interesting that Peter should consider Paul **hard to be understood!** He does not say that all of Paul is difficult, only certain things in his epistles (most of which would be written by this time and would already have been read and known according to this statement). What those things are we can only guess, but Paul also had a great deal to say about the Second Coming, and since that is the point here, we could assume the connection. Those who had the most problem with Paul's writings (and Peter's too) were the **unlearned** (Gr *amathēs*), which is a rare word meaning literally "not a learner," and, as the opposite of "disciple" (Gr *mathētēs*), means here a non-Christian. Compare I Corinthians 1:18; 2:14. These difficult passages in Paul are also a problem for the **unstable** (Gr *astēriktos*), meaning those who needed support in their faith. Paul often used this word (in its positive form) in praying for God to "strengthen" or "stabilize" his readers, and Peter uses it in I Peter 5:10; II Peter 1:12, and also in the next verse (3:17). The are said to **wrest** (Gr *strebloō*), literally "twist," or "torture," **also the other scriptures.** The mention of **scriptures** shows not only that others existed, but that they were early regarded as the Word of God, equal to the prophetic Word of the Old Testament, and the apostolic preaching (see 1:16, 20,

21). The result of contradicting and opposing the Scripture, or the teaching of the apostles as the false teachers had done, was **destruction.**

V. CONCLUSION. 3:17-18.

17 Ye therefore, beloved, seeing ye know *these things* before, beware lest ye also, being led away with the error of the wicked, fall from your own stedfastness.

18 But grow in grace, and *in* the knowledge of our Lord and Saviour Jesus Christ. To him *be* glory both now and for ever. Amen.

17-18. Peter encourages them to be on their guard **beware,** (Gr *phylassō,* meaning "guard," or "protect" yourselves) that they do not get dragged off with these false teachers and fall from their own **steadfastness.** He encourages them rather to **grow in grace, and in the knowledge of our Lord and Savior Jesus Christ.**

BIBLIOGRAPHY

Barnes, Albert. James, Peter, John and Jude. In *Notes on the New Testament, Explanatory and Practical.* Grand Rapids: Baker, 1951.

Brown, John. *Expository Discourses in the First Epistle of the Apostle Peter.* Grand Rapids: Sovereign Grace, reprint of 1848 ed.

English, E. Schuyler. *The Life and Letters of Saint Peter.* New York: Our Hope, 1941.

*Green, E. M. B. Second Epistle General of Peter and the General Epistle of Jude. In *Tyndale New Testament Commentary.* Grand Rapids: Eerdmans, 1968.

Hiebert, D. Edmond. *An Introduction to the Non-Pauline Epistles.* Chicago: Moody Press, 1962.

Jowett, John. *The Epistles of St. Peter.* Grand Rapids: Kregel, 1970.

Kelly, William. *The Epistles of Peter.* London: Hammond, n.d.

*Leighton, Robert. *A Practical Commentary upon the First Epistle General of Peter.* Grand Rapids: Kregel, reprinted, 1972.

Lillie, J. *Lectures on the First and Second Epistles of Peter.* New York: Scribner's, 1869.

Meyer, F. B. *Tried by Fire.* London: Marshall, Morgan & Scott, 1955 reprint of 1890 ed.

Paine, Stephan. Epistle of Peter. In *Wycliffe Bible Commentary.* Chicago: Moody Press, 1962.

Plummer, Alfred. Second Epistle General of Peter. In *Elicott's Commentary on the Whole Bible.* Grand Rapids: Zondervan, reprinted, n.d.

*Selwin, Edward. *First Epistle of St. Peter.* London: Macmillan, 1961.

*Stibbs, Alan. The First Epistle General of Peter. In *Tyndale New Testament Commentary.* Grand Rapids: Eerdmans, 1960.

Thomas, W. H. B. *The Apostle Peter: Outline Studies in His Life, Character and Writings.* Grand Rapids: Eerdmans, 1950.

The First Epistle Of
JOHN

INTRODUCTION

Although this writing does not display the usual features of a letter, nevertheless it has always been classified as an epistle. Like Hebrews, it lacks an opening salutation, but in addition it lacks the epistolary conclusion of a letter. No formal mention of thanksgiving for the readers is given in the opening sentences (a practice never violated by Paul except in Galatians). It does not contain a single proper name (except that of Jesus Christ). In addition it does not locate itself historically, geographically, or personally. Nothing in the epistle is specific or local. The contents of this epistle clearly show that it was intended for a local audience. However, on the basis of contents alone it has properly been judged a letter (not a sermon).

Authorship. Although the author does not identify himself directly in any of the three epistles traditionally ascribed to him, the consensus of scholars is that they are all from the pen of the Apostle John, the son of Zebedee.

Tradition and internal evidence make it hard to deny the united assumption that John is the author. There is reference to the gospel and epistles of John in the Muratorian Canon. Various allusions to the epistles are found in Clement of Rome, the Didache, and the Epistle to Diognetus. Polycarp quotes I John and Papias also used it.

There are obvious similarities between the epistles and the gospel. The themes of light and darkness, life and death, Christ and antichrist, love and hate are all prevalent in both. The author claims to be an eyewitness (I Jn 1:1-3) and speaks with authority using "we" as if to include himself with the other apostles.

Date and place of writing. There are no indications in the epistle which assist us in fixing a definite time for its composition. The tone and writer's paternalistic attitude toward his readers suggests an old man is writing to a younger generation. The fact that the destruction of Jerusalem in A.D. 70 is not mentioned would mean that the epistle was either written before the city fell or a sufficient time afterward to make common reference to its destruction unnecessary. Generally, a date around A.D. 90 is accepted as accurate.

There is no hint as to where John was when he wrote this epistle, but since the latter years of the apostle's life were spent in Ephesus, it seems most likely that this is the place of writing. No evidence exists to the contrary.

Purpose. The purpose of the Gospel of John was "that ye might believe that Jesus is the Christ, the Son of God; and that believing ye might have life . . ." (Jn 20:31). The purpose of the first epistle is, "that your joy may be full" (I Jn 1:4), and, "that ye may know that ye have eternal life" (I Jn 5:13). Joy and assurance seem to be the attitudes John wishes to encourage in his readers.

The readers were already believers in Jesus Christ and they worshiped and fellowshiped in rather well-defined churches with membership rolls and local pastors. Evidently false teachers (not unlike those in II Peter and Jude) had caused some basic doctrinal problems (I Jn 1:10). With the emphasis on light and darkness, and the incarnation, and knowing, there must also have been an incipient quasi-gnostic movement afoot. John, at any rate, with apostolic concern, writes to encourage the believers to joy and assurance in purity of life as they wait for the appearance of Christ.

OUTLINE

COMMENTARY

THAT which was from the beginning, which we have heard, which we have seen with our eyes, which we have looked upon, and our hands have handled, of the Word of life;

2 (For the life was manifested, and we have seen *it*, and bear witness, and shew unto you that eternal life, which was with the Father, and was manifested unto us;)

3 That which we have seen and heard declare we unto you, that ye also may have fellowship with us: and truly our fellowship *is* with the Father, and with his Son Jesus Christ.

4 And these things write we unto you, that your joy may be full.

5 This then is the message which we have heard of him, and declare unto you, that God is light, and in him is no darkness at all.

6 If we say that we have fellowship with him, and walk in darkness, we lie, and do not the truth:

7 But if we walk in the light, as he is in the light, we have fellowship one with another, and the blood of Jesus Christ his Son cleanseth us from all sin.

I. INTRODUCTION. 1:1-4.

1:1-4. That which was from the beginning. We must take verses 1-4 as one long, involved, elliptical sentence, and look for the key main verb, which seems to be **and show unto you** in 1:2 (Gr *apanggellō*). The word means "declare," "announce," or "make known." What is being "made known" in this letter is the object of the verb here and is multifaceted: it is something which existed from eternity, it is something with which the writer has the most detailed personal acquaintance. It could be called the "Word of Life"; it has made a real appearance in the world of men. Others besides the author have seen it and can prove it. Finally, it existed earlier in close association with the Father and then made its appearance into the world. That object which is now being "made known" more fully in this letter is, of course, Jesus Christ. More succinctly, the author is saying that in this letter, "We are declaring Jesus Christ."

The purpose for this declaration is also given in duplicate form: **that ye also may have fellowship with us** (vs. 3), and **that your joy may be full** (vs. 4). Several of the verbs in this sentence are repeated for emphasis and clarity, and those which support the eyewitness nature of his testimony are given in the Greek perfect tense to stress the certainty of the facts. This should be brought out in the translation; for example, ". . . we have actually heard, in fact have seen him with our own eyes. . . ." **That ye also may have fellowship with us** is the purpose, but not the ultimate purpose, for fellowship with the apostles without fellowship with the **Father, and with his Son Jesus Christ,** would be mundane. Verse 4 should read "that our joy may be truly complete," rather than **your** joy. This makes little difference in the sense, however, since the joy of the apostles is truly complete when the believers have real **fellowship** (Gr *koinōnia*) with the Father and Son.

II. Fellowship with God. 1:5-2:8.

A. Walking in the Light. 1:5-7.

5-7. John has made it clear that the purpose of his writing is that the believers might have true fellowship; he now proceeds to make some subtle philosophical implications about fellowship with God which will apply to the present circumstances of the believers. **God is light, and in him is no darkness at all.** Here are the two great symbols suggesting moral purity and evil; John says literally that there is not even one bit of darkness in God. Therefore, **If we say** introduces the protasis of a general condition used as the premise of a syllogism; the first negative conclusion (vs. 6) is **we lie.** It is obvious that if there are false teachers or any others who claim to have **fellowship** (Gr *koinōnia*) with God (having something in common with God), and at the same time (both verbs are in the progressive present in Greek) continue to live according to the standards of darkness only, there is no way around the conclusion that they are lying! "Walking" (Gr *peripateō*) is the regular metaphor for "living" or "conducting one's life" in these epistles. Now, John may have come right to the point; he is probably dealing with a real situation where there are those who claim that you can have fellowship with God and live any way you please. Exactly this situation had existed earlier, and occasioned the writing of II Peter and Jude. More sophistication had probably been added, but these false teachers or incipient gnostics showed signs of having the same warped logic which would permit practicing known and willful sin. John now states the positive form of the conclusion to the syllogism: **we have fellowship one with another.** The grammar here is ambiguous, but the context makes it obvious that **one with**

another means we who walk in the light have fellowship with God. Thus, it is clear that the epistle deals with **fellowship** as fellowship in the life eternal. John's evidences of fellowship are not proofs of whether a believer is right with God, but are proofs of whether one is saved at all! Fellowship here refers to being born again. **And the blood of Jesus Christ his Son cleanseth us from all sin.** If it were not for the atoning death of Christ (the original reading was "Jesus his Son") fellowship with God would be impossible according to the syllogism because of the opposing symbols of light and darkness. What makes the difference is the **blood of . . . Christ,** His atoning death, which **cleanseth us from all sin;** this makes the darkness (here specified as **sin**) into light.

B. Walking in Sin. 1:8-10.

8 If we say that we have no sin, we deceive ourselves, and the truth is not in us.

9 If we confess our sins, he is faithful and just to forgive us *our* **sins, and to cleanse us from all unrighteousness.**

10 If we say that we have not sinned, we make him a liar, and his word is not in us.

8-10. Sin must be dealt with; it is a fact. Note the simple style of the Hebrew parallelism, saying the same thing in two different ways, and the repetition of ideas. The correct way of dealing with sin is not to deny it, but to acknowledge it and allow God to cleanse it. **If we confess** (Gr *homologeō*, meaning "acknowledge" or "agree with") **our sins, he is faithful and just** (He can be faithful to us and fulfill His promise, as well as just in accordance with His own righteousness and require the punishment of sin in Christ) so that (non-final clauses with Gr *hina* are possible in John) He forgives our sins, and cleanses **us from all unrighteousness. If we say that we have not sinned** (vs. 10). This is different from saying that we **have no sin** in verse 8. In verse 8 it is a matter of recognizing what can be classed as sin in our lives; in verse 10 it is a matter of denying that we have ever really (perfect tense in Greek) sinned at all. **We make him a liar, and his word is not in us.**

C. Walking with the Advocate. 2:1-2.

CHAPTER 2

MY little children, these things write I unto you, that ye sin not. And if any man sin, we have an advocate with the Father, Jesus Christ the righteous:

2 And he is the propitiation for our sins: and not for ours only, but also for *the sins of* **the whole world.**

2:1-2. My little children. These words are, of course, not written merely to little children; this is an idiom of endearment, as if to say, "My dear friends." On the other hand, John is assuming apostolic authority and responsibility for these his spiritual children. **These things I write unto you, that ye sin not.** Again, John is assuming some threat that would lure the believers away from Christ (perhaps false doctrine). Obviously, in the light of chapter 1, he is not saying that his writing will enable them to avoid committing their first sin. But, **if any man sin,** that is if any believer who has already acknowledged that he was a sinner, and has already been cleansed from his sin by the atoning sacrifice of Christ, if this person should be led off into sin, would he be eternally lost? He could sin, but he would not be hopelessly lost, because **we have an advocate.** Advocate (Gr *paraklētos*) is the word John used four times in his gospel for the Holy Spirit as the "Comforter." It is not so much "comfort" as "encouragement" or "help" which is usually meant by this word, and the help sought is pictured as an **advocate** (which word comes from the Latin equivalent of our Greek word here) or "attorney." **With the Father** means that He will stand and face the Father for us; the very same words are used of Christ in 1:2 (and in Jn 1:1). If we sin, our trouble with the Father will be darkness or unrighteousness, and we will be out of **fellowship** (1:6) with Him; but our Advocate who is to get us out of the difficulty is **the righteous** One.

And he is the propitiation for our sins. This very important biblical word **propitiation** (Gr *hilasmos*) denotes the price which must be paid to avoid the divine punishment upon sin. It is, therefore, the "fine" we must pay in court to avoid going to jail. In the Bible, there are other synonyms for this concept of the "fine," such as the "atonement" or "ransom" or "sin offering." One really should study all these words throughout the Old and New Testaments to get the full picture of this important redemptive term. Here, Christ is not only the Righteous Lawyer who is on very familiar terms with the Father (Judge), but he pays our "fine," or, more properly according to the text, He *is* the "fine" or "atonement" for our sins. Exactly in what sense Jesus Christ is the **propitiation** for our sins, John does not say; he assumes this knowledge from 1:7, and from a thorough discussion of the passion of Christ in the gospel. **For the sins of the whole world** does not mean that the application of the atonement is automatic for all the individuals in the world, but simply that if anyone in the world will believe in Christ and confess his sin, he too will find the atonement sufficient. Christianity is not exclusive like Gnosticism; anyone can know Him if they want to.

D. Walking under Commandment. 2:3-8.

3-4. And hereby means "in this way," and is used often in the epistle. **We do know that we know him.** The last occurrence of **know** is in the perfect tense in the original stressing the certainty of the action; we should translate, "In this way we know that we *really* know Him," or, "By this we may be sure that we know Him." **If we keep his commandments.** This is another simple syllogism (major premise, minor premise, and conclusion): "Everyone who truly knows Christ keeps His commandments; a certain person does not keep His commandments (regardless of his verbal claim that he truly knows Him); conclusion? Simple: he is a liar!"

3 And hereby we do know that we know him, if we keep his commandments.
4 He that saith, I know him, and keepeth not his commandments, is a liar, and the truth is not in him.

5-6. Next, John shows how the syllogism applies with a positive minor premise: keeping His commandments (living according to His moral standards) means not only that we have true knowledge of Him, but also that **love of God** (objective genitive) is **perfected** in him (that is, he is a true Christian). **He that sayeth he abideth in him** (talk is cheap) **ought** to walk (live) **even as he** (Christ) **walked.** All of this sounds as if it was meant to deal with the antinomian, gnostic false teachers.

5 But whoso keepeth his word, in him verily is the love of God perfected: hereby know we that we are in him.
6 He that saith he abideth in him ought himself also so to walk, even as he walked.

7-8. I write no new commandment unto you, but an old commandment which ye had from the beginning. We must keep in mind that John wrote with his immediate readers and their problems in view. He is reminding them of the preaching of the other apostles. What he writes is not new in that sense; it is the Word which they heard from the apostles. Note the emphasis in chapter 1 on terms like **witness, declare,** and **message.** Note also that in 1:5, the content of the message is "that God is light and in Him is no darkness at all." Now observe that **commandment** (2:7-8) is another didactic term like **message,** and has a content which is quite similar to the content in 1:5, that darkness is vanishing, and true light is already shining. In one sense these readers must accept nothing new (like a new teaching or commandment from false teachers), and in just that sense John's message is not new; it is old. The **old commandment is the word which ye have heard (from the beginning** is not original). The **word** (Gr *logos*) is not, it seems, a verse of Scripture which we know, but the **word** in the sense of the "preaching" of the apostles (cf. "the preaching of the cross," I Cor 1:18). There is also another sense in which John's readers need a new **commandment,** a new **word,** and they must receive it not from quasi-gnostic false teachers, but from the apostle himself. The new **word** is true with respect to them, or (in a different sense) with respect to Christ. The new commandment is, "Darkness is vanishing and the true light is now shining." This new **word** is in fact the major premise for John's third syllogism. How it applies to Christ is left to the reader's ingenuity (obviously He is the Light of the World, etc.); how it applies to the believers is the subject of 9-11.

7 Brethren, I write no new commandment unto you, but an old commandment which ye had from the beginning. The old commandment is the word which ye have heard from the beginning.
8 Again, a new commandment I write unto you, which thing is true in him and in you: because the darkness is past, and the true light now shineth.

III. FELLOWSHIP WITH LIGHT AND DARKNESS. 2:9-28.

A. Walking in Love. 2:9-17.

9 He that saith he is in the light, and hateth his brother, is in darkness even until now.

10 He that loveth his brother abideth in the light, and there is none occasion of stumbling in him.

11 But he that hateth his brother is in darkness, and walketh in darkness, and knoweth not wither he goeth, because that darkness hath blinded his eyes.

9-11. First, the negative application (vs. 9): if every believer has the True Light shining in his life (major premise), then the person who continually hates (Greek progressive present; his life is characterized by hate) his brother (minor premise: his life is all darkness), is still in darkness (conclusion) to this very moment, and thus is not a believer at all. Next, the positive application (vs. 10) which is just the opposite in its conclusion: the person whose life is characterized by love and light is a true believer. In verse 11, John goes back to negative application of the light-and-love premise in order to emphasize that hatred (perhaps he has in mind some aspect of the problem with the false teachers) creeps over one's life like the darkness, affecting his walk, and even his knowledge (**knoweth not whither he goeth**), making him in fact spiritually "blind." See II Peter 1:9, where false teachers were also a problem.

12 I write unto you, little children, because your sins are forgiven you for his name's sake.

13 I write unto you, fathers, because ye have known him *that is* from the beginning. I write unto you, young men, because ye have overcome the wicked one. I write unto you, little children, because ye have known the Father.

14 I have written unto you, fathers, because ye have known him *that is* from the beginning. I have written unto you, young men, because ye are strong, and the word of God abideth in you, and ye have overcome the wicked one.

12-14. I write unto you little children. John is not, of course, writing to literal children, young men, and fathers in this passage. These are metaphors which refer to the various levels of spiritual maturity among his readers. In one sense, all the believers are like **children** to him (cf. 2:1, 18; 3:7; 5:21). In another sense, John can include himself with them as **children** of God (3:1). In still another sense, as in this passage, some of the believers are less mature (having just recently been converted) than others who may have been saved from the beginning and are in a sense **fathers** in the faith to them. The metaphorical use of age for maturity is not at all unusual in the New Testament. The problem of the changes in tense where **I write** (Gr *graphō*) occurs in these verses is not significant; the six instances all refer to the present letter as he is writing it (the Greek aorist being epistolary). John, however, uses the perfect tense in Greek to stress the certainty of the reality of Christianity for each of the six metaphors (sins have "really been forgiven," they have "truly known," "have actually conquered," etc). In this way John assures the readers of his confidence in them, while in the same letter he repeatedly exposes the false teachers for what they really are.

15 Love not the world, neither the things *that are* in the world. If any man love the world, the love of the Father is not in him.

16 For all that *is* in the world, the lust of the flesh, and the lust of the eyes, and the pride of life, is not of the Father, but is of the world.

17 And the world passeth away, and the lust thereof: but he that doeth the will of God abideth for ever.

15-17. Love not the world, neither the things that are in the world. This prohibition (present tense in the original, and thus progressive action) would literally be translated, "Don't continue your love for the world . . ." (meaning after you have been saved). This introduces the next (fourth) syllogism on how to tell a real believer from a phony. The major premise is found in verse 17; in the lives of those who really love God, **the world passeth away.** Note that **passeth away** (Gr *paragomai*) is the same word used of the darkness in the last syllogism, and that **world** is the same in meaning as **darkness** (cf. 2:8). It follows then, that one who continues his love for the world while he claims to know and love the Father (vs. 15) is a phony. Loving the world (lust, greed, pride, etc.) is the opposite of doing the will of God. With a positive minor premise (vs. 17), the conclusion is positive: he is a true believer rather than a false prophet, and he **abideth for ever.**

B. Walking with Apostates. 2:18-28.

18 Little children, it is the last time: and as ye have heard that antichrist shall come, even now are there many antichrists; whereby we know that it is the last time.

19 They went out from us, but they were not of us: for if they had been of us, they would *no doubt* have continued with us: but *they went out*, that

18-19. John now moves into his fifth test (another syllogism) by which the believers may determine whether the self-authenticating teachers are true or false. First, it is to be expected that false prophets will arise since **it is the last time.** The coming of Christ marked the beginning of the "last days" (cf. I Cor 10:11; I Pet 4:7; Heb 9:26); God's promises of blessing were fulfilled, but there were also prophecies of apostasy and the Antichrist yet to come (II Thess 2:3; I Tim 4:1; II Tim 3:1; 4:3;

they might be made manifest that they were not all of us.

20 But ye have an unction from the Holy One, and ye know all things.
21 I have not written unto you because ye know not the truth, but because ye know it, and that no lie is of the truth.
22 Who is a liar but he that denieth that Jesus is the Christ? He is antichrist, that denieth the Father and the Son.
23 Whosoever denieth the Son, the same hath not the Father: *[but] he that acknowledgeth the Son hath the Father also.*
24 Let that therefore abide in you, which ye have heard from the beginning. If that which ye have heard from the beginning shall remain in you, ye also shall continue in the Son, and in the Father.

25 And this is the promise that he hath promised us, *even* eternal life.
26 These *things* have I written unto you concerning them that seduce you.
27 But the anointing which ye have received of him abideth in you, and ye need not that any man teach you: but as the same anointing teacheth you of all things, and is truth, and is no lie, and even as it hath taught you, ye shall abide in him.

28 And now, little children, abide in him; that, when he shall appear, we may have confidence, and not be ashamed before him at his coming.

II Pet 2:1; 3:3; Jude 18; I Jn 4:1). In one sense, then, the prophecies are already fulfilled in these false teachers, for they are **antichrists,** that is they are against Christ. **They went out from us, but they were not of us.** The meaning of this play on words is obvious: they associated with the believers but they were not real believers. John uses a contrary-to-fact condition in Greek to express his proof that the false teachers are impostors.

20-24. But ye have an unction. This is the key concept in the major premise; the word **unction** (Gr *chrisma*) denotes literally the "oil" or "unguent" with which a person has been anointed. In the Old Testament, kings were "anointed" as a part of the inaugural ceremony (I Sam 16:6-13); it involved simply pouring oil on the head of the chosen person. The chosen person then had the "oil" on him and was called the "anointed" (Heb *meshiach,* Gr *christos*). Thus, throughout the New Testament, God's chosen King, the Messiah, is designated the **Christ,** meaning in translation, "the Anointed One" or the one who had the "oil" (Gr *chrisma*). The baptism of Christ (Mt 3:13-17, et al.), with the Spirit coming upon him, and the voice with its messianic pronouncement, is symbolic of the King's coronation, and announced Him to the world as the anointed King.

The verb form **anoint** (Gr *chriō*) is also used several times in the New Testament to allude to the anointing of Christ, but once it is used of Christians, who are also in a sense (obviously a lesser sense than Christ) **anointed** (II Cor 1:21); in this passage it is clear that the "oil" with which we are **anointed** is the same as that with which Christ was anointed, namely the Holy Spirit (cf. II Cor 1:22). This, in fact, is the meaning behind the name "Christian," for believers are "little christs," "little anointed ones." When John, therefore, uses this word **unction** (Gr *chrisma*), or, as it occurs twice in verse 27, **anointing,** he simply means to say that all believers have the Holy Spirit. Since believers have the Holy Spirit, they have an "edge" on unbelievers and can "know" certain things that unbelievers cannot. So, John says in verse 20, **ye know all things.** Do the gnostic false teachers claim to "know"? Here is truth they cannot know, which even the simplest believer "knows" because he has the Spirit. The truth which makes it possible to tell Christians from **antichrists** is the truth that Jesus is the **Christ.** This is the message which the believers had **heard from the beginning** (compare this clause of verse 24 with verse 7, and note the emphasis on hearing and receiving the Word of God from the apostles, as well as holding to that same **commandment,** or letting it **remain in you**). The major premise of John's syllogism can be rephrased: "Every believer has been anointed with the Holy Spirit, and therefore *knows* that Jesus is the Christ." Add the negative minor premise, "The false teacher **denieth that Jesus is the Christ** (vs. 22)," for the obvious conclusion: "He is a **liar** and an **antichrist.**"

25-27. In case anyone has not been able to follow the logic of it all through the many subtle implications and plays upon words, John states plainly in verse 26, that this is a test to be used on false teachers: **These things have I written unto you concerning them that seduce** (lit. "try to deceive") **you.** It is clear from verse 27 that they do not need to listen to these false teachers; they have been taught the Word of God by the apostles, and they have the indwelling Holy Spirit who will give them assurance and teach them to live by that Word.

28. John's exhortation to them is to the effect that they should continue to live in Christ (Greek present tense), ignore the false teachers, and look forward to the second coming of Christ with joyous confidence.

IV. FELLOWSHIP AND LOVE. 2:29-4:21.

A. Identification of Believers. 2:29-3:10.

29 If ye know that he is righteous, ye know that every one that doeth righteousness is born of him.

29. Every one that doeth righteousness is born of him. This is the summary of the sixth major premise and test to be applied to the false teachers. It is important to note first that **doeth** (Gr *poieō*) is progressive present in the original; this means that John is not talking about a person who performs one or two righteous acts, but about a person whose conduct can be characterized as righteous. Of such a person it may be said that he is **born** (Gr *gennaō*), or rather "has been truly born" (perfect tense) of God.

CHAPTER 3

BEHOLD, what manner of love the Father hath bestowed upon us, that we should be called the sons of God: therefore the world knoweth us not, because it knew him not.

2 Beloved, now are we the sons of God, and it doth not yet appear what we shall be: but we know that, when he shall appear, we shall be like him; for we shall see him as he is.

3:1. That we should be called the sons of God. Note that **sons** (Gr *teknon*) is the word usually translated "children" in the New Testament, and stresses the fact that we are members of God's family by birth; this relates 3:1 to 2:29. John stresses that we are *now* the children of God.

2. It doth not yet appear what we shall be. What we shall be along with all John's stress upon true **birth** and **children** of God, gives us reason to believe that besides the emphasis on knowledge, the false teachers also believed in some kind of esoteric spiritual rebirth. The argument is that if they do not live righteous lives, they are not born of God; they are, of course, somebody's children, the devil's!

3 And every man that hath this hope in him purifieth himself, even as he is pure.
4 Whosoever committeth sin transgresseth also the law: for sin is the transgression of the law.
5 And ye know that he was manifested to take away our sins; and in him is no sin.

3-5. Every man that hath this hope. The **hope** (Gr *elpis*) is not a "hope-so" chance for the Christian, but a "know-so" expectation which is part of the "knowledge" we have because of the indwelling Holy Spirit. It is because of this "sure expectation" that we "purify" our lives. But the implications here for the false teachers are: they do not purify their lives because they do not have the hope; they do not have the hope because they do not have the Holy Spirit; they do not have the Holy Spirit because they are not children of God, which is obvious because they do not live righteous lives.

6 Whosoever abideth in him sinneth not: whosoever sinneth hath not seen him, neither known him.

6. Whosoever abideth in him sinneth not. Sinneth not (Gr *hamartanō*, progressive present) does not mean that once a person is saved he never sins again! It does mean, however, that once a person is saved he no longer lives in sin; his life is no longer characterized by sin (as the lives of the false teachers here are). This is just the other side of the coin of 2:29. To say, "No one who is alive in Christ lives in sin" is the same as saying, "Everyone who is truly born of God lives righteously."

7 Little children, let no man deceive you: he that doeth righteousness is righteous, even as he is righteous.
8 He that committeth sin is of the devil; for the devil sinneth from the beginning. For this purpose the Son of God was manifested, that he might destroy the works of the devil.

7-8. Let no man deceive you. It is obvious, again, that the false teachers fail the test; they are not **born of God** (vs. 9) at all, whatever they may have claimed. Their lives, characterized by sin, show that they have not really seen, or truly known God. Living in sin is the opposite to Christianity, for Christ came to take away sin (vs. 5). Sin is a characteristic of the devil, and Christ came to destroy (Gr *luō*) the works of the devil (vs. 8).

9 Whosoever is born of God doth not commit sin; for his seed remaineth in him: and he cannot sin, because he is born of God.
10 In this the children of God are manifest, and the children of the devil: whosoever doeth not righteousness is not of God, neither he that loveth not his brother.

9. It is clear that the false teachers are not children of God at all, like John's readers, but are in reality the children of the devil.

10. Whosoever doeth not righteousness is not of God, neither he that loveth not his brother. Being **of God** or of the devil can be determined in another way, to deal more fully with a proposition introduced earlier (2:10); a man cannot make claim to righteous living if he does not love his brother. The word **brother** cannot be restricted always to mean only a true, born-again Christian, as is obvious if the logic is pressed here. It has always been part of the Word that was preached, as well as the Old Testament Word, that love is the fulfillment of the law of God. We are to love God with all our hearts; we are to love our neighbor as ourselves.

B. Living with the Believers. 3:11-24.

11 For this is the message that ye

11-12. This is the message that ye heard from the begin-

heard from the beginning, that we should love one another.

12 Not as Cain, *who* was of that wicked one, and slew his brother. And wherefore slew he him? Because his own works were evil, and his brother's righteous.

13 Marvel not, my brethren, if the world hate you.

14 We know that we have passed from death unto life, because we love the brethren. He that loveth not *his* brother abideth in death.

15 Whosoever hateth his brother is a murderer: and ye know that no murderer hath eternal life abiding in him.

16 Hereby perceive we the love *of God*, because he laid down his life for us: and we ought to lay down *our* lives for the brethren.

17 But whoso hath this world's good, and seeth his brother have need, and shutteth up his bowels *of compassion* from him, how dwelleth the love of God in him?

18 My little children, let us not love in word, neither in tongue; but in deed and in truth.

19 And hereby we know that we are of the truth, and shall assure our hearts before him.

20 For if our heart condemn us, God is greater than our heart, and knoweth all things.

21 Beloved, if our heart condemn us not, *then* have we confidence toward God.

22 And whatsoever we ask, we receive of him, because we keep his commandments, and do those things that are pleasing in his sight.

23 And this is his commandment, That we should believe on the name of his Son Jesus Christ, and love one another, as he gave us commandment.

24 And he that keepeth his commandments dwelleth in him, and he in him. And hereby we know that he abideth in us, by the Spirit which he hath given us.

CHAPTER 4

BELOVED, believe not every spirit, but try the spirits whether they are of God: because many false prophets are gone out into the world.

ning, that we should love one another. The same expression, almost verbatim, appears in 1:5, "This then is the message which we have heard of him. . . ." It appears again at 2:7 and 2:25. The formula stresses that what is expressed was an important part of the Word of God. John had also expressed in his Gospel (13:34-35) that love for one another should be an identifying characteristic of Christians. Cain is given as a negative example, and would probably have been suggested by the ruthless attitude of the false teachers.

13-16. If every believer lives righteously and loves his brother, then it is easy to deduce that these people who persist in hatred are not believers. On the other hand, the positive minor premise applied to the principle will give assurance that **we have passed from death unto life** (Gr *metabainō*, perfect tense shows certainty of the fact). John uses the supreme example of sacrificial love here (as he did in Jn 13:34-35) to show what love is ultimately, **he laid down his life for us.** Here, the word **for** (Gr *hyper*) shows the vicarious nature of the atonement; Christ died in our place, and suffered the punishment for us. This is made the basis for the obligation of Christian love.

17-21. **Whoso hath this world's good.** This translation of the original idiom should not be taken to mean that a person must be rich before he is obligated; the text says only that he has the "sustenance" that his brother needs, understands the need, and refuses to help. Again, the conclusion is obvious: this person does not have the love of God living in him, or to put it another way, he is not a true believer. **Hereby we know that we are of the truth, and shall assure our hearts before him.** The result of the test when applied to the true believer, on the other hand, is comforting assurance, and enables us to look forward to his coming with joyous confidence.

22. Our prayers are likewise answered **because we keep his commandments, and do those things that are pleasing in his sight.** "Keeping" his commandments alludes to "doing righteousness" in 2:29 which is the major premise in this syllogism. **Pleasing** (Gr *arestos*) is also a basic part of the righteousness of believers. This was a common way of expressing this "heart attitude" of Christians; in John 8:29 these words come from the lips of Our Lord Himself. This is not at all like legalism, any more than it is like antinomianism; the believer just naturally wants to do the will of God.

23-24. **His commandment** is not any one word to which our attention is now directed, but it is simply his will or desire for us (cf. John 6:29 where instead of **commandment** we find **work**). His will for us involves trusting in Him, loving one another, and in general, living the Christian life ("abiding" means living), and enjoying the gift of the Holy Spirit (especially in our confrontation with the false prophets, to which subject he now turns).

C. Warning to the Believers. 4:1-6.

4:1. **Believe not every spirit. Spirit** does not, of course, refer to merely spiritual or supernatural beings; these could not be tested by John's readers. John has just made mention of the fact that believers are indwelled and led by the Spirit of God; the false prophets also claimed spiritual leading. John warns against believers' accepting from these teachers things that are contrary to what they have already received from the apostles. **But try the spirits. Try** (Gr *dokimazō*) means to check out by a pattern or standard that never changes; the standard intended is the Word of God. John has, in this letter, been reminding them of that Word, and the principles by which these false prophets should be checked. Here he repeats one of them.

2 Hereby know ye the Spirit of God: Every spirit that confesseth that Jesus Christ is come in the flesh is of God:

3 And every spirit that confesseth not that Jesus Christ is come in the flesh is not of God: and this is that *spirit* of antichrist, whereof ye have heard that it should come; and even now already is it in the world.

4 Ye are of God, little children, and have overcome them: because greater is he that is in you, than he that is in the world.

5 They are of the world: therefore speak they of the world, and the world heareth them.

6 We are of God: he that knoweth God heareth us; he that is not of God heareth not us. Hereby know we the spirit of truth, and the spirit of error.

7 Beloved, let us love one another: for love is of God; and every one that loveth is born of God, and knoweth God.

8 He that loveth not knoweth not God; for God is love.

9 In this was manifested the love of God toward us, because that God sent his only begotten Son into the world, that we might live through him.

10 Herein is love, not that we loved God, but that he loved us, and sent his Son *to be* the propitiation for our sins.

11 Beloved, if God so loved us, we ought also to love one another.

12 No man hath seen God at any time. If we love one another, God dwelleth in us, and his love is perfected in us.

13 Hereby know we that we dwell in him, and he in us, because he hath given us of his Spirit.

14 And we have seen and do testify that the Father sent the Son *to be* the Saviour of the world.

15 Whosoever shall confess that Jesus is the Son of God, God dwelleth in him, and he in God.

16 And we have known and believed the love that God hath to us. God is love; and he that dwelleth in love dwelleth in God, and God in him.

17 Herein is our love made perfect, that we may have boldness in the day of judgment: because as he is, so are we in this world.

18 There is no fear in love; but perfect love casteth out fear: because fear hath torment. He that feareth is not made perfect in love.

19 We love him, because he first loved us.

20 If a man say, I love God, and hateth his brother, he is a liar: for he that loveth not his brother whom he

2-5. Hereby know ye the Spirit of God, that is the truly Christian teacher who has the Word of God. **Every spirit that confesseth that Jesus Christ is come in the flesh is of God.** This test is equal to that already given in 2:22; the inference to be made here is that the gnostic or quasi-gnostic teachers denied the incarnation and refused to believe that Jesus was God in the flesh. The deduction to be made concerning the false teachers, then, is that they are not inspired by the Spirit as they claim, but are against Christ, and of the same character as the Antichrist (cf. 2:18).

6. We are of God: he that knoweth God heareth us. Here John includes himself with the other apostles as **spirits** who follow the Spirit of Truth, and thus proclaim the truth. The readers, who truly know God, will recognize and willingly accept the word of the apostles for what it really is, the Word of God (cf. I Thess 2:13).

D. Love and the Believers. 4:7-21.

7-10. Let us love one another. Again John returns to the theme of love, but this time it is as a direct exhortation to the believers in order to show that they are different from the false teachers. Once more the principle is stated that **every one that loveth is born of God, and knoweth God.** The negative minor premise is **He that loveth not knoweth not God.** The major premise is listed both here and in verse 16 (where it is followed by the positive minor premise) **God is love.** This should be compared to 1:5 where "God is light." The proof of God's love to us is clearly seen in that He sent His only Son into the world to die on the Cross as our **propitiation** (cf. 4:10 with 2:2, and see the comments there). **That we might live through him,** shows the purpose and design of the atonement, as well as the fact that life (that is the new quality of life for the Christian) does not come by knowledge, but rather through the atonement of Christ alone.

11-16. The love of God to us makes us obligated to love one another, for this is the only way we can show that we really have love. Claiming to love God is meaningless without showing love to each other. **Because he hath given us of his Spirit.** This is repeated from 3:24, except that here the word given (Gr *didōmi*) is in the perfect tense in the original, showing the certainty of the fact that the apostles rather than the false teachers are moved by the Spirit of God, and are united in their testimony about Christ. **We have seen and do testify** refers again to the testimony of the apostles; this is the same way the epistle started (see 1:1-4). The testimony of Christ is here more general, to include that God has sent the Son as the Saviour of the world.

17-19. Herein is our love made perfect, that we may have boldness in the day of judgment: because as he is, so are we in this world. This verse does not mean to say that we can become perfect in fulfilling the command of love. First, the original does not say, **our love** but "love with us." It is because God is love, and because He lives in us, that love can be truly accomplished with us. God is love, so in a sense, we are love (we are all the world will ever see of love). The whole point is that **We love . . . because he first loved us.**

20-21. The principle of love is repeated here, and once again it is demonstrated that the false teachers do not pass the test. How can they claim to love God if they do not love a brother

hath seen, how can he love God whom he hath not seen?

21 And this commandment have we from him, That he who loveth God love his brother also.

CHAPTER 5

WHOSOEVER believeth that Jesus is the Christ is born of God: and every one that loveth him that begat loveth him also that is begotten of him.

2 By this we know that we love the children of God, when we love God, and keep his commandments.

3 For this is the love of God, that we keep his commandments: and his commandments are not grievous.

4 For whatsoever is born of God overcometh the world: and this is the victory that overcometh the world, *even* our faith.

5 Who is he that overcometh the world, but he that believeth that Jesus is the Son of God?

6 This is he that came by water and blood, *even* Jesus Christ; not by water only, but by water and blood. And it is the Spirit that beareth witness, because the Spirit is truth.

7 For there are three that bear record in heaven, the Father, the Word, and the Holy Ghost: and these three are one.

8 And there are three that bear witness in earth, the spirit, and the water, and the blood: and these three agree in one.

(person) who is right there before their eyes with a real need. Love in "word" is not real; it remains to be demonstrated.

V. FELLOWSHIP AND ASSURANCE. 5:1-17.

A. Assurance of Victory. 5:1-8.

5:1-3. Whosoever believeth that Jesus is the Christ is born of God. Is born (Gr *gennaō*) should rather be translated, "has been truly born," since it is perfect tense in the original. This is another test for the believers to use on the false teachers. Every person who believes (John does not mean merely intellectual assent, for that would contradict the total message of his writings) that Jesus is the Christ is a real Christian (see again on 2:22; 4:2). He now moves on to reiterate several of the tests in their connections to each other. Since the true believer loves God (the begetter, active voice of Gr *gennaō*, meaning to give birth to), it follows that he will also love other believers (**loveth him also that is begotten of him,** is passive voice of the same verb; in this context John is not referring to Christ, though he does in 5:18). The tests are mixed: **By this we know that we love the children of God, when we love God, and keep his commandments.** Love to God is again defined, it is keeping His commandments which are not **grievous** (Gr *barys*), that is they are not difficult to fulfill because we are truly "born of God" and have therefore easy victory.

4-5. Whatsoever is born of God overcometh the world. Overcometh (Gr *nikaō*) denotes gaining victory over; it is used four times in these two verses (4-5). Its first occurrence is present tense in the original, giving the sense: "The true believer is always victorious over the world." Victory is normal and natural, and that is why His commandments are not difficult. **This is the victory that overcometh** (gnomic aorist) **the world, even our faith.** This could be put, "Our faith is the key to victory over the world." **Faith,** in verse 4, is defined as "believing" that Jesus is the Son of God; the words are cognate and reiterate the same test found in 2:22; 4:2; and 5:1. This faith, saving faith, is what makes us true children of God, which in turn assures us of victory over the world.

6-8. John now gives a description of Jesus Christ as **he that came by water and blood.** No one knows (now) exactly what John had in mind when he used these two symbols. Tertullian's guess seems to fit the facts best: the **water** is a reference to His baptism or inauguration, where the Voice from heaven declared, "This is my beloved Son," and established that Jesus was the Christ. The **blood** is a common symbol for His death, where there were also supernatural miracles to cause even the confirmed and cruel Roman centurion to realize that this man (Jesus) was more than a mere man (Mt 27:54); also, by the Resurrection, the Father confirmed Jesus as the Son of God (Rom 1:4). This interpretation also fits the facts concerning the gnostic-type beliefs of Cerinthus who taught that the Christ came upon Jesus at the baptism but left Him before the Cross; John could have been refuting some such heresy. It is interesting that John called attention to **the water, and the blood** which came from the side of Jesus on the cross (Jn 19:34-35). At any rate, these were important symbols or witnesses to the deity of Christ in John's mind. He also adds a third witness, the indwelling **Spirit.** Thus, according to John's count here, **there are three that bear record.** The rest of verse 7 and the first nine words of verse 8 are not original, and are not to be considered as a part of the Word of God (refer to the marginal notes in any reference Bible). John's three witnesses then are: **the spirit, and the water, and the blood: and the three agree in one. Agree in one** is an idiom which is properly translated simply, **agree.** Only two or three witnesses were needed to establish the truth of a fact (Deut 19:15; Jn 8:17).

9 If we receive the witness of men, the witness of God is greater: for this is the witness of God which he hath testified of his Son.

10 He that believeth on the Son of God hath the witness in himself: he that believeth not God hath made him a liar; because he believeth not the record that God gave of his Son.

11 And this is the record, that God hath given to us eternal life, and this life is in his Son.

12 He that hath the Son hath life; and he that hath not the Son of God hath not life.

13 These things have I written unto you that believe on the name of the Son of God; that ye may know that ye have eternal life, and that ye may believe on the name of the Son of God.

14 And this is the confidence that we have in him, that, if we ask any thing according to his will, he heareth us:

15 And if we know that he hear us, whatsoever we ask, we know that we have the petitions that we desired of him.

16 If any man see his brother sin a sin which is not unto death, he shall ask, and he shall give him life for them that sin not unto death. There is a sin unto death: I do not say that he shall pray for it.

17 All unrighteousness is sin: and there is a sin not unto death.

18 We know that whosoever is born

B. Assurance of Eternal Life. 5:9-13.

9. The witness of God is greater. It is greater because he is God; if numbers are important (and John did stress the numbers in Jn 8:17-18, where Christ's own testimony is counted with the Father's for the necessary two), God's testimony is three in one. The point is only that there is plenty of evidence to confirm the fact that Jesus is the Christ. **Which he hath testified** (Gr *martyreō*); the Greek perfect tense is used for this word to stress the certainty of the fact of God's witness.

10. He that believeth on the Son of God hath the witness in himself; by believing, a person mystically lives in Christ, and Christ lives in the believer. The believer also has the Spirit who is once more a third witness. **Because he believeth not the record that God gave of his Son.** There is a play upon the cognate forms **record** (Gr *martyria*), and **gave** (Gr *martyreō*), here, with the latter being in the perfect tense stressing again the absolute certainty of the truth of the witness; the allusion is to the apostolic preaching of which the content is now specified in brief.

11-12. The message of the apostles was essentially, **God hath given to us eternal life, and this life is in his Son.** The one who has the Son, that is in the sense of believing in Him (2:22; 4:2; 5:1), **hath life; and he that hath not the Son of God hath not life.** See again 1:1-4 on giving the testimony or "preaching."

13. In summary and conclusion, John wants to make his purpose clear; **These things have I written unto you that believe on the name of the Son of God.** Note the similarity to John 20:31: ". . . that ye might believe. . . ." which was the purpose there, is changed to . . . **that ye may know. . . .** The letter is written so that believers might have "knowledge" or assurance about eternal life. In these last few verses, John refers to "knowledge" nine times by means of four synonyms; it must be clear that there were false teachers who were engrossed in a quasi-Gnosticism.

C. Assurance of Answered Prayer. 5:14-17.

14-17. This is the confidence (Gr *parresia*). This word originally meant "speaking out" boldly, but later came to denote the boldness or confidence without reference to the "speaking." In this book, it means "joyous confidence" toward God; in 2:28 it can be seen as the opposite of shame. **If any man see his brother sin a sin which is not unto death.** It is important to keep the context in mind while focusing on the meaning of the **sin . . . not unto death.** It has been emphasized by John that believers have passed over from death into life (3:14). It is quite possible that John is still on the same track; his concern could be over believers who might have already been influenced by heresy, and are living in sin because they think it has nothing to do with worship of God. He would stress that God would answer prayers like this and restore such backsliders to life in Christ. It may be, too, that some who were in the church and considered to be brothers in Christ (although they were not, they **went out from us, but they were not of us** 2:19) have been so influenced by the false teachers that they have, speaking figuratively, now already passed back over from **life** into death. In this sense the **sin unto death** would be rejection of God's truth to the point that one died in unbelief. Others suggest that the sin unto death is not a particular act of sin, but any sin that occasions one's untimely death. Therefore, a living person need never fear that he has already committed the sin unto death, since he is still alive. Only total rejection and rebellion against God, and rebellion to God's laws, may cause one to sin **unto death.**

VI. CONCLUSION. 5:18-21.

18. Whatsoever is born of God sinneth not reiterates the

of God sinneth not; but he that is begotten of God keepeth himself, and that wicked one toucheth him not.

19 *And* we know that we are of God, and the whole world lieth in wickedness.

20 And we know that the Son of God is come, and hath given us an understanding, that we may know him that is true, and we are in him that is true, *even* in his Son Jesus Christ. This is the true God, and eternal life.

21 Little children, keep yourselves from idols. Amen.

principle which has been stated in many different ways throughout the book, that if a person is genuinely born of God (Gr *gennaō* is used in the perfect tense), he will not live in sin (Gr *hamartanō* is used in the present tense to imply a life characterized by sin, rather than an isolated act of sin). John again plays upon the word **born** by using it to refer to Christ; **he that is begotten of God keepeth himself** should rather be translated, "The One who was born of God keeps him." It is because Christ keeps the believer that the evil one cannot touch him.

19-21. The theme of assurance and true knowledge continues its intensity to the very end of the epistle as John repeats in the perfect tense, **we know** (for sure!) **that we are of God . . . we know** (for sure!) **that the Son of God** has come (for sure!), **and hath give us an understanding** (for sure!). The purpose for all this assurance and certainty is, "so that we might enjoy knowledge (Greek present tense denoting not just coming to know, but enjoying continually) of the True One." In place of the benediction is the closing exhortation, **keep yourselves from idols. Amen.**

(see page 780 for Bibliography to I, II, and III John)

The Second And Third Epistles Of
JOHN

INTRODUCTION

These two letters, II and III John, have the distinction of being the shortest books of the Bible. Each of these epistles contains less than three hundred Greek words and was no doubt written on a single sheet of papyrus.

These two brief letters give insight into the hospitality of Christians to fellow travelers. Since inns in the first century were notoriously flea-infested and rapacious, where would a Christian stay while traveling? The answer was in the home of another Christian. "For example, Paul was entertained by Lydia in Philippi, Jason in Thessalonica, Gaius in Corinth, Philip the evangelist in Caesarea and the Cypriot Mnason in Jerusalem (Acts 16:15; 17:7; Rom 16:23; Acts 21:8, 16)" (John R. W. Stott, *The Epistles of John*, pp. 198-199).

Authorship. Again, the author of II and III John is accepted as being the Apostle John. Such was the belief of the Church Fathers. Eusebius listed these two brief books among the *antilegomena* (*Eccl. Hist.* III. 25). Irenaeus twice quotes from II John in his *Against Heresies*. Clement of Alexandria speaks of John's "longer epistle" which would probably indicate that he was aware of some shorter epistles that John had written.

Date and place of writing. Like the First Epistle of John, these writings offer no hint as to the date of their writing. Their close affinity to I John would probably suggest that they were written shortly after the first epistle.

The common assumption is that they were written from Ephesus, as the first epistle. This is based on the history of John's life after receiving the care of our Lord's mother at the cross (Jn 19:26-27). John was called to be the pastor at the church of Ephesus and there apparently labored until he died, with the exception of the brief interlude on the island of Patmos.

Purpose. It appears that the great purpose of II John was to warn the believers not to give indiscriminate hospitality to strangers or traveling evangelist-teachers. Those who did not meet the sure test of sound doctrine were to be refused hastily.

III John seems to have been penned in order to gain the services of Gaius on behalf of the missionary representative John was sending out. Gaius is encouraged not only to continue in his good work, but to learn from the worthy example of Demetrius and the unworthy example of Diotrephes.

OUTLINE

I. Introduction. 1-3.
II. Exhortation to Love. 4-6.

III. Exhortation to Doctrine. 7-11.
IV. Conclusion. 12-13.

COMMENTARY

I. INTRODUCTION. 1-3.

THE elder unto the elect lady and her children, whom I love in the truth; and not I only, but also all they that have known the truth;

1. Only a hint of the identity of the author is given when John calls himself here **the elder** (Gr *presbyteros*). The word is synonymous to "pastor" and "bishop" in New Testament literature. Being used with the article, it implies that John has a superior position of leadership and respect in the Christian community. John the Apostle writes to **the elect lady**. **Lady** (Gr *kyria*) is the same word as "Lord" in the New Testament, except that it is feminine here (and in vs. 5), and refers not to a literal "lady" but to the "congregation" or "church" in a figurative sense. The church is a **lady** in much the same way as we refer to a ship as "she." As the bride of Christ, it is proper to refer to the church as "she." The adjective **elect** is more important; it defines the church "chosen," and implies the metaphor of the church as "bride of Christ." **And her children**, would mean, of course, the members of the church, i.e., the people who make up the church (churches are never merely buildings in the New Testament). **Whom I love in truth.** The references here to truth, love, and knowledge show the similarity to especially I John. **Also all**

they that have known the truth. Known is perfect tense in the original, stressing the certainty of the fact of the knowledge; it does not mean all who have ever known the truth in any way, but rather all who "really know the truth," that is, real believers.

2-3. The reason that real believers love each other is because of the indwelling truth (which is the Holy Spirit, the Spirit of Truth). Grace . . . mercy, and peace are part of the standard, Christian greeting formula (cf. I Tim 1:2; II Tim 1:2).

2 For the truth's sake, which dwelleth in us, and shall be with us for ever.
3 Grace be with you, mercy, *and* peace, from God the Father, and from the Lord Jesus Christ, the Son of the Father, in truth and love.

II. EXHORTATION TO LOVE. 4-6.

4 I rejoiced greatly that I found of thy children walking in truth, as we have received a commandment from the Father.

4. I rejoiced greatly that I found. I found is the same as saying "I learned," and may even mean simply "I heard." This is a way of starting the letter in a positive tone; what follows is the real conciliatory message. Evidently the same problems faced this particular congregation as those to whom I John was written. There were ruthless and immoral teachers who claimed authority and spirituality over the believers and threatened to lead some of them astray. Walking in truth is here and elsewhere in the New Testament the same as "living righteously." As we have received a commandment. This would be the preaching of the apostles which was recognized by the various churches as the Word of God, and so is here spoken of as coming from the Father.

5 And now I beseech thee, lady, not as though I wrote a new commandment unto thee, but that which we had from the beginning, that we love one another.
6 And this is love, that we walk after his commandments. This is the commandment. That, as ye have heard from the beginning, ye should walk in it.

5-6. What John is writing is not a new commandment in the sense that it is different from that apostolic message. This was an important point to make, since the message of the false teachers was new and different rather than being part of the original message. Love, and walking according to God's commandments are the same message as was given all along.

III. EXHORTATION TO DOCTRINE. 7-11.

7 For many deceivers are entered into the world, who confess not that Jesus Christ is come in the flesh. This is a deceiver and an antichrist.

7. The reason given for the exhortation to love and righteous living is that many deceivers are entered into the world, who confess not that Jesus Christ is come in the flesh. The deceivers (Gr *planos*) are the apostolic impostors who are trying to lead astray those who are true believers. They are the same false teachers in view throughout John's first letter. The deceivers have not just entered into the world, but according to the original reading of the text, have "gone out into the world," the sense of which is more fully explained in comparison to I John 2:19, where they were professing Christians as became obvious when they left the church. Another of John's descriptions for the impostors is those who confess not that Jesus Christ is come in the flesh. Another translation has, ". . . who will not acknowledge the coming of Jesus Christ in the flesh." The words is come are in the original a supplemental participle in indirect discourse; however, there may be some of the Old Testament apocalyptic flavor remaining in this word, and John may be alluding to the rejection of the Messiah as the "Coming One." At any rate, the deceivers, because they will not agree to this basic truth, are antichrists (cf. I Jn 2:18, 22; 4:2; 5:1).

8 Look to yourselves, that we lose not those things which we have wrought, but that we receive a full reward.

8. Look to yourselves simply means "Watch out!" Two alternative possibilities are laid out with the warning in regard to the false teachers. That we lose not those things which we have wrought. The text should probably read, "that you do not lose what we have accomplished." It is the apostles who have preached and thus fulfilled the Commission and made great gain (salvation) possible for the believers; the apostles will not lose anything themselves, but the believers stand to lose all the blessings of Christianity if they listen to the false teachers. It is the believers also who will receive the reward, which is not a reward for something done, but the gift of salvation by grace.

9 Whosoever transgresseth, and abideth not in the doctrine of Christ, hath

9. Whosoever transgresseth (Gr *proagō*, rather than *parabainō*) should be translated "Whoever goes too far and refuses to

not God. He that abideth in the doctrine of Christ, he hath both the Father and the Son.

live by the teaching," **hath not God.** Now the standard by which the false teachers are to be tested is called the "teaching," which is another technical term to denote the message or preaching of the apostles. The application of a positive minor premise to this syllogism would change the conclusion to the positive, "has both the Father and the Son," which means that he is a true believer rather than one of the impostors.

10 If there come any unto you, and bring not this doctrine, receive him not into *your* house, neither bid him God speed:
11 For he that biddeth him God speed is partaker of his evil deeds.

10-11. If there come any unto you, and bring not this doctrine. This reveals an interesting characteristic of the primitive church, the itinerant prophets or teachers. These circuit-riding preachers depended upon the people of God in each town along their route for food and sustenance; they could not survive without the help and support of Christians. Any of these who do not bring the distinctively Christian message of the apostles, John says, should not be "received," which means that he must not be supported; the hope is that he will be starved out of his diabolical mission. John says that even a greeting is too good for them! **Bid him God speed** (Gr *chairo*) means only to say "Hello." It was a greeting as common in that day as our "Hi!"

IV. CONCLUSION. 12-13.

12 Having many things to write unto you, I would not *write* with paper and ink: but I trust to come unto you, and speak face to face, that our joy may be full.
13 The children of thy elect sister greet thee. Amen.

12-13. Having many things to write unto you. II John is a mini-version of I John. The author is saying that although he could go on and write much more, he prefers to be with them and speak to them **face to face** (which in the first-century idiom is vividly "mouth to mouth") in order that he might, as it were, restore them to spiritual life in Christ. The greeting from the **elect sister** is, of course, another congregation, perhaps a larger one where John lived.

(see page 780 for Bibliography to I, II, and III John)

OUTLINE

COMMENTARY

I. INTRODUCTION. 1.

THE elder unto the well-beloved Gaius, whom I love in the truth.

1. The author's identity is given in the same way as it is in II John 1:1 (see comments there). The letter is addressed to **the well-beloved Gaius,** an individual rather than a church congregation as in II John. Since Gaius was a common name, it cannot be said with certainty that this Gaius identifies with Gaius of Derbe (the traditional view, cf. Acts 20:4), Gaius of Macedonia (Acts 19:29), or Gaius of Corinth (I Cor 1:14; Rom 16:23). The traditional view is quite possible; at least we know that this Gaius was a leader in the church; he was very hospitable, and that he was a dear friend, perhaps a convert of John's. The word **well-beloved** (Gr *agapetos*) is simply the adjective "loved," and would quite naturally translate into, "To my dear friend Gaius"; the same word is found referring most probably to the common bond in the one message of the apostolic preaching; the same words were used in the address to the congregation in II John 1.

2 Beloved, I wish above all things that thou mayest prosper and be in health, even as thy soul prospereth.
3 For I rejoiced greatly, when the brethren came and testified of the truth that is in thee, even as thou walkest in the truth.
4 I have no greater joy than to hear that my children walk in truth.

II. PRAYERS FOR THE BELOVED. 2-4.

2-4. Beloved, I wish above all things that thou mayest prosper and be in health, even as thy soul prospereth. This is John's wishful prayer for Gaius. The word **prosper** (Gr *euodoō*), which occurs with **soul** as well as with respect to physical well-being, means literally to "have a pleasant trip," and came to denote "getting along well." John hopes that his letter may find everything going well, and Gaius in good health physically as he is spiritually. **For I rejoiced greatly,** expresses the reason and basis of John's knowledge of Gaius' "prosperous soul." He knows that Gaius is doing well spiritually because of the situation he is about to describe. **Brethren came and testified.** The use of the progressive present tense in the original here indicates that this was not a one-time witness; from "time to time" brethren have come to John and testified of how Gaius had helped them along their way. **The truth that is in thee, even as thou walkest in the truth.** The evidence that the truth is in Gaius is that he **walks** (Gr *peripateō*) in the truth, meaning that he lives according to the message of the apostles, rather than just giving mental assent to it. John has **no greater joy** than hearing that his **children walk in truth.** The use of the word **children** with Gaius may indicate that he was a convert of John's; tradition has it that John later appointed Gaius as the first bishop of Pergamum.

III. EXAMPLES OF THE BELIEVERS. 5-8.

5 Beloved, thou doest faithfully whatsoever thou doest to the brethren, and to strangers;

5. Beloved, thou doest faithfully. This indicates the value of the service which has been performed; another translation has, "It is a loyal thing you do. . . ." **Whatsoever thou doest to the brethren, and to strangers.** But these are not to be understood as two separate groups; the brethren are the **strangers** (Gr *xenos*), or those to whom the "hospitality" (Gr *philoxenia*, a cognate) is shown. It is important that aspiring bishops show this quality among others (I Tim 3:2).

6 Which have borne witness of thy charity before the church: whom if thou bring forward on their journey after a godly sort, thou shalt do well:

6. Which have borne witness of thy charity (Gr *agapē*), which is rather "love" as a proof of Gaius' genuine Christianity. The mention of the **church** is perhaps a reference to the larger congregation from which John writes; this also gives some indication of the conduct of meetings where missionaries gave reports and testified before the group. Another indication of the life of the early church is the use of the technical term to denote missionary support, "send forward" (Gr *propempō*), which is translated here as **if thou bring forward on their journey.** The phrase **after a godly sort** is an idiom meaning that Gaius' support is deserved by the missionaries in the Christian system, since they have given themselves to serve as God's representatives.

7 Because that for his name's sake they went forth, taking nothing of the Gentiles.

7. Because for his name's sake they went forth. This "going out" is missionary service; it is the corresponding opposite to the "going out" of the false teachers (cf. I Jn 2:19; 4:1; II Jn 10). The itinerant missionaries went out in the name of the Lord (literally, "in behalf of the Name") and unlike representatives of other religious cults, they did not receive anything **of the Gentiles. Gentiles** (Gr *ethnikos*), although it usually signifies Gentiles in contradistinction to Jews, here means non-Christians; God's people have the privilege and responsibility to support God's workers.

8 We therefore ought to receive such, that we might be fellow-helpers to the truth.

8. We therefore ought to receive such. Such missionaries are to be **received** by the Christians, meaning that they are to be given food, supplies, and money to help them along their way. By doing this the Christians at the home base become **fellow helpers** (Gr *synergos*, a technical term for missionaries and workers for the Lord in distinction to laity; used exclusively by Paul except for this one use in John) **to the truth** (**truth** is personified here as God, so that Gaius is working with God).

IV. DIOTREPHES AND THE BRETHREN. 9-10.

9 I wrote unto the church: but Dī-ŏt're-phĕs, who loveth to have the preeminence among them, receiveth us not.

9. I wrote unto the church. Exactly what was written, we have no way of knowing, since the letter must have been destroyed by Diotrephes or otherwise lost. This indicates something of John's position as an elder who evidently had some kind of supervision of the churches and local bishops. Probably Gaius and Diotrephes were teachers or preachers in the same congregation, although they could have had neighboring churches in the same community. At least they were rivals and Diotrephes was far different in character from Gaius. **Diotrephes, who loveth to have the pre-eminence.** To apply some of the tests given in I and II John, Gaius measures up as a true believer: he walks in the truth (lives righteously), serves God faithfully and obeys the commands, he demonstrates that the love of God is fulfilled in him as he loves and ministers to others. Diotrephes, on the other hand, measures up as a false teacher, an impostor! He loves himself more than anyone else; the word **loveth to have the pre-eminence** (Gr *philoprōteuō*) means literally, "to love first place." He does not receive the word of the apostles as the Word of God, but instead continues to reject it personally (cf. I Thess 2:13, where a cognate word for **receiveth us not** appears). His works are evil, and he shows hate rather than love for the missionaries as well as the members who want to help them.

10 Wherefore, if I come, I will remember his deeds which he doeth, prating against us with malicious words: and not content therewith, neither doth he himself receive the brethren, and forbiddeth them that would, and casteth *them* out of the church.

10. I will remember his deeds which he doeth, prating against us with malicious words. Diotrephes not only refuses to acknowledge the authority of the Apostle John, he is in active opposition to him. **Prating** (Gr *plyareō*) means "to talk nonsense," and is used in the present tense here to denote the way Diotrephes always treats the Word of God through the apostles. He mocks it like the false teachers in II Peter 3:3 who are called "scoffers." **Not content therewith.** There is more to show that he is a false teacher: he not only refuses to receive, welcome, and care for the missionaries himself, but he further shows his malicious nature by attempting to prevent (conative present in Greek) real Christians from doing it, and excommunicating them from the church.

V. DEMETRIUS AND HIS BELIEF. 11-12.

11 Beloved, follow not that which is evil, but that which is good. He that doeth good is of God: but he that doeth evil hath not seen God.

11. Beloved is singular and vocative; it again addresses Gaius directly, probably as a younger or aspiring bishop. He must not **follow** (Gr *mimeomai*), meaning to "mimic," an evil pattern, but a good one. Again one of John's syllogisms is applied to Diotrephes in contradistinction to **Demetrius** a real believer, and probably another bishop in the congregation or community: **he that doeth evil hath not seen God. Not seen** is in the perfect tense in the original, and emphasizes the negative certainty of the action here, ". . . has never really seen God at all." Diotrephes is not even a believer! How can he be a leader of believers? He certainly should not be respected, obeyed, or allowed to influence Gaius who aspires to be a minister.

12 De-mē'trĭ-us hath good report of all *men*, and of the truth itself: yea, and we *also* bear record; and ye know that our record is true.

12. Demetrius, on the other hand, would be a good pattern; he checks out all right. **Hath good report** (Gr *martyreō*), the same word that is used for preaching, or testifying to the truth of the gospel; the perfect tense is used in the Greek to show the certainty of the testimony concerning Demetrius both by all the believers, and by the truth (which is demonstrated in his life). **And we also bear record; and ye know that our record is true. We bear record** is the same word as **report.** John means that in this letter he is now giving his word concerning the genuine Christian character of Demetrius.

VI. CONCLUSION. 13-14.

13 I had many things to write, but I

13-14. I had many things to write, but I will not with ink and pen write unto thee. The same idea is expressed here as in the

will not with ink and pen write unto thee:

14 But I trust I shall shortly see thee, and we shall speak face to face. Peace *be* to thee. *Our* friends salute thee. Greet the friends by name.

close of II John, but here the desiderative imperfect tense in Greek occurs with a different verb (had), and a slight variation in vocabulary provides a change in style. The same desire to speak face to face (or as the original idiom has it, "mouth to mouth") is present. **Our friends salute thee. Greet the friends by name.** Friends (Gr *philos*) is used here in place of "children of your elect sister" in II John 13, but this is merely another name for "brethren" or "saints." Jesus called his disciples his friends (Jn 15:13-14). It is easy to see why John would use this term if it is remembered that the literal meaning is "loved ones"; it is a synonym for the word **beloved** in verse 2. **By name** hints that the churches were quite small which must have promoted close, personal, and sincere fellowship and love. "By this shall all men know that ye are my disciples, if ye have love one to another" (Jn 13:35).

BIBLIOGRAPHY

Alexander, Neil. *The Epistles of John: Introduction and Commentary*. New York: Macmillan, 1962.

Boice, J. M. *The Epistles of John*. Grand Rapids: Zondervan, 1979.

Bruce, F. F. *The Epistles of John*. London: Pickering & Inglis, 1970.

*Candlish, Robert. *The First Epistle of John*. Grand Rapids: Zondervan, reprinted, n.d.

Conner, Walter. *The Epistles of John*. Nashville: Broadman Press, 1957.

Cotton, John. *An Exposition of First John*. London: 1657.

Dodd, C. H. *The Johannine Epistles*. New York: Harper & Brothers, 1946.

Drummond, R. and Leon Morris. Epistles of John. In *New Bible Commentary*. Grand Rapids: Eerdmans, 1954.

*Findlay, George. *Fellowship in the Life External*. Grand Rapids: Eerdmans, 1955 reprint of 1909 ed.

Ironside, H. A. *Addresses on the Epistles of John and Exposition on the Epistle of Jude*. New York: Loizeaux Brothers, 1954.

King, Guy. *The Fellowship*. London: Marshall, Morgan & Scott, 1954.

Law, Robert. *The Tests of Life: A Study of the First Epistle of St. John*. Grand Rapids: Baker, 1968.

*Lenski. *The Interpretation of the Epistles of St. Peter, St. John, and St. Jude*. Columbus: Wartburg Press, 1938.

Plummer, Alfred. The Epistles of St. John. In the *Cambridge Greek Testament*. Cambridge: University Press, 1894.

Ross, Alexander. The Epistles of James and John. In the *New International Commentary on the New Testament*. Grand Rapids: Eerdmans, 1954.

Ryrie, Charles. Epistles of John. In the *Wycliffe Bible Commentary*. Chicago: Moody Press, 1962.

*Stott, John R. W. The Epistles of John. In the *Tyndale New Testament Commentary*. Grand Rapids: Eerdmans, 1964.

Strauss, Lehman. *The Epistles of John*. New York: Loizeaux Brothers, 1962.

Vine, William. *The Epistles of John*. Grand Rapids: Zondervan, reprinted, n.d.

*Westcott, B. F. *The Epistles of St. John*. Grand Rapids: Eerdmans, 1966 revised edition of 1883 ed.

White, R. E. O. *An Open Letter to Evangelicals: A Devotional and Homiletical Commentary on the First Epistle of John*. Grand Rapids: Eerdmans, 1964.

The General Epistle Of
JUDE

INTRODUCTION

Authorship. In the normal manner, this author identifies himself in the salutation as Jude, the brother of James. This means that he was also the brother of our Lord (Mt 13:55; Mk 6:3). He preferred not to mention the family relationship to Jesus directly; perhaps the mention of James, who was a leading figure in the church in Jerusalem, was enough to give weight to his identity. His boast, like that of Peter and Paul, was that he was a "slave" of Jesus Christ.

Jude was listed as a disputed book by both Origen and Eusebius; this means only that there were some who did not accept it, but Origen himself quoted it as Scripture, and even states that it was "divine Scripture." However, external evidence for this book is strong. It was quoted by several early church Fathers (Polycarp, Clement of Rome, etc.), and is listed in the second-century Muratorian Canon.

The outstanding reason for disputing the authenticity of Jude in ancient and modern times has been the fact that Jude quotes from the apocryphal Enoch, evidently accepting that he is the seventh from Adam. Another problem is the amount of duplication from II Peter, although there could have been a common oral or written source behind both. There is no real reason for not accepting the traditional canonical status of Jude.

Occasion and purpose. Jude, like Peter, writes to encourage believers to continue to hold to the faith against the diabolical attack of false teachers. The Old Testament Scriptures and the common apostolic preaching are the authorities which predict both the presence and the doom of the scoffers. His letter has the stated purpose of encouraging his readers to contend for the faith (vs. 3). The letter assumes an existing danger of apostasy into immorality and deep sin because of the influence of shrewd and greedy teachers. Jude writes to correct this.

Date and place of writing. Whether before or after II Peter, Jude is at least in the same general period. There is the possibility that both draw heavily from a contemporary oral or written source which is no longer extant. The fact that Jude is more definite in his reference to the false teachers as a present reality to his readers (vs. 4) suggests that he wrote after Peter when the problem had more fully developed.

No hint of who the readers are is given in the book, except that they are perhaps in the Palestine area so that they will know who James (vs. 1) is; they may be Jews or Gentiles. The date must then lie somewhere between about A.D. 65 and 80, perhaps A.D. 67-68. The place of writing is not indicated but quite likely is Jerusalem.

Characteristics. The book is characterized by the strongest apocalyptic condemnation of the ungodly and immoral false teachers. Jude, like Peter, refers to the Old Testament to prove his point about the judgment of God upon sin; unlike Peter, he freely refers also to the apocryphal works that were current. Of all New Testament writers, Jude is more noted for this, but he is not alone in doing it. Matthew, Paul, and the writer of Hebrews all do things with quotations which require strained explanations if we judge their literary practices by twentieth century western standards. The book is definitely in character with the other apostolic writings and there is no reason not to accept it as authoritative today.

OUTLINE

COMMENTARY

I. INTRODUCTION. 1-2.

JUDE, the servant of Jesus Christ, and brother of James, to them that are

1-2. Jude. The salutation is normal and unpretentious. The author identifies himself as the brother of James (who was well known as the leader of the church in Jerusalem), but more

sanctified by God the Father, and preserved in Jesus Christ, *and* called.

2 Mercy unto you, and peace, and love, be multiplied.

importantly to him, as the **servant of Jesus Christ.** The word **servant** (Gr *doulos*) is literally "slave" and conveys the picture of a bondslave who belonged to another person. Even though, as the brother of James, Jude was the brother of Christ, he prefers that we know him as the "slave" or property of Christ. Peter (II Pet 1:1) and Paul (Rom 1:1) also spoke of themselves in this way; it is a metaphor of complete dedication. Of the readers, we know only that they were **sanctified . . . preserved,** and **called,** and that they must have lived somewhere in the vicinity of Palestine in order to know who James was. There is a variant in the text which should read "well-loved" rather than **sanctified,** and an acceptable translation would be, "To those who are called, beloved in God the Father and kept for Jesus Christ."

II. OCCASION OF THE EPISTLE. 3-4.

A. Change of the Purpose. 3.

3 Beloved, when I gave all diligence to write unto you of the common salvation, it was needful for me to write unto you, and exhort *you* that ye should earnestly contend for the faith which was once delivered unto the saints.

3. Beloved, when I gave all diligence to write unto you. This **diligence** (Gr *spoudē*) is really "eagerness" here and is the object of a circumstantial participle in the original, which seems to be a polite concession in order to introduce the real purpose for writing. It is like saying, "Although I've been wanting to write to you for a long time about our common salvation, I now find that there is a compelling necessity, I must write." **Common salvation** is an abstract term like Christianity. Peter begins the first General Epistle with a discussion of salvation, as he does in his second epistle; so does Paul in all his epistles, and Hebrews and James assume salvation. None of the epistles are primarily evangelistic; they are not like "gospel tracts," but are written to Christians who have some specific need for correction, reproof, encouragement, or instruction. Here Jude sees that **it was needful for me to write unto.** The word **needful** (Gr *anangkē*) implies a compelling, pressing need; a serious problem has come up among the believers, and it must be dealt with. He had to write to encourage them to **earnestly contend** (Gr *epagōnizoman*) for the faith. This word means "fight for" someone; here Jude is writing to encourage whatever "agonizing struggle" might be necessary to defend the good name of the **faith.** The **faith** (vs. 3) is synonymous with "common salvation" or Christianity; they are to "fight for" the honor of the *faith.* Note that the emphasis is not on contention, but on the faith which is now described further as **once delivered unto the saints.** The faith is shown to be synonymous with the apostolic preaching by the use of **delivered** (Gr *paradidō*) which is a technical term for the preaching or handing down of the gospel message by the apostles (the word is used twice in I Corinthians 15:3 for the message which Paul "delivered" after having "received" it himself). What is being promoted here is the apostolic preaching, that is, the Word of God, not an attitude of constant fighting with other believers. This is reinforced by the use of **once,** which is not the word for "once upon a time" assuming a considerable passage of time, but rather means "once for all," and refers to the fact that the apostles preached this Word as a final and authoritative message which cannot now be changed by the false teachers.

B. Purpose of the Change. 4.

4 For there are certain men crept in unawares, who were before of old ordained to this condemnation, ungodly men, turning the grace of our God into lasciviousness, and denying the only Lord God, and our Lord Jesus Christ.

4. For there are certain men crept in unawares. Jude here (vs. 4) explains why he had to write giving this encouragement; false teachers had sneaked in (Gr *pareisduō;* denotes a "sneak" or furtive attack) and they must continue their fight for the purity of the Word. The same idea had been used by Peter (II Peter 2:1) and by Paul (Gal 2:4) to alert believers to the presence of heresy. Jude says (and so had Peter) that such people as these stand under the condemnation of the Old Testament itself: **who were before . . . ordained to this condemnation** (here and elsewhere in this letter Jude seems to allude to Deuteronomy

13:1-11, where people who lure others away from true worship of God are condemned in the strongest possible terms). The false teachers are further identified with the enemies of God in all apocalyptic literature by the word **ungodly** (Gr *asebēs*); these are by no means Christian brothers with a different opinion. What they have done is called **turning the grace of our God into lasciviousness.** The word **turning** (Gr *metatithēmi*) means "transfer" but what these people have done is called negative transfer; they have "misapplied" the grace of God. While God accepts us and forgives our sin, we cannot and dare not misapply this grace and say that therefore we can sin all we want and still enjoy forgiveness. So that there will be no doubt, these people are further described as those who deny **the only Lord God, and our Lord Jesus Christ.** Note that the titles here both refer to the one person Jesus Christ. These false teachers denounce Him and want no part of being "Christian."

III. THE APOSTATE PAST. 5-7.

A. Israelite Apostasy. 5.

5. I will therefore put you in remembrance. Jude now gives three examples of how Deuteronomy 13:1-11 has applied in history and resulted in death and destruction for the offenders. First, those who **believed not** were destroyed (Num 14:35). That great tragedy, you will remember, was called the "day of bitterness," or "day of testing" in the wilderness before the entrance into the Promised Land. The greatest responsibility was upon those "spies" or scouts who brought the "evil report." They not only disbelieved themselves, but they caused the people of God to despair and disbelieve the Word of God. They were **destroyed.**

B. Angelic Apostasy. 6.

6. Then there were the **angels which kept not their first estate, but left their own habitation** whom he has **reserved** (perfect tense in Greek to show the certainty of the fact) to the Day of Judgment. On this compare Genesis 6:1-4, the apocryphal interpretation of which both Peter (II Peter 2:4, 9) and Jude accept, at least for the sake of the illustration.

C. Pagan Apostasy. 7.

7. The third example is taken from the fiery destruction of the cities of **Sodom and Gomorrah** and the surrounding cities which committed fornication and went **after strange flesh.** The use of **fornication** (Gr *ekporneuō*), which occurs only here in the New Testament, with "strange flesh" refers to the distinctive and terrible sin of Sodom, homosexuality, for which God destroyed the whole area. The point in this passage is that the people of God were lured away from the true worship of God by the homosexual cities (cf. Gen 18-19) and they were therefore destroyed. In the Bible, the most serious sins are those which draw others away from the true worship of God or hinder others from believing in Christ (cf. Deut 13:1-11; Mk 9:42).

IV. THE APOSTATE PRESENT. 8-16.

A. Activity of the Apostates. 8-10.

8-10. Jude now shows the complete and total corruption of these false teachers to prove their identity with the kind of people mentioned in the above three examples. **Likewise also these filthy dreamers.** The word **filthy** is not in the original text but is mistakenly supplied; **dreamers** (Gr *enypiazomai*) means that they are prophets, or actually false prophets, who claimed to get their teachings by revelation or dreams (cf. Deut 13:1-5). That they are filthy is not to be denied but is brought out by the fact that they **defile** flesh which seems to mean men as opposed

5 I will therefore put you in remembrance, though ye once knew this, how that the Lord, having saved the people out of the land of Egypt, afterward destroyed them that believed not.

6 And the angels which kept not their first estate, but left their own habitation, he hath reserved in everlasting chains under darkness unto the judgment of the great day.

7 Even as Sodom and Go-mŏr'rha, and the cities about them in like manner, giving themselves over to fornication, and going after strange flesh, are set forth for an example, suffering the vengeance of eternal fire.

8 Likewise also these *filthy* dreamers defile the flesh, despise dominion, and speak evil of dignities.
9 Yet Michael the archangel, when contending with the devil he disputed about the body of Moses, durst not bring against him a railing accusation, but said, The Lord rebuke thee.
10 But these speak evil of those things which they know not: but what

they know naturally, as brute beasts, in those things they corrupt themselves.

to angels, and also connects them with the people of Sodom who went **after strange flesh.** So bold in their false teachings are these men that they **despise** (which means "reject") **dominion** (probably God's rule) **and speak evil of dignities.** These false prophets evidently openly rejected God's Word and all spiritual powers, and were so audacious that Michael the Archangel beside them looks timid! On blaspheming **those things which they know not,** compare Paul's words in I Timothy 1:7. **But what they know naturally, as brute beasts, in those things they corrupt themselves.** Here in a very cryptic sentence would seem to be another reference to their wickedly perverted conduct (homosexuality and gluttony) in which they become completely corrupt, and for which they are to be justly destroyed (both meanings are possible for the Gr *ptheirō*).

B. Warning of the Apostates. 11-16.

11 Woe unto them! for they have gone in the way of Cain, and ran greedily after the error of Balaam for reward, and perished in the gainsaying of Cŏ're.

12 These are spots in your feasts of charity, when they feast with you, feeding themselves without fear: clouds *they are* without water, carried about of winds; trees whose fruit withereth, without fruit, twice dead, plucked up by the roots;

13 Raging waves of the sea, foaming out their own shame; wandering stars, to whom is reserved the blackness of darkness for ever.

14 And Ē'noch also, the seventh from Adam, prophesied of these, saying, Behold, the Lord cometh with ten thousands of his saints,

15 To execute judgment upon all, and to convince all that are ungodly among them of all their ungodly deeds which they have ungodly committed, and of all their hard *speeches* which ungodly sinners have spoken against him.

16 These are murmurers, complainers, walking after their own lusts; and their mouth speaketh great swelling *words,* having men's persons in admiration because of advantage.

17 But, beloved, remember ye the words which were spoken before of the apostles of our Lord Jesus Christ;

18 How that they told you there should be mockers in the last time, who should walk after their own ungodly lusts.

19 These be they who separate themselves, sensual, having not the Spirit.

11-13. Woe unto them! They are doomed as certainly as **Cain . . . Balaam . . . and Korah.** These false teachers are denounced as being as worthless as **spots** (blemishes) **in your feasts** (vs. 12), rainless **clouds** (vs. 12), fruitless **trees** that have been **plucked up by the roots** (vs. 12), **Raging waves** (vs. 13), and **wandering stars** (stars out of orbit, vs. 13).

14-16. Verses 14 and 15 are quoted from Enoch 1:9 (and 60:8) verbatim. They stress typically the ungodliness of the sinners (**ungodly** recurs four times) and the judgment they deserve and get at the Lord's coming. A clearer translation of verse 16 would be, "These grumblers and malcontents follow their own lusts; their bloated words are nothing but flattery."

V. EXHORTATIONS AGAINST APOSTATES. 17-23.

A. Exhortation by the Apostles. 17-19.

17-19. Remember ye the words which were spoken before of the apostles of our Lord Jesus Christ. Spoken before (Gr *proeipon*) has been taken to mean that Jude is a late author writing in another generation than that of the apostles; this is not a valid inference, since the word does not necessarily mean "a long time ago." Paul often used this word to refer to his own previous statements made only weeks or months before; once, in Galatians 1:9, he uses it to refer to his statement in the previous verse! The whole purpose of the letter is to remind them that the Word of God was given once and for all by the apostles. The words were not, of course, spoken **of the apostles** (objective genitive), but "by the apostles," as is obvious from the next verse as well as from the grammatical construction of the original. **There should be mockers in the last time.** There are close verbal correspondences with II Peter 3:3 and I Timothy 4:1 which seems to hint at some kind of oral formula in apostolic times (see II Pet 3:3).

B. Exhortation by Warning. 20-21.

20 But ye, beloved, building up yourselves on your most holy faith, praying in the Holy Ghost,

21 Keep yourselves in the love of God, looking for the mercy of our Lord Jesus Christ unto eternal life.

20-21. But ye, beloved, building up yourselves. This is now the positive exhortation of the letter. The main imperative verb is **Keep yourselves in the love of God. Keep** (Gr *tēreō*) means "guard" or "reserve," and its object is **yourselves.** The meaning here seems to be "keep yourselves from being dragged off into a life that is different from what God wants for you." The **love of**

God may be objective genitive, meaning the true worship of God; again compare Deuteronomy 13:3; ". . . for the Lord your God proveth you, to know whether ye love the Lord your God with all your heart and with all your soul." The main exhortation to **keep yourselves** in the love of God is supplemented with three circumstantial participles of means in the original; they answer the question, "How does one keep himself in the love of God?" By **building up yourselves** in the faith, which means learning more about the faith, or growing in the grace and knowledge of the Lord and Saviour. He adds, **by praying in the Holy** Spirit, which may be simply worshiping God as led by the Holy Spirit rather than listening to these false prophets who do not have the Spirit at all (vs. 19). And, thirdly, keep yourselves by **looking for the mercy of our Lord Jesus Christ unto eternal life. Looking for** (Gr *prosdechomai*) means to "anticipate." What is meant here is probably the same exhortation as was given by Paul when he used this very word in a similar connection in Titus 2:13, "Looking for that blessed hope, and the glorious appearing of the great God and our Savior Jesus Christ." It is interesting that Paul also used the word **mercy** in a reference to the Second Coming, "The Lord grant unto him that he may find mercy . . . in that day" (II Tim 1:18). Peter also closed his second epistle with a triple use of a synonym, asking his readers to **look for** the coming of the Day of God.

C. Exhortation by Example. 22-23.

**22 And of some have compassion, making a difference:
23 And others save with fear, pulling** *them* **out of the fire; hating even the garment spotted by the flesh.**

22-23. Jude seems to have some mercy himself for the false teachers (more likely, for some of the brethren who may have been influenced by them) and we would translate, "Have mercy on those who waver in doubt; save those you can by snatching them, as it were, from the flames. Show mercy in godly fear, although you hate the clothes they wear, stained as they are by the flesh."

VI. CONCLUSION. 24-25.

24 Now unto him that is able to keep you from falling, and to present *you* **faultless before the presence of his glory with exceeding joy,
25 To the only wise God our Saviour,** *be* **glory and majesty, dominion and power, both now and ever. Amen.**

24-25. In closing Jude gives one of the most balanced and beautiful benedictions in the New Testament. It is a prayer fitting for his readers who are threatened both with **falling** and with **fault** because of the false teachers who are trying to lure them into sin with claims of false revelation. Only by recalling the Word of God, i.e., the Old Testament, and especially the preaching of the apostles which showed it to be fulfilled in Jesus Christ, can they be "kept" **from falling,** and "presented" **faultless before the presence of his glory with exceeding joy.**

BIBLIOGRAPHY

Coder, Maxwell. *Jude: The Acts of the Apostates.* Chicago: Moody Press, 1958.

*Green, E. M. B. Second Epistle General of Peter and the General Epistle of Jude. In the *Tyndale New Testament Commentary.* Grand Rapids: Eerdmans, 1968.

Jenkyn, Williams. *An Exposition Upon the Epistle of Jude.* London: Bohn, 1653.

*Manton, Thomas. *An Exposition of the Epistle of Jude.* London: Banner of Truth, 1958 reprint of 1677 ed.

*Mayor, Joseph. *The Epistle of St. Jude and the Second Epistle of St. Peter.* Grand Rapids: Baker, 1965.

Robertson, R. Jude. In the *New Bible Commentary.* Grand Rapids: Eerdmans, 1954.

Wallace, David. Jude. In the *Wycliffe Bible Commentary.* Chicago: Moody Press, 1962.

Wolff, Richard. *A Commentary on the Epistle of Jude.* Grand Rapids: Zondervan, 1960.

The Book Of
REVELATION

INTRODUCTION

The name of the book. It is definitely not "The Revelation of St. John the Divine" (AV). Better is "The Revelation of John." Best is "The Revelation of Jesus Christ" (cf. 1:1).

Authorship. The author of the book is John, the son of Zebedee, author of the Gospel of John and I, II, and III John (cf. 1:1, 4, 9; 22:8). Donald Guthrie (*New Testament Introduction,* p. 933) has stated: ". . . There are few books in the New Testament with stronger early attestation." Apostolic authorship was questioned by Dionysius, Eusebius of Caesarea, the Council of Laodicea (ca. A.D. 360), and the Peshitta Version (early fifth century).

1. *Arguments for apostolic authorship are:*

a. *External evidence.* Those who witnessed to belief in apostolic authorship in the second and early third centuries were Justin, Irenaeus, Clement, Origen, Tertullian, and Hippolytus.

b. *Internal evidence.*

(1). He was known by the name John to the seven churches of Asia, and knew the activities of each church.

(2). He writes with authority, expecting the churches to accept what he has written as a message from God.

(3). His book, belonging to the style of apocalypse, is different from the noncanonical Jewish types. It is not attributed to an ancient worthy like Enoch or Baruch.

(4). The writer is conscious of divine inspiration (1:1, 11, 19; 10:10; 22:6-9, 18ff.).

(5). Similarities of thought indicate a close relationship between the Apocalypse, the Gospel of John, and I, II, and III John. The affinities are seen in common ideas, theology, and wording (cf. Jn 1:1 with Rev 19:13; Jn 4:10-14ff.; Jn 7:38 with Rev 7:17; 21:6; 22:17; Jn 10:1ff. with Rev 7:17; Jn 4:21 with Rev 21:22). There is a marked use of antithesis in both books, e.g., the power of God and the power of the world; light and darkness; truth and falsehood.

2. *Arguments against apostolic authorship (pro John the Elder) are:*

a. *Linguistic differences.* No one denies there are differences in language between the Revelation and the other works of John. Explanations have been given to account for these:

(1). There was an interval of a score of years between the gospel and the Revelation. However, different grammatical constructions appear by choice.

(2). Revelation differs from the gospel because as prophecy it follows Old Testament patterns.

(3). There is no proof for the use of amanuenses. Guthrie (op. cit., p. 942): "It should be noted, incidentally, that in spite of linguistic and grammatical differences the Apocalypse has a closer affinity to the Greek of the other Johannine books than to any other New Testament books."

b. *There are no apostolic claims.* Since John's apostleship was not disputed (unlike Paul), there was no need to stress his office.

c. *Non-johannine features.* The doctrines of God, Christ, the Spirit, and future things are said to be different from the gospel. Differences do not indicate incompatibility. There is progress in doctrine and necessary additions to doctrine already revealed.

d. *The conflicting traditions of the apostle's death.* One holds that death occurred in his old age at Ephesus and another earlier at the time of martyrdom of James (Acts 12). The first is the stronger and more reliable tradition.

As to authorship by a John the Elder, there is no solid evidence that such a person ever lived. The view that the author was John the prophet is no more tenable than the position just given.

Place and date of writing. Patmos, where the Apostle John was exiled for the faith (1:9). Patmos, a small rocky island in the Mediterranean Sea, is about thirty-five miles southwest of Miletus. During the time of the Roman Empire, it was used as a place of banishment. Because of John's exile here, the island was esteemed during subsequent times, although it was depopulated by pirates.

The date of the book is ca. A.D. 95/96 in the reign of the Roman emperor Domitian, which is the most generally accepted view. Most authorities feel the background of persecutions (1:9; 2:10, 13; 3:10; 6:9; 18:24) best fits the reign of Domitian (A.D. 51-96). The date in the reign of Nero (A.D. 37-68) has little to commend it.

Canonicity. A canonical book is one which carries divine authority and is normative for Christian belief and behavior. Revelation was early considered as part of the canon, but not all were persuaded. Justin, Melito of Sardis, Irenaeus, Tertullian, among others, accepted the book as the work of the Apostle John. On the other hand, the Eastern Church expressed doubts on the question and did not accord the Revelation canonicity until the fourth century. Luther, Zwingli, and Erasmus did consider it apostolic; Calvin did not address the question. But in the light of uniform ancient tradition, the book must be accorded canonical status (H. C. Thiessen, *Introduction to the New Testament,* pp. 318-319).

Destination. The indicated destination of the book, as given in chapters 1-3, was certain churches in Asia, specifically, Ephesus, Smyrna, Pergamos, Thyatira, Sardis, Philadelphia, and Laodicea. But unquestionably, it was intended for other churches of that day and the church universal of all ages. The promise of blessing (1:3) cannot be restricted.

Place in the canon. It is in every sense of the word the capstone of the Bible, and its significance cannot be overestimated. It is indeed the grand consummation of all God's earthly and heavenly plans and the supreme vindication of Christ's person and work.

Use of the Old Testament. The Apostle John,

steeped in Old Testament truth, drew his concepts and symbols from Daniel, Ezekiel, Isaiah, and Zechariah, as well as Exodus, Jeremiah, and Joel (D. Guthrie, op. cit., pp. 964-967). Although the apocalypse does not quote directly, its four hundred four verses contain about five hundred fifty references to the Old Testament (B. F. Westcott and F. J. A. Hort, *Greek New Testament*, pp. 184ff.).

Interpretation. There are four main interpretive approaches to the book:

1. The Historical Method. This view claims the book covers the entire history of the church, picturing the antagonism of the forces of evil in the world against the church.

2. The Praeterist. This approach sees the greater part of the prophecies as fulfilled in the past, especially in the confrontation of the church with the Roman Empire. The victory of the church is foretold and assured.

3. The Spiritual. This method of interpretation holds that the book manifests the ultimate and permanent triumph of truth over error.

4. The Futurist Approach. This approach maintains that from chapter 4 on all is predictive (1:3, 19).

Purpose of the book. The book exhibits a threefold purpose:

1. To encourage believers. In the times of the Roman persecutions of the early church this book aimed to assure believers of the final victory of Christ.

2. To enlarge upon and add to the Old Testament. This book explained prophetic truth, especially in the area of the consummation of human history.

3. To present Christ as He enters His purchased possession. The Revelation is a vivid unveiling of the Lord Jesus Christ throughout creation.

Style of the book. It is a message in symbolic language; e.g., "signified," i.e., conveyed the message by sins (1:1). The book can only be properly understood in light of the scores of symbols and figures from the Old Testament.

Characteristics. The book is an apocalypse, i.e., an unveiling or disclosure. This type of literature is found in Isaiah 24-27, 65, 66; Joel 2:1-11, 28-32; Zechariah 9-14; and especially in Daniel. There are certain general characteristics of apocalypse which distinguish this literature from prophecy in general. Prophecy and apocalyptic differ as to content. The predictive element in prophecy is more prominent in apocalyptic, covers longer periods of time, and is more comprehensive in its view of the world. Both prophecy and apocalypse tell of the coming of the Messiah, but in the latter it has a broader reference. In prophecy, the rule of Messiah is mainly related to Israel; in apocalypse, it is seen in relation to the dominant powers of the world (cf. Dan 7:13, 14; Rev 11:15). The prophet as a preacher of righteousness used prediction as a guarantee of his divine mission or as a display of the natural result of rebellion against God. The apocalyptist assigns great importance to prediction.

Prophecy and apocalyptic differ as to form. Prophecy uses visions; but they are implied, rather than described. In apocalyptic the vision is the vehicle whereby the prediction is presented. In prophetic visions the symbols used are natural, e.g., the bones of Ezekiel 37. The visions of apocalyptic are arbitrary, e.g., the horns of the goat of Daniel 8. They have no basis in nature. Whereas the prophets wrote in a style that bordered on poetry, the apocalyptists always used prose.

Theme. The glorious theme of the book is the Lord Jesus Christ Himself as He enters upon His purchased possession. Specifically, He is revealed in representative chapters as follows:

1. Ch. 1—The medium of God's revelation (vss. 1, 5).
2. Ch. 2—The coming Ruler of the nations (vs. 27).
3. Ch. 5—The Lion of the tribe of Judah (vs. 5)—The slain Lamb (vs. 6).
4. Ch. 7—The Lamb the Shepherd (vs. 17).
5. Ch. 14—The Lamb on Mount Zion (vs. 1).
6. Ch. 18—The Judge of Babylon (vs. 8).
7. Ch. 19—The Bridegroom (vss. 7-9)—King of Kings and Lord of Lords (vs. 16).
8. Ch. 20—The Reigning Christ (vss. 4-6).
9. Ch. 21—The Alpha and the Omega (vs. 6).
10. Ch. 22—The Root and Offspring of David, the Morning Star (vs. 16).

Critical questions. See under *Place and date of writing* and *Authorship.*

Plan of the book (1:19).

1. The things John saw (ch. 1).
2. The things which are (chs. 2-3).
3. The things which shall occur after these things (chs. 4-22; cf. Dan 9:27).
   a. Tribulation Period (chs. 4-19).
   b. Millennial reign (ch. 20).
   c. Eternal glory (chs. 21-22).

OUTLINE

I. The Vision of the Risen Christ. 1:1-20.
  A. The Introduction. 1:1-8.
    1. Title of the book. 1:1.
    2. Means of communication. 1:1-2.
    3. The promised blessing. 1:3.
    4. Messages to the seven churches. 1:4-8.
      a. Salutation from the triune God. 1:4-6.
      b. The visible return of Christ. 1:7.
      c. The Author of the messages. 1:8.

  B. The Vision on Patmos. 1:9-20.
    1. The recipient of the vision. 1:9.
    2. The place of the vision. 1:9.
    3. The Revealer of the vision. 1:10.
    4. The destination of the message. 1:11.
    5. The content of the vision. 1:12-16.
      a. The seven golden candlesticks. 1:12.
      b. The Son of Man. 1:13.
      c. His head, hair, and eyes. 1:14.
      d. His feet and voice. 1:15.

e. The seven stars, a sharp sword, and His face. 1:16.
6. John's reaction. 1:17a.
7. Assurance for John. 1:17b-18.
8. The command to write. 1:19.
9. Interpretation of the seven stars and seven candlesticks. 1:20.

II. The Letters to the Seven Churches. 2:1-3:22.
A. The Letter to the Church of Ephesus. 2:1-7.
1. The description of Christ. 2:1.
2. Commendation of the church. 2:2-3.
3. Rebuke of the church. 2:4-6.
4. The command to hear. 2:7a.
5. The promise to the overcomer. 2:7b.
B. The Letter to the Church of Smyrna. 2:8-11.
1. The description of Christ. 2:8.
2. Commendation of the church. 2:9.
3. The coming trial and call to faithfulness. 2:10.
4. The command to hear and the promise to the overcomer. 2:11.
C. The Letter to the Church of Pergamos. 2:12-17.
1. The description of Christ. 2:12.
2. Commendation of the church. 2:13.
3. Rebuke of the church. 2:14-15.
4. Call to repentance. 2:16.
5. The command to hear and the promise to the overcomer. 2:17.
D. The Letter to the Church of Thyatira. 2:18-29.
1. The description of Christ. 2:18.
2. Commendation of the church. 2:19.
3. Rebuke of the church. 2:20-21.
4. Warning to the church. 2:22-23.
5. Counsel to the godly. 2:24-25.
6. Promise to the overcomer. 2:26-28.
7. The command to hear. 2:29.
E. The Letter to the Church of Sardis. 3:1-6.
1. The description of Christ. 3:1.
2. Call to repentance. 3:2-3.
3. Reward for the worthy. 3:4.
4. Promise to the overcomer. 3:5.
5. The command to hear. 3:6.
F. The Letter to the Church of Philadelphia. 3:7-13.
1. The description of Christ. 3:7.
2. Commendation of the church. 3:8.
3. Reward for faithfulness. 3:9-10.
4. Exhortation to steadfastness. 3:11.
5. Promise to the overcomer. 3:12.
6. The command to hear. 3:13.
G. The Letter to the Church of Laodicea. 3:14-22.
1. The description of the church. 3:14.
2. Rebuke of the church. 3:15-17.
3. Counsel for the church. 3:18.
4. Call to repentance. 3:19.
5. Invitation to accept Christ. 3:20.
6. Promise to the overcomer. 3:21.
7. The command to hear. 3:22.

III. The Vision of the Throne in Heaven. 4:1-5:14.
A. The Creator on the Throne. 4:1-11.
1. The call to ascend. 4:1.
2. The throne and its Occupant. 4:2-3.
3. The twenty-four elders and thrones. 4:4.

4. Activity before the throne. 4:5.
5. Four creatures around the throne. 4:6-7.
6. Worship by the four creatures. 4:8-9.
7. Worship from the twenty-four elders. 4:10-11.
B. The Redeemer on the Throne. 5:1-14.
1. The book with seven seals. 5:1.
2. The Lion of Judah and the book. 5:2-5.
3. The Lamb and the book. 5:6-7.
4. The worship of the creatures and the elders. 5:8-10.
5. All creatures worship the Lamb. 5:11-14.

IV. The Seal Judgments. 6:1-17.
A. The First Seal: The White Horse. 6:1-2.
B. The Second Seal: The Red Horse. 6:3-4.
C. The Third Seal: The Black Horse. 6:5-6.
D. The Fourth Seal: The Ashen Horse. 6:7-8.
E. The Fifth Seal: The Martyrs. 6:9-11.
F. The Sixth Seal: Upheaval in Nature. 6:12-17.

V. A Parenthesis. 7:1-17.
A. The Sealed Remnant of Israel. 7:1-8.
B. Tribulation Saints. 7:9-17.

VI. The Seventh Seal and Four Trumpet Judgments. 8:1-13.
A. The Seventh Seal. 8:1-2.
B. The Angel with a Golden Censer. 8:3-5.
C. First Trumpet Sounded. 8:6-7.
D. Second Trumpet Sounded. 8:8-9.
E. Third Trumpet Sounded. 8:10-11.
F. Fourth Trumpet Sounded. 8:12.
G. Announcement of Woe Judgments. 8:13.

VII. The Fifth and Sixth Trumpets. 9:1-21.
A. Fifth Trumpet Sounded. 9:1-12.
B. Sixth Trumpet Sounded. 9:13-21.

VIII. A Parenthesis. 10:1-11:14.
A. The Angel with the Little Book. 10:1-11.
B. The Two Witnesses. 11:1-13.
C. Announcement of Third Woe. 11:14.

IX. The Seventh Trumpet (Third Woe). 11:15-19.

X. Chief Participants in the Tribulation. 12:1-14:20.
A. The Woman, the Red Dragon, and the Child. 12:1-6.
B. War in Heaven. 12:7-17.
C. The Beast from the Sea. 13:1-10.
D. The Beast from the Earth. 13:11-18.
E. The Lamb and a Remnant on Mount Zion. 14:1-5.
F. The Angel with the Eternal Gospel. 14:6-7.
G. Babylon's Fall Announced. 14:8.
H. Judgment on Worshipers of the Beast. 14:9-12.
I. The Blessed Dead. 14:13.
J. Reaping Earth's Sin. 14:14-20.

XI. The Seven Vial Judgments. 15:1-16:21.
A. Preparation for the Judgments. 15:1-8.
1. Seven angels with seven plagues. 15:1.
2. The godly victors. 15:2-4.
3. The temple in heaven. 15:5-8.
B. Six Vials of Judgment. 16:1-12.
1. Command to empty the vials. 16:1.
2. Plague on the earth. 16:2.
3. Plague on the sea. 16:3.
4. Plague on the rivers and waters. 16:4-7.
5. Plague on the sun. 16:8-9.
6. Plague on the beast's seat. 16:10-11.

7. Plague on the Euphrates River. 16:12.
C. Preview of Armageddon. 16:13-16.
D. The Seventh Vial. 16:17-21.
  1. Plague on the air. 16:17-18.
  2. The fall of Babylon. 16:19.
  3. Nature in upheaval. 16:20-21.
XII. Judgment on Babylon. 17:1-18:24.
  A. Doom of the Harlot. 17:1-18.
    1. Her position. 17:1.
    2. Her sin. 17:2.
    3. Her seat on the scarlet beast. 17:3.
    4. Her clothing. 17:4.
    5. Her name. 17:5.
    6. Her bloodthirstiness. 17:6.
    7. The mystery of the woman. 17:7.
    8. Identity of the beast. 17:8-13.
    9. The victory of the Lamb. 17:14-18.
  B. Fall of Babylon. 18:1-24.
    1. The glorious angel. 18:1.
    2. Babylon's fall realized. 18:2.
    3. Babylon's guilt. 18:3.
    4. Call to flee the doomed city. 18:4-8.
    5. The mourning of kings and merchants. 18:9-20.
    6. The finality of her doom. 18:21-23.
    7. The reason for her fall. 18:24.
XIII. The Supper of the Lamb and the Supper of God. 19:1-21.
  A. Alleluias in Heaven. 19:1-6.
  B. The Marriage of the Lamb. 19:7-10.
  C. The Visible Coming of Christ. 19:11-16.
  D. The Supper of God: Armageddon. 19:17-19.
  E. Judgment of the Beast and False Prophet. 19:20-21.
XIV. The Millennial Reign of Christ. 20:1-15.
  A. The Binding of Satan. 20:1-3.
  B. The Resurrection and Reign of the Saints. 20:4-6.
  C. The Final Doom of Satan, the Beast, and the False Prophet. 20:7-10.
  D. The Great White Throne Judgment. 20:11-15.
XV. The New Heaven and Earth. 21:1-27.
  A. Passing of the Old Heaven and Earth. 21:1.
  B. New Jerusalem. 21:2-7.
  C. The Portion of the Ungodly. 21:8.
  D. The Wife of the Lamb. 21:9.
  E. Description of the New Jerusalem. 21:10-27.

  1. Its origin. 21:10.
  2. Its brilliance. 21:11.
  3. Its wall. 21:12.
  4. Its gates. 21:13.
  5. Its foundation stones. 21:14.
  6. Its measurements. 21:15-17.
  7. Its materials. 21:18-21.
  8. Its temple. 21:22.
  9. Its illumination. 21:23.
  10. The presence of the nations and their kings. 21:24.
  11. Continuous access. 21:25.
  12. The glory and honor of the nations. 21:26.
  13. The absence of sin and presence of the redeemed. 21:27.
XVI. The Paradise of God. 22:1-21.
  A. The River of the Water of Life. 22:1.
  B. The Tree of Life. 22:2.
  C. The Removal of the Curse. 22:3a.
  D. The Throne of God and of the Lamb. 22:3b.
  E. The Bliss of the Godly. 22:3c-4.
  F. The Absence of Darkness. 22:5a-5b.
  G. The Saints' Reign. 22:5c.
  H. The Validity of the Message. 22:6.
  I. The Coming of Christ. 22:7a.
  J. The Blessedness of the Obedient. 22:7b.
  K. John's Reaction to the Revelation. 22:8-9.
    1. His reception of the messages. 22:8a.
    2. His worship of the interpreting angel. 22:8b.
    3. The angel's warning and advice. 22:9.
  L. The Angel's Final Words. 22:10-19.
    1. Book to remain unsealed. 22:10.
    2. The irreversible states of ungodly and godly. 22:11.
    3. Christ's coming with His rewards. 22:12.
    4. His eternal character. 22:13.
    5. The blessedness of the redeemed. 22:14.
    6. The ungodly excluded. 22:15.
    7. The Authenticator of the book. 22:16.
    8. Invitation to the unsaved. 22:17.
    9. Warnings against tampering with the prophecy. 22:18-19.
  M. The Testimony of Christ to His coming. 22:20.
  N. Benediction. 22:21.

COMMENTARY

I. THE VISION OF THE RISEN CHRIST. 1:1-20.

A. The Introduction. 1:1-8.

1. Title of the book. 1:1.

The correct title for the book indicates that it is not a revelation of John, but of Jesus Christ. The unveiling tells what He will accomplish in consummating time and ushering in eternity.

2. Means of communication. 1:1-2.

THE Revelation of Jesus Christ, which God gave unto him, to shew unto his

1:1-2. So significant is the truth embodied in the message of the book that there is a fivefold avenue of transmission of the

servants things which must shortly come to pass; and he sent and signified *it* by his angel unto his servant John:

2 Who bare record of the word of God, and of the testimony of Jesus Christ, and of all things that he saw.

3 Blessed *is* he that readeth, and they that hear the words of this prophecy, and keep those things which are written therein: for the time *is* at hand.

4 JOHN to the seven churches which are in Asia: Grace *be* unto you, and peace, from him which is, and which was, and which is to come; and from the seven Spirits which are before his throne;

5 And from Jesus Christ, *who is* the faithful witness, *and* the first begotten of the dead, and the prince of the kings of the earth. Unto him that loved us, and washed us from our sins in his own blood,

6 And hath made us kings and priests unto God and his Father; to him *be* glory and dominion for ever and ever. Amen.

7 Behold, he cometh with clouds; and every eye shall see him, and they *also* which pierced him: and all kindreds of the earth shall wail because of him. Even so, Amen.

8 I am Alpha and Omega, the beginning and the ending, saith the Lord,

word: the Father to the Son to the mediating angel to John the apostle/prophet to God's servants. Emphasis is laid on the fact that John not only heard messages, but he saw visions as well (Gr *hosa eiden*).

Things which must shortly come to pass. This statement gives no basis for the historical interpretation of the book. Events are seen here from the perspective of the Lord and not from the human viewpoint (cf. II Pet 3:8). The same Greek words appear in Luke 18:7-8 (Gr *en tachei*), where the delay is clearly a prolonged one.

He sent and signified it by his angel. He signified (Gr *esēmanen*) the message; that is, He conveyed it by signs to the angel. In both the Old and New Testament the ministry of angels is employed with regard to future events (Ezk 1:5ff.; Dan 8:16; Zech 1:9; Acts 8:26; 10:3, 7).

3. The promised blessing. 1:3.

3. Only this book in the Bible pronounces a blessing on **he that readeth** (singular because with few copies of the Scriptures in those days, one read while many could hear), and **they that hear** and **keep** (obey) **those things which are written.** Scripture can only be effective when applied in the life. It is vital to notice that the book is called the **prophecy.** Future things are at the heart of the book. **The time is at hand.** These words (Gr *ho kairos engus*) appear only twice in the Revelation. Neither reference indicates the possible length involved. Again, all is seen from the perspective of God.

4. Messages to the seven churches. 1:4-8.

a. Salutation from the triune God. 1:4-6.

4. John to the seven churches which are in Asia. The writer is the Apostle John (see Introduction), who is mentioned besides here in 1:1, 9; 22:8. Asia does not refer to the continent of Asia, but rather to the Roman province of Asia Minor. There were other churches in the province (e.g., Colossae), but these were chosen because of specific characteristics in them. The salutation combines both the Greek (**grace**) and Hebrew (**peace**) elements found in the New Testament books, and issues from all the Godhead: the sevenfold fullness of the Holy Spirit (cf. Isa 11:2), the eternal Father, and Jesus Christ the Mediator.

5. Christ is seen in His threefold office as prophet, priest, and king. The Father is on the throne; the Spirit is before the throne; and the Son is connected with the earth as supreme Ruler. The doxology is carried through from this verse to the next. It is directed to Christ in His ever-present love (**loved us**) and accomplished release of His own from sin by the work of Calvary.

6. As redeemed ones, believers constitute a kingdom and are **kings and priests unto God.** Since Christ is both king and priest, His own partake of His nature and offices. Notice the emphasis on **glory and dominion,** a dual objective of the entire book (cf. Rev 20:6; also II Tim 2:12).

b. The visible return of Christ. 1:7.

7. The second coming of Christ to earth in fulfillment of Old Testament prediction (cf. Dan 7:13) will be seen by **all kindreds of the earth** at the time, Israel and the nations. The time is that spoken of in Zechariah 12:10. But believers also now long for that coming.

c. The Author of the messages. 1:8.

8. The three persons of the Trinity put their authoritative seal to the message.

which is, and which was, and which is to come, the Almighty.

9 I John, who also am your brother, and companion in tribulation, and in the kingdom and patience of Jesus Christ, was in the isle that is called Patmos, for the word of God, and for the testimony of Jesus Christ.

10 I was in the Spirit on the Lord's day, and heard behind me a great voice, as of a trumpet,

11 Saying, I am Alpha and Omega, the first and the last: and, What thou seest, write in a book, and send it unto the seven churches which are in Asia; unto Ĕph′e-sus, and unto Smyrna, and unto Pĕr′ga-mos, and unto Thȳ-a-tī′ra, and unto Sardis, and unto Philadelphia, and unto La-od-i-ce′a.

12 And I turned to see the voice that spake with me. And being turned, I saw seven golden candlesticks;

13 And in the midst of the seven candlesticks one like unto the Son of man, clothed with a garment down to the foot, and girt about the paps with a golden girdle.

14 His head and his hairs were white

B. The Vision on Patmos. 1:9-20.

1. The recipient of the vision. 1:9.

9. John, already seen in verse 4, identifies himself with his readers as **your brother, and companion in tribulation, and in the kingdom and patience of Jesus Christ.** The tribulation referred to is not the one so fully described in the Revelation, but those trials common to all believers in this life (cf. Acts 14:22), and more particularly, endured in that day under the widespread persecutions of Domitian the Roman emperor. The kingdom mentioned may indicate that of verse 6 or more probably the kingdom on earth to be established through the coming of the Lord Jesus to earth. The perseverance spoken of is that patience and steadfastness required in the midst of persecutions.

2. The place of the vision. 1:9.

The isle that is called Patmos. Indeed, John was writing that very hour from a lonely island where he had been banished for his fidelity to the Word of God.

3. The Revealer of the vision. 1:10.

10. Just as all Scripture is given by the inspiration of the Spirit, so John was under the control of the Spirit when the vision was revealed to him. What is meant by **the Lord's day?** J. A. Seiss (*The Apocalypse,* pp. 17-19), among others, considered that the phrase could mean only the Day of the Lord, referred to so many times in the Old Testament and elaborated on in the Revelation. However, the majority of expositors are surely correct in understanding the reference to be to the first day of the week, Sunday. A. T. Robertson (*Word Pictures in the New Testament,* Vol. VI, p. 290) has written: "Deissmann has proven (*Bible Studies,* p. 217ff.; *Light,* etc., p. 357ff.) from inscriptions and papyri that the word *kuriakos* was in common use for the sense 'imperial' . . . and from papyri and ostraca that *hēmera Sebastē* (Augustus Day) was the first day of each month. . . . It was easy, therefore, for the Christians to take this term, already in use, and apply it to the first day of the week in honour of the Lord Jesus Christ's resurrection on that day. . . . In the N.T. the word occurs only here and I Cor. 11:20 (*kuriakon deipnon* the Lord's Supper). It has no reference to *hēmera kuriou* (the day of judgment, II Pet 3:10)."

A great voice is that of Christ (vs. 15) and is likened to a **trumpet** sound to indicate that the message was a matter of great public importance.

4. The destination of the message. 1:11.

11. The seven churches (vs. 4) to whom the book is sent, are named in the order messengers would carry letters, going from northwest to northeast and southeast.

5. The content of the vision. 1:12-16.

a. The seven golden candlesticks. 1:12.

12. There is an allusion to the **candlesticks** in the tabernacle and Temple, the difference being they were all united there, whereas they are separate here, with Christ in the midst in the place of preeminent authority. The churches are seen in their sphere of earthly authority.

b. The Son of Man. 1:13.

13. Christ is revealed as the High Priest coming in judgment, yet as the serving One (the **golden girdle**).

c. His head, hair, and eyes. 1:14.

14. His head . . . hairs . . . white as snow; and his eyes were as a flame of fire. This description of the Lord Jesus

like wool, as white as snow; and his eyes *were* as a flame of fire;

15 And his feet like unto fine brass, as if they burned in a furnace; and his voice as the sound of many waters.

16 And he had in his right hand seven stars: and out of his mouth went a sharp twoedged sword: and his countenance *was* as the sun shineth in his strength.

17 And when I saw him, I fell at his feet as dead. And he laid his right hand upon me, saying unto me, Fear not; I am the first and the last:

18 *I am* he that liveth, and was dead; and, behold, I am alive for evermore, Amen; and have the keys of hell and of death.

19 Write the things which thou hast seen, and the things which are, and the things which shall be hereafter;

20 The mystery of the seven stars which thou sawest in my right hand, and the seven golden candlesticks. The seven stars are the angels of the seven churches: and the seven candlesticks which thou sawest are the seven churches.

Christ is reminiscent of the judgment scene of Daniel 7:13-14. What is stated in Daniel of "the Ancient of days" (the Father) is true of the Son, because they are both truly divine.

d. His feet and voice. 1:15.

15. In judgment Christ will trample the winepress of God's wrath (Isa 63:1-5). His powerful **voice** will not be lifted to quiet the troubled sea, but to call down the judgment of God on the wicked.

e. The seven stars, a sharp sword, and His face. 1:16.

16. The **seven stars** (to be explained in vs. 20) are securely under His complete control. The **two-edged sword** is His Word (cf. Heb 4:12; Rev 19:15, 21), which will be active in the coming judgments. **His countenance.** As for His blessed face, here are brilliance, splendor, and holy **strength.**

6. John's reaction. 1:17a.

17a. Though John had fellowshiped with the Lord in His earthly ministry, the vision of the risen Christ was so glorious and overpowering that John **fell at his feet as dead.**

7. Assurance for John. 1:17b-18.

17b-18. Fear not. John is reassured by Christ's word concerning His person and nature. He is the eternal One; He dominates time: **I am he that liveth.** He lived, lives, and lives forever; He has supreme authority over death (the body) and Hades (the soul).

8. The command to write. 1:19.

19. Write the things which thou hast seen . . . which are . . . which shall be hereafter. This is the key verse of the book; it indicates the threefold plan of the prophecy (see Introduction); and it is the only safe guide to its correct interpretation.

9. Interpretation of the seven stars and seven candlesticks. 1:20.

20. The angels of the seven churches are not literal angels, nor believers in general; but, as chapters 2-3 show, they are pastors, or ministers, of the local churches in places of authority and responsibility. Local congregations are likened to **seven candlesticks** in order to convey their function of testimony and to spread the light of the gospel.

II. THE LETTERS TO THE SEVEN CHURCHES. 2:1-3:22.

A. The Letter to the Church of Ephesus. 2:1-7.

There are seven churches chosen, because in Scripture seven is the number of completion. In these seven letters the Spirit gives a complete picture of the moral and spiritual history of the church, along with other truths. The letters have seven exhortations to hear them, yet they are sadly neglected. The messages have spiritual, historical, and prophetic value. Since chapter 1 dealt with the things John saw—the risen Christ—and chapters 2-3 treat of the things that are, then they are pertinent to the church age from Pentecost to the Rapture. Each letter has four elements: (1) The manner in which Christ presents Himself; (2) the commendation (or condemnation) He gives; (3) the reward He promises; and (4) the exhortation to hear. The messages refer to distinct, historical churches in the province of Asia; hence, they are timely. They also apply to types of believers in every age; hence, they are timeless. Ephesus may be characterized as the church of departed love.

CHAPTER 2

UNTO the angel of the church of Ĕph'e-sus write; These things saith he that holdeth the seven stars in his right hand, who walketh in the midst of the seven golden candlesticks;

2 I know thy works, and thy labour, and thy patience, and how thou canst not bear them which are evil: and thou hast tried them which say they are apostles, and are not, and hast found them liars:

3 And hast borne, and hast patience, and for my name's sake hast laboured, and hast not fainted.

4 Nevertheless I have *somewhat* against thee, because thou hast left thy first love.

5 Remember therefore from whence thou art fallen, and repent, and do the first works; or else I will come unto thee quickly, and will remove thy candlestick out of his place, except thou repent.

6 But this thou hast, that thou hatest the deeds of the Nĭc-o-lā'i-taneś, which I also hate.

7 He that hath an ear, let him hear what the Spirit saith unto the churches; To him that overcometh will I give to eat of the tree of life, which is in the midst of the paradise of God.

8 And unto the angel of the church in Smyrna write; These things saith the

---

1. The description of Christ. 2:1.

2:1. In the history of the church, this congregation speaks of the apostolic period. **Ephesus** was the main center of Grecian culture and heathen idolatry. Here was located the temple of the goddess Artemis (Diana), adorned and ornamented by all of Asia, one of the seven wonders of the ancient world (cf. Acts 19). Aquila, Priscilla, and Apollos labored in this city; and Paul preached here for three years at one time. In Ephesus John, having left his home in Jerusalem, ministered for thirty years.

Christ is seen here in His proper place of guiding, controlling, and ruling over all. His servants are secure, since He holds them firmly in His right hand. Outwardly, everything is in proper order.

2. Commendation of the church. 2:2-3.

2-3. I know thy works . . . labor . . . patience. In each letter it is indicated that Christ has absolute knowledge of what transpires in each local congregation. Deeds, toil, and perseverance are all virtues. Moreover, the Ephesians put to the test those claiming apostolic authority. The apostles were dying, and perhaps John was the only one left. The Ephesians kept their doctrine pure.

Further commendation is stated in verse 6, because the Ephesians hated the deeds of the Nicolatanes (lit., conquerors of the people). It is not known who they were, although some interpreters try to connect them with some sect. Archbishop Richard C. Trench states simply, "Nicolaitanism is clerisy" (*Lectures on the Book of Revelation*, p. 52).

3. Rebuke of the church. 2:4-6.

4. In spite of all the commendable qualities of this church, there was one vital lack: they had left their **first love.** This was true of the church whose name means "desired." Their hearts were drifting away from Christ. The first love is marked by its all-engrossing quality, fervency, and constancy. It can be seen in the words of Philippians 1:21. The first danger sign for any believer is to grow cold toward Christ. A church may have great zeal and activity, soundness of doctrine and practice, yet have its first love for Christ on the decline. It is subtle. Love looks for love, and meticulous care with doctrine and discipline will not take its place. Loss of first love can be so easily followed by evils in doctrine and practice. Christ will have all the believer's love or none (cf. Lk 10:38-42).

5. The church is commanded to **repent** or suffer removal. This does not mean that individuals lose their salvation, but the church can forfeit its place of light-bearing and witness. Ephesus is a city now wrapped in the mantle of Islam. The light of the church has indeed been moved.

6. See above notes on 2:2-3.

4. The command to hear. 2:7a.

7a. He that hath an ear. It is clear that the message and warning of this church were for all in that day, but the admonition is pertinent to all believers today.

5. The promise to the overcomer. 2:7b.

7b. The paradise of God expresses the blessedness of heaven. Possibly, Ephesus had tried to make her Paradise here on earth and so allowed her love to grow cold (cf. Col 3:1-2).

B. The Letter to the Church of Smyrna. 2:8-11.

1. The description of Christ. 2:8.

8. The letter to **Smyrna** is the shortest of the letters; that to Thyatira is the longest. Smyrna was originally an Ionian settle-

first and the last, which was dead, and is alive;

ment that passed into decline in the process of time. Rebuilt by Alexander the Great and Antigonus I, it became immediately wealthy and famous. It was about forty miles north of Ephesus. In some respects, it was the rival of Ephesus. Because of its natural and commercial situation, its wealth, commerce, and splendid buildings, it was called "the beautiful." It was not far behind Ephesus in idolatry. This city is not named in the Acts or the epistles of Paul; so it is not known when the gospel was first preached there. The Roman imperial laws against Christianity were strenuously enforced in Smyrna. The persecutions of believers in Asia Minor were centered here. Polycarp, friend of John and the last disciple who knew the apostle personally, is said to have been slain here in A.D. 168. It is generally believed that Polycarp was **the angel of the church in Smyrna.**

Christ's eternal nature and deity are expressed in absolute terms. The infinite Saviour is supreme before all things and all time. He is also the last as the goal of all things (cf. Rom 11:36). His great triumph over death is next stated. He has destroyed death and its power. How important that Christ should be revealed in this light to the suffering and persecuted church. It was the period of the Roman persecutions of the church which lasted for two centuries. Smyrna means "myrrh," which must be crushed to give forth its fragrance. In the martyr age the church yielded a sweet fragrance to God (cf. II Cor 2:14-16).

2. Commendation of the church. 2:9.

9 I know thy works, and tribulation, and poverty, (but thou art rich) and *I know* the blasphemy of them which say they are Jews, and are not, but *are* the synagogue of Satan.

9. The Lord informs them that He knows their **works, and tribulation** (Gr *thlipsis*, a word that conveys the idea of pressing grapes until the juice comes forth). Christ has gone to the utmost depths of suffering and death. He sometimes permits trials in order to rekindle lost first love (Ps 119:67). Furthermore, He knows their **poverty** (cf. II Cor 8:9); they had, like Hebrew believers of a former time (Heb 10:34), suffered the loss of everything. Confiscation of goods attended and followed persecution. But they are reminded that though poor in worldly goods, they were rich in faith (cf. I Cor 3:21-23). Then Christ informs them that He knows the reviling of **the synagogue of Satan.** The reference is not to the Jewish nation in general. What is meant is the legalizing, Judaizing movement of the early Christian era. It was Galatianism which made its appearance in the apostolic and sub-apostolic age, because men tried to dilute the grace of God with legalism and ceremonialism. Satan's synagogue is in opposition here to the church of God. Satan attacked this church from without by persecution and from within by perversion of doctrine. The evil had evidently not made inroads into this church, for there is no censure or command to repent.

3. The coming trial and call to faithfulness. 2:10.

10 Fear none of those things which thou shalt suffer: behold, the devil shall cast *some* of you into prison, that ye may be tried; and ye shall have tribulation ten days: be thou faithful unto death, and I will give thee a crown of life.

10. It is interesting that there is no word that the Smyrnans would escape their suffering. But even more, they are told their trials would be increased. They were tortured, exposed to wild bulls and lions that tore them to pieces. In the Roman Empire, imprisonment was not a form of punishment as today, because the government was not willing to support a multitude of prisoners. A man in prison was either awaiting his trial or death. As for the ten days, there were ten persecutions from Nero to Diocletian (A.D. 312). They were under Nero, Domitian, Trajan, Antoninus, Severus, Maximian, Decius, Valerian, Aurelian, and Diocletian. Too, Diocletian's persecution lasted ten years.

They are encouraged to **be thou faithful unto death,** not just as long as they lived, but even if it cost them their lives. The call speaks not of extensiveness, but of intensity. In the Old Testament saints were delivered from death (cf. Job 2:6; Dan 3:19-30; 6:16-24), but in the New Testament they triumph over death. Their hope was to be dependent on the Lord. The reward was to

11 He that hath an ear, let him hear what the Spirit saith unto the churches; He that overcometh shall not be hurt of the second death.

12 And to the angel of the church in Per'ga-mos write; These things saith he which hath the sharp sword with two edges;

13 I know thy works, and where thou dwellest, *even* where Satan's seat *is:* and thou holdest fast my name, and hast not denied my faith, even in those days wherein Ān'ti-pas *was* my faithful martyr, who was slain among you, where Satan dwelleth.

be a crown of life. Christ Himself, faithful until death, was crowned with life on resurrection morning. Believers may be rewarded with one or more of five crowns (2:10; 4:4; II Tim 4:8; Jas 1:12; I Pet 5:4).

4. The command to hear and the promise to the overcomer. 2:11.

11. The second death is eternal death (cf. 20:6, 14; 21:8). It is the portion of all the unsaved. Notice how well this promise is suited to those who were threatened with the first death.

C. The Letter to the Church of Pergamos. 2:12-17.

1. The description of Christ. 2:12.

12. Pergamos lay north of Smyrna and was considered one of the finest cities of Asia. It had little or no commerce but was remarkable for its learning, refinement, and science, especially medicine. A number of kings made this their royal residence. Its famous library, second only to that of Alexandria, consisted of 200,000 books. Ephesus and Smyrna were evil cities, but Pergamos was especially so in its idolatry. Here was to be found the renowned temple of Aesculapius in which the most prominent object was the wreathed serpent. The early science of medicine was identified with the worship of Satan who usurped the place and dignity of Christ, for they called Aesculapius, the Preserver and Saviour.

As Ephesus was the church of departed love and Smyrna the church of fiery persecutions, so Pergamos (meaning marriage) was the church of worldly alliance. This was the period in the history of the church when she was elevated to a place of power and married the world. It was the era when church and state came together under the reign of Constantine (A.D. 313) and his successors. After the reign of Diocletian, there was a power struggle between Constantine and Maxentius, with victory going to the former, who claimed he had a vision of a cross with these words (in Latin): "In this sign conquer." Upon his accession to the throne of Rome, Constantine declared Christianity the official religion.

Christ is revealed as the One **which hath the sharp sword with two edges.** This is undoubtedly the Word of God (cf. Jn 5:22, 27; Heb 4:12). Since this church is tolerating error, it needs to have the measuring rule of God's Word brought into action.

2. Commendation of the church. 2:13.

13. Satan's throne speaks of his usurped world power. He is identified in Scripture as the prince of this world (cf. Mt 4:8-9; II Cor 4:4). In the Smyrna age Satan tried to destroy the church by persecution. In the next centuries he tried to ruin her testimony by patronage without and false principles within. Constantine's attitude toward the church brought into it many who were pagan at heart. Gibbon, in his famous work on the decline and fall of the Roman Empire, stated: "The salvation of the common people was purchased at an easy rate, if it be true that in one year 12,000 men were baptized at Rome, besides a proportionable number of women and children, and that a white garment with twenty pieces of gold had been promised by the emperor to every convert." In many cases, heathen were won over by adoption of pagan rites and festivals as parts of Christian worship. The union of church and state has wrought havoc wherever introduced, as attested in ancient times and to this day.

Holdest fast my name may well refer to the Arian controversy, which lasted for over a century and was finally settled in A.D. 325 by the Council of Nicaea (southeastern France on the Mediterranean Sea). They did not deny Christ's name, for the essential deity of the Lord Jesus Christ was maintained. The

14 But I have a few things against thee, because thou hast there them that hold the doctrine of Balaam, who taught Balac to cast a stumblingblock before the children of Israel, to eat things sacrificed unto idols, and to commit fornication.

15 So hast thou also them that hold the doctrine of the Nĭc-o-lā′i-tanĕs, which thing I hate.

16 Repent; or else I will come unto thee quickly, and will fight against them with the sword of my mouth.

17 He that hath an ear, let him hear what the Spirit saith unto the churches; To him that overcometh will I give to eat of the hidden manna, and will give him a white stone, and in the stone a new name written, which no man knoweth saving he that receiveth *it*.

18 And unto the angel of the church in Thȳ-a-tī′ra write; These things saith the Son of God, who hath his eyes like unto a flame of fire, and his feet *are* like fine brass;

commendation of **Antipas** (lit., against all), **my faithful martyr,** is explicit indeed. He is unknown to us, but God knows all His faithful witnesses.

3. Rebuke of the church. 2:14-15.

14. In Ephesus there was one cause of censure; here Christ says **a few things.** Pergamos was one of the fulfillments of Paul's warning in Acts 20:29-30. Notice the decline from Ephesus where the deeds of the Nicolatanes were hated, to Pergamos where their teaching was held and tolerated. It appears that the teaching of **Balaam** and that of the Nicolatanes are distinct, but they have the same disastrous results. Numbers 25:1-9 gives a clear picture of the union of church and state. Balaam taught **Balak** how to draw Israel away from their position of separation (Num 23:9).

15. The doctrine of the Nicolatanes, as already noticed in the church of Ephesus, has reference to clericalism, which developed rapidly in this era of the church. There is no basis in Scripture now for a special class of priests, such as God instituted in Israel (cf. Lev 8). The ultimate claim of Nicolatanism is infallibility.

4. Call to repentance. 2:16.

16. Repent; or else I will come unto thee quickly. The church was called upon to exercise its discipline. The coming mentioned is a judicial visitation in speedy judgment according to the Word of God.

5. The command to hear and the promise to the overcomer. 2:17.

17. Manna (lit., What is it?) in the Old Testament was not hidden. For 12,500 mornings the Lord rained this bread from heaven for His people. It was later preserved (cf. Ex 16:33; Heb 9:4). Notice the contrast between **the hidden manna** (type of Christ, Jn 6) and the public glory of union with the world. To go to the place of separation with Christ, the hidden manna, is greater gain than consorting with the world. The **white stone** speaks of the custom of casting such a stone into a voter's urn with the name of a candidate, indicating the approval of the one who cast it. Special divine approval will be the portion of the godly nucleus in Pergamos.

D. The Letter to the Church of Thyatira. 2:18-29.

1. The description of Christ. 2:18.

18. Thyatira lay southeast of Pergamos. Ephesus, Smyrna, and Pergamos were more noted than Thyatira, which, nevertheless, has an interest of its own. The city is first mentioned in connection with Paul's missionary labors in Europe. His first convert on that continent was a woman of Thyatira, Lydia, a seller of purple, a commodity for which the city was famous (cf. Acts 16:14). The city was founded by Seleucid I, the first of the Seleucid dynasty (early fourth century A.D.), although it had been inhabited before that time and, indeed, was when John wrote. It came to be a garrison city and military post because of its unfavorable natural condition—an open valley with great sloping hills of moderate elevation—which had to be strengthened in the interest of security. It is the longest of all the letters. It marks the beginning of the second group of letters in which the moral history goes on to the second coming of Christ. In this and the following letters the call to hear comes after the promise. The title **the Son of God** is used only here in the Revelation.

Thyatira, which means continual sacrifice, is the church of clerical domination. It designates the period in the history of the church from the sixth or seventh century to the Reformation in the sixteenth century. The dominant church of that period promoted continual sacrifice in its services.

When anyone is permitted to usurp the place of Christ, the emphasis must be placed on Him as **Son of God,** rather than the son of Mary. The title is meant to convey power and authority. The Saviour is revealed as searching, penetrating, and judging. **His eyes like unto a flame of fire** discern evil, for He cannot tolerate it. **His feet are like fine brass** indicates that He stamps out evil with judgment (cf. as a parallel Isa 63:1-6).

2. Commendation of the church. 2:19.

19. This church has much evil in it, but Christ looks first at what can be commended. These are the strongest words of commendation addressed to any of the churches. **Faith, and thy patience, and thy works.** Devotion and zeal did exist in the Middle Ages in spite of the apostasy and corruption of the majority. **The last to be more than the first.** The darker the night, the more ardent was the company of the godly minority.

3. Rebuke of the church. 2:20-21.

20. That woman Jezebel (cf. I Kgs 19-21) was the wife of Ahab and the source of idolatry in Israel. Balaam attacked Israel from without; she, from within. Recall that she was a stranger in Israel; she was responsible for the worst idolatry in the nation, and she persecuted the servants of God. **Which calleth herself** (never called of God) **a prophetess,** claiming infallibility in setting forth doctrine and new revelation from God. The dogmas of papal Rome are clearly discerned. This church leads people astray by her teaching; it points them away from divine authority to man's. But there is still a remnant of the faithful bond servants of Christ. As a counterpart of Jezebel of old, there is a godless consorting with the world and an intricate system of worship of idols.

21. Space to repent . . . she repented not. In His grace and forbearance God gave this church time to repent. Godly men called upon the church to repent, but she refused to do so. Therefore, there is no call to repent in this letter. Only judgment remains. This church remains apart from the truth of God until she is joined with all the systems of religious evil of the world (cf. chs. 18-19).

4. Warning to the church. 2:22-23.

22. Except they repent of their deeds. In this portion there are three groups: Jezebel, those who dabble with her system perhaps from a spirit of tolerance or unity, and her children, i.e., her adherents. Notice that her judgment is in the very place of her corruption.

23. I will give unto every one of you according to your works. The lesson given is both individual (to Thyatira) and general (to **all the churches**).

5. Counsel to the godly. 2:24-25.

24. The rest in Thyatira are evidently a godly remnant who did not follow the corruptions of the church, but rather denounced its unbiblical ways. In compassion, the Lord would lay **none other burden** on them; they were suffering much for the truth.

25. Hold fast till I come. Since there is no hope that the corrupt church will repent, the godly in her can only look for the coming of the Lord in faithful holding to the truth. The fact that the Thyatira saints are seen to go on to the time of Christ's coming reveals that the church as such goes on beyond its original period in the Middle Ages.

6. Promise to the overcomer. 2:26-28.

26. He that overcometh. Those who refuse the advantages of the world, which the ungodly prematurely enjoy, will yet enter

---

19 I know thy works, and charity, and service, and faith, and thy patience, and thy works; and the last *to be* more than the first.

20 Notwithstanding I have a few things against thee, because thou sufferest that woman Jĕz′e-bel, which calleth herself a prophetess, to teach and to seduce my servants to commit fornication, and to eat things sacrificed unto idols.

21 And I gave her space to repent of her fornication; and she repented not.

22 Behold, I will cast her into a bed, and them that commit adultery with her into great tribulation, except they repent of their deeds.

23 And I will kill her children with death; and all the churches shall know that I am he which searcheth the reins and hearts: and I will give unto every one of you according to your works.

24 But unto you I say, and unto the rest in Thȳ-a-tī′ra, as many as have not this doctrine, and which have not known the depths of Satan, as they speak; I will put upon you none other burden.
25 But that which ye have *already* hold fast till I come.

26 And he that overcometh, and

keepeth my works unto the end, to him will I give power over the nations:

27 And he shall rule them with a rod of iron; as the vessels of a potter shall they be broken to shivers: even as I received of my Father.

28 And I will give him the morning star.

29 He that hath an ear, let him hear what the Spirit saith unto the churches.

CHAPTER 3

AND unto the angel of the church in Sardis write; These things saith he that hath the seven Spirits of God, and the seven stars; I know thy works, that thou hast a name that thou livest, and art dead.

2 Be watchful, and strengthen the things which remain, that are ready to die: for I have not found thy works perfect before God.

into the ample privileges provided for them by Christ (cf. II Tim 2:12). Theirs will be a blessed portion in the coming kingdom of Christ on earth.

27. Even as I received of my Father. Since this is not usurped authority, it will be enjoyed and will endure (cf. Ps 2:7-9). Mark you, the authority granted the faithful will come from God the Father, as did Christ's.

28. The morning star (cf. II Pet 1:19; Rev 22:16) is the promise of being with Christ before the day breaks; it is the promise of the Rapture. Israel awaits the Sun of righteousness (cf. Mal 4:2); the church looks for the Morning Star (cf. Rev 22:16).

7. The command to hear. 2:29.

29. He that hath an ear. The message to this church, as all the rest, has an application to all believers at all times.

E. The Letter to the Church of Sardis. 3:1-6.

1. The description of Christ. 3:1.

Sardis is about twenty-seven miles due south of Thyatira. It was one of the oldest and greatest cities of western Asia. In ancient times it was a proud, wealthy city, the capital of the kingdom of Lydia. It had a history of many wars, and it was the city of the wealthy Croesus. The patron deity of the city was Cybele, whose form appeared on their coins. She was represented as half-human and was regularly associated with a pair of lions or single lion. The deity was supposed to have power to restore the dead. The city fell before Cyrus the Great of Persia in the sixth century B.C. In A.D. 17 the city suffered greatly from an earthquake. When John wrote this letter, the city was a city of the past. Later, it was restored and continued to flourish until A.D. 1400-1403, when the Tartar Tamerlane swept over the area and destroyed everything. The city has never recovered from this desolation.

Sardis (probably meaning remnant) was the church of empty profession. This period in the history of the church was that of the Reformation. The moral and spiritual corruption of the church of the Middle Ages, together with the evangelical preaching of certain godly leaders, brought about needed reform.

3:1. The seven Spirits of God. Paul speaks of the unity of the person of the Spirit (cf. Eph 4:3); John emphasizes the diversity of His attributes and actions as well as the fullness of His power (cf. Isa 11:2). In the different creeds of Christendom, it will be remembered, the Holy Spirit was not given His rightful place. **The seven stars** are an allusion to the way Christ was revealed to the Church of Ephesus. The Reformation itself was God's work; the resulting ecclesiastical systems were of man. Man is ever prone to error, so the results of the period reveal the presence of error and shortcoming. **I know thy works.** Sadly, the Lord commends nothing in this church. The measure of its privilege and profession was the measure of its responsibility. It was full of empty profession; hence, it was **dead.** Again, the union of church and state brought about more profession than life.

2. Call to repentance. 3:2-3.

2. The call to **be watchful** and wakeful was directed to the spiritual leaders to carry out their responsibility. They were exhorted to **strengthen the things which remain,** because they had the testimony of the Word of God more fully than those who were engulfed in the ecclesiastical formalism of the former period. It may surprise many to learn that not all truth was recovered in the Reformation, but this verse indicates that all was not **perfect before** (complete in the sight of) **God.** It was not a complete return to the apostolic church. Areas of doctrine and behavior were left incomplete, i.e., truths found in the epistles to the Ephesians and Colossians were not emphasized by the reformers. How much of the truth of the Holy Spirit was there? of life truth? of prophetic truth?

3 Remember therefore how thou hast received and heard, and hold fast, and repent. If therefore thou shalt not watch, I will come on thee as a thief, and thou shalt not know what hour I will come upon thee.

3. Remember therefore how thou hast received and heard. Sardis believers are alerted to recall how much of recovered truth they had, and to **hold fast** the good they had received. Also, they needed to **repent** of the inadequate use they were making of it. If the church did not awake, they were in danger of meeting Christ when they were not ready. Mark you, the Lord does not come to believers **as a thief,** but to professors only.

3. Reward for the worthy. 3:4.

4 Thou hast a few names even in Sardis which have not defiled their garments; and they shall walk with me in white: for they are worthy.

4. In spite of all appearances, there was a godly remnant in this church **which have not defiled their garments** (cf. Jas 1:27). **They are worthy.** The worthiness spoken of is a reckoning of grace; they had been made such by Christ.

4. Promise to the overcomer. 3:5.

5 He that overcometh, the same shall be clothed in white raiment; and I will not blot out his name out of the book of life, but I will confess his name before my Father, and before his angels.

5. There are actually three promises here. **Clothed in white raiment.** Garments are made white only in the blood of the Lamb (cf. 7:14). The promise not to **blot out his name out of the book of life** is strong assurance of the eternal security of the believer in Sardis. Moreover, Christ will delight to recognize (**confess his name**) as His own all overcomers. The method of overcoming is clear throughout the Word (cf. I Jn 5:4).

5. The command to hear. 3:6.

6 He that hath an ear, let him hear what the Spirit saith unto the churches.

6. This is a simple call to a simple act, but it is so seldom heeded.

F. The Letter to the Church of Philadelphia. 3:7-13.

1. The description of Christ. 3:7.

7 And to the angel of the church in Philadelphia write; These things saith he that is holy, he that is true, he that hath the key of David, he that openeth, and no man shutteth; and shutteth, and no man openeth;

7. The city was named after its founder, Attalus Philadelphus, king of Pergamos (159-138 B.C.), because he was loyal to his brother Eumenes. It was situated twenty-five miles south of Sardis. Its modern name is *Allah Shehr* (city of God). The remains of early Christian times are more numerous here than in any other of the cities named by John. It was a missionary city in the Greek world, promoting unity of spirit, customs, and loyalty within the kingdom (cf. W. M. Ramsay, *The Letters to the Seven Churches,* pp. 391-412). It is the only one of the seven churches whose name has been preserved to this day. The Pennsylvania city named Philadelphia was founded by William Penn. This church is the church of the faithful remnant; the reference appears to speak of no distinct church period. There are no words of censure for them. **Philadelphia** (brotherly love) may cover the times of revivals and missions that began in the eighteenth and nineteenth centuries after the deadening effect of doctrinal controversies and state-church union in the midst of professing Protestantism, but the letter is manifestly to faithful individuals in all groups of professing Christians.

He that is holy, he that is true. The One speaking is holy in life and true in doctrine, holy in character and true in action. Christ is not revealed by this characteristic in chapter 1. He is seen here not in His judicial nature, but in His personal character and attributes. **The key of David** is mentioned in connection with the treasurer of David's house in Isaiah 22:22. **He that openeth** by His Spirit the truths of the Word, **no man shutteth;** to hardened spirits He **shutteth and no man openeth.** Christ is also the key to the Word of God. His administrative authority is revealed here as well; He opens and shuts doors of ministry (cf. Acts 16:6-10). Connected with David, He is depicted in His messianic, kingly office.

8 I know thy works: behold, I have set before thee an open door, and no man can shut it: for thou hast a little strength, and hast kept my word, and hast not denied my name.

2. Commendation of the church. 3:8.

8. The **open door** is that of witness and testimony, including the worldwide mission field. To be sure, it is not a matter of human power and ingenuity; for these believers had **a little strength.** But no individual or group has power to frustrate the service of those joined to Christ. Their weakness is their defense (cf. II Cor 12:10). Smyrna and Philadelphia are the only churches without reproof; the one is a suffering church, the other, a weak one. **Hast kept my word, and hast not denied my name.** Moreover, this church kept Christ's Word, speaking of their obedience and submission (cf. Jn 14:23). Nor have they denied the name of Christ: obedience and no apostasy.

9 Behold, I will make them of the synagogue of Satan, which say they are Jews, and are not, but do lie; behold, I will make them to come and worship before thy feet, and to know that I have loved thee.

10 Because thou hast kept the word of my patience, I also will keep thee from the hour of temptation, which shall come upon all the world, to try them that dwell upon the earth.

3. Reward for faithfulness. 3:9-10.

9. Synagogue of Satan. Since there is a return to the first principles in this assembly, Satan again marshals his old attacks. He injects legalism; it is the Judaizing system in its opposition to the truth of grace. However, this Judaizing is not true Old Testament theology.

10. Because thou hast kept the word of my patience, the promise is that they will be kept **from** (not through) **the hour of temptation,** which is the Tribulation Period (chs. 6-19) that is to **come upon all the world** of those who have completely settled **upon the earth** (Gk is not merely *oikeō*, to dwell, but *katoikeō*, to settle down, which is contrary to the pilgrim nature of the church, cf. Phil 3:18-20; I Pet 2:11).

11 Behold, I come quickly: hold that fast which thou hast, that no man take thy crown.

4. Exhortation to steadfastness. 3:11.

11. Behold, I come quickly. Because Christ will come suddenly, they were not to surrender one iota of Christ's word that they then possessed. **That no man take thy crown.** If the truth is relinquished, the crown is lost. Notice the word is not that anyone would take their salvation, but their crown. A faithless servant may lose his crown, but not eternal life. Lost opportunities will result in lost crowns.

12 Him that overcometh will I make a pillar in the temple of my God, and he shall go no more out: and I will write upon him the name of my God, and the name of the city of my God, *which is* new Jerusalem, which cometh down out of heaven from my God: and *I will write upon him* my new name.

5. Promise to the overcomer. 3:12.

12. Notice the repetition of **my God.** The promises are full of identification and appropriation. The **pillar** is a reminder of the two in the temple of Solomon (cf. I Kgs 7:21) and connotes stability, strength, and permanence. Those who have been with Christ in the day of His rejection will realize the glory of the day of His enthronement.

13 He that hath an ear, let him hear what the Spirit saith unto the churches.

6. The command to hear. 3:13.

13. A command to believers to hear is never out of place, because it is a long spiritual exercise to be quick to hear.

G. The Letter to the Church of Laodicea. 3:14-22.

1. The description of the church. 3:14.

Laodicea is about forty miles southeast of Philadelphia. Built by the Seleucid monarch, Antiochus II (261-246 B.C.), it was named after his wife, Laodice. It was a city of considerable size, trade, and wealth, specializing in the manufacture of wool. It was a bone of contention in Asia Minor under the Romans and under the Turks. In later times it was a Christian city of importance and was the residence of a bishop, as well as the meeting place of church councils. Pride and self-satisfaction characterized the people and made their impression on the church as well. The city was destroyed by the Moslems in the Middle Ages, and today the site of the once wealthy city is a mass of ruins.

14 And unto the angel of the church of the Lā-ŏd-i-cē'ans write; These

14. Laodiceans. The church at Laodicea (rights of the people) is the church of insipid lukewarmness. It describes the

things saith the Amen, the faithful and true witness, the beginning of the creation of God;

moral condition of the church at the close of the church age. The people demand their rights with democracy and almost anarchy as the result (cf. II Tim 4:3). There is nothing to commend in this church, although it thinks it is perfect (cf. vs. 17). Christ refers to Himself as **the Amen,** the One who establishes all God's promises. He is the Last Word, the Ultimate Authority, the Finality of all things. When the church in her closing days will be unfaithful and untrue, He is seen as the **faithful and true witness** (cf. 1:5). All God's witnesses have failed at one time or other, but Christ never. Moreover, He is **the beginning of the creation of God.** This does not invalidate His eternality. It indicates that He is Head of the new creation (cf. II Cor 5:17).

2. Rebuke of the church. 3:15-17.

15 I know thy works, that thou art neither cold nor hot: I would thou wert cold or hot.

15. The fault with this church is that it is **neither cold nor hot;** there is neither zeal for God nor absolute repudiation of the Lord. Lukewarmness (lukewarm water is an emetic) is hot and cold together: in Laodicea there are great humanitarian and cultural projects without the saving grace of the gospel. Here is their attitude toward Christ; they are totally indifferent. It is worse to be lukewarm (evangelical but not evangelistic, as many say) than to be one who abandons all profession. An active, positive opposition (notice Paul on the Damascus road) could be faced with better results.

16 So then because thou art lukewarm, and neither cold nor hot, I will spue thee out of my mouth.

16. I will spew thee out of my mouth. Spitting the church out of Christ's mouth has no reference to loss of salvation, but removal from a place of witness. When believers are raptured, the Laodicean Church will remain on earth, spewed out by Christ to endure the Tribulation Period.

17 Because thou sayest, I am rich, and increased with goods, and have need of nothing; and knowest not that thou art wretched, and miserable, and poor, and blind, and naked:

17. This church claims it has need of nothing; it is self-satisfied and self-complacent. Boasting of wealth and methods of organization, it fails to realize the absence of spiritual life in its midst. Christ informs them that they are utterly insensitive to their condition.

3. Counsel for the church. 3:18.

18 I counsel thee to buy of me gold tried in the fire, that thou mayest be rich; and white raiment, that thou mayest be clothed, and *that* the shame of thy nakedness do not appear; and anoint thine eyes with eye-salve, that thou mayest see.

18. For their threefold need (poverty, nakedness, and blindness), they are advised to buy, without money and price to be sure (cf. Isa 55:1), gold, which speaks of divine righteousness, **white raiment,** which denote practical righteousness, and **eyesalve,** which points to spiritual discernment. Their trouble was that they had never really seen themselves as sinners.

4. Call to repentance. 3:19.

19 As many as I love, I rebuke and chasten: be zealous therefore, and repent.

19. As many as I love, I rebuke and chasten. The reason for the rebuke and counsel was His love. If not for this, He would have forsaken her. The mass will not heed these words, but individuals will (so the singular Gk verbs). Grace is still open to individuals.

5. Invitation to accept Christ. 3:20.

20 Behold, I stand at the door, and knock: if any man hear my voice, and open the door, I will come in to him, and will sup with him, and he with me.

20. Here is a tragic, but true, picture. It is a group professing the name of Christ, but keeping Him on the outside. He is knocking at the door of the church for an individual to let Him in (**sup with him**). Christ may disown the church as a whole, but He still makes His plea to the individual heart.

6. Promise to the overcomer. 3:21.

21 To him that overcometh will I grant to sit with me in my throne, even as I also overcame, and am set down with my Father in his throne.

21. To sit with me in my throne. To sit with Christ on His throne is indicative of royal authority, power, and glory. Kingdom participation is in view here. Christ will have His throne (cf. II Sam 7:13; Lk 1:31-33; Mt 25:31). He is now **set down with my Father in his throne** (cf. Ps 110:1; Heb 1:3; 8:1; 10:12-13; 12:2). The overcomer will reign with the victorious Christ on His blessed glorious throne.

22 He that hath an ear, let him hear what the Spirit saith unto the churches.

CHAPTER 4

AFTER this I looked, and, behold, a door *was* opened in heaven: and the first voice which I heard *was* as it were of a trumpet talking with me; which said, Come up hither, and I will shew thee things which must be hereafter.

2 And immediately I was in the spirit: and, behold, a throne was set in heaven, and *one* sat on the throne.

3 And he that sat was to look upon like a jasper and a sardine stone: and *there was* a rainbow round about the throne, in sight like unto an emerald.

4 And round about the throne *were* four and twenty seats: and upon the seats I saw four and twenty elders sitting, clothed in white raiment; and they had on their heads crowns of gold.

---

7. The command to hear. 3:22.

22. The tireless Spirit of God still pleads with the individual heart.

III. THE VISION OF THE THRONE IN HEAVEN. 4:1—5:14.

A. The Creator on the Throne. 4:1-11.

1. The call to ascend. 4:1.

Thus far, the first two divisions of the prophecy have been covered (cf. 1:19): the things John saw (ch. 1) and the things which are during the church age (chs. 2-3). The largest section of the book (chs. 4-22) is divisible into three parts: (1) chapters 4-19; (2) chapter 20; and (3) chapters 21-22, all relating to the things that are to be **hereafter,** subsequent to the church period. The same words (Gr *meta tauta*) appear once in 1:19 and twice in 4:1. Chapters 4-19 cover the Seventieth Week of Daniel (cf. Dan 9:27), known as the Tribulation Period. Recall that if the consistent chronology of the Revelation is to be followed, all this is to be fulfilled in the future after the church is taken home to heaven. It is clear how many times the word **church** has appeared in the first three chapters; it does not occur again until 22:16. The **bride** of chapter 19 is the **church,** but no other references occur with that word during the time of trial on earth.

4:1. Come up hither. John is commanded to come up to heaven, so that he may see and understand the things that are to transpire on earth from that vantage point. Christ Himself has changed His position: in chapters 1-3 He was seen among the **candlesticks** on earth. Now He is in heaven. A number of expositors see the call to John as that of I Thessalonians 4:16-17 namely, the Rapture of the church. H. A. Ironside has put it concisely: "Of this the rapture of the apostle is the symbol" (*Lectures on the Revelation*, p. 80), a view held by many others. It is the position of this commentary that the Rapture does occur after chapter 3, but there are more compelling reasons than the one just stated, as will be shown below.

2. The throne and its Occupant. 4:2-3.

2. The **throne . . . set in heaven** occupies the attention of John first, as it will the adoration of the redeemed. The throne is occupied by the Son (cf. Jn 5:22), though neither the Father nor the Spirit is excluded.

3. When heavenly things are spoken of, the description beggars earthly speech, so beautiful and durable are the precious stones introduced (cf. ch. 21). **Jasper** is of various brilliant colors, and **sardine** is a red color. These stones were the first and last precious stones in the breastplate of the high priest (cf. Ex 28:17-20). **Emerald** is green. The **rainbow** reveals God in covenant relation with nature (cf. Gen 9:16); He does not forget His promises. Many judgments in this book will be poured out on the earth, but it is not God's purpose to bring about earth's utter destruction.

3. The twenty-four elders and thrones. 4:4.

4. As important as 3:10 is for the pretribulation Rapture, so is this crucial verse. In fact, it is decisive in the matter. How so when it only speaks of **four and twenty elders** and **four and twenty seats?** The reasons are these: (a) The elders are enthroned (cf. 3:21). (b) Their number is important. The Levitical priesthood had twenty-four courses (shifts) in Israel (cf. I Chr 24:7-19). The church is a priesthood (cf. I Pet 2:5-9; Rev 1:6). (c) Their office is indicative; it is an eldership, a representative office, showing they are not to be understood in an individual capacity (cf. Acts 15:2; 20:17). (d) Their testimony is distinctive (cf. 5:9-10). This is true only of the church. (e) They display spiritual insight and are acquainted with the counsels of God (5:5; 7:13; Jn 15:15). (f) Their garments indicate they have been redeemed (cf. 3:18). (g) Perhaps as determinative of all these reasons is the fact that they are crowned. Only saints of the church age are promised **crowns of gold** as rewards. They have already received them, and that means the judgment seat of Christ has taken place (II Cor 5:10). The Rapture, let it be remembered, is not a reward; it is of grace, just as salvation is.

4. Activity before the throne. 4:5.

5. It is significant that from and before the throne there are **lightnings and thunderings and voices: and . . . seven lamps of fire.** Here the throne is one of judgment, not of grace. Judgment is pending and ready to break.

5. Four creatures around the throne. 4:6-7.

6. The **sea of glass** is reminiscent of the laver in the Mosaic tabernacle and the bronze sea of the Solomonic temple (cf. II Chr 4:2-6). Holiness is now a fixed state, as in 15:2. Much discussion has centered about the four living creatures (not **beasts** as in AV). Some connect them with the four Gospels, as did some of the early church fathers; others see in them the cherubim. Still others consider them as representative of the basic forms of the divine government. They are God's instruments for the carrying out of His judgments. They indicate the attributes of God and the principles of His actions represented by angelic beings. The fullness of eyes denotes the omniscient perception of God in His judgments. All is under His infinite wisdom. Four is the number of universality (cf. Walter Scott, *Exposition of the Revelation of Jesus Christ*, pp. 125-126).

7. The **lion** represents power and majesty; the **calf**, endurance; **man**, intelligence; the **eagle**, speed in execution of judgment. The parallel with Ezekiel 1 is inescapable.

6. Worship by the four creatures. 4:8-9.

8. They rest not day and night. Untiringly and without interruption, they worship, ascribing holiness to the triune God in the Trisagion of Isaiah 6:3. The eternality of the Godhead is emphasized again.

9. They so enter into the purposes of God that they can **give glory and honor and thanks to** Him for all that will proceed from His throne.

7. Worship from the twenty-four elders. 4:10-11.

10. Worship him. The church in heaven will occupy herself with worship, the highest function of any creature of God. In this exercise the rewards (**crowns**) will find their greatest use.

11. Thou hast created all things . . . for thy pleasure. The focus and worship here center on the fact of God's claims as Creator. There is another basis upon which God can rest His judgments of man and creation; it is His right as Redeemer, a truth enunciated in chapter 5.

B. The Redeemer on the Throne. 5:1-14.

Chapters 4-5 are introductory to, and explanatory of, the remainder of the Apocalypse. This chapter carries on the scene from the previous chapter.

1. The book with seven seals. 5:1.

5:1. One must first disabuse his mind concerning the meaning of the **book,** because it has no relation to modern bookbinding. **A book written within and on the backside.** It was in fact a

---

5 And out of the throne proceeded lightnings and thunderings and voices: and *there were* seven lamps of fire burning before the throne, which are the seven Spirits of God.

6 And before the throne *there was a* sea of glass like unto crystal: and in the midst of the throne, and round about the throne, *were* four beasts full of eyes before and behind.

7 And the first beast *was* like a lion, and the second beast like a calf, and the third beast had a face as a man, and the fourth beast *was* like a flying eagle.

8 And the four beasts had each of them six wings about *him;* and *they were* full of eyes within: and they rest not day and night, saying, Holy, holy, holy, Lord God Almighty, which was, and is, and is to come.

9 And when those beasts give glory and honour and thanks to him that sat on the throne, who liveth for ever and ever,

10 The four and twenty elders fall down before him that sat on the throne, and worship him that liveth for ever and ever, and cast their crowns before the throne, saying,

11 Thou art worthy, O Lord, to receive glory and honour and power: for thou hast created all things, and for thy pleasure they are and were created.

CHAPTER 5

AND I saw in the right hand of him that sat on the throne a book written within and on the backside, sealed with seven seals.

2 And I saw a strong angel proclaiming with a loud voice, Who is worthy to open the book, and to loose the seals thereof?

3 And no man in heaven, nor in earth, neither under the earth, was able to open the book, neither to look thereon.

4 And I wept much, because no man was found worthy to open and to read the book, neither to look thereon.

5 And one of the elders saith unto me, Weep not: behold, the Lion of the tribe of Juda, the Root of David, hath prevailed to open the book, and to loose the seven seals thereof.

6 And I beheld, and, lo, in the midst of the throne and of the four beasts, and in the midst of the elders, stood a Lamb as it had been slain, having seven horns and seven eyes, which are the seven Spirits of God sent forth into all the earth.

7 And he came and took the book out of the right hand of him that sat upon the throne.

8 And when he had taken the book, the four beasts and four and twenty elders fell down before the Lamb, having every one of them harps, and golden vials full of odours, which are the prayers of saints.

9 And they sung a new song, saying, Thou art worthy to take the book, and to open the seals thereof: for thou wast slain, and hast redeemed us to God by thy blood out of every kindred, and tongue, and people, and nation;

10 And hast made us unto our God kings and priests: and we shall reign on the earth.

scroll which was so full of information that it took both sides, front and back. Moreover, it was firmly **sealed with seven seals,** so that the contents could not be known until God's appointed time. R. H. Charles (*The Revelation of St. John,* I, pp. 137-138) states: "A will . . . in Roman law bore the seven seals of the seven witnesses on the threads that secured the tablets or parchment. . . . Such a Testament could not be carried into execution till all the seven seals were loosed." The scroll was not a book of prophecy, or even the Book of Revelation, because they would not require worthiness to open it. It is the title deed to the earth, to which Christ has the right of ownership, both by way of creation and, even more, by way of redemption at Calvary. The book was **in the right hand of him that sat on the throne** (the Father) and is the same as that in 10:2.

2. The Lion of Judah and the book. 5:2-5.

2-3. The **strong angel** is not further identified, but his question points up the dilemma connected with the book. No one of the angelic host or the human race or the demonic host could open the seals or look into the book.

4. No man was found worthy. The failure was not merely lack of power, but of worthiness. The book must involve a matter of importance for the apostle to have **wept much.**

5. Weep not. Weeping is turned to joy when one of the elders points out the One able to open the book and the seals. The designation of **Lion of the tribe of Judah** and the **Root of David** directly relate Him to Israel (cf. 22:16; Mt 22:42-46).

3. The Lamb and the book. 5:6-7.

6. Notice that the Lion is the Lamb (cf. Jn 1:29, 36). He will always bear the marks of His suffering and death in His glorified, resurrected body. He overcame as a Lamb (cf. Isa 53:7), and all can overcome through His blood (cf. Rev 12:11). He now sits at the right hand of the Father (cf. Heb 1:3), but in that day He will stand (cf. Isa 3:13). **A Lamb as it had been slain.** He was slain but is alive now forever. The **seven horns** point to His fullness of power (cf. Ps 89:17, 24); the **seven eyes** speak of complete wisdom (cf. Zech 4:10), a characteristic of the fullness of the Spirit, which was uniquely His. Thus, the Lamb's three qualifications are: (1) He was sacrificed for man's sins; (2) He has all power to overcome every foe; and (3) He enjoys all wisdom and intelligence to foresee and oversee.

7. He came and took the book. The act described here represents and includes all that the Revelation will yet unfold. It is that for which creation (that is, the world of humanity) and the church especially have been waiting through all the centuries.

4. The worship of the creatures and the elders. 5:8-10.

8. Now will be answered the **prayers of saints** of all ages, symbolized by the **golden vials full of odors** (incense). It is the saints holding up their own prayers to Christ, those for one another and those for all the redeemed.

9. They sung a new song, but it is the old, old story. The worthiness of the Lamb is clearly stated as a result of His work on Calvary (**thou wast slain**), which **redeemed** to God every trusting heart. Notice the three circles of praise (vss. 9-13). The redeemed in heaven are the closest to the throne, and from them praise goes out in ever-widening circles.

10. Many claim that the **reign** of the saints **on the earth** is a fancy. It is claimed that it is carnal and Jewish. The saints in heaven, who are made **kings and priests** (1:6), do not so regard

11 And I beheld, and I heard the voice of many angels round about the throne and the beasts and the elders: and the number of them was ten thousand times ten thousand, and thousands of thousands;
12 Saying with a loud voice, Worthy is the Lamb that was slain to receive power, and riches, and wisdom, and strength, and honour, and glory, and blessing.
13 And every creature which is in heaven, and on the earth, and under the earth, and such as are in the sea, and all that are in them, heard I saying, Blessing, and honour, and glory, and power, *be* unto him that sitteth upon the throne, and unto the Lamb for ever and ever.
14 And the four beasts said, Amen. And the four *and* twenty elders fell down and worshipped him that liveth for ever and ever.

CHAPTER 6
AND I saw when the Lamb opened one of the seals, and I heard, as it were the noise of thunder, one of the four beasts saying, Come and see.

2 And I saw, and behold a white horse: and he that sat on him had a bow; and a crown was given unto him: and he went forth conquering, and to conquer.

3 And when he had opened the sec-

it. That reign is not first spoken of in 20:4, because it has been stated in 3:21 in a promise and here in praise (cf. Mt 25:31).

5. All creatures worship the Lamb. 5:11-14.

11. Many angels. Both in verse 9 and here, a vast multitude of redeemed are seen in heaven. It must be noticed that the angels do not indicate they have been redeemed. They have been preserved, not saved.

12. Power, and riches, and wisdom, and strength, and honor, and glory, and blessing. Sevenfold accrual is the Lamb's because of Calvary and the unfathomable agony endured there.

13. Every area of creation—heaven, earth, subterranean, and sea—is included (cf. Phil 2:10-11). Both the Father and the Son are recipients of the acclaim.

14. Every creature. Now the four living creatures and the elders respond, **Amen**, in unanimity. The psalmist was right: "Praise is becoming to the upright" (Ps 33:1).

IV. THE SEAL JUDGMENTS. 6:1-17.

Chapters 4-5 were occupied with heaven; in chapter 6 events of the earth, with which most of the Apocalypse deals, come before the reader. The method by which the truth of chapter 5 is carried out is presented here: Christ's entering in upon the purchased possession. The Day of the Lord, the time of God's judgments on earth before the visible reappearing of the Lord Jesus, is the subject in this and the following chapters.

A. The First Seal: The White Horse. 6:1-2.

6:1. The Lamb opened one of the seals. At this point it is well to make an important distinction. When the Tribulation Period is spoken of, reference is to all the Seven Years of Daniel 9:27. The Great Tribulation covers only the last three and a half years of the period. Expositors are far from agreement on when the latter part of the trials on earth will begin. The present writer holds that the final part of the Tribulation Period coincides with the events of Matthew 24:15ff. Thus, the first six seals occur during the first half of Daniel's Seventieth Week. They are the beginning of sorrows (cf. Mt 24:8). The first four seals are broken in connection with the four living creatures, but it is the Lamb who has the power and authority to break the seals. As He does so, more of the contents of the scroll are brought into view.

2. The rider on the **white horse** has been identified with Christ (cf. ch. 19), or even a false Christ. To identify the rider as any specific person is not in keeping with the interpretation of the other horses, which symbolize conditions and not individuals. This rider and horse refer to the attempts of many to bring in permanent peace (cf. I Thess 5:3). It is verifiable from many times in the past, and especially in this century, that before some of the greatest conflicts between nations, there have been powerful attempts at man-made peace. The text indicates the desire to conquer in this area, but does not state that the objective was achieved. In this passage horses speak of the powerful providential actions connected with the government of the earth. Speed is also a factor (cf. Zech 1, 6). **White** speaks of victory and triumph, a bloodless victory for the moment.

B. The Second Seal: The Red Horse. 6:3-4.

3-4. The **second beast** or living creature is connected with the breaking of the **second seal.** Unquestionably, this seal

ond seal, I heard the second beast say,
Come and see.

4 And there went out another horse
that was red: and *power* was given to
him that sat thereon to take peace from
the earth, and that they should kill one
another: and there was given unto him
a great sword.

5 And when he had opened the third
seal, I heard the third beast say, Come
and see. And I beheld, and lo a black
horse; and he that sat on him had a pair
of balances in his hand.

6 And I heard a voice in the midst of
the four beasts say, A measure of
wheat for a penny, and three measures
of barley for a penny; and *see* thou hurt
not the oil and the wine.

7 And when he had opened the fourth
seal, I heard the voice of the fourth
beast say, Come and see.

8 And I looked, and behold a pale
horse: and his name that sat on him
was Death, and Hell followed with him.
And Power was given unto them over
the fourth part of the earth, to kill with
sword, and with hunger, and with
death, and with the beasts of the earth.

9 And when he had opened the fifth
seal, I saw under the altar the souls of
them that were slain for the word of
God, and for the testimony which they
held:

10 And they cried with a loud voice,
saying, How long, O Lord, holy and
true, dost thou not judge and avenge
our blood on them that dwell on the
earth?

11 And white robes were given unto
every one of them; and it was said unto
them, that they should rest yet for a
little season, until their fellowservants
also and their brethren, that should be
killed as they *were*, should be fulfilled.

speaks of war, bloodshed. **There went out another horse that
was red.** Man's attempts at world **peace** have failed miserably
and carnage is the result (cf. Mt 24:6-7). The **great sword**
indicates war's ravages will be let loose on a universal scale
throughout the earth.

C. The Third Seal: The Black Horse. 6:5-6.

5. A pair of balances in his hand. The rider of the **black
horse** is holding a symbol of commerce. Too, when there is
abundance, there is no minute weighing of common articles of
food (cf. Ezk 4:10, 16). Worldwide war is followed by worldwide famine (cf. Mt 24:7b), because the soil is abused and men
are not free to work it as necessary.

6. The scarcity of the time is underscored by the inflated
price of necessities. One man's **measure of wheat** will take a
day's wage; **three measures of barley** (the food for cattle and
horses) can be bought for a day's wage. These are starvation
conditions. Wheat and barley are necessities of life, but why the
mention of **oil and the wine?** They are luxuries (cf. Ps 104:15;
Prov 21:17) for the rich. The wealthy will apparently not be
touched at the first, but ultimately they will undergo suffering as
well (cf. W. Scott, *op. cit.*, p. 150).

D. The Fourth Seal: The Ashen Horse. 6:7-8.

7-8. The livid or **pale horse** clearly speaks of death, probably
by pestilence and plague. **Death** is the place of the body of the
departed and is synonymous with the grave; **Hell** is the abode of
the departed spirit (cf. Ezk 14:21; see Mt 24 for the same order
as in the horses). Notice that one-fourth of the earth is involved.
When in human history has such a pestilence overtaken man?

E. The Fifth Seal: The Martyrs. 6:9-11.

In verses 2-8 of this chapter the first four seals are grouped,
and the remaining seals are conceived of as united. The provi-
dences of verses 2-8 have occurred in other ages also, but not
with such severity as in the age of judgment under consideration.

9. The scene is now of the Temple, incidentally another
indication that Israel is in the fore in these dealings with earth.
The **altar** was the appointed place of sacrifice, because these
martyrs had been slain as burnt offerings for the Word of God
and their **testimony.** John on Patmos could understand something of their experience. The **souls** are the Jewish martyrs of
that period.

10. Their cry for vengeance is in keeping with an age of
judgment. **How long** is the well-known prayer of Jewish saints,
so often found in the imprecatory and other psalms. These
departed saints must not be confused with the saints of this age,
who have already been seen as seated and crowned in heaven.

11. These souls are not unredeemed, crying out for revenge
on their persecutors. **White robes were given** to each. This
indicates they are justified and accepted by God. Then they are
told something of God's counsels. They are to rest a short while
longer **until their fellow servants also and their brethren** of the
last part of the Tribulation Period will have been slain. In grace
God desires the witnesses of other martyrs to be added to theirs
already given.

F. The Sixth Seal: Upheaval in Nature. 6:12-17.

Interpreters are divided as to whether all this judgment is to
be taken literally or symbolically. The best hermeneutical principle is to take all elements of a passage literally, unless such a
procedure issues in conflict with other literal passages of Scripture and the demands of reason. Too, it must always be remembered that in the Apocalypse, symbols and signs are normative
and not an intrusion (cf. 1:1). The features under the sixth seal

could well speak of literal occurrences, which in their universal effects must have social, emotional, and spiritual implications for all men involved. In these instances parallel passages are very helpful. Earthquakes, changes in the heavenly bodies, falling stars, and the movement of mountains and islands from their places are striking and terrifying phenomena of nature.

12. Earthquake . . . the sun became black . . . the moon became as blood. Our Lord had predicted earthquakes (cf. Mt 24:7); Isaiah had foretold the darkening of the sun (cf. 50:3); and Joel had prophesied the change in the moon (cf. 2:30, 31).

13. Stars of heaven fell unto the earth. The Olivet Discourse mentions the falling of the stars (cf. Mt 24:29 with Isa 34:4).

14. Every mountain and island were moved out of their places. With such comprehensive upheavals in nature, no part of the physical universe could remain untouched. Earthquakes alone could be responsible for violent changes in mountains and islands, but in that day the phenomena will be greatly heightened in their effects.

15-16. Hide us . . . from the wrath of the Lamb. How could society go on in an orderly manner? There will be unsettling religious and social forces. Human life will be in chaos and turmoil. But in that day there will be no escape. None will be exempt. The terror will be universal. Notice that the cause of the miseries is not lost on those undergoing them. All understand that the trials of the Tribulation Period are traceable to the Father and the Lamb. The reference here is not to the judgment of chapter 20, nor is it a judgment of saved and unsaved alike. These individuals are beyond the day of grace.

17. Who shall be able to stand? They cry out, not for salvation or the intervention of God on their behalf, but for an end to their miseries.

V. A PARENTHESIS. 7:1-17.

That there is a parenthesis, or hiatus, in this chapter is clear from a comparison of 6:12 and 8:1. This chapter does not carry on the episodes of Daniel's Seventieth Week in a chronological way, for there is a break between the sixth and seventh seals. In the midst of wrath God remembers mercy for His own (cf. Charles, op. cit., p. 203).

A. The Sealed Remnant of Israel. 7:1-8.

All interpreters have seen two groups in this chapter, one mentioned in verses 1-8 and another in verses 9-17. In fact, they are so distinct that some have even considered that they do not belong in the same chapter. But to believe that would be to disregard the unity of the passage.

7:1. The four angels are not prominent creatures, or they would have been specified with more detail. They are God's providential restraining forces against judgment until the sealing is completed. **Winds** are known to be God's agencies to carry out His purposes (cf. Ps 148:8).

2. The **angel** in this verse is quite different by description and performance. Just as today the seal is the Holy Spirit (cf. Eph 1:13; 4:30), so it will be in the Tribulation Period. Only Christ can perform this sealing by the Spirit. He is the Angel of the Lord and the Angel of the Covenant of the Old Testament, another incidental proof that these events are related to Israel's age. **The seal of the living God** probably includes a special impartation of the Holy Spirit for their specific service for God.

3. Have sealed the servants of our God in their foreheads. In a period when ownership and security are vital factors (cf. 9:4; 14:1; 13:16), the seal of God on the **foreheads** of His **servants** is essential to their ministry.

4-8. I heard the number of them which were sealed.

---

12 And I beheld when he had opened the sixth seal, and, lo, there was a great earthquake; and the sun became black as sackcloth of hair, and the moon became as blood;

13 And the stars of heaven fell unto the earth, even as a fig tree casteth her untimely figs, when she is shaken of a mighty wind.

14 And the heaven departed as a scroll when it is rolled together; and every mountain and island were moved out of their places.

15 And the kings of the earth, and the great men, and the rich men, and the chief captains, and the mighty men, and every bondman, and every free man, hid themselves in the dens and in the rocks of the mountains;

16 And said to the mountains and rocks, Fall on us, and hide us from the face of him that sitteth on the throne, and from the wrath of the Lamb:

17 For the great day of his wrath is come; and who shall be able to stand?

CHAPTER 7

AND after these things I saw four angels standing on the four corners of the earth, holding the four winds of the earth, that the wind should not blow on the earth, nor on the sea, nor on any tree.

2 And I saw another angel ascending from the east, having the seal of the living God: and he cried with a loud voice to the four angels, to whom it was given to hurt the earth and the sea,

3 Saying, Hurt not the earth, neither the sea, nor the trees, till we have sealed the servants of our God in their foreheads.

4 And I heard the number of them

which were sealed: *and there were* sealed an hundred *and* forty *and* four thousand of all the tribes of the children of Israel.

5 Of the tribe of Juda *were* sealed twelve thousand. Of the tribe of Reuben *were* sealed twelve thousand. Of the tribe of Gad *were* sealed twelve thousand.

6 Of the tribe of Ā'ser *were* sealed twelve thousand. Of the tribe of Nĕph'tha-līm *were* sealed twelve thousand. Of the tribe of Ma-năs'sĕs *were* sealed twelve thousand.

7 Of the tribe of Simeon *were* sealed twelve thousand. Of the tribe of Levi *were* sealed twelve thousand. Of the tribe of Ĭs'sa-char *were* sealed twelve thousand.

8 Of the tribe of Zăb'u-lon *were* sealed twelve thousand. Of the tribe of Joseph *were* sealed twelve thousand. Of the tribe of Benjamin *were* sealed twelve thousand.

Strangely, at this point there is much divergence of views as to the identity of the company in verses 4-8. Some take an allegorical interpretation, but this allows for great latitude for the imagination and provides nothing firm upon which to rest one's interpretation. Some indicate the group must be the first fruits of the church ("the Israel of God," cf. H. Alford, *The Greek Testament*, Vol. IV, Part II, pp. 623-625). Still others hold they are the Jewish nation in general. First, that they are of Israel is manifest from their identity (vs. 4); they are from **all the tribes of the children of Israel.** Second, they cannot be reckoned as the church; for that body is never called Israel (even in 6:16, where the issue is legalizers over against genuine believers in Israel, who are the elect remnant in the church, Rom 11:5). Third, they cannot be Israel in general; for God would not place His seal upon unbelievers for service to Him. Finally, these servants are from the tribes of Israel, literally so, redeemed by God and sealed for service when the church has been raptured to heaven (cf. 14:4).

As to the number **a hundred and forty and four thousand,** some take it literally and others symbolically. If it is understood symbolically, it appears strange that there is such a detailed enumeration of the tribes. If the number appears too small for the magnitude of the task, one needs only to remember that twelve apostles and their converts in the early church turned the world upside down in the first century (cf. Acts 17:6). The fact that Levi is included in the enumeration has intrigued readers of the Apocalypse (he was never given a portion in the land under Joshua, only forty-eight cities in the territories of the other tribes). Also, the list substitutes Joseph for Ephraim; and, most puzzling, it omits Dan. There is no ground for dogmatic assertion here, although many opinions have been offered to explain the omission. One position is that Dan is omitted because the Antichrist will come from that tribe, judging from Genesis 49:17. Built on so many imponderables, such a view can scarcely be called valid. Notice also, 49:16 is a strong promise. Another explanation is that Dan does not appear in the list because it was the first tribe to embrace idolatry (cf. Jud 18). But nowhere is this serious departure from the Lord evaluated as worse than the idolatries of the other tribes. Moreover, in the distribution of the land in the reign of Christ in Jerusalem, Dan is in fact given his inheritance (Ezk 48:1-2).

The time of the sealing is important, even if it can be determined only approximately. Judging from the fact that the sealing is accomplished before the breaking of the seventh seal (8:1), it probably will take place before the last seal, thus before the second half of the Tribulation Period when Satan's forces will be arrayed against the godly and the witnesses will indeed need the added protection of God for their work. They are a special group commissioned for a specific mission.

B. Tribulation Saints. 7:9-17.

Again, various opinions have been advanced for the identity of this group. First, it can be stated with confidence that they are not the same group that is mentioned in the first part of the chapter. It is clearly set forth that this second company is from all the nations of the earth, whereas it was clearly presented that the 144,000 were from one nation alone, Israel. To mingle the groups would confuse identities that the Scriptures are careful to distinguish. Second, they are not the church; they are separate from the elders (vss. 11, 13). Third, nothing is intimated concerning death or resurrection; thus, they are probably (to be seen later) on earth. Fourth, they are redeemed, as indicated in verses 13-14. Fifth, the time of their salvation is after the Rapture (vs. 14). How they came to saving faith is not expressly stated, but the highest probability is that they were redeemed through the preaching of the 144,000 witnesses. It is difficult to

9 After this I beheld, and, lo, a great multitude, which no man could number, of all nations, and kindreds, and people, and tongues, stood before the throne, and before the Lamb, clothed with white robes, and palms in their hands;

10 And cried with a loud voice, saying, Salvation to our God which sitteth upon the throne, and unto the Lamb.

11 And all the angels stood round about the throne, and about the elders and the four beasts, and fell before the throne on their faces, and worshipped God,

12 Saying, Amen: Blessing, and glory, and wisdom, and thanksgiving, and honour, and power, and might, be unto our God for ever and ever. Amen.

13 And one of the elders answered, saying unto me, What are these which are arrayed in white robes? and whence came they?

14 And I said unto him, Sir, thou knowest. And he said to me, These are they which came out of great tribulation, and have washed their robes, and made them white in the blood of the Lamb.

15 Therefore are they before the throne of God, and serve him day and night in his temple: and he that sitteth on the throne shall dwell among them.

16 They shall hunger no more, neither thirst any more; neither shall the sun light on them, nor any heat.

17 For the Lamb which is in the midst of the throne shall feed them, and shall lead them unto living fountains of waters: and God shall wipe away all tears from their eyes.

discern why the two groups are placed in juxtaposition in this chapter if this is not the case.

9. The **great multitude** is innumerable, whereas the witnesses from Israel were exactly numbered, even with subdivisions in each case. They have access to **the throne,** the presence of God, and **the Lamb, clothed with white robes,** the garments of righteousness. Moreover, the **palms in their hands** speak of victories over the enemy.

10. Their praise accords with the similar exercise of the redeemed ones in this book.

11-12. Angels . . . elders and the four beasts join in the symphony of praise to God.

13. One of the elders (since he is part of the church in heaven, he knows the answer, cf. I Cor 13:12) asked John the identity of the great company, evidently to focus attention on their essential nature.

14. If they are the church, it would be amazing that John could not recognize them as such. The elder identifies them as redeemed ones, **they which came out of great tribulation** (Gr *ek tēs thlipeōs tēs megalēs,* out of the Tribulation, the great one).

15. Where are these redeemed standing? Some declare they are in heaven; others, on earth. It seeems that the second is the true view, because this verse mentions that they are **before the throne of God** and speaks of serving **day and night.** According to 21:25 and 21:22 of this book, there is no night or temple in heaven (cf. F. W. Grant, *The Revelation of Christ,* Part II, pp. 80-81 et al.). Isaiah 66:19-21 teaches that there will be a temple in the Millennium, and Isaiah 4:5-6 predicts a tabernacle as well (for the details of the temple cf. Ezk 40-48).

16. They shall hunger no more, neither thirst. (see Isa 49:10). The reason many cannot conceive of these things happening in the Millennium is their lack of understanding of the glories of that wonderful age and reign, when the Lord Jesus Christ visibly rules the earth from His headquarters and capital in Jerusalem.

17. For the Lamb shall feed them . . . lead them . . . and God shall wipe away all tears from their eyes. In view of the unprecedented agonies these redeemed have endured through the Great Tribulation, the words of promise in verses 15-17 are all the more welcome. The truth of Romans 8:18 will be found as true for them as it is for the church today.

VI. THE SEVENTH SEAL AND FOUR TRUMPET JUDGMENTS. 8:1-13.

When the seventh seal is opened, the entire scroll is open to view. The seventh seal includes the seven trumpets, a fact which would preclude the seal and trumpet judgments being simultaneous or concurrent. Apart from two parentheses (chs. 7 and 10:1-11:14), the events of chapters 4-11 are in sequence. With the beginning of chapter 12, events are again viewed with reference to Israel especially and the chief participants of the last days of Israel's age. As for the vial judgments of chapters 15-16, they appear to be the scroll reversed (cf. 5:1). It must be emphasized that the seal, trumpet, and vial judgments are not contemporaneous, but successive. As events move on to a consummation, there is no marking time or retrogression.

With the seal judgments, the mass of humanity on earth view them as providential acts only, like those that have occurred in history previously, although not with such severity. With the blasts of the trumpets, the judgments take on a severer and more judicial aspect. In the vial judgments the concentrated and unmixed wrath of God is poured out; and the trumpet judgments are treated from 8:2-11:18.

The Scriptures reveal that trumpets accompany significant events. There was a trumpet at the giving of the Law at Sinai (Ex 19:19). There were trumpets appointed in Israel for both worship and warning (Num 10:1-10); at Jericho the walls fell flat at the blasts of the trumpets (Josh 6:13-20); the Midianites were routed under Gideon when the trumpets were blown (Jud 7:16-22); and the Rapture of the church will occur at the blowing of the trumpet of God (I Thess 4:16; I Cor 15:52). It is the very nature of the case that a trumpet is blown when something of great significance transpires, which must have widespread attention; and Messiah's reign will be prepared for by trumpet judgments on the ungodly.

A. The Seventh Seal. 8:1-2.

8:1-2. No events are recorded with the breaking of **the seventh seal**. But an ominous **silence** pervades all nature, which is indicative of the solemnity of the things that are about to take place. It is the calm before the storm. **The space of half an hour** is not a reckoning according to a heavenly chronometer, but it does indicate a very brief period.

There are **seven angels** entrusted with the service of blowing the **seven trumpets** of judgment. Since they are not further described, there is no warrant to identify them with extrabiblical angels found in apocryphal books of Tobit or Enoch, where Uriel, Raphael, Raguel, Michael, Sariel, Gabriel, and Remeiel are named. Speculation in such matters is futile.

B. The Angel with a Golden Censer. 8:3-5.

3-5. This **angel** is entirely separate from the seven angels mentioned in verse 2, not so much because of added description, but by the very nature of the work involved. It is undoubtedly the Lord Jesus Christ. The Bible knows of no other than Him who does the work of mediating **the prayers of all saints**, symbolized by the incense (cf. 5:8; see also Ottman, *The Unfolding of the Ages*, p. 201 and Lincoln, *Lectures on the Book of Revelation*, I, p. 137). Again, it is vital to realize that **the golden altar, much incense**, and a **golden censer** remind one of Old Testament worship, another proof that attention is centered on Israel's (not the church's) age. Here He is not functioning as the Advocate of the church's saints, because she is already in heaven. He is invoking the judgments of God on the oppressors of the remnant of Israel. In chapter 6 the altar was the bronze altar, because sacrifice of life was in view; here it is the golden altar, because intercession is in mind. This is the work of no mere human being or angel (other references where Christ is seen as **another angel** are 10:1 and 18:1). There was no intercession in 6:9, but there is here; grace is needed by the living, not the dead. **The prayers of the saints** must be for judgment on their oppressors (in keeping with a time of judgment, but not in this day of grace), because this is the nature of the answer.

Fire . . . voices, and thunderings, and lightnings, and an earthquake all constitute a formula for catastrophe of universal proportions.

C. The First Trumpet Sounded. 8:6-7.

6-7. Once the mediating Angel has performed His work, the seven angels ready themselves for their important task. All interpreters express difficulty in explaining the trumpet judgments. The visitations do remind one of the plagues of Egypt in Exodus, but the present judgments are much more severe and universal. Scott states (*The Book of the Revelation*, p. 188): "The

CHAPTER 8

AND when he had opened the seventh seal, there was silence in heaven about the space of half an hour.
2 And I saw the seven angels which stood before God; and to them were given seven trumpets.

3 And another angel came and stood at the altar, having a golden censer; and there was given unto him much incense, that he should offer *it* with the prayers of all saints upon the golden altar which was before the throne.
4 And the smoke of the incense, *which came* with the prayers of the saints, ascended up before God out of the angel's hand.
5 And the angel took the censer, and filled it with fire of the altar, and cast *it* into the earth: and there were voices, and thunderings, and lightnings, and an earthquake.

6 And the seven angels which had the seven trumpets prepared themselves to sound.
7 The first angel sounded, and there followed hail and fire mingled with blood, and they were cast upon the earth: and the third part of trees was

burnt up, and all green grass was burnt up.

8 And the second angel sounded, and as it were a great mountain burning with fire was cast into the sea: and the third part of the sea became blood;
9 And the third part of the creatures which were in the sea, and had life, died; and the third part of the ships were destroyed.

10 And the third angel sounded, and there fell a great star from heaven, burning as it were a lamp, and it fell upon the third part of the rivers, and upon the fountains of waters;
11 And the name of the star is called Wormwood: and the third part of the waters became wormwood; and many men died of the waters, because they were made bitter.

interpretation of the Seals is a simple matter compared to that of the Trumpets." With the trumpets there is more of the element of mystery. The trumpet judgments, like the seal, are divided into two groups of four and three, indicating the number of the world, i.e., the four points of the compass, and the number of the Trinity. The last three trumpet judgments have the added designation of woe judgments because of their severity. Some interpret the judgments literally, which is the correct starting point hermeneutically, whereas the majority take them symbolically, a method impossible to rule out in view of the symbolical character of the Apocalypse.

As symbols, **hail** speaks of sudden judgment from God (cf. Isa 28:2, 17); **fire**, of God's wrath (cf. Deut 32:22 and numerous other times); and **blood**, of death (cf. Ezk 14:19). **Cast upon the earth.** The casting of them (they did not just fall) to the earth indicates omnipotent power. The third part is referred to several times in this chapter, and it has been understood as a reference to the revived Roman Empire of the end time. However, there is insufficient evidence to be so specific at this point. **Trees** and **grass** have been understood symbolically to refer to the high and low in society, but the literal sense is surely potent enough to convey horrendous decimation of natural elements so necessary for ongoing human existence on earth.

D. Second Trumpet Sounded. 8:8-9.

8-9. With the sounding of the second trumpet, something like a **great mountain burning with fire was cast into the sea.** It is usually held that the **mountain** is to be taken symbolically because of the expressed comparison (simile). To what is the reference made? In Scripture a mountain is used to speak of a great kingdom power (cf. Isa 2:2; Zech 6; especially Jer 51:25). Some students of the passage have even named the kingdom, Babylon, probably on the basis of the Jeremiah passage. But with a minimum of scriptural characterization, it is not wise to be so specific because of the wide range of possibilities. Seiss (op. cit., p. 195), who takes the mountain symbolically, understands the **sea** as probably the Mediterranean Sea, the prominent sea of the Bible because of its relation to the Land of Promise. If the sea if symbolical, it is known in Scripture as a symbol of people in general (cf. Ps 2:1) and of restlessness among them (Rev 17:15). The trumpet judgment could well refer to a great upheaval in nature (as with the first trumpet), with disastrous results for the waters of the sea, making them unfit for human use, marine life, and commerce. Though in each instance only a third is involved, it is enough to disrupt life beyond recognition.

E. Third Trumpet Sounded. 8:10-11.

10-11. But the wrath of God is still not fully expended on the wicked of earth. Water is such an indispensable element of life that again waters and springs are affected, as the sea was under the second trumpet judgment. **A great star from heaven, burning . . . fell.** It is understandable that stars can refer to important personalities. For example, today there are sports stars of all descriptions, entertainment stars, and a host of others. Scripture uses the term symbolically of our Lord Jesus (cf. Num 24:17). Some interpreters find an apostate ruler or dignitary here, perhaps even a church leader who falls from a high position. The symbolic explanation has credence because of the figurative name given the star. If so, then the contamination of the waters must indicate the corruption of the spiritual life of the masses. **Wormwood** (Gr *apsinthos*), that which makes water no longer potable, is a bitter and poisonous herb. When used without control, it can produce convulsions, paralysis, and even death. In fairness to all views, it must be indicated that, if the falling

12 And the fourth angel sounded, and the third part of the sun was smitten, and the third part of the moon, and the third part of the stars; so as the third part of them was darkened, and the day shone not for a third part of it, and the night likewise.

13 And I beheld, and heard an angel flying through the midst of heaven, saying with a loud voice, Woe, woe, woe, to the inhabiters of the earth by reason of the other voices of the trumpet of the three angels, which are yet to sound!

CHAPTER 9
AND the fifth angel sounded, and I saw a star fall from heaven unto the earth: and to him was given the key of the bottomless pit.

2 And he opened the bottomless pit; and there arose a smoke out of the pit, as the smoke of a great furnace; and the sun and the air were darkened by reason of the smoke of the pit.

star refers to a celestial phenomenon, it is difficult to see how it could contaminate so large an area.

F. Fourth Trumpet Sounded. 8:12.

12. When earth, sea, ships, rivers, and springs of waters have been touched, there are other areas that have not been involved. **Sun . . . moon . . . stars . . . the third part of them was darkened.** This reference is to the heavenly bodies. Notice once again the specific enumeration of one third. It is as though in infinite patience God touches just a part in order to bring it to repentance before everything is involved. Literal and symbolical interpretations of this section have long vied for attention. Some who have explained the judgment symbolically have gone far afield into naming specific areas of land, people, rulers, religious leaders, doctrines, and much more. If taken literally, the objection has been that the obscuring of the heavenly bodies would not result in darkness for only two-thirds of the time. It may be pointed out that in Scripture certain signs and symbols go beyond the range of the natural (as the beasts of the book of Daniel and the Revelation) in order to bring out certain truths of revelations. Then the symbols are admittedly arbitrary.

G. Announcement of Woe Judgments. 8:13.

13. The reading of **angel** here is doubtless to be discarded in view of the strong testimony of Codices Sinaiticus, Alexandrinus, Vaticanus, and a host of eminent authorities (cf. Seiss, op. cit., pp. 200-201). The reading of "eagle" (NASB) underscores the swiftness of the coming judgment (cf. Mt 24:28). Ample warning is given again. So terrifying are the last three trumpet judgments that they have the added nomenclature of woe judgments. Once more, it is announced that the judgments are intended for those who have settled down on the earth (a characterization of the ungodly, cf. for contrast with 3:10; the verb in both cases is *katoikeō*, not simply *oikeō*). Man can never claim he has not been sufficiently warned of coming judgment. As with the judgment on sin in Eden before the Flood in Noah's day, and in every age since, God is infinitely patient and compassionate toward those deserving of His wrath.

VII. THE FIFTH AND SIXTH TRUMPETS. 9:1-21.

A. Fifth Trumpet Sounded. 9:1-12.

The last three trumpet judgments (also called the woe judgments) are equally as difficult to interpret as the first four. The last woe trumpet is to be found in 11:15-18.

9:1. The first of the woe judgments is directed from Satan against the ungodly in Israel (cf. vs. 4); the second is from the east upon idolatrous Gentiles (vss. 14-15, 20). The star in mind had already fallen from heaven, the seat of authority. It appears to be the same as in 8:10, but important details are added here. It is the great apostate leader of the third trumpet. Some suggest it is the Antichrist, but to become that specific here without further particulars is unwarranted. Why is a literal star not in view? It refers to a living person, for the work performed is that of a human or living being. On the basis of 12:12, A. C. Gaebelein (*The Revelation*, p. 63; so also Seiss, op. cit., pp. 202-203) maintains it was Satan himself. If it is a false teacher, then Satan works through him, as is clear from numerous other occasions in the history of mankind. **The key of the bottomless pit** (abyss, so the Greek) was entrusted to him.

2. What is the **bottomless pit** of the abyss? Is it Hades (Sheol), Tartarus, or Gehenna? The full discussion of the phrase will be found in this commentary at chapter 20. For the moment, let it be said that it is the detention place of Satan and the demons (cf. Lk 8:31; Rev 20:3). When the abyss is opened, **a smoke out of the pit, as the smoke of a great furnace** issues

3 And there came out of the smoke locusts upon the earth: and unto them was given power, as the scorpions of the earth have power.

4 And it was commanded them that they should not hurt the grass of the earth, neither any green thing, neither any tree; but only those men which have not the seal of God in their foreheads.

5 And to them it was given that they should not kill them, but that they should be tormented five months: and their torment was as the torment of a scorpion, when he striketh a man.

6 And in those days shall men seek death, and shall not find it; and shall desire to die, and death shall flee from them.

7 And the shapes of the locusts were like unto horses prepared unto battle; and on their heads were as it were crowns like gold, and their faces were as the faces of men.

8 And they had hair as the hair of women, and their teeth were as the teeth of lions.

9 And they had breastplates, as it were breastplates of iron; and the sound of their wings was as the sound of chariots of many horses running to battle.

10 And they had tails like unto scorpions, and there were stings in their tails: and their power was to hurt men five months.

11 And they had a king over them, which is the angel of the bottomless pit, whose name in the Hebrew tongue is A-băd'don, but in the Greek tongue hath his name A-pŏl'ly-on.

---

from it. The blinding effect of smoke is well-known; here it refers to moral blinding. The reference is to that strong delusion that leads to perdition (cf. II Thess 2:11-12). Their whole spiritual horizon will be **darkened** by the false system let loose, obscuring the true light from God. All the apostate, pagan systems are leading to this dire situation, culminating in the Tribulation Period.

3-4. There came out of the smoke locusts, which have **power, as the scorpions of the earth.** It is immediately clear that these are not ordinary, earthly locusts. They are symbolic, not literal, because they do not feed on the natural food of locusts, such as grass, greenery, trees; indeed, they do not seem to eat at all, but rather injure men. They do no harm to nature; but they torture men, especially the ungodly in the land of Israel (cf. vs. 4 last clause with 7:1-3).

5. Their function is **that they should not kill,** but **torment.** Here, as in the book of Job (cf. 1:9-12), Satan must operate within the authority permitted of God. The torment is for **five months,** a limited time. This is the natural life of a literal locust, that is, from May to September. The pain from the **torment** (sting) **of a scorpion,** though not always fatal, is often so; it is perhaps the most intense that any animal can inflict on the human body. These forces with malign intent thus overrun the Holy Land and the unsealed portion of Israel.

6. Men seek death, and shall not find it. So great will the torment of those with sin-laden and guilty consciences be, that men will seek relief in self-destruction; but suicide will be impossible. There will be no rest of heart or peace of mind.

7-10. Now a detailed description of these supernatural locusts follows. In their strength and irresistible onslaught they are likened to **horses prepared unto battle.** Further, they will be victorious; for **on their heads** they wear **crowns like gold.** As to facial features, they resemble **faces of men,** indicating human intelligence. Another symbolic detail indicates their **hair as the hair of women** in attractiveness. **Teeth of lions** remind us that they are fierce and rapacious in their destructiveness. Nor are they to be halted in their designs, for they have the protection of **breastplates of iron.** Stubborn resistance and impenetrable qualities are indicated here. Locusts would be expected to have **wings,** so these locusts have them; but they are of such number and power that they sound like **horses running to battle** and chariots rushing on to combat.

The portrayal thus far, has been fearful enough, but more is yet to come. As in verse 5, they are compared to **scorpions** with **stings in their tails** capable of inflicting excruciating pain. No dimensions are given for them, but in view of the other details of the picture, they must be of extraordinary proportions. They have a certain degree and measure of intelligence; they do not hurt the ones with the seal of God, and they are able to understand and execute the commands given to them. They combine characteristics of **horses, chariots, lions, men,** and **scorpions.** This full description is sufficient in itself to demonstrate that the locusts cannot be literal, but are symbolic. Mark you, they are nonetheless real because of their figurative character.

11. A king over them. Although locusts have no king (cf. Prov 30:27), these revelatory locusts have one who is identified as the **angel of the bottomless pit.** Moreover, this king's name is given in both Hebrew (*Abaddon*) and Greek (*Apollyon*). Some interpreters believe the angel of the abyss is someone other than Satan, whereas others hold that they are one and the same being. Probably the latter is to be preferred; at any rate, their objectives are undoubtedly the same. The names of this creature mean Destruction or Destroyer. **Abaddon** is first because his blighting influence falls on Israel first, as in the first woe trumpet (cf. vs. 4). **Apollyon** signifies that his judgment will next light on

12 One woe is past; *and,* behold, there come two woes more hereafter.

13 And the sixth angel sounded, and I heard a voice from the four horns of the golden altar which is before God,

14 Saying to the sixth angel which had the trumpet, Loose the four angels which are bound in the great river Eū'phrā'tēś.

15 And the four angels were loosed, which were prepared for an hour, and a day, and a month, and a year, for to slay the third part of men.

16 And the number of the army of the horsemen *were* two hundred thousand thousand: and I heard the number of them.

17 And thus I saw the horses in the vision, and them that sat on them, having breastplates of fire, and of jacinth, and brimstone: and the heads of the horses *were* as the heads of lions; and out of their mouths issued fire and smoke and brimstone.

18 By these three was the third part of men killed, by the fire, and by the smoke, and by the brimstone, which issued out of their mouths.

19 For their power is in their mouth, and in their tails: for their tails *were* like unto serpents, and had heads, and with them they do hurt.

20 And the rest of the men which were not killed by these plagues yet repented not of the works of their hands, that they should not worship devils, and idols of gold, and silver, and brass, and stone, and of wood: which neither can see, nor hear, nor walk:

21 Neither repented they of their murders, nor of their sorceries, nor of their fornication, nor of their thefts.

the gentile world. The first title connects him with unbelieving Jews; the second, with apostate Christendom.

12. One woe is past . . . two woes more hereafter. The Spirit states that only one of the woe judgments have been fulfilled; two others will be also.

B. Sixth Trumpet Sounded. 9:13-21.

13. The **golden altar** in the Temple, and in the tabernacle as well, was placed directly before the veil, which hid the Holiest of all from human gaze. This verse is the answer to the prayers of 8:3-4. The voice is that of God or one of His delegated messengers. **The four horns** indicate the whole strength of the altar of intercession exerted to answer the prayers of the persecuted saints.

14. The four angels here are not those of 7:1-3. The first (7:1-3) are at the ends of the earth; these of chapter 9 are in the limited region of the Euphrates. Those of chapter 7 restrain; these do the opposite: they release. The **Euphrates** is usually spoken of as **the great river;** it is 1780 miles long. It will be referred to in 16:12. It is the longest and most important river of western Asia. It will be remembered that the River of Egypt (the Wadi el Arish) and the Euphrates are the bounds of the Promised Land (cf. Gen 15:18). The Euphrates was the boundary of the eastern powers and of the old Roman Empire.

15. Four angels were loosed . . . to slay the third part of men. A specific time had arrived in the counsels of God; all proceeds on proper schedule with Him. The mission on which the four angels are sent is to accomplish a vast carnage.

16-17. The number of the army (cf. Ps 68:17) is 200,000,000. It is an immense army, far beyond calculation. John did not count them, but he was told their number. The armies of **horses** and **horsemen** will be involved in waves of invasions. The horses evidently have riders upon them, but the horsemen are not of primary importance. They only serve to state the protection for their bodies. **The heads of the horses were as the heads of lions,** and from their mouths **fire and smoke and brimstone issue.** The fire will burn, and the smoke and brimstone (sulphur) will choke and stifle to death. The combination here has been called the "defensive armor of hell." Jacinth (hyacinth) is a deep blue like that of a flame, but it is the blue of the pit and not the blue of heaven (cf. Gen 19:24 for fire and brimstone in judgment).

18-19. The fire, . . . smoke, and . . . brimstone are so deadly that they are now called **plagues** (vs. 20). They decimate one-third of mankind, a visitation not known in history apart from the Flood of Noah's day. But the physical havoc is not all; symbolically, the smoke can indicate the moral, blighting delusion of the pit. The teachings and lies of Satan will be manifold. **The tails like unto serpents** speak of deceit and falsehood. The tails are described as possessing **heads;** that is, they are intelligently guided.

20-21. Men which were not killed by these plagues yet repented not. If ever human obduracy and perversity were pictured, it is here. Those who are spared the visitations just set forth will neither repent of their wickedness nor their worthless idolatries, which are totally useless. Verse 20 tells of their **worship;** verse 21, of their **works.** Is it possible that boasted civilization will revert to basest idolatry? It is unmistakably stated that it will. The second woe is far worse than the first, but there is no repentance. The ungodly are incorrigible in their murders, sorceries, and immorality. Punishment does not soften wicked hearts; only the love of God can.

VIII. A PARENTHESIS. 10:1-11:14.

Just as there was a parenthesis in chapter 7 between the sixth and seventh seals, so now from 10:1-11:14 there is a parenthetical section between the sixth and seventh trumpets. There is a very brief parenthesis (cf. 16:15) between the sixth and seventh vial judgments. This shows the orderly arrangement of the Revelation.

A. The Angel with the Little Book. 10:1-11.

10:1. Another mighty angel. Of primary importance is the identity of the strong angel. Happily, there are details which reveal that He is the "angel of the Lord" of the Old Testament, the Lord Jesus Christ. He sealed the 144,000 (cf. 7:2-3); He offered incense with the prayers of the saints (cf. 8:1-6); He is **clothed with a cloud,** a heavenly clothing; **his face was as it were the sun** (cf. 1:16); **a rainbow was upon his head** (cf. 4:3); **his feet as pillars of fire** tallies with the description in 1:15. Why does Christ appear in the Apocalypse as an angel? Is this retrogression in doctrine, rather than progress? He appears as an angel because reference is made to conditions in Israel before their Messiah had been revealed to them in His incarnation. He takes the same position as He occupied in Old Testament times, another proof that the Tribulation Period is a part of the Jewish age and will remain unfinished at the first coming of Christ.

2. Attention is next directed to **a little book open** in the **hand** of the Angel. There are three views as to the identity of the little book: (1) It is the same book as the seven-sealed book of 5:1; (2) it is the aggregate of Old Testament prophecy concerning Israel (it is strange that a little book could contain so much prophetic truth); and (3) it is the part of the Revelation that is subsequent to the sounding of the seventh trumpet (i.e., 11:19-19:21). We prefer the first position (cf. also Ironside, op. cit., pp. 175-176). The reason is that in a book of symbols it would be confusing to have a detail in chapter 5 appear again in chapter 10 with another meaning and without some explanation. The reference then, is, to the title-deed to the earth. Here He makes His indisputable claim to all creation as His inalienable right. Further proof is forthcoming in the Angel's action. **He set his right foot upon the sea, and his left foot on the earth.** In the Old Testament such an act signified taking possession of that place (cf. Deut 11:24; Josh 1:3).

3. **And cried with a loud voice, as when a lion roareth.** The voice of the Angel was like the roaring of a lion, for He is the Lion of the tribe of Judah (cf. 5:5). A lion always roars when he has caught his prey (cf. Amos 3:4). In chapter 5 He was seen in the role of Lamb; here He is pictured in His wrath as a Lion (cf. 6:16). Again, **seven thunders** speak of God's activity in judgment.

4. **Seal up those things . . . and write them not.** At this point John was **about to write** the import of the **seven thunders,** but the Lord did not permit it. The manner in which all takes place is not revealed (cf. Deut 29:29). In this book of disclosures this is the only detail sealed.

5-7. **And sware by him . . . who created heaven . . . the earth . . . the sea, and the things which are therein.** The solemnity of the transaction is underscored. He swears by the God of all creation. What is the subject of the oath? Simply, it is that there will be delay no longer. The translation of "delay" (Gr *chronos*) as **time** is unfortunate (so AV), because it is inaccurate (cf. NASB). There is here no announcement of the end of time and the ushering in of eternity, for that comes over 1000 years later. The Angel is stating, rather, that there will be no more delay in rectifying the wrong government of the earth. Sin has held sway long enough. God's secret dealings are over, and His public judgments begin. Heaven is silent no longer, and man's day is about to close. **The seventh angel** is the one who sounds the seventh trumpet. What is the **mystery of God** that is finished? Reference is to His permission for evil to go on in its present course with seeming impunity. God appears to be silent

---

CHAPTER 10
AND I saw another mighty angel come down from heaven, clothed with a cloud: and a rainbow *was* upon his head, and his face *was* as it were the sun, and his feet as pillars of fire:

2 And he had in his hand a little book open: and he set his right foot upon the sea, and *his* left *foot* on the earth,

3 And cried with a loud voice, as *when* a lion roareth: and when he had cried, seven thunders uttered their voices.

4 And when the seven thunders had uttered their voices, I was about to write: and I heard a voice from heaven saying unto me, Seal up those things which the seven thunders uttered, and write them not.
5 And the angel which I saw stand upon the sea and upon the earth lifted up his hand to heaven,
6 And sware by him that liveth for ever and ever, who created heaven, and the things that therein are, and the earth, and the things that therein are, and the sea, and the things which are therein, that there should be time no longer:
7 But in the days of the voice of the seventh angel, when he shall begin to sound, the mystery of God should be finished, as he hath declared to his servants the prophets.

in the whole conflict between good and evil. According to a Jewish proverb, "Michael flies with but one wing, and Gabriel with two." In short, God is quick in sending angels of peace, and they fly swiftly. But the messengers of wrath come slowly. But they do come!

8-11. Now John is told to become actively involved in the unveiling of coming events. He is charged to **take the little book which is open in the hand of the angel.** The reply of the Angel in verse 9 reminds one of the experience of Ezekiel in his ministry (cf. Ezk 2:8-3:3). The eating of the scroll is done by faith through meditation and reflection. To **eat** is to incorporate into one's being (cf. Jn 6:49-58). The study of the prophetic Word, and its central emphasis on Christ and His ultimate victory has a twofold effect: **sweet** and **bitter.** It both gladdens and saddens. The truth of the Lord's reign and triumph was sweet to John, but the judgments and plagues by which that consummation will be brought about will be bitter indeed.

What is the meaning of the command to **prophesy again** concerning kings and nations? It will be remembered that only the first and second series of septenary judgments have been covered in the chapters thus far. There remains the last series (the vial judgments) to be unfolded. Furthermore, there are other disclosures in chapter 12 to the end of the book concerning Satan, a final political leader, the Antichrist, the world system of godlessness, the reign of Christ, judgment, resurrection, and the new heaven and new earth. It is an approach to the subjects of chapters 1-11, but with many significant details added. The truth of the book is duplicated, just as Pharaoh's dream of the famine (cf. Gen 41:32) was repeated to him.

8 And the voice which I heard from heaven spake unto me again, and said, Go *and* take the little book which is open in the hand of the angel which standeth upon the sea and upon the earth.

9 And I went unto the angel, and said unto him, Give me the little book. And he said unto me, Take *it,* and eat it up; and it shall make thy belly bitter, but it shall be in thy mouth sweet as honey.

10 And I took the little book out of the angel's hand, and ate it up; and it was in my mouth sweet as honey: and as soon as I had eaten it, my belly was bitter.

11 And he said unto me, Thou must prophesy again before many peoples, and nations, and tongues, and kings.

CHAPTER 11

AND there was given me a reed like unto a rod: and the angel stood, saying, Rise, and measure the temple of God, and the altar, and them that worship therein.

2 But the court which is without the temple leave out, and measure it not; for it is given unto the Gentiles: and the holy city shall they tread under foot forty *and* two months.

B. The Two Witnesses. 11:1-13.

11:1-2. Again, the mention of the **temple of God, and the altar, . . . the court, . . . and the holy city** alerts the reader that events continue on Jewish ground. Yet there are some eminent students who claim that verses 1-14 are one of the most difficult portions of the Revelation (cf. H. Alford, in loco). Much of the confusion is attributable to the fact that they inject the church here, whereas she has been seen in heaven since chapter 4.

This chapter, through verse 14, is the continuation of the parenthesis begun in 10:1 between the sixth and seventh trumpets. The background of chapter 11 is essential. The nation Israel is returned to their land in unbelief. They had made a covenant with a sinister political leader of the time (cf. Dan 9:27), who promises them political protection and religious freedom. The Temple is rebuilt with an attempt at restoring the Mosaic ritual. It may be well to review the status of the Temple in Israel here and then touch on a preview of what is yet in store. The tabernacle of Moses (cf. Ex 25ff.) was the pattern, greatly enlarged to be sure, for the majestic temple of Solomon (cf. I Kgs 7-8). With its destruction in 586 B.C. by Nebuchadnezzar of Babylon and the subsequent exile, Israel was without a Temple. More than a score of years went by before the restoration Temple was built under Zerubbabel, a scion of the Davidic house, who built it with the spiritual motivation provided by the prophets Haggai and Zechariah near the end of the sixth century B.C.. During the reign of Herod under Roman suzerainty, the Temple was renovated over a period of time (cf. Jn 2:20), only to be destroyed by the armies of Titus at the end of the Judaeo-Roman War of A.D. 66-70. Israel has not had, and does not now have, a temple in Jerusalem. Judaism knows only worship in synagogues around the world. (Reformed Jews speak of their places of worship as temples, but in no sense do they imply any relationship to the temples already discussed here.) When the church has been taken to heaven in the Rapture (an event that may transpire at any moment—"in a moment," I Cor 15:52) and Israel is returned to their land, they will build a temple in Jerusalem. It may be called the Tribulation Temple (the Scripture references are clear: 11:1-2; Dan 9:27; 11:31; 12:11; Mt 24:15; Mk 13:14; II Thess 2:3-4). There is yet to be another temple constructed, and it will be built by the Lord Jesus Christ. It is the millennial temple (cf. Isa 66:20-23; Ezk 40-48; Zech 6:12-13). In the New Jerusalem there will be no temple (cf. Rev 21:22).

Rise, and measure. John's people are in view; so he is commanded to measure the temple, the altar, and the worshipers. The altar is that of burnt offering, God's first provision for Israel's drawing nigh to Him. The measuring reminds one of Revelation 21:15ff; Ezekiel 40; and Zechariah 2. Measuring conveys the concept of marking off for one's own possession. God does recognize and claim a godly, worshiping remnant in Jerusalem in the time of the Tribulation. The measuring must be symbolical in that the worshipers are included. **The court which is without the temple leave out.** The outer court, it is explicitly stated, is to be excluded. In the temples in Israel in the past this was the court of the Gentiles. Now it is indicated that the Gentiles will not only command this area as their own, but for **forty and two months** (i.e., the three and a half years of the Great Tribulation) they will overrun Jerusalem as well. During the domination of the beast and the Antichrist (cf. ch. 13) Jerusalem will not enjoy autonomy. The rejected court speaks of the mass of the nation being in apostasy and rejection, as well as their being the prey of the nations. It is Jerusalem's greatest hour of agony.

3-4. Prophesy a thousand two hundred and threescore days, clothed in sackcloth. But God never allows Himself to be without a witness. The very period of the trampling down of Jerusalem will be the time of their testimony, i.e., 1260 days. Their clothing of sackcloth shows their afflicted condition regarding the spiritual desolation about them. Notice that they preach with power. Since they were identified only by the description in verse 4, which is general indeed, various identifications have been suggested by interpreters. Some claim the **two witnesses** are Elijah and Enoch, who did not experience death in order to see death here. Others say they are Moses and Elijah. This has much to commend it in the light of Malachi 4:4-5 and the nature of the works that they perform (see vs. 6 of this chapter). A good number prefer to think of them as a godly remnant in Israel and not two men, since two are required to insure competent witness (cf. Deut 17:6; Jn 8:17). Some are uncertain in identifying the witnesses, but the opinion of the majority is that the witnessing ministry and miracles are like those of Moses and Elijah.

Their function is stated in verse 4 as being similar to **the two olive trees, and the two candlesticks** before the Lord in Zechariah 4:14. In that passage the reference was to two specific men, Joshua the son of Jehozadak, the high priest, and Zerubbabel the son of Shealtiel, the governor, one representing governmental power and the other religious. Through them the light and message of God were mediated to the people of Israel in those post-captivity days. The two witnesses of the Great Tribulation serve in a royal and priestly capacity, witnessing to the soon coming of the King of the earth.

3 And I will give *power* unto my two witnesses, and they shall prophesy a thousand two hundred *and* threescore days, clothed in sackcloth.
4 These are the two olive trees, and the two candlesticks standing before the God of the earth.

5 And if any man will hurt them, fire proceedeth out of their mouth, and devoureth their enemies: and if any man will hurt them, he must in this manner be killed.
6 These have power to shut heaven, that it rain not in the days of their prophecy: and have power over waters to turn them to blood, and to smite the

5-6. Also, they have power to accredit and authenticate their mission to unbelieving Israel. Miracles like those of Moses and Elijah will confirm their divine empowering. Israel will be in a state of slavery, as in Egypt (now under the domination of the first beast); and she will also be in a condition of apostasy, as in Elijah's day (now under the delusion of the false prophet, the second beast, cf. 13:1-18). Because they testify for God, they will be hated by the ungodly. But they will be invincible and immortal until their ministry is completed. Notice the range of

earth with all plagues, as often as they will.

7 And when they shall have finished their testimony, the beast that ascendeth out of the bottomless pit shall make war against them, and shall overcome them, and kill them.

8 And their dead bodies *shall lie* in the street of the great city, which spiritually is called Sodom and Egypt, where also our Lord was crucified.

9 And they of the people and kindreds and tongues and nations shall see their dead bodies three days and an half, and shall not suffer their dead bodies to be put in graves.

10 And they that dwell upon the earth shall rejoice over them, and make merry, and shall send gifts one to another; because these two prophets tormented them that dwelt on the earth.

11 And after three days and an half the Spirit of life from God entered into them, and they stood upon their feet; and great fear fell upon them which saw them.

12 And they heard a great voice from heaven saying unto them, Come up hither. And they ascended up to heaven in a cloud; and their enemies beheld them.

13 And the same hour was there a great earthquake, and the tenth part of the city fell, and in the earthquake were slain of men seven thousand: and the remnant were affrighted, and gave glory to the God of heaven.

14 The second woe is past; *and*, behold, the third woe cometh quickly.

15 And the seventh angel sounded; and there were great voices in heaven, saying, The kingdoms of this world are

their authority in verse 6: to smite the earth with all plagues, as often as they will.

7-10. When they shall have finished their testimony, the beast . . . shall make war against them. Once the testimony of the witnesses is completed, they will glorify God even to death, being slain by the beast. This is the first mention of the beast of Revelation 13:1ff. He actually carries on warfare against them until they are martyred. Evidently, the populace will assent to the work of the beast, because in their anger against the two witnesses they do not allow their dead bodies to be put in graves, an indignity of immense proportions in the East. With satanic cunning and deception, the beast that ascendeth out of the bottomless pit has won over the masses to himself.

Jerusalem is characterized mystically (not literally) as Sodom, because of its wickedness, and as Egypt, because of its oppression and enslavement of the people of God. Both names appear repeatedly in Scripture as the objects of God's unrelenting wrath. Lest any reader misunderstand the geographical place intended because of the use of symbolism, the passage identifies the place as Jerusalem, where also our Lord was crucified. That Christ is designated as their Lord is proof that the two witnesses are not representative of masses of individuals, nor are they angelic beings. They are redeemed men on earth.

The three days and a half of verse 9 are obviously intended to be literal days. Now the utter depravity of the dwellers on earth is manifested. They refuse decent burial for the witnesses; but even more, they want to celebrate the cessation of that witness that was so irksome and tormenting to them in their incorrigible godlessness. They will carry out their merriment in feasts, banquets, and exchange of gifts, so galling had been the testimony of the godly messengers.

11-13. Come up hither. And they ascended up to heaven in a cloud. But the hour of vindication arrives at last. Their indecent merriment would redound upon the heads of the insensitive wicked. The witnesses are resurrected in the sight of all their enemies. But even more, a heavenly voice calls them into the presence of the Lord; they are afforded an ascension in the presence of their foes. What an honor! Even Paul and the apostles were not so rewarded. Furthermore, the ungodly experience a final stroke of God's displeasure at the very hour of the ascension of the witnesses, an earthquake strikes the city of Jerusalem with lethal results: seven thousand people are slain in the disaster. Even the blindest spiritually could not escape the meaning of the earthquake and the decimation of the population. The remnant mentioned are those who were spared. Their reaction was terror, the result of human fear with no practical outcome. Outwardly, they gave glory to the God of heaven; but their hearts are not genuinely touched, as future events will clearly attest.

C. Announcement of Third Woe. 11:14.

14. The second woe is past; and, behold, the third woe cometh quickly. The parenthesis which began with 10:1 ends here. It further confirms that the reader is not to expect an improvement or amelioration in conditions on earth; for without change in men's hearts, God's righteous judgments must continue. Six trumpet judgments (including two woes) are concluded; there remains only fearful looking forward of more judgment, especially the seventh trumpet or third woe visitation.

IX. THE SEVENTH TRUMPET (THIRD WOE). 11:15-19.

15. Verses 15-18 return to the trumpet judgments, last dealt with at 9:21. It is immediately evident that under this trumpet many particulars of the events of the Tribulation Period are not

become *the kingdoms* of our Lord, and of his Christ; and he shall reign for ever and ever.

16 And the four and twenty elders, which sat before God on their seats, fell upon their faces, and worshipped God,

17 Saying, We give thee thanks, O Lord God Almighty, which art, and wast, and art to come; because thou hast taken to thee thy great power, and hast reigned.

18 And the nations were angry, and thy wrath is come, and the time of the dead, that they should be judged, and that thou shouldest give reward unto thy servants the prophets, and to the saints, and them that fear thy name, small and great; and shouldest destroy them which destroy the earth.

19 And the temple of God was opened in heaven, and there was seen in his temple the ark of his testament: and there were lightnings, and voices, and thunderings, and an earthquake, and great hail.

treated. Verse 19, it is generally agreed, belongs to the next chapter and the additional details that follow in the subsequent chapters. The seventh seal and the seventh trumpet are similar in that no judgment is directly announced under them (cf. 8:1; 11:15-18). Nothing is spoken of as coming from the sounding of the seventh trumpet; it is wrapped in silence. But loud voices in heaven have a vital declaration to make before the details of the last trumpet are revealed in the seven vials (bowls) of wrath in chapter 16. The heavenly announcement proclaims that **the kingdoms of this world** (Gr *basileia* is singular, as in the NASB, not plural as in the AV) **are become the kingdoms of our Lord and of his Christ.** The seventh trumpet does not bring in the kingdom; it only shows its proximity. The kingdom should be in the singular, because under earth's final sinister political leader there will be an amalgamation of all kingdoms into one universal kingdom. Christ's reign will be eternal. If His rule is eternal, then how can it be a thousand years, millennial reign? He rules a thousand years (cf. 20:1-7) in time to vindicate and execute God's purposes for earth; then that kingdom is merged into the eternal kingdom. Verse 15 speaks of the kingdom anticipatively, as a preview; the actual realization is to be seen in chapters 19-20.

16-18. As in chapter 4, the **four and twenty elders,** the church in heaven, **worshiped God.** Unstinted praise is rendered that God has finally consummated events on earth and reigns in omnipotence. So certain is it that it is spoken of as already accomplished. Five significant factors are fulfilled at that time. (1) The rage of the nations. They have exhibited defiance and arrogance against God many times before, but now it has reached its culmination (cf. 16:13-16; 19:19; Ps 2). Here is an epitome of Armageddon. (2) The wrath of God. No longer will the patience of God be manifest. The hour of His vengeance will have arrived (cf. Ps 2:5; II Thess 1:7-8). (3) The judgment of the dead. This is probably a reference to the future Great White Throne judgment (cf. ch. 20). (4) The rewarding of the godly. This will occur for the church at the Rapture; for other saints it will take place at the resurrection of the righteous in the first resurrection (cf. ch. 20). (5) The destruction of the destroyers of the earth. The reference amply covers those who carry out their diabolical purposes in the Tribulation Period. What a summary this is!

19. The temple of God was opened in heaven. With this verse John resumes the entire history from a different viewpoint, i.e., that of the chief participants in the soon-coming events. A good number of scholars connect this verse with the next three chapters, thus making yet another parenthesis, from 11:19-14:20, before the unveiling of the vial judgments in chapters 15-16. There is much to be said in favor of this position. God resumes His relationship with Israel (**his temple, the ark of his testament**), but there is still judgment ahead as evidenced by the **lightnings, voices, thunderings, earthquake, and great hail.**

X. CHIEF PARTICIPANTS IN THE TRIBULATION.
12:1-14:20

From chapter 12 on, a new beginning and fuller details are presented. Chapters 12-14 constitute a connected and important prophecy in the book. Chapters 12-13 depict the principal agents for good and evil in the end time. Chapter 14 gives the consummation preparatory to the setting up of the kingdom. From 12:5 to 14:20 a great sweep of history is covered from the birth of Christ to the time of His treading the winepress of God's wrath. In chapter 12 alone, there is a grouping of events second to none in this book. The chapter takes the reader farther back than any other in the Revelation.

CHAPTER 12

AND there appeared a great wonder in heaven; a woman clothed with the sun, and the moon under her feet, and upon her head a crown of twelve stars:

2 And she being with child cried, travailing in birth, and pained to be delivered.

3 And there appeared another wonder in heaven; and behold a great red dragon, having seven heads and ten horns, and seven crowns upon his heads.

4 And his tail drew the third part of the stars of heaven, and did cast them to the earth: and the dragon stood before the woman which was ready to be delivered, for to devour her child as soon as it was born.

A. The Woman, the Red Dragon, and the Child. 12:1-6.

12:1-2. The **great wonder in heaven** is something pointing to a definite subject or object. The **woman** is actually on earth; but the wonder or sign is seen in heaven, so that God's purposes concerning her may be made known from heaven. Two distinct features are indicated concerning her: her clothing and her condition. **The sun . . . the moon . . . a crown of twelve stars.** She is clothed brilliantly with the heavenly bodies and a crown; she is a mother **with child** and is in labor. When the Revelation is studied, it will be seen that the book pictures four women, all of them in a representative capacity. In 2:20 the woman **Jezebel** was seen, not in her individual and historic position, but as representing the clerical system at its highest, i.e., the papal system. In 17:1 **the great whore,** as will be shown later, is all corrupt, apostate religious systems, especially professing Christendom. **The wife,** the church in heaven, is indicated in 19:7.

The fourth woman is considered in verses 1-2. Various views of her identity have been put forth. There are three positions as follows: (1) She is the virgin Mary. Nowhere in Scripture is Mary pictured as in verse 1. She is not portrayed in the Gospels as verse 4 indicates. There is no biblical ground to believe Mary underwent the experience of verse 6. Moreover, how could verse 17 apply to her? She does not fit the picture. (2) She is the church. This view has many adherents and defenders. H. Alford (op. cit., in loco); Matthew Henry (*Commentary*, VI, 1160); J. A. Seiss (in loco) represent this view, along with numerous others. The difficulty here is that the church did not give birth to Christ; He is the builder of the church (cf. Mt 16:18) and its foundation (cf. I Cor 3:11). (3) Many hold the woman is Israel. A. T. Robertson (op. cit., in loco) holds that John must have had Isaiah 7:14 in mind. Even more, under the direction of the Spirit, he knew Isaiah 9:6; 66:7-8; Micah 5:2; and Romans 9:4-5. The **sun, moon,** and **stars** indicate a complete system of government and remind the reader of Genesis 37:9. God had caused royal dignity to rest in Israel in the line of David. The number **twelve** appears with the twelve patriarchs, twelve disciples, and twelve thrones (cf. Mt 19:28). In verse 1 Israel is seen, not as she has been or is now, but as she will be. It is the nation as God had intended her to be, a condition that will be fulfilled in the reign of her Messiah. When the **child,** who is Christ, was born, the people of Israel were not in a place of power and dignity, but under the galling yoke of Roman domination.

3-4. The scene now shifts to heaven where **another wonder** is closely observed. The symbol is **a great red dragon.** It is called **great** because it is not a minor or insignificant creature. He has great power. He is **red** because he is eager and ready to shed blood. A **dragon** is a winged (for speed) serpent (for deception). The figure is meant to bear out great cruelty and hatred. Undoubtedly, this is Satan (cf. vs. 9 and 20:2). This is the first place in the Bible where Satan is called a dragon. But the description is enlarged: (1) he has **seven heads;** (2) **ten horns;** and (3) **seven crowns.** Some try to connect the **seven heads** with the seven great world monarchies of Egypt, Assyria, Babylon, Persia, Greece, Rome, and the Roman Empire in its restored condition (cf. J. A. Seiss, op. cit., in loco). This is artificial and arbitrary, for the seventh kingdom is not a separate one from the Roman Empire of history. A head is a symbol of wisdom; seven speaks of fullness and completion. Satan is indeed wise and powerful. **Horns** represent power in Scripture (cf. I Sam 2:1; Zech 1:18-21; especially Dan 7:7-8, 24-25; Rev 13:1; 17:3, 12-16). **Ten** is the number of universality, and the goal of Satan is nothing less than world domination. Such is his objective, as will be seen in chapter 13. The **seven crowns** indicate Satan's objective to be crowned; he would reign over all men at all costs.

The **tail** symbolizes delusive power (cf. Isa 9:15), which Satan uses to accomplish the moral ruin of those in highest position. But he is not successful with all, only a third. Upon whom was the venom of Satan to be poured out? The answer is clear: the woman's **child as soon as it was born** (cf. Mt 2 with Gen 3:15). Herod was merely a tool of Satan's power, but he was nevertheless responsible.

5 And she brought forth a man child, who was to rule all nations with a rod of iron: and her child was caught up unto God, and to his throne.

6 And the woman fled into the wilderness, where she hath a place prepared of God, that they should feed her there a thousand two hundred and threescore days.

5-6. The identity of the woman and her child is assured beyond question in verse 5. The **man child** is to **rule** (Gr *poimainō*, to shepherd) **all nations with a rod of iron:** He is unmistakably the Lord Jesus Christ (cf. Ps 2:7, 9). As the Son of Man, He has sovereign rights of world rulership (cf. Ps 8; Dan 7:13-14). What is remarkable is that the entire period in the life of Christ from His birth until His ascension is omitted here. But, as has been seen many times in Scripture, the record contains not only history, but divine history, and that from a specific viewpoint. History as such is not the aim, but the moral and spiritual purpose of God in the earth. The church age is omitted also in verse 6 because the purpose of God in Israel is at the center of the book. What the woman in Genesis 3 was not able to accomplish, namely, victory over Satan, the woman here did effect in her all-victorious, ascended Lord.

Again, a large span of history is not mentioned, that is, from the ascension of the Saviour to the flight of Israel in the Tribulation Period. Here is proof again that from the vantage point of the Old Testament the entire church age is an unrevealed mystery (cf. Eph 3:1-7). The same satanic fury unleashed at the birth of Christ is still operative against the godly of the nation that gave Him birth. **A place prepared of God, that they should feed her.** The same faithful Father, who watched over His people in the time of the Saviour's birth, provides a place and nourishment from the relentless fury of the dragon. A **wilderness** is a place lacking human resources. It may have reference to Ezekiel 20:35, but there is no valid reason why it cannot refer to the literal wilderness east of the holy city, Jerusalem. The time is the latter half of the Tribulation (1,260 days), what Daniel refers to as the "final period of the indignation" (NASB) In the AV Daniel 8:19 reads "the last end of the indignation." Chronologically, verses 7-12 occur before the flight of the woman into the wilderness and explain, at least in part, the reason for the flight.

B. War in Heaven. 12:7-17.

This conflict is not said to be a sign, because the presence of Satan in heaven is a reality (cf. Eph 6:10-12). The first step in the execution of the final judgment on Satan is depicted here.

7 And there was war in heaven: Michael and his angels fought against the dragon; and the dragon fought and his angels,

8 And prevailed not; neither was their place found any more in heaven.

7-8. In this section of the chapter another important personality of the Tribulation is introduced, namely, **Michael** the archangel. Notice these features: (1) His name. It means "Who is like God?" This bears testimony to the uniqueness of the God he serves. (2) He is clearly designated as "the archangel" (cf. Jude 9). Nowhere in Scripture is there a plural to this noun (cf. I Thess 4:16; Jude 9). (3) He has the added description of "the great prince" (cf. Dan 12:1). (4) He has power even to challenge Satan (cf. Jude 9). (5) He has angels at his command (cf. 12:7). (6) He will be present at the Rapture of the church (cf. I Thess 4:16). (7) He is the champion of Israel and the espouser of their cause (cf. 12:7; Dan 12:1). He appears when they are in question and their interests are involved. His presence immediately alerts the reader that the events relate to Israel and her enemies.

It is unusual to read of **war in heaven,** a place where peace and bliss prevail. But here the ultimate doom of **Satan** must begin, just as his first sin did (cf. Isa 14:12-14; Ezk 28:12-15). In pre-time, his early fall was from the immediate presence of God to the second heaven (cf. Eph 6:10-12). Just as Michael has a retinue of angels at his command, Satan has his followers. The

9 And the great dragon was cast out, that old serpent, called the Devil, and Satan, which deceiveth the whole world: he was cast out into the earth, and his angels were cast out with him.

10 And I heard a loud voice saying in heaven, Now is come salvation, and strength, and the kingdom of our God, and the power of his Christ: for the accuser of our brethren is cast down, which accused them before our God day and night.

11 And they overcame him by the blood of the Lamb, and by the word of their testimony; and they loved not their lives unto the death.

12 Therefore rejoice, ye heavens, and ye that dwell in them. Woe to the inhabitants of the earth and of the sea! for the devil is come down unto you, having great wrath, because he knoweth that he hath but a short time.

13 And when the dragon saw that he was cast unto the earth, he persecuted the woman which brought forth the man child.

14 And to the woman were given two wings of a great eagle, that she might fly into the wilderness, into her place, where she is nourished for a time, and times, and half a time, from the face of the serpent.

15 And the serpent cast out of his mouth water as a flood after the woman, that he might cause her to be carried away of the flood.

16 And the earth helped the woman, and the earth opened her mouth, and swallowed up the flood which the dragon cast out of his mouth.

17 And the dragon was wroth with the woman, and went to make war with the remnant of her seed, which keep the commandments of God, and have the testimony of Jesus Christ.

battle will be no dress rehearsal or sham encounter; it will be mortal conflict. But Satan, already defeated at Calvary, is no match for **Michael and his angels**.

Neither was their place found any more in heaven. The weaker foe will be permanently dislodged, never to regain access to heaven. Doubtless, Christ foresaw this in Luke 10:17-18. Satan's forceful eviction from heaven is a chief cause of the Great Tribulation. The three steps in Satan's ultimate doom are in 12:9; 20:3; and 20:10.

9. Twice it is stated that **Satan . . . was cast out,** and once that **his angels were cast out with him.** Now he will be identified to the full. First, he is **the great dragon.** Here power and cruelty are to the fore. Second, as **that old serpent, called the Devil,** he is the master of cunning, as with Eve in Eden. The added characterization, **old** (some versions have "ancient" or "original"), directly relates him to Genesis 3. In the Greek **Devil** conveys the force of slanderer or false accuser. Recall his blasphemous insinuations concerning God in tempting Eve. **Satan** means the adversary or opposer. All these attributes are employed toward the one great objective of all his activities, namely, to deceive the entire world.

10-12. In the Apocalypse, when earth mourns (cf. 18:11; 19:1), heaven rejoices, an indication of how out of tune with heaven the earth is. The **loud voice . . . in heaven** is not identified, but the message is filled with good news. The consummation of God's gracious purposes for His own draws nearer. Satan is called **the accuser of our brethren,** and he is tirelessly at his occupation (cf. Job 1:11; 2:5; Zech 3:1; Lk 22:31; see also I Jn 2:1 with its implications). The godly of all ages have been the target of his slanders. Surely, the 144,000 and the godly Gentiles (cf. ch. 7), with other redeemed ones of that time, will be especially the objects of his unbounded fury for his expulsion from heaven.

The manner of the victory of the godly over Satan, different from the victory of Michael and his angels, will be threefold: **the blood of the Lamb** (their justification before God on that basis), **the word of their testimony** (faithful witness) to the work and grace of God, and their willingness to be martyred (**loved not their lives**) for their faith. No wonder heaven is called upon to **rejoice.** No earth-originated faith could accomplish this. But a warning is sounded. **Woe to the inhabiters of the earth and of the sea** (heaven now being inviolate without the sinister presence of Satan and his own), in view of the increased wrath of the devil **because he knoweth that he hath but a short** time.

13-17. Verses 7-12 explain why the woman had to flee and why Satan is so furious on earth. In short, verse 13 resumes the thread of thought in verse 6. If further proof were needed, it is to be found in a comparison of the notations of time in verses 6 and 14. They treat of the same time, namely, the Great Tribulation; the 1,260 days are identical with the three and a half years. (Note: for purposes of computation, the Bible reckons a year as 360 days.) Throughout the account it is clear that the objective of the hatred of the dragon is the woman, Israel. What he could not accomplish at the birth of Christ, i.e., the extermination of the Saviour, he now seeks to compensate for by the persecution of Israel (vs. 13) and the remnant of her descendants (vs. 17).

But as the Lord undertook for Israel at the incarnation, so He does now. **The wings of a great eagle** are known for their strength; here they represent God's enablement of the godly in Israel (perhaps the result of the witness of the 144,000 among them also). In Exodus 19:4 God indicated to Israel that He had borne them on eagles' wings and had brought them into the wilderness from the hostile Egyptians. Here He will grant them eagles' wings to flee from Jerusalem to the wilderness to escape the deadly venom of their archenemy Satan. His past faithfulness is a pledge of His fidelity in the then present hour. **She is**

nourished for a time. Nourishment (same as in vs. 6) will be afforded her in her extremity. Since the eagles' wings are intended to be understood symbolically in Exodus and in this passage, they may refer to friendly persons and nations who will espouse the cause of Israel.

And the serpent cast out of his mouth water as a flood. Satan does not relinquish his evil schemes so easily. In a final desperate thrust, he now tries to engulf the godly in Israel as by a **flood.** Continuing the symbolism, this may refer to Satan's activating hostile nations on earth against the Jews. Again, he will be foiled by the alertness and activities of those who come to Israel's aid. Defeated repeatedly, Satan's rage will be unbounded. His goal now is to annihilate **the remnant of her seed** who remained in Jerusalem. That they are redeemed ones is manifest from the characterization of them in the last words of the chapter.

C. The Beast from the Sea. 13:1-10.

The apostle continues the delineation of the chief participants of the end time in this chapter, adding two more to those given in chapter 12. A study of Daniel 7; 9; and 11 is essential to the understanding of this vital chapter of the Apocalypse.

13:1. In 19:20 the two beasts of this chapter are designated as the **beast** and the **false prophet.** With the **dragon** (vs. 2), they form a horrendous trio of evil. The beasts are the chief wicked instruments of Satan. Here is the culmination of the world's desire for the amalgamation and merger of political and religious power, a combination of church and state. The Roman Beast and the Antichrist (man of sin of II Thess 2:3) will fulfill the longing of the ungodly.

The better manuscripts read "he stood," instead of **I stood** in verse 1. It is still the dragon spoken of in chapter 12. He stands **upon the sand of the sea** in order to motivate the rise of the beast from the sea. The verse first gives the origin of the beast and then offers a general description of his appearance. In Scripture, **the sea** represents multitudes of nations in tumult and unrest (cf. 17:15; 20:8; Ps 2:1). Interpreters of the Revelation differ as to the identity of the two beasts of this chapter. Some hold that the first beast (vss. 1-10) is the Antichrist, a political leader; and the second beast (vss. 11-18) is an apostate Jew, a religious leader (cf. F. C. Ottman, op. cit., p. 321ff.). Others maintain that the first beast is the Roman Beast, a political leader; and the second beast is the False Prophet or Antichrist (cf. *New Scofield Reference Bible*, p. 1364, fn. 2; H. A. Ironside, op. cit., pp. 219-252). As the commentary proceeds, it will be seen that this writer holds to the latter view.

The first beast represents the revived Roman Empire (vs. 3), the ten toes of Daniel 2, which have not been historically fulfilled. So united with Satan is this beast-like leader that what is written of Satan in 12:3 is here ascribed to the political leader (cf. Dan 7:8).

2. This verse throws much light on Daniel 7:1-12. There the first beast was a lion (eagles' wings are added to bring out added truth), namely, Babylon; the second was a bear, that is, Medo-Persia; the third was a leopard (birds' wings and heads are included to set forth additional truths), i.e., Greece. The fourth beast is not likened to any known animal in nature; hence, it is called the nondescript. Now it is clear why the fourth beast is not named, because there is no beast that combines the features of a **leopard, bear,** and **lion.** But the revived Roman Empire will incorporate the features of the preceding three empires. Ancient Rome boasted that no matter how many powers she subjugated in her conquests, she could always assimilate them into her hegemony. That political power is being emphasized here is certain from the mention of **his power, and his seat** (i.e., the whole earth), **and great authority.**

CHAPTER 13

AND I stood upon the sand of the sea, and saw a beast rise up out of the sea, having seven heads and ten horns, and upon his horns ten crowns, and upon his heads the name of blasphemy.

2 And the beast which I saw was like unto a leopard, and his feet were as the *feet* of a bear, and his mouth as the mouth of a lion: and the dragon gave him his power, and his seat, and great authority.

3 And I saw one of his heads as it were wounded to death; and his deadly wound was healed: and all the world wondered after the beast.

3. His deadly wound was healed. Rome did suffer political decline. The city of Rome fell in A.D. 476, and to this hour the Roman Empire has ceased to exist. But it will rise again, as this chapter reveals. Since World War II and Churchill's statement concerning the United States of Europe, there have been strong currents to build a confederation of nations in Europe as a sort of buffer between the superpowers of the East and West. Ten kingdoms will arise in western Europe (cf. 17:12). The ancient Roman Empire never existed in this form. It will represent a strong attempt to centralize political and economic power (17:13). The ruler over the federated kingdoms will be the "little horn" of Daniel 7:8 (cf. also Dan 9:27). The first beast of chapter 13 is the "little horn" (signifying political power) of Daniel 7:24-25. **All the world wondered after the beast.** Because the turn of events will be beyond normal expectation, the whole world will be astounded and, feeling there is the exhibition of supernatural power, will give their allegiance to the beast. Their wonder will turn to worship, because the world has not witnessed such a sight as the revived Roman Empire. Once more Satan will attempt to usurp God's place.

4 And they worshipped the dragon which gave power unto the beast: and they worshipped the beast, saying, Who is like unto the beast? who is able to make war with him?

4. And they worshiped the dragon which gave power unto the beast. Realizing that the political leader is exercising **power** delegated from Satan, the world will turn to worship the source of that authority. In doing so, they ascribe omnipotence and invincibility to the beast. The insolent questions are to be answered in 19:11-16.

5 And there was given unto him a mouth speaking great things and blasphemies; and power was given unto him to continue forty and two months.

5. Notice that here, and in verse 7, the words **given unto him** occur four times. All is under the permissive direction of God, as with Job and Satan long ago (cf. Job 1-2). Only **great things and blasphemies** issue from the mouth of this beast (also vs. 1, **name of blasphemy;** cf. Dan 7:8, 11, 20, 25). This latter part of the Tribulation Period, called the Great Tribulation (cf. 7:14), is so important that it is referred to explicitly by days (12:6), years (12:14), and **months** (here).

6 And he opened his mouth in blasphemy against God, to blaspheme his name, and his tabernacle, and them that dwell in heaven.

6. By definition, **blasphemy** is irreverent speech against God; but this beast is not satisfied with maligning God and His blessed character. He includes, as well, all the saints who are with the Lord in heaven. How could he have failed to realize the importance of the great event of the Rapture of the church?

7 And it was given unto him to make war with the saints, and to overcome them: and power was given him over all kindreds, and tongues, and nations.

7. As Daniel had prophesied (cf. 7:21-22), this vile political leader was permitted **to make war with the saints** still living on earth. Notice the wide range of his authority; in verse 15 he is enabled to kill all who do not worship his image.

8 And all that dwell upon the earth shall worship him, whose names are not written in the book of life of the Lamb slain from the foundation of the world.

8. With the display of such unprecedented power, it is easy to see how **all that dwell upon the earth** (cf. 3:10; 13:12) will be quick to enlist themselves as worshippers of him. The times of the Gentiles began with man-worship (cf. Nebuchadnezzar in Dan 3); and they will end the same way, as is clearly stated here. Only those who have trusted Christ as Saviour, whose names are eternally recorded **in the book of life of the Lamb,** will refuse the beast the worship that belongs only to God. If occurrences foretold here seem incredulous, let it be remembered that the deification of Roman emperors in the past is well-attested in history. They assumed divine titles, commanded divine honors, and built temples for the worship of themselves.

9 If any man have an ear, let him hear.
10 He that leadeth into captivity shall go into captivity: he that killeth with the sword must be killed with the sword. Here is the patience and the faith of the saints.

9-10. The sway of the beast will be worldwide; so the call to **hear** is similarly broad. Retributive justice will be experienced in that day. In that day, the godly on earth, especially the remnant in Israel, are called upon to refrain from employing the **sword** (carnal weapons; cf. the three witnesses in Dan 3). God's **saints** must have **patience,** thus exhibiting their sole **faith** in God.

D. The Beast from the Earth. 13:11-18.

The first beast comes from the sea, hence, it is a Gentile; the second has his origin from the earth (or land) or the Land of

Promise. As indicated earlier in this chapter, those who identify this beast with the Antichrist (which is the position of this writer) claim the second beast is an apostate Jew. Is this conclusion regarding his national origin a compelling one? It is true that Jews would not accept a non-Jew, as their Messiah, and history witnesses that they have received some scores of false Messiahs already (cf. Jn 5:43; Acts 5:36-37). But the portrayal of the Antichrist in Daniel 11:36-45; Zechariah 11:15-17; Matthew 24:15-28; John 5:43; II Thessalonians 2:1-12; and here in Revelation is such that the one called "the man of sin" is not likely to be compelled by truth as to his national origin, any more than he adheres to the facts in claiming to be God Himself (cf. II Thess 2:4). Falsehood is one of the staples of his stock in trade. Thus, he will arise from the Land of Promise and will falsely claim to be of the nation of promise and the promised Messiah.

11. Like Satan, this **beast,** the third member of the evil trio of the Tribulation Period, traffics in counterfeiting. He has **horns like a lamb;** Satan's agents are able to pass themselves off as messengers of light (cf. II Cor 11:13-15). F. W. Grant (cf. *The Numerical Bible,* in loco) has suggested that this beast seeks to imitate the kingly and prophetic ministries of Christ. **Spake as a dragon.** But his speech betrays him as a tool of Satan; he pretends meekness and humility as a lamb, but in actuality is a masterpiece of the devil. He is stationed in Jerusalem (cf. II Thess 2:4); but he owes his position and power to the first beast, who resides in Rome (cf. Dan 11:38-39, especially the words "god of forces" and "strange god"). With the military help of his superior, he can command universal compliance with his demands.

12. As stated, **the first beast** is willing to sponsor the Antichrist (he is also **the false prophet,** cf. 19:20), with the understanding that the coadjutor direct all **worship** to the first beast. What a singular stroke of Satan that all this transpires at the focal point of the world's three monotheistic religions, namely, in Jerusalem.

13. Because God never sent a prophet of His without proper attestation with miracles (cf. Moses and Elijah as examples), Satan must counterfeit this feature also in order to carry through the greatest deception of the ages. Notice that the miracles are characterized as **great wonders,** and one is specified (**fire come down from heaven**) which could deceive men into thinking that the Antichrist has power even in heaven.

14. It is known that a lackey will often overdo his role. So the Antichrist, in working his **miracles,** commands that **an image** (idol) **to the beast** be made for universal homage. Christ referred to this in Matthew 24:15. It is the ultimate in man's search to be like God. Satan tried it; those at the Tower of Babel attempted it; now the Antichrist puts the finishing touches to the gruesome blasphemy (cf. Mt 24:24-25; II Thess 2:9-10).

15. And he had power to give life unto the image of the beast. Even more, God permits a power which is not seen elsewhere in Scripture. The Antichrist wants to make the deception as strong as possible. So the image is given breath to speak, to command worship, and to mete out capital punishment to those who refuse adoration of the idol. When political power and man's religion are so wedded, Satan is indeed the master of ceremonies.

16-17. All is despotic tyranny without consideration for divine or human rights. It is one thing to suffer social ostracism, political deprivation, or religious persecution; but to link idolatrous worship with economic deprivation is a master stroke of Satan. Boycott is a potent use of force. In order to obtain the elements for livelihood, it will be necessary for everyone to be branded in a visible place **in their right hand, or in their foreheads** with the mark of the beast, either his **name . . . or the number of his name** given in verse 18.

11 And I beheld another beast coming up out of the earth; and he had two horns like a lamb, and he spake as a dragon.

12 And he exerciseth all the power of the first beast before him, and causeth the earth and them which dwell therein to worship the first beast, whose deadly wound was healed.

13 And he doeth great wonders, so that he maketh fire come down from heaven on the earth in the sight of men,

14 And deceiveth them that dwell on the earth by *the means of* those miracles which he had power to do in the sight of the beast; saying to them that dwell on the earth, that they should make an image to the beast, which had the wound by a sword, and did live.

15 And he had power to give life unto the image of the beast, that the image of the beast should both speak, and cause that as many as would not worship the image of the beast should be killed.

16 And he causeth all, both small and great, rich and poor, free and bond, to receive a mark in their right hand, or in their foreheads:

17 And that no man might buy or sell, save he that had the mark, or the name of the beast, or the number of his name.

18 Here is wisdom. Let him that hath understanding count the number of the beast: for it is the number of a man; and his number *is* Six hundred threescore *and* six.

18. His number is Six hundred threescore and six. It is almost impossible to list the number of suggestions for 666; they range all the way from Nero in ancient Rome to persons in this day. Probably the most that can be gleaned is that since seven is the biblical number of completion, six, which falls short of it, is man's failure at its worst. Man's worship of man is, indeed, spiritual insanity to the highest degree.

E. The Lamb and a Remnant on Mount Zion. 14:1-5.

Chapter 14 is the sequel and God's answer to the wickedness of the persons in chapter 13. God intervenes in grace and judgment. As stated earlier, chapters 12-14 form a series of their own and are placed between the trumpet and vial judgments, intending to emphasize the individuals who are prominent in the end time. R. H. Charles claims: "The entire chapter is *proleptic* in character. That is, the orderly development of future events as set forth in the successive visions is here . . . abandoned, and all the coming judgments from xvi. 17 to xx. 7-10, are summarized in xiv. 6-11, 14, 18-20" (*The Revelation of St. John*, II, p. 1).

CHAPTER 14

AND I looked, and, lo, a Lamb stood on the mount Sion, and with him an hundred forty *and* four thousand, having his Father's name written in their foreheads.

2 And I heard a voice from heaven, as the voice of many waters, and as the voice of a great thunder: and I heard the voice of harpers harping with their harps:

3 And they sung as it were a new song before the throne, and before the four beasts, and the elders: and no man could learn that song but the hundred *and* forty *and* four thousand, which were redeemed from the earth.

4 These are they which were not defiled with women; for they are virgins. These are they which follow the Lamb whithersoever he goeth. These were redeemed from among men, *being* the firstfruits unto God and to the Lamb.

5 And in their mouth was found no guile: for they are without fault before the throne of God.

14:1-5. And, lo, a Lamb stood on the mount Zion. All the persons mentioned in verse 1 have appeared before the reader earlier in the book. The **Lamb** is Christ, so designated by John as the favorite appellation for the Saviour. **A hundred forty and four thousand, having his Father's name written in their foreheads.** The Father needs no explanation. The 144,000 are undoubtedly those of chapter 7, the godly witnesses during the Tribulation, sealed and marked out for God. **Mount Zion,** is the literal city of David, entirely consistent with the godly remnant for Israel.

The scene in verses 2 and 3 changes to **heaven,** from which comes forth a remarkable **voice** which sounds like **many waters, . . . great thunder: and . . . harps.** Who are the harpists and singers? By elimination, it is evident that they are not the four living creatures, nor the elders, nor the 144,000 who had need to learn the song. The singing was done before the three already-named groups. Ottman (op. cit., p. 339) suggests that they may be those who are martyred under the rampages of the beast. This proposal is as good as any other, because details for ascertaining the identity of these godly ones are general.

First, they are noted for their testimony; in their witness they were not ashamed to bear the name of their God (when puny, wicked man was claiming divine prerogatives) on **their foreheads.** Second, they kept themselves separated from the defilement of the world. The **virgins** of the AV (Gr *parthenoi*) is a correct, literal translation; but the connotation is misleading. There is no intent to advocate celibacy over against marriage (cf. Heb 13:4), but only to emphasize their chastity in life as virgins are. They have kept themselves from the idolatry so blatantly fostered by the Roman **beast** and the **false prophet** (ch. 13). Repeatedly in the Old Testament, idolatry is likened to fornication and adultery (cf. the book of Hosea for an extended example). Third, they have chosen the highest fellowship in the universe; they are constantly in the company of the spotless Lamb of God. Fourth, they are honored to be first fruits to God and Christ. The Lord Jesus is the first fruits in resurrection (cf. I Cor 15:20); the church is the "firstfruits of his creatures" (cf. Jas 1:18); here are the first fruits of the coming kingdom age (cf. Ironside, op. cit., p. 256). Finally, in a day of wholesale falsehood and deception perpetrated by Satan and the Antichrist, these will keep themselves unblemished (not sinlessly perfect) by avoiding all lying.

F. The Angel with the Eternal Gospel. 14:6-7.

6 And I saw another angel fly in the midst of heaven, having the everlasting

6-7. In the next seven verses of the chapter, three angels with different announcements are introduced. If voices are silenced

gospel to preach unto them that dwell on the earth, and to every nation, and kindred, and tongue, and people,

7 Saying with a loud voice, Fear God, and give glory to him; for the hour of his judgment is come: and worship him that made heaven, and earth, and the sea, and the fountains of waters.

on earth by devilish agents, God is not thwarted in His purposes to send forth His message to needy men. Gaebelein (op. cit., p. 87) and Ottman (op. cit., pp. 344-346) maintain that a literal angel is not in view here, but witnesses during the Tribulation Period who preach the gospel of the kingdom, that is, preparation by repentance for the coming of Messiah. The passage indicates nothing concerning the gospel of the kingdom (as John the Baptist preached it and the apostles as well before the crucifixion of Christ), but rather speaks of an eternal gospel. Nor is there basis for assuming that the angel represents witnesses during the Tribulation Period. Moreover, this is not the gospel preached during the church age for the purpose of gathering out a bride for the Redeemer. It is specifically "good news" (Gr *euangelion*) of an eternal character intended for those who inhabit (not the same Greek word as in 3:10) the earth from all nations. Verse 7 seems to contradict the concept of good news, for the contents appear to announce only judgment. This is a hasty conclusion. The dual appeal in the message is to reverence God, giving Him glory, and to worship Him as Creator of the universe (cf. Rom 1:20 with Ps 19:1-6). This gospel proclaims that God is the sovereign Maker, and blessing is only in obedience to His will. It is **everlasting** because it has abided through the ages. It is in effect a call to come from the worship of the Roman Beast, a creature, to God the Creator. But the element of good news is definitely here: the declaration of soon-coming **judgment** is made in view of the time still granted to turn to God. If the die were already cast, then the element of good tidings would be absent; but such is not the case here.

G. Babylon's Fall Announced. 14:8.

8 And there followed another angel, saying, Babylon is fallen, is fallen, that great city, because she made all nations drink of the wine of the wrath of her fornication.

8. **Babylon is fallen.** The second angel has an announcement unrelated to any offer of grace. In broad outlines, it states the fall of Babylon the Great, who has seduced all the nations with her immorality. Drawing on many Old Testament passages, the reader is able to transfer the figure of physical uncleanness to that of spiritual defection from God to idolatry (cf. Jer 51:8). Interpreters differ on the identity of this Babylon. There is a general consensus that the Babylon introduced here proleptically is that of chapters 17-18. R. H. Charles maintains that the fall of Rome is announced (op. cit., II, p. 14). Scott holds: "But what is before us now is the mystic Babylon, that huge system of spiritual adultery and corruption which holds sway over the whole prophetic scene. It is scarcely possible to conceive of a huge system of wickedness eagerly embraced by the nations once called Christian. It will nevertheless be so. Babylon here is the full development of the state of things under the Thyatiran condition of the Church (chap. 2:18-23)" (op. cit., p. 299). R. C. H. Lenski (*The Interpretation of St. John's Revelation*, p. 432), after designating the first beast of chapter 13 as "antichristian power" and the second beast as "antichristian propaganda," feels that "All those who do this constitute Babylon, *the antichristian world city or empire*, which is named 'Babylon the Great' after the Old Testament Babylon . . . the great enemy of Israel, Jerusalem, Zion." He elucidates further by way of summary (p. 434): "The preterists regard Babylon as a reference to pagan Rome alone; the historical interpreters as a reference to papal Rome; the futurists as a reference to the capital of the antichrist who is yet to come, either Rome or Jerusalem. Babylon . . . is *the entire antichristian* empire throughout the whole New Testament Era. Both pagan and also papal Rome would then be included." Since the mention of Babylon here is admittedly anticipatory to the detailed treatment in chapters 17-18, the entire subject will be dealt with at that place. This is the first mention of Babylon in the Revelation, but already her widespread influence and her wickedness are clearly set forth.

9 And the third angel followed them, saying with a loud voice, If any man worship the beast and his image, and receive *his* mark in his forehead, or in his hand,

10 The same shall drink of the wine of the wrath of God, which is poured out without mixture into the cup of his indignation; and he shall be tormented with fire and brimstone in the presence of the holy angels, and in the presence of the Lamb:

11 And the smoke of their torment ascendeth up for ever and ever: and they have no rest day nor night, who worship the beast and his image, and whosoever receiveth the mark of his name.

12 Here is the patience of the saints: here *are* they that keep the commandments of God, and the faith of Jesus.

13 And I heard a voice from heaven saying unto me, Write, Blessed *are* the dead which die in the Lord from henceforth: Yea, saith the Spirit, that they may rest from their labours; and their works do follow them.

14 And I looked, and behold a white cloud, and upon the cloud *one* sat like unto the Son of man, having on his head a golden crown, and in his hand a sharp sickle.

15 And another angel came out of the temple, crying with a loud voice to him that sat on the cloud, Thrust in thy sickle, and reap: for the time is come for thee to reap; for the harvest of the earth is ripe.

16 And he that sat on the cloud thrust in his sickle on the earth; and the earth was reaped.

17 And another angel came out of the temple which is in heaven, he also having a sharp sickle.

18 And another angel came out from the altar, which had power over fire; and cried with a loud cry to him that had the sharp sickle, saying, Thrust in thy sharp sickle, and gather the clusters of the vine of the earth; for her grapes are fully ripe.

19 And the angel thrust in his sickle

H. Judgment on Worshipers of the Beast. 14:9-12.

9-12. They have no rest day nor night. The third angel has a message of unrelieved judgment. Both verses 9 and 11 designate the objects of the divine visitation to be the worshipers of the beast and his image and the recipients of his mark. The judgment depicted is horrendous indeed. It will be intoxication with the unmitigated **wine of the wrath of God,** torment **in the presence of the holy angels, and . . . the Lamb,** and unceasing restlessness, namely, eternal **torment.** Those who hold that the unrepentant wicked will be ultimately restored to bliss (they are known as restitutionists) find no confirmation in verse 11. In fact, the words used in the New Testament for the eternality of God are found here (Gr *eis aiōnas aiōnōn*; cf. 22:11 also). Their trust in the power and authority of the beasts (ch. 13) will not stand them in good stead in that coming day. Finally, as in 13:10 (last clause), perseverance and faith will be called for in the days when believers on earth are undergoing affliction and trials (W. Hendriksen, *More Than Conquerors*, pp. 186-187).

I. The Blessed Dead. 14:13.

13. Blessed are the dead which die in the Lord. It must be remembered that not all will share the experience of the 144,000 sealed ones. Many will suffer martyrdom in the period under consideration. Although it is always blessed to die in Christ (cf. Phil 1:21 with II Cor 5:6, 8), it will be peculiarly so in this time; for the blessedness will be near. Too, to die will be preferable to living, because they will be spared the remaining portion of the Great Tribulation. The alternatives will be either worship the beast and live, or resist him and be killed to die in the Lord. God will take full notice of their faithful works; their rewards are assured.

J. Reaping Earth's Sin. 14:14-20.

14-16. God's judgment of the ungodly on earth is now delineated under two figures: **the harvest of the earth** (vss. 14-16) and **the vine of the earth** (vss. 17-20). Careful consideration of the scene will reveal that the Great White Throne judgment is not in view here, but rather the judgment of the nations of Matthew 25:31-46, the tribunal at the end of Israel's age referred to in Matthew 13:40. The Judge is the Lord Jesus Christ, as the portrayal indicates (cf. 1:13; 10:1). The designation "a (not "the," as in the AV, for the Greek text does not have the definite article) son of man" (NASB) identifies Him with the events of Daniel 7:13-14, and all the references to Son of man in the New Testament. The evidence of John 5:22, 27, is weighty. The **golden crown** speaks of His royal prerogative to judge. The **sharp sickle** can only remind us of reaping activity. The sickle is mentioned only twelve times in the Bible, and seven occurrences are in this portion of the Revelation (cf. W. R. Newell, *The Book of the Revelation*, p. 228).

Notice that the angel of verse 15 proceeds from the **temple** in heaven, another indication that the age is related to Israel, not the church. Apparently, the angel conveys the signal of God the Father to the Son of Man to begin the work of harvesting. No sooner is the will of the Father declared than the Son performs it with obedience and power. The earth was ripe for judgment.

17-20. In verse 17 another angel is seen leaving the temple in heaven, and he is equipped with a sharp sickle. A caution is needed at this point. Some students of the book claim the reaping is of both saints and sinners. Surely, the entire context of the book would lead the reader to see "that this Revelation scene is purely one of *judgment*" (Newell, op. cit., p. 229). In Scripture, **fire** is a common figure for purifying by fire as a means of judgment (cf. 20:10, 15, the lake of fire; God in His purity is likened to fire, Heb 12:29). The reference to altar has already been found in 6:9 and 8:3. Again, an angel conveys the

into the earth, and gathered the vine of the earth, and cast *it* into the great winepress of the wrath of God.

20 And the winepress was trodden without the city, and blood came out of the winepress, even unto the horse bridles, by the space of a thousand *and* six hundred furlongs.

message to begin the work of judgment; but this time it is not a reaping of a harvest, but the gathering of the vintage into the winepress of the wrath of God. Just as the **harvest** was **ripe** (vs. 15), so the **vine** (vs. 19). Though the judgment in this chapter includes both Jews and Gentiles, verse 20 indicates where the center of events will be. The city is unquestionably Jerusalem. Instead of grape juice flowing from the winepress, it will be the blood of men. But the fearful picture is even more explicit; **and blood came out . . . unto the horse bridles**, estimated to be about four feet. Yet more, this river will stretch for two hundred miles (Gr *stadia*, i.e., the total of 1,600 *stadia* or furlongs). This is the distance from Bozrah (Edom) in the south (cf. Isa 63:1-6) to the Valley of Jehoshaphat at Jerusalem (cf. Joel 3:1-3, 9-14) to Megiddo in the north (cf. Rev 16:14, 16). It is generally conceived that **Armageddon** will be a battle; this stems from the translation in AV, RSV, NIV, and NEB of "battle" for the Greek *polemos*. This gives too simplified a picture of the conflict. The rendering in ASV and NASB of **war** is correct (cf. H. G. Liddell and R. Scott, *A Greek-English Lexicon*, Vol. II, col. 2), because the first meaning of the word is war. Thus, Armageddon is not an isolated battle, but part of a larger picture of encounters in different parts of the land. The name of the war is called Armageddon, because the terrain there is better suited for warfare than anywhere else in the land. However, the climax of the War of Armageddon is at Jerusalem (cf. Zech 14:1-5, 12-15) with the visible appearing of the Lord Jesus.

XI. THE SEVEN VIAL JUDGMENTS. 15:1-16:21.

A. Preparation for the Judgments. 15:1-8.

The chapters now under consideration form a literary unit that follows logically after chapter 11, giving the third series of the septenary judgments of God. Why need there be three series of these judgments? They evidently follow the pattern of warfare as men know it: first, the initial encounter; then, the intensive assaults; finally, the consummating blows. Undoubtedly, the vial judgments take place in the Great Tribulation in its last stages. The implication seems to be that they will transpire in a very brief period of time. They will be both rapid and severe. The Revelation does deal repeatedly with judgment, but not exclusively so; for the final prospect is bright indeed.

1. Seven angels with seven plagues. 15:1.

15:1. In 10:7 it was stated that the mystery of God was finished, but no details were given. They are now seen in chapters 15-16. To introduce these fearful judgments called **plagues**, John is shown a **sign in heaven** (cf. 12:1, 3), which is characterized as **great and marvelous**. The concept of greatness is here, because in scope and intensity there has been nothing previous to this to compare with them. The idea of marvel is introduced, because the inflictions will excite amazement and wonder. These plagues are marked as last, because in them the wrath of God is fully spent upon ungodly mankind.

2. The godly victors. 15:2-4.

2-4. Before judgment falls, John saw a company of victors with harps of God. They are the ones mentioned in 14:2-3. Why the reference to **a sea of glass?** These who have triumphed over the beast (cf. ch. 13) have paid the supreme price and have entered into bliss. The sea may have reference to the bronze laver in the tabernacle of Moses and the bronze sea in the Temple. Here its waters are not disturbed any longer; it is that which is unalterable and firm. Purity is indicated here, but it has been attained at the cost of trials under the beasts (so the fire). As in 14:2, they have harps to accompany their praise to God.

CHAPTER 15

AND I saw another sign in heaven, great and marvellous, seven angels having the seven last plagues; for in them is filled up the wrath of God.

2 And I saw as it were a sea of glass mingled with fire: and them that had gotten the victory over the beast, and over his image, and over his mark, *and* over the number of his name, stand on the sea of glass, having the harps of God.

3 And they sing the song of Moses the servant of God, and the song of the Lamb, saying, Great and marvellous *are* thy works, Lord God Almighty; just

and true *are* thy ways, thou King of saints.

4 Who shall not fear thee, O Lord, and glorify thy name? for *thou* only *art* holy: for all nations shall come and worship before thee; for thy judgments are made manifest.

5 And after that I looked, and, behold, the temple of the tabernacle of the testimony in heaven was opened:

6 And the seven angels came out of the temple, having the seven plagues, clothed in pure and white linen, and having their breasts girded with golden girdles.

7 And one of the four beasts gave unto the seven angels seven golden vials full of the wrath of God, who liveth for ever and ever.

8 And the temple was filled with smoke from the glory of God, and from his power; and no man was able to enter into the temple, till the seven plagues of the seven angels were fulfilled.

CHAPTER 16

AND I heard a great voice out of the temple saying to the seven angels, Go your ways, and pour out the vials of the wrath of God upon the earth.

2 And the first went, and poured out his vial upon the earth; and there fell a noisome and grievous sore upon the

The theme of their harp playing is the song of Moses and the song of the Lamb (cf. Ex 15:1-18). What do these songs have in common? They both celebrate redemption and deliverance. In the first case, it was God's physical release of Israel from Egyptian servitude through the Passover Lamb; here it is liberation spiritually from the bondage of Satan and his agents through "Christ our passover" (cf. I Cor 5:7). In their singing they extol God's great and marvelous works, His righteousness and truth, His sovereignty over the nations, His holiness, and ultimate reception of universal worship through the disclosure of His righteous dealings.

3. *The temple in heaven. 15:5-8.*

5-8. In order to underscore the holiness of God in His righteous judgments on sinful man, John is granted a view **of the tabernacle of the testimony in heaven.** Ready to perform their duties, **the seven angels** (cf. vs. 1) proceed from the temple fully equipped for their tasks. They are priests as well as angels, because their attire of **pure and white linen** and **golden girdles** marks them as God's priests (cf. 1:13 of Christ). Seiss has aptly indicated (op. cit., p. 370): "They appear as priests, because they come for the sacrificing of a great sacrifice to the offended holiness and justice of God."

Notice how all is pervaded with gold, an emblem of the holiness and righteousness of God (cf., e.g., the cherubim of gold over the ark of the covenant in the Holy of Holies). One of the four living creatures at the command of God presented the **seven angels seven golden vials full of the wrath of God.** The **vials** of the AV (derived from the Gr *phialē*) is too weak to convey the idea that the receptacles were bowls, like those used for pouring libations in the Old Testament. (Cf. Zech 12:2 where the translation "cup" is inadequate; "bowl" is intended from the Heb word employed.)

The **smoke** filling the temple came from the incense of the priests' censers (cf. 8:5). Two attributes of God are now underscored: His **power** and His **glory.** Where God's glory is manifested, man is unable to abide the sight. So it was with Moses (cf. Ex 40:34-35) and in Solomon's day (cf. I Kgs 8:10-11). So solemn and grave is the action that **no man was able to enter into the temple, till the seven plagues of the seven angels were fulfilled** (the chapter beginning and ending with the concept of finality and irretrievability).

B. Six Vials of Judgment. 16:1-12.

1. *Command to empty the vials. 16:1.*

16:1. It is quite instructive to compare the plagues of this chapter with those recorded of Egypt in Exodus 7:20-12:30. The **great voice out of the temple** is evidently that of God who authorizes the fearful final pouring out of His **wrath** on all nature and man. Notice throughout the chapter how the ultimate objects of the visitations are men (cf. vss. 2-3, 8-11, 14, 21). Moreover, the increased intensity and range of the plagues are easily seen in this final series of God's dealings in judgment with ungodly men. In previous judgments it was common to learn that the inflictions touched a third part of the earth; the areas were limited. But no such restriction is recorded concerning the vial judgments. There is an unmistakable finality about all the transactions. The pouring out indicates an overflowing measure without stint or reserve. **Vials** or bowls of the temple employed for purposes of grace are now used for judgment.

2. *Plague on the earth. 16:2.*

2. **The first went . . . and there fell a noisome and grievous sore.** The first visitation reminds at once of the sixth plague in Egypt (cf. Ex 9:10-11). The contents of this **vial** were loath-

men which had the mark of the beast, and *upon* them which worshipped his image.

3 And the second angel poured out his vial upon the sea; and it became as the blood of a dead *man:* and every living soul died in the sea.

4 And the third angel poured out his vial upon the rivers and fountains of waters; and they became blood.

5 And I heard the angel of the waters say, Thou art righteous, O Lord, which art, and wast, and shalt be, because thou hast judged thus.
6 For they have shed the blood of saints and prophets, and thou hast given them blood to drink; for they are worthy.
7 And I heard another out of the altar say, Even so, Lord God Almighty, true and righteous *are* thy judgments.

8 And the fourth angel poured out his vial upon the sun; and power was given unto him to scorch men with fire.
9 And men were scorched with great heat, and blasphemed the name of God, which hath power over these plagues: and they repented not to give him glory.

10 And the fifth angel poured out his vial upon the seat of the beast; and his kingdom was full of darkness; and they gnawed their tongues for pain,
11 And blasphemed the God of heaven because of their pains and their sores, and repented not of their deeds.

some, unsightly, and malignant (cancerous) sores, which afflicted all **men which had the mark of the beast, and upon them which worshiped his image.** Ulcers will outwardly reveal their inner corrupt moral and spiritual condition. Since no symbolism is indicated, the plague must be considered as literal as the corresponding judgment on Egypt of old.

3. Plague on the sea. 16:3.

3. Every living soul died in the sea. Under the second trumpet (cf. 8:8) only a third of the sea was involved; here the picture is of the whole sea. Some expositors prefer to understand the verse symbolically, but it is confusing to shift from literal to symbolic without some basis for doing so. Water, a source for the sustenance of life, is here made an agent of death. So it was with the water of Egypt in the first plague of Exodus 7:17-25. All marine life died immediately. Coagulated **blood** is death-dealing and emits an unbearable stench.

4. Plague on the rivers and waters. 16:4-7.

4. The rivers and fountains of waters . . . became blood. Again, the similarity with the plagues of Egypt is undeniable (cf. Ex 7:19-21). In 8:10-11, under the third trumpet, only a third of the waters was involved; here, there is no limitation whatever. Water, an indispensable commodity for life, is once more the object of God's judgment, as in verse 3.

5-7. It is interesting that so many subjects in the Apocalypse have their special angel. **The angel of the waters** has authority over this area of nature, and the judgment strikes his sphere of rule. But he justifies the judgment of God. God is as righteous in judgment as He is in blessing. Because men have heedlessly poured out the blood of God's servants, He operates on the principle of what the Latins termed *lex talionis,* the law of recompense in kind. It is attested to in numerous portions of Scripture. They deserved exactly the visitation God brought on them. Even **the altar,** symbolically to be sure, vindicates the wrath of God. Evidently, there is a connection here with the altar of burnt offering in 6:9-11.

5. Plague on the sun. 16:8-9.

8-9. William Barclay has correctly stated (op. cit., p. 165): "In Hebrew thought every natural force—the wind, the sun, the rain, the waters—had its directing angel. These angels were the ministering servants of God, placed by God in charge of various departments of nature in the universe." With the fourth trumpet judgment (8:12) the sun was darkened, along with the moon and the stars; but only a third part of them was affected. Now, only the sun is touched, but in a totally different way. Instead of the sun being darkened, its rays were heightened in heat **to scorch men with fire.** The **sun,** the source of such blessing and essential to plant and animate life on earth, is now a medium of God's wrath. **They repented not to give him glory.** Three times in this awesome chapter (vss. 9, 11, 21), it is declared that men reacted to their punishments with blasphemy against God and not with repentance. These judgments are not remedial or corrective in effect, but they reveal the corruption of those undergoing them all the more. The judgments are punitive; the dwellers on earth are incorrigible. Men who will not be drawn by God's love will not be attracted by His wrath, either.

6. Plague on the beast's seat. 16:10-11.

10-11. The fifth vial judgment is poured out **upon the seat of the beast.** W. Hendriksen (op. cit., p. 195) writes: "This throne of the beast is the center of anti-christian government. Cf. Nah 3:1; Hab 3:12-14." Adhering to an undeviating symbolism often results in generalities which leave the student of the book with few certainties of a specific nature. **The seat of the**

beast (evidently, the first one of ch. 13) is Rome, his capital city. This plague is God's unequivocal answer to the insolent question of 13:4; that arrogance is further met with finality in 19:19-21. The **darkness** is another allusion to the plague of darkness in Egypt (cf. Ex 10:21-23). **Gnawed their tongues for pain** is the only expression of its kind in the Bible and speaks of the most intense agony and suffering. There is no repentance, but rather a further degradation. In verse 9 the name of God was blasphemed; here He Himself is derogated. Is there any question as to whether there will be repentance in hell?

7. *Plague on the Euphrates River. 16:12.*

12 And the sixth angel poured out his vial upon the great river Eū-phrā′tēs; and the water thereof was dried up, that the way of the kings of the east might be prepared.

12. The great river Euphrates. This important river has been introduced earlier in connection with the sixth trumpet judgment. As noticed earlier, the river is 1,800 miles long, from 3 to 1,200 yards wide, from ten to thirty feet deep (cf. Seiss, in loco). History records what hindrance the river has been to military operations. Reminding one of the drying up of the Red Sea, this river will be dried up to allow passage of inimical forces into the Middle East area for the final conflict. The kings of the east referred to (Gr *apo anatolēsēliou*, lit., from the sunrising) are the Asiatic lands like China, Japan, and the nations of the Far East.

C. Preview of Armageddon. 16:13-16.

13 And I saw three unclean spirits like frogs *come* out of the mouth of the dragon, and out of the mouth of the beast, and out of the mouth of the false prophet.
14 For they are the spirits of devils, working miracles, *which* go forth unto the kings of the earth and of the whole world, to gather them to the battle of that great day of God Almighty.

13-14. Verses 13-16 are evidently an integral portion of that which transpires at the pouring out of the sixth vial. When verses 12 and 14 are compared, the conclusion that the action of the first verse is related to that of the second as cause and effect is compelling. Notice the evil trio—**dragon, beast** (13:1), and **false prophet** (13:11)—are out in full force, ready for mortal combat for the final consummation. All three are characterized by the same uncleanness and corruption. The **three unclean spirits** are not said to be frogs, but **like frogs.** They are further explicated as **spirits of devils working miracles,** but of such magnitude and convincing quality that they are capable of motivating and energizing, not only the kings of the Far East but **the kings of the earth and of the whole world.** What is the objective of this vast enterprise? Simply stated, it is the summoning of all of them to the War of Armageddon, captioned here as **the battle of that great day of God Almighty.** The mind can scarcely conjure up or fathom the scene and its vast implications for the world of mankind (cf. for further light I Kgs 22:19-38; Ps 2:1-3; Joel 3:9-11; Mt 24:24-25; I Tim 4:1).

15 ¶Behold, I come as a thief. Blessed *is* he that watcheth, and keepeth his garments, lest he walk naked, and they see his shame.

15. Before a concluding word about this unparalleled conflict, the Spirit indicates a parenthetical word in verse 15. It is Christ speaking and declaring that He will **come as a thief.** Nowhere in Scripture are believers warned against the coming of the Saviour as a thief. In II Thessalonians 5:1-8, notice how carefully the Spirit distinguishes believers ("children of the day") from unbelievers ("children . . . of night"). Because of the intensification of demon activity, just stated in verses 13-14, the godly of the Tribulation are warned against defilement from the widespread corruption, issuing in their shame.

16 And he gathered them together into a place called in the Hebrew tongue Är-ma-gĕd′don.

16. And he gathered them together. There is no question that this verse carries on the thought of verse 14, because the same verb (Gr *sunagō*, to gather together) is found in both contexts. **A place called . . . Armageddon.** The additional information of verse 16 is that the place of the conflict is named in Hebrew, *Har-Magedon.* The conflict has been foretold in various passages in the Old and New Testament (e.g., Ps 2:1-3), but now the geographical location is added. The more popular name is Armageddon (the Greek noun has a rough-breathing equivalent to the letter *H*). *Har* is a well-known common noun for "mountain." **Megiddo** comes from a verb, meaning "to slaughter" (Heb *gadad;* its basic concept is to cut off, cf. KB,

Lexicon, s.v.). The site was the great battleground of the Old Testament. It was the place of the victory of Deborah and Barak (cf. Jud 5:19); Josiah met his death before Pharaoh Nechoh in the Valley of Megiddo (cf. II Chr 35:22-24). Since the subject will be treated more fully in chapter 19 below, it will suffice to state that Megiddo is the mountain overlooking the Valley of Esdraelon (Gr for Jezreel), the great plain in the northern part of Palestine. Napoleon I is credited with having said of Megiddo: "What an excellent place into which all the armies of the world could be maneuvered."

D. The Seventh Vial. 16:17-21.

1. Plague on the air. 16:17-18.

17 And the seventh angel poured out his vial into the air; and there came a great voice out of the temple of heaven, from the throne, saying, It is done.

17. When the seventh vial was poured out, it was **into the air**. This is the domain of Satan as prince of the power of the air (cf. Eph 2:2). Though cast out of the highest heaven in his pre-time rebellion against God (cf. Isa 14; Ezk 28), Satan has had access to the second heaven (cf. Eph 6:12; Rev 12:7). When cast down to the earth (12:8-9) after his complete expulsion from the heavenly spheres, he could have limited activity over the air immediately above the earth. All this is with the authorization of God and in keeping with His holiness, **out of the temple of heaven, from the throne.** The voice from heaven utters one word (Gr *Gegonen*, **It is done**), which declares that all God's plagues have thus been exhausted. By contrast, the word of the Lord Jesus on Calvary (Gr *Tetelestai*, "It is finished" in Jn 19:30) has all the blessedness of a finished redemption for sinful men.

18 And there were voices, and thunders, and lightnings; and there was a great earthquake, such as was not since men were upon the earth, so mighty an earthquake, *and* so great.

18. Since all judgments are completed with this vial plague, it is valid to see the remaining chapters concerning God's visitations (i.e., chs. 17-19) as summarized here. When the seventh vial has done its intended work, all judgment will have been accomplished. Verse 18 easily reminds one of similar expressions in 4:5; 8:5; 11:19 (cf. W. Lincoln, II, p. 86). Always, there is an intensification of the trials and agonies. Yet more, an **earthquake, such as was not since men were upon the earth,** occurs. It is characterized by the words **great** (twice) and **mighty.** Its scope, mark well, is unlimited.

2. The fall of Babylon. 16:19.

19 And the great city was divided into three parts, and the cities of the nations fell: and great Băb′y-lon came in remembrance before God, to give unto her the cup of the wine of the fierceness of his wrath.

19. The cities of the nations fell. This is the second mention of judgment on **great Babylon** (cf. 14:8). It is remarkable in that two chapters (17-18) are occupied at length with Babylon and her fate. In chapters 14 and 16 the city is described as **great**; the same is true of the portrayal in the following chapters. Expositors are divided as to whether **the great city** in verse 19 is the same as the **Babylon** of the same verse. They are definitely divided also as to the identity of Babylon, now mentioned for the third time in the book. One group of commentators equate **the great city** and **Babylon** with Jerusalem (cf. 11:8); others, with Rome (whether political, religious, or papal). When reliable expositors differ so widely, it is presumptuous to be dogmatic. Furthermore, all would greatly desire more details before making a final decision. As the reader of this commentary has already noticed, this writer prefers, as a principle in both extra-biblical and biblical writings, to understand the subject under discussion as staying the same unless there is clear basis for the introduction of another element. If the great city is other than Babylon, whose identity will be dealt with at length in he following two chapters, why is Babylon introduced here without further introduction? Moreover, the catastrophe will strike not only Babylon the Great, but the metropolises of the nations. J. A. Seiss sees a gradation in severity of judgment and doom: Jerusalem was two-thirds destroyed; the cities of the nations

20 And every island fled away, and the mountains were not found.
21 And there fell upon men a great hail out of heaven, *every stone* about the weight of a talent: and men blasphemed God because of the plague of the hail; for the plague thereof was exceeding great.

completely; finally, Babylon with the greatest onus of sin and guilt, suffering most poignantly (cf. op. cit., in loco).

3. *Nature in upheaval. 16:20-21.*

20-21. Verse 20 must not be made to teach the destruction of matter, which is neither biblical nor scientific. All that need be understood is that there will be a shifting and upheaval in the island and mountainous areas. Whether or not these changes are to be directly related to the earthquake mentioned in verse 18 (so H. Alford, op. cit., in loco), it is not essential to determine.

And there fell upon men a great hail out of heaven. Hailstones have already been mentioned in the Apocalypse, but not like those that are indicated here. Their magnitude and severity are emphasized. Each hailstone weighed about one hundred pounds. It takes little imagination to picture the destruction these would cause to houses and structures and, most agonizing of all, upon human beings, especially children. Does man fathom the depth of his alienation from God and earnestly seek to be reconciled to his Judge? The more severe the judgment, the greater the blasphemy.

XII. JUDGMENT ON BABYLON. 17:1-18:24.

A. Doom of the Harlot. 17:1-18.

That the theme of Babylon is an important one in the Revelation can be seen from the fact that the Spirit of God devotes two chapters in this essential book of prophecy to the subject. From Genesis 10:10 (Babel is from the Akkadian *Bab-ilu,* gate of God), which is the first mention, to 18:21, which is the last reference, this subject of biblical revelation and prophecy is given extraordinary prominence. The student of the Word of God is wise to stress what the Spirit underscores. All the so-called major prophets (Isa-Dan) have important disclosures concerning Babylon). Isaiah refers to the city some thirteen times, Ezekiel, some seventeen times, but Jeremiah most of all with one hundred and sixty-eight citations. In the Revelation, besides chapters 17-18 which are entirely devoted to the subject of Babylon, the first occurrence of the word is in 14:8, the second, in 16:19. Both passages briefly indicate the fall and doom of Babylon. In a true sense, chapters 17-18 are an elaboration of 16:19.

Because so much has been written on the matter and so many differing views have been advanced, it is helpful to clear up certain positions at the outset. First, no student of the Bible, theological or otherwise, doubts that in historic times there has existed a literal city called Babylon on the plain of Shinar (cf. Gen 10:10).

Second, large numbers of reverent students of Scripture understand Genesis 11 as teaching the inception of idolatry at Babel (Heb from *balal,* to confound, from which Eng *"babble"* is derived) and the confusion of men's languages (cf. Gen 11:7, 9).

Third, the city of Babylon was the seat of a great empire, dominating the ancient world from the fall of the Assyrian Empire with the capture of Nineveh in 612 B.C. until the demise of the Babylonian Empire through the capture of Babylon by Cyrus of Persia in 536 B.C. The city continued until about A.D. 100 (cf. *ZPEB,* I, pp. 439-448, art. by D. J. Wiseman). Today there are a number of cities, like Hilla, which have utilized the sun-dried and kiln-baked bricks of the ancient city to build new walls, houses, and dams (cf. Isa 13:19-22; Jer 50:23-26; 51: 24-26; *Wycliffe Bible Encyclopedia,* I, pp. 187-190, art. by F. E. Young).

Fourth, it is well-known how idolatrous Babylon has been; both biblical and secular sources leave no room for doubt in the matter.

Fifth, it must be kept in mind that Revelation 17-18 is not dealing with literal, historical Babylon, so that the question of the rebuilding of a future Babylon is irrelevant in the interpretation of these chapters. Proof is forthcoming from verse 9 (Babylon was situated in a plain, not on seven mountains); 18:24 (such a wide range could not be true of literal Babylon); and especially verses 5 and 7 (**MYSTERY**, which indicates something hitherto not made known, but now revealed, cf., Rom 16:25-26; Eph 3:4-7. The import of the word is that a sense other than literal is to be understood; cf. 11:8 where Gr *pneumatikōs* is translated **spiritually** in the AV and "mystically" in the NASB).

CHAPTER 17

AND there came one of the seven angels which had the seven vials, and talked with me, saying unto me, Come hither; I will shew unto thee the judgment of the great whore that sitteth upon many waters:

1. Her position. 17:1.

17:1. John the apostle/prophet is invited by **one of the seven angels, which had the seven vials** (bowl judgments), to witness the judgment of (1) **the great whore** and (2) her position (**that sitteth upon many waters**). The reader is not left to his own resources in the interpretation of this important chapter, but he must scrutinize every clue given. Harlotry is amply explained in passages of the Old and New Testaments (cf. Ezk 16:15; Hos 1-3; Jas 4:4; II Pet 2:14). Both adultery and harlotry are sins of physical immorality which are made to represent spiritual defection and apostasy. Wherein her harlotry consists is explained in verses 4-6 of this chapter and in 18:3-5, among other passages. **The many waters** upon which she sits are interpreted explicitly (stated in vs. 15) as **peoples** and **nations**.

2. Her sin. 17:2.

2 With whom the kings of the earth have committed fornication, and the inhabitants of the earth have been made drunk with the wine of her fornication.

2. Her dominant position over the nations could be political or spiritual. Those interpreters who believe the domination is political identify the harlot as the Roman Empire. Those expositors who consider the rule and subjugation are spiritual/religious, among whom the present writer is one, identify her as a corrupted papal Rome, with the inclusion under her hegemony of all systems and sects which are basically anti-Christian, not excluding apostate Christendom. So grievous were her acts of immorality (mentioned twice in this verse) that the results are likened to a drunken stupor.

3. Her seat on the scarlet beast. 17:3.

3 So he carried me away in the spirit into the wilderness: and I saw a woman sit upon a scarlet coloured beast, full of names of blasphemy, having seven heads and ten horns.

3. In verse 1 the position of the harlot was described in its wide scope, all nations and peoples; here she is seen sitting (dominating and domineering) **upon a scarlet-colored beast.** Is the harlot the same person as this woman? Context and logic demand an affirmative reply. The meaning of her riding the scarlet beast, replete with **names of blasphemy,** and **having seven heads and ten horns,** is that the religious system is controlling and subjugating the political power (cf. 13:1 for the connection with the beast from the sea). In short, at Rome the political power is under the absolute sway of the religious system. This was revealed supernaturally to John by the inditing Spirit. The **scarlet color** indicates the glory and splendor of the political power, but it cannot hinder the suppressive control of the religious leaders.

4. Her clothing. 17:4.

4. Some six elements are introduced to demonstrate the wealth, luxury, and extravagance of the harlot. But all is utilized toward the one end—her uncleanness and immorality (cf. 18:9-19 for a picture of extensive wealth). The **golden cup** here is related to the enticements spoken of in verse 2.

4 And the woman was arrayed in purple and scarlet colour, and decked with gold and precious stones and pearls, having a golden cup in her hand full of abominations and filthiness of her fornication:

5. Her name. 17:5.

5. There is no mistaking her identity, for her **name** is written **upon her forehead.** Roman harlots in their brazenness wore a label with their names on their foreheads (cf. R. H. Charles, op.

5 And upon her forehead was a name written, MYSTERY, BABYLON THE GREAT, THE MOTHER OF HARLOTS

AND ABOMINATIONS OF THE EARTH.

cit., II, p. 65). The name contains a mystery, a disclosed secret for this time. Her widespread influence is underscored by the repeated references to her greatness. She is the source of godlessness and idolatrous practices throughout the world (cf. for a lengthy sketch, H. A. Ironside, op. cit., pp. 285-302). In the Greek text of the United Bible Societies her name is in normal lower case except for the *B* in "**Babylon**"; AV, ASV, NASB, and NIV use the upper case. What is the intended meaning of this verse? It is stating that literal Babylon of old is typical, symbolical of religious Babylon (cf. Jer 50:38; 51:7). For a parallel usage, see 11:8 of Revelation. MYSTERY, BABYLON is in fact the mystery of iniquity in its final form (cf. II Thess 2:7).

6. *Her bloodthirstiness.* 17:6.

6 And I saw the woman drunken with the blood of the saints, and with the blood of the martyrs of Jesus: and when I saw her, I wondered with great admiration.

6. To this point one may feel that the harlot system is guilty of atrocities in the moral and spiritual realms alone. But she is culpable of much more. The blood of the saints and witnesses for Christ has stained her hands. In 18:24, the climax of the two chapters on Babylon, she is again charged with being **drunken with the blood of the saints** who have been martyred on earth. Thus, the harlot cannot be literal Babylon nor papal Rome alone; it must comprehend all godless systems, consummating at last in this hideous figure. Here it is professing Christendom with her motley followers persecuting and slaying the saints of God; it is not now pagan emperors as in the days of the early Christian centuries. No wonder John was amazed. He was astonished that the professing church of his day could become so degenerate in a coming day.

7. *The mystery of the woman.* 17:7.

7 And the angel said unto me, Wherefore didst thou marvel? I will tell thee the mystery of the woman, and of the beast that carrieth her, which hath seven heads and ten horns.

7. What the Apostle John saw still needed to be explained to him in its details. Since the disclosure was granted him, not to perplex but to instruct him, the angel (cf. vs. 1) promises to clarify **the mystery of the woman, and of the beast.**

8. *Identity of the beast.* 17:8-13.

8 The beast that thou sawest was, and is not; and shall ascend out of the bottomless pit, and go into perdition: and they that dwell on the earth shall wonder, whose names were not written in the book of life from the foundation of the world, when they behold the beast that was, and is not, and yet is.

8. There is a consensus among interpreters that the **beast** (the same as 13:1) is the Roman Empire: its historic appearance, its long disappearance, and its future reappearance. As to its motivation in reappearing, it will come from **the bottomless pit,** devilish empowering, and finally find its end in perdition. The ancient Roman Empire was destroyed in its imperial form in John's time in A.D. 476. That political power is not in existence today. But Satan will see that it is revived to fulfill his purpose. Notice that, as to his human origin, the beast is from the nations (cf. 13:10); but as to its supporting power, it is a satanic revival. Such a resurrection of the old Roman Empire, almost endlessly scoffed at by unbelievers and even many believers, will amaze the earth-dwellers, who are plainly stated to be unbelievers. John **wondered** (vs. 6); the world of a coming day also **shall wonder.**

9 And here *is* the mind which hath wisdom. The seven heads are seven mountains, on which the woman sitteth.

9. It is immediately stated that it takes God's **wisdom** to understand the disclosure. The **seven mountains** (or hills) are proof that mystical Babylon cannot be ancient, literal Babylon, which was situated in a plain and not on mountains. However, it is known that Rome is built on seven hills (e.g., the Quirinal, Capitoline, Palatine); classical writers familiarly spoke of "the city of seven hills" (cf. Charles, op. cit., II, p. 69).

10 And there are seven kings: five are fallen, and one is, *and* the other is not yet come; and when he cometh, he must continue a short space.

10. If there has been a variety of views to this point, it has surely been increased to confusion in verses 10-11. Who are the **seven kings?** The text plainly states that five are past, one is present, and the last is future. R. H. Charles (op. cit., II, p. 69; followed by Barclay, op. cit., p. 181 et al) names them as Augustus, Tiberius, Caligula, Claudius, and Nero, then Vespa-

sian, and finally Titus. The reign of the last is held to be a short one, thus fulfilling the text. However, much discussion has been expended on the state of the original manuscript and a Nero *redivivus* (resurrected) for 17:8, 11, 14. It is poor exegesis to find fault with the condition of the original Greek when the interpretation does not fit the exigencies of the case. History will verify that in Roman rule six types of government are to be found: kings, consuls, dictators, decemvirs, and military tribunes; the sixth is the imperial form, which was in existence when John was on Patmos. The seventh type is the Roman Empire under a new head (cf. 13:1). This government will have ten kingdoms (cf. Dan 2 and 7), never equalled before and all subject to the beast (cf. Gaebelein, in loco; also Ottman, pp. 309-311), whose tenure of office will be brief.

11 And the beast that was, and is not, even he is the eighth, and is of the seven, and goeth into perdition.

11. The human revival of the empire (cf. 13:1) in the Tribulation Period will be followed by the hellish revival (cf. vs. 8), which is so complete in itself as to be called an **eighth** feature (eight is the number of resurrection). There will be an organic connection between the last two stages of the Roman Beast in his sovereignty. He will be one of the seven, but distinct enough to be considered the eighth (cf. Dan 7:7-8, 23-26).

12 And the ten horns which thou sawest are ten kings, which have received no kingdom as yet; but receive power as kings one hour with the beast.

12. The **ten kings** kingdom (cf. 13:1) is the form in which the Roman Empire will be revived. It has never existed thus before (cf. Dan chs. 2 and 7). Verses 10 and 12 both stress the shortness of this rule: **a short space** and for **one hour**. The precise time has been given earlier in the book more than once.

13 These have one mind, and shall give their power and strength unto the beast.

13. The confederated kings of the revived Roman Empire will have **one mind** and purpose: total subservience to the Roman Beast.

9. The victory of the Lamb. 17:14-18.

14 These shall make war with the Lamb, and the Lamb shall overcome them: for he is Lord of lords, and King of kings: and they that are with him *are* called, and chosen, and faithful.

14. What is the goal of the confederated powers? Nothing less than **war with the Lamb.** Recall the war in heaven between Michael and his angels (cf. 12:7ff.) and the dragon and his angels—quite an unequal combat. But here the balance of power is infinitely against the ungodly armies. **The Lamb shall overcome them . . . and they that are with him are called, and chosen, and faithful.** The issue is never in doubt; it is victory for the Lamb and His redeemed (not angels) in heaven, as can be discerned from the three adjectives that conclude the verse. Notice the honorific, well-deserved title of the Lamb. Here, by anticipation, is another preview of Armageddon, yet to be fully set forth in 19:14-21.

15 And he saith unto me, The waters which thou sawest, where the whore sitteth, are peoples, and multitudes, and nations, and tongues.

15. Peoples, and multitudes, and nations, and tongues. In an apocalyptic book with rich symbolism and a multiplicity of participants, there is need for occasional explanation; so this verse identifies the waters of verse 1.

16 And the ten horns which thou sawest upon the beast, these shall hate the whore, and shall make her desolate and naked, and shall eat her flesh, and burn her with fire.

16. Here illumination is given concerning the **beast** and his underlings who were dominated by the apostate system (vs. 3). In some way not stated, the subservient ones turn the tables and vent their hatred against the harlot. So thoroughgoing will their judgment on her be, that it must be expressed by four concepts: desolation, nakedness, consumption (cannibalism), and burning (cf. with the fate of Jezebel of old, II Kgs 9:30-37).

17 For God hath put in their hearts to fulfil his will, and to agree, and give their kingdom unto the beast, until the words of God shall be fulfilled.

17. Overruling all the feelings of the enemies of the harlot, it will ultimately be God who directs them to execute His judgment on her. All He has given in the prophetic word **shall be fulfilled.**

18 And the woman which thou sawest is that great city, which reigneth over the kings of the earth.

18. The **woman** of this verse is the same as the one in verse 16, and indeed throughout the chapter. This verse is not an unnecessary addendum to the chapter. It reveals (1) that the woman (harlot), though a colossal system of apostasy and idolatry, is also to be thought of in terms of **that great city** of her headquarters, namely, Rome; and (2) that her reign is worldwide (**over the kings of the earth**).

B. Fall of Babylon. 18:1-24.

This chapter carries on the subject of God's judgment on Babylon. Strangely enough, some writers have understood chapter 17 to speak of one person and system, and chapter 18 to deal with a totally different individual. The Scriptures use multiple figures, and the careful student will have sufficient clues to come to the proper understanding of each passage. Since the church is the Bride of Christ and a city, the New Jerusalem (cf. 21:9-10), there is no valid reason to deny that the harlot Babylon *is* a city (cf. 18:10). It is proper to think of Babylon in chapter 17 as a vast religious (ecclesiastical) system (cf. vss. 2, 4, 6), and also in chapter 18 as a huge interlocking commercial system (cf. vss. 3, 11-17). The present chapter pictures the doom of so-called Christian civilization in its social and commercial aspects. Civilization ever since the time of Cain has followed a path apart from God. See Genesis 4:16-24: cities, property, music, skilled art, polygamy, violence, and murder (cf. W. R. Newell, op. cit., pp. 281-285, for his masterful treatment of "The Character of Commerce" and his inclusion of the equally able, extended quotation from J. A. Seiss, *The Apocalypse*). Since the Hebrew ephah is emblematic of commerce, compare Zechariah 5:5-11 (esp. vs. 11: "in the land of Shinar") with the present chapter in the Revelation.

1. The glorious angel. 18:1.

CHAPTER 18

AND after these things I saw another angel come down from heaven, having great power; and the earth was lightened with his glory.

1. Although this **angel** is introduced by the general word **another,** he is not one connected with the bowls of wrath mentioned in 17:1. Two features indicate his importance: (1) **great power** (there are degrees of authority among the angels), and (2) the ability to illuminate **the earth . . . with his glory.** The strong probability is that Christ is meant here as in 8:3 and 10:1. In the first reference He is the Angel-Priest; in the second He is the Angel-Redeemer; here He is the Angel-Avenger of His own.

2. Babylon's fall realized. 18:2.

2 And he cried mightily with a strong voice, saying, Babylon the great is fallen, is fallen, and is become the habitation of devils, and the hold of every foul spirit, and a cage of every unclean and hateful bird.

2. **Babylon the great is fallen.** In 14:8 the announcement of the fall of Babylon was proleptic; similarly, in 16:19 the statement was brief and anticipatory. But here God's purpose concerning her is actualized. True, in chapter 17 Babylon's doom is brought about by the ten kingdoms and the Roman Beast (the political power); here, her downfall is seen as issuing directly from Christ. Surely, there is no discrepancy here; for 17:17 clearly states God's sovereign, righteous employment of the human factors in accomplishing His purpose. Just as idolatry came into the human sphere in Genesis 11 with Babylon of old (there is no record of idolatry before the flood of Noah), so it will have its hideous, unclean, hateful consummation in the Babylonish system of the future. **The hold of every foul spirit, and a cage.** All Satan's evil agencies will congregate in her. There will be no freedom there, as words used for "prison" are mentioned twice (NASB). It is a veritable cesspool of corruption.

3. Babylon's guilt. 18:3.

3 For all nations have drunk of the wine of the wrath of her fornication, and the kings of the earth have committed fornication with her, and the merchants of the earth are waxed rich through the abundance of her delicacies.

3. **All nations.** Again, the universality of her sway is underscored as in 17:1, 2, 15, 18. All the nations are pointed out here as the subjects of her deceptions and seductions. Godless religion knows how to capture the attention of the unwary world by display, ritual, easy means of redemption, and vast amounts of wealth. **The kings of the earth** referred to now are not those included in the ten kingdom confederation; these kings are outside that conglomerate. An additional element is introduced by the **merchants** (Gr *emporoi*, to which the Eng emporium is related) **of the earth,** and their riches and wealth are set forth (along with sensuality). There is a commercial side to MYSTERY, BABYLON.

4 And I heard another voice from heaven, saying, Come out of her, my people, that ye be not partakers of her sins, and that ye receive not of her plagues.
5 For her sins have reached unto heaven, and God hath remembered her iniquities.

6 Reward her even as she rewarded you, and double unto her double according to her works: in the cup which she hath filled fill to her double.
7 How much she hath glorified herself, and lived deliciously, so much torment and sorrow give her: for she saith in her heart, I sit a queen, and am no widow, and shall see no sorrow.
8 Therefore shall her plagues come in one day, death, and mourning, and famine; and she shall be utterly burned with fire: for strong is the Lord God who judgeth her.

9 And the kings of the earth, who have committed fornication and lived deliciously with her, shall bewail her, and lament for her, when they shall see the smoke of her burning,
10 Standing afar off for the fear of her torment, saying, Alas, alas that great city Babylon, that mighty city! for in one hour is thy judgment come.

11 And the merchants of the earth shall weep and mourn over her; for no man buyeth their merchandise any more:
12 The merchandise of gold, and silver, and precious stones, and of pearls, and fine linen, and purple, and silk, and scarlet, and all thyine wood, and all manner vessels of ivory, and all manner vessels of most precious wood, and of brass, and iron, and marble,
13 And cinnamon, and odours, and ointments, and frankincense, and wine, and oil, and fine flour, and wheat, and beasts, and sheep, and horses, and chariots, and slaves, and souls of men.
14 And the fruits that thy soul lusted after are departed from thee, and all things which were dainty and goodly are departed from thee, and thou shalt find them no more at all.
15 The merchants of these things, which were made rich by her, shall

4. Call to flee the doomed city. 18:4-8.

4-5. The **voice** now is not that of the angel of verse 1. It is directed to God's people. Before judgment falls on the wicked (cf. Noah and his family, Gen 6:13-22; Lot and his daughters, Gen 19:12-22; and, as has been shown in this book, the church in the Rapture before the Tribulation Period, 4:1ff.), God mercifully warns His own in order to deliver them from the coming catastrophe. Thus, as far as the apostate system is concerned, the call is applicable at all times (cf. Heb 13:13). It will be all the more applicable in the time under consideration in this chapter. In short, both believing Jews and Gentiles will heed the warning and will escape the burning destruction.

Ancient, literal Babylon wanted to build a "tower" (ziggurat for their gods), as stated in Genesis 11:4. Here her mystical counterpart piled up her **sins . . . unto heaven,** an affront to the thrice holy God of heaven and earth. While it is indicated that **God hath remembered her iniquities,** it is not that He had forgotten them previously. It is the biblical way of stating that the hour of reckoning and judgment had arrived.

6-8. Double unto her double according to her works. Because Babylon's sins have accumulated over so long a period of time, and she has been impervious over the centuries to God's loving entreaties to repent, the Mosaic law of recompense in kind is doubled (cf. Ex 21:23-25). In the light of I Corinthians 6:2, the summons in verses 6-7 could well be addressed to the church. The root of Babylon's degeneration was her pride, self-security, godlessness, and glorification of wealth and luxury, all directed toward self-exaltation. The Lord God in His omnipotence will be her Judge (cf. Isa 47:9-11). The visitation is detailed in five particulars: **plagues, . . . death and mourning, and famine; and . . . fire.** All this will come upon her in **one day.**

5. The mourning of kings and merchants. 18:9-20.

9-10. In the verses under consideration (vss. 9-20), weeping and mourning are repeated as a theme in a sonata. First, **the kings of the earth,** who have the most to lose in any economic or commercial collapse, **shall bewail . . . and lament** inconsolably over the torment and demise of the wicked system, which has interlocking interests throughout the civilized world. They cry out woe upon the great and strong city, whose judgment has overtaken her. The **one day** of verse 8 is now **one hour,** a clear indication that mathematical precision is not intended. It will be in a very short time. Fair-weather friends that they are, the kings bewail Babylon's calamity, but stand at a distance lest they become involved in her misery and agony.

11-17a. The merchants, who are directly involved in day-by-day transactions with her, mourn over the economic collapse of that vast system with its many commercial ramifications. The cargoes include some twenty-eight distinct items. Here there is a combination of the religious with the commercial, for it begins with **gold** and ends with human lives (vs. 14). The list includes costly ornaments, costly raiment, costly furniture, costly perfumes, costly food, costly equipages, and men's souls and bodies (cf. W. Pettingill, *The Unveiling of Jesus Christ,* p. 80). The wealth of the world will be thrown into confusion and hopeless collapse.

stand afar off for the fear of her torment, weeping and wailing,

16 And saying, Alas, alas that great city, that was clothed in fine linen, and purple, and scarlet, and decked with gold, and precious stones, and pearls!

17 For in one hour so great riches is come to nought. And every shipmaster, and all the company in ships, and sailors, and as many as trade by sea, stood afar off,

18 And cried when they saw the smoke of her burning, saying, What *city is* like unto this great city!

19 And they cast dust on their heads, and cried, weeping and wailing, saying, Alas, alas that great city, wherein were made rich all that had ships in the sea by reason of her costliness! for in one hour is she made desolate.

20 Rejoice over her, *thou* heaven, and *ye* holy apostles and prophets; for God hath avenged you on her.

21 And a mighty angel took up a stone like a great millstone, and cast *it* into the sea, saying, Thus with violence shall that great city Babylon be thrown down, and shall be found no more at all.

22 And the voice of harpers, and musicians, and of pipers, and trumpeters, shall be heard no more at all in thee; and no craftsman, of whatsoever craft *he be*, shall be found any more in thee; and the sound of a millstone shall be heard no more at all in thee;

23 And the light of a candle shall shine no more at all in thee; and the voice of the bridegroom and of the bride shall be heard no more at all in thee: for thy merchants were the great men of the earth; for by thy sorceries were all nations deceived.

24 And in her was found the blood of prophets, and of saints, and of all that were slain upon the earth.

17b-19. Moreover, the fall of commercial Babylon has serious consequences for maritime projects, involving shipmasters, sailors, and passengers. All will be crippled **in one hour** (cf. vss. 17, 19). The losses will be irretrievable.

20. Rejoice over her, thou heaven. What a change is now before the reader. The scene is shifted to heaven and God's perspective. The dwellers there—"saints and apostles and prophets" (NASB), believers of every station—are summoned to rejoicing. Earth mourns, but heaven rejoices (cf. 19:1-6). This reveals how out of tune with heaven earth dwellers can be. When on their pilgrimage on earth, the saints suffered grievously at the hands of the apostate system; but now, in their hour of vindication, they exult in God's justice.

6. The finality of her doom. 18:21-23.

21-23. Her ruin is final, complete, and irreversible. The symbolism in verse 21 is related to Jeremiah 51:63-64, which bears out the impossibility of recovery from this judgment. Along with the passing of the city, there will be an end of music, crafts, housekeeping (**sound of a millstone**), illumination, and the joys of marriage. The cause of it all is her deception of all the nations with her religious sorcery, an activity promoted by demons and Satan. Included is the entire system of ungodliness from the beginning of man's sojourn on earth.

7. The reason for her fall. 18:24.

24. Any pity or compassion on her is misspent and misdirected, for she is worthy of all the misery and judgment God pours out on her. She is guilty of the blood of martyred **prophets, and of saints, and of all that were slain upon the earth.** This inclusive statement shows that more than one apostate organization is meant; it involves the totality of all of them, from man's appearance on earth until the coming of the Son of man to earth.

XIII. THE SUPPER OF THE LAMB AND THE SUPPER OF GOD. 19:1-21.

The events toward which the book of Revelation has steadily been leading are recorded here. Until the usurper on earth (the harlot) is judged, the bride (the church) is not made manifest. The harlot and the bride do not occupy the scene of action at the same time.

A. Alleluias in Heaven. 19:1-6.

19:1-2. It is after the doom of mystical Babylon (**after these things**—see the same Gr wording in 4:1), fully detailed in chapters 17-18, that the invitation to rejoice in 18:20 can be fulfilled. Those participating are indicated only as **much people (a great**

CHAPTER 19

AND after these things I heard a great voice of much people in heaven, saying, Alleluia; Salvation, and glory, and honour, and power, unto the Lord our God:

2 For true and righteous *are* his judgments: for he hath judged the great whore, which did corrupt the earth with her fornication, and hath avenged the blood of his servants at her hand.

3 And again they said, Alleluia. And her smoke rose up for ever and ever.

4 And the four and twenty elders and the four beasts fell down and worshipped God that sat on the throne, saying, Amen; Alleluia.
5 And a voice came out of the throne, saying, Praise our God, all ye his servants, and ye that fear him, both small and great.

6 And I heard as it were the voice of a great multitude, and as the voice of many waters, and as the voice of mighty thunderings, saying, Alleluia: for the Lord God omnipotent reigneth.

multitude in vs. 6). There is no profit in seeking to particularize here, when the designation is so broad. It is all the redeemed in heaven, including the twenty-four elders and the four living creatures (vs. 4). The rejoicing begins with the word **Alleluia**, which occurs four times in this chapter (vss. 1, 3, 4, 6). It is a transliterated (not translated) Hebrew word, found no other place in the New Testament. In fact, even in the Old Testament, especially in the book of Psalms, it is correctly translated "Praise the Lord!" It is thus interesting that four times in the Revelation the Hebrew word (actually two words) should be found. It is indeed a beautiful word known worldwide, which needs no translation. Augustine said that both the feeling and saying of the word incorporate all the blessedness of heaven (cf. J. A. Seiss, in loco). Earth knows much of blasphemy and vile vituperation against God and His blessed Name, but heaven gloriously rings with His praises. Three attributes of God are singled out for acclamation: **Salvation, and glory, and honor.** W. Barclay has well stated: "Each of these three great attributes of God should awaken its own response in the heart of man, and these responses taken together constitute real praise. The *salvation* of God should awaken the *gratitude* of man. The *glory* of God should awaken the *reverence* of man. The *power* of God is always exercised in the love of God, and should, therefore, awaken the *trust* of man. Gratitude, reverence, trust—these are the constituent elements of real praise" (op. cit., II, p. 218).

The attributes of truth and righteousness have been clearly witnessed in the judgment of the great harlot. The latter part of verse 2 could well apply to the martyrs, though the language is couched in the third person.

3. Apparently, the same company utter the second **Alleluia.** They give praise for the finality, the completeness, and eternal character of Babylon's judgment.

4. The reader is here immediately reminded of those who worship and praise God in chapter 4. They join the heavenly **Alleluia** chorus.

5. With so much praise and adoration filling the scene, one would not expect further summons to praise and extol God. But even after the third **Alleluia,** it must be stressed that God is worthy of nothing less than eternal **praise.** All God's bond servants, of whatever rank or position, **both small and great,** are included in the invitation to praise Him; for the word of invitation comes from the seat of God's government.

6. With this verse a crescendo appears to be reached, as the wording indicates. In his oratorio of "The Messiah," Handel has correctly caught the climax: "Hallelujah! for the Lord God omnipotent reigneth." This is the hour for which the church has prayed and longed, and all creation has groaned (cf. Rom 8:18-23). Before Christ assumes His rightful throne on earth, Babylon must be judged on earth and His marriage celebrated in heaven. The first is past (chs. 17-18); the second follows here. What was stated by way of anticipation in 11:15 is now realized.

B. The Marriage of the Lamb. 19:7-10.

Of all the provisions of God for man's well-being and joy on earth, marriage, God's first social institution, ranks second only to that of salvation. Both Old and New Testament give ample evidence of the importance of this symbolism. Hosea spoke of it from a traumatic experience in his own life (cf. Hos 2:19-20); Isaiah spoke glowingly of it (cf. Isa 54:5); Jeremiah dwelt on the theme (cf. Jer 3:14; 31:31-32); and Ezekiel portrayed it with fullness (cf. Ezk 16). The New Testament speaks of the marriage feast (cf. Mt 22:2), the bridal chamber and wedding garment (cf. Mt 22:10-11), the sons of the bridal chamber (cf. Mk 2:19), the bridegroom (cf. Mt 25:1; Mk 2:19), and the friends of the bridegroom (cf. Jn 3:29). Paul writes of the church as the

7 Let us be glad and rejoice, and give honour to him: for the marriage of the Lamb is come, and his wife hath made herself ready.

8 And to her was granted that she should be arrayed in fine linen, clean and white: for the fine linen is the righteousness of saints.

9 And he saith unto me, Write, Blessed *are* they which are called unto the marriage supper of the Lamb. And he saith unto me, These are the true sayings of God.

10 And I fell at his feet to worship him. And he said unto me, See *thou do it* not: I am thy fellowservant, and of thy brethren that have the testimony of Jesus: worship God: for the testimony of Jesus is the spirit of prophecy.

11 And I saw heaven opened, and behold a white horse; and he that sat upon him *was* called Faithful and True, and in righteousness he doth judge and make war.

betrothed virgin of Christ (cf. II Cor 11:2) and of the pattern of the relationship between husband and wife (cf. Eph 5:21-33; also Barclay, *The Revelation of John*, pp. 222-223).

7. The wording of verse 7 is unusual and must not be overlooked. In normal parlance the wedding is spoken of as the marriage of the bride, but here it is **the marriage of the Lamb.** And rightly so, for the chief joy is His. It takes place in heaven, and no details are given. Care is to be exercised in speaking of the relationship of Israel and the church with reference to marriage, so that biblical norms are not violated. Israel is the unfaithful, yet to be reclaimed, wife of the Lord in the Old Testament; the church is the bride of Christ the Lamb in the New Testament. Once the wife or bride is mentioned, there is no further reference in the book to elders as in verse 4.

8. For this glorious occasion the bride of necessity had to make herself ready. The preparation includes: (1) acceptance of the marriage offer of the Lamb, which is regeneration; (2) the desire to be properly clothed for the wedding; (3) a willingness to receive what is given her for the joyous event. When the bride clothes herself, it is with the finest of apparel. Her basic clothing is the garment of salvation, which she received at her acceptance of the Lamb's gracious offer of marriage (cf. Isa 61:10). Now, in addition to the initial clothing, she has **granted** to her (still all of grace) **fine linen, clean and white.** It is identified as the righteous acts (Gr is plural, *dikaiōmata*) of the saints. How has she obtained these? It is inescapable that the judgment seat of Christ has already been held in order to grant rewards to the saints for faithful service to Christ (cf. II Cor 5:10). What a recognition day that will be!

9. But another important element of every wedding is the guests, so John is instructed to indicate **Blessed are they which are called unto the marriage supper of the Lamb.** These are the friends of the Bridegroom (cf. Jn 3:29); the guests are seen in another figure as the virgins, the companions of the bride (cf. Ps 45:9, 14). They are probably all Old Testament saints. All others than the church are the guests at the marriage supper. Lest some reader consider these words to be too good to be true, the mediating angel (cf. 1:1) informs the apostle that the words are sure and certain; they come from God.

10. **I fell at his feet to worship him.** The disclosure of truth was so marvelous, and perhaps the appearance of the angel was so striking, that John was moved to worship at his feet. When John did this at Christ's feet (cf. 1:17), he received no rebuke, but was rather delivered from fear. But in this verse, and in 22: 8-9, the apostle is forbidden such worship; for no creature in heaven, on earth, or under the earth is permitted to receive man's worship. Men may receive honor and respect (cf. Rom 12:10; 13:7), but no creature may receive worship. Angels are servants on the basis of creation; believers are servants on the basis of redemption. All homage and worship belong to Jesus, to whom all prophecy points. The last sentence in verse 10 is one of the most important in all Scripture. **For the testimony of Jesus is the spirit of prophecy.** Plainly stated, it declares that the witness and testimony that are borne to Jesus are the motivating and underlying purpose of all prophecy. **Prophecy** is meant to convey an indispensable witness to Jesus.

C. The Visible Coming of Christ. 19:11-16.

11. **And I saw heaven opened.** Now heaven is opened to the gaze of John; he had seen it open several times before (cf. 4:1 et al), but never on such a sight as this (cf. Acts 1:11; esp. Rev 1:7). Here John sees the One with dyed garments from Bozrah of Isaiah's prophecy, the Righteous Branch and King of Jeremiah's prediction, the returning Shekinah Glory of Ezekiel's foretelling, the Stone cut out without hands of Daniel's announcement, the Lord coming with His saints of Zechariah's

prophecy, and the appearing of the Son of Man of the Saviour's own prophecy (cf. Mt 24:29, 30). The **white horse** symbolizes victory and triumph. He is **Faithful and True** in His character and every deed. Indeed, He is the mighty Warrior who will right the world's every ill (cf. Acts 17:31). **He doth judge and make war** under the same principle, that is, **righteousness.**

12 His eyes *were* as a flame of fire, and on his head *were* many crowns; and he had a name written, that no man knew, but he himself.

12. The description of His glorious Person continues. That **His eyes were as a flame of fire** indicates penetrating scrutinizing omniscience. On that blessed **head,** once crowned at Calvary for sinful men, **were many crowns.** His is supreme authority. Saints have crowns; He has **many crowns.** The Roman beast (cf. 13:1) has crowns also, but only because he assumes absolute authority. But how can one head have many crowns? They are in tiers, one above another, indicating highest majesty and authority. Many things have been divulged in the Apocalypse so far, and more will follow to the end of the book; but there are certain elements which must remain hidden from man (cf. Deut 29:29). From scriptural usage it is known that the **name written** indicates His own essential glory, which expresses the fullness of His divine nature.

13 And he *was* clothed with a vesture dipped in blood: and his name is called The Word of God.

13. The Redeemer does not come now to save, but to judge. **A vesture dipped in blood** points to the activity in Isaiah 63:1-6 (see vs. 15). The judgment of Christ will be exercised to the full. **His name is called The Word of God** and shows that He is the full expression (as a word is of the thought in the mind) of God, but now in judgment (cf. II Thess 1:7-10).

14 And the armies *which were* in heaven followed him upon white horses, clothed in fine linen, white and clean.

14. Who are **the armies . . . upon white horses, clothed in fine linen, white and clean?** Good men differ as to their identity. All are agreed that they are believers, redeemed ones; some even include the angels. It appears that they are, first, the church, second, the Tribulation saints, then the Old Testament saints. Jude 14-15 will then be fulfilled.

15 And out of his mouth goeth a sharp sword, that with it he should smite the nations: and he shall rule them with a rod of iron: and he treadeth the winepress of the fierceness and wrath of Almighty God.

15. The description continues, not merely to fill out the portrait, but to reveal the activity with which the Lord of glory is occupied. The **sharp sword** issuing from His mouth is undoubtedly the Word of God (cf. Isa 11:4; Heb 4:12), but specifically in judgment. **The nations,** the objects of His rule, will be ruled with **a rod of iron** (cf. Ps 2:9; Rev 12:5). The rule will be stern and inflexible, but always absolutely righteous. He has ample power to implement His every command. Besides the mention of the sword and rod of iron, there is now the figure of the winepress. Again, this is the figure of the vintage (cf. 14:19-20; Isa 63:1-6).

16 And he hath on *his* vesture and on his thigh a name written, KING OF KINGS, AND LORD OF LORDS.

16. In addition to the two names connected with the returning Lord Jesus (cf. vss. 12-13), there is another **on his vesture and on his thigh. KING OF KINGS, AND LORD OF LORDS.** It has been introduced already in 17:14, but in reverse order. It is His full majestic name in His glorious position relative to the earth, visible for all to read. Such a title was arrogantly assumed by men in the ancient Near East. Conquering kings allowed their subjugated, royal enemies to retain their former title in order to convey the idea that they, the victorious ones, were the highest and supreme above all. To be sure, this was empty boasting, but not so with the conquering Christ.

D. The Supper of God: Armageddon. 19:17-19.

17 And I saw an angel standing in the sun; and he cried with a loud voice, saying to all the fowls that fly in the midst of heaven, Come and gather yourselves together unto the supper of the great God;

17. Actually, the picture of Armageddon continues on through verse 21, but the account narrows down in verses 20-21 to the two principal offenders of the time, **the beast** and **the false prophet.** Although the record is not an extended one, it is the last treatment of the subject of Armageddon, the former two references (cf. 14:18-20 and 16:13-16) being anticipatory and on the whole general. One must not expect a recital of a war such as is found in extra-biblical works, because the objective in Scripture is quite different. The details of the war are given under the figure of a supper in contrast to the marriage supper of the

18 That ye may eat the flesh of kings, and the flesh of captains, and the flesh of mighty men, and the flesh of horses, and of them that sit on them, and the flesh of all *men, both* free and bond, both small and great.

Lamb. The invitation is addressed **to all the fowls that fly in the midst of heaven.** The vultures remind of Matthew 24:27-28, as well as Isaiah 34:2-6.

18. Notice the inclusiveness of those who are involved in the conflict: **kings, . . . captains, . . . mighty men, . . . horses, . . . them that sit on them, . . . all men, both free and bond, both small and great.** Five times the word **flesh** is found in this verse; a vast feast of carrion is envisaged. No wonder; for it takes place on an ideal battlefield, the most famous in the world. Among the battles fought there are: Sisera against Barak (cf. Jud 5:19-20); Gideon against the Midianites (cf. Jud 6:33-34); Saul and Jonathan against the Philistines (cf. I Sam 31); King Josiah against Pharaoh Nechoh (cf. II Kgs 23:20); on the western border Elijah contended with the prophets of Baal (I Kgs 18:39-40); Ahaziah died there (cf. II Kgs 9:27). It has been the scene of conflict from ancient times to modern days. The relevant Scripture passages are Psalm 2:1-3; Ezekiel 38-39; Joel 3:9-16; Zechariah 12:1-9; 14:1-4, besides others in the Old and New Testaments. In the Revelation, 9:13-18; 14:14-20; and 16:12-14, 16 have already prepared the way for the final treatment in this chapter. In view of the foregoing comments, it is difficult to understand how an able scholar can state: "Since Megiddo is not associated with any eschatological expectation, it is possible some corruption underlies this word" (cf. R. H. Charles, op. cit., II, p. 50). Another writer feels that "such a Mount does not appear elsewhere in Scripture or in other ancient literature" (cf. R. C. H. Lenski, op. cit., p. 479). Yet another comments: "Har-Magedon is the symbol of every battle in which, when the need is greatest and believers are oppressed, the Lord reveals his power in the interest of his distressed people and defeats the enemy" (cf. W. Hendriksen, op. cit., p. 96). Some men are driven to such extremes when they forsake the literal interpretation of prophecy.

19 And I saw the beast, and the kings of the earth, and their armies, gathered together to make war against him that sat on the horse, and against his army.

19. The Roman political leader (cf. 13:1) musters his following among the **kings of the earth,** with their respective **armies** to do battle with Christ and His followers (cf. vss. 14-15). There will be no need for the redeemed to fight. The encounter will be both short and decisive.

E. Judgment of the Beast and False Prophet. 19:20-21.

20 And the beast was taken, and with him the false prophet that wrought miracles before him, with which he deceived them that had received the mark of the beast, and them that worshipped his image. These both were cast alive into a lake of fire burning with brimstone.
21 And the remnant were slain with the sword of him that sat upon the horse, which *sword* proceeded out of his mouth: and all the fowls were filled with their flesh.

20-21. Now the chief antagonists, **the beast** (cf. 13:1) and **the false prophet** (cf. 13:11), are seized and thrown alive into the **lake of fire.** The false prophet (the Antichrist, religious leader) is singled out, because it was he who worked miracles to seduce and deceive men (cf. II Thess 2:1-12). It is remarkable that these two ungodly leaders find their final place of judgment even before Satan does (cf. 20:7-10). Their followers are slain by the **sword** of Christ; notice the wording of II Thessalonians 2:8: ". . . the Lord shall consume with the spirit of His mouth" to learn the literalness of these events. The final word is that the supper of God **filled** the appetite of all the **fowls.** Horrendous carnage it will be.

XIV. THE MILLENNIAL REIGN OF CHRIST. 20:1-15.

This chapter serves as a Continental Divide of Scripture. If one follows a single, consistent hermeneutical principle in interpreting Scripture, it will lead him to one perspective on this chapter. If, on the other hand, one should employ a dual hermeneutic (one for non-prophetic portions of Scripture and another for the prophetic parts), it will carry him to a totally different interpretation of this pivotal chapter. Premillennialists (also known as chiliasts from the Greek word for 1000) use a single interpretive principle and find in this vital chapter that, after the visible coming of Christ in chapter 19, He will set up His earthly kingdom and reign with His saints for a thousand years, while Satan, the Roman Beast, and the Antichrist are confined to the bottomless pit. Later, the evil trio are cast into the lake of fire to remain there forever. Amillennialists employ a dual hermeneutic in interpretation and find no earthly reign of Christ either predicted in the Old or New Testament or realized in a thousand-year kingdom. For them Satan was bound by Christ (contra I Pet 5:8) and is imprisoned throughout the church age. As to the two resurrections of chapter 20, one is said to be spiritual and the other literal and final. There is an admission on the part of some that in the early church the millennial view was dominant, if not general, because of the Jewish view of the messianic rule of the Son of God, fortified, they say, by the teaching of the apocalyptic works which arose between the Old and New Testaments. But when Christian doctrine became more explicit, chiliasm was rejected. The fact is that chiliasm was dominant until Augustine rebelled against it and introduced his spiritualizing method of interpreting prophecy. For a full discussion of the question, see the present writer's *Millennialism: The Two Major Views*, Moody Press, 1980 and 1982.

A. The Binding of Satan. 20:1-3.

20:1-3. This chapter follows the events of the previous chapter. Though unseen by mortal eye, Satan has been on earth since 12:9, carrying on his blighting work. The angel is probably the Lord Jesus Christ, for He alone is a match for Satan (Michael is not, cf. Jude 9). The scene is admittedly symbolic (cf. 1:1), because a spirit being is not susceptible to treatment by keys and chains. The **key** is to lock, and the **chain** is to bind. In the last analysis, God has authority over **the bottomless pit.**

The purpose of the **angel** is to bind **Satan** for **a thousand years. Dragon** indicates cruelty; **serpent** speaks of guile; **Devil** indicates him as the tempter of man; and **Satan** indicates he is the adversary of Christ and His people. From verse 2-7 there are six mentions of 1000 years. If this number is symbolic, of what is it a symbol? It cannot mean that which is endless, because the Greek language, as well as the Hebrew, has ample means to convey endlessness without ambiguity.

Thrown into the abyss, Satan is incarcerated, so that he is unable to deceive the nations for the length of that period, namely, the Millennium. The sealing is for security, as elsewhere in Scripture. He is adequately curbed and restrained. What a boon to mankind is this! Deception has characterized Satan from Genesis 3 to the time now under consideration (cf. II Cor 4:3, 4). In God's purpose Satan will be **loosed a little** after the allotted time. Why? Simply, God would reveal to us that he has not changed his nature, and that man still is susceptible to his wiles and stratagems. The result of the loosing is indicated in verses 7-8.

B. The Resurrection and Reign of the Saints. 20:4-6.

4. What was seen in 11:15 by way of anticipation is here realized. It is understood that Christ will sit on His throne and reign as the legitimate Son of David, and that is clearly stated in the last clauses of this verse. Who are the occupants of the **thrones?** From the combined testimony of Scripture, they will be New Testament saints (cf. I Cor 6:2) who reign as the Queen of the King. Too, there will be Old Testament saints who will rule as viceregents of the King and Queen (cf. Deut 28:1, 13; Mt 19:28). The martyred through the Tribulation Period, and those who resisted the idolatry worship of the beast, will also reign. These will come to life (only a literal, not spiritual, resurrection will meet the demands of the context, in which individuals have been beheaded) and reign with Christ for the Millennium.

5. The rest of the dead do not experience resurrection **until the thousand years were finished.** Thus, it is pointless and baseless to speak of a general resurrection in order to avoid the

---

CHAPTER 20

AND I saw an angel come down from heaven, having the key of the bottomless pit and a great chain in his hand.

2 And he laid hold on the dragon, that old serpent, which is the Devil, and Satan, and bound him a thousand years,

3 And cast him into the bottomless pit, and shut him up, and set a seal upon him, that he should deceive the nations no more, till the thousand years should be fulfilled: and after that he must be loosed a little season.

4 And I saw thrones, and they sat upon them, and judgment was given unto them: and *I saw* the souls of them that were beheaded for the witness of Jesus, and for the word of God, and which had not worshipped the beast, neither his image, neither had received *his* mark upon their foreheads, or in their hands; and they lived and reigned with Christ a thousand years.

5 But the rest of the dead lived not again until the thousand years were finished. This *is* the first resurrection.

intervening period of 1000 years, as amillennialists do. The order of the **resurrection** can be gleaned from these Scriptures: I Corinthians 15:23-24; Revelation 20:4-6; Daniel 12:1-3; and Luke 20:34-36. The word **first** is found in verses 5 and 6. If this means there is but one resurrection, words are emptied of meaning. There are definite stages in the first resurrection; the chief one is Christ Himself (cf. I Cor 15:20).

6 Blessed and holy *is* he that hath part in the first resurrection: on such the second death hath no power, but they shall be priests of God and of Christ, and shall reign with him a thousand years.

6. Blessed and holy are all who have part in the **first resurrection**, i.e., of the righteous. **Blessed** tells of their condition; **holy** speaks of their character. They are **priests** and kings (cf. 1:6; I Pet 2:5), exactly as Christ combines the two offices (cf. Zech 6:13). The reign with Christ, prophesied in Old and New Testament alike, will endure **a thousand years.** Over these righteous ones the second death (the lake of fire, vs. 14) has no sway; it holds no terror for them through the all-sufficient work of the Saviour.

C. The Final Doom of Satan, the Beast, and the False Prophet. 20:7-10.

7 And when the thousand years are expired, Satan shall be loosed out of his prison.

7. After the Millennium **Satan shall be loosed** from his imprisonment in the abyss. This loosing it is for the last exhibition of his venom and the last test of man.

8 And shall go out to deceive the nations which are in the four quarters of the earth, Gog and Mā'gŏg, to gather them together to battle: the number of whom *is* as the sand of the sea.

8. After Christ's glorious mediatorial reign on earth for 1000 years, Satan stages a rebellion through his deceptions. Notice, first of all, it is on a universal scale, namely, **the nations which are in the four quarters of the earth.** How could this occur? It must be remembered that there will be procreation in the Millennium on the part of those who have entered the kingdom (cf. Mt 25:31-46) in unresurrected bodies; but their progeny will not be born redeemed any more than this has transpired at any time in the history of man (cf. Isa 65:20). Furthermore, many will give only feigned obedience to the ruling King (cf. Ps 66:3 in the NASB).

Are the **Gog and Magog** here the same as those of Ezekiel 38-39? Definitely not, for four reasons: (1) The chronological factor. The events of Ezekiel 38-39, take place before the Millennium in Israel's latter days (cf. the present writer's *The Book of Ezekiel*, Moody Press, 11th printing, 1982, pp. 218-239). The rebellion of Revelation 20 occurs after the Millennium. (2) The geographical factor. More than once Ezekiel clearly states that Gog and Magog come from the uttermost parts of the north of the Land of Promise. Here John explicitly locates the nations involved as coming from the four corners of the earth. (3) The actuating factor. It is true that Satan can be faulted for much of the ungodliness in the world, but there are also the elements of the flesh and the world (cf. Eph 2:1-3). It cannot be denied that Satan is behind the invasion of Ezekiel 38-39, but not in so clearly a stated manner as here. (4) The interpretive factor. The reader of the Apocalypse will certainly assent by this time that John uses common nouns, even proper nouns, in a symbolic manner. Witness the use of Jezebel (cf. 2:20), Sodom and Egypt (cf. 11:8), and Babylon (cf. the most extended use of symbolism in a name in chs. 17-18). Thus, the student of the Revelation need not be surprised to find the names Gog and Magog used symbolically here. (Cf. W. F. Arndt and F. W. Gingrich, *A Greek-English Lexicon of the New Testament*, p. 167, col. 2.) Sad, indeed, it is that after such a benevolent and beneficent rule of the Lord of glory, there should be a following of Satan like the sand of the sea.

9 And they went up on the breadth of the earth, and compassed the camp of the saints about, and the beloved city: and fire came down from God out of heaven, and devoured them.

9. These nations will be banded together for one purpose and will press on toward one goal, namely, to destroy the capital city of the King, Jerusalem, and work havoc among His faithful subjects. God delights in Jerusalem and calls it **the beloved city,** because outside its walls the Son of God accomplished redemption for the world in the will of the Father, and then has reigned

10 And the devil that deceived them was cast into the lake of fire and brimstone, where the beast and the false prophet *are,* and shall be tormented day and night for ever and ever.

in righteousness in that city for 1000 years. The judgment of God with **fire** on the invaders is swift and final.

10. Now the instigator to sin ever since the Garden of Eden is dealt with. His final doom is **the lake of fire**—unthinkable torment. It will be eternal and irreversible, because the **beast** and **false prophet,** who were cast into the lake of fire before the Millennium, are still there. They will be preserved in judgment, but not annihilated. There will be never-ending mental agony and physical suffering. Unbelievers scoff at the concept of anyone or anything being preserved in fire. The same God who placed consuming power in fire can, if He wills, counteract that power. He has done so in the past (cf. the Hebrew youths in the fiery furnace, Dan 3:27) and will do so in the future (cf. Mk 9:49). If the torment is forever, why are day and night introduced here? There will be no day or night in eternity according to our chronological reckoning; but this is the clearest way to convey it to our minds, which are accustomed to concepts of time and space.

D. The Great White Throne Judgment. 20:11-15.

Our amillennialist brethren, who are operating on a unitary principle of one covenant, one people of God, one resurrection, and one judgment, carry through this hermeneutic here also. For them, there will be the coming of Christ, a general resurrection, and a general judgment. Actually, the biblical doctrine of judgment is not so simplistic, if all the scriptural data are to be taken into account. True, the judgment in these verses is the final one; but it is *not* the only one. The Bible reveals seven distinct judgments: one past, one present, and five future. Because of the tyranny of time and space, the first six will be dealt with briefly, and the last one more fully. First, there is the judgment of the Cross. It was a judgment in two senses: (1) man's sins were judged at Calvary (cf. II Cor 5:21; Gal 3:13; Rom 8:1), and (2) Satan was judged there also (cf. Col 2:14, 15, with Jn 16:11). It is a judgment that is past and will never be repeated. Second, there is the judgment of the sinning believer (cf. I Cor 11:30-32), if he does not judge himself. The more often this judgment is experienced, the better. Third is the judgment of the believer's works (cf. 22:12; Rom 14:10; I Cor 3:10-19; 4:5; II Cor 5:10). This takes place at the Rapture (cf. II Tim 4:8) at the judgment seat (*bēma*) of Christ in heaven. It is for rewards or suffering loss (cf. I Cor 3:14-15). Fourth, there is the judgment upon Israel (cf. Ezk 20:33-38; Mt 24:9-10). It takes place after the Tribulation Period; those who continue to reject their Messiah will not enter the kingdom; those who have received Him will enter it (cf. Rom 11:26). Fifth, there will be a judgment of the nations (cf. Joel 3:11-16; Mt 25:31-46). It will occur after the Tribulation Period; it will be on the basis, as always, of acceptance or rejection of Christ, manifested in their treatment of the earthly brethren of our Lord. The righteous enter the kingdom and eternal life; the wicked are excluded from both. Sixth, this judgment will come upon fallen angels and Satan (cf. II Pet 2:4; Jude 6; Rev 20:10). Time and place are not specified for the angels; the beast and false prophet will be judged before the reign of Christ and Satan after the 1000 years. Because of their relentless rebellion against God, they will suffer eternal fire. The seventh judgment is now under consideration in 20:11-15. It is properly called The Great White Throne Judgment.

11 And I saw a great white throne, and him that sat on it, from whose face the earth and the heaven fled away; and there was found no place for them.

11. This is the judgment of the wicked dead, distinct from all the previous ones just considered. It is described as **great** because it is the most awesome assize ever held. The characterization **white** has reference to the purity and holiness with which it will be conducted. The **throne** indicates that majestic authority is involved. The One who sits on the throne is the Lord Jesus Christ (cf. Jn 5:22, 27; II Tim 4:1). To underscore the gravity of

12 And I saw the dead, small and great, stand before God; and the books were opened: and another book was opened, which is *the book* of life: and the dead were judged out of those things which were written in the books, according to their works.

13 And the sea gave up the dead which were in it; and death and hell delivered up the dead which were in them: and they were judged every man according to their works.

14 And death and hell were cast into the lake of fire. This is the second death.

15 And whosoever was not found written in the book of life was cast into the lake of fire.

CHAPTER 21

AND I saw a new heaven and a new earth: for the first heaven and the first earth were passed away; and there was no more sea.

the proceedings, John states that **the earth and the heaven fled away from His presence, and there was found no place for them.** This does not mean the annihilation of the earth and heaven. It is rather that the Great White Throne Judgment will take place between the passing of the Millennial scene and the entrance on the new heaven and earth.

12. Stand before God. Where will the subjects of the judgment stand? They will be upheld by God in space. This is a deeply solemn scene that merges into eternity. The judgment is final and eternal; for all that are circumscribed, that is, earth and heaven, have passed away. The high and low of rank on earth will be there. The sinner is now brought face-to-face with God the Son, from whom he cannot escape. The distinctions of this verse are vital: notice that there are **books . . . and another book.** Could not the latter be included in the former? By no means, because both entities are defined. The book is **the book of life,** in which all who have trusted Christ are inscribed. Here it is introduced to show that the subjects of the judgment are unsaved. The books contain the record of their **works** (cf. vss. 12-13). Why is there any need to consult their works, if they are lost? It is intended to reveal the number and gravity of their sins to determine degrees of their punishment (cf. carefully Lk 12:47-48).

13. Even the unsaved who have died on the seas, whose bodies have never been recovered, will not be exempt from this august tribunal (cf. Jn 5:28, 29). **Death** (used here for the grave) gives up the bodies; **hell** gives up the souls. No one is said to escape or enter eternal bliss. All the unsaved will suffer their eternal doom (cf. 20:6).

14. Death and hell, brought into existence by man's sin, end where all sinners do, namely, **the lake of fire.** This means an actual, eternal separation from God in conscious, unceasing torment.

15. Whosoever. There is no indication that any individual at the Great White Throne ever escapes judgment. The cause of their final doom—not that they did not accumulate sufficient good deeds in the books—is that their names were not found written in the Lamb's **book of life** (cf. 3:5; 13:8; 21:27). This is all-inclusive, from Cain to the end of human history.

XV. THE NEW HEAVEN AND EARTH. 21:1-27.

A. Passing of the Old Heaven and Earth. 21:1.

21:1. Prophecy does not deal at length with the eternal state; therefore, it is difficult for any man to answer the many questions posed by those who long for details. Even Paul, who was caught up to the third heaven, which is the throne of God, was not permitted to divulge what he saw and heard (cf. II Cor 12:3-4). Prophecy carries the reader to the end of the Millennium. References to the eternal state are few: Isaiah 65:17; 66:22; I Corinthians 15:24-28; Ephesians 3:21; and II Peter 3:13, together with the disclosures here in chapters 21-22.

Verse 1 of this chapter is to be connected with 20:11 (cf. II Pet 3:13). Scripture does not teach the annihilation of the material universe. God annihilates nothing, let alone human beings, as some erroneously teach. Earth and heaven will be completely purified. During the Millennium the earth is renovated (cf. Isa 35:1ff.; Mt 19:28 ["regeneration" in this text has nothing to do with spiritual matters, but with the renovation of the earth]). Apparently, the **new heaven** will be the home of believers of this age; the **new earth** will be the residence of redeemed ones apart from the church. It is not to be expected that believers in these areas will not have constant communication and communion with each other. Both will be populated with redeemed, cleansed souls. Righteousness suffers now (the godly suffer, cf. II Tim 3:12); in the Millennium it will reign

2 And I John saw the holy city, new Jerusalem, coming down from God out of heaven, prepared as a bride adorned for her husband.

(cf. Isa 11:9; 32:1); in the eternal state it will dwell (cf. II Pet 3:13). John indicates that **there was no more sea.** This will give so much more land space in the eternal earth for the peoples on earth.

B. New Jerusalem. 21:2-7.

2. The holy city, new Jerusalem. In popular thinking, all mentions of **Jerusalem** in the Bible are thought to refer to the same city. This is not true. Multiplied references in Scripture do speak of the literal, earthly city, the one David made his capital. But there are other references that do not have that city in view at all. How is one to distinguish in these cases? The Spirit of God, Master of language that He is, gives the student definite clues. For instance, in Galatians 4 Paul writes of "Jerusalem which now is" (cf. vs. 25) and "Jerusalem which is above" (cf. vs. 26). He is not speaking of cities at all; symbolically, he is contrasting the principles of law and grace. The writer of the Epistle to the Hebrews speaks of Abraham's looking for a city whose architect is God (cf. Heb 11:10, 16); then he mentions (cf. Heb 12:22) "the heavenly Jerusalem," which is doubtless the one of 21:2, as will be shown below. There is a millennial Jerusalem predicted in Isaiah 2:1-4, to which all the nations will flow, a true confluence of peoples. But there is yet another Jerusalem designated as the **new Jerusalem**, with the added description that it is **the holy city.** Popular opinion equates the New Jerusalem with heaven; this is an error. The New Jerusalem comes down from heaven from God; even more, the city is called (vss. 9-10) **the bride, the Lamb's wife.** Why? Because she is its most prominent inhabitant. Thus, it is clear that when other than the literal city is intended, the Spirit adds qualifying and descriptive words to make this known. Recall that Babylon will be both a harlot (cf. ch. 17) and a city (cf. ch. 18). Apparently, **The holy Jerusalem, descending out of heaven from God** in verse 10 is at the beginning of the Millennium; the **coming down from God** in verse 2 is at the end of the Millennium, extending into the eternal state. The church will be seen throughout all eternity as an adorned bride. The picture stresses the positional; because the New Jerusalem, somewhat in the way of a midway house, will be the meeting place of all the redeemed, as the city is suspended, from all appearances, above the millennial Jerusalem.

3 And I heard a great voice out of heaven saying, Behold, the tabernacle of God *is* with men, and he will dwell with them, and they shall be his people, and God himself shall be with them, *and be* their God.

3. The tabernacle of God is with men. God dwelling among men was the purpose of the tabernacle of old (cf. Ex 25:8); indeed, it was the object of the incarnation (cf. Jn 1:14), Immanuel (God with us) in the most universal and complete sense (cf. 7:15). A tabernacle suggests moving about; the saints will have access to all part of God's creation. Undoubtedly, there will be communication between the earthly, millennial Jerusalem and the mystical, or New, Jerusalem. God will dwell with men; there will be no change in the eternal state.

4 And God shall wipe away all tears from their eyes; and there shall be no more death, neither sorrow, nor crying, neither shall there be any more pain: for the former things are passed away.

4. All sin's effects will be obliterated (cf. 7:17). The **eyes,** called the **living fountains of waters,** will be dry forever.

5 And he that sat upon the throne said, Behold, I make all things new. And he said unto me, Write: for these words are true and faithful.

5. The One on the throne is the Father; for the kingdom has been delivered over to Him by the Son, the Mediator (cf. I Cor 15:24-28).

6 And he said unto me, It is done. I am Alpha and Omega, the beginning and the end. I will give unto him that is athirst of the fountain of the water of life freely.

6. I am the Alpha and Omega, the beginning and the end. God is indeed the source and end of all glory (cf. Rom 11:36). He is the First (**Alpha**) and the Last (**Omega**). After their sin in Eden, Adam and Eve were prohibited from taking of the tree of life; here, all are invited to take **of the water of life freely** through the redemption of Christ. Since Christ thirsted on Calvary when dying for us no one will thirst in eternity. It is still a valid offer from God today.

7 He that overcometh shall inherit all things; and I will be his God, and he shall be my son.

7. The overcomer here, as in chapters 2-3, is the believer, the one who has drunk of the water of life. For him there is sonship with God forever.

C. The Portion of the Ungodly. 21:8.

8 But the fearful, and unbelieving, and the abominable, and murderers, and whoremongers, and sorcerers, and idolaters, and all liars, shall have their part in the lake which burneth with fire and brimstone: which is the second death.

8. For the unrepentant, who are designated under some eight categories, there will not be bliss, but burning in the lake of fire, **the second death** (cf. 20:6, 14). A believer may be called on to pass through one death, i.e., physical death (and if the Rapture intervenes, he will forego that death, cf. I Cor 15:51, 52); an unbeliever faces two deaths: physical death and the second death. Why are the cowardly and liars spoken of in two categories? The first are afraid to accept Christ and bear the ridicule of the world. The second are those who have denied their sin and need of Christ as Saviour.

D. The Wife of the Lamb 21:9.

9 And there came unto me one of the seven angels which had the seven vials full of the seven last plagues, and talked with me, saying, Come hither, I will shew thee the bride, the Lamb's wife.

9. It is gracious of God to allow one of the **angels** who was commissioned to pour out the most horrendous plagues earth has ever known, the privilege of inviting John to a special view of **the bride, the Lamb's wife.** For the remainder of the chapter a symbolic description of **the bride** in all her millennial glory will be presented. Her relationship to Christ continues on into the eternal ages. Because the millennial picture approximates heaven, many have equated them. This is an error, for there are some in the Millennium whose hearts have not been touched for God who will enlist under Satan's banner in his rebellion against Christ (cf. 20:8, 9) at the end of that glorious reign. Amillennialists see this age of grace merging into the age of glory at the coming of Christ. Premillennialists believe that the age of grace will be followed by the age of righteousness (where Christ will be vindicated in time as He was rejected in history), which will then merge into the age of glory.

E. Description of the New Jerusalem. 21:10-27.

1. Its origin. 21:10.

10 And he carried me away in the spirit to a great and high mountain, and shewed me that great city, the holy Jerusalem, descending out of heaven from God,

10. Mark that John is transported by **the spirit to a great and high mountain,** a vantage point where he can see the holy city, Jerusalem, in all her beauty and glory. It is wonderful to read of Jerusalem as a holy city; the prophets inveighed against her in centuries past, for she was just the opposite (cf. Isa 1:4, 15, 18, 21; 5:7). It is unmistakably stated that this city proceeds from the heavenly realm; it is **out of heaven from God.** However, it is not to be equated with heaven, as indicated above.

2. Its brilliance. 21:11.

11 Having the glory of God: and her light *was* like unto a stone most precious, even like a jasper stone, clear as crystal;

11. **Jasper stone.** The description is given under the figure of precious stones, because (1) they are costly, and (2) they are durable. The Spirit uses language best adapted to our limited comprehension. The city will be brilliant and glorious.

3. Its wall. 21:12.

12 And had a wall great and high, *and* had twelve gates, and at the gates twelve angels, and names written thereon, which are *the names* of the twelve tribes of the children of Israel:

12. The **wall** indicates that all will be secure within the city, and it will be separate from all that is unlike it in holiness. Notice that the foundation of the church was laid in **Israel.**

4. Its gates. 21:13.

13 On the east three gates; on the north three gates; on the south three gates; and on the west three gates.

13. **Gates** were places of judgment. Here is the fulfillment of Matthew 19:28.

5. Its foundation stones. 21:14.

14 And the wall of the city had twelve foundations, and in them the names of the twelve apostles of the Lamb.

14. The world may forget, and has, that it was **the twelve apostles** who laid the foundation for the church upon the foundation Stone, Christ Himself (cf. Eph 2:20). But God never forgets.

15 And he that talked with me had a golden reed to measure the city, and the gates thereof, and the wall thereof.
16 And the city lieth foursquare, and the length is as large as the breadth: and he measured the city with the reed, twelve thousand furlongs. The length and the breadth and the height of it are equal.
17 And he measured the wall thereof, an hundred *and* forty *and* four cubits, *according to* the measure of a man, that is, of the angel.
18 And the building of the wall of it was *of* jasper: and the city *was* pure gold, like unto clear glass.
19 And the foundations of the wall of the city *were* garnished with all manner of precious stones. The first foundation was jasper; the second, sapphire; the third, a chalcedony; the fourth, an emerald;
20 The fifth, sardonyx; the sixth, sardius; the seventh, chrysolyte; the eighth, beryl; the ninth, a topaz; the tenth, a chrysoprasus; the eleventh, a jacinth; the twelfth, an amethyst.
21 And the twelve gates *were* twelve pearls; every several gate was of one pearl: and the street of the city *was* pure gold, as it were transparent glass.
22 And I saw no temple therein: for the Lord God Almighty and the Lamb are the temple of it.

23 And the city had no need of the sun, neither of the moon, to shine in it: for the glory of God did lighten it, and the Lamb *is* the light thereof.

24 And the nations of them which are saved shall walk in the light of it: and the kings of the earth do bring their glory and honour into it.

25 And the gates of it shall not be shut at all by day: for there shall be no night there.

6. Its measurements. 21:15-17.

15-17. From the measurements given it is clear that the city is a cube 1,500 miles in each direction.

7. Its materials. 21:18-21.

18-21. The **gold** (cf. vss. 18, 21) speaks of divine glory, as in the tabernacle of old where the cherubim of gold were called the cherubim of glory. All the stones named are known for their value, beauty and enduring quality.

8. Its temple. 21:22.

22. Contrary to the long history of temples in Israel, there will be **no temple** in the New Jerusalem. Does this indicate an element of secularism? God forbid. Rather, it means there will be free access to God; it will be for all (recall that only priests could enter the sanctuary proper and that only the High Priest could enter the Holy of Holies, and that on one day a year). It will be immediate access, and it will be without barrier (witness the calamity that befell Uzziah of Judah when he tried to offer incense in the holy place; cf. II Chron 26:16-21).

9. Its illumination. 21:23.

23. God the Father and the Lamb will be the all-sufficient light for the city. Therefore, there will be **no need of the sun, neither of the moon; the Lamb** will meet every requirement. Remember that in the Temple, as in the tabernacle, there were three means of illumination. For the outer court, the illumination of the sun by day and the moon by night was ample. For the inner sanctuary, the candlesticks lighted all the furniture, because the light of sun and moon did not penetrate there. For the Holy of Holies, the Shekinah provided all; this typified the blessed light of the Lamb (cf. Jn 1:4, 9; 9:5).

10. The presence of the nations and their kings. 21:24.

24. The New Jerusalem, with the church, will be the center of the governments of the earth. There has never been a rule like it.

11. Continuous access. 21:25.

25. The gates of it shall not be shut. There will be unhindered access and no setting sun, but full noon always. Ever since Adam and Eve sinned, there has been a barrier to access. They could no longer enjoy the Garden of Eden. Even Adam feared communication with God and hid himself. When Israel accepted the yoke of the Law (cf. Ex 19), immediately they were not allowed access to Mount Sinai on pain of death. When the tabernacle, and later the Temple also, was constructed, God placed the symbol of His Presence (the Shekinah, lit., the Dwelling-Presence of God) in the innermost compartment, as far from sinful man as possible; and he could only come through his representative, the High Priest, with the blood of an offering. Now, in the New Jerusalem all blockages to access are removed forever.

12. The glory and honor of the nations. 21:26.

26 And they shall bring the glory and honour of the nations into it.

26. This verse builds on the truth of verse 24. But notice its **glory**. In the worship of Israel no Gentile could enter into the holy precincts without serious repercussions. Remember the persecution Paul suffered when some inferred that he had brought a Gentile into the Temple (cf. Acts 21:22-29). But no barriers will be found in the New Jerusalem.

13. The absence of sin and presence of the redeemed. 21:27.

27 And there shall in no wise enter into it any thing that defileth, neither *whatsoever* worketh abomination, or *maketh* a lie: but they which are written in the Lamb's book of life.

27. Sin, in all its hideous forms, will be entirely excluded. The never-ending beauties of the New Jerusalem are indescribable, but they are such because of the Lord Jesus and His presence there.

XVI. THE PARADISE OF GOD. 22:1-21.

Apparently, the scene is shifted from the New Jerusalem above the earth to heaven itself. This chapter reveals beautifully that what was lost in Genesis is regained in the Revelation, a true "Paradise Regained."

CHAPTER 22

AND he shewed me a pure river of water of life, clear as crystal, proceeding out of the throne of God and of the Lamb.

A. The River of the Water of Life. 22:1.

22:1. The **pure river of water of life,** flowing from the **throne of God and of the Lamb,** speaks of fullness of refreshment, life, and joy (cf. Ps 36:8). In Genesis, the tree of life was mentioned first; here, the river of life is referred to first. There are heavenly and earthly streams of blessing: earthly in Ezekiel 47:1 and Zechariah 14:8; heavenly in this passage. All come from the seat of His blessed government.

B. The Tree of Life. 22:2.

2 In the midst of the street of it, and on either side of the river, *was there* the tree of life, which bare twelve *manner of* fruits, *and* yielded her fruit every month: and the leaves of the tree *were* for the healing of the nations.

2. Was there the tree of life. Satisfying fruit will be there in abundance; the saints will partake of it. Even the leaves will promote the sustained health of the nations.

3 And there shall be no more curse: but the throne of God and of the Lamb shall be in it; and his servants shall serve him:

C. The Removal of the Curse. 22:3a.

3a. The **curse** brought on the human family through the disobedience of Adam (cf. Gen 3:14-19; Rom 5:12) will be wiped out completely. It was paid for at Calvary.

D. The Throne of God and of the Lamb. 22:3b.

3b. There can be no curse where **the throne of God and of the Lamb** exist. These are spiritual irreconcilables of infinite proportions.

E. The Bliss of the Godly. 22:3c-4.

4 And they shall see his face; and his name *shall be* in their foreheads.

3c-4. God's **servants shall serve him,** an unsullied, gladsome, eternal service without failure or weariness and with fullness of joy and praise. **And they shall see his face.** Many question whether saints in heaven will see God's face. The Scripture here is plain; they assuredly will. Reread Exodus 24:9-11 (a remarkable vignette). Did not John the apostle lie on Christ's bosom at the Last Supper, hear His heart beat, and look into His face? (cf. Jn 13:23). Was it not this same beloved disciple that bore witness of what he had heard, had seen with his eyes, and had handled with his hands, even the Word of Life? (cf. 1 Jn 1:1). But, someone has said, mortal man cannot look upon the face of God. This can be true of man in his sinful state and in his condition before his resurrection. But, when he is glorified with the Saviour, it will be entirely different (cf. Rom 8:28-30). In eternity there will always be a difference between deity and redeemed humanity, but this truth does not preclude the "beatific vision," as it has been called. The **name** of God **in**

their foreheads indicates public acknowledgement of belonging to Him, as well as conformity to His blessed nature.

F. The Absence of Darkness. 22:5a-5b.

5a-5b. How early in life does a child learn to fear darkness; in advanced age it appears again (cf. Eccl 12:1-5). For the believer, darkness will be banished forever. Darkness always flees in the presence of **light** (cf. Jn 1:5). God and Christ are the eternal light of the world.

G. The Saints' Reign. 22:5c.

5c. And they shall reign for ever and ever. The millennial reign and the eternal reign are united. Saints will never cease to reign, as long as there will be subjects (cf. Rom 5:17). Why do earthly reigns come to an end? They are terminated, either by injustices, fraud, ineptitude, or by death. None of these will be present when Christ the King reigns with His Bride. Why, then, should not the millennial phase of His reign merge into the eternal phase? Verily, it will!

H. The Validity of the Message. 22:6.

6. These sayings are faithful and true. In a sense, this text is a recapitulation of 1:1. If any questioner thinks these disclosures are too good to be authentic, let him now hear yet another confirmation of their reliability and truth.

I. The Coming of Christ. 22:7a.

7a. Behold, I come quickly. The soon-coming, without delay, of the Lord Jesus is stated three times in this chapter, in verses 7, 12, 20. This neatly ties in the end of the book with its beginning (cf. 1:3). After all, this is the dominant theme of the book: the coming revelation of the Lord Jesus (cf. 1:7).

J. The Blessedness of the Obedient. 22:7b.

7b. Blessed is he. Blessedness is promised to those who treasure, preserve, and live in the light of this prophetic book.

K. John's Reaction to the Revelation. 22:8-9.

1. His reception of the messages. 22:8a.

2. His worship of the interpreting angel. 22:8b.

3. The angel's warning and advice. 22:9.

8-9. Again, because of the surpassing wonder of the disclosures he has witnessed and heard, John seeks to worship the creature who mediated these truths to him. Worship of the creature (cf. 19:10), rather than the Creator, is *never* justified (cf. Rom 1:25). The more seemingly worthy the creature, the greater is the danger.

L. The Angel's Final Words. 22:10-19.

1. Book to remain unsealed. 22:10.

10. Seal not. Contrast these instructions with those of Daniel 12:4. In Daniel the time was far off; here it is near (cf. 1:3).

2. The irreversible states of the ungodly and godly. 22:11.

11. No one will be so foolish as to understand this verse as an invitation to pursue ungodliness. Actually, there are more exhortations to godliness in the text than the reverse. The passage states that character tends to become fixed and unchangeable. The common saying is true: "Sow a thought and reap an act. Sow an act and reap a habit. Sow a habit and reap a character. Sow a character and reap a destiny." As one is found in that day, so will he be eternally. Death or the coming of the Lord fixes one's character and eternal destiny.

---

5 And there shall be no night there; and they need no candle, neither light of the sun; for the Lord God giveth them light: and they shall reign for ever and ever.

6 And he said unto me, These sayings *are* faithful and true: and the Lord God of the holy prophets sent his angel to shew unto his servants the things which must shortly be done.

7 Behold, I come quickly: blessed *is* he that keepeth the sayings of the prophecy of this book.

8 And I John saw these things, and heard *them.* And when I had heard and seen, I fell down to worship before the feet of the angel which shewed me these things.
9 Then saith he unto me, See *thou do it* not: for I am thy fellowservant, and of thy brethren the prophets, and of them which keep the sayings of this book: worship God.

10 And he saith unto me, Seal not the sayings of the prophecy of this book: for the time is at hand.

11 He that is unjust, let him be unjust still: and he which is filthy, let him be filthy still: and he that is righteous, let him be righteous still: and he that is holy, let him be holy still.

12 And, behold, I come quickly; and my reward *is* with me, to give every man according as his work shall be.

13 I am Alpha and Omega, the beginning and the end, the first and the last.

14 Blessed *are* they that do his commandments, that they may have right to the tree of life, and may enter in through the gates into the city.

15 For without *are* dogs, and sorcerers, and whoremongers, and murderers, and idolaters, and whosoever loveth and maketh a lie.

16 I Jesus have sent mine angel to testify unto you these things in the churches. I am the root and the offspring of David, *and* the bright and morning star.

17 And the Spirit and the bride say, Come. And let him that heareth say, Come. And let him that is athirst come. And whosoever will, let him take the water of life freely.

18 For I testify unto every man that heareth the words of the prophecy of this book, If any man shall add unto these things, God shall add unto him the plagues that are written in this book:

19 And if any man shall take away from the words of the book of this prophecy, God shall take away his part out of the book of life, and out of the holy city, and *from* the things which are written in this book.

20 He which testifieth these things saith, Surely I come quickly. Amen. Even so, come, Lord Jesus.

21 The grace of our Lord Jesus Christ *be* with you all. Amen.

2720

3. Christ's coming with His rewards. 22:12.

12. My reward is with me. For the saints, the rewards will come at the judgment seat of Christ. For the nations, they will come at the judgment of Matthew 25:31-46. For the wicked dead, they will come at the Great White Throne.

4. His eternal character. 22:13.

13. As though the intimate the blessed Trinity, there is a threefold declaration of the eternality of God.

5. The blessedness of the redeemed. 22:14.

14. The AV has unhappily utilized a Greek text here that is faulty and teaches what the rest of the Bible denies, that is, salvation by keeping the commandments. Rather, salvation comes by symbolically washing their robes in the blood of the Lamb (cf. 7:14).

6. The ungodly excluded. 22:15.

15. There is always a need to warn the unbelieving of the gravity of their condition. Those excluded are in the same company as the ones designated in 21:8.

7. The Authenticator of the book. 22:16.

16. Here is a reminder that the message of the book is for the churches; yet how they have neglected this very message! **The root** connects Christ with Israel and **David** (cf. Rom 1:3); **the bright and morning star** (cf. II Pet 1:19) links Him with the church. The Old Testament ends with Christ as the "Sun of righteousness" (cf. Mal 4:2) to "arise with healing in his wings" in millennial blessing; the New Testament closes with Him as **the bright and morning star.** He will come for His saints before He comes with them to reign, just as the morning star appears before the sun.

8. Invitation to the unsaved. 22:17.

17. The Spirit and the bride say, come. And let him that heareth say, Come. There are actually three invitations in this important text. The Bible will not close before an opportunity is given for the unsaved to trust Christ. The first two invitations are for the coming of the Lord, although they may be interpreted as a call from the Spirit and the church to the unsaved. **Whosoever will.** The third is clearly for the sinner to come and partake of life in Christ.

9. Warnings against tampering with the prophecy. 22:18-19.

18-19. The message of the Bible is complete and needs no collaboration from anyone. Here is a most solemn warning, one which is true of all the Word of God (cf. Deut 12:32), but especially so here. What a rebuke to those who treat the message carelessly. There is too much at stake here.

M. The Testimony of Christ to His Coming. 22:20.

20. These things refers to the contents of the entire book; all the message is from Christ personally. He has promised to **come quickly** (cf. Heb 10:37). If the reckoning were on God's chronometer, hardly two days are gone (cf. II Pet 3:8). **Amen. Even so, come, Lord Jesus.** The answer of John represents that of the church. Thank God, more are saying it than ever before.

N. Benediction. 22:21.

21. The Old Testament closed with a threatened curse (cf. Mal 4:6); the New Testament concludes with a benediction of